Tiley and Collison's
UK Tax Guide 2009

Tiley and Collison's UK Tax Guide 2009–10

27th edition

Keith M Gordon,
MA (Oxon), FCA, CTA (Fellow),
Barrister, Atlas Chambers

Ximena Montes-Manzano,
BSc,
Barrister, Atlas Chambers

John Tiley,
CBE, MA, BCL, *Professor of the Law of Taxation, University of Cambridge*
Fellow of Queens' College, Cambridge
Barrister

Specialist contributors

Part IV:
Anne Fairpo,
MA (Oxon), CTA (Fellow), Solicitor

Part IX:
Patrick Cannon,
CTA, LLB, BCL, Barrister

Part X:
Charles Barcroft,
CTA

Tiley and Collison's UK Tax Guide 2009-10

Members of the LexisNexis Group worldwide

United Kingdom	LexisNexis, a Division of Reed Elsevier (UK) Ltd, Halsbury House, 35 Chancery Lane, London, WC2A 1EL, and London House, 20-22 East London Street, Edinburgh EH7 4BQ
Argentina	LexisNexis Argentina, Buenos Aires
Australia	LexisNexis Butterworths, Chatswood, New South Wales
Austria	LexisNexis Verlag ARD Orac GmbH & Co KG, Vienna
Benelux	LexisNexis Benelux, Amsterdam
Canada	LexisNexis Canada, Markham, Ontario
Chile	LexisNexis Chile Ltda, Santiago
China	LexisNexis China, Beijing and Shanghai
France	LexisNexis SA, Paris
Germany	LexisNexis Deutschland GmbH, Munster
Hong Kong	LexisNexis Hong Kong, Hong Kong
India	LexisNexis India, New Delhi
Italy	Giuffrè Editore, Milan
Japan	LexisNexis Japan, Tokyo
Malaysia	Malayan Law Journal Sdn Bhd, Kuala Lumpur
Mexico	LexisNexis Mexico, Mexico
New Zealand	LexisNexis NZ Ltd, Wellington
Poland	Wydawnictwo Prawnicze LexisNexis Sp, Warsaw
Singapore	LexisNexis Singapore, Singapore
South Africa	LexisNexis Butterworths, Durban
USA	LexisNexis, Dayton, Ohio

© Reed Elsevier (UK) Ltd 2009
Published by LexisNexis

All rights reserved. No part of this publication may be reproduced in any material form (including photocopying or storing it in any medium by electronic means and whether or not transiently or incidentally to some other use of this publication) without the written permission of the copyright owner except in accordance with the provisions of the Copyright, Designs and Patents Act 1988 or under the terms of a licence issued by the Copyright Licensing Agency Ltd, Saffron House, 6–10 Kirby Street, London, EC1N 8TS. Applications for the copyright owner's written permission to reproduce any part of this publication should be addressed to the publisher.
Warning: The doing of an unauthorised act in relation to a copyright work may result in both a civil claim for damages and criminal prosecution.

Crown copyright material is reproduced with the permission of the Controller of HMSO and the Queen's Printer for Scotland. Parliamentary copyright material is reproduced with the permission of the Controller of Her Majesty's Stationery Office on behalf of Parliament. Any European material in this work which has been reproduced from EUR-lex, the official European Communities legislation website, is European Communities copyright.
A CIP Catalogue record for this book is available from the British Library.

ISBN 9781405742498

Printed in the UK by CPI William Clowes Beccles NR34 7TL

Visit LexisNexis at www.lexisnexis.co.uk

Preface

My preface last year ended with the hope that the administration of the tax system could "only get better". Perhaps I was being too optimistic, but at least for most of the year it did not become significantly worse.

The tax system is inevitably at the heart of the country's battle with economic recession. Hence, short-term fiscal incentives (such as the ill-conceived temporary cut in VAT) will soon be replaced by future tax rises, subtly poised to come into effect after the imminent General Election.

Once again, the tax code is being unjustifiably overburdened with new material. Although this year's Budget Speech proved to be a non-event, we nevertheless found ourselves with a Finance Act containing 458 pages and including 61 Schedules. The Act also includes new compliance powers that were introduced without any consultation or even warning, notwithstanding a long-standing dialogue between the Government and the professional bodies on the development of HMRC powers.

Counting pages is an easy way to measure the increasing complexity of a tax system. However, even this is misleading because, in the past two years, Parliament has chosen to omit the standard "repeals" schedule, so as to reduce the page count slightly. In addition, Finance Acts are more commonly containing so-called Henry VIII provisions that permit the consequential amendments that one would ordinarily expect to find in a Finance Act to be made by secondary legislation.

With HMRC under orders to collect the maximum amount of tax, many readers will find that they will continue to be busy in the coming year. On this note, it is worth remarking (with regret) two further developments that do not bode well for the future. The first is the proposed abolition of the equitable liability practice, a lifeline for the taxpayer who has found him/herself with an excessive assessment which is too late to challenge by normal means. In 1995, the then Inland Revenue stated that to collect tax that was known to be excessive would be "unconscionable"; it is unclear why that is no longer the case.

Secondly, a summertime consultation document announces a proposal to tax many self-employed subcontractors as if they were employees. Although the document is packaged as a way to tackle avoidance in the construction industry, the proposal appears to be designed solely to raise tax that is not properly due. It is not clear why the construction industry has been singled out for this treatment or whether, if the proposal is implemented, the same treatment will be applied to other sectors in the future.

Finally, it is worth marking the forthcoming demise of the Tax Law Rewrite Project. Its popularity with the tax profession has not been universal although it has been well received in many quarters. As someone who has been personally involved in the project for a decade, I feel it is inappropriate for me to enter into the debate. However, whatever one's views about the success of the project, I believe that all will agree that it stood for all that can be good in the tax system:

Preface

- there was a desire to make the law as accessible as possible;
- there was frank dialogue between HMRC and taxpayers (mainly through the professional bodies); and
- the project was staffed by dedicated professionals from both within HMRC and the private sector.

Whilst the project will fold during the coming year, it is to be hoped that what it stood for will continue.

Keith M Gordon
August 2009

Contents

Preface   v

PART I FUNDAMENTALS

1	Sources of tax law	5
2	Tax administration – an overview	69
2A	Tax administration – the mechanics	117
3	Avoidance—judicial principles	205
4	Anti-avoidance legislation	231

PART II INCOME TAX

5	Income tax—general	265
6	Allowances and reliefs	293
7	Employment income	337
8	Income from trades, professions and vocations	499
9	Capital allowances	661
10	Property income	731
11	Savings income	761
12	Miscellaneous income	805
13	Trusts	829
14	Estates in the course of administration	857
15	The Settlement Code	867

PART III CAPITAL GAINS TAX

16	Gains and chargeability	901
17	Assets, exemptions and reliefs	945
18	Disposal	971
19	Death	1019
20	Settled property	1031
21	Shares and companies	1057
22	Business and partnerships	1083
23	Land	1125
24	Taper relief, indexation allowance and rebasing	1161

Contents

PART IV CORPORATION TAX

25	Profits and chargeability	1177
26	Distributions	1225
27	Loan relationships, foreign exchange and intellectual property	1247
28	Groups, consortia and substantial shareholdings	1275
29	Close companies	1321
30	Investment companies	1335

PART V SAVINGS

31	Savings products with tax exemptions or reliefs	1351
32	Pensions	1383

PART VI THE INTERNATIONAL DIMENSION

33	Connecting factors	1435
34	Enforcement of foreign revenue laws	1479
35	Foreign income and capital gains of residents	1487
36	The foreign taxpayer and the United Kingdom tax system	1555
37	Double taxation relief	1565

PART VII INHERITANCE TAX

38	Introduction	1607
39	Transfers of value by disposition	1623
40	Death	1655
41	Gifts with reservation	1685
42	Settled property	1703
43	Exempt transfers	1755
44	Business property relief and other reliefs	1777
45	Valuation	1815
46	Liability for payment of IHT	1847
47	Foreign element	1863

PART VIII NATIONAL INSURANCE CONTRIBUTIONS

48	The contributory scheme	1883
49	The employed earner	1895
50	Employment earnings	1915

51	Employer and employee contributions	1953
52	The self-employed earner	1985
53	Interaction with benefits	1997
54	The international dimension	2009
55	Administration	2033

PART IX STAMP TAXES

56	Stamp duty—general	2043
57	Heads of charge	2077
58	Stamp duty in specific situations	2109
59	Companies—stamp duty (and stamp duty reserve tax)	2119
60	Companies—reliefs	2133
61	Stamp duty reserve tax	2147
62	Stamp duty land tax	2175

PART X VALUE ADDED TAX

63	Introduction	2235
64	Registration	2299
65	The charge to tax	2321
66	Tax credits, repayments and refunds	2373
67	Accounting and payment	2417
68	Exemption	2435
69	The zero rate	2467
70	The reduced rate	2501

Tables and index

Table of cases	2511
Table of statutes	2619
Index	2699

Butterworths Tolley Taxation Service

Information on the UK taxation system is also provided in the following looseleaf works:

1. Simon's National Insurance Contributions (Simons NIC).
2. Simon's Tax Planning Service (STP).
3. De Voil Indirect Tax Service.
4. Foster's Inheritance Tax.
5. Simon's Taxes.
6. Sumption: Capital Gains Tax.
7. Sergeant and Sims on Stamp Duties.

Part I
Fundamentals

1

Sources of tax law
The power to tax
EC law
Abuse of rights
Reviewing the law
Human rights law
Statutes and statutory interpretation
Scotland and Northern Ireland
Case law
Revenue practice
The tax year
The Provisional Collection of Taxes Act 1968

2

Tax administration – an overview
HM Revenue and Customs
Appeals against HMRC decisions
Appeals from the tribunal
Judicial review
Other remedies against HMRC
Evasion and fraud
HMRC prosecution powers
Serious fraud
Enforcement powers
Other compliance powers

2A

Tax administration – the mechanics
The taxpayer—making the return (and claiming tax credits)
Paying the tax (and getting tax credits)
Interest
Surcharges
Verification, enquiries and interventions
Information powers
Assessments
Correction by a taxpayer
Penalties

3

Avoidance—Judicial principles
Construction and fact finding: *Barclays*
Other recent cases
The taxpayer and the doctrine
Conclusions and current cases

4

Anti-avoidance legislation
General rule or specific legislation
Dividend stripping and bond washing
Sale and repurchase of securities
Manufactured dividends
Transactions in securities
Sale by individual of income derived from his personal activities
Statutory provisions introduced as a consequence of disclose of a tax mitigation scheme
Manufactured capital losses

1

Sources of tax law

The power to tax	PARA 1.01
EC law	PARA 1.02
Abuse of rights	PARA 1.13
Reviewing the law	PARA 1.14
Human rights law	PARA 1.21
Statutes and statutory interpretation	PARA 1.23
Scotland and Northern Ireland	PARA 1.28
Case law	PARA 1.29
Revenue practice	PARA 1.30
The tax year	PARA 1.31
The Provisional Collection of Taxes Act 1968	PARA 1.32

The power to tax

[1.01] The power to levy taxes is but one manifestation of the sovereignty of Parliament. The Bill of Rights provides that no charge on the subject shall be levied by pretence of prerogative without the consent of Parliament.[1] The Bill of Rights is not pure history; in the 1992 decision in the *Woolwich Building Society* case it was invoked by Lord Goff as one reason for granting restitution.[2] By contrast the Court of Appeal recently said it would make a mockery of the law to suggest that a fraudster can escape with impunity by piously invoking the benefit of the Bill of Rights.[3]

Parliament means the UK Parliament at Westminster; it should be noted that the Parliament of Scotland, sitting in Edinburgh, has a tax-varying power.[4] There is a presumption that express statutory authority is needed before a tax can be imposed;[5] this does not apply to a charge levied for services.[6] Within Parliament no motion requiring the expenditure of money will be received unless a motion is moved by a Minister of the Crown. Further, the powers of the House of Lords are limited in relation to a money Bill.[7] The power to tax extends even over a stonemason despite the fact that he may regard his supreme authority as the Master Mason.[8]

Tax legislation distinguishes the UK from the rest of the world. The UK includes England, Wales, Scotland and Northern Ireland—and the Scilly Isles[9]—but not the Channel Islands nor the Isle of Man.[10]

The EC has the power to raise taxes. As from 1975 the financial basis of the Community is entirely provided out of the revenues of the Community—and consists of agricultural levies, customs duties and proportion of VAT; that proportion is equivalent to 1.27% applied to a VAT base limited to 50% of GNP.[11] This basis was first settled by the European Council Meeting of February 1988.[12] The EC's power to raise taxes rests on the various member states agreeing to do so unanimously.[13]

5

[1.01] Sources of tax law

The Westminster Parliament's right to levy taxes must not be exercised in a way which breaches EC law. Taxes levied in breach of such law are ineffective owing to the twin doctrines of the supremacy of EC law and the direct effect of EC law. Where a tax breaches EC law the UK authority's effort to enforce the tax will be dismissed and any tax already paid may be recovered under principles of restitution; in appropriate cases compensation may be ordered. See further infra, §§ **1.02** et seq.

The Westminster Parliament's right to levy taxes is also affected by the European Convention on Human Rights. The UK became a signatory to the Convention in 1966 but did not incorporate it into domestic law—and then only partially—until the Human Rights Act 1998 which came into force on 2 October 2000.[14] If a UK law breaches the convention rights as set out in the Human Rights Act the UK courts may not override the statute, as they can for breach of EC law, but may simply make a declaration of incompatibility—and then only if the court is of sufficient seniority.[15] The High Court is sufficiently senior but the Special and General Commissioners are not. Before the court makes a declaration of incompatibility it must see if it can achieve an answer compatible with convention rights by the process of construction.[16]

The Human Rights Act impacts on the tax system in other ways too: see further infra, §§ **1.13** et seq.

Simon's Taxes A1.101–107.

---

[1] 2 Will and Mar sess. 2 c. 2 art 4.
[2] [1992] STC 657, 677.
[3] *C and E Commissioners v Total Network* (2007) EWCA Civ 39; [2007] STC 1005 at para 31.
[4] Scotland Act 1998, ss 73–80.
[5] *A-G v Wiltshire United Dairies* (1921) 37 TLR 884. Cf Emergency Powers (Defence) Act 1939, ss 1(3) and 2. On (non) limitation by international law, see *Cheney v Conn* [1968] 1 All ER 779, 44 TC 217. However, in *Aston Cantlow v Wallbank* [2001] EWCA Civ 713, [2002] STC 313, it was recognised that a parochial church council has a power to tax arising from common law: see infra, § **1.15** footnote 1. The Court of Appeal ruled that the particular tax charge was incompatible with the Human Rights Act 1998; although the decision was reversed by the House of Lords on other grounds this does not alter the proposition that it is possible for a 'tax' to be imposed by common law and not by statute.
[6] *China Navigation Co Ltd v A G* [1932] 2 KB 197.
[7] Parliament Act 1911, s 1. Since 2003, the House of Lords has had a committee to consider a Finance Bill. Its role, although influential, is, however, advisory.
[8] *Lloyd v Taylor* (1970) 46 TC 539.
[9] TA 1988, Sch 30, paras 6(2)(*b*), 21. See also FA 1986, s 108 on definition of UK relating to oil taxation.
[10] The United Kingdom and the Isle of Man are, however, a single area for the purposes of value added tax: Isle of Man Act 1979, s 6(1).
[11] Reduced from a 55% ceiling by Council Decision 94/728 of 31 October 1993, OJ 1993 L293; on changes to VAT percentages see Council Decision 00/597 OJ 2000 L253.

[12] See now Council Decision 2000/597 of 29 September 2000, OJ 2000, L253/42. On EC provision re budget see EC Treaty Arts 268–280 and especially Art 269.
[13] EC Treaty Arts 90-95 especially Art 95 (2).
[14] Between 1966 and 2000, where a UK tax law broke the Convention, complaint could be made to the European Human Rights Commission and, if necessary, the associated Court in Strasbourg. By 2000 the Commission had disappeared and only the Court remained—and still remains—as the ultimate arbiter on these matters.
[15] Human Rights Act 1998, s 4.
[16] Human Rights Act 1998, s 3; on duty of court to strive hard to do this see speeches in the House of Lords in *Ghaidan v Godin-Mendoza* [2004] UKHL 30 (HL), [2004] 2 AC 557.

EC law

[1.02] The EC Treaty limits the rights of member state legislatures to levy taxes.

As Hoffmann J reminded us in 1991:

> The [EC] Treaty is the supreme law of this country, taking precedence over Acts of Parliament . . . entry into the Community was a high act of social and economic policy, by which the partial surrender of sovereignty was seen as more than compensated by the advantages of membership.[1]

This supremacy only applies to those areas in which sovereignty has been ceded. Taxation is not at present one of those areas, and unless or until harmonisation takes place, remains a matter for the legislatures of member states.[2]

However, supremacy issues do arise in connection with UK legislation. The UK Parliament may find that its legislation conflicts with principles of the EC Law[3] or that it has not followed the proper procedure by not consulting the Commission so that in either case its legislation is of no effect.[4] However, they may also arise when an individual taxpayer is accorded rights under EC law through the doctrine of direct effect.[5] Provisions of EC law having direct effect may include both rights under the Treaty and rights under other parts of EC law. A provision giving rise to direct effect must be clear and concise; it must be unconditional and unqualified and not subject to the taking of any further measures on the part of a Community or national authority and must leave no substantial discretion in its implementation to a Community or national authority.[6] In the tax field many provisions on the four freedoms recognised by EC law have been given direct effect (see infra, § **1.03**). The European Commmunities Act 1972, s 2 requires a court to see first whether it can interpret UK legislation in a way which does not conflict with EC principles. If this is not possible the UK legislation may have to be disapplied.[7]

Further issues arise in connection with Directives. These are instructions to member states, agreed at the Council and so, in the case of tax, agreed unanimously, under which the states agree to introduce legislation within their own legal systems to carry out the proposals in the Directive. As legislation

[1.02] Sources of tax law

which is subordinate to the Treaty, Directives will only be valid if they conform to EC law.[8] If the state does not implement the proposals by the due date the direct effect doctrine will apply to enable the taxpayer to assert the rights set out in the Directive against the member state.[9] In addition, the citizen may be able to recover damages from the state under the principle in *Francovich v Italy*[10] for failure to implement the Directive—this right may arise even though the principles required for direct effect are not satisfied.[11] In tax matters, the effect of a decision that a tax was not due at all is to give rise to a right to restitution of the amount wrongly paid. Where the tax was levied prematurely the restitutionary claim will be the same as the claim for interest.[12]

Several restitutionary claims for interest have been litigated.[13] In the combined *Hoechst* and *Metallgesellschaft* cases, the ECJ delivered its judgment on 8 March 2001.[14] Under UK rules the payment of advance corporation tax (ACT) normally due when a dividend was paid could be deferred if the payment was by a subsidiary to a parent—provided the two companies were both resident in the UK, ie both within the UK tax net. This territorial restriction was held to break the non-discrimination rules. The current case is based in restitution, the ground being that the payment had been made under a mistake of law. Under s 2 of the Limitation Act 1980, the normal limitation period, on which the Revenue relied, would be six years before the parties began the action claiming compensation or restitution. However, they argued that under s 32(1)(c) of the 1980 Act, the limitation period where an action is brought for relief from the consequences of a mistake begins to run only when the claimant discovered the mistake or could with reasonable diligence have discovered it. That period would begin on the date of the judgment of the ECJ or, at worst, that of the opinion of the Advocate General. The House of Lords held that recovery of tax was not governed exclusively by the 'unlawful demand principle' established in *Woolwich v IRC*[15] and that therefore a claim would lie where the payment had be made under a mistake. They also agreed that there had a sufficient mistake here though for divergent reasons.[16] The fundamental principles of restitution were also in issue. If it were to transpire that the UK law of restitution was not adequate to give the taxpayers a remedy they would presumably have a right to recover under EC law for breach of their treaty rights anyway.

The Revenue were, quite rightly, not confident of victory and so with effect from 8 September 2003, statute[17] disapplies s 32 of the Limitation Act 1980 from any taxation matter under the care and management of the Commissioners of Inland Revenue. Section 32 does still apply to litigation launched before 8 September. The limitation period for a sum paid under a mistake of fact is six years from the end of the company's accounting period.[18] The period runs from six years from the date of payment and not from the date the mistake was discovered; FA 2007, s 107 imposes this rule for actions brought before that date unless there is a House of Lords decision before 6 December 2006 or the action is part of a Group Litigation order. It remains to be seen whether this restriction will meet the requirement of EC law that the local (ie UK) remedy must be effective.

In *Deutsche Morgan Grenfell v IRC* the House of Lords has held that money paid under a mistake of law may be recovered in an action for restitution.[19] This was one of a stream of cases which have entered the lists; many stem from decisions of the European Court of Justice since these have given rise to decisions which were unexpected. Some might think that saying that the tax was paid under a "mistake" was a rather odd use of language, but it enables the court to hold that the taxpayer has a ground for a remedy in restitution without having to decide the big question whether the claimant needs to show a ground or can instead rely on some general overarching principle of unjust enrichment. In *Deutsche Morgan Grenfell* The House held that there was no special exemption for tax and it made no difference that the payments had been made under a settled understanding of the law (a matter very relevant to TMA 1970, s 33 but not here). The House held that sums were paid under a mistake because they had been paid in the belief that a group income election was not open to the taxpayers. That had only became clear when the ECJ gave its decision in the *Metalgesellschaft* case in 2001[20] and so the limitation period in only began to run as from that date. As seen above this limitation rule has now been changed.

The question of the relationship between a claim in restitution for recovery of a payment made under a mistake of law and the regime in TMA 1970, s 33 for error and mistake claims was not considerd in *Deutsche Morgan Grenfell*. It has however reached the Court of Appeal in *Monro v HMRC*.[21] The Court held that where a claim under TMA 1970, s 33 was barred by the defence in subs (3) – viz. that HMRC could rely on the fact that the payment was in accordance with the general practice prevailing at the time – there could be no claim in restitution either. This entirely sensible approach will, one hopes, be upheld on final appeal.

The principal articles on tax are considered at supra, §1.04. The articles on state aid are also relevant for some tax matters and are considered at supra, §1.03. Other articles of the treaty may also arise in tax disputes and recent case law has illustrated the importance of art 18 on the right of citizens to free movement and residence of persons who are not economically active.[22]

In proceedings brought by *Turpeinen*[23] the taxpayer (T) was domiciled in Finland where she worked. In 1998 she retired and moved to Belgium; a year later she settled permanently in Spain. Her Finnish pension paid in Finland was at first subject to progressive income tax at 28.5%. The Finnish tax office then tried to tax her as at 35% as she had not been domiciled in Finland for three consecutive years. This attempt failed not under art 39 (free movement of workers) – she was not a worker – but under art 18 (see para **1.18** et seq). Art 18 EC gave every citizen in the Union the right to move and reside freely within the territory of member states. The Finnish tax rules in question placed some of its nationals at a disadvantage simply because they had exercised that freedom (eg para 22); there was no justification (para 32 et seq).

---

[1] *Stoke-on Trent City Council v B and Q plc* [1991] 4 All ER 221 at 223. On forms of legislation see EC Treaty Art 249.
[2] *R (on the application of Professional Contractors Group Ltd) v IRC* [2001] EWCA Civ 1945, [2002] STC 165 at para 82.
[3] As in the famous *Factortame* case—*R v Secretary of State for Transport, ex p Factortame Ltd (No 2)* C-213/89 [1991] 1 AC 603, ECJ.

[1.02] Sources of tax law

4 As in *R v Customs and Excise Comrs, ex p Lunn Poly Ltd* [1998] STC 649 at 659–664 affirmed [1999] STC 350 CA.
5 (Case C-26/62) *van Gend en Loos v Nederlandse Tariefcomissie* [1963] ECR 1.
6 Edward and Lane *European Community Law*, 2nd edition, para 133.
7 See eg *Vodafone 2 v HMRC* [2009] EWCA Civ 446.
8 On Directives see EC Treaty Art 249. For a plausible but unsuccessful challenge to the Parent/Subsidiary Directive see (Case C-58/01) *Oce van der Grinten v IRC* [2003] STC 1248, paras 90–103.
9 The so-called 'vertical' direct effect of Directives allows the enforcement of rights against the member state but not against other citizens—Edward and Lane, loc. cit.
10 (Cases C 6/90, 9/90) *Francovich v Italy*, [1991] ECR I-5357. Edward and Lane, para 141. See also the cases cited at para 33 of the ECJ judgment in *Hoechst* cited below.
11 (Case C-91/92) *Faccini Dori v Recreb* [1994] ECR I–3325.
12 eg *Deutsche Morgan Grenfell v IRC and A-G* [2006] UKHL 49, [2007] STC 1 arising out of (Cases C-397/98 and C-410/98) *Metallgesellschaft Ltd and Hoechst AG v IRC ECJ Judgment*, 8 March 2001 [2001] STC 452 paras 77–96.
13 *Deutsche Morgan Grenfell Group plc v IRC and A-G* supra.
14 See supra, note10.
15 [1993] AC 70.
16 eg Virgo [2007] BTR 27.
17 FA 2004, s 320.
18 FA 1998, Sch 18, para 51(1)(c).
19 [2006] UKHL 49; [2007] STC 1; [2003] STC 1017. For comments see Virgo [2007] BTR 27; the house was able to clarify its remarks in *Kleinwort Benson v Lincoln City Council* [1999] 2 AC 349.
20 [2001] STC 452. See also, in relation to a claim for interest arising out of a claim for restitution, *Sempra Metals (formerly Metallgesellschaft) v IRC* [2004] STC 1178.
21 2007] EWHC 114 (Ch); [2007] STC 1182.
22 See also (Case C-76/05) (Case C-318/05) *Schwarz and another v Finanzamt Bergisch Gladbach EC Commission v Germany* [2008] STC 1357 on school fees and (Case C-104/06) *EC Comm v Sweden* [2008] STC 2546.
23 (Case C-520/04) [2008] STC 1.

State aid

[1.03] Articles 87–89 of the EC Treaty concern state aid; case law clearly establishes that tax provisions which are in substance state aid fall foul of these provisions and so are of no effect unless clearance has been obtained from the Commission under Article 88.[1] A relatively recent example arose when the UK Parliament increased the rate of insurance premium tax for certain types of insurance sold through travel agents without obtaining clearance from the Commission; the English court held that this differential taxation would distort competition and intra-community trade and so breached Article 87.[2] However, the fact that undertakings are treated differently does not of itself amount to state aid; to be unlawful it must favour one undertaking over its competitors.

EC law [1.04]

The state aid rules apply both to direct and indirect taxes. These rules differ from those rules about discrimination (see infra, §§ 1.03 ff) in one very important respect. A state aid can be approved by the Commission and so be saved from Article 87;[3] a discriminatory rule breaking the fundamental freedoms contained in Articles 39–58 cannot be saved from invalidity by any act of the Commission.

The first element of a state aid requiring notice to the Commission under Article 87 is that the aid is granted by a member state or through the resources of a member state. The second is that there should be a tax advantage; a tax disadvantage is not caught by the state aid rules. The problem of deciding whether a rule is advantageous or normal is a complex one requiring the court to look at the general tax system of the member state. For an advantage to be a state aid it must be an advantageous deviation from the general nature of the tax system; it follows that an advantage which emerges from the logic of the tax system itself is not an unlawful state aid.[4] Further, the prohibition is on state aid in certain situations or to certain taxpayers. There is no prohibition on a state giving aid generally—such as a tax relief available to all.[5] The distinctions are subtle. FA 2008 changes the limits for reliefs for venture capital trusts (VCT) Corporate Venturing Scheme (CVS) and for Enterprise Investment Schemes (EIS). EIS requires state aid approval but the others do not.[6]

The state aids issue has to be distinguished from the ongoing programme by member states to review all their rules in an effort to stamp out harmful tax competition. See further infra, § 1.11.

[1] On state aids there is a useful summary of law and Commission practice in OJ C 384 of 10 December 1998 and see EC Commission Report 9 February 2004, C(2004)131
[2] *R v Customs and Excise Comrs, ex p Lunn Poly Ltd* [1999] STC 350, CA; on implementation see Customs and Excise Business Brief, 31 March 1999, *Simon's Weekly Tax Intelligence* 1999, p 740.
[3] For analysis of state aids in general see Lasok *Law and Institutions of the European Union* (7th edn, Ch 30 (pp. 705–720)) and, in relation to tax law, Schoen [1999] CML Rev 911. See also Commission Report IP/03/1605, 26 November 2003, *Simon's Tax Weekly Intelligence* 2003, p. 2234.
[4] *R (on the application of Professional Contractors Group Ltd) v IRC* [2001] EWCA Civ 1945, [2002] STC 165.
[5] eg *Marks & Spencer plc v Halsey* [2003] STC (SCD) 70.
[6] Budget Technical Note BN16 12 March 2008

The Treaty Articles on tax

[1.04] Articles 90–93 of the Treaty concern tax. So Article 90 prohibits discrimination against imports from other member states through the levy of charges higher than those on domestic products. Article 91 prohibits refunds on exports exceeding the actual taxation imposed on the goods. The original Article 97 introduced a single tax on imports and uniform average rates of refund on exports and was repealed, its work done. Article 92 required the Commission to consider how the legislation of turnover taxes could be

[1.04] Sources of tax law

harmonised, a process which has given us the famous Sixth Directive which gave a common tax base to VAT throughout the Community. This was enacted in the UK as VATA 1983, now consolidated as VATA 1994. Directives under Article 92 require unanimity in the Council. This surrender of sovereignty in relation to turnover taxes does not extend to taxes which are not turnover taxes, eg insurance premium tax.[1]

Article 92 extends the principle of Article 91 to direct taxation and prohibits member states from operating systems of compensation for the effects of direct taxation on intra-Community trade. However, as with Article 87, this is subject to a right of derogation provided the government obtains authorisation, although this time the authorisation must come from the Council acting by a qualified majority on a proposal from the Commission.

Article 94 empowers the Council of the EC to issue Directives "for the approximation of such law, regulations or administrative provisions of the Member States as directly affect the establishment of functioning of the common market". It is on this basis that the Commission has tried to achieve harmonisation of company taxes. There is, however, nothing in this Article to force adherence against the wishes of a member state. Legislation under Article 94 requires unanimity in the Council.

Interestingly the Commission recently brought a case against the Council to determine whether a particular regulation on administrative cooperation was correctly passed under Articles 93 or under Article 9, both of which which require unanimity, or under Article 95, which allows qualified majority voting. The Court dismissed the Commissions' complaint holding that it was a 'fiscal' provision and so outside Article 95.[2]

[1] R v Customs and Excise Comrs, ex p Lunn Poly Ltd [1998] STC 649 at 664–666.
[2] (Case C-533/03) European Commission v EU Council [2006] SWTI 234.

Implementing EC legislation

[1.05] Most years see the passing of some UK legislation to implement Directives, eg the duty to provide information about liabilities to tax in another member state.[1] The Single Market programme provided its own impetus leading to the Ruding Committee's 1992 report on the distortions caused by different tax systems, the extent to which those could be removed by market forces and the desirability of legislation towards harmonisation should those forces not be enough.[2] The Commission has an ongoing review of cross border company tax obstacles.[3] Two 1990 Directives were approved in 1992—the Parent-Subsidiary Directive (see infra, § **27.05**) and the Mergers Directive (infra § **25.51**) being designed to grant to cross-border transactions the same favourable treatment (usually a deferral of liability) as is provided for equivalent purely domestic transactions. The UK provided the appropriate implementing legislation but the Revenue conceded that the Directives would probably have had direct effect anyway.[4] Proposals for improving both these Directives were made in 2003 and the amending Directives have now been implemented. The first Directive on the Taxation of Savings Income in the form of Interest Payments came into effect on 1 January 2005 subject to transitional arrangements in some countries.[5] The Commission must report on the operation of the Directive to the Council on a regular three year cycle. The Directive for a common system of taxation for interest and royalty payments between associated companies of different member states; this came into effect on 1 January 2004. These two Directives were announced as part of a package to curb harmful tax competition; the third element in that package was a Code of Conduct for Business Taxation.[6] The Royalty Directive has already been amended.[7]

There is a quite distinct multilateral convention on transfer pricing which the UK has ratified and a council regulation on administrative co-operation in the field of indirect taxation.[8] 2006 saw a Council Resolution setting up a code of conduct on transfer pricing documentation; this has been followed by a Communication by the Commission.[9] A Directive on mutual assistance in direct tax matters has been in force since 1977.[10] Mutual enforcement was applied to indirect taxes, duties and certain levies in 1976;[11] this has now been extended to direct taxes as from the passing of FAs 2002 and 2004.[12] Co-operation to counter VAT fraud was strengthened by a new regulation in 2003.[13]

Ever closer co-operation within the European Single Market is undermining many traditional assumptions and techniques of international tax; the UK is developing a half-way house between international tax and domestic tax to cope with the EC. Among suggestions are proposals for the consolidation of cross-border losses although this was withdrawn in December 2003, presumably to await the outcome of the ECJ's decision in the *Marks and Spencer* case.[14] The Commission has also issued guidance to member states explaining how their tax rules should apply to foreign dividends in the light of other ECJ decisions though this area has since been the subject of more decisions.[15] Subjects of recent work by the Commission include transfer pricing, thin capitalisation and headquarters costs. The Commission has worked on the co-ordination of tax treaties. It is recognised[16] that the Commission should not interfere in what are essentially bilateral negotiations but there is thought to be a role for the Commission in looking at matters such as limitation-of-benefit clauses.[17]

At the moment the most significant work is that being done to achieve a consolidated common corporate tax base. A major staff working paper "Company Taxation in the Internal Market" was published in October 2001 and much work has been done since.[18] It is quite possible that a common base will be agreed and operated by a number of the states under the enhanced cooperation rules in EU Treaty, Art 27A, and with the UK remaining resolutely outside.

The Commission also intends to be more proactive and targeted in initiating legal action against member states whose tax measures infringe community law—in the Commission's view.

Among the many sources of primary EC tax law material particular mention should be made of the annual volumes selected and edited by Professor Kees van Raad for the International Tax Centre, Leiden.

Simon's Taxes A1.107, A2.1302.

[1.05] Sources of tax law

[1] FA 1990, s 125.
[2] See generally Gammie, *The Ruding Committee: an initial response* IFS Commentary 30.
[3] eg IP/03/1/593, *Simon's Weekly Tax Intelligence* 2003, p. 2231.
[4] C Direct Tax Measures, A Consultative Document, December 1991, para 2.13.
[5] IP/03/1214 *Simon's Weekly Tax Intelligence* 2003, p 1603 and IP/03/1418 *Simon's Weekly Tax Intelligence* 2003, p 1859. Directive 2003/48/EC; the transitional and review requirements are in articles 17 and 18. The UK legislation was enacted in FA 2004, ss 97–106, enacting the EU Interest and Royalties Directive (Council Directive 2003/49/EC) of 3 June 2003 and is considered at infra, § **11.13**.
[6] IP/03/787, *Simon's Weekly Tax Intelligence* 2003, p. 1057.
[7] IP/04/105, *Simon's Weekly Tax Intelligence* 2004, p. 266.
[8] *Simon's Tax Intelligence* 1992, p 161.
[9] 20 June 2006, 9738/06. On Communication see COM(2007) 71.
[10] EC Council Directive 77/799; for a rare case see (Case C-420/98) *W N v Staatssecretaris van Financiën* [2001] STC 974.
[11] EC Council Directive 76/308; implemented in UK by FA 1977, s 11.
[12] EC Council Directive 2001/44 amending the 1976 Directive; implemented in UK by FA 2002, s 134 and F(No 2)A 2005, s 68: see infra, § **34.01** & **34.08**.
[13] IP/03/1350, *Simon's Weekly Tax Intelligence* 2003, p. 1799.
[14] COM/90/595; see comments by CFE 22 April 1992, *Simon's Tax Intelligence* 1992, p 490.
[15] IP/03/1350, *Simon's Weekly Tax Intelligence* 2004, p. 1220.
[16] IP/04/25, *Simon's Weekly Tax Intelligence* 2004, p. 122.
[17] *Simon's Tax Intelligence* 1993, p 350.
[18] COM (2001) 582, published 23 October 2001. COM (2003) 726 European Tax Survey SEC 2004, 1128/2 and Report of CEPS Task Force Brussels, November 2005.

Non-discrimination principles of EC law

[1.06] The principle of non-discrimination is at the heart of the European Treaty and the law, including case law, which has followed from it. As seen in supra, § **1.02**, although income tax law has not been harmonised, the tax laws of the member states must not infringe this principle. EC law, in the tax context, is usually concerned with discrimination on the grounds of residence, sometimes on grounds of nationality and occasionally on grounds of sex. When passages in EC directives talk about non-residents they are actually concerned only with nationals of the EC; discrimination against citizens of or companies resident in countries outside the EC is not usually governed by EC law.[1] A report for the European Parliament published in March 2008 and dealing with material down to December 2007 not only assesses the court judgments in this area but tries to assess how far the members states have amended their laws in response to the court's decisions.[2] There has been much new writing in this area.[3]

As AG Leger has put it in the recent case of *Cadbury Schweppes v IRC*[4] the ways in which restrictions on the exercise of treaty rights have been struck down have taken different forms. There may be overt discrimination on the basis of nationality or, in the case of a company, its seat. They can also take the form of 'indirect discrimination', namely measures which apply irrespective of the company's seat and are based on conditions which apply without distinction which result essentially in placing nationals from other member states at a disadvantage, such as the criterion of fiscal residence. Finally, in its more recent case law, the Court does not inquire into whether the measure in question is to be classified as direct or indirect discrimination. It merely states that there is a difference in tax treatment which creates a disadvantage for economic operators who have exercised the rights conferred by Article 43 EC and could deter them from exercising such rights. Following the "new approach" (infra, § **1.07**) of which *Cadbury Schweppes* is one example, courts are now again talking of indirect discrimination.[5]

In paying heed to the effects of such restrictions the Court was ensuring that tax law was treated the same as other areas of law under its jurisdiction where discrimination issues arose. The law thus went through a stage of development and enlargement which may have been appropriate to the free movement of goods or services but which simply opened up opportunities for advisers and their clients to claim back years of tax.

The result was a series of cases in which member states were held to have broken EC law in ways they could not necessarily have predicted and so were obliged to repay very large sums of money for claims going back over many years often to the surprise of the client and the delight of the adviser.[6] In turn the member states gave serious attention to the idea of removing direct tax from the jurisdiction of the court, a change to the treaty which would have required unanimity. One might have thought that a simpler solution would have been to change the treaty so that court decisions in direct tax cases were only prospective. The court has been toying with the circumstances in which its decisions would be prospective but the idea has not yet been applied in any case.[7]

The Court was all too aware of the criticisms and in 2005, following the departure of one or two particular judges, set about creating a new approach (infra, § **1.07**). One price paid for the new approach is that tax is no longer necessarily treated quite the same way as other areas of law. There is move back from the restriction approach to something resembling the older discrimination. There is a greater awareness of the need to maintain a balanced allocation of taxing rights between states and a development of justifications for restrictive rules on the basis of countering 'abuse'. It is a nice question how far 2005 marks a retreat and how it is better seen a watershed. None of the old cases has been overruled. What has happened is that more extreme ideas have been rejected (see, eg *Re D*, infra, § **1.07**).

Many of the cases which follow involve a reference by a national court to the ECJ for an opinion under what is now Article 234. Only a court can make such a reference; the Special Commissioners are a court for this purpose.[8]

The principle of non-discrimination is embodied for tax purposes in four freedoms—the free cross-border movement of employees (Article 39), freedom of establishment for businesses (Article 43, extended to companies by Article 48), freedom to provide services (Article 49), and free movement of capital

[1.06] Sources of tax law

(Article 56). Recent case law has shown a significant increase in the cases brought under Art 56 and the willingness of the Court to give that provision just as much scope as its companions, but only when it applies (infra, § **1.11**).

Tax provisions which break, or may break, these provisions may be challenged by court action; they are also the subject of complaint to and investigation by the Commission. In assessing breaches of the non-discrimination principle the court looks first to see whether there is in fact and law any difference of treatment and then invites the member state to justify that difference on objective grounds. Where the discrimination is overtly on the basis of nationality, justification must be sought within the terms of the treaty itself; Article 46 states that discrimination may be allowable if it is justified on grounds of public order, public safety and public health. In the tax context this formal position has been repeated in *Royal Bank of Scotland v Greece*.[9] Where the discrimination is covert, eg because the rule is framed in terms of residence rather than nationality, the court looks to wider grounds of justification, including the need to protect the cohesion of the tax system in issue and the effectiveness of fiscal supervision. However the court's willingness to find new justifications does not mean that it will approve national rules. The court has insisted on the principle of proportionality and in particular that the means adopted by the member state to achieve the permitted goal are the least restrictive available. In practice the court has looked at these wider grounds of justification in cases involving direct discrimination but has avoided open conflict with the formal view by avoiding ruling on whether the national rule is discriminatory. The unsatisfactory nature of the position has been pointed out by Advocate General Jacobs who has invited the court to reconsider the matter in his opinion in *Danner Case C-136/00*.[10] Sadly, this invitation was declined.[11]

The UK Parliament may pass pre-emptive corrective legislation and it is now a routine feature of Finance Bills. Some older examples will show the width of these corrections. The 1995 legislation extending the benefits of share schemes to part-time employees[12] and of TESSAs to relevant European institutions should be seen as moves to head off investigation by the Commission.[13] In 1992 the Commissioner in charge of taxation indicated that the restriction of the qualifying maintenance deduction to orders made by UK courts might infringe Community law;[14] amending legislation was passed.[15] In 2009 a change is made to inheritance tax extending certain rules on agricultural property and woodlands to land in any EEA state.[16]

Simon's Taxes A1.107, A2.102.

[1] See (Case C-264/96) *ICI v Colmer* [1998] All ER EC 585, [1998] STC 874.
[2] The Impact of the Rulings of European Court of Justice in the Area of Direct Taxation (Lead author Malherbe). Policy Department Economic and Scientific Policy PE404.888.
[3] Kingston (2007) 44 Common Market Law Review 1321 and Sir Andrew Park, [2006] *British Tax Review* 322-344. See also Vanistedael (ed), *EU Freedoms and Taxation* EATLP International Tax Series Vol 2 (IBFD 2006); Schoen (ed) *Tax Competition in Europe* EATLP IBFD; Ghosh, *Principles of the Internal Market and Direct Taxation*, Key Haven 2007 and Weber, *The Influence of European Law on Direct Taxation*, Kluwer 2007.

4   (Case C-196/04) [2004] 3 CMLR 325, [2005] SWTI 1496, at para 63.
5   Eg (Case C385/05) *Talotta v Belgium* [2008] STC 3261.
6   Notably in *Bosal Holding BV v Staatssecretaris van Financiën* [2003] STC 1483, ECJ Case C-168/01. In *Banco Popolare di Cremona* ECJ Case C-475/03, the amounts were almost astronomical but the court managed to held there had been no breach of EC law.
7   On possible principles see the opinion of Advocates General in *Banco Popolare di Cremona* Case C-475/03
8   In *Re Schmid* [2002] ECR I-4573, Case C-516/99 an appeal chamber of a regional finance authority was held not to be a court: see especially paras 34 and following.
9   [2000] STC 733 Case C-311/97 at para 32; see also *Ciola v Land Vorarlberg* [1999] ECR I-2517, Case C-224/97 at para 16.
10 Case C-136/00; opinion delivered 21 March 2002.
11 [2002] STC 1283.
12 FA 1995, s 137.
13 TA 1988, s 326A as amended by FA 1995, s 63.
14 OJ 92/C89, 9 April 1992, *Simon's Tax Intelligence* 1992, p 479.
15 F(No 2)A 1992, s 61.
16 Bill Clause 121.

The 'new approach'

[1.07] As suggested above recent decisions of the Court, often sitting as a Grand Chamber of 13, have been seen by some as marking a new realism on the part of the court. It is true that they show a greater willingness to analyse tax rules in their context and to undertake a deeper exercise when considering justifications for rules which at first sight break EC principles. How far this is a new approach is matter of much debate; what is clear is that there is a new and more cautious use of language. There are fewer extravagant broad sweeps of principle. The court has come to accept the need for a "balanced allocation of taxing powers" between the member states. It has meant a softening of the test under which a restriction would be struck down as discriminatory if it made trans-border operations less attractive.[1] It has been accompanied by a recognition that a state has a legitimate interest in protecting its tax base from 'wholly artificial' arrangements entered into to avoid tax.

The new approach begins in 2005 with the case of D[2] and concerns the scope of relieving provisions in a double tax treaty. A German taxpayer (D) had land in the Netherlands; the land represented 10% of his assets, the rest being in Germany where he was resident. Germany (G) had no wealth tax but the Netherlands (N) did. N taxed those resident in N on their world wide wealth and gave various allowances. N taxed non-residents, like D, on their wealth in N but gave allowances only if 90% of the assets were in N.

The court first considered whether this was a breach of free movement of capital. It concluded that while the rules clearly had a restrictive effect, D could not complain since he had too few assets in N to be comparable to a resident (paras 36, 38).

The court then considered whether D could invoke the treaty between N and Belgium (B). B did not have a wealth tax either but the treaty would have given a Belgian resident a right to the allowance in N. The court said the appropriate comparison for D was not with a resident of N but with another non-resident (paras 53–58). Thus the court does not take the restriction approach but goes back to discrimination. The approach of the court was to regard a Double Tax Convention as representing an allocation of taxing power, giving an overall balance based on reciprocal rights and obligations. The court also cites older case law as recognising that member states were free to determine the connecting factors for the purpose of allocating powers of taxation and that differences in tax treatment between nationals of two member states resulting from that allocation is not discrimination (paras 53 and 61).[3]

The second major case was the *Marks and Spencer* case on group loss relief (infra, § 1.09) and the third was *Cadbury Schweppes* on CFCs (infra, § 1.10). Other recent cases on dividends and thin capitalisation are considered at infra, § 1.19.

[1] The test stemmed from Case C–55 /94 *Gebhard* [1996] ECR I–1416, para 37 extended to tax in (Case C–234/01) *Gerritse v Finanzamt Neukolln-Nord* [2003] ECR I-5933. Doubts can be traced to the opinion of Adv General Tizzano Case C–442/02 *Caixa-Bank v Ministère de l'Économie, des Finances and de l'industrie* [2004] ECR I-8961.
[2] (Case C-376/03) *D v Inspecteur van de Belastingdiens buitenland te Heerlen* [2005] STC 1211. On treaties see also the pioneering work of Hinnekens, EC Tax Law Review 1994, pp 146–166.
[3] Citing (Case C-336/96) *Gilly v Directeur des Services Fiscaux du Bas-Rhin* [1998] STC 1014 and (Case C-307/97) *Compagnie de Saint-Gobain, Zweigniederlassung Deutschland v Finanzamt Aachen-Innenstadt* [1999] ECR I-6161, [2000] STC 854.

The non-discrimination case law of the ECJ in tax matters

[1.08] It is time to look at the older, but still relevant, case law of the ECJ.[1] We take two cases – one on Article 43, freedom of establishment, and one on Article 39, free movement of workers. Workers means "employed". The self-employed may not use Article 39 and so must Article 43. Freedom of establishment entails the freedom to carry on an economic activity on an on-going basis, and not just a letter box activity.[2] In the *French Tax Credits* case[3] an Italian insurance company had set up a branch in France. The branch received dividend income from French sources. Under French tax law, companies could reclaim the tax credit accompanying the dividend from the French revenue; however, repayment was withheld if the company was not resident in France. The refusal was held to break what is now Article 43. Even if the disadvantage to the Italian company under the present rule was compensated for by other advantages, those could not justify this breach of the duty under Article 43, which was to accord foreign companies the same treatment as was accorded to French companies. The extent of the disadvantage could not be in issue since Article 43 prohibits all discrimination, even if only of a limited nature. Moreover, the fact that the Italian company could have got the benefit of the credit if it had established a French subsidiary (rather than a branch) was irrelevant since this interfered with the freedom to trade in another member state in a vehicle of its own choice—whether branch or subsidiary. The court's insistence that a subsidiary and a branch must be treated alike is at the root of much of the, at that time, quite surprising, decisions which have followed. Although this text used to say that only the reversal of the French tax credits case would enable the national governments to recover the ground they had lost there are signs that, as suggested above at 1.07 the court is now paying closer attention to the arguments put forward by member states to justify tax rules which breach these principles.

Article 39 guarantees freedom of movement for workers and bans any discrimination based on nationality between workers of the member states as regards employment remuneration, and other conditions of work and employment. The article has been extended by case law to ban covert forms of discrimination which, by the application of criteria of differentiation other than nationality, lead to the same result. In *Biehl v Administration des Contributions du Grand-Duche de Luxembourg*[4] a provision of the Luxembourg tax code denying a PAYE repayment to persons ceasing to be resident was struck down because it worked against taxpayers who were nationals of other states.[5] This was so even though there was an administrative procedure which gave much the same result—an administrative discretion was no substitute for rights.

Simon's Taxes A1.107, A2.102.

[1] See Lyons [1994] BTR 554–571 and Stanley [1997] CMLR 713.
[2] See eg cases below at 1.13 (abuse of rights), 1.15 (CFC) and 1.19 (thin cap).
[3] (270/83) *EC Commission v French Republic* [1986] ECR 273, ECJ. For a recent example see Case 231/05 Oy AA R. Older cases include (Case C-118/96) *Safir v Sfattemyndigheten i Dalarnas Län* [1998] STC 1043 and (Case C-311/97) *Royal Bank of Scotland v Greece* [2000] STC 733.
[4] (Case C-175/88) [1991] STC 575, ECJ. The principle of equal treatment with regard to remuneration would be rendered ineffective if it could be undermined by discriminatory national provisions on income tax; hence Regulation 1612/68, art 7.
[5] (C-175/88) [1991] STC 575, ECJ, paras 11–14.

Cross-frontier workers: employed (Article 39) and self-employed (Article 43)

[1.09] Much of the case law under these articles has been concerned with the problem of cross-frontier workers—where X, a person resident in A, is employed in B. Country B will usually tax non-residents on a basis less favourable than its own residents refusing, for example, to grant X any personal allowances or deductions for pension contributions or favourable family taxation under an aggregation or quotient system, leaving all those deductions and adjustments to A, the country of residence. B's attitude, while conforming to established international tax norms, may have unfortunate effects if X has no income other than that arising in B. If, as is common in continental Europe, A does not tax foreign income at all, X will have a tax liability in B but not in A while getting deductions in A but not in B. The problem is that while the ECJ agrees that B may tax non-residents differently from residents, the effect is sometimes to deprive X of the economic value of

[1.09] Sources of tax law

the right to work across the border. One solution is to define those circumstances in which the economic disadvantage to X is so severe as to amount to a breach of Article 39. However, the cases put the matter the other way round—given that state B is not taxing this worker in the same way as its residents, can B justify the different treatment on objective differences taking full account of EC doctrines such as proportionality. The difference is that under the second approach the rule will be struck down whenever it is unjustified, not when the problem is severe—the difference is shown in the *Asscher* case.[1]

Deductions and Aggregation: In *Finanzamt Köln-Altstadt v Schumacker*[2] Germany (country B in the above illustration) was compelled to grant a taxpayer (X in the above example) both aggregation of spousal income and relief for certain losses and for certain insurance payments (old-age sickness and invalidity) where the taxpayer derived his income entirely or almost entirely from Germany, although he was resident in (and a national of) Belgium. Germany could not justify the difference simply on the basis of non-residence. In the analogous case of *Wielockx v Inspecteur der Directe Belastingen*[3] the court compelled Germany to grant a self-employed person who was working in Germany but resident in Belgium the benefit of Germany's rules permitting deduction of a pension contribution; the precise percentage of income earned in Germany is not clear but was probably more than 90%.

Rates: This broad approach was followed in *Asscher v Staatssecretaris*[4] where the issue concerned not the availability of deductions but the rate of tax. If X had been resident in B or if 90% of X's income had been taxable in B, the rate would have been the normal progressive rate (13%); instead it was a flat rate of 25%. The court held that X was entitled to the lower rate in B. Two points were underlined. First, although residents and non-residents could be taxed differently the fact that the income earned in B, while not taxed in A, was taken into account in determining total income for progression in A made it reasonable for X to be able to use the progressive rate scale in B. Second, the fact that the 13% rate would have applied under B's law if X had paid social security contributions, so making the 13% rate compensation for paying those contributions, was not sufficient to justify the difference.

Later cases have continued this line of thinking. *Zurstrassen v Administration des Contributions Directes*[5] is a major case only in that a full panel was convened to hear it; the decision does not come as a surprise. Under Luxembourg tax law, spouses who were living together were only entitled to be assessed jointly if they were resident in Luxembourg. The taxpayer, Z, and his wife were Belgian nationals. Although he resided in Luxembourg, where he worked during the week, his wife and their children resided in Belgium. Weekends were spent together in Belgium. 98% of the household income derived from Z's earned income in Luxembourg, whilst the remaining 2% was derived from his teaching in Belgium. On this basis the Luxembourg rule denying him the benefit of joint assessment was held to conflict with EC Treaty Article 39(2) (formerly Article 48(2)) and also with Article 7(2) of EC Council Regulation 1612/68 of 15 October 1968.

Zurtsrassen shows that member states which grant tax reliefs on the basis of residence must also make provision for cross border workers. In *Gschwind v*

Finanzamt Aachen-Außenstadt[6] the court found that the German provisions for cross border workers were sufficient and justifiable and so refused to interfere to allow a person who was resident in the Netherlands but worked in Germany to use the EC treaty to gain German tax benefits when that person's German income tax circumstances fell short of the threshhold set in the German legislation. That threshold had two alternatives; (1) that not less than 90% of the worldwide income was taxable in Germany, or (2) that the income received abroad and not taxable in Germany was less than 24,000DM.

The essentially – but necessarily – negative nature of the court's jurisdiction in these cases is well brought out in *FWL de Groot v Staatssecretaris van Financiën*.[7] This outlawed a particular form of the system of exemption with progression but declined to say what specific requirements a government could take into account.

A recent case, much cited in the new approach, is *Schempp v Finanzamt München V*;[8] here a German national sought to deduct maintenance payments made to his former wife now resident in Austria. He would have been so entitled if she had still been resident in Germany or in any other country where the payment was subject to tax. The court first agreed with the taxpayer by holding that this was not a purely internal German tax law matter (para 25). However, they then held that there was no relevant discrimination under Article 12 of the EC Treaty since the taxpayer's case rested on the wrong comparisons (para 35). They also dismissed the taxpayer's argument based on EC Treaty Article 18 on free movement of persons since the German rule did not interfere with *his* right to move (paras 44–46).

1 (Case C-107/94) *Asscher v Staatssecretaris van Financiën* [1996] STC 1025.
2 (C-279/93) [1995] STC 306, ECJ.
3 (Case C-80/94) [1995] STC 876.
4 (Case C-107/94) [1996] STC 1025. See Stanley [1997] CMLR 713–725; Lyons [1996] BTR 641.
5 (Case C-87/99) [2001] STC 1102.
6 (Case C-391/97) [2001] STC 331.
7 (Case C-385/00) [2002] ECR I-11819, esp at paras 108–115.
8 (Case C-403/03) [2005] STC 1792.

Business Articles 43, 48 and 49

[1.10] Article 43 of the Treaty of Rome guarantees freedom of establishment and expressly bans restrictions on the setting up of agencies, branches or subsidiaries by nationals of any member state in the territory of any other member state. This is extended to companies and firms by Article 48. Article 49 provides freedom for persons to provide services in other member states. Like the other articles, Article 43 has been interpreted broadly so as to ban not only overt discrimination by reason of nationality or, in the case of a company, its seat, but all covert forms of discrimination which by the application of other criteria of differentiation lead to the same result.[1] Its wide scope has already been seen in the *French Tax Credits* case. The taxpayer also won in *R v IRC, ex p Commerzbank AG*.[2] Here a German bank with a UK branch had successfully argued that it was entitled to exemption from UK tax on interest

[1.10] Sources of tax law

received from US corporations;[3] its claim to repayment supplement was successful even though the UK domestic legislation clearly did not allow repayment supplement to a non-resident. The UK had argued that it was entitled to withhold the repayment supplement since *Commerzbank*, unlike resident companies, was exempt on the income originally in issue. This was swept aside. "The argument cannot be upheld. The fact that the exemption in question was available only to non-resident companies cannot justify a rule of a general nature withholding the benefit. That rule is therefore discriminatory."[4] In *Halliburton Services BV v Staatssecretaris van Financiën*,[5] the court required an exemption from a Dutch transaction tax which was given to a corporate reorganisation involving two Dutch companies to be given where the transfer of property involved a Dutch and a German company.

The same trends could be seen in the court's decision in *ICI plc v Colmer*.[6] The case concerned the UK rule that consortium relief for losses, now in TA 1988, ss 402 and 413, could be claimed only where the holding company's 90% subsidiary trading companies were also companies resident in the UK. The challenge was made under Article 43. The main point made by the court was that the restriction was not justifiable under EC law as it stood. The restriction to UK resident companies was an obvious breach of Article 43 and therefore would have to be struck down unless the UK could justify it. The UK could not justify it. In response FA 2000, s 97 contains rules extending consortium and group relief to all non-resident companies while s 75 contains rules regulating the way in which capital allowances for machinery and plant are given to non-residents.

In the *Saint-Gobain*[7] case the German branch of a French company sought to take advantage of certain clauses in treaties made by Germany with other states (ie not France). The court held that the French branch was entitled to do so. While the language is typically expansive the issue only arose because of a provision of German domestic tax law which gave relief by reference to the treaties. Despite this narrow point the UK legislature took it as its cue to extend various double taxation reliefs to UK branches of foreign companies.[8] This broad UK response was most probably justified since the court's whole sense of mission is to act broadly. In *Sempra Metals v IRC* (which was formerly known as *Metallgesellschaft Ltd and Hoechst AG v IRC*),[9] the ECJ continued in its *French Tax Credits* mode. On a reference by the High Court, the ECJ looked at the rule which then allowed the UK subsidiary of a company resident in the UK to pass a dividend to its parent without having to pay advance corporation tax (ACT). The court noted that this conferred a cash flow advantage. The case concerned a UK resident subsidiary of a non-UK parent, which successfully argued that it was contrary to EC law for the UK to withhold the same cash flow advantage in these circumstances. The UK legislation has already removed this problem by abolishing ACT as from 1 April 1999 (infra, § **26.16**) but there are other issues awaiting resolution. In the meantime one must just note yet again the court's insistence on asserting the principles of community law over the subtle refinements of domestic systems.

One of those issues arose in *Pirelli Cable Holdings NV v IRC*.[10] Here the UK resident companies had paid ACT but now sought compensation or restitution in the form of interest for the period between the repayment of ACT and its set off against mainstream corporation tax or, if no mainstream ACT liability had arisen, compensation equal to that unused sum. Under the dividend article of the relevant tax treaty the non-resident shareholder companies were entitled to a tax credit on the dividends paid by their UK subsidiary; they were liable to UK tax on the aggregate of the tax credit and the dividend and to the payment by the Revenue for any of the excess of the credit. Could these payments be treated as relevant "countervailing advantages" which could be used to offset the claims brought by the UK resident companies? The Court of Appeal upheld the judgment of Park J,[11] who rejected the Revenue arguments. The relevant treaty payments by the Revenue were due whether or not there was a group income election. The House of Lords dismissed the Revenue appeal and remitted the case to the Commissioners to decide the crucial question of fact which was whether the companies would have made the group income election.[12] The company has made further but so far unsuccessful appeals.[13]

Other cases posed very considerable threats to the international tax order as previously understood. Moreover, the steps to which member state are put to correct any breaches may themselves be bad. In the *Bosal* case,[14] a Dutch finance subsidiary company sought to deduct interest on a loan incurred by a parent to finance a subsidiary in another member states. The Dutch government refused this on the ground that Dutch law only gave an interest deduction where the company in question was subject to Dutch corporation tax. The Court treated this as a breach of Article 43. *Lankhorst-Hohorst*[15] mentioned infra, at § **1.13** was even more distressing for traditionalists. A Dutch parent had a German subsidiary. The German subsidiary had a loan from an independent third party at commercial rates of interest and was in some difficulty, so the Dutch parent made it a softer loan so that it could pay off the third party. The interest from the German company to the Dutch parent was recharacterised as dividend (under "thin capitalisation" rules). The Commission argued that this was contrary to EC law because the interest payment would be taxed twice through being recharacterised as dividend. The ECJ held that the difference in treatment arose because of the Dutch residence of the parent company and that this could not be justified on any of the usual grounds. As the Dutch rule was not aimed at artificial arrangements the argument that the rule was a necessary anti-avoidance measure failed. The case failed on the cohesion ground because while there was a disadvantage there was no offsetting advantage anywhere. A considerable number of companies in the UK are potentially affected by the ECJ decision in *Lankhorst-Hohorst*. On 30 July 2003, a Group Litigation Order was made in the High Court to hear claims which seem to challenge the UK capitalisation provisions on the basis of the ECJ decision. The slightly surprising outcome of the litigation is reported infra, at § **1.13**.[16]

Other examples continue to flow. In *Gerritse v Finanzamt Neukolln-Nord*, a provision of the German tax code imposing a flat rate tax on visiting entertainers and sportsmen was held to break Article 43.[17] In the *Skandia* case a Swedish rule allowing a particular form of tax relief for payments to a retirement insurance policy only if the company were resident in Sweden was held to break Article 49 because there were circumstances in which the overall effect was less favourable.[18] In *Hughes de Lasteyrie du Saillant* a French rule directing a deemed disposal of assets for capital gains purposes when there

[1.10] Sources of tax law

was change of residence was held to break Article 43 when the move was to another EC member state.[19] Reconciling this decision with that in the Daily Mail Trust case is interesting.[20]

The issue of succession duty rights for an EC national who had moved his residence, the equivalent of the UK deemed domicile rules, was held not to break EU law in the *Barbier* case.[21] Finally there is the *Lindman* case where the court held that Finland could not tax a Finnish resident on winnings from a Swedish lottery ticket when winnings from a Finnish lottery ticket would not be taxable.[22]

Other recent cases include CLT-UFA SA where the court looked at the German tax on profits of the German branch of a foreign company. The point of particular interest is that the court compared the burden of that tax with that on the distributed profits of German company.[23]

---

1   Judgment of the European Court in *Commerzbank* para 4, citing (Case 152/73) *Sotgiu v Deutsche Bundespost* [1974] ECR 153 at para 11. (Case C-30/91) *R v IRC, ex p Commerzbank AG* [1993] STC 605, ECJ, at 621 (para 14).
2   [1993] STC 605, ECJ. For subsequent action see *Simon's Tax Intelligence* 1993, pp 1091, 1264.
3   *IRC v Commerzbank AG* [1990] STC 285.
4   (C-330/91) [1993] STC 605 at 622, ECJ. The right to repayment supplement was extended to individuals resident in another member state, by concession: Extra-statutory concession A82: the concession applies also to partnerships, the trustees of a settlement and personal representatives.
5   (Case C-1/93) [1994] STC 655.
6   Case C-264/96 [1998] All ER (EC) 585, [1998] STC 874. For the subsequent decision of the House of Lords see [1999] STC 1089.
7   (Case C-307/97) *Compagnie de Saint-Gobain, Zweigniederlassung Deutschland v Finanzamt Aachen-Innenstadt* [2000] STC 854.
8   FA 2000, s 104 and see infra, § **37.04** ff.
9   (Cases C-397/98 and C-410/98) ECJ Judgment, 8 March 2001 [2001] STC 452. The ECJ judgment was incorporated into the judgment of the Court of Appeal, with the case re-named *Sempra Metals Ltd v IRC* [2005] EWCA Civ 389, [2005] STC 687.
10 [2003] EWCA Civ 1849, [2004] STC 130.
11 [2003] EWHC 32 (Ch), [2003] STC 250.
12 [2006] UKHL 4, [2006] STC 548.
13 *Pirelli Cable Holding NV and others v Revenue and Customs Commissioners (No 2)* [2008] EWCA Civ 70, [2008] STC 508 upholding Rimer J [2007] EWHC 583 (Ch), [2008] STC 144.
14 (Case C-168/01) *Bosal Holding BV v Staatsecretaris van Financien* [2003] STC 1483, ECJ, ECJ.
15 (Case C 324/00) *Lankhorst – Hohorst Gmbh v Finanzamt Steinfurt* [2003] STC 607.
16 (Cse C-364/1) *Barbier's Heirs v Inspecteur van de Belastingdienst Particulieren/Ondernemingen Buitenland te Heerlen* [2004] 1 CMLR 1283; (Case C-5103) *van Hilten-van der Heijden v Inspecteur van de Belastingdienst/Particulieren/Ondernemingen buitenland te Heerlen* [2006] All ER (D) 349 (Feb).

[17] (Case C-234/01) *Gerritse v Finanzamt Neukolln-Nord* [2003] ECR I-5933.
[18] (Case C-422/01) *Forsakringsaktebolaget Skandia (publ) v Riksskatteverket* [2003] STC 1361.
[19] (Case C-9/2) *De Lasteyrie du Saillant v Ministere de l'Economie, des Finances et de l'Industrie* [2004] SWTI 890.
[20] *R v HM Treasury ex parte Daily Mail and General Trust plc* [1988] STC 787; see Airs *Tax Journal* Issue 852, 11 September 2006, pp. 9–11.
[21] (Cse C-364/1) *Barbier's Heirs v Inspecteur van de Belastingdienst Particulieren/Ondernemingen Buitenland te Heerlen* [2004] 1 CMLR 1283; (Case C-5103) *van Hilten-van der Heijden v Inspecteur van de Belastingdienst/Particulieren/Ondernemingen buitenland te Heerlen* [2006] All ER (D) 349 (Feb).
[22] (Case C–42/02) *Lindman v Skatterattelsnamnden* [2005] STC 873, [2004] 1 CMLR 1220.
[23] C–253/03 [2007] STC 1303.

Cases on Treaty of Rome Article 56: Freedom of movement of capital

[1.11] EC rules on freedom of movement of capital were at first rudimentary as compared with the other three freedoms. This changed with the adoption of the 1988 Directive requiring full liberalisation by 1 July 1990. This change was accelerated by the Treaty of Maastricht which came into force on 1 January 1994 and which assimilated the rules on movement of capital and those on movement of payments as well as making other major changes.[1] The current rules are in Articles 56 et seq. Minor changes will be made by the Treaty of Lisbon when it is ratified. A very recent example is *Européenne et Luxembourgeoise d'investissments SA (ELISA) v Directeur général des impôts and Another* (Case C-451/05). French law levied an annual tax on the commercial value of property held in France by "legal persons". Those resident in France were exempt in certain circumstances. A Luxembourg holding company persuaded the ECJ that it too was entitled to the exemption. Under the French rule a non-resident company was only exempt if there was a convention between France and the non-resident's state. The conditions for exemption thus made investment in immovable property in France less attractive for non-resident companies and therefore constituted a restriction on the free movement of capital that was in principle prohibited by Article 56 EC unless it was justified.

These articles have given the courts some problems. First Article 56, unlike its neighbours, protects not only the free movement of capital not only between member states but also, subject to a condition, that between member states and third countries. The condition, also known as the grandfathering or standstill rule and found in Article 57, relates to restrictions existing on 31 December 1993; these old rules cannot be attacked under Article 56 by third countries.[2] Next Article 58 directed that Article 56 was without prejudice to the rights of member states to apply provisions of their tax law which distinguished between taxpayers who were not in the same situation with regard to their place of residence or with regard to where their capital was invested. Further,

[1.11] Sources of tax law

Article 56 was to be to without prejudice to the rights of member states to take all requisite measure to prevent infringement of national law with regard to various specific areas including taxation.

These points might have made the courts wary in applying Article 56 but instead the courts have treated the scope of discrimination just as broadly as in the other articles.[3] However while the court has taken this broad approach it has been quite strict in drawing a line between Article 56 and the other rules where both might apply. Faced with a case which could have been decided under Articles 43, 49 or 56 the court could simply have declined to rule on the application under Article 56 on the ground that the court's decision was already covered by the others. However the court has gone further and developed boundary rules such as that where the case concerned a shareholding which gave a significant amount of control – not necessarily 50% – then the case belonged under Article 43 and not Article 56 and so cannot be used by a company in a non member state.[4] Conversely where there is no element of control, Article 43 cannot apply and so the only question is whether Article 56 does, as in the recent *ELISA* case.[5] In the FII case the court started another line of reasoning to the effect that the justification which a court might accept might be different where the transfer was to a third country.[6] This point was picked up by the subsequent Commission paper.[7] What the words in the FII case may mean is that where a particular justification is put forward by a member state to prevent being in breach of the treaty article in issue, the terms of that justification may be harder to meet when a member state is involved. This is because relations between the member states take place against a common legal background, characterised by the existence of Community legislation, such as Directive 77/799 and Community harmonisation measures on company accounts.[8] Where a non-member state is involved this may not be so.

One of the first tax cases decided solely on the basis of freedom of movement of capital was *Staatssecretaris van Financiën v BGM Verkooijen*.[9] In this case V, a Dutch resident, received dividend income from a Belgian company which was subject to 25% withholding in Belgium in the usual way. If the dividends had been from a company with its seat in the Netherlands V would have been entitled to an exemption on the first NLG 1,000 of dividend income. V appealed on the basis that EC law did not allow Dutch tax law to restrict the exemption to companies resident in the Netherlands but should apply to companies resident in all member states. On a reference from the Hoge Raad under Article 234 the ECJ agreed with V.

The purpose of the exemption (para 11) was firstly to increase interest in equity shareholdings—and so the amount of capital subscribed to Dutch companies—and secondly to compensate in some small way for the effect of the Dutch classical system of corporate taxation which meant that no part of the corporate was imputed through to the shareholder. This was treated by the court as a clear breach of EC law since it constituted an obstacle to a Belgian company raising capital in the Netherlands.

The interest in this case is partly in its decision and partly in the vigorous but unsuccessful support given to the Dutch by the UK government (see paras 47 and 53). No doubt this support was given because of other matters which may be argued before the court and which relate to certain features of the UK system, some now repealed. The case is also of interest because of its comment on the *Bachmann* case.[10]

The lessons of this case were clearly taken into account by the government in fixing the ceiling for foreign tax on dividends at 45% (see infra, § **37.30**).

In *EC Commission v Belgium*[11] the court held that the Belgian government had broken EC law by issuing certain bonds on terms which allowed interest to be paid gross (ie without a withholding tax) but which prevented their purchase by persons resident in Belgium. The *Belgium* case is curious in that both Belgium and the Commission appeared to believe that while the Treaty had vertical direct effect it did not have horizontal direct effect.

Belgium has featured in a more recent case: *Ministre des Finances v Weidert*[12] is a short and relatively straightforward case on free movement of capital. The taxpayers, a married couple resident in Luxembourg, had subscribed for 200 shares in a Belgian company. If they had acquired shares for cash in fully taxable capital companies resident in Luxembourg, they would have been entitled to a relief from Luxembourg income tax. The court held that the relief was discriminatory and so the taxpayers were entitled to the benefit of the relief. The effect of the Luxembourg rules was to discourage Luxembourg nationals from investing their capital in companies established in another member state; the provision also constituted an obstacle to a Belgian company seeking to raise capital in another member state (at para [14]).

The boundary between freedom of establishment and freedom of capital was nicely shown by the *Baars* case.[13] Here a Dutch national held a controlling interest in an Irish company making cheese in Ireland. He was subject to Dutch wealth tax which gave an exemption for such holdings but only in Dutch companies. The ECJ held that the restriction on Dutch companies broke the rules on freedom of establishment and that those on freedom of capital were not relevant. By contrast, in *Verkooijen* the payment of dividends to an ordinary shareholder was a matter for the rules on movement of capital. The boundary between freedom of establishment and this freedom where a subsidiary company is concerned depends on the extent of the interest.[14] On dividend cases see infra, § **1.13**.

A difference between residents and non-residents in the way in which property was valued for succession duty was considered as a freedom of movement of capital issue in the *Barbier* case.[15] The court held that the difference broke that freedom.

In *Manninen*[16] the court considered one aspect of the imputation system of corporate taxation in the context of free movement of capital. Finnish law provided that the tax credit on dividends was only available if the company paying the dividend was established in the same member state as the person receiving it. More fully, those people liable to full tax in Finland were subject to income tax at the rate of 29% on dividends received—whether from Finnish or foreign companies. As with the now repealed UK system, dividends from Finnish companies came with a tax credit, here equal to 29/71ths of the dividend. This credit would settle the income tax liability and would mean that the tax paid on distributed profits at company and shareholder level would be

27

[1.11] Sources of tax law

29%. Mr Manninen's dividends came from a Swedish company. Under the Finland/Sweden double tax treaty Sweden charged a 15% withholding tax. This was given effect in Finland by a deduction from the amount of the dividends and not by a full credit for the Swedish tax. Mr Manninen therefore argued that under the free movement of capital provisions he should not be liable to pay the Finnish tax on the Swedish dividend. Of course, Finland did not get any of the Swedish corporate tax. On dividends see further infra, §§ 1.16 et seq.

Using the traditional direct link test for the cohesion argument the court concluded in favour of the taxpayer:

> 48. In the case at issue in the main proceedings here, however, the factual context is different. At the time when the shareholder fully taxable in Finland receives dividends, the profits thus distributed have already been subject to taxation by way of corporation tax, irrespective of whether those dividends come from Finnish or from Swedish companies. The objective pursued by the Finnish tax legislation, which is to eliminate the double taxation of profits distributed in the form of dividends, may be achieved by also granting the tax credit in favour of profits distributed in that way by Swedish companies to persons fully taxable in Finland.

---

1   Directive 88/361/EEC of 24 June 1988. See generally chapter 13 of *Law of the Single European Market* (ed. Barnard and Scott), written by Peers.
2   See eg Case C 101/05 *Sketterverket v A*. Matter remitted to Swedish Court.
3   Eg (Case C-101/05) *Skatteverket v A* [2009] STC 405.
4   See the non-tax case of (Case C/452/04) *Fidium Finance* and also (Case 196/04) *Cadbury Schweppes v IRC* [2006] STC 1908, para 32; (Case C-251/98) *Baars* and (Case C-436/00) *X and Y*.
5   (Case C-451/05) *Européenne et Luxembourgeoise d'investissements SA v Directeur général des impôts and another* [2008] STC 1762.
6   Case–C446/04 para 121.
7   See COM 2007 785 Direct Taxation Communication on the application of anti-abuse measures.
8   (Case C-101/05) *Skatteverket v A* [2009] STC 405, paras 60 and 61.
9   (Case C-35/98) [2002] STC 654. Delivered in open court in Luxembourg on 6 June 2000.
10 (C-204/90) [1994] STC 855: see infra, § **1.08**.
11 [2000] STC 830.
12 (Case C-242/03) [2005] STC 1241.
13 (Case C-251/98) [2000] ECR I-2787.
14 For recent difficulties see Morgan and Bridges *Tax Journal*, 19 March 2007 Issue 877, pp 7–9.
15 (Case C-364/01) *Barbier's Heirs v Inspecteur van de Belastingdienst Particulieren/Ondernemingen Buitenland te Heerlen* [2004] 1 CMLR 1283.
16 (Case C-19/02) *Proceedings brought by Manninen* [2004] STC 1444.

Limits on the principle: taxpayer defeated

[1.12] Taxpayers do not always succeed in invoking these Articles since it is always open to a member state to justify the discrimination on grounds allowed by the Treaty or some other source of EC law—provided it meets the other tests of EC law such as that of proportionality—or for the court itself to find that there is no discrimination or, even more irresponsibly, to make no finding on the discrimination issue. Some of these arguments have succeeded and others not. In many cases the justification has failed because of the principle of proportionality – which means here that the measures adopted by the member state to achieve the permitted goal are the least restrictive available.

One argument that succeeded was that an area of community law was insufficiently developed. Ths explains the *Daily Mail* case.[1] Here a UK resident company failed to circumvent the then UK rule requiring the company to obtain Treasury consent before emigrating. The court held that the UK's need to protect its tax base was sufficient especially as the company's claimed freedom of movement for companies was not made out in view of the still undeveloped nature of European company law rules on that freedom.[2]

One that has had, at least until recently, limited success is the need to prevent tax avoidance.

was also emphasised in the 2002 decision of the Court of Appeal in *R (on the application of Professional Contractors Group Ltd) v IRC*[3] concerning the UK's FA 2000 legislation on personal service companies. The Court of Appeal first held there was no discrimination and then went on to consider whether the prevention of tax avoidance (as opposed to fiscal supervision and fiscal cohesion, two other expressions which recur in Community jurisprudence) can be a proper ground of justification. As Robert Walker LJ put it:

> The issue about tax avoidance resolved itself, in the course of argument, into whether the Court of Justice was in *EC Commission v France* and in *Imperial Chemicals Industries plc v Colmer (Inspector of Taxes)*[4] holding that all measures against tax avoidance, or only discriminatory measures against tax avoidance, were inadmissible by way of justification. The crucial texts are paras 24 and 25 of the former judgment and paras 24 to 29 of the latter. In my view it is clear that the court was referring only to discriminatory measures. I note also that in para 26 of *Imperial Chemicals Industries plc v Colmer* the suggestion that the more artificial the tax avoidance which has to be countered the easier it may be to find justification. IR35 is aimed at relatively artificial avoidance since it counters only activities which are the provision, in the guise of self-employment (normally through a corporate vehicle), of employee-like services.

There is a general principle (mentioned in *Syndesmos ton en Elladi Touristikon kai Taxidiotikon Grafeion v Ergasias*[5] that economic aims cannot be a justification for measures which offend fundamental principles of Community law. That principle is in a sense obvious, since a member state cannot rely on its own economic interests to flout the principles on which the common market is founded. But the principle must be understood in its context. It cannot be used to undermine the principle that direct taxation is at present, and unless and until harmonisation takes place, a matter for the legislatures of member states. Diminution of tax revenue cannot be a justification for unequal treatment (see *Imperial Chemicals Industries plc v Colmer* para 28) but the general prohibition on economic aims does not seem to take the argument any further.

Another that succeeded at least initially is the cohesion principle. The cohesion principle was established by the ECJ's decision in *Bachmann v Belgian State*.[6]

[1.12] Sources of tax law

Although it was for along time fashionable for the court to do everything it could to narrow the principle, it is enjoying a period resuscitation now that the new approach has been accepted. Arguments based on the correct allocation of taxing powers between states seem to suggest that Bachmann is now revived but at a higher level of activity.[7] In *Bachmann* itself State B allowed X to deduct sickness and invalidity insurance contributions only if paid to a company recognised by the authorities in B. B established an objective reason for the refusal; under B's law any income eventually paid out under the policies would be taxed in B and this could be monitored by restricting the deduction to contributions made to a Belgian company. Moreover, where contributions had not been deducted the sums paid out were not subject to tax. The restriction of the right to deduct to payments made in B was therefore justified in the interests of the cohesion of its tax system. No less crucially B had established that there was no other way of protecting that cohesion; where, in a later case, double tax treaty provisions were in place the court said those provisions were sufficient to protect the cohesion of B's system.[8]

The *Bachmann* case was narrowed—and distinguished—in the *Verkooijen* case (see supra, § 1.07). The ECJ said that in *Bachmann* there had been a direct link in the case of one and the same taxpayer between the grant of the tax advantage and the offsetting of that tax advantage by a fiscal levy, both of which related to the same tax. The direct link argument also appears in *Sempra Metals v IRC* (formerly known as *Metallgesellschaft Ltd and Hoechst AG v IRC*).[9] Here the issue was whether a UK tax rule confined to companies resident in the UK broke the EC non-discrimination principles. This was the rule allowing dividends to be passed by one group company to another under a group dividend election without having to pay the now repealed advance corporation tax (ACT); the effect of the election was to give a deferral of tax and so a tax advantage. The United Kingdom argued that there was a link between the non-exemption from ACT for non-resident companies and their non-residence. This was rejected by the Court.[10]

Some see the approach of the court in cases like *Marks and Spencer v Halsey*[11] where it talks of the balanced allocation of taxing powers as a reassertion of the cohesion justification. It will also be remembered that in that case the Advocate General suggested in that case that *Verkooijen* was too strict.[12]

Another argument which has succeeded relates to tax treaties. The court has said that these articles do not prevent states from making tax treaties which allocate tax jurisdiction on the basis of nationality, at least where they are in accordance with international norms. This has been reasserted by the court in its ground breaking decision in *Re D* where the court recognised the need for a balanced allocation of taxing powers between the states. Moreover it recognised that a treaty gave rise to reciprocal rights and obligations for residents of the two states concerned; the rights could not be invoked by someone resident in a third country.[13] *Re D* involved the Dutch wealth tax; the taxpayer was resident in Germany and was trying, unsuccessfully, to invoke the benefit of treaty made between the Netherlands and Belgium. Ghosh sees the reasoning as articulated in this case as inconsistent with other decisions of the court.[14]

This approach may be seen as justification for the older case of *Gilly v Directeur des Services Fiscaux Bas Rhin*.[15] As seen above in connection with

Re D and below with the outbound dividend ACT decision (supra, § **1.07** and infra, § **1.17**) the court has held that these articles do not prevent states from making tax treaties which allocate tax jurisdiction on the basis of nationality. So the taxpayer lost in *Gilly v Directeur des Services Fiscaux Bas Rhin*.[16] (The case concerns the French-German Double Tax Treaty and frontier workers. Mr and Mrs G lived in France but while Mr G, a French national, worked in France, Mrs G, a German national worked in Germany. Mrs G, who had acquired French nationality on marriage and so was a dual national, paid tax in Germany at a rate higher than she would have had to pay under French law—because the German system was more steeply progressive and the family quotient system applicable in France, the state of residence, did not apply in Germany, the state of source. The tax treaty provided her with a credit in France for the tax paid in Germany but only up to the rate applicable in France. This left some German tax still unrelieved—she could not reclaim it from France under EC law. The court first held that the duty on the member states imposed by Article 220 (now Article 293) to eliminate double taxation within the Community was not capable of having direct effect.) On the main point they held that in the absence of harmonisation, it was open to member states to define the criteria for allocating taxing powers between themselves with a view to eliminating double taxation, there was nothing objectionable in a tax treaty making distinctions on the basis of nationality—ie no breach of Article 48 (now Article 39). This conclusion owed much to the fact that the Treaty was based on international practice as represented by the OECD model. The Court also held that as the object of the tax treaty was to prevent double taxation, not to ensure that the tax paid in one state was no higher than would have been paid in the other, there was nothing contrary to Article 48 in these arrangements.

(Unfortunately, the boundary between *Gilly*, on the one hand, and *Schumacker* and *Wielockx*, on the other, was not easy to determine.[17] The view taken here is that the Court quite deliberately, and, some might say, wisely, backed off from a decision which could have been used to unpick the tax treaty network. *Re D* follows that approach.) Other recent cases on treaties include *Bouanich v Skatteverket* and *Columbus Container Services BVBA Fianzamt Bielefeld–Innenstadt* where the court placed great reliance on *Gilly*.[18]

Then there is the need for effective supervision of tax matters. Mention should also be made of *Futura Participations SA, Singer v Administration des Contributions*,[19] where the court upheld the taxing government's argument in part based on a principle that a state could justify a rule by reference to the need for supervision to be effective. In the case the argument was accepted in principle but then not applied for reasons of proportionality. The taxpayer was the Luxembourg branch of a French company. In such circumstances Luxembourg only taxed the profits attributable to the branch (or permanent establishment) and did not insist that accounts be kept in Luxembourg. Stricter rules applied, however, when the branch sought to use trading losses from a previous year. Here Luxembourg insisted that accounts had to be kept in Luxembourg. The Court held that this did breach Article 43 as necessary to achieve the legitimate purpose advanced by the tax authorities. It did not, however, follow that Luxembourg had to accept a simple apportionment basis. Although the need to provide effective fiscal supervision looks initially promising from the

[1.12] Sources of tax law

member state's point of view it must be remembered that the court takes the view that the exchange of information powers in double tax treaties or under EC law may well suffice.[20]

Then there is territoriaility. In *Futura Participations SA*, the court also enunciated a principle of territoriality; Luxembourg insisted that the loss had to be economically related to the income and it should not be compelled to allow the company to carry the losses forward. The court held that this did not breach Article 43 as the Luxembourg position was completely reasonable. However this potentially sensible doctrine was not applied by the court in *Bosal*.[21] In *Marks and Spencer* the Advocate General suggested that the principle is designed to prevent conflicts of tax jurisdiction between member states and so may be part of the doctrine of cohesion.[22] The Court considered the territoriality issue (see supra, § **1.09**) but did not consider the relationship with cohesion. In the court's decision this becomes the famous phrase about the need for the court to protect a balanced allocation of the taxing powers between the member states.[23]

(6) Interpretation of national law stills a matter for national court. In *ICI plc v Colmer*[24] the House of Lords was faced with two ways of interpreting UK tax law. The first would have prevented a breach of EC law; the second would not. The European Court ruled that there was no EC law obligation on a national court to prefer the first construction to the second.

(7) Nationals of MS only. In general the purpose of the treaty and so of this case-law is to protect nationals of other member states; residence has been equated with nationality because most non-residents will be nationals of other member states, so that covert discrimination is revealed. Nationals of states outside the European Community are not entitled to protection under these rules as shown by the recent UK litigation involving NEC, a Japanese company.[25] Therefore, a US company with a branch in the UK cannot complain about being discriminated under, say, French law. However, some care is needed where subsidiaries are involved. If a US company establishes a UK subsidiary it will be open to the subsidiary to complain of discrimination under French law since, as a company established under UK law, it has UK nationality. The reason that this paragraph begins with the words "in general" is to remind one that the free movement of capital article can affect non-EC countries.

[1] *R v HM Treasury and IRC, ex p Daily Mail and General Trust plc* [1988] STC 787.
[2] [1988] STC 787 at 807, para 21.
[3] [2002] EWCA Civ 1945, [2002] STC 165; note that the court refused to refer the matter to the ECJ under Article 234 (formerly Article 177) see para 91.
[4] [1998] STC 874 at 892, [1999] 1 WLR 108 at 126.
[5] (Case C-398/95) [1997] ECR I-3091.
[6] (Case C-204/90) [1994] STC 855.
[7] And see (Case C-446/03) *Marks and Spencer*, Adv General Maduro building on comments of Adv General Kokott in the *Manninen* case (Case C-392/02) at para 35.
[8] (Case C 80/94) *Wielockx* [1995] STC 876.
[9] (Cases C 397/98 and C 410/98) judgment given 8 March 2001 [2001] STC 452. The ECJ judgment was incorporated into the judgment of the Court of Appeal, with the case re-named *Sempra Metals v IRC* [2005] EWCA Civ 389, [2005] STC 687.

[10] Judgment, paras 61–76.
[11] Case C446/03 paras 43 et seq.
[12] Adv General Maduron's suggestions are at para 71 of his opinion.
[13] Case C–376/03 *D v Inspecteur ven de Belastingen. . .Heerlen* [2005] STC 1211.
[14] *op cit* p 73.
[15] Case C–336/96 [1998] All ER EC 826; [1998] STC 1014; see comments in [1998] IBFD Journal 328.
[16] (Case C–336/96) [1998] All ER EC 826, [1998] STC 1014.
[17] See, generally, Hedemann-Robinson [1999] BTR 128, 135–38; see also JFAJ [1999] BTR 11 suggesting that if Gilly is right, and the Schumackers had been resident in France, the Schumacker decision would have been different for the year in which Mrs Schumacker had some earned income, but the same for the year in which she had none. On failure of the court to clarify matters in Case C–391/97 *Gschwind* see JGFAJ [2000] BTR 195.
[18] (Case C-265-04)*Bouanich v Skatteverket* [2008] STC 2020; (Case C-298/05) *Columbus Container Services BVBA Fianzamt Bielefeld –Innenstadt* [2008] STC 2554.
[19] (Case C-250/95) [1997] ECR 1-2471, [1997] 3 CMLR 483, [1997] STC 1301, ECJ.
[20] Eg (Case C-443/06) *Hollmann v Fazenda Puiblica* [2008] STC 1876.
[21] Case C168/01 *Bosal Holding BV v Staatssecretaris van Financien* [2003] STC 1483, para 37 et seq.
[22] (Case C-446/03) Adv General Maduro paras 58–64.
[23] Case 446/03 para 43.
[24] Case C–264/96 [1998] All ER (EC) 585; [1998] STC 874; on treatment of outstanding cases, see Inland Revenue Press Release, 26 February [1999] *Simon's Weekly Tax Intelligence* 312.
[25] Now called *Boake Allen and other v HMRC* [2007] UKHL 25; [2007] STC 1265; compare of course the Test Claimants of the *FII Group Case* 446/04 2006 ECJ 326.

Abuse of rights

[1.13] One of the most interesting developments of the new approach by the court is to recognise more subtly the right of the state concerned to counter avoidance (or as the court prefers to say abuse, sometimes adding "of rights") ie the right of the taxpayer to carry on business in a tax-efficient manner. The court recognises the taxpayer's right but then adds, as in *Cadbury Schweppes* (supra, § **1.15**), that it must not be abused. It is not yet clear whether "abuse" is to take its place alongside concepts such as "proportionality" as cornerstones of EC law. It is more likely that it will develop in particular areas – and may not do so at all in others.

In *Halifax plc v Customs and Excise Comrs*[1], *BUPA Hospitals Ltd v Customs and Excise Comrs*[2] and *University of Huddersfield v Customs and Excise Comrs*[3], the ECJ sitting as a Grand Chamber of 13 enunciated a doctrine of abuse of rights which went a long way to limit some of the more expansive versions of the doctrine.[4] In some ways, the approach of the Court echoes that of the House of Lords in *Barclays*. There are no absolute principles except at a level of abstraction which is so high that they clash. There is a distinct

[1.13] Sources of tax law

reluctance to let loose in the law a principle of uncertain scope; everything must proceed on a principle by principle, case by case basis—and that basis is nothing like as favourable to the Revenue authorities as they might have wished.

The court first reiterated (paras 56 and 57) that the terms defining taxable transactions under the Sixth Directive were all objective in nature and applied without regard to the purpose or results of the transactions, even where transactions were entered into solely to avoid VAT. The transactions qualified as supplies made in the course of their economic activities, (esp paras 51–54). An obligation on the tax authorities to carry out inquiries to determine the intention of the taxable person would be contrary to the objectives of the common system of VAT of ensuring legal certainty and facilitating the application of VAT by having regard, save in exceptional cases, to the objective character of the transaction in question. It was true that the law would look differently at tax evaded by means of untruthful tax returns or the issue of improper invoices but those was very different situations.

The court then turned to 'abusive practices'. The court began (para 67) by noting that the problems stemmed, at least in part, from national rules allowing taxable persons to undertake at the same time taxed and untaxed transactions, or only untaxed transactions, to transfer leases of immovable property to another entity under its control, which is entitled to opt for taxation of the letting of that property and thereby to deduct the total input VAT paid on construction or renovation costs.

While Community law could not be relied on for abusive or fraudulent ends, a court had to ensure that Community legislation was certain and its application foreseeable by those subject to it. This was all the more necessary where the rules were liable to entail financial consequences. The court then endorsed the choice principle (para 74): where the taxable person chose one of two transactions, the Sixth Directive did not require him to choose the one which involved paying the highest amount of VAT. On the contrary, as the Advocate General observed in point 85 of his Opinion, taxpayers may choose to structure their business so as to limit their tax liability.

It followed that a practice was abusive only if the transactions concerned resulted in a tax advantage the grant of which would be contrary to the purpose of those provisions (this is one of those echoes of *Barclays*). Moreover, the question whether the essential aim of the transactions concerned was to obtain a tax advantage had to be apparent from a number of objective factors. They expressly approved the Advocate General's observation (point 89 of his Opinion) that the prohibition of abuse is not relevant where the economic activity carried out may have some explanation other than the mere attainment of tax advantages. Finally, at this general level, the Court said (para 76) that it was for the national court to verify in accordance with the rules of evidence of national law, provided that the effectiveness of Community law is not undermined, whether action constituting such an abusive practice has taken place in the case before it. The Court then made further observations on the approach to the particular VAT issues (paras 78–86).

The Court also made some interesting points (paras 92–98) further limiting the doctrine. So the national courts should not go further than is necessary to prevent fraud and must not undermine the neutrality of the tax. The finding of abusive practice should not lead to a penalty since a clear and unambiguous legal basis was required for that. A simple obligation to repay the input VAT would suffice. In this way the abusive transactions were redefined so as to re-establish the situation that would have prevailed in the absence of the transactions constituting that abusive practice.

There is nothing new in the court developing fundamental legal principles, such as human rights,[5] proportionality or legitimate expectations. However abus de droit is in some ways a more slippery concept. A French legal commentator has written: "Le droit cesse là où l'abus commence". This has been translated as: "The law ends where abuse begins". This appears, at least prima facie, to be directly contrary to the basic proposition of English law that: "if conduct is presumptively unlawful, a good motive will not exonerate the defendant, and that, if conduct is lawful apart from motive, a bad motive will not make him liable".[6]

The abuse of right doctrines are used to protect the citizen against a member state or Community institution.[7] However, the doctrine was enunciated in the *Centros* case[8] and can be applied where a person relies on an EC right to get round a national law rule; the test is full of impressive epithets—"it would be unreasonable to derive, to the detriment of others, an improper advantage, manifestly contrary to the objective pursued by the legislator in conferring that particular right on the individual".

A bridge between the approach in English law and this continental concept is provided by Advocate General La Pergola:

> the problem of abuse is resolved in the last analysis by defining the material content of the particular situation and thus the scope of the right conferred on the individual concerned. In other words it is claimed that to determine whether or not a right is actually being exercised in an abusive manner is simply to define the material scope of the right in question.[9]

A second and different test, stemming from the *EMU Tabac* case,[10] is based on an absence of economic purpose. It applies as Peacock puts it "where a person carries out transactions not for an economic purpose but to obtain the benefits of EC law". Since the grant of the benefit has been created artificially the EC right can be withheld.

---

1   [2006] STC 919, ECJ Case C-255/02. The decision of the court of first instance, the London Tribunal Centre on 1 February 2001 is unreported. For an interesting consideration of abuse of rights in a wider, European context, see Hui Ling McCarthy *Abuse of Rights — Europe's Legal Elephant* [2007] BTR 160.
2   Case C-419/02 unreported.
3   [2006] STC 980, ECJ Case C-223/03.
4   Such as *WHA Ltd v Customs and Excise Comrs* [2003] EWHC 305 (Ch), [2003] STC 648, *Blackqueen Ltd v Customs and Excise Comrs* (2002) VAT Decision 17680, and *BUPA Hospitals Ltd v Customs and Excise Comrs* (2002) VAT Decision 17588.
5   (Case 26/69) *Stauder v City of Ulm* [1969] ECR 419.
6   Planiol *An Elementary Treaty of Civil Law* (1899). This is quoted by Robert Venables QC in his interesting and useful article "Abuse of Rights in EC Law" in

[1.13] Sources of tax law

Tax Adviser, October 2003 pp 16–19. The statement on English law is taken from *Rogers, Winfield & Jolowicz on Tort*, (15th edn, 1999) p 55, as approved by Lord Steyn in *Three Rivers District Council v Bank of England* [2000] 2 WLR 1220 at 1230. Consider also Lord Halsbury LC in *Bradford Corpn v Pickles* [1895] AC 587 at 594: "If it was a lawful act, however ill the motive might be, he had a right to do it. If it was an unlawful act, however good his motive might be, he would have no right to do it. Motives and intentions in such a question as is now before your Lordships seem to be absolutely irrelevant."

[7] *Tax Adviser* July 2002 p 24.
[8] (Case C-212/97) [1999] ECR I-1459.
[9] Para 20 of the Advocate General's opinion in (Case C-212/97) *Centros Ltd v Erhverus-og Selskabsstyrelsen* [1999] ECR I-1459, ECJ.
[10] (Case C-296/95) [1998] ECR I-1605.

Reviewing the law

Losses: Marks & Spencer v Halsey

[1.14] *Marks & Spencer plc v Halsey*,[1] a case on relief for losses, began with the Special Commissioners, as they saw it, declining a daring invitation to change the UK international loss relief rules in the cause of EC non-discrimination.

Their view was so clear that they declined to refer the matter to the ECJ as they had power to do under Article 234. However, this was reversed on appeal and we now have the decision of the Court in Luxembourg. The result is something of a score-draw with the taxpayers in the case able to claim some relief but with clear statements by the court that other taxpayers with losses would not be so lucky. There was much relief in government circles in the member states but it is too early to know whether that relief is justified.[2] The UK legislation (TA 1988, Sch 18A) is added by FA 2006, s 27 (infra § **28.05**). The court, faced with submissions from many of the member states, was forced to confront some of the consequences of its loose language and unconvincing reasoning in earlier cases. The decision of the Court is much shorter than that of the Advocate General.

The case concerns losses of subsidiaries in other member states. Under UK tax rules these losses could not be set off against UK profits. The first argument for the taxpayer was that it was contrary to EC law for the UK to apply different treatment as between (1) a UK company with an EU branch and (2) a UK company with an EU subsidiary (losses being relieved under (1) but not under (2)). Taking the same line as the Special Commissioners the Advocate General rejected this argument, stating that branches and subsidiaries could be treated differently—the difference in the tax treatment did not merely comprise the loss of a specific benefit as a result of the option being made in favour of the establishment of foreign subsidiaries but stemmed from a difference in the tax regimes applicable to different types of establishment.[3] The Court did not even comment on this aspect of the case.

Reviewing the law [1.14]

The taxpayer's second argument was that it was unlawful for the UK to apply different treatment as between (1) a UK company with a UK subsidiary (losses can be relieved) and (2) a UK company with an EU subsidiary (losses being relieved under (1) but not under (2)). The Court accepted this argument, stating that this amounted to a hindrance on a company wishing to establish subsidiaries in other member states, and therefore breached EC law.[4]

The court accepted that the UK rules were in conformity with the principle of territoriality—Marks & Spencer plc had no jurisdiction over the foreign subsidiary—but that was not enough to justify the UK rules. The Court's conclusion was that Articles 43 EC and 48 EC did not preclude provisions of a member state which generally prevent a resident parent company from deducting from its taxable profits losses incurred in another member state by a subsidiary established in that member state although they allow it to deduct losses incurred by a resident subsidiary. However, it was contrary to those Articles to prevent the resident parent company from doing so where the non-resident subsidiary had exhausted the possibilities available in its state of residence of having the losses taken into account for the accounting period concerned by the claim for relief and also for previous accounting periods and where there were no possibilities for those losses to be taken into account in its state of residence for future periods either by the subsidiary itself or by a third party, in particular where the subsidiary has been sold to that third party. The English courts are now considering how to implement this decision. The views of Park J and the Court of Appeal are considered at infra, § **28.05**.

The court's conclusion is an amalgam of points made when considering the arguments put forward by the member states (the UK and others) as to whether the infringement could be justified (paras 43–55). The arguments put forward by the states rested on a general point that matters of profits and losses were two sides of the same coin and must be treated symmetrically in the same tax system in order to protect a balanced allocation of the power to impose taxes between the different member states concerned. To allow companies the option to have their losses taken into account in the member state in which they are established or in another member state would significantly jeopardise a balanced allocation of the power to impose taxes between member states, as the taxable basis would be increased in the first state and reduced in the second to the extent of the losses transferred. Secondly there was the risk that losses could be given relief twice. Third, and last, if the losses were not taken into account in the member state in which the subsidiary is established there would be a risk of tax avoidance. Here the court accepted that the UK rules prevented various practices, which might be inspired by the realisation that the rates of taxation applied in the various member states vary significantly. From this it followed that the restrictions pursued legitimate objectives. So the court had to decide whether the rules went beyond what was necessary to attain those objectives.

The court said later (para 57) that member states were free to adopt or to maintain in force rules having the specific purpose of precluding from a tax benefit wholly artificial arrangements whose purpose is to circumvent or escape national tax law.[5] It is not clear whether para 57 is meant to narrow the earlier point or to stand separately.

37

[1.14] Sources of tax law

On territoriality, the Court and the Advocate General rejected the UK's argument that the principle of territoriality allowed the UK not to take account of the losses of EU subsidiaries because such subsidiaries were not within the charge to UK tax.[6]

On cohesion, as seen below, the Advocate General invited the court to make a new beginning.[7] On this the court itself was silent but its approach is consistent with this approach. The Advocate General considered how the risk of double relief could be verified.[8] He acknowledged that it might be difficult for the UK to establish this but member states had the EC-wide rules on exchange of information to assist them.[9]

There have been several other ECJ cases on losses building on *Marks & Spencer*. In that case the ECJ identified three factors which would allow a court to uphold a restriction of relief for a loss sustained by a foreign subsidiary. These were a) the need to protect a balanced allocation of the power to impose taxes between the different member states concerned; b) the need to avoid double relief for losses; and c) the risk of tax avoidance. So, in para 55, the non-resident subsidiary should have exhausted the possibilities of loss relief in its state of residence, whether for that or previous accounting periods or if necessary by transferring those losses to a third party. Moreover there should be no possibility for the foreign subsidiary's losses to be taken into account in its state of residence for future periods either by the subsidiary itself or by a third party, in particular where the subsidiary has been sold to that third party (para 55). The case law of 2008 shows that the three justifications can operate independently of one another.[10]

---

[1] (Case C-446/03) judgment delivered 13 December 2005; the Special Commissioners decision is reported at [2003] STC (SCD) 70. For comments see Vajda and Holmes *Tax Journal* Issue 820, 16 January 2006 p 7; Cussons *Tax Journal* Issue 821, 23 January 2006 p 9. For the earlier loss relief decision in the *AMID* case see supra, § **1.06**.
[2] See Morgan and Bridges *Tax Journal* Issue 825, February 2006 p 5.
[3] Adv General Maduro 7 April 2005 para 49.
[4] Court Paras 31–34.
[5] Citing (Case C-264/96) *Imperial Chemical Industries plc v Colmer (Inspector of Taxes)* [1998] STC 874, para 26, and (Case C-9/02) *de Lasteyrie du Saillant v Ministère de l'Économie, des Finances et de l'Industrie* [2005] STC 1722, [2004] ECR I-2409, para 50.
[6] Court para 39 and 40; A G paras 50–55.
[7] Paras 58–64, especially 63.
[8] Para 74.
[9] Para 81.
[10] (Case C-410/06) *Lidl Belgium Gmbh and Co KG v Finanzamt Heilbronn* [2008] STC 3229, para 40 citing (Case C-231/05) *OyAA, Proceedings brought by* [2008] STC 991 and (Case C-379/05) *Amurta v Inspecteur van de Belastingdienst* [2008] STC 2851. See also (Case C-347/04) *Rewe Centralfinanz v FinanzAmt Koln-Mitte* [2008] STC 2785 and (Case C-157/07) *Finanzamt für Körperschaften III in Berlin v Krankenheim Ruhesitz am Wannsee-Seniorenheimstatt GmbH* [2009] STC 138.

CFCs: Cadbury Schweppes v IRC

[1.15] *Cadbury Schweppes plc and Cadbury Schweppes Overseas Ltd v IRC*[1] concerns the UK's controlled foreign company (CFC) legislation. Generally, a UK resident parent company is not taxed on the profits of its subsidiaries as they arise but only where the profits are passed to the parent eg as interest or dividends. This general rule is excluded if the CFC rules apply. This is the first of a series of CFC cases currently governed by a Group Litigation order. This one concerned profits for the year 1996 arising from a subsidiary established in Ireland, in the International Financial Services Centre, Dublin.

The Special Commissioners asked the court whether the legislation constituted either discrimination or a restriction on freedom of movement and, if so, whether it could be justified as countering tax avoidance. This would require the court to consider whether setting up the subsidiary in another state to enjoy a more favourable tax regime was an abuse of freedom of establishment, whether the UK CFC rules hindered the exercise of that freedom and whether the hindrance could be justified. The short answer is that the application of the rules could be justified in certain circumstances and so it was up to the Special Commissioners to examine each case separately in the light of the court's guidance; that was that the rules had to be confined to artificial arrangements intended to circumvent national tax law. If the courts could not restrict the CFC rules in this way the CFC rules would be in breach of EC law.

The opinion of Advocate General Leger was commented on in the 2006–07 edition. Now we have the Court's decision which, like the Advocate General builds on the Marks and Spencer case.

Like the Advocate General the court sought the answer in terms of freedom of establishment (Articles 43 and 48), rather than on the free movement of capital (Article 56) and on the freedom to provide services (Article 49) (paras 29–34).

It was clear that the UK's treatment of the subsidiary amounted to a restriction on freedom of establishment (para 46) and so was permissible only if justified by overriding reasons of public interest. It was further necessary, in such a case, that its application be appropriate to ensuring the attainment of the objective thus pursued and not go beyond what is necessary to attain it (para 47). A national measure restricting freedom of establishment could be justified where it specifically relates to wholly artificial arrangements aimed at circumventing the application of the legislation of the member state concerned (para 51).

The purpose of freedom of establishment was to allow a Community national to participate, on a stable and continuing basis, in the economic life of a member state other than his state of origin and to profit therefrom. This it presupposed actual establishment of the company concerned in the host member state and the pursuit of genuine economic activity there.

The UK could therefore apply its CFC rules in so far as they were aimed at conduct involving the creation of wholly artificial arrangements which did not reflect economic reality, with a view to escaping the tax normally due on the profits generated by activities carried out on national territory.

The court insisted that this question had to be resolved by the use of objective factors (para 67). The crux comes at paras 72 and 73:

[1.15] Sources of tax law

In this case, it is for the national court to determine whether, as maintained by the United Kingdom Government, the motive test, as defined by the legislation on CFCs, lends itself to an interpretation which enables the taxation provided for by that legislation to be restricted to wholly artificial arrangements (in which case the UK legislation is compatible with EC law) or whether, on the contrary, the criteria on which that test is based mean that, where none of the exceptions laid down by that legislation applies and the intention to obtain a reduction in United Kingdom tax is central to the reasons for incorporating the CFC, the resident parent company comes within the scope of application of that legislation, despite the absence of objective evidence such as to indicate the existence of an arrangement of that nature (in which case the UK CFC rules are not compatible).

There is therefore a two stage test; the legislation is effective in so far as it deals with wholly artificial arrangements, as defined, but the taxpayers must be given an opportunity to show on the basis of objective factors that their arrangements were not such.

In paragraph 68 the court had given an example:

If checking those factors leads to the finding that the CFC is a fictitious establishment not carrying out any genuine economic activity in the territory of the host member state, the creation of that CFC must be regarded as having the characteristics of a wholly artificial arrangement. That could be so in particular in the case of a 'letterbox' or 'front' subsidiary.

The UK courts have also considered CFC issues stemming from *Cadbury Schweppes* in relation to the Vodafone company.[2] The Court of Appeal has ruled that it was permissible to use the motive test in the CFC legislation in deciding whether the company was entitled to the protection of Article 43 on freedom of establishment. This was achieved by treating the problem as one of interpretation of the UK and so not of disapplication.

In a later case the court held that the particular application on German CFC rules broke EC law.[3] The facts presented to the court were not sufficient to justify the rules. Interestingly the effect of the German CFC rules was to move the company from an exemption system to a UK-style system of full taxation but with credit for any foreign tax paid.

---

[1] (Case C-196/04) [2006] STC 1908.
[2] Eg the litigation involving Vodafone; (Case C-203/05); now *Vodafone 2 v HMRC* [2009] EWCA Civ 446 reversing Evans Lombe J [2008] EWHC 1569 (Ch), [2008] STC 2391.
[3] (Case C-298/05) *Columbus Container Services BVBA*.

The dividend (and thin capitalisation) cases

[1.16] There are three recent cases involving the UK, each part of a Group Litigation Order. The UK cases on ACT[1] and thin capitalisation[2] have very interesting suggestions by the Advocate General Geelhoed for a new approach to these issues. He reaches the same answers as the Court but the Court's reasoning is sometimes not as clear nor as bold. The two UK dividend cases arose as an indirect result of *Metalgesellschaft*.[3] There the Court had looked at a UK

Reviewing the law [1.17]

rule which allowed payments flowing between group members resident in the UK to pass without having to pay ACT—the so called 'group income' payments. The court held that the cash flow advantages of not having to pay ACT in UK group situation breached EC law.[4] These taxpayer successes encouraged the present litigation.

[1] Cases C-374/04 and C-446/04.
[2] Test Claimants in the Thin Cap Group Litigation v IRC [2007] STC 906, Case C-524/04.
[3] [2001] STC 452, ECJ.
[4] Case C-397/98 and Case C-410/98 [2001] STC 452.

Outbound dividends

[1.17] In Test Claimants in Class IV of the ACT Group Litigation[1] the court considered the compatibility of the UK rules on taxation of outbound dividends with EC principles under Articles 43 and 56. It upheld the right of the UK to refuse credits on such dividends. Since this part of the recent litigation concerns rules which are mostly still in force it is dealt with first.

The essence of the case was an argument by the companies that there was a difference in treatment between that accorded to payments to other UK resident companies (TA 1988, s 208 made them exempt) and to non-resident companies (where s 208 did not apply). The court examined TA 1988, s 233 and concluded that the real effect of that section was that the UK simply did not attempt to tax the outbound dividend at all. This was acceptable to the court. Incidentally it is this which distinguishes the UK case from the Denkavit case on dividends outbound from France. In Denkavit[2] by contrast the French system taxation of dividends differed depending on whether they were going to domestic parent companies or foreign parent companies; this was held contrary to Article 43 of the EC Treaty.[3]

In this case the Italian company (Pirelli) had a minority holding but as it was at least 10% holding, it received favourable treatment under the double tax treaty. The other two companies owning 100% of the relevant UK subsidiaries; the companies were resident in the Netherlands but were 100% subsidiaries of companies based in Germany and Japan; because of the foreign ownership these companies were excluded from the benefit of the UK-Netherlands double tax treaty. In the Class IV case the court noted the various tax credits under double tax treaties, sometimes full and sometimes partial.

On the general point the court said it was for each member state to organise, in compliance with Community law, its system of taxation of distributed profits and, in that context, to define the tax base as well at the tax rates which apply to the company making the distribution and/or the shareholder to whom the dividends are paid, in so far as they are liable to tax in that state (paras 49 and 50). Requiring that profits distributed to a non-resident shareholder were not liable to a series of charges to tax or to economic double taxation, would mean in point of fact that that state would be obliged to abandon its right to tax a profit generated through an economic activity undertaken on its territory (para 59). Moreover, any procedure for preventing or mitigating economic

[1.17] Sources of tax law

double taxation by the grant of a tax advantage to the ultimate shareholder, was best done by the member state in which the latter is resident as it is best placed to determine the shareholder's ability to pay (para 60).

On the point of the variety of credits and treatments such differences did not worry the court. Articles 43 EC and 56 EC did not preclude a situation in which a member state does not extend the entitlement to a tax credit provided for in a double taxation convention concluded with another member state for companies resident in the second state which receive dividends from a company resident in the first state to companies resident in a third member state with which it has concluded a double taxation convention which does not provide for such an entitlement for companies resident in that third state (paras 85-94). The court noted that the Parent Subsidiary Directive only applied once the holding was 25%; it must therefore be open to member states to do as they wished below that threshold.

Outbound dividends were also considered in the recent *Amurta* case, decided under Article 56. The court tok a fairly simple approach. It held that resident and non-resident shareholders in the company were in a comparable position. It followed that a withholding tax which was charged on non-resident shareholders but not charged on residents broke EC law.[4]

---

[1] Case C-374/04, [2007] STC 404, judges Pirelli, Essilot and Sony.
[2] Case 170/05.
[3] On *Denkavit* see Cussons *Tax Journal* Issue 868 15 January 2007 pp 10-12.
[4] Case C-379/05.

Inbound dividends

[1.18] In turning to the treatment of inbound dividends for the years in question it is necessary to return to the ACT system (repealed 1999). The decision in *Test Claimants FII*[1] is a major, but not complete, victory for the companies. Many issues have been referred back to the UK courts. Under the ACT rules then in force and repealed in 1999, when a UK company making a qualifying distribution, eg a dividend, to shareholder, the company had to pay Advance Corporation Tax (ACT). The company could use the ACT against its own liability to mainstream corporation tax on its profits for the period in respect of which the dividend had been paid. A problem arose if the company had foreign income which benefited from a foreign tax credit relief—the effect of the credit, especially if the taxpayer had a holding of at least 10% and so benefited from the credit relief for tax on the underlying profits, would be that there would be no mainstream corporation tax against which to set the ACT. This was the surplus ACT problem.

There was also the franking problem. If the shareholder was a company resident in the UK and made a distribution of its own it could, for example, set the credit accompanying the dividend (called franked investment income) against its own liability to pay ACT when it made its own dividend payment so 'franking' the dividend; there were other ways of using the credit eg in relation to losses but what the company could not generally do was to reclaim the tax from the Revenue. The franking problem was a timing problem.

Reviewing the law [1.18]

One argument in the case was that the court should reject the whole UK two track approach which distinguished so sharply between purely domestic dividends and foreign dividends. As we shall see the Court upheld the two track approach but with conditions which will be, as far as the UK Revenue are concerned, expensive.

The case also involved the Foreign Income Dividend scheme. This was introduced in 1994 (FA 1994, Sch 16) to help companies with surplus ACT problems. A company was allowed to match the FID with foreign profits. However, the company had first to pay the ACT in the usual way and then when it matched the foreign dividend it could get the ACT repaid by the Revenue—but not until the mainstream corporation tax became due, usually nine months after the end of the period. The vulnerability of this scheme to an argument based on the cash flow advantage which succeeded in *Metalgesellchaft*[2] is obvious. However, the companies went further and argued that some companies should be compensated for enhanced dividend they had to pay to those shareholders, eg pension funds, who lost out on the tax credits normally accompanying the dividends (and which were not available to foreign income dividends).

In *Test Claimants FII*[3] the only major point of comfort for the Revenue was that the court allowed the two track approach in. The Court held that having an exemption system for domestic distributions (s 208) while subjecting incoming dividends to the UK's imputation system might break EC principles in Articles 43 and 56. The question was to be answered by looking at the tax burden. The UK rules would satisfy Articles 43 and 56 if the rate on inbound dividends was not greater than that on domestic dividends AND that that the credit was at least equal to the amount paid in the member state of the company making the distribution up to the limit of the tax charged in the MS on the company receiving the dividends (para 57).

The court identified one situation in which there would be a breach of Article 56. This is where the shareholder had less than 10% stake and so would not benefit from the full credit (para 74). Another taxpayer victory was in relation to the ACT advantage of the franked investment income system which clearly favoured domestic over foreign source dividends; the cash flow disadvantage broke Articles 43 and 56 (paras 94, 112 and 139).

The court also held that the foreign divided income scheme broke Articles 43 and 56 because of (a) the cash flow advantage and (b) the denial of the tax credit (para 173). The question of the appropriate remedy and, in particular, whether the UK was liable in damages was left to the UK courts—as were very many other loose ends.[4]

The UK asked the court to limit the temporal effects of the judgment. Some of the claims went back to 1973 and the UK argued that the court should take account of the fact that, since the adoption of the domestic legislation in 1973, its compatibility with Community law has never been challenged and, secondly, to the serious financial implications, estimated at £4,700m, which the applications brought before the national court would have for the UK. The figure of £4,700m was disputed by the companies. However, the court pointed out that the figure was based on the assumption that the UK would lose on all

[1.18] Sources of tax law

the points. It seems unfortunate that there was no way in which the UK could come back with figures corrected in the light of the court's quite complicated judgment.

The inbound dividend problem has generated much litigation, including *Verkooijen* and *Manninen* both cited above at **1.11**. Other cases include *Lenz* (Case C-315/02) and *Kerchaert Morres* (Case C 513/04)), *Meilicke and others v Finanzamt Bonn-Innenstadt* (Case C-292/04) and *Amurta v Inspecteur van den Belastingdienst* (Case C-379/05).

On UK case law on the FII case see *Test Claimants in the FII Group Litigation v Inland Revenue* (Case C-446/04)[5].

[1] Case C-446/04.
[2] [2001] STC 452, ECJ.
[3] Case 446/04.
[4] See Morgan, Bridges and Fichardt *Tax Journal* Issue 867 8 January 2007 pp 8–10 and Morgan and Bridges *Tax Bulletin* Issue 868 15 January 2007 pp 13–14.
[5] [2006] ECR I-11753 (ECJ); [2008] EWHC 2893 (Ch); (2009) STC 254 (Chancery Division).

Thin capitalisation

[1.19] In the *Thin Cap Group Litigation Test Case*[1] the court used its customary approach asking whether the rules were a restriction, could they be justified and whether they were proportionate. There were three sets of UK rules. The original rule in TA 1988 directed that where the thin capitalisation rules applied the whole payment was treated as dividend and not as interest. This bizarre all-or-nothing rule was held to break EC law.

The original rule was amended by FA 1995 which concentrated on the amount of interest as opposed to the rate and directed that only the excess over the amount that would have been paid if there had been no connection between the parties was to be treated as interest. These rules were in turn amended by FA 2004 following the decision of the Court rejecting the German thin capitalisation rules in *Lankhost-Hohorst GmbH v Finanzamt Steinfurt*.[2] The 2004 changes use the transfer pricing rules instead of a separate provision and apply to certain domestic situations as well.

The court did not reject the 1995 rules as necessarily contrary to EC law principles. Rather they used the abuse approach developed in *Cadbury Schweppes*.[3] The taxpayers had a right to arrange intra group finance as they wished but the states have interests in preventing artificial transfers of profit across borders. Taxpayers must be allowed to show that non arms length can be justified commercially. So as in *Cadbury Schweppes* the rule must be applied on a case-by-case basis. The court has not yet considered the 2004 rules. Some hope for their repeal in the light of this decision.

The case has other important—and controversial—comments on the scope of Article 56 as opposed to Article 43 and on the new role of the justification of cohesion.[4]

Two later cases require mention. *Lasertec v Finanz amt Emmingem*[5] is important on the boundary between Articles 43 and 56. The argument on

44

Article 56 failed and Article 43 was not available because of the part Swiss ownership of the company. In *Lammer v Van Cleeff*[6] the Belgian rules were held inapplicable because they were too wide.

[1] Case C-524/04, [2007] 2 CMLR 765.
[2] (Case 324/00) [2003] STC 607.
[3] (Case C-196/04) [2006] STC 1908.
[4] See Morgan and Bridges *Tax Journal* Issue 877 19 March 2007 pp 7 et seq.
[5] Case C-429/04.
[6] Case C-105/07.

Other aspects of Community law

Interpretation

[1.20] European courts treat law as a matter of principle and purpose; the court states the principle and then works down to the facts. When applying EC law, UK courts adopt a purposive interpretation as they say they now do in UK tax law generally. Moreover, in EC law literal interpretations are rejected in favour of the purpose of the Directive;[1] only if all else fails do the courts proceed to a literal approach.[2] This approach comes naturally where UK courts face the problem of interpreting EC law as such or UK rules based on EC Directives. However, the schizophrenic state under which tax matters were to be tested on a literal basis in a domestic context and on a purposive basis in a European context became unstable and may be one reason for the change in English law.

The court sometimes refers to Article 10 (formerly Article 5) which imposes a duty to co-operate in good faith. So, in *ICI v Colmer*,[3] the House of Lords asked whether this duty extended to persons resident in non-member states. More specifically, the House of Lords asked whether, if the legislation at issue in the case was incompatible with Community law in denying relief for subsidiary companies with seats in member states, it ought also to grant relief where the subsidiaries had their seat in non-member countries. The ECJ said there was no such obligation since the situation fell outside the scope of Community law.

[1] Eg recent case of (Case C-104/06) *EC Comm v Sweden* [2008] STC 2546.
[2] (Case 139/84) *Van Dijk's Boekhuis BV v Staatssecretaris van Financiën* [1986] 2 CMLR 575, ECJ, distinguishing the creation of a new article from the thorough repair of an old.
[3] (Case C-264/96) [1998] STC 874.

The role of the Commission and its views

As the Commission has enforcement powers under the Treaty one must pay particular attention to its views.[1] One view is that current EC law does not oblige a member state to grant automatically the withholding tax rate of its most favourable bilateral agreement to taxpayers of another state, which is not covered by the agreement. The mere fact that the Commission holds this view does not mean that it is correct, merely that the Commission itself is unlikely to take that point to the Court. As we have seen the point has now been decided by the Court itself.[2]

[1] See Lyal *Tax Journal* Issue 847 24 July 2006 pp 9–10.
[2] On Commission views see Written Answer, 9 November 1992, Qn 647/92, OJ C40/93 reported in *Simon's Tax Intelligence* 1993, p 302.

(Harmful and other) tax competition

Tax competition raises two distinct but related points. First, at a general and political level, it is clear that there is a division in the Community between those countries which believe that the necessary cliché of the level playing field will have to be imposed by the centre, and those who believe that it is sufficient to attain approximation rather than harmonisation and that this can be achieved by tax competition.

Second, we have had in both international, ie OECD, and EC tax circles, a change of view about what non-discrimination rules should be trying to do. Ever since the Second World War the view, which is expressed in the EC case law, has been concerned to make sure that the non-national is treated at least as favourably as the national. In the circles just mentioned attention has now been switched to the opposite problem—where the non-resident is treated more favourably. On this view we have to recognise and then address the problem of unacceptable tax competition in favour of non-residents. On this approach state C may not have to have a 30% corporation tax rate but a rate of only 10% for foreign owned start-up companies; C may, however, have a 10% rate for all companies or a 10% rate for start-up companies regardless of ownership.[1] A related phenomenon is the practice already seen in the UK legislation implementing the Mergers Directive to ensure that cross-border transactions are not favoured at the expense of purely domestic ones.[2]

Both the OECD and the EU have produced plans for dealing with these problems.[3] The problem was considered by the House of Lords Select Committee on European affairs.[4] UK legislative reaction includes new information agreements with other countries including the UK's own overseas territories and Crown Dependencies.[5] Meanwhile a Code of Conduct was reaffirmed in 2003.[6] A Code on Conduct on Transfer Pricing Documentation was agreed in 2006.[7]

The EU conducted its own Survey of Harmful Practices currently adopted by member states; progress is being made by member states repealing their condemned rules. The OECD has issued a report on "Progress on identifying and eliminating harmful tax practices" which was welcomed by the UK government.[8] It is very easy to see these efforts at OECD level as the rich countries ganging up on the small in a high minded protection of their tax systems while refusing to grant those same poor countries access to their markets, especially in agricultural products.

[1] See Easson OECD and EU on harmful tax competition [1998] ECTJ 3/1 at 1 and 1998 European Taxation 96. This did not stop the Commission from arguing in support of the taxpayer in the *Gilly* case (supra, § **1.02**, note 17).
[2] Inland Revenue: EC Direct Measures—A Consultative Document 1991, paras 2.4, 2.5, 2.10.
[3] A full list of the practices considered by the EC was published by the Council in SN 4901/99, 23 November 1999. See also *Keeling and Shipwright* [1995] ELR 580 for list of UK rules expressed including requirements in term of UK residence. The 1999 list included the following UK provisions: International Holding Cos (repealed), Film industry, Enterprise zones, 100% relief for N Ireland, ships balancing charges deferral, Independent Investment managers, Scientific Research allowances and 40% FYA for SMEs.
[4] House of Lords Session 1998/99. House of Lords paper 92.
[5] Inland Revenue press release 20 March 2000, *Simon's Weekly Tax Intelligence* 2000, p 499.
[6] IP/03/787, *Simon's Weekly Tax Intelligence* 2003, p 1057.
[7] Council Resolution 20 June 2006, 9738/06. See supra § **1.05** footnote 9.
[8] Statement by the Paymaster General, *Simon's Weekly Tax Intelligence* 2000, p 943.

Human Rights Law

[1.21] Human rights law is relevant to tax law in three ways. First, there is the European Convention on Human Rights. Although the UK signed the European Convention on Human Rights in 1950 it saw no need to incorporate it into domestic law—no doubt because it was thought that rights were sufficiently well protected through existing judicial and political procedures. Finally in 1998 the Convention was given some direct effect in domestic law by the Human Rights Act 1998—as from 2 October 2000. Even before 2 October 2000 legislators had to ensure that their actions conformed to the requirements of the Convention.[1]

The second way in which the Convention is important is the influence which it has already had on the development of UK law, especially in administrative law matters.[2] With the incorporation of the Convention into UK law this process may well accelerate, although the form in which it has been incorporated may discourage the courts from challenging parliamentary sovereignty too directly. A recent example is the law of breach of confidence.[3]

Finally there is the influence of the Convention in the development of fundamental principles of EC law, principles said to emerge in part from the common traditions of the member states. The importance here is that these fundamental principles are capable of direct effect and therefore, thanks to the supremacy of EC law, will override Diceyan parliamentary sovereignty in those areas where EC law holds sway.[4] In this connection one should note that the German constitution specifically prohibits retroactive legislation.[5]

The rights protected by the Convention and the 1998 Act are set out in the First Schedule to that Act. They are those contained in the Convention itself and in two protocols, the first and the sixth. The only mention of taxes comes

[1.21] Sources of tax law

in the first article of the first protocol where the protection of property is not to impair the right of the state to secure the payment of taxes. An indirect mention may also be found in Article 4 of the main convention where the prohibition of slavery and forced labour is not to prevent any work of service which forms part of normal civic obligation.[6] Other convention rights include the right to life (Article 2), the prohibition of torture (Article 3) the prohibition of slavery and forced labour (Article 4), the right to liberty and security (Article 5), to a fair trial (Article 6), to no punishment without law (Article 7), respect for private and family life (Article 8), freedom of thought, conscience and religion (Article 9) freedom of expression (Article 10), freedom of assembly and association (Article 11), the right to marry and found a family (Article 12) and the prohibition against discrimination in the exercise of any of these rights (Article 14). Article 17 disallows any reliance on the convention for acts aimed at destroying any of the rights and freedoms set out, while Article 18 makes the very important point that any restrictions permitted under the conventions are to be applied only for the purposes prescribed. The First Protocol lists the protection of property, the right to education and the right to free elections. The Sixth Protocol is concerned with the death penalty.

The 1998 Act imposes on courts an obligation to read and give effect to all legislation in a way which is compatible with Convention rights (s 3). If a court cannot do this it can, if sufficiently senior, issue a declaration of incompatibility (s 4); the court does not have the power to annul the legislation. The High Court may issue a declaration; the Commissioners may not. All courts have extensive powers to grant remedies for breach of the Act (s 8)); however this is to be done on the principles to be found in the Convention and in particular that of "just satisfaction", below.

The courts did not at first appear to be zealous in finding ways of protecting these rights through interpretation. Thus the Divisional Court[7] saw no reason to view the right of a client to confidentiality in dealings with his lawyer (legal professional privilege) as some sort of absolute right; a different view was taken in certain dicta in the House of Lords.[8] That more interventionist approach was echoed in the 2004 decision of the House in the non-tax case of *Ghaidan v Godin-Mendoza*[9] where Lord Steyn was particularly critical of judges who opted to make declarations of incompatibility rather than using their powers to construe the statutes and the court construed the term 'spouse' to include a member of a same sex couple in the context of housing legislation. However, it is a matter of context as was shown one year later the House declined to interpret 'widow' in TA 1988, s 262 to include widower in the tax case of *R (on the application of Wilkinson) v IRC*.[10]

> The reason, which turns on the scope of s. 6(2) of the Human Rights Act was explained by Lord Hoffmann as follows "Although Human Rights Act s 6(1) requires a public authority to give effect to the rights set out in the act—by making it unlawful for them to act in a way incompatible with a convention right—it does not compel the public authority to act in a way which is clearly contrary to the relevant UK legislation. This is set out in s 6(2).
>
> Subsection (1) does not apply to an act if—(a) as the result of one or more provisions of primary legislation, the authority could not have acted differently; or (b) in the case of one or more provisions of, or made under, primary legislation which cannot

be read or given effect in a way which is compatible with the Convention rights, the authority was acting so as to give effect to or enforce those provisions.

It was in reliance on these words that the House refused to compel the Revenue to grant relief to the widower by extra statutory concession.[11] The court also refused him any compensation. The basis for allowing compensation (or just satisfaction of the claim) is to put the person in the position he would have been in if he had gone to Strasbourg; it is not to create a new right of action for breach of statutory duty. As Parliament could have met the discrimination problem by abolishing the relief for widows, as it later did, no damages were necessary to put him in the position he would have been if there had been compliance with his Convention rights.[12] This position has been repeated by the Strasbourg Court.[13] These points show that Convention rights are much weaker than those arising under EC law.

The Strasbourg Court has sometimes shown a reluctance to intervene in tax matters, an approach expressed as allowing the states a 'margin of appreciation'. One of the most interesting cases comes from long before 1998 and involves the UK. This is *A, B, C and D v UK* where a Strasbourg organ upheld a retrospective provision. The taxpayers complained that FA 1978, s 31, which introduced legislation back to 1976, interfered with their right to property under the First article. The Commission said the measure was necessary to prevent avoidance and was not disproportionate.[12] In *National and Provincial Building Society v United Kingdom*[14] the Strasbourg Court declined to interfere with the UK legislature's reversal of the *Woolwich* case with retroactive effect so far as concerned building societies other than the Woolwich itself. However, while at first sight it appears to leave a high "margin of appreciation" to the signatory states in fiscal matters the decision is narrow in scope. It proceeds on an interpretation of the facts which is distinctly favourable to the Revenue. It deals with a case in which Parliament had tried to amend the law and the subordinate law making process had got it wrong first time; so the UK system was allowed a second chance to do by primary legislation what it had certainly wanted to do the first time because this was obviously consistent with the legislature's intent. One may comment that since the purpose of human rights is to protect people against the state, including the legislature, this looks rather weak. Further, the case does not tell us anything about the attitude of the court if the UK legislation had tried to remove the fruits of victory from the Woolwich Building Society itself.

The question as to which bits of tax legislation are vulnerable to being declared incompatible with the European Convention is still an open one. In *R (on the application of Professional Contractors Group Ltd) v IRC*,[15] a group representing taxpayers sought judicial review of UK statutory provisions[16] on the grounds that the provisions were contrary to Article 1 of Protocol 1 of the Human Rights Convention which guarantees the peaceful enjoyment of possessions. Burton J held that the particular legislation in issue, that dealing with personal service companies (see infra, § **8.27**), could not be attacked on these grounds; although the legislation imposed a higher burden of tax and because the legislation was unclear and imposed significant compliance costs, the argument that it amounted to a breach of the treaty was not even arguable.[17]

[1.21] Sources of tax law

In *King v United Kingdom (No 3)*[18] the Strasbourg Court held that the taxpayer in the particular case suffered an infringement to his rights because his case had not been dealt with sufficiently promptly and so he had been denied his right to trial within a reasonable time under Article 6(1). However, they denied him compensation for his pecuniary losses because there was no clear causal connection between the violation and the pecuniary losses; he was also denied compensation for non-pecuniary losses as he had been partly at fault for the delay; he was awarded reasonable costs.

The Court of Human Rights (and the now disbanded Commission on Human Rights) have indicated a willingness but only in principle to use Article 1 of the First Protocol to strike down an entire tax in an appropriate case. The Convention bans confiscation and there must come a point at which excessive taxation becomes confiscation.[20] In *Aston Cantlow v Wallbank*,[19] the Court of Appeal held that a common law rule which they defined as a tax was contrary to Article 1 of the First Protocol. As the right did not arise under statute there was no difficulty in simply holding that the council's claim was invalid. The charge was an arbitrary one which had long since lost its factual and legal basis. This was a historical legacy rather than a considered system, voted upon by a representative legislature familiar with contemporary social conditions. Even if it did not breach Article 1, the court held that it breached Article 14 of the Convention as being discriminatory.[21]

Sadly perhaps, the House of Lords reversed the Court of Appeal on the ground that the tax is levied by a Parochial Church Council and this, in their judgement, is not a core public authority and therefore not subject to Article 6.[22]

The Strasbourg Court has also indicated a willingness to use Article 1 and Article 14, the non-discrimination article, and condemned a UK rule in TA 1988, s 259, which was restricted to men whose wives were incapacitated under that head;[23] s 259 was immediately changed.[24]

In *Holland v IRC*,[25] the presiding Special Commissioner turned down the submission by taxpayer's counsel that the Human Rights Act 1998 requires that an unmarried cohabiting couple enjoy the same inheritance tax exemption as married spouses.

> We conclude that persons who live together as man and wife without being married are not in an analogous situation to married persons and that the difference in treatment in s 18 of the 1984 Act is objectively justified. There is therefore no breach of Article 14 and we are not obliged by s 3 of the 1998 Act to give a wider interpretation to the meaning of the word spouse in s 18.

The issue of the scope of the inheritance tax exemption for transfers between spouses also arose in *Burden v United Kingdom*.[26] Here the taxpayers were unmarried sisters who had lived in and owned a house in joint names. As in Holland the claim was based on discrimination which interfered with the family life and the peaceful enjoyment of their possessions. The full ECHR has now held that they were not entitled to redress from the court as the matter was within the wide margin of appreciation left to national authorities. The taxpayers' case was helped by the fact that the exemption was now extended to civil partners but not helped enough. At a lower level the court was sharply divided—four to three, the three condemning the UK rules as "unfair". The Grand Chamber preferred to found its decision on the lack of analogy between those who have entered into a legally binding marriage or civil partnership agreement, on the one hand and those, such as the applicants, who are in a long-term relationship of cohabitation, on the other (para 47).

The question of the scope of the now obsolescent rules on deductions for maintenance payments arose in *PM v United Kingdom*.[27] Today there is no longer a right to deduct maintenance payments (unless the payer was over 65 in 2000). Before 2000, TA 1988, s 347B(1) gave such a right but only if the payer was married to the mother. The present claim related to 1997–98 and so had to be taken direct to Strasbourg rather than through the UK courts. The ECHR ruled that s 347(1)(b) interfered with the taxpayer's right to enjoy his possession under Article 1 and did so in a way which was discriminatory—the government had not provided an objectively justifiable basis for the difference (para 28). The court awarded damages equal to the loss of the benefit of the deduction (para 38). One should note also that the court held that there was no violation of Article 13 of the Convention (para 34). What mattered in this case was that the court was considering the taxpayer as parent—not as spouse. The court does recognise that some discrimination between married and unmarried is justifiable even with regard to parents eg the non tax case of *McMichael v United Kingdom* where the UK rule refusing automatic parenthood to unmarried fathers was upheld.[28]

The Convention may also become relevant when considering procedures adopted by the Revenue in administering tax law; see, for example, *R v Allen*, infra, § **1.14**.

In *R v Dimsey*[79] the appellant argued that TA 1988, s 739 breached the convention if as the Revenue argued the provision gave the Revenue the power to choose whether to tax the transferor or the transferee—or both. This too was rejected by the House of Lords as being well within the margin of appreciation left to member states in respect of tax legislation. Lord Scott said:[30]

> The tax liability being imposed on the tax avoider does not depend on his having actually received any benefit from the income or assets of the transferee. The liability may be regarded as having a penal character and as intended to discourage United Kingdom residents from seeking to avoid tax by transferring assets abroad. The imposition of such a tax liability is, in my opinion, well within the margin of appreciation allowed to member states in respect of tax legislation.

---

1 Hence the statement by the Chancellor of the Exchequer at the start of each of Finance Bill since 1999. On the Convention generally in relation to tax matters see *Baker* [2000] BTR 211-377. The taxpayer cannot, however, require a court to apply the provisions of the Human Rights Act to defeat an action by the Revenue that was taken before 2 October 2000, even if that action determines the liability of the taxpayer over periods after that date: *Al Fayed v Advocate General for Scotland* [2002] STC 910 per The Lord Justice Clerk (Gill) at 942b.
2 See eg Klug and Starmer [1997] Public Law 223-233.
3 *Campbell v MGN Ltd* [2004] UKHL 22, [2004] 2 All ER 995.

[1.21] Sources of tax law

[4] See eg Hartley, *Foundations of European Community Law*, chapter 5 and essays in *Droits sans Frontières: Essays in Honour of L Neville Brown* (1991) by Jacobs 235–242, Ellis 265–276 and Usher 277–293.
[5] On such legislation see Loomer [2006] *British Tax Review* pp 64–9.
[6] On Article 4 see *Murat v IRC* [2004] EWHC 3123 (Admin), [2005] STC 184 citing *Van der Mussele v Belgium* (1983) 6 EHRR 163.
[7] *R (on application of Morgan Grenfell & Co Ltd) v Special Commr of Income Tax* [2000] STC 965.
[8] [2002] STC 786, HL.
[9] [2004] UKHL 30 (HL), [2004] 2 AC 557, [2004] 3 WLR 113.
[10] *R (on the application of Wilkinson) v IRC* [2005] UKHL 30, [2006] STC 270, especially paras [14] to [19] at 275a–276b.
[11] Para 22.
[12] Paras 24–28.
[13] *Hobbs and others v United Kingdom (Applications 63684/00, 63475/00, 63484/00 and 63468/00)* [2008] STC 1469 Fourth Section; or just satisfaction see 61 et seq agreeing with the House of Lords.
[12] *A, B, C and D v The United Kingdom (Application 8531/79)*.
[14] [1997] STC 1466.
[15] [2001] EWHC Admin 236, [2001] STC 629.
[16] FA 2000, s 60, Sch 12, also Welfare Reform and Pensions Act 1999, ss 75, 76 and subsidiary legislation.
[17] *R (on application of Professional Contractors Group Ltd) v IRC* [2001] EWHC Admin 236, [2001] STC 629 at 673g. No human rights argument was raised at the Court of Appeal level: [2002] STC 165.
[18] *King v United Kingdom (No 3)* [2005] STC 438.
[20] *Svenska Management Grupen AB v Sweden* (1985) 45 DR 211, EC of HR.
[19] *Aston Cantlow and Wilmcote with Billesley Parochial Church Council v Wallbank* [2001] EWCA Civ 713, [2002] STC 313, see infra, § **1.15**.
[21] *Aston Cantlow and Wilmcote with Billesley Parochial Church Council v Wallbank* [2001] EWCA Civ 713, [2002] STC 313 at 326b. Nothing in the court judgment distinguished between a tax imposed by a common law or a tax imposed by statute insofar as the ability of the court to overturn it. Moreover, the common law was recognised by statute in Ecclesiastical Dilapidations Measure 1923, which established the procedure under which the charge is levied by the parochial church council.
[22] [2003] UKHL 37, [2003] 3 All ER 1213.
[23] *MacGregor v United Kingdom* (application No 30548/96) (3 December 1997, unreported), ECtHR.
[24] FA 1998, s 26.
[25] [2003] STC (SCD) 43. Steven Oliver QC and Dr Nuala Brice, at [92].
[26] Application 13378/05 [2007] STC 252 and, full court, [2008] STC 1305.
[27] Application 6638/03 [2005] STC 1566.
[28] [1995] 2 FCR 718 (esp para 98).
[29] [2001] UKHL 46, [2001] STC 1520, in particular para 71.
[30] [2001] UKHL 46, [2001] STC 1520, at 1534a to 1535j, in particular 1535e–f.

Human rights procedural issues in tax cases

[1.22] The European Court of Human Rights, which sits in Strasbourg, has had quite a lot to say about tax procedures.[1] These may be broken down into three main areas.

First, the court and the now disbanded Commission have used Article 8 of the Convention on protection of a person's private and family life, home and correspondence to examine a search with warrant under French law, French law at that time not requiring a warrant.[2] The court placed considerable emphasis on the types of interference permitted by Article 8(2). Second, they have considered Article 6(1) (the right to a fair trial) and held that the determination of a tax liability itself is not a matter of determining a person's "civil rights and obligations".[3] This very unsatisfactory decision may one day be reversed but as it is a 2001 decision with a full hearing this may be optimistic. The dissatisfaction is reflected in the fact that the court was sharply divided, that the court may not have understood the background to the Convention properly and that its decision looks odd when put with its earlier decision that Article 6(1) did apply to social security appeals.[4] The UK courts have accepted that position.[5]

A quite different approach has been take in Article 6(2). Meanwhile the court has held that the imposition of a tax penalty can be treated as a "criminal charge", and so within that Article. They have therefore looked at a 100% tax penalty[6] (and awarded damages) and rejected a state's right to claim a penalty for a tax fraud committed by someone else.[7] They have also considered whether a tax investigation for tax fraud which took eight and a half years was too long and so was a breach of Article 6.[8] The question whether the proceedings amount to a criminal charge depend on the domestic classification of the offence, the nature of the offence and the nature and degree of severity of the potential or actual penalty.[9]

Thirdly, and in the same vein, the court has held that a right which originates in a tax matter, such as a right to repayment of tax or of indemnity against another person, may be a "civil right or obligation". Appeals against civil evasion penalties under VATA 1994, s 60 and for penalties for fraud or neglect under TMA 1970, s 95 have been held to be criminal for the purpose of Article 6; however, in one of these cases there is a dictum that the serious misdeclaration penalty under VATA 1994, s 63 would be regarded as regulatory rather than criminal.[10] In *Sharkey v Revenue and Customs Comrs*,[11] Etherton J considered a penalty notice for £50 issued under TMA 1970, s 97AA for breach of s 19A (failure to produce documents). He agreed with the Special Commissioner that the primary objective of the £50 penalty is to procure production of the documents and this was not enough to make it a criminal charge (para [37])). He emphasised that he was concerned only with the £50 penalty and not the daily penalty which could arise later (para 38).

Human rights issues were raised at the House of Lords level in *R v Allen*,[12] a prosecution for conspiring to cheat the public revenue. In *Allen* the taxpayer's human rights argument was that he had been deprived of his privilege against self incrimination. He had been asked for certain information and then under the well known 'Hansard' procedure, threatened with prosecution if he did not tell and induced by a promise of non-prosecution to provide a schedule of assets. All this was, he argued, in breach of his right to a fair trial and so his conviction for conspiring to cheat the public revenue was unsafe. These arguments were rejected by Lord Hutton, who gave the only substantial reasoned speech. First, the events had occurred before the 1998 Act came into force and the Act is not retroactive.[13] Secondly, the state had a right to ask for this information[14] and, thirdly, any inducement was irrelevant because the accused had not provided accurate information but continued to give false information.[15] The third point may be seen as a pyrrhic victory for the Revenue because it means that where the taxpayer provides information in response to the Hansard statement there may well be a breach of Convention Rights if the Revenue proceed to make use of it at any later trial or when seeking penalties.[16]

In *R v Gill*,[17] the Hansard procedure was considered not in the context of human rights legislation but in the context of the Police and Criminal Evidence Act 1984. The Human Rights Act was not relevant as the events occurred before that Act came into force. However, the court noted[18] that the Strasbourg Court of Human Rights had rejected an application by Allen that the Hansard procedure breached the Convention as amounting to a breach of the right to silence and his privilege against self incrimination; it also held that there was no improper inducement. This was done on the basis of the facts.

On *R (on the application of Wilkinson) v IRC*, see supra, § 1.21.

The UK tax system may find many human rights issues taken over the next few years. Two contradictory points should be borne in mind. The first is that although many tax issues have been raised in the Strasbourg jurisprudence not many have succeeded, not least because that court likes to leave a margin of appreciation to the member state. The other is that while the Strasbourg court may, for sensible political reasons, wish to leave a margin of appreciation to the member state there is no reason why a court of that member state should. Whether the enthusiasm with which the UK courts adapted themselves to EC law will, after *Ghaidan v Godin-Mendoza*[19], be matched by a similar enthusiasm for human rights remains to be seen. It should not, however, be forgotten that the ECJ has declared that human rights can be part of EC law and so be relevant—and of direct effect—in those matters subject to EC law.

The Joint Committee of the Houses of Parliament on Human Rights considers, among other things, whether legislation is compatible with the Convention. The Committee decided that the income tax charge on pre-owned assets (infra, § 12.13) introduced by FA 2004 did not break the convention but this view has been criticised.[20]

---

[1] See generally the article by Baker [2000] BTR 211–377.
[2] *Funke v France* (1993)16 EHRR 297 see also cases cited by Baker loc cit at pp 332 and 357.
[3] *Ferrazini v Italy Application 44759/98* [2001] STC 1314.
[4] *Schouten and Meldrum v Netherlands* (1994) 19 EHRR 432.
[5] eg *Significant Ltd v Farrel* [2005] EWHC 3434 (Ch), [2006] STC 1626.
[6] *JJ v Netherlands* (1998) 28 EHRR 168.
[7] *AP, MP and TP v Switzerland* (1997) 26 EHRR 541, ECHR.
[8] *Hozee v Netherlands* (1998) unreported.

[9] In *Georgiou v United Kingdom* [2001] STC 80 (ECHR). See also *Han v Customs and Excise Comrs* [2001] EWCA Civ 1040, [2001] STC 1188 and *King v Walden* [2001] STC 822. See generally Baker loc cit at pp 228–238.
[10] *Han v Customs and Excise Comrs (VAT)* [2001] EWCA Civ 1040, [2001] STC 1188 (on s 63 see para 81); and *King v Walden* [2001] STC 822.
[11] [2006] EWHC 300 (Ch) [2006] STC 2026, relying especially on *Engel v the Netherlands* [1976] ECHR 51000/71 and on *Han v Customs and Excise Comrs* (above).
[12] [2001] UKHL 45, [2001] 4 All ER 768, [2001] STC 1537.
[13] [2001] STC 1537 at 1549d [para 23].
[14] [2001] STC 1537 at 1554e [para 30].
[15] [2001] STC 1537 at 1556h [para 35].
[16] On the legitimacy of pretrial procedures there is an interesting article by Ormerod in [2001] BTR 194–206.
[17] [2003] EWCA Crim 2256, [2003] STC 1229.
[18] At paras 26–28.
[19] [2003] EWCA Civ 814, [2003] STC 1113.
[20] 12th Report 2003–04 Session especially at paras 1.48 and 1.50; for criticism see Chamberlain and Whitehouse Pre Owned Assets, para 1.22.

Statutes and statutory interpretation

Statutes

[1.23] The statute law for a particular tax is to be found in the statute which introduced it as subsequently amended.[1] Sometimes amendments are made to the text of the original Act; at other times a new provision is introduced to exist alongside the original Act. The result might be described as a patchwork were it not for the overtones of antique cosiness that go with that word; it is better described as a shambles.

Sometimes the text relating to a particular tax is consolidated, eg income tax in the 1918, 1952, 1970 and 1988 acts, corporation tax in 1970 and 1988, CGT in 1979 and 1992, corporation tax on capital gains in 1970 and 1992, VAT in 1983 and 1994 and CTT (now IHT) in 1984, but the perfection of consolidation is often marred within weeks. We now have to cope with the work of the Tax Law Rewrite Project. Statutes produced from the toil of this Committee are not consolidations, but the re-expression of statutory principles in a manner that, by codification and expansion of the text aims to guide the reader to relevant provisions and to state the provisions more clearly. Statutes so far produced are Capital Allowances Act 2001, Income Tax (Earnings and Pensions) Act 2003, Income Tax (Trading and Other Income) Act 2005 and Income Tax Act 2007 and the Corporation Taxes Act 2009. A second Corporation Tax act is expected to reach the statute book in 2010 to be followed by a Taxation (International and other provisions) Act which will cover most of the remaining parts of income tax and corporation tax. It is not clear whether rewrite work will continue beyond that date. The characteristic of these Acts that is most noticeable to the seasoned practitioner is the removal

[1.23] Sources of tax law

of reference to tax Schedules, without the abandonment of the Schedular system. Thus, Schedule D Case VI becomes "Miscellaneous income". Schedule E becomes "Employment income, pension income and Social security income".

Income tax is an annual tax and the charge is reimposed by Parliament each year in the Finance Bill (Income Tax Act 2007, s 4), see supra, § **1.32**. The result is that the Tax Acts are really in the nature of an Income Tax Clauses Act and apply whenever any Act imposes an income tax.[2] The Finance Bill also amends the rules for the other taxes. The resulting combination of measures of great economic importance and matters of great technical subtlety discussed against the background of the hurly burly of Parliamentary procedure is, not surprisingly, capable of error.

Simon's Taxes A1.103.

---

[1] The Court of Appeal has reminded us that it is also constitutionally possible for a tax to be imposed under common law: *Aston Cantlow v Wallbank* [2001] EWCA Civ 713, [2002] STC 313, CA.

[2] Per Atkin LJ in *Martin v Lowry* (1926) 11 TC 297 at 317.

Statutory interpretation

[1.24] The modern approach to interpreting and applying tax statutes was set out by the House of Lords in the *Barclays* case.[1] The nature of the composite transaction rule (or approach) is discussed in Chapter 3. Here we concentrate on the wider aspects of the purposive approach. In doing so we must not overlook what Lord Hoffmann has said extra judicially, "It is one thing to give a statute a purposive construction. It is another to rectify the terms of highly prescriptive legislation in order to include provisions which might have been included but are not actually there."[2] In the light of this it would be premature to discard altogether material from older times.

In *Barclays* Lord Nicholls speaking for the entire committee said:

> [27] It is no doubt too much to expect that any exposition will remove all difficulties in the application of the principles because it is in the nature of questions of construction that there will be borderline cases about which people will have different views. It should however be possible to achieve some clarity about basic principles.
>
> [28] As Lord Steyn explained in *IRC v McGuckian*[3], the modern approach to statutory construction is to have regard to the purpose of a particular provision and interpret its language, so far as possible, in a way which best gives effect to that purpose. . . .
>
> [29] The *Ramsay* case[4] liberated the construction of revenue statutes from being both literal and blinkered. It is worth quoting two passages from the influential speech of Lord Wilberforce. First[5] on the general approach to construction:
>
> 'What are "clear words" is to be ascertained on normal principles; these do not confine the courts to literal interpretation. There may, indeed should, be considered

the context and scheme of the relevant Act as a whole, and its purpose may, indeed should, be regarded: . . .'

[30] Second[6] on the application of a statutory provision so construed to a composite transaction: 'It is the task of the court to ascertain the legal nature of any transaction to which it is sought to attach a tax or a tax consequence and if that emerges from a series or combination of transactions, intended to operate as such, it is that series or combination which may be regarded.'. . .

[32] The essence of the new approach was to give the statutory provision a purposive construction in order to determine the nature of the transaction to which it was intended to apply and then to decide whether the actual transaction (which might involve considering the overall effect of a number of elements intended to operate together) answered to the statutory description.

The traditional UK view has been that a citizen is not to be taxed unless he is designated in clear terms by the taxing Act as a taxpayer and the amount of his liability is clearly defined.[7] Now, Lord Wilberforce's point in para 29 above should be borne in mind.

The traditional view of strict interpretation was well stated by Rowlatt J:[8]

In a taxing Act one has to look merely at what is clearly said. There is no room for any intendment. There is no equity about a tax. There is no presumption as to a tax. Nothing is to be read in, nothing is to be implied. One can only look fairly at the language used.

However well stated, it cannot stand against the words of the House of Lords in *Barclays*. Yet Lord Hoffmann's words may mean that there are times when a purposive approach will not give the Revenue the success they crave. There may still be good sense in some contexts to follow the judge who said, in 2000, that where a taxpayer sought to take advantage of a rule a judge should only refuse to give effect to that plan if there was some express or implied prohibition, such implication being made only where it is necessary or the statute unambiguously so requires.[9]

The problem of seemingly meaningless legislation (or legislation that does not seem to give a clear meaning in a particular context) is a problem that has faced the courts throughout the history of modern taxation and the problem remains despite the new purposive approach. As early as 1876, Brett J[10] declared as a rule of statutory interpretation:

It is a canon of construction that, if it be possible, effect must be given to every word of an Act of Parliament or other document; but that, if there be a word or a phrase therein to which no sensible meaning can be given, it must be eliminated.

This concise statement of the principle impressed Lord Bridge[11] in the House of Lords in 1984, but in the end he decided that, however intractable the problem the section had to give up its arcane meaning.

The literal interpretation has (or had) two consequences. The first is that it is for the Crown to establish that the subject falls within the charge.[12] This means that if the words were ambiguous the subject was entitled to the benefit of the doubt. But the principle was not that the subject is to have the benefit if, on any argument that ingenuity can suggest, the Act does not appear perfectly accurate but only if, after careful examination of all the clauses, a judicial mind

[1.24] Sources of tax law

still entertains reasonable doubts as to what the legislature intended:[13] if there was no ambiguity the words must take their natural meaning.[14] Nowadays the words have to be interpreted purposively but, as already suggested, the problem of ambiguity remains.

The second consequence was that strict interpretation applies to the taxpayer just as much as to the Revenue. So if a literal interpretation produces a construction whereby hardship falls on innocent beneficiaries by the rights, monstrous or otherwise, conferred on the Revenue, that interpretation must be adhered to and the hardship produced is not a relevant consideration.[15] Further where an exception from taxation is given by a statute, that exception is to be construed strictly and any ambiguity construed against the taxpayer.[16] It is to be hoped that here too the advent of purposive construction will lead to change.

[1] *Barclays Mercantile Business Finance Ltd v Mawson* [2004] UKHL 51 [2005] STC 1.
[2] 'Tax Avoidance' Lecture given at the Centre for Commercial Studies Queen Mary London printed 2005 *British Tax Review* 195 at 205.
[3] [1997] STC 908 at 915, [1997] 1 WLR 991 at 999.
[4] [1981] STC 174, [1982] AC 300.
[5] [1981] STC 174 at 179, [1982] AC 300 at 323.
[6] [1981] STC 174 at 180, [1982] AC 300 at 323–324.
[7] Per Lord Wilberforce in *Vestey v IRC* [1980] STC 10 at 18: but contrast *Floor v Davis* [1979] 2 All ER 677, [1979] STC 379 (in which Lord Wilberforce dissented).
[8] *Cape Brandy Syndicate v IRC* [1921] 1 KB 64 at 71, 12 TC 358 at 366.
[9] Peter Gibson LJ in *Carr v Armpledge Ltd* [2000] STC 410 at 416c, CA.
[10] *Stone v Yeovil Corpn* (1876) 1 CPD 691 at 701.
[11] *Gubay v Kington* [1984] STC 99 at 108f.
[12] Per Parke B in *Re Micklethwaite* (1855) 11 Exch 452 at 456, approved by Lord Halsbury LC in *Tennant v Smith* [1892] AC 150 at 154.
[13] Per Kindersley V-C, in *Wilcox v Smith* (1857) 4 Drew 40 at 49.
[14] eg Nourse LJ (dissenting) in *Palmer v Moloney* [1999] STC 890 at 900.
[15] Per Danckwerts J in *Re Joynson's Will Trusts, Gaddum v IRC* [1954] Ch 567 at 573 and see *IRC v Hinchy* [1960] 1 All ER 505, 38 TC 625.
[16] Per Cohen LJ in *Littman v Barron* [1951] 2 All ER 393 at 398, 33 TC 373 at 380.

[1.25] Anti-avoidance provisions phrased in broad language which deliberately eschews legal terms of art were construed broadly long before *McGucklian* (1997).[1]

While the judges have wrestled with legislation of great complexity, there have been warnings that it is possible that the obscurity of an enactment or the uncontrollable width of its language—or of the discretion needed to implement it—may compel a court to find that no reasonable construction is available and that the taxpayer is therefore not to be charged.[2] The House of Lords has shown itself capable on the one hand of depriving a provision of any effect[3] and on the other of imposing double taxation.[4] The first of these decisions might now be rejected but the second may fall within Lord Hoffmann's category of highly prescriptive legislation which cannot be rectified.

Statutes and statutory interpretation [1.26]

Simon's Taxes Division A2.

1 Eg Lord Reid in *Greenberg v IRC* [1972] AC 109 at 137; however, see also Nourse J in *Pilkington Bros Ltd v IRC* [1981] STC 219 at 235; see also *Mangin v IRC* [1971] AC 739 at 746.
2 *Customs and Excise Comrs v Top Ten Promotions Ltd* [1969] 3 All ER 39 at 93, HL, per Lord Donovan and at 95 per Lord Wilberforce; *Vestey v IRC* [1980] AC 1148, [1980] STC 10.
3 *IRC v Ayrshire Employers Mutual Insurance Association Ltd* [1946] 1 All ER 637, 27 TC 331, HL.
4 *Cleary v IRC* [1967] 2 All ER 48, 44 TC 399; infra, § **4.19**.

[**1.26**] The court may look at the purpose and history of the relevant legislation and to this end reference may be made to the state of the law, and the material facts and events with which it is apparent that Parliament was dealing.[1] In *Pepper v Hart*[2] the House of Lords, reversing centuries of case law, held that the court could consult *Hansard* in order to interpret the words of the legislation. As Lord Browne-Wilkinson put it:

. . . subject to any question of Parliamentary privilege,[3] the exclusionary rule should be relaxed so as to permit reference to Parliamentary materials where:

(a) legislation is ambiguous or obscure, or leads to an absurdity;
(b) the material relied on consists of one or more statements by a minister or other promoter of the Bill together if necessary with such other Parliamentary material as is necessary to understand such statements and their effects; and
(c) the statements relied on are clear.[4]

In this case the House looked at Hansard and concluded that a reading of Hansard showed that in 1976 a particular statement by the minister in charge of the Bill took the view that in determining the measure of cost incurred by an employer in providing an in-house benefit in kind one should pay attention to marginal cost not overall cost. It followed that that was how the provision should be construed. Hansard has been cited to the court in later cases but not with decisive effect. In *Wilson v First County Trust* Lord Nicholls treated the rule as allowing the courts to look at Ministerial statements, if clear and umabiguous, as part of the background to the legislation.[5]

Simon's Taxes A2.104.

1 See Lord Macdermott in *IRC v Rennell* [1964] AC 173 at 198 and Lord Macdermott in *Madras Electric Supply Corpn Ltd v Boarland* [1955] AC 667 at 686, 35 TC 612 at 640, [1955] 1 All ER 753 at 760.
2 [1992] STC 898.
3 At 926 he concluded that there was no problem with privilege. He rehearsed the standard textbook position on privilege, citing Erskine May. "It is for the courts to decide whether a privilege exists and for the House to decide whether such privilege had been infringed." Here ". . . neither the Clerk of the Commons nor the Attorney General have identified or specified the nature of any privilege extending beyond that protected by the Bill of Rights. In the absence of a claim to a defined privilege as to the validity of which your Lordships could make a determination, it

would not be right to withhold from the taxpayers a decision to which, in law, they were entitled."

4   1992] STC 898 at 922, 923.
5   [2004] 1 AC 816 at para [58].

Some rules

[1.27] Some rules are as follows:

(1) Statute must be read and given effect in a way that is compatible with the rights and fundamental freedoms in the convention for the protection of human rights.[1]
(2) The Act must be read as a whole. Where there is an ambiguity the scheme of the Act may resolve it.[2]
(3) The words of the legislation must be construed in their context. Until a person has read the whole of a document or statute he is not entitled to say that it, or any part of it, is clear and unambiguous.[3]
(4) Arguments based on competing anomalies do not find favour.[4]
(5) Where a statutory provision is enacted but is based upon a misconception of what the law then was, the law remains as it was and does not share the misconception of the legislature.[5]
(6) There is a presumption that provisions dealing with the machinery of taxation do not impose a charge.[6] The courts will not construe a machinery provision so as to defeat the charge;[7] however the absence of machinery has been used to qualify a charge.[8]
(7) There is a presumption that words used in the same contexts in different statutes are used in the same sense.[9]
(8) Where a particular interpretation would give the Revenue a discretion power to allocate the burden of tax between taxpayers, the courts will reject it.[10]
(9) When interpreting a consolidated enactment, the court should not in general refer to the earlier Acts. However, the court is entitled to have regard to the fact that a subsection was later added to the original section.[11]
(10) The Taxes Acts[12] are equally applicable in England and Wales, Scotland and for most of them, Northern Ireland. It follows that the language which they employ ought to be construed so as to have, as far as possible, uniform effect in all four countries alike.[13]
(11) When the provisions are ambiguous the court may consider the effect of subsequent legislation only when the two views of the original statute are equally tenable and there are no indications favouring one rather than the other. The argument advanced on the basis of this rule is that the new provision could only have been needed if one view was held by Parliament rather than the other.[14]
(12) Where, as sometimes happens, statutes deem certain things to be as they are not, the court must consider for what purposes and between what persons the statutory fiction is to be resorted to.[15] However, this does not require the court to abandon the golden rule of construction, that the grammatical and ordinary sense of the words should be adhered to

unless that would lead to absurdity or inconsistency in which case the grammatical and ordinary sense of the words may be modified to avoid that absurdity and inconsistency but no further.[16]

(13) The courts do not place much weight on arguments from redundancy ie that if this argument is correct then another provision would not have been included. It is not unusual for Parliament to say expressly what the courts would have inferred anyway.[17]

---

[1] Human Rights Act 1998, s 3.
[2] Per Lord Halsbury in *IRC v Priestley* [1901] AC 208 at 213.
[3] Viscount Simonds in *A-G v Prince Ernest Augustus of Hanover* [1957] AC 436 at 463.
[4] Per Lord Normand in *Dale v IRC* [1953] 2 All ER 671 at 676, 34 TC 468 at 488, HL.
[5] *Davies, Jenkins & Co Ltd v Davies* [1967] 1 All ER 913 at 915, 922, 44 TC 273 at 287, HL and per Robert Walker LJ in *Plumbly v Spencer* [1999] STC 677 at 684c.
[6] Per Lord Macmillan in *Straits Settlements Comr of Stamps v Oei Tjong Swan* [1933] AC 378 at 389.
[7] *IRC v Longmans Green & Co Ltd* (1932) 17 TC 272 at 282.
[8] *Colquhoun v Brooks* (1889) 14 App Cas 493 at 506, 2 TC 490 at 500.
[9] Per Lord Reid in *Gartside v IRC* [1968] AC 553 at 602, [1968] 1 All ER 121 at 131. But this is only a presumption; see Atkin LJ in *Martin v Lowry* [1926] 1 KB 550 at 561, 11 TC 297 at 315.
[10] *Vestey v IRC* [1980] AC 1148, [1980] STC 10.
[11] *IRC v Joiner* [1975] 3 All ER 1050, [1975] STC 657 but note the more restrictive approach of Lord Diplock and see the discussion by Baxter in (1976) Conv, 336 at 343.
[12] Defined in TA 1988, ss 831, 832.
[13] Viscount Simon in *IT Comrs for General Purposes (City of London) v Gibbs* [1942] 1 All ER 415 at 422, 24 TC 221 at 236, 244, HL. Hence the English courts will follow Scottish decisions—per Lord Evershed MR in *Wiseburgh v Domville* [1956] 1 All ER 754 at 758, 36 TC 527 at 538–539, CA.
[14] Per Oliver LJ in *Finch v IRC* [1985] Ch 1 at 15, [1984] STC 261 at 272, CA; and Hoffman J in *Westcott v Woolcombers Ltd* [1986] STC 182 at 191.
[15] Per Nourse J in *IRC v Metrolands (Property Finance) Ltd* [1981] STC 193 at 208.
[16] Peter Gibson J in *Marshall v Kerr* [1993] STC 360 at 365, CA.
[17] Per Lord Hoffmann in *Walker v Centaur Clothes Group Ltd* [2000] STC 324 at 331.

Scotland and Northern Ireland

[1.28] The Taxes Acts apply to the whole of the United Kingdom, thus, they are to be implemented under the three separate legal systems of, first, England and Wales, second, Scotland and, third, Northern Ireland.

The way in which the Taxes Acts are worded in order to achieve this result was analysed by Lord Macnaghten. Lord Macnaghten analysed the manner in

[1.28] Sources of tax law

which a statute that applies to the whole of the United Kingdom is given effect in each of the separate jurisdictions as the employment of three classes of technique:[1]

> It seems to me that statutes which apply to Scotland as well as to England, and which touch upon matters commonly dealt with in legal language, may be divided into three classes. Sometimes, but very rarely, all legal terms are carefully avoided[2]. . .every legal term according to English law is immediately followed by its equivalent in Scotch legal phraseology, and where no exact equivalent is to be found a neutral and non-legal expression is adopted.[3] But in some cases certainly, and especially in the legislation of former days, the statute proclaims its origin and speaks the language of an English lawyer, with some Scotch legal phrases thrown in rather casually. The Income Tax Acts, I think fall within this class. How are you to approach the construction of such statutes?. . .You must. . .reason by analogy; that is. . .you must take the meanings of legal expressions from the law of the country to which they properly belong, and in any case arising in the sister country you must apply the statute in an analogous or corresponding sense, so as to make the operation and effect of the statute the same in both countries. Thus you get 'a consistent sensible construction'.

In construing statutes that fall within his third class, Lord Macnaghten noted that the approach he outlined for construction of the statute must be adopted, even though it "may do violence to some of the best established doctrines of Scots law".[4]

More recently, Lord Walker has said that the fact that the legislation has to apply in Scotland is a good reason for not being swayed by highly technical arguments from English land law. He also said that when asked to deal with a flaw in the legislation he would always tend to favour a statutory analysis under which the taxable results corresponded with the actual results, ie, the commercial (or economic) consequences.[5]

A totally separate question is the forum for proceedings. A criminal act committed in Scotland is prosecuted before a court in Scotland; a criminal act in England, before an English court. If a trader in Brighton knowingly enters on a tax return figures that are false, he may be committing a criminal offence when he delivers that return to a HMRC office. HMRC has established some processing centres in Scotland. If the trader in Brighton posts his document to Scotland to a HMRC office with a Scottish address, the offence is likely to be committed where the document is received and acted upon. This means that any criminal prosecution that arises will be before the Scottish courts and not the English courts, even though the trader may have no other connection with Scotland.[6]

Statute[7] provides 'relevant place of business' rules in respect of General Commissioners' hearings in relation to corporation tax and an election procedure for both an appellant corporation taxpayer and the Revenue to select the location of an appeal from those places.[8] The superior court (the High Court in England, the Court of Session, sitting as the Court of Exchequer in Scotland) that will have jurisdiction over an appeal from the General Commissioners is determined by the location of the General Commissioners who heard the case. An appeal from the General Commissioners in England is to the High Court. An appeal from the General Commissioners is to the Court of Session.[9]

But there were no such rules for the Special Commissioners. The jurisdiction of the Special Commissioners was a United Kingdom wide jurisdiction. Both TMA 1970 and now the Tribunals, Courts and Enforcement Act 2007 are statutes of UK wide application. It does not segment the Special Commissioners' jurisdiction into separate jurisdictions for England, Scotland and Northern Ireland.[10] The location of hearings of the Special Commissioners is a matter of pure administrative convenience. A hearing in London can consider points of Scots private law,[11] for example.

[1] *IT Special Comrs v Pemsel* (1891) 3 TC 53 at 93/94.
[2] Lord Macnaghten gave as his example Succession Duty Act 1857. The more recent example is IHTA 1984, s 3(1), (2), and see Megarry J in *Sargaison v Roberts* [1969] 3 All ER 1072 at 1077, 45 TC 612 at 617.
[3] Lord Macnaghten gave as his examples the Bills of Exchange Act 1882 and the Partnership Act 1890. A more recent example is IHTA 1984, s 199(4).
[4] Per Lord Macnaghten in *Lord Advocate v Countess of Moray* [1905] AC 531 at 540, HL.
[5] Lord Walker in *Jerome v Kelly* [2004] UKHL 25; [2004] STC 887, para 28.
[6] See further at infra, § **2.27**.
[7] TMA 1970, s 44(1) & Sch 3.
[8] TMA 1970, Sch 3, para 4(3).
[9] TMA 1970, s 46 contains no provisions analogous to the now repealed rules for General Commissioners in s 44 or Sch 3.
[10] See the judgment of Julian Ghosh in *Spring Salmon & Seafood v R & C Comrs* [2005] STC (SCD) 830, paras 40 & 41 at 843e–844b.
[11] See the judgment of Julian Ghosh in *Spring Salmon & Seafood v R & C Comrs* [2005] STC (SCD) 830, para 46 at 843g.

Case law

[1.29] Cases are authorities in the usual way according to the rule of precedent save that tax is a UK law and so English courts will accept Scottish decisions and vice versa. However, in assessing the value of a precedent in tax law, special complications arise from the fact that the appeal structure in the UK allows the courts to reverse a decision of the Commissioners only for error of law or because it cannot be supported on the evidence: infra, § **2A.35**.

Since January 1995 decisions of the Special Commissioners have been published.[1]

[1] See Special Commissioners (Jurisdiction and Procedure) Regulations 1994, SI 1994/1811, para 20; this regulation is made under TMA 1970, s 56D, inserted by F(No 2)A 1992, Sch 16, para 4, it applies as from 1 September 1994.

Revenue practice

[1.30] Although not law, statements of Revenue practice are of great importance in the practical administration of the system and the Revenue; major changes of policy in recent years have led to a great increase in the amount of information being made available. These statements are of different sorts. One feature of the Tax Law Rewrite Project has been to take as many of the concessions and practices etc as possible onto the statute book.

First, there are extra-statutory concessions. These are few, tightly written and almost legislative in form. One crucial difference from a statutory provision was that the Revenue could withhold the benefit of the concession if they were so minded without legal—as distinct from political or administrative—consequences. However, the development of administrative law remedies suggests that an assessment made on the basis of withholding a concession could be quashed on the basis of breach of the duty to act fairly as between different taxpayers.[1] Such a situation would only arise where the taxpayer could bring himself within the scope of the concession and in this connection it is important to note that the list of concessions is prefaced with a general statement that a concession will not be given where an attempt is made to use it for tax avoidance.[2] In a note to a new concession the Revenue stated that concessions are used "to deal with what are, on the whole, minor or transitory anomalies . . . and to reduce cases of hardship at the margins of the code when a statutory remedy would be difficult to devise or would run to a length out of proportion to the intrinsic importance of the matter".[3] Judicial comment on an extra statutory concession was made by Sir Richard Scott V-C in *Steibelt v Paling*[4] where he quoted extra statutory concession D24 as being the way in which a court would probably have constructed the statutory language and commented: "I am not satisfied that in publishing D24 the Revenue is making any concession at all".[5]

The Revenue's power to make extra statutory concessions has been much discussed in constitutional law. In the latest case, *R (on the application of Wilkinson) v IRC*[6] the House of Lords held that the department could not be compelled to grant a concession so as to give effect to a right arising under the Human Rights Act 1998. Concessions arising from the need to collect tax pragmatically with minor or transitory anomalies, cases of hardship at the margin or cases in which a statutory rule was difficult to formulate or its enactment would take up a disproportionate amount of parliamentary time.[7] The power to make concessions is usually based on HMRC's responsibility, originally under Inland Revenue Regulation Act 1890 and now under TMA 1970, s 1, for the collection and management of the various taxes. In the Wilkinson case it was suggested that the power was not as wide as previously thought (by HMRC). By FA 2008 the Treasury may make statutory instruments to give concessions and practices statutory effect. It is expected that this power will be used only where there is a doubt whether the concession etc comes within TMA 1970, s 1.[8]

Second, HMRC publish statements of practice; these are only slightly less formal than the concessions. These, too, have been gathered together in booklet IR 131. The Revenue position often prefers a broad legislative rule which can then be interpreted "liberally" or not. The disadvantages of this are that such a rule may be interpreted unevenly and there is the possibility, however unlikely, of abuse. Statements of practice are now supplemented by published Revenue interpretations; these interpretations are heavily qualified and the Revenue will not necessarily regard themselves as bound by them. In proceedings for judicial review the court has ordered discovery of such documents but only on the basis that the taxpayer relied on having been informed that there was a Revenue view of the correct construction of a provision and that that construction was in his favour.[9]

Third, there are advance rulings in individual cases. For certain specified types of transaction, HMRC have a statutory duty to give a ruling on a proposed transaction.[10] For other types of transaction, the Revenue have no duty imposed on them to express a view in advance of action being taken. However, in practice advice is often available provided there is a detailed scheme; the Revenue usually insist on knowing the identity of the taxpayer concerned.[11] The Revenue are not there to provide a free legal aid clinic, but it is in the Revenue's interests to be helpful.[12] Where an application for judicial review is made on the basis of a ruling, the Revenue will only be bound in the case of an informal approach if the taxpayer gave full details of the specific transaction on which he sought the Revenue's ruling, indicated the ruling sought and made it plain that a fully considered ruling was sought, and indicated the use he intended to make of any ruling given, and the ruling or statement made was clear, unambiguous and devoid of qualification.[13] Where the Revenue gives a decision contrary to that sought by the taxpayer, on a matter that is not the subject of a statutory clearance, the court will not admit a challenge to the pre-transaction advisory opinion of the Revenue.[14] This is not because of a lack of jurisdiction; the refusal is based on the recognition that the public interest is served by the Revenue giving pre-transaction advice and this advice would be curtailed if it were subject to judicial challenge.[15] A breach of a representation by the Revenue will not amount to an abuse of power if the taxpayer knows that clearance at local level is not to be treated as binding on the Revenue or if the taxpayer has not fully disclosed all relevant material to the inspectors.[16] There is not necessarily full disclosure merely because sufficient information has been disclosed to enable inferences to be drawn. It is not yet clear whether obtaining a ruling on the status of a taxpayer will necessarily protect the taxpayer from assessment to tax on a transaction if that transaction was not disclosed.[17]

From November 1991 to February 1994, Inland Revenue Tax Bulletin contained "Inland Revenue Decisions". No decisions have been published since February 1994. However, "Revenue Interpretations", which also started in November 1991, continue to be published.

Fourth, since April 1998 a taxpayer has been able to apply to the Revenue for a post-transaction ruling as to the tax treatment of a transaction that has been completed. This includes a procedure for the taxpayer—or his agent—to supply full details of a valuation that is suggested for an asset, either at the date of disposal or at 31 March 1982. The Revenue will then rule as to whether the taxpayer's valuation is acceptable in the context of the particular transaction that has taken place.[18] Application must be made on HMRC form CG34. It is hoped that a form of advanced rulings for corporations will begin in 2007 or 2008.[19]

[1.30] Sources of tax law

Fifth, HMRC staff manuals are available to the public. By mid-1998, 46 Revenue manuals had been published. Some paragraphs that appear in the manuals issued to staff are not published in the version provided to the public at large, it being considered that it is not in the public interest for certain operational instructions to be disclosed. It is understood that much of the material that is suppressed is guidance to Inspectors on the response to be adopted to certain claims made on behalf of taxpayers or other areas where the Revenue's stance is frequently at odds with the view taken by tax practitioners. (It is interesting to note that within this excluded category falls a significant part of the instructions on Revenue practice in relation to residence.) Both the amount of detail and the precision vary greatly from one manual to another and the manuals are criticised for their poor indexing. However, the manuals can provide information on Revenue practice. In proceedings, they cannot be relied upon directly in relation to a question of liability to tax.

While these various pronouncements are of great value to the tax professional and Revenue alike they do not have the force of law and cannot, in the Revenue's view, require appropriate action by the taxpayer. One consequence of this has led to legislation in 1999 in the CGT area—see infra, § **16.01**.

[1] eg the unsuccessful applications in *R v IRC, ex p J Rothschild Holdings* [1987] STC 163, *R v Inspector of Taxes, ex p Brumfield* [1989] STC 151 and *R v IRC, ex p Kaye* [1992] STC 581.
[2] This general anti-avoidance statement was used by the Revenue to defeat a move to quash an assessment for breach of natural justice in *R v IRC, ex p Fulford-Dobson* [1987] STC 344.
[3] Inland Revenue press release, 16 February 1989, Simon's Tax Intelligence 1989, p 74.
[4] [1999] STC 594.
[5] [1999] STC 604 c.
[6] [2005] UKHL 30, [2006] STC 270, [2003] EWCA Civ 814, [2003] STC 1113.
[7] At para 21.
[8] FA 2008, s 154, HMRC Note BN85, 12th March 2008; the case was *R (Wilkinson) v HMRC* above.
[9] *R v IRC, ex p J Rothschild Holdings plc* [1986] STC 410; upheld [1987] STC 163, CA.
[10] The main statutory clearances are: share exchanges, TCGA 1992, s 138; reconstructions, TCGA 1992, s 139(5); demergers, TA 1988, s 125; company purchase of own shares, TA 1988, s 225; transactions in securities, TA 1988, s 707.
[11] The terms on which advice is available are set out in ICAEW Memorandum TR 818, see Simon's Tax Intelligence 1990, p 893; see also later correspondence in ICAEW Memorandum TR 830, reproduced in Simon's Tax Intelligence 1991, p 404.
[12] On judicial review see infra, § **2A.64**.
[13] *R v IRC, ex p MFK Underwriting Agencies Ltd* [1989] STC 873; also *R v IRC, ex p Camacq Corpn* [1989] STC 785.
[14] *R v IRC, ex p Bishopp* [1999] STC 531.
[15] Per Dyson J, *R v IRC, ex p Bishopp* [1999] STC 531 at 546f.
[16] *Matrix-Securities Ltd v IRC* [1994] STC 272, HL. See also text of letter from the Inland Revenue dated 3 June 1994 and reprinted in Simon's Tax Intelligence 1994,

p 729.
[17] *R v IRC, ex p Howmet Corpn* [1994] STC 413, QBD.
[18] Inland Revenue Code of Practice 10, Simon's Weekly Tax Intelligence 1998, p 572; see also Simon's Weekly Tax Intelligence 1997, p 184.
[19] HMRC response to the Vardy Report on Links with Business HMRC Press Release November 2006.

The tax year

[1.31] For income tax and CGT, the tax year runs from 6 April to 5 April,[1] so that the year from 6 April 2008 to 5 April 2009 is known as the tax year 2008–09. Different rules apply to corporation tax.[2] The reason for these dates is that the financial year originally began on Lady Day, 25 March; this was changed in 1752 when the calendars were changed.[3] Almost any dating is arbitrary and change now would simply substitute the apparently rational for the attractively picturesque; there are, however, advantages to having similar periods when calculating statistics.

It is customary for Parliament to empower HMRC to collect income tax for one year at a time. So FA 2009 provides that tax is to be charged for 2009–19 and sets the rates for the year. The Income Tax Act 2007 provides that income tax is charged for a year only if an Act of Parliament so provides and that every assessment must be made for a specified tax year.[4]

Simon's Taxes A1.104, 105.

[1] Income Tax Act 2007, s 4.
[2] And, before its abolition, to DLT, see DLTA 1976, s 13.
[3] Royal Commission 1920 App 7(o).
[4] Income Tax Act 2007, s 4.

The provisional collection of Taxes Act 1968

[1.32] Since income tax is an annual tax[1] and is imposed by a charge in each year's Finance Act, difficulties arise where the Finance Act has not become law by the start of the tax year (6 April). Tax could not be levied lawfully simply on the basis of a resolution of the House of Commons.[2] However, by the Provisional Collection of Taxes Act 1968 temporary statutory effect will be given to resolutions of the House of Commons. The resolutions, if passed in March or April, expire on 5 August next and if passed in any other month expire after four months. New taxes are expressly excluded.

With the change to a unified Budget in 1994, Royal Assent was needed by 5 May.[3] Matters have reverted to the older timetable under the present (New) Labour administration.

[1.32] Sources of tax law

1 Supra, § 1.24. Corporation tax is, also, an annual tax: TA 1988, s 8(6). By contrast, CGT is imposed until parliament declare otherwise: TCGA 1992, s 1(1), as is stamp duty: FA 1973, s 50 and VAT: VATA 1994, s 1.
2 *Bowles v Bank of England* [1913] 1 Ch 57. The Finance Acts of 1909, 1910 and 1911 reached the statute book 13, 7 and 7 months after the start of the financial year. Mr Bowles was an opposition backbencher. The Chancellor of the Exchequer was Lloyd George.
3 PCTA 1968, s 1 as amended by FA 1993, s 205. The background to the 1994 timetable is explained in Government White Paper on Budgetary Reform Cm 1867 and, more specifically in HM Treasury press release, 31 December 1992, *Simon's Tax Intelligence* 1993, p 160.

2

Tax administration – an overview

HM Revenue and Customs	PARA 2.01
Appeals against HMRC decisions	PARA 2.09
Appeals from the tribunal	PARA 2.18
Judicial review	PARA 2.23
Other remedies against HMRC	PARA 2.24
Evasion and fraud	PARA 2.25
HMRC prosecution powers	PARA 2.27
Serious fraud	PARA 2.30
Enforcement powers	PARA 2.37
Other compliance powers	PARA 2.41

HM Revenue & Customs

Duties of the Department

[2.01] HMRC is a non-ministerial government department.[1] The Department is responsible for:[2]

(a) The collection and management of revenue (ie taxes, duties and national insurance contributions), formerly the responsibility of the Commissioners of Inland Revenue.

(b) The collection and management of revenue (ie taxes, duties and levies), formerly the responsibility of the Commissioners of Customs and Excise.

(c) The payment and management of tax credits, formerly the responsibility of the Commissioners of Inland Revenue.

(d) All other functions (save those vested in the Director of Revenue and Customs Prosecutions),[3] formerly vested in the Commissioners of Inland Revenue.

In exercising their functions, the Commissioners must comply with any directions of a general nature given to them by HM Treasury.[4]

Statute gives to HM Revenue & Customs the collection and management of taxes. This is statutorily defined[5] to have the same meaning as the previous statutory duty for the "care and management of the taxes". The Court of Session has interpreted this provision as meaning that the Revenue is obliged to collect tax in accordance with the statutory provisions. The House of Lords has further restricted the scope of any administrative discretion by holding that ameliorating extra-statutory practices might be ultra vires.[6]

[2.01] Tax administration – an overview

1. HM Revenue & Customs was created by the merger of Customs & Excise and Inland Revenue on 18 April 2005. The merger was effected by Commissioners for Revenue and Customs Act 2005, s 53; and Commissioners for Revenue and Customs Act 2005 (Commencement) Order, SI 2005/1126, art 2. The legislative framework is set out in the Commissioners for Revenue and Customs Act 2005 (CRCA 2005). CRCA 2005 provides for the appointment of Commissioners for Her Majesty's Revenue and Customs (who are referred to in the Act simply as "the Commissioners") and staff. CRCA 2005 brings together a few management provisions of general application throughout the department but leaves most of the Taxes Management Act 1970 and the Customs and Excise Management Act 1979 untouched.
2. CRCA 2005, s 5.
3. CRCA 2005, ss 5(3), 35. For the Revenue and Customs Prosecution Office, see infra, § **2.05**.
4. CRCA 2005, s 11.
5. Former Inland Revenue Regulation Act 1890, ss 1, 13 and 39; TMA 1970, s 1.
6. *R v Inland Revenue Commissioners, ex parte Wilkinson* [2005] UKHL 30. This has led to a re-examination of all such practices with legislation being introduced in FA 2008, s 160 enabling practices having effect before 21 July 2008 to be codified by Treasury order.

Tax collected

[2.02] The amounts collected in 2007/08, and the cost of collection, for the taxes dealt with in this book are:[1]

Tax	Total Collected £m	Cost of Collection pence per £ collected
Income Tax	155,100	1.16
National Insurance Contributions	98,200	0.37
Value Added Tax	84,900	0.56
Corporation Tax	46,800	0.73
Stamp Taxes	13,700	0.12
Inheritance Tax	3,900	0.64
Capital Gains Tax	5,500	0.85
Total	408,100	

1. Tax collected statistics taken from HM Revenue & Customs 2007–08 Accounts (HC674). Cost of collection statistics taken from HM Revenue & Customs Annual Departmental Autumn Performance Report 2008.

Direct taxes

[2.03] HM Revenue & Customs is organised into four business areas:

(1) *Operations*
 12 area offices, plus criminal investigations, serious civil investigations, detection and intelligence, as well as customer contact, compliance, debt management and processing units;
(2) *Product and process groups*
 Focusing on products eg taxes, duties, credits and benefits, and the processes that deliver them;
(3) *Customer units*
 Large businesses and employers, small and medium enterprises and employers, individuals and frontiers;
(4) *Corporate functions*
 Including a strategy unit and an anti-avoidance group, as well as other support services.

The larger part of the work in connection with income tax, corporation tax and capital gains tax is undertaken by the 12 area offices.

In recent years, there has been a move to centralise the administration of specialist areas of income tax and capital gains tax. Thus, the taxation of trusts is dealt with by five specialist trust units and there is a specialist compliance unit to deal with Lloyd's Underwriters. There are also specialist compliance units for industrial sectors where, it is considered, there is a risk of significant loss of tax to the Revenue—such as agricultural gang workers and the rag trade. Inheritance tax, stamp duties and national insurance contributions are administered by separate executive agencies, each having its own administrative structure.

Simon's Taxes Division A3.1.

Indirect taxes

[2.04] HMRC has responsibility for:
(1) The collection of VAT and excise duties.[1]
(2) The collection of customs duties and agricultural levies for the EU.
(3) The enforcement of prohibitions and restrictions on imports and exports.
(4) Tasks connected with foreign trade (eg trade statistics) carried out on behalf of other government departments.[2]

In direct contrast to the situation for all other taxes dealt with in this work, the Isle of Man is within the United Kingdom for the purpose of the imposition of Value Added Tax. Hence, the sending of goods to the Isle of Man is not treated as an export[3] and a VAT group registration can include a company in the Isle of Man.[4] However, as the Isle of Man is a separate administration, answerable to the Parliament to the Isle of Man and not to Westminster, the Isle of Man has its own independent service for VAT matters.[5]

The local administration of VAT is carried out separately from other HMRC work. Local VAT offices (LVO) are situated in principal towns throughout the

[2.04] Tax administration – an overview

country. A typical LVO is headed by an Assistant Collector and divided into eight or ten districts, each headed by a Surveyor. Individual districts deal with internal office procedures (eg registration, enquiries and keeping traders' files), collection of outstanding tax, and making routine control visits to traders.

VAT Central Unit is responsible for issuing tax returns, receiving returns and remittances and maintaining a register of taxable persons. An increasing number of administrative functions in relation to VAT are being centralised on a national or regional basis. Thus, for example, registration is now centralised in Carmarthen, Grimsby, Newry and Aberdeen with a Non-established Taxable Persons Unit in Aberdeen. Recent changes include centralisation of refunds under the do-it-yourself builders relief arrangements in Birmingham and reorganisation of the Large Business Group, where the geographic regions have been disbanded to form a national organisation based on trade sectors.

De Voil Indirect Tax Service V1.262–264.

1   VATA 1994, Sch 11, para 1(1).
2   81st Annual Report, Cm 1223, para 1.2 and Appendix F.
3   Isle of Man Act 1979, s 6(1).
4   The Value Added Tax (Isle of Man) Order 1982, SI 1982/1067, para 4 enacted under the authority of Isle of Man Act 1979, s 6(2)(g).
5   The Value Added Tax (Isle of Man) Order 1982, SI 1982/1067, para 7 enacted under the authority of Isle of Man Act 1979, s 6(2)(f).

HM Revenue and Customs Prosecution Office

[2.05] The Director of Revenue and Customs Prosecutions has power to institute and conduct criminal proceedings in England and Wales relating to criminal investigations carried out by HMRC.[1] He is appointed by the Attorney General. He has a duty to provide such advice as he thinks appropriate relating to those proceedings and investigations.[2] He thereby assumes functions previously within the responsibility of both the Commissioners of Inland Revenue and the Customs and Excise Prosecutions Office.[3]

1   CRCA 2005, s 34.
2   CRCA 2005, s 35.
3   The Customs and Excise Prosecutions Office was created in April 2003 and operated under the terms of a Memorandum of Understanding between the Attorney General, Treasury Ministers and the Commissioners of Customs and Excise. Mr Justice Butterfield recommended that the Office should be placed on a statutory footing: see *The Review of Criminal Prosecutions Conducted by HM Customs and Excise* (15 July 2003). This recommendation was accepted by Ministers in December 2003.

Exchange of information

[2.06] It is a criminal offence[1] for any Revenue officer to disclose information relating to the tax affairs "of any identifiable person", other than disclosure of information made:

(a) with a lawful authority,
(b) with a consent of any person in whose case the information is about a matter relevant to tax,
or
(c) which has been lawfully made available to the public before the disclosure is made.[2]

The sanctions imposed[3] extend to imprisonment for up to two years.

These provisions operate, in general, to prohibit the Revenue passing information to other Government departments. Prior to April 1999, the effect of these provisions was to limit quite severely co-ordination between the activities of the Inland Revenue, in relation to income tax, and the Contributions Agency, in relation to National Insurance Contributions. However, on 1 April 1999, the 8,000 staff of the Contributions Agency were integrated with the 50,000 Inland Revenue staff, the Revenue having taken over responsibility for both operational and policy matters in respect of National Insurance Contributions. Thus, from 1999 onwards, there was no statutory prohibition on information regarding an individual's National Insurance Contributions being available to the Revenue officer considering the income tax liability of that individual, and vice versa. Indeed, a government press release states: 'The transfer of the Contributions Agency to the Inland Revenue is aimed at achieving better service and better compliance'.[4] The statutory provisions for the transfer specifically provide for such exchange of information.[5]

The merger in April 2005 of Inland Revenue and HM Customs & Excise into HMRC has the consequence that there is no statutory bar to the transfer to, say, the Revenue officer dealing with a company's corporation tax affairs information discovered by, say, officers on a VAT control visit. Indeed, the revised powers of HMRC officers will mean that many enquiries and inspections will take a distinct multi-disciplinary feel.

The Tax Credits Act 2002, Sch 5 provides for the exchange of information between HMRC and authorities administering certain benefits, and the provision of information by HMRC for health and education purposes.

Simon's Taxes A3.1.

---

[1] FA 1989, s 182(1). The provisions of this section came into effect on the repeal of the Official Secrets Act 1911, s 2, which had previously provided criminal sanctions against the unauthorised passing on of information obtained from employment in a Revenue department, as elsewhere in government service.
[2] FA 1989, s 182(5).
[3] FA 1989, s 182(8).
[4] DSS press release, 26 November 1999, *Simon's Weekly Tax Intelligence* 1998, p 1699. This is, in effect, a repeat of the statement made by the Chancellor of the Exchequer on Budget Day, 17 March 1998; *Simon's Weekly Tax Intelligence* 1998,

[2.06] Tax administration – an overview

p 475. There continues to be a greater level of protection in respect of National Insurance benefits. SSAA 1992, s 122 permits the Inland Revenue to pass information to the DSS, but only where there are civil or criminal proceedings, see SSAA 1992, s 122(3)(b).

5 Social Security Contributions (Transfer of Functions etc) Act 1999, s 5.

Duty of fairness

[2.07] The Board of HMRC is under a duty to collect income tax. It is considered that the Revenue is not guilty of an abuse of power if it enters into a special arrangement absolving a particular taxpayer or a group of particular taxpayers from liability to tax, the Revenue view being that this authority stems from the wording of CRCA 2005, s 5(1), where HMRC is given "collection and management" of taxes. However, the judgment of the Court of Session in *Al Fayed v Advocate General for Scotland*[1] is that the Revenue is failing in its statutory duty[2] if it enters into an agreement with a particular taxpayer that leads to collection of a cash sum without the computation of the taxpayer's actual liability under statute.

Revenue practice is to repay tax on a claim made after the statutory time limit where the overpayment of tax has arisen because of an error by HMRC or another Government department.[3]

There is statutory authority[4] for HMRC to use its discretion to "mitigate any penalty, or stay or compound any proceedings for a penalty and may also, after judgment, further mitigate or entirely remit the penalty".

A similar position applies to VAT. Thus, HMRC can enter into administrative arrangements with individual taxpayers in accordance with specific powers[5] or by virtue of their responsibility for the care and management of VAT.[6] Their powers in relation to penalties and proceedings extend to the restoration of forfeited goods and the early release of anyone imprisoned for a VAT offence.[7]

In *IRC v National Federation of Self-Employed and Small Businesses Ltd*,[8] the court held that a taxpayer does not have the ability to ask the court to investigate the way in which HMRC applies its management powers in relation to the tax affairs of another taxpayer. However, in carrying out the duty laid on it HMRC must act with administrative common sense.[9]

HMRC also has a duty under common law to act fairly. This duty may be infringed by treating similarly placed taxpayers differently.[10] HMRC must perform the duties given to it by statute. They are not bound by a promise given by government, where this is contrary to their statutory duties.[11]

R v Inland Revenue Commissioners, ex parte Wilkinson[12] suggests that HMRC may not deviate from statute by introducing extra-statutory practices that are not justified on grounds of administrative common sense. That case concerned a claim by a widower for an allowance that was available to widows. It was accepted that the statute then in force was discriminatory; however, the House of Lords held that the case was an example of widows being unfairly advantaged rather than widowers being unfairly disadvantaged.

Therefore, the House of Lords refused to "level up" the allowances, noting that the statute had since changed by the withdrawal of the allowance altogether. It remains to be seen how a court would react in cases where a person is unfairly disadvantaged by a discriminatory statutory provision and whether they would go further than merely to give declaratory relief under the Human Rights Act 1998, s 4.

As there is no estoppel against the Crown, the general rule is that no reliance[13] can be placed on statements by HMRC. However, this principle is considerably weakened by the operation of judicial review. In *Matrix-Securities Ltd v IRC*[14] Lord Griffiths commented that compensation may be possible if the Revenue withdraws a clearance that has been properly given. Compensation can also be obtained through the Parliamentary Commissioner for Administration.[15]

Like other government departments the Revenue was party to the Citizen's Charter.[16] In *Kempton v Special Comrs and IRC*[17] a taxpayer relied on the Citizen's Charter to argue that no reasonable inspector with the Charter in mind would have issued a notice seeking information from the taxpayer in the wide terms that were used. However, in that case, the taxpayer failed on the facts.

In 1993, a Revenue Adjudicator was appointed, to act independently of HMRC when a taxpayer has not been satisfied with the way in which HMRC have treated a complaint. The first Revenue Adjudicator was Elizabeth Firkin, who served until April 1999 and who was succeeded by Dame Barbara Mills DBE QC. Since 2009, the role has been undertaken by Judy Clements OBE. Since April 1995, the powers of the Revenue Adjudicator have extended to indirect taxes as well as direct taxes.

Simon's Taxes Division A3.1.

---

[1] *Al Fayed v Advocate General for Scotland* [2002] STC 910; the decision was upheld on appeal: [2004] STC 1703, Ct Sess. In 1980, the House of Lords declared that the Revenue does not have discretion in allocating tax liabilities amongst taxpayers: per Lord Wilberforce in *Vestey v IRC* [1980] STC 10 at 19.

[2] Extra-statutory concession A19, see Inland Revenue press release, 26 April 1994, *Simon's Tax Intelligence* 1994, p 579.

[3] Extra-statutory concession B41. The concession states that it is only applied 'where there is no dispute or doubt as to the facts'.

[4] TMA 1970, s 102.

[5] For example, under VAT Regulations, SI 1995/2518, regs 67, 102.

[6] VATA 1994, Sch 11, para 1. For an example, see *Labour Party v Customs and Excise Comrs* (2001) VAT decision 17034.

[7] CEMA 1979, s 152; VATA 1994, s 72(12).

[8] [1981] 2 All ER 93, [1981] STC 260 (Fleet Street amnesty not illegal).

[9] For a recent example, see *R (on the application of Freeserve.com plc) v Customs and Excise Comrs (America Online Inc, interested party)* [2003] EWHC 2736 (admin), [2004] STC 187 and contrast *R v A-G ex p ICI plc* (1984) 60 TC 1.

[10] See *R (on the application of British Sky Broadcasting Group plc) v Customs and Excise Comrs* [2001] EWHC Admin 127, [2001] STC 437 at paras 8–10.

[11] The judgment in *R v HM Treasury, ex p Service Authority for the National Crime Squad* [2000] STC 638 indicates that the Treasury is not bound to honour the

[2.07] Tax administration – an overview

Government's promises to relieve people from tax; this is an Exchequer matter and the courts will not interfere with the Treasury's reasons for not granting relief, whether or not those reasons are justified.

12   [2005] UKHL 30.
13   Per Lord Edmund Davies, in *Vestey v IRC* [1980] STC 10 at 35. See also *Southend on Sea Corpn v Hodgson (Wickford) Ltd* [1962] 1 QB 416, [1961] 2 All ER 46; see however *R v IRC, ex p J Rothschild Holdings plc* [1987] STC 163 where an estoppel issue was raised in judicial review proceedings but it failed on the facts. For a case concerning VAT, see, for example, *Bennett v Customs and Excise Comrs (No 2)* [2001] STC 137.
14   [1994] STC 272 at 284.
15   Wade and Forsyth, *Administrative Law* (10th edn pp 281–285); see also comments of Lord Griffiths in *Matrix-Securities Ltd v IRC* [1994] STC 272, HL at 284 on possible compensation claims if the Revenue withdraw clearance.
16   Inland Revenue press release, 13 August 1991, *Simon's Tax Intelligence* 1991, p 771; see also Inland Revenue press release, 11 February 1992, *Simon's Tax Intelligence* 1992, p 178.
17   *Kempton v Special Comrs and IRC* [1992] STC 823.

HMRC charter

[2.08] Following concerns about increased powers given to HMRC and a lack of corresponding statutory safeguards for taxpayers, a campaign was launched (with much support from the Chartered Institute of Taxation) for the introduction of a charter, a document that would set down a minimum standard of behaviour that could be expected from HMRC officers. Having persuaded ministers to formulate such a charter, the next stage was to ensure that the charter had statutory backing. Eventually, the Government acceded to such requests, the charter being enshrined in CRCA 2005, s 16A (as inserted by FA 2009, s 92).

The ongoing consultations in respect of the wording of the eventual charter suggest that the finished product will be little more than an aspirational statement of HMRC's behaviour allied with a mission statement; it also states HMRC's expectations with regards to the behaviour of taxpayers (and others with whom it has to deal). How the charter evolves remains to be seen. What is also unclear is the reaction by the courts to any charter in cases where behaviours have fallen short of the aspirational standards set down.

Appeals against HMRC decisions

Introduction

[2.09] Following the introduction of the new unified appeals system, the system relating to appeals against decisions taken by HMRC will be the same irrespective of the underlying tax in issue. The term 'appeal' will be used with different meanings, depending on the particular context.[1]

In the first instance, a taxpayer (or other interested party) can register a formal disagreement with a determination or assessment made by HMRC. That disagreement, known as an appeal, will usually need to be made in writing to the HMRC officer making the assessment or determination within 30 days.

At that stage, HMRC and taxpayers will have the opportunity to continue discussing the point informally. Alternatively, the dispute can then be subject to an internal review and/or resolution by the tribunal. Any such hearing by the tribunal will also be called an appeal, the taxpayer almost invariably being the appellant in such circumstances. Where one or more party is unhappy with the decision of the tribunal, a further appeal can often be made.

The tribunal is divided into two tiers, the First-tier Tribunal and the Upper Tribunal. The vast majority of appeals are heard initially by the First-tier Tribunal, with the Upper Tribunal assuming an appellate function. However, the most complex of tax cases can be heard at first instance by the Upper Tribunal. Both tiers are themselves divided into different 'chambers' – each chamber having an area of speciality.[2] Tax matters will be heard almost exclusively in the Tax Chamber of the First-tier Tribunal and the Finance and Tax Chamber of the Upper Tribunal.[3] However, cases involving tax credits and social security matters will be heard in the Social Entitlement Chamber of the First-tier Tribunal and the Administrative Appeals Chamber of the Upper Tribunal.[4]

---

[1] It has been suggested that the confusion that this can cause was considered by HMRC, but they were reluctant to allow a new term to be introduced to one of the stages because it would have led to a major rewriting of HMRC literature.
[2] Tribunals, Courts and Enforcement Act 2007.
[3] The First-tier Tribunal and Upper Tribunal (Chambers) Order 2008, SI 2008/2684, arts 5A, 8.
[4] The First-tier Tribunal and Upper Tribunal (Chambers) Order 2008, SI 2008/2684, arts 3(c), 7(a).

Internal reviews

[2.10] FA 2008 introduced powers that would permit regulations to introduce a formal internal review process. Such a process would apply in respect of decisions made by the Commissioners themselves or any officer of Revenue and Customs. The purpose of the scheme is to permit taxpayers the opportunity to have decisions reviewed internally before commencing any formal appeal process. The precise mechanics of the internal review process have been introduced into the legislation by SI 2009/56, with the rules depending on the particular tax in issue.

The effectiveness of the internal review procedure remains to be seen.

The legislation concerning the conduct of internal reviews and also regarding the notification of any remaining dispute to the tribunal is subject to time limits. If these are not adhered to, the taxpayer will lose the automatic right to having the appeal heard. Late appeals will be accepted, however, if either

HMRC agree (ie agree to waive the delay) or if the tribunal gives permission.[1] HMRC are required to give permission if the taxpayer makes written application for the appeal to be heard, HMRC are satisfied that there was reasonable excuse for the appeal notice not being given within the statutory timeframe and if HMRC are satisfied that the application was made without delay after the reasonable excuse ceased to apply.[2]

This was applied by the High Court (albeit on the previous wording of the section) in *R (on the application of Cook) v General Commissioners of Income Tax*[3] where the High Court held that the Commissioners' decision to refuse an appeal against a tax assessment out of time by a taxpayer facing bankruptcy was not irrational because they had taken into account all the relevant material considerations in reaching their decision.

The court further concluded that as it was in the public interest to achieve finality in tax matters and that it was important for HMRC to be able to close their books in respect of the taxpayer without the threat of an appeal out of time from a taxpayer that faced a bankruptcy order but that had failed to file tax returns or appeals in time.

[1] TMA 1970 s 49(2).
[2] TMA 1970, s 49(3)–(6).
[3] [2009] EWHC 590 (Admin).

Direct taxes

[2.11] An appeal may be made against a Revenue notice or assessment by giving notice to the officer within 30 days of its issue.[1] The time limit is an absolute requirement and the court has no power to extend it.[2]

An appeal can be against:

(a) an assessment on the individual;[3]
(b) a notice;[4]
(c) an HMRC amendment of the self-assessment;[5]
(d) a penalty assessment;[6]
(e) a notice requiring the production of documents;[7]
(f) delay in completing enquiries into a self-assessment.[8]

Once an appeal has been made (and provided that the case has not been referred to the tribunal) the dispute can be subject to an internal review by HMRC (by a different part of HMRC from that making the original decision). The internal review can be initially requested by the taxpayer or offered by HMRC.[9]

If the taxpayer requests the review, HMRC must set out their initial position within 30 days of the request.[10] They then have 45 days[11] or such other period as may be agreed to reconsider their position.[12] The reconsidered position then replaces the original decision.[13] The taxpayer will be deemed to have accepted the revised view unless a further appeal is made direct to the tribunal within 30 days of the date on which the conclusion of the review is sent to the taxpayer.[14] Late notifications to the tribunal can be accepted out of time, but only with the permission of the tribunal.[15]

Alternatively, HMRC may offer a review. In such cases, the offer should include in writing HMRC's initial position.[16] In such cases, the taxpayer is deemed to accept the HMRC position unless within 30 days of the date of HMRC's statement of their position the taxpayer either accepts the offer or notifies the Tribunal of the disputed matter.[17] As is the case with reviews requested by taxpayers, HMRC have 45 days to conduct the review and the conclusions are deemed to be the final position between the parties unless the tribunal is notified of the appeal within 30 days or later, subject to the tribunal's permission.

Other methods of appeal include seeking the opinion of the court (as in *A-G v National Provincial Bank Ltd*).[18] It is also sometimes possible to enter an originating summons as in *Buxton v Public Trustee*[19] which concerns the charitable nature of trusts. An originating summons was, however, refused in *Argosam Finance Co Ltd v Oxby*[20] on the grounds that this was vexatious. There was no provision for arbitration [21] but the tribunals rules since 1 April 2009 now accommodate alternative dispute resolution.

The duty of the former Commissioners was limited by Goulding J in *Wicker v Fraser*[22] when distinguishing their role from that of an inquisitorial tribunal concerned to approach the primary facts de novo and to perform the same office as an officer initially making an assessment.

The fact that an appeal is under group litigation order (GLO)[23] does not change the procedure for jurisdiction. The first hearing is before the tribunal; it is not possible for the High Court to act as the first instance trial court.[24] However, it is likely that most new GLOs will be permitted to start at the Upper Tribunal, which is at the same judicial level to the High Court.

If determination of an appeal requires a ruling on European law, the Commissioners (or the judge) can refer the question to the ECJ. Questions of UK domestic law are to be decided by the appropriate UK court before any reference to the ECJ.[25]

Simon's Taxes E1.268.

---

1 TMA 1970, s 31. The General Commissioners dispose of about 75,000 cases each year. In 2000, the Special Commissioners disposed of 142 cases; the VAT and Duties Tribunal disposed of 3,207, although only about 700 were actually heard: Tax Adviser, November 2001 p 25.
2 *New World Medical Ltd v Cormack* [2002] EWHC 1787 (Ch), [2002] STC 1245.
3 TMA 1970, s 31.
4 TMA 1970, s 32.
5 TMA 1970, s 31(1). The High Court allowed an appeal by the taxpayers against a closure notice in *Tower MCashback LLP 1 & Another v Revenue & Customs Commrs* [2008] EWHC 2387, pointing out that an appeal against a closure notice did extend the scope of the appeal into an enquiry into the entire tax return. The scope and subject of the appeal would be limited to the conclusions stated in the notice and the amendments (if any) made to the return. It was further held that

the duty of the Tribunal on appeal was not to review or adjudicate upon the inspector's reasons for issuing the notice.

[6] TMA 1970, s 29(8).
[7] TMA 1970, s 19A(6).
[8] TMA 1970, s 28A(6).
[9] TMA 1970, s 49A.
[10] TMA 1970, s 49B(2), (5) or such longer period as is reasonable.
[11] 90 days in cases where the original decision was made before 1 April 2009 and the review date is before 1 April 2010, SI 2009/56, Sch 3, para 5.
[12] TMA 1970, s 49E(5).
[13] TMA 1970, s 49F.
[14] TMA 1970, s 49G.
[15] TMA 1970, s 49G(3).
[16] TMA 1970, s 49C(2).
[17] TMA 1970, s, 49C(3), (6), 49H.
[18] (1928) 14 TC 111.
[19] (1962) 41 TC 235.
[20] (1964) 42 TC 86.
[21] See Sheridan [1978] BTR 2435.
[22] [1982] STC 505 at 511.
[23] Under r 19.10–19.15 of the Civil Procedure Rules.
[24] *Re Claimants under Loss Relief Group Litigation Order* [2005] STC 1357, HL. The House of Lords overturned the Court of Appeal [2004] STC 1054, CA and restored the judgment of Park J: [2004] STC 594.
[25] *Trustees of BT Pension Scheme v Revenue and Customs Comrs* [2005] EWHC 3088 (Ch), [2006] STC 1685 per Park J at para [31] at 1693b.

National Insurance contributions

[2.12] After 1 April 1999, in conjunction with the transfer of responsibilities from the then DSS (now the Department for Work and Pensions) to what is now HMRC, NIC appeals have been heard by the General and Special Commissioners. From 1 April 2009, such appeals have been heard by the Social Entitlement Chamber of the First-tier Tribunal.

Many business people have always assumed that the system now in place has always existed in respect of contribution disputes. In fact, until the change in 1999, a dispute could be "determined" only by the Secretary of State for Social Security with appeal by only the employer or contributor to the High Court and then on a point of law only.

The following are the subject of a decision by an officer of HMRC:[1]

(1) whether a person is or was an earner and the category if so;
(2) whether a person is or was an employer for industrial injuries benefit purposes;
(3) whether a person is or was liable to pay contributions of a particular class and if so the amount;
(4) whether a person is entitled to pay contributions, notwithstanding that there is no liability (eg Class 3);

Appeals against HMRC decisions **[2.12]**

(5) whether contributions of a particular class have been paid in respect of a period;
(6) any issue in connection with entitlement to statutory sick pay, statutory maternity pay, statutory paternity pay or statutory adoption pay;
(7) other decisions in connection with statutory sick pay or statutory maternity pay;
(8) personal liability of directors, etc for company contributions under SSAA 1992, s 121C (introduced from 6 April 1999 by SSA 1998, s 64);
(9) issues under the Jobseekers Act 1995, s 27 (employment of long-term unemployed: deductions by employers);
(10) whether a person is liable to pay interest and the amount thereof;
(11) whether a person is liable to a penalty and the amount thereof;
(12) any other matters prescribed by regulations made by HMRC.

Issues under 12 above have been prescribed from 8 October 2002[2], as follows:

(1) whether a notice should be given under reg 3(2B) and if so the terms of such notice;
(2) whether a notice given under reg 3(2B) should cease to have effect;
(3) whether a direction should be given under reg 31 and if so the terms of the direction;
(4) whether the condition in reg 50(2) is satisfied;
(5) whether late applications under reg 52(11), reg 54(3) or reg 55(3) for the refund of (respectively) contributions generally, Class 1 contributions paid at the wrong rate or Class 1A contributions should be admitted;
(6) whether, where a secondary contributor has failed to pay primary contributions that failure was with the consent or connivance of the primary contributor, as is mentioned in reg 60;
(7) whether the condition in reg 61(2) is satisfied;
(8) whether in the case of Class 2 contributions remaining unpaid at the due date, the reason for non-payment is the contributor's ignorance or error, and if so whether that is due to failure to exercise due care and diligence (reg 65(2));
(9) whether the reason for non-payment of Class 3 within the prescribed period is the contributor's ignorance or error, and if so whether that is due to failure to exercise due care and diligence (reg 65(3));
(10) whether the reason for non-payment of Class 3 within two years of the end of the year to which the contributions relate is the contributor's ignorance or error, and if so whether that is due to failure to exercise due care and diligence (reg 65(4));
(11) whether a late application under reg 110(3) for the return of a special Class 4 contribution should be admitted;
(12) whether a contribution (other than a Class 4 contribution) has been paid in error (Reg 52(1)(*a*));
(13) whether there has been a payment of contributions in excess of the amount specified in reg 21 (reg 52(1)(*b*));
(14) whether certain delays are reasonable;

(15) whether the delay in making payment of primary Class 1 contributions was neither with the consent or connivance of the primary contributor;[3]

(16) whether in the case of a contribution paid after the due date, the failure was due to ignorance or error and not failure to exercise due care and diligence.[4]

Whilst the Department for Work and Pensions (DWP) retains policy responsibility for statutory sick pay and statutory maternity pay, enforcement is carried out by HMRC. Until 2009, this led to appeals being heard by the General and Special Commissioners and not through the benefit appeal procedures. Now such matters are heard by the Social Entitlement Chamber of the First-tier Tribunal.

Following a decision by an officer of HMRC, aggrieved parties may appeal in writing within 30 days after the date on which the decision was issued.[5] There is no specific form provided for this purpose. Such matters are subject to the same internal review procedures as apply for tax purposes (see above).[6]

---

[1] Social Security Contributions (Transfer of Functions, etc) Act 1999, s 8.
[2] Social Security (Contributions) (Amendment No. 3) Regulations 2002, SI 2002/2366, reg 18, *Simon's Weekly Tax Intelligence* 2002, p 1295.
[3] Social Security (Crediting and Treatment of Contributions, and National Insurance Numbers) Regulations 2001, SI 2001/769, reg 5.
[4] Social Security (Crediting and Treatment of Contributions, and National Insurance Numbers) Regulations 2001, SI 2001/769, reg 6.
[5] Social Security Contributions (Transfer of Functions, etc) Act 1999, s 11.
[6] Social Security Contributions (Decisions and Appeals) Regulations 1999, SI 1999/1027, reg 7 applying TMA 1970, ss 49A to 49I with only consequential modifications of the terminology.

Tax credits

[2.13] Under s 38 of the Tax Credits Act 2002 (all section numbers below referring to that Act) appeals can be made against:

(1) An initial decision on an award (s 14(1)).

(2) A revised decision on an award following a notification of a change in circumstance (s 15(1)) which increases the maximum rate of tax credit.

(3) A revised decision on an award, where HMRC have reasonable grounds for believing that the rate of tax credit that has been awarded differs from the rate at which the claimant(s) is entitled for the period (s 16(1)).

(4) A final decision on an award (s 18).

(5) A decision following an enquiry into an award (s 19(3)).

(6) A decision to revise an award following a revision to an income tax liability (s 20(1)).

(7) A decision to revise an award where there are reasonable grounds for believing that a conclusive decision relating to entitlement is not correct and that this is attributable to fraud or neglect (s 20(4)).

Appeals against HMRC decisions **[2.14]**

(8) Revisions to decisions following official error (s 21).
(9) A charge to interest on overpayments of tax credits attributable to fraud or neglect (s 37(1)).
(10) A penalty determined under paragraph 1 of Schedule 2 to the Act. These are penalties for:
  (a) fraudulently or negligently incorrect statements,
  (b) continuing failure to comply with requirements (where a penalty for failure to comply has already been imposed by the General or Special Commissioners—see below),
  (c) a failure to notify certain changes in circumstances, and
  (d) failures by employers to make correct payments (but note that all payments via employer ceased during 2005–06).

Also, claimant(s) applying for a direction for an enquiry to be closed have their applications heard and determined in the same way as an appeal.[1]

Notice of appeal must generally be given within 30 days[2] (though there are provisions for late appeals in certain circumstances) and once the appeal has passed to the appeals tribunal specific regulations determine the procedures to be followed.[3]

Until 31 March 2009, jurisdiction for tax credits appeals was split between the General and Special Commissioners and the Unified Appeals Service, which considered other social security appeals. From 1 April 2009, all appeals are heard by the Social Entitlement Tribunal of the First-tier Tribunal, with onward appeals being heard by the Administrative Appeals Chamber of the Upper Tribunal.

[1] TCA 2002, s 19(10) and see supra, § **2A.49**.
[2] TCA 2002, s 39(1).
[3] Tax Credits (Appeals) Regulations 2002, SI 2002/2926; Tax Credits (Notice of Appeal) Regulations 2002, SI 2002/3119; Tax Credits (Appeals) (No 2) Regulations 2002, SI 2002/3196; Social Security Commissioners (Procedure) (Tax Credit Appeals) Regulations 2002, SI 2002/3237.

Value added tax

The VAT and Duties Tribunal

[2.14] A new tribunal was established in 1972 to hear appeals in connection with VAT. It was originally known as the VAT Tribunal. This name was changed to the VAT and Duties Tribunal in 1994 when the tribunal's jurisdiction was extended to include other taxes, duties and levies that were then under the care and management of HM Customs and Excise.[1] The tribunal was abolished on 1 April 2009 and replaced by the new tribunal.

Where a decision is made by HMRC, the person affected has a 30-day period in which to make a written appeal.[2]

At the same time that an appeal is made, HMRC must offer a review.[3] During the statutory 30-day appeal period, the taxpayer may accept the offer or notify

[2.14] Tax administration – an overview

the tribunal of the matter in dispute.[4] Following any review, the taxpayer has a 30-day period in which to notify the tribunal of any continued dispute.[5]

Late appeals may be permitted by the Tribunal.[6]

De Voil Indirect Tax Service V1.288.

[1] FA 1994, s 7.
[2] VATA 1994, s 83G(1).
[3] VATA 1994, s 83A.
[4] VATA 1994, s 83C.
[5] VATA 1994, s 83G(3)-(5).
[6] VATA 1994, s 83G(6).

Costs in the tribunal

[2.15] Generally, each party bears its own costs of proceedings before the tribunal. Where a party has acted unreasonably in bringing or defending the case, the tribunal may order that party to pay the other side's costs. In cases categorised by the tribunal as a "complex case", the winner of any appeal may apply for its costs in the appeal. In such cases, however, the taxpayer has the right to opt out of this rule within 28 days of the case categorisation, in which case each party will bear its own costs subject to the other party's conduct being found to be unreasonable. Applications for costs should be made in writing within 28 days of the final determination of the matter by the tribunal.[1,2]

There are no statutory provisions that permit costs orders to be given by the Social Entitlement Chamber. Thus in such cases, the parties are responsible for their own costs, notwithstanding the conduct of the other side.

[1] The Tribunal Procedure (First-tier Tribunal) (Tax Chamber) Rules 2009, SI 2009/273, rule 10.
[2] Prior to 1 April 2009, costs were available only in cases where a party had acted "wholly unreasonably". That rule continues to apply in respect of appeals before the tribunal at 31 March 2009 which were not concluded by that date. For a commentary on the application of this more restricted rule, see the 2008–09 edition of this book.

Jurisdiction

[2.16] An appeal lies to a VAT and Duties Tribunal against a decision by HM Revenue and Customs in relation to the matters listed in VATA 1994, s 83. These matters include questions relating to registration; the rate of VAT chargeable on a supply, acquisition or importation; input tax, refunds and repayments; assessments for VAT, default surcharge, penalties and interest; and requirements for security.

A tribunal has no inherent supervisory jurisdiction. Thus, for example, it has no jurisdiction in relation to the conduct of customs officers,[1] or to the

Appeals against HMRC decisions **[2.17]**

application of an extra-statutory concession in an individual case.[2] That said, however, its statutory jurisdiction frequently involves applying a test of reasonableness to decisions made by HM Revenue and Customs[3] and, in some cases, its powers are specifically confined to consideration of this question.[4] Moreover, when hearing an appeal over which it has jurisdiction, a tribunal can consider an earlier decision over which it has no jurisdiction. However, it may do so only if the decision under appeal depended upon the prior decision.[5]

De Voil Indirect Tax Service V5.401–406.

[1] *Marks & Spencer plc v Customs and Excise Comrs* [1999] STC 205; *Customs and Excise Comrs v National Westminster Bank plc* [2003] EWHC 1822 (Ch), [2003] STC 1072.
[2] See *Cando 70 v Customs and Excise Comrs* [1978] VATTR 211; *Shepherd v Customs and Excise Comrs* [1994] VATTR 47.
[3] See, for example, *John Dee Ltd v Customs and Excise Comrs* [1995] STC 941, CA.
[4] See, for example, VATA 1994, s 84(4A) as inserted by FA 1999 s 16.
[5] VATA 1994 s 84(10). For examples, see *Customs and Excise Comrs v Arnold* [1996] STC 1271; *Customs and Excise Comrs v National Westminster Bank plc* [2003] EWHC 1822 (Ch), [2003] STC 1072.

Rules for the conduct of appeal hearings

[2.17] For any appeal hearing before the First-tier Tribunal, the conduct of the appeal is governed by rules enacted by the following statutory instruments:

Tax matters: The Tribunal Procedure (First-tier Tribunal) (Tax Chamber) Rules 2009.[1]

Social security matters: The Tribunal Procedure (First–tier Tribunal) (Social Entitlement Chamber) Rules 2008.[2]

The rules in the Upper Tribunal apply across all chambers and are found in The Tribunal Procedure (Upper Tribunal) Rules 2008.[3]

An appeal cannot be entertained if the appellant's VAT returns, or any payments due from him in respect of them, are in arrears.[4] Moreover, specified classes of appeal cannot be entertained unless the disputed VAT, surcharge, penalty or interest has been paid. However, HMRC, or (if they refuse) the tribunal, can waive this requirement on the grounds of hardship.[5]

A number of procedural matters must be dealt with before an appeal comes to a hearing. Both parties must serve a list of any documents and a copy of any witness statements to be produced at the hearing.[6] HMRC must also serve a statement of case.[7] There are procedures for making and setting aside a witness summons[8] and service of further and better particulars.[9] Either party may apply for a direction in relation to the appeal.[10]

Simon's Taxes E1.268; De Voil Indirect Tax Service V5.411–489.

[1] SI 2009/273.

[2] SI 2008/2685
[3] SI 2008/2698.
[4] VATA 1994, s 84(2).
[5] VATA 1994, s 84(3).
[6] SI 1986/590 rr 20 and 21.
[7] SI 1986/590 rr 7 and 8.
[8] SI 1986/590 r 22.
[9] SI 1986/590 r 9.
[10] SI 1986/590 r 19.

Appeals from the tribunal

[2.18] Matters that were determined prior to 1 April 2009 may be appealed to the High Court in England and Wales or to the Court of Session in Scotland. (Very occasionally, appeals from the Special Commissioners could be certified so as to go straight to the Court of Appeal.) For matters determined on or after 1 April 2009, however, appeals from the First-tier Tribunal would invariably be heard by the Upper Tribunal.

Appeals from the Upper Tribunal are made to the Court of Appeal (or the Court of Session in Scotland) with the English High Court now being excluded from such regular tax matters. For those occasional matters that are first heard by the Upper Tribunal, the appellate court is still the Court of Appeal or Court of Session.

Any further appeal will then be heard by the House of Lords (soon to be replaced by the Supreme Court.[1]

[1] Under the Constitutional Reform Act 2005.

Function of the appellate court or tribunal

[2.19] The role of the court, on appeal, is limited to a question of law. A court has no jurisdiction on a question of fact. The court cannot reverse an earlier decision simply because the appellate judge would have reached a different conclusion.[1]

In *Edwards v Bairstow and Harrison*,[2] the House of Lords considered a determination made by the General Commissioners. The taxpayers had purchased second-hand industrial plant with the intention of resale. The resale duly took place at a profit. The Commissioners ruled that this transaction was not trading and discharged the assessment under what was then Schedule D, Case I. In his leading judgment, Viscount Simonds said:

> I do not find in the careful and indeed exhaustive statement of facts any item which points to the transaction not being an adventure in the nature of trade. Everything pointed the other way.[3]

In this case, which is generally considered to be the leading case on the authority of a court to intervene on a finding of fact by the Commissioners, the role of the court was succinctly stated in his judgment by Lord Radcliffe:

> . . . it may be that the facts found are such that no person acting judicially and properly instructed as to the relevant law could have come to the determination under appeal. In those circumstances, too, the Court must intervene. It has no option but to assume that there has been some misconception of the law and that this has been responsible for the determination. So there, too, there has been error in point of law. I do not think that it much matters whether this state of affairs is described as one in which there is no evidence to support the determination or as one in which the evidence is inconsistent with and contradictory of the determination or as one in which the true and only reasonable conclusion contradicts the determination. Rightly understood, each phrase propounds the same test.[4]

In his judgment, in the same case, Viscount Simmonds said:

> To say that a transaction is or is not an adventure in the nature of trade is to say that it has or has not the characteristics which distinguish such an adventure. But it is a question of law, not of fact, what are those characteristics, or, in other words, what the statutory language means. It follows that the inference can only be regarded as an inference of fact if it is assumed that the tribunal which makes it is rightly directed in law what the characteristics are and that, I think is the assumption that is made. It is a question of law what is murder: a jury finding as a fact that murder has been committed has been directed on the law and acts under that direction. The Commissioners making an inference of fact that a transaction is or is not an adventure in the nature of trade are assumed to be similarly directed, and their finding thus becomes an inference of fact.[5]

In *Clarke v British Telecom Pension Scheme Trustees*,[6] the Court of Appeal held that an error in law made by the Commissioners should be disregarded if it had no real causal connection with the conclusion.

The fact that the General Commissioners did not deliberate on a issue, is not a ground for setting aside the decision of the General Commissioners.[7]

Simon's Taxes A3.517.

[1] *Bean v Doncaster Amalgamated Collieries Ltd* (1944) 27 TC 296 at 307 per Du Parcq LJ.
[2] (1955) 36 TC 207.
[3] (1955) 36 TC 207 at 224.
[4] (1955) 36 TC 207 at 229.
[5] (1955) 36 TC 207 at 225.
[6] [2000] STC 222.
[7] In *McCullough v Ahluwalia* [2004] EWCA Civ 889, [2004] STC 1295, the General Commissioners did not deliberate on issues because neither the Revenue nor the taxpayer asked them to do so (para 49 at 1305f). Per Jonathan Parker LJ: 'The fact that the decision was not opposed on behalf of the taxpayer cannot deprive it of its status as a determination for the purposes of the taxes axe'.

Issue of fact or issue of law

[2.20] The question whether an issue is one of fact or law is not always immediately apparent, nor easy.[1] The distinction is a product of history, as explained by Lord Hoffmann in *Carmichael v National Power plc*:[2]

> I add a few words only on the troublesome distinction between questions of fact and questions of law.
>
> The difficulties which have risen in this area are, I think, attributable to the historical origin of the distinction in trial by jury and the pragmatic way in which the courts have applied it. In his Hamlyn Lectures on Trial by Jury, Lord Devlin said:[3]
>
>> The questions of law which are for the judge fall into two categories: first, there are questions which cannot be correctly answered except by someone who is skilled in the law; secondly, there are questions of fact which lawyers have decided that judges can answer better than juries.
>
> Included in the second category is the construction of documents in their natural and ordinary meaning. An uninitiated person might have thought that, for example, the interpretation of a letter written by a layman, stating the terms upon which he offered work to someone else, should be a question of fact, best decided by an employment tribunal, which was likely to be more familiar with the relevant background than a judge. But the opposite is the case.[4] This rule may be part of the explanation for the otherwise remarkable fact that the Employment Appeal Tribunal has a majority of lay members although it has jurisdiction to hear appeals only on questions of law. The rule was adopted in trials by jury for purely pragmatic reasons. In mediaeval times juries were illiterate and most of the documents which came before a jury were deeds drafted by lawyers. In the 18th and 19th centuries the rule was maintained because it was essential to the development of English commercial law. There could have been no precedent and no certainty in the construction of standard commercial documents if questions of construction had been left in each case to a jury which gave no reasons for its decision. Thus the rule that the construction of documents is a question of law was well established when industrial tribunals were created and has been carried over into employment law.
>
> On the other hand, it does not apply when the intention of the parties, objectively ascertained, has to be gathered partly from documents but also from oral exchanges and conduct. In the latter case, the terms of the contract are a question of fact. And of course the question of whether the parties intended a document or documents to be the exclusive record of the terms of their agreement is also a question of fact.

Hart J considered the legislation on intermediary companies:[5]

> The inquiry which reg 6(1)[6] directs is in the first instance an essentially factual one. It involves identifying, first, what are the 'arrangements involving an intermediary' under which the services are performed, and, secondly, what are the 'circumstances' in the context of which the arrangements have been made and the services performed. The legal hypothesis which then has to be made is that the arrangements had taken the form of a contract between the worker and the client. To the extent that 'the arrangements' are in the particular case to be found only in contractual documentation, it may be true to say that the interpretation of that documentation is a question of law. Even in that case, however, the findings of the fact-finding tribunal will be determinative of the factual matrix in which the interpretative process has to take place, and influential to a greater or lesser degree in enabling the essential character of the arrangements to be identified. Where, on the other hand,

the arrangements cannot be located solely in contractual documentation, their identification and characterisation is properly to be described as a matter of fact for the fact-finding tribunal. The fact that the tribunal is then asked to hypothesise a contract comprising those arrangements directly between the worker and the client does not, by itself, convert the latter question from being a question of mixed fact and law into a pure question of law.

The significance of the point is, of course, that if the question is characterised as one fact, or of mixed fact and law, this court can only interfere if it concludes that the decision reached by the commissioners is an impossible one on the facts found by them or that they have misdirected themselves.

Difficulties arise where the first-instance Tribunal, having decided the true meaning of the statute in issue, has to apply that meaning to the facts. The difficulties are of two sorts.

The first difficulty is the familiar problem of primary and secondary facts, the latter being inferences drawn from the former. In general, such inferences are matters of fact and the courts are reluctant to substitute their own views, the more so since the tribunal, unlike the court, has seen the witnesses. The view that secondary facts are findings of fact was emphatically restated by Lord Brightman in *Furniss v Dawson*.[7] Thus the question of whether a trade is being carried on is one of fact. The tribunal must not only decide the primary facts such as what transactions were carried on when but also form its own conclusion as to whether these activities amounted to a trade or not, a conclusion which must depend on a whole range of circumstances and impressions.[8] However, the question of the meaning of trade is one of law. So the question whether an isolated transaction can come within the meaning of trade is one of law, whether this one does is one of fact.

The second difficulty is that the legal system has to accept that if a particular issue is one of fact, cases on almost identical facts may fall either side of the line. Some judges may be tempted to say in such circumstances that the two differently constituted tribunals cannot both be right and extricate themselves from the mess by characterising the issue as one which is of mixed law and fact.[9] Such judges are incorrect in their premise and so in their conclusion. Other judges show greater humility.[10] The third difficulty is that the law can be formulated in such a way as to leave more or less to the tribunal to decide depending on the level of abstraction employed. Thus in employment cases the issue may be: "is it a reward for services?" or, more simply: "is it an emolument?" Clearly the latter leaves more to the tribunal and reduces the court's power to intervene.

It is the task of the tribunal to make the findings of fact on the evidence before it[11] and the parties are entitled to expect that the tribunal will report in its decision its findings of fact which are relevant to the arguments adduced or intended to be adduced on appeal. However, the tribunal cannot be instructed to find facts or to make its findings in any particular way. This can cause problems in the subsequent court hearing, as is illustrated in *Fitzpatrick v IRC*.[12] The court may sometimes remit the case to the tribunal for additional findings of fact. However, this will only be done if such findings are material to some tenable argument, at least reasonable upon the evidence adduced and not inconsistent with findings already made.[13]

Simon's Taxes A1.115, 116.

1. See Lord Simon in *Ransom v Higgs* [1974] STC 539 at 561.
2. [1999] 1 WLR 2042, HL at 2048–2049, quoted by Hart J in *Synaptek Ltd v Young* [2003] EWHC 645 (Ch), [2003] STC 543 at para [9], 553d–554c.
3. (1956) at p 61.
4. See *Davies v Presbyterian Church of Wales* [1986] 1 WLR 323.
5. *Synaptek Ltd v Young* [2003] EWHC 645 (Ch), [2003] STC 543 para [11] at 554f.
6. Social Security Contributions (Intermediaries) Regulations 2000, SI 2000/727.
7. [1984] STC 153 at 167.
8. *IRC v Hyndland Investment Co Ltd* (1929) 14 TC 694 at 700 per Lord Sands.
9. eg *Fitzpatrick v IRC (No 2)* [1994] STC 237, HL, per Lord Templeman at 242e, 246g.
10. *Fitzpatrick v IRC (No 2)* [1994] STC 237, HL, per Lord Jauncey at 248, and Lord Mustill at 255.
11. It is also the duty of the Commissioners to decide the law. See *Esslemont v Marshall* [1996] STC 1086 n at 1086f. However, decisions of law, unlike decisions of fact, can be reversed by the court on appeal.
12. [1991] STC 34.
13. *Consolidated Goldfields plc v IRC* [1990] STC 357 at 361 per Scott J. The court will not remit a case back to the Commissioners simply because the taxpayer wishes to present his case differently: *Denekamp v Pearce* [1998] STC 1120. See, for example, *Revenue and Customs Commissioners v Wright* [2007] EWHC 526 (Ch). That case concerned the employment status of three workers. The judge on appeal, Lewison J, held: "It is not for me to substitute my view of the facts for the view which they take. But, for the reasons I have given, I am satisfied that the General Commissioners did apply the wrong legal test and in those circumstances I must allow the appeal and remit the question to the General Commissioners."

Order of the court

[2.21] When the court has heard an appeal by way of case stated it may make such order as to the court may seem fit.[1] This has been interpreted widely, enabling the court to uphold an assessment as if it had been made under a different section or to remit the matter to the Tribunal with a direction to uphold it as if it had been made under a different section. This power has been exercised to order the disclosure of documents previously withheld from the Revenue.[2]

The limited nature of the jurisdiction of the court emerges from a sharp divergence of judicial views in *Fitzpatrick v IRC (No 2)*.[3] Dealing with an issue of the deductibility of expenses incurred in connection with employment, Lord McCluskey proceeded to list various issues of fact which he regarded as important to such cases and then criticised the case stated for failing to address them sufficiently; such deficiencies opened the way for him to substitute his own decision on the ground that the Commissioners had made an error of law.[4]

Lord McCluskey was alone in his view. The more orthodox view was expressed by Lord Hope:

In my opinion this approach is at variance with the law and practice to be applied by this court . . . . The onus is on the taxpayer to satisfy the Commissioners that the assessment he has appealed against is wrong, and the question at this stage is whether on the facts found by the Commissioners they were entitled to arrive at their decision that the onus had not been discharged. It is not the practice for the Commissioners to set out the facts which were not established by the evidence and I believe that it would be unreasonable to expect the Commissioners to have addressed the facts as listed by Lord McCluskey since nobody, so far as I am aware, has previously analysed [the section] in that way.[5]

Lord Templeman in his judgment in the House of Lords repudiated Lord McCluskey's attempt to rewrite the provision in his own words.[6]

Simon's Taxes A1.116.

[1] TMA 1970, s 56(6).
[2] *IRC v McGuckian* [1994] STC 888, NI CA.
[3] [1992] STC 406.
[4] [1992] STC 406 at 443a.
[5] [1992] STC 406 at 439e.
[6] [1994] STC 237, HL at 243d.

Costs in the higher courts

[2.22] The decision of the Court of Appeal[1] in *Agassi v Robinson*[2] gives a comprehensive examination of the costs which can, and those which cannot, be recovered by a successful party in court proceedings where counsel is instructed under the Bar's Licensed Access Scheme (now known as BarDirect). Andre Agassi was held by the Special Commmissioners[3] to be assessable to UK income tax as a non-resident[4] in respect of payments connected with his activities in the UK as sportsman. The decision was upheld by the High Court[5], but reversed by the Court of Appeal.[6] Christopher Mills (a chartered tax adviser) instructed counsel under the Bar's Licensed Access' scheme. Tenon, of which Christopher Mills was a partner, had acted for the appellant for many years and, moreover were experts in tax law. The tax point at issue in the current litigation was a short point of statutory interpretation. There was no evidence to be marshalled and no witnesses were to be called. The appellant considered that it was more efficient to use Tenon rather than a firm of solicitors.

Dyson LJ, in his judgment, commented:

> In principle, it is obviously desirable that members of organisations such as the Chartered Institute of Taxation who are responsible and skilled persons should be encouraged to use the Licensed Access Scheme. As we have said (at [16], above), the Lord Chancellor has approved the arrangements by which they may instruct barristers direct in a limited range of cases as a new and a better way of providing advocacy services. The advantages of these arrangements are clear. These persons have specialist expertise in the field of tax law, often far exceeding that of solicitors. We were told by our assessor that the fees charged by a firm of solicitors for the work done in respect of these two appeals might well have been three times as high as Tenon's charges.[7]

[2.22] Tax administration – an overview

The taxpayer's right to conduct litigation derived solely from CPR 48.6, his right to recover costs from the opposing party had to be found in CPR 48.6 and not under the general rules as to costs.

Dyson LJ[8] said, in his judgment:

> A clear distinction has always been recognised between disbursements made and work done by a legal representative. It follows in our view that the appellant is not entitled to recover costs as a disbursement in respect of work done by Tenon which would normally have been done by a solicitor who had been instructed to conduct the appeal. This means that the appellant is not entitled to recover for the cost of Tenon providing general assistance to counsel in the conduct of the appeals. But it seems to us that it does not necessarily follow that the appellant is not entitled to recover costs in respect of the ancillary assistance provided by Tenon in these appeals. Mr Mills is an accountant who has expertise in tax matters, especially in the kind of issues that arose in the present case. It may be appropriate to allow the appellant at least part of Tenon's fees as a disbursement. It may be possible to argue that the cost of discussing the issues with counsel, assisting with the preparation of the skeleton argument etc is allowable as a disbursement, because the provision of this kind of assistance in a specialist esoteric is not the kind of work that would normally be done by the solicitor instructed to conduct the appeals. Another way of making the same point is that it may be possible to characterise these specialist services as those of an expert, and to say for that reason that the fees for these services are in principle recoverable as a disbursement.

With the introduction of the Upper Tribunal (so far as England and Wales is concerned), this decision will now be relevant only to cases being heard by the Court of Appeal and those last remaining appeals from the Commissioners still to be heard by the High Court.

The BarDirect scheme does not extend to appeals before the House of Lords and it is suspected will not apply in cases before the Supreme Court due to replace the judicial function of the Lords.

[1] The judgment was given by Dyson LJ who said: 'This is the judgment of the court, to which all its members have contributed' (para [1]). The members of the Court were: Brooke LJ, Dyson LJ and Carnwath LJ sitting with Master Hurst, Senior Costs Judge, as assessor.
[2] [2005] EWCA Civ 1507, [2006] STC 580, CA.
[3] *Set, Deuce and Ball v Robinson* [2003] STC (SCD) 382.
[4] Under TA 1988, s 556.
[5] *Agassi v Robinson* [2004] EWHC 487 (Ch), [2004] STC 610.
[6] *Agassi v Robinson* [2004] EWCA Civ 1518, [2005] STC 303, CA.
[7] [2006] STC 580, CA, para [80] at 600f–g.
[8] [2006] STC 580, CA, para [74], [75] and [76] at 599a, g–j.

Judicial review

[2.23] Two other ways of challenging a tribunal's decision judicially require mention. One is by judicial review, a remedy equally applicable to the decision of the Revenue. The most usual obstacle is that the court will not allow an applicant to use judicial review where the point should be dealt with by appeal.[1] It should also be noted that the Chancery Division of the High Court does not have jurisdiction to review a claim for tax relief based on the principle of a legitimate expectation created by HMRC, such a claim can only be entertained by the Administrative Court in judicial review (although that function can be delegated to the Upper Tribunal under the Tribunals, Courts and Enforcement Act 2007, section 15).[2]

Conversely, allegations of unfairness in the conduct of the appeal by a tribunal on matters for judicial review are not for appeal.[3]

The remedies available to a successful applicant for judicial review are: a declaration, an injunction, a quashing order, a mandatory order and/ or a prohibiting order depending on the particular facts of the case and the complaint made (Civil Procedure Rules 54.2 and 54.3). In addition, a claim for judicial review may include a claim for damages, restitution or the recovery of a sum due but these remedies may not be sought alone: *R (on the application of Bamber) v R & C Comrs* [2007] EWHC 798 (Admin). The reason behind this rule is that a claimant who has a good claim in private law (civil courts) for recovery of a sum should not rely on a public law remedy.

When judicial review is sought the rules of judicial review must be followed; so where review is sought for a Revenue failure to decide between two courses of action with regard to an assessment the remedy is a mandatory order to compel the Revenue to decide and not an order quashing the original assessment.[4] In *R (on the application of Sagemaster plc) v Customs and Excise Comrs*,[5] the applicant was assessed to recover input tax. The applicant appealed against the assessment and also applied for permission to apply for judicial review on the grounds that it had a legitimate expectation that it would be entitled to input tax credit if it complied with Customs' guidelines. Although the VAT and Duties Tribunal can apply the Community doctrine of legitimate expectation, this doctrine applies where an attack is made on legislation enacted by a member state. In this case, the complaint was an abuse of power by individual officers of a public authority. This falls within the English doctrine, in respect of which the tribunal had no jurisdiction. Permission was granted because it was strongly arguable that the complaint could only be made by way of judicial review.

In the recent case of *R (on the application of BMW AG & Ors) v R & C Comrs* [2008] EWHC 712 (Admin), the taxpayer, a repayment trader, sought permission to apply for judicial review of a decision by the Revenue requiring it to make quarterly VAT returns in line with its associated supplier. The taxpayer argued that the decision ought to be quashed on two grounds: firstly that the Revenue had no power to make the direction issued, and secondly, if it did have the power, the decision was irrational. The Court held that the Revenue has power to issue a direction requiring repayment traders to make quarterly returns instead of monthly returns pursuant to Reg 25 of the Value Added Tax Regulations 1995, SI 1995/2518, and consistently with the purpose of the Sixth Council Directive 77/388/EEC. Reg 25 gives the Revenue power to direct or allow a trader to make monthly returns but not in perpetuity and as such the Revenue has liberty to withdraw it as they think fit. In terms of irrationality, the Court gave permission to apply for judicial review

[2.23] Tax administration – an overview

on the basis that since the main concern of the Revenue was unjustified and unintended cash flow advantages for traders at its expense, the application of its policy and the decision-making process were flawed for the following reasons:

(a) the Revenue should have considered whether there was a commercial reason why the taxpayer completing a quarterly return instead of a monthly return would cause them significant administrative difficulties or expense;

(b) the Revenue did not consider whether the export through an associated repayment trader resulted in a significant cash flow advantage for the taxpayer that it would not obtain if it were itself the exporter, and so the repayment trader.

The second is by arguing that the assessment is ultra vires.[6] This line of argument has been used—unsuccessfully—to argue that the profits of prostitution could not be taxable since, as a matter of law, the profits of an illegal activity cannot be subject to tax. The judges will no doubt keep this use of the ultra vires doctrine under very tight control to prevent it from becoming another avenue of appeal. An inspector does not act ultra vires merely because he makes a mistake of law.

In *R (on the application of Federation of Technological Industries) v Customs and Excise Comrs*,[7] the applicants were given permission to apply for a declaration that the provisions relating to joint and several liability and security introduced by FA 2003, ss 17 and 18 were not authorised by Community law and that the issue of authority should be referred to the Court of Justice.

A County Court does not have the power to vary a determination of the tribunal.[8]

Judicial review has strict time limits, that is, a claim form must be filed with the Administrative Court *promptly and in any event not later than 3 months after the grounds to make the claim first arose*.[9] A slothful claimant will have to present good reasons for any delay to the Court in order to avoid permission being refused on the grounds of undue delay. In the case of *R (on the application of BMW AG & Ors) v R & C Comrs* [2008] EWHC 712 (Admin), two applications for permission to apply for judicial review by Jaguar Cars and Land Rover exports were refused at first instance for undue delay of over 10 months even though their substantive arguments were as strong as those of BMW.

In general terms, grounds for judicial review first arise on the date a final decision or assessment has been issued by the HMRC or the tribunal. In VAT cases, a claimant is entitled to wait until the notification of an assessment before taking steps to bring proceedings for judicial review, even if it has been clear from correspondence there is an imminent assessment.[10]

Simon's Taxes A5.301, 302.

---

[1] In *R v IRC, ex p Preston* [1985] STC 282, HL, Lord Scarman said: 'a remedy by way of judicial review is not to be made available where an alternative remedy exists

'... Where parliament has provided by statute an appeal procedure, as in the taxes statutes, it will only be very rarely that the courts will allow the collateral process of judicial review to be used to attack an appealable decision', see also *Re McGuckian* [2000] STC 65, NI CA. However, see also *R (Davies) v HMRC* [2008] EWCA Civ. In that case, the Court of Appeal restored the claimant's application for permission for judicial review where the basis of the challenge was the alleged reneging from published guidance and, the Court held, to deal with the substantive appeal before consideration of the taxpayer's legitimate expectations would have effectively restricted the role of the Administrative Court on any subsequent judicial review.

2   *R v IR Commrs ex parte MFK Underwriting Agents Ltd & Ors* [1989] BTC 561; *Steibelt (HMIT) v Paling* [1999] BTC 184; *Hatt v Newman (HMIT)* [2000] BTC 42, *Venables & Ors v Hornby (HMIT)* [2003] BTC 559; *Demibourne Ltd v HMRC* (2005) Sp C 486 and most recently *Refson v R & C Comrs* (June 2008, unreported).
3   *Mellor v Gurney* [1994] STC 1025n.
4   *Wang v Commissioner of Inland Revenue* [1994] STC 753, PC.
5   [2004] EWCA Civ 25, [2004] STC 813.
6   *IRC v Aken* [1990] STC 497, CA.
7   [2004] EWHC 254 (admin), [2004] STC 1008.
8   *McCullough v Ahluwalia* [2004] EWCA Civ 889, [2004] STC 1295.
9   Civil Procedure Rules 54.5(1).
10 See *R (on the application of Software Solutions Partners Ltd) v R & C Comrs* [2007] EWHC 971 (Admin).

Other remedies against HMRC

[2.24] There will also be occasions in which the Revenue will be acting as a private party. Typically, this will be in cases where the Revenue and a taxpayer enter into a contract settlement for the resolution of a dispute. Although the terms of such settlements often entitle, in the event of a breach by the taxpayer, the Revenue to recommence (or continue) assessment proceedings, the Revenue will often be entitled in the alternative to any outstanding sums as liquidated damages. Proceedings under the latter category will be for breach of a contract. Where it is the Revenue that appears to have breached the terms of a contract, there will conversely be contractual rights that the taxpayer might enforce. That would be best done (depending on the precise facts) by the taxpayer seeking an injunction or other declaratory relief from the High Court to restrain the behaviour complained of.[1] There are arguments to suggest that such actions ought to be commenced by judicial review, as they relate to the exercise of the Revenue's public powers. However, given that judicial review is intended to be an approach of the last resort[2] and the dislike of such fine distinctions by the judiciary, it is suggested that a defence based solely on the form of the claim made will not find the favour of the judge.

The Revenue will also be liable to taxpayers (and others) in tort law for other civil wrongs committed. However, the scope of such actions is very tightly prescribed. For the Revenue to be liable in negligence, the claimant must show

[2.24] Tax administration – an overview

that HMRC owed it a duty of care. The carrying out of statutory functions does not give rise to such a duty.[3] However, in exceptional circumstances, a duty will be owed. In *Neil Martin Ltd v R & C Comrs* [2007] EWCA Civ 1041, the Court of Appeal has confirmed a duty of care can be owed.[4] For an authority to show that a bank does not owe a duty of care to the Revenue in respect of a charge the Revenue holds over unpaid tax, see *HM Customs & Excise v Barclays Bank plc* [2006] UKHL 28.

---

[1] For an example of an unsuccessful attempt by a taxpayer to seek such relief see *Stockler Charity (a firm) v R & C Comrs* [2007] EWHC 2967 (Ch).

[2] In the case of *R (on the application of Davies & Anor) v Revenue & Customs Commrs* [2008] EWCA Civ 933 in the Queen's Bench Division of the High Court, the taxpayers argued that they had a legitimate expectation that their arrangements were not liable to UK tax, because they were not resident within the United Kingdom for the relevant tax year. Their contention that they had such an expectation was based on their reliance upon IR 20. The claim for judicial review was that the Revenue in those guidance notes set out very clear criteria (91–day test) for non-residents that the claimants complied with, therefore it would be wrong for the Revenue to depart from the test and the apparent satisfaction of the test set out in the guidance notes. The High Court allowed the judicial review claim to go ahead before the appeal to the Special Commissioners had been determined notwithstanding the fact that judicial review is – in normal circumstances – a remedy of last resort. The reason for this departure from normal procedure was that the Court considered that there was a real risk that a decision by the Special Commissioners may be seen as stifling a claim for judicial review. Once a Commissioners' decision had been established that the taxpayers were, as a matter of fact, resident during the relevant period, a statutory duty on the Revenue to collect tax due would become effective. A Court in a judicial review application would not have been confident to direct the Revenue not to collect tax which was held to be due.

[3] *Stovin v Wise* [1996] AC 923.

[4] In that case, an employee at HMRC negligently completed an application form for the Construction Industry Scheme without the permission of the taxpayer concerned. Exceeding the statutory duty in those circumstances was sufficient to give rise to the duty of care.

Evasion and fraud

Avoidance or evasion

[2.25] The difference between avoidance and evasion is crucial. Dennis Healey, when Chancellor of the Exchequer, famously described the distinction as "the thickness of a prison wall". Avoidance is arranging one's affairs, or structuring a transaction to reduce the tax liability which arises. Evasion is pretending that assets or a transaction are other than they are in truth. In other words, evasion is a type of fraud.

A useful corrective to some woolly thinking that has sometimes attempted to blur this vital distinction was given by Dawn Primarolo, the Paymaster General, in the House of Common on 29 June 2000:

> The Right Hon. Member for Wells asked about tax advisers who gave advice on avoidance schemes that failed. A failed scheme whose details are not hidden from the Revenue amounts not to tax evasion, but to tax planning . . . The Government may not like some of that planning and may legislate against it, but, as it is not hidden, it does not fall within the remit of the measure . . . avoidance is not evasion; there are separate laws to deal with the latter. The Right Hon. Gentleman asked when avoidance became evasion. Unless he can give an example, I cannot think of such an eventuality.[1]

Historically, the provisions for dealing with evasion and fraud have differed according to the differing taxes.

In its investigations, the Revenue makes use of information supplied by informants. From time to time, the Revenue makes payment for information supplied. The existence of this practice forms the subject of *R (on the application of Churchhouse) v IRC*.[2] In that case, an informer had been paid for information supplied on tax avoidance by a large company but the Revenue declined to make a second payment for further information. In this judicial review case, the informer failed in his attempt to obtain a direction from the court that a second payment should be made to him.

---

[1] The statement was made during the debate on what is now FA 2000, s 144.
[2] [2003] EWHC 681 (Admin), [2003] STC 629.

Nature of fraud or negligent conduct

[2.26] The onus of proving fraud or negligent conduct is on the Crown and there is no presumption of such a state of mind arising from mere proof of an omission to disclose profits, although the tribunal is entitled to conclude that there was.[1] This is reconciled with the rule that the burden of proof of upsetting an assessment rests on the taxpayer, by imposing the burden on the taxpayer to show the default assessment is incorrect, once the Revenue have established fraud or wilful default.[2] It is not necessary for the Crown to show that the profits relate to one or other source of income; this is a matter which the taxpayer can dispute by appealing against the assessment.[3] Moreover, it has been said that when the Crown succeeds in proving just one instance of fraud or wilful default, the tribunal could infer that the taxpayer had been guilty of fraud or wilful default in each of the years for which assessment is in issue.[4] This is, however, perhaps better viewed as an illustration of the principle that it is for the tribunal to make findings of fact.

The test which distinguishes mere neglect from wilful default is that the latter demands knowledge or simply not caring whether the return is accurate.[5]

Conscious carelessness as to whether or not one is doing one's duty is wilful default.[6] So where a husband made a return of his wife's income not knowing of a particular source, it was held that he was not guilty of fraud or wilful

[2.26] Tax administration – an overview

neglect, whereas a simple refusal to declare some of his wife's income would be wilful default.[7] On the other hand, there is wilful default where a person fails to make a return and simply pays the tax demanded in an estimated assessment knowing that the sum demanded is insufficient.[8]

The fraud or negligent conduct must have been committed by the taxpayer or on his behalf. It has been held that if an agent is guilty of fraud or negligent conduct, that fraud or negligent conduct is on behalf of the principal even if he is not privy to it.[9]

Simon's Taxes A4.325.

---

[1] Hillenbrand v IRC (1966) 42 TC 617. In a very detailed judgment, the Special Commissioner in Chartered Accountant v Inspector of Taxes [2003] STC (SCD) 166 considered an entry for interest relief made by the taxpayer in his personal tax return when he knew he was not entitled to the relief: "In our view that is fraudulent conduct as it involved dishonesty and the appellant knew what he was doing. It is also negligent conduct." (at para 141, 192j)
[2] Amis v Colls (1960) 39 TC 148.
[3] Hudson v Humbles (1965) 42 TC 380 at 387 per Pennycuick J.
[4] Nicholson v Morris [1976] STC 269.
[5] Wellington v Reynolds (1962) 40 TC 209 at 215 per Wilberforce J, but cf Salmon LJ in Frederick Lack Ltd v Doggett (1970) 46 TC 524 at 535, CA.
[6] Clixby v Pountney (1968) 44 TC 515 at 520 per Cross J.
[7] Brown v IRC (1965) 42 TC 583 at 589 per Stamp J.
[8] Amis v Colls (1960) 39 TC 148 at 163 per Cross J.
[9] Clixby v Pountney (1968) 44 TC 515.

HMRC prosecution powers

Direct taxes

[2.27] The Taxes Acts provide for penalties to be imposed for a variety of failures and offences (see supra, §§ **2A.90–2A.97**). In severe cases HMRC may opt to press criminal charges in the criminal courts, such as under the Theft Act 1968, s 32(1) or the common law offence of cheating the revenue. A criminal prosecution does not exclude civil penalties.[1] HMRC prefer the penalty procedure to criminal prosecution because HMRC considers that prosecution is a drastic step which ought to be reserved for really serious cases and because of practical matters such as the burden of preparing cases. The decision to prosecute in a particular case is amenable to judicial review.[2] It is possible, although rare, for the Crown Prosecution Service to take criminal proceedings if HMRC have accepted a contract settlement and decided not to prosecute.[3]

The peculiar nature of these powers may be illustrated by a number of special rules. First, negligence will be assumed if an error remains uncorrected.[4] Second, the death of the taxpayer does not end the proceedings.[5] Third, contrary to the normal rules of evidence, any statements made by the taxpayer are admissible, even where an inducement has been given by HMRC.[6] Fourth, there are time limits for the recovery of penalties.[7] Fifth, HMRC have the power to mitigate penalties even after the courts have pronounced.[8] These provisions apply to both criminal and civil proceedings. As is stated in HMRC booklet IR 73, HMRC practice is to tell the taxpayer that HMRC is prepared to accept a pecuniary settlement and that the sum payable under such a settlement will be reduced if full disclosure is made.

Simon's Taxes A1.117.

[1] Statement of practice SP 2/88.
[2] *R v IRC, ex p Mead and Cook* [1992] STC 482.
[3] *R v W* [1998] STC 550, CA at 557g.
[4] TMA 1970, s 97.
[5] TMA 1970, s 100A.
[6] TMA 1970, s 105.
[7] TMA 1970, s 103.
[8] TMA 1970, s 102.

Contract settlement

[2.28] The practice of HMRC is to favour a contract settlement whereby, at the end of a back duty investigation, the taxpayer pays a single sum, on receipt of which, HMRC agree to waive its entitlement to all tax, penalties and interest covered by the settlement.

In terms, the sum in settlement is offered by the taxpayer and the contract is made by HMRC accepting the offer. In practice, the investigating officer often drafts the letter of offer from the taxpayer, specifying an amount which would be acceptable to the Board.

Where there is a contract settlement of a taxpayer's back duty, it is usual for HMRC to completely mitigate (that is, choose not to charge) the fixed sum penalties given in statute for failures to make returns.[1]

Once a settlement has been entered into, the sum that it payable under the settlement is no longer a payment of tax, but is a payment due under a contract, quite separate from the payment of tax, interest and penalties from which the contractual debt is calculated.[2] The courts have held that this is not an illegal contract.[3] Since the settlement is an agreement between the parties, HMRC may not claim as a preferential creditor in respect of the sums agreed.[4]

The conduct of back duty cases is a skilled art. HMRC may have been tipped off or may simply disbelieve the taxpayer's return. Sources of information that are used include returns made by banks, etc, evidence given in court,[5] government contracts, a customer suspicious on being asked for a bearer cheque,[6] and even a reported robbery;[7] informers may be rewarded.

Once alerted HMRC may require a complete statement of means and a satisfactory explanation of all sums appearing in bank accounts or supporting a luxurious lifestyle. To this end HMRC are reported to keep records of all horse racing results and details of wins on the National Lottery.

[2.28] Tax administration – an overview

Park J describes the process of back duty and the use of capital statements:

> Sophisticated points of tax law rarely arise in back duty cases. Back duty is the area where the Revenue, having conducted an investigation into a taxpayer, form the view that the income which he had been declaring for tax was lower than his true income. In back duty investigations the Revenue frequently prepare (as they did in this case) 'capital statements'.
>
> Capital statements are useful. It is a fact—unfortunate but true—that there are people who cheat on their taxes, and capital statements are a technique which ferrets out the case where the taxpayer has had more money to spend than his declared income suggests he should have had.[8]

Sometimes an exhaustive back duty inquiry will lead to exoneration of the taxpayer. In such circumstances the Revenue may reimburse the taxpayer his costs but only if there was a serious error on the part of the department.[9]

A contract settlement does not restrict the evidence permitted to be called at any proceedings before Commissioners.[10]

Contract settlements are to be negotiated in cases of tax credit enquiries and examinations.[11]

Simon's Taxes A1.117.

---

[1] See, for example, TMA 1970, s 93(1)(a).
[2] *A-G v Midland Bank Executor and Trustee Co Ltd* (1934) 19 TC 136.
[3] Rowlatt J described it as "a beneficial and merciful practice" in *A-G v Johnstone* (1926) 10 TC 758.
[4] *IRC v Woollen* [1992] STC 944, CA.
[5] However, in a matrimonial case, the court ordered the Revenue to destroy all copies of a judgment given in an ancillary relief case, the judgment holding, as a question of fact, that tax evasion had taken place. The court's judgment had been made available to the Revenue by an aggrieved third party: *S v S (No 2) (Disclosure of Material)* [1997] STC 759.
[6] *Rosette Franks (King Street) Ltd v Dick* (1955) 36 TC 100.
[7] *Crole v Lloyd* (1950) 31 TC 338.
[8] *Hurley v Taylor* [1998] STC 202 at 213f, g.
[9] See statements of practice SP A28 and A31; supplemented by ICAEW Memorandum TR 788, *Simon's Tax Intelligence* 1990, p 43.
[10] TMA 1970, s 105(1) amended by FA 2003, s 206.
[11] See Revenue manual, New Tax Credits Claimants Compliance Manual, CCM8230 and CCM21360.

Stamp duty land tax

[2.29] FA 2003, s 93 and Sch 13 govern the powers of HMRC to call for documents and information for the purposes of stamp duty land tax. HMRC may authorise an officer of theirs to inspect any property in order to ascertain its market value or for any other relevant matter.[1]

FA 2003, s 95 creates the statutory criminal offence of a person being knowingly concerned in the fraudulent evasion of SDLT by him or any other person. If found guilty the person is liable on summary conviction to imprisonment for a term not exceeding six months or a fine not exceeding the statutory maximum (or both) and on conviction on indictment to imprisonment for a term not exceeding seven years or a fine (or both). This section is based on and largely copies FA 2000, s 144 which was introduced to make prosecution of PAYE and NIC fraud involving payment of wages by cash in hand without deducting tax more effective. When that provision was introduced into the Finance Bill 2000 at a late stage unease was expressed about the imprecision inherent in the phrases "knowingly concerned" and "fraudulent evasion". In response the Paymaster General explained the use of these phrases as follows:

> I will deal with the important point about the words 'knowingly' and fraudulent evasion. . . . My officials will smile when they hear this, but initially I said to them, 'Surely evasion is fraud', and asked why it needed to be qualified as 'fraudulent evasion'. I have received assurances which I will pass on to the Committee. The juxtaposition of the words 'knowingly' and 'fraudulent evasion' reinforces exactly which offences the provision is aimed at.
>
> Let us take the question of someone who is knowingly concerned in the evasion of income tax. I want to make it clear that it is not enough for this purpose to show that a person should have suspected that someone was evading tax. The person must have knowledge and involvement in the fraud. For example, he could help someone evade tax by helping to produce false business records.
>
> People may ask why we have put the words 'fraudulent' and 'evasion' together. I am reliably informed by people who know better than I do that, in English usage, 'to evade' can mean to dodge, without any dishonest intent. Although 'evasion' has come to imply dishonesty in the context of tax, the Bill needs to be drafted tightly. 'Fraudulent' may not appear to add much to 'evasion', but the expression 'fraudulent evasion' is well precedented and subject to interpretation by the courts.

---

[1] FA 2003, s 94.

Serious Fraud

Documents held by a tax accountant

[2.30] An inspector may call for documents in the possession of a tax accountant.[1] In order to apply for service of a s 20A notice on a tax accountant, the inspector must be able to show:

(a) that the agent has been convicted of an offence in relation to tax by or before any court in the UK. The reference to "tax" is within the context of the Taxes Acts, and not being extended by definition, therefore would not include VAT. The reference to conviction by or before a court connotes a criminal charge, eg fraud, whereby the tax accountant has been found guilty and duly convicted. The full appeal procedure against the conviction must have been exhausted before a notice can be sought; and

(b) that the tax agent has had awarded against him a penalty under TMA 1970, s 99, ie a penalty of up to £3,000 for assisting in or inducing the making or delivery of a knowingly incorrect return or accounts for tax purposes. A s 20A notice cannot be sought by the inspector while any appeal is pending against the making of such an award, this restriction does not apply to an appeal simply against the amount of any penalty awarded. The distinction is, of course, between an appeal against the finding of the Commissioners that the circumstances for the award of a penalty existed, and otherwise an appeal on the grounds that, the fault having been found, the penalty awarded was excessive.

---

[1] TMA 1970, s 20A. HMRC views on the scope of its power to obtain documents from a tax accountant and the type of document that is immune from an order under s 20B by virtue of professional privilege is given in Inland Revenue Tax Bulletin April 2000, pp 743–746.

The new system

[2.31] HMRC can exercise a number of statutory powers in the course of carrying out a criminal investigation. For historical reasons, the scope and extent of HMRC's statutory powers differ in relation to VAT on one hand and direct taxes on the other. These powers were ring-fenced when the former revenue departments were merged.

In 2005, the Government launched a review of powers, deterrents and safeguards.[1] The first outcome of this review is a system of criminal investigation powers applicable to both direct and indirect taxes. Separate legislation applies to England and Wales,[2] Scotland,[3] and Northern Ireland.[4] It came into force on 8 November and 1 December 2007.[5]

In essence, FA 2007 makes the following changes to primary legislation in order to bring about the new system in England and Wales:

(1) Subject to a number of exceptions,[6] powers in relation to VAT and direct tax cease to be ring-fenced.[7]
(2) Powers in relation to VAT and direct taxes broadly follow the equivalent powers exercised by the police. The primary legislation comprises: (a) the Police and Criminal Evidence Act 1984, ss 8, 14A, 14B[8] and such other provisions as may be specified (with or without modification) by an order made under s 114(2); (b) the Criminal Justice and Police Act 2001, ss 50, 67 and such other provisions in Part 2 (ss 51–70) as may be specified (with or without modification) by an order made under s 67;[9] and (c) Criminal Justice and Public Order Act 1994 ss 136–139.[10]
(3) In so far as provisions of TMA 1970, CEMA 1979, VATA 1994, Tax Credits Act 2002, Proceeds of Crime Act 2002 and FA 2003 Sch 13 are superseded by the legislation in head (2), they are repealed.[11]

As regards Scotland and Northern Ireland, the new system is brought about by amending the corresponding legislation in force in those countries.

1   See Economic and Fiscal Strategy Report, para 5.110. For consultations, see in particular, *Criminal Investigation Powers* (HMRC, August 2006).
2   See FA 2007, ss 81, 83, 85, 86 and Sch 22.
3   See FA 2007 s 84–86 and Sch 23.
4   See FA 2007, ss 82, 83, 85, 86 and Sch 22.
5   The Finance Act 2007 (Sections 82 to 84 and Schedule 23) (Commencement) Order 2007, SI 2007/3166.
6   FA 2007 s 83(3).
7   FA 2007, s 83(1), (2).
8   As amended or inserted by FA 2007, ss 81, 85.
9   As amended by FA 2007, Sch 22, para 2.
10 As applied and modified by FA 2007 s 86.
11 By FA 2007, Sch 22, paras 3, 4, 5, 8, 14, 15, 16.

Procedure in a criminal investigation: PACE

[2.32] The Police and Criminal Evidence Act 1984 (PACE 1984) specifies procedures that are to be followed in a criminal investigation. These procedures include Code C, which requires a caution and tape recording of any interview. PACE 1984, s 67(9) makes it clear that its provisions apply to any persons in the discharge of a duty of investigating offences.

Code C of PACE (as amended in 1995) states:

> A person whom there are grounds to suspect of an offence must be cautioned before any questions about it (or further questions if it is his answers to previous questions which provide the grounds for suspicion) are put to him regarding his involvement or suspected involvement in that offence if his answers or his silence (ie failure or refusal to answer a question or to answer satisfactorily) may be given in evidence to a court in a prosecution.

The Court of Appeal[1] has held that these procedures apply when HMRC officers undertake an investigation with a view to a criminal prosecution, the, so called, "Hansard interview".

In 1984 and again in 1994 the Revenue questioned tax returns submitted by Sewa Gill and Paramjit Gill. On 8 March 1995 the two brothers were interviewed by three members of what was then known as the Special Compliance Office (SCO). SCO commenced the interview by reading out a reply to a Parliamentary Question given by the Chancellor of the Exchequer (Mr John Major) on 18 October 1990 ("the Hansard extract"), which states:

> The practice of the Board of Inland Revenue in cases of tax fraud is as follows:
>
> (1) The Board may accept a money settlement instead of instituting criminal proceedings in respect of fraud alleged to have been committed by a taxpayer.
> (2) They can give no undertaking that they will accept a money settlement and refrain from instituting criminal proceedings even if the case is one in which the taxpayer had made a full confession and has given full facilities for investigation of the facts. They reserve to themselves full discretion in all cases as to the course they pursue.

[2.32] Tax administration – an overview

(3) But in considering whether to accept a money settlement or to institute criminal proceedings, it is their practice to be influenced by the fact that the taxpayer has made a full confession and has given full facilities for investigation into his affairs and from examination of such books, papers, documents or information as the Board may consider necessary.

The above statement of practice should be regarded as replacing the one given by the then Chancellor of the Exchequer on 5 October 1944.

The SCO followed the ordinary practice in this case. It asked the appellants to agree to an interview and asked them a number of questions. It also asked them to answer a set of standard questions as follows:

(1) In regard to any business with which you have been concerned either as a director, partner or sole proprietor,
 (a) Have any transactions, receipts or expenses been omitted from or incorrectly recorded in the books thereof?
 (b) Are the accounts sent to the Inland Revenue correct and complete to the best of your knowledge and belief?
 (c) Are all taxation returns correct and complete to the best of your knowledge and belief?
(2) Are all your personal taxation returns correct and complete to the best of your knowledge and belief?
(3) Are you prepared to allow an examination of all business books, business and private bank statements and other business and private records in order that the Revenue may be satisfied that your answers to the first two questions are correct?

The Gill brothers then answered questions on income they had received.

It was subsequently ascertained that the answers given by the Gill brothers were incorrect. The loss of tax arising from the incorrect statements made after the Hansard extract had been given amounted to £534,635. The Gill brothers were prosecuted by the then Inland Revenue. Sewa Gill was sentenced to three years imprisonment, Paramjit Gill was sentenced to 20 months imprisonment. The Gill brothers appealed to the Court of Appeal.[1]

The trial judge had said that evidence was admissible since the interview was all part of a civil proceedings to collect tax; the proceedings were not criminal and so the interview was not part of a criminal investigation. The Court of Appeal did not agree. Clarke LJ said:

We hold that Code C applied in the Hansard interview conducted on 8 March 1995 and that the appellants should have been cautioned and a tape recording made of the interview.[2]

The court noted that the accused had been warned of the possibility of criminal proceedings and so that the case was likely to go beyond simple penalties under the Taxes Management Act 1970. The court also noted that this decision would necessitate a redrawing of the Revenue's Code of Practice 9.[3]

However the Court of Appeal (Criminal Division) went on to decide that the admission of answers had had no adverse effect on the fairness of the proceedings and so the convictions stood. In deciding that the conviction should still stand, the court noted that, while the breach of the code was 'significant', it had been committed in good faith. The purpose of the rule was to protect the accused from making admissions; here however the Revenue used the interview to show that the accused had continued to tell lies.[4] The court also noted that the accused had been advised to get legal representation[5]

Serious Fraud [2.32]

that they must have known they were not obliged to answer[6] and that a full note was made by the revenue officers.[7]

The present status of the Code as it applies to tax matters is subtle. PACE 1984, s 67 deals first with the steps to be followed by the Secretary of State when issuing a code of practice. These steps have been amended by the Criminal Justice and Police Act 2001 and the Criminal Justice Act 2003. Section 67(8) as enacted in 1984 stated that a police officer is liable to disciplinary proceedings for a failure to comply with any provision of the code—unless precluded by s 104. This draconian provision was found to be ineffective and was repealed in 1994. There was no suggestion that an officer of the Inland Revenue was a police officer for the purposes of s 67(8). Section 67(9) states that person other than police officers who are charged with a duty of investigating offences or charging offenders shall in the discharge of that duty have regard to any relevant provision of the code; this was the provision in issue in *Gill*. Section 67(10)(*b*) states that the failure of a person under a duty does not of itself make the person liable in criminal or civil proceedings. Section 67(11) states that the code is to be admissible in civil or criminal proceedings and if any provision of the code appears to be relevant to any question it shall be taken into account in those proceedings.

Thus s 67 does not say that breaches of the code mean that the evidence is on that ground alone inadmissible; these matters are left to the general power under s 78 for the judge to exclude evidence which would have such an adverse effect on the proceedings that the court should not admit it. Section 78 does not in terms impose a duty on the judge to exclude it. These provisions replace the old informal "Judges Rules" which also left the courts with a discretion. However commentators note that the judges have been much more willing to punish the police and others for breaches of the codes than they were under the old rules.[8]

Gill shows that HMRC officers fall within the scope of these codes but this had been conceded by a Parliamentary answer in 1986.[9] Also caught are certain Bank of England officials, store detectives and commercial investigators.

As a consequence of the Court of Appeal judgment, HMRC completely revised their procedure to deal with the case of serious fraud. Termed the "new civil fraud procedure",[10] this applies across all indirect and direct tax regimes. The intention is not to prosecute for the fraud under the new civil procedures. There is, however, a prosecution sanction but only for making a materially false disclosure (including deliberate false statements during the course of the investigation or furnishing false documents at the conclusion of that investigation).

The Police and Criminal Evidence Act 1984 has been amended[11] to apply to all taxes administered by HMRC.

1   *R v Gill* [2003] EWCA Crim 2256, [2003] STC 1229.
2   At [40].
3   See [40], [34] and [35].
4   At [42].
5   At [47].

105

[2.32] Tax administration – an overview

[6] At [48].
[7] At [51].
[8] Zander, *The Police and Criminal Evidence Act 1984* (4th edn) para 6.15.
[9] Hansard vol 100 23 June 1986 col 51—see Zander, above.
[10] HM Revenue Practice—New civil investigation of fraud procedures—updated Notice COP9, *Simons Weekly Tax Intelligence* 2005, pp 1558–1559.
[11] PACE 1984, s 114 amended by FA 2007, s 81.

Procedure in a criminal investigation: human rights

[2.33] The UK PACE 1984 and associated Northern Ireland Orders are concerned with the investigation of criminal offences in England, Wales, Scotland and Northern Ireland and provide their own protection for such investigations. As seen supra, § **1.20**, however, the ECtHR in Strasbourg has taken a much wider view of the meaning of the term 'criminal charge' in arts 6(2) and (3) of the European convention on Human Rights concerning the burden of proof and minimum rights such as a right to an explanation of the charge in a language the accused can understand, the right to silence and legal aid. So the Court has stated that the expression has an autonomous meaning and can cover an administrative penalty for negligent or fraudulent conduct.[1]

The effect of a tax procedure being classified as involving a criminal charge is particularly important in the context of Art 6 because it also means that Art 6(1) applies. This guarantees the right to a court, to an independent and impartial tribunal, to a determination within a reasonable time and the right to a public hearing. As seen supra, § **1.16**, the ECtHR has determined that the determination of a tax liability is not a determination of civil rights and obligations within art 6(1).

[1] See Baker [2000] BTR 211 at 235 et seq citing the leading case of *Engel v Netherlands* (1976) 1 EHRR 647 and *Benendoun v France* Application 12547/86, *AP, MP and TP v Switzerland* 19958/92 and *Vastaberga Taxi v Sweden* 36985/97. See also *King v Walden* [2001] STC 822, *Georgiou v United Kingdom* [2001] STC 80 (also Application No 40042/98), *Customs and Excise Comrs v Han* [2001] STC 1188.

Does a criminal sanction indicate a criminal act?

[2.34] It is widely considered that any tax-geared penalty is the determination of a criminal charge for the purposes of the ECHR. The safeguards in art 6 would then apply to the investigation leading to the imposition of the penalty. If the penalty at the end of the process is a criminal sanction, is the act for which it was imposed a criminal act?

If so, this has wide implications for the conduct of an interview to investigate any suspected under-declaration of tax, not only by what is now HMRC Special Civil Investigations but also by local compliance offices.

The conduct giving rise to an understatement or overstatement of tax may amount to the commission of a criminal offence under the VAT legislation,[1] customs legislation,[2] general criminal legislation,[3] or at common law.[4] HMRC has two choices where the criminal standard of proof is met:

(1) They may prosecute. Where this is done, the collection of any fines imposed is the responsibility of the court.
(2) They may compound proceedings,[5] ie accept a pecuniary penalty in lieu of prosecution. In this case, a debt arises under the contract made between them and the trader and is collected as a debt due to the Crown.[6]

Offences specific to VAT are as follows:

(1) Being knowingly concerned in the fraudulent evasion of VAT.
(2) Taking steps with a view to the fraudulent evasion of VAT.
(3) Producing, furnishing, sending or making use of any document which is false in a material particular with intent to deceive.
(4) Furnishing any information known to be false in a material particular.
(5) Making any statement known to be false in a material particular.
(6) Recklessly making a statement which is false in a material particular.
(7) Conduct which must have involved the commission of one or more of the foregoing offences.
(8) Acquiring possession of VAT-evaded goods.
(9) Dealing with VAT-evaded goods.
(10) Accepting the supply of VAT-evaded services
(11) Receiving or supplying goods or services without providing security.

The new offence of "fraud or evasion of income tax" was created by FA 2000, s 144. The first case under this new offence was prosecuted in January 2004.[7] A self-employed taxi driver was convicted of fraudulently evading tax of £2,428.99 by failing to inform HMRC that he was in business.

There is also an offence of fraud under the Tax Credits Act.[8] A person commits an offence if he is knowingly concerned in any fraudulent activity undertaken with a view to obtaining payments of a tax credit by him or any other person. Conviction on indictment carries a sentence of up to seven years or a fine or both. Summary conviction carries up to six months imprisonment or a fine or both.

De Voil Indirect Tax Service V5.261, 341, 343, 361–365.

---

[1] ie VATA 1994, s 72(1)–(11). See *R v McCarthy* [1981] STC 298, CA; *R v Asif* (1985) 82 Cr App Rep 123, CA; *R v Howard* [1990] STI 351, CA; *R v Dealy* [1995] STC 217, CA; *R v Ike* [1996] STC 391; *R v Choudhury* [1996] STC 1163, CA; *R v Collier* [1997] SWTI 474, CA.
[2] ie CEMA 1979, ss 167, 168, 171(4).
[3] eg under Theft Acts 1968 and 1978.
[4] ie. cheating the public revenue. This is expressly retained as an offence by Theft Act 1968, s 32(1)(a). See *R v Mavji* [1986] STC 508, CA; *R v Redford* [1988] STC 845, CA; *R v Fisher* [1989] STI 269, CA.
[5] ie. under CEMA 1979, s 152; VATA 1994, s 72(12). See Notice No. 12.
[6] See Report of the Committee on Enforcement Powers of the Revenue Departments (Cmnd. 8822), para 16.4.2.

[7] *R v Mark Michael Brown*, reported in Inland Revenue Tax Bulletin, February 2004, p 1096.
[8] TCA 2002, s 35.

Where a prosecution is made

[2.35] If a criminal offence is alleged to have been made in Scotland, the matter is normally prosecuted before the Scots courts under the terms of Scots Law. An offence in England will be prosecuted under English law and an offence in Northern Ireland under Northern Irish law. However, statute[1] provides that a VAT offence can be tried in the courts of any one of the three constituent parts of the United Kingdom, irrespective of the place where the offence has been committed.

There is no such equivalent provision for the direct taxes. This has a practical effect now that HMRC has established processing offices in Scotland that deal with information sent by taxpayers, particularly employers, in England. If an employer in Brighton makes a false statement on his year end PAYE return and posts this to a processing centre in Scotland, the offence is made where the document has been received and acted upon. This means that any prosecution for the submission of the false document will take place before a Scots court under the terms of Scots Law. HMRC is not a prosecuting authority in Scotland and any decision on such a prosecution would be made by the Crown office, Scotland. In such an instance, there would appear to be no procedure available for transferring jurisdiction to England as no criminal offence has been committed in England.

[1] CEMA 1979, s 148.

Prosecution by Assets Recovery Agency

[2.36] Statute[1] empowers the director of the Assets Recovery Agency to assess and collect any or all of: income tax; capital gains tax; corporation tax; national insurance contributions; statutory sick pay; statutory maternity pay; statutory paternity pay; statutory adoption pay; student loans.[2] In order to collect any or all of these taxes, what statute refers[3] to as "general Revenue functions" are vested in the director of the Assets Recovery Agency but only in relation to the person named in a notice that the director serves on HMRC.[4]

In order to exercise such Revenue functions, the director is required to have reasonable grounds to suspect that income arises (or a gain accrued to) a person as a result of criminal conduct either by that person or by another person.[5] This is not merely a limitation of the actions of the Assets Recovery Agency, it is a reflection of a purpose that is fundamentally different from that of HMRC. HMRC is charged by statute with the care and management of income tax, corporation, capital gains tax, and other taxes.[6] By contrast, the director of the Assets Recovery Agency is directed by statute[7] to exercise his functions "in the way in which he considers is best calculated to contribute to the reduction of crime". There is, thus, no requirement on the Assets Recovery Agency to collect tax in every case. Conversely, there could be circumstances in which the Assets Recovery Agency seeks to impose a tax charge when no charge would be levied by HMRC. The traditional analysis of income tax has been that this is charged only where there is a source that falls within one of the schedules.[8] By contrast, statute[9] specifically authorises the Assets Recovery Agency to act even though they cannot identify a source for any income. This provision may be of less effect than has been suggested by some commentators[10] as the only way the director of the Assets Recovery Agency can act is by acquiring functions vested by statute in HMRC.[11] If it is correct that the Revenue cannot assess income tax unless there is a source, it is difficult to see how the acquisition of the Revenue's functions by the Assets Recovery Agency in any particular case empowers that agency to collect income tax where there is no source. This is, no doubt, a matter that will be brought before the courts.

Appeals against an assessment by the director of the Assets Recovery Agency are to the Tax Chamber of the First-tier Tribunal (taking over the work from the Special Commissioners).[13]

In the first two reported cases, the presiding Special Commissioner sat with a second Special Commissioner. In *Harper v Director of the Assets Recovery Agency*[14] the Special Commissioners declared that the methodology adopted by the Assets Recovery Agency seems to have been sound and authorised the raising of the assessment. In *Khan v Director of Assets Recovery Agency*[15] a raft of submissions were made dealing with jurisdiction, human rights and other matters. Again, the Special Commissioners confirmed the assessment.

By contrast, in *Rose v Director of the Assets Recovery Agency*[16] the Special Commissioners quashed the assessments, saying[17] that "on the balance of probabilities there was no trade [of drug dealing] carried on by Mr Rose."

[1] Proceeds of Crime Act 2002, s 317(3).
[2] Proceeds of Crime Act 2002, s 323(1).
[3] Proceeds of Crime Act 2002, s 317.
[4] Proceeds of Crime Act 2002, s 317(2).
[5] Proceeds of Crime Act 2002, s 317(1)(*a*); the equivalent provisions for corporation tax when crime has given rise to a company's profits are given by s 317(1)(*b*).
[6] TMA 1970, s 2(1); see the discussion at supra, § **2.03**.
[7] Proceeds of Crime Act 2002, s 2(1).
[8] See infra, § **5.03**. The schedular system is, however, no longer applied for employment income by virtue of ITEPA 2003.
[9] Proceeds of Crime Act 2002, s 319(1).
[10] See, for example, the article by Tamara Solecki, Taxation 27 November 2002, p 216.
[11] Proceeds of Crime Act 2002, s 232(1) & (2). However, certain functions of the Revenue in relation to inheritance tax cannot be exercised by the Assets Recovery Agency: PCA 2002, s 232(3).
[13] The First-tier Tribunal and Upper Tribunal (Chambers) Order 2008, SI 2008/2684, art 5A.
[14] [2005] STC (SCD) 874.
[15] [2006] STC (SCD) 154.

[16] [2006] SWTI 1631, [2006] STC (SCD) 472.
[17] [2006] STC (SCD) 472 para 19 at 476d.

Enforcement powers

Proceedings in courts

[2.37] Where the tax that is payable under any assessment is less than £2,000, that tax is recoverable summarily as a civil debt by proceedings in a Magistrate's Court commenced in the name of the collector.

When tax is payable by instalments, the limit of £2,000 is applied to the individual instalment that is in arrears.[1]

The sum recovered by this process can, in practice, significantly exceed £2,000 as the monetary limit is applied to the tax that is due. Penalties and interest can be added to this, while still remaining within the jurisdiction of the Magistrate's Court.

TMA 1970, s 66 provides that tax due and payable under any assessment may be sued for and recovered as a debt due to the Crown by proceedings in a county court commenced in the name of the collector.

From 1 July 1991, a county court has jurisdiction under this section whatever the amount involved.[2] However, the normal practice of HMRC is that, where the amount recoverable is £50,000 or more, proceedings are normally taken in the High Court.[3] Normal practice where the amount involved is £2,000 to £25,000 is for action to lie in the county court; between £25,000 and £50,000, application is made to either the county court or the High Court, depending on circumstances, the proximity of the appropriate court and the whim of the collector. Where proceedings are commenced in the county court, they can be transferred to the High Court.[4] The County Court has no jurisdiction to vary a Commissioner's determination of the amount of tax due.[5]

In Scotland, proceedings are taken in the Court of Sessions sitting as the Court of Exchequer.

The Insolvency Act 1986 abolishes the Crown's status as a preferential creditor in respect of taxes assessed on the taxpayer. However, the Act retained the Crown preference for recovery of taxes in cases where the taxpayer acted as an agent for the Revenue, notably in respect of PAYE, National Insurance contributions and withholding tax on payments to subcontractors.[6] This Crown preference was finally abolished by the Enterprise Act 2002, s 251 with effect from 15 September 2003.

VAT due from any person is specified by statute[7] as being recoverable as a debt due to the Crown.

Simon's Taxes A1.7.

---

[1] TMA 1970, s 65(1). The limit of £2,000 was made by FA 1994, s 196 for 1996–97 and subsequent years. For prior years the limit is £1,000.

2   High Court and County Courts Jurisdiction Order 1991, SI 1991/724, art 2.
3   Under TMA 1970, s 68, the HMRC can take proceedings in the High Court for the collection of tax of any amount.
4   County Courts Act 1984, ss 40(2), 41(1).
5   *McCullough v Ahluwalia* [2004] EWCA Civ 889, [2004] STC 1295.
6   Insolvency Act 1986, Sch 6, paras 1–7.
7   VATA 1994, Sch 11, para 5(1). This provision allows Customs & Excise to sue in accordance with Crown Proceedings Act 1947, ss 13–15: see infra, § **66.04** note 9.

Distraint

[2.38] If a person neglects or refuses to pay the sum charged, HMRC is empowered to distrain.[1]

A justice of the peace may issue a warrant in writing authorising a collector to break open, in the daytime, any house or premises, calling to his assistance any constable.

In *Nixon v Freeman*[2] the court held that a bailiff in collecting tax was entitled to enter premises through an open window, and may also further open a window which was already partly open. However, three years later, in *Hancock v Austin*[3] it was held that a bailiff was not entitled to open a window catch without a warrant authorising him to "break open" the premises. The saga continued in *Miller v Tebb*[4] where the court held that a bailiff was entitled to enter premises through a partially open skylight. In *Long v Clark*[5] the court held that a bailiff had no right to break into premises without a warrant but, even without a warrant, was entitled to climb over a wall or fence from adjoining premises.

Certain items cannot be distrained. In *Morley v Pincombe*[6] it was held that food is exempt from distraint, on the grounds that, being perishable, it is incapable of being returned in the same condition as when distrained upon. In *Nargett v Nias*[7] it was held that distraint could not be levied on a trader's tools.

Voluminous detail is given in the Revenue Staff manuals on Revenue procedure in relation to enforcement.

UK Revenue Departments can apply to the court for an order to distrain in order to collect a tax liability due in another EC state.[8] UK tax liabilities can, likewise, be collected in other EC jurisdictions under the procedures available to collect domestic tax liabilities in those jurisdictions.[9]

Simon's Taxes A4.141.

1   For direct taxes, the power is given by TMA 1970, s 61(1), (2). For VAT, the power is given by Distress for HMRC Duties and Other Indirect Taxes Regulations SI 1997/1431: see infra, § **67.04**. Any breach of a walking possession order gives rise to a civil penalty under VATA 1994, s 68. The equivalent provisions for Scotland are given by FA 1997, s 52 and Debtors (Scotland) Act 1987.
2   (1860) 5 H & N 647.
3   (1863) 14 CBNS 634.

[2.38] Tax administration – an overview

[4] (1893) 9 TLR 515, CA.
[5] [1894] 1 QB 119, CA.
[6] (1848) 2 Exch 101.
[7] (1859) 1 E & E 439.
[8] FA 2002, s 134 and Sch 37: see infra, § **34.01**.
[9] EC Directives 76/308/EEC, 79/1071/EEC.

Validity of assessments

[2.39] In *IRC v Pearlberg*[1] the Revenue took court proceedings to recover unpaid tax. In those proceedings, the defendant contended that the assessments on which the tax liability arose were incorrect. The Court of Appeal held that the question of the validity of the assessments was a matter which could not be raised in proceedings for recovery of the tax, as this was a matter for the General or Special Commissioners (now the First-tier Tribunal) and not for the court. This doctrine was followed in *IRC v Soul*.[2] In that case the defendant contended, during the course of recovery proceedings in court that the income that had been assessed was not his income but was enjoyed by his trustee in bankruptcy. The Court of Appeal held that the correct procedure to be followed is for the taxpayer to appeal to what is now the Tribunal against the assessment on the grounds stated. The court could consider only the question on the basis of a decision of the appropriate Tribunal.

Simon's Taxes A5.301.

[1] (1953) 34 TC 57.
[2] (1976) 51 TC 86.

Enforcement of NIC contributions

[2.40] The former DSS had recognised for some years that its enforcement powers were less comprehensive and effective than those of the then Inland Revenue. To this end measures were included in the Social Security Act 1998 to remedy this and to "mirror" the Inland Revenue. The original Bill had been drafted some considerable time before the transfer of the CA was announced and the various measures had been planned to come into effect on 6 April 1999. However, the transfer on 1 April 1999 had the effect that the new body in charge of the administration of contributions already had the required powers because it was that body's powers (those of the Inland Revenue) themselves upon which a number of the provisions were modelled. In particular, this encompassed the charging of fixed and tax-related penalties for late and/or incorrect end-of-year returns (although many thought that this power extended to the then DSS and CA, it did not in fact do so) and distraint upon goods for unpaid debts without recourse to the county court.

The combined effects of the Social Security Act 1998 and the transfer to the Inland Revenue, whilst tortuous to follow through, can be summarised as follows:

Enforcement powers [2.40]

(1) A number of contribution offences were decriminalised and are now subject to civil remedy.
(2) Fixed-rate and tax-geared penalties may be applied to the contribution aspects of end-of-year returns and can now be applied by HMRC.
(3) Distraint upon the assets of businesses which fail to meet their debts is available under TMA 1970 powers. Poinding action is applicable in Scotland.

In addition some new penalty provisions in the 1998 Act now, in consequence of the transfer, are operated by HMRC in relation to contribution matters, and apply from 6 April 1999, as follows:

(1) Penalties and interest are due in respect of late paid Class 1A contributions in respect of 1999–2000 and earlier years, where application was made to use the Alternative Payment Method, and in respect of contributions paid by centrally paying employers, such as government departments, HM Forces and other public sector agencies.[1] (For Class 1A liabilities in respect of 2000–01 onwards, the provisions mentioned above, suitably modified, apply to the universal method of accounting for and paying Class 1A.)
(2) A criminal offence arises in the case of "any person who is knowingly concerned in the fraudulent evasion of any contributions". A person guilty of such an offence may be imprisoned for up to seven years, fined or both. Note the very wide nature of this provision; it could extend to a junior payroll clerk or the tax staff in an accountants' practice.[2]
(3) In certain circumstances, the unpaid contribution debt, together with accrued and future interest, may be transferred to one or more company officers and thereafter treated for enforcement purposes as the personal debt of the director or officer concerned.[3] Although official announcements suggested that this provision was aimed at "phoenix" companies and "phoenix" directors, the legislation itself is not confined to companies in administration or liquidation, and can also apply to the first occasion where an officer is involved in a failure to pay.

Further provisions relating to penalties for breach of regulations, eg failure to record employees' National Insurance numbers on year-end returns, even though there may not be any underpayment of contributions, have yet to come into effect and no start date has yet been advised by the authorities.[4]

[1] Social Security Act 1998, s 57 and SI 1999/975.
[2] SSAA 1992, ss 114.
[3] SSAA 1992, s 121C.
[4] SSAA 1992, s 113.

Other compliance powers

Duties of senior accounting officers

[2.41] Although a review of HMRC powers had been conducted for several years in conjunction with the professional bodies, FA 2009 contained a number of unexpected measures, which had not been subject to any prior consultation.

The first obliges senior accounting officers of 'qualifying companies' to take personal responsibility for the companies' compliance with their tax obligations. The lack of prior discussion (and the ensuing furore about the new obligations) meant that the rules had to be redrafted in a hurry during the Finance Bill's passage through Parliament and a radical reduction in the number of affected companies. This is discussed below.

The second allows HMRC to publish details of people who have been subject to a penalty for deliberate errors in their tax returns and associated documents. This second measure is discussed at § **2A.98**.

The main duty of a senior accounting officer

[2.42] Under the rules (located in FA 2009, Sch 46), the senior accounting officer 'must take reasonable steps to ensure that the company establishes and maintains appropriate accounting arrangements'.[1]

This is statutorily expanded to ensure that the officer takes reasonable steps 'to monitor the accounting arrangements of the company' and 'to identify any respects in which those arrangements are not appropriate tax accounting arrangements'.[2]

'Appropriate tax accounting arrangements' is defined as 'accounting arrangements that enable the company's relevant liabilities [being all tax liabilities] to be calculated accurately in all material respects'. Accounting arrangements are defined so as to include arrangements for keeping accounting records.[3]

For each financial year, the senior accounting officer must provide a certificate to HMRC which:

(1) states whether or not the company had appropriate tax accounting arrangements throughout the financial year; and

(2) if not, explains how the arrangements were not appropriate.[4]

Generally, the certificate must be provided by the due date of the company's accounts. But a later date may be allowed by HMRC.[5]

---

[1] FA 2009, Sch 46, para 1(1).
[2] FA 2009, Sch 46, para 1(2).
[3] FA 2009, Sch 46, para 14.
[4] FA 2009, Sch 46, para 2(1), (2).
[5] FA 2009, Sch 46, para 2(3)(b).

Other compliance powers **[2.45]**

The senior accounting officer

[2.43] In the case of companies that are not members of a group, the senior accounting officer is the director or officer who, in the company's reasonable opinion, has overall responsibility for the company's financial accounting arrangements.[1]

In the case of group companies, the senior accounting officer is the director or officer (of that company or another member of the group) who, in the company's reasonable opinion, has overall responsibility for the company's financial accounting arrangements.[2] Thus a group may have one senior accounting officer for each group company or different group companies may have different senior accounting officers.

[1] FA 2009, Sch 46, para 16(1).
[2] FA 2009, Sch 46, para 16(2).

Qualifying companies

[2.44] Companies are qualifying companies if they exceed one or both thresholds:

- Turnover - £200m;
- Balance sheet total - £2bn.[1]

For group companies, the thresholds apply to the aggregate of the group.[2]

The test is applied in respect of the results of the previous financial year.[3] Regulations can specify that certain companies are excluded from the definition of qualifying company.[4]

[1] FA 2009, Sch 46, para 15(2).
[2] FA 2009, Sch 46, para 15(3).
[3] FA 2009, Sch 46, para 15(4).
[4] FA 2009, Sch 46, para 15(8).

Procedural obligations

[2.45] For each financial year, qualifying companies must notify HMRC of the senior accounting officers during the course of the year. Such notifications should generally be provided by the due date of the company's accounts, but a later date may be allowed by HMRC.[1]

[1] FA 2009, Sch 46, para 3.

[2.46] Tax administration – an overview

Penalties payable

[2.46] Penalties of £5,000 are payable in the following circumstances:

Circumstance	Person liable for the penalty
The senior accounting officer fails to comply with the main duty.	The senior accounting officer.[1]
The senior accounting officer fails to provide a certificate.	The senior accounting officer.[2]
The certificate contains a careless or deliberate inaccuracy.	The senior accounting officer.[3]
The certificate contains an inaccuracy that was neither careless nor deliberate but the senior accounting officer did not take reasonable steps to inform HMRC after discovering inaccuracy.	The senior accounting officer.[4]
The company fails to notify HMRC of its senior accounting officers by the due date.	The company.[5]

Note: A penalty notice may be the subject of an appeal.[6]

---

[1] FA 2009, Sch 46, para 4.
[2] FA 2009, Sch 46, para 5(1)(a).
[3] FA 2009, Sch 46, para 5(1)(b).
[4] FA 2009, Sch 46, para 5(4).
[5] FA 2009, Sch 46, para 7.
[6] FA 2009, Sch 46, para 10.

2A

Tax administration – the mechanics

The taxpayer—making the return (and claiming tax credits)	PARA 2A.01
Paying the tax (and getting tax credits)	PARA 2A.14
Interest	PARA 2A.32
Surcharges	PARA 2A.44
Verification, enquiries and inspections	PARA 2A.46
Information powers	PARA 2A.53
Assessments	PARA 2A.60
Correction by taxpayer	PARA 2A.68
Penalties	PARA 2A.78

The taxpayer—making the return (and claiming tax credits)

Overview

[2A.01] All taxes dealt with in this work require the taxpayer to assess himself, to a very substantial extent. Of the taxes we are here considering, the tax with the longest history of self-assessment is Stamp Duty. Since its introduction in 1694[1] the onus has been on the persons producing a document to present the document for stamping, a procedure that forms the foundation of the system of collecting stamp duties that continues today. For most of the history of stamp duties, the taxpayer has sent the document to the Stamp Office with a statement of the stamp duty calculated by the taxpayer as due. The stamp office returns the document, stamped with the sum declared by the taxpayer, even if, on the information given on the face of the document itself, the amount the taxpayer has calculated is wrong. This procedure of a paper document being posted and returned with a physical stamp is still available. However, most share transfers and land transfers are now stamped by electronic submission of what is, in effect, the taxpayer's self-assessment.[2]

The National Insurance Act 1946, which imposed a charge to national insurance contributions commencing two years later, required contributions to be computed by the employer for his employees. The self-assessment procedure for NIC has continued, substantially unchanged, although widened in scope.[3]

From its introduction in the UK on 1 April 1973,[4] VAT has been a fully self-assessed tax, with its system of quarterly returns by traders and the traders' own calculation of the payment due.[5]

Capital Transfer Tax, later renamed Inheritance Tax,[6] was introduced with a substantial self-assessment requirement in that the taxpayer must compute the IHT payable on the estate at death and send the initial return with the sum he computes, in so far as it relates to the deceased's free estate, but does not attract instalment option.[7] Unlike other taxes considered in this work, there remains for inheritance tax a significant role for assessments raised by the Revenue in the routine administration for tax that is payable on lifetime transfers and for instalment property at a death.

A historically recent development has been the complete overhaul of the administration system for income tax and capital gains tax, with the introduction of self-assessment with effect from 1996–97.[8] The legislation, when first enacted in 1994, contained the provisions necessary to require self-assessment of corporation tax. This was brought into effect for accounting periods ending on or after 1 July 1999,[9] with amendments that had been made in the intervening period,[10] although the previous system of Pay and File,[11] which came into force on 1 October 1993, had significant elements of self-assessment in it.

Tax credit claims are made to the HMRC by the claimant.[12]

Capital Taxes Office is now the only section of the two government Revenue departments that has to raise assessments in order for tax to be collectable. The role of HMRC has, thus, become that of a recipient of cash payments and a supervisor of taxpayers' compliance in assessing and paying tax liabilities, and a deliverer of cash payments in the form of tax credits.

[1] Stamp Duty Act 1694 Will and Mary c 21.
[2] Unlike all other taxes considered in this work (other than bearer instrument duty: see infra, § **61.11**), there is no direct statutory requirement to send a document to be stamped for stamp duty. Instead, certain actions—such as registration of title to land and court proceedings—cannot take place unless a document has been stamped: see infra, § **56.20**. The statutory framework for stamp duty land tax is in complete contrast. This adopts the structure for all other main taxes. It is the transaction (not the document) which is taxable and the taxpayer has an obligation to pay the tax: FA 2002, s 76.
[3] Arguably, the self-assessment of NIC commenced with the National Insurance Act 1907, which was concerned with contributions to approved Friendly Societies.
[4] FA 1976, ss 1–51.
[5] See infra, § **67.03**.
[6] FA 1986, s 100(1)(*a*).
[7] IHTA 1984, s 226(2).
[8] FA 1994, s 178.
[9] FA 1994, section 199 (Appointed Day) Order 1998, SI 1998/3173.
[10] FA 1998, Sch 18.
[11] F(No 2)A 1987, s 95(2).
[12] See infra, § **6.51** et seq.

Income tax and capital gains tax

[2A.02] Any person in receipt of income, from which a liability to pay tax arises, which has not been otherwise discharged, is required to make a return of the income.[1]

Making the return [2A.03]

For a person subject to income tax, the procedure can be summarised, as follows:

(1) A person liable to income tax or capital gains tax may be served with a tax return;
(2) The due date for a return issued to a taxpayer depends on the method adopted for filing the return.[2] A return of income and capital gains for 2009–10 must be submitted to HMRC by 31 October 2010 or by 31 January 2011 if the return is filed online. A person is liable to a penalty if he fails to return his return by the due date;[3]
(3) If no return is issued, a person liable to income tax or capital gains tax for 2009–10 must notify HMRC of that fact by 5 October 2010. A person is liable to a penalty if he fails to notify HMRC by the prescribed date.[4]

The information shown on the return includes the income and gains chargeable to income tax and capital gains tax, the reliefs and allowances claimed, a self-assessment and a declaration that the return is correct. Different returns are prescribed for trusts and estates.

All returns must show a self-assessment of the net amounts chargeable to income tax,[5] Class 4 National Insurance contributions[6] and capital gains tax.[7]

If the return for 2009–10 is returned after 31 October 2010, the return must also include a self-assessment of the amount payable by way of income tax and capital gains tax.[8] If the 2009–10 return is submitted before 1 November 2010, the taxpayer can leave the calculation of the liability to income tax and CGT (but not to corporation tax) for HMRC to undertake. Leaving the Revenue to undertake the calculation does not stop the Revenue enquiring into the return, nor does it influence the selection of a return for enquiry.

The use in statute of the words "on his behalf" makes the Revenue officer an agent of the taxpayer. See further infra, § **2A.16**.

The penalty rules for the late or non-delivery of returns are to be revised with effect from 2010 (FA 2009)).

---

[1] TMA 1970, s 7(1). If the person has received a return document, the liability to report the income arises under TMA 1970, s 8(1).
[2] TMA 1970, ss 8, 8A & 12AA amended by FA 2007, ss 87, 88 & 89. Exceptionally, if the notice requiring the submission of return is issued by the Revenue after 31 July, the due date for the submission of a paper return is three months after the date of the notice.
[3] TMA 1970, s 93.
[4] TMA 1970, s 7(8).
[5] TMA 1970, s 8(1).
[6] SSCBA 1992, s 15.
[7] TMA 1970, s 8(1).
[8] TMA 1970, s 9(1)(*a*).

Reporting capital gains

[2A.03] Capital gains made by individuals, trustees and personal representatives are reported on the self-assessment tax return. When the chargeable gains

[2A.03] Tax administration – the mechanics

are less than the annual exempt amount available to the taxpayer and the aggregate consideration received does not exceed four times the annual exempt amount available, no declaration is required.[1] Any enquiry into the gain is made by opening an enquiry into that particular tax return.[2] When a capital gain is made on the disposal of a partnership asset, the sale proceeds are declared on the partnership statement. A proportion of each gain is then taken into the self-assessment of an individual partner. Any enquiry into a partnership gain is made by means of an enquiry into the partnership statement.[3]

The taxpayer (or representative partner of a partnership) is required to calculate any gain.[4] The provision for requiring a Revenue calculation of the balancing payment arising under self-assessment[5] enables the taxpayer to leave to the Revenue the task of adding together the aggregate of net gains he has calculated with the income he has reported.

It is possible to send the HMRC details of a valuation that it is proposed to incorporate in a CGT computation with a request that the Revenue agree the valuation in advance of the tax return being submitted.[6] Such an application can only be made after the disposal of an asset.[7] The effect of this arrangement is that it is possible for correspondence agreeing a valuation to take place over a period of up to 22 months prior to the due date for submission of the tax return reporting the gain that has been crystallised. The Revenue have stated that where an enquiry is held open pending agreement on a valuation they will not take advantage of the open enquiry to raise new issues—unless new facts come to light.[8]

Simon's Taxes C1.109.

[1] TCGA 1992, s 3A, inserted by FA 2003, Sch 28, para 1.
[2] TMA 1970, s 9A.
[3] TMA 1970, s 12AC.
[4] TMA 1970, s 8(1).
[5] TMA 1970, s 9(2).
[6] Using Form CG 34.
[7] The procedure is specified in Inland Revenue press release, 4 February 1997; *Simon's Weekly Tax Intelligence* 1997, p 184.
[8] Statement of practice SP1/99; Inland Revenue press release, 28 January 1999, *Simon's Weekly Tax Intelligence* 1999, p 219.

Using an estimate to calculate a capital gain

[2A.04] It is of the essence of self-assessment that the taxpayer is required to assess himself by 31 January following the fiscal year. Where a capital gain is computed by reference to the market value, eg of an asset on 31 March 1982, it is inevitable that the taxpayer's self-assessment is dependent on a judgmental figure. Where such a figure is used, the tax return form issued by the Revenue requires that it is identified as such by a "tick box". If further information is made available to the taxpayer that causes him to believe that the judgmental figure is incorrect, the taxpayer may notify the Revenue of an amendment to his return.[1] Where such an amendment is made, the Revenue are empowered by TMA 1970, s 9A to enquire into the amendment at any time up to

Making the return [2A.04]

12 months after the end of the quarter in which the amendment is made, or until 31 January following the normal filing date in any case.

Where an amendment is made, any adjustment to the tax payable or repayable carries interest from the due date of payment, normally 31 January following the fiscal year, not from the date of the amendment. The liability to interest is not affected by any considerations, such as care exercised by the taxpayer or the taxpayer's good faith in submitting the judgmental figure. Such considerations are, however, relevant when considering any liability to surcharges or penalties.[2] A penalty is payable in respect of an incorrect return only where it can be demonstrated that the return had been delivered "fraudulently or negligently".[3] Finding that a figure is wrong, does not mean that its use in the return was negligent. The best statement of the law in this respect is probably that of Goulding J in *Dunk v General Comrs for Havant*.[4] The Revenue have stated in correspondence that, in their view, this statement is equally valid for the self-assessment regime as previously. In his judgment Goulding J said:[5]

> What the taxpayer has to declare is 'that the return to the best of his knowledge is correct and complete'. If . . . a taxpayer finds particular circumstances that make the best of his knowledge more than usually unreliable, it is open to him to put against his figure for a particular item of income such words as 'estimated' and 'see accompanying memorandum', or something of that kind, and explain the circumstances. If he has done his best and, of course, he is under a duty to use all proper sources of knowledge—he will not, in my view, be guilty of making a false statement providing, as I say, he puts in a genuine estimate and, if necessary, explains that is not reliable.

The Revenue's view in this area is given in Revenue booklet SAT2, which states:[6]

> There will be occasions on which some information cannot be finalised within the formal self-assessment time limits despite the taxpayer's best efforts to do so. In such cases the taxpayer should include a 'best estimate' of the information in the return and, if appropriate, a corresponding estimate of the tax due. The estimate should be clearly identified as such in the return and where appropriate should be accompanied by a note saying how the estimate was calculated and when the final figure is likely to be available. A return containing any such provisional figure will not be regarded as incomplete.

The extent to which such statements can prevent a subsequent discovery are discussed at infra, § **2A.62**.

Simon's Taxes C1.105.

---

[1] TMA 1970, s 9(4)(*b*), inserted by FA 1994, s 179.
[2] TMA 1970, s 95 for years up to 2007/08; FA 2007, Sch 24 from 2008/09.
[3] TMA 1970, s 95(1). On appeal against a penalty for undeclared profits, the standard of proof to be applied by the tribunal is the civil standard, on the balance of probabilities. See *Revenue & Customs Commrs v Khawaja* [2008] EWHC 1687 (Ch).
[4] [1976] STC 460.
[5] [1976] STC 460 at 461.
[6] Revenue booklet SAT2 (1995) para 2.53.

[2A.05] Tax administration – the mechanics

Reporting a tax avoidance scheme

[2A.05] FA 2004 contains rules requiring a promoter[1] to provide the Revenue with information about notifiable arrangements and proposals for notifiable arrangements.[2] Arrangements are notifiable if they come within any description prescribed by Treasury regulations and enable, or might be expected to enable, any person to obtain a tax advantage in relation to any tax so prescribed in relation to the arrangements. It is also necessary that the main benefit or one of the main benefits that might be expected to arise from the arrangements is the obtaining of that advantage. Some of these terms are defined in ways strongly reminiscent of the rules in ITA 2007, Pt 13, Ch 1; there are extensive regulation making powers.[3] The provision applies to a wide range of direct taxes under HMRC's jurisdiction, including inheritance tax and stamp duties but not National Insurance contributions.[4] The regulations not only contain details of arrangements that are caught but also of those which are not, eg ISAs and finance leasing.

The promoter must inform the Revenue when the notifiable proposal is available for implementation or, if earlier, when the promoter becomes aware of any transaction forming part of the proposed arrangements.[5] The promoter does not have to notify if someone else has already done so.[6] Where a promoter is resident outside the UK and no promoter is resident within the UK, the obligation to report falls on the client.[7] Where there is no promoter, the duty to notify falls on those entering into any transaction which is part of the notifiable arrangements.[8]

Nothing in this part of the Act requires any person to disclose to HMRC any privileged information ie anything to which a claim to legal privilege or its Scottish counterpart could be maintained in legal proceedings.[9]

For failing to notify, statute[10] provides a maximum penalty of £5,000 plus £600 a day; this potential penalty liability excludes a number of other penalty provisions. Prior to 1 April 2009, jurisdiction was reserved to the Special Commissioners.[11] A separate provision authorises the Revenue to direct how the information is to be provided.[12] In *Mercury Tax Group v HMRC*[13], a Special Commissioner heard a taxpayer's appeal against the imposition of a penalty for the non-disclosure of a particular scheme. In the event, the Special Commissioner (Dr John Avery Jones) held that the scheme did not fall within the scope of the disclosure rules. However, he considered the alternative outcome and held that, in the circumstances, the appellant had acted sufficiently carefully by relying upon Counsel's advice by not disclosing. He therefore held that, were a penalty due, it should be reduced to nil.

The duty extends to national insurance arrangements from 1 May 2007. Where an arrangement needs to be notified for both base and national insurance purposes only one notification need be made but it must make clear that it relates to both imposts.[13]

---

[1] Defined in FA 2004, s 307.
[2] Defined in FA 2004, s 306.
[3] FA 2004, s 317.
[4] FA 2004, s 318(1) ('tax').

⁵ On multiple promoters and multiple proposals see FA 2004, s 308(4) and (5).
⁶ FA 2004, s 308(3).
⁷ FA 2004, s 309.
⁸ FA 2004, s 310.
⁹ FA 2004, s 314. Details are given in the Tax Avoidance Schemes (Proscribed Descriptions of Arrangements) Regulations SI 2004/1863, as subsequently amended. The subsequent amendment has the effect of moving onto the client the duty of disclosing a tax avoidance scheme where the promoter can claim legal privilege. In these circumstances, it is open for the client to authorise the promoter to waive legal privilege and make the statutory declaration. For a useful analysis see Philip Baker, QC, "Legal Professional Privilege and Tax Avoidance Disclosure" Tax Adviser, January 2005, pp 11–13.
¹⁰ TMA 1970, s 98C inserted by FA 2004, s. 315.
¹¹ FA 2004, s 315(3); s 315(2) excludes TMA 1970, s 100.
¹² FA 2004, s 316.
¹³ (2008) SpC 737.
¹³ National Insurance Act 2006, s 7; National Insurance Contributions (Application of Part 7 of the Finance Act 2004) Regulations 2007, SI 2007/785.

Corporation tax

Reporting company profits—Corporation Tax Self Assessment (CTSA)

[2A.06] A company is required to compute its own liability to tax.¹ Statute² empowers HMRC to issue a notice requiring a company to deliver a return. HMRC practice is to issue a very brief notice, leaving it to the company (or, more usually, its agent) to obtain and deliver the appropriate return. If no notice is received from HMRC, the company has an obligation to give notice that it is chargeable to corporation tax within 12 months of the end of its accounting period.³

A company tax return is for the company's accounting period. Various events, such as the cessation of the trade, trigger the end of one accounting period and the start of another; where this is the case, a separate return is required for each accounting period.⁴

Statute⁵ provides that certain claims, notably to repayment and for credits, are not competent unless they are included in the company's return.

A curiosity of the corporation tax self-assessment procedure is that the due date for submission of a company's tax return is later than the due date of the payment of the tax (see infra, § **2A.20**). The filing date for the company tax return is the last of three alternative dates: (i) 12 months from the end of the accounting period; (ii) if the company has a period of account with the length of less than 18 months, 12 months from the end of that period; (iii) 30 months from the beginning of the period of account, or (iv) 3 months from the date on which the notice requiring of the return was served.⁶

Statute gives provisions equivalent to those that apply for income tax, for the repair of a company tax return⁷ and an enquiry into a company tax return.⁸

[2A.06] Tax administration – the mechanics

These provisions cover not only corporation tax as such but also related sums such as charges under TA 1988, s 419 (loans to participators, infra, § **29.10**) and s 747 (the controlled foreign company legislation, infra, § **35.64**).

Under CTSA interest paid by a company for late payment of tax is deductible in the corporation tax computation; interest paid to a company by HMRC for overpayment of corporation tax, is part of the profits of the company and is taxable.[9]

Like the income tax self-assessment regime the corporation tax system is based on "process now—check later"; once the enquiry window of 12 months has passed the corporation tax return becomes final. Other provisions which are similar to those for income tax are the company's right to ask the Commissioners to order the Revenue to end an enquiry, Revenue information powers and the Revenue right to make discovery assessments in certain circumstances.

CTSA differs from income tax self-assessment in several ways. A company cannot opt for the Revenue to calculate its tax liability and the return requires the submission of accounts. Corporation tax has a separate penalty regime, which is based on the former pay and file rules including automated tax-related penalties whether or not the return has been delivered. From 2010, a harmonised penalty regime will be introduced under FA 2009.

Clubs, unincorporated associations and property management companies

Clubs and unincorporated associations are subject to corporation tax on income, other than income from mutual trading (see infra, § **8.35**). For many clubs, unincorporated associations and property management companies the only taxable income is a small amount of bank interest. Where the annual corporation tax liability of the club is not expected to exceed £100 and the club is run exclusively for the benefit of its own members, then HMRC practice is not to require a corporation tax return, nor to require payment of the tax liability but to treat the club, etc, as dormant, subject to a review at least every five years.[10]

The same practice is applied by HMRC to a property management company if the following conditions are fulfilled:

(a) the company's business consists of the management, on a non profit making basis, of a block(s) of flats or apartments for the owners, lessees or tenants of the flats or apartments;

(b) the company's articles of association contain rules to ensure only the persons having an interest in the property under management own the shares in the company;

(c) the company must not be entitled to receive any income from an interest in land; and

(d) the company must pay no dividend or make any other distribution of profit.

---

[1] FA 1998, Sch 18, para 7(1)
[2] FA 1998, Sch 18, para 3.
[3] FA 1988, Sch 18, para 2.
[4] FA 1988, Sch 18, para 5(2).

[5] FA 1988, Sch 18, para 9 & 10.
[6] FA 1998, Sch 18, para 14. For a consideration of the legislation on filing dates, see *R & C Comrs v La Senza* [2007] STC 901.
[7] FA 1988, Sch 18, para 16.
[8] FA 1988, Sch 18, paras 24–35.
[9] TMA 1970, ss 90(2), TA 1988, s 826(5A) & FA 1996, s 100(4).
[10] This is based on a statement made by the financial secretary to the Treasury in the House of Commons during the debate on 2 May 2006 on Finance Bill 2006. HMRC Press Release, 25 August 2006, *Simon's Weekly Tax Intelligence* 2006, p 2146.

Inheritance tax

Lifetime dispositions

[2A.07] In the case of a chargeable transfer a transferor must give an account of all such transfers unless some other person liable for the tax, eg the transferee, has already done so. A return to HMRC is not required for a potentially exempt transfer.[1] When a chargeable transfer is made, this is reported to the Capital Taxes Office on HMRC form IHT100. This is a multipurpose form that is used for the periodic charge and exit charge arising to trustees, as well as a chargeable transfer by an individual. The return is made by appending one of the alternative sets of supplementary pages to the main form IHT100, the choice of supplementary pages depending on the event that is being reported and the property to which it relates.

Simon's Taxes I11.211; Foster's Inheritance Tax L2.11.

[1] IHTA 1984, s 216.

Death

[2A.08] Personal representatives must make an account of the property forming the estate of the deceased person.[1] The account is made to the Capital Taxes Office in HMRC form IHT200, which must be delivered before the grant of representation can be obtained and the tax must be paid at the time of submitting the account on non-instalment property in the free estate. Personal representatives may make a provisional account where the exact value of the property cannot be ascertained. The personal representatives must report any transfer that was a potentially exempt transfer when made but, by virtue of the death within seven years thereafter, has become a chargeable transfer.[2] Transfers that were chargeable transfers when made, such as a transfer into a discretionary trust, are also to be reported.

This rule creates a practical problem in that the personal representatives have to pay the tax but, not yet having the grant of probate, cannot prove title to a purchaser. Tax may therefore be funded by a loan from the beneficiaries, or the sale of assets for which probate need not be produced, or the appropriate use of a life policy (ie one not belonging to the deceased's estate) or, if necessary, a loan from a bank.[3]

Where no UK grant of representation has been obtained within 12 months of the death those in whom the property is vested (at the time of death or since) or those beneficially entitled to an interest in possession are under a duty to account; this extends to the actual beneficiaries of a discretionary trust.[4]

[1] IHTA 1984, s 216.
[2] For a death on or after 9 March 1999, personal representatives are under a statutory obligation to report failed PETs; IHTA 1984, s 216(3) as amended by FA 1999, s 105(1). Previously, the request for details in the HMRC account did not have statutory force.
[3] On relief from interest see infra, § **14.02**.
[4] IHTA 1984, s 216(2).

Excepted estate

[2A.09] A return at death to the HMRC is not required for an "excepted estate".[1] Separate provisions apply according to whether the deceased is or is not, at the date of death, domiciled within the UK.

Where the deceased died domiciled within the UK, an excepted estate is one for which the following conditions are satisfied:

(1) the gross value of the estate, including the deceased's interest in joint property, plus lifetime transfers that become taxable by virtue of death does not exceed £300,000;
(2) where the deceased has an interest in possession in a settlement, this did not exceed £150,000 in value;
(3) the non-UK assets in the estate do not exceed £100,000 in value;
(4) lifetime transfers that become chargeable by virtue of the death consist of cash or quoted shares or securities or land and buildings (with contents as appropriate) and do not exceed £150,000;
(5) the deceased had not at any time made a gift with reservation with benefit;
(6) the deceased did not have an alternatively secured pension fund.

Where the deceased is domiciled outside the UK, his estate is an "excepted estate" if:

(1) the value of UK situs assets in the estate does not exceed £150,000;
(2) the UK situs assets consist only of cash or quoted shares or quoted securities;
(3) the deceased had never been domiciled within the UK at any time during his life.

In every other case, where there is a chargeable transfer an account is required, even though the transfer may be within the nil rate band. The account must be delivered within 12 months or, if later, three months from the date on which he first becomes liable for the tax. Similar rules apply to trustees.

There is no implied limitation based on territoriality. If a person such as a trustee is liable for the tax then such a person is also under a duty to comply with the administrative machinery preceding the payment of the tax.[2]

Making the return [2A.09]

The obligation is to report chargeable transfers. Hence, there is no obligation to report a potentially exempt transfer until a death within the cumulation makes it a chargeable transfer. It is then the transferee's duty to report it.[3] The same applies to gifts with reservation.[4] In each case the account must be delivered not later than 12 months after the end of the month in which death occurred.[5] A similar rule applies when the termination of an interest in possession is a potentially exempt transfer.[6]

The obligation is to deliver an account specifying to the best of his knowledge and belief all appropriate property and the value of that property. Knowledge means personal knowledge including information contained in documents in that person's possession. There is, however, no obligation to seek information from others (even servants or agents).[7] In *Robertson v IRC*[8], the Revenue sought to impose a penalty[9] on an executor for incorporating estimated values in the IHT account at death, which the executor voluntarily increased when the property was sold. The Special Commissioner held that the executor had fulfilled his statutory duty and no penalty was payable.[10] In a further hearing[11], a Special Commissioner held that the Revenue acted totally unreasonably in connection with this hearing and awarded costs against the Revenue.[12]

Simon's Taxes Division I11; Foster's Inheritance Tax L1.03; L2.12, 31.

---

[1] IHTA 1984, s 256 as amended by FA 2004, s 293. Inheritance Tax (Delivery of Accounts) (Excepted Estates) Regulations 2006, SI 2006/2141, *Simon's Weekly Tax Intelligence* 2006, p 2098. The statutory instrument applies to Scotland and Northern Ireland as well as to England and Wales. The test whether or not the estate is an excepted estate is applied without consideration of any deed of variation. The position is neatly summarised by a Revenue example:

> Let us consider the estate of a husband and wife. The husband owns assets worth £50,000 in his own right, the wife £60,000. Their home is owned jointly as beneficial joint tenants and has an open market value of £350,000. They each leave their whole estate to the other.
>
> The husband dies first. On his death, his IHT estate is valued at £225,000 (being £50,000 plus one half of the house), so the estate qualifies as an excepted estate and IHT200 is not required. The widow inherits the whole estate and becomes sole owner of the house by survivorship.
>
> When the widow dies, her estate is worth £460,000. To make use of both nil-rate bands, the beneficiaries of her estate execute an IoV (before applying for probate) to redirect the husband's estate and his share of the joint property to themselves. The effect of the IoV is to reduce the widow's estate for IHT purposes to £235,000. But this does not alter the fact that, in reality, at the date of her death the widow's estate was valued at £460,000. Her estate is therefore outside the excepted estate regulations.
>
> Form IHT200 should be completed by the widow's personal representatives declaring the true gross value of the estate in sections F & G. Then to give effect to the IoV, the assets that are being redirected away from the estate should be deducted in the 'Exemptions and reliefs' boxes. This way, the correct value for the gross and net estate is carried forward to form D18 and to the probate papers and the taxable value of the estate for IHT purposes is also correctly calculated. (*Inland Revenue IHT Newsletter*, August 2004, p 7.)

[2] *Re Clore (No 3), IRC v Stype Trustees (Jersey) Ltd* [1985] STC 394.
[3] IHTA 1984, s 216(1)(*bb*). For a death on or after 9 March 1999, the lifetime transfer must also be reported by the personal representatives; IHTA 1984, s 216(3) amended by FA 1999, s 105(1).

[2A.09] Tax administration – the mechanics

[4] IHTA 1984, s 216(1)(bc).
[5] IHTA 1984, s 216(6)(aa), (ab).
[6] IHTA 1984, s 216(1)(bd).
[7] Re Clore (No. 3), IRC v Stype Trustees (Jersey) Ltd [1985] STC 394.
[8] [2002] STC (SCD) 182.
[9] Under IHTA 1984, s 247(1). The Revenue sought to charge a penalty of 10% of the "culpable tax", being the increase in the tax liability consequent on the increase in the valuation.
[10] J Gordon Reid QC, sitting as Special Commissioner, said of the executor: 'What he did was, in my view, consistent with standard practice in the legal profession in Scotland and indeed with common sense.' (at 194f) 'I do not consider the account to be incorrect. The valuation was an estimate, ie an approximation, and was not stated to be the exact value. The exact value, in so far as such a valuation can ever be "exact", was greater than the estimate, but that does not necessarily mean that an incorrect account has been negligently delivered, furnished or produced' (at 196j).
[11] Robertson v IRC (No 2) [2002] STC (SCD) 242.
[12] [2002] STC (SCD) 242 at 246d.

National Insurance contributions

Reporting liabilities

[2A.10] The essence of the national insurance scheme is that it requires payment of contributions in return for benefits. Nearly £100bn[1] is paid by employers, under the statutory requirement imposed on them[2] to deduct contributions from employees when making salary payments and add to them their own liabilities, being calculated in accordance with NI tables that have statutory effect.

Any taxpayer who is self-employed is required[3] to pay weekly Class 2 contributions and to incorporate his Class 4 liability in his self-assessment of income tax, CGT and NIC for the year.[4]

Payment of Class 3 contributions is voluntary.[5]

[1] Government Actuary's Report, January 2007.
[2] Social Security (Contributions) Regulations 2001, SI 2001/1004, Part 7 and Sch 4.
[3] SSCBA 1992, s 2(1)(b) and s 11.
[4] SSCBA 1992, s 15(2).
[5] SSCBA 1992, s 13(1).

Tax credits

[2A.11] Those entitled to tax credits must make a claim to the HMRC on a Form TC600. This gives the claimant the opportunity to report his/her income for the previous tax year[1] and state his/her personal circumstances at the date of claim. Tax credit claims can only be backdated by three months at the maximum[2] so to get a full entitlement for 2009–10 claimants must submit the form by 6 July 2009.

Because tax credits are ultimately based on current year income, and because it is impossible to know current year income at the start of a year, those who fear a fall in their income (to tax credit entitlement levels) should make a "protective claim". This will lead to an award of nil.[3] When the award is finalised[4] the nil rate will either be confirmed or, if the suspected income fall has occurred, an award of tax credits for the full year will be given.

Once part of the tax credits system, claimants have an obligation to notify certain changes in circumstances which might affect their award.[5] Failure to notify a change in the claiming unit, or a fall in childcare of £10 a week or more, or a fall in childcare to nil, within three months, carry a £300 penalty.[6] The Revenue have agreed that such penalties will not be charged where a claimant is on a nil award.[7] Other changes in circumstances which might increase an award (for example the birth of a child, starting work, working longer hours, starting childcare) should be notified within three months to ensure a claimant does not lose out under the three month backdating rule.[8] Changes in circumstances which decrease an award are automatically backdated to the date of change. Changes in income are not governed by these rules and will usually be dealt with when a tax credit award is finalised after the end of the tax year. A claimant may notify a change in income in-year if he or she so wishes, a reason for doing this being either to get the extra credits due at an earlier date, or to avoid the running up of a tax credits overpayment.[9]

When a tax credit award is made or amended the claimant gets a new award notice. Several of these may be received in one tax year, according to the number of changes in circumstances (or perhaps income) reported. After the end of the tax year the claimant will receive a renewal pack asking him/her either to declare their actual income for the year just ended, or, if the award is not income contingent, to confirm that their income is within a band where changes would make no difference to their tax credits award. Those in the latter category are known as "auto-renewal" cases and their awards, of family element only, will continue into the next year with no further action by them. Those in the first category are known as "reply-required" cases and their awards will only be fully renewed when their up-to-date income details are returned. In both cases claimants are invited to confirm (in auto-renewal cases, by default) that their personal circumstance details are also up to date.[10] If their circumstances are not up to date the claimants must notify the Revenue of all changes not previously notified, at this point of renewal and finalisation. The other step in the renewals process is to finalise the award. For more on this see infra § **6.53**. The notice inviting claimants to renew their award and return their previous year's income will give a date by which the return must be made, or if the claimants are "auto-renewal" cases, a date by which they will be treated as having declared that their circumstances are as stated. By regulation[11] the date must not be later than 30 September following the end of the tax year, or 30 days after the date on which the notice is given, if later. If the claimant can only provide an estimate of their income by this date, they must return accurate figures by another date, similarly specified by regulations as 31 January following the end of the tax year, or 30 days after the date on

[2A.11] Tax administration – the mechanics

which the notice is given, if later.[12] These dates are the "relevant section 17 dates" for the purposes of the time limits for enquiries (see infra § **2A.48**).

Regulations also specify how notices under section 17 are treated as claims for the coming year.[13] In view of the fact that the section 17 dates can be after the usual three month time limit the regulations allow the claim to be backdated to the preceding 6 April where the declaration is made by 30 September. Where the declaration is made after 30 September but before 31 January the claim is backdated to the preceding 6 April providing, in the opinion of HMRC, the claimant had good cause for not making the declaration earlier. If there is no good cause or the declaration is made after 31 January the claim will only be backdated by the usual three months.

---

[1] See infra, § **6.51**.
[2] Tax Credits (Claims and Notifications) Regulations 2002, SI 2002/2014, reg 7.
[3] TCA 2002, s 14(3).
[4] TCA 2002, s 18.
[5] TCA 2002, s 6.
[6] Tax Credits (Claims and Notifications) Regulations 2002, SI 2002/2014, reg 21 and see infra, § **2A.49**
[7] See CIOT website at http://www.tax.org.uk/showarticle.pl?id=1750&n=
[8] Tax Credits (Claims and Notifications) Regulations 2002, SI 2002/2014, reg 25.
[9] See infra § **6.54**.
[10] The terms "auto-renewal" and "reply required" are terms spawned by the fact that TCA 2002, s 17 allows the Revenue either to provide a notice informing the persons that they will be treated as having declared that their income and circumstances were as specified or to provide a notice requiring them to provide details of income and circumstances.
[11] TCA 2002, ss 17 and 22(1)(b) and Tax Credits (Claims and Notifications) Regulations 2002, SI 2002/2014, reg 33(a) as amended Tax Credits (Miscellaneous Amendments) Regulations 2004, SI 2004/762, reg 3.
[12] TCA 2002, ss 17 and 22(1)(b) and Tax Credits (Claims and Notifications) Regulations 2002, SI 2002/2014, reg 33(b) as amended by Tax Credits (Miscellaneous Amendments) Regulations 2004, SI 2004/762, reg 3.
[13] Tax Credits (Claims and Notifications) Regulations 2002, SI 2002/2014, reg 11(3) as amended by Tax Credits (Miscellaneous Amendments) Regulations 2004, SI 2004/762, reg 3.

Stamp duties

Delivering documents for stamping

[2A.12] For the taxpayer's duties in relation to stamp duty see infra, §§ **56.20–56.25**. For the taxpayer's duties in relation to stamp duty reserve tax see infra, §§ **61.16–61.18**. For the taxpayer's duties in relation to stamp duty land tax see infra, § **62.23**.

Value added tax

Reporting supplies

[2A.13] The reporting of supplies,[1] on which a liability to value added tax may arise, can be by a variety of methods, including:

(1) periodic returns (normally quarterly) for taxable persons (which include tax chargeable on supplies and acquisitions and credit for input tax);
(2) special returns by representatives (eg receivers);
(3) everyone importing goods makes a declaration (eg coming through the red channel at an airport or green form on a small value postal packet) or entry (ie a customs declaration);
(4) non-taxable persons notify HMRC when acquiring new means of transport from another EU member state;
(5) claims for repayment or refund of tax.

---

[1] For the requirements of a business to report supplies subject to VAT, see infra, §§ 67.01–67.03.

Paying the tax (and getting tax credits)

Income tax and capital gains tax

Balancing payment

[2A.14] Under self-assessment, the principal payment of income tax, capital gains tax and Class 4 National Insurance is in a single sum, as a balancing payment, due 31 January following the fiscal year.

The taxpayer is required to make a payment of the amount due for the year, less any income tax paid by deduction at source and less any payments on account made (infra, § 2A.17).[1]

The balancing payment is normally due on 31 January following the fiscal year.[2] Payment later can give rise to automatic charge to interest, with the possibility of surcharges and penalties.

There is only one exception to the general liability for payment to be made by 31 January. This arises where a tax return has not been received by a taxpayer, but the taxpayer has, by 5 October following the fiscal year, notified the inspector that he has a liability to income tax and/or capital gains tax. It is necessary for the notification to have specified the source of each item of income giving rise to the liability, but not for details to be given of the amount of income. If having received such notification, the inspector fails to issue the taxpayer with a tax return until after 31 October, the due date for payment of the balancing liability is then three months after the date on which the tax return is ultimately issued to the taxpayer.[3]

131

It should be noted that the Revenue consider that where statute requires a notice to be "given", the date that notice is given is taken as the date of its receipt by a Revenue officer. Hence, in order to trigger a later date for payment, it is necessary for the notification to be sent to the Revenue in time for it to be received by 5 October. The date that determines the due date is then the date the tax return is issued by a Revenue officer, not the date on which it is received by the taxpayer.

The effect of this provision is shown in the example below.

EXAMPLE: EFFECT OF TMA 1970, S 59(3)(B)

Notice of chargeability given by taxpayer	2 Sep 09	6 Oct 09	4 Oct 09	23 July 09
Tax return issued	3 May 10	3 May 10	29 Oct 09	2 Nov 09
Due date for payment of tax	3 Aug 10	31 Jan 10	31 Jan 10	2 Feb 10

Where the interim payments exceed the liability to income tax due for the fiscal year, the overpayment reduces any payment of capital gains tax that is required. Where there is no capital gains tax liability, or where the income tax repayment exceeds the capital gains tax liability, repayment is due from the Revenue. This repayment carries interest from the due date, normally 31 January following the fiscal year.

It is possible for the tax deducted at source, plus any interim payments made, to exceed the total liability that is calculated for the fiscal year. In this case, the balancing payment is, in effect, negative. Repayment is then due. Where a self-assessment tax return has been issued, the mechanism for claiming the repayment is to make a calculation as if there were balancing payment, demonstrating that this is a negative sum which is then due to the taxpayer. If repayment is made after 31 January following the fiscal year, it carries interest from that date.[4]

Simon's Taxes Division E1.2.

[1] TMA 1970, s 59B(1).
[2] TMA 1970, s 59B(4).
[3] TMA 1970, s 59B(3)(*b*).
[4] TMA 1970, s 59B.

PAYE underpayments

[2A.15] A taxpayer, or his agent, can undertake the self-assessment on the basis that a PAYE underpayment of up to £2,000 will be collected by adjustment of the following year's coding notice, as long as the return is submitted to the Revenue by 31 October following the fiscal year.[1]

[1] TMA 1970, s 59B(8); SI 2003/2682, reg 186.

Revenue calculation of balancing payment

[2A.16] When a taxpayer delivers his tax return by 31 October following the year for which the return is made, the return can be submitted without the taxpayer's self-assessment of the balancing payment.[1]

Where the notice to deliver a tax return is issued after 31 July following the fiscal year, advantage of this provision can be taken if the return is submitted by a date two months after the date of issue.

TMA 1970, s 9(3) gives direction to the Revenue as:

an officer of HMRC shall . . .

(a) make the assessment on his behalf on the basis of the information contained in the return . . . and . . .
(b) send him a copy of the assessment so made.

A number of points arise from this.

First, the Revenue is instructed to make the self-assessment solely on the basis of items in the return. It has frequently been stated by the Revenue that this is not an offer of a tax return completion service provided by a Government department. What is undertaken by the Revenue is simply transcription of numbers already put on the return and a few rudimentary calculations being performed with those numbers.

Second, what is produced by the Revenue is the taxpayer's own self-assessment. All the statutory positions relating to the taxpayer's self-assessment apply to a Revenue calculation. In particular, leaving the Revenue to undertake the calculation does not stop the Revenue enquiring into the return, nor even influences the selection of that return for enquiry.

Third, the use of the words "on his behalf" makes the Revenue officer an agent of the taxpayer. The law of agency, thus, applies. The taxpayer is responsible for the acts of his agent. If there is a fault, he cannot avoid liability by showing it arose from an incorrect act by his agent. (In *Mankowitz v Income Tax Special Comrs and IRC*[2] the court upheld penalties imposed on the taxpayer, holding that the alleged negligence of his agent did not remove culpability from the principal, nor did it serve to reduce the level of penalties awarded.) Under the law of agency, a principal has a right against his agent for restitution. It is considered, therefore, that if the Revenue officer making the self-assessment on behalf of the taxpayer makes a mistake and that mistake leads to pecuniary loss for the taxpayer, the taxpayer then has a right of restitution from the Revenue. This right is completely separate from the liability to pay any tax, interest or penalties on that being a liability that remains with the taxpayer whatever the error of the Revenue.

Fourthly, whilst the due date for the payment of tax is sometimes postponed in cases where a tax return is issued late, payments on account of the following year's liabilities are not so postponed.

Simon's Taxes E1.256.

---

1   TMA 1970, s 9(2).
2   (1971) 46 TC 707.

Payment on account

[2A.17] The balancing payment made is reduced by the two payments on account the taxpayer is required to make by 31 January during the fiscal year and 31 July following the fiscal year.[1] Each of the two payments on account is calculated as 50% of the total liability to income tax and Class 4 National Insurance (but not to capital gains tax) for the preceding year, less income tax that was deducted at source for that preceding year.[2]

It must be noted that the payment on account required is never higher than that given by this calculation. That is, the maximum payment required is computed by reference to the remaining liability for the previous year. This is irrespective of any change in the taxpayer's circumstances.

No payment on account is required in any of the following circumstances:

(a) in the preceding year, the taxpayer was not subject to UK income tax (perhaps because he was not resident in the UK);
(b) for the preceding year the taxpayer satisfied his liability to income tax through PAYE;
(c) for the preceding year the taxpayer satisfied his liability to income tax through tax deducted at source;
(d) the total liability for the previous year less the tax deducted at source does not exceed £500;[3]
(e) more than 80% of the preceding year's liability to income tax was collected by deduction at source.[4]

A taxpayer has the right to make a claim under TMA 1970, s 59A(4) that he makes a payment on account of less than the sum computed as in supra, § **2A.14**. In making the claim, he is stating that he has a belief that the amount to which he will be assessed to income tax for the year in respect of which the payment on account is made, exceeds the amount of income tax deducted at source by an amount which is less than the relevant amount.

In principle, a fraudulent or negligent statement by the taxpayer in claiming a reduced payment on account renders him liable to a penalty not exceeding the difference between the "relevant amount" (as defined) and the amount actually paid. However, of more usual practical importance is that any reduction in the payment on account that is made which proves ultimately not to have been applicable attracts interest from the due date for the payment on account until the deficiency is made good.

Simon's Taxes E1.250, 251.

---

[1] TMA 1970, s 59B(1)(*b*).
[2] TMA 1970, s 59A(1), (2).
[3] As defined in TMA 1970, s 59A(1)(*c*).
[4] TMA 1970, s 59A(5).

Other mechanisms for collecting tax

[2A.18] In addition to self-assessment, there are various statutory arrangements whereby a payer is required to account for tax to the Revenue:

Paying the tax (and getting tax credits) **[2A.19]**

(1) Pay As You Earn[1] (see infra, §§ **7.133–7.139**) which is extended by the IR35 system[2] (infra, § **8.26**).
(2) Deduction at source on paying interest, and royalties or an annuity[3] (see infra, §§ **11.37–11.47**).
(3) Tax withheld on payment to a subcontractor[4] (see infra, § **2A.19**).
(4) Tax withheld on rent paid to a non-resident[5] (see infra, § **36.11**).
(5) Tax withheld on fees paid to a non-resident sportsperson or entertainer[6] (see infra, § **36.10**).

[1] TA 1988, s 203.
[2] FA 2000, Sch 12.
[3] ITA 2007, Pt 15.
[4] FA 2004, ss 57–58.
[5] ITA 2007, ss 971-972.
[6] ITA 2007, ss 965–970.

Construction Industry Tax Deduction Scheme

[2A.19] In response to perceived widespread evasion of tax by self-employed workers in the construction industry, in 1975[1] a scheme was introduced under which a person making a payment to a subcontractor is obliged to withhold tax[2] from the payment. In 1995,[3] and, again, in 1998,[4] substantial changes were made to the operation of the scheme in an effort to control widely reported abuse of subcontractors' certificates of exemption. A completely new Scheme started on 6 April 2007.[5]

The obligation to withhold tax is lifted if the subcontractor is registered with HMRC. The scheme does not depend on registration cards; instead, the payer will normally contact HMRC online. HMRC will check their records to see if the subcontractor is registered and then tell the contractor to pay the subcontractor gross, net of a deduction at the standard rate or net of a deduction at the higher rate. The higher rate will apply if HMRC have no record of the subcontractor's registration or are unable to verify the details for any other reason. HMRC will give a verification reference number for each subcontractor.

The scheme of deduction of tax from payments is not restricted to payments to an individual. It also applies to a payment made to a company[6] or to a partnership.[7] A subcontractor is defined as a person who:[8]

(a) is under a duty to the contractor to carry out the operations, or to furnish his own labour (that is to say, in the case of a company, the labour of employees or officers of the company) or the labour of others in the carrying out of the operations or to arrange for the labour of others to be furnished in the carrying out of the operations; or
(b) he is answerable to the contractor for the carrying out of the operations by others, whether under a contract or under other arrangements made or to be made by him.

This is specifically stated to include "any person carrying on a business which includes construction operations."[9]

(i) when his average annual expenditure on construction operations in the period of three years ending with the end of the last period of account before that time exceeds £1,000,000, or

(ii) if he was not carrying on the business at the beginning of that period of three years, one-third of his total expenditure on construction operations for the part of that period during which he has been carrying on the business exceeds (£1,000,000).[10]

In addition, payments by local authorities and specified governmental bodies are specifically brought within the scheme.

A subcontractor, whether an individual or a partnership or a company, can obtain a certificate of exemption from HMRC, production of which allows payment to be made to that person without deduction of tax.

The issue of exemption certificates is controlled by regulations.[11] The main requirements to be met by an individual[12] in order to obtain an exemption certificate are:

(i) His business must be carried on in the UK involving construction operations.
(ii) The business must be carried on to a substantial extent by means of a bank account.
(iii) Proper records must be kept, especially with a view to meeting income tax and national insurance contributions obligations.
(iv) The business must be carried on from proper premises and with proper equipment, stock and other facilities.
(v) There must have been compliance with income tax and national insurance obligations in the three years ending with the date of the application for the certificate (unless the Revenue accept that any failure was minor and technical), and an expectation of compliance in the future.
(vi) The turnover threshold must be satisfied, which means that annual turnover, excluding the cost of materials, must exceed £30,000 per annum, applying either the six-month or the three-year test.

For a partnership, equivalent conditions are imposed[13] in respect of the business requirements, the annual turnover threshold being £30,000 multiplied by the number of partners, or £200,000 if lower.

For a company, there are equivalent provisions requiring a history of tax compliance for the company itself and also, in the case of a close company, for the individuals who are its directors.[14] The annual turnover threshold for a company is £30,000 multiplied by the number of "relevant persons",[15] or £200,000 whichever is lower.

Appeal can be made to the General or Special Commissioners against the Revenue's refusal to issue, or renew, registration under the construction industry scheme.[16] In the latter part of 2005, a clutch of appeals against General Commissioners' decisions on old-style CIS certificates was heard by the High Court, plus one reported decision of the Special Commissioners. The issue common to all these cases was a consideration by the Court as to whether the compliance failings by the taxpayer were sufficiently serious to justify the Revenue refusing a CIS certificate. In *Woods (Inspector of Taxes) v Lightpower Ltd*[17] the taxpayer succeeded and the court ordered the issue of the CIS certificate. In *Templeton (Inspector of Taxes) v Transform Shop Office and Bar Fitters Ltd*[18] the High Court refused to overturn a decision of the General Commissioners ordering the Revenue to issue a certificate. In *London*

Recruitment Services v Revenue and Customs Comrs[19] the Special Commissioner ordered the Revenue to issue a CIS certificate, following an analysis of the contractual arrangement under which the taxpayer company provided services. In *Revenue and Customs Comrs v Oriel Support Ltd*[20] the High Court overturned the decision of the Special Commissioner and a CIS certificate was issued to the taxpayer company.

The taxpayer failed in *Hudson Contract Services Ltd v Revenue and Customs Comrs*,[21] *Glaze & Frame v Revenue and Customs Comrs*,[22] *Barnes (Inspector of Taxes) v Hilton Main Construction Ltd*,[23] *Cormack (Inspector of Taxes) v CBL Cable Contractors Ltd*,[24] *Mundial Invest SA v Moore*,[25] *Arnold (Inspector of Taxes) v G-CON Ltd*,[26] *R (Corr) v General Comrs of Income Tax*,[27] *R & C Comrs v Smith*,[28] *Gabem Management Ltd v C*[29] *and Revenue and Customs Comrs v Facilities and Maintenance Engineering Ltd*.[30]

In *Shaw v Vicky Construction Ltd*,[31] the Court rejected the submission of taxpayer's Counsel that the refusal of the Revenue to issue a certificate under the Construction Industry Tax Deduction Scheme was a breach of the taxpayer's right to peaceful enjoyment of possessions, granted by the Human Rights Act 1998.[32]

---

1 F(No 2)A 1975, s 69.
2 Originally at 35%; since 1 August 1999 at 18%.
3 FA 1995, s 139, Sch 29.
4 FA 1995, ss 55 to 57 and Sch 8, the provisions of which were brought into force on 1 August 1999.
5 The statutory framework for the Scheme is given in FA 2004, ss 57–77 and Schs 11 & 12. A brief guide to the arrangements that have now been delayed until 6 April 2007 is given in HMRC Press Release 2006, New Construction Industry Scheme—An Introduction to the Changes, *Simons Weekly Tax Intelligence* 2006, pp 152–157. In addition, HMRC has published nine fact sheets, CIS 351 to 349: www.hmrc.gov.uk/new-CIS/CIS341.pdf, plus a booklet CIS 340 "Construction Industries Scheme—Guide for Contractors and Subcontractors".
6 The issue of a subcontractor's certificate to a company is governed by TA 1988, s 565. The procedures adopted by the Revenue are given in HMRC Construction Industry Manual paras FC450 to 605 and 641 to 643. If an application by a company is approved, the Revenue issues a 714P certificate. The refusal by the Revenue may be appealed.
7 The issue of a subcontractor's certificate to a partnership is governed by TA 1988, s 564. The Revenue view of the application of the turnover test is given in Inland Revenue Tax Bulletin December 1998, page 615.
8 TA 1988, s 560(1).
9 TA 1988, s 560(2)(*a*).
10 TA 1988, s 560(2)(*f*).
11 Income Tax (Sub-Contractors in the Construction Industry) Regulations 1993 SI 1993/743, made under the authority of TA 1988, s 566. These regulations have been substantially amended by the Income Tax (Sub-Contractors in the Construction Industry) Amendment Regulations SI 1998/2633.
12 TA 1988, s 562.
13 TA 1988, s 564.
14 TA 1988, s 565.

[2A.19] Tax administration – the mechanics

15 A "relevant person" is a director of the company plus, in the case of a close company, every beneficial owner of shares in the company; TA 1998, s 565(2)(a).
16 TA 1988, s 561(9).
17 [2005] EWHC 1799 (Ch), [2006] STC 759.
18 [2005] EWHC 1558 (Ch), [2006] STC 900.
19 [2006] STC (SCD) 502
20 [2007] STI 111.
21 [2005] STC (SCD) 740. Appeal dismissed by the High Court: [2007] EWHC 73 (Ch).
22 [2005] STC (SCD) 757.
23 [2005] EWHC 1355 (Ch), [2005] STC 1532.
24 [2005] EWHC 1294 (Ch), [2006] STC 38.
25 [2005] EWHC 1735 (Ch), [2006] STC 412.
26 [2006] STC 1516, CA.
27 [2006] STC 709.
28 [2002] EWHC 2659 (Ch), [2002] STC 1544.
29 [2007] STI 537.
30 [2007] STC (SCD) 247.
31 [2006] STC 1887.
32 Under Article 1 of the First Protocol to the European Convention on Human Rights and Fundamental Freedoms 1950, as set out in the Human Rights Act 1998, Sch 1.

Corporation tax

[2A.20] Traditionally corporation tax has been due at the end of nine months after the end of the company's accounting period and this is still the case for small and medium sized companies, although the return will not normally be due until 12 months after the end of the period.[1] A company may well not know its correct tax liability at the time and so will have to exercise some judgment as to whether to lean towards overpayment rather than underpayment, especially since any eventual claim for repayment will carry interest at a lower rate than that charged on an underpayment. If, after the initial payment at the end of the nine months, it emerges that there has been an underpayment, the company is free to reduce its interest exposure by making a payment at that time without waiting for an assessment. Equally, if the opposite proves to be the case it may seek repayment.

The mechanism by which these things are done is, however, important. Where the nine-month period has passed and the company wishes to make an extra payment on account this is all that it does; if the Revenue wish to insist upon payment they must make an assessment which can, of course, be appealed against in the usual way. If the company wishes to amend its return to show an extra liability it makes an amended return;[2] the tax due and on which interest runs is the amount shown on the return. Interest still runs as from the end of the nine-month period until the amount is paid; the tax is due to the collector at once and there is no need for the Revenue to make an assessment.

A company can pay its tax liability in euros.[3]

138

Corporation tax is levied on the profits of a company that arise during liquidation. The corporation tax liability arising on the profits of a company after the start of a winding up is an expense of the winding up and is payable in priority to the claims of creditors.[4]

In practice[5] no action is taken by HMRC to collect a corporation tax liability of less than £100 that arises from the activities of a club or unincorporated association that is run exclusively for the benefit of its members, or a property management company that satisfies certain criteria (see supra, § **2A.06**).

[1] TMA 1970, s 59D. "Large" companies are required to make payments in quarterly instalments. See infra, § **2A.21**.
[2] FA 1998, Sch 18, para 15.
[3] Inland Revenue leaflet "The Euro—Tax and National Insurance Options for UK Businesses from 1 January 1999". *Simon's Weekly Tax Intelligence* 1999, p 25. A survey by the Inland Revenue during 1998 concluded that of the 700,000 companies that are liable to pay UK corporation tax, only 20 planned to make payment in euros: Inland Revenue press release, 31 July 1998. *Simon's Weekly Tax Intelligence* 1998, p 1152.
[4] Re Toshoku Finance plc [2002] UKHL 6, [2002] STC 368, HC.
[5] For full details see supra, § **2A.06**. This is based on a statement made by the financial secretary to the Treasury in the House of Commons during the debate on 2 May 2006 on Finance Bill 2006. HMRC Press Release, 25 August 2006, *Simon's Weekly Tax Intelligence* 2006, p 2146.

Quarterly instalments

[**2A.21**] A system of payment of corporation tax in instalments applies for "large" companies.[1] The quarterly instalment regime applies to tax due in respect of profits of companies after deducting tax paid under the sub-contractors regulations but including sums in respect of loans to participators (taxable under TA 1988, s 419) and the controlled foreign companies legislation.[2] Payment by instalments applies only to "large" companies. A company is large if its profit exceeds the upper limit for small profits relief ie £1.5m.[3] There is, however, a de minimis exception if the total liability does not exceed £10,000.[4] To protect growing companies a company is not large if its profits did not exceed £1.5m the previous year and its total cumulative profits do not exceed £10m.[5] The Revenue have stated that they intend to operate the system flexibly: "The QIP system is best thought of as treating a running balance of payments and liabilities, not a series of free-standing liabilities."[6]

Groups of companies may pay on a group-wide basis.[7] The group must enter into a formal contract with HMRC and all details must be agreed two months before the first instalment. The regulations contain rules on the surrender of excessive instalment payments within groups.[8]

The tax is due in four instalments. Where there is a 12-month accounting period, payments are due on the fourteenth day of months 7, 10, 13 and 16.[9] Underpayments attract an interest charge;[10] deliberate or reckless underpayments attract a penalty of twice the interest charge.[11]

[2A.21] Tax administration – the mechanics

The intention behind the scheme is that the four instalments made by the company equal, in aggregate, the total liability of the company for the accounting period. If a company decides that it has under/overestimated its potential liability to corporation tax it may simply pay more/less in a later quarter, with consequent risks of an interest charge.[12] If, however, it has paid a great deal more than it should and this is due to a change in the circumstances of the company since the payments were made it may seek a repayment from HMRC[13]—with interest.[14] Fraudulent or negligent repayment claims attract a penalty of twice the interest charge.[15] Interest is paid to the company if the company has made quarterly payments but it turns out not to have been a large company in the accounting period concerned.[16] The regulations also make provision relating to the production and inspection of information and records.[17]

Simon's Taxes D1.1301, D1.1346.

---

[1] Corporation Tax (Instalment Payments) Regulations 1998, SI 1998/3175, *Simon's Weekly Tax Intelligence* 1999, p 200 made under TMA 1970, s 59E added by FA 1998, s 30.
[2] SI 1998/3175, reg 2(3).
[3] SI 1998/3175, reg 3(1); see also reg 3(4) and (5).
[4] SI 1998/3175, reg 3(2). As amended by the Corporation Tax (Instalment Payments) Amendment Regulations SI 2000/892, reg 2 with effect from 1 July 2000.
[5] SI 1998/3175, reg 3(3)—on meaning of last year for new companies see sub-para (6).
[6] Inland Revenue Tax Bulletin, February 2000, pp 723–726.
[7] Arrangements are made under FA 1998, s 36; for details see Inland Revenue Guide to Self Assessment (1999) Chapter 14.
[8] SI 1998/3175, reg 9.
[9] SI 1998/3175, reg 5(3). The regulation specifies the dates of payment for accounting periods that are less than 12 months and provides that profits are apportioned to different accounting periods.
[10] SI 1998/3175, reg 7. See the Taxes (Interest Rate) Regulations 1989, SI 1989/1297, paras 3ZA, 3ZB, 3BA and 3BB added by the Taxes (Interest Rate) (Amendment No. 2) Regulations 1998, SI 1998/3176, paras 6 and 8. *Simon's Weekly Tax Intelligence* 1999, p 162. These provide for interest to be payable by the taxpayer company at 1% above the reference rate (reg 3ZA) and repayments to attract interest at 0.25% below the reference rate (reg 3BA). Once the old due date has passed (nine months after the year end) the base rates revert to those used for companies not caught in the quarterly payment scheme.
[11] SI 1998/3175, reg 13. On practice see Inland Revenue press release, 11 June 1999, *Simon's Weekly Tax Intelligence* 1999, p 1021.
[12] SI 1998/3175, reg 7.
[13] SI 1998/3175, reg 6.
[14] SI 1998/3175, reg 8.
[15] SI 1998/3175, reg 13. For practice see note 11, supra.
[16] SI 1998/3175, reg 8(1)(*b*). FA 1999, s 89 applies interest computed under TMA 1970, s 98.
[17] SI 1998/3175, paras 10–13 and 15.

Paying the tax (and getting tax credits) [2A.22]

Liability for another company's tax

[2A.22] A company is not normally liable for the payment of another company's corporation tax; if a subsidiary company in a group fails to pay its tax liability, HMRC do not have a general power to obtain payment for its holding company.[1] However, statute[2] provides rules under which either another company[3] or specified individuals[4] can be required to pay a corporation tax liability.[5] These rules apply where it appears to HMRC that there has been a change in the ownership[6] of a company (T), and corporation tax assessed on T for an accounting period beginning before the change remains unpaid more than six months from the date on which it was assessed.[7] This enables HMRC to collect the tax[8] from defined persons in defined circumstances. Such a payment cannot be deducted in computing profits but the payer is given a right of indemnity against T.[9]

The defined persons are those who within a specified time had control[10] of T or of any company which had control of T. Broadly the period is three years before the change in the ownership unless there was a change in ownership during that time in which case only the period since the change is relevant.

There are three sets of circumstances enabling HMRC to collect tax from the defined persons. The first is where T's business activities have ceased or become small or negligible in scale at any time during the three years before the change in ownership of T and no significant revival before that change occurs.[11] The second is where at any time after the change in ownership, but under arrangements made before the change, the activities of a trade or business of that company cease or the scale of those activities become small or negligible.[12]

The third condition is more complex because it is designed to catch transactions similar to but broader than the first two. This is where at any time during the six years beginning three years before the change in ownership there is a major change in the nature or conduct of a trade or business of that company;[13] there must also be a transfer of T's assets to a person with control or someone connected[14] with such a person or to any person under arrangements which enable any of those assets, or assets representing those assets, to be transferred to such a person. The transfer[15] must occur during the three years before the change in ownership or after that change but under arrangements made before that change. The rules can apply where there is more than one transfer but in any event the transfer or transfers must cause the major change.[16]

The 1997 changes introduce new provisions which are to sit alongside the existing ones and make use of them.[17] They are designed to counter schemes under which the tax liability of the company crystallises after the date of the change of ownership by use of claims for capital allowances or capital gains rollover relief. The new rule begins by looking at the terms of the transactions entered into in connection with the change of ownership and asking whether it would be reasonable to infer from the terms of those transactions that at least one of the transactions was entered into on the assumption that a potential liability to tax would not be met.[18] A potential tax liability is one which might arise on the transferred company (or any associated company[19]) after the change in ownership in circumstances either reasonably foreseeable at

141

[2A.22] Tax administration – the mechanics

the time of the change or of which there was a reasonably foreseeable risk.[20] A transaction is defined so as to include a transaction entered into as part of a series of transactions or schemes.[21] The period goes back three years before the change in ownership of the company or, if shorter, to the last previous change of ownership.[22] The persons liable to be assessed are persons with control of the company during that period.[23]

The words of the 1997 rules are very wide. Taxpayers will have to take such comfort as they can from the words of the Treasury that HMRC will not interpret the section in a way as to assess on the vendor liabilities wholly unrelated to the changes of ownership of the company in question.[24] There is a wide information power enabling the Revenue by notice to require any person to supply them with documents in that person's possession or power which appear to HMRC to be relevant for determining specified matters; or any particulars which appear to them to be so relevant.[25] The matters specified include whether the seller is, or may become, liable and the extent of any liability.[26]

---

1   For exceptions where someone other than the company realising the gain may be accountable see TCGA 1992, ss 189 (shareholder following capital distribution of gain), 190 (recovery from another group member), 139(7), (tax on transfer of assets following reconstruction or amalgamation) and 137(4) (share for share exchange outside protection of bona fide commercial reasons zone). There are also special provisions for groups of companies: FA 1998, s 36 and, more recently, provisions concerning unpaid tax of UK branches of foreign companies where other group members may find themselves liable: FA 2000, Sch 28.
2   TA 1988, ss 767A, 767B added by FA 1994, s 135 and extended by FA 1998, s 114. For Revenue practice see HMRC interpretation RI 90.
3   TA 1988, s 767A(2)(*b*).
4   TA 1988, s 767A(2)(*a*).
5   TA 1988, s 767C gives the Revenue wide powers to obtain information from any person, not merely those connected with the defaulting company.
6   Defined by reference to TA 1988, s 769 but note addition of TA 1988, s 769(2A) and exclusion of sub-s (8) by sub-s (9).
7   TA 1988, s 767A(1), (9); the assessment can be made within three years from the date on which T's liability is finally determined; s 767A(10). On time limit note also TA 1988 s 768(8) applied by s 767B(9).
8   The amount of tax must not exceed the amount of the tax which, at the time of that assessment, remains unpaid by T—TA 1988, s 767A(8).
9   TA 1988, s 767B(2).
10 Control is to be construed in accordance with TA 1988, s 416 as slightly modified by s 767B(5), (6).
11 TA 1988, s 767A(4).
12 TA 1988, s 767A(5).
13 Defined by TA 1988, s 767B(7) as including any change mentioned in TA 1988 s 245(4)(*a*)–(*d*) and a change falling within any of those paragraphs which is achieved gradually as the result of a series of transfers.
14 Defined by reference to TA 1988, s 839.
15 Widely defined in ss 767A(6), 767B(8) and including the giving of any business facilities with respect to it.

[16] TA 1988, s 767A(6), (7). On Revenue practice see HMRC interpretation RI 90.
[17] TA 1988, s 767AA introduced by FA 1998, s 114; s 115 adds s 767C which contains information powers and s 116 makes tidying up amendments to the existing provisions. For Report on consultation exercise see Inland Revenue press release, 19 August 1998, *Simon's Weekly Tax Intelligence* 1998, p 1301.
[18] TA 1988, s 767AA(2).
[19] Defined in s 767AA(8).
[20] TA 1988, s 767AA(3).
[21] TA 1988, s 767AA(6), (7).
[22] TA 1988, s 767AA(5).
[23] TA 1988, s 767AA(4); assessments are made in the name of the company—sub-s (9); on the period for making the assessment see sub-s (10).
[24] Inland Revenue Notes on Finance Bill Clause 112; Inland Revenue press release, 17 February 1998, *Simon's Weekly Tax Intelligence* 1998, p 245.
[25] TA 1988, s 767C(2); the matters are specified in sub-s (3).
[26] TA 1988, s 767C(3). The power extends to associated companies.

Inheritance tax

Due date for payment

[2A.23] Tax is in general due six months after the end of the month in which the transfer takes place; for potentially exempt transfers six months after the month in which death occurred.[1] However, tax due on a chargeable lifetime transfer made between 6 April and 30 September is not due until the end of April in the following year.[2]

Tax due from personal representatives[3] as a prerequisite to obtaining probate must be paid on delivery of the account to the Probate Registry. Payment can be made from the bank account of the deceased direct to HMRC, even though probate has not been granted.[4] This does not apply to tax on instalment property or on property for tax on which the personal representatives are not primarily liable, eg potentially exempt transfers and tax on settled property.

Interest runs from these dates whether or not a notice of determination has been issued. Tax may therefore be paid on account.

For confirmation that no further IHT is due, see infra, § **46.07**.

Simon's Taxes Division I11.4.

---

[1] IHTA 1984, s 226(3A) added by FA 1986, Sch 19, para 30(2).
[2] IHTA 1984, s 226(1).
[3] IHTA 1984, s 226(2).
[4] Banks and building societies that have chosen to participate in the scheme accept an instruction on form D20 from an applicant for a grant of probate to transfer funds to the Revenue to satisfy that liability to IHT that has to be satisfied before probate is granted; for details of the operation of the scheme, see Inland Revenue IHT Newsletter April 2003, p 1 and August 2003, p 4, Inland Revenue Press Release, 11 March 2003; *Simons Weekly Tax Intelligence* 2003, p 523.

[2A.24] Tax administration – the mechanics

Payment by instalments

[2A.24] IHT may be paid by instalments if it is attributable to certain types of property and the transfer is either:

(1) on death; or
(2) is a lifetime transfer with the donee paying the tax; or
(3) the charge relates to settled property and either
    (a) the property remains settled (eg it passes to another life tenant); or
    (b) the tax is borne by the beneficiary.[1]

The taxpayer must elect in writing. The tax is payable by ten equal yearly instalments. The first instalment is due when the whole of the tax would otherwise have been payable; in the case of a transfer on death six months after the end of the month in which death occurred.

The taxpayer may at any time pay off the outstanding tax and must do so if the property is sold or, in the case of a partnership he receives a sum in satisfaction of his interest, in the case of a lifetime transfer if there is a further lifetime chargeable transfer of the property or in the case of settled property it ceases to be comprised in the settlement. Where only a part of the property is sold or transferred only a proportionate part of the tax becomes due.

The property qualifying for this treatment is (a) land and buildings situated in or out of the UK, (b) certain shares and securities (see infra, § 2A.25), (c) the net value of a business or an interest in a business provided it is carried on for gain (ie not as a hobby),[2] and (d) timber.[3] The introduction in 1992 of the 100% relief for certain property within (b) and (c) has reduced the importance of the present relief.

The instalment method is available to tax on potentially exempt transfers which become chargeable because the transferor dies within seven years and to the additional tax due because the transferor of a chargeable transfer dies within seven years only if certain conditions are satisfied.[4] The transferee[5] must own the property, whether land or shares,[6] throughout the period from the date of the transfer down to the date of the death of the transferor (or his own earlier death); alternatively the property must have been replaced by property falling within the replacement rules for business or agricultural property reliefs.[7] If the property consists of unquoted shares or unquoted securities they must remain unquoted.[8]

Simon's Taxes Division I11.5; Foster's Inheritance Tax Division L5.

[1] IHTA 1984, s 227.
[2] IHTA 1984, s 228.
[3] IHTA 1984, s 229.
[4] IHTA 1984, s 227(1A) amended by FA 1987, Sch 8, para 15.
[5] Defined in IHTA 1984, s 227(1B).
[6] IHTA 1984, s 228(3A) added by FA 1987, Sch 8, para 16.
[7] IHTA 1984, ss 113B or 124B.
[8] IHTA 1984, s 228(3A) added by F(No 2)A 1992, Sch 14.

[2A.25] IHT can be paid in instalments if it is in respect of shares and securities that satisfy the following conditions:[1]

(1) they gave control of the company immediately before the transfer. Control means having a majority of the votes on all issues affecting the company as a whole; at one time it sufficed to have a majority on any particular question affecting the company as a whole but this gave rise to avoidance devices. Where husband and wife have shares or securities each is deemed to have control if they have control together.

(2) they are unquoted and do not give control but undue hardship would otherwise result; this is extended—and no hardship need be shown—where the transfer is on death and the person liable for the tax shows that at least 20% of the tax for which he is liable is attributable to unquoted shares or securities or other property in respect of which instalment relief is available).

(3) they are unquoted shares (but not other securities) and the value transferred is more than £20,000 and the shares constitute at least 10% of the nominal value of all the shares then issued by the company or they are ordinary shares and their nominal value is at least 10% of all the ordinary shares then issued.

As from 10 March 1992 shares are only quoted if they are quoted on a recognised Stock Exchange (and so not if they are quoted on the USM) or the alternative investment market.[2]

For the calculation of interest when the instalment option is available, see 2.43.

Simon's Taxes Division I11.5; Foster's Inheritance Tax L5.11–14.

[1] IHTA 1984, s 228.
[2] IHTA 1984, ss 227(1AA), 228(5) added by F(No 2)A 1992, Sch 14, para 6 and Inland Revenue press release, 20 February 1995, *Simon's Weekly Tax Intelligence* 1995, p 343.

National Insurance contributions

[2A.26] The duty imposed on the employer as regards Class 1, Class 1A and Class 1B Contributions is, in effect, to report and pay simultaneously.[1]

[1] See supra, § **2A.10**.

Tax credits

[2A.27] Working tax credit (other than the childcare element) must be paid by the employer if a tax credit claimant is an employee.[1] In the 2004 Budget the Chancellor announced he would consult on ways to phase out payment by employers to reduce the regulatory burdens on businesses.

[2A.27] Tax administration – the mechanics

The self-employed are paid direct by HMRC. If both members of a couple are working 16 hours or more they can nominate which one of them is to receive the working tax credit on their tax credit claim form.

Child tax credit and the childcare element of working tax credit are paid direct by HMRC to the child's main carer. A couple can nominate which one of them is the main carer on their tax credit claim form. Credits can be paid weekly or four weekly where they are not being paid by the employer.[2]

It is not infrequent for tax credits to be overpaid, particularly where payment depends on profit of a self-employment which cannot be calculated until after the end of the tax year. The various methods available for an individual to repay an overpayment are described in HMRC Code of Practice 26.[3]

[1] The rules as to how employers pay tax credits (including provision for funding) are contained in Working Tax Credit (Payment by Employers) Regulations 2002, SI 2002/2172 as amended by SI 2003/715 and SI 2004/762.
[2] See The Tax Credits (Payments by the Board) Regulations 2002, SI 2002/2173 as amended by SI 2003/723 and SI 2004/762.
[3] The system, with the alternatives available, is usefully summarised in Inland Revenue Tax Bulletin, December 2004, pp 1164–1165.

Stamp duty

[2A.28] In general, payment is required when submitting a document for stamping.[1] When adjudication is necessary[2] payment of the duty is required within 30 days of the decision of the Stamp Office.[3]

[1] See supra, § **2A.12**.
[2] See infra, § **56.21**.
[3] SA 1891, s 12. The HMRC is empowered to grant a date for payment more than 30 days after its decision, s 12A.

Stamp duty reserve tax

[2A.29] Stamp duty reserve tax is due and payable on the accountable date.[1]

The 0.5% charge on agreements to transfer chargeable securities is no longer deferred until the expiration of two months beginning with the day on which the agreement is made (or, where the agreement is conditional, the day on which the condition is satisfied). Instead, there is now an immediate 0.5% charge in respect of agreements to transfer chargeable securities (see infra, § **61.02**) which may be cancelled where the transaction is completed by a duly stamped transfer within six years of the agreement being made or becoming unconditional (see infra, §§ **61.21** ff.). The accountable date is the fourteenth day following the transaction where it is effected by means of a relevant system[2] (such as CREST) or where it is reported to an exchange or recognised body unless another date has been agreed between HMRC and the operator of

Paying the tax (and getting tax credits) [2A.31]

such a system. If the transaction could have been so reported but was not, the accountable date is the fourteenth day following the transaction. In any other case, the accountable date is the seventh day of the month following the month in which the charge to tax occurred.[3]

EXAMPLE

A agrees to transfer registered shares to B on 1 February. The charge arises on 1 February. Stamp duty reserve tax is due and payable on 15 February or other agreed date if the transaction is effected by means of a relevant system (such as CREST) or if it is reported to an exchange or recognised body. If the transaction could have been so reported but was not, stamp duty reserve tax is due and payable on 15 February. In any other case, stamp duty reserve tax is due and payable on 7 March.

Sergeant and Sims A2.6 [134]–[139], Division D [5023]–[5044].

[1] Stamp Duty Reserve Tax Regulations 1986, SI 1986/1711, regs 2, 3.
[2] See the Uncertificated Securities Regulations 1995, SI 1995/2372, reg 2(1).
[3] SI 1986/1711, reg 2 as amended by the Stamp Duty Reserve Tax (Amendment) Regulations 1997, SI 1997/2430, reg 3.

Stamp duty land tax

[2A.30] Stamp duty land tax in respect of a land transaction must be paid not later than the filing date for the tax return ie 30 days from the effective date of the land transaction. Any tax payable as the result of the withdrawal of either group relief, reconstruction or acquisition relief and charities relief must be paid not later than the filing date for the tax return ie 30 days from the date of the disqualifying event.[1]

[1] FA 2003, s 86 as amended by FA 2007, s [79].

VAT

[2A.31] In general, VAT is payable by the end of the month following the return period.[1] A period covered by a return may be one month, three months or twelve months.[2] If the annual accounting scheme is used, the date of payment is two months after the end of the annual accounting period, with a requirement to make either quarterly or monthly sums if the excess of output tax over input tax for the preceding period exceeds specified limits.[3]

[1] See infra, §§ **67.04–67.05**.
[2] Value Added Tax Regulations 1995, SI 1995/2518. regs 25(1), 50, amended by SI 2002/1142.
[3] SI 1995/2518, reg 51, amended by SI 2002/1142. For the annual accounting scheme, see infra, § **63.43**.

Interest

Income tax, capital gains tax and NICs

Unpaid tax

[2A.32] Interest is charged in respect of the period from the due date of payment to the actual date of payment for:

(a) a payment on account of an income tax liability;
(b) tax payable on an assessment raised by HMRC;
(c) the balancing payment of income tax and capital gains tax;
(d) tax payable as a consequence of an amendment to a self-assessment;
(e) unpaid PAYE;
(f) a surcharge imposed;
(g) a penalty imposed;
(h) national insurance contributions.[1]

The rate of interest on late payment of tax is given by statutory instrument.[2] This provides for interest to be calculated each month, the rate being 2½% above bank base rate.

Under the rewritten version of TMA 1970, s 86, interest runs in every case from "the relevant date". This is:

(a) for a payment on account—31 January in the fiscal year and 31 July in the fiscal year;[3]
(b) balancing payment—31 January following the fiscal year;[4]
(c) PAYE—19 April following the fiscal year;[5]
(d) surcharges and interest—30 days after imposition.[6]

Simon's Taxes E1.256.

---

[1] FA 1992, Sch 1, paras 6(2) and (3).
[2] SI 1989/1297 reg 3, amended by SI 1996/3187.
[3] TMA 1970, s 86(2) amended by FA 1995, s 110 applying s 59A(2).
[4] TMA 1970, s 86(2)(b) amended by FA 1995, s 110 applying s 59B(4) unless the Revenue's delivery of the return is delayed, in which case it is three months after the return is sent to the taxpayer—s 86(2)(a) applying s 59B(3).
[5] SI 1993/744, reg 51(3) issued under the authority of TA 1988, s 203(2)(dd).
[6] TMA 1970, s 59C(6) and s 103A brought into effect from 9 March 1998 by SI 1998/311, *Simon's Weekly Tax Intelligence* 1998, pp 215, 314.

Overpaid tax

[2A.33] TA 1988, s 824,[1] provides for repayment supplements to be paid by HMRC at a rate that is specified by statutory instrument.[2]

From repayments of tax relating to fiscal year 1996–97 and subsequent years, repayment supplement is calculated from the date the tax was paid,[3] at a rate calculated[4] as:

$$(RR + 2.5)\frac{(100 - BR)}{100}$$

Interest [2A.34]

where:

RR is bank base rate;
BR is the basic rate of tax.

Repayment supplement is available in respect of:

(a) payments on account found to be excessive;
(b) a balancing charge found to be excessive;
(c) repayment of any other income tax charge paid by or on behalf of an individual;
(d) a surcharge subsequently reduced;
(e) a penalty subsequently reduced.

[1] As rewritten by FA 1994, s 119(2).
[2] Issued under the authority of FA 1988, s 178.
[3] TA 1988, s 824(3) amended by FA 1997, s 92. Tax deducted at source is treated as if it were paid on 31 January following the fiscal year: TA 1988, s 824(3)(b).
[4] Taxes (Interest Rate) Regulations 1989 SI 1989/1297 reg 3AB as inserted by SI 1996/3187.

Corporation tax

[2A.34] The rate of interest on unpaid/overpaid corporation tax depends on whether the company has to pay corporation tax under the quarterly payment scheme.[1] For "large" companies caught under this scheme the rates have been brought into line with commercial rates for the period between the first instalment and the date on which the corporation tax has traditionally been payable, ie nine months after the end of the accounting period. Interest accrues on a running balance based from each instalment date at base plus 1%[2] and base minus ¼% for under/over payments of tax respectively. Nine months after the end of the accounting period the rates revert to the more penal rates of base plus 2½% and base minus 1% which also applies to companies who still have their normal due date nine months after the end of the account period.[3]

Income tax on company payments (now less of an issue for companies) less income tax suffered on any receipts is due 14 days after the end of the period for which a CT61 return is required (normally a calendar quarter).[4]

Interest credited on a repayment forms part of the profits of a company subject to corporation tax. Interest charged on late payment of corporation tax, is an expense of the company and, therefore, leads to a reduction in the corporation tax payable for the accounting period in which the interest is paid.[5]

[1] TMA 1970, s 59E, SI 1998/3175.
[2] From 20 April 2000.
[3] TMA 1970, s 87A applying FA 1989, s 178. 6.5% from 21 May 2007.
[4] TMA 1970, s 87.
[5] FA 1998, ss 33 and 34, which reverse the previous treatment of interest as being outside the charge to tax, with effect from accounting periods ending on or after

1 July 1999. In order to reflect this change, interest in respect of corporation tax that is credited/charged on or after 14 October 1999 is calculated without adjustment for tax in the interest rate formula. Interest Rate (Amendment Number 4) Regulations (SI 1999/2637) amending The Taxes (Interest Rate) Regulations 1989 (SI 1989/1297) regulation 3AA.

Inheritance tax

[2A.35] Unpaid tax carries interest on all transfers.[1] Interest runs from the date the tax fell due and is not affected by changes in rates of tax.

The rate is calculated as:

$$(RR + 2)\frac{(100 - BR)}{100} - 1$$

(For the meaning of RR and BR, see supra, § **2A.33**.)

If tax is overpaid interest is paid on the repayments; interest is calculated from the date of payment to the date of repayment. Such interest is not taxable as income of the recipient. The rate is the same as that for underpayment.

Interest ceases to run from the offer date where property is accepted in satisfaction of tax on the basis of an offer date valuation.

Simon's Taxes Division I11.4; Foster's Inheritance Tax L4.05.

---

[1] IHTA 1984, s 233. The interest rate is specified in Taxes (Interest Rate) Regulations 1995, SI 1989/1297, reg 4, made under IHTA 1984, s 233.

Rates are:

6 Oct 94 to 5 Mar 99 5%
6 Mar 99 to 5 Feb 00 4%
6 Feb 00 to 5 May 01 5%
6 May 01 to 5 Nov 01 4%
6 Nov 01 to 5 Aug 03 3%
6 Aug 03 to 5 Dec 03 2%
6 Dec 03 to 5 Sep 04 3%
6 Sep 04 to 5 Sep 05 4%
6 Sep 05 to 5 Sep 06 3%
6 Sep 06 to date 4%

Interest on instalments

[2A.36] Where the instalment option is available (infra, § **46.14**), interest is calculated from the day the instalment falls due in so far as the tax is attributable to the value of shares, securities, an interest in a business, agricultural property or woodlands.[1] This treatment applies where the tax is payable by virtue of death, a chargeable transfer or a periodic charge/exit charge in respect of a settlement.

Where tax payable is attributable to the value of any other property, interest is calculated from the normal due date that would apply if the instalment option had not been chosen.[2]

Exceptionally, interest is calculated from the normal due date and not from the date for payment of the instalment, where the instalment is attributed to the value of shares or securities in a company whose business is dealing in stocks, shares or securities, a market maker, a discount house or dealing in land or buildings or making or holding investments.[3]

Simon's Taxes Division I11.5; Foster's Inheritance Tax L5.31, 32.

[1] IHTA 1984, s 234(1).
[2] IHTA 1984, s 233(1).
[3] IHTA 1984, s 234(2)–(4).

National Insurance contributions

[2A.37] Interest is charged on overdue Class 1, Class 1A and Class 1B contributions at the same rate as for income tax. If the payment of NI contributions is made electronically, interest is charged for any payments made after 22 April; otherwise, interest is charged from 19 April after the end of the tax year.[1] Interest is charged on overdue Class 4 contributions under self-assessment as for income tax.

[1] Social Security (Contributions) Regulations 2001, SI 2001/1004, regs 76–79 and Sch 4, paras 17–21.

Tax credits

[2A.38] Interest is only chargeable on overpaid tax credits where the overpayment is attributable to fraud or neglect.[1]

[1] TCA 2002, s 37.

Stamp duty

[2A.39] Interest is payable under SA 1891, new s 15A if an instrument chargeable with ad valorem duty is not duly stamped within 30 days of execution and is charged on the unpaid duty from the end of the 30-day period until the duty is paid. Under SA 1891, old s 15(3) if an instrument was executed outside the UK, interest and penalties only began to run if the stamp duty was not paid within 30 days of the instrument being first received in the UK. Under SA 1891, old s 15(2)(*a*), even when the instrument had been executed in the UK, no interest and penalties arose if the instrument was submitted for adjudication within 30 days of execution.

However, under SA 1891, new s 15A interest is chargeable from 30 days after execution in relation to any unpaid ad valorem duty regardless of where the instrument was executed and whether it has been submitted for adjudication

[2A.39] Tax administration – the mechanics

within 30 days of execution. Hence, it is necessary in practice when submitting a document which is or may be liable to ad valorem duty for adjudication, to lodge an estimate of the duty payable in order to forestall an interest charge and SA 1891, new s 15A(2) gives statutory recognition to the concept of lodging an estimate of the amount of duty with HMRC. Where payable, interest is calculated at the usual rate under FA 1989, s 178 and is rounded down to the nearest multiple of £5 and is not payable if less than £25.

Stamp duty reserve tax

[2A.40] Interest is charged on tax paid late but in their "Notes for Guidance" (February 1998) the Stamp Office state that they will not seek interest in relation to transfers of securities held outside CREST if a duly stamped instrument or transfer is produced by the later of seven days after the end of the month in which the charge arises or 30 days after the agreement. This has now been extended to 60 days from the date on which the charge arises by concession as explained in the former Inland Revenue's Tax Bulletin of October 1998 and confirmed by section 13.18 of the Stamp Office Manual published on 20 March 2000 and updated in March 2002.

Stamp duty land tax

[2A.41] Interest is payable on the amount of any unpaid SDLT after 30 days from the effective date[1] of the transaction. In the case of the withdrawal of group relief, reconstruction or acquisition relief or charities relief giving rise to tax, interest is charged after 30 days following the disqualifying event.[2] In the case of tax deferred under FA 2003, s 90[3] interest is charged after 30 days from when the deferred payment is due.[4] However, where contingent, uncertain or unascertained consideration is not deferred under FA 2003, s 90 interest on any tax that becomes payable under FA 2003, s 80 (adjustment where the contingency ceases or consideration becomes ascertained) runs from the effective date of the transaction.[5] An amount of tax lodged with the HMRC in respect of the tax will reduce the interest payable accordingly.[6]

[1] See infra, § **62.04**.
[2] See infra, §§ **62.17** and **62.20**.
[3] See infra, § **62.06**.
[4] FA 2003, s 87.
[5] FA 2003, s 87(5) and see infra, § **62.04** for "effective date".
[6] FA 2003, s 87(6).

Value added tax

VAT recoverable by assessment

[2A.42] An amount of tax[1] carries interest from the reckonable date[2] until payment if:[3] (a) it is assessed under VATA 1994, s 73; or (b) the amount liable

Interest [2A.43]

to be so assessed is paid before such an assessment is made.[4] Interest runs for a maximum period of three years.[5] The rate in force from 6 September 2006 is 7.50%.[6]

Interest is assessed.[7] The amount assessed is treated as an amount of tax due from the trader and is thus recoverable as a debt due to the Crown.[8] A right of appeal is given in respect of the amount of interest assessed.[9] HMRC assesses interest only if it represents commercial restitution.[10] Interest is assessed on voluntary declarations only if the net underdeclaration exceeds £2,000.[11]

Interest is paid without deduction of income tax.[12]

De Voil Indirect Tax Service V5.361–365.

---

[1] For the amount carrying interest where two or more voluntary disclosures have been made, see *Camden London Borough v Customs and Excise Comrs* [1993] VATTR 73; *Mackenzie v Customs and Excise Comrs* (1993) VAT decision 11597; *SGS Holdings UK Ltd v Customs and Excise Comrs* (1996) VAT decision 13918.
[2] Defined in VATA 1994, s 74(5).
[3] VATA 1994, s 74(1), (2). For the conditions imposed in relation to tax assessable under VATA 1994, s 73(1), see VATA 1994, s 74(1)(a)–(c).
[4] See *P and O Ferries v Customs and Excise Comrs* [1991] VATTR 327, [1991] 3 CMLR 683.
[5] VATA 1994, s 74(3). For the calculation, see *Shokar v Customs and Excise Comrs* [1998] V & DR 301.
[6] VATA 1994, s 74(1), (2), (4). The rate of interest in force for the time being is specified in orders made by the Commissioners under FA 1996, s 197(5). From 6 September 2005 to 5 September 2006 the rate was 3%. For the rates in force for earlier periods, see Air Passenger Duty and Other Indirect Taxes (Interest Rate) Regulations, SI 1998/1461, reg 4(1) and Table 3 as amended by SI 2000/631.
[7] VATA 1994, s 76(1)(b). For the period assessed, see VATA 1994, s 76(3)(d), (4). For the date to which interest is assessed, see VATA 1994, s 76(7), (8). For the time limits, see VATA 1994, s 77(1)–(5).
[8] VATA 1994, s 76(9), Sch 11, para 5(1).
[9] VATA 1994, ss 83(q), (r), 84(6). For jurisdiction in relation to the decision whether or not to assess interest, see *Camden London Borough v Customs and Excise Comrs* [1993] VATTR 73.
[10] Customs and Excise Press Notice No. 34/94 dated 7 September 1994. *RMSG (a partnership) v Customs and Excise Comrs* [1994] VATTR 167.
[11] Customs and Excise Press Notice No. 9/95 dated 31 January 1995.
[12] VATA 1994, s 74(7).

VAT overpaid due to official error

[2A.43] HMRC are liable to pay interest if, due to an error[1] on their part, a trader has accounted for output tax which is not due or failed to deduct input tax to which he was entitled.[2] Interest must be claimed. Claims must be made in writing no later than three years after the time when HMRC authorised payment of the output tax or input tax concerned.[3] The rate in force from 6 September 2006 is 4%.[4] Interest is not compounded.[5] A right of appeal is given in relation to claims.[6]

Interest runs from the date when tax for the relevant prescribed accounting period was paid, repaid or set off.[7] Any period of delay arising from the claimant's conduct is left out of account in calculating the period for which interest runs.[8]

HMRC may recover overpaid interest by way of assessment.[9]

De Voil Indirect Tax Service V5.196.

---

[1] For "error", see *North East Media Development Trust Ltd v Customs and Excise Comrs* [1995] V & DR 240; *Chartered Institute of Bankers v Customs and Excise Comrs* (1998) VAT decision 15648.
[2] VATA 1994, s 78(1)(*a*), (*b*).
[3] VATA 1994, s 78(10), (11) (as inserted by FA 1997, s 44).
[4] VATA 1994, s 78(3). The rate of interest in force for the time being is specified in orders made by the Commissioners under FA 1996, s 197(5). From 6 September 2005 to 5 September 2006 the rate was 3%. For the rates in force for earlier periods, see Air Passenger Duty and Other Indirect Taxes (Interest Rate) Regulations, SI 1998/1461, reg 5(1) and Table 7 as amended by SI 2000/631.
[5] *National Council of YMCAs Inc v Customs and Excise Comrs* [1993] VATTR 299.
[6] VATA 1994, s 83(s).
[7] VATA 1994, s 78(4), (5). See *North East Media Development Trust Ltd v Customs and Excise Comrs* [1995] V & DR 240.
[8] VATA 1994, s 78(8), (8A), (9) as substituted by FA 1997, s 44.
[9] VATA 1994, s 78A(1)–(4), (6), (8) as inserted by FA 1997, s 45. For an example, see *Customs and Excise Comrs v DFS Furniture Co plc* [2003] EWCA Civ 243, [2004] STC 559.

Surcharges

Income tax, capital gains tax and NICs

[2A.44] Where income tax, capital gains tax and NIC is due to be assessed on a taxpayer's self-assessment and the tax remains unpaid 28 days after the due date, the taxpayer is liable to a surcharge of 5% of the unpaid tax. Where the liability remains unpaid six months after the due date, a further 5% surcharge is added, making a total of 10%.[1] A payment on account cannot attract a surcharge, nor is a surcharge made where there is a tax geared penalty.[2]

Interest accrues on an unpaid surcharge (supra, § **2A.32**).

On 15 February 1995 the Financial Secretary to the Treasury was asked whether there would be a surcharge imposed where the taxpayer discovered he has made a mistake in his self-assessment and volunteered a correction of that mistake to the Revenue. After saying that additional tax due would carry interest, the Financial Secretary to the Treasury continued:

> provided that the taxpayer volunteers the information and pays the amount promptly, a surcharge would not be imposed by the Board.[3]

Surcharges [2A.45]

A surcharge is not levied where the taxpayer has a "reasonable excuse" for late payment.[4] In *Bancroft v Crutchfield*,[5] the Special Commissioner held that: "a reasonable excuse implies that a reasonable taxpayer would have behaved in the same way".[6] In that case, a surcharge was imposed on a firm of solicitors. In the words of the Special Commissioner: "The taxpayers were playing brinkmanship in paying tax on the last possible date but they had not read the rules properly." The Special Commissioner rejected the submission by taxpayer's counsel that the imposition of the surcharge was contrary to Human Rights Act 1998 saying:[7]

> I must, in accordance with s 3 of the Human Rights Act 1998 'so far as it is possible to do so', read and give effect to the legislation in a way that is compatible with the taxpayer' convention rights. It seems to me that if Parliament says that I may set aside the surcharge if I find that there is a reasonable excuse but that if I do not so find I may confirm the imposition of the surcharge, even the widest possible reading consistent with the 1998 Act cannot result in my doing the opposite. Perhaps 'may' is used because there are two alternatives but having found that there is no reasonable excuse it can only mean 'must'.

It is possible for reliance on an agent to be a "reasonable excuse". In *Rowland v Revenue and Customs Comrs*[8] Mrs Rowland relied on a specialist firm of accountants to advise on her on the action she should take in connection with a film scheme tax mitigation arrangement, on which she had no pre-existing knowledge. The Special Commissioner found that it was reasonable for Mrs Rowland to rely on her accountants and that it was this reliance that led to the underpayment. He quashed the surcharge.

Simon's Taxes E1.254.

1   TMA 1970, s 59C(2), (3) inserted by FA 1994, c 194. Payment on the 29th day is not adequate to avoid surcharge, see *Thompson v Minzly* [2002] STC 450.
2   TMA 1970, s 59C(4).
3   HC Official Report, Standing Committee A, 15 February 1994, col 235, Simon's Tax Intelligence 1994, p 239.
4   TMA 1970, s 59C(9)(*a*).
5   [2002] STC (SCD) 347.
6   [2002] STC (SCD) 347 at 349j, para 5.
7   [2002] STC (SCD) 347 at 350c, para 6.
8   [2006] STC (SCD) 536 applying *Thorne v Sevenoaks General Comrs and IRC* [1989] STC 560, 62 TC 341 and *Enterprise Safety Coaches v Customs and Excise Comrs* [1991] VATTR 74.

Value added tax

[2A.45] A trader is liable to default surcharge if he fails to furnish a VAT return, or pay any tax shown to be due thereon, in respect of a prescribed accounting period falling within a "surcharge period" notified to him in a surcharge liability notice.[1] For default surcharge in relation to VAT, see infra § **67.08**.

De Voil Indirect Tax Service V5.371–380.

[1] VATA 1994, s 59(1)–(3).

Verification, enquiries and interventions

Introduction

[2A.46] FA 2008 introduced wholesale reforms to the powers of HMRC to ensure compliance with the tax code. They came into effect on 1 April 2009 and applied initially to income tax, capital gains tax, corporation tax, VAT and overseas taxes in relation to states where mutual enforcement arrangements had been entered into with the United Kingdom.[1] FA 2009 extended the rules to all other UK taxes with effect from a date to be announced. It is worth noting that the new rules severely curtailed the rights of taxpayers and they have been widely criticised by the professional bodies.[2]

[1] FA 2008, Sch 36, para 63.
[2] It was reported in Taxation, 9 October 2008, that HMRC had thought that the new package of powers was balanced in that, whilst powers in respect of direct taxes had increased, powers had decreased in respect of VAT on the basis that HMRC now have to act "reasonably".

Self-assessment

[2A.47] The purpose of self-assessment is to save administrative costs by getting taxpayers to do the work (and incur the costs) of calculating their tax liabilities so that the revenue departments can deploy their resources on verifying the quantum of income, gains, etc declared by taxpayers.

In the past, Inland Revenue and HM Customs & Excise have adopted different approaches to verification. This is in part historical and in part due to the different nature of direct and indirect taxes.

Inland Revenue has historically relied on office based procedures—using information gathered from statutory returns (eg by banks, etc) to check whether income has arisen or transactions have taken place, and credibility testing as regards quantum (eg on profits of the self-employed).

By contrast, for VAT, Customs and Excise have historically relied on periodically checking accounting records at business premises. In recent years, assurance work has become more targeted. Individual traders are now targeted by risk factors and intelligence gathering. Thus, larger traders are visited more frequently and smaller traders hardly at all. Traders in high risk areas (eg cut and trim) are specifically targeted. Low risk traders may be controlled by office-based procedures (eg looking at the latest set of accounts). Some visiting arises from computer checks—the computer reckons that something funny has happened in a return submitted, the risk is manually assessed and a visit made or telephone enquiry made.

Verification, enquiries and interventions [2A.48]

Direct taxes work on the basis of a finality to a taxpayer's return which can only be upset by the raising of a formal "enquiry",[1] or, if the "enquiry window" has closed,[2] by way of a "discovery".[3] Thus, there are statutory procedures for determining tax liabilities and a time limit for opening up a taxpayer's return for investigation. A determination can only be set aside if a "discovery" is made. HMRC are, however, now experimenting with informal, non-statutory "interventions".[4]

There is no procedure for VAT that is equivalent to a Revenue enquiry, or a discovery. There is merely a three-year time limit for making assessments which is extended to 20 years in cases of dishonesty. Thus, verification is an on-going process but there is a time limit for recovering any understated tax discovered.

For tax credits there is a power to enquire into an entitlement after the tax year end[5] and the ability to revise a tax credit decision where there is a discovery.[6] HMRC also use their powers in various sections of the Act, concerned with decisions on tax credits, to 'enquire' into tax credit claims in-year.[7] These enquiries have become known as tax credit "examinations" to distinguish then from year-end enquiries although this term is not used anywhere in the Tax Credits Act 2002.

---

[1] TMA 1970, s 9A(1).
[2] TMA 1970, s 9A(2).
[3] TMA 1970, s 29; see infra, § **2A.60**.
[4] See infra, § **2A.48**.
[5] TCA 2002, s 19.
[6] TCA 2002, s 20.
[7] TCA 2002, ss 14(2), 15(2), 16(2), (3).

Enquiries under self-assessment (and tax credits)

General

[2A.48] It is of the essence of self-assessment that the taxpayer makes his own assessment and payment follows from the self-assessment, not from action by the Revenue.[1] Even where the taxpayer makes his return but leaves the Revenue to calculate the tax, this is, nevertheless, the taxpayer's self-assessment, not the Revenue's assessment. The corollary to self-assessment by the taxpayer is a statutory regime for the Revenue to test the veracity of self-assessments by a process of Revenue enquiries.

About one tax return in every one thousand returns submitted is selected at random for a Revenue enquiry. This selection process takes place before tax returns are sent to taxpayers with selection being based on stratified sampling applied to the previous year's returns. By this method, the Revenue centrally collects information on compliance by around 7,500 taxpayers, of which 3,200 are business cases and the remainder non-business cases. It is on this random sample that the Revenue estimate the extent of any tax loss, the frequency of overpayment and make judgements as to any alterations that may be appropriate in the wording of a tax return form for a future year.

Many more enquiries commence as a result of either information on the tax return or information from a third party. The Revenue staff manual instructs local districts to consider cases for enquiry by applying three criteria: cases that were pre-selected because of information held before the receipt of the return; cases that display features that have been identified by the local compliance officer; and cases where information indicates risk of error or evasion.

The HMRC staff manual instructs local districts to review every tax return, with a view to opening an enquiry, that is within certain specified categories.[2] The categories for which a review is required are: a non-compliant taxpayer; a high risk taxpayer; a taxpayer with large income or with capital gains; a taxpayer about whom certain third party information is held; "permanent review cases" and "the 500 highest risk cases".

An enquiry under self-assessment is a formal procedure that commences with written notification served on the taxpayer by the Revenue officer.[3] Such notification can only be given during the "enquiry window" which for the 2007–08 return, and returns for later years, starts with the date of receipt of the self-assessment return by the Revenue and ends 12 months after the date of receipt of the return.[4] Where, the return is submitted late, the "enquiry window" extends to the end of the calendar quarter twelve months after the date on which the return is made.[5]

A notice received after the end of the "enquiry window" is not a valid notice.[6] After the closing of the "enquiry window", the only way in which further tax can be collected is by the Revenue raising a "discovery assessment". The distinction between an enquiry and a discovery is that an enquiry can be commenced without any requirement to show cause; the latter requires the Revenue officer to be able to demonstrate that he "could not have been reasonably expected, on the basis of the information made available to him before that time, to be aware that [tax was under-charged]".[7]

An enquiry, which is a statutory procedure, must be distinguished from an informal "intervention". HMRC has, since 2006, piloted a scheme of contacting taxpayers and asking if they are willing to co-operate with either a "Real Time Health Check" or a "Real Time Records Review". Around 13,000 taxpayers were contacted in the initial pilot, of whom 9,000 agreed to participate.[8] It is important to appreciate that this procedure has no statutory basis.

Tax credits also have an enquiry window. The difference is that tax credits are awarded in the tax year (and, often, amended after the end of the year). Hence, an enquiry can be opened at any time after the submission of the claim and ends either with the date the self-assessment return becomes final[9] (if the claimant has been required to make such a return) or, in any other case, one year after the last date on which the claimant could have provided the information necessary to finalise his award[10] (see supra, § **A2.08**).

---

[1] See TMA 1970, s 9(1) inserted by FA 1994, s 179.
[2] Inland Revenue Manual—Enquiry Handbook, paras 58, 260–264 and 1025–1026.
[3] TMA 1970, ss 9A, 12AC and FA 1998, Sch 18, para 24, as amended by FA 2007, s 95 with effect from returns for tax year 2007–08 for income tax and corporation

tax and with effect from accounting periods ending after 31 March 2008 for corporation tax.
[4] Previously, there was a fixed period ending on the second 31 January after the end of the tax year (or later in cases of tax returns submitted late). However, this was perceived to discourage early submission of tax returns. In *Holly v Inspector of Taxes* [2000] STC (SCD) 50 the special commissioner held that a notice posted by the Revenue on Monday 25 January 1999 by second class post was not a valid notice of commencement of enquiry under TMA 1970, s 9A as it was not actually received until 3 February 1999. In *Wing Hung Lai v Bale* [1999] STC (SCD) 238, the special commissioner applied as the test the Royal Mail's code of practice. The notice was posted by the Revenue on Wednesday 27 January 1999 by second class post. Under the code of practice, delivery of that notice would be in the ordinary course of post on Monday 1 February. On this basis, the notice was held to be invalid. On the Revenue's interpretation of the 31 January filing date and the effect of the special commissioners' decisions quashing the notices of enquiry, see Inland Revenue Tax Bulletin Special Issue April 2000 reported in *Simon's Weekly Tax Intelligence* 2000, pp 682–687. In *Langham v Veltema* [2002] EWHC 2689 (Ch), [2002] STC 1557, the Court held that the Revenue had no power to raise an additional assessment after the enquiry window had closed, even though the valuation of a house that was the subject of an entry in the taxpayer's tax return had been agreed at a higher figure than had been declared in the return.
[5] TMA 1970, s 9A(2).
[6] As confirmed in the case of *Morris & Anor v Revenue and Customs Comrs* [2007] EWHC 1181 (Ch) where it was held that the six-year time limit for raising an assessment to income or capital gains tax in TMA 1970, s 34 did not apply to self-assessments or subsequent amendments.
[7] TMA 1970, s 29(5). This is discussed at supra, § **2A.47**. The meaning of the requirement that the officer could not have been "reasonably expected" has been considered by the Special Commissioners in *Osborne v Dickinson* [2004] STC (SCD) 104 and by the Court of Appeal in *Langham v Veltema* [2004] STC 544.
[8] HMRC published a 272 page evaluation report on interventions on 25 April 2007. It can be accessed at www.hmrc.gov.uk/new-interventions/index.htm
[9] TCA 2002, s 19(4)(*a*).
[10] TCA 2002, s 19(4)(*b*).

Conduct of the enquiry

[2A.49] On giving notice under TMA 1970, s 9A(1), s 11B(1) or s 12AC(1), a Revenue officer is empowered to require the taxpayer to produce to the officer "such documents as are in the taxpayer's possession or power and as the officer may reasonably require for the purpose of determining whether and, if so, the extent to which the return is incorrect or incomplete or the amendment is incorrect".[1] The notice from the Revenue must specify the time in which the taxpayer is required to produce the documents. The time given to the taxpayer, must not be less than 30 days.[2] This time limit is interpreted strictly. A notice that gave 30 days from the date it was posted by the Revenue was held to be invalid, as the taxpayer could not have had 30 days from the date of receipt of that notice.[3]

[2A.49] Tax administration – the mechanics

The taxpayer may provide copies rather than originals, subject to the right of the Revenue officer to require that the original be provided for his inspection.[4]

In conducting a tax credit enquiry HMRC may require the claimant to provide any information or evidence which HMRC consider they may need for the purposes of the enquiry[5] and they may require any person of a prescribed description to provide any information or evidence of a prescribed description which HMRC consider they may need for those purposes.[6] To date the only types of person so prescribed are employers and childcare providers.[7] The time given for response to such notices is to be not less than 30 days.[8]

A taxpayer is required to retain "all such records as may be requisite for the purpose of enabling him to make and deliver a correct and complete return".[9]

In the case of a person carrying on a trade, profession or business alone or in partnership, the nature of the records to be retained is specified more precisely as records of all amounts received and expended in the course of the trade, including sales and purchases that are made, with "all supporting documents".[10]

There are two alternative time limits specified in statute for which records are to be retained. For a taxpayer who carries on a trade, profession or business either alone or in partnership, records are to be retained until the fifth anniversary of the 31 January next following the year of assessment.[11] It is to be noted that this requirement extends to all records supporting such a taxpayer's tax return. Thus, an individual who carries on a trade is required to retain records supporting entries for his investment income, for example, for this lengthened period.

For all other taxpayers, the requirement to maintain records is until "the first anniversary of the 31 January next following the year of assessment".[12]

Where a claim was incorporated in a tax return, the provisions of TMA 1970, ss 9A, 12AC provide authority for a Revenue officer to make enquiries into that claim.

Where the taxpayer makes a claim which is not incorporated in a tax return, TMA 1970, Sch 1A, para 5 empowers a Revenue officer to enquire into the claim, in terms that echo the provisions of TMA 1970, s 9A.

Simon's Taxes A3.151.

---

[1] TMA 1970, s 19A(2) inserted by FA 1994, s 187.
[2] TMA 1970, s 19A(2A).
[3] *Self-assessed v Inspector of Taxes* [1999] STC (SCD) 253.
[4] TMA 1970, s 19A(3).
[5] TCA 2002, s 19(2)(*a*).
[6] TCA 2002, s 19(2)(*b*).
[7] Tax Credits (Claims and Notifications) Regulations 2002, SI 2002/2014, regs 30, 31.
[8] SI 2002/2014, reg 32.
[9] TMA 1970, s 12B(1)(*a*) inserted by FA 1994, Sch 19, para 3.
[10] TMA 1970, s 12B(3) inserted by FA 1994, Sch 19, para 3.

[11] TMA 1970, s 12B(2).
[12] TMA 1970, s 12B(2) inserted by FA 1994, Sch 19, para 3 and amended by FA 1995, s 105(2).

Notices requiring documents

[2A.50] TMA 1970, s 19A provided the Revenue, and in particular one of its officers dealing with an enquiry[1], with a power to make a written request for accounts, books and other information for the purpose of determining such an enquiry[2]. This power has since been subsumed within FA 2008, Sch 36, para 1 which is considered in more detail below. For a full discussion of the previous wording, see the 2008/09 edition of this work.

[1] TMA 1970, s 19A(1).
[2] TMA 1970, s 19A(2).

Completion of the enquiry

[2A.51] At the completion of an enquiry, the Revenue officer is required to issue a "closure notice" informing the taxpayer that he has completed his enquiry and stating his conclusions.[1] The closure notice must either state that no amendment of the return is required or makes an amendment of the return. The effect of a "closure notice" is, thus, to amend the taxpayer's self-assessment without any action by the taxpayer.

The taxpayer can then make an appeal against the amendment of his self-assessment.

For tax credits the enquiry is brought to a close by HMRC making a decision on entitlement.[2] The claimant has a right of appeal against such a decision.[3]

[1] TMA 1970, s 28A(1) as substituted by FA 2001, Sch 29, para 8. FA 2001 completely rewrites the procedure to be adopted at the end of an enquiry. It has effect for any enquiry that is in progress on 11 May 2001 and any enquiry commenced thereafter. For an enquiry into a partnership return or a claim not included in the return, parallel provisions are provided in TMA 1970, s 28B as inserted by FA 2001, Sch 29, para 9 and by TMA 1970, Sch 1A amended by FA 2001, Sch 29, para 10.
[2] TCA 2002, s 19(8).
[3] TCA 2002, s 38(1).

Taxpayer's right to end an enquiry

[2A.52] A taxpayer who has a tax return under enquiry, has the right to apply to the Commissioners for an order requiring that the enquiry be brought to a closure within a period of time specified by the taxpayer.[1] Statute[2] directs the Commissioners to direct the Revenue to complete their enquiry and issue a closure notice, within the time specified, unless there are reasonable grounds for not issuing the closure notice in the period specified.

In practice, the Special Commissioners have interpreted their powers rather more widely than the wording of statute may suggest. In *Jade Palace v Revenue and Customs Comrs*[3] an enquiry had been open for four years. The Special Commissioner said:[4]

> The period necessary will vary with the circumstances and complexity of the case and the length of the enquiry. The longer the period of the enquiry, the greater the burden on the Revenue to show reasonable grounds as to why a time for closure should not be specified.

The Commissioner directed the Revenue to issue a closure notice within four months.

Similarly in *Eclipse Film Partners No 35 LLP v R & C Commrs*[5], an enquiry into a limited liability partnership which had entered into certain transactions in relation to the licensing and distribution of film rights, the Special Commissioner held that what was required of a HMRC officer was that he should have reached a point in his enquiry where it was reasonable for him to make an informed judgment as to the matter in question, so that, exercising that judgment he could then state his conclusions and duly make any amendments to the return. Although the Special Commissioner considered that the officer had reached that point in that case, he gave HMRC a three-month 'grace period' to complete their enquiry and issue a closure notice.

In *Doyle v Revenue and Customs Comrs*,[6] however, the taxpayer claimed, inter alia, that the Revenue's failure to provide a closure notice was in conflict with the principle of proportionality in Human Rights legislation.[7] This was rejected by the Special Commissioner.

A taxpayer can apply to the Commissioners and the Commissioners have the ability to require an enquiry to be brought to a close irrespective of the nature of the enquiry. In *Revenue and Customs Comrs v Vodafone 2*[8] the Revenue enquired into the possibility of the controlled foreign company legislation[9] giving a tax liability on the UK taxpayer company that was not stated on the company self-assessment tax return. From an early stage it seemed likely that a reference to the European Court would be required to determine the case, as the taxpayer company considered that the UK legislation was not in accordance with European Law. The Court of Appeal held that the Special Commissioners had acted properly in issuing a direction requiring the Revenue to close the enquiry.

After reference to the ECJ by the Special Commissioners in *Vodafone 2*, the ECJ gave judgment in the reference in the case of *Cadbury Schweppes plc v Revenue & Customs Commrs*[10] which also concerned the compatibility of the controlled foreign company legislation with EC law. The judgment was to the effect that the legislation was in fact not compatible and the ECJ asked the Special Commissioners whether they wished to withdraw their reference and direct the Revenue to issue a closure notice. The Commissioners refused to withdraw their reference and on the taxpayer's appeal to the High Court, Evans-Lombe J[11] held that as the legislation was incompatible with EC law and would have to be disapplied, the Revenue's enquiry into the tax return for the relevant period had no legitimate purpose and should be closed at once. This decision, however, was overturned by the Court of Appeal.[12]

---

[1] TMA 1970, s 28A(4) for an enquiry into an individual's or a trustee's tax return; TMA 1970, s 28B(7) for an enquiry into a partnership tax return; FA 1998, Sch 18 para 33(1) for an enquiry into a company tax return.
[2] TMA 1970, s 28A(6) for an enquiry into an individual's or a trustee's tax return; TMA 1970, s 28B(4) for an enquiry into a partnership tax return; FA 1998, Sch 18 para 33(3) for an enquiry into a company tax return.
[3] [2006] STC (SCD) 419.
[4] [2005] STC (SCD) 419 paras 42 & 43 at 424g.
[5] (2009) Sp C 736.
[6] [2005] STC (SCD) 775.
[7] Under Article 1 of the First Protocol of the Convention for the Protection of Human Rights and Fundamental Freedoms 1950 (see supra, § **1.16**). [2005] STC (SCD) 775 at 778h.
[8] [2006] EWCA Civ 1132, [2006] STC 1530, CA.
[9] TA 1988, ss 747–756, see infra, §§ **35.64–35.74**.
[10] (Case C-196/04).
[11] *Vodafone 2 v Revenue & Customs Commrs* [2008] EWHC 1569 (Ch).
[12] [2009] EWCA Civ 446: at the time of writing, it is widely understood that the company will make a further appeal to the House of Lords.

Information powers

Power to enter premises

[2A.53] VAT is a self-assessed tax and it is therefore not surprising that the legislation makes provision for the periodic inspection of traders' records and the verification of returns. The normal method of audit is known as an "assurance visit".

FA 2008, Sch 36 contains harmonised rules dealing with HMRC's right to information.

Taxpayer notices

[2A.54] Paragraph 1 merges the provisions that were formally within TMA 1970, ss 19A and 20 (and in FA 1998, Sch 18 for corporation tax) and relates to information that can be demanded from taxpayers. In short, it provides that an HMRC officer may give a written notice that requires the recipient to provide information or produce a document provided that the information or document is reasonably required by the officer for the purpose of checking the recipient's tax position.

[2A.54] Tax administration – the mechanics

It will be seen that the provision of information extends beyond merely forwarding an existing document but could go to a person's reasons for entering into a particular transaction.

One principal change under the provisions is that HMRC can now request this information before a taxpayer has even submitted the relevant tax return. In fact, the rules cover a person's past, present and future tax liabilities.[1]

The rules also cover information and documents that are reasonably required to check a person's penalties, claims, elections, applications and notices relating to any tax covered by the Schedule.[2]

---

[1] FA 2008, Sch 36, para 64(1)(a).
[2] FA 2008, Sch 36, para 64(1)(b),(c).

Interaction with self-assessment

[2A.55] In the case of income tax, capital gains tax and corporation tax, there are some additional procedural hurdles that HMRC have to overcome concerning the timing of taxpayer notices if a return for the period under review has been submitted.

Provided that the return can still be subject to a valid enquiry (see § **2A.48** above), then a taxpayer notice may not be given unless an enquiry has actually been opened.[1] Once the enquiry window has expired (or any enquiry that had been opened has been closed) a taxpayer notice may not be given unless the HMRC officer has reason to suspect that tax has been underpaid.[2] The statutory wording does not go so far as the restriction imposed under the previous legislation in TMA 1970, s 20(1) by Stanley Burnton J in R *(on the application of Johnson and others) v Branigan (HMIT)*[3] at paras 14 and 15 where the Judge held that an information notice (outside the scope of a formal enquiry) could not be issued unless there was "a sensible or reasonable possibility" of it leading to a discovery assessment. In other words, it would not have been sufficient to show that tax had been underpaid but that the other requirements for a discovery assessment (being either evidence of negligent or fraudulent conduct or an insufficiency of disclosure of information on or in connection with the return and the absence of the "prevailing practice" defence) were met. It is suggested that the test laid down by Stanley Burnton J would continue to apply as it would be most improper for a taxpayer to be required to provide information once the enquiry window had passed in circumstances where it was not realistic to assume that a discovery assessment to follow.

---

[1] FA 2008, Sch 36, para 21(1),(2),(4),(5).
[2] FA 2008, Sch 36, para 21(6).
[3] [2006] EWHC 885 (Admin).

Appeals

[2A.56] Taxpayers can appeal to the First-tier Tribunal against taxpayer notices, except in cases where the request is for the provision of any information or any document that forms part of the taxpayer's statutory records.[1] In cases where HMRC do not wish taxpayers to appeal against taxpayer notices, they can arrange for the taxpayer notice to be pre-approved by the Tribunal.[2]

The approach to be taken by the First-tier Tribunal is likely to follow that taken by the Special Commissioners and the High Court in cases concerning the provision of documents under the former statutory powers in TMA1970, s 19A when considering whether something is "reasonably required" by the officer. In the case of *Sokoya v Revenue & Customs Commrs*[3], the High Court upheld a s 19A notice pointing out that the Revenue's ability to enquire into a tax return was not restricted to positive entries made by the taxpayer; if there was an affirmation of nil returns from the taxpayer, it was appropriate for the Revenue to enquire into whether the tax return was complete and accurate.

It is, however, essential for the notice to be correctly drawn up by HMRC. In *Jacques v R & C Comrs*[4] the Special Commissioner set aside a notice as invalid as too much uncertainty was introduced by the wrong date and misdescription.

The conclusion to be drawn from the case law to date is that a taxpayer notice will be upheld wherever the document is reasonably required for the purpose of enquiring into the return, irrespective of any legal protection the document may otherwise have. In *Guyer v Walton*[5] the Special Commissioner said:[6] 'The provisions of section 19A override the contractual duty of confidence'. However, in *Spring Salmon and Seafood Ltd v R & C Comrs*[7] the Special Commissioner amended the Revenue notice, setting aside the requests for trading and loan accounts as they were not relevant to the question of the commercial bona fides of the transaction under which the company acquired the trade and assets of the partnership. The request for correspondence between the company and accountants, auditors and solicitors were also set aside as they were subject to legal professional privilege. Otherwise the documents gave rise to a reasonable concern that the material transactions were between related parties and the notice was confirmed, in respect of these particular documents. In his decision, the Special Commissioner, Julian Ghosh said:[8]

> In relation to the requirement of reasonableness, this has two facets. Firstly, the documents and information specified in a notice of enquiry must be 'reasonable' in that to obtain them must not be too onerous for the company subject to the notice of enquiry. Secondly, the documents and information must be 'reasonable' in a different way, namely that it must be 'reasonable' for the Commissioners to consider them 'relevant' to the company's tax affairs. It is important to remember that this hearing is not to determine the substantive points as to liability in respect of particular assessments. Rather it is to determine whether the Revenue is entitled to sight of documents or information relevant to the appellant's corporation tax liability.

In *R (Murat) v IRC*[9] the High Court upheld the decision of the Special Commissioner[10] in refusing to quash a Revenue notice requiring production of documents. The Special Commissioner had made a thorough review of the scope of s 19A. The case was an application by an accountant in practice, seeking an order from the Commissioners setting aside a Revenue notice requiring production of certain documents in respect of his practice. The decision gives rulings on five different matters:

[2A.56] Tax administration – the mechanics

(a) a section 19A notice can not only require existing documents to be produced but can also request the preparation of documents, such as income and expenditure accounts or balance sheets and the furnishing of other particulars which may not be contained in existing documents;
(b) a section 19A notice can require production of records for which there is no statutory duty to retain for a six-year period;[11]
(c) a section 19A notice requires production of such documents "as the officer may reasonably require"[12]; it is not open to the taxpayer to substitute other documents;
(d) it was reasonable for the inspector, in this case, to require production of the taxpayers personal bank and building society accounts[13] and the undesignated clients account kept in the practice;
(e) it was reasonable for the inspector to require the accountant to construct a balance sheet, even though he had not prepared one as part of his annual accounts.

---

[1] FA 2008, Sch 36, para 29(1), (2); para 62 defines statutory records as those records required to be kept under a statutory authority so far as they relate to a person's business.
[2] Paras 3, 29(3).
[3] [2008] EWHC 2132 (Ch).
[4] [2006] STC (SCD) 40.
[5] [2001] STC (SCD) 75.
[6] [2001] STC (SCD) 75 at 82d.
[7] [2005] STC (SCD) 830.
[8] Para 28 at 841d.
[9] [2005] STC 184.
[10] Sub-nom *Accountant v Inspector of Taxes* [2000] STC (SCD) 522. The same taxpayer also argued against production of documents: *Murat v Ornoch* [2004] STC (SCD) 115.
[11] Listed in TMA 1970, s 12B.
[12] TMA 1970, s 19A(2)(*a*).
[13] In Taxation 17 January 2002, p 361 Antony Bassett reports a case where the General Commissioners quashed a Revenue request for sight of taxpayer's private bank statements on the basis that the Revenue officer had not demonstrated that they were reasonably required for the enquiry into this particular taxpayer's tax return.

Third-party notices

[2A.57] Similar powers are available to HMRC to require persons (third parties) to provide information or documents concerning other persons' tax position.[1] Such notices cannot be issued without the consent of the Tribunal.[2] Generally, the taxpayer should be sent a copy of any third-party notice but this requirement can be dispensed with by the Tribunal provided if the officer has reasonable grounds for believing that providing a copy might prejudice the assessment or collection of tax.[3]

Paragraph 5 permits HMRC to request third parties to provide information or documents in cases where the HMRC officer does not know the individual identity of the taxpayer concerned. Such requests may not be made without the prior approval of the First-tier Tribunal.[4]

Such notices may be appealed against on the grounds that it would be unduly onerous to comply with the notice.[5] However, third parties (in respect of known taxpayers cannot use this ground in cases where the document or information forms part of the taxpayer's statutory records or where the tribunal has pre-approved the notice.[6]

Simon's Taxes A5.119.

[1] FA 2008, Sch 36, para 2.
[2] FA 2008, Sch 36, para 3(1).
[3] FA 2008, Sch 36, para 4.
[4] FA 2008, Sch 36, para 5(3).
[5] FA 2008, Sch 36, paras 30(1), 31.
[6] FA 2008, Sch 36, para 30(2), (3).

Inspection powers from 1 April 2009

[2A.58] The new inspection powers are also set out in FA 2008, Sch 36, which rewrites (and extends) HMRC's powers to visit premises. Although the legislation refers to "business premises", that is defined as anywhere that an HMRC officer has reason to believe are being used in connection with the carrying on of a person's business.[1] The only real exception is premises used solely as a dwelling,[2] but it is unclear the extent to which home offices will be subject to inspections. It should be remembered, though, that human rights law will often protect taxpayers from inspections at home, even if they are carrying on a business there.[3] However, HMRC will not necessarily respect this until the matter is challenged in the courts.

Care needs to be taken concerning the timing of visits. In theory, HMRC can severely prejudice taxpayers who exercise their few rights in this regard. It should be noted, however, that taxpayers do not have the right to appeal against any proposed or actual inspection: where an inspection is unlawful, judicial review is their only remedy (perhaps with an emergency injunction in the meantime). Inspections can take place:

- at any reasonable time with at least seven days' notice; or
- at any time by agreement; or
- at any time if the inspection is carried out by or with the agreement of an authorised officer.[4]

They need not be pre-sanctioned by the First-tier Tribunal. However, an authorised officer can seek (or agree that a more junior officer may seek) pre-approval of the tribunal for the inspection.[5] Where an inspection has been pre-approved, penalties for obstruction can be imposed.[6]

Under FA 2009, amendments have been made so that a number of third parties may be inspected. However, the most extensive new power is a right to inspect premises – theoretically any type of premises – of any person to check another person's valuation. Thus, if a person buys an asset from an individual and the valuation of the asset was relevant to the CGT liability of that individual (or any other person, perhaps the person from whom the individual acquired the asset), HMRC may claim the right to visit the purchaser's premises and bring along a valuation expert.[7]

---

[1] FA 2008, Sch 36, para 10.
[2] FA 2008, Sch 36. para 10(2).
[3] See 'Inspections at Home-Offices under the new Schedule 36 Powers: What would the European Court of Human Rights say?', by Tom Wesel, *The Personal Tax Planning Review* [2009] Vol 12, Issue 3.
[4] FA 2008, Sch 36, para 12.
[5] FA 2008, Sch 36, para 13.
[6] See **2A.59** below.
[7] FA 2008, Sch 36, para 12A.

Penalties

[2A.59] Penalties can be imposed for failures to respond to taxpayer and third-party notices. They are fixed penalties of £300 and daily penalties of up to £60.[1] Similar penalties can be charged under those provisions against any person who deliberately obstructs an officer in the course of an inspection that has been pre-approved by the tribunal.

Penalties can be appealed against to the First-tier Tribunal[2] and a defence of reasonable excuse exists.[3]

---

[1] FA 2008, Sch 36, paras 39–40.
[2] FA 2008, Sch 36, para 47.
[3] FA 2008, Sch 36, para 45.

Assessments

Introduction

[2A.60] Prior to April 2005 there was a difference between the powers granted to the two separate revenue departments to make assessments. The difference may be explained on historical grounds.

The former Inland Revenue historically relied on a six-year time limit for assessment with a system of civil penalties for fraud, wilful default or neglect (later changed to fraudulent and/or negligent conduct). This changed with self-assessment. An assessment may now be made on any grounds if the enquiry is opened up within 12 months. In other cases, an assessment may normally be made only if fraudulent or negligent conduct is proved. Although some statutory offences have always existed, they were less than satisfactory—and seldom used—reliance being placed on the common law offence of cheating the public revenue. A new offence was introduced in FA 2000 to fill the most obvious gap.

Customs and Excise, on the other hand, traditionally relied on criminal prosecution. Prior to 1985, all transgressions were offences and a penalty thus arose only if there was a criminal prosecution. This situation changed following the Keith Committee report. Most of the offences were repealed and replaced by civil penalties. There is now a carefully graduated response to different levels of default:

(1) assessment of tax and interest in the case of a voluntary disclosure;
(2) assessment of tax, interest and different levels of penalty for dishonesty, one-off large misdeclaration, repeated misdeclaration;
(3) assessment of tax and interest and penalty imposed by the courts for various classes of dishonest conduct.

Since 2002 confiscation powers[1] have been available to the Assets Recovery Agency to recover the proceeds of crime. In this work, the Assets Recovery Agency works closely with HMRC to attempt to collect a liability to tax that may have arisen as a consequence of, or a corollary to, the criminal activity.

The techniques of investigation have also traditionally differed. Until the mid-1970's, the Inland Revenue approach was largely geared to the preparation of capital statements. Since then, a much greater reliance has been placed on mark-up computations and similar techniques for calculating "off sales" of the self-employed and thereby estimate undisclosed income. Customs and Excise have always placed reliance on mark-up computations and similar techniques.

The approach of investigators has also differed. The Revenue's big stick has always been a "Hansard" interview. The Customs and Excise equivalent has been an interview under caution under similar rules (actually an adaptation of the same rules) to those used by the police.[2]

---

[1] Proceeds of Crime Act 2002: see supra, § **2.33**.
[2] On the necessity for a "police caution" when investigating evasion of direct taxes, see supra, § **2.32**.

Revenue assessments

Minor discrepancies in assessments

[2A.61] TMA 1970, s 114(1) provides that an assessment (or determination, warrant or other proceeding) is not void "for want of form, . . .by reason of a mistake, defect or omission therein, if the same is in substance and in effect in conformity with or according to the intent and meaning of the Taxes Acts". In particular, an assessment is declared not to be affected "by reason of a mistake therein as to (i) the name of a person liable or (ii) the description of any profits or property or (iii) the amount of the tax charged or by reason of any variance between the notice and the assessment or determination".[1]

In the case of *Pipe & Ors v R & C Comrs*² the High Court held that continuing daily penalties imposed for failure to deliver tax returns on time were lawful notwithstanding the dates specified in the penalty notices did not fall within the correct period authorised by a direction given by the General Commissioners. It was further held that a mistake about dates of this type was a 'variance' for the purposes of the section. However, the court has proved reluctant to uphold an assessment containing a significant error. In *Baylis v Gregory*,³ the Court of Appeal held that an assessment issued for the wrong year could not be saved by TMA 1970, s 114, even though the taxpayer was not and could not have been misled. In *IRC v McGuckian*,⁴ the Northern Ireland Court of Appeal refused to allow the alteration of an assessment to correct a misapprehension under which the inspector had suffered, on the grounds that the inspector had not made a mistake since he had intended to do what he had, in fact, done.

1   TMA 1970, s 114(2).
2   [2008] EWHC 646 (Ch).
3   [1987] STC 297.
4   [1994] STC 888, NI CA.

'Discovery' assessment

[2A.62] Under self-assessment, there are formal procedures for an enquiry to be raised into a tax return.¹ Such an enquiry can lead to an amendment of the self-assessment,² which creates a legally enforceable debt for an additional payment of tax, where the amendment is to increase the tax liability. However, an enquiry cannot be commenced more than 12 months after the due date for submission of a return, unless the return was submitted late, in which case the "enquiry window" closes 12 months after the end of the calendar quarter in which the return was actually submitted.³ If an enquiry is not raised within the specified time limit, the Revenue are not able to collect any tax that is subsequently found to be due unless the conditions for a "discovery" are fulfilled.⁴

If a Revenue officer "discovers" that profits have not been assessed or the assessment has become insufficient or that excessive relief has been given, he may make an assessment.⁵ Where the taxpayer has made a self-assessment return, no "discovery assessment" can be made unless one of two alternative conditions is fulfilled. The first alternative is that the self-assessment charges too little tax (or overstates a claim) as a result of fraudulent or negligent conduct by the taxpayer or a person acting on his behalf.⁶ The second alternative is that at the end of the period allowed for an enquiry (or the completion of the enquiry, where there was one) the Revenue officer could not have been reasonably expected, on the basis of information supplied to him, to be aware that the self-assessment charges too little tax (or overstates a claim).⁷ This assessment is subject to the same time rules as original assessments. The term discovery has been given a wide ambit by the courts; the words are apt to cover any case in which for any reason it newly appears that the taxpayer has been undercharged.⁸ So an assessment may be made where HMRC decide that a company should be treated as a dealing company rather than an investment company[9] or where a new inspector takes a different view of the law from his predecessor[10] or to correct an arithmetical error in the computation. Since the validity of the new assessment is a question of law, HMRC may justify its validity even though it refers to an incorrect provision.[11] It is open to HMRC to issue a second (additional) assessment rather than seeking an increase in the first on appeal.[12]

For a "discovery assessment" to be valid, the circumstances must be such that the Revenue officer "could not have been reasonably expected, on the basis of the information made available to him before that time, to be aware that [tax was under-charged]".[13] In *Osborne v Dickinson*,[14] the taxpayer had sent all the details of a disposal to the Revenue, with a request for the market value at acquisition to be agreed.[15] The Revenue agreed the value but the taxpayer then failed to submit a tax return reporting the gain. The Special Commissioners held that the provision of all the information on the sale to the Revenue officer dealing with the agreement of market value did not estop the officer dealing with compliance (or lack of it) raising a "discovery assessment". In *Langham v Veltema*,[16] the taxpayer's family company transferred a house to him. The transfer was duly reported by the company on its annual return of benefits supplied[17] and reported by the taxpayer on his annual tax return. On both documents, the value was given as £100,000, in accordance with advice received from a firm of chartered surveyors. After the closure of the tax return "enquiry window",[18] the Inspector was informed by the District Valuer that he considered the value to be £160,000. The value was ultimately agreed at £145,000. The Inspector raised a "discovery assessment". The Court of Appeal upheld the assessment. Auld LJ said:[19]

> Applying the proper statutory test, there was no basis upon which [the General Commissioners] could have found that the Inspector ought reasonably to have been aware . . . of the insufficiency of the [self-]assessment on the basis of the information contained in Mr Veltema's tax return or, even if relevant, in the P11D Form . . . There was nothing to suggest that the information was unreliable.

Where an assessment is made under these powers, and is not to make good a loss due to fraudulent or negligent conduct, a new rule applies to claims by the taxpayer. The taxpayer may make any claim for further relief for that year within one year from the end of the chargeable period in which an assessment is made.[20]

The *Veltema* case puts into sharp focus a problem that has been identified but not fully explored since the advent of self-assessment. How much, and what information is it necessary to display on a self-assessment tax return in order to achieve finality at the end of the enquiry window and avoid the possibility of a discovery assessment many years later? In response to questions raised by professional bodies, the former Inland Revenue issued a guidance note on this topic.[21] In the light of the potential areas of dispute on relevance of the settlement code to remuneration and dividends paid by a company owned by husband and wife, or shares of profit enjoyed by a husband and wife partnership, the Revenue statement in the section entitled: "Taking a different view" is particularly useful:

> It is open to a taxpayer properly advised to adopt a different view of the law from that published as the Revenue's view. To protect against a discovery assessment after

the enquiry period the Return would have to indicate that a different view had been adopted. This might be done by entering in the Additional Information space comments to the effect that they have not followed Revenue guidance on the issue or that no adjustment has been made to take account of it. This would offer an opportunity to the Revenue to take up the return for enquiry. In the Revenue's view it is not necessary for the taxpayer to provide with the Return enough information for the inspector to be able to quantify any resulting under assessment of tax.

A current example of this is the Revenue's guidance on Settlements Legislation in s 660A. The guidance on discovery is that taxpayers should enter in the Additional Information space: . . . 'Revenue guidance indicates that s 660A may apply. No adjustment has been made'.

The Veltema judgment does not require the provision of enough information to quantify the effect on the self-assessment.

Provided the point at issue is clearly identified and the stance adopted is not wholly unreasonable, the existence of an under-assessment or insufficiency is demonstrated by the statement that a different view of the law was followed. It is not necessary to provide all the documentation that the inspector might need to quantify that insufficiency if he chose to enquire into the Return. In these circumstances the taxpayer achieves finality if no enquiry is opened within the twelve-month time limit.

The *Veltema* judgment was considered by a Special Commissioner, Charles Hellier, in a case in 2008.[22] That case highlighted the absurdity of adopting Auld LJ's *obiter* comments literally because the Judge seemed to require tax returns to highlight their own inadequacies if they are to be protected from discovery assessments. Mr Hellier has suggested that the return make it clear that the return is incorrect on the balance of probabilities. It is the authors' view that this is still not the correct test and, it is expected, that the Courts will be required to focus their attention on this in due course.[23]

The burden of proving entitlement to raise a discovery assessment falls on HMRC.[24] In practice, however, HMRC do not always follow the procedures to ensure that the statutory conditions are met.[25]

If the lawfulness of a discovery assessment is to be challenged, it must be by way of appeal to the Commissioners subject to the normal time limits.[26] It is submitted that an appeal against the validity of a discovery assessment should not, in the majority of cases, be considered in isolation of the technical issues. In the interests of justice, administrative convenience and saving costs, one single hearing dealing with both the validity of a discovery assessment and its technical merits will usually be the preferred option. See *Hankinson v HMRC* (2007) SpC 619 and *Walker v R & C Commissioners* (2007) SpC 626.

Where a taxpayer had made a return on what was then the generally prevailing basis, a discovery assessment may not be made if it subsequently turns out that that basis was incorrect.[27] However, it is for the taxpayer to prove the prevailing nature of the previous basis.[28]

Once the lawfulness of a discovery assessment has been proven by HMRC, the burden of discharging the assessment reverts to the taxpayer as is the case with most other appeals against assessments.[29]

Where a person's income tax liability is revised and the Board, as a consequence, have reasonable grounds for believing that a conclusive decision relating to the entitlement to tax credit is not correct, HMRC may revise that decision under discovery powers in the Tax Credits Act.[30] A revised decision can only be made if it is too late to enquire into the award or it is less than 12 months since the income tax liability was revised.[31] Similarly HMRC may revise a conclusive decision where they have reasonable grounds for believing that it is not correct and it is attributable to the fraud or neglect of any person (either the claimant or any person acting for them).[32] A revised decision in the latter case can only be made if it is too late to enquire into the award or it is less than five years after the end of the tax year to which the conclusive decision relates.[33]

There is a similar code for corporation tax[34] and Stamp Duty Land Tax.[35]

[1] TMA 1970, s 9A: see supra, § **2A.30**.
[2] TMA 1970, s 9A(2).
[3] TMA 1970, ss 28A(7), 59B(1).
[4] TMA 1970, s 29.
[5] See TMA 1970, s 29(3) inserted by FA 1994, ss 191, 199 replacing the old version of s 29, with effect from 1996–97 for income tax and capital gains tax.
[6] TMA 1970, s 29(4).
[7] TMA 1970, s 29(5).
[8] Per Viscount Simonds in *Cenlon Finance Co Ltd v Ellwood* [1962] 1 All ER 854 at 859, 40 TC 176 at 204.
[9] *Jones v Mason Investments (Luton) Ltd* (1966) 43 TC 570, [1967] BTR 75 JGM.
[10] *Parkin v Cattell* (1971) 48 TC 462.
[11] *Vickerman v Personal Representatives of Mason* [1984] STC 231.
[12] *Duchy Maternity Ltd v Hodgson* [1985] STC 764.
[13] TMA 1970, s 29(5)
[14] [2004] STC (SCD) 104.
[15] On Revenue form 34CG.
[16] [2004] EWCA Civ 193, [2004] STC 544.
[17] On Revenue form P11D.
[18] See TMA 1970, s 9A(2)(*a*) considered supra, § **2A.48**.
[19] [2004] EWCA Civ 193, [2004] STC 544 at para 555d.
[20] TMA 1970, ss 43A, 43B added by FA 1989, s 150: it appears that this does not apply when the assessment is an original (but late) assessment as distinct from an additional assessment.
[21] Inland Revenue Guidance Note 24, December 2004: *Discovery following the Veltema Judgment, Simon's Weekly Tax Intelligence* 2005, pp 12–19.
[22] *Corbally-Stourton v HMRC* (2008) SpC 692.
[23] See, for example, 'Discovery assessments – the consequences of the decision in Corbally-Stourton', *The Personal Tax Planning Review* [2009] Vol.12(3), pp45–67.
[24] *HMRC v Household Estate Agents Limited*[2007] EWHC 1684 (Ch).
[25] See for example the Special Commissioners' decision in *Jones v Garnett*.
[26] TMA 1970, s 29(8).
[27] TMA 1970, s 29(2)
[28] *HMRC v Household Estate Agents Limited*.
[29] TMA 1970, s 50(6). See also *Momin & Others v R & C Commissioners* [2007] EWHC 1400 (Ch). In *Hurley v Taylor*, the High Court held that the taxpayer

[2A.62] Tax administration – the mechanics

nevertheless loses the right to be heard first in such circumstances. However, it is respectfully submitted that that conclusion will not always be right particularly in cases where the evidence needed by the taxpayer to deal with the substantive issue can be separated from the evidence required by HMRC to support the discovery assessment itself.

[30] TCA 2002, s 20(1).
[31] TCA 2002, s 20(3).
[32] TCA 2002, s 20(4).
[33] TCA 2002, s 20(5).
[34] FA 1998, Sch 18, Paras 41–45.
[35] FA 2003, Sch 10, Paras 28–30.

Estimated assessments

[2A.63] Prior to self-assessment, it was commonplace for a Revenue inspector to issue an estimated assessment, this being the Revenue's interpretation of the statutory requirement on an inspector "to make an assessment to tax to the best of his judgement".[1] Although considerably less frequent, estimated assessments continue to have a place in the regime under self-assessment. If a Revenue officer discovers that tax has been lost, statute instructs the officer or HMRC to make an assessment in the amount "which ought in his or their opinion to be charged in order to make good to the Crown the loss of tax".[2]

The inspector may make alternative assessments but not cumulative ones. When alternative assessments have become final the Revenue may not recover both amounts due by way of tax.[3] This is illustrated by *IRC v Wilkinson*,[4] where alternative assessments to CGT and income tax under TA 1988, s 776 were made in respect of the same transaction.

[1] TMA 1970, s 29(1)(*b*) (old version).
[2] TMA 1970, s 29(1) (new version).
[3] TMA 1970, s 32.
[4] [1992] STC 454, CA.

PAYE—Determination

[2A.64] Where an employer has not accounted to the Revenue for PAYE, "the inspector may determine the amount of PAYE due to the best of his judgement, and shall serve notice of his determination on the employer".[1] Regulation 49(7) provides that this determination is subject to the same statutory provisions for enforcement as applied to an assessment. This has the effect that interest (supra, § **2A.32**) and penalties are payable, as well as allowing distraint by the collector.

[1] IT (Employments) Regulations 1993, SI 1993/744, reg 49(2).

Discharging an assessment

[2A.65] An assessment once made may be disturbed only by appeal, by judicial review,[1] or by agreement pending appeal[2] and so not by the unilateral

Assessments [2A.65]

act of the inspector.[3] The House of Lords held in *Scorer v Olin Energy Systems Ltd*[4] that, for this purpose, an inspector is taken to have agreed to something if he accepts a computation put forward by the taxpayer, since he must have directed his mind to it. The Revenue view on the effect of the decision in this case is given in an HMRC Statement of Practice.[5] In order for section 54 to have effect, the Revenue and the taxpayer must "come to an agreement". There is no agreement if the taxpayer remains silent and is content not to correct the Revenue's obvious mistake.[6]

Where the agreement is based on an assumption that the statements made by the taxpayer, eg as to trading profits, are correct and it later emerges that those statements were not correct there is nothing in TMA 1970, s 54 to prevent the inspector from making a further assessment to correct the mistake.[7] The agreement used to settle an appeal has been described as "a binding legal contract or something close thereto".[8] The ordinary law of contract applies to such an agreement.[9] It follows that if the document recording the contract does not do so accurately it may be rectified.[10] In order for an appeal to be settled by agreement, it is necessary for one party to make an offer and for the other party to accept that offer.

The effect of an agreement under s 54 can be to stop the taxpayer subsequently making an error or mistake claim under TMA 1970, s 33.[11] However, an amendment of a self assessment is not an "agreement under s 54" and does not preclude an error or mistake claim under s 33.[12]

For tax credits it is possible for an award to be revised in favour of the claimant if it is incorrect by reason of an official error.[13] Regulations define official error for tax credit purposes.[14]

Simon's Taxes Divisions A4.2, 4.3.

---

1 An assessment may be saved from invalidity despite errors by TMA 1970, s 114; see *Fleming v London Produce Co Ltd* [1968] 2 All ER 975, 44 TC 582 and *Baylis v Gregory* [1987] STC 297; in the latter case the Court of Appeal held that an assessment issued for the wrong year could not be saved by s 114 even though the taxpayer was not and could not have been misled. The conclusion seems quite ritualistic. See also *IRC v McGuckian* [1994] STC 888, NI CA when again a court refused to allow the alteration of an assessment when the inspector had been under a misapprehension but had not made a mistake since he had intended to do what he had done.
2 TMA 1970, s 54; on extent of agreement see *Tod v South Essex Motors (Basildon) Ltd* [1988] STC 392. On authority of an accountant to agree on behalf of a taxpayer, see *IRC v West* [1991] STC 357n, CA. On the consequence of an agreement prohibiting a further Revenue assessment, see *Newidgets Manufacturing Ltd v Jones* [1999] STC (SCD) 193.
3 *Baylis v Gregory* [1987] STC 297.
4 [1985] STC 218.
5 Statement of practice SP 8/91.
6 *Schuldenfrei v Hilton* [1999] STC 821.
7 *Gray v Matheson* [1993] STC 178. *Scorer v Olin* was quite different in that there the taxpayer had made a sufficient claim that it was entitled to set off accumulated losses against the income of an engineering business and it was the assessment based

175

[2A.65] Tax administration – the mechanics

on those accounts which was the subject matter of the agreement—per Vinelott J at 187c.
8   Neuberger J in *Schuldenfrei v Hilton* [1998] STC 404 at 420d. In his judgment, Neuberger J was reviewing a decision previously given in the High Court. In this part of his review, Neuberger J considers what he regards as a "more limited view" of the previous decision. The tenor of his comments would seem to indicate that Neuberger J considers that an agreement under s 54 has all the characteristics of a contract.
9   Per Popplewell J in *R v Inspector of Taxes, ex p Bass Holdings Ltd* [1993] STC 122 at 132.
10 *R v Inspector of Taxes, ex p Bass Holdings Ltd* [1993] STC 122 (group relief to be allowed once not twice).
11 *Eagerpath Ltd v Edwards* [2000] STC 26, CA.
12 *Wall v IRC* [2002] STC (SCD) 122.
13 TCA 2002, s 21.
14 Tax Credit (Official Error) Regulations 2003, SI 2003/692.

Time limit for a Revenue assessment

[2A.66] The normal time limit for making an assessment is six years from the end of the year to which it relates;[1] so an assessment for 2007–08 must be made by 5 April 2014. Any objection to an assessment on the basis that the time limit has expired must be made by way of appeal against the assessment and so, presumably, not by way of judicial review.[2] Claims for repayment of tax where there is no dispute or doubt about the facts and the overpayment is due to Revenue error are allowed, by concession, outside the six year period.[3]

The normal time limit for raising an assessment is set aside in cases of fraudulent or negligent conduct. The assessment may then be made at any time not later than 20 years from the end of the period to which it relates.[4] There is express provision for giving effect to any reliefs or allowances which the taxpayers could have claimed.[5] The effect of this is that a relief which would not normally be time-barred can be claimed against an assessment raised to collect tax on a default assessment.

The insistence upon an element of "conduct" raises the question whether omissions will suffice to trigger this power to assess beyond the normal six year limit.[6] Practitioners have noted that HMRC officers appear to act on the basis that an omission is an item of conduct.

See infra, § **2A.94** for the time limits for amending tax credit awards.
Simon's Taxes A4.325.

1 TMA 1970, s 34.
2 In *R v IRC, ex p Preston* [1985] STC 282 Lord Scarman said; 'a remedy by way of judicial review is not to be made available where an alternative remedy exists'.
3 Inland Revenue press release, 10 February 1992, *Simon's Tax Intelligence* 1992, p 134.
4 TMA 1970, s 36(1) substituted by FA 1989, s 149.
5 TMA 1970, s 36(3) substituted by FA 1989, s 149.

[6] Prior to the rewriting of TMA 1970, s 36 by FA 1989, s 149, the statutory provisions specifically provided for an omission to be a ground for the extended time limit.

VAT assessments

[2A.67] HMRC may assess the amount due from the trader if his return appears to be incomplete or incorrect. The assessment must be made to the best judgement of HMRC[1] and notified to the person assessed.[2] Making and notifying an assessment are separate operations and they may therefore take place at different times.

The legislation does not draw a distinction between the decision to make an assessment and the making of that assessment. Nor does it need to do so. Whether an assessment has been made is resolved objectively by reference to what has been done. If, on an objective analysis, the officer has made an assessment, there is no room for any further enquiry whether he decided to do what he did. On the other hand, if the officer's actions did not amount to the making of an assessment, his state of mind is irrelevant.[3]

The procedure for making an assessment is an internal matter for the Commissioners. The date on which it is made is a matter of fact. Thus, the steps taken in an individual case, and the dates on which they were taken, should be verifiable by reference to contemporary documentary evidence. An assessment is normally made when form VAT 641 is signed off.[4]

HMRC may assess tax for individual prescribed accounting periods,[5] but are not bound to do so. An assessment (referred to as a "global assessment") may be validly made in respect of a defined period comprising two or more prescribed accounting periods whether or not individual assessments could be made for the individual periods concerned.[6]

The amount to be assessed may depend upon a determination of the underlying legal issues. Thus, one amount may be due if the issues are decided in one way and a different amount if they are decided in another way. HMRC may validly issue separate assessments for each amount in this situation. The assessments must be made in the alternative so as to be mutually exclusive.[7]

HMRC may reduce or withdraw an assessment.[8] Whether an assessment has been withdrawn turns upon an objective view of: (a) the nature of the act relied upon as constituting the withdrawal, and (b) (if the act is unclear or ambiguous) whatever admissible evidence there might be throwing light on the purpose of the act relied on. The fact that a later assessment repeats the figures in an earlier assessment does not, by itself, indicate that the earlier assessment has been withdrawn by the later assessment.[9]

HMRC may also make an additional assessment (if further evidence of facts[10] have come to light since making the original assessment) or a supplementary assessment (in other cases),[11] and may replace an assessment with a new one.[12] The distinction between additional and supplementary assessments is important because the time limit for making the assessment is governed by the provision under which it is made.[13] A tribunal can correct an understated assessment by giving a direction specifying the correct amount.[14]

[2A.67] Tax administration – the mechanics

An assessment must be made within two years after the end of the prescribed accounting period concerned or within one year after evidence justifying an assessment came to light.[15] An assessment under the one year time limit may not be made more than three years after the prescribed accounting period concerned.[16] The three-year time limit is increased to 20 years in specified circumstances.[17] However, if an individual dies, an assessment may be made at any time in the three years after death if an assessment would have been in time at the date of death.[18] The time limits for a global assessment run from the end of the earliest prescribed accounting period included in the assessment.[19]

HMRC practice is not to assess tax in the following circumstances:[20]

(1) A trader has been misled by HMRC to the detriment of the taxpayer.
(2) A genuine misunderstanding has arisen in connection with matters not clearly covered by published guidance or by specific instructions given to a trader.
(3) An incorrect declaration claiming eligibility for zero-rating has been given by a customer.
(4) A change of policy, of which a trader could not be aware, is introduced by the Commissioners following an internal review or a decision by the court or a tribunal.

De Voil Indirect Tax Service V5.132–135.

---

1 For best judgement, see particular *Van Boeckel v Customs and Excise Comrs* [1981] STC 290; *Rahman (trading as Khayam Restaurant) v Customs and Excise Comrs* [1998] STC 826; *Rahman (trading as Khayam Restaurant) v Customs and Excise Comrs (No 2)* [2003] STC 150, CA; *Customs and Excise Comrs v Pegasus Birds Ltd* [2004] STC 1509, CA.
2 VATA 1994, s 73(1). For notification, see in particular *House v Customs and Excise Comrs* [1996] STC 154, CA and the statement of practice in Notice No. 915.
3 *Courts plc v Customs and Excise Comrs* [2005] STC 27, CA.
4 *Courts plc v Customs and Excise Comrs* [2005] STC 27, CA.
5 Input tax is assessed for the period in which the VAT is deducted: *Customs and Excise Comrs v Croydon Hotel and Leisure Co Ltd* [1996] STC 1105, CA.
6 *S J Grange Ltd v Customs and Excise Comrs* [1979] STC 183, CA; *International Language Centres Ltd v Customs and Excise Comrs* [1983] STC 394; *House v Customs and Excise Comrs* [1996] STC 154, CA.
7 *University Court of the University of Glasgow v Customs and Excise Comrs* [2003] STC 495; *Courts plc v Customs and Excise Comrs* [2005] STC 27, CA.
8 VATA 1994, s 73(9).
9 *Courts plc v Customs and Excise Comrs* [2003] EWHC 2541 (Ch), [2004] STC 690 at paras 72, 75 affd [2005] STC 27, CA at para 113.
10 For "evidence of facts", see in particular *Mervyn Conn Organisation Ltd v Customs and Excise Comrs* (1990) VAT decision 5205.
11 *Roberts v Customs and Excise Comrs* (1998) VAT decision 15759. For further assessments, see VATA 1994, s 73(6). For supplementary assessments, see VATA 1994, s 77(6).
12 See *Bennett v Customs and Excise Comrs (No 2)* [2001] STC 137.
13 For the time limits, see VATA 1994, ss 73(6), 77(1)(a), 77(1), (5), (6); *Roberts v Customs and Excise Comrs* (1998) VAT decision 15759.

14 VATA 1994, s 84(5). For the exercise of this power, see *Elias Gale Racing v Customs and Excise Comrs* [1999] STC 66.
15 VATA 1994, s 73(6). For the one-year time limit, see in particular *Pegasus Birds Ltd v Customs and Excise Comrs* [1999] STC 95. An assessment is made when the Commissioners have carried out their statutory power to assess: *Classicmoor Ltd v Customs and Excise Comrs* [1995] V & DR 1 at 10.
16 VATA 1994, s 77(1) as amended by FA 1997, s 47.
17 VATA 1994, s 77(4) as amended by FA 1997, s 47.
18 VATA 1994, s 77(5)(b).
19 *S J Grange Ltd v Customs and Excise Comrs* [1979] STC 183, [1979] 2 All ER 91, CA. See also *International Language Centres Ltd v Customs and Excise Comrs* [1983] STC 394; *Barratt Construction Ltd v Customs and Excise Comrs* [1989] VATTR 204.
20 Notice No. 48 (December 1999) paras 3.4, 3.5, 3.11; Business Brief (Issue 14/94), 6 July 1994.

Correction by taxpayer

Revising the tax return

[2A.68] The taxpayer has the right to amend his self-assessment after its submission.[1] The time limit for a taxpayer amendment is the same time limit as is applied for a Revenue enquiry.[2] Thus, for tax returns for 2007–08 and subsequent years, an amendment can be made at any time during the 12 months from the date of submission of the return.[3]

In the case of a group relief claim, statute[4] requires a claim for group relief to be included in a company tax return. If a claim has validly been made, it can be amended, but only by withdrawing the previous claim and replacing it with another claim; this is effected by amending the company tax return.[5] This has the effect that the time limit for amendment of a claim is the same as the time limit for the submission of the original tax return: that is, 24 months after the end of the period of account, unless there is a short period of account.[6]

1 TMA 1970, ss 9ZA & 12ABA.
2 See supra, § **2A.48**.
3 TMA 1970, ss 9ZA & 12ABA amended by FA 2007, s 90(2) & (3).
4 FA 1988, Sch 18, para 67.
5 FA 1998, Sch 18, para 73.
6 vide FA 1998, Sch 18, para 74(1).

Statutory relief

[2A.69] When a taxpayer discovers that he has made an error in the tax return and this has lead to an overpayment of income tax, capital gains tax or corporation tax, the taxpayer can claim repayment of the tax that has been overpaid by virtue of his error.[1]

The time limit for the statutory claim is, for income tax and CGT, three years following the 31 January in the year after the fiscal year of the return[2] and for corporation tax, four years after the end of the accounting period.[3]

Relief cannot be claimed where the return was made in accordance with "prevailing practice". That is, statute excludes relief for:[4]

> an error or mistake as to the basis on which the liability of the claimant ought to have been computed where the return was in fact made on the basis or in accordance with the practice generally prevailing at the time when it was made.

This statutory provision cannot provide repayment of tax where the error or mistake was made in a claim included in the return.[5]

The denial of a tax repayment where the tax was computed in accordance with prevailing practice can be harsh. In *Rose Smith & Co Ltd v IRC*,[6] the company followed the decision of the Special Commissioners in another case and apportioned the charges paid under an HP agreement on a basis that gave lower income in earlier years than the basis used previously, which spread the charges evenly over the period of the hire purchase agreement. The Special Commissioner rejected the claim for repayment of tax that arose from the reapportionment, as the company had had a "prevailing practice" of even apportionment of expenditure in prior years. In *Carrimore Six Wheelers Ltd v IRC*[7] the company had included rents in its trading income, so that the rents were assessed under Schedule D Case I. A claim for the correct statutory treatment of taxing rents under Case A was rejected. In *Arranmore Investment Co Ltd v IRC*[8] the Revenue changed its interpretation on a point of law. The Court of Appeal rejected the company's error or mistake claim, saying that the previous view of the law constituted the "prevailing practice" under which the profits were originally returned. In *Monro v Revenue and Customs Comrs*[9] Mr Monro completed his 1999–2000 tax return incorporating the gain he made on the exercise of an employee share option. That gain was computed by deducting from the proceeds of sale (£7,386,955) the base cost attributable to the 900,000 shares sold (£2,115,000) as provided for by TCGA 1992, s 120. In December 2002 the Court of Appeal concluded that such a computation was wrong in law.[10] Thus he had paid £846,000 more in tax than was properly due from him. The court rejected the claim for repayment of tax as, in 1999–2000, the practice prevailing was to deduct the base cost, and not the market value as was subsequently decided to be the correct approach. On appeal against this decision, the taxpayer contended that the decision below was in breach of his right to property.[11] The Court of Appeal unanimously upheld the decision of the High Court explaining that the jurisprudence of the Convention gave a large margin of discretion to the national authorities in determining what was proportionate in the field of tax. As s 33 provided for the recovery of overpayments of tax within the reasonable limits of the legislature and as the taxpayer had a right to appeal there was no violation of his right to property.[12]

There are narrow limits to the taxpayer's ability to correct a wrong under these provisions. Where a figure, thought to be correct, has been entered in to accounts but subsequent events show the figure to be inaccurate, statutory relief for mistake does not permit the reopening of the accounts. In *British Mexican Petroleum Co Ltd v Jackson*,[13] the taxpayer company had incurred a large liability in year 1; in year 3 the creditor released a part of it. The House of Lords held that the release could not alter the amount of the liability entered for the year 1.

In *Symons v Weeks*[14] staged payments to architects involved a substantial element of payment in advance but the exact whole fee could not be known until the work was completed. In accordance with accounts which had been properly drawn up only a portion of the sum received in a year was shown as a trading receipt. Warner J said that it was not open to the Revenue to amend the figures retrospectively and the taxpayer was right in seeking to be taxed on the figures in the accounts.

---

1   TMA 1970, s 33 for income tax and CGT; FA 1998, Sch 18, para 51 for corporation tax.
2   TMA 1970, s 33(1) (as amended by FA 2008, Sch 39 with effect from 1 April 2010).
3   FA 1998, Sch 18, para 51(1)(c) (as amended by FA 2008, Sch 39 with effect from 1 April 2010).
4   TMA 1970, s 33(2A)(a); FA 1998, Sch 18, para 51(3)(a).
5   TMA 1970, s 33(2A)(b); FA 1998, Sch 18, para 51(3)(b).
6   (1933) 17 TC 586. The claim was made under FA 1923, s 24, the precursor of TMA 1970, s 33 and was refused under s 24(2) proviso, the wording of which refuses relief for "prevailing practice" in substantially the same terms as in TMA 1970, s 33(2A)(a). The "other case", on the basis of which the claim was made is unreported and unnamed—vide the decision of the Special Commissioners (1931) 17 TC 586 para 4 at 588.
7   (1944) 26 TC 301.
8   [1973] STC 195, CA.
9   [2007] EWHC 114 (Ch), [2007] SWTI 290.
10 *Mansworth v Jelley* [2002] EWHC 442 (Ch), [2003] STC 53, CA, see infra, § **18.28**.
11 Under Article 1 of the first protocol to the European Convention of Human Rights.
12 [2008] EWCA Civ 306.
13 (1932) 16 TC 570; and see Atkinson J in *Jays the Jewellers Ltd v IRC* [1947] 2 All ER 762 at 768, 29 TC 274 at 284.
14 [1983] STC 195 (Warner J pointed out that if the Revenue had not insisted on a change from cash basis to earnings basis they could have got what they wanted).

Restitution

[2A.70] Where a taxpayer requires repayment of tax, an alternative to the statutory claim can be the application of the law of restitution. This is a comparatively recent development by the courts of a principle of common law. The essence of the principle was stated by Lord Gough in *Lipkin Gorman (a firm) v Karpnalel Ltd*[1] as:

> The recovery of money in restitution is not, as a general rule, a matter of discretion for the court. A claim to recover money at common law is made as a matter of right;

and even though the underlying principle of recovery is the principle of unjust enrichment, nevertheless, where recovery is denied, it is denied on the basis of legal principle. It has been argued[2] that the modern law of restitution is recognition of the rights of the person under Bill of Rights Act 1689, Art. 4: 'levying money for or to the use of the Crown, by pretence of prerogative, without grant of Parliament, for longer time, or in other manner than the same is or shall be granted is illegal'.

Restitution can give a remedy when the time limit for statutory relief has expired, as the time limit for the common law remedy of restitution is six years from the discovery of the mistake,[3] which may, in particular instances, be a considerably longer time limit than the limit for the statutory claim, being (in effect) five years from the due date of payment of the tax. A claim under the law of restitution is, also, appropriate where tax has been wrongly paid, but there has not been a mistake by the taxpayer.[4] However, in *Monro v Revenue and Customs Comrs*[5] Morritt J ruled that a claim under the law of restitution cannot be made if a claim under the statutory provisions[6] is excluded by the "prevailing practice" proviso:

> It would be inconsistent with TMA 1970, s 33 to recognise a common law remedy in precisely the circumstances postulated by subsection (1) but free of the limitation contained in subsection (2A). Accordingly the claim in so far as it was based on a restitutionary claim to recover tax paid under a mistake of law would be rejected.

The law of restitution is founded on three principles:

(1)   Restitution aims to remove unjust enrichment.
(2)   Restitution aims to correct a wrong doing.
(3)   Restitution is a vindication of property rights.

The concept of "unjust enrichment" is that the sum that is paid in a successful suit for restitution is the profit that was made by the defendant; it is not the loss suffered by the claimant. In the context of a tax claim, the amount of "unjust enrichment" enjoyed by the state when tax has been wrongly paid is the amount of the tax paid plus the benefit obtained by the state in retaining that sum since the time of wrongful payment. In contrast to other civil actions, it is considered that a court can award compound interest in satisfying a claim for restitution.[7]

A claim for restitution is brought in the High Court, not before the Commissioners.[8]

Restitution was used as a basis for a claim to a repayment of tax paid erroneously as early as 1774.[9] A more recent example of its use is *Deutsche Morgan v IRC*.[10] In this case, the company was a subsidiary of a German parent company. Between 1993 and 1996 it paid ACT[11] on dividend paid to its German parent company, as UK statute[12] did not allow a group income election between a UK resident company and a foreign company.

On 8 March 2001, the ECJ issued its decision in *Metallgesellschaft Ltd v IRC and A-G*.[13] The ECJ ruled that it was unlawful for the UK to limit a group income election to UK companies as this unfairly discriminated against companies in other states of the EU. Evidence was given, and accepted, that Deutsche Morgan would have made a group income election if its officers had known that the restriction to UK companies given by statute was unlawful.

Correction by taxpayer [2A.70]

The House of Lords, in overruling the decision of the Court of Appeal and restoring the decision of Park J in the High Court, granted restitution to Deutsche Morgan for the benefit properly enjoyed by the Crown for the use of the cash paid in ACT from the time of payment to the time that the ACT was offset against the main stream liability.[14] As Lord Hope said:[15]

> The proposition that money paid under a mistake is recoverable is based on the principle that, prima facie, its receipt by the defendant will lead to his unjust enrichment. There is no reason to distrust a proposition based on such an elementary principle just because it is simple. Now that the common law world has recognised that there is a general right of recovery whether the mistake is of fact or law, it should be careful not to disturb its purity and its simplicity unless there is a clear basis on grounds of principle or policy for doing so.

A more recent case relating to the ECJ ruling in *Metallgesellschaft* was *Europcar UK Ltd v Revenue & Customs Commrs*[16]. In that case, a Group Litigation Order (GLO) was made to enable the orderly and efficient disposal of the resulting litigation. Nineteen claimants relied upon this decision to claim in mistake-based restitution against the Revenue and made claims before 8 September 2003. The Chancery Division of the High Court held that the individual claim forms had the basic pleading requirement of setting out the material facts relied upon and the causes of action to which they related. Any subsequent amendments to the claim would be barred from adding new claims (or if they did, adding claims that arose out of the same or substantially the same facts as the original claim). The consequence of this was that 18 of the claims were allowed to be amended and continue under the old rules (pre-September 2003) and one, because the changes effectively amounted to a new claim, fell within the provisions of FA 2004, s 320.

---

1 [1991] 2 AC 548.
2 See G. Virgo, *Principles of the Law of Restitution*.
3 Applied by Limitation Act 1980, s 32(1)(c).
4 Such as in *Deutsche Morgan v IRC* [2007] STC 1, HL.
5 [2007] EWHC 114 (Ch), [2007] SWTI 290.
6 TMA 1970, s 33, see supra, § **2A.67**.
7 Per Graham Virgo. In *Principles of the Law of Restitution* Virgo subdivides the requirement to show unjust enrichment as:
(i)   enrichment
(ii) at the expense of the claimant
(iii) unjust within one of the recognised grounds of restitution
(iv) no available defences.
8 *Autologic Holdings plc v IRC* [2005] UKHL 54, [2005] STC 1357, HL.
9 *Campbell v Hall* (1774) 1 Cowp 204.
10 [2007] STC 1, HL.
11 By virtue of TA 1988, s 14 revoked with effect from 6 April 1999 by FA 1998, s 31.
12 TA 1988, s 247.
13 [2001] STC 452.
14 Under TA 1988, ss 239 & 240, subsequently revoked by FA 1998, s 31.
15 [2007] STC 1 para [41] at 16e.
16 [2008] EWHC 1363 (Ch).

Rectification

[2A.71] Sometimes the taxpayer's mistake is in a document. In the commercial world, such mistakes can be easily corrected by entering into a supplementary contract. Such a means of correction is not possible if the document is an irrevocable deed, such as a deed creating a trust. Even commercial contracts cannot always be corrected so easily from a taxation point of view, particularly when a significant period of time has elapsed between the execution of the contract and the discovery of the mistake. Payments may have been made or received in that period. In taxing or relieving those payments, the provisions in the original contract should be taken at their face value, even though the parties agree that the provisions are a mistake.

In *Toronto-Dominion Bank v Oberoi*[1] a foreign bank signed a lease for a house in London for one of its senior employees. The rent on the lease was declared to be £345,000 for a 22 month period. This sum was declared in the court to be "far too large to be rent; there is only any commercial sense in the transaction if it is to be regarded as a premium". Relabelling £345,000 as "premium", rather than the "rent", dramatically reduced the benefit in kind charged on the employee.

Where there is a mistake, an application can be made to the court for the equitable remedy of rectification under which the court orders the correction of a document so that its text, as rectified, expresses the actual agreement of the parties. The order for rectification enables the parties to point to the *as rectified* text as governing all the acts carried out under the contract, even if those acts took place before the date of the order.

For the court to order rectification, there are five conditions:[2]

(1) a prior firm accord, usually outwardly expressed;
(2) a common continuing intention up to the time of the execution of the agreement;
(3) clear evidence ("strong irrefutable evidence") that the agreement as executed did not reflect that common intention;
(4) that the wording contended for by the claimant will accurately reflect the agreement; and
(5) that there is an issue between the parties capable of being contested.

The court has discretion as to the order it makes. Thus, in *Toronto-Dominion Bank v Oberoi* the court rectified the tenancy agreement so that the first payment of £32,500 fell to be treated as rent and the balance of £312,500 was a premium.

It is acceptable for tax to be the motive for the application for rectification,[3] but the application will fail unless there is evidence that the clear intention of the parties was other than is reflected in the words of the deeds. Thus, in *Racal Group Services Ltd v Ashmore*[4] there was evidence that the deed of covenant in question had been made with the clear intention that each payment to be made under it should qualify as a charitable covenant that would be a charge on income for the payer. Unfortunately, the payment dates actually chosen covered a period of less than four years, so the deed could not qualify and the payments could not be deductible as charges on income. There was no evidence to show that the parties had intended to pay on any other dates, so there could be no rectification.

An agreement between a taxpayer and the Revenue can be the subject of a successful application for rectification.[5]

Some applications are for rectification of a simple, such as a typing, error, such as in *Seymour & Another v Seymour*.[6] Other cases, by contrast, are where the execution of an entire document is a mistake. In *Green v Cobham*[7] the court set aside a trustees appointment of capital as the trustees made the appointment in ignorance of the fact that retirement of a professional trustee had the effect that the trust became a UK resident trust and the appointment of capital triggered a substantial UK tax liability. When setting aside an entire deed (or the entire action of a party) the court follows the doctrine in *Re Hastings-Bass, Hastings-Bass v IRC*.[8] In that case, Buckley LJ said:[9]

> In our judgement, where by the terms of a trust (as under Trustee Act 1925, s 32) a trustee is given a discretion as to some matter under which he acts in good faith, the court should not interfere with his action notwithstanding that it does not have the full effect which he intended, unless (1) what he has achieved is unauthorised by the power conferred on him, or (2) it is clear that he would not have acted as he did (a) had he not taken into account considerations which he should not have taken into account, or (b) had he not failed to take into considerations which he ought to have taken into account.

The *Hastings-Bass* doctrine was followed in *Burrell v Burrell*.[10] In that case a deed of appointment was executed which generated considerable inheritance tax liabilities. Mann J set aside the appointment, saying:[11]

> The trustees in the case before me can still fulfil the requirements of the [*Hastings-Bass*] principle. In my view, both the trustees and their advisers were in breach of duty when they were considering the deed of appointment. Mrs Sharman never really addressed fiscal matters; she relied on others to do so. Mr Burrell was aware that there was a tax point, but relief at least in part on his own imperfect understanding of the position, failed to give clear instructions to his solicitors (or anyone else) to consider the matter, and failed to appreciate that he had not asked for, and was not in possession of, a full picture of the tax consequences of what was proposed.
>
> The trustees failed to take a highly relevant consideration into account, and had they taken it into account they clearly would not have acted as they did.

---

[1] [2004] STC 1197.

[2] *Joscelyne v Nissen* [1970] 2 QB 86.

[3] *Whiteside v Whiteside* [1950] Ch 65 (payments would have been deductible for surtax) and *Re Slocock's Will Trusts* [1979] 1 All ER 358 (CTT saving). Other cases where a document has been rectified and a beneficial tax consequence achieved are *Burroughes v Abbott* [1922] 1 Ch 86; *Jervis v Howle and Talke Colliery Co Ltd* [1937] Ch 67; *Fredensen v Rothschild* (1941) 20 ATC 1; *Van der Linde v Van der Linde* [1947] Ch 306 and *Whiteside v Whiteside* [1949] 2 All ER 913, CA; *Royal College of Veterinary Surgeons v Meldrum* [1996] SSCD 54; *Matthews v Martin & Others* [1991] BTC 8048 and *Lake v Lake* [1989] STC 865.

[4] [1995] STC 1151. CA.

[2A.71] Tax administration – the mechanics

5   R v Inspector of Taxes, ex p Bass Holdings Ltd [1993] STC 122.
6   [1989] BTC 8043.
7   [2002] STC 820 see infra, § **33.40**.
8   [1974] STC 211, CA.
9   At 221f.
10 [2005] EWHC 245 (Ch), [2005] STC 569.
11 [2005] EWHC 245 (Ch), [2005] STC 569 paras 23 & 24 at 580c–g. Other cases where the *Hastings-Bass* principle has been followed include *Abacus Trust Co (Isle of Man) Ltd v National Society for the Prevention of Cruelty to Children* [2001] STC 1344 and *Green v Cobham* [2002] STC 820.

Inheritance tax

[2A.72] HMRC has power to take proceedings for the recovery of tax[1] and to accept property in satisfaction of a liability to tax and interest.[2] The value may be taken either at the day the property is offered or that on which it is accepted. If the former is chosen, the interest is due after that date.[3]

HMRC has extensive powers to obtain information,[4] including information relating to a liability to a tax of a member state of the European Communities other than the UK if the tax is similar in character to inheritance tax and in relation to which a specified Directive applies.[5] The normal privilege given to communications between a solicitor and his client is respected but the solicitor may be required to disclose the name and address of his client and, where that client is a non-resident involved in forming companies or making settlements, that client's clients.[6] There is a further power where a person (other than a barrister) is concerned in making an inter vivos settlement with a UK domiciled settlor but non-resident trustees; such a person must inform HMRC of the names and addresses of the settlor and the trustees within three months of the settlement being made.[7]

Simon's Taxes Division I11; Foster's Inheritance Tax L2.21, 31; L4.09.

1   IHTA 1984, s 242.
2   IHTA 1984, s 230.
3   IHTA 1984, s 233(1A), SP 6/87; Inland Revenue press release, 8 April 1987, *Simon's Tax Intelligence* 1987, p 302—for acceptance for IHT after 16 March 1987, this has been extended to CTT and estate duty by F(No. 2)A 1987, s 97.
4   IHTA 1984, ss 219 and 219A (added by FA 1999, s 94). From 1999 the request for documents is made by a Revenue officer. The person who has delivered the account then has the power to appeal to the Special Commissioners (but not the Court) for the request to be defeated on the grounds that it is unreasonable (s 219B).
5   FA 1990, s 124(3); the Directive is No. 77/99/EEC, dated 19 December 1977.
6   This power is subject to the consent of a Special Commissioner who must be satisfied that HMRC are justified in seeking to use this power; IHTA 1984, s 219 (1A) added by FA 1990 s 124.
7   IHTA 1984, s 218.

National Insurance contributions

[2A.73] Most National Insurance contributions are collected through the PAYE system or in the case of Class 4 contributions through income tax self-assessment.

The former process of closer working between PAYE auditors and DSS Inspectors was completed following the transfer to the [then] Inland Revenue on 1 April 1999 of the administrative functions of the former Contributions Agency.

An issue which gives rise to difficulty when a settlement is proposed concerns the common situation where unreported benefits made available to employees are identified but the employer agrees to meet the tax liabilities which would arise. The tax settlement will then require a grossing up at the average marginal tax rate of the employees concerned. But whether or not the benefits themselves are liable to NICs, the former DSS always considered that a liability for NICs arises on the tax settled by the employer on behalf of the employees. This is on the grounds that a personal tax liability of the employee is being met by the employer and the payment is therefore additional earnings of the employee under the decision in *Hartland v Diggines*.[1]

However, this is not a correct construction of the position. In particular, the tax settlement is made to avoid the employee having a tax liability. The employee's tax liability remains contingent and is never in fact assessed. The payment to HMRC under the settlement does not discharge the employee's tax liability but is consideration for HMRC agreeing not to pursue the employee.[2] The former DSS always resisted such reasoning but the points made are nonetheless valid.

Given the introduction of Class 1B contributions on 6 April 1999 whereby the meeting of any personal tax liability is circumvented by use of a PAYE Settlement Agreement and gives rise to a liability under that class of contribution, the opportunity for this issue to be challenged legally is diminished, but by no means extinguished, as the point is still applicable in settlement cases.

Where, following employer compliance visits, irregularities come to light, HMRC will require recovery of arrears, normally for the tax year in which the inspection takes place and for the preceding six years. This approach to recovery treats the unpaid contributions in the same way as unpaid PAYE and rests on the regulation which requires Class 1 contributions to be paid, accounted for and recovered in like manner as income tax is deducted under PAYE.[3] In any event the former DSS considered that it was normally precluded by the Limitation Act 1980, s 9(1) from seeking recovery of arrears of Class 1, Class 1A and Class 2 contributions more than six years after the date on which such contributions first become overdue. The Inland Revenue, since the Transfer in April 1999, also appeared to accept that this is the case. This is on the basis that NICs are not a tax, the recovery of which by the Crown is exempt from the application of the Limitation Act 1980.[4] Exceptions will be cases where the contributor has deliberately concealed from the authorities facts relevant to the recovery of the arrears of contributions,[5] or where the contributor within the previous six years has acknowledged liability for arrears accruing before the start of that six-year period.[6]

As an alternative method of recovery, the authorities are entitled to require payment of Class 1 contributions by means of direct collection. Moreover the remedies available for recovery of unpaid contributions are not confined to those available in respect of unpaid PAYE.[7]

[1] [1926] AC 289, 10 TC 247, HL.
[2] See Technical Release TAX 21/92 para 107 issued by the Tax Faculty of the ICAEW.
[3] Social Security (Contributions) Regulations 2001, SI 2001/1004, reg 67; Sch 4.
[4] Limitation Act 1980, s 37(2)(*a*).
[5] Limitation Act 1980, s 32.
[6] Limitation Act 1980, s 29(5).
[7] SI 2001/1004, reg 68.

Stamp duty

[2A.74] Stamp duty has a special status as there is no automatic penalty for the failure to stamp a document. Instead, an instrument that is not properly stamped is not admissible in court proceedings.[1]

[1] See infra, § **56.29**.

Stamp duty reserve tax

[2A.75] HMRC has the power to take proceedings for the recovery of the tax and to obtain information.[1]

[1] Stamp Duty Reserve Tax Regulations 1986 SI 1986/1711.

Stamp duty land tax

[2A.76] FA 2003, s 93 and Sch 13 govern the powers of HMRC to call for documents and information for the purposes of stamp duty land tax. HMRC may authorise an officer of theirs to inspect any property in order to ascertain its market value or for any other relevant matter.[1]

FA 2003, s 95 creates the statutory criminal offence of a person being knowingly concerned in the fraudulent evasion of SDLT by him or any other person. If found guilty the person is liable on summary conviction to imprisonment for a term not exceeding six months or a fine not exceeding the statutory maximum (or both) and on conviction on indictment to imprisonment for a term not exceeding seven years or a fine (or both). This section is based on and largely copies FA 2000, s 144 which was introduced to make prosecution of PAYE and NIC fraud involving payment of wages by cash in hand without deducting tax more effective. When that provision was introduced into the Finance Bill 2000 at a late stage unease was expressed about the imprecision inherent in the phrases "knowingly concerned" and "fraudulent evasion". In response the Paymaster General explained the use of these phrases as follows:

> I will deal with the important point about the words 'knowingly' and fraudulent evasion. . . . My officials will smile when they hear this, but initially I said to them, 'Surely evasion is fraud', and asked why it needed to be qualified as 'fraudulent evasion'. I have received assurances which I will pass on to the Committee. The juxtaposition of the words 'knowingly' and 'fraudulent evasion' reinforces exactly which offences the provision is aimed at.
>
> Let us take the question of someone who is knowingly concerned in the evasion of income tax. I want to make it clear that it is not enough for this purpose to show that a person should have suspected that someone was evading tax. The person must have knowledge and involvement in the fraud. For example, he could help someone evade tax by helping to produce false business records.
>
> People may ask why we have put the words 'fraudulent' and 'evasion' together. I am reliably informed by people who know better than I do that, in English usage, 'to evade' can mean to dodge, without any dishonest intent. Although 'evasion' has come to imply dishonesty in the context of tax, the Bill needs to be drafted tightly. 'Fraudulent' may not appear to add much to 'evasion', but the expression 'fraudulent evasion' is well precedented and subject to interpretation by the courts.

[1] FA 2003, s 94.

Equitable liability

[2A.77] As a final safeguard available to taxpayers, a practice known as equitable liability was developed by the former Inland Revenue. The practice recognised that taxpayers might find themselves with tax debts that are legally payable, in that they are no longer subject to any appeal procedure, but can be shown to exceed the true tax liability (being the amount that would have been payable had the Revenue been in possession of all the relevant facts at the time that they assessed or determined the tax payable).

The practice was of particular use to vulnerable and other unrepresented taxpayers, especially those whose tax compliance fell below the ideal standards due to health, family or other financial issues.

Although it had existed since before 1986, the practice was first publicized widely in the August 1995 edition of Tax Bulletin in which the Revenue accepted that in such cases it would be "unconscionable to insist on collecting the full amount of tax assessed and legally due".[1]

The timing of the Tax Bulletin article was prompted in part by an undertaking by the then chairman of the Inland Revenue when giving evidence to a Parliamentary Select Committee to ensure that more tax practitioners were aware of the practice. The timing also ensured that the Revenue could make a statement about how the then imminent system of self-assessment would interact with the extra-statutory practice. The article explained that it was thought unlikely that the system of determinations in the absence of a return would mean any need for the practice; however, where the conditions for the practice were nevertheless fulfilled, the Revenue would be prepared to consider extending their practice to meet such cases.

The role of extra-statutory practices, however, has since been reviewed following the decision of the House of Lords in *R v Inland Revenue Commissioners, ex parte Wilkinson*[2] and HMRC now propose to withdraw the practice with effect from 1 April 2010.[3]

---

[1] Originally, the practice ensured that the Crown Preference then available to the Revenue would not lead to excessive tax liabilities being paid ahead of and to the disadvantage of other creditors in the case of a bankruptcy. However, as the Tax Bulletin article made clear, the practice had been extended to protect the taxpayers themselves from excessive tax bills.
[2] [2005] UKHL 30; see supra, § **2.01** (Ch 2 not 2A).
[3] HMRC website announcement 22 May 2009: http://www.hmrc.gov.uk/news/statement220509.htm.

Penalties

FA 2007, s 96 and Sch 24 (as amended by FA 2008) impose a unified penalty regime that applies to Introduction

[2A.78] The HMRC Powers Review has realigned the penalty provisions for the various taxes under HMRC's control. The initial changes were to the system of tax-geared penalties for errors contained in returns and associated documents. These were introduced by FA 2007, s 96 and Sch 24 for income tax, capital gains tax, corporation tax and VAT. No penalty can be imposed under this new regime until returns that are to be made on or after 1 April 2009. The following sections describe the provisions that apply to penalties imposed before that date.[1]

FA 2008, Sch 40 extended FA 2007, Sch 24 so that it would cover all other taxes and other situations not covered by the original version of the rules. The extended version of Sch 24 will come into effect for returns that are to be made on or after 1 April 2010.[2]

Other changes, to take effect in future years, have been introduced by FA 2009. As they are not yet in force, they will be discussed in future editions. The text below reflects the rules currently in place (first as introduced by FA 2007, Sch 24 for incorrect returns and then the penalties for other failings).

---

[1] The Finance Act 2007, Schedule 24 (Commencement and Transitional Provisions) Order 2008, SI 2008/568.
[2] The Finance Act 2008, Schedule 40 (Appointed Day, Transitional Provisions and Consequential Amendments) Order 2009, SI 2009/571.

Penalties for errors on tax returns

[2A.79] These rules apply for the purposes of income tax, capital gains tax, corporation tax and VAT.[1] For returns due on or after 1 April 2010, they will be extended to cover insurance premium tax, inheritance tax, SDLT, stamp duty reserve tax, petroleum revenue tax, aggregates levy, climate change levy, landfill tax, air passenger duty and other duties and excises charged on leisure activities.

There are three types of culpable error:

- errors on returns etc;
- deliberate withholding of information or provision of false information which leads to an error on a return;
- failure by a taxpayer to correct an under-assessment by HMRC.

[1] FA 2007, Sch 24, para 1.

Errors on tax returns etc

[2A.80] An error will give rise to a penalty if:

- it is contained on a document of type specified in the legislation;
- it amounts to or leads to an understatement of the tax liability of a person (P);
- it is P who gives HMRC the document containing the error; and
- the error was careless or deliberate.

In such cases, it will be P who is liable for the penalty.[1]

Where a document contains more than one error, a penalty will be payable for each.[2]

[1] FA 2007, Sch 24, para 1.
[2] FA 2007, Sch 24, para 1(4).

Careless or deliberate errors

[2A.81] The terminology used in the legislation is new. Previously, the legislation would refer to negligent or fraudulent conduct.

Paragraph 3 defines carelessness as failure to take reasonable care. Arguably, therefore, the meaning of "careless" is not that different from "negligent" and it is likely that the courts will apply the standard laid down by Baron Alderson in *Blyth v Birmingham Waterworks Company*[1]:

> Negligence is the omission to do something which a reasonable man, guided upon those considerations which ordinarily regulate the conduct of human affairs, would do, or doing something which a prudent and reasonable man would not do. The defendants might have been liable for negligence, if, unintentionally, they omitted to do that which a reasonable person would have done, or did that which a person taking reasonable precautions would not have done.

One will expect HMRC to apply different standards of reasonable care to different scenarios although the dictum of Baron Alderson and the legislation do not necessarily accommodate that. For example, a financially literate taxpayer might be expected to expend more care on the preparation of his or her tax return than a less sophisticated individual.

The meaning of deliberate errors is not specified in the legislation although its meaning is straightforward. However, it should be noted that, when determining the severity of the error (and, therefore, the type of penalty payable) deliberate errors are subject to two classifications:

- deliberate but not concealed – where an error is deliberate but P does not make any arrangements to conceal the error; and
- deliberate and concealed – where P makes arrangements to conceal the error.[2]

The legislation provides an example of what can be deliberate and concealed: occasions where P submits false evidence to support an inaccurate figure. It remains to be seen whether the courts will start to tolerate a wider meaning.

---

[1] (1856) 11 Ex Ch 781.
[2] FA 2007, Sch 24, para 3(1).

Non-culpable errors

[2A.82] Although implicit under the regime that was in place before 2009, HMRC have been at pains to make it clear that there is (initially at least) no penalty payable for errors that are genuine mistakes. HMRC guidance defines those as including:

- a reasonably arguable view of situations that is subsequently not upheld;
- an arithmetical or transposition inaccuracy that is not so large either in absolute terms or relative to overall liability, as to produce an obviously odd result or be picked up by a quality check;
- following advice from HMRC that later proves to be wrong, provided that all the details and circumstances were given when the advice was sought;
- acting on advice from a competent adviser which proves to be wrong despite the fact that the adviser was given a full set of accurate facts;
- accepting and using information from another person where it is not possible to check that the information is accurate and complete.

In addition, HMRC will consider a person to have taken reasonable care if:

- arrangements or systems (such as comprehensive internal accounting systems and controls with specific reference to tax sensitive areas) exist that, if followed, could reasonably be expected to produce an accurate basis for the calculation of tax due by the internal tax department, or external agent; and
- despite the above, inaccuracies arise in processing or coding items through the person's accounting system which result in a mis-statement of tax liability; and
- the effect of the inaccuracies is not significant in relation to the person's overall tax liability for the relevant tax period.[1]

This, however, is subject to two caveats:

- Elsewhere in the HMRC manuals, it is asserted that where there is an error in a person's tax return, "there is a prima facie case for the view that the error or omission is at least negligent and possibly fraudulent".[2] Such a view seems to be at odds with the approach of the courts. For example, the High Court held that in such cases, in the absence of sufficient evidence of culpability by the taxpayer, "the benefit of the doubt as to negligence should be given to the taxpayer".[3]
- Additionally, where a taxpayer subsequently discovers the error but does not take reasonable steps to inform HMRC of the error, the error (however innocent initially) is subsequently to be classified as a careless error and hence liable for a penalty.[4]

[1] Compliance Handbook CH81130.
[2] Enquiry Manual EM5126.
[3] Jacob J in *King v Walden* (2001) High Court.
[4] FA 2007, Sch 24, para 3(2).

Specified types of document

[2A.83] The types of document specified by the legislation are tax returns (including PAYE returns), accounts, any statements or declarations in connection with a tax return and any document which is likely to be relied upon by HMRC to determine a question about a taxpayer's tax liability, payments of or in connection with tax, any other payments by the taxpayer (including penalties), repayments or any other kind of payment or credit to the taxpayer.[1]

[1] FA 2007, Sch 24, para 1, Table.

Errors due to third parties

[2A.84] For returns due on or after 1 April 2010, third parties will be liable to penalties if they deliberately withhold information or deliberately provide inaccurate information from taxpayers with the intention of the taxpayer giving HMRC a specified document (see above) with an inaccuracy that would lead to an understatement of tax (or an inaccurate loss or repayment claim).[1]

Such penalties will be in addition to any penalty payable by the taxpayer for the same error.[2]

[1] FA 2007, Sch 24, para 1A(1), (2).
[2] FA 2007, Sch 24, para 1A(3).

Under-assessment by HMRC

[2A.85] The third situation covered by Sch 24 is where HMRC make an assessment of tax which proves to be insufficient and the taxpayer fails to take reasonable steps within the 30 days (beginning with the date of the assessment) to notify HMRC of the under-assessment.[1]

[2A.85] Tax administration – the mechanics

In its manuals, HMRC suggest that this penalty will be applicable only in cases where they issue a determination in the absence of a timely return from the taxpayer.[2] Thus, it appears that HMRC do not propose to apply a penalty in cases where a taxpayer receives a discovery assessment that proves to be insufficient. However, it is arguable that determinations in the absence of a self-assessment are not themselves assessments within the meaning of Sch 24.[3] Consequently, it would appear that penalties can be appealed against on this basis.

[1] FA 2007, Sch 24, para 2.
[2] Compliance Handbook CH81170.
[3] TMA 1970, s 28C(3) provides that determinations are to be treated as assessments only for certain specified purposes of that Act.

Amount of penalties

[2A.86] Until 2009, HMRC (and the courts) could raise a penalty of between nil and 100% of the tax lost due to negligence or fraud. Although the courts have occasionally tried to assess what they consider the appropriate level of penalty for the particular case[1], HMRC felt that it would be fairer to ensure that the legislation contains statutory guidelines as to the range of penalties to be charged.

Ordinarily, the penalty would be based upon the tax lost as a result of the error ('potential lost revenue'), applying as a percentage of that figure.[2]

However, when a loss has been overstated (to the extent that it has not caused the incorrect reduction of any tax payable), the penalty will be calculated on the basis of 10% of the overstated loss.[3] Where there is no reasonable prospect of the loss being used, there is deemed to be no tax lost for these purposes.[4]

If an error simply results in an amount of tax being declared later than would otherwise be the case, the deemed tax lost is calculated as 5% of the tax lost per annum.[5] So a sale that is wrongly posted into a later quarter for VAT purposes, delaying output tax of £10,000, would be treated as potential lost revenue of £125.

[1] See, for example, *HMRC v Mercury Tax Group Ltd* (2009) Sp C 737.
[2] FA 2007, Sch 24, para 5.
[3] FA 2007, Sch 24, para 7.
[4] FA 2007, Sch 24, para 7(5).
[5] FA 2007, Sch 24, para 8

Range of penalties

[2A.87] Once the potential tax lost has been ascertained, the penalty is calculated as a percentage of that figure.

The legislation determines the maximum percentage applicable for each type of error and minima, depending on whether the taxpayer disclosed the error to

HMRC with or without "prompting". A disclosure is stated to be unprompted if, at the time, the taxpayer had no reason to believe that HMRC would have discovered the error; otherwise it is prompted.[1]

A disclosure must involve telling HMRC about the error, giving HMRC reasonable help in quantifying it and allowing HMRC access to records to ensure that the error is fully corrected.[2]

The ranges of percentages applicable are set out in the table below:[3]

Type of error	Maximum	Minimum
Careless	30%	15% if prompted 0% if unprompted
Deliberate but not concealed	70%	20% if prompted 35% if unprompted
Deliberate and concealed	100%	30% if prompted 50% if unprompted

For these purposes, penalties under paragraph 1A (third parties) are treated as deliberate and concealed.[4]

[1] FA 2007, Sch 24, para 9(2).
[2] FA 2007, Sch 24, para 9(1).
[3] FA 2007, Sch 24, para 10.
[4] FA 2007, Sch 24, para 4(1A).

Suspension of penalties

[2A.88] One innovation within Sch 24 is the possibility of having penalties suspended for up to two years.[1] The stated purpose of the suspension is to give taxpayers the opportunity to invest in systems that will prevent a recurrence of the error. For this reason, HMRC policy is not to permit the suspension of a penalty for a one-off error.[2]

Nevertheless, it is arguable that this approach is contrary to the legislation which provides that a suspension must be accompanied by conditions that would help the taxpayer avoid being liable in future to penalties for careless inaccuracies.[3] Whilst a totally one-off inaccuracy would fall outside this category, it is likely that many one-off errors (such as failure to report a capital gain) should nevertheless be subject to suspension.

Suspension is not available for any deliberate errors.[4]

[1] FA 2007, Sch 24, para 14.
[2] Compliance Handbook CH83130.
[3] FA 2007, Sch 24, para 14(3).
[4] FA 2007, Sch 24, para 14(1).

Failure to notify chargeability

[2A.89] FA 2008, Sch 41 provides a further set of penalties. Paragraph 1 imposes a penalty in cases where taxpayers fail to notify HMRC of chargeability to any tax within the statutory time limit.

[2A.89] Tax administration – the mechanics

Again, the amount of the penalty is stated to be a percentage of the potential lost revenue[1]; again, there are different degrees of culpability and the percentages reflect these.[2] However, there is no concept of innocent error. Any failure that is not deliberate will attract a maximum 30% penalty. However, there is no penalty if the person has a reasonable excuse for the failure.[3]

Once again, reductions are available in cases of disclosure.[4] But there is no scope for the suspension of penalties.

---

[1] FA 2008, Sch 41, para 6.
[2] FA 2008, Sch 41, paras 5, 6.
[3] FA 2008, Sch 41, para 20.
[4] FA 2008, Sch 41, paras 12, 13.

Income tax and capital gains tax

[2A.90] The main penalty is that where a taxpayer fraudulently or negligently delivers an incorrect return or any incorrect accounts in connection with his liability to income tax or capital gains tax a penalty of 100% of the tax loss can be charged.[1] The tax loss is defined as the difference between the income tax plus capital gains tax that would have been payable if the return, etc, was correct and the amount actually paid.[2] The Revenue are given power to mitigate the penalty.[3] In practice, HMRC use the mitigation power extensively so that the percentage of loss tax that is actually charged as a penalty is related to the perceived gravity of the taxpayer's error, his cooperation and whether the tax loss was disclosed by the taxpayer.[4]

In addition to tax geared penalties, statute provides fixed penalties, which include:

- failure to make a return by the due date—£100;[5]
- continuing failure to make a return—£60 per day;[6]
- failure to produce documents—£50;[7]
- failure to supply information on "special return"—£300;[8]
- supply of incorrect information on a "special return"—£3,000;[9]
- supply of incorrect information on a "special return"—£3,000;[10]
- failure to make a sub-contractor's return—£100 per 50 sub-contractors;[11]
- assisting in the preparation of an incorrect return—£3,000.[12]

All penalties attract interest in the case of late payment.[13]

The fact that an application has been made to the European Commission of Human Rights and the European Court has not yet heard the application is not a ground for quashing or deferring penalties.[14]

TMA 1970, s 114 is also applicable to the determination of penalties and penalty notices issued accordingly. See *Pipe & Ors v R & C Comrs*.[15]

Simon's Taxes A4.502.

---

[1] TMA 1970, s 95(2).

² TMA 1970, s 95(2).
³ TMA 1970, s 102.
⁴ The practice adopted by the Revenue in mitigating penalties is given in Revenue Booklets IR73, 74 and 75.
⁵ TMA 1970, s 93(1)(a); the penalty is increased to £200 if the tax return is more than six months late. 775,000 individuals paid a £100 penalty for failing to submit the 1996/97 tax return by 31 January 1998, of which 400,000 were required to pay a second £100 penalty as their returns were still outstanding at 31 July 1998.
⁶ TMA 1970, s 93(1)(b).
⁷ TMA 1970, s 97AA inserted by FA 1994, s 196.
⁸ TMA 1970, s 98(1)(i).
⁹ TMA 1970, s 98(1)(ii).
¹⁰ TMA 1970, s 98(2).
¹¹ TMA 1970, s 98A(3).
¹² TMA 1970, s 99.
¹³ TMA 1970, s 103A inserted by FA 1994, Sch 19, para 33.
¹⁴ *Slater v IT General Comrs for Beacontree (No 2)* [2002] EWHC 2676 (Ch), [2004] STC 1342 per Park J at 1344e.
¹⁵ [2008] EWHC 646 (Ch).

Corporation tax

[2A.91] Penalties for corporation tax are levied on a similar basis to that which applies to individuals, etc for income tax and capital gains tax. A company that fraudulently or negligently delivers an incorrect return can have a penalty imposed on it of 100% of the tax lost,[1] calculated in the same way as for income tax, etc. The same 100% of tax lost is the penalty for failure to notify chargeability.[2] HMRC has, and uses, its power to mitigate these penalties to encourage cooperation.[3]

There are a variety of fixed penalties that can be imposed on a company. Following failure of a company to deliver a corporation tax return the penalty is:

(a) if the first or second offence:
return delivered less than three months late—£100 penalty
return delivered more than three months late—£200 penalty.
(b) third or subsequent offence:
return delivered less than three months late—£500 penalty
return delivered more than three months late—£1,000 penalty.[4]

There are also tax geared penalties[5] of 10% of any tax unpaid 18 months after the end of the return period, which rises to 20% of the tax unpaid 24 months after the end of the return period.[6] This is in addition to any fixed-rate penalties.

¹ FA 1998, Sch 18 para 20.
² FA 1998, Sch, 18, para 2.
³ TMA 1970, s 102.

⁴ FA 1998, Sch 18, para 17. This provision was described in *Lessex v Spence* [2004] STC (SCD) 79 para 37 at 87e:

> Para 17(4) does not make sense at it stands. If we look at the 'ordinary' words . . . and we put them together with para 17(3) in the way we are directed, the result is nonsense . . . . The result has meaning but is a patent absurdity.

The decision continues (para 41 at 88c):

> I consider that there is clear authority permitting me to reject nonsensical or absurd literal interpretations in favour of an interpretation that makes sense of the paragraph as a whole in its context.

The court levied a penalty of £1,000.

⁵ FA 1998, Sch 18, para 18(2)(*a*)
⁶ FA 1998, Sch 18, para 18 (2)(*b*).

Inheritance tax

[2A.92] The penalty regime for inheritance tax is in line with that for income tax and capital gains tax, representing a significant tightening up compared to the previous penalty regime, at least in a number of important areas.

Generally, the due date for submitting an account to the Capital Taxes Office is twelve months after the death, or other chargeable event. A penalty of £100 (or the tax, if less) is chargeable for failure to deliver a return in the 12-month period, the penalty being doubled if the return is more than 18 months after the death or other chargeable event.[1] No penalty is charged if the person due to deliver the account demonstrates a reasonable excuse[2] for the failure to deliver an account. It is suggested, however, that this provision is likely to be applied very restrictively and there are few occurrences that would qualify as a reasonable excuse in this context.

If a Court or the Special Commissioners have made an order requiring delivery of an account, an additional penalty of £60 is levied for each day the delivery is delayed after the date specified in the order.[3]

Where the account has not been delivered within 24 months of the death or other chargeable event, the penalty increases to £3,000.[4] This penalty, unlike the others, is not limited to the tax found to be due.

If a deed of variation has the effect of increasing the inheritance tax payable, the personal representatives and the parties to the instrument are required to notify HMRC accordingly within six months of the date of the deed.[5] Failure to submit within the six month period attracts a penalty of £100,[6] or the amount of the increase in tax, if less. Failure to submit the deed of variation within 12 months, attracts a penalty of up to £3,000, which is not automatically reduced by the tax payable.[7]

Negligent provision of incorrect information attracts a penalty of up to 100% of the tax lost.[8] In addition, and in recognition of the special role played by the professional agent in inheritance tax matters, a penalty of up to £3,000 can be charged on a professional advisor for negligently or fraudulently supplying incorrect information or documentation.[9]

¹ IHTA 1984, s 245(2)(*a*), (3).
² IHTA 1984, s 245(7).
³ IHTA 1984, s 245(2)(*b*).
⁴ IHTA 1984, s 245(4)(*b*).
⁵ IHTA 1984, s 218A.
⁶ IHTA 1984, s 245A(1A).
⁷ IHTA 1984, s 245A(1B).
⁸ IHTA 1984, s 247(2).
⁹ IHTA 1984, s 247(3).

National Insurance contributions

[2A.93] A penalty of 100% of the NICs unpaid through fraud or negligent conduct is chargeable;¹ in addition, fixed penalties include a penalty of £100 per 50 employees for each month (or part month) in which a Class 1 return is late.² A penalty applies in the case of a late Class 1A return, equivalent to the penalty for form P11D.³

¹ SSCBA 1992, Sch 4, para 16 applies the income tax regime of TMA 1970, s 95 to NIC.
² FA 1989, s 165(1).
³ SI 2001/1004, reg 82.

Tax credits

[2A.94] Penalties of up to £3,000 can arise where a person fraudulently or negligently makes incorrect statements in connection with their tax credits claim.¹ A penalty not exceeding £300 can be imposed where a person fails to give a required notification of change of circumstances.² A penalty not exceeding £300, followed by a daily penalty not exceeding £60 per day can be imposed where there is a failure to comply with any requirements under the tax credit legislation (such as providing information or evidence in support of a claim, or returning a notice under section 17).³

There are also penalties of up to £3,000 where an employer refuses, or repeatedly fails, to make payments of tax credits to an employee or where the employer fraudulently or negligently pays the incorrect amount.⁴

¹ TCA 2002, s 31.
² TCA 2002, s 32(3) and supra, § **2A.48**ff.
³ TCA 2002, s 32.
⁴ TCA 2002, s 33.

Stamp duty and stamp duty reserve tax

[2A.95] A penalty is payable under SA 1891, s 15B on an instrument which is not presented for stamping within 30 days after:

(1) if the instrument is executed in the UK, or relates to land in the UK: the day on which it is executed;

(2) if the instrument is executed outside the UK, and does not relate to land in the UK: the day on which the instrument is first received in the UK.

The maximum penalty is £300 (or the amount of unpaid duty if less) if the instrument is presented for stamping within one year of the 30-day period in 1 or 2 above. If the instrument is not presented for stamping until after the end of one year from the 30-day period mentioned in 1 or 2 above, the maximum penalty is the greater of £300 or the unpaid duty. The Commissioners may mitigate or remit any penalty and no penalty is payable if there is a reasonable excuse for the delay in presenting the instrument for stamping.[1]

An appeal against the penalty payable on late stamping lies to the Special Commissioners rather than the High Court.[2]

Equivalent provisions apply to stamp duty reserve tax.[3]

Administrative fines have largely been replaced by penalties. The general level of penalties (other than on late stamping) was increased and a modern collection and appeals structure was introduced.[4] These penalties relate to various administrative offences including a failure to provide information, refusal to allow the inspection of documents and fraudulent acts or omissions. In most cases the penalty is £300 but this is increased to £3,000 where fraud is involved. All penalties may be mitigated by the Commissioners. An appeal against a penalty determination lies to the Special Commissioners.

Perhaps the two most important penalties in practice are those of £3,000 in relation to SA 1891, s 5 (failure to disclose the facts and circumstances affecting liability to duty) and of £300 in relation to SA 1891, s 17 (registrar enrolling instrument not duly stamped).

The Treasury are empowered to make regulations under FA 1999, Sch 17, Part III applying the Taxes Management Act 1970 in relation to the collection and recovery of penalties. Regulations have been made under which a person in default of a stamp duty penalty will be charged the costs of distraint action.[5] Regulations have also been made allowing for the recovery of a penalty determined by the Special Commissioners for failure to comply with a direction or summons in appeal proceedings relating to stamp duty as though it was a penalty other than a late stamping penalty, determined by the Commissioners and due and payable.[6]

Sergeant and Sims A18.5.

---

[1] SA 1891, s 15B(4) and (5), as amended by FA 2002, s 114, and see The Stamp Office Manual para 3.30 et seq and the SO Customer Newsletter of February 2001 for details of their mitigation policy.

[2] SA 1891, ss 13(4) and 13A.

[3] See TMA 1970, ss 93, 95, 97, 99, 100–105 and 118(2) as modified, applied and restated in SI 1986/1711.

[4] FA 1999, s 114 and Sch 17.
[5] The Distraint by Collectors (Fees, Costs and Charges) (Stamp Duty Penalties) Regulations SI 1999/3263.
[6] The Special Commissioners (Jurisdiction and Practice) (Amendment) Regulations SI 2000/288.

Stamp duty land tax

[2A.96] Penalties carry interest from the date they are determined until payment.[1] A repayment of SDLT (including an amount lodged under FA 2003, s 87(6)) carries interest at the rate applicable under FA 1989, s 178 between the payment of the tax and the repayment (unless it is a payment made in consequence of a court order or judgment of a court having power to allow interest on the payment). Any such interest paid is not income for tax purposes.[2]

[1] FA 2003, s 88. Interest is charged at the rate applicable under FA 1989, s 178.
[2] FA 2003, s 89.

Value added tax

Generally

[2A.97] The VAT penalty regime distinguishes three situations involving misdeclarations of VAT:[1]

(1) conduct involving dishonesty.
(2) Misdeclarations for a prescribed accounting period exceeding a specified threshold.
(3) Misdeclarations exceeding a specified threshold taking place during a "penalty period" specified in a "penalty liability notice".

These penalties will be replaced from an appointed day[2] by a new penalty regime in respect of careless or deliberate inaccuracies applicable to income tax, capital gains tax, corporation tax and VAT.[3]

A person is also liable to a penalty in respect of the following matters:

(1) Providing an incorrect certificate relating to zero-rating.[4]
(2) Material inaccuracy in an EC sales statement or a statement in respect of supplies of gold to which the reverse charge applies.[5]
(3) Failure to submit an EC sales statement or a statement in respect of supplies of gold to which the reverse charge applies.[6]
(4) Failure to notify liability to registration.[7]
(5) Failure by a non-taxable person to notify acquisition of a new means of transport or goods liable to excise duty.[8]
(6) Issuing a VAT invoice when not entitled to do so.[9]
(7) Breach of a walking possession agreement,[10] specified regulatory provisions,[11] record-keeping requirements relating to transactions in gold,[12] or record-keeping requirements imposed by directions.[13]

Penalties are assessed.[14] The amount assessed is treated as an amount of tax due from the trader and is thus recoverable as a debt due to the Crown.[15] A right of appeal is given in respect of any liability to penalty or the amount thereof.[16]

De Voil Indirect Tax Service V5.000.

[1] VATA 1994 ss 60, 61, 63, 64.
[2] FA 2007, s 96(2)–(4).
[3] FA 2007, Sch 24.
[4] VATA 1994, s 62(1).
[5] VATA 1994, s 65(1), (7).
[6] VATA 1994, s 66(3), (10).
[7] VATA 1994, s 67(1)(*a*).
[8] VATA 1994, s 67(1)(*b*).
[9] VATA 1994, s 67(1)(*c*).
[10] VATA 1994, s 68(3).
[11] VATA 1994, ss 69(1).
[12] VATA 1994, s 69A(2).
[13] VATA 1994, ss 69B(1).
[14] VATA 1994, s 76(1)(*b*).
[15] VATA 1994, s 76(9); VATA 1994, Sch 11, para 5(1).
[16] VATA 1994, s 83(*n*), (*q*).

Publishing details of tax defaulters

[2A.98] Despite having previously dismissed the idea of a 'naming and shaming provision', FA 2009, s 94 contains provisions that permit HMRC to publish details of persons who have incurred certain tax penalties ('relevant tax penalties').

The details will not be published unless the potential lost revenue[1] is more than £25,000 (either singly or in aggregate).[2] By aggregating, it can be seen that a £5,000 error over six years can trigger the provisions.

The details that may be published are:

- the person's name (including former names, pseudonyms and any trading names);
- the person's address (and also registered office);
- the nature of the person's business (if any);
- the amount of the penalty and the potential lost revenue;
- the periods or times to which the penalty relates; and
- any other such information that HMRC consider it appropriate to make clear the person's identity.[3]

[1] See § **2A.86** above.
[2] FA 2009, s 94(1)(*b*).
[3] FA 2009, s 94(4).

Relevant tax penalties

[2A.99] The penalties that can attract the naming and shaming are:

- penalties for inaccurate returns[1] (see § **2A.79** above), in cases of deliberate errors[2];
- penalties on third parties (who withhold information or provide false information) leading to inaccurate returns[3] (see § **2A.84** above)[4];
- penalties for failure to notify chargeability to tax[5] (see § **2A.89** above)[6]; and
- penalties for various VAT and duties contraventions (including the deliberate issue of unauthorised VAT invoices).[7]
No details may be published in cases where a penalty has been subject to the maximum reduction available for disclosure.[8]

---

[1] Under FA 2007, Sch 24, para 1.
[2] FA 2009, s 94(2)(*a*).
[3] Under FA 2007, Sch 24, para 1A.
[4] FA 2009, s 94(2)(*b*).
[5] Under FA 2008, Sch 41, para 1.
[6] FA 2009, s 94(2)(*c*).
[7] FA 2009, s 94(2)(*d*).
[8] FA 2009, s 94(10).

Procedures before publication

[2A.100] it was widely thought that the person would have the opportunity to appeal the proposed publication. However, that appears to have been an optimistic reading of the press release which announced the new rules. Although the elements of the penalty will be subject to appeal under the rules above, the actual intention to publish the details of the default are not subject to any separate appeal.

Before publication, however, HMRC must tell the person of their intentions to publish the information. They should also give the person the opportunity to make representations about whether or not the information should be published.[1] However, in the absence of appeal procedures, a person's only remedy would be by way of judicial review (possibly on an emergency basis if publication is imminent).

Information may not be published until after the final date for appealing any decision concerning the amount of the penalty.[2] This does not take into account the possibility of appeals being heard late.[3]

---

[1] FA 2009, s 94(6).
[2] FA 2009, s 94(7).
[3] FA 2009, s 94(11).

[2A.101] Tax administration – the mechanics

Time limits for publication

[2A.101] Once a penalty has become final (albeit subject to a late appeal being heard), HMRC have one year to publish the details for the first time.[1]

The information may not be published (or continue to be published) for more than a year after first publication.[2] This second time limit does not, of course, prevent third parties from keeping the information on their websites (for example, archives of newspapers). Thus, once the information is published, it will be next to impossible for the taxpayer to ensure that it will ever cease to be publicly available.

[1] FA 2009, s 94(8).
[2] FA 2009, s 94(9).

3

Avoidance—judicial principles

Construction and fact finding: *Barclays*	PARA **3.01**
Other recent cases	PARA **3.06**
The taxpayer and the doctrine	PARA **3.22**
Conclusions and current cases	PARA **3.23**

Construction and fact finding: Barclays

Three cases: Barclays, Campbell and Scottish Provident

[3.01] In *Barclays Mercantile Business Finance Ltd v Mawson*[1] the Judicial Committee of House of Lords has provided some overdue clarification of the basic principles applicable in this area. On the same day an identically constituted Committee provided further guidance in *IRC v Scottish Provident Institution.*[2]

What emerges from these cases is a process of cleansing in which excrescences (or even errors) already revealed in cases such as the distinction between commercial concepts and legal concepts suggested by Lord Hoffmann in *MacNiven v Westmoreland Investments Ltd*[3] are removed and we are left with the simple fact that tax law is about interpreting statutes and that statutes should be interpreted purposively. There is less intellectual chaos since there is agreement on basic principles. The full mantra is that the words must be interpreted purposively and in their context. This will not of itself produce certainty since it is in the nature of questions of construction that there will be borderline cases about which people will have different views.[4] *MacNiven* showed that there was no general overriding judicial anti-avoidance rule of law (or doctrine) to be applied like a principle of EC law. *Barclays* shows that there is no general overriding judicial anti-avoidance approach to construction. *Scottish Provident* shows that the House of Lords are not going to use their new approach to *Ramsay* to take us back to the 1960s and 1970s.

The major case law beginning with *Ramsay* and ending earlier in 2004 is upheld – but simply as exercises in construction. It is to be noted that since the *Barclays* decision the House of Lords has upheld the Revenue's claims in three other avoidance cases, viz *Macdonald (Inspector of Taxes) v Dextra Accessories Ltd*[5] and *West (Inspector of Taxes) v Trennery.*[6] It may be that the Law Lords, having spent much of their intellectual energy rejecting Revenue efforts to persuade them to create a judicial anti-avoidance doctrine, are keen to show that they are not some pro-taxpayer Mafia but can be trusted to reach realistic, sensible and balanced constructions of the legislation coming before them.

[3.01] Avoidance—judicial principles

Jones v Garnett, also known as the *Arctic Systems* case, is consistent with this view since the Revenue won the part of the case dealing with the scope of the settlement provisions.[7]

One should also note that in *Barclays Mercantile v Mawson*, the House of Lords went out of their way to praise[8] the approach of the Special Commissioners to *Lord Campbell v IRC*.[9] Previous editions have included lengthy extracts but it probably now suffices to refer the reader to paras 69 et seq of the decision.

---

[1] [2004] UKHL 51, [2005] STC 1, HL reversing [2002] EWCA Civ 1853, [2003] STC 66, CA reversing [2002] EWHC Civ 1527, [2002] STC 1068.

[2] [2004] UKHL 52, [2005] STC 15 reversing [2003] STC 1035.

[3] [2001] UKHL 6, [2001] STC 237; on Lord Hoffmann's distinction see also the extracts quoted in the 200405 edition of UK Tax Guide at § 3.02 from Collector of Stamp Revenue v Arrowtown Assets Ltd Court of Final Appeal of the Hong Kong Special Administrative Region, 4 December 2003. The Hong Kong Government provides an excellent service in posting onto a website the complete text (in English and Chinese) of every judgment of a senior Hong Kong court, the judgment being available within 72 hours of being made. English language versions of judgments can be accessed at www.judiciary.gov.hk/en/legal_ref/judgements.htm

[4] *Barclays Mercantile Business Finance Ltd v Mawson* [2004] UKHL 51, [2005] STC 1, para 27.

[5] [2005] UKHL 47, [2005] 4 All ER 107, [2005] STC 1111 see infra, §7.22.

[6] [2005] UKHL 5, [2005] 1 All ER 827, [2005] STC 214, see infra, §19.04.

[7] [2007] UKHL 35, 2007 STC 1536.

[8] In *Barclays Mercantile v Mawson* [2004] UKHL 51, [2005] STC 1 para 38 at 13f, Lord Nicholls refers us to "the perceptive judgement of the Special Commissioners (Theodore Wallace and Julian Ghosh) in *Campbell v IRC* [2004] STC (SCD) 396".

[9] [2004] STC (SCD) 396.

Barclays Mercantile v Mawson

[3.02] Reduced to their post-House of Lords simplicity, an Irish company, BGE, had built a pipeline. They sold the pipeline to the taxpayers, BMBF, for £91.3m. BMBF leased the asset back to BGE which granted a sub lease onwards to its UK subsidiary. The question was whether BMBF was entitled to a capital allowance in respect of the £91.3 m spent, as BMBF argued, to acquire an asset used in its business of finance leasing. The simple finance deal was then hedged around with many complex money flows; BMBF argued that the purpose of these arrangements was to ensure that the sums due from BGE under the lease arrangements would actually come through. Barclays thought their primary concern in drawing up arrangements was not to avoid tax but to ensure that the bank met the capital adequacy rules laid down by the UK banking regulatory authorities.

Although, seen from the point of view of BMBF, these were just 'security arrangements', the Revenue did not accept that view and argued that if one looked at the scheme as a whole, they were nothing of the sort. They so protected the position of BMBF as to prevent BMBF from incurring any expense at all and so took it outside the scope of the relevant provision.[1] On this view the expense was incurred neither (a) on the provision of machinery and plant nor (b) the purposes of BMBF's trade nor (c) incurred at all.[2]

The crux of the decision of the House of Lords was that the only person on whom the court should concentrate was the finance lessor (BMBF), not the finance lessee (BGE). The statutory requirements were concerned entirely with the acts and purposes of the lessor. The Act said nothing about what the lessee should do with the purchase price, how he should find the money to pay the rent or how he should use the plant. It followed that they agreed with Carnwath LJ – and not with Park J. For them there was nothing in the statute to suggest that "up-front finance" for the lessee was an essential feature of the right to allowances. The statutory test was based on the purpose of the lessor's expenditure, not the benefit of the finance to the lessee (para [42]).

In reaching this conclusion the House said (at para [32]):

> The essence of the new approach was to give the statutory provision a purposive construction in order to determine the nature of the transaction to which it was intended to apply and then to decide whether the actual transaction (which might involve considering the overall effect of a number of elements intended to operate together) answered to the statutory description. Of course this does not mean that the courts have to put their reasoning into the straitjacket of first construing the statute in the abstract and then looking at the facts. It might be more convenient to analyse the facts and then ask whether they satisfy the requirements of the statute. But however one approaches the matter, the question is always whether the relevant provision of statute, upon its true construction, applies to the facts as found.

Legislation amending the capital allowance rules for finance leases was passed in 2006; see infra, § **9.53**.

---

[1] Then CAA 1990, ss 24(1) (now CAA 2001, s 11(4)). Contrast Park J's analysis in the High Court: [2002] STC 1068 at [14]–[34] with the analysis of the Court of Appeal [2003] STC 66, CA at [26]–[36].
[2] [2003] STC 66, CA at [25].

IRC v Scottish Provident

[3.03] In *IRC v Scottish Provident*[1] the taxpayer company was trying to take advantage of an apparent gap in the transitional rules when the loan relationship rules came into force. In the simplified form as set out in the House of Lords it bought a right, not an obligation, to buy 5-year gilts at 90% of their par value—in return for a premium; it sold a right, not an obligation, to buy 5-year gilts at 70% of their par value. The company's idea was that the premium would not be taxable because it was a mutual company and the deal would be carried out before the new rules came into force in 1996 while the related (but netted out) loss of £20m would be allowable because it was timed so as to fall the under new rules.

Taking, as the House had just directed itself to in *Barclays*, the relevant provision (FA 1994, s 150A(1) (as inserted by the 1996 Act)) the question was whether the body had a 'debt contract' ie a contract under which a qualifying

[3.03] Avoidance—judicial principles

company had an "entitlement . . . to become a party to a loan relationship". A "loan relationship" includes a government security. So the short question was whether the option gave it an entitlement to gilts. As the House describes the scheme, especially para 6, the essentials of the scheme were settled before various other steps were inserted to make sure that there really was a transaction in gilts. These extra steps were put into the plan before it was agreed and, in due course, implemented. The effect of these extra steps was crucial.

To the Special Commissioners (para 24) the effect was to produce a chance that the scheme would not go through and so prevent the steps being a preordained transaction in the *Craven v White* sense.

> If the chance of the price movement occurring was similar to an outsider winning a horse race we consider that this, while it is small, is not so small that there is no reasonable or practical likelihood of its occurring; outsiders do sometimes win horse races.

The House disagreed.

> [I]n our opinion the Special Commissioners erred in law in concluding that their finding that there was a realistic possibility of the options not being exercised simultaneously meant, without more,[2] that the scheme could not be regarded as a single composite transaction. We think that it was and that, so viewed, it created no entitlement to gilts and that there was therefore no qualifying contract.

The House pointed out that the scheme could just as well have fixed it at 80 and achieved the same tax saving by reducing the Citibank strike price to 60. It would all have come out in the wash. Thus the contingency upon which SPI rely for saying that there was no composite transaction was a part of that composite transaction; moreover it had been chosen not for any commercial reason but solely to enable SPI to claim that there was no composite transaction. It is true that it created a real commercial risk, but the odds were favourable enough to make it a risk which the parties were willing to accept in the interests of the scheme.

So the House went on:

> [23] We think that it would destroy the value of the *Ramsay* principle of construing provisions such as s 150A(1) of the 1994 Act as referring to the effect of composite transactions if their composite effect had to be disregarded simply because the parties had deliberately included a commercially irrelevant contingency, creating an acceptable risk that the scheme might not work as planned. We would be back in the world of artificial tax schemes, now equipped with anti-Ramsay devices. The composite effect of such a scheme should be considered as it was intended to operate and without regard to the possibility that, contrary to the intention and expectations of the parties, it might not work as planned.

For the recent decision of the Special Commissioners in *Astall v HMRC* see below at 3.24.

We now note the impact of these cases on the older case law.

---

[1] [2004] UKHL 52, [2005] STC 15.
[2] Italics supplied.

MacNiven v Westmoreland Investments Ltd, 2001

[3.04] Westmoreland (WIL) was a property company that owed £70m including £40m arrears of interest on loans from a pension fund, which were also its only shareholders. If the interest could be paid, WIL would be able, thanks at that time to TA 1988, s 338, to use that payment as a charge on income and so create a loss which could be set against any later profits the company might earn in later years. If the terms of TA 1988, s 768 were met, the set off might even be against profits earned following a change of ownership. The scheme enabled this payment to be made. The pension fund shareholders lent the money to WIL, which used the loan to pay the arrears of interest. The facts thus disclosed a preordained series of transactions carried out in order to secure a payment of interest and a tax advantage in that WIL now had an allowable loss. The Revenue invoked the preordained composite transaction doctrine to deny WIL this loss.

In the House of Lords[1] the Revenue formulated its argument as follows:[2]

> When a Court is asked
>
> (i) to apply a statutory provision on which a taxpayer relies for the sake of establishing some tax advantage
>
> (ii) in circumstances where the transaction which is said to give rise to the tax advantage is, or forms part of, some preordained, circular, self-cancelling transaction
>
> (iii) which transaction though accepted as perfectly genuine (ie not impeached as a sham) was undertaken for no commercial purpose other than the obtaining of the tax advantage in question
>
> then (unless there is something in the statutory provisions concerned to indicate that this rule should not be applied) there is a rule of construction that the condition laid down in the statute for the obtaining of the tax advantage has not been satisfied.

This extreme version of the preordained composite transaction doctrine was dismissed by Lord Hoffmann.

> My Lords, I am bound to say that this does not look to me like a principle of construction at all. . . . This cannot be called a principle of construction except in the sense of some paramount provision subject to which everything else must be read, like s 2(2) of the European Communities Act 1972. But the courts have no constitutional authority to impose such an overlay upon the tax legislation and, as I hope to demonstrate, they have not attempted to do so.

---

[1] [2001] UKHL 6, [2001] STC 237, HL.
[2] At para 28.

The speeches

[3.05] The reason why this case was important was Lord Hoffmann's distinction[1] between terms which should be construed juristically from those which should be interpreted commercially.

The distinction drawn by Lord Hoffmann between "juristic terms" and "commercial terms" was played down by the House in *Barclays Mercantile Business Finance Ltd v Mawson*.

[3.05] Avoidance—judicial principles

38. This is not an unreasonable generalisation, indeed perhaps something of a truism, but we do not think that it was intended to provide a substitute for a close analysis of what the statute means. It certainly does not justify the assumption that an answer can be obtained by classifying all concepts a priori as either 'commercial' or 'legal'. That would be the very negation of purposive construction: see Ribeiro PJ in *Arrowtown* at paras 37 and 39 and the perceptive judgment of the Special Commissioners (Theodore Wallace and Julian Ghosh) in *Campbell v IRC* [2004] STC (SCD) 396.

One should not overlook the speech of Lord Nicholls in MacNiven. Lord Nicholls was to chair the Committee in *Barclays* and did so in *MacNiven*. Although expressly agreeing with Lord Hoffmann, he refrained from using terms such as juristic and commercial and explained in simple language that the meaning of the word payment could not vary according to the purpose for which the payment of interest is made.[2]

---

[1] Thus consider the speech of Lord Hoffmann in *Charter Reinsurance Co Ltd v Fagan* [1997] AC 313, especially at 393 discussing the words "actually paid" in a reinsurance contract. Lord Hoffmann (as obiter) approved the decision of Langley J in ruling that the payment of a bonus to a director was a payment in money and attracted NIC, when the way in which the bonus was paid was to give the director ownership of a quantity of platinum sponge held at a bank, with arrangements in place for the sale of the sponge for money: *NMB Holdings Ltd v Secretary of State for Social Security* (2000) 73 TC 85. See also *DTE Financial Services Ltd v Wilson* [2001] STC 777, CA ("payment" to be construed commercially in the context of PAYE).

[2] At para 15. Lord Hoffmann makes the same point, at much greater length, at para 67. The other judges to give reasoned speeches were Lords Hope and Hutton. When one adds the silent Lord Hobhouse one finds four of the five judges with names beginning with H, which makes for some sort of record.

Other recent cases

DTE Financial Services v Wilson, 2001

[3.06] In *DTE Financial Services v Wilson*[1] D, the employer, wanted to provide a £40,000 bonus for E, a director: they both wanted to avoid NIC and postpone PAYE. D used a contingent reversionary interest under settlement to get money to E. The scheme had four steps:

(1) Scheme operator creates a reversionary interest of the desired value on the basis of figures supplied by D.
(2) D takes an assignment of the reversionary interest for £40,600.
(3) D assigns the interest to E.
(4) E's interest falls into possession and £40,000 is remitted to E's bank account.

PAYE would have been due if (a) the reversionary interest had been a tradeable asset within s 203F or, (b) more broadly, the whole scheme was simply a payment of £40,000 cash by D to E.

The Court of Appeal held in favour of the Crown on ground (b).[2]

---

[1] [2001] EWCA Civ 455, [2001] STC 777.
[2] See especially Jonathan Parker LJ at 788e–h.

IRC v John Lewis Properties plc, 2002

[3.07] The Court of Appeal decision in *IRC v John Lewis Properties plc*[1] may be seen as anticipating the House of Lords decision in *Barclays*. The case involved an avoidance scheme which was stopped by FA 2000 (see infra, § **10.16**).[2]

The taxpayer company, JLP, was a property holding company which let property out to trading companies in return for rent. It sold its right to receive rents for a five year period to a Dutch bank with which it was not otherwise connected and received a lump sum payment from the bank in exchange. JLP wanted to use the money to fund capital expenditure on various stores. If the payment was held to be capital the transaction would be treated as a part disposal of the land and the company would be able to defer any liability through a claim for rollover relief. If however the receipt was of an income nature it would be taxable as part of JLP's profits, no holdover relief could be claimed and there would be no claim for capital allowances because of the nature of the building.

Lightman J distinguished *McGuckian*. JLP was giving up an income stream in return for an up-front capital sum. The price was no mere relabelling; it was a distinct sum paid out of the resources of the bank under a transaction which had commercial reality. He decided not to follow the Australian decision in *Federal Comr of Taxation v Myer Emporium Ltd*.[3]

The Court of Appeal dismissed the Revenue's appeal.[4] The reasoning of Dyson LJ with whom Schiemann LJ concurred, focuses almost entirely on the distinction between income and capital and sets out a number of factors which in his view explained why the payments were capital; Arden LJ also treated the issue as one of capital or income but reached a different conclusion.

---

[1] [2001] STC 1118.
[2] TA 1988 ss 43A–43G, now superseded by TA 1988, ss 774A–774G, added in 2006.
[3] (1987) 163 CLR 199, Aust HC.
[4] [2002] EWCA Civ 1869, [2003] STC 117 at [80]–[87].

Carreras Group Ltd v Stamp Comr, 2004

[3.08] In *Barclays* the House mentions with approval the recent Privy Council stamp duty appeal from Jamaica, *Carreras Group Ltd v Stamp Comr*.[1] This

[3.08] Avoidance—judicial principles

decision is symptomatic of the new approach to *Ramsay*. The Jamaican stamp duty legislation granted an exemption for the shares transferred as part of a reorganisation of share capital. On 27 April shares were exchanged for debentures which were to be redeemed on 7 May (actually redeemed 11 May). The Privy Council treated the exchange and the redemption as one transaction and so held to be not within the exemption. Lord Hoffmann dealt with one question of uncertainty as follows:

> [15] Mr Goldberg submitted that a factual inquiry into what constituted the relevant transaction for the purposes of para 6(1) would give rise to uncertainty. He was disposed to accept that if the representative of Carreras had handed the share certificates over the desk in exchange for the debenture and the representative of Caribbean had then handed it back in exchange for a cheque, it would be hard to say that the relevant transaction should not be characterised as an exchange of shares for money. But what if the debenture had been redeemed a year later? Why should a fortnight be insufficient to separate the exchange from the redemption?

> [16] One answer is that it is plain from the terms of the debenture and the timetable that the redemption was not merely contemplated (the redemption of any debenture may be said to be contemplated) but intended by the parties as an integral part of the transaction, separated from the exchange by as short a time as was thought to be decent in the circumstances. The absence of security and interest reinforces this inference. No other explanation has been offered. In any case, their Lordships think that it is inherent in the process of construction that one will have to decide as a question of fact whether a given act was or was not a part of the transaction contemplated by the statute. In practice, any uncertainty is likely to be confined to transactions into which steps have been inserted without any commercial purpose. Such uncertainty is something which the architects of such schemes have to accept.

In *Barclays* (para 35) the House said "In *Carreras* the transfer of shares in exchange for a debenture with a view to its redemption a fortnight later was not regarded as an exempt transfer in exchange for the debenture but rather as an exchange for money. . . . [T]he court looked at the overall effect of the composite transactions by which . . . the vendors in *Carreras* received cash."

[1] [2004] UKPC 16, [2004] STC 1377, PC.

Collector of Stamp Revenue v Arrowtown Assets Ltd

[3.09] In the above case[1] the seller was issued with and retained 100,000 "B" shares. These shares carried a right to a dividend only if the profits exceeded a fantastic figure equivalent to (about) US $12.8 quadrillion. A right to a distribution on a winding up of the company could only arise if the assets exceeded a similar sum. There was, however, a commercially sensible right to appoint a director of the company. The company had the right to repurchase the "B" shares at par value at any time; there was no equivalent right in the seller to compel the company to buy. The relevant stamp duty rule gave an exemption for share transfers in which at least 90% of the target company's issued share capital continued to be owned by the transferor's corporate group. The court held that (per Lord Millett): "The words 'issued share capital' in the [exemption] section, properly construed, mean share capital issued for a commercial purpose, and not merely to enable the taxpayer to claim that the requirements of the section have been complied with." The "B" shares, which were not issued for a commercial purpose, must be disregarded in applying the exemption, he said.

[1] Court of Final Appeal of the Hong Kong Special Administrative Region, 4 December 2003.

Terminology: avoidance, evasion and mitigation

Avoidance and evasion

[3.10] Tax avoidance, which is lawful, must be distinguished from tax evasion, which is illegal. If a person marries in order to reduce his tax burden he is practising tax avoidance; if he tells the Revenue that he is married when he is not, he is guilty of tax evasion, and may well be prosecuted. There is also an important distinction between a scheme under which no liability to tax arises—tax avoidance—and one under which a charge arises but the tax cannot be collected.[1]

[1] See *Roome v Edwards* [1979] STC 546 at 561–565, [1979] BTR 261.

Mitigation; a dying concept?

[3.11] For some years the judges, and especially Lord Templeman,[1] distinguished tax avoidance from tax mitigation. This was first done for the purpose of interpreting a general anti-avoidance provision in New Zealand law.[2] Lord Hoffmann criticised the distinction in *Westmoreland*. The term mitigation is not mentioned at any point in *Barclays*.

As Lord Nolan put it in *IRC v Willoughby* in 1997: "The hallmark of tax avoidance is that the taxpayer reduces his liability to tax without incurring the economic consequences that Parliament intended to be suffered by any taxpayer qualifying for such reduction in his tax liability. The hallmark of tax mitigation, on the other hand, is that the taxpayer takes advantage of a fiscally attractive option afforded to him by the tax legislation, and genuinely suffers the economic consequences that Parliament intended to be suffered by those taking advantage of the option."[3] In that case Lord Nolan considered the application of TA 1988, s 741 (now ITA 2007, s 739) which provided an exemption from s TA 1988, s 739 (now ITA 2007, s 720) if avoiding a liability to tax was not one of the purposes of the transaction. He concluded that it would be absurd in the context of s 741 to describe as tax avoidance the acceptance of an offer of freedom from tax which Parliament has deliberately made. Tax avoidance within the meaning of s 741 is a course of action designed to conflict with or defeat the evident intention of Parliament. He also said that where the taxpayer's chosen course was held to involve tax avoidance (as opposed to tax mitigation), it followed that tax avoidance must be at least one of the taxpayer's purposes in adopting that course, whether or not the taxpayer has formed the subjective motive of avoiding tax.

[3.11] Avoidance—judicial principles

The trouble with this explanation is that while it provides a coherent reason for saying in a particular case that the facts do not amount to avoidance and so do not trigger the application of some rule it does not provide a way of telling whether those particular facts fall one side of the line or the other—it is a conclusion not a test and so it restates the problem rather than solving it.

However this is not necessarily the end of the concept. First, Lord Hoffmann conceded that the distinction had a role in cases such as *IRC v Willoughby* where the legislation in question used the term tax avoidance. Secondly, it is tempting to say that, since the essence of the distinction is a point of construction as to when *Ramsay* applied and when it did not, it will resurface in the post-*Barclays* world of construction. However, that depends on what points counsel choose to take.

Simon's Taxes A1.118, A5.501, 203.

---

[1] Per Lord Templeman in *IRC v Challenge Corpn Ltd* [1986] STC 548 at 555. The New Zealand provision was Income Tax Act 1976, s 99 renders void for tax purposes arrangements entered into for purposes of tax avoidance.
[2] See eg Lord Templeman in *Ensign Tankers (Leasing) Ltd v Stokes* [1992] STC 226 at 240–241 and Lord Goff at 244–245.
[3] [1997] STC 995 at 1003–1004; the question whether the transaction was exempt as a bona fide commercial transaction was deliberately left open.

IRC v Duke of Westminster, 1936

[3.12] There are different layers to the famous *Westminster* case. It represents an approach to the statutes and facts the overall effect of which is distinctly pro-taxpayer. Its approach to the statutes is literal rather than purposive. Its approach to facts is unimaginative or worse. It is therefore terribly old fashioned and out of date. In *Barclays Mercantile v Mawson*, Lord Nicholls draws[1] on the explanation of Lord Steyn in *IRC v McGuckian*:[2]

> Until the *Ramsay* . . . revenue statutes were remarkably resistant to the new non-formalist methods of interpretation. The particular vice of formalism in this area of the law was the insistence of the courts on treating every transaction which had an individual legal identity (such as a payment of money, transfer of property, creation of a debt, etc) as having its own separate tax consequences, whatever might be the terms of the statute. As Lord Steyn said, it was:

> . . . those two features—literal interpretation of tax statutes and the formalistic insistence on examining steps in a composite scheme separately—[which] allowed tax avoidance schemes to flourish . . .

Lord Steyn was on the Committee of the House of Lords in *Barclays Mercantile v Mawson*.[3]

It is, therefore, highly unlikely that any modern court would say, as Lord Tomlin did in *IRC v Duke of Westminster*.[4]

> Every man is entitled if he can to arrange his affairs so that the tax attaching under the appropriate Acts is less than it otherwise would be. If he succeeds in ordering

them so as to secure that result, then, however unappreciative the Commissioners of Inland Revenue or his fellow taxpayers may be of his ingenuity, he cannot be compelled to pay an increased tax.

In *IRC v Burmah* Lord Diplock commented that the dictum told us little or nothing as to what methods of ordering one's affairs would be recognised by the courts as effective to lessen the tax that would attach to them if business transactions were conducted in a straightforward way.[5]

In *IRC v Westminster* the Duke covenanted to pay an employee a sum of £1.90 per week; the covenant was to last seven years whether or not he remained in the Duke's service. The employee had a wage of £3 a week and he was told that while he would be legally entitled to the full £3 it was expected that in practice he would take only the balance of £1.10. The purpose of the scheme was to enable the Duke to deduct the payment in computing his total income for surtax.[6] The scheme succeeded; the true construction of the document showed that these sums were income of the employee, not employment income (then under Schedule E), but under Schedule D, Case III, (now ITTOIA 2005, Pt 5, Ch 7) as an annuitant.

In reaching this conclusion the court was entitled to look at all the circumstances of this case, including the fact that the taxpayer had received a letter containing the expectations of the Duke already referred to. However, the court was also entitled to look at the fact that the legal right to payment would continue even though the employment ceased. The majority of the court said that they were not entitled to conclude that, just because money passed from employer to employee, therefore it must be Schedule E income if it was, in law, income under Schedule D, Case III. Lord Atkin, dissenting, thought the letter amounted to a contractual term and not just an expectation. Lord Templeman would have agreed with Lord Atkin.[7]

Simon's Taxes A1.118.

[1] [2004] UKHL 51, [2005] STC 1, at [28].
[2] [1997] STC 908, HL at 915.
[3] [2002] EWHC 1527 (Ch), [2002] STC 1068. The decision of the House of Lords in this case is given as a single opinion of the five Law Lords. It must, therefore, be assumed that Lord Steyn, as one of the five, was quoting his own words with approval.
[4] [1936] AC 1, 19 TC 490.
[5] [1982] STC 30 at 32f
[6] Such payments are not now effective: see infra, §§ 15.01 and 15.30.
[7] See *Ensign Tankers (Leasing) Ltd v Stokes* [1992] STC 226 at 235, HL.

The Westminster doctrine

[3.13] There is, however, another layer to the *Westminster* case and this is that taxpayers and Revenue are bound by the legal results which the parties have achieved. If the facts showed that the payments were in law annual payment rather than employment income then that conclusion had to be accepted and one could not go to some underlying 'reality' or 'substance' to change that outcome. This doctrine is still the formal position of UK tax law. As the House of Lords has said repeatedly since *Craven v White* in 1988 the court cannot disregard those facts just because of the tax avoidance purpose which may have led the parties to create those facts in the first place. Sometimes those legal facts may be decisive of the fiscal consequences, as in the cases on the boundary between the contract of service and contract for services which marks the line between ITEPA 2003 (Schedule E) and ITTOIA 2005, Part 2 (Schedule D, Case I or Case II). Sometimes, as in *Westminster*, these legal facts while not in themselves conclusive may point decisively in the direction of one particular tax consequence or characterisation. Hence in *Westminster* the fact that, if the gardener had been dismissed or had left the Duke's employment he would still have been entitled to the sums under the covenant for the balance of the seven year period, swayed the majority to their conclusion. As Lord Atkin would not have reached that decision he was led to a different conclusion. In a case in 1986, *Reed v Young*[1] the House of Lords held that as the parties had created a limited partnership the courts were bound to give effect to a tax saving scheme based upon that legal structure. There is no mention of *Reed v Young* in *Westmoreland* or *Barclays*, but that is no reason to doubt that the decision in *Reed v Young* continues to be good law.

The *Westminster* doctrine was sometimes expressed in the form that the court must look to the form of the transaction and not its substance. This formulation is, however, misleading in that it tends to suggest that the form of a transaction, a matter which may be within the control of the taxpayer, will be conclusive for tax purposes. Often, however, the legal form used by the parties is not conclusive as a matter of tax law and here it is accepted that the court must look at the substance of the matter in order to determine the true tax consequences of the transaction in the legal form adopted by the parties. Thus by looking at the substance it could conclude that this form attracted tax just as much as another. In these instances the court was not putting upon the transaction a legal character which it did not possess but was trying to discover the true character in tax law of the transaction entered into.[2] So the court might hold that a trade is carried on by a partnership even though the only document states that there was none,[3] that a trader is still trading even though he says he is not,[4] or that the person claiming to trade is simply the means by which the trade is carried on by someone else.[5] In such contexts the documents cannot be used to deny proven facts. Where, however, both the facts and the legal arrangements point in the same direction, the court might not disregard them.[6] It follows that the name given to a transaction by the parties concerned did not necessarily decide the nature of the transaction.[7] So a verbal description of a series of payments as an annuity or a rentcharge does not determine their character for tax purposes.[8]

Simon's Taxes A2.115.

---

[1]   [1986] STC 285.
[2]   Per Sir Wilfrid Greene MR in *IRC v Mallaby-Deeley* [1938] 4 All ER 818 at 825; 23 TC 153 at 167.
[3]   *Fenston v Johnstone* (1940) 23 TC 29.
[4]   *J and R O'Kane & Co Ltd v IRC* (1922) 12 TC 303.
[5]   *Firestone Tyre and Rubber Co Ltd v Lewellin* [1957] 1 All ER 561, 37 TC 111.

[6] *Ransom v Higgs* [1974] 3 All ER 949, [1974] STC 539.
[7] *Secretary of State in Council of India v Scoble* [1903] AC 299, 4 TC 618.
[8] *IRC v Land Securities Investment Trust* [1969] 2 All ER 430, 45 TC 495.

Sham transactions

[3.14] Neither the *Westminster* doctrine nor the *Barclays* approach give any effect to a sham transaction, ie where the acts done were intended to give the appearance of creating legal rights different from those which were actually created. Such schemes still fail for the simple reason that the tax falls to be levied on the basis of the actual legal rights created. This argument although frequently advanced by the Revenue did not meet with great success[1]. However, the new approach based on the decision of the House of Lords in *Furniss v Dawson*[2] encouraged the courts to give the Revenue occasional glimpses of success. So, in *Hitch's Executors v Stone*[3] the Court of Appeal upheld a finding by the Commissioners that documents purporting to grant long leases were a sham. In *Sherdley v Sherdley*[4] Sir John Donaldson, MR thought that an order to pay school fees to a school on behalf of a child and made at the suit of the parent against whom the order would have been made would be a sham. This use of the sham argument is highly questionable and probably erroneous. The decision was later reversed by the House of Lords, but without discussion of this point.[5] Since then the orthodox narrow definition of a sham transaction has prevailed.[6]

The problems of determining whether there is a sham transaction are shown by the recent case of *Hitch's Executors v Stone*[7] where the Court of Appeal reversed the High Court which had in turn reversed a finding by the Commissioners; the end result was that the transaction was a sham. In the Court of Appeal counsel for the Revenue made the useful distinction that while an artificial transaction was intended to be carried out even in an unnecessarily complex way, in the case of a sham transaction the parties did not intend to carry the transaction out at all. Arden LJ then set out her—and the court's—principles for sham transactions.

> [64] The particular type of sham transaction with which we are concerned is that described by Diplock LJ in *Snook v London and West Riding Investments Ltd* [1967] 2 QB 786. It is of the essence of this type of sham transaction that the parties to a transaction intend to create one set of rights and obligations but do acts or enter into documents which they intend should give third parties, in this case the Revenue, or the court, the appearance of creating different rights and obligations. The passage from Diplock LJ's judgment set out above has been applied in many subsequent decisions and treated as encapsulating the legal concept of this type of sham.. . . An inquiry as to whether an act or document is a sham requires careful analysis of the facts and the following points emerge from the authorities.
>
> [65] First, in the case of a document, the court is not restricted to examining the four corners of the document. It may examine external evidence. This will include the parties' explanations and circumstantial evidence, such as evidence of the subsequent conduct of the parties.
>
> [66] Second, as the passage from *Snook* makes clear, the test of intention is subjective. The parties must have intended to create different rights and obligations

217

[3.14] Avoidance—judicial principles

from those appearing from (say) the relevant document, and in addition they must have intended to give a false impression of those rights and obligations to third parties.

[67] Third, the fact that the act or document is uncommercial, or even artificial, does not mean that it is a sham. A distinction is to be drawn between the situation where parties make an agreement which is unfavourable to one of them, or artificial, and a situation where they intend some other arrangement to bind them. In the former situation, they intend the agreement to take effect according to its tenor. In the latter situation, the agreement is not to bind their relationship.

[68] Fourth, the fact that parties subsequently depart from an agreement does not necessarily mean that they never intended the agreement to be effective and binding. The proper conclusion to draw may be that they agreed to vary their agreement and that they have become bound by the agreement as varied (see for example *Garnac Grain Co Inc v HMF Faure and Fairclough Ltd* [1966] 1 QB 650 at 683–684 per Diplock LJ, which was cited by Mr Price).

[69] Fifth, the intention must be a common intention (see *Snook*).

However the court also held that it was not necessary that every party to the act or document should be a party to the sham; so that a document might, in unusual circumstances, be held to be a sham in part only.

Simon's Taxes A1.118.

---

[1] eg *IRC v Fleming & Co (Machinery) Ltd* (1951) 33 TC 57 at 62. For an interesting commentary on the differing approach to the concept of sham taken in different jurisdictions, see David Russell, *International Developments in Relation to Sham Trusts.*
[2] [1984] STC 153, [1984] 1 All ER 530.
[3] [2001] EWCA Civ 63, [2001] STC 214, reversing the decision of the High Court at [1999] STC 431.
[4] [1986] STC 266 at 273. Balcombe LJ disagreed (at 278) and Neill LJ made no comment.
[5] [1987] STC 217.
[6] See eg Lord Goff in *Ensign Tankers (Leasing) Ltd v Stokes* [1992] STC 226 at 245h, HL.
[7] [2001] EWCA Civ 63, [2001] STC 214; reversing [1999] STC 431.

Ramsay v IRC, 1981

[3.15] *Ramsay v IRC* concerned capital gains taxation. A had a large gain and wished to create an allowable loss which could be set against the gain and so remove his liability for tax. Under the scheme he bought shares in a company and proceeded to make it two loans each of £218,750 at 11%; the loans were made with the aid of the funds borrowed from a bank associated with the vendors of the scheme. A had the right once to decrease the rate of interest on one loan and make a corresponding increase on the other; this he exercised causing the rate on one loan to drop to nil and on the other to rise to 22%; the latter loan he sold for £391,481, a gain of £172,731. The other loan was repaid at par by the company but the shares in the company were sold at a large consequential loss. The narrow ratio of the House of Lords decision was that the gain on the sale of the debt was a chargeable gain because the debt was a debt on a security (a chargeable asset) and not a simple debt (a non-chargeable asset). However, the wider and more important ratio was that the court was entitled to look at the whole transaction and so to conclude that the taxpayer had suffered a loss only of some £3,000. As Lord Wilberforce said:[1]

> [The approach for which the Crown contends] does not introduce a new principle; it would apply to new and sophisticated legal devices, the undoubted power and duty of the courts to determine their nature in law and to relate them to existing legislation. While the techniques of tax avoidance progress are technically improved, the courts are not obliged to stand still.

In *Westmoreland* Lord Hoffmann said:

> My Lords, it seems to me that what Lord Wilberforce was doing in *Ramsay* was no more (but certainly no less) than to treat the statutory words 'loss' and 'disposal' as referring to commercial concepts to which a juristic analysis of the transaction, treating each step as autonomous and independent, might not be determinative. What was fresh and new about *Ramsay* was the realisation that such an approach need not be confined to well recognised accounting concepts such as profit and loss but could be the appropriate construction of other taxation concepts as well.[2]

Lord Steyn's words in *Barclays* on the vice of formalism have been quoted above.

Simon's Taxes A2.116.

---

[1] [1981] STC 174 at 181.
[2] [2001] UKHL 6 at [36], [2001] STC 237 at [36]; see also [32].

IRC v Burmah Oil Co Ltd, 1982

[3.16] After *Ramsay v IRC* it was possible to argue that the decision affected simply circular self-cancelling transactions, leaving the *Westminster* principle intact for other transactions. Doubts about this narrow view were raised by the decision of the House of Lords in *IRC v Burmah Oil Co Ltd*.[1] In this case the company, B, had transferred property to a subsidiary, S, but left the money outstanding. As the property had declined in value and was the only substantial asset held by S, it was clear that the debt was worthless. By means of a loan from a fellow subsidiary bank, SB, S was enabled to repay the original loan to B and, by means of a rights issue, attracted further money from B with which to pay off SB. S was then liquidated.[2] The effect was to substitute equity (a chargeable asset) for simple debt (a non-chargeable asset).[3]

Two further facts should be borne in mind. The first was that B still held the property so that in due course a genuine disposal of that property to an outside purchaser could give rise to an allowable loss. The second was that there were outside shareholders or creditors of S. The House of Lords, applying the *Ramsay* doctrine, refused to allow B to deduct the payments made under the rights issue in computing its loss on the shares of S when S was liquidated.

There were superficial differences from *Ramsay* in that the scheme was designated just for B instead of being bought "off the shelf", and that B used its own money in making the various payments instead of borrowing it—but these differences were of no real importance.

Burmah gave rise to particular difficulties in *Westmoreland* since the cases appeared identical; in each case an existing unfavourable tax situation was transformed into a favourable tax situation by a circular transaction entered into for no reason other than the avoidance of tax.

In *Barclays Mercantile v Mawson*, *Burmah* was treated as a case where a series of circular payments which left the taxpayer company in exactly the same financial position as before was not regarded as giving rise to a 'loss' within the meaning of the legislation.[4]

Simon's Taxes A2.116.

---

[1] [1982] STC 30.
[2] In the terms in which the case was argued this event triggered the tax advantage but may not have had to form part of the series of transactions; see Gammie, *Strategic Tax Planning*, Part D, p 17.
[3] The Commissioners had found that the steps would, almost inevitably, have been carried through.
[4] [2004] UKHL 51, [2005] STC 1, at [35].

Furniss v Dawson, 1984

[3.17] *Furniss v Dawson*[1] marked the furthest and most unruly extension of the *Ramsay* approach; the language in which the decision is couched shows a desperate wish not to pre-empt future developments and so opened the way to great uncertainty. As narrowed in *Craven v White* (see infra, § **3.18**) the case is manageable. As explained by Lord Nicholls in *MacNiven* (see supra, § **3.04**) it ceased to be any form of 'rule' and was simply a useful approach in the particular circumstances of the case.

In *Furniss v Dawson* a shareholder wished to sell his stake in Company A to Company C. He followed what Lord Brightman called "a simple and honest scheme which merely seeks to defer payment of tax until the taxpayer has received into his hands the gain which he has made". The shares in Company A were exchanged for shares in Company B and Company B then sold the shares in Company A to Company C. The House of Lords held that, although there was an express finding that all the steps were genuine, nonetheless the effect of the transactions for tax purposes was that the shareholder had disposed of his shares in Company A to Company C in return for consideration paid to Company B.

Lord Brightman, after stressing that no distinction was to be drawn in fact, because none existed in reality, between a series of steps carried through under a non-binding arrangement and those carried through under a contract, stated that the preconditions for the applicability of the *Ramsay* principle were:

> First, there must be a preordained series of transactions; or, if one likes, a single composite transaction. This composite transaction may or may not include the

achievement of a legitimate commercial (ie business) end . . . Secondly, there must be steps inserted which have no commercial (business) purpose apart from the avoidance of a liability to tax—not 'no business effect'.

It followed that the courts had the power to ignore (ie excise) the steps inserted for no commercial purpose. So here the preordained series of transactions began with the sale by the taxpayer to Company B and ended with the sale by Company B to Company C. This led to the excision of the intervening steps and therefore the whole scheme fell to be treated as a sale by the taxpayer direct to Company C in return for money paid to Company B, thereby excising Company B from this affair until the very end.

The analysis in *Barclays* was that the composite transaction is used to ascertain the true parties (the taxpayer and company C) and to ascertain the true dealing in a transaction which was a non-exempt disposal to C and so not a tax exempt disposal to B.[2]

Furniss v Dawson had received close attention in *Westmoreland*. Lord Hoffmann looked for the relevant fiscal concept and went on to say:

> In *Furniss (Inspector of Taxes) v Dawson*, this was the concept of a disposal by one person to another. For that purpose, and for that purpose only, the disposal to Greenjacket was disregarded. But that does not mean that it was treated, even for tax purposes, as if it had never happened. The payment by Wood Bastow was undoubtedly to Greenjacket and so far as this might be relevant for tax or any other purposes, it could not be disregarded.[3]

Perhaps anticipating *Barclays* Lord Nicholls was more circumspect.[4]

> . . . as I am sure Lord Brightman would be the first to acknowledge, the *Ramsay* approach is no more than a useful aid. This is not an area for absolutes. The paramount question always is one of interpretation of the particular statutory provision and its application to the facts of the case. Further, as I have sought to explain, *Ramsay* did not introduce a new legal principle. It would be wrong, therefore, to set bounds to the circumstances in which the *Ramsay* approach may be appropriate and helpful.

Simon's Taxes A1.547.

---

[1] [1984] 1 All ER 530, [1984] STC 153, HL.
[2] *Barclays Mercantile v Mawson* [2004] UKHL 51, [2005] STC 1, at [35].
[3] [2001] UKHL 6 at [48], [2001] STC 237 at [48].
[4] [2001] UKHL 6 at [48], [2001] STC 237 at [48].

Craven v White, 1988

[3.18] In *Craven v White* (and associated appeals)[1] the House of Lords had to consider the status of *Furniss v Dawson* and the intellectual chaos it had created by looking at its application to three sets of facts. The facts were argued exclusively in terms of the preordained composite transaction doctrine and the degree of pre-ordination required. In *IRC v Bowater Property Developments Ltd* the court was dealing with a development land tax (DLT) fragmentation scheme. A company which was a sister company to the taxpayer

[3.18] Avoidance—judicial principles

company was contemplating a sale to X. The sale did not materialise and the land was sold to the taxpayer for 97 1/2% of its market value. Subsequently, in order to take advantage of the rule that allowed each disponer, for DLT purposes, to claim an exemption on the first slice of realised development value (at that time £50,000), the taxpayer transferred the land in question to five other companies in the same group. This transfer had corporation tax consequences for the taxpayer company. A year later X reopened negotiations and, 19 months after the disposal by the taxpayer to the five companies, contracts were exchanged between the five companies and X. Could this be treated as a disposal by the taxpayer company to X, thus giving the companies only one exemption rather than five? The House of Lords unanimously said No.

In *Baylis v Gregory* the taxpayer was contemplating the sale of his company to Y; he went through a *Furniss v Dawson* operation and transferred the shares in his company to an Isle of Man company in exchange for shares in that company. However Y, unlike Wood Bastow, did not complete the sale. A year or so later a quite new company, Z, appeared and, after a further eight months, the sale to Z went through. Since the taxpayer had an intention to use the same provision as that which the taxpayers were trying to use in a *Furniss v Dawson* scheme, did it follow that the eventual sale to Z was by the taxpayer rather than by the Isle of Man company? Again, a unanimous House of Lords said No

In *Craven v White* the taxpayer owned all the shares in Q and were advised that they should seek either a merger or a sale. As a first step the taxpayers carried through a *Furniss v Dawson* style share for share exchange with an Isle of Man company. At that time there was the prospect of either a merger with C or a sale to O. If the merger had gone through there would have been a deferral of liability under the reorganisation provisions anyway. If, however, the sale to O took place the facts were close to *Furniss v Dawson*. At the time of the share exchange the prospects for the sale to O did not look good but on the same day O asked for a further meeting. After further negotiations, including one "stormy meeting", the sale to O went through. The Commissioners rejected the taxpayers evidence that their sole intention in carrying through the exchange was to merge with C and said that the primary objective was the sale to O and that they were keeping their options open. By a bare majority the House of Lords held that the taxpayers were not to be taxed as if they had sold their shares direct to O; the entity making the disposal to O was the Isle of Man company. Two issues faced the court. The first was whether the earlier decision in *Furniss v Dawson* should be taken as the start of the development of a general anti-tax avoidance jurisprudence. On this basis the fact that when the share exchanges and the transfer of the land took place the motive of the taxpayer was to save tax should be sufficient to enable the court to undo all the later developments. This argument was quickly and decisively rejected. Amongst many matters which troubled the House, as they had troubled the Court of Appeal, was what would be the legal status of the first transaction while one waited to see what might ensue, and, in particular, the status of any assessments to tax which might have been made on the basis of that first transaction (as might have occurred in the *Bowater* case).

The second was what degree of certainty there had to be before the steps could be said, to use Lord Brightman's word, to be "preordained". For the majority Lord Keith said that steps could be said to be preordained if, and only if, at the time the first of them was entered into the taxpayer was in a position for all practical purposes to secure that the second also is entered into. Lord Jauncey was tempted by a formulation in terms of whether there was no real likelihood that the second step would not go through but felt that this might be too rigid; the temptation to be a parliamentary draftsman was resisted. This is the point at which *Barclays* and *Scottish Provident* become relevant again. There is no suggestion that the House of Lords of 2005 would reach a different decision but just a warning against absolutes.

Lord Templeman and Lord Goff dissented on *Craven v White* but not in the other two appeals. For Lord Goff the matter could not be dealt with on the practical certainty test. While the interruption in *Bowater* and the unformed plan in *Baylis v Gregory* obviously dictated the conclusion in those cases, *Craven v White* was different as the sale to O was a primary purpose of the share exchange. Lord Templeman felt that the three majority speeches went too far in narrowing *Furniss v Dawson* and would revive a surprised tax avoidance industry; he thought *Craven v White* was indistinguishable from *Furniss v Dawson*.[2]

Lord Nicholls' reaffirmation of *Craven v White* has been mentioned above in connection with the *Scottish Provident* case (see supra, § **3.03**).

Simon's Taxes A2.116.

---

[1] [1988] STC 476.
[2] However, it is interesting to compare his test at [1988] STC 476 at 490 with that of Lord Oliver at 507.

Ensign Tankers (Leasing) Ltd v Stokes, 1992

[3.19] The next House of Lords case, chronologically, is *Ensign Tankers (Leasing) Ltd v Stokes*. The decision of the House of Lords embodies a matter of approach rather than a rule. This approach allows (and probably requires) the courts to examine the reality of the situation reaching the correct tax characterisation of the facts. This may mark the reconciliation, at least at the formal level, of the New Approach with the *Westminster* doctrine since, of course, under that doctrine the labels given by parties did not matter and the courts have long been required to determine the true legal character of the transactions. What may matter just as much is the emphasis given by Lord Templeman to the obligation of the courts to ensure that the taxpayer does not pay too much tax, not just too little.[1] Neither the taxpayer nor the Crown should be deprived of the fiscal consequences of the taxpayers' activities properly analysed.

Under a complex set of arrangements what V, a limited partnership and therefore E, one of the limited partners, hoped to achieve was that in return for putting up £3.25m, less than[2] 25% of the cost, they would be able to receive capital allowances on the total cost of production (£14m); at that time the rate of corporation tax rate was 50% and the rate of the relevant allowances was 100% of the expenditure. The Crown's attack was no less extreme; this was not a trading transaction and therefore E was not entitled to any allowance at all, not even the expenditure of $3.25m which had been incurred.

The House of Lords, held that this was a trading transaction.[3] V and therefore E were entitled to capital allowance on the expenditure actually incurred. However the expenditure which had been incurred was $3.25m not $14m. This conclusion involved a close analysis of the facts to determine their true legal effect.[4] The scheme would not be allowed to have the apparently magical effect of creating expenditure for tax purposes of $14m while incurring real expenditure of only $3.25m. The expenditure of the remaining $10.75m was really incurred by L. The House of Lords proceeded to penalise the taxpayers for attempting a scheme which "brought no credit" on their advisers[5] by making them pay all the costs of the appeal.[6]

In *Arrowtown* Lord Millett made the point that one effect of the reasoning in *MacNiven* might be that *Ensign Tankers* could be decided the other way.[7] However, this is probably to be seen as part of Lord Millett's critique of the approach of Lord Hoffmann in *MacNiven* rather than a likely result.

Simon's Taxes A2.116; STP Introduction [31]–[90].

[1] [1992] STC 226 at 236.
[2] After taking account of the overrun which was also financed by non-recourse loan.
[3] Infra, § **8.11**.
[4] Infra, § **9.04**.
[5] [1992] STC 226 at 234.
[6] [1992] STC 226 at 244.
[7] Para 138; we are indebted to Philip Wylie of the University of Wales, Cardiff Law School for drawing this to our attention.

Fitzwilliam v IRC, 1993

[3.20] *Fitzwilliam v IRC*[1] is discussed further at infra, § **39.33**. This case established that if the Crown wished to use the New Approach to create a charge to tax, the mere fact that a scheme was preordained was not of itself sufficient. The court has to consider whether it was possible realistically and intellectually to treat the scheme as a whole. If the Crown's case required the court to pick and choose different bits of the scheme and treat them in different ways the court could not realistically or intellectually treat the scheme as a whole and therefore refused to do so.[2] The case was cited to the court in *Westmoreland* and *Barclays* but is not mentioned in any of the speeches in either case.

Simon's Taxes A2.3116.

[1] [1993] STC 502, HL.
[2] See also *Young v Phillips* [1984] STC 520.

IRC v McGuckian, 1997

[3.21] The importance of the *McGuckian*[1] decision in 1997 is that Lord Steyn, using words echoed in *Barclays*, described the *Ramsay* case as an intellectual breakthrough in which the courts escaped from their literal approach to the statutes and from their self imposed insistence of treating each step of a composite transaction as separate and distinct.[2]

The actual case is well summarised for present purposes by the Special Commissioners in *Campbell*[3] at para 74.

> 74. Thirdly, the *Ramsay* doctrine has been applied to ascertain the true nature of a receipt in the hands of a taxpayer. So where a taxpayer, entitled to a dividend which has been declared, sells the right to that dividend to a third party for a sum which is funded by the very dividend payment itself, the receipt by the assignee is income, not capital, for the purposes of s 478 of the Income and Corporation Taxes Act 1970: *IRC v McGuckian*, as explained by Lord Hoffmann in *Westmoreland*, supra, paras 51 to 57, especially paras 54, 55 and by Lord Millett in *Arrowtown*, para 147.

The second reason why the case is important is that both Lord Steyn and Lord Cooke would have held the payment to the trust for the right to the dividend to be income not capital, without reference to the *Ramsay* principle at all.

Lord Cooke, while not saying he agrees with the actual decision in the *Duke of Westminster*, clearly indicates a degree of unease. However, the unease stems from the concept of "a wage", which is probably the same as the basis of Lord Atkin's well known dissent in that case, rather than on the use of the *Ramsay* approach.

Simon's Taxes A2.116.

---

[1] [1997] STC 908
[2] at 915
[3] [2004] STC (SCD) 396; see HL para 38.

The taxpayer and the doctrine

[3.22] Now that we know the basis of the case law on statutory construction, it ought to follow that the courts will apply a purposive approach to terms, whether this is sought by the taxpayer and not by the Revenue. At one time it appeared that the matter might be resolved by the litigation in *Whittles v Uniholdings Ltd (No 3)*[1] the taxpayers had taken out a dollar bank loan to finance a sterling acquisition. In order to reduce their exposure to currency exchange risks the taxpayer also took out a forward contract with the same bank to buy the same number of dollars at the end of the period of the loan at a fixed sterling price. The issue was whether this will be treated as one single transaction or as two; in the latter, some absurd but well known fiscal consequences accrue. The Revenue argued that the transactions should be taxed separately; the taxpayer that they constituted a single composite agreement between it and the bank under which it could not deal with forward

[3.22] Avoidance—judicial principles

contract without the consent of the bank. Sir John Vinelott held that there was a single composite transaction because that was the true contractual effect of the arrangement. In the Court of Appeal the Crown argued that there were two transactions whether or not there was a contractual nexus. Aldous LJ would have dismissed the appeal but was outvoted by Nourse LJ and Sir John Balcombe. For Nourse LJ what mattered was that but for the *Ramsay* case, which he persisted in calling "the fiscal nullity doctrine", he would have attached great weight to the House of Lords decision in *Aberdeen Construction Group Ltd v IRC*.[2] He then said:

> One thing may, however, be asserted without fear of contradiction. While . . . the principle, . . . one of statutory construction, is capable of being invoked by a taxpayer in certain circumstances, it is clear that if it had never before been thought of, it would not have been invented to enable the company to succeed in this case. More decisively still, it could not attribute to two transactions with no contractual link between them fiscal consequences different from those resulting from two transactions between which there was such a link.

Simon's Taxes A2.116.

[1] [1996] STC 914; 68 TC 528, 594.
[2] [1978] STC 127.

Conclusions and current cases

[3.23] The case law culminating in *Barclays* can be seen as a perfect example of the common law judicial process. New ideas are floated and expanded then contracted and then widened again. Eventually a new principle evolves and is generally accepted. The classic example from the law of tort is the evolution of the tort of negligence. *Donoghue v Stevenson* [1932] AC 562 was followed by a period of narrowing judicial decisions before being allowed to develop into the principle tort lawyers recognise today. In *Westmoreland* the House of Lords gave us a clear—and constitutionally sustainable—basis for the case law but at the cost of having to repudiate much of the language used in those older cases and creating a whole new range of uncertainty. This process has been carried further in *Barclays*. The result is less chaos but more uncertainty. Recent cases show the courts adopting a purposive approach when interpreting coherent sets of statutory rules and so reaching results which are favourable to HMRC (see infra, § **3.24**). However judges will not – and cannot – achieve this result where the taxpayer has simply taken advantage of gaps between different sets of rules (see infra, § **3.25**). Mention is also made of two of Lord Hoffmann's Hong Kong cases (see infra, § **3.26**).

Current cases

Revenue victories

[3.24] Recent litigation before the Special Commissioners shows that this is still an area of considerable activity. *Astall v HMRC*[1] is a further illustration of the points made by the House of Lords in *IRC v Scottish Provident* (above). The Commissioners, Gordon Reid QC and Dr Avery Jones, were faced with what the taxpayers argued was a loss arising from a transfer or relevant discounted securities within FA 1996, Sch 13, Para 3 (now ITA 2007). The Commissioners held that two elements in the terms governing the transaction – one a condition relating to a change in the market and the other a decision not to seek a purchaser for the security until after it had been issued – should be disregarded. Peter Smith J upheld the Special Commissioners' decision and dismissed the appeal to the High Court saying that there were no grounds for suggesting that the Commissioners had come to factual conclusions they were not entitled to and there was nothing to suggest that they had misapplied the relevant law.[2]

For the taxpayers to succeed the particular provision required there to be a deep gain. However it was "practically certain", to use the words reaffirmed in *IRC v Scottish Provident*[3], that there would be a loss on the sale of the security. Like the Special Commissioners the judge took a purposive approach to the meaning of "discounted security". He had to consider real possibilities of redemption, not those written into the document creating the security that the parties and any reasonable person having the knowledge available to the parties, knew would never occur. The difference between the issue price and the redemption price had to give rise to a possibility of making a gain that could be objectively seen to exist. The security never had that possibility; it was a practical certainty that there would be a loss (paras 42–44).

In *Scottish Widows plc v HMRC*[4], the same two Commissioners considered whether sums described in the accounts as "transfer from capital reserves, were to be take into account as receipts in computing the company's profits or losses for corporation tax in the early 2000s. The issue arose under the insurance company taxation rules in force at that time (FA 1989, s 83). The facts arose from the demutualisation of the Scottish Widows insurance company; the amounts transferred over three years of came to £876m. One issue was whether the relevant value of the fund was a) the market value used to determine the solvency of the company or b) the sum given by an actuarial investigation to be taken to determine the amount of surplus available for distribution to the policy holders or the shareholders. The Commissioners held in favour of b). There was a further issue as to how the decision in favour of b) should be taken into account for tax purposes which, they held, should be as a Case I receipt of the business so that the company lost. The decisions are replete with references to purposive interpretation.

In *Prudential v HMRC*[5], Sir Andrew Morritt C, sitting in the Chancery Division, has dismissed the taxpayer's appeal from the Special Commissioners.[6] The principle question was whether a "front end" payment was a "qualifying" payment for the purpose of foreign exchange rules then in force (FA 1994); if it were, it would be deductible, so giving rise to the advantage sought by the taxpayer company (C). The essential reasoning begins at para 36 and the consequences are set out at 54–58. He held that a payment could only be a qualifying payment if made "to secure the making of the contract"; here the payment was not made by way of inducement to enter into the contract but

[3.24] Avoidance—judicial principles

in fulfilment of the contract (para 54) and no amount of mislabelling could alter the facts (para 55). He agreed with the reasoning of Sir Stephen Oliver and Mr Wallace.[7]

The Commissioners had also considered whether the company had established that the payment was properly attributed to a particular period. This was matter of accounting evidence and the Commisioners decided in favour of the Revenue. In their view the accounts had neither recognised nor computed any payment. Sir Andrew Morritt C expressed no opinion (para 44).

Finally – and perhaps more interestingly – was the main purpose for which the company was party to that agreement a tax advantage purpose, so that s 168A applied? Once more they held in favour of the Revenue. On the evidence the company was not simply finding a use for £65 million of idle currency. Rather it had implemented the scheme in the manner prescribed by the accountants and using as much cash as was available for the purpose. Many will be studying this very subjective approach to see how to arrange their affairs in future. Again, Sir Andrew Morrit C expressed no opinion (para 44).

HMRC v Limitgood Ltd; Revenue and Customs Commissioners v Prizedome Ltd[8] is an interesting case on the corporation tax rules barring pre-entry capital losses. Blackburne J allowed the HMRC appeal from the Special Commissioners, who had been divided. The view of Dr Avery Jones in favour of HMRC was upheld by Blackburne J, but he did not agree with all the reasoning (paras 64 et seq). The taxpayer's argument would give a decision closer to the words of the section, but the HMRC case was closer to its purpose (especially paras 53–63). The Court of Appeal has dismissed the taxpayer's further appeal.[9]

The particular question involved TGCA 1992, s 170 and Sch 7A. The taxpayer companies, L and P, which were subsidiaries of A, then acquired shares in A. Next a wholly owned subsidiary of GL acquired shares in L and P; this meant first that they ceased to be members of the A group and joined the GL group; and secondly that they were deemed to have disposed of their assets so realising large losses which were pre-entry losses vis-a-vis the GL group. Gains were then realised by another company in the GL group – and passed to L and P under TGCA 1992, s 171A. The GL group was then acquired by another group, referred to in the case correctly but confusingly as the GH group. Later still GH was acquired by H. The question was whether the particular group for the relevant provision comprised GH and H, as HMRC contended, or whether it comprised GH, H and GL, as L and P argued. The precise answer would determine whether the particular loss was a pre-entry loss, and as it has already been said, the answer given by Blackburne J was in favour of the HMRC view (see especially the conclusions at paras 53 et seq). The precise reasoning is too detailed to be set out here. What is important is that the case is a classic example of the new 2008 purposive construction as opposed to a more literal approach. What is not clear is how the case would have been decided in a) 1998, b) 1988 or c) 1978.

In the Court of Appeal Mummery LJ gave the only reasoned judgement and one which was, for this area of law, relatively short – and much shorter than those of the judges below. He held that the taxpayers were entitled to the relief sought under TGCA 1992, Sch 7A, para 1(6) only if two conditions were met and one of them was not satisfied. He went out of his way (para 36) to emphasise his agreement with the ampler reasons given by Dr Avery Jones and Blackburne J.

1   SpC 628 [2008]; STC (SCD) 142.
2   [2008] EWHC 1471 (Ch); [2008] STC 2920.
3   [2004] UKHL 52; [2005] STC 15; [2005] All ER Rev.
4   (2008) SpC 664.
5   (2008) SpC 636; [2008] STC 239. For comment see Fazzini, *Tax Journal*, 8 October 2007 and 5 November 2007, and Shiers, 19 November 2007.
6   [2008] STC 2820; [2008] EWHC 1839, Ch.
7   (2008) SpC 636; [2008] STC 239. For comment see Fazzini, *Tax Journal* 8 October 2007 and 5 November 2007, and Shiers, 19 November 2007.
8   [2008] EWHC 19 (Ch); [2008] STC 361.
9   [2009] EWCA Civ 177; [2009] STC 980.

Revenue defeats

[3.25] These two HMRC successes do not mean that they will always win appeals. While the judges are adopting a purposive approach to interpreting coherent sets of statutory rules, and so reaching results which are favourable to HMRC as just seen, they will not – and cannot – achieve this result where the taxpayer takes advantage of gaps between different sets of rules. This can be seen first in *Revenue and Customs Commissioners v Bank of Ireland Britain Holdings Ltd*.[1] The case involved a provision (TA 1988, s 730A) tackling schemes under which taxpayers turned taxable income into a capital sum; the legislation then turned them back into taxable income. Here, however, the scheme did not turn income into capital, but arranged matters so that the income accrued to a non-resident company outside the charge to corporation tax (High Court para 41). Counsel did not claim that there was any fiscal or economic merit in the result for which they contend; they simply submitted that the relevant legislation admitted of only one construction, and if the result was not to the Revenue's liking, then the Revenue has only itself to blame for procuring the enactment of such complex deeming provisions without giving enough thought to the consequences (High Court para 4). The Court of Appeal agreed.[2]

The taxpayer has also succeeded in *Revenue and Customs Commissioners v D'Arcy*.[3] This case concerned the accrued income scheme (TA 1988, s 710, now ITA 2007, Pt 12 (s 615 et seq). Under a scheme, the taxpayer (D'A) had made a sale and repurchase of gilts, a "repo" transaction. Henderson J dismissed the Revenue's appeal from the Special Commissioner. The taxpayer had taken advantage of an unintended gap left by the interaction between two different sets of statutory provisions – TA 1988, ss 710 and 737A. Section 737A, now ITA 2007, Pt 11, Ch 4, allowed D'A to claim a deduction. What the Revenue were really complaining about was that the accrued income scheme did not give rise to a charge which counterbalanced D'A's deduction

[3.25] Avoidance—judicial principles

under s 737A. This did not entitle him to construe s 710 differently to fill the gap. There is also material on the relationship between different parts of the income rules.

[1] [2007] EWHC 941 (Ch); [2008] STC 253.
[2] [2008] EWCA Civ 58; [2008] STC 398.
[3] [2007] EWHC 163 (Ch); [2008] STC 1329.

Hong Kong and Lord Hoffman

[3.26] Readers are also directed to the comments of Lord Hoffmann in the recent Hong Kong Case of *CIR v HIT Finance Ltd*.[1] In the first part of the case the court held that scheme would succeed, as it had in Westmorland, and Barclays. However the general anti-avoidance provision (Inland Revenue Ordinance Cap.112) (s 61A) was a different matter. Lord Hoffmann concluded that the borrowing and repayment had been introduced into the transaction for the sole or dominant purpose of avoiding tax. The evidence to suppose that there was some other purpose was somewhat sparse.[2] In his analysis of s 61A he referred to his earlier decision in *CIR v Tai Hing Cotton Mill Development Ltd*.[3]

[1] FACV No 8 and 16 of 2007.
[2] Para 20.
[3] FACV No 2 of 2007.

4

Anti-avoidance legislation

General rule or specific legislation	PARA **4.01**
Dividend stripping and bond washing	PARA **4.07**
Sale and repurchase of securities	PARA **4.10**
Manufactured dividends	PARA **4.15**
Transactions in securities	PARA **4.18**
Sale by individual of income derived from his personal activities	PARA **4.30**
Statutory provisions introduced as a consequence of disclose of a tax mitigation scheme	PARA **4.32**
Manufactured capital losses	PARA **4.33**

General rule or specific legislation

[4.01] Unlike many countries, the UK has no general provision that schemes which save tax shall be void against the Revenue. Further, the doctrine laid down by the House of Lords in *IRC v Duke of Westminster* prevented the courts from going behind the legal effect of a transaction and taxing it as if the transaction had some different legal effect. The problems raised by this rule for the Revenue were compounded by the judicial approach to the interpretation of tax legislation which placed on the Revenue the burden of showing that the taxpayer fairly fell within the scope of the charge.[1] To this one could add the judicial neutrality observed by those judges who saw nothing inherently evil in tax avoidance as distinct from tax evasion.[2] Much might have been changed as a result of the decision of the House of Lords in *Furniss v Dawson*[3] but very few of the many specific anti-avoidance provisions have as yet been repealed on the basis that they are unnecessary and the decision in *Craven v White*[4] rejects any possible wide scope of the New Approach in favour of a narrowly defined step transaction doctrine.

Statute[5] places an obligation on a "promoter"[6] of certain specified categories of tax avoidance scheme[7] to notify the Revenue (see supra, § **2A.02**). In addition, any person[8] concerned with the making of an overseas settlement by a UK-domiciled individual is required to report the creation of the settlement to the Revenue.[9]

Simon's Taxes A2.115–116.

---

[1] Contrast Lord Sumner in *IRC v Fisher* [1926] AC 395 at 412 and in *Levene v IRC* [1928] AC 217 at 227 and Lord Clyde in *Ayrshire Pullman Motor Services and Ritchie v IRC* (1929) 14 TC 754 at 763 with the wartime utterings of Lord Simon in *Latilla v IRC* [1943] AC 377 at 381 and Sir Wilfred Greene MR in *Lord Howard de Walden v IRC* [1942] 1 KB 389 at 397. See also Lord Simon in *Ransom v Higgs* (1974) 50 TC 1 at 94. "For the Courts to try to stretch the law to meet hard cases

[4.01] Anti-avoidance legislation

(whether the hardship appears to bear on the individual taxpayer or on the general body of taxpayers as represented by the Inland Revenue) is not merely to make bad law but to run the risk of subverting the rule of law itself." For further discussion of this area, see *Simon's Tax Planning* Introduction: The *Ramsay* Principle.

[2] On dividend stripping compare Upjohn LJ in *J P Harrison (Watford) Ltd v Griffiths* (1961) 40 TC 281 at 290 with Lord Morris in *Bishop v Finsbury Securities Ltd* [1966] 3 All ER 105 at 110; 43 TC 591 at 625.

[3] [1984] STC 153.

[4] [1988] STC 476 (supra, § **3.18**).

[5] FA 2004, ss 306–319. See supra, §§ **2A.05**.

[6] Defined in FA 2004, s 307 as (broadly) a person engaged in a profession providing services relating to taxation. There is no exemption for barristers. Where the promoter is overseas, or there is no promoter, the obligation falls on the person entering into the scheme: FA 2004, ss 309 & 310.

[7] The categories of scheme are specified in a statutory instrument: Tax Avoidance Schemes (Prescribed Descriptions of Arrangements) Regulations 2004 issued under the authority of FA 2004, ss 306(1)(*a*) and 317. A first draft of this SI was published on 17 May 2004 and amendments thereto published on 23 June 2004: *Simon's Weekly Tax Intelligence* 2004 pp 1250 and 1510.

[8] Excluding a barrister. In contrast to the provisions in FA 2004, ss 306–319, there is no obligation to declare an overseas trust if another person has made a report to the Revenue, or if the settlement is created by will: IHTA 1984, s 218(2).

[9] Within three months of the making of the settlement: IHTA 1984, s 218(1).

[4.02] To counter the problems so raised the Revenue in this and other countries have adopted various solutions which were classified by the Carter Commission in four groups.[1]

(1) The sniper approach, which contemplates the enactment of specific provisions which identify with precision the type of transaction to be dealt with and prescribes with precision the tax consequences of such a transaction. This has been the traditional pattern of UK legislation. One example is the rule for business entertainment expenses.[2]

[1] Carter Report, vol 3, App A at p 552.
[2] ITTOIA 2005, s 45 (income tax), TA 1988, s 577 (corporation tax) (infra, § **8.133**).

[4.03] (2) The shotgun approach, which contemplates the enactment of some general provision which imposes tax on transactions which are defined in a general way. The difference from the sniper approach lies in its conscious rejection of certainty. Of this TA 1988, s 703 probably represents the most obvious example, but others are TA 1988, ss 775, 776. All these sections create penumbral areas although the areas are circumscribed.

Simon's Taxes D9.101–104.

[4.04] (3) The transaction not at arm's length approach, which provides that the tax consequences shall be different from what they would be by treating the transaction as if it had taken place between parties at arm's length. Typical examples are the rules substituting market value for the price if any actually received for disposal of capital assets[1] and sales between associated persons for income tax.[2] Technically this is a means of carrying out one of the other approaches rather than a separate approach since the circumstances in which the technique is to be applied can be described with more or less precision.

Simon's Taxes B2.225.

---

[1] Infra, § **18.47**.
[2] TA 1988, Sch 28AA and TA 1988, s 541(3).

[**4.05**] (4) The "administrative control approach" which contemplates the grant of wide powers to an official or an administrative tribunal in order to counteract tax avoidance transactions. There is no such provision in UK law. Such a provision was included in the excess profits tax during the Second World War.[1] However, that scheme was less than fully effective.

---

[1] FA 1941, s 35. For an example of its application see *Crown Bedding Co Ltd v IRC* [1946] 1 All ER 452, 34 TC 107, CA.

[**4.06**] If one rejects the case for a general anti-avoidance provision, and one accepts the case for a sniper as distinct from the shotgun approach, one has to accept all the consequences of that approach. If the argument is based on the Rule of Law, the concept of certainty and the rejection of official discretion, then one must also reject any discretion in the Revenue to soften the application of a particular rule in hard circumstances. All too often critics of the Revenue really want the best of both worlds, a Revenue bound hand and foot by red tape in its efforts to get taxes but with unfettered power to waive tax due.

Dividend stripping and bond washing

Introduction

[**4.07**] Since a company is a legal entity distinct from its shareholders tax advantages accrue. Thus an individual trader will be liable to tax on his profits as they accrue; whereas, if he trades through a company, he may accumulate profits in the company and then withdraw as appropriate, either in the income form of dividends or management fees or in the capital form of further shares treated as paid up out of the profits, which shares he can then sell and thus realise a capital gain, or through the eventual winding-up or outright disposal of the concern. The basic distinction between the company and its shareholders has been accepted by UK tax law, although some manoeuvres are checked in the general interest of equity. Two such practices are dividend stripping and bond washing.

[4.08] Anti-avoidance legislation

Dividend stripping

[4.08] When a taxpayer transfers shares in a company, the tax system is normally content to accept that income payments made by the company after a sale of shares must be taxed according to the tax circumstances of the new owner of the shares, and the fact that the previous owner had a higher marginal tax rate does not entitle the Revenue to tax the new owner at his predecessor's rates. However, if the new owner is able to extract all the surplus cash in the company without incurring any liability to tax, to strip the company of its cash, the Revenue have caused the legislature to come to their aid.

This stripping can be achieved in the following way. A has shares in company X. A sells those shares to B. B uses his voting power to compel the company to pay a large dividend to B. B then sells the shares back to A or to someone else. At first sight there is nothing inequitable about this. If B's marginal rate is simply lower than that of A there is a loss of tax. This lower rate may be achieved if B is either an exempt person or is simply less well off than A. If however B is a dealer in securities he may claim that, while the dividend paid out is undoubtedly his income, that must be set off against the loss he incurs when the shares he had bought are resold, the loss being due to the payment out of the cash reserve of the company. The effect is that the payment will have been drawn out free of tax, while A has received a sum which reflects the value of those cash reserves and that sum will be treated as a capital payment only.

Attempts to obstruct these schemes have been ineffective unless drastic. Thus it was not clear whether the courts would hold that the transaction of buying in order to resell at a loss was a trading transaction.[1] If it was not a trading transaction, no relief could be given in respect of the loss and the scheme would fail. However, the UK courts at first accepted the arguments on behalf of B and so allowed the whole dividend stripping industry to get under way.

Some legislation was designed to prevent the accumulations from arising in the first place, this being the purpose of the close company legislation. Then the Revenue tried by a quite separate avenue to undo the tax advantages of stripping. Such devices, however, have always been subject to exceptions which exemplify the ambivalent attitudes of government to small, and therefore largely unregulated businesses. At first legislation was designed to interfere with the sales to security dealers and exempt persons but in 1960 the legislature aimed at transactions in securities generally.

Simon's Taxes D9.104.

---

[1] This is not a happy field for believers in precedents. The final view seems to be that this is not a trading transaction—see *FA and AB Ltd v Lupton* [1971] 3 All ER 948, 47 TC 580 but earlier cases especially *Griffiths v J P Harrison (Watford) Ltd* [1962] 1 All ER 909, 40 TC 281, were distinguished not overruled and the whole area was examined in *Coates v Arndale Properties Ltd* [1984] STC 124, CA, where the *Harrison* case was distinguished. These cases are cited in the litigation leading to *Ensign Tankers (Leasing) Ltd v Stokes* [1992] STC 226, HL (infra, § **8.11**).

Bond washing

[4.09] Dividends and interest payments become income only when they are due and payable[1] and there is no apportionment of that dividend over the period in respect of which it is declared.[2] Further, time usually elapses between the announcement of a proposed dividend by the company and its becoming payable. If during this time a high rate taxpayer sells his securities to one paying tax at a lower rate, the purchase price which he receives, although reflecting the value of the impending payment, cannot be segregated into an amount on account of capital and another amount on account of the dividend so as to tax the latter.[3]

This is still the law although legislation has been passed to prevent too blatant abuses; for anti-avoidance legislation dealing with accrued interest from securities, see infra, §§ **11.08** ff. One abuse is where the vendor sells the shares to his purchaser who collects the dividend taxed at his lower rate and who then sells them back to the original purchaser, all this being planned under the original agreement. In this way the bond or shares are said to be washed of their dividend. On the treatment of certificates of deposit and of rights to have such certificates issued see infra, § **12.14**.

Simon's Taxes Divisions D9.2, D9.10.

[1] Infra, § **26.02**.
[2] *Wigmore v Thomas Summerson & Sons Ltd* [1926] 1 KB 131, 9 TC 577.
[3] *Thompson v Trust and Loan Co of Canada* [1932] 1 KB 517, 16 TC 394.

Sale and repurchase of securities

[4.10] In 1937[1] a more serious attempt was made to counteract one type of tax avoidance involving the sale and repurchase of securities. This applies where a high rate taxpayer agreed to transfer securities[2] and either in the same or a collateral[3] agreement there was an agreement to buy back, or an option to buy back those or similar securities. If the result of such a transaction was that any interest, a term defined to include a dividend, became payable in respect of the securities and was receivable by someone other than the vendor, it was deemed to be the vendor's income. Thus the legislation was primarily intended to nullify any advantage to the vendor.

This statutory provision has been taken over by the accrued income scheme.[4]

Simon's Taxes Divisions D9.3, D9.10.

[1] FA 1937, s 12.
[2] Formerly TA 1988, s 729.
[3] See *Re Athill, Athill v Athill* (1880) 16 Ch D 211 at 222.
[4] ITA 2007, ss 616–681, see infra, § **11.08**.

[4.11] Curiously the 1937 legislation failed to cover the situation where the vendor sold not the shares but simply the right to the dividend. In *Paget v IRC*[1]

[4.11] Anti-avoidance legislation

the taxpayer held Hungarian bonds which carried the right to interest payable in sterling in London. Hungarian legislation altered the terms of the bonds making the interest payable in pengos through the Hungarian National Bank in London but the money could be spent only for certain limited purposes in Hungary. It was held that the fact that the pengos were on deposit for Miss Paget in London did not constitute the receipt of interest by her since the bank was not acting as agent for her and that she was not taxable on the purchase price received by her when she sold the coupons to a coupon dealer.

What is now TA 1988, s 730[2] was therefore passed in 1938[3] to catch the sale of the right to receive any interest payable in respect of securities without selling or transferring the securities themselves. The interest is deemed to be that of the vendor.

One may note that in *IRC v McGuckian*[4] the House of Lords treated the payment of a price for the right to dividends as income for the purposes of what is now ITA 2007, Pt 13, Ch 2 (transfers of assets abroad).

Simon's Taxes Division D9.10.

---

[1] [1938] 2 KB 25, 21 TC 677; on deduction of tax from interest see Inland Revenue Tax Bulletin Issue 20, December 1995.
[2] Amended by F(No 2)A 2005, Sch 7, para 2.
[3] FA 1938, s 24.
[4] [1997] STC 908 (supra, § **3.21**).

[4.12] The rules on the distinction between interest and other payments are refined by specific provisions dealing with the sale and repurchase of securities (known as "repo" transactions).[1] Under such a transaction the vendor's repurchase price is fixed at the time of the first transfer so putting the risk of change in market value on the original holder.

Under a repo transaction the difference between the sale and repurchase price, called the price differential, is to be treated as interest and, where a company is concerned, within the 1996 loan relationship rules.[2] The legislation goes on to direct that the differential will be taxable income of the recipient and deductible by the payer.[3] So if, as will usually be the case, the repurchase price is greater than the original sale price the difference is treated as interest made by the repurchaser; to complete the fiction the interest is treated as arising from a deemed loan from the interim holder on an amount equal to the sale price. Conversely, if the sale price exceeds the repurchase price there is a loan from the repurchaser and the interim holder is treated as paying the interest. This system applies where the original owner is required to buy back the securities; it applies also if the repurchase is to be by a person connected with the original owner and whether the obligation arises under the original agreement, a related agreement or an option acquired under that original or related agreement.[4] The treatment of the payment as interest is expressly made to apply also to TA 1988, s 209(2)(*d*), (*da*) so that any excess interest can be treated as a distribution.[5]

Specific legislation[6] deals with the stripping and reconstitution of gilts. Stripping a security of its right to income might save tax. This is the process of selling the right to the income without selling the underlying security.

Sale and repurchase of securities [4.14]

A thorough analysis of transactions under gilt-repro arrangements and the tax treatment of the transactions is given in the decision of the Special Commissioners in *Bank of Ireland Britain Holdings v Revenue and Customs Comrs*.[7] The Special Commissioners' decision was upheld both in the High Court and most recently in the Court of Appeal.[8]

Simon's Taxes Division D5.120–127, D9.10.

[1] ITA 2007, ss 593–594. See *D'arcy v Revenue and Customs Comrs* [2006] STC (SCD) 543.
[2] ITA 2007, s 607 (income tax); for corporation tax, the provisions were replaced by those in FA 2007, Sch 13.
[3] ITA 2007, s 578(3).
[4] ITA 2007, s 569(4).
[5] ITA 2007, s 575.
[6] ITTOIA 2005, ss 443–452.
[7] SpC 544, [2006] STC (SCD) 477.
[8] [2008] EWCA Civ 58.

[4.13] TA 1988, s 729[1] applied to disallow the purchaser's loss where there was a duty or right to resell to the original vendor and so did not apply where there was a right to resell to some other person. Nor did it restrict the rights of persons other than traders. A series of provisions was introduced in 1959,[2] to widen the net but these rules are excluded by the more powerful accrued income scheme introduced by FA 1985 and were eventually repealed by FA 2008 on the grounds that the mischief targeted by them was covered elsewhere.[3]

These provisions extended to three main groups of persons, dealers in securities, persons entitled to exemption from income tax such as charities, and persons other than dealers in securities who, having trading losses, are close to being exempt persons. The purpose of the provisions was to prevent the purchase of shares cum dividend to persons in these three groups who would receive the dividends subject to deduction of tax and then having resold them ex-dividend, recover the tax already paid.

Simon's Taxes Divisions D9.2, D9.10.

[1] Repealed by FA 1996.
[2] Which became TA 1988, ss 731–734.
[3] ITA 2007, ss 616–677, see infra, § **11.08**.

[4.14] Where a company dealing in securities obtains a holding of more than 10% in another company and then there is one or more distributions by that other company the net effect of which is materially to reduce the value of the holding, TA 1988, s 736 directed that the reduction in the value of the holding was to be added to the value of the security.[1] The purpose of this was to counteract the tax advantage obtained in a typical dividend strip by simply wiping out the loss on the shares which the dealing company would hope to put against the distribution. As the Revenue are today using the powers in TA

[4.14] Anti-avoidance legislation

1988, s 703 in preference to TA 1988, s 736, the latter was repealed by FA 2008. The Revenue may also use the enhanced CGT value shifting rules (TCGA 1992, ss 30 et seq).

Simon's Taxes D9.1101.

[1] Cf TCGA 1992, s 177; infra, § **28.31**.

Manufactured dividends

The scope of the provisions

[4.15] Many provisions have been produced in recent years to deal with the problem of manufactured payments. These are payments due under a contract or other arrangements for the transfer of shares and represent dividend or interest. Tax is charged in various sets of circumstances on the amount representing the dividend or interest; the definition of that amount is made according to precise rules in each set of circumstances. The charge only arises if the manufacturer is not itself entitled to the dividend or interest payment.

The rules apply to manufactured dividends on UK equities,[1] interest on UK securities[2] and foreign income dividends.[3] All try to apply to the manufactured payment at least some of the rules which would apply to actual payments of dividend or interest. The rules also apply to certain deemed manufactured payments arising from the sale and repurchase of securities.[4] There is also special provision for deemed manufactured payments in the case of stocklending.[5] In all instances there are duties on the person making the payment to supply the appropriate information for tax purposes. A charge under these rules excludes any charge under the accrued income scheme.[6]

These rules are an updated version of a provision first introduced in 1960. At that time it was described as dealing with something "which the ordinary layman could fairly describe as a swindle at the expense of the honest taxpayer—not a criminal conspiracy but a racket".[7] Briefly, a vendor (V) would sell a stock on The Stock Exchange "cum-div" but would not buy the stock until later, when it had gone ex-div. V would then hand over to the purchaser (P) the stock together with a net amount of the dividend and a voucher showing the tax deducted. Thus P would receive the dividend net of income tax which he might be able to reclaim. Yet no tax would have reached the Treasury since the operator was not required to account for the tax and he would make a profit since the difference between the price cum-div and price ex-div would be more than the net amount of dividend after tax had been deducted.

Since 1960 there have been many developments in the way in which investment markets are run. In 1998 the Revenue described some manufactured dividends in slightly less threatening terms describing them as being commonly made (a) "by a borrower of equities to a lender to compensate him for the dividend he would have received had he not lent those equities" and (b) "to someone who had bought equities on terms entitling him to receipt of the dividend but where the equities delivered do not come with that dividend." Whatever the motivation for the transactions, the gap in the tax base if these rules did not exist would be used ruthlessly.

There is an extensive regulation-making power which may modify the effect of these provisions where the dividend manufacturer either is not resident in the UK, carries on a trade through a branch or agency here, or is a member of a recognised investment exchange.[8] These may grant or withhold reliefs and prescribe the way in which tax is to be accounted for.

Simon's Taxes Division D9.7.

[1] ITA 2007, s 573.
[2] ITA 2007, s 578.
[3] ITA 2007, s 581.
[4] ITA 2007, ss 601–605.
[5] ITA 2007, s 596.
[6] ITA 2007, s 647.
[7] HC Official Report 1960, Vol 624, col 451 (Sir Edward Boyle).
[8] ITA 2007, s 582.

The manufactured payments provisions

[4.16] The manufactured payments provisions are as follows:

(1) **UK equities.**[1] Here the amount representing the dividends is treated as a dividend if the manufacturer of the payment is a company resident in the UK. With the abolition of ACT in 1999 manufacturers and recipients will not be accountable for any notional ACT for dividends paid on or after 6 April 1999. All recipients of manufactured dividends are treated as receiving dividends of the company whose equities are involved irrespective of the status of the manufacturer. The payer is specifically prohibited from obtaining a trading deduction for the payment.

(2) **Interest on UK securities.**[2] Here the amount is treated as an annual payment. It is not yearly interest of the recipient (though it is deemed to be interest) nor is it payable wholly out of profits or gains brought into charge to income tax—thus it is as if it came within s 349 not s 348 although this is not actually spelt out. There is, however, an obligation to account for tax at the lower rate in TA 1988, s 1A; this means that the actual receipt has to be grossed up and tax accounted for at 20% on that grossed up figure. The payer is given a right to deduct the gross sum. There is no obligation to deduct if the manufacturer is not resident unless the amount is paid in the course of a trade carried on in the UK through a branch or agency; if, in these circumstances the payer is not obliged to deduct the tax a resident recipient may be accountable instead. Where the payment relates to gilt edged securities there is no obligation to deduct tax. Loan relationships are the subject of equivalent legislation.

[4.16] Anti-avoidance legislation

(3) **Overseas Dividends.**[3] Here the payment made by the manufacturer is treated as an annual payment within TA 1988, s 349. The deduction is to be at a rate not exceeding any relevant withholding tax, unless regulations so provide. There are rules for foreign elements similar to those dealing with interest on UK securities. The effect is that there is no charge if the manufacturer is not resident in the UK and the manufactured dividend is paid otherwise than in the course of a trade carried on through a branch or agency in the UK. Again a resident recipient may be liable instead.

(4) **Irregular payments.**[4] There is also a catch-all provision to sweep up any sums which exceed the amount of the real dividend. The excess is not to be treated as a dividend under any of these rules but as a separate fee for entering into the contract—and taxed separately as well. The converse is true in that where the actual payments are less than the real dividend; only the actual sums are allowed by way of deduction.

(5) **Sale and repurchase of securities.**[5] The manufactured payments scheme is extended to the situation in which a person (T) agrees to sell securities and under the same or a related agreement T (or a connected person) is either required to buy them (or similar securities) back or has an option to do so. The rules apply if a dividend is payable in respect of the securities and goes to someone other than T; however, they are excluded if there is no obligation on anyone to pay T an amount representative of the dividend. The rules only apply if, as will usually be the case, it is reasonable to assume that in arriving at the repurchase price account was taken of the fact that someone other than T was going to collect the dividend. These matters are judged as at the date the repurchase money is due. The rules are adapted where connected persons are involved.

The dividend manufacturing rules are applied as if X, the person from whom T buys back the securities, was to pay T an amount representative of the dividend. Where the repurchase price is reduced to compensate for the loss of the dividend the amount is the real dividend. There are further rules for interest and for overseas securities and further adjustments to take account of sums treated as falling under the deemed manufacture rules.

One should also note that qualifying distributions do not give rise to a tax credit if the person is a borrower under a stock-lending arrangement or the interim holder under a repurchase agreement only if the manufactured dividend to which it relates is paid on or after 6 April 1999. The last condition shows that this is best seen as an anti-avoidance measure to prevent people exploiting the change to the new regime. There is a similar, and similarly timed, rule where there is a sale and repurchase agreement under which the original owner receives a manufactured dividend under the repo agreement.

An anti-avoidance provision[6] applies, designed to stop companies obtaining a tax advantage by entering into a range of artificial schemes involving manufactured payments. The Treasury press release announcing this provision states:

> a range of artificial schemes have recently come to light to which companies contrive to make, or begin to make, manufactured payments which rank as a deduction for tax purposes, but which ensure that any counter-balancing profits or gains are not

taxed at all.. . . [the intention of the new provisions is to] block these schemes by providing that a company is not entitled to tax relief irrespective of a manufactured payment to the extent that the arrangements under which the payment is made have an unallowable purpose.

An unallowable purpose is one that is not a business or other commercial purpose of the company concerned. The Revenue has published,[7] in considerable detail, its view of the way in which the new provisions operate.

Simon's Taxes A4.336, 405 and Division A9.7.

[1] ITA 2007, s 573.
[2] ITA 2007, s 578.
[3] ITA 2007, s 581.
[4] ITA 2007, ss 583–585.
[5] ITA 2007, ss 593–594.
[6] TA 1988, Sch 23A, para 7A(1)(*b*).
[7] Inland Revenue Tax Bulletin, August 2004, pp 1132–1137.

[4.17] A regulation-making power[1] has been granted to the Treasury to enable the new gilt repo market to operate effectively despite the thicket of rules.[2] Where a transaction contains both a price differential as defined under the repo legislation and a manufactured payment, the regulations will enable the manufactured payment to be identified and taxed. Perhaps of greater interest is another regulation-making power which will enable manufactured payments and the price differential arising from a repo transaction to be exempt from tax if relating to certain pension arrangements. This applies only to UK equities and securities.[3]

Simon's Taxes Division D9.7.

[1] ITA 2007, s 612(1); it applies also to TA 1988, s 730A (supra, § **4.12**) and ITA 2007, s 654 (exclusion of repo transactions from accrued income scheme which was itself added by FA 1995, s 79)—see Inland Revenue press release, 27 March 1995, para 10, *Simon's Weekly Tax Intelligence* 1995, p 548.
[2] ITA 2007, ss 593–594.
[3] Inland Revenue press releases, 27 March 1995, para 10, 5 April 1995, *Simon's Weekly Tax Intelligence* 1995, pp 548, 624.

Transactions in securities

[4.18] The technique used in these sections is to allow the Revenue to issue a notice counteracting tax advantages gained in certain circumstances prescribed in language of uncertain scope.[1] The effect of the notice is to undo the transaction but only for tax purposes. Briefly, (a) the tax advantage must have been obtained as a result of a transaction in securities, and (b) it must fall within one of the four (previously, five) sets of circumstances set out in statute.[2] It is, however, open to the taxpayer to show that the transaction was carried

[4.18] Anti-avoidance legislation

out either for bona fide commercial reasons or in the ordinary course of making or managing investments and, in either event, not with the obtaining of a tax advantage as its main or one of its main objects. In *Bird v IRC*[3] Vinelott J said that it was not open to the Revenue to rely on *Furniss v Dawson* and statute in the same transaction. In the same case the Court of Appeal held that the taxpayer could not use use the new approach to disregard a step which statute said had to be taken into account.[4] In *IRC v McGuckian*,[5] the minority of the House of Lords felt able to bring the facts within these provisions without having to rely on the new approach.

These provisions which follow are among the most difficult in the UK tax law. They are, generally speaking, the most obscure, the penalties for infringing them are the most severe, and they are barely touched upon by published statements of Revenue practice.[6] A further difficulty is the absence of any provision governing the interaction with CGT. Where the proceeds of sale of shares fall within these provisions, Revenue practice is to allow the tax as a credit against CGT.[7] There is a clearance procedure.[8]

There is a special tribunal to hear appeals.[9] The tribunal has jurisdiction to rehear the case on application by either the taxpayer or Revenue. While the tribunal has power to strike out an appeal for abuse of process it has held that certain statements made in the House of Commons in 1960 were not to be taken as limiting the circumstances in which the Revenue were enabled to take an appeal—the statements were simply illustrations of situations in which an appeal might be made and contained no undertakings that appeals would not be made in others.[10] Appeal from that tribunal is on a point of law only and is still by way of case stated.[11]

One example is *IRC v Wiggins*.[12] A company restored and sold picture frames. One frame was found to contain a valuable painting, The Holy Family, by Poussin.[13] Rather than simply sell the painting and distribute the profits as dividend the company first sold all its other stock to one company after which another company bought the shares of the first company for £45,000. The courts held that the £45,000 represented the value of trading stock so that para D applied, and the £45,000 could be treated as income of those who had sold their shares.

Simon's Taxes D9.101–136.

---

[1] However, the Revenue are under a duty to exercise their power fairly: *R v IRC, ex p Preston* [1983] STC 257.
[2] ITA 2007, ss 682–713 (income tax); TA 1988, s 704 (corporation tax).
[3] [1985] STC 584.
[4] [1987] STC 168; the point was not taken in the House of Lords; [1988] STC 312. Lord Keith (at 318) said that it was open to the Revenue to choose whether to use s 703 or the new approach as a means of applying what is now ITA 2007, ss 682–713.
[5] [1997] STC 908, HL.
[6] Nolan, IFS Conference (28 June 1974), p 25, para 3.
[7] See *IRC v Garvin* [1981] STC 344 at 349, 353.
[8] ITA 2007, s 701,702 (income tax); TA 1988, s 707 (corporation tax); see *Balen v IRC* [1978] STC 420 and statement of practice SP 3/80.

[9] ITA 2007, s 704 (income tax); TA 1988, s 706 (corporation tax).
[10] *Marwood Homes Ltd v IRC* [1998] STC (SCD) 53.
[11] ITA 2007, s 707 (income tax); TA 1988, s 705A (corporation tax). For Northern Ireland appeals see ITA 2007, s 711 (income tax); TA 1988, s 705B (corporation tax).
[12] [1979] STC 244, [1979] 2 All ER 245.
[13] The frame was bought in 1955 for £50; the picture was found to be by Poussin ten years later—value £130,000.

A tax advantage

[4.19] This is defined[1] (a) a relief or increased relief from or a repayment or increased repayment of tax, or (b) the avoidance or reduction of an assessment to tax or the avoidance of a possible assessment thereto, whether the avoidance or reduction is effected by receipts accruing in such a way that the recipient does not pay or bear tax on them or by a deduction in computing profits or gains. A "tax advantage" is defined to include the receipt of a tax credit. Before 1990–91 a husband was assessable in respect of a tax advantage accruing to his wife.[2]

The question whether a relief is to be distinguished from an exemption has been answered in different ways by different judges. However, the present position is that there is no distinction and so a tax advantage can arise from either.[3] So if a company issues shares in favour of charitable trustees and other shareholders waive their rights to a dividend, so that all the dividends accrued to the trustees, the trustees' repayment claim can be stopped by s 703.

Curiously the word "tax" is undefined. When the provision was first introduced there was no CGT[4] so presumably that is excluded as is corporation tax in respect of the capital gains of companies. However, the tax system has changed in other respects since 1960 so that this must be open to question. Section 703 applied to ACT even though that tax was unknown in 1960.[5]

The definition of tax advantage suggests that there must be a contrast of the actual case where there is an accrual in a non-taxable way with a possible accrual in a taxable way.[6] So where a company had issued and later redeemed bonus debentures there was an avoidance of tax in that had the money been distributed as dividends it would have been taxable.[7] However, whether it is the issue or the redemption that constitutes the tax advantage is still unclear.[8] In *Cleary v IRC*[9] it was argued that the words "avoidance of a possible assessment thereto" indicated that Parliament had in mind the reduction of profits available for dividends and not the reduction of physical assets for that purpose, so that there would be no tax advantage if a company simply used its cash resources to buy shares in another company. However, this view was rejected by the House of Lords. In the case two sisters owned the shares of two companies and they extracted the cash from one company by allowing that company to buy their shares in the other. They thus avoided the possible assessment that would have arisen if the cash had been paid out by way of dividend.[10] The fact that this would have been the worst possible procedure, and so unlikely to happen, did not matter. This case is disturbing since, when

[4.19] Anti-avoidance legislation

the purchasing company in turn made its distribution no credit could be claimed for the tax already exacted.[11] The fact that there is an abnormal dividend is, of itself, not sufficient to create a liability under s 703 but it may be a strong contributory factor. In *Trustees of the Omega Group Pension Scheme v IRC*,[12] the amount received by the taxpayer was normal for what he sold. In *IRC v Trustees of the Sema Group Pension Scheme*,[13] the Court of Appeal held that the court did not have the power to overturn the finding of fact by the Commissioners that the dividend received was not normal.

Similarly in *Emery v IRC*[14] where a company had made a large trading profit the taxpayer was held to have derived a tax advantage when he sold his shares because he could have got the company to declare a dividend or go into liquidation.

In *Bird v IRC*[15] it was held that the quantum of the advantage was ascertained by contrasting the non-taxable receipt with a similar receipt that might have accrued in some other, taxable, way. Further, the House of Lords held that in determining what should be done to counter such an advantage there was an obligation to make an accurate measure of the tax advantage obtained. When the taxpayer had to make good the liability of another person that should reduce the tax advantage obtained.

Recently the Revenue negotiated a settlement where directors of a company had sold company shares to a small self-administered pension scheme. Under the settlement the directors repurchased the shares.[16]

Simon's Taxes D9.103, 111.

[1] ITA 2007, s 683 (income tax); TA 1988, s 703 (corporation tax).
[2] TA 1988, s 703(7) repealed by FA 1988, Sch 14, Part VIII; *Green v IRC* [1975] STC 633, CA.
[3] *IRC v Universities Superannuation Scheme Ltd* [1997] STC 1 which distinguished *Sheppard v IRC (No 2)* [1993] STC 240.
[4] On overlap with CGT see *IRC v Garvin* [1981] STC 344 especially per Lord Wilberforce at 349.
[5] *Cedar plc v Inspector of Taxes* [1998] STC (SCD) 78.
[6] Per Lord Wilberforce in *IRC v Parker* [1966] AC 141 at 178–9.
[7] *IRC v Parker* [1966] 1 All ER 399, 43 TC 396; cf *Anysz v IRC* [1978] STC 296.
[8] See *IRC v Parker* [1966] 1 All ER 399, 43 TC 396.
[9] [1967] 2 All ER 48, 44 TC 399.
[10] See *Hague v IRC* [1968] 2 All ER 1252, 44 TC 619. In a judgment not easy to reconcile with *IRC v Parker* or *Cleary v IRC*, the Court of Appeal refused to accept as a possible assessment one that would arise if spouses opted for separate assessments, a possibility scarcely more fanciful than that envisaged by the House of Lords in *Cleary v IRC*. This was later reversed; TA 1988, s 703(7); this provision has now been repealed; see FA 1988, Sch 14, Part VIII.
[11] In the Court of Appeal Lord Denning said that 'the courts are well able to take care of that contingency'. However, there is no legislation analogous to TA 1988, s 419(4) or TA 1988, s 427(4). It is therefore hard to see what his Lordship had in mind.
[12] [2001] STC (SCD) 121.
[13] [2002] EWCA Civ 1857, [2003] STC 95.

[14] [1981] STC 150.
[15] [1988] STC 312 at 317 per Lord Keith.
[16] Inland Revenue decision RD 6.

Transaction

[4.20] Transaction is defined[1] as including transactions of whatever description relating to securities and in particular, (a) the purchase, sale or exchange of securities, (b) the issuing or securing the issue of or applying for or subscribing for new securities, and (c) the altering or securing the alteration of the rights attached to securities. The term "transaction in securities" has a "very wide meaning".[2] Hence repayment of share capital as a reduction is a transaction[3] as is the payment of the purchase price for shares by instalments, at least when the instalments were related to dividends,[4] and perhaps even if not so related.[5]

The payment of a dividend on the liquidation of a company is not, of itself, a transaction in securities.[6] As stated by Lord Millett:[7]

> Whether the company is in liquidation or continuing to carry on business as a going concern, therefore, the distribution of the undistributed profits of a company to the shareholders entitled thereto merely gives effect to the rights attached to the shares. The funds are released, in the one case from the liquidator's discretion to retain them for the purpose of the winding up, and in the other from the directors' discretion to retain them for the purposes of the undertaking. Given that the former is not 'a transaction relating to securities', neither in my opinion is the latter. The relationship between the payment and the shares in respect of which it is paid is the same in both cases.

By contrast, when a liquidation is combined with a transaction, that may be a transaction in securities.[8]

Simon's Taxes D9.103, 111.

[1] ITA 2007, s 713 (income tax); TA 1988, s 709(2) (corporation tax).
[2] Per *Lord Reid in Greenberg v IRC* (1971) 47 TC 240, HL. In *IRC v Parker* [1966] AC 141 at 172–3, Lord Guest said that "it is not qualified in any way".
[3] *IRC v Brebner* [1967] 1 All ER 779, 43 TC 705.
[4] *Greenberg v IRC* [1972] AC 109, [1971] BTR 1319.
[5] *Greenberg v IRC* per Lord Reid at 137.
[6] *IRC v Laird Group plc* [2003] UKHL 54, [2003] STC 1349, para 42 at 1359e.
[7] ITA 2007, s 684(3) (income tax) (or TA 1988, s 703(2) (corporation tax)) appears to be drafted on the premise that a liquidation of a company is not a transaction of securities: see comments by Lord Dilhorne and Diplock in *IRC v Joiner* [1975] STC 657, HL.
[8] *IRC v Joiner* [1975] STC 657, HL.

Securities

[4.21] This is defined to include shares and stock and, in relation to a company not limited by shares (whether or not it has a share capital) includes a reference to the interest of a member of the company as such. Thus debentures and securities are included and their redemption is a transaction in securities. A loan note even though unsecured is a security;[1] likewise the receipt of a loan from and repayable to a controlled company is a transaction in securities.[2]

Simon's Taxes Division D9.1.

---

[1] Per Lord Wilberforce in *IRC v Joiner* [1975] 3 All ER 1050 at 1056. What if in *Cleary v IRC*, the assets sold had been buttons not shares?
[2] *Williams v IRC* [1980] 3 All ER 321, [1980] STC 535, HL.

The four (previously five) sets of circumstances

[4.22] (A) The first[1] concerns abnormally high dividends where in connection with the distribution of profits of a company or in connection with the sale or purchase of securities followed by the purchase or sale of the same or other securities, the person in question receives an abnormal amount by way of dividend and the amount so received is taken into account for the purposes of (a) any exemption from income tax, (b) the setting-off of losses against profits or income, or (c) the giving of relief for interest payments.

A dividend is regarded as abnormal[2] if (a) it substantially exceeds a normal return on the consideration provided paid for securities or (b) it is a dividend at a fixed rate and substantially exceeds the amount which the recipient would have received if the dividend had accrued from day to day and he had been entitled only to so much of the dividend as accrued while he held the securities. This special rule applies only if he sells or acquires a right to sell those or similar securities within six months.

The word profit is defined to include income, reserves or other assets. This is unfortunate when compared with standard accountancy definitions, but indicates the wide scope of the section.[3]

A charity or pension fund that receives an abnormally high dividend can be treated under these provisions as having obtained "relief" from tax, even though it enjoys an exemption from tax in respect of ordinary dividends.[4]

Simon's Taxes Division D9.1.

---

[1] ITA 2007, s 686 (Income tax); TA 1988, s 704-A (corporation tax).
[2] ITA 2007, ss 692–694 (income tax); TA 1988, s 709(4)-(6) (corporation tax). For example see Inland Revenue *Tax Bulletin*, Issue 5, November 1992; see also *Cedar plc v Inspector of Taxes* [1998] STC (SCD) 78.
[3] Cf Lord Upjohn in *Cleary v IRC*.
[4] *IRC v Universities Superannuation Scheme Ltd* [1997] STC 1.

[4.23] (B) This concerned the drop in the value of securities[1] as a result of the dividend. The purpose here was to catch the stripper who does not receive an abnormal dividend but who simply claims a loss. In *IRC v Kleinwort*

Benson Ltd[2] a dealing company bought debentures on which interest was in arrears; subsequently, that interest was paid off and the debentures redeemed on the same day—and by one cheque, it was held that there was no "fall in the value of the debentures" by reason of the payment of the interest and so no liability under TA 1988, s 703; rather the stock had simply ceased to exist. But had the interest been paid off even one day before there would have been such a fall in value since the market price would have fallen. This circumstance was repealed with effect from 1 April 2008 by FA 2008.

Simon's Taxes Division D9.1.

[1] ITA 2007, s 687 (income tax); TA 1988, s 704-B (corporation tax).
[2] [1969] 2 All ER 737, 45 TC 369.

[4.24] (C) This deals with the opposite side of the transaction[1] from that covered by (A) and former (B). Following the amendments made by FA 2008, this circumstance reads as follows:

(1) This section applies in relation to a person ("A") if subsections (2), (3) and (6) apply.
(2) A receives consideration which—
    (a) is or represents the value of—
        (i) assets which are available for distribution by a company by way of dividend, or
        (ii) assets which would have been so available apart from anything done by the company,
    (b) is received in respect of future receipts of a company, or
    (c) is or represents the value of trading stock of a company.
(3) The receipt is in consequence of a transaction whereby another person ("B")—
    (a) subsequently receives, or has received, an abnormal amount by way of dividend (see section 692).
"Available for distribution by way of dividend" means legally available, not commercially available.[2]

In the ordinary dividend strip or bond washing operation it was not to be supposed that all the economic advantage would be confined to the purchaser. Thus in one instance[3] a company had 15,000 unclassified £1 shares. These were converted into 300,000 5p shares and a once for all dividend of £2.37½ was declared. These shares were sold to superannuation funds and to charities at £3.37½ which then reclaimed the tax paid on the dividend. After the dividend the shares were worth about 15p each. The funds and charities had paid £3.37½ for shares worth only about £2.37½, an operation that only made sense on the basis that they collected tax of about £1.50 per share thanks to their exempt status. Thus the vendor collected £1 and the funds 50p per share—free of tax. Hence paragraph (C).

Simon's Taxes Division D9.1.

[1] ITA 2007, s 688 (income tax); TA 1988, s 704-C (corporation tax).

[2] *IRC v Brown* [1971] 3 All ER 502, 47 TC 236, even though current liabilities exceed current assets. See now Companies Act 2006, ss 830, 841(2).
[3] HC Official Report 1960, Vol 624, col 626 (Sir Edward Boyle).

[4.25] This paragraph also catches two other devices, known as forward stripping and "scissors" or stock stripping. Forward stripping occurred when a company was about to make a large profit.[1] Special shares were created carrying a high rate of dividend and these would be sold to a dealing company for a capital sum. The dealer would then set off the loss on resale against the predicted dividend that had subsequently accrued.

Stock stripping occurs when a company has stock on its books at the correct conservative figure of cost or market value whichever is the lower. Should the stock be realised there would be a considerable income receipt. Enter the finance company which also deals in stock. The company buys both stock and shares at book value. The increased price obtained by sale at market value is offset by the drop in the value of the shares. Thanks to (iii) above the original company, if it is allowed its loss, will be subject to tax as having obtained a tax advantage.

For paragraph (C) to apply the Revenue must not only establish each element but also show that the transaction and the abnormal dividend or whatever it may be are causally linked; this flows from the word "whereby".[2] In deciding the scope of the transaction the court may take a broad view and is not limited to the immediate cause of the dividend but still the causal connection must be shown.[3] Where, as is usually the case, more than one step is involved this causal connection can be established even though the taxpayer does not take part in each one.[4] It has also been decided that the causal link can be found in the purpose and design of those who, for a fee and instructed by the taxpayers, controlled the operation of the schemes.[5]

Simon's Taxes Division D9.1.

[1] See *Greenberg v IRC* [1972] AC 109, [1971] 3 All ER 136, 47 TC 240, HL.
[2] *Bird v IRC* [1985] STC 584.
[3] *IRC v Garvin* [1981] STC 344.
[4] *Emery v IRC* [1981] STC 150.
[5] *Bird v IRC* [1985] STC 584.

[4.26] (D) This[1] has given the courts the most difficulty:

(1) This section applies in relation to a person if subsections (2) to (4) apply.
(2) The person receives consideration in connection with—
   (a) the distribution, transfer or realisation of assets of a relevant company (see section 691), or
   (b) the application of such assets in discharge of liabilities.
(3) The consideration:
   (a) is or represents the value of:
      (i) assets which are available for distribution by way of dividend by the company, or

> > (ii) assets which would have been so available apart from anything done by the company,
> (b) is received in respect of future receipts of the company, or
> (c) is or represents the value of trading stock of the company.
> (4) The person so receives the consideration that the person does not pay or bear income tax on it.

This superb example of legislation by reference was, when the Finance Bill 1960 was first presented, originally a part of (C); hence perhaps the reference. The companies in question are those under the control of five or fewer persons and all unquoted companies, unless under the control of a quoted company. Like (C) it applies to the vendor rather than the purchaser, but unlike (C) there is no requirement that conditions (A) or (B) should also be present. Moreover, there is no requirement that the amount of any dividend should be abnormal. These matters give paragraph (D) its wide ambit.

The phrase "distribution of profits" is very widely defined; thus profits include references to income, reserves or other assets and references to distribution include references to transfer or realisation including an application in discharge of liabilities. Thus the capitalisation of undistributed profits followed by a reduction in capital is a distribution for this purpose,[2] as are a reduction in capital followed by capitalisation,[3] an issue and redemption of debentures,[4] and even the purchase of one company's shares by another.[5] There may be a distribution of profits without diminution of assets.[6]

Control must be shown to exist. This will trigger liability whether it exists at the time the asset is realised or at the time of the subsequent distribution but it is not enough for the Revenue simply to prove control when the sum is received.[7]

Paragraph (D) requires that the sum be received "in connection with" the distribution of profits. This imposes a less definite causal link than the word "whereby" in paragraph (C).[8]

IRC v Wiggins (see supra, § **4.18**) is an example of paragraph (D). The purchase price paid for the shares in the company owning the picture represented the value of that company's trading stock so that the taxpayer received consideration of the proscribed type; the company was controlled, a tax advantage obtained and there was a transaction in securities.

Simon's Taxes Division D9.1.

---

1. ITA 2007, s 689 (income tax); TA 1988, s 704-D (corporation tax).
2. *Hague v IRC* [1968] 2 All ER 1252, 44 TC 619.
3. *IRC v Horrocks* [1968] 3 All ER 296, 44 TC 645.
4. *IRC v Parker* [1966] 1 All ER 399, 43 TC 396.
5. *Cleary v IRC* [1967] 2 All ER 48, 44 TC 399.
6. *Cleary v IRC* [1967] 2 All ER 48, 44 TC 399.
7. *IRC v Garvin* [1981] STC 344.
8. *Emery v IRC* [1981] STC 150.

[4.27] (E) This paragraph[1] was added in 1966 and applies where there are two or more paragraph (D) companies and where the taxpayer receives non-taxable consideration in the form of share capital or a security issued by a paragraph (D) company and does so "in connection with the transfer directly or indirectly of assets" of one paragraph (D) company to another such company, and the consideration is or represents the value of assets available for distribution by such a company. If the consideration is non-redeemable share capital the liability arises when the share capital is repaid. If it takes any other form, liability arises upon receipt. It is very unclear whether this adds anything to the other paragraphs. In *Williams v IRC* the Court of Appeal held that where a transaction falls within both (D) and (E), paragraph (E) should apply. This point was not taken in the House of Lords.

Simon's Taxes Division D9.1.

[1] ITA 2007, s 690 (income tax); TA 1988, s 704-E (corporation tax).

Defences

[4.28] The income tax treatment does not apply if the taxpayer shows[1] that the transaction was carried out for bona fide commercial reasons, or in the ordinary course of making or managing investments, and that no transaction had as its main object or one of its main objects to enable tax advantages to be obtained.[2] It is perhaps interesting, in view of the decision of the House of Lords in *FA and AB Ltd v Lupton*,[3] to note that this defence presupposes that a transaction whose main object was the obtaining of a tax advantage could be in the ordinary course of making investments or have bona fide commercial reasons.

Perhaps correctly, this is the only part of the legislation in which the courts have shown any sympathy for the taxpayer. In determining what are bona fide commercial reasons, the word commercial includes non-financial reasons. Hence a view that to retain family control of a company is important for the future prosperity of the company, whether in the context of company–customer or employer–employee relationships can be good commercial reasons so that steps taken to preserve that control will escape TA 1988, s 703.[4] In *Marwood Homes v IRC*,[5] a Special Commissioner held that the main object of an intra-group transfer of shares followed by the payment of dividends totalling £1,040,000 from subsidiary companies, the payment being outside a group income election, was to enable the reserves in the subsidiaries to be passed through to the taxpayer company in order to strengthen the financial position of the taxpayer company. However, this decision was later reversed by the tribunal set up under s 706.[6]

Deliberate, and careful, tax planning does not, of itself, make the obtaining of a tax advantage one of the main objects, when there is a commercial reason for the sale. In *Lewis v IRC*[7] the trustees of a pension fund held shares in a company that was shortly to be floated. After flotation, the value of that shareholding would have been over 35% of the assets in the pension fund, which was considered by the trustees to be an unacceptably high percentage. The trustees sold part of the shareholding to the company for £2,532,937. By making a capital sale to the company, the tax saved by the pension fund was

£633,234. The Special Commissioner quashed an assessment in this sum, holding that the trustees "were aware of the possible tax benefits of choosing this option but the obtaining of a tax advantage was not the main object . . . the tax benefit was 'the cherry on the cake'".[8] The main object was the desired reduction in the size of the shareholding. The trustees "reacted to the situation by taking the simplest and cheapest option available to them and in doing so in our judgement were acting in the ordinary course of managing investments".[9]

In deciding whether there are commercial reasons it is not necessary for the taxpayer to show that those reasons are connected with the company concerned. So in *Clark v IRC*[10] the taxpayer, a farmer, decided to sell shares in a controlled company in order to raise money with which to buy another farm; his claim to use this defence was upheld. When the Revenue invoke TA 1988, s 703 it may be that they may not also invoke the decision in *Furniss v Dawson*.[11]

Simon's Taxes D9.101, 133, 134.

---

[1] On the importance of onus of proof note *Hasloch v IRC* (1971) 47 TC 50 where the transaction was instituted by a board of directors of which he was not a member. The transaction was the redemption of certain preference shares, a move which would improve the capital structure of the company but also confer a tax advantage on the taxpayer who failed to persuade the Commissioners that the latter was not an object. The case also shows that ITA 2007, ss 682–713 apply even though the intention to mitigate tax exists only for some of the time.
[2] ITA 2007, s 685 (income tax); TA 1988, s 703(1) (corporation tax); for a recent example see *Laird Group plc v IRC* [1999] STC (SCD) 86.
[3] [1971] 3 All ER 948, 47 TC 580 (infra, § **8.11**).
[4] *IRC v Goodwin* [1976] STC 28, HL.
[5] [1997] STC (SCD) 37.
[6] [1999] STC (SCD) 44.
[7] [1999] STC (SCD) 349.
[8] [1999] STC (SCD) at 361e.
[9] [1999] STC (SCD) at 362e.
[10] [1978] STC 614, [1979] 1 All ER 385; the Special Commissioners had ruled that there was a bona fide commercial motive but that it had to be intrinsic to the transaction.
[11] The question was left open by Vinelott J in *Bird v IRC* [1985] STC 584 at 647.

[4.29] Most litigants have argued that the obtaining of a tax advantage was not one of the main objects. The test is subjective and the question is one of fact.[1] If a business operation is carried out in two distinct phases, one of which is purely commercial and the other of which had the tax advantage as one of its main objects, it is a question of fact for the Commissioners whether there was one transaction or two. The House of Lords has commended a "broad common sense view" to the Commissioners.[2]

In *IRC v Brebner*[3] the respondent and his colleagues were resisting a takeover bid and so made a counter offer for the shares. This was financed by a loan from a bank on terms requiring early repayment. After two unsuccessful

[4.29] Anti-avoidance legislation

attempts to persuade the minority interests to sell out, the original counter offer was accepted by a majority of the shareholders. The company then resolved first to increase its capital by £75,000 by capitalising its reserves and then reducing them by the same amount thus causing £75,000 to come out of the company to the new shareholders who used them to pay off the loans from the bank. The Commissioners held that the whole was one transaction and that it did not have as one of its main objects the obtaining of a tax advantage. A notice to counteract the advantage therefore failed. The House of Lords held that there was ample evidence to support the findings. Lord Upjohn said that a choice of a method which carried less tax than another did not necessarily mean that one of its main objects was to obtain a tax advantage.[4]

It has also been said that a charity does not have a tax advantage as one of its main objects simply because, in reaching a decision, it is influenced by its privileged tax status.[5]

Other defences are that the transaction was effected before 6 April 1960[6] and that the assessment was made out of time (ie more than six years after the chargeable period to which the tax advantage relates).[7]

Simon's Taxes Division D9.1.

[1] Per Lord Upjohn in *IRC v Brebner* [1967] 2 AC 18 at 30, [1967] 1 All ER 779 at 784, 43 TC 705 at 718 and Lord Pearce at 26, 781, 715. In all five reported cases the Commissioners' decision on fact has (eventually) been upheld—Apart from *IRC v Brebner* these are *IRC v Hague* [1968] 2 All ER 1252, 44 TC 619; *Hasloch v IRC* (1971) 47 TC 50 (supra), *IRC v Goodwin* (supra) and *Clark v IRC* (supra).
[2] Lord Pearce in *IRC v Brebner*, supra at 26, 781, 715 respectively. See also *Lloyd v R & C Comrs* (2008) SpC 671.
[3] Supra.
[4] Supra.
[5] Per Cross J in *IRC v Kleinwort Benson Ltd* [1969] 2 All ER 737 at 743, 45 TC 369 at 382. If this is correct there is still some scope for TA 1988, s 729 (supra, § **4.13**).
[6] TA 1970, s 468(1) on which see *IRC v Brebner*, supra. This was repealed in 1987 as a pre-consolidation amendment presumably for obsolescence.
[7] ITA 2007, s 698 (income tax); TA 1988, s 703(12) (corporation tax).

Sale by individual of income derived from his personal activities

[4.30] This is the famous Beatles or constellation clause which was introduced in 1969[1] to prevent one form of converting future taxable income into present untaxable capital. This form was the sale of the right to an individual's future services to a company in return for shares or an option over shares, a practice particularly prevalent in the entertainment industry, whose practitioners of course were more likely than others to suffer from the absence of any proper averaging clause in the UK tax system. Suppose that a film is about to be made and that £1m is available for the star's services. A company acquires his services in return for an option to take shares. It would pay him say

£50,000 by way of living allowance so as to cover his expenses, these being taxable to the individual as employment income but deductible by the company. The company would sell the star's services to the film company in return for £1m, would receive that sum and would suffer corporation tax. Likewise if a company was formed to promote the career of a potential star over a number of years. Again the company would acquire exclusive rights for a number of years; then, when the star was well launched, he would sell out his shares in the company to another company at a large capital gain. Before the sale the company would be a close one[2] but would argue the need to retain earnings for the future in a highly uncertain trade.

Simon's Taxes E1.120.

[1] Originally enacted as FA 1969, s 31 & Sch 16, now ITA 2007, ss 773–789.
[2] At that time the rules for close companies were stricter than they are now—infra, Chapter 29. The effect of the schemes was to reduce tax from 91.25% (income tax) to something like 60% (corporation tax and CGT)—[1970] BTR 84 (Potter). The tax payable on the emoluments received would be corporation tax and income tax, and often higher than 60%. For examples of such schemes see *Crossland v Hawkins* [1961] 2 All ER 812, 39 TC 493 (infra, § **15.07**), *IRC v Mills* [1974] STC 130, [1974] 1 All ER 722 (infra, § **15.03**) and *Black Nominees Ltd v Nicol* [1975] STC 372 at 411. These schemes were unsuccessful on other grounds.

[4.31] The scope of the tax charge is much wider than the covering of these devices in the entertainment industry. It applies where (a) arrangements are made to exploit the earning capacity of an individual by putting some other person (eg the company) into a position to receive the income from his activities, and (b) as part of the arrangement the individual or any other receives a capital amount, provided (c) that the main object or one of the main objects was the avoidance of tax.[1] Since the purpose of the provision appears to be to stop rather than to regulate this kind of contract, the whole capital sum is made subject to income tax and there is no provision for top-slicing or any other form of relief. Historically, it was treated as earned income, a concept that is no longer of any relevance, but does not attract a liability to National Insurance contributions. Further the section applies to all persons regardless of their residence provided that the occupation is carried on in whole or in part in the UK,[2] and to any indirect methods of enhancing the value of property.[3] It is interesting to note that the Revenue manual[4] lists occupations to which these provisions are more likely to be applied in practice as jockeys, actors, pop stars, golfers, tennis players, footballers and boxers.

The section does not apply to a capital amount obtained in respect of the disposal of assets (including any goodwill) of a profession or vocation or shares in a company so far as the value is attributable to the value of the business as a going concern.[5] However, an exception is made where the value of the business as a going concern is derived to a material extent from the individual's activities and for which he does not get full consideration.

The definition of capital amount is very wide and vague. It means any amount in money or money's worth which would not otherwise fall to be included in any computation of income for the purpose of the Tax Acts.[6] The justification

[4.31] Anti-avoidance legislation

for this legislation must turn on the way in which the Revenue apply it. The charge is backed up by various powers, one of which allows the Revenue to require a payment to be made under deduction of tax at basic rate if the payee is non-resident.[7]

Simon's Taxes E1.201–1208.

---

[1] Presumably this has a subjective meaning—cf the use of the same test in the transactions in securities provisions, (supra, § **4.29**).
[2] ITA 2007, s 777.
[3] ITA 2007, s 778, 779.
[4] Inspector's Manual para IM4682. The application of the provisions to arrangements in respect of an accountant's practice run as an incorporated entity are discussed by Keith Gordon in Taxation, 27 February 2003, pp 513–515.
[5] ITA 2007, s 784(4). The meaning of this exemption is obscure. If a lawyer or an accountant runs his practice as an incorporated entity, is the capital distribution on the winding up of the company exempted by virtue of the entire value passing to the shareholders? Or does ITA 2007, s 776 potentially apply as the distribution is made on the winding up and not by reference to a valuation of a going concern? Does the position vary according to whether the practice ceases activity or sells its goodwill to a third party?
[6] ITA 2007, s 775(*b*). Consider unremitted partnership profits when the remittance basis applies. Is there a charge at once under ITA 2007, s 776 and again under ITTOIA 2005, s 832 when the profits are remitted?
[7] ITA 2007, s 944 on weakness in which see *Entergy Power Development Corp v Pardoe* [1999] STC (SCD) 165.

Statutory provisions introduced as a consequence of disclosure of a tax mitigation scheme

[4.32] The introduction of the requirement to report a tax mitigation scheme[1] has quickly led to amendments of statutory provisions to block the schemes. With effect from 16 March 2005, statutory provisions[2] are designed to close a number of loopholes and block a number of avoidance schemes disclosed to the Revenue.

The disclosed schemes are stated by The Treasury as 'exploiting legislation relating to financial products and arrangements of the types for which disclosure of schemes is required'.[3] The main categories of affected schemes are ones which:

(1) convert interest type income into a capital gain or an untaxed receipt;
(2) exploit a loophole in the loss-buying rules;
(3) involve capital redemption bonds and the creation of artificial losses;
(4) exploit the 15-year cut off in the rent factoring rules;
(5) attempt to claim a double deduction under both the manufactured interest rules and the accrued income scheme;

(6) exploit perceived weaknesses in the arm's length rule for loan relationships and the group continuity rules for them and for derivative contracts;
(7) use strips of corporate bonds to create discount which is not taxable under existing legislation, and strips of annuities and annual payments to exploit existing anti-avoidance legislation.
(8) Tax arbitrage between national tax codes.

Subsequent Finance Acts have similarly contained measures apparently highlighted by the disclosure rules.

---

[1] FA 2004, ss 306–319; see supra, § **2A.05**.
[2] Items 1 to 7 are attacked by F(No 2)A 2005, Sch 7; item 8 is attacked by F(No 2)A 2005, ss 24–31 & Sch 2: see infra, § **35.74**.
[3] Treasury Notes to F(No 2)A 2005, Sch 7.

Manufactured capital losses

[4.33] Statute[1] excludes from the definition of "allowable loss"[2] a loss arising "directly or indirectly in consequence of, or otherwise in connection with, any arrangements [where] the main purpose, or one of the main purposes, of the arrangements is to secure a tax advantage.

This provision has effect for capital gains tax and also corporation tax on chargeable gains.[3] The Revenue statement[4] states that:

> the measure applies to 'contrived' capital losses arising on disposals . . . Transactions where a tax advantage is not one of the main purposes will not be caught by the Targeted Anti-Avoidance Rule. Ordinary transactions made in the normal course of managing investments that give rise to a real loss as a result of a real disposal will not be affected by the Targeted Anti-Avoidance Rule.

If the conditions in this provisions are satisfied, any loss that arises is not an "allowable loss" for CGT purposes; and it is automatically removed from capital losses that can be relieved against income.[5]

In order for the provision to have effect, it is necessary to identify an "arrangement". Whether a transaction forms part of a series of transactions, or a scheme, or an arrangement is in general a question of fact, but this conclusion will follow in any case where on transaction would not have taken place without another transaction, or would have taken place on different terms without that other transaction. However, it is not necessary that transactions must depend on each other in this way in order that they form part of a scheme or arrangements.

The provision has the effect when arrangement leads to a "tax advantage". This expression is defined as "relief or increased relief from tax, repayment or increased repayment of tax, the avoidance or reduction of a charge to tax or an assessment to tax, or, the avoidance of a possible assessment to tax".[6] For this purpose, "tax" has a restricted meaning as capital gains tax, corporation tax or income tax.[7] The Revenue guidance states:[8]

[4.33] Anti-avoidance legislation

The purpose of the arrangements is determined by the purpose of the participants in entering into the arrangements. If any participant has a main purpose of achieving a tax advantage, that will constitute a main purpose of the arrangements.

There is no one factor that determines whether the obtaining of a tax advantage is a main purpose of an arrangement. All the circumstances in which the arrangements were entered into need to be taken into consideration. The circumstances might include:

- The overall commercial objective: this should be considered not only from the perspective of individual participants in the arrangements, but also from any wider perspective, such as that of the settlor or beneficiaries of a settlement whose trustees were participants: for these purposes a commercial objective does not include tax motivated reasons;
- Whether this objective is one which the parties involved might ordinarily be expected to have, and which is genuinely being sought;
- Whether the objective is being fulfilled in a straightforward way or whether the introduction of any additional complex or costly steps would have taken place where it not for the tax advantage that could be obtained.

The existence of a tax advantage, such as obtaining a deduction for tax purposes, is not enough in itself to show that the arrangements have a main purpose of obtaining a tax advantage.

For instance, where there is evidence that a person considered two ways to achieve a commercial objective and chose on commercial grounds to pursue one of them, the fact that there was a beneficial difference in tax treatment for the chosen route would not meet the main purpose test. Where the potential tax treatment was a factor in choosing between alternative arrangements, then it would still be necessary that securing a tax advantage was a main purpose to the arrangements. There may be situations where the tax advantage secured through undertaking one arrangement rather than another is so significant that this indicates that achieving a tax advantage was a main purpose. This is unlikely to be the case where the arrangements chosen do not involve addition, complex or costly steps included solely to secure or enhance a tax advantage.

Hence it will be relevant to draw a comparison in order to consider whether, in the absence of the tax considerations:

- The transaction giving rise to the advantage would have taken place at all;
- If so, whether the tax advantage would have been of the same amount; and
- Whether the transaction would have been made under the same terms and conditions.

Nothing in the new legislation prevents relief for losses where a genuine loss has been incurred on an asset which has been lost or extinguished, etc, or where an asset has genuinely become of negligible value. Nor will the new set off against a person's own gains, including the case where, before the real disposal that gives rise to the genuine loss, the person acquires the relevant asset from a spouse or civil partner at no gain/no loss under section 58.

This legislation will not apply where there is a genuine commercial transaction that gives rise to a real commercial loss as a result of a real commercial disposal. In these circumstances there will be no arrangements with a main purpose of securing a tax advantage. Conversely, where there is either no genuine commercial disposal, or no real commercial loss, or no real commercial disposal or any combination of the foregoing, then there are likely to be arrangements in place with a main purpose of securing a tax advantage so the legislation will apply.

Examples of arrangements that, in the view of HMRC, create a disallowable loss under this provision are:[9]

EXAMPLE 1 – LOSS ON SECOND-HAND LIFE INSURANCE POLICY

An individual, C, acquires a life insurance policy "second-hand" for £1 million. The policy had been issued a few days earlier to a third party for a single premium of (say) £990,000. The policy falls within the income tax regime for "chargeable event gains".

C surrenders 95% of the policy back to the insurance company, receiving (say) £955,000 for the surrender. A few days later C surrenders the remaining 5% of the policy, receiving (say) £55,000 in final settlement.

EXAMPLE 2 – CAPITAL LOSS SET AGAINST INCOME

An individual, F, subscribes £20 for 20 ordinary shares in a company which meet the requirements for any loss on disposal of the shares to be relievable against F's income (TA 1988, s 574).

To generate a significant loss F arranges to sell the shares for their current value to a third party [P]. F also grants P an option to sell the shares back for their market value at the time the option is exercised.

EXAMPLE 3 – ARTIFICIAL LOSS FROM MATCHED OPTIONS, ETC

An individual, or a body of trustees, W, takes out two options or futures, designed so that one will yield a loss and the other a corresponding (or similar) gain, depending on how the value of the underlying assets has changed. The contracts are completed so that a loss and a matching (or similar) gain arise.

---

[1] TCGA 1992, s 16A inserted by FA 2007, s 77 with effect from 6 December 2006. This provision replaces the anti-avoidance provision of TCGA 1992, s 8(2A) inserted only for corporation tax by FA 2006, s 69 with effect from 5 December 2005.
[2] See infra, 16.26 et seq.
[3] TCGA 1992, s 8(2) amended by FA 2007, s 27(2).
[4] Issued 6 December 2006.
[5] Under ITA 2007, s 133 for individuals; TA 1988, s 573 for companies.
[6] TCGA 1992, s 16A(2) inserted by FA 2007, s 27.
[7] TCGA 1992, s 16A(2) inserted by FA 2007, s 27.
[8] HMRC Statement, 6 December 2006, paras 10–15 & 18.
[9] HMRC Statement, 6 December 2006, paras 24, 25, 28, 29, 32.

Part II
Income Tax

For payment of income tax, returns, enquiries, appeals and other administrative matters, see Chapter 2 and 2A.

5

Income tax—general
The charge to tax
Rates of tax
The Schedular system
History
History's legacy
The heads of charge
Timing
Non-taxable income
Prohibited deductions
Earned income and investment income
Savings income
Calculation of tax

6

Allowances and reliefs
The tax unit
Property jointly owned by spouses and civil partners
Personal allowances
Allowances for non-residents
Claiming relief
Loss relief
Maintenance payments
Gifts to charities
Interest relief
Averaging
Top slicing
Tax credits

7

Employment income
Charging base of employment income
Earnings of UK resident and domiciled employee
Earnings of employee resident or domiciled outside the UK
Office or employment
Employment income: the causation test
Types of income
Compensation payments for claims against employers
Benefits in kind—general
Particular benefits
Employee share schemes
Enterprise management incentives

Employee share ownership plans
Employees earning £8,500 per annum or more and directors
The benefits code
Particular benefits in the benefits code
Expenses and deductions from earnings
Pay as you earn
PAYE and self-assessment

8

Income from trades, professions and vocations
Trade, profession or vocation
Distinction between (1) trade and (2) profession or vocation
Is there a trade?
Basis of assessment
Partnerships
The measure of income
Spreading adjustments
Trading receipts
Exempt trading income
Expenses
Timing of transactions
Trading stock
Commission, cashbacks and discounts
Mining

9

Capital allowances
Introduction
What is capital expenditure?
When expenditure is incurred
Method of giving capital allowances
Industrial buildings
Dwelling-houses let on assured tenancies
Plant and machinery
Mining
Dredging
Agricultural land and buildings
Other allowances

10

Property income
The charge to tax
A 'UK property business'

Borderline between Property Income and Trading Income
Calculation of income
Property income of a partnership
Energy saving expenditure
Interest paid—income tax
Non-resident landlord
Furnished lettings
Rent a room
Furnished holiday lettings
Taxation of premiums as income

11

Savings income
The charge to tax
Savings income not charged to tax
Interest—meaning
Accrued interest
Yearly interest—meaning
Deduction at source
Deeply discounted securities
Gilt strips
Annuities and annual payments
Deduction at source: basic rate
Consequence of failing to deduct tax
Payments 'free of tax'
Rule in *Re Pettit*
Maintenance payments

12

Miscellaneous income
Scope of this chapter
Income taxed under ITTOIA 2005 Chapter 8
Foreign questions
Computation
Pre-owned assets

13

Trusts
Introduction
Bare trustee
Trusts with a vulnerable beneficiary
Taxation of the trustee
The two trust rates

Settlor-interested trusts
Taxation of the beneficiary
Capital or income
Charities

14

Estates in the course of administration
Income of the deceased
Income arising after death

15

The settlement code
The code in statute
A settlement
Settlor
Change on income arising
Charge on the settlor
Parental settlements on unmarried minor children
Capital sums paid to the settlor
Settlements of income
Jones v Garnett

5

Income tax—general

The charge to tax	PARA 5.01
Rates of tax	PARA 5.02
The Schedular system	PARA 5.03
History	PARA 5.04
History's legacy	PARA 5.05
The heads of charge	PARA 5.08
Timing	PARA 5.14
Non-taxable income	PARA 5.17
Prohibited deductions	PARA 5.19
Earned income and investment income	PARA 5.20
Savings income	PARA 5.26
Calculation of tax	PARA 5.29

Income tax is charged at the rates in force for a particular year of assessment on the income attributed by the tax system to that year. The tax system thus has to set the rates of tax, which may vary according to the type of income, to define what is meant by income, to define when it arises and, because of international rules, where it arises and on occasion to whom it arises. These issues so simply stated form the subject of Part II of this book as supplemented by Parts V and VI.

For payment of income tax, see §§ 2A.14–2A.19

The charge to tax

[5.01] The main tax statutes (ITEPA 2003, ITTOIA 2005 and ITA 2007) do not, in terms, impose a charge to income tax. They merely provide the framework under which income tax will be administered, if Parliament chooses to impose a charge for the year. In every year since 1842, Parliament has chosen to impose a charge to income tax, although technically, each year's charge is imposed as a temporary measure: ie a charge only lasts for a single fiscal year. Income tax for 2009–10 is imposed by Finance Act 2009, s 1(1).

The charge to income tax is not restricted to individuals. Income tax is charged on income received by any person, except where the Taxes Acts exclude the charge. Hence, income tax is payable by trustees and by personal representatives. A company is required to pay income tax on its income, where the income is not within the charge to corporation tax. Thus, a non-resident company that does not have a permanent establishment in the UK pays UK income tax (not corporation tax) on its UK-source income.[1]

[5.01] Income tax—general

[1] FA 2003, s 151 has the effect that a non-resident company without a permanent establishment in the UK is not subject to income tax on interest or dividend income (although any tax credits and tax deducted at source are not repayable to such a company).

Rates of tax

[5.02] The terms used in describing the rates of income tax have been made more complicated by recent legislation. The arithmetic process required to compute the total tax burden is more complex than at any time since the 1973 reforms. This complexity, based upon politically-motivated obfuscation, is inconsistent with the philosophy behind self-assessment which requires simplicity in the basics of the income tax system. Today the taxpayer has to identify the nature of the income in order to calculate the tax due. For 2009–10, the basic rate remains at 20%. However, to the extent that an individual's top slice of income is savings income (as defined) other than dividend (or similar) income then a 10% rate applies for the first £2,440 of taxable income.[1]

Income that consists of dividends and similar income is taxed at the dividend ordinary rate of 10% where it is part of taxable income but does not exceed the basic rate limit of £37,400.[2]

All other income is taxed at the basic rate of 20% up to the basic rate limit of £37,400. Where income is above the basic rate limit, the higher rate of 40% applies (unless it is dividend, etc income which then attracts tax at the dividend upper rate of 32.5%).[3]

The starting rate limit and the basic rate limit are computed by indexing the limits for the preceding year, as Parliament has not enacted otherwise.[4]

The rates of tax on trusts reflect the rates for individuals, except that the rate depends on the type of trust and not on the amount of income. For this purpose, there are two types of trust. The first type is a trust within ITA 2007, s 479. This is a trust where the trustees have the power to decide on amounts to be distributed or/and the power to accumulate income. Such trusts pay income tax at 32 1/2% on dividend income and 40% on all other income.[5] The income on which this charge is levied is the income over which the trustees have discretion and/or the power to accumulate. It, thus, does not include income that is extended as "trust management expenses".[6] The second type of trust is a trust where one or more individuals has the right to income as it arises. Dividends received by trustees of such a trust are subject to tax at 10% and other income at 20%.

[1] ITA 2007, s 12 as amended by Income Tax (Indexation) (No 3) Order 2008, SI 2008/3023, art 3.
[2] ITA 2007, s 8(1) and 12(1) as amended by FA 2009, s 2(1) (overturning the Income Tax (Indexation) (No 3) Order 2008, SI 2008/3023, art 2).
[3] ITA 2007, s 8(2).

[4] ITA 2007, s 21.
[5] ITA 2007, s 9. The first £1,000 of trust income is, however, charged to tax at basic rate only: ITA 2007, s 491: see infra, § **13.17**.
[6] The term "trust management expenses" is that which was used in TA 1988, s 686(2A). After tax law rewrite, ITA 2007, s 484 uses the term: "allowable expenses". This change of nomenclature indicates a complete change in the structure of the tax charge. Under TA 1988, it was possible to argue that the income subject to what was then termed "the rate applicable to trusts" could only be income after trustees had made payments for their expenses, as the charge was on "income available to be accumulated or payable at the discretion of the trustees" and income expended on expenses, whatever their nature, is not available to the trustees to do anything with. After the tax law rewrite, the charge is on a statutory formula. That is, the total taxable income received less expenses that are specified as being allowable. See infra, § **13.12**.

The schedular system

[5.03] The Finance Act 1803 established a set of Schedules, with each item of income categorised under a Schedule. The rule for the measurement of income was specified in the Schedule, different Schedules being subject to different rules.[1] Income tax was then charged on the income falling within the Schedules; any income that did not fall within a Schedule did not attract a charge to income tax. This basic scheme continued until 2003. Each year's Finance Act imposed a charge on "profits or gains" described or comprised in the different Schedule.[2] A charge under one Schedule excludes a charge under another section for that Schedule for that same item of income.[3] There is no general aggregation of income but rather a sum of the plus figures obtained under each Schedule, with a loss under a Schedule being taken into account only where this is permitted by legislation.[4]

The principle underlying the exclusivity of the income tax schedules is given in the speech of Lord Radcliffe in *Mitchell and Edon v Ross:*[5]

> Before you can assess a profit to tax you must be sure that you have properly identified its source or other description according to the correct Schedule: but, once you have done that, it is obligatory that it should be charged, if at all, under that Schedule and strictly in accordance with the rules that are there laid down for assessments under it. It is a necessary consequence of this conception that the sources of profit in the different Schedules are mutually exclusive.

Prior to the enactment of Income Tax (Earnings and Pensions) Act 2003, this could be interpreted as providing that the profits described in the then remaining Schedules A, D, E and F were mutually exclusive, by virtue of what was TA 1988, s 1(1).

Income Tax (Earnings and Pensions) Act 2003 rewrote the law relating to the profits previously charged to income tax under Schedule E. Income Tax (Trading and Other Income) Act 2005 continued the process for income sources previously charged under Schedules A, D and F. Consequently, with effect from 6 April 2005, the schedular system has been abolished for income

[5.03] Income tax—general

tax purposes. It should be noted, however, that the schedular system currently remains intact for corporation tax purposes.

TA 1988, s 1(1) now exists as ITA 2007, s 3. The section provides for income tax to be charged (first) on the amounts charged under the Parts of ITEPA relating to employment income, pension income and social security income, and (secondly) on the amounts charged under the Parts of ITTOIA 2005 relating to trading income, property income, savings and investment income and miscellaneous income. The three categories "employment income", "pension income" and "social security income" are, broadly, the successor categories to the former Schedule E; "trading income" represents what were Cases I and II of Schedule D; "property income" represents the former Schedule A; "savings and investment income" represent what were previously Schedule D, Case III and Schedule F. However, there is not always a direct alignment between one former Schedule (or Case) and the new headings. For example, overseas income previously charged under Case IV or V of Schedule D now comes under the heading appropriate to the type of income (eg trading or property), In addition, "miscellaneous income" covers income formerly assessable under Cases III, V and VI of Schedule D as well as assessable income not previously within the schedular system.

An Inland Revenue legal consultant has stated[6] that, in the Revenue view, the principle of exclusivity of the income tax schedules given in the speech of Lord Radcliffe in *Mitchell and Edon v Ross* will continue to apply, not to Schedules but to the new seven categories of income.

A recent decision that rests on the allocation of income to Schedules is *Property Co v Inspector of Taxes*.[7] Income arose to a company from let property. Rental income, and defined categories of income related to letting, was taxable under Schedule A. However, the contract under which this particular income arose was held to be void. The Special Commissioner ruled that income arising from a void contract cannot properly be regarded as rent and could not fall within Schedule A. The income was, therefore, taxable under the residual Schedule D, Case VI.

Income tax is charged on income for the tax year. Each year is taken separately and there is no general averaging provision. Such income is not necessarily the income actually arising within that 12-month period since some income categories have a system of assessment on the basis of the income arising in a 12-month period that ends in the tax year of assessment.[8]

---

[1] Different Schedules tax income of different periods. Thus, for many years income tax under Schedule D Case I and II was the profits arising in a period ending in the previous fiscal year, whereas dividend income, for example, has always been income of the current fiscal year. The distinction continues, despite the adoption of the, so called, "current year basis": infra, §§ **5.16** and **8.43** et seq.

[2] TA 1988, s 1(1).

[3] *Salisbury House Estates Ltd v Fry* (1930) 15 TC 266, HL.

[4] *Griffiths v Jackson* [1983] STC 184; *Gittos v Barclay* [1982] STC 390. See further infra, § **11.07**.

[5] (1961) 40 TC 11, 61.

[6] Letter from the legal consultant to Tax Rewrite Project to the Chartered Institute of Taxation, dated 12 February 2004.
[7] [2005] STC (SCD) 59, see particularly the Special Commissioner's comments at 87j.
[8] See infra, § **8.43**.

History

[5.04] Income tax began, ironically, as a means of giving relief from another tax. By an Act of 1797 Pitt imposed the so-called Triple Assessment, a tax based on property and expenditure; this involved a sharp increase on the tax levied on that basis in the previous year; the full increase was to be charged on those whose income was more than £50 the previous year and there were smaller increases for those with income below that figure; further the tax payable was not to exceed 10% of total income. The process was not a success and the following year Pitt introduced the Property and Income Tax Act to be effective from January 1799. The tax was based on a general return by the taxpayer of his income for the year, a return which could be challenged by the Surveyors who could ask for details under 19 different heads. The tax was charged at 10p in the £ on all income over £200 with a graduated rate between £60 and £200 and exemption below £60. Among permitted deductions were allowances for children, interest payments and life assurance. This tax was a only partial success and was completely overhauled.

Henry Addington's Act of 1803, under which income that was to suffer taxation was classified into five Schedules: Schedule A (income from land and buildings), Schedule B (farming profit), Schedule C (public annuities), Schedule D (self-employment and other items not covered by the other Schedules) and Schedule E (salaries, annuities and pensions). Tax was charged at 5% (which rose to 10% in 1806) and the words "income tax" were deliberately avoided, the Act being styled as a "contribution of the profits arising from property, professions, trades and offices". Practitioners will recognise that the specification of the schedules by Addington in 1803 is substantially the same as the specification that until recently applied for income tax and that remains for corporation tax, there having being remarkably little change over the intervening 202 years. Although income tax was repealed after the defeat of Napoleon in 1815 and the belief that the demand on the Parliamentary purse could be satisfied without a tax on incomes, the reintroduction of income tax by Sir Robert Peel in 1842 was effected by a reintroduction of Henry Addington's Schedules, although Sir Robert Peel, in opposition, had argued against the schedular system.

There is still no statutory definition of income, beyond the statement that income is taxable if it falls within one or other of the income categories.

A further irony is that the introduction of the schedular system was justified as a system of the taxation of separate categories of income as opposed to total income, with the abandonment of the requirement for an individual to make a general return of his total income. The rationale behind the schedular system was explained in 1885 as:[1]

[5.04] Income tax—general

As the former duty was imposed on a general account of income from all sources, the present duty is imposed on each source, by itself, in the hands of the first possessor, at the same time permitting its diffusion through every natural channel in its course to the hands of the ultimate proprietor. Instead of the landlord and the various claimants upon him in succession, it looks to the occupier only.[2] Instead of the creditor, it looks to the fund from which the debt is answered.[3] In the place of a complicated account collected from various sources from which the income of an individual is derived, it applies to the source itself to answer for its increase. By these means its object is attained with more facility and celerity, and with less intricacy and disclosure, diminishing the occasion of evasion by means of exaction; thus the charge is gradually diffused from the first possessor to the ultimate proprietor, the private transactions of life are protected from the public eye and the Revenue is more effectually guarded.

There is now a requirement on a taxpayer to not only disclose all sources of income but to calculate his self-assessment income tax based on the totality of his income. Nevertheless, the schedular system was retained and continues today in all but name.

[1] 28th Report C. 4474 (1885) page 30.
[2] This refers to the old Schedule A.
[3] This refers to what is now ITA 2007, s 874. This was extended to Schedule C in 1806.

History's legacy

[5.05] This passage highlights three central features of the Victorian tax system which remain with us today: the division of different types of income into different categories, the doctrine of the source and the system of deduction at source:

(1)   There is no provision in the income tax acts stating that income tax is levied on a person's income. ITA 2007, s 3(1) states simply that income tax is charged under the provisions listed in that section; Chapter 2 of Part 2 of that Act states that basic rate income tax is levied on income and then that if an individual's total income exceeds a certain figure income tax may be levied at higher rates; Chapter 3 determines how an individual's tax liability is calculated. From this stems the distinction between income and total income and the conceptual difficulties over the taxation of trusts.

(2)   If there is no source, there is no taxable income. This central concept of the British tax system provided the rationale for the arrangement whereby the gift, made abroad, of the proceeds of foreign income arising to a non-domiciled individual avoids tax when remitted to the UK by the recipient, frequently a UK domiciled spouse.[1] The legislator has attempted to restrict the planning opportunities by introducing timing rules so that a receipt is linked with a previous source, notably for earnings paid after the cessation of an employment,[2] and in respect of remittances by non-UK domiciled individuals[3] but the legislator has never revoked the central doctrine of source.

(3) Provisions allow the assessment of persons receiving or entitled to income: ITTOIA 2005, ss 8 (trading income), 271 (property income) and 371 (interest income) are examples of this rule. Neither of these terms has been authoritatively expounded by the courts but their function and therefore scope in the Victorian system which rejected the notion of a total return of income may be different from that in today's system where such a return is accepted.

---

[1] See infra, § **35.22**.
[2] ITEPA 2003, ss 17 and 30. See infra, § **7.22**. The doctrine of source also forms the foundation of the causation test which is of paramount importance in considering the application of ITEPA 2003: see infra, § **7.17**.
[3] FA 2008, Sch 7.

[5.06] Where income falls within a category[1] of income it falls to be computed in accordance with the rules in that category and no other.

In *Fry v Salisbury House Estate Ltd*[2] the company received rents from unfurnished offices in a building. The company also provided services for the offices such as heating and cleaning at an additional charge. The rents were chargeable under Schedule A, although the basis of assessment at that time was not simply the rents minus costs of maintenance but the annual value of the premises, which were revalued every five years, minus a statutory allowance for running costs. The company agreed that its profits from the ancillary services fell within Schedule D, Case I, but resisted the Revenue's argument that it was liable to tax on the actual rent received under Schedule D, Case I rather than the notional rent under Schedule A. The Revenue conceded that it would have to make an allowance in computing tax under Schedule D, Case I for the tax due under Schedule A.[3] The House of Lords found for the company. Although the company could be said to be carrying on a trade and therefore fall within Schedule D, Case I, the Schedules were mutually exclusive and each Schedule was dominant over its own subject matter. The charge under Schedule A therefore excluded the charge under Schedule D, Case I (see infra, § **10.07**). Lord Atkin said:[4]

> Specific income must be assets under the specific schedule . . . The dominance of each Schedule A, B, C and E over its own subject matter is confirmed by reference to the Sections and Rules which respectively regulate them in the Act of 1842. They are therefore a complete code for each class of income, dealing with allowances and exemptions, with the mode of assessment and, with the officials whose duty it is to make the assessments.

Simon's Taxes A2.112.

---

[1] Prior to 2003, a category of income was a Schedule, or a Case within a Schedule. The work of the Tax Law Re-write Project in producing first, ITEPA 2003 and then ITTOIA 2005 removes Schedules from income tax that is covered by those Acts, and in place of Schedules, creates a larger number of categories. The principle, however, continues that the computation of taxable income is determined by the rules of the category in which that income falls.
[2] [1930] AC 432, 15 TC 266. Decision reversed by FA 1940, ss 13–18.

[3] See *Russell v Aberdeen Town and County Bank* (1888) 2 TC 321.
[4] *Salisbury House Estates Ltd v Fry* (1930) 15 TC 266, HL.

[5.07] Just as income is specific to a category, so a loss arises from an activity within a particular category. The relief (if any) available for the loss is determined by the rules for the category under which it arises. There is no general set off of losses in the UK tax system. Certain, restricted, types of loss (notably a loss arising on a UK based trade)[1] can be off set against total income,[2] which is the aggregate of the income arising under the different categories of income.

[1] ITA 2007, s 64(1). See infra, § **6.15**.
[2] ITA 2007, s 23 *Step 1*. See infra, § **6.52**.

The heads of charge

[5.08] The various heads of charge are now set out.

Employment; pension and social security income (ITEPA 2003, s 6)

[5.09] Until 2003, Schedule E taxed emoluments from an office or employment. ITEPA 2003 now charges employment income, pension income and social security income without reference to a schedule. Tax is due on a current year basis and is usually collected by PAYE. See infra § **7.02**. A receipts basis is normally used.
Simon's Taxes A1.139.

Trading income (ITTOIA 2005, Pt 2)

[5.10] The trading income part of ITTOIA 2005 (Pt 2) taxes annual profits arising from a trade, profession or vocation. Under the former schedular system, there was a technical distinction (albeit not one that latterly had any practical effect) between trading income (assessable under Case I of Schedule D) and income from professions or vocations (assessable under Case II). Whilst some rules still differ between these two types of income, they have now been brought under the single heading of trading income. The trading income Part also deals with trades, professions and vocations carried on overseas.
Simon's Taxes A1.135.

Property income (ITTOIA 2005, Pt 3)

[5.11] Property income was rewritten for income tax in 1995 (and, with small variations, for corporation tax in 1998). It taxes the annual profits arising from what the legislation refers to as a property (formerly "Schedule A")

The heads of charge [5.11]

business.[1] Whereas a Schedule A business had (and for corporation tax must continue) to be carried on for the exploitation of an estate interest or rights in or over land in the UK[2], Pt 3 of ITTOIA 2005 covers UK and overseas land. However, income from UK land forms a single "UK property business" and overseas income a separate "overseas property business". The charge for these two types of business extends beyond mere rents under a lease to sums paid for licences to use land, to rent charges and, sometimes, to a part of a sum paid by way of a premium on the grant of a lease.

Income from a property business is computed by bringing together in all rents, premiums and other income arising from land in the UK (in the case of a UK property business) or from all land outside the UK (in the case of an overseas property business). From the relevant aggregates are deducted all expenses incurred in respect of that aggregate income.[3]

Expenditure relating to the income is then deducted from the aggregate of income received, not from specific items of income. Whilst the statute refers to the resulting sum as income from property business, this income is, however, not business income on which pension contributions can be paid (except in so far as it relates to furnished holiday lettings).

Tax is chargeable not on the income received, or even the income due, in the particular year but on the income attributable to the tax year. So if rent is payable in half-yearly instalments in advance on 1 January and 1 July, the sum paid on 1 January 2010 will be attributed partly to the year 2009–10 and partly to the year 2010–11; a strict allocation means that 95/181 of the rent is brought to charge in 2009–10 and 86/181 to 2010–11.

The Revenue have stated that the designation of property income as being treated as arising from a single property "business" is a formulation that is relevant only within the assessment boundaries. Hence, a self-assessment partnership return is not issued to a property owning partnership, unless the activity is, in its own right, of such a nature as to constitute a "business".[4]

Whilst ITTOIA 2005, Pt 3 mainly contains the provisions for sources formerly assessable under Schedule A (or Schedule D, Case V in the case of an overseas property business), the Part also contains the rules relating to other property-based income charges that were formerly charged under Schedule D, Cases III and VI. These include post-cessation receipts, rents received from "section 12(4) concerns" (which include mines, quarries, tolls) and electric-line wayleaves.[5]

Simon's Taxes A1.132.

---

[1] ITTOIA 2005, s 276; see also ITA 2007, ss 118 & 120 (losses) and CAA 2001, s 15 (allowances for plant and machinery).
[2] TA 1988, s 15.
[3] ITTOIA 2005, ss 260 and 265.
[4] Inland Revenue interpretation RI 137.
[5] ITTOIA 2005, s 260(1).

Savings and investment income (ITTOIA 2005, Pt 4)

[5.12] Part 4 of ITTOIA 2005 brings together the rules for interest, annuities and other annual payments (formerly Schedule D, Case III), dividends (formerly Schedule F) and their overseas equivalents, together with some types of income formerly assessable under Schedule D, Case VI.

Simon's Taxes A1.140.

Schedule B (TA 1988, s 16) and Schedule C (TA 1988, s 17)

[5.13] The above headings correspond loosely with former Schedules E, part of Schedule D, Schedule A and some of the rest of Schedule D and Schedule F. The other Schedules were B and C.

Schedule B taxed the occupation of woodlands in the UK managed on a commercial basis.[1] The charge to tax under this Schedule was abolished with effect from 6 April 1988 subject to transitional provisions.[2]

Schedule C taxed income from public revenue dividends paid in the UK.[3] This Schedule was abolished for 1996–97 and subsequent years.[4] Such dividends are not taxed as "interest".[5]

Simon's Taxes A1.133, 134.

---

[1] TA 1988, s 5(1) (now repealed). Under the 1803 Act, Schedule B taxed farming profits.
[2] FA 1988, s 65, Sch 6.
[3] TA 1988, s 17 (now repealed).
[4] ITTOIA 2005, ss 365(1)(a) & 369.
[5] FA 1996, Sch 7, para 4.

Timing

[5.14] The issue of timing is important for several obvious reasons. Income tax is assessed on income of a year of assessment and payment of the tax liability is required on the due dates for that year. As income tax is a charge for the fiscal year and is levied by a Finance Act enacted for a specified year, the tax treatment may differ according to whether the income is income of year 1 or income of year 2.[1] Some reliefs are geared to a maximum percentage of a person's income for a year, as is the case with retirement annuity premiums or pension plan contributions (see infra, § **31.26**).[2] The taxpayer is under an obligation to report his income year by year[3] so that penalties may arise if he errs in the timing of a particular receipt. The effective rate of tax may vary according to the time it becomes chargeable; this is because the taxpayer's marginal rate of tax may vary from one year to the next and because UK tax law still contains no general averaging provision. A further reason is that in general it will be the value at the time the income arises that is relevant for tax purposes; subsequent changes in value are in general ignored.[4] Further, reliefs may be available against the income of a particular year.[5]

The timing of the receipt can cause it not to be assessable. This arises from the doctrine, which is central to the concept of the system that treats separately the different types of income so that, in order to be subject to income tax, every piece of income must have a source and tax case reports abound with references to fruit and tree. The doctrine was applied to exempt certain types of income which clearly ought to have been taxed. These payments escaped tax because since income tax was an annual tax, it followed that not only must the income arise within the tax year, but the source must also exist in that tax year. Hence, before there was specific statutory provision, it was decided that the post-cessation receipts of a trade were not taxable. The classical formulation was given by Rowlatt J.[6]

> When a trader or a follower of a profession or a vocation dies or goes out of business . . . and there remain to be collected sums owing for good supplies during the existence of the business or for sums rendered by the professional man during the course of his life or his business, there is no question of assessing those receipts to income tax.

Thus, under the classical formulation, income cannot be assessed to tax if the source of income does not exist for that particular year of assessment. Thus, until 1960, it was commonplace for a barrister on ceasing practice, whether on promotion to a juridical post or otherwise, to receive fees after his cessation without any charge to income tax. In order to impose a charge to income tax, specific legislation now charges post-cessation trading receipts.[7] In *Bray v Best*[8] it was held that payments made after an employment has ceased but for services rendered as an employee could not be retrospectively attributed to the years of service. As with post-cessation receipts, specific legislation has been introduced to charge receipts after an employment has ceased.[9] Of continuing relevance, is a charge on a remittance basis. If money is brought into the UK in a year after that in which the source ceases, no tax is payable.[10]

However, the issue of timing is also relevant to a subtler matter, namely the non-correlation of the rules with regard to receipts with those for expenses. One cannot be taxed on income one does not acquire; once income has been acquired a deduction for paying it back will be allowed only if permitted by the deduction rules appropriate to that category of income. So preventing the income from arising will avoid tax whereas a receipt followed by a disposal will not.

In *Way v Underdown (No 2)*[11] an insurance agent gathered in a premium and subsequently paid back to the insured an amount equal to his commission on the premium. It was held that as there was no obligation to repay he could not deduct the sum in computing his taxable profits; he was therefore taxable on the commission. However, had he simply not collected the premium in full in the first place he might well not have been taxed.

Simon's Taxes A1.126.

---

[1] As in *Strick v Longsdon* (1953) 34 TC 528 (special contribution for 1947–48).
[2] The maximum retirement annuity premium that can be paid is the percentage specified for the age of the individual applied to his net relevant earnings for that year: TA 1988, s 619. The maximum premium that can be paid to a personal pension plan is the percentage specified for the individual's age applied to the

[5.14] Income tax—general

highest total income in the year of contribution, or any of the preceding five years: TA 1988, s 640.
3   TMA 1970, s 8.
4   This is of crucial importance when dealing with payments in kind or payments in foreign currency; for authority in the latter instance see *Payne v Deputy Federal Comr of Taxation* [1936] AC 497, [1936] 2 All ER 793 and *Greig v Ashton* [1956] 3 All ER 123, 36 TC 581.
5   As in *Parkside Leasing Ltd v Smith* [1985] STC 63.
6   *Bennett v Ogston* (1930) 15 TC 374 at 378. See also *Stainer's Executors v Purchase* [1951] 2 All ER 1071, 32 TC 367, *Carson v Cheyne's Executors* [1958] 3 All ER 573, 38 TC 240.
7   FA 1960, s 32 which applies to receipts arising after 5 April 1960 and is now ITTOIA 2005, Pt 2, Ch 18 (income tax) and TA 1988, s 103 (corporation tax).
8   [1989] 1 All ER 969, [1989] STC 159, HL.
9   ITEPA 2003, ss 17 and 30.
10 Infra, § **35.15**.
11 [1975] 2 All ER 1064, [1975] STC 425, CA; affg. [1974] 2 All ER 595, [1974] STC 293 (Pennycuick V-C).

[5.15] Timing questions are resolved by allocating each item of income to a specified fiscal year. Each category of income has its own rules to achieve this result. The employment income rule, for example, is, in general, to require payment of tax for the year in which income is received; thus, if the agreement for the termination of an employment provides that the former employee will have free use of a company car for some years into the future, the benefit of the free use is brought into the charge to tax in the year in which it is enjoyed, not the year of termination of the employment.[1]

This revitalises the old and much abused dictum that "receivability without receipt is nothing". This dictum has been applied to the payment of arrears of interest causing payments for six years to be treated as the taxable income of one[2] although relief is available for retrospective increases in pensions.[3] This principle raises the question of what amounts to receipt. Where trustees or personal representatives receive income, that receipt may be treated as receipt by the beneficiaries,[4] as may receipt of income by an agent for a principal or by one partner for the other[5] although it has been held that the mere receipt of a cheque is not a receipt of income.[6] Where a taxpayer directs payment to a third party, so that the taxpayer never actually receives payment himself, the economic control shown by the direction is still sufficient to amount to receipt.[7] The crediting of an account which act enures to the benefit of the account-owner will also be a receipt.[8] A payment made direct to a third party to discharge the taxpayer's obligations to that third party[9] is also a receipt. Where a payer is under a duty to deduct the recipient's tax on that income, the sum withheld is treated as having been received by the taxpayer.[10]

There is a statutory definition of receipt for Employment Income.[11]

Certain foreign income is taxable not because it has accrued but because—and so only when—it is remitted to this country: see infra, § **7.07** and § **35.12**.

Under self assessment, the same approach is taken for reliefs that are related back to an earlier year. Thus, for example, if a farmer claims a reduction in the income assessable in a previous year by virtue of the averaging provisions,[12] the previous year assessment is not reopened but, instead, the tax payable following the making of the claim is reduced to reflect the tax effect on the previous year of the claim that is made; this can lead to a repayment from the Revenue for that new year.[13]

Simon's Taxes B3.304.

---

[1] ITEPA 2003, s 403. The question of allocation to the fiscal year of trading income is the interaction of statutory rules and the principles of commercial accounting: see infra, § **8.64**.
[2] *Leigh v IRC* [1928] 1 KB 73, 11 TC 590 (Schedule D, Case IV).
[3] ITEPA 2003, s 840 (formerly Extra-statutory concession A55).
[4] Infra, § **13.12**.
[5] *IRC v Lebus' Executors* (1946) 27 TC 136 at 147.
[6] *Parkside Leasing Ltd v Smith* [1985] STC 63.
[7] Lord Hansworth MR, in *Dewar v IRC* [1935] 2 KB 351 at 367, 19 TC 561 at 577.
[8] *Dunmore v McGowan* [1978] 2 All ER 85, [1978] STC 217 discussed at [1982] BTR 23, the point there taken being approved in *Macpherson v Bond* [1985] STC 678. *Dunmore v McGowan* was followed in *Peracha v Miley* [1990] STC 512, CA but distinguished in *Girvan v Orange Personal Communications Services Ltd* [1998] STC 567.
[9] Cf *Salter v Minister of National Revenue* (1947) 2 DTC 918.
[10] ITA 2007, s 848(1); infra, § **11.40**.
[11] ITEPA 2003, s 687; infra, § **7.22**.
[12] ITTOIA 2005, s 223.
[13] TMA 1970, Sch 1B, paras 3 and 4.

Basis period

[5.16] Apart from income arising from a trade, profession or vocation, the basis period for all income is the fiscal year; that is, income from 6 April 2009 to 5 April 2010 is brought into the taxpayer's self-assessment for 2009–10.

For interest and savings income this is income paid in that period.[1] For employment income, it is usually income received in the year.[2] For property income, it is income arising in the year.[3]

For the charge to tax in respect of trading income, the basis period is determined by the accounting date. Accounting date is defined as a date in the tax year to which accounts are made up. Where there are two or more such dates in a fiscal year, it is the last of those dates.[4]

The accounting date is, thus, determined by the actions of the taxpayer in that it is the taxpayer who makes up his accounts, not the Revenue. The Revenue do not have the power to require accounts to be made up to any specified accounting date and cannot ignore an accounting date, except as is authorised by ITTOIA 2005, s 216(4) which applies only when a taxpayer changes his accounting date.

Where accounts are made up for a period of 12 months ending in an accounting date in the fiscal year, the accounts to that accounting date form the basis period of assessment for the fiscal year in which the accounting date falls.[5]

For periods of account that are longer or shorter than 12 months, whether due to commencement, change of accounting date or to cessation, see infra §§ **8.48–8.50** and §§ **8.54–8.58**.

Simon's Taxes B4.101.

---

[1] See, in particular, ITTOIA 2005, ss 370 and 384.
[2] ITEPA 2003, ss 15(2), 21(2), 25(2) and 27(2).
[3] ITTOIA 2005, s 270; see infra, § **10.06**.
[4] ITTOIA 2005, s 197(1).
[5] ITTOIA 2005, s 198(1).

Non-taxable income

[5.17] The concept of income is narrowed in five main ways. First, it is clear that unless a particular receipt comes within one or other of the categories of income it is not taxable income.

Second, although ITTOIA 2005, s 683 charges income tax on "annual payments that are not [otherwise] charged to income tax" and s 687 includes a residuary case to catch receipts not caught by the other Parts of that Act or by any other Act, the courts have construed these provisions in a limited way—generally, profits are only income if they possess a quality of recurrence[1]—and have confined them to profits similar to those caught by the other more specific provisions, infra, § **12.04**. In particular the courts have taken a restrictive view of what is income by drawing a line between income and capital.

Third, the interpretation of the income categories is governed by the doctrine of the source. To be taxable in a fiscal year, every piece of income must have a source in that year.[2]

Fourth, in order to be income, the receipt must be from another person. In the UK tax system, this is taken to exclude from a charge to tax, income that is generated within an entity. Thus, income from mutual trading is not taxable, see infra, §§ **8.35–8.41**. This concept serves to exclude from a charge to tax not only members' clubs but, also, mutual assurance companies, many of which are very large and have significant surpluses.

Finally, the basic distinction between income and capital is central to the system, although the legislature has occasionally intervened, as with premiums for leases, infra, § **10.16**, the proceeds of certain life assurance policies, infra, § **31.22** and golden handshakes, infra, § **7.36**. The reason for this acceptance by the legislature is probably the high value placed by the legislature on the requirement of certainty in the sense of enforceability or practicality, even at the expense of equity.

As a consequence of these rules, non-taxable receipts include gambling winnings,³ instalments of capital,⁴ most gifts⁵—including the remission of a debt⁶—and loans.⁷

Simon's Taxes A1.121, 122.

1 *Moss Empires Ltd v IRC* [1937] AC 785, 21 TC 264. This does not prevent single payments from being caught—eg the Schedule D Case VI case of *Ryall v Hoare* (1923) 8 TC 521.
2 eg *Brown v National Provident Institution* [1921] 2 AC 222 at 246, 8 TC at 89, per Lord Atkinson; and *Leeming v Jones* [1930] 1 KB 279 at 297, 15 TC 333 at 349–50, per Lord Hanworth. See also supra, § **3.12**.
3 The gambling industry pays many taxes but the exemption for the individual winner is a remarkable exception to the approach generally adopted by the legislator of taxing when there is an ability to pay.
4 Infra, § **11.32**.
5 But see infra, § **7.24**, § **8.75** and § **11.20**.
6 But see infra, § **8.146**.
7 A loan is not income. Statute, however, provides an income tax charge on the receipt of certain loans that fall within the anti-avoidance rules for settlements see infra, § **15.23**.

[5.18] Certain types of receipt are exempt from liability to income tax:

(1) *Short-term Social Security benefit*¹
    Adoption pay
    Maternity allowance
(2) *Social Security benefits in respect of children*
    Child benefit
    Child dependency additions²
    Child tax credit
    Child's special allowance
    Guardian's allowance³
    One-parent benefit
(3) *Industrial injury Social Security benefits*
    Constant attendance allowance
    Industrial death benefit
    Industrial disablement benefit
    Pneumoconiosis, byssinosis and miscellaneous disease benefits
    Reduced earnings allowance
(4) *War disablement Social Security benefits*
    Constant attendance allowance
    Disablement pension
    Severe disablement allowance
(5) *Other Social Security benefits*⁴
    Attendance allowance
    Bereavement payment
    Christmas bonus
    Cold weather payments
    Council tax benefit

[5.18] Income tax—general

        Disability living allowance
        Earnings top-up
        Housing benefit
        Income-related employment and support allowance
        Incapacity benefit for the first 28 weeks
        Income support[4]
        Jobfinder's grant
        Redundancy payment
        Social fund payments
        Television licence payment
        Vaccine damage (lump sum)
        War pensions
        Widow's payment
        Winter fuel payment
        Working tax credit

(6) An annuity paid as a result of a claim under permanent health insurance policy.[5]

(7) Certain pensions for disabled employees.[6]

(8) Scholarship income arising from a scholarship held by a person receiving full time instruction at a university, college, school, or other educational establishment (ITTOIA 2005, s 776 and see statement of practice SP 4/86, revised 1992).[7] Certain education allowances under the Overseas Aid Act Schemes are exempt by extra-statutory concession A44.

(9) Foreign service allowance for civil servants (ITEPA 2003, ss 228 and 299).

(10) Interest on damages payable for personal injuries (ITTOIA 2005, s 751). A similar exception applies to annuities (including the assignment of such annuities) payable under structured settlements of claims for such injuries or in respect of payments from certain trusts in respect of such settlements (ITTOIA 2005, ss 732 and 734).

(11) Interest and bonuses on National Savings Certificates (ITTOIA 2005, s 692) and terminal bonuses on save as you earn contracts (ITTOIA 2005, s 702).

(12) Housing grants paid by local authorities (ITTOIA 2005, s 769).

(13) The first £70 of interest on National Savings Bank deposits. As separate taxpayers husband and wife may each claim £70 (ITTOIA 2005, s 691).

(14) Interest on Government securities held by non-resident central banks (TA 1988, s 516).

(15) Various payments to members of visiting forces (ITEPA 2003, ss 228 and 303).

(16) Annuities and pensions payable to victims of National Socialist persecution under the laws of West Germany or Austria (ITEPA 2003, s 642) and interest arising on any deposit (ITTOIA 2005, s 756A(1), FA 2006, s 64(2)).

(17) Pensions for wounds and disability (ITEPA 2003, s 641).

(18) Allowances, bounties and gratuities paid for additional service in the armed forces (ITEPA 1988, ss 297 and 298).

(19) Annuities and additional pensions to holders of gallantry awards ITEPA 2003, s 318).
(20) Grants under the European Assembly (Pay and Pensions) Act 1979, s 3 and certain related payments together with similar payments for Ministers, MPs, the Mayor of London and members of the Greater London Assembly (ITEPA 2003, s 291 as amended by the FA 2008).
(21) Income arising within an ISA (replacing personal equity plans and TESSAs (SI 1998/1870, reg. 22; see infra, §§ **31.01**)).
(22) Payments made by way of compensation for loss suffered by a person who took out, or contributed to, a personal pension scheme, the payments were made as a result of bad investment advice received (FA 1996, s 148).
(23) Interest attached to certain repayments of student loans to the student (ITTOIA 2005, s 753).
(24) Payments under the New Deal 50 Plus (ITTOIA 2005, s 781).
(25) Payments under the Employment Zones programme (ITTOIA 2005, s 782).
(26) Certain income of a non-resident company (ITA 2007, s 815).
(27) Fees paid to a foster carers, subject to limits (ITTOIA 2005, Pt 7, Ch 2).[8]
(28) A payment to an adopter made under Adoption Act 1976 (ITTOIA 2005, s 744).[9]

Income of certain persons is exempt from liability to income tax (and also corporation tax):

(1) Diplomats.[10]
(2) The Issue departments of the Reserve Bank of India and the State Bank of Pakistan (ITA 2007, s 839).
(3) Various Commonwealth and foreign representatives (ITEPA 2003, ss 228, 300, 333, ITA 2007, 841).[11]
(4) The Crown[12] and local authorities (ITA 2007, s 838 & TA 1988, s 519(1)(*b*)).
(5) Health service bodies (TA 1988 s 517A)
(6) International Organisations.[13]
(7) The London Organising Committee of the Olympic Games Ltd[14]

Certain persons are exempt from income tax on certain categories of receipt:

(1) Charities.[15]
(2) Pension funds.[16]
(3) Non-residents.[17]
(4) Income arising from participation in the London Olympics for specified competitors and staff.[18]

In assessing the base of the income tax a number of general points stand out. First, there are still a number of exemptions for payments received eg redundancy payments and the first £30,000 of golden handshakes infra, § **7.34**. Second, there are still a number of deductions which have long remained sacrosanct; today mortgage interest payments are no longer deductible but contributions to pension funds still are. One result of this is the sharply differing tax treatments of different forms of savings and investment.

Third, there is great insistence in the UK tax system on deduction of tax at source, a system which has at one time or another covered almost all payments other than the profits of a trade or profession and short interest. The legislature was, for a long time, reluctant to tax payments that could not be conveniently taxed at source. In recent years, there has been a move to providing relief at source.[19]

Lastly there is the problem of capital gains. Nigel Lawson's 1988 changes went a long way to reducing the importance of this distinction; in particular, he ensured that gains were to be taxed at the income tax rates that would have applied had the gains been income. However, Gordon Brown's taper relief has changed this with the effective rates of capital gains tax often being lower than the equivalent marginal income tax rate. Alistair Darling's ill-judged reforms in FA 2008 have taken the matter full circle to the pre-1988 position with a single flat rate of tax irrespective of the individual's income tax position. It is still the case that differences remain as may be seen from contrasting the treatment of an asset which is the subject of an adventure in the nature of trade (and so subject to income tax as trading income) and a capital asset. Tax on the capital asset is due on realisation; pre-1982 gains are ignored and there is an annual exemption of £10,100. Tax on the trading asset will again be due on realisation although if it qualifies as trading stock and goes down in value there will be immediate relief (infra, § **8.154**; there is no relief for increase in value before 1982; there is neither indexation nor taper relief and there is no £8,800 annual exemption. There are further differences with regard to the treatment of losses. A capital loss cannot be set off against ordinary income—or vice versa; although trading losses can be relieved against capital gains.[19]

Simon's Taxes Division E4.3.

---

[1] By contrast, the following Social Security benefits are treated as taxable social security income:

Bereavement allowance
Incapacity benefit after the first 28 weeks
Industrial death benefit pensions
Invalid care allowance
Jobseeker's allowance
Retirement pension
Statutory adoption pay
Statutory maternity pay
Statutory paternity pay
Statutory sick pay
Widowed mother's allowance
Widow's pension

[2] The child dependency addition escapes taxation if it is paid with retirement pension, widow's benefit, incapacity benefit, invalidity benefit, invalid care allowance, severe disablement allowance, higher-rate industrial death benefit, unemployability supplement and sickness (or, formerly, unemployment benefit) if beneficiary over pension age.

[3] Adoption allowance paid under the Adoption Allowance Regulations 1991, or, the equivalent in Scotland, are not subject to tax by virtue of Extra-statutory concession A40.

4   Other than payments made to people who had to sign on or strikers before 7 October 1996: introduction of jobseeker's allowance. In practice, payments to an unemployed person who was (a) aged 60 or over, (b) a lone parent with a child under 16, or (c) someone staying at home to look after a severely disabled person, were not taxed: Revenue booklet IR41 "Income Tax and the Unemployed".
5   ITTOIA 2005, s 735.
6   Extra-statutory concession A62.
7   The need for revision arose as a result of *Walters v Tickner* [1992] STC 343.
8   Relief is given for two elements; a fixed amount of £10,000 per annum plus a sum for each children fostered, being £200 a week for a child under 11 and £250 a week for an older child. See *Simons Weekly Tax Intelligence* 2003, p 1625 for an exhaustive explanation of the relief and Revenue guidance on the completion of the self-assessment tax return.
9   Or the equivalent statutes in Scotland and Northern Ireland, viz: Adoption (Scotland) Act 1978 or Adoption (Northern Ireland) Order 1987 or Adoption of Children Act 2002. Exemption is given for payments under these statutory provisions. The payments fall within the following categories:

(a)   payments authorised by the court to a person who has adopted or intends to adopt a child;
(b)   payments of legal or medical expenses of such a person;
(c)   payments of allowances to such a person;
(d)   financial support given under ACA 2002, ss 2(6) & (7) and 4;
(e)   payments under ACA 2002, Sch 4, para 3(1).

10 Diplomatic Privileges Act 1964, s 4. For the interpretation of the exemption in relation to an employee of a diplomatic mission see *Jimenez v IRC* [2004] STC (SCD) 371.
11 In *Caglar v Billingham* [1996] STC (SCD) 150, the Special Commissioners held that the exemption given to representatives of foreign states is restricted to those states that are recognised by Her Majesty's Government.
12 This was explicitly provided by TA 1988, s 829(2) but this provision was excluded from ITA 2007 on the basis that the contextual change meant it was no longer required. However, the private estates of the Crown are subject to tax: Crown Private Estates Act 1862.
13 ITA 2007, s 979.
14 FA 2006, s 65.
15 See infra, § **13.22**.
16 See infra, § **32.18**.
17 See infra, § **36.01**.
18 The types of income and the classes of the person to enjoy the exemption are to be specified by statutory instrument issued under the authority of FA 2006, s 68.
19 For many years, tax relief on a contribution by an employee to his employer's pension scheme has been given by deducting the payment before applying PAYE (TA 1988, s 593). From 6 April 2001, all contributions made to a personal pension scheme by an individual (whether employed or self-employed) are made net of basic rate tax, the Revenue paying to the scheme an amount equal to the tax deducted on the scheme member's contribution. Contributions by an employer to an employee's personal pension scheme are, however, made gross: Personal Pension Schemes (Reliefs at Source) Regulations 1988 (SI 1988/1013) reg 4, as amended by Personal Pension Schemes (Reliefs at Source) (Amendment) Regulations 2000 (SI 2000/2315) reg 4, see *Simon's Weekly Tax Intelligence* 2000, p 1325.

Prohibited deductions

[5.19] The legislation sometimes provides that certain sums are not to be deductible in computing income under various heads. There are now four such types of provision. The first deals with business entertainment expenses (ITTOIA 2005, s 45 for trading and property income, ITTOIA 2005, s 867 for other Parts of ITTOIA 2005 and ITEPA 2003, s 356 for employment income).

The second provides that no deduction shall be made for any expenditure incurred in making a payment, the making of which constitutes the commission of a criminal offence.[1] Perhaps oddly it does not apply to CGT. Examples given in the Inland Revenue press release[2] are bribes contrary to the Prevention of Corruption Acts and payments which are contrary to the Prevention of Terrorism Acts. These examples are much narrower than the potential ambit of the section which seems to encompass any act which amounts to the offence of aiding and abetting the commission of an offence by another. One may assume that a criminal offence means an act or omission which is an actual offence under the criminal law of some relevant part of the UK rather than under some foreign jurisdiction although this is not clear from the legislation. If this view is correct considerable attention may have to be paid to the territorial scope of those criminal offences. FA 1994 added to this list of prohibited crime related payments expenditure incurred in making a payment induced by blackmail.[3]

Simon's Taxes B2.301.

---

[1] ITTOIA 2005, ss 55 (for trading and property income) and 870 (for other income) (income tax); TA 1988, ss 577 and 577A (corporation tax).
[2] Inland Revenue press release, 11 June 1993, *Simon's Tax Intelligence* 1993, p 957.
[3] Now in ITTOIA 2005, ss 55(2) (for trading and property income) and 870(3) (for other income) (income tax); TA 1988, s 577A (corporation tax).

Earned income and investment income

[5.20] Until 1984 investment income was taxed more heavily than earned income.[1] The distinction between earned and investment income was important in that before 1990–91 a wife could be taxed separately from her husband in respect of her earned but not her investment income. The distinction was also important for the wife's earned income relief. Today the distinction remains important for relief in respect of pension contributions.[2] The most common types of investment income are interest, dividends and rent. Income from furnished holiday accommodation is expressly treated as earned income.[3] Property income is computed under trading profit principles but is not trading income; it remains investment income.

Since 1996–97, a more important distinction has been that between "savings income" and other income. See Chapter 11.

Simon's Taxes E1.107.

1. FA 1971, s 32(1) (repealed by TA 1988, s 844, Sch 31).
2. Infra, Chapter 51.
3. ITA 2007, s 127.

Definitions

[5.21] "Earned income" is no longer defined as a category by statute.[1] Instead, income is categorised by the act that imposes the income tax charge. ITEPA 2003 charges income tax[2] on:

(a) employment income;
(b) pension income;
(c) social security income.

ITTOIA 2005 imposes charges to income tax[3] on:

(a) trading income;
(b) property income;
(c) savings and investment income;
(d) certain miscellaneous income.

Income tax is also charged by other acts on:

(a) registered pension schemes;[4]
(b) social security pension lump sums;[5]
(c) charitable trust;[6]
(d) accrued income profits;[7]
(e) tax avoidance.[8]

Simon's Taxes E1.107.

1. TA 1988, s 833(4) was repealed with the tax law rewrite that produced ITA 2007. This is one of the changes in the legislation identified by the Tax Law Rewrite Project (change 125). See also the Explanatory Notes para 2515-2517.
2. ITEPA 2003, s 1(1).
3. ITTOIA 2005, s 1(1).
4. FA 2004, ss 204–242.
5. F(No 2)A 2005, s 7.
6. ITA 2007, ss 518–564.
7. ITA 2007, ss 616–677.
8. ITA 2007, ss 682–809ZD.

Employment income

[5.22] Statute[1] defines "employment income", rather unhelpfully, as, "earnings within ITEPA 2003 Part III Chapter 1 plus any amount treated as 'earnings' or any amount which counts as 'employment income'". Although not specified by statute, I suggest that any income that has been categorised in case law as "earned income" which comes from employment is "employment income", within the meaning of ITA 2007. On this basis, the essence of employment income is that it is a reward for services.

In *Dale v IRC*[2] annuity payments to a trustee "so long as he acts as trustee" were held by the House of Lords to be earned income. In that case the trustee was to receive the payments. It was said that the amount and value of the work actually done was irrelevant.[3] The Revenue argued that since a trustee was not entitled to remuneration for his services as distinct from the reimbursement of expenses, the annuity was a conditional gift. However, it was held that since the condition of the annuity was compliance with the testator's condition of serving as a trustee[4] the income was earned.

The form in which the income is received is irrelevant. Hence dividends may be earned income, despite technically coming within the category of savings and investment income and not employment income, provided they are a reward for services. In *White v Franklin*[5] the taxpayer was assistant managing director of a company. His mother and brother settled 50% of the issued share capital to trust to pay the income to the taxpayer "so long as he shall be engaged in the management of the company," with remainder to the mother and others. It was held that his income from the trust was earned income. The Commissioners had found that the settlement had been made as an inducement to him to remain with the company, and so the income accrued to him because, not simply while, he was an active director.[6] It was also important that the trust held a large block of shares in the employing company so that the taxpayer's work would produce direct results. These, however, are matters of fact to support the inference that the purpose of the settlement was to keep the taxpayer interested in the company and not simply an arrangement in a family settlement distributing income arising from family property to persons with certain qualifications.[7] This appears to be a borderline case.[8]

If a payment of income is not only in return for services but also for some other consideration, there can be no apportionment of the income so as to treat even a part of it as earned.[9] The question is one of the construction of the arrangement.

Simon's Taxes E1.107, Division E4.4.

1 ITEPA 2003, s 7(2).
2 [1953] 2 All ER 671, 34 TC 468.
3 Per Lord Normand, 34 TC 468 at 493.
4 Per Lord Normand, 34 TC 468 at 491.
5 [1965] 1 All ER 692, 42 TC 283, [1965] BTR 152.
6 Case stated: 42 TC 283 at 284.
7 [1965] 1 All ER at 699, 42 TC at 297.
8 See Vinelott J in *O'Leary v McKinlay* [1991] STC 42 at 53.
9 And hence, presumably, "employment income": *Hale v Shea* [1965] 1 All ER 155, 42 TC 260.

Pension income and social security income

[5.23] Statute[1] defines "pension income" as 'pensions, annuities and income of other types' within 14 specified sections of ITEPA 2003. This would appear to exclude any reference to previous case law on the scope of the [then] Schedule E charge on pension income. "Social Security benefits" are defined similarly.[2]

[1] ITEPA 2003, s 566(2).
[2] ITEPA 2003, s 657(2).

Trading income

[5.24] The trade must have been carried on by the individual[1]. In *Fry v Shiels Trustees*[2] trustees legally owned and managed a business the income of which was held for infant beneficiaries. It was held that the income was not earned since the profits were earned by the trustees and so by individuals who certainly did not own them. More difficulty has come from the requirement that the profit must be derived immediately from the business, since it suggests that other profits equally taxable under one of these Schedules are not derived immediately, but only incidentally. An example is *Northend v White, Leonard and Corbin Greener*[3] where Templeman J, held that interest accruing to a solicitor on money deposited at a bank on general deposit account was investment income. The reason was that the source was not the carrying on of the profession but rather the loan deposit with the bank.

[1] Cf TA 1970, s 122(2)(b) (repealed by FA 1974) and see the comments of Lindsay J in *Koenigsberger v Mellor* [1993] STC 408 at 414.
[2] 1915 SC 159, 6 TC 583.
[3] [1975] STC 317, 50 TC 121, the interest belonged to the solicitor thanks to Solicitors Act 1965, s 8(2).

Miscellaneous income

[5.25] Certain types of income are declared to be employment income. These are income in respect of a Civil List pension, voluntary pensions,[1] and golden handshakes (see infra, § **7.36**).

Trading income includes post cessation receipts, income from the sale of patent rights for an invention actually devised by the taxpayer, infra, § **9.64**, business start-up payments[2] (formerly enterprise allowance payments) and income from furnished holiday lettings.[3]

Retirement income of a self-employed person will generally be investment income. This is mitigated in three ways. First, he may have been able to take advantage of the retirement annuity schemes, annuities payable being earned income, infra, § **32.31**. Second, he may take advantage of ITTOIA 2005, s 717 (income tax) or TA 1988, s 656 (corporation tax) and treat a part of a purchased annuity payment as the repayment of capital, infra, § **31.31**; the portion which is treated as income is investment income. Alternatively, or in addition, he may arrange a consultant's post with his former firm.

[1] ITEPA 2003, ss 570 and 633.
[2] ITTOIA 2005, s 207(2).
[3] ITA 2007, s 127.

Savings income

Rate of tax on 'savings income'

[5.26] Between 1996–97 and 2007–08 "savings income" was charged at different tax rates from other income. For 2007–08 an individual with savings income has a starting rate of 10% on the first £2,230 of total income.[1] Above this threshold savings income was taxed not at the then basic rate of 22% but at the savings rate of 20%.[2] This applied until the top of the basic rate band of £34,600 (now £34,800) is reached.[3] Since 2008–09, the distinction has been relevant only in respect of an individual's first slice of taxable income (for 2009–10, the first £2,440).[4]

Special rates of 10% and 32.5% apply for dividend income.[5] Dividend income arising in the UK also differs from other savings income in that the 10% tax credit accompanying the dividend cannot be repaid to the taxpayer—so while a personal relief may be used to receive tax withheld at source on a payment of interest, no such claim may be made for a dividend from a UK resident company.

One of the most bizarre aspects of the differing rates is the rate of tax applied to a foreign dividend. If the recipient is a basic rate taxpayer resident in the UK and domiciled within the UK, the foreign dividend attracts UK income tax at 10%.[6] If the overseas dividend is received by an individual resident in the UK but subject to the remittance basis, the foreign dividend, insofar as it is remitted to the UK, attracts tax in the hands of a basic rate taxpayer at a rate of 20%.[7] Between 6 April 2005 and 5 April 2008, there was no distinction in the higher rate charged on dividends. This arose from an inadvertent change made to the law when ITTOIA 2005 was drafted.[8] The previous regime, giving the higher charge on remitted income has now been restored by FA 2008, s 65(1), which defines the charge for the "dividend upper rate" (ie 32 1/2%) as excluding "relevant foreign income".[9]

In determining whether such "savings income" falls within a particular rate band, "savings income" is treated as the highest part of an individual's income, other than termination payments and chargeable events.[10]

Where the taxpayer has other income that exceeds the upper limit of the basic rate band, the "savings income" is assessed at higher rate.[11] In so far as it has been received under deduction of tax at 20%, there is, thus, a further 20% to be accounted for in the taxpayer's self-assessment. Where the taxpayer's other income is less than the upper limit of the basic rate band, but the addition of the "savings income" takes the taxpayer above that band, tax at the lower rate is charged on the amount of income required to bring the rate up to the upper limit of the basic rate band and tax at the higher rate is charged on the excess.

Similar processes apply where the taxpayer has more than one type of income and the starting rate is concerned.

Where payments are required to be made after deduction of tax, the rate of tax to be applied is the savings lower rate of tax,[12] where the payment is "savings income" in the hands of the recipient.[13]

Dividends carry a tax credit at 10%.[14] This tax credit is not repayable, other than under a double taxation agreement. The rate of tax applied to such savings income received by a basic rate taxpayer is, similarly, reduced to 10%.[15] A higher rate taxpayer is subject to tax on such savings income at 32 1/2%. This rate structure applies also to equivalent foreign income.[16] These two rates are known as the dividend ordinary rate and the dividend upper rate.[17]

Simon's Taxes E1.101.

---

[1] ITA 2007, ss 8 & 23 (prior to FA 2008).
[2] ITA 2007, ss 12, 13, 14 & 23 (prior to FA 2008).
[3] ITA 2007, ss 13, 14, 16 & 18 (prior to FA 2008).
[4] ITA 2007, s 12 (as substituted by FA 2008, Sch 1, para 5).
[5] ITA 2007, s 8.
[6] ITA 2007, s 8.
[7] ITA 2007, s 10(2) charges tax at basic rate (which is specified by each year's Finance Act, eg FA 2007, s 1(*b*) specifies 22%). All income in the basic rate band is charged at this rate, unless statute otherwise determines. ITA 2007, s 13 charges the dividend ordinary rate, unless it is "relevant foreign income" charged under ITTOIA 2005, s 832 (the remittance basis): vide ITA 2007, s 13(1)(*c*).
[8] HMRC Tax Bulletin August 2006, p 1303.
[9] ITA 2007, s 13(2).
[10] ITA 2007, s 16.
[11] 40% for 2007–08; ITA 2007, s 10.
[12] 20% for 2007–08.
[13] ITA 2007, s 851(2).
[14] ITTOA 2005, s 397(1).
[15] ITA 2007, s 13.
[16] ITA 2007, s 19(3).
[17] ITA 2007, s 8.

Definition of savings income

[5.27] "Savings income" is:[1]

(a) Interest.[2]
(b) Purchased life annuity payments.[3]
(c) Income from deeply discounted securities.[4]
(d) Accrued income.[5]
(e) Chargeable gains on life assurance (for an individual or personal representative, only).[6]

---

[1] ITA 2007, s 18.
[2] Charged under ITTOIA 2005, ss 369–371.
[3] Charged under ITTOIA 2005, ss 422–426.
[4] ITTOIA 2005, ss 427–460.

[5.27] Income tax—general

[5] ITA 2007, ss 616–677.
[6] ITTOIA 2005, ss 461–546.

Remittance basis

[5.28] The special treatment applied to "savings income" does not apply to any income assessed as it is received in the UK, as opposed to income assessed on an arising basis; see infra, §§ **35.12** ff. Hence, an individual subject to tax at basic rate who brings to the UK all interest credited to his account at a bank overseas is subject to tax at 20% on that interest if he is domiciled within the UK, but at 22% if he is domiciled or ordinarily resident outside the UK and subject to the remittance basis[1]. The availability of the remittance basis was severely curtailed by FA 2008.

Simon's Taxes E1.101.

[1] The 20% rate of tax is applied only to "savings income". "Savings income" is defined by ITA 2007, s 18(2)(b) as excluding "relevant foreign income charged under ITTOIA 2005, s 832" (remittance basis).

Calculation of tax

[5.29] The calculation of income tax due is complicated by a number of factors. First, there is the problem of calculating the amount of income; this sometimes involves grossing up a sum received to reflect the fact that tax has been deducted at source. Second, there is a bewildering variety of deductions which must be distinguished. Some are deductions in computing income from a particular source, others are deductions in computing income or total income, others are deductions from particular groups of income. These must in turn be distinguished from deduction from income or from total income. Relief may also be given by way of relief from tax or by reduction of tax or by credit against tax. Third, while basic rate tax is levied on income, lower rate tax and higher rate tax are charged on an individual's total income. Fourth, there is the problem that income tax is paid not only by individuals but also by trusts, by estates in administration and by partnerships. What follows concentrates on the taxation of an individual. Finally, there are problems arising from the government's love of gimmicks, especially in relation to the lower rate of tax on dividend income and to taxing some "savings income" at 10% rather than 20% (see supra, §§ **5.25–5.27**).

Total income

[5.30] Total income means the total income of that person from all sources estimated in accordance with the provisions of the Income Tax Acts.[1]

Various items are included in total income.

(1) Income from each source according to the rule of each category of income (ITA 2007, s 3). Sums deductible in computing income eg allowable expenses in respect of property income are taken into account in computing the amount of income under that heading. If the figures show a loss, the amount to be included is nil.[2]
(2) Income subject to deduction under the PAYE scheme is included at its gross amount.
(3) Income subject to deduction at basic rate at source must be grossed up to reflect that fact; the taxpayer is then given credit for the tax withheld. Grossing up is carried out by multiplying the figure by the fraction 100/(100–TAX) where TAX is the rate of tax applicable.
(4) Bank interest and building society interest. Tax on interest is usually deducted at source and so added back to calculate the income.
(5) Dividends together with the accompanying tax credit which is now geared to the 10% dividend ordinary rate: ITTOIA 2005, s 398(1) (infra, § **26.12**).
(6) The taxpayer's share of partnership income.
(7) Income deemed to be his under the provisions of ITTOIA 2005, eg under the settlement code (ss 19–648).
(8) Income to which he is entitled as beneficiary under a trust.
(9) Income of an unadministered residuary estate in which he has a life interest in possession or an absolute interest.
(10) Any income of another which must be treated as his, eg under the anti-avoidance rules discussed infra, Chapter 15.

Simon's Taxes Division E1.8.

---

[1] ITA 2007, s 23 *Step 1*.
[2] ITA 2007, s 23, *Step 2*.

Deductions in calculating total income

[5.31] The legislation contains a bewildering assortment of formulae for calculating deductions:

(1) Interest on a qualifying loan.[1]
(2) Some pension contributions are deducted from the employment income itself.[2]
(3) By contrast, relief from others is given as a deduction from total income.[3]
(4) Loss relief: The taxpayer may claim relief from income tax on an amount of his income equal to the loss.

Simon's Taxes Division E1.8.

---

[1] ITA 2007, s 383.
[2] TA 1988, s 619, FA 2004, s 193.
[3] FA 2004, s 194 (in accordance with Step 2 in ITA 2007, s 23TA 1988, s 639.

Order of making deductions

[5.32] The general rule is that deductions are to be made in the order that will result in the greatest reduction of liability to income tax.[1] This rule is of course subject to express provision to the contrary.

Deductions for personal reliefs, that is deductions authorised by ITA 2007, Pt 3 or TA 1988, Part VII, Ch I,[2] are made after any other deductions.

[1] ITA 2007, s 25(2).
[2] Including reliefs for life assurance premiums under contracts made before 14 March 1984.

6

Allowances and reliefs

The tax unit	PARA **6.01**
Property jointly owned by spouses and civil partners	PARA **6.02**
Personal allowances	PARA **6.04**
Allowances for non-residents	PARA **6.10**
Claiming relief	PARA **6.12**
Loss relief	PARA **6.14**
Maintenance payments	PARA **6.35**
Gifts to charities	PARA **6.36**
Interest relief	PARA **6.39**
Averaging	PARA **6.46**
Top slicing	PARA **6.50**
Tax credits	PARA **6.51**

The tax unit

[6.01] UK income tax applies not only to individuals but also to entities such as trusts and partnerships as well as companies not resident in the UK. Partly for this reason the system, unlike others, does not automatically exempt an initial slice of taxable income.

The adjustment of the burden of income taxation is a task which is carried out by allowing deductions, known as personal allowances, which may be claimed by individuals, but not other persons, in computing taxable income.

An initial problem is the choice of the taxable unit. That unit may be the individual, a couple (and, if so, whether this should be restricted to married couples and those within civil partnerships), such couples together with any minor children, or some wider grouping. Prior to 6 April 1990, the income of married women was aggregated with that of their husbands and assessed on the husbands. The year 1990–91 saw the introduction of the system of independent taxation. Under this regime husbands and wives (and, consequently, civil partners) are taxed as separate individuals. Each has her or his own single person's allowance. From 1990–91 to 1999–2000, a married couple was entitled to the married couple's allowance, which was originally equal to the difference between the pre-1990 married allowance and the single person's allowance. The rate at which the allowance was granted was steadily reduced and is abolished from 2001–02 onwards, other than for those born before 6 April 1935 (see infra, § **6.07**).

From 1969–70 to 1971–72, all investment income of children, whether or not derived from their parents, had to be aggregated.[1] Since 1972, statute has required the aggregation of a child's income (above a de minimis level) where the income has been derived from an asset provided by its parents,[2] but general aggregation is not required.

[6.01] Allowances and reliefs

From 5 December 2005, it is possible for a same-sex couple to register a civil partnership.[3] Statutory instruments[4] have striven to ensure that tax provisions apply equally to civil partners as they apply to spouses.[5]

---

[1] FA 1968, s 15 (repealed by FA 1971).
[2] ITTOIA 2005, s 629, see infra, § **15.21**.
[3] Civil Partnership Act 2004.
[4] Tax and Civil Partnership Regulations, SI 2005/3229, *Simons Weekly Tax Intelligence* 2005, p 1907, Tax and Civil Partnership (No 2) Regulations, SI 2005/3230, *Simons Weekly Tax Intelligence* 2005, p 1936, Civil Partnership Act 2004 (Tax Credits, etc) (Consequential Amendments) Order, SI 2005/2919, *Simons Weekly Tax Intelligence* 2005, p 1779.
[5] A useful summary of the effect of the provisions relating to civil partners is given in HMRC Tax Bulletin 80, December 2005, pages 1251–1259. A perusal of this study gives an interesting perspective of the disparate (and, perhaps marginal) role that marriage now plays in the UK tax system.

Property jointly owned by spouses and civil partners

[6.02] Where property is held in the joint names of a married couple or civil partners who are living together, income from that property is divided equally between them, irrespective of the proportion in which the income is divided between them, or the ownership of the property from which it is derived.[1]

This provision does not apply in six situations:

(1) to income to which neither individual is beneficially entitled;[2]
(2) where the income is beneficially owned in unequal shares (including one having no beneficial interest) and an election (see infra) has been validly made;[3]
(3) to income derived from property that is held by a partnership in which the husband and wife are partners;[4]
(4) (until 5 April 2010) income from furnished holiday lettings;[5]
(5) where the income arises from a shareholding in a close company;[6]
(6) where income is deemed by statute to be that of the other member of the couple.[7]

In any of these six cases, the division of income between the couple is the division of the ownership of the property from which the income arises. That is, in the case of a partnership, the division of partnership profits and in the other cases, the division of beneficial ownership of the property.

Unless the income falls within one of these six categories, the statutory treatment of income arising from joint ownership of the couple is that one half of such income is assessable on each, as long as they are living together at some time during the tax year. Thus, a property purchased for letting which is financed by, and owned by, the wife to the extent of 99% and the husband to the extent of 1% gives rise to an equal division of the assessable income arising, even though the capital gain on the ultimate sale will be allocated between wife and husband in the ratio 99:1.

Jointly-owned property [6.02]

This treatment applies only where property is owned jointly. It can be that both names appear on the Land Registry certificate but the beneficial ownership is entirely that of one member of the couple.[8] If this is the case, the deeming provisions do not apply and the income arising is assessable wholly on the actual beneficial owner.

If the property is jointly owned by the couple in unequal shares (including one having no beneficial interest in the income), statute[9] allows them to make a joint election for income tax to be levied on the basis of the income being divided between them in proportion to the actual proportions in which they own the property.[10] No election can be made for an allocation of income that is other than the division of the actual beneficial ownership.[11]

This election cannot be made where neither member of the couple is beneficially entitled, eg where they hold property as trustees.[12] Nor can it be made in respect of income to which one member is entitled beneficially but which the legislation treats as the income of the other or of a third party.[13]

Where an asset is owned by the couple in unequal shares, the couple have a free choice whether or not to make the election. If the couple is subject to income tax at different rates and the larger share of the asset is owned by the member who is subject to tax at the higher rate, the aggregate income tax liability would be increased by the couple if they chose to make an election.

The election has no effect for capital gains tax, nor inheritance tax. In determining the liability to CGT on the sale of a jointly held asset, the gain is computed by reference to the actual division of the beneficial ownership of the asset. If the actual division is unclear, Revenue practice is to treat the asset as being owned equally.

Simon's Taxes E5.103A.

---

[1] ITA 2007, s 836(2).
[2] ITA 2007, s 836(3) Exception A.
[3] ITA 2007, s 836(3) Exception B.
[4] ITA 2007, s 836(3) Exception C. The Revenue consider that a property owned by a couple is not owned by them in partnership unless there is "a business" (see Partnership Act 1890, s 1(1)). Revenue guidance states: "to accept that a partnership exists you would have to be satisfied of the existence of a similar degree of business organisation as in an ordinary commercial business" (Inland Revenue Property Income Manual, para PIM1030). The notes in the Revenue manual indicate that the Revenue accepts that a property owned as an incidental part of a partnership carrying on a trade gives a presumption that the letting of that property is partnership business. This in contrast with a property owned without a trade. However, *Griffiths v Jackson* [1983] STC 184 suggests that a single property may sometimes constitute a business.
[5] ITA 2007, s 836(3) Exception D. The 2009 Budget proposed the abolition of the furnished holiday lettings rules from 6 April 2010.
[6] ITA 2007, s 836(3) Exception E.
[7] ITA 2007, s 836(3) Exception F.
[8] The sole beneficial ownership of an asset registered in joint names is recognised in Inland Revenue Press Release, 21 November 1990: Independent Taxation—Capital

[6.02] Allowances and reliefs

Gains Tax on jointly owned assets, which states: 'A couple may for instance have agreed that one partner is merely a nominee and has no beneficial interest in the asset; and where land and buildings are jointly owned, there may be a legal agreement between the partners about their respective rights. Where the split of ownership is not clear cut (as will often be the case with investments such as shares and securities) the Revenue will normally accept that the couple hold the asset in equal parts.'

[9] The election is on HMRC form 17, which is a statutory form governed by ITA 2007, s 837. The conditions imposed by statute are strict and HMRC staff are under instruction not to allow any variation from the strict statutory provisions. Notice of election must be given to the inspector within 60 days beginning with the date of the declaration (s 837(3)(*b*)). Declarations do not have retroactive effect. A declaration once made remains in force (s 837(5)). There is no provision for revocation of a declaration. If the couple ceases to live together, both the statutory presumption of equality and any declaration cease to apply and thereafter income will be attributed according to their entitlements. It is expressly provided that the declaration automatically ceases to be effective if the beneficial interests in the income or the property cease to accord with the declaration (s 837(5)). The declaration of the division of ownership being in unequal shares, made for income tax purposes, as providing "a presumption that the same split applies for capital gains tax purposes" (Inland Revenue Press Release, Independent Taxation—Capital Gains Tax on Jointly Owned Assets, 22 November 1990).

[10] Form 17.
[11] ITA 2007, s 837.
[12] ITA 2007, s 836(3) Exception B & s 836(3) Exception A.
[13] ITA 2007, s 836(3) Exception F.

Anti-avoidance—income from property from other member of couple

[6.03] Where one member of the couple has an interest in property settled (eg by gift) by the other, income arising under the settlement will be treated as that of the settlor rather than the recipient, unless there has been an outright gift of the capital asset that generates the income and the gift is substantially more than a mere gift of a right to income.[1] (See further Chapter 15.)

Simon's Taxes E5.103B.

[1] ITTOIA 2005, ss 624 & 626(1). For the provisions relating to pension rights, see ITTOIA 2005, s 627(2)(*c*).

Personal allowances

[6.04] There are two distinct types of allowance:

(1) A fixed sum, which is deductible from total income of an individual in calculating taxable income. Allowances of this type are:

- The principal personal allowance (see infra, § 6.07)
- Age-related allowance (see infra, § 6.08)
- Blind person's allowance (see infra, § 6.09)

(2) A reduction in the income tax liability of an individual. The allowances currently available of this type are:
- Married couple's allowance[1]
- The qualifying maintenance deduction of £2,540 where either payer or recipient was born before 6 April 1935 (see infra, § 11.45)
- Relief under the enterprise investment scheme (see infra, § 31.06)
- Investment into a venture capital trust (see infra, § 31.17)

Both types of allowance can be claimed only by individuals as opposed to, for example, trusts, and therefore are distinguishable from other deductions such as interest payments. Further, to claim a personal allowance, the individual must either fulfil a test of residence, being resident in the UK or fall within a category specified in statute (such as an EEA national).[2] Allowances are available only for the year of assessment; allowances which are not used in one year cannot be rolled forward (or backwards) to another year. Most allowances may not be assigned.

The principal personal allowance and the blind person's allowance were traditionally fixed sums; the age-related allowances and the married couple's allowance vary in amount depending on the income of the year. However, FA 2009 has introduced provisions that cause the principal personal allowance to be tapered away to nil for those taxpayers with "adjusted net income" in excess of £100,000 with effect from 2010–11. In such cases, the allowance is reduced by £1 for every £2 of income in excess of this limit. This has the effect of adding by a half the marginal rate of tax suffered during the effect of the taper. For example, an individual with income of £100,000 would ordinarily be paying income tax at a marginal rate of 40%. However, an additional £2 of income would render that individual to tax on an extra £3 (the additional £2 plus the £1 lost allowance). This would mean an additional £1.20 of tax on an additional £2 of income, an effective marginal rate of tax of 60%.

The value of the personal allowances is tied to changes in the retail prices index each year but it is open to Parliament to override these effects.[3]

---

[1] The name for this allowance has been retained despite the introduction of civil partnerships.
[2] See infra, § 6.10 for non residents who are entitled to personal allowances.
[3] ITA 2007, s 57; the relevant date at which the RPI is calculated is September in the preceding year.

The principal personal allowance

[6.05] The principal deduction or allowance allows a claimant a deduction from his total income.[1] In 2009–10, it is £6,475 (FA 2009, s 3). Since 2001–02, this amount has been aligned with what is now the NICs primary threshold (an alignment that is in practice quite illusory but has some sort of political

[6.05] Allowances and reliefs

attraction to it). However, a backbench rebellion at the beginning of the 2008–09 tax year led to a sudden and last-minute increase in the basic personal allowance. This lack of synchronisation has continued into 2009–10.[2]

Simon's Direct Tax Service E2.201.

[1] ITA 2007, s 235.
[2] See infra, § **6.06**.

Income-related increase of the personal allowance on account of age

[6.06] An individual who is aged 65 or more at the end of the fiscal year may claim an increased personal allowance[1]; for 2009–10 that figure is £9,490.[2] This figure is enhanced to £9,640 for a taxpayer who is aged 75 or more at the end of the fiscal year.[3] In the case of a taxpayer who dies during the fiscal year, the test is applied in respect to the age that individual would have attained by the end of that fiscal year.[4] The relief depends exclusively on the age of the claimant.

However, where the individual's "adjusted net income"[5] for that year exceeds a specified limit, the additional allowance given on account of age is reduced by one-half of the excess of total income over the specified limit. For 2009–10 that limit is £22,900.[6] Given a basic rate of tax of 20%, the effect of the restriction in age allowance is to give a marginal rate of tax of 30%. The benefit of the age 65+ allowance disappears altogether when income exceeds the specified limit by twice the extra age allowance.[7]

A new pensioner can elect to defer the receipt of his state retirement pension.[8] Anyone who makes this election receives a one-off lump sum payment.[9] This lump sum is taxed, but does not count in calculating the reduction in age-related personal allowance.[10]

[1] For a comparison between the UK and 14 other countries see Gordon Keenay and Edward Whitehouse *The role of the personal tax system in old-age support: a survey of 15 countries*, Fiscal Studies (2003) vol 24, No 1. p 1.
[2] ITA 2007, s 36 (as amended by Income Tax (Indexation) (No 3) Order 2008, SI 2008/3023, art 4(b)).
[3] ITA 2007, s 37 (as amended by Income Tax (Indexation) (No 3) Order 2008, SI 2008/3023, art 4(c)).
[4] ITA 2007, s 55(2).
[5] Defined in ITA 2007, s 58.
[6] Income Tax (Indexation) (No 3) Order 2008, SI 2008/3023, art 4(h).
[7] For figures showing points at which reliefs cease to have value see Simon's Taxes, Binder 1: (table 17) p 7025.
[8] Pensions Act 2004.
[9] SSCBA 1992, s 55 & Sch 5.
[10] F(No 2)A 2005, s 7(2)(*b*).

Married couple's allowance for those born before 6 April 1935

[6.07] Married couple's allowance is a reduction in the income tax liability of a person who is married or a member of a civil partnership if either member of the couple was born before 6 April 1935.[1] This date has not changed in the last five years; hence, the allowance is obsolescent.

The allowance is available as long as the couple live together for at least part of the tax year.[2]

Where the above conditions are fulfilled[3], an allowance of £2,670 is available, irrespective of income.[4] The allowance is given at 10% only.[5] The allowance operates to reduce the liability to tax; there cannot be a repayment.

A higher allowance is available, depending on the claimant's income. For 2009–10, the maximum married couple's allowance is £6,965 where at least one spouse is aged 75 or over at 5 April 2010.[6] The allowance is reduced by one-half of the income over £22,900, subject to the minimum allowance.

In the case of a marriage that took place before 5 December 2005, it is the husband who is primarily entitled to the allowance.[7] For marriages entered into on or after 5 December 2005 and civil partnerships, the allowance is primarily given to the member of the couple with the higher net income for the tax year.[8]

However, the other member of the couple may, unilaterally, claim one-half of the reduction[9] or both parties may jointly elect that the reduction should be given wholly to that other person.[10] In general an election to transfer all or half of the allowance must be made before the start of the year in which it is to have effect and lasts for that year and for all subsequent years until it is withdrawn.[11] The election does not change the amount of the relief. Hence, if a husband aged 75 years has minimal income, an election to transfer the allowance to the wife reduces the wife's tax liability by the full amount of £696.50 even if the wife is a higher rate taxpayer.[12]

---

[1] ITA 2007, s 42.
[2] ITA 2007, ss 45(2)(a) and 46(2)(a). Spouses and civil partners are living together unless they are separated under an order of a court of competent jurisdiction or by a deed of separation or are in fact separated in such circumstances that the separation is likely to be permanent; ITA 2007, s 1011. *Holmes v Mitchell* [1991] STC 25 applying the divorce test formulated in *Hopes v Hopes* [1949] P 227, [1948] 2 All ER 920, CA.
[3] For a discussion of the conditions, see the 2000–01 and earlier editions of this work.
[4] ITA 2007, s 46(4); Income Tax (Indexation) (No 2) Order 2008, SI 2008/3023, art 4(c).
[5] ITA 2007, s 45(1).
[6] Income Tax (Indexation) (No 2) Order 2008, SI 2008/3023, art 4(f)(I) and (g)(I).
[7] ITA 2007, s 45(1).
[8] ITA 2007, s 46(2)(e); where the couple's income is identical then it is incumbent on the couple to make a joint election to nominate the initial recipient of the allowance.
[9] ITA 2007, s 47(1).
[10] ITA 2007, s 48.

[6.07] Allowances and reliefs

[11] ITA 2007, s 50(2)(b).
[12] Calculated as £6,965 @10%.

Effect of chargeable events on age allowances

[6.08] When an insurance bond is encashed, a special regime applies to calculate the income tax liability.[1] The effect of this regime is to identify the rate of tax by treating as an addition to income the gain made on the encashment, divided by the number of years for which the bond has been held. A credit is then given at basic rate. The effect is, thus, that an individual with other income of, say, £15,000 who makes a gain of £30,000 on a bond that has been held for 10 years has no liability to income tax on the encashment of that bond.

An unfortunate effect of the legislation is that such an individual, although not charged to income tax, will suffer the abolition of the additional age allowance. Age allowance is reduced by one half of the amount by which the taxpayer's "adjusted net income" exceeds £22,900.[2] "Adjusted net income" is defined[3] by totalling income, without regard to the top slicing provisions which apply for taxing a gain on an insurance bond.

[1] See infra, §§ 31.26–31.30. ITTOIA 2005, ss 461–546.
[2] ITA 2007, s 36(2) as amended by Income Tax (Indexation) (No 3) Order 2007 SI 2008/3023, art 4(h).
[3] ITA 2007, s 58.

Blind person's allowance

[6.09] A registered blind person is entitled to an allowance; in 2008–09 this is £1,890 and, like the ordinary personal allowance takes effect at the taxpayer's marginal rate.[1] The deduction may be claimed by a fully-sighted individual whose spouse or civil partner living with him is blind. Should they both be blind each has the allowance. The person must be registered with a local authority for at least a part of the year; this excludes non-residents. If the eye condition develops in one year but registration is not completed until the next, the relief may be given for the first year.[2]

If the claimant is married any unusable part of the allowance may be transferred to the other spouse.

[1] ITA 2007, s 23, 38; Income Tax (Indexation) (No 3) Order 2008 SI 2008/3023, art 4(d).
[2] Previously by concession. From 2007–08 ITA 2007, s 38(4).

Allowances for non-residents

[6.10] Individuals who are not resident[1] are entitled to personal reliefs only if they fall within certain categories. The categories[2] are:

(a) an individual who is resident in the Channel Islands or Isle of Man;
(b) an individual who has previously resided within the UK but who is compelled to live abroad for reasons of health or the health of a member of his or her family resident with him or her;
(c) an individual who is or has been employed in the service of the Crown;
(d) a widow whose late husband (or widower whose late wife or a bereaved civil partner whose late civil partner) was in the service of the Crown;
(e) an individual who is employed in the service of any missionary society;
(f) an individual who is in the service of any territory under Her Majesty's protection;
(g) until 2009–10 only, a Commonwealth citizen;
(h) an EEA national;[3]
(i) a citizen of a country who can claim personal allowances by virtue of a "non-discrimination" clause in a double taxation treaty between the UK and his country of citizenship.[4]

The abolition by FA 2009, Sch 1 of the allowances for Commonwealth citizens (who did not also qualify under another heading) was collateral damage inflicted by the Human Rights Act.

Simon's Taxes E6.2.

---

[1] The non-residence is that of the taxpayer; the residence of dependants for whom he claims is usually irrelevant.

[2] Categories (a) to (f) (and from 6 April 2008, (h)), where the personal allowance is given by virtue of either residence or employment, are enacted by ITA 2007, s 56(3). Category (g) (and, until 5 April 2008, (h)), which gives personal allowance by virtue of nationality, are enacted by TA 1988, s 278(2)(a), which has been retained and has not been rewritten into ITA 2007: vide ITA 2007, Sch 1, para 40.

[3] That is a national of any of the member states of the European Economic Area, which is the European Union plus Iceland, Liechtenstein and Norway.

[4] This is a provision of Article 24(1) of the OECD Model Agreement. Non-discrimination clauses are found in many agreements between the UK and other territories, particularly those that have been entered into in recent years, such as Article 23(1) of the agreement with Azerbaijan (SI 1995/762) and Article 25(1) of the agreement with China (SI 1975/425). In both cases, sub-clause (3) states that this provision does not oblige either contracting state to extend personal allowances to persons not resident. However, in the author's view, the correct reading of this is that sub-clause (3) is subsidiary to sub-clause (1). There is an obligation not to discriminate. If the taxing authority does not grant personal allowances to its own citizens who are not resident, citizens of the other contracting state cannot claim personal allowances against their tax liabilities in the state in which they are not resident; however, if the taxing authority does grant personal allowances to its own citizens who are not resident, personal allowances cannot be denied to citizens of the other contracting state against their tax liabilities in the state in which they are not resident.

[6.11] Allowances and reliefs

Charges on income

[6.11] Where an individual makes a gift aid contribution to a charity, or is treated as paying his part of a partnership annuity, tax relief is given as a charge on income. A charge is against total income. The payment is made after deduction of tax at basic rate.[1] The recipient thus receives the sum with the accompanying tax credit, which is repayable.

The individual making the payment obtains relief against the higher rate charge through the self-assessment system.

Simon's Taxes E1.8.

---

[1] ITA 2007, s 414; and see infra, § **11.43**.

Claiming relief

[6.12] Reliefs, and many deductions, are obtained by the taxpayer "making a claim". In most cases, a claim is made by the taxpayer as an integral part of his self-assessment tax return.[1] The effect of the claim is incorporated by the taxpayer himself in his self-assessment calculation. It is, however, still permissible to make a claim that is not included in a return. There is then a mechanism for the Revenue to act in respect of that claim; the effect of the provision is that a Revenue officer is given equivalent powers in enquiring into the claim as he would have were the enquiry mounted into a tax return incorporating that claim.[2]

Once a claim is made to the Revenue, it is not necessary for the inspector to take any action, either in accepting that claim or in satisfying himself that the claim is correctly made. FA 1996, s 133 and Sch 19 thus remove from the statute the many provisions in the Taxes Act that were known internally in the Revenue as "inspectors' discretions". Now, claims are made by unilateral action by the taxpayer. The principal claims are:

(1) Claim for remittance basis (ITA 2007, s 809B).[3]
(2) Relief for an investment under an Enterprise Investment Scheme or into a Venture Capital Trust (ITA 2007, s 205).
(3) Post cessation expenditure (ITA 2007, ss 96 and 125).
(4) Emoluments for duties performed outside the UK (ITEPA 2003, s 38).
(5) Accommodation excluded from a benefit charge (ITEPA 2003, s 99).
(6) Pool cars (ITEPA 2003, s 167).
(7) Exclusion of benefit charge on certain loans (ITEPA 2003, s 180).
(8) Entitlement to age allowance (ITA 2007, s 35 & 36).
(9) Married couples allowance for those born before 6 April 1935 (ITA 2007, ss 45 & 46).
(10) Blind person's allowance (ITA 2007, s 38).
(11) Personal allowances for non-residents (ITA 2007, s 56(3)).
(12) Relief for losses (ITA 2007, ss 64, 71, 72, 83, 89 & 96).
(13) Holiday letting accommodation (ITTOIA 2005, s 326).
(14) Relief for unremittable overseas income (ITTOIA 2005, s 842).

A taxpayer's self-assessment does not require the submission with the return of any certificates issued in respect of income received. However, statute requires a taxpayer to have obtained a certificate before he is entitled to make a claim for many of the reliefs. Thus, for example, a pre-condition for a taxpayer receiving relief in respect of the Enterprise Investment Scheme is that he has received a certificate from the company certifying that the shares to which he has subscribed are eligible shares under the terms of the Enterprise Investment Scheme.[4]

Where the making of a claim provides relief for more than a single year, or where the effect of a claim is to reduce tax payable for an earlier year, TMA 1970, Sch 1B provides a mechanism whereby there is an effective repayment of tax without the necessity of reopening a taxpayer's self-assessment from an earlier year.

Simon's Taxes E1.260.

[1] TMA 1970, s 42.
[2] TMA 1970, Sch 1A.
[3] See infra, § **33.19**.
[4] ITA 2007, s 204.

Time limit

[6.13] The general time limit for making claims provides that, unless statute requires otherwise for a specific claim, any claim must be made by the end of five years following 31 January after the fiscal year to which it relates.[1]

Additional time is given where the claim arises as a result of an assessment that is made late. In that case, the claim can be made up to any time after the end of the fiscal year following that in which the assessment is made.[2]

Where statute requires a claim to be made, provisions are provided under which a claim is held to be valid, unless these are specifically altered by provisions relating to the particular type of claim.[3]

A claim should normally be made to the taxpayer's normal tax office. A diminishing number of statutory provisions require a claim to be made to HMRC (meaning the "Board" themselves). In practice, this is addressed to the local tax office. Revenue internal procedures, however, often specify a particular procedure to be followed within the Revenue in receipt of a claim addressed to the Board. Typically, the internal procedures of the Revenue require that a claim that is made to the Board be accepted or rejected by a more senior officer of the Revenue.

Simon's Taxes E1.265.

[1] TMA 1970, s 43(1).
[2] TMA 1970, s 43(2).
[3] TMA 1970, s 42.

[6.14] Allowances and reliefs

Loss relief

[6.14] In closely prescribed circumstances a loss may give rise to a relief from tax by being set against an equivalent amount of income and relieving that income from any liability to tax.

Simon's Taxes Division E1.11.

Relief for trading losses

Trading loss set off against general income

[6.15] If one sustains a loss in one's trade, profession or vocation the correct figure for the profits chargeable to income tax for the year is nil. Relief for the loss can then (sometimes, but not always) be obtained by putting the loss against the income. Where the loss arises on a trade (or professional or vocation), there are potentially two different claims that can be made for relief of the loss: (a) set the loss against the taxpayer's total income for the year;[1] (b) carry the loss forward against profits from the same trade in future years.[2] If the loss is in the early years of a business,[3] or is immediately before the cessation of the business,[4] other reliefs are available. There is also the potential of setting a loss against capital gains[5] and carrying it forward to a company where the business is incorporated.[6]

A person who sustains trading losses may elect to put the loss against his total income for the tax year in which the loss arises. The relief must be claimed.[7] The deadline for making the claim is 31 January in the second fiscal year after that in which the loss arises. It seems that if a claim is made it must be for the whole of the loss which can be set against the income—one cannot make a claim for such part of the income as reduces one's income to the amount of one's personal reliefs. If a loss would come into two fiscal years, eg on commencement or a change of accounting date the loss belongs to the first year.

Relief for the loss can be against the income of the year in which the loss arises, or the preceding year.

---

[1] ITA 2007, s 64.
[2] ITA 2007, s 83.
[3] ITA 2007, s 72; see infra, § **6.21**.
[4] ITA 2007, s 89; see infra, § **6.22**.
[5] ITA 2007, s 71; see infra, § **6.17**.
[6] ITA 2007, s 86; see infra, § **6.20**.
[7] On importance of claim see *Richardson v Jenkins* [1995] STC 95n. On relief for a Lloyds name see *Holliday v De Brunner* [1996] STC (SCD) 85. On a claim being made out of time see *Richardson v Jenkins* [1995] STC 95.

Temporary extension of loss relief

[6.16] FA 2009 provides temporary relief for losses incurred in 2008–09 or 2009–10, allowing some losses to be carried back for up to three years. The rules are highly prescriptive and their effect has been criticised. (See, for example, 'For this relief' by Mike Truman, *Taxation*, 14 May 2009.)

Trading loss set against capital gains

[6.17] Where the person's trading loss cannot be set against general income of that year and relief has not been given in any other way, it may be set against chargeable capital gains realised in that year.[1] Relief is given against the gain computed before applying taper relief.[2] This relief must be claimed and may not be claimed in part. In computing the chargeable gains against which the trading loss is to be set, no deduction is to be made for the annual exempt amount.

It is still not possible to set capital losses against trading profits.

[1] ITA 2007, s 71 and TCGA 1992, ss 261B & 261C.
[2] TCGA 1992, s 1(2)(*a*): on procedure for making claim note Inland Revenue interpretation RI 47.

Restrictions on loss relief — film partnerships, LLPs and part-time trades

[6.18] In the limited liability partnership the capital contributed by each partner (and so the amount of risk he bears) is limited. The agreement may nonetheless provide that the trading loss of the partnership should be attributed to the limited partners in full. In *Reed v Young*[1] it was held that sideways relief could be claimed even where the loss so attributed exceeded the amount of capital at risk. This gave rise to a number of film schemes, in which the individual provided capital for the making of a film by a partnership of which he was a limited partner. The majority of films do not make a profit, especially if the producer, production crew and actors are all paid full salaries for the work they undertake. The loss arising was then apportioned among the partners, the lion's share going to the limited partner who has, thereby, generated a large trading loss for a relatively small amount of capital spent. This trading loss is, then, available to be put against the individual's total income for the year.

With effect from 10 December 2003, statute[2] provides for a charge to income tax when "an exit event" occurs. The charge to income tax is the sum of the disposal consideration and the excess of any relief loss over the taxpayer's capital contribution to the film partnership. An exit event occurs in any of three circumstances: (a) the taxpayer receives non-taxable consideration for the disposal of his rights; (b) losses claimed exceed the taxpayer's capital contribution; (c) there is a further increase in the amount by which the losses claimed exceed the capital distribution.

These provisions are extended with effect from 12 March 2008. If an individual spends on average of less than 10 hours per week in a trade, loss relief is capped to £25,000.[3]

These restrictions apply to sideways relief (see infra, § **6.21**) and some capital gains tax reliefs (see supra, § **6.17**). Thus any loss in excess of a capped amount will qualify for carry-forward relief in the event that future profits are made.

[6.18] Allowances and reliefs

Simon's Taxes B7.130.

[1]   [1986] STC 285.
[2]   ITA 2007, ss 107 & 115 amended by FA 2007, Sch 4.
[3]   ITA 2007, s 74A.

Trading loss carried forward

[6.19] To the extent that relief for the allowable loss has not been given against general income either sideways relief or some other provision the loss may be carried forward and set off, not against the general income of subsequent years, but only against the future profits (if any) of the trade.[1] The relief must be given against the earliest profits available.[2] Where the trade has received income taxed by deduction at source such as interest or dividends the loss carried forward can be set off against that taxed income.[3]

The right to roll losses forward is available only so long as the taxpayer carries on the trade, and so is lost if there is a discontinuance of the trade. Provision is made, however, for two situations where the discontinuance is technical rather than commercial (see infra, § **6.24**).

Simon's Taxes E1.1120–1126.

[1]   ITA 2007, s 83; see *Gordon and Blair Ltd v IRC* (1962) 40 TC 358.
[2]   ITA 2007, s 83(4).
[3]   ITA 2007, s 85. See *Nuclear Electric plc v Bradley* [1996] STC 405, HL.

Trading loss carried forward on incorporation of business

[6.20] If the business is transferred to a company and the sole or main consideration is the transfer of shares of the company to the individual or his nominees, an accumulated loss may be carried forward.[1] This provision applies whether the business is incorporated or taken over by an existing company. The section does not allow the company to claim relief against the future profits of the trade but rather allows the individual to claim relief against income derived by him from the company, whether by dividend or otherwise, for example under a service agreement, but the loss must be set off against earned income before being set off against distributions. In this way the trading loss can be set against income from the company no matter how the company makes its profits, eg from other trades. It is not necessary that the individual or his nominees own all the shares in the company. The relief may be claimed only so long as the company carries on the business and the individual pays tax.

In addition, the individual must be beneficially entitled to the shares throughout the tax year for which he claims relief.[2] Curiously there seems to be no requirement that the beneficial ownership be unbroken, only that it last throughout the year of assessment in question. If therefore he sells the shares but then buys them back he should be able to resume his loss claim in the year subsequent to that in which he bought them back.

Simon's Taxes E1.1123.

[1] ITA 2007, s 86.
[2] ITA 2007, s 86(3). During the first year of trading, the requirement is that beneficial ownership must have extended from the date of incorporation to the end of the tax year.

Early year trading loss carried back

[6.21] A carry back of a trading loss[1] is allowed where the loss arises in the year of assessment in which the trade is first carried on or the next three years of assessment;[2] it thus applies to losses arising in the first four years of business. The loss may be carried back and set off against *general* income for the three years before that in which the loss is sustained. Income of an earlier year is taken first, so a loss incurred in 2009–10 can be carried back to 2006–07. When the accounting period of the business goes past the end of the year of assessment in which the trade begins the loss in that period is apportioned.

Partial claims for loss relief may not be made. It should also be noted that with the relief being given by reference to the basis period and not to the fiscal period the choice of accounting date will determine how far back one can go.[3]

If a trade is acquired from a spouse the four tax years run from the date that the spouse began to trade.[4] However, this restriction applies only when the claimant acquired the trade from a spouse to whom he was then married and with whom he was then living; it follows that this restriction does not apply where he succeeds to a trade on the death of the other spouse.

When a loss arises during one of the first three years of trading, the taxpayer can choose whether to claim against total income from that year, or to carry back the loss to pre-trading years. The taxpayer has to choose; the loss cannot be apportioned[5] and relief for a loss can only be given once.[6]

The calculations involved in deciding whether or not to claim this relief must take into account capital allowances and the basis of assessment for opening years.

Relief is restricted for non-active partners.[7] If a partner spends less than ten hours per week[8] personally engaged in activities carried on for the purpose of the trade of the partnership the relief for trade losses is restricted to the partner's capital contribution. This involves comparing the cumulative total of losses allowed against general income and chargeable gains at the end of the year[9] to the partner's capital contribution to the trade, as at the end of the year.[10]

Inland Revenue has published[11] its view of the manner in which these revisions operate. The Revenue view is that time spent by a partner in a management or servicing role, such as personnel, accountancy or purchasing counts when calculating whether the individual spends ten hours per week but time spent making decisions concerning the investment in the partnership does not.

Simon's Taxes E1.1131.

[1] ITA 2007, s 72: the relief is also available for a loss arising in a profession or vocation.

[6.21] Allowances and reliefs

[2] It is the loss that arises in the accounting period that forms the basis fiscal year that is relievable. Thus, the statutory provisions that have applied the "current year basis of assessment" for tax years since 1997–98 have reversed the decision in *Gascoine v Wharton* [1996] STC 1481 in which the taxpayer unsuccessfully argued for reliefs that would now be granted to him by statute.
[3] Inland Revenue booklet SAT 1 (1994) s 4.24.
[4] ITA 2007, s 74.
[5] *Butt v Haxby* [1983] STC 239.
[6] *Gamble v Rowe* [1998] STC (SCD) 116.
[7] ITA 2007, s 104.
[8] ITA 2007, s 112.
[9] ITA 2007, s 110.
[10] ITA 2007, ss 110 & 111.
[11] Inland Revenue press release 26 March 2004 "Tackling avoidance—income tax: manipulation of partnership losses" *Simon's Weekly Tax Intelligence* 2004, p 881.

Loss on ceasing a trade

[6.22] Once a trade, profession or vocation has been permanently discontinued, there can ex hypothesi be no carry forward of a loss. A terminal loss may, however, be carried *back* and set off against the profits charged under Schedule D in respect of the trade for the three years last preceding that in which the trade ends.[1] Relief is given as far as possible from the assessment of a later rather than earlier year.[2] Assessments may thus have to be reopened. Assessments may thus have to be reopened.

EXAMPLE
Terminal loss relief

A trader ceases his trade on 31 October 2009. His results for the four years to 30 April 2009 and for the final six months were as follows:

Year ended	30 April 2006	£12,000
	30 April 2007	£11,000
	30 April 2008	£12,000
	30 April 2009	£4,000
	1 May 2009 to 31 October 2009	–£14,000

Relief will be available for setting off as follows:

2009–10		£4,000	leaving nil taxable
2008–09		£10,000	leaving £2,000 taxable
		£14,000	

(A further reduction is available by virtue of overlap profit relief.)

Only terminal losses can be used in this way, ie a loss, sustained in the year of assessment in which the trade is permanently discontinued and in that part of the preceding year of assessment beginning 12 months before the date of discontinuance.

Simon's Taxes E1.1132.

¹ ITA 2007, s 90(1).
² ITA 2007, s 91.

[6.23] Interest on investments arising during any relevant period but which are excluded from the computation of profits because taxed at source may be used as profits against which the terminal loss may be set.¹ The period relevant will be that of the year in which the trade ceases or any of the three preceding years of assessment. It will be noted that the dividend or interest is taxed on an arising basis.

Simon's Taxes E1.1132.

¹ ITA 2007, s 92. See *Bank Line Ltd v IRC* [1974] STC 342 and *Nuclear Electric plc v Bradley* [1996] STC 405, HL.

[6.24] Where payments have been made during the relevant years by the trader under deduction of tax, the profits are treated as reduced by the gross amount of such payments.¹ Similarly, in computing the terminal loss the figure otherwise obtained is to be reduced by the amount of any such payments. In both instances relief has already been given.

Where a partner retires there is a deemed discontinuance of the partner's notional trade and a terminal loss is calculated for the retiring partner only. This loss is set off against that part of the partnership income which was included in his total income for each relevant year. His share of the loss is governed by his share of the profits at the date of discontinuance.²

¹ See infra, § 11.43.
² ITA 2007, s 62, 89.

Is the loss from a trade?

[6.25] Loss relief is important not only to the genuine trader but also to others who have used it as the basis of schemes. To claim relief the trader must have been carrying on a trade and his allowable expenses must exceed his trading receipts. In addition the trade must be carried on on a commercial basis and with a view to the realisation of profit.¹

Further, the trade must have been carried on in a commercial way for the whole of the year of assessment whether or not there has been a change in the manner in which the trade was being carried on and whether or not there has been a change in the persons running the trade if at least one person was running it for the whole year. If the trade was set up or discontinued (or both) in a year of assessment the test is applied to those parts of the year in which the trade was in being.

By concession relief can be claimed in respect of maintenance expenses of owner-occupied farms not carried on on a commercial basis.²

Losses on dealings in commodity futures are restricted where partnerships are involved.³ There are also restrictions relating to film partnerships; here, the

[6.25] Allowances and reliefs

restriction is that the rate of tax at which capital allowance is given in one year is applied to the balancing charge when it arises in the subsequent year, even though the taxpayer may then have a lower rate of tax to which he is generally subject, or may be outside the scope of UK tax.[4]

Simon's Taxes E1.1132.

---

[1] ITA 2007, s 66; *Walls v Livesey* [1995] STC (SCD) 12, *Wannell v Rothwell* [1996] STC 450 and *Delian Enterprises (A partnership) v Ellis* [1999] STC (SCD) 103. See also *Ensign Tankers Leasing Ltd v Stokes* [1992] STC 226, HL and *FA and AB Ltd v Lupton* [1971] 3 All ER 948, 47 TC 580, infra, § **7.11** as to what is a trading transaction.
[2] Extra-statutory concession B5.
[3] ITA 2007, s 81.
[4] ITA 2007, s 109.

[6.26] "With a view to profit". A loss is not relievable unless the trade that was being carried on was on a commercial basis and with a view to the realisation of profits.[1] In *Walls v Livesey*,[2] the Special Commissioner considered that what is now sideways relief for losses occurred in early years is available where profits may be expected a reasonable time after the four year period provided for claims. The Revenue have stated that they do not construe the section in this way, although that particular case did not turn on this point.[3] In the Revenue's view, what constitutes a "reasonable time" depends on the facts and, in particular, the nature of the loss making activity. The Revenue see this as normally being a fairly short period, but accept that in the context of capital intensive activities a loss claim may be competent where the reasonable and realistic expectation of profits is within five years from the date of commencement of the activities. In the authors' view, this rigid formulation cannot be supported on the wording of statute. Whilst there is, clearly, a denial of loss relief if there is not a realistic expectation of profit, a claim remains competent, even if the expected move into profitability is considerably longer than the period envisaged by the Revenue. It may be that the enterprise is too small to make a profit; in *Walsh v Taylor*[4] a farm of 25.48 acres was described by the Commissioner as "too small to be viable" and relief for the loss arising was denied on the basis that profits could not reasonably be expected.[5]

It is important to note that the question as to whether a particular activity constitutes a trade and the question whether this trade is carried on with a view to profit are both questions of fact and, hence, solely within the jurisdiction of the Tribunal. The evidence that is supplied to the Tribunal is vital. The phrase "with a view to . . ." directs attention to the state of mind of the taxpayer when the activity is commenced. It is, therefore, evidence of intention at that time that is of greatest value. In this context, the Revenue have stated: 'We would expect a written business plan to be prepared at the outset . . . The figures in such a plan must be credible'.[6]

Simon's Taxes E1.1111.

---

[1] ITA 2007, s 66.

² [1995] STC (SCD) 12 (taxpayer wins). Note also the taxpayer victory in *Delian Enterprises (a partnership) v Ellis* [1999] STC (SCD) 103.
³ Inland Revenue Tax Bulletin October 1997, p 473.
⁴ [2004] STC (SCD) 48
⁵ A paraphrase of the statutory requirement for loss relief in ITA 2007, s 74.
⁶ Inland Revenue Tax Bulletin October 1997, p 473.

Loss from furnished holiday lettings

[6.27] Loss relief is available when a letting is within the definition of furnished holiday lettings (see infra, § **10.15**).¹ In *Brown v Richardson*² the Special Commissioners considered a claim for loss relief on the basis that property had been acquired to be "let on a commercial basis and with a view to the realisation of profits".³ An accountant and his wife had purchased a property in Cornwall, the entire purchase being funded by a mortgage secured on the couple's main residence. A partnership agreement was drawn up between husband and wife so that profits arising on the letting of the Cornish property were split equally between husband and wife, but any losses were allocated wholly to the husband. Losses arose, primarily because of significant finance charges.

The taxpayer argued that the requirement in ITTOIA 2005 s 323(2)(*b*) for there to be a view to the realisation of "profits", is to be tested by applying the definition of "profit" as used in the Taxes Acts; that is, a sum that falls for assessment before the deduction of charges on income and any other reliefs. This approach was rejected by the Special Commissioner, who held that in s 323(2) "profits" means commercial profits and not tax adjusted profit. In considering whether an activity can reasonably be expected to produce a commercial profit, it is necessary to look at the anticipated surplus or deficit after finance charges. The Special Commissioner noted that the letting was carried on in a commercial manner, with the employment of an agent and the charging of full market rents. However, on the facts, he decided that the letting was effected with a view to generating income to offset costs, rather than with a view to the realisation of profits.

The 2009 Budget announced the proposed abolition of the furnished holiday lettings rules from 6 April 2010.

Simon's Taxes B8.605.

¹ ITA 2007, s 127.
² [1997] STC (SCD) 233.
³ ITTOIA 2005, s 323(2).

Partnership loss

[6.28] Loss relief is always granted to a "person". Thus, where there is a partnership that produces a loss, the loss is apportioned amongst the partners and each individual partner may choose to make whatever claim is appropriate for his individual circumstances. (This treatment is afforded to Scottish partnerships as well as English partnerships.¹) Thus, partner A may wish to set

[6.28] Allowances and reliefs

his share of the trading loss against his other income; partner B may choose to carry forward his loss against trading profits of a later year.

For the restriction of loss relief for a partnership see supra, § **6.18**. For restriction of loss relief for a non-active partner see supra, § **6.21**.

Simon's Taxes E1.1124.

---

[1] ITA 2007, s 62.

[6.29] Hobby farming. Where losses are sustained in a trade of farming or market gardening, relief is not available, other than by carry forward, if a loss was incurred in each of the five prior years.[1] It should be remembered that all farming, but not market gardening, is treated as one trade[2] so that a loss on one farm may be set off against the profits of another. Special provision is made for the genuine farmer who has a reasonable expectation of profit but whose business is taking longer than six years to come right.

Simon's Taxes E1.1111.

---

[1] ITA 2007, s 67. For an extension of the relief in response to the foot and mouth crisis, see extra-statutory concession B55.
[2] ITTOIA 2005, s 9(1).

Relief for a non-trading loss

Employment loss

[6.30] Statute[1] refers to a loss sustained in an employment (although not to offices). However, the Revenue do not accept that a claim can ever arise—even when expenses exceed emoluments.[2] This is because ITEPA 2003, ss 328–338 allows expenses to be deducted only if they are defrayed "out of" emoluments.

---

[1] ITA 2007, s 128.
[2] See *Taxation* 1989, p 74.

Loss from a foreign trade or a miscellaneous income

[6.31] A loss arising from a trade or profession carried on wholly overseas can be given relief, but only against other foreign income.[1]

Losses from the letting of foreign property are relieved in the same manner as losses from the letting of property within the UK.[2] Thus, all rental income arising from overseas property is pooled and expenses incurred in generating that income are deducted therefrom. This has the effect that loss relief is immediately given for a deficit of income on a particular property where another property has produced a surplus. An overall deficit is carried forward to a subsequent year.[3] The pool of overseas letting income assessable is, however, separate from the pool of UK letting income. There is, thus, no offset of loss from one to the other.

If allowable cost exceed miscellaneous income[4] the loss created can be relieved against the total of miscellaneous income for the year,[5] with the unrelieved apportion being carried forward to later years' miscellaneous income.[6]

Simon's Taxes Division B9; E1.1140, 1141.

[1] ITA 2007, s 95.
[2] ITA 2007, s 117.
[3] ITA 2007, s 118.
[4] Taxed under ITTOIA 2005, ss 687–689.
[5] ITA 2007, s 152.
[6] ITA 2007, s 153.

Loss on property income

[6.32] The general rule is that the rents from all properties in the UK are aggregated and expenditure is deducted from the aggregate.[1] This automatically provides loss relief for a deficit on a single property, where there is other property let to provide a surplus. Any net losses may be rolled forward indefinitely and set off against any profit of a UK property business carried on in a subsequent year.[2]

In two circumstances, a loss arising from a property business can be set against general income. First, for this purpose, and for many other purposes, a business of furnished holiday lettings in the UK is treated as if it were a trade[3] and the reliefs, such as loss relief, available to a trade[4] can be used (see supra, § 6.27).

Second, the property loss can be relieved against general income in either of the following circumstances:[5]

(a) the loss includes capital allowances treated as expenses of the business,[6] or
(b) the loss arises from an agricultural estate and the loss includes agricultural expenses.[7]

The loss relievable is the lower of[8] (i) the amount of the loss, and (ii) the net capital allowances/agricultural expenses.

A relief is given by deducting the loss from the general income of the tax year in which the loss arises. Any surplus loss is then carried forward to the next tax year.[9]

"Allowable agricultural expenses", are defined in statute[10] as: "any expenses attributable to the estate which are deductible in respect of maintenance, repairs, insurance or management of the estate", excluding loan interest.[11]

[1] ITTOIA 2005, s 268.
[2] ITA 2007, s 118.
[3] ITA 2007, s 127. The 2009 Budget announced the proposed extension of the rules to cover such lettings elsewhere in the EEA (for 2009–10) and the complete withdrawal of the rules from 2010–11.

[6.32] Allowances and reliefs

[4] See supra, §§ 6.15–6.27.
[5] ITA 2007, s 120(1).
[6] ITA 2007, s 123(2).
[7] ITA 2007, s 123(3).
[8] ITA 2007, s 122(2).
[9] ITA 2007, s 120(2)(b).
[10] ITA 2007, s 123(5)(a).
[11] ITA 2007, s 123(5)(b).

Interest, etc or dividend income

[6.33] No relief is possible, since the tax legislation does not permit any deductions.

Income tax relief for a capital loss

Losses on unquoted shares in trading companies

[6.34] Although capital losses are the province of CGT and may not be set off against income, an exception is made where the loss arises from the disposal of unquoted shares in a trading company or member of a trading group. The relief is available only in respect of shares for which the individual or his spouse subscribed[1] —as distinct from those acquired through gift, inheritance or purchase. The shares must be ordinary share capital.[2] The company must be a "qualifying trading company". A company qualifies only if it satisfies complex criteria as to what it has been doing (eg trading—but not in forbidden items such as shares or land)[3] and for how long (six years if previously an investment company or a dealer in forbidden items). In addition the company must not have its shares quoted on a recognised stock exchange[4] and must be resident in the UK.

The loss is computed on CGT principles;[5] in addition the disposal must be an arm's length sale for full consideration or a distribution on winding up or the deemed disposal which arises when shares have become of negligible value.[6] Relief is denied even for such disposals if there is a share exchange for non-commercial reasons[7] or value shifting[8] has occurred.

This relief may be claimed for the year in which the loss is realised or the preceding year.[9] Any unused loss can then be set only against capital gains. Where the taxpayer also has a trading loss, precedence is given to relief for the loss on unquoted shares.[10]

Further rules apply where there are mixed holdings, eg where some shares were acquired by subscription and others by inheritance; those rules restrict the loss to what would have been the deductible cost if mixing had not occurred. The mixing rules can be avoided by issuing different types of shares.[11] Special rules apply also to reorganisation.[12] Legislation now affirms "beyond doubt" the Revenue view that the withdrawal of funds from share accounts with Building Societies or Industrial and Provident Societies cannot give rise to this relief.[13]

Simon's Taxes E1.1142.

¹ ITA 2007, s 131.
² ITA 2007, s 134.
³ ITA 2007, s 137.
⁴ ITA 2007, s 143. Losses on shares dealt in on the Alternative Investment Market will qualify for relief; Inland Revenue press release, 20 February 1995, *Simon's Weekly Tax Intelligence* 1995, p 343.
⁵ ITA 2007, s 133.
⁶ ITA 2007, s 131(3).
⁷ ITA 2007, s 136.
⁸ ITA 2007, Sch 1, para 309 (infra, § **17.05**).
⁹ ITA 2007, s 133. A claim is essential. For a sad case where a claim had not been made see *Marks v McNally* [2004] STC (SCD) 503. The decision in this case gives an interesting review of the manner in which what is now ITA 2007, ss 131–151 operate.
¹⁰ ITA 2007, s 133
¹¹ ITA 2007, s 147,148
¹² ITA 2007, s 131(3); mixing is the same as pooling for CGT.
¹³ Inland Revenue press release, 3 July 1987, *Simon's Tax Intelligence* 1987, p 462.

Maintenance payments

[6.35] From 6 April 2000, no relief for maintenance payments made is available unless one of the parties to the marriage was born before 6 April 1935.¹ Where one of the parties to the marriage was born before that date, the payer is entitled to a reduction in income tax, which is calculated as 10% of the amount paid in the year, or £2,670, whichever is less.² In contrast to the position in 1999–2000 and earlier years, the amount actually paid is not available as a deduction, even where the obligation arose prior to 1988.³

The deduction is not to be greater than the sum needed to reduce the payer's tax liability to nil, ie it cannot generate a repayment claim.

In determining the amount of income tax to which the payer would be liable and against which the deduction is to be set no account is to be taken of any income tax reduction under the rules for personal reliefs or any relief for double taxation whether under an agreement with another country or unilaterally.⁴

¹ ITA 2007, s 454(3)
² ITA 2007, s 453 applying the limit in s 45 amended by Income Tax (Indexation) (No 2) Order 2008, SI 2008/3023, art 4(e).
³ For a discussion of the detailed provisions relating to this restricted relief for maintenance payments, see Tiley & Collison's UK Tax Guide 1999–2000 § **9.80**.
⁴ eg under TA 1988, ss 788 or 790.

Gifts to charities

Gift Aid

[6.36] A donation is treated as a qualifying donation if it meets various conditions and the donor gives an appropriate declaration in relation to it to the charity.[1] The same treatment is afforded to a single payment and a series of payments, whether made under the terms of a covenant or not. A declaration differs from a certificate in that it may be made orally or electronically as well as in writing. The donor must be resident in the UK or in some other way be subject to UK tax on the profits out of which the donation is made.[2] The donation may be given relief either against income tax or against capital gains tax.[3] The payment must not already be the subject of relief such as a payment under the payroll deduction scheme.

A donation does not qualify under the Gift Aid legislation where it is made by means of releasing a loan that had previously been made to the charity.[4] Relief is given for the year in which the gift is made,[5] or the taxpayer can elect for relief in the preceding tax year.[6] The payment must not be subject to repayment: it must not be conditional on or associated with or part of an arrangement involving the acquisition of property by the charity otherwise than by way of gift from the donor or a person connected with him.

The gift is treated as grossed up at the basic rate of income tax;[7] for this purpose it does not matter what the source of the payment is. Where the donor has not been assessed in respect of the tax treated as deducted from the donation under the grossing up process, a direct assessment may be made to recover the shortfall.[8]

If the donor is a non taxpayer, or has income that is only subject to tax at 10%,[9] the tax repayable by the charity on the donation will exceed the tax suffered by the donor. As dividends received by a basic rate taxpayer have a tax credit of 10% and no further liability, this situation is not uncommon amongst retired people who live on their investment income. In this circumstance, the way in which the tax calculation works on the self-assessment tax return is that the shortfall is automatically recouped by an increase in the balancing payment due for the year. Where the donor is not within the self-assessment system, the Revenue can collect the tax by direct assessment or by restricting personal allowances in any PAYE code that is applied, for example, to an occupational pension.[10]

In *St Dunstan's v Major*, the Special Commissioners considered a frequently used arrangement whereby a deed of variation diverted part of the residue of an estate to a charity.[11] It was not in dispute that the inheritance tax exemption was available on the £20,000 variation. The residuary legatee claimed that this sum also qualified for gift aid relief as, for income tax purposes, a deed of variation is correctly treated as a "gift by an individual". The Special Commissioner ruled that the £20,000 failed to attract Gift Aid relief as the effect of the deed of variation was to reduce the burden of inheritance tax on the residue. Hence, a benefit had arisen "in consequence of making the gift",[12] the effect of which was to deny relief for Gift Aid. This case leaves unanswered the situation where a legatee entitled to receive only a fixed sum under the will of the deceased enters into a deed of variation diverting the legacy to a charity. As the reduced inheritance tax liability benefits the residue and not such a legatee, it would appear to be the case that such an arrangement continues to be effective for providing both the inheritance tax relief and Gift Aid relief.

The effect of the gift being a qualifying donation is that the gift is treated as having been made after deduction of basic rate tax; the donor's basic rate tax band is increased by the amount of the gift.[13] So a payment of £800 is treated as a gift of £1,000 and the basic rate band extends to £35,800 instead of £34,800. The donor must pay income tax at the basic rate in the usual way on the £1,000.

The charity would ordinarily recover £200 tax from the Revenue.[14] This is not affected by the fact that the donor may be liable only to lower rate tax. However, as a transitional measure to reflect the reduction of the basic rate from 6 April 2008, Gift Aid donations made between that date and 5 April 2011 will be treated (in the charity's hands) as if basic rate at 22% had been deducted. Thus a net gift of £800 would in fact be worth £1,025 to the charity.[15]

The Income Tax Act contains the usual elaborate rules as to disregarding various charges, reliefs and set offs.[16] Where the donor is entitled to the enhanced personal or married couples' allowances that person's total income is reduced by the grossed up amount of the gift when considering whether the tapering rules apply.[17]

The taxpayer can elect for payments made one year to be treated as if they were Gift Aid payments made in the previous year.[18] The election must be made by the date on which the individual submits his self-assessment tax return (the election normally being part of the return) or, if earlier, 31 January following the tax year.[19] The making of the election does not affect the charity, which recovers tax by reference to the date on which the payment was actually made.[20]

A gift to a registered "Community Amateur Sports Club" attracts the same tax reliefs as a gift to a charity.[21]

A system has been introduced under which a taxpayer can direct the Revenue to make a repayment of tax directly to a charity specified by the taxpayer, this payment being treated as a gift aid payment by the taxpayer.[22]

The same arithmetical effect as gift aid is afforded to the donor by the payroll deduction scheme.[23] The employer withholds a part of the salary of the employee and pays this to a charity specified by the employee. The employee's income tax liability (and PAYE deducted) is computed on the net amount paid, after the charitable donation.

There are detailed regulations[24] for paperwork required of a charity in accepting gift aid. A charity can refuse to accept an oral gift aid declaration, without the necessity of sending a written confirmatory statement, as long as specific explanations are given when the declaration is made by the donor. The intention of this provision, is to allow for gift aid on a donation (usually by credit card) telephoned to the charity, as has become commonplace in major national appeals in recent years.

[6.36] Allowances and reliefs

Gift aid applies only to a gift of money. However, it is possible for an individual to hand goods to charity shops on the basis that the proceeds of the sale of the goods constitute a gift aid donation to the charity. The goods must remain the property of the potential donor until they are sold; it is the donor who is selling the goods not the charity.[25]

Simon's Taxes D1.320, E1.811.

1. ITA 2007, s 416(1).
2. ITA 2007, s 416(2).
3. ITA 2007, s 414(1).
4. *Battle Baptist Church v IRC and Woodham* [1995] STC (SCD) 176n. This particular case was, however, decided on the preliminary point that the release of the loan was not made under seal and was, hence, unenforceable in law and was, thus, incapable of amounting to a gift of any sort.
5. ITA 2007, s 414(2).
6. ITA 2007, s 426.
7. ITA 2007, s 415.
8. ITA 2007, s 424(1).
9. By virtue of total income being in the band for the lower rate, or by virtue of the income being dividend income.
10. ITA 2007, s 424(1). It is thought that, in practice, the Revenue do not usually take steps to recover the underpayment of tax in these circumstances, although no relief is afforded to those within the self-assessment system.
11. [1997] STC (SCD) 212.
12. Which falls foul of the conditions in ITA 2007, s 416(7) Condition F.
13. ITA 2007, s 414(2)(b).
14. ITA 2007, s 520(1).
15. FA 2008, Sch 19.
16. ITA 2007, s 423.
17. ITA 2007, s 423(5).
18. ITA 2007, s 426.
19. ITA 2007, s 426(6).
20. ITA 2007, s 426(7).
21. ITA 2007, s 430(1)(d).
22. ITA 2007, s 429, which allows a tax repayment arising from the 2007–08 tax return to be treated as a gift aid donation for 2007–08.
23. ITEPA 2003, s 713.
24. Donations to Charity by Individuals (Appropriate Declarations) Regulations 2000, SI 2000/2074, substantially amended by Donations to Charity by Individuals (Appropriate Declarations) (Amendment) Regulations 2005, SI 2005/2790, *Simons Weekly Tax Intelligence* 2005, p 1721. A useful guide to the current requirements on a recipient charity is given in Taxation, 17 November 2005, pp 174–177 and a follow-up article on 26 January 2006, p 422.
25. HMRC Statement, 28 November 2006, *Simon's Weekly Tax Intelligence* 2006, p 2556. This statement also gives practical suggestions for charity auctions and a donation that allows visitors the right to free admission to view charity property.

Benefit received

[6.37] The general principle is that in order for a deduction to be available under the gift aid scheme, there must have been a donation, that is, an act of bounty, not a payment for services received. Thus, if a church puts on a concert and charges £8 admission, the purchase of the admission ticket cannot be regarded as a gift aid donation.[1] By contrast, if there is no charge for admission but an individual puts £8 into the church's collecting box when he comes to attend the concert, the £8 can then be properly regarded as a gift aid donation.

Statute relaxes the strictness of this rule in three ways.

First, Parliament has enacted provisions designed to help charities such as The National Trust and The Royal Society for the Protection of Birds. Any charity that has as one of its purposes the preservation of property, or the conservation of wildlife can treat as gift aid a sum it receives for admission to the property.[2] It is the condition for this relaxation of the strict rule, that the charity gives rights of admission for such a "qualifying donation" to members of the public, and not to a restricted class of persons.[3]

Second, a donation to any charity can be treated as under the gift aid scheme where the value of the benefit[4] does not exceed:

(a)   25% of the gift, if the gift does not exceed £100.
(b)   £25 if the gift is £100 to £1,000.
(c)   5% of the gift if the gift is £1,000 to £10,000.
(d)   £500 if the gift exceeds £10,000.[5]

This second statutory relaxation does not, however, change the treatment illustrated by the person attending the church concert. Even if it can be established that the "benefit" of attending the concert is less than £2, the payment of £8 for a ticket is a payment for a service received and not a gift.

Third, a charity can accept a gift aid donation instead of an admission fee.[6]

---

[1] This is in contrast to the treatment for VAT. HM Customs & Excise agreed that VAT was levied on a small proportion only of the ticket price for the Band Aid concert at Wembley Stadium, on the basis that the dominant motivation of those attending was to make a charitable donation.
[2] ITA 2007, s 420.
[3] ITA 2007, s 420(4).
[4] ITA 2007, s 418 (donation by an individual), TA 1988, s 339 (donation by a company), both amended by FA 2007, s 49, which includes the value of a benefit received by a connected person.
[5] FA 1990, s 25(4) & (2)(e).
[6] ITA 2007, s 420. There are detailed statutory conditions to be satisfied. A Revenue guide to these provisions has been published: Inland Revenue Guidance Note, 22 September 2005, *Simons Weekly Tax Intelligence* 2005, pp 1625–1630.

Gifts of land, shares or securities to a charity

[6.38] Income tax relief may be claimed not only where the individual makes a gift of cash, as under the Gift Aid scheme, but also where the gift is of shares

[6.38] Allowances and reliefs

or securities or of land in the UK.[1] Corporation tax relief is, similarly, available for a gift by a company. A donor making a gift of a qualifying asset is entitled to an income tax deduction in computing total income equal to the relevant amount ie the market value of the asset, defined as for CGT, increased by any associated costs of disposal.[2] Relief is thus given at both basic rate and higher rate.

Investments qualify if they are quoted shares or securities, units in an authorised unit trust, shares in an OEIC or an interest in an offshore fund.[3]

The relief is reduced by any consideration or benefit received, as where the benefactor sells the shares to the charity at a low price.[4]

The relief is limited to the "net benefit to the charity"[5], which is defined in statute[6] as the market value of the investment[7] reduced by liabilities assumed by the charity.[8]

Where a trader makes a gift to a charity, or to an educational establishment, of an item he has manufactured, or in which he deals, no account is taken of the value of the item gifted, when computing profits.[9]

---

[1] ITA 2007, s 431.
[2] ITA 2007, s 434.
[3] ITA 2007, s 432.
[4] ITA 2007, ss 434 & 436.
[5] ITA 2007, s 434.
[6] ITA 2007, s 437.
[7] Defined as including holdings of connected persons: ITA 2007, s 434(1).
[8] ITA 2007, s 437.
[9] ie statute disapplies the decision in *Sharkey v Wernher* [1955] 3 All ER 493, HL (now codified by FA 2008) and the value of the item gifted is not treated as increasing the turnover of the business: ITTOIA 2005, s 108(2). The relief is also available in gifts to designated bodies, such as the British Museum.

Interest relief

[6.39] A limited number of categories of payment by way of interest are deductible in computing income.[1] Interest is deductible if it is payable on one of the following categories of loan:

(a) a loan to buy plant or machinery for partnership use[2] (see infra, § **6.41**);
(b) a loan to buy plant or machinery for employment use[3] (see infra, § **6.41**);
(c) a loan to buy interest in close company[4] (see infra, § **6.42**);
(d) a loan to buy interest in employee-controlled company[5] (see infra, § **6.42**);
(e) a loan to invest in partnership[6] (see infra, § **6.42**);
(f) a loan to invest in co-operative[7] (see infra, § **6.42**); and
(g) a loan to pay inheritance tax.[8] (see infra, § **6.43**).

In addition, interest payments may be deductible in computing income from a particular source, eg profits arising from a trade.

The reason for allowing interest as a general deduction from income is that tax is levied on income and in computing income all charges on that income including interest should be deducted. This used to be the general rule for UK tax law and gave rise to much complexity not least due to the machinery by which it was implemented. Since 1974 interest payments have been deductible in computing income only if the interest is on a loan to defray money applied for certain defined purposes.

No relief is available for interest on a loan to purchase a main residence. See infra, § **10.11** for interest paid on a loan to fund the purchase or improvement of let property and infra, § **8.132** for interest on a loan for a trade.

Simon's Taxes Division E1.8.

1   ITA 2007, s 383.
2   ITA 2007, s 388.
3   ITA 2007, s 390.
4   ITA 2007, s 392.
5   ITA 2007, s 396.
6   ITA 2007, s 398.
7   ITA 2007, s 401.
8   ITA 2007, s 403.

General rules

[6.40] In order to obtain a deduction for interest for any of the specified purposes, a number of general rules must be satisfied:

(a)   Relief is not available if the interest is incurred in overdrawing an account or debiting the holder of a credit card.[1]
(b)   The interest paid must be in respect of a loan to the taxpayer; sums paid in respect of a guarantee of a loan to another do not qualify.[2] Where a loan account is created by the consolidation of and transfer from overdrawn accounts nothing is actually paid to defray money applied for a particular purpose and so no relief is due.[3]
(c)   Where the rate of interest exceeds a reasonable commercial rate, no relief is given for the excess.[4]
(d)   Special rules apply to old loans to provide annuities (category 4 above).
(e)   Where only a part of a debt qualifies, relief may be given for that proportion of interest.

Simon's Taxes Division E1.8.

1   ITA 2007, s 384; on what is an overdraft see *Walcot Bather v Golding* [1979] STC 707.
2   *Hendy v Hadley* [1980] 2 All ER 554, [1980] STC 292. See further infra, § **9.37**.
3   *Lawson v Brooks* [1992] STC 76.
4   ITA 2007, s 384.

[6.41] Allowances and reliefs

Purchase of machinery or plant for use by a partnership or as an employer

[6.41] A partner, or employee, may claim relief for interest he has paid on a loan to purchase machinery and plant which is for use in the business of his partnership or his employer.[1] This relief is, however, available only in the year in which the advance is made and the next three years of assessment.

It is usually more desirable for a partnership to make a purchase of machinery or plant. There is then no time limit on the relief for interest paid on the purchase, this being available as an ordinary business expense. Furthermore IHT business property relief at 100% will normally be available, compared to 50% BPR on machinery or plant owned by an individual partner.[2]

Simon's Taxes E1.826.

[1] ITA 2007, s 390.
[2] See infra, § **43.06**, category 5.

Acquisition of an interest in close company, co-operative, employee-controlled company or partnership[1]

[1] See also ITA 2007, ss 392, 396 & 398. See *Major v Brodie* [1998] STC 491 for a consideration of the operation of the statutory provisions in relation to a Scottish partnership. In *Lancaster v IRC* [2000] STC (SCD) 138 at 142h, a partner in a professional partnership claimed that paying for an annual holiday constituted a payment of interest to his wife on a loan she had made to his partnership. The Special Commissioner held there was no business element in the entire arrangement, other than the obtaining of a reduction in tax liability. The claim was rejected.

[6.42] Interest is allowable if the loan is used to acquire a material interest (ie more than 5%)[2] in a close company with no capital repayment or in lending money to the company for use in its trade (or to repay an eligible loan). The company must exist wholly or mainly for the purpose of carrying on a trade.[3] Relief may also be claimed if the borrower works for the greater part of his time in the actual management or conduct of the company irrespective of the size of his shareholding.[4] Relief is still available if the company was close when the interest in the company was acquired, but is no longer close when the interest is paid. By concession, the relief will be continued even after a partnership has been incorporated or shares in one company are exchanged for shares in another provided a new loan would have satisfied all these conditions.[5] Relief is not available if the person acquiring the shares claims relief under the enterprise investment scheme.[6]

Similar relief is available to buy an interest in a partnership[7] or co-operative or to lend money to such a body and to purchase ordinary share capital of an employee-controlled company.[8] The loan must still be for use in the trade of the entity in which an interest is acquired.[9]

Interest relief is not usually available if the business consists of the occupation of commercial woodlands.[10]

The receipt of sums from the company may be treated as a repayment of the loan, so bringing about a reduction or extinction of the claim.[11]

---

[2] ITA 2007, s 394. Shares held by associates are aggregated for this test, but shares held in profit-sharing schemes do not qualify.
[3] See *Lord v Tustain* [1993] STC 755.
[4] ITA 2007, s 393 and see Inland Revenue interpretation RI 62.
[5] Extra-statutory concession A43.
[6] ITA 2007, s 392(3); semble relief is withheld even if the claim for EIS relief subsequently fails (eg because the trade is not a qualifying trade)—ICAEW Memorandum TR 759, *Simon's Tax Intelligence* 1989, p 718.
[7] ITA 2007, s 398. Relief is not available when the individual has ceased to be a partner before the interest is paid—Inland Revenue interpretation RI 41.
[8] ITA 2007, s 396.
[9] *Major v Brodie* [1998] STC 491 and *Lancaster v IRC* [2000] STC (SCD) at 142h. In this case, it was held that the £30,000 paid into a partnership was to cover the debt of the same sum created the same day; it was not new funds contributed. See also infra, § **6.45**.
[10] ITA 2007, s 411(1).
[11] ITA 2007, s 407on which see Inland Revenue interpretation RI 12.

Payment of IHT

[6.43] It is usually necessary for personal representatives to take out a loan to fund the payment of inheritance tax that is required on non-instalment property in the deceased's free estate when an application for probate is made, as the personal representatives have no access, at that time, to the funds in any bank accounts left by the deceased. Interest on a loan to pay IHT during a period of 12 months from the date of the loan is deductible against income arising to the personal representatives.[1]

---

[1] ITA 2007, s 403.

Preserved relief for old loan—purchase of a life annuity secured on land

[6.44] A loan taken out before 9 March 1999 to buy a life annuity continues to attract relief.[1]

The conditions are stringent. At least nine-tenths of the loan must have been applied in the purchase; the annuity must be a single or joint life annuity; the borrower (or each of them) must have been 65 years of age at the time of the loan; the loan must be secured on land in the UK or the Republic of Ireland and the borrower must have an interest in the land. The interest must be payable by the borrower or by one of the annuitants and where the loan exceeds

[6.44] Allowances and reliefs

£30,000[2] relief is not given for the excess.[3] Various rules which applied for mortgage interest relief must have been satisfied here also—eg the MIRAS system, and those for loans on former residences[4] and for substituted security arrangements[5].

Although relief has been applied only at basic rate since 1998–99, FA 2000 provides that relief will continue to be given at the old (ie 1999–2000) basic rate of 23% and not the current rate of 20%.[6]

FA 1999 prevents the use of this relief for new loans by providing that relief may be given only for loans made before 9 March 1999.[7] The relief may, however, be given if the loan was made after that date if it was made in pursuance of an offer, in writing or appropriately evidenced, and the offer was made by the lender before 9 March 1999.[8]

FA 1999 relaxes the rules for qualifying loans in two respects as from 27 July 1999. First, entitlement to relief does not end just because the property is no longer used by the borrower as a residence;[9] so the relief may still be claimed if the borrower goes into a nursing home.[10] Second, that entitlement does not end just because the borrower re-mortgages the property—even if they increase the size of the loan (subject to the £30,000 limit).[11]

Simon's Taxes E1.833.

---

[1] TA 1988, s 365.
[2] TA 1988, s 365(3).
[3] TA 1988, s 353(4), (5).
[4] TA 1988, s 365(1A), (1B), see also the 1999–2000 edition of this book at § **5.32**.
[5] TA 1988, ss 357A, 357B, 357C; see also the 1999–2000 edition of this book at § 5.33.
[6] TA 1988, s 353(1AA).
[7] TA 1988, s 365(1)(*aa*).
[8] TA 1988, s 365(1AA).
[9] TA 1988, s 365(1)(*d*).
[10] Inland Revenue notes to Finance Bill 1999, Clause 37.
[11] TA 1988, s 365(1AB), (1AC) and (1AD).

Anti-avoidance

[6.45] Three anti-avoidance points should be noted.

(1) If a transaction is associated with the lending of money, TA 1988, s 786 applies to deprive the transaction of its normal tax consequence. So a payment of an annuity is treated as a payment of yearly interest. Similarly the transfer of an income earning asset with a duty to sell back may result in the income of the asset being treated as that of the transferor as will the assignment, surrender or waiver of any income. But for these rules the income could be shifted to the transferee, the lender, in whose hands it would be taxable as income just as if it had been interest, but not taxable—and so in effect deductible—so far as the borrower was concerned.

(2) TA 1988, s 787 denies relief in respect of interest paid after 8 June 1976 when a scheme has been made and the sole or main benefit that might be expected to accrue was the obtaining of a reduction in tax liability by means of the relief. This was particularly designed to deal with schemes whereby an individual would pay a substantial sum by way of (allowable) interest in advance and then sell the right to the capital. As a result the court looks at the scheme overall and not at each separate payment of interests.[1]

(3) One should note the decision of the Court of Appeal in *Cairns v MacDiarmid*[2] that interest payable under a scheme was not interest for the purposes of a deduction under these rules.

Simon's Taxes E1.824.

[1] *MacNiven v Westmoreland Investments Ltd* [2001] UKHL 6, [2001] STC 237.
[2] [1983] STC 178.

Averaging

[6.46] There is no general averaging procedure in the UK tax system whereby income is averaged out over a number of years. Rather the system takes the view that income tax is an annual tax and therefore taxes only the income arising in that year. Averaging is thus allowed over the year—but not beyond it.

This is unjust in a number of ways but much less unjust now that the progressive nature of the tax system has been so drastically reduced. However, it remains inequitable for individuals whose income fluctuates around the bottom of the tax scale, since unused personal allowances may not be rolled forward to subsequent years. The arguments against allowing such rolling forward are largely administrative; it would also make the yield from taxes more difficult to predict.

Arguably, the absence of an averaging clause causes injustice to the individual who suddenly receives an exceptional sum which the tax system treats as income. These abnormal receipts are different from the problem of fluctuating incomes from one source not least in that the receipt may be isolated and subjected to special treatment by the tax system.[1]

For many years, averaging has been available for farming income. With effect from 2001–02, averaging is also available in respect of the trade, profession or vocation of creating literary, dramatic, musical, or artistic works or designs.[2]

Simon's Taxes E1.100.

[1] Such as a lease premium: TA 1988, s 34, ITTOIA 2005, s 277 or a chargeable event: ITTOIA 2005, ss 461 & 484.
[2] ITTOIA 2005, s 221.

[6.47] Allowances and reliefs

Averaging for farming and creative works

Computation

[6.47] Averaging is available for two kinds of activities. First, for the profits of the trade of farming.[1] Second, for the profit of the profession or vocation of a "creative artist",[2] which is defined by statute as one where the taxpayer's profits are derived wholly or mainly from "literary, dramatic, musical or artistic works or designs created by the taxpayer personally or if the trade is carried on in partnership, by one or more of the partners personally".[3]

The computational provisions for both categories are identical.[4]

---

[1] ITTOIA 2005, s 221(2)(a) & (b).
[2] ITTOIA 2005, s 221(2)(c).
[3] ITTOIA 2005, s 221(3).
[4] ITTOIA 2005, s 223.

[6.48] The profits of two years are compared. If the profits of either year are nil or less than 70% of the other, the profits may be equalised. Averaging is not permitted in the first or last years of assessment.[1]

EXAMPLE

Tax adjusted profits are:

2007–08 £10,000
2009–10 £50,000
2010–11 £28,000

First alternative:

A claim can be made to average 2007–08 and 2009–10, subjecting £30,000 to tax in each of those years. No claim can, then, be made to average 2009–10 and 2010–11, as the profits of the latter year are greater than 70% of the profit that is subjected to tax for the former year, after the averaging given above.

Second alternative:

A claim can be made to average 2009–10 and 2010–11, subjecting £39,000 to tax in each of those years. No claim can, then, be made to average 2007–08 and 2009–10, as this is barred.

If the profit of one year is between 70% and 75% of that of the other, averaging, as specified above, is not available but a claim can be made to adjust the profits of the two years by shifting from the higher year to the lower year an amount equal to three times the difference between the two, less 3/4 of the higher figure.

EXAMPLE

2003–04 £7,200
2004–05 £10,000

The difference is £2,800 so the amount to be shifted is:
(3 × £2,800) − (75% × £10,000) = £900

Thus, after the claim, assessable profits are:

2003–04 £8,100
2004–05 £9,100

Simon's Taxes B5.170.

1   ITTOIA 2006, s 222(4)(a).

Method of obtaining relief

[6.49] Effect is given to a claim for averaging by the taxpayer adjusting his self-assessment for the later of the pair of years that is being averaged.

The taxpayer adjusts the profits by averaging a pair of years. The profits thus computed for the second (later) year are then brought into the self-assessment for that year. For the preceding year, the taxpayer is required to recompute what his tax liability would have been if the averaged profit had been brought into his self-assessment. The difference between the tax that was actually computed on the self-assessment for the earlier year and the tax which would have been computed had the average profits been taken is then treated as an adjustment to tax payable (or repayable) on the later year's self-assessment. This can, of course, be either an increase in tax payable, or a decrease. Where it is a decrease and this decrease is greater than the total tax remaining payable for the taxpayer's total income in the later year, a repayment arises which is due from the Revenue.[1]

Interest on the additional payment or repayment runs from the normal due date for the payment of tax for the later year.[2]

The relief must be claimed not later than 12 months after 31 January after the end of the second year of assessment; but a further year is given if there is a further adjustment because the second year is the first year of another pair. Claims under other provisions (eg loss relief) can be revoked within the period.[3]

The operation of these provisions can be illustrated:

EXAMPLE

A painter has tax adjusted profits:

2009–10   £40,000
2010–11   £6,000

and other income:

2009–10   £30,000
2010–11   £30,000

He makes a claim under ITTOIA 2005, Pt 2, Ch 16 to average the profits of 2009–10 and 2010–11. Hence, his taxable profit for each of those years is £23,000.

His self-assessment for 2010–11 is:

[6.49] Allowances and reliefs

	£
Painting profits averaged [£40,000 + £6,000] ÷ 2	23,000
Other income	30,000
	53,000
Tax thereon	13,632
Less: relief in respect of 2009–10 arising from averaging £40,000–£23,000 @ 40% (Note 1)	(6,800)
Tax payable 31 January 2012 (Note 2)	7,985

Note:

(1) The relief is given in the 2010–11 self-assessment but is calculated at 2009–10 rates.

(2) The effect of the relief is a reduction in tax payable on the normal due date for 2010–11. Interest on tax repayable runs from that normal due date (31 January 2012) not from the due date for the year in respect of which relief is calculated.

Simon's Taxes B5.170.

[1] TMA 1970, Sch 1B, paras 3, 4.
[2] TMA 1970, s 86.
[3] ITTOIA 2005, s 224(4).

Top slicing

[6.50] When a capital sum is received on the encashment of a non-qualified life policy, a charge to tax arises in the year of encashment, by reference to the excess of the proceeds over the original cost, which is called the "chargeable event".[1] Income and gains made within a non-qualifying assurance fund are subject to corporation tax. Hence, the principle applied in taxing chargeable events is that there is a deemed tax credit at basic rate, so that there is no further charge to tax in so far as the chargeable event is within the basic rate band and the charge on a higher rate taxpayer is 20%, being the difference between higher rate and basic rate.

The tax charge is applied when the capital sum is received. Hence, if the non-qualifying policy has been held for many years, it is very likely that the gain that is brought into the charge to income tax would take even a taxpayer on modest income into higher rates. A rough and ready relief from this effect is provided by the technique of top slicing. This can be illustrated as follows:

EXAMPLE

A chargeable event arises in 2009–10 producing a gain of £20,000 on a policy held for 10 years.
The taxpayer's other income is £35,000, after personal allowance and all reliefs.

Step 1: Top slice	
£20,000 ÷ 10 years =	£2,000
Step 2: Tax on £2,000 when added to other income of £35,000:	
£1,000 @ 20% =	200
£1,000 @ 40% =	400
	600
Step 3: Deduct £2,000 × 20%	(400)
	200
Step 4: Tax is £200 × 10 policy years	£2,000

The top slicing calculation is performed by reference to the single year in which the chargeable event arises. No attempt is made to calculate the tax liability that would arise if the chargeable event were actually spread across the years for which the policy was held.

Simon's Taxes B8.667

---

[1] ITTOIA 2005, s 491.

Tax credits

Integrating tax and benefits

[6.51] The Tax Credits Act 2002 (TCA 2002) introduced two new tax credits, working tax credit and child tax credit.[1] These replaced children's tax credit (a personal allowance given under TA 1988,[2] which worked as an income tax reducer); working families' tax credit and disabled person's tax credit (two credits originally paid by the DSS and viewed by many as social security benefits); and various elements of certain social security benefits representing payments in respect of children and particular types of work.[3]

Working tax credit (WTC) and child tax credit (CTC) are administered entirely by HM Revenue and Customs (HMRC), and such appeals are held before a different chamber (Social Entitlement Chamber) of the Tribunals system.[4]

The Tax Credits Act and its associated regulations (of which there are very many) represent a first real attempt to integrate the tax and benefits system. The measure of income for tax credit purposes is based on the income tax rules[5] and the credits are given by reference to the income tax year.[6]

The new tax credit system also attempts to be responsive to the needs of claimants, so that the first award for a tax year, often referred to as the "initial award",[7] is initially based on the previous year's income but then is revised to current year's income, either when the claimant provides an estimate of that income or when the award is finalised after the tax year-end.[8] Likewise, the personal circumstances, on which the award is based, are those of the current tax year and the award can be changed in-year, or post year-end, to reflect changes in those circumstances.[9] All this makes the tax credit system quite

[6.51] Allowances and reliefs

complicated, and very dependent on claimants keeping HMRC advised of changes to their personal circumstances.

One way in which the tax credits system differs fundamentally from the tax system, however, is the unit of claim. In the case of a man and a woman who are married to each other, or living together as husband and wife, the claim must be made by the couple.[10] Same sex couples, including registered civil partners are, similarly, required to make a joint claim.[11] This means that both individual's incomes are aggregated and, via the means test inherent in tax credits, used to reduce the tax credits award. A single person, including a lone parent, will have their award reduced only to the extent of their one income. To many commentators this is an erosion of independent taxation. In the case of a polygamous marriage the income of all the parties to the marriage are aggregated![12]

---

[1] TCA 2002, s 1(1).
[2] TA 1988, s 257AA.
[3] TCA 2002, s 1(3).
[4] TCA 2002, s 63 and the First-tier Tribunal and Upper Tribunal (Chambers) Order 2008 (SI 2008/2684), arts 5 and 5A.
[5] Tax Credit (Definition and Calculation of Income) Regulations 2002, SI 2002/2006 as amended by SI 2003/732, 2003/2815, 2004/762, 2004/2663, 2005/2919, 2006/745 and 2006/766.
[6] TCA 2002, s 5 and Tax Credits (Income Thresholds and Determination of Rates) Regulations 2002, SI 2002/2008.
[7] The term initial award is not used in the Tax Credits Act but derives from s 14, the section by which the Board make the first award, which is called "Initial decisions". At the start of each new tax year HMRC make "provisional payments" of tax credits based on the last known entitlement for the tax year just finished (something permitted under TCA 2002, s 24(4)) to ensure that no-one has to wait for their payments until their tax credit claim is renewed.
[8] TCA 2002, ss 7, 17 and 18.
[9] TCA 2002, s 6.
[10] TCA 2002, s 3(3)(a).
[11] Civil Partnership Act 2004 (Tax Credits, etc) (Consequential Amendments) Order, SI 2005/2919, *Simons Weekly Tax Intelligence* 2005, p 1779.
[12] TCA 2002, s 3(3)(aa) inserted by SI 2003/742, reg 4(b).

Qualifying conditions for tax credits

[6.52] Tax credit claimants must be aged at least sixteen and "in the United Kingdom".[1] Eligibility for tax credits is also affected by European Law with a differing treatment for child tax credit and working tax credit, the former being a family benefit and the latter being affected by the rules regarding freedom of workers within the EC.[2] For most claimants, however, being in the UK means being physically present here at a time when they are also "ordinarily resident".[3] There are special provisions for those who are subject to immigration control.[4] These rules do mean that those who make a claim to tax credits whilst "in the UK" but then leave the UK for more than eight weeks normally, or twelve weeks in the case of illness of death in the family,[5] must notify that there is a change in the tax credits claiming unit.[6]

To claim working tax credit a claimant without children or disabilities must normally be working at least 30 hours per week and be aged at least 25. If such a claimant is part of a couple these 30 hours cannot be shared between them; one claimant must work at least 30 hours.

If the claimant has children, or is disabled, the requirement is to work only 16 hours per week and the claimant need be only 16 years of age. Such a claimant will also get a 30 hour element added to their award if they work 30 hours, or, if they have children, if they and their partner between them work 30 hours.

Certain claimants who are over 50 years of age, and are returning to work after a period on benefits, are also required to work only 16 hours a week, and receive extra benefit if they work 30 hours or more.

Additional elements of working tax credit are paid to disabled claimants, to lone parents and to couples. There is a childcare element where qualifying childcare costs are incurred and for couples where 16 hours per week are worked by both claimants.[7]

To qualify for child tax credit there is no work requirement. A claimant merely has to be aged at least 16 and "be responsible for one or more children or qualifying young persons".[8] A child is defined as being under the age of 16 and, broadly, a qualifying young person is one between the ages of 16 and 20 and still in full-time education or approved training.[9]

The child tax credit consists of a basic family element paid to those whose income does not rise above a higher threshold of income. A higher family element is paid where one child in the family is under one year old. Then there are separate elements for each child (not age related) and additional elements for children who are disabled. These individual child elements are tapered away after a much lower threshold of income, and will remain in payment only to low income families, or families with a larger number of children and/or substantial childcare costs.

---

[1] TCA 2002, s 3 and Tax Credits (Residence) Regulations 2003, SI 2003/654.
[2] See Inland Revenue Manual TCTM02007.
[3] "Ordinarily resident" here does not mean "ordinarily resident" for direct tax purposes. The concept is one used for social security law. For more on the meaning of "being in the United Kingdom", including the provisions for temporary absences, see Inland Revenue Manual TCTM02003 et seq.
[4] TCA 2002, s 42 and Tax Credits (Immigration) Regulations, SI 2003/653.
[5] For detail on temporary absences for tax credits see Tax Credits (Residence) Regulations 2003, SI 2003/654, reg 4.
[6] See supra, § **2A.11**.
[7] For the detailed rules on entitlement to Working Tax Credit see Working Tax Credit (Entitlement and Maximum Rate) Regulations 2002, SI 2002/2005 as amended by SI 2003/701, 2004/762, 2004/941, 2004/1276, 2004/2663, 2005/681, 2005/769, 2005/2919 and 2006/766.
[8] TCA 2002, s 8(1).
[9] For the detailed rules on entitlement to Child Tax Credit see Child Tax Credit Regulations 2002, SI 2002/2007 as amended by SI 2003/738, 2004/762, 2004/941,

[6.52] Allowances and reliefs

2005/681, 2006/222, 2006/766, 2006/963 and 2006/1163. The upper age limit was amended to 20 years by Child Tax Credit (Amendment) Regulations, SI 2006/222, art 4, *Simons Weekly Tax Intelligence* 2006, p 411.

The calculation of credits

[6.53] The amount of tax credit a claimant will receive is dependent on their income,[1] unless they are in receipt of certain social security benefits in which case the maximum credits are paid.[2] The credits are tapered away as income rises.

Although the tax credit regulations specify separate calculations for the two credits[3] the fact that the threshold for one can be affected by the threshold for the other[4] means that for those entitled to both, a single calculation is the easiest way of doing the calculations, with an order of tapering of credits applied. For those entitled to only one credit then an individual threshold is applied.

As mentioned above, the first tax credit award is based on the previous year's income.[5] So, for example, a single person aged 25 on 6 April 2009 working 35 hours per week and earning in 2009–10 a salary of £9,000 will receive the following amount of tax credit initially in 2009–10:

EXAMPLE

WTC – basic element		£1,890
WTC – 30 hour		775
		2,665
2009–10 income	£9,000	
Threshold	(6,420)	
	2,580 @ 39%	1,006
Total credits due (approx £31.49 per week)		£1,659

Strictly tax credits should be calculated using daily amounts and multiplying the amounts by the number of days in the "relevant period". A "relevant period" is a period for which the maximum rate of tax credits remains the same (except in the case of childcare this is where the elements of the tax credit remain the same[6]). Where there are changes of circumstance new relevant periods begin and the computations get more complicated.

After the end of the tax year the claimant will be invited to renew his tax credit award for the coming year and will have his previous year's award finalised. Assuming that there have been no changes in his or her circumstances (eg getting married or entering into a civil partnership, starting to live with someone as if a married couple or civil partners, becoming disabled, taking responsibility for a child, and so forth) then the previous initial award is finalised by comparing the income used for that year (ie the income from the year before that) with the actual income for the year in question. The first £25,000 increase in income is ignored,[7] so that in this example, if by an extraordinarily fortunate turn of events the final 2008–09 income was, say, £35,000 only £10,000 would be counted in the finalised award. The final tax credits due for 2009–10 will be:

EXAMPLE

WTC – basic element		£1,890
WTC – 30 hour		775
		£2,665
2009–10 income	£10,000	
Threshold	(6,420)	
	3,580 @ 39%	£1,396
Total credits due		1,279
Total credits paid		1,659
Overpayment		£380

Overpayments are collected using a Code of Practice[8] and are generally recovered from future awards. If this is not possible, ie because the claimant is no longer entitled to tax credits, or because the claiming unit has changed (eg the claimant was previously single but has now started a relationship and is making a joint claim with his or her partner), overpayments are generally collected by direct assessment. There is also provision in the Tax Credits Act for payment to be recovered by collection through PAYE, but this has never been implemented.[9] If in the above example the claimants' income had decreased than an underpayment would have arisen. This is paid in a lump sum at the end of the tax year.[10]

If a claimant is entitled to both tax credits the order of taper of the credits is as follows:

(1) The non-childcare elements of working tax credit first.
(2) Then the childcare element of working tax credit (WTCC).
(3) Then the individual elements of child tax credit.
(4) Finally the family element of child tax credit (with a different, and lower, rate of taper applying).

The example below shows a computation in the case of a claim for both credits.

EXAMPLE

Martin and Mary have two children aged 5 and 7. Both parents work 16 hours a week. They incur qualifying childcare costs of £50 per week and in 2009–10 their total tax credits income is £19,000. Their income in 2008–09 was £18,000. Their final award for 2009–10 will be:

WTC – basic element		£1,890
WTC – couple		1,860
WTC – 30 hour		775
WTC – childcare, £50 × 52 × 80%		2,080
CTC – child element 2,235 × 2		4,470
		£11,075
2008–09 Income*	£18,000	

[6.53] Allowances and reliefs

Threshold	(6,420)	
	11,580 @ 39%	£4,516
Credits due (£4,470 of CTC and the balance in WTC)		6,559
CTC – family element (tapered only if income exceeds £50,000²)		545
Total credits due		£7,104

[*] the 2008–09 income figure is used in the finalised award as the 2008–09 income figures is not greater by more than £25,000.

---

[1] TCA 2002, s 7. For useful practical advice on Tax Credits and their calculation see Liz Lathwood: "Tax Credits—renewals, rewards and overpayments", Tax Adviser, March 2004 and Liz Lathwood: "Tax Credits—where are we now?" Tax Adviser, September 2004, pp 11–14.

[2] TCA 2002, s 7(2).

[3] See Tax Credits (Income Thresholds and Determination of Rates) Regulations 2002, SI 2002/2008, regs 7, 8.

[4] See Tax Credits (Income Thresholds and Determination of Rates) Regulations 2002, SI 2002/2008, reg 8(3), Step 4.

[5] For 2003–04 claims to tax credits the previous year was deemed to be 2001–02, so that claims could be set up before the start of the tax year (see Tax Credits (Claims) (Transitional Provision) (Amendment) Order 2002, SI 2002/2158).

[6] See Tax Credits (Income Thresholds and Determination of Rates) Regulations 2002, SI 2002/2008, regs 7(2), 8(2).

[7] Tax Credits (Income Thresholds and Determination of Rates) Regulations 2002, SI 2002/2008, reg 5. For tax years before 2006–07 the amount prescribed under this regulation was £2,500. The considerable increase to £25,000, announced in the December 2005 pre-Budget report, was in response to general criticism about the high level of overpayments in the tax credits system. It was anticipated that the increase in the level of disregard, by effectively removing the cause of income-related overpayments, would in time reduce the total volume of overpayments by one-third.

[8] Code of Practice 26 *What happens if we have paid you too much tax credit?* and see Tax Credits (Payments by the Board) Regulations 2002, SI 2002/2173, reg 12A as inserted by Tax Credits (Miscellaneous Amendments) Regulations 2004, SI 2004/762, reg 18. The Code of Practice has itself been the subject of much controversy in the way in which overpayments arising from official error are collected. Section 28(1), (5) of the Tax Credits Act 2002 gives HMRC complete discretion to decide whether or not overpayments must be repaid. COP26 states that an overpayment arising from official error will not be recovered if the claimant could 'reasonably' have thought that their payments were correct. There is no independent right of appeal against HMRC's decision on the matter. This 'reasonableness test' has been widely criticised on the grounds that the lack of appeal rights gives HMRC the right to be judge and jury in its own cause. In addition, the test is only applied at the instance of the claimant; if HMRC's computer identifies an overpayment, it begins collection automatically and it is up to the claimant to object. Both these factors have been cited by representative bodies as contrary to natural justice and probably unlawful in consequence.

[9] TCA 2002, s 29.
[10] TCA 2002, s 30.

The calculation of tax credits income

[6.54] As stated earlier one of the hopes of the new tax credits system was to move towards an integrated tax and benefits system (see supra, § **6.51**) and, to that extent, to have an income measure that was very similar to that used for tax. Instead of just using the taxable figure of income in all cases, however, tax credits law introduces a new set of regulations to measure tax credit income.[1]

Part of the need for these arose from the fact that if the claim is made by a couple (or by a polygamous unit), both (or all) incomes have to be aggregated.[2] Other reasons for having a separate set of rules is that not all tax reliefs were deemed suitable for tax credits (carry back of losses, top-slicing relief on chargeable event gains, to name but two), and it was thought necessary to include all worldwide income, not just that taxable in the UK.[3]

There are also anti-avoidance-type provisions to stop claimants inflating their tax credits claim by depriving themselves of income,[4] or by not applying for income to which they would be entitled,[5] or by providing services to other persons at less than full earnings.[6]

In many cases, therefore, detailed study of the income regulations will be necessary to ensure that a tax credits income figure is correct. It is beyond the scope of this book to go into these regulations in detail but apart from the differences already mentioned above readers may wish to note that relief for trading losses is quite different under tax credits (only sideways and carry forward relief is possible, but this does go against income of the spouse as well as income of the lossmaker[7]), there is no averaging of profits of farmers and creative artists,[8] many common benefits in kind (such as living accommodation, medical insurance, etc) are left out of employment income—although car and car fuel benefits are included,[9] and reliefs for items like Gift Aid and pension contributions are given as a deduction from the aggregated total income of the claiming unit.[10] It should be noted that Gift Aid relief cannot be carried back for tax credits purposes even though it can be so relieved for income tax.[11]

[1] Tax Credit (Definition and Calculation of Income) Regulations 2002, SI 2002/2006 as amended by SI 2003/732, 2003/2815, 2004/762, 2004/2663, 2005/2919, 2006/745, 2006/766.
[2] See Tax Credit (Definition and Calculation of Income) Regulations 2002, SI 2002/2006, reg 3(1) as amended by SI 2003/732.
[3] See Tax Credit (Definition and Calculation of Income) Regulations 2002, SI 2002/2006, reg 3(4), (5), (5A) and (6) as amended by SI 2003/732 and 2003/2815.
[4] Tax Credit (Definition and Calculation of Income) Regulations 2002, SI 2002/2006, reg 15.
[5] Tax Credit (Definition and Calculation of Income) Regulations 2002, SI 2002/2006, reg 16 as amended by SI 2004/762.
[6] Tax Credit (Definition and Calculation of Income) Regulations 2002, SI 2002/2006, reg 17.

[6.54] Allowances and reliefs

[7] See Tax Credit (Definition and Calculation of Income) Regulations 2002, SI 2002/2006, reg 3(1), Step 4 as amended by SI 2003/732 and 2003/2815.
[8] Tax Credit (Definition and Calculation of Income) Regulations 2002, SI 2002/2006, reg 6.
[9] See Tax Credit (Definition and Calculation of Income) Regulations 2002, SI 2002/2006, reg 4 as amended by SI 2003/732, 2003/2815 and 2004/762 for the detail on employment income included in the tax credit claim.
[10] Tax Credit (Definition and Calculation of Income) Regulations 2002, SI 2002/2006, reg 3(7) as amended by SI 2003/732, 2003/2815 and 2006/766.
[11] Tax Credits (Definition and Calculation of Income) Regulations 2002, SI 2002/2006 reg 3(7)(b).

7

Employment income

Charging base of employment income	PARA 7.02
Earnings of UK resident and domiciled employee	PARA 7.04
Earnings of employee resident or domiciled outside the UK	PARA 7.06
Office or employment	PARA 7.08
Employment income: The causation test	PARA 7.17
Types of income	PARA 7.23
Compensation payments for claims against employers	PARA 7.30
Benefits in kind—general	PARA 7.40
Particular benefits	PARA 7.48
Employee share schemes	PARA 7.77
Enterprise management incentives	PARA 7.82
Employee share ownership plans	PARA 7.95
Employees earnings £8,500 per annum or more and directors	PARA 7.99
The benefits code	PARA 7.102
Particular benefits in the benefits code	PARA 7.110
Expenses and deductions from earnings	PARA 7.122
Pay as you earn	PARA 7.144
PAYE and self-assessment	PARA 7.150

[7.01] Income tax is charged under the employment income provisions of ITEPA 2003 (Parts 2 to 7) on "general earnings" and "specific employment income" from any office or employment.[1] Pension income and social security income is taxed under Parts 9 and 10 of ITEPA 2003.[2] It may also be extended to certain other categories eg workers supplied by agencies.[3]

"Earnings" in relation to an employment means "any salary, wages or fee", any gratuity or other profit or incidental benefit of any kind obtained by the employee if it is money or money's worth" or "anything else that constitutes an emolument of the employment".[4] Case law makes it clear that not all payments from employers to employees fall within this definition and that some payments from non-employers do.[5] The test is one of causation; an emolument is a payment in return for acting as or being an employee.[6]

"Money's worth" is defined[7] as something which is "of direct monetary value to the employee or capable of being converted into money or something which is of direct monetary value to the employee".

Employees earning £8,500 a year or more and directors are, in general, taxable on the cost of a benefit provided by an employer, not solely its money's worth.[8]

Expenses are deductible from employment income if they are incurred necessarily in the performance of the duties of this office or employment and, except in the case of travel, either wholly and exclusively so incurred or satisfy a test introduced in 1998 relating to travel to or from a temporary workplace.[9] In December 2003 the Revenue published a useful article on the treatment of expenses and benefits received by employees working at home, and what expense deductions might be allowable for such "teleworkers".[10]

[7.01] Employment income

Capital allowances may be claimed by the employee in respect of machinery and plant, other than motor cars, if incurred necessarily.[11]

Statute provides deduction for certain expenses but ITEPA 2003, s 329 restricts the deduction by saying that it "may not exceed the earnings from which it is deductible". A loss is arithmetically impossible.[12] Earnings paid by the employer are subject to a system of deduction of tax at source—the PAYE system.[13] Whether subject to that system or not, income is assessed on a current year basis. It is taxed when it is received or becomes due, whichever is the earlier; it is not, since 1989, backdated to the year in which the service was performed.[14]

Where income falls within the charge under the employment income rules of ITEPA 2003, it cannot be charged under another Schedule. In *Ainslie v Buckley*,[15] the Special Commissioner rejected the approach taken by a taxpayer in completing his self-assessment tax return, under which he treated part of the payments he received from his employer as Schedule A income for the use of his office at home, against which he attempted to put deductions appropriate to Schedule A.

An employee may receive a payment made by his employer in respect of a right he has under statute. The source is then the statutory right and not the employment; hence, the receipt is not within the employment income charge.[16]

Simon's Taxes E4.4.

---

[1] ITEPA 2003, s 6. Until 1922 what was then described as Schedule E was confined to income from a *public* office or employment. A director of a company held a public office. Overseas remuneration from non-public office or employment remained in Schedule D, Case V until FA 1956, s 10.

[2] A pension is a taxable subject matter distinct from the office or employment—per Viscount Simon LC, in *Tilley v Wales* [1943] AC 386 at 392, 25 TC 136 at 149. Pensions in respect of other overseas service now come within Part 9 of ITEPA 2003 if the source is foreign. A reduction of 10% is applied to foreign pensions by ITEPA 2003, s 575(2)(a) and TA 1988, s 65. See *Esslemont v Marshall* [1996] STC 1086, CA for an unsuccessful attempt to argue that pension payments were not subject to what was then Schedule E of TA 1988.

[3] ITEPA 2003, ss 7, 44 and 48; on which see Revenue Manual EIM 11815 and ESM 2000 et seq.

[4] ITEPA 2003, s 62. A perquisite, a term used in the original Schedule E legislation, is merely a casual emolument additional to regular salary or wages: per Lord Guest in *Owen v Pook* [1970] AC 244 at 225, [1969] 2 All ER 1 at 5.

[5] Infra, § **7.40**.

[6] Per Lord Radcliffe in *Hochstrasser v Mayes* [1960] AC 376 at 389, 392; the test goes beyond one of simple reward for services but must still be referable to the performance of duties under the contract.

[7] By ITEPA 2003, s 62(3).

[8] Chapters 3 and 6 to 10 of Part 3 of ITEPA 2003 (see infra, § **7.89**).

[9] ITEPA 2003, ss 328 et seq (see infra, § **7.111**).

[10] Tax Bulletin Issue 68, December 2003, p 1068.

[11] CAA 2001, s 15(1)(i). The availability of capital allowances for an employee is severely limited: see ss 20(1) and (2), 36(2), 251 and 262. Prior to 2002–03, it was

possible for an employee to obtain capital allowances for a vehicle he provided for the purposes of his employment or office. The claim was under CAA 2001, s 80, which was repealed with effect from 6 April 2002 by FA 2001, ss 59 and 110. The allowance available for an employee in respect of motoring costs has its own, separate, code, see infra, § **7.120**.

[12] See TA 1988, s 380 (see supra, §§ **6.15** and **6.30** and infra, § **7.111**).
[13] See ITEPA 2003, s 682 et seq (see infra, § **7.133**). On the identity of the employer when an employee is seconded see *Caldicott v Varty* [1976] 3 All ER 329, [1976] STC 418.
[14] ITEPA 2003, Sch 7, para 8(4) (see infra, § **7.22**).
[15] [2002] STC (SCD) 132.
[16] *Mimtec v IRC* [2001] STC [SCD] 101. See also dicta of Lord Wolfe in *Mairs v Haughey* [1993] STC 569 at 577 and of Lord Radcliffe in *Hochstrasser v Mayes* (1957) 38 TC 673 at 707.

Charging base of employment income

Income taxable

[7.02] For charging base of employment income generally see ITEPA 2003, ss 6, 7 and 10. The operation of the tax charge under the employment income Parts of ITEPA 2003 is set out in Chapters 3 to 6 of Part 2. What were the previous "Cases of Schedule E" are replaced by specific charging provisions in Chapters 4 and 5. These cover the charge on "general earnings" which is limited according to the residence status of the recipient. The detail is summarised in the Table below with the section numbers being those of Chapters 4 and 5 of ITEPA 2003. The charge on "specific employment income" (eg termination payments and share related income) depends on the terms of the relevant provision.[1]

Chapter 3 of ITEPA also sets out how to calculate the "net taxable earnings" (taxable general earnings less deductions) and "net taxable specific income" (specific employment income less deductions).[2]

Duties performed wholly in UK	Duties performed partly in UK, partly abroad	Duties performed wholly abroad	Person domiciled in the United Kingdom OR employer resident in the United Kingdom

1 Resident in UK *and* ordinarily resident in UK

[7.02] Employment income

	Duties performed wholly in UK	Duties performed partly in UK, partly abroad	Duties performed wholly abroad	Person domiciled in the United Kingdom OR employer resident in the United Kingdom
	All earnings (ss 15, 21)	(a) All earnings of UK duties *plus* (b) All earnings of duties abroad (ss 15, 21)	All earnings (ss 15, 21)	In UK
2 Resident in UK but *not* ordinarily resident in UK Abroad				
	All earnings (s 25)	← →	Remittances (s 26)	3 Not resident in UK
	All earnings (s 27)	← →	Outside scope of UK tax	Person domiciled abroad AND employer resident abroad
4 Resident in UK *and* ordinarily resident in UK				
In UK	All earnings (s 21)			
		5 Resident in UK but *not* ordinarily resident in UK		
Abroad	All earnings (s 21) Remittances (s 22)			
	All earnings (s 25)	← →	Remittances (s 26)	6 Not resident in UK
	All earnings (s 27)	← →	Outside scope of UK tax	

From April 2005, a new pensioner can elect to defer the receipt of his state retirement pension.[3] Anyone who makes this election receives a one-off lump sum payment.[4] This lump sum is taxed, but does not count in calculating the reduction in age-related personal allowance (see supra, § **6.06**).[5]

Simon's Direct Tax Service E4.102.

---

[1] Infra, § **7.36**.

[2] ITEPA 2003, s 9–12
[3] Pensions Act 2004.
[4] SSCBA 1992, s 55 & Sch 5.
[5] F(No 2)A 2005, s 7(2)(b).

Definitions

[7.03] *Place of performance of duties.*[1] In determining whether duties are performed wholly outside the UK, duties performed in the UK but which are purely incidental to the performance of duties abroad are ignored.[2] Certain duties are declared to be performed in the UK such as certain duties on board ships and aircraft and certain employments of a public nature under the Crown and payable out of public revenue.[3] These rules are varied when one comes to the deductions for seafarers' earnings.[4]

Simon's Taxes E4.102, 111–116.

[1] See *Taylor v Provan* [1974] 1 All ER 1201 at 1208, [1974] STC 168 at 175, *Barson v Airey* (1925) 10 TC 609.
[2] ITEPA 2003, ss 39, TA 1988, s 335, *Robson v Dixon* [1972] 3 All ER 671, [1975] BTR 466, *Taylor v Provan* [1973] 2 All ER 65 at 74.
[3] ITEPA 2003, ss 25, 27, 28, 40 and 304, *Graham v White* [1972] 1 All ER 1159, 48 TC 163.
[4] ITEPA 2003, s 378 et seq.

Earnings of UK resident and domiciled employee

[7.04] Where the employee is resident, ordinarily resident and domiciled in the UK, statute[1] charges general earnings which are received in the tax year. The earnings are chargeable in full wherever the duties are performed.

Sections 16 and 17 of ITEPA 2003 give the meaning of earnings "for" a tax year for the purposes of this Chapter and deal with the situation where earnings are for a year in which the employment is not held. Sections 18 and 19 give the rules for determining when money and non-money earnings are treated as received for the purposes of this Chapter.

Simon's Taxes E4.112.

[1] ITEPA 2003, s 15.

100% reduction for seafarers

[7.05] The 100% relief for earnings arising from duties performed overseas during a "qualifying period" was abolished for qualifying periods after 17 March 1998 except for seafarers.[1]

[7.05] Employment income

The conditions to be satisfied for seafarers to obtain this relief[2] are described in the 1997–98 edition of Tiley and Collison's UK Tax Guide §§ **6.05–6.08**, except that a qualifying period for a seafarer permits a period in the UK of up to 183 days, with a fraction of one-half being applied for the cumulative test.

Simon's Taxes E4.123.

---

[1] FA 1998, s 63.
[2] ITEPA 2003 in Chapter 6 of Part 5, ss 378 et seq.

Earnings of employee resident or domiciled outside the UK

[7.06] Part 2 of ITEPA deals with employees who are either:

(a)   resident and ordinarily resident, but not domiciled in the UK
(b)   resident but not ordinarily resident in the UK, or
(c)   not resident in the UK.

Section 21 charges general earnings of employees who are resident and ordinarily resident but not domiciled in the UK but only to the extent that earnings are not "chargeable overseas earnings". Chargeable overseas earnings are broadly earnings for a year in which the employee is resident and ordinarily resident but not domiciled in the UK, where the employment is with a foreign employer and where the duties are performed wholly outside the UK.[1]

Section 25 charges general earnings of employees who are resident but not ordinarily resident in the UK but only in respect of duties performed in the UK. Such a person is not taxable under this section in respect of duties wholly performed outside the UK; although he may come within s 26.

Where the duties of a single employment are performed both in and outside the UK, it is necessary to apportion the emoluments to determine the quantum that is attributable to UK duties and assessable under s 25 and the quantum on which the tax charge only arises on a remittance under s 26. Revenue practice is to accept time apportionment, based on the number of days worked abroad and the number of days in the UK.[2]

In such a case, the Revenue interpretation of the judgment in *Sterling Trust Ltd v IRC*[3] is that remittances of income to the UK that relate to the emoluments paid should be treated as arising firstly from the amount assessable under s 25 for that year. Hence, the s 26 assessment is restricted to the excess of the aggregate over the s 25 assessment.[4]

Simon's Taxes E4.115.

---

[1] ITEPA 2003, s 23.
[2] Inland Revenue Statement of Practice SP5/84 para 2.
[3] (1925) 12 TC 868.
[4] Inland Revenue Statement of Practice SP5/84 para 5.

[7.07] (1) Section 22 of ITEPA 2003, Chapter 5 charges general earnings of an employee who is resident and ordinarily resident but not domiciled in the UK but only to the extent that the earnings are "chargeable overseas earnings".[1] Section 26 charges general earnings of an employee who is resident but not ordinarily resident in the UK but only to the extent that they are not in respect of duties performed in the UK. Section 27 charges general earnings of an employee who is not resident in the UK but only in respect of duties performed in the UK. Under all three sections the remittance basis applies.

When there is a single contract of employment for duties that are performed partly in the UK and partly outside the UK, the normal basis applied for dividing the emoluments is by reference to the number of days worked abroad and the number of days worked in the UK.[2] This apportionment can, however, be defeated by the particular facts in a particular instance, such as, for example, where the number of hours worked per day differs or the degree of responsibility assumed is significantly greater according to the location of the performance of the duties. Revenue practice is to regard the liability under the remittance basis as limited to the excess of earnings remitted to the UK (plus benefits enjoyed in the UK) over the amount assessable under the received basis.[3]

(2) Sections 29 and 30 of ITEPA 2003 give the meaning of earnings "for" a tax year for the purposes of this Chapter and deal with the situation where earnings are for a year in which the employment is not held. Sections 31 to 34 give the rules for determining when money and non-money earnings are treated as received or remitted for the purposes of this Chapter.

Where a non-UK domiciled person works for a foreign employer and renders services both here and abroad it may well be worth his while to have two separate contracts of employment, the one for work in the UK (charged under s 21) and the other for work overseas—charged on the remittance basis. If the earnings for the latter are unreasonably inflated, ITEPA 2003, s 24 restricts the amount chargeable under s 23.

One must not overlook the effect of double tax treaties on one who is not resident in the UK; these may grant exemption from the employment income charge.[4]

Simon's Taxes E4.116.

[1] ITEPA 2003, s 23 and supra, § **7.06**.
[2] Statement of practice SP 5/84
[3] SP 5/84, para 5. See also infra, § **35.12**.
[4] Infra, § **37.12**.

Office or employment

[7.08] The employment income provisions of ITEPA tax income from an office or employment, both of which words are further defined.[1] These definitions are derived from case law. An office denotes "a subsisting, permanent, substantive position which has an existence independent of the person who fills it, and which is filled in succession by successive holders".[2] Examples include a director of a company,[3] even if he has a contract of employment and owns all the shares, a trustee or executor,[4] a company auditor,[5] a National Health service consultant[6] and a local land charges registrar.[7] By contrast in *Edwards v Clinch*[8] a person appointed to act as an inspector at a public inquiry did not hold an office since the post had no existence independent of him; there was neither continuity nor permanence. The Court of Appeal in that case also held that an office and an employment were not mutually exclusive.[9] It is not necessary that an office should be constituted by some enactment or other instrument nor that it should have any public relevance; however, an office is more than just a job description.[10] It thus seems that the essence of an office is the independence of its existence from the identity of the present holder.[11] It is from this element of independence that the element of continuity may be said to derive.[12]

An employment was once described as a post and as something "more or less analogous to an office"[13] but modern cases take a different tack and equate employment with a contract of service. If the arrangement under which sums are paid to a taxpayer is one for services, it falls outside the employment income provisions. The test is whether the person performing the services is in business on his own account.[14] In making this judgment one cannot gain much assistance by looking at the facts of previous cases and comparing them to see what facts are common, what are different and what particular weight was given to the facts which are common. The approach is stated succinctly by Lightman J:

> There is no one test which is conclusive for determining into which category a particular engagement falls. There are a number of badges of one or other of the relationships and these badges depending on the context may carry greater or lesser weight. The proper course for the court in each case . . . is to form an overall view giving due weight to the relative significance of the various badges in the particular context.[15]

It is open to a fact-finding tribunal to conclude that a person is in business on his own account when all that he provides are personal services.[16] A ship's master, a chauffeur and a reporter on the staff of the newspaper are all employed under a contract of service and so come within the employment income provisions whereas a ship's pilot, a taxi-man and a newspaper contributor are employed (by the owner, the hirer or the newspaper) under a contract for services[17] and so do not. A consultant under the National Health Service is taxed under the employment income provisions in respect of that employment or office whether the arrangement is whole time or part time.[18] Again, a teacher working whole time for a local education authority is taxed as an employee.[19] In the Revenue's view, an actor now falls within the employment income provisions and so within the PAYE system.[20] By contrast a person under contract to provide clerking services to a set of barristers' chambers was held to be an independent contractor on the particular facts.[21] If no services are to be performed, the contract is not one of employment; however, the remuneration may be brought within employment income by virtue of it arising from "an office".[22]

North Sea divers are excluded from the employment income provisions.[23]

Office or employment [7.08]

Whether a person is an employee or a self-employed person is a question of fact.[24] The fact that the contract is illegal cannot of itself convert an employee into a self-employed person. Problems sometimes arise if an employee is seconded to work for another firm. Where the employee is seconded to work for a charity on a temporary basis there is express provision allowing the employer to deduct the costs as if the employee had remained working for the employer.[25]

Simon's Taxes E4.201, 202.

---

[1] ITEPA 2003, ss 4, 5 and Note 1 of Annex 2. The distinction between office and employment can be crucial. Thus by TA 1988, s 291(2) a person is connected with a company, and so disqualified from holding shares under the EIS scheme if he is an employee and not, apparently, if he holds an office. One should, however, note that a director is, subject to s 291A, expressly disqualified by s 291.

[2] Rowlatt J in *Great Western Rly Co v Bater* [1920] 3 KB 266 at 274, 8 TC 231 at 235. See generally Napier [1981] Industrial Law Journal 52 and Ward [1989] BTR 281 at 283–295. This is not a "complete" definition: per Lord Atkin in *McMillan v Guest* [1942] AC 561 at 564, 24 TC 190 at 201.

[3] *Lee v Lee's Air Farming Ltd* [1961] AC 12, [1960] 3 All ER 420, PC. The posts of director and managing director may be separate offices *Goodwin v Brewster* (1951) 32 TC 80.

[4] *Dale v IRC* [1951] 2 All ER 517, 34 TC 468, *A-G v Eyres* [1909] 1 KB 723.

[5] *Ellis v Lucas* [1966] 2 All ER 935, 43 TC 276.

[6] *Mitchell and Edon v Ross* [1961] 3 All ER 49, 40 TC 11.

[7] *Ministry of Housing and Local Government v Sharp* [1970] 2 QB 223, [1969] 3 All ER 225.

[8] [1981] STC 617; duties of a public nature did not necessarily make the post an office.

[9] [1980] STC 438. As might be inferred from the dictum of Lord Normand in *Dale v IRC* [1954] AC 11 at 26.

[10] Per Scott J in *McMenamin v Diggles* [1991] STC 419 at 430, 431.

[11] Ward [1989] BTR 281 at 287.

[12] Ward [1989] BTR 281 at 294.

[13] Per Rowlatt J in *Davies v Braithwaite* [1931] 2 KB 628 at 635; see Ward [1989] BTR 281 at 295–300.

[14] *Andrews v King* [1991] STC 481. For an unsuccessful attempt by a taxpayer to argue that a catering business constituted a Schedule E employee, see *McManus v Griffiths* [1997] STC 1089.

[15] *Barnett v Brabyn* [1996] STC 716 at 724c, approving *Hall v Lorimer* [1994] STC 23.

[16] *Hall v Lorimer* [1994] STC 23, CA.

[17] *Stevenson, Jordan and Harrison Ltd v Macdonald and Evans* [1952] 1 TLR 101 at 111, per Lord Denning (this case concerned copyright not tax). On what is a contract of service, see also *Ready-Mixed Concrete (South East) Ltd v Ministry of Pensions* [1968] 2 QB 497, [1968] 1 All ER 433 and *Hall v Lorimer* [1994] STC 23, CA.

[18] *Mitchell and Edon v Ross* [1959] 3 All ER 341, 40 TC 11 (Upjohn J) and [1960] 2 All ER 218, 40 TC 11, CA; [1961] 3 All ER 49, 40 TC 11, HL.

[19] *Fuge v McClelland* (1956) 36 TC 571.

[7.08] Employment income

[20] See HC Written Answer, 11 June 1990; *Simon's Tax Intelligence* 1990, p 541. On practical application of rules, see ICAEW Memorandum TR 796; *Simon's Tax Intelligence* 1990, p 607. On deductibility of Agents' fees see Inland Revenue press release, 6 July 1990 and FA 1990, s 77 adding ITEPA 2003, ss 328 and 352.

[21] *McMenamin v Diggles* [1991] STC 419.

[22] *Clayton v Lavender* (1965) 42 TC 607. It is on the basis that Schedule E charges "an office", that payments by an Oxford or Cambridge college to its fellows are held to be subject to Schedule E, despite it being specifically provided that a college fellowship has no duties whatsoever attached to it.

[23] ITEPA 2003, s 6(5) and TA 1988, s 314; see **Simon's Taxes E5.701**.

[24] *Cooke v Blacklaws* [1985] STC 1 (the illegality of the arrangement was a factor, but not a conclusive one). The Revenue Manual SE 535–704 contains many pages of guidance to inspectors as to what is meant by these terms. On instruction to inspectors to watch out for suspect Schedule D Cases but to handle them with care see SE 786–787; on list of possible questions, which must not be issued in writing, see SE 900.

[25] TA 1988, s 86. From 1 April 1997, relief under this provision is not available for the salary costs of an employee seconded to an educational establishment, unless the establishment is a charity: s 86(3).

Managed service company

[7.09] From 2001–02 to 2006–07 inclusive, the, so called, "IR35 rules"[1] had the effect that an intermediary company (or partnership) was obliged to account for PAYE as if the fees it had received had been paid directly to an individual. The test applied to decide whether or not the IR35 rules operated was to postulate a contract between the end client and the worker supplied by the intermediate company and to decide whether such a postulated contract would be a contract of employment.[2]

From 6 April 2007, the "IR35 rules" are replaced[3] by new provisions for a "managed service company" (see infra, § **8.27**).

[1] ITEPA 2003, ss 48–61 (formerly FA 2000, Sch 12).

[2] ITEPA 2003, s 49(1)(*c*).

[3] ITEPA 2003, s 48(2)(*aa*) inserted by FA 2007, Sch 3, para 3 dissapplies Chapter 8 (ss 48–61) whenever the conditions for "a managed service company" are applied. The provisions for "managed service companies" FA 2007, Sch 3, have effect from 6 April 2007: FA 2007, s 25(2). The "IR35 rules" are, thus, not revoked. It is technically possible for a company to fall within the IR35 rules but not within the managed service company rules, however that is, in practice, unlikely.

An employment and a profession

[7.10] A taxpayer may have more than one source of income; the existence of a day-time employment is not incompatible with the co-existence of a trade or profession.[1] Moreover the activity or skill which is used in the employment may be the same as that used in the trade or profession. So a doctor may be a part-time employee of a Hospital Board and carry on a part-time private practice, his pay under the former source will be taxed as employment income while that from the latter will be taxed as trading income.[2] Similarly a barrister with a day-time income as trading income may also have evening employment as a lecturer within the employment income provisions.[3]

Simon's Taxes E4.202.

[1] Per Rowlatt J in *Davies v Braithwaite* [1931] 2 KB 628 at 635, 18 TC 198 at 203.
[2] The tax law rewrite committee has chosen the phrase "trading income" to encompass income arising from a trade, a profession or a vocation: see ITTOIA 2005, ss 3 & 24.
[3] *Sidey v Phillips* [1987] STC 87.

Employment or self-employment?

[7.11] Where a person holds an office he can only be taxed under the employment income provisions so that a series of offices is just that and is not a profession.[1] However, in relation to a series of employments one can discern two quite distinct approaches. In *Davies v Braithwaite*[2] the taxpayer was Miss Lilian Braithwaite, the actress. Between 1924 and 1928 she acted in the UK in a number of plays, films and wireless programmes. She also recorded for the gramophone. She had separate contracts for each play and wireless appearance. She also appeared in a play on Broadway, New York. The performance in New York being completely outside the UK, she argued that it was an employment so that she would be taxable at that time only on such sums, if any, as she remitted to the UK. The Revenue argued that it was merely one engagement in her profession as an actress, a profession carried on inside and outside the UK so that she was taxable on an arising basis under Schedule D, Case II. The Revenue won; Rowlatt J said:[3]

> Where one finds a method of earning a livelihood which does not contemplate the obtaining of a post and staying in it, but essentially contemplates a series of engagements and moving from one to the other . . . then each of those engagements could not be considered an employment, but is a mere engagement in the course of exercising a profession, and every profession and every trade does involve the making of successive engagements and successive contracts and, in one sense of the word, employments.

This test, by starting with the general scheme of the taxpayer's earnings and then seeing where a particular contract fits, is totally different from the approach of Pennycuick V-C, in *Fall v Hitchen*.[4] In this case a professional ballet dancer was held to be liable to tax under Schedule E in respect of a contract with one particular company because that contract looked at in isolation was one of service and not one for services. Pennycuick V-C, held that this concluded the matter.[5]

On this divergence two points should be noted. The first is that in *Davies v Braithwaite* neither Rowlatt J nor counsel for the Revenue seems to have been concerned with the question whether the contract was one of service or one for services.[6] The second is that the two approaches may not be quite so far apart since some cases suggest that one of the factors in determining the classification of the contract is whether that person carries on business on his own account.[7]

Davies v Braithwaite was resurrected in *Hall v Lorimer*.[8] Here the Court of Appeal held that while the distinction between a contract of service and one for services was critical this did not of itself enable one to tell whether the particular contract should be classified as one or the other. In deciding that a vision mixer who worked for 80 days over a four-year period all on one- or two-day contracts was taxable under Schedule D rather than under the employment income provisions, Nolan LJ cited both *Davies v Braithwaite* and *Fall v Hitchen*. Meanwhile one should note that in *Fall v Hitchen* the one contract in issue was for rehearsal time plus 22 weeks. The approach of the Court of Appeal does not sit easily with that of the House of Lords in either *IRC v Brander and Cruickshank* or *Mitchell and Edon v Ross*.

While the best starting point is to ask whether the person is in business on his or her own account this may, on some facts, be little more than a way of reformulating the question. There is no infallible criterion[9] and there can be many borderline cases. One may note that in *Davies v Braithwaite* neither Rowlatt J nor counsel for the Revenue seems to have been concerned with the question whether the contract was one of service or one for services.[10]

In determining whether a contract is one of service or one for services a useful rule of thumb is whether the taxpayer gets a salary or is paid so much an hour for work actually done. The traditional test was one of control but that is not a sufficient condition of a contract of service. One must now consider whether he provides his own equipment, or hires his own helpers, what degree of financial risk he runs, what degree of responsibility he has and how far he has an opportunity to profit from sound management.[11]

The question whether a contract is one of service or for services appears to be one of law so far as the identification of the criteria is concerned but the balancing process of applying those criteria seems to be left to the Commissioners as a question of fact.[12]

The Revenue have waged campaigns to bring many people within the employment income provisions by threatening to make the payer responsible for the payment of income tax under the PAYE system.

HMRC Internal Instructions[13] give ample evidence of the Revenue attitude. The HMRC employment status manual, and its supplement issued in mid 2001, has been extensively criticised. The coverage in the manual of *Barnet v Brabyn*[14] is highly selective. Important cases where the taxpayer has won his argument for self-employment are omitted. These include *BSM (1257) Ltd v Secretary of State for Social Services*,[15] where driving instructors were held to be self-employed largely as a consequence of a declaration of a self-employment; *McMenamin v Diggles*[16] in which a barrister's clerk was held to be self-employed and *Swan (Hellenic) Ltd v Secretary of State for Social Services*,[17] where the finding of self-employed rested on a declaration by the parties as to who would except liability for tax and national insurance.[18]

The "IR35 rules" require one to decide whether if there were a contract between the end client and the worker supplied by the intermediate contract that postulated contract would be a contract of employment.

Office or employment [7.11]

Cases where the Special Commissioner has held that the postulated contract is one of employment are *Battersby v Campbell*,[19] *F S Consulting Ltd v McCaul*,[20] *Synaptek v Young*[21], *Future Online v Faulds*[22], *Usetech Ltd v Young*[23] and *Dragonfly Consulting v R & C Commrs*[24] and upheld at the High Court reported at [2008] EWHC 2113 (Ch). Cases where the taxpayer company established where the postulated contract did not have the hallmark of employment are *Lime-IT Ltd v Justin*,[25] *Tilbury Consulting v Gittins*,[26] and *Ansell Computer Services Ltd v Richardson*.[27]

Simon's Taxes E4.206.

---

[1] *IRC v Brander and Cruickshank*, (see infra, §§ 7.12 and 7.15); compare *Marsh v IRC* [1943] 1 All ER 199, 29 TC 120. By extra-statutory concession A37, however, emoluments received for the office of auditor or as a director of a company, are subject to assessment under Schedule D Case II if they are paid into a professional partnership of which the director is a partner, or paid to a company and the conditions specified when the extra-statutory concessions apply. Where extra-statutory concession A37 operates, travelling expenses are not treated as a benefit: extra-statutory concession A4 and Inland Revenue interpretation RI 105.

[2] [1931] 2 KB 628, 18 TC 198. For a slightly more modern example, see *Household v Grimshaw* [1953] 2 All ER 12, 34 TC 366.

[3] [1931] 2 KB 628 at 635, 18 TC 198 at 203.

[4] [1973] 1 All ER 368, [1973] STC 66; no appeal was made. See *Simon's Tax Intelligence* 1990, p 173.

[5] [1973] 1 All ER 368 at 374; the taxpayer had no other contracts at that time (unlike Miss Braithwaite), indeed, his was a full-time contract and one which prohibited him from taking on outside activities without his employer's consent.

[6] See [1931] 2 KB 628 at 631–2. In *Mitchell and Edon v Ross* in the Court of Appeal, Lord Evershed distinguished *Davies v Braithwaite* as not involving a contract of service (!): [1960] Ch 498 at 521, 40 TC 11 at 43. Compare with *Davies v Braithwaite, Bennett v Marshall* [1938] 1 KB 591, [1938] 1 All ER 93, 22 TC 73.

[7] *Market Investigations Ltd v Minister of Social Security* [1969] 2 QB 173 at 185.

[8] [1994] STC 23, CA.

[9] See eg Nolan LJ in *Hall v Lorimer* [1994] STC 23 at 30e.

[10] The test comes from Cooke J in *Market Investigations Ltd v Minister of Social Security* [1969] 2 QB 173 at 185. See [1931] 2 KB 628 at 631–2. In *Mitchell and Edon v Ross* in the Court of Appeal, Lord Evershed distinguished *Davies v Braithwaite* as not involving a contract of service(!): [1960] Ch 498 at 521, 40 TC 11 at 43. Compare with *Davies v Braithwaite, Bennett v Marshall* [1938] 1 KB 591, [1938] 1 All ER 93, 22 TC 73.

[11] *Ready Mixed Concrete (South East) Ltd v Minister of Pensions* [1968] 2 QB 497, [1968] 1 All ER 433. See also *Sidey v Phillips* [1987] STC 87.

[12] *O'Kelly v Trusthouse Forte plc* [1984] QB 90, [1983] 3 All ER 456, CA, approved by Nourse LJ in *Beauchamp v F W Woolworth plc* [1988] STC 714 at 718, CA. cf Lord Widgery CJ, in *Global Plant Ltd v Secretary of State for Social Services* [1972] 1 QB 139 at 154, 155. See criticism by Pitt [1985] LQR 217.

[13] HMRC ES Manual. A useful decision of Revenue practice is given in ICAEW Tax Practice Supplement "Employment Status", February 2007. There is now an online tool "employment status indicator" provided by HMRC. It is not a highly sophisticated tool, but considers the basic indicators and gives an opinion which is

349

not presently legally binding. It is used internally by HMRC staff to arrive at decisions about employment status.

[14] [1996] STC 716.
[15] [1978] ICR 894.
[16] [1991] STC 419.
[17] 18 January 1983, unreported.
[18] For the economic impact of the categorisation, see Judith Freeman "Employed or self-employed? Tax classification of workers in the changing labour market" published by the Institute of Fiscal Studies, February 2001.
[19] [2001] STC (SCD) 189.
[20] [2002] STC (SCD) 138.
[21] [2003] EWHC 645 (Ch), [2003] STC 543.
[22] [2004] STC (SCD) 237. The finding of the Special Commission was upheld by the High Court: [2004] EWHC 2597 (Ch), [2005] STC 198.
[23] [2004] STC (SCD) 213. The finding of the Special Commission was upheld by the High Court: [2004] EWHC 2248 (Ch), [2004] STC 1671.
[24] (2007) Sp C 655.
[25] [2003] STC (SCD) 15.
[26] [2004] STC (SCD) 72.
[27] [2004] STC (SCD) 472.

Consequences of income being categorised as employment income

[7.12] The consequences of coming within the employment income provisions as opposed to trading income are extensive, and rest on the doctrine that the Schedules are mutually exclusive (the employment income provisions were originally Schedule E). In *IRC v Brander and Cruickshank*, Lord Donovan said that the doctrine was quite unreal and served no useful purpose. Indeed its application in that case would cause administrative chaos.[1]

[1] [1971] 1 All ER 36 at 46–9. The concessionary relief at A37, should also be noted—tax treatment of directors' fees received by partnerships and other companies; Revenue Manual SE 2500.

[7.13] (1) An overseas employment may fall to be taxed on a preferential basis whereas if it is simply an incident in the carrying on of a profession by a UK resident the receipts will be taxed in full (as in *Davies v Braithwaite*, and see supra, § 7.03).

[7.14] (2) Expenses incurred for an office or employment under the employment income provisions will only be deductible if they conform to the strict test laid down in ITEPA 2003, s 336 (in Chapter 2 of Part 5);[1] expenses incurred for a trade or profession will be deductible on a different and less niggardly test.[2]

In *Mitchell and Edon v Ross*[3] the taxpayer, Ross, held an appointment as a consultant radiologist under the Birmingham Regional Hospital Board, and served at a number of hospitals under that authority. He was also in private practice as a consultant radiologist, which practice he carried on at his home in Rugby. The Revenue admitted that Ross was correctly assessed under Schedule D, Case II in respect of his private practice but argued that income accruing from the Hospital Board should be assessed—and so calculated—under what was then Schedule E and is now the employment income provisions.

At first instance and in the Court of Appeal[4] the taxpayer argued unsuccessfully that the positions with the Hospital Board were not offices. He further argued that if he was correctly assessable under Schedule E (now employment income), the employment should nonetheless also be seen as part of his profession under Schedule D, Case II (now trading income) so that the Schedule D rules for deduction of expenses should apply. This rested on a finding by the Commissioners that these employments were a necessary part of his profession as consultant radiologist and merely incidental to that profession.[5]

Only the second point was argued in the House of Lords and the taxpayer lost. If the employment was assessable under Schedule E, expenses in respect of that employment could be allowed only if they conformed to the requirements of the Schedule; the appointment could not be treated for tax purposes as part inside and part outside the Schedule (and what is now the employment income provisions).[6]

Simon's Taxes E4.222.

[1] Infra, § **7.111.**
[2] Infra, § **7.131.**
[3] [1961] 3 All ER 49, 40 TC 11.
[4] [1959] 3 All ER 341, 40 TC 11; and [1960] 2 All ER 218, 40 TC 11, CA.
[5] Suppl. Case stated, 40 TC 11 at 32.
[6] On concordat reached between the Revenue and the medical profession; see **Simon's Taxes E4.233**, and for treatment of retirement benefit provision see extra-statutory concession A9.

[7.15] (3) Terminal payments in connection with the ending of an office or employment may escape tax in whole or in part;[1] compensation for the loss of a trading asset will usually be a trading receipt.[2]

In *IRC v Brander and Cruickshank*[3] the House of Lords held that where a firm of Scottish advocates with a substantial general legal business also acted as secretaries and/or registrars for some 30 to 40 companies, each appointment was a separate office and therefore, thanks to the employment income rules, sums received on the termination of two such appointments, escaped tax.[4]

In an earlier case, *Blackburn v Close Bros Ltd*[5] the taxpayer was a merchant banking company which derived income from acting as managers, secretaries and registrars of various companies. One appointment with a particular company was terminated and Pennycuick J, held the sum paid by way of compensation to be a trading receipt within Schedule D, Case I.

In *IRC v Brander and Cruickshank*, Lord Guest,[6] with whom Lord Upjohn agreed, doubted the correctness of *Blackburn v Close Bros Ltd* but Lord

[7.15] Employment income

Morris regarded the facts of the earlier case as being quite different[7] and thought the offices were not trading assets. Lord Donovan would have followed the earlier case if there had been a finding of fact that the taxpayer had sought the office as part and parcel of his trade or profession.[8] On such a finding Lord Donovan would have been prepared to hold that income payments fell within what was then Schedule E and terminal payments within Schedule D. Lord Reid dismissed the appeal "for the reasons given by your Lordships".[9]

Given the logic of *Mitchell and Edon v Ross*[10] it is hard to understand any conclusion other than that of Lord Guest.[11] If an office falls exclusively within the employment income provisions it does not cease to be an office simply because it was sought; while if different payments from the same source can fall under two different sets of provisions, as Lord Donovan suggested, the selection of the applicable rules from the range offered by the two sets of provisions seems as arbitrary as the selection of an Easter bonnet.

Simon's Taxes E4.202, 222.

---

[1] Under ITEPA 2003, ss 401–416 (infra, § **7.36**).
[2] But it may still escape tax as a gift or a capital payment and not a trading receipt (see infra, § **8.75**).
[3] [1971] 1 All ER 36, 46 TC 574.
[4] ITEPA 2003, ss 401–416 apply when the payment is not otherwise chargeable to tax (see s 401(3)). The finding that the post was an office and so within the employment income rules meant that the payment was not chargeable to tax under some other provision, thus enabling s 403 to operate.
[5] (1960) 39 TC 164.
[6] [1971] 1 All ER 36 at 45, 46 TC 574 at 593.
[7] At 42, 590.
[8] At 47, 595.
[9] At 40, 588.
[10] If the taxpayer was not carrying on a profession, the payment might have fallen within Schedule D, Case VI, but this seems to be excluded by the conclusion that the post was an office and so within the employment income provisions.
[11] One consequence of Lord Guest's view is that a company can hold an office and so have that income computed under the employment income provisions.

[7.16] (4) The costs of acquiring the office will not be deductible under the employment income rules; they will usually be deductible if the income is correctly treated as trading income.[1]

(5) Solicitor trustees receiving annuities from the trust fund for acting as trustee have traditionally been taxed on the recipient as trading income with deduction at source.[2] However, as an office, the post of trustee falls within the employment income provisions.[3] (**Simon's Taxes E4.230.**)

(6) Employment income is assessed on a current year basis and under PAYE; Schedule D uses a current year basis but with problems of overlap profits periods, has no PAYE but does have self-assessment and payment on account.[4]

(7) The capital allowance structure is much wider for trades than for employments.

Simon's Taxes E4.222.

1   Cf Pennycuick J in *Blackburn v Close Bros Ltd* (1960) 39 TC 164 at 173.
2   TA 1988, ss 348, 349.
3   Supra, § **7.08**.
4   Infra, § **8.43**.

Employment income: The causation test

[7.17] ITEPA 2003, s 6 taxes general earnings and specific employment income from the office or employment. The test to be applied in determining whether a payment is taxable as employment income has been set out by Lord Templeman in *Shilton v Wilmshurst*.[1] He said,

> Section [19] is not confined to 'emoluments from the employer' but embraces all 'emoluments from employment'; the section must therefore comprehend an emolument provided by a third party, a person who is not the employer. Section [19] is not limited to emoluments provided in the course of the employment; the section must therefore apply first to an emolument which is

This passage shows very clearly that what the court is asked to do is to look for the reason for the payment; the question, to use the term adopted in earlier cases, is one of causation. This is traced back to the words of the statute by stating that the earnings or income must be *from* the office or employment.[2] However, it is not clear to what extent this formulation is meant to be a summary of existing case law and to what extent it is meant to mark a new point of departure.

The words italicised show that the test must be read closely. It is not enough for the first limb that the payment should be paid as a reward for past services; it must also be an inducement to continue to perform services. Similarly, in the second limb it is not enough that an emolument is paid as an inducement to enter into a contract of employment; it must also be paid as an inducement to perform services in the future.

Three other comments should be made before passing on to the rest of the case law. The first is that it seems wrong for the taxpayer to have conceded that the £75,000 was an emolument when his argument was that it was not "from" the employment. The *Oxford English Dictionary* defines an emolument as a payment from an office or employment; if a payment is not from an employment it cannot be an emolument. (Emolument was the term used to cover virtually all chargeable amounts under what was then Schedule E. ITEPA 2003 has removed the word emolument, except in the formulation of what constitutes earnings.[3]) Second, the result of the case gives rise to some very fine distinctions (see infra, § **7.33**). Third, perhaps the real interest in the litigation in *Shilton v Wilmshurst* lies in the explicit effort of the Revenue to argue that the test in terms of reward for services emerging from *Hochstrasser v Mayes* was no longer sufficient, a view based on the decision in *Hamblett v Godfrey* (see infra, § **7.28**). This seems to have been unsuccessful.

[7.17] Employment income

The approach in the *Shilton* case was followed by the Special Commissioners in *Antelope v Ellis*[4] and in the cases of *Bootle v Bye* and *Wilson v Bye*.[5] In the first of these cases, Stephen Antelope appealed against an assessment under what was then Schedule E in the sum of £349,360. Some two-thirds of this sum was received as an inducement for the taxpayer to leave a particular employment and accept another employment. The Special Commissioner ruled that the sum received was fully assessable and the termination payment provisions did not apply. In the latter pair of cases, there was an attempted hostile takeover of the US parent of Safeway Food Stores Ltd. A US company in the Safeway Group made payments of £176,790 and £175,605 respectively to two directors of the Safeway UK Company. These payments were made "to foster and encourage the continued attention and dedication of the directors to their duties during the potentially disturbing circumstances arising from the possibility of a change in control of Safeway Foodstores Ltd". No services were required to be performed for the sums received, nor were any rights surrendered by the directors. It was held that the sums received were, nevertheless, "emoluments from employment" and, hence, subject to Schedule E.

Earlier cases went back to the words of Upjohn J in *Hochstrasser v Mayes*:[6]

> . . . the payment must be made in reference to the services the employee renders by virtue of his office and it must be something in the nature of a reward for services past, present or future.

In the House of Lords in that case Viscount Simonds accepted this as entirely accurate subject only to the observation that the word "past" might be open to question.[7] In *Laidler v Perry* Lord Reid expressed doubts on the use of the word "reward" saying:[8]

> It is not apt to include all the cases that can fall within the statutory words. To give only one instance, it is clear that a sum given to an employee in the hope that he will produce good service in the future is taxable.

This last observation has been applied in two decisions of the House of Lords before *Shilton v Wilmshurst*. In *Brumby v Milner*[9] sums of money held in a profit sharing scheme were distributed when the scheme was wound up. The House held that this payment, like the previous income payments, arose from the employment and from no other source; it was therefore taxable. In *Tyrer v Smart*[10] the taxpayer applied for shares in his employing company, having preferential right of application as an employee. The House held that he was taxable on the advantage gained.

It is still open to a court to distinguish *Shilton v Wilmshurst* on the facts as was done in *Mairs v Haughey*.[11] Here the business of the employer was being bought out by a new company. The taxpayer employee was offered an employment by the new employer on condition that he did not take the redundancy payments due to him from the old employer under a non-statutory redundancy scheme but should, in the event of the buy-out being successful, receive an ex-gratia sum from the company which was the sole shareholder in the new employer. Part of that sum was equal to a fraction of what would have been received for redundancy under the old scheme. The Special Commissioner began by splitting the sum received into a part which was for becoming an employee with the new company and a second part which was compensation for loss of redundancy rights and held the latter did not fall within s 19. The House of Lords, like the Court of Appeal for Northern Ireland before it, dismissed the Crown's appeal. The House first held that whether one looked at the documents by themselves or at the substance and reality of the situation the payments were made for two separate and identifiable considerations; it was quite impossible to regard the two sums in aggregate as inducements to become employed for the new company; apportionment was possible and had been correctly carried out.[12] It also held that there was no liability to income tax under what was then s 19 of TA 1988 for a payment made in lieu of a right to receive a non-statutory redundancy payment. A redundancy payment has a real element of compensating or relieving an employee for the consequences of not being able to earn a living in the former employment. It is distinct from damages for breach of contract and from deferred payment of wages (since entitlement to a redundancy payment is never more than a contingent entitlement which both parties normally hope will never accrue). It is not an emolument from the employment but compensation for not being able to receive emoluments from the employment. As such it must be distinguished from a payment made to all employees whether or not they became redundant.[13]

Compensation for unfair dismissal awarded by an employment tribunal is accepted by the Revenue as outside the charge in ITEPA 2003, s 6.[14] In *Wilson v Clayton*[15] the Court of Appeal held that a payment made under a compromise agreement to halt proceedings before an employment tribunal is, similarly, outside the charge in that section.[16]

The source of the payment is to be judged by reality. In *O'Leary v McKinlay*[17] a football club made a long loan to trustees who held the money for a player. The income from the resulting investments was held to be income from the employment and so within employment income provisions and not income from a loan which would have brought it within Schedule D, Case V.

One remaining issue is whether the question of whether a payment is an emolument is one of law or of fact. In *Hochstrasser v Mayes* Upjohn J took the question to be one of inference from primary fact and of legal inference at that, thus making the question one of law. In *Tyrer v Smart*, however, the inference seems to have been treated as one of fact and so within the sole jurisdiction of the Commissioners. The position is as confused as it is unfortunate; the earlier view seems preferable.

The general principle is weakened by a number of what were concessions but have now become part of statute in ITEPA. These are payments under a suggestion scheme[18] and meals provided for employees.[19]

Simon's Taxes E4.403, 405.

1 [1991] STC 88; for facts see infra, § **7.33**.
2 ITEPA 2003, s 9.
3 ITEPA 2003, s 62 and Note 13 in Annex 2.
4 [1995] STC (SCD) 297.
5 [1996] STC (SCD) 58. See also *Teward v IRC* [2001] STC (SCD) 36, in which a payment by a new employer to compensate a new recruit for the rights under a

[7.17] Employment income

share scheme he had lost by leaving his previous employment was held to be an emolument within TA 1988, s 19(1).
6   [1959] Ch 22 at 33.
7   See infra, § **7.20**.
8   [1966] AC 16 at 30, 42 TC 351 at 363. See also Browne Wilkinson VC in *Shilton v Wilmshurst* [1990] STC 55 at 59 and 61, CA (see supra, § **7.01**, note 5).
9   [1976] 3 All ER 636, [1976] STC 534, but distinguish *Tyrer v Smart* [1976] 3 All ER 537, [1976] STC 521.
10 [1979] 1 All ER 321, [1979] STC 34.
11 [1993] STC 569, HL.
12 [1993] STC at 576j–577b.
13 *Allan v IRC* [1994] STC 943, Ct of Sess.
14 See comments reported in the judgement of Patten J in *Wilson v Clayton* [2004] EWHC 898 (Ch), [2004] STC 1022 para [4] at 1029a.
15 [2004] EWCA Civ 1657, [2005] STC 157.
16 But it is within the charge in ITEPA 2003, s 403: *Wilson v Clayton* [2004] EWHC 898 (Ch), [2004] STC 1022 para [28] at 1039h–1040d.
17 [1991] STC 42.
18 ITEPA 2003, ss 321 and 322; for the Revenue's own suggestion scheme see *Simon's Tax Intelligence* 1991, p 1086.
19 ITEPA 2003, ss 266 and 317.

Consequences of the test being causation

[7.18] Since the question is one of causation, and not consideration, the court is not confined to any expressions of consideration in any service contract. So in *Pritchard v Arundale*[1] a payment expressed in the contract of service to be in consideration of that service escaped tax. Conversely in *IRC v Duke of Westminster*, Lord Atkin would have held the payment to be an emolument notwithstanding that the service was expressed not to be the consideration.[2]

A second consequence of the rule of causation is that a payment caused by something other than services must escape tax. Moreover the onus is on the Revenue to show that the payment is an emolument.[3] A question that the courts have not yet dealt with is that of multiple causes. Where a payment is caused by service and by something else, principle would suggest an apportionment of the payment, at least where this is practicable.[4]

Third, it is clear that the payment may be an emolument even though it is made by someone other than the other party to the contract of employment. Moreover in such cases it is established that the person making the payment may be required to deduct tax under the PAYE system.[5]

Fourth, one must look for the real cause. In *Bridges v Bearsley*[6] property (shares in the employer company) was transferred by other shareholders (X and Y) to an employee, B, under a deed which said the transfer was in consideration of B remaining a director of the company. When the court looked at the circumstances surrounding the transfer it was clearly due to a wish to honour a promise made to B by the father of X and Y that the father would leave the shares to B by will and so not B's taxable emolument under what was then s 19 of TA 1988; since the test is one of causation the court could look at all the circumstances.

Simon's Taxes E4.401.

1   [1971] 3 All ER 1011 (see infra, § **7.28**).
2   [1936] AC 1 (see supra, § **3.12**).
3   Per Viscount Simonds in *Hochstrasser v Mayes* [1959] Ch 22, supra.
4   See infra, § **7.35**.
5   *Booth v Mirror Group Newspapers plc* [1992] STC 615.
6   (1957) 37 TC 289, CA.

[7.19] The reference by Lord Templeman in *Shilton v Wilmshurst* to a payment made "to provide assistance to a home buyer" is presumably to the decision of the House of Lords in *Hochstrasser v Mayes*[1] itself. Here the taxpayer worked for ICI Ltd, a large concern with factories in different parts of the UK. To encourage its employees to remain in the service of the company if asked to move to a different part of the country, the company would make good any loss incurred by the employee through a fall in the value of a house which the employee owned. This scheme was restricted to married employees and also to houses not exceeding £2,000 in value. (Note: this is at 1951 prices.) On being moved from Hillhouse to Wilton, the taxpayer sold his house in Fleetwood for £1,500; it had originally cost £1,850. ICI reimbursed him this loss of £350 and the Revenue sought to assess him on the £350; they failed.

The Revenue argued that all payments by employers to their employees as such were taxable unless they were payments in return for full consideration in money or money's worth other than his services under the employment. The first difficulty with this proposition is the vagueness inherent in the notion of a payment to an employee as such. When Parker LJ, had adopted a similar approach in the Court of Appeal he would have excepted gifts to the employee in a personal capacity.[2] The second difficulty is the problem of deciding whether a payment was for full consideration or not and Viscount Simonds eschewed such a task. In the House of Lords this approach was rejected unanimously. It was not disputed that the company would not have made this payment if the taxpayer had not been an employee and it was clear that the company thought that it was going to benefit by having a more settled work force if a scheme like this were in operation. Moreover, because the taxpayer had a perfectly standard wage, it could not be said that this was disguised remuneration.

The House of Lords[3] held that the payment was not in respect of his services to the company but rather to compensate him for the loss which he had sustained, and was therefore not taxable.

The first set of difficulties concerns other possible payments. As the Revenue's counsel put it, to be recouped a loss by someone else is plainly a profit. If these profits escaped tax, which profits would not?

It was agreed that if Mayes had suffered a bereavement and the company had seen fit to grant him something from its benevolent fund of course such payment would not have been taxable.[4] But if Mayes had been compensated for a loss on an investment on the Stock Exchange it would be surprising that he should not be liable to tax in respect of such a payment. Only Lord Denning gave reasons why an indemnity of the last type would be taxable.[5] Unfortunately this example was premised on the view that the indemnity would be by way of reward for services, a premise which automatically makes the sum taxable. His Lordship went on to say that the sum would be taxable because the losses were his own affair and nothing to do with his employment, but this would be equally true of the hypothetical bereavement. Despite these doubts a court has since held that a taxpayer is not liable to tax in these circumstances.[6]

The second set of difficulties concerns the case itself.[7] Other housing benefits are taxed and show how isolated the decision is. If ICI had provided him with rent-free accommodation, he would have been taxable, as he would if he had gone into private rented accommodation and the employers had paid the rent; likewise if ICI had guaranteed him against any increase in rent. Perhaps if they had guaranteed him against an increase in mortgage rates such payments would have been taxable. This case gave rise to a practice (now replaced by a statutory provision) for relocation expenses.[8]

One may note that the company was getting the best of both worlds. Not only was the sum not taxable in the hands of its employee but also it was deductible by the company in computing its profits. This is legally correct but encourages planning.

However, one should also note that it was not in dispute that Mayes was receiving the correct salary for the job he was doing, so that it was not a case of disguised remuneration, that he worked for a blue chip company and the scheme was restricted to houses of less than £2,000 in price so that it was not available to very senior employees;[9] quite how relevant these points are is highly debatable.

The case is authority for three important propositions:

(1) that service must be the causa causans and not simply the causa sine qua non of the payment if it is to be a taxable emolument;[10] so
(2) the categories of non-taxable payments are not closed;
(3) the onus in such cases is on the Revenue to show that the payments fall within the scope of the taxing statutes.[11]

---

[1] (1960) 38 TC 673. On current Revenue practice see Manual SE 1246b.
[2] (1960) 38 TC 673 at 697.
[3] (1960) 38 TC 673 per Viscount Simonds at 707.
[4] (1960) 38 TC 673 per Lord Radcliffe at 707.
[5] At 396. Quaere if the loss were on shares of the employer company which he was obliged to sell on leaving the company (see infra, § **7.54**).
[6] *Wilcock v Eve* [1995] STC 18.
[7] Both Viscount Simonds and Lord Radcliffe (at 707) thought the case was near the line although the former had little doubt as to the side of the line on which it fell. In *Laidler v Perry* Lord Hodson said that *Hochstrasser v Mayes* was a decision on its peculiar facts: [1966] AC 16 at 36, 42 TC 351 at 366.
[8] See infra, § **7.51**.

[9] Quaere whether the payment would have fallen within what was then TA 1988, s 154 and is now in the benefits code, see infra, § **7.97** et seq, if the employee's income had exceeded (now) £8,500. In *Jennings v Kinder* [1959] Ch 22, 38 TC 673, CA the Revenue's attempt to tax it under what is now ITEPA 2003, s 70—as a payment in respect of expenses—failed. In *Wicks v Firth* [1983] STC 25, HL, the House of Lords held (prior to statutory provisions) that payments to children of higher paid employees were not part of the emoluments of the parents, when the payment was made to assist with costs of attending a University course.

[10] See [1960] AC 376, per Viscount Simonds at 389; per Lord Cohen at 395; in the vernacular Lord Radcliffe at 392. In *Brumby v Milner* (see supra, § **7.17**), Lord Simon criticised the use of these phrases and preferred to ask whether these payments arose relevantly from the employment; this, with respect, seems to get one absolutely nowhere.

[11] Per Viscount Simonds at 389.

Services past

[7.20] The liability to income tax of payments for services past was left open by Viscount Simonds in *Hochstrasser v Mayes*[1] but in the light of the words of Lord Templeman in *Shilton v Wilmshurst* such payments will be taxable if also intended as an inducement to continue to perform future services. So it has been held that a tip to a taxi driver is taxable even though given only at the end of the service.[2] A bonus payment to an employee[3] and a payment on completion of, say, 25 years service with the company[4] are likewise taxable although in these cases, since the employment had not yet terminated, the payments might be seen as incitements to even greater service and loyalty in the future. By what was a concession[5] an award in the form of a tangible article or shares in the employing company (or certain other benefits) is tax-free if the cost is reasonable, ie if it does not exceed £50 per year of service. The employee must have been in service for at least 20 years and not have received any other award within the previous ten years. The service must be with the same employer unless there has been a change of employer of the kind described in subsection (5) of ITEPA 2003, s 323. Statute[6] provides for the long service exemption to extend to any possible charge to income tax.[7]

Such authority is only indirect since none of these cases appears to turn on the question of payment for past services but it may be taken as some authority for their liability to tax since the payments must have escaped tax had the point not been accepted.[8] The fact that past consideration is no consideration is quite irrelevant since the test is one of causation and not of consideration. The true line seems to be not one between services future and services past but between a gift for personal or other reasons and a payment for services past or future. The fact that the service is past is but one factor in enabling this line to be drawn.[9] So in *Moore v Griffiths*[10] the fact that the payment was not known about until after the services had been rendered tended to show that it was a testimonial and so not taxable.

[1] Supra, § **7.17**.
[2] *Calvert v Wainwright* (see infra, § **7.25**).

[7.20] Employment income

³ *Radcliffe v Holt* (1927) 11 TC 621. However, will the emphasis on inducement as to future service mean that ordinary tips paid to a taxi driver, who to the knowledge of the payer is about to retire, escape tax?
⁴ *Weston v Hearn* (1943) 25 TC 425.
⁵ What was extra-statutory concession A22 is rewritten as ITEPA 2003, s 323. The limit of £20 per year was increased to £50 per year by SI 2003/1361 from 13 June 2003; but on long service awards to firemen see *Simon's Tax Intelligence* 1985, p 178.
⁶ ITEPA 2003, s 228.
⁷ See change 79 in Annex 1 of ITEPA Explanatory Notes.
⁸ See per Evershed MR, in *Henley v Murray* [1950] 1 All ER 908, 31 TC 351 at 366—"nor was it a reward for his past service"—not taxable. Similarly Lord Warrington in *Hunter v Dewhurst* (1932) 16 TC 605 at 643.
⁹ As in *Cowan v Seymour* [1920] 1 KB 500, 7 TC 372; *Denny v Reed* (1933) 18 TC 254.
¹⁰ Infra, § 7.26 [1972] 3 All ER 399, 48 TC 338.

Capital

[7.21] Certain payments which escape ITEPA 2003, s 6 have been described as capital payments.¹ It is not clear whether such payments escape ITEPA 2003, s 6 because they are capital payments or whether they escape tax because not in return for services and could conveniently but irrelevantly or even inaccurately be described as capital sums. The latter view appears preferable.² It is axiomatic that income tax is a tax on income but since what is income is defined in each Schedule and Case or rewritten law provision it ought to follow that earnings of an office or employment are by definition income. The decision in *Brumby v Milner* (see supra, § 7.17) now appears to hold, although without apparent argument, that this is correct. It is, to say the least, significant that in no case has the classification of a payment as capital been the prime reason for holding that the payment is not taxable, the description capital is therefore best regarded simply as a convenient label for certain types of non-earnings.³

Simon's Taxes E4.403.

¹ eg Lord Denning MR in *Jarrold v Boustead* [1964] 3 All ER 76 at 81. Lord Simon in *Tilley v Wales* [1943] AC 386 at 393, 25 TC 136 at 149.
² Finlay LJ, in *Prendergast v Cameron* (1939) 23 TC 122 at 138.
³ See also Walton J in *Brumby v Milner* [1975] STC 215 at 227 and Lord Coulsfield in *IRC v Herd* [1992] STC 264 at 286.

Timing

[7.22] The rules for determining when employment income arises were changed in 1989 to use a receipts basis, ie to charge tax by reference to earnings as and when they are received.

Unless the remittance basis applies (supra, §; **7.02**), income tax is charged on a receipts basis: that is, on the full amount of the emoluments received in the year in respect of the office or employment concerned.[1] (However, the status of the payment, and the availability of any relief, may be determined by the year for which it is payable; see infra, § **7.36** for termination payment.) In *White v IRC*,[2] a policeman successfully challenged the Royal Ulster Constabulary for payment of housing allowance from when he joined the force in 1994. The payment was made to him in August/September 1997. The Special Commissioner held that the entire payment formed part of the employment income assessable in 1997–98 and could not be treated as additions to the income of the years on the basis on which it was calculated. Moreover this basis of charge is to apply whether the earnings are for that year or for some other year of assessment. In a major reversal of earlier law, including the decision of the House of Lords in *Bray v Best*,[3] it is not necessary that the employee should hold the office in the year in which the sums are received.[4] This last rule has to be elaborated. It is therefore provided that in such circumstances if in the year concerned the office has never been held the earnings are to be treated as earnings for the first year in which the office is held; conversely if the office or employment is no longer held they are to be treated as earnings of the last such year.[5] To this extent the legislation retains the doctrine of the source. The statute does not address the problem arising if a person holds an office, resigns it and then resumes and receives a payment between the two periods of tenure. In such circumstances the answer presumably turns on the question "which period of tenure is the payment from?".

The question what amounts to a receipt is not left to case law development but is the subject of detailed provision. Generally earnings are to be treated as received at the earlier of (a) when the payment is made of or on account of the earnings, and (b) when the person becomes entitled to payment of or on account of earnings.[6] The meaning of the expression "on account of" is not amplified. Where the person becomes entitled to payment but does not receive the payment, eg through the insolvency of the company, there is no provision giving relief.[7] These rules apply also to PAYE.[8]

In addition special rules apply if the person is a director at any time during the year of assessment and the earnings relate to an office or employment with that company (whether or not that office or employment is the directorship).[9] Where sums on account of earnings are credited in the company's accounts or records, that date is to be preferred whether or not there is any fetter on the right to draw the sum.[10] Likewise if the amount to be paid for a period is determined before the period ends, the payment will be treated as chargeable when that period ends even though no payment has yet been made. Where the amount for the period is not known until later eg when the bonus is finalised, the date of that determination will be taken. Where more than one of these rules, including the general rules in the previous paragraph apply, the earliest date will be taken. The questions of when a payment is credited to the company's accounts or records and of what amounts to a determination of the amount of the earnings are left to future litigation.

These rules are not to override the special statutory timing rules for cash or non-cash vouchers, credit tokens and payments of compensation on retirement or removal from office.[11] The new rules are also excluded for the beneficial

[7.22] Employment income

occupation rules (see infra, § **7.49**) and the rules governing benefits and expenses payments for directors and employees earning £8,500 pa or over (see infra, §§ **7.88** ff).

In a further change of theoretical, and practical, interest, there is to be no deduction for the employer under Schedule D, Cases I and II on account of earnings until the earnings would be brought into charge as employment income but not paid within nine months of the end of the period of account in which the employer would otherwise be entitled to the deduction.[12] There is, also, no benefit received by the employee when the payment is made more than nine months after the employer's year end.[13]

Tax is charged on earnings taxed under the remittance bases on the full amount of the earnings received in the UK in the year.[14] As with non-remittance based income, this is to apply whether the earnings are for that year or any other year of assessment. Also as with non-remittance based income it is not necessary for the office or employment to exist in the year in which they are received in the UK and provision is made for payments received in periods during which the office or employment is not held.[15]

Simon's Taxes E4.108.

---

[1] ITEPA 2003, ss 18, 19, 31 & 32. See also ICAEW Memorandum TR 759, *Simon's Tax Intelligence* 1989, p 716.
[2] [2003] STC (SCD) 161.
[3] [1989] STC 159.
[4] ITEPA 2003, ss 15, 21, 22, 25, 26 and 27.
[5] ITEPA 2003, ss 17 and 30.
[6] ITEPA 2003, ss 18 and 31; for origins, see Committee on Enforcement of Revenue Powers (Cmnd. 8822 the Keith Committee), pp 141–145.
[7] Contrast the position in Schedule D, Cases I and II: TA 1988, s 74(1)(*j*).
[8] FA 1989, s 45. For detailed guidance see Inland Revenue press release, 28 July 1989, *Simon's Tax Intelligence* 1989, p 633 and ICAEW Guidance note Tax 11/93, *Simon's Tax Intelligence* 1993, p 1069.
[9] ITEPA 2003, ss 18, 31; the term director is defined in sub-ss 18, 31 and 686. On problems in earlier years see ICAEW Memorandum TR759, *Simon's Tax Intelligence* 1989, p 718.
[10] ITEPA 2003, ss 18 and 31.
[11] ITEPA 2003, ss 19, 32 and 403(2).
[12] TA 1989, s 43.
[13] *Macdonald v Dextra Accessories* [2003] EWHC 872 (Ch), [2003] STC 749.
[14] ITEPA 2003, ss 33 and 34.
[15] ITEPA 2003, ss 21, 22, 25, 26 and 27.

Types of income

Money's worth—discharge of employee's obligation

[7.23] Payments applied for the benefit of the taxpayer are just as much his income as moneys paid directly to him.[1] Section 62 of ITEPA 2003, which defines earnings, also specifically includes "money's worth" and a definition of money's worth is given in subsection (3). So where an employer discharges a pecuniary obligation of his employee the sum paid is treated as income of the employee even if it is income tax as in *Hartland v Diggines*.[2] This applies equally where both employer and employee are jointly liable.[3] The fact that the employer was under no obligation to make the payments was irrelevant.

A promise to pay a salary "without any deductions and taxes which will be borne by" the employer is interpreted as an agreement to pay such sums as after deduction of tax gives the net salary after deduction of tax.[4] The principle was applied in *Nicoll v Austin*[5] to future obligations. The taxpayer was life director of and had a controlling interest in his employing company. Under his contract of service he was to continue to reside in his own house but the company would pay all outgoings in respect of his house, including rates, taxes and insurance and the costs of gas, electric light and telephone and of maintaining the house and gardens[6] in proper condition, but the house remained the taxpayer's. Finlay J, reversing the Commissioners, held that the payments made by the company constituted money's worth to the taxpayer who was therefore taxable. By concession this rule does not apply to the heating, lighting, cleaning and gardening costs of certain clergymen.[7]

However, the rule in *Nicoll v Austin* does not apply if after leaving the employer and before being used to discharge the liability of the employee it has become the income of someone else. In *Barclays Bank Ltd v Naylor*[8] ICI had set up a discretionary trust out of which payments could be made to assist in the cost of educating the children of employees working for overseas companies in the ICI group. Grants were made by the trust to a child of one of the employees and the sums were paid to the child's account with Barclay's Bank which as his agent sought repayment of the tax deducted at source. This claim would succeed if the payments were annual payments within Schedule D, Case III, but fail if the payments were emoluments of the child's father's employment. Cross J held that the payments had become the income of the child and the fact that income had been used to discharge the father's legal obligation to pay the school fees was insufficient to turn the income of the child into the income of the parent.

The tax avoidance possibilities thus opened up are however limited. First the payment under the trust must be a genuine payment.[9] Secondly if there is a rule that children's investment income is aggregated with that of their parents the end result may be worse for the employee.[10] Thirdly if the employee earns over £8,500 from that and connected employments or is a director, the payment will be taxable under the relevant part of the benefits code and ITEPA 2003, s 211 et seq[11] since, after 14 March 1983, the payment cannot be treated as exempt under TA 1988, s 331 as scholarship income.[12]

[7.23] Employment income

The payment of an expense in connection with the provision of a parking place is expressly excluded.[13]

Simon's Taxes E4.402, 415.

---

1. eg *Drummond v Collins* [1915] AC 1011, 6 TC 525.
2. [1926] AC 289, 10 TC 247. See also *IRC v Miller* [1930] AC 222, 15 TC 25; *IRC v Leckie* (1940) 23 TC 471. An underdeduction of a director's PAYE which is accounted for to the Revenue by his employer is taxed under ITEPA 2003, s 223, infra, § **7.110**.
3. *Richardson v Worrall* [1985] STC 693 (quaere whether this will not be so if the primary liability and the primary benefit are the employer's).
4. *Jaworski v Institution of Polish Engineers in Great Britain Ltd* [1951] 1 KB 768, [1950] 2 All ER 1191. But cf *Jennings v Westwood Engineering Ltd* [1975] IRLR 245. Tax-free remuneration for directors is now prohibited by Companies Act 1985, s 311; on definition of director see Companies Act 1985, s 741. The net sum paid is to be treated as a gross sum but see **Simon's Taxes E4.453**.
5. (1935) 19 TC 531.
6. For a doubt about the gardens, see Lord Evershed MR, in *Wilkins v Rogerson* (1961) 39 TC 344 at 353 and infra, § **7.43**.
7. Extra-statutory concession A61.
8. [1960] 3 All ER 173, 39 TC 256. Under an earlier scheme an allowance was paid directly to the employee—such an allowance was taxable. See also *Constable v Federal Taxation Comr* (1952) 86 CLR 402.
9. Cross J emphasised that the Crown had not argued that the trust was not a genuine discretionary trust nor that the payment was not a proper exercise of the discretion. The former point, if substantiated, would presumably give rise to liability since the trust would be treated as a sham. However, if the latter point was substantiated the correct result ought to be that the employee was obliged to return the sum to the trustees and so no charge on the employee.
10. Before 6 April 1984 the income, being investment income, was liable to the investment income surcharge.
11. Infra, § **7.109**.
12. Reversing the effect of the decision of the House of Lords in *Wicks v Firth* [1983] STC 25.
13. ITEPA 2003, ss 237 and 266

Examples of what are earnings

[7.24] Payments for services include not only ordinary wages and salaries but less obvious payments such as those to mark a period of service with the employer.[1] Also included are bonus payments whether contracted for or not,[2] even if paid at Christmas.[3] A sum paid "to preserve an employer's good name and good staff relations" was held to be taxable even though it was designed to compensate staff for the withdrawal of a tax-free benefit in kind.[4]

A payment for service to an employer may be taxable even though the service was not within the scope of his duty. So in *Mudd v Collins*[5] a director who negotiated the sale of a branch of the company's business was held taxable on the sum of £1,000 granted him by the company as commission. All that had occurred was that the office had been enlarged.

However, if the taxpayer can show that the payment is not for services but a testimonial[6] he will escape tax. Thus in *Cowan v Seymour*[7] a company was being wound up and the former secretary of the company acted as liquidator without remuneration. When the liquidation was nearly complete the shareholders resolved to give the liquidator £586. The Commissioners held that he was taxable in respect of that sum, as did Rowlatt J, but that decision was reversed by the Court of Appeal, where it was emphasised that the duties of the liquidator had virtually ceased[8] and that the payment was made not by the employer but the shareholders.[9] However, neither of these points is conclusive.[10] The question is one of fact and the decision must today be considered doubtful.[11]

A payment by an employer to reimburse an expense incurred by the employee is part of general earnings against which it is open to the employee to claim an allowable deduction.[12] This is so even if the employee would not have been able to deduct the expense himself under any of the provisions listed in ITEPA 2003, s 72(3); however, it is assumed that this applies only to expenses incurred in connection with the employment.[13] The reimbursement of an expense must be distinguished from an expense allowance; such an allowance is treated as earnings.[14]

Shares issued to an employee when his employer partnership converts to a company have been held to be emoluments, taxable as general earnings.[15]

Simon's Taxes E4.465.

---

[1] *Weston v Hearn* [1943] 2 All ER 421, 25 TC 425
[2] *Denny v Reed* (1933) 18 TC 254. See ITEPA 2003, s 323. (Payments up to £50 for each year of service, minimum period 20 years and no similar award in the last ten years, are not taxed.)
[3] *Laidler v Perry* [1965] 2 All ER 121, 42 TC 351. On Christmas parties see ITEPA 2003, s 264; *Simon's Tax Intelligence* 1988, p 768; the limit is now £150 following SI 2003/1361.
[4] *Bird v Martland* [1982] STC 603. Payments for suggestion schemes are governed by ITEPA 2003, ss 321, 322.
[5] (1925) 9 TC 297; Rowlatt J. See also *Radcliffe v Holt* (1927) 11 TC 621.
[6] Infra, § **7.31**.
[7] [1920] 1 KB 500, 7 TC 372.
[8] Per Lord Sterndale MR, at 509, 379; per Atkin LJ at 511, 381.
[9] Per Younger J at 516, 384.
[10] Supra, note 7.
[11] *Cowan v Seymour* was distinguished in *Shipway v Skidmore* (1932) 16 TC 748 and in *Patrick v Burrows* (1954) 35 TC 138 but was, surprisingly, followed in *IRC v Morris* (1967) 44 TC 685, when the Court of Session held that there was evidence to support the Commissioners' findings. Payments in excess of £30,000 might at first sight appear to be caught by TA 1988, ss 148 and 188(4), but this applies only if they are "in consequence of the termination of the office".
[12] ITEPA 2003, ss 7, 70 and 72 reverses the decision in *Owen v Pook* [1969] 2 All ER 1, 45 TC 571 but see Lord Simon (dissenting) in *Taylor v Provan* [1975] AC 194

at 218; see also *Donnelly v Williamson* [1982] STC 88. Reimbursement of car parking expenses when the parking space is at or near the place of work is not taxable—ITEPA 2003, ss 237 and 266 added by FA 1988, s 46(4), (5).

[13] Thus, in *Richardson v Worrall* [1985] STC 693 a reimbursement of the cost of petrol obtained for private use was taxable; but in *Donnelly v Williamson* (supra) a reimbursement of a teacher's costs for doing something outside the contract of service (attending a parents' evening) was not.

[14] *Perrons v Spackman* [1981] STC 739.

[15] *McLoughlin v R & C Comrs* [2006] STC (SCD) 467.

Payment for services or gifts on personal grounds

[7.25] Earnings must be distinguished from a gift which is for reasons unconnected with the employment. Thus a payment may be made to relieve poverty[1] or as a mark of personal esteem, or to mark some particular occasion such as the passing of an examination,[2] or as a reward for some service; only the last is taxable as earnings. There is now a statutory exemption for gifts of up to £250 in a year when they are received from third parties.[3]

The mere fact that the donor is the employer will not suffice to make the gift general earnings, but neither is the fact that the donor is not the employer sufficient to prevent the gift from being earnings. The question is whether the payment is made because of the services rendered by the employee in the course of his employment. On this basis Atkinson J held in *Calvert v Wainwright*[4] that a tip to a taxi driver was taxable but added that a tip of £10 would not be taxable if it was paid at Christmas or when the driver was going on holiday and was intended to acknowledge the driver's qualities and faithfulness. Such a payment would be different from one given in the ordinary way as remuneration for services rendered.[5]

In *Moorhouse v Dooland* Jenkins LJ, stated four principles:[6]

(1) the test of liability to tax on a voluntary payment made to the holder of an office or employment is whether, from the standpoint of the person who receives it, it accrues to him by virtue of his office or employment or, in other words, by way of remuneration for his services;

(2) if the recipient's contract of employment entitled him to receive the voluntary payment that is a strong ground for holding that it accrues by virtue of the office, or, in other words is a remuneration for his services;

(3) the fact that the voluntary payment is of a periodic or recurrent character affords a further, though less cogent ground for the same conclusion;

(4) on the other hand, a voluntary payment may be made in circumstances which show that it is given by way of present or testimonial on grounds personal to the recipient, as for example a collection made for the particular individual who is at the time vicar of a given parish because he is in straitened circumstances, or a benefit held for a professional cricketer in recognition of his long and successful career in first class cricket. In such a case the proper conclusion is likely to be that the

voluntary payment is not a profit accruing to the recipient by virtue of his office or employment but a gift to him as an individual paid and received by reason of his personal needs or by reason of his personal qualities or attainments.

These principles were stated in a case which concerned a payment by a third party. At least where the payer is the employer one should also consider the intentions of the payer.[7] The amount of the payment is also relevant.[8]

In *McBride v Blackburn*,[9] John McBride was chairman of an association formed to conduct litigation against Lloyds. The post was unpaid. When, ultimately, the litigation was successful, the grateful Names who had benefited from the Lloyds settlement made ex gratia payments to John McBride, which totalled £280,000. The Special Commissioners held these ex gratia payments were "for or in respect of services which had been rendered"[10] and, hence, were correctly regarded as emoluments within the charge to employment income.

One area where the courts have had to distinguish between gifts and earnings concerns the clergy. It was early decided that grants from a sustention fund to supplement the incomes of clergy in poorly endowed parishes were emoluments.[11] The payments were not admittedly from their employers but they were still earnings because they were paid for services; they were paid to the clergy by virtue of their offices. The fact that such a payment was voluntary was quite irrelevant. What mattered was that the reason for the payments was to augment stipends and not to make grants to clergy because they were poor. In *Blakiston v Cooper*[12] the House of Lords held that Easter offerings which by custom and episcopal prompting were used not for the general purposes of the church as decided by the particular parish but given to the vicar, were also taxable. It may appear startling that those who on a particular Sunday—and that one of the most significant in the Christian year—contribute to the collection in their church, should be rendering unto Caesar nearly 22% of contributions, but so undoubtedly it is.[13] Such payments are given to the vicar as incumbent and are therefore taxable.[14] The giving may be voluntary but it is not spontaneous and there is an element of recurrence.[15] The fact that he may get more than a previous vicar because his congregation like him better merely underlines the fact that the payment is for services. Of course not all payments to vicars by members of their congregation are earnings. If the gift had been of an exceptional kind, such as a golden wedding present[16] or a testimonial or a contribution for a particular purpose, as to provide a holiday or a subscription due to the personal qualities of the particular clergyman, it might be a mere present.[17] On this reasoning a gift by a parishioner to the parish vicar so that he may hire a car while on holiday might not be taxable but a gift to assist with his car costs in the parish certainly would be.

Simon's Taxes E4.467, 468.

---

1   *Turton v Cooper* (1905) 5 TC 138.
2   *Ball v Johnson* (1971) 47 TC 155 (not taxable even though the bank required the employee to take this bankers examination); however, the payment is viewed by the Revenue as coming within TA 1988, s 154 if the employee is paid at a rate of

[7.25] Employment income

£8,500 pa or higher; ICAEW Memorandum TR 786, *Simon's Tax Intelligence* 1990, p 205.
[3] ITEPA 2003, s 324 as uprated by SI 2003/1361.
[4] [1947] 1 All ER 282, 27 TC 475; on Revenue practice see *Simon's Tax Intelligence* 1984, p 187 and *Simon's Tax Intelligence* 1985, p 187.
[5] At 529, 283, 478. The question is one of fact and degree. Christmas presents will be taxable if customary: *Wright v Boyce* [1958] 2 All ER 703, 38 TC 167, CA, or indiscriminate: *Laidler v Perry* [1966] AC 16, [1965] 2 All ER 121, 42 TC 351. A company gave each of its employees a £10 voucher at Christmas, regardless of their rate of remuneration or personal circumstances. A senior employee earning more than £2,000 a year thought the payment a charming Christmas gesture rather than as a payment for services, but this did not prevent the vouchers from being taxable under what was then s 19 of TA 1988 and were taxed at £10 in view of the wide range of goods for which they could be exchanged. Among the facts which supported this conclusion were that the vouchers of the same amount were given to nearly all staff and that this pattern of giving was past its eleventh year, indeed it was only a cash equivalent for the Christmas turkey which each employee had received before a scarcity of supplies made such munificence impossible.
[6] *Moorhouse v Dooland* [1955] Ch 284, 36 TC 1.
[7] Per Lord Hodson in *Laidler v Perry* [1966] AC 16 at 35, 42 TC 351 at 366; and see Brightman J in *Moore v Griffiths* [1972] 3 All ER 399 at 411 (employer's gift; third party's gift). If the company had in return for their payment used the footballer's name to advertise their products that payment would have been taxable under Schedule D, Case VI (see infra, § **12.10**). Quaere whether allowing one's receipt of a gift to be used for advertisement will not also fall within Schedule D, Case VI.
[8] Thus the difference between the wage and the benefit in *Seymour v Reed* and the £10 tip in *Calvert v Wainwright*. See also Lord Denning MR in *Laidler v Perry* [1965] Ch 192 at 199, 42 TC 351 at 361.
[9] [2003] STC (SCD) 139.
[10] At [62], 152d and [93], 159j/160a. The Commissioners also held that the payments were not received in connection with the termination of the holding of an office and, hence, did not fall to be taxed under the provisions of ITEPA 2003, s 403(1), nor were they employment related benefits within the scope of ITEPA 2003, s 201 (at [93] 160a).
[11] *Herbert v McQuade* [1902] 2 KB 631, 4 TC 489.
[12] [1909] AC 104, 5 TC 347.
[13] See the comment by Lord Evershed in *Moorhouse v Dooland* [1955] Ch 284 at 299.
[14] So Whitsun gifts to the curate are also taxable: *Slaney v Starkey* [1931] 2 KB 148, 16 TC 45.
[15] Per Lord Phillimore in *Seymour v Reed* [1927] AC 554 at 569, 11 TC 625 at 653.
[16] Per Lawrence J in *Corbett v Duff* [1941] 1 KB 730 at 740, 23 TC 763 at 779.
[17] Per Lord Loreburn in *Blakiston v Cooper* [1909] AC 104 at 107.

Sporting achievements—bonus or appreciation

[7.26] In *Seymour v Reed*[1] Seymour, the taxpayer, was a professional cricketer employed by Kent County Cricket Club. In 1920 he was awarded a benefit season which meant inter alia that members of the club subscribed money to a fund for him and that he was to receive the gate money at one of the home matches of that season. The gate money came to £939 16s and this was held by trustees together with the subscriptions until Seymour had found a farm. The money was then paid over to him and used by him for the purchase of the farm. The Revenue attempted to tax only the £939 16s and to tax it for the year when it was paid over. The attempt failed. The payment was a personal gift and not employment income. He had no right to a benefit season, the benefit would usually be towards the close of a man's career and was intended to provide an endowment on retirement; it was intended as an appreciation for services past rather than an encouragement for services to be rendered.[2]

In *Moorhouse v Dooland*[3] on the other hand the Revenue successfully claimed tax. Dooland was a professional cricketer employed by the East Lancashire Cricket Club. Under club rules he was entitled to talent money of one guinea for every time he scored 50 runs or more or took six wickets or did the hat-trick. (Until 1950 the league rules had also required collections to be taken for meritorious performances.) In the 1950 and 1951 seasons Dooland qualified for talent money and the resulting public collection, six and eleven times respectively. The Revenue successfully claimed tax in respect of the public collections. *Seymour v Reed* was distinguishable on almost every point. Dooland had a contractual right to a collection; Seymour had no such right to his benefit. Dooland had a collection whenever he performed well; Seymour had his one benefit. Dooland's payments were small compared with his salary; Seymour's were very great.

It does not follow that all collections for special feats would fall within the definition of earnings. Thus if Dooland had no contractual right to a collection but had scored 50 runs and then taken all ten wickets in a match so that the achievement was exceptional,[4] such a collection might not be taxable. In *Moore v Griffiths*[5] payments made by the Football Association to mark England's victory in the World Cup in 1966 were held not taxable. The payment was intended to mark the Association's pride in a great achievement and it would be more in keeping with the character and function of the Football Association to construe the payment as a testimonial or mark of esteem. Brightman J added darkly but presciently that the payment had no foreseeable element of recurrence.[6]

Simon's Taxes E4.469.

[1] [1927] AC 554, 11 TC 625.
[2] This is a question of fact and proof—see esp Lord Phillimore in *Seymour v Reed* [1927] AC 554, 11 TC 625 at 572, 655 and see *Corbett v Duff* [1941] 1 All ER 512, 23 TC 763—footballers' benefits more frequent than once in a career and perhaps after only five years held taxable.
[3] [1955] Ch 284, [1955] 1 All ER 93, 36 TC 12.
[4] Per Lord Evershed MR [1955] Ch 289 at 298.
[5] [1972] 3 All ER 399 at 411; quaere whether this meant that recurrence was not foreseeable for these players.
[6] [1972] 3 All ER 399 at 411; quaere whether this meant that recurrence was not foreseeable for these players.

Surrender of an advantage

[7.27] A payment by way of compensation for giving up some advantage rather than by way of reward for services is not taxable as earnings. This principle is applied even though the surrender of the advantage is a necessary consequence of taking the employment save where the advantage or right being surrendered is inseparable from the employment. Where the payment is made in return for an undertaking the effect of which is to restrict the employee as to his conduct or activities the payment may be taxable under ITEPA 2003, s 225.

Simon's Taxes E4.481.

Reward for services or compensation?

[7.28] In deciding this question the Commissioners are not apparently tied to the words of the contract. There are strong policy reasons for such a line since, as Megarry J observed in *Pritchard v Arundale*,[1] the days of the skilled draftsman are not past, but the decision that the question whether a particular payment is for services or by way of compensation can be judged according to the reality and not mere words is one more qualification of the decision of the House of Lords in *IRC v Duke of Westminster*.[2]

Where an employer makes a payment to an employee at the commencement of his service it is a question of fact whether it is a payment for future services or by way of compensation for some loss. A payment does not cease to be taxable because it is a premium or other initial payment in return for entering into a contract for services. Remuneration for services is still remuneration for services even if paid in a lump sum in advance.[3] Whereas it would be very difficult to demonstrate that periodical payments are anything but employment income, the fact that the payment is a lump sum is a factor that can be taken into account.[4]

In *Pritchard v Arundale* the taxpayer was in practice as a senior chartered accountant when a business friend of his persuaded him to leave the practice and to join him in business, as joint managing director of a company. The taxpayer received a full salary at the commercial rate but insisted upon a stake in the business. The friend who owned all but three of the 51,000 shares in the company transferred 4,000 to the taxpayer. The transfer of shares was held to be not taxable as employment income. Although the contract of service stated that the friend agreed to transfer the shares in consideration of the taxpayer undertaking to serve the company, a contractual expression of consideration was not conclusively determinative of causation, and anyway that expression did not mean that that was the sole consideration.[5] Other factors[6] were the date of the transfer being six months before service started, the out and out nature of the transfer, that the transferor was not technically the employer but only the principal shareholder of the employer, and that the taxpayer's surrender of his existing livelihood was expressed elsewhere in the contract. These points were emphasised by Walton J in *Glantre Engineering Ltd v Goodhand*[7] when holding that a payment to an employee who had given up an employment elsewhere was taxable. This leaves open the question of whether the distinction is between employment and self-employment or is simply one of fact; the latter is to be preferred. Where the payment is to induce the person to leave an employment the sum may be taxable under ITEPA 2003, s 401 et seq.

Another illustration of this principle relates to rugby players. Until recently, rugby league was for professional players; rugby union was for amateur players. Once a person had joined a rugby league club he was barred from ever again playing for, or even visiting a rugby union club. If discovered on a rugby union ground as a spectator he would have been asked to leave. Now, if he signs as a professional for either code he will be barred from competing as an amateur in, for example, amateur athletics.[8]

In *Jarrold v Boustead*[9] the taxpayer joined Hull Rugby League Club and was to receive in addition to a wage related to the team's performance, the sum of £3,000 on signing as a professional for the club. He successfully argued that the £3,000 was compensation for the loss of these various social and recreational activities, this conclusion being accepted by the Commissioners and by the Court of Appeal, leave to appeal to the House of Lords being refused.

In *Riley v Coglan*[10] however, the sum was not £3,000 but £500, of which £100 was to be paid on signing professional forms and the balance on taking up residence in York. The player agreed to serve for the remainder of his playing career or for 12 years if longer. If he failed to serve the whole stipulated period a proportionate part of the £500 was to be repaid by way of ascertained and liquidated damages. The Commissioners followed *Jarrold v Boustead* but on appeal that case was distinguished by Ungoed-Thomas J, who concluded that the £500 was to be a running payment for making himself available to serve the club when required to do so.[11]

The distinction is one of fact. Coglan's contract nowhere mentioned the abandonment of amateur status, but neither did Boustead's. Boustead's contract provided for the payment of £3,000 on signing professional forms from which the court inferred that the payment was for loss; Coglan's for £500 at the same time but with the proviso that £400 was to become payable only when he took up residence in York, a factor suggesting that the payment was for services to the club. These however are minor differences. The principal distinction is that in Boustead's case no part of the £3,000 was returnable, whereas Coglan might have to return some of his £500. In *Pritchard v Arundale* the transfer was out and out.

It is significant that in *Jarrold v Boustead* the disqualification of the player from rugby union and amateur athletics was for life. On parity of reasoning if a church organist were required to give up Sunday golf as one of the conditions of his employment and was paid £500 compensation, that sum would not be taxable as employment income.[12] If, however, the condition was against playing golf at those times when he ought to be playing the organ, the payment would only be a thinly disguised remuneration. More difficult is the question whether such a sum would be taxable if the disqualification against Sunday golf or against playing rugby union were binding only so long as he was church organist or played rugby league. It may be significant that in *Pritchard v Arundale* where there was nothing to prevent the taxpayer from resuming his practice as a chartered accountant on leaving his employment, Megarry J stressed the difficulties which a person of the taxpayer's age would find in building up his practice again.[13] The taxability of any such payment under ITEPA 2003, s 225, infra, § **7.29** has not yet been considered.

Compensation for loss of a general personal liberty such as amateur status or the playing of golf may thus be outside the employment income rules. However, payment in return for the surrender of a right which is part of the employer-employee relationship, eg the surrender of a right to commission payments,[14] clearly falls within employment income. The right to join a trade union was held to fall within this second group of rights in *Hamblett v Godfrey* which concerned the surrender of rights by employees at GCHQ. Here the Court of Appeal distinguished the surrender of rights and advantages closely connected with the employment from the giving up of social advantages.[15]

This decision was accepted by Lord Templeman in *Shilton v Wilmshurst* as being in recognition of the loss of rights that were not personal rights but that were directly connected with the employment. It followed that the source of the payment was the employment.[16]

The decision of the House of Lords in *Shilton v Wilmshurst*[17] leaves intact the tax-free status of the payment in *Pritchard v Arundale*. *Jarrold v Boustead* was not cited but presumably remains in place for the same reason. The Commissioners had expressly found that the payment in this case was not compensation for loss of rights enjoyed at Nottingham Forest.

In *Mairs v Haughley*, *Shilton v Wilmshurst* was expressly distinguished by the Court of Appeal in Northern Ireland[18] on the basis that in that case the payment was made in order to compensate for loss of rights under the former employer's redundancy scheme and not as an inducement to enter into the new contract of employment. *Hamblett v Godfrey* was distinguished on the basis that there the payment was made in return for the employee continuing as an employee. In the House of Lords these points of distinction were not articulated. However, Lord Woolf discerned in *Shilton v Wilmshurst* a clear view that payments for the relief of distress would not fall within employment income and that payments to compensate for redundancy would therefore not be taxable.[19] He also said that prima facie a payment made after the termination of employment is not earnings from the employment unless for example it is simply deferred remuneration.[20]

Simon's Taxes F4.404.

---

[1] [1971] 3 All ER 1011 at 1002.
[2] Supra, §§ **3.12** ff.
[3] See eg Lord Greene MR, in *Wales v Tilley* (1942) 25 TC 136 at 142.
[4] *Pritchard v Arundale* [1971] 3 All ER 1011 at 1022, 47 TC 680 followed in *Vaughan-Neil v IRC* [1979] STC 644, [1979] 3 All ER 481.
[5] [1971] 3 All ER 1011 at 1022.
[6] Quaere how substantial these really are.
[7] [1983] STC 1.
[8] *Jarrold v Boustead* [1964] 3 All ER 76 at 781, 41 TC 701 at 704.

[9] [1964] 3 All ER 76, 41 TC 701.
[10] [1968] 1 All ER 314, 44 TC 481.
[11] Cf the signing on payment in *Cameron v Prendergast* [1940] AC 549, [1940] 2 All ER 35.
[12] Lord Denning MR in *Jarrold v Boustead* [1964] 3 All ER 76 at 80, 41 TC 701 at 729.
[13] [1971] 3 All ER 1011 at 1023 c. Curiously, this point was *not* emphasised in *Glantre Engineering Ltd v Goodhand* [1983] STC 1.
[14] *McGregor v Randall* [1984] STC 223, [1984] 1 All ER 1092 (see infra, § **7.34**).
[15] [1987] STC 60, [1987] 1 All ER 916, CA.
[16] [1991] STC 88 at 95.
[17] [1991] STC 88; the details are set out at § **7.33**.
[18] [1992] STC 495, NI CA.
[19] *Mairs v Haughey* [1993] STC 569, HL, at 579h.
[20] *Mairs v Haughey* [1993] STC 569, HL, at 579j.

Restrictive covenants

[7.29] Statutory provisions were introduced[1] to reverse the decision of the House of Lords in *Beak v Robson*.[2] In that case a director agreed to continue serving the company at a salary of £2,000 a year and received £7,000 in return for an agreement not to compete with the business within a radius of 50 miles for five years. The £7,000 was held not taxable. This section applies wherever consideration is provided by the employer, whether to the employee or someone else, in return for an undertaking, whether binding or not, the tenor and effect of which is to restrict the employee as to his activities. The undertaking may be given before, during or after the employment. For the section to apply it must also be shown that the payment was made "in respect of" the undertaking. It has been held that this was not satisfied where the undertaking involved taking on the very duties inherent in and inseparable from the office or employment itself. In *Vaughan-Neil v IRC*[3] a barrister undertook to cease to practice at the planning bar on taking up his employment with a building contractor; the payment in return for that undertaking escaped the section.

The tax treatment of the value of the consideration, a phrase which includes consideration in kind, depends on the date on which the undertaking was given. If this occurred after 8 June 1988 the whole is subject to income tax at basic or higher rates in the usual way[4] and the income is to be treated as taxed for example for the purposes of TA 1988, s 348. If, however, it occurred before this date the whole was taxed in an unusual way—it was subject only to excess liability.[5]

The reasons for the 1988 changes were a wish to remove tax advantages in the system as part of the general reduction in tax rates and also a wish to counter the tax advantages of the device under the old regime. This section enabled an employer to make a tax-free payment to his lower paid employees and payments free of basic rate tax to his senior employees. It may not have proved popular because of the decision of the Court of Appeal in *Associated Portland Cement Manufacturers Ltd v Kerr*[6] that the employer could not deduct such payments in computing his profits. However, in that case the covenants were to last for life and it became common for employers to take covenants for shorter periods so that they could achieve a result of having the covenant taxed at a nil or low rate in the hands of the employee while being deductible by the employer. This result was not satisfactory to the Revenue. However, while making the payments fully taxable on the employee, the payment is deductible by the payer.

Simon's Taxes E4.481.

---

[1] The provisions now within ITEPA 2003, s 225 were introduced by FA 1950, s 16. The purpose of backdating the section for payments within s 34(4)(a) was to catch payments made to the managing directors of Austin and Morris Motor Companies. See Sabine, *A History of Income Tax*, p 116.
[2] [1943] 1 All ER 46, 25 TC 33.
[3] [1979] 3 All ER 481, [1979] STC 644.
[4] ITEPA 2003, ss 7 and 225.
[5] ITEPA 2003, s 225.
[6] [1946] 1 All ER 68, 27 TC 103 (see infra, § **8.129**).

Compensation payments for claims against employers

[7.30] ITEPA 2003, s 6 charges payments made which are either "general earnings" (s 6(1)(a)) or "specific employment income" (s 6(1)(b)). Both types of payment must arise "from" the employment (see s 9). It follows that sums paid by the employer where the employee has a cause of action against the employer will only be chargeable under this rule if arising from the employment.[1] So if an employee owns property adjoining his employer's factory sums paid by way of compensation under a claim for nuisance will not be taxable.[2]

Two statutory relaxations should be mentioned under this particular heading. First, payments under the statutory redundancy schemes are excluded from ITEPA 2003, s 6 but not from s 401.[3] Sections 401 et seq are part of Part 6 of ITEPA 2003 and are thus "specific employment income" rather than "general earnings". Second, payments by an employer in providing advice to an employee in connection with the ending of the office or employment are excluded from employment income altogether.[4] The legislation excludes the provision of the qualifying services, the payment or reimbursement of fees for such services to the employee, and the payment or reimbursement of related allowable travelling expenses.[5]

Compensation for loss of such voluntary rights may also escape[6] but payments made to all employees whether or not they were to be made redundant may not.[7]

Problems arise where the right being surrendered is a right under the contract of employment; in principle such payments escape tax under ITEPA 2003, s 6(1)(a) and s 62 as earnings unless they are made in return for services. It would have been easy for the courts to follow the line taken under Schedule D,

Cases I and II and to hold that sums paid in lieu of income are themselves income;[8] this however the courts have not done. The cases to be considered all turn on their own facts and, in particular, on the construction of the agreements reached, but certain principles do emerge.

Simon's Taxes Division E4.8.

---

[1] If the compensation takes the form of annual payments it will be taxable as income under Schedule D, Case III: *Asher v London Film Productions Ltd* [1944] KB 133, [1944] 1 All ER 77. See also *Taxation Comr (Victoria) v Phillips* (1937) 55 CLR 144.
[2] Although redundancy payments are exempt from income tax they are taken into account under s 401: ITEPA 2003, s 309.
[3] ITEPA 2003, s 309. On Revenue practice see Revenue Manual SE 13760 et seq.
[4] ITEPA 2003, s 310; advice for which this provision applies is exhaustively defined in s 310(2)–(6).
[5] ITEPA 2003, s 310(1).
[6] *Mairs v Haughey* [1993] STC 569, HL (see supra, § **7.17**).
[7] *Allan v IRC* [1994] STC 943, Ct of Sess.
[8] See infra, § **8.79**. *Chibbett v Robinson* (1924) 9 TC 48.

Payments in lieu of notice

[7.31] In *EMI Group Electronics Ltd v Coldicott*[1] the Court considered a payment made by an employer in lieu of notice ("PILON"). Two senior employees of EMI were each given PILON equal to six months pay. Each employee had a contract with the company which stated: 'The company will give [the employee] six months notice of its intention to terminate employment . . . The company reserves the right to make payment of the equivalent of salary in lieu of notice.'

The Revenue contended that the payment was within what was then s 19(1) of TA 1988, being a payment "from" an employment. The company, which had appealed against an assessment charging PAYE on the entire payment, argued that the payments were within what was s 148 of TA 1988 and, hence, enjoyed the £30,000 tax exemption (now in ITEPA 2003, s 403). The courts upheld the Revenue's contentions.

Such cases turn on the terms of the contract when the employment commences (unless later varied). It is, of course, trite law that contract is not solely what is written but is also what is understood between the parties, including the expectation that arises from the way in which that particular employer customarily treats its employees. In the Court of Appeal Chadwick LJ reviewed the case law on termination payments and quoted, with approval, the following statement by his predecessor Lawrence LJ in 1930:[2]

> In my judgement, the determining factor in the present case is that the payment to the Respondent, whatever the parties may have chosen to call it, was a payment which the company had contracted to make to him as part of his remuneration for his services as a director. It is true that payment of this part of his remuneration was deferred until his death or retirement or cesser of office, and that in the articles it is

[7.31] Employment income

called 'compensation for loss of office'. It is, however, a sum agreed to be paid in consideration of the Respondent accepting and serving in the office of director, and consequently is a sum paid by way of remuneration for his services as director.

In the light of the particular employment contract given by EMI, Chadwick LJ concluded[3]:

> Notice of intention to terminate—or a payment in lieu of notice—is not intended to relieve the hardship consequent upon becoming unemployed. It is no substitute for a redundancy payment. Indeed, it is something to which the employee is entitled in addition to a redundancy payment—as the present case itself illustrates. Notice of intention to terminate—or a payment in lieu of notice—gives recognition to the obvious fact that it is likely to take time to find other employment; and that a prudent employee enters into employment on terms that, when the time comes for that employment to end, he will have the security of a continued right to receive his salary (or a payment in lieu) while he finds other employment.
>
> I am satisfied, therefore, that there is nothing in the authorities which requires this court to reach the conclusion that a payment in lieu of notice, made in pursuance of a contractual provision, agreed at the outset of the employment, which enables the taxpayer company to terminate the employment on making that payment, is not properly to be regarded as an emolument from that employment. In my view, for the reasons which I have set out, such a payment is an emolument from the employment. That was the view reached by the commissioners and by the judge. I am satisfied that they were correct.

[1] [1999] STC 803, CA, upholding the decision of Neuberger J [1997] STC 1372.
[2] *Henry v Foster* (1930) 16 TC 605 at 632, CA.
[3] [1999] STC 803 at 820, CA.

[7.32] (1) A sum paid by way of commutation of pension rights is not within ITEPA 2003, s 6.[1] This is not technically a matter which involves the compromise of a right arising under the contract of employment since while the right may have its sources in such a contract the pension itself is a taxable entity quite distinct from the office or employment.[2]

Simon's Direct Tax Service E4.805.

[1] *Tilley v Wales* [1943] AC 386, [1943] 1 All ER 280, 25 TC 136.
[2] Per Viscount Simon LC [1943] AC 386 at 392, 25 TC 136 at 149.

[7.33] (2) A payment by way of compensation on the termination of the contract of employment whether after judgment or by settlement is not within ITEPA 2003, s 6(1)(*a*).[1]

Payments for breach of the contract must however be distinguished from three other situations. The first is where it is agreed between employer and employee that the contract shall cease with effect from a future date and the contract is allowed to run its natural course until that date. Since the contract still exists and services are performed, sums paid under the contract are within ITEPA 2003 s 6(1)(*a*) and s 62.[2] A payment conditional on continued service for a short period consistent with the reasonable needs of the employer will also not escape ITEPA 2003, s 6(1)(a) and s 62, such sums being treated as terminal bonuses.[3] Such facts must in their turn be distinguished from the situation in which the employment is to cease but the remuneration is still to be paid after the date of termination; in such circumstances the remuneration is not within ITEPA 2003, s 6(1)(a) and s 62.[4]

The second situation to be distinguished is that in which the contract of employment stipulates the sum to be paid in the event that the contract does not run its full course. The payment of that sum in accordance with the contract is earnings.

In *Dale v De Soissons*[5] the company exercised its right under the contract to terminate it after one year on payment of £10,000. The payment was held to be taxable. As Lord Evershed put it,

> The contract provided that he should serve either for three years at an annual sum or, if the company so elected, for a shorter period of two years or one year at an annual sum in respect of the two years or one year, as the case might be, plus a further sum, that is to say it was something to which he became entitled as part of the terms upon which he promised to serve.[6]

It also follows from *Dale v De Soissons* that a clear, but perhaps unfortunate, distinction arises between those who have the forethought to stipulate in advance what sums shall be due in the event of early termination of the contract, and those who are content to await events, between—to take a completely inappropriate analogy—the wise virgins (who are taxed for their wisdom) and the foolish virgins (who escape a tax charge).

It should be noted that statutory redundancy payments are exempt from tax[7] and that non-statutory but genuine redundancy payments are regarded as falling outside ITEPA 2003, s 6.[8] Ex-gratia payments for the surrender of such non-statutory rights may also escape[9] but payments made to all employees whether or not they were to be made redundant may not.[10]

The third situation is that which occurred in *Shilton v Wilmshurst*[11] (see supra, § 7.17). A payment which is not to compensate for the termination of one employment but for the start of another will be treated as taxable earnings of the new employment.

Shilton v Wilmshurst concerned the transfer of Peter Shilton, then and for a long time thereafter the England goal keeper, from Nottingham Forest to Southampton in 1982. Under the deal Shilton was paid a signing on fee of £80,000 by Southampton which, it was agreed, was taxable in full under what is now ITEPA 2003, s 6(1)(a) and s 62. He was also paid a fee of £75,000 by Nottingham Forest as an inducement to leave the club—and so go off their payroll.

The House of Lords, reversing both Morritt J and the unanimous Court of Appeal, held that the sum was taxable in full as part of the emoluments from the employment with Southampton (even though paid by Nottingham Forest). The idea of Shilton being subject to tax because, while he was saving goals for Southampton against Nottingham Forest, he had been paid by Nottingham Forest to render services to Southampton is so ridiculous that further explanation is needed.

Morritt J had held that the payment was an emolument "for" entering into the contract with Southampton rather than "from" that employment and that a payment by a third party would only be "from" the employment if that third party had some interest in the performance of the contract. Applying that test he held that Nottingham Forest had no interest in how Shilton performed for Southampton. The judgments in the Court of Appeal were similar; the payment had to be "referable to" the performance of services under the contract; Nottingham Forest has no interest in the performance as distinct from the formation of the contract.[12]

This test of interest was rejected by Lord Templeman in typical style. What sort of interest would suffice; why should a payment be taxable if it were by a director of Southampton but not if it were from Nottingham Forest? Lord Templeman concluded that the payment from Nottingham Forest should be treated the same way as that from Southampton.[13] In reaching this conclusion Lord Templeman used the test set out supra, § 7.17.

The case highlights the unsatisfactory boundary between payments taxable under ITEPA 2003, s 6(1)(a) and s 62 and compensation claims. A payment by an employer for breach of a contract of employment (a golden handshake) is not taxable under ITEPA 2003, s 6(1)(a) and s 62 because it is not paid under the contract but for breach of it. So if an employer breaks the contract and pays compensation the payment will fall outside general earnings. Yet if he acts as a good employer and finds a new employment for the employee before dismissing him the payment will be taxable if it is for taking up the new employment. All turns on the reason for the payment (and the evidence needed to establish it). There is much sense in the argument for Shilton that his was a payment to cease to be an employee of Nottingham Forest; however, this was not so on the facts as found.

If the employee decides to start his own business the parting payment has not previously been treated as a receipt of the new trade or profession yet the argument of Lord Templeman could be applied by analogy here also. If, of course, the new business is incorporated, so that the new source of income is from employment with the company rather than self-employment, the case may fall within *Shilton v Wilmshurst*.

There may be good sense in abolishing the special treatment for golden handshakes altogether. Lord Templeman's speech may be seen as a step towards achieving this objective by reducing the credibility of the distinctions in this area. Meanwhile employees and their advisers know that if they want to bring the payment within ITEPA 2003, s 401 they must be extremely careful; they may also take note of a rather guarded ministerial statement on the costs of re-employment counselling and training[14] although statute now excludes a tax charge on certain payments.[15]

Simon's Taxes E4.404, 405, 511.

---

[1] See *Henley v Murray* [1950] 1 All ER 908 at 909, 31 TC 351 at 363.
[2] See, for example, *Richardson v Delaney* [2001] STC 1328 and *Ibe v McNally* [2005] STC 1426.
[3] Statement of practice SP 1/94.

⁴ *Clayton v Lavender* (1965) 42 TC 607, not following *Hofman v Wadman* (1946) 27 TC 192.
⁵ [1950] 2 All ER 460, 32 TC 118, CA; and see *Henry v Foster* (1931) 16 TC 605, CA and *Williams v Simmonds* [1981] STC 715. Quaere if the company refused to pay alleging some default by the employee, and a compromise payment was later made to the employee.
⁶ [1950] 2 All ER 460 at 462, 32 TC 118 at 127.
⁷ ITEPA 2003, s 309.
⁸ Statement of practice SP 1/94.
⁹ *Mairs v Haughey* [1993] STC 569, HL (see supra, § **7.17**).
¹⁰ *Allan v IRC* [1994] STC 943, Ct of Sess.
¹¹ [1991] STC 88.
¹² STC 55 at 62. For comment on the CA decision see [1990] BTR 313–318.
¹³ [1991] STC 88 at 94.
¹⁴ HC Written Answer, 2 June 1992, see *Simon's Tax Intelligence* 1992, p 584.
¹⁵ ITEPA 2003, s 310. The statutory exclusion is subject to restrictive conditions.

[7.34] (3) A payment for the modification of the contract of employment ought in principle to be capable of escaping the general earnings charge in the same way as a payment for termination. However, in practice, where the contract of employment continues, it is very difficult to persuade the courts that the payment is one for giving up a right under the contract as distinct from a payment for the services still to be rendered.

In *Hunter v Dewhurst*¹ the taxpayer wished to retire and live in Scotland but the company wished him to continue as a director, although doing less work—for less pay. This rearrangement would mean a reduction in a sum payable under a clause in the company's articles prescribing compensation of a sum equal to five years' earnings. The taxpayer agreed to continue as a director but received a lump sum of £10,000 under an agreement in which he renounced all rights to the compensation payment. The House of Lords held that this payment escaped tax, largely on the ground that it was compensation for the surrender of his contingent rights under the clause in the articles.²

By contrast in *Tilley v Wales*³ the taxpayer agreed to take a reduced salary of £2,000 a year in return for a payment taken to be £20,000.⁴ It was held that this was referable to the agreement to continue to serve as managing director at a reduced salary, so was advance remuneration and so within what was then s 19(1) of TA 1988.

Hunter v Dewhurst is a decision which has been more often distinguished⁵ than followed⁶ and it must now be taken as confined to its special facts.⁷ However there does appear to be a clear distinction in principle between the surrender of rights under the contract which may after all be taken as analogous to the surrender of pension rights in *Tilley v Wales*, and a payment in consideration of refraining from resigning.

In *Holland v Geoghegan*,⁸ refuse collectors had had their right to sell salvaged property lawfully terminated; they went on strike but returned to work on payment of £450 compensation for loss of earnings due to the termination of the scheme. Foster J reversing the Special Commissioners, held that as the right to sell salvaged property had been lawfully terminated the payment was not one of compensation for loss of a right but an inducement to return to work and so taxable.

In *McGregor v Randall*[9] the difficulty of persuading the court to treat compensation for variation of terms of employment was well-shown. The taxpayer had been entitled to commission on profits; he received compensation in return for the loss of this right. In all other respects the employment continued. Scott J held that what was then s 19(1) applied; he confined *Hunter v Dewhurst* to its special facts and distinguished *Tilley v Wales* and *Du Cros v Ryall*[10] on the basis that the rights lost there would not or could not be enjoyed while the employment was current.

Simon's Taxes E4.405, 406.

---

[1] (1932) 16 TC 605. In the three courts, four judges found for the taxpayer and five for the Revenue but the taxpayer had three in the House of Lords.
[2] This is emphasised in the explanations of *Hunter v Dewhurst* in *Cameron v Prendergast* [1940] 2 All ER 35, 23 TC 122.
[3] [1943] 1 All ER 280, 25 TC 136.
[4] The sum paid was £40,000 but this was apportioned between the loss of pension rights and the reduction in salary.
[5] *Cameron v Prendergast* [1940] 2 All ER 35, 23 TC 122; *Tilley v Wales* [1943] 1 All ER 280, 25 TC 136; *Leeland v Boarland* [1946] 1 All ER 13, 27 TC 71; *Bolam v Muller* (1947) 28 TC 471; *Holland v Geoghegan* [1972] 3 All ER 333, 48 TC 482.
[6] *Duff v Barlow* (1941) 23 TC 633 and *Tilley v Wales* appear to be the only reported cases in which *Hunter v Dewhurst* has been applied but in the former *Cameron v Prendergast* [1940] 2 All ER 35, 23 TC 122 was not cited.
[7] eg Sir Raymond Evershed MR, in *Henley v Murray* [1950] 1 All ER 908 at 911, 31 TC 351 at 366.
[8] [1972] 3 All ER 333, 48 TC 482.
[9] [1984] STC 223, [1984] 1 All ER 1092.
[10] (1935) 19 TC 444.

[7.35] Another difficulty concerns apportionment where a payment is made for two causes, the one future services and the other compensation for loss of office or of some other right. In *Tilley v Wales* the House of Lords was relieved of the task of deciding whether an apportionment should be made because of agreement between the parties.[1] In principle apportionment is possible.[2] Whether there will be an apportionment if the sum is paid for two causes neither of which can be valued remains unclear.[3] If one can be valued without insuperable difficulty the balance is taken as due to the other.

---

[1] [1943] AC 386 at 394, 25 TC 136 at 150.
[2] *Carter v Wadman* (1946) 28 TC 41.
[3] This was left open by the Court of Appeal in *Shilton v Wilmshurst*: see [1990] STC 55.

Taxation of termination payments

[7.36] Payments or benefits[1] received on retirement or removal from office or employment which are not earnings under general principles[2] are subject to a special scheme of taxation and are taxable when, and only when, they exceed £30,000.[3] This special scheme is a separate charging provision and can therefore apply even though the taxpayer left the UK and was neither resident nor ordinarily resident in the UK in the year in which the employment ended and the payment made.[4] Payments and benefits caught are those received directly or indirectly in consideration of, or in consequence of, or otherwise in connection with, the termination or change.[5] For instance, the Special Commissioners held in the case of *Brander & Ors v R & C Comrs* (2007) SpC 610, that payments, on termination of employment of the directors of a company, labelled 'pension contributions' and 'loss of share option rights' payments were received in connection with or as a consequence of that termination of employment and therefore fell under TA 1988, s 148[6] and the £30,000 exemption applied to each of those payments. If the payment or benefit fits the description it is immaterial whether it is paid in pursuance of a legal obligation or not.[7] It is caught even if made to the personal representatives of the holder or past holder of the office or employment, even if it is paid to the spouse or any relative or dependant of his, as is a payment on his behalf or to his order;[8] the employee is taxable even if the benefit is received by another.[9] If the payment fits the description, it is immaterial whether the payment is made by the employer, a former employer, or any other person.[10]

There are reporting requirements.[11]

Timing. Cash receipts are treated as received when the payment is made or the recipient is entitled to call for it. A non-cash benefit is treated as received when it is used or enjoyed.[12]

Exclusions. There are exclusions for payments on death, disability or injury,[13] certain superannuation benefits or gratuities, payments exempt under the relocation expenses rules, payments in respect of employee liabilities and indemnity insurance, payments to members of Her Majesty's forces, and certain payments in relation to services for a government of an overseas territory within the Commonwealth.[14] A payment which is not a retirement benefit, but rather one for wrongful dismissal, can come within ITEPA 2003, s 401 but Revenue practice requires a close examination of the facts to determine the genuineness or otherwise of the claim.[15] Certain payments in respect of foreign service can be exempt or are reduced by 50%.[16]

If the payment is not otherwise exempt it still will escape tax if it is not more than £30,000.[17] In calculating the £30,000 one must include any redundancy payment or ex-gratia payment but not certain supplementary contributions to retirement schemes.[18] Two payments for the same employment or two payments for different employments with the same or associated employers[19] are aggregated. Payments for distinct employments with unassociated employers are not aggregated. Where payments are aggregated the aggregation is cumulative from year to year, the £30,000 exemption being applied to earlier payments before later ones. There are also valuation rules.[20]

[7.36] Employment income

A payment outside ITEPA 2003, s 6(1)(a) but within the charge under ITEPA 2003, s 401 does not count as "final earnings" in calculating the ceiling for pension rights.

This regime applies to certain payments to Members of Parliament, members of the European Parliament, the Scottish Parliament and the devolved assemblies for Wales and Northern Ireland.[21] It also applies to certain payments to ministers, the Mayor of London and members of the Greater London Assembly on ceasing to hold office.[22]

By concession the Revenue will not use ITEPA 2003, s 401 to charge certain legal costs properly incurred by the employee and reimbursed by the employer.[23]

The regime in ITEPA 2003, ss 401 to 416 applies only when there is not a charge to income tax under general principles.[24] The first stage is, thus, to analyse the contract of employment to discover whether the payment at termination arises as a contractural right (when tax will be charged[25] on the total received), or whether it arises without a contractural right (when the furst £30,000 is free of tax and tax will be charged[26] on the excess above £30,000). In *SCA Packaging Ltd v R & C Comrs*[27] the Special Commissioner had to analyse an unwritten contract of employment implied by custom and practice. He concluded that payments made were, in part, contractural and, in part, not contractural. Conversely, in *Resolute Management Services Limited v HMRC and Haderlein v HMRC*[28], the Special Commissioner held that a £150,000 payment made to the former employee was truly ex gratia and, therefore, the first £30,000 was excluded from the tax charge. (As it happens, the operation of the US–UK Double Tax Treaty meant that the subsequent £120,000 also escaped UK tax.)

Simon's Taxes E4.801.

---

[1] Defined in ITEPA 2003, s 402.

[2] In *Bluck v Salton* [2003] STC (SCD) 439, Special Commissioners confirmed that relief under what is now ITEPA 2003, s 403 only applies where the sum is not otherwise chargeable to tax. In *Wilson v Clayton* [2004] EWCA Civ 1657, [2005] STC 157, the Court of Appeal held that compensation paid by Birmingham City Council to Mr Clayton for withdrawal of his essential car use allowance was not an emolument within the basic charging provison of ITEPA 2003, s 6 and, hence, it fell to be assessed under ITEPA 2004, s 403. For a useful summary of decided cases on the taxation of sums arising under an agreement to terminate employment (ie whether charged under ITEPA 2003, s 6 on the full amount, or under ITEPA 2003, s 403 on the amount that exceeds £30,000), see the decision of Malcolm J F Palmer in *Porter v R & C Comrs* [2005] STC (SCD) 803.

[3] ITEPA 2003, s 403. For an example of the operation of the provision, see *Walker v Adams* [2003] STC (SCD) 269. For an example of the operation of the charge before its amendment by FA 1998, s 58, see *George v Ward* [1995] STC (SCD) 230. In *Bluck v Salton* [2003] STC (SCD) 439, it was held that the entitlement granted to the employee was taxable under the share option legislation. The provisions for termination payments were, therefore, not applicable

[4] *Nichols v Gibson* [1994] STC 1029.

[5] ITEPA 2003, s 401.

[6] Now ITEPA 2003, ss 401(1)(3), 403(1)(4) and 404.
[7] TA 1988, s 148(5)(b) and see Note 42 in Annex 2 of the Explanatory Notes of ITEPA 2003.
[8] ITEPA 2003, s 401.
[9] ITEPA 2003, s 403.
[10] TA 1988, s 148(5)(a) and see Note 42 in Annex 2 of the Explanatory Notes of ITEPA 2003.
[11] On reporting requirements see Income Tax (Employments) (Amendment No 2) Regulations, SI 1990/70, *Simon's Weekly Tax Intelligence* 1999, pp 180 and 234.
[12] ITEPA 2003, s 403.
[13] ITEPA 2003, s 406; see *Horner v Hasted* [1995] STC 766.
[14] ITEPA 2003, ss 405–412.
[15] Statement of practice SP 13/91 as amplified by note by Law Society, 7 October 1992, *Simon's Tax Intelligence* 1992, p 869.
[16] ITEPA 2003, ss 413 and 414; see HMRC Schedule E Manual para SE13700; on need to define a place of service, see *Wienand v Anderton* [1977] STC 12.
[17] ITEPA 2003, s 403.
[18] Statement of practice SP 2/81.
[19] ITEPA 2003, ss 403 and 404.
[20] ITEPA 2003, s 415; on loans see s 416.
[21] ITEPA 2003, s 291.
[22] ITEPA 2003, s 291 as amended by the FA 2008.
[23] Extra-statutory concession A81.
[24] ITEPA 2003, s 401(3).
[25] Under ITEPA 2003, ss 9(2) & 6(1)(a) as "general earnings".
[26] Under ITEPA 2003, s 403(1).
[27] [2006] STC (SCD) 426.
[28] (2008) Sp C 710.

Termination payments: contrast between an employee and a trader

[7.37] The contrast between the treatment under ITEPA 2003 and the treatment for a receipt by a self-employed individual is highlighted by the position of sub-postmasters. The monthly sums paid to a sub-postmaster are, by long standing Revenue practice, paid without deduction of PAYE and are treated as receipts of the trade carried on by that person, typically involving running a village stores in the same shop as the village post office.

The Post Office is currently looking to reduce the number of sub-post offices and is offering a compensation payment to each sub-postmaster whose post office is closed.

If the payment is made to an employee, the first £30,000 would escape an income tax charge.[1]

By contrast, if the payment is from a trading contract that is terminated, the whole of any termination payment is taxable as a trading receipt[2] and there is no exemption for the first £30,000 of the receipt. It was for this reason that a firm of lawyers contended in *IRC v Brander & Cruickshank*[3] that they were entitled to be assessed under Schedule E on payments received on the termination of company registrarships, even though in earlier years the income had been taxed under Schedule D Case II. Their argument was accepted by the House of Lords. On the authority of this decision, a taxpayer who receives income from an office has the right to insist on taxation as "employment income", even if in prior years the profits from the sub-postmaster business have been taxed under Schedule D. The whole of the tax year must be one of the two alternative treatments; it is not possible for some of the year to be treated under Schedule D and only the part in which the position terminates to be assessed as employment income.

Exceptionally, a termination receipt can be treated as a capital receipt liable to CGT if the contract in respect of which it is made governs the whole profit-making structure of the taxpayer's business.[4]

[1] See supra, § 7.36.
[2] *Kelsall Parsons & Co. v IRC* (1938) 21 TC 608; *Deeny v Gooda Walker Ltd* [1996] STC 299, HL.
[3] (1970) 46 TC 574.
[4] *Van Den Berghs Ltd v Clark* (1935) 19 TC 390, HL.

Termination payment being a payment to a non-approved retirement benefits scheme

[7.38] ITEPA 2003, s 386 charges as income of an employee a sum paid by an employer in accordance with a non-approved retirement benefits scheme. There is no £30,000 exemption. Such a payment may be any lump sum, gratuity or other like benefit given or to be given on retirement or on death.

The charge under ITEPA 2003, s 386 does not arise where the payment is made under an "approved scheme".[1] An employer who wishes to make an ex gratia payment that would otherwise fall to be charged to tax under ITEPA 2003, s 386 can apply for approval of the single lump sum payment as constituting an "approved scheme". Application is made on form SF 60.[2] In order to grant such approval, HMRC require the following conditions to be satisfied:

(a) There is no lump sum relevant benefit potentially payable from another approved scheme.
(b) The amount payable is within the normal requirements for tax approval of a pension scheme,[3] being, on retirement, no higher than 3/80ths of final salary for each year of service or, on death, not higher than four times salary.

An employer can make a payment of up to £7,950, without prior approval being required, as long as the employee is not part of another approved scheme or a relevant statutory scheme.[4]

[1] ITEPA 2003, s 386(1)(*a*).
[2] Application should be made to Pension Schemes Office, Yorke House, PO Box 62, Castle Meadow Road, Nottingham, NG2 1BG.

³ The limit is 1/12th of the earnings cap for personal pension schemes, £99,000 for 2003–04.
⁴ Inland Revenue Statement of Practice SP13/91, para 8.

Continuing benefits provided in a termination payment

[7.39] It is commonly the case that a termination package includes the right granted to the employee to continue to enjoy a particular benefit. Thus, for example, an employee with a company car may be allowed to retain the car for his private use for a further specified period. Where an employer has a sports facility for employees, it is not infrequently the case that those employees made redundant are allowed to continue to use the sporting facilities for a lengthy period after termination of the employment.

Any cash paid after termination of an employment is brought into charge to tax for the year in which it is received.[1] Where a termination package includes a continuing benefit, statute provides that the benefit is brought into the income tax assessment for the year in which it is used or enjoyed and subject to tax at the rate applicable to the individual taxpayer for the year in which it is used or enjoyed.[2]

[1] ITEPA 2003, s 403, overruling *George v Ward* [1995] STC (SCD) 230.
[2] ITEPA 2003, s 403.

Benefits in kind—general

[7.40] The general principle that money's worth is income applies also to benefits in kind—but with difficulty. Where an employer transfers a benefit in kind to his employee any tax system has two sets of problems. The first is that of defining the benefits to be taxed. Thus the provision of a more luxurious office or of greater secretarial assistance would not at first sight give rise to a taxable benefit. To state a test in terms of causation will give rise to problems like *Hochstrasser v Mayes*[1] while to state one in terms of a but-for test of causation then gives rise to the need to state exceptions.

The second set of problems concerns the valuation of the benefit. One basis is to tax the employee on the cost to the employer, a basis which applies in the UK where the employee earns £8,500 or more a year or is a director (see infra, § **7.99**). A second basis is to tax the employee on the value to him, a test which raises very acute problems where the same benefit is conferred on employees of differing tastes and circumstances. A third basis is to take the market value of the benefit, but this is ambiguous since it could mean the price which the employee would have had to pay to acquire the asset for himself or the price which he could have obtained for the asset if he had chosen to sell it secondhand. A further problem is whether to take the resulting figure or to gross it up. What follows concerns only the income tax treatment of benefits in kind; these benefits are not subject to Class 1A national insurance contributions.

[7.40] Employment income

In order to be assessable as a benefit of employment, the payment must be made in respect of employment. The Revenue accept that benefits extended to retired ex-employees under a group medical scheme are not assessable as a pension is not an employment.[2] The distinction between employment income and pension income is made explicit in ITEPA 2003, which treats them as separate classes of income.[3] However, if the medical benefit is provided as a specific part of the pension or as part of a termination package, it is taxable as such.[4]

Simon's Taxes E4.4.

---

[1] (1959) 38 TC 673.
[2] HMRC Employment Manual para EIM21764.
[3] The Revenue view is that the doctrine of the exclusivity of schedules now applies to the separate categories of income identified by ITEPA 2003: see *Mitchell and Edon v Ross* (1961) 40 TC 11, HL, considered at supra, § **5.03**.
[4] HMRC Employment Manual para EIM21764.

[7.41] The general principle adopted in the UK is the second variation of the third basis, the secondhand value of the benefit, a principle which has the logical consequence that, if the benefit cannot be converted into money or turned to pecuniary account, it is not taxable, unless it is accommodation. It is now subject to statutory modification (a) for employees not in lower paid employments (see infra, § **7.97**), and (b) for all employees if the benefit is provided by means of a voucher. The general principle, however remains the starting point. It was laid down by the House of Lords in *Tennant v Smith*.[1]

In *Tennant v Smith* the taxpayer was agent for the Bank of Scotland at Montrose. He was bound as part of his duty to occupy the bank house as custodian for the whole premises belonging to the Bank, and also for the transaction of any special bank business after bank hours. He was not allowed to vacate the house even for a temporary period unless with the special consent of the directors who in that case sanctioned the occupation of the house by another official of the bank during the absence of the agent. The agent, besides dealing with business after bank hours, had to lock up the bank and attend to the security of the safe. There was a night bolt from the agent's bedroom to the bank's premises. He was not allowed to sublet the bank house nor to use it for any purpose other than the bank's business. The bank house was suitable accommodation for him but as Lord Macnaghten observed, "his occupation is that of a servant and not the less so because the bank thinks proper to provide for gentlemen in his position in their service accommodation on a liberal scale".[2] His total income from other sources came to £375 and the value of his occupation of these premises was placed at £50. Where a taxpayer's income was below £400 he was entitled to an abatement.[3] The House of Lords held that he was not assessable under Schedule D or Schedule E as it then was[4] in respect of his occupation of the premises and so was entitled to the abatement. Lord Halsbury stated that the thing sought to be taxed "is not income unless it can be turned to money".[5] The bank agent's occupation of the premises was not capable of being converted into money since he could not let it.[6]

For the purpose of a charge to tax, a benefit is treated as provided when it becomes available to be enjoyed by the taxpayer. Thus, in *Templeton v Jacobs*[7] a future employer paid for the conversion of the taxpayer's loft into an office, which he was to use after he had entered into employment. The taxpayer's argument that the cost of conversion was not assessable as at the time of conversion he was not in that employment, was rejected. The Court held that the converted loft was enjoyed by the taxpayer once he commenced employment, being the office from which he carried on that employment. Hence, it was employment income of the year in which the employment commenced, being the year in which the taxpayer first enjoyed the benefit.

Simon's Taxes E4.402.

[1] [1892] AC 150, 3 TC 158, HL.
[2] [1892] AC 150 at 162, 3 TC 158 at 169.
[3] 5 & 6 Vict. c. 35, s 163.
[4] Nor was he assessable under the priniciples then applied by Schedule A since it was not he but the Bank that was the occupier; per Lord Watson, at 158, 166; per Lord Macnaghten, at 162, 169.
[5] At 156, 164; to the same effect Lord Watson, at 159, 167; per Lord Macnaghten, at 163, 170; per Lord Field, at 164, 171 and per Lord Hannen, at 165, 172. Lord Morris concurred.
[6] With the bank's tacit consent he used the premises for an insurance business but this was ignored. At one time it was thought that where a person was in beneficial occupation but that occupation was not convertible (into money or money's worth) then if the employer paid the Schedule A tax in respect of that occupation, the employee was not taxable in respect of that payment under what was then Schedule E: *M'Dougall v Sutherland* (1894) 3 TC 261, but this was overruled in *IRC v Miller* [1930] AC 222, 15 TC 25.
[7] [1996] STC 991.

Convertibility

[7.42] A benefit may be converted in ways other than simple sale. In *Abbott v Philbin*[1] an employee was said to be taxable in respect of the value of an option to acquire shares even though the option was expressed to be non-assignable because the employee could have turned the value of the option into money in other ways notably by raising money on the right to call for the shares.[1]

A benefit can also be turned into money by being surrendered, or by not being accepted. In *Heaton v Bell*[2] an employee was loaned a car by his employers and went on to what was called an amended wage basis. The House of Lords held that the correct construction of the agreement was that there was no change in his wage but the employers were entitled to deduct each week a sum in respect of the use of the car. It followed that tax was due on the gross wage each week with no deduction for tax purposes for the sum withheld on account of the car. Yet if the correct construction had been that the employee took a lower wage and received the free use of a car, a majority of the House would have held that

[7.42] Employment income

he was taxable in respect of the use of the car on the amount he would have received had he surrendered that use.[3] Such statements are obiter.

It has since been held[4] that when an employee could, and did, use a non-chargeable method of obtaining a benefit, the fact that he could have chosen a different method which could have resulted in liability was enough to give rise to liability. So when an employee has a choice between an allowance and the benefit in kind it might be argued, on the basis of the dicta in the House of Lords in *Heaton v Bell*,[5] that as the employee could surrender his benefit in kind and take the (taxable) allowance in lieu he should pay tax on the value of the allowance whether he takes the benefit or the allowance.

The principle is modified by a concession allowing all agricultural workers free board and lodging to remain free of tax despite his right to take a higher cash sum in lieu.[6] This concession does not apply if the employment is one falling within the main parts of the benefits code of ITEPA 2003, excluding the parts not applicable to those in lower paid employments (see infra, § 7.88).

The treatment of the offer of an alternative to a car is now the subject of specific legislative treatment.[7] Where a car is made available to the employee under the rules for directors and employees earning over £8,500 (see infra, § **7.105**) and an alternative to that benefit is offered, the mere fact that the alternative is offered does not make the benefit of the car chargeable to tax under general principles. The effect is that the employee will be taxed on the benefit chosen. Similarly, statute[8] exempts the first £500 of the cash equivalent of the benefit of computer equipment being supplied by an employer for the private use of an employee, even when the employee has chosen to take the equipment rather than a cash alternative offered.

Simon's Taxes E4.402, 403.

---

[1] Per Lord Radcliffe [1961] AC 352 at 378–9, 39 TC 82 at 125.
[1] Per Lord Radcliffe [1961] AC 352 at 378–9, 39 TC 82 at 125.
[2] [1969] 2 All ER 70, 46 TC 211.
[3] Per Lord Morris of Borth-y-Gest, at 753, 84, 253 and per Lord Diplock, at pp 767, 96, 265. To the same effect but by a different route Lord Reid, dissenting, at 746, 79, 247. While the first two Lords would have quantified the benefit as the sum subtracted each week × 52 (the number of weeks in the year) Lord Reid would have taken the same sum × 50 since two weeks notice has to be given before returning to the scheme. So while Lord Morris and Lord Diplock appear to tax the benefit foregone, Lord Reid would appear to tax the benefit that could be obtained. The latter seems more correct.
[4] *Westall v McDonald* [1985] STC 693 at p 721.
[5] [1969] 2 All ER 70, 46 TC 211.
[6] Extra-statutory concession A60.
[7] ITEPA 2003, s 119; see Inland Revenue press release, 21 July 1994, *Simon's Tax Intelligence* 1994, p 888.
[8] ITEPA 2003, s 320 amended by FA 2004, s 79.

[7.43] Another problem concerns the reason why the assets may not be convertible. In *Tennant v Smith* Lord Halsbury said that a thing could be treated as money's worth where the thing was capable of being turned into money "from its own nature".[1] Yet in *Tennant v Smith* the only reason why the agent could not turn his occupation of the house into money was the *fiat* of his employer. Clearly the loopholes in the tax net will be greatly widened if it is left to the employer to decide whether a benefit is convertible and so assessable. The courts have indicated that while restrictions imposed by employers may be treated as an effective restriction[2] this will not be so if the conditions are not genuine.[3] However, Lord Diplock has gone further in the defence of the Revenue and in *Heaton v Bell* said that limitations on use arising from a contract collateral to the contract of employment into which the employee entered of his own volition would not escape tax.[4] It remains to be seen whether this approach will be accepted and whether, if it is, the courts will treat a clause in a contract of employment as giving rise to a collateral contract.[5] It is also worth noting in the context of convertibility the wording used in the definition of "money's worth" in ITEPA 2003.[6]

Simon's Taxes E4.402, 403.

[1] [1892] AC 150 at 156, 3 TC 158 at 164.
[2] eg *Ede v Wilson and Cornwall* [1945] 1 All ER 367, 26 TC 381—shares subject to a condition that they would not be sold without employer's permission—held that valuation must take account of the restriction on effect of a term forbidding assignment of a debt; for effect of a prohibition on assignment of a chose in action see *Helstan Securities Ltd v Hertfordshire County Council* [1978] 3 All ER 262.
[3] Lord Reid in *Heaton v Bell* [1969] 2 All ER 70 at 79, 46 TC 211 at 247.
[4] At 95, 264.
[5] Cf the test that an expense, to be deductible, must be required by the job, and not simply by the employer (see infra, § **7.127**).
[6] ITEPA 2003, s 62(3)(*b*) and supra, § **7.01**.

Extent of liability

[**7.44**] Convertibility provides the test not only of liability but also of its extent; the employee is chargeable on the amount of money into which he could turn the benefit.[1] In *Weight v Salmon*[2] where the employee was given the right to apply for shares at less than market price he was held assessable on the difference between the market price and the price he paid.

In *Wilkins v Rogerson*[3] the employee was provided with a suit; he was held assessable on the second hand value of the suit, which was only one third of the purchase price, a fact which involved "no reflection on the tailor" because "it is notorious that the value of clothing is very much reduced the moment that it can be called second hand". Where on the other hand an employee was provided with a voucher which he could spend at a great number of stores it was held that because of the range of objects which he was enabled to buy the face value should be taken.[4] Special legislation now applies to vouchers (see infra, § **7.47**).

The value is ascertained at the date the benefit is enjoyed, rather than when the asset is received;[5] although a special rule now applies to certain share options,

[7.44] Employment income

other options are subject to the general rule. If an asset is received in non-convertible form but later becomes convertible, there is little reason why a charge should not arise at the latter time.

A further anomaly is the borderline between the rule in *Nicoll v Austin* and that in *Tennant v Smith*. If an employer buys each of his employees a new suit at Christmas, the employee is taxable only on the second hand value of the suit. If however the employee has already bought a suit but not yet paid for it and his employer settles the debt for him, he is taxable on the amount paid to the tailor. In *Wilkins v Rogerson*[6] the employer arranged for a tailor to provide some of its employees with clothes suitable for wear at the office, the employee to choose from a suit, overcoat or raincoat, up to a maximum cost of £15. One employee chose a suit costing £14.75 and the Revenue sought to charge him with that sum. The Court of Appeal however held that he was chargeable only on the second hand value of the suit, £5. It would appear from the reasoning of Lord Evershed MR, in that Court and of Danckwerts J at first instance that if the employer had given Rogerson a voucher with which to buy the suit he would have been taxable on the cost of the suit, £14.75, since in that case he would have acquired not a suit but a right to spend up to £15 on a suit. The reasoning of Donovan LJ, is slightly different; he rejected the Crown's argument because the employee never became liable to pay the £14.75 to the tailor. The question of whose is the liability to be discharged, rather than what right the employee acquired, is a clearer way of explaining what remains a most technical area of law. Yet its clarity leads to further anomalies. Thus would the taxpayer's liability be for £14.75 if he made the contract but only for £5 if he made the contract as agent for his employer who then gave him the suit? To escape liability a genuine agency would have to be shown. This is a question of fact; when an employee drives into a garage and begins to pump petrol into his car he may be an agent for his employer or he may be acting on his own account.[7] If the employer is an undisclosed principal the employee is personally liable on the contract so his liability may be for tax on £14.75.[8]

Simon's Taxes E4.461.

[1] This will relate to the way in which the benefit is convertible (see supra, § **7.41**).
[2] (1935) 19 TC 174.
[3] [1961] 1 All ER 358, 39 TC 344.
[4] *Laidler v Perry* [1965] 2 All ER 121, 42 TC 351.
[5] Statute has reversed the timing rule in *Abbott v Philbin* (see infra, § **7.53**).
[6] [1961] 1 All ER 358, 39 TC 344.
[7] *Richardson v Worrall* [1985] STC 693.
[8] The presence of joint liability on the part of employer and employee does not necessarily mean that discharge by the employer will be taxable earnings—see *Richardson v Worrall* at 718.

Vouchers and credit tokens

[7.45] These anomalies have led to legislation concerning vouchers and credit tokens. First, a voucher that can be exchanged for cash is treated as earnings (and subject to the PAYE system).[1] Second, a voucher, including a "cheque voucher",[2] that can be exchanged for money, goods or services—including transport—gives rise to liability on an amount equal to the cost to the person at whose cost the voucher and the money, goods or services for which it can be exchanged are provided in or in connection with that provision.[3] As the cost to the employer is taken on the basis of charge the value of the benefit is ignored. The liability arises when the expense is incurred[4] or, if later, when the voucher is received although the appropriation of the voucher (eg by sticking it on a card held for him) is treated as receipt by the employee. Travel concessions for lower paid employees of passenger transport undertakings[5] and the provision of a works bus service, or the loan of a bicycle and/or bicycle safety equipment are still free of tax, as are the provision of car or motor cycle or bicycle parking at or near the place of work and entertainment which is, to use broad terms, provided by someone not connected with the employer.[6] Third, similar rules apply to credit tokens and credit cards.[7] When the employee uses the token to obtain money, goods or services he is charged to income tax on earnings equal to the expense involved[8] although the costs of providing the token and of any interest charges are ignored.[9]

Relief is given when the vouchers or credit token are used to meet proper business expenses[10] or where the employee makes good the cost involved.[11]

These rules would now catch *Wilkins v Rogerson* but only if a voucher or credit token were used. So the charge would be avoided if the employer accompanied the employee to the shop—or sent an agent, perhaps even the employee himself. For the practice where incentive award schemes are provided by way of voucher see statement of practice SP 6/85 and Revenue Manual SE 2050 et seq.

By concession, there is no charge where a voucher or token is given to an employee by a person who is not the employer, nor a person connected with the employer, and the value is less than £250.[12]

[1] ITEPA 2003, s 81.
[2] ITEPA 2003, s 84.
[3] ITEPA 2003, s 87 and see s 89 for the reduction of 15p per working day for meal vouchers.
[4] For cheque vouchers the year is that in which the voucher is handed over in exchange for the goods etc see ITEPA 2003, s 88.
[5] ITEPA 2003, s 86.
[6] ITEPA 2003, s 266 (see infra, § **7.118**).
[7] ITEPA 2003, ss 90–94 and see s 267 for the exemption where credit tokens are used for exempt benefits. Credit token is no longer defined by reference to Consumer Credit Act 1974, s 14.
[8] ITEPA 2003, s 94(3).
[9] These charges were originally to give rise to liability—FA 1981, s 71—but this was removed by FA 1982, s 45.
[10] ITEPA 2003, ss 362 and 363. On vouchers for in-house sports facilities see infra, § **7.94**.
[11] ITEPA 2003, s 87(2)(*b*) and s 94(2)(*b*).
[12] ITEPA 2003, s 324 and s 270, as uprated by SI 2003/1361. From 6 April 2005, childcare vouchers are exempt: FA 2004, s 78.

Childcare and childcare vouchers

[7.46] Income tax is not charged on the benefit provided by a workplace nursery,[1] or childcare provided at the employer's expense,[2] provided that a large number of stringent conditions are fulfilled (see infra, § **7.102**). Where the employer provides a voucher for childcare,[2] the childcare voucher is defined, in principle, as a non-cash voucher that forms part of the earnings of the employee.[3]

The first £50 per week of the childcare voucher is exempt from tax.[4] As with exemption for the charge on the benefit of workplace nursery, the exemption for the voucher is subject to stringent conditions. An employee is only entitled to one exempt amount, irrespective of the number of children[5] and the exemption for a voucher is not available if the benefit of employer-supported childcare is also provided.[6]

[1] ITEPA 2003, s 318.
[2] ITEPA 2003. Defined in s 84(2A).
[2] ITEPA 2003. Defined in s 84(2A).
[3] ITEPA 2003, s 87. To prevent a double charge to tax from occurring, where the benefit of a voucher is taxed, no account is taken of the goods or services obtained by using the voucher: s 95(3A).
[4] ITEPA 2003, s 270A.
[5] ITEPA 2003, s 270A(8).
[6] ITEPA 2003, s 270A(9).

PAYE and fringe benefits—tradeable assets

[7.47] In order to reduce the tax attractions of fringe benefits, successive Finance Acts have extended the scope of PAYE.

First, there are rules for earnings taking the form of tradeable assets.[1] An asset is tradeable if it can be sold or realised on a market—whether a recognised investment exchange or the London Bullion Market or on a market to be specified in PAYE regulations. In these cases the market value is taken to be the value of the asset.[2]

An asset is also tradeable if "trading arrangements" exist in relation to it when the asset is provided. These are defined as arrangements for the purpose of enabling the person to whom the asset is provided to obtain an amount similar to the expense incurred in the provision of the asset.[3] The purpose here is to catch assets which are not immediately marketable but where the employer arranges for the employees to convert them into cash.[4] The Revenue have a regulation-making power to exclude assets; this power has been exercised to exclude shares and options over shares.[5]

An asset is defined by exclusion. It does not include any payment actually made of, or on account of, assessable income, any non-cash voucher, credit-token or cash voucher (as defined in Chapter 4 of Part 3 of ITEPA 2003, ss 73–96); or any description of property for the time being excluded from the scope of this section by PAYE regulations. Subject to these exclusions, which are designed to leave existing PAYE targets in place, it is provided that the term "asset" does include any property and in particular any right or interest falling within any paragraph in the Financial Services Act 1986, Sch 1, Part I.

In these circumstances the employer is deemed to make a payment; tax must be deducted from any actual payments of income and if that does not suffice the employer must account to the Revenue direct.[6] If the employee does not make good the amount of that tax to the employer within 90 days, the payment of tax is treated as income of the employee assessable to tax as employment income.[7]

These rules are backed up by further provisions which are designed to catch tradeable assets provided by means of vouchers and credit tokens.

The first provision affects non-cash vouchers. It applies if the voucher is capable of being exchanged for goods which, when the voucher is provided, can be sold or realised on a market as just described or if trading arrangements exist.[8] It also applies if the market or trading arrangements exist in relation to the voucher itself.[9] The provision of the voucher is treated as a notional payment with the usual consequences.[10] Similar provisions then apply to credit tokens[11] and to cash vouchers.[12]

FA 1994 also includes rules widening the scope of the PAYE scheme to cover payments by intermediaries (see infra, § **7.135**).

Simon's Taxes E4.905.

[1] ITEPA 2003, s 696; for an avoidance scheme that nearly succeeded see *DTE Financial Services Ltd v Wilson* [2001] STC 777, IIL.
[2] ITEPA 2003, s 702.
[3] See ITEPA 2003, s 702.
[4] See Inland Revenue press release, 30 November 1993, *Simon's Tax Intelligence* 1993, p 1525.
[5] ITEPA 2003, s 702; Income Tax (Employments) (Notional Payments) Regulations 1994, SI 1994/1212; Inland Revenue press release, 4 May 1994, *Simon's Tax Intelligence* 1994, p 594. The 1994 regulations were amended in 1998: *Simon's Weekly Tax Intelligence* 1998, p 1235, SI 1998/1891.
[6] ITEPA 2003, s 710.
[7] ITEPA 2003, ss 7, 222, as amended by FA 2003, s 144. See *Ferguson v IRC* [2001] STC (SCD) 1.
[8] ITEPA 2003, s 694.
[9] ITEPA 2003, s 694(4).
[10] ie ITEPA 2003, ss 7 and 222, as amended by FA 2003, s 144.
[11] ITEPA 2003, s 695; on quantum see ITEPA 2003, s 94(2).
[12] ITEPA 2003, s 693; on quantum see ITEPA 2003, s 81(2).

Particular benefits

Living accommodation

[7.48] Where living accommodation is provided for a person or for his family or household[1] by reason of his employment, he is chargeable whatever the level of his income and whether or not he is a director.[2] So if a non-domiciled person owns his house through a non-resident company, a favourite way of avoiding IHT, there will be a charge to income tax under this rule if he is a director, which he usually will be.[3] The rule is not to apply where by some other provision the accommodation is made the subject of any charge to him by way of income tax. An employee will be otherwise chargeable if he comes within the general principle of convertibility (see supra, § **7.41**): he will be chargeable on the profit which he could make by sub-letting the property or granting licences.

Whether living accommodation is provided by reason of the employment is a question of fact; however it is deemed to be so provided if it is provided by the employer. This deeming is avoided if it is shown that (a) the employer is an individual and he makes the provision in the normal course of his domestic, family or personal relationships[4], or (b) it is provided by a local authority for an employee of theirs and on terms which are no more favourable than those for non-employees similarly circumstanced[5], a rule which means that a council house tenant is not to be charged with extra rent simply because he works for the council.

The terms in (a) are defined by reference to the rules relating to those chargeable under all of the benefits code; (see infra, § **7.91**). Under this rule a secretary who fills the more personal role of mistress to her employer is able to escape tax on the flat which he provides for her. This rule only applies, however, where the employer is an individual, presumably because only an individual can have domestic family or personal relationships; this leaves open the case of a family business run by a trust, perhaps because the owner of the business has died and his estate has not yet been administered, unless one says that a trust is capable of being an individual.

If the accommodation is provided by someone other than the employer and so escapes the deeming provision, it may still give rise to tax if it is shown that the accommodation was in fact provided by reason of the employment, as may well be the case if it is provided by an associated company or trust.

This charge applies to the provision of living accommodation.[6] It does not apply to the provision of ancillary services; such services will not usually be capable of being turned into money and so will not give rise to any charge. However, they will give rise to a charge on employees earning £8,500 pa or more and directors under ITEPA 2003, s 201 (see infra, § **7.100**); when these come within the three categories of non-beneficial occupation the charge is not to exceed 10% of the total earnings. The costs of providing living accommodation are not further defined although liability in respect of rates, now Council Tax, is not to give rise to a charge when the occupation is within the three categories of non-beneficial occupation.

An employee who is taxable under the ITEPA 2003 living accommodation rules is either charged under s 105, or s 106 where the cost of the accommodation is over £75,000 (see infra, §§ **7.49, 7.50**).

ITEPA 2003, ss 105 and 106 apply to "shadow" directors.[7]

Simon's Taxes E4.412–415.

[1]   ITEPA 2003, s 97. On Revenue practice see Revenue Manual SE 2200 et seq.
[2]   ITEPA 2003, s 216.
[3]   By reason of the definition in ITEPA 2003, s 67. The fact that the individual receives no other benefit or remuneration is irrelevant.
[4]   ITEPA 2003, s 97(2).
[5]   ITEPA 2003, s 98.
[6]   ITEPA 2003, s 97.
[7]   *R v Allen* [2001] STC 1537, HL.

Exceptions—non beneficial occupation

[7.49] If the accommodation is provided by reason of the employment, the cost will still not be chargeable if the taxpayer comes within any of three situations which correspond broadly with the old cases of representative occupation. These are:

(a)   where it is necessary for the proper performance of the employee's duties that he should reside in the accommodation;[1]
(b)   where the employment is one of the kinds of employment in which it is customary to provide living accommodation and the accommodation is provided for the better performance of the duties of the employment;[2]
(c)   where, there being a special threat to his security, special security arrangements are in force and he resides in the accommodation as part of those arrangements.[3]
(d)   where the living accommodation provided by a company to a director or other officer of the company or a member of their family or household is outside the UK (FA 2008).

Exceptions (a) and (b) are excluded so that a charge to income tax will arise if the taxpayer is a director of the company providing the accommodation unless he is a full-time working director and he does not have a material interest in the company[4] (see infra, § **7.89**).

Those coming within 1 will include caretakers, the hotel manager, and other staff who are compelled to live in the hotel and the bank manager in *Tennant v Smith*;[5] for this group the necessity has to be found in the relationship between the duties and the accommodation and not in the personal exigencies of the taxpayer.[6] HMRC accepts that managers of public houses satisfy the conditions for this exemption.[7]

For exemption (b), there are two tests to satisfy—"the customary test" and "the better performance test". The Revenue accept that amongst the classes of employee to satisfy the exemption under (b) are managers of newspaper shops which have paper rounds and managers of traditional off licence shops.[8]

Group (b) is very wide covering farmworkers, miners and even university teachers; the requirement that it should be customary to provide the accommodation in that kind of employment is an interesting one since it is presumably a flexible one and so can take account of changes in practice and can be satisfied even though occupation is not required by the employer; the requirement that the provision be for the better performance of the duties is presumably a question of fact and is to be determined objectively paying attention to—but without being bound by—the terms of the employment and the views of the employer.

There is a certain amount of case law that gives guidance as to the interpretation to be placed on the statutory provisions. In *Butter v Bennett*,[9] the Court of Appeal considered the services provided to the manager of Bridgend Paper Mills Limited. (The case was specifically concerned with the question of what was then a Schedule E charge arising by virtue of the coal, electricity and services of a gardener provided for the accommodation.) In that case, Lord Denning, MR said:[10]

> Mr Bennet is employed by the Bridgend Paper Mills Limited, as the manager of a paper mill. He is paid more than £2,000 a year. He has a house near the mill in which he is required by the company to live, and in which it is necessary for him to live in order to carry out his duties as manager. . . . He was required to live in this mill house, the manager's house; it was necessary for him to do it in respect of his duties; and therefore, he is exempt from taxation in regard to expenses incurred by the company 'in or in connection with the provision of living accommodation' for him.

In that case, the Court of Appeal held that "the expense which is exempt is the expense of providing accommodation . . . as distinct from the expense of inhabiting the accommodation."

In the case stated[11] three reasons are given for Mr Bennett's residence in the manager's house being 'necessary'. The reasons that were accepted by the Commissioners and upheld by the Court of Appeal were:

(a)   Mr Bennett had no deputy manager and was the only person with the necessary technical knowledge at the mill to keep it running and he had on many occasions been called into the mill at night. He had to be available night and day, including weekends.
(b)   The making of paper is a craft and one of the main responsibilities of the manager is to decide whether the paper that is being produced conforms approximately to the quality that has been ordered.
(c)   The mill worked during the weekends as well as the normal 5 1/2 day week.

The meaning, in the context of s 154(4)(a), of the word "necessary" was given by the Court of Appeal in *Brown v Bullock*[12] by Donovan LJ as:

> the test is not whether the employer imposes the expense but whether the duties do, in the sense that, irrespective of what the employer may prescribe, the duties cannot be performed without incurring the particular outlay.[13]

The Court considered the situation of an export sales supervisor, whose employer required him to live in Central London, so as to be readily available to entertain prospective purchasers who arrived from overseas. Trevor McKie had a house in Hertfordshire. He and his wife chose a flat in London; his employer paid part of the rent and he paid the balance. The Court held that the occupation of a property, whilst convenient, was not "necessary" and the Court held that partial reimbursement of the employee's rent constituted a benefit.

A similar approach was taken by the Court in *Vertigan v Brady*[14] where the manager of a nursery for growing plants was provided with accommodation by his employer. By contrast to the house for the manager of the paper mill, the evidence given to the Commissioners in *Vertigan v Brady* was that "any dwelling within a five mile radius of Mill Lane Nursery would have sufficed".[15] In his judgment, Knox J said of FA 1977, s 33(4) [now ITEPA 2003, ss 99, 100 and 314]:

> the paragraph in question is directed to a necessity based on the relationship between the proper performance of the duties and the dwelling house, not to a necessity based on the personal exigencies of the taxpayer in the shape of his inability to finance the acquisition of suitable accommodation. Where, as here, there are rather more than 78 square miles of inhabited countryside in which geographically and physically suitable accommodation existed, it seems to me impossible to contend that it was necessary for the proper performance of the taxpayer's duties for him to reside where he did.[16]

In *Vertigan v Brady*, the Court heard that the taxpayer failed also because the provision of accommodation for his particular occupation was not sufficiently common to be "customary". The Court was unimpressed by statistical evidence, preferring "customary" to be given a qualitative, rather than a quantitative meaning.

Accommodation provided to government ministers and to some diplomats is clearly exempted from charge by the exemption in (c) as a residence provided as part of security arrangements. In *Lord Hanson v Mansworth*[17], it was held that the exemption applies to accommodation provided by a private employer.

Exemption (d) will apply only if:

(1) the company providing the living accommodation outside the UK is wholly owned by a director or other officer of the company (or him and other individuals but not as part of partnership property) and
(2) the company has been the 'holding company of the property' at all times after the relevant time.

A company is a 'holding company of the property' if it (or a wholly owned subsidiary) has a proprietary interest which is its main or only asset and the only activities undertaken by the company are incidental to the ownership of that proprietary interest. The relevant time is defined as the time the company first owned a proprietary interest in the property but only if none of the director's interests in the company existed at the time or were acquired from a person connected with the director. There are, however, exceptions to exemption (d) which exclude properties acquired from a connected company at an undervalue, or which expenditure has been incurred by a connected company or when any borrowing of the company from a connected company is outstanding. The exception also excludes tax avoidance arrangements for living accommodation outside the UK. This exemption has retrospective effect from 6 April 2003.

[7.49] Employment income

Simon's Taxes E4.412.

1. ITEPA 2003, ss 99(1).
2. ITEPA 2003, ss 99(2).
3. ITEPA 2003, s 100.
4. ITEPA 2003, s 9(3)–(5).
5. [1892] AC 150, 3 TC 158, HL.
6. See *McKie v Warner* (1961) 40 TC 65.
7. HMRC Manual para SE11342.
8. HMRC Manual para SE11351.
9. (1962) 40 TC 402.
10. (1962) 40 TC 402 at 411, 412
11. (1962) 40 TC 402 at 403.
12. (1961) 40 TC 1 at 10.
13. (1961) 40 TC 1 at 65.
14. [1988] STC 91 at 99f.
15. [1988] STC 91 at 99j.
16. [1988] STC 91 at 102a (see also the comments of the Special Commissioner at 97j, 98a).
17. [2004] STC (SCD) 288. Such cases are, probably rare. The Commissioners' decision was that the only reason Lord Hanson could have been a terrorist target was because he was the executive chairman of Hanson plc and because of the way in which he did that particular job. "The appellant lived and moved and had his being as chairman of Hanson plc": para 72 at 308d/e.

The basic charge

[7.50] The charge is on the cash equivalent of the benefit of the accommodation for the taxable period.[1] The cash equivalent depends on whether the cost of providing the accommodation does or does not exceed £75,000.[2]

For accommodation costing £75,000 or less the cash equivalent is the difference between the "rental value of the accommodation" for the taxable period, and any sum made good by the employee to the person at whose cost the accommodation is provided. Section 105 of ITEPA 2003 provides that this must be properly attributable to the provision of the accomodation.[3] Rent paid by the employee is therefore deductible. Benefits in kind provided in return may also, in principle be taken into account but only if they clearly relate to the accommodation.[4]

The "rental value of the accommodation" is the rent which would have been payable for that period if the property had been let to the employee at an annual rent equal to the annual value.[5] The annual value is given by s 110 of ITEPA 2003 as:

> the rent which might reasonably be expected to be obtained on a letting from year to year if the tenant undertook to pay all taxes, rates and charges usually paid by a tenant, and the landlord undertook to bear the costs of the repairs and insurance and the other expenses (if any) necessary for maintaining the property in a state to command that rent.

The annual value is treated as being equal to the rateable value (s 110 of ITEPA 2003 draws on the wording of s 23 of the General Rate Act 1967 which was repealed in 1988).[6] Estimated values will be used for new properties following the replacement of rates by the short-lived community charge.[7] In the absence of any provision directing otherwise, it is to be assumed that in calculating the annual rent hypothetically payable account is taken of all the terms of the occupation, even those imposed in connection with the office or employment.

If those at whose cost the accommodation is provided pay rent which is higher than the annual value, that higher figure is to taken as the "rental value of the accommodation".[8]

The employee may deduct from the value as ascertained any sums allowable under Chapter 2 or 5 of Part 5 of ITEPA 2003.[9]

Simon's Taxes E4.412.

[1] ITEPA 2003, s 102.
[2] ITEPA 2003, s 103.
[3] ITEPA 2003, s 105(2)(b).
[4] *Stones v Hall* [1989] STC 138.
[5] ITEPA 2003, s 105(3).
[6] See Explanatory Notes 403 to 411 of ITEPA 2003. In Scotland, an amount equal to the 1978 rates valuation figure will be used, instead of the much higher values set in the 1985 revaluation: Extra-statutory concession A56
[7] Inland Revenue press release, 19 April 1990, *Simon's Tax Intelligence* 1990, p 382.
[8] ITEPA 2003, s 105(4).
[9] ITEPA 2003, s 364.

The additional accommodation charge

[7.51] An employee who is provided with living accommodation which cost more than £75,000 is taxable under ITEPA 2003, s 106. The charge is calculated in four Steps. Step 1 takes the charge under s 105[1]. Step 2 calculates "the additional yearly rent", which is:

[(cost of providing accommodation − £75,000) × appropriate %]

The cost of providing the accommodation is the purchase price plus improvement expenditure, less any amount paid by the employee as reimbursement for the expenditure or as consideration for the tenancy. If, however, the employee first occupies the accommodation after 30 March 1983 and the person providing the accommodation has held an estate or interest in the property for the previous six years, the market value at the date on which the employee first occupies the property is substituted for the purchase price.[2] Market value is defined.[3]

The "appropriate percentage" is the official rate of interest set for the purpose of calculating the benefit of low-interest and interest-free loans to employees earning £8,500 pa or more and directors,[4] in force on 6 April beginning the year of assessment; for 2005–06 the percentage is 5%.[5]

[7.51] Employment income

Step 3 calculates the rent which would have been payable for the taxable period if the property had been let to the employee for the additional yearly rent calculated under Step 2. Step 4 adds the results of Steps 1 and 3 and deducts the "excess rent".

"Excess rent" is the amount by which any rent paid by the employee exceeds the rental value of the accommodation under s 105; (see supra, § **7.49**).

EXAMPLE

A is an employee earning over £8,500 pa On 6 April 1997 he began to occupy a house provided by his employer. The house was purchased by the employer on 9 November 1992 for £196,000 and the employer spent £8,000 on improvements. A reimbursed £1,000 of the expenditure and pays a rent which exceeds by £2,000 the rental value of the accommodation. The official rate of interest is 5%.

The cost to the employer of providing the property is:

(£196,000 + £8,000) − £1,000 =   £203,000

The charge for the living accommodation under s 106 to A is:

[(£203,000 − £75,000) × 5%] − £2,000 =   £4,400

A is therefore taxed on a benefit of £4,400. There is no charge under Step 1 because all of the rental value is eliminated by the rent paid.

If the employer had purchased the property in 1987, the market value of the property on 6 April 1997 would have been substituted for the purchase price.

Where a company provides luxury accommodation for an employee it may be worthwhile comparing the tax charge arising on the employee when the company pays a high rent with the tax charge that would arise if the company purchased the property. In *Toronto-Dominion Bank v Oberoi*[6] the employer bank had undertaken to pay the income tax liability of its senior employee and entered into a scheme whereby a premium of £345,000 was paid for a two year lease at a peppercorn rental, instead of the bank paying rent of about £11,000 per month. The essence of the scheme was that a charge arose on the employee under [now ITEPA 2003, s 106] of £345,000 × 5% = £17,250 (based on the premium paid by the employer) per annum, as opposed to a charge under ITEPA 2003, s 105 of £132,000 per annum (the rent paid by the employer).

---

[1] Supra, § **7.49**.
[2] ITEPA 2003, s 107; on pre 31 March 1983 occupation see Sch 7, para 21.
[3] ITEPA 2003, s 107(3) and (4).
[4] Infra, §§ **7.101–7.102**.
[5] Inland Revenue press release, 12 December 2002, *Simon's Weekly Tax Intelligence* 2002, p 1800.
[6] [2002] EWHC 3216 (Ch), [2004] STC 1197. This case was an action for rectification, the lease having been wrongly drafted, referring to the premium as "rent" and containing clauses inconsistent with the proposed arrangement. Nicholas Warren QC, sitting as a deputy judge of the High Court and formerly the Revenue junior gave rectification in part. The case has a number of points of interest, including representation. The defendant did not appear and was not

represented at the hearing but the Inland Revenue were joined to the proceedings and represented by Counsel.

Relocation benefits and expenses

Relocation

[7.52] Under the statutory provisions, removal expenses and removal benefits must meet certain criteria to be eligible for exemption from income tax.[1] They must then fall into certain categories to be within the exemption provided by Chapter 7 of Part 4 of ITEPA 2003.[2] The Treasury have power to extend the list of eligible expenses and benefits by regulations[3] and "to include such supplementary, incidental or consequential provisions as appear to the Treasury to be necessary or expedient".[4]

Benefits and expenses within Chapter 7 are:

(a) disposal of the old residence;[5]
(b) acquisition of the new;[6]
(c) abortive acquisition;[7]
(d) transporting belongings;[8]
(e) travelling and subsistence;[9]
(f) bridging loan,[10] including a beneficial bridging loan; and[11]
(g) replacement of domestic goods.[12]

To be eligible for exemption the expenses must be reasonably incurred by the employee in connection with a change of the employee's residence which meets the conditions in ITEPA 2003, s 273.[13] In addition they must be incurred on or before the limitation day.[14] The limitation day is that on which the relevant year ends and that, subject to a discretion in the Board to extend the period, means the year of assessment following the year in which the new employment or the new place of employment occurs.[15] An eligible removal benefit is similarly defined. It must be provided for the employee or for members of his family or household, be on the list of exempt benefits and be reasonably provided in connection with the change of residence and provided on or before the limitation day.[16]

Section 273 provides that the expense or benefit must be sufficiently connected with the employment. This requires first that the change of residence must result from the employee becoming employed by an employer, or from an alteration in the employee's duties (without a change of employer) or an alteration in the place at which those duties are carried out.[17] It also requires that the change must be made wholly or mainly to allow the employee to have his residence within a reasonable daily travelling distance of the place where the duties are to be performed.[18] The employee's former home must not be within a reasonable daily travelling distance from the place where the new duties are to be performed.[19] There is no need actually to sell the old residence to qualify for this relief[20]—it is sufficient that it is no longer the main residence (as where the old house is rented out or used only at weekends). ITEPA 2003, s 276(1) provides that if an employee has more than one residence, the exemption is only given by reference to the main residence.

[1] ITEPA 2003, ss 271–276. On Revenue practice see Revenue Manual SE 3100 et seq.
[2] ITEPA 2003, ss 277–285.
[3] ITEPA 2003, s 286(1).
[4] ITEPA 2003, s 286(2)
[5] ITEPA 2003, s 279.
[6] ITEPA 2003, s 277.
[7] ITEPA 2003, s 278.
[8] ITEPA 2003, s 280.
[9] ITEPA 2003, s 281.
[10] ITEPA 2003, s 284.
[11] ITEPA 2003, s 288.
[12] ITEPA 2003, s 285.
[13] ITEPA 2003, ss 272(3)(a). Section 273 gives three conditions: A, B and C.
[14] ITEPA 2003, s 272(3)(b).
[15] ITEPA 2003, s 274.
[16] ITEPA 2003, s 272(1).
[17] ITEPA 2003, s 273(2) Condition A.
[18] ITEPA 2003, s 273(3) Condition B.
[19] ITEPA 2003, s 273(4) Condition C.
[20] See Revenue Manuals EIM 3014 and SE 3104.

[7.53] The limit on exemption for any particular change of residence is set at £8,000[1]. In determining whether this limit has been reached one aggregates the sums paid in respect of expenses (treated as earnings under ITEPA 2003, Part 3, Chapter 3) and the cash equivalent of the benefits determined as if they fell within the benefits code of ITEPA 2003.[2] In the case of living accommodation this is the cash equivalent less any amount deductible under ITEPA 2003, s 364[3]. Exemption is given on the first £8,000 of this total with only the excess being taxable.

Provision is also made for the situation in which a relocation package includes a beneficial loan on which tax is chargeable (see infra, §§ **7.101–7.102**). Such loans are brought within the ambit of this relief by it being provided that if the employee has not used up his £8,000 exemption on the other costs of moving house he can bring the bridging loan or part of it into play in order to use up the total relief available. This is achieved by removing days from the period for which tax is chargeable in respect of the loan.[4]

It is expressly provided that no exemption is available where earnings are chargeable under ITEPA 2003, ss 22 and 26 (see supra, § **7.07**)[5]. These are earnings only charged on the remittance basis.

[1] ITEPA 2003, s 287
[2] See infra, §§ **7.88** ff.
[3] ITEPA 2003, s 287(5).
[4] ITEPA 2003, ss 288, 289.
[5] ITEPA 2003, s 271(2).

Securities given to employees

General principles

[7.54] Earnings are declared to be "any salaries, wages . . . gratuities . . . or incidental benefits . . . or anything else that constitutes an emolument of the employment".[1] Thus, where, in return for services, an employee receives shares in his employing company, tax is chargeable on the value of those shares. In *Weight v Salmon*[2] an employer gave his employee shares. The market value on the date of receipt was taken as the taxable amount since they could be sold at that price.

For the employer, giving shares as emoluments is attractive. There is no immediate cash cost for the employer, just a dilution of the interest of the existing shareholders. In theory at least, the share price reflects the success of the company; granting shares that an employee can sell at a later date is, thus, offering a direct incentive to the employee to make the company more successful. It is not surprising, therefore, that giving shares as part of an employment package is now commonplace. Frequently, what is passed to the employee is not a shareholding but an option to acquire shares, or rights over shares, at future date. Often, the shares are in the holding company rather than the company that employs the individual.

The tax code has always struggled with the income tax charge to be levied on an employee in respect of share rights. There are now two different approaches taken in statute. There are certain share schemes that are "approved" and subject to a particular statutory regime.[3] Where there is not a statutory approved scheme, FA 2003, Sch 22 completely rewrote the tax charge that applies.[3]

The Revenue has identified, from the disclosure of tax mitigation schemes, what is regarded by the Revenue as abuse of the statutory reliefs. This has led to a large number of detailed amendments to the statutory code.[4]

---

[1] ITEPA 2003, s 62(2).
[2] (1935) 19 TC 174.
[3] By completely rewriting ITEPA 2003, ss 417 to 484. As a commentator has pointed out, FA 2003, Sch 22, enacting these rewritten sections, is, itself, as long as an entire Finance Act of a generation ago.
[3] By completely rewriting ITEPA 2003, ss 417 to 484. As a commentator has pointed out, FA 2003, Sch 22, enacting these rewritten sections, is, itself, as long as an entire Finance Act of a generation ago.
[4] F(No 2)A 2005, Sch 2.

Securities

[7.55] Prior to FA 2003, statutory provisions applied, generally, only to shares or rights over shares. Now, the granting of rights in any securities can be treated as employment income. "Securities" are defined as:

(a) shares in any body corporate wherever incorporated or in any unincorporated body constituted under the law of a country or territory outside the UK;

(b) debentures, debenture stock, loan stock, bonds, certificates of deposit and other instruments creating or acknowledging indebtedness;
(c) warrants and other instruments entitling their holders to subscribe for securities (whether or not in existence or identifiable);
(d) certificates and other instruments conferring rights in respect of securities held by persons other than the persons on whom the rights are conferred and the transfer of which may be effected without the consent of those persons;
(e) units in a collective investment scheme;
(f) futures; and
(g) rights under contracts for differences or contracts similar to contracts for differences.[1]

[1] ITEPA 2003, s 420 inserted by FA 2003, Sch 22, para 2.

By reason of employment

[7.56] The income tax charge on employment income (and also an NIC liability) is imposed where the rights over securities have been obtained "by reason of employment".[1] This is given a wide meaning to include any right or opportunity made available by the employer, or by a person connected with the employer[2] and employment includes current, former or prospective employment,[3] except that the provision is by reason of an employment but where:

(a) the person providing shares is an individual; and
(b) the shares are transferred in the normal course of domestic family or personal relationships.[4]

Despite the width of the charging provision, it remains possible to argue that an individual is acting in his capacity as an investor when he acquires shares, even though he may be an employee. This can be the situation, for example, where an individual invests in an unquoted trading company, perhaps under EIS[5] and seeks to protect his investment by being appointed by the board of directors.

"Lock in" restrictions create potential difficulties. It is commonplace on a takeover of a small company for the core individuals to receive cash or securities in exchange on condition that these are retained for a specified period. The taxation of an individual shareholder who has obtained shares by virtue of employment is the subject of published correspondence between the Chartered Institute of Taxation and Inland Revenue.[6]

[1] ITEPA 2003, s 421B(1) inserted by FA 2003, Sch 22, para 2.
[2] ITEPA 2003, s 421B(3).
[3] ITEPA 2003, s 421B(2)(*b*).
[4] ITEPA 2003, s 421B(3).
[5] See infra, § **31.06** et seq.
[6] CIOT press release, 16 November 2004, *Simon's Weekly Tax Intelligence* 2004, pp 2409–2412.

Market value

[7.57] The CGT definition[1] is applied in determining the market value of any security given to an employee. This means that the provisions under which information is deemed to be available in assessing market value[2] are applied to income tax in the same way as to CGT and it is not possible to argue for a minimal value on the grounds that the restrictions make an actual market for the shares virtually impossible.[3]

In practice, a typical owner-managed company is only willing to allow employees to become shareholders if the family shareholders are satisfied that the employees cannot force the company to act against the perceived interests of family members. This leads to a wide variety of arrangements to restrict the rights of employee shareholders. The way in which the statutory provisions operate in such a wide variety of arrangements practice is far from clear.[4]

This was clearly demonstrated in the case of *Company A v R & C Comrs*[5]. In that case, the managing director of the appellant taxpayer had owned some shares in the taxpayer's parent company. Under a shareholders' agreement, the managing director would receive a disproportionate share of any sale proceeds if the company were (as it ultimately was) sold. HMRC argued that this triggered the provisions in ITEPA 2003, s 446Y which apply if a disposal is for a consideration exceeding the market value. The Special Commissioner dismissed the taxpayer's appeal although the decision has not escaped criticism.[6]

1   TCGA 1992, s 272 and 273.
2   TCGA 1992, s 273(3).
3   *A-G v Jameson* [1905] 2 IR 218; see Palles CB at para 61.
4   There has been considerable, and there continues to be, correspondence between Inland Revenue and the Chartered Institute of Taxation on this point.
5   (2007) SpC 602.
6   See, for example, *Taxation*, 10 January 2008.

Options to acquire securities

[7.58] Frequently, an employer does not simply allocate shares to an employee but instead, grants the employee the right to purchase shares at a future date, typically at the value of the shares on the date the option is granted. Not infrequently, the option right is subject to the employee continuing in employment up to the option date. Many option schemes are entered into in the expectation that the employee will not retain the shares when he exercises the option but, instead, will arrange with a third party financer to sell the shares simultaneously with his exercising the option.

Unless the option is made available to an individual in the normal course of domestic, personal or family relations any option made available to an employee by a person's employer, or a person connected with him, is deemed to be made by reason of his employment.[1]

Income tax is not charged on the grant of a securities option[2] instead, the principal chargeable event is the exercise of the option; this takes place when beneficial ownership of the securities is acquired and not, if different, at the time at which the securities are conveyed or transferred.

There is also a chargeable event where the option is assigned for consideration otherwise to an associated person or where consideration is received following the release of the option by an associated person.

Finally, there is a chargeable event where an associated person (which in this context includes the option holder him or herself) receives a benefit in money or money's worth in connection with the option. This would include sums received for varying an option or in compensation for the loss of an option, but specifically excludes sums received on account of disability under the Disability Discrimination Act 1995.

Benefits in money or money's worth received for agreeing not to acquire securities under the option or granted to another person who has a right to acquire securities which are subject to the option are regarded as received in connection with the securities option.[3]

In the normal case, where the event is the acquisition of the securities (ie the exercise of the option), the gain is simply the excess of the market value of the securities at the date of the acquisition over the amount paid for the securities—ie the option exercise price.[4] Anything paid for the option itself is not deductible here, but relief is given under s 480.

These rules are overridden by the specific provisions in the EMI option legislation.

Where the chargeable event is the assignment or release of the option, the amount of the gain is the consideration given for the assignment or release. Where the chargeable event is the receipt of a benefit in connection with the option, the amount of the gain is the amount or market value of the benefit.

These two latter events are subject to an anti-avoidance provision.

Where the consideration or benefit consists in the provision of securities or an interest in securities—this would include any securities, not simply the securities over which options have been granted—and the value of those securities has been devalued by at least 10% in the last seven years by things done otherwise than for genuine commercial purposes, the consideration or benefit is calculated as if that devaluation had not taken place.

A non-commercial 'thing' includes (but is not limited to) anything done wholly or mainly as part of a scheme for the avoidance of tax or national insurance, and also includes non-arm's-length transactions between group companies other than payments for group relief.

---

[1] ITEPA 2003, s 471(3) inserted by FA 2003, Sch 22, para 10.
[2] ITEPA 2003, s 475(1) with the exception of options granted at a discount under an approved CSOP scheme (ITEPA 2003, s 526).
[3] ITEPA 2003, s 477.
[4] ITEPA 2003, s 479.

Restricted securities

[7.59] A major exemption to the income tax charge on the grant of securities is made in respect of restricted securities.

The basic proposition is that it would be wrong to tax an employee on the acquisition of shares where his interest in those shares was conditional on some future event. Instead, the tax charge is postponed until the future event happens. If the effect of that future event is that the employee obtains the shares unconditionally, he is taxed on the value of the shares at that point. If he lost the shares, he is not charged to tax.

This special and, frequently highly beneficial, treatment is given where the securities acquired by the employee are within the statutory definition[1] of "restricted securities" which, broadly, is that the value of the employment related securities is less than the market value by virtue of any contract, etc, under which the right to the securities will be forfeited by the employee (or there would be enforced transfer or reversion of the securities).[2]

Where restricted securities, which are subject to forfeiture, are awarded on terms such that they will cease to be subjected to forfeiture within five years of the acquisition date, no charge to income tax arises at the date of issue.[3] It is important to note that a distinction is to be drawn here between shares subject to forfeiture and shares which have restricted rights. It is only the former which are free of income tax at the point of award. An employee might be awarded shares which he can only dispose of to other employees. Those shares are restricted securities but exemption will not apply and they will be taxed on award in the normal way.

As an alternative, the employer and employee can jointly elect for the securities to be taxed at the time of award,[4] on their market value at that date. The effect of this is to spread the tax liability on the award. Some tax would be paid on acquisition but, as will be seen, credit for this is given when computing the tax on subsequent chargeable events.

The basic concept of the restricted securities legislation is that when a chargeable event occurs, a liability to income tax arises.[5] The liability is treated as employment income for the tax year in which the chargeable event occurs.

The first chargeable event is where the securities cease to be restricted securities but where the employee continues to hold them.[6] This would be the case in a typical LTIP scheme, where shares are awarded subject to performance conditions and those conditions are met.

The second event is where there is a variation of any of the restrictions in the terms on which the securities are held, but the securities continue to be restricted securities.[7] The removal of a restriction is treated as a variation of a restriction.

The third event, is the disposal of the securities to a non-associated person for consideration at a time when they are still restricted securities.[8]

A company created for the commercial exploitation of a scientific discovery is frequently structured so that the academic credited with the scientific discovery is given restricted and convertible securities. Statute[9] provides that the transfer of intellectual property into such a company does not trigger an immediate income tax charge on the holders of shares, where the shareholder is actively engaged in research relating to that intellectual property.[10]

---

[1] ITEPA 2003, s 423 inserted by FA 2002, Sch 22, para 3.
[2] There are some important exceptions to the basic definition. Shares are not restricted securities merely because they are unpaid or partly paid and could be forfeited for non-payment of calls (provided there is no restriction which could prevent the calls being paid). Securities are not restricted if they are subjected to forfeiture where the holder ceases employment because of misconduct or where the shares are redeemable for payment. These tests are alternatives rather than all-or-nothing tests. For example, a share which is redeemable for payment will still be a restricted security if it falls within one of the other tests. Note that a security which has to be forfeited on cessation of employment where there is no misconduct is not within the exemption and is potentially—depending on the circumstances—a restricted security. This is a change from the old conditional share award rules, where an award on such terms would not have been treated as a conditional share award.
[3] ITEPA 2003, s 425(2).
[4] ITEPA 2003, 425(3). The election is irrevocable and must be made within 14 days of the acquisition, in a form approved by HMRC. There is no requirement to submit the election to HMRC.
[5] ITEPA 2003, s 426(2) & (3).
[6] ITEPA 2003, s 427(3)(a).
[7] ITEPA 2003, s 427(3)(b).
[8] ITEPA 2003, s 427(3)(c).
[9] With effect from 2 December 2004: ITEPA 2003, s 451–460 inserted by FA 2005, s 20. There are also transitional rules to deal with pre-2 December 2004 cases: FA 2005, s 21.
[10] ITEPA 2003 s 458 inserted by FA 2005, s 20(1).

Planning using restricted securities

[7.60] The nature of the charge on grant of restricted securities to an employee gives the possibility of substantially reducing the income tax arising and avoiding national insurance contributions.

One variant of an arrangement that was used prior to 2 December 2004[1] is for the employer to create a new subsidiary into which the employer passes cash equal to the amount it would expect to pay as a discretionary bonus to a category of employees. The employees were then offered shares[2] in the new subsidiary on terms so that the employee would forfeit his shares if he leaves employment and, in any case, after a period specified as less than five years.

As the shares are subject to forfeiture, they count as employment related restricted shares and no income tax charge arises on the issue of the shares to the employee. The subsidiary then declares a dividend which exhausts the entire resources of the subsidiary. After that, the shares are then surrendered by the employees. Income tax under Schedule F[3] is paid by the employee on the dividend he receives. The surrender of the shares is a chargeable event. The shareholding is then in a company with no assets, as all the cash that was formerly in the company has been paid as a dividend. Hence, no tax is payable by virtue of this chargeable event.

For an exhaustive analysis of an arrangement for using a loan to negate the tax charge on restricted securities given to an employee, see *Campbell v IRC*.[4]

[1] Anti-avoidance provisions were introduced by F(No 2)A 2005, Sch 2, paras 3–7.
[2] The shares issued to employees are typically non-voting shares. The employer holds all the voting shares in the captive subsidiary and appoints the directors who make the decision to pay the planned dividend.
[3] At an effective rate of 25% of the cash received, in contrast to a tax charge at 40% which would apply on the grant of securities that were not restricted securities.
[4] [2004] STC (SCD) 396. For further suggestions on the tax efficient issue of share to employees, see Nigel Doran and Dan Pipe "Blossoming Rights" Taxation, 20 May 2004, pp 188–192.

Convertible securities

[7.61] Since 1999, there has been a special code applied to shares acquired by reason of employment, which are subsequently converted into another class of share. There is a tax charge on the acquisition of the shares and also on the increase in value arising from the conversion.

Convertible securities are securities which confer on the holder an immediate or conditional entitlement to convert them into securities of a different description.

Convertible securities are taxable on acquisition.[1] The taxable acquisition value is computed without taking any account of the right to convert.

There is, then, a second tax charge on the accounts of a chargeable event.[2]

There are four categories of chargeable events. The first is the conversion of the securities into securities of a different description where an associated person has a beneficial interest in the securities before and after conversion.[3]

The second chargeable event is the disposal for consideration—other than to a connected person—of the securities while they remain convertible securities.[4]

The third chargeable event is the release for consideration of the entitlement to convert the security.[5] This is a necessary anti-avoidance device. Without it, it would be possible to award low-value securities with a right to convert.

The fourth chargeable event is the receipt by an associated person (which would, as explained above, include the original holder) of a benefit in money or money's worth in connection with the right to convert.[6]

The charge is the gain on the chargeable event less the consideration given for the entitlement to convert plus any expense incurred by the holder in connection with the conversion, disposal, release or receipt.[7]

[1] ITEPA 2003, s 437 inserted by FA 2003, Sch 22, para 4. Anti-avoidance provisions were introduced by F(No 2)A 2005, Sch 2, paras 8–11.

[7.61] Employment income

2   ITEPA 2003, s 438(2).
3   ITEPA 2003, s 439(3)(a).
4   ITEPA 2003, s 439(3)(b).
5   ITEPA 2003, s 439(3)(c).
6   ITEPA 2003, s 439(3)(d).
7   ITEPA 2003, s 440(1) to (3).

Notional loan on acquisition of employee securities

[7.62] Where an employee acquires a security without payment, or by making a payment that is less than the market value of the securities acquired, statute[1] deems the employee to have received an employment related loan.

All of the normal tax rules relating to employment-related loans (de minimis amount, averaging, tax relief etc) also apply to this notional loan.[2]

The two main cases where this notional loan arises are, therefore, the acquisition of securities partly paid, or the exercise of share options by employees not resident nor ordinarily resident in the UK. Such employees will not be charged to income tax on the acquisition of the securities under the option securities regime (see below) and, therefore, will be within the charge.

The notional loan is deemed to have been discharged when the securities are actually paid for in full. The effect of the securities being paid for in full is that any charge comes to an end at that point. The charge also comes to an end if the employee dies.

Where the securities are disposed of, or the obligation to pay the amount due on non-fully paid up securities is transferred, released or adjusted so that it no longer binds any connected person, there is a discharge of the notional loan. This would be the case, for example, if an employee was issued with non-fully-paid up securities and the employer later waived the amount due on the shares.

In the cases outlined in the previous paragraph the amount of the notional loan outstanding immediately before the disposal or release is treated as employment income of the year of disposal/release.[3]

---

1   ITEPA 2003, s 446S inserted by FA 2003, Sch 22, para 7.
2   These are given in ITEPA 2003, s 175 (benefit of taxable cheap loan treated as earnings), s 178 (exceptions for loans where interest qualifies for tax relief), s 180 (threshold for benefit of loan to be treated as earnings), s 182 (normal method of calculation; averaging), s 183 (alternative method of calculation), s 184 (interest treated as paid), s 185 (apportionment of cash equivalent in case of joint loan etc), and s 187 (aggregation of loans by close company to director).
3   ITEPA 2003 s 446U(2).

PAYE and NIC on shares given to employees

[7.63] If an asset is a readily convertible asset any employment income derived from that asset is within the scope of PAYE.[1]

Shares which are traded on any market are, clearly, readily convertible assets and, hence, the PAYE charge applies. This encompasses not only listed securities but also securities for which there is a market, such as AIM or a foreign equivalent. Statute² deems all employment related securities to be readily convertible assets and, hence, PAYE to be imposed, unless, exceptionally, they are not readily convertible under general principles and the company would be entitled to a corporation tax deduction under Sch 23 in respect of the shares.³ This means that, in practice, it will be difficult to find circumstances, in all but the most straightforward cases, in which employment-related securities which are within Sch 22 will not be subject to PAYE.

If the employee pays his own National Insurance Contributions arising in relation to restricted and convertible employment-related securities and also the secondary contributions payable by the employer, income tax relief is given to the employee for the secondary contributions paid.⁴

Statute⁵ empowers HMRC to issue a notice requiring details of shares given to employees. From 2003–04 to 2005–06, the Revenue used its powers under this section to routinely require the issue of form 42. In December 2006⁶ HMRC announced that it no longer requires submission of form 42.⁷

---

1   ITEPA 2003, s 696(1).
2   ITEPA 2003, s 702(5A) inserted by FA 2003, Sch 22, para 15.
3   ITEPA 2003, s 702(5B).
4   ITEPA 2003, ss 442A and 428A. Inserted by FA 2004, Sch 16. There are also consequential amendments for corporation tax and also for the CGT base cost for the employee.
5   ITEPA 2003, s 421J.
6   HMRC Tax Bulletin December 2006, p 1327.
7   HMRC states that the compliance cost of completing form 42 was £200 for each employer.

Share option and incentive schemes

History

[7.64] If, in return for services, an employee receives shares in his employing company, tax is chargeable on the value of those shares.¹ If the shares are ordinary shares the market value on the date of receipt will be taken as the taxable amount since they could be sold at that price.²

The basis of chargeability is that the employee is receiving a benefit by virtue of the employment. This reasoning would apply also where the employee is given priority in a public offer and so ends up with more shares than he would have got as a member of the public, assuming that the values at allocation exceeded the price paid. Special rules have been introduced to exclude the charge in such cases.³ Under these rules the amount reserved for the priority allocation must not exceed 10% of the shares.⁴ Further, all applicants must be on level terms.⁵ These requirements are relaxed where shares in more than one company are offered to the public at the same time and employees of one company are offered shares in another. In these circumstances the aggregate value of priority allocations of shares in all the companies involved are taken into account in determining whether the level terms have been achieved.⁶

Further amendments have been made to cater for the situation arising where a public offer consists of a package of shares in two or more companies (eg the two electricity generating companies) and while the public offer relates to all the companies the offer to the employees gives priority rights to allocations in just one (or more but not all) of the companies involved); here exemption is given where the 10% test is met with regard to each company in the offer.[7]

When the employee is allowed to buy at a discount, the original effect was to tax both the benefit conferred by the discount and that conferred by the priority right. Now only the discount right will attract tax—provided not more than 10% of the shares are offered to the employees in priority.[8] Further provision is made for the situation in which the offer to the public consists of a number of different elements, eg a fixed price offer and a tender offer.[9] Provision is also made for the situation in which an offer in two or more companies is made to the public but employees receive priority rights in some but not all of the companies.[10]

If the employee receives an option to buy shares, tax is due on the value of the option, which would be the difference between the price payable under the option and the market value of the shares on the date of receipt of the option. In *Abbott v Philbin*[11] the employee received an option to buy shares at £3.42 1/2 each, the market value at the date of the option, and he exercised the option in a subsequent tax year when the market value of the shares was £4.10. The House of Lords held that the emolument arose in the year the option was acquired and at that time he received no benefit from it since he was merely given an option to buy at what was then full market value. The fact that the emolument subsequently increased in value did not mean that that increase in value was an emolument.

Legislation followed in 1966 (see infra, § **7.54**) but this was largely avoided by the device of giving not an option to acquire shares but shares subject to restriction and not yet fully paid up. In 1978 under the Lib–Lab pact a new form of share scheme, called profit sharing, was introduced (see infra, § **7.76**) and another form was approved by the Conservative government in 1980 (see infra, § **7.75**). In 1984, the concept of an approved discretionary share option scheme was revived (see infra, § **7.68**). Since that time there have been new tax incentives for profit-related pay introduced in 1986 and for ESOPs (see infra, § **7.84**) introduced in 1989. In considering those rules one must also remember the possible impact of TA 1988, ss 160, 162 (see infra, §§ **7.101–7.103**).

The last Conservative administration dealt a great blow to approved share options schemes by capping the amount of the benefit in FA 1996 which restricted the value of share over which unexercised share options could be held to £30,000. The present Labour administration has reviewed the entire area, a process culminating in legislation in FA 2000 which introduces one new general share scheme of some complexity called the Employee Share Ownership Plans and another, different, much narrower and much more generous share option scheme called Enterprise Management Incentives. All the old schemes remain save that the approved profit sharing scheme is to be phased out; the last appropriation to such schemes must take place before 6 April 2002.

Particular benefits **[7.65]**

There are many reasons for using these plans as part of a remuneration package. They encourage some identification of interest by the employee with the company, they usually cost the company (as opposed to other shareholders) very little and sometimes attract no national insurance contribution; they may also be very advantageous in income tax terms but this depends upon the type of plan used. They may also be used in their more selective forms to attract or retain key employees; in their more general forms they are part of the drive to create a more widespread share ownership.

The value of a right to exercise an option is not a taxable benefit under TA 1988, s 19.[12]

Simon's Taxes Division E4.5.

[1] *Weight v Salmon* (1935) 19 TC 174.
[2] Where the shares are subject to special conditions, see supra, § **7.52**.
[3] ITEPA 2003, ss 542 and 544, see *Simon's Tax Intelligence* 1987, pp 716, 866.
[4] ITEPA 2003, ss 542 and 544.
[5] ITEPA 2003, ss 542, 544 and 546. The employee may however vary the entitlements according to remuneration, length of service or similar factors.
[6] ITEPA 2003, s 546.
[7] ITEPA 2003, ss 544, 545 and 547.
[8] ITEPA 2003, ss 543 and 545.
[9] ITEPA 2003, ss 542 and 544.
[10] ITEPA 2003, ss 543 and 545.
[11] [1961] AC 352, [1960] 2 All ER 763, 39 TC 82 (see supra, § **7.41**).
[12] *Wilcock v Eve* [1995] STC 18.

Options to acquire shares: charge on exercise of option

[7.65] Where a gain is realised by the *exercise* of the option, income tax is to be charged[1] on the difference between the price paid under the option, including the price of the option,[2] and the market value of the shares acquired under the option.[3] This charge excludes any liability on the grant of the option;[4] the option must be exercised within ten years.[5] From 19 March 1986, the receipt of consideration in money or money's worth by an employee in return for allowing an option to lapse or granting a second option or right is also treated as a taxable event.[6]

This provision is an independent charging section and therefore applies whether or not the benefit of the option can be converted into cash.[7]

Simon's Taxes E4.510–516.

[1] ITEPA 2003, s 471. On Revenue practice on unapproved share options and shares acquired under such options see Revenue Manual SE 2800 et seq. For options granted before 3 May 1966, see TA 1988, s 136(4), which excepts the gain attributable to an increase in market value up to that date.
[2] This is not to include the value of the services rendered: ITEPA 2003, ss 479, 480 and 484 proviso.
[3] ITEPA 2003, ss 479, 480 and 484.

⁴ ITEPA 2003, s 474 eg under the decision in *Weight v Salmon*. This is without prejudice to the rules for approved share option schemes in TA 1988, s 185.
⁵ This is presumably to protect the charge under ITEPA 2003, s 475(1).
⁶ ITEPA 2003, ss 471, 477, 478, 479 and 480.
⁷ *Ball v Phillips* [1990] STC 675.

Charge on grant of option exercisable beyond ten years

[7.66] If the option can be exercised more than ten years after its grant, tax is chargeable at the time of the *grant* on the value of the benefit granted, any tax so charged being deducted from any tax subsequently chargeable on the exercise of the option.[1] To avoid any argument based on *Abbott v Philbin*[2] the value of the benefit granted is stated to be not less than the market value at the time the right is obtained of the shares that can be acquired less the value of the consideration for which the shares are to be acquired. If the consideration is variable only its lowest value is taken.[3] Tax cannot be avoided by assigning the option to a person with whom the employee is connected nor if the assignment is otherwise than by way of bargain at arm's length; in such circumstances the assignor is chargeable in respect of the gain realised by the assignee.[4]

These charges arise when the option was granted to that person "as director or employee" a phrase which is defined as a grant by reason of the office or employment.[5] The grant may have been to that person or another. This is to prevent the obvious avoidance device of granting the option to the employee's spouse or nominee.

Simon's Taxes E4.514.

[1] ITEPA 2003, ss 475 and 478. For an illustration of the effect of the unamended provisions, see *Williamson v Dalton* [1981] STC 753.
[2] [1961] AC 352, 39 TC 82 (see supra, § **7.41**).
[3] ITEPA 2003, ss 475 and 478.
[4] ITEPA 2003, ss 471, 477, 478, 479 and 480, but a special rule applies if the assignment was on bankruptcy, s 477. More devious arrangements fall within s 483. Exercises of the option after the employment has ceased fall within ss 471 and 473.
[5] ITEPA 2003, ss 471 and 473.

Planning

[7.67] The effect of these rules is to make share option schemes unattractive in tax terms. So long as an option is exercisable within seven years there will be no tax charge on the grant of the option but any gain made on the exercise of the option is treated as income and it may therefore be necessary for the employee to sell some of the shares to raise the money to pay the tax.

The scheme also involves some dilution of equity. For these reasons so called "phantom" schemes have been devised by which, on the exercise of the option, the company pays money to a trust which then buys shares for the employee and transfers them to him—while this does not avoid ITEPA 2003, s 471 it does avoid the need to sell shares (as only the net-of-tax sum is invested) and so also reduces equity dilution. A better way of avoiding ITEPA 2003, s 471 is to take advantage of the statutorily approved exceptions from that section.

Share purchase incentive schemes

[7.68] The essence of these schemes was that they sidestepped the rules relating to share options. Instead of being given an option to buy a share for £1, the current market value of the share, which might in due course be worth £3, the employee would be issued with a share which ordinarily would have had a current market value of £3 but which was subject to restrictions which meant that it was only worth £1. At a later date the restrictions would be removed. The increase in value could not be subject to the share option rules since the employee did not realise a gain by exercising a right to acquire shares—the shares were already owned. Such schemes might further involve using partly paid up shares. If the company capitalised its profits to pay them up there would be a charge under ITEPA 2003, s 201 on the employee on the amount so spent but this would usually be a lot less than the gain realised.

Faced with these schemes the legislature has provided two sets of rules. The one of greater theoretical interest was added in 1998 and clarifies the treatment of conditional acquisitions of shares and the conversion of convertible shares. The other is ITEPA 2003, s 488 (see supra, §§ **7.61** ff) and charges tax on certain growths in value.

Conditional acquisitions

[7.69] Under many long-term share incentive schemes benefits accrued only if performance conditions attached to the options were satisfied. The assumption that there was no charge on the grant of such shares, but only when the conditions were satisfied and benefits received, rested, until 1998, on general principle rather than express provision. It could, contrary to the general assumption, be argued, on the basis of *Abbott v Philbin* that there should be a charge on the grant of the option based on a prediction, ie a guess, as to the chance that the particular employee would derive a benefit in the fullness of time thanks to the success of the company or the stock market's assessment of the company. On this basis the charge based on guesswork at the time of the grant would exclude any charge when the conditions were removed. So in 1998 rules were enacted validating the general assumption.

ITEPA 2003, s 422 applies to what are termed "conditional acquisitions of shares". The acquisition must be as a director or employee.[1] There are elaborate rules as to when an acquisition is conditional.[2]

If the condition attached to the shares must be satisfied (or not) within five years there may be no charge on the grant of the shares.[3] If, however, the condition may be satisfied beyond the five-year period there was, under TA 1988 s 140A(2) (which was part of the rules as enacted in 1998), an immediate charge when the shares are obtained.[4] It was soon found that the immediate charge could give rise to unintended double taxation. So if the employee exercised an option over shares which could still be subject to a risk of forfeiture after more than five years there will be a charge under ITEPA 2003, s 471 in addition to the immediate charge. To solve the problem the immediate charge was abolished for shares acquired on or after 27 July 1999.[5] There will be a charge under ITEPA 2003, s 427 when or, rather, if and when, the holding becomes unconditional on any earlier sale of the shares or of any interest in them.[6] The charge is on the market value of the shares (when the holding becomes unconditional on prior disposal) less allowable deductions.[7] Any liability on the grant of the shares, including any under the now repealed TA 1988 s 140A(2), will be taken into account to prevent a double charge.[8] The charge does not arise if the holding is unconditional or if the only conditions concern forfeiture for non-payment of calls, the exercise of pre-emption rights or where a sum must be paid to redeem them.[9] FA 1999 widens these exclusions by providing that, for shares acquired on or after 27 July 1999, the shares will not be treated as conditional if the shares are to be forfeited on the occasion of dismissal for misconduct.[10] This Act also widens the scope of the pre-emption exemption and provides for exemption from s 140A where the share could be forfeited for more than one of these permitted reasons.[11]

Simon's Taxes Division E4.5.

---

[1] Defined in ITEPA 2003, ss 423, 434 and 436; there are information powers in s 432. The rules apply to conditional interests in shares acquired on or after 17 March 1998: ITEPA 2003, s 424.
[2] ITEPA 2003, ss 424 and 434; on similar treatment for NICs see National Insurance press release, 5 May 1998, *Simon's Weekly Tax Intelligence* 1998, p 729.
[3] ITEPA 2003, s 426 is subject to ITEPA 2003, s 479 (unapproved share options) and ITEPA 2003, s 195 (deemed loan for non fully paid up shares).
[4] TA 1988, s 140A(2).
[5] FA 1999, s 42(2) repealing TA 1988, s 140A(2).
[6] ITEPA 2003, ss 7, 10 and 427.
[7] ITEPA 2003, ss 7, 10 and 428; allowable deductions are defined in ITEPA 2003, ss 428 and 429.
[8] ITEPA 2003, s 428.
[9] ITEPA 2003, s 424.
[10] ITEPA 2003, s 424.
[11] ITEPA 2003, s 424.

Convertible shares: charge on conversion

[7.70] Although the growth in value charge in FA 1988, s 78 was effective for many purposes it did not necessarily apply where one class of shares was converted into another. A further charge[1] arises where the person has acquired shares as a director or employee,[2] and the shares carry a right or a possible entitlement to convert the shares into shares of a different class.[3] The charge is on the market value of the new shares following conversion less any deductible amounts.[4]

Among the interesting features of the statutory provision is the exclusion of a conversion of shares of one class only ("the original class") into shares of one other class only ("the new class"). To meet this exclusion all the shares of the original class must be converted into shares of the new class and satisfy either of two alternative tests.[5] One is that immediately before the conversion the company is employee-controlled by virtue of holdings of shares of the original class. The other is more complicated and is that immediately before the conversion the majority of the company's shares of the original class are held otherwise than by or for the benefit of directors or employees of the company; this is extended to an associated company of the company or directors or employees of such an associated company. The explanatory notes to the 1998 Finance Bill state that the effect of these rules is that an employee should not be taxed when the conversion happens "as a result of, say, a company reconstruction."

Simon's Taxes E4.527.

[1] ITEPA 2003, s 444.
[2] On which see ITEPA 2003, ss 423, 434 and 436.
[3] ITEPA 2003, s 435; on National Insurance Contributions see supra, § **7.58**, note 2.
[4] ITEPA 2003, s 439; the terms are defined in the rest of s 435 and s 442 (which mirrors s 429).
[5] ITEPA 2003, s 440.

The growth in value charge

[7.71] There had been legislation before 1988 imposing other charges. These remain in force. Rules were introduced in 1972 (now TA 1988, s 138)—which still apply, although in limited form, to some shares acquired before 26 October 1987.[1] Events on or after that date can still give rise to a charge under these rules in their modified form[2] (see supra, § **7.63**). Shares acquired on or after that date are subject to different—and more relaxed—rules in FA 1988.[3]

The 1988 rules differ from the 1972 rules in two principal ways. First, they try to reduce the charge so that it applies only to the extent that value is being conferred by the removal of the restrictions and not to catch the general underlying increase in value attributable to the growth of the business. This represents a change of view of these schemes—from being purely a tax avoidance device to being a legitimate way of involving employees in the fate of their company. Second, they try to extend the new approach to companies which are subsidiaries so that employees can acquire shares in their company rather than in the head group company; this is achieved by distinguishing dependent subsidiaries from others.

[1] ITEPA 2003, Sch 7, para 57.
[2] See *Butterworths UK Tax Guide 1987–88*, § **6.57**.
[3] ITEPA 2003, ss 447, 449, 452, 453, 456, Sch 7, para 55.

Shares acquired by reason of employment

[7.72] ITEPA 2003, ss 449 and 452 impose three charges where shares have been acquired in pursuance of a right conferred on him or an opportunity offered to him by reason of his office or employment by that or any other company.[1] None can apply where the shares are acquired in pursuance of an offer made to the public.[2] The frequently used terms "acquisition" and "disposition" cover increases and decreases in a person's interest in the shares.[3]

[7.72] Employment income

The first charge to tax arises if a chargeable event occurs provided that the employee still owns or, technically, has any beneficial interest in, the shares.[4] A person who acquires the shares otherwise than under a bargain at arm's length with an unconnected person is deemed to continue to hold them until there is a disposal of them by a bargain at arm's length to an unconnected person. A separate set of rules applies if the company is a "dependent subsidiary";[5] (see supra, § 7.64) hence if the company is a subsidiary but not a dependent one the following rules apply.

The list of chargeable events covers the removal or variation of any restrictions[6] on the shares and the creation of rights or restrictions on them. It also covers the imposition of restrictions on other shares in the company since such events equally cause a shift in value between the groups of shares.[7] The amount to be charged is the increase in value accruing from these events[8] and not simply the increase in value during the period of ownership. There is no automatic charge at the end of seven years.

Four situations are excluded from this charge. The first is where the shareholder has not been an employee or director of that or any associated company in the last seven years.[9] The second is where the employees hold a minority of the shares whose value is increased.[10] The third is where the company is employee-controlled by virtue of the class of shares affected[11] and the fourth is where the shares affected are a single class and the company is a subsidiary which is not a dependent subsidiary.[12]

Simon's Taxes E4.526.

---

[1] If he acquires the right as a person connected with a director or employee, it is caught by ITEPA 2003, s 447; the term acquisition covers increases in a person's interest in the shares— ITEPA 2003, s 464. On Revenue practice see Revenue Manual SE 2900 et seq.
[2] ITEPA 2003, s 448.
[3] ITEPA 2003, s 464.
[4] ITEPA 2003, ss 449 and 452.
[5] ITEPA 2003, ss 449, 452 and 453.
[6] Widened by ITEPA 2003, s 450.
[7] ITEPA 2003, ss 7, 10, 449 and 451.
[8] ITEPA 2003, ss 7, 10, 449 and 451.
[9] ITEPA 2003, ss 452; if he acquired the shares as an employee of another company he must also not have been an employee of the first company.
[10] ITEPA 2003, ss 450 and 469.
[11] ITEPA 2003, ss 450 and 469; employee control is defined in ss 468 and 718.
[12] ITEPA 2003, ss 450 and 469.

[7.73] The second charge arises where the shares are shares in a "dependent subsidiary". The term dependent subsidiary is defined by exclusion. A subsidiary is dependent unless its business is wholly or substantially with persons who are not members of the group and there has been either no, or only a minimal, increase in the value of the company which stems from intra-group activities. The directors and auditors must certify that these conditions are satisfied.[1]

Where the company is such a subsidiary, whether at the time of the acquisition or during his ownership of the shares, rules much closer to those of 1972 apply. There will be a charge either at the end of seven years or if he ceases to own them before that time. The charge is on the increase in value over this period since acquisition.[2] The charge will be reduced if the taxpayer's interest is less than full beneficial ownership[3]; if he has to provide more consideration since acquisition in accordance with the terms of acquisition[4]; or if in accordance with the terms of the acquisition he ceases to own them by disposing of them for less than full consideration.[5]

These rules are adapted where the company was not a dependent subsidiary at the time of acquisition but became one before he ceased to own the shares.[6] Here there will be a chargeable increase if the value when the company became a dependent subsidiary is less than its value at the earliest of the following dates: (a) the passing of seven years, (b) the person ceasing to own the shares, (c) the company ceasing to be a dependent subsidiary.[7] There will be no charge under this head if he was not a director or employee of that or any associated company within the seven years before the company became a dependent subsidiary.[8]

The Revenue view is that these are pragmatic rules to provide the new, more generous, approach only where the subsidiary is operating more or less independently of its group.[9] In other circumstances the Revenue feel that it is just too easy for value to be shifted around the group and so into the shares of the lucky employees or directors.

Simon's Taxes E4.526.

[1] ITEPA 2003, s 467. On problems in defining dependant subsidiary see ICAEW Memorandum TR 739, *Simon's Tax Intelligence* 1989, p 40.
[2] ITEPA 2003, ss 453 and 454.
[3] ITEPA 2003, ss 7, 10, 453, 455.
[4] ITEPA 2003, s 455.
[5] ITEPA 2003, s 455.
[6] ITEPA 2003, s 453.
[7] ITEPA 2003, ss 453 and 454.
[8] ITEPA 2003, s 456; if he acquired the shares as an employee of another company he must also not have been an employee of that company.
[9] *Simon's Tax Intelligence* 1987, p 799.

[7.74] The third charge is when the shareholder receives special benefits.[1] The benefit will be special if it is received when the company is a dependent subsidiary and the shares are of a single class.[2] It will also be special if when it becomes available it is not available to at least 90% of the persons who then hold shares of the same class as those which, or an interest in which, the person holds.[3]

This represents a relaxation of the original rule which required that the benefit should be actually received and that that receipt should be in respect of all the shares of the relevant class if it was to escape special benefit treatment. This relaxation could lead to abuse if the benefit were available nominally in respect of all shares but in fact received only by employees and directors. Therefore the remaining sets of conditions are tightened up.[4] In their new form they provide that for a benefit to escape special benefit status it must also satisfy any one of three sets of conditions of increased elaboration.[5] The first is that when the benefit is received the majority of the shares in respect of which the benefit is received are held otherwise than for the benefit of the directors or employees of the company, an associated company or the directors and employees of that associated company. The second is where the company is employee-controlled by virtue of this class. The third is where the company is a subsidiary but not a dependent subsidiary and the majority of the shares in respect of which the benefits are received are held otherwise than by or for the benefit of directors or employees of the company, a company which is an associated company but not its parent company[6] or directors or employees of a company which is an associated company of the company.[7] The charge is excluded if the shareholder has not been a director or employee of that or any associated company within the last seven years.[8]

Simon's Taxes E4.526.

---

[1] ITEPA 2003, s 457; for explanation see Inland Revenue press release, 12 November 1991, *Simon's Tax Intelligence* 1991, p 1035. This rule applies where the shares have been acquired by a person connected with a director or employee: s 83(4). The same provision carries over the rule that a person who acquires the shares otherwise than under a bargain at arm's length with an unconnected person is to be deemed to continue to hold the shares until there is a disposal of them by a bargain at arm's length to an unconnected person.
[2] ITEPA 2003, s 458.
[3] ITEPA 2003, s 458.
[4] For explanation see supra, note 1.
[5] ITEPA 2003, ss 458 and 469.
[6] Defined as a company of which the other is a subsidiary; ITEPA 2003, s 458.
[7] ITEPA 2003, ss 458 and 469.
[8] ITEPA 2003, s 460; if he acquired the shares as an employee of another company he must also not have been an employee of that company.

Taxation of the company with a share incentive plan trust

[7.75] The payment made by a company to its share incentive plan trust is deductible in computing the company's liability to corporation tax.[1] This deduction is dependent on the company payment being used by the trustees to purchase shares in the company, such purchase to amount to at least 10% of the total ordinary share capital in the company.[2] The corporation tax relief is clawed back if shares are not distributed to employees within five years.[3]

While the shares are held by the trustees of the SIP, dividends paid the trustee are exempt from income tax[4] and the capital gain arising on the allocation of shares is exempt from capital gains tax.[5]

---

[1] With effect from 6 April 2003: Employee Share Scheme Act 2002, s 1(3). The decision is given by FA 2003, s 141 and Sch 23: see infra, § **25.06**.
[2] ESSA 2002, s 1(3).

³ ESSA 2002, s 1(4).
⁴ As long as the shares have not been held in the SIP trust for more than ten years: FA 2000, Sch 8, para 88 amended by ESSA 2002, s 3(2).
⁵ FA 2000, Sch 8, para 98 amended by ESSA 2002, s 3(3).

Share options for internationally mobile employees

[7.76] It has been estimated that shares to a value of some £50,000,000 are granted each year by UK resident companies to non-resident employees, mostly by the larger companies. The scheme of the UK legislation is to relate the share option to the employment. This means that an employee who retires and moves overseas before he exercises a share option he obtained whilst in employment in the UK, is treated under the UK legislation as receiving Schedule E emoluments from a UK employment, even though he has ceased to be resident in the UK by the time he exercises the option. The approach taken by the foreign jurisdiction where he is resident at the time of exercise may, however, be different and, hence, double taxation can occur.

There is also the problem to be faced when a share option is granted by a multi-national company to an employee who has exercised his employment in different jurisdictions during the course of his working life, although for a single employer. Thus, for example, the employee may have worked for an employer for 20 years, 10 years spent working in the UK and 10 years in a variety of other countries, some of which may have double tax agreements with the UK. Broadly, UK statute is designed to bring such cases within a charge to UK income tax. It is then a matter of construing double taxation agreements and for unilateral relief to be given in the absence of an agreement, often by Revenue concession. The role of double taxation relief in these circumstances is discussed at infra, § **37.32**.

A further area of difficulty on the granting of share options internationally is the potential for transfer pricing issues to arise. These were considered by the Special Commissioners in *Waterloo v IRC*.[1] In that case, a UK resident company lent £97,000,000 interest free to an employee share option trust. The trust used the funds to acquire shares in the UK plc in order to satisfy options granted to employees. As Waterloo Plc carried on a worldwide business, many of its employees moved in and out of UK residence. The Special Commissioners held that the granting of the interest free loan was "the giving of business facilities"[2] and transfer pricing principles applied to impute an interest receipt by the UK resident company in respect of the funds used to grant options to non-resident employees.

The Revenue interpret[3] the *Waterloo* decision by distinguishing between a plan under which a company satisfies the share options granted to its employees by purchasing shares (a non-dilutive plan) and a plan where the employees' options are satisfied by the issue of new shares (dilutive plan). This is not a distinction that accords with the commercial reality of company operations. Typically, a larger company will not specify in advance whether shares will be purchased on the market (non-dilutive) or newly issued (dilutive); rather, the company will respond to its share price on the market taking the first route when it judges the price to be low and the second route when it judges the price to be high.

[7.76] Employment income

[1] [2002] STC (SCD) 95.
[2] Under TA 1988, s 773(4). This legislation has been superceded by TA 1988, Sch 28AA; however, it is likely that the concept of "transactions" or "series of transactions" within the new provisions would be construed by the court as giving rise to the same consequence for transfer pricing. See infra, § **8.153**.
[3] Inland Revenue Tax Bulletin October 2001, pp 883–887 and August 2004 pp 951–951, updated April 2005 pp 1193–1199. See also Inland Revenue Interpretation 21 April 2005, *Simon's Weekly Tax Intelligence* 2005, p 858. The view of HMRC on the liability to pay National Insurance contributions on share options granted to internationally mobile employees is given in a Special Edition of HMRC Tax Bulletin, May 2005: "NICs and Shares".

Employee share schemes

[7.77] The following approved employee share schemes are currently in existence:[1]

(1) Approved Profit Sharing Schemes (7.78);
(2) Savings-Related Share Option Schemes (7.79);
(3) Company Share Option Plan (7.80);
(4) Discretionary Share Option schemes (7.81);
(5) Enterprise Management Initiatives (7.82);
(6) Share Incentive Plan (7.88).

Employees who acquire shares from an approved all-employee share scheme (ie Approved Profit Sharing Scheme, Savings-Related Share Option Scheme, or Share Incentive Plan) may transfer them directly into a stocks and shares component of an Individual Savings Account (ISA).[2]

[1] The material on share schemes that are no longer available to be established is based substantially on Inland Revenue Guidance Note, 2 August 2004; employee share schemes, *Simon's Weekly Tax Intelligence* 2004, pp 1808–1810.
[2] 2 See infra, § **31.02**.

Approved Profit Sharing Schemes

[7.78] Special tax treatment for share awards to employees under Approved Profit Sharing (APS) schemes started in 1978, but was phased out following the introduction of Share Incentive Plans (see infra, § **7.88**). No new profit sharing schemes were approved after 5 April 2001. Awards under existing schemes ceased by 31 December 2002, although employees continue to hold tax-advantaged shares from past appropriations.

To obtain approval for a scheme, a company had to set up a trust and make cash payments to it. The trustees then had to use the money both to buy shares in the company that they appropriated to its employees and to meet the expenses of the trust. If the money was used in this way, a corporation tax deduction for the payment should have been available for the company.

Employees did not pay income tax or National Insurance on the value of shares when appropriated to them by the trustees, but they had to agree to leave their shares with the trustees for at least two years. If the shares are sold in the third year after appropriation, there is an income tax charge on 100% of their value at appropriation. If they are sold in the fourth year after appropriation, or later, there is no income tax charge, but there may be a liability to capital gains tax.

APS was intended as an all-employee share scheme—it had to be open to any employee (whether full-time or part-time) whom the company had employed for at least five years. Other employees may have been included in the scheme if the company wished, but all employees who took part had to do so on similar terms. The value of the shares appropriated to an employee in any tax year had not to exceed £3,000 or 10% of the employee's earnings, whichever was the greater, subject to a ceiling of £8,000.

Savings-Related Share Option Schemes

[7.79] Tax relief for approved Savings-Related Share Option schemes was introduced in 1980. The scheme allows a company to give employees the right ("option") to buy at a future exercise date, a certain number of shares in the company at an exercise price that is fixed when the option is granted. The exercise price must not be less than 80% of the value of the underlying shares at that time. Participating employees are required to save between £5 and £250 per month under a Save as You Earn (SAYE) savings contract with either a bank for building society. These contracts last for three or five years. Employees with five-year SAYE contracts may decide at the outset whether to take the proceeds after the fifth anniversary or leave the savings for another two years to earn an additional bonus. The bonus or interest earned on these savings is tax-free.

The lump sum resulting from the SAYE contract can be used to buy the shares if the employee chooses to exercise their options after three, five or seven years, depending on the terms of the option. Employees are not obliged to exercise their options and they may not want to do so if the current share price is less than the exercise price at which the option entitles the employee to buy shares in their employer. If the option is not exercised, the employee receives the proceeds of the SAYE contract in the normal way.

Under an approved Savings-Related Share Option Scheme, the employee does not pay income tax or National Insurance on:

(1) the grant of options;
(2) the bonus or interest received under the SAYE contract:
(3) the benefit from being able to buy shares at a discounted price;
(4) any increase in the market value of underlying shares between the dates on which the option was granted and exercised.

Capital gains tax may be payable if shares aquired at option exercise are later sold.

Savings-Related Share Option schemes are intended as all-employee schemes. As was the case with APS, the scheme must be open to any employee who has been employed by the company for at least five years. Other employees may be included in the scheme if the company wishes, but all employees who take part must do so on similar terms.

Discretionary Share Option Schemes

[7.80] Tax relief for Discretionary Share Option schemes was introduced in 1984 and ceased in 1996, when no futher options could be granted. Employees were given the right ("option") to buy at a future date a certain number of shares at an exercise price fixed when the option was granted. Granting of options under these schemes was discretionary in that the company was free to decide which employees or full-time directors could participate. Options did not have to be linked to any kind of savings arrangement and employees are not obliged to exercise their options. The value of options that could be held by an individual was limited to the greater of £100,000, or four times the individual's salary for the current or the preceding year.

Under an approved Discretionary Share Option scheme, the employee had no income tax or National Insurance to pay on the grant of an option or any increase in the market value of the underlying shares between the dates on which the option was granted and exercised. (Capital gains tax may be payable if the shares acquired at option exercise are later sold). To obain this beneficial treatment, the options could not be exercised less than three years or more than ten years after the grant date. In addition, there also had to be a three-year interval between successive exercises of approved options. Until 2005–06, options granted under approved Discretionary Share Option schemes may, therefore, continue to attract income tax and National Insurance relief on gains at exercise.

Company Share Option Plans

[7.81] Discretionary Share Option schemes were replaced in 1996 by a new type of discretionary scheme called Company Share Option Plan (CSOP). Under CSOP there is a limit of £30,000 on the value of the shares under option that may be held by an employee at any one time (taking into account the value of shares in options held under the Discretionary Share Option scheme). Also, options may not be offered at a discount (ie the exercise price must not be manifestly less than the market value of the underlying shares on the option grant date).

The tax and National Insurance treatment of CSOP was the same as applied for Discretionary Share Option schemes (see supra, § 7.80) until 9 April 2003, when the condition requiring a three-year interval between different options exercises to qualify for relief was rescinded, In addittition, since 10 April 2003, CSOP options exercised within three years of grant have been subject to National Insurance contributions and Pay As You Earn.

Enterprise management incentives

[7.82] The most recent type of approved share option scheme is the enterprise management incentive scheme. The main features of this are:

(a) A qualifying company is able to grant EMI options to a maximum of 15 key employees.
(b) Each employee is able to hold options over shares worth up to £100,000 at the time of grant.
(c) In order to qualify, the company must be an independent company trading in the UK, with gross assets not exceeding £30 million.
(d) The company can be quoted or unquoted.
(e) There are no scheme approval procedures—companies enter into individual EMI share option agreements with each employee, which are notified to HMRC.
(f) Normally no tax or NICs are payable by the employee when the options are exercised nor is there normally any NIC charge on the employer.
(g) When the shares are sold, the gain arising usually qualifies for the more generous business asset taper relief and, in addition, this relief starts from the date when the options are granted.

[7.83] Enterprise management incentives (EMIs) are designed to help small companies attract and retain the people they need and to reward employees for taking a risk by investing their time and skills in helping small companies achieve their potential. An option only qualifies if granted for commercial reasons in order to recruit or retain a key employee in a company; it must not be part of a scheme or arrangement the main purpose of which is the avoidance of tax.[1] With limits of £3,000,000 in total and £100,000 for any employee[2] the company may grant EMI share options. Where an employee holds options over £100,000, EMI treatment will apply to the first £100,000. The £100,000 limit applies to a three-year period beginning with the date of the grant; so if an employee is given £100,000 of share options in year one and exercises them in year three, no new options may be taken out until year four when the third anniversary of the grant comes round.

This scheme is meant to apply to small high-risk companies. The company must be a qualifying company,[3] ie one which is an independent[4] trading[5] company with gross assets not exceeding £30 million.[6] The company may be listed or unlisted but must meet qualifying conditions and in particular must not be involved in certain prohibited types of trade.[7] The receipt of substantial sums by way of royalty or licence fee will disqualify a company, unless the intellectual property rights were created by the company or another group company.[8] If the company is not in a group, the company must exist for the purpose of carrying on a trade in the UK but the company need not be resident here.[9] If the company is the holding company of a group the condition is satisfied if any group member exists for the purpose of carrying on a trade in the UK.[10] Only qualifying companies can form a group; only the parent can grant EMI options. Subsidiaries will prevent the parent from granting EMI options unless each subsidiary meets all these requirements.[11] The relief also applies to a company carrying on activities of research and development from which it is intended that a qualifying trade will emerge.[12] In addition, there is a requirement on the number of employees a qualifying company may have. In

[7.83] Employment income

the case of a single company, the number of full-time employees must be less than 250 and in the case of parent company the sum of its full-time employees and the full-time employees of each of its qualifying subsidiaries must be less than 250. Directors are regarded as employees for this purpose but employees on maternity or paternity leave and students on vocational training should be excluded from the calculation[13].

[1] ITEPA 2003, Sch 5, para 4.
[2] ITEPA 2003, Sch 5, para 5–7. Prior to 6 April 2001, there was a limit of 15 employees who could receive EMI's and an overall limit of £1,500,000 of EMI share options issued.
[3] ITEPA 2003, s 719, Sch 5, paras 8–14.
[4] ITEPA 2003, s 719, Sch 5, para 9.
[5] ITEPA 2003, Sch 5, paras 13, 14.
[6] ITEPA 2003, Sch 5, para 12.
[7] The following are excluded activities: dealing in land or shares, etc, banking, insurance etc, leasing, legal or accountancy, property development, farming or market gardening or woodlands, hotels or nursing homes: ITEPA 2003, Sch 5, paras 15–23. The FA 2008 added shipbuilding, producing coal and producing steel to the list of excluded activities.
[8] ITEPA 2003, Sch 5, para 19.
[9] ITEPA 2003, Sch 5, paras 13, 15.
[10] ITEPA 2003, Sch 5, paras 14, 15.
[11] ITEPA 2003, s 717, Sch 5, paras 10, 11.
[12] ITEPA 2003, Sch 5, para 15. The provisions for subsidiaries are amended by ITEPA 2003, Sch 5, paras 11A and 11B inserted by FA 2004, s 96 and paras 8,10 and 11 amended by FA 2004, s 96, with effect from 17 March 2004.
[13] FA 2008.

The employee

[7.84] Eligible employees[1] must work for the company for a substantial amount of their time, ie 25 hours or, if less, 75% of their working time;[2] they may be inventors, scientists or experts in raising finance. Companies may offer up to £3 million[3] worth of share options to help them recruit and retain the high calibre people that they need to make their company successful and grow.

The employee may also hold SRSOP options but not shares under the all employee share plan (see supra, § 7.76).[4] The employee must not have a material interest, ie control of 30% or more of the ordinary share capital.[5]

The option must be capable of being exercised within ten years;[6] a charge arises if it is not exercised within the period.[7] The option may be conditional provided the condition can occur within the period. The option must be over the ordinary share capital of the company.[8]

The shares must also be fully paid up and neither redeemable nor convertible; the option must be non-assignable;[9] the terms must be agreed in writing.[10] However there are no rules directing the conditions under which the share may be issued; so the shares may be non-voting or subject to pre-emption rights on the part of the company. This is to allow the company to protect its independence.[11]

[1] ITEPA 2003, ss 549–554, Sch 5, paras 24–33.
[2] ITEPA 2003, Sch 5, paras 26, 27.
[3] ITEPA 2003, Sch 5, para 7.
[4] ITEPA 2003, Sch 5, paras 5, 6.
[5] ITEPA 2003, ss 549–554, Sch 5, paras 28, 29, 30, 31, 32, 33.
[6] ITEPA 2003, Sch 5, para 36.
[7] ITEPA 2003, s 529.
[8] ITEPA 2003, Sch 5, para 35.
[9] ITEPA 2003, Sch 5, para 35.
[10] ITEPA 2003, Sch 5, para 37.
[11] Inland Revenue Memorandum 4.7 and 4.9.

Income tax treatment

[7.85] If the option is granted at current market value there is no income tax liability on either the grant or on a single exercise of the option.[1] However, if the option price is below market value there will be a Schedule E charge on the value of the discount.[2] The option may be at a nil cost; in this case a charge arises under TA 1988, s 135 by reference to the value when the option is granted or, if lower, when it is exercised.[3] The company may grant options at a price above market value if it wishes.

[1] ITEPA 2003, ss 528 and 530.
[2] ITEPA 2003, s 531.
[3] ITEPA 2003, s 531.

Disqualifying events

[7.86] The precise effect of a disqualifying event[1] depends on its nature. The events are:

(1) loss of independence (ie becoming a 51% subsidiary of another company or otherwise coming under the control of another company);
(2) ceasing to meet the correct trading activities requirements;
(3) ceasing to meet the eligible employee requirements (eg the 75% working time conditions);[2]
(4) alterations in the terms of the option the effect of which is to increase the value of the shares or to break the rules as to qualifying options;
(5) any relevant alteration in the share capital of the company;[3]
(6) any relevant conversion of the shares;[4]
(7) granting the employee an option under the condition set out in infra, § **7.76** if this would take the employee over the £100,000 maximum level.[5]

[7.86] Employment income

The shares must be valued at the date of the disqualifying event.[6] Relief on the value down to that event continues to be available. However, any later increase in value is subject to a charge under ITEPA 2003, s 471.[7]

[1] ITEPA 2003, ss 534–539 and 429; on (non) effects of disqualifying event happening to the old company following company reorganisation, see s 534.
[2] ITEPA 2003, s 535.
[3] ITEPA 2003, s 537.
[4] ITEPA 2003, s 538.
[5] ITEPA 2003, s 539.
[6] ITEPA 2003, ss 532 and 420.
[7] ITEPA 2003, s 541.

Other share option rules

[7.87] ITEPA 2003, ss 192 to 197, which would otherwise deem a loan if the option price is below market value, is excluded.[1] However, various charges may arise after the shares have actually been acquired. So nothing in the new rules will prevent a charge from arising on the release of rights attached to shares acquired under a qualifying option, if the shares are convertible.[2] There will also be a charge under TA 1988, s 135 if a sum is received for the release of rights under the option itself.[3]

Capital gains tax[4] will be payable when the shares are sold but as they count as business assets they will benefit from the taper relief. The taper period will begin at the date the options are granted. When combined with the FA 2000 reduction in the taper period for business assets this means that the CGT burden will be much less than any income tax charge. Where there is a rights issue in respect of shares acquired under these options there is no amalgamation of the two holdings for CGT purposes.[5]

Further rules apply to the effect of a company reorganisation, as where the company in which the employee had the relevant options is taken over and new replacement options are given by the new company.[6]

The scheme must be acceptable to the Revenue but this takes the form of notification and not approval.[7] Of course the company then runs the risk that the Revenue will argue that the qualifying conditions have not been met.

[1] ITEPA 2003, s 540.
[2] ITEPA 2003, s 439.
[3] ITEPA 2003, s 541.
[4] FA 2000, Sch 14, paras 56, 57.
[5] FA 2000, Sch 14, para 58 excluding TCGA 1992, ss 127–130.
[6] ITEPA 2003, s 719, Sch 5, paras 39–43; note also ss 529 and 534.
[7] ITEPA 2003, Sch 5, paras 44–50; the details required in the notice are set out in para 44.

Share Incentive Plan

[7.88] The Finance Act 2000 introduced yet another scheme, now called a Share Incentive Plan ("SIP"). If the conditions are observed, all shares in the plan, held for two years,[1] will be completely free of income tax and CGT while so held.

The plan may contain three elements each with its own rules.[2] These are called free shares, partnership shares and matching shares; there is also a fourth category comprising dividend shares.

The plan may be on a group basis.[3] It needs to be approved by the Revenue.[4] It must have a purpose, as defined by the legislation, to provide benefits to employees in the nature of shares which give them a continuing stake in the company; it must not have features which are neither essential nor reasonably incidental to that purpose.[5]

The plan must be available to all employees within Schedule E, Case I who meet certain conditions of eligibility, although a minimum period of employment not exceeding eighteen months, can be imposed.[6] There must be no preferential treatment of directors, no further conditions and no loan arrangements.[7] Where there is more than one plan, all limits are applied by aggregating the various plans.[8] The employee must not have a material interest, ie control of more than 25% of the ordinary share capital.[9]

There are also conditions as to equal treatment to ensure that all are eligible to participate and that those who do so, participate on similar terms.[10] However, this does not prevent discrimination on the basis of hours worked, remuneration or length or service; nor does it prevent plans from being performance related. Group plans must not favour directors or higher paid employees.[11]

The shares must also be fully paid up and neither redeemable nor convertible.[12] However, there are no rules directing the conditions under which the share may be issued; so the shares may be non-voting or subject to pre-emption rights on the part of the company.[13] The company must either be listed or not be controlled by any other company,[14] ie it must be the appropriate type of company.

---

[1] FA 2000, Sch 8, para 88.
[2] ITEPA 2003, s 488, Sch 2, paras 2, 3.
[3] ITEPA 2003, Sch 2, para 4.
[4] ITEPA 2003, Sch 2, paras 81, 82.
[5] ITEPA 2003, Sch 2, para 7.
[6] ITEPA 2003, Sch 2, paras 7, 14, 15.
[7] ITEPA 2003, Sch 2, para 10.
[8] ITEPA 2003, Sch 2, para 18A(1) inserted by FA 2003, Sch 21, para 2.
[9] ITEPA 2003, Sch 2, paras 19–24.
[10] ITEPA 2003, Sch 2, paras 8, 9.
[11] ITEPA 2003, Sch 2, para 9.
[12] ITEPA 2003, Sch 2, paras 25–28.
[13] ITEPA 2003, Sch 2, paras 30, 32, 99.
[14] ITEPA 2003, Sch 2, para 29.

The free share plan

[7.89] Employers can give up to £3,000 of shares to employees. Employers do not have to treat all employees alike but may discriminate amongst them eg for reaching performance targets and so rewarding "personal, team or divisional performance". These plans resemble approved profit sharing schemes, however, unlike those schemes, the award of free shares may be linked to performance provided the criteria are objective and fair to all employees ie the targets set are broadly comparable.[1] Comparable does not mean identical and under one variant up to 80% can be awarded on the basis of performance as long as the highest reward is not more than four times greater than the award to an employee on similar terms.[2] There are also rules about the information to be given to employees.[3]

Free shares are held by trustees and appropriated to the participant.[4] The shares must remain with the trustee for a period of at least three and not more than ten years.[5] The shares must be transferred to any employee leaving the employment (even within the three-year period) and a charge may then arise; however, the terms of the plan may require that the share be forfeited when a plan is terminated.[6] The charge is on the full market value of the shares on leaving.[7] The shares may be withdrawn tax-free within the three-year period if the employment ends because of redundancy or disability etc.[8] If the shares are withdrawn between years three and five there is a charge either on the value when transferred or on the value when the option was given, whichever is the lower.[9]

[1] ITEPA 2003, Sch 2, paras 39–42.
[2] ITEPA 2003, Sch 2, para 41.
[3] ITEPA 2003, Sch 2, para 40.
[4] On powers and duties see ITEPA 2003, Sch 2, paras 71–80, 99.
[5] ITEPA 2003, Sch 2, para 37; amended by ESSA 2002, s 3(1).
[6] ITEPA 2003, Sch 2, para 90.
[7] ITEPA 2003, ss 7, 10, 505.
[8] ITEPA 2003, s 498.
[9] ITEPA 2003, ss 7, 10, 505.

Reinvestment of cash dividends (dividend shares)

[7.90] Dividends accruing on the plan shares may either be distributed in the usual (taxable) way or reinvested in "dividend shares".[1] There is a ceiling of £1,500 a year in any tax year.[2] The shares have their own three-year holding period.[3] Once the three years have passed there is no income tax charge on these shares. The share may be left in the plan or transferred as the employee wishes. If the holding period rules are broken the dividend used to pay for the shares becomes taxable.[4] Certain amounts which are not reinvested may be retained by the trustees and then paid out if not used.[5]

[1] ITEPA 2003, Sch 2, paras 62, 64–69.
[2] ITEPA 2003, Sch 2, para 64.
[3] ITEPA 2003, Sch 2, para 67.

[4] ITEPA 2003, Sch 2, para 67.
[5] ITEPA 2003, Sch 2, para 68.

Capital gains tax

[7.91] A CGT liability may accrue if the employee having had the shares transferred, then sells them. No liability arises on the appropriation or on withdrawal,[1] nor is there any liability on a disposal of rights under a rights issue.[2] Since the base cost of the shares will be the value when they are transferred to the employee[3] little if any liability will arise if the employee sells them immediately. So long as the shares remain in the plan the employee is treated as beneficially entitled to them as against the trustee.[4] Once the shares have been withdrawn by the employee—something required after five years anyway—they become chargeable assets and potentially liable to CGT. However, the shares will be business assets for taper relief; taper relief begins when the shares are withdrawn.

CGT holdover reliefs are available not only to trustees where funds are transferred to one of these funds from a qualifying ESOP[5] but also to existing shareholders wanting to sell their shares to a new plan trust for the benefit of employees.

When computing CGT on the disposal of shares, the base cost is the market value of the shares at the date the option was exercised.[6] Thus, the amount by which the market value exceeds the consideration given by the employee escapes taxation.

[1] FA 2000, Sch 8, para 101.
[2] FA 2000, Sch 8, para 104.
[3] FA 2000, Sch 8, para 101(1).
[4] FA 2000, Sch 8, para 99.
[5] ITEPA 2003, Sch 2, para 78.
[6] *Mansworth v Jelley* [2002] EWCA Civ 1829, [2003] STC 53. See infra, § **18.28**. For the refusal of a claim for repayment that would arise if the principle in *Mansworth v Jelley* were applied, see *Monro v R & C Comrs* [2007] STI 290.

The partnership share plan

[7.92] Employees may buy shares out of their pre-tax monthly salary or weekly wages[1] up to a maximum of £1,500 a year or £125 a month.[2] There is also a maximum limit of 10% of salary,[3] while another rule requires the employee to be informed about the possible effect of these rights on benefit entitlement.[4] The rules give the employee a tax deduction for the sums spent on the purchase of the shares. The payments must be deducted from the employee's salary.[5] The plan may allow for money to be accumulated; if it does not, the sums must be invested within 30 days.[6] Sums may not be accumulated beyond 12 months.

As the employee has paid for the share there is no minimum period during which the share must be retained and the employee will face no charge if the shares are left in the plan for five years. If shares are removed before three years

[7.92] Employment income

have passed the employee must pay income tax on the value of the shares when they are removed.[7] There is no deduction for the original price since it was tax free. If shares are removed between years three and five the employee must pay income tax on the sums used to buy the shares or the value when removed.[8] Charges may also arise if share money is paid over to the employee or if sums are paid to the employer on cancellation of the agreement.[9] Sums set aside by the employee in this way are tax free yet are not deductible from salary in computing relevant earnings for pensions limits.[10] Dividend shares may arise here; the rules are the same as for free shares above.

[1] ITEPA 2003, Sch 2, paras 43–57.
[2] ITEPA 2003, Sch 2, para 46; there is also a minimum of £10 a month: para 47.
[3] ITEPA 2003, Sch 2, para 46; on salary see para 43.
[4] ITEPA 2003, Sch 2, para 48.
[5] ITEPA 2003, Sch 2, para 45.
[6] ITEPA 2003, Sch 2, para 50; on plans with accumulation powers see para 52.
[7] ITEPA 2003, ss 7, 10 and 506.
[8] ITEPA 2003, ss 7, 10 and 506.
[9] ITEPA 2003, ss 7, 10, 503 and 504.
[10] ITEPA 2003, s 492.

Matching (partnership) shares

[7.93] These allow employers to match "partnership" shares by giving employees up to two free shares for each partnership share they buy. They must be on the same terms and carry the same rights as the partnership shares; they must be appropriated at the same time,[1] and to all employees on the same basis. There are rules about giving employees information. The holding period rules are the same as for free shares; further rules allow the company to require forfeiture of the shares when the employee leaves employment.[2] Income tax and CGT rules are the same as for free shares. The rules for dividend shares apply here also.

[1] ITEPA 2003, Sch 2, paras 58–61.
[2] ITEPA 2003, s 505.

[7.94] Employers may deduct the costs of setting up and running the plan and for the market value of any free and matching shares used in the plan.[1] The trustees are given a power to borrow money to buy the shares or subscribe for rights issues.[2]

The impact of NICs where employees withdraw partnership shares within three years is the subject of consultation. This review has been caused by the extreme volatility of prices in the technology sector.

[1] FA 2000, Sch 8, paras 105–113 extended by FA 2001, Sch 13, para 3.
[2] ITEPA 2003, Sch 2, para 76.

Employee share ownership plans

[7.95] FA 1989 contained rules for a further incentive for employee share ownership plans; this scheme remains in force. Shares may be transferred from this older scheme to a new scheme without incurring an income tax charge.[1] In essence these arrangements combine a share participation scheme with a trust for the benefit of the employees. The legislation ensures that the company obtains a corporation tax deduction when making its contribution to the trust and for the costs of setting a trust up. In essence this amounts to a two-tier structure with an employee benefit trust funded primarily by contributions by the company acquiring shares for subsequent distribution to an approved profit-sharing scheme.[2] FA 1994 contains provisions relaxing some of the rules as from 3 May 1994.[3]

An ESOP comes under these special rules if there is a qualifying employment share ownership trust. This is defined at length. The trust must be established under a deed. The trust must be established by a company which is not controlled by any other company and is resident in the UK.[4] The deed must appoint the first trustees and contain various rules as to the trustees eg as to having a majority independent of the founding company.[5]

It is the rules as to the trustees which are widened by the 1994 legislation.[6] Previously the trust had to have three or more UK resident trustees. Three further conditions had to be fulfilled: (a) one had to be a trust corporation, solicitor, or a member of professional body approved by the Revenue, (b) a majority had to be employees of the company or group elected by such a majority and a majority of them must not be or have ever been directors of the company setting up the ESOP or of a group company. As from 3 May 1994 there is a second structure. Under this the trustees must still number at least three UK resident trustees. One of them must be a professional trustee (ie equates with the old (a)) but with the proviso that a person is disqualified through being a director or employee of the company setting up the ESOP or of a group company; this person must be selected by the other (non-professional trustees). In addition at least one half of the other non-professional trustees must be employees of the founding company or of a group company and must be selected by those employees or by persons elected by them. The new legislation also allows a third option; a corporate trustee ie a single trustee which is a UK resident company controlled by the company setting up the ESOP with a board of directors set up in the same way as the second option. There will be consequential regulatory changes to the Financial Services legislation.[7]

There are rules as to beneficiaries—certain employees must be included (eg those who have been with the company or any other company within the group for at least five years and from 1 May 1995 whether full-time or part-time) but others may be beneficiaries; those who are part-time directors or have material interests or who have worked for the company for less than one year must be excluded.[8] Thus, employees of subsidiaries can qualify. The trust deed must spell out various duties of the trustees eg as to their functions in receiving money from the company and investing it in the appropriate securities within the appropriate period and dealing with the securities promptly.[9] Thus they must invest the money in ordinary shares of the founding

[7.95] Employment income

company or spend it on some other qualifying purpose within nine months;[10] they must be told not to invest if the company is then controlled by another company and that any acquisitions must be at a price at or below current market value; special restrictions on the shares are not permitted but this has to be achieved by expressly stating that the trustees may not buy shares which are subject to such restrictions.[11] The trustees are permitted to vary the basis of allocation only by reference to the basis of level of remuneration or length of service.[12] When the trust disposes of its shares it must do so either directly to the employees or to an approved profit-sharing scheme; any other transfer will be a chargeable event and this restriction must be spelt out in the trust.[13]

Apart from the acquisition of shares in the founding company the purposes for which the trustees are permitted to use the money are limited to matters such as the repayment of loans taken out to acquire the shares, the payment of interest on such loans, payments to employees and the payment of trust expenses.[14] The deed must not contain features which are not essential, or reasonably incidental, to these primary purposes.[15] A trust which ceases to satisfy some of these conditions ceases to be a qualifying ESOP.

There is now a clearance procedure to enable trustees to obtain confirmation that their trust satisfies these rules.[16]

Simon's Taxes D2.528–542.

[1] ITEPA 2003, Sch 2, para 65.
[2] See generally Williams, *Taxation of employee share schemes* (3rd edn) Chapter 6, pp 125–216.
[3] FA 1994, s 102.
[4] FA 1989, Sch 5, para 2.
[5] FA 1989, Sch 5, para 3.
[6] FA 1989, Sch 5, paras 3A–3C.
[7] Treasury press release, 5 April 1994, *Simon's Tax Intelligence* 1994, p 494.
[8] FA 1989, Sch 5, para 4; material interest is defined in FA 1989, Sch 5, para 16.
[9] FA 1989, Sch 5, paras 5–10.
[10] FA 1989, Sch 5, para 7.
[11] FA 1989, Sch 5, para 9.
[12] FA 1989, Sch 5, para 6.
[13] FA 1989, Sch 5, para 5(2)(c), (d); the chargeable event is specified in s 69(1)–(3).
[14] FA 1989, Sch 5, para 6(3).
[15] FA 1989, Sch 5, para 10.
[16] Inland Revenue press release, 9 May 1990, *Simon's Tax Intelligence* 1990, p 443.

The consequences

[7.96] FA 1989 contains rules allowing the company to claim a deduction for contributions to an ESOP and then provides complicated rules as to the clawback of the benefit. It will be noted that there is no CGT relief on a sale of the shares. The company may deduct a payment to the trustees if the trust is still a qualifying ESOP, at that time at least some of the employees are eligible to benefit, the company is resident in the UK, a sum is spent on a qualifying purpose within nine months and a claim for relief is made.[1]

Employee share ownership plans [7.96]

When a chargeable event occurs the benefit of the corporation tax deduction is clawed back from the trustees. The Revenue view is that this will be the rate appropriate to trusts, currently 34%. The charge is under Schedule D, Case VI. The company may be liable to pay if the trustees fail to pay within six months.[2]

The chargeable events are related very closely to the matters which the trustees are or are not permitted to do. So the trustees must not make a non-qualifying transfer (ie a transfer to someone other than a beneficiary or an approved profit sharing scheme)[3] or a transfer on non-qualifying terms.[4] They must not spend the money on a non-qualifying purpose.[5] They are also barred from retaining securities for more than seven years.[6] The amount brought into charge for expenditure on a non-qualifying purpose is the sum so spent. Otherwise it is the capital gains base cost (without any allowance for indexation relief) of the security retained or transferred.[7]

In computing the sum to be charged a further adjustment is made in order to achieve the legislative object of clawing back the relief rather than simply penalising the trustee. First, one adds the present sum to be charged to the total of any previous charges.[8] This is then set against the amounts deductible for corporation tax by the company (whether or not any claim for relief has actually been made). The sum to be charged is chargeable only to the extent that it exceeds the deductible amounts.

A further charge will arise in a combination of circumstances. The first is that a sum could have been charged—because it arose on a chargeable event—but it was not charged because of an adjustment. The second is that at that time the trustees had borrowed money. If any of the borrowings are subsequently repaid the trustees are chargeable under Case VI on the amount repaid.[9]

There are extensive information powers.[10] There are special rollover relief rules for the disposal of assets to such trusts.[11]

There are provisions for applying PAYE to collect the tax charge.[12]

Simon's Taxes D2.528–542.

---

[1] FA 1989, s 67. See generally ICAEW Memorandum TR 759, *Simon's Tax Intelligence* 1989, pp 723–726.
[2] The mechanics are set out in FA 1989, s 68; see Hansard Standing Committee G, col 311.
[3] FA 1989, s 69(2), (3). The list of events which are qualifying events and so do not give rise to a charge now includes a share exchange within TCGA 1992, s 135(1); see FA 1989, s 69(3A).
[4] FA 1989, s 69(4), (6).
[5] FA 1989, s 69(5).
[6] See FA 1989, s 69(1)(c), (7)–(12).
[7] FA 1989, s 70.
[8] FA 1989, s 72(2).
[9] FA 1989, s 71.
[10] FA 1989, s 73.
[11] TCGA 1992, ss 227–235, discussed infra, § **17.20**.
[12] ITEPA 2003, s 684.

Exemption for training schemes, scholarship and apprentice schemes at universities and technical colleges

[7.97] Expenditure incurred by an employer in providing training is deductible in computing the liability to tax on the profits of the employer.[1] It is also not treated as assessable earnings for the employee.[2] In *Silva v Charnock*,[3] the Special Commissioner held that a bonus of £18,000 paid to an individual on resuming her duties after unpaid leave to study for an MBA was exempt under this provision, being reimbursement of the employee's MBA fees.

One exemption is given for expenditure reimbursed or incurred by the employer in connection with retraining courses. The course must be attended on a full-time (or substantially full-time) basis; the employee must have been employed for two years and the opportunity to take the course must be available either generally to employees and former employees or to a particular class of such persons.[4] So the owner of a firm cannot use this simply to provide a child of his with a training at the state's subsidy just by taking him on to the books for a few days and then sending him off to a course. The course must be designed to impart or improve skills or knowledge relevant to and intended to be used in the course of gainful employment (including self-employment) of any description and the course must be entirely devoted to the teaching and/or practical application of such skills or knowledge. In addition the course must not last more than one year.[5]

The course must be undertaken by an employee (or former employee) with a view to retraining. This test stands as one of purpose, presumably in the light of the objective test used by the House of Lords in *Mallalieu v Drummond* (see infra, § **8.96**). However, the legislation also states that the course cannot be regarded as undertaken with a view to retraining unless it is begun while employed by the employer or within one year of ceasing to be so; it is also necessary that the employee should in any event cease to be so employed within two years of the end of the course.[6] This last rule underlines the purpose of the provision. It is designed to encourage employers and employees to get retrained and then re-employed or self-employed elsewhere.

Where the employee attends a full-time course at a university or technical college payments by the employer may qualify as scholarship income under TA 1988, s 331. A statement of practice sets out the conditions to be observed.[7]

---

[1] See TA 1988, s 588 for retraining courses and see infra, § **8.139**.
[2] ITEPA 2003, ss 250–260 and s 311.
[3] [2002] STC (SCD) 426.
[4] ITEPA 2003, s 311—the two year employment condition means two years before he starts the course or ends the employment whichever is the earlier.
[5] ITEPA 2003, s 311.
[6] ITEPA 2003, s 311; re-employment within two years is a breach of the conditions; any breach of these conditions has to be reported within 60 days of the employer coming to know of it (ITEPA 2003, s 312(4)) and the normal six year time limit for assessments runs from the end of the year in which the breach occurred (ITEPA 2003, s 312); there are also Revenue information-gathering powers in ITEPA 2003, s 312(5).

[7] Statement of practice SP 4/86. On Revenue practice see Revenue Manual SE 6200 et seq.

[7.98] The rules in ITEPA 2003, s 250 exclude liability for certain work related training provided by employers while, as just seen, those in ITEPA 2003, s 312 exclude liability for retraining received around the time of leaving an employment. Where these rules do not apply ITEPA 2003, s 255 may provide relief. These are the new Individual Learning Accounts set up under the Skills and Learning Act 2000; the tax legislation refers to that Act for many of its definitions. The effect of ITEPA 2003, ss 250 and 255 is to prevent a benefits-in-kind charge where the employer pays the training provider directly or the employer reimburses the costs. These rules extend also to any related costs, ie incidental expenses arising wholly and exclusively from undertaking the qualifying education and training.[1] The Revenue notes to the Finance Bill suggest that this test would allow additional expenses arising directly from undertaking the training, such as extra travel and additional childcare paid for or reimbursed by the employer but not preliminary or everyday expenses such as routine childcare costs. Similarly the Revenue would allow the costs of an assessment or examination and the costs of registering a qualification. The cost of an award would be exempt if it were simply a recognition of achievement.

Learning from the experience of NVQs, ITEPA 2003, ss 253 and 257 withhold the exemption to the extent that the education or training is actually for entertainment, recreation or reward.[2] Hence skid-pan training offered as part of the staff's annual outing (and so meeting the fair opportunity rules) would not be exempt under ITEPA 2003, s 255 or s 250. Likewise golfing lessons offered to those sales representatives meeting sales targets would not be exempt. It will be possible to apportion such expenditure in appropriate cases.

The rules allow suitable travel and subsistence costs[3] and the costs of supplying suitable materials for the training.[4] There is even a specific exemption for things made by the trainee during training; the Revenue's example is a cake made on a catering course.

The tax exemption for the Individual Learning Account Training only applies if the employer makes those contributions available to all employees on similar terms under "fair opportunity arrangements".[5] Regulations are to be made so that different categories of Crown servants can be treated separately for these purposes; large companies are left to their own devices.

Further rules apply equivalent relief where the training is funded by third parties.[6]

---

1 ITEPA 2003, ss 250 and 255.
2 ITEPA 2003, ss 253 and 258.
3 ITEPA 2003, ss 252 and 257.
4 ITEPA 2003, ss 254 and 259.
5 Defined in ITEPA 2003, s 260.
6 ITEPA 2003, ss 250 and 255.

Employees earning £8,500 per annum or more and directors

[7.99] One product of the rule in *Tennant v Smith*[1] was a substantial amount of tax avoidance. What would otherwise be remuneration was dressed up as an expense allowance or paid in the form of benefits in kind. Expense allowances in so far as they exceeded the sums actually spent by the recipient on behalf of his employer[2] would be taxable, but difficult to trace, while benefits in kind insofar as they could be traced would be taxable only if convertible into money or money's worth. Yet these expenses or allowances would be deductible by the employer in computing the profits of his business. For these reasons special legislation was introduced in 1948.

Simon's Taxes E4.601–604.

[1] [1892] AC 150, 3 TC 158, HL (see supra, § **7.40**).
[2] Such sums only escaped tax if deductible under what was then TA 1988, ss 198 or 201.

[7.100] The charges that arise in this section were introduced by FA 1948 as a code for bringing into tax benefits supplied to the highest earning employees and directors. This was a code for this limited group of people who were thought to be in a position to take advantage of the generally restricted nature of what was then the Schedule E charge by being able to arrange to have remuneration packages that would otherwise be of untaxed benefit. The code was applied to employees who, in 1948–49, earned over £2,000 per annum. This was at a time that the average earnings in the UK were £305 per annum, thus the code only applied to those earning more than 6 1/2 times the national average. If the limit had stayed in line with the increase in average earnings the code would now apply to those earning more than £188,000 per annum.[1] The £2,000 limit was increased to £5,000 in 1975–76[2], to £7,500 in 1978–79[3] and then to £8,500 in 1979–80.[4] Subsequently the Government has steadfastly refused to change the limit, which now stands at 36% of national average earnings. Hence, the code in the following section applies to the majority of employees, as well as to directors.[5] It is difficult to understand why the following code is not merged with the code that charges all employees, irrespective of earnings.[6] It is noted that ITEPA 2003 deals with the division between those who are chargeable and those who are not by excluding from the relevant parts of the benefits code those in "lower paid employments" (see Chapter 11 of Part 3).

The charges are imposed on a "shadow director", even though, under company law, the individual may have no office and under employment law is not regarded as an employee of the company.[7]

Also excluded from the definition of director are those who are directors of non-profit making bodies and charities provided they have no material interest in the company.[8]

In computing the employee's earnings for the £8,500 the cash value of benefits is included;[9] this is to prevent avoidance by means of a low salary and large expenses or benefits in kind. Dubiously there is no deduction in making this computation for expenses allowable, although an inspector may give a notice of nil liability[10] in respect of a benefit or allowance where he is satisfied that no extra charge to tax would arise. Such notices, however, are not issued where the effect would be to take the employee below the £8,500 threshold.[11] An expense which the employer meets directly will not be taken into account. Deduction is permitted for approved pension contributions, and contributions under approved payroll giving schemes.[12]

An employer may not avoid these rules by dividing up an employee's functions into different employments,[13] and similar rules apply if the second employment is with a controlled company. A director of a company may also be an employee but these provisions apply to him whether or not his income from the employment reaches £8,500,[14] save where he is a full-time working director. If he is a director (other than a full-time working director without a material interest) of one controlled company and an employee of another, these rules apply to him in respect of *both* situations.

Simon's Taxes E4.602, 603.

---

[1] The Office for National Statistics Annual Abstract of Statistics 1948 gives average earnings for all operatives in all industries at October 1948 of £5.87 per week. The Government Office, National Statistics gives the average earnings, UK, all industries at April 2000 as £418 per week. National Statistics Monthly Index of Average Earnings was rebased at 100 as at April 2000; at February 2007, the index is 132.1.

[2] FA 1974, s 18.

[3] FA 1977, s 35(3).

[4] FA 1978, s 23.

[5] A director of a charitable company is not charged to the benefits discussed below, where the value of those benefits would not cause the total emoluments to be above £8,500: ITEPA 2003, s 216(3). A full-time working director who does not have a material interest in the company only comes within these provisions if his earnings, with benefits come to £8,500 or more.

[6] See supra, §§ 7.39–7.87. There is no £8,500 threshold for charging the benefits of accommodation provided, or for charges arising from the share option legislation. It is difficult to see why an employee earning less than £8,500 should be charged for the receipt of these benefits but not for the benefit of receiving a company car.

[7] R v Allen [2001] UKHL 45, [2001] STC 1537, HL.

[8] ITEPA 2003, s 216.

[9] ITEPA 2003, ss 218 and 219. The Revenue claim that the purpose of this last rule is to maintain equity between one who is paid a gross salary out of which deductible expenses are met and another who receives a lower salary but separate reimbursements of deductible expenses. This claim is unsound since equity could be achieved equally well by allowing both persons to deduct their expenses and because it creates inequity between these two and the third person who receives a lower salary but who incurs no deductible expenses because his employer meets them directly. FA 2007, s 61 removes the double counting that previously arose when an employee was given a voucher (such as a company credit card) with which he could purchase private petrol. However, this has not addressed the basic anomaly.

[10] ITEPA 2003, s 65; On Revenue practice see Revenue Manual SE 3800 et seq.

[11] Quaere whether the Revenue have the power to do this.

[12] ITEPA 2003, s 218.
[13] ITEPA 2003, s 220.
[14] ITEPA 2003, s 220.

Payments for expenses and expense allowances

[7.101] Any payment[1] made by reason of the employment[2] in respect of expenses is, unless otherwise chargeable to tax, to be treated as income of the director or employee. The section applies not only to expense allowances but also to reimbursement of expenses actually incurred since here too there is payment in respect of expenses; the only expenses not caught are those which the employer meets himself. The recipient may however deduct sums actually expended if they satisfy the tests laid down in ITEPA 2003, s 327.[3] The section thus catches payments that would not otherwise be caught since under *Owen v Pook* the reimbursement of an expense is not an emolument;[4] further the sum must be reported as income and then claimed as an expense.

The section also applies to sums put at the employee's disposal and paid away by him.[5] So sums are caught even though the money does not at any time become the property of the employee.[6]

The employer has to report all such payments. In order to avoid too much circuity where the sum would be deductible under those sections, the inspector, having received a statement from the employer, and being satisfied that no additional tax falls to be charged under this chapter, may issue notice of nil liability directing that the chapter shall not apply.[7] The concession for the reimbursed expenses of certain living costs of members of the clergy does not apply if that member earns £8,500 pa or more.[8]

Simon's Taxes E4.604.

[1] See *Jennings v Kinder* [1958] 1 All ER 369, 38 TC 673.
[2] All sums paid by the employer are deemed to be paid by reason of the employment unless the employer is an individual and the payment is made in the normal course of the employer's domestic, family or personal relationships; ITEPA 2003, s 71.
[3] The burden of proof rests on the taxpayer to show that the expense comes within these provisions—*McLeish v IRC* (1958) 38 TC 1. On reimbursement of fees for solicitors practising certificates, see a statement by the Law Society, 24 February 1993, *Simon's Tax Intelligence* 1993, p 341.
[4] Royal Commission Cmd 9474 (1955) § **226** and supra, § **7.24**, note 13.
[5] ITEPA 2003, s 70(2).
[6] ITEPA 2003, s 70. The effect of the whole section is to make almost any employee with financial responsibility subject to the chapter.
[7] ITEPA 2003, s 65. Dispensations are not given for allowances fixed at a "round sum": Inland Revenue leaflet IR 480 (1998) § **2.2**.
[8] Extra-statutory concession A61.

The benefits code

[7.102] Chapter 2 of Part 3 of ITEPA sets out "the benefits code". This covers all charges other than basic "earnings" and includes the items formerly known as "benefits in kind". Chapters 4 and 5 cover vouchers and credit tokens and living accommodation which are chargeable on all employees (vide supra, § 7.45). Chapter 3 covers expenses payments (as above) chargeable only on those not in lower paid employments. Chapters 6 to 10 of Part 3 of ITEPA 2003 cover the rest of the "benefits in kind", again chargeable on those not in lower paid employments.

Chapter 10 sweeps up the non-specific benefits by treating as earnings of the director or employee the cash equivalent of an "employment-related benefit". This is defined as a benefit or facility of any kind, other than an excluded benefit, provided for an employee or for a member of his family or household.[1] It would include prizes for passing examinations.[2] An excluded benefit is one to which Chapters 3 to 9 of the benefits code would apply (but for an exception) or a benefit consisting of the right to receive earnings dealt with under ITEPA 2003, s 221 (payments because of sickness or disability).[3]

Section 203 charges the cash equivalent of the benefit and defines this as the cost of the benefit less any part of that cost made good by the employee to the persons providing the benefit. The section is not confined to benefits in kind but can apply to cash. However, there must be some benefit to the employee; the receipt of a sum which was a fair valuation for loss of rights could not be a benefit.[4]

The persons providing a benefit are the person or persons at whose cost the benefit is provided.[5] If the same benefit would give rise to a charge as "earnings" under ITEPA 2003, s 62, s 64 provides that the benefits charge should only be on any excess. Thus if the benefit could be converted into cash but only for less than its cost, the cash is chargeable as earnings under *Tennant v Smith* and the balance is treated as earnings under the benefits code. (In practice the amount chargeable under the benefits code is not distinguished.[6]) If, however, the resale value is higher than cost, s 64(2) enables the Revenue to charge the whole of that resale value as earnings under *Tennant v Smith*. ITEPA 2003, s 64 does not apply to living accommodation or where the notional loan rules on acquisition of shares for less than market value apply.

An expense has been made good by the employee either by the payment of cash or by the provision of some other consideration (except for the provision of services under the contract of employment).[7]

ITEPA 2003, s 201 applies only where the benefit is provided by reason of the employment. However, all provision for an employee, or for members of his family or household, by his employer are deemed to be made by reason of the employment unless it can be shown that the employer is an individual and that the provision was made in the normal course of his domestic, family or personal relationship.[8]

A benefit is treated as provided by the employer if it is provided at his cost. In *Wicks v Firth*[9] scholarships awarded by trustees were held to be provided at the cost of the employer as the trustees used money supplied by the employer and were only performing duties imposed on them by the employer.

[7.102] Employment income

If the deeming provision does not apply s 201 will apply if the benefit is provided "by reason of the employment". This test may involve a causa sine qua non—in which case it is different from the general test of causation under the employment income rules.[10]

Statute provides that the provision by an employer of certain child care facilities is not taxed as a benefit received by the employee.[11]

TA 1988, s 201 talks simply in terms of the provision of certain benefits or facilities. It does not require that the employee should receive the exclusive benefit; so when the service benefits both employer and employee, s 201 applies. It is quite immaterial that the employee, left to himself, would have spent less on the service.

In *Rendell v Went*[12] a company incurred expenses of £641 in the (successful) defence of one of its directors on a charge of causing death by dangerous driving. That sum was chargeable to the director under what was then s 154. The expense was incurred "in the provision of a benefit to" the director regardless of the fact that there might be good commercial reason for the expenditure and regardless of the fact that the director, left to himself, would have spent no more than £60 and no-one suggested that he could have received free legal aid.

Since the section then talked of the provision of a service it was presumably irrelevant that no benefit accrued (it is interesting that the term "service" has been dropped in ITEPA 2003); so the director in *Rendell v Went* would be chargeable in respect of the £641 even if he had been found guilty and been given the maximum sentence. Likewise, where a facility (the term used in ITEPA 2003) is provided, it is presumably irrelevant that the employee would rather not have the benefit. Thus the cost of providing a seat in a party for the FA Cup Final would be taxable to the employee even if he detests football and would rather be at Covent Garden to attend a performance of Götterdämmerung—or vice versa.[13]

However, it is presumably necessary that the employee should accept or acquiesce in the provision of the benefit. So, for Lord Reid, in *Rendell v Went* it was important that the director knew and accepted what was being done on his behalf even though he may not have realised how much it was costing and Lord Reid would express no opinion on the case of a company spending a large sum of money without the director's knowledge to procure a benefit that he did not want.[14]

Simon's Taxes E4.611–613.

---

[1] ITEPA 2003, s 201
[2] ICAEW Memorandum TR 786, *Simon's Tax Intelligence* 1990, p 205.
[3] ITEPA 2003, s 202. In *Wicks v Firth* [1983] STC 25, HL, the House of Lords held that although a scholarship awarded to the taxpayer's child by his employer was a benefit provided to the taxpayer by reason of his employment, it was exempt under TA 1988, s 331 as scholarship income. However, the effect of this decision has been reversed by ITEPA 2003, s 212 (see infra, § **7.109**). See also Explanatory Note 805 on ITEPA 2003 and Note 25 in Annex 2.
[4] *Mairs v Haughey* [1992] STC 495, NI CA. This point was not argued before the House of Lords—see [1993] STC 569 at 576b.

⁵ ITEPA 2003, s 209.
⁶ See Revenue Manual SE 21640.
⁷ If the employee pays a sum equal to the cost of providing the benefit he escapes a tax charge, even though the market value is higher: ITEPA 2003, s 203. Quaere whether a tenant paying a full market rent thereby "makes good" to the lessor any sums spent by the lessor even though those sums exceed the rent. See *Luke v IRC* [1963] 1 All ER 655, 40 TC 630. Lord Reid took this view at 578, 647 but contra Lord Guest at 586, 652. On making good see also Revenue Manual SE 21120 et seq. *Mairs v Haughey* [1992] STC 495, NI CA.
⁸ ITEPA 2003, s 201(3). Quaere if the business is held in a family trust so that the body of trustees is the employer. This provision could not apply *Mairs v Haughey* [1992] STC 495, NI CA as the court said that a payment made by someone other than the employer could not have been paid by reason of the employment.
⁹ [1983] STC 25.
¹⁰ [1982] STC 76 per Lord Denning MR at 80. This point was left open by the House of Lords; see [1983] STC 25, HL per Lord Templeman at 32.
¹¹ ITEPA 2003, ss 318, 318A, 318B, 318C and 318D. These provisions are substantially rewritten by FA 2004, Sch 14, with effect from 6 April 2005. See infra, § **7.104**.
¹² [1964] 2 All ER 464, 41 TC 641; on apportionment see supra, § **7.99**.
¹³ Such discrimination is ruled out by Donovan LJ in *Butter v Bennett* (1962) 40 TC 402 at 414.
¹⁴ At 466, 655.

Statutory exemptions from benefits charged

[7.103] Certain benefits provided by the employer are excluded:

(1) An expense incurred in the provision of accommodation supplies or services used in premises occupied by the employer is excluded, provided these are used by the employee solely in performing the duties of his employment. Thus a director is not chargeable on sums spent on an expensive secretary or on luxurious office furniture.¹ These rules proved to be unrealistic where the employee was able to make private use of work benefits but the amount involved was small; special rules were added by FA 2000 (see supra, § **7.95**) and the original exception repealed.²

(2) Meals served in canteens which are made available to the staff generally.³ The provision of vouchers for use in a separated part of a restaurant run independently of the employer might well fall within this exception and although vouchers for use in any restaurant would not, those for use in a particular restaurant might well escape the charges in ITEPA 2003, ss 82 et seq.

(3) Expenses incurred in the provision of any pension, annuity, lump sum, gratuity or other like benefit to be given to the director or employee or his spouse children or dependants on his death or retirement.⁴

(4) Travel warrants for H.M. forces.⁵

(5) Medical insurance for foreign visits and medical treatment, the need for which arises while the director or employee is abroad.⁶

[7.103] Employment income

(6) As a result of the decision of the House of Lords in *Wicks v Firth*, a provision rendering a payment non-taxable as income may also impliedly exempt the employee from liability under the benefits code, whether the payment is made either to the employee or a member of his family.[7] The particular exemption in that case (TA 1988, s 331) has now been the subject of special legislation (see infra, § **7.109**) but the principle remains.[8]

(7) The provision of a parking place for cars or motor cycles or facilities for bicycles at or near the employee's place of work.[9]

(8) The provision of entertainment by someone unconnected with his employment.[10]

(9) The supply to miners of coal and allowances in lieu of coal.[11]

(10) Incidental overnight expenses.[12]

(11) Annual parties and functions.[13]

(12) A gift made to an employee by a person who is neither the employer nor a person connected with the employer where the value of all such gifts from that person does not exceed £250 in the fiscal year.[14]

(13) Mobile telephones.[15]

(14) Employees' eye tests and special glasses.[16]

(15) The loan of a bicycle or bicycle safety equipment for use on qualifying journeys.[17]

(16) The provision of a works bus service or of support for public transport bus service for use for qualifying journeys.[18]

(17) Childcare financed by the employer (see infra, § **7.104**).

(18) Voucher for childcare (see supra, § **7.46**).

---

[1] ITEPA 2003, s 316.
[2] FA 2000, s 156.
[3] ITEPA 2003, s 317. On Revenue practice see Revenue Manual SE and EIM 21670 et seq.
[4] ITEPA 2003, s 307 which also gives the relief previously given by extra-statutory concession A72 where the benefit is for a member of the employee's family or household, as defined in ITEPA 2003, s 712(4), (5), the family being the employee's spouse, children, parents and others who are the dependants of the employee, plus spouses of his/her children.
[5] ITEPA 2003, s 296.
[6] ITEPA 2003, s 325.
[7] [1983] STC 25, HL
[8] Unless the House of Lords follows its own (bad) precedent in *Thomson v Moyse*.
[9] ITEPA 2003, s 237 added by FA 1988, s 46(3); this exclusion has retroactive effect when liability was settled before 15 March 1988.
[10] ITEPA 2003, ss 265 and 718.
[11] ITEPA 2003, s 306.
[12] ITEPA 2003, ss 240, 241 (see infra, § **7.130**).
[13] ITEPA 2003, s 264.
[14] ITEPA 2003, ss 270 and 324.
[15] ITEPA 2003, s 319 amended by FA 2006, s 60(3).
[16] ITEPA 2003, s 320A inserted by FA 2006, s 62(2).

[17] ITEPA 2003, s 244 (infra, § **7.131**).
[18] ITEPA 2003, ss 242 and 243 (infra, § **7.131**).

Exemption for childcare

[7.104] No income tax arises on the provision of childcare by an employer for a child of an employee[1] if certain conditions are met.

The child must be a child or step-child of the employee maintained (wholly or partly) at the employee's expense who either resides with the employee or for whom the employee has parental responsibility.[2] The childcare must be provided on registered premises,[3] which are not a private dwelling.[4] The childcare can be provided by the employer alone or in partnership with other employers.[5] The childcare must be provided to all employees employed at a particular location.[6]

Although the tax exemption is commonly referred to as "workplace nursery", the care can be for any child up to age 15[7] (extended to 16, if the child is disabled).[8]

The care that can be provided is widely defined, but excludes normal schooling.[9] It has been noted that the definition is wide enough to cover tuition in abseiling for 14-year olds. The care must be provided by registered persons.[10]

If the care is provided by the employer, either alone or in partnership with other employers, there is no financial limit to the cost borne by the employer for the provision of childcare. If the childcare is provided by others, at the employer's expense, the exemption extends to £50 per employee only, the excess above this figure being a taxable benefit.[11] The £50 relates to the employee, irrespective of the number of children that employee has.

[1] ITEPA 2003, s 318(1).
[2] ITEPA 2003, s 318(3). Parental responsibility is defined in s 318B.
[3] ITEPA 2003. s 318(4)(*b*), (5).
[4] ITEPA 2003, s 318(4)(*a*).
[5] ITEPA 2003, s 318(6), (7).
[6] ITEPA 2003, s 318(8). The cost of administering the voucher scheme are also exempt from income tax: ITEPA 2003, s 270A amended by FA 2005, s 15.
[7] ITEPA 2003, s 318B(2).
[8] ITEPA 2003, Defined in s 318B(3).
[9] ITEPA 2003, s 318C(2)(*b*).
[10] ITEPA 2003, s 318C(2) for England. Sub-section 318C(3), (4) and (5) for Wales, Scotland and Northern Ireland respectively.
[11] ITEPA 2003, s 318A(*c*).

Exemption for in-house sports facilities

[7.105] There is also a statutory exemption for in-house sports facilities, identified in ITEPA 2003 as recreational benefits.[1] Where the exemption applies there is a similar exclusion from liability in respect of a non-cash voucher which can be exchanged only for such a benefit.²

The exempted benefit is the right or opportunity to make use of any sporting or other recreational facilities provided such facilities are available to employees generally.

Certain facilities are proscribed—an interest in or the use of mechanically propelled vehicles is outside the exemption unless regulations provide otherwise.³ The term "vehicle" expressly includes any ship, boat or other vessel, any aircraft and any hovercraft; since this is the definition of the term "vehicle" it ought to follow that the provision of such a vehicle without mechanical propulsion, eg a sailing dinghy or even, perhaps,⁴ a glider is not outside the exemption.

Also excluded is an interest in or use of any holiday or overnight accommodation or any facilities provided in association with a right or opportunity to make use of such facilities.⁵ A benefit is also taxable if it consists of a facility provided on domestic premises.⁶

Other prohibitions are designed to ensure that the benefit is restricted to employees. So the benefit is taxable if the facility is provided so as to be available to or for use by members of the public generally;⁷ hence subscriptions for employees to sports clubs will not be exempt. Similarly the benefit will be taxable if it is used neither wholly nor mainly by persons who derive their right or opportunity from the employment (although they may be run by two or more employers jointly).⁸ For the purposes of this last rule the right derives from a person's employment if and only if it derives from being or having been an employee of a particular employer or a member of the family or household of such a person.⁹

The Treasury is empowered to make regulations to grant exemption to benefits which are proscribed and may do so conditionally.¹⁰

---

1   ITEPA 2003, ss 261 to 263; see also Inland Revenue press release, 19 March 1993, *Simon's Tax Intelligence* 1993, p 438. On Revenue practice see Revenue Manual EIM 21825 and SE 22850 et seq.
2   ITEPA 2003, ss 261 and 266; non-cash voucher is defined by reference to ITEPA 2003, ss 7, 82, 87, 88, and 95.
3   ITEPA 2003, s 262.
4   The doubt stemming from the need to launch the glider in the first place.
5   ITEPA 2003, s 262(1)(*a*)(i).
6   ITEPA 2003, s 262(1)(*b*); domestic premises are defined in s 262(2).
7   ITEPA 2003, ss 261(4).
8   ITEPA 2003, s 261(5).
9   ITEPA 2003, s 261(6).
10 ITEPA 2003, s 263.

Minor benefits derived in performing duties of employment

[7.106] ITEPA 2003, s 316 excludes certain private benefits derived from assets and services used in performing the duties of the employment. If these are provided on the employer's premises they will be exempt from tax provided the use for private purposes is not significant.[1] Simultaneous use for both employment and private purposes is treated as use for private purposes.[2] Where the benefit is provided elsewhere one must also show that the sole purpose of providing the benefit was to enable the employee to perform the duties of his employment and that it is not an excluded benefit.[3] A benefit is excluded if it is so designated by Treasury regulations or the benefit is the use of a motor vehicle, boat or aircraft.[4] A benefit is also excluded if it consists of an extension or alteration to living accommodation or to buildings relating to living accommodation.[5] See also the tax treatment of employer provided equipment to teleworkers and the interaction with ITEPA 2003, s 316. The Revenue will treat a telephone line, broadband internet access, and the provision of computer equipment in excess of £500 (see supra, § **7.98**) as exempt under this provision.[6]

[1] ITEPA 2003, s 316(2).
[2] ITEPA 2003, s 316(3).
[3] ITEPA 2003, s 316(4).
[4] ITEPA 2003, s 316(5)(*a*).
[5] ITEPA 2003, s 316(5)(*b*).
[6] Tax Bulletin Issue 68, December 2003, page 1068.

Extent of charge

[7.107] The legislation states simply that the cost of an employment-related benefit is "the expense incurred in or in connection with provision of the benefit (including a proper proportion of any expense relating partly to provision of the benefit and partly to other matters)".[1] This causes problems where an employer provides a service in house. Let us suppose that an airline employer provides an employee with a free seat on a flight from London to New York. One view is that cost means opportunity cost ie that if the airline could have sold the seat to an ordinary passenger at £500, it would have had an opportunity cost of £500; it forwent the opportunity of making that sum. It is generally thought such a cost is not "incurred". A second view, which was generally thought to be the correct one, was that cost means the marginal cost of carrying this passenger, ie the cost of providing another meal together with the amount of fuel needed to carry the extra weight. In *Pepper v Hart*[2] the Revenue argued against marginal cost and in favour of actual cost. Therefore to continue with the example outlined above the airline must average the entire cost of the journey over all the passengers. However, this cost would itself be a matter of dispute since one has to consider how much of the overhead cost should be included, thus should it be (a) the marginal cost to the airline of running this flight, so spreading the cost over the number of passengers on this flight (a matter of some interest if for example the employee were the only passenger on the flight), or (b) the appropriate proportion of the cost of the entire operations of that month (or year), so perhaps treating the employee as receiving a benefit far higher than the normal fare? The Revenue lost in the House of Lords.

[7.107] Employment income

The *Pepper v Hart* case actually concerned the provision of education at a private school (Malvern College) for the child of a member of the teaching staff. The member of staff paid a fee equal to one-fifth of the normal fee; that was more than enough to cover the marginal cost to the school but was substantially less than the average cost found by spreading the entire costs of the school for the year over all the pupils. That average cost was rejected by the House of Lords.[3]

Benefits in kind are seen as tax-efficient. If the cost of the benefit is £100 and the taxpayer's marginal rate is 40%, he will acquire the benefit (£100) but pay tax of £40. Yet if he had had to pay for the benefit out of his own pocket his salary would have had to be increased by £167 to give him the £100 net of tax with which to acquire an equivalent benefit. The amount charged is the same whether the employee receives £100 under an expense allowance which he spends on the object or receives the object as a benefit in kind. This example can be criticised for failing to compare like with like as one is comparing tax of £40 leaving him with the benefit in kind and tax of £67 leaving him with £100 but this is not the way most employers or employees think. There is a less contentious point that benefits in kind generally only attract national insurance contributions for the employer.[4]

If no expense is incurred in providing the benefit, no charge can arise under ITEPA 2003, ss 201 and 203. The provision of a service at a charge lower than market value does not seem to have a cash equivalent—unless perhaps the employer could have provided the service at full cost to a stranger who was anxious to buy it. So an interest-free loan does not give rise to liability; for this reason special legislation now applies (see supra, §§ 7.111–7.112). A cost under ITEPA 2003, ss 203 and 204 might have arisen if the employer had realised a particular asset to provide the loan and so forgone income from that asset.[5]

Where an employee sells or transfers an asset to the employer and the cost to the employer exceeds the market value of the asset, a charge under these rules may arise. By what was originally a concession but is now enacted in ITEPA 2003, the Revenue do not include the transaction costs incurred, such as legal fees, in making the relevant calculations.[6] However, costs normally incurred by the transferor or which are borne by someone other than the employee are not within the exemption.

Simon's Taxes E4.613.

---

[1] ITEPA 2003, s 204.
[2] [1992] STC 898.
[3] On practical consequences see Inland Revenue press release, 21 January 1993, *Simon's Tax Intelligence* 1993, p 196.
[4] On Class 1A contributions on taxable benefits in kind see infra, § 51.13.
[5] HC Official Report, 18 December 1975, Vol 902, cols 1622, 1623 and note TA 1988, s 548(3)(a)(ii). But quaere if he sold shares which then dropped in market price would the fall in capital value be set off against the dividend income forgone and when could the fall in capital value be computed? What if the share value had increased? These speculations may suggest that income foregone is not a cost.
[6] ITEPA 2003, s 326; see also Explanatory Notes to the Act, change 80 in Annex 1.

[7.108] Where the asset remains the property of the person providing the benefit, the cost of the taxable benefit is the higher of (a) the annual value of the use of the asset, and (b) the annual amount of the sums paid by those providing the benefit by way of rent or hire, together with any other expense incurred in providing the asset other than the cost of producing or acquiring the asset.[1]

The annual value of the use of the asset varies according to the benefit. In the case of land it is the "annual rental value", which is separately defined for this purpose[2] but draws on the definitions used for the general living accommodation charge (see supra, § **7.49**); for other assets the figure is 20% of the market value at the time the asset was first applied as an employment-related benefit.[3] So if an employer provides his employee with a cat the cash equivalent will be the sum of (a) 20% of the cost plus (b) the full cost of food and any veterinary services paid for by the employer.

The costs of acquisition or production of the asset are excluded from (b) presumably because they are taken into account under (a). Acquisition and production have been construed widely. Expenditure resulting in the replacement or renewal of the asset as distinct from its maintenance is excluded; on this basis sums spent on supplying a house with a new water main were not part of (b) and so escaped tax.[4]

If the asset is subsequently transferred to the employee the normal rule is to charge the employee on the market value of the asset when it is so transferred.[5] However, an alternative rule will now apply if it would give rise to a higher charge. The problem arises when an asset is transferred to the employee and it has depreciated in value since it was acquired, as where an employer acquires a hi-fi system, allows the employee the use of it for two years and then transfers it to him. The cash equivalent for the first two years will be calculated on the basis of the rules already considered. The cash equivalent on the transfer to the employee is now to be the greater of (a) the asset's market value at that time less any price paid for it by the employee, and (b) the market value when it was first provided but with a deduction for amounts already taxed and any sum paid for it.[6] This alternative does not apply to cars.

EXAMPLE

X provides E with a hi-fi costing £600. After two years X sells the system to E for £150, its then market value being £250. E is liable on the higher of:

(a) £250 − £150 = £100 and (b) £600 − (2 × 20% × £600) − £150 = £210.

Simon's Taxes E4.613.

---

[1] ITEPA 2003, s 205, other expenses would include repair and insurance, for example.
[2] ITEPA 2003, s 207.
[3] ITEPA 2003, s 205(3)(b).
[4] *Luke v IRC* [1963] 1 All ER 655, 40 TC 630 (see supra, § **7.102**).
[5] ITEPA 2003, s 206(2); transaction costs incurred by the transferor are ignored.
[6] ITEPA 2003, s 206(3)–(5).

Apportionment

[7.109] If the expense is incurred by the employer partly to provide a benefit for the employee and partly for other purposes, ITEPA 2003, s 203 will tax only a proper proportion of the expense so incurred.[1] However, where a particular expense confers benefits both on the employer and on the employee and no part of the expenditure is on something which benefits the employer exclusively, no apportionment can be made.

In *Westcott v Bryan*[2] the managing director wished to live in London but the company insisted that he live in a large rambling house set in two acres of garden close to the factory which lay in a rural area of North Staffordshire. He paid the company a rent of £140 pa and £500 pa for services. He paid the rates. In the tax year the company spent £1,017 on gas, electricity, water, insurance of contents, telephone, cleaning, window cleaning, gardener's wages and maintenance. The house was bigger than the taxpayer either needed or desired, but no specific area was set aside for the entertainment of the company's guests. It was held by the Court of Appeal that an apportionment under what was then TA 1988, s 156(2) should be made even though the expenses could not be clearly severed either on a temporal or spatial basis. The method of apportionment was not canvassed in the Court of Appeal[3] but at first instance Pennycuick J had said that it could only be done on a rough and ready basis, to determine what proportion of the total expense was fairly attributable to the use or availability for use of the house by the company.[4]

The decision is to be distinguished from that in *Rendell v Went*[5] where no apportionment could be made. In that case the employer had spent a sum of money in the provision of a benefit when the employee would have spent less, and no part of the sum was spent on something which did not benefit him.[6] In *Westcott v Bryan* the expenditure was made for two distinct purposes only one of which was of benefit to the director.

ITEPA 2003, ss 204 and 205 direct an apportionment of the expense. ITEPA 2003, s 203 limits its charge to so much of the expense as is not made good by the employee. Where therefore a sum is to be apportioned and the employee makes a payment for the benefit, the question arises whether the expense is apportioned first and then the payment is set off against that apportioned figure or rather the set-off occurs first and the apportionment is then applied to that reduced figure. The former would seem more correct.[7]

Simon's Taxes E4.613.

---

[1] ITEPA 2003, ss 204 and 205.
[2] [1969] 3 All ER 564, 45 TC 467.
[3] But see Sachs LJ at 571, 493.
[4] 45 TC 467 at 487.
[5] Supra, § **7.103**.
[6] [1964] 2 All ER 464 at 467, 41 TC 641 at 659; this distinction is criticised by Kerridge [1986] BTR 36.
[7] But in *Westcott v Bryan* the latter view appears to have been accepted.

Particular benefits in the benefits code

Living accommodation: ancillary services

[**7.110**] The provision of living accommodation for a person by reason of his employment is governed by ITEPA 2003, s 102 (see supra, § **7.47**). The provision of certain ancillary services falls within ITEPA 2003, ss 201 and 203. However, where the occupation is non-beneficial and the employee comes within the terms of the exception[1] (see supra, § **7.48**), the amount taxable is subject to a limit. Sums in respect of (a) heating, lighting or cleaning the premises, (b) repairs (other than structural repairs)[2] maintenance or decoration, and (c) the provision of furniture or other appurtenances or effects which are normal for domestic occupation, are not to exceed 10% of the earnings of the employment.[3]

Where the accommodation is provided for a part of the year but the employment for longer (or shorter), the percentage is applied to the earnings attributable to the period of occupation. Any sums made good by the employee are deducted from the 10%.

The earnings are not to include the cost of the services notionally fixed at 10%; this avoids a circular problem. There will be included all earnings including benefits caught by the benefits code of ITEPA 2003 but deduction of expenses allowable under ITEPA 2003, s 232, or Part 5 or TA 1988, ss 592(7), 594 and 619(1)(a) and CAA 2001 s 262 is permitted to ascertain the figure of which 10% is to be taken.[4]

This limit does not apply where the ancillary services are other than those listed; liability in respect of such services is without limit. The specific exception of structural repairs is presumably because the Revenue accept the view expressed in *Luke v IRC*[5] that these are part of the cost of acquiring or producing the asset under what was then TA 1988, s 156(5)(b).[6] Costs to the owner of owner's cost such as insurance and feu duty, are presumably part of the cost of providing the living accommodation and so fall within ITEPA 2003, s 97 et seq.[7]

---

[1] As a director with a material interest in a company cannot avail himself of the exclusion in ITEPA 2003, s 99, the limit to the charge on ancillary services does not apply to such directors, other than the very rare case that the director can show he is within the exemption of ITEPA 2003, s 100, being required to live in the accommodation for reasons of personal security.

[2] Including repairs which would be the landlord's responsibility under a lease within the Landlord and Tenant Act 1985, ss 11, 16, 36 and see ITEPA 2003, s 313.

[3] ITEPA 2003, s 315.

[4] ITEPA 2003, s 315(5), Step 3.

[5] [1963] 1 All ER 655; 40 TC 630; FA 1976, s 62(5).

[6] This was the line taken by Lord Guest and Lord Pearce and by Lord Reid (this is a case of any port in a storm, 578, 665, 646) and by Lord Dilhorne at 572, 661, 643. The consequence of the repair will be an increase in the annual value of the premises. To hold that the expense of repair did not fall within what was then s 156(5)(b) (and is now in ITEPA 2003 at s 205(4)(a) and 313(2)(a)) and then to

[7.110] Employment income

      increase the annual value would be a flagrant case of double taxation.
7 See, however, *Luke v IRC* on the forerunner of what was TA 1988, s 154 and is now in the part of the benefits code of ITEPA 2003 that applies to all those not in lower paid employments.

Low interest loans

[7.111] Directors and employees not in lower paid employments are taxable on the cash equivalent of employment-related loans[1] which are taxable cheap loans provided by reason of their employment. A loan is a loan and so within these rules whether or not there is any other benefit or advantage to the employee.[2] An interest free equity loan, under which the borrower has to repay not the exact sum received but a proportion of the proceeds of sale of property bought with the aid of the loan, is still a loan.[3]

The charge is not to apply if the total of all such loans does not exceed £5,000;[4] this de minimis exception is complicated if there are qualifying and non-qualifying loans (see below).

Interest on loans made on ordinary commercial terms is excluded from ITEPA 2003, Part 3, Chapter 7. The rules for this exclusion were rewritten by FA 2000. Previously the loan had to be made by an employer whose business includes the making of loans. From 2000–01 an ordinary commercial loan may also be made by any employer who supplies goods or services on credit.

For original loans it is also necessary to show that comparable loans were available to all who might be expected to avail themselves of these services, that a substantial proportion of those loans are made to members of the public and that the terms on which the loans are made to the employee must be comparable to the terms of loans to the public at the same time.[5] The FA 2000 rules also deal with the problem of variations but take variations made before 2000–01 separately from those made later. The "later" variations must comply with a condition that the right to vary must be open to all members of the public as well as to employees.[6] The essence of these rules is that the ordinary commercial loans exemption will apply where loans to employees are varied to bring them into line with such terms without, as previously, requiring the loan to be paid off and a new one made.[7]

In deciding whether rights to vary a loan or the loans themselves are held on the same terms certain matters are ignored. These are penalties or interest due on the variation and any fees, commission etc paid to obtain the loan.[8]

Chapter 7 of Part 3 of ITEPA 2003 also excludes loans where all the interest qualifies for tax relief.[9] This simplification could be made because of the final removal of the partial relief for mortgage interest. Broadly, loans are qualifying loans if the interest on them would qualify for tax relief whether under TA 1988, s 353 or as deductions in computing trading profits.

The rules treat the employee as having paid interest on the loan in that year of the same amount as the cash equivalent;[10] naturally this deeming does not create a tax liability on the part of the lender.[11] The timing rule is that the interest is treated as accruing during, and as paid by the employee at the end of, the year; however, this will be displaced by the period of employment if he is no longer in employment at the end of the year.

Certain loans can be treated as one single loan for the purpose of ascertaining the cash equivalent. These are all the loans between the same lender and borrower in the same currency where (a) there is a time in the tax year when each loan is outstanding and the lender is a close company and the borrower is a director of that company, (b) the loans are not qualifying loans, and (c) at all times in the tax year the rate of interest on the loans is less than the official rate. The lender must elect for aggregation to apply, for that tax year in the case of that borrower, before 7 July after the end of the tax year.[12]

The de minimis formulation relates to the aggregate of loans outstanding in the year. The cash equivalent is not to be treated as earnings of the employment if at no time in the year the amount outstanding on all the employment-related loans does not exceed £5,000 or if the aggregate of such loans which are not qualifying loans does not exceed £5,000.

The charge will arise whether the loan is made to the employee or to a relative of his; relative is defined differently from family and means spouse, lineal ascendant or descendant, brother or sister of the employee or the spouse and the spouse of such people.[13] It is, however, open to the employee to show that he derived no benefit from the loan made to a relative.[14]

The charge remains so long as the loan made by reason of the employment is outstanding and the borrower continues in the employment;[15] however, it does end on the death of the employee.[16] It appears that a loan to an ex-employee will not be caught.

Where a loan was made otherwise than by reason of employment and, on the employment beginning, the rate of interest is reduced, no charge appears to arise.[16]

Simon's Taxes E4.631–633.

---

[1] On advances to meet expenses see ITEPA 2003, s 179. *Williams v Todd* [1988] STC 676 (advance of salary held to be a loan). See also *Gold v Inspector of Taxes* [1998] STC (SCD) 222 (a form of credit) and *Grant v Watton* [1999] STC 330, Ch D. The charge arises regardless of the date of the loan; ITEPA 2003, Sch 7, para 25(1). In another tax context it has been held that a loan requires consensus so that a misappropriation by a director does not give rise to a loan—*Stephens v T Pittas Ltd* [1983] STC 576; infra, § **28.12**. On Revenue practice see HMRC Manual SE 26100 et seq.

[2] *Williams v Todd* [1988] STC 676.

[3] *Harvey v Williams* [1995] STC (SCD) 329 and *Gold v Inspector of Taxes* [1998] STC (SCD) 222. The facts, as reported, assume that the house would go up in value; it is unclear whether the lender would have had to bear a share of any loss if that value had gone down.

[4] ITEPA 2003, s 180.

[5] ITEPA 2003, s 176.

[6] ITEPA 2003, s 176(6).

[7] Under the old rules the loan was treated as made when it was advanced and not when its terms were varied: *West v Crossland* [1999] STC 147.

[7.111] Employment income

[8] ITEPA 2003, s 176(8) and (9).
[9] ITEPA 2003, s 178.
[10] ITEPA 2003, s 184(2) and see supra § **7.102** as to what is the cash equivalent.
[11] ITEPA 2003, s 184(5).
[12] ITEPA 2003, s 187.
[13] ITEPA 2003, s 174(6).
[14] ITEPA 2003, s 174(5)(*b*).
[15] ITEPA 2003, s 175.
[16] This contrasts with the charge on loan waivers (see supra, § **7.102**) which continues notwithstanding termination of employment.

[7.112] The cash equivalent of the loan is the difference between the amount of interest that would have been paid at an official rate and any interest actually paid.[1] The payment is "for" the year and so does not have to be paid during the year. Where two or more employees are chargeable to tax in respect of the same beneficial loan, the charge shall be apportioned between them in a fair and reasonable manner.[2]

Loans between the same borrower and lender can be aggregated (see above where loans are by a close company to a director); others are not—a matter of importance where different rates of interest are paid on different loans.[3] The amount of interest due at the official rate is calculated first by taking a simple average of the loan outstanding at the beginning and end of the tax year, multiplying this by the number of months of the loan in the year and divided by 12 and then applying the official rate to it.[4] However, either the taxpayer or the Revenue may elect that the interest be calculated on a day to day basis, a matter of importance where the amount of the loan fluctuates during the year.[5] Further provisions deal with the calculation of the interest where an employment-related loan is replaced, directly or indirectly by a further employment-related loan, or by a non-employment-related loan which in turn is, in the same year of assessment or within 40 days thereafter, replaced, directly or indirectly, by a further employment-related loan. In these circumstances the rules are applied as if the replacement loan or loans were the same as the first employment-related loan.[6]

EXAMPLE

A has borrowed £10,000 from his employer just before the start of the year of assessment. On 30 June he repays £3,000 but on 3 September he borrows another £4,000. The amount outstanding at the end of the year of assessment is £11,000. A pays £200 in interest. The official rate is 5%.

(1) Simple calculation.

$$\text{Average amount outstanding during the year } \frac{£11{,}000 + 10{,}000}{2} = £10{,}500$$

Official rate at 5% gives £525

(2) More precise calculation:

First period $\quad 10{,}000 \times \dfrac{85}{365} \times 5\% \quad £116.44$

Second period	$7{,}000 \times \dfrac{65}{365} \times 5\%$	£62.33
Third period XE	$11{,}000 \times \dfrac{215}{365} \times 5\%$	£323.97
		£502.74

So cash equivalent is £1,206.57 – £200 = £302.74

The official rate is determined by reference to commercial mortgage rates.[7] For 2007–08 the official rate is 6.25%.[8] Where a loan is made for a fixed period at a fixed rate, which is not less than the then official rate, Chapter 7 is not to apply when the official rate later rises.[9]

Special rules provide for the calculation of the official rate of interest where the loan is made in the currency of a foreign country. For this rule to apply the employee must normally live in that country and have done so at some time within the period of six years ending with the year of assessment. Where these conditions are satisfied, regulations apply.[10] Regulations have been made for loans in Japanese Yen and Swiss francs.[11]

Simon's Taxes E4.631–633.

[1] ITEPA 2003, s 175.
[2] ITEPA 2003, s 185.
[3] ITEPA 2003, s 175(4).
[4] ITEPA 2003, s 182.
[5] ITEPA 2003, s 183.
[6] ITEPA 2003, s 186; a loan is employment-related if the benefit of the loan was obtained by reason of the employment; a loan is a further employment-related loan if it was obtained by reason of the same or other employment with the person who is the employer in relation to the first employment-related loan or with a person connected with that employer (on connection see TA 1988, s 839 by virtue of ITEPA 2003, s 718).
[7] SI 1989/1297, *Simon's Tax Intelligence* 1989, p 695 and 1991, p 434.
[8] Taxes (Interest Rate) (Amendment No 3) Regulations 2001, SI 2001/3860, *Simon's Weekly Tax Intelligence* 2001, p 1788.
[9] ITEPA 2003, s 177.
[10] ITEPA 2003, s 181(2).
[11] Taxes (Interest Rate) (Amendment) Regulations 1994, SI 1994/1307 and Taxes (Interest Rate) (Amendment No 2) Regulations 1994, SI 1994/1567. For 1998–99 the rates are: Japanese yen 3.9%, Swiss francs 5.5%. See Inland Revenue press release, 9 April 1999, *Simon's Weekly Tax Intelligence* 1999, p 781.

Loan waivers

[7.113] Where the whole or part of a loan is released or written off, there is a charge on the amount so released or written off.[1] This applies whether or not the loan is chargeable under the previous rule; so the charge will arise even

[7.113] Employment income

though the loan released was used for a qualifying purpose. The release of a loan to a relative comes within this rule unless the employee can show that he derived no benefit from it.[2] The charge arises even though the loan was released or written off after the employment ceased[3] but not if this is deferred until after death.[4] Where a loan is replaced the new loan used to fall within the rules outlined at supra, §7.101.[5] This ceases to apply as from 6 April 1995 regardless of the date of the loan but new rules are put in place to prevent abuse. The replacement loan remains subject to the charge just outlined and arising when a loan is released or written off. Where there was a loan and the employment later terminates or ceases to be within these rules but the loan continues, any subsequent replacement loan will also be subject to these rules—unless it is itself under these rules as having been obtained by reason of another employment.[6]

Where arrangements have been made with a view to protecting the holder of shares from a fall in their market value, benefits received are not chargeable under this rule.[7] This is designed to protect those who acquired shares under incentive schemes which contained so called stop-loss clauses; these schemes had been approved by the Revenue and it was thought wrong to alter the tax basis upon which they had been made.

Simon's Taxes E4.638.

[1] ITEPA 2003, s 188.
[2] ITEPA 2003, s 174 and because s 188 applies to all employment-related loans.
[3] ITEPA 2003, s 188(2).
[4] ITEPA 2003, s 190(2).
[5] TA 1988 s 160(5)(*b*) repealed by FA 1995 s 45(2), (5), Sch 29, Pt VIII(3).
[6] ITEPA 2003, s 188(3).
[7] ITEPA 2003, Sch 7, para 25(2).

Share purchase schemes: deemed loans

[7.114] Where shares are acquired by a director or employee not in lower paid employment as a right or opportunity offered by reason of his employment with that or any other company and the shares were issued at less than market price or in other than fully paid up form, the tax system decrees a notional loan of the difference between the amount paid for the shares and their then market value.[1] So long as this loan remains outstanding, interest at the official rate is treated as earnings. Conversely any payment of a call is treated as a repayment of the loan.

When such shares are acquired on such a notional loan or on a real loan and the loan is discharged or released by any arrangement involving the disposal of the shares, the aggregate amount paid for them minus any consideration received on the disposal is compared with the market value at the time of acquisition and the amount by which the latter exceeds the former is treated as earnings. The market value at the time of the disposal is quite irrelevant, the purpose of this provision being to catch so-called "stop loss" arrangements under which employees would offer to accept payment at current value as satisfying the debt.

[1] ITEPA 2003, ss 193–200. The market value ignores any restriction other than those applying to all shares of that class.

Cars and fuel

[7.115] Motor cars. A car is defined as any mechanically propelled road vehicle except vehicles of a construction primarily suited for the conveyance of goods etc; those of a type not commonly used as a private vehicle and unsuitable to be so used; and motor cycles and invalid carriages.[1]

Statute[2] excludes a tax charge if the car is an emergency vehicle.[3]

The car benefit charge is obtained by multiplying the price of the car for tax purposes (in most cases, its list price plus accessories less capital contributions) by the "appropriate percentage".[4]

The appropriate percentage is based on the car's approved CO[5] emissions figure. If the car's CO_2 emissions figure does not exceed the lower threshold for that year the appropriate percentage is 9% (previously 15%) ('the basic percentage') and if the figure does exceed the lower threshold it is either the basic percentage increased by one percentage point for each 5 grams per kilometre ("g/km") by which the CO_2 emissions figure exceeds the lower threshold for the year or 35% whichever is the lesser. The lower threshold for 2008–09 or 2009–10 was reduced by FA 2008 to 135 g/km and for 2010–11 to 130 g/km. FA 2009 amended the lower threshold for 2011–12 and subsequent years to 125 g/km.

There are some supplements and reductions to take account of different fuels. The rules governing the supplements and reductions are:

Type of fuel	Code	Standard adjustment	Other adjustments
PetrolP	none	none	Diesel (not Euro IV)
D	supplement 3%[a]	none	Diesel (EURO IV) first registered on or before 31 December 2005
L	none	none	Diesel (Euro IV) first registered on or after 1 January 2006
L	supplement 3%[b]	none	Electric only

457

[7.115] Employment income

Type of fuel	Code	Standard adjustment	Other adjustments
E	reduction 6%	none	Hybrid electric
H	reduction 3%	none	Gas only
use lowest CO^2 figure Bi-fuel conversion, or other bi-fuel not within type BB	reduction 2%	none	Bi-fuel with CO^2 emissions figure for gas[c]
CB	reduction 2%	none	none

[a] Subject to the overall maximum appropriate percentage of 35%.

[b] Cars which were type approved as bi-fuel cars and were first registered on or after 1 January 2000. These cars have two approved CO_2 emissions figures, one each for petrol and gas (though only one may appear on the Vehicle Registration Certificate, V5C).

[c] Cars which were type approved as bi-fuel cars and were first registered on or after 1 January 2000. These cars have two approved CO^2

Supplements and reductions only apply to cars first registered on or after 1 January 1998. They apply to all such cars, whether or not they have an approved CO_2 emissions figure.

A key definition is the "price of a car" which is the car's list price, being the price published by the car's manufacturer, importer or distributor as the inclusive price appropriate for a car of that kind as sold in the UK singly in a retail sale in the open market immediately before the day of the car's first registration. If there is no list price, the price of the car is taken as that of the equivalent car if sold in the UK on the same basis. Until 2010–2011 the price is capped at £80,000, so that the maximum benefit is £28,000 pa.[6] There are complex rules where accessories are included, the main rule being that the list price of those accessories is added to the list price of the car to arrive at the price of the car.[7] Where accessories are added after the car is first made available to an employee, the list price of those accessories is added into the price of the car, unless the list price of any accessory is less than £100.[8] The inclusive price includes delivery charges, tax (customs duty, VAT etc) but not the administration fee of £25.[9] In the case of an accessory any fitting charge must be included. From 2009–10, where an employee with a disabled person's badge has an automatic car (and requires the car to be automatic because of the disability), the price taken is that of the equivalent manual car (if lower).[10]

There are two sections that deal with replacement issues. One deals with the situation where an accessory replaces another so that the price of the new accessory is substituted for the replaced accessory.[11] The other situation covered is where the main car is unavailable for a period of less than 30 days.[12] If the replacement car is similar or there is no intention to provide an employee with a better car, the benefit in kind is calculated as if the main car continues to be used by the employee throughout.

Where for any part of the relevant year the car is unavailable the taxable benefit otherwise applying is reduced on a time apportionment basis for the period of unavailability.[13]

The sharply increased scale of charges in recent years has reduced the benefit of this perk; perhaps it is time to record the fact that most employers do not provide this benefit without reason and that in the days of a reduced public transport system the car is often an indispensable tool of business. The effect of recent changes has been to make the value of this benefit highly marginal in certain circumstances. However, it is also the case that the company car is a more widespread benefit in the UK than in other advanced economies.

On treatment of mileage allowance payments, see infra, § **7.132**.

---

[1] ITEPA 2003, s 115 and see SE 23040 to 23043 for Revenue comment, especially where a vehicle has been modified. A motorhome sold as leisure vehicle provided by employer but used as mobile office and for collecting goods is a 'car' for purposes of the car and fuel benefit provisions: Country *Pharmacy Ltd v Revenue and Customs Comrs* [2005] STC (SCD) 729.

[2] ITEPA 2003, s 248A inserted by FA 2004, s 81 with effect from 6 April 2004. This was enacted in response to the decision in *Gurney v Richards* [1989] STC 682 where it was held that a car with a flashing emergency light permanently fitted to the roof is "of a type not commonly used as a private vehicle and unsuitable to be so used" and, hence, no assessable benefit arose on the employee for whose use this vehicle was provided. Road Vehicles Lighting Regulations 1984, SI 1984/182, regs 11(2), 13 and 15(1) which make unlawful the use of such cars by members of the public on a public road.

[3] "Emergency vehicle" is defined as one with a flashing light for use in emergencies, or, interestingly, a vehicle used by the police, fire or ambulance services for "undercover" emergency work: ITEPA 2003, s 248A(3) & (4).

[4] A detailed guide is available for employees in the IR 203 self-assessment helpsheet (www.hmrc.gov.uk/helpsheets/ir203.pdf) and for employers in booklet 480 (www.hmrc.gov.uk/guidance/480.pdf).

[5] ITEPA 2003, s 248A inserted by FA 2004, s 81 with effect from 6 April 2004. This was enacted in response to the decision in *Gurney v Richards* [1989] STC 682 where it was held that a car with a flashing emergency light permanently fitted to the roof is "of a type not commonly used as a private vehicle and unsuitable to be so used" and, hence, no assessable benefit arose on the employee for whose use this vehicle was provided. Road Vehicles Lighting Regulations 1984, SI 1984/182, regs 11(2), 13 and 15(1) which make unlawful the use of such cars by members of the public on a public road.

[6] ITEPA 2003, ss 121 and 122 to 124; FA 2009, Sch 28, para 2.

[7] ITEPA 2003, ss 121(1), Step 2 and 125–131. Equipment designed solely for use by a chronically sick or disabled person is ignored: s 125(2)(c) and s 172.

[8] ITEPA 2003, s 126.

[9] ITEPA 2003, ss 123 and 171(1).

[10] ITEPA 2003, s 124A.

[11] ITEPA 2003, s 131.

[12] ITEPA 2003, s 145.

[13] ITEPA 2003, s 143 and see s 145 where car temporarily replaced.

[7.116] Further rules for a car provided by an employer. Given the many circumstances that arise in practice, the legislation must contemplate these to arrive at a proper measure of benefit. It is debatable whether, in some cases, fairness is achieved.

One particular example is where an employee contributes to the cost of the car.[1] An employee could contribute in many ways, such as simply making a payment to his employer towards the cost of the car that is sunk on payment, possibly to be repaid if the car is ever sold, either in whole or in part. Alternatively the employer and employee could agree to purchase a car jointly and no doubt there are many other permutations. In principle, the measurement of the car benefit in the way set out above only applies if a car is made available without any transfer of the property in it. This has led to the suggestion that if an employer sells an interest in the car to the employee, then the measure of the benefit should be calculated in the same way as an asset other than a car, which in most cases is likely to produce a much lower charge. It is clear, though, that the Revenue do not accept this argument[2] although it is difficult to follow their reasoning entirely on this. The Revenue's approach is on the lines that the contribution rules would not be relevant otherwise, those rules providing that the contribution of a capital sum by an employee to expenditure on a car (or accessories) reduces the price of the car by the smaller of the capital sum and £5,000. The Revenue also go on to say that if the contribution is repaid in full when the car is sold, then it is not a capital contribution that can reduce the price of the car. On the other hand, if an employee receives an appropriate part of the sale proceeds on sale to a third party, this itself would not prevent the reduction of the price by such a contribution.[3] None of this is set out in the statutory rules and hence the room for differing views. It does, though, seem unfair that if an employee owns a car equally with his employer that the maximum sum that reduces the price of the car is £5,000.[4]

Instead of, or possibly in addition to, a capital sum, an employee could pay money to his employer for the use of the car. In that case, the amount paid by the employee for that use reduces the cash equivalent of the benefit but only where such payment is a condition of the car being available for private use. This is largely a question of evidence and ensuring that contractual arrangements are properly put in place.[5]

These car rules are generally far reaching and so a special exception has to be made for pooled cars. The definition of such a car is very restrictive, requiring that the car is made available to and actually used by more than one employee; that the car is not in the year ordinarily used by one to the exclusion of the others; that any private use must be incidental to other use; and that the car is not normally kept overnight on or in the vicinity of any residential premises where any of the employees was residing (unless kept overnight on premises occupied by the employer).[6]

The price of a classic car (being a car which has a market value for the year of £15,000 or more) is based on the market value of the car. This only applies to cars whose age is 15 years of more at the end of the tax year. Similar rules apply to capital contributions and accessories as for other cars.[7]

Given that an employee can be assessed on a benefit provided for himself or other members of his family, it would be quite possible for the Revenue to tax one employee on the benefit provided to another member of the family working for the same employer. ITEPA has enacted the concession in this situation so that the employee actually using the car is taxed provided the terms of the concession are met. In particular, the car must be available to that employee in his or her own right and either equivalent cars are provided in a similar way to other employees or in accordance with normal commercial practice.[8]

---

[1] ITEPA 2003, s 132.
[2] SE 23053.
[3] SE 23163.
[4] In *Vasili v Christensen* [2004] EWHC 476 (Ch), [2004] STC 935, the employer paid 95% of the cost of the car provided for the employee and the employee, himself, paid the remaining 5%. Reversing the decision of the Special Commissioner [2003] STC (SCD) 428. Pumfrey J in the High Court held that joint ownership can give a charge under the car benefit legislation.
[5] ITEPA 2003, s 144.
[6] ITEPA 2003, s 167. The reference to incidental use is interpreted in a qualitative sense. See Statement of practice SP 2/96.
[7] ITEPA 2003, s 147.
[8] ITEPA 2003, s 169.

[7.117] Car accessories. The relevant percentage is applied to the price of the car, a concept which is itself elaborately defined but which is basically the list price plus accessories, delivery charge, VAT and car tax. The price of a car as regards a year is its list price, ie the inclusive price appropriate for a car of that kind if sold in the UK singly in a retail sale in the open market.[1] The list may be provided by the manufacturer, the importer or the distributor and the relevant date is that immediately before the date of registration; taxes (VAT and car tax but not vehicle excise duty) are included.[2] The list price supersedes any price at which the employer actually buys the car. The date of the car's first registration is defined by reference to the car's first registration under the Vehicle Excise Registration Act 1994 or corresponding foreign legislation,[3] so that not only is the price fixed by reference to that registration date rather than subsequent registration in the UK following its import but it is also related to the UK price at that time notwithstanding that the level of prices in the UK is notoriously high. If the car has no list price, a notional price is taken. This is what it would have been if the manufacturer or supplier had published one, taking an equivalent car if necessary.[4]

If, when the car is first made available to the employee,[5] it includes accessories,[6] these too have to be brought into account.[7] Accessories which are included in the list price of the car, which are known as standard accessories, will already have been brought into account, so these rules apply to optional accessories, eg those made available as an option by the manufacturer.[8] The price of the car will have to be increased to take account of the list price of accessories as set by the manufacturer or distributor where this is available—including VAT, delivery and fitting charges.[9] Where a list price is not available a notional price is used.[10] When a car is converted for use by a chronically sick or disabled person, the accessories used in that conversion are

[7.117] Employment income

ignored.[11] Accessories ignored are not only those designed for use only by the disabled but also generally available accessories, such as power steering, where the employee is an orange badge holder and needs the accessory by reason of disability.[12]

Further rules apply where the accessory is made available after the car is first made available.[13] The list price of accessories over £100 (including VAT, fitting and delivery) is included in the price of the car as regards that year in which they are fitted and all subsequent years—the removal of the accessory does not seem to have been contemplated by the legislation although the replacement of an accessory is covered by s 131 of ITEPA 2003—one wonders whether a removal can be equated with a replacement by nothing. The £100 figure may be raised by Treasury regulation.

If the employee makes a capital contribution to the provision of the car or accessory the sum reduces the price of the car—not the cash equivalent. There is a maximum of £5,000 which may be taken into account although this sum may be raised by Treasury regulation.[14]

The maximum market value which can be taken for a car whether classic or not is £80,000; the figure of £80,000 may be raised by Treasury regulation. These rules make the current maximum cash equivalent £28,000.[15]

Special rules apply to so-called classic cars, ie where the value of the car exceeds £15,000 and is higher than the manufacturer's list price when it was first registered, ie its price for the year, and the car is more than 15 years old at the end of the tax year.[16] In such circumstances the cash equivalent is found by applying the relevant percentage to the open market value of the car (and accessories) at the end of the tax year or, if different, the last day on which it was available to the employee.[17] Contributions towards the cost of the car or accessories can be deducted up to a limit of £5,000.[18]

Simon's Taxes E4.627A.

1. ITEPA 2003, ss 121, 122, and 123; on timing of availability, see s 116.
2. ITEPA 2003, ss 123, 124, and 171.
3. ITEPA 2003, s 171(2).
4. ITEPA 2003, s 124.
5. On timing see ITEPA 2003, s 116.
6. Note ITEPA 2003, s 125, defining accessories (but excluding the provision of a mobile phone).
7. ITEPA 2003, o 121, Stop 2.
8. ITEPA 2003, s 126.
9. ITEPA 2003, ss 127–129.
10. ITEPA 2003, s126(4)(*b*) and 130.
11. ITEPA 2003, s 125(2)(c) and s 172; see HC Official Report, Standing Committee D, (Seventh sitting), cols 197–202, *Simon's Weekly Tax Intelligence* 1995, p 267.
12. ITEPA 2003, s 172; see Inland Revenue press release, 28 March 1995, *Simon's Weekly Tax Intelligence* 1995, p 555.
13. ITEPA 2003, s 126.
14. ITEPA 2003, ss 132 and 170.
15. ITEPA 2003, s 121.

[16] ITEPA 2003, s 147(1).
[17] ITEPA 2003, s 147(3), (4).
[18] ITEPA 2003, ss 147(5)–(7), 170.

[7.118] Car fuel. A special scale charge applies where the employer provides free petrol for private motoring in company cars: anomalously there is no reduction in charge if the employee reimburses the employer as part of the cost. To cancel the scale charge, payment by the employee for private fuel must be made in the tax year in which fuel is provided.[1] In *Impact Foiling v Revenue and Customs Comrs*[2] full reimbursement was made on 31 January 2005 for fuel used in 2002–03 and 2003–04. The full fuel charge was levied for 2002–03 and 2003–04 as reimbursement was not made in the year in which the fuel was provided.

The benefit charged on the employee for fuel supplied by his employer is related to the CO2 emissions of the car.[3]

A problem arises if an employee has, say, a salary of £8,000 and potential charge of £450; so far he is not within the charge to tax as he is below the £8,500 limit. Suppose, however, that he uses a credit card to pay for £200 of repairs. By ITEPA 2003, s 90 he is taxable on £200, but on crossing the £8,500 threshold he finds that the £200 is taken out of charge again. To break this loop it is provided that car expenses that would be charged if ITEPA 2003, Part 3, Chapter 6 did not apply will be taken into account in determining whether an employee is over the limit of £8,500; it will then be assessed either on the scale benefit or on the relevant expense as appropriate.

Simon's Taxes E4.629.

[1] ITEPA 2003, s 151(2). Rates from 1 August 2007 are:

	Petrol	*Diesel*	*LPG*
1400cc or less	10p	10p	6p
1401–2000cc	13p	10p	8p
2000cc+	18p	13p	10p

HMRC announcement, 27 June 2007, *Simon's weekly Tax Intelligence 2007*, page 1759
[2] [2006] STC (SCD) 764 per Avery-Jones at 767g.
[3] ITEPA 2003, ss 149–153.

[7.119] Vans. There is a separate code for the benefit of an employer providing a van[1] and van fuel[2].

Where an employee is given a choice of a van or a higher salary, statute[3] now provides that the tax charge is on the choice accepted, not on the amount of salary sacrificed.[4]

For 2006–07 the cash equivalent of the benefit of a van supplied by an employer for private use is £500 for a van less than four years old at the end of the tax year and £350 for older vans.[5] However, if private use is restricted for use for travel from home to work, there is no charge for the benefit provided.[6] Periods of unavailability can lead to a reduction in the scale charged,[7] as can sharing a van[8] where the employee makes a payment for private use, the cash equivalent of the benefit is reduced by the payment made.[9]

Fuel provided by an employer gives rise to a tax charge being treated as earnings, which, thus, attracts National Insurance Contributions.[10] The cash equivalent of van fuel benefit is £0 for 2006–07[11], but the new statutory provisions[12] have effect from 6 April 2005.

Revenue practice whereby a vehicle provided to more than one member of the same family is charged on one person only, thereby removing the double charge, is given statutory effect[13] in the case of the employee van benefit.

There is no benefit charge for a parking space provided at workplace for the van.[14]

---

[1] ITEPA 2003, s 155–159, completely rewritten by FA 2004, Sch 14.
[2] ITEPA 2003, s 160–164. rewritten by FA 2004, Sch 14.
[3] ITEPA 2003, s 119.
[4] The rule in *Heaton v Bell* (1969) 46 TC 211 is, thus, excluded.
[5] ITEPA 2003, s 155(3)(*a*). This rises to £3,000 for 2007–08 and subsequent years.
[6] ITEPA 2003, s 155(4), (5).
[7] ITEPA 2003, s 156.
[8] ITEPA 2003, s 157.
[9] ITEPA 2003, s 158.
[10] ITEPA 2003, s 160(1).
[11] £500 for 2007–08: ITEPA 2003, s 161B.
[12] FA 2004, Sch 14.
[13] ITEPA 2003, s 169A.
[14] ITEPA 2003, s 237(3)(*a*).

Scholarships

[7.120] The general exemption from tax of scholarship income[1] is restricted to the person holding the scholarship.[2] This reverses the effect of the decision of the House of Lords in *Wicks v Firth*.[3] A director or employee earning £8,500 pa or more receives a taxable benefit if a scholarship is provided to a member of his family or household under arrangements made by his employer or a person connected with the employer.

No taxable benefit arises if the scholarship is awarded under a trust or scheme to a person receiving full-time education and not more than 25% of the payments made under the trust in that year would have been taxable were it not for this provision,[4] ie taxable as benefits in kind. If the connection between the award of the scholarship and the employment is fortuitous, the 25% test will be applied so as, perhaps, to enable the award to escape tax but to ensure that, in calculating the 25%, all scholarships awarded by reason of employment are taken into account (whether or not taxable eg an award to the child of an employee earning less than £8,500, or the child of an overseas employee). In deciding for this purpose whether scholarships are awarded by reason of employment, the special deeming rules are ignored.[5]

Simon's Taxes E4.618.

---

[1] Under TA 1988, s 331.
[2] ITEPA 2003, s 215. On Revenue Practice see Revenue Manual SE 6200.
[3] [1983] STC 25 (see supra, § **7.102**).
[4] ITEPA 2003, s 213.
[5] ITEPA 2003, s 213.

Tax paid by employer

[7.121] If an employer fails to deduct tax from a director's earnings under PAYE but that tax is accounted for to the Revenue by someone other than the director, there is a chargeable benefit equal to the tax accounted for.[1] The benefit is reduced by the amount of any reimbursement made by the director. An amount accounted for after the employment ends is treated as a benefit of the last year of assessment in which the director was employed by the company, unless it was accounted for after the director's death.[2]

The provision applies only to directors; it does not extend to other employees. It does not apply, however, if the director has no material interest in the company (ie not more than 5%) and he is a full-time working director or the company is non-profit making or a charity.[3]

Simon's Taxes E4.619.

---

[1] ITEPA 2003, s 223. See IR 480, chapter 19.
[2] ITEPA 2003, s 223(5) and (6).
[3] ITEPA 2003, s 223(8) and s 67.

Expenses and deductions from earnings

Basic rules for expenses

[7.122] ITEPA 2003, s 336 and ss 337–342 allows holders of offices or employments to deduct expenses which they are obliged to incur if those expenses are either:

(a) travel expenses, or
(b) any amount other than travel expenses incurred wholly exclusively and necessarily in the performance of the duties of the office or employment.[1]

There are four rules:

[7.122] Employment income

(a) an expense must relate to an employment;[2]
(b) the emoluments must be subject to tax in the UK;[3]
(c) the expense must have actually been incurred;[4]
(d) the expense must be incurred in the year in which the employment was exercised.[5]

Section 329 stipulates that the amount of any deduction under Part 5 of ITEPA 2003 may not exceed the earnings from which it is deductible. There is an exception for expenses of ministers of religion under ITEPA 2003, s 351 and specific reference if a loss arises under TA 1988, s 380.[6]

The basic expenses rules were rewritten in 1998. However, most of the concepts of the previous rules are preserved. The principal change is the introduction of a second category of travelling expense to deal with costs of travel and subsistence incurred in travelling to or from a temporary workplace. This change was designed to make the law clearer but its effect is not always clear; it may be seen as a refinement rather than a repudiation of previous case law. The minor presentational change is the removal of the reference to the costs of keeping a horse to enable employees to perform their duties.[7] The view expressed by the Revenue is that this does not make any change in practice, as the cost of keeping a horse is deductible if the cost is a travel expense. It is understood that clergy in rural parishes obtain tax relief for the cost of keeping a horse on this basis.

Where the expense is incurred overseas, or in travel from the UK to a foreign country, there are special rules (see infra, §§ **7.133–7.135**).

Members of Parliament have their own rules.[8]

For home workers expenses, see infra, § **7.142**.

Simon's Taxes E4.701.

---

[1] See Chapter 2 of Part 5 of ITEPA 2003 which allows deductions for employee's expenses.
[2] In *Harrop v Gilroy* [1995] STC (SCD) 294, a taxpayer unsuccessfully argued for expenses to be relieved against unemployment benefit.
[3] Where earnings are charged on a remittance basis, for an expense to be deductible it must be linked to a remittance; apportionment may be required: ITEPA 2003, ss 334 & 335.
[4] In *Bevins v McLeish* [1995] STC (SCD) 342, the taxpayer unsuccessfully argued for relief for expenditure that had not actually been made.
[5] In *Hinsley v Revenue and Customs Comrs* [2007] STC (SCD) 63, Airtours International paid for a pilot's training course. Mr Hinsley left the employment of the company 11 months after the course and was required to reimburse the company of the cost of the course. Relief was denied.
[6] ITEPA 2003, s 329(4), (6).
[7] The horse was introduced in 1853—see 16 and 17 Vict c. 34 s 51; on its Trojan characteristics see Lord Reid in *Taylor v Provan* [1974] STC 168 at 175, [1974] 1 All ER 1201 at 1206. For another view of the horse, see Pollock MR in *Ricketts v Colquhoun* [1925] 1 KB 725 at 732. See also *Elderkin v Hindmarsh* [1988] STC 267.
[8] ITEPA 2003, s 292.

Express deductions

[7.123] A payment by an employer to a homeworker to defray additional household expenses is exempt from income tax if it is within a specified limit.[1]

Payments to pension schemes are deductible under the relevant legislation.[2]

In a major departure from orthodox tax theory an employee is allowed to deduct from his pre-tax pay contributions to charity under a payroll deduction scheme.[3] The scheme has effect both for the measure of employment income, pension income, social security income and for PAYE.[4]

Statute provides specific deduction for certain expenses incurred by:

(a) Members of Parliament, Members of the Scottish Parliament and the devolved assemblies for Wales and Northern Ireland;[5]
(b) Ministers of religion;[6] and
(c) Entertainers.[7]

Simon's Taxese E4.704, 719.

---

[1] ITEPA 2003, s 316A inserted by FA 2003, s 137 with effect from 6 April 2003. The limit is set by order. The limit is currently £2 per week. See also Tax Bulletin Issue 68, December 2003, p 1068 for the Revenue's further explanation of this relief including how the employer could pay more than £2 per week and still preserve the relief.
[2] See infra, Chapter 32.
[3] ITEPA 2003, s 713. Payment can be made through an agency charity approved by the Revenue.
[4] ITEPA 2003, ss 11(1), 12(1), 567(3), 658(3) and Part 12.
[5] ITEPA 2003, ss 292, 293 and 295 (although the latter is an exemption for Government ministers from a charge, rather than a deduction). Also deductible is the cost of visits to European Community institutions—but only in Brussels, Luxembourg or Strasbourg (ITEPA 2003, s 294).
[6] ITEPA 2003, s 351. Statute allows the deduction of one-quarter of rent paid for a domestic dwelling in which the minister of religion perform his duties of employment.
[7] ITEPA 2003, s 352. This gives a deduction for agency fees, in so far as they do not exceed 171/2 % of the emoluments. The application of this statutory provision is explored in *Madeley and another v R & C Comrs* [2006] STC (SCD) 513, in which the presenters of a television programme ("Richard and Judy") were declared to be "theatrtical artists".

Travel expenses

[7.124] Travel expenses fall into two categories.

(a) Established law. Repeating the old law word for word, the first category consisted of amounts necessarily expended on travelling in the performance of the duties of the office or employment. The statute does, however, go on to provide expressly that expenses of travel by the holder of an office or employment between two places at which he performs duties of different offices or employments under or with companies in the same group are to be treated as necessarily expended in the performance of the duties which he is to perform at his destination and so as deductible.[1] A 51% subsidiary test is used here to determine when companies are members of the same group.[2]

(b) New law. The statute was extended in 1988 to add a second category of qualifying expenses—other expenses of travelling which (i) are attributable to the necessary attendance at any place of the holder of the office or employment in the performance of the duties of the office or employment, but (ii) which are not expenses of ordinary commuting or private travel.[3] (i) was designed to clarify the law concerning the costs of travel between home and a temporary workplace while (ii) was designed to prevent (i) from opening the door too wide.

Category (a) will be considered first as it provides much of the background to (b). However, it must be stressed that the two categories are alternatives; it is enough for the sum to come within one of them to be deductible.

---

[1] ITEPA 2003, s 340.
[2] ITEPA 2003, s 340; one may be a 51% subsidiary of the other or both 51% subsidiaries of a third company.
[3] Ordinary commuting or private travel is defined in ITEPA 2003, s 338.

Category (a)—travelling in the performance of the duties of the office or employment

[7.125] The strict rule in ITEPA 2003, s 337 means that "concessions" are made for particularly hard cases. The most interesting is the exemption of extra travel and subsistence allowances when public transport is disrupted by strikes or other industrial action or the employee has to work late[1] or is severely disabled.[2] Under ITEPA 2003, s 248 the exception is widened to cover payments by employers where car sharing arrangements have broken down.[3] Others have been superseded by new statutory rule (b).[4]

To be deductible the cost must be incurred in the performance of the duties of the office—and necessarily so incurred. The Revenue do not require that the shortest possible route be taken—the question is whether the route was chosen for good business reasons.[5]

The costs of travelling to work from home are in general not deductible.[6] This is because the costs are not incurred in the course of performing the duties but in order to get to the place where the duties are to be performed. This non-deductibility applied right down to the extra costs of an employee's having to travel to work by car because the car is needed for his work once he gets there.[7]

In deciding whether an expense is incurred necessarily the courts began with an objective test. In *Ricketts v Colquhoun* Lord Blanesburgh said that the expense had to be one which each and every occupant of the particular office is necessarily obliged to incur.[8] Thus the necessity must emerge from the job rather than from the personal circumstances of the employee.

However this view, although making some sense in the context of a long established statutory office with very particular duties, is inconsistent with the modern bargaining process under which the goals of the contract may be coloured by the interests of both employer and employee. This inevitably brings about a need to pay more attention to the needs of the employees particularly when individual contracts are being negotiated with senior employees.[9] As two later decisions of the House of Lords show, in determining whether the expense would be incurred by each and every occupant of the office one must now look and see who could be appointed to hold the office. If the range of reasonable appointees is restricted the test must be applied in relation to such potential appointees and one must ask whether each of these persons if appointed would have to incur the expense; if the answer is yes then the expense is deductible notwithstanding that some other person, who would not be a suitable appointee, might not have to incur it; this is *Owen v Pook*.[10] In an extreme case it may be possible to show that the taxpayer is the only person in the world who can carry out the duties; this is *Taylor v Provan*.[11] These three House of Lords cases are now considered in more detail.

In *Kerr v Brown*[12] the Special Commissioner held that no benefit arises in respect of a journey by a fireman to the fire station in a car provided by the fire service.[13]

---

[1] ITEPA 2003, ss 245 and 248.
[2] ITEPA 2003, ss 246 and 247.
[3] ITEPA 2003, s 248(3).
[4] ITEPA 2003, s 305.
[5] Inland Revenue interpretation RI 99.
[6] *Cook v Knott* (1887) 2 TC 246; *Revell v Elsworthy Bros & Co Ltd* (1890) 3 TC 12; *Andrews v Astley* (1924) 8 TC 589; *Ricketts v Colquhoun* [1926] AC 1, 10 TC 118. The costs may also be disallowed under (b). In *Jackman v Powell* [2004] EWHC 550 (Ch), [2004] STC 645, it was held that a milkman's place of work was the 35 roads in his milk round. Travel from his home to that place of work was not allowable.
[7] *Burton v Rednall* (1954) 35 TC 435. It is interesting to compare the position in tort when the question is whether an employee is acting in the course of his employment—see *Smith v Stages* [1989] AC 928, [1989] 1 All ER 833, HL.
[8] [1926] AC 1 at 7, 10 TC 118 at 135 (cf Lord Salmon in *Taylor v Provan* [1975] AC 194 at 227).
[9] Ward [1988] BTR 6.
[10] Infra, § **7.126**.
[11] Infra, § **7.127**.
[12] [2002] STC (SCD) 434.
[13] This case turns on its own particular facts. The fire officers had standby duty hours, during which they were allowed to be at home and carry on with a normal life but were required to attend a fire for which they received a call during that standby period. The Special Commissioners applied an apportionment of the benefit, by reference to the aggregate number of the taxpayer's rest and leave days per year, compared to the duty days. The method of measuring the charge that arose in the

case is the subject of a further decision of the Special Commissioner: *Kerr v Brown (No 2)* [2003] STC (SCD) 266.

Three House of Lords cases

[7.126] In *Ricketts v Colquhoun*[1] the taxpayer (R) lived in London and was a practising member of the London bar. He was taxable under Schedule D, Case II in respect of his earnings at the bar. He was also Recorder of Portsmouth and was taxable under the employment income rules in respect of his earnings from this source. He sought to deduct the costs of travelling from his home to Portsmouth. The House of Lords rejected his appeal on two main grounds. First, when travelling to his place of work he was travelling not in the course of those duties but in order to enable him to perform them.[2] His duties only began at Portsmouth. Second, the expenses could not be said to have been incurred necessarily.[3] Since a Recorder could have lived in Portsmouth, the costs of travel from London were not necessary. A further point was that his choice of abode in London was a personal matter and the expenses consequent on that choice were therefore personal expenses.

In *Owen v Pook*[4] the taxpayer (O) was a medical practitioner who resided at Fishguard. He also held part-time appointments as obstetrician and anaesthetist at Haverfordwest 15 miles away. Under these appointments he was on "stand-by duty" two weekends a month and on Monday and Friday nights, at which times he was required to be accessible by telephone. If he was called at home he would give advice by phone, sometimes set out at once and at other times await further reports. He was responsible for his patient as soon as he received the telephone call. Although he received a payment for travelling expenses this was only for the last ten of his 15 miles. He was assessed in respect of the payments received for the ten miles and denied his claim for deduction in respect of the five miles. His appeal to the courts against this assessment was successful. Since he had two places where his duties were performed, the hospital and his residence with the telephone, the expenses of travel between the two places were deductible.[5] Lord Wilberforce said that the job as actually constituted and the purpose for which he incurred the expenses differed greatly from *Ricketts'* case.[6]

---

[1] [1926] AC 1, 10 TC 118.
[2] Per Lord Cave, LC, at 4, 133.
[3] Per Lord Blanesburgh, at 7, 135. cf Lord Salmon in *Taylor v Provan* [1974] 1 All ER 1201 at 1223, [1974] STC 168 at 190.
[4] [1969] 2 All ER 1, 45 TC 571. *Owen v Pook* was distinguished in *Bhadra v Ellam* [1988] STC 239 and *Parikh v Sleeman* [1988] STC 580 (upheld on narrower grounds [1990] STC 233, CA) and *Knapp v Morton* [1999] STC (SCD) 13 (all cases concerning the NHS).
[5] See Lord Guest 45 TC 571 at 590, Lord Pearce at 591 and Lord Wilberforce at 596.
[6] 45 TC 571 at 596; see Ward [1988] BTR 6 at 14, 15.

[7.127] Exceptionally the personal qualifications of the taxpayer may supply the material to satisfy the objective test of necessity. In *Taylor v Provan*[1] the taxpayer (T) was a Canadian citizen living in Toronto. He was the acknowledged expert in the brewing world on successful expansion by means of amalgamation and merger. He agreed to become a director of an English company which merged with others in 1958 to become United Breweries Ltd, which merged with Charringtons in 1962 which in turn merged to form Bass Charrington Ltd in 1967. The taxpayer did most of his work in connection with the English amalgamations in Canada and the Bahamas but he made frequent visits to England. He had extensive Canadian interests for which he worked from his offices in Toronto and the Bahamas. He agreed to serve as director of the companies "for reasons of prestige", although this had the unfortunate effect of bringing him within what are now the benefit code provisions of ITEPA 2003. He received no fees for his services since he regarded it as a business recreation, but his travelling expenses were reimbursed. The House of Lords held unanimously that the reimbursements were sums spent on behalf of the company and were taxable under what was then TA 1988, s 153 and is now Chapter 3 of Part 3 of ITEPA. The House held (by 3–2) that the expenses were deductible. Of the majority Lord Morris[2] and Lord Salmon[3] held that the taxpayer's duties were performed both in the UK and in Canada so that there were at least two places of work. Travel to England could not therefore be dismissed as travel from home to a place of work and so were allowable as incurred in performing the duties of the employment.

Lord Reid, however, gave a rather different account of *Owen v Pook*:[4]

> I think that the distinguishing fact in *Owen's* case was that there was a part-time employment, and that it was impossible for the employer to fill the post otherwise than by appointing a man with commitments that he would not give up. It was therefore necessary that whoever was appointed should incur travelling expenses.

On this approach, which goes much wider than any pronouncement in recent years and undermines both the decision of the House of Lords in *Ricketts v Colquhoun* and much of the practice of the Revenue, the expenses were deductible in *Taylor v Provan* because the taxpayer was the only person who could do this job which he was only willing to do from Canada, and that he did some of the work in Canada. It was not enough that he insisted on working in Canada (so satisfying requirement 1); what was crucial was that he was the only person who could do the work (so satisfying requirement 2).

The question arises whether Lord Reid's approach undermines the earlier decision in *Ricketts v Colquhoun*. No member of the majority in *Taylor v Provan* wished to question the result of that earlier decision but Ricketts' post as Recorder of Portsmouth was a part-time one and anyone appointed would have had to be a member of the bar. However, Ricketts was not the only member of the bar who could have been appointed and it was possible that another appointee would have lived in Portsmouth. Another explanation could be that Rickett's home was not a place of work. This would conclude the matter if as may well be the case,[5] Lord Reid's explanation of *Owen v Pook* rests on the assumption that there were two places of work.

---

[1] [1974] 1 All ER 1201, [1974] STC 168.
[2] [1974] 1 All ER 1201 at 1210 and 177.
[3] [1974] 1 All ER 1201 at 1224 and 191.

[4] [1969] 2 All ER 1 at 1207 and 174.
[5] This emerges from [1974] 1 All ER 1201 at 1207 and 174.

An alternative explanation

[7.128] Central to *Owen v Pook* and *Taylor v Provan* is a finding of a dual place of employment. When then is home a place of employment? A director's house could not become a place of employment simply because he entertained clients there, even if his employer ordered him to do so. Unless however the home is a place in which work should, as opposed to could, be done, it is hard to see when a home is a place of work. The explanation of *Owen v Pook* and *Taylor v Provan* may therefore be not that home was one of the places of work but that in each case their employment was in a sense itinerant. In *Owen v Pook* there was no reason why the employment should have been located in the taxpayer's home. What mattered was that he assumed responsibility for the patient when he received the telephone message. If he were out with friends for the evening and had given their telephone number instead of his own, that would not necessarily make his friend's house one of his places of work. The point was *when* did his duties commence rather than *where*. In the same way in *Taylor v Provan* the House of Lords seemed to be concerned with the question "was he travelling in the performance of his duties" rather than "was his office a home and, if not, did he travel from his office or from his home". On this approach one can reconcile the earlier decision of *Nolder v Walters*[1] where an airline pilot sought unsuccessfully to deduct the cost of travelling from his home to the airport. The fact that he was summoned by his employer made no difference. While travelling to the airport he was not under his employer's command. He was travelling to his office not from one office to another.

If this approach is right one is paying far more attention to the subjective circumstances of the parties to the contract than was apparent from the approach of Lord Blanesburgh in *Ricketts v Colquhoun*.[2]

In order to obtain the deduction under this head, it is necessary that work is performed at both locations. In *Warner v Prior*[3] the Special Commissioner accepted that Mrs Warner, a supply teacher, had a place of work at her home,[4] but denied relief for travel from home as the location of that place of work had no bearing on her appointment to her job or her ability to perform it.[5]

[1] (1930) 15 TC 380.
[2] See generally Ward [1988] BTR 6.
[3] [2003] STC (SCD) 109.
[4] At [8], 112a.
[5] At [14], 114a. The Commissioner distinguished *Owen v Pook*, where, he said, the location of the doctor's secondary place of work was dictated by the hospital job.

Category (b)—travel to and from a temporary workplace

[7.129] From 6 April 1998, statute specifies the treatment to be applied where an employee travels directly from home to a temporary workplace which is at a different location from the permanent workplace.[1] The rules allow a deduction to be claimed for expenses of travelling which are attributable to the necessary attendance at any place which are not expenses of ordinary commuting or of private travel.[2] This allows for a deduction of all the costs incurred and not, as was originally enacted, the additional costs of travel which meant deducting any saving realised by not having to incur the costs of ordinary commuting travel.[3]

The effect of the rules can be illustrated:[4]

EXAMPLE

Alan has his permanent workplace in Bristol, where he is a lathe operator. One day he has to travel from home to Bath to look at a new machine. He is entitled to relief for the full cost of his return journey from home to Bath because it is a journey to a temporary workplace.

Betty lives in Cheltenham and each day drives to her permanent workplace in Swindon where she works as a trainee accountant. No relief is available for the journey from Cheltenham to Swindon as this is ordinary commuting.

Clive lives and works in Dagenham but goes to Devon for the weekend to stay with friends. He remains in Devon on the Monday, which he spends on some work that he has taken with him from the office. He is not entitled to relief for the cost of the journey from Dagenham to Devon as it is private travel.

Derek normally works at his employer's offices in Edinburgh, travelling each day from home in East Kilbride. One day he has to visit Perth to undertake some work in Perth for his employer. The cost of the return journey from East Kilbride to Perth is £34. Derek is entitled to relief for £34, being the full cost of the business travel.

Emma is an engineer who works on installing machines at the premises of her employer's various clients throughout the United Kingdom. Emma has no permanent workplace and attends each temporary workplace for a short period only. One week she travels between her home in Folkestone to work at an employer's client's premises in Falkirk, where she stays in a hotel for four nights and then returns to Folkestone. The cost of the Folkestone to Falkirk return journey is £130. The cost of four nights in the hotel plus meals is £300. Emma is entitled to relief for £430, being the full cost of her business travel.

Where there are two or more separate employments, relief is not available for the cost of travelling from the workplace for one employment to the workplace for the other employment. Exceptionally, however, where an individual is a director or an employee of two or more companies within a group of companies, relief is available for the cost of a journey between the different workplaces for the performance of duties of the different companies. For this treatment to apply, there must be a 51% shareholding link between the companies concerned. This link can be direct or indirect.[5]

A recent Special Commissioner's decision has highlighted the meaning of the temporary workplace rules.[6] An agency construction worker with three separate contracts to work at three different sites could not treat the sites as three different temporary workplaces within one employment. They were three separate employments and travel to and from each was "ordinary commuting". In the second case another agency worker had had a temporary job and then a permanent job with the same employer at the one site. Because he had worked at the same site continually for more than 24 months his travel was, again, "ordinary commuting" rather than travel to a temporary workplace.

Many teleworkers no longer use the employer's office as a permanent workplace, and providing certain conditions are satisfied, these workers will often have no ordinary commuting costs. Travel to the employer's office will be travel to a temporary workplace and qualify for tax relief.[7]

The legislation requires an objective test as to what travel is required by the employment. Thus, a subjective decision by an employee as to where he will undertake certain duties does not, of itself, give rise to relief. However, the cost of business travel will not normally have any bearing on the availability of relief. Specifically, HMRC do not seek to disallow first class rail travel on the grounds that only standard class was necessary to make the journey.[8] This does not allow relief where the mode of transport is some sort of reward as opposed to it being attributed to business travel.[9]

An employee may deduct expenses which are attributable to his necessary attendance at a place in the performance of his duties unless the journey is ordinary commuting or private travel.[10]

Ordinary commuting is defined[11] as travel between the employee's home (or any other place that is not a workplace) and a permanent workplace. Unhelpfully, permanent workplace is defined[12] as a place that the employee visits regularly in the performance of the duties of the employment which is not a temporary workplace. Thus, travel to a temporary workplace is not ordinary commuting and the expenses of the travel are deductible even if the journey starts off and finishes at the employee's home.

Statute[13] defines a temporary workplace as a place the employee attends to perform a task of limited duration, or for some other temporary purpose. In the Revenue view[14] if there is no identifiable task of limited duration, or other temporary purpose for the employee's visit, then the place cannot be a temporary workplace and if the employee visits the place regularly the expenses of the journey will not be deductible.

If there is an identifiable task of limited duration, or some other temporary purpose for the employee's visit, there are two other rules which may prevent a place from being a temporary workplace; (a) the 24 months rule and (b) the fixed-term appointment rule.[15]

The 24 months rule denies as a temporary workplace any workplace at which the employee has continuing work lasting for more than 24 months or, when it is reasonable to assume that the work will last at that place for more than 24 months. In the Revenue view[16] the "reasonable to assume" test means that account must be taken of change in circumstances. If an employee is sent to work at a place to perform a task which is expected to take 20 months and which does, in fact, take 20 months, that will be a temporary workplace. However, if there are delays which mean that the task in fact takes more than 24 months, the workplace ceases to be a temporary workplace from the point when it becomes known that the 24 months limit is going to be exceeded. That could well happen before the original anticipated 20 months has passed. Conversely, if the task is expected to last for 30 months, that workplace is a permanent workplace from the start of the period. If, in fact, it turns out that the task takes less than 24 months, the status of the workplace changes to a temporary workplace only at the point at which the change of duration becomes known.

The fixed-term appointment rule says that a place cannot be a temporary workplace if the employee's attendance is either (a) in the course of a period of continuous work comprising all or almost all of the period for which the employee is likely to hold the employment or (b) if it is at a time when it is reasonable to assume that it will be in the course of such a period. Particular difficulty is found with the fixed-term appointment rule, when the employer is a composite service company such as is commonly found in the construction industry, IT, supply of teachers and medical workers. If the relationship between the employee and the composite service company is a series of discrete employment contracts, each one involving attendance at a single site and lasting only as long as an assignment at which the employee is engaged, then none of the places visited will be a temporary workplace. Hence, travel to that workplace is not deductible. By contrast, where the relationship between the employee and the composite service company is an overarching contract employment covering all the assignments that he undertakes for the company, the fixed-term appointment rule will not apply, but the other tests are required to be passed in order to obtain the exemption for travel.

There are special rules for foreign travel.[17]

---

[1] ITEPA 2003, ss 338 and 339. These provisions supersede the many separate local agreements between different tax offices and particular employers to deal with journeys that have a mixed private and business nature.

[2] ITEPA 2003, s 338(1)(b) taken with (2) and (4); see *Kirkwood v Evans* [2002] EWHC 30 (Ch), [2002] STC 231.

[3] See TA 1988, s 198A repealed by FA 1998, s 61 without having come into force. However, for many years before 1998 the Revenue would not allow the total cost as such but would take account of the amount which the taxpayer saved by being away. The practice was defended by Rowlatt J in *Nolder v Walters* (1930) 15 TC 380 at 388. The rules were relaxed save where the taxpayer is a single person ordinarily living in a hotel or club; see Simon's Tax Intelligence 1974, p 319. On limits, see *Collis v Hore* (1949) 31 TC 173.

[4] Considerable guidance is given on the Revenue interpretation of these rules in the HMRC booklet "Employee Travel, Tax and NIC Guide for Employers" issued 1998, now known as leaflet 490 "Employee travel: A tax and NICs guide for employers". The illustrations are based on examples given in para 1.9 of this booklet.

[5] ITEPA 2003, s 340.

[6] *Phillips v Hamilton* and *Macken v Hamilton* [2003] STC (SCD) 286.

[7] Tax Bulletin Issue 68, December 2003, p 1069.

[8] HMRC booklet 490 "Employee Travel, A Tax and NIC Guide for Employers" para 5.14.

[9] HMRC booklet 490 "Employee Travel, A Tax and NIC Guide for Employers" para 5.15.

[10] ITEPA 2003, ss 338 and 339.

[11] ITEPA 2003, s 338(3).

[12] ITEPA 2003, s 339(2).

[13] ITEPA 2003, s 339(3).

[14] Given in Inland Revenue Tax Bulletin, December 2004, pp 1166–1168.

[15] ITEPA 2003, s 339(5).

[16] Given in Inland Revenue Tax Bulletin, December 2004, pp 1166–1168.
[17] ITEPA 2003, ss 328, 331, 335, 341, 342, 370–376 (see supra, § **7.121**).

Incidental overnight expenses

[7.130] ITEPA 2003, ss 240 and 268 provide statutory exclusion for certain incidental overnight expenses. The exclusion is effective for ITEPA 2003, ss 7, 82, 87, 88 and 95 (non-cash vouchers) ITEPA 2003, ss 7, 90, 94 and 95 (credit tokens) and ITEPA 2003, ss 7, 70 and 72 (the charge under ITEPA 2003, s 201).[1]

The broad effect of the new provisions is to exclude these charges where the overnight accommodation costs associated with them would be allowable deductions under the various travel rules, whether the travel is in the UK, or is foreign travel. In the source legislation the deductibility of travelling costs was listed out. To simplify matters ITEPA 2003 refers instead to expenses "deductible under Part 5 (otherwise than under any of the excepted foreign travel provisions)".[2] There is a maximum of £5 per night for expenses in the UK and £10 elsewhere but these limits may be varied by statutory instrument.[3] These limits are spread over the period of absence rather than being applied to each night separately but the effect of exceeding the maximum is that the whole sum becomes taxable.

An allowable incidental overnight expense is one which is paid wholly and exclusively for the purpose of paying or reimbursing expenses which are incidental to the employee's absence from the place where he normally lives, relate to a continuous period of such absence in relation to which the "overnight stay conditions" are met, and would not be deductible if the employee incurred and paid them and Chapter 2 of Part 4 did not apply (mileage allowances and passenger payments).[4]

The "overnight stay conditions" are that the employee is obliged to stay away from the place where he normally lives, the period includes at least one overnight stay and each such overnight stay is at a place the expenses of travelling to which meet condition A or B (for which see s 240(5) and (6)).[5]

Simon's Taxes E4.441.

[1] ITEPA 2003, ss 240, 241 and 268.
[2] ITEPA 2003, ss 240(5). The "excepted foreign travel provisions" are listed in subsection (7).
[3] ITEPA 2003, ss 241 and 716.
[4] ITEPA 2003, s 240(1); not every provision allowing the deduction of travel deduction opens the door to s 240—those which do not are ITEPA 2003, s 376 (board and lodging), and ss 371 and 374 (accompanying spouse or child).
[5] ITEPA 2003, s 240(4).

Further reliefs for travel to or during work

[7.131] FA 1999 introduced five provisions to prevent the tax system from getting in the way of environmentally sensible ideas on the part of employers.

First, ITEPA 2003, ss 242 and 266(2) remove any charge to tax if an employer provides a works bus service.[1] Such a service has to be provided by means of a bus, ie one with a seating capacity of 12 or more or a mini-bus (a seating capacity of 9, 10 or 11).[2] The service must be one for conveying employees on qualifying journeys; the employees may belong to one or more employers.[3] Journeys qualify not only if they are between one workplace and another but also, and in complete contrast to the rules in ITEPA 2003, s 337 et seq, between home and workplace.[4] In either case the journey must be in connection with the performance of the duties of the office or employment. In addition the service must be available to employees generally and the main use of the service must be for qualifying journeys by those employees.[5]

The exemption is only available where "the service is used only by the employees for whom it is provided or their children (defined widely but excluding those aged 18 or over) or is substantially used only by those employees or children."[6] This means that the exemption will not be lost just because of some other occasional purpose. One must, however, distinguish the service from the bus itself. If therefore the bus is used both for qualifying journeys and for separate non-qualifying journeys there will be a charge for the latter; if, however, there are non-qualifying aspects to a single journey there will be a charge unless the qualifying aspects form the substance of the matter (or whatever substantially may mean).

Second, ITEPA 2003, ss 243 and 266(2) remove any charge to tax where an employer provides financial or other support for public bus services. Again the employees may belong to one or more employers and the service must be for qualifying journeys.[7] Third, the various exemptions from tax for car parking spaces are extended to spaces for parking motor cycles and facilities for parking cycles.[8] Quite why cycles need facilities and motor cycles only need spaces is unclear. Presumably this wording is intended to cover facilities for locking bicycles up.

Fourth, ITEPA 2003, ss 244 and 266(2) remove any charge to tax where an employer lends an employee a cycle or a cyclist's safety equipment.[9] The benefit or facility must be available to employees generally. The employee must use it mainly for qualifying journeys.[10] Safety equipment is not defined but presumably includes both lights and safety helmet; it is unlikely to cover fancy gears (which will be part of the cycle anyway) or rain-cape or locks. Some softening of these boundaries may occur in practice. There is a definition of "cycle" and "cyclist" for this section.[11]

---

[1] ITEPA 2003, s 242.
[2] ITEPA 2003, ss 242(3) 249.
[3] ITEPA 2003, s 242(2).
[4] ITEPA 2003, ss 242(1)(*b*), 249.
[5] ITEPA 2003, ss 242(1)(*a*), (*b*), 249.
[6] ITEPA 2003, s 242(1)(*c*).
[7] ITEPA 2003, ss 243 and 249.
[8] ITEPA 2003, s 237. See Note 29 in Annex 2 of the Explanatory Notes of ITEPA 2003—the definitions of a motor cycle and a cycle are not rewritten because they are considered unnecessary for the meaning of a parking space for a motor cycle or facilities for a cycle.

[9] ITEPA 2003, ss 244 and 266.
[10] ITEPA 2003, ss 244 and 249.
[11] ITEPA 2003, s 244(5).

Authorised mileage allowances

[7.132] For many years the Revenue have specified mileage rates that could be paid to employees for the use of their own car on business, known as the fixed profit car scheme. By operating the scheme, the Revenue is looking to tax as a benefit only a payment that is in excess of the specified mileage rate. This scheme was initially applied almost exclusively to the public sector. In 1990 the rates were openly published and all employers encouraged to use the fixed profits car scheme. Until 6 April 2002, the rates were designed to reflect the actual cost of motoring. With effect from 6 April 2002 this system has been put on a new statutory basis, with no attempt to reflect actual costs for larger cars.[1] This can be seen as another plank in the government's approach to environmental matters. For 2002–03 and subsequent years the maximum that can be paid tax free to an employee for business travel is 40p per mile for the first 10,000 miles and 25p per mile thereafter. This rate also applies to vans. Motor-cycle travel can be reimbursed at a rate of up to 24p per mile, irrespective of engine size or cost.[2] As can be seen, the car rates apply irrespective of the size of the car, thus favouring the smaller car.

There is no objection in principle to an employer paying higher mileage rates but the consequence is that the excess will be taxed on the employee, irrespective of the actual running cost. The employee cannot make a claim for those additional costs.[3] On the other hand, if the employer reimburses at a lower rate than the statutory amounts the employee can make a claim for the difference to be deducted from his emoluments.[4]

It would be very easy in some cases to circumvent the 10,000 mile yearly limit by arranging for an employee to charge other entities in the same ownership. To prevent this, it is expressly provided that business travel in relation to the employment and any associated employment by car or van in the tax year in question is aggregated. Employers are associated if the employer is the same; the employers are partnerships or bodies and an individual or another partnership or body has control of both of them; or the employers are associated companies within the meaning of TA 1988, s 416.[5]

Prior to 2002/03 in addition to the more generous mileage rates, any employee could also claim for the business element of interest on a loan applied in acquiring a car. That is no longer possible because one of the conditions for that relief is that the employee must be entitled to capital allowances on the car and the provisions for capital allowances on vehicles owned by employees were withdrawn with effect from 6 April 2002.[6]

To encourage the sharing of cars, an employer can now make what is called an approved passenger payment to the employee of up to 5p per mile where one or more qualifying passengers are carried in a car or van while being used for business travel. The passenger must also be an employee on business travel to qualify. Moreover, the employee must either receive mileage allowance payments for use of the car or be taxed on the benefit where the car is made available by the employer. The approved passenger payment amount is based on the number of business miles travelled by the employee for which a qualifying passenger is carried in the year. This is applied separately for each qualifying passenger. An employee cannot make a deduction from the emoluments if the employer does not make a passenger payment.[7]

Dispensations for mileage allowances have automatically been withdrawn with effect from 6 April 2002 in view of these new provisions.[8]

In a further gesture to "green travel", an employer can pay up to 20p per mile to an employee who uses his bicycle to perform duties of his employment.[9] This exemption is available for the employee who chooses to travel by tricycle, or any machine that is more than three wheels as long as the motive power is the taxpayer's muscles not an internal combustion engine.[10] The exemption is not, however, available to the monocyclist. An employee who chooses to travel on his employer's business on a circus monocycle is subject to tax on the full sum received from his employer, less the actual cost of monocycle travel.

[1] ITEPA 2003, ss 229, 230.
[2] ITEPA 2003, s 230. Business travel means travelling expenses that would fall within ITEPA 2003, ss 337–342 (see ITEPA 2003, s 236(1)).
[3] ITEPA 2003, s 359.
[4] ITEPA 2003, ss 231, 232.
[5] ITEPA 2003, s 230(3)–(5).
[6] FA 2001, s 59 substituting a new CAA 2001, s 36.
[7] ITEPA 2003, ss 233, 234.
[8] ITEPA 2003, Sch 7 paras 16, 20.
[9] ITEPA 2003, s 230.
[10] This is a consequence of ITEPA 2003, s 235(5) adopting the definition of "cycle" in the Road Traffic Act 1988, s 192(2) which requires the machine to have two or more wheels to qualify as a "cycle".

Foreign expenses

[7.133] (1) *Initial and final travel expenses.* Where the duties of the employment are carried out wholly outside the UK the cost of travel to take up the post and return from it is not allowable under the general principle[1] since such expenses are incurred not in the performance of the duties but to enable one to carry them out or return from having carried them out. So special legislation is needed and applies where the employee is resident and ordinarily resident in the UK and, where the earnings are from a foreign employer, the employee is domiciled in the UK. The employee may deduct the costs of travel from a place in the UK to take up the employment and of travel to a place in the UK on its termination. The reference to "a place in" the UK is presumably to ensure where an employee flies from Glasgow to the US via Heathrow he can deduct the costs of the flight from Glasgow to London and not just the costs of travel from the airport of departure from the UK.[2]

(2) *Board and lodging.* Expenses of board and lodging to enable an employee to carry out the duties of an employment performed wholly outside the UK are

deductible if they were met (a) directly by the employer, or (b) by the employee and he was then reimbursed by the employer.[3] It will be seen that no deduction is allowed where the employee meets the expenses himself and is not reimbursed; this is presumably because in those situations in which deduction is allowed the employer will claim to deduct these sums in computing his profits and so the Revenue can check the sums claimed by the employer against the sums claimed by the employee. The employee must be resident and ordinarily resident in the UK, and if the employer is a foreign employer, the employee must be domiciled in the UK. Where the expense is incurred partly for a non-employment purpose, apportionment of the cost is permitted.[4]

(3) *Travel between multiple employments.* Travel costs are also deductible where the employee has more than one employment the duties of at least one of which are performed wholly or partly outside the UK.[5] Travel from one job to another could not be said to be in the performance of the duties of either and so a special rule treats the expense as incurred in performing the duties of the employment to which he is going. This rule applies to journeys both from and to the UK and where both the place of departure and destination are outside the UK but the employee must be resident and ordinarily resident in the UK, and if the employer is a foreign employer, the employee must be domiciled in the UK.[6] Apportionment is authorised where there is more than one purpose.[7]

(4) *Intermediate and family travel.* The rules so far outlined do not cover return journeys while the duties of the employment are being carried out nor do they provide for the deduction of the costs of travel by the employee's family. These matters are regulated separately—by a different and more restrictive rule.[8]

First, for the costs of family travel to qualify the employee must be absent from the UK for a continuous period of at least 60 days,[9] whether or not in the year of assessment, for the purpose of performing the duties of the employment. Second, the cost must be either paid or reimbursed by the employer as in the board and lodging rule.[10] Third, the rule only extends to two outwards and two inwards journeys in any year of assessment. The child must not be over 17[11] at the beginning of the outwards journey.

Where the duties are performed partly in and partly out of the UK they must be such that those being performed overseas can only be performed there and the journey must be wholly and exclusively for the purpose of performing those duties (in the case of an outward journey) or (in the case of an inbound journey) returning after performing such duties.[12] Where the duties are of one or more employments a similar rule applies. The employee can deduct the costs of travel for any journey from and to a place in the UK[13] provided the duties can only be performed outside the UK and the absence from the UK was occasioned wholly and exclusively for the purpose of performing the duties concerned.[14] The condition that the duties can only be performed outside the UK is relaxed for seafarers.[15]

(5) *Employees not domiciled in the UK.* Employees not domiciled in the UK but paid for duties performed here have a special rule.[16] To qualify for this rule the following conditions must be satisfied:

Expenses and deductions from earnings [7.133]

(a) The employee must be domiciled in a state other than the UK and receive earnings from duties of an office or employment performed in the UK (in all cases).
(b) The cost of travel must be borne or reimbursed by (or on behalf of) the employer and be an assessable emolument of the employee (in all cases).
(c) The employee must be present in the UK for the purpose of performing the duties of one or more offices or employments for a continuous period of 60 days or more (for relief for family members' travel and expenses).
(d) The journey has to be undertaken by the family to either:
 (i) accompany the employee at the beginning of the continuous period of 60 days or more, or
 (ii) visit the employee during such a period or to return afterwards (for relief for family members' travel and expenses).
(e) The journey must be made within five years of a qualifying arrival in the UK by the employee (in all cases).
(f) The person must not have been resident in the UK for either of the two years preceding the year of assessment in which he arrived or must not have been in the UK for any purpose during the two years ending with the date of his arrival (in all cases).[17]

When these conditions are fulfilled, the cost of travel to and from his usual place of abode, if paid by the employer or reimbursed separately,[18] is deductible; that is, no tax is payable on the benefit received.

Once here the employee is entitled to the benefit of these rules for a period of five years beginning with the date of arrival.[19]

By concession, the Revenue treat an employee as satisfying the 60 days rule where:

(a) he spends at least two thirds of their working days in the UK over a period of 60 days or more; and
(b) he is present in the UK for the purpose of performing the duties of their employment both at the start and at the end of this period.[20]

The concession is issued so that the tax treatment more accurately reflects employment in international business whilst preventing a deduction for travelling expenses of an employee's family where the employee simply makes frequent short business trips to the UK.

Simon's Taxes E4.115.

---

[1] ITEPA 2003, ss 336(1)(*b*) and 337(1)(*b*) require the cost to be incurred in the performance of the duties. Hence, there is no deduction under the general rule for the cost of getting to the place where the employee performs his duties.
[2] ITEPA 2003, s 341.
[3] ITEPA 2003, ss 369 and 376.
[4] Apportionment is authorised by ITEPA 2003, s 376(3).
[5] ITEPA 2003, ss 342 and 721.
[6] ITEPA 2003, s 342 Conditions E and F.
[7] ITEPA 2003, s 342(8).
[8] The travel may be from or to "a place in" the UK; ITEPA 2003, s 370.

[7.133] Employment income

⁹ ITEPA 2003, s 371(3). On costs of travel by wife to accompany a director or employee in precarious health see extra-statutory concession A4(*d*). (The phraseology of this concession is flagrantly sexist.)
¹⁰ ITEPA 2003, s 371(1).
¹¹ A person reaches 18 at the start of the day which is his 18th birthday; Family Law Reform Act 1969, s 9.
¹² ITEPA 2003, s 370 (see Conditions A, B or C).
¹³ ITEPA 2003, s 370 (see Conditions A, B or C).
¹⁴ ITEPA 2003, s 370. On "wholly and exclusively" in a slightly different context see *Mallalieu v Drummond* [1983] STC 665 (see infra, § **8.96**).
¹⁵ ITEPA 2003, s 372.
¹⁶ ITEPA 2003, ss 373, 374 and 375.
¹⁷ This rule may operate harshly, for instance, when an employee visits the UK with a view to seeing whether he wishes to come here to work.
¹⁸ ITEPA 2003, ss 373(1)(*b*) and 374(1)(*b*).
¹⁹ ITEPA 2003, ss 373, 374 and 375.
²⁰ Inland Revenue Tax Bulletin, December 2001, p 900. This treatment can be applied to fiscal year 2001–02, and subsequent years. The treatment can also be applied to 2000–01 if the taxpayer makes a claim by 31 January 2003 for amendment of his self-assessment return.

[**7.134**] In addition to expenses deductible under the general rules, employees who are not domiciled in the UK and are employed by a foreign employer may attract further deductions for "corresponding payments".[1] Payments are "corresponding" if they are similar to payments which would be deductible if all the relevant elements were in the UK. This could include contributions to a foreign pension fund which corresponds to a UK pension fund for which relief could be given.[2]

Such payments are allowable only if made out of earnings from the employment and, save for pension contributions, Revenue practice may require proof that there is not sufficient overseas income (on which UK tax is not payable) to enable him to make the payments without having recourse to the foreign earnings.[3]

Simon's Taxes E4.115.

---

[1] ITEPA 2003, s 355.
[2] Schedule E Manual, para 32661 et seq.
[3] Schedule E Manual, para 32661 et seq.

Employees seconded to work in the UK

[**7.135**] When an individual who normally works abroad comes to the UK to work for a period, the initial question to ask is whether the work in the UK is carried out at a "temporary workplace". If all, or almost all, of the period for which the employee is likely to hold the employment is the time spent in the UK, then the UK base is not a "temporary workplace".[1] In applying this test, it is necessary to consider whether the secondment is part of the duties of a continuing employment or whether it involves taking up different employment.[2]

As long as the hurdle in the preceding paragraph is passed, the basic rule is that a workplace can be treated as a temporary workplace where it is reasonable to assume that an employee's attendance for that workplace in the course of the continuing employment will not exceed 24 months.[3] It is possible that there is a change in circumstances that altered the expected length of the secondment. In the Revenue view, the workplace is a temporary workplace during any time in which the reasonable expectation (viewed in the light of all the available evidence, whether or not committed to writing) is that the secondment would be for a period that does not exceed 24 months.[4]

If it is established that the UK site is a temporary workplace, the cost of business travel that is allowed without triggering a benefit charge includes not only travel between the employee's home and the location of the secondment but also accommodation and subsistence, for the duration of the secondment.

HMRC practice is to allow relief for the cost of hotel accommodation of a quality that reflects the seniority of the employee concerned. Where furnished or unfurnished living accommodation is supplied, in preference to hotel accommodation, no benefit arises from the supply of such an alternative, as long as the total cost incurred by the employee is appropriate to the business need.[5] The relief then extends to costs associated with accommodation, such as utility bills and personal expenditure attributable solely to the business travel, as well as the cost of travel between the temporary accommodation and the temporary workplace.[6] In addition, a payment of up to £5 per night can be made for expenses incidental to the business travel.[7]

The employer can apply for a "notice of nil liability", commonly termed a dispensation.[8]

[1] ITEPA 2003, s 339.
[2] Inland Revenue Tax Bulletin December 2000, p 806. This bulletin contains further information on the Revenue approach, including nine worked examples.
[3] ITEPA 2003, s 339(5).
[4] Inland Revenue Tax Bulletin December 2000, p 807.
[5] Inland Revenue Tax Bulletin December 2000, p 807.
[6] Inland Revenue Tax Bulletin December 2000, p 809.
[7] ITEPA 2003, ss 240 and 268; £10 per night for any time the employee spends out of the UK.
[8] ITEPA 2003, s 65. The conditions that the Revenue require to be satisfied before issuing a dispensation are in HMRC Manual, para SE30055.

Other expenses

[7.136] The principles applicable to travel expenses apply with equal force to other expenses which, however, must also satisfy the test that they were wholly and exclusively incurred. The words of ITEPA 2003, s 336 were described by Vaisey J as:[1]

> . . . notoriously rigid, narrow and restricted in their operation. In order to satisfy the terms of the rule it must be shown that the expenditure incurred was not only necessarily but wholly and exclusively incurred in the performance of the relevant

[7.136] Employment income

official duties. And it is certainly not enough merely to assert that a particular payment satisfies the requirements of the rule without specifying the detailed facts upon which the finding is based. An expenditure may be necessary for the holder of an office without being necessary to him in the performance of the duties of that office; it may be necessary in the performance of those duties without being exclusively necessary referable to those duties; it may perhaps be both necessarily and exclusively but still not wholly so referable. The words are indeed stringent and exacting; compliance with each and every one of them is obligatory if the benefit of the rule is to be claimed successfully. They are to my mind, deceptive words in the sense that when examined they are found to come to nearly nothing at all.

The exemption provided by ITEPA 2003, s 316A (see supra § **7.129**) for teleworker's household expenses is not regarded by the Revenue as giving any extension to these principles. Citing the case of *Kirkwood v Evans*[2] they regard most employees who work at home as doing so by choice and so not entitled to a deduction under ITEPA 2003, s 336 for any unreimbursed additional household expenses.[3]

---

[1] *Lomax v Newton* (1953) 34 TC 558 at 561–562. In *Revenue and Customs Comrs v Decadt* (2007) Times, 4 June, [2007] SWTI 1434, [2007] All ER (D) 139 (May) the High Court refused relief for the cost incurred by a medical registrar in obtaining a Certificate of Completion of Specialist Training, on the grounds that this was not necessary to the performance of the duties of employment, even though holding the Certificate was an obligation of the contract of employment.

[2] 74 TC 481

[3] Tax Bulletin Issue 68, December 2003, p 1069.

Rules for deduction of expenses

In the performance of duties

[7.137] A sharp distinction is drawn between expenditure incurred *in the performance* of the duties of an office and expenditure incurred in order either to enable oneself to do the job initially[1] or to enable oneself to perform the duties of that office more efficiently. Thus the cost of a housekeeper to look after one's family and so enable one to go out to work is not deductible.[2] Similarly, no deduction could be claimed for any part of the employee's community charge even though a part of the home was used for employment purposes.[3]

An actor is now allowed to deduct agent's fees, including payments to bona fide co-operatives.[4]

A school teacher who attended a series of weekend lectures in history at a college for adult education for the purposes of improving his background knowledge could not deduct those expenses.[5] There is a distinction between qualifying to teach and getting background material on the one hand and preparing lectures for delivery on the other hand.[6] Likewise a clerk obliged to attend late meetings of the council and who bought himself a meal before the meeting was not allowed to deduct the cost of the meal;[7] he had been instructed to work late, not to eat. Again, a clerk to the General Commissioners who took out a mortgage to buy premises used partly as an office and partly as a pied-a-terre was not entitled to deduct the mortgage interest, even though he had been allowed to deduct three quarters of the running costs.[8] On similar grounds an employee was not allowed to deduct the costs of a record player and gramophone records which he had purchased for the purpose of providing a stimulus of good music while he worked especially late at night.[9] As Cross J drily observed, "it may well be that (he) was stimulated to work better by hearing good music, just as other people may be stimulated to work better by drink . . ."[10]

There is a fundamental distinction between expenditure incurred in the performance of the duties of the office (which may be a deductible) and expenditure which is incurred to prepare oneself to carry out those duties (which is not). In *Smith v Abbott*[11] four journalists claimed[12] in respect of expenditure on newspapers and periodicals. The Commissioners held in relation to each of them that the reading of the material was a necessary part of their duties as staff photographer, sports reporter, news sub-editor and picture editor; it was inherent in their jobs. They therefore concluded that the expenses were deductible. This was upheld by Warner J[13] and by the Court of Appeal[14] but reversed (by a majority) by the House of Lords.[15]

Lord Templeman giving the longest majority speech in the House of Lords pointed out that the reading was not done at their place of work but at home and while travelling to and from work and in the employee's own time;[16] the fact that there was no contractual obligation to buy and read these papers was irrelevant.[17] Under these circumstances the journalists did not purchase and read the newspapers in the performance of their duties but for the purpose of ensuring that they would carry out their duties efficiently.[18] The work of the journalists did not begin until they reached the office.[19]

Lords Jauncey and Mustill, were much more circumspect in concluding that while there were differences in evidence they were not in the end sufficient to justify a different decision.[20] The dissentient, Lord Browne-Wilkinson concluded that the court had no power to overrule the findings of the Commissioners.[21]

In *Snowdon v Charnock*[22] a fully qualified medical practitioner and psychiatrist wished to undertake specialist training in adult psychotherapy. He was given employment as a registrar trainee. The employing National Health Service trust required him, as part of his training, to undergo personal psychotherapy sessions. The Special Commissioner held, on the authority of *Smith v Abbott*, that his attendance at these training courses was not in the performance of his duties and, hence, no tax deduction was allowed for the expenses incurred thereon by Dr Snowdon. In *Consultant Psychologist v R & C Comrs*[23] relief was denied for the cost of professional training as this was identified as equipping this psychologist for further duties, such as those he may undertake if he went into private practice but not for the duties he was currently undertaking; thus, the expenditure was not incurred in the performance of the duties of the employment.[24]

---

[1] *Lupton v Potts* [1969] 3 All ER 1083, 45 TC 643; *Elderkin v Hindmarsh* [1988] STC 267.

[7.137] Employment income

2   *Bowers v Harding* [1891] 1 QB 560, 3 TC 22; *Halstead v Condon* (1970) 46 TC 289.
3   Inland Revenue press release, 10 November 1989, *Simon's Tax Intelligence* 1989, p 838.
4   ITEPA 2003, s 352.
5   *Humbles v Brooks* (1962) 40 TC 500.
6   40 TC 500 at 504. Even if this distinction had been ignored the expenditure might have failed on the ground of necessity since it was possible that a properly qualified history teacher could have been appointed who would not have needed to attend the course.
7   *Sanderson v Durbidge* [1955] 3 All ER 154, 36 TC 239; nor could the Recorder in *Ricketts v Colquhoun* [1926] AC 1, 10 TC 118.
8   *Baird v Williams* [1999] STC 635.
9   *Newlin v Woods* (1966) 42 TC 649.
10 (1966) 42 TC 649 at 658.
11 [1991] STC 661.
12 Technically they were claiming under what was then TA 1988, s 198 (and is now ITEPA 2003, s 336) in order to escape from a charge under what was then TA 1988, s 153 (and is now ITEPA 2003, s 70) in respect of an allowance to cover these items.
13 *Smith v Abbott* [1991] STC 661.
14 *Smith v Abbott* [1993] STC 316, CA.
15 *Smith v Abbott* [1994] STC 237, HL.
16 [1994] STC 237, HL, at 245b, 244a and 247d respectively.
17 [1994] STC 237, HL, at 245j.
18 [1994] STC 237, HL, at 243b.
19 [1994] STC 237, HL, at 244a.
20 [1994] STC 237, HL, at 248, 255; the fifth member of the Committee, Lord Keith, agreed with Lord Templeman.
21 [1994] STC 237, HL, at 254.
22 [2001] STC (SCD) 152. In her decision, Dr Nuala Brice took as her authority *Fitzpatrick v IRC (No 2)* [1994] STC 237, HL, which was heard by the House of Lords in conjunction with *Smith v Abbot*. The point was also taken, in respect of legal expenses, in *Ben Nevis v IRC* [2001] STC (SCD) 144; again, the taxpayer was unsuccessful in obtaining a deduction.
23 [2006] STC (SCD) 653.
24 [2006] STC (SCD) 653.

Necessarily

[7.138] The cases do not distinguish clearly the requirement that the expense be incurred in the performance of the duties of the office from the requirement that it be necessarily so incurred. It is, however, clear that the test of necessity is objective, as already seen.[1] Hence an employee with defective eyesight cannot recover the cost of his glasses.[2] Some softening of this objective test is discernible in *Taylor v Provan*. It is not necessary for the Commissioners to record a finding that the duties of the office could not be performed without the holder incurring the expenditure in question. In *Smith v Abbott* Warner J felt that their statements entailed a finding that "any and every holder of the employment" would have to incur it.[3]

Expenses and deductions from earnings **[7.139]**

The fact that the employer requires the particular expenditure is not decisive.[4] The employer will require the employee to come to work but that does not make the costs of travel to work deductible. As Donovan LJ has put it, "The test is not whether the employer imposes the expense but whether the duties do, in the sense that irrespective of what the employer may prescribe, the duties cannot be performed without incurring the particular outlay".[5] So a student assistant in the research laboratories of a company who was required to attend classes in preparation for an external degree from the University of London was not allowed to deduct his expenses,[6] any more than a soldier was obliged to share in the costs of the mess.[7]

In *Brown v Bullock*,[8] a bank manager was not allowed to deduct the cost of his subscription to a London club even though it was "virtually a condition of his employment". But in *Elwood v Utitz*[9] a director of a company in Northern Ireland who was obliged to travel to and stay in London frequently was allowed to deduct the costs of his subscription to a London club since he was buying accommodation and the fact that he chose to buy it at a club rather than a hotel was immaterial.

---

[1] *Ricketts v Colquhoun* [1926] AC 1 at 10 (see supra, § **7.126**). But if the taxpayer is the only person capable of doing the job, different questions arise: *Taylor v Provan* (see supra, § **7.127**).
[2] *Roskams v Bennett* (1950) 32 TC 129.
[3] [1991] STC 661 at 684. There is no further comment in the House of Lords.
[4] But the fact that an employer has not sanctioned it greatly weakens the taxpayer's case; see *Owen v Burden* [1972] 1 All ER 356 at 358, and *Maclean v Trembath* (1956) 36 TC 653 at 666.
[5] *Brown v Bullock* (1961) 40 TC 1 at 10.
[6] *Blackwell v Mills* [1945] 2 All ER 655, 26 TC 468. He was not performing his duties as a laboratory assistant when he was listening to the lecture, at 470.
[7] *Lomax v Newton* [1953] 2 All ER 801, 34 TC 558; *Griffiths v Mockler* [1953] 2 All ER 805, *35 TC 135*. Major in Royal Army Pay Corps would have been subject to disciplinary action if he had not paid but mess membership not necessarily in performance of duties as an officer.
[8] [1961] 1 All ER 206, 40 TC 1. Counsel for the bank manager conceded that his client could still perform the duties of a bank manager even though he had not been a member of the club.
[9] (1965) 42 TC 482.

Wholly and exclusively

[7.139] Many of these cases could as easily be explained on the ground that the expenditure was not incurred wholly and exclusively for the employment. Thus in the mess cases there was some element of personal benefit[1] while in *Brown v Bullock* the bank manager derived personal benefit from the membership of the club. Unlike the test of necessity, the requirement of "wholly and exclusively" is not wholly objective.[2] Thus the expenditure may satisfy this test if its sole object is the performance of duties regardless of the fact that it may bring about some other incidental result or effect.[3]

[7.139] Employment income

Where a person wears ordinary clothes but of a standard required by his employer, no part of the cost is deductible. However, where a car is being used sometimes for business purposes and sometimes for personal purposes some apportionment is possible. The distinction between the two cases is that when the car is being used for business purposes it is being used only for those purposes whereas when the clothes are worn at work they have a dual purpose, part-business, part-personal.[4] So where a telephone is used partly for business calls the taxpayer can deduct the business calls but not the others and he may not deduct any part of the telephone rental.[5] However, some softening of this position may be detectable in practice.[6]

[1] *Griffiths v Mockler* (1953) 35 TC 135 at 137.
[2] Per Lord MacDermott CJ, in *Elwood v Utitz* (1965) 42 TC 482 at 498.
[3] 42 TC 482 at 497, relying on cases decided under Schedule D, Case II.
[4] *Hillyer v Leake* [1976] STC 490; *Woodcock v IRC* [1977] STC 405, 121 Sol Jo 575 and *Ward v Dunn* [1979] STC 178.
[5] *Lucas v Cattell* (1972) 48 TC 353.
[6] See the facts in *Baird v Williams* [1999] STC 635 where three quarters of the running costs were allowed by the inspector.

Liability insurance and uninsured liabilities

[7.140] Statute[1] provides relief for liability insurance and for uninsured liabilities. More formally, it allows a deduction for money spent either on discharging a qualifying liability together with associated costs and expenses, or on a premium for a qualifying contract of insurance relating to an indemnity against a qualifying liability. The expense must not exceed the earnings of the office or employment[2]. The effect is to remove liability on the employee where these costs are met by the employer[2] and to give relief for the employee's own expenditure.

Separate relief is given for expenditure up to six years after the year in which the employment ends.[3]

A qualifying liability is one imposed for acts or omissions of the employee either as the holder of the office or employment or in some other capacity in which he acts in the performance of the duties of that office or employment. It may also be for a liability arising out of related proceedings eg legal costs. It is immaterial whether the liability is owed to the employer or someone else. The conditions to be satisfied by the insurance policy are also elaborately set out but include the rule that the period may not exceed two years (except by virtue of renewals each for a period of two years or less) and may not require renewal.[4] Where a policy covers more than one risk only one of which is a qualifying risk an apportionment of the premium may be carried out.[5] There is no deduction if it would have been unlawful for the employer to effect the insurance.[6]

Post-employment deductions may be set against total income.[7] The relief may, like post-cessation business expenses, be set against CGT.[8] The deduction extends to qualifying sums spent in the period beginning when he ceased to hold the relevant office or employment and ending with the sixth year of assessment after that year.

Expenses and deductions from earnings **[7.141]**

The burden must fall on the employee rather than the employer. A liability met out of relevant retirement benefits or post-employment emoluments is regarded as falling on the employee. A burden is treated as falling on the employer if it falls on certain others eg a successor to the business, a person under a liability to that successor or any connected person.

---

1   ITEPA 2003, s 346. For the Revenue interpretation of the provisions, see Revenue Interpretation RI 131.
2   ITEPA 2003, s 329, and s 72 in respect of reimbursements.
3   ITEPA 2003, ss 555–564 (Part 8 of ITEPA 2003).
4   ITEPA 2003, ss 348–350, 559–561.
5   ITEPA 2003, ss 346(3)(*b*) and 558(3)(*b*).
6   ITEPA 2003, ss 346(2) and 558(2).
7   ITEPA 2003, s 555(2).
8   ITEPA 2003, s 555(6).

Summary

[7.141] The test of deductibility under ITEPA 2003, s 336 is, thus, strict, even severe. A particularly strong example of this is *Eagles v Levy*[1] where the employee had to sue his employer to recover wages due to him and was not allowed to deduct the costs of the action. Such costs were not incurred in the course of the performance of his duties.

The restrictive nature of the test of deductibility has often been commented upon, usually adversely,[2] and it remains true that the test is very much stricter than that laid down under Schedule D, Cases I and II where the requirement is that the expenditure be wholly and exclusively for the purposes of the business.[3]

A good example of the discrepancy is *Hamerton v Overy*[4] where a full-time anaesthetist sought to deduct the cost of maintaining a telephone, a maid to take messages, his subscription to the Medical Defence Union and the excess of his car running expenses over his allowance received from his employers. All these items would have been deductible had he been in private practice under Schedule D, Case II; none were deductible under what was then Schedule E and is now the employment income part of ITEPA; had he succeeded in establishing two places of work as the taxpayer did in *Owen v Pook*[5] the first and the last might well have been deductible.

However, the discrepancy can be exaggerated. Many expenses disallowed under Schedule D are likewise disallowed under the employment income rules. Thus travelling expenses from home to work are disallowed under both,[6] as are other expenses of a personal nature, such as living expenses. Second, it must be noted that some expenses allowed under Schedule D may subsequently be recouped by the Revenue as for example where trading stock is bought and later sold or valued at market value on discontinuance.[7] Again the cost of a home office which is allowed under the employment income rules will not affect the exemption of the principal private residence from CGT whereas the same allowance under Schedule D may result in a partial loss of that exemption. Third, there remains the crucial difference between an employment

[7.141] Employment income

and a profession or trade, between being a servant and being an owner. If an employee incurs expense for his employer, he may ask his employer to reimburse him, a trader can only seek payment from himself. Whether the reimbursement will itself be taxable will turn on the form of reimbursement and the subtleties of taxation of benefits in kind.

One approach to the problem is to keep the present strict rule and provide exceptions for particular situations such as the child minding expenses disallowed in *Halstead v Condon*[8] or the fees payable in *Lupton v Potts*.[9] ITEPA has made statutory some of the expenses in fact allowed by the Revenue.[10] There are still non-statutory exemptions such as the non-taxation of allowances for teachers in respect of books[11] or the home study allowance.[12] Legislation has been passed to deal with relocation expenses. The present system appears to have regional differences; such erratic administration is unfair.

Simon's Taxes E4.701.

---

[1] (1934) 19 TC 23. Cf Schedule D, Cases I and II (see infra, § **8.95**, note 1).
[2] Rowlatt J in *Ricketts v Colquhoun* (1924) 10 TC 118 at 121; Croom Johnson J in *Bolam v Barlow* (1949) 31 TC 136 at 129; Danckwerts J in *Roskams v Bennett* (1950) 32 TC 129 at 132; Harman LJ in *Mitchell and Edon v Ross* [1960] 2 All ER 218 at 232 and 40 TC 11 at 51, [1960] Ch 498 at 532. But cf Lord Radcliffe in *Mitchell and Edon v Ross* [1962] AC 814 at 841, [1961] 3 All ER 49 at 56, 40 TC 11 at 62; and Rowlatt J in *Nolder v Walters* (1930) 15 TC 380 at 389.
[3] See Lord Evershed MR in *Brown v Bullock* (1960) 40 TC 1 at 9.
[4] (1954) 35 TC 73.
[5] Supra, § **7.126**.
[6] Infra, § **8.102**.
[7] TA 1988, s 100.
[8] (1970) 46 TC 289.
[9] [1969] 3 All ER 1083, 45 TC 643.
[10] ITEPA 2003, ss 367, 368 (fixed sum deductions). For Revenue flowchart see Revenue Manual SE 32730a. Other reliefs depend on agreements between the Revenue and various Unions, the results being made available to their members.
[11] See Revenue Manual SE 70700 et seq for the tax treatment of teachers, lecturers and tutors.
[12] This was thought to be outside ITEPA 2003, s 336 in *Roskams v Bennett* (1950) 32 TC 129, but inside in *Elwood v Utitz* (1965) 42 TC 482 at 495.

Unreimbursed homeworking expenses

[7.142] Statute[1] provides relief for expenses that an employee is obliged to incur and pay wholly, exclusively and necessarily in the performance of the duties of the employment. For an expense to be deductible under ITEPA 2003, s 336 it must be one that the employee is obliged to incur solely because he holds the employment, and not because of any reasons personal to him or herself. Thus any element of personal choice as to whether the employee works at home or at the employer's premises will prevent a deduction under s 336 for those employees who choose to work from home.

Revenue practice is specified in HMRC Internal Instruction Manual as reducing the underlying law to two non-statutory tests. They are (i) that the duties that the employee performs at home are substantive duties of the employment; and (ii) that there is an objective requirement that those duties should be carried out at the employer's home and nowhere else.

Revenue practice is to accept that employees who work at home are entitled to a deduction under ITEPA 2003, s 336 for their additional household expenses where all the following circumstances apply:

(a) the duties that the employee performs at home are substantive duties of the employement. "Substantive duties" are duties that an employee has to carry out and that represent all or part of the central duties of the employment (this condition is unchanged);
(b) those duties cannot be performed without the use of appropriate facilities;
(c) no such appropriate facilities are available to the employee on the employer's premises (or the nature of the job requires the employee to live so far from the employer's premises that it is unreasonable to expect him or her to travel to those premises on a daily basis);
(d) at no time either before or after the contract is drawn up is the employee able to choose between working at the employer's premises or elsewhere.[2]

HMRC practice is to give relief for only the following expenses: (i) the additional unit costs of gas and electricity consumed while a room is being used for work, (ii) the metered cost of water used "in the performance of the duties" (if any), (iii) the unit costs of business telephone calls (including "dial up" internet access).[3]

---

[1] ITEPA 2003, s 336; see supra, § **7.122**.
[2] HMRC Tax Bulletin October 2005, pp 1231–1235. The Revenue give 12 examples where relief for homeworking expenses is allowed.
[3] A deduction of £2 per week (exclusive of business telephone calls) is given without proof of expenditure. The Revenue require a taxpayer to have a record of expenditure available if a higher sum is claimed.

Professional subscriptions

[7.143] On general principles, a subscription to a professional body paid by a county medical officer of health was disallowed as a deduction, as the subscription was not "necessary", in that other individuals could have performed the duties of the particular office without being a member of the professional body.[1] Whilst this finding was almost certainly correct in the light of the statutory requirement that any expenditure should be "necessary", the effect is to go against the encouragement that is thought should be given to a professionally qualified individual to keep himself up to date in developments within his own particular field. The position was then reversed by statute[2] and subscriptions to approved societies are now deductible. Deduction is, however,

[7.143] Employment income

only allowed if the society is named on the HMRC approved list of societies.[3] Any professional body can make application to HMRC for admission to the list.[4]

The deduction for a subscription to a professional body can only be made against earnings from employment. Although pensions are assessed under ITEPA 2003, this does not make an occupational pension an "emolument". If the only earned income of an individual is pension, no relief for a professional subscription is available.[5]

---

[1] *Simpson v Tate* [1925] 2 KB 214, 9 TC 314, Rowlatt J. On Revenue practice see HMRC Manual SE 32880 et seq.
[2] ITEPA 2003, ss 343, 344, 345.
[3] The current list was published on 18 December 1996 and can be obtained from HMRC, or viewed on the HMRC web site.
[4] ITEPA 2003, s 344.
[5] *Singh v Williams* [2000] STC SCD 404.

Pay as you earn

[7.144] For pay as you earn generally see ITEPA 2003, ss 682–712 (Part 11).[1]

The UK has a system of withholding tax at source. Such a system, it has been said, 'combines the expedient and the objectionable. It is a rough and ready system which virtually garnishees taxpayers' incomes, sometimes for debts they do not owe but subject in this event to refund . . . It is surprising that this withholding system, to which strong objections may be raised on grounds of principle, has aroused so little comment. It has probably done more to increase the tax collecting power of central governments than any other one tax measure of any time in history.'[2] The PAYE system imposes a duty on the employer[3] to account once a month (but quarterly for certain employers)[4] for the tax that he has or ought to have deducted when making a payment.[5] Where an emolument is paid by a third party that third party person making the payment may be required to deduct tax under the PAYE system.[6] Construction workers supplied by an agency are within the PAYE scheme.[7] For extension to certain tradeable assets see supra, § **7.47**.

If the employer fails to deduct, the Revenue may, in certain circumstances, proceed against the overpaid employee. One of those circumstances is where it appears to the Board that the employer's failure to comply with the PAYE Regulations was wilful and the employee knew that the employer had wilfully failed to deduct the tax due.[8] It has been held that where the Revenue seek to use this power in county court collection proceedings it is open to the defendant-employee to raise the public law defence that on no view of the evidence could the Board reach that conclusion.[9] If the Revenue proceed against the employer he may not in his turn recover from the employee.[10] This was because the employee is not a trustee of the payment for the employer and because the old action for money had and received would not lie. It was, however, suggested that the employer could withhold the sums from any later payment due to the employee.[11] It is unclear whether the employer can now use the new principles of restitution to recover such a payment from the overpaid employee.[12]

The definition of payment is the same as that under the timing rule set out at supra, § **7.22**.[13] The Revenue often publish practice arrangements, eg for casual harvest workers.[14] When the PAYE system has been applied to income the Crown may make an assessment as regards income in the light of the practice generally prevailing;[15] however it has to do so within 12 months following the year for which the assessment was made, a rule which binds the Revenue and does not affect the taxpayer's right of appeal.[16]

There are provisions where an employer makes a lump sum settlement of PAYE that it is estimated should have been deducted on wages paid.[17]

Where PAYE is not deducted by an employer, the Revenue can make a determination of the PAYE payable.[18] If the employer fails to pay the tax so determined within 30 days, the Revenue may then recover the tax from the employee.[19] PAYE operates on the transfer of a trade debt from an employer so that the debtor pays an employee directly.[20]

Where PAYE is paid to the Revenue later than 14 days after the month of paying the employee, interest is charged.[21]

A large employer[22] is required to pay the PAYE to the Revenue electronically.[23] In order to attract electronic payment by small employers, HMRC makes a payment to each employer with fewer than 50 employees, if the annual return is submitted online. The payment for the return for 2007/08 is £100.[24]

PAYE operates by the issuing of a "PAYE code" to each employee, the higher the code the less tax is deducted. A PAYE code number can be the subject of an appeal. In *Blackburn v Keeling*[24] the High Court upheld the taxpayer's right to require a PAYE code to be increased so as to give relief for the losses he had suffered as a Lloyd's Name but the Court of Appeal reversed this decision, holding that there was no right to a loss in the coding notice until the loss was actually "sustained".[25]

PAYE income includes pension income and social security income.[26]

Simon's Taxes, Division E4.9.

---

[1] The primary legislation for the operation of PAYE is ITEPA 2003, ss 682–712 (Part 11), which enables the detailed operation of the system to be determined by regulations. The major framework of the system is specified in Income Tax (Employments) Regulations 1993, SI 1993/744, which has been frequently amended, and Income Tax (Employments) (Notional Payments) Regulations, SI 1994/1212. For an account of the introduction of the PAYE system see an excellent article by John Jeffrey-Cook "The Birth of PAYE", Taxation, 2 May 2002, pp 124–127, the date of publication being 60 years (all but three days) after the first use of the expression "pay as you earn" was used in the House of Commons. The Tax Law Rewrite Project have just rewritten the PAYE regulations which are now the Income Tax (Pay As You Earn) Regulations 2003, SI 2003/2682 and are operative from 6 April 2004.

[7.144] Employment income

[2] MacGregor, [1956] 4 Can Tax Jo 171 at 173; Carter, Study 16, p 17.
[3] eg *Glantre Engineering Ltd v Goodhand* [1983] STC 1, [1983] 1 All ER 542.
[4] SI 1993/744, regs 40, 41 as amended by SI 1999/284, Income Tax Employments (Amendment No 2) Regulations, *Simon's Weekly Tax Intelligence* 1999, p 557.
[5] On meaning of payment see *Paul Dunstall Organisation Ltd v Hedges* [1999] STC (SCD) 26. The employer is not liable if he took reasonable care to comply with the PAYE regulations and the under-deduction was made in good faith; PAYE reg 42(2). On application of tronc rules (reg 5), see *Figael Ltd v Fox* [1990] STC 583; upheld [1992] STC 83, CA.
[6] *Booth v Mirror Group Newspapers plc* [1992] STC 615.
[7] ITEPA 2003, s 44 and Sch 7, para 14.
[8] Reg 42(3) on which see also *R v IRC, ex p Sims* [1987] STC 211 and *R v IRC, ex p Cook* [1987] STC 434.
[9] *Pawlowski v Dunnington* [1999] STC 550, CA.
[10] *Bernard & Shaw Ltd v Shaw* [1951] 2 All ER 267.
[11] Note the very special facts in *Philson & Partners Ltd v Moore* (1956) 167 Estates Gazette 92.
[12] In *Kleinwort Benson Ltd v Lincoln City Council* [1997] 2 AC 349, [1998] 4 All ER 513, the House of Lords allowed recovery for sums paid under a mistake of law; previously recovery had been permitted only for sums paid under a mistake of fact.
[13] ITEPA 2003, s 686.
[14] Older schemes modified—Inland Revenue press release, 29 May 1991, *Simon's Tax Intelligence* 1991, p 549.
[15] ITEPA 2003, s 709.
[16] *Walters v Tickner* [1993] STC 624, CA.
[17] ITEPA 2003, s 703 et seq.
[18] Income Tax (Employments) Regulations 1993, SI 1993/744, reg 49; **Simon's Direct Tax Service, Division H2.**
[19] Reg 49(5). For an unsuccessful appeal against collection of tax from an employee, see *R v IRC, ex p McVeigh* [1996] STC 91 and *DTE Financial Services Ltd v Wilson* [2001] EWCA Civ 455, [2001] STC 777.
[20] ITEPA 2003, s 696.
[21] SI 1993/744, regs 50–52.
[22] Defined as an employer with 250 or more employees on the payroll.
[23] FA 2003, s 203. The detailed operation is specified by regulations and directions issued under the authority of Income Tax (Pay As You Earn) Regulations 2003, SI 2003/2682, regs 190(1) & 209(1). The Commissioners of Her Majesty's Revenue & Customs have issued Commissioners' Directions specifying 29 October 2006 as the date on which an employer's size will be determined, by reference to the number of employees subject to PAYE, for the purposes of mandatory electronic payment by large employers in respect of 2007–08 returns.
[24] The payment is made by the employer deducting the sum from the quarterly payment after the end of the tax year. Payments for other years are:

2005–06:	£250
2006–07:	£150
2008–09:	£75

²⁵ [2003] STC 639 for High Court decision; [2003] STC 1162 for Court of Appeal. TA 1988, s 380 is triggered when a taxpayer "sustains a loss".
²⁶ ITEPA 2003, s 683.

Court's approach to PAYE liability

[7.145] One should also note the decision of the House of Lords in *IRC v Herd*.¹ A charge to tax had arisen under the employment share option rules on the unrealised gain on shares acquired as an employee. The issue was whether, as the taxpayer-employee, but not the Revenue, contended, the employer was under an obligation to deduct tax under PAYE. In upholding the Revenue's position that the employee was not so bound, Lord Mackay said that what was then the Schedule E charge was not on the amount paid but on the net gain and this involved questions of the market value of shares which are not publicly quoted and so could involve considerable calculation and perhaps even more important substantial judgments on matters of opinion.² In the absence of a clear direction that the PAYE regulations did apply the court should not hold that they did. He went on to emphasise that his view applied only where a particular payment is treated only in part as assessable to income tax under the employment income rules; it would not prevent a payer being under an obligation to deduct tax where it was clear that there were two or more payments made together some of which were employment income while others were not.³

¹ [1993] STC 436.
² [1993] STC at 442e.
³ [1993] STC at 443d.

[7.146] As part of the 1994 scheme to widen PAYE,¹ payments by certain intermediaries are brought into the scheme. In future where any payment of, or on account of, assessable income of an employee is made by an intermediary of the employer, the employer is treated for PAYE purposes as making the payment—unless the intermediary deducts and accounts for the tax under PAYE regulations. The concept of a payment by an intermediary is widely defined and covers payments made by a person acting on behalf of the employer and at the expense of the employer or a person connected with him, or by trustees holding property for any persons or class of persons which includes the employee.² In these circumstances the employer is treated as making a notional payment;³ tax must be deducted from any actual payments of income and if that does not suffice the employer must account to the Revenue direct.⁴ If the employee does not make good the amount of that tax to the employer within 30 days, the payment of tax is treated as income of the employee assessable to tax under the employment income rules.⁵

The *Ramsay* principle can be applied here to identify the relevant transaction. It was so used to bring facts within this extension of the PAYE scheme to the intermediary where sums were paid by way of interests in non-resident trusts.⁶ Regulations have been made, particularly but not exclusively concerning timing.⁷

[7.146] Employment income

Where an employee works for someone other than the employer and that someone, known as the relevant person, pays the employer, one or other of these will operate the PAYE system. The Revenue now have power to direct the relevant person to apply the system if it appears to the Revenue that tax will not be deducted or accounted for as usual.[8] The provision giving this power carries the title "PAYE: mobile UK workforce".

Simon's Taxes E4.905.

[1] On PAYE liabilities in respect of tradeable assets see supra, § **7.47**.
[2] ITEPA 2003, s 687 and *R (on the application of Oriel Support Ltd) v Revenue & Customs Commrs* [2008] EWHC 1304 (Admin) on definition of connected person, see TA 1988, s 839.
[3] ITEPA 2003, s 710.
[4] ITEPA 2003, s 710.
[5] ITEPA 2003, s 222.
[6] See *DTE Financial Services Ltd v Wilson* [1999] STC 1061.
[7] Income Tax (Employments) (Notional Payments) Regulations 1994, SI 1994/1212; Inland Revenue press release, 4 May 1994, *Simon's Tax Intelligence* 1994, p 594. The power is contained in ITEPA 2003, s 710 added by FA 1994, s 128.
[8] ITEPA 2003, s 691, see also Inland Revenue press release, 11 April 1994, *Simon's Tax Intelligence* 1994, p 490.

[7.147] The system is one of cumulative withholding over the year. Full account is taken of the employee's income from this source and of such personal allowances as he may be entitled to. In essence he is allowed 1/52 of his allowances each week, or 1/12 each month. At the end of any week taxable income is discovered by subtracting the accumulated 1/52 shares of the allowances from the taxable pay to date. If the income rises over the year the tax will rise with it; if it falls, eg because of a change of job or a strike, a repayment may be made by the employer or lower tax paid for the rest of the year.

The system applies to all earnings paid by an employer. Earnings include expenses, expenses allowances and benefits in kind. Where the system does not apply, eg in the case of a non-resident employer, direct assessment on the employee is used.

Although the system applies to ITEPA 2003 income only it can in effect be used to collect tax in respect of other sources. This is achieved by directing that the taxpayer's allowances shall be attributed to those other sources of income, thus reducing the allowances to be set against the employment income, pension income or social security income and so gathering the tax from the ITEPA source. The system can also be used to collect underpayments of tax from that or a previous year as well as to refund overpayments.

[7.148] The obligation on an employer to operate the PAYE system arises if he has a sufficient tax presence in the UK. For this purpose a non-resident company carrying on business in the UK through a branch or agency has a sufficient presence.[1]

Where an employee works for a person based in the UK but the actual employer is based overseas (and so outside the PAYE regulations) the person for whom the employee is working can be made to apply the PAYE system on behalf of the employer. The same burden falls on the person for whom the work is done where someone other than the employer makes the payment and is also outside the UK.[2]

Simon's Taxes E4.909.

---

[1] *Clark v Oceanic Contractors Inc* [1983] STC 35 (where the branch was deemed to be in the UK by what is now TCGA 1992, s 276(7)).
[2] ITEPA 2003, s 689; see also Inland Revenue press release, 11 April 1994, *Simon's Tax Intelligence* 1994, p 490.

[7.149] Where an employee is not resident in the UK or, if resident is not ordinarily resident here, the PAYE system is designed to apply only to those earnings which are for work done in the UK. The problem is that when the payments are made it may well be unclear just how much of the remuneration will be taxable. Employers may ask for a direction as to the proportion to be subject to PAYE; if no direction is sought the whole payment is subject to the system.[1]

---

[1] ITEPA 2003, s 690; see also Inland Revenue press release, 11 April 1994, *Simon's Tax Intelligence* 1994, p 490.

PAYE and self-assessment

[7.150] In principle, the primary charge to income tax is the charge under self-assessment. PAYE is simply a method of withholding tax, which is brought into the calculation of the balancing payment. However, where the underpayment in the year amounts to £2,000 or less and arises solely in respect of earnings to which PAYE is applied, the underpayment can be collected by adjustment of the PAYE code.

A particular problem under self-assessment is that a director or employee who receives benefits in kind and to whom a self-assessment tax return is not issued, is not in a position to know whether the Revenue are proposing to collect tax on the benefits in kind through amendment of the PAYE code for the following year, or whether he should notify chargeability in order to make his own self-assessment. Under statute, penalties could be imposed if the employee does not notify chargeability.

The Revenue accept that employees who receive such a copy of the information on a P11D can assume any items on it which are not already taken into account for PAYE "will be" taken into account for PAYE, so that there is no need to notify chargeability because of them. This does not, however, apply where the particular employee knows that the P11D return has not, in fact, been submitted to the Revenue.[1]

Simon's Taxes E1.1205.

[7.150] Employment income

[1] Statement of practice SP 1/96.

8

Income from trades, professions and vocations

Trade profession or vocation	PARA **8.01**
Distinction between (1) trade and (2) profession or vocation	PARA **8.07**
Is there a trade?	PARA **8.09**
Basis of assessment	PARA **8.43**
Partnerships	PARA **8.61**
The measure of income	PARA **8.64**
Spreading adjustments	PARA **8.69**
Trading receipts	PARA **8.73**
Exempt trading income	PARA **8.94**
Expenses	PARA **8.95**
Timing of transactions	PARA **8.143**
Trading stock	PARA **8.151**
Commission, cashbacks and discounts	PARA **8.170**
Mining	PARA **8.171**

Trade profession or vocation

[8.01] Until the abolition of the Schedules for income tax by ITTOIA 2005, there was a technical (albeit latterly insignificant in practice) distinction between income from trades and that from the carrying on a profession or vocation. The former were taxed under Schedule D, Case I whereas the latter fell within Case II.

Part 2 of ITTOIA 2005 taxes all such income under one heading.[1] However, the few marginal differences between trades on the one hand and professions and vocations on the other are retained. For example, the rules dealing with animals kept for the purposes of a business (in s 30) which deem the animals to be trading stock are disapplied in respect of professions and vocations.[2] These exceptions, however, are expected to be of no practical significance. For this reason the legislation and the commentary below when referring to "trades" will mean "trades, professions and vocations" except where the contrary is expressed. For consequential non-statutory differences between trades and professions and vocations see infra, § **8.08**.

The profits of a company arising from a trade remain taxed under Schedule D, Case I and, to the extent that companies can carry on professions or vocations, profits from such activities are taxed under Schedule D, Case II.[3]

---

[1] ITTOIA 2005, s 5.

[8.01] Income from trades, professions and vocations

² ITTOIA 2005, ss 24, 30(4).
³ TA 1988, s 18(3).

[8.02] Part 2 of ITTOIA 2005 taxes the profits of a trade wherever it is carried on.¹ This Case charges only annual profits and is therefore not a capital gains tax,² although the width of the definition of trade may make it appear like one at times.

Simon's Taxes B1.401.

¹ ITTOIA 2005, s 6(1). For trades carried on overseas, see infra, § **35.02**.
² On Revenue power to make alternative assessments see *Bye v Coren* [1985] STC 113 and *IRC v Wilkinson* [1992] STC 454, CA.

[8.03] Trade is defined statutorily as including every trade, manufacture, adventure or concern in the nature of trade.¹ Judicial definitions of trade have been given reluctantly. However, in *Erichsen v Last* Brett LJ said, 'Where a person habitually does and contracts to do a thing capable of producing profit and for the purpose of producing profit, he carries on a trade or business.'² More recently Lord Reid said in *Ransom v Higgs* that the word 'is commonly used to denote operations of a commercial character by which the trader provides to customers for reward some kind of goods or services,' and in the same case Lord Wilberforce said, 'Trade normally involves the exchange of goods or services for reward . . . there must be something which the trade offers to provide by way of business. Trade moreover presupposes a customer'.³ Other judges have suggested that what amounts to a commercial deal is a trade and therefore caught by Part 2 of ITTOIA 2005⁴ while others again have asked what the operation is if it is not trade, to which the answer that it is investment will be sufficient if that can be established.

Simon's Taxes B1.1401.

¹ TA 1988, ss 831, 832. On the relations between the last words and the nouns, see *Johnston v Heath* [1970] 3 All ER 915, 46 TC 463.
² (1881) 8 QBD 414 at 420, 4 TC 422 at 425.
³ [1974] 3 All ER 949 at 955, per Lord Reid, and per Lord Wilberforce, at 964.
⁴ Lord Radcliffe in *Edwards v Bairstow and Harrison* [1955] 3 All ER 48 at 58, 36 TC 207 at 230.

[8.04] The question whether there is a trade, as defined, is one of fact. This means that it is for the Commissioners not only to determine the primary facts, such as what transactions were carried out, when, by whom and with what purpose, but also to conclude that the transaction was or was not a trade as defined.¹ Although this conclusion is an inference it is usually treated as one of fact. Where the findings are inconsistent it is for the court to judge.²

It should be remembered that it is not always to the advantage of the Revenue to argue that a particular transaction is an adventure in the nature of trade, since losses resulting from an adventure may be eligible for loss relief.³

Simon's Taxes B1.1402.

---

[1] *Leeming v Jones* [1930] 1 KB 279, 15 TC 333, CA; affd sub nom *Jones v Leeming* [1930] AC 415, 15 TC 333, HL; *Hillerns and Fowler v Murray* (1932) 17 TC 77.
[2] *Simmons v IRC* [1980] STC 350, [1980] 2 All ER 798.
[3] *Stott v Hoddinott* (1916) 7 TC 85 but cf *Lewis Emanuel & Son Ltd v White* (1965) 42 TC 369.

Liability—who is trading?

[8.05] The trade must be carried on by the person whom it is sought to charge; the tax is levied on the trader and not on the transactions. Hence if an individual carries out three transactions each with a different partner, it is possible to conclude that in view of the frequency of the transactions he was carrying on a trade but that his partners were not.[1] The boundary between enabling someone else to carry on a business and carrying it on oneself is a fine one.[2] On partnerships, see infra, § **8.60**.
Simon's Taxes B1.405.

---

[1] *Pickford v Quirke* (1927) 13 TC 251; *Marshall's Executors v Joly* [1936] 1 All ER 851, 20 TC 256.
[2] *Alongi v IRC* [1991] STC 517.

[8.06] Where no profit accrues to the person by whom the trade is carried on no charge can be made on that person.

In *Ransom v Higgs*[1], land was owned by a company owned by H and his wife. H agreed to a scheme by which the company developed the land and paid the profits to a discretionary trust. It was held that the trade of developing the land was not carried on by H. As Lord Reid put it, 'He did not deal with any person. He did not buy or sell anything. He did not provide anyone with goods or service for reward. He had no profits or gains'.[2] There was no evidence that the trade carried on by the company was in fact carried on by H. H had not compelled but merely persuaded the company to conduct a trading operation and so could not be said to be the trader.

In deciding who is trading the court looks to the facts. In *Smart v Lowndes*[3] a half share in land owned by the taxpayer's wife was held to be the taxpayer's trading stock. Where a trading operation is carried out by a company there is authority for the view that the gain realised on the sale of shares in the company can be a trading receipt: *Associated London Properties Ltd v Henriksen*.[4] Although the Court of Appeal was clear that the decision turned on its facts, it is not completely clear what these facts were. If the facts had been that the new company was simply the agent of its owners so that in fact the trade was carried on by them and not by the company, the case could be treated as just a useful illustration of a general principle; however the case appears to involve a fine disregard of the separate legal personality of the company. The decision has not been much used by the Revenue despite its potentialities to counter tax avoidance.

Simon's Taxes B1.404.

1. [1974] STC 539, [1974] 3 All ER 949, see Twitley, [1974] BTR 335
2. [1974] STC 539 at 545, [1974] 3 All ER 949 at 955.
3. [1978] STC 607 narrowing still further *Williams v Davies* [1945] 1 All ER 304, 26 TC 371.
4. (1944) 26 TC 46, distinguished in *Fundfarms Development Ltd v Parsons* [1969] 3 All ER 1161, 45 TC 707.

Distinction between (1) trade and (2) profession or vocation

[8.07] Part 2 of ITTOIA 2005 also charges income tax on the profits of any profession or vocation. Neither term is defined. The term profession involves the idea of an occupation requiring either purely intellectual skill, or of manual skill controlled, as in painting and sculpture or surgery, by the intellectual skill of the operator; such an occupation is distinct from one which is substantially the production or sale or arrangements for the production or sale of commodities.[1] So a journalist and editor carries on a profession but a newspaper reporter carries on a trade.[2] The question is one of fact and degree and the crux is the degree of intellectual skill involved. So one who ran a service for taxpayers seeking to recover overpaid tax or to reduce assessments was held by the Commissioners to be carrying on a trade and the Court of Appeal felt there was no error of law.[3]

A vocation is analogous to a calling, a word of great signification meaning the way in which a man passes his life.[4] A dramatist,[5] a racing tipster[6] and a jockey[7] have all been held to be carrying on a vocation but not a perennial gambler[8] nor a film producer.[9]

Where an individual is carrying on a profession, the assessment on the profits of that profession will encompass profits on transactions that are closely linked to the professional activity, even though the transactions, if undertaken on their own, would be the carrying on of a trade. In *Wain v Cameron*[10] Professor Wain had carried on the profession of a writer for at least 33 years. Professor Wain then sold Edinburgh University Library manuscripts and working papers for his books, retaining the copyright. The court held that the gain made on the sale of the documents arose from the profession of author carried on by the taxpayer and, hence, were part of the undivided professional business carried on by the taxpayer.

Simon's Taxes B8.301, 302.

1. *IRC v Maxse* [1919] 1 KB 647 at 656, 12 TC 41 at 61.
2. [1919] 1 KB 647 at 656, 12 TC 41 at 61.
3. *Currie v IRC* [1921] 2 KB 332, 12 TC 245. Other traders include a stockbroker: *Christopher Barker & Sons v IRC* [1919] 2 KB 222; and a photographer: *Cecil v IRC* (1919) 36 TLR 164.

[4] Per Denman J in *Partridge v Mallandaine* (1886) 18 QBD 276 at 278, 2 TC 179 at 180.
[5] *Billam v Griffith* (1941) 23 TC 757.
[6] *Graham v Arnott* (1941) 24 TC 157.
[7] *Wing v O'Connell* [1927] IR 84.
[8] *Graham v Green* [1925] 2 KB 37, 9 TC 309.
[9] *Asher v London Film Productions Ltd* [1944] 1 All ER 77, [1944] KB 133.
[10] [1995] STC 555. In *Salt v Fernandez* [1997] STC (SCD) 271, the Special Commissioner distinguished between the profession being carried on by Dr Salt as an author and the trade of publishing, which was also carried on by Dr Salt. Cash accounts were accepted for the former but earnings accounts required for the latter.

[8.08] For a few specific purposes only, it is necessary to distinguish between a profession and a trade:

(1) the provisions of ITTOIA 2005, Pt 2, Ch 11A (the provisions that codified the rule in *Sharkey v Wernher*) do not apply to professions;[1]
(2) an isolated transaction may be an adventure in the nature of trade, but income from an isolated service cannot be taxed as professional income.[2]
(3) exemption from CGT for compensation for personal injury is confined to professions and vocations.[3]

[1] Infra, § **8.154**.
[2] It cannot fall within Part 2 of ITTOIA 2005 but can be treated as "miscellaneous income"; see Chapter 12.
[3] TCGA 1992, s 51(2).

Is there a trade?

Illegality

[8.09] The question whether the profits of an illegal trade are taxable has produced conflicting dicta but the answer clearly ought to be, and on balance of authority now is, yes.[1] It was decided in *Partridge v Mallandaine*[2]. that a bookmaker's profits were taxable notwithstanding that wagering contracts were unlawful, and in *Lindsay, Woodward and Hiscox v IRC*[3] that profits of illegal contracts were taxable. These cases merely decide however that the profits of a contract which the law will not enforce are nonetheless taxable. No such explanation can be advanced for the decision of the Privy Council in *Minister of Finance v Smith*[4] that the profits of illegal brewing during the prohibition era were taxable. Today the true principle is that the taxpayer cannot set up the unlawful character of his act against the Revenue.[5]

The profits from a criminal activity, carried on consistently, are profits of a trade. Thus, in *Forbes v Director of the Assets Recovery Agency*,[6] an assessment was upheld charging income tax on the profits made by Michael

[8.09] Income from trades, professions and vocations

Forbes in obtaining money by deception. The decision of the Court of Appeal in 1990 in *IRC v Aken*[7] suggests that the approach of the Court today would be to recognise any organised activity as potentially constituting a trade, even if the activity is criminal or contracts entered into are legally void. Any other conclusion may lead to distinctions between acts illegal per se and acts which are merely incidental to the carrying on of a trade. There may be difficulty in calculating profits[8] as there is a civil obligation to restore the goods to their owner and it should be remembered that a consistently unprofitable trade may not be a trade at all.

On the prohibition of the deduction of payments[9] which amount to criminal offences see supra, § **3.16**.

Simon's Taxes B1.420.

---

[1] *IRC v Aken* [1988] STC 69, (prostitution a trade); affd [1990] STC 497, CA.
[2] (1886) 18 QBD 276, 2 TC 179
[3] (1933) 18 TC 43.
[4] [1927] AC 193.
[5] *Southern v AB* [1933] 1 KB 713, 18 TC 59; *Mann v Nash* [1932] 1 KB 752, 16 TC 523; contra *Hayes v Duggan* [1929] IR 406.
[6] [2007] STC (SCD) 1. This counters the previous statement by Lord Sands in *Lindsay v IRC* (1932) 18 TC 43 at 56.
[7] [1990] STC 497, CA.
[8] ITTOIA 2005, s 55 (income tax) and TA 1988, s 577A (corporation tax) deny a deduction for a payment, the making of which constitutes the commission of a criminal offence. When computing, for tax purposes, the profits of the trade of burglary, a distinction needs to be made between expenditure (such as the purchase of a jemmy) which, of itself, is lawful and which can be deducted in the computation and expenditure (such as a payment to an accomplice to force open a safe) which is not lawful and which cannot be deducted for tax purposes.
[9] A fine on a taxpayer is not a deductible expense: *IRC v Alexander von Glehn & Co Ltd* [1920] 2 KB 553, 12 TC 232.

The badges of trade

[8.10] The question whether there is a trade or an adventure in the nature of trade is one of fact.[1] What follows is an attempt to synthesise the many cases and to indicate not only what factors the courts take into account but also the frail nature of those factors.

It is often necessary to decide whether transactions are properly regarded as acquisitions and disposals of investments (and, hence, generally subject to capital gains tax) or whether they are incidents in the conduct of a trade (and, hence, generally subject to income tax).[2] The approach that the courts have found most useful in making this distinction is to consider what have become known as the "badges of trade". The Royal Commission of 1955[3] listed six "badges of trade":

First badge –	the subject-matter of the realisation.
Second badge –	the length of period of ownership.
Third badge –	the frequency or number of similar transactions by the same person.
Fourth badge –	supplementary work on or in connection with the property realised.
Fifth badge –	the circumstances that were responsible for the realisation.
Sixth badge –	motive.

These badges are principally important in determining what is an adventure in the nature of trade. In considering the borderline between an employee and a self-employed independent contractor, Lightman J said: 'There are a number of badges of one or other of the relationships, these badges depending on the context may carry greater or lesser weight. The proper course for the court in each case, no doubt after first identifying the individual badges of potential significance, is to form an overall view giving due weight to the relative significance of the various badges in the particular context.'[4]

In 2002, in *Rosemoore Investments v Inspector of Taxes*[5] the Special Commissioner examined the company's activities under consideration by reference to nine badges of trade:[6]

First badge–	a one off transaction can be an adventure in the nature of trade but the lack of repetition points towards there being no trade.
Second badge–	a transaction related to the trade of the taxpayer is more likely to be a trade.
Third badge–	the nature of the subject matter may be a valuable pointer.
Fourth badge–	the way in which the transaction was carried through.
Fifth badge–	the source of finance.
Sixth badge–	whether work was done on the object purchased for resale.
Seventh badge–	whether the object purchased for resale was broken down into lots.
Eighth badge–	whether the purchaser intended to resell at the time of purchase.
Ninth badge–	whether the object purchased and resold provided employment or an income pending resale.

The nine badges of trade considered in *Rosemoore* are adopted as a structure for infra, §§ **8.12–8.24** below.

---

[1] In *Rangatira Ltd v IRC* [1997] STC 47, the Privy Council overturned the New Zealand Court of Appeal, which had endeavoured to substitute its own finding of fact as to whether the taxpayer had been trading. The Privy Council restored the decision at the first instance, where the evidence on which the finding of fact was based was given to the hearing.

[8.10] Income from trades, professions and vocations

2   For a company, both gains on investment and trading are subjected to corporation tax, but the manner of calculation is determined as to whether the transactions are investment transactions or trading transactions.
3   1955 Cmd 9474 para 116.
4   *Barnett v Brabyn* [1996] STC 716 at 724c.
5   [2002] STC (SCD) 325.
6   [84] to [91], 345c to 346f.

[8.11] An intention to make a profit is not a necessary ingredient of a trade but its presence helps to establish a trading transaction.[1] Operations of the same kind as, and carried out in the same way, as those which characterise ordinary trading are not the less trading operations because they make a loss or there is no intention to make a profit.[2] However, a scheme which inevitably involves a loss may not be a trading transaction.[3] So losses on loan transactions with no commercial element in them have been disallowed.[4] Once however one gets beyond cases which have no commercial purpose it is important to pay attention to actions rather than to words. In *Ensign Tankers (Leasing) Ltd v Stokes* the House of Lords held that the investment of funds in the production of a film was a trading transaction even though much of the motivation was to obtain a tax advantage. The transaction was not a sham and could have resulted in either a profit or a loss; there was real expenditure of real money.[5] In the Court of Appeal it had been held that there was an intention to gain a fiscal advantage. In such circumstances the Court of Appeal required the Commissioners to weigh the fiscal elements against the non-fiscal to decide whether the transaction was entered into (a) for essentially commercial purposes but in a fiscally advantageous form, or (b) essentially for the purpose of obtaining a fiscal advantage under the guise of a commercial transaction.[6] However, in the House of Lords Lord Templeman said, surely correctly, that neither the Commissioners nor the courts were competent or obliged to decide such issues.[7]

Lord Templeman said of *FA and AB Ltd v Lupton* that there the tax avoidance scheme negatived trading because on the true analysis of the transaction the trader did not trade at all; there was neither profit nor loss. The House in that case had not addressed the problem of what was to happen where, as in *Ensign* itself, there was actual expenditure.[8]

Simon's Taxes B1.404.

1   *Torbell Investments Ltd v Williams* [1986] STC 397.
2   See Lord Reid in *J P Harrison (Watford) Ltd v Griffiths* (1960) 40 TC 281; affd sub nom *Griffiths v J P Harrison (Watford) Ltd* [1962] 1 All ER 909, 40 TC 281, and cases there cited. See also *Building and Civil Engineering Holidays Scheme Management Ltd v Clark* (profit but not trading) (1960) 39 TC 12. A related issue is whether a particular transaction carried out by one who clearly is trading forms part of the trade even though a loss must result.
3   *FA and AB Ltd v Lupton* [1971] 3 All ER 948, 47 TC 580.
4   *Overseas Containers Finance Ltd v Stoker* [1989] STC 364, CA.
5   *Ensign Tankers (Leasing) Ltd v Stokes* [1992] STC 226 at 243j.
6   Browne-Wilkinson V-C in *Ensign Tankers (Leasing) Ltd v Stokes* [1991] STC 136 at 147–149.

⁷ [1992] STC 226 at 241.
⁸ [1992] STC 226 at 236.

[8.12] One must distinguish a trade from a merely charitable endeavour. In *Religious Tract and Book Society of Scotland v Forbes*,[1] the question was whether colportage, that is the sending out of colporteurs whose job was to sell Bibles and to act as cottage missionaries, was a trade. The Court of Exchequer (Scotland) ruled that the activity, which could not possibly be carried on at a profit, could not be a trade, with the result that the losses on colportage could not be set off against what were undoubtedly trading profits from the society's book shops. It would therefore appear that while the impossibility of profit will prevent the activity from being a trade, the absence of a profit motive will not.

Where numerous operations are undertaken and the activities are intertwined, it is necessary to look at the activities as a whole to decide whether or not a trade is carried on.[2]

If there is an intention to make a profit but then to apply it in some worthy way, there is a trading activity. The tax system is concerned with the acquisition and not with the distribution of profit.[3]

Simon's Taxes B1.416; C5.122, 523.

[1] (1896) 3 TC 415.
[2] *British Olympic Association v Winter* [1995] STC (SCD) 85.
[3] *Mersey Docks and Harbour Board v Lucas* (1883) 8 App Cas 891, 2 TC 25.

First badge of trade—repeated actions

[8.13] The frequency of transactions is only one factor; an investor is still an investor even though he changes his investments. In *J. Bolson & Son Ltd v Farrelly* where the taxpayer company ran a passenger service but bought a large number of boats in a short time for the service and resold them after modification, Harman J agreed that the Commissioners' finding that there was a trade was inevitable. He said, 'A deal done once is probably not an activity in the nature of trade, though it may be. Done three or four times it usually is. Each case must depend on its own facts.'[1]

However, while it is clear that repeated transactions may support the inference of a trade and that an isolated transaction many nonetheless be an adventure in the nature of trade, there is also authority that where a transaction is repeated the court may use that fact to place the label of trade on to the original transaction. In *Leach v Pogson*[2] the taxpayer had set up a driving school in early 1954; the business was incorporated. In December 1955 he transferred it to a newly formed company in return for cash and shares. He subsequently started other schools which he likewise transferred to companies. It was agreed that he was liable to income tax on the profits from the subsequent transactions but the taxpayer argued that he was not liable in respect of the profit on the first. It was held that he was so liable and that the subsequent transactions could be used to support that conclusion. It is probably of great importance that in that case, while he had no intention of embarking upon the business of establishing and selling motoring schools when the first one was set up, he did have that intention before he sold it. The case would thus appear to be correctly decided although perhaps more appropriately dealt with as a case of a change in the character of the transaction.

Simon's Taxes B8.112; B1.405.

[1] (1953) 34 TC 161 at 167. See also *Foulds v Clayton* (1953) 34 TC 382 at 388. Likewise *Pickford v Quirke* (1927) 13 TC 251.
[2] (1962) 40 TC 585.

[8.14] A fast buck is the essence of a deal. A long period between the acquisition of an asset and its disposal may corroborate an intention to hold it as an investment.[1] Conversely, a quick sale invites a scrutiny of the evidence to see whether the acquisition was with that intent.[2] One element of an investment is that the acquirer intends to hold it at any rate for some time, with a view to obtaining either some benefit in the way of income in the meantime or obtaining some profit, but not an immediate profit by resale.[3] In *Eames v Stepnell Properties Ltd*[4] the Commissioners' finding that there was no trade was reversed by the courts. Land subject to zoning for school use in the county development plan was held by a firm of civil engineers and building contractors. The firm had agreed in principle to sell it to the council, but then sold it at its agricultural value (£2,100) to the taxpayer company which was intended to be an investment company. About that time the basis for valuation in compulsory purchase cases was altered from existing use to market value. After much delay in obtaining a ruling from the Minister as to alternative development, a matter crucial to valuation, the land was sold to the county council for £50,000. As Harman LJ put it:[5]

> This sort of property is not of any use to a building company nor can it be described as a form of investment of any sort for as it was, and without purchase by the county council it was a mere piece of agricultural land yielding about 2% on its price . . . This . . . was land earmarked for sale, and earmarked for sale at a profit.

However, while an asset acquired on a short-term basis[6] will often be the subject of an adventure, it does not follow that this will always be so. Thus in *IRC v Reinhold*[7] the taxpayer admitted that he acquired the property with the intention of reselling it and that he had instructed his agents to sell whenever a suitable opportunity arose. The land was sold after three years. This isolated transaction escaped income tax. Much more doubtful, however, is the decision of Danckwerts J in *McLellan, Rawson & Co Ltd v Newall*[8] in which the Commissioners' decision that there was a taxable profit was reversed, even though the taxpayer had entered into an arrangement to sell the woodlands while he was still negotiating for their purchase.

Simon's Taxes B1.431, 432.

[1] Per Donovan J in *Harvey v Caulcott* (1952) 33 TC 159 at 164.

² Per Cross J in *Turner v Last* (1965) 42 TC 517 at 522-3.
³ Per Buckley J in *Eames v Stepnell Properties Ltd* (1966) 43 TC 678 at 692.
⁴ [1967] 1 All ER 785, 43 TC 678.
⁵ At 794 and 701.
⁶ eg *Wisdom v Chamberlain*; infra, § **8.18**.
⁷ (1953) 34 TC 389.
⁸ (1955) 36 TC 117.

Second badge of trade—other activities of the taxpayer

[8.15] Where a single transaction is involved and is of a nature close to, but separate from, what is undoubtedly a trade carried on by an individual, it is likely that the courts will conclude that the transaction is an adventure in the nature of a trade.¹ In *T Beynon & Co Ltd v Ogg*² where the company acted as agents for the purchase of wagons and bought some on their own account, the profits on the resale of those wagons were held taxable, as they were in *Cape Brandy Syndicate v IRC*³ where South African brandy was acquired for blending and resale in this country by three persons who happened to be members of certain firms engaged in the wine trade. In these cases the taxpayer was held assessable on the profits of the adventure in the nature of trade, but the profits did not form part of his general trading activities, but rather a distinct taxable source.

The second way in which the individual may become important is if he possesses some special skill. There is some authority that if a person has a skill and makes money by it, the profit is more likely to be taxable⁴ but today the absence of a skill appears to be neutral.⁵

The third way in which the individual may become important is his conduct in carrying out the activity he claims to be a trade. In *Wannell v Rothwell*⁶ the taxpayer claimed loss relief on the basis that his buying and selling of shares amounted to a trade. Accepting the finding of fact by the Special Commissioners, in the High Court it was accepted that the taxpayer was not buying shares to hold them as investments but that he aimed at a quick turnover at a profit. On this basis, the taxpayer was regarded as trading. The fact that he had no customers and always dealt as the customer of a broker, did not conflict with this finding of fact. However, loss relief was denied to the taxpayer in this particular case as the Special Commissioner held that the trade was not conducted on a commercial basis, the evidence given was that the taxpayer was less than attentive to share price movements and the manner in which he conducted his trade was not that which would have been employed by one who was acting solely with the view to profit.

Simon's Taxes B1.405.

¹ Per Lord Normand in *Cayzer and Irvine & Co v IRC* (1942) 24 TC 491 at 496.
² (1918) 7 TC 125.
³ [1921] 2 KB 403, 12 TC 358.
⁴ Per Scott LJ in *Smith Barry v Cordy* (1946) 28 TC 250 at 260 but doubts as to the correctness of this decision were raised in *Ransom v Higgs* [1974] STC 539, [1974] 3 All ER 949.

⁵ Per Goff J in *Johnston v Heath* [1970] 3 All ER 915 at 921.
⁶ [1996] STC 450.

Third badge of trade—nature of the subject matter

[8.16] Second, if the object does not yield income but can be enjoyed in kind so that there is pleasure or even pride in its possession,¹ as where a person buys a picture for purposes of aesthetic enjoyment, any profit on resale will escape income tax. Conversely, the purchase of a commodity which gives no such pleasure and which cannot be turned to account except by a process of realisation, may well give rise to a taxable profit.² Examples of this turn not only on the nature of the commodity, such as the railway wagons in *Gloucester Railway Carriage and Wagon Co Ltd v IRC*³ but also on the quantity as in *Rutledge v IRC*⁴ where there were one million rolls of lavatory paper; however, as always, these are questions of fact and it was important also that the taxpayer had no intention other than to resell the property at a profit.⁵

Land is another asset which can easily yield taxable profits.⁶ If one owns a house and lives in it, the house is unlikely to be trading stock. However, occupation is not conclusive and courts are reluctant to disturb a finding by the Commissioners that there was an adventure in the nature of trade. In *Page v Pogson*⁷ the taxpayer had built a house for himself and his wife and then sold it six months after completing it. He then built another house nearby but had to sell it when his job was moved from the South to the East of England. He was held taxable on the profits of the sale of the second house and Upjohn J felt himself unable to reverse that finding although doubting whether he would have reached that decision himself.

Simon's Taxes B1.405.

¹ See Lord Normand in *IRC v Fraser* (1942) 24 TC 498; quaere how a trust can enjoy such an object-in which case one should consider the liability of pension funds which purchase pictures.
² Consider the tax position of unit holders in trusts which are to make investments in commodities as distinct from in companies producing commodities.
³ [1925] AC 469, 12 TC 720.
⁴ (1929) 14 TC 490 and see also *Martin v Lowry* (44 million yards of aeroplane linen), [1927] AC 312, 11 TC 297.
⁵ *Mamor Sdn Bhd v Director General of Inland Revenue* [1985] STC 801 at 806, PC.
⁶ Infra, § 23.29.
⁷ (1954) 35 TC 545; cf *Sharpless v Rees* (1940) 23 TC 361 and *Shadford v H Fairweather & Co Ltd* (1966) 43 TC 291.

Fourth badge of trade—the manner of the transaction

[8.17] The number of steps taken to dispose of the asset is a fragile indicator of a trade.¹ The purchase of goods in bulk and their resale in smaller quantities is the essence of a wholesale-retail trading operation. So in *Cape Brandy*

*Syndicate v IRC*² one of the factors in favour of a trade was that the brandy was disposed of in some 100 transactions spread over 18 months. On the other hand, the fact that a large number of disposals of land occurred did not make them trading transactions in *Hudsons Bay Co Ltd v Stevens*.³

Conversely, a single disposal can nonetheless amount to an adventure in the nature of trade.⁴

Simon's Taxes B1.405.

---

1 Per Lord Russell in *IRC v Reinhold* (1953) 34 TC 389 at 395.
2 [1921] 2 KB 403 at 417, 12 TC 368, at 376. For another example *Martin v Lowry* (1926) 11 TC 297 at 320.
3 (1909) 5 TC 424.
4 eg *T Beynon & Co Ltd v Ogg* (1918) 7 TC 125.

Fifth badge of trade—source of finance

[8.18] In *Wisdom v Chamberlain*¹ the taxpayer had assets worth between £150,000 and £200,000. Fearing that sterling might be devalued his accountant concluded that silver bullion would be a suitable hedge and tried to buy £200,000's worth. However, the brokers would only sell £100,000 worth, a transaction which was financed on a loan from the brokers of £90,000 at 3% above bank rate. Five months later the accountant managed to get £200,000 worth of bullion from the brokers on the basis that the original purchase would be repurchased by the brokers, at a loss to the taxpayer of £3,000. The new deal was financed by loans of £160,000 from a bank and £40,000 from the brokers, both for a maximum period of one year and at high rates of interest. The brokers were under an obligation to buy back for £210,000 within a certain period. Between October 1962 and January 1963 the bullion was disposed of at a profit of £48,000 after deducting interest payment of £7,000.

The Commissioners held that this was a transaction in the nature of trade and the Court of Appeal held that they were amply justified in reaching that conclusion. For Harman LJ this was 'a transaction entered into on a short term basis for the purpose of making a profit out of the purchase and sale of a commodity and if that is not an adventure in the nature of trade I do not really know what it is'.² Salmon LJ observed that if the taxpayer had realised his other assets and used the proceeds to finance the purchase of the silver the case might have been quite different. The facts of the case however presented a trading adventure—"and a very sensible and successful one. I for my part cannot see that it is any the less a trading adventure because you describe it as something to offset the loss incurred by a fall in the value of sterling or as a hedge or insurance against devaluation".³

Simon's Taxes B1.405.

---

1 [1969] 1 All ER 332, 45 TC 92; cf *Marson v Morton* [1986] STC 463.

² [1969] 1 All ER 332 at 336, 45 TC 92 at 106.
³ [1969] 1 All ER 332 at 339, 45 TC 92 at 108.

Sixth badge of trade—work done

[8.19] The presence of an organisation through which the disposal of the asset is carried out is one of the hallmarks of a trade, not least because the expenses of such an organisation will be deductible in computing the net profit on the deal.[1] Equally another factor in deciding whether or not a trade has been discontinued is whether the trade organisation has ceased to exist in an identifiable form.[2] However, the presence or absence of an organisation is anything but conclusive in deciding whether or not there has been an adventure in the nature of trade. As Lord Wilberforce said in *Ransom v Higgs*: 'Organisation as such is not a principle of taxation, or many estimable ladies throughout this country would be imperilled'.[3] Thus in *West v Phillips*[4] where the taxpayer built certain houses for letting and subsequently set up an estate agency business run by a separate company for the purposes of selling the houses that action was regarded as simply a convenient method of realising investment property consisting of a large number of component parts. On the other hand, in *Hudson v Wrightson*[5] where the appellant was a retired druggist who had bought some houses and later sold them but had never had an office or staff, the Commissioners concluded that there was a trade and their decision was not reversed.

Simon's Taxes B1.425.

[1] Lord Radcliffe in *Edwards v Bairstow and Harrison* [1955] 3 All ER 48 at 58, 36 TC 207 at 230.
[2] *Andrew v Taylor* (1965) 42 TC 557.
[3] [1974] 3 All ER 949 at 966; note extra-statutory concession C4.
[4] (1958) 38 TC 203 at 213; see also *Rand v Alberni Land Co* (1920) 7 TC 629.
[5] (1934) 26 TC 55. Cf *Bradshaw v Blunden* (1956) 36 TC 397.

Seventh badge of trade—breaking the purchase into lots

[8.20] The alteration of the asset by the taxpayer may suggest that there is an adventure in the nature of trade. So if a purchaser were to carry through a manufacturing process which changed the character of the article, as where pig-iron is converted into steel, there is likely to be a trade, but merely to put the asset into a condition suitable for a favourable sale, such as cleaning a picture or giving a boat a general overhaul, would not suggest a trade. In the case from which these illustrations are taken, *IRC v Livingston*,[1] the taxpayer, a ship repairer, together with a blacksmith and a fish salesman's employee, purchased a cargo vessel which they converted into a steam drifter and then sold without themselves using it for fishing. The alterations took nearly four months and were carried out by two of the three for wages. The Court of Session held that the profit was taxable.

The mere enhancement of value, as by obtaining planning permission,[2] is not sufficient nor will be the normal use of the asset. So whereas the planting of rubber trees did not indicate a trade in *Tebrau (Johore) Rubber Syndicate Ltd v Farmer*,[3] the blending of brandy in the *Cape Brandy Syndicate* case did.[4]

Jenkinson v Freedland[5] must be regarded as a most unusual case. There the taxpayer bought two stills which were coated with a resinous substance and succeeded in removing it by a process of his own devising. It was held that there was no trade on the particular facts but this turns largely on the eventual sale of the stills by the taxpayer to his own company.

Simon's Taxes B1.431.

[1] 1927 SC 251, 11 TC 538.
[2] *Taylor v Good* [1974] STC 148, [1974] 1 All ER 1137.
[3] (1910) 5 TC 658.
[4] [1921] 2 KB 403, 18 TC 358.
[5] (1961) 39 TC 636.

Eighth badge of trade—intention to re-sell

[8.21] The motive attending the acquisition of an asset is a factor which, when there is doubt, is to be thrown into the balance.[1] An acquisition under a relative's last will and testament is clearly different from a purchase with a view to speedy re-sale.[2] If the taxpayer embarks on an adventure which has the characteristics of trade his purpose or object cannot prevail over it. But if his acts are equivocal his purpose or object may be very material.[3] So if a bank acquires the shares of a customer who was in difficulties not intending to hold the shares as circulating assets the transaction will be on capital account.[4]

The acquisition of an asset with the intention of making a profit on the resale does not inevitably signify an adventure in the nature of trade since whether a person is hoping to carry out a deal or hoping to make a good investment some capital appreciation is anticipated.[5] The time at which resale is foreseen is of greater importance.

However, if the taxpayer argues that it was not his intention to make a profit through resale the onus is on him to produce some plausible explanation for his purchase, such as that he intended to enjoy the income before reselling.[6] Further, the taxpayer's assertion that he intended to buy an asset for investment purposes, whether as an investment fund for old age or as a hedge against devaluation[7] will not be allowed to stand against other facts. The Revenue thus get the best of both worlds; the taxpayer's state of mind can make up for equivocal acts while unequivocal acts cannot be distorted by intent.[8]

In assessing these matters the case stated must be examined in the round. A finding that the taxpayer had no predetermined intention to sell one property when buying another is only one finding.[9]

If there is no prospect of immediate profit through resale this may suggest that the acquisition is not an adventure in the nature of trade.[10] However, whatever the taxpayer's original intention may have been that may change.

[8.21] Income from trades, professions and vocations

The difficulties in this area are well illustrated by the decision in *Kirkham v Williams*.[11] The General Commissioners found that the taxpayer, a general dealer, bought land for use principally as an office and for storage space for equipment used in his trade. He did not intend to live there nor would all the land be used for the purposes specified. He did intend to carry on certain limited farming activities. Shortly after acquiring the property he applied for planning permission first for an agricultural worker's cottage and when that was unsuccessful for a house for himself. He built the house, moved in and then sold all the land and the house and went off to begin farming.

On these facts the Commissioners held that there was an adventure in the nature of trade. Vinelott J said that this conclusion was consistent with the facts and dismissed the appeal.[12] In the Court of Appeal Ralph Gibson LJ agreed with Vinelott J although not for precisely the same reasons.[13] However, Nourse and Lloyd LJJ allowed the appeal. Nourse LJ said that the acquisition on its own was equivocal and so account had to be taken of purpose; here the development purpose (which had not been found to be a trading purpose) was too subsidiary to outweigh the principal capital purpose. Lloyd LJ said that the subsidiary purpose had not been designated as a trading purpose by the Commissioners; the same went for farming. The Commissioners had therefore not concluded that either subsidiary purpose was a trading purpose and therefore it was not open to them to go against the primary purpose; the transaction was not equivocal. Leave to appeal to the House of Lords was refused.

Simon's Taxes B1.404.

[1] As in *Lucy and Sunderland Ltd v Hunt* [1961] 3 All ER 1062, 40 TC 132 and *West v Phillips* (1958) 38 TC 203.
[2] But distinguish *Pilkington v Randall* (1965) 42 TC 662 where one beneficiary bought the interest of another.
[3] Per Lord Reid in *Iswera v IRC* [1965] 1 WLR 663 at 668.
[4] *Waylee Investment Ltd v Comr of Inland Revenue* [1990] STC 780, PC; see also *Beautiland v Comr of Inland Revenue* [1991] STC 467, PC.
[5] *IRC v Reinhold* (1953) 34 TC 389.
[6] *Reynold's Executors v Bennett* (1943) 25 TC 401.
[7] *Wisdom v Chamberlain*, supra.
[8] eg *Mitchell Bros v Tomlinson* (1957) 37 TC 224.
[9] *Kirkby v Hughes* [1993] STC 76.
[10] Supra, § **8.14**.
[11] [1991] STC 342.
[12] *Cronin (t/a Cronin Driving School) v Customs and Excise Comrs* [1991] STC 333.
[13] [1991] STC 342 at 353.

[8.22] A separate question concerns companies which, as legal persons, have their capacity limited by their objects. The court, in deciding whether there is an adventure or not, may look at the objects of the company,[1] but a statement therein limiting the company's powers to investment is not conclusive against liability to tax on its income.[2] On the other hand, if a company is set up which has the power to purchase land and to turn it to account, such operations are likely to be regarded as trading operations³ and it has been suggested that the mere setting up of a company points to a trading intention because of the implied continuity of the company.⁴

Simon's Taxes B1.405.

1   *Cooksey and Bibbey v Rednall* (1949) 30 TC 514 at 521.
2   *Eames v Stepnell Properties Ltd* [1967] 1 WLR 593, 43 TC 678; affd [1967] 1 All ER 785, 43 TC 678, CA; *Emro Investments Ltd v Aller* (1954) 35 TC 305.
3   *IRC v Reinhold* (1953) 34 TC 389 and see *IRC v Korean Syndicate Ltd* [1921] 3 KB 258, 12 TC 181 and *Ruhamuh Property Co Ltd v FCT* (1928) 41 CLR 1648; see also *Lewis Emanuel & Son Ltd v White* (1965) 42 TC 369.
4   Per Lord Carmont in *IRC v Reinhold* (1953) 34 TC 389.

[8.23] The question of motive reappears in *Clarke v British Telecom Pension Scheme Trustees*,¹ a major case on the taxation of pension schemes. The taxpayers were trustees administering pension schemes and as such were exempt from tax on various forms of investment income including underwriting commissions charged under Chapter 8 of Part 5 of ITTOIA 2005, but not if charged under Part 2.² The Revenue made assessments on the basis that the commissions were chargeable as trading income. On the evidence, their transactions were frequent and with a relative lack of risk that the sub-underwriters would be left with the shares.³ The Commissioners had described the trustees' entry into these arrangements as "habitual, organised, for reward, extensive and business-like".

Having decided that the transactions were, in principle, capable of being as either trading income or within the residual category covered by Pt 5, Ch 8⁴ and having reviewed decided case law on the question of trading,⁵ the Commissioners said: 'in our judgment the crucial factor is motive viewed not only subjectively but objectively in the light of the surrounding circumstances'.⁶ The trustees of the pension scheme were engaged in administering a very substantial portfolio of shares. The Commissioners held that the sub-underwriting that was in question "formed an integral part of the investment process and took its colour therefrom".⁷ The basic investment process carried out by the pension trustees was the subject of the specific statutory exemption,⁸ which extended to transactions within Chapter 8 but not those taxed as trading income. The Commissioners held that the sub-underwriting activities, viewed in this way, did not constitute a trade but fell within what is now Chapter 8 so that the statutory tax exemption was, thus, available.⁹

In the High Court¹⁰ Lightman J analysed the facts found by the Commissioners in a two stage process to determine the question of trading and ruled that the only conclusion which the Commissioners could have reached if properly directed in law was that the pension trustees were trading.¹¹ In the Court of Appeal¹² Robert Walker LJ reviewed the approach taken by the Commissioners and re-established their finding that the transactions are within Case VI and Case I¹³ stating:¹⁴

> The commissioners had a difficult task in determining this important appeal, but they approached their task in a very responsible and thorough manner . . . I

consider that it is rarely helpful for the appellate tribunal (or indeed for the commissioners in their initial evaluation) to divide the process into two stages, as the judge . . . Where there is any element of ambiguity the inquiry must look at all relevant facts and circumstances in the round. A two-stage approach is akin to looking at a video film twice, first with the sound off and then with the sound on . . . These considerations persuade me that there were substantial grounds for the commissioners' conclusion that the sub-underwriting activities did form an integral part of the investment process and took its colour from the process.[15]

It is likely that if these transactions had been carried out by an ordinary individual liability would have arisen under Case I. However, ordinary individuals do not have the same overall investment responsibilities as trustees and one must wait and see whether the higher courts are persuaded that this makes a difference. Rather than considering "motive", the Revenue looks to the "purpose" of a transaction when considering how to tax the profits from a currency swap.[16] An individual, or an unincorporated entity,[17] may use an interest rate swap to reduce risk of sudden change, or a currency swap or another form of credit derivative. In the Revenue's view,[18] receipts or payments under a swap contract form part of the profits assessable as part of a trade where either (a) the swap forms part of the circulating capital of a financial trade being carried on or (b) the swap transaction is ancillary to a trading transaction, such as a swap to hedge borrowing undertaken for trade purposes.[19]

Simon's Taxes E7.233.

---

[1] [2000] STC 222, CA.
[2] TA 1988, s 592(3).
[3] It is true that the underwriting commissions all related to companies in which the trustees held shares but the opportunity to earn those commissions does not seem to have come to them because they owned the shares and this may afford only a slender basis of distinction.
[4] [1998] STC (SCD) 14 at 33j.
[5] [1998] STC (SCD) 14 at 34 to 35.
[6] [1998] STC (SCD) 14 at 36a.
[7] [1998] STC (SCD) 14 at 39a.
[8] TA 1988, s 592(2) and (3).
[9] [1998] STC (SCD) 14 at 39j.
[10] [1998] STC 1075.
[11] [1998] STC 1075 at 1115a to 1117a.
[12] [1998] STC 1075 at 1118h.
[13] [2000] STC 222 CA.
[14] [2000] STC 222 at 235c.
[15] [2000] STC 222 at 234g to 235a and b, 234e.
[16] Inland Revenue Tax Bulletin August 2003, p 1054.
[17] No distinction is necessary for a company or unincorporated association, as transactions in swaps are then dealt with under the loan relationship provisions of FA 1996, whether or not they form part of the trade.
[18] Inland Revenue Tax Bulletin August 2003, p 1055, para 6.
[19] The "purpose" analysis is extended in this Revenue discussion to treat transactions in swaps as subject to tax under ITTOIA 2005, Pt 3 where the swap was taken out of head interest payments which are deductible in computing the profits or losses of

a property business (para 7) and to treat a swap as an investment giving rise to exempt income for a pension scheme where the swap is not held in conjunction with a business activity by the pension scheme (paras 14 to 18). Where a swap is held as an investment, the gain arising on transactions in the swap is assessable under Pt 5, Ch 8. See infra, § **12.06**.

[**8.24**] "Some explanation, such as a sudden emergency or opportunity calling for ready money, negatives the idea that any plan of dealing prompted the original purchase."[1] There are few reported cases in which the point has been successfully made. In *Mitchell Bros v Tomlinson*[2] a decision to sell houses originally bought for letting was motivated by changes in rent control legislation which made letting uneconomic, the rising costs of repairs and the need to realise partnership assets on the death of a partner, but the court held that the only reasonable conclusion was that the trade had commenced before the death of the partner and even before some of the houses had been bought, let alone sold. In *Stott v Hoddinott*[3] an architect was obliged as a term of a contract to take up shares in the company granting him the contract. He subsequently sold those shares in order to provide funds to take up shares under later contracts with other companies. It was held that this was a capital transaction so that he was not entitled to relief in respect of the loss which he sustained.

Simon's Taxes B1.1425.

[1] RC 1955, Cmd 9474, § 115.
[2] (1957) 37 TC 224. See also *Page v Pogson*, supra, § **8.16**.
[3] (1916) 7 TC 85.

Ninth badge of trade—income provided or employment generated

[**8.25**] The courts take the view that some commodities are more likely to be acquired as investments than as the subject of a deal. There are two main groups of examples. Objects recommended for investment in the light of these cases include wine, gold coins and reversionary interests. Antiques and works of art are likewise recommended provided they are retained for some time and not sold by commercial methods.

First, if the object yields income, whether in the form of rent or dividends, that object is more likely to be an investment than is one which yields no income.[1] Where the court can see some fruit, the source of the fruit is likely to be a tree. A subtle case is *Snell v Rosser Thomas & Co Ltd*[2] where the taxpayer, a developer, bought a house and 53/4 acres of land. The house produced rent from tenants but the land produced no income and was therefore stock in trade.

In determining whether or not there is income the court has looked not simply at the flow of money to the taxpayer but also at any outflow. So in *Wisdom v Chamberlain*[3] the interest payments were of importance while in *Cooke v Haddock*[4] rent of £167 a year had to be set against the £320 a year interest.

This approach was questioned in *Marson v Morton*[5] where it was said that it was no longer self-evident that unless land is producing income it cannot be an investment. The legal principle cannot change but life could. "Since the arrival of inflation and high rates of tax on income new approaches to investment have emerged putting the emphasis on the making of capital profits at the expense of income yield".[6]

Property which produces income may none the less be trading stock so that the proceeds of sale must enter a profit and loss account. The question depends on the individual circumstances of the case. Thus stocks and shares bought by a bank in order to make good use of funds in hand and subsequently disposed of in order to finance repayments to depositors are treated as trading stock of the banking business.[7] Equally a company which in addition to building ships ran a passenger service and bought and sold four ships for that service in rapid succession was held taxable on the profits from the resales of the passenger ships.[8]

Simon's Taxes B1.405.

[1] *Salt v Chamberlain* [1979] STC 750.
[2] [1968] 1 All ER 600, 44 TC 343 and consider the factory in *W M Robb Ltd v Page* (1971) 47 TC 465.
[3] [1969] 1 All ER 332, 45 TC 92; supra, § **8.18**.
[4] (1960) 39 TC 64.
[5] [1986] STC 463.
[6] *Marson v Morton* [1986] STC 463 per Browne-Wilkinson V-C at 472.
[7] *Punjab Co-operative Bank Ltd v Amritsar IT Comr Lahore* [1940] 4 All ER 87, [1940] AC 1055; a similar rule applies to insurance companies. *General Reinsurance Co Ltd v Tomlinson* [1970] 2 All ER 436, 48 TC 81 discussed in *General Motors Acceptance Corpn v IRC* [1985] STC 408.
[8] *J Bolson & Son Ltd v Farrelly* (1953) 34 TC 161.

Intermediate company

[8.26] In the building industry and in the computer industry, it has been common practice for an individual to establish a company to receive fees for work undertaken by that individual alone. The customer does not have to apply PAYE as he is paying a company. The company itself applies PAYE (and NIC) only on the amount that is taken out by the individual as remuneration; NIC and employment income can be avoided by taking out funds by means of dividend or by retaining the funds in the company, for ultimate distribution as a capital gain on winding up the company.

In some instances, this arrangement has continued for many years between a single customer and a single individual, with the services of that individual being supplied by his intermediate "personal" company. Particularly in the computer industry, it is not unusual to find a group of people working together where some members of the group are paid under PAYE as employees and some members are supplied by their personal companies, without there being any difference in their hours of work or the working conditions visible to their colleagues.

Is there a trade? [8.26]

The Revenue sought to attack such arrangements by the issue of a "Regulation 29" notice.[1] The situation in the building industry was then targeted by the introduction of the subcontractors scheme[2], which required the payer to deduct tax at basic rate from specified payments to any individuals and companies that did not hold subcontractors' certificates.

From 2000–01 to 2006–07 the imposition of PAYE and Class 1 NIC was achieved by what has become known as "the IR35 rules".[3] The essence of these rules was to extract PAYE and NIC from the intermediate company. These provisions charged PAYE and NIC on (broadly) 95% of the fees received by the intermediate company. The rules operated by considering the relationship between the individual supplied by the intermediate company and its customer. If the relationship between the customer and the individual undertaking the work would have been a contract of employer–employee (supra, § **7.08**), "the IR35 rules" operated and the intermediate company was obliged to operate PAYE and charge Class 1 NIC on the payments it received from the customer, subject to specified deductions.[4]

The "IR35 rules" provided difficulty for the Revenue. A number of cases before the courts were found in favour of the taxpayer[5] and the process of obtaining information proved difficult for the Revenue, as did the problem of determining the terms of a deemed—and, hence, non-existent—contract.

---

[1] So called, as the authority for the direction was reg 29 of SI 1973/334. This has been re-enacted as Income Tax (Employments) Regulations, SI 1993/744, reg 49 and is now found in the Income Tax (Pay As You Earn) Regulations, SI 2003/2682, reg 80.

[2] See TA 1988, ss 559-567, TMA 1970, s 98A and SI 1993/743.

[3] ITEPA 2003, ss 48-61.

[4] For a fuller discussion of the IR35 rules see Tiley & Collison 2006-07 Edition. ITEPA 2003, ss 48-61 have not been revoked. Technically, therefore, it is possible for the IR35 rules to apply after 5 April 2007. However, these provisions are disapplied where the managed service company provisions operate (ITEPA 2003, s 48(2)(*aa*) inserted by FA 2007, Sch 3, para 3). In practice it is difficult to envisage a situation where an intermediate company is within the IR35 rules but is not a managed service company, within the meaning of the new ITEPA 2003, ss 61A-61J.

[5] *Lime-IT Ltd v Justin* [2001] STC (SCD) 189, *Tilbury Consulting v Gittins* [2004] STC (SCD) 72, *Ansell Computer Services v Richardson* [2004] STC (SCD) 472. By contrast, a deemed contract was held to be a contract of employment and, hence, the IR35 rules applied in *Battersby v Campbell* [2001] STC (SCD) 189, *F S Consulting Ltd v McCaul* [2002] STC (SCD) 138, *Synaptek Ltd v Young* [2003] STC (SCD) 15, *Usetech v Young* [2004] STC 1671, *Future Online v Faulds* [2005] STC 198, *Netherlane Ltd v York* [2005] STC (SCD) 305. A case worthy of note is that of *Dragonfly Consulting v R & C Commrs*. The Special Commissioner (as reported at [2007] Sp C 655) reinterpreted the nature of the hypothetical contract and his approach was not overturned on appeal before the High Court (reported at [2008] EWHC 2113 (Ch)).

Managed service company

[8.27] From 6 April 2007, PAYE is payable (and all other provisions relating to taxation of employment income applied)[1] on a "deemed employment payment" by a management service company to the worker.[2]

A "deemed employment payment" is a payment (or/and a benefit) that the worker, or an associate of the worker, receives (from any person) which can reasonably be taken to be in respect of the services provided by the managed service company, where the payment or benefit is not earnings within ITEPA 2003, s 62.[3]

A company is a "managed service company" if:

(a) its business consists wholly or mainly of providing (directly or indirectly) the services of an individual to other persons;
(b) payments are made (directly or indirectly) to the individual (or associates of the individual) of an amount equal to the greater part or all of the consideration for the provision of the services;
(c) the way in which those payments are made would result in the individual (or his associates) receiving payments of an amount (net of tax and national insurance) exceeding that which would be received if every payment in respect of the services were employment income of the individual; and
(d) a person who carries on a business of promoting or facilitating the use of companies to provide the services of individuals ("an MSC provider") is involved with the company.[4]

The provision in (d) is widely drawn. Statute[5] states that an MSC provider is involved with the company if he or an associate:

(a) benefits financially on an ongoing basis from the provision of the services of the individual;
(b) influences or controls the provision of those services;
(c) influences or controls the way in which payments to the individual (or associates of the individual) are made;
(d) influences or controls the company's finances or any of its activities; or
(e) gives or promotes an undertaking to make good any tax loss.

There are limited exemptions. A person is not an MSC provider merely by virtue of providing legal or accountancy services in a professional capacity[6] and the placing of the workers by an employment agency is also excluded.[7]

---

[1] Other than deduction from employment issues and mileage allowance reliefs ITEPA 2003, s 619(3) inserted by FA 2007, Sch 3, para 4.
[2] ITEPA 2003, s 61G(1) inserted by FA 2007, Sch 3, para 4.
[3] ITEPA 2003, s 61D(1) & (2) inserted by FA 2007, Sch 3, para 4.
[4] ITEPA 2003, s 61B(1) inserted by FA 2007, Sch 3, para 4.
[5] ITEPA 2003, s 61B(2) inserted by FA 2007, Sch 3, para 4.
[6] ITEPA 2003, s 61B(3) inserted by FA 2007, Sch 3, para 4.
[7] The Government states that this is the effect of ITEPA 2003, s 61B(4) inserted by FA 2007, Sch 3, para 4, see Finance Bill 2007: Explanatory Notes, March 2007 issued by HM Treasury.

Sales by personal representatives and liquidators

[8.28] A personal representative may be empowered to carry on the deceased's business by the terms of the will, however his acts may nevertheless amount to carrying on a trade whether or not there is such a power.[1] As personal representative his job is to realise the assets of the estate and distribute them among the beneficiaries. There is therefore a presumption that if all he did was to realise the asset in a way advantageous to the estate then he was not carrying on a trade.[2]
Simon's Taxes B1.426.

[1] Weisberg's Executrices v IRC (1933) 17 TC 696.
[2] Per Sargant LJ in Cohan's Executors v IRC (1924) 12 TC 602 at 620; approved by Greene MR in Newbarns Syndicate v Hay (1939) 22 TC 461 at 472.

[8.29] Whether the acts amount to carrying on a trade is a matter of degree and must depend on the nature of the trade, as two cases concerning farming show.

In *Pattullo's Trustees v IRC*[1] the taxpayers were the representatives of a tenant farmer who also carried on the trades of cattle breeder and feeder. The farm and the cattle dealing business were bequeathed specifically so that the only asset to be realised was the feeding business. The deceased died in November at which season the cattle would already be on the land of other farms feeding from it and manuring it. The trustees felt they had to complete these contracts for economic reasons. They also bought more cattle in order to consume the remaining feedstuffs on these farms. The cattle were all sold by the following June. The Commissioners held that the trustees were carrying on the business of cattle feeding and were not simply preparing the assets for sale, even though this was their motive. The Court of Session held that there was evidence to support the Commissioners' finding.

However, in *IRC v Donaldson's Trustees*[2] the Commissioners held there was no trading and their conclusion was supported by the Court of Session. In this case the deceased was a farmer whose sole interest was a pedigree herd of Aberdeen Angus cattle. He died in March 1955 and the trustees were advised to sell the heifer calves in September 1955 and the bull calves in February 1956. This they did but had to keep the cattle alive and well in the meantime. The manager was told that the cattle were to be sold and the farm was rearranged for preparing them for sale instead of grazing and breeding. It was held that the occupation of the farm was simply for the termination of husbandry and there was no trade.

It is thus a question of fact and degree whether the acts amount to the realisation of the asset or to trade.[3] However, if the acts are equally consistent both with the carrying on of a trade and with mere realisation, the act will be mere realisation since to hold otherwise would deprive the executors of their right vis-à-vis the Revenue to realise their testator's assets in the ordinary way.[4] In *Donaldson's Trustees* the personal representatives were able to show a positive change from the normal pattern of farming. In *Pattullo's Trustees* the Revenue could show, by the purchase of extra cattle, a continuation or development of the trade.

Simon's Taxes B1.426.

1   (1955) 36 TC 87.
2   (1963) 41 TC 161.
3   *Wood v Black's Executor* (1952) 33 TC 172.
4   Per Greene MR in *Newbarns Syndicate v Hay* (1939) 22 TC 461 at 476.

[8.30] Where the deceased was carrying on a trade in partnership with others, his executors may insist that on his death the assets should be realised so that they may administer the estate. Where such assets are realised the court may hold that as far as the estate is concerned the process is one of mere realisation as in *Marshall's Executors, Hood's Executors and Rogers v Joly*;[1] it was proved that the executors did not consent to the continuation of the trade but insisted upon their share of the assets. In the absence of such a finding the court will uphold a finding by the Commissioners that there was a continuation of the trade. In *Newbarns Syndicate v Hay*[2] not only did the process of realisation take ten years but the executor attended all partnership meetings as a voting participant, something he was not entitled to do as the mere executor of a deceased member; there was thus an implied agreement to continue the trade.

Simon's Taxes B1.426.

1   [1936] 1 All ER 851, 20 TC 256.
2   (1939) 22 TC 461.

Liquidation

[8.31] The liquidator's duty, like the personal representative's, is to realise the assets.[1] Here too the courts ask the question: what reason is there to suppose that the winding up was done for any purpose other than the normal carrying out of the duties of a liquidator?[2] There is a presumption that a mere disposal is not a trading operation. In *Wilson Box (Foreign Rights) Ltd v Brice*[3] the company was formed to turn patent rights to account. However, no trade of dealing in patents was commenced. During liquidation certain patent rights were sold. The Special Commissioners held that there was a trading operation but the Court of Appeal held that there was no evidence to support this. On the other hand the payment to the liquidator of sums in respect of trading contracts made before the date of liquidation will be trading receipts.[4]

Simon's Taxes B1.425

1   Per Atkin LJ in *IRC v Burrell* [1924] 2 KB 52 at 73, 9 TC 27 at 42. In these cases it is irrelevant that the assets were the trading stock of the company or represented undivided profit.

The same principles apply to trustees holding on an assignment for the benefit of creditors (*Armitage v Moore* [1900] 2 QB 363, 4 TC 199, supplying steam power is trading not realising asset) and to a receiver for debenture holders (*IRC v Thompson* [1936] 2 All ER 651, 20 TC 422).

2   *Wilson Box (Foreign Rights) Ltd v Brice* [1936] 3 All ER 728, 20 TC 736, esp. per Lawrence J at 742, and per Slesser LJ at 747; and per Ungoed-Thomas J, in *John*

Mills Production Ltd v Mathias (1964) 44 TC 441 at 456.
[3] [1936] 3 All ER 728, 20 TC 736].
[4] *IRC v Oban Distillery Co Ltd* (1932) 18 TC 33.

Retirement

[8.32] To dispose of trading stock after announcing one's retirement may well be trading, since the moment when trade ceases is a question of fact. Declarations by the trader are not of themselves decisive. In *J and R O'Kane Ltd v IRC*[1] the taxpayers had carried on the business of wine and spirit merchants. They announced their intention to retire in early 1916 but did not complete the disposal of their stock until late 1917, an operation which was carried out mostly in 1917 and which took the form of many small sales. The only purchases made for the business after the announcement of their retirement were under continuing contracts with distillers. The Special Commissioners held that the trade did not end in early 1916 and that the proceeds of the disposal sales were therefore taxable as the profits of the trade. The House of Lords held that there was abundant evidence for the Commissioners' findings.

Simon's Taxes B1.425.

[1] (1922) 12 TC 303.

[8.33] Problems also arise on the completion of executory contracts entered into before retirement. In *Hillerns and Fowler v Murray*[1] the trade was run by a partnership which was dissolved by lapse of time under the terms of the partnership deed. At that time the partners held trading stock and they acquired other stock after that time under contracts entered into before the dissolution. The trading stock was used to fulfil orders placed by customers before the dissolution but no new contracts whether for purchase or sale were entered into after dissolution. The Commissioners held that there was evidence of trading after the dissolution. Although Rowlatt J reversed their decision, the Court of Appeal held that there was evidence to support their conclusion. The mere declaration by the partners that offices would remain open only for the carrying out of existing contracts could not give them immunity from the Income Tax Acts. The argument was put that this was simply the best way of realising the assets of the partnership. Romer LJ after pointing out that the realisation of the assets to best advantage might involve trading, went on "in most cases, in the winding up of a partnership it is necessary for the proper getting in of the assets and winding up of the affairs of it, to carry on the business for a short time, or to carry on the business to a limited extent".[2] So the presumption that is said to exist that a sale by an executor is a realisation of an asset and not a trading activity, does not apply.

Simon's Taxes B1.425.

[8.33] Income from trades, professions and vocations

¹ (1932) 17 TC 77.
² At 92, and see Lord Hanworth, at 87.

[8.34] Where a trader sells his trade to another, he ceases to trade. Whether his successor, in selling former trading stock commences to trade or simply realises assets is a matter of fact.¹ If the successor is a company which is under some obligation to hand over the whole or part of the profits of the trade to the predecessor, it may be that new owner is simply the agent of the old, so that the former owner does not cease to trade.² An alternative conclusion on the facts may be that the old trade has ceased but the former owner has commenced a new trade through the agency of the new owner.³ The choice between the two solutions is not merely academic since apart from the commencement and cessation provisions there are such questions as unused loss relief and capital allowances which will be lost under the second solution.⁴
Simon's Taxes Division B1.3.

¹ *Lucy and Sunderland Ltd v Hunt* [1961] 3 All ER 1062 at 1066, 40 TC 132 at 139.
² *Baker v Cook* [1937] 3 All ER 509, 21 TC 337.
³ *Southern v Watson* [1940] 3 All ER 439, 23 TC 566; see also *Parker v Batty* (1941) 23 TC 739.
⁴ Infra, § **8.53**.

Mutual trading

[8.35] It is necessary to distinguish a profit from a trade from an excess of contribution over expenditure. If I allow myself £10 a week for housekeeping but spend only £9, no one would contend that the £1 saved was taxable profit. The immunity of the £1 from tax rests on two principles, either of which is sufficient; the one is that no man can trade with himself and the other is that the sum does not represent a profit.

This immunity has been applied to groups of people who combine for a purpose and contribute towards expenses, as in the case of a golf club whose members pay a club subscription. Here too any excess of income from subscriptions over expenses is free from tax.¹ Each member is entitled to a share of the surplus and it is irrelevant that there is only a limited liability to contribute to any deficiency.² Wherever therefore there is identity³ of contributors to the fund and the recipients from the fund, it is impossible that the contributors should derive profits from contributions made by themselves to a fund which could only be expended or returned to themselves.⁴ Even if the club had a bar at which drinks were served at prices which yielded a profit there is no liability to tax since the bar is merely a part of the club, and is open only to members who thus make certain additional contributions to the fund. A different situation arises if the bar is open to the public,⁵ since there is now no identity of contributors to the fund with recipients from it; profits from the bar would be taxable even if the rest of the club ran at a loss. Liability would also arise if the facts showed that the bar was a distinct trading venture separate from the rest of the club.

The mutuality principle has been used to exempt a local authority[6] from liability to tax on its rates but today its scope is limited to mutual insurance companies, institutions like the BBC[7] and members' clubs.[8]

Simon's Taxes B1.436–440.

[1] Carlisle and Silloth Golf Club v Smith [1913] 3 KB 75, 6 TC 48 and 198; dist, Carnoustie Golf Course Committee v IRC 1929 SC 419, 14 TC 498.
[2] Faulconbridge v National Employers Mutual General Insurance Association Ltd (1952) 33 TC 103.
[3] But not equality, per Lord Macmillan in Municipal Mutual Insurance Ltd v Hills (1932) 16 TC 430 at 448; as long as the relationship is reasonable.
[4] See per Lord Normand in English and Scottish Joint Co-operative Wholesale Society Ltd v Assam Agricultural IT Comr [1948] 2 All ER 395 at 400; [1948] AC 405 at 419. IRC v Eccentric Club Ltd [1924] 1 KB 390, 12 TC 657 and Finlay J in National Association of Local Government Officers v Watkins (1934) 18 TC 499 at 506.
[5] Grove v Young Men's Christian Association (1903) 4 TC 613.
[6] See Lord Thankerton in IRC v Forth Conservancy Board [1931] AC 540 at 554, 16 TC 103 at 123; contrast IRC v Stonehaven Recreation Ground Trustees 1930 SC 206, 15 TC 419.
[7] BBC v Johns [1964] 1 All ER 923, 41 TC 471.
[8] Originally FA 1933, s 31.

[8.36] The principle of mutuality applies even though the contributions are made to a separate legal entity,[1] such as a company, so long as the company exists simply for the convenience of its members and as an instrument obedient to their mandate as is the case with members of a mutual insurance company.[2] Income from investments is taxable in the usual way. Any excess of premium income over liabilities will also be the income of the company. However, so long as such income is returnable to the members either in the form of bonuses or by way of reduction of premiums, that income is exempt from tax since although the company is trading[3] this sum is not a profit to its members.[4] Should a member surrender his policy he will lose his entitlement to future bonuses even though he has contributed to them. Likewise if a person becomes a member of the company by taking out a policy he may become entitled to a portion of the surplus contributed by someone else. Such possibilities do not prevent there being mutuality, since the excess of contributions must go back to the policy holders as a class even if not precisely in the proportions in which they have contributed to them.[5]

It is, however, essential that such companies should be mutual companies, that is one where only the policy holders are the members of the company. If the company has shareholders who do not hold life policies but who are entitled to the profits of this business the company is not a mutual company.[6] Today a body corporate—and an unincorporated association—are subject to corporation tax and TA 1988, s 490 ensures that distributions to members will be charged to income tax as dividend income. However, this applies only to distributions out of profits chargeable to corporation tax and so the principle of mutuality remains.

[8.36] Income from trades, professions and vocations

[1] See Rowlatt J in *Thomas v Richard Evans & Co Ltd* [1927] 1 KB 33 at 47, 11 TC 790 at 823.
[2] For criticism, see RC 1955, Cmd 9474, § 22, and [1961] BTR 398.
[3] See Lord Cave in *IRC v Cornish Mutual Assurance Co Ltd* [1926] AC 281 at 286-7, 12 TC 841 at 866-7, criticising Lord Watson in the Styles case, at 393, 471.
[4] See eg Lord Macmillan in *Municipal Mutual Insurance Ltd v Hills* (1932) 16 TC 430 at 448. In *Westbourne Supporters of Glentoran Club v Brennan* [1995] STC (SCD) 137, the Special Commissioners ruled that equality of voting rights is not a basic essential of the mutuality principle. In that particular case, the club had ordinary members and associate members. An associate member has no vote at a general meeting. However, the Special Commissioners commented (at 141g): 'It is clear from oral evidence that associate members . . . are able to make their views known on such important matters as the prices of drinks.' The Special Commissioners ruled that no liability to tax arose from the club's trading with its associate members as this constituted mutual trading in just the same way as applied to trading with ordinary members.
[5] On position of newcomers see Upjohn J in *Faulconbridge v National Employers Mutual General Insurance Association Ltd* (1952) 33 TC 103 at 121 and 124-5.
[6] *Last v London Assurance Corpn* (1885) 10 App Cas 438, 2 TC 100, but see now TA 1988, s 433.

[8.37] The mutuality doctrine is not without its limits. First, as just indicated, it applies only to the mutual dealings between the contributors. Mutual insurance companies are taxable on the ordinary income accruing from transactions with non-members. Thus in *New York Life Insurance Co v Styles*[1] where the House of Lords held that the company was not taxable on its profits from premium income from members' participating policies, it was agreed that the company was taxable on its profits from policies for fixed sums without profits and from its general annuity business with strangers, since they were not members of the company, just as it was taxable on its investment income. Exemption is afforded not to the profits from members but to the non-profit of mutual dealings.

Simon's Taxes B1.436.

[1] (1889) 14 App Cas 381, 2 TC 460; see also *Municipal Mutual Insurance Ltd v Hills* (1932) 16 TC 430, HL.

[8.38] Second, the doctrine applies only if there is genuine mutuality. In *Fletcher v IT Comr*[1] a members' club owned a bathing beach in Jamaica. They permitted guests at certain hotels to use the beach on payment of an entrance fee. The club was clearly taxable on the profits of these fees since they were carrying on a trade with non-members. They then altered their arrangements, abolishing the payment of a fee by the hotel guests and making the hotels voting members of the club.[2] However, each hotel member, like each individual, held only one share. The hotels were, like the individual members, to pay a sum by way of subscription, and in addition a sum which was based on the number of its guests using the beach. The gross receipts were £1,750. The Revenue sought to tax the club on the profit element in the relevant proportion of the hotel membership subscription. Lord Wilberforce said that if mutuality was to have any meaning, although a uniform fee was not essential, "there must be a reasonable relationship, contemplated or in result, between what a member contributed and what, with due allowance for interim benefits of enjoyment, he may expect or be entitled to draw from the fund; between his liabilities and his rights".[3] The great use of the beach made by hotel guests was not sufficient allowance and so the mutuality principle did not apply.

This decision forms the unstated basis for a Revenue interpretation on profits arising from green fees at a golf club. The profit arising from fees paid by a member is not taxable, that from fees paid by a non-member is taxable. Temporary membership will not be enough unless their rights as temporary members are similar to those of full members.[4]

Simon's Taxes B1.440.

[1] [1971] 3 All ER 1185, [1972] AC 414.
[2] An earlier scheme had made the hotels members but without voting rights and it had been held that this scheme failed because the hotels were not truly members.
[3] [1971] 3 All ER 1185 at 1191.
[4] Inland Revenue interpretation RI 84.

[8.39] Third, as *Municipal Mutual Insurance v Hills*[1] showed, not all business between a company and its members is mutual business. A business cannot escape tax on its profits for a year simply because at the end of the year it discovers that all its business has been with its members. A mutual insurance company carries on a trade with its members but its principal function is as a mere entity for the convenience of its members.[2] The mutuality principle is satisfied because nothing belongs to the corporation which is severable from what belongs to the aggregation of individuals.[3] When a company has share capital with a chance of dividends and, to one side of that, dealings with people who happen to be the owners of the share capital affording benefits to those people one by one individually, there is no reason to ignore the incorporation. In *English and Scottish Joint Co-operative Wholesale Society Ltd v Assam Agricultural IT Comr*[4] a company was set up to own and manage a tea estate with the bulk of its produce going to its two shareholders who advanced money by way of loan to be set off against the price due for the tea supplied by the company to its shareholders. It was held that the company had earned profits from dealings with its shareholders and so was taxable. This conclusion could not have been avoided by restricting the company's business to sales to its members.[5] A different result might have been reached if the business had not been incorporated and a different practical result would have been achieved if the price paid for the tea had been fixed so that no profit would have been earned.[6]

Simon's Taxes B1.436.

[1] (1932) 16 TC 430; supra, § **8.34**.
[2] Per Lord Normand in *English and Scottish Joint Co-operative Wholesale Society Ltd v Assam Agricultural IT Comr* [1948] 2 All ER 395 at 399, [1948] AC 405 at 417.

³ Per Rowlatt J in *Liverpool Corn Trade Association Ltd v Monks* (1926) 10 TC 442 at 453. See also Lord Watson in *New York Life Insurance Co v Styles* (1889) 14 App Cas 381 at 393, 2 TC 460 at 471.
⁴ [1948] 2 All ER 395, [1948] AC 405.
⁵ [1948] 2 All ER 395 at 399, [1948] AC 405 at 417.
⁶ At 421, 401 (perhaps by treating the application of profit as a discount reducing the price); see *Pope v Beaumont* [1941] 3 All ER 9, 24 TC 78.

Legislation

[8.40] An attempt was made in 1933[1] to tax the profits of mutual companies from dealings with members by directing that such profits or surplus should be treated as if those transactions were transactions with non-members. Since it was the mutuality of the transaction rather than the fact that it was with a member which gave immunity from taxation, the House of Lords, in a somewhat unimaginative construction of the statute, ruled that even if the transactions had been with non-members they would be exempt from tax and thus deprived the statute of any force.[2] The section remained on the statute book unamended until the pre-consolidation changes of 1987.[3] When such companies became the subject of profits tax in 1937[4] the legislature was more direct and simply taxed the profits of the trade of mutual companies. This more direct approach succeeded until the abolition of profits tax in 1958.[5] Since 1958, the surplus arising from mutual trading has not been subjected to tax.

¹ FA 1933, s 31.
² *Ayrshire Employers Mutual Insurance Association Ltd v IRC* [1946] 1 All ER 637 at 640, 27 TC 331 at 347 note comments in *Fothergill v Monarch Airlines Ltd* [1981] AC 251.
³ See FA 1987, Sch 16, Part III.
⁴ Profits tax originated with the "national defence contribution", which was introduced in 1937-38 and became "excess profits tax": F(No 2)A 1939, s 12. Excess profits tax was drastically reduced by F(No 2)A 1945, s 29 and abolished by FA 1946.
⁵ Profits tax continued until its abolition by FA 1965, s 81, with the introduction of corporation tax as the charge on company profits from 6 April 1965.

[8.41] The exemption from tax afforded by mutual dealings does not operate to prevent certain contributions being claimed as deductions in computing the taxable income of the contributor.[1] Thus a payment to a fire insurance scheme is deductible whether or not the scheme is mutual. If the mutual business then ceases there will be a repayment to the contributor of any surplus, but without any charge to tax so that he can in effect recover more than he has paid.[2] If for example, he made a contribution of £100 and has a marginal tax rate of 50%, he saves the payment of £50 in tax; if the business is wound up and he gets back £100 he is not subject to tax. Without special legislation this device could be used to build up tax free reserves. ITTOIA 2005, s 104 (income tax) and TA 1988, s 491 (corporation tax) now provide that where a body corporate is being wound up or dissolved and a non-taxable sum is paid to one who was allowed to deduct that payment in computing the profits or gains or losses of a trade, profession or vocation, the receipt is treated as a trading receipt of the trade or, if the trade has ceased, as a post-cessation receipt. In deciding whether the receipt is a trading one or post-cessation, technical discontinuances under TA 1988, s 337 (corporation tax)[3] are ignored. In either event the payment is treated as earned income so long as the income from the trade was earned. If it is a post-cessation receipt advantage may be taken of any unrealised losses or capital allowances.

This section applies where the company is being wound up and the receipt is an asset of the corporation or is part of the consideration for the transfer of those assets as part of a scheme of amalgamation or reconstruction or a sum received for the transfer of a right to such asset or such reconstruction.

The section is confined to situations where the mutual business is carried on by a company.

Simon's Taxes B1.439.

---

[1] *Thomas v Richard Evans & Co Ltd* [1927] 1 KB 33, 11 TC 790.
[2] *Stafford Coal and Iron Co Ltd v Brogan* [1963] 3 All ER 227, 41 TC 305, HL.
[3] TA 1988, s 491(4) (corporation tax); the previous reference to deemed discontinuances for income tax purposes in TA 1988, s 113 is no longer necessary.

Use of land and trade

[8.42] Income derived from the exploitation of property is property income rather than trading income.[1] Income arising under this heading which is treated in many ways as if it were a trade is nonetheless not trading income and remains taxable as property income. So income from furnished lettings is taxable as property income.[2] Income from caravan sites where there is both trading and associated letting income can all be treated as trading income.[3]

All farming and market gardening in the UK is taxed as a trade[4] and all farming carried on by any particular person or partnership or body of persons is to be treated as one trade.[5] As from 29 November 1994 the cultivation of short rotation coppice is regarded as farming not forestry.[6]

The occupation of land for purposes other than farming or market gardening managed on a commercial basis and with a view to realisation of profits, is likewise considered a trade:[7] actual occupation is required; granting a licence to someone else to occupy is not enough.[8] Woodlands were subject to a separate regime under Schedule B.[9] The profits arising from a commercial woodland are now outside the charge to income tax and corporation tax.[10] Actual occupation is required for this rule; simply having a licence to fell and remove timber or clear the land for replanting is not enough.[11] In *Jaggers v Ellis*[12] the court upheld a finding of a Special Commissioner that a plantation of Christmas trees did not constitute "woodlands". Hence, the profits are assessable as trading income and not exempt as within the scope of the former Schedule B. Lightman J said:[13]

> As it seems to me, the term 'woodland' connotes a wood, a sizeable area of land to a significant extent covered by growing trees of some maturity, height and size . . .

[8.42] Income from trades, professions and vocations

Whether the tree is on a particular area of land such as to entitle it to be regarded as woodlands is very much a matter of impression and personal judgment for the viewer. He may find it difficult (if not impossible) to give his definition of woodlands as he would of an elephant, but he will know when he has had the pleasurable experience of seeing either. The site with its Christmas trees did not strike the Commissioner as woodlands and would not strike me for a moment, or (I think), anyone acquainted with the English language as a wood or woodlands.

Profits from mines, quarries and other specified concerns including ferries and canals are also to be treated as trading profits.[14]

Simon's Taxes Division B5.2.

---

[1] *Webb v Conelee Properties Ltd* [1982] STC 913.
[2] *Gittos v Barclay* [1982] STC 390.
[3] ITTOIA 2005, s 20. Before 6 April 2005, this was provided for by Extra-statutory concession B29.
[4] ITTOIA 2005, s 9(1) (income tax); TA 1988, s 53(1) (corporation tax). On the scope of market gardening, see *Bomford v Osborne* (1940) 23 TC 642 at 660, especially per Scott LJ. Originally farmers had been within Schedule B, infra, § **10.05**, and remained there partly because of the difficulty farmers had in keeping accounts.
[5] ITTOIA 2005, s 9(2) (income tax); TA 1988, s 53(2) (corporation tax)—hence if X has a farm A with accrued losses and unused capital allowances and buys farm B he may set those losses and allowances against the profits of B even if he later sells A; see *Bispham v Eardiston Farming Co (1919) Ltd* [1962] 2 All ER 376, 40 TC 322 noted [1962] BTR 255. This provision does not appear to apply to market gardening.
[6] ITTOIA 2005, s 876(3) (income tax); FA 1995, s 154 (corporation tax); this is for the purposes of income tax, corporation tax and CGT but not for IHT.
[7] ITTOIA 2005, s 10(1) (income tax); TA 1988, s 53(3) (corporation tax). See *Sywell Aerodrome Ltd v Croft* [1942] 1 All ER 110, 24 TC 126. If the land is not managed on a commercial basis a charge may arise under Pt 5, Ch 8 (income tax) or Schedule D, Case VI (corporation tax), infra, § **12.11**.
[8] *Webb v Conelee Properties Ltd* [1982] STC 913.
[9] TA 1988, s 54.
[10] ITTOIA 2005, ss 11 and 768(1) (income tax); FA 1988, Sch 6, para 3(2).
[11] TA 1988, s 16(6).
[12] [1997] STC 1417.
[13] At 1423j to 1424c.
[14] ITTOIA 2005, s 12 (income tax); TA 1988, s 55 (corporation tax).

Basis of assessment

Continuing business

[8.43] A continuing business that makes up its accounts for a 12-month period is assessable on the tax adjusted trading profits of the period that ends during the fiscal year.[1] Thus, if accounts are consistently made up to

31 January, the basis period for 2005–06 is the year ended 31 January 2006; if accounts are to 30 June, the basis period is the year ended 30 June 2005. This applies whether or not the trade or profession is carried on in the UK. In computing the tax adjusted profits, capital allowances are treated as trading expenses of the accounting period and not for the fiscal year.[2]

Where the taxpayer has suffered overseas taxes, relief is obtained by reference to the overseas tax charged for the period of account that is brought into assessment, not the fiscal year. Thus, if accounts are consistently made up to 30 June, the basis period for 2005–06 is the year ended 30 June 2005 and the overseas tax is that for the period 1 July 2004 to 30 June 2005, not for the period 6 April 2005 to 5 April 2006.

Where a trade or profession is carried on in partnership, each individual partner is treated as if he has commenced a trade at the time he joins the partnership and has ceased that trade at the time he leaves the partnership.[3] However, the individual partner cannot choose his accounting period. This has to be the period to the accounting date of the partnership. A return of income is made for the partnership and this return specifies the basis period and the income arising to each individual partner in respect of that basis period.[4] The individual partner is then required to bring into his individual self-assessment the income for that period. He is not able to make any alteration to the income.[5] Any expenditure he has incurred personally, therefore, in the conduct of the partnership trade, etc, must be brought into the partnership return.

Simon's Taxes B3.106, E1.101, 220.

[1] ITTOIA 2005, s 198(1)
[2] CAA 2001, s 247.
[3] ITTOIA 2005, s 852.
[4] TMA 1970, s 12AA.
[5] TMA 1970, s 8(1B), (1C).

Commencement of trade

[8.44] Where a trade, etc, is commenced, the income assessable for the fiscal year in which the trade is commenced is the income arising in that year.[1] Where accounts are not drawn up to 5 April (or 31 March, and from 2005–06, 1–4 April), the profit for the fiscal year of commencement is normally computed by time apportioning the profit of an accounting period.

For the second year of assessment, the basis period is always a 12-month period. The basis period is:

(a) if accounts are made up for a period of 12 months or more to any date in the second fiscal year, the basis period is 12 months ending at the accounting date in the second fiscal year;

(b) if accounts are made up for a period of less than 12 months, to a date in the second fiscal year, the basis period is the period of 12 months from the date of commencement of the trade or profession;

(c) if there is a change of accounting date such that the new date in the second fiscal year is less than 12 months after the commencement of the trade, the basis period is the period of 12 months from the date of commencement of the trade or profession;
(d) in any other case, the basis period is the second fiscal year.[2]

The convention whereby accounts to 31 March are treated as accounts of the fiscal year is given statutory effect.[3]

The effect of these rules is that some income can be taxed in the fiscal year in which the trade commences and, again, in the second fiscal year. This gives what is referred to in statute as an "overlap period". Relief for the charging of tax twice on profits generated in the overlap period is given at cessation of the trade (or earlier, if there is a change of accounting date).

Where overseas taxes are paid, double taxation relief is given in each fiscal year in respect of the basis period for that fiscal year. The effect of this is to give relief twice for profits generated during the "overlap period". This "excess" relief is clawed back at the cessation of the trade. Where a trade or profession is carried on in partnership, clawback of the individual partner's share of the overseas tax is given on the retirement of that individual partner, despite the continuance of the trade of the firm. Particular attention will need to be paid to this in practice.

Simon's Taxes B4.101, 102, 103.

---

[1] ITTOIA 2005, s 198.
[2] ITTOIA 2005, s 200.
[3] From 2005-06, ITTOIA 2005, s 209 provides that an accounting year that ends on 31 March or 1 or 2 or 3 or 4 April be treated as if it were the year to 5 April, so that no overlap relief arises and small apportionments are avoided.

Change of accounting date

[8.45] A taxpayer is free to change his accounting date to any date he specifies and to make as many changes as he desires, where the new accounting date falls within any of the first three fiscal years in which the trade is carried on.[1]

Where the change is made later, the change will only be taken into account for fiscal purposes if all the following conditions are fulfilled:

(a) the accounting period to the new date does not exceed 18 months;
(b) notice of the change of accounting date is given to HMRC by 31 January following the year of assessment (the date for submission of the relevant tax return);
(c) the accounting date was not changed during any of the five fiscal years preceding the year in which the change is made.[2]

Where the first two conditions are satisfied, but there has been a change in the preceding five-year period, a further change can be made if HMRC are satisfied that the further change is made for commercial reasons, and notice of that reason was given by 31 January following the change.[3] HMRC are given 60 days in which to reject the application; an appeal against rejection can be made to the Commissioners.[4]

The Revenue state that each year about 3% of businesses change their accounting date and one-sixth of all businesses make a change in the accounting date at some time in the life of the business.

Simon's Taxes B4.101, 110.

[1] ITTOIA 2005, s 215.
[2] ITTOIA 2005, ss 216, 217.
[3] ITTOIA 2005, ss 217(2), (6)(b) and 218(3)(a).
[4] ITTOIA 2005, s 218(3)(b).

Triggering use of overlap profit relief

[8.46] Where a change of accounting date brings into assessment in a fiscal year a period longer than 12 months all or part of the overlap profit is treated as a deduction from the profit brought into assessment.[1] Thus, if 15 months' profit is brought into assessment, overlap relief will be from three months of an earlier year; where 13 months is brought into assessment, overlap profit relief will have derived from one month. The effect is always to reduce the period assessed during a fiscal year to twelve months.

The deduction is, however, the proportion of profits generated in that earlier period. The deduction is not a scaling down of current profits. Where the overlap profit relief available is substantial, it may be advantageous to change the accounting date so as to obtain deduction for the potential relief at an early stage, rather than waiting for cessation of the trade. In this way, exceptionally high profits can be reduced, possibly avoiding a charge to tax at a higher rate.

Simon's Taxes B4.101.

[1] ITTOIA 2005, s 220.

Year of cessation

[8.47] Profits brought into assessment for the fiscal year in which a trade, etc, ceases are the profits of the period that starts the day after the end of the accounting period that was assessed in the previous fiscal year up to the date of cessation.[1]

Cessation does not cause any change to be made on the basis period, nor to the assessment, for any year prior to the fiscal year of cessation.

In many instances, the profits brought into assessment in the year of cessation will have been generated over a longer period than the trade has been carried on during that final fiscal year.

Relief for overlap profits is commonly available against the profits brought into charge in that year of cessation.[2]

The effect of the system of overlap profit relief is that where a trade, etc, was established after 5 April 1994, all profit made during the life of the trade will, at the end of the day, have been assessed once and once only. This contrasts

[8.47] Income from trades, professions and vocations

with the effect of the basis period rules under the old regime, where some profit could be assessed up to three times and profits arising in periods of trade before cessation escaped assessment.

Where relief for overlap profits has previously been given on the occasion of a change of accounting date, the relief available at cessation is reduced by the quantum of relief that was previously applied.

Relief for overlap profits can reduce the assessment for the final fiscal year to £nil. Also, as relief is given as an expense of the trade, it can create or augment an existing loss, to be relieved in the normal way.

Under general principles, a taxpayer may cease to be resident in the UK but may continue his trade, despite his change of residence. This is particularly the case for a taxpayer who continues to carry on the same professional activities after his departure from the UK as he previously carried on in the UK. The granting of overlap profit relief is dependent on their being a "permanent discontinuance" of the trade. ITTOIA 2005, s 17[3] ensures that the benefit of overlap profit relief is not lost for a taxpayer who is emigrating by deeming a change of residence into or out of the UK to be a permanent discontinuance of the trade, profession or vocation.

Where there are overlap profits, relief for the same payment of overseas tax may be allowed twice, in different years of assessment.[4] Where this has occurred, there is a clawback of excess relief in the year of cessation.[5] This clawback is effected by a charge on the taxpayer for the year of cessation.[6] It is possible, given certain profit profiles, for relief not to have been given for all overseas tax paid. Where this arises as a result of the basis period rules, there is provision for a balancing credit to be given in the year of cessation.[7]

Simon's Taxes B4.101.

[1]   ITTOIA 2005, s 202(1).
[2]   ITTOIA 2005, s 205. See supra, § **8.44** for the creation of overlap profits.
[3]   Rewriting TA 1988, s 110A (inserted by FA 1995, s 124).
[4]   TA 1988, s 804(1).
[5]   TA 1988, s 804(5A).
[6]   TA 1988, s 804(5B)(a).
[7]   TA 1988, s 804(5B)(b).

[8.48] Deemed overlap profit: This simple equation of profit generated and profit assessed does not, however, apply where a trade was commenced prior to 6 April 1994. In such a case, the profit brought into assessment for 1996–97 is under the transitional period rules, normally a method of averaging profit for, typically, a 24-month period. For such a trade, the effect of the new rules is that, on cessation, the profit that is brought into assessment has arisen over a longer period than that which the trade is carried on in the year of cessation. A measure of relief is given for this by deducting from the assessable profit for the year of cessation—a deemed "overlap profit". This is calculated by treating a period as if it were an overlap profit period. The statutory provision is:

> For the purposes of Chapter 15 of Part 2 [of ITTOIA 2005] 'overlap profit' includes the amount of profits or gains of the basis period for the year 1997–98 which–

(a) arose after the end of the basis period for the year 1996–97 . . . and,
(b) arose before 6th April 1997.[1]

The effect of the alternative provisions for a new trade and for an old trade is that, in both cases, the profits brought into assessment in the year of cessation have deducted from them the number of months' profit that is necessary to reduce the period to the length of time that the trade, etc, is carried on during the final fiscal year. The elegance of this is, however, more apparent than real. Current year profits are reduced by deducting profits generated many years previously, without any allowance for inflation. Whilst the methodology applied to a new trade has an underlying logic, the identification of overlap profit for an old trade is, at best, a measure of rough and ready justice. The effect of the deeming provision is that, at the end of the day, profits generated for a period prior to 6 April 1997 by an old trade escape taxation.

The manner in which deemed overlap profit relief, as described above, is calculated provided an opportunity for a trader to arrange his affairs so that profit was recognised in the period that, ultimately, escaped taxation. Certain actions that would have achieved this result were the subject of anti-avoidance rules.[2]

---

[1] ITTOIA 2005, Sch 2, para 52(2).
[2] FA 1995, Sch 22 paras 3-5 and 14-17. For a discussion of these anti-avoidance rules, see Tiley & Collison's UK Tax Guide 1999-2000 and previous editions.

When does trade commence?

[8.49] It is important to determine when a trade commenced, partly because of ITTOIA 2005, ss 199, 200 but also because expenditure incurred before that time is only deductible as a result of specific provisions.[1] An expense incurred in the seven years before trading is treated as an expense incurred on the day of commencement. Such an expense must, however, have been incurred by the trader; the benefit is lost if the business is incorporated.[2] Similarly, if group company A incurs an expense while group company B carries on the trade, neither can deduct—A never trades and B does not incur the expense.[3]

It is a question of fact not only whether there is an adventure in the nature of trade but also when it begins—and ends. In *Birmingham & District Cattle By-Products Co Ltd v IRC*[4] Rowlatt J recited the history of a company:

> It was incorporated on the 20th June [1913]. The company took over agreements. Then they entered into a contract for the erection of works . . . That is preparatory . . . Then they purchased machinery and plant for carrying on the business. That was getting ready. Then they entered into agreements for the purchase of products. But no materials came in, nor were any sausage skins made. In October [1913], having looked round, and having got their machinery and plant, and having also employed their foreman, and having . . . generally got everything ready, then they began to take the raw materials to turn out their product.

Rowlatt J held that the trade commenced in October 1913.

By contrast, in *Cannop Coal Co Ltd v IRC*[5] where the trade was to be the mining of coal by sinking pits in the Forest of Dean, the company had, since

[8.49] Income from trades, professions and vocations

1909, extracted a certain amount of coal from a drift nearby for use in its machines and, finding it had extracted more than it needed, sold the excess to the public, the company was held to have commenced trading when it sold the excess coal to the public and not when, in 1912, coal began to emerge from the pits. In his judgement[6], Sankey J said that it was clearly a fact that the coal company was engaged in a trade in those three years and it was too fine a point to say that the trade in those years was different from the mining of coal from the pits. Thus the mere formation of an intention to commence trading is not the moment of commencement, nor is the incurring of capital expenditure for the purpose of preparing to trade.

A difficult question concerns the use of small-scale pilot projects involving resale to the public to decide precisely what product to make. It was important in *Cannop Coal Co Ltd v IRC* that the sales were substantial[7] and it may therefore be that pilot projects are not trading.

The approach in *Birmingham & District Cattle By-Products Co Ltd v IRC* has been followed in a number of cases.[8] In *Mansell v Revenue and Customs Comrs*[9], the Special Commissioner rejected the argument that Mr Mansell commenced his trade before 6 April 1994 saying: 'Operations did not begin with the agreeing of the heads of terms because nothing was acquired, nothing was expended or risked, nothing was ventured and nothing won until, at the earliest, the option agreement was made'.[10]

It is important to separate the question whether a trade has begun from the question whether any income has arisen from it.[11] Where an asset is acquired and subsequently disposed of, it is open to the court to conclude from the evidence that the whole transaction was an adventure in the nature of trade. It is, however, also, open to the court to conclude that an asset was acquired with the intention of retaining it as an investment but that trading subsequently commenced so that the profit accruing on resale will be taxable.[12]

At any one time the asset must either be trading stock or a capital asset; it cannot be both.[13] It is also clear that a case stated must be examined in the round.[14]

In computing the profit where the trade is begun subsequently to the asset being acquired, the asset arguably must be brought into the account at its market value at that time.[15]

---

[1] In *City of London Contract Corpn Ltd v Styles* (1887) 2 TC 239, it was held that there was no deduction available for an expense incurred before the commencement of trade. Relief is now given by statute: ITTOIA 2005, s 57 (income tax); TA 1988, s 401 (corporation tax).

[2] Revenue interpretation RI 32.

[3] Revenue interpretation RI 32.

[4] (1919) 12 TC 92 (an excess profits duty case).

[5] (1918) 12 TC 31 (another excess profits duty case). In both instances the Revenue won.

[6] In one year 68% of the coal was resold and in another 84%.

[7] At 40.

[8] *Cordy v Barry (Inspector of Taxes)* [1946] 2 All ER 396, 28 TC 250, CA, *Gartry v The Queen* 94 DTC 1947 (TCC), *Khan v Miah* [2001] 1 All ER (Comm) 282,

536

[2001] 1 All ER 20, [2000] 1 WLR 2123, HL, *Kirk and Randall Ltd v Dunn (Inspector of Taxes)* (1924) 8 TC 663, *Miller v The Queen*, 2001 CanLII 593 (TCC), *Slater v Commissioner of Inland Revenue* [1996] 1 NZLR 759, *Spiro v Glencrown Properties Ltd* [1991] Ch 537, [1991] 1 All ER 600.
[9] [2006] STC (SCD) 605.
[10] [2006] STC (SCD) 605, para 106 at 623e.
[11] See *Eckel v Board of Inland Revenue* [1989] STC 305, PC.
[12] *Taylor v Good* [1973] STC 383, [1973] 2 All ER 785.
[13] *Simmons v IRC* [1980] STC 350, [1980] 2 All ER 798.
[14] *Kirkby v Hughes* [1993] STC 76.
[15] *Simmons v IRC* [1980] STC 350, [1980] 2 All ER 798. This is the converse of Sharkey v Wernher (infra, § **8.152**). See also TCGA 1992, s 161. Cases in which this rule should have been applied include *Leach v Pogson* (supra, § **8.23**) and *Mitchell Bros v Tomlinson* (supra, § **8.20**). However, given the subsequent question marks over the principle in *Sharkey v Wernher*, this rule must now be due for reconsideration.

Commencement—new trade or development of existing one

[8.50] There is no rule of law that a person, whether or not a company, cannot carry on more than one business and it is immaterial that there is one consolidated balance sheet. The question is one of fact and degree. As Rowlatt J put it in a case where the two activities had both been bought from another company, "the real question is, was there any inter-connection, any interlacing, any interdependence, any unity at all embracing those two businesses".[1] So if a trader commences a new trade alongside his established one, the two trades are treated separately,[2] even for purposes of loss relief and capital allowances; the sources are distinct. It is a question of fact whether a particular development is an expansion of an existing trade[3] or the commencement of a new one; it may happen that the amalgamation of two trades is to be treated as the cessation of both and the commencement of one new trade.[4]

A relatively modern example is *Seaman v Tucketts Ltd.*[5] In 1956 control of the company was acquired by a new group. The company carried on the trade of manufacture and sale of confectionery; this included the purchase and resale of such goods from other manufacturers, which ended early in 1958. In September 1958 the two retail shops were closed and in November 1958 manufacture ceased. By April 1959 the existing stocks and the factory had been sold. The company which had previously bought sugar and cellophane for its own business now bought these for resale to the new parent company at cost plus 10%. Two years later it began to supply confectionery again. Reversing the Commissioners, Pennycuick J held that the only true and reasonable conclusion was that, at the end of 1958 when the manufacture had ceased, a new trade of sugar merchants, including the buying and selling of cellophane paper, had been commenced and the case was remitted to the Commissioners to determine whether the confectionery trade had been discontinued or had been merely quiescent.

The question is one of fact and degree. *Seaman v Tucketts Ltd* shows that not only may there be a termination of one trade and the commencement of another but there may also be a contraction of one trade and the commencement of another, even though that other deals with a commodity employed in the original trade. There is also authority that a substantial change in management policy can lead to a discontinuance and a new commencement.[6] However a barrister does not, on taking silk, start a new profession.[7]

The basic rule in ITTOIA 2005, s 860(2) requiring there to be a change in the person running the trade assumes that the trade carried on by the previous owner is continued under the new partnership. If the new owner does not carry on the existing business but starts one there will be a discontinuance. This may raise the familiar question whether there is an expansion of an existing business or the commencement of a new one. A recent example arose where taxpayers with one shop bought another one. In *Maidment v Kibby* [8] the taxpayers ran a fish and chip shop in Chepstow; they then bought a shop in Caldicott and ran the new shop in their own style under their own name with a single system for buying materials and with one set of accounts. The Revenue argued that the Caldicott shop had retained its identity, that there had therefore been a change of persons running the trade and so a discontinuance. The Commissioners rejected the argument and Sir Donald Nicholls V-C held that it was open to them to do so.

A television producer who was freelance for part of his time and received gross fees of between £1,000 and £5,000 per annum was held to merely continue his existing business when he gave up his employment and worked freelance the whole of his time, receiving gross fees between £60,000 and £210,000 per annum.[9]

---

[1] *Scales v George Thompson & Co Ltd* (1927) 13 TC 83 at 89.
[2] *Fullwood Foundry Ltd v IRC* (1924) 9 TC 101.
[3] *Howden Boiler and Armaments Co Ltd v Stewart* (1924) 9 TC 205 and *Cannon Industries Ltd v Edwards* (1965) 42 TC 151.
[4] *George Humphries & Co v Cook* (1934) 19 TC 121.
[5] (1963) 41 TC 422.
[6] See Rowlatt J in *Kirk and Randall Ltd v Dunn* (1924) 8 TC 663 at 670.
[7] *Seldon v Croom-Johnson* [1932] 1 KB 759, 16 TC 740.
[8] [1993] STC 494.
[9] *Edmunds v Coleman* [1997] STC 1406.

Discontinuance

[8.51] There is a discontinuance if the trader ceases to carry on his trade; this will also occur if he ceases to trade in the way in which he had previously traded.[1] It is a question of fact whether the particular change is the ceasing of one trade and the commencement of another or is simply a normal development of his previous trade.

Where a taxpayer has, say, two offices and closes down one of them it is a nice question whether the continuing office is continuing the trade. Clearly this will be so if the original business was not one but two separate businesses each run from its own office, in which case the continuing office continues its trade as before.² As stated above in connection with commencement this is a matter of fact and degree.³ In *Rolls Royce Motors Ltd v Bamford* the original Rolls Royce Ltd had developed and built motor cars since 1906; since 1915 it had been involved in the manufacture of aero engines. In 1971 a large project, the RB211 engine, went seriously wrong; the aero engine side was put into a new company and the motor company business was put into the taxpayer separate company. The Commissioners' decision that the taxpayer had not been carrying on the same trade as Rolls Royce Ltd was held by Walton J to be the only rational conclusion and so the taxpayer could not use the losses incurred on the RB211 project.

Simon's Taxes B4.101, E1.3.

1   Supra, § **7.47**.
2   *C Connelly & Co v Wilbey* [1992] STC 783.
3   Supra, § **7.47**.

[8.52] A trade does not cease if it is merely in abeyance. Thus a mere interruption in production does not cause a discontinuance[1] nor does a disposal of assets[2] nor even the appointment of a receiver.[3] Business is not confined to being busy and long periods of inactivity may occur.[4] It is however, a question of fact whether a particular trade has lapsed into a period of quiescence or has ceased. A trade may be treated as permanently discontinued notwithstanding that the former trader later commences a new trade which is in all respects identical with the previous ceased trade.

In *Kirk and Randall Ltd v Dunn*[5] the new owners of a trading company obtained no new contracts and tried to sell the premises; they then had their works and plant requisitioned during the First World War. However, the Managing Director tried to obtain contracts overseas. Rowlatt J, reversing the Commissioners, held that the company was still trading as there was evidence of business activity resulting in expenditure and loss.

However, in *J G Ingram & Son Ltd v Callaghan*[6] where the period was much shorter the Court of Appeal upheld the Commissioners' finding that there was not just unprofitability but inactivity and so a discontinuance. In this case the company had by May 1961 ceased to produce rubber goods, had sold off its stock and dismissed its staff, the plan being to switch to plastics. From September 1961 to June 1962 products were manufactured by another subsidiary of the owner and sold over the company's name. In this way the goodwill was kept alive but the operations of the company were confined to little more than bookkeeping and perhaps debt collecting; the trade was not kept alive between those dates. A similar conclusion was reached in *Rolls Royce Motors Ltd v Bamford*[7] where there was a discontinuance even though the company was actually reverting to its former narrow trade. This may be due to the fact that the revertor was due to a sudden crisis which the company solved by disposing of many of its activities.

Simon's Taxes B1.432.

1   *Merchiston Steamship Co Ltd v Turner* [1910] 2 KB 923, 5 TC 520.

[8.52] Income from trades, professions and vocations

[2] *Aviation and Shipping Co Ltd v Murray* [1961] 2 All ER 805, 39 TC 595; see also *Watts v Hart* [1984] STC 548.
[3] *Wadsworth Morton Ltd v Jenkinson* [1966] 3 All ER 702.
[4] *South Behar Rly Co Ltd v IRC* [1925] AC 476, 12 TC 657; cf *Morning Post Ltd v George* (1941) 23 TC 514.
[5] (1924) 8 TC 663. See also *Robroyston Brickworks Ltd v IRC* (1976) 51 TC 230.
[6] [1969] 1 All ER 433, 45 TC 151, CA. The same conclusion was reached in *Tryka Ltd v Newall* (1963) 41 TC 146, Ch D, noted [1964] BTR 286, and *Goff v Osborne & Co (Sheffield) Ltd* (1953) 34 TC 441.
[7] (1976) 51 TC 319.

Effects

[8.53] When a trade, profession or vocation is permanently discontinued, the basis of assessment is determined by ITTOIA 2005, s 202.[1] However, there are special rules concerning relief for losses and capital allowances which may, contrary to the usual rule, be carried back on discontinuance.[2] Insofar as these losses or capital allowances exceed the income of the period over which they are taken back they are lost save for post-cessation receipts and cannot be used by anyone else, even a successor to the trade. Another rule directs the valuation of trading stock. Certain sums paid just before discontinuance may be non-deductible because not spent in order to keep the business in being;[3] a statutory exception is made for certain redundancy payments.[4]

Simon's Taxes B4.101.

[1] Supra, § **8.46**.
[2] Supra, § **6.22**.
[3] Infra, § **8.56**.
[4] ITTOIA 2005, s 79 (income tax); TA 1988, s 90 (corporation tax), see Inland Revenue interpretation RI 103.

Succession

[8.54] Problems of commencement also arise where a trade which has been carried on by one person is transferred to another; such a transfer is called a succession and must be distinguished from the mere purchase of the assets used in the trade. In the case of such a transfer there is a discontinuance by the old trader and a commencement by the new one, so that the closing years of the old trader fall within ITTOIA 2005, s 202 and the opening years of the new trader fall into ITTOIA 2005, s 199. If the transferee simply absorbs the trade into an existing trade s 199 will not apply, although s 202 will apply to the transferor.[1]

Simon's Taxes Division B1.6.

[1] Other relevant provisions are TA 1988, s 343 (loss reliefs) and CAA 2001, s 557.

Effects on new trader

[8.55] The opening years of the new trader fall within ITTOIA 2005, s 199 unless he is going to absorb the acquired trade into his existing one and even though it is in truth one business.

Effects on old trader

[8.56] Where a succession to a trade occurs, neither losses nor unused capital allowances incurred by the first trader can be used by the successor.[1]

One other point concerns the former trader. Generally, expenditure incurred shortly before a discontinuance may not be for the purposes of the continuing trade and so may not be deductible but the case law on this point is now more favourable to deductibility.[2] So expenditure made with a view to the trade after transfer may be incurred for the purposes of the trade and not for the purposes of the present trader and so deductible by the first trader despite the succession.[3] The reason for this departure from the general rule is that the deemed discontinuance and commencement is a statutory innovation; the older principle was therefore treated as having been abrogated only to the extent needed to bring into operation what are now ITTOIA 2005, ss 199 et seq into their current or former (TA 1988, ss 61–63) form.

Simon's Taxes B1.604, 613.

---

[1] eg *Rolls-Royce Motors Ltd v Bamford* [1976] STC 162.
[2] *Godden v Wilson's Stores (Holdings) Ltd* (1962) 40 TC 161, CA distinguished in *O'Keeffe v Southport Printers Ltd* [1984] STC 443 and not followed in *IRC v Cosmotron Manufacturing Co Ltd* [1997] STC 1134 (PC); see also Inland Revenue Interpretation RI 200.
[3] Per Lord Clyde in *IRC v Patrick Thomson Ltd* (1956) 37 TC 145 at 157.

Rules to decide whether there has been a succession

[8.57] (1) A succession to a trade must be distinguished from the purchase of the assets of a trade. Thus where a company which had a tramp shipping business bought a ship second hand from another trader there was no succession to that person's trade, but only the purchase of a ship.[1] These are, however, questions of fact and it was important in that case that the purchaser acquired no list of customers along with the ship, that the ship had no special route along which and only along which she used to ply her trade and that no goodwill came with the ship.

Since the origin of the concept of succession lay in the application of the rule that profits be measured by the average of three previous years business, there had to be a "very close identity" between the business in the former proprietorship and the business in the new proprietorship.[2] A very close identity is, however, not the same as a complete identity. Thus a successor to a business with say 50 shops may choose to shut up some of them, make alterations in the goods that he sells, change his supplier or may cut out a particular class of customer or a particular area.[3] The question whether such changes prevent there being a succession to the business is one of fact.

[8.57] Income from trades, professions and vocations

There may be a succession even though there is no purchase of the entire assets.[4] In one case a circular was distributed to the former trader's customers that the new owners had acquired the "trading connection" of the former traders. The Commissioners held that there was no succession; the courts felt unable to reverse that conclusion.[4] Conversely in another case where a circular to the public described the new firm as successors, but they took over no books, no lists of customers and none of the staff except a few workpeople, they were held to be successors by the Commissioners and the courts again declined to intervene.[5]

Simon's Direct Tax Service B1.606.

[1] *Watson Bros v Lothian* (1902) 4 TC 441. Compare *Bell v National Provincial Bank of England* [1904] 1 KB 149, 5 TC 1.
[2] Per Rowlatt J in *Reynolds, Sons & Co Ltd v Ogston* (1930) 15 TC 501 at 524, approved by Lord Hanworth MR at 527.
[3] Per Sir Wilfrid Greene MR in *Laycock v Freeman, Hardy and Willis Ltd* (1938) 22 TC 288 at 297.
[4] *Reynolds, Sons & Co Ltd v Ogston* (1930) 15 TC at 524.
[4] *Reynolds, Sons & Co Ltd v Ogston* (1930) 15 TC at 524.
[5] *Thomson and Balfour v Le Page* (1923) 8 TC 541.

[8.58] (2) There can be no succession to a part of a trade. However, as Rowlatt J said, 'I do not think that it means that if what is succeeded to is not the same extent of trade or even does not include a particular line of customers, it necessarily follows that there cannot be a successor to a trade'.[1]

Simon's Taxes B1.607.

[1] *James Shipstone & Son Ltd v Morris* (1929) 14 TC 413 at 421; and see *Stockham v Wallasey UDC* (1906) 95 LT 834.

[8.59] (3) There is no succession through the accidental acquisition by a trader who continues in business, of custom left by another who goes out of business. For there to be a succession there must be a transfer by one trader to another of the right to that benefit which arises from connection and reputation.[1] Thus if a trader goes out of business and his former rival captures his customers there is no succession; however if there were a transfer of the business and its goodwill to the rival, there would be.

Simon's Taxes B1.607.

[1] *Thomson and Balfour v Le Page* (1923) 8 TC 541 at 548.

[8.60] (4) There is no succession if the trade has ceased before being acquired by its new owner, nor if the new owner closes it down immediately he acquires it. Thus if a business has gone bankrupt and remained in the hands of the trustee in bankruptcy for 12 months before the assets were sold, it is likely that such a sale would be treated as a sale of assets rather than of the business.[1]

Indeed there is authority that where a business has been making heavy losses and practically has to sell to avoid shutting down, it is likely that there is no succession.[2] However, where a business suffered extensive fire damage and ceased to trade with the public but kept together its employees and various pieces of equipment, a delay of seventeen months between the fire and the acquisition of the business by a new owner did not prevent there being a succession.[3]

The question for the Commissioners is "whether it is true and fair to say that the business in respect of which the successor is said to be making profits is the business to which he succeeded". In *Laycock v Freeman, Hardy and Willis Ltd*[4] the respondent company bought shoes from wholesalers and resold them to the public. Some 20% to 30% of its supplies came from two subsidiary companies which it controlled. In 1935 the subsidiary companies went into voluntary liquidation and the liquidator assigned all the assets and goodwill to the respondent company which also took over all the staff. The respondent company took all the products of the factories previously owned by the subsidiary companies and sold them in their shops. It was held that there was no succession. The business of the subsidiary companies was that of wholesale manufacturing concerns; that business had ceased; manufacturing was still carried on but the business of wholesale manufacturing was not. This decision has recently been criticised on the ground that the distinction between manufacturing for sale wholesale and manufacturing goods for sale is a false one.[5] Millett J has criticised this decision on the ground that the distinction between manufacturing for sale wholesale and manufacturing goods for sale retail is a false one. "It is impossible to discern any sensible fiscal policy for differentiating, for the purpose of applying the opening year provisions, between the acquisition of a manufacturing business by a wholesaler and the acquisition of a similar business by a retailer. They are both examples of vertical integration."[6]

Laycock v Freeman, Hardy and Willis was distinguished in *Briton Ferry Steel Co Ltd v Barry*[7] where the appellant company produced steel bars which were then supplied to six wholly owned subsidiary companies, which in turn converted the bars into blackplate and tinplate. Sales were handled by another wholly owned subsidiary. In 1934 the six subsidiary companies were wound up and the conversion of the bars into blackplate and tinplate was carried on by the appellant company using the plant and workforce of the former companies. The Commissioners held that there was a succession to the trades carried on by the subsidiaries. The fact that the company through its shares already controlled them was irrelevant, as was the fact that another subsidiary company controlled their sales.[8] The Court of Appeal refused to interfere with that decision. *Laycock v Freeman, Hardy and Willis* was distinguished. In that case the business of the subsidiaries, that of making profits by wholesale sales, had ceased, and one of retail manufacturing begun. In the present case the business of the subsidiary companies, that of making profits by the conversion of steel bars into blackplate and tinplate and resale still existed, but was being carried on by someone else,[9] and the retail side was handled by a separate legal entity. The fact that someone had previously supplied the steel bars was irrelevant.

A further problem concerns the calculation of the profit of the trade acquired. In *Laycock v Freeman, Hardy and Willis* the Court of Appeal held that it was "wholly illegitimate" to invent a notional sale from the wholesale stage of the enterprise to the retail stage at a price which would yield a notional "wholesale profit".[10] But in *Briton Ferry Steel Co Ltd v Barry* the same Court, having again rejected a notional sale, directed that the transfer of the steel bars from the one artificial side of the trade to the other should be treated as carried out at the actual cost of production. This ensures that the profit from the whole operation would be attributable to the newly acquired sector of the trade.[11] One cannot help feeling that the court was being a little ingenuous.

Falmer Jeans v Rodin concerned TA 1988, s 343 and the transfer of losses to a new company in the same ownership. A made jeans for B which B sold. B supplied the materials to A and B paid for A's services on a cost plus basis. When A started making losses it stopped trading and transferred its trade and assets to B. Manufacturing appeared as a separate cost centre in B's accounts. Millett J, allowing B's appeal, from the Commissioners, held that B was carrying on A's trade.

Simon's Taxes B1.607.

---

[1] Per Greer LJ in *Reynolds, Sons & Co Ltd v Ogston* (1930) 15 TC 501 at 528.
[2] Per Rowlatt J in *Wilson and Barlow v Chibbett* (1929) 14 TC 407 at 413.
[3] *Wild v Madame Tussauds (1926) Ltd* (1932) 17 TC 127.
[4] Per Sir Wilfrid Greene MR in *Laycock v Freeman, Hardy and Willis Ltd* [1938] 4 All ER 609 at 614, 22 TC 288 at 298.
[5] See generally the comments of Millet J in *Falmer Jeans v Rodin* [1990] STC 270 at 279, 280.
[6] See *Falmer Jeans v Rodin* [1990] STC 270 at 279, 280.
[7] [1939] 4 All ER 541, 23 TC 414, applied *IRC v Spirax Manufacturing Co Ltd* (1946) 29 TC 187.
[8] Per Macnaghten J [1938] 4 All ER 429 at 434-5, 23 TC 414 at 431, 432.
[9] Per Sir Wilfrid Greene MR at 479, 547 and 431.
[10] Per Sir Wilfrid Greene MR [1938] 4 All ER 609 at 616, 22 TC 288 at 300.
[11] Per Sir Wilfrid Greene MR [1939] 4 All ER 541 at 550, 23 TC 414 at 434.

Partnerships

[8.61] It is a question of fact whether a particular person is a partner in an enterprise or merely a senior employee. In so far as this involves a question of construing a document, it will raise questions of law. Although the receipt by a person of a share of the profits is prima facie evidence that he is a partner further evidence may be needed to establish exactly when the partnership begins to trade.[1] In *Fenston v Johnstone*[2] the appellant wished to buy some land but lacked finance. He therefore agreed with another person to share the profits and losses and to assist in the development of the land. The document said that there was no partnership and described the appellant's share of the profits as a fee for introducing the other person to the vendor. It was held that there was a partnership. On the other hand in *Pratt v Strick*[3] there was held to be no partnership where a doctor sold his practice to another but agreed as part of the sale to stay in his house with the purchaser for some three months introducing the purchaser to the patients and sharing receipts and expenses over that period. In both these cases the decisions of the Commissioners were reversed.

Simon's Taxes B7.101–104, 201.

---

[1] *Saywell v Pope* [1979] STC 824.
[2] (1940) 23 TC 29.
[3] (1932) 17 TC 459; see also *Bulloch v IRC* [1976] STC 514.

Taxation of partnership profits

[8.62] The application of the current year basis meant a complete rewriting of the basic rules. The partnership is no longer treated for the purposes of the Tax Acts as an entity which is separate and distinct from those persons. Instead profits are to be computed as if the partnership were an individual and a partner's share in the profits for a period are to be determined according to the interests of the partners during that period.[1]

To implement this the legislation deems each partner to have his own trade carried on by him alone which was commenced by him when he became a partner.[2] If the actual trade was previously carried on the deemed trade is taken to begin when the actual trade began.[3] Proceeding symmetrically the law states that the deemed trade is to end when he ceases to be a partner or, where the actual trade is subsequently carried on by him alone, the time when the actual trade or profession is permanently discontinued.[4]

These rules apply to trades and professions[5] and to claims for losses[6], as well as to tax on profits and to non-trading income of the partnership.[7]

These changes mean that partners are individually liable for tax on their own shares of the profits and that the taxable share is related to the actual share and not the profit sharing ratio in force in a subsequent year. Moreover once the trade has begun there will be no deemed discontinuance by reason of a change in the partners. There were also other changes consequential on the phased ending of the preceding year basis.[8]

Where a partnership includes a company, the profits of the trade are computed as if the partnership were a company and the member company's shares ascertained and subjected to corporation tax.[9] Income tax is chargeable on the shares of individual partners.[10] There is no transfer of a trade on a change of a corporate partner.

Simon's Taxes B7.101, E1.220.

---

[1] ITTOIA 2005, ss 848, 850(2).
[2] ITTOIA 2005, s 852(2)(a).
[3] ITTOIA 2005, s 852(2)(b).
[4] ITTOIA 2005, s 852(4).

[5] ITTOIA 2005, s 847(2).
[6] ITTOIA 2005, ss 849 et seq.
[7] ITTOIA 2005, s 854.
[8] eg the repeal of TA 1988, s 277 and various amendments to TA 1988, ss 114, 115.
[9] TA 1988, s 8(2). This means that the loan relationships legislation of FA 1996, ss 80-105 (see infra, §§ **27.04–27.10**) apply to the corporate partner and the whole partnership is treated as a party to a loan relationship: Inland Revenue statement of practice SP4/98.
[10] TA 1988, s 114.

Limited liability partnerships

[8.63] A limited liability partnership is treated in law as a "body corporate"[1] and is subject to aspects of company law. However, for tax purposes, the same treatment is applied to the assessment of the profits enjoyed by individual partners as would be applied if the partnership were not a limited liability partnership.[2] That is, a limited liability partnership is treated as transparent for tax purposes and each partner is assessed to tax on his individual share of the limited liability partnership's income.[3] An individual who is a partner in a limited liability partnership is entitled to claim interest relief on a loan raised in order to provide capital for the partnership.[4] However, a partner's undrawn profits in a limited liability partnership are a debt of that entity and are not part of the individual partners' capital, unless there is an agreement between the partners to override the general provision. Consequently, when calculating any loss relief available to an individual partner, the ceiling[5] is applied without reference to the individual partner's undrawn profits.

Where there is a liability to negligence, for which an individual partner takes personal responsibility, the capital contribution made by that individual partner to the limited liability partnership is treated as an addition of capital subscribed for the purpose of computing loss relief.[6]

Where an ordinary partnership converts to a limited liability partnership, the conversion is ignored for tax purposes.[7] Hence, the individual partners' overlap profit relief continues, unaffected by the change of legal liability.[8] If, conversely, a limited liability partnership is created to take over only a part of a former partnership's trade, such an event can trigger the cessation provisions, unless the business acquired by the limited liability partnership is recognisably "the business" that was previously carried on by the unlimited partnership,[9] or the continuing activity in the old partnership constitutes a continuation of "the business".

Any continuing "adjustment charge"[10] that arose as a result of a change from cash basis to earnings basis by the former unlimited partnership, can be carried forward and treated as an addition to the profits of a limited liability partnership, that is created as a successor to the unlimited partnership.[11]

The Revenue require a single partnership tax return for the fiscal year in which an unlimited partnership converts to a limited liability partnership.[12] This return will show the aggregate of profits for the 12-month period, irrespective of the entity by which the profits were made.

A limited liability partnership may be formed to carry on the business of a property investment or, perhaps, life assurance business. Where the business of the LLP is investment, rather than trading, the treatment of the income enjoyed by the individual partners is, broadly, the same as would be applied to income arising directly to the partner.[13]

Simon's Taxes E7.130.

---

[1] Limited Liability Partnership Act 2000, s 1; ITTOIA 2005, s 863 (income tax); TA 1988, s 118ZA (corporation tax).
[2] Limited Liability Partnership Act 2000, s 10.
[3] ITTOIA 2005, s 852(1) (income tax); TA 1988, s 114 (corporation tax).
[4] TA 1988, s 362(1) and Inland Revenue Tax Bulletin December 2000, p 801. Extra-statutory concession A43, which deals with interest for investment in partnerships, does not, however, apply to limited liability partnerships.
[5] TA 1988, ss 117 and 118ZA-118ZL.
[6] See supra, §§ **8.44–8.48**.
[7] Inland Revenue Tax Bulletin December 2000, p 802.
[8] Inland Revenue Tax Bulletin December 2000, p 802. The treatment in statement of practice SP 9/86 applies.
[9] ITTOIA 2005, s 205 provides for overlap profits to be deducted from profits in the year in which the taxpayer "permanently ceases to carry on a trade". Continuing a trade as a LLP is not a permanent cessation.
[10] Inland Revenue Tax Bulletin December 2000, p 803.
[11] Inland Revenue Tax Bulletin December 2000, p 803.
[12] Inland Revenue Tax Bulletin December 2000, p 803.
[13] Detailed provisions are given in FA 2001, Sch 25.

The measure of income

[8.64] Income tax in respect of trades, professions and vocations is charged on "profits".[1] The measure of income assessable in respect of property businesses is, similarly, defined by reference to "profits".[2] For a company, corporation tax is chargeable on the "total profits".[3] In contrast to the approach taken in a number of continental countries, the UK Taxes Acts do not provide a formulation of the measure of profit.[4]

The earliest judicial formulation as to what constitutes "profit", as a measure on which a tax liability is to be charged, was given in 1888 by Lord Herschell:

> The profit of a trade or business is the surplus by which the receipts from the trade or business exceed the expenditure.[5]

For an economist, an attempt to define "income" is "chasing a will-o'-the-wisp".[6] McDonald comments:

> Profit is an abstraction; it is not something given in nature . . . Profit measurement is a purposive activity, the measurement, whilst being a measure of something, is determined not by what is measured but by the purpose for which the measurement is undertaken.[7]

Case law gives two distinct approaches to the relationship between questions of law and principles of accountancy. One asserts that the court should first look to see what accountancy says and then see whether any rule of law contradicts it;[8] the other that the court should first determine the question as a matter of law, then see whether accountancy gives a different answer and then determine which should prevail. It will be appreciated that the former gives much greater weight to accountancy practice than the latter. In 1993 the Court of Appeal doubted whether any judge-made rule could override a generally accepted rule of commercial accountancy which (a) applied to the situation in question, (b) was not one of two or more rules applicable to that situation, and (c) was not shown to be inconsistent with the true facts or otherwise inapt to determine the true profits or losses of the business.[9] This new approach has already been followed.[10] However, as Freedman has noted, 'The arguments for the taxpayer were too stark and left important issues unexplored. These issues were not explored because of the weight given to SSAP 21. To accept a standard without investigation of its objectives and effects is . . . an abdication of responsibility by the court'.[11]

A decision in which the courts made a ruling in an area where there was no one single recognised practice is *Willingale v International Commercial Bank Ltd*.[12] The taxpayer bank held a number of bills of exchange issued by borrowers all over the world and maturing over periods from one to ten years. The issue was whether the bank should bring the proceeds of such bills into the account only when the bills matured (or were disposed of) or whether, following the practice applied to the clearing banks, it should bring in a part of the expected profit each year. The House, upholding all the lower tribunals, held that although the bank had made up its accounts on the practice stated it was entitled to insist that for tax purposes the other basis should be taken as this would be in conformity with a fundamental principle that profits should not be taxed until ascertained. The decision was by a bare majority and has been heavily criticised. On one view, the decision in this case has been distinguished by subsequent cases where the court has taken as its starting point the accounts that have been drawn up by the taxpayer, only allowing adjustments to these accounts where statute makes specific direction or where it is established that the accounts were not in accordance with an accepted accountancy practice (see infra, § **8.65**). The statement by Lord Fraser that the accounts which excluded the accrued discounts would have given a true and fair view of the state of the bank's business and would have been just as satisfactory for commercial purposes as accounts which included them is almost certainly wrong.[13]

Exchange rate fluctuations have provided much debate. For corporation tax, the treatment is now provided by statute.[14] For income tax, it is still necessary to apply basic principles to determine whether a fluctuation relates to revenue (and, thus, gives an increase or a decrease in taxable profit) or relates to capital (when it may give an increase or decrease in the capital allowance but is more likely to have no tax effect). The Revenue have issued a statement of practice[15] which relies heavily on the decision of the House of Lords in *Pattison v Marine Midland Ltd*.[16]

The principle that the decision is for the court is neatly stated by Lord Denning MR who said:[17]

It is well established that the question whether a particular payment is a payment of a capital nature or of a revenue nature must be answered in accordance with sound accountancy principles. Skilled accountants may well be much better qualified than most Judges to formulate and explain such principles; but nevertheless in every case of this kind it is the Judge and not the witness who must decide whether a witness's evidence in fact exemplifies sound accountancy principles. A Judge may reject the accountant's evidence, or he may accept it. This accords with what was said by Salmon LJ:[18]

> Where there is evidence which is accepted by the court as establishing a sound commercial accounting practice conflicting with no Statute, that normally is the end of the matter. The court adopts the practice, applies it and decides the case accordingly.

I emphasise the words 'which is accepted by the Court as establishing a sound commercial accounting practice'. It must be axiomatic that the evidence of no witness cannot be conclusive on a question of law. In the state of the evidence in this case, Goulding J saw no reason to reject Mr Bailey's evidence, which consequently should be accepted as exemplifying sound principles of commercial accountancy.

In *Comr of Inland Revenue v Secan Ltd*[19] the Court had to consider the case where a company prepared its accounts in accordance with an accounting principle that is generally accepted and then sought to apply a different principle to compute the tax liability. The judgement of Lord Millett NPJ, sitting as a judge of the Court of Appeal, Hong Kong, in that case is neatly summarised by Dr Nuala Brice and John Walters QC as:

> There was no basis on which a taxpayer could challenge an assessment based on its own financial statements so long as those were prepared in accordance with ordinary accounting principles, showed a true and fair view of its affairs, and were not inconsistent with the statute.[20]

The clearest statement of the central relevance of a "true and fair view" is given in the leading judgment of Lord Hoffmann in the House of Lords in *Revenue and Customs Comrs v William Grant & Sons Distillers Ltd*.[21] He said:

> My Lords, the method of computing trading profits for the purposes of income and corporation tax has been settled for many years. First you compute the profits on a basis which gives a true and fair view of the taxpayer's profits or losses in the relevant period. Then you make any adjustments expressly required for tax purposes.

Lord Hoffmann upheld the methodology used by the taxpayer company in measuring stock, saying that no adjustment was required for tax purposes. All four other Law Lords expressed their "full agreement".[22]

Simon's Taxes B8.311.

---

[1] ITTOIA 2005, s 5 (income tax); TA 1988, s 18(1) (corporation tax).
[2] ITTOIA 2005, s 268 (income tax); TA 1988, s 15(1) (corporation tax) (see infra, § **10.09**).
[3] TA 1988, s 6(1).
[4] Some provisions, most notoriously ITTOIA 2005, s 34(1) (income tax) and TA 1988, s 74 (corporation tax), list items that are not to be included as expenses and other provisions possible for specified deductions (such as capital allowances), but

no attempt is made to formulate either income or expenditure. This is in contrast to the approach in, for example, Germany where the fiscal code enumerates the categories into which a receipt must fall if it is to be recognised as a taxable credit and the categories within which a payment must fall if it is to be recognised as a tax-deductible debit.

5   *Russell v Aberdeen Town and County Bank* (1888) 2 TC 321 at 327.
6   Hicks, "Value and Capital", (1946, Clarendon Press), reprinted in "Readings in the Concept and Measurement of Income" (R. H. Parker & G.C. Harcourt eds.) (Cambridge University Press, 1969).
7   In "Matching Accounting and Taxable Profits" [1995] BTR 484.
8   eg Salmon J in *Odeon Associated Theatres Ltd v Jones* [1972] 1 All ER 681 at 689, 48 TC 257 at 283A and Lord Haldane in *Sun Insurance Office Ltd v Clark* [1912] AC 433 at 455, 6 TC 59 at 78; Lord Clyde in *Lothian Chemical Co Ltd v Rogers* (1926) 11 TC 508 at 520; also Tucker Report 1951, Cmd 8189 § 135.
9   *Gallagher v Jones* [1993] STC 537, CA; see especially Sir Thomas Bingham MR at 555-556. However, see also the scathing criticisms by Freedman [1993] BTR 468.
10 *Johnston v Britannia Airways Ltd* [1994] STC 763 on which see [1995] BTR 499. Following this case, ICAEW wrote to the Inland Revenue for clarification of the Revenue's interpretation of this decision. In its response, the Revenue confirmed that provisions for future payments under warranty claims, or of anticipated closure costs or for likely costs of disputed legal actions are deductible for tax purposes if the provision is made in accordance with commercial accounting principles. The Revenue's answer states: "*James Spencer* is now seen simply as an answer, on a specific set of facts and reached without the benefit of accountancy input, to the question of whether the provision is sufficiently accurate to be acceptable for tax". Commercially, there is often more than one accounting policy that can validly be followed by an enterprise. The Revenue state: 'In general the Revenue will accept a generally accepted accounting policy which does not violate any rules of tax law'. The correspondence is published in ICAEW press release, 12 April 1995, Guidance Note TAX 10/95, *Simon's Weekly Tax Intelligence* 1995, p 703. See also *Sycamore plc and Maple Ltd v Fir* [1997] STC (SCD) 1.
11 [1993] BTR 468, 477.
12 [1978] STC 75, [1978] 1 All ER 754; see also Vinelott J in *Pattison v Marine Midland Ltd* [1981] STC 540.
13 See 52 TC at 272 and *White* [1987] BTR 292 at 295.
14 FA 1993, ss 92 to 94A, FA 1996, ss 80 to 105 and FA 2002, Sch 26.
15 Statement of Practice 2/02 issued 30 September 2002, see Simons Weekly Tax Intelligence 2002, p 1318.
16 [1984] STC 10, HL.
17 In *Heather v P-E Consulting Group Ltd* (1972) 48 TC 293 at 323C-H.
18 *Odeon Associated Theatres Ltd v Jones* (1978) 48 TC 257, CA at 283A.
19 (2000) 74 TC 1, Court of Final Appeal of the Hong Kong Special Administrative Region.
20 Part of the Special Commissioner's decision in *Mars UK Ltd v Small* [2004] STC (SCD) 253 para 89 at 271h.
21 [2007] STC 680, HL. In this case, Lord Hoffmann criticised the decision of Lord Millett in Secan.
22 [2007] STC 680 paras [27], [40], [41] and [42] at 688a, 690j, 691a and 691b. The House of Lords, thereby, overruled the Court of Appeal: *Small v Mars (UK)* [2005]

EWHC 553 (Ch), [2005] STC 958; *IRC v William Grant & Sons Distillers* [2006] STC 69.

Taxation based on 'generally accepted' accounting practice

[8.65] Statute requires that, in computing a liability to tax, the profits of a trade, profession or vocation are to be measured in accordance with "generally accepted accounting practice"[1]. These words were inserted by FA 2002, replacing a requirement for accounts used for tax purposes to give "a true and fair view". The change is, arguably, most significant for unincorporated businesses. Accountants have long regarded the requirement of "a true and fair view" as the paradigm of accounts preparation. The truth and fairness of accounts for the purposes of its users may, it is argued, best be achieved by adopting an accounting policy that is specifically tailored to the users of those particular accounts, which may not be the policy followed by published financial reporting standards. The change in the statutory requirement made in 2002 brings in what most would regard as a technical phrase with a specific meaning. "Generally accepted accounting practice" is widely regarded as synonymous with the application of all Financial Reporting Standards that are current.[2]

Financial Reporting Standards (FRS) are issued by the Accounting Standards Board. Over the next five years, there is a substantial programme of introducing international accounting standards (IASs) issued by the International Accounting Standards Board (ISAB). Generally, IASs will be required for listed companies only.

It is common for a FRS to state that its provisions do not apply to an entity adopting the financial reporting standard for small entities (FRSSE).[3] However, paragraph 2.1 of FRSSE[4] states that an entity preparing accounts under FRSSE[5] is required by para 2.1 of that Statement to recognise, in its accounts, all assets identified by the relevant FRSs, although the disclosure notes may not be necessary. The view is generally taken that the effect of FRSSE, para 2.1 taken with ITTOIA 2005, s 25(1) and FA 1998, s 42 (as amended) is that all enterprises, including small partnerships and sole traders, are required to reflect the provisions of all FRSs insofar as these determine the measure of profit that is to be subject to tax.

There is a tension between the approach of the Accounting Standards Board (and the ISAB), on the one hand, and the measure under a profit for tax purposes, on the other hand. The ASB and ISAB are acting to further the interest of the investor in an enterprise; in other words, the focus is on what is appropriate in the accounts of a listed company. Only a tiny percentage of the companies in the UK are listed; by definition, the 2,500,000 unincorporated businesses are not. We, thus, have an extreme example of the listed tail wagging the tax dog.

A pertinent example of the inappropriateness of the ASB's approach to the taxation of small enterprises is afforded by FRS 5 "Revenue Recognition" and the application note of that standard issued on 13 November 2003. A member of ASB has commented: "after 700 years of double entry bookkeeping, we still don't know what revenue is". ASB attempted to grapple with the problem that a few listed companies were reporting a higher turnover figure than was justified, in the view of ASB. To give guidance on this, ASB issued Application Note G on 13 November 2003 which stated that revenue should be recognised if, and only if, work that had been done gave a right to receive remuneration. If the effect of FRSSE, para 2.1 is correctly stated above, the treatment given in Application Note G is to be applied in measuring profits of every sole practitioner, even though the focus of ASB's activity is on listed companies. What does this mean to the sole practitioner accountant or solicitor in the High Street? If the contracts the professional has with his clients provide for work to be billed when it is completed, Application Note G probably has little effect. The professional's accounts will, for tax purposes, show work in progress measured by reference to cost and no account is taken of the partner's time. By contrast, if the practitioner has a contract with his client whereby he can bill all the time he has expended on a job, whether or not work is completed, the effect of Application Note G is probably to create an asset on the balance sheet, called by some "accrued revenue", which states the amount that the practice can reasonably expect to receive for the work undertaken under such a contractual arrangement. It is well established that work in progress (being a category of expenditure) must not, for tax purposes, include the proprietor's own time. No such analysis applies to "accrued revenue", being a category of debtor rather than expenditure. The consequence of ASB issuing Application Note G is, thus, arguably, that two professional practices that viewed commercially would be regarded as of equal worth and generating equal profits are shown as substantially different in their accounts if one practice operates on the basis of time based billing alone and the other on the basis of project billing.[6]

Those responsible for setting standards view their aim as achieving "representational faithfulness". A long-term aim of the standard setting bodies has been stated to be the measurement of all assets and liabilities at fair value. The advantage for the investor analysing a company's performance is apparent. The difficulty in using such concepts to define a sum on which tax is levied is equally clear. This difficulty is made all the greater by the rapid change of financial reporting standards that we are experiencing in these earlier years of the twenty-first century. An entity should know the tax base that will be applicable to a transaction when it enters into that transaction. With the rapid development of UK financial reporting standards and the replacement of these by international accounting standards, it is unclear to many enterprises, particularly in the financial services field, how transactions will be reported. If the reporting of a transaction determines the tax liability, an undesirable degree of uncertainty is experienced.

The other side of the argument is, of course, that it is widely considered that a tax charge should reflect the commercial reality. If the commercial world measures profits in a certain way, then this should be the basis for tax on those profits.

In June 2001 the Revenue published an important statement which reversed their previous approach:[7]

The measure of income [8.65]

Our understanding of the law

Recent court decisions have presented an evolving view of the interaction of tax and accountancy. It has been well established that there is no rule of law stating that expenditure is tax deductible as it is paid or incurred. For timing purposes, the starting point for tax is the measure of accounting profits as shown by accounts drawn up under general accounting practice.

This means that expenditure which is revenue in terms of tax law, but which is deferred (or 'capitalised') and shown somewhere on the balance sheet under correct accounting practice, can only be relieved for tax purposes as and when it is posted to the profit and loss account in accordance with generally accepted accountancy practice. Generally this will be when the expenditure is amortised or depreciated. (FRS15, 'Recognition, measurement and depreciation of tangible fixed assets', may be relevant.)

So a computational adjustment to obtain earlier relief on a paid or incurred basis for this kind of expenditure, which is posted to the balance sheet, is no longer acceptable. This treatment, of course, only applies to bona fide revenue expenditure. It is well established in law that capital expenditure is inadmissible for tax purposes, whatever the accounting treatment might be.

Where a depreciation charge includes both revenue and capital elements, any reasonable method of identifying the revenue element will be accepted, provided it is consistently applied, and excludes amounts for which relief has already been given.

The judgement in the *Herbert Smith* case[8] supports the trend in aligning tax and accounting. We issued a Press Release[9] in July 1999 following the *Herbert Smith* case which explained that, broadly, deductions (for provisions for allowable revenue expenditure) were to be allowed for tax, if they followed generally accepted accounting practice, but that no expenditure could be relieved more than once.

Practical Measures

We want to get everybody on the same footing because differing practices have grown up over the years on how to deal with deferred revenue expenditure. But we recognise that there can be practical difficulties in achieving this. Specifically, there may have been doubt over how to deal with revenue expenditure that is posted to fixed assets, as opposed to current assets. We now know that it is irrelevant for tax purposes where revenue expenditure, that is deferred, is held on the balance sheet.

The cut off

We propose to treat 30 June 1999 as the cut off date from which the correct view of the law should be applied.

The evolving relationship between accounting income and taxable income, with proposals for future developments is discussed in a Discussion Paper of the Institute of Fiscal Studies: "The Taxation of Business Income: Aligning Taxable Income with Accounting Income".[10]

It is important to note that a financial reporting standard often permits a variety of treatment, with the enterprise being instructed to choose an accounting policy that is appropriate to its particular circumstances.

FRS 18 "Accounting policies"[11] permits a choice of accounting policy. The choice is, however, constrained by requiring the policy chosen to properly reflect the fundamentals of accountancy, which are described as the two concepts of the going concern assumption and accruals[12]. These, in FRS 18, are stated as playing a pervasive role in financial statements, and hence in the selection of accounting policies[13].

The tax effect of a change of accounting policy can be spread over three to six years (see infra, § **8.69**).

---

[1] For a period of accounts beginning on or after 1 January 2005, FA 2004 s 50, amplified by FA 2005, ss 80–84, gives two alternative statutory definitions of "generally accepted accounting practice". If the entity prepares IAS accounts, statute defines "generally accepted accounting practice" accounts in accordance with international accounting standards. For any other entity "generally accepted accounting practice" means the generally accepted accounting practice for UK companies that is intended to give a true and fair view.

[2] Statute now specifies that the generally accepted accounting practice with respect to accounts of UK companies is applicable to unincorporated entities, for measuring income for taxation purposes: FA 2004, s 50.

[3] For example, FRS5 at para 13A states that this particular FRS is not applicable to an entity preparing its accounts under FRSSE.

[4] Generally, an entity with a turnover of less than £5,600,000.

[5] This is the principle neatly demonstrated in *Oram v Johnson* [1980] STC 222, where the taxpayer sought to have a deduction in a CGT computation for the time he had expended on building the house that he later sold and thereby triggered a capital gain. The court held that the concept of "expenditure" denoted the paying out of money or of money's worth. An unincorporated entity is the proprietor himself (or the partners themselves) and there is no paying out of money or money's worth in the work, of the proprietor(s) himself/themselves.

[6] This is, necessarily, a brief summary of the debate occasioned by the issuing of Application Note G. The practical effect may well not be as great as some have claimed. When recognising in the accounts the right to income that has arisen, prudence demands that adequate provision be given for the possibility of irrecoverability. In many instances this may give a figure that is not materially different from the figure used for work in progress. An interesting debate has also arisen on the nature of the change that may arise through Application Note G. The Revenue have stated in correspondence that they consider the adoption of Application Note G to be a change of accounting policy. If so, the opening position needs to be restated under FRS 18 and any increase in the opening position is a sum assessable under ITTOIA 2005, s 229 (income tax) or Schedule D Case VI: FA 2002, Sch 22, para 4(2) (corporation tax). This view appears to be incorrect. ISB has not made a change to FRS 5. Application Note G is, in terms, simply guidance by ASB as to how FRS 5 should always have been operated. Hence, it is not a new accounting policy and an enterprise that makes up its accounts to a subsequent date by reference to Application Note G is not adopting a new accounting policy. The complexity of the issue is well illustrated by the fact that Abstract 40 has now been issued to explain the manner in which Application Note G should be interpreted.

[7] Inland Revenue Tax Bulletin, June 2001, p 859.

[8] [1999] STC 173.

[9] PR138/99.

[10] Published April 2002 for the Tax Law Review Committee by the Institute of Fiscal Studies, TLRC Discussion Paper No 2.

[11] Issued in 2001 as a replacement for SSAP2 "Disclosure of Accounting Policies". SSAP2 set out four fundamental concepts of accountancy:

(1) **Prudence:** The principle that revenue is not to be anticipated and is only to be included when realised.
(2) **Consistency:** Consistent accounting policies are to be adopted from one period to the next.
(3) **Matching:** Revenue and expenses are to be accrued and, if related, are to be matched.
(4) **Going concern:** It is assumed that an enterprise will continue to operate for the foreseeable future.

[12] It is interesting to see the central place that is given to accruals. Those who set accounting standards reject the "cash basis" that was generally in use until 1999 to draw up the accounts of the majority of professional partnerships.

[13] FRS 18 then continues to give guidance in considerable detail on the way in which accounting policies should be selected for a particular enterprise.

Statutory recognition of accounting practice

[8.66] In FA 2000 Parliament used the concept of "normal accounting practice" to enact anti-avoidance leglisation.[1] Certain companies have entered into an arrangement whereby the right to future rental income has been transferred and it has been argued that the amount received is assessable as a capital gain, not rental income. Statute counters this device by requiring a company to draw up its accounts for tax purposes in accordance with the accounting practice that is applicable in the United Kingdom,[2] whether or not the company is incorporated in the UK,[3] thus the approach of the Accounting Standards Board in distinguishing revenue from capital is given statutory effect.[4]

Since, 2000, the concept has been used in statute, but the formulation changed in FA 2002 to "generally accepted accounting practice". This is thought to automatically import the effect of accounting standards into the tax code. The concept is used in two separate ways in legislation. First, there is a requirement to apply "generally accepted accounting practice" in measuring the profits that are subjected to tax.[5] Second, "generally accepted accounting practice" is adopted as the determinant of whether an item qualifies for a statutory relief, notably for research expenditure.[6]

---

[1] TA 1988, s 43A inserted by FA 2000, s 110. See also the provision on goodwill in FA 2002.
[2] TA 1988, s 43A(2).
[3] TA 1988, s 43A(4).
[4] The Treasury notes to Finance Bill 2000 state that the new legislation, which inserts TA 1988, s 43A, has been drafted on the assumption that the ASB will issue a Financial Reporting Standard on the basis of the provisions in the ASB discussion paper of December 1999, "Leases: Implementation of the New Approach". The way that the statutory provision has been drafted has the effect that, when Finance Bill 2000 was published it gave statutory effect to the "normal accounting practice" in FRS 5 but a statement, at any time, by ASB that FRS5 has been superseded by a new statement would automatically cause the "normal accounting practice"

[8.66] Income from trades, professions and vocations

required by statute to be the practice in the new statement and the practice in FRS 5 would no longer be permitted.
[5] ITTOIA 2005, s 25.
[6] TA 1988, s 837A(2) inserted by FA 2000, Sch 19, para 1.

Accounting provisions

[8.67] FRS 12 "Provisions Contingent Liabilities and Contingent Assets" was issued by the Accounting Standards Board in September 1998 and is mandatory for accounting periods ending on or after 23 March 1999.

FRS 12 had its origin in the concern of the Accounting Standards Board that businesses were making large provisions for future restructuring (so-called "big bath" provisions, since everything was thrown into them) where in many cases the only event that had occurred at the balance sheet date was an unpublished decision of the directors. However, FRS 12 goes much wider than restructuring provisions; its basis is that provisions must satisfy the definition of liabilities as "obligations of an entity to transfer economic benefits as a result of past transactions or events". Mere anticipation of future expenditure, however probable and no matter how detailed the estimates, is not enough, in the absence of an obligation at the balance sheet date.

FRS 12 lays down a complete code prescribing when provisions must be made, and when they must not, and also lays down rules for the quantification of provisions. Where businesses have made, or not made, provisions in the past on a basis which does not accord with FRS 12, they will need to change their accounting policies.

"Provisions" are defined by FRS 12 as "liabilities of uncertain timing or amount". A provision must be made when, and only when, at the balance sheet date a business has a present obligation (legal or constructive) as a result of a past event and it is probable that a "transfer of economic benefits" (ie expenditure) will be required to settle the obligation and a reliable estimate can be made of the amount of the obligation.

The Revenue view on the allowability for tax purposes of provisions determined in accordance with FRS 12 is that a provision made in accounts will be allowable for tax purposes if (and only if):

(1) it is in respect of allowable revenue expenditure (and not, for example, in respect of capital expenditure);
(2) it is required by UK generally accepted accounting practice ("GAAP");
(3) it does not conflict with any specific tax rule governing the time at which expenditure is allowed; and
(4) it is estimated with sufficient accuracy.

Where (1)–(3) are satisfied but (4) is not then the Revenue view is that no deduction can be allowed for tax purposes until there is a sufficiently accurate estimate.[1]

In recent years the courts have shown a tendency to accept accountancy evidence to substantiate a set of accounts that has been properly drawn up in accordance with accounting standards. Courts have tended to avoid constructing rules for tax computations that differ from the approach taken for commercial accounts. In *Herbert Smith v Honour*,[2] a solicitors firm occupied four offices in London as tenant. On 26 January 1990, the firm entered into a lease of new premises with the intention of transferring the whole of the firm's operation to those new premises. The move was made during 1990 and completed by the end of that calendar year. In the accounts for the 12-month period ended 30 April 1990, provision was made for the excess of rent the firm would be liable to pay in the future in respect of the old premises. In subsequent years, further deductions were claimed as the original estimate proved to have been insufficient. The Revenue contended that such provisions were not deductible for tax purposes when made but, rather, deduction was available in a later year, when there was an actual payment. Lloyd J, in his judgment, gave an extensive review of the case law on provisions and concluded:

> While I would not say that the judge-made rule as to the relevance of accounts prepared in accordance with generally accepted principles of commercial accounting does not permit non-statutory exceptions beyond those already recognised in decided cases, I am not able to hold that the relevance of such accounts is subject to a general exception prohibiting the deduction of sums entered in the debit side of the accounts by way of a provision in accordance with the prudence concept as set out in para 14(d) of SSAP 2.[3]

The court upheld the similar approach adopted by special commissioners who allowed a deduction for the provision for the cost of repairs that were necessary to be undertaken in the future.[4] Similarly, in *Tapemaze v Melluish*[5] accounts were drawn up in accordance with FRS 3 so that the write-back of a provision for rentals paid in advance and a provision for deferred maintenance, a total of £5,189,609, was treated in the accounts as an increase in the profit of the final year of trading. The Court upheld the Special Commissioners' decision to reject the taxpayer's application that this sum should be treated for tax purposes as income of the company for later years and not for the single year in which it was recognised for accounting purposes. The approach currently taken by the courts is to favour a tax charge based on the accounting practice that has been adopted by the taxpayer and to reject amendments made unless clearly required by tax statute. Hence, in *Commissioner of Inland Revenue v Secan Ltd*,[6] the Privy Council held that the capitalisation of interest that had been undertaken by the company in three previous years gave the required tax relief and the company could not argue that relief was available in the later year when the interest was actually paid.

---

[1] Inland Revenue Tax Bulletin, December 1999, p 707. See also Inland Revenue Press Release, 23 July 1999, which was issued after the Revenue decided not to appeal the decision in two cases concerning provisions made by businesses in computing profits: *Herbert Smith (a firm) v Honour* [1999] STC 173 on provisions for future rents and *Jenners Princes Street Edinburgh Ltd v IRC* [1998] STC (SCD) 196 on provision for repairs.

[2] [1999] STC 173.

[3] [1999] STC 173 at 204d.

[4] *Jenners Princes Street Edinburgh Ltd v IRC* [1998] STC (SCD) 196.

[5] [2000] STC 189.
[6] (2000) 74 TC 1, PC. The case was decided under the Hong Kong Ordinance. It is of particular interest in that it appears to have led directly to the issuing by the Revenue of the June 2001 statement reproduced at supra, § **8.66**.

[8.68] Regard should be had to the current law on the differences between tax law and accounting. The courts accept, even in *Jones v Gallagher* that while the ordinary principles of commercial accounting must, as far as is practicable, be observed, income tax law must not be violated.[1]

(1) The courts have consistently held that the question whether an expenditure is a capital or revenue account is one of law—whatever the accounting view.[2] By treating these issues as questions of law the courts have enabled themselves to keep complete residual control.

(2) Depreciation. It is an elementary accountancy principle that capital expenditure on a depreciating asset must be written off over the lifetime of the asset. However, the tax law allows the deduction of capital expenditure only if that expenditure falls within the capital allowances system (infra, Chapter 9).

(3) Abortive expense. Prudent accountancy practice writes off abortive expenditure as a revenue expense but for tax law abortive capital expenditure is not deductible.[3]

(4) ITTOIA 2005, s 34 (income tax); TA 1988, s 74 (corporation tax). Certain expenditure which is clearly revenue rather than capital is nonetheless not deductible because it is barred by ITTOIA 2005, s 34 or TA 1988, s 74, eg because it is not incurred "wholly and exclusively for the purpose of earning a profit" or because it is not directed to the earning of profits.

(5) Other express provisions. Certain items of expenditure are deducted in commercial accounts but are disallowed by an express statutory provision.[4]

(6) Timing. However, the courts have not confined their decisions on points of accountancy to those situations where an express statutory provision is in point. The courts have also ruled on such questions as the correct method of assessing work in progress,[5] and the correct method of valuing stock in trade,[6] matters where there is no express provision. In the latter case the courts have ruled that there is such a thing as the correct method, even though accountancy knows of many methods. Differing methods tend to produce similar results overall when applied consistently from year to year and perhaps the one thing upon which there is uniform accountancy opinion is that there must be consistency from year to year. The Revenue have not felt inhibited about seeking to change the basis from year to year, eg cash to earnings basis, and have challenged accounts on bases which they have previously accepted over a period of many years.[7]

(7) Nothings. Bona fide commercial payments and receipts sometimes fall outside the tax system; they cannot fall outside the accounting system.[8]

Taking a simple view of the problem one can see a defined role for ITTOIA 2005, s 25 (income tax) and TA 1988, s 42 (corporation tax). Determining the net profit of a business involves three sets of issues. The first is to determine the items which should be taken into account. The pre-1999 approach, exemplified in the case law, was to determine the profits of a period by computing the taxable (ie trading) receipts of that period and then deducting the allowable (revenue) expenditure. The balance was the profit (or loss) of the trade for that period. This approach will continue subject to the need to show that ITTOIA 2005, s 25 (income tax) and TA 1988, s 42 (corporation tax) have been observed. The extent to which these sections will have much to say on these issues of classification of receipts and expenditures is as yet unclear. The fact that the accounting practice is subject to "adjustments required or authorised by law" suggests that the courts' determination to treat such issues as matters of law will not only prevail but also continue.

The second set relates to timing. It is easier to compute the total profit or loss of a trade from its commencement to its discontinuance than it is to compute that figure for a particular artificial accounting period such as a year. Rules already absorbed by case law from accounting practice apply to deal with the transfer of unsold trading stock from one period to another. Other timing issues have arisen in which an established accounting practice can be decisive.[9] ITTOIA 2005, s 25 (income tax) and TA 1988, s 42 (corporation tax) may be taken to have reinforced this trend.

The third set relates to issues of valuation, eg discounting. While it must be conceded that there are different methods of income measurement,[10] this seems pre-eminently an area in which accounting evidence will be accepted by the courts.

Simon's Taxes B2.107.

[1] *Viscount Simonds in Ostime v Duple Motor Bodies Ltd* [1961] 2 All ER 167 at 169, 39 TC 537 at 566.
[2] *Beauchamp v F W Woolworth plc* [1989] STC 510; here the tax treatment coincided with the accountancy treatment. See also *Associated Portland Cement Manufacturers Ltd v Kerr* [1946] 1 All ER 68, 27 TC 103 (decision against accounting evidence) and *Heather v P E Consulting Group* [1973] 1 All ER 8, 48 TC 320 (decision consistent with accounting evidence).
[3] *Southwell v Savill Bros Ltd* [1901] 2 KB 349; 4 TC 430.
[4] Such as business entertaining expenses, ITTOIA 2005, s 45 (income tax); TA 1988, s 577 (corporation tax).
[5] *Ostime v Duple Motor Bodies Ltd* [1961] 2 All ER 167, 39 TC 537.
[6] eg the prohibition of LIFO.
[7] eg *BSC Footwear Ltd v Ridgway* [1970] 1 All ER 932, 47 TC 511 (practice accepted for 30 years) and *Ostime v Duple Motor Bodies Ltd* [1961] 2 All ER 167, 39 TC 537 (practice accepted for 28 years).
[8] Such as in *Beauchamp v F W Woolworth plc* [1989] STC 510; however, this would now be treated within the forex provisions for companies.
[9] See Walton J in *Willingale v International Commercial Bank Ltd* [1976] STC 188 at 194-5 and *Symons v Weeks* [1983] STC 195.
[10] Thus in *Southern Railway of Peru Ltd v Owen* [1956] 2 All ER 728, 36 TC 602 (supra, § **7.149**), the House of Lords felt that the accountancy figures were not sufficiently reliable.

Spreading adjustments

Change of accounting policy

[8.69] On two occasions in recent years a group of taxpayers has suffered a significant increase in its tax burden by the imposition of a change of accounting policy. The first was changing the accounting policy imposed by statute,[1] requiring accounts to be used for income tax purposes to be drawn up on the accruals basis (see infra, § **8.70**). The consequence of this was that many professional partnerships brought into a charge to tax work in progress and debtors that previously had not been recognised until converted into receipts. The second change does not have its origin in statute but in a reinterpretation of a long-standing financial reporting standard, FRS5. This reporting standard addresses a perennial problem of how to reflect in annual accounts contracts that do not fit neatly into a 12-month period. It has long been recognised in the accounting profession that when an enterprise undertakes a contract that will take several years to complete, then it is appropriate to recognise in each annual accounting period a proportion of the profit that it is thought, on the basis of a prudent estimate, will arise on the contract taken as a whole. How that is achieved numerically has been the subject for great debate and difference of opinion in the accounting profession. With a view to limiting the range of treatments and the potential for misrepresenting profits, particularly in the financial reports of listed companies in the construction and defence industries, on 13 November 2003 the accounting standard board issued its interpretation of the manner in which profit on contracts that span an accounting year end should be allocated to the two or more years in which the profit can be considered as being generated (see supra, § **8.65**). The ASB "Application Note G" went much further than specifying a treatment for what is traditionally regarded as a long term contract. The application note stated that adherence to FRS5 requires recognition of profit in one accounting period for any billable work undertaken on a contract commenced in that accounting period, which continues into the next period. Thus, a typical matter undertaken by a firm of solicitors where work is billed on a time basis gives profit to be recognised in the accounts in year 1 even though the work will extend over a few months and will not normally be billed until year 2. This is achieved by, in effect, valuing the work in progress and at selling price (after appropriate provision). For an unincorporated business, this turns on its head the principle that the value of time expended by the sole trader or any partner must not be recognised in work in progress. Even the partner's time appears in the accounts at selling price. We no longer say: "No man can pay himself".

Faced with significant increases in taxable profit arising, in general, to the same group of people who suffered an additional tax charge on the charge for cash basis, for which spreading off the tax charge over 10 years is available,[2] Parliament has again made provision for spreading the burden of the tax charge,[3] The spreading is over a period of up to six years and is not specifically linked to the recognition of profit in work in progress; it is available for any change of accounting policy that takes place in a period of accounts ending on or after 22 June 2005,[4] the date from which UITF 40[5] is operative.

Spreading adjustments [8.70]

In each of the first three years, following the adoption in the taxpayer's accounts of UITF 40, one-third of the "adjustment income" is compared with one-sixth of the normal business profits for that year and the extra tax charge is limited to the lower of:

(a) one-third of the original amount of the 'adjustment income'; or
(b) one-sixth of the profits of the business.

There is sweep-up of any outstanding 'adjustment income' in Year 6.

[1] FA 1998, s 42.
[2] FA 1998, Sch 6.
[3] FA 2006, s 102 & Sch 15.
[4] FA 2006, Sch 15, para 1(1).
[5] In March 2005, the Urgent Issues Task Force of the Accounting Standards Board issued UITF 40 which clarified the principles governing the recognition of revenue in accounts and the treatment of work in progress. UITF 40 applies to accounts prepared for accounting periods ending on or after 22 June 2005. UITF 40 is expected to result in substantial upward adjustments for some taxpayers.

Change from cash basis to earnings basis

[8.70] Prior to 1999–2000, many professionals, including some very large professional partnerships, drew up their accounts on what was termed as a "conventional" basis. In practice, there were many different accounting bases that were adopted. Some partnerships drew up true "cash accounts"; that is, no income was recognised until it was received and no expenditure until it was paid—this meant there was no work in progress, debtors or creditors. More commonly, creditors and debtors were recognised but not work in progress. In some cases, accounts were drawn up recognising creditors but not debtors nor work in progress. Where work in progress was recognised, the accounting treatment ranged from a valuation at charging rates for all work undertaken, including that by the principals, to a purely nominal sum that had its basis in history and nothing else. Good arguments could be—and were—put forward for the use of such accounting concepts. For barristers, for example, the fact that it is not possible to sue for fees charged for representation at proceedings provided a justification that the only proper way of accounting was to recognise those fees only when they were received. Over the years, the courts accepted a "conventional basis" for a professional to draw up his accounts.[1] Revenue acceptance of "cash accounting", and its many variants, was stated publicly,[2] although the Revenue sought, probably without legal authority, to require a profession to adopt the "earnings basis" for the first three years from the date of setting up.

From 2000–01, a profession is required to draw up its accounts, for tax purposes, using opening and closing balance sheets that are in accordance with accounting standards.[3] The effect of this is that the accounts for the period that forms the first period under the new rules are drawn up with the opening position being the closing balance sheet for the preceding period.[4] The closing position is, however, a balance sheet in accordance with Accounting Standards. Where a conventional basis has been used in the past the effect of this is that the profit of the basis period for the first period under the new rules is increased by the difference between the balance sheet total at the end of that period and the total that would have been computed had the conventional basis been followed. This is termed the "adjustment charge".[5] This "adjustment charge" may, however, be spread over ten years.[6]

In each of the first nine years an addition is made to taxable profits, the addition being the lower of one-tenth of the "adjustment charge" and one-tenth of the profits that would otherwise be assessable for that year.[7] In the tenth year, the balance of the "adjustment charge" that has not been subject to tax is brought into charge.[8] Where the business is permanently discontinued before the expiry of ten years, the "adjustment charge" allocated to subsequent years continues to be charged in those years even though no profits are enjoyed.[9] This treatment is applied even after the death of the partner, the personal representative being assessable on the annual instalments of the adjustment charge,[10] although an election to discharge all remaining liability can be made.[11] The taxpayer can elect that the amount brought into charge in any one year be increased.[12] This may be beneficial if the individual's income moves from one rate of tax to a higher rate, or where the taxpayer wishes to maximise the pension payments he is entitled to make. Where the profits are profits of a partnership, the election must be made jointly by all partners.[13]

Barristers and advocates may claim exemption from s 42 for the seven years beginning with the date they first hold themselves out as available for fee-earning work.[14] During this period they may be taxed either on a cash basis or on the basis that income is received when the fees are agreed or a fee note delivered; the chosen basis must be applied consistently.[15] They may choose at any time during the seven years to switch to the general rule in s 42; such an election is irrevocable.[16]

Simon's Taxes B8.311.

[1] See *McCash and Hunter v IRC* (1955) 36 TC 170 and *D & G R Rankine v IRC* (1952) 32 TC 520. For a modern case where a cash basis was accepted, see *A Firm v Honour* [1997] STC (SCD) 293.
[2] Inland Revenue Press Release, 11 November 1969.
[3] FA 1998, s 42.
[4] The calculation of the adjustment is specified in FA 1998, Sch 6, para 3. The description given here gives the effect of the para 3 calculation, without adopting its formulation, which is given in the rather long-winded style suggested by the Tax Law Rewrite Project.
[5] FA 1998, Sch 6, para 2(1).
[6] FA 1998, Sch 6, para 4.
[7] FA 1998, Sch 6, para 4(4). Now, for barristers and advocates, ITTOIA 2005, s 238(2).
[8] FA 1998, Sch 6, para 4(5). Now, for barristers and advocates, ITTOIA 2005, s 238(4).
[9] FA 1998, Sch 6, para 4(6). Now, for barristers and advocates, ITTOIA 2005, s 238(5). The 1998 statute (as did its replacement in 2002) refers to the profession being permanently discontinued. The Partnership Act 1890 treats the retirement of

an individual partner as constituting the discontinuance of the partnership. Presumably, the charge to the balance of the "adjustment charge" is not triggered as the new partnership created out of the continuing partners continues the profession. ITTOIA 2005 refers to the individual ceasing to carry on the profession.

[10] FA 1998, Sch 6, para 7. Now, for barristers and advocates, ITTOIA 2005, s 240.
[11] FA 1988, Sch 6, paras 7(b) and 5. Now, for barristers and advocates, ITTOIA 2005, s 240(3).
[12] FA 1998, Sch 6, para 5. Now, for barristers and advocates, ITTOIA 2005, s 239.
[13] FA 1998, Sch 6, para 6. (Not relevant to barristers and advocates.)
[14] Now, ITTOIA 2005, s 160(1), (2).
[15] Now, ITTOIA 2005, s 160(3), (4).
[16] Now, ITTOIA 2005, s 160(5), (6).

[8.71] A business may decide to change from one accounting policy to another. For accounting purposes, the business is required to state the results of the current period by applying the new accounting policy to the whole of that period, amending the opening figure as necessary. The transition is made from the previous period, in which a different accounting policy was adopted, by a "prior year adjustment".

This approach is in conflict with the desire under self-assessment to finalise the tax liability of an individual or a company. Hence, the approach taken by the Taxes Acts is to measure the effect of the change of accounting policy and to treat the sum thus measured as an increase or decrease in the taxable profits of the year in which the new accounting policy is adopted. Professional partnerships that had prepared their accounts on a "cash basis" (see supra, § **8.70**) were forced to change the accounting policy on which their accounts were based, for fiscal year 1999–2000; for this change, a form of "spreading" of the charge arising from the change is provided.[1]

If the change occurs in an accounting period that ends after 31 July 2002, ITTOIA 2005, Pt 2, Ch 17 (income tax) and FA 2002, Sch 22 (corporation tax) provide a complete statutory code for the tax effect of the change. The schedule is written in the new, irritating style adopted by the Tax Law Rewrite Project, instructing the taxpayer to calculate an "adjustment" by applying a "First step" of identifying profits that were understated on the old basis and then a "Second step" of deducting from that sum the amounts by which profits were overstated on the old basis.[2]

If the adjustment is positive, the timing of the adjustment depends on the tax. For income tax, it is chargeable to tax (for corporation tax purposes, under Schedule D, Case VI)[3] as income arising on the last day of the first period for which the new basis is adopted.[4] For income tax, the adjustment is not taxed as part of the profits from the professional so do not carry an NIC liability.

If a positive adjustment is chargeable to corporation tax purposes, it is charged under Schedule D, Case VI[5] as income arising on the first[6] day of the first period for which the new basis is adopted.

Curiously, statute requires that an adjustment arising to a partnership be allocated amongst the partners in proportion to their profit shares for the preceding period.[7] This seems bizarre and may be enacted by mistake. Partners

[8.71] Income from trades, professions and vocations

in the previous period clearly have no interest in the adjustment, particularly if they have retired from the partnership at the end of the previous period.

If the adjustment is negative, it is a deduction in computing profits for the first period in which the new policy is adopted.[8]

The adjustment is relevant earnings, earned income and profits against which a loss can be put, despite not being assessable to NIC.[9]

---

[1]   FA 1998, Sch 6 para 4; see supra, § **8.70**.
[2]   ITTOIA 2005, s 231 (income tax); FA 2002, Sch 22, para 2 (corporation tax).
[3]   ITTOIA 2005, s 233.
[4]   FA 2002, Sch 22, para 4(2)(a). This reverses the previous treatment (given by FA 1998, Sch 6, para 2(2)(a)). For the problems associated with the previous requirement for the adjustment to be treated as arising on the first day of the accounting period, see Tiley & Collison: UK Tax Guide 2001–02 § **8.139**.
[5]   FA 2002, Sch 22, para 4(2)(b).
[6]   FA 2002, Sch 22, para 4 amended by F(No 2)A 2005, Sch 6, para 1.
[7]   ITTOIA 2005, s 860(4) (income tax); FA 2002, Sch 22, para 13(2)(a) (corporation tax). It is suggested that this may be a legislative mistake as the provision applies both to a current change to accounting policy and to the enforced change from a conventional basis to an earnings basis imposed by FA 1998, s 42. In the latter case, it is, no doubt, assumed that a partner who retires at that time would receive the benefit of work in progress and debtors that had not previously appeared in the accounts. By contrast, a partner who retires immediately before his firm voluntarily changes its accounting policy (or, perhaps, is forced to do so by pronouncement of the Accounting Standards Board) is most unlikely to receive any financial benefit from the adoption of the new policy for the following period of account. Nevertheless, the curiosity has been preserved under the Rewrite of these provisions into ITTOIA 2005.
[8]   ITTOIA 2005, s 228(3) (income tax); FA 2002, Sch 22, para 5(1) (corporation tax).
[9]   ITTOIA 2005, s 232(4).

[8.72] For any period of account ending on or after 22 June 2005, in which there has been a change in accounting policy in order to conform with UITF 40,[1] the taxpayer can elect to spread the income tax (or corporation tax) effect of the charge of accounting policy.

Statute[2] specifies how to calculate "adjustment income". The maximum amount of adjustment income taxed in each of the first three tax years in which the adjustment income is spread is the lower of (i) one-third of the original amount of adjustment income and (ii) one-sixth of the profits of the business for the tax year.[3]

In the fourth or fifth years, the maximum amount taxed in either of those years is the lowest of (i) any amount not previously taxed (ii) one-third of the original amount of adjustment income and (iii) one-sixth of the profits of the business for the tax year.[4]

If the whole of the adjustment income has not been taxed by the end of the fifth tax year, the remainder is to be taxed in the sixth tax year.

An election[5] is available to bring forward the adjustment income so that more of it is taxed in a tax year than would otherwise be required.

For a partnership, the adjustment income is to be calculated at partnership level under income tax rules.[6] For the first tax year, the adjustment income is to be divided according to the arrangements for sharing the profits of the business for the twelve month period preceding the first period of account in which the changed accounting policy was applied. For the second and subsequent tax years, the adjustment income is to be divided amount the partners for the 12-month period preceding the corresponding anniversary of the start of the first period of account.[7]

---

[1] FA 2006, Sch 15, para 1(5). Guidance agreed between HMRC and ICAEW on the tax implications of UITF 40 was published on 6 October 2006: ICAEW TAXGUIDE 8/06.This can be viewed at www.icaew.co.ukl/index.cfm?route=142494
[2] ITTOIA 2005, s 231.
[3] FA 2006, Sch 15, para 2(2).
[4] FA 2006, Sch 15, para 2(4).
[5] FA 2006, Sch 15, para 4.
[6] FA 2006, Sch 15, para 7(2).
[7] FA 2006, Sch 15, para 7(3).

Trading receipts

Rule 1—trading stock

[8.73] A payment arising from the disposal of trading stock in the normal course of business is normally a trading receipt. Trading stock is not defined[1] but means (a) raw materials, (b) finished products, and (c) work in progress. It does not extend to plant nor to mere utensils as distinct from raw materials nor to a source of trading stock.[2] In *Willingale v International Commercial Bank Ltd* the bills of exchange were not trading stock. It follows that the question whether an item is trading stock must depend on the nature of the trade. In *Abbott v Albion Greyhounds (Salford) Ltd*[3] a greyhound racing company argued that the dogs used in their races were trading stock.[4] This was rejected by Wrottesly J on the ground that the saleable value of the kennel was at no time a commercial picture of the company's success or failure. Had the company bought and sold dogs by way of trade the answer would have been quite different.

Simon's Taxes Division B1.30.

---

[1] But for ITTOIA 2005, ss 173 and 174 (income tax); TA 1988, s 100, see sub-s (2) (corporation tax); see also infra, § **8.78**.
[2] Infra, § **8.127**.

[3] [1945] 1 All ER 308, 26 TC 390; see also *General Motors Acceptance Corpn v IRC* [1985] STC 408.
[4] And so should be valued at the end of the year.

Rule 2—business or business assets

[8.74] By contrast with rule 1, a sum arising from the disposal of the business itself or of a business asset is normally a capital receipt and so not a trading receipt. So in *British Borneo Petroleum Syndicate Ltd v Cropper*[1] a sum received in return for the surrender of a royalty agreement was held to be a capital receipt.

The terms on which an asset is sold may however give rise to a taxable profit. So in *Lamport and Holt Line Ltd v Langwell*,[2] A, a shipowner, sold shares in B, a company trading as fuel suppliers, to C, another company of fuel suppliers; the contract provided that A should receive a part of the commission which C should receive for supplying oil to A; these part-commissions were held to be trading receipts of A.

In *Tanfield Ltd v Carr*,[3] sums totalling £400,000 were received in respect of a motor fuel supply agreement. These sums were held by the Special Commissioner to constitute revenue receipts, on the basis that the restrictions for which the payment was made did not affect the whole structure of the taxpayer's business; they concerned only a small part of it.

In judging whether a receipt arises from the trade of the taxpayer and, hence, part of assessable profits, the receipt has the nature given to it by the circumstances at the time it arises. Subsequent unanticipated events that change the nature of the taxpayer's business cannot be used to recharacterise the receipt.[4]

Simon's Taxes A1.208, B1.431.

[1] [1969] 1 All ER 104, 45 TC 201.
[2] (1958) 38 TC 193; see also *Orchard Wine and Spirit Co v Loynes* (1952) 33 TC 97.
[3] [1999] STC (SCD) 213.
[4] *Tapemaze Ltd v Melluish* [2000] STC 189.

Rule 3—payment for non trade purposes

[8.75] While a payment in return for goods or services will normally be a trading receipt a payment made for reasons other than trade will not be a trading receipt.

A voluntary payment may be a trading receipt, eg the payment of an extra sum for work already paid for;[1] however, a testimonial or solatium is not. The latter, although perhaps in recognition of past services is not paid in respect of them nor for future services.[2] The question is one of fact; in deciding this issue it is the nature of the payment rather than the motive of the payer that prevails.

In *Murray v Goodhews*[3] a brewing company decided to end a number of tenancy agreements with the taxpayer and chose to make voluntary payments of some £81,000 over two years. These payments were held to be not trading receipts partly because, although an ex-gratia payment had been mentioned early on in the negotiation, there was no disclosure of the basis on which the payment was calculated, there had been no subsequent negotiations between the parties on this point and the amount had not been calculated by reference to profit earned.

Payments escaping tax on this basis have included one to a firm of accountants on not being reappointed to act as auditors to a company which had changed ownership, the sum being equivalent to one year's salary[4] and a payment to an insurance broker on the ending of a relationship with a client when that client was taken over by another company.[5] In practice, a prize awarded to an author for his literary work is not treated as taxable.[6]

On the other hand a payment to assist a taxpayer club to improve its curling facilities was held to be a trading receipt as the purpose of the payment was to enable the club to keep in business, *IRC v Falkirk Ice Rink Ltd*;[7] likewise a payment to compensate an estate agent for the loss of a fee-earning opportunity *McGowan v Brown and Cousins*.[8]

The matter is one of fact. In *Murray v Goodhews* the payment escaped tax despite the continued trading relationship between the parties, whereas in *McGowan v Brown and Cousins* the payment was taxable even though the trading relationship had ended. In *Rolfe v Nagel*[9] on the other hand, a payment was held taxable when made by one diamond broker to another because a client had transferred his business. The facts were unusual in that such a broker is unable to earn commission from a client until the client has been accepted as "an active client", a process taking a number of years. Other facts supported this conclusion; thus the two brokers agreed to accept whatever a third broker should think suitable and the sum, £15,000, was not paid until the client became "active".

The fact that a testimonial escapes tax is consistent with the rules for employment income.

The payment may, as a capital receipt, be liable to CGT. In practice the Revenue may treat it as a payment for goodwill and so eligible for the business asset rate of taper relief.

Simon's Taxes B2.223.

---

[1] *Temperley v Smith* [1956] 3 All ER 92, 37 TC 18; *Isaac Holden & Sons Ltd v IRC* (1924) 12 TC 768, and *Australia (Commonwealth) Taxation Comr v Squatting Investment Co Ltd* [1954] 1 All ER 349, [1954] AC 182.

[2] Per Buckley LJ in *Murray v Goodhews* [1978] STC 207 at 213, [1978] 2 All ER 40 at 46.

[3] Supra, note 2. On deduction by the brewers see *Watney Combe Reid & Co Ltd v Pike* [1982] STC 733.

[4] *Walker v Carnaby, Harrower, Barham and Pykett* [1970] 1 All ER 502, 46 TC 461.

[5] *Simpson v John Reynolds & Co (Insurances) Ltd* [1975] STC 271, CA.

[6] *Simon's Tax Intelligence* 1979, p 76.

[7] [1975] STC 434, 51 TC 42.
[8] [1977] STC 342, [1977] 3 All ER 844.
[9] [1982] STC 53.

Rule 4—incidental payments

[8.76] A payment arising incidentally in the course of a trade may be a trading receipt; the recurrence of the transaction will make this conclusion more likely. The cases concern items which are used (or used up) in the running of the trade without being clearly either capital or trading stock. They arise in the course of the conduct of the business and by and large, from that business as being carried on in the ordinary way. The cases where payments for compensation have been treated as trading receipts may be seen as further examples.

Know-how

Statute now provides that all payments in return for know-how are trading receipts if the know-how has been used in the trade and the trade is still carried on.[1]

Earlier case law decided that where a trader possessed a patent or know-how sums received in return for permitting the use of these assets would be income[2] since all that was happening was that some part of the capital of the trade was being put to use in a profit earning way.[3] Where the know-how was disposed of along with other assets of a trade in a foreign country, sums received in return for the know-how were capital receipts as part of the disposal of the trade.[4] Where, however, the company had to supply know-how as a condition of entering into a trading arrangement in a country with which there had been no previous trade, the receipt was one on revenue account as the transaction did not materially affect the company's profit making structure.[5]

Statute also now provides that where a person disposes of a trade or part of a trade, any consideration for know-how is generally to be dealt with on both sides, as a payment for goodwill. However, this is not so if the parties jointly elect otherwise or if the trade was carried on wholly outside the UK (in which latter case the old case law still applies).[6]

Simon's Taxes Division B5.3.

[1] ITTOIA 2005, s 193(2) (income tax); TA 1988, s 531(1) (corporation tax).
[2] See *IRC v Desoutter Bros Ltd* (1945) 29 TC 155 at 162 but cf *IRC v Iles* (1945) 29 TC 225.
[3] On patent royalties as deductions, see infra, § **8.130**. On know-how, see *Rolls Royce Ltd v Jeffrey* [1962] 1 All ER 801, 40 TC 443; *Musker v English Electric Co Ltd* (1964) 41 TC 556; infra, § **9.56**.
[4] *Evans Medical Supplies Ltd v Moriarty* [1957] 3 All ER 718, 37 TC 540.
[5] *Coalite and Chemical Products Ltd v Treeby* (1971) 48 TC 171 followed in *John & E. Sturge Ltd v Hessel* [1975] STC 573, 51 TC 183, 208.
[6] ITTOIA 2005, s 193(3) (income tax); TA 1988, s 531(3) (corporation tax).

Contracts for supply of trading stock

[8.77] In *George Thompson & Co Ltd v IRC*[1] a shipping company found that some of its ships had been requisitioned by the Australian Government and was left with contracts for the supply of coal in excess of its needs. It therefore transferred the benefit of the contract to another company—not in the form of an assignment but a transfer of the right to take delivery at a premium first of 6s a ton and then of 10s a ton. Although they had only rarely sold coal before, Rowlatt J had no difficulty in holding that this was a revenue receipt of the trade. The coal had not been bought as capital on capital account, but as a thing which they needed to buy and use as consumable stores. The purchase of the coal had been arranged as a part of their business so that it could not be treated as a separate business.

Simon's Taxes B2.602.

---

[1] (1927) 12 TC 1091.

Foreign currency

[8.78] The rule that a receipt must be a receipt of that trade has had some effect where a trader invests in foreign exchange which he later realises at a gain (or loss).[1] In *Imperial Tobacco Co (of Great Britain and Ireland) Ltd v Kelly*[2] the company bought tobacco leaf in America and to this end bought dollars over the year. With the outbreak of the Second World War the company, at the request of the Treasury, stopped buying American leaf and thereafter its dollars were acquired by the Treasury at a profit to the company. It was held that this was a profit of the trade. It did not matter that the company did not carry on the trade of dealing in foreign exchange. What mattered was that the dollars had been bought as the first step in an intended commercial transaction. One can thus view the dollars as equivalent to raw materials.

On the other hand in the earlier case of *McKinlay v H T Jenkins & Son Ltd*[3] a firm of builders who would shortly have to buy some marble in Italy had bought some lire for £16,500. The lira then rose in value against the pound and the holding was sold in order that a profit might be realised on the exchange.[4] The sale price was £22,870, a net profit of about £6,700. The value of the lira then fell and the firm bought the currency needed for £19,386 which sum was allowed as a deduction in computing the profits. Rowlatt J upheld the Commissioners' decision that the £6,700 was not taxable as a profit of the trade.

There was no evidence that the lire in *McKinlay v H T Jenkins & Son Ltd* were initially bought simply as a speculation[5] but rather, like the dollars in *Imperial Tobacco Co Ltd v Kelly*, as the first step in an intended commercial transaction. However, there was evidence that the decision to sell was simply motivated by the desire for a quick profit. In *Imperial Tobacco Co Ltd v Kelly* the Court of Appeal left open the correctness of Rowlatt J's decision. Today it seems likely that the profit would be taxable, either because the case cannot stand with the later decision of the Court of Appeal or because the decision to withdraw the lire holding from the ambit of the trade would cause the rule[6] in *Sharkey v Wernher*[7] to operate thus ensuring that the profit accruing up until the moment of the decision to withdraw should be a trading receipt, whether actually realised or not, leaving the balance of the profit on realisation to be taxed either as a capital gain[8] or as a separate adventure in the nature of trade. It is, however, open to the trader to show that on the particular facts the money was not trading stock.

In *Davies v Shell Co of China Ltd*[9] sums deposited with the taxpayer by its agents were repaid in foreign currency which had depreciated against sterling; the resulting profit was not a trading receipt but a capital profit.

A similar problem arose in *Pattison v Marine Midland Ltd*.[10] Here a bank raised a fund of dollars by way of loan and proceeded to lend dollars in the course of its banking business. When the original funding loan was repaid the dollar had strengthened against sterling but the House of Lords held that the bank was not taxable on the sterling profit that arose on the withdrawal of the money from the bank's lending fund since the fund had never been converted into sterling and had been translated into sterling only for balance sheet (as distinct from profit and loss account) purposes. As the fund had never been converted into sterling, the money was like an asset held by the company and generating income by being hired out; the asset might be specific or, as in *Pattison v Marine Midland Ltd*, fungible.

The 1993 changes with regard to the tax treatment of foreign exchange provide that where a company carries on a trade its profits are to be computed and expressed for corporation tax in sterling, save that a company may elect, in prescribed circumstances, that a different currency be used.[11] These changes do not apply to income tax.

Simon's Taxes B4.304.

[1] On treatment of financial futures and options see statement of practice SP 14/91.
[2] [1943] 2 All ER 119, 25 TC 292; and see *Landes Bros v Simpson* (1934) 19 TC 62 and *O'Sullivan v O'Connor* [1947] IR 416.
[3] (1926) 10 TC 372.
[4] (1926) 10 TC 376.
[5] See Rowlatt J's subsequent explanation in *George Thompson & Co Ltd v IRC* (1927) 12 TC 1091.
[6] Since codified by FA 2008.
[7] Infra, § **8.154**.
[8] *Wisdom v Chamberlain*, supra, § **8.18**.
[9] (1951) 32 TC 133.
[10] [1984] STC 10, HL.
[11] FA 1993, ss 92-94.

Investment of cash

[8.79] Investments of spare cash on a short term basis have been held to give rise to trading receipts as part of the trade of a bank or insurance company[1] and as part of a separate trade of another sort of company.[2]

Simon's Taxes B2.607.

[1] *General Reinsurance Co Ltd v Tomlinson* (1970) 48 TC 81, see also *Nuclear Electric plc v Bradley* [1995] STC 285.
[2] *Cooper v C and J Clark Ltd* [1982] STC 335.

Rule 5—restriction of activities

[8.80] A payment received as the price for a substantial restriction on one's business or as compensation for the sterilisation of a capital asset is a capital receipt, but as will be seen in rule 6 at infra, § **8.81**, a payment received as a surrogatum for trading profit is itself a trading receipt. The boundary between these two is easier to state than to apply.

In applying these two principles the court's task is complicated by the fact that a payment may come within this head even though the measure used by the parties to determine the level of payment is loss of profit—the measure does not determine the quality of the payment. The leading modern authority on rule 5 is *Higgs v Olivier*.[1] Mr Laurence Olivier (as he then was), a well-known actor, had entered into a covenant that he would not for a period of 18 months appear as an actor in or act as producer or director of any film to be made anywhere by any other company. In return he received £15,000. The covenant was with the company which had just made the film of Henry V starring Mr Laurence Olivier. The reason for this deal appears from the Case Stated, 'He was quite a popular film actor, appearing in quite the ordinary kind of films, and the company thought that if he made a more ordinary film than Henry V, the public would go to that instead'. The covenant was made after the film had been completed and indeed released in England where alas it was not making much money; it was only hailed a success after its release in New York. Thus the covenant was quite separate from the original contract to make the film. The Court of Appeal held that the payment was for a restriction extending to a substantial portion of the professional activities that were open to him, and so not a trading receipt; it may thus be seen as an expression of rule 3, supra, § **8.75**. The court also stressed that the covenant could not possibly be regarded as being in the ordinary run of the vocation of actors. The receipt would now be subject to CGT.

By contrast in *White v G and M Davies (a firm)*[2] the receipt of a premium payment by a farmer under an EEC scheme was held to be a trading receipt. In return for the payment the farmer undertook not to sell milk products for four years and to ensure that dairy cattle accounted for no more than 20% of his herd. Browne-Wilkinson J distinguished *Higgs v Olivier* on the basis that the present restrictions controlled the taxpayer as to the way in which he carried on his business whereas this had not been so in the earlier case. A similar result was reached in *IRC v Biggar*.[3]

Rule 5 was applied in *Murray v Imperial Chemical Industries Ltd*[4] where the company received a capital sum in return for agreeing not to trade in a certain country. This "keep-out" payment was made under an agreement whereby the company allowed another firm to use its patent in that country. The principle was, however, not applied in *Thompson v Magnesium Elektron Ltd*[5] where a company producing magnesium and therefore needing chlorine, agreed to buy chlorine from another company and agreed not to manufacture chlorine or caustic soda (a by product of the manufacture of chlorine) beyond its own needs; the company was to receive payments calculated on the amount of caustic soda it would have produced. It was held that the payments simply affected the price the company was paying for its chlorine. It would appear that if the payment had been a lump sum it would not have been a trading receipt,[6] as the form of the payment would have suggested that it was for not making caustic soda instead of for receiving chlorine.

Simon's Taxes A1.210–212.

[1] [1952] 1 Ch 311, 33 TC 136.
[2] [1979] STC 415; the judge noted the unfairness of treating the payment as income of one year.
[3] [1982] STC 677.
[4] [1967] 2 All ER 980, 44 TC 175. For Revenue practice note Inland Revenue interpretation RI 52.
[5] [1944] 1 All ER 126, 26 TC 1.
[6] As in *Margerison v Tyresoles Ltd* (1942) 25 TC 59.

Rule 6—surrogata for trading profits—compensation payments

[8.81] A sum received in respect of trading stock is income whether it is the proceeds of sale, or damages for breach of contract or for tort, or compensation on compulsory acquisition. The occasion for the receipt is immaterial. Lord Clyde illustrated this in *Burmah Steamship Co Ltd v IRC*:[1]

> Suppose someone who chartered one of the Appellant's vessels breached the charter and exposed himself to a claim of damages . . . there could, I imagine, be no doubt that the damages recovered would properly enter the Appellant's profit and loss account for the year. The reason would be that the breach of the charter was an injury inflicted on the Appellant's trading, making (so to speak) a hole in the Appellant's profits, and damages recovered could not be reasonably or appropriately put . . . to any other purpose than to fill that hole. Suppose on the other hand, that one of the taxpayer's vessels was negligently run down and sunk by a vessel belonging to some other shipowner, and the Appellant recovered as damages the value of the sunken vessel, I imagine that there could be no doubt that the damages so recovered could not enter the Appellant's profit and loss account because the destruction of the vessel would be an injury inflicted, not on the Appellant's trading, but on the capital assets of the Appellant's trade, making (so to speak) a hole in them, and the damages could therefore . . . only be used to fill that hole.

In *Burmah Steamship Co Ltd v IRC* the appellants had bought a ship which required extensive repairs before it could put to sea. The repairer was in breach of contract in that he did not complete the repairs until some five months after the due date. The appellant recovered £1,500 damages for late delivery, the sum being an estimate of the loss of profit. The sum was held to be income. The purchase price of the ship would however have been a capital item and therefore it ought to follow that had the purchaser arranged for a reduction in price that reduction would have meant a lower capital price and not a taxable income receipt.[2] So a payment for the *use* of a capital asset is a revenue receipt, but one for its realisation is a capital receipt.[3] In *Able (UK) Ltd v Revenue and Customs Comrs*[4] the taxpayer company received £2,185,000 for the loss of use of land as compensation under s 31(3) of the Land Compensation Act 1961. Brigg J held that where there had been only a temporary interference with the taxpayer's use of its fixed asset; the general rule was that compensation for such interference (even if it was associated with a change in the precise nature of the business or with a depreciation in the value of the capital asset) was likely to be classified as income.

Where both the lost profits and the damages are taxable no account is taken of the tax situation in assessing the damages, save for the exceptional case where justice demands it.[5]

Simon's Taxes A1.213.

---

[1] (1930) 16 TC 67 at 71, 72.
[2] Per Lord Sands (1930) 16 TC 67 at 73. See also *Crabb v Blue Star Line Ltd* [1961] 2 All ER 424, 39 TC 482 (proceeds of insurance policy against late delivery held capital). On treatment of compensation payments for compulsory slaughter of farm animals, see extra-statutory concession B11.
[3] *Greyhound Racing Association (Liverpool) Ltd v Cooper* [1936] 2 All ER 742, 20 TC 373.
[4] [2006] EWHC 3046 (Ch), [2006] SWTI 2345, [2006] All ER (D) 241 (Oct).
[5] *Deeny v Gooda Walker Ltd* [1995] STC 439.

[8.82] The rule that a surrogatum for loss of profit is an income receipt has been consistently applied. It has been applied where a company which had acquired a licence to take Noel Coward's *Cavalcade* on tour in the UK received damages because a film of that show was released to the detriment of the profits of the tour,[1] where a firm who made steam ships received damages from a purchaser in return for the cancellation of an agreement to buy ships,[2] where timber which was the trading stock of a company was destroyed by fire and sums were received from an insurance company equal to the replacement value of the timber[3] and likewise where sums were payable under an insurance policy against loss of profit.[4] Payments by the state for loss of profit while serving on a jury or local authority are considered to be taxable receipts.[5] Slightly less obviously it has been applied where a company received a large sum under a life policy they held on one of their key employees,[6] the services of the employees being regarded as being as much part of the trading activities of the business as the goods which were its trading stock and the court noticing that sums paid to induce the resignation of a director had been held to be income expenditure.[7] More recently a company whose jetty was damaged by the negligent navigation of a tanker was held taxable on the damages received in so far as they represented damages for loss of the use of the jetty during repairs but not the much larger sum needed to repair the jetty.[8] What would have happened had there been no clear apportionment of the damages is unclear.

Where damages are received for loss of profit, the fact that the damages are used to write down certain capital expenditure incurred during the contract is irrelevant; the payment is nonetheless an income receipt.[9]

When the payment is a capital receipt, it may well give rise to CGT.[10]

The rule that a surrogatum for loss of profit is an income receipt has also been applied to compensation for increased revenue expenditure.[11]

Simon's Taxes A1.213; B2.601.

[1] *Vaughan v Archie Parnell and Alfred Zeitlin Ltd* (1940) 23 TC 505. It follows that no deduction for tax can be made in assessing the damages. *Diamond v Campbell-Jones* [1960] 1 All ER 583, [1961] Ch 22.
[2] *Short Bros Ltd v IRC* (1927) 12 TC 955.
[3] *J Gliksten & Son Ltd v Green* [1929] AC 381, 14 TC 364.
[4] *R v British Columbia Fir and Cedar Lumber Co Ltd* [1932] AC 441, see also *Mallandain Investments Ltd v Shadbolt* (1940) 23 TC 367.
[5] Inland Revenue interpretation RI 18.
[6] *Williams Executors v IRC* [1942] 2 All ER 266, 26 TC 23, but see Harris and Hewson, *Life Assurance and Tax Planning*, pp 9–28, 102. It appears that in general it is Revenue practice not to treat lump sum proceeds as trading receipts if no claim was made to deduct the premiums as trading expenses. But it does not follow that the company can opt to have the proceeds treated as capital by not claiming relief for the premiums. The proper tax treatment of the proceeds must be considered on its own merits.
[7] *B W Noble Ltd v Mitchell* (1926) 11 TC 372.
[8] *London and Thames Haven Oil Wharves Ltd v Attwooll* [1967] 2 All ER 124, 43 TC 491.
[9] *IRC v Northfleet Coal and Ballast Co Ltd* (1927) 12 TC 1102.
[10] Under TCGA 1992, s 22; see *Lang v Rice* [1984] STC 172, CA.
[11] *Donald Fisher (Ealing) Ltd v Spencer* [1989] STC 256, CA.

[8.83] There is no relation between the measure that is used for the purpose of calculating a particular result and the quality of the figure that is arrived at by means of the application of that test. In *Glenboig Union Fireclay Co Ltd v IRC*[1] the taxpayer company held leasehold rights in certain fireclay seams with the right to remove minerals. The seam ran under the railway track of the Caledonian Railway Company. The railway company obtained an interdict to prevent the taxpayer from removing fireclay from the seam pending the hearing of their case against the company in which they claimed that although the lease granted the right to remove minerals, fireclay was not a mineral. The railway company lost its case and then exercised its powers compulsorily to prevent the fireclay company from exercising its rights. Eventually it was agreed that a large sum should be paid to the fireclay company for loss of the fireclay. The House of Lords held that the sum was a capital receipt. The case concerned excess profits duty and it was the Revenue who argued that the receipt was capital.[2] The company argued that as that seam would have been fully worked out in two and a half years the sum paid was nothing but a surrogatum for profits lost. Lord Buckmaster regarded that argument as fallacious:[3]

In truth the sum of money is the sum paid to prevent the Fireclay Company obtaining the full benefit of the capital value of that part of the mines which they are prevented from working by the railway company. It appears to me to make no difference whether it be regarded as the sale of the asset out and out, or whether it be treated merely as a means of preventing the acquisition of profit which would otherwise be gained. In either case the capital asset of the company to that extent has been sterilised and destroyed, and it is in respect of that action that the sum . . . was paid . . . It is now well settled that the compensation payable in such circumstances is the full value of the minerals that are left unworked, less the cost of working, and that is of course the profit that would have been obtained were they in fact worked. But there is no relation between the measure that is used for the purpose of calculating a particular result and the quality of the figure that is arrived at by means of the application of that test.

See also the Privy Council's decision in *Lutchumun v Director General of the Mauritius Revenue Authority*[4].

Simon's Taxes A1.211–213.

[1]   Per Lord Buckmaster (1922) 12 TC 427 at 464, HL.
[2]   The higher the company's profits before 1914, the lower the excess profits duty.
[3]   (1922) 12 TC 427 at 464.
[4]   [2008] UKPC 53.

Compensation as capital

[8.84] Compensation for the sterilisation of a capital asset is a capital payment (supra, § 8.80) but this leaves the question what is a capital asset. Goodwill is a capital asset and therefore damages payable for injury to goodwill are a capital receipt.[1] Extraction industries have always been odd for tax purposes since the process of their trade turns fixed into circulating capital.[2] Thus in *Glenboig* had the railway company accidentally destroyed the fireclay after it had been extracted it would appear that the sums payable by way of damages would have been a trading receipt.

Another question left unanswered is the duration of the restriction. In *Glenboig* the House of Lords did not have to consider a further point, namely the correct tax treatment of the damages for wrongous interdict.[3] The Court of Session held that the sum was a capital receipt on the ground that it was the reimbursement of expenditure of a capital nature—capital because it proved to be totally fruitless owing to the expropriation proceedings.[4] The parties settled this aspect of their liability before going to the House of Lords. If this payment was held to be a revenue receipt[5] one has the droll result that (a) the payment computed by reference to loss of profit was a capital payment while this one, not so computed, but which is for loss of profit, is a trading receipt while (b) a payment relating to a period of three years would be an income payment whereas that relating to the two and half years that it would have taken to exhaust the fireclay was a capital payment.

When compensation is received from an insurance policy, the purpose in taking out that insurance can determine the taxability of the receipt. In *Greycon Ltd v Klaentschi*,[6] keyman insurance had been taken out on the life

[8.84] Income from trades, professions and vocations

of Dr Goulimis. He died and the dispute was whether or not the £585,999 received from the insurance was or was not subject to corporation tax as profits of the company. The Special Commissioner identified that the company's reason for taking out the keyman insurance was that it was a condition precedent for an agreement by which a third party invested in the company.[7] On that basis, the receipt was declared to be a capital receipt, not part of the company's profits, and did not attract a charge to corporation tax.

Simon's Taxes A1.211–213.

---

[1] eg Lord Evershed MR, in *Wiseburgh v Domville* [1956] 1 All ER 754 at 758, 36 TC 527 at 539.
[2] Per Lord Radcliffe in *Taxes Comr v Nchanga Consolidated Copper Mines Ltd* [1964] AC 948 at 964, [1964] 1 All ER 208 at 212.
[3] The amount payable to the fireclay company in respect of expenses of keeping the seam open but unused while the interdict prevented them from working it.
[4] Per Viscount Cave LC in *British Insulated and Helsby Cables Ltd v Atherton* [1926] AC 205 at 211; *Southern v Borax Consolidated Ltd* [1940] 4 All ER 412, 23 TC 597.
[5] eg Lord Clyde in *Burmah Steamship Co Ltd v IRC* (1930) 16 TC 67 at 72 although in the Glenboig case Lord Clyde had thought it a capital receipt: 12 TC at 450.
[6] [2003] STC (SCD) 370.
[7] See para 23 at 381d.

Contracts relating to structure of business

[8.85] Damages paid for breach of a contract to make good the loss of profit from that contract will usually be income under rule 6; in such instances it makes no difference what the importance of the contract is to the trade. However, one must distinguish profit-earning contracts from those relating to the whole structure of the profit-earning apparatus of the trade. In *Van den Berghs Ltd v Clark*[1] the appellant company entered into an agreement with a competing Dutch company in 1912. The agreement provided for the sharing of profits, the bringing in of any other margarine concerns they might acquire and the setting up of a joint committee to make arrangements with outside firms as to prices and limitation of areas of supply of margarine. The agreement was intended to last until 1926 at the earliest and later variations extended that to 1940. The outbreak of the First World War upset the arrangements of the Dutch company and eventually that company agreed in 1927 to pay the appellant company £450,000 for cancellation of the agreement. The House of Lords held that the sum was paid for loss of future rights under the agreement which was a capital asset and therefore was a capital receipt. Lord Macmillan said:[2]

> The . . . agreements which the Appellants consented to cancel were not ordinary commercial contracts made in the course of carrying on their trade; they were not contracts for the disposal of their products or for the engagement of agents or other employees necessary for the conduct of their business; nor were they merely agreements as to how their trading profits when earned should be distributed between the contracting parties. On the contrary the cancelled agreements related to the whole structure of the Appellants profit making apparatus. They regulated the

Appellants' activities, defined what they might and what they might not do, and affected the whole conduct of their business. The agreements formed part of the fixed framework within which their circulating capital operated; they were not incidental to the working of their profit making machine but were essential parts of the mechanism itself. They provided the means of making profits, but they themselves did not yield profits.

Simon's Taxes A1.210.

---

[1] (1935) 19 TC 390, HL.
[2] 19 TC 390 at 431, 432.

[8.86] Sums paid on the *variation* of an agreement which relates to the whole structure of the profit-making apparatus are also capital. In *Sabine v Lockers Ltd*[1] the taxpayers held the main distributorship for the Austin motor company in the Manchester area; they were not allowed to enter into any agreement with any other manufacturer. Sums paid for variation of that contract were held capital receipts. The distributorship lasted only for one year with a right of renewal for a further year but there was reasonable prospect of further yearly renewals.

In both *Van den Bergh's Ltd v Clark* and *Sabine v Lockers Ltd* the agreements related to the framework of the company's business rather than one for the disposal of the company's products. It is less easy, but apparently not impossible,[2] for a contract of the latter type to be treated as a capital asset. However, the mere fact that a trader arranges his work on the basis of a particular contract is insufficient to make that contract one relating to the structure of his business. Thus a shipbuilding company may only make a few ships a year but an order for a ship is profit yielding contract; damages for breach will therefore be an income receipt.[3] A similar result was reached on cancellation of an agreement between a film star and a company owning the right to his services.[4]

In *Glenboig* an item of fixed capital was sterilised. This must be distinguished from the prevention of the acquisition of profit.[5]

Simon's Taxes B2.308.

---

[1] (1958) 38 TC 120.
[2] Note Ungoed-Thomas J in *John Mills Productions Ltd v Mathias* (1964) 44 TC 441 at 453.
[3] *Short Bros Ltd v IRC* (1927) 12 TC 955.
[4] *John Mills Productions Ltd v Mathias* (1964) 44 TC 441.
[5] eg *Waterloo Main Colliery Co Ltd v IRC* (1947) 29 TC 235.

Agency contracts

[8.87] The restriction, even though temporary, of one's profit making apparatus is very different from the mere loss of trading opportunity such as occurs when an agency contract on commission ends and a lump sum is received for the cancellation. At first sight it would seem that such contracts, producing

[8.87] Income from trades, professions and vocations

income, must be capital assets[1] but they are usually treated as revenue assets since their acquisition and replacement is one of the normal incidents of the business. They are disposal contracts in that the company is disposing of services. Such a contract is not a capital asset and the sum received will be taxed as a mere trading receipt. In *Shove v Dura Manufacturing Co Ltd*[2] Lawrence J gave three reasons why there was nothing of a capital nature about the contract, 'No money was spent to secure it; no capital asset was acquired to carry it out; its cancellation was only an ordinary method of modifying and realising the profit to be derived from it'.[3]

In *Kelsall Parsons & Co v IRC*[4] the appellants commenced business in Scotland as manufacturer's agents and engineers in 1914 when one of their two agencies was for a firm in Birmingham making electric switch gear. A series of agency agreements was made with the firm the last of which was for three years from 30 September 1932 but this was terminated by agreement on 30 September 1934 the firm agreeing to pay £1,500 compensation to the appellants. The Court of Session held that the sum was a trading receipt. It was true that the appellants had built up a considerable technical organisation to handle this particular agency agreement[5] but that was insufficient to bring the facts within the principle in *Van den Berghs Ltd v Clark*. In reaching this conclusion it was important to Lord Normand and Lord Fleming that the agreement had only one year to run; as Lord Normand put it this was not a case where 'a benefit extending over a tract of future years is renounced for a payment made once and for all'.[6]

Simon's Taxes B2.207.

---

[1] Per Lord Evershed MR in *Anglo-French Exploration Co Ltd v Clayson* [1956] 1 All ER 762 at 766, 36 TC 545 at 557.
[2] (1941) 23 TC 779.
[3] At 783.
[4] (1938) 21 TC 608 applied in *Creed v H and M Levinson Ltd* [1981] STC 486.
[5] Case stated para (9), 21 TC 608 at 615.
[6] 21 TC 608 at 620.

[8.88] An exceptional case the other side of the line is *Barr Crombie & Co Ltd v IRC*[1] where the appellants managed ships, 98% of its business came from an agreement with one company for a period of 15 years from 1936 which was terminated in 1942 when the shipping company went into liquidation, and a large sum paid in respect of the eight years left of the agreement. The payment was held to be a capital receipt. Taking all the facts into account Lord Normand thought that the effect on the company's structure and character was such as to bring the facts within *Van den Berghs Ltd v Clark*.

The difficulty with *Barr Crombie & Co Ltd v IRC* is that it shows how unclear is the distinction between a contract which is merely one created in the ordinary life of the business and one which relates to its profit-making structure.

These are essentially matters of degree and circumstance. One must distinguish the situation in which the rights and advantages surrendered on cancellation are such as to destroy or materially to cripple the whole structure of the recipient's profit-making apparatus, involving the serious dislocation of the normal commercial organisation and resulting perhaps in the cutting down of staff previously required, from that in which the benefit surrendered was not an enduring asset and where the structure of the recipients business is so fashioned as to absorb the shock as one of the normal incidents to be looked for and where it appears that the compensation received is no more than a surrogatum for future profits surrendered.[2] These are, however, only explanations and illustrations. There was no reduction in the staff employed as a result of the cancellation of the agreement in *Van den Berghs Ltd v Clark* but the fact that the work force had to be reduced after the cancellation was insufficient to turn the compensation into a capital receipt in *Elson v James G Johnston Ltd*.[3] In *Barr Crombie* itself Lord Normand stressed that none of the factors which distinguished the case from *Kelsall, Parsons & Co v IRC* were of themselves conclusive but the combination was.[4] What *Barr Crombie* does however is to establish that compensation may be a capital receipt even though the contract is a disposal contract. However, there is also authority for the proposition that a pure disposal contract will not be a capital asset no matter how big it is.[5] Therefore one must conclude that in *Barr Crombie* the contract was a capital asset primarily by reason of its duration and because the business had been built around that contract. It was not a mere disposal contract.[6] The particular agency had been the company's principal asset since the trade commenced so that it could not be said that its loss was a normal incident of the business. Further the loss of the agency necessitated the complete reorganisation of the taxpayers' business, a reduction in staff and the taking of newer and smaller premises.

Simon's Taxes A1.210, B2.207.

[1] (1945) 26 TC 406. See also *California Oil Products Ltd v FCT* (1934) 52 CLR 28—company formed to operate one agency and liquidated following its cancellation-compensation on cancellation was a capital receipt.
[2] Per Lord Russell in *IRC v Fleming & Co (Machinery) Ltd* (1951) 33 TC 57 at 63.
[3] (1965) 42 TC 545.
[4] (1945) 26 TC 406 at 412.
[5] Per Ungoed-Thomas J in *John Mills Productions Ltd v Mathias* (1964) 44 TC 441 at 456.
[6] Cf Ungoed-Thomas J 44 TC 441 at 755.

Subsidies

[8.89] Payments in the nature of a subsidy from public funds made to an entrepreneur to assist in the carrying on of his trade or business are trading receipts.[1]

When a subsidy takes the form of a payment to bring the receipt for a product up to a certain level and that product is trading stock, the payment is clearly a trading receipt.[2] Where a subsidy is paid in advance and may therefore have to be repaid, in whole or in part, the question is whether the payment is a loan or a receipt. The court looks to the business nature of such payments and treats them as trading receipts at the time of payment if they were intended to be used in the business.³ So payments to enable the trader to meet his trading obligations are trading receipts when made but where the payments were made to assist with a specific project of a capital nature it was held that unemployment grants were not trading receipts.⁴ A payment to maintain employment is neither clearly capital nor clearly revenue.⁵

The subsidy may come from another company. So in *British Commonwealth International Newsfilm Agency Ltd v Mahany* a payment to a subsidiary company as a supplement to its trading revenue and in order to preserve its trading stability was a trading receipt.⁶

---

1. Per Viscount Simon in *Pontypridd and Rhondda Joint Water Board v Ostime* [1946] AC 477 at 489, 28 TC 261 at 278; see also *Poulter v Gayjon Processes Ltd* [1985] STC 174. TA 1988, s 93 expressly makes grants under the Industrial and Development Act 1984 and similar Acts trading receipts unless clearly capital.
2. *Lincolnshire Sugar Co Ltd v Smart* (1935) 20 TC 643 at 667. See also *Higgs v Wrightson* (1944) 26 TC 73 (ploughing subsidies-trading receipts); *Burman v Thorn Domestic Appliances (Electrical) Ltd* [1982] STC 179.
3. *Lincolnshire Sugar Co Ltd v Smart* (1935) 20 TC 643 at 667. See also *Higgs v Wrightson* (1944) 26 TC 73 (ploughing subsidies-trading receipts); *Burman v Thorn Domestic Appliances (Electrical) Ltd* [1982] STC 179.
4. *Seaham Harbour Dock Co v Crook* (1930) 16 TC 333 as explained in *Poulter v Gayjon Processes Ltd* [1985] STC 174.
5. *Ryan v Crabtree Denims Ltd* [1987] STC 402; although the judgement in this case focuses on the purpose for which the payment is applied it is to be assumed that one looks first at the purpose for which the payment was made.
6. [1963] 1 All ER 88, 40 TC 550, HL. Cf *Moss' Empires Ltd v IRC* [1973] AC 785, 21 TC 264.

Rule 7—property of the trader

[8.90] A receipt which still belongs to someone else and has not yet become the property of the trader is not yet a trading receipt.

Where a trader receives sums of money from customers on their behalf, the receipt is not a trading receipt and so is not to be brought into account. This remains the case even though the trade is carried on by a partnership and the sums held for the customers are allocated to the partners as a domestic arrangement for book keeping purposes.¹ If, however, the sums originally repayable to the customers cease to be so by reason of the Limitation Act, they become trading receipts of the period when the claims are barred.² The question whether the money belongs to the customers or to the trader must depend on the facts. Where a sum is paid to a trader by way of part payment, it is still the customer's money whereas if the money is paid by way of deposit it immediately becomes the property of the trader and is irrecoverable by a purchaser in default; a deposit is therefore a trading receipt,³ subject, however, to the correct treatment under accountancy principles.⁴

Simon's Taxes B2.502.

1   Morley v Tattersall [1938] 3 All ER 296, 22 TC 51 (the limitation period did not begin to run in this case in respect of any of the payments: 29 TC 274 at 284).
2   IRC v Jay's the Jewellers Ltd [1947] 2 All ER 762, 29 TC 274.
3   Elson v Price's Tailors Ltd [1963] 1 All ER 231, 40 TC 671.
4   Herbert Smith (a firm) v Honour [1999] STC 173.

Rule 8—payment falling under different heading

[8.91] A payment falling under some other category of income is not a trading receipt.

Income correctly taxed as arising from a UK property business or employment, social security or pension income ought not to be taxed as trading income and so cannot enter into the computation. Thus rental income in respect of land in the UK is assessable as part of the profits of a UK property business,[1] while income from office or employment is usually taxed as employment income and, if that is done, cannot be assessed as trading income.[2] A line must also be drawn between trading receipts and payments falling as interest; a payment which forms part of the trading activities of the recipient cannot be pure income profit in his hands and so cannot be interest. So a payment incorrectly received under deduction of tax[3] must form part of the trading profits while one that was correctly so received cannot be a trading receipt.[4] If, however, a particular receipt can be taxed as trading income and under another heading (but not where the income arises from a UK property business or is employment, social security or pension income), it cannot be assessed to tax twice; until 6 April 2005, the Revenue had to choose under which heading to make the assessment.[5] From 6 April 2005, however, the statute provides (in accordance with previous practice) that the income should be assessed as trading income.[6]

Where dividends are involved, this rule extends the practice previously applied to traders dealing in investments. For such dealers, statute previously provided that the dividends are to be treated only as trading receipts, with no claim to repayment of (or to make any other use of) any tax credits.[7]

Simon's Taxes B2.308.

1   ITTOIA 2005, s 4(1) (income tax); TA 1988, s 18 (corporation tax); Infra, § **10.17**. See also *Lowe v J W Ashmore Ltd* [1971] 1 All ER 1057, 46 TC 597; sales of turf by farmer Case I not Schedule A; noted [1970] BTR 416 (PL).
2   ITTOIA 2005, s 4(2); *Thompson v Trust and Loan Co of Canada* [1932] 1 KB 517, 16 TC 394.
3   Under TA 1988, ss 348-350; infra, § **11.37**.
4   *British Commonwealth International Newsfilm Agency Ltd v Mahany* [1963] 1 All ER 88, 40 TC 550.
5   *Liverpool and London and Globe Insurance Co v Bennett* [1913] AC 610, 6 TC 327 and, latterly TMA 1970, s 9D.
6   ITTOIA 2005, ss 261, 366(1), 575(1).

[8.91] Income from trades, professions and vocations

7   ITTOIA 2005, s 366(1) (income tax); TA 1988, s 95 as amended by F(No 2)A 1997, s 24 (corporation tax); see infra, § **26.12**.

Rule 9—market value

[8.92] In deciding the amount to be included as a trading receipt regard must be had to the rules substituting market value for any price agreed between the parties, especially transfer pricing if one party controls the others infra, § **8.153** and the rule in *Sharkey v Wernher* (now codified as ITTOIA 2005, Pt 2, Ch 11A), infra, § **8.154**.

Rule 10—Release of a debt

[8.93] Where in computing a tax liability a debt has given rise to a deduction, the subsequent release of the debt is treated as a trading receipt.[1] The length of time between the deduction for the debt and the release is irrelevant. By contrast, where assets and liabilities of a company are transferred into a group, the Revenue consider a charge under there provisions does not arise[2] but failure to pay, or the bankruptcy of the debtor does not automatically cause a charge.[3]

In *Wildin & Co (a firm) v Jowett*,[4] the operation of the statutory provisions was comprehensively considered by the Special Commissioner in respect to debt between a partnership and a service company owned by the partners, the service company having gone into liquidation.

1   ITTOIA 2005, s 97 (income tax); TA 1988, s 94 (corporation tax).
2   ICAEW Technical Release 799, June 1990.
3   Inland Revenue interpretation RI 50.
4   [2002] STC (SCD) 390.

Exempt trading income

[8.94] The trading profits of a charity are exempt from income tax if the carrying on of a trade is a primary purpose of the charity,[1] or is carried on by the beneficiaries of the charity[2] or is income from a lottery whose profits are applied solely to the purposes of the charity.[3] In addition, income from certain small scale fundraising events has, by concession, been treated as exempt.[4]

From 6 April 2000[5] there is a statutory exemption for any trading income of a charity where the gross income, before deduction of expenses, is not greater than 25% of the charity's total receipts for the year (or £50,000, if this is less).[6] Where the charity's incoming receipts are less than £20,000, trading income is exempt if the gross income from the trade does not exceed £5,000.[7]

The exemption applies to income assessed under any of the provisions listed in TA 1988, s 836B (income tax) or Schedule D, Case VI (corporation tax),[8] where the assessment is under that case by virtue of the general principles. This will exempt, for example, the fee paid to a charity for the use of its logo. However, income assessed under any provision of the provisions listed in FA 2000, s 46(2A) (miscellaneous anti-avoidance provisions) is not granted this exemption.[9]

[1] TA 1988, s 505(1)(e)(i). This exempts, for example, the profits of a school that is run as an educational charity.
[2] TA 1988, s 505(1)(e)(ii). This exempts, for example, the profits of a factory run by a charity for the purpose of providing employment to disabled people.
[3] TA 1988, s 505(1)(f).
[4] Extra-statutory concession C4 revised 31 March 2000.
[5] 1 April 2000 in the case of an incorporated charity.
[6] FA 2000, s 46(1).
[7] FA 2000, s 46(4).
[8] FA 2000, s 46(1).
[9] FA 2000, s 46(2) which excludes it from the exempt income assessed under TA 1988, ss 214, 547, 703, 776, 788, 790 and 804, FA 1998, Sch 18 para 52(4) and ITTOIA 2005, Pt 4, Ch 9 and Pt 5, Ch 5. The Act also makes provision for other charges to be excluded from the exemption by statutory instrument.

Expenses

[8.95] The right to deduct expenses in computing taxable profit rests not on any express statutory provision but rather on the absence of any express prohibition; the right to deduct is inferred from the fact that it is the profit, not the receipts, of a trade that are taxed.[1] It should be noted that this rule has not been explicitly rewritten into ITTOIA 2005 for income tax purposes.

The right to deduct is limited by a number of rules:

(1) the expense must have been incurred for business purposes—the principle of remoteness;
(2) it must have been incurred only for business purposes—the principle of duality;
(3) it must have been incurred for the purpose of earning profit—the rule in *Strong & Co of Romsey Ltd v Woodifield*;
(4) it must be an expense of earning profit and not a division of profit;
(5) it must be of an income nature as opposed to a capital nature; it must be a revenue expense; and
(6) it must not be expressly barred by some statutory provision.

In answering all these questions the court has regard to established commercial accounting principles.[2]

It is also necessary that the expense is incurred by the taxpayer.[3] In *Rutter v Charles Sharpe & Co Ltd*[4] the company made payments to trustees of a fund held for the benefit of its employees. It was held that as the company could at any time wind up the scheme and then enforce the return of the payments, it followed that the sums could be recalled at will by the company and so could not be allowable deductions. For the same reason a payment will not be deductible if it can be recouped from another person.[5]

Simon's Taxes Division B2.3.

---

[1] TA 1988, s 817 prohibits all deductions save those expressly authorised; ITTOIA 2005, s 34 (for example) and TA 1988, s 74 do not authorise deductions but forbid them. On the difficulties in this formulation see Romer LJ in *Anglo Persian Oil Co Ltd v Dale* [1932] 1 KB 124 at 144, 16 TC 253 at 272.
[2] Per Lord Sumner in *Usher's Wiltshire Brewery Ltd v Bruce* [1915] AC 433 at 468, 6 TC 399 at 436.
[3] See *Abbott v IRC* [1996] STC (SCD) 41n, where there was no evidence of the taxpayer's wife being paid the wages for which a deduction was claimed.
[4] [1979] STC 711.
[5] *Bolton v Halpern & Woolf (a firm)* [1979] STC 761 at 770; revsd for other reasons [1981] STC 14, CA.

Rules 1 and 2: wholly and exclusively—remoteness and duality

[8.96] Rules 1 and 2 are derived from what is now ITTOIA 2005, s 34 (income tax) and TA 1988, s 74(1)(a) (corporation tax) which prohibits the deduction of "expenses not incurred wholly and exclusively for the purposes of the trade . . ."[1] The word "wholly" refers to the quantum of the money expended while the word "exclusively" refers to the motive or object accompanying it. The question whether the expenditure was incurred exclusively for business purposes is one of fact and purpose. However, if the sole purpose is business promotion the expenditure is not disqualified because the nature of the activity necessarily involves some other result or the attainment or furtherance of some other objective since the latter is necessarily inherent in the act.[2]

The leading case is the decision of the House of Lords in *Mallalieu v Drummond*[3] in which a lady barrister sought to deduct the cost of clothes bought for wear in court, such clothes being required by court etiquette. The undisputed evidence was that the taxpayer's expenditure was motivated solely by thoughts of court etiquette and not at all by mere human thoughts of warmth and decency. Counsel for the taxpayer disclaimed any reliance on his client's dislike of black clothing and the question was reduced to this: if clothing is purchased for use only on business occasions and such clothes are only so used (or for proceeding to and from work) is the expense deductible? The House of Lords said no. In addition to the business purpose there were the other purposes of warmth and decency. As Lord Brightman said 'I reject that notion that the object of a taxpayer is inevitably limited to the particular conscious motive in mind at the moment of expenditure'.

Earlier cases had decided that the courts could ignore an incidental benefit to the taxpayer. This is reformulated by Lord Brightman in his distinction between the object of the taxpayer in incurring the expenditure and the effect of the expenditure. "An expenditure may be made exclusively to serve the purposes of the business, but it may have a private advantage. The existence of that private advantage does not necessarily preclude the exclusivity of the business purpose." His Lordship gave an example of a medical consultant flying to the south of France to see a patient; if a stay in the south of France was a reason, however subordinate, no deduction could be claimed whereas if it were not a reason but an unavoidable effect the deduction could be made.

While there may be substance in what the House said there are uncomfortable questions of degree to be resolved. Thus Lord Brightman would have allowed expenditure by a self-employed nurse on clothing dictated by the practical requirements of the act of nursing and the maintenance of hygiene, and even that by a self employed waiter on the provision of "tails", this being the particular design of clothing required in order to obtain engagements. For similar reasons presumably the Revenue were disposed to concede expenditure on wig, gown and bands in the instant case.

Following *Mallalieu v Drummond* it has been held that the cost of modest lunches eaten by solicitors during office meetings was not deductible[4] and rent for living accommodation provided with a public house is not deductible.[5]

The present position thus is that (a) expenditure incurred solely for a business purpose is deductible, (b) expenditure partly for a business purpose is not deductible, and that while for (b) the court will ignore a purely incidental purpose, which the court calls an effect, they will not ignore a merely subordinate non-business purpose, and for both (a) and (b) the test of purpose is applied subjectively but with a dash of common sense; evidence of the uppermost purposes in a person's mind is not to exclude common sense inferences as to other but unarticulated purposes.

This approach was endorsed, but glossed, by the House of Lords in *McKnight v Sheppard*.[6] Here the taxpayer, S, was held to be entitled to deduct legal expenses incurred by him in resisting charges for breach of professional rules. If found guilty he could have been suspended from carrying on his profession or expelled altogether. The commissioner found that the sole purpose was the preservation of his trade and that considerations of personal reputation were effects rather than purposes. As Lord Hoffmann put it after referring to Lord Brightman's example of the medical consultant:[7]

> If Lord Brightman's consultant had said that he had given no thought at all to the pleasures of sitting on the terrace with his friend and a bottle of Côtes de Provence, his evidence might well not have been credited. But that would not be inconsistent with a finding that the only object of the journey was to attend upon his patient and that personal pleasures, however welcome, were only the effects of a journey made for an exclusively professional purpose. This is the distinction which the commissioner was making and in my opinion there is no inconsistency between his conclusion of law and his finding of fact.

The case depends crucially on the findings of fact. Had the commissioners found that concern for personal reputation had been a purpose and not an effect it is unlikely that an appeal by S would have succeeded. Quite why decency and clothing should be subconscious purposes in *Mallalieu v Drummond* while personal reputation was only an effect here is unclear; this disregard of the obvious is however consistent with that of the Court of Appeal

[8.96] Income from trades, professions and vocations

in *Vodafone Cellular Ltd v Shaw*.[8] Here Millett LJ, dealing with a case in which a company had incurred payments which had benefited itself and other group members, said:[9]

> Although the taxpayer's subjective intentions are determinative, these are not limited to the conscious motives which were in his mind at the time of the payment. Some consequences are so inevitably and inextricably involved in the payment that unless merely incidental they must be taken to be a purpose for which the payment was made.
>
> To these propositions I would add one more. The question does not involve an inquiry of the taxpayer whether he consciously intended to obtain a trade or personal advantage by the payment. The primary inquiry is to ascertain what was the particular object of the taxpayer in making the payment. Once that is ascertained, its characterisation as a trade or private purpose is in my opinion a matter for the commissioners, not for the taxpayer. Thus in *Mallalieu v Drummond* the primary question was not whether Miss Mallalieu intended her expenditure on clothes to serve exclusively a professional purpose or partly a professional and partly a private purpose, but whether it was intended not only to enable her to comply with the requirements of the Bar Council when appearing as a barrister in court but also to preserve warmth and decency.
>
> Similarly, in my opinion, the present case does not involve an inquiry whether the directors who resolved to enter into the fee cancellation agreement consciously intended to obtain a benefit thereby for one company rather than another. The primary inquiry is to ascertain the particular object which the directors sought to achieve by it. Once that is ascertained the characterisation of that object as serving the purposes of the trade of one particular company or another is not a finding of primary fact, but a conclusion based upon the primary facts.

Simon's Taxes B2.316, 319.

---

[1] For recent decisions see *Redkite Ltd v Inspector of Taxes* [1996] STC (SCD) 501, *Executive Network (Consultants) Ltd v O'Connor* [1996] STC (SCD) 29 and *Taylor v Clatworthy* [1996] STC (SCD) 506.

[2] See Romer LJ in *Bentleys, Stokes and Lowless v Beeson* [1952] 2 All ER 82 at 85, 33 TC 491 at 504 and see *Dollar v Lyon* [1981] STC 333 infra, § **8.102**.

[3] [1983] STC 665, [1983] 2 AC 861, HL.

[4] *Watkis v Ashford Sparkes & Harward* [1985] STC 451; infra, § **8.97**.

[5] *McLaren v Mumford* [1996] STC 1134. The duality principle was also applied to defeat the deduction of a life assurance premium in *Beauty Consultants Ltd v Inspector of Taxes* [2002] STC (SCD) 352.

[6] [1999] STC 669.

[7] At 671f.

[8] [1997] STC 734; see infra, § **8.98**, note 3.

[9] At 742.

[8.97] *Mallalieu v Drummond*[1] also raises the problem of conference expenses. The costs of food and lodging must be incurred at least partly because one has to eat and sleep (or are these just unavoidable effects of the initial decision to attend the conference?) The problem was considered in two cases before *Mallalieu v Drummond*. In *Bowden v Russell and Russell*[2] the sole partner of a firm of solicitors attended meetings of the American Bar

Association in Washington and the Empire Law Conference in Ottawa. He went in an unofficial capacity and was accompanied by his wife, although no claim was made in respect of those expenses attributable to her. He admitted that there were holiday and social purposes. He argued that his attendance was in order to maintain the firm's efficiency, to obtain new clients and to improve the office organisation. The Revenue argued that the rule of remoteness barred the deduction, the purpose of the visit being social not business and, alternatively, that, if there was a business element the deduction was barred by the rule of duality. The Revenue won.[3] On the other hand in *Edwards v Warmsley, Henshall & Co*[4] a partner in a firm of chartered accountants went to represent the firm at the International Congress of Accountants in New York. There was no evidence of any other purpose. The expenses were held deductible. In this case it was said that he had only met those whom he was meant to go and see. This however, while it may go to credibility, does not in theory affect the issue of deductibility. Had he agreed to go to the conference and while in New York decided to visit a relative in Boston simply because he was over there, this could not affect the deductibility of the expenses of travel to and from New York and it would make no difference that he had had that intention before deciding to obey the instruction of his firm. The question is one of motive and not of effect.

In *Watkis v Ashford Sparkes & Harwood*[5] Nourse J accepted the latter decision was still good law—despite *Mallalieu v Drummond*—and held that the cost of overnight accommodation at the annual conference of a firm was deductible and that no distinction could be drawn between the costs of accommodation and the costs of food and drink consumed. This was despite the fact that in the same case expenditure on meals taken at a time when the taxpayers would normally have eaten was held to be incapable of being incurred exclusively for business purposes. The moral seems to be that if one wishes to secure deduction of meal expenditure one has to have accommodation as well. The test in such cases is whether the expense is incurred as a business person or as a human being. This decision has now been followed in *Prior v Saunders*.[6]

Simon's Taxes B2.476.

[1] [1983] STC 665, [1983] 2 AC 861, HL.
[2] [1965] 2 All ER 258, 42 TC 301. See also *Knight v Parry* (1973) 48 TC 580.
[3] They agreed to allow him to deduct the conference fee but only by concession and without prejudice to the argument of remoteness.
[4] [1968] 1 All ER 1089, 44 TC 431.
[5] [1985] STC 451; on acceptance of this decision and practice for lorry drivers see Inland Revenue interpretation RI 51.
[6] [1993] STC 562.

Duality—apportionment (not allowed) and dissection (allowed)

[8.98] The duality rule prevents the deduction of expenditure for mixed purposes. This usually arises where the expenditure has mixed business and personal purposes. However, it has been applied with no less severity where a company incurs expenditure partly for its own trading purposes and partly for the trading purposes of another company, even of another member of the same group.[1] This ridiculous conclusion may be avoided by establishing that although the expenditure benefits both companies nonetheless the purpose was only to benefit one[2] or, according to recent Court of Appeal guidance, that it was incurred for the "trading entity" as a whole without giving any conscious thought to the position of individual companies.[3]

However, the duality rule does not prevent the dissection of expenditure and subsequent deduction of that part of the expenditure which is wholly and exclusively for business purposes. Thus, if a professional man uses one of his rooms in his house as an office, the expenses of that office are deductible, and this will be so even though the electricity, rates and other bills apply to the house as a whole and have to be dissected in order to discover the part attributable to the office. In these cases, the sum is dissected in order to discover that part which is wholly for business purposes, wholly being a matter of quantum, and the test of exclusive business purpose is then applied to that part.[4] The rule is frequently applied when a business loan is obtained and part of the sum borrowed is used for personal expenditure, which may be evidenced by excess drawings being made from the business.[5] Dissection has also been applied where an unreasonable amount of remuneration was paid to an employee, the court allowing the employer to deduct that part which would have been reasonable.[6] However, it could not be applied in *Bowden v Russell and Russell* since one could not identify the precise point in mid-Atlantic at which the solicitor ceased to be travelling for personal reasons and began to travel for business reasons.[7]

The present position is unsatisfactory since the Revenue do, in practice, allow an apportionment in a situation like that in *Bowden v Russell and Russell*. For example, the Revenue have stated:

> Generally where a property is used partly for domestic purposes and partly for non-domestic purposes, the different parts will be subject to council tax and business rates respectively, but there may be some situations where a mixed use property is only subject to council tax. This means that in some situations landlords and traders may pay council tax for property which they rent out or use for trading purposes.
>
> In these cases, traders and landlords will normally be able to claim a deduction for the part of the council tax which is attributable to the trade or letting.[8]

Another example is afforded by the well-known Revenue practice of allowing a deduction of a part of the expense of garaging a car when that car is used partly for personal and partly for business purposes. However, the present position appears to provide little scope for appeal to the Commissioners.

Simon's Taxes B2.319, 320

---

[1] *Garforth v Tankard Carpets Ltd* [1980] STC 251 and *Commercial Union Assurance Co plc v Shaw* [1998] STC 386; the point was not argued in the Court of Appeal: [1999] STC 109. The same point arose in *Lawson v Johnson Matthey plc* [1990] STC 149 at 158-159, but was not argued on appeal.
[2] *Robinson v Scott Bader Co Ltd* [1980] STC 241.
[3] *Vodafone Cellular Ltd v Shaw* [1997] STC 734; explained by Harman J in *Commercial Union Assurance Co plc v Shaw* [1998] STC 386 at 402 on the basis

that the sum was paid to discharge a liability of the one company only so that the benefit to the other companies was indirect.

4   This dissection was applied in *Gazelle v Servini* [1995] STC (SCD) 324 to property expenses where the home was used as an office.
5   See, for example, *Silk v Fletcher* [1999] STC (SCD) 220 and *Silk v Fletcher (No 2)* [2000] STC (SCD) 565.
6   *Copeman v William J Flood & Sons Ltd* [1941] 1 KB 202, 24 TC 53—but contrast *Earlspring Properties Ltd v Guest* [1993] STC 473.
7   For a highly critical account of and a different view of the present law see Kerridge [1986] BTR 36; and for a contrary but also critical view see Ward [1987] BTR 141.
8   Inland Revenue Press Release, 16 March 1993, *Simons Weekly Tax Intelligence* 1993, p 443.

[8.99] Expenditure for the purpose of two separate trades of one person is in theory deductible from neither[1] but it is unlikely that this absurd result would be applied by the Revenue. However, this situation must be distinguished from that of two separate persons with similar trades, eg two companies in a group.[2] Where an expense is incurred by one company for the other it is not deductible; whether it is so incurred is a question of fact. Where one company in a group takes over trading stock from another company in the group the costs of the acquisition are deductible even though the group or the other company may have motives of their own; what is important is the motive of the company making the expenditure.[3]

Where one company in a group is about to cease trading, payments to employees may be for the purpose of the orderly conduct of its trade, or for other purposes such as the interests of other companies in the group or the fulfilment of contractual or statutory duties connected with the cessation. Which it is turns on the company's purpose and so is a question of fact.[4]

The opposite problem arises where the trader purchases supplies from a subsidiary or related company and a part of the profit accruing to the other company will return to the trader. In *IRC v Europa Oil (NZ) Ltd*[5] the profit accruing would return to the trader as tax-free dividend and the price was fixed in advance to ensure the exact return to the trader. The Privy Council held that the expenditure was not incurred exclusively in the purchase of trading stock and to that extent could not be allowed. The difficulty for UK law is that there is no warrant for making an apportionment so that the whole should be disallowed. By contrast in *Europa Oil (NZ) Ltd v IRC*[6] the Privy Council held that the relations between the trader and the supplier were such that the former had no legal right to the profit and so the whole sum was allowed.

Simon's Taxes B1.404.

1   See Walton J in *Olin Energy Systems Ltd v Scorer* [1982] STC 800.
2   See cases cited at § **7.93**, note 1, supra, and *Watney Combe Reid & Co v Pike* [1982] STC 733.
3   *Torbell Investments Ltd v Williams* [1986] STC 397.
4   *O'Keeffe v Southport Printers Ltd* [1984] STC 443.

[1971] AC 760.
[1976] STC 37.

[8.100] Difficulties have also arisen in connection with partnerships. Since, in English tax law, a partnership is not a taxable entity it follows that the purposes to be investigated are those of the partners. This can seem unreal where a firm has, say, 98 partners and it is therefore tempting to equate such partnerships with companies which have separate legal personality. If such temptation is not resisted it will follow that expenditure incurred to reimburse a partner for his costs of removing his personal belongings, when moving his place of work from one part of the country to another at the request of his partners, will be deductible as was held by the Court of Appeal in *MacKinlay v Arthur Young McClelland Moores & Co*, however this conclusion has now been resoundingly rejected by the House of Lords.[1] The conclusion reached by the Court of Appeal rested on the basis that the partnership was like a company and a company could, of course, deduct such payments to an employee. Logically, however, if it is correct to say that such an expense when incurred by a sole trader cannot be deducted[2]—since it is incurred at least for dual purposes if not solely for personal purposes—it must follow that there is at least a similar element when it is incurred by the partners. If logic is rejected it would seem to make no difference whether the partners are 98 or 2 in number. The decision of the House of Lords is therefore to be welcomed.

Logic does not require the non-deductibility of payments in return for goods or services supplied by the partner to the partnership. So where the partner has granted the partnership a lease of property which he owns, there is no reason why the rental payments should not be incurred wholly and exclusively for business purposes;[3] they will of course be taxed in the hands of the partner/landlord.

It would seem to be more satisfactory either to make special tax rules for partnerships equating them with companies, including subjecting them to corporation tax and NICs as employers, or to hold that such payments to partners are either not deductible or are fully taxable to the partner as being an allocation of profit not an expense of earning it (infra, § **8.106**).

Simon's Taxes B2.463.

[1] [1989] STC 898, HL; reversing [1988] STC 116, CA. This was followed in *AB (a firm) and Revenue and Customs Comrs* [2007] STC (SCD) 99, where a deduction in the accounts of a partnership of solicitors for the cost of conducting litigation for an individual partner was denied.
[2] The Court of Appeal, however reluctantly, decided the case on this assumption.
[3] *Heastie v Veitch & Co Ltd* [1934] 1 KB 535, 18 TC 305. See also Lord Oliver in *MacKinlay v Arthur Young* [1989] STC 898 at 905.

[8.101] Expenditure in the form of subscriptions to charity are the generous acts of good citizens. There is, therefore, a duality of capacity about the payment, part as trader, part as citizen.[1] However, whether the explanation is remoteness or duality they are rarely deductible.[2] The same reasoning bars payments for political purposes.³ Gifts other than to charity also fall within ITTOIA 2005, s 45 (income tax); TA 1988, s 577 (corporation tax) (infra, § **8.133**).

Subscriptions to trade associations are according to case law deductible to the extent that the expenditure by the association would have been deductible if incurred directly by the subscriber.⁴ In practice, however, the Revenue grant complete deduction for the subscription in return for the taxability of the association.⁵ Contributions to approved local enterprise agencies, training and enterprise councils, local enterprise councils and urban regeneration companies are now deductible.⁶

Simon's Taxes B2.441, 450, 459, 474.

---

1   See Romer LJ in *Bentleys, Stokes and Lowless v Beeson* [1952] 2 All ER 82 at 85, 33 TC 491 at 505. For another reason, see infra, § **8.106**.
2   *Bourne and Hollingsworth Ltd v Ogden* (1929) 14 TC 349 (annual subscription to hospital used by employees deductible in practice but two special large subscriptions not deductible); *Hutchinson & Co (Publishers) Ltd v Turner* [1950] 2 All ER 633, 31 TC 495. See extra-statutory concession B7, and extra-statutory concession B32 on expenses of running a payroll giving scheme.
3   *Joseph L Thompson Ltd v Chamberlain* (1962) 40 TC 657; cf *Morgan v Tate and Lyle Ltd*; infra, § **8.104**.
4   *Lochgelly Iron and Coal Co Ltd v Crawford* (1913) 6 TC 267.
5   See **Simon's Taxes B2.441**. On the non-taxability of the association, see *Joseph Adamson & Co v Collins* [1938] 1 KB 477, 21 TC 400.
6   ITTOIA 2005, s 82 (income tax); TA 1988, ss 79, 79A and 79B (corporation tax).

Personal expenditure

[8.102] Expenditure for personal reasons is not deductible. One example is *Bowden v Russell and Russell* (supra). Others are (a) meals—one eats in order to live, not to work¹, and (b) a pied à terre over the office.² These cases have been decided primarily under TA 1988, s 74(1)(*a*) (now, for income tax, ITTOIA 2005, s 34) although many have been argued under TA 1988, s 74(1)(*b*) in the alternative. There is no reported case of an expense being deductible under (*a*) but not under (*b*). TA 1988, s 74(1)(*b*) has since been repealed from 6 April 2005 as redundant.

Medical expenditure is incurred primarily to put right that which is medically wrong and so not for business purposes. In *Murgatroyd v Evans-Jackson*³ the taxpayer was a trademark agent. He fell ill and was treated in a private nursing home for five weeks, his reason for selecting private care being that he required a separate room from which to conduct his business, a facility not available under the National Health Service. He claimed only 60% of the cost, a matter which admitted duality of expenditure, but Plowman J also held that had the taxpayer claimed the whole of his costs he would still not have been able to deduct the expense since one reason for going into the nursing home was to receive treatment. However, one might argue that since the choice was not between a greater and a lesser expense but between no expense at all under the National Health Service and this expense as a private patient, the whole expense was in fact for business purposes. Moreover, the decision does cause some fine distinctions. Thus, if he had had a bed in a room with other patients but had also rented another room as an office, the rent of that other room would have been deductible. One must distinguish from *Murgatroyd v Evans-Jackson* the case in which the operation itself is for business purposes.[4]

Payments for personal physical security, whether in the provision of an asset or a service are expressly deductible.[5]

Expenditure for family reasons is not deductible. So in *Dollar v Lyon*[6] sums paid to children were held to be not deductible since they were, subject to one exception, in the nature of pocket money rather than payments for services on the taxpayer's farm. A similar problem arose in *Earlspring Properties Ltd v Guest*.[7] Here an unincorporated business owned by the husband paid sums to a company owned by the wife; the wife's company then made payments to her as director of the company. The services performed by her for her company were mostly social but extended to necessary legal work such as signing leases. The company had no premises or staff and sub-contracted all tasks such as rent collection and consultancy to the husband. Vinelott J held that the Commissioners were justified in finding that sums paid by the company to the wife were not incurred wholly and exclusively for the purpose of the business; it would have been surprising and even perverse if they had reached any other conclusion.

In *Carney v Nathan*[8] a self-employed graphic designer working from home sought to deduct as a business expense the cost of caring for her child as, without this expense, it was impossible to carry on the business. The taxpayer argued that tax relief should be given, as expenditure by an employer on providing childcare for employees is deductible by statute[9] and to deny a deduction for a self-employed person was in contravention of the right to respect for private and family life given in the Convention for the Protection of Human Rights that is applied in UK legislation by the Human Rights Act 1998. The Special Commissioner held that the duality of purpose defeated the deduction and that a self-employed person paying childcare expenses herself was not in a similar situation to an employer paying for an employee and, hence, there was no discrimination that was outlawed by the Human Rights Act 1988.[10]

Expenditure on a child's nanny is not deductible; expenditure for secretarial services is deductible. Payments to a nanny for secretarial services are therefore deductible, where the facts are established.[11]

Where an employer requires his employee to work from home, a payment to the employee to defray the increase in household expenses that arises from his home working is a deductible expense for the employer.[12] It may also be a tax free receipt for the employee, if the conditions of ITEPA 2003, s 316A are satisfied.

Simon's Taxes B2.471

---

[1] See *Caillebotte v Quinn* [1975] STC 265, [1975] 2 All ER 412.
[2] *Mason v Tyson* [1980] STC 284.
[3] [1967] 1 All ER 881, 43 TC 581, noted [1967] BTR 285 (Wallace); and see *Norman v Golder* [1945] 1 All ER 352, 26 TC 293.

[4] See Pennycuick J in *Prince v Mapp* [1970] 1 All ER 519 at 525, 46 TC 169 at 176.
[5] FA 1989, ss 112, 113. On Revenue views of scope, see ICAEW Memorandum TR 759.
[6] [1981] STC 333.
[7] [1993] STC 473.
[8] [2003] STC (SCD) 28.
[9] Now ITEPA 2003, s 318.
[10] [2003] STC (SCD) 28 at 34b.
[11] Inland Revenue interpretation RI 82.
[12] Under general principles – the payment is part of the cost of employing that individual.

Travelling expenses

[8.103] Travelling expenses will be deductible in computing the profits of the business if they are incurred wholly and exclusively for the purposes of the trade and are of a revenue as opposed to a capital nature.[1] Expenses incurred by a barrister in travelling from his home to his chambers are not deductible,[2] even though he uses his home for work and is granted a "study allowance".[3] On the other hand a solicitor with an office in two towns may deduct the cost of travel between the two offices.[4] The reason for the distinction is that although the barrister does his work in both places it is clear that he carries on his profession in his chambers; his chambers, not his home, are his base of operations and so travel from his chambers to his home in the evening is not motivated wholly and exclusively by the desire to do more work. The expense is thus at least in part a personal living expense and not a business expense.[5] Likewise, the solicitor is not able to deduct the cost of travelling from his home to his office. However, if the solicitor were to go to the nearer office first then to the further and then back to the nearer, he would be allowed to deduct both journeys between the offices. Such a conclusion rests on the fact that the office is a place where he carries on his profession. So where a dental surgeon visited his laboratory (L) on his way through from his home (H) to his surgery (S) he was not allowed to deduct the cost of travel from L to S.[6] The purpose of the expenditure was to get from H to S; the fact that it also enabled him to stop at L could not affect that purpose.

Where, however, a person's home is his base of operations different rules apply. In *Powell v Jackman*,[7] a self-employed milkman was held to have his place of business at his home. On that basis, his travel to collect the milk was a business expense, as was his travelling from sale to sale. If his travel is purely itinerant, he is allowed to deduct the cost of travel between his home and the places to which he travels as in the case of an independent contracting bricklayer.[8] However, when the occupation is itinerant only within a certain area but the taxpayer lives outside that area, the costs of travel at least as far as the border of that area would not be deductible.[9]

The rules for mileage allowances[10] do not inhibit the deduction of motoring costs incurred in the conduct of a business. A sole trader (or a partner in a partnership) will deduct the actual cost of motor travel in the course of his business, even if this cost is greater than the 40p per mile. If an employer pays an employee a mileage rate that is greater than 40p per mile, but which, nevertheless, represents the true cost of motoring, the total amount paid to the employee is an expense deductible in computing the profits of the employer for income tax (or corporation tax).

Incorporation of a business, thus, requires consideration of the subsequent treatment of motoring costs of the proprietor, as he is henceforth subject to the restricted regime for recovery of motoring costs from his company. Prior to 6 April 2002, it was frequently advantageous for the car to be retained outside the company, the shareholder/director charging the company for the cost of motoring incurred on the company's business. Where the running costs of the car exceed 40p per mile, the effect of such arrangement in 2002/03 and subsequent years is that the reimbursement of cost by the company will give rise to a taxable benefit for the recipient.

Simon's Taxes B2.476.

---

[1] *Sargent v Eayrs* [1973] STC 50, [1973] 1 All ER 277. It should be noted that the rules on travel expenses in ITEPA 2003, ss 328-334, 336-338 and FA 1998, Sch 10 (supra, §§ 7.112–7.117) are not directly relevant when preparing accounts in respect of trades, professions or vocations.
[2] *Newsom v Robertson* [1952] 2 All ER 728, 33 TC 452.
[3] Under ITTOIA 2005, s 34 (income tax); TA 1988, s 74(1)(c) (corporation tax). Strictly, s 74(1)(c) was not rewritten into ITTOIA 2005 on the basis that it was covered by ITTOIA 2005, s 34(2).
[4] Per Somervell LJ at 730, 462.
[5] Per Denning LJ at 731, 464.
[6] *Sargent v Barnes* [1978] STC 322, [1978] 2 All ER 737.
[7] [2002] STC (SCD) 488.
[8] *Horton v Young* [1971] 3 All ER 412, 47 TC 60.
[9] Per Brightman J [1971] 2 All ER at 356.
[10] Now found in ITEPA 2003, s 230; see supra, § 7.120.

Rule 3—the purpose of earning profits

[8.104] In *Strong & Co of Romsey Ltd v Woodifield* Lord Davey said, 'It is not enough that the disbursement is made in the course of or arises out of or is connected with the trade or is made out of the profits of the trade. It must be made for the purpose of earning profits.'[1] This gloss on the statute seems to have little effect in the practice of the Revenue but enables the Revenue to grant by concession that which ought to be deducted as of right.

The taxpayer company carried on the businesses of brewers and innkeepers. A chimney at one of their inns fell in and injured a guest. The guest sued and recovered damages of £1,490 which the company sought to deduct in computing its profits. Today the case is remembered principally for Lord Davey's dictum. However, for Lord Loreburn and the other members of the House (but not for Lord Davey) the critical provision was what is now ITTOIA 2005, s 34 (income tax) and TA 1988, s 74(1)(e) (corporation tax) which prohibits the deduction of any loss not connected with the trade, profession or vocation. Whether the expense was barred by s 74(1)(a) or (1)(e) is in one sense immaterial (and both rules have been incorporated into ITTOIA 2005, s 34 for income tax): the expense may not be deducted. In an unhappily apt phrase Lord Loreburn said that losses could not be deducted "if they fall on the trader in some character other than that of trader". So here he thought that the loss fell on the trader in its character as householder not as trader. One may suppose that one reason why this decision has not been reversed is that businesses now insure their premises, such premiums being deductible.² The fineness of the distinction inherent in the House of Lords approach may be seen from two examples given by Lord Loreburn: 'losses sustained by a railway company in compensating passengers for accident in travelling might be deducted. On the other hand if a man kept a grocer's shop, for keeping which a house is necessary, and one of the window shutters fell upon and injured a man walking in the street the loss arising thereby ought not to be deducted'.³

Not only are these examples unclear but they can be made to suggest that deduction should have been allowed in the instant case. First it is not clear what point is being made. On the one hand the example of the grocer's house is reasonably clear if the house is separate from the shop then there is a distinction between trading expenses and personal expenses, and the same might be true if the premises were all in one and the shutter fell off the residential part of the premises. If, however, the point is the distinction between trading and personal expenses then surely the expense should have been deductible in the instant case. Yet if the distinction is that between trading and householding, between at that time Schedule D, Case I and Schedule A, that suggests a very restricted scope to be given to the example of the railway company and could mean that the company could deduct if the engine was driven negligently with a resulting accident but not if injury occurred when a piece of a station platform gave way. What would happen if there were a defect in a piece of static equipment like a signal is again unclear. Lord James expressed doubts about the application of the principle to a customer within the inn but would have had no doubts about the non-deductibility of an injury to a stranger walking down the street outside the inn. Such a distinction seems today quite incredible.

In *Macdonald v Dextra Accessories Ltd*,⁴ payments were made to an offshore trust, the trustees of which had discretion as to whether they were to be paid to employees, or used otherwise. The company was refused a deduction for the payments into trust.

Simon's Taxes B2.317.

---

1 [1906] AC 448 at 453, 5 TC 215 at 220. This decision was based largely on what is now TA 1988, s 74(1)(e) (infra, § **8.131**), but is generally treated as an authority on TA 1988, s 74(1)(a) eg *Morgan v Tate and Lyle Ltd* [1954] 2 All ER 413, 35 TC 367; infra, § **8.116**.
2 *Usher's Wiltshire Brewery Ltd v Bruce* [1915] AC 433, 6 TC 399.
3 [1915] AC 433 at 452, 6 TC 399 at 419.
4 [2005] STC 1111, HL.

[8.105] In order to judge whether an item of expenditure is deductible in computing profits, it is necessary to look at the nature of the action of the taxpayer in incurring that expenditure. In *AB Bank v Inspector of Taxes*[1] the London branch of a foreign co-operative bank made a loss of some £30,000,000 on a loan to its subsidiary. After exhaustive inspection of the actions of the two companies, AB Bank (the lender) and its subsidiary (the borrower), the Special Commissioners held that AB Bank's actions were those of a banker acting as a banker and not those of an owner acting as a shareholder. The loss was, therefore, allowable as a deduction in computing the profits of the banking trade.

Sums spent for the purpose of earning profit will be deductible even though no profit is expected that year;[2] moreover since the test is one of purpose the sums will be deductible even though no profits accrue at all.[3] Losses incurred which are incidental to the carrying out of the business are likewise deductible.[4] Damages for libel can be held deductible when the libel is published in the course of a newspaper business; such damages must be distinguished from those payable for a libel not incidental to the business[5] and from penalties imposed by a court.[6] Penalties, fines and interest charges in respect of the VAT legislation are expressly non-deductible.[7] The House of Lords has held that fines imposed by a professional body are not deductible but that this bar does not extend to legal expenses incurred in defending those charges.[8]

Damages for wrongful dismissal of employees are in practice allowed although this is hard to reconcile with Lord Davey's dictum. Legal expenses are also deductible even though not for the direct purpose of earning profits provided they are incurred in the running of the business.[9]

Advertising expenses although originally in doubt,[10] are now clearly deductible,[11] as are sponsorship costs provided, in practice, that the sole purpose is to provide the sponsor with a benefit commensurate with the expenditure.[12] So wide has the principle of deductibility become that the dictum in *Strong & Co of Romsey Ltd v Woodifield* should either be repealed or be regarded as having force only in the light of the frequently quoted statement of Viscount Cave LC:

> ... a sum of money expended, not of necessity and with a view to a direct and immediate benefit to the trade, but voluntarily and on the grounds of commercial expediency, and in order indirectly to facilitate the carrying on of the business, may yet be expended wholly and exclusively for the purposes of the trade.[13]

However, the principle can be applied. In *Knight v Parry*[14] a solicitor was not allowed to deduct the costs of defending (successfully) an action in which professional misconduct and breach of a former contract of employment were alleged. The court held that the sums were spent, at least in part, to ensure that he was not precluded from carrying on his practice and this was not the same as expenditure referable to the carrying on of his practice. In *McKnight v Sheppard*,[15] the House of Lords upheld the finding of fact by the Special Commissioner that the payment of fines levied on a stockbroker and accompanying legal costs was to avoid the destruction of the taxpayer's business and, hence, the fines and legal costs were deductible for tax purposes. At first, Lightman J had explored the notion that the taxpayer could not deduct expenses because he had been acting outside the scope of his trade. This was rejected by the Court of Appeal,[16] but the House of Lords did not have much to say. The House of Lords did not explore this point in detail.

1   *AB Bank v Inspector of Taxes* [2000] STC (SCD) 229.
2   *Vallambrosa Rubber Co Ltd v Farmer* (1910) 5 TC 529; *James Snook & Co Ltd v Blasdale* (1952) 33 TC 244. However the timing is subject to relevant accounting principles—*Gallagher v Jones* [1993] STC 537, CA.
3   *Lunt v Wellesley* (1945) 27 TC 78.
4   *Golder v Great Boulder Proprietary Gold Mines Ltd* (1951) 33 TC 75. A sum paid in settlement of a civil claim in connection with the formation of a company held to be deductible because it was not paid for any proven infraction of the law. On losses resulting from the collapse of BCCI see Inland Revenue interpretation RI 57.
5   *Fairrie v Hall*(1947) 28 TC 200.
6   *IRC v Von Glehn & Co Ltd* [1920] 2 KB 553, 12 TC 232.
7   ITTOIA 2005, s 54 (income tax); TA 1988, s 827(1) (corporation tax).
8   *McKnight v Sheppard* [1999] STC 669.
9   See *Spofforth and Prince v Golder* [1945] 1 All ER 363, 26 TC 310.
10 See Kelly CB in *Watney & Co v Musgrave* (1880) 1 TC 272 at 277.
11 *Morley v Lawford & Co* (1928) 14 TC 229.
12 HL Written Answer, 26 October 1987, Vol 489, col 405. If the taxpayer enjoys ballooning does this enable his company to deduct the sponsorship costs of a balloon journey across the Atlantic? What if he is a sole trader?
13 *British Insulated and Helsby Cables Ltd v Atherton* [1926] AC 205 at 211.
14 [1973] STC 56, 48 TC 580.
15 [1999] STC 669.
16 [1997] STC 846, CA overruling [1996] STC 627, Ch D.

Rule 4—division of profits or expense of earning profits

[8.106] A sum paid in the course of earning a profit is clearly distinct from a distribution of the profit made. A dividend by a company or a payment under a profit-sharing arrangement is a distribution of profit made and not an expense of earning it;[1] by contrast a payment of interest will usually be a deductible expense. The question whether a payment is one of interest or a distribution of profits is one of substance.[2]

The rule has been applied to render non-deductible certain payments by a company purporting to be by way of remuneration to directors or employees. So remuneration based on a percentage of profits must be distinguished from a distribution of profits and while a resolution at an annual meeting to pay a bonus as an appropriation of profit will be conclusive[3] the absence of such a resolution is not conclusive the other way.[4] Excessive remuneration has generally been dealt with under the wholly and exclusively rule but this rule could have been applied instead.

Payments by a partnership to its employees will likewise be treated as deductions but the division of profits between the partners must be just that and no payment to a partner in return for services[4] can qualify as a deductible emolument.[5]

So a partnership can deduct the cost of the salary of an employee but not the share of profits accruing to a partner. However, rent paid by the partnership to a partner is deductible unless excessive.[6]

[8.106] Income from trades, professions and vocations

The correct treatment of a payment towards a partner's personal removal has now been settled by the House of Lords.[7] Such payments being personal in nature cannot be deducted.

A payment by a company to an approved profit-sharing scheme is an allowable deduction.[8]

---

[1] See *Eyres v Finnieston Engineering Co Ltd* (1916) 7 TC 74; *Utol Ltd v IRC* [1944] 1 All ER 190; infra, Chapter 26 on meaning of distributions.
[2] *AW Walker & Co v IRC* [1920] 3 KB 648.
[3] As in *Pegg and Ellam Jones Ltd v IRC* (1919) 12 TC 82.
[4] See per Lord Maughan in *Indian Radio and Cable Communications Co Ltd v IT Comr Bombay* [1937] 3 All ER 709 at 713–14, and *British Sugar Manufacturers Ltd v Harris* [1938] 2 KB 220, 21 TC 528. See also *Union Cold Storage Co Ltd v Adamson* (1931) 16 TC 293; *Overy v Ashford Dunn & Co Ltd* (1933) 17 TC 497.
[5] Salaried partners who have the right to receive a specified sum, even if the partnership makes a loss are treated as employees not partners.
[6] *Heastie v Veitch & Co* [1934] 1 KB 535, 18 TC 305.
[7] *MacKinlay v Arthur Young McClelland Moores & Co* [1989] STC 898.
[8] TA 1988, s 85.

[8.107] The rule was also applied to prevent the deduction of sums paid out of the totalisator fund to racecourse owners to assist in improving amenities at racecourses and to provide subsidies to owners and trainers.[1] The distinction inherent in the rule is a fine one but turns on the precise definition of the trade. In that case the trade was that of running totalisators at racecourses and the expenditure in question was not incurred for the purpose of that trade.

---

[1] *Young v Racecourse Betting Control Board* [1959] 3 All ER 215, 38 TC 426.

[8.108] The rule has been applied also to prevent the deduction of taxes on profits, whether imposed by the UK[1] or some foreign government.[2] However, other taxes may be deductible. Thus rates[3] may be deductible, as are road licences and stamp duty[4] in all instances depending upon the actual circumstance of the case. In *Harrods (Buenos Aires) Ltd v Taylor-Gooby*[5] the taxpayer company operated in Argentina and was liable to an annual local tax levied on the capital of the company. The courts reversed the Commissioners and held that the tax was deductible since it was not a tax that depended upon the company having earned any profits but was simply an essential cost of trading in that country. The actual circumstances may show that the particular tax is a capital expense in which case it will not be deductible.[6]

Simon's Taxes B2.472.

---

[1] Lord Halsbury in *Ashton Gas Co v A-G* [1906] AC 10 at 12.
[2] *IRC v Dowdall O'Mahoney & Co Ltd* [1952] 1 All ER 531, 33 TC 259. On deduction of overseas tax, see now TA 1988, s 811 (TA 1970, s 516) and infra, § **37.03**.

3   *Smith v Lion Brewery Co Ltd* [1911] AC 150, 5 TC 568.
4   Semble per Buckley J in *Harrods (Buenos Aires) Ltd v Taylor-Gooby* (1963) 41 TC 450.
5   (1963) 41 TC 450.
6   eg stamp duty on conveyance of land forming part of the fixed capital of the trade or if the payment in *Harrods (Buenos Aires) Ltd v Taylor-Gooby* had been a once only payment for the right to trade in Argentina.

[8.109] More controversially the rule has been applied to prevent the deduction of expenses incurred by a company in appealing, successfully, against an assessment to tax on profits. The expense of preparing the documents needed to be filed under the Companies Act would clearly be deductible as would the preparation of accounts for internal management.[1] However as Lord Simonds put it:[2]

> What profit he has earned he has earned before ever the voice of the tax-gatherer is heard. He would have earned no more and no less if there was no such thing as Income Tax. His profit is no more affected by the exigibility of tax than is a man's temperature altered by the price of a thermometer, even though he starts by haggling about the price of it.

In practice, HMRC allow certain costs of handling an enquiry. The current attitude is stated as:[3]

"**Accountancy expenses arising out of self-assessment enquiries.**

It is the practice to allow, in computing profits assessable under Case I and II of Schedule D, the normal accountancy expenses incurred in preparing accounts or accounts information and in assisting with the self-assessment of tax liabilities. Additional accountancy expenses arising out of an enquiry into the accounts information in a particular year's return will not be allowed where the enquiry reveals discrepancies and additional liabilities for the year of enquiry, or any earlier year, which arises as a result of negligent or fraudulent conduct. Where, however, the enquiry results in no addition to profits, or an adjustment to the profits for the year of enquiry only and that adjustment does not arise as a result of negligent or fraudulent conduct, the additional accountancy expenses will be allowable."[3]

Simon's Taxes B2.472, 461.

1   *Worsley Brewery Co Ltd v IRC* (1932) 17 TC 349 esp. per Romer LJ at 360.
2   In *Smith's Potato Estates Ltd v Bolland* [1948] 2 All ER 367 at 374, 30 TC 267 at 293.

One criticism is that expenditure in order to preserve the company's assets is deductible; see *Morgan v Tate and Lyle*, supra, § **8.104**. However, the expense must avoid rule 4 as well as rule 3; the motive for the payment cannot turn a profit into an expense. But this reasoning seems to be contrary to that of the Court of Appeal in *Heather v PE Consulting Group Ltd* [1973] 1 All ER 8, 48 TC 320. The position cannot therefore be clearly stated.

3   The HMRC Enquiry Manual, para 9010, reported in HMRC Tax Bulletin 37, October 1998, being Statement of practice A28, as modified by SP 16/91; Inland Revenue interpretation RI 192.

Rule 5—capital expenditure

[8.110] Capital expenditure is not deductible in computing profits even though incurred wholly and exclusively for business purposes; such expenditure may qualify for relief under the capital allowance system.

The task of distinguishing revenue from capital expenditure is not easy; and the problem has been made difficult by the inevitable fact that words or formulae that have been found useful in one set of facts may be neither relevant nor significant in another.[1] While the courts have provided different tests at different times, none is paramount.[2]

Two tests are to be discerned in the older cases, although these have now been to some extent superseded. The first distinguished fixed capital from circulating capital;[3] expenditure on the former was capital expenditure while that on the latter was not. Fixed capital is retained in the shape of assets which either produce income without further action, eg shares held by an investment company, or are made use of to produce income, eg machinery in a factory. Circulating capital is that which the company intends should be used by being temporarily parted with and circulated in the business only to return with, it is hoped, profit, eg money spent on trading stock.[4] The difficulty with this test is that it sometimes begs the very question at issue.[5]

The second test was enunciated by Viscount Cave in *Atherton v British Insulated and Helsby Cables Ltd* and became known as the enduring benefit test. He said:[6]

> When an expenditure is made not only once for all, but with a view to bringing into existence an asset or advantage for the enduring benefit of a trade, I think there is very good reason (in the absence of special circumstances leading to an opposite conclusion) for treating such an expenditure as properly attributable not to revenue but to capital.

The principal difficulty with this test was that many sorts of expenditure have an enduring effect and not all of them are of a capital nature. Thus a payment to be rid of an unsatisfactory employee or agent is a revenue expense but one to be rid of a term of a lease is a capital expense.[7] A payment to a trust for the benefit of certain employees where the amount and the duration of the fund were uncertain and the whole fund could be distributed at any time was held to be a revenue expense.[8] A payment to persuade an institution to buy the worthless shares of a subsidiary was likewise held to be revenue since the expenditure did not bring any asset into existence or procure any advantage for the enduring benefit of the trade but was, rather, to remove the threat to the taxpayer's whole trade resulting from the subsidiary's insolvency.[9]

The latest test, reinforced by the House of Lords in *Tucker v Granada Motorway Services Ltd*[10] requires first that one isolate the asset on which the sum has been spent; sums spent on an asset of a capital nature may be capital while sums spent on other things will not be. If that asset is of a capital nature, one then considers the nature of the particular expense; so sums spent on acquiring the capital asset will be capital while sums spent maintaining or repairing it will be revenue. At this point the earlier tests may reappear as in *Walker v Joint Credit Card Co Ltd*[11] and *Whitehead v Tubbs (Elastics) Ltd*.[12]

This text has now been used in connection with liabilities. If the liability is on capital account, a loss, eg an exchange loss, incurred on repayment of the loan, will be a capital loss whereas it would have been a revenue loss if the loan had been a revenue transaction.[13]

This approach was followed by the Privy Council in *Auckland Gas v CIR*.[14] Gas leaked from old iron pipes. Instead of repairing the iron pipes, a network of polyethylene pipes was installed. The work was capital.

This test is not without difficulties. The place of the asset within the business is not usually too difficult to determine, indeed it is similar to the old distinction between fixed and circulating capital; but problems arise where the asset is not discernible as part of the assets of the business, as where one is dealing with trading arrangements with other traders or with the modification of a company's charter or articles of association. Thus is money spent in removing restrictions on a company's business a capital expense?[15] Care must also be taken in defining the asset accurately.[16] Similar problems arise with the idea of an advantage. Thus, if a taxpayer borrows money for a period does he simply receive cash or does he obtain a furtherance of the trade for the period of the loan?[17] Apart from this there remains the difficulty of deciding whether the particular expense is of a capital or a revenue nature. It would, however, be foolish to reject the asset test simply because it does not provide an answer to all cases; the danger is that it will be applied, as have its predecessors, without regard to the variety of facts or, again like its predecessors, without regard to the disclaimer of universality uttered by its formulators.

Another test (or, perhaps a variant of this test) was applied by the Special Commissioner in *Transco plc v Dyall*.[18] In that case, the Special Commissioner found that the character of the pipeline had not been altered by installing polyethylene piping where previously there had been metal pipes. The expenditure was revenue, not capital.

Expenditure on training is income expenditure where the course is an adjunct to or "refresher" to the taxpayer's existing activities; where the course equips the taxpayer with new skills, the expenditure is capital.[19]

When considering a financial instrument, the approach followed to determine where an item was capital or income in *Kato Kagaku Co v Revenue and Customs Comr*[20] was to analyse the transaction; the taxpayer's purpose was not determinative.

Statute[21] specifically permits tax relief for research and development expenditure that is treated for accounting purposes as an addition to the cost of an intangible asset, such as a patent, know-how, or goodwill.

Simon's Taxes B2.307–311.

---

[1] Per Lord Radcliffe in *Taxes Comr v Nchanga Consolidated Copper Mines Ltd* [1964] 1 All ER 208 at 212, [1964] AC 948 at 959.
[2] See *Caledonian Paper plc v IRC* [1998] STC (SCD) 129 at 134, citing passages from *Regent Oil Co Ltd v Strick* [1965] 3 All ER 174, 43 TC 1.
[3] The dual reference to capital is unfortunate but it refers to the capital of the company and so the source from which the expenditure is funded.

[8.110] Income from trades, professions and vocations

⁴ See per Swinfen Eady LJ in *Ammonia Soda Co v Chamberlain* [1918] 1 Ch 266 and per Romer LJ in *Golden Horseshoe (New) Ltd v Thurgood* [1934] 1 KB 548, 18 TC 280; *Pattison v Marine Midland Ltd* [1981] STC 540. This is not a question of pure fact per Lord Evershed MR in *Pyrah v Annis & Co Ltd* (1956) 37 TC 163 at 173.
⁵ See Lord MacMillan in *Van den Berghs Ltd v Clark* (1934) 19 TC 390 at 432.
⁶ [1926] AC 205 at 213, 10 TC 155 at 192.
⁷ See *Anglo Persian Oil Co Ltd v Dale* (1931) 16 TC 253 which was followed in *Croydon Hotel and Leisure Co Ltd v Bowen* [1996] STC (SCD) 466. See also *Southern Counties Agricultural Society Ltd v Blackler* [1999] STC (SCD) 200.
⁸ *Jeffs v Ringtons Ltd* [1985] STC 809, [1986] 1 All ER 144.
⁹ *Lawson v Johnson Matthey plc* [1992] STC 466 at 470, HL distinguished in *Stone & Temple Ltd v Waters; Astrawall Ltd v Waters* [1995] STC 1.
¹⁰ [1979] STC 393, [1979] 2 All ER 801.
¹¹ [1982] STC 427 at 437.
¹² [1984] STC 1, CA.
¹³ *Beauchamp v F W Woolworth plc* [1988] STC 714 at 721c; decision reversed by HL [1989] STC 510.
¹⁴ 2000] STC 527, PC.
¹⁵ It was held not to be a capital expense in *IRC v Carron Co* 1968 SC 47, 45 TC 18, HL.
¹⁶ See *Bolton v International Drilling Co Ltd*, infra, § **8.116**.
¹⁷ See *Beauchamp v F W Woolworth plc* [1989] STC 510.
¹⁸ [2002] STC (SCD) 199.
¹⁹ *Dass v Special Comrs* [2006] EWHC 2491 (Ch), SCD, [2007] STC 187.
²⁰ [2007] SWTI 1181.
²¹ FA 2004, s 53.

[**8.111**] Some other formulations may be helpful.

In *Vallambrosa Rubber Co Ltd v Farmer* Lord Dunedin said that capital expenditure was something that was going to be spent once and for all and income expenditure was a thing that was going to recur every year,¹ while in *Ounsworth v Vickers Ltd* Rowlatt J said that the distinction was between expenditure that was to meet a continuous demand and expenditure made once and for all.²

In *Taxes Comrs v Nchanga Consolidated Copper Mines Ltd*³ Lord Radcliffe said that there was a demarcation between the cost of creating, acquiring or enlarging the permanent (which does not mean perpetual) structure of which the income is to be the produce or fruit and the cost of earning that income itself or performing the income earning operations; he added that this was probably as illuminating a line of distinction as the law by itself is likely to achieve.

In *McClymont v Glover*⁴ Shell paid a cash sum to the taxpayers, which was used by them to purchase a petrol filling station. The Commissioner held that the intention was that the cash be used for the purchase⁵ and, as such, it was in the nature of a capital receipt, not a revenue receipt.

¹ (1910) 5 TC 529 at 536.
² (1915) 6 TC 671 at 675.

[3] [1964] 1 All ER 208, [1964] AC 948.
[4] [2004] STC (SCD) 54.
[5] See the comments in para 16 at 59.

[8.112] In deciding these difficult questions the court's task is to determine the true profits of the business but the court is hampered by the fact that a deductible expense must be entered when the expense is incurred and therefore cannot be spread over a number of years. It follows that to allow a major item of expenditure as a deduction in one year when its benefits will be spread over many will necessarily give a distorted picture of the profitability of the company.[1] Moreover many of these cases were decided when the taxation of capital gains was not a feature of the UK tax system and it would have been anomalous to allow the deduction of an item as a revenue expense when a receipt on the disposal of the same item would not be a trading receipt.

There is no rule whereby the treatment of the expenditure in the hands of the payer predetermines its character in the hands of the payee. So an item can be a revenue expense and a capital receipt or a capital expense and a revenue receipt.[2] The payment must be looked at in respect of the taxpayer alone and in relation to the actual situation of the taxpayer.[3]

Simon's Taxes B3.204.

[1] See Lord Reid in *Regent Oil Co Ltd v Strick* [1965] 3 All ER 174 at 181, 43 TC 1 at 31.
[2] *Regent Oil Co Ltd v Strick* [1965] 3 All ER 174, 43 TC 1.
[3] *Vodafone Cellular Ltd v Shaw* [1995] STC 353.

Acquisition of a business (capital) or running a business (revenue)

[8.113] The costs of acquiring a business are capital expenses. Expenses shortly after acquiring a business will not be deductible if they are part of the acquisition cost,[1] especially where the expense is the sums paid on the termination of the contract of employment of a senior employee.[2] See also supra, §§ **8.48–8.60**. The matter is however one of fact.[3]

The costs of running a business are clearly revenue expenses so payments to employees for their services are deductible. Many of these expenses will be in the form of salaries or wages[4] which will therefore be taxable as income of the employee. A director's salary is also deductible. To allow such payments to be taxable in the hands of the employee but not deductible by the employer would amount to double taxation. There is, however, no correlation between these two and it is possible for a payment to be deductible by the employer and not taxable to the employee,[5] as in the case of certain benefits in kind.

Deductible sums include not only salaries proper but also pensions[6] and retirement gratuities. There is no rule that to be deductible the payment must relate to services rendered in that year.[7]

FA 1989 introduced an important timing rule for the deduction of emoluments. Broadly, these are not to be deductible for trading purposes until the sum is brought into charge on the employee as employment income.[8]

Simon's Direct Tax Service B2.407, 414, 416, 419, 460.

1. Royal Insurance Co v Watson [1897] AC 1, 3 TC 500.
2. Bassett Enterprises Ltd v Petty (1938) 21 TC 730.
3. IRC v Patrick Thomson Ltd (1956) 37 TC 145. In *Commissioner of Inland Revenue v NZ Forest Research Institute* [2000] STC 522, PC, the new company assumed actual contingent liabilities of the Crown in respect of employees who transferred to employment with the new company, which was created under a New Zealand statute to take over the operations of the Crown Research Institute. The Court held that payments that arose in consequence were capital expenditure, being part of what was paid for the acquisition of the Crown of the trade acquired.
4. But not sums paid to the Revenue in respect of tax not deducted under the PAYE scheme; *Bamford v ATA Advertising Ltd* [1972] 3 All ER 535, 48 TC 359. Incentive payments are deductible even if they are to enable the workforce to buy control of the employer: *Heather v PE Consulting Group Ltd* [1973] 1 All ER 8, 48 TC 320; see the discussion of this case in *E Bott Ltd v Price* [1987] STC 100 at 106. Payment of an employee's community charge was a deductible expense if a bona fide part of the employee's remuneration package: Inland Revenue press release, 10 November 1989, *Simon's Tax Intelligence* 1989, p 838.
5. Supra, § **7.17**. For the converse position, see *Weight v Salmon* (1935) 19 TC 174, supra, §§ **7.55–7.56**.
6. *Smith v Incorporated Council of Law Reporting for England and Wales* (1914) 6 TC 477.
7. *Hancock v General Reversionary Society and Investment Co Ltd* [1919] 1 KB 25, 7 TC 358.
8. ITTOIA 2005, s 36 (income tax); FA 1989, s 43 (corporation tax).

Facilities for and reorganisation of business (capital)

[8.114] The facilities are clearly capital of the business so expenditure on them may be capital. Thus the building of a factory is a capital expense and there will also be so classified ancillary works such as the provision of a water supply,[1] of drainage[2] and roads.[3] Likewise the cost of sinking a mine shaft is a capital expense[4] as is the cost of reconverting an oil rig at the end of its lease period[5] or the cost of acquiring a waste tipping site,[6] although legislation now permits the deduction of both restoration payments and preparation expenditure in closely defined circumstances.[7] Capital allowances will sometimes be available for such expenditure but the availability of capital allowances excludes the revenue deduction for restoration payments and preparation expenditure on waste disposal projects.

The expense of moving from one set of business premises to another is a capital expense[8] although the costs of removing trading stock are not so regarded. In practice removal costs which are forced on the trader, as on the expiration of a lease are allowed. Where, however, the general rule applies it prevents the deduction of ancillary costs such as conveyancing expenses.

Once for all expenditure on reorganisation may be capital. This was so in *Watney Combe Reid & Co Ltd v Pike* where a brewery made ex-gratia payments to tenants under a scheme by which separate management companies were substituted for tenants; the purpose was to make the assets more profitable[9] but it was important that the scheme involved a new corporate structure and a new way of doing business.

Facilities may be financial as well as physical. So the question whether an exchange loss on a borrowing is deductible may turn on whether the borrowing is part of the taxpayer's revenue transactions or an accretion to capital. The latter has some degree of permanence, the former is essentially short term. A fixed five-year loan was held to be on capital account—so that a foreign exchange loss on repayment was not an allowable deduction.[10] In 1997, a number of old established building societies, whose members were those depositing money on "share accounts", converted to banks (being quoted companies) the members then holding conventional voting shares. In 2000, the Special Commissioners heard appeals from four such newly created banks[11] in relation to the very considerable expenditure[12] required to effect the conversion. The Special Commissioners identified that the advantage obtained by the payments was a change in the regulatory regime applicable to the building society/bank such that it was able to trade in the same way but with fewer restrictions:

> The expenditure on the conversion costs was calculated to effect a transfer from a restrictive regulatory regime to a more flexible regulatory regime. This was undertaken for the purposes of the trade of the Halifax. In particular, the building society wanted to borrow above the wholesale funding limits and could not do so. The only remedy available to the building society under the BSA was the transfer of its business to a commercial company. The Halifax Building Society did not necessarily want to be a public limited company but that was the only way it could escape from the restrictive regulatory regime. The business of the Halifax was carried on in the same way, and by the same people, before and after the conversion. . . . Having considered the practical and business effect of the transactions we conclude that the conversion costs were of a revenue nature.[13]

Simon's Direct Tax Service B2.308, 309, 311, 407, 464, 478, B5.416.

[1] *Boyce v Whitwick Colliery Co Ltd* (1934) 18 TC 655.
[2] *Bean v Doncaster Amalgmated Collieries Ltd* [1944] 1 All ER 621, 27 TC 296.
[3] *Pitt v Castle Hill Warehousing Co Ltd* [1974] 3 All ER 146, [1974] STC 420. See also *Ounsworth v Vickers Ltd* [1915] 3 KB 267, 6 TC 671.
[4] *Bonner v Basset Mines Ltd* (1912) 6 TC 146.
[5] *RTZ Oil and Gas Ltd v Elliss* [1987] STC 512.
[6] *Rolfe v Wimpey Waste Management Ltd* [1989] STC 454, CA (Special Commissioner reversed).
[7] ITTOIA 2005, ss 165(2) and 168(2) (income tax); TA 1988, ss 91A, 91B (now only for corporation tax) added by FA 1990, s 78 and modified by FA 1993, s 110 to allow the deduction of pre-trading expenditure for trades begun on or after 1 April 1993. See Inland Revenue interpretation April 1998, *Simon's Weekly Tax Intelligence* 1998, p 692.
[8] *Granite Supply Association Ltd v Kitto* (1905) 5 TC 168.
[9] [1982] STC 733.
[10] *Beauchamp v F W Woolworth plc* [1989] STC 510; this was despite by the fact that the borrowing had been treated as an accretion to capital on the company's accounts.

[8.114] Income from trades, professions and vocations

[11] *Halifax plc v Davidson* [2000] STC (SCD) 251, *Woolwich plc v Davidson* [2000] STC (SCD) 302, *Northern Rock plc v Thorpe* [2000] STC (SCD) 317, *Alliance and Leicester plc v Hamer* [2000] STC (SCD) 332.
[12] The expenditure in dispute in the four cases totals £359.6 million.
[13] *Halifax plc v Davidson* [2000] STC (SCD) 251 at 298a-299a.

Expansion of a business (capital) or maintenance of a business (revenue)

[8.115] The expense of an application for planning permission over land is generally capital since the land is a capital asset and this expense is more than mere maintenance.[1] Likewise the premises are capital assets and so where a brewer applies for a licence for new premises the legal cost of applying for the new licence is not deductible[2] any more than would be the legal costs of acquiring the new premises or the costs of moving his plant and stock.[3]

A licence governing the terms of one's trade is different from a tax incurred in running it. So in *Pyrah v Annis*[4] it was held that the costs of an unsuccessful application to vary an existing public carrier's licence by increasing the number of vehicles from four to seven was capital expenditure because the licence was an asset retained by the trader which produces income. However, in *IRC v Carron Co* a company was entitled to deduct the legal costs of altering its charter so as to remove restrictions on ordinary business operations.[5] This distinction is somewhat fine.

Simon's Taxes B2.434.

[1] *ECC Quarries Ltd v Watkis* [1975] STC 578, [1975] 3 All ER 843. A land developer can deduct such expenses since the land is not capital.
[2] *Morse v Stedeford* (1934) 18 TC 457.
[3] *Granite Supply Association Ltd v Kitton* (1905) 5 TC 168, see also *Pendleton v Mitchells and Butlers Ltd* [1969] 2 All ER 928, 45 TC 341.
[4] [1956] 2 All ER 858, 37 TC 163.
[5] (1968) 45 TC 18.

Preservation of capital (revenue)

[8.116] Sums paid in order to preserve the capital or capital assets of the business are revenue expenses. So sums spent on a software project to ensure that an existing computer system can cope with the millennium will be regarded as revenue expenditure unless part of a major new project instituting other changes and that project is itself capital in nature.[1]

In *Cooke v Quick Shoe Repair Service*[2] the firm had bought a business and arranged for the vendor to settle outstanding liabilities to suppliers and employees. When he failed to do so the firm paid off the creditors and was held entitled to deduct the sums so paid because they were paid to preserve the goodwill of the business and not to buy it.

Sums paid in order to protect title to capital assets have been held to be revenue expenses. The reason for this is that the expenses are incurred in maintaining the company's capital and so are just as deductible as expenses of repair and maintenance on the fixed assets of the company.[3] The expenditure results in neither the improvement nor the acquisition of any fixed capital asset.[4] So expenses incurred in resisting an unfounded allegation of misrepresentation have been held deductible as have sums paid by way of settlement of a civil claim against the trade.[5] It is clear that sums paid by way of fines or penalty are not deductible but this is because the expense is not incurred wholly and exclusively for the purposes of trade.[6] It is, however, of importance since it suggests that expenditure to preserve the company's entire trading apparatus can be revenue expenditure.

However, in *Bolton v International Drilling Co Ltd*, where a company's sole income earning asset was originally acquired subject to another person's option to reacquire it, a sum paid for release of the option was not revenue expenditure.[7] This is because until that time the trade's right in the asset was not one of complete ownership; hence the payment did not preserve the original title but improved it.

The importance of looking at the assets is also shown by *Walker v Joint Credit Card Co Ltd* where sums paid not just to preserve goodwill, but to improve it were held to be capital expenditure.[8]

A controversial application of that principle occurred in *Morgan v Tate and Lyle Ltd*[9] where the company successfully claimed to be entitled to deduct expenses incurred in a publicity campaign to defeat the proposed nationalisation of the company. The form of nationalisation proposed for the sugar industry was not the compulsory acquisition of its shares but the compulsory acquisition of its assets and on this basis the House of Lords held that the costs of the campaign were deductible. If the company had been faced with a takeover of its business by a group of persons anxious to acquire control through the purchase of its shares it was clear that the costs of resisting such a takeover would not have been deductible, the threat in such a case being to the existing management rather than to the assets or trade of the company. Those reading the advertisements issued during the campaign might be forgiven for not appreciating that the company was resisting not nationalisation in general but merely one form of nationalisation on terms thought disadvantageous to the shareholders.

In all these cases it is essential to show that the payment was for the preservation of capital. In *Lawson v Johnson Matthey plc*[10] it was held that where an expense had been incurred in order to preserve the company's trade the court could ignore the means by which it was done (which was by the disposal of worthless shares in a subsidiary company). The House of Lords held that, on the facts, that money was paid, and paid solely, to enable the taxpayer company to continue in business.

Simon's Taxes B2.444.

---

[1] Inland Revenue interpretation RI 180, *Simon's Weekly Tax Intelligence* 1998, p 690.
[2] (1949) 30 TC 460—"an odd case" per Walton J in *Garforth v Tankard Carpets Ltd* [1980] STC 251 at 259, 260. See also *Walker v Cater Securities Ltd* [1974] STC 390, [1974] 3 All ER 63 (taxpayer owned shares in a customer-company; X had

[8.116] Income from trades, professions and vocations

option to buy these shares; sum paid by taxpayer to X for release of option held revenue expense; this conclusion supported by Revenue evidence; payment considered in substance to be to keep an important customer, not just to acquire a capital asset-see *Bolton v International Drilling Co Ltd* [1983] STC 70 at 92).
[3] Distinguish *Pitt v Castle Hill Warehousing Co Ltd* [1974] STC 420, [1974] 3 All ER 146.
[4] *Southern v Borax Consolidated Ltd* [1940] 4 All ER 412, 23 TC 597.
[5] *IT Comr Bihar and Orissa v Singh* [1942] 1 All ER 362.
[6] Supra, § **8.104**.
[7] [1983] STC 70.
[8] [1982] STC 427.
[9] [1954] 2 All ER 413, 35 TC 367. Cf *Hammond Engineering Co Ltd v IRC* [1975] STC 334.
[10] [1992] STC 466, HL; reversing [1991] STC 259, CA.

Costs of loan capital

[8.117] The costs of raising, servicing and repaying loan capital are the subject to a mixture of case law and statute. Statute permits the deduction of incidental costs of loan finance (ITTOIA 2005, s 58 (income tax only[1])) and interest is the subject of a special set of rules; infra, § **8.132**. The deduction is made in computing the profits of the period during which the finance was obtained.[2] This leaves the issue of the deductibility of an exchange loss on the repayment of a loan. In *Pattison v Marine Midland Ltd*[3] a bank borrowed a large sum in US dollars by way of unsecured loan stock issued to its parent, the lender. Vinelott J held that the loss was not deductible. The loan represented a long term obligation entered into for the purpose of raising money employed by the company to enable it to commence trading; the use of the funds could not alter their capital nature. This matter was not raised on the further appeals in that case.

In *Beauchamp v F W Woolworth plc*[4] the taxpayer company, with an annual turnover of some £300m, borrowed 50m Swiss francs for a five-year period; the loan was immediately converted into sterling. The following year the taxpayer incurred a second such loan, which was also converted. In due course the loans were repaid but, owing to the decline of sterling against the Swiss franc, at a large loss. The House of Lords held that the loan was an accretion to capital and not a revenue transaction and therefore the loss was not allowable. The precise ratio is not easy to determine. At one point Lord Templeman talks of the loan having to be temporary and fluctuating and incurred in meeting the ordinary running expenses of the business.[5] However, this was said in the context of distinguishing *Regent Oil v Strick* and stress was being laid on the question whether the petrol tie or loan could be said to be an ordinary incident of marketing. A more abstract statement by Lord Templeman was that the loan would only be on revenue account if it were part of the ordinary day to day incidence of carrying on a business.[6] The latter seems to be the more promising starting point but for corporation tax only.

Simon's Taxes B2.433, B4.304.

[1] For corporation tax, relief is given within the loan relationship rules.

² *Cadbury Schweppes plc v Williams* [2002] STC (SCD) 115.
³ [1981] STC 540.
⁴ [1989] STC 510. This case predates both the loan relationships (see infra, § **27.01**) and the FOREX legislation (see infra, § **27.11** ff).
⁵ [1989] STC 510 at 518.
⁶ [1989] STC 510 at 517.

Examples

Ending onerous obligations and restrictions

[8.118] A payment for getting rid of a permanent disadvantage or onerous burden may be an enduring benefit and so a capital expense. The problem here is that whereas it is well settled that a payment to dismiss an unsatisfactory employee is a revenue expense, it is equally well settled that certain other payments will be a capital expense. One starting point is to ask whether the payments made under the liability being got rid of would themselves be revenue expenses.¹ So in *Alexander Howard & Co Ltd v Bentley*² the taxpayer paid a lump sum to be rid of a contingent liability to pay an annuity to the widow of its governing director; the annuity payments would not have been deductible since not paid wholly and exclusively for trade purposes but rather as an adjunct to shares; it followed that the lump sum payment was not deductible either.

In principle an expense incurred to be rid of a revenue expense ought to be deductible; just as a surrogatum for loss of profit is a trading receipt so a commutation of deductible outlay should be a revenue expense. However, while it appears to be true that payments to get rid of liabilities which are *not* revenue expenses will be treated as not deductible, payments to get rid of revenue expenses are not always so. One must distinguish getting rid of a charge against revenue from acquiring a capital asset which enables one to get rid of such a charge. So the purchase of labour-saving machinery is a capital expense and cannot be converted into a revenue expense simply because it can be shown to reduce the wage bill.³

Whereas expenditure incurred on the maintenance of a physical asset of the company is revenue, expenditure on replacing that asset will be capital expenditure. Thus if a channel is continually being silted up and the trader decides to replace the silting channel with a concrete one, that is capital expenditure even though the costs of clearing the silt would have been a revenue expense.⁴

A payment to settle a capital liability is clearly a capital payment. So where a company had agreed to buy a ship to use in its trade a payment made on cancellation of the contract was a capital expense.⁵

Simon's Taxes B2.455.

1 Per Simon LJ in *Bean v Doncaster Amalgamated Collieries Ltd* (1944) 27 TC 296 at 312.
2 (1948) 30 TC 334. It does not follow that this expense was capital-simply that it was not for trading purposes and so not deductible.

[8.118] Income from trades, professions and vocations

³ Per Rowlatt J in *Anglo-Persian Oil Co Ltd v Dale* (1931) 16 TC 253 at 261.
⁴ Per Rowlatt J in *Mitchell v B W Noble Ltd* [1927] 1 KB 719 at 728, 11 TC 372 at 415.
⁵ *Countess Warwick Steamship Co Ltd v Ogg* [1924] 2 KB 292, 8 TC 652.

[8.119] Difficulties arise over payments to vary or terminate leases. These difficulties stem from the nature of the lease for tax purposes in that while payments of rent under the lease would clearly be revenue expenses, the payment of a premium would not even if paid by instalments¹ provided the lease itself formed part of the capital structure of the business. It followed that where a company had a lease of a shop for five years and the company ceased to use that shop after two years, the rent would still be deductible in computing its profits assuming, as was the case, that the trade itself was still conducted from other premises.²

Where the lease is a capital asset of the business a payment to vary the terms of the lease will be a capital expense. This may be because the payment rendering the lease either more advantageous or less disadvantageous improves the lease and so comes within the next example—supra, § **7.116**. In *Tucker v Granada Motorway Services Ltd*³ the landlord (the Minister of Transport) was entitled to rent from the lessees of a motorway service station together with an additional rent based on takings, the latter to include an element for tobacco duty. As tobacco duty rose the lessees found it difficult to make a profit and so it was agreed to exclude the tobacco duty from the calculation in return for a lump sum. The House of Lords held that the lump sum was a capital expense; it was quite irrelevant that the purpose of the expenditure was to increase profit.

A fortiori a payment for the *surrender* of the lease in commutation of the liability to pay rent is a capital expense and not deductible.⁴

Simon's Taxes B2.405, 465, 479.

¹ *IRC v Adam* (1928) 14 TC 34—see Tucker Report 1951, Cmd 8189 § 247.
² *IRC v Falkirk Iron Co Ltd* (1933) 17 TC 625.
³ [1979] STC 393 [1979] 2 All ER 801.
⁴ *Cowcher v Richard Mills & Co Ltd* (1927) 13 TC 216; *Mallett v Staveley Coal and Iron Co Ltd* [1928] 2 KB 405, 13 TC 772; see also *IRC v William Sharp & Son* (1959) 38 TC 341; *Bullrun Inc v Inspector of Taxes* [2000] STC (SCD) 384. *IRC v John Lewis Properties plc* [2002] EWCA Civ 1869, [2003] STC 117.

[8.120] Payment to be rid of a director whose continuance in office would be detrimental to the company is a revenue expense.¹ This is because the company receives no enduring advantage; one cannot point to any asset of the company which is enhanced; an employee is not a permanency and the satisfactory state of the workforce is not regarded as part of the capital of the business.

In *Anglo-Persian Oil Co Ltd v Dale*² this was extended to allow deduction of substantial payments to agents to terminate an agency agreement with eleven years to run. This decision equates an agency with a contract of employment and rests on the statement by Lawrence LJ in the Court of Appeal that the cancellation "merely effected a change in the company business methods and internal organisation leaving its fixed capital untouched".[3]

Simon's Taxes B2.426.

---

[1] *Mitchell v B W Noble Ltd* [1927] 1 KB 719, 11 TC 372.
[2] [1932] 1 KB 124, 16 TC 253.
[3] [1932] 1 KB 124 at 141, 16 TC 253 at 272.

[8.121] In *Whitehead v Tubbs (Elastics) Ltd*[1] a payment was made to secure the release of a term in a loan agreement which had significantly limited the company's power to borrow money. This payment was held to be capital. By contrast, in *IRC v Carron Co*[2] the court had held that a payment to secure the alteration of a company's constitution was a revenue expense. This case was distinguished in *Whitehead v Tubbs (Elastics) Ltd* on the basis that the restrictions in that case were attributable not to any asset of the company but to its constitution, the alteration of which would normally have been effected as part of its day to day management; moreover in *IRC v Carron* no asset was brought into existence and nor was there any expenditure on any asset or liability of the company.

Simon's Taxes B2.437, 455.

---

[1] [1984] STC 1, CA.
[2] (1968) 45 TC 18, HL.

Repairs (revenue) and Improvements (capital)

[8.122] TA 1988, s 74(1) expressly disqualifies in para (d): "any sums expended for repairs of premises occupied . . . for the purposes of the trade beyond the sum actually expended for the purpose", a provision which restricts deductions to sums actually spent and therefore prohibits the deduction of sums set aside by way of reserve for future expenditure; while para (g) prohibits the deduction of any capital employed in improvements of premises occupied for the purposes of the trade profession or vocation. At first sight this paragraph would seem to be directed to the source from which the trader chooses to finance his improvements, however, it is generally taken to mean that sums spent on improvements are capital payments and therefore not deductible, while sums spent on the repair of capital assets are deductible.

Neither of these provisions has been rewritten into ITTOIA 2005 for income tax purposes and one can infer that they are probably redundant for corporation tax too. This aspect of para (d) was felt to be redundant following the Special Commissioners' decision in *Jenners Princes Street Edinburgh Limited v IRC*.[1] The provisions from para (g) were thought to be covered by the general prohibition against deductions in respect of capital expenditure now found in ITTOIA 2005, s 33.

Improving the building of a factory is a capital cost because it is a material improvement of the land.[2] Money spent on the replacement of one kind of rail

[8.122] Income from trades, professions and vocations

by a superior kind is not deductible, since it increases the value of the railway line.[3] Expense incurred in increasing the number of sleepers under each rail was admitted to be capital expense in *Rhodesia Railways Ltd v Bechuanaland Protectorate IT Collector*,[4] but the railway company was allowed to deduct as repairs the cost of works in renewing 74 miles of railway track by replacing rails and sleepers. This was not an improvement since it only restored the worn track to its normal condition and did not increase the capacity of the line in any way. Money spent on pulling down a chimney and building a new bigger and better chimney[5] or on renovating a factory with a higher roof line and so more space is not deductible.[6] The question whether work is a repair or an improvement is one of fact.[7]

Where an improvement is carried out no deduction may be claimed for such part of the expenditure as would have been needed to pay for mere repair. In *Thomas Wilson (Keighley) Ltd v Emmerson*,[8] Danckwerts J commented, 'It seems to me to be a hardship and something which is calculated to discourage manufacturers from making the best use of their property'. The theoretical reason for disallowing apportionment is clear enough but one may notice that in respect of a property business the Revenue will by concession allow such part of the cost as would have been needed to carry out the repair work.[9] On the other hand if the work consists of a number of separate jobs it may be possible to distinguish between the different items thus allowing some of the expense so in *Conn v Robins Bros Ltd*[10] the construction of "a ladies toilet" was held to be an improvement but the insertion of steel joists a repair.

These rules are not confined to physical assets. Sums spent on training courses for proprietors are regarded as capital if intended to give them new expertise, knowledge or skill as distinct from mere updating.[11]

Simon's Taxes B2.409.

---

[1] (1998) SpC 166, [1998] STC (SCD) 196.
[2] For capital allowances, see infra, Chapter 9.
[3] *Highland Rly Co v Balderston* (1889) 2 TC 485; and see *LCC v Edwards* (1909) 5 TC 383.
[4] Admitted by taxpayer [1933] AC 368 at 372; but see Lord Cooper in *Lawrie v IRC* (1952) 34 TC 20 at 25.
[5] *O'Grady v Bullcroft Main Collieries Ltd* (1932) 17 TC 93.
[6] *Thomas Wilson (Keighley) Ltd v Emmerson* (1960) 39 TC 360; *Lawrie v IRC* (1952) 34 TC 20; *Mann Crossman and Paulin Ltd v IRC* [1947] 1 All ER 742, 28 TC 410.
[7] *Conn v Robins Bros Ltd* (1966) 43 TC 266 at 274.
[8] (1960) 39 TC 360 at 366.
[9] Extra-statutory concession B4.
[10] (1966) 43 TC 266.
[11] Inland Revenue interpretation RI 1.

[8.123] Renewals or repairs. As Buckley LJ said in *Lurcott v Wakely and Wheeler*,[1] not a revenue case:[2]

'repair' and 'renew' are not words expressive of clear contrast . . . repair is restoration by renewal or replacement of subsidiary parts of a whole. Renewal, as distinguished from repair, is reconstruction of the entirety, meaning by the entirety not necessarily the whole but substantially the whole subject matter under discussion.

Thus the replacement of a slate on a roof[3] would be a repair, but the rebuilding of a retort house in a gas works would be a renewal.[4]

This test presupposes a satisfactory definition of the unit repaired or renewed. In *O'Grady v Bullcroft Main Collieries Ltd*[5] a chimney used to carry away fumes from a furnace had become unsafe and so the company built a new one. Rowlatt J said that in his view the chimney was not a part of the factory but an entirety. Similarly, in *Margrett v Lowestoft Water and Gas Co* the replacement of a reservoir by a new one was a renewal, not a repair. On the other hand in *Samuel Jones & Co (Devonvale) Ltd v IRC*[6] the costs of replacing an unsafe chimney at a factory were held deductible. In the Court of Session which reversed the Special Commissioners Lord Cooper said that the factory was the entirety, the chimney therefore only a part of the entirety. The court also stressed the low cost of the replacement of the chimney relatively to the insured value of the factory, a point not taken in *O'Grady v Bullcroft Main Collieries Ltd*. The distinction between a part and the entirety thus appears to be a convenient method of describing a conclusion rather than a helpful test.

The question seems to be one of the size and importance of the work. One big job may be capital whereas a combination of small jobs may be revenue. In *Phillips v Whieldon Sanitary Potteries Ltd*[7] the replacement of a barrier protecting a factory from water in a canal was held to be a renewal and so capital expenditure, the court taking into account the extent of the work, the permanent nature of the new barrier and the enduring benefit it would confer on the business by preserving a part of the fixed capital. In that case Donovan J followed the *Bullcroft* case and reversed the Commissioners.

An expenditure may be in respect of a repair as opposed to a renewal even though it is carried out some time after the need has first arisen. Thus the costs of keeping a channel dredged would be income expenditure even though the dredging was done only once every three years or so.[8] There is no need to take away every grain of sand as it comes.

Simon's Taxes B2.419, 479; B3.210.

---

[1] [1911] 1 KB 905 at 923, 924 cited eg by Lord MacMillan in *Rhodesia Railways Ltd v Bechuanaland Protectorate IT Collector* [1933] AC 368 at 374.
[2] The case concerned the construction of a lessee's covenant to keep in thorough repair and in good condition.
[3] Per Rowlatt J in *O'Grady v Bullcroft Main Collieries Ltd* (1932) 17 TC 93 at 101.
[4] Per Donovan J in *Phillips v Whieldon Sanitary Potteries Ltd* (1952) 33 TC 213 at 219.
[5] (1932) 17 TC 93; the ratio was that the chimney was an addition, there being no evidence that the old one was pulled down, see also *Wynne-Jones v Bedale Auction Ltd* [1977] STC 50, 51 TC 426 (cattle ring, not whole complex, the relevant unit): criticised [1977] BTR 184 (Baxter).
[6] (1951) 32 TC 513; see also *Margrett v Lowestoft Water and Gas Co* (1935) 19 TC 481.

[8.123] Income from trades, professions and vocations

[7] (1952) 33 TC 213; contrast *Conn v Robins Bros Ltd* (1966) 43 TC 266.
[8] Per Rowlatt J in *Ounsworth v Vickers Ltd* (1915) 6 TC 671.

[8.124] Initial repairs. Where a trader acquires an asset which requires extensive repairs before it is in a usable condition, the expenses of those repairs are not deductible since they are as much capital expenditure as the costs of acquiring the asset itself. Were the rule otherwise a trader could convert at least a part of the prospective capital expense into a revenue item by buying the asset in an incomplete state and finishing the work himself, perhaps by employing the person who had worked on it before its acquisition.

In *Law Shipping Co Ltd v IRC*[1] a shipping company bought a ship which was at that date ready to sail with freight booked. The Lloyd's survey was then overdue but with the consent of the insurers, the ship was allowed to complete the voyage. The ship cost £97,000 and the company had to spend an extra £51,558 on repairs in order for the vessel to pass the survey. Of that sum some £12,000 was in respect of repairs caused by deterioration during the voyage and was allowed by the Revenue, the balance of £39,500 was not, correctly as the Court of Session held.

Simon's Taxes B2.404, 409, 419.

[1] 1924 SC 74, 12 TC 621 see also *IRC v Granite City Steamship Co Ltd* 1927 SC 705, 13 TC 1 and the expenditure on the branch line in *Highland Rly Co v Balderston* (1889) 2 TC 485.

[8.125] However, it is not every repair incurred to put right something occurring before an asset is acquired that is disallowed. The *Law Shipping* case applies where the expenditure is required to make the asset commercially viable; a different rule applies where the asset is already so viable. In *Odeon Associated Theatres Ltd v Jones*[1] the company bought a cinema in 1945. Only small sums had been permitted to be spent in the previous five years and restrictions on repair work lasted for some time after the war. The cinema was open to the public and was a profit earning asset. The Court of Appeal held that sums spent subsequently to the acquisition in respect of the deferred repairs were deductible. The primary reason was that such would be in accordance with the normal principles of commercial accountancy, as the Commissioners had made a finding not made in the *Law Shipping* case. However, there were other differences. Although in the *Law Shipping* case the ship had been permitted to complete one voyage it was clear that after that a full insurance survey would be needed and the price showed that substantial expenditure would be needed before the ship would again be a profit earning asset. By contrast the cinema was an immediate income earning asset and it appeared that the price had not been affected by the fact of disrepair. Two other facts are material. First, even if the vendors had wished to carry out the repair work before the sale they would have been unable to do so because of the restrictions. Second, there was no indication that the taxpayer had in fact been put to greater expense by reason of the deferred repairs. The precise extent of the case is uncertain.

Simon's Direct Tax Service B2.404, 419.

[1] [1972] 1 All ER 681, 48 TC 257, CA. See also *Whelan v Dover Harbour Board* (1934) 18 TC 555. This decision must cast doubt on *Jackson v Laskers Home Furnishers Ltd* [1956] 3 All ER 891, 37 TC 69.

Allowable capital expenditure—the renewals basis

[8.126] The distinction between repair and renewal is blurred by the Revenue practice of allowing the cost of replacing machinery and plant as a revenue expense. This practice is quite distinct from the capital allowances system. There appear to be two distinct legal bases for this practice which, confusingly, is called a renewals allowance. One is the general theory of profit which would equate a renewal with a repair and would regard both as maintaining intact the capital originally invested in the physical assets of the business. The disadvantage of the explanation is that it is quite inconsistent with the cases just considered and would presumably apply to a range of expenditures other than those on machinery and plant.[1]

The second explanation rests on TA 1988, s 74(1)(d) which disallows sums spent on the "supply, repairs or alterations of any implements, utensils or articles employed, for the purposes of a trade, profession or vocation, beyond the sum actually expended for those purposes". As drafted this simply prohibits the deduction of reserves for future expenditure and so may be taken to allow actual expenditure; further it draws no distinction between initial and replacement utensils. Moreover it would confine the allowance to implements, utensils and articles and thus not necessarily cover all types of machinery and plant.[2]

It seems best to regard this as an extra-statutory concession dating from the days when there were no capital allowances. This not only avoids the problems mentioned but also justifies the Revenue's insistence that some renewals allowances are to be made only over a period of two or three years.

These provisions of TA 1988, s 74(1)(d) were not fully rewritten into ITTOIA 2005 for income tax purposes and one can infer the rest is probably redundant for corporation tax too. Under the rewritten rules, a deduction is available in respect of capital expenses incurred on replacing or altering any implement, utensil or article used for the purposes of a trade where the capital nature of the expenditure would otherwise preclude a deduction.[3] The rest of the expenditure covered by TA 1988, s 74(1)(d) is believed to qualify for relief under normal rules.

Where the renewals basis is adopted the allowance given is the cost of the new article (excluding additions or improvements) less the scrap or realised value of the replaced article. The cost of the new article may be greater or less than that of the old.

Successfully to claim a renewals allowance is to classify the expenditure as revenue. However, this is not to prevent a later switch to the capital allowance system. The two systems of relief are alternatives.[4]

Simon's Taxes B3.307.

[1] But note Revenue practice in relation to shop fronts.

² See *IRC v Great Wigston Gas Co* (1946) 29 TC 197. An item may be capital expenditure even though on utensils—see *Hinton v Maden and Ireland Ltd* [1959] 3 All ER 356, 38 TC 391.
³ ITTOIA 2005, s 68.
⁴ See extra-statutory concession B1.

Trading stock—the tree and the fruit

[8.127] The purchase of trading stock is generally a deductible revenue expense. However, care is needed to distinguish the purchase of trading stock from the purchase of an asset bearing trading stock.¹ Thus the purchase of a mine for extraction purposes is an item of capital expenditure and not the purchase of trading stock.² So in *IRC v Pilcher*³ a fruit grower was not allowed to deduct the cost of purchasing a cherry orchard, not even that part which represented the value of the nearly ripe crop. The contract had expressly included "this year's crop" but that meant only that the vendor was not to be entitled to pick the crop ripening between contract and completion.⁴ The grower had purchased an income earning asset and not two separate items namely the trees and the crop.

In these cases since one is distinguishing trading stock from capital considerable care is needed in defining the trade; thus in one case sums spent by a timber merchant on the purchase of standing timber were not deductible⁵ whereas in another case the costs of standing timber bought by a dealer in standing timber were held deductible.⁶

The methodology used in valuing stock has been the subject of *Revenue and Customs Comrs v William Grant* and *Small v Mars (UK) Ltd*,⁷ which were heard together by the House of Lords. In his leading judgment, with which all four other Law Lords expressed their "full agreement",⁸ Lord Hoffmann upheld the methodology used by the taxpayers companies in measuring stock,⁹ saying that the companies' accounts give a true and fair view and the Taxes Acts do not give any express requirement to adjust the profits for tax purposes.

Simon's Taxes B2.604.

¹ Supra, § **8.109**.
² *Alianza Co Ltd v Bell* [1906] AC 18, 5 TC 172; *Stratford v Mole and Lea* (1941) 24 TC 20.
³ [1949] 2 All ER 1097, 31 TC 314.
⁴ Quaere how far the case turns on the distinction between *fructus naturales* and *fructus industriales*.
⁵ *Hood Barrs v IRC (No 2)* [1957] 1 All ER 832, 37 TC 188 noted [1957] BTR 174 (Silberrad); see also *Kauri Timber Co Ltd v IT Comr* [1913] AC 771; *Hopwood v C N Spencer Ltd* (1964) 42 TC 169 and *Taxation* vol 79, p 10.
⁶ *Murray v IRC* (1951) 32 TC 238.
⁷ [2007] STC 680, HL. Other cases on the valuation of stock, which turn on their own particular facts have been *Terry and Terry (Trading as C & J Terry & Sons) v Revenue and Customs Comrs* [2005] STC (SCD) 629 and *Triage Services Ltd v R & C Comrs* [2006] STC (SCD) 85.
⁸ [2007] STC 680 paras [27], [40], [41] and [42] at 688a, 690j, 691a and 691b.

⁹ The House of Lords, thereby, overruled the Court of Appeal: *Small v Mars (UK) Ltd* [2005] EWHC 553 (Ch), [2005] STC 958; *IRC v William Grant & Sons Distillers Ltd* [2006] STC 69.

[8.128] The purchase of a business is a capital expenditure and a purchase of trading stock as part of that purchase is also capital expenditure. Normally separate entries will take care of trading stock stricto sensu, but this will not take care of incidental profit making sources. In *John Smith & Son v Moore*¹ the taxpayer had inherited his father's business in return for a sum which included a figure of £30,000 for specific unexpired contracts for the supply of coal. The son was not allowed to deduct this £30,000. Viscount Haldane held that the contracts formed part of his fixed capital and that it was the coal which was the circulating capital,² and Lord Sumner held that the business was not that of buying and selling contracts but buying and selling coal and that the price paid was the price of acquiring the business.³

The decision clearly needs some explanation since contracts for the supply of trading stock can lead to trading profits in ways other than taking delivery of trading stock.⁴ In *Taxes Comr v Nchanga Consolidated Copper Mines Ltd*⁵ Viscount Radcliffe explained the decision as resting on two important elements in the facts of the case. One was that an aggregate price had been paid for the entire business as it stood. The other was that the son did not acquire stock in trade.⁶ However, the facts suggest that the son was not carrying on business on his own account before his father's death, in which case it is a simple case of pre-trading expenses and leaves the court free to dissect the price paid where the business is taken over by one already trading.

Simon's Taxes B2.410.

¹ [1921] 2 AC 13, 12 TC 266.
² At 20 and 282, 283.
³ At 20 and 282, 283.
⁴ *Thompson v IRC* (1927) 12 TC 1091.
⁵ [1964] 1 All ER 208, [1964] AC 948.
⁶ See *Whimster & Co v IRC* (1925) 12 TC 813; and see Lord Reid in *Regent Oil Co Ltd v Strick* [1965] 3 All ER 174 at 185, 43 TC 1 at 36.

Trading arrangements

[8.129] Sums paid to regulate the structure of the business tend to be capital although the duration of the arrangement is of importance.¹ So a sum paid in instalments to secure a customer for ten years were held to be capital² as was a payment to a trade association to prevent the sale of the business of a member of the association to a non-member.³

Payment to a retiring employee for a covenant not to compete was held not deductible.⁴ It can be argued that such expenses are made in order to preserve the business and so should be deductible; however, a significant advantage is gained and so the payment is of capital.⁵ On balance it would seem that since the expense of buying up a rival business in order to suppress it is capital, the same should apply to a long term agreement to the same effect. Such arrangements relate to the commercial structure of the business. The question is, however, one of fact and degree. It is decisions in this area that are most open to review as a result of *Tucker v Granada Motorway Services Ltd* as it is often hard to see any identifiable business asset.

Simon's Taxes B2.426, 444, 462.

1   See *Taxes Comr v Nchanga Consolidated Copper Mines Ltd* [1964] 1 All ER 208, [1964] AC 948 (one year-revenue expense). Cf du Parcq LJ in *Henriksen v Grafton Hotel Ltd* [1942] 2 KB 184 at 196, 24 TC 451 at 462.
2   *United Steel Companies Ltd v Cullington* (1939) 23 TC 71.
3   *Collins v Joseph Adamson & Co* [1937] 4 All ER 236, 21 TC 400.
4   *Associated Portland Cement Manufacturers Ltd v Kerr* [1946] 1 All ER 68, 27 TC 103.
5   Note Lord Reid in *Regent Oil Co Ltd v Strick* [1965] 3 All ER 174 at 183, 43 TC 1 at 35.

Petrol ties

[8.130] After 1945 the petrol trade was arranged at the retail level on the basis that a garage would sell several brands of petrol. Around 1950, however, there commenced the "exclusivity war" and the petrol companies began to acquire ties over individual garages whereby the garage owner would promise to sell only that company's products and in return the company would offer to pay for minor improvements at the garage and perhaps a discount on the petrol supplied. Originally these agreements lasted for a short time with low discounts but as the war increased the garage owners demanded better terms. In *Bolam v Regent Oil Co*[1] Danckwerts J held that the expense incurred by the petrol company was still a revenue expense even though the tie was to last five years. There a round sum was paid in advance and based upon estimated sales. The expense was incurred in order to earn profits and being based upon the estimated sales was as much a revenue expense as would have been the cost of supplying the petrol at a lower cost.

The exclusivity war was not confined to the UK. In *BP (Australia) Ltd v Taxation Comr*[2] the oil company paid sums by way of a "development allowance" to garage owners in return for a five year tie, the amount being related to the estimated gallonage. The Privy Council holding that the payments were revenue expenses drew attention to the changing pattern of the petrol trade and its use of longer-term arrangements and talked in terms of fixed and circulating capital. The length of the agreements was simply a matter of degree, the fact that they were to last longer than one year immaterial.

The garage owners' own tax liability was affected by these payments. In so far as they were payments for their reimbursement of capital expenditure they were capital receipts,[3] as where the petrol company paid for substantial new buildings, but in so far as they were reimbursements of revenue expenditure, eg sales promotion, they would be revenue receipts.[4] Further, if the amounts were related to gallonage they might be treated as rebates on trading stock and so revenue payments.[5] On the other hand the garage owner might successfully invoke the principle in *Glenboig Union Fireclay Co Ltd v IRC*[6] and say that the payment was in return for the restriction of his trading opportunities, an argument that succeeded in a case involving a ten-year tie.[7] In order to make sure that the sums received were capital receipts there was evolved the system of the lease and lease back. The garage owner would grant a lease to the oil company which would promise to pay a nominal rent and a large premium. The company would then sub-lease the garage to the owner who would covenant to sell only the company's products, on breach of which the sublease would end. The premium would be a capital receipt by the garage owner, although now subject to tax in part by ITTOIA 2005 s 277 (income tax) and TA 1988, s 34 (corporation tax).[8]

This scheme was considered by the House of Lords in *Regent Oil Co v Strick*,[9] their judgment being given on the same day as the Privy Council in *BP (Australia) Ltd v Taxation Comr* with identical judges and no mention of the one case in the other. Payments under the scheme by Regent Oil were based upon estimated gallonage and the period ranged from five years to 21 years. It was stated that the company had 5,000 agreements in the UK, mostly of the older variety without a lease. The House of Lords unanimously held that the payments in respect of the lease arrangements were capital expenditure and so not deductible. The distinction between a five year tie of the old sort the expenditure on which was a revenue item and a five year lease, the premium on which was a capital item, means that the distinction must be sought in the nature of the asset acquired by the company. Under the lease scheme not only did the company acquire an interest in the land, but also a better security since if the owner broke the covenant they could terminate the sublease and take possession under the lease. The commercial needs of the company in a changing market which had affected the Privy Council were ignored by the House of Lords. An argument that the ties were payable out of circulating capital because they were to secure orders and would therefore come circulating back which had impressed the Privy Council was trounced by the House of Lords.

The present position is, to say the least, uncertain. A tie accompanied by a lease would seem to be capital but Lord Reid in *Regent Oil Co v Strick* thought that payments for very short leases, say two or three years might be revenue.[10] A tie unaccompanied by a lease will usually be a revenue expense even if it lasts for five years. There is authority that such a tie for twenty years will not be a revenue expense since it lacks the element of recurrence, but where the line is to be drawn between five and twenty remains to be seen, although in *Bolam v Regent Oil* a six year tie had been classified as revenue. The stress in the House of Lords on the nature of the asset acquired suggests that a premium payment in respect of a lease will be a capital item. One reason for this was that the payment would be capital in the hands of the recipient, an erroneous reason made the more absurd by the subsequent decision by the legislature to tax part of the premium as income of the recipient. Whether a premium in respect of a short lease would be treated as a revenue item remains to be seen.

In *Beauchamp v F W Woolworth plc* Lord Templeman, in explaining these cases, said that where the expenditure had been held to be a revenue account it was because the petrol tie had become an integral method of trading and an ordinary incident of marketing.[11] These cases were therefore immaterial in considering the status of a five year loan.[12]

---

[1] (1956) 37 TC 56; for a general discussion of the cases see *Whiteman* [1966] BTR 115; the leading cases were cited in *Rolfe v Wimpey Waste Management Ltd* [1988] STC 329.
[2] [1965] 3 All ER 209, [1966] AC 224.
[3] *IRC v Coia* (1959) 38 TC 334.
[4] *Evans v Wheatley* (1958) 38 TC 216.
[5] *Evans v Wheatley* (1958) 38 TC 216. *Bolam v Regent Oil* was approved only on this ground in *Regent Oil v Strick* by Lord Morris [1965] 3 All ER 174 at 191, 43 TC 1 at 43.
[6] Supra, § **8.83**.
[7] *IRC v Coia* (1959) 38 TC 334.
[8] Infra, § **10.16**.
[9] [1965] 3 All ER 174, 43 TC 1.
[10] See 43 TC 1 at 38; note also the Revenue view that a lump sum spent on computer software will be treated as revenue expenditure if the software has a useful economic life of less than two years—Inland Revenue interpretation, RI 56.
[11] See [1989] STC 510 at 518.
[12] See supra, § **7.111**.

Rule 6—prohibited expenditure

[8.131] TA 1988, s 74 lists many prohibited deductions, now for corporation tax only. For income tax, these prohibited deductions feature in Chapters 4 and 5 of Part 2 of ITTOIA 2005. Many of these are clearly not allowable on normal accountancy principles, but the list antedates those principles and its retention was recommended in order that inspectors of taxes might have something in black and white to show small shopkeepers who are "among the class of persons most apt to suppose that they might charge some of their domestic expenses against their business receipts".[1]

Section 74(1)(*b*) prohibited the deduction of sums for the maintenance of the parties, their families in establishments or any sum expended for other domestic or private purposes distinct from the trade, profession or vocation. Whether the first limb prescribes a purely objective test is as yet unsettled. It has been held that the expression "maintenance" while not restricted to domestic maintenance is confined to the ordinary necessities of life.[2] The rule, however, has been repealed from 6 April 2005 as redundant.

TA 1988, s 74(1)(*c*) (corporation tax only) prohibits the rent of domestic office and dwellinghouses. Strictly, s 74(1)(*c*) was not rewritten into ITTOIA 2005 on the basis that it was covered by ITTOIA 2005, s 34(2).

TA 1988, s 74(1)(*d*) (corporation tax only) concerns the repair of premises and the supply, repair and alteration of articles and utensils and limits the deductions to sums actually so spent (supra, § **8.122**). The provisions of TA 1988, s 74(1)(*d*) were not fully rewritten into ITTOIA 2005 for income tax purposes and one can infer the rest is probably redundant for corporation tax too. Under the rewritten rules, a deduction is available in respect of capital expenses incurred on replacing or altering any implement, utensil or article used for the purposes of a trade where the capital nature of the expenditure would otherwise preclude a deduction.[3] The rest of the expenditure covered by TA 1988, s 74(1)(d) is believed to qualify for relief under normal rules.

TA 1988, s 74(1)(e) (corporation tax only) prevents the deduction of any loss not connected with or arising out of the trade, profession or vocation. This was the provision which provided the ratio for the majority of the House of Lords in *Strong v Woodifield* (supra § **8.104**). A loss is different from an expense in that it does not come from the trader's pocket but comes upon him ab extra. Thus money stolen from a till is a loss but money spent on legal advice is an expense or disbursement.[4] The provision also means that a loss sustained in a transaction not forming part of the trade cannot be deducted.[5] For income tax, the provisions of s 74(1)(e) have been incorporated into ITTOIA 2005, s 34 (which also rewrites TA 1988, s 74(1)(a)).

ITTOIA 2005, s 33 (income tax) and TA 1988, s 74(1)(f) prohibit the deduction for any items of a capital nature. This includes (and in TA 1988, this prohibition is expressed as covering) any capital withdrawn from, or any sum employed or intended to be employed as capital in the trade, but with an express allowance for interest.[6] The opening words refer particularly to capital losses in connection with loans and guarantees financing the trade. There is, however, a distinction between a capital loss and a revenue loss. Losses on money advanced by a consortium to a colliery company were held to be capital,[7] but losses incurred when a solicitor guaranteed a client's overdraft were held to be revenue, the distinction being that the guarantee was a normal incident of the profession.[8] Today the section operates to prohibit the deduction of a premium due on the redemption of preference shares or the repayment of loan capital. The section does not appear to apply to an exchange loss incurred on repayment of a loan in foreign currency; this section applies only to the loans themselves.[9]

TA 1988, s 74(1)(g) (corporation tax only) prohibits the deduction of capital employed on improvements of business premises (supra, § **8.122**). For income tax, this prohibition is covered by ITTOIA 2005, s 33.

TA 1988, s 74(1)(h) (corporation tax only) prohibits any deduction for interest which might have been made if any of the sums previously mentioned had been laid out as interest. The previous mention refers to s 74(1)(f), (g). This bars notional interest but not actual interest. Section 74(1)(c) was not rewritten into ITTOIA 2005 on the basis that it was thought to be redundant now that accounts are to be prepared in accordance with generally accepted accounting practice.

ITTOIA 2005, s 35 (income tax) and TA 1988, s 74(1)(j) concern debts not shown to be bad (infra, § **8.146**).

TA 1988, s 74(1)(k) (corporation tax only) bars any average loss beyond the actual amount of loss after adjustment and concerns insurers.

ITTOIA 2005, s 106 (income tax) provides that any capital sum recovered by a trader under an insurance policy or indemnity contract is to be brought into

[8.131] Income from trades, professions and vocations

account as a trading receipt. TA 1988, s 74(1)(*l*) (corporation tax) is written so as to prohibit the deduction of any sums recoverable under an insurance or indemnity. This is surprisingly limited and does not cover sums recoverable for example in tort, although any sums actually recovered will be taken into account.

TA 1988, s 74(1)(*m*)–(*p*) (corporation tax). The rule that business expenses are deductible has to be adjusted when it comes into collision with the delicate system of deduction of tax at source which applies to annuities or other annual payments payable out of profits or gains, any royalty or other sum paid in respect of the use of a patent.[10] That adjustment is made by providing that no deduction may be made on account of such payments when the profits are computed. This leaves the trader with the right to deduct tax when making the payment and, if the facts fall within TA 1988, s 348 keeping the tax for himself and so recovering the tax relief in respect of the expenditure. Each category of payments must however be considered. It will be noted that payments for bona fide commercial reasons in connection with an individual's trade profession or vocation are not affected by the changes made to the scope of what was Schedule D, Case III in 1988.[11] ITTOIA 2005, s 51 rewrites TA 1988, s 74(1)(*p*) for income tax; TA 1988, s 74(1)(*m*) and (*o*) have not been rewritten for income tax.

Annuities or other annual payments are not to be deductible as a business expense if, in addition to satisfying all the usual tests of such payments, they are payable out of profits or gains. This had been taken to mean that they must form a charge on the profits as opposed to being an element in computing those profits,[12] so that sums are a deductible expense if deductible in computing those profits.

Where the business consists of the grant of annuities those annuities are not payable out of profits or gains so that the payments will be deductible in computing the profits or gains.[13] On the other hand an annuity payable to the widow of a deceased partner would be payable out of profits or gains.

The phrase "any royalty or other sum paid in respect of the user of a patent", is misleadingly wide. Since the reason for the prohibition of deduction is because of the relationship with TA 1988, ss 348, 349, an expense will only fall within this prohibition if it has the quality of income in the hands of the recipient. Further the expense must be for the use, as distinct from the acquisition, of a patent so that for example a right to restrain the patent holder from exercising his patent in a particular area is more than a mere right of user.[14]

Statute[15] denies a deduction for interest charged on late payment of tax due under the Sub-contractors Tax Deduction Scheme.

Simon's Taxes Division B3.13.

---

[1] Report of the Committee on the Taxation of Trading Profits (1951) Cmd 8189 para 137.
[2] *Watkis v Ashford Sparkes & Harwood* [1985] STC 451; (b) was also considered briefly in *Prince v Mapp* (1970) 46 TC 169.
[3] ITTOIA 2005, s 68(2)

4   Per Finlay J in *Allen v Farquharson Bros & Co* (1932) 17 TC 59 at 64. See also *Roebank Printing Co Ltd v IRC* (1928) 13 TC 864 and Bamford v ATA Advertising Ltd [1972] 3 All ER 535, 48 TC 359. Distinguish petty pilfering by an employee.
5   eg *FA and AB Ltd v Lupton*, supra, § **8.11**.
6   This reverses *European Investment Trust Co Ltd v Jackson* (1932) 18 TC 1.
7   *James Waldie & Sons v IRC* (1919) 12 TC 113; for a fuller example see *Beauchamp v F W Woolworth plc* [1987] STC 279, supra, § **8.117**.
8   *Hagart and Burn-Murdoch v IRC* [1929] AC 386, 14 TC 433, HL; *Jennings v Barfield and Barfield* [1962] 2 All ER 957, 40 TC 365.
9   *Beauchamp v F W Woolworth plc* [1988] STC at 718c; it follows from his decision that the earlier decision in *European Investment Trust Co Ltd v Jackson* (1932) 18 TC 1, which disallowed interest under this provision, was to be explained solely on the ground that there was disregarded a concession as to the meaning of the statute—see [1988] STC at 718a. In other words the decision should be disregarded. This issue was not touched on by Lord Templeman in the House of Lords [1989] STC 510.
10 ITTOIA 2005, s 51 (income tax); TA 1988, ss 74(1)(p) (corporation tax), 348, 349.
11 TA 1988, s 347A(2).
12 *Paterson Engineering Co Ltd v Duff* (1943) 25 TC 43.
13 *Gresham Life Assurance Society v Styles* [1892] AC 309, 3 TC 185.
14 Per Lord Watson in *Gresham Life Assurance Society v Styles* [1892] AC 309 at 320, 3 TC 185 at 192, supra; *British Salmson Aero Engines Ltd v IRC* [1938] 2 KB 482, 22 TC 29.
15 TA 1988, s 566(1A).

Interest

[8.132] A person carrying on a trade can, in computing the profits, deduct the interest payments he incurs in that trade. Such payments will be deductible on general accounting principles and so deductibility is distinct from the special rules in supra, §§ **6.43**, **6.44**. Before 6 April 2005, there were some special provisions.

Business gifts and entertainment expenses

[8.133] ITTOIA 2005, s 45 (income tax) and TA 1988, s 577 (corporation tax) prohibit the deduction of expenses—including incidental expenses—incurred in providing business entertainment, a phrase defined to include hospitality of any kind;[1] these sections also extend to the provision of gifts, subject to the de minimis exception of £50 pa.[2] The disallowance turns on the facts not the purpose of the trader.[3] Normally this disallowance affects computation of profits of trades, property businesses and in respect of miscellaneous income.[4] Where an asset is used for business entertainment purposes any capital allowance otherwise claimable is disallowed.[5]

ITTOIA 2005, s 47(3) (income tax) and TA 1988, s 577(8) (corporation tax) relax the provisions in respect of gifts so as to allow inexpensive articles carrying a conspicuous advertisement for the donor. Gifts to charities are, however, exempted by ITTOIA 2005, s 47(5) (income tax) and TA 1988, s 577(9) (corporation tax). Extra-statutory concession B7 extends this exemption to gifts for "benevolent" purposes provided that certain conditions regarding a close connection with the donor's business are met. If the employer pays the employee an allowance purely for entertainment purposes, the employer may not deduct the allowance in computing his profits; the employee is taxable on the allowance but may deduct his expenditure, even though it may not be deductible in computing the tax liability of his employer. If, however, the employer pays the employee a general allowance to cover terms which include entertainment the position is reversed. The employer may deduct the cost of the allowance, assuming that it also satisfies the other rules (eg ITTOIA 2005, s 34 (income tax) and TA 1988, s 74(1)(a) (corporation tax)) but the employee may deduct only such entertainment costs as satisfy the conditions in ITEPA 2003, ss 328 ff.[6]

An overseas trading company may employ a representative in the UK but nevertheless be not resident in the UK for tax purposes. Its profits, whilst chargeable to tax in its own country, are not subject to UK tax. In that case there can be no disallowance on the company under s 577(1)(a) so ITEPA 2003, s 357 cannot operate to protect the employee, and ITEPA 2003, s 356 denies the employee a deduction for business entertainment expenses irrespective of whether the expenses are, or are not, reimbursed by the employer. This can, and often does, result in such employees being taxed under ITEPA 2003 in respect of their reimbursed entertainment expenses with no possibility of an off-setting deduction under ITEPA 2003, ss 328 ff.

The Revenue have for many years accepted that if the profits of a business would have been taxed in the UK but for the terms of a double taxation agreement, s 577(1)(a) can be regarded as having operated to disallow the entertainment expenses before the double taxation agreement comes into play. The employees of such a business are therefore regarded as being protected from ITEPA 2003, s 356 (by the operation of ITEPA 2003, s 357) even though their employer has paid no UK tax on their trading profits. Entertainment expenses which are paid out of money supplied by, or reimbursed by the employer for that purpose will therefore qualify for a deduction if they satisfy the conditions of ITEPA 2003, ss 328–330, 333–338.[7]

Simon's Taxes B2.432.

---

[1] ITTOIA 2005, s 45(4)(b) (income tax); TA 1988, s 577(5) (corporation tax).
[2] ITTOIA 2005, s 47(3) (income tax); TA 1988, s 577(8) amended by FA 2001, s 73 (corporation tax).
[3] *Fleming v Associated Newspapers Ltd*, infra, § **8.134**.
[4] See also (for income tax) ITTOIA 2005, ss 272 and 867.
[5] CAA 2001, s 269(1).
[6] ITEPA 2003, s 357. This reverses the normal process under ITEPA 2003, ss 7, 70, and 72, which charges the employee but allows the employer to deduct.
[7] Inland Revenue Tax Bulletin, Issue 42, August 1999, p 681.

Exceptions to entertainment expenses rules

[8.134] (1) Business entertainment expenses used to be deductible if incurred in the entertainment of an overseas customer, meaning a non-resident trading

Expenses [8.134]

overseas who might use the goods or services of the entertainer, or an agent for such a non-resident trader or overseas government or public authority, a definition to assist British exporters—not importers. In these instances the entertainment had to be of a kind and on a scale which is reasonable in all the circumstances.[1] This exception is repealed for expenditure incurred after 14 March 1988 save when it is incurred under a contract made before 15 March 1988.[2]

(2) Expenses incurred in the entertainment of bona fide members of staff are deductible. Curiously the requirement of reasonableness is absent here.[3] The exception does not apply when the entertainment is incidental to the provision of entertainment for outsiders.

(3) Expenses are deductible if they are for small gifts carrying conspicuous advertisements, such as calendars and diaries.[4]

(4) Expenses are deductible if (a) incurred in the provision of that which it is his trade to provide if it is provided by him in the course of his trade for payment, or (b) gratuitously if with the object of advertising to the public generally.[5] Examples of expenses within group (a) would be the provision of food by a restaurateur or of theatre tickets by a theatre owner and of those within group (b) free samples of products or complimentary theatre tickets for the press, although not for friends.

The exception is limited to the provision of "anything which it is his trade to provide". "Anything" has been construed to mean business entertainment so that it must be his trade to supply such entertainment. Hence, a newspaper man who provided drinks for potential sources of information or meals for the softening up of contributors did not fall within the exception.[6] It was his trade to produce newspapers not refreshment. It would follow that if he offered not drinks but a copy of his paper that expense might be deductible.

Another problem is whether he must supply the entertainment himself. Thus if the owner of a fried chicken shop provides business entertainment in his own shop with his own fried chicken he can clearly deduct his costs, but it is not clear whether he could deduct the costs of entertaining the same people at the Ritz. In this latter instance he is supplying that which it is his trade to supply, but one cannot help feeling that the sums would not be deductible merely because of the coincidence of the entertainment provided with his own trade. It is probable that the expense is only deductible if his trade supplies the entertainment.

(5) Expenses incurred in making a gift to a charity, including the Historic Buildings Commission and the National Heritage Memorial Fund are excluded from ITTOIA 2005, s 45 (income tax) and TA 1988, s 577 (corporation tax).[7] This leaves the taxpayer with the task of ensuring that the gift also escapes from ITTOIA 2005, s 34 and TA 1988, s 74(1)(a).[8]

Simon's Taxes B2.432.

---

[1] TA 1988, s 577(2) repealed by FA 1988, s 72.
[2] FA 1988, s 72.
[3] TA 1988, s 577(5).

[8.134] Income from trades, professions and vocations

[4] ITTOIA 2005, s 47(3) (income tax); TA 1988, s 577(7) (corporation tax). The cost to the donor must not exceed £50 per donee per year, ITTOIA 2005, s 47(3)(b); TA 1988, s 577(8)(b).
[5] ITTOIA 2005, s 47(2) (income tax); TA 1988, s 577(10) (corporation tax).
[6] *Fleming v Associated Newspapers Ltd* [1972] 2 All ER 574, 46 TC 401.
[7] ITTOIA 2005, s 47(5) (income tax); TA 1988, s 577(9) (corporation tax).
[8] Supra, § **8.101**.

Reverse premiums

[**8.135**] Reverse premiums, known by the more appropriate name of lease inducement payments in Canada,[1] were held to be capital receipts, and so non-taxable, in the 1998 Privy Council decision on the New Zealand appeal in *IRC v Wattie*.[2] This produced a lack of symmetry in that the payment would often be made by a property developer so that the sums paid would be deductible while the sum received was not taxable. The decision has now been superseded by FA 1999, Sch 6 which, in broad terms, applies to premiums received on or after 9 March 1999.[3] Such payments are now taxable—regardless of their treatment in the hands of the person making the payment.

The rule catches payments or other benefits, although here we will talk only of payments to X. Examples of other benefits are contributions to X's costs in fitting out the building or relocating a business, and taking over X's liabilities under an old lease of the premises.[4]

The payment must be made by way of inducement in connection with a "relevant transaction" but the transaction may be being entered into by X himself or a person connected with X. A transaction is relevant if it is one under which X or a person connected to X becomes entitled to an estate or interest in, or a right in or over, land. The payment must come from the grantor of the estate, G, interest or right or a person connected with G or a nominee of, or a person acting on the directions of, G or a person connected with G.[5] The purpose is to catch the reverse premium paid when the lease is granted; it is not intended to catch a payment by a lessee to someone to persuade them to take over a lease later on when the lease has become onerous.[6] However, the Revenue view is that the provisions catch a premium payable to an assignee where it is in substance an inducement to take a grant of a lease dressed up as an assignment.[7]

The tax treatment of T depends on T's tax status. If the relevant transaction is entered into by T for the purposes of a trade, profession or vocation carried on or to be carried on by T, the reverse premium enters the profits of that trade, profession or vocation.[8] In any other circumstances, as where the transaction is not for T's trade or the trade is being carried on by the connected person, the sum is treated as a receipt of a transaction entered into by T for the exploitation, as a source of rents or other receipts, of an estate, interest or right in or over the land in question ie the relevant property business.[9] In any event the sum is treated as a revenue receipt.[10] However, the effect of this rule is to go further and to contain a timing rule. Under the principles of commercial accounting, which are to apply to business profits and property businesses, the receipt will be spread over the period of the lease or, if shorter, until the first rent review.[11] Where the premium has been taken into account in calculating the allowable expenditure for capital allowance purposes, by reducing the allowable expenditure it is not to be taken as chargeable under these rules. This is to prevent what would be in effect a double charge.[12]

Taxability under this rule is excluded if the transaction relates to an individual's only or main residence,[13] or if the matter already falls within TA 1988, s 779 or s 780 as a sale and leaseback.[14] Special rules apply to insurance companies.[15]

The timing rule of spreading is excluded where the arrangements are not at arm's length ie some or all of the parties to the relevant arrangements are connected persons and the terms of those arrangements are not such as would reasonably have been expected if those persons had been dealing at arm's length.[16] Here the whole sum must be taxed at once or, as the statute more precisely puts it, in the first relevant period of account.[17] Thus if the trade has not yet begun it will be treated as taxable in the first period of account of that trade.

The Revenue view on the operation of the reverse premium rules is that all cash payments are "caught", as are taxable inducements such as contributions towards specified tenant's costs, for example fitting out, start up or relocation. Sums paid to third parties to meet obligations of the tenant, such as rent to a landlord under an old lease, or a capital sum to terminate such a lease are also within the terms of the provisions, as is the effective payment of cash by other means, eg the landlord's writing off a sum which the tenant owes.[18] However, an inducement is not caught where it does not represent actual outlay. In the Revenue guidance, the following examples are given of inducements that do not give rise to a tax charge:

(1) The grant of a rent free period of occupation and replacement by agreement of an existing lease at a rent which a change in market conditions has made onerous by a new lease at a lower rent.

(2) Replacement by agreement of an existing lease containing some other provision the tenant has found onerous by a new lease without the onerous condition.[19]

Simon's Taxes B9.221.

---

1   See generally Carr (1998) 46 Can Tax Jo 953—991.
2   [1998] STC 1160—the decision is equally applicable to UK tax-per Lord Nolan at p 1169j and 1170e.
3   ITTOIA 2005, Sch 2, para 28 (income tax); FA 1999, s 54(2) (corporation tax); the treatment does not apply if the person was entitled to the payment immediately before that date.
4   Inland Revenue Notes to Finance Bill, para 31.
5   ITTOIA 2005, s 99(4) (income tax); FA 1999, Sch 6, para 1 (corporation tax); on connected person status see s 103 and para 1(7) respectively both referring to TA 1988, s 839.
6   Inland Revenue Notes to Finance Bill, para 33. The Revenue view is that a rent-free period is another reverse premium but that no notional charge arises.

[8.135] Income from trades, professions and vocations

[7] Inland Revenue Notes to Finance Bill, para 33.
[8] ITTOIA 2005, s 101(2) (income tax); FA 1999 Sch 6, para 2(2) (corporation tax).
[9] ITTOIA 2005, s 101(3) (income tax); FA 1999 Sch 6, para 2(3) (corporation tax).
[10] ITTOIA 2005, s 101(1) (income tax); FA 1999 Sch 6, para 2(2) (corporation tax).
[11] Inland Revenue Notes to Finance Bill, para 32.
[12] ITTOIA 2005, s 100(1) (income tax); FA 1999, Sch 6, para 5 (corporation tax); Inland Revenue press release, 19 May 1999, *Simon's Weekly Tax Intelligence* 1999, p 946.
[13] ITTOIA 2005, s 100(2) (income tax); (not relevant for corporation tax).
[14] ITTOIA 2005, s 100(3) (income tax); FA 1999, Sch 6, para 7 (corporation tax) —see infra, § 8.136.
[15] FA 1999, Sch 6, para 4.
[16] Defined in ITTOIA 2005, s 102(2) (income tax); FA 1999, Sch 6, para 3(4) (corporation tax).
[17] ITTOIA 2005, s 102(3) (income tax); FA 1999, Sch 6, para 3(1) (corporation tax).
[18] Inland Revenue Tax Bulletin, December 1999, p 712.
[19] Inland Revenue Tax Bulletin, December 1999, p 712. The Tax Bulletin then gives extensive elaboration of the Revenue views of the practical effect of the provisions.

Sale and leaseback—TA 1988, ss 779, 780

[8.136] Leasebacks of land. Where rents in excess of the commercial rent are paid under a leaseback arrangement, the excess is not deductible.[1] Where the asset sold is a lease for a term not exceeding 50 years and it is leased back for a term not exceeding 15 years a part of the sale consideration which would otherwise be capital is taxed as income.[2] That part is 16–n/15 when n is the term of the new lease. Top-slicing relief used to be available[3] but this is repealed for 1989–90 and later years.[4]

Simon's Taxes B5.247.

[1] TA 1988, s 779.
[2] TA 1988, s 780.
[3] TA 1988, s 780(5).
[4] FA 1988, s 75.

[8.137] Leased assets other than land. Where, before the sale and leaseback, the asset was used in the trade the allowable deduction is limited to the commercial rent.[1] Disallowed rental payments may however be rolled forward and used in later periods when the rent paid is below the commercial rent.

Where the asset was not so used and the payer, having received a tax deduction for his rent, then receives a capital sum under the lease, the deduction is clawed back to the extent of that sum;[2] the clawback is reduced when part of the rent has been disallowed. This rule applies also where the lessor's interest belongs to an associate of the payer and the associate receives a capital sum; in this case the charge is on the associate.

Simon's Taxes B5.410, 411, 413.

[1] TA 1988, s 782.
[2] TA 1988, s 781; capital sum includes insurance proceeds.

Other expressly prohibited deductions

[8.138] Payments of penalties, interest and surcharges under the VAT legislation are non-deductible.[1]

Simon's Taxes B2.439.

[1] ITTOIA 2005, s 54 (income tax); TA 1988, s 827 (corporation tax).

Permitted expenditure

[8.139] Certain types of expenditure are deductible by statute. These include payments under certified and statutory redundancy schemes,[1] revenue expenditure on scientific research,[2] applications for patents,[3] the cost of training courses for employees[4] payments to superannuation funds,[5] rents paid for tied premises,[6] employer's redundancy payments,[7] payments by market boards to reserve funds,[8] certain capital expenditure by a cemetery or cremation authority,[9] deductions in computing post-cessation receipts,[10] premiums payable in respect of business premises when the landlord is chargeable[11] and certain payments under schemes for rationalising industry.[12] In addition certain payments may be deducted under the quite separate capital allowance system.[13] Sums spent in establishing share option or profit-sharing schemes or ESOPs as well as payments into approved share schemes or ESOPs for employees are also deductible even though representing a division of profits,[14] as are incidental costs of loan finance,[15] contributions to approved local enterprise agencies and to an urban generation company,[16] local enterprise companies, training and enterprise councils (TECs) and business-link organisations,[17] and the costs of seconding employees to charities.[18] Payments to personal pension schemes,[19] payments to an employee under a restrictive covenant under ITEPA 2003, ss 7 and 225[20] and the costs of employees seconded to various educational bodies[21] or sent away for training are also deductible.[22] Payments by football pool businesses to certain trusts are made expressly deductible.[23] Statute provides relief for the costs of providing counselling services to employees in connection with the termination of their employment[24] and contributions to agent's expenses paid in connection with the payroll deduction scheme for charitable gifts by employees.[25]

The capital costs incurred by a company in cleaning up contaminated land acquired for the purpose of the company's trade attracts a deduction from profits calculated as 150% of the capital cost incurred.[26] Relief is available against trading income or the profits of a UK property business.[27] If the relief exceeds the taxable income, a payment is made to the company.[28] All relief is denied if the company, itself, contaminated the land.[29]

The costs incurred in "euroconverting" a trading company's shares or securities are deductible for corporation tax.[30]

629

[8.139] Income from trades, professions and vocations

Simon's Taxes Division B2.4.

1. TA 1988, ss 568, 572.
2. See the enhanced allowance available for revenue expenditure on research and development, infra, § **8.140**.
3. ITTOIA 2005, ss 89, 90 and 600 (income tax); TA 1988, ss 83, 526 (corporation tax).
4. ITTOIA 2005, s 74 (income tax); TA 1988, s 588 (corporation tax); for the exclusion of the employee benefit see ITEPA 2003, s 250: infra § **7.98**.
5. TA 1988, s 592(4).
6. ITTOIA 2005, s 19 (income tax); TA 1988, s 98 (corporation tax).
7. ITTOIA 2005, ss 77(2), 79(3) (income tax); TA 1988, s 579(2) (corporation tax).
8. TA 1988, s 509.
9. ITTOIA 2005, s 170 (income tax); TA 1988, s 91 (corporation tax).
10. ITTOIA 2005, s 254 (income tax); TA 1988, s 105 (corporation tax). Expenses incurred after the cessation of trading can only be deducted against revenue received after the cessation of trade-an ungenerous approach.
11. ITTOIA 2005, ss 61(1), 64(3) (income tax); TA 1988, s 87 (corporation tax).
12. TA 1988, s 568.
13. Infra, Chapter 9.
14. TA 1988, s 85 and FA 1989, s 67(2); TA 1988, ss 84A, 85A.
15. ITTOIA 2005, s 58(1) (income tax only).
16. ITTOIA 2005, s 82(2) (income tax); TA 1988, ss 79 and 79B inserted by FA 2003, s 180 with effect from 1 April 2003 (corporation tax).
17. ITTOIA 2005, s 82(2) (income tax); TA 1988, ss 79A (corporation tax).
18. ITTOIA 2005, s 70(2) (income tax); TA 1988, s 86 (corporation tax).
19. ITEPA 2003, s 308.
20. See supra, § **7.32**.
21. ITTOIA 2005, s 70(2) (income tax); TA 1988, s 86(1) (corporation tax).
22. ITTOIA 2005, s 74(1) (income tax); TA 1988, s 588 (corporation tax); see also extra-statutory concessions A63, A64; see *Silva v Charnock* [2002] STC (SCD) 426.
23. ITTOIA 2005, s 162(3) (income tax); FA 1991, s 121(2) (corporation tax).
24. ITTOIA 2005, s 73 (income tax); TA 1988, s 589A(8) (corporation tax).
25. ITTOIA 2005, s 72 (income tax); TA 1988, s 86A (corporation tax).
26. FA 2001, s 70 and Schs 22 and 23.
27. FA 2001, Sch 22, para 13.
28. FA 2001, Sch 22, para 16.
29. FA 2001, Sch 22, para 1(5).
30. SI 1998/3177 European Single Currency (Taxes) Regulations 1998, reg 5.

Enhanced allowance for R & D expenditure

[8.140] A comprehensive account of the way in which the Revenue consider these provisions operate is given in a special edition of Inland Revenue Tax Bulletin December 2002.[1]

A deduction of 175%[2] of expenditure incurred can be claimed for expenditure on research and development[3] by a "small or medium-sized enterprise"[4], where the expenditure is related to a trade of the enterprise or from which it is intended that a trade to be carried on is to be derived.[5] A company (but not an unincorporated enterprise) that is too large to fall within the definition of a "small or medium-sized enterprise" has available a deduction of 125% of expenditure on research and development.[6] This novel approach to subsidising investment compliments the enhanced capital allowances available, which are granted on 150% of the expenditure incurred on research and development assets (infra,§ **9.59**). For an enterprise to be eligible for the enhanced deductions, the enterprise must spend at least £10,000 on research and development in a 12-month period, or a pro rata sum in a shorter accounting period.[7] Furthermore, the FA 2008 has added a cap of 7.5 million euros on the total R & D aid (as calculated in accordance with the formula specified elsewhere in the FA 2008) in respect of expenditure by the company attributable to any project. A further novel feature of the enhanced deduction, which makes it equivalent to a subsidy, is that an enterprise that does not make a profit has a choice between creating a loss by the enhanced expenditure and relieving the loss by group relief or carry forward or, alternatively, by surrendering the loss in exchange for a cash sum paid by the Revenue, being 16% of the surrendered loss.[8]

If the research is related to AIDS and HIV, the 150% relief is available, irrespective of the size of the company.[9] Statute[10] specifically permits tax relief for research and development expenditure that is treated for accounting purposes as an addition to the cost of an intangible asset, such as a patent, know-how, or goodwill.

The FA 2008 introduced a provision preventing companies from claiming R & D relief tax credit or if it is not a going concern. A company is a going concern if its latest published accounts were prepared on a genuine going concern basis and not on the expectation that it would receive R & D or vaccine research relief accordingly. Moreover, if the company ceases, for any reason, to be a going concern after making a claim for relief, such a claim will be invalidated.

A similar set of rules is available for vaccine research relief as contained in Sch 13 of the FA 2002 (as amended by the FA 2008).

---

[1] Inland Revenue Tax Bulletin December 2002 is devoted solely to tax incentives for research and development in respect of:

- the R and D tax credit for small and medium companies (FA 2000, Sch 20)
- the R and D tax credit for large companies (FA 2000, Sch 12)
- the vaccines research relief (FA 2000, Schs 13 and 14).

FA 2004, s 141 amends FA 2000, Sch 20, para 6 to include expenditure on computer software, water, fuel and power. The enhanced allowances for these additional items are available for expenditure incurred on or after 1 April 2004: Finance Act 2004, section 141 (Appointed Day) Order 2005, SI 2005/123. A further amendment allows payments to the subject of clinical trials as being treated as eligible research and development expenditure: FA 2006, s 28.

[2] Before FA 2008 this deduction was 150%.

[3] In keeping with the new approach in statute (see supra § **8.65**), "research and development" is not defined, other than by stating that it means activities that fall to be treated as research and development in accordance with normal accounting practice: TA 1988, s 837A(2) inserted by FA 2000, Sch 19, para 1.

[8.140] Income from trades, professions and vocations

[4] Defined in accordance with the criteria adopted by the European Commission: FA 2000, Sch 20, para 2(1). Thus, references to turnover and balance sheet totals are in euros, not pounds. This approach generated 2,900 words of comment at the committee stage: Hansard 13 June 2000: HC Standing Committee H cols 645–659.

For the purpose of granting these enhanced 150% allowances, statute adopts the European Commission recommendation. As from 1 January 2005, this is EC Recommendation 2003/36 which defines enterprises as:

Small
    Less than 50 employees, and
    Turnover less than €10 million or balance sheet total less than €10 million
Medium sized
    Less than 250 employees, and
    Turnover less than €50 million or balance sheet total less than €43 million
    The test is applied by aggregating all "linked" enterprises. An enterprise is linked if one entity has 25%+ of the voting rights in the other entity, or 25%+ rights to capital or controls it by virtue of a shareholders' agreement. (Investment by a "venture capitalist" not exceeding €1,250,000 is ignored for this purpose).

[5] FA 2000, Sch 20, para 4(1).
[6] FA 2002, Sch 12.
[7] Reduced from £25,000 by FA 2003, Sch 31, para 2 amending FA 2000, Sch 20, para 1(1).
[8] FA 2000, Sch 20, para 15.
[9] FA 2002, Schs 13, 14.
[10] FA 2004, s 53.

Gifts to educational establishments and charities etc

[8.141] An individual or a company can obtain tax relief for a gift to a charity of an interest in land or quoted shares and securities.[1] In addition, a trader can obtain a tax deduction for certain gifts made to a charity or to an educational establishment,[2] the tax deduction overriding the rule in *Sharkey v Wernher*,[3] now codified in ITTOIA 2005, Pt 2, Ch 11A, so that any cost of providing the gift is an allowable expense in computing profits but the value of the gift is not brought into the receipts of the trade.

The relief is to be lost if the donor, or any person connected with him, receives any benefit which is attributable to the making of the gift.[4] This rule is very widely drawn. On a plain reading even the benefit flowing from publicity surrounding the gift will cause the relief to fail; yet this conclusion would be fatal to the whole purpose of the section. There is no requirement that the benefit should be subsequent to the gift.

The gift may be of an article produced by the donor in the course of the trade in which case no amount is to be brought into the accounts of the business; otherwise the market value would have to be brought in. It may be inferred that all the costs associated with the production of the article remain deductible. The legislation does not in terms cover the provision of services even though it does extend to professions and vocations; one may therefore infer a Revenue view that, at the very least, *Sharkey v Wernher* did not extend to the provision of services in a profession or vocation.

Alternatively the gift may be of an item used as machinery and plant in respect of which capital allowances have been claimed; in this case no amount need be brought in as disposal value.[5] The effect is not only to prevent any recapture by way of a balancing charge but to allow for the recognition of the remaining expenditure. For corporation tax only, there are further restrictions in that the activities of the educational establishment are to be treated as if they amounted to the carrying on of a trade and the asset must then qualify for capital allowances as machinery and plant.[6] It is thought that items qualifying will include photocopiers, computers, typewriters, televisions, vans, mini-buses, much laboratory equipment, furniture, books and so on.[7] This restriction was deliberately not reproduced for income tax purposes when ITTOIA 2005 was introduced.

When the gift is of medical supplies or equipment, the relief is available, even if the recipient is not a charity. This relief is available only to companies.[8]

Simon's Taxes B2.442.

[1] ITTOIA 2005, s 108, FA 1990, s 25; TA 1988, ss 83A, 587B and 587C, see supra, §§ **6.41, 6.42**. For the list of institutions designated by the Secretary of State for Education as "educational establishments" for the purpose of the relief, see Taxes (Relief for Gifts) (Designated Educational Establishments) Regulations 1992, SI 1992/42; see also Revenue Interpretation RI 151.

[2] ITTOIA 2005, s 108(1)(*a*), (*b*) (income tax); TA 1988, ss 83A(3)(*a*) & 84(3)(*a*) (corporation tax).

[3] (1956) 36 TC 275.

[4] ITTOIA 2005, s 109(1) (income tax); TA 1988, s 587B amended by FA 2004, s 139 (corporation tax).

[5] ie under CAA 2001, s 61; see infra, § **9.37**.

[6] TA 1988, s 84(2).

[7] HC Official Report, Standing Committee B, 20 June 1991, col 343.

[8] FA 2002, s 55. Some comments from the Revenue on the practical effect of this legislation are given in Inland Revenue Tax Bulletin October 2000, p 975.

Receipts after discontinuance

[8.142] A profession (or trade) that ceased prior to 6 April 1999 may have made up accounts under the cash basis with the result that receipts after cessation are not brought into account. ITTOIA 2005, s 242 (income tax) and TA 1988, s 103 (corporation tax) provide that all sums received after the discontinuance and arising from the carrying on of the trade are chargeable provided their value had not been brought into computing the profits of any period before the discontinuance. For corporation tax, the charge arises under Schedule D, Case VI.[1]

In computing the charge, only the deductions permitted in ITTOIA 2005, s 254(2) (income tax) and TA 1988, s 105 (corporation tax) may be made; the amount brought into charge is not computed under the rules that apply ordinarily to trading profits.[2]

Where a debt has been allowed in the computation of the profits of a trade since discontinued and the whole or any part of the debt is later released, the amount released is treated as a sum received.[3] Presumably a covenant by the creditor not to sue, being analytically distinct from a release, will not cause a charge to tax. A release forming part of a voluntary arrangement under the Insolvency Act 1986 does not give rise to a trading receipt.[4]

Certain sums are excluded,[5] namely sums received by a person beneficially entitled thereto who is not resident in the UK representing income arising from a country or territory outside the UK; a lump sum paid to the personal representatives of the author—but not the author himself—of a work as consideration for the assignment by them of the copyright or public lending rights, wholly or in part,[6] and, finally, sums received on the transfer of trading stock or work in progress, which provision is needed to prevent an overlap with ITTOIA 2005, Pt 2, Ch 12 (income tax) and TA 1988, ss 100, 101 (corporation tax)[7] and to avoid depriving the exceptions in those sections from any effect.

The taxpayer can choose to have the receipt taxed for the year in which it arises or, alternatively, for the receipt to augment the profits of the last period of trading.[8]

---

[1] TA 1988, s 103(1), (2)(a).
[2] *Gilmore v Inspector of Taxes* [1999] STC (SCD) 269.
[3] ITTOIA 2005, s 249(1), (2) (income tax); TA 1988, s 103(4) (corporation tax). This provision is not happily drafted; it refers to the amount released when it presumably ought to refer to the release in respect of a debt "so far as allowed as a deduction". See per Megarry J in *Simpson v Jones* [1968] 2 All ER 929 at 936, 44 TC 599 at 609.
[4] ITTOIA 2005, s 249(1)(c) (income tax); TA 1988, s 103(4)(b) as amended by FA 1994, s 144(2) (corporation tax) for releases on or after 30 November 1993.
[5] ITTOIA 2005, ss 252, 253 (income tax); TA 1988, s 103(3) (corporation tax). There may also be a gap in that these sections do not appear to catch a sum paid before the discontinuance but which does not appear in the accounts, as in *Symons v Weeks* [1983] STC 195.
[6] Thus preserving the immunity from tax in the *Haig* case, infra, § **12.08**.
[7] Infra, § **8.152**.
[8] ITTOIA 2005, s 257. The election cannot be made if the post cessation receipt is received more than six tax years after the trade was permanently discontinued.

Timing of transactions

When does a transaction occur?

[8.143] Questions of timing are now largely a matter of the application of commercial accounting principles (see supra, §§ **8.64–8.67**). However, some statutory rules override accountancy principles by requiring an adjustment to the profit that has been declared in financial statements. A more difficult question is whether the case law that has been established and revered by its age is now relevant or whether it has given way to the statutory provision of ITTOIA 2005, s 25 (income tax) or FA 1998, s 42 (corporation tax), which require that accounts be drawn up for the purpose of imposing an income tax charge in accordance with "generally accepted accounting practice".

A recent case where the court was required to consider the timing of a transaction is *Thomas Cook (New Zealand) Ltd v IRC*[1]. In this case, the Privy Council was required to consider a New Zealand statute containing the phrase: "the date on which the money has become payable".[2] In his judgment, Lord Brown made reference to only one precedent, and that being solely on the point that no cause of action arises against a bank until a customer demands payment.[3] Lord Brown gave the decision of the Privy Council:

> . . . the point is, however, that the word 'payable' is used to mean simply that, as between the company and its shareholders, the money is due to the shareholders. They are entitled to it, whether it has been demanded or not.

---

[1] [2004] UKPC 53, [2005] STC 297.
[2] Unclaimed Money Act 1971 (New Zealand) s 4(e).
[3] *Joachimson v Swiss Bank Corp* [1921] 3 KB 110, CA.

[8.144] The particular provisions of a contract under which a taxpayer trades may determine the period for which an item of income or expenditure is treated as arising for taxation purposes. In 1921, in *J P Hall & Co Ltd v IRC*[1] it was held that profit could not be recognised until it was ascertained at the conclusion of a contract. In *Johnson v W S Try Ltd*[2] it was held that compensation could not be recognised until a final agreement under which it was payable.

The traditional view[3] was that accounts were drawn up on the basis of provisional estimates when actual figures were not known, with the accounts being reopened and tax liabilities reassessed when the actual sum is ascertained. This approach has almost certainly given way to the concept that accounts are finalised when they are laid before the members of a company, or adopted by the partners of a partnership. Any adjustment that is required in the light of further experience is then recognised in the accounts of a subsequent period.

In recent years, the courts have increasingly adopted the approach that the profit that is to be subjected to tax for each period of account is that which is shown in the commercial accounts of the enterprise, with the only adjustments permissible being those that are specifically required by statute.[4] The consequence is that there now appears to be little scope for arguing that an entry made in the accounts in one year should be brought as a share to tax in another year.

---

[1] [1921] 3 KB 152, 12 TC 382.
[2] [1946] 1 All ER 532, 27 TC 167.
[3] See for example *IRC v Gardner, Mountain and D'Ambrumenil Ltd* (1947) 29 TC 69 and *Isaac Holden & Sons Ltd v IRC* (1924) 12 TC 768.

[8.144] Income from trades, professions and vocations

[4] See supra, §§ **8.64–8.67**, in particular the comprehensive Revenue statement in § 8.65.

Relating forward—payment in advance

[8.145] The decision in *Johnston v Britannia Airways Ltd*[1] would appear to be authority for saying that the matching principle allows a payment received to be brought into a charge to tax in the later year, not in the year in which it is received. This can, thus, be seen as distinguishing the decision in *Elson v Price's Tailors Ltd*,[2] where deposits were brought into account when received.

[1] [1994] STC 763.
[2] [1963] 1 All ER 231, 40 TC 671.

Default of debtor

[8.146] Statute requires that an adjustment for the default of a debtor is made when the default occurs and is not related back. No deduction may be taken for any debts except:

(a) a debt which is bad;
(b) a debt or part of a debt estimated to be bad;
(c) a debt to the extent it is released wholly and exclusively for the purposes of his trade, profession or vocation as part of a voluntary arrangement.[1]

For corporation tax, no deduction may be taken for any debts except:

(a) a bad debt;
(b) a debt or part of a debt released by the creditor wholly and exclusively for the purposes of his trade, profession or vocation as part of a relevant arrangement or compromise;
(c) a doubtful debt to the extent estimated to be bad, meaning, in the case of the bankruptcy or insolvency of the debtor, the debt except to the extent that any amount may reasonably be expected to be received on the debt.[2]

Of these (b) is new and (c) has been rewritten. The reason for the introduction of (b) was that the previous version allowed debts to be deducted only when and to the extent that they were proved to be bad ie irrecoverable. This would not allow the deduction of debts released as part of the new insolvency practice. For similar reasons (c) now provides that a deduction may be taken where the debt is a doubtful debt to the extent that it is estimated bad.[3]

It should be noted that ITTOIA 2005, s 35 and TA 1988, s 74(1)(j) deal only with deductions and does not say what debts are to be brought into account nor at what value. The value of a debt, is a matter of fact and is not necessarily its face value, even if not proved to be a bad debt. In *Absalom v Talbot*[4] the taxpayer was a speculative builder. His purchasers might, after payment of a deposit and a sum borrowed from a building society, leave the balance outstanding on granting the taxpayer a second mortgage on the house, the sum to be repaid with interest over a period of 20 years.

The Revenue have issued an interpretation of s 74(1)(j).[5]

[1] ITTOIA 2005, s 35.
[2] TA 1988, s 74(1)(j).
[3] FA 1994, s 144(1).
[4] [1944] 1 All ER 642, 26 TC 166.
[5] Inland Revenue Interpretation RI 81.

Timing of liabilities

[8.147] On an earnings basis expenses are deductible when incurred and not when paid, but not simply because the need for that work has arisen. So in *Naval Colliery Co Ltd v IRC*[1] a company's mines were damaged during a strike which ended on 2 July 1921; no element for the costs of reconditioning the mine could be included for the period ending 30 June 1921. The denial of the deduction for future payments was most vigorously stated in *James Spencer & Co v IRC*.[2] However, this decision must now be seen in the light of the finding in *Johnston v Britannia Airways Ltd*.[3] The Inland Revenue stated: 'James Spencer is now seen simply as an answer, on a specific set of facts and reached without the benefit of accountancy input, to the question of whether the provision is sufficiently accurate to be acceptable for tax.'[4]

An interesting case forbidding the anticipation of a loss is *Edward Collins & Sons Ltd v IRC*.[5] Here the taxpayer had entered into contracts for the delivery of raw materials in the following year. The market price of those materials had dropped substantially by the end of his trading year. It was held that he could not anticipate his loss by deducting the excess of the contract price over current market value. Two things must be noted. First, the taxpayer did not seek to deduct the whole price due under the contract, but only the predicted loss. He was right not to claim this since the obligations to pay had not yet arisen. Second, had the raw materials been delivered it would have become trading stock and so the loss would have become eligible for relief under the rules for valuation of trading stock.[6] These rules could not however be extended to merely executory contracts for the delivery of trading stock.

The issue of the timing of expenses has been comprehensively reviewed by the Court of Appeal in *Gallagher v Jones*.[7] The question was whether expenses should be timed as they accrued or whether tax law should follow accounting principles and require them to be spread.

The former principle, articulated clearly by Harman J in the first court of instance, was that expenditure made in the course of and properly referable to the trade in any year is deductible in computing the profits for that year whether or not they can be attributed to the production of goods in that year and so even where this would be contrary to ordinary principles of commercial accounting.[8] Harman J based that principles on *Vallambrosa Rubber Co Ltd v Farmer*. In that case the company sought to deduct the costs of superintendence, weeding, and control of pests and similar expenditure on a rubber estate even though rubber trees take seven years to start producing rubber and so only one in seven of the rubber trees was actually in production; the claim succeeded.[9] The case itself was concerned mainly with the distinction between capital and revenue. It does not appear that the Crown argued that the expenses should be allowed only when the trees began to produce. The Court of Appeal's recent decision leaves the case as one in which expenses were allocated to the period in which they were incurred and as an instance of expenses being deductible even though not referable to any profits made in that year. However, the case does not lay down a broad principle.[10]

In *Gallagher v Jones*[11] the position concerned finance lease and SSAP 21. The Revenue had indicated in 1991 that they accepted SSAP 21 and that payments under finance leases were deductible for tax purposes as they were allocated under SSAP 21 and not simply by reference to the date they fell due.[12] Here the company failed in its claim to deduct sums paid under a finance lease as they were made. The lease provided for payments during an initial period of 24 months of a large initial payment followed by 17 monthly instalments; in the secondary period which began after 24 months a nominal rent was due. The Revenue argued that the initial payment and the 17 monthly instalments should be spread evenly over the 24 month period as suggested in SSAP 21. Reversing Harman J, the Court of Appeal held that SSAP 21 should be followed. The uncontradicted evidence before the Commissioner given by an eminent accountant was that the taxpayers' simple approach would give a completely misleading picture of their trading results. Under these circumstances, it would be extraordinary if any judge-made rule could override a generally accepted rule of commercial accountancy which: (a) applied to the situation in question; (b) was not one of two or more rules applicable to that situation; and (c) was not shown to be inconsistent with the true facts or otherwise inapt to determine the true profits or losses of the business.[13]

Gallagher v Jones has been followed in various cases of which the most recent is *Herbert Smith (a firm) v Honour*.[14]

Simon's Taxes B2.504–506.

[1] (1928) 12 TC 1017; see also *James Spencer & Co v IRC* (1950) 32 TC 111.
[2] (1950) 32 TC 111.
[3] [1994] STC 763.
[4] ICAEW Guidance Note TAX 10/95, 12 April 1995, *Simon's Weekly Tax Intelligence* 1995, p 703.
[5] 1925 SC 151, 12 TC 773; see also *Whimster & Co v IRC* 1926 SC 20, 12 TC 813 and *J H Young & Co v IRC* 1926 SC 30, 12 TC 827.
[6] Infra, § **8.151**.
[7] [1993] STC 537, CA.
[8] See [1993] STC 537, CA, at 544f and [1993] STC 199 at 213 where Harman J suggests that the principle might be based on the words of Lord Reid in *Ostime v Duple Motor Bodies Ltd* (1961) 39 TC 537 at 571.
[9] (1910) 5 TC 529.
[10] [1993] STC 537, CA, at 547f.
[11] [1993] STC 537, CA.

[12] Statement of practice SP 3/91 (for leases entered into on or after 11 April 1991).
[13] Sir Thomas Bingham MR [1993] STC 537, CA, at 556.
[14] [1999] STC 173.

Contingent liabilities

[8.148] The question whether one can make a deduction for a contingent liability must be answered first by reference to sound principles of accountancy practice. Such evidence was not forthcoming in *Peter Merchant Ltd v Stedeford*.[1] The taxpayer ran a canteen for a factory owner and was under a contractual obligation to replace utensils; owing to wartime scarcities it was not possible to replace them. The accountant recommended that the amounts owing under the liability to replace should be deducted each year. However, he had committed an error of law by construing the contract to mean that there was a liability to replace the stock each year rather than at the end of the contract; it followed that deduction could not be allowed each year.

When an obligation matures over a number of years or is contingent it is proper to make provision year by year if, and only if, reliable figures can be established. In *IRC v Titaghur Jute Factory Co Ltd*[2] a company was obliged by foreign statute to make provision for gratuities to be paid to employees on leaving the company service; the amount would depend on the final salary and the length of service. The Court of Session allowed the company to deduct a sum set aside to meet this obligation. Similarly in *Johnston v Britannia Airways Ltd*[3] the court allowed a company's major overhaul costs in respect of aero engines to be spread over the period of three or four years leading up to the overhaul. This decision depended on the recognition of the treatment as being in accordance with the accepted principles of commercial accountancy and follows the general approach to such questions taken in *Gallagher v Jones*.[4]

By contrast, in *Southern Railway of Peru Ltd v Owen*[5] the taxpayer could not justify its figures and so was not allowed any deduction. By Peruvian law it was bound to pay its employees certain sums of money on redundancy, retirement or death. The payments were to be of one month's salary for each completed year of service, the salary being computed according to the rates in force at the time of redundancy or other cause, with certain protection for employees whose salaries declined. No payments were due, however, if an employee on a fixed term contract resigned before the term had expired nor where an employee was dismissed for just cause. The Revenue argued that the correct method of computing profits was to deduct payments actually made during the period. The company, however, argued that it should charge against each year's receipts the cost of making provision for the retirement benefits that they would ultimately have to pay and conceded that as a corollary they would not be able to deduct the actual payments made each year. It was clearly impractical to regard the setting aside of these sums as provisional payments and adjust them retrospectively as each employee became entitled to his share. The House of Lords held that the company's method was far more likely to give a true picture of the company's annual profit but that this object could only be achieved if the figures were sufficiently reliable. The figures for which the company was arguing were thus explained by Lord Radcliffe, 'It has calculated what sum would be required to be paid to each employee in respect of retirement benefit if he retired without forfeiture, at the close of the year'. This process was defective in that it failed to take account of the length of time that would pass before the payments would become due, a factor which could be met by a discounting process, secondly in that it failed to recognise that the legislation which had created the present system could also vary it and thirdly in that there was the possibility that a certain number of employees would forfeit their rights to payments. For these reasons the figure which the company was trying to deduct, although correctly deducted in order to give a "true and fair" view of the profits, and necessarily so for the purposes of the Companies Acts, was not sufficiently precise for the Income Tax Acts.

It should be noted that the issue in *IRC v Titaghur Jute Factory Co Ltd* concerned the year in which the initial liability was imposed on the company; no attempt was made to make provision for obligations which had matured in previous years—any such obligation should have been provided for in the earlier years.

Simon's Taxes B2.504.

1   (1948) 30 TC 496.
2   [1978] STC 166.
3   [1994] STC 763.
4   [1993] STC 537, CA.
5   [1956] 2 All ER 728, 36 TC 602 and see also the decision of Lush J, allowing the deduction of future expenses of maintaining graves: *London Cemetery Co v Barnes* [1917] 2 KB 496, 7 TC 92.

Receipts in kind

[8.149] The only difference between a payment in money and a payment in kind is that the value of the former is more obvious. Where, therefore, a trading receipt is received otherwise than in sterling, whether in foreign currency or in kind a value must be put on the receipt at the time it becomes a trading receipt ie when it is delivered or, if earlier, when it is due. Subsequent changes in value should be ignored.[1]

It is no objection to such valuation that the benefit in kind cannot in fact be realised. So in *Gold Coast Selection Trusts Ltd v Humphrey*[2] the trust had sold certain rights in a gold mine concession in exchange for shares in a company and was held taxable on the value of the shares so received even though it would be quite impossible to obtain a reasonable price for them if all were sold at one go on the Stock Exchange. Where, as in this case, the shares would become part of the trading stock of the company, adjustments to their value would have to be made each year under the principle of cost or market whichever is the lower.

Where a dealing company receives shares they will be valued as trading receipts only when they represent the end of a trading transaction as opposed to a step in the course of one. The central idea was expressed by Rowlatt J:[3]

While an investment is going up or down for income tax purposes the Company cannot take any notice of fluctuations, but it has to take notice of them when that state of affairs comes to an end when the investment . . . ceases to figure in the company's affairs, when it is known exactly what the holding of the investment has meant, plus or minus to the Company, and then the Company starts as far as that portion of its resources is concerned with a new investment.

So in *Gold Coast Selection Trusts Ltd v Humphrey*[4] there was a realisation. In *Varty v British South Africa Co*, by contrast, where a company had an option to subscribe for shares in company C at par and decided to exercise that option, there was no realisation and so no taxable profit at the time.[5] The question in all cases is one of fact and substance, but the *Varty* case appears to be the only reported instance involving securities where the court has held there was no realisation. So even an exchange of shares under a company amalgamation scheme has constituted a realisation[6] as has the exchange of mortgage bonds against one company for debenture stock in a new one when the first company's finances were being restructured.[7] Even the exercise of an option in a government savings scheme to convert the holding into a new government stock was held to be a realisation.[8]

On this basis where securities—the original holding—are held as circulating capital, trading receipts arise when they are disposed of and allowable expense on their reinvestment in the new holding. If, however, they were held as fixed capital a form of rollover relief might apply so postponing liability in respect of the resulting capital gain. To further the policy behind the CGT relief, ITTOIA 2005, s 150 (income tax) and TA 1988, s 473 (corporation tax) provide that where that relief would apply if the assets were such that the proceeds of sale would not be trading receipts, then the original holding is not treated as disposed of and the new holding is treated as the same asset.

Simon's Taxes B2.222.

[1] *Greig v Ashton* [1956] 3 All ER 123, 36 TC 581.
[2] [1948] 2 All ER 379, 30 TC 209. See [1970] BTR 150.
[3] In *Royal Insurance Co Ltd v Stephen* (1928) 14 TC 22 at 28.
[4] Supra. See also *Californian Copper Syndicate Ltd v Harris* (1904) 5 TC 159.
[5] [1965] 2 All ER 395, 42 TC 406.
[6] *Royal Insurance Co Ltd v Stephen* (1928) 14 TC 22.
[7] *Scottish and Canadian General Investment Co Ltd v Easson* (1922) 8 TC 265.
[8] *Westminster Bank Ltd v Osler* [1933] AC 139, 17 TC 381.

[8.150] Trading receipts in kind have received rather different treatment in the very different statutory environment in Australia where considerable emphasis has been placed on convertibility. However, the courts have also distinguished a receipt in kind from being relieved of an expense. In *Federal Comr of Taxation v Cooke and Sherden*[1] the taxpayers, who were two independent couples operating in different states, sold drinks from door to door on a self-employed basis. They rented a truck from the drink manufacturer and in each case the male respondent drove the truck and delivered the orders. Each winter each taxpayer was given a week's holiday by the manufacturer—in Queensland or outside Australia in the Pacific Ocean. This was arranged by the manufacturer as reward for those agents who reached their quotas. It was described as "a discretionary holiday scheme for the retailer and wife, not a negotiable reward. Our objective is to give the retailer's wife a holiday as much as the retailer. If the wife cannot go or if the retailer is single (unattached) a second ticket may be issued to a lady companion in lieu of a wife, provided the committee considers that this person is genuinely in lieu of a wife and not just a fill-in for someone because the retailer thinks there is a free ticket to be used." In holding the value of the holidays to be non-taxable the full Federal Court spent some time on what the UK would regard as employment income cases on non-convertibility of benefits in kind. After noting that these benefits could not be converted on any of those tests, the Court then said: 'It is immaterial that the respondents would have had to expend money themselves had they wished to provide a holiday for themselves. If the receipt of an item saves a taxpayer from incurring expenditure, the saving is not income; income is what comes in, it is not what is saved from going out.'

Such cases have not yet arisen in the UK although the final sentence is exactly the rule which underlies the mutuality principle. In the UK they might come within the solatium principle which has enabled certain benefits to escape tax under rule 3 at supra, § **8.56** as a recognition of past service but this is not certain since the finding that these arrangements were not rewards seems odd to UK eyes. If the benefits do not escape tax under the solatium principle it will be interesting to see whether a UK court would hold that they were non-taxable for the reasons given by the Australian court.

[1] (1980) 10 ATR 696.

Trading stock

[8.151] Trading stock gives rise to a number of special rules which are dealt with together.

Rule 1—substitution of market value

In general, where trading stock is disposed of, the sum to be entered into the accounts will be the actual price realised on the disposal. If the goods have been given away perhaps for reasons of advertisement there will be no sum to be entered at all. Neither the Revenue nor the taxpayer are in general allowed to substitute a fair market price for that in fact obtained.[1] To this principle, however, there are three exceptions:

(1) The statutory transfer pricing provisions.[2]
(2) The transfer of goods from one trade to another, where the trades are under common ownership.[3]
(3) The transfer to personal use of goods held as trading stock.[4]

Simon's Direct Tax Service B2.616; D9.205.

[1] *Craddock v Zevo Finance Co Ltd* [1946] 1 All ER 523, 27 TC 267 at 288.
[2] TA 1988, Sch 28AA, see infra, § **8.153**.
[3] *Watson Bros v Hornby* [1942] 24 TC 506, see infra, § **8.154**.
[4] From 12 March 2008: ITTOIA 2005, Pt 2, Ch 11A; formerly, this rule was based upon the decision in *Sharkey v Wernher* (1955) 36 TC 275, see infra, §§ 8.154–8.157.

Transfer-pricing—TA 1988, Sch 28AA

[8.152] The first exception is when the statutory provisions[1] on transfer pricing require substitution of an arm's length price in place of the sum actually receivable. The provisions now[2] apply to transfers between UK entities as well as transactions between a UK entity and a foreign entity. For unincorporated entities, the statutory provisions apply only if the entity is of a size that, if it were incorporated, would make it a medium or large company.[3]

[1] TA 1988, Sch 28AA as amended by FA 2004, ss 30-37 & Sch 5. The provisions are fully discussed in relation to companies at infra, § **25.07**.
[2] With effect from 6 April 2004: FA 2004, s 37(4).
[3] An enterprise is not within the scope of these provisions if it would satisfy the conditions for a small company: TA 1988, Sch 28AA, para 5B inserted by FA 2004, s 31(3). An enterprise that would satisfy the conditions for a medium sized company can be given a Revenue direction to apply these provisions: TA 1988, Sch 28AA, para 5C inserted by FA 2004, s 31(3).

For the purpose of granting these enhanced 150% allowances, statute adopts the European Commission recommendation. As from 1 January 2005, this is EC Recommendation 2003/36 which defines enterprises as:

Small
Less than 50 employees, and
Turnover less than €10 million or *balance sheet total less than €10 million*
Medium sized
Less than 250 employees, and
Turnover less than €50 million or *balance sheet total less than €43 million*

The test is applied by aggregating all "linked" enterprises. An enterprise is linked if one entity has 25%+ of the voting rights in the other entity, or 25%+ rights to capital or controls it by virtue of a shareholders' agreement. (Investment by a "venture capitalist" not exceeding €1,250,000 is ignored for this purpose).

Watson Bros v Hornby

[8.153] This is the second exception. Where one trader has two distinct trades[1] and transfers goods from one trade to the other the transfer must be treated as a sale and purchase at a reasonable price. In *Watson Bros v Hornby*[2] on the transfer from a trade then taxed under Schedule D, Case I, that of chicken breeder and hatcher to a farm which at that time was taxed under Schedule B, the market value was less than the cost of production and so the taxpayer succeeded in establishing a trading loss. The case was decided on the basis of a notional sale at a reasonable price.[3]

[8.153] Income from trades, professions and vocations

1 TA 1988, s 770 only applies where there are two traders.
2 **Simon's Taxes B2.215.** [1942] 2 All ER 506, 24 TC 506; see also *Long v Belfield Poultry Products Ltd* (1937) 21 TC 221.
3 Sale of Goods Act 1893, s 8.

Sharkey v Wernher

[8.154] This is the third exception. The Revenue turned their defeat in *Watson Bros v Hornby* to good use in *Sharkey v Wernher*.[1] Lady Zia Wernher carried on the business of a stud farm; she also rode horses for pleasure. She transferred a horse reared at the farm to her personal use and entered the costs incurred in respect of the horse until the date of its transfer as a credit item in the account of the stud farm. There was thus no attempt to take tax advantage of the deductions she had already been allowed. The Revenue successfully contended that the horse should be entered not at cost but at market value. The rule is that where a trader disposes of trading stock otherwise than in the course of trade, he is deemed to dispose of it at market value and that figure must be entered as a credit in his accounts. This principle applies whether he supplies the goods to himself or to some other person unless the disposal is a genuine commercial transaction. The value entered in the books of the transferor is also entered in the books of any trader acquiring the stock.[2]

The rule is subject to two technical objections. First, the profit alleged to be made comes from a course of dealing with oneself; it is precisely because this is alleged to be impossible that no charge to tax arises from mutual dealings. In reply Viscount Simonds said that 'the true proposition is not that a man cannot make a profit out of himself but that he cannot trade with himself',[3] a principle which was not to apply where trading stock was removed from the trade for a man's own use and enjoyment. However, this is not consistent with other formulations of the mutuality principle.[4]

Second, the decision appears to conflict with the fundamental principle that a person is taxed on what is actually earned and not on what he might have earned. However, in *Sharkey v Wernher* the taxpayer received value; the question therefore is the figure to be entered in the accounts. Lord Radcliffe rejected the idea of taking the cost figure on the grounds that market value "gives a fairer measure of assessable trading profit" and was "better economics".[5] For a trader who was concerned with the profitability of his trade it would be better book-keeping to include market value. However, the issue is not what is good book-keeping but the correct basis for taxation. In this regard it may be noted that the cost figure was in conformity with then accepted accountancy practice.[6]

The validity of the rule has recently been questioned.[7] The underlying doubts were based upon two key factors: first, the House of Lords had not been able to take into account accounting evidence and, consequently, their judgment had to be considered as merely provisional on that basis; secondly, the importance of accounting standards became yet more emphatic following the enactment of FA 1998, s 42 (now ITTOIA 2005, s 25). But for these questions the rule would have been codified upon the enactment of ITTOIA 2005. And, but for those questions, that would have been a sensible policy as it would have been wholly within the spirit of the Rewrite Project for such important rules to be immediately apparent to new users of the legislation. However, given the objections, the former Inland Revenue made the sensible decision to withdraw the proposal:

> We see no reason to doubt that the principles explained in *Sharkey v Wernher* continue to apply to the calculation of business profits. But it would be wrong to enact those principles while others doubt the position. The only way to preserve the law is to continue to rely on case law in this area."[8]

The highly publicised doubts about the validity of the rule seemed to encourage accountants to challenge the HMRC position and to withhold suggestions that adjustments be made to taxpayers' self assessments. Ultimately, so it seems, the Government could not risk the rule being overturned in the Special Commissioners. Consequently, the Budget 2008 press notices included the announcement that the rule would be codified with effect from 12 March 2008. For income tax purposes, the provisions are more or less identical to those previously consulted on in the draft Income Tax (Trading and Other Income) Bill and are now found in ITTOIA 2005, Pt 2, Ch 11A.

Simon's Taxes B2.215.

---

[1] [1955] 3 All ER 493, 36 TC 275.
[2] *Ridge Securities Ltd v IRC* [1964] 1 All ER 275, 44 TC 373. See [1964] BTR 168 (Crump). This means that the transferee gets the whole profit free of tax but a double charge to tax is avoided; contrast *Skinner v Berry Head Lands Ltd* [1971] 1 All ER 222, 46 TC 377, when the transferee was fixed with the whole gain.
[3] [1955] 3 All ER 493 at 496, 36 TC 275 at 296.
[4] Supra, § **8.13**.
[5] [1955] 3 All ER 493 at 506, 36 TC 275 at 307.
[6] See Lord Oaksey (dissenting).
[7] See, for example, Roger Kerridge's article in the *British Tax Review* [2005] BTR 287 and Keith Gordon's article in Taxation, 24 July 2003.
[8] Tax Law Rewrite Responses to the draft Income Tax (Trading and Other Income) Bill, para 179 (23 September 2004).

The limits of the rule in Sharkey v Wernher

[8.155] The most serious criticism of the decision of the *Sharkey v Wernher* rule is simply that of the uncertainty as to the scope of the notional income. It would appear first that the rule is confined to trading income. Thus landlords who allow themselves to occupy their houses would not be treated as owing themselves an economic rent for the purposes of a property business.

[8.156] It is not clear whether the rule applies to professions. In *Mason v Innes*[1] the author, Hammond Innes, had written a book called *The Doomed Oasis*. Shortly before completing the manuscript he had assigned the copyright to his father by way of gift. It was agreed that the market value of the copyright at that date was £15,425. The rule in *Sharkey v Wernher* was not applied. The effect in *Mason v Innes* was that not only did the Revenue see their share of the copyright vanish but they were still left bearing the loss of tax resulting from the deduction of expenses incurred by the author in the creation of the copyright.

Lord Denning MR, said that there are three reasons for making a distinction. First, a professional man was different from a trader and suggested that a picture painted by an artist was somehow different from a horse produced on a stud farm. Second, this professional man was taxed on a cash basis whereas a trader was taxed on an earnings basis, a distinction which ought to be irrelevant since it goes to calculating liability to tax rather than deciding what items should be taxable.[2] Third, was the set of anomalies that would result notably in contrast with the rules that allowed spreading of copyright income[3] and the taxation of post cessation receipts both of which provisions must have been passed on the basis that notional sales could not arise from the transfer of the copyright.[4] On the other hand the area is full of anomalies anyway.

A more convincing reason for the decision of the Court of Appeal is given by Potter:[5]

> ... the whole point of *Sharkey v Wernher* was that some figure had to be entered in the trading account because an item of trading stock that stood in that account at cost was taken out. An author does not however enter his copyrights in his professional account. He does not deal in copyrights. His earnings are in essence fees for services, not proceeds of sale of assets. He pays tax on what he receives or is entitled to receive, no account being taken of opening or closing stock.

On this basis *Mason v Innes* was correctly decided but it may mean a closer examination of the boundary between a profession and a trade.[6] Thus an artist who sells his own pictures might be regarded as carrying on the profession of an artist and the trade of a picture dealer. In this event the value of the paintings will be entered into his trading account at their then market value.

It would also mean that the rule only applies to dispositions of trading stock[7] and so does not extend to things which are the assets of a profession, nor to disposal of certain items in a trade. Thus the disposal of an agency at an undervalue would not be a disposal of trading stock.

Simon's Taxes B8.301.

---

[1] *Mason v Innes* [1967] 2 All ER 926, 44 TC 326; assignments of copyright may fall within TA 1988, s 775, supra, § **4.31** and be subject to CGT and IHT.
[2] See however Russell LJ in *Mason v Innes* at 341.
[3] Previously in TA 1988, s 534.
[4] Now in ITTOIA 2005, Pt 2, Ch 18 (income tax); TA 1988, s 104 (corporation tax) (formerly: TA 1970, s 144).
[5] [1964] BTR 438 at 442.
[6] Supra, § **8.07**.
[7] See Russell LJ in *Mason v Innes* at 341.

[8.157] The rule does not apply to a sale at a fairly negotiated price. In *Jacgilden (Weston Hall) Ltd v Castle*[1] a property developer acquired the right to buy a hotel for £72,000. He later transferred that right to a company for

£72,000 although at the time the hotel was worth £150,000; the company then sold the hotel for £155,000. The company sought to have the hotel entered into the books of the company at its market price as opposed to the actual cost price—and failed. There was no question of the contract for sale being an illusory or colourable or fraudulent transaction; it was a perfectly straightforward and honest bargain between the developer and the company.

The rule may not apply to a transfer on discontinuance to one carrying on a trade in the UK and in whose accounts the cost of the stock transferred will appear as a revenue deduction.[2] The statutory rules in ITTOIA 2005, Pt 2, Ch 12 (income tax) and TA 1988, s 100 (corporation tax) may here exclude *Sharkey v Wernher*.

Three concluding points ought to be made. The first is that a system which provided for no figure to be entered into the accounts by way of credit on the occasion of a self-supply[3] would give the self-supplier a great tax advantage. Although in *Sharkey v Wernher* the taxpayer was arguing that the figure should be cost, thus surrendering the benefit of the deductions she had been able to claim, no such surrender was offered in *Mason v Innes*.

The second is that in view of the general dislike of the rule evinced by lower courts[4] the decision may be reversed although whether this could be done through expert evidence of accountancy practice, a matter which had not weighed much with the House in *Sharkey v Wernher*, or through the exercise of the power to reverse earlier decisions remains to be seen. Any such challenge will, of course, be limited by the decision to codify the rule in FA 2008.

The third is that these transactions may give rise not only to income tax but also to CGT and IHT. Thus in the *Jacgilden* case it would be hard for the seller to bring himself within IHTA 1984, s 10; infra, § 39.14 since he controlled the company; moreover CGT might well be assessed by reference to market value; infra.

Simon's Taxes D9.205.

---

[1] [1969] 3 All ER 1110, 45 TC 685. In *Julius Bendit Ltd v IRC* (1945) 27 TC 44 the test seems to have been whether the deal was a bona fide trading transaction (which it was); the same result was reached in *Craddock v Zevo Finance Co Ltd* [1944] 1 All ER 566, 27 TC 267. These cases might be decided differently today but the principle which they represent is probably sound.
[2] *Moore v R J MacKenzie & Sons Ltd* [1972] 2 All ER 549, 48 TC 196.
[3] On self-supply for VAT see VATA 1994, s 5 (VATA 1983, s 3), and infra, §§ 65.31–65.35.
[4] The Revenue did not put the principle at risk by appealing in Mason v Innes (supra, § 8.156).

Gifts of trading stock to charities

[8.158] Many large towns have "soup kitchens" that provide meals for the homeless. These charities generally acquire the food supply by donations of surplus stock from retail and manufacturing food outlets. When a trader donates stock that he has manufactured to a charity or an educational establishment, statute provides that the value of the stock that is to be brought into account shall be £nil.[1] However, there is not an equivalent relief for donations to charities generally. Provided that the trading stock was originally manufactured and/or purchased for sale in the ordinary course of trade, its donation to charity will not cause its cost to be disallowed for tax purposes.[2] If the gift is of medical supplies or equipment, this treatment is applied for corporation tax purposes, even if the recipient is not a charity.[3]

Where a donation is made in the course of a trade, the amount to be credited in the trader's account for tax purposes will be the actual disposal proceeds, that is £nil. The Revenue have stated that they will accept that a donation is made in the course of a trade where a donation is "the most effective commercial way of disposing of the stock where, for example, it would not be commercially effective to sell surplus perishable food".[4] Where a donation is not made in the course of trade, the amount to be credited in the accounts of the donor is the market value of the stock at the date of disposal.[5] This is interpreted by the Revenue as "the amount the stock could reasonably be expected to have realised in a market commercially available to the trader". The Revenue accept that where no market commercially available to the trader exists for the stock, the market value is £nil.[6]

Simon's Taxes B2.441.

[1] ITTOIA 2005, s 108 (income tax); TA 1988, ss 83A, 84 (corporation tax).
[2] Inland Revenue interpretation RI 151.
[3] FA 2002, s 55.
[4] Inland Revenue interpretation RI 151.
[5] *Sharkey v Wernher* (1955) 36 TC 275.
[6] Inland Revenue interpretation RI 151.

Rule 2—end of year valuations

[8.159] The value of trading stock unsold at the end of the first period is entered into the account of the year as a receipt and into the account of the second period as an expense; it is thus sold from one year to the next. The figure entered is cost or market value—whichever is the lower.[1] The effect is that losses may be anticipated—but not profit—a sound conservative accounting principle.

Income tax is charged upon the profit of the trade over a particular period, usually the accounting year of the business. The true profit for the period—ignoring overheads—is not simply sums for goods sold received minus sums spent, but sums received for goods sold minus sums spent on those goods. Thus suppose that a retailer sells shoes. In the first year he spends £10,000 on shoes, and sells half of them for £10,000. The second year he sells the other half for £10,000 but buys no more stock. The naif view that the profit for his first year was nil but for his second year £10,000 would give a very distorted view of the profitability of his business. Hence the rule which takes £5,000 as a receipt for the first year and an expense of the second. Over the two year period the naif view and the correct one produce the same total profit. They differ in the methods of determining the profit of a particular artificial period during the life of the business.

In valuing stock the Revenue will accept any method which is recognised by the accountancy profession so long as it does not violate the taxing statutes as interpreted by the courts.[2] That interpretation now has to take account of the greater force given to accounting principles in *Gallagher v Jones*.[3]

Simon's Taxes B2.611.

---

[1] *Whimster & Co v IRC* (1926) 12 TC 813.
[2] Statement of practice SP 3/90. See also Inland Revenue interpretation RI 98. On change of method, see infra, § **8.167**.
[3] [1993] STC 537, CA. On effects for motor dealers buying in used cars at inflated prices in order to sell a new car see Inland Revenue interpretation RI 83.

Trading stock

[**8.160**] The first problem is to decide the range of assets to which this valuation should apply. It clearly applies to trading stock but equally clearly does not apply to capital assets. Stock not yet delivered is not trading stock,[1] nor is it permissible to anticipate a loss on the hiring of ships on time charter,[2] since such charters are not trading stock. In *Willingale v International Commercial Bank Ltd*[3] there was no suggestion that the bills were trading stock; otherwise the Revenue would have won. Thus one may not anticipate any loss save that on trading stock proper.

Simon's Taxes B2.602.

---

[1] *Edwards Collins & Sons Ltd v IRC* (1925) 12 TC 773, supra, § **8.147**.
[2] *Whimster & Co v IRC* (1926) 12 TC 813 and see *Scottish Investment Trust Co v Forbes* (1893) 3 TC 231 and *Lions Ltd v Gosford Furnishing Co and IRC* (1961) 40 TC 256 (future hiring receipts not stock in trade).
[3] Supra, § **8.64**.

[**8.161**] The next problem is to determine what trading stock is to be valued. While our small shoeshop may be able to determine precisely which shoes were unsold at the end of the year, it is less practicable to expect a coal merchant to be able to say just how many tons of coal he had in stock at the end of work on the last day of his accounting period, and there is in fact no obligation on him to weigh his stock at the end of that day before resuming his business. The Revenue appear content to rely on an annual stocktaking with any adjustments necessary.

The cost of the goods is complicated if the goods are fungibles and prices alter in the course of the trading period. Three principal types of formulae are used by accountants. The first, is first in first out (FIFO), ie last in still there. If prices are rising this means using the cheaper stock first so that the cost of the goods sold is low. The stock remaining at the end of the year, a plus item in the accounts, will therefore be the dearer items. The FIFO system has the advantage that the closing stock will be valued at the more recent prices and so, depending on the rapidity of turnover and the rate of price change, at a figure more or less close to replacement cost. It has, however, the converse disadvantage that it matches past costs with current receipts and thus, in an era of inflation, an over-optimistic picture of profitability.

The second formula, which was rejected for tax purposes by the Privy Council in *Minister of National Revenue v Anaconda American Brass Ltd*[1] is the opposite of the first, last in first out (LIFO). The third method—the weighted average—is a compromise. This looks at the different prices paid for the stock over the period and weights the price according to the quantity of stock bought at each price.

The different methods of determining the stock to be valued yield different results and so different profit figures for each accounting period. However, over the lifetime of the business all three methods will give the same figure of profits if applied consistently since the same total amount will have been spent on stock and the same total amount received on sales and any remaining stock is valued under ITTOIA 2005, Pt 2, Ch 12 (income tax) and TA 1988, ss 100, 102 (corporation tax).

Aberrations will occur where there is a change in the method of valuing stock during the lifetime of the trade. For tax purposes too there will be the same total profit to be taxed although different tax rates and, for individuals, the complexities of the gaps and overlaps of the commencement and cessation period will mean that the total tax charged may well vary according to the method chosen.

Simon's Taxes B2.611.

[1] [1956] 1 All ER 20, [1956] AC 85.

Cost

[8.162] The cost is that at the original acquisition. Expenses incurred in keeping the goods in good condition are ignored;[1] these expenses properly belong to the time they were incurred since their value will not be recouped later.

Simon's Taxes B2.611.

[1] Per Lord Reid in *Ryan v Asia Mill Ltd* (1951) 32 TC 275 at 298.

Market value

[8.163] Stock is valued at lower of cost and market value. Market value means generally net realisable value, and not replacement cost. Thus where a retail shoeshop values trading stock the correct figure for market value should be the normal retail price rather than the price the shop would have to pay wholesale to replace that item. On the other hand if the trade were that of a wholesale supplier of shoes the figure would be that which the trader would receive on a wholesale disposal.

In *BSC Footwear Ltd v Ridgway*[1] the House of Lords held that a retail shoe shop should value unsold stock by reference to the value to be expected in a sale and with a deduction for the salesperson's commission but without any allowance for the general expenses of the business for later periods of account; so no deduction could be made for the normal retail mark-up. As Lord Pearson put it:

> The correct principle is that goods should not be written down below cost price unless there really is a loss actual or prospective. So long as the fall in prevailing prices is only such as to reduce the prospective profit the initial valuation at cost should be retained.[2]

Simon's Taxes B2.613.

---

[1] [1971] 2 All ER 534, 47 TC 495.
[2] [1971] 2 All ER 534 at 550, 47 TC 511 at 540.

The formula applied

[8.164] In applying the formula cost or market value whichever is the lower, each item may be treated separately so that one may be valued at cost and another at market value.[1] This is consistent with the idea of anticipating losses but not profits. Where stock is acquired by gift[2] the receipt is treated as being at market value. When the transfer falls within the rule in *Sharkey v Wernher* the value at which the transferor is taken to dispose of it is taken as the acquisition cost to the transferee.

Where different methods of computing the cost or market value are available the same method must be used at the end of the year as was used at the beginning.[3] However, the method used at the opening of the second period need not be that used at the closing of the first.[4] Where such a change occurs there will be either a double charge or no charge at all on the difference between the closing stock of the first period and the opening stock of the second period.

Simon's Taxes B2.613.

---

[1] *IRC v Cock Russell & Co Ltd* [1949] 2 All ER 889, 29 TC 387.
[2] See per Lord Greene MR in *Craddock v Zevo Finance Co Ltd* [1944] 1 All ER 566, 27 TC 267.
[3] *Steel Barrel Co Ltd v Osborne (No 2)* (1948) 30 TC 73.
[4] Although the Revenue will not generally allow this without good reason. The Revenue do not seem to insist upon consistency in their own behaviour, eg *Ostime v Duple Motor Bodies and BSC Footwear Ltd v Ridgway* (infra, § **8.167** and supra, § **8.163**).

Rule 3—ground rents and rentcharges

[8.165] Where a builder grants the house purchaser a long lease and charges both a premium and a ground rent, there is no outright realisation of the builder's interest in the land.¹ His previous freehold interest is now subject to a leasehold interest in the householder. It follows that the reversion remains part of the builder's stock and must therefore be entered each year at cost or market value, whichever is the lower.²

The cost of the reversion must include a part of the building cost. The formula used to ascertain that part is $A/(A+B)$ where A is the market value of the reversion (traditionally calculated as a multiple of the rent payable) and B is the premium.³

Very different is the situation where the builder sells the freehold interest but reserves to himself a rentcharge,⁴ chief rent or, in Scotland, a ground annual.⁵ Here the House of Lords has held that there is a realisation of the interest in the land for money (the price) and money's worth (the rent). The market value of the rentcharge must therefore be entered as a trading receipt in the year of sale and the rent payable will likewise be treated as a trading receipt. On the other hand the eventual disposal of the rentcharge will not give rise to a trading receipt unless the court holds that there is a trade of dealing in rent charges.

Simon's Taxes B2.229–232, 603.

[1] *B G Utting & Co Ltd v Hughes* [1940] 2 All ER 76, 23 TC 174.
[2] *Heather v G and J A Redfern & Sons* (1944) 26 TC 119.
[3] See case stated, para V, in *J Emery & Sons Ltd v IRC* [1937] AC 91, 20 TC 213 at 219.
[4] *Broadbridge v Beattie* (1944) 26 TC 63.
[5] *J Emery & Sons Ltd v IRC* [1937] AC 91, 20 TC 213.

Rule 4—work in progress

[8.166] Where the trader is a manufacturer and there is work in progress at the end of the accounting period as well as finished trading stock, the work in progress must be taken into account. One problem is that of determining just what is its cost—a problem of some difficulty. In *Duple Motor Bodies v Ostime*¹ the company made motor bodies and had since 1924 used the "direct cost" of ascertaining the cost of the work in progress, meaning that only the cost of materials used and labour directly employed in the manufacture were included. This gave a loss of £2,000. The Revenue argued that the cost should be computed on the "on-cost basis" meaning that there should also be included the proportion of overhead expenditure, with the effect that the profits for the year would be increased since the deductible expenses would be offset by the extra item on the credit side of the balance sheet. This gave an extra profit of £14,000. This would have the odd result that if work were slack so that the same quantity of overheads would have to be spread over fewer items, the "cost" of the work in progress would be increased so that while his receipts dropped his taxable profits in respect of work in progress would be increased. The accountancy profession was divided on the issue of which method should be adopted. The House of Lords held that the Revenue had failed to show that the "direct cost" was wrong especially in this case where it had been used for so long and dismissed the Revenue's appeal. They declined to lay down any general principle—the real question was what method best fitted the circumstances of the particular business.

ITTOIA 2005, s 25 (income tax) and FA 1998 s 42 (corporation tax) require all taxpayers carrying on a trade to report their income in accordance with generally accepted accounting practice. Certain professions have previously adopted rather different bases. There are a number of different bases that have been adopted in this respect. Some partnerships do not recognise debtors, on the grounds that income is uncertain until it is received. Some partnerships do not recognise work in progress; others value work in progress by treating it as a constant percentage of the previous year's turnover.

For the periods of account beginning on or after 6 April 1999 and subsequent years, the income subjected to tax in respect of trades, professions and vocations must be measured from a set of accounts "calculated in accordance with generally accepted accounting practice".[2] Between 1998 and 2002, the statute required the accounts to be prepared on an accounting basis that gave a "true and fair view". This phrase derives from the wording of an audit certificate and denotes that the accounts have been drawn up in accordance with recognised (and published) Accounting Standards.[3]

Work in progress should, thus, normally be measured in accordance with SSAP9; that is, the valuation should reflect employees' time spent up to the balance sheet date plus attributable overheads, less any provision that should prudently be made for time spent in excess of that which will ultimately be charged to the client. Where there is a long term contract, the provisions of SSAP22 should be applied; the effect of this is to bring into charge to tax a proportion of profits that it is anticipated will be made at the completion of a long term project.

The question as to which overheads should properly be attributed to work in progress is a question that, in the authors' view, requires consideration to be given to the particular nature of the professional practice. It is not necessarily either appropriate or required that all overheads should be reflected in WIP. Indeed, a good case can be made that some expenditure, such as rent, is incurred irrespective of the level of activity of employees and, hence, should be fully written off in the year in which the expenditure is incurred, rather than being partially carried forward as part of a WIP valuation.

Although it may be useful for management purposes to include in the WIP valuation time spent by partners (or by the proprietor in the case of a sole practitioner) this is clearly an incorrect basis on which to compute a liability to income tax as it conflicts with the principle that a man cannot pay himself.[4]

Simon's Taxes B2.618.

[1] [1961] 2 All ER 167, 39 TC 537.
[2] ITTOIA 2005, s 25 (income tax); FA 1998, s 42(1) (corporation tax); see supra, § 8.64.
[3] The statutory provisions have been criticised because the Accounting Standards are drawn up to specify accounting conventions which are appropriate for a company; these may not be appropriate for an unincorporated business.

⁴ Consider, for example, the denial of a deduction in the CGT computation for the value of the taxpayer's own labour in *Oram v Johnson* [1980] STC 222.

[8.167] Accountancy principles require that a loss be shown in the accounts as soon as it is recognised. This applies to work in progress, as well as obsolete stock.¹

Simon's Taxes B2.618.

¹ On this analysis, the decision in *Duple Motor Bodies v Ostime* (1961) 39 TC 537 is distinguished. In that case Lord Reid said that there must be some way of doing it.

Rule 5—valuation of trading stock on discontinuance

[8.168] When a trade had been discontinued the general rule (rule (a)) is that stock is entered at market value.¹ However, where the stock is sold or transferred for valuable consideration to a person who carries on or intends to carry on a trade in the UK and the cost will fall to be deducted in computing that person's profits, the general rule normally yields to the facts and the figure for any trading stock belonging to the trade at discontinuance is to be the sale price or the value of the consideration. (rule (b)).² However, rule (b) could lead to manipulation and so, if the parties are connected and the discontinuance occurs on or after 29 November 1994, the price to be taken is that which would have been obtained in a transaction between independent persons dealing at arm's length (rule (c)).³ The new rule is subject to exceptions; so rule (b) still applies if the stock consists of parts of a production herd.⁴ Probably of greater importance is the provision under which rule (b) may also still apply by election of the parties if the figure given under (c) exceeds both the price paid by the parties and the "acquisition value" of the stock.⁵ The acquisition value is the amount that would be taken into account as its cost if there had been an open market sale.⁶ The point of this exception is to allow the parties to avoid the charge on unrealised profits which would otherwise arise.⁷ Whatever figure emerges from these rules is then taken as the cost of the stock to the purchaser.⁸

The general rule is designed to prevent a person from discontinuing his business, bringing his stock into account at cost value and then reselling it at the much higher market value so securing to himself a large gain free of income tax, as nearly happened in *J & R O'Kane & Co Ltd v IRC*.⁹

The rule applies whenever a trade is discontinued including those situations made discontinuance by TA 1988, s 337(1). Perhaps because it is an anti-avoidance provision it does not apply where a trade carried on by a single individual is discontinued by reason of his death.¹⁰ The market value will however be taken for IHT.

Similar rules apply to work in progress at the discontinuance of a profession. The phrase "the amount that would have been paid for a transfer as between parties at arm's length" is substituted for market value.¹¹ Where this amount exceeds the actual cost of the work the taxpayer may elect to pay no tax now and submit to having sums actually received later taxed as post cessation receipts under ITTOIA Pt 2, Ch 18 (rather than Ch 12) (income tax) or TA 1988 s 103 (not s 104) (corporation tax).[12]

Simon's Taxes B2.617.

[1]   ITTOIA 2005, s 175(4) (income tax); TA 1988, s 100(1)(b) (corporation tax).
[2]   ITTOIA 2005, s 176 (income tax); TA 1988, s 100(1A) (corporation tax). See *Moore v R J Mackenzie & Sons Ltd* [1972] 2 All ER 549, 48 TC 196; supra, § **8.158**. Trading stock is defined in s 137(4).
[3]   ITTOIA 2005, s 177 (income tax); TA 1988, s 100(1A)(*b*) added by FA 1995, s 140 (corporation tax); for definition of connected persons see ITTOIA 2005, s 179 (income tax) or TA 1988, s 100(1F) (corporation tax).
[4]   ITTOIA 2005, s 175(3) (income tax); TA 1988, s 100(1B) (corporation tax).
[5]   ITTOIA 2005, s 178(1)-(4) (income tax); TA 1988, s 100(1C) (corporation tax).
[6]   ITTOIA 2005, s 178(5) (income tax); TA 1988, s 100(1D) (corporation tax).
[7]   Inland Revenue press release, 29 November 1994, *Simon's Tax Intelligence* 1994, p 1479.
[8]   ITTOIA 2005, s 180 (income tax); TA 1988, s 100(1E) (corporation tax).
[9]   (1922) 12 TC 303; supra, § **8.32**.
[10] ITTOIA 2005, ss 173(4), 182(3) (income tax); TA 1988, s 102(2) (corporation tax).
[11] ITTOIA 2005, s 184(2) (income tax); TA 1988, s 101(1) (corporation tax).
[12] ITTOIA 2005, s 185 (income tax); TA 1988, s 101(2) (corporation tax).

Farm animals

[8.169] Special rules apply down on the farm. Generally animals kept by a farmer for the purpose of his farming are to be treated as trading stock.[1] This applies to related trades like animal breeding, dealing in cattle or milk and so on.[2] Certain animals are excluded from this treatment, namely animals kept wholly or mainly for public exhibition or for racing or for other competitive purposes,[3] and animals kept wholly or mainly for the work they do in connection with farming,[4] such as sheep dogs.

Where animals which would under this rule be treated as trading stock form part of a production herd, the farmer may instead elect[5] that the herd be treated as a capital asset. As tangible movable wasting assets such animals are exempt from CGT.[6] The rules for income tax flowing from an election for herd basis were thus summarised by the Inland Revenue:[7]

(A) The initial cost of the herd and the cost of additions

Neither the initial cost of the herd nor the cost of any animals which are added to the herd to increase its numbers (as distinct from animals which replace those which die or are taken out of the herd) will be deducted as an expense in calculating profits or losses . . .

(B) Replacement of animals in the herd

When an animal is replaced in the herd (for example, when it dies or is culled), the sale price of the old animal, or of its carcass, will be included and the cost of the new animal will be deducted in arriving at the profit or loss, but if the new animal is of better quality than the old one, the extra cost of the new animal due to the element of improvement will not be deducted. If the new animal is home-bred, the cost of rearing it will already have been deducted as part of the expense of labour, feeding stuffs, etc, and no further deduction will be necessary . . .

(C) Replacement of the whole herd (see also sub-paragraph (D) below)

If a farmer sells a herd and buys another herd of the same kind, sub-paragraph (B) above will apply to the number of animals equal to the number in the smaller of the two herds, ie, the sale price of that number of animals will be included as a receipt and the cost of that number of animals deducted as an expense (except that the extra cost of any new animals of better quality will not be deducted). If the new herd is larger than the old herd, the cost of the additional animals will not be deductible as an expense. If the new herd is smaller than the old herd, the profit or loss arising from the sale of the animals which have not been replaced will be taken into account for tax purposes. There is, however, an exception to this last rule where the new herd is substantially smaller than the old herd (see sub-paragraph (D) below): in that case, the profit or loss arising from the sale of the animals which have not been replaced is not taken into account for tax purposes . . .

(D) Sale of the whole herd, or a substantial part of the herd, without replacement

If the whole of a herd is sold within a period of twelve months without replacement, any profit or loss on the sale will not be taken into account for tax purposes. Any profit or loss on the sale of a substantial part of the herd within a period of twelve months will be treated in the same way. (It will depend on the facts of the case whether a particular reduction in numbers is substantial, but the Board of Inland Revenue will normally be prepared to consider a reduction of 20 per cent or more as substantial.)

[Special rules apply if a new herd is begun within five years.]

(E) Sale of individual animals which are not replaced

If an animal (or a part of a herd which is not substantial) is sold out of the herd and is not replaced, any profit or loss on the sale will be taken into account.

The Revenue have now published guidance on the question as to when an animal is a replacement.[8]

This treatment applies only to a "production herd", which means[9] a herd of animals of the same species (irrespective of breed) kept by the farmer wholly or mainly for the products obtainable from the living animal which the animals produce for the farmer to sell. The term does not include cattle kept for disposal such as beef cattle, these being pure trading stock.

An immature animal is not generally treated as forming part of a production herd.[10] Where such an animal is transferred to the herd on reaching maturity, the transfer is treated as taking place at its total cost to that point. Since such an animal will have been treated previously as trading stock those expenses will have been deductible as revenue expenses; this rule provides for the recapture of those expenses before the animal passes out of the income tax net. An election for herd basis is irrevocable.[11] When a trade is passed to another taxpayer (such as by incorporation), the new taxpayer has the choice whether or not to elect for the herd basis.

For the valuation of shares in a stallion syndicate see **Simon's Taxes B2.620.**

Following the legislating of extra-statutory concession B37, the herd basis now applies (and is deemed always to have applied) where an animal is shared.[12]

Simon's Taxes B5.111–135.

---

[1] ITTOIA 2005, s 30(1) (income tax); TA 1988, Sch 5, para 1(1) (corporation tax).
[2] ITTOIA 2005, s 111(3) (income tax); TA 1988, Sch 5, para 9(1) (corporation tax).
[3] ITTOIA 2005, s 30(1) (income tax); TA 1988, Sch 5, para 9(5) (corporation tax).
[4] ITTOIA 2005, s 30(1)(a) (income tax); TA 1988, Sch 5, para 7 (corporation tax).
[5] The election period is extended following the abolition of stock relief to allow farmers who may have considered stock relief more advantageous to reappraise the position.
[6] Infra, § **17.18**.
[7] Taken from HMRC leaflet IR 9 (1984), § 7.
[8] Revenue interpretation RI 91.
[9] ITTOIA 2005, s 112(1)(c) (income tax); TA 1988, Sch 5, para 8(3) (corporation tax).
[10] ITTOIA 2005, s 112(3) (income tax); TA 1988, Sch 5, para 8(2) (corporation tax).
[11] Inland Revenue interpretation RI 19; *Simon's Direct Tax Service, Division H5.4*.
[12] ITTOIA 2005, s 112(7)(*b*) (income tax); TA 1988, Sch 5, para 9(4)(*b*) (corporation tax). Formerly extra-statutory concession B37; FA 2000, s 76(2).

Commission, cashbacks and discounts

[8.170] The tradition in the insurance industry has been to remunerate its agents and intermediaries by means of commission; it is now frequent practice that a part of the commission is passed on to the customer who purchases the insurance product. Furthermore, a customer for a home mortgage or for a hire purchase contract may receive a cashback as an inducement to favour a particular lender with his custom. Following consultation with the insurance industry and professional bodies, on 27 November 1997 the Inland Revenue issued a statement giving its view of the tax treatment appropriate to the more common arrangements.[1]

Ordinary retail customers who receive a commission, discount or cashback when purchasing goods, investment or services at arm's length are not liable to income tax or capital gains tax in respect of the receipt. Thus, if an ordinary retail customer negotiates to receive from the salesperson part of the commission he earns on the sale of a car to that customer, there is no income tax charge on the customer in respect of that commission.

By contrast, where the provision of services remunerated by commission, etc, is on a sufficiently commercial, regular and organised basis to amount to a trade or profession, commissions and similar sums are properly treated as part of the receipts in the trade or profession. When part of the commission, etc, is passed on to a client, it is, nevertheless, the gross sum received that is brought into the accounts of the business. Where the commission is passed to the customer as an inducement for that customer to enter into a transaction, the commission passed on is deductible if laid out wholly and exclusively for the trade or profession. This statutory test is very likely to be satisfied if the customer required the commission to be passed on as a condition of entering into the transaction or if the transaction was one between independent parties acting at arm's length.

Where the trader is entitled to commission, but instructs the provider to pass the commission direct to the customer, this does not change the analysis. Any commission to which the trader is entitled, forms part of the receipts of the business and the corresponding deduction must, in principle, be justified on the basis specified above.

By contrast, where a discounted purchase price is paid or extra value is added to the goods, there is no receipt by the trader and no addition requires to be made to the profits of the business. Thus, for example, where bonus units in a unit trust are issued to a customer, this does not cause an increase in the receipts of the business that negotiated the purchase of the unit trust.

Where a business asset is purchased, such as a car purchased for business purposes, the deduction in the business accounts (or the sum on which capital allowances are claimed) is required to be net of any cashbacks, etc.

A business person may receive commission in respect of a private transaction. Thus, where an accountant in practice instructs a stockbroker to purchase or sell shares for his personal portfolio, the broker will normally pay a specified part of the broking commission to the accountant. In the view of the Revenue, such a payment made to the accountant in his private capacity is a taxable business receipt; however, by concession, the Revenue agree that such a payment can be excluded from taxable profits insofar as it does not exceed the maximum amount that a trader or professional person can reasonably have been expected to pass on to an arm's length customer on the same transaction.[2]

Where an employee receives commission, a cashback or a discount, and the employee is employed on a salary of £8,500 or more a year, the employee is assessable under ITEPA on the commission, etc, if the commission is received by the employee in his capacity as such. Where, as part of the normal framework of the employer's business, the employee shares commission with another party, the Revenue accept that a deduction can be claimed for the commission shared.[3]

Where an employee receives a cashback from his employer or a third party there is no employment income liability if the cashback is received on the same basis as is available to members of the general public.[4]

Where a contribution is made to a personal pension plan or a retirement annuity policy, tax relief is available on the amount paid into the policy. If the payment is of a discounted amount, it is the amount after the discount. If the payment is followed by commission being received, the receipt of commission does not reduce the amount on which tax relief is granted. Where extra value is added to the policy, such as by the allocation of bonus units, relief is given for the payment ignoring the bonus.[5]

Where a chargeable event is computed by reference to premiums paid, the calculation is by reference to the actual amount paid. That is, any commission received back is ignored but any discounted premium is treated as the discounted payment that was made.[6]

Simon's Taxes B8.406.

1   Statement of practice SP4/97. See also Inland Revenue Tax Bulletin 33, February 1998, pp 485–489.
2   Statement of practice SP4/97, para 16.
3   Statement of practice SP4/97, para 33.
4   Statement of practice SP4/97, para 32.
5   Statement of practice SP4/97, para 39.
6   Statement of practice SP4/97, para 38.

Mining

[8.171] Special rules apply to mining. Income from land is taxed as a receipt of a property business but profits from mines, quarries and other concerns are taxed as trading income and mining[1] rents and royalties are charged under Pt 3 of ITTOIA 2005 (income tax) or Schedule D (corporation tax).[2]

Owing to technological advances which have made the extraction of minerals a much more rapid process, and because the costs were so high that a lease in return for royalties was a better method of arranging the business than a fixed capital sum, special rules now provide that where a person resident or ordinarily resident in the UK is entitled to receive mineral royalties under a mineral lease or agreement, one half of the proceeds are to be treated as income and one half as capital gains.[3] The land concerned may be in the UK or overseas.

Simon's Taxes Division B5.6.

1   ITTOIA 2005, s 12 (income tax); TA 1988, s 55 (corporation tax).
2   ITTOIA 2005, s 337 (income tax); TA 1988, s 119 (corporation tax). The obligation to deduct tax under TA 1988, ss 348 or 349 was removed by FA 1995, s 145.
3   ITTOIA 2005, s 340 (income tax); TA 1988, s 122(1) (corporation tax).

9

Capital allowances

Introduction	PARA 9.01
What is capital expenditure?	PARA 9.04
When expenditure is incurred	PARA 9.06
Method of giving capital allowances	PARA 9.07
Industrial buildings	PARA 9.11
Dwelling-houses let on assured tenancies	PARA 9.22
Plant and machinery	PARA 9.23
Mining	PARA 9.55
Dredging	PARA 9.58
Agricultural land and buildings	PARA 9.59
Other allowances	PARA 9.62

Introduction

[9.01] Expenses incurred in the acquisition of a capital asset are not deductible in computing the profits of a trade.[1] If that asset may have a limited life, its value to the business will decline. The causes of this decline may be physical, such as wear and tear on plant and machinery, or economic such as obsolescence or a change in trading policy. To anticipate the eventual loss depreciation is deductible for accounting purposes but no provision was originally made for tax purposes as the tax was thought to be temporary.

The tax system has relaxed this strict approach by making allowances for certain defined types of capital expenditure. When claimed, these allowances displace the deductibility of expenditure on renewals.[2] The structure of the present system goes back to the Income Tax Act 1945. This Act defined certain types of capital expenditure which qualified for allowances and specified different rates of allowance. Broadly speaking the list is the same today although there have been changes in the way in which the allowances are made. The legislation is now consolidated in the Capital Allowances Act 2001.

The statutory scheme is to provide writing down allowances at differing rates for the differing types of capital expenditure. For some assets (such as plant and machinery), the allowance is on a reducing balance of a pool; for other assets (such as relief for business premises renovation), the allowance is straight line and given for each asset separately. In addition, various governments have sought to promote investment by granting an accelerated allowance in the year of acquisition. For plant and machinery, this is termed a first year allowance; prior to 1986, first year allowances were available generally. For buildings, the accelerated allowance is called an initial allowance.[3] The Government has used initial allowances to attract investors into supplying funds for the rejuvenation of decaying areas, such as London Docklands. These areas have been designated Enterprise Zones and an initial allowance of

661

[9.01] Capital allowances

100% is available for the first purchaser of new commercial property in such a zone. This remains, see CAA 2001, s 39.

In 1997, first year allowances were again made available for the purchase of machinery, but only by a small or medium sized business. The 50% first year allowance introduced on 2 July 1997 was designed for one year. After 17 March 1998, the allowance was reduced to 40%. This was declared to be a permanent rate. Subsequent Finance Acts have lifted the rate to 50%, for small enterprises only, for temporary periods. However, from 1 April 2008 (or 6 April 2008 for income tax), the 50% and 40% first year allowances have been withdrawn in favour of a scheme permitting businesses to write down the first £50,000 of their annual expenditure on plant or machinery.[4]

A further major change was announced in the 2007 Budget speech and effected in the FA 2007 and FA 2008. Industrial building allowances and agricultural buildings allowances are to be withdrawn over a four year period, starting in April 2007, with the allowances being unavailable from 1 April 2011.[5] The only change for 2007–08 was the abolition of balancing adjustments (see infra, § **19:17** and the removal of an allowance for the successor for an industrial or an agricultural building.[6] From April 2008, allowances will be reduced by one quarter, a further quarter from April 2009 and by a third quarter from April 2010.

Capital allowances are only available where tax is computed on the basis of profits. If the shipping company elects to pay corporation tax based on tonnage,[7] capital allowances are denied.[8]

Simon's Taxes Division B3.1.

[1] *Coltness Iron Co v Black* (1881) 6 App Cas 315, 1 TC 311.
[2] Supra, § **8.126**.
[3] The initial allowance regime is the successor to the investment allowance introduced in 1954. Unlike capital allowances this was a tax free subsidy and was not taken into account for the purpose of any balancing allowance or charge. The new provisions are CAA 2001, ss 305–308.
[4] CAA 2001, ss 38A and 51A–51N.
[5] FA 2007, s 36(1).
[6] HM Treasury Finance Bill 2007 Explanatory Notes, Clause 35, para 16 and Budget Press Release BNO2, 21 March 2007 *Simon's Weekly Tax Intelligence* 2007, p 883. This note also stated that the Government's intention to reduce the plant and machinery writing down allowance from 25% to 20% from 2008–09, a measure subsequently enacted in FA 2008.
[7] FA 2000, Sch 22, see infra, § **25:08**.
[8] FA 2003, Sch 32 amending FA 2000, Sch 22, paras 89 to 102.

[9.02] Many types of capital expenditure do not qualify for any allowance. In order to obtain an allowance, it must be claimed: it is sometimes advantageous not to claim them.

[9.03] Historically the system of allowances has provided for three steps:

(1) An initial or first year allowance of a substantial percentage of the capital expenditure.

(2) A writing down allowance during the life of the asset, an allowance that obviously does not apply if there is a 100% initial allowance.

(3) A balancing allowance or charge at the end of the trade or the life of the asset. The scheme of capital allowances is designed to provide relief that equates with the actual expense. To achieve this, when an asset is sold, the sale proceeds are put against the expenditure reduced by allowances previously granted and the balance is a balancing allowance or charge. Where the legislation provides for a single asset to be treated alone, the total allowances given over the life of the asset do, indeed, equate to the net expenditure incurred by the business. However, plant and machinery generally is treated on a pool basis. Where the pool is substantial, the disposal of individual items of plant usually affects only continuing allowances and does not trigger a balancing charge or allowance. Hence, where there is a pool, capital allowances only equate with expenditure if one computes over the entire life of a business.

Where an asset is sold for more than it has cost, the balancing charge claws back allowances given. The excess that remains is then a matter for capital gains tax (or corporation tax on the capital gain). There is no provision whereby the balancing charge may be spread over the number of years for which the allowance was claimed; so an individual may pay more tax on the charge than he saved on the allowance. A balancing charge is treated as a trading receipt.[1]

EXAMPLE

A buys an asset for £1,000 and has claimed £500 allowances when he sells it for (a) £600; (b) £450; (c) £1,200. Ignoring pooling with other assets, in (a) there is a balancing charge of £100; in (b) a balancing allowance of £50; and in (c) a balancing charge of £500 the remaining £200 being left to CGT.

Simon's Direct Tax Service Division B3.

[1] CAA 2001, s 247.

What is capital expenditure?

[9.04] This is defined as excluding any sums allowable as deductions in computing the profits or gains of the trade profession or employment carried on by the person incurring the expense;[1] this boundary is not precise. No allowance can be claimed for sums reimbursed by others if the others can obtain capital allowances or a deduction in computing profits[2] or for subsidies from public or local authorities, save for certain grants under the Industry Acts and the Industrial Development Act 1982.[3] Provision is, however, made for allowances for contributions to the capital expenditure of others.[4] When a subsidy is made in respect of machinery and plant by a contributor for the contributor's trade, profession or vocation, a new trade is deemed to have begun.[5] This is to accelerate the benefit of the allowance but also creates a separate pool for giving the allowance.

The capital expenditure must have been incurred on the construction of the building or on the provision of the machinery and plant, etc. In *Ben-*

[9.04] Capital allowances

Odeco Ltd v Powlson[6] the taxpayer was going to carry on a trade of hiring out an oil rig. In order to finance the construction of the rig it had to borrow money and for this had to pay commitment fees (£59,002) and interest (£435,988). These sums were charged to capital (correctly) in the company's accounts. However, the House of Lords held that the sums were spent not on the provision of machinery and plant but on the provision of money and so did not qualify for capital allowances. This case was distinguished in *Van Arkadie v Sterling Coated Materials Ltd*[7] where the extra (sterling) cost of a price to be paid by instalments but in foreign currency was treated as allowable expenditure.

It was critical in this case that the contract provided for payment to be made by instalments; a different conclusion would have been reached if the contract had provided for a single payment which had been made with the aid of a loan from a bank which the purchaser paid off in instalments.

Simon's Taxes B3.103, 104, 306.

[1] CAA 2001, s 4(2)(a); eg *Rose & Co (Wallpaper and Paints) v Campbell* [1968] 1 All ER 405, 44 TC 500 (pattern books of current wallpaper stock not capital expenditure).
[2] CAA 2001, s 536.
[3] CAA 2001, ss 532–536 and *Birmingham Corpn v Barnes* [1935] AC 292, 19 TC 195. For an exception to s 153 see FA 1990, s 126(4): payments to football clubs out of reduced betting duty. Where a grant is repaid, extra-statutory concession B49 treats the amount repaid as expenditure by the trader, on which capital allowances may be given. FA 1990 s.126(4) has not been repealed, therefore it remains an exception to s 532 of CAA 2001.
[4] CAA 2001, ss 537–541.
[5] CAA 2001, s 538(3). This does not seem to be the same provision as its predecessor (CAA 1990, s 155(6)). The new consolidation provides that any expenditure must be allocated to a single asset pool.
[6] [1978] STC 460, [1978] 2 All ER 1111.
[7] [1983] STC 95.

[9.05] The present status of expenditure financed by non-recourse loans is unclear owing to the opaque speech of Lord Templeman in *Ensign Tankers (Leasing) Ltd v Stokes*.[1] In principle, as Millett J had held at first instance, the fact that a borrower who obtains a non-recourse loan incurs no personal liability to repay the lender is irrelevant; the capital allowance legislation is concerned with the taxpayer's ability to spend it in acquiring the asset, not with his liability to repay the lender.[2] In the House of Lords Lord Goff explained that the non-recourse nature of the loan was only one of the elements which enabled him to conclude that this expenditure had not been incurred by the taxpayer; other factors included the fact that the lender was L, the US film producer company, that the money was paid into a special bank account opened at a bank nominated by L and that when the money was paid in by L an identical sum was repaid by the taxpayer to L out of the same account on the same day. On such facts Lord Goff found it impossible to conclude that the money paid into the account by L was in any meaningful sense a loan; the payment was simply money paid in as the first step in a tax avoidance scheme.³ Lord Templeman however, with whom all the other judges agreed, said that:

> by reason of the non-recourse provision of the loan agreement the loan was not repayable by [the taxpayer] or anyone else. A creditor who receives a participation in profits *in addition* to the repayment of his loan is of course a creditor. But a creditor who receives a participation in profits instead of the repayment of his loan is not a creditor. The language of the document in the latter case does not accurately describe the true legal effect of the transaction which is a capital investment by the 'creditor' in return for a participation in profits.⁴

1   [1992] STC 226, HL (see supra, § **3.18**). For treatment of security arrangements in relation to films see SP 1/85, paras 66–68.
2   [1989] STC 705 at 769.
3   [1992] STC 226 at 246.
4   [1992] STC 226 at 233.

When expenditure is incurred

[9.06] Two rules apply as to when the expenditure is incurred. First, one looks to the date on which the obligation to pay becomes unconditional.¹ Where the purchaser acquires title before the obligation becomes unconditional the expenditure will be treated as incurred in the period in which title passed provided the obligation becomes unconditional not more than one month after the end of that period.²

The second rule looks to the date on which the expenditure became payable.³ This rule applies if the due date for payment is more than four months after the obligation to pay has become unconditional. The first rule is also excluded if it does not apply where the old rule deems an expenditure to be delayed, eg capital expenditure incurred before a trade is commenced is deemed incurred on the day of commencement.⁴

Special timing rules apply to VAT liabilities and rebates under the capital goods scheme.⁵

1   CAA 2001, s 5(1)–(3); see also Inland Revenue interpretation RI 54.
2   CAA 2001, s 5(4)(*c*)
3   CAA 2001, s 5(5).
4   CAA 2001, s 4.
5   CAA 2001, ss 235, 236, 238, 240, 346, 347, 348, 349, 350, 351 and 547–551. See also Sch 3, para 46(2).

[9.07] Capital allowances

Method of giving capital allowances

[9.07] Now that both income tax and corporation tax use a current year basis of assessment as opposed to the old preceding year basis, capital allowances are to be given effect in taxing the trade or property business,[1] or, where there is no trade or rent, by deduction.[2]

Where the allowance is to be given effect in taxing the trade it is to be treated as a trading expense for the period of account to which it relates; similarly a balancing charge is treated as a trading receipt.[3] So the correct profits figure will be profit less capital allowances and any excess allowances will automatically generate a trading loss. Claims for allowances are to be made in the tax return.[4] Any property business is taxed in the same way.[5]

The allowance is to be "treated as" a trading expense rather than being an expense. Hence a taxpayer is under no obligation to take allowances available but has a discretion whether or not to take them.[6] When a non-resident company is involved there are rules directing the separation of sources subject to income tax from those subject to corporation tax.[7]

Allowances are computed by reference to qualifying expenditure and disposals in each period of account.[8] Since allowances are given on an annual basis they will be increased or reduced if the chargeable period is greater or less than 12 months. For income tax the concept of the period of account has replaced the old concept of the basis period.[9] The old concept was needed because of the preceding year basis under which the profits of some periods were used twice as a basis of taxation and others not at all. Although the old system could tolerate revenue expenses and receipts being treated in this way it did not think it appropriate for capital allowances.

Today the chargeable period now means the accounting period of a company or the period of account of someone liable to income tax.[10] Where the allowance is made in taxing the trade, the period of account is usually any period for which accounts are made up for the purposes of the trade.[11]

Where, as in the opening two years, two periods of account overlap, the period common to both shall be deemed to fall in the first period of account only and if there is an interval between two periods of account, the interval shall be deemed to be part of the first period of account.[12] Conversely if there is a gap between periods of account (eg because accounts are not made up for that period) the gap is treated as belonging to the prior period.[13] In this way the allowance—or charge—is given once and only once. Any period of account greater than 18 months is subdivided; the first subdivision begins with the commencement date of the original period and later ones at 12-month intervals.[14]

It can happen that a particular capital expense falls within more than one category of allowance. In the absence of any express provision the taxpayer can choose the most favourable category.[15]

Simon's Taxes B3.102, 106.

---

[1] ie under CAA 2001, s 247.

² CAA 2001, s 262.
³ CAA 2001, s 247; for scientific research allowances see ss 2(1), 450; on widening the definition of trade to include toll road undertaking, see s 352(2).
⁴ CAA 2001, s 3(2), (3); For self-assessment under corporation tax see FA 1998, Sch 18, Part IV.
⁵ CAA 2001, ss 352(1), 353(2)–(4) (see supra, § **9.03**).
⁶ *Elliss v BP Oil Northern Ireland Refinery Ltd* [1987] STC 52, CA. (CAA 1968, s 73 contains the word "shall" but this was interpreted in a non-mandatory sense.) The decision was applied to loss reliefs in *Carr v Armpledge* [2000] STC 410, CA.
⁷ CAA 2001, s 566.
⁸ CAA 2001, s 6(2)–(5).
⁹ CAA 2001, s 6(2)–(5).
¹⁰ CAA 2001, s 6(1).
¹¹ CAA 2001, s 6(2).
¹² CAA 2001, s 6(4)–(6).
¹³ CAA 2001, s 6(4), (5).
¹⁴ CAA 2001, s 6(6).
¹⁵ CAA 2001, ss 7–10(2).

[9.08] A capital allowance differs from a deductible expense:

(1) it must be an item of capital expenditure as distinct from revenue;
(2) whereas a revenue expense is deductible unless statute otherwise directs, a capital allowance is only made if the statute permits;
(3) whereas an allowance may be claimed in respect of expenditure incurred before a trade commences, although only when the trading begins,[1] an expense so incurred is only deductible if incurred within seven years of the trade beginning;
(4) an expense incurred partly for trade and partly for other purposes is not deductible whereas such duality results in an apportionment of capital expenditure;[2]
(5) a revenue expense is deductible at once and in full whereas allowances are made only at specified rates and often over several years.

Simon's Taxes B3.106.

¹ CAA 2001, s 306(4).
² eg *G H Chambers (Northiam Farms) Ltd v Watmough* [1956] 3 All ER 485, 36 TC 711 where an extravagant choice of motor car for personal reasons led to a reduction in the allowance.

[9.09] The amount of a balancing charge or allowance clearly depends upon the amount received. The actual sale price will be taken unless either (a) the buyer is a body of persons[1] over whom the seller has control,[2] or vice versa or both buyer and seller are under the control of some other person, or (b) it appears that the sole or main benefit which might have been expected to accrue was the obtaining of an allowance or deduction in which case market value is substituted unless the parties elect—as permitted for (a) but not for (b)—to take the residue of the seller's expenditure.[3] The purpose behind (a) is to allow the transfer of the property between connected persons in such a way that no balancing adjustment need take place. This election is not available when capital allowances and charges cannot be made on both parties.[4] The election must now be made within two years of the sale.[5] This election is not open to a dual resident investment company.[6] Similar provisions apply for machinery and plant.[7] This election applies also to qualifying hotels, commercial buildings and structures within an enterprise zone and qualifying research expenditure.[8] Know-how has its own provision.[9]

Special rules apply when the sale involves an asset in respect of which allowances have been claimed and another asset. The net proceeds of sale are to be apportioned and the Commissioners are not bound by any apportionment made by the parties.[10]

The rules as to timing also include an anti-avoidance rule to deal with the situation in which the obligation to pay becomes unconditional on a date earlier than that which accords with normal commercial usage and the sole or main benefit to be derived is the obtaining of the allowance.[11]

Simon's Taxes B3.108.

---

[1] Defined in TA 1988, s 832(1).
[2] CAA 2001, s 574.
[3] CAA 2001, s 569(4) and TA 1988, s 839; CAA 2001, s 570(1).
[4] CAA 2001, s 570(2)–(4).
[5] CAA 2001, s 569(7).
[6] CAA 2001, s 570(2)–(4) (infra, § **33.25**).
[7] CAA 2001, s 213.
[8] CAA 2001, s 569.
[9] TA 1988, ss 531(7), 532(5)(b).
[10] CAA 2001, s 562, eg *Fitton v Gilders and Heaton* (1955) 36 TC 233; *A Wood & Co Ltd v Provan* (1968) 44 TC 701.
[11] CAA 2001, s 5(6).

Successions

[9.10] In general where a trader discontinues his trade, a balancing charge or allowance is made. Any capital allowances still unused cannot be carried forward if one trade ends and another one begins.[1] If the trade is transferred to someone else, the new trader may be able to claim allowances in respect of his own capital expenditure including that in respect of items bought from his predecessor; that expenditure may give rise to balancing charges or allowances to the vendor. The transfer of a UK trade by one company to another, where one is resident in one member state and the other in another, does not give rise to any allowance or charge if the parties elect.[2]

As part of the phasing out of industrial buildings allowance and agricultural buildings allowance, a successor post-20 March 2007 is not eligible for industrial buildings allowance or an agricultural buildings allowance,[3] unless the contract under which he succeeds to ownership of the asset was made before 21 March 2007[4] or the allowance is for expenditure in a qualifying enterprise zone.[5]

Simon's Taxes B3.109, 110.

1 See supra, § **8.56**; infra, § **25.05**.
2 CAA 2001, s 561.
3 CAA 2001, s 311 amended by FA 2007, s 36(2).
4 FA 2007, s 36(7).
5 CAA 2001, s 311(2) amended by FA 2007, s 36(3).

Industrial buildings

[9.11] Industrial allowances are available when a person incurs capital expenditure on the construction of an industrial building or structure which is to be occupied for the purposes of a trade.[1] When the building is to be occupied by a lessee or licensee[2] it is the occupier's trade that is relevant.[3] The conditions for the much more important writing down allowance require that the person be entitled to an interest in the building or structure, that that interest be a "relevant" interest and that the building should be an industrial building at the end of the relevant period.[4] Since the allowances are confined to the expenses of construction, the cost of the land is excluded.[5] Provision is made for any additional VAT falling due under the capital goods scheme to be treated as capital expenditure.[6] The costs of certain preliminary works such as cutting, levelling and tunnelling may be claimed if, but only if, they are to prepare the land for the installation of machinery or plant.[7]

Industrial allowances are in the process of being phased out with effect 1 April 2011 (6 April 2011, income tax). For details of the transitional measures see infra § **9.21**.

Simon's Taxes B3.222, 227.

1 CAA 2001, s 271.
2 See also infra, § **9.14**.
3 CAA 2001, s 305(1), (2), Sch 3, para 64 and see statement of practice SP 4/80 (separate lettings of workshops for small businesses).
4 CAA 2001, ss 309–313.
5 CAA 2001, s 272(1).
6 CAA 2001, s 346(1)–(3), (5), Sch 3, paras 75, 76, 347(1)–(3), 311(1)–(3), 349(1), (2).
7 CAA 2001, s 273(1); "cutting" received a narrow construction in *McIntosh v Manchester Corpn* [1952] 2 All ER 444, 33 TC 428.

[9.12] The allowance may only be claimed if the building is an industrial building or structure, which is elaborately defined. The general effect of the definition is to confine allowances to productive, as opposed to distributive industries. A building in use for the purposes of a trade carried on in a mill, factory or other similar premises is an industrial building as is a building for the purposes of a trade which consists in the taking and catching of fish or shellfish.[1] A building is a factory only if something is made there; so a repair

[9.12] Capital allowances

depot normally cannot qualify.[2] However, a building used for the maintenance or repair of goods will qualify if the goods or materials are employed in a trade or undertaking which itself qualifies.[3] Other trades specified are the ploughing or cultivating of land (unless the trader occupies the land in which case he qualifies for agricultural allowances), the working of mineral deposits or a foreign plantation, transport, dock, inland navigation, water, electricity or hydraulic power undertaking, a tunnel, any road, a highway concession or bridge undertaking, the manufacturing or processing of goods or materials, or subjecting goods or materials to any process,[4] the storage[5] of goods which are to be so used or the end product while it awaits delivery to a customer and the storage of goods on arrival by any means of transport in any part of this country from outside.[6] Stockists can claim allowances, provided they carry on the trade of storing goods.[7] The test is whether the building is used for the purposes of a trade which consists in the storage of the qualifying goods and not whether the building is used for the storage of such goods. An allowance can therefore be claimed for a building even though it is in part used for the storage of other goods.[8] An allowance is not available if the storage is merely ancillary to a retail shop.[9] Whether the storage area is a warehouse in its own right or merely ancillary to a shop, must be decided by consideration of the nature of the activities that take place in the building and to the degree to which they are separate to the activities in the shop.[10]

In *Bestway (Holdings) Ltd v Luff*[11] a building was used for the storage of goods during a process of manufacturing. The business of the company consisted of a single trade, of which storage was merely an aspect. The claim for industrial buildings allowance was denied. The case of *Crusabridge Investments Ltd v Casings International*[12] was distinguished as the collection and storage of tyres was an essential part of the business in that case.

Similarly, in *Maco Door and Window Hardware (UK) Ltd v Revenue and Customs Comrs*[13], where the Special Commissioner decided that the taxpayer was entitled to industrial buildings allowance because the building was used for storage, the storage was a part of the taxpayer's trade and the products stored in the warehouse were goods or materials "to be used in the manufacture of other goods or materials". That decision was later reversed on appeal in the High Court[14] by Patten J, where he held that storage was not "a part" of the trade in the required sense because it merely supported the taxpayer's trade and was not "a trading or commercial activity in itself". The Court of Appeal overturned the decision by Patten J restoring the favourable decision of the Special Commissioner emphasising the danger of overcomplicating a simple statutory test and the need to give words in the statute their ordinary meaning. However, by a 3-2 majority, the House of Lords upheld HMRC's appeal, restoring the decision by Patten J. Although the case was therefore decided against the taxpayer company, taxpayers can take one crumb of hope from the case. Lord Walker, who gave the leading speech for the majority, emphasised that the use of a different corporate structure would have overcome the problem ultimately faced by Maco. His Lordship explicitly reinforced the view that the use of different corporate entities can validly change the tax consequences of transactions "even if the economic results are the same from the consumer's point of view". It is the authors' view that this

Industrial buildings [9.12]

dictum should kill off arguments by HMRC that the structuring of arrangements using subsidiaries is necessarily tax avoidance.[15]

In *Buckingham v Securitas Properties Ltd*[16] a security firm constructed a special area in which bulk coins and notes were broken down into individual wage packets. The court held that the notes and coins were not "goods"; if they had been goods the court would have held that they were not being subjected to any process.

It is not necessary that the building be constructed in this country, indeed foreign plantations are expressly mentioned and defined. However the profits or gains of the foreign trade must be assessable in accordance with the rules for UK trades.[17]

This definition specifically excludes any building used as, or as part of, a dwellinghouse, retail shop, showroom, hotel or office and of any building ancillary to the purposes of those excluded;[18] ancillary means subservient or subordinate.[19] In determining what is an office the courts have not been blinded by terminology. Thus a drawing office is no more an office than a machine shop is a shop;[20] likewise a document processing centre may not be an office.[21] It should be noted, however, that where an office is built in a designated enterprise zone it will qualify for special 100% initial allowances together with 25% writing down allowances as appropriate.[22] This allowance is extended to the provision of sports pavilions,[23] whether or not the trade falls within the qualifying list. Expenditure on safety at sports grounds may qualify for a more generous machinery and plant allowance.[24]

Simon's Taxes B3.203–213.

---

1 CAA 2001, s 271(1); see also ss 274(1), Tables A and B and 284.
2 *Vibroplant Ltd v Holland* [1982] STC 164.
3 CAA 2001, s 274(1). This would not have helped in the *Vibroplant* case (see note 2 above) as the trade of plant hire would not qualify under CAA 2001, s 271(1), Table A.
4 For a macabre case see *Bourne v Norwich Crematorium Ltd* [1967] 2 All ER 576, 44 TC 164; this expenditure would seem now to qualify as plant (*IRC v Barclay, Curle & Co Ltd*, infra § **9.29**). For an unsuccessful attempt to argue that a banking operation is a process for this purpose, see *Girobank plc v Clarke* [1998] STC 182, CA. An argument that a freezer room connected with a cash and carry supermarket was a building used for a process was equally unsuccessful in *Bestway (Holdings) Ltd v Luff* [1998] STC 357.
5 See *Dale v Johnson Bros* (1951) 32 TC 487 and *HMRC v Maco Door and Window Hardware (UK) Ltd* [2006] SWTI 1919.
6 This received a narrow construction in *Copol Clothing Co Ltd v Hindmarch* [1984] STC 33, [1984] 1 WLR 411, CA, the expression being confined to buildings in the vicinity of an airport or seaport, and in *Carr v Sayer* [1992] STC 396, where the provision was confined to facilities needed in the ordinary process of physically transporting goods and so not extending to quarantine kennels.
7 This will be the case even where the stockist does not subject the materials to the industrial process himself see *Crusabridge Investments Ltd v Casings International Ltd* (1979) 54 TC 246 (a case concerning an action for breach of a covenant in a lease in which the term industrial building was held to cover a

671

warehouse used for the storage of tyres before they were sold for remoulding) and the Inland Revenue press release, 26 March 1982, *Simon's Tax Intelligence* 1982, p 145.

[8] *Saxone Lilley and Skinner (Holdings) Ltd v IRC* [1967] 1 All ER 756, 44 TC 122.
[9] CAA 2001, s 277(1), (5). *Bestway (Holdings) Ltd v Luff* [1998] STC 357.
[10] *Sarsfield v Dixons Group plc* [1998] STC 938.
[11] [1998] STC 357.
[12] (1978) 54 TC 246.
[13] [2008] UKHL 54.
[14] [2006] BTC 829
[15] Neutral citation [2008] UKHL 54, judgment delivered on 30 July 2008.
[16] [1980] STC 166.
[17] CAA 2001, s 282.
[18] CAA 2001, s 277(1), (5).
[19] *Sarsfield v Dixons Group plc* [1998] STC 938.
[20] *IRC v Lambhill Ironworks Ltd* (1950) 31 TC 393 (where the office qualified because of its essentially industrial character).
[21] *Girobank plc v Clarke* [1998] STC 182, CA.
[22] CAA 2001, s 271: on the position of purchaser of unused buildings see extra-statutory concession, published 16 December 1991; but for events on or after 16 December 1991, see F(No 2)A 1992, Sch 13 (see infra, § **9.15**). F(No 2)A 1992, Sch 13 has been substantially amended by CAA 2001, ss 294–296, 298, 299, 302 and 307. Specifically on the issue of unused buildings, see s 294.
[23] CAA 2001, ss 271(1), 280 and see **Simon's Taxes B32.310**.
[24] CAA 2001, ss 30–32.

[9.13] If only a part of a building qualifies for an allowance an apportionment is made save where the cost of the non-qualifying part does not exceed 25%[1] of the total cost, in which case the whole cost is allowed.[2] This raises the difficult problem of defining the building. If a building includes an office the cost of which is less than 25% an allowance is made in respect of the whole cost. If, however, the office is a separate building, no allowance can be made even though its cost is 25% or less of the total cost of the buildings. Separate blocks, which are not physically integrated, do not form one building.[3]

30% of the area of a factory building is used as a showroom, and the capital expenditure on the showroom area is 20% of the total. The expenditure was incurred in January 1985.

The expenditure on the showroom is less than 25% of the total cost, so no apportionment is necessary.

Simon's Taxes B3.210.

[1] Now CAA 2001, s 283(2)—currently 25%.
[2] CAA 2001, s 283(1), (2), Sch 3, para 59.
[3] *Abbott Laboratories Ltd v Carmody* [1968] 2 All ER 879, 44 TC 569.

The relevant interest—who can claim the allowances?

[9.14] An initial allowance can be claimed by the person who incurs the cost of the building. Writing down and balancing allowances may be claimed by the person with the relevant interest.[1]

The "relevant interest" means the interest in that building to which the person who incurred the expenditure was entitled when he incurred it.[2] So if a lessee spends money improving property he can claim the allowance—but his landlord cannot. From 21 March 2007 onwards, if the relevant interest is transferred, the transferee cannot take over the claim to allowances.[3]

If the owner of the freehold incurs the expense and later leases the building to someone else he will be able to set the allowances against his rental income.[4] It is, however, essential that the lessee use the building for qualifying purposes.[5]

This rigid insistence on the relevant interest could cause injustice if, for example, a pension fund (which paid no tax and therefore to which the allowance was useless) wanted to finance the construction of a building which would then be used by a tenant under a long lease. So, where a long lease is granted and both lessor and lessee so elect, the lessee is to be able to claim the allowances even though the expenditure was incurred by the lessor. The mechanism for this change is that the newly created lease is designated the relevant interest in place of the reversionary interest.[6] The same applies where a long sub-lease is created out of a lease. Any capital sum paid by the lessee (or sub-lessee) becomes the sum in respect of which the allowance can be claimed. It follows that the grant of such a lease may cause a balancing allowance or charge to accrue to the lessor. A long lease is defined as one exceeding 50 years; the rules in TA 1988, s 34 (see infra, § **10.19**) apply.[7]

This rule does not apply where lessor and lessee are connected persons[8], The rule is also excluded if it appears that the sole or main benefit which might be expected to accrue is the obtaining of a balancing allowance.[9] It appears that the sole object of obtaining a balancing charge, perhaps to soak up other reliefs, does not prevent the rule from operating.

If the building has not been used before the lease is granted, the lessee may claim not only the writing down allowance but also the initial allowance. This is of particular importance where the lessor is an exempt person such as a local authority, or charity since it is only the lessee who will have taxable income against which to set the allowance.

If the relevant interest is a lease, the holder of that interest is entitled to the allowances even after his lease has ended if he holds over with the consent of his landlord[10] or takes a new lease in pursuance of an option in the first lease.[11]

Where the lease is surrendered and so becomes merged in another interest that other interest becomes the relevant interest so that the right to the allowance is not lost;[12] likewise if the lessee acquires the reversionary interest.

If the relevant interest is a lease and the lease ends but the landlord pays the lessee a sum, eg for improvements carried out by the lessee, matters are treated as if the lease had been surrendered.[13] So also if the landlord grants a new lease to a different person and the new lessee pays a sum to the first lessee then the

673

leases are treated as one and the same so that the new lessee has the "relevant interest".[14] This scheme makes no allowance for the situation in which the new lease is granted to the original lessee otherwise than under a right in the original lease. In this situation a balancing allowance or charge is made.

Injustice also occurred where industrial property was not let but instead occupied by someone for the purposes of his trade under a licence as he has no property interest and so no industrial buildings allowances could be claimed. A licence is particularly useful to those starting-up small workshops and businesses as the obligations of a licensee are normally less than those of a lessee, an important consideration where there are cash problems, so the legislation has been extended and where an owner or a lessee grants a licence his interest will be treated as if it is subject to a lease thus allowing him to claim the allowances.[15] Claims for allowances can also be made where the premises are occupied by more than one licensee so long as all the licensees are carrying on industrial businesses such as to make the building an industrial building.[16]

A person entitled to a highway concession in respect of a toll road is treated as having an interest in the road and that interest can be a relevant interest.[17]

Simon's Taxes B3.225.

---

[1] CAA 2001, s 271(3). On the situation where the expense is shared, see CAA 2001, s 537.
[2] CAA 2001, s 286.
[3] FA 2007, s 36.
[4] CAA 2001, ss 258, 352, 353 and ss 259, 260.
[5] CAA 2001, ss 271, 286.
[6] CAA 2001, ss 290, 291. Claims must be made within two years of the date the lease takes effect, s 291(4).
[7] CAA 2001, s 291(3)—looks to TA 1988, s 38(1)–(4), (6) without regard to CAA 2001, s 359(3).
[8] CAA 2001 s 291(1).
[9] See *Barclays Mercantile Industrial Finance Ltd v Melluish* [1990] STC 314.
[10] CAA 2001, s 359(1), (2).
[11] CAA 2001, s 359(1), (3).
[12] CAA 2001, ss 288(1), 289.
[13] CAA 2001, s 359(1), (4).
[14] CAA 2001, s 359(1), (5).
[15] CAA 2001, s 305(1), (2), Sch 3, para 64.
[16] CAA 2001, s 278, Sch 3, para 57.
[17] CAA 2001, s 342(1). On definitions see s 274(1), Table B, item 6.

Initial allowance

[9.15] An initial allowance of 100% was available for the cost of purchase or construction of a commercial building in an enterprise zone.[1] Enterprise zones were declared for 10 year periods, all of which have now expired.

Simon's Taxes B3.108, 223, 238, 261–265.

[1] For a discussion of initial allowances in enterprise zones, see Tiley & Collison: UK Tax Guide 2001–02 edition § **9.15**. The method of calculating the amount of expenditure was considered in *Enterprise Zone Syndicate v Inspector of Taxes* [1996] STC (SCD) 336.

Writing down allowance

[9.16] Writing down allowances are made to the person entitled to the relevant interest provided that the building is used as "an industrial building" at the end of the chargeable period.[1] The allowance is 4% of the cost for a full year but this is to be reduced or increased if the chargeable period is less or more than 12 months.[2] These may be made during periods of temporary disuse.[3]

Simon's Taxes B3.234, 236.

[1] CAA 2001, s 271(1), (3).
[2] CAA 2001, s 310(1), (2), Sch 3, para 66.
[3] CAA 2001, s 285(1), (2).

Balancing allowance and charge

[9.17] Prior to 21 March 2007, a balancing allowance or charge arose if within 25[1] years of the building being first used, the relevant interest is sold or the building is demolished or destroyed or altogether ceases to be used. No such allowance or charge arises in respect of any event on or after 21 March 2007, unless it occurs before 1 April 2011 in pursuance of a contract made before 31 March 2007.[2]

Simon's Taxes B3.237–239.

[1] CAA 2001, ss 314–326. Repealed with effect from 21 March 2007, by FA 2007, s 36(1).
[2] Repealed with effect from 21 March 2007 by FA 2007, s 36(1) and (7).

Transitional measures before 2011

Writing down allowances

[9.18] During the period from 1 (or 6) April 2008 until 31 March (or 5 April 2011), industrial buildings allowances are being phased out. In a nutshell, writing down allowances are being reduced by 25% for the financial year 2008 (or, for income tax, the 2008–09 tax year) by 50% for the following year and by 75% in the third year of the transitional phase.[1]

In many cases, this will amount to writing down allowances of 3% in 2008–09, 2% in 2009–10 and 1% in 2010–11. (For any pre-5 November

[9.18] Capital allowances

1962 expenditure, the rates will be 1 1/2%, 1% and 1/2% respectively.) However, for taxpayers that have acquired second hand buildings, their percentage rate for writing down allowances will not usually be 4% per annum but a fraction relating to the residue at the purchase date and the remaining period of the writing down period. Thus in these cases, it is important to consider the allowance that would have been available and then to reduce it by the appropriate percentage.

For taxpayers whose chargeable periods straddle the dates of 1 April (or 6 April), the percentage reduction must be adjusted proportionately – by reference to the number of days before and those on or after the relevant date.[2]

Thus, a taxpayer otherwise entitled to a writing down allowance of £10,000 in respect of the chargeable period for the year to 30 September 2008 will actually be entitled to an allowance of:

(a) for income tax purposes: £10,000 × (188 × 100% + 178 × 75%)/366 = £8,784
(b) for corporation tax purposes: £10,000 × (183 × 100% + 183 × 75%)/366 = £8,750.

This rule does not apply for enterprise zone expenditure.[3]

Simon's Taxes B3.234, 236.

---

[1] FA 2008, s 82(3).
[2] FA 2008, s 82(4).
[3] FA 2008, s 82(2).

Writing down allowances for enterprise zone expenditure

[9.19] A special rule has been enacted for enterprise zone expenditure.

In such cases, the restriction on writing down allowances applies only in respect of chargeable periods which end on or after 1 April 2011 (or, for income tax purposes, 6 April 2011).

Where a writing down allowance would be given for such a chargeable period, the amount given is restricted by reference to the proportion of days in that chargeable period that fall before the relevant date.[1]

---

[1] FA 2008, s 83.

Anti-avoidance measure connected with transitional rules

[9.20] Given that the writing down allowances are reduced by reference to the dates of a taxpayer's chargeable period, it would be possible for the impact of the reduction to be mitigated by taxpayers transferring industrial buildings to related parties whose accounting period ends earlier than the transferor. This measure is blocked with effect from 12 March 2008 if:

(a) there is a sale of the relevant interest;
(b) the buyer and seller have different chargeable periods;

(c) the parties satisfy the control test in CAA 2001, s 567 (broadly, the parties are connected or under common control);
(d) a tax advantage was the or one of the main purposes of the sale.

In such cases, the buyer's writing down allowances are reduced to reflect only the percentage of the chargeable period for which it is entitled to the relevant interest.[1]

[1] CAA 2001, s 313A.

Hotel buildings and extensions

[9.21] Hotels do not qualify for industrial buildings allowances, as such, since a hotel does not come within the list of trades permitted.[1] However, a capital allowance is given on the cost of a hotel building in a similar way as for an industrial building. There is an annual writing down allowance of 4% on a straight line basis.[2] Subsequent holders of the relevant interest may write off the residue of the expenditure over the balance of the 25 year period.[3] The temporary 20% initial allowance applied as it did to industrial buildings[4] for expenditure incurred or treated as incurred between 1 November 1992 and 31 October 1993.

Where a person buys a qualifying hotel unused, he is treated as having incurred expenditure on its construction when the purchase price becomes payable.[5]

The hotel must be a "qualifying hotel", a concept which is elaborately defined;[6] The hotel may be outside the UK but the trade must be taxed under as a UK trade. The costs of dwelling accommodation for the owner are not allowable but such costs would be allowable if the trade were incorporated and the accommodation were for a director or employee.

Capital allowances for fire safety and thermal insulation fall under the rules for machinery and plant (see infra, § **9.23**, note 1).

Simon's Taxes B3.251–254.

[1] See supra, § **9.12**.
[2] CAA 2001, s 310(1); there was previously a 20% initial allowance but this was repealed by FA 1985, s 66 as from 1 April 1986.
[3] CAA 2001, s 311(1)–(3).
[4] CAA 2001, s 310(1).
[5] CAA 2001, s 296.
[6] CAA 2001, s 279(1), (9); on need to offer breakfast and dinner see statement of practice SP 9/87.

Dwelling-houses let on assured tenancies

[9.22] Allowances may be given for the cost incurred before 1 April 1992 in the construction of[1] "qualifying dwelling-houses" which broadly speaking

[9.22] Capital allowances

must be let on assured tenancies within the meaning of the Housing Act 1980, s 56 or its successor in Part I of the Housing Act 1988.[2] Although it is not necessary for the landlord to be a company for the purposes of the assured tenancy scheme, from (in general) 5 May 1983, the landlord must be a company if capital allowances are claimed under these provisions.[3] Expenditure will qualify for this allowance if the company was committed to it before 15 March 1988 and the purpose was to provide dwellings let on the terms of the 1980 Act.[4]

Where a dwelling-house has qualified it remains a qualifying dwelling-house even if the landlord is no longer an approved body so long as it is subject to a regulated tenancy or a housing association tenancy.[5] A dwelling-house will not qualify if the landlord and tenant are connected persons, if the tenant is a director of a company which is, or is connected with, the landlord, if the landlord is a close company and the tenant is a participator or associate of a participator, or if there is an arrangement between landlords or owners whereby one landlord grants a tenancy which would prevent the dwelling-house qualifying if it was granted by the other.[6] It is not possible for a co-operative housing association[7], or a self-build society within the Housing Associations Act 1985 to qualify.[8] The allowance is available on the first £40,000 (£60,000 in Greater London) of such expenditure only.[9] Where a building contains one or more qualifying dwelling-houses the cost must be apportioned to each unit and the cost of the communal parts can be apportioned but this can not exceed one tenth of the apportioned cost of the dwelling-house.[10]

A writing down allowance of 4% per annum is given[11] and balancing allowances and charges apply as appropriate.[12] Where the chargeable period is greater or less than 12 months the 4% is increased or reduced proportionately.[13] Expenditure for which capital allowances have been given under these provisions is not deductible when computing any allowable loss for CGT purposes on the disposal of the building.[14]

Simon's Taxes B3.902, 903, 906, 908.

---

[1] CAA 2001, ss 490, 491. These allowances now come within the definition of "Capital Allowances Acts" in TA 1988, s 832(1) and so can give rise to a claim for group relief: FA 1990, Sch 13, para 7. There was an *initial* allowance but, like the initial allowance for industrial buildings, this allowance was phased out by 1986.
[2] CAA 2001, s 504.
[3] CAA 2001, s 504.
[4] CAA 2001, s 490(3). This was needed because the Housing Act 1988 introduced a new "assured shorthold tenancy" which was to be outside the scope of this allowance—s 95(4). The Housing Act 1988 received the Royal Assent on 15 November 1988.
[5] CAA 2001, ss 490(2), (4), 491(1)–(3).
[6] CAA 2001, ss 491(2), (3), 504(1), 505(1).
[7] See TA 1988, s 488.
[8] CAA 2001, s 505(1).
[9] CAA 2001, s 511.
[10] CAA 2001, s 511(2).

[11] CAA 2001, s 508(1).
[12] CAA 2001, ss 501–522.
[13] CAA 2001, s 508(1), (2).
[14] TCGA 1992, s 41(4).

Plant and machinery

[9.23] The present scheme of capital allowances applies to expenditure incurred after 26 October 1970 but it has been much amended.[1] Today expenditure generally qualifies for an annual writing down allowance.[2] First year allowances have been intermittently available but since April 2008, such allowances were to be restricted to expenditure on certain environment-friendly assets (see infra, § **9.32**ff). Replacing the more complex regime of first year allowances for small and medium-sized enterprises (which were introduced in 1997) is a new system giving businesses an annual investment allowance. Nevertheless, first-year allowances were temporarily reintroduced with effect from April 2009 by FA 2009 in order to stimulate growth in the economy (see infra, § **9.32**).

Expenditure on a part of machinery or plant[3] or on a share in such assets[4] qualifies for an allowance.

The allowances apply to commercial trades, professions, vocations, employments and offices and to estate management under a UK property business, furnished holiday lettings.[5] The expenditure must be on machinery and plant wholly and exclusively for the purposes of the trade.[6] This brings in the rules discussed in connection with trading expenditure (see supra, § **8.96**) with regard to the nature of purpose (on which see *Mallalieu v Drummond*)[7] but there is a system of apportionment where expenditure is incurred for dual purposes.[8]

Where the allowance is claimed against employment income it must also be shown that the machinery and plant was *necessarily* provided for use in the performance of the duties of the office or employment.[9] The term "necessarily" is interpreted as under ITEPA 2003, ss 328 et seq so that a finding that another holder of the office could have performed his duties without incurring this expense is fatal to the claim for the allowance.[10] Special rules apply to restrict first year allowances where the machinery or plant continues to be used for the purposes of a trade carried on by the seller or it appears that the sole or main benefit which might otherwise have been expected to accrue to the parties was the obtaining of the allowance or when there is a sale between connected persons. The first year allowance is withdrawn and a writing down allowance is given to the purchaser by reference to the disposal value brought into account by the vendor.[11] This applies also to agreements for sale, sale and leaseback etc[12]

The amount of expenditure for which the taxpayer is entitled to claim is not usually a problem where the asset is bought. If the person brings machinery or plant into use in the trade and he had originally bought the asset for other purposes or if the asset is acquired by way of gift, it used to be the market value

[9.23] Capital allowances

of the asset when it was brought into the use of the trade which was taken as the amount of expenditure incurred.[13] However, where the relevant event occurs on or after 21 March 2000, the allowance will be based on the lower of that market value and the (unindexed) original cost.[14] So, if a world class violinist buys a Stradivarius for his collection and later decides to use it for public performance the allowance will be given by reference to original cost; of course the term cost has to be taken in its statutory context so that if the violinist inherited the violin, the market value at the time of the inheritance would be used rather than the cost. If the event occurred between 1 November 1992 and 31 October 1993 inclusive, the 40% temporary first year allowance was potentially available. However, if the asset is brought into the trade after 13 April 1993 having been used for a non-qualifying purpose, the matter is treated as an acquisition from a connected person so that first year allowances will not generally be due.[15]

Where the allowance is given for a trade the expression trade extends to a UK property business, furnished holiday lettings and certain leasing activities.[16] These rules are not usually expressly confined to entities resident in the UK but the precise treatment of a non-resident carrying on taxable activities in the UK through a branch or agency has been clarified by FA 2000 with effect from 21 March 2000.[17] Entitlement to the allowance depends on liability to UK tax. So where only a part of the trade is subject to UK tax only an equivalent part of the allowance may be claimed; to achieve this the UK part of the trade is treated as a separate trade. Consequential rules have to apply if there are any changes in the amount of UK trade, so that the portion of the trade attributable to the UK part declines.[18]

Simon's Taxes Division B3.3.

---

[1] Equivalent relief is given for expenditure on thermal insulation CAA 2001, s 28, safety at sports grounds CAA 2001, ss 30, 31 and on personal security measures CAA 2001, s 33. See also extra-statutory concession B16 concerning expenditure on fire safety in Northern Ireland and by lessors. However, while these attract capital allowances they do not give rise to balancing charges.

[2] CAA 2001, s 11(4).

[3] CAA 2001, s 571(1).

[4] CAA 2001, s 270(1), (2).

[5] TA 1988, s 32, CAA 2001, s 15(1).

[6] CAA 2001, ss 15(1)(a), 19.

[7] [1983] STC 665, HL.

[8] CAA 2001, s 205, infra, § 9.32, note 1.

[9] On Case III see ITEPA 2003, ss 328–330, 335, 353 and 354.

[10] *White v Higginbottom* [1983] STC 143.

[11] CAA 2001, ss 213–218; to cover not only the situation in which the machinery or plant continues to be used in the seller's trade but also that when it is used in the trade of a person connected with the seller without having been used in any other trade in the interim (except the trade of leasing). On ss 213–218 see *Barclays Mercantile Industrial Finance Ltd v Melluish* [1990] STC 314.

[12] CAA 2001, s 213(1), (2) and ss 214–218.

[13] CAA 2001, s 13; the gift is treated as a purchase from the donor for this amount for the purposes of s 75.

[14] CAA 2001, s 13(4), (5).
[15] CAA 2001, ss 13(2), (3), (7), 14(2), (3), (5), 46(2); the first year allowance will be available only if s 22(3B) applies.
[16] CAA 2001, s 15 and ss 502, 503.
[17] CAA 2001, s 105; naturally s 83(2A) does not apply to those parts of the CAA which already refer to activities outside the UK – ie Chapter V(39–50), s 64A, 75–78.
[18] CAA 2001, s 208.

Limitation on backdating of claims

[9.24] A 1994 provision was intended to limit the extent to which a taxpayer could backdate claims for allowances on the basis of challenges to the accepted scope of machinery and plant allowances.[1] The rule required that notice of the expenditure was given to the inspector, in such form as the Board might require, not later than three years after the end of that period.[2] The notification requirement was repealed by FA 2000 for chargeable periods for which the three-year period ended on or after 1 April 2000, ie chargeable periods ending on or after 1 April 1998 for corporation tax and 6 April 1998 for income tax.[3] Normally the claim is affected by inclusion of plant and machinery additions in the calculation of taxable trading profit reported in a self-assessment tax return.[4]

Simon's Taxes B3.106.

[1] CAA 2001, s 58(4).
[2] CAA 2001, s 58(4).
[3] FA 2000, s 73.
[4] Inland Revenue Statement of Practice SP 6/94, para 6, and Revenue Interpretation RI 1832.

[9.25] The asset must belong to the person in consequence of the payment.[1] This requirement has caused many problems and legislation has been needed to undo the effects of this rule on the areas of fixtures, computer programmes, production sharing contracts[2] and hire purchase.

The word "belong" is interpreted strictly by reference to property law concepts. So in *Stokes v Costain Property Investments Ltd*[3] where plant (lifts) was installed by a tenant and immediately became the property of the landlord under general land law principles, the tenant was not entitled to the allowances as the lift did not belong to the tenant. This case is no authority on fixtures which remain the property of the tenant. It has now been held in *Melluish v BMI (No 3) Ltd* that where the asset becomes a fixture it cannot still belong to the person installing it. The concept of a fixture which remains personal property is a contradiction in terms and an impossibility in law.[4] It follows that a contractual right to remove the fixture cannot prevent it becoming part of the land and so ceasing to belong to the installer.

In *Melluish v BMI (No 3) Ltd*,[5] the House of Lords considered a claim for capital allowances in respect of central heating, boilers, lifts and similar equipment leased by the taxpayer company to local authorities. This equipment was incorporated into the structure of buildings owned by the lessees of the plant. In consequence, the equipment became fixtures. Under general law, chattels fixed to land become the property of the owner of the land. The House of Lords held that the correct interpretation of the transaction was that the plant became fixtures before the lease was entered into and hence, at no time during the leasing of that plant can the plant be said to have "belonged to" the taxpayer claimant. Hence, capital allowances were denied. In so far as *Melluish* decided that lessors could obtain allowances where plant was leased to non-taxpayers such as charities or local authorities the decision was reversed by FA 1997—save where the lessor had an interest in the land.[6]

The words "in consequence of" were held to be satisfied where a payment was made by the taxpayer to induce the holder of an option to reacquire the property to release that option.[7]

The situation resulting from *Stokes v Costain Property Investments Ltd* was seen to be unjust and a new scheme applies for expenditure incurred after 11 July 1984. The fixture is now treated as belonging to the lessee (or similar person) who incurred the expenditure in providing the machinery or plant for the purposes of a trade carried on by him (or for leasing otherwise than in the course of a trade) if the machinery or plant becomes in law a part of this land and at that time he has an interest in the relevant land.[8] The rules also cover the case where the plant becomes a fixture before the capital expenditure is incurred. The lessee's allowance excludes the lessor's but a lessor who contributes to the expenditure is not excluded.[9] There are special provisions to deal with disputes as to whether the item is a fixture,[10] for expenditure (and disposals) by equipment lessors[11] and for the transfer of the right to an allowance to a lessee.[12] The definition for qualifying expenditure by an equipment lessor is widened by FA 2000 to cover leased assets under the Affordable Warmth programme.[13] There are also rules applying where an interest in the land is sold and the price is referable to the fixture[14] and when the fixture ceases to belong to a particular person.[15] These rules are to be taken at face value. The allowances are not confined to cases where the user is liable to tax.[16] The definition of fixture has been amended by FA 2000 so as to include boilers and radiators even though these are (relatively) easy to remove; as this was always thought to be the law the change has retroactive effect.[17]

As a result of the 1997 changes the rules limit the amount qualifying for allowances to the original cost of the fixtures and prevent multiple claims.[18] There are also rules to prevent the acceleration of allowances.[19] On a more helpful note the 1997 legislation allows vendor and purchaser of the property to allocate a part of the purchase price to fixtures.[20]

Simon's Taxes B3.106.

---

[1] See also infra, § **9.45**.
[2] CAA 2001, ss 167–170.
[3] [1984] STC 204, [1984] 1 All ER 849, CA; contrast the "relevant interest" rules for industrial buildings (see supra, § **9.14**). See also *Melluish v BMI (No 3) Ltd* [1994] STC 315.
[4] [1994] STC 802, CA.

[5] [1995] STC 964.
[6] CAA 2001, s 177(1)–(3) and s 179(1), (2).
[7] *Bolton v International Drilling Ltd* [1983] STC 70.
[8] CAA 2001, ss 173–175.
[9] CAA 2001, ss 172(5), 537.
[10] CAA 2001, s 175(2). On disposal value see CAA 2001, s 196.
[11] CAA 2001, ss 172–177.
[12] CAA 2001, ss 183–186.
[13] CAA 2001, ss 177(1), (2), (5), 180(1), (2),(3), 203(1)–(4).
[14] CAA 2001, ss 181, 182.
[15] CAA 2001, ss 188, 190–192.
[16] *Melluish v BMI (No 3) Ltd* [1994] STC 802, CA.
[17] FA 2000, s 38 consolidated as CAA 2001, ss 172(1) and 173(1).
[18] CAA 2001, ss 181–186.
[19] CAA 2001, s 197.
[20] CAA 2001, s 198; on which see Inland Revenue interpretation RI 184.

What is plant or machinery?

[9.26] Neither plant nor machinery is defined in the Act, and the question whether an item is machinery or plant depends on the facts of the case. It is clear that an expenditure may qualify for both the plant and machinery and industrial building allowances[1] but in such an event it is likely that only the former will be claimed.[2] Parliament has attempted to provide some clarification on the boundary between plant and its setting but with what success remains to be seen (see infra, § **9.28**).

Different definitions have been suggested for specific instances. In *Yarmouth v France*[3] a claim was brought by a workman under the Employers' Liability Act 1880 for damages for injuries sustained due to a defect in his employer's plant, in that case a vicious horse. Lindley LJ said:[4]

> in its ordinary sense (plant) includes whatever apparatus is used by a business man for carrying on his business—not his stock-in-trade, which he buys or makes for sale; but all goods and chattels, fixed or movable, live or dead, which he keeps for permanent employment in his business.

This test has been found helpful but not exclusive[5] in capital allowance cases.

This test is viewed by the Revenue as covering fixtures and fittings of a durable nature. So railway locomotives and carriages[6] and tramway rails[7] have been held to be plant as have knives and lasts used in the manufacture of shoes,[8] but not the bed of a harbour[9] nor stallions for stud purposes,[10] nor an underground electrical substation[11] nor a car wash.[12]

It is now clear that machinery and plant is not confined to things used physically[13] but extends to the intellectual storehouse of the trade or profession eg the purchase of law books by a barrister.[14] Whether plant can include things lacking physical manifestation (eg computer software) is still unclear although special legislation now applies to computer software.[15] This leads to a substantial and regrettable lack of clarity with regard to expenditure on

683

[9.26] Capital allowances

many types of intellectual property. The Revenue view is that a thing must have physical manifestation to qualify as plant. It is not, however, necessary that the object be active, although a passive object may be less obviously plant.[16]

On the boundary between plant and structure see infra, § **9.28**.

Capital allowances cannot be claimed when another person has previously been entitled to the allowance in respect of expenditure on the asset.[17]

A caravan on a holiday caravan site qualifies for capital allowances as plant[18] if it is provided mainly for holiday lettings and is part of the pseudo trade of holiday lettings. By contrast, a caravan that is let for the whole trade to one individual who uses it as his private residence does not attract a capital allowance as the caravan then fails to perform the function of plant and there is, moreover, no trade.

Simon's Taxes B3.305.

[1] IRC v Barclay Curle & Co Ltd (see infra, § **9.29**); however, the area of overlap is reduced by the reasoning in *Wimpy International Ltd v Warland* [1989] STC 273, CA.
[2] Double allowances are excluded by CAA 2001, ss 7–10(2).
[3] (1887) 19 QBD 647.
[4] (1887) 19 QBD 647 at 658.
[5] Lord Donovan in *IRC v Barclay Curle & Co Ltd* [1969] 1 All ER 732 at 751, 45 TC 221 at 249.
[6] *Caledonian Rly Co v Banks* (1880) 1 TC 487.
[7] *LCC v Edwards* (1909) 5 TC 383.
[8] *Hinton v Maden and Ireland Ltd* [1959] 3 All ER 356, 38 TC 391 (expected to last only three years): noted [1959] BTR 454.
[9] *Dumbarton Harbour Board v Cox* (1918) 7 TC 147.
[10] *Earl of Derby v Aylmer* [1915] 3 KB 374, 6 TC 665.
[11] *Bradley v London Electricity plc* [1996] STC 1054.
[12] *Attwood v Anduff Car Wash Ltd* [1997] STC 1167, CA.
[13] Per Cross J in *McVeigh v Arthur Sanderson & Sons Ltd* [1969] 2 All ER 771 at 775, noted [1969] BTR 130.
[14] *Munby v Furlong* [1977] STC 232, [1977] 2 All ER 953.
[15] Infra, § **9.28**.
[16] *Jarrold v John Good & Sons Ltd* [1963] 1 All ER 141, 40 TC 681.
[17] *West Somerset Railway plc v Chivers* [1995] STC (SCD) 1.
[18] CAA 2001, s 23(1), list C, item 19. This replaces Revenue Extra Statutory Concession B50.

Computer software

[9.27] Where capital expenditure[1] is incurred on the outright acquisition of computer software the normal plant and machinery allowance is available. However, where a capital sum is paid for a licence to use the software or for the provision of software by electronic means problems arise. In the first instance it cannot be said that the software belongs to the taxpayer while in the second it may lack the degree of tangibility necessary for plant to exist. To circumvent such problems a special rule now applies for expenditure incurred on or after 10 March 1992.[2] Software acquired under a licence is treated as belonging to the trader as long as he is entitled to the right,[3] while computer software is treated as being machinery or plant.[4]

Consequential changes are made for such rights granted on or after 10 March 1992 so as to ensure that proper provision is made for the calculation of writing down allowance and balancing adjustments,[5] the calculation of disposal value[6] and whether that disposal value exceeds the capital expenditure incurred.[7]

The meaning of "computer software" is to be determined by the courts.[8]

Simon's Taxes B3.341.

[1] On boundary between capital and revenue note Inland Revenue interpretation RI 56.
[2] CAA 2001, s 71.
[3] CAA 2001, s 71(2).
[4] CAA 2001, s 71(1).
[5] CAA 2001, s 72.
[6] CAA 2001, s 72(3), Table, items 1–3.
[7] CAA 2001, s 73(1)–(3).
[8] HC Official Report, Standing Committee B, 25 June 1992, col 351. Quaere whether the courts will use the definition in the Copyright, Designs and Patents Act 1988.

Fixtures: plant or setting? The statutory provisions

[9.28] The boundary between plant and machinery, which attract a high rate of capital allowance, and the structure of the building, which attracts either no capital allowance or a low rate, is now the subject of statutory elaboration[1]. This elaboration is not to affect a number of special provisions which treat specified expenditure as if it were machinery or plant—thermal insulation, computer software, films, tapes and discs, fire safety, sports grounds and security.[2] It is also provided that nothing in the list is to affect the question whether expenditure on the provision of any glasshouse which is constructed so that the required environment (ie air, heat, light, irrigation and temperature) for growing plants is provided automatically by means of devices which are an integral part of its structure is, for the purposes of this Act, expenditure on the provision of machinery or plant.[3]

The stated purpose of this change is to provide that buildings and structures cannot qualify as plant (although it is also stated that the broad aim is that expenditure on buildings and structures which already qualify as plant should continue to do so).[4] Of the twelve cases reported between 1975 and 1997 seven were cases in which the Revenue successfully appealed against a Commissioners' determination that the items were plant, one was a successful appeal by a taxpayer against a Commissioners' decision in favour of the Revenue, in two the court agreed with the Commissioners that the items were plant and in two the Commissioners had decided that some items were plant but the court decided that more items were plant. Of those items which the court decided were plant one or two have now been taken into the non-plant category by the statutory list.[5] However, for the most part the list may be taken to reflect what the courts have achieved. The effect of the change is partly to provide detailed guidance and partly simply to prevent the judges from changing the law themselves.

The list deals first with buildings and excludes from the category of "machinery or plant" any expenditure on the provision of a building. It defines building as including any asset in the building which is incorporated into the building, or which, by reason of being moveable or otherwise, is not so incorporated, but is of a kind normally incorporated into buildings.[6] This abstract statement is supplemented by a table with two columns of items; all items are then swept into the definition of buildings. Items in the first column cannot be machinery or plant; items in the second column may.[7] Cold stores, caravans provided mainly for holiday lettings and any moveable building intended to be moved in the course of the trade may also be plant. The legislation leaves it to the taxpayer to establish that these items are plant under existing law. To make things clearer it is provided that an asset cannot come within column 2 if its principal purpose is to insulate or enclose the interior of the building or provide an interior wall, a floor or a ceiling which (in each case) is intended to remain permanently in place.[8] Examples of items in column 1 are walls, floors, ceilings, doors, gates, shutters, windows and stairs and in column 2 gas and sewerage systems provided mainly to meet the particular requirements of the trade, or provided mainly to serve particular machinery or plant used for the purposes of the trade.

A structure is defined as a fixed structure of any kind, other than a building. Again the legislation begins with a prohibition—expenditure on the provision of machinery or plant does not include any expenditure on the provision of structures or other specified assets or any works involving the alteration of land. Again there is a table with two columns and items in the first column cannot qualify whereas items in the second may do so. Examples from the first column include any dam, reservoir or barrage (including any sluices, gates, generators and other equipment associated with it), any dock and any dike, sea wall, weir or drainage ditch; the column ends ominously with any structure not within any other item in this column. The second column includes expenditure on the provision of towers used to support floodlights, of any reservoir incorporated into a water treatment works, of silos used for temporary storage or on the provision of storage tanks, of swimming pools, including diving boards, slides and any structure supporting them and of fish tanks or fish ponds. This second column had to be substantially widened in the course of debate.[9]

Finally the list turns to land and provides that expenditure on the acquisition of any interest in land cannot qualify as plant. This bar also extends to any asset which is so installed or otherwise fixed in or to any description of land as to become, in law, part of that land.[10]

Being incorporated in the list of items in the statute does not change the fundamental principle. In order for plant and machinery allowance to be available the item must have the function of plant and machinery in the particular business. Thus, in *IRC v Anchor International Ltd*[11] the High Court upheld the finding of the Special Commissioner who accepted that synthetic grass carpet that provided a five-a-side football pitch was correctly regarded as plant and machinery for a company whose trading activity was the provision of five-a-side football pitches.

Simon's Taxes B3.303.

[1] CAA 2001, ss 21–24.
[2] CAA 2001, s 23(1), (2).
[3] CAA 2001, s 23, List C, item 17.
[4] Inland Revenue press release, 30 November 1993, *Simon's Tax Intelligence* 1993, p 1539.
[5] eg the windows in *Leeds Permanent Building Society v Procter* [1982] STC 821 whether the dock in Barclay Curle itself is redesignated depends on whether "any dock" includes a dry dock.
[6] CAA 2001, ss 21(3), 23(3).
[7] CAA 2001, s 23(3), List C, items 18–21; on scope see *Family Golf Centres Ltd v Thorne* [1998] STC (SCD) 106.
[8] CAA 2001, s 22(3).
[9] See Inland Revenue press release, 9 March 1994, *Simon's Tax Intelligence* 1994, p 339.
[10] CAA 2001, s 24; the definition of land in the Interpretation Act 1978 is modified—see CAA 2001, s 22(3)(*b*).
[11] [2005] STC 411.

Case law principles

[9.29] Plant does not include the place where the business is carried on; "plant" is that with which the trade is carried on as opposed to the "setting or premises" in which it is carried on.[1] Plant carries with it a connotation of equipment or apparatus, either fixed or unfixed. It does not convey a meaning wide enough to cover buildings in general. It may cover equipment of any size. Equipment does not cease to be plant merely because it discharges an additional function such as providing the place in which the business is carried on, eg a dry dock,[2] but these categories are not necessarily mutually exclusive and the different rates of allowance make correct classification of great practical importance. So it has been held that special partitioning used by shipping agents to sub-divide floor space to accommodate fluctuating office accommodation requirements were plant; some stress was laid on the fact that office flexibility was needed.[3] Something which becomes part of the premises, as opposed to merely embellishing them, is not plant, save where the premises are themselves plant,[4] as in *IRC v Barclay, Curle & Co Ltd*.

The test is one of function, not appearance or construction. In *Shove v Lingfield Park 1991*[5] the Court of Appeal considered a claim for plant and machinery allowances on expenditure of £2,962,650 in constructing an All-Weather Race Track, which included track draining, 'equitrack' surfacing and safety fencing. Mummery LJ said:[6]

> The All-Weather Race Track functions as premises for horse racing, as does the grass racecourse running parallel to it. . . .. The AWT is not land in its natural state. It is synthetic in nature. It has a limited life. . .. The AWT is not a building affording shelter or security. Those features of the AWT do not, however, prevent the AWT from functioning as premises on or in which the trade of horse racing is conducted.

The unit must be defined. In cases such as these it is often crucial whether the various items are taken separately or treated as one installation. This is a question of fact, and so for the Commissioners to decide, subject to the tests in *Edwards v Bairstow and Harrison*. In *Cole Bros Ltd v Phillips*[7] the taxpayer had spent money on electrical installations in a large department store at Brent Cross shopping centre. The Revenue agreed that wiring to certain items such as alarms and clocks was plant but said that (a) transformers, switchgear and the main switchboard and (b) specially designed lighting fittings, were plant. The Commissioners decided that the transformers were plant but not the other items under (a) or any of (b). The Court of Appeal held that the switchboard was plant because of the fact that some of the wiring had been agreed to be plant. The House of Lords agreed with the Court of Appeal in treating the remaining items as matters for the Commissioners' decision as matters of fact.[8] An alternative argument advanced by the taxpayer was that the whole electrical installation was one item. This was rejected by the Commissioners; the appellate courts treated the issue as a matter of fact for the Commissioners but the discomfort shown by the speeches in the House of Lords is marked.[9] The issue arose more recently in *Attwood v Anduff Car Wash Ltd* where the question was whether car wash sites were single units of plant. The Commissioners held that it was but the appellate courts held that neither the whole site nor the wash hall alone could be treated as a single unit.[10]

While there is a clear distinction between the shell of a building and the machinery currently used in it, there are considerable difficulties where a large and durable structure is created for a specific purpose. This occurred in the leading case of *IRC v Barclay, Curle & Co Ltd*.[11] The taxpayer had constructed a dry dock, a process requiring the excavation of the site and the construction of a concrete lining. The Revenue agreed that such expenditure as that incurred on the dock gate and operating gear, the cast iron keel blocks and the electrical and pumping installations related to plant, but argued that while the expenses of excavation and concreting might relate to industrial building they did not relate to plant and machinery. The Revenue lost. It will be noted that while a dock is now classified in the statutory scheme as a structure and so not capable of qualifying for allowances as plant, a dry dock is classified differently. The expenditure on the concrete lining was held to be in respect of plant because it could not be regarded as the mere setting in which the trade was carried on but was an integral part of the means required for the trading operation. Hence a structure which fulfils the function of plant is, prima facie, plant.[12]

The costs of excavation were likewise held to be incurred in the provision of plant because what was indubitably plant, namely the dock itself, could not have been made before the excavation had taken place. This "but for" test is not, however, without limits and, by analogy with the express provision in relation to industrial buildings, costs incurred on the acquisition of the land could not fall within the allowance. Where capital expenditure is incurred on

Plant and machinery [9.29]

alterations to an existing building incidental to the installation of machinery or plant for the purposes of trade, allowances may be claimed in respect of such expenditure just as if the works formed part of the machinery or plant. This would appear to follow from the decision of the House of Lords but is expressly provided in CAA 2001, s 67. This provision was thought by the members of the majority to be merely for the avoidance of doubt.

The mere fact that an item has a business use (the business test) does not make it plant; an item cannot be plant if its use is as the premises or place on which the business is conducted (the premises test).[13] In *Wimpy v Warland* the taxpayer sought (unsuccessfully) to claim allowances for expenditure on shop fronts, wall panels, suspended ceilings, mezzanine floor, decorative brickwork, wall finishes and a trapdoor and ladder. As Fox LJ said:[14]

> There is a well established distinction, in general terms, between the premises in which the business is carried on and the plant with which the business is carried on. The premises are not plant. In its simplest form that is illustrated by [the] example of the creation of atmosphere in a hotel by beautiful buildings and gardens on the one hand and fine china, glass and other tableware on the other. The latter are plant; the former are not. The former are simply the premises in which the business is conducted.

In *Gray v Seymours Garden Centre (Horticulture) (a firm)*,[15] a case that involved what might loosely be called a high-tech glasshouse used in a garden centre, Nourse LJ said:

> While the cold frames which formerly provided a similar function to that of the planteria might well have been plant, the same cannot be said of the planteria itself. It is a structure to which plants are brought already in a saleable condition, albeit that some of them tend to be in there for quite considerable periods and others require special treatment . . . The fact that the planteria provides the function of nurturing and preserving the plants while they are there cannot transform it into something other than part of the premises in which the business is carried on. The highest it can be put is that it functions as a purpose-built structure. But . . . that is not enough to make the structure plant.

The distinction between setting and plant depends in part upon the degree of sophistication to be employed in the concept of a setting.[16] The problem is acute when electrical apparatus and wiring are concerned. The matter has to be resolved by the use of the functional test and so, for example, while lighting would not usually be plant it would become so if it is of a specialised nature, as where it is designed to provide a particular atmosphere in a hotel; this must be judged by reference to the intended market.[17] The Revenue consistently refused to treat wiring leading to such apparatus as plant; the statutory list[18] placed mains services and systems of electricity generally in the category of assets which cannot qualify as plant while allowing electrical systems provided mainly to meet the particular requirements of the trade or to serve particular machinery or plant used for the purposes of the trade.[19] From April 2008, electrical and lighting systems have fallen within the heading of integral features and therefore qualify as plant.

---

[1] Per Pearson LJ in *Jarrold v John Good & Sons Ltd* [1963] 1 All ER 141, 40 TC 681 at 696.
[2] See Sir Donald Nicholls V-C in *Carr v Sayer* [1992] STC 396 at 402.

[9.29] Capital allowances

3. *Jarrold v John Good & Sons Ltd*. The decision of the Commissioners was left intact. If a new agency were taken on, a new department would have to be created.
4. Per Fox LJ in *Wimpy International Ltd v Warland* [1989] STC 273 at 279e, CA.
5. [2004] EWCA Civ 391, [2004] STC 805.
6. paras 23 and 24 at 811g-j.
7. [1982] STC 307 HL and [1981] STC 671, CA.
8. But note the doubts of Lord Russell [1982] STC 307 at 316d.
9. See eg Lord Hailsham at 312–313, Lord Wilberforce at 314f and Edmund Davies at 316a.
10. [1997] STC 1167, CA and [1996] STC 110.
11. [1969] 1 All ER 732, 45 TC 221.
12. Lord Reid, [1969] 1 All ER 732 at 740, 45 TC 221 at 239.
13. Per Hoffmann J in *Wimpy International v Warland* [1988] STC 149 at 171b.
14. [1989] STC 273 at 279, 61 TC 51 at 96.
15. [1995] STC 706 at 711b. For a general Revenue view on glasshouses see Inland Revenue interpretation RI 33.
16. *Imperial Chemical Industries of Australia and New Zealand v Taxation Comr of the Commonwealth of Australia* (1970) 120 CLR 396.
17. *Cole Bros Ltd v Phillips* [1982] STC 307, HL; *Hunt v Henry Quick Ltd* [1992] STC 633; *IRC v Scottish and Newcastle Breweries Ltd* [1982] STC 296 note that the light fitting was allowed in *Wimpy International Ltd v Warland* [1988] STC 149 at 176.
18. In CAA 2001, s 21.
19. The Revenue relied strongly on *J Lyons & Co Ltd v A-G* [1944] Ch 281, [1944] 1 All ER 477. The essence of the decisions is reflected in electricity supply systems being excluded from plant and machinery allowances by CAA 2001, s 21(3), list A, item 2, whilst permitting expenditure in electrical systems meeting the particular requirements for qualifying activity as potentially attracting plant and machinery allowances, by virtue of CAA 2001, s 23(4), list C, item 2 (pre FA 2008) but note also head 1 in column 2.

[9.30] The case law distinction between buildings and apparatus is thus indistinct. Relatively recent cases have shown that items which cannot be plant under the case law test include a prefabricated building at a school used to accommodate a chemistry laboratory,[1] a canopy over a petrol station[2] (although this has since been doubted[3]), an inflatable cover over a tennis court,[4] a floating ship used as a restaurant.[5] These failed the business test—they performed no function in the trade. Many of these cases now appear in the statutory list of assets which cannot qualify as plant. Permanent quarantine kennels,[6] putting greens at a nine-hole golf course,[7] a car washing facility operated on a conveyor belt system[8] and a new racetrack[9] probably met the business test but certainly failed the premises test.

On the other hand it has been held that a silo used in the trade of grain importing was not simply part of the setting and could not be considered separately from the machinery and other equipment within it.[10] Likewise a swimming pool at a caravan site was held to be plant since it was part of the apparatus of the business,[11] as were decorative screens placed in the windows of a building society's offices as the screens were not the structure within which the business was carried on,[12] and, perhaps surprisingly, mezzanine platforms installed by a wholesale merchant to increase storage space.[13] In the celebrated House of Lords case of *IRC v Scottish and Newcastle Breweries Ltd*[14] murals designed to attract customers were held to be plant as was a metal seagull sculpture, kilts and sporran hung on the walls and other items designed to create "ambience".[15]

These cases prove the old adage that an ounce of evidence (before the Commissioners) is worth a ton of law.

[1] *St John's School (Mountford and Knibbs) v Ward* [1974] STC 69; on appeal [1975] STC 7 (note the astonishingly harsh refusal by Templeman J to allow an apportionment between the building and the equipment).
[2] *Dixon v Fitch's Garage Ltd* [1975] STC 480, [1975] 3 All ER 455.
[3] *Cole Bros Ltd v Phillips* [1982] STC 307 per Lord Hailsham at 311 but see the pointed comment of Walton J in *Thomas v Reynolds* [1987] STC 135 at 140.
[4] *Thomas v Reynolds* [1987] STC 135.
[5] *Benson v Yard Arm Club Ltd* [1979] STC 266, [1979] 2 All ER 336.
[6] *Carr v Sayer* [1992] STC 396, 65 TC 15.
[7] *Family Golf Centres Ltd v Thorne* [1998] STC (SCD) 106.
[8] *Attwood v Anduff Car Wash Ltd* [1997] STC 1167, CA.
[9] *Shove v Lingfield Park 1991 Ltd* [2003] EWHC 1684 (Ch), [2003] STC 1003.
[10] *Schofield v R and H Hall Ltd* [1975] STC 353.
[11] *Cooke v Beach Station Caravans Ltd* [1974] STC 402, [1974] 3 All ER 159.
[12] *Leeds Permanent Building Society v Procter* [1982] STC 821.
[13] *Hunt v Henry Quick Ltd* [1992] STC 633 at 644 and 645 (note doubts of Vinelott J at 644).
[14] [1982] STC 296, HL.
[15] See also *J D Wetherspoon plc v R & C Comrs* (2008) SpC 665.

Integral features

[9.31] Some of the issues relating to the boundary of plant or premises have become less relevant following the introduction of CAA 2001, s 33A with effect 1 April 2008 (6 April 2008, for income tax). The distinction between plant and premises has been further confused by statute. CAA 2001, s 33A provides that expenditure on integral features (as defined) is treated as if incurred on plant or machinery provided that the purpose of the feature is not to insulate the interior of a building or to provide an interior wall, floor or ceiling which is intended to remain permanently in place.

The meaning of integral feature includes some assets that were previously treated as plant but also some that were previously excluded from the definition of plant. Integral features are defined as the following:

(a) an electrical system (including a lighting system);
(b) a cold water system;
(c) a space or water heating system, a powered system of ventilation, air cooling or air purification and any floor ceiling comprised in such a system;
(d) a lift, escalator or moving walkway; and
(e) external solar shading.

[9.31] Capital allowances

Section 33B treats certain repair costs as if they were incurred on the replacement of integral features (and therefore not entitled to a revenue deduction.[1] This applies if the repair costs exceed half the replacement cost that would otherwise have been incurred. To ensure that repair costs are not artificially split, CAA 2001, s 33B(4) ensures that one must aggregate repair costs if:

(i) the first expenditure is less than 50% of the replacement cost and
(ii) further expenditure in the next 12 months takes the overall total above 50%.

---

[1] ITTOIA 2005, s 55A (income tax); TA 1988, s 74(1)(*da*) (corporation tax).

First year allowances

[9.32] First year allowances are available for the following categories of capital expenditure, as long as the items are not used for leasing:[1]

(1) Motor cars with low CO_2 emissions or are powered by electricity—100% allowance.[2]
(2) Energy efficient plant and machinery and plant and machinery for a gas refuelling station—100% allowance.[3]
(3) Environmentally beneficial plant or machinery—100% allowance.[4]

Once the first year has passed the normal 10% or 20% writing down allowance applies on any unrelieved expenditure. The first year allowance is not available for sea going ships, railway assets or for various leasing transactions or in the final year of the business.[5]

Other types of first year allowance expenditure were introduced for temporary periods expiring before April 2008.

In April 2009, a 40% first-year allowance was introduced at a rate of 40%. It applies to expenditure incurred in the year from 1 April 2009 (for corporation tax) or from 6 April 2009 (for income tax) provided that it complies with the restrictions in CAA 2001, s 46(2), it does not already attract 100% first-year allowances, and the expenditure is not allocated to the special rate (10%) pool.[6] Given the retention of the annual investment allowance (see supra, § **9.36**) which covers expenditure of up to £50,000 in a year, the temporary first-year allowance will particularly benefit larger businesses.

Simon's Taxes B3.330.

---

[1] CAA 2001, s 46(2). See infra, § **9.46**.
[2] CAA 2001, s 45D inserted by FA 2002, Sch 19 for expenditure incurred between 17 April 2002 and 31 March 2008 extended by FA 2008 to 31 March 2013.
[3] CAA 2001, ss 39, 45A. In order to qualify for the 100% allowance, expenditure on plant and machinery for a gas refueling station must be incurred between 17 April 2002 and 31 March 2008: FA 2002, Sch 20. See infra, § **9.33**.
[4] CAA 2001, s 45H inserted by FA 2003, Sch 30, para 3. CAA 2001, s 45I specifies the procedure for certification of environmentally beneficial plant and machinery.

[5] CAA 2001, s 46.
[6] FA 2009, s 24.

Energy efficient plant and machinery

[9.33] Capital expenditure on new plant and machinery incurred on or after 1 April 2001 attracts 100% first year allowance if the expenditure is on items that are certified as meeting energy saving criteria.[1] The 100% allowance is available for any size of enterprise. In order to qualify, the plant and machinery must be within the following categories of technologies, which form the energy technology list:

(1) Boilers;
(2) Motors and drives;
(3) Refrigeration;
(4) Heat pumps;
(5) Radiant and warm air heaters;
(6) Compressed air equipment;
(7) Solar thermal systems
(8) automatic monitoring and targeting equipment
(9) air-to-air energy recovery equipment,
(10) compact heat exchangers;
(11) heating, ventilation and air conditioning zone controls.[2]

To have a product included on the energy technology list, the manufacturer must complete an application either online or on a paper form which can be obtained from the Carbon Trust.[3] The application must include the product specification and evidence of appropriate internal testing procedures to prove that the product passes the required energy efficiency criteria. Each product type has a different set of eligibility criteria, which are listed on the website and included in the producers' pack distributed by the Carbon Trust. For example, condensing economisers are heat exchangers that raise the fuel efficiency of boilers, and for one to qualify the manufacturer must demonstrate that it increases a boiler's fuel efficiency by at least 9%.

If the Carbon Trust is satisfied that the product meets the criteria, it will send the manufacturer an acceptance letter. This confirms that the product qualifies for an enhanced capital allowance from the date of the letter. If the product is rejected, the Trust will provide reasons for the decision and invite the manufacturer to resubmit the product with further information if necessary. The whole process takes about 30 days, and the energy technology list[4] is updated each month with the details of newly approved products.

Where an item of plant is made up of various components, some of which comply with the requirements for energy saving plant and machinery, the capital allowance is given of such an amount that is specified by the Treasury order. This, therefore, overrides the usual statutory just apportionment[5] that would otherwise apply.

Energy efficiency capital allowances are not available for ships, nor railway assets.[6] However, unlike the usual treatment, a first year energy efficient capital allowance of 100% is available for an asset used for leasing.[7]

[9.33] Capital allowances

By its very nature, much energy saving plant is fixed to a building. Statute provides that the person incurring the expenditure is entitled to claim the 100% allowance, even where the plant and machinery is installed in another person's premises.[8] Special provision is, therefore, provided to overrule the normal requirement that an interest in the land is required in order to claim a capital allowance.[9] In order for this arrangement to operate, it is necessary for the claimant to enter into an energy service agreement, with a joint election being made by the energy services provided and the person claiming the capital allowances.[10]

Where property is sold with energy saving plant and machinery attached, the plant, etc, is treated as ceasing to belong to the energy services provider. A proportion of the expenditure by the purchaser of the building can be apportioned to the energy saving plant and qualify for allowances.[11]

Expenditure of up to £1,500 by a landlord in installing cavity wall and loft insulation is deductible in full from the rent receivable for the letting of the property.[12]

---

[1] CAA 2001, s 45A(1). Expenditure on energy saving items for let property is deductible, if it does not otherwise attract a capital allowance: ITTOIA 2005, s 312 (income tax), TA 1998, s 31ZA inserted by FA 2007, s 17(1), see infra, § **10:10**.
[2] Statutory instruments are issued under the authority of CAA 2001, s 45B. There were initially seven categories of technologies within the energy technology list from 1 April 2001, which were defined by statutory instrument SI 2001/2541. Four additional categories were added by SI 2002/1818 with effect from 5 August 2002; one was added by SI 2003/1744 with effect from 5 August 2003. Other items were substituted or omitted by SI 2004/2093 (with effect from 26 August 2004) and SI 2006/2233 (with effect from 7 September 2006).
[3] The Carbon Trust, 9th Floor, 3 Clement's Inn, London WC2A 2AZ, tel: 0202 7170 7033 or 020 7170 7000, fax: 020 7170 7020, email: eca@thecarbontrust.co.uk. All queries regarding the energy technology list can also be dealt with by the Action Energy line: 0800 585794.
[4] The energy technology list can be interrogated through the enhanced capital allowances website: www.eca.co.uk
[5] CAA 2001, s 562(3).
[6] CAA 2001, ss 45A(1)(c) and 46.
[7] FA 2002, s 62 with effect from 17 April 2002.
[8] CAA 2001, s 182A.
[9] CAA 2001, s 175A.
[10] CAA 2001, s 180A.
[11] CAA 2001, ss 192A and 195A.
[12] TA 1988, ss 31A and 31B inserted by FA 2004, s 143(1) for the period 6 April 2004 to 5 April 2009 only.

Environmentally beneficial plant and machinery

[9.34] Capital expenditure incurred on or after 1 April 2003 on new plant and machinery attracts a 100% first year allowance if the expenditure is on items that are certified as "environmentally beneficial plant or machinery".[1]

This 100% allowance is available for any size of enterprise and the scheme is closely modelled on that introduced to you earlier for energy efficient plant and machinery.[2] As with previous provisions, the items for which the allowance is available are those prescribed by treasury order.

The statutory provisions allow the Treasury to certify items that have any type of beneficial effect or are judged to have any type of beneficial effect on the environment. However, the Revenue 2003 Budget statement[3] makes it clear that the official thinking is that this allowance will be granted for "designated plant and machinery to reduce water use and improve water quality". The Revenue state that the scheme will apply initially to the following designated technology classes, provided the equipment meets the strict water saving/efficient criteria:

(1) meters and monitoring equipment;
(2) flow controllers;
(3) leakage detection;
(4) efficient toilets; and
(5) efficient taps.

It is possible to claim the 100% allowance for a component of a piece of plant or machinery, where the component is judged to be environmentally beneficial, irrespective of the operation of the total machine.[4]

---

[1] CAA 2001, s 45H inserted by FA 2003, Sch 30, para 3. CAA 2001, s 45I specifies the procedure for certification of environmentally beneficial plant and machinery.
[2] CAA 2001, s 45A, see supra, § **9.33**.
[3] Inland Revenue Press Release Rev BN26, 9 April 2003, *Simon's Weekly Tax Intelligence* 2003, p 436.
[4] CAA 2001, s 45J inserted by FA 2003, Sch 30, para 3.

First year tax credits

[9.35] FA 2008 introduced Schedule A1 to CAA 2001. That provides that companies (not individuals) may convert losses into repayable tax credits. The losses must arise from first year allowances in respect of expenditure incurred on energy-saving plant or machinery between 1 April 2008 and 31 March 2013.

The credit is equal to 19% of the loss or (if lower, the higher of £250,000 and the company's total PAYE and NIC liabilities in the year).

Annual investment allowance

[9.36] Finance Act 2008 contained measures that were intended to simplify the tax procedures for smaller businesses by giving them, in many cases, an immediate write-off for capital expenditure. The rules replaced the regime of 40% and 50% first-year allowances that were previously available to small and medium-sized enterprises. (The regime allowing certain environment-friendly expenditure to qualify for 100% first-year allowances remains.)

[9.36] Capital allowances

Although the measures are intended to benefit the smaller business, the rules apply to all. However, the financial cap on the allowance means that the measures will be more of a nuisance than a benefit to larger enterprises.

In a nutshell, the measures provide for an annual allowance (the annual investment allowance) of £50,000. Businesses are entitled to an immediate write-off of up to £50,000 of their qualifying expenditure in any year. Any balance of expenditure will be allocated to the pools and would qualify for writing-down allowances in the ordinary way.

The AIA is available in respect of qualifying expenditure incurred on or after:

(a) 1 April 2008 for corporation tax purposes; and
(b) 6 April 2008 for income tax purposes.[1]

---

[1] CAA 2001, s 38A(4).

Who qualifies for the annual investment allowance?

The AIA is available to individuals and companies. It is also available to partnerships if all the members are individuals.[1]

Therefore, trustees and partnerships with corporate partners will not be eligible for the annual investment allowance.

---

[1] CAA 2001, s 38A.

When AIA is not available

Despite the intention to bring simplifications to small businesses, the AIA rules occupy eleven pages of legislation most of it dealing with restrictions on its availability. The AIA is not available in the following cases.

(1) In the chargeable period in which the qualifying activity is permanently discontinued.
(2) In respect of capital expenditure on a car.[1]
(3) In respect of expenditure incurred wholly for the purposes of a ring-fence trade.
(4) Where there is a change in the nature or conduct of the qualifying activity and obtaining the AIA might objectively be seen as a main benefit of making the change.
(5) Where the plant or machinery was acquired for other purposes, for long-funding leasing or where it was acquired as a gift.[2]

Subject to these exceptions, the AIA is available whether or not the expenditure qualifies for writing down allowances at the 20% rate or at the 10% rate.

---

[1] Car is defined in CAA 2001, s 81 so as to include motorcycles.
[2] CAA 2001, s 38B.

Claiming the AIA

The AIA is equal to £50,000 (or the amount of AIA qualifying expenditure if lower).[1]

If the taxpayer's chargeable period is longer or shorter than a year, the value of the AIA is proportionately adjusted.[2]

If the AIA is allocated to expenditure on plant or machinery that will not be used wholly for the purposes of the qualifying activity, then the AIA is subject to a just and reasonable reduction.[3]

Unused AIA may not be carried forward. Conversely, the AIA is not compulsory. Consequently taxpayers who would rather defer the allowances until a later year are not required to claim the AIA in full or at all. However, even in such circumstances, any unused element may not be carried forward. Instead, expenditure will be relieved by way of writing down allowances in the usual way.

[1] CAA 2001, s 51A(5). See 9.06 as to when capital expenditure is treated as incurred.
[2] CAA 2001, s 51A(4).
[3] CAA 2001, s 205.

AIA and businesses under common control

Individuals and partnerships

For individuals and partnerships, an AIA is generally available in respect of each qualifying activity carried on. Therefore, supposing an individual owned a confectioner's, ran a private tuition service and was also a partner (with another individual) in a farming business, that individual would be entitled to two AIAs in addition to the AIA available to the partnership.

However, there are restrictions if there are two or more qualifying activities which are:

(a)   carried on by a partnership or an individual;
(b)   controlled by the same person; and
(c)   related to each other.

Where this applies, there will be a single AIA available to the person(s) carrying on the qualifying activities.

Qualifying activities are related if either:

(i)   they are carried on from the same premises; or
(ii) they are within the same "NACE classification" under European Law.[1]

[1] CAA 2001, s 51J.

Companies

Companies are subject to four restrictions.

[9.36] Capital allowances

(1) First, companies are entitled to only one AIA, irrespective of how many qualifying activities they carry on.[1]
(2) Secondly, groups of companies are entitled to only one AIA.[2]
(3) Groups of companies under common control are entitled to only one AIA if they are related to each other.[3]
(4) Other companies under common control are entitled to only one AIA if they are related to each other.[4]

As with unincorporated taxpayers, companies are related if at the end of the chargeable period, they carry on qualifying activities from the same premises.

However, the other definition of related differs slightly from that applying with respect to unincorporated businesses. Companies are also related if more than 50% of each company's turnover is derived from qualifying activities within the same NACE classification.[5]

---

[1] CAA 2001, s 51B.
[2] CAA 2001, s 51C.
[3] CAA 2001, s 51D.
[4] CAA 2001, s 51E.
[5] CAA 2001, s 51G.

When restrictions apply

When the AIA is restricted amongst multiple taxpayers, they can choose how to allocate the allowance between them.

Writing down allowance

[9.37] This allowance, which is given on a 20% (until April 2008, 25%) reducing balance basis, applies where the person incurs[1] capital expenditure on the provision of machinery and plant wholly and exclusively for the purposes of the trade. In consequence of the expenditure the asset must belong to him.[2] It is not necessary that the asset should have been brought into use in the trade. If the chargeable period is greater or less than 12 months the figure of 20% is increased or reduced accordingly.[3]

Where an asset is acquired partly for business purposes and partly for other purposes the allowance is reduced to such extent as is just and reasonable in the circumstances; particular attention is directed to the use to which the asset is put.[4] Rules are provided for an asset originally acquired solely for business purposes being used partly for non-business purposes and vice versa.

Generally all plant and machinery used in the trade is placed in one pool and the writing down allowance is applied to the value of the pool.[5] However, certain items have their allowance calculated on an individual asset basis. These are:

(1) assets used partly for non-business purposes,[6]
(2) expensive road vehicles;[7] and
(3) ships[8] (here the law allows deferments of writing down allowances at will).

Plant and machinery [9.37]

However, a separate pool of assets has existed since FA 1997 for expenditure on long life assets (see **9.43**). That historically attracted a rate of writing down allowances of 6% but was otherwise subject to identical rules to the "main pool". FA 2008 has made three changes to the long life asset pool.

(a) It has rebranded the long pool the "special expenditure pool".
(b) It requires expenditure on integral features to be allocated to this pool rather than the main pool.
(c) It has increased the rate of writing down allowances to 10%.[9]

Where a taxpayer carries on more than one trade, each trade has a separate main pool.[10] The effect is not to create a separate pool for each such asset but to create a separate pool for all assets of that class.

A separate pool was created for each of the following types of asset: (a) motor cars with original cost price below £12,000[11], (b) assets for leasing outside the UK[12], and (c) leases used other than in the course of a trade.[13] The reasoning behind separate pools for (a) and (b) was that these assets were not entitled to first year allowances; with the reduction in the scope of first year allowances it became less sensible to maintain these rules and so 16 years after Nigel Lawson's decision to remove most of the first year allowances, FA 2000[14] enacts that with effect from 6 April 2000 (1 April for corporation tax) the requirement of a separate pool was removed; the balance of the separate pool was merged with the main pool, subject to the taxpayer being able to defer the change for a year.[15]

Assets can be treated separately and the writing down allowance calculated on the cost of the individual asset, if the taxpayer so elects and the asset is not excluded by statute from being treated as a short life asset.[16]

Writing down allowances may be claimed in part whether by an individual or by a company.[17] Under self-assessment any claims can be made varied or withdrawn for a period of one year from the end of the first anniversary of the filing date or such longer period as the Revenue may allow.[18]

The qualifying expenditure includes that on related alterations to buildings[19] and demolition costs.[20]

Where a first year allowance is taken the taxpayer could not also claim a writing down allowance for that first year in respect of any expenditure in excess of the allowance. This is less relevant now that all first year allowances are available at a rate of 100%. However, where a reduced allowance is taken in the first year, the 20% allowance applies to the balance of the expenditure remaining after the first year allowance.

A balancing adjustment may be made where a non-resident trades through a branch or agency in the UK and the proportion of the total trade represented by the UK branch or agency changes downwards (ie is reduced).[21]

No allowance may be claimed for the period during which permanent discontinuance takes place; only a balancing allowance (or charge) is made.[22] If the base period is less than one year an appropriate proportion of the allowance is given.

The writing down allowance is given at 25% of the balance of the pool each year.

[9.37] Capital allowances

EXAMPLE

If an asset cost £10,000, and it was the only asset in the pool, the allowance would be £2,000 in the first year, but 20% of (10,000–2,000) ie £1,600 in the second.

Suppose that an asset was bought in year 1 for £10,000, that a second asset was bought in year 2 for £92,000, and that in year 3 the first asset was sold for £10,000. The allowances would be year 1 £2,000 and year 2 £20,000. At the start of year 3 the qualifying expenditure would be £102,000–(2,000+20,000) or £80,000. This must be reduced by the £10,000 disposal so that in year 3 the allowance will be 20% of (80,000–10,000)=£14,000.

Where more items come into the pool, the writing down allowance is 20% of the excess of sums spent over sums so far allowed whether under a first year allowance or a writing down allowance plus disposal value.

Simon's Taxes B3.332.

---

[1] CAA 2001, ss 4, 5. For VAT see ss 235 and 238(1)–(3).
[2] See supra, § **9.25** and CAA 2001, s 69 (hire purchase), s 70, Sch 3, para 17 (leased assets).
[3] CAA 2001, s 56(3).
[4] CAA 2001, s 205.
[5] CAA 2001, s 56. The pooling rule is examined in clause 2.8 of the Tax Law Rewrite project Capital Allowance Part 3.
[6] CAA 2001, s 205.
[7] CAA 2001, ss 74–78, 107 (see infra, § **9.50**).
[8] CAA 2001, s 127 onwards.
[9] CAA 2001, ss 104C, 104D.
[10] CAA 2001, s 53.
[11] CAA 2001, s 107(2) and s 105.
[12] CAA 2001, ss 81, 107 (see infra, § **9.52**).
[13] CAA 2001, s 19.
[14] CAA 2001, s 107.
[15] FA 2000, s 74(5).
[16] CAA 2001, ss 83, 84 (see infra § **9.42**).
[17] FA 1998, Sch 18, para 82 (corporation tax); there are further rules if the Revenue make an enquiry.
[18] FA 1998, Sch 18, Part IX (corporation tax).
[19] CAA 2001, s 25. That treats as part of the cost of plant and machinery any expenditure incidental to the installation of plant or machinery. In *J D Wetherspoon plc v R & C Comrs* (2008) SpC 665, it was held that this provision was to be construed narrowly so as not to include costs that were merely consequential on the installation of the plant or machinery. For example, the wipe-clean walls in a pub's kitchen were consequential on the installation of the sinks but not incidental thereto. However, an exception was given in respect of expenditure so closely related to the plant or machinery itself (for example, the partitions around a toilet).
[20] CAA 2001, s 26.
[21] CAA 2001, s 208.
[22] CAA 2001, Sch 3, para 47(6).

Special rate expenditure

[9.38] For expenditure on or after 1 April 2008 (corporation tax) or 6 April 2008 (income tax), certain expenditure must be allocated to the special rate (10%) pool rather than the main pool. The only exception is where the expenditure must be allocated to a single asset pool (because, for example, the asset is not used wholly for the purposes of the qualifying activity[1]).

These rules apply to:

(a) expenditure on thermal insulation which is treated as if incurred on plant or machinery;
(b) expenditure on integral features; and
(c) long-life asset expenditure.

Such expenditure is known as "special rate expenditure"[2]. Where only part of capital expenditure on plant and machinery is special rate expenditure, it is treated for capital allowances purposes as expenditure on separate items of plant or machinery, with a just and reasonable apportionment of expenditure as necessary[3].

---

[1] Even in those cases CAA 2001, s 104D(2) provides that writing down allowances are given at a rate of 10%.
[2] CAA 2001, s 104A.
[3] CAA 2001, s 104B.

Small pools allowance

[9.39] A simplification measure was introduced in FA 2008. CAA 2001, s 56A permits balances (before writing down allowances) of £1,000 or less to be written off immediately. However, this applies only in the main pool or the special rate pool. It does not apply to any single asset pool. Whilst that makes sense in some ways (it avoids write downs of aspects of private expenditure or, in the case of cars, it prevents an acceleration of relief), this distinction will mean that many unincorporated businesses will not be able to obtain any relief (since many assets are in single asset pools because of private use). Consequently, the measure (whilst well-intentioned) will not assist many of the taxpayers at which it was directed.

Disposal

[9.40] When an enterprise disposes of plant and machinery on which capital allowances have been granted, the disposal value[1] is brought into the calculation of capital allowances so that, at least in concept, there is either clawback of allowances or grant of additional allowances to provide an aggregate allowance for the enterprise equal to the expenditure on which the allowance is granted. The principle is, however, conceptual rather than real where assets are pooled, as the adjustment to the allowances is only finally determined when the pool is extinguished.[2]

Disposal value becomes relevant when:[3]

[9.40] Capital allowances

(1) the asset ceases to belong to the claimant;[4]
(2) if he loses possession of it in circumstances in which it is reasonable to assume the loss is permanent;
(3) the asset ceases to exist as such (as a result of destruction, dismantling or otherwise);
(4) the asset begins to be used wholly or partly[5] for purposes other than those of the trade; or
(5) the trade is permanently discontinued.

The disposal value to be brought into account depends upon the event by reason of which it falls to be taken into account,[6] but it cannot exceed the capital expenditure incurred on that item, any such excess being subject to capital gains legislation. The disposal value to be deducted from the pool is not to exceed the cost of the plant to the person disposing of it. However, when the plant was acquired as a result of a transaction or series of transactions between connected persons the greatest acquisition expenditure incurred in any of the transactions concerned is the maximum disposal value;[7] this rule applies not only on a disposal to a connected person or to an acquisition from a connected person but extends to an acquisition as a result of some transaction between connected persons, with whom the disposer need not be connected.[8] If the asset has been sold,[9] the proceeds of sale are taken and if that sale has been affected by some event, for example, if the asset has been damaged, account is also taken of any insurance or compensation money received. Market value will, if greater, be substituted for the proceeds of sale unless there is a charge to tax under ITEPA 2003 or the buyer can in turn claim a capital allowance in respect of machinery or plant or a scientific research allowance.[10] The reason for the latter exemptions is that the low sale price will give rise in turn to low allowances. However, the functional definition of plant and machinery may prevent this matching, as where the asset was plant and machinery of the vendor but is an industrial building to the purchaser, there market value will be taken for the disposal value while the purchaser's capital allowance will be geared to the actual price. There is also a bar on taking an undervalue if the buyer is a dual resident investment company—as part of the general drive against such companies.[11]

If the event is the demolition or destruction of the asset the disposal value is the sums received for the remains together with any insurance or compensation, and in other instances of permanent loss, for example theft, is simply any insurance or compensation. In all other cases market value is taken.

If the event is the permanent discontinuance of the trade and that is followed by the sale, demolition, destruction or permanent loss of the asset the disposal value on discontinuance is that specified for the event although a special election may apply if there is a succession to a trade by a connected person.[12] The predecessor's written down value overrides other provisions referring to market value.[13] The right to elect is restricted to cases where both parties are within the charge to UK tax on the profits of the trade and is subject to a time limit of two years starting with the date of the transaction.[14] The election can be made by a partnership.[15] In all other cases market value is taken.[16] For the period in which permanent discontinuance occurs neither first year nor writing down allowances are given, everything being settled by the balancing allowance or charge.

Plant and machinery [9.41]

In appropriate cases the disposal proceeds may be apportioned.[17]

Provision is also made for a rebate of VAT under the capital goods scheme.[18]

Where a qualifying gift is made to an educational establishment there is a nil disposal value.[19]

Special rules apply to computer software.[20]

Simon's Taxes B3.334.

---

[1] CAA 2001, s 61(2), Table (see infra § **9.42**).
[2] CAA 2001, s 56(7).
[3] CAA 2001, s 60 and, in relation to computer software, CAA 2001, s 72.
[4] CAA 2001, ss 67(4), 68(1), (2), (4).
[5] Or partly ceasing to be so used see CAA 2001, s 11(4).
[6] CAA 2001, s 61(2).
[7] CAA 2001, s 62(2), (3).
[8] CAA 2001, s 511.
[9] See *IRC v West* (1950) 31 TC 402.
[10] CAA 2001, s 61(2).
[11] CAA 2001, s 61(2).
[12] CAA 2001, s 266.
[13] CAA 2001, s 266(1)–(7), Sch 3, para 52.
[14] CAA 2001, s 266(1), (2), (3).
[15] CAA 2001, s 266(6).
[16] CAA 2001, s 265; on succession on death note CAA 2001, s 268(5)–(7).
[17] CAA 2001, ss 562–564.
[18] CAA 2001, ss 238, 239.
[19] See supra, § **8.141**.
[20] CAA 2001, ss 72, 73.

Balancing charge—anti-avoidance provisions

[9.41] With effect from 7 November 2002, a specific anti-avoidance rule applies so that a balancing allowance is denied if the market value of property of which there is a balancing event is artificially depressed as a result of a tax avoidance scheme. The counter-measure has a deterrent effect because any subsequent capital allowances claim by the purchaser would be limited to the amount the purchaser had actually paid (just as it would have been had a balancing allowance been made to the vendor).[1]

The anti-avoidance rule was introduced in order to counter an arrangement in relation to industrial buildings allowances. The allowance is claimed at 4% a year on the "straight-line basis" on the capital expenditure on the construction of the building. The disposal of the building triggers a balancing event. Where the market value of the building is less than its written down value for tax, an extra allowance, called a balancing allowance, is made in respect of the difference (ie that extra fall in value) to the person making the disposal.

The device sought to depress the market value of a property to obtain an accelerated balancing allowance.

The new rules apply to capital allowances for industrial buildings, mineral extraction, flat conversions, agricultural buildings and assured tenancies.

[1] CAA 2001, s 570A inserted by FA 2003, s 164(1) with effect for any balancing event occurring on or after 7 November 2002, unless it is as a consequence of a contract entered into before that date. (The exemption is applied where the pre November 2002 contract was an option, or similar, which is exercised on or after 27 November 2002.)

Short life assets—the non-pooling option

[9.42] The effect of the reducing balance basis being used for the writing down allowance is that about 90% of the cost will be written off over eight years. Because some assets have a shorter life expectancy the rules have been amended to allow such assets to be kept out of the main pool.[1] One advantage is that if the asset is disposed of any balancing allowance is given immediately instead of waiting for the overall effect on a pool—but only if it is disposed of within, approximately, five years.

The asset is kept in a pool of its own. Any first year allowance and the normal subsequent 25% writing down allowance is then applied to that pool.[2] The (irrevocable) election must be made within two years of the year of acquisition.[3]

The asset remains in its pool for five years beginning with the year of acquisition. If the asset still belongs to the taxpayer at the end of that period the unrelieved balance of the expenditure is transferred to the main pool.[4] Until this time the short life asset remains separate and, for example, one cannot set that asset's relief against a charge otherwise arising on the main pool of assets. Special rules apply to disposals before the end of the period to connected persons etc[5] and to notional disposals where a leased asset ceases to be used for a qualifying purpose.[6]

The election is not open to those assets which are required to be pooled separately anyway.[7]

Statute requires a separate capital allowance calculation for each asset. However, in practice, where a sufficient number of assets have similar anticipated lives, the Revenue will accept a calculation for an aggregate of assets.[8] This practice is commonly applied to computer software. If a practice of the business is to discard software after three years on average, it is normally acceptable to the Revenue for capital allowances to be prepared on the basis that a year's expenditure on software is treated as being scrapped for no consideration after a three-year period.

Simon's Taxes B3.343.

[1] CAA 2001, ss 83–89.
[2] CAA 2001, ss 65(2), 86(1).
[3] CAA 2001, s 85(1)–(4).
[4] CAA 2001, s 86(2)–(4); on computer software note discretion to ignore CAA 2001, s 72.

[5] CAA 2001, ss 88, 89.
[6] CAA 2001, s 87(1), (2). This is confined to short term assets used for leasing.
[7] CAA 2001, s 84.
[8] Inland Revenue Statement of Practice SP 1/86.

Long life assets

[9.43] With the privatisation of public utilities, attention has been drawn to the very substantial disparity between the rapid rate at which capital allowances are given and the slow rate at which plant such as reservoirs and power stations is written down in the financial accounts of the newly privatised companies. Until 2007–08, the writing down allowance for plant and machinery was 6% per annum, calculated on a reducing balance basis, where it is reasonable to expect that the plant and machinery will have a useful economic life of at least 25 years. From April 2008, long life expenditure is allocated to the special rate pool qualifying for 10% writing down allowances. Existing long life asset pools are transferred to the new special rate pool.[1]

Certain assets are excluded from these rules. These include fixtures in a dwelling-house, retail shop, showroom, hotel or office and any mechanically propelled road vehicle.[2] The test as to the likely life of an asset is the reasonable expectation when the asset is new. This treatment is not applied unless the taxpayer has expenditure of over £100,000 in a twelve month basis period on such plant.[3]

Where this treatment is applied, the long life asset is treated as creating a pool separate from other assets.

There are provisions for apportioning composite expenditure between a long life asset and an asset with a shorter life.[4]

This treatment only applies to assets purchased on or after 26 November 1996. Assets purchased after that date where expenditure is incurred prior to 1 January 2001 are also excluded if the contract to purchase the asset was concluded prior to 26 November 1996.[5]

Ships are brought into these provisions, where the expenditure is incurred on or after 1 January 2011.[6]

The Revenue have published their view as to what constitutes a long life asset.[7] The examples given display a theme. The test is always to be applied at the time of first bringing the asset into use; hindsight cannot be applied. Also, the length of time chosen for depreciation in the commercial accounts of the taxpayer company does not determine the tax treatment. The Revenue accept as not long life assets not only assets that are expected to be worn out within 25 years but also assets purchased for a specific production run that is not likely to last for 25 years, or where the product is likely to be obsolete within that period, as long as the asset is not expected to be readily saleable at the end of that period. Where the asset is purchased to serve a specific contract that is likely not to be renewed to run over the 25-year period, the Revenue accept that the asset is not a long life asset. Different treatment can be applied to

[9.43] Capital allowances

different entities that operate together. The example is given of jets for long haul flights depreciated over 20 years but, based on past experience of similar aircraft, it is likely that the planes will continue in service for more than 25 years, perhaps with non-UK airlines. Such jets would be considered to be long-life assets. However, if the engines for these jets are depreciated over fifteen years (being the projected life of the engine in flying hours divided by the planned use per annum) these engines would be accepted as not being long life assets. The Revenue consented to an agreement with the British Air Transport Association[8] under which certain aircraft are stated not to be treated as long life assets. The Revenue's approach to aircraft outside the BATA agreement has also been published.[9]

Simon's Taxes B3.344.

[1] FA 2008, s 80.
[2] CAA 2001, ss 93–95.
[3] CAA 2001, ss 97–100.
[4] CAA 2001, ss 90–92.
[5] CAA 2001, Sch 3, para 20.
[6] CAA 2001, s 94.
[7] Inland Revenue Tax Bulletin, August 1997, pp 445–450.
[8] Inland Revenue Tax Bulletin, June 1999. This has been extended for a further five years to 31 December 2008 (Inland Revenue Tax Bulletin, December 2003, p 1074). Forms for the claiming of allowances on aircraft covered by the BATA agreement are available from Inland Revenue large business offices at Nottingham and Manchester.
[9] Inland Revenue Tax Bulletin, December 2003, p 1075.

Ships

[9.44] Ships have for many years been treated specially for capital allowance purposes. If the expenditure qualifies for a first year allowance the allowance may be postponed or reduced in whole or in part;[1] the amount deferred can be claimed as a first year allowance in a later year.[2] This freedom to depreciate applies to writing down allowances also. The writing down allowance may be deferred in whole or in part in prescribed circumstances.[3] Expenditure on ships is not pooled.

There is no statutory definition of a ship but there have been many decisions on its meaning under the Merchant Shipping Acts. So a floating gas container without power and not fitted for navigation was held not to be a ship[4] but a hopper barge without engine or sail was held to be a ship.[5] There is, however, a statutory definition of qualifying ships for the purpose of the 1995 rules on deferment of balancing charges—the vessel must be of a sea-going kind of at least 100 g.r.t.[6] and meet certain registration requirements and certain vessels (eg hovercraft) are specifically excluded. To be a qualifying ship it must be registered in the UK, a dependent territory, a Crown dependency, the Isle of Man or Channel Islands or another state within the EU or EEA.

FA 1995, ss 94–98 and FA 1996, Sch 35 contain new rules on the treatment of balancing charges, the broad effect of which is to allow such charges arising on the disposal of qualifying ships[7] to be rolled over for a period of up to three years to be set off against subsequent expenditure[8] on new ships within that period. This treatment is analogous to rollover relief for capital gains tax. The amount that can be rolled forward is that needed to ensure that there is no tax liability in the year. Tax deferred may be recovered if, for example, the new ship is not bought or does not meet the terms of the provisions. The ship may have been owned by the taxpayer previously but there must be a six-year gap.[9]

Subject to EU approval, the new provisions apply to chargeable periods ending on or after 21 April 1994.[10]

Simon's Taxes B3.351–353.

[1] CAA 2001, s 130(1), (3)–(5).
[2] CAA 2001, s 131(1), (2), (4).
[3] CAA 2001, ss 129–133.
[4] *Wells v Gas Float Whitton No 2 (Owners)* [1897] AC 337, HL; see also *Wirth Ltd v SS Acadia Forest* [1974] 2 Lloyds Rep 563.
[5] *The Mac* (1882) 7 PD 126, CA.
[6] This limit does not apply if the ship is lost at sea or irreparably damaged: CAA 2001, ss 151–154.
[7] CAA 2001, s 151.
[8] CAA 2001, s 146.
[9] CAA 2001, ss 147(1), 148.
[10] CAA 2001, ss 132, 145.

Hire purchase

[9.45] Where machinery or plant is purchased on hire purchase or conditional sale contracts first year and writing down allowances may be claimed in respect of the capital element.[1]

The machinery or plant is treated as belonging to him and not to any other person while he is entitled to the benefit of the contract; capital expenditure to be incurred by him under the contract after the machinery or plant has been brought into use in the trade is treated as incurred by him at that time; he is thus treated as incurring the full capital cost at that time. Where this rule deems the asset to belong to X but the special rules for fixtures deemed it to belong to Y, the fixtures rule prevails;[2] although this was introduced by FA 2000 it is deemed always to have had effect. Where the hire purchase rule deems the asset to be X's and it then becomes a fixture and so belongs to Y, X is treated as selling the asset to Y. This rule is not retroactive and applies to assets becoming fixtures after Royal Assent; FA 2000 does not specify the price at which the sale is treated as taking place.

There are special provisions when the option under the contract is not exercised.[3]

The actual words of this provision go wider than just hire purchase. They refer to situations in which the person carrying on a trade incurs capital expenditure on the provision of machinery or plant for the purposes of the trade "under a

[9.45] Capital allowances

contract providing that he shall or may become the owner of the machinery or plant on the performance of the contract". While this naturally applies to hire purchase contracts, and such contracts are referred to in the side note, that side note also contains the words "etc". The Revenue have pointed out that these words are therefore apt to cover situations in which capital expenditure is incurred on goods which are never owned, eg a deposit paid for goods which are then not supplied.[4]

Simon's Direct Tax Service B3.340

---

[1] CAA 2001, s 67. A hirer under such an agreement is very different from a mere lessee—see Inland Revenue press release, 27 October 1986, *Simon's Tax Intelligence* 1986, p 680. The tax position of lessees (and lessors) is not affected by SSAP 21; statement of practice SP 3/91.
[2] CAA 2001, s 69.
[3] CAA 2001, s 67(4).
[4] Inland Revenue interpretation RI 10.

Leasing

[9.46] Where a person carries on a trade of leasing, plant and machinery that is leased to others can attract writing down allowances in the normal way but first year allowances are not available.[1] A capital allowance is available to the purchaser even where the arrangements made for leasing the asset are such that the purchaser's expenditure is immediately refunded.[2]

An item of plant and machinery that is leased by a person who is not carrying on a trade of leasing is treated in the same way, with writing down allowance being available but no first year allowance, except that the item leased is treated as being in a pool of its own, separate from any items of plant and machinery that are used by that person in his own trade.[3] The capital allowances that arise cannot be set off against the general profits of the lessor but only against the income from the notional separate trade of leasing.[4] The question whether the asset is provided wholly and exclusively for the notional trade is determined according to the facts.[5]

In *Baldwins Industrial Services plc and Barr Ltd*[6] it was held that the supply of a crane with a crane driver was not the trade of leasing plant and machinery as the standard construction and plant hire association contract, which was used in this case, includes the condition that the driver "shall be under the control of the hirer". Hence, in this case, a first year allowance was available to the supplier of the crane. This has lead to the Revenue changing its view and stating that first year allowances will now be granted to small and medium sized businesses where plant and machinery is supplied with an operator, on condition that the operator remains with the equipment during its use and it is operated by him or her alone, except in exceptional circumstances.[7]

---

[1] CAA 2001, s 46(2); general exclusion 6. For a dispute over a lease where the availability of capital allowances is critical, see *Gold Fields Mining and Industrial Ltd v GKN UK Plc* [1996] STC 173.

[2] *Barclays Mercantile Business Finance Ltd v Mawson* [2004] UKHL 51, [2005] STC 1. In that case, Barclays Mercantile spent £250,000,000 purchasing a gas pipeline running from Scotland to Ireland, financed by European Union money and bank loans. Lease agreements were entered into, the effect of which was to reimburse Barclays Mercantile its entire expenditure, reimbursement being the same day as the expenditure was incurred. The House of Lords upheld Barclays' claim to a capital allowance of £91,542,000. The case is further considered at supra, § **3.02**. By contrast, in *DMBF (No 24) v IRC* [2002] EWHC 2466 (Ch), [2002] STC 1450, capital allowances were denied as the company did not acquire legal title to the equipment.
[3] CAA 2001, s 65(1).
[4] CAA 2001, s 258(4).
[5] See CAA 2001, s 35 for expenditure on plant or machinery in a dwelling house.
[6] [2002] EWHC 2915 (TCC), [2003] CILL 1949.
[7] Inland Revenue Tax Bulletin, August 2003, p 1054.

Operating lease and finance lease

[9.47] In accounting practice a distinction is made between an "operating lease" and a "finance lease". A typical example of the former is a tenant who occupies a factory and pays a fixed amount each month to the landlord. The monthly sums are normally fixed over the period of the lease, or over a period of years between pre-specified rent review dates. At the end of the lease period the owner has an asset that he would expect to be able to let: the tenant does not expect further use of the asset without payment of a periodic rent that is similar to that charged previously. By contrast, a finance lease is a pre-determined series of payments for what is, in commercial terms, the purchase by the lessee of the asset concerned. Typically, a finance lease is entered into by a business that requires an expensive item of machinery which is likely to be used by the business for the larger part of the expected useful life of the machine. Many farmers acquire a combine-harvester on a finance lease as an alternative to an outright purchase financed by means of a bank loan. Accounting practice[1] requires the treatment of payments and receipts under a finance lease to reflect the underlying commercial reality that the asset is treated in the business as if the asset were owned by the business and a loan had been taken out to purchase the acquisition.

Where expenditure is incurred on the provision of plant and machinery for leasing out under a finance lease, capital allowances are given by reference to the period over which the plant and machinery is leased out.[2] Thus, for example, if expenditure is incurred three months before the end of the accounting period, the writing down allowance is 3/12 of the annual amount. This is achieved by reducing the expenditure that is treated as qualifying expenditure in that accounting period by multiplying the actual expenditure by the number of days from the date on which an allowance is available to the end of the accounting period divided by the number of days in the accounting period.[3]

A capital allowance is not available until the later of the date on which expenditure is incurred and the date on which machinery or plant belongs to the taxpayer.[4] Not infrequently, in the case of a finance lease, these dates will be different for the taxpayer entitled to capital allowances. If the plant or machinery is first used in the trade in a period later than that in which expenditure is incurred, the capital allowance is first granted in that later period.[5] However, pre-trading expenditure on a finance lease attracts capital allowances from the date of the expenditure being incurred, if the trade commences during the same accounting period. Under general law, a hire purchase contract does not give ownership of the asset until a payment is made for ownership—typically the payment of a nominal sum at the end of the HP period. For capital allowance purposes, a trader who obtains plant or machinery under a HP contract is treated as qualifying for a capital allowance on the later of the date that the contract is made and the date on which the plant or machinery is brought into use in the trade. However, when a finance lessor buys an asset for leasing on hire purchase, the capital allowance available is restricted to the amount of expenditure actually incurred.[6]

There are anti-avoidance provisions, which operate by applying special treatment where the lessor and the lessee are connected persons. A common arrangement in a group of companies is for one member of the group to provide finance to other members, including the provision of finance leases. Such arrangements come into the anti-avoidance provisions[7] by virtue of the finance company and its client being connected persons.[8] The anti-avoidance provisions apply where there is an actual sale of the asset,[9] a deemed sale,[10] or the benefit of a contract is transferred,[11] the allowances are then restricted to the lower of the cost price to the lessor and the cost price to the lessee.[12] Where the item of plant and machinery is subsequently sold to another taxpayer, the limit that is applied under the anti-avoidance measures continues to apply, even though the purchaser may not be a connected person to the original lessor.[13] There is a clearance procedure.[14]

Where there is a sale of finance leaseback, the disposal value is restricted to the lower of the market value of the plant or the notional written down value, so that the vendor's capital allowances are not clawed back.[15] There is then a partial disallowance of the tax deduction for rents payable under the leaseback.[16]

---

[1] Statement of Standard Accounting Practice SSAP 21.
[2] CAA 2001, s 220.
[3] CAA 2001, s 220.
[4] CAA 2001, s 11(4).
[5] CAA 2001, ss 172, 174.
[6] CAA 2001, s 229(3).
[7] CAA 2001, ss 221–227.
[8] TA 1988, s 839(5).
[9] CAA 2001, s 213.
[10] CAA 2001, s 213.
[11] CAA 2001, s 213. The Revenue consider that as this section is an anti-avoidance provision it should, "be given a wide reading to cover the kinds of mischief against which it is aimed", but does not cover novation (Inland Revenue Tax Bulletin, June 1998, p 542).
[12] CAA 2001, ss 221, 224, 228.

[13] CAA 2001, s 226.
[14] The Revenue is prepared to give its view on whether CAA 2001, s 222(4) will apply to any proposed arrangements, if a detailed technical description of the arrangements accompanied by "a plain English summary" is sent to Inland Revenue Special Investigation Section (Inland Revenue Tax Bulletin, June 1998, p 544).
[15] CAA 2001, s 222.
[16] CAA 2001, ss 228B—228H. Inserted by FA 2004, s 134 with effect from 17 March 2004 and amended subsequently. There are transitional provisions for leases that span that date: FA 2004, Sch 23.

Restrictions on allowances—leasing

[9.48] There are other restrictions on using the allowances whether first year allowances or writing down allowances. First, for income tax, although not for corporation tax, losses arising from leasing, whether from first year or writing down allowances, can only be set against general (ie non-leasing) income if the lessor carries on a trade of leasing, does so for at least six months, and devotes substantially the whole of his time to it.[1] The effect of this is to make equipment leasing an unattractive proposition, save when it is a full-time business.

Second, there is a restriction where a leasing partnership was involved. For example X, Y and Z Ltd are partners who buy plant and claim allowances. X and Y then withdraw from the partnership leaving Z to face the balancing charge, but Z is a non-resident company. Relief under ITA 2007, ss 64 and 72 is now denied where a scheme has been entered into with a company partner in prospect. This applies to allowances:

(1) granted to an individual when the plant concerned was acquired for leasing in the course of a trade carried on by the individual *and*, at the time of incurring expenditure on the plant, he was carrying on the trade in partnership with a company, or arrangements had been or were later made for him to do so; or
(2) given
    (a) in connection with a trade carried on by a partnership (either at the time the expenditure was incurred or later) or transferred to a person connected with the individual otherwise entitled to the relief; or
    (b) in respect of an asset later transferred by the individual either at undervalue or to a person connected with him; *and*
    (c) in both (a) and (b) it is apparent that, as a result of arrangements made either then or later, the sole benefit that the individual is likely to receive as a result of the acquisition of the plant is a reduction in his tax liability.[2]

Third, when a non-trading company claims capital allowances on plant leased to a non-trader, the allowances can only be set against income from letting plant.[3] Group relief is not available in such circumstances.[4]

Simon's Taxes B3.366.

[9.48] Capital allowances

1. TA 1988, s 384(6)–(8).
2. CAA 2001, Sch 2, para 30.
3. CAA 2001, s 258(4).
4. CAA 2001, s 260(7).

Machinery and plant on lease—lessee's expenditure

[9.49] A special provision deals with capital expenditure by a lessee on the provision of machinery or plant for the purposes of his trade under the terms of his lease.[1] The asset is treated as belonging to the lessee so long as his trade continues. The asset in fact belongs to the lessor and as from the determination of the lease the rules as to disposal value and balancing charges are applied as if the original expenditure had been incurred by the lessor. Thus the allowance is given to the lessee but any balancing charge may be levied on the lessor. As a result of the rules stemming from *Stokes v Costain Property Investments Ltd*[2] this does not now apply to machinery and plant that becomes part of a building on other land.

Simon's Taxes B3.385.

1. CAA 2001, s 70(1)–(5), Sch 3, para 17.
2. [1984] STC 204, [1984] 1 All ER 849, CA (see supra, § **9.25**).

Motor vehicles

[9.50] Expenditure on certain types of road vehicle can be treated as ordinary expenditure on machinery and plant. The favoured vehicles are:[1]

(1) goods vehicles of a construction primarily suited to the carriage of goods or burden of any description;
(2) vehicles of a type not commonly used as private vehicles and unsuitable to be so used, for example works buses and minivans;[2]
(3) vehicles provided wholly or mainly for hire to, or for the carriage of members of the public in the ordinary course of a trade;[3] and
(4) 4 Motor cars with low CO_2 emissions or powered by electricity—100% allowance.[4]

For condition 3 the number of consecutive days for which it was on hire to or used for the carriage of the same person would normally be less than 30 and the total number of days in any period of 12 months will normally be less than 90. The vehicle is also favoured if it is hired to a person who will himself use it wholly or mainly for hire to members of the public in this way. This is an effort to distinguish the ordinary car rental business from the increasingly common leasing arrangement whereby a (new) car is leased to a person for two or three years. An exception is made for cars leased to persons receiving mobility allowance.[5]

Expenditure on cars outside these favoured categories and costing less than £12,000 is to be pooled separately from other assets but to form one single

Plant and machinery [9.50]

pool.[6] Where however the capital expenditure on such a car exceeds £12,000, each car is treated as a separate asset and the allowance is limited to a maximum of £3,000. The maximum will be reduced if the period for which the allowance is claimed is less than one year or the use is subsidised.[7] The effect of the £3,000 limit is to defer the benefit of the relief. These figures of £3,000 and £12,000 are reduced or increased proportionately if the chargeable period is less or greater than 12 months.[8]

When a car costing more than £12,000 is leased, further special rules apply to restrict the relief normally given in computing profit for hiring charges.[9] These special rules do not apply if the car has low CO emission, or is powered by electricity.[10] The restriction also does not apply where the car is subject to a hire purchase agreement under which the hirer has an option to buy the car for an amount equivalent to 1% (or less) of the retail price of the car when new.[11]

When a car, other than a favoured car is leased, the deduction available for the rent paid under the lease is reduced in the proportion which the £12,000 plus half the amount by which the retail price of the vehicle when new exceeds £12,000, bears to that retail price. Thus suppose that the car cost £18,000 new and that the rent is £5,600, the amount claimable for tax is:

$$\frac{12{,}000 + (18{,}000 - 12{,}000)/2}{18{,}000} \text{ or } \frac{5}{6} \times £5{,}600 = £4{,}666$$

£12,000 + £18,000

2 × £18,000 × rent paid

This has the effect of giving tax relief on 5/6ths of the rent paid. The missing 1/6 will never qualify for relief.

Simon's Taxes B3.342.

---

[1] CAA 2001, s 81.
[2] *Roberts v Granada TV Rental Ltd* [1970] 2 All ER 764, 46 TC 295.
[3] CAA 2001, s 82(2), (3).
[4] CAA 2001, s 45D inserted by FA 2002, Sch 19 for expenditure incurred between 17 April 2002 and 31 March 2008. This was extended by FA 2008 until 2013 but with a reduction in the CO_2 emissions figure from 120g/km to 110 g/km.
[5] CAA 2001, s 82(4).
[6] CAA 2001, ss 65(2), 74(1).
[7] CAA 2001, ss 75, 76, Sch 2, para 52.
[8] CAA 2001, ss 74–79.
[9] CAA 2001, Sch 2, para 52. On the meaning of "hire" for the purpose of this restriction, see *Lloyds UDT Finance Ltd v Chartered Finance Trust Holdings plc* [2002] EWCA Civ 806, [2002] STC 956. On the effect of rebate of hire charge, see extra-statutory concession B28.
[10] FA 2001, s 59 for expenditure incurred between 17 April 2002 and 31 March 2008 on a car first registered after 16 April 2002.
[11] CAA 2001, Sch 2, para 52.

Capital allowances for an employee

[9.51] In principle, an employee can obtain capital allowances to put against employment income in respect of machinery and plant provided by the employee for use in his employment.[1]

However, no capital allowances are available in respect of expenditure on a motor car, a cycle or cycle safety equipment.[2] Instead, tax relief is provided through the system of motoring allowances (see supra, § **7.120**).

If an employee provides any item of machinery or plant other than a mechanically propelled road vehicle or a cycle or cycle safety equipment, a capital allowance is only available if a machinery or plant "is necessarily provided for use in the performance of the duties" of the employment.[3] Hence, the possibility of another individual performing the duties of the employment without that item of machinery is fatal to the granting of the capital allowance. This is of particular importance in relation to computers used by employees. For most employments, it is not possible under statute to claim a capital allowance for a computer/word processor purchased by an employee for use in his employment as it would be possible to perform the duties of that employment by the use of pen, paper and brain as opposed to the use of the computer/word processor. Not infrequently, the argument is put by the Revenue that the fact that it is the employee, not the employer, who provides the equipment is evidence that the item is not "necessary" for the employment. (Arguably, the position of an office holder assessable under ITEPA 2003 is better than that of his employee colleague. As the source of income is the office he occupies, rather than an employer, the argument should centre on whether the duties of the office necessitate the purchase of the item in question.)

There are, however, local agreements for particular groups of employees. For example, an agreement is in operation whereby the relevant tax district accepts that the "necessary" test is demonstrated as having been satisfied in the case of a university teacher where the employer university or college reimburses a part of the university teacher's expenditure on a computer/word processor. Capital allowances are then granted to the university teacher on the balance of the expenditure that he has incurred personally.

---

[1] CAA 2001, s 15(1)(*e*).
[2] CAA 2001, s 36 rewritten with effect from 6 April 2002, by FA 2001, s 59(1). CAA 2001, s 80 which provided for capital allowances being granted for expenditure on vehicles used for the purpose of employment is repealed by FA 2001, s 59(2) with respect to expenditure incurred on or after 6 April 2002.
[3] CAA 2001, ss 20(2), 36(2).

Assets leased overseas

[9.52] The 25% pa allowance for assets leased outside the UK was a favourable rate and often used to subsidise deals which had no real connection with the UK. As a result, the allowances available with respect to expenditure on the provision of machinery and for leasing to persons who are not resident in the UK and do not use the machinery or plant for the purposes of a trade carried on in the UK or for earning profits or gains which are taxed in the UK, have been reduced to 10%.[1] Where there is a chain of leases the Revenue can now apply these rules to each lessee and not, as previously, only to the final lessee.[2]

For leases entered into on or after 16 March 1993 these rules are widened in two ways. First, the restriction to 10% applies unless the person is using the asset exclusively for the purposes of earning profits which are chargeable to tax in the UK. Second, profits or gains chargeable to UK tax do not include those arising to a person who can claim relief under a double taxation agreement, eg the UK branch of a foreign company.[3] This does not apply to short-term leasing nor to the leasing of a ship, aircraft or transport container used for a qualifying purpose.[4] The Revenue view appears to be that a container which has a function of movement as part of its design is not a transport container; this means that only 10% allowances are available for railway wagons and trailers designed, for example, for cross-channel operations.[5]

Where the lease could be for more than 13 years, or consecutive payments are more than a year apart or of varying amounts or collateral payments are made, or payments connected to the value of the machinery or plant at the expiry of the lease there could be possibilities for tax avoidance and entitlement to allowances may be suspended.[6] First year writing down and balancing allowances already given may be withdrawn.[7]

Expenditure on these assets is pooled separately.[8] There are rules about joint leases and information.[9]

Where an asset has qualified for an allowance, whether a writing down allowance or a first year allowance on the basis that it will be used for a qualifying purpose (and only so used) for the requisite period, any breach of the conditions during the period leads to restriction or withdrawal of the allowances. The requisite period was originally fixed at ten years,[10] and this period was applied to assets leased abroad. There was some doubt as to the position where an asset was originally used for a qualifying purpose within the UK and then leased abroad; it is now established that the period should be ten years.[11]

Simon's Taxes B3.345.

1 CAA 2001, s 105.
2 Revenue interpretation April 1999, *Simon's Weekly Tax Intelligence* 1999, p 834. For the Court of Appeal's analysis where there is a multi-party lease, see *BMBF (No 24) Ltd v IRC* [2003] EWCA Civ 1560, [2004] STC 97.
3 CAA 1990, s 50(2) added by FA 1993, s 116 for leases.
4 CAA 2001, s 109(2).
5 See *Simon's Tax Intelligence* 1991, p 1138(8).
6 CAA 2001, s 110.
7 CAA 2001, s 114(1)–(3).
8 CAA 2001, s 114(4).
9 CAA 2001, ss 111–120.

[10] CAA 2001, s 213.
[11] CAA 2001, ss 87(1)(c) and 132(1)(b).

Ships and aircraft leased on charter

[9.53] When the new provisions for leased assets were introduced in 1980 it was necessary to protect shipping and aircraft transactions to some extent because of the large sums involved. Thus where UK residents purchased ships or aircraft to be let out on charter, the capital allowance was preserved[1] even though the charter was with an overseas company, if the UK company was responsible for the ship's navigation and management. Today the 25% writing down allowance is still available in such circumstances. However, if the main object, or one of the main objects, for letting the ship or aircraft on charter is to obtain a 25% writing down allowance in respect of the expenditure, whether by the lessor or by some other person the 25% allowance is not available.[2] The purpose is not a qualifying purpose and so only a 10% allowance may be available.[3]

Simon's Taxes B3.351.

[1] CAA 2001, s 123(1)–(3)
[2] CAA 2001, s 123(4), Sch 3, para 23.
[3] CAA 2001, ss 105(2), (3), 109(2).

Films, tapes and discs

[9.54] The rules relating to expenditure on master copies of films, tapes and discs were radically altered in 1982, relaxed in 1992 and further relaxed in 2005. Previously, investment in such master copies had qualified for 100% first year allowances. Today, 100% allowances are available only for expenditure on certain British films costing less than £15m to make.[1] The expenditure must be incurred on or after 2 July 1997 and before 10 October 2005.[2]

Expenditure incurred after 10 March 1982[3] is treated as a normal expense, but written off over the life of the film, tape or disc. The taxpayer has the right to allocate additional expenditure to a particular period.[4] These provisions do not apply where the film etc would in any event be treated as trading stock under the general law (see supra, § **8.151**). Sums received from the disposal of the film, etc will be treated as receipts of a revenue nature.[5]

The terms used in these rules are clarified by FA 2000. Thus the definition of expenditure is simplified by the removal of the requirement that the expenditure would otherwise have been capital expenditure. The rights to be acquired along with the master are defined more closely.

Certain expenditure on qualifying films payable on or after 10 March 1992 now benefits from a relaxed regime. The essence of the new reliefs is to recognise the long time gap between the incurring of expenditure on a film and the film's release.[6] The present rules give the taxpayer the option to take a

Plant and machinery [9.54]

capital allowance on capital expenditure or to take a revenue deduction either steadily over the life of the film or pound for pound as income arises. The new rules bring forward the date at which relief can be given, but this is a matter of election.[7]

Relief for preliminary expenditure of a revenue nature[8] is given. This takes the form of a tax deduction for the costs of developing prospective films as they are incurred. In essence any expenditure incurred prior to a firm decision being taken to proceed with the film (called the first day of principal photography) will attract this relief up to a limit of 20% of total budgeted expenditure as calculated on that day.[9] Abortive expenditure qualifies. Various provisions try to restrict this relief to expenditure on films that would be qualifying films if completed.[10]

Relief for production expenditure of a revenue nature,[11] so far as not already written off as preliminary expenditure, is written off over a three-year period at a flat rate.[12] This rule applies also to the costs of acquisition expenditure.[13] FA 2000 clarifies what must have been done by 10 March 1992.[14]

Simon's Taxes B1.613.

---

[1] F(No 2)A 1997, s 48 amended by FA 2005, ss 58–71. In order to qualify for the 100% first year allowance, the film must be certified as a "British film" by the Secretary of State for Culture, Media and Sport: Films Act 1985, Sch 1, para 9. For an unsuccessful application for a court order requiring a certificate see *Peakviewing (Interactive) Ltd v Secretary of State for Culture, Media and Sport* [2002] EWHC 1531 (Admin), [2002] STC 1226. In that case, an unsuccessful application was made in respect of five-minute films that were described by the court as more akin to advertisements than products for the cinema. FA 2002, s 99(1) now denies the 100% first year allowance unless there is an intention at the time the film is completed of exhibiting the film to the paying public in the commercial cinema, although there are strange exceptions under transitional provisions for expensive drama films that were commissioned before 17 April 2002. The intention appears to be that the enhanced first year allowances are not available after the end of the transition period for any production that is for television and not for the cinema.

[2] F(No 2)A 1997, s 48(2)(a) extended by FA 2005, s 58.
[3] CAA 2001, Sch 2, para 82.
[4] CAA 2001, Sch 2, para 82.
[5] CAA 2001, Sch 2, para 82; see statement of practice SP 1/98.
[6] Inland Revenue press release, 23 June 1992, *Simon's Tax Intelligence* 1992, p 638.
[7] CAA 2001, Sch 2, para 82.
[8] CAA 2001, Sch 2, para 82.
[9] F(No 2)A 1992, s 41.
[10] F(No 2)A 1992, s 41(3), (4).
[11] CAA 2001, Sch 2, para 82.
[12] CAA 2001, Sch 2, para 82.
[13] CAA 2001, Sch 2, para 82.
[14] CAA 2001, Sch 2, para 82.

Mining

Qualifying expenditure

[9.55] Qualifying expenditure is defined both by inclusion[1] and exclusion.[2] Thus the expense of an abortive application for planning permission is allowed[3] but that on the acquisition of a site on which expense qualifying for relief will be carried out will not.[4] Expenditure on machinery and plant is usually left to the machinery and plant system of allowances but this will not work where the expense is a pre-trading expense and the asset is disposed of before the trade begins; such expense may therefore be qualifying expenditure.[5] There is a similar rule for pre-trading exploration expenditure.[6] Also included are certain payments by mining concerns for site comfort and development outside the UK.[7] Expenditure on restoring a site at the end of the operation also qualifies.[8]

Simon's Taxes B3.406–408.

[1] CAA 2001, s 400.
[2] CAA 2001, s 399(2)–(6)
[3] CAA 2001, s 396(2)–(3).
[4] CAA 2001, s 399.
[5] CAA 2001, s 402.
[6] CAA 2001, s 401.
[7] CAA 2001, s 415.
[8] CAA 2001, s 416.

The allowance

[9.56] When qualifying expenditure is incurred for the purposes of the trade of mineral extraction, a writing down allowance is given by reference to the amount by which the qualifying expenditure exceeds any disposal proceeds received during the period. The scheme is a simple reducing balance so that previous allowances reduce the qualifying expenditure. For pre-trading expenditure on machinery and plant disposed of before the trade begins and pre-trading exploration expenditure, the figure is 10%; for other qualifying expenditure it is 25%.[1] The allowance is given in taxing the trade.[2]

Disposal proceeds include the disposal value of an asset which ceases permanently to be used for the trade of mineral extraction. Capital sums reasonably attributable to qualifying expenditure must be brought into account.[3]

Where allowances and disposal proceeds exceed expenditure, there is a balancing charge equal to the excess but this is not to lead to a charge greater than the allowances already given.[4] Balancing allowances may arise principally in the period when the trade of mineral extraction ends and there are special rules for situations in which work on a particular mining deposit ceases and when disposal proceeds arise.[5] Pre-trading expenses on machinery and plant and exploration are treated as balancing allowances.[6] Balancing allowances may also arise where an asset is lost, ceases to exist or begins to be used for a purpose other than mineral extraction (in whole or in part).[7] Expenditure on mineral exploration and access is treated as incurred for the purpose of the trade[8] and demolition costs are to be added to qualifying expenditure when the asset in question may give rise to a balancing allowance or charge.[9]

Simon's Taxes B3.420, 421.

[1] CAA 2001, s 418.
[2] CAA 2001, s 432.
[3] CAA 2001, ss 421–423.
[4] CAA 2001, ss 417, 418.
[5] CAA 2001, ss 428(1)–(3), 431.
[6] CAA 2001, s 430(1).
[7] CAA 2001, ss 426, 427.
[8] CAA 2001, s 400(2).
[9] CAA 2001, s 433.

Limitations of qualifying expenditure

[9.57] There are a number of rules restricting the amount of expenditure that would otherwise qualify for the relief. First the cost of land is excluded; the valuation is carried out by assuming no source of mineral deposits and only existing or authorised use allowed.[1] There is a similar valuation for calculating the disposal proceeds.[2]

Where the expenditure is incurred in the purchase of an asset which has already been used by a previous trader in the mineral extraction business, the purchaser is usually required to take over the previous trader's position even if the purchase is not directly from that person. So where the previous trader was not entitled to any relief it is the previous trader's qualifying expenditure that is taken rather than the price paid by the taxpayer[3] and where an allowance or charge has already been made to or on the previous trader, that too must be taken into account.[4]

Where the purchase is of mineral deposits and part is attributable to exploration and access, an apportionment is directed.[5] For similar reasons, expenditure on Petroleum Act licences must be restricted to the price paid by the original licensee[6] and where a mineral asset is transferred within a group it is the transferor's qualifying expenditure that matters.[7]

Where a person incurs expenditure on mineral exploration and access and he sells assets representing that expenditure but does not himself carry on a mineral extraction trade, the qualifying expenditure is not the price paid to him by the purchaser but his expenditure.[8]

Simon's Taxes B3.410–414.

[1] CAA 2001, s 404.
[2] CAA 2001, s 424.

³ CAA 2001, ss 407, 411.
⁴ CAA 2001, s 411(3).
⁵ CAA 2001, s 407.
⁶ CAA 2001, s 410.
⁷ CAA 2001, s 412.
⁸ CAA 2001, ss 408, 409(1).

Dredging

[9.58] Allowances are given in respect of capital expenditure incurred on dredging if the trade consists of the maintenance or improvement of the navigation of a harbour, estuary or waterway or the dredging is for the benefit of vessels coming to, leaving or using any dock or other premises occupied for the purpose of the trade.[1] Dredging refers only to acts done in the interests of navigation.[2] In general the allowance is similar to that for industrial buildings.

The allowance is made in taxing the trade.[3] The initial allowance was 15%; the straight line writing down allowance is 4%.[4] If the trade is permanently discontinued before the expenditure has been written off there is an immediate write-off of the balance.[5] There is no balancing charge.

Simon's Taxes B3.801–807.

¹ CAA 2001, ss 485(1), 487(1), (2), Sch 3, para 103 undoing *Dumbarton Harbour Board v Cox* (1919) 7 TC 147.
² CAA 2001, s 484(3), (4).
³ CAA 2001, s 488(1), (3)–(5).
⁴ CAA 2001, s 488(1), (2).
⁵ CAA 2001, s 488(1), (2).

Agricultural land and buildings

[9.59] For expenditure in 2007–08[1] and earlier years, an allowance may be claimed by a person with a major interest in agricultural land who incurs capital expenditure on the construction of farmhouses, farm buildings, cottages, fences and other works, eg drainage.[2] The allowance takes the form of a writing down allowance over 25 years, ie 4% pa straight line.[3]

The allowance is set primarily against agricultural income.[4] The quite separate industrial buildings allowance may sometimes be available.[5]

The expenditure must have been incurred for the purposes of husbandry[6] on the agricultural land but an apportionment is made where the expenditure is only partly for that purpose.[7] Where the expenditure is on a farmhouse, one third is allowable and a smaller proportion being substituted if the accommodation and amenities of the farmhouse are out of due relation to the nature and extent of the farm.[8] It is probably the case that there only be one farmhouse on a farm.[9] A house is designated "a farmhouse" by virtue of its use on the farm, not by virtue of the individual who occupies it.[10]

In *Lindsay v IRC* the only house on a sheep farm was occupied by a shepherd and the owner resided in the United States but it remained the farmhouse. In *IRC v John M Whiteford & Son*[11] the fact that the occupier was one of the partners running the farm did not mean that his house was necessarily a farmhouse; rather it could be an agricultural cottage and so entitled to the full allowance. The proper criterion is not the status of the occupant but the purpose of the occupation of the premises.[12] In that case there was evidence that the farm was run from the house of the other partner. In both cases the decision of the Commissioners was upheld. If it is of a scale extravagantly large for the purpose for which it was being used, it might be entitled to no allowance whatsoever.[13]

Simon's Taxes B3.503, 507.

[1] As part of the phasing out of agricultural buildings allowances, a successor post-20 March 2007 is not eligible for an agricultural buildings allowance, unless the contract under which he succeeds to ownership of the asset was made before 21 March 2007: FA 2007, s 36(7).
[2] CAA 2001, ss 361, 369, 370, 371.
[3] CAA 2001, s 373(1).
[4] CAA 2001, s 392.
[5] CAA 2001, s 274.
[6] CAA 2001 s 362(1)(a).
[7] CAA 2001, ss 361, 369(1)–(5).
[8] CAA 2001, ss 361, 369(1)–(5).
[9] In *IRC v John M Whiteford & Son* (1962) 40 TC 379, the farming partnership consisted of father and son, who lived together in a single farmhouse. The son married and moved to a new house, also on the farm. The court held that the son's house was a cottage and not the farmhouse.
[10] In *Lindsay v IRC* (1952) 34 TC 289, there was only one house on a sheep farm. This was occupied by a shepherd, the owner residing in the United States. The court held that the house in which the shepherd lived was the farmhouse as he was the person running the farm.
[11] (1962) 40 TC 379.
[12] Per Lord Clyde, at 384.
[13] Per Lord Clyde, at 384.

[9.60] The details of the allowance are similar to those for industrial buildings. So expenditure on the acquisition of land or rights over land is excluded.[1]

Prior to 21 March 2007, a balancing allowance or charge arose if within 25[2] years of the agricultural building being first used, the relevant interest is sold or the building is demolished or destroyed or altogether ceases to be used. No such allowance or charge arises in respect of any event on or after 21 March 2007, unless it occurs before 1 April 2011 in pursuance of a contract made before 31 March 2007.[3] Other transitional measures connected with the withdrawal of the allowance are discussed below.

[9.60] Capital allowances

Simon's Taxes B3.503, 509–511.

1   CAA 2001, s 363.
2   CAA 2001, ss 314–326. Repealed with effect from 21 March 2007 by FA 2007, s 36(5).
3   Repealed with effect from 21 March 2007 by FA 2007, s 36(5) and (7).

Transitional measures before 2011

Writing down allowances

[9.61] During the period from 1 (or 6) April 2008 until 31 March (or 5 April 2011), agricultural buildings allowances are being phased out. In a nutshell, writing down allowances are being reduced by 25% for the financial year 2008 (or, for income tax, the 2008–09 tax year) by 50% for the following year and by 75% in the third year of the transitional phase.[1]

For taxpayers whose chargeable periods straddle the dates of 1 April (or 6 April), the percentage reduction must be adjusted proportionately – by reference to the number of days before and those on or after the relevant date.[2] Only days in which the taxpayer was entitled to the relevant interest are taken into account in this calculation.[3]

1   FA 2008, s 82(3).
2   FA 2008, s 82(6).
3   FA 2008, s 82(7).

Other allowances

Research and development

[9.62] Research and development allowances, previously called scientific research allowances, are available[1] for capital expenditure on scientific research, provided it is related to the trade carried on (or to be carried on). The allowances are not available against profits of a profession or vocation.[2] The research may be carried on by someone other than the trader provided it is on behalf of the trader, an expression which requires something close to agency.[3] The allowance does not extend to the costs of creating a training centre since research is confined to natural or applied science for the advancement of knowledge.[4] Costs in acquiring rights in scientific research are not allowed. No allowance can be claimed for expenditure incurred after 31 March 1985 on the acquisition of land or rights over land (as distinct from buildings) or on the acquisition of a dwelling, although apportionment is permitted.[5] Apportionment of expenditure is permitted.[6]

Research and development is defined[7] by reference to accounting practice, but with a Treasury power to change this, whether by inclusion or exclusion, by

Other allowances [9.62]

statutory instrument.[8] Oil and gas exploration and appraisal receive special mention because while they are to continue to qualify for this allowance they are not to qualify for the new credit. Appeal on these matters now lies within the ordinary tax appeal structure and not as previously with the Secretary of State for Trade and Industry.[9]

There are balancing allowances and charges but only if the asset ceases to be used for scientific research and is then (or later) sold (or destroyed).[10] VAT under the capital goods scheme is also taken into account.[11] The relevant chargeable period is that in which the expenditure was incurred save that for pre-trading expenditure the chargeable period beginning with the commencement is taken.[12]

For expenditure incurred after 31 March 1985[13] these allowances and charges arise when the asset ceases to belong to the person whether through sale, destruction or any other event.[14]

Sums paid to approved research associations, universities and institutions may be deductible as if they were revenue expenditure.[15]

When there is a transfer from one person to another of an asset on which research and development allowances have been given, the parties can choose to elect to transfer the asset at its tax written down value (see supra, § **9.08**).[16]

Uniquely, an allowance of 150% is given for expenditure on research and development by small and medium companies, as long as it is not capital expenditure.[17]

Simon's Taxes B3.703, 704, 706.

[1] CAA 2001, s 437.
[2] CAA 2001, ss 439(1). For rejection of a claim for allowances on the ground that there was no trade, see *Salt v Golding* [1996] STC (SCD) 269.
[3] CAA 2001, ss 439(1); *Gaspet Ltd v Elliss* [1985] STC 572.
[4] CAA 2001, ss 437(2) applying TA 1988, s 837A. On meaning of when an asset is sold, see CAA 2001, s 451.
[5] CAA 2001, s 440.
[6] CAA 2001, s 439(4), Sch 3, para 89.
[7] TA 1988, s 837A(2)–(5); this brings in SSAP 13.
[8] TA 1988, s 837A(3).
[9] CAA 2001, ss 219, 226.
[10] CAA 2001, ss 442–444.
[11] CAA 2001, ss 447, 438, 449.
[12] CAA 2001, ss 441(2), 447(3).
[13] FA 1985, s 63; the old rules remain for expenditure incurred before that date and for expenditure incurred after that date but before 1 April 1987 under a contract entered into before 13 March 1984.
[14] On values to be taken see CAA 2001, ss 443(4), 577(1).
[15] CAA 2001 ss 441(1), 438.
[16] CAA 2001, s 569(3), (4).
[17] FA 2000, Sch 21, para 3(2). See supra, § **8:140**.

Patents and know-how

[9.63] Since 1945 there has been a special regime to treat sums derived from the disposal of patents as income and conversely to allow expenditure on acquiring patent rights. The capital cost of purchasing patent rights was, broadly speaking, allowed by equal annual instalments over 17 years.[1] For expenditure incurred on or after 1 April 1986, this is replaced by an annual writing down allowance of 25% (reducing balance basis[2]); this regime also applies to the costs of acquiring knowhow,[3] a term defined as information likely to assist in the manufacture or processing of goods or materials.[4] There are balancing allowances and charges if the rights come to an end or are disposed of.[5] Royalties payable under a patent agreement to a non-resident are subject to deduction at source under TA 1988, s 349.

Capital payments received for the disposal of patent rights are taxed as income and spread over six years. If the individual dies before the six year period ends any remaining instalments may be spread back; similar rules apply on discontinuance or on the winding up of a company.[6]

Simon's Taxes B3.605, 606, 616, 617, B5.333, 336.

[1] CAA 2001, Sch 3, para 92–96.
[2] CAA 2001, ss 468–472.
[3] CAA 2001, ss 454–462.
[4] ITTOIA 2005, s 192. The term "know how" also encompasses any industrial information and techniques likely to assist working a source of mineral deposits (including the searching for, discovery or testing of deposits or the winning of access thereto), or carrying out of any agricultural, forestry or fishing operations.
[5] CAA 2001, Sch 3, paras 92–100.
[6] ITTOIA 2005, ss 587 & 590.

Conversion of business premises into flats

[9.64] In his Budget statement on 7 March 2001, Gordon Brown said: 'to help revitalise our high streets, we will provide 100% first year capital allowances for bringing empty flats over shops back into the residential market'.[1] The new provisions were recommended by the Urban Task Force, chaired by Lord Rogers, in the report "Towards an Urban Renaissance"[2] and the intention of the legislation is described by the Treasury as enabling property owners and occupiers "to obtain up front tax relief for their capital expenditure on recycling former residential space over shops. . .(being) part of a package of measures being introduced to encourage the regeneration of urban areas".[3]

The statutory scheme[4] is modelled on that for industrial buildings allowances[5] but is self-standing and does not impose a balancing charge (nor is there a balancing allowance) if there is a disposal of the property after it has been let (or has been available for letting) for a seven year period[6] and, unlike IBAs, the allowances are not transferable to the purchaser.

Although Revenue Press Releases refer to "flats over shops"[7] allowances are available for the conversion of any commercial building within the parameters designated; there is no requirement for the building to be, or be above, a shop.

The allowance is given to a person who has a "relevant interest" in property that is converted into a "qualifying flat" and who incurs "qualifying expenditure". Where the conditions are fulfilled, that person is entitled to claim an initial allowance of 100% of the qualifying expenditure.[8] The claim can be made for an initial allowance of any sum less than 100%.[9] Where reduced initial allowance claim is made, the balance of allowance due is granted by means of a writing down allowance of 25% of the qualifying expenditure,[10] which can, itself, be reduced to a lower figure specified by the taxpayer, at his option.[11] The allowance is calculated as 25% of the initial expenditure, not the reducing balance. Hence, if the claim for initial allowance is reduced to 50% of the initial expenditure, the balance of the expenditure will be relieved by writing down allowances over the next 24 months.

A taxpayer is treated for the purpose of this allowance as having a "relevant interest" if he holds the freehold, including a reversionary interest for a freehold subject to a lease, or if he holds any leasehold interest, or if he acquires an interest in the flat as a result of the completion of the conversion.[12]

A qualifying building is one whose construction was completed before 1 January 1980,[13] the ground floor of which[14] is authorised for business use.[15]

The intention behind the legislation is, clearly, to grant an allowance for the creation of low price, privately let accommodation. This is achieved by the restrictive definition of a "qualifying flat", being one within a qualifying building,[16] with its own entry,[17] having not more than four rooms,[18] that is suitable for letting as a dwelling and held for the purpose of short-term letting.[19] In addition, the flat must be such that the rent that could reasonably be expected for a shorthold letting[20] to an unconnected tenant[21] is less than £480 per week, if in Greater London, or £300 per week if elsewhere in the UK (lower limits are imposed for flats of less than four rooms).[22] In addition, the flat must not be created or renovated as part of a scheme whereby other flats are created that would attract rents above the limit specified[23] and must not be actually let to a connected person.[24]

"Qualifying expenditure" is capital expenditure incurred on, or in connection with, the conversion or renovation of part of a qualifying building into a qualifying flat,[25] including incidental repairs[26] but excluding the cost of the land[27] and the cost of any furnishings.[28] Capital expenditure is any expenditure that would not be deductible as a Revenue expense for the purpose of calculating the profits from a property business.[29]

If within seven years of the time when the flat was first suitable for letting as a dwelling, the flat is sold, any capital allowance given to the vendor is treated as an income receipt of the vendor at the time of sale, up to the limit of the sale proceeds received.[30] The charge is imposed whenever there is "a balancing event" within the seven year period.[31] In addition to a sale, the following are treated as a balancing event if within the seven year period:

(a) the grant for long lease;

[9.64] Capital allowances

(b) the ending of the leasehold interest held by the person who obtained the allowance;
(c) the demolition of the flat;
(d) the flat ceasing to be a "qualifying flat".[32]

The balancing charge is, in each case, the allowance that has been given (whether by initial allowance or balancing allowance), up to the maximum of the proceeds receivable, except for category (b) where it is the market value of the interest in the flat that comes to an end.[33]

It is also possible for a balancing event to give a balancing allowance. This will arise when the full 100% initial allowance is not claimed and the flat is destroyed, with the insurance proceeds (if any) being less than the qualifying expenditure.[34] There is also a balancing allowance given at the death of the person who incurred the qualifying expenditure, if there is then any qualifying expenditure for which an allowance has not been given.[35]

---

[1] *Simon's Weekly Tax Intelligence* 2001, p 369.
[2] Published 29 June 1999 by Department of Environment, Transport and The Regions.
[3] H M Treasury Explanatory Notes to the Finance Bill 2001, 30 March 2001.
[4] CAA 2001, ss 393A–393W inserted by FA 2001, Sch 19.
[5] See supra, §§ **9.11–9.22**.
[6] CAA 2001, s 393M(4).
[7] For example Budget Note 15/01, *Simon's Weekly Tax Intelligence* 2001, p 445.
[8] CAA 2001, s 393H(1), (2).
[9] CAA 2001, s 393H(3).
[10] CAA 2001, s 393K(1).
[11] CAA 2001, s 393J(4).
[12] CAA 2001, ss 393F and 393G.
[13] CAA 2001, s 393G(1)(d).
[14] Or most of the ground floor: CAA 2001, s 393G(1)(d).
[15] This is defined for England or Wales as used within class A1, A2, A3, B1 or D1(a) specified in the Schedule to the Town and Country Planning (Use Classes) Order 1987, SI 1987/764, with equivalent categories for Scotland by reference to the Town and Country Planning (Use Classes) (Scotland) Order 1997, SI 1997/3061 and for Northern Ireland by reference to the Planning (Use Classes) Order (Northern Ireland) 1989, Northern Ireland Statutory Rule 1989/290: CAA 2001, s 393C(2).
[16] CAA 2001, s 393G(2).
[17] CAA 2001, s 393D(1)(a).
[18] CAA 2001, s 393D(1)(d).
[19] CAA 2001, s 393D(1)(c). Kitchen, bathroom and entry rooms less than 5 square meters are ignored: s 393D(3).
[20] In Scotland, a short assured tenancy.
[21] CAA 2001, s 393E(2)(d).
[22] The notional rent limits are:

Other allowances [9.65]

Number of rooms in flat (ignoring, kitchen, bathroom and hallway)	Flats in Greater London	Flats elsewhere
1 or 2 rooms	£350 per week	£150 per week
3 rooms	£425 per week	£225 per week
4 rooms	£480 per week	£300 per week

CAA 2000, s 293E(5).
[23] CAA 2001, s 393D(1)(g).
[24] CAA 2001, s 393D(1)(h).
[25] CAA 2001, s 393B(1)(a), (b).
[26] CAA 2001, s 393B(1)(c).
[27] CAA 2001, s 393(3)(a).
[28] CAA 2001, s 393(3)(d).
[29] CAA 2001, s 393B(4), see infra, § **10.08**.
[30] CAA 2001, ss 393M(4), 393N(1)(a) and 393O(1) (Balancing event 1) and 393P(3) and (4).
[31] CAA 2001, s 393M(1)(b) and (4).
[32] CAA 2001, s 393N(1)(b), (c), (e) and (f).
[33] CAA 2001, s 393O(1).
[34] CAA 2001, ss 393P(1), (2) and 393O(1) (Balancing event 5).
[35] CAA 2001, ss 393P(1), (2) and 393O(1) (Balancing event 4).

Contaminated land

[9.65] Capital expenditure by a company on what statute describes as "remediation of contaminated land" attracts a special capital allowance of 150%[1] granted in the year in which the expenditure is incurred.[2] Pre-trading remediation expenditure is treated as incurred on the first day of trading.[3] The relief is available to a company which carries on a trade (or will do so) or who has lettings assessable as property income).[4]

In order to attract the allowance, five conditions must be satisfied:

(i) The expenditure is on land that is, in all or part, contaminated.[5]
(ii) The expenditure is on work undertaken by the company itself or by someone acting on its behalf.[6]
(iii) The expenditure consists of employees costs or of materials or payments to sub-contractors.[7]
(iv) The expenditure would not have been incurred if the land had not been contaminated.[8]
(v) No subsidy is obtained for the expenditure.[9]

Employee costs can be capitalised and attract the allowance.[10] The employee must be directly involved in the remediation work; salaries paid to secretarial or administrative staff do not qualify.[11] There is provision for allocating part of an individual's salary cost to remediation work, as long as the individual spends more than 20% of his total working time on the relevant land remediation.[12]

The expenditure that attracts the allowance is the additional expenditure incurred because of the contamination; this includes the cost of operations

[9.65] Capital allowances

preventing or minimising the effects of any harm or pollution and for restoring the land or waters to their formal state. Normal site preparation costs do not qualify for remediation relief.[13]

Where a company pays a sub-contractor who is a connected person, the relief is granted by reference to the expenditure by the sub-contractor, not the charge levied on the company.[14]

1. FA 2001, Sch 22, para 13.
2. FA 2001, Sch 22, para 12(2).
3. FA 2001, Sch 22, para 1(3).
4. FA 2001, Sch 22, para 1(1)(*a*) and Sch 23, para 1.
5. FA 2001, Sch 22, paras 2(2) and (3).
6. FA 2001, Sch 22, paras 2(3) and (4).
7. FA 2001, Sch 22, paras 2(4), (5), (6) and (11)
8. FA 2001, Sch 22, paras 2(5) and (7).
9. FA 2001, Sch 22, para 2(6) and (8).
10. FA 2001, Sch 22, para 5.
11. FA 2001, Sch 22, para 5(4).
12. FA 2001, Sch 22, para 5(3).
13. FA 2001, Sch 22, para 7.
14. FA 2001, Sch 22, para 10.

Renovation of business premises in disadvantaged areas

[9.66] A 100% initial capital allowance is available[1] for capital expenditure on bringing qualifying business premises into productive use. This allowance is given in place of plant and machinery allowances and any industrial buildings allowance or agricultural buildings allowance that would be due. Expenditure on commercial buildings, such as offices and shops, attracts the allowance, although no capital allowance would previously have been available.

In order to qualify for the allowance, the expenditure must be incurred, on, or in connection with, the conversion[2] of a building or structure[3] into premises to be used,[4] or to be let for use, for the purpose of a trade, profession or vocation.

The allowance is only available where the premises are situated within one of the 1,999 areas designated as disadvantaged areas.[5]

As long as the premises are suitable and available for use in a trade, profession or vocation for a period of seven years, no balancing charges arise on the disposal of the premises and the allowances are not transferable to a subsequent purchaser.

1. CAA 2001, ss 360A–360Z4, inserted by FA 2005, Sch 6. These provisions take effect from the date that state aid is authorised for this purpose.
2. CAA 2001, s 360B(1), inserted by FA 2005, Sch 6, para 1.
3. CAA 2001, s 360C(1), inserted by FA 2005, Sch 6, para 1.
4. CAA 2001, s 360D(1), inserted by FA 2005, Sch 6, para 1.

[5] The disadvantaged areas are those specified for stamp duty land tax disadvantaged area relief under FA 2003, Sch 6, except that the Treasury has the power to make statutory instruments adding or removing other areas from this list: CAA 2001, s 360C(2) inserted by FA 2005, Sch 6, para 1.

10

Property income

The charge to tax	PARA **10.01**
A 'UK property business'	PARA **10.02**
Borderline between Property Income and Trading Income	PARA **10.07**
Calculation of income	PARA **10.08**
Property income of a partnership	PARA **10.09**
Energy saving expenditure	PARA **10.10**
Interest paid—income tax	PARA **10.11**
Non-resident landlord	PARA **10.12**
Furnished lettings	PARA **10.13**
Rent a room	PARA **10.14**
Furnished holiday lettings	PARA **10.15**
Taxation of premiums as income	PARA **10.16**

The charge to tax

[**10.01**] As stated earlier (Chapter 5), from 6 April 2005 the schedular system was abolished for income tax but not for corporation tax. This chapter will use predominantly the income tax terminology although, except where otherwise stated, the rules will equally apply for corporation tax purposes.

For income tax purposes, the provisions are in ITTOIA 2005, Pt 3 "Property Income". Under this part, income is charged[1] in respect of:

(1) the profits of a UK property business
(2) the profits of an overseas property business
(3) analogous income, such as rent from mines, fees received for fishing rights, etc[2]
(4) rent receivable for UK electric-line wayleaves.

Part 3 also contains rules dealing with post-cessation receipts arising from a UK property business and cases where a person subject to the remittance basis is in receipt of overseas property income.[3]

For corporation tax, the rules for UK property are dealt with predominantly in Schedule A. The rules for overseas income are under Schedule D Case V. Some minor matters under Schedule D also relate to UK property.[4]

For relief when the "property business" produces a loss, see supra, §§ **6.27**, **6.32**.

---

[1] ITTOIA 2005, s 260.
[2] ITTOIA 2005, s 260(1)(c) imposes a charge on what it unmemorably calls "a UK section 12(4) concern". ITTOIA 2005, s 12(4) lists the concerns to which it relates as:

[10.01] Property income

4 The concerns to which this section applies are—

(a) mines and quarries (including gravel pits, sand pits and brickfields),
(b) ironworks, gasworks, salt springs or works, alum mines or works, waterworks and streams of water.
(c) canals, inland navigation, docks and drains or levels,
(d) rights of fishing,
(e) rights of markets and fairs, tolls, bridges and ferries,
(f) railways and other kinds of way, and
(g) a concern of the same kind as one specified in paragraph (b), (c), (d) or (e).

[3] ITTOIA 2005, s 260(1).
[4] TA 1988, ss 15 and 18.

A 'UK property business'

[10.02] Statute requires that all income arising from land and buildings in the UK to any one person be aggregated and measured as "the profits of a UK property business" (or "Schedule A business" for corporation tax purposes).[1] The computation is the same, whether the charge is to income tax or to corporation tax; however, the regime for companies is, however, more beneficial in that rental business losses can be offset against future income of all descriptions and can be included within the claim for group relief.[2]

For income tax purposes, a strict current year basis is applied; that is, all income is measured on a basis period from 6 April to 5 April.[3] For corporation tax purposes, the company's income is measured in accordance with its accounting period.

The computation is in accordance with the rules that apply for trading income.[4]

Nevertheless, the income categories (and, for corporation tax purposes, the Schedules) remain distinct; income from property is not trading income. So, while the computational rules for the post-cessation receipts apply, the receipts are not earned income.[5] Similarly, property income cannot be relevant earnings for pension contribution rules.[6]

Simon's Taxes B9.101.

[1] ITTOIA 2005, s 264 (income tax); TA 1988, s 15(1), Sch A, para 1(3) (corporation tax).
[2] TA 1988, s 103(1)(b). There is, however, a distinction between income tax and corporation tax for the treatment of interest. For a taxpayer within the charge to corporation tax, interest paid is within the loan relationship rules and losses are given relief in the same way as excess management charges of investment companies (TA 1988, s 392A).
[3] ITTOIA 2005, s 270(1).
[4] ITTOIA 2005, s 272 (income tax); TA 1988, s 21A (corporation tax).
[5] ITTOIA 2005, ss 349 & 256 treat post-cessation receipts as earned income only if the profits prior to cessation were earned income.
[6] FA 2006, s 189(2).

[10.03] A UK property business consists of every business which a person carries on exploiting an estate, interest or right in or over any land in the UK as a source of rents or other receipts.[1] In order to be within this category, the payment must be made in respect of rights over land. An individual may not treat sums received by virtue of his employment as property income.[2]

Electric line wayleaves form part of a UK property business when they are for an easement over land within the "business".[3] Lest the term business be considered too restrictive the definition has a second limb which covers transactions entered into for such exploitation, the transaction being deemed to have been entered into in the course of such a business.[4] The profits of a "UK property business", including the business treated as arising under the second limb, are subject to tax.[5]

The words "exploiting . . . as a source of rents or other receipts" replace the idea of receipts arising by virtue of ownership. It is at yet unclear whether this is simply a modernisation of language for a more managerial age. The words "as a source of rents or other receipts" are expressly stated to include:

(1) payments for a licence to occupy or otherwise to use land;
(2) the exercise of any other rights over land; and
(3) rent charges and other annual payments reserved in respect of, or charged on or issuing out of land;[6]
(4) capital sums from rent factoring.[7]

Income from land outside the UK forms the profits of an "overseas property business" (for corporation tax, taxed under Schedule D, Case V) but such income is calculated in the same way as for UK property.[8]

Simon's Taxes B9.101.

---

[1] ITTOIA 2005, s 264(*a*) and 266(1) (income tax); TA 1988, s 15(1), para 1(1) 1998 version (referring to "exploitation as a source of rents or other receipts") (corporation tax).
[2] In *Ainslie v Buckley* [2002] STC (SCD) 132, the taxpayer, when constructing his self-assessment tax return, treated part of the income he received from his employer as property income, against which he put the cost of running part of his home as an office. The Special Commissioner held that the payments made by the employer arose from the taxpayer's employment and could not be regarded as property income.
[3] ITTOIA 2005, s 345 (income tax); TA 1988, s 120 (corporation tax).
[4] ITTOIA 2005, s 264(*b*) (income tax); TA 1988, s 15(1), para 1(2) 1998 version (corporation tax).
[5] ITTOIA 2005, s 368 (income tax); TA 1988, s 832(1) (corporation tax).
[6] ITTOIA 2005, s 266(3) (income tax); TA 1988, s 15(1), para 1(4) (corporation tax).
[7] TA 1988, s 785A inserted by FA 2004, s 135 with effect from 2 July 2004. The Revenue view of how the provision works in practice is given in Inland Revenue Press Release 17 August 2004, *Simon's Weekly Tax Intelligence* 2004, p 1931. This section has been reinforced by TA 1988, ss 785B–s 785E, inserted by FA 2008 with effect from 13 December 2007.
[8] ITTOIA 2005, s 272(1) (income tax); TA 1988, s 70A(5) (corporation tax).

[10.04] Property income

[10.04] Rent is not defined for tax purposes. Its general meaning[1] is a payment due from a tenant to his (land)lord by reason of tenure; it must be reserved as rent. However, it has been held that a payment can be rent even though there is no right to distrain for it.[2] The rent is a sum payable for the lease and the obligation to pay passes to an assignee; the payment of a premium in instalments is not rent.[3]

Payments falling within 3, above, include such items as licence fees for advertisement hoardings, parking fees and service charges which are not reserved as rent and are not in respect of services constituting a trade.[4] Thus a separate charge for meals would fall within the heading of trading income, whereas if a lease provides for the provision of a service for which no separate payment is made, eg heating, the rent constitutes property income and the cost of heating is an allowable expense. Where payments were made by an employer to an employee for the use of an employee's garage to store samples and stock for use in the employee's work, the payments were held to be what is now employment income, not property income.[5] Some situations will be impossible to classify. Where a farmer sold turf from his land he was held taxable under what was then Schedule A but also, in the alternative, under Schedule D, Case I.[6] Rental income from caravan sites may be amalgamated with associated trading income.[7]

Damages for trespass to land and loss of rent are not liable to income tax as rent.[8] Some such payments have, in another jurisdiction, been held to be income under general principles[9] in which case they may be taxable as property income. If the payments are not taxable at all it follows that in assessing damages the court will take account of the tax which the plaintiff has not had to pay and grant only the net sum under the rule in *British Transport Commission v Gourley*.[10] This situation must be distinguished from that in which an action is brought for arrears of rent since such sums are form part of a property business.

One may also note the practice whereby a trader, who lets a part of the building in which he carried on a business, may treat the rents as trading income.[11]

Rent under a lease which includes the use of furniture is now dealt with as part of the property business and not, as previously, as a separate source of income under Schedule D, Case VI.[12]

In order for income to be within the charging provision of property income[13] the taxpayer must own the land during the tax year in which the income falls into charge. In *Property Co v Inspector of Taxes*[14] the company received sums of money by virtue of ownership of land in the past. The Special Commissioner held that these current receipts cannot fall within Schedule A and were therefore, assessable under Schedule D, Case VI.[15]

Simon's Taxes B9.105.

---

[1] On general meaning see Gray, *Elements of Land Law*, 2nd ed, pp 701–706.
[2] T and E Homes Ltd v Robinson [1979] STC 351.
[3] But it may, in whole or in part, be taxed as if it were rent: TA 1988, s 34(1) (corporation tax) (see infra, § **10.15**).

4 George, *Taxation of Property Transactions* (3rd edn), p. 48. For an excellent example of the problem see the Revenue note on the taxation of caravan sites in *Simon's Tax Intelligence* 1984, p. 386 and extra-statutory concession B29.
5 *Beecham Group Ltd v Fair* [1984] STC 15.
6 *Lowe v Ashmore Ltd* (1970) 46 TC 597 (see also supra, § **8.41**).
7 ITTOIA 2005, s 20 (income tax). Prior to 6 April 2005 for all purposes and since that date for corporation tax purposes, this rule is strictly concessionary: Extra-statutory concession B29.
8 *Hall & Co v Pearlberg* [1956] 1 All ER 297n, [1956] 1 WLR 244.
9 *Raja's Commercial College v Gian Singh & Co Ltd* [1976] STC 282, [1976] 2 All ER 801, PC (damages for almost six years; occupation after end of lease, damages equal to excess of market rent over rent under former lease).
10 [1955] 3 All ER 796, [1956] AC 185. In *Hall v Pearlberg* the rate of tax used was that at the time of the judgment but this appears to be wrong since the rates of tax for the years in issue were known.
11 Inland Revenue leaflet IR 27 (1984), § 17 (but not where the business consists of rendering services to the tenants, § 107).
12 ITTOIA 2005, s 308 (income tax); TA 1988, s 15(1), para 4 (corporation tax). Prior to the amendments made by FA 1995 (income tax) and FA 1998 (corporation tax), income from furnished lettings was assessed under Schedule D, Case VI.
13 Schedule A for corporation tax.
14 [2005] STC (SCD) 59.
15 ITTOIA 2005 has changed the categories from Schedule A and Schedule D, Case VI for income tax purposes only to "property income" and "other income", respectively.

[10.05] Specifically *excluded* from the charge are:[1]

(1) any profits arising from the occupation of land;[2]
(2) any profits charged to tax in respect of farming or market gardening, mines, quarries and sand and gravel pits, mining and other royalties or tied premises;[3]
(3) certain corporation tax matters.[4]

In respect of corporation tax, tax is charged under Schedule A if the source, the land, is in the UK. Income from foreign land will be taxed to a UK resident under Schedule D, Case V.[5]

1 ITTOIA 2005, s 267 (income tax); TA 1988, s 15(1), para 2 (corporation tax).
2 ITTOIA 2005, s 267(*b*) (income tax); TA 1988, s 15(1), para 2(1) (corporation tax).
3 ITTOIA 2005, ss 267(*a*), (*c*) and 273(2) (income tax); TA 1988, s 15(1), para 2(2) (corporation tax). But *some* payments for electric wayleaves are taxable as property income; see ITTOIA 2005, s 345 and TA 1988, s 120(2).
4 TA 1988, s 15(1), para 2(3).
5 TA 1988, s 18(3).

[10.06] Tax on property income is a tax on income and not on capital gains.[1] A premium accruing on the grant of a lease giving possession of premises would, but for special legislation (in ITTOIA 2005, ss 276–307 for income tax, TA 1988, ss 34–36 for corporation tax), fall outside the charge. Still however, a gain accruing from the assignment, as distinct from the grant of a lease,[2] or the grant of a lease of shooting rights, is capital rather than income. Likewise a sum payable in return for the grant or release of an easement would normally escape a charge to income as has a one-off payment for allowing a motorway contractor to tip sub-soil onto the taxpayer's land.[3]

A "reverse premium" or lease-inducement payment is brought within the charge by FA 1999 if the land is in the UK and the payment is not taxed under as trading income[4] (see supra, § **8.134**).

Simon's Taxes Division B9.2.

---

[1] See, for example, the arguments raised (unsuccessfully) in *Jeffries v Stevens* [1982] STC 639 and *Lowe v J W Ashmore Ltd* (1970) 46 TC 597.
[2] Unless the original lease is granted at an undervalue: ITTOIA 2005, s 282 (income tax); TA 1988, s 35 (corporation tax) (see infra, § **10.23**).
[3] *McClure v Petre* [1988] STC 749.
[4] ITTOIA 2005, ss 101 and 311 (income tax); FA 1999, s 54 and Sch 6 (corporation tax).

Borderline between property income and trading income

[10.07] The line between property income and that taxed as trading income can be hard to draw. The former covers annual profits arising from a "[business] exploiting land".[1] Every business (unless it is somehow carried on in cyberspace) requires land. Does this mean that an individual who carries on the business of manufacturing widgets in a factory building he owns should be assessed to tax under the heading of property income for a part of his profits that are somehow attributed to the exploitation of the land and buildings required for the carry on of the business, with the balance being subject to tax as trading income? That this is not the case is implicit in the wording of statute (even after its Rewrite), which declares that property income covers income arising from "exploiting [the land] as a source of rents or other receipts".[2] Following the statutory principle, the wording "other receipts" is limited, *ejusdem generis*, to receipts that are akin to "rent", the word that precedes the conjunction. The principle that profits of a business cannot be split between property and trading arises from the doctrine of the mutual exclusivity of Schedules.[3] In rejecting just such an apportionment, Lord Atkin said:[4]

> Specific income must be assets under the specific schedule . . . The dominance of each Schedule A, B, C and E over its own subject matter is confirmed by reference to the Sections and Rules which respectively regulate them in the Act of 1842. They are therefore a complete code for each class of income, dealing with allowances and exemptions, with the mode of assessment and, with the officials whose duty it is to make the assessments.

This doctrine does not, however, exclude the possibility of there being two separate supplies of services for the same customers. Thus, in the *Salisbury House Estate* case, it was accepted, in advance of the hearing, that the supply of cleaning services to tenants was a trade, irrespective of the manner of assessment of the other receipts from tenants which were in dispute.[5]

The businesses of farming, market gardening, and mining and quarrying are specifically excluded from property businesses, as are receipts from tied premises that are treated as trading receipts.[6] Receipts for the provision of furniture, supplies in a furnished letting, are specifically included as part of the property business.[7] In 1920, the House of Lords held that the governors of the Rotunda Hospital were carrying on a trade in letting out a hall for entertainments, with seats, lighting, heating and attendance. The profits fell to represent trading income.[8] On the other side of the line, the income received by Sywell Aerodrome Ltd from garage rents, housing and landing fees and a percentage of money from the sale of ice-cream was, in 1942, held to be assessable as property income.[9] Lawrence J said:

> The land is used primarily for the purpose of landing and taking off in aeroplanes. For that purpose, land is at present essential. No doubt, it may be a more profitable form of occupation of land than farming, but so may keeping thoroughbred stallions. The amount of the profit is irrelevant, except insofar as it affects the annual value. The only activities in the present case which might, I think, be said to be distinct from the occupation of land are the repairs of aeroplanes, the selling of petrol and the selling of ices, but, in my view, these activities are merely ancillary to the main purpose of the aerodrome.[10]

In *Griffiths v Jackson*,[11] Vinelott J said that the answer turned on the question: "Who is in occupation?":[12]

> In the *Rotunda Hospital* case the taxpayers retained legal occupation of the entertainment rooms and retained control over them. The income was not derived from their property in the rooms, as it would have been if they had parted with legal occupation to someone who had carried out the activities of providing the rooms for public entertainment. That was the ground on which the *Rotunda Hospital* case was distinguished in the *Salisbury House Estate* case.
>
> The *Rotunda Hospital* case, in fact, is a useful illustration of the way in which the owner of land may, without parting with his occupation of it, exploit his rights of property and occupation by carrying on a trade.
>
> That, I think, affords the answer to the alternative argument of counsel for the taxpayer. He drew an analogy between the position of these taxpayers and that of an hotel owner or the landlord of a lodging house. It was the analogy of a lodging housekeeper which led Rowlatt J to conclude in *Salisbury House Estate Ltd v Fry*[13] that the taxpayer was carrying on a trade. However, as Lord Russell of Killowen pointed out in *Westminster City Council v Southern Rly Co*,[14] the landlord of a lodging house remains in occupation and:
>
>> for the purpose of that business he has a continual right of access to the lodgers' rooms and . . . in fact, retains the control of ingress and egress to and from the lodging house, notwithstanding that the power of ingress and egress at all times is essential to the lodger.
>
> That was a rating case but in *Dawson v Counsell*[15], Scott L J pointed out that 'the occupier for tax purposes is broadly the same kind of occupier as the occupier for rates'. The distinction between a hotelier or a lodging housekeeper, on the one hand, and the owner of property who lets furnished rooms and provides services is no doubt in practice a narrow one, more particularly in these days of self-service hotels

and motels, but the principle is clear and in the present case there can be no doubt on which side of the line the taxpayers' activities fall. It is quite clear from the terms of the tenancy agreements and the taxpayers' form of letter that they let rooms furnished to tenants, albeit with shared facilities and some services.

It was this distinction, that, in 1953, led to an assessment under Schedule D on Middlesbrough Corporation[16] in respect of receipts from fees charged for the use of the Town Hall for holding meetings, dancing and rollerskating.

Occupation can be as tenant or as licensee.[17]

A lot of work by the taxpayer in connection with a letting does not convert property income to profits from a trade.[18] This led Vinelott J to comment:[19]

> I may perhaps be permitted to add that I am not without sympathy for the taxpayers. It is a peculiar feature of United Kingdom tax law that the activity of letting furnished flats or rooms, while it may be a business and, in this case, a demanding and time-consuming business, is not a trade . . . It is not too easy to see why in the modern world a business consisting of the exploitation of the right of property in land should be treated differently from a business consisting of the exploitation of other assets. However, the principle is now too deeply embedded in the law to be altered except by legislation.

A case that is often quoted is *Gittos v Barclay*.[20] In that case, Mrs Gittos had registered a business name for the letting of holiday villas near Looe in Cornwall. The taxpayer and his wife travelled to Cornwall taking blankets and house linen and prepared the villas at the beginning of each season and also dealt with all the administration necessary for holiday lets. The commissioners held that the income arising was assessable as property income and was not the profits of a trade. Goulding J, in his judgment, comments that he "might or might not myself have come to the same conclusion" but ruled that the commissioners had not misdirected themselves as to the law or arrived at a wholly unreasonable conclusion.[21] At the end of the day, the judgment in *Gittos v Barclays* can be viewed as an illustration of the principle that questions of fact are for the commissioners and not for the court,[22] rather than a clear statement as to the borderline between what constitutes property or trading income. Nevertheless, the decision in *Gittos v Barclay* led to enactment of the furnished holiday letting legislation, which treats property income that is so designated as attracting certain reliefs that are normally only available to a trade.[23]

Published statements by the Revenue say surprisingly little on the Revenue view as to, firstly, the identification in practice of the borderline between property and trading income and secondly, identifying as a separate trade the services provided by a landlord to his tenants. The difficulty experienced by the Revenue, in practice, is, perhaps, well illustrated by the instruction given by local districts to consult the relevant Inland Revenue Technical Division whenever a local inspector cannot agree the correct head of charge with the taxpayer or his agent and the matter seems likely to proceed to a contentious hearing.[24]

The Revenue instruction to its inspectors states:[25]

> If the provision of services is to be treated as a separate trade, then those services would have to go beyond those which landlords normally provide.

If regular meals are provided, it may be more likely that the whole activity is a trade, including the letting element.

It is not conclusive, but it is more likely to be appropriate to treat the services as being provided in the course of a separate trade if there is a separate charge for them. But this would not necessarily be the case, especially if the tenants have no option to pay the rent only, and do without the services and the service charge.

The Revenue view as to the kinds of services that landlords commonly provide and, hence, which do not lead to treatment as trading income is given in the Revenue publication "Taxation of Rents A Guide to Property Income" as "the cleaning of stairs and passages in multi-unit premises, the provision of hot water and heating, supervision involving rent collection and arranging new tenancies and arranging for repairs to the property".[26]

This, the Revenue contrast with the following examples of services that, if provided by a landlord, would probably amount to a trading activity: "the regular cleaning of rooms when they are let and not just between changes of tenant, the regular supply of clean linen and the regular provision of meals".[27]

---

[1] ITTOIA 2005, s 266(1) (income tax). For corporation tax, the statute reads "business carried on for the exploitation . . . [of] land in the United Kingdom" (TA 1988, s 15(1) para 1(1)).

[2] ITTOIA 2005, s 266(1) (income tax). For corporation tax, the statute continues to read "the exploitation, as the source of rents or other receipts" (TA 1988, s 15(1) para 1(1)).

[3] See supra, § **5.06**.

[4] *Salisbury House Estates Ltd v Fry* (1930) 15 TC 266 at 319, HL.

[5] *Salisbury House Estates Ltd v Fry* (1930) 15 TC 266 at 273–274.

[6] ITTOIA 2005, ss 267 and 273 (income tax); TA 1988, s 15(1) paras 2(2)(*a*) and (*b*) (corporation tax).

[7] ITTOIA 2005, s 308 (income tax); TA 1988, s 15(1) para 4(1) (corporation tax).

[8] *Governors of Rotunda Hospital Dublin v Coman* (1920) 7 TC 517, HL.

[9] *Sywell Aerodrome Ltd v Croft* (1942) 24 TC 126.

[10] (1942) 24 TC 126 at 133.

[11] [1983] STC 184.

[12] [1983] STC 184 at 193.

[13] (1929) 15 TC 266 at 282.

[14] [1936] AC 511 at 530.

[15] (1938) 22 TC 149, CA.

[16] *Jennings v Middlesbrough Corpn* (1953) 34 TC 447.

[17] If a taxpayer is licensee, TA 1988, s 15(1) para 4 is not applicable. However, a licensee can be the "occupier" and, hence the property income charging provisions apply. Per Goulding J: "I think the question whether the occupying holidaymakers were tenants or licensees is at most of only slight importance", *Gittos v Barclay* [1982] STC 390 at 394d; Lord Greene MR: "nor do I think in the end that it is critical to the decision of the controversy", *Sywell Aerodrome Ltd v Croft* (1942) 24 TC 126 at 139.

[18] See, for example, *Webb v Conelee Properties Ltd* [1982] STC 913 and *Gittos v Barclay* [1982] STC 390.

[19] *Griffiths v Jackson* [1983] STC 184.

[20] [1982] STC 390.

[21] [1982] STC 390 at 395h–j.
[22] In *Edwards v Bairstow* (1955) 36 TC 207, it was held that the court must intervene where the decision of the commissioners was such "that the facts found are such that no person acting judicially and properly instructed as to the relevant law could have come to the determination under appeal"—per Lord Radcliffe at 229. If this test is not satisfied, the court cannot reverse findings of fact by the commissioners (see supra, § **2A.66**).
[23] See infra, § **10.15**.
[24] Inland Revenue Property Income Manual, para 330. The relevant technical division is Business Taxes.
[25] Inland Revenue Property Income Manual, para 330.
[26] Revenue publication IR150, para 514.
[27] Revenue publication IR150, para 516.

Calculation of income

[10.08] While the charging words of Schedule A (now relevant only for corporation tax purposes) refer to income arising, in computing income the principles for trading income apply.[1] This is now even more explicit for income tax as ITTOIA 2005, s 268 imposes a charge on the profits of a property business.

The legislation also makes it clear that various trading income computational rules apply.[2] These are for income tax purposes:

(1)   ITTOIA 2005, s 25 (generally accepted accounting practice);
(2)   ITTOIA 2005, s 26 (losses calculated on same basis as profits);
(3)   ITTOIA 2005, s 27 (receipts and expenses);
(4)   ITTOIA 2005, s 28 (items treated under CAA 2001 as receipts and expenses);
(5)   ITTOIA 2005, s 29 (interest);
(6)   ITTOIA 2005, s 33 (capital expenditure);
(7)   ITTOIA 2005, s 34 (expenses not wholly and exclusively for trade and unconnected losses);
(8)   ITTOIA 2005, s 35 (bad and doubtful debts);
(9)   ITTOIA 2005, ss 36 and 37 (unpaid remuneration);
(10) ITTOIA 2005, ss 38 to 44 (employee benefit contributions);
(11) ITTOIA 2005, ss 45 to 47 (business entertainment and gifts);
(12) ITTOIA 2005, ss 48 to 50 (car or motor cycle hire);
(13) ITTOIA 2005, s 51 (patent royalties);
(14) ITTOIA 2005, s 52 (exclusion of double relief for interest);
(15) ITTOIA 2005, s 53 (social security contributions);
(16) ITTOIA 2005, s 54 (penalties, interest and VAT surcharges);
(17) ITTOIA 2005, s 55 (crime-related payments);
(18) ITTOIA 2005, s 57 (pre-trading expenses);
(19) ITTOIA 2005, ss 58 and 59 (incidental costs of obtaining finance);
(20) ITTOIA 2005, s 68 (replacement and alteration of trade tools);
(21) ITTOIA 2005, ss 69 (payments for restrictive undertakings);

and for corporation tax purposes:

Calculation of income [10.08]

(1)   TA 1988, s 72 (apportionment);
(2)   most of TA 1988, ss 74–99, ie all the provisions of Chapter V of Part IV (computational provisions relating to the Schedule D charge) (for exceptions see below);
(3)   TA 1988, s 577 (business entertainment expenses);
(4)   TA 1988, s 577A (expenditure involving crime);
(5)   TA 1988, ss 579 and 580, ITEPA 2003, s 309 (redundancy payments);
(6)   TA 1988, ss 588 and 589, ITEPA 2003, ss 311 and 312 (training courses for employees);
(7)   TA 1988, ss 589A and 589B (counselling services for employees);
(8)   FA 1988, s 73(2) (consideration for restrictive undertakings);
(9)   FA 1989, s 43 (timing rule on deductions in respect of certain emoluments);
(10) FA 1989, s 76 (expenses in connection with non-approved retirement benefit schemes); and
(11) FA 1998, ss 42 and 46(1) and (2) (provisions as to computation of profits and losses).

In addition (corporation tax), TA 1988, s 74(1)(*d*) which disallows provisions for future repairs is made to apply to Schedule A by treating the reference to premises occupied for the purposes of the trade as if it were to premises held for the purposes of the Schedule A business.[3]

The provisions of TA 1988 which are excluded for corporation tax purposes are[4] s 87 (treatment of premiums taxed as rent) and s 98 (tied premises: receipts and expenses treated as those of trade). The first contains rules which are superseded by other rules in Schedule A while the latter refers to matters which are excluded from Schedule A.

Non-computational rules in TA 1988 which are made to apply to Schedule A (ie for corporation tax purposes)[5] are most of the post cessation rules, ie ss 103–106 and 110; s 337(1) (effect of company beginning or ceasing to carry on trade); and s 401(1) (pre-trading expenditure). In addition the rules on change of accounting basis (now in FA 2002, s 64 and Sch 22) apply.

For income tax, Part 3 of ITTOIA deals explicitly with such rules in:

(a)   s 310 (change in persons carrying on business);
(b)   s 329–334 (change of accounting basis);
(c)   s 349–356 (post-cessation receipts);
(d)   s 361 (change of trustees or personal representatives).

The first requirement in the income tax list (item 12 in the corporation tax list) is a requirement to compute the profits of property business in accordance with generally accepted accounting practice. This would seem to require the computational effect of each and every Financial Reporting Standard be applied, where this has relevance to rental, etc income. Thus for income tax, the revenue is rents receivable, not solely those received, and rent for a period that spans 5 April[6] must be apportioned between accounts for two tax years. Generally accepted accounting practice is, however, specifically disapplied in respect of lease premiums, which are subject to tax for the accounting period in which they arise.[7]

[10.08] Property income

Receipts will include not only rent but also service charge contributions from tenants. However, if the property is residential the landlord's duty to keep the money in a separate account may prevent this.[8]

Expenditure must be recognised according to an acceptable accounting basis. This clearly requires recognition of creditors. However, it does not necessarily require the recognition of accruals. A premium on an insurance policy is customarily treated as accruing over the period for which the insurance cover is provided. This may not necessarily be the appropriate accounting basis where, as will commonly be the case, no part of the premium is returnable if a claim is made. In this case it may be more appropriate for certain expenditure to be recognised when it falls due. This principle extends, in appropriate circumstances, to the recognition of expenditure once it has been ascertained and determined even before there has been any financial outlay or work, for which payment is to be made, has commenced. In *Jenners Princes Street Edinburgh Ltd v IRC*[9] the Special Commissioners held that in accordance with accounting practice it was permissible for the company to make provision for the full cost of repairs when the contract was put out to tender and that this was not barred by TA 1988, s 74(1)(*d*). As a result of this decision, that part of s 74(1)(*d*) was not rewritten for income tax purposes (see Explanatory Notes accompanying ITTOIA 2005, s 68).

Since the source is the business of exploiting land it is no longer necessary, as it was under the old law, to treat different properties as different sources; expenses incurred on different properties will be pooled regardless of whether they are still owned. However, it should not be forgotten that expenditure incurred in whole or in part for non-commercial reasons should not now be allowable at all; this could lead to problems under the duality principle.

The charge applies to the person receiving, or who is entitled to, the profits, a formula which is the same as for trading income.[10] The income is charged on the full amount of the profits arising in the tax year, a current year basis.[11] The tax is paid as part of the taxpayer's self-assessment. For corporation tax, TA 1988, s 9 ensures that income tax principles apply for corporation tax and, to the extent that they are necessary for this purpose, the Schedules are held to continue to exist for income tax.

While most of the computational provisions for trading income apply, the basis rules (ITTOIA 2005, Pt 2, Ch 15) do not. This means that there is no place in the new Schedule A for the basis of assessment rules and that a current year period from 6 April to 5 April is used, unless the property income arises to a partnership that carries on a trade.[12]

Simon's Taxes Division B5.

---

[1] ITTOIA 2005, s 272(1) (income tax); TA 1988, s 21A(1) (corporation tax).
[2] ITTOIA 2005, s 272(1) (income tax); TA 1988, s 21A(2) (corporation tax).
[3] TA 1988, s 21A(3).
[4] TA 1988, s 21A(4).
[5] TA 1988, s 21B.
[6] For corporation tax, there is apportionment where the rental period spans the accounting date.

[7] ITTOIA 2005, s 277(3) (income tax); TA 1988, s 34(1) (for corporation tax). This treatment also applies to a receipt for assignment of a lease (s 35) and a sale subject to a reconveyance (s 36) (for income tax purposes: ITTOIA 2005, ss 282(3) and 284(3) respectively).
[8] Landlord and Tenant Act 1987, s 43(2)(*b*)—see de Souza 1998: Private Client Business 267 at 270.
[9] [1998] STC (SCD) 196, restricts certain deductions to sums actually expended but this was held to mean expended in an accounting sense.
[10] ITTOIA 2005, s 271.
[11] ITTOIA 2005, s 270(1).
[12] Where this is the case, the basis period for the property income is the period used for the trading income: ITTOIA 2005, ss 854–856.

Property income of a partnership

[10.09] Where a trading partnership is in receipt of other income, including property income, the basis period for income arising to the partnership and then apportioned to individual partners is income arising in the period of account that forms the basis period for the year of assessment under the rules that apply to the relevant trading income.[1] This treatment provides overlap profits for all income, including property income. Relief for these overlap profits is given at any subsequent change of accounting date or on the cessation of the partnership or earlier retirement of the individual from the partnership.

There is a distinction between the term "business" as used in Partnership Act 1890 and the concept of a "property business" (introduced originally as "Schedule A business" by FA 1995). Exceptionally, the exploitation of property can constitute a business and, if carried on by persons jointly, is correctly regarded as a partnership with the consequence that the self-assessment regime requires income to be reported on a partnership statement and the accounting period is the basis period. Such cases are, however, rare. Joint ownership of property does not, of itself, create a partnership. Co-owners are required to declare their separate portions of the income arising from the property on their separate individual self-assessment tax returns. In this case, no partnership return is required and the provisions relating to partnership basis periods are not applicable.[2]

The potential for partnership property income being assessed with a different basis period from that applied to the income of individuals acting singly, means that it is important to correctly identify whether income from jointly owned property constitutes partnership income. There are at least five alternative situations. As the joint ownership very often occurs with married couples, the five alternatives are illustrated by reference to Mr and Mrs Smith, who each have a 50% interest in property. The relationship between the two individuals does not, however, change the treatment; the same principle is applied if a 40% interest in the property is owned by Mr Smith, a 50% interest by Mr Jones and a 10% interest by Mr Mackintosh.

The five situations are:

[10.09] Property income

(1) Mr and Mrs Smith jointly own a property, for which rent is received. In this case, Mr Smith enters one half of the rental receipts and one half of the rental expenses on his personal tax return and his wife does likewise. There is no partnership statement. The basis period is the fiscal year.

(2) Mr and Mrs Smith carry on a business in partnership, that business generates some property income and some trading income. This will be the case when, for example, they own a block of flats and each tenant pays not only rent for the flat, but also a monthly charge for providing a porter, a cleaner for the communal areas and services for the individual flats. In this case, a partnership statement is required. Both sources of income are shown on the partnership assessment and are assessable using the basis period that applies for trading income.[3]

(3) Mr and Mrs Smith have rental income and they also have trading income, but these arise from separate activities each of which is carried on in partnership. The Revenue view of this situation is that there are then two separate partnerships, albeit between the same two individuals. Two separate partnership statements are required. Income from the partnership carrying on the trade is assessed using the basis period that applies under the trading income rules. Property income arising to the partnership is assessable under a fiscal year basis.

(4) Mr and Mrs Smith jointly own the freehold of a property. The ground floor of the property is used as a retail shop they run in partnership. The first floor of the property is let to a third party. In this case, the income from the shop is income of a trading partnership but the rental income is income received by co-owners. The income generated by the ground floor shop is shown in a partnership statement. The rental income from the first floor does not appear in a partnership statement, but, instead, each spouse enters on his/her personal tax return one half of the rental income arising and one half of the attributable expenses.

(5) Mr and Mrs Smith own a four storey office block. Most of the office block is occupied by staff they employ for the carrying on of the business of the professional firm they run in partnership. Three rooms on the top floor are, however, let to an unconnected third party. In this case, Mr and Mrs Smith can choose to apply the extra-statutory concession in Inland Revenue booklet IR 27, para 107 and include the rental receipts in the turnover from which the professional profits are calculated, such receipts being small in relation to the fees generated.

Concern was expressed by professional bodies that enquiries into a co-owner's tax return could raise questions that could not reasonably be answered by that co-owner where the co-owner was not personally engaged in the letting of the property. In correspondence, a senior Revenue officer stated:

> We shall avoid as far as possible carrying out what would amount to an audit of the managing co-owners' books solely through the medium of enquiries into a passive co-owner's return. Thus, where we institute enquiries into the return of a taxpayer in receipt of income from co-owned property and those enquiries extend to that source, our enquiries will normally be extended to other co-owners thereby enabling the managing co-owner to provide the relevant information. Of course, we may need

to make some enquiries first to establish basic facts (such as who the other co-owners are).

---

[1] ITTOIA 2005, s 851.
[2] Inland Revenue interpretation RI 137, *Simon's Weekly Tax Intelligence* 1996, p. 26. Inland Revenue Property Income Manual directs inspectors: "Most cases of jointly owned property will fall short of the degree of business organisation needed to constitute a partnership. To accept that a partnership exists you would have to be satisfied that a similar degree of business organisation as in an ordinary commercial business . . . .. On the other hand, where it has been accepted that a partnership already exists and has in it property belonging to the partnership, the presumption would normally be that the letting is part of the partnership and there is more than mere joint ownership." (PIM1030.)
[3] ITTOIA 2005, ss 854 to 856.

Energy saving expenditure

[10.10] Statute[1] provides a deduction for a landlord against rental income of an amount spent on capital expenditure incurred in the installation of hot-water system insulation, draught-proofing, solid wall insulation, floor insulation, loft insulation, cavity wall insulation in dwelling houses that are let unfurnished. Where the relief is claimed, capital allowances are not available on the same expenditure.

This special allowance is available for expenditure between:

(a) 6 April 2004 and 5 April 2015[2] only (income tax); or
(b) 8 July 2008 and 31 March 2015 (corporation tax)[3].

The amount of the deduction is restricted to £1,500 per property.[4]

Simon's Taxes B9.101

---

[1] ITTOIA 2005, s 312.
[2] Extended from 2009 to 2015 by FA 2007, s 18(3) amending ITTOIA 2005, s 312(1)(c).
[3] TA 1988, s 31ZA and Energy-Saving Items (Corproration Tax) Regulations 2008, SI 2008/1520.
[4] Energy Saving Items (Deductions for Expenditure etc) Regulations, SI 2004/2664, reg 2 made under the authority of ITTOIA 2005, s 314(1).

Interest paid—income tax

[10.11] Interest is deductible or not according to the rules in ITTOIA 2005, Pt 2, as they apply to trading income. This means that interest is deductible by reference to the date it falls due rather than the date of payment. This also

[10.11] Property income

means not only that there is a duty to withhold basic rate tax in the circumstances prescribed but also that the duality rules in ITTOIA 2005, s 34 will become relevant, a matter of particular importance if the property is not let at a commercial rent. If property is let at a commercial rent for part of the year and at a non-commercial rent for the rest of the year apportionment of the interest would seem to be possible.

Interest is deducted in the computation of the taxable income arising from the property business by applying normal commercial accounting principles. In the same way as in the computation of trading income, a loan that is used partly for private purposes and partly for the business is apportioned so that the interest deducted is that which relates to the business part only; the interest relating to the loan used for private purposes is not deducted. Withdrawal of capital from a business is not a private purpose. The Revenue recognise that proprietors of businesses are entitled to withdraw their capital from the business even though substitute funding then has to be provided by interest bearing loans.[1]

Simon's Taxes B9.101.

---

[1] Inland Revenue Business Income Manual para BIM 45700. The manual gives an illustration:

Mr A owns a flat in central London, which he bought ten years ago for £125,000. He has a mortgage of £80,000 on the property.

He has been offered a job in Holland and is moving there to live and work. He intends to come back to the UK at some time. He decides to keep his flat and rent it out while he is away. His London flat now has a market value of £375,000.

The opening balance sheet of this rental business shows:

Mortgage	£80,000	Property at MV	£375,000
Capital account	£295,000		
	£375,000		£375,000

He renegotiates his mortgage on the flat to convert it to a buy to let mortgage and borrows a further £125,000 which he then uses to buy a flat in Rotterdam.

The balance sheet at the end of year 1 shows:

Mortgage	£205,000	Property at MV	£375,000
Cap acc b/f	£295,000		
Less: drawings	(125,000)		
Carry forward	£170,000		
	£375,000		£375,000

Although he has withdrawn capital from the business, the interest on the mortgage loan is allowable in full because it is funding the transfer of the property to the business at its open market value at the time the business started. The capital account is not overdrawn.

For a further discussion of the consequences of the Revenue interpretation see Dean Wootten, Interest in Property, *Taxation*, 3 March 2005, pp 539–542.

Non-resident landlord

[10.12] Where rent for land and buildings in the UK (or any other payment in respect of a UK property business or chargeable under Schedule A) is paid direct to a person whose usual place of abode is outside the UK, the payers must deduct a sum from the payment equal to the basic rate of income tax and account to the Revenue for this deduction.[1]

However, no deduction of tax is required on the payment of rent to a non-resident, whether directly by the tenant or through an agent, if the non-resident holds a Revenue certificate issued under the "non-resident landlord scheme". Revenue practice is to issue a certificate under the scheme allowing the payment of rents gross where the non-resident landlord has either had no liability to UK tax in the immediately prior years, or has "a good tax history . . . and a commitment to comply fully with the requirements of self-assessment and to follow the self-assessment procedures".[2] The Revenue are entitled to withdraw the certification where the non-resident fails to make a return of profits, or otherwise causes the Board to "cease to be satisfied that the non-resident will comply".[3]

The withholding rule does not apply where the income is paid to the UK branch of a non-resident company which is chargeable to corporation tax.[4]

This procedure does not require notice by either the landlord or the Revenue to the tenant on whom is therefore cast the duty of knowing the landlord's usual place of abode. The right to deduct tax is lost as soon as the payment is made gross.[5] There is no right to make good the failure to deduct by making a deduction from a later payment, even one falling within the same tax year.[6]

Simon's Taxes B9.503.

---

[1] ITA 2007, s 971 and Taxation of Income from Land (Non-Residents) Regulations, SI 1995/2902, para 8(2).
[2] SI 1995/2902.
[3] Regulation 19. A useful guide to the workings of the system is given in Inland Revenue booklet IR 140.
[4] SI 1995/2902, para 8(3).
[5] *Tenbry Investments Ltd v Peugeot Talbot Motor Co Ltd* [1992] STC 791.
[6] [1992] STC 791.

Furnished lettings

[10.13] Rent for the occupation of the property forming part of a UK property business extends also to situations where the rent includes the use of furniture.[1] Further rules apply if the rent fulfils the conditions for furnished holiday lettings.

Capital allowances are not available for machinery and plant in a dwellinghouse that is let.[2] Concessionary relief is therefore given for wear and tear on furniture in furnished lettings; broadly the tenant (T) may elect between the actual costs of replacement on the "renewals" basis or take a 10% deduction from the net rent received. The rent must also be reduced for any council tax or water rates which the landlord pays.[3] Taking the 10% deduction does not prevent T from claiming renewals allowance for renewing fixtures which are an integral part of the building.

An exception to the rule excluding capital allowances for expenditure on items in a dwelling-house is statutory relief[4] for the cost of installing cavity wall and loft insulation.[5]

For relief when a furnished lettings "property business" produces a loss, see supra, § 6.27.

[1] ITTOIA 2005, s 308 (income tax); TA 1988, s 15(1), para 4 (corporation tax). The Law Commission previously rejected a proposal to move rent from furnished lettings into Schedule A partly because the variable amounts from such furnished lettings make the Schedule A machinery less appropriate: 1971 Cmnd. 4654 § 61. The advent of self-assessment removed this problem.

[2] CAA 2001, s 35(2).

[3] Extra-statutory concession B47; T must also deduct any payments for services normally borne by a tenant.

[4] Income tax: ITTOIA 2005, s 312 for the period 6 April 2004 to 5 April 2015 only (corporation tax), TA 1988, s 31ZA–31ZC inserted by FA 2007, s 17(1) for the period to 31 March 2015 only, see supra, § 10.10.

[5] Relief is given against rents receivable and is given in full in the year in which it is incurred, but is limited to expenditure of up to £1,500 per dwelling.

Rent a room

[10.14] The purpose behind this complicated relief is to provide an incentive to those who have spare rooms in their homes to let them out.[1] A qualifying individual who receives "rent-a-room receipts"[2] in respect of the individual's only or main residence may elect to be exempt from income tax on the "rent-a-room receipts" up to a limit of £4,250.[3] These receipts can cover the use of furnished accommodation in the residence (or residences) or any connected goods or services.[4] Goods and services are relevant if they are, or are similar in nature to, meals, cleaning and laundry.[5] If the individual has any other receipts from the same residence (or residences) relief is not available.[6] The Revenue view is that this relief does not extend to income from uses other than as furnished living accommodation.[7]

The exemption is given in respect of relevant sums, which are, as already seen, defined in terms of sums accruing and so not taking account of any allowable deductions. The exemption is given up to a basic amount which is, as also already seen, currently £4,250. This applies to the basis period and subsequent 12-month periods.[8] This amount is reduced by 50% (to £2,125) if at any time during the year sums accrue to any other person or person's in respect of the residential accommodation or relevant goods or services and at that time the residence is the individual's only or main residence.[9] This rule applies where for example A and B share a house and jointly let a room in it to C or A lets a room to D and B to E. However, this rule applies only where A and B receive money; if A and B arrange affairs so that all the income accrues to A or to B the limit will be £4,250); if it is shared the limit will be £2,125. In determining the gross sums received account must be taken of any balancing charge falling due in respect of machinery and plant by including that amount as part of the gross receipt.[10]

The relief is in respect of sums accruing and account is not generally to be taken of any capital allowances or balancing charges or of any other expenses.[11] Two sets of elections flow from this. First, the taxpayer may elect that the relief should not apply;[12] this will be valuable if for example the allowable expenses and other deductions give rise to a loss.

Secondly, the taxpayer may choose between being taxed on the whole *profit* in the usual way and an alternative basis consisting of being taxed on the gross receipts so far as they exceed £4,250;[13] this is designed for the situation in which the gross receipts exceed £4,250 but not by much. This alternative basis will be applied only if the taxpayer elects it.[14]

Simon's Taxes B9.111.

---

[1] Inland Revenue press release, 18 June 1992, *Simon's Tax Intelligence* 1992, p. 617.
[2] "Rent-a-room receipts" are defined by ITTOIA 2005, s 786(1) as "receipts in respect of the use of furnished accommodation in a residence in the United Kingdom or in respect of goods or services supplied in connection with that use . . . accruing to the individual . . . [if that] residence is the individual's only or main residence and . . . the receipts would otherwise be brought into account in calculating the profits of a trade or UK property business or chargeable under Chapter 8 of Part 5 (income not otherwise charged)".
[3] ITTOIA 2005, s 789(4).
[4] ITTOIA 2005, s 786(1).
[5] ITTOIA 2005, s 786(2).
[6] ITTOIA 2005, ss 785(1)(*b*).
[7] See Inland Revenue interpretation RI 80.
[8] ITTOIA 2005, s 790(2).
[9] ITTOIA 2005, s 789(3).
[10] ITTOIA 2005, s 788(1).
[11] ITTOIA 2005, s 788(1).
[12] ITTOIA 2005, s 799.
[13] ITTOIA 2005, ss 795–798.
[14] ITTOIA 2005, s 800.

Furnished holiday lettings

[10.15] Statute[1] provides favoured treatment for furnished holiday lettings. Where there is a furnished holiday letting, the following rules (otherwise applicable only to trades) apply:

[10.15] Property income

(1) the income is treated as earned income (§ **5.24**);
(2) loss relief rules apply as for trades (§ **6.31**, § **25.19**);
(3) the profits constitute qualifying earnings for personal pension plan and retirement annuity purposes (§ **32.32**);
(4) capital allowances are available (§ **9.23**);
(5) rollover relief for CGT (§ **17.05**);
(6) retirement relief for CGT (§ **17.05**);
(7) CGT relief for gifts of business assets (§§ **18.41** ff);
(8) bad debt relief for loans to traders (§ **17.05**);
(9) relief for pre-trading expenditure; and
(10) taper relief at the business asset taper rate is applied.

There are stringent conditions to be satisfied before letting is treated as a furnished holiday letting. It was previously the case that the property must be in the UK. However, in 2009, the Government accepted that this requirement breached EC law and this requirement is no longer enforced. However, in the same announcement the Government announced the repeal of the rules from 6 April 2010.

Other conditions are that the letting must be on a commercial basis and with a view to the realisation of profit and the tenant must be entitled to the use of the furniture. The property must be available for letting to the general public during the season, must be available for not less than 140 days, must be let for at least 70 days and:

(a) for income tax purposes: it must not be in the same occupation for more than 31 days for periods totalling more than 155 days;
(b) for corporation tax purposes: for a period of at least seven months it must not normally be in the same occupation for continuous periods exceeding 31 days.[2]

Where these conditions are fulfilled in relation to one property but not another the taxpayer may elect to have the properties averaged. Thus if property 1 is let for 80 days and property 2 for 68 days, an averaging election will make both properties let for 74 days and so both qualify.

These conditions have to be satisfied by reference to periods of 12 months, being the year of assessment for an individual and the accounting period of a company. Special rules apply where the accommodation was not within these rules in the previous year—the 12-month period runs from the date of the first letting; in the converse situation the period begins on the last date of letting.

A loss arising from a furnished holiday letting can be relieved under the provisions available for a trading loss.[3] However, the three year carry back rule for losses in the first three years of a trade (ITA 2007, s 74) applies only if the accommodation let has been owned as let property for less than three years.[4] This prevents such a loss relief claim where the loss arises in a year in which the property qualifies as a furnished holiday let having been let on a long lease previously.

The treatment of income from furnished holiday lettings is akin to that from a trade. It is not, however, necessary to demonstrate the "badges of trade" in order to obtain the advantages of the treatment afforded to furnished holiday lettings but there must be a realistic likelihood of a profit.[5]

The furnished holiday letting provisions apply for income tax and capital gains tax. The provisions have no application for inheritance tax; the property does not attract IHT business property relief.

Simon's Taxes B9.111.

---

[1] ITTOIA 2005, ss 323–326 (income tax); TA 1988, ss 503, 504 and 504A (corporation tax).
[2] ITTOIA 2005, s 325 (income tax); TA 1988, s 504(3) (corporation tax).
[3] TA 2007, s 127 gives specific authority for the loss reliefs given for trades in ITA 2007, ss 59–126 to be available for a deficit of income arising from furnished letting. ITA 2007, s 75 (restriction on loss releasing activity) is disapplied: ITA 2007, s 127(4). There is specific provision for apportionment of a loss when the property business consists, in part, of furnished holiday lettings and, in part, of other letting: ITA 2007, s 127(7).
[4] ITA 2007, s 127(6).
[5] *Brown v Richardson* [1997] STC (SCD) 233. See discussion in supra, § **6.28** for the Revenue's view.

Taxation of premiums as income

[10.16] Since the rules for property businesses tax only the annual profits and not the capital gains arising from land, the payment of a premium by a tenant to his landlord would escape tax as income[1] even though this resulted in a lower rent and so a lower income for the landlord. Statute[2] brings into the charge to tax as income a portion of the premium on a lease for a term not exceeding 50 years.

Companies found that they could obtain a tax advantage by selling the rights to future rental income in circumstances which were in economic terms little more than bank loans. These became known as "rent factoring schemes"[3] and legislation to stop them was introduced in 2000[4] and extended in 2005.[5] The legislation brings these receipts into tax under Schedule A—but only for corporation tax.

On taxation of reverse premiums see supra, § **7.130**.

Simon's Taxes B9.201.

---

[1] *O'Connor v Hume* [1954] 2 All ER 301, [1954] 1 WLR 824. Conversely payment of the premium by the lessee was a capital expense: *Green v Favourite Cinemas Ltd* (1930) 15 TC 390.
[2] ITTOIA 2005, Pt 3, Ch 4 (income tax); TA 1988, ss 34–39 (corporation tax).
[3] See *IRC v John Lewis Properties plc* [2002] EWCA Civ 1869, [2003] STC 117, in which the Court of Appeal confirms that, before the FA 2000 legislation, the sum received by John Lewis Properties Ltd is correctly regarded as a capital receipt.
[4] TA 1988, ss 43A–43G.
[5] TA 1988, ss 43A–43G amended by F(No 2)A 2005, Sch 7, para 1.

A premium

[10.17] A premium is defined so as to include[1] "any similar sum payable to the immediate or a superior landlord or to a person connected[2] with such person". Thus a payment required by a landlord on the grant of a lease to a tenant would fall within this rule but a payment required by the tenant on the assignment of his interest would not. A payment exacted by the tenant on the grant of a sub-lease would be caught. Case law provides a further definition as any sum of money paid by the tenant to the landlord in consideration of the grant of a lease.[3] In *Toronto-Dominion Bank v Oberoi*[4] a premium was wrongly described in the lease document as "rent". The courts had no difficulty in identifying it as a premium and ordered rectification.

The sum need not be mentioned in the lease document. A sum paid in or in connection with the granting of a lease eg key money is presumed to be a premium but it is open to the taxpayer to show some reason for the payment other than the grant.[5]

Simon's Taxes B9.105.

---

1. ITTOIA 2005, s 307(1) (income tax); for corporation tax purposes, the definition in TA 1988, s 24(1) reads "including any like sum whether payable to the immediate or superior landlord or to a person connected with the immediate or superior landlord". On pre-1963 leases, see s 39(1).
2. Defined in TA 1988, s 839, applied for income tax by ITTOIA 2005, s 878(5). It is likely that a payment to a third party other than a connected person is a premium; such a payment is a premium for the Landlord and Tenant (Rent Control) Act 1949: *Elmdene Estates Ltd v White* [1960] AC 528, [1960] 1 All ER 306. A premium in non-monetary form is caught: TA 1988, s 24(4).
3. Per Walton J in *Clarke v United Real (Moorgate) Ltd* [1988] STC 273 at 299 (a CGT case).
4. [2002] EWHC 3216 (Ch), [2004] STC 1197.
5. ITTOIA 2005, s 306(1)–(3) (income tax); TA 1988, s 24(2) (corporation tax). Quaere whether payment by the lessee of the lessor's legal costs is a premium—semble not.

Duration of lease

[10.18] These rules apply only where the duration of the lease does not exceed fifty years.[1] The definition of a 50 year lease takes full account of the commercial realities. Thus if a tenant has a 40-year lease with an option to extend it for a further 20 years, account may be taken of the circumstances making it likely that the lease will be so extended. Likewise if a tenant, or a person connected with him, has the right not to extend the existing lease but instead has the right to a further lease of the same premises or part of them, the term may be treated as not expiring before the end of the further lease. Both these provisions, by lengthening the lease, favour the landlord but another rule does not. This provides that if any of the terms of the lease (whether relating to forfeiture or to any other matter) or any other circumstances render it unlikely that the lease will continue beyond a date falling short of the expiry of the term of the lease, the lease shall be treated as if it ended not later than that date, provided that the premium would not have been substantially greater had the lease been expected to run its full term.[2] Thus a 51-year lease with an option to the landlord to terminate it after five years would be treated as a five-year lease, as would one which provided that after five years the rent, originally a full commercial rent, should be quintupled.

The question of what is unlikely is judged at the time the lease is granted.[3] The rule by focusing on what is likely or unlikely means that a lease for lives can fall within these rules if the life is unlikely to last more than 50 years despite the imposition of a 99-year lease by virtue of the Law of Property Act 1925, s 149.

Simon's Taxes B9.203.

[1] ITTOIA 2005, s 277(1)(a) (income tax); TA 1988, s 34(1) (corporation tax).
[2] ITTOIA 2005, ss 303–304 (income tax); TA 1988, s 38 (corporation tax). These rules apply only to leases granted after 24 August 1971.
[3] ITTOIA 2005, s 304(1) (income tax); TA 1988, s 38(2) (corporation tax).

Taxing the premium

[10.19] A premium payable in respect of a lease not exceeding 50 years is treated as payable by way of rent and as part of the property business;[1] if it is payable to someone other than the landlord the recipient is treated as carrying on a separate property business and it is taxed as that person's income.[2] The landlord or other person is treated as becoming entitled when the lease is granted.[3]

Without modification this rule could first cause a sharp distinction between a 49-year lease and a 51-year lease. This problem is solved by the fractional reduction of the premium that fraction being related to the duration of the lease, as defined; the longer the lease the less the chargeable sum.[4] The premium is reduced by 1/50 for each complete period of 12 months (other than the first) comprised in the duration of the lease.[5] Only complete years are taken into account so that a premium on a lease for two years less a day would be chargeable in full. The sum by which the premium is reduced is not taxable in any subsequent year.[6]

If the premium is payable by instalments the taxpayer may spread the taxable fraction of the premiums over a period allowed by the Revenue. This period is not to exceed eight years or until the last instalment of the premium becomes due, if shorter.[7]

Simon's Taxes B9.202.

[1] ITTOIA 2005, s 276(1) (income tax); TA 1988, s 34(1) (corporation tax).
[2] ITTOIA 2005, s 279(2) (income tax); TA 1988, s 34(6) (corporation tax).
[3] Quaere how one grants an agreement for a lease; see further *City Permanent Building Society v Miller* [1952] Ch 840 at 853, [1952] 2 All ER 621 at 628.
[4] ITTOIA 2005, s 277(3), (4) (income tax); TA 1988, s 34(1) (corporation tax).

[5] This could have been more elegantly expressed by saying the fraction chargeable shall be 50 minus the number of years of the lease plus one over 50.
[6] The part not taxed as a premium may nonetheless be chargeable to tax: as income, if the lessor deals in land, or otherwise to CGT.
[7] ITTOIA 2005, s 299 (income tax); TA 1988, s 34(8) (corporation tax).

Anti-avoidance provisions—piercing the disguise

Improvements

[10.20] ITTOIA 2005, s 278 (income tax) and TA 1988, s 34(2) (corporation tax) provide that if the terms subject to which the lease is granted impose on the tenant an obligation to carry out any work on the premises[1] then the amount by which the value of the landlord's estate immediately after the commencement of the lease exceeds the value which it would have had if no such obligation had been imposed on the tenant, is treated as a premium. The measure of liability is the benefit received, not the cost incurred—a matter of particular importance if the landlord is a lessee and his lease ends shortly after the sub-lease. Since the provision applies whenever there is an obligation to carry out work, there is a specific exclusion where the works are such that the costs would be deductible by the landlord as an expense of the landlord's property business if he had to do them, for example works of maintenance.[2]

Simon's Taxes B9.204.

[1] This premium does not extend to work on other property belonging to the landlord; nor does it apply when the tenant does work under an obligation outside the lease.
[2] ITTOIA 2005, s 278(4), (5) (income tax); TA 1988, s 34(3) (corporation tax).

Commutation of rent or surrender of lease

[10.21] Any sums which become payable by the tenant in lieu of rent *or* as consideration for the surrender of the lease but only if these sums are payable under the terms of the lease are treated as a premium.[1] A payment in lieu of rent is attributed to the period covered by the payment. So if there is a ten-year lease under which the tenant is to pay rent of £700 pa but with the right at any time after the first year to pay £5,000 and a rent of only £200 pa and the right is exercised, the £5,000 would be treated as a premium.

In calculating the charge to tax on sums in lieu of rent the duration of the lease is the period for which the payment is being made. Thus, if the right in the previous example is exercised when there are eight years left, the calculations assume an eight-year lease.

Simon's Taxes B9.205.

[1] ITTOIA 2005, s 279 (income tax); TA 1988, s 34(4) (corporation tax).

Variations and waivers

[10.22] A sum payable by a tenant on the surrender of a lease, where that sum is not stipulated in the original lease, is similarly treated as if it were a premium, as is any consideration for the variation or waiver of any terms of the lease.[1] A waiver means the abandonment of a right in such a way that the other party is entitled to plead the abandonment by way of confession and avoidance if the right is later asserted. It is not confined to total abandonment of the right. So when a tenant's option to renew a lease had lapsed, a sum paid to the landlord for the reinstatement of the option was a payment for the variation or waiver of a term of the lease,[2] whether such sums were stipulated in the lease or not. Payments within this section are chargeable in the tax year in which the contract of variation is entered into[3] and not, when it becomes payable by the tenant.[4] Further, payments within s 34(5) if paid to someone other than the landlord are only chargeable if paid to a person connected with the landlord, there being no such restriction for payments within s 34(4).[5] Pre-1963 leases are also caught.[6]

Simon's Taxes B9.204–206.

---

[1] ITTOIA 2005, s 281 (income tax); TA 1988, s 34(5) (corporation tax).
[2] *Banning v Wright* [1972] 2 All ER 987, 48 TC 421, HL where the option lapsed owing to a breach of covenant by the lessee.
[3] ITTOIA 2005, s 281(3) (income tax); TA 1988, s 34(5)(*b*) and (7A) (corporation tax).
[4] As is the case under ITTOIA 2005, ss 279(3) and 280(3) (income tax) and TA 1988, s 34(4)(*b*) and (7A) (corporation tax).
[5] ITTOIA 2005, s 281(1)(*b*) (income tax); TA 1988, s 34(7) (corporation tax).
[6] TA 1988, s 39(2).

Assignment of a lease granted at an undervalue.

[10.23] Although in general payments by an assignee of the lease to the assignor escape tax, this will not be so if the lease was granted to the assignor or some predecessor in title at an undervalue.[1] If A grants a lease to B at a rent plus a premium, the provisions already discussed will charge the premium to income tax. If A grants the lease to X who assigns it to B and X is obliged to pay A money for the privilege of assignment, the sum will be taxed to A under ITTOIA 2005, ss 279–281 (income tax) or TA 1988, s 34(4) or (5) (corporation tax). If X is not obliged to pay A money for the privilege, the economic benefit may still accrue to A if, for example, X is a connected person or a family company. It is therefore provided in ITTOIA 2005, s 282 (income tax) or TA 1988, s 35 that (a) if the original[2] grant of the lease was at an undervalue, and (b) the lessee subsequently assigns the lease for a profit, then the lessee must bring a proportion of the premium into account as a receipt of the property business.[3]

The amount brought in as income is:

$$P \times (50 - Y) / 50$$

[10.23] Property income

where

P is the lower of:

(a) the profit on the assignment; and
(b) the amount by which the undervalue exceeds the total of the profits made by previous assignments; and

Y is the number of complete years (except the first) comprised in the effective duration of the lease.[4]

The amount is treated as a receipt of the property business for the tax year in which the consideration for the assignment is payable.[5]

This rule cannot be avoided by X assigning to Y without permission who then assigns to B at a premium, since ITTOIA 2005, s 282 and TA 1988, s 35 apply to *any* assignment of the lease. So Y would be liable to tax on the excess of the premium paid to him by B over any premium paid by him to X. This process continues until the amount that has been rendered chargeable equals the amount forgone.

The amount chargeable is that before the percentage reduction; the reduction is calculated by reference to the initial duration of the lease and so remains constant.

EXAMPLE

In 2000 A granted B a lease for 26 years at a premium of £1,000 and a peppercorn rent; the lease is worth £80,000. A is chargeable under Pt 3 on £1,000 less 50% = £500.

In 2002 B assigned the lease to C for £10,000. B is chargeable under Pt 3 on £10,000 less £1,000 already charged, less 50% = £4,500.

In 2004 C assigns the lease to D for £9,000. C is not chargeable as the premium he receives is less than the one he paid.

In 2006 D assigns the lease to E for £200,000, its current market value. D is chargeable on £80,000 original value less £1,000 charged to A and £9,000 charged to B, less 50% = £35,000.

It will be seen that the charge is on the assignor, not the grantor, but that it applies whenever the original grant was at an undervalue and that it is not confined to situations where the lessee is a person connected with the grantor. The section applies when the sum is payable to a person other than the assignor although the charge will still fall on the assignor.

Simon's Taxes B9.212.

---

[1] Nor if he takes a short lease back: ITTOIA 2005, s 285 (income tax); TA 1988, s 36 (corporation tax).

[2] And only the original grant. If the original grant was for full value the fact that a subsequent assignment was not for full value does not create a potential charge under ITTOIA 2005, s 282 or TA 1988, s 35.

[3] The fractional reduction and top-slicing rules apply. For corporation tax, this represents a Schedule A charge arising under TA 1988, s 15 (TA 1988, s 35(2)). The charge was moved from Schedule D, Case VI to Schedule A by FA 1998.

[4] ITTOIA 2005, s 282(4) (income tax); TA 1988, s 35(2) (corporation tax). Any excess may be liable to CGT.

[5] ITTOIA 2005, s 282(3) (income tax); TA 1988, s 35(2) (corporation tax).

Sale with right of reconveyance.

[10.24] Despite ITTOIA 2005, s 277–282 and TA 1988, ss 34, 35 it would still be possible to exact the equivalent of a premium from a "tenant" by the device of conveying to him not a lease but the entire interest of the vendor and reserving to the vendor a right to reacquire the property at some future date. Thus instead of giving B a seven-year lease for £4,000, A might convey the land to B for £6,000 and reserve a right to buy it back from B for £2,000 after seven years. ITTOIA 2005, s 284 and TA 1988, s 36 are designed to cure this. They apply when the terms subject to which an estate or interest is sold provide that it shall be or may be required to be reconveyed to the grantor or to a person connected with him.[1] The amount by which the sale price exceeds the repurchase price is charged to the vendor—not the connected person—as part of the vendor's income from a property business[2] the amount being assessed at the time of the sale and not of the repurchase. The sum so charged is not described as a premium, but the fractional reduction for the length of the "lease" will apply and thus reduces the amount chargeable by 1/50 for each complete year after the first between the sale and the reconveyance.[3] If the sale does not fix the date of the reconveyance but does fix the price, it is assumed that the reconveyance will occur at the earliest possible date.[4] If the sale does not fix the date of the reconveyance and the price varies with the date, the sum to be taxed is computed on the assumption that the price on reconveyance shall be the lowest obtainable.[5]

Should the terms of the sale provide that the purchaser is to lease the property back to the vendor, rather than reconvey it, a notional premium may arise. If the lease is later, then the seller must bring into account a similar proportion of the total of the premium (if any) for the lease back and the value at the date of the sale of the right to receive a conveyance of the reversion immediately after the lease begins to run. Thus one deducts from the original sale price not only the value of the reversion on the lease but also any premium paid.[6]

No notional premium arises if the lease is granted and begins to run within one month after the sale, a provision to protect the normal commercial transaction of the sale and lease back.[7]

Simon's Taxes B9.213.

---

[1] Defined in ITA 2007, s 993 (income tax); TA 1988, s 839 (corporation tax).
[2] ITTOIA 2005, s 284(3) (income tax); TA 1988, s 36(1) invoking the Schedule A charge under TA 1988, s 15(1), para 1(2) (corporation tax).
[3] ITTOIA 2005, s 284(3) (income tax); TA 1988, s 36(1) (corporation tax). These provisions cause difficulty in the common case where a landowner sells mineral rights but with an option to buy back at the land's agricultural value. It should also be noted that, strictly, in corporation tax cases, the 1/50 reduction applies after two complete years.
[4] ITTOIA 2005, s 284(1)(*b*) (income tax); TA 1988, s 36(1) (corporation tax).
[5] ITTOIA 2005, s 284(1)–(3) (income tax); TA 1988, s 36(2)(*a*) (corporation tax).
[6] ITTOIA 2005, s 285 (income tax); TA 1988, s 36(3) (corporation tax).
[7] ITTOIA 2005, s 285(2) (income tax); TA 1988, s 36(4) (corporation tax).

Franking the premium on a sublease

[10.25] If a charge to tax has arisen on a payment within ITTOIA 2005, ss 277–282 or TA 1988, ss 34 or 35 (but not ITTOIA 2005, ss 284 and 285 or TA 1988, s 36), that payment can be used to frank in whole or in part a similar charge arising from a dealing with the interest granted. This is designed to prevent a double charge to tax. Thus if A grants a lease for 46 years to X, and X pays a premium of say £10,000 that premium will be caught for tax by ITTOIA 2005, s 277 or TA 1988, s 34(1), the amount chargeable being £1,000. If X assigns the lease to Y, normally[1] no charge will arise, but if X grants Y a sublease for, say, nine years and exacts a premium of, say, £1,200, he is liable to be taxed on £1,008 under ITTOIA 2005, s 277 or TA 1988, s 34(1). Relief is given for the sublease premium.[2] The amount chargeable on the grant by A to X, £1,000, is called (in respect of corporation tax) "the amount chargeable on the superior interest" and the amount chargeable on the grant by X to Y, £1,008, is referred to as "the later chargeable amount". The amount charged to X on the grant of the sublease is reduced by the appropriate fraction of the amount chargeable on the superior interest.[3] The numerator of this fraction is the period in respect of which the later chargeable amount arose (nine years) and the denominator is the period in respect of which the earlier amount arose (46 years)[4] so that the fraction will be 9/46 of £1,000 = £196. The later chargeable amount is therefore reduced by £196 and X's chargeable amount is therefore £1,008 − 196 = £812.

If the second sum, that payable by Y to X, is payable by instalments X's relief will be to treat those instalments as rent.

The purpose of the relief is presumably to avoid a double charge to tax and preserve the tax neutrality between an assignment of a lease and the grant of a sublease. Thus the longer the sublease the greater the appropriate fraction of the first sum chargeable that can be set off against the new charge.

This procedure is no longer available for sums charged under ITTOIA 2005, ss 284 and 285 or TA 1988, s 36. Schemes were entered into specifically so as to create large sums deductible under s 37 or 87 (what are now for income tax, ITTOIA 2005, ss 288 and 60–67). An interest in land would be sold off with a provision for reconveyance at a reduced price. Now where a vendor is assessed under ITTOIA 2005, ss 284 and 285 or TA 1988, s 36 on the notional extra rent, the purchaser can no longer set that off against any tax he has to pay on the grant of a sublease (ITTOIA 2005, ss 288 or (corporation tax) TA 1988, s 37)—nor may he deduct the notional rent under ITTOIA 2005, ss 60–67 or (corporation tax) TA 1988, s 87.

---

[1] See ITTOIA 2005, s 285 (income tax); TA 1988, s 35 (corporation tax) (lease at undervalue) (see supra, § **10.23**).
[2] ITTOIA 2005, ss 287 and 288 (income tax); TA 1988, s 37(2) (corporation tax).
[3] ITTOIA 2005, s 288(2), (3) (income tax); TA 1988, s 37(5) (corporation tax).
[4] ITTOIA 2005, s 288(4) (income tax); TA 1988, s 37(7) (corporation tax).

Premium set against rent

[10.26] If a tenant grants a sublease he is taxable in respect of the rent received under that sublease but may deduct the rent he himself pays under his lease. If he paid a premium charged under ITTOIA 2005, ss 277–282 (income tax) or TA 1988, ss 34 or 35 (corporation tax) but not ITTOIA 2005, ss 284 and 285 or TA 1988, s 36—he is allowed to deduct a part of that from the rent derived from the sublease.[1]

EXAMPLE

If A grants B a lease for 25 years paying a premium of £10,000 and B sublets to C for £600 a year, B is allowed to deduct from his receipts the sum of 1/25 × £10,000 × (50 − 24)/50=5,200/25 or £208 plus any rent paid to A. The set-off is thus limited to that part which is taxable in A's hands. If B assigns the lease to X, X may also use the £208 each year. Where the sub-lease is also at a premium, B may deduct the taxable element of the premium paid to A from the taxable element of the premium which he receives from C. Where the sublease is at a premium and a rent, the part of the premium paid to A is set off against the taxable element of the premium in priority to the rent.

[1] ITTOIA 2005, s 291 (income tax); TA 1988, ss 37(4) and 37A(1) (corporation tax).

Interaction with trading income

[10.27] There are three specific rules relating to particular aspects of the interrelationship between property income and trading income:

(1) Where the tenant can deduct the rent paid in computing the profits of his business, whether because the lease is of business premises or is trading stock, he may deduct the proportion of any premium charged under ITTOIA 2005, ss 277–282 (income tax) or TA 1988, ss 34 or 35 (corporation tax).[1] That proportion is spread over the duration of the lease.

(2) Rental income accruing to a dealer in land ought to be charged as property income but if small in relation to other income, is treated as part of the trading income computation.[2]

(3) Where a dealer in land receives a payment which is taxable as a premium under ITTOIA 2005, ss 277–285 (income tax) or TA 1988, s 34(1), (4) or (5) or ss 35 or 36 (corporation tax) and a part is chargeable under those sections,[3] that part is so charged and only the excess is treated as trading income. Where an individual trades in land therefore he will be entitled to top-slicing relief to the extent of the fractionally reduced sum, but is taxable in full on the amount of the reduction.

[1] ITTOIA 2005, ss 60–67 (income tax); TA 1988, s 87 (corporation tax).
[2] A practice published in *Tax Bulletin* February 1994 legislated for income tax by ITTOIA 2005, s 21 from 6 April 2005.
[3] ITTOIA 2005, s 158 (income tax); TA 1988, s 99(2), (3) (corporation tax). But note the qualification in ITTOIA 2005, s 158(4) (referring to ss 301 and 302) in respect

[10.27] Property income

of repayments arising under ss 284 and 285 (income tax) and in TA 1988, s 99(3) relating to s 36(2)(b) (corporation tax).

11

Savings income

The charge to tax	PARA **11.01**
Savings income not charged to tax	PARA **11.02**
Interest—meaning	PARA **11.05**
Accrued interest	PARA **11.07**
Yearly interest—meaning	PARA **11.12**
Deduction at source	PARA **11.13**
Deeply discounted securities	PARA **11.17**
Gilt strips	PARA **11.19**
Annuities and annual payments	PARA **11.20**
Deductions at source: basic rate	PARA **11.36**
Consequence of failing to deduct tax	PARA **11.40**
Payments 'free of tax'	PARA **11.42**
Rule in *Re Pettit*	PARA **11.43**
Maintenance payments	PARA **11.45**

This chapter looks at the taxation of what statute refers to as 'Savings Income'. See Chapter 31 for a discussion of savings products with specific tax exemptions.

The charge to tax

[11.01] Income tax is levied under Pt 4 of ITTOIA 2005 in respect of savings income. This covers:

(1) interest (ITTOIA 2005 Chapter 2);
(2) dividends from UK resident companies (ITTOIA 2005 Chapter 3);
(3) dividends from non-UK companies (ITTOIA 2005 Chapter 4);
(4) stock dividends from UK resident companies (ITTOIA 2005 Chapter 5);
(5) the release of loans to participators in close companies (ITTOIA 2005 Chapter 6);
(6) purchased life annuity payments (ITTOIA 2005 Chapter 7);
(7) profits from deeply discounted securities (ITTOIA 2005 Chapter 8);
(8) life insurance and other similar gains (ITTOIA 2005 Chapter 9);
(9) distributions from unauthorised unit trusts (ITTOIA 2005 Chapter 10);
(10) transactions in deposits (ITTOIA 2005 Chapter 11);
(11) disposals of futures and options involving guaranteed returns (ITTOIA 2005 Chapter 12);
(12) sales of foreign dividend coupons. (ITTOIA 2005 Chapter 13);

In respect of corporation tax, a charge is levied under Schedule D, Case III on:[1]

[11.01] Savings income

(1) interest on money, whether yearly or otherwise, or any annuity or other annual payment falling outside TA 1988, ss 347A or 347B whether such payment is payable within or outside the UK[2], either as a charge on property of the person paying the same by virtue of any deed or will or otherwise, or as a reservation out of it, or as a personal debt or obligation by virtue of any contract, or whether the same is received and payable half yearly or at any shorter or more distant periods but not including any payment chargeable under Schedule A;
(2) discounts, other than on Bills and deep gain securities (which are taxed in a special way);
(3) income from securities bearing interest payable out of public revenue.

Before the introduction of ITTOIA 2005, it was expressly provided in TA 1988, s 64 that no deductions can be made in respect of these sources of income. This statement has not been reproduced for income tax on the basis that there are no provisions allowing such a deduction. The words are pro tem retained for corporation tax purposes.[3]

Income assessed under ITTOIA 2005, Part 4 is defined as "savings" income and may use the 10% starting rate; until 5 April 2008, savings income above the starting rate limit was taxed at the *lower* rate of 20% where such income forms part of the total income of an individual falling within the basic rate band;[4] the basic rate[5] did not apply. From 2008/09, the basic rate has replaced the 20% savings rate and the distinction between the types of income is relevant only for the residual 10% starting rate band. Where savings income is part of taxable income which exceeds the basic rate band the normal *higher* rate of 40% applies. For these purposes the savings income is treated as the top slice[6] so that if an employed taxpayer has taxable total income (ie total income after deduction of personal reliefs) of £2,000 more than the basic rate band, the employment income will be taxed at basic rate and the £2,000 savings income at higher rate.

Investment income which consists of dividend and similar income is taxed at the *dividend ordinary rate* of 10%[7] if it is within the individual's basic rate band (£34,800) and at 32 1/2% if it is part of the taxable income exceeding the limit of the basic rate band. On savings and investment income for trusts see infra, § **13.11**.

The recipient of these income payments thus becomes liable to income tax which will generally be under self assessment. However, if the payment is an annuity or other annual payment, basic rate income tax is not directly assessed on the recipient but is deducted by the person making the payment, the scheme being regulated by ITA 2007, Pt 15 (see infra, § **11.36**).

The scope of what was Schedule D, Case III was substantially reduced by FA 1988 which introduced TA 1988, ss 347A, 347B. The general effect of those reforms was to make new non-charitable covenants non-deductible for tax purposes. To compensate for the removal of the right to deduct, these payments ceased to be taxable income. Before FA 1988 such income had been taxable but with an offsetting right, sometimes limited, for the payer to deduct the sums in computing total income (see the 1999–2000 edition of this book, § **9.33**).

The overall effect was greatly to reduce the importance of Schedule D, Case III in the personal sector. However, the concepts and, regrettably, the machinery in what is now ITA 2007, ss 448 & 449 remain of importance where either (a) the payment is of a type specifically excluded from the new scheme, or (b) the payer is a person other than an individual (so again the new rules do not apply). FA 2000 continued the pattern of reducing the importance of these rules by removing charitable covenants both from the scope of what is now ITA 2007, ss 448 & 449 and from Schedule D, Case III;[8] the machinery for claiming the deduction is the same as for Gift Aid (see supra, § **6.33**). The reform package, while immensely important, of itself did little to reduce the conceptual junkheap of the tax system: the 1996 rewriting of the rules for the taxation of interest was confined to corporation tax.

From 1997–98, when savings and investment income arises to an individual, it is brought into the individual's self-assessment on a strict current year basis. That is, income assessable for 2008–09 is income arising from 6 April 2008 to 5 April 2009.[9]

Exceptionally, however, where a trading partnership is in receipt of other income, such as interest, the basis period for income arising to the partnership and then apportioned to individual partners is income arising in the period of account that forms the basis period for the year of assessment under the rules that apply to the trading income.[10] This treatment provides overlap profits for all income, including savings and investment income. Relief for these overlap profits is given at any subsequent change of accounting date or on the cessation of the partnership or earlier retirement of the individual from the partnership.

Simon's Taxes B8.402.

---

[1] TA 1988, s 18. Other provisions cause income to be taxed under Case III—eg TA 1988, s 119. For list see **Simon's Taxes B8.403.**
[2] These words focus on where the sum is payable; if the source of the interest is a foreign source then the income falls under Schedule D, Case IV (see infra, § **35.10**) and not Case III.
[3] See ITTOIA 2005, ss 370(1), 424(1) and 428(1) (income tax); TA 1988, s 70(1) (corporation tax); see also *Soul v Caillebotte* (1964) 43 TC 657.
[4] ITA 2007, ss 12(10) & 7.
[5] 22% in 2007–08.
[6] ITA 2007, ss 16.
[7] ITA 2007, ss 8, 23.
[8] FA 2000, s 41.
[9] ITTOIA 2005, ss 370(1), 424(1) and 428(1).
[10] ITTOIA 2005, ss 854–856.

Savings income not charged to tax

Interest, etc received by a non-resident

[11.02] Interest and dividends[1] are excluded from the charge to income tax when received by a company that is not resident in the UK.[2]

Interest and dividends received by an individual is not subject to income tax when the individual is not resident in the UK, although the effect of receiving the income, etc, can be to reduce the personal allowance that would otherwise be available against other income.[3]

---

[1] Also income assessable under Chapters 7, 8, 10 and 11 of Part 3, some royalties income and income assessable under Chapters 4 and 7 of Part 5.
[2] FA 2003, s 151. This provision continues the treatment under FA 1995, s 128. The Paymaster General stated in the 2003 Finance Bill debates that the statutory change was simply a consequential adjustment designed to replicate exactly the effect of the formal provision. The change became necessary following the change from "branch or agency" to "permanent establishment" that was introduced by FA 2003, s 148 (Hansard, 20 May 2003, col 151).
[3] ITA 2007, s 811.

Payments by an individual

[11.03] Any annual payment made by an individual is excluded from tax[1] unless it is:

(i) a payment of interest;
(ii) a payment made for commercial reasons in connection with the individual's trade, profession or vocation eg, partnership retirement annuities;[2] and
(iii) a maintenance or alimony payment on the breakdown of a marriage;[3] and
(iv) a reverse premium.[4]

Also outside the new regime are all those payments categorised as savings income and which are made by other entities, ie companies (which have their own rules as to deduction of tax and deductibility for corporation tax) and trusts.[5] The legislation further provides that in computing foreign income no deduction may be made on account of an annuity which would not have been within the following provisions of ITTOIA 2005: Chapter 10 of Part 4, s 579 or Chapters 4 and 7 of Part 5 (income tax) or Schedule D, Case III (corporation tax) if it had arisen in the UK.[6] This non-deduction is applied also to certain income arising in Ireland[7] and foreign emoluments from a non-resident employer.[8]

Maintenance payments are neither deductible by the payer nor chargeable income of the payee.

Simon's Taxes B8.420.

[1]   ITTOIA 2005, s 727, (income tax): TA 1988, s 347A, (corporation tax).
[2]   ITTOIA 2005, s 728.
[3]   ITTOIA 2005, s 729.
[4]   ITTOIA 2005, s 729.
[5]   On Scottish partnerships, see TA 1988, s 347A(6).
[6]   ITTOIA 2005, s 839.
[7]   ITTOIA 2005, s 839(6).
[8]   ITTOIA 2005, s 839(5), ie, payments under ITEPA 2003, ss 328, 329, 334 and 355. Inland Revenue press release, 8 June 1992, *Simon's Tax Intelligence* 1992, p 582.

Permanent health insurance

[11.04] Many individuals pay a premium to an insurance company so that, in the event of long term illness, the insurance company pays a regular monthly sum to the insurer. In the absence of the specific provision, the monthly receipts would fall to be taxed under either ITTOIA 2005, s 683 or 689. However, statute[1] provides a wide range of exemption from tax for regular payments under insurance policies providing benefits in the event of accident, sickness, disability, infirmity or unemployment. The exemption covers payments made by both domestic and foreign insurers.

For the exemption to apply, four conditions must be satisfied:

(a)   the insurance must be partly or wholly against:
    (i)   a "health risk", which is defined[2] as one which insures against the insured becoming subject to any physical or mental illness, disability, infirmity or defect (or to any deterioration in a condition resulting from such illness, disability, infirmity or defect; or
    (ii)   an "employment risk"—ie the risk of unemployment (including the cessation of self-employment);
    (iii)   the terms of the policy providing cover against the risk in question must be "self-contained" or do not differ significantly from those that would apply had the policy only covered health or employment risks;[3]
(b)   the policy must only provide benefits for the period throughout which one of a number of "conditions of payment" are satisfied; these conditions[4] are:
    (i)   the insured continues to suffer from the illness etc insured against (including convalescence or rehabilitation);
    (ii)   the insured is out of work in the circumstances covered by the policy;
    (iii)   the insured's income (excluding the policy benefits) is reduced on account of the circumstances insured against;
    (iv)   the period immediately following the death of the insured in a period within (i)–(iii) (this allows the exemption to continue in respect of benefits paid to a surviving spouse or dependant);

(c) the terms of the policy covering the risk in question must expose the insurer to the risk of a significant underwriting loss in relation to the premiums charged and the investment return therefrom; for this purpose the transfer of risk by way of reinsurance is ignored,[5] and the test is to be applied to the individual policy so that, implicitly, the elimination of risk to the insurer by the aggregation of a sufficient number of similar contingent risks is also disregarded; this last condition denies the exemption to what might in essence be savings type policies.[6]

Simon's Taxes B8.4.

---

[1] ITTOIA 2005, s 735.
[2] ITTOIA 2005, s 736.
[3] ITTOIA 2005, ss 739, 740.
[4] ITTOIA 2005, s 737.
[5] ITTOIA 2005, s 738.
[6] House of Commons Official Report, Standing Committee E, 22 February 1996, col 452.

Interest—meaning

[11.05] There is no statutory definition of interest. In *Bennett v Ogston*, Rowlatt J defined it as "payment by time for the use of money".[1] *Halsbury* defines it as "the return or compensation for the use or retention by one person of a sum of money belonging to, or owed to, another".[2] In *Riches v Westminster Bank*[3], Lord Wright said that:

> the essence of interest is that it is a payment which becomes due because the creditor has not had his money at the due date. It may be regarded either as representing the profit he might have made if he had had the use of the money, or, conversely the loss he suffered because he had not that use. The general idea is that he is entitled to compensation for the deprivation.

This theme was expanded upon in *Euro Hotel (Belgravia) Ltd*[4]. Megarry J said that as a general rule, there are two requirements that must be satisfied for a payment of interest. First, there must be a sum of money by reference to which the payment is to be ascertained; second, that sum of money must be due to the person entitled to the alleged interest.

It is clear from these cases that entitlement is an essential feature of interest. An entitlement to interest arises under common law where there is an express agreement to pay interest or such agreement can be inferred from the circumstances.

Thus a payment on a loan may be interest but a dividend on a share is not. The use of the word "interest" is not conclusive; so where the "interest" was due shortly after the loan and exceeded the principal sum, the court had little difficulty in holding that the payment was not interest.[5] The courts have stressed that the payment must be just recompense and so held that an excessive payment could not be interest.[6]

Compensation for delay in payment must be distinguished from compensation for delay in performing some other obligation, and payments by time for the use of money from payments by time for non-performance of obligations—the fact that time is used to measure a payment does not suffice to make the payment interest when there is no principal debt.[7] So, suppose that A buys whisky in bond for £100 and A then gives B an option to buy that whisky at any time within six months for £100 plus "interest" at the rate of 12% per annum from the time A bought the whisky until B exercises the option. If B exercises the option after three months and pays £103 this would be a simple purchase for £103 and not a purchase for £100 plus £3 interest.[8]

It is unclear whether a payment by a guarantor in respect of interest due from the principal debtor is itself interest,[9] but a payment under a contract of indemnity has been held to be interest when the guarantor expressly guaranteed payment of this interest on a promissory note as distinct from accepting a general obligation to make good the general contractual defaults of the principal.[10]

The question whether a payment is interest is relevant to the payee in determining his income and to the payer in determining his claim to a deduction (see supra, § **6.39, 6.40**). In *Cairns v MacDiarmid* the Court of Appeal used the *Ramsay* principle to disallow a claim for deduction whether or not the payment was technically one of interest under these rules.[11]

If A lends B money for a fixed period, A may insist not only on the current general rate of interest but also on some extra payment. He might charge extra interest or he might ask for a larger sum to be paid back than was lent, viz a premium. Alternatively, he might issue promissory notes but sell them for less than their face value—a discount. Where a company issues debentures at less than face value the Revenue have never argued that the difference between the issued price and the price at which the debenture is redeemed is an interest payment.[12] However, if a lender offers a loan of £90 without interest on condition that the borrower pays £100 in 12 months, the extra £10 will be interest. Moreover if interest is charged but at an unreasonably low rate and the extra sum is geared to the length of the loan, the courts have held the extra sum to be interest even though the parties called it a premium.[13] This does not breach the "form versus substance" rule since the court is saying that the description given by the parties is not conclusive of its legal form and the test is whether £10 or the extra sum represents payment by time for the use of money.

In *Davies v Premier Investment Co Ltd*[14] a company issued unsecured promissory notes at par without interest but offered to redeem them at a premium of 30% after six years with the alternative of a premium calculated at 5% pa should the company redeem the notes or go into voluntary liquidation before six years. The premium was held to be interest though this conclusion might not have been reached had the premium been 30% regardless of when the notes were redeemed.

When compensation is paid, there is frequently an enhancement element. This is found, for example, in compensation for mis-selling of mortgage endowment policies. Here, one would expect the enhancement element to be designed to

[11.05] Savings income

put the investor back into the position he would have been in had the particular mortgage endowment policy not been purchased. Typically, thus, the amount paid is the premiums paid for the product plus an additional amount to compensate for the time the investor did not have use of the money. In such circumstances, whatever label may be put on this enhancement, it would seem to bear the hallmarks of interest, as defined in *Riches v Westminster Bank* and *Euro Hotel (Belgravia) Ltd*. The enhancement element is calculated by reference to the refunded premiums and there is clearly entitlement that is recognised by the payment of the compensation.[15]

Where normal commercial rates of interest are charged the question whether any "premium" or discount is taxed as interest is determined according to the following rules laid down in *Lomax v Peter Dixon*:[16]

(1) supra, if interest is charged at a rate that would be reasonably commercial on a reasonably sound security there is no presumption that a "discount" or a "premium" is interest;
(2) the true nature of the payment is a matter of fact rather than of law;
(3) among the factors relevant will be, the contract itself, the term of the loan, the rate of interest expressly stipulated for, the nature of the capital risk, the extent to which, if at all, the parties expressly took or may reasonably be expected to have taken the capital risk into account in fixing the terms of the contract.

In such cases the court is trying to distinguish payment for the use of money from insurance against the risk of loss of capital; one may wonder whether there is a real distinction here. One should also note that in *Lomax* the payments were made by a foreign company and under the foreign law the payments probably were interest (and so deductible under that law).

Simon's Taxes B8.404–406.

[1] (1930) 15 TC 374 at 379.
[2] Halsbury's Laws of England (4th edn), Vol 32, para 106.
[3] (1947) 28 TC 159, HL.
[4] [1975] STC 682, 51 TC 293.
[5] *Ridge Securities Ltd v IRC* [1964] 1 All ER 275, 44 TC 373; cf *Chevron Petroleum (UK) Ltd v BP Development Ltd* [1981] STC 689.
[6] *Cairns v MacDiarmid* [1982] STC 226 but on appeal Sir John Donaldson MR thought that on the facts the payment might be just; [1983] STC 178.
[7] *Re Euro Hotel (Belgravia) Ltd* [1975] STC 682, [1975] 3 All ER 1075.
[8] Sir Robert Megarry VC in *Chevron Petroleum (UK) Ltd v BP Development Ltd* [1981] STC 689 at 695j.
[9] See *Westminster Bank Executor and Trustee Co (Channel Islands) Ltd v National Bank of Greece SA* (1970) 46 TC 472 at 485 (CA saying it was) but cf 494 (point left open by HL).
[10] *Re Hawkins, Hawkins v Hawkins* [1972] Ch 714, [1972] 3 All ER 386 (this is different from the question whether the payment is interest "on a loan", a matter of importance for deduction under TA 1988, s 353, see supra, § Chapter 6).
[11] [1983] STC 178 (semble that the payment could be income of the payee but this point was not raised).

[12] See per Lord Greene MR in *Lomax v Peter Dixon & Son Ltd* [1943] 2 All ER 255 at 259, 25 TC 353 at 363.
[13] *IRC v Thomas Nelson & Sons Ltd* (1938) 22 TC 175.
[14] *Davies v Premier Investment Co Ltd* [1945] 2 All ER 681, 27 TC 27.
[15] The Revenue view is given in Inland Revenue Tax Bulletin, August 2004, pp 1131–1132. This article gives the Revenue's rejection of arguments that have been advanced to treat the enhancement as not subject to tax. It should be noted that the exemption for taxation provided for compensation for mis-selling of pensions is a consequence of a specific statutory exemption: FA 1996, s 148.
[16] Supra, note 1, at 262, 367.

Interest and damages

[11.06] The notion that interest is a sort of service charge for the use of money may explain the initial reluctance of the judges to treat as interest for income tax purposes sums awarded by them by way of interest when awarding damages—such sums were treated as extra damages.[1] In *Riches v Westminster Bank Ltd*,[2] however, this approach was held to be wrong. In that case the taxpayer successfully sued a business partner for his share of the profit on a transaction (£36,255) which the partner had concealed. The judge also awarded him £10,028 as interest at 4% since the original deception, exercising his discretion under the Law Reform (Miscellaneous Provisions) Act 1934, s 3. It was held by the House of Lords that the £10,028 was interest. As Lord Simon put it, "It is not capital. It is rather the accumulated fruit of a tree which the tree produces regularly until payment."[3]

Legislation now exempts certain interest on damages for personal injuries;[4] separate legislation was needed to deal with personal injury damages in the form of periodical payments.[5]

Simon's Direct Tax Service B8.409.

[1] Eg *IRC v Ballantine* (1924) 8 TC 595.
[2] (1947) 28 TC 159, [1947] 1 All ER 469.
[3] (1947) 28 TC 159 at 188, [1947] 1 All ER 469 at 471.
[4] ITTOIA 2005, s 751.
[5] ITTOIA 2005, s 751.

Accrued interest

Accrued interest—general position before 1986

[11.07] Interest accrues from day to day even if payable only at intervals and is therefore apportionable in point of time between persons entitled in succession to the principal.[1] However, if a person owning a security sells that security with the right to any accrued interest, the price received for the security is just that and cannot be dissected into an element representing the

[11.07] Savings income

principal and another element representing the unpaid but accrued interest;[2] it follows that the purchaser is liable to tax on the whole of the interest paid.[3] These rules gave rise to the sale of gilts before these stocks go ex-div and the consequent conversion of income into capital gain.

The theoretical analysis devised by the courts was carried further when the courts held that the right to the interest could be sold separately from the securities themselves and the purchase price would be for the sale of a right and not an interest payment even though the date for payment had arrived before the sale.[4] Legislation to counter these decisions in certain tax saving situations is considered in supra, §§ **4.09** ff.

Simon's Taxes B8.407.

---

[1] Halsbury's Laws of England (4th edn), vol 32, para 106.
[2] *Wigmore v Thomas Summerson & Sons Ltd* [1926] 1 KB 131, 9 TC 577.
[3] *Schaffer v Cattermole* [1980] STC 650.
[4] *IRC v Paget* [1938] 1 All ER 392, 21 TC 677; supra, § **4.09**.

The Accrued Income Scheme

[11.08] The provisions outlined at supra, §§ **4.09–4.15**, were not effective to counter the practice of bond washing. For a long time the Treasury, presumably anxious to do nothing to inhibit the sale of gilts, were content with the large revenue loss that stemmed from the freedom to convert accrued income into capital gain even though the purchaser might be a tax-free pension fund and the vendor safe from CGT by reason of the annual exemption or having held the securities for at least 12 months. This changed in 1986[1]: presumably the Treasury was then confident about its ability to sell gilts and therefore more able to proclaim its belief in tax neutrality. These rules excluded liability under TA 1970, s 30 which was later repealed, and TA 1988, s 29 (see supra, § **4.10**). These rules are replaced by "the accrued income scheme".

In essence, the accrued income scheme is simple. Despite its essential simplicity, the accrued income scheme is, in the experience of the author, arguably the most irritating matter in the Taxes Act for the routine preparation of tax returns. Part of the irritation is the small amounts involved. On questioning as to the reason for such apparently unnecessary provision, a senior member of the Revenue stated that it was enacted solely to deal with very large holdings of government stock held by Lloyds underwriters. Where securities bearing interest are disposed of the tax system will treat the interest as accruing from day to day. Therefore on the sale of such securities cum-div the vendor will have to pay tax on the interest that accrues to that date and the purchaser will deduct that amount from the interest payment he receives so that only the interest accruing after the purchase will be charged to tax. When the purchase is made ex-div the converse rules apply.

Securities are defined[2] widely and include any loan stock at a fixed or variable rate of interest[3] whether issued by a public body, a company or any other body. There are specific exclusions for ordinary or preference shares, national and war savings certificates, bills of exchange and other bills and certificates of deposit.

On a transfer[4] with accrued interest the transferor is treated as entitled to a sum equal to the "accrued amount" which is a time apportioned part of the later interest payment.[5] For the purposes of the time apportionment, the transferor is treated as entitled to interest accruing for the number of days up to and including the date of settlement.[6] An interest period is not to exceed 12 months.[7]

The accrued proportion of the interest on the securities payable for the period is A+B where A is the number of days in the interest period up to and including settlement day and B is the number of days in the interest period.

EXAMPLE

A security has interest payment dates of 15 January and 15 July. It is quoted ex-div on 28 December and 27 June. The six monthly interest payment is £500.

If X sells the security cum-div in a period ending with settlement day on 15 December he will not actually receive the interest payment due on 15 January, but for tax purposes he is treated as receiving:

$$\frac{153}{184} \times £500 = £415.76$$

On a transfer without accrued interest the transferor is treated as entitled to relief on the "accrued income losses" and the transferee is treated as entitled to that amount.[8] The rebate amount is calculated in a similar way to the accrued amount but is of course the converse figure.[9]

The figures conform to the words of the legislation but not to Stock Exchange practice; this is to take the number of days from the last interest payment to the date of the settlement date and divide it by 365 (366 in a leap year). This factor is then applied to the year as a whole. It is understood that these figures, which are shown on contract notes, are accepted by the Revenue.

If in the previous example X had sold ex-div with a settlement day on 2 January he would have received the whole interest payment on 15 January but would be entitled to treat a fraction of it as capital; the fraction would have been

$$\frac{(184 - 171)}{184}$$

which applied to £500 gives a rebate of £35.33.

Where securities are issued in tranches the rules as originally framed failed to catch a device in which the size of an existing issue was increased by the issue of further securities of the same stock without distinguishing between the original issue and the new one. Under this device the price of the new securities would include a sum representing interest on the existing securities. That sum is now subject to the apportionment system.[10]

Where under these rules a person is treated as entitled to a sum, he is treated as receiving that amount by way of income on the last day of the interest

[11.08] Savings income

period[11]. The charge is at the rate for savings income.[12] An interest period is a period ending with an interest payment day[13] but any period in excess of 12 months is divided so that no period can exceed 12 months;[14] in this way an interest period can end without an interest payment day.

It is central to the scheme that the party not treated as receiving income is granted relief. The relief is set against any sums he is treated as receiving under these rules[15] and is then set against the sums actually received by way of interest during the interest period.[16] Where the interest period does not end with an interest payment day and there is no deemed income under these rules the relief may be rolled forward to the next interest period.[17]

Simon's Taxes B8.407, 408.

[1] Introduced by FA 1985, ss 73–75, with effect from 28 February 1986.
[2] ITA 2007, s 619(1). The accrued income scheme applies to UK securities, foreign securities, secured and unsecured, irrespective whether the security has fixed or variable rates of interest and whether the securities are certified or in bearer form, ITA 2007, s 619(2).
[3] The term "interest" is defined in ITA 2007, s 671. For a calculation under the accrued income scheme where interest payable is specified amounts on specified dates see *Cadbury Schweppes v Williams* [2005] STC (SCD) 151. This case is an attempt to circumvent the accrued income tax charge. In a carefully argued judgement, the Special Commissioners rejected the taxpayers' arguments and held that the tax scheme was ineffective. The Commissioner's decision was upheld by the High Court: [2006] STC 210 and by the Court of Appeal, by a majority: [2007] STC 106, CA.
[4] Defined in ITA 2007, s 620 as including sale, exchange and gift.
[5] ITA 2007, s 632.
[6] Defined in ITA 2007, s 674.
[7] See ITA 2007, s 673(1).
[8] ITA 2007, s 633.
[9] ITA 2007, s 633(5).
[10] ITA 2007, s 649.
[11] ITA 2007, s 628.
[12] ITA 2007, ss 18(3)(*d*) & 7.
[13] ITA 2007, s 673.
[14] ITA 2007, s 673(1)(*b*).
[15] ITA 2007, o 628.
[16] ITA 2007, s 629.
[17] ITA 2007, s 637(2).

[11.09] These rules are excluded in a number of situations. Where this occurs there will be no deemed income for the one party. The exceptions are:[1]

(1) where the transferor is trading and the transfer is taken into account in computing his profits;

(2) where the transferor is an individual[2] and on no day in the year of assessment in which the interest period ends (or the previous year) does the *nominal*[3] value of securities held by him exceed £5,000 (for this rule, when income from the securities is deemed to be the income of another person, the securities are treated as belonging to *both*[4]);
(3) a provision similar to 2 for estates in administration;
(4) a provision similar to 2 for a trust for a disabled person;[5]
(5) the transferor is not resident[6] in the UK for any part of the chargeable period nor ordinarily resident for that period (unless the transferor carries on a trade in the UK, when stock held for the purpose of the trade is incorporated into the accrued income scheme);[7]
(6) where the transferor is an individual entitled to the remittance[8] basis and any interest in the year of transfer would be taxed on that basis under ITTOIA 2005, s 832;
(7) the interest arises from stock lending transactions;[9]

The exclusion of the transferor from tax on an accrued amount in respect of a sale cum-div does not in itself deny the transferee relief for that amount.

There are special rules for unremittable interest on foreign securities,[10] for appropriations to and from trading stock,[11] for conversion of securities,[12] for variable rate securities[13] and for situations in which the interest is in default.[14]

The accrued income scheme does not apply to a transfer of securities if there is an obligation in that or some related agreement to buy the same or similar securities back or if there is an option to reacquire them and that option is subsequently exercised.[15]

Finally, there are rules concerning the effect of these charges on double taxation relief. DTR for any foreign tax is given by way of credit if the income falls or would have fallen within the types of income listed in ITTOIA 2005, s 830 ("relevant foreign income"). When an actual payment of interest is reduced for tax purposes by a relief under these rules any foreign tax credit may also be reduced.[16]

Simon's Taxes Division B8.4.

---

[1] ITA 2007, ss 638–647
[2] Husband and wife living together are one person.
[3] Defined in ITA 2007, s 676 as the value by reference to which the interest is calculated or the original issue price.
[4] ITA 2007, s 639.
[5] Defined by reference to TCGA 1992, Sch 1.
[6] Defined by ITA 2007, s 643.
[7] ITA 2007, s 643(3).
[8] ITA 2007, s 644.
[9] ITA 2007, s 653.
[10] ITA 2007, s 668, 669, 615.
[11] ITA 2007, s 623, 624.
[12] ITA 2007, s 620, 621, 673.
[13] ITA 2007, ss 627 & 635.
[14] ITA 2007, s 659.

[15] ITA 2007, s 654.
[16] TA 1988, s 807.

Accrued interest scheme—death

[11.10] The charge at death is excluded where the death is after 5 April 1996.[1] For a death after that date, the personal representatives are responsible for any tax arising by virtue of transfers made by the deceased during his lifetime but the interest that has accrued in the stock up to the date of death is not subject to tax. Similarly, where a transfer is made by the personal representatives to the beneficiaries entitled under the will or intestacy of the deceased, this transfer is not an occasion of charge for the accrued income scheme. The basis of valuing the estate for inheritance tax purposes is not changed. Such a valuation includes the income accrued in the stock.

Where interest is paid on a stock during the period of administration, the interest is assessable on the personal representatives, but at basic rate only.[2]

Simon's Taxes D9.413.

[1] FA 1996, s 148.
[2] See infra, § **14.02**.

Companies

[11.11] A company that is within the charge to corporation tax is not subject to the accrued income scheme. Accrued interest is brought into charge under the loan relationship provisions (see infra, §§ **27.04–27.10**).

Yearly interest—meaning

[11.12] It is sometimes necessary to distinguish yearly or annual interest from other interest.[1] Yearly interest, which presumably means the same as annual interest, is not defined in the statutes. The distinction between yearly and short interest depends on the intention of the parties.[2] If a banker makes a loan to a customer to be repaid at the end of three months the interest payable is not annual.[3] If on the other hand a mortgagor executes the usual form of mortgage, under which he becomes liable at law to pay the amount borrowed at the end of six months, the interest payable is nonetheless annual.[4] A technical explanation for this distinction may be that in the bank loan the contract specifies that the repayment of capital with interest is to be on a fixed day and there is no law which, without a new contract by the parties, says that interest is payable thereafter as a matter of right.[5] A simpler explanation is commercial reality. Mortgages are not usually repaid at the end of six months. Both parties envisage that the mortgage may well last longer than 12 months and thus the loan is in the nature of an investment as opposed to a short loan on moneys presently payable but held over.[6]

In determining whether interest is yearly, the courts have regard to substance so that a three month loan does not carry yearly interest merely because the rate is expressed in annual terms.[7] A loan of no fixed term carries yearly interest even though that interest is payable half yearly, quarterly or weekly.[8] Following the same approach, interest may be yearly even though the principal is payable after less than a year[9] or even on demand.[10] Interest may be yearly even though the amount borrowed and the rate of interest both fluctuate.[11] It will also be yearly if the period of the loan is expressed and intended to be one year only.[12]

It is hard to see why, given the above approach, interest awarded on damages should be yearly[13] or why interest payable by a purchaser on an outstanding contract[14] should be yearly, at least in the absence of some positive intention on the part of the vendor to treat the outstanding amount as an investment rather than a nuisance. These are, however, examples of yearly interest.

It therefore appears that interest payable on loans or other sums which are expressed or intended to last 12 months or longer is yearly interest, while interest on loans both expressed and intended to last less than 12 months is not.

A trader is permitted to charge interest at a statutory rate, when payment is delayed on certain contracts for goods or services,[15] even where interest is not specifically provided in the contract. The Revenue have stated:[16]

> . . . that it is not (the intention of the Late Payment Act) nor will it normally be its effect, to provide interest of money over a long period. Accordingly we consider that interest payable under the Act will not constitute 'yearly' interest, and that no obligation therefore arises to the payer to deduct tax from the payment under Section 349(2). This same view extends to interest especially provided for under the terms of a contract for goods or services, where that contract is one to which the contract would have applied but for the prior contractual right to interest.

However, the "loan relationships"[16] legislation applies, so that interest should be brought into account on an accruals basis if the charge is to corporation tax.[17]

Simon's Taxes A4.415, B8.411.

---

[1] A company or a local authority is obliged to deduct tax when making a payment of yearly interest, but not on paying interest that is not yearly interest: ITA 2007, s 874(1).
[2] *Cairns v MacDiarmid* [1983] STC 178 at 181, CA.
[3] *Goslings and Sharpe v Blake* (1889) 23 QBD 324, 2 TC 450.
[4] *Re Craven's Mortgage, Davies v Craven* [1907] 2 Ch 448.
[5] Per Lord Esher in *Goslings and Sharpe v Blake*, at 328, 454.
[6] Per Rowlatt J in *Garston Overseers v Carlisle* [1915] 3 KB 381, 6 TC 659. For a modern emphasis on the reality of the transaction see *Minsham Properties Ltd v Price* [1990] STC 718.
[7] *Goslings and Sharpe v Blake*. See also *Cairns v MacDiarmid* [1982] STC 226.
[8] *Re Janes' Settlement, Wasmuth v Janes* [1918] 2 Ch 54.
[9] As in a mortgage. See also *Mink v Inspector of Taxes* [1999] STC (SCD) 17.
[10] *Corinthian Securities Ltd v Cato* [1969] 3 All ER 1168, 46 TC 93, noted [1970] BTR 144.

[11] *IRC v Hay* (1924) 8 TC 636.
[12] *Ward v Anglo-American Oil Co Ltd* (1934) 19 TC 94 (quaere if repayable in 365 days).
[13] *Jefford v Gee* [1970] 2 QB 130 at 149, [1970] 1 All ER 1202 at 1210; the facts were unusual in that the sale was deferred for more than 12 months.
[14] *Bebb v Bunny* (1854) 1 K & J 216. On practical problems, see [1971] BTR 333.
[15] The Late Payment Of Commercial Debts (Interest) Act 1998.
[16] Inland Revenue Tax Bulletin August 1999, p. 687.
[17] FA 1996, s 100(2) and (4).

Deduction at source

Until the abolition of the 20% savings rate with effect from 2008–09, deduction was usually required to be effected at the 20% rate. However, some provisions required tax to be deducted at the basic rate (see 11.36).

Relevant deposits

[11.13] The system of deducting tax at source is applied to interest on "relevant deposits" made with a "deposit-taker". "Deposit-taker" is, broadly, any bank.[1] A deposit is "relevant" if the person beneficially entitled to it is an individual (provision is made for concurrent interests) or a personal representative as such.[2] There then follows a long list of deposits which are not to be considered "relevant".[3] The list includes general client account deposits[4] and a premium trust fund of a Lloyd's underwriter[5] and "qualifying deposits".[6] Every deposit is to be assumed to be a relevant deposit until the deposit taker has satisfied himself that it is not.[7]

An individual not ordinarily resident in the UK can make a declaration on a statutory form, the consequence of which is that his bank deposit is not "a relevant investment"[8] and, hence, interest is paid gross. There are equivalent provisions for personal representatives and trustees.[9]

A payment of interest or royalty is made without deduction of tax[10] if the following four conditions are all fulfilled:

(1) the payment is made by a UK company or a UK permanent establishment of an EU company;[11]
(2) the beneficial owner of the income is an EU company or its permanent establishment;[12]
(3) both the payer and the recipient are 25% associates;[13]
(4) where the payment is of interest, Inland Revenue has issued an exemption notice.[14]

This exemption is subject to provisions regarding excessive interest and royalty payments due to a special relationship between the party[15] and there is an anti-avoidance rule dealing with arrangements to take advantage of the exemption.[16]

Simon's Taxes D7.719.

[1] The list of companies regarded as "deposit-takers" for the purpose of this legislation is given in ITA 2007, s 853, with the addition of bodies so specified in statutory instruments issued under the authority of what is now ITA 2007, s 854(2): Income Tax (Prescribed Deposit-takers) (No 1) Order, SI 1984/1801, the Income Tax (Composite Rate) (Prescribed Deposit-takers) Order, SI 1985/1696 and the Income Tax (Prescribed Deposit-takers) Order, SI 1992/3234.
[2] ITA 2007, s 856; on Scottish partnerships see ITA 2007, s 856.
[3] ITA 2007, ss 863–870.
[4] Added by ITA 2007, s 863(1).
[5] ITA 2007, s 867.
[6] A "qualifying time deposit" is a deposit of a loan of at least £50,000 where repayment is within a specified time, not greater than five years from the date of the deposit: ITA 2007, s 866(2).
[7] ITA 2007, s 857.
[8] ITA 2007, s 858. The declaration can be made for any investment, not solely a bank deposit account. There is equivalent provision for interest paid to a Scottish partnership that is not ordinarily resident in the UK: ITA 2007, s 859.
[9] ITA 2007, ss 860 & 861.
[10] ITTOIA 2005, ss 757–767 (rewriting FA 2004, ss 97–106 which enact the EU Interest and Royalties Directive (Council Directive 2003/49/EC) of 3 June 2003).
[11] ITTOIA 2005, s 758(2).
[12] ITTOIA 2005, s 758(3).
[13] ITTOIA 2005, s 758(4). 25% associates are defined by ITTOIA 2005, s 761 as one company holding at least 25% of either the capital rights or the voting rights in the other or, alternatively, a third company directly holding 25% of either the capital rights or the voting rights in each of the two companies.
[14] ITTOIA 2005, s 758(5). The conditions for the issue of a tax exemption notice are given in ITTOIA 2005, s 100.
[15] ITTOIA 2005, ss 763 and 764.
[16] ITTOIA 2005, s 765.

[11.14] Certain payments of interest, annuities or royalties are subject to deduction at source.[1] The rate of tax for interest and royalties was the lower rate of tax on savings income[2], but for annuities was the basic rate.[3] For 2008–09, deduction is at the standard basic rate of 20%.

Where the interest payment is to be made subject to deduction, the payer must account for the tax to the Revenue,[4] complete with the obligation to provide a certificate of deduction.

Any payment of interest made by a company or by a local authority[5] is made without deduction of tax at source if the recipient is a UK resident company[6] (including an incorporated charity[7]), a partnership of UK companies,[8] a non-resident company that is chargeable to UK corporation tax on the profits of trade in the UK carried on through a branch or agency,[9] a company entitled to receive interest gross under the terms of the double tax agreement,[10] a tax-exempt body,[11] a PEP, ISA,[12] a partnership where each partner would be entitled to receive payment gross[13] or is a royalty payment to a non-resident person who has registered under the cross-border royalty scheme.[14]

[11.14] Savings income

All payments of interest are made without deduction of tax, if the payment is by a person carrying on the business of dealing in financial instruments and is authorised under the Financial Services and Markets Act 2000.[15]

Interest is paid gross if it is interest payable in the UK on an advance from a bank carrying on a bona fide banking business in the UK[16] or the interest is paid by such a bank in the ordinary course of its business, a question answered by reference to ordinary UK banking practice at the time; yearly interest paid by a bank where the borrowings relate to the capital structure of the bank will not qualify.[17]

In addition to the deduction of tax on interest payments, certain other payments require deduction of tax. Historically, some deductions were effected at different rates: see infra, §§ **11.36–11.44**. The distinction was removed when the 20% savings rate was abolished and the basic rate reduced to 20%.

---

1. ITA 2007, s 874, 875.
2. ITA 2007, s 902(4).
3. ITA 2007, s 902(2).
4. If the tax deducted at source is deducted by a company, payment is required each quarter, using the system specified in ITA 2007, s 947: vide ITA 2007, s 901(5)(a). If the deduction at source is made by an individual, the individual accounts to the Revenue for the tax deducted in his self-assessment tax return: vide ITA 2007, ss 900(3) & 964.
5. ITA 2007, s 931(1).
6. ITA 2007, s 930 and 933.
7. HM Treasury Explanatory Notes, Finance Bill 2001.
8. ITA 2007, s 931.
9. ITA 2007, s 931.
10. Although exceptions are made here also UK Double Taxation Agreements provide for interest to be paid without deduction of tax to residents of all other EC countries and also persons resident in Bulgaria, Falkland Islands, Iceland, Kuwait, Malawi, Norway, Nigeria, Russian Federation, Switzerland, Ukraine, USA and countries of the former USSR. In order to obtain the relief granted by Double Taxation Agreement it is necessary to follow the procedure specified by that agreement. In particular, a company is only permitted to pay interest gross under the terms of an agreement if authority has been obtained from Inland Revenue in advance of the payment of interest.
11. ITA 2007, s 930.
12. ITA 2007, s 935.
13. ITA 2007, s 937.
14. ITA 2007, s 911, 912.
15. ITA 2007, s 885(1), 874.
16. See *United Dominions Trust Ltd v Kirkwood* [1966] 1 QB 783, [1965] 2 All ER 992 and *Hafton Properties Ltd v McHugh* [1987] STC 16.
17. On meaning see *Royal Bank of Canada v IRC* (1971) 47 TC 565 and statement of practice SP 12/91.

Discounts

[11.15] Under a Treasury Bill, the government borrows the money paid for the bill for a certain period and pays a larger sum at the end of the period. The extra is a profit or a discount and is taxable on receipt.[1] Taxable discounts may arise on bills other than Treasury Bills. If there is a regular business of discounting, the discounts are instead taxed as trading income as in *Willingale v International Commercial Bank Ltd.*[2]

The discount on a Treasury Bill just described looks very like an interest payment. The distinction between a debt of £x with a discount of £y and a debt of £x – y with a premium of y is a fine one; in each case the total sum eventually paid is £x. However:

> In the interest account, interest upon the amount is charged upon each bill until it is actually paid; but when a bill is discounted, the interest to be deducted is calculated up to the time when it becomes due and for no longer period.[3]

Liability arises when the income is realised, that is when the bill reaches maturity or when it is sold prior to maturity. In *Ditchfield v Sharp*[4] trustees bought an interest-free promissory note with a guarantee from the vendor that they would receive not less than 75% of the face value. The profit accruing on maturity was held liable to tax under Schedule D, Case III as this was an income receipt from a discounting transaction. In that case the taxpayers were not allowed to argue that, as the notes were long term, the profit could be capital; such a point should have been taken before the Commissioners.

In *Ditchfield v Sharp*, the Court of Appeal said that if the whole gain could be liable to tax as arising from a discount [the whole gain should be so taxed], notwithstanding that, on another analysis, at least a part of the gain could be said to be interest.[5]

Simon's Taxes Division B8.4.

---

[1] Per Lord Haldane in *Brown v National Provident Institution* [1921] 2 AC 222 at 232, 8 TC 80 at 83.
[2] [1978] STC 75.
[3] Per Holroyd J in *Thompson v Giles* (1824) 2 B & C 422 at 432; and see *Torrens v IRC* (1933) 18 TC 262.
[4] [1982] STC 124, upheld on appeal [1983] STC 590, CA.
[5] Quaere the payer's legal position if he ought to withhold tax on an interest payment.

[11.16] The traditional way in which discounts are taxed is not immediately obvious. Suppose a company issues bonds at £70 and promises to redeem them in three years' time at £100. As far as the company is concerned there will be a loss of £30 and the tax system, while allowing the company to claim that loss, does so only when the loss is realised—ie when the bonds are redeemed for £100. The tax system aims at symmetry of treatment for the bond holder. So if X buys the bond on issue at £70 he is taxed on the income gain arising from the transaction when in three years' time the bond is redeemed at £100. If, however, towards the end of year 2 X sells the bond to Y for, say, £92

[11.16] Savings income

X's gain of £22 is not treated as an income profit of £22 but as a capital gain of that amount while, when at the end of the third year, Y receives £100 he is then treated as receiving income not of £8 but of £30. Such a system lasted because the structure of the tax system ensured that there were always knowledgeable vendors and purchasers with widely differing tax circumstances. Thus, if Y had reliefs which he could not otherwise use he might pay no tax on the gain of £8 which he actually made on the £30 which the tax system treated him as receiving.

Deeply discounted securities

(formerly "relevant discounted securities")

[11.17] In place of the traditional treatment for taxing discounts, statute[1] now imposes a charge to income tax on the disposal (generally, a transfer or redemption) of a "deeply discounted security". The amount brought into charge is the profit arising on the disposal (ie the proceeds of transfer or redemption less the amount paid on acquisition). One may also deduct the costs incurred in connection with the acquisition, transfer or redemption if these were incurred before 27 March 2003.[2] Additionally, later costs may be deducted in respect of securities owned continuously since before 27 March 2003 and listed on a recognised Stock Exchange at any time before that date.[3] For a gilt strip, the amount brought into charge is the publicly quoted price, without reference to any charge or restriction on the particular strip.[4]

The charge arises in respect of the fiscal year in which there is a transfer. The transfer may be by redemption, sale, exchange, gift "or otherwise".[5] Death is treated as an occasion of transfer.[6] When a transfer takes place by means of a conditional contract, the transfer is treated as taking place when the condition is satisfied.[7] Conversion of a security is also treated as an occasion of charge, the proceeds of the transfer being the market value of the securities acquired.[8]

The charge is specifically brought within the scope of the provisions charging on a UK resident income arising to a person domiciled overseas, where the UK resident has power to enjoy that income.[9]

The charge on relevant discounted securities is exceptional for savings and investment income in that there is relief for costs and losses. However, the availability of such relief was severely curtailed by FA 2003 from 27 March 2003 (see above). Where a relievable loss is sustained on disposal, relief can be claimed against total income. Such relief must be claimed by 31 January, 22 months after the end of the fiscal year.[10]

Transfers between connected persons are treated at market value,[11] as are transfers for a consideration that is not money or money's worth.[12]

When the security is held by trustees, the charge is computed on the basis outlined in supra, § **11.10**. The tax trust rate is applied to the charge.[13]

Prior to 27 March 2003 schemes were used whereby deeply discounted securities were issued to an employee in conjunction with a loan, which created a loss to cancel the tax charge. Such a scheme was considered by the Special Commissioner in *Campbell v IRC*[14] (see also supra, § **7.58**).

Simon's Taxes B8.401.

1   ITTOIA 2005, s 427.
2   ITTOIA 2005, s 439(4).
3   ITTOIA 2005, s 455.
4   ITTOIA 2005, s 450. This provision applies to disposals on or after 15 January 2004 and was introduced to counter the gilt strip scheme, where a tax-allowable loss was generated by selling a gilt strip with the liability to repay a loan taken out to fund its purchase.
5   ITTOIA 2005, s 437(1).
6   ITTOIA 2005, s 437(3).
7   ITTOIA 2005, s 438.
8   ITTOIA 2005, ss 437(1)(c) and 440(4).
9   ITTOIA 2005, s 459 invoking TA 1988, ss 739, 740.
10 ITTOIA 2005, s 454.
11 ITTOIA 2005, s 440(1), (2)(b).
12 ITTOIA 2005, s 440(1), (2)(c).
13 ITA 2007, s 482 Type 6.
14 [2004] STC (SCD) 396.

Definition of 'deeply discounted security'

[11.18] A "deeply discounted security" is one where the redemption price exceeds or might exceed the issue price by more than 1/2% of the redemption price times the number of years between issue and redemption (capped at thirty years). If the security is issued for a period longer than thirty years, it is a "deeply discounted security" if the discount exceeds 15% irrespective of the number of years.[1] A security within this definition remains a "deeply discounted security" for each subsequent purchaser of the security, irrespective of the difference between the redemption terms and the price paid by the subsequent purchaser. Gilt strips are specifically included in the definition of "deeply discounted security"[2] but the following are excluded: company shares,[3] gilts,[4] a security where the amount payable on redemption is linked to the value of chargeable assets[5] life assurance and capital redemption policies.[6] In addition, securities are excluded from the definition if they are issued under the same prospectus as other securities that have been issued previously and which are not deeply discounted securities.[7]

The definition of a deeply discounted security is modified for securities transferred on or after 15 February 1999 and where the holder becomes entitled to any payment on redemption.[8] A discount was only relevant if a comparison gave rise to a deep gain. This comparison was originally made by looking at the amount payable on redemption and by reference to the amount payable on the earliest possible redemption date. If the holder had an option to redeem at par or at a very small discount the security would not be "relevant" since it would not be deep enough. In turn this enabled the holder to defer any tax until redemption as opposed to intermediate transfer (ie be under the old pre-1984 rules) while the issuing company could get a deduction year by year because of the corporation tax loan relationship rules.

[11.18] Savings income

To correct this lack of symmetry FA 1999 provided that for transfers or redemptions on or after 15 February 1999 one is to look at every possible occasion and not just the earliest; if the gain is or would or might be deep on any one of those occasions the security is "deeply discounted"[9] and so comes within these rules. An exception is made where the holder's option to redeem arises because of a default by the issuer—provided a redemption is unlikely.[10]

During the legislative process it was realised that the words could cover targets different from those intended where the discount was not very deep, such as those which included provision for a premium to be paid if the issuer chooses to redeem early in circumstances which were likely to occur. The bill was therefore amended to exclude redemptions which were not at the option of the holder;[11] this exclusion does not apply if the issuer and holder are connected,[12] or the main or one of the main benefits of the redemption is to obtain a tax advantage.[13] The exception for holder redemptions is also extended to events which are unlikely to happen and where the provision for redemption is included to ensure that the holder's interests are not adversely affected by the events.[14]

Because the amendments provide that a security is, in many cases, only a deeply discounted security if the holder and issuer are connected, it is necessary to deal with the cases where a security is acquired after issue by a holder connected with the issuer,[15] and where a holder becomes connected with the issuer after he has acquired a security.

---

[1] ITTOIA 2005, s 430(1). Where the security is issued in connection with the earn out, the definition is extended: ITTOIA 2005, s 442.
[2] ITTOIA 2005, s 443. "Gilt strips" are defined in ITTOIA 2005, s 444.
[3] ITTOIA 2005, s 432(1)(a).
[4] ITTOIA 2005, s 450. This provision applies to disposals on or after 15 January 2004 and was introduced to counter the gilt strip scheme, where a tax-allowable loss was generated by selling a gilt strip with the liability to repay a loan taken out to fund its purchase.
[5] ITTOIA 2005, s 437(1).
[6] ITTOIA 2005, s 432(1)(c), (d).
[7] ITTOIA 2005, ss 432(4), 434 and 435(1), subject to the anti-avoidance provisions of s 436.
[8] FA 1999, s 65 (now repealed); see also Inland Revenue press release, 15 February 1999, *Simon's Weekly Tax Intelligence* 1999, p. 253. The post-1999 rules are now in ITTOIA 2005, s 431.
[9] ITTOIA 2005, s 430(1).
[10] ITTOIA 2005, s 431(1)–(3).
[11] ITTOIA 2005, s 431(2).
[12] ITTOIA 2005, s 431(2)(b).
[13] ITTOIA 2005, s 431(2)(c); tax advantage is defined in TA 1988, s 709(1) (ITTOIA 2005, s 460(2)).
[14] ITTOIA 2005, s 431(3).
[15] ITTOIA 2005, s 431(5).

Gilt strips

[11.19] With effect from 15 January 2004, gilt strips are removed from the general treatment as "deeply discounted securities" where there is a scheme or arrangement to obtain a tax advantage.[1] This statutory provision is designed to bring an end to a marketed tax avoidance scheme under which an individual purchases a gilt strip with borrowed funds and then sells the gilt strip to a third party, the gilt being charged by the borrowing. The income tax loss thus arising, before the statutory change, could then be put against the individual's total income for the year.

Where these provisions apply, the income tax charge is computed by reference to a specially defined "market value" of the gilt strip. The statutory rule[2] requires market value of a quoted holding to be the quoted price, without any discount for any restrictions; for an unquoted holding, restrictions are ignored in assessing the value.

[1] ITTOIA 2005, s 449(1), (2).
[2] ITTOIA 2005, s 450(1) inserted by FA 2004, s 138.

Annuities and annual payments

Annuity

[11.20] Annuity is not defined. It has been judicially described as meaning "where an income is purchased with a sum of money and the capital has gone and has ceased to exist, the principal having been converted into an annuity".[1] The precise boundary between an annuity and an annual payment is one which the courts have not had to mark out. Statute[2] assumes that an annuity payable by an individual is an annual payment. The scope of these rules will be greatly reduced in due course.

An annuity must be distinguished from the payments of a debt by instalments.[3] In an annuity the capital has gone and, in the normal annuity contract, payments will continue so long as the annuitant lives; an annuity is thus an insurance against outliving capital. On the other hand, where a debt is being paid by instalments, the debt remains and liability is not usually affected by the death of either party.

[1] Per Watson B in *Foley v Fletcher and Rose* (1858) 3 H & N 769 at 784. Purchased annuities are now dissected if they come within TA 1988, s 656.
[2] Supra, §§ **11.01** ff.
[3] Infra, §§ **11.27** ff.

[11.21] Where a person goes to an annuity office and buys an annuity with cash it is clear that he receives an annuity and that tax is due on the payments he receives. Several cases have been concerned with attempts to get payments

[11.21] Savings income

of the same economic value as an annuity out of an annuity company while making sure that the payments are not themselves annuities. The crux is that under an annuity the principal sum is liquidated.

In *Perrin v Dickson*[1] the taxpayer paid premiums under a policy of assurance to an assurance society for six years from 1912 to 1917 and the company undertook to pay an "annuity" for seven years from 1920 to 1927 to the taxpayer's son if he should so long live. If the son did not live until 1927, the total amount paid by the taxpayer was to be returned to him without interest although less any amount paid out under the annuity. Rowlatt J and the Court of Appeal, held that, since the taxpayer could not possibly lose his money, the transaction was one of deposit rather than annuity so that the payments under the "annuity", which included an increment for interest, should be dissected into interest and capital.

The opposite result was reached on different facts in *Sothern-Smith v Clancy*.[2] Here, in return for a single premium of $65,243 the company agreed to pay an annuity of $6,510 but promised that if he should die before the amount repaid reached the amount invested, the society would continue to pay out to specified beneficiaries until full repayment had been made. The purchaser died when $39,203 remained outstanding and this sum was paid to his sister who argued that she should not pay tax. The sum was held to be an annuity. *Perrin v Dickson* was distinguished on appeal on the ground that that case was really one of the investment of capital, the fruits of which were to come out only if the payments fell to be made to the son and so were not wholly income payments.

These cases have been described as very special and the reasoning of the first as hard to follow.[3] Another decision treated sums borrowed as loans not annuities.[4] The first has had its particular purposes defeated by the rule that income from a settlement by a parent on an infant must be treated as that of the parent.[5] All one can say is that every case must be determined on its own facts. Many advances by insurance companies are now taxed.

Simon's Taxes B8.420, 429.

---

[1] [1930] 1 KB 107, 14 TC 608.
[2] [1941] 1 All ER 111, 24 TC 1 cited in *IRC v Plummer* [1979] STC 793 at 798.
[3] By Lord Greene MR in *IRC v Wesleyan and General Assurance Society* [1948] 1 All ER 555, 30 TC 11.
[4] *IRC v Wesleyan and General Assurance Society*.
[5] ITTOIA 2005, s 629 (see infra, § 15.21).

Other annual payments

[11.22] Quite apart from exemptions provided by statute, case law shows that, in order to be an annual payment:

(1) there must be some legal obligation to pay the sum;
(2) the payment must possess the essential quality of recurrence implied by the description annual;

(3) the payment must be pure income profit in his hands;
(4) the income must belong to the payee;
(5) the payment must form part of the income of the payee as opposed to being a capital payment to him;

Rule 1—the obligation

[11.23] Such an annual payment must be due under an enforceable obligation; the obligation is the source. This is quite distinct from the question whether or not the obligation is created for valuable and sufficient consideration.[1]

A series of voluntary gifts cannot be an annual payment; nor can ultra vires payments by a company.[2] Dividend payments by companies are not annual payments, since a company is under no obligation to pay a dividend.[3]

The obligation may be involuntary, eg a court order or a statute.[4]

Where trustees have an express discretion to make payments to an object, sums paid under that discretion to objects of the trust[5] are not regarded as voluntary. In *Drummond v Collins*[6] trustees exercised a power of maintenance in respect of children who had a contingent interest in the trust capital. Although the children had no enforceable right to the payments, Lord Loreburn said that they were not 'voluntary in any relevant sense. They were payments made in fulfilment of a testamentary disposition for the benefit of the children in the exercise of a discretion conferred by the will.'[7] This principle has since been applied where, under a will, trustees exercised their discretion to give a surtax payer a voluntary allowance of £600 a month,[8] and where trustees had a discretion to have recourse to capital in order to maintain the value of an annuity.[9] In these cases the payee was an object of the trust, either in the sense that he had a vested right under the trust[10] as well as being a potential beneficiary under the discretion, or that as such a potential beneficiary the trustees were under a duty at least to consider whether or not to exercise that discretion in his favour.[11] Payments by trusts are not within the new regime and therefore remain taxable income of the recipient.[12]

This requirement is easily satisfied. In *Dealler v Bruce*[13] the taxpayer's mother had bequeathed shares to trustees and directed that they should pay an annuity to the taxpayer's sister out of the income. The trustees were given the power to sell the shares in order to raise funds sufficient for the annuity but the taxpayer who was a director of the company was given the right to have all the dividends paid to him if and so long as he should pay the annuity himself anyway. As it turned out, the dividends yielded no income but he paid the annuity. It was held that the payment of the annuity to the sister was not voluntary. He obtained good consideration in that he made sure that the shares were not sold.

This conclusion seems hard to justify since this advantage showed why the taxpayer acted as he did but did not impose any legal obligation on him to act.

Simon's Taxes B8.425.

---

[1] *Smith v Smith* [1923] P 191 at 197, per Lord Sterndale and at 202, per Warrington LJ.

[11.23] Savings income

2 *Ridge Securities Ltd v IRC* [1964] 1 All ER 275, 44 TC 373.
3 *Canadian Eagle Oil Co Ltd v R* (1945) 27 TC 205 at 245, [1945] 2 All ER 499 at 504.
4 See note 4, supra.
5 A payment by a charitable trust would however be regarded as voluntary since the beneficiary under the trusts is charity and not the person benefited: per Romer LJ in *Stedeford v Beloe* [1931] 2 KB 610 at 626.
6 [1915] AC 1011, 6 TC 525 (a decision on Case V).
7 [1915] AC 1011 at 1017, 6 TC 525 at 539.
8 *Lord Tollemache v IRC* (1926) 11 TC 277 (Rowlatt J).
9 *Lindus and Hortin v IRC* (1933) 17 TC 442 (Finlay J); *Cunard's Trustees v IRC* [1946] 1 All ER 159, 27 TC 122.
10 Distinguish *Stedeford v Beloe* [1932] AC 388, 16 TC 505, where the object of the trust was the school, not the individual headmaster. Cf *Duncan's Executors v Farmer* (1909) 5 TC 417.
11 Per Lord Greene MR in *Cunard's Trustees v IRC* [1946] 1 All ER 159 at 163, 27 TC 122 at 133 and Finlay J in *Lindus and Horton v IRC* (1933) 17 TC 442 at 448. Voluntary pensions are now taxable under ITEPA 2003, s 570.
12 ITTOIA 2005, s 727(1)(a) (income tax) and TA 1988, s 347A(2) (corporation tax) are confined to payments by individuals.
13 (1934) 19 TC 1.

Rule 2—recurrence

[11.24] It is the word "annual" which indicates that a payment which falls within ITTOIA 2005, Pt 5, Ch 7 must, like interest on money or an annuity, have the quality of being recurrent or being capable of recurrence.[1] For this reason an obligation which cannot last longer than 12 months cannot create an annual payment.[2] On the other hand if the obligation can endure so long, it is quite irrelevant that the payment is expressed as a variable sum. It is irrelevant that the sum paid may vary; so payment of such a sum as after tax at the basic rate in force in the year of payment shall equal £5 is an "annual payment". It is also irrelevant that the obligation is contingent so that no sum may be payable under the obligation at all. For example, a guarantee that one will provide funds to enable a company to pay a fixed dividend should the company have insufficient profits, will create a liability to make annual payments even though in any year the company may have sufficient profits so that no sums become payable under the guarantee.[3] The purpose of the rule seems to be to exclude payments which are casual and temporary and therefore fall more easily into ITTOIA 2005, Pt 5, Ch 8 than into ITTOIA 2005, Pt 5, Ch 7.[4] To fall within Chapter 8, the income has no requirement of recurrence.

Weekly payments are "annual". The annual payment in this case is the weekly sum multiplied by the number of weeks in the year, which may be 52 or 53 depending upon the day of the week on which the obligation falls.[5]

Simon's Direct Tax Service B8.424.

1 Per Lord Maugham in *Moss Empires Ltd v IRC* [1937] AC 785 at 795, 21 TC 264 at 299.

[2] Per Lord Sterndale in *Smith v Smith* [1923] P 191 at 196.
[3] *Moss Empires Ltd v IRC*.
[4] Per Lord Radcliffe in *Whitworth Park Coal Co Ltd v IRC* [1959] 3 All ER 703 at 716, 38 TC 531 at 575.
[5] *Re Janes' Settlement, Wasmuth v Janes* [1918] 2 Ch 54.

Rule 3—pure income profit

[11.25] It is inconsistent with the scheme of deduction at source that income assessable under ITTOIA 2005, Pt 5, Ch 7 should include payments that are likely to be *gross* receipts of the payee and not his pure income.[1] It follows that if the payee is entitled to deduct expenses from the receipt as where he promises to provide the payer with goods or services in return for the income, the payment should not fall within Chapter 7, an idea expressed in the requirement that the payment should be pure income profit[2] in the hands of the payee.

Simon's Taxes B8.423.

[1] Per Lord Radcliffe, in *Whitworth Park Coal Co Ltd v IRC* [1959] 3 All ER 703 at 715, 38 TC 531 at 575.
[2] In *IRC v London Corpn (as Conservators of Epping Forest)* Lord Normand said that the formula would lose nothing by the omissions of the words "pure" and "profit": [1953] 1 All ER 1075 at 1081, 34 TC 293 at 320.

[11.26] **A trading receipt cannot be an annual payment.** Scrutton LJ provided a famous example in *Howe v IRC*:[1]

> If a man agrees to pay a motor garage £500 a year for five years for the hire and upkeep of a car, no one suggests the person paying can deduct income tax from each yearly payment. So if he contracted with a butcher for an annual sum to supply all his meat for a year, the annual instalment would not be subject to tax as a whole in the hands of the payee, but only that part of it which was profits.

In these instances the trader would be entitled—and bound—in computing his profits to deduct the cost to him of the car or of the meat, so it could not be said that the payment was pure income.

In *Howe v IRC* the taxpayer had mortgaged his life estate in certain properties and had to mortgage also a life assurance policy. He sought to deduct the premiums which he was legally obliged to pay in computing his income for surtax, but failed. The payment was not pure income in the hands of the insurance company but merely a receipt which would be taken into account in computing its profits. The quality of the payment is not however determined by its place in the accounts. The question is whether it is a trading receipt or an annual payment.

Simon's Taxes B8.421

[1] [1919] 2 KB 336 at 352, 7 TC 296 at 303, see also *Re Hanbury, Comiskey v Hanbury* (1939) 38 TC 588.

[11.27] Savings income

[11.27] In the same way a payment which is a receipt of the payee's profession will not be an annual payment within ITTOIA 2005, Pt 5, Ch 7. Here too expenses may be written off against the sum received so that it is not all income. So where a solicitor trustee was entitled to charge for his services under a charging clause, such payments were not within what was then Schedule D, Case III (and now ITTOIA 2005, Pt 5, Ch 7) even though by agreement with the beneficiaries and other trustees they took the form of a percentage of the trust income.[1] On the other hand an annuity of £100 for a trustee for acting as trustee has been held to be an annual payment.[2] Both payments are acts of bounty on the part of the settlor, the trustee having no right to charge for his time and trouble but only a quite independent indemnity for his expenses which is unaffected by the annuity; however the former is ex hypothesi a receipt of the firm for services rendered whereas the latter is not. More recently it has been held that such an annuity is earned income,[3] a finding which throws doubt upon the annuity's status as an annual payment although the point was expressly left open and the Revenue do not appear to have pressed it. Likewise any annuities or annual payments which are charged under other headings fall outside ITTOIA 2005, Pt 5, Ch 7.[4]

Simon's Taxes B8.421.

---

[1] *Jones v Wright* (1927) 13 TC 221.
[2] *Baxendale v Murphy* [1924] 2 KB 494, 9 TC 76.
[3] *Dale v IRC* [1953] 2 All ER 671 at 676, 34 TC 468 at 493.
[4] ITTOIA 2005, s 683(1), (2).

Other payments

[11.28] "One must determine in the light of all the relevant facts, whether the payment is a taxable receipt in the hands of the recipient without any deduction for expenses or the like, or is simply gross revenue in the recipient's hands, out of which a taxable income will emerge only after his outgoings have been deducted".[1]

When a non-trading body is concerned, the presence of some counter-stipulation may deprive the payment of its character of pure income benefit. The difficulty is to know where precisely this line is to be drawn. At one time it was thought that the presence of any counter-stipulation or condition would be fatal[2] but this view was rejected by the House of Lords in *Campbell v IRC*.[3]

Today the presence of a counter-stipulation or condition deprives the payment of a quality of pure bounty but not necessarily of its character as pure income profit. Thus the purchaser of an annuity from an insurance company has to pay for his annuity; again where a person sold the right to use a secret process in return for a percentage of the profits those payments had the quality of pure income[4] as they did when an employee gave up all existing rights to remuneration in return for a percentage of the profits of a particular film.[5] In *Campbell v IRC* Lord Denning MR put the following case "Suppose a man gives a covenant for seven years to his old school and in return there is a private understanding that his son, who is a dunce, will be given a place".[6] In the Court of Appeal, Lord Denning, acting on the old view that a counter-stipulation would be fatal, held that such a payment would not be pure income, but in the House of Lords both Lord Hodson and Lord Donovan[7] thought that such payment would fall within Case III, although Lord Donovan added what was probably implicit in Lord Hodson's speech, that the full fees would be payable for the dunce son. In all these examples the consideration was executed before the annual payments began but Lord Donovan pointed out that in *Westminster v IRC* Lord Macmillan had said that if, in return for the annuity, the employee had promised to work for lower wages the payments would still be within what was Schedule D, Case III, a view with which Lord Wright had agreed.[8]

These problems were discussed in connection with covenants in favour of charities, which sometimes offer inducements in order to obtain those covenants. Statute now regulates the advantages which a charity may offer if the covenant is to be classified as a qualifying donation.[9] The fact that the payee is a charity cannot affect the question whether the covenant is an annual payment.[10] In *IRC v National Book League*[11] the charity provided a central lending library, arranged exhibitions, ran a book information service and made available to members various rooms at its headquarters such as sitting rooms, a restaurant and a cocktail bar. Payments under covenants in its favour were held not to be pure income profit. The correct basis of the decision is that the covenants were simply a club subscription in return for the annual provisions of goods and services.[12] The question of what inducements can be offered remains therefore a matter of doubt.

The provision of such facilities as private viewing days for Friends of a particular museum or priority booking for certain performances by a theatre or opera company is probably not sufficient to prevent the payments from being the pure income profit of the charity. The offer of seats at reduced prices was fatal in one first instance decision[13] decided before, and not commented upon in, *Campbell v IRC*. However, whether they prevent the payments being covenanted payments to charity is a separate question.[14] This separate question was later clarified at least in part by FA 1989, s 59, but only for charities for the preservation of property or the conservation of wildlife for the public benefit.[15]

Simon's Taxes B8.423

---

1   Per Lord Donovan in *Campbell v IRC* (1968) 45 TC 427 at 475, [1968] 3 All ER 588 at 606; and see [1969] BTR 68.
2   Eg the judgments of the Court of Appeal in *IRC v National Book League* [1957] 2 All ER 644, 37 TC 455 and in *Campbell v IRC* [1967] 2 All ER 625, 45 TC 427.
3   *Campbell v IRC* (1968) 45 TC 427, [1968] 3 All ER 588.
4   *Delage v Nuggett Polish Co Ltd* (1905) 92 LT 682.
5   *Asher v London Film Productions Ltd* [1944] KB 133, [1944] 1 All ER 77.
6   [1967] 2 All ER 625 at 629, 45 TC 427 at 447; see also *Essex County Council v Ellam* [1989] STC 317, CA.
7   [1968] 3 All ER 588 at 599, 45 TC 427 at 467.
8   [1968] 3 All ER 588 at 606, 45 TC 427 at 474.
9   FA 1990, s 25.
10 [1968] 3 All ER 588, 45 TC 427.

[11.28] Savings income

[11] 37 TC 455, [1957] 2 All ER 644.
[12] *Campbell v IRC* [1968] 3 All ER 588 at 594, 45 TC 427 at 462 and per Morris LJ in *IRC v National Book League*, at 475, 652.
[13] *Taw and Torridge Festival Society Ltd v IRC* (1959) 38 TC 603, [1960] BTR 61.
[14] See [1988] BTR 231.
[15] Bodies listed in ITA 2007, s 430(1) qualify. See *Ghosh v Robson* [1993] BTR 496.

Rule 4—income of the payee

[11.29] The payment must be income of the payee and not that of someone else; it will not be his income if he is under a legally enforceable obligation to hand it on to someone else.

In *Campbell v IRC* a payment by A to B under a covenant of a sum equal to 80%[1] of net profits which B had to pay to C, who paid it back to A was not income of B. The scheme was to enable B, a charity, to acquire the goodwill of A's business.

The scheme failed because the legally enforceable obligation to use the same amount of money to pay for the goodwill, deprived the payment of the character of pure income profit,[2] and/or because the payments were capital in B's hands, a conclusion resting on the need to look at the quality of the payment in the hands of the recipient and not the payer. The second view expressed by Lords Dilhorne, Hodson, Guest and Upjohn,[3] was that the legally enforceable obligation to use the same amount of money to pay for the goodwill deprived the payment of its character of pure income profit. Lords Hodson and Upjohn expressly left open this opinion of what would have happened if the obligation had not been legally enforceable.[4]

A similar principle was applied in *McBurnie v Tacey* where Peter Gibson J held that where a wife received supplementary benefit for a child and the husband was ordered to pay sums to the Secretary of State for Social Services; the payments by the husband were not small maintenance payments to the wife and so were not deductible by him. The Secretary of State was not like B in the *Campbell* case.[5]

Simon's Direct Tax Service B8.423

---

[1] 80% was chosen because the covenant was not deductible for profits tax and 20% was needed to pay that tax.
[2] Lord Upjohn [1970] AC 77 at 108, [1968] 3 All ER 588 at 603 and 45 TC 427 at 472. Quaere if there had been no legally enforceable obligation.
[3] Lord Dilhorne at 99, 595, 463; Lord Donovan at 110, 604 and 473; Lord Hodson at 102, 598 and 466; Lord Guest at 104, 600 and 468.
[4] 45 TC at 466D, 470A.
[5] [1984] STC 347. An ancillary reason was that what is now ITEPA 2003, s 645 prevented the payments to the wife from being taxable income in her hands; quaeri whether the "new approach" could lead to a different result, making this payment taxable income of the wife and deductible by the husband.

Rule 5: capital or income—or some of each

[11.30] An annual payment is taxable within ITTOIA 2005, Pt 5, Ch 7 only if it is income. Where, therefore, a series of payments is made, the law has to decide whether the payments are the income of the recipient or merely a payment of capital by instalments. If the former, each payment is an annual payment; if the latter, each is capital and so not an annual payment. Sometimes the answer is that the payment is partly income and partly capital but in this instance the income element is not an annual payment but rather one of interest.

The question for the court is the true legal nature of the transaction which the parties have entered into.[1] In answering that question evidence dehors the contract is admissible, particularly in order to explain that which the contract often does not explain, namely the quality of the sums in question.[2]

The test is whether, as a matter of substance, the payments are instalments of the purchase price or pure income payments.[3] This is not regarded as breaking the principle laid down in *Duke of Westminster v IRC*[4] because the test does not involve putting upon a transaction between parties a character which in law it does not possess, but rather involves discovering what is the true character in law of the transaction which was entered into.[5]

Simon's Direct Tax Service B8.428

---

[1] *IRC v Church Comrs for England* [1976] STC 339, [1976] 2 All ER 1037. An agreement may contain two different types of payment, as in *IRC v British Salmson Aero Engines Ltd* [1938] 3 All ER 283, 22 TC 29.
[2] Per Lord Wilberforce in *IRC v Church Comrs for England* [1976] 2 All ER 1037 at 1044.
[3] *Brodie's Will Trustees v IRC* (1933) 17 TC 432 at 440.
[4] Supra, § **3.06**.
[5] Per Sir Wilfrid Greene MR in *Mallaby-Deeley v IRC* [1938] 4 All ER 818 at 825, 23 TC 153 at 167.

[11.31] Certain matters are clear although they tend to add to the confusion. First, the fact that a payment is made out of capital in no way affects the question whether the payment is income of the recipient. Therefore annuity payments are taxable even though under the terms of the will or settlement giving rise to it the trustees are empowered to have recourse to capital in order to pay the sum and the trustees exercise the power.[1] For the same reason an investment of capital in the purchase of an annuity gives rise to payments which are pure income, although here special legislation now provides that the payments are mixed capital and income if the annuitant and the purchaser are the same individual.[2]

Secondly, the label which the parties choose to give to the payment is not conclusive. Thus an "annuity" payment has been held to be capital,[3] and the payment of a purchase price by instalments has been held not to create pure capital payments.[4]

Thirdly, the courts have stressed that the question in every case is one of the true legal nature of the transaction[5] and that every case is to be decided on its own facts. A particular fact may have been the dominating factor in a case but that is not the same as a conclusive test.[6]

Fourthly, the courts have said that they cannot regard the conduct of the parties as conclusive but that they may draw comfort from discovering that the decision of the court corresponds with that conduct.[7] When the Revenue are parties to the litigation the courts tend to look at what the parties have done; whether they have, by deducting tax or not, shown that they regarded the payments as income or capital.

Simon's Taxes B8.428

---

[1] Infra, § **13.21**.
[2] ITTOIA 2005, s 717 (income tax); TA 1988, s 656 (corporation tax) (see infra, § **31.31**).
[3] *Secretary of State in Council of India v Scoble* [1903] AC 299, 4 TC 618.
[4] *Vestey v IRC* [1961] 3 All ER 978, 40 TC 112.
[5] *IRC v Church Comrs for England*; (see infra, § **11.35**).
[6] *Dott v Brown* [1936] 1 All ER 543.
[7] Per Lord Normand in *IRC v Hogarth* (1940) 23 TC 491 at 500.

Principles for Rule 5

[**11.32**] **Principle 1.** Where a definite sum of money is due and the payment of that sum in one lump would be a capital receipt of the payee, as where it is in return for an asset, the same quality attaches to the payment even though it is paid by instalments; so they will not be annual payments.

In *Foley v Fletcher and Rose*,[1] the taxpayer was one of two tenants in common of certain lands who agreed to sell the land for £99,000.[2] £6,770 was paid immediately and it was agreed that the balance of £92,230 was to be paid in half yearly instalments of £1,537 16s. over the next 30 years. The payer's claim to deduct tax in respect of each instalment as being a payment of an annuity was rejected by the Court of Exchequer.

Some judges thought that there was no method by which these payments could be dissected into capital and income elements,[3] but this is not correct today. Another view was that this was not a contract to pay an annuity but to pay a principal sum of money;[4] an annuity arises where the income is purchased with a sum of money and the capital has gone and has ceased to exist.[5] A further view was that these payments were not profits derived from property but the price of it. The fact that a part of the instalments could be regarded as the price of the inconvenience of getting the payment postponed, and thus perhaps a profit, did not mean that the whole payment thereby became a profit.[6]

In *Mallaby-Deeley v IRC*[7] an individual had undertaken to pay £33,000 to assist in the publication of Burke's Complete Peerage and to pay by equal quarterly instalments. He then made a covenant in which he was to make larger instalment payments in the earlier years and smaller payments in the later years. These payments were held to be capital.

The same result may be reached even though no fixed sum is agreed when the instalments commence, provided a formula for ascertaining the amount is fixed.

In *Ramsay v IRC*[8] the taxpayer had agreed to buy a dental practice. A primary price of £15,000 was agreed but the taxpayer agreed to pay it in the form of £5,000 at once and then to pay each year for ten years a sum equal to 25% of the net profits of that year. These were described as capital payments and no interest was payable. It was held that the payments were not annual payments but capital instalments so that the taxpayer could not deduct income tax when making the payments. It is probably also relevant that this decision involving the Revenue corresponded with the conduct of the parties.

Guidelines have now been agreed between the Revenue and the Association of British Insurers as to when compensation for personal injuries in the form of periodical payments will be treated as being tax free.[9]

Simon's Taxes B8.428–430

[1] (1858) 3 H & N 769.
[2] The total amount is probably about double the sums which would have been paid if paid at once: per Bramwell B at p. 782.
[3] Semble, per Pollock CB at 769; per Bramwell B at 783 and per Watson B at 784, but contra Channell LJ at 788.
[4] Per Pollock CB at 779.
[5] Per Watson B at 784.
[6] Per Pollock CP at 779.
[7] [1938] 4 All ER 818, 23 TC 153.
[8] (1935) 20 TC 79, distinguished in *IRC v Hogarth* (1940) 23 TC 49, (see infra, § 11.34).
[9] See *Law Society's Gazette*, 26 July 1989, p. 32 and **Simon's Direct Tax Service** B8.429.

[11.33] Principle 2. However, where the bargain was always thought of in income terms, and was concluded in income terms, and there is nothing in the documents to give the transaction a capital character, the payments will be pure income. This is even more likely to be the case where the payments are expressed in terms strongly suggestive of income, such as a rentcharge.

In *IRC v Church Comrs for England*,[1] a charity sold a reversion on a lease to the tenant in consideration of rentcharges payable annually for ten years and amounting in aggregate to £96,000 each year. It was clear that at no time was the purchaser willing to purchase for a single lump sum. The House of Lords held that these payments were pure income and could not be dissected into capital and interest payments.

Simon's Taxes B8.428–430.

[1] [1976] STC 339, [1976] 2 All ER 1037. This case may be taken as an a fortiori example of principle (3) since the calculation of the sum involved a wish to maintain an income equivalent to the rent for the remainder of the lease and to establish a fund which could then yield that sum in perpetuity.

[11.34] Savings income

[11.34] Principle 3. Where, despite principle 1, a series of payments are made in exchange for a right to income payments, the payments are likely to be pure income.

In *IRC v Hogarth*[1] the partners agreed to pay one of them who was retiring not only his share of the capital account and assets of the firm but also a sum equal to one fourteenth part of the net profits of the business for the three years ending 31 December 1937, 1938 and 1939, under deduction of tax. The partners making this payment sought to deduct these sums from their income for surtax purposes, something they could only do if the payments were income of the recipient. The Court of Session held that they were income, first because a statement that the payments were to be made under deduction of tax indicated it, and secondly because the payments were in satisfaction of a claim to annual profits or gains.

In *Chadwick v Pearl Life Insurance Co.*[2] the plaintiff owned a lease which had ten years to run. The total income from the sublease was £1,925 pa and the rent payable under the lease was £300, leaving a rental income of £1,625. The plaintiff sold his interest to the defendant for £1,000 and a covenant by the defendant to pay £1,625 pa for ten years. No sum was fixed as the total amount due on the sale, although that total sum could clearly have been ascertained (£17,250). Since the intention of the transaction was that the plaintiff should continue to receive as income to the end of the term the same amount that he had previously received as rent Walton J concluded that the payments were income, although he observed that the distinction was a fine one.

Simon's Taxes B8.428, 432.

---

[1] (1940) 23 TC 491; see also *Jones v IRC* [1920] 1 KB 711, 7 TC 310, doubted by Scott LJ in *Dott v Brown* [1936] 1 All ER 543.
[2] [1905] 2 KB 507.

[11.35] Principle 4. If the payment is not pure income, it may be dissected into capital and interest. This will be done if the parties, who are buying and selling a capital asset, having agreed on a price then make provision for payment of that price by instalments, the amount of which is so calculated, and shown to be so calculated, as to include an interest element.[1]

In *Secretary of State in Council of India v Scoble*[2] the East India Company bought a railway from a company and was empowered to pay outright or in instalments over a period of 46 years; the instalments, although called an annuity, were dissected. The only question in this case was whether the payments were pure income or could be dissected.

Where no lump sum purchase price has been agreed upon the power to dissect is debatable. However, the question whether a lump sum is involved is to be decided after looking at the transaction as a whole. This may explain the most extreme example of dissection: *Vestey v IRC*.[3] The taxpayer sold shares worth £2m for £5 1/2m, the sum to be paid in 125 yearly instalments of £44,000. The agreement stated that the price of £5 1/2m was to be without interest. The

Revenue sought to charge the taxpayer to surtax either on the whole payment as an annuity or on a part of it as interest. Cross J upheld the second claim. However, the enthusiasm with which Cross J preferred the second approach to the first is not to be found in the decision of the House of Lords in *IRC v Church Comrs for England*.[4] The facts of that case fell on the other side of the line principally because the transaction was thought of throughout in income tax terms, see principle 2, and because there was no evidence that the parties had ever settled on a firm lump sum price. Yet Lord Wilberforce accepted the *Vestey* decision as correct despite the fact that the only figure agreed on by the parties was the overall price of £51/2m.[5]

Today it is likely that, when the parties have agreed on a fixed sum, the sum will be dissected and will not be pure capital unless the period is short and the contract in a common form. Dissection into interest and principal was directed in *Vestey* where the period was 125 years, but not in *Ramsay* where the period was ten years and the contract was for the disposal of a business, the price being ascertained on a common and reasonable basis. In *Foley v Fletcher and Rose* the period was 30 years but today it seems inconceivable that there would be no dissection on such facts.

Simon's Taxes B8.428–430.

[1] Per Lord Wilberforce in *IRC v Church Comrs for England* [1976] STC 339 at 345, [1976] 2 All ER 1037 at 1043.
[2] [1903] AC 299, 4 TC 623.
[3] [1961] 3 All ER 978, 40 TC 112, (Phillips).
[4] [1976] 2 All ER 1037, especially per Lord Wilberforce at 1043.
[5] Actuarial report made to the trustees referred to in the case stated in *Vestey* (1961) 40 TC 112 at 115.

Deduction at source: basic rate

Payments within the scheme

[11.36] Annuities and other annual payments come within this scheme provided they are taxable as the recipient's income under ITTOIA 2005, Pt 5, Ch 7. The types of such payments falling within this category were greatly reduced in 1988. Annuities and other annual payments which would otherwise be within the scheme after 1988 are nonetheless excluded if they are (a) charged on land—chargeable as property income, (b) made under a source sited outside the UK—chargeable as income from overseas, (c) from a source sited inside the UK but in favour of a non-resident and exempt under a double tax treaty.[1] However, deduction at basic rate at source continues to be applied to annual payments[2] of patent royalties.

The scheme of deduction at source originally applied not only to most annuities and annual payments but also to payments of yearly interest and in effect to dividends.[3] Today, most interest payments are outside the scheme and dividend income is the subject of a special regime.

[11.36] Savings income

Simon's Taxes A4.405, 415.

[1] eg royalty payments under art 12 of the US/UK Double Tax Agreement, SI 2002/2848.
[2] ITA 2007, s 903.
[3] Income Tax Act 1918—All Schedules Rule 20.

Machinery

[11.37] When A makes a payment to B out of income which has been brought into charge to income tax and the payment is an annuity or annual payment, and so B's income is taxable, statute[1] obliges A to deduct basic rate tax. So if A is due to pay B £100 he must deduct £20 and pay only £80. The authority for this is ITA 2007, Pt 15. Payments which were removed from the charge to tax (under what was then Schedule D, Case III) by FA 1988 are not subject to this rule (see infra, § **11.38**).

A deducts income tax at basic rate. This has long been the law. The introduction of the lower rate of tax on savings income in 1996 led to some changes. Deduction at basic rate continues to apply to annuities and annual payments other than interest and to payments in respect of patent royalties; all other payments within the scheme in ITA 2007, Pt 15 suffered deduction at the lower rate of 20%.[1] The following account deals with an annuity or other annual payment and so the rate at which tax is withheld has generally been the basic rate. From 2008–09, with the reduction of the basic rate to 20% and the abolition of the lower rate, this distinction has disappeared.

Under ITA 2008, s 848 the amount deducted is treated as income tax paid by B.[2] It follows that if B's marginal rate of tax is the same as the rate of the deduction there is nothing more to be done. If, however, B's rate is 0% B may recover the tax by making a repayment claim to the Revenue (not A). If B's rate is 40% there is additional tax to pay. Quite anomalously, while there is a duty on the payer to supply a certificate to show that tax has been deducted,[3] there is no penalty for non-compliance, a matter of considerable practical importance.

However Pt 15 not only allows A to act as tax collector for B, it also allows him to keep the tax for himself. This is the mechanism whereby A's payment to B is treated as an assignment of A's income to B with result that it is deductible—or not taxable in A's hands.[4]

The scheme thus has two functions. The first is to make a provisional assessment on B by allowing A to deduct tax at source; this may be called the withholding function. The second is to give effect to A's right to deduct this payment in computing total income by first making A pay tax on this part of his income and then permitting A to recoup that tax on making this payment; this may be called the relief function.

This scheme applies where payment is made out of income that has been brought into charge to income tax. If the tax has not yet been paid, an assessment will be made. That provision also directs that, subject to other provisions of the Act, the rate of tax to be paid by A will be basic rate—and only basic rate. This means that he is not liable to higher rate tax.

It will not be forgotten that A is not entitled to personal relief on that slice of his income which has been assigned to B; it follows that he will pay tax at the basic rate on that slice and then recoup that tax under Pt 15.

Simon's Taxes A4.402, 403.

---

[1] The obligation is given by a different statutory section, according to the type of payment: vide ITA 2007, ss 900(2) (commercial payment), 901(3)(a) & (4) (annual payment by a person other than an individual), s 903(5)(a) & 6(a) (payment of patent royalties).
[2] ITA 2007, s 448.
[3] TMA 1970, s 106(1).
[4] ITA 2007, s 952.

The payer

[11.38] The person making the payment is obliged to deduct income tax when making the payment,[1] but only at the basic rate.[2] If the payments are made late, the rate of tax to be deducted is that in force when the payment falls due.[3]

"On making the payment" includes payment by cheque or by transfer of a marketable security and can be[4] by the making of credit entries in books of account.[5] There must however be some effective act by the payer which transfers the right to the money[6] so that the mere capitalisation of unpaid interest by the lender is not payment of interest by the borrower.[7] Where the payee is also a debtor of the payer, payment may be made by the payee extinguishing the payer's liability.[8]

The duty to deduct is imposed on the person "by or through whom" it is made. Where therefore solicitors held funds for one obliged to make a payment the solicitors were held accountable.[9]

If therefore in *Stokes v Bennett* (see infra, § **11.39**) the husband had remitted the sums to his solicitors in England to be paid over to the wife, the solicitors would have been assessable had they received the sums gross and then failed to deduct.[10] The words "through whom" are apt to cover any agent even a bank.

Simon's Taxes A4.410.

---

[1] See supra, § **11.37**, footnote 1.
[2] Unless the payment is savings income in the hands of the recipient.
[3] *IRC v Crawley* [1987] STC 147.
[4] *Minsham Properties Ltd v Price* [1990] STC 718.
[5] Per Lord Wright MR, in *Rhokana Corpn Ltd v IRC* [1937] 1 KB 788 at 808; on appeal [1938] 2 All ER 51, 21 TC 552 at 573; see also *IRC v Plummer* [1979] STC 793, [1979] 3 All ER 775.

[11.38] Savings income

6   See also *Re Vernon, Edwards v Vernon* (1946) 175 LT 421, and *Momm v Barclays Bank International* [1976] 3 All ER 588.
7   *IRC v Oswald* [1945] 1 All ER 641, 26 TC 448.
8   *Butler v Butler* [1961] P 33, [1961] 1 All ER 810.
9   *Rye and Eyre v IRC* [1935] AC 274, 19 TC 164 and see *Howells v IRC* [1939] 3 All ER 144, 22 TC 501.
10 Quaere whether they would have been assessable if the husband had remitted to them only the net sum—semble not.

Tax deducted—immunity of payee from basic rate liability

[11.39] Under statute, the payee is treated as having paid the amount of income tax which has been deducted.[1]

If the payer has deducted tax the payee is regarded as having paid basic rate income tax and so is safe from direct assessment whether or not the payer accounts for the tax to the Revenue.[2] In *Stokes v Bennett*,[3] a man resident in Brazil was under a liability to pay his former wife sums under an order made on their divorce by an English court. The husband made the payments but deducted tax. Having no UK income he was within the obligation to deduct tax but did not account to the Revenue for the tax deducted. Upjohn J held that no direct assessment could be made on the wife as she had already suffered tax. Had the payment been under an order of a foreign court the payments would have constituted foreign income, and former TA 1988, s 349 would not have applied.[4]

Simon's Taxes A4.416.

1   ITA 2007, s 448(5).
2   On the position where the payer fails to deduct (see infra, § **11.41**).
3   [1953] 2 All ER 313, 34 TC 337.
4   *National Bank of Greece SA v Westminster Bank Executor and Trustee Co (Channel Islands) Ltd* [1971] 1 All ER 233, 46 TC 491 suggests that this is unlikely and that Case III is to be confined to obligations arising in the UK. TA 1988, s 18 was not so confined but cf *Colquhoun v Brooks* (see infra, § **35.02**). On location of source of interest see Inland Revenue interpretation RI 58.

Consequences of failing to deduct tax

HMRC and the parties

[11.40] In *Re Sharp, Rickett v Rickett*,[1] trustees of a settlement failed to deduct tax when paying certain annuities. This was a breach of trust because they had overpaid the annuitant at the expense of the other beneficiaries and were therefore compelled to make good the loss.

The deduction is to be treated as income tax paid by the person to whom the payment is made.[2] Therefore if no deduction is made, no tax can be treated as having been paid. It seems to follow that if tax is not deducted a direct assessment may therefore be on the payee.³ The Revenue view is that no repayment claim can be made by the payee but this is subject to concessionary relief for maintenance payments which takes the odd form of allowing the payer to deduct the payment in computing his income.⁴

It is clear that if tax is deductible but the tax is not deducted, the Revenue may make a direct assessment on the payee.⁵ However the payer is obliged, not entitled, to deduct tax, and to account for it to the Revenue; he therefore remains liable.⁶ The amount on which the payer is assessable is the amount payable. If he makes a covenanted payment of £100 but fails to deduct the £22 tax, he may be charged with the tax of £22. There is no rule which treats him as having paid the £100 *net* of tax so as to cause that figure actually paid to be grossed up to £128.20.⁷

Simon's Taxes A4.416, 433.

1. [1906] 1 Ch 793.
2. ITA 2007, s 448(5).
3. TA 1970, s 52(1)(*a*) precluded any direct assessment on the payee but in 1973 this was replaced by what is now ITA 2007, Pt 15. Direct assessment on the payer is now possible and is common where the payee is subject to higher rate liability, whether or not the payee deducts tax.
4. Extra-statutory concession A52; for a critical comment see [1985] BTR 329.
5. *Grosvenor Place Estates Ltd v Roberts* [1961] 1 All ER 341, 39 TC 433 (JGM).
6. *Lord Advocate v Edinburgh* Corpn 1905 7 F (Ct of Sess) 1972.
7. *IRC v Watson* (1943) 25 TC 25.

The parties inter se

[11.41] If the payer (A) fails to deduct tax, and so pays more than necessary, A will be able to recover the overpayment from B whether the mistake is one of fact or one of law. Until 1998 only sums paid under mistake of fact could be recovered. However, in 1998 the House of Lords held that restitution for unjust enrichment is not excluded by mistake of law;¹ it also held that the new rule applied to payments made before 1998 even though at the time of payment the older rule was firmly established. The 1998 case is an example of the development of the new principles of restitution. The new principle contains a number of defences the details of which will have to be worked out by the courts.

Under the old law A was treated as making a gift which, being complete, could not be undone. It followed that no action would lie against the overpaid B for recovery of the sum and A had no right to withhold later payments to secure reimbursement.² This is changed by the 1998 decision. It was also held that if the payment had been one of a series of payments within the tax year and some of those payments remained to be made, A could not make good the loss by making the deduction from one of the later payments;³ this too has changed. To make matters worse for A it was also held that where a sum had been paid and A did not then notify B of any deduction, A was treated as having failed to deduct tax.⁴

[11.41] Savings income

However, the payer may have been able to take some comfort under one or more of the following qualifications:

(1) A failure to deduct in respect of a past payment did not prejudice his right to deduct in respect of later ones.

(2) The general rule applied to payments that had been made; it followed that he could deduct in respect of payments to be made even though the due date for payment had passed.[5] Further it may be that a payment made "on account" or expressed to be made provisionally would not have been treated as having been made and so as entitling the payer to adjust the account when making later payments.[6]

(3) The general rule did not apply to payments made under a mistake of fact. So when a deduction system applied under Schedule A and the tenant failed to deduct income tax in respect of rent because he thought the lease was for ten years—and so outside the deduction system—when it was in fact for 99 years, the court held that his mistake was one of fact and permitted him to recover his loss.[7] In such instances it is a matter for the payer whether he recovers the sums from the payee or withholds from subsequent payments under the general principles of set-off.

(4) Where payments were made by personal representatives under a mistake of law they may—contrary to the general rule—deduct the amount of tax which they should have deducted from earlier payments from later ones and thus make good the loss to the estate. This was on the ground that in the administration of an estate the court would wherever possible correct errors of account between the estate and the beneficiaries.[8] The position may be different if the trustee was also the beneficiary who had been underpaid.[9] It was in any case doubtful whether the loss could be made good by recovery from the beneficiary directly,[10] save where property could be traced into his hands, he was a constructive trustee of the property or an action lay under the principle in *Ministry of Health v Simpson*.[11]

(5) Where the failure to deduct was due to the fact that the rate of tax had not then been fixed, former TA 1988, s 348 expressly allowed the payer to make good the deficiency on making later payments; if there were no more payments to be made he could recover the sum by action.

(6) Failure to deduct basic rate tax could not affect the payer's right to deduct the payments in computing his total income for purposes of higher and additional rate liabilities.

Simon's Taxes A3.416.

---

[1] *Kleinwort Benson Ltd v Lincoln City Council* [1999] 2 AC 349, [1998] 4 All ER 513, HL.

[2] *Warren v Warren* (1895) 72 LT 628 applied in *Re Hatch, Hatch v Hatch* [1919] 1 Ch 351.

[3] This applied both to former TA 1988, s 348, *Johnson v Johnson* [1946] P 205, [1946] 1 All ER 573, CA, and to s 349 *Tenbry Investments Ltd v Peugeot Talbot Motor Co* [1992] STC 791.

[4] *Hemsworth v Hemsworth* [1946] 1 KB 431, [1946] 2 All ER 117.

5   See cases at note 2 supra and *Taylor v Taylor* [1937] 3 All ER 571, [1938] 1 KB 320.
6   Perhaps payments to be made in instalments might come within this principle too.
7   *Turvey v Dentons (1923) Ltd* [1952] 2 All ER 1025, [1953] 1 QB 218.
8   *Re Musgrave, Machell v Parry* [1916] 2 Ch 417.
9   *Re Horne, Wilson v Cox Sinclair* [1905] 1 Ch 76; see also *Re Ainsworth, Finch v Smith* [1915] 2 Ch 96.
10 *Re Robinson, McLaren v Public Trustee* [1911] 1 Ch 502.
11 [1951] AC 251, [1950] 2 All ER 1137.

Payments 'free of tax'

Validity of agreements

[11.42] Any *agreement* for the payment of interest, rent or other annual payment in full without allowing the deduction of income tax shall be void.[1] This invalidates the part relating to non-deduction and not the whole agreement.[2] So if P agrees to pay Q £100 a year without deduction, P is nonetheless entitled to deduct tax or bound to do under ITA 2007, Pt 15. It applies only to agreements,[3] not to wills nor to orders of the court.[4] In appropriate cases the court will rectify an agreement to avoid the agreement being void.[5]

Where there is an agreement that P shall pay Q £100 "free of tax", the House of Lords held in *Ferguson v IRC*, overriding a long line of authority, that P must pay Q such sums as after deduction of income tax leaves £100;[6] such a construction means that the agreement does not fall foul of s 106(2). However, it also means that Q is entitled to £100 free of his marginal rate of tax; if that rate is 20%, he will be entitled to £125 gross, ie £100 net. It is not clear whether the decision of the House of Lords means that the agreement is to pay free of such higher rates as Q may be liable to or only basic rate; the point was not in issue. The decision brings the rule of construction for agreements into line with that for court orders.[7]

1   TMA 1970, s 106(2).
2   *Booth v Booth* [1922] 1 KB 66.
3   *Re Goodson's Settlement, Goodson v Goodson* [1943] Ch 101, [1943] 1 All ER 201.
4   An agreement to carry out an order of the court is subject to s 106(2). *Blount v Blount* [1916] 1 KB 230; the converse is not; *Massey v Massey* [1949] WN 422.
5   *Burroughes v Abbott* [1922] 1 Ch 86, distinguished in *Whiteside v Whiteside* [1950] Ch 65, [1949] 2 All ER 913.
6   [1969] 1 All ER 1025, 46 TC 15.
7   Infra, § **11.43**.

The rule in re Pettit

[11.43] Where P is to pay Q £100 "free of tax", P will make a payment of £100; this is equivalent to £128.20 gross and Q's income is therefore taken to include not £100 but £128.20.

If Q has no other income he will be able to reclaim £28.20 from the Revenue on account of his personal reliefs. If he were allowed to keep the sum, he would have benefited to the tune of £128.20 and not £100 as undertaken by P; Q is therefore directed by the rule in Re Pettit, Le Fevre v Pettit[1] to hold the sum recovered from the Revenue on trust for P. Q is therefore under an obligation to make the repayment claim.[2]

If Q has other income, the value of the personal reliefs has to be shared between the annuity and the other income. It follows that the rule applies to that proportion of the reliefs which the gross amount of the annuity bears to Q's total income. So if Q is entitled to a personal relief of £4,895 and has other UK interest income of £1,000 gross or £800 net Q will have a repayment claim for £228.20 of which £128.20/1,128.20 or £24.75 will be refunded to P. This matter becomes important where Q's total income moves above the level of his personal reliefs.

In every reported case Q has been entitled to a repayment of tax. However, the principle should apply wherever Q is entitled to set a relief from tax against his annuity income in whole or in part—and not simply when he makes a repayment claim. Any other conclusion would mean that the rule would apply where for example Q's other income was dividend income of £2,000 but not if it was employment income. In this context the withdrawal of any right to repayment of the tax credit in connection with dividends in 1999 should be remembered.

Q is obliged to account for relief from tax not only in respect of personal allowances but also for loss relief claimed under TA 1988, s 380.[3] Although Q is under a duty to make the claim for a repayment when it is due it would appear that he is not obliged to claim relief under TA 1988, s 380 rather than under TA 1988, s 385.

The obligation to account causes problems in adjusting the total income of P and Q; thus is the sum due to be handed back as annual payment to P by Q so that ITA 2007, Pt 15 applies and the gross sum treated as P's income? To make matters yet more complex one need only recall that Q would not be entitled to claim personal reliefs on that part of his income which he is under a duty to pay over.[4] It has been held that the liability to repay does not affect Q's total income nor his repayment claim.[5] The Revenue are therefore not entitled to refuse repayment simply because Q is bound to hand it over. No authority exists on the effect on P but the Revenue practice is to treat him as entitled to additional income equivalent to the grossed up sum he is repaid.[6]

The rule in Re Pettit is one of trust law and applies whenever the construction of the agreement, trust or will requires it. The question is whether the agreement is that Q should benefit to the extent of £100, and only that sum, in which case the rule applies or whether Q is to receive £100 net from P regardless of the actual tax Q may have to pay, if any.[7] The rule therefore applies whenever there is a fixed increase in Q's spendable income. There is thus a clear distinction between £100 "free of tax" to which the rule applies and "such sum as after deducting tax at the current rate shall leave £100"—known as a formula deduction covenant—to which the rule does not apply; the former indicates the extent to which Q is to benefit while the latter does not. Where the annuity is free of tax the annuitant is assured of a constant net sum and the payer of a constantly fluctuating liability; where the deduction formula applies, the payer is assured of a constant net outflow and the payee of constantly fluctuating net receipts. Where the annuity is free of tax, the liability of the payer will vary according to the financial position of the payee; where the deduction formula is used the benefit to the payee varies with his financial position. The rule in *Re Pettit* applies to free of tax clauses but not to a deduction formula covenant.

The rule has not been applied where Q was to receive "a clear annuity of" £100 nor £100 "free of all deductions";[8] on the other hand it was applied where Q was to receive "such sum as would leave in her hands" £100.[9]

The rule applies to agreements, estates and trusts. However, its status in Scotland is unclear. Illogically the rule does not apply to court orders[10] with the result that the same words will have one effect in an agreement and a different one in an order.

Simon's Taxes E1.1960, 961–967.

[1] [1922] 2 Ch 765.
[2] *Re Kingcome, Hickley v Kingcome* [1936] 1 All ER 173, [1936] Ch 566. On position of non-residents see *Re Jubb, Neilson v King* (1941) 20 ATC 297. In *Re Batty, Public Trustee v Bell* [1952] 1 All ER 425, [1952] Ch 280. Vaisey J held that a wife could be made to elect for separate assessment so as to be compelled to make the repayment claim; on appeal it was held that the rule in *Re Pettit* did not apply so this issue was not discussed; however if the husband held any repayment on trust for the wife (*Re Cameron, Kingsley v IRC* [1965] 3 All ER 474, 42 TC 539) it ought to follow that the payer could compel the wife to compel the husband to make the claim. See also *Re Tatham, National Bank Ltd and Mathews v Mackenzie* [1945] Ch 34, [1945] 1 All ER 29.
[3] *Re Lyons, Barclays Bank Ltd v Jones* [1952] Ch 129, [1952] 1 All ER 34.
[4] Supra, § **6.53**.
[5] *IRC v Cook* [1945] 2 All ER 377, 26 TC 489.
[6] On the effect on P when P is an estate see *Re Twiss, Barclays Bank Ltd v Pratt* [1941] Ch 141, [1941] 1 All ER 93.
[7] *Re Batley, Public Trustee v Hert (No 2)* [1952] Ch 781, [1952] 2 All ER 562.
[8] *Re Skinner, Milbourne v Skinner* [1942] Ch 82, [1942] 1 All ER 32.
[9] *Re Maclennan, Few v Byrne* [1939] Ch 750, [1939] 3 All ER 81. See also *Re Jones, Jones v Jones* [1933] Ch 842 and *Re Eves, Midland Bank Executor and Trustee Co Ltd v Eves* [1939] Ch 969.
[10] *Jefferson v Jefferson* [1956] 1 All ER 31, [1956] P 136.

[11.44] Savings income

Construction of court orders

[11.44] Since the rule that an agreement for payment without deduction of income tax does not apply to court orders, the courts have long felt able to construe an order to pay £x "free of tax" as an order to pay such sum as after deduction of income tax at the basic rate leaves £x.[1] If the order is to pay "£x less tax," it is construed as an order to deduct basic rate tax on £x under ITA 2007, Pt 15 and to pay the balance.

Simon's Taxes E4.126.

---

[1] *Spilsbury v Spofforth* [1937] 4 All ER 487, 21 TC 247.

Maintenance payments

[11.45] No relief for maintenance payments made is available unless one of the parties to the marriage was born before 6 April 1935.[1] Where one of the parties to the marriage was born before that date, the payer is entitled to a reduction in income tax, which is calculated as 10% of the amount paid in the year, or £2,150 whichever is less.[2] For details of the qualifying maintenance deduction see supra, § **6.35**.

In contrast to the position in 1999–2000 and earlier years, the amount actually paid is not available as a deduction, even where the obligation arose prior to 1988.[3]

---

[1] ITA 2007, s 454(3).
[2] The amount is equal to the minimum age-related married couple's allowance: ITA 2007, s 453(3) applying ITA 2007, s 43 amended by Income Tax (Indexation) (No 2) Order 2006, SI 2006/3241, art 2(4)(d), *Simon's Weekly Tax Intelligence* 2006, p 2776.
[3] For a discussion of the detailed provisions relating to this restricted relief for maintenance payments, see Tiley & Collison's UK Tax Guide 1999–2000, § **9.80**.

12

Miscellaneous income

Scope of this chapter	PARA **12.01**
Income taxed under ITTOIA 2005 Chapter 8	PARA **12.06**
Foreign questions	PARA **12.12**
Computation	PARA **12.13**
Pre-owned assets	PARA **12.15**

Scope of this chapter

[12.01] This chapter is concerned with two broad categories of miscellaneous income:

(1) income subject to income tax under ITTOIA 2005, Pt 5, Ch 8 (or, if received by a company, subject to and, for companies, TA 1988, s 18(3) corporation tax under Schedule D Case VI);

(2) an income tax charge levied on the enjoyment of a pre-owned asset.

[12.02] Before the introduction of ITTOIA 2005, income tax was charged under Schedule D, Case VI on any annual profits or gains not falling under any other Case of Schedule D, not charged under Schedules A and F nor charged as employment income, pension income or social security income.[1] Schedule D, Case VI was thus the residual case in the residual Schedule. In addition the Taxes Acts often directed that a particular type of payment which is brought into charge to income tax was to be charged under Schedule D, Case VI.[2] Where certain relatively small amounts of trading income accrue to a charity, the legislation introduced by FA 2000 and excluding a charge under Schedule D, Case I, takes great pains not to exclude many of these heads of charge which, for income tax, were assessable under Case VI.[3]

Following the introduction of ITTOIA 2005, the residual charge to income is covered by ITTOIA 2005 ss 687–689.[4] The charging provision (to income tax) in ITTOIA 2005 is: "Tax is charged under this Chapter on income from any source that is not charged to income tax under . . . any other provision of this Act or any Act".[5] The declared intention of the tax law rewrite scheme is to maintain the charging provision exactly as in the predecessor's statute. On this basis, case law on the interpretation of the charge to Schedule D Case VI in TA 1988 and its predecessors is relevant. From this body of case law, four principles may be laid down: (a) the profit must be annual, (b) it must be of an income nature, (c) must not be gratuitous and (d) must be analogous to some other head of charge under what was previously Schedule D.

For corporation tax, Schedule D Case VI remains the charging provision.

Simon's Taxes B8.601, 602.

[12.02] Miscellaneous income

1   TA 1988, s 18(3). The cumbersome phrase "employment income, pension income or social security income" is now necessary to denote income charged by ITEPA 2003, which abolishes the neat designation "Schedule E".
2   eg TA 1988, ss 660C (settlements) and 761 (offshore income gains); for a list see **Simon's Direct Tax Service B8.602**. Following the introduction of ITTOIA, the references to Schedule D Case VI have been removed as far as income tax is concerned leaving a freestanding charge to tax.
3   Now in ITA 2007, s 527(2).
4   Although the miscellaneous (predominantly anti-avoidance) provisions are covered elsewhere in that Act and (for the time being) in the Taxes Act.
5   ITTOIA 2005, s 687(1).

Principle 1—annual profits

[12.03] Case law[1] declares that to be taxed under this head, the income must have the nature of "annual profits". Casual profits may therefore be caught but only if they are of an income, as opposed to a capital, nature.[2] As Rowlatt J observed, "Annual can only mean calculated in any one year and . . . 'annual profits or gains' means 'profits or gains in any year as the succession of years comes round".[3] The word does not therefore add very much by way of definition. This is not however surprising since the other cases of the former Schedule D all taxed annual profits or gains and Case VI was analogous to them.

Simon's Taxes B8.604, 605.

1   Per Viscount Dunedin in *Jones v Leeming* [1930] AC 415 at 422, 15 TC 333 at 359; see also Rowlatt J in *Townsend v Grundy* (1933) 18 TC 140 at 148.
2   *Jones v Leeming*; for a complex example see *Black Nominees Ltd v Nicol* [1975] STC 372.
3   In *Ryall v Hoare* [1923] 2 KB 447 at 455; also "the plant is not annual—it is the sowing that is annual" (at 454). The mere fact that the profit arises within the course of one calendar year only and does not recur is not sufficient to exclude it from the category of annual profits": per Lord Warrington in *Jones v Leeming* [1930] AC 415 at 425, 15 TC 333 at 361; and see Lord Inglis in *Scottish Provident Institution v Farmer* (1912) 6 TC 34 at 38: "There is nothing said in the Act about a gain being necessarily within the year of assessment."

Principles 2, 3 and 4—income eiusdem generis

[12.04] To fall within the charge on miscellaneous income (for corporation tax, Case VI) a receipt must be of an income nature, must not be gratuitous and must be analogous to those profits or gains caught by the preceding Cases of Schedule D.[1] A profit derived from the sale of an asset will either be income from an adventure in the nature of trade and so taxable under what was Schedule D, Case I or be of a capital nature and so outside both Case I and Case VI.[2]

To be of the nature of income a receipt must have a source and be distinct from that source. Hence a gift, the casual finding of a thing[3] or the receipt of gambling winnings do not fall to be taxed as income under Case VI any more than does a capital gain. On the other hand a receipt in return for services rendered will be caught by Case VI if not by some other case.

Simon's Taxes B8.611

---

[1] Per Lord Dunedin, in *Jones v Leeming* [1930] AC 415 at 422, 15 TC 333 at 359.
[2] *Jones v Leeming*.
[3] By contrast, the Revenue have been reported to regard recurrent use of a metal detector to look for "finds" as potentially within the charge under Chapter 8. If there is sufficient organisation to the activity of metal detection, this could constitute a trade. The Revenue's reported approach is consistent with our analysis at infra § **12.05**.

Gambling and distinguishable transactions

[**12.05**] Such transactions[1] are merely irrational agreements. The event which entitles the gambler to his winnings does not of itself produce the profit. There is no increment, no service, but merely an acquisition.[2] This has to be distinguished from an organised seeking after profits which may create a trade and so a subject matter which bears fruit in the shape of profits or gains. Hence it has been held that while gambling may be a way of life—indeed in *Graham v Green* it was the taxpayer's sole means of livelihood—it is not a trade and so its winnings escape tax. Such views however do not prevent courts from holding that a bookmaker is carrying on a vocation and is therefore taxable as trading income, the distinction being that a bookmaker has an organisation.[3]

Also to be distinguished from mere gambling winnings are winnings incidental to a taxable activity. Thus in *Norman v Evans*[4] the taxpayer leased horses bred at his stud to other persons to be raced by them and would receive one half of all sums received in respect of the horses' winnings. The Revenue did not argue that he was carrying on the trade of racing horses. Hence if he had raced these horses himself (as a hobby) any winnings would have been non-taxable. Yet it was held that his one half of the winnings were taxable. On the other hand where a bet is on professional skill it is still a bet and therefore not taxable. A borderline case is *Down v Compston*[5] where a golf professional taxable under what is now employment income was held not taxable in respect of money won on bets with other persons with whom he played golf. This decision should be contrasted with certain Commonwealth cases in which gains from betting which is associated with other taxable horse racing activity have been subjected to income tax as part of that other activity—by a horse owner,[6] by a horse trainer,[7] by a registered bookmaker[8] and even by a horse owner who leased racehorses and had a stud farm for breeding horses.[9] The question must be one of fact. *Down v Compston* was distinguished in *Burdge v Pyne*[10] when the proprietor of a gambling club was held taxable on the profits of his gambling at his club as part of his trading income.

Also to be distinguished from mere gambling is speculation. Thus a person who buys shares on the stock exchange or cotton futures[11] in the hope of an increase in capital value is a speculator and not a gambler—the distinction being that the contract to buy or sell the cotton is a very real one from the point of view of the vendor and gives rise to very real contractual rights whereas in a gambling transaction both parties regard the matter as a mere wager.[12] Thus the profits of speculation in commodity futures may be taxable if there is a sufficient substratum of activity to give rise to the finding that there is a trade and so a source taxable as trading income.

Also to be distinguished are payments for the provision of services. So a man carrying on the consistent trade of tipster is taxed on the profits of his profession as trading income.[13] The income of an occasional tipster may fall within the residual heading of Chapter 8 as the meaning of professional income contains no concept equivalent to an adventure in the nature of trade.[14]

Simon's Taxes B8.607, 615.

---

[1] *Graham v Green* [1925] 2 KB 37, 9 TC 309.
[2] See per Rowlatt J at 39; 312 who draws a parallel with finding and gift.
[3] *Partridge v Mallandaine* (1886) 18 QBD 276, and *Graham v Green* (n. 1, supra), at pp 42, 314.
[4] [1965] 1 All ER 372, 42 TC 188 (Buckley J).
[5] [1937] 2 All ER 475, 21 TC 60 (Lawrence J).
[6] *Knight v Taxation Comr* (1928) 28 SR NSW 523.
[7] *Holt v Federal Taxation Comr* (1929) 3 ALJ 68.
[8] *Vandenberg v Taxation Comr New South Wales* (1933) 2 ATD 343.
[9] *Trautwein v Federal Taxation Comr* (1936) 56 CLR 196.
[10] [1969] 1 All ER 467, 45 TC 320.
[11] *Cooper v Stubbs* [1925] 2 KB 753, 10 TC 29, followed in *Townsend v Grundy* (1933) 18 TC 140.
[12] Per Warrington LJ at 769, 52 and per Atkin LJ at 770–771; 53–54.
[13] *Graham v Arnott* (1941) 24 TC 157.
[14] The Taxes Acts do not define "profession". By contrast TA 1988, s 832(1) defines "trade" as including "an adventure in the nature of trade". The Oxford English Dictionary defines "profession" as: "a vocation in which a professed knowledge of some department of learning is used in its application to the affairs of others, or in the practice of an art founded upon it"; there is no suggestion here that any type of adventure would be part of a profession.

Income taxed under ITTOIA 2005 Chapter 8

[12.06] As befits the case of the residual charge, the categories of income which the courts have held to fall within its scope forms something of a motley bunch. Apart from those items that statute specifically brings within this category, case law has determined that what is now Chapter 8 taxes a cluster of activities, including:

(i) Underwriting commission payments received by a pension fund.[1]
(ii) Sale of cotton futures.[2]
(iii) Shipping dues.[3]

(iv)   Racehorses let for share of prize moneys.[4]
(v)   Fee for an overdraft guarantee.[5]
(vi)   Underwriting commission.[6]
(vii) Fee for negotiating a sale of shares.[7]
(viii) Commission from assurance company.[8]
(ix)   Commission for introduction.[9]
(x)   Sale of rights in life story to newspaper.[10]

The Revenue regard currency swaps, interest rate swaps and certain kinds of credit derivatives as falling within the charge on miscellaneous income.[11] when carried on by an individual or trust,[12] if the swap does not form part of the circulating capital of financial trade nor is ancillary to a trade transaction on current account.[13] The charge extends to lump sums, as well as profits or losses arising on the swap itself.[14] One consequence of the Revenue's treatment of swaps by a non-corporate is the profits the charity enjoys on these are chargeable, whereas investment income, received by a charity is exempt.[15]

[1] Clarke v British Telecom Pension Scheme Trustees [2000] STC 222, CA.
[2] Cooper v Stubbs (1925) 10 TC 29, CA.
[3] IRC v Forth Conservancy Board (1931) 16 TC 103, HL.
[4] Norman v Evans (1964) 42 TC 188.
[5] Ryall v Hoare (1925) 8 TC 521.
[6] Lyons v Cowcher (1926) 10 TC 438.
[7] Grey v Tiley (1932) 16 TC 414, CA and Bloom v Kinder (1958) 38 TC 77.
[8] Hugh v Rogers (1958) 38 TC 270.
[9] Brocklesby v Merricks (1934) 18 TC 576, CA and Bradbury v Arnold (1957) 37 TC 665.
[10] Hobbs v Hussey (1942) 24 TC 153 and Housden v Marshall (1958) 38 TC 233.
[11] Inland Revenue Tax Bulletin August 2003, p 1055, para 5.
[12] Income from swaps by a company or an unincorporated association within the charge to corporation tax is dealt with under the FA 1996 relationships provisions: see infra, § **27.01** et seq.
[13] If the swap forms part of the circulating capital or is ancillary to a trading transaction, it is regarded by the Revenue as part of the profits from the trade; if it is ancillary to property income, the Revenue regard it as part of the "profits" of the property business: Inland Revenue Tax Bulletin August 2003, p 1055, para 6.
[14] Inland Revenue Tax Bulletin August 2003, p 1055, para 10.
[15] ITA 2007, ss 531 (charities exemption from property income), 532 (charities exemption for savings and investment income). The exemption enjoyed by a charity from a tax charge on miscellaneous income is restricted to income from royalties, wayleaves, annual payments and foreign distributions: ITA 2007, s 536: see infra, § **13.25**.

[**12.07**] Liability in respect of trading profits differs from that in respect of miscellaneous sources of income in a number of respects:

(1)   the basis period for trading profits is generally a 12-month accounting period ending in the fiscal year of assessment but with complications if there are profits arising in an overlap period; the basis period for Chapter 8 is the fiscal year, from 6 April to following 5 April;[1]

[12.07] Miscellaneous income

(2) losses suffered in respect of a trade may be set off against general income of that and the next year but then only against later profits of the same trade; losses under Chapter 8 may only be set off against other Chapter 8 income but can be rolled forward against all such income of later years;[2]

(3) the trading income of a charity is exempt from tax if certain conditions are met; a charity is not exempt from tax on miscellaneous income, except in very restricted circumstances[3] or the total assessable income is within the de minimis exemption.[4]

(4) miscellaneous income does not form part of net relevant earnings for the purpose of computing a pension contribution.[5]

(5) trading profits are generally computed on an earnings basis. It would appear from case law,[6] that amounts taxable as miscellaneous income are computed on a cash basis; however, Revenue practice is to accept a calculation under the earnings basis for a sum chargeable under ITA 2007, s 755 (transactions in land).[7]

The contrast may be illustrated by the plight of the owners of stately homes who open their homes to visitors. If this is done on a commercial basis, liability arises as trading income; if not then under Chapter 8. Under the latter, the only costs allowable will be those involved in showing the house, such as those on the wages of guides, additional cleaning, advertising and the purchase of souvenirs; if however the matter comes within the scope of a trade, one will be able to deduct these items and the costs of upkeep of the building and its gardens, the wages of caretakers, gardeners, heating, lighting and insurance. Allowances may also be claimed for expenditure on car parks, and plumbing, refreshment rooms and access roads. In practice it is difficult to bring oneself within a trade without heavy capital expenditure; yet it is only if one is sure to be within the scope of a trade that one can (perhaps) afford the expenditure.

Simon's Taxes B8.620, 621.

---

[1] ITTOIA 2005, ss 198(1) and 688(1).
[2] ITA 2007, s 152(2) (see supra, § 6.31).
[3] ITA 2007, ss 527(2)(e) & 536(3) and infra, § 13.22.
[4] ITA 2007, s 528. See infra, § 13.25.
[5] TA 1988, ss 619(2) and 640(1)(b).
[6] *Pearn v Miller* (1927) 11 TC 610 at 614; *Grey v Tiley* (1932) 16 TC 414.
[7] See infra, § 23.25. As the statutory requirement to produce accounts on an earnings basis has arisen since the cases mentioned above and, also, in the intervening periods there has been a greatly increased judicial acceptance of accounting standards, it is likely that these cases could be distinguished and an assessment in respect of such miscellaneous income on an earnings basis would now be upheld by the courts.

Casual authorship

[12.08] In *Hobbs v Hussey*[1] the taxpayer, a solicitor's clerk who had not carried on the profession of author, agreed to write his memoirs and to assign the copyright in return for payment and was held taxable on the proceeds under what is now Chapter 8.

In *Earl Haig's Trustees v IRC*,[2] however, trustees who held the copyright in certain diaries and who allowed an author to use the materials in those diaries "so far as the public interest permitted" in return for a half share in the profits of the book, were held not taxable. The Court of Session there held that the sums were capital payments in return for the partial realisation of assets and so escaped income tax and not, as the Special Commissioner had held, remuneration for the use of and access to the diaries by the author, and so taxable under what is now Chapter 8 as being income derived from property. The question is whether the transaction is really a sale of property or the performance of services. A transaction may be one for the performance of services even though it may involve some subsidiary sale of property, eg dentures supplied by a dentist.[3] Hence in *Hobbs v Hussey* the payments were held to be income even though as part of the contract the taxpayer transferred his copyright in the articles. So also, in *Alloway v Phillips*[4] where memoirs were ghosted, the fact that she promised not to write for any other publisher was not sufficient to take the matter out of what is now Chapter 8 as this restriction was simply an adjunct of the main contract.

It has not been easy for taxpayers to place themselves on the *Haig* side of the line, which is of course inherently vague. Thus when in *Housden v Marshall*[5] a jockey agreed to make available to a reporter his reminiscences and supporting documents together with the right to use a facsimile of his signature, payments to the jockey were held taxable. The situation is complicated by two further factors. First, the test of what is income as opposed to capital seems to be different under what is now Chapter 8 from that prevailing in respect of the receipts of professional authors where sums received for the sale of copyright have been held to be income receipts.[6] Second, the Solicitor-General commented in *Hobbs v Hussey*[7] that he was not to be taken as admitting that the *Haig* case was rightly decided. However, it would appear to follow from the present authorities that had Hobbs and Marshall written their reminiscences first and then allowed them to be published, sums received in return for the sale would have escaped tax under what is now Chapter 8. What was fatal to their case was that under the contract they agreed to perform services, in the one case to write his memoirs and in the other to supply information.

Simon's Taxes B8.606, 612.

[1] [1942] 1 All ER 445, 24 TC 153.
[2] (1939) 22 TC 725.
[3] See Lawrence J in *Hobbs v Hussey* [1942] 1 All ER 445 at 446, 156. For the converse case where the court disregarded a trifling service, see *Bradbury v Arnold* (1957) 37 TC 665 and the *Earl Haig case* (1939) 22 TC 725.
[4] [1980] STC 490, [1980] 3 All ER 138.
[5] [1958] 3 All ER 639, 38 TC 233, where Harman J reversed the Special Commissioners.

[12.08] Miscellaneous income

[6]   *Howson v Monsell* [1950] 2 All ER 1239, 31 TC 529 (Schedule D, Case II). Cf *Beare v Carter* [1940] 2 KB 187, 23 TC 353 (Schedule D, Case VI).
[7]   [1942] 1 KB 491 at 495, 24 TC 153 at 155.

Introduction fees

[12.09] One who introduces a potential purchaser to a vendor may expect some appreciation in pecuniary form. If the introducer has a right to sue for these sums he will be taxable on them as miscellaneous income (unless the activity amounts to a trade, when it is taxed as trading income). If, however, he has no right to sue then it was held in *Dickinson v Abel*[1] the sums escape tax just like any other gifts, the law not concerning itself with the motive of a donor.

On the other hand in *Brocklesby v Merricks*[2] the taxpayer, an architect, met at a social occasion a landowner who expressed interest in selling his land. Later the taxpayer arranged a meeting between the landowner and a developer who then arranged to buy the land. The taxpayer then agreed with the developer to endeavour to dispose of the land and to assist in negotiations in return for one fourth of the net profit of the sale. The Court of Appeal held that the taxpayer was chargeable under what is now ITTOIA 2005, Chapter 8 on the share of the profit received.

The agreement to act in the negotiation for resale was fatal to the taxpayer's case. Yet had he been content with a cash payment from the developer for the introduction to the landowner he might well have escaped tax. Further, as *Scott v Ricketts*[3] suggests, if he had been offered a sum for the introduction and then commuted it into a share of the profits after the developer had bought the land, and had he taken this share of profits as his introduction fee rather than for his work on the negotiations on the resale, he would presumably have escaped tax.

[1]   [1969] 1 All ER 484, 45 TC 353.
[2]   (1934) 18 TC 576. The possibility of a charge under Schedule D, Case II was reserved by the Crown. Experience would suggest that the use of remuneration for an agent to sell a property is likely to be in the range of 1% to 3%. The approach of the court was almost certainly coloured by the fact that the commission agreed was 25% of the profit. See also *Bloom v Kinder* (1958) 38 TC 77.
[3]   (1967) 44 TC 303, CA.

Miscellaneous sources

[12.10] Commission payments received by a director for guaranteeing the company's bank overdraft have been held taxable under what is now Chapter 8 because they were received by virtue of services which had been rendered.[1] The same result followed when a solicitor guaranteed an overdraft of a third party for the commission was earned by the pledging of credit.[2] In each case there was a contractual right to the payment. Whether such sums should be taxed as trading or miscellaneous income is one of fact. Such receipts are held taxable and are not treated as capital payments because the source from which the income flows is not the service but the individual's efforts and those efforts are capable of recurring.[3]

There is some doubt whether the income of a prostitute is taxable as trading income or as miscellaneous income. It has been reported that prostitutes have accepted a Revenue assessment under what is now miscellaneous income and the running of a brothel has been a subject of a charge as trading income. The activities of a single prostitute would appear to be most appropriately charged as income assessable under ITTOIA Part 2 as being income from a profession or, perhaps, from a vocation. However, an assessment of such profits as trading income has been upheld by the Court of Appeal.[4]

Simon's Taxes B8.606.

[1] *Ryall v Hoare* [1923] 2 KB 447, 8 TC 521. See 1977 Can. Tax Jo. 26.
[2] *Sherwin v Barnes* (1931) 16 TC 278; but cf *Trenchard v Bennet* (1933) 17 TC 420 where in reality shares received were not for the guarantee but in order to gain control of a company—a capital asset—and so were not taxable.
[3] *Whyte v Clancy* [1936] 2 All ER 735, 20 TC 679.
[4] *IRC v Aken* [1990] STC 497, CA.

The analogy of income from property

[12.11] Schedule D in addition to taxing the annual profits of a trade or a profession or vocation also taxed "the annual profits or gains arising or accruing . . . from any kind of property whatever".[1] Although the cases under the former Case VI have not always been decided expressly on this analogy, it would appear that many of the cases can be so rationalised and indeed that much of the talk of a "source" is an implicit recognition of the analogy. Thus stud fees received for the services of a stallion[2] could be caught on this analogy. Sums derived from the sale of a right to nominate a particular dam for whom the stallion should stand are taxed, the analogy of the sale of property being specifically rejected.[3] Again sums received for the use as distinct from the disposal of information,[4] or for the display of property such as Earl Haig's diaries[5] or the pledging of one's credit[6] or leasing a horse[7] could all fall intelligibly within this analogy, which has the further advantage of focusing attention on the sums earned by the property which would be income as distinct from the sums received on the disposal of the property which would be capital.

Where the property concerned is land, income received is usually taxable as property income. In its simplified form now applicable to both corporation tax and income tax (albeit under different Acts) this will usually be so. In the old days income outside Schedule A and caught by Schedule D, Case VI included sums received for car parking or visitors' green fees at a golf club.[8]

Income which might fall within the charge to miscellaneous income when arising on dealings in commodity and financial futures and traded options was taken away by the income tax charge and put under the CGT regime by FA 1985.[9] This change does not affect income arising from dealing in assets in such a way as to give rise to liability as trading income.[10]

[12.11] Miscellaneous income

Simon's Taxes Division B8.6.

1. TA 1988, s 18(1)(a)(i).
2. As in *Earl of Derby v Bassom* (1926) 10 TC 357.
3. *Benson v Counsell* [1942] 1 All ER 435, 24 TC 178.
4. As in *Housden v Marshall* [1958] 3 All ER 639, 38 TC 233.
5. See Lord Normand in *Earl Haig's Trustees v IRC* 1939 SC 676 at 682, 22 TC 725 at 732.
6. eg *Wilson v Mannooch* [1937] 3 All ER 120, 21 TC 178.
7. eg *Norman v Evans* [1965] 1 All ER 372, 42 TC 188.
8. *Coman v Governors of the Rotunda Hospital Dublin* [1921] 1 AC 1, esp. at 12–14, 7 TC 517, at 559, 560. See also *Forth Conservancy Board v IRC* [1931] AC 540, 16 TC 103.
9. Now ITTOIA 2005, s 779 (income tax), TA 1988, s 128 (corporation tax).
10. ITTOIA 2005, s 779(1) (income tax); TA 1988, s 128(1) (corporation tax).

Foreign questions

[12.12] In accordance with the general principles of the tax system, gains accruing to those not resident and which would be taxable as miscellaneous income are so taxable where the source is in the UK.[1] It is of considerable practical importance when considering a gain made on the sale of land. If a non-resident sells land outright to a developer, a capital gain arises but no charge to UK tax, as a non-resident is (generally) outside the charge to UK capital gains tax.[2] If, on the other hand, the non-resident contracts with the developer to receive a sum that is computed by reference to the developer's profits, the gain enjoyed by the non-resident may well fall within the charge under ITA 2007, s 755 (transactions in land) and, hence, be subject to income tax.

In *Alloway v Phillips*[3] a person resident in Canada who agreed to provide information in Canada about her life as the wife of one of the Great Train Robbers was held taxable under what is now Chapter 8 because the contract was made, was enforceable, and provided for payment in England by a person resident in England.

Where the source is outside the UK but the income arises in favour of a UK resident the charge presumably arose under Case IV or V rather than under Case VI.[4] Any other conclusion would remove the remittance basis[5] from any income within what was Case VI while leaving it intact for income within other Cases. This approach has been adopted in ITTOIA 2005. Whilst ITTOIA 2005, s 688 prima facie taxes miscellaneous income on an arising basis, ITTOIA 2005, s 830(2)(o) allows such income from a foreign source to be treated as "relevant foreign income". This, in turn, ensures that the remittance basis is available in respect of such income.[6]

Prior to ITTOIA, offshore income gains were assessable to income tax under Schedule D, Case VI. A Case VI charge remains for corporation tax; for income tax, such gains are now subject to a freestanding charge to tax (see infra, § **35.45**).

1 As in *Curtis-Brown Ltd v Jarvis* (1929) 14 TC 744.
2 TCGA 1992, s 10(1); infra, §§ **23.25–23.33**.
3 [1980] STC 490, [1980] 3 All ER 138.
4 *Colquhoun v Brooks* (1889) 14 App Cas 493, 2 TC 490, HL (see infra, § **35.02**) and note *Lilley v Harrison* (1951) 33 TC 344, CA.
5 TA 1988, s 65(4) (see infra, § **35.15**).
6 ITTOIA 2005, s 831.

Computation

[12.13] When assessing receipts under Chapter 8, the assessment is after deducting associated payments.[1]

When furnished letting income was assessable under Case VI, the approach taken by the Revenue was to assess on the purely cash basis. Hence, an expense paid in the fiscal year in which there was no income received was not relievable.[2] This approach arose from the unsatisfactory case of *Grey v Tiley*[3] where the Court felt bound by *Leigh v IRC*[4] and counsel for the Crown conceded that the taxpayer could not be taxed for the year when money becomes due but only when it was received. The Revenue approach has now changed and the Revenue accept that it is appropriate to adopt the normal accounting principle of matching income and expenditure. There is, thus, no prohibition on deducting expenditure on an accruals basis. In practice, the Revenue accepted income being recognised when it arises and not when it is received.

All tax charged as miscellaneous income is taxed on a current year basis. Apportionment of income is on the basis of days not months.[5] Any loss under a transaction[6] treated as miscellaneous income may be set off against income from any other transaction treated as miscellaneous income of that or any later year,[7] subject however to express statutory direction as in transactions involving house premiums.[8] Miscellaneous income losses may not be set off against income under another heading of the same year.

Simon's Taxes, Division D9.1, E1.1131.

1 *Curtis-Brown Ltd v Jarvis* (1929) 14 TC 744.
2 This was the personal experience of the author in the mid 1970s. Some 10 years later, however, the relevant Inland Revenue headquarters technical specialist stated in conversation with the author that the district involved had acted incorrectly. Nevertheless, until the creation of a concept of profits of "Schedule A business" by FA 1995, s 39, the norm was to report income from furnished lettings on a cash basis.
3 (1932) 16 TC 414.
4 [1928] 1 KB 73, 11 TC 590 (Case IV).
5 TA 1988, s 72(2) as amended by FA 1995, s 121 (corporation tax). There would now appear to be no equivalent provision for the computation of miscellaneous income subject to income tax.

[12.13] Miscellaneous income

⁶ On meaning of transaction, see *Barron v Littman* [1951] 2 All ER 393, 33 TC 373.
⁷ ITA 2007, s 152(3).
⁸ ITA 2007, s 152.

Certificates of deposit

[12.14] The tax treatment of the profit arising from a certificate of deposit (CD) is an example of the statutory use of the former Schedule D, Case VI to catch certain profits which fall through the tax net. Under general tax law any profit from the sale of a certificate was exempt from CGT[1] while no income tax charge could arise unless the holder was a dealer and so liable in respect of trading profits. There was no liability under Schedule D, Case III since the gain was not in the nature of interest and the profit on a discount was charged to the person holding the certificate on maturity.[2] Statute therefore intervened and provided that the profit should be charged under what was (and remains for corporation tax) Schedule D, Case VI.[3] The effect is that all profit will be charged to tax whether it be interest, capital gain on disposal or on maturity. Interest on CDs of £50,000 or more may be paid without deduction of tax at source.[4]

This is now supplemented where there is an arrangement under which there is a right to receive an amount (with or without interest) in pursuance of a deposit of money. When the right comes into existence there is no certificate of deposit in respect of that right but the person for the time being entitled to the right is entitled to call for a certificate of deposit.[5] This is presented as a kindness to enable paperless CDs to be treated the same way as paper ones to the benefit of the Central Moneymarket Office of the Bank of England.[6]
Simon's Direct Tax Service D9.1104.

[1] By TCGA 1992, s 251.
[2] Supra, §§ **11.14–11.15**.
[3] ITTOIA 2005, s 551 (income tax); TA 1988, s 56 (corporation tax); "certificate of deposit" receives a wide definition—TA 1988, s 56(5).
[4] TA 1988, s 710(3)(*da*) added by F(No 2)A 1992, Sch 8, para 5.
[5] ITTOIA 2005, s 552(1)(*c*) (income tax); TA 1988, s 56A (corporation tax); originally added by F(No 2)A 1992, Sch 8.
[6] Inland Revenue press release, 10 March 1992, *Simon's Tax Intelligence* 1992, p 322.

Pre-owned assets

[12.15] From 2005–06 onwards, a new type of income tax charge is levied[1] on an individual where there is continuing enjoyment of an asset that was previously owned by the individual, but is no longer in that individual's ownership.

The rationale behind the new charge was given at the time of the 2004 Budget as[2]:

The Government is aware that various schemes designed to avoid inheritance tax have been marketed in recent years. These use artificial structures to avoid the existing rules and gifts made with reservation. As a result, people have been removing assets from their taxable estates but continue to enjoy all the benefits of ownership. The Government is determined to block this sort of avoidance and announced in the Pre-Budget Report that people who benefit from these sorts of schemes would be subject to an income tax charge from April 2005, to reflect their additional taxable capacity from receiving these benefits at low or no cost.

Subsequently, the Secretary to the Treasury, Dawn Primarolo, said in the 2004 Finance Bill debate:[3]

> Provision implements one aspect of the anti-avoidance measures that we announced in the Pre-Budget Report last year, directed at avoidance involving the contrived use of trusts. We are concerned specifically with the range of schemes that allow wealthy taxpayers to give their assets away, or achieve the appearance of doing so, and so benefit from the inheritance tax exemption for life-time gifts, while in reality retaining continuing enjoyment of and access to those assets, much as before . . .. The schedule provides for an either/or situation. It will either allow the inheritance tax rules to operate as they should without the contrived schemes, or if the scheme is used and the taxpayer does not want to unwind that scheme—or simply elects for it to disapply, which the schedule provides for—an assessment will be made each year when they have benefited from use of an unearned asset that comes into taxable capacity, in exactly the same way as the benefiting kind legislation operates.

This is probably the first time that a charge to tax has been created solely to fill gaps in the charge of a totally unrelated tax. It is, however, a mistake to analyse the income tax charge on pre-owned assets simply by reference to inheritance tax matters. FA 2004, Sch 15 enacts a freestanding income tax charge. The income tax charge arises where the provisions of the schedule are satisfied, whether or not the taxpayer has entered into a form of inheritance tax avoidance scheme. There are, furthermore, IHT avoidance schemes that do not trigger a charge to income tax under the pre-owned assets regime.

In their worthwhile book "Pre-owned assets: capital tax planning in the new era", Emma Chamberlain and Chris Whitehouse say:[4]

> The starting point in evaluating the Regime technically is to realise that it is built on shaky foundations, because it involves the grafting of a mini code—the regime—onto another mini code—the reservation of benefit rules—which was itself ineptly grafted onto the basic IHT legislation.

The charge is first levied for enjoyment of property on or after 6 April 2005. The Government has, thus, termed the charge as not retrospective. However, its effect is highly retrospective, being charged by reference to property owned at any time on or after 18 March 1986,[5] which was the date from which the inheritance gift with reservation rules[6] have effect.

---

[1] By FA 2004, Sch 15.
[2] Inland Revenue press release, 17 March 2004, "Tax Treatment of Pre-Owned Assets" (REVBN40): *Simon's Weekly Tax Intelligence*, 2004, p 812.
[3] Hansard HC 18 May 2004 Cols 237 & 239.
[4] At para 1-08.

[12.15] Miscellaneous income

[5] FA 2004, para 3(2)(a).
[6] FA 1986, s 102.

Categories of asset

[12.16] The pre-owned asset regime applies to three categories of asset:

(1) land occupied by the individual, either alone or with others;[1]
(2) chattels either possessed by or used by the individual, either alone or with others;[2]
(3) intangible property in a settlement in which the settlor (or/and his spouse) has retained an interest.[3]

[1] FA 2004, Sch 15, para 3(1)(a), see infra, § **12.17**.
[2] FA 2004, Sch 15, para 6, see infra, § **12.18**.
[3] FA 2004, Sch 15, para 8(1), infra, § **12.19**.

Land

[12.17] Any interest in land can give rise to this income tax charge.[1] Hence, leases, co-ownership and licenses are clearly included.

A charge to income tax is imposed for a tax year if the taxpayer is in occupation of the land at any time during that year and either what statute terms "the disposal condition"[2] or "the contribution condition"[3] is met.

The disposal condition is met if:

(1) the taxpayer owned an interest in the land at any time on or after 18 March 1986. The disposal condition is thus satisfied, even if the interest previously held by the taxpayer was not the same as the interest that is currently held;
(2) some time on or after 18 March 1986, the taxpayer disposed of that interest or a part of it. There is no de minimis exemption, even a small disposal can trigger the charge;
(3) the disposal was not by an excluded transaction (see infra, § **12.20**).

In addition, there is a tracing process so that the sale of one property and the purchase of another with the proceeds of that sale causes the income tax charge to apply by virtue of occupation of the property into which the proceeds have been traced.[4] The explanatory notes issued by the Treasury to Finance Bill 2004 refer simply to the taxpayer having previously owned an interest in the other property which "funded" the acquisition of the land. A strict reading of the statutory provision, however, would seem to limit its application to where there has been a disposal of the whole of the property and not just an interest in it. If this strict reading is correct, then the tracing provision can, perhaps, properly be regarded as merely a replication of the "contribution condition".

The contribution condition is satisfied[5] if:

(1)   another person acquired an interest in the land now occupied by the taxpayer, and
(2)   the taxpayer directly or indirectly provided all or any of the consideration given by that other person for the acquisition, and
(3)   that provision was not by way of an excluded transaction (see infra, § **12.20**).

Thus, in a simple case where father gives daughter cash and daughter uses that cash to purchase a property in which father then lives, the income tax charge then arises on father. It is notable that this is in direct contrast to the provision for inheritance tax, where a gift of cash is not traced into a subsequent purchase of property.[6] The gift does not have to be of cash, any property gifted can be traced into this subsequent purchase of land.

If, on the facts, the money used to buy an interest in the land by another person cannot be traced back to the taxpayer who occupies, neither the disposal condition nor the contribution condition is satisfied. Thus, there is no income tax charge, even though the taxpayer's estate may have been diminished. This should be contrasted with indirect provision, which satisfies the contribution condition and leads to the income tax charge. Such indirect provision could encompass routing through a third party, but it is suggested that that third party must then be accountable to the person who makes the land purchase, or at the very least, there must be an expectation that he will pass on the gift.[7]

No definition of "occupies" is given. Presumably, it means occupation in the legal sense and, hence, staying as a guest of the occupier does not trigger the charge. Where occupation is for only part of the year, the charge is scaled pro rata.

Statute uses the term "owned", without definition. In particular, the extended definition of the word used in inheritance tax legislation is not demonstrably applied. However, case law authority[8] would suggest that the interest of a life tenant of a trust in settled property is within the definition of "owned" for this purpose. This would appear to be the Revenue view.

"Provided" is a key term in the contribution condition. Case law on the settlement code[9] equates "provided" with an element of bounty. Commonly, a transaction without an element of bounty will be within the definition of an excluded transaction (see infra, § **12.20**), however, if there is full consideration but the transaction was not of a kind that would be made between persons at arm's length, there is, it is suggested, an element of bounty and the contribution condition can be satisfied by the property being thereby "provided".

Where a charge arises by virtue of occupation of land, the taxpayer is treated as receiving taxable income equal to rent which would have been payable if the property had been let to the individual on a lease providing that the tenant undertakes to pay all taxes, rates and charges usually paid by a tenant and the landlord undertakes to bear the cost of repairs, insurance and other customary landlord expenses,[10] less the rent (if any) that the taxpayer actually pays.

Where the property is occupied on 6 April 2005, the market rent is assessed at that date and this rent, without alteration, determines the quantum of the tax charge for five years,[11] if occupation continues during that period. The market

[12.17] Miscellaneous income

rent will, thus, next be assessed on 6 April 2010. If occupation ceases at any time, the rent is re-assessed on the date of any resumption of occupation.[12]

If the property is occupied for only part of the tax year, the income tax charge is measured by reference to the period of occupation.[13] It appears that the income tax charge is always a pro rata apportionment of the rent that would be chargeable for a whole year. Thus, if mother has given son cash with which he buys a holiday home, which he lets for the six months of summer, but allows mother to occupy during the six winter months, the income tax charge would appear to be one half of the annual rent that is assessed, even though a winter let would, commercially, attract a much lower rent.

Where more than one person lives in a property, the income tax charge is on the rent that would be payable by the individual charged. Hence, if father gives son cash to fund the entire purchase by son of a property which is then occupied by father and son together, one would expect the income tax charge on father to be calculated by reference to one half of the market rent that would arise. Statute does not give any guidance as to whether the rent in such circumstances should be calculated by taking account of the fact that there is a co-occupier.[14]

---

[1] FA 2004, Sch 15, para 1 applies the definitions of "land" and "interest in land" that are stated to apply to IHTA 1984, which, in turn, applied the definition in Interpretation Act 1978, Sch 1.
[2] FA 2004, Sch 15, para 3(2).
[3] FA 2004, Sch 15, para 3(3).
[4] FA 2004, Sch 15, para 3(2)(*a*)(ii).
[5] FA 2004, Sch 15, para 3(3).
[6] FA 1986, Sch 20, para 2(2)(*b*).
[7] vide *Yuill v Wilson* [1979] STC 486 per Buckley LJ and *Potts Executors v IRC* (1950) 32 TC 211, HL.
[8] vide *R v IRC, ex p Newfields Development Ltd* [2001] STC 901 at 906.
[9] vide *IRC v Leiner* (1964) 41 TC 589, and *IRC v Plummer* [1979] STC 793, HL.
[10] FA 2004, Sch 15, paras 4 & 5.
[11] Charge to Income Tax by Reference to Enjoyment of Property Previously Owned Regulations 2005, SI 2005/724, regs 2 & 4(1), *Simon's Weekly Tax Intelligence* 2005, p 674. See also Ministerial Statement on 7 March 2005, *Simon's Weekly Tax Intelligence* 2005, p 372.
[12] Charge to Income Tax by Reference to Enjoyment of Property Previously Owned Regulations 2005, SI 2005/724, regs 2 & 4(2), *Simon's Weekly Tax Intelligence* 2005, p 674. See also Ministerial Statement on 7 March 2005, *Simon's Weekly Tax Intelligence* 2005, p 372.
[13] FA 2004, Sch 15, para 4(3), (6).
[14] What would an unconnected third party pay as rent to occupy a property on an undivided basis with an existing occupier? It may be that a lower rent is justified on the basis of arguments akin to those advanced in *Arkwright v IRC* [2004] STC (SCD) 89 and [2004] STC 1323.

Chattels

[12.18] The income tax charge on pre-owned assets applies where the taxpayer is in possession of a chattel or has use of the chattel and either the disposal condition or the contribution condition is satisfied. These conditions are effectively the same as apply for land (see supra, § **12.17**).

Where the taxpayer gives full consideration for his possession or use of a chattel, no charge arises. This is an important exclusion as the market rent for use of a chattel will often be less than the sum calculated under the formula statute imposes under the pre-owned asset regime.

Where there is a charge under the pre-owned asset regime, the quantum is calculated by valuing the chattel and applying the "prescribed rate of interest" to this value.[1]

Where a chattel is possessed by, or in the use of, a taxpayer on 6 April 2005, the market value of the chattel is assessed at that date. If the chattel continues to be possessed or used, the market value at that date is used as the measure of tax charge for five fiscal years; thus, the next valuation date is 6 April 2010.[2] Where possession or use of the chattel commences at a date after 6 April 2005 (or there is a period when it is not used and there is resumption of possession/use) the valuation date is the date on which the chattel is first possessed/used (or is brought back into possession/use).[3]

The prescribed rate of interest is the official rate of interest.[4] For 2007–08 this is 5%.

For a discussion on the valuation of chattels, and of the market rent for use of chattels, see 45.04.

---

[1] FA 2004, Sch 15, para 6.
[2] Charge to Income Tax by Reference to Enjoyment of Property Previously Owned Regulations 2005, SI 2005/724, regs 2 & 4(1), *Simon's Weekly Tax Intelligence* 2005, p 674. See also Ministerial Statement on 7 March 2005, *Simon's Weekly Tax Intelligence* 2005, p 372.
[3] Charge to Income Tax by Reference to Enjoyment of Property Previously Owned Regulations 2005, SI 2005/724, regs 2 & 4(2), *Simon's Weekly Tax Intelligence* 2005, p 674. See also Ministerial Statement on 7 March 2005, *Simon's Weekly Tax Intelligence* 2005, p 372.
[4] As defined in ITEPA 2003, s 181.

Intangible property

[12.19] Unlike the charges in respect of land and chattels, "intangible property" only gives rise to a pre-owned asset income tax charge if it is in a settlement where the settlor is deemed to have retained an interest for himself or his wife.[1] A strange definition of "intangible property" is given for this purpose,[2] as any property other than chattels or land, thus, cash and shares, if held in a settlor interest settlement are "intangible property" for the purpose of the pre-owned asset regime.

[12.19] Miscellaneous income

To fall within the charge, the settlement must be one the income of which is assessed on the taxpayer under ITTOIA 2005, s 625, except that no pre-owned asset regime charge arises where the only interest is that of the settlor's spouse.[3]

In practice, it is thought that the charge on intangible property in a settlement will arise only in a relatively few instances and probably only in relation to sophisticated tax planning exercises that have been undertaken. In a simple situation, where property has been put into a settlor interested settlement, the gift with reservation that then arises for income tax purposes[4] excludes the income tax charge under the pre-owned assets regime.[5]

The charge under the pre-owned asset regime for intangible property is the value of the property multiplied by the prescribed rate, calculated in the same way as for chattels.[6]

Where the pre-owned assets regime imposes an income tax charge in relation to intangible property in a settlement, there will already have been a charge on income actually arising in the settlement.[7] The tax payable under that provision[8] reduces the amount charged under the pre-owned assets regime. The greatest effect of the pre-owned assets regime in respect of intangible property is thus, where there is a "dry" settlement, which does not produce any income. However, where there is income, there will still be liability arising as the deduction is of the tax paid, not the amount assessable.

For this provision, the definition applied to "the settlement" is the definition for inheritance tax[9] and not that for income tax.[10]

---

[1] FA 2004, Sch 15, para 8(1)(*a*).
[2] FA 2004, Sch 15, para 1.
[3] FA 2004, Sch 15, para 8(1)(*b*).
[4] FA 1986, s 102.
[5] FA 2004, Sch 15, para 11(5)(*a*).
[6] Under ITTOIA 2005, s 624(1).
[7] FA 2004, Sch 15, para 9(1).
[8] ITTOIA 2005, s 624(1) and also any tax charged under ITTOIA 2005, ss 461–468 or ITA 2007, s 714 or TCGA 1992, s 77 or 86. Conceptually, this is bizarre. We have an income tax charge defined by reference to inheritance tax and the deemed income is reduced not only by income tax paid, but also by capital gains tax paid.
[9] FA 2004, Sch 15, para 1.
[10] ITTOIA 2005, ss 624–627 operate on the basis of the income definition of settlement. There is thus, a mismatch between the two provisions.

Excluded transactions

[12.20] If the disposal by the taxpayer of land or of chattels was by means of an excluded transaction, no charge under the pre-owned asset regime applies.[1]

A transaction is excluded if it is a disposal of the whole of the taxpayer's interest and is at arm's length with an unconnected person.[2] Hence, a normal commercial sale will be an excluded transaction.

Where the sale is made to a connected person[3] the transaction is only treated as an excluded transaction if it is one that "might be expected to be made at arm's length between persons not connected with each other".[4] This requires us to look at the transaction in its entirety with, it is suggested, any actions directly related to the transaction.

An arrangement that has been entered into to mimic that in *Ingram v IRC*[5] without falling foul of the subsequent anti-avoidance provision[6] is for a freehold encumbered by a highly onerous lease to be sold for the greatly reduced market value that applies by virtue of the onerous conditions of the lease. Typically, the sale consideration is expressed as being payable at some future distant date, or perhaps, on the death of the vendor. A transaction between unconnected persons would not be expected to have the provision that the consideration was only paid at a distant, or unforecastable, date. Hence, such a sale, although for the full market value, is not an excluded transaction. Another arrangement that has been entered into has involved property being sold to Trust 1 in return for an IOU which is then settled in Trust 2. Again, the IOU is expressed to mature at a distant date, or the death of the vendor. Such a two trust arrangement in that form is, thus, likely to trigger a charge under the pre-owned asset regime.

A gift of land or chattels is an excluded transaction if it is to a settlement in which a spouse or former spouse has an interest in possession.[7] Thus, in this one respect, the income tax pre-owned asset regime mimics the approach taken by inheritance tax in exempting inter-spouse transfers. Two further IHT exemptions are imported as excluded transactions: (a) a disposition for the maintenance of the family,[8] and (b) a gift within the annual exemption or gifts exemption.[9]

An important exclusion is given for an outright gift of money. This is an excluded transaction in relation to the contribution condition if the gift of money was made at least seven years before the taxpayer first occupied the land, or used the chattel.[10] The exclusion is strictly applied to a gift of cash, which may be a foreign currency, and does not apply for a gift of, for example, shares, even though they may have been immediately sold and converted into cash. The seven-year period is not linked to the commencement of the pre-owned asset regime. Thus, a cash gift in 1998 that is used to purchase a property in 2004 is not an excluded transaction in relation to the pre-owned asset charge that commences in 2005.

Regulations[11] exempt from the pre-owned asset regime property occupied where there has been a part disposal on arms length terms prior to 7 March 2005. This is designed to exclude for the charge equity release schemes, whether with a commercial lender or intra-family.[12]

---

1 FA 2004, Sch 15, paras 3(2)(*b*) and 6(2)(*b*).
2 FA 2004, Sch 15, para 10(1)(*a*)(i).
3 The definition of "connected persons", is that used for inheritance tax: vide IHTA 1984, s 270. It is thus, wider than the definition for income tax (TA 1988, s 839) as it includes an uncle, aunt, nephew or niece.
4 FA 2004, Sch 15, para 10(10)(*a*)(ii).
5 [1999] STC 37, HL.
6 FA 1986, s 102A inserted by FA 1999, s 104 with effect for disposals made after 8 March 1999.

[12.20] Miscellaneous income

[7] FA 2004, Sch 15, para 10(1)(*a*).
[8] IHTA 1984, s 11.
[9] IHTA 1984, s 19 and 20.
[10] FA 2004, Sch 15, para 10(2)(*c*).
[11] Charge to Income Tax by Reference to Enjoyment of Property Previously Owned Regulations 2005, SI 2005/724, reg 5, *Simon's Weekly Tax Intelligence* 2005, p 674. See also Ministerial Statement on 7 March 2005, *Simon's Weekly Tax Intelligence* 2005, p 372.
[12] Ministerial statement by Dawn Primarolo, the Paymaster General, HC, 7 March 2005, column 99S, printed in *Simon's Weekly Tax Intelligence*, 2005, pp 372–373.

Exemptions

[12.21] No income tax charge under the pre-owned asset regime arises if one of the four exemptions applies:

Exemption One: Within the taxpayer's estate for IHT purposes.

The income tax charge does not arise if the property is treated as part of the taxpayer's estate by virtue of the gift with reservation provisions.[1]

The charge will also not apply if the property is within the taxpayer's estate by virtue of it having been given back to the taxpayer, or is deemed to be within the taxpayer's estate by virtue of the taxpayer having an interest in possession in it.[2]

This exemption is also given for traced property.[3]

The IHT exemptions[4] apply to the pre-owned asset regime.[5] Hence, if there has been an unforeseen change in the circumstances of the donor such that the donor is unable to maintain himself through old age, infirmity or otherwise, and the property gifted is provided for occupation by the donor by the donee, being a relative, such provision is reasonable in all the circumstances, the pre-owned asset regime does not apply.

There is, however, no exemption from the income tax charge where property is within the taxpayer's estate as it is part of the trust fund in which the taxpayer has the interest in possession, but no IHT will be charged as the terms of the trust are that the property reverts to the settlor at the taxpayer's death (see infra, § **12.23**).

[1] FA 2004, Sch 15, para 11(5).
[2] FA 2004, Sch 15, para 11(1).
[3] FA 2004, Sch 15, para 11(4).
[4] Ie those given in FA 1986, Sch 20, para 6(1)(*b*).
[5] FA 2004, Sch 15, para 11(5)(*d*).

Exemption Two: Co-occupation.

Where a gift of a part share has been made to a co-occupier and the property is then occupied by its co-owners, no charge under the pre-owned asset regime applies.[1]

This exemption is linked with the IHT exemption[2] where there is no reservation of benefit if the following conditions are satisfied:

(1) the donor has made the gift of the undivided share in an interest on or after 9 March 1999;
(2) the donor and the donee occupy the land; *and*
(3) the donor does not receive any benefit other than a negligible benefit provided by or at the expense of the donee for some reason connected with the gift.

This is an important exemption. The statutory provision for inheritance tax came into effect in 1999 and was an enactment of the Revenue practice stated in the House of Commons by Peter Brook, Secretary to the Treasury, on 10 June 1986.[3] Where the gift to create co-owning occupiers was made prior to 9 March 1999, the pre-owned asset regime charge is excluded if the gift was within the terms of the ministerial statement which, broadly, follow those in the subsequent statutory provision.

---

[1] FA 2004, Sch 15, para 11(5)(*c*)
[2] FA 1986, s 102B(4).
[3] Hansard, Treasury Standing Committee G, 10 June 1986, Col 425:

It may be that my Honourable Friend's intention concerns the common case where someone gives away an individual share in land, typically a house, which is then occupied by all the joint owners including the donor. For example, an elderly parent may make unconditional gifts of undivided shares in their house to their children and the parents and the children occupy the property as their family home, each owner bearing his or her share of the running costs. In those circumstances, the parent's occupation or enjoyment of the part of the house that they have given away is in return for similar enjoyment of the children of the other part of the property. Thus the donor's occupation is for full consideration.

Accordingly, I assure my honourable friend that the gift with reservation rules will not be applied to an unconditional gift of an undivided share in land merely because the property is occupied by all the joint owners or tenants in common, including the donor.

Exemption Three: Annual value under £5,000.

This is a de minimis exemption.

If, after aggregating all possible tax charges arising under the three arms of the pre-owned asset regime the total is £5,000 or less, no income tax liability arises.[1] If, however, the aggregation is £5,001, the charge is on the entire sum. In order to calculate whether the exemption is available, charges are aggregated *before* making any deductions for rent paid.[2] This is of considerable practical importance as it means that to avoid the income tax charge it is necessary to pay the full market rent.

---

[1] FA 2004, Sch 15, para 13(1).
[2] FA 2004, Sch 15, para 13(2). The formulation is to aggregate "the appropriate rental value as determined under para 4(2)"; the formulation for the sum in which

income tax is charged is "the appropriate rental value, less the amount of any payments"; vide para 4(1).

Exemption Four: Election for imposition of inheritance tax.

The pre-owned asset regime does not apply if the taxpayer elects that the property concerned be treated as if it were within his estate for inheritance tax purposes.[1] If the property concerned otherwise subject to pre-owned asset regime on 6 April 2005, the election must be made by 31 January 2007.[2] If circumstances are such that the pre-owned asset regime first applies to the particular property at a subsequent date, the election must be made by 31 January following the fiscal year in which the charge first arises. There is a statutory form for the election;[3] it is assumed that this will normally be made as part of the self-assessment income tax return for the year.

[1] FA 2004, Sch 15, paras 21–23.
[2] FA 2004, Sch 15, para 23(1)(3).
[3] FA 2004, Sch 15, para 23(2).

Non-domiciled taxpayer

[12.22] An individual not resident in the United Kingdom for a tax year is not subject to the pre-owned assets regime for that year.[1]

An individual resident in the United Kingdom for a fiscal year but not domiciled within the United Kingdom is subject to the pre-owned asset regime in respect of property situated within the United Kingdom, but not in respect of property situated outside the UK.[2]

In addition, a limited form of exemption from the pre-owned asset charge is given in relation to settled property treated under IHT rules as excluded property. For the purpose of IHT,[3] foreign property in a settlement where the settlor was not domiciled within the UK on the date of settlement is excluded property. Where such property is enjoyed by an individual resident in the UK, the income tax pre-owned asset regime does not apply if the individual who enjoys the property either is domiciled outside the UK or has at any time previously been domiciled outside the UK.[4] Hence, the settlor will, himself always be excluded from the income tax charge by this provision but the charge could apply to any other beneficiary such as the child of the settlor, if the child is born with a UK domicile which has never changed. This is in contrast to the IHT exemption that would be enjoyed by the child.

For the purpose of this exemption from income tax charge under the pre-owned asset regime, the inheritance tax definition of domicile is used,[5] not the income tax definition. This is a very important restriction of the exemption as it means that, after 16 years residence in the UK, the income tax charge is applied on a foreign domiciliary as if the foreign domicile had been lost.[6]

[1] FA 2004, Sch 15, para 12(1).
[2] FA 2004, Sch 15, para 12(2).

[3] IHTA 1984, s 48(3)(*a*).
[4] FA 2004, Sch 15, para 12(3).
[5] FA 2004, Sch 15, para 12(4).
[6] IHTA 1984, s 267.

Reverter to settlor trust

[12.23] Statute[1] provides that, when a person who is beneficially entitled to an interest in possession in settled property dies while the settlor is still living, and the property reverts to the settlor, its value is left out of account in determining the value of the person's estate. The value is also left out of account if the living spouse of the settlor[2] (or the civil partner) becomes beneficially entitled to the settled property; or if the settlor's UK-domiciled widow or widower (or surviving civil partner) becomes beneficially entitled to it where the settlor has died less than two years earlier. The same exemptions apply where the interest in possession comes to an end during the life of the person beneficially entitled to it.[3]

Prior to 2006, the reverter to trust regime could be used to side-step both IHT and the pre-owned asset income tax charge. For example:[4]

(a) B owns an asset, say a house, which he wants to carry on using. B gives it to S, who would otherwise inherit on B's death;
(b) S then settles an interest in possession in the house back on B for life, with the condition that it reverts to S on B's death;
(c) for IHT purposes, B is therefore treated as owning the house.[5]

Thus, the income tax pre-owned asset charge is excluded.[6]

However, although the house is part of B's estate for IHT purposes, there is no IHT charge on B's death by virtue of the exemption. Exemption given for property that reverts to the settlor.[7]

Before 5 December 2005, reverter to settlor trusts were thus potentially an available method of avoidance of both IHT and pre-owned assets income tax in relation to any gift where a donee had acquired an asset absolutely, including many carve-out or "Ingram" schemes (ie where a lease is retained by the donor and the freehold given away), and many reversionary lease schemes, as well as the simpler types of gift as in the above examples. It is not surprising that there has been a clampdown.

With effect from 5 December 2005,[8] the exemption from the income tax pre-owned asset charge does not apply where the property in question (or any derived property) is in the chargeable person's estate for IHT purposes by virtue of the chargeable person being beneficially entitled to an interest in possession in it.[9]

The provisions are not specifically tied to whether the reverter to settlor exception would apply on the chargeable person's death.[10] The taxpayer can elect[11] not to suffer the income tax charge but to disapply the IHT reverter to settlor exemption, so that the property is treated as part of his estate at death.

[1] IHTA 1984, s 54(1).

[12.23] Miscellaneous income

2 IHTA 1984, s 54(2).
3 IHTA 1984, s 53(3) and 53(4).
4 The example is taken from The Treasury Notes to Finance (No 2) Bill 2006, clause 80.
5 By virtue of IHTA 1984, s 49.
6 Sch 15, para 11(1).
7 IHTA 1984, s 54(1).
8 FA 2006, s 80(8). The intention to make this change was announced on 5 December 2005, and this provision applied from that date. The effect is, however, retrospective in that, like the remainder of the pre-owned asset regime, it taxes arrangements entered into at any time after 17 March 1986.
9 FA 2004, Sch 15, para 11(11) & (12)(a) inserted by FA 2006, s 80(2).
10 ITA 2007, s 11(1) states: "income tax is charged at the basic rate on the income of persons other than an individual".
11 FA 2004, Sch 15, para 22(2)(b)(iii) inserted by FA 2006, s 80(4).

13

Trusts

Introduction	PARA **13.01**
Bare trustee	PARA **13.02**
Trusts with a vulnerable beneficiary	PARA **13.04**
Taxation of the trustee	PARA **13.08**
The two trust rates	PARA **13.10**
Settlor interested trusts	PARA **13.14**
Taxation of the beneficiary	PARA **13.15**
Capital or income	PARA **13.20**
Charities	PARA **13.22**

Introduction

[13.01] A trust is a financial intermediary which causes considerable difficulty in any tax system.

The first approach is that where trustees receive income, the law might charge the trustees to income tax as agents of the beneficiary taking into account all the personal circumstances of the beneficiary, including personal allowances and any other taxable income. The UK tax system adopts this model in one situation: trustees holding assets for a person under incapacity are taxed as agent for that person.[1]

The second approach is that the tax system might treat the trust as an independent entity like a company which is fit to be taxed in its own right. If it chooses to adopt this second approach it must then select one of a number of different methods of implementing it. So it could have a severe classical system which regarded trustee and beneficiary as completely separate entities or it might seek some imputation system. If some imputation is sought, the system could give credit at the beneficiary level for the tax paid by the trustees or, perhaps, allow the trustees to deduct those parts of the trust income which become income of the beneficiary.

The general approach in the UK has been to opt for the second approach. Trustees are subjected to a two tier procedure. The first tier is that trustees are liable to basic rate tax on income arising during the administration of the trust (but lower rate in the case of savings income and the dividend ordinary rate for dividend income). The second tier, which does not apply to all trusts, is to charge what is now known as "the trust tax rate" (see infra, § **13.08**).

When the beneficiary receives income from a trust, he is given the appropriate rate of tax as a tax credit, which goes against his personal income tax liability.

In December 2003 proposals were put forward that would have moved the UK tax system away from the second approach. The proposals were not enacted,

[13.01] Trusts

except that the first approach is now adopted in a regime for trusts with a vulnerable beneficiary (infra, § **13.04**), which moves the UK tax system to the first approach for this category of trust. A second outcome of the consultation is the amelioration of the higher rates charged on trustees by excluding the first £1,000 of income from the trust rates (infra, § **13.10**).

Simon's Taxes Division C4.2.

---

[1] TMA 1970, s 72; *IRC v McIntosh* (1955) 36 TC 334.

Bare trustee

Bare trustees for minor or incapacitated person

[13.02] A trustee having the direction, control or management of property held on bare trusts for a minor is assessable and chargeable to income tax in respect of income arising from that property. The liability is calculated as if the income arose directly to the minor himself and no regard is taken of the personal circumstances of the individual trustee. It is thus possible for the trustees to claim repayment of income tax by reference to the personal allowance available to the minor.

The trustee of a minor is subject to any liability to higher rates of tax, calculated with respect to the total income of that minor.[1] Furthermore, in relation to such a charge, a trustee is answerable for all matters required to be done by the Income Tax Acts for assessment and payment of income tax on behalf of the minor.[2]

These provisions also apply equally where the beneficial owner is a person of unsound mind, a lunatic, an idiot or an insane person.[3]

Further, where the beneficial owner is a minor, his parent, guardian or, in Scotland, his tutor is liable, not only for tax levied in respect of the minor's income but also in respect of any payment arising from neglect or refusal to pay that tax.[4] He is therefore liable to pay any interest and any penalties imposed.

The above provisions can be regarded as giving statutory effect to the decision in *IRC v McIntosh*.[5] In this case, the court had to consider whether the charge to surtax was on the total income arising to the curator bonis or whether it was that sum less the curator's commission and the auditor's fee. The Court of Session held that the essential purpose of the appointment of a curator bonis to an incapax was to supersede the latter in the management of his estates: it did not divest the incapax of his estates and transfer them to the curator as a trustee. It was thus necessary to look at the position that would have arisen if the beneficial owner had been capax. On this footing, the expenses of the trustee were held not be deductible.

---

[1] TMA 1970, s 72(1).

[2] TMA 1970, s 72(2).
[3] TMA 1970, s 118(1).
[4] TMA 1970, s 73.
[5] (1955) 36 TC 334.

Nominee or bare trustee for an adult for a person sui juris

[13.03] Where the beneficial owner of the property that gives rise to the income is sui juris, the provisions of TMA 1970, s 72 have no application. The general rule is that the nominee is ignored and the income taxed on the beneficial owner.

In *Corbett v IRC*[1] Sir Wilfred Greene stated:

> where trustees are in receipt of income which is their duty to pay over to beneficiaries, either with or without deduction of something for trustees' expenses on the way, that income is at its very inception the beneficiaries' income.

This does not, however, necessarily preclude an assessment to income tax on the nominee. Income tax in respect of property income can be charged not only on the persons entitled to rental income but also on the persons receiving it.[2] There is an equivalent provision in respect of trading and savings income.[3]

In practice, the Revenue assess the beneficial owner of income, rather than his nominee. It is suggested that, if an assessment were raised on a bare trustee of a person sui juris, the tax charge would be limited to basic rate only, as statute[4] applies the higher rate of tax to the total income of an individual. A bare trustee is not an individual. This is in contrast to the situation of a bare trustee of a minor, where there is a specific charging provision[5] applying higher rate tax where appropriate.

[1] (1938) 21 TC 449, CA at 460.
[2] ITTOIA 2005, s 271.
[3] ITTOIA 2005, ss 8.
[4] ITA 2007, s 10 (ITA 2007, s 11(1) states: "income tax is charged at the basic rate on the income of persons other than individuals").
[5] TMA 1970, s 72(1).

Trusts with a vulnerable beneficiary

[13.04] Statute[1] provides a special tax regime for a trust with a vulnerable beneficiary that satisfies the statutory requirements.[2] The provisions only apply where there is an election.[3] The election can be retrospective, and apply from a date specified by the trustees and beneficiaries jointly.[4] The date does not have to be at the start of a tax year. The election can be made at any time up to 31 January in the two years after the tax year in which the date falls, thus, an election for the special regime to apply from 6 April 2004 can be made at any time up to 31 January 2007.

[13.04] Trusts

This regime is introduced in recognition that the rate applicable to trusts and the dividend trust rate has an adverse effect on trusts with vulnerable beneficiaries, particularly trusts for disabled people and for children who have lost a parent.[5]

Where the election is made, the income tax liability of the trustees is calculated by reference to the circumstances of vulnerable beneficiary. That is, the tax payable equates to the tax that would have been payable by the beneficiary had he received the income directly. The trustees can take account of the vulnerable beneficiary's personal allowances, his starting rate band and his basic rate income tax band.[6] For income tax, the treatment is applied whether or not the trustees are resident in the UK.

The regime applies irrespective of whether or not payment of the income is actually made to the vulnerable beneficiary. Thus, if permitted under the trust deed, income can be accumulated without this attracting the higher rates of tax

---

[1] FA 2005, ss 23–45.
[2] The requirements to be fulfilled for the trust: FA 2005, s 24; the requirements to be fulfilled for the beneficiary: FA 2005, ss 34–35.
[3] FA 2005, s 37.
[4] FA 2005, s 37(2)(b).
[5] Finance Bill 2005 Treasury Note clauses 39–61 para 120.
[6] The calculation is given in FA 2005, s 26 in terms of relief being applied to the trustee's income tax liability to reduce it to the liability that would arise if the income received directly by the vulnerable beneficiary.

Trust for a disabled person

[13.05] An election for a trust to be treated within these provisions can be made where the trust terms provide that throughout the lifetime of the disabled person, or sooner, when the trust terminates, any property held in the trust cannot be advanced other than for the benefit of the disabled person and no income arising in the trust can be applied for the benefit of any person other than the disabled person.[1]

A beneficiary is treated as a disabled person for the purpose of this regime[2] if, either (a) he/she by reason of mental disorder[3] is incapable of administering his/her property or managing his/her affairs, or (b) he/she receives either attendance allowance or disability living allowance.[4]

---

[1] FA 2005, s 34.
[2] FA 2005, s 38.
[3] Within the meaning of Mental Health Act 1983.
[4] In order to qualify, either allowance must be paid at either the highest or middle rate.

Trust for a minor

[13.06] Where a trust has as its beneficiary a person under age 18 one of whose parents has died, an election can be made for income arising to be taxed in accordance with this regime.[1]

In order to be eligible for treatment under this regime, the trust must be established either under the rules of intestacy,[2] or under the will of a deceased parent[3] or under the Criminal Injuries Compensation Scheme.[4]

The terms of the trust must provide that property is held in trust until the beneficiary attains age 18 and when the beneficiary is below that age no capital advancement nor payment of income can be made to any other person.[5]

[1] FA 2005, s 39.
[2] FA 2005, s 39(1)(a): a trust arising under Administration of Estates Act 1925, ss 46 and 47(1).
[3] FA 2005, s 35(2)(a). This includes the possibility of a trust arising under a deed of variation.
[4] FA 2005 s 35(2)(b), being an arrangement under the Criminal Injuries Compensation Act 1995, or an arrangement prior to that date (for Northern Ireland under Criminal and Injuries (Northern Ireland) Order 2002, SI 2002/796.
[5] FA 2005, s 35(3).

Election for the application of the regime

[13.07] The election must be made on a statutory form[1] and be made by the trustees and the vulnerable beneficiary jointly.[2] The election is irrevocable.[3]

[1] FA 2005, s 37(2).
[2] FA 2005, s 37(1).
[3] FA 2005, s 37(4).

Taxation of the trustee

[13.08] The basis for the liability of the trustee to income tax under the UK system must be sought both in the present legislation and in history. Income tax in respect of most forms of income is charged on the person receiving or entitled to the profits so charged;[1] that in respect of unauthorised unit trusts is charged on the person receiving the income in respect of which it is charged.[2], The charge in respect of UK dividend income is on the person who is entitled to or receiving the distribution.[3] Trustees come within each of these rules even though they are not entitled to the income beneficially; they are entitled to the income in that they can sue for it and they may be said to receive it. Moreover this approach of taxing the person in receipt is fully consistent with the original notion of income tax as a flat rate tax largely deducted at source.

The present rate structure is more complicated because of the decision to have three types of income each with their own rates.[4] Trusts have two sets of rates

[13.08] Trusts

depending on the type of trust concerned. For trusts not subject to the "trust rates"[5] the relevant rates are the *basic rate* of 22%, the *lower* rate of 20% for savings income qualifying for that rate and the *dividend ordinary rate* of 10% for UK dividend, and equivalent foreign, income. So rental income or trading income will be taxed at 22%, interest at 20% and UK dividends at 10%. The starting rate of 10% has no relevance to trusts and the higher rates that are charged on individuals do not apply.[6]

Trusts subject to the trust rate and the dividend trust rate are subject to tax at 321/2%[7] on UK dividend income and at 40% on all other income. Statute[8] now gives a formulation for the amount of trust income on which the two trust rates are charged.

Trustees are assessable to income tax regardless of the personal tax circumstances of the beneficiary or of themselves. They are assessable and chargeable not as agent for the beneficiary nor as trustee as such but simply because they receive income.[9] This is so even if there is only one beneficiary and he is *sui juris*.[10]

It follows that if the circumstances of the trustees (or those of them whom it is sought to tax) are such as to take them out of the charge to tax they cannot be taxed. In *Dawson v IRC*[11] there was a discretionary trust and no beneficiary was entitled to the income. The administration of the trust was carried on outside the UK and the principal beneficiaries were resident outside the UK. No income was remitted to the UK. There were three trustees only one of whom was resident in the UK. The Revenue attempted to tax the single UK resident trustee; this failed as they could not show that the trustee had sufficient control[12] over the income for it to be said that the income had accrued to him. This decision rejected an established Revenue practice and is now reversed by legislation.[13]

In calculating the total income of the trustees and so of their personal tax liability, the trust income is not added to their personal incomes; conversely their personal incomes are ignored in computing their liability as trustees.

The trust may not claim any personal reliefs of the trustees; nor, since it is not an "individual",[14] may it claim any personal reliefs for itself. On the other hand it may be entitled to various reliefs which are available to "persons", such as loss relief or deductions on account of interest.

Simon's Taxes C4.201.

---

[1] ITTOIA 2005, ss 8, 230, 245, 271, 332, 338, 348, 352, 360, 371, 404(1), 425, 554, 573, 581, 611, 616, 605, 609.
[2] ITTOIA 2005, s 549.
[3] ITTOIA 2005, s 385.
[4] TA 2007, s 3, 4, 6, 10, 11, 20, 23, 21, 17, 12, 13, 14, 18, 19, 7, 8. These rates are charged on income received, whether or not by an individual and hence, these rates apply to trustees unless displaced by the rate specified in TA 1988, s 686(1A)(*b*).
[5] ITA 2007, s 9 introduces the terms "trust rates" and "dividend trust rates". These replace the term "rate for trusts" that we have known, but not loved, in TA 1988, s 686.
[6] ITA 2007, s 11. Exceptionally, the dividend trust rate of 321/2% is applied for certain types of receipt, even where the trust is not normally subject to "the trust

rates". Receipts to which the dividend trust rate is applied are specified in ITA 2007, s 482, being:

Type 1 A payment made by a company on the redemption, repayment or purchase of shares in the company or on the purchase of rights to acquire such shares. (The charge is on the receipt less the subscription price.)

Type 2 Accrued income profits taxed by ITA 2007, s 628(5) or 630(2).

Type 3 Offshore income gains taxed by TA 1988, s 761(1).

Type 4 Income tax charges relating to FA 1989, s 68(2) or 71(4) (employee share ownership trusts).

Type 5 A sum to which ITTOITA 2005, ss 276–307 (which provides for certain amounts to be treated as receipts of a property business) applies.

Type 6 A profit in relation to which the trustees are liable for income tax under ITTOIA 2005, s 429 (profits from deeply discounted securities).

Type 7 A gain in relation to which the trustees are liable for income tax under ITTOIA 2005, s 467 (gains from contracts for life insurance etc) other than a gain to which subsection (7) of that section applies.

Type 8 A profit or gain in relation to which the trustees are liable for income tax under ITTOIA 2005, s 554 (transactions in deposits).

Type 9 A profit or gain (a) in relation to which the trustees are liable for income tax under ITTOIA 2005, s 557 (disposals of futures and options) and (b) which does not meet any of conditions A to C in ITTOIA 2005, s 568.

Type 10 Proceeds in relation to which the trustees are liable for income tax under ITTOIA 2005, s 573 (sales of foreign dividend coupons).

Type 11 Income treated as arising to the trustees under ITA 2007, ss 752–772 (tax avoidance: transactions in land).

[7] The rates of 321/2% and 40% apply from 6 April 2004; previously the rates were 25% and 34%: ITA 2007, s 9.
[8] ITA 2007, ss 484(5) & (6) & 486. Steps 1 to 6: see infra, § **13.11**.
[9] Per Viscount Cave in *Williams v Singer* [1921] 1 AC 65 at 71, 7 TC 387 at 411. See also *Reid's Trustees v IRC* 1929 SC 439, 14 TC 512; trustees assessable under what was Schedule D because they were receiving or entitled to the income within what is now ITTOIA 2005, s 371.
[10] *Hamilton Russell's Executors v IRC* (1943) 25 TC 200.
[11] [1989] STC 473, HL. In the Court of Appeal [1988] 3 All ER 753, [1988] STC 684 considerable emphasis was placed on the joint nature of the title and responsibility of trustees.
[12] There was a negative control in that the trustee's consent was needed before the discretions could be exercised but this was held not to be sufficient.
[13] One should note that none of the income accrued to the trustees from sources in the UK. The decision is of importance for its insistence on finding a basis for liability in the words of the taxing statutes (eg ITTOIA 2005, s 371) rather than in established practice.
[14] ITA 2007, ss 35–38 permit claims for the various types of personal allowance only by an individual. A trust is not "an individual".

Exceptions to general liability of trustees

Income accruing to beneficiary

[13.09] Since the trustee is assessable simply because income accrues to him, it follows that where income accrues not to him but directly to the beneficiary, the trustee is not assessable. By TMA 1970, s 76 a trustee who has authorised the receipt of profits by the person entitled thereto or his agent is only required to make a return of the name, address and the profits of that person. This section is concerned only with the trustee's duty to supply information with regard to the assessment *of the beneficiary*. In *Williams v Singer*[1] income from investments held in the United States was, at the direction of the trustees, who were resident in the UK, paid directly to the beneficiary who was domiciled and resident outside the UK. The beneficiary, if taxable at all, would only have been taxed on a remittance basis and since no income was remitted to this country no tax was due from her. The Revenue tried to charge tax on the trustees. The attempt failed. The trustees had not themselves received any income and were not assessable. They were not "in actual receipt and control" of the income.[2]

Simon's Taxes A1.441, C4.202, E1.487.

[1] [1921] 1 AC 65, 7 TC 387. See also *Dawson v IRC* [1988] 3 All ER 753, [1988] STC 684, CA.
[2] [1921] 1 AC 65, 7 TC 387 at 71, 411. See also *Drummond v Collins* (infra, § **13.11**).

The two 'trust rates'

First £1,000 of income

[13.10] The two trust rates (as discussed in infra, §§ **13.11** and **13.12** below) do not apply to the first £1,000 of trust income.[1] This exemption, originally set at £500, was introduced in 2005–06,[2] largely as a means of reducing the very substantial compliance cost of dealing with the trust tax returns. During the preceding consultation period, the Revenue reported that one third of all trusts dealt with by HMRC have income of less than £500 a year. Having the exemption means that trustees of trusts that are identified as consistently having small income are taken out of the routine self-assessment regime and are not required to complete an annual tax return, unless the trustees discover that income exceeds the limit for the year. The limit was increased from £500 to £1,000 for 2006–07 and subsequent years.[3]

From 6 April 2006, the exemption for each settlement is reduced,[4] when a settlor has made more than one settlement. The exemption is the higher of: (a) £1,000 divided by the total number of settlements; (b) £200.

[1] ITA 2007, s 491.
[2] FA 2005, s 14(1).

[3] FA 2004, Sch 13, para 4.
[4] ITA 2007, s 492(1) & (2).

Income in excess of £1,000

[13.11] Neither the starting rate band[1] nor the higher rate of tax applies to trustees since they are not "an individual"; income tax is therefore charged only at the basic rate (or, in the case of savings income, the lower rate)—subject to what is about to follow.[2]

Although the additional rate no longer applies to individuals, ITA 2007, s 479 provides that the trustees are liable at the special rate now known as "the trust rate" and "the dividend trust rate".[3] The latter is a rate of 32 1/2% charged on dividends[4] and the former a rate of 40% charged on all other income.[5] Deducting the basic rate, this gives a surcharge of 22 1/2% on dividends, 20% on other savings income and 18% on non-savings income. This rate applies not only to discretionary trusts but also where beneficiaries have contingent interests and Trustee Act 1925, s 31 empowers the trustees to apply income for their maintenance. It is, thus, applicable to a statutory trust during the minority of the beneficiary, an accumulation and maintenance trust prior to the right to income vesting and to a protective trust where the discretionary trust has arisen.[6]

Statute[7] applies the trust tax rate (and the dividend trust tax rate) to income received by the trustees less "allowable expenses". This change of nomenclature indicates a complete change in the structure of the tax charge. Under TA 1988, it was possible to argue that the income subject to what was then termed "the rate applicable to trusts" could only be income after trustees had made payments for their expenses, as the charge was on "income available to be accumulated or payable at the discretion of the trustees" and, income expended on expenses, whatever their nature, is not available to the trustees to do anything with. After the tax law rewrite, the charge is on a statutory formula.

"Allowable expenses" are defined[8] as: "Expenses of the trustees, properly chargeable to income, ignoring the express terms of the settlement". Excess allowable expenses can be carried forward.[9] An expense can be allocated between income and capital.[10]

A stock dividend[11] is treated as income for this purpose and this additional tax charge is levied on a stock dividend received by discretionary trustees.[12]

Now that there are so many different rates of tax applicable to different types of income, rules are needed to direct the order in which deductions are made. The order is (a) income taxed at lower rate from UK sources and the release of close company loans to participators; (b) equivalent income from overseas; (c) other savings income taxed at lower rate; and (d) other income chargeable at basic rate. Expenses are disallowed if the trustees or the beneficiary are not liable to tax.[13] Where the discretionary trust is not resident in the UK the expenses which can be relieved in this way are limited to the fraction equivalent to the proportion of the trusts' total income which is subject to UK

[13.11] Trusts

tax; for this purpose trust income which escapes UK tax by reason of the trustees being non-resident or able to use double taxation relief is not subject to UK tax.[14]

The purpose of this provision is to increase the cost of accumulation and discretionary trusts which have significant tax advantages as shelters in which income can be generated but taxed only at the rates appropriate to trustees rather than the marginal rates of the individual beneficiaries. Many small accumulation trusts for children have been set up in recent years under unit trust schemes. Paradoxically the tax bill will now often be lower if the parent is entitled to some interest under the settlement so that the income is to be treated as his.

The rate applicable to trusts does not to apply to income of an estate of a deceased person during administration;[15] however, if the personal representatives pay sums to trustees of a discretionary, etc, trust, a charge under s 686 is levied on the trustees on the sum received from the personal representative. Non-resident trustees are liable to additional rate under s 686 on UK source income, even though they may not be liable to basic rate tax on that income,[16] by virtue of the tax credit on a UK company dividend.

The tax collected by self-assessment is due on 31 January following the end of the year of assessment in which it arose.[17]

---

[1] ITA 2007, s 6.
[2] Before 1973 trusts were not entitled to earned income relief so this change can be exaggerated.
[3] See also ITA 2007, s 9.
[4] ITA 2007, s 9(b).
[5] ITA 2007, s 9(a).
[6] IRC v Berrill [1981] STC 784.
[7] ITA 2007, s 484.
[8] ITA 2007, ss 479, 480.
[9] ITA 2007, ss 479, 480.8 ITA 2007, s 484(5). The definition reflects the decision in Carver v Duncan [1985] AC 1082, [1985] STC 356, HL that life insurance premiums and fees for investment advice are not deductible despite specific authority in the trust deed for such charges to be made against income. (Quaere whether they were "expenses" anyway.)
[10] ITA 2007, s 485.
[11] See infra, § 26.18.
[12] Howell v Trippier [2004] STC 1245, CA. See also Revenue Interpretation February 2005, Simon's Weekly Tax Intelligence 2005, p 276.
[13] ITA 2007, s 486.
[14] ITA 2007, s 487(4).
[15] ITA 2007, s 463(1).
[16] IRC v Regent Trust Co Ltd [1980] STC 140; this is odd because the credit for s 686 tax against s 687 liability is not available on a literal interpretation of s 687(3)(a).
[17] TMA 1970, s 59B(4).

Effect of the rate applicable to trusts

[**13.12**] A rate of 32 1/2% is applied to UK dividend income where the trust is subject to tax at the rate applicable to trusts. This is called the *dividend trust rate*. The tax credit on dividends is at 10%.

Since 6 April 1999, a beneficiary of a discretionary trust that receives dividends has been at a significant disadvantage. A dividend paid by a UK company is treated as having a tax credit of 10%, which satisfies liability at basic rate, but this credit is not refundable and cannot be used to frank payments by the trustees to a beneficiary. The disadvantage can be illustrated as follows:

EXAMPLE

	£
Dividend declared by company	10,000
If this dividend were paid directly to a basic rate taxpayer:	
Net cash received	10,000
If the dividend is paid to trustees of a s 686 trust:	
Tax calculation by trustees: Gross equivalent £10,000 × 100/90	11,111
Tax @ 32 1/2%	3,611
Less: Tax credit on dividend	(1,111)
Tax payable	2,500
Maximum distribution that can be made to a beneficiary:	
Distribution	6,000
Accompanying tax credit (40% of gross)	4,000
Net cash receipt enjoyed by basic rate beneficiary:	
Tax due £10,000 × 22%	(2,200)
Tax Credit	4,000
Tax repayment to beneficiary	1,800
Cash received from trustees	6,000
Cash ultimately received by beneficiary	7,800

On the basis of this illustration, the beneficiary receives £2,200 less by the dividend being routed through the discretionary trust rather than paid to him directly. This is equivalent to an additional tax charge of 22%. The equivalent calculation for a higher rate taxpayer is that the additional liability is 15% of the net dividend.[1]

A possible solution to this problem, albeit partial, is for the trustees to choose not to pay income to a beneficiary but, instead, to make payments of capital. On the basis of the figures in the above illustration, the trustees have a net sum of £7,500 available. If an amount equal to this is passed to a beneficiary (whether basic rate or higher rate) by means of a capital distribution, no charge to income tax arises.[2]

In *Stevenson v Wishart*,[3] the Court of Appeal held that eight monthly payments, each of £5,000, made by trustees of a discretionary settlement to

[13.12] Trusts

Mrs Henwood in order to pay for her nursing home fees could correctly be regarded as a capital payment as the trustees had made a declaration to that effect. On the authority of this case, it would appear that well-advised trustees who make appropriate declarations can choose to make capital payments in most circumstances.[4]

---

[1] Note that a change in 2004–05 in the trust tax rate does not affect the final position for the beneficiary. If the rate is 100%, or 0%, or any figure in between, the disadvantage remains at 22%.

[2] If the trust fund at the preceding 10 year anniversary (or the sum settled, if the distribution is made during the first 10 years of the trust's life) exceeds the inheritance tax nil rate band, an IHT exit charge will be payable: See infra, § **42.41**.

[3] [1987] STC 266, CA. Fox LJ said (at 271h): 'it is, I think, necessary to bear in mind throughout that the trustees were disposing of capital under a power to appoint capital. Mrs Henwood was, it is true, an object of certain trusts of income in the settlements, but the trustees were not exercising or purporting to exercise such powers.'

[4] The decision in *Stevenson v Wishart* was followed by the Special Commissioners in *Sugden v Kent* [2001] STC (SCD) 158, where it was held that regular annual payments of £20,000 made by trustees of an offshore insurance trust created under an arrangement and under which the taxpayer was entitled to receive such sums, were correctly regarded as capital and not income as the documentation had been drawn up to give them the character of capital.

Trustees' 'allowable expenses'

[13.13] The "trust rate" and "dividend trust rate" are charged on the income received by the trustees, less the £1,000 reduction (see supra, § **13.10**) less "expenses of the trustees . . . properly chargeable to income, ignoring the expressed terms of the settlement".[1] HMRC has published an extensive note giving the Revenue view as to what constitutes expenses properly chargeable to income.[2]

In managing a trust the trustees may incur expenses in the course of exercising their duties and powers. These are to be distinguished from payments made to beneficiaries (distributions).

For an expense to be properly chargeable to income the expense must be (a) not a distribution to (or for) a beneficiary, (b) not an expense in generating income (such expenses are brought into account in measuring income to be taxed), (c) an expense of the trustees, and (d) an expense that the trustees are authorised to charge to the income fund.

In *Carver v Duncan*[3] Lord Templeman explains that there are two issues—the trust question of the incidence of trust expenditure as between income and capital; and the tax question of the deductibility of expenses for the purpose of calculating income chargeable to what is now the trust rate.

The general rule in trust law is that income "must bear all ordinary outgoings of a recurrent nature, such as rates and taxes, and interest on charges and encumbrances" while capital "must bear all costs, charges and expenses incurred for the benefit of the whole estate".

An "ordinary outgoing" is "some payment which must be made in order to secure the income of the property".[4]

The fact that something is recurrent does not necessarily mean it is of an income nature. The annual premiums in *Carver v Duncan* were "a recurrent charge but not an ordinary outgoing", and remained capital. Expenditure incurred for the benefit of the whole estate is a capital expense.

As stated in the HMRC Note, there is no suggestion in case law that there is any basis for apportioning into income and capital costs expenses that are incurred for the benefit of the whole estate. This is a trust law principle affecting both accumulation/discretionary trusts and IIP trusts. Thus, annual fees paid to a firm of investment advisers to keep under review and to advise changes in investments comprised in the trust fund are also capital, as established in *Carver v Duncan*. Such fees "are incurred for the benefit of the estate as a whole because the advice of the investment advisers will affect the future value of the capital of the trust fund and the future level of income arising from the capital".[5]

By contrast income bears the cost of "ordinary outgoings", which are payments made "in order to secure the income of the property". That is, they are not made in order to distribute the income or apply it in any way, but to "secure" it.

The general principle as stated by Lord McLaren in *Aikin v Macdonald's Trustees*[6] is: "The only kind of deduction allowed is expenditure incurred in earning the profits. There is no deduction under any circumstances allowable for expenditure incurred in managing profits which have already been earned and reduced into money".[7]

When calculating income subject to the trust tax rate, statute[8] provides that the provisions of the trust deed should be ignored when looking at expenses. Relief is given in the tax year in which the liability for the expenses incurred.[9] (This is a change of law effected by the enactment of ITA 2007.)

The HMRC Note provides the following summary:[10]

> In looking at TMEs for the purposes of taxing accumulation/discretionary trustees, it is necessary to consider—
> - whether a particular cost is an expense at all, as opposed to a distribution;
> - if so, whether it is an expense of the trustees;
> - if so, whether it is "properly chargeable to income", that is an income expenses according to general trust law principles (and ignoring what the trust deed says);
> - if so, whether it is also an expense for the purposes of Section 686(2AA);
> - if so, whether it was defrayed (ie paid) in the tax year in question.

The Revenue's view on the following specific categories of expenses is of interest:[11]

Cost of having trust accounts prepared

A part of the costs of having trust accounts prepared will be properly chargeable to income, on the basis of a just and reasonable apportionment. Such an apportionment is best made by the person who prepares the accounts.

[13.13] Trusts

Cost of preparing trust tax return

If only income is returned in one year all of the costs are allowable trust management expenses. If both income and capital gains are returned the allowable trust management expenses are those that relate to income, apportioned on a just and reasonable basis.

Cost of obtaining tax advice

Tax advice is an allowable trust management expense only where it relates to directly to the preparation of income tax returns.

Distributing income – cost of

The incidental costs of making distributions such as the cost of posting a cheque to a beneficiary are not properly chargeable to income because they are not concerned with the securing of the trust income. These costs are therefore not allowable trust management expenses.

Interest

In certain instances interest can be an allowable trust management expense, where it is paid to secure the income of the trust. For example where interest is paid on a loan taken out in order to purchase an income-bearing asset for the trust, the interest should be regarded as an expense of income.

Legal costs

Legal costs are not allowable trust management expenses, unless they relate exclusively to the IIP beneficiary.

Trustees' fees

In the Revenue's view trustees' fees are properly payable out of capital. The contrary view is that trustees' fees are annual recurrent expenses. The annual fee reflects work done on behalf of both income and capital. Thus, a proportion of the fees should be charged to income.

The principles of the decision in *Carver v Duncan* were reviewed by the High Court in *Revenue and Customs Comrs v Trustees of the Peter Clay Discretionary Trust*[12], In that case, overturning the decision of the Special Commissioners, Lindsay J held that the principles of general trust law overrode any allocation of an expense by the trustees. If an expense was incurred for the benefit of the estate as a whole it was "inescapably assigned to capital".

Lindsay J held that the same principle should apply to trustees' fees even though they were not in issue in Carver v Duncan. In his Lordship's mind, the starting point for such fees is that they should be regarded as incurred for the benefit of the whole estate, and therefore capital. For the alternative conclusion to be reached, ie that some of the fees can be regarded as deductible from income, "a heavy evidential burden" must be satisfied.

The trustees appealed to the Court of Appeal[13] arguing that his Lordship had made an error in failing to recognise that trustee's fees and remuneration were in part incurred not for the benefit of capital but for the benefit of income and that, as such, part of the burden of those fees should be charged to income. Their Lordships held that as the Special Commissioners had made no finding as to the proportion of the non-executive trustees' time spent in dealing with matters exclusively for the benefit of the income of the beneficiaries, they had erred in deciding that the nature of fixed fees was a factor precluding correct apportionment. In the absence of time records, it was unsatisfactory to say that the determination of the proportion of time devoted by the trustees for the benefit of income would be imprecise. Their Lordships stressed that it is open to the Special Commissioners to make a realistic estimate in such circumstances.

1   ITA 2007, s 484(2) & (5). Prior to ITA 2007, the sums eligible for deduction were termed "trust management expenses".
2   HMRC Press Release 2 February 2006, *Simons Weekly Tax Intelligence* 2006, pp 302–319.
3   [1985] STC 356, HL.
4   Per Lindley LJ in *Re Bennett, Jones v Bennett* (1896) 1 Ch 778 at 784 cited by Lord Templeman in *Carver v Duncan* at 364e.
5   Per Lord Templeman: *Carver v Duncan* [1985] STC 356, HL at 364c.
6   (1894) 3 TC 306.
7   At 309.
8   ITA 2007, s 484(5)(b)
9   ITA 2007, s 484(1).
10 HMRC Press Release, 2 February 2006 "Trust Management Expenses Guidance", para 4.21.
11 This is a summary of the view expressed in HMRC Guidance Note of 2 February 2006, paras 9.5 to 9.45.
12 [2007] EWHC 2661 (Ch).
13 [2008] EWCA Civ 1441.

Settlor-interested trusts

[13.14] From 6 April 2006 the trustees of a settlor-interested trust are subject to the trust rate and the dividend trust rate.[1] The calculation of the trustees' liability for any trust where the settlor retains an interest[2] is, thus, carried out in the same way as for a discretionary trust.

Income which is treated as income of the settlor for tax purposes, whether from a trust or from a settlement, will retain its character in the hands of that person. Income is chargeable[3] in the same way as would have been the case had the income arisen directly to that person. It is therefore chargeable at that person's marginal rates and carries a credit for any tax paid by trustees—this could be 10%, 20%, 22,% 32 1/2% or 40% depending on the nature of the trust and income.

1   TA 1988, s 686(2)(*b*) amended by FA 2006, Sch 13, para 2, then re-enacted in its amended form by ITA 2007, s 480(1) & (3)(*a*). The meaning of the amended and re-enacted provision is a little obscure. However, it is stated in HMRC Tax Bulletin

[13.14] Trusts

August 2006, p 1306 as: "ICTA 1988, s 686(2)(b) has been amended and from 6 April 2006 the trustees of settlor-interested trusts are no longer taken out of the charge to the special trust rates. The normal rules for accumulation and discretionary trusts will therefore apply in these cases, so that dividend income is assessable at 321/2% and all other income is assessable at the rate applicable to trusts, currently 40%. As a result boxes 13.1 to 13.6 in Question 13 of the Trust and Estate return will be removed."

[2] ITA 2007 s 479.
[3] ITTOIA 2005, s 619.

Taxation of the beneficiary

Is the beneficiary taxable?

[13.15] Where the trustees have paid the tax and administration expenses and the balance belongs to a beneficiary as income, as where he has a vested life interest in the income, that income is liable to income tax in his hands. The amount received is grossed up at basic, lower or dividend rates to take account of the tax paid by the trustees. So savings income of £80 will be grossed up at 20% to £100. If the beneficiary's rate of tax is nil he will recover £20 from the Revenue; no recovery is allowed for the 10% dividend credit. While this is clear the underlying theory is not.

Where a beneficiary is currently entitled to the income under the trust the result of the decision of the House of Lords in *Baker v Archer-Shee*[1] is that he is entitled to—and so taxable on—the income as and when it arises, whether or not he receives it from the trustee. This may have the further consequence that he will be taxable under the income heading appropriate to the income as it arises.[2] Different principles apply where there is an annuity under the trust, the annuitant in this instance being chargeable under ITTOIA 2005, s 683 although an assessment will usually be precluded—as far as basic rate is concerned—by the prior deduction of basic rate income tax by the trustees.[3] Different principles also apply where the beneficiary is entitled to an interest in the residue of an estate in the course of administration, it being well settled that *Baker v Archer-Shee* does not apply in such an instance and so special rules apply.[4]

The importance of the distinction between the liability of the trustees and that of the beneficiary is nicely shown by *Sinclair v Lee*.[5] Here an allocation of shares to a trust on a demerger gave rise to no tax liability on the trustee because of an express provision. It was only prevented from being taxable income of the income-beneficiary by being classified by the court as capital.

Simon's Taxes C4.221, 222.

[1] [1927] AC 844, 11 TC 749. For facts, see infra, § **35.12**. The facts of this case were most favourable to the Revenue's contentions. Not only was the beneficiary sole life tenant but she had also been given the power to nominate trustees and was herself

involved with the management of the fund to the extent that her consent was needed for any change of investments. The majority decision may be criticised for failing to distinguish between an active from a passive trust and it may be suggested that the decision does not apply to an active trust. See also the explanations in *Reid's Trustees v IRC* 1929 SC 439, 14 TC 512.
[2] However, in determining whether the income is earned or investment income, the question is whether it was earned by the beneficiary and not whether it was earned by the trustees, see supra, § **5.20**.
[3] Supra, § **11.36**.
[4] Infra, § **14.03**.
[5] [1993] Ch 497.

Vested rights in income

[13.16] A beneficiary is currently entitled to the trust income if the trustees are under a duty to pay the income to the beneficiary and he is then absolutely entitled to it or is entitled to have income applied for his benefit.[1] Benefits in kind are caught and questions whether the benefit is convertible into money are completely irrelevant.[2] If the beneficiary's title to the income is contingent or vested subject to being divested,[3] it is not taxable as his income.

Where a trustee receives income from investments held for a tenant for life each sum received is the income of the tenant for life as soon as it is received and regardless of the date on which it is paid over to the beneficiary. This is because the income is immediately under the beneficiary's control.[4]

The payments which a beneficiary receives under a Scottish interest in possession trust are technically annual payments assessable under ITTOIA 2005, s 683. This would not generally matter as far as the tax system was concerned but for the introduction of the lower rate of tax on dividends in 1993–94. One effect of that change on the Scottish rule would be that the beneficiaries would receive income deriving from dividends which was not technically dividend income and so would still carry a basic rate tax credit. To solve this problem, it is provided that where English law would treat the beneficiary as having an equitable right in possession the rights of the beneficiary are to be treated in the same way—despite the general Scottish position.[5] This rule does not apply if the trustees are not resident in the UK.

Where a trust is under English law, statute[6] provides that accumulation is only permitted for a maximum of 21 years, or a shorter period specified in the trust deed. After 21 years have passed, the trustees are obliged to distribute income.

[1] *Tollemache v IRC* (1926) 11 TC 277; *Miller v IRC* [1930] AC 222, 15 TC 25. For the Revenue's interpretation of a beneficiary's entitlement to income and, hence, the question as to whether the special rate for trusts is levied on that income, see Inland Revenue interpretation RI 162.
[2] *Lindus and Hortin v IRC* (1933) 17 TC 442.
[3] *Stanley v IRC* [1944] 1 All ER 230, 26 TC 12; *Brotherton v IRC* [1977] STC 73.
[4] Per Megarry J in *Spens v IRC* [1970] 3 All ER 295 at 299, 46 TC 276 at 285, citing *Hamilton Russell's Executors v IRC* (1943) 25 TC 200 at 207–8, and *Dreyfus v IRC* (1963) 41 TC 441 at 448. See also *Stern v IRC* (1930) 15 TC 148, HL.

[5] ITA 2007, s 464(1) & (2); for explanation see Inland Revenue press release, 9 July 1993, *Simon's Tax Intelligence* 1993, p 1048.
[6] Perpetuities and Accumulation Act 1964, s 13(1). This provision has its origin in the Accumulation Act 1800, commonly called the Thellusson Act, which was described by Lord Cranworth, Lord Chancellor in 1850, as "one perhaps of the most ill-drawn acts found in our statute book". Parliament passed this Act as a reaction to Mr Thellusson providing in his will for the investment of £750,000, which was to be accumulated at compound interest during the lives of his sons, grandsons and great-grandchildren living at his death, with the first distribution taking place at the death of the survivor of this class of persons. In 1988, the Law Commission published a report proposing the abolition of the statutory restriction on accumulation, other than for charitable trusts, allowing accumulation throughout the perpetuity period for a trust. It is understood that the Lord Chancellor's office has accepted this proposal but no legislation has yet been placed before Parliament. For a discussion of the history of the statutory prohibition on accumulations see Christopher Sokol "Why accumulations?" in STEP Journal February 2004, p 12.

Grossing up: trustees' income different from beneficiary's

[13.17] (a) **Expenses.** Sums received by the beneficiary are grossed up to reflect the basic or other rate tax paid by the trustees. However, this grossed up income will not necessarily be the same as the trustee's income. This is because of *Macfarlane v IRC*[1] which is authority for the rule that while trust expenses are non-deductible in computing the trustees' income,[2] such expenses are deductible in computing that of the beneficiary.

One may wonder whether this rule is correct; certainly the basis of the rule is suspect. *Macfarlane v IRC* rests on an earlier case[3] in 1926 in which the Court of Session held further that the beneficiary's income was the sum received net of tax paid by the trustees and then minus expenses, making a sum of £68 in our example. The reasoning on this point was destroyed by the decision of the House of Lords in *Baker v Archer-Shee* but on the main point was reaffirmed by *Macfarlane v IRC*.[4] The reason given for deduction was that the expenses were incurred before the beneficiary received the money and not by anyone she employed but rather by the trustees appointed by the settlor.[5] This is inconsistent with the notion that the income is the beneficiary's as soon as it is received by the trustee.[6] The anomaly may be the prohibition on allowing the trustees to deduct their expenses in computing their liabilities at basic and lower rate.[7]

(b) **Other deductions and reliefs.** There are other concerns about the difference between trust income under trust law and the beneficiary's income for tax purposes. Thus trust law knows nothing of capital allowances (or balancing charges) or relief for losses from earlier years. A trust may be able to charge depreciation or other expenses expressly prohibited for tax purposes. These do not usually cause a difference between the income of the trustee for tax purposes and the income of the beneficiary for tax purposes except for expenses; the position with regard to capital allowances is not clear.[8] One situation is particularly difficult. An enhanced stock dividend may be income or capital of the trust or may give rise to an obligation on the trustees to take the payment as capital but to compensate the life tenant for the loss of the dividend. Revenue practice is to accept the treatment decided upon by the trustees—provided it is supportable on the facts.[9]

Simon's Taxes C4.225.

[1] 1929 SC 453, 14 TC 532.
[2] Supra, § **13.02**.
[3] *Murray v IRC* (1926) 11 TC 133.
[4] Cited with approval by Lord Blanesburgh in *Baker v Archer-Shee* (1926) 11 TC 749 at 786.
[5] Per Lord Sands at 138.
[6] Cf Lord Sands in *Macfarlane v IRC* (1929) 14 TC 532 at 540.
[7] These expenses are deductible in computing the trust's liability to the applicable rate for accumulation trusts: ITA 2007, ss 484,486.
[8] See generally Venables *Comments on the Consultative Document*, App C.
[9] See Statement of Practice SP 4/94; this Statement of Practice continues in operation, despite the decision in TA 1988, s 686(1A). Thus, it would appear, the Revenue distinguish between a stock dividend provided as an alternative to a cash dividend (when the entire stock dividend attracts the higher rate) and an enhanced stock dividend (when the enhancement element does not).

No vested right in income—accumulations

[13.18] Income will only be treated as the income of a beneficiary if he has a vested and indefeasible interest in that income; his rights in capital may be different. In *Stanley v IRC*[1] the appellant had a vested life interest in certain property but the trustees had a power under Trustee Act 1925, s 31 to accumulate the income during his minority. This power was exercised until the appellant reached the age of majority, when he became entitled to the accumulated income. When the appellant reached that age, the Revenue sought to levy additional assessments to cover the years in which the income had been accumulated. Trustee Act 1925, s 31 provided that when a person died before reaching the age of majority,[2] the accumulated income was to be paid not to that person's estate, as would be the case if his title to that income was absolute, but was to be added to capital. It followed that although the infant beneficiary had a vested life interest he only had a contingent right to the income or, at best, a right that was vested subject to being divested if he failed to reach the age of majority. Since there would be no guarantee that he would reach that age and so no certainty that he would be entitled to the income it could not be said that the income was his in the years as it arose.

The case also shows that when the beneficiary under an accumulation trust reaches the age of majority, or whatever event is specified in the trust, and so becomes entitled to the accumulated income, that income cannot be taxed as his in the year of receipt because it is then a capital payment to him and not the income of that year.

[1] [1944] 1 All ER 230, 26 TC 12.
[2] 18 for settlements made and wills executed after 31 December 1969: Family Law Reform Act 1969, s 1.

[13.19] Trusts

[13.19] The tax liability of the beneficiary depends on the nature of his right in the income. First, if this interest is *vested*, he will be taxed like any other beneficiary with such an interest. The income—less trust expenses—is taxed as the beneficiary's income even though it is in fact accumulating in the hands of the trustees. Moreover the fact that he has such a right will mean that the trustees do not have to pay the special rate applicable to trusts.[1] This will occur when a contingent beneficiary reaches the age of majority since s 31 gives him a right to subsequent income even though his interest in capital remains contingent.

Second, if his interest is *contingent* as when he is still under 18 the income cannot be treated as his unless and until actually made his eg under a power.[2] It will be remembered that income which is advanced is to be grossed up at the basic and additional rates in force in the year of the payment and the resulting figure enters the beneficiary's total income.

Simon's Taxes C4.235.

[1] Because it is his income **before** it is distributed ITA 2007, ss 479, 480.
[2] *Drummond v Collins* [1915] AC 1011, 6 TC 525.

Capital or income

[13.20] Loan. These rules only apply where the receipt by the beneficiary properly falls to be treated as his income and so not where it is a capital payment. Where therefore the trustees make a loan to a beneficiary eligible for the receipt of income, the receipt cannot be treated as his income, and no tax will be due. However, where the trustees have no power to make the loan the courts have treated the payments as income.[1] Further, whether a payment is a loan or income is a question of fact.[2]

Simon's Taxes C4.203.

[1] *Esdaile v IRC* (1936) 20 TC 700; the lack of power could not be cured by agreement between the trustees and some only of the beneficiaries.
[2] *Williamson v Ough* [1936] AC 384, 20 TC 194. Cf *Peirse-Duncombe Trustees v IRC* (1940) 23 TC 199.

Capital as income

[13.21] Where trustees hold property on trust but have to pay an annuity, or other annual payment, the trustees are under a duty to deduct tax.[1] This duty survives the 1988 changes since those only apply to annual payments made by individuals.[2]

Whether the payments are to be regarded as an annuity or as a series of payments of capital depends upon the rights of the recipient and not on the source of the payments. In *Brodie's Will Trustees v IRC*[3] the annuity was charged on both income and capital so that the trustees were under a *duty* to have recourse to capital. The payments were annuities and so wholly taxable as income of the recipient. In *Lindus and Hortin v IRC*[4] the trustees had a *discretion* to have recourse to capital to make good any shortfall in the trust income, and the payments were still annuities. This principle was then applied in *Cunard's Trustees v IRC*[5] where the trustees had power to use capital to supplement the income of the tenant for life. In all these cases there was a series of recurrent payments over a substantial period of time. Where trustees have a discretion to resort to capital, the effect of exercising that discretion may be to cause the payment to fall within TA 1988, s 687, since the sum is received by the annuitant as income and was not his income before the discretion was exercised.

These cases were taken by the Revenue to justify the position that any payment out of the capital of a trust fund which is intended to be used by a beneficiary for an income purpose (eg payment of school fees) is income of the beneficiary.[6] However, this approach was rejected by the Court of Appeal in *Stevenson v Wishart*[7] who held that payments made in exercise of a power over capital[8] were not payments of income and could not be turned into income simply because it was applied to an income purpose. The decision in *Stevenson v Wishart* was followed in *Sugden v Kent*,[9] thereby giving judicial approval to a tax avoidance scheme. A similar result had earlier been reached in *Lawson v Rolfe*.[10] There a tenant for life was under the law applicable to the settlement entitled to all bonus shares issued by corporations in which the trust held shares. Issues of such shares were not infrequent and the Revenue argued that the frequency of these payments meant that they should be treated as income payments and so taxable in the hands of the beneficiary. This argument was rejected by Foster J. There was all the difference in the world between a series of payments by the trustees under the terms of the will and these distributions by companies which so far as the trust was concerned were purely fortuitous and unplanned.

Simon's Taxes C4.224, 226.

[1] *Brodie's Will Trustees v IRC* (1933) 17 TC 432.
[2] ITA 2007, ss 900, 901.
[3] (1933) 17 TC 432.
[4] (1933) 17 TC 442.
[5] [1946] 1 All ER 159, 27 TC 122.
[6] See Venables, Tax Planning Through Trusts, at **20.19**.
[7] [1987] STC 266, [1987] 2 All ER 428. See also supra, § **13.07**.
[8] This case is a strong authority as the beneficiary was also an income beneficiary and the payments were made at monthly intervals to pay for nursing home fees.
[9] [2001] STC (SCD) 158. The facts are outlined in supra, § **13.07**.
[10] [1970] 1 All ER 761, 46 TC 199.

Charities

Reliefs—general

[13.22] Income and capital gains[1] accruing to charities[2] receive privileged treatment. First, various types of income are exempt from income tax.[3] These are:

(1) rents and profits of any lands belonging to a hospital,[4] public school[5] or almshouse[6] or vested in trustees for charitable purposes so far as they are applied to charitable purposes only;[7]
(2) investment and savings income (interest, purchased life annuity payments, deeply discounted securities and distributions from unauthorised unit trusts, royalties, telecommunication rights or other annual payments) and if received by (or for) a charity or which is applicable to charitable purposes only and is so applied;[8]
(3) certain trading income[9] (see infra, § 13.23);
(4) certain lottery profits;[10]
(5) offshore income gains;[11]
(6) gift aid,[12] a term which includes what were formerly covenanted donations to charity; and
(7) trading income or income assessable under any of the provisions listed in the table in TA 1988, s 836B (or, for companies, income under Schedule D, Cases I and VI) up to a certain limit (infra, § **13.25**).
(8) receipt from a real estate investment trust[13]

This list does not exhaust the range of taxable income and so the charity is chargeable on any income it may receive, for example such that is not either interest or other annual payments. The exemption applies only where the income is actually applied for charitable purposes only; this gives the Revenue a policing role. There are also wider exemptions for certain specified public charities.[14]

Second, there are reliefs which assist or encourage the donor. Thus under the Gift Aid scheme gifts, of any amount, provide relief from income tax (see supra § **6.37**) and are treated as grossed up at 22%.[15] The relief is extended to gifts of shares, securities and land. There is also a relief from capital gains tax for a gift by an individual to a charity. The charity may recover the payer's basic rate income tax.[16] For the payer, qualifying donations are deductible in computing income for higher rates.[17]

A similar relief applies to companies, including close companies (see infra, § **25.18**). A company that is owned by a charity can make donations under gift aid to its "parent" charity up to nine months after the end of the accounting period.[18] On treatment of dividends see infra, § **26.12**.

A payroll deduction scheme is available.[19] Statute provides for the deduction in computing trading income of costs incurred in sending employees to work for charities[20] and removes the application of ITTOIA 2005, s 45 (including as applied by s 272) (income tax) and TA 1988, s 577 (corporation tax) (but not other rules such as ITTOIA 2005, s 34 and TA 1988, s 74(1)(a)) from gifts to charities.[21]

Charities [13.22]

Tax is not charged on gains made by a charity.[22] A charity also enjoys IHT exemptions: see infra, § **43.12**.

No repayment of tax credit on a dividend is available to a charity where the dividend is paid after 5 April 1999.[23]

The consequence of the removal of a reclaimable tax credit on dividends is that there is an advantage for a charity to receive interest on government stock or to receive rental income, rather than dividend income.

Simon's Taxes Divisions C1.4, C5.1.

---

[1] TCGA 1992, s 256. If the charity is incorporated and so liable to corporation tax, similar relief is provided; TA 1988, s 9(4).

[2] Defined as any body of persons or trust established for charitable purposes only. On this meaning of charitable purposes see Pettit, *Equity and the Law of Trusts* (8th edn), Chapter 14; the English law of charities is to be applied in Scotland: *IRC v City of Glasgow Police Athletic Association* [1953] 1 All ER 747, 34 TC 76. On position of contemplative orders see extra-statutory concession B10.

[3] TA 1988, s 505(1) and corporation tax TA 1988, s 9(4); on CGT see infra, § **17.05**; on IHT see infra, § **43.12**. There are also reliefs from rates under Local Government Finance Act 1988, ss 43(5), (6), 45(5), (6) for 80% relief; see also s 47(2) for concessionary 100% relief. From VAT under VATA 1994, Sch 8, Group 15 and from stamp duty; see infra, § **56.37**.

[4] See *Royal Antediluvian Order of Buffaloes v Owens* [1928] 1 KB 446, 13 TC 176.

[5] See *Girls Public Day School Trust Ltd v Ereaut* [1931] AC 12, 15 TC 529.

[6] See *Mary Clark Home Trustees v Anderson* [1904] 2 KB 645, 5 TC 48.

[7] On application for charitable purposes, see *IRC v Helen Slater Charitable Trust Ltd* [1981] STC 471, CA; the scope of that decision is however greatly restricted by the new rules outlined infra, § **13.26**.

[8] ITA 2007, s 532.

[9] Only certain trading activity is exempt from tax: see infra, § **13.23**.

[10] ITA 2007, s 530.

[11] ITA 2007, s 535.

[12] ITA 2007, ss 520 & 522.

[13] ITA 2007, s 531(2A) and TA 1998, s 505(1)(*aa*) inserted by FA 2007, Sch 17, paras 17 & 18.

[14] ITA 2007, s 530(1).

[15] It should be noted that although the FA 2008 has lowered the basic rate to 20%, in order to avoid penalising certain charities the Government has allowed charities to continue treating Gift Aid scheme gifts as grossed up at 22% for the years 2008 09 to 2010 11.

[16] ITA 2007 s 520(2) (see supra, § **6.37**; for payments by corporations, see TA 1988, s 339.

[17] ITA 2007, s 414(2)(*b*).

[18] TA 1988, s 339(7AA).

[19] ITEPA 2003, s 713.

[20] ITTOIA 2005, s 70 (income tax); TA 1988, s 86 (corporation tax).

[21] ITTOIA 2005, s 47(5)(*a*) (income tax); TA 1988, s 577(9) (corporation tax).

[22] TCGA 1992, s 256.

[23] F(No 2)A 1997, s 35(2).

Trading income of a charity

[13.23] If a charity carries on a trade, it is exempt from the tax on the profits of that trade if the profits are within the statutory de minimis exemption (see infra, § **13.25**) but, otherwise, only if the profits are applied solely for the purposes of the charity, and the trade is within the statutory definition of "trade". A "charitable trade" is either where (i) the trade is exercised in the course of the actual carrying out of a primary purpose of the charity or (ii) the work in connection with the trade is mainly carried out by beneficiaries of the charity.[1]

In considering whether money is applied for charitable purposes, the court looks to see how the money has been applied.[2] However, if a charity established for the public benefit gives all its income to the children of employees of a particular firm which is connected with the managers of the charity, this requirement is not met.[3]

Requirement (i) is that the trade is exercised in the course of the actual carrying out of a primary purpose of the charity. So if a charity runs a law surgery and one of its objects is the provision of lectures and general legal education, the profits of conferences for solicitors escape tax. Likewise, if a school or college carries on the trade of education and charges fees, or presumably an old people's home charges for its services, the trade is exercised in the course of the actual carrying out of a primary purpose of the charity. Requirement (ii) contemplates "the basket factory of a blind asylum, the blind inmates being the beneficiaries by whose work the trade of manufacturing baskets for sale mainly, is carried on".[4] However, it has been extended to a charitable association which organised a competitive music festival, the competitors being treated as the beneficiaries.[5] More obviously the profits of a school run by nuns have been held exempt, the nuns, and not just the pupils, being regarded as the beneficiaries.[6] But it does not follow that ordinary school masters are beneficiaries.[7]

It is possible for a single trade to be carried out, in part, to perform the primary purpose of the charity and, in part, otherwise. Statute[8] requires the receipts and expenses of such a trade to be apportioned so that relief is only given for the part that relates to performance of the primary purpose of the charity. Where the exemption is not obtained by reference to the primary purpose but by reference to the trade being carried out by beneficiaries of the charity, a similar apportionment is required if the trade is carried out partly by beneficiaries of the charity and partly by others.

Simon's Taxes C5.122, 123.

---

[1] ITA 2007, s 525. Introduced by FA 1920, s 30(1)(c) to reverse *Coman v Governors of the Rotunda Hospital* [1921] 1 AC 1.
[2] Per Buckley J in *Campbell v IRC* (1966) 45 TC 427 at 443, 444.
[3] *IRC v Educational Grants Association* [1967] 2 All ER 893, 44 TC 93.
[4] Per Lord Clyde in *IRC v Glasgow Musical Festival Association* (1926) 11 TC 154 at 163.
[5] Per Lord Clyde in *IRC v Glasgow Musical Festival Association* (1926) 11 TC 154 at 163.

⁶ *Brighton Convent of the Blessed Sacrament v IRC* (1933) 18 TC 76.
⁷ Per Lord Buckmaster in *Brighton College v Marriott* [1926] AC 192 at 203, 10 TC 213 at 234.
⁸ ITA 2007, s 525(4).

[13.24] It will be seen that commercially orientated trading such as the sale of Christmas cards or the organisation of the sales of gifts give rise to taxable, not exempt profits, such sales not being integral parts of the charity's purposes. However, by concession the profits from bazaars or jumble sales run by voluntary organisations were not generally charged to tax.¹ A result similar to complete exemption of trading income from income tax can be achieved by the device of letting the trade be carried on by a company whose shares are held by the charity and which then makes gift aid payments to the charity equal to its profits; such payments are charges on income and so are deductible (see infra, § **27.23**). Theoretically such arrangements are vulnerable to attack under the *Ramsay* principle, especially in the light of *Furniss v Dawson* but the Revenue have indicated that such schemes will not usually be challenged provided no circularity is involved such as when the charity provides an interest-free loan to the trading entity or the trader effectively controls the charity using it as a tax-free money box.²

Where a charity makes a loss on its charitable but non trading activities, it cannot set that loss off against its profits from a taxable trade.³ However, if a charity carries on two trades one exempt, on which it makes a loss, and the other taxable, on which it makes a profit, it may be that the loss can be relieved.⁴ This view seems doubtful but has not been tested in the courts. The charity would in any case have to surmount TA 1988, s 384 first.⁵ On the other hand, it is perfectly permissible for a loss on a taxable trade to be set off against the profit of another taxable trade.

Simon's Taxes C5.122, 123.

1 Extra-statutory concession C4. On lottery profits see TA 1988, s 505(1)(*f*).
2 *Simon's Tax Intelligence* 1985, p 572. Of course the company must comply with the requirements of TA 1988, Sch 16.
3 *Religious Tract and Book Society of Scotland v Forbes* (1896) 3 TC 415.
4 Such as under ITA 2007, s 64 (see supra, § **6.15**), or ITA 2007, s 83 (see infra, § **16.19**), or ITA 2007, s 72 (see supra, § **6.21**). Where the charity is incorporated, the equivalent corporation tax reliefs are potentially available: vide TA 1988, s 393 (see infra, § **25.23**) and TA 1988, s 393A (see infra, § **25.28**).
5 ITA 2007, s 66: see supra, § **6.25**.

Exemption for small receipts

[13.25] To avoid putting charities to the cost of using companies as described in supra, § **13.24**, there is an exemption from tax in respect of trading income or income assessable under any of the provisions listed in the table in ITA 2007, s 106¹ (corporation tax: TA 1988, s 836B). The exemption applies where the receipts that would otherwise give rise to profits assessable under this provision are less than 25% of the charity's total incoming resources[2] (subject to an absolute limit of £50,000). This exemption also applies where the charity had a reasonable expectation, judged at the beginning of the tax year, that it would not exceed that limit.[3]

It has been noted that the exemption is for trading profits or receipts after associated expenses that would be assessable under the provisions listed. However, the test to see whether the exemption can be applied is formulated in terms of gross receipts, before any deduction for trading expenditure or applicable costs.

---

[1] The exemption is granted by ITA 2007, ss 527(1), (4) & (5).
[2] ITA 2007, s 528(6).
[3] ITA 2007, s 528(1)(b).

Restriction of charity exemptions: non-charitable purposes

[13.26] Charities, with the tax exemptions available to them, were widely used for tax avoidance schemes. In order to stop what was regarded as an unacceptable use of charitable status, in 1986 Parliament enacted a provision[1] which removes the income tax exemption[2] from a charity insofar as the charity uses its funds for non-charitable purposes. As is commonly the case with anti-avoidance legislation, the provisions are widely drawn and can catch the unwary. The charity's tax exemption can be lost (or reduced) by investing the charity's funds otherwise than as what are specified as "qualifying investments".[3] This is a significant problem for a charity that has a trading subsidiary. The shares the charity holds in its subsidiary will be "non-qualifying investments" and any loan made by the charity to its subsidiary to fund its activities will be a "non-qualifying investment".[4] It is also possible that donations made outside the UK can unwittingly fall foul of these provisions.

The tax exemptions to which the charity is entitled are restricted if any expenditure by the charity during the chargeable period is incurred otherwise than for exclusively charitable purposes. Expenditure which is not incurred for charitable purposes only is referred to as "non-qualifying expenditure", and "qualifying expenditure" is expenditure incurred for charitable purposes only. A payment made to a body outside the UK is treated as non-qualifying expenditure unless the charity has taken such steps as are reasonable in the circumstances to ensure that the payment will be used for charitable purposes only.[5]

All investments are also treated as non-qualifying expenditure unless the investment is "an approved charitable investment".[6] "Approved charitable investment" is defined by statute[7] as:

Type 1	Securities issued by bodies listed in statute.[a] This includes those issued by EU Governments, by building societies, by open ended investment companies and by companies listed on a recognised stock exchange.[b]

Charities [13.26]

Types 2, 3 & 4	Common investment funds established under Charities Act 1960, 1993, or equivalent
Type 5	Land
Type 6	UK Government bills, certificates of tax deposit, savings certificates and tax reserve certificates
Type 7	Northern Ireland Treasury Bills
Type 8	Unit trust holdings
Type 9	Bank deposit
Type 10	A deposit with the National Savings Bank, a building society or a credit institution
Type 11	Certificates of deposit
Type 12	A loan or other investment as to which an officer of Revenue and Customs is satisfied, on a claim, that it is made for the benefit of the charitable trust and not for the avoidance of tax (whether by the trust or any other person).

[a] ITA 2007, s 559.
[b] Defined in ITA 2007, s 1005.

Tax relief is withheld from the amount by which a charity "relevant income and gains" exceeds its "qualifying expenditure" to the extent that this amount does not exceed the "non-qualifying expenditure" incurred by the charity in that chargeable period.[8] The charity may specify the items of relevant income and gains which are to be treated as attributable to the non-exempt amount.[9]

If the charity's total expenditure in a chargeable period exceeds its relevant income and gains so that part of the non-qualifying expenditure has not been taken into account under these provisions, that part may be attributed to earlier chargeable periods.[10]

The Special Commissioners have considered an arrangement whereby a charity has consistently made loans to its wholly owned trading subsidiaries, those loans being equal to the sums paid by the subsidiary to the parent charity under deed of covenant. In the circumstances of that particular case, the decision of the Special Commissioners was that the loans were properly made, they did not amount to "non qualifying expenditure" and, hence, tax relief was available on the payments made under the deed of covenant.[11]

---

[1] TA 1988, ss 505, 506. The purpose is to prevent schemes such as those behind *IRC v Helen Slater Charitable Trust Ltd* [1981] STC 471, CA. A lively, non technical account of the events which caused the Parliamentary backlash is given in Nigel Tutt, The Tax Raiders: The Rossminster Affair, publ: Financial Training Publications Ltd, 1985.

[2] The exemption is also from CGT: TCGA 1992, s 256(1) applying TA 1988, s 505(3).

[3] TA 1988, Sch 20, paras 1–9.

855

[4] It is possible for the charity to apply to the Revenue for the loan to be classified as a "qualifying investment" under the discretion given to the Revenue by TA 1988, Sch 20, para 10(d). This is a cumbersome procedure and the policy adopted by the Revenue is that the favoured classification is only granted if the terms of the loan replicate those that would be provided on a loan at arm's length terms to an unconnected third party, not the usual terms for an intra-group loan. Unless the loan is thus classified, the effect of the provisions is to bring into charge to tax income (or gains) up to the amount of the capital loaned.

[5] ITA 2007, s 547.
[6] ITA 2007, s 543(1)(i).
[7] ITA 2007, s 558.
[8] ITA 2007, s 540, 562.
[9] ITA 2007, s 541, 542.
[10] ITA 2007, s 563.
[11] *Nightingale Ltd v Price* [1996] STC (SCD) 116.

Restriction of charity exemptions: transaction with substantial donor

[13.27] Statute[1] removes the charity exemption from an amount of income equal to any payment made by the charity to a substantial donor, unless the payment is within one of the statutory exceptions.[2] A substantial donor is one who has given either (i) £25,000 or more to the charity in any 12 month period of which the charity's year is the whole or part, or (ii) a person who has given £100,000 or more during a period of six years, where the six year period includes all or part of the charity's accounting period.[3]

Transactions for substantial donors do not cause restriction of the charity's tax reliefs where the transaction falls into one of the categories specified by statute.[4] This allows the donor to sell to the charity goods, services and property in the course of his business, as long as the terms of business are no less beneficial to the charity than those that might be expected in a transaction at arms length and do not form part of an arrangement for the avoidance of any tax.

[1] ITA 2007, s 551(1) applying the treatment given by ITA 2007, s 543 as if the payments were non-charitable expenditure.
[2] ITA 2007, s 554.
[3] ITA 2007, s 549(2). A company wholly owned by the charity is not regarded as a substantial donor, even if it gifts profits over these limits: ITA 2007, s 555(1).
[4] ITA 2007, s 554(1)–(3).

14

Estates in the course of administration

Income of the deceased   PARA **14.01**
Income arising after death   PARA **14.02**

Income of the deceased

[14.01] Personal representatives have to settle the liability of the deceased person to income tax on the income that accrued to him during his lifetime.[1] In computing this liability the personal reliefs of the deceased for the year of death are allowed in full—there is no reduction for dying before 5 April. If the deceased was carrying on a trade his death will involve a discontinuance. Personal representatives can obtain a tax return without waiting until the end of the fiscal year and can request confirmation that the Revenue will not mount an enquiry into the return, without waiting until the closure of the "enquiry window" (see infra, § **14.10**).[2]

Income payable after, but in respect of a period before, the death of the deceased is treated as that of the personal representatives, not of the deceased.[3] However, the income is apportioned for IHT purposes, so that the payment may both be charged with IHT as a debt due to the deceased and also be charged to income tax as income of the personal representatives arising in the period of administration. Once distributed, it becomes income of the beneficiary with credit for tax paid by the personal representatives. In computing any higher rate tax charge on the beneficiary, income arising from the residue is taken as reduced by the amount of IHT payable in respect of that income.[4]

Simon's Taxes C4.102.

---

[1] TMA 1970, s 74 and note s 40(1).
[2] Inland Revenue press release, 4 April 1996, *Simon's Weekly Tax Intelligence* 1996, p 663.
[3] *IRC v Henderson's Executors* (1931) 16 TC 282. Distinguish the situation in which the dividend is payable before, but is paid after, the death *Potel v IRC* [1971] 2 All ER 504, 46 TC 658.
[4] ITTOIA 2005, s 669.

Income arising after death

Taxation of the personal representatives

[14.02] Like trustees, personal representatives are assessable to income tax at the lower rate on savings income, the dividend rate on dividend income and basic rate on other income. Personal representatives are never subjected to the trust rate, nor the dividend trust rate.[1] If the will creates a trust and the terms of the trust attract these trust rates, the liability to pay the trust rates falls on the trustees when they receive income paid to them by the personal representatives, typically at the end of the period of administration.[2] Like trustees they are not subject to tax at either the starting rate or the higher rate.[3] They cannot use any personal allowances of the deceased. They may, however, claim relief in respect of interest payments or in respect of any loss which *they* incur in running a business. Interest in respect of unpaid IHT is not deductible,[4] but relief is available for interest on a loan to pay IHT if the loan is made to the representatives and relates to tax payable on personalty before the grant of representation. Only interest arising during the period of 12 months from the date of the loan is deductible.[5] Excess interest can be carried back; if it is still not relieved, the unrelieved part can then be carried forward.[6]

On liability to tax on trading income, see supra, § **8.28**.

Simon's Taxes C4.106.

---

[1] The charge to tax is given by ITA 2007, s 11, personal representatives being "other persons" within the meaning of that section. The trust rate and the dividend trust rate are imposed by ITA 2007, s 479 on trustees only.
[2] ITA 2007, s 483.
[3] ITA 2007, s 6 specifies the starting rate and the higher rate for individuals; trustees are not individuals.
[4] *Lord Inverclyde's Trustees v Millar* (1924) 9 TC 14.
[5] ITA 2007, s 403.
[6] ITA 2007, s 405.

Taxation of the beneficiary

[14.03] Until the administration is complete, no beneficiary has any rights in the property of the estate or to the income from it;[1] it follows that no beneficiary is liable to income tax on the income of the personal representatives.[2] The question whether administration is complete is a matter of fact, the issue being whether the residue has been ascertained.[3] In many cases, the event that triggers the end of the period of administration is the determination of the inheritance tax payable on the estate. In some cases, particularly where the estate is less than the IHT nil rate band, the end of the period of administration will be triggered by the determination of liabilities to third parties as at the date of death; in principle, the determination of the value of an asset could be later than the determination of liabilities, although in practice this is rarely found. A prolonged administration can see a fund administered with expertise but taxed only at the relevant rate of tax rather than the higher rate; conversely if the prospective beneficiaries had low incomes and so unused personal allowances, it may be beneficial to expedite the administration.

Simon's Taxes C4.105.

1   *Stamp Duties Comr (Queensland) v Livingston* [1964] 3 All ER 692, [1965] AC 694.
2   *R v IT Special Purposes Comrs, ex p Dr Barnardo's Homes National Incorporated Association* [1920] 1 KB 26, 7 TC 646; *Corbett v IRC* [1937] 4 All ER 700, 21 TC 449; see also *Prest v Bettinson* [1980] STC 607 and statement of practice SP 7/80, but contrast extra-statutory concession A14.
3   *George Attenborough & Son v Solomon* [1913] AC 76.

UK estates and foreign estates

[14.04] The rules taxing the beneficiary vary according to whether the estate is a UK estate or a foreign estate. A UK estate is defined as one where the income of which comprises only income which has borne UK tax or for which the representatives are directly assessable. However, an estate is not a UK estate if the personal representatives are exempt from tax by reason of residence outside the UK.[1] An estate which is not a UK estate is a foreign estate.[2] In applying these rules certain amounts are ignored—these are foreign income dividends, stock dividends, the release of a loan from a close company and certain gains on life policies.[3]

Simon's Taxes C4.107, 116.

1   ITTOIA 2005, s 651 (income tax); TA 1988, s 701(9) (corporation tax).
2   ITTOIA 2005, s 651(1) (income tax); TA 1988, s 701(10) (corporation tax).
3   ITTOIA 2005, s 651(4) (income tax); TA 1988, s 701(10A) (corporation tax).

Specific legacy

[14.05] Where a personal representative vests a specific legacy in the legatee, intermediate income accruing during the administration is related back and so assessed on the beneficiary as at the times that income had accrued to the property.[1]

Where a legacy carries interest, the beneficiary is liable to tax on that interest if it has become his income. An attempt to disclaim the interest failed where a sum had been set aside to pay the legacy.[2] From this it should follow that where no sums have been set aside, the legatee may have a right to interest but is not taxable in respect of it. When he receives the legacy with its interest, it is an open question whether the payment relates back.

Income of a legatee who is not resident or not ordinarily resident in the UK may, by concession, be treated as if it arose directly from the various sources, even though the estate is a UK estate (eg sole assets are UK government securities).[3]

Simon's Taxes C4.122.

[1] IRC v Hawley [1928] 1 KB 578, 13 TC 327.
[2] Spens v IRC [1970] 3 All ER 295, 46 TC 276; cf Dewar v IRC [1935] 2 KB 351, 19 TC 561.
[3] Extra-statutory concession A14; as revised 1999, Simon's Weekly Tax Intelligence 1999, p 727.

Residuary beneficiary

[14.06] Where the administration of an estate is completed, a beneficiary brings income that has accrued during the period of administration into his individual self-assessment in the year in which he receives such income.[1]

Simon's Taxes C4.118.

[1] ITTOIA 2005, s 661(1) (income tax); TA 1988, s 695 (corporation tax).

Limited interest

[14.07] A person has a limited interest if he does not have an absolute interest but would have a right to income if administration were complete.[1] It is an open question whether a person whose interest is vested subject to being divested is entitled to the income.[2]

Any sums which are actually paid[3] during the administration period in respect of the limited interest are grossed up[4] at the applicable rate and treated as his income for the year of assessment in which the sum was paid or, if the interest has ceased, as income for the year of assessment in which it ceased.[5] Income from a foreign estate is grossed up to reflect the UK tax paid.[6]

The applicable rate means the basic or lower or dividend rate according to the type of income of the residuary estate out of which the amount is paid, ie basic rate for general interest and the dividend ordinary rate for dividend income.[7] Where dividend income is treated as having borne tax at its ordinary rate the normal rules apply.[8] The beneficiary may then use the tax charged at the applicable rate as a credit against his own tax liability, including the right to repayment of any tax overpaid. The beneficiary cannot make any repayment claim in respect of any dividend income but may use such income to frank payments falling within TA 1988, s 348 or 349.[9] Further rules apply to ensure the appropriate tax treatment where the income is distributed to a discretionary or other trust subject to the special rate of tax applicable to trusts.[10]

Rules are needed to determine the source of any income distributed. So distributions are treated as coming first from income taxed at basic rate then income taxed at lower rate and finally dividend income.[11]

Different rules apply to certain types of income which have not borne tax. These are stock dividends, release of loans made to a participator in a close company and certain gains on life policies.[12] When amounts are allocated to individual beneficiaries these types of income are allocated last.[13] These amounts are treated as having borne tax at the dividend ordinary rate save that

Income arising after death [14.07]

the life policy gains are treated as having borne tax at the lower rate.[14] No repayment of tax may be made; however, the tax is available as a credit against the beneficiary's own tax liability in respect of the limited interest arising from a foreign estate and it is this credit which represents the change from earlier rules. Dividend income is brought within the list of these amounts so as to prevent any right to repayment of tax but is then taken out again so as to allow the use of such income to frank payments.[15]

When the administration is completed any sums in the estate remaining payable to the beneficiary are income of the year in which the administration is completed. This is subject to one minor qualification; if the interest of the beneficiary ended before the year in which administration was completed, as will be the case if the beneficiary died, it is treated as income of the year in which the interest ceased instead.[16] This is in complete contrast to the rules for earlier years which required a spreading back of the remaining sums over the period of administration.[17] The new rule is simpler to apply (and more appropriate to self-assessment) but it means that income will be concentrated in one year.

The income on which the beneficiary is taxed may, and almost certainly will, bear little relation to the actual income of the estate in respect of which the personal representatives are chargeable. This is partly because administration expenses are deductible in computing the beneficiary's income, but not in computing the estate income, but also because the fluctuation in rates of tax and the variation in the estate income mean that the estate income may arise at times different from the dates of payment.

The personal representatives have a duty to provide information about the amount of tax at the applicable rate which the income is deemed to have borne.[18]

---

1 ITTOIA 2005, s 650(2) (income tax); TA 1988, s 701(3) (corporation tax).
2 The doubts stem from *Stanley v IRC* (supra, § **13.12**).
3 Widely defined—ITTOIA 2005, s 681 (income tax); TA 1988, s 701(12) (corporation tax).
4 Benefits in kind must be grossed up: *IRC v Mardon* (1956) 36 TC 565.
5 ITTOIA 2005, s 661(1) (income tax); TA 1988, s 695(2) (corporation tax).
6 ITTOIA 2005, s 657 (income tax); TA 1988, s 695(5) (corporation tax).
7 ITTOIA 2005, s 663 (income tax); TA 1988, s 701(3A) (corporation tax).
8 ITTOIA 2005, s 383 and ITA 2007, ss 8 and 14.
9 ITA 2007, s 1026.
10 ITA 2007, s 483 (infra, § **14.09**).
11 ITTOIA 2005, s 679(3) (income tax); TA 1988, s 701(3A)(*b*) (corporation tax).
12 ITTOIA 2005, s 680(3)(*b*) and (4): ie income falling within ITTOIA 2005, ss 410(4), 419(2) and 466(2).
13 ITTOIA 2005, s 679(4) (income tax); TA 1988, s 699A(2)(*b*) referring to TA 1988, s 701(3A) (corporation tax).
14 ITTOIA 2005, s 680(3)(*b*), (4) (income tax); TA 1988, s 699A(3), (4) (corporation tax).
15 TA 1988, s 348(4)(*e*) and ITTOIA 2005, s 680(3)(*a*), (5) (income tax); TA 1988, s 699A(1A) (corporation tax).

[14.07] Estates in the course of administration

[16] ITTOIA 2005, ss 654(3), (4) and 674(4), (5) (income tax); TA 1988, s 695(3) (corporation tax).
[17] TA 1988, s 695(3) (original version).
[18] TA 1988, s 700(5), (6).

Absolute interest

[14.08] A beneficiary has an absolute interest in residue if, on the hypothesis that the administration were then complete, he would be entitled to the capital or a part of it in his own right.[1] It is unclear whether a person entitled to capital but subject to the payment of an annuity is entitled to it "in his own right".

Sums actually paid[2] during the administration period are grossed up at the applicable rate and treated as the beneficiary's income of the year of payment.[3] Tax on income of a foreign estate is adjusted to reflect any UK tax paid.[4] The rules for calculating the applicable rates and for grossing up as necessary where the particular UK income is not taxed in the UK are the same as for limited interests.[5] Since, however, he is also entitled to the capital this treatment applies only to the extent of the aggregated income entitlement of that person for that year, any excess being treated as capital. A person's aggregate income entitlement is defined as the amount which would be the aggregate of the amounts received for that year of assessment and all previous years of assessment in respect of the interest if that person had a right in each year to receive, and had received in the case of a UK estate, his residuary income for that year less income tax at the applicable rate for that year. In the case of a foreign estate this calculation assumes that he has received his residuary income for that year.[6] The applicable rate varies according to the type of income and the rules are the same as those set out in supra, § **14.07** for limited interest. The beneficiary cannot make any repayment claim in respect of any dividend income but may use such income to frank payments falling within TA 1988, ss 348 or 349.[7] Rules are needed to determine the source of any income distributed. So distributions are treated as coming first from income taxed at basic rate then income taxed at lower rate and finally dividend income.[8]

Residuary income is defined as the aggregate of income received but with a deduction for interest, annuities and other annual payments charged on the residue and management expenses of the personal representatives in so far as they are properly chargeable to income.[9] If these deductions exceed the sums paid as income the deficit may be carried forward.[10]

Where the administration is completed after 5 April 1995 one must compare the amount paid out during administration with the aggregate income entitlement down to and including that year. If that amount is less than the entitlement the balance is treated as income paid immediately before the end of the period of administration.[11] This balance will have to be grossed up as necessary. Adjustments are also necessary if the benefits received turn out to be less than the aggregate residuary income. This may occur if for example debts payable out of residue are discovered late in the administration period. Any such reduction is carried out first against the income of the year of completion of the administration; any remaining reductions take effect against the income of earlier years.[12]

Where the residuary beneficiary is exempt from income tax, he will be entitled to a repayment. Further rules apply to ensure the appropriate tax treatment where the income is distributed to a discretionary or other trust subject to the special rate of tax applicable to trusts.[13]

Dividend income may not give rise to a right to repayment of tax although the payer may use such income to frank payments.[14]

Concessionary treatment of income of a non-resident from a UK estate which is dealt with at supra, § **14.05**, applies here also.[15]

The personal representatives are under an obligation, enforceable at the suit of the person making the request, to respond to a request in writing of details of the deemed income.[16]

Simon's Direct Tax Service C4.118, 124.

[1] ITTOIA 2005, s 650(1) (income tax); TA 1988, s 701(2) (corporation tax).
[2] Widely defined in ITTOIA 2005, s 681 (income tax) and TA 1988, s 701(12) (corporation tax).
[3] ITTOIA 2005, s 660(1) (income tax); TA 1988, s 696(3) (corporation tax).
[4] ITTOIA 2005, s 657(4) (income tax); TA 1988, s 696(3A) (corporation tax).
[5] ITTOIA 2005, s 657 (income tax); TA 1988, s 696(6), (7) (corporation tax).
[6] ITTOIA 2005, s 657(3), (4) (income tax); TA 1988, s 699A, especially s 699A(3) (corporation tax).
[7] ITA 2007, s 1026 together with ITTOIA 2005, s 680 (income tax) and TA 1988, s 699A(1A) (corporation tax).
[8] ITTOIA 2005, s 679(3) (income tax); TA 1988, s 701(3A)(*b*) (corporation tax).
[9] ITTOIA 2005, s 666(1), (2) and (5) (income tax); TA 1988, ss 696(3B) and 697(1) (corporation tax).
[10] ITTOIA 2005, s 666(2)(*d*), (6) (income tax); TA 1988, s 697(1A) (corporation tax).
[11] ITTOIA 2005, s 665(1), (2) and (3) (income tax); TA 1988, s 696(5) (corporation tax).
[12] ITTOIA 2005, s 668 (income tax); TA 1988, s 697(2) (corporation tax). On power to make assessments see ITTOIA 2005, s 682 (income tax) and TA 1988, s 700 (corporation tax).
[13] ITTOIA 2005, s 655 (income tax); TA 1998, s 698(3) (corporation tax) (infra, § **14.09**).
[14] ITA 2007, s 1026 together with ITTOIA 2005, s 680 (income tax) and TA 1988, s 699A(1A) (corporation tax).
[15] Extra-statutory concession A14.
[16] TA 1988, s 700(5), (6).

Other interests in the estate

[14.09] If the residue is held on discretionary trusts, neither of the provisions so far considered applies, since there are neither absolute nor limited interests. In such cases, the rules follow those used for limited interests.[1] Where income is paid indirectly through a trustee any payment to the trustee is treated for the purpose of the rules as income paid of the trustee.[2]

Provision is also made for the possibility that the beneficiary himself dies before administration is complete. If the beneficiary had an absolute interest,

[14.09] Estates in the course of administration

that interest passes to his personal representatives and the income of the first estate will now form part of the beneficiary's estate; the personal representatives are treated as succeeding to the absolute interest despite their representative status.[3]

Where successive interests in the residue arise for some other cause such as assignment or disclaimer, different rules apply.[4] Where successive limited interests[5] follow each other they are treated as being one and the same.[5] While this means that the whole residuary income will be divided between those successive holders, allowance will be made for sums due to the first holder which are paid to that holder after the assignment, such sums being treated as income of the first holder.

If a limited interest is followed by an absolute interest, the absolute interest is treated as having always existed.[6] Statutory provisions[7] dealing with an absolute interest are then applied as if the payment made to the holder of the limited interest had been made to the holder of the absolute interest; this does not undo the liability of the holder of the limited interest but ensures that all the income is properly taxed to one or other of them and that each is taxed on what each actually receives.

Successive absolute interests in the residue may arise as by assignment. Here the change in beneficiary is ignored. The aggregate income entitlement is calculated in the usual way. The effect is that each is taxed on what each received. If any adjustment has to be made at the end of the administration period this will fall primarily on the second holder of the interest.[8]

Simon's Taxes C4.115.

[1] ITTOIA 2005, s 662 (income tax); TA 1988, s 698(3) (corporation tax) applied also to payments made via discretionary trusts; statement of practice SP 4/93.
[2] ITTOIA 2005, s 680A.
[3] ITTOIA 2005, s 650(5) (income tax); TA 1988, s 698(1) (corporation tax).
[4] ITTOIA 2005, ss 671–674 (income tax); TA 1988, s 698(1A) (corporation tax).
[5] ITTOIA 2005, s 675 (income tax); TA 1988, s 698(1B) (corporation tax).
[6] ITTOIA 2005, s 672 (income tax); TA 1988, s 698(1A), (1B) (corporation tax).
[7] ITTOIA 2005, s 665.
[8] ITTOIA 2005, s 671 (income tax); TA 1988, s 698(2) (corporation tax).

Revenue enquiries and personal representatives

[14.10] When the estate at death has been ascertained, it is the duty of the personal representatives to distribute the assets to the beneficiaries. The personal representatives also have a duty to make a return of income (and capital gains) arising during the period of administration,[1] accompanied by the personal representatives' self-assessment in respect of that income (and capital gains).[2] In turn, the Revenue have the right to enquire into the return made by the personal representatives. The length of the period during which, under statute, the Revenue have a right to raise an enquiry into a self-assessment creates practical difficulties for personal representatives, who may not wish to distribute assets of the estate while there remains a possibility that the Revenue will seek to amend the self-assessment and, thereby, require a payment out of funds that are no longer under their control. On the basis of the statutory provisions, this period of uncertainty is of a very long duration. If, for example, the period of administration is brought to an end in summer 1997, it is possible for a further tax liability to arise by amendment of the personal representatives' self-assessment for the final period of administration as a result of an enquiry that commences at any time up to 31 January 2000.[3]

The Inland Revenue have announced that where a period of administration has come to an end, they will, on request, issue a tax return without waiting until the end of the tax year.[4] Further, the Revenue are prepared, on request, to give early written confirmation that they do not intend to enquire into the return. However, if the Revenue subsequently discover that the return is incomplete or incorrect, the Revenue declare that in "these exceptional circumstances", they reserve the right to enquire into the return.[5]

This "fast track" treatment is also available, on request, in respect of the tax return made for an individual for the year of death, or for a tax return made by trustees for the year in which a trust is wound up.

Simon's Taxes A6.401, E1.240.

[1] TMA 1970, s 7(1).
[2] TMA 1970, s 9 if a notice is delivered under s 8. In practice, a declaration of chargeability made under s 7 will trigger the Revenue issuing a notice under s 8 and hence the personal representatives are obliged to make a self-assessment.
[3] TMA 1970, s 9A(2)(*a*).
[4] Inland Revenue press release, 4 April 1996, Note 6, *Simon's Weekly Tax Intelligence* 1996, p 664.
[5] Inland Revenue press release, 4 April 1996, Note 7, *Simon's Weekly Tax Intelligence* 1996, p 664.

15

The Settlement Code

The code in statute	PARA **15.01**
A settlement	PARA **15.02**
Settlor	PARA **15.07**
Charge on income arising	PARA **15.09**
Charge on the settlor	PARA **15.19**
Parental settlements on unmarried minor children	PARA **15.21**
Capital sums paid to the settlor	PARA **15.23**
Settlements of income	PARA **15.30**
Jones v Garnett	PARA **15.31**

The code in statute

[15.01] The "settlement code"[1] is a series of statutory provisions designed for four purposes. The first is to restrict the use of other taxable entities, particularly trusts, as piggy banks, in which income can be taxed at the rates appropriate to that entity, rather than at the settlor's marginal rates, and so grow more rapidly before being passed back for the settlor or his spouse to enjoy. The second is to stop tax saving by moving income whilst retaining the capital value of the source. The fourth is to restrict the income splitting opportunities within the family as between parents and minor children. The third is to restrict the income assignment possibilities created by the system for taxing covenants (see supra, § **11.31**), that system remains in place despite the abolition of the general right to deduct sums paid under many covenants.

The technique used by the legislature is to provide that where one of these arrangements, which are now all described as settlements, is made, the income arising under the arrangement instead of being the income of the entity in whose hands it arises, shall be treated as the income of the person who made the arrangement, the settlor.[2] The settlor is given a right to recover the tax from the entity concerned.[3]

When income is treated as that of the settlor under one of these rules, the correct legal analysis is that the income arises first in the hands of the settlement and then is transferred to, or back to, the settlor by parliamentary transfer. This can have surprising results, especially if the disposition which is treated as a settlement is the creation of a right to annual payments by a covenant. In *Ang v Parrish*[4] the taxpayer made a covenant in favour of his parents in law which fell foul of the now repealed TA 1988, s 683. The taxpayer only had earned income out of which to make the payments. Walton J held that the payment came back to him as investment income and so was subject to the additional rate, even though the payment was originally made out of earned income. This rather silly decision left the taxpayer's final state worse than the first. It is one more example of the folly of the system of

867

deduction at source, which is, now, thankfully, greatly reduced. A rational system of taxation would have prescribed deductions eg payments under covenants, and then listed the circumstances in which deduction was not permitted. This aspect of the system has not been changed.

A study of these rules might leave one with the impression that a trust is never effective for tax purposes. This is quite untrue. Income may be accumulated or distributed and the settlor may specify relatives, other than his wife or minor unmarried children as objects of the trust, without any adverse income tax consequences under these rules. Indeed he may even be a trustee and himself control the selection of beneficiaries, again other than his wife or infant children, under a discretionary trust or a power of appointment.

Simon's Taxes C4.301.

[1] ITTOIA 2005, ss 619-648.
[2] ITTOIA 2005, s 622.
[3] ITTOIA 2005, s 646.
[4] [1980] STC 341, [1980] 2 All ER 790, para 1.

A settlement

[15.02] The statutory provisions that constitute "the Settlement Code" were originally enacted in Finance Act 1936. In 1939, the High Court[1] held that the concept of "settlement" in this code has a breadth of meaning far wider than "a settlement": "settlement" includes outright gifts, and even the creation of a company can be a settlement for the purpose of the Code. In *Copeman v Coleman*, two children of Mr and Mrs Coleman each subscribed £10 for a preference share in a company established by Mr Coleman. They received dividends which were substantially larger than the amounts paid for the shares. Lawrence J said:[2]

> In my opinion, it is impossible to come to any other conclusion but that this was not a bona fide commercial transaction, and it appears to me that there was a disposition or an arrangement in the nature of a disposition within the meaning of [the statutory provision] . . . I am also of opinion that the Respondent was a settlor. I am unable to see how the word 'indirectly' can be limited in the way which is suggested so as to exclude the settlements which are made through the interposition of a company.

The continued reference to "settlements" is unfortunate as it gives overtones of the ladies of Jane Austen. The law would look remarkably foolish if it took the view that income splitting should be countered only where it took place behind devices akin to the strict settlement and the law does not take such a view. So the term "settlement" "includes any disposition, trust, covenant, agreement, arrangement or transfer of assets (except that it does not include a charitable loan arrangement)".[3]

It has been said that the word "settlement" is not a dominating word which colours the others and that the word "arrangement" is not a term of art.[4] Many acts have been held to be settlements, including the setting up of corporate structures (an arrangement) and the disclaimer of an interest by a remainderman (a disposition). The courts have held that the word "arrangement" is limited to a case where there is bounty. This was first articulated in *IRC v Leiner*,[5] where Plowman J said:[6]

> The arrangement in my view must be looked at as a whole, and looked at in this way, I find it impossible to say that the Respondent did not provide the trustees with an income of £2,040 a year in the sense in which the word 'provided' is used in s 401 of the Act; that is to say, as importing an element of bounty.

Hence, in *Bulmer v IRC*[7] an arrangement (in the general sense of that term) with another company under which the third party company received dividends was not an "arrangement" within the statutory definition as it was a commercial arrangement in order to head of an unwelcome takeover campaign and involved no element of "bounty".[8]

[1] Copeman v Coleman (1939) 22 TC 594.
[2] At 601.
[3] ITTOIA 2005, s 620(1).
[4] Greene MR in *IRC v Payne* (1940) 23 TC 610 at 626. Cf *Shop and Store Developments Ltd v IRC* [1967] 1 All ER 42, [1967] 1 AC 472 (stamp duty).
[5] (1964) 41 TC 589.
[6] At 596.
[7] (1966) 44 TC 1.
[8] See also *IRC v Plummer* [1979] STC 793, [1979] 3 All ER 775, *Chinn v Collins* [1981] STC 1 and *Ewart v Taylor* [1983] STC 721.

Two old cases

[15.03] In *IRC v Mills*[1] the taxpayer was a child film star. In order to make sure that her earnings were "legally protected", her father formed a company and settled the shares of that company on trust for the taxpayer with various contingent remainders over. The taxpayer then signed a service contract with the company giving the company the right to her exclusive services for a period of five years at a salary of £400 a year. The company received large sums for the films she made. A substantial proportion was retained in the company and part was distributed in the form of dividend to the trustees. Since the trustees did not distribute the income the question arose whether the income accumulated by the trust could be treated as hers. The House of Lords held that there was a settlement, that she was the settlor and that the source of the dividends was the money paid for her work so that she had by her work provided the settlement with income indirectly. The result was that income accumulated by the trustees was deemed to be hers under what is now ITTOIA 2005, s 624. Today, the whole of the income would be treated as hers whether accumulated or not.

[1] [1974] 1 All ER 722, [1974] STC 130. Where a stranger provides trustees with advice as a result of which the income of the fund is increased it appears that this

section cannot apply since the stranger provides advice not funds, see *Mills v IRC* 49 TC 367 per Viscount Dilhorne at 408.

[15.04] In *IRC v Buchanan*[1] property was settled by X on A for life with remainder to B for life on protective trusts with remainder to B's children. The settlement also provided that if B should disclaim her life interest, the property should be administered at the moment when B's interest would have fallen into possession as if B were dead, thus avoiding the discretionary trusts that would otherwise have arisen on A's death following the disclaimer. B disclaimed her interest and the next day A released his interest. The Court of Appeal held that the destruction of an interest was a disposition. B had a disposable interest in that she had the right to income after A's death and could end that entitlement or not as she chose. The result was that the disclaimer was a settlement and so income arising in favour of B's infant children was deemed to be hers under what was TA 1988, s 663; the income would now be caught by ITTOIA 2005, s 629.

[1] [1957] 2 All ER 400, 37 TC 365.

[15.05] If there is no element of bounty the transaction is not a settlement; this follows even if the transaction is not carried out for commercial reasons.

So in *IRC v Levy*[1] an interest-free loan by a taxpayer to a company wholly owned by him, a transaction which the Commissioners had found to contain no element of bounty, was not a settlement. As Nourse J said:[2]

> A commercial transaction devoid of any element of bounty is not within this definition. The absence of any correlative obligation on the part of him who is on the receiving end of the transaction may be material, but is not conclusive in determining whether it contains an element of bounty or not.

FA 2000 (now ITTOIA 2005, s 630) makes express provision for the favourable treatment of loans to charities (see infra, § **15.18**). In *IRC v Plummer*[3] a charity paid £2,480 to the taxpayer who covenanted to pay the charity a sum which net of tax at basic rate would amount to £500 each year for five years. The purpose of the scheme was to enable the taxpayer to reduce his liability to surtax. The payments were annual payments being income of the charity under what was then Schedule D, Case III and, in consequence, deductible under TA 1988, s 835. The difference between £500 grossed up at basic rate and £500 were thus relieved from surtax thus enabling the taxpayer to keep the benefit of the tax relief himself. Despite the fact that the arrangement was made solely to obtain the tax advantage the House of Lords held that as there was no bounty as between the parties it was not a settlement. Such reverse annuity schemes were originally stopped by statute. The House of Lords has now held that in the new era of *IRC v Ramsay* and its succeeding cases the decision in *Plummer* is wrong—it is simply inconsistent with later cases.[4] It followed that the payments were not annual payments. This leaves *Plummer* as an example of the no-bounty test.

One may doubt the validity of the bounty test. If X settles property for two years upon trust for X absolutely if X survives the period and, if not, for Y and

Y provides full consideration for his interest, *IRC v Plummer* seems to say there is no settlement and yet this is the very type of avoidance at which provisions like the old TA 1988, s 673 were aimed.[5]

In applying the test the courts look at the transaction as a whole. In *Chinn v Collins*[6] trustees exercised a power of appointment in favour of a beneficiary who later assigned his contingent interest under that exercise as part of a scheme to avoid tax. It was argued that there was no element of bounty about the appointment or the subsequent transaction. However, the House of Lords held that the appointment and the subsequent activities made an arrangement and that the benefit accrued to the taxpayer as a result of the original act of bounty by the settlor in creating the settlement; the settlor's bounty remained incomplete until the appointment was made and the trustees then conferred bounty on the beneficiary.

The test of bounty was applied in *Butler v Wildin*.[7] Parents who were architects had worked for a company without fee. They had arranged for shares to be held by their infant children. Vinelott J, reversing the Special Commissioner, held that there was a settlement. The children had contributed nothing of substance and were not exposed to any risk. Income arising from the company in the form of dividends was therefore not the income of the children and the claim for repayment of income tax because they had unused personal allowances failed.

---

[1] [1982] STC 442.
[2] [1982] STC 442 at 457.
[3] [1979] STC 793, [1979] 3 All ER 775.
[4] Moodie v IRC [1993] STC 188; see generally Gillard, *In the Name of Charity* (1987).
[5] Venables, *Tax Planning Through Trusts*.
[6] [1981] STC 1, [1981] 1 All ER 189 and see discussion in *IRC v Levy* [1982] STC 442.
[7] [1989] STC 22.

[15.06] The term settlement is so widely defined that the more crucial question[1] is to determine what property is comprised in the settlement. The key statutory concept is that property is settled if it originates from the settlor; this is elaborately defined by reference to property originating from the settlor.

References to property comprised in the settlement refer only to property originating from that settlor[2] and references to income arising include only income originating from that settlor.[3] References to property originating from a settlor refer to (a) property which S has supplied directly or indirectly for the purposes of the settlement, (b) property representing that property and (c) so much of any property as represents both property so provided and other property as, on a just apportionment, represents the property so provided,[4] It is expressly provided that property representing accumulated income is caught.[5]

In *Chamberlain v IRC*[6] the settlor transferred assets to a company which he controlled and trustees acquired ordinary shares issued by the company. The trustees paid for the shares with money given to them by the settlor. The settlor later gave them more money with which to buy further shares. It was held that the property comprised in the settlement was the money given by the settlor and the shares purchased with that money—but not the assets of the company itself.

[1] Per Lord Thankerton in *Chamberlain v IRC* [1943] 2 All ER 200 at 203, 25 TC 317 at 329.
[2] ITTOIA 2005, s 644(3)(*a*).
[3] ITTOIA 2005, s 644(3)(*b*).
[4] ITTOIA 2005, s 645(1).
[5] ITTOIA 2005, s 645(4).
[6] Per Lord Thankerton in *Chamberlain v IRC* [1943] 2 All ER 200 at 203, 25 TC 317 at 329. In *Young v Pearce* [1996] STC 743, Sir John Vinelott analysed the *Chamberlain* case and held that an arrangement whereby wives obtained preference shares was correctly analysed as husbands providing their wives with "income arising under a settlement" and, hence, the income arising was properly assessable under what was then TA 1988, s 674A.

Settlor

[15.07] A settlor is defined[1] as any person by whom the settlement was made. In addition a person is deemed to have made a settlement if he has made or entered into a settlement directly or indirectly, a phrase which is then made the subject of a non-exclusive example—by having provided or undertaken to provide funds, directly or indirectly for the purposes of the settlement.[2] So in *IRC v Buchanan*[3] B made the settlement, and so was a settlor, when she disclaimed her interest. Similarly there was an indirect provision of funds in the case of the film star in *IRC v Mills*.[4] A person makes a settlement if he carries out any steps of that settlement. So where the taxpayer had carried out one step and later a scheme was devised and carried out by his solicitors and accountants, it was held to be part of his settlement even though he was not consulted or present at any meetings.[5] An infant can make a settlement.[6]

The notion of a settlor is then widened to include one who has made a reciprocal arrangement with another person for that other person to make or enter into the settlement. The purpose here is to catch the obvious device whereby A makes a settlement on B's children and in return B makes a settlement on A's children; in such instances there must be a reciprocal arrangement.[7] However, there must be a reciprocal arrangement. If X gives property to Y who transfers it to a settlement, Y is the settlor and X is not—unless there is some conscious association between X and the proposed settlement.[8]

Where funds are provided for a settlement a very strong inference is to be drawn that they are provided for that purpose,[9] an inference which will be rebutted if it is established that they were provided for another purpose. So in *IRC v Mills* the infant provided funds for the purposes of a settlement even if unconsciously.

Simon's Direct Tax Service C4.303.

1. ITTOIA 2005, s 620(1). This is wider than the definition given of "settlor" income tax, generally: ITA 2007, s 467; for capital gains tax: TCGA 1992, s 68A; or for inheritance tax: IHTA 1984, s 44.
2. ITTOIA 2005, s 620(2), (3).
3. [1957] 2 All ER 400, 37 TC 365.
4. [1974] STC 130, [1974] 1 All ER 722, 49 TC 367.
5. *Crossland v Hawkins* [1961] 2 All ER 812, 39 TC 493.
6. Semble in *IRC v Mills* no argument was raised by the infant to have the arrangement set aside on the grounds of its invalidity by reason of her infancy.
7. eg *Hood Barrs v IRC* [1946] 2 All ER 768, 27 TC 385.
8. Per Lord Keith in *Fitzwilliam v IRC* [1993] STC 502, HL, at 516.
9. *IRC v Mills* [1974] 1 All ER 722 at 727, [1974] STC 130 at 135.

Whose income?

[15.08] The breadth of the definition of settlement and of settlor means that more than one person may be a settlor in relation to a particular settlement.[1] Two issues arise: (a) are there two settlors? (b) if so, what are the consequences?

The legislation directs that where there is more than one settlor these rules are to apply to each settlor as if he were the only settlor.[2] Given the definition of settlement it follows that there are two or more settlors if income arising under the settlement originates from two or more persons. References to property comprised in the settlement refer only to property originating from that settlor and references to income arising include only income originating from that settlor.[3] As already seen references to property originating from a settlor refer to property which S has supplied directly or indirectly for the purposes of the settlement and property representing that property. Where the property originating from the settlor is not the only property in the settlement an apportionment is made.[4] It is expressly provided that property representing accumulated income is caught.[5] Income originates from the settlor if it is income from property originating from S or income provided directly or indirectly by S (eg under a covenant).[6]

In *IRC v Mills*[7] it was held that while the father was clearly a settlor, so also was the taxpayer and, since it was the taxpayer's services which supplied the company with funds from which to pay dividends to the trust, she indirectly provided the income for the settlement; hence all the income originated from her. The problem of the two settlors did not therefore arise in relation to the taxpayer and her father, and what would happen in such a case was left undecided by the House of Lords. In the Court of Appeal, Orr LJ suggested that this was simply a case in which it is left to the Revenue authorities to act reasonably:[8] a solution which may be illustrated by *IRC v Buchanan*.[9] In that case the Revenue argued that the income accrued to B's children in consequence of her disposition. Yet if A had not released his interest no income would actually have accrued to the children. The Revenue won but did not make any assessment for any year before that in which A died. One should note that the Court of Appeal treated A as not being a settlor for this purpose, a conclusion difficult (but not impossible) to reconcile with *Chinn v Collins*.[10]

This decision was followed in *d'Abreu v IRC*.[11] In simplified terms, property had been settled by P on his daughters J and A; each moiety was held for life with remainders over to children in default of appointment and in default of children the moiety was to pass to the other. In 1959 J, who never married, released her power to appoint in favour of any husband she might marry; A then released and assigned her contingent interest in J's moiety to the trustees of her moiety and then exercised the power of appointment in favour of her children. The result was that when J died in 1963 the income from her moiety accrued to A's children who were still infants.

Oliver J held that, as in *Buchanan*, the whole of the income accruing to A's children did so in consequence of A's acts and so fell within what became TA 1988, s 663 and is now superseded by ITTOIA 2005, s 629. However, he went on to say that even if J were also a settlor the provisions directed that the section was to apply to each settlor as if he were the only settlor; all the income therefore originated from A and one could not apportion on the basis of an actuarial valuation of their interests in 1959. Two comments may be made. First, the decision draws a sharp and so unfortunate distinction between successive and other interests. Thus if A and J had under the Variation of Trusts Act 1958 extracted capital sums which they had then jointly settled on A's children it is at least arguable that the income from J's fund would not fall within the section. Second, difficulties remain. Thus, suppose that there are successive life interests for H and W and they both release their interests in favour of their infant children. One could not say that they were both settlors and so tax the income twice. It is no answer to say that W's income is treated as H's since this does not stop the income being potentially liable twice and in any case the issue arises again if the spouses separate. The appropriate answer would be to apportion on the basis of actuarial valuation of their interests but this was rejected in *d'Abreu v IRC*.

To treat the matter as turning on the reasonableness of the Revenue is to make liability turn on administrative discretion, the very view rejected by the House of Lords in *Vestey v IRC*.[12] It is therefore to be hoped that *d'Abreu v IRC* is not the last word.

---

[1] As set out in ITTOIA 2005, s 644.
[2] ITTOIA 2005, s 644(1).
[3] ITTOIA 2005, s 644(3).
[4] ITTOIA 2005, s 645(1)(c).
[5] ITTOIA 2005, s 645(4).
[6] ITTOIA 2005, s 645(2). There are special rules for settlements of infant children—s 644(3)-(4).
[7] [1974] STC 130, [1974] 1 All ER 722, 49 TC 367.
[8] [1973] STC 1 at 22, [1972] 3 All ER 977 at 998.
[9] [1957] 2 All ER 400, 37 TC 365.
[10] [1981] STC 1, [1981] 1 All ER 189.
[11] [1978] STC 538.
[12] [1980] STC 10, [1980] AC 1148.

Charge on income arising

Income arising

[15.09] "Income arising under a settlement" includes "any income chargeable to income tax, by deduction or otherwise".[1] It thus makes no allowance for any trust management expenses. The phrase also includes any income which would have been so chargeable if it had been received in the UK by a person domiciled, resident and ordinarily resident in the UK. This creates a hypothetical remittance to a hypothetical resident and so catches all income wherever it arises.[2] An exception has therefore to be made and this is where the settlor is not domiciled or resident or ordinarily resident in the UK and the settlor would by reason of that not be chargeable to UK tax on that income.[3] This exception is then qualified to deal with the situation in which the income is remitted. Such remitted income is treated as arising in the year of remittance if the settlor would have been taxable in the UK by reason of his residence.[4]

Simon's Taxes C4.335.

[1] ITTOIA 2005, s 648(1)(a).
[2] Reversing *Astor v Perry* [1935] AC 398, 19 TC 255.
[3] ITTOIA 2005, s 648(2), (3).
[4] ITTOIA 2005, s 644(4), (5).

The first charging provision—settlor retaining interest in settled property

[15.10] ITTOIA 2005, s 624 begins by deeming all income arising under a settlement to be income of the settlor for all purposes of the Income Tax Acts and not as the income of any other person. It then goes on to exclude this deeming treatment where the income arises from property in which the settlor has no interest.[1] In deciding whether this exclusion is satisfied a settlor is to be regarded as having an interest in property if that property or any related property is, or will or may become, payable to or applicable for the benefit of the settlor or his spouse in any circumstances whatsoever.[2] Related property means income from that property or any other property directly or indirectly representing proceeds of, or of income from, that property or income therefrom.[3]

[1] ITTOIA 2005, s 624(1)(b).
[2] ITTOIA 2005, s 625(1).
[3] ITTOIA 2005, s 625(5).

Illustration of the first general provision—revocable settlement

[15.11] If a settlement can be revoked and, on that revocation, the property reverts to the settlor or to his spouse the terms of the principal charging provision will be satisfied and income arising is treated as that of the settlor

[15.11] The Settlement Code

from the very beginning.[1] If, on revocation, only a part of the property will so revert, only that part of the trust income arising is treated as the settlor's income. Under the earlier rules, which referred specifically to revocable settlements it was held that a power to advance the whole of the settled capital was a power to revoke the settlement.[2] Similarly a power to diminish the property comprised in the settlement or the income which people other than the settlor or his wife might receive from it, was treated as a power to revoke. If in such circumstances the rights of the settlor or his spouse are increased the new provision will apply. Since the language refers to the possibility of the income arising in any circumstances whatsoever it is presumably immaterial whether it is the settlor or some other person who has the power to revoke and it is likewise immaterial whether the power to revoke is exercisable with or without the consent of any other person.

[1] A supplemental deed is not retroactive—*Taylor v IRC* [1946] 1 All ER 488n, 27 TC 93.
[2] *Kenmare v IRC* [1957] 3 All ER 33, 37 TC 383.

[15.12] However, it was not every chance of the reduction in the trust assets that gave rise to an application of the old provision but only a power to be found in the settlement and derived directly therefrom. In *IRC v Wolfson*[1] the settlement was of shares in a company which was controlled by the settlor. He was thus in a position to deprive the trust of its income. This was held not to amount to a power of revocation. However, if the company had been set up as part of the scheme of settlement a different result might have followed and it would have been permissible to look at the structure of the company to determine whether there was a power of revocation.[2] So if a settlement is expressed to endure only so long as the company exists, and the settlor has the power to cause the company to go into liquidation, the new provision may apply.[3] When property was in the UK, the old provision operated regardless of the fact that the settlor and the trustees are non-resident;[4] the same result seems to arise today.

[1] [1949] 1 All ER 865, 31 TC 158.
[2] But note Lord Simonds at 868, 169.
[3] By analogy with *IRC v Payne* (1940) 23 TC 610. Cf *Chamberlain v IRC* [1943] 2 All ER 200, 25 TC 317.
[4] *Kenmare v IRC* [1957] 3 All ER 33, 37 TC 383.

'In any circumstances'—case law on the meaning of the statutory words

[15.13] The language of ITTOIA 2005, s 625(1) is marginally narrower than its predecessor (TA 1988, s 660A(2) which was based on that found in the now repealed TA 1988, s 673). Section 625(1) provides that a settlor is treated as having an interest in property "if there are any circumstances in which the property or related property [might be payable or applicable to the settlor or the settlor's spouse]". The repealed provisions said that a settlor retained an interest if, "in any circumstances whatsoever", any income or property could become payable to or applicable for the benefit of the settlor or the settlor's spouse.

Examples of s 673, and s 660A applying included the failure to transfer the settlor's entire beneficial interest with a consequent resulting trust,[1] or where the settlor retained a general power of appointment or a special power of which he was one of the objects. This was carried further in *Glyn v IRC*[2] where the power was to be exercised jointly by the settlor and his son. Although the Revenue admitted that the section would not have applied if the power had been vested in the son alone, the court held that the settlor was subject to s 673. This conclusion seems surprising in view of the fact that the son's concurrence was needed for the exercise of the power, but it may be regarded as having been realistic since s 673 was concerned only to charge income which was accumulated. If no appointment could be made without the settlor's consent he could thereby determine whether or not the income was accumulated. It is unclear whether the fact that the settlement itself was brought about by a joint arrangement with the son forms part of the ratio; it certainly provides a means of distinction.

[1] *Hannay's Executors v IRC* (1956) 37 TC 217, as nearly happened in *IRC v Bernstein* [1961] 1 All ER 320, 39 TC 391, and *Pilkington v IRC* [1962] 3 All ER 622, 40 TC 416.
[2] [1948] 2 All ER 419, 30 TC 321.

[15.14] Case law has placed some limits on the scope of the phrase "in any circumstances". First, it was held that where the power of the settlor over the assets is fiduciary rather than beneficial, no interest is retained. So in *Lord Vestey's Executors v IRC*[1] a power to direct investments granted to the settlor and another and not to the trustees did not cause TA 1988, s 673 to operate. Likewise the possibility that the settlor may become a trustee of another settlement to which the first settlement transfers funds should not have that effect.

Second, the section did not apply if the property may only come back to the settlor through the independent act of a third party. Pennycuick J said that although TA 1988, s 673 was in very wide terms it must be confined to cases where income or property will or might become payable to or applicable for the benefit of the settlor either under the trusts of the settlement itself or under some collateral arrangement having legal force.[2] So the possibility that a beneficiary to whom funds are properly paid may then decide to make a gift to the settlor should not be taken into account. The same would hold good if the beneficiary chose to leave his property to the settlor by will. However, where the settlor's position as heir gives him the right to succeed not as beneficiary under his son's will or intestacy but because the remainder is given by the settlement to those falling within the class, TA 1988, s 673 applied[3] and so ITTOIA 2005, s 624 would apply.

Third, the possibility that the property will come back to the settlor's estate and not during his lifetime is too remote.[4]

Fourth, in *Muir v IRC* Pennycuick J said that the mere fact that there was some present doubt about the validity of the trust could not cause the section to apply.[5] Eventually the doubt would be resolved one way or the other and then the issue could be determined. A different problem might arise under the wait-and-see rule for perpetuities since the validity of the remainder will not be resolved until some future date. It is presumed that the statutory direction[6] that the gift is to fail only when it becomes clear that vesting cannot occur within the perpetuity period, and that the gift is to be treated as valid until that time, is effective for tax purposes, thus excluding TA 1988, s 673.

Fifth, it was held that the possibility that the settlor may derive some incidental benefit in the course of a commercial transaction should be ignored.[7] This contains many difficulties, not the least of which is the lack of any clear guidance as to what is "incidental" in this context. Finally one should presumably ignore the possibility of subsequent legislation or the migration of the trust to a country which would regard the trust (or part of it) as invalid.[8] The Revenue originally took the view that a settlor retained an interest if the trustees could, or had the power to, pay the CTT (now IHT) due on the transfer. This was because the property in the settlement could be used to meet a liability that was his—even though jointly. This view has now been abandoned.[9]

---

1. [1949] 1 All ER 1108, 31 TC 1. It may be relevant to note that this case was decided on the basis of TA 1988, s 673, the wording of which was that a settlor retained an interest if "in any circumstances whatsoever" income or property could become payable to the settlor or his spouse. ITTOIA 2005, s 625 uses a different formulation. However, the intention and the creation of ITTOIA 2005 is to retain the meaning unchanged and, thus, *Lord Vesty's Executors v IRC* should be available to be taken as authority for the interpretation of the new statute.
2. *Muir v IRC* [1966] 1 All ER 295 at 305, 43 TC 367 at 381. See also Lord Keith in *Fitzwilliam v IRC* [1993] STC 502, HL, at 516 on an analogous provision.
3. *Barr's Trustees v IRC* (1943) 25 TC 72.
4. *IRC v Gaunt* [1941] 2 All ER 82, 24 TC 69. It is unclear whether now his wife must also predecease the return of the asset to his estate; semble not since she will benefit, if at all, only through his generosity in leaving her an interest in his estate.
5. *Barr's Trustees v IRC* (1943) 25 TC 72.
6. Perpetuities and Accumulations Act 1964, s 3(1). Halsbury's Statutes (4th edn) perpetuities.
7. See *Wachtel v IRC*; and note Lord Morton in *Lord Vestey's Executors v IRC* (1949) 31 TC 1 at 114, who said that while a loan at a commercial rate of interest might benefit a person by tiding him over a difficult period, it was not money lent "for the benefit of" the debtor within s 447.
8. Quaere if the trust contained an express power to migrate to a country with such a rule.
9. Statement of practice SP 1/82 (for years 1981–82 and following).

'In any circumstances'—statutory limits

[15.15] **Spouses; wife or husband; inter-spousal gifts.** A "spouse" of the settlor does not include (a) a spouse from whom the settlor is separated under an order of a court, or under a separation agreement or (b) a spouse from whom the settlor is separated where the separation is likely to be permanent, or (c) the widow or widower of the settlor, or (d) a person to whom the settlor is not for the time being married but may later marry.[1]

Of these (d) is a statutory provision[2] enacted to deal with the disproportionally harsh effect of the decision in *Unmarried Settlor v IRC*,[3] where a capital gain was charged on the settlor on the basis that the deed did not exclude a future spouse. The settlor was aged in his 80s, a bachelor and gave evidence that he was homosexual. The Special Commissioner ruled (on the basis of the law before the statutory enactment) that neither the age nor the sexual orientation of the taxpayer could be taken into account, he was legally able to marry and the terms of the trust deed did not exclude from benefit any future wife there may be. Provisions (b) and (c) are in recognition of the fact that the marriage is at an end and (c) is in line with earlier case law since an ex-spouse is not a spouse.[4]

The general rule in ITTOIA 2005, s 625(1) would deprive gifts between spouses of any effect for income tax. Not wishing to inhibit such generosity but anxious to prevent the exploitation of the separate taxation of spouses the legislation directs that an outright gift of property by one spouse to the other is not to be treated as a settlement for these rules unless either the gift does not carry a right to the whole of that income, or the property given is wholly or substantially a right to income.[5] A gift is stated not to be an outright gift if it is subject to conditions, or if the property given or any derived property is or will or may become, in any circumstances whatsoever, payable to or applicable for the benefit of the donor.[6] In *Young v Pearce*,[7] it was held that an arrangement that involved the issue of preference shares in a close company was correctly analysed as an attempted gift of income without a corresponding gift of capital as the substantial value remained with the donor. In *Jones v Garnett*[8] the House of Lords held that the ordinary share (with customary rights) acquired by Mrs Jones was not substantially a right to income.[9]

Payments on family breakdown are also outside these provisions. More formally s 624(1) does not apply to income arising under a settlement made by one party to a marriage by way of provision for the other after the dissolution or annulment of the marriage, or while they are separated under an order of a court, or under a separation agreement or in such circumstances that the separation is likely to be permanent.[10] This applies only to the extent that the income arising is payable to or applicable for the benefit of that other party.

Simon's Taxes C4.311.

1 ITTOIA 2005, s 625(4).
2 ITTOIA 2005, s 62(4)(*d*) (for CGT: TCGA 1992, s 77(3)(*a*)).
3 [2003] STC (SCD) 274. Regulations for civil partners have the effect that settlements legislation only applies, in this respect, from the date of the registration of the civil partnership; that is, a deed that does not exclude a future civil partner will not have income taxed on the settlor by virtue of the settlement code unless and until an individual who can benefit from the settlement actually becomes a civil partner of the settlor.
4 *Lord Vestey's Executors v IRC* [1949] 1 All ER 1108, 31 TC 1.

[5] ITTOIA 2005, s 626. This is illustrated in *Meredith-Hardy v McLellan* [1995] STC (SCD) 270 where a husband purported to assign his state retirement pension to his wife. The Special Commissioner held that a direction to the DSS to pay the pension into his wife's bank account did not constitute a disclaimer of the pension and did not relieve him of his liability to tax.
[6] ITTOIA 2005, s 626(4).
[7] [1996] STC 743.
[8] [2007] UKHL 35. See **15.31**.
[9] See, in particular, the speech of Lord Hope of Craighead.
[10] ITTOIA 2005, s 627(1).

Permitted interests

[15.16] Certain types of interest may, however, be retained by the settlor without causing a charge under ITTOIA 2005, s 624; these are not quite identical to the old exceptions. No charge arises if and so long as none of that property, and no related property, can become payable or applicable for the settlor except in the event of (a) the bankruptcy of some person who is or may become beneficially entitled to the property or any related property; or (b) an assignment of or charge on the property or any related property being made or given by some such person; or (c) the charging of (or in Scotland, the granting of a right in security over) the property or related property of such a person; or (d) in the case of a marriage settlement, the death of both the parties to the marriage and of all or any of the children of the marriage; or (e) the death at any age of a child of the settlor who had become beneficially entitled to the property or any related property at any age not exceeding 25.[1] It will be seen that (e) refers to death at any age whereas the earlier law had referred to death under 25.

It will be seen that these conditions are alternatives so that s 624 is avoided if any one of them is satisfied. However, the legislation goes on to say that s 624 is also avoided if and so long as some person is alive and under the age of 25 during whose life that property, or any related property, cannot become payable or applicable as mentioned in that subsection except in the event of that person becoming bankrupt or assigning or charging his interest in the property or any related property.[2]

The difference between the first group of provisions and the longer provision is that the four events listed in the first paragraph above are alternatives but those in the second paragraph are not. Thus a settlement on trust to accumulate the income until X reaches the age of 25 and then for X for life determinable on X's bankruptcy and then to revert to the settlor, will not satisfy the conditions in the first paragraph but will satisfy the conditions in the second paragraph. Had the accumulations been directed to end at 28, not 25, the accumulated income would have been treated as that of the settlor only in the years after X reached 25.

[1] ITTOIA 2005, s 625(2).
[2] ITTOIA 2005, s 625(3).

Gifts to charity

[15.17] A trust may make gifts to charity without triggering any liability under the provisions discussed in this chapter.[1] Income qualifies if it is to be accumulated, is payable at the discretion of the trustees or any other person (whether or not there is a power to accumulate) or which before being distributed belongs to any person other than the trustees. The former phrase covers discretionary trusts, the latter interest in possession trusts; in the former case the charity is an object of the discretion and in the latter it is entitled to income under the terms of the trust. The trustees must be resident in the UK and this condition must be satisfied when the income arises.

The rules in this chapter are excluded if the income belongs to the charity under the trust or is given by the trustees to the charity during the year. However, this does not mean that there are no income tax issues. What it means is that the qualifying income is treated as that of the trust as opposed to the settlor. This opens the way for the liability of the trustee and beneficiary to be determined in the normal way under the rules in Chapter 13.

If the trust is a bare trust the rules in the present chapter do not apply anyway; any gift by the trust in these circumstances is treated as a gift by the individual beneficiary under the normal Gift Aid rules.

Where the trust is an interest in possession trust and the charity is entitled to the income, the trustees pay the income tax in the usual way qua trustees and then hand the sum net of tax income to the charity. The charity can then reclaim the tax already paid by the trustee.[2] Where the source is a dividend the charity cannot make a claim for repayment of the tax credit.

Where the trust is not an interest in possession trust but eg a discretionary trust, the trustee will have to settle the liability to the trust rate (at 40%). So, if the trust income is £1,000 the trustees will have £600 to pay to the charity and the charity will recover £400 from the Revenue in respect of the credit arising under s 687.

A problem arises if the qualifying income given away to charity is less than the income arising. Where this occurs the charity's income is drawn rateably from the different types of income eg dividend income taxed at 10%, savings income at 20% and rental income taxed at 22%.[3] Naturally, this yields to any express provision in the settlement. It will be interesting to see whether it becomes normal practice to include clauses directing where charitable payments should be made from—and how quickly the fiscal assumptions underlying those clauses will change. Sections 628(5) and 630(4) simply refer to a "requirement" that a particular source be used.

Relief is to be given for management expenses to the extent that the gift to charity is treated as coming from qualifying income.[4] Suppose that a charitable interest in possession trust from which the settlor is not entirely excluded has £1,000 of qualifying savings income and £100 of management expenses so that £900 is left over. The trustees pay £200 in income tax, leaving them with £700. If they give £350 to charity the charity will be able to reclaim £100 from the Revenue ie will be able to reclaim the credit not only on the £350 received but also on the £50 spent on management expenses.

[15.17] The Settlement Code

[1] ITTOIA 2005, ss 628(1), 630(1).
[2] ITA 2007, s 520(2) treats the charity as receiving the gift grossed up by basic rate tax. The charity then reclaims the tax under ITA 2007, s 520(1), as it is exempt from tax on gift aid income. See supra, § **6.36**.
[3] ITTOIA 2005, ss 628(4), 630(3).
[4] ITTOIA 2005, s 646A inserted by ITA 2007, Sch 1, para 560.

Loans

[15.18] The charge on the settlor under ITTOIA 2005, s 624 does not apply where an individual makes an interest free, or low interest, loan of money to a charity.[1]

[1] ITTOIA 2005, s 620(5).

Charge on the settlor

[15.19] From 6 April 2006 the trustees of a settlor-interested trust are subject to the trust rate and the dividend trust rate.[1] The calculation of the trustees' liability for any trust where the settlor retains an interest[2] is, thus, carried out in the same way as for a discretionary trust.

Income which is treated as income of the settlor for tax purposes, whether from a trust or from a settlement, retains its character in the hands of that person. Income is chargeable[3] in the same way as would have been the case had the income arisen directly to that person. It is therefore chargeable at that person's marginal rates and carries a credit for any tax paid by trustees—this could be 10%, 20%, 22%, 32½% or 40% depending on the nature of the trust and income.

[1] TA 1988, s 686(2)(b) amended by FA 2006, Sch 13, para 2, then re-enacted in its amended form by ITA 2007, s 480(1) & (3)(*a*). The meaning of the amended and re-enacted provision is a little obscure. However, it is stated in HMRC Tax Bulletin August 2006, p 1306 as: "ICTA 1988, s 686(2)(b) has been amended and from 6 April 2006 the trustees of settlor-interested trusts are no longer taken out of the charge to the special trust rates. The normal rules for accumulation and discretionary trusts will therefore apply in these cases, so that dividend income is assessable at 32½% and all other income is assessable at the rate applicable to trusts, currently 40%. As a result boxes 13.1 to 13.6 in Question 13 of the Trust and Estate return will be removed."
[2] Under ITTOIA 2005, ss 619–648.
[3] Under ITTOIA 2005, ss 623(2).

[15.20] Although often the settlor will have a marginal rate higher than that of the beneficiary, it may happen that the reverse is the case and in that event

ITTOIA 2005, s 624, which directs the income to be treated as that of the settlor, may actually reduce the amount of tax otherwise payable. However, there are limits. In *Becker v Wright*[1] the payee was resident in the UK but her father-in-law, the payer, was resident in Trinidad. The covenant was to last only three years and the payee's husband was assessed to tax under Schedule D, Case V. He argued that the effect of what is now ITTOIA 2005, s 624 was to deem the income to be the payer's "for all the purposes of the Income Tax Acts", and so not his. Stamp J, however, accepted the Crown's argument that this effect of the settlement code would deem there to be income of a non-resident arising outside the UK which was contrary to the general principles of the tax system. Such a person cannot have such income "for the purpose of the Income Tax Acts". No assessment could be made on the payer nor did what is now Chapter 5 as such create any power to assess.

[1] [1966] 1 All ER 565, 42 TC 591.

Parental settlements on unmarried minor children

[**15.21**] In general the UK income tax system does not aggregate the income of a child with that of his parent. Since 1936 an exception has been made to prevent income splitting when the income is derived from the parent. Such income is attributed to the parent but only so long as the child is unmarried and under the age of majority, ie 18, so that income arising in favour of adult children escapes this rule.[1]

The rule contained in ITTOIA 2005, s 629 is that any income arising under a settlement as previously defined and which does not fall within the general rule in s 624 but which is paid during the life of the settlor to or for the benefit of an unmarried minor child of the settlor is treated as that of the settlor.[2] There is a de minimis exception of £100 from all sources within this section of the code.[3] The rule applies whenever the settlement was made—whether before or after 1995. An outright gift is a settlement.[4]

Section 629 applies whether the income arises under an ordinary trust or a bare trust.[5] It appeared that the rule did not apply where income arose under a bare trust created by the parent where the income arising was retained by the trustees but not formally accumulated by them. This extension applies to settlements made or on or after 9 March 1999 and for income arising from property added on or after that date.[6] The £100 de minimis exception applies.[7]

"Child" is defined as "including a stepchild and an illegitimate child".[8] The 1995 definition (adopted by the rewritten legislation in 2005), unlike its predecessor, does not mention an adopted child, presumably because an adopted child is to be treated as the child of the adoptive parents.[9] Whether this includes a foster child remains to be seen although this seems unlikely since the two examples in the statutory definition are precise legal relationships.

Where a settlor is assessable to tax under ITTOIA 2005, s 629, any tax paid by the trustees at the rate applicable to trusts in respect of the income

[15.21] The Settlement Code

distributed is available to the settlor as a credit.[10] By concession, this treatment is applied also to non-resident trusts.[11]

[1] ITTOIA 2005, s 629(7)(b).
[2] ITTOIA 2005, s 629(1); references to payments include payments in money or money's worth—s 629(7)(c).
[3] ITTOIA 2005, s 629(3).
[4] *Thomas v Marshall* [1953] 1 All ER 1102, *34 TC 178*.
[5] ITTOIA 2005, s 629(1)(b); Inland Revenue press release 9 March 1999, *Simon's Weekly Tax Intelligence* 1999, p 459.
[6] FA 1999, s 64(5); apportionments are to be made on a just and reasonable basis.
[7] ITTOIA 2005, s 629(3).
[8] ITTOIA 2005, s 629(7)(a), TA 1988, s 832(5).
[9] Adoption Act 1976, s 39.
[10] ITA 2007, s 494.
[11] Extra-statutory concession A93.

Accumulation settlements

[15.22] If income arising under a settlement is retained or accumulated by the trustees, no charge arises under ITTOIA 2005, s 629 (unless it is a bare trust)—as distinct from ITTOIA 2005, s 624 where that provision applies. Similarly no charge arises if income has not been retained or accumulated and a capital payment is made. However, once income has been retained or accumulated any subsequent payment made by virtue or in consequence of the settlement (or any relevant enactment) to or for the benefit of an unmarried minor child of the settlor falls within s 629 income if or to the extent that there is available retained or accumulated income.[1]

In deciding whether there is retained or accumulated income available one first calculates the aggregate income which has arisen under the settlement since it was begun and then deducts three categories of payment.[2] The first category is income which has already been treated as income of the settlor or a beneficiary. The second is income which has been paid (whether as income or capital) to or for the benefit of a beneficiary other than an unmarried minor child of the settlor. It will be seen that it is only actual payments which are taken into account—and only payments out of income. The third is income properly spent on trust expenses or, more formally, income applied in defraying trust expenses of the trustees which were properly chargeable to income (or would have been so chargeable but for any express provisions of the trust). The definition of this third category is the same as for TA 1988, s 686.[3]

The legislation also makes express provision for an offshore income gain[4] accruing in respect of a disposal of assets made by a trustee holding them for a person who would be absolutely entitled as against the trustee but for being minor. In such circumstances the income treated as arising by reference to that gain is deemed to be paid to that person.[5]

[1] ITTOIA 2005, s 631(1)–(3).

² ITTOIA 2005, s 631(4), (5). There is a fourth category relating to income for an unmarried minor child prior to 6 April 1988. ITTOIA 2005, s 631(5)(d), (6), (7).
³ On which see supra, § 13.11.
⁴ ITTOIA 2005, s 632; an offshore gain is one within the meaning of TA 1988, Part XVIII, Ch V.
⁵ The reference to income is to that arising under TA 1988, s 761(1).

Capital sums paid to the settlor

[15.23] The paragraphs that follow outline rules that were resurrected in the course of the 1995 Finance Bill debates. One does not greet this resurrection with much joy but the rules do have two advantages. The first is that they are tolerably well known; the second is that they are significantly better than the rules proposed in the Finance Bill. If income has been accumulated and a capital sum is paid by the trustees directly or indirectly to the settlor, that sum is under ITTOIA 2005, s 633 treated as the income of the settlor if it was not paid for full consideration in money or money's worth.[1] This applies whenever there is income "available"[2] in the trust, ie both when accumulated income exists in the fund when the sum is paid and, subject to limits, when the accumulation arises subsequently.

In one instance however sums paid for full consideration cause a charge. If the trustees lend money to the settlor or his spouse there would be a promise to repay and so full consideration and yet also the risk that the repayment terms might not be enforced at least so long as the settlor was alive. In this way a settlor could create a fund which would be taxed only at basic and additional rates and yet enjoy what was once his money at the same time. The section therefore defines capital sum as any sum paid by way of a loan and goes on to extend this to any sum paid (by the trustees to the settlor or the settlor's wife) by way of repayment of a loan.[3]

A capital sum does not give an income tax charge on the settlor; it can only be payable to the settlor on the death of a child of the settlor at an age under 25[4], or on the bankruptcy of a beneficiary or, in the case of a marriage settlement, on the death of both parties to the marriage plus one, or more, children of the marriage.[5]

As drafted the section did not catch payments to third parties to whom the settlor owed money.[6] This and other loopholes are now sealed, the term capital sum extending to:

(1) any sum paid to the settlor (or the spouse of the settlor) jointly with another person;
(2) any sum paid to a third party at the settlor's direction;
(3) any sum paid to a third party by virtue of the assignment by him of his right to receive it; and
(4) any sum otherwise paid or applied by the trustees for the benefit of the settlor.[7]

The section applies to capital payments made directly or indirectly to the settlor.[8]

[15.23] The Settlement Code

Simon's Taxes C4.321–323.

1. ITTOIA 2005, s 634(1)(*b*)(ii).
2. Defined in ITTOIA 2005, s 635.
3. ITTOIA 2005, s 634(1)(*a*).
4. ITTOIA 2005, s 634(3)(*b*).
5. ITTOIA 2005, s 625(2) applied by s 634(3)(*a*).
6. *IRC v Potts* [1951] 1 All ER 76, 32 TC 211.
7. ITTOIA 2005, s 634(5), (7).
8. ITTOIA 2005, s 633(1)—quaere whether these words add anything; *IRC v Wachtel* [1971] 1 All ER 271, 46 TC 543.

Loans and repayments

[15.24] The concept of "loan" is central to ITTOIA 2005, s 633 yet the term is not further defined. Case law shows that it is not confined to the common law relationship of debtor and creditor and applies equally where there is an equitable right to reimbursement.[1] A loan need not be in cash and a secured loan is still a loan. A loan is a loan even though the person giving it may view the transaction as an investment.[2]

Once the loan is repaid it ceases to be subject to s 633 for years subsequent to that in which the repayment takes place.[3] So if a loan was made in 2000–01, is repaid in 2004–05 and income is accumulated for the first time in 2007–08, s 633 will have no effect. Furthermore, if the settlor receives a loan of say £5,000 which he then repays only to take a further loan of £5,000 he will be liable to a charge only on £5,000.

Section 633 applies also where a loan by the settlor to the trustees is repaid.[4] Analogous mitigating rules apply. So where the loan has been repaid but the settlor then makes a further loan of an amount not less than the original loan, s 633 does not apply.[5] This provision is curious in that it applies only where the original loan has been completely repaid; there is no proportionate relief for a partial repayment. However, while the rule requires complete repayment this does not necessarily mean repayment in full; an agreement by a settlor to accept a lesser sum in complete discharge of the original loan will presumably suffice.

Simon's Taxes C4.321–323.

1. *De Vigier v IRC* (infra, § **15.29**).
2. *McCrone v IRC* (1967) 44 TC 142.
3. ITTOIA 2005, s 638(1).
4. See *Piratin v IRC* [1981] STC 441.
5. ITTOIA 2005, s 638(4), (5).

The charge

[15.25] Since a capital sum is here in issue, and since the whole purpose of the legislation is to prevent a settlor from deriving benefit for himself from property the income of which may be taxed at a lower rate than if it were still his, ITTOIA 2005, s 633 only applies to the extent that the payment could have been made from income, that is to the extent that the income arising under the trust since it was created[1] is greater than the sums distributed or which although not distributed, have already been treated as his together with the tax on these payments.[2] Perhaps because the payment is made to the settlor himself he is given no statutory right to be reimbursed out of the trust funds, in respect of the tax; for the same reason, any repayment of tax by reason of the settlor's personal relief may be retained by him.[3] These acts of apparent generosity are however more than offset by the fact that there is no way of refunding the tax when the settlor, or his estate, repay the loan.[4]

Simon's Taxes C4.321–323.

---

1   Or since the year 1937–38 if shorter.
2   ITTOIA 2005, s 635.
3   ITTOIA 2005, s 623(2). Cf supra, § **15.23**.
4   Cf TA 1988, s 419(4) (infra, § **29.10**).

[15.26] Chapter 5 applies with equal vigour to a capital sum received by the settlor from a body corporate connected with the settlement, eg a loan from the company.[1] A body corporate is connected with a settlement if it is at any time in the year either (a) a close company (or not a close company only because it is not resident in the UK) and the participators then include the trustees of the settlement, or (b) controlled by such a company.[2]

Partly because of the habit of using accumulation trusts to receive dividend income from private companies which income was not needed by the family owners, these provisions (formerly in TA 1988, s 677) were a lethal trap whenever the settlor would think of making a loan to the company, or vice versa. In order therefore to limit the operation of these rules to those situations in which it could fairly be said that the settlor was deriving some benefit from the accumulation, s 641(1)(b) requires there also to be an "associated payment", that is a payment by the trustees to the company in a period of five years ending or beginning with the date on which the payment is made to the settlor. Further, s 641 is not to apply if the loan is repaid within 12 months and the period for which loans are outstanding in any five year period does not exceed 12 months.[3]

The 1995 legislation made one minor change to the rules. By repealing s 678(7) it tried to ensure that when a capital payment is made to the settlor by a company and that payment precedes the making of an associated payment from the trustees to the company the settlor is not taxed until that associated payment is made.[4]

Simon's Taxes C4.321–323.

---

1   ITTOIA 2005, s 641(1). For reason, see Lord Reid, infra, § **15.28**, note 1.

[15.26] The Settlement Code

² ITTOIA 2005, s 643(2) invoking the definition in ITTOIA 2005, s 643(2). This means that whenever a trust has shares in a family company the settlor must beware, ITTOIA 2005, s 633 and TA 1988, s 419 (infra, § **29.10**) whenever he takes or makes a loan.
³ ITTOIA 2005, s 642.
⁴ Inland Revenue press release, 28 March 1995, para 4; *Simon's Weekly Tax Intelligence* 1995, p 549.

[15.27] The sum which is charged on the settlor is the undistributed income grossed up at the basic rate plus the rate applicable to trusts.¹ Credit is given for such tax as has been charged on the trust.² Trustees who have made payments to the settlor which fall within ITTOIA 2005, s 633 must therefore be anxious to distribute all the trust income each year until the settlor dies or the 11-year period, see infra, § **15.28**, expires.

If the settlor emigrates it would appear that, the source being within the UK, the charge to tax remains although if he has little other UK income his tax bill may be reduced.

A further problem is that the sum is treated as the income of the settlor in the year of payment notwithstanding that it may have been accumulated over many years. It is small wonder that most trusts now contain a clause making it a breach of trust to pay any capital sum to the settlor or his spouse; this is simply a reminder to trustees since if payments are made they will fall within these provisions even though in breach of trust.

Simon's Taxes C4.321–323.

¹ ITTOIA 2005, s 640.
² ITTOIA 2005, s 640(2).

[15.28] Should the capital sum paid exceed the undistributed income, the excess is carried forward and charged to the settlor in the next year to the extent that there is undistributed income available up to the end of that year, and so on for succeeding years subject to a maximum of 11 years. There is no 11-year maximum to the carry-back rule where the income has been accumulated before the capital sum is paid. An allowance is made for sums already charged under ITTOIA 2005, s 633.¹

Once the 11-year limit has passed it falls out of account for s 633 but it cannot then reduce the amount of available income which may be matched against a subsequent capital payment.

Simon's Taxes C4.321–323.

¹ On previous law see Lord Reid in *Bates v IRC* [1967] 1 All ER 84 at 90, 44 TC 225 at 261.

[15.29] The capricious nature of the section has caused much adverse comment as when an innocent transaction is caught by the section. In *De*

Vigier v IRC[1] trustees held property for two infant children contingently upon their attaining the age of 25 years, with a power to accumulate and maintain. The trustees had wished to take advantage of a rights issue by a company whose shares they held but they had no money and no power to borrow. The trustees were the settlor's wife and a solicitor. The settlor's wife therefore paid £7,000 into the trust bank account to pay for the shares and within nine months that sum had been repaid in two equal instalments. The settlor was held taxable on the grossed up equivalent of £7,000, £12,174 at that time. It was a sum paid by way of repayment of a loan. The fact that her right to the repayment arose from the equitable right of an indemnity given to a trustee who incurs expenses on behalf of the trust rather than the common law claim on a contract of loan made no difference. Yet had the trust had the power to borrow and had she merely guaranteed that loan, no charge would have arisen.[2]

In the Court of Appeal Russell LJ, suggested that had she been a sole trustee there could have been no loan. However, in the House of Lords Lord Upjohn said 'the mere fact that under the old forms of pleading, in the circumstances of this case, an action of debt for return of a loan would not lie does not prevent the transaction being properly described as a loan'.[3] The point was that an advance of money was made to the trust upon the terms that it was to be repaid out of the trust fund. That was a loan.

Simon's Taxes C4.323.

[1] [1964] 2 All ER 907, 42 TC 24.
[2] Per Russell LJ, 42 TC 24 at 33, CA.
[3] [1964] 2 All ER 907 at 915, 42 TC 24 at 41.

Settlements of income

[15.30] An obvious form of tax mitigation would appear to be for a higher rate taxpayer to sign the income arising from his investments to members of his family who are subject to tax at basic rate or, even better, have insufficient income to use the personal allowance to which they are entitled. Prior to 14 March 1988 it was, indeed, possible to make this arrangement by entering into a covenant in favour of another family member. The covenant diverted income but left the asset generating the income in the ownership of the covenantor. A covenant in favour of an adult child could be useful and once the age of majority was reduced to 18, such covenants to support children at university became commonplace. A covenant in favour of a minor child did not produce the desired effect as statute[1] caused the income payable to the minor child to be assessed on the covenantor parent (see supra, § **15.21**). At that time, no fiscal advantage was obtained by a covenant in favour of a spouse as a married couple's income was aggregated and assessed on the husband.[2]

The advent of independent taxation in 1990–91 lead to the focus of tax mitigation within the family group being put on arrangements designed to give income to a spouse taxable at basic rate, rather than to a spouse at higher rate.

[15.30] The Settlement Code

The effect of ITTOIA 2005, s 625(1) is that income arising from property gifted is taxed on the donor if the donor's spouse can have any benefit from the property in any circumstances whatsoever. Clearly, thus, under the general rule, a purported diversion of income from one spouse to another has no tax effect. The exception to this is given by ITTOIA 2005, s 626 which removes from the definition of settlement and (hence the retention of the tax liability with the donor):

> an outright gift by one spouse to the other of property from which income arises, unless—
> (a) the gift does not carry a right to the whole of that income, or
> (b) the property given is wholly or substantially a right to income.

The provision has been in statute since 1936[3] but was of limited practical relevance until the advent of independent taxation in 1990. Until around 2003 it was rare for the Revenue to challenge arrangements in a family company by reference to this provision.[4]

Some matters are clear. Settling a life interest on a spouse is ineffective as a life interest is wholly a right to income.

In *Hadlee v Commissioner of Inland Revenue*[5] a solicitor in partnership with others, appointed to his wife a share of income that arose to him. This was ineffective, as the appointment was wholly or substantially a right to income without a gift of the capital asset from which the gift arose.

In *Young v Pearce*[6] a company controlled by husband created a special class of shares with a right to dividend but no rights in a winding up and no votes. These shares in this special class were issued to the wife. It is not surprising that the court identified these special shares with restricted rights as property that is substantially a right to income and the issue by the company controlled by the husband as being effectively a settlement by the husband. It followed that the dividends declared on the wife's shares were assessed on the husband.

What is much less clear is the situation in thousands of small family companies where husband and wife both hold ordinary shares in the company, bearing equal rights. If the company activity is to exploit the skills of one spouse, is the effect of the Settlement Code to tax all dividends on the spouse with the skill? This was the question at the heart of the test case *Jones v Garnett*.[7]

---

[1] [Now] ITTOIA 2005, s 629.
[2] Prior to 1990 there was an election available for the separate taxation of a wife's earnings, but this did not affect the taxation of the wife's investment income (such as dividends from the family company), which were always taxed on the husband.
[3] FA 1936, s 21.
[4] The Revenue has stated that they customarily look at about 50 cases each year where they consider a question arises as to a settlement of income.
[5] [1993] STC 294, PC.
[6] [1996] STC 743.

[7] Special Commissioners' decision: [2005] STC (SCD) 9; High Court decision: [2005] STC 1667; Court of Appeal decision: [2006] STC 283, CA; House of Lords decision: [2007] UKHL 35.

Jones v Garnett

[15.31] In the case of *Jones v Garnett*[1] Geoffrey Jones and his wife Diana Jones acquired an off-the-shelf company in 1992, Arctic Systems Ltd.[2] The company had two shares in issue, Geoffrey held one; Diana held the other. The company had a sole director, Geoffrey Jones. The business of the company was to supply the services of Geoffrey Jones as a consultant in the field of information technology. Diana Jones undertook administrative duties for the company. Geoffrey Jones and Diana Jones both took modest salaries from the company. The company's profits were distributed by means of dividend, Geoffrey Jones and Diana Jones each receiving the same dividend by virtue of the single share held by each. In 1999–2000, for example, the company's receipts were £78,355. Mr Jones took £6,520 as salary and Mrs Jones £3,600. The company paid dividends of £25,767.25 to each of the shareholders.

The Revenue raised assessments on the basis that the issue of the share to Diana Jones was a settlement by Geoffrey Jones and the charge was not exempted from the Settlement Code by the exclusion given for an outright gift between spouses.[3] Hence, in the Revenue's view, the dividend paid to Diana Jones was assessable on Geoffrey Jones.

The House of Lords held[4] that the issue of one share to Mr Jones and one share to Mrs Jones was a settlement. As Lord Hoffmann said[5]:

> Mrs Jones could not have been issued with a share without the agreement of her husband and when he agreed to that arrangement, it was expected that he would take a low salary and that substantial dividends would be distributed. That was the advice which they had received from the accountant. And that was what happened. Each year the salaries were set at a level suggested by the accountant and the rest retained or distributed as dividend. The decisions were tax driven and not commercially driven. And it was necessary, in order to gain the tax benefit, that Mr Jones should, in a broad sense, transfer some of his earnings to his wife.
>
> "Authority for taking a broad and realistic view of the matter may be found in several cases of which the most relevant is *Crossland v Hawkins*[6]...
>
> "I cannot agree that this was a 'normal commercial transaction between two adults'. It made sense only on the basis that the two adults were married to each other. If Mrs Jones had been a stranger offering her services as a book keeper, it would have been a most abnormal transaction. It would not have been an arrangement into which Mr Jones would ever have entered with someone with whom he was dealing at arms' length. It was only 'natural love and affection' which provided the consideration for the benefit he intended to confer upon his wife. That is sufficient to provide the necessary 'element of bounty'.

Statute[7] exempts from the charge on the settlor income that arises from an outright gift by one spouse to the other of property that carries a right to the

[15.31] The Settlement Code

whole of the income generated by that property as long as the property is "not wholly or substantially a right to income". The Revenue argued that the share acquired by Mrs Jones was substantially a right to income. Hence, in the submission of Revenue counsel, the exclusion did not apply and the dividend paid to Mrs Jones was to be taxed as income of Mr Jones. This was firmly rejected by all five judges in the House of Lords. As Lord Hoffmann said:[8]

> It is true that the value in the share arose from the expectation that it would generate income. But that is true of many shares, even in quoted companies. The share was not wholly or even substantially a right to income. It was an ordinary share conferring a right to vote, to participate in the distribution of assets on a winding up, to block a special resolution, to complain under section 459 of the Companies Act 1985. These are all rights over and above the right to income. The ordinary share is different from the preference shares in *Young v Pearce*[9], which conferred nothing except the right to 30% of the net profits before distribution of any other dividend and repayment on winding up of the nominal amount subscribed for their shares. Those shares were substantially a right to share in the income of the company.
>
> "In my opinion, [the arrangement in *Jones v Garnett*] falls within the exception in [now ITTOIA 2005, s 626].

The nature of a share being more than a mere right to income was expanded by Lord Hope:[10]

> For the reasons my noble and learned friends have given, an arrangement by which one spouse uses a private company as a tax-efficient vehicle for distributing to the other income which its business generates is likely to constitute a 'settlement' on the other spouse within the meaning of [now ITTOIA 2005, s 624]. But so long as the shares from which that income arises are ordinary shares, and not shares carrying contractual rights which are restricted wholly or substantially to a right to income, the settlement will fall within the exception created by [now ITTOIA 2005, s 626]. This is an important point of general public interest on which I should like to add these brief comments.
>
> "The rights which attach to shares in a company depend on the contractual relations between the holders of those shares as defined by the articles of association of the company. It is the articles of association that determine questions between ordinary and preference shareholders as to the right to income in the form of dividends, and the right to the repayment of capital and to participate in the distribution of surplus assets in the event of a winding up of the company. They also determine questions as to the right to attend and to vote at general meetings of the company. The general rule is that the profits of a company belong to the ordinary shareholders, subject to the payment of any preference dividend. Then there is the question how surplus assets not required for the discharge of the company's liabilities or the return of paid up capital to the shareholders are to be distributed in the event of a winding up. The rights of the preference shareholders in any particular case will depend on what the articles of association provide. This is because the rights of the shareholders are determined by the terms of the bargain which they made with the company and with each other. The articles must be taken as a complete statement of the rights of the preference shareholders in the winding up: *Scottish Insurance Corpn Ltd v Wilsons and Clyde Coal Co Ltd*.[11]

It is interesting to note the robust criticism of the Revenue action in bringing the case made by Carnwath LJ in the Court of Appeal:[12]

> The lack of a clearly ascertainable legislative purpose underlines the need for caution in extending the concept of settlement beyond the scope of existing jurisprudence.

The Revenue's position in this case seems to me a significant extension. For the first time, they seek to apply the concept to what has been found to be a normal commercial transaction between two adults, to which each is making a substantial commercial contribution, albeit not of the same economic value. Such a difference, by itself, is not enough to my mind to take the arrangement into the realm of 'bounty', as it has been understood in the existing cases. If the legislature wishes such an arrangement to be brought within a special regime for tax purposes, clearer language is necessary to achieve it.

Within 24 hours of the decision in the House of Lords, the Government announced its intention to introduce legislation to reverse the effect of the case.[13] Draft legislation was published on 6 December 2007. That, had it been enacted, would not have modified the settlements code but would have been a new layer of complexity, requiring couples (and others) to ascertain whether or not they had effected a tax-saving by using arrangements that were not carried out on an arm's length basis (thereby linking into Lord Hoffmann's speech in *Jones v Garnett*). It was announced on Budget Day (12 March 2008) that the new legislation would not be introduced with effect from 6 April 2008 but would be included in the Finance Bill 2009 instead.[14]

---

[1] [2007] UKHL 35 upholding the decision of the Court of Appeal (but on different grounds): [2006] STC 283, CA, which reversed the decision of Park J, [2005] STC 1667.

[2] Although the company was not a party to the litigation, the case was often referred to as "*Arctic Systems*".

[3] Now ITTOIA 2005, s 626.

[4] Lord Hoffmann, Lord Hope, Lord Walker and Lord Neuberger had no hesitation in declaring the issue of the share to Mrs Jones to be a settlement. Baroness Hale had some hesitation on the point, saying ([2007] UKHL 35 at para 71): "it only becomes a 'settlement' within the meaning of [now ITTOIA 2005, s 624(1)] because of expectations about later events which are too uncertain and fluid to be included as part of the initial arrangement. However, in view of our unanimous conclusion that the appeal should be dismissed, it would be presumptuous of me to reach a different conclusion on the settlement point."

[5] [2007] UKHL 35 at paras 10, 11 & 24.

[6] (1961) 39 TC 493, [1961] Ch 537.

[7] ITTOIA 2005, s 626(1)-(3), see supra **15.15**.

[8] [2007] UKHL 35 at para 30.

[9] [1996] STC 743, (1996) 70 TC 331

[10] [2007] UKHL 35 paras 34 & 35

[11] [1949] AC 462, per Viscount Maugham at p 481, Lord Simonds at p 488.

[12] [2006] STC 283, CA para [108] at 309i/310a.

[13] Written Answers to Parliament 26 July 2007.

[14] The clear implication was that any new legislation would be introduced with effect from 6 April 2009. However, the Budget Day statement, if read closely, does not preclude an earlier commencement date. In view of the universal lack of popularity of the proposed new rules, however, some commentators now expect the legislation to be shelved indefinitely.

Part III

Capital Gains Tax

For payment of capital gains tax, returns, enquiries, appeals and other administrative matters, see Chapter 2.

16

Gains and chargeability
Outline
Consideration
Allowable expenditure
Foreign taxes paid
Wasting assets
Losses
Assets of negligible value
Payment of capital gains tax by instalments
Persons chargeable
Rates of tax and annual exempt amount
Spouses and civil partners
Charities
Gift to a charity

17

Assets, exemptions and reliefs
Assets
Exemptions and reliefs
Valuation

18

Disposal
Meaning of disposal
Time of disposal
Part disposals
Compensation and insurance payments
Use of assets
Mortgages and bankruptcy
Options
Gifts, bargains not at arm's length and other gratuitous transactions
Holdover relief
Gratuitous transfers of value
Connected persons

19

Death
Basic rule: acquisition without disposal
Deed of variation
Inheritance (Provision for Family and Dependants) Act 1975

Disposal to legatee
Death of a life tenant of settled property
Losses
Disposals during period of administration

20

Settled property
Introduction
Settlor retains an interest
Identifying the settlor
Avoiding the charge on the settlor
Meaning of 'settled property'
Transfer into trust
Disposals during trust period
Deemed disposals
Trust with a vulnerable beneficiary
Non-resident trusts

21

Shares and companies
Securities—identification
Capital distribution by a company
Conversion of securities
Company reconstructions and amalgamations
Miscellaneous

22

Business and partnerships
Capital allowances
Stock in trade
Trading losses: CGT set-off
Transfer of a business to a company
Rollover relief
Deferral relief
Gifts of business assets—holdover relief
Partnerships
European Economic Interest Grouping (EEIG)
Non-residents trading in the UK

23

Land
Definition of land
Capital gain or a trading transaction?
Part disposal
Exchange of joint interests
Furnished holiday lettings
Main residence
Leases
Reverse premiums
Mineral royalties
ITA 2007, Pt 13, Ch 3 / TA 1988, s 776

24

Taper relief, indexation allowance and rebasing
Introduction
Taper relief
Indexation allowance
Rebasing to March 1982 election
Time apportionment—assets held at 6 April 1965

16

Gains and chargeability

Outline	PARA 16.01
Consideration	PARA 16.05
Allowable expenditure	PARA 16.16
Foreign taxes paid	PARA 16.23
Wasting assets	PARA 16.25
Losses	PARA 16.26
Assets of negligible value	PARA 16.33
Payment of capital gains tax by instalments	PARA 16.38
Persons chargeable	PARA 16.39
Rates of tax and annual exempt amount	PARA 16.40
Spouses and civil partners	PARA 16.41
Charities	PARA 16.45
Gift to a charity	PARA 16.49

For payment of capital gains tax, see supra, §§ **2A.14–2A.19**.

Outline

History

[16.01] Despite a history of over 40 years, the nature of CGT is still unsettled. Is it an attempt to charge tax on a commercial gain? Or is it, like development land tax, a charge on an arithmetic formula? Is the tax levied because Parliament considers that it is right to tax a capital gain? Or is it in existence mainly to preserve the integrity of a tax on income, by stopping devices that would otherwise change a taxable income receipt into an untaxed capital increase? Why does Parliament consider that it is right to tax an individual at a flat rate on a "paper gain", but a company is to be taxed on the whole of a "real gain"? There is a logic in the tax charge being at the shareholder level and a company being treated as merely an intermediate stage; but why is this treatment applied when the company sells a substantial shareholding, but not when the company sells a small shareholding?

The conceptual basis of the tax may be unclear but the computational complexity is abundantly clear to any practitioner. CGT is an expensive tax to administer. Official statistics[1] state that the cost to the Revenue of collecting CGT is 0.92% of the tax collected, making it the third most expensive tax to collect. (For 2002–03, it cost the Revenue 2.73% of the tax collected, making it, then, the most expensive tax to collect. This was the last year for retirement relief; perhaps the real reason for its abolition was the cost to the Revenue of policing the relief.) Some commentators have estimated that by adding to the

[16.01] Gains and chargeability

Revenue costs the compliance costs of fees levied by the tax profession on the payers of CGT, the cost of administering tax could be 25% of the tax collected.

In 1965 CGT was introduced initially as a tax on long-term gains; gains made within 12 months were then charged to income tax under Schedule D, Case VII. Case VII was abolished in 1971.[2] The concept of CGT was a tax at a rate separate from other taxes charged on the difference between consideration received and expenditure incurred, with a rough and ready formulation to avoid charging pre-1965 gains. Death was a chargeable disposal from 1965 until 1971. The 1971 decision to abolish the CGT charge at death,[3] while keeping the acquisition by the personal representatives, and through them the beneficiaries, at market value at death meant that estate duty (later to be superseded by CTT and IHT) became the sole tax on death; it also meant that the concept of charging all gains during an individual's lifetime was dropped. In 1982, the concept changed again with the introduction of indexation relief;[4] so that the gain subjected to tax became the difference between actual sale proceeds and a cost adjusted by reference to an index of living costs, which has never been an index of asset prices. This move away from a gain as measured in commercial accountancy towards a charge based on an arithmetic difference continued in 1988 with the general adoption of the base as an indexed 1982 market value.[5] The charge to tax bore little real relation to the commercial gain enjoyed as the statutory provisions for market value produce widely differing values for shares in the same company, according to the size of the individual's shareholding. In 1988 too, the concept of CGT being a separate tax with its own tax rate was abandoned; the rate at which CGT was paid being aligned with the income tax rate[6]—a major change which reduced much avoidance planning.

In 1998 we had a further change in the concept of taxing capital gains. Indexation allowance was replaced by taper relief—but not for companies.[7] At the time that the UK moved from price-adjustment costs to taper relief, Spain moved away from taper relief to price-adjusted cost. The scheme chosen by the UK is not dissimilar to that used in France for taxing capital gains, except that the UK taper stops after ten years, whereas in France the taper continues so that no charge is levied on the disposal of an asset held for more than 22 years. In 1999 the rate structure was changed yet again so that the rates of tax replicated that applying for savings income (10%, 20% and 40%).

Calls for simplification of the CGT regime were repeatedly ignored: each gain being measured by applying indexation allowance to the first period and taper period to the second period, with a bonus given if the taxpayer happened to hold the asset as the Chancellor was speaking on 17 March 1998, but only if the asset sold is not a business asset.

Then, when simplification was proposed in October 2007 (to take effect from April 2008), the proposals brought only more complexity (and, possibly worse, confusion). Under the rules applying since 6 April 2008, all gains (whether business assets or not) are taxed at a flat rate of 18% (irrespective of the period of ownership and equally irrespective of the taxpayer's marginal income tax rates). It should be noted, however, that only the rules for capital gains tax have changed; the taxation of chargeable gains of companies remains as it has been since 1988.

The CGT legislation was first introduced in 1965 and is now showing its age, having passed through two Consolidation Acts.[8] and is backed up by the usual array of concessions and statements of practice, Revenue interpretations and a very detailed Revenue Manual. These informal arrangements sometimes allow taxpayers to defer a charge. Naturally the Revenue assume that the taxpayer will declare and pay the deferred tax in due course but the fact that the deferral was given on the basis of a concession rather than strict law meant that there was often no legal obligation on the taxpayer to do so. It says much for UK taxpayers that most made their returns in due course submitting to the deferred charge. However, some did not and so statute provides[9] that where a person has taken advantage of a concession, widely defined, deferring tax there is now a legal obligation to pay the deferred tax in due course; a charge is imposed on the amount of the gain relieved for the earlier period.[10] The charge is a reserve power in that it is imposed only if the taxpayer fails to observe the terms of the concession. The charge cannot be for less than the gain deferred by way of concession; it is unclear whether, for gains before 6 April 2008 which were subject to the tapering relief rules, it could sometimes be for more. Self-assessment requires clearly defined obligations on the taxpayer to operate a system that is precisely defined and comprehensible by a taxpayer making the self-assessment. Capital gains tax falls far short of this paradigm. A system relying on concessions is not consistent with assessment by the taxpayer. There are too many areas of uncertainty. The greatest criticism must, surely, be the complexity of the calculation required for many common, straightforward transactions. The cost for the taxpayer in obtaining the services of an adviser competent to compute capital gains is often out of proportion to the tax payable.

Prior to 1998, if the value of an asset increased in line with inflation, no tax was payable.[11] Between 1998 until 2008, if an asset was purchased for £100,000 and sold after 10 years for the same amount in real terms, tax of £11,526 was payable[12] (£4,800 if a business asset).[13] At least the aim of the 2008 changes was simplification. But it reversed the policies introduced in 1982 and 1998 taking the tax back to the relative simplicity of the 1965 rules. The difficulty with that approach is that capital gains are (more often than not) made in respect of assets held over the longer term and taxpayers are finding that commercial decisions made in accordance with the then prevailing orthodoxy are suddenly finding themselves penalised when politicians have a change of heart. Of course, whilst simplification is a laudable aim, closer examination of the Budget Report shows that the consequential increase in the tax receipts could not have been an added attraction to the Treasury.[14]

Simon's Taxes Division C1.1; Sumption CGT, Division A1.

---

1   HM Revenue & Customs Annual Report 2005/06: see supra, § 2.02.
2   FA 1971, s 56(1).
3   FA 1971, s 59.
4   FA 1982, s 86.
5   FA 1988, s 96.
6   FA 1988, s 98.
7   FA 1998, s 121.

[16.01] Gains and chargeability

[8] The first consolidation was the Capital Gains Tax Act 1979. The second consolidation, which also incorporates the corporation tax charge on capital gains made by companies is the Taxation of Chargeable Gains Act 1992.

[9] TCGA 1992, ss 284A and 284B added by FA 1999, s 76; see also Inland Revenue press release, 9 March 1999, *Simon's Weekly Tax Intelligence* 1999, p 463 and Inland Revenue Tax Bulletin, October 1999, p 700.

[10] Concessions given statutory effect by ss 284A and 284B are D15 (see infra, § **22.15**), D16 (see infra, § **22.13**), D22 (see infra, § **22.15**) and D39 (see infra, § **23.17**).

[11] Pre 1998:

The calculation is:	£
Sale proceeds	148,024
Indexed cost:	
£100,000 × (1.04)^{10}	(148,024)
Gain	nil

[12] Post 1998:

The calculation is:	£
Sale proceeds	148,024
Cost:	(100,000)
	48,024
Gain after taper relief	nil
£48,024 × 60%	28,815
CGT payable @ 40%	£11,526

[13] If a business asset:

The calculation is:	£
Gain after taper relief	
£48,024 × 25%:	12,006
CGT payable @ 40%	£4,800

[14] Budget Report Table A.2 anticipates annual savings of £250m in 2008–09 increasing to £500m in 2010/11).

Interpretation

[16.02] Courts have had difficulty with the concept of a "gain". As recently as 1993, the Special Commissioners and the Court of Appeal held that the word "gain" takes its meaning from its context,[1] whereas the High Court and the House of Lords held that the word "gain" has a meaning independent of its context.[2] The approaches taken by the court can appear to lack consistency. On the one hand, one has highly detailed legislation often interpreted by the judges in a mechanistic, way.[3] On the other hand, one has decisions such as *Ramsay v IRC*[4] and *Furniss v Dawson*[5] where senior judges say that capital gains tax must live in "the real world". One may also cite *Marren v Ingles*[6] where the court adopted an imaginative construction of the legislation in defeating a technical argument on behalf of the taxpayer. As a further example of this second view, we find Lord Wilberforce in *Aberdeen Construction Group v IRC*[7] attempting to express the nature of capital gains tax by saying that any interpretation of the statutory provisions must have a "guiding principle", that the purpose of the legislation is to tax capital gains and make allowance for capital losses "each of which ought to be arrived at on normal business principles". Insofar as this statement is intended to mean that a court should hesitate before accepting results which are paradoxical and contrary to business sense (as Lord Wilberforce also said) the statement is welcome but it has to be said that the courts have not always heeded this advice.

Although Lord Wilberforce was anxious to establish that capital gains tax was not simply a tax on arithmetical differences, that is the thought that emerges from a literal examination of the statutory framework and that is the approach which has often been adopted by the courts. Courts have frequently ignored any concept of a commercial gain in interpreting the legislation. So in *Bentley v Pike*,[8] dealing with the acquisition of a foreign asset, the court held that CGT is levied on the difference between disposal proceeds and the acquisition cost, each expressed in sterling at the relevant time, and without regard to the question whether there was or was not a gain in terms of the foreign currency involved. This is not to say that the decision is wrong—simply that there is a gap between the result in the case and the concept of commercial gain or, indeed, the gain as perceived by an individual taxpayer.

TCGA 1992, Part II (ss 15–57) entitled "General provisions relating to computation of gains . . ." provides rules for determining sums that are to be treated as "consideration" and sums to be treated as "acquisition costs". Although statute does not direct the taxpayer to deduct the second from the first, that is the only sensible reading of capital gains legislation. It follows that whenever statute refers to "gain", it means this numerical difference. It does not mean what commercial accountancy practice may regard as a gain. In this respect, CGT legislation is to be contrasted with income tax legislation as the latter has as its starting point a concept of "income" that is external to the legislation.

Whatever semblance there may have been of "normal business principles" in the scheme introduced in FA 1965, the rebasing provisions of FA 1988 take us very far away from a tax based on the sum that would be identified as a gain in constructing financial accounts. The gain for tax purposes is increased from a purely artificial base point, which gives a measure of gain that is not even comparable to that which would be calculated when preparing current cost accounts. Perverse results arise in relation to unquoted shares, and also to intangible assets (see also comments in infra, § **22.40**). When a business is sold, the ability to deduct a base cost for self-generated goodwill depends on whether the business started before March 1982 and what was the position of the business at that date. As early as 1966, a Swedish commentator said of CGT:

> Never was Britain a more self-evident centre of interest for tax experts around the world. I leave it to the audience to say whether the role of guinea pigs for the tax paying world is an enviable one or not.[9]

[16.02] Gains and chargeability

Simon's Direct Tax Service C1.101.

1. Charles Potter QC sitting as Special Commissioner in *Smith v Schofield* in 1989; unanimous judgment of Glidewell LJ, Beldam LJ and Nolan LJ [1992] STC 249, CA.
2. Hoffmann J [1990] STC 602, in the High Court in *Smith v Schofield*; Lord Templeman, Lord Goff, Lord Jauncey, Lord Mustill and Lord Woolf [1993] STC 268, in the House of Lords. In the Court of Appeal, Revenue counsel stated that the Revenue had computed that the effect of this decision on outstanding cases was a total of £10,000,000 of tax payable. In *MEPC Holdings v Taylor* [2000] STC (SCD) 504, the decision in *Smith v Schofield* was used by the Special Commissioner as authority for holding that "profits" in corporation tax legislation on group relief means a sum computed by including capital gains after deduction of brought forward capital losses. This approach was favoured by the House of Lords [2003] UKHL 70, [2004] STC 123 but only after being rejected by the High Court and Court of Appeal. But perhaps with different arguments: see Lord Hoffmann's judgment at para 22 regarding TA 1988, s 403(8).
3. In *Goodbrand v Loffland Bros North Sea Inc* [1998] STC 1930, CA, the Court of Appeal upheld an assessment that was £9,500,000 greater than the commercial gain made by the company. In *Whittles v Uniholdings Ltd (No 3)* [1996] STC 914, CA, the Court of Appeal, by a majority, upheld an assessment that divided a single commercial operation into a loan and a forward contract that were commercially a single transaction, with the result that the company did not obtain tax relief for a loss of £2,950,565.
4. [1981] STC 174, HL.
5. [1984] STC 153, HL.
6. [1980] STC 500, HL.
7. [1978] STC 127 at 131c.
8. [1981] STC 360.
9. Professor Leif Muten, [1966] BTR 138 at 146.

Basic elements of capital gains tax

[16.03] For a liability to capital gains tax to arise:

(1) there must be a disposal of a type relevant to CGT;
(2) of an asset of a type relevant to CGT;
(3) by a person chargeable to the tax;
(4) on which a chargeable gain which is computed under the Act arises.

The scheme of the legislation is to distinguish a gain from a chargeable gain. It is only the latter that is subjected to tax. The legislation does not specify how a gain should be computed. Rather, it specifies what costs can be deducted from the consideration.[1] Finally, one should deduct any relief that arises by virtue of the nature of the asset (such as main residence relief) or a relief that arises from the use of the proceeds (roll-over relief, deferral relief). Prior to 6 April 2008, when calculating the raw gain, taxpayers were entitled to deduct indexation allowance in respect of any asset owned before 1 April 1998 to reflect the effects of inflation between the time that the asset was acquired and its disposal. Furthermore, for gains realised between 6 April 1998 and 5 April

2008, the final figure reached (after taking into account any other reliefs) could be reduced by 'taper relief' in order to compute the chargeable gain.

Simon's Taxes Division C1.1.

---

[1] TCGA 1992, s 38.

Scheme of Capital Gains Tax

[16.04] Capital gains tax (CGT) is charged on chargeable gains "accruing to" a person, other than a company, during a year of assessment.[1]

Chargeable gains accrue only on chargeable disposals of chargeable assets. Certain events are treated as disposals, eg the complete loss or destruction of an asset.[2]

Although a number of the machinery provisions relating to returns, self-assessments, appeals and so on, are common to both taxes, CGT is a tax separate from income tax. This was still the case, notwithstanding the unification of the rates of CGT and income tax between 1988–89 and 2007-08.[3] Any gain liable to income tax is excluded from CGT[4] and losses available for set off against income are not allowable losses for CGT. Conversely, an excess of capital losses cannot be set off against income liable to income tax.[5] Further, deductions that are or would be allowable for income tax are not generally allowable for CGT.[6]

Although CGT was introduced in 1965, since 2008–09 it is imposed only on gains accruing since 31 March 1982.[7] Until 5 April 2008, taxpayers had a limited right to be taxed on a historical gain (or even, in cases of assets owned before 6 April 1965, a share of the historical gain). The pre-2008 rules were beneficial to taxpayers whose actual historical costs exceeded the value of their asset as at 31 March 1982. However, with effect from 6 April 2008, all assets held at 31 March 1982 are automatically rebased to the value as at that date (whether or not this is in the taxpayer's interest).

Simon's Taxes C1.101; C2.301; Sumption CGT A1.01.

---

[1] TCGA 1992, s 1. On the taxation of offshore income gains see infra, § **35.41**.
[2] TCGA 1992, s 24(1).
[3] See infra, § **16.31**.
[4] TCGA 1992, s 37.
[5] But see FA 1991, s 71 and TA 1988, s 574 for exceptions to this: supra, §§ **6.17** and **6.34**.
[6] TCGA 1992, s 39. As to the deduction of trading losses from chargeable gains, see infra, § **22.09**.
[7] TCGA 1992, s 35.

Consideration

[16.05] Unless statute otherwise provides, the consideration for the disposal is the actual amount received, in money or money's worth.

Any receipt is potentially liable to be treated as consideration. In *Stanton v Drayton Commercial Investment Co Ltd*,[1] the House of Lords considered an agreement whereby investments were to be purchased from an insurance company for a consideration that consisted in the taxpayer company issuing 2,461,226 ordinary shares at 160p per share. The agreement was conditional on permission being obtained for the shares to be dealt with on the Stock Exchange. Agreement was subsequently obtained and, hence, on 11 October 1972 the agreement became unconditional. The following day, the shares were first quoted on the Stock Exchange at the price of 125p per share. Following the subsequent sale of the shares, the Revenue raised an assessment using 125p per share as the base cost. The company contended that the shares should be valued at 160p each, being the issue price noted in the agreement. The House of Lords upheld the taxpayer's computation on the basis that this was what was shown in an arm's length agreement and there was no reason for going behind this agreed value. It was accepted the market value was lower, but it was held that this was only relevant when no agreed value was available.

Where there is a complex arrangement for the disposal, such as frequently arises on commercial deals when companies are sold or reorganised, the approach to be adopted was given by Lightman J in *Spectros International plc v Madeen*[2] as:

> The critical issue is to identify the consideration agreed and allocated to the disposal of the shares. . . . I must approach the question before me as a matter of construction of the composite of the three documents . . . I must identify and give effect to the form of transaction which the parties have entered into and which they have sought to do; and in this process I must have regard first and foremost to the terms and language of the composite documents read as a whole in their proper context, but I am also to take into account business sense and reality and most particularly the value of the shares.

Where the consideration includes an asset (eg a right) that will be valued at the date of the first disposal. The value of the disposal consideration will then become the acquisition cost of the asset eg *Marren v Ingles*.[3]

The valuation of any consideration must be taken as at the date of disposal; hindsight is not permitted. In *Fielder v Vedlynn Ltd*,[4] the court considered a sale by Vedlynn Ltd of eight subsidiary companies to a third party. The subsidiary companies had incurred capital losses, which had not at that stage been agreed with the Revenue. The sale agreement provided that Vedlynn Ltd received £19,529, but that the purchaser provided a guarantee to procure that each of the eight subsidiaries should pay Vedlynn Ltd in addition a sum equal to 7.5% of the losses finally agreed. Two years later, the losses were agreed at £19.5m and the sums due under the payment were paid. The Revenue assessed Vedlynn Ltd for the accounting period covering the date of the original sale on the basis that the sum subsequently paid constituted a sale consideration. The Special Commissioner upheld Vedlynn Ltd's appeal that the consideration was the sum of £19,529 actually received and the guarantees under which the further consideration was received were at the date of the sale of no additional value.

Simon's Taxes C2.101.

[1] [1982] STC 585.
[2] [1997] STC 114 at 138b.
[3] [1980] STC 500.
[4] [1992] STC 553.

Consideration that cannot be valued

[16.06] Where there is a disposal of an asset "wholly or partly for a consideration that cannot be valued, or in connection with his own or another's loss of office or employment or diminution of emoluments, or otherwise in consideration or recognition of his or another's services or past services in any office or employment or of any other service rendered or to be rendered by him or another", the market value of the asset disposed of is treated as the consideration.[1]

Simon's TaxesC2.101.

[1] TCGA 1992, s 17(1)(b). For transfer on divorce, see infra, § **16.32**. See also *Mansworth v Jelley* [2002] EWHC 442 (Ch), [2002] STC 1013.

Deferred consideration

[16.07] In a computation of the gain consideration for the disposal should be brought into account without any discount for the delay in the receipt of the disposal consideration, nor for the risk of any part of the consideration being irrecoverable.[1] However, if, in the event, part of the consideration "subsequently proved to be irrecoverable, there should be made and a claim to be made to that effect, such adjustment, whether by way of discharge or repayment of tax or otherwise, as is required in consequence".[2] If consideration is payable by instalments and later instalments prove to be irrecoverable, perhaps by virtue of bankruptcy of the payer, the capital gains computation is retrospectively amended to incorporate only those instalments that were receivable. This rule is applied strictly and has no application where events other than irrecoverability of later instalments reduce the consideration received. In *Goodbrand v Loffland Bros North Sea Inc*[3] a company had disposed of an interest for instalment consideration paid in dollars. The company argued that as the instalments yielded fewer pounds than had been used as the basis for the original calculation of the CGT liability it should get relief because the sum had become irrecoverable; however, the Court of Appeal held that change in the value of the consideration was not the same as part of it becoming irrecoverable.

[16.07] Gains and chargeability

Where a consideration is payable by instalments over a period exceeding 18 months, the taxpayer can request that the capital gains tax liability be paid by instalments[4] over a period not exceeding eight years after the normal due date of payment. Full payment is due on the date on which the last instalment of consideration is payable to him.

Where capital gains tax is paid by instalments which have been agreed with the Revenue, no interest is payable if the instalment is paid on the agreed date.[5]

This treatment does not apply where the sale agreement operates so that the full sum is paid at the time of the sale, but some or all of the sale consideration is then lent back to the purchaser. In *Coren v Keighley*,[6] there was a sale of land for £3,750 and a loan back to the purchaser of £2,250 repayable by monthly instalments. Capital gains tax on the entire £3,750 was payable at the normal due date. Where the deferred consideration takes the form of shares in or debentures of the acquiring company, TCGA 1992, s 138A provides for shares in the acquiring company to be identified with the shares in the target company, so that no gain arises until there is a disposal of the shares acquired on the earn out.[7]

Simon's Taxes C2.106.

[1] TCGA 1992, s 48.
[2] TCGA 1992, s 48.
[3] [1998] STC 930.
[4] TCGA 1992, s 280.
[5] Revenue procedure is given in HMRC Assessed Taxes Manual para AT6.611.
[6] (1972) 48 TC 370.
[7] This treatment was previously given by extra-statutory concession D27.

Foreign currency

[16.08] A gain must be computed in sterling. Where the consideration is in a foreign currency, this is translated into sterling at the rate of exchange that applies at the time of the consideration. Thus, the consideration paid for the acquisition of an asset is translated from the foreign currency into sterling at the rate of the time of acquisition, the consideration received for disposal is converted into sterling at the rate applicable on the date of disposal. Where the foreign currency concerned has strengthened against sterling between the date of acquisition and the date of disposal, the gain that is computed in sterling will be greater than that which would have been computed had the computation been in the foreign currency. Conversely, where the foreign currency has weakened against sterling, a smaller sterling gain is brought into charge.

In *Bentley v Pike*,[1] the court held that a gain made on the sale of land in Germany, which had been inherited by the taxpayer's wife under the will of her German father, was computed by translating the sale consideration from the foreign currency into sterling at the rate applicable at the date of sale and deducting therefrom the market value of the land at the date of the taxpayer's wife's father's death, translated into sterling at the rate ruling at the date of his death. The point is emphasised where an individual acquires an overseas asset wholly from moneys borrowed in the same foreign currency. If the asset is sold for the same sum as it cost, no commercial gain arises, as the proceeds will simply be used to repay the foreign currency loan. However, a tax gain or loss arises if the exchange rate is different at acquisition from the rate at a disposal.

This is to be contrasted with the treatment of trading profits, where regard can be taken to a matching pool of foreign currency assets and liabilities.[2]

The decision in *Bentley v Pike*[3] was followed in *Capcount Trading v Evans*.[4]

Where a consideration is received in a foreign currency and the taxpayer chooses to keep the funds in that currency before converting it into sterling at a later date, it is likely that the rate of exchange enjoyed by the taxpayer will be different from that applied in computing the sterling equivalent of the consideration when it arose. The difference between the sterling receipt that is actually obtained and that which is brought into the capital gains computation for the disposal of the asset is, itself, a gain subject to UK capital gains tax or an allowable loss. For the purposes of the capital gains tax legislation, foreign currency is an asset, it is not money.[5]

Simon's Taxes C2.101.

[1] [1981] STC 360.
[2] *Pattison v Marine Midland Ltd* [1984] STC 10.
[3] [1981] STC 360.
[4] [1993] STC 11.
[5] *Capcount Trading v Evans* [1993] STC 11.

Consideration consisting of a right

[16.09] It is not infrequent for a contract to provide that the vendor be paid further consideration on the occurrence of a defined event. Thus, the vendor of shares in a private company may receive an additional sum if the profits of that company exceed a target in the following year. The right to receive the further consideration is part of the consideration for the first disposal. It requires to be valued and incorporated in that CGT computation along with other sale consideration. The value that is determined for this first computation is then the base cost for a second CGT computation, the sale proceeds of which are the amount that ultimately arises under the right that was obtained.[1]

In *Marren v Ingles* the court considered the following situation. In 1970 a taxpayer sold shares in a private company for £750 per ordinary share, plus the right to receive a further cash payment. This cash payment was to be calculated by reference to the market value of shares following the flotation of the company. In the event, the taxpayer received a further £2,825 per ordinary share as a result of the flotation. The House of Lords, upholding the Court of Appeal, analysed the transaction as the receipt by the taxpayer in 1970 of consideration that consisted of two parts. First, there was the cash sum of £750 per ordinary share; second, there was the right to receive a further sum of money in the future. In 1972 there was a second CGT disposal by the taxpayer, being consideration of £2,825 per ordinary share less the acquisition cost, which was the value of the right to receive that sum, valued at the time of acquisition of the right in 1970, this being the value that had previously been brought in as consideration for the previous disposal.

Lord Fraser said:

> The first question is whether the right to half the profit is properly to be regarded as a separate asset . . . In my opinion (this) is correct. 'Asset' is defined in [now TCGA 1992, s 21(1)] in the widest terms, to mean all forms of property . . . It is therefore apt to include the incorporeal right to money's worth . . . The vendors could have disposed of the right at any time after 15 September 1970 by selling it or giving it away in assigning it . . . In fact they did not dispose of the right, but they held it until it matured on 5 December 1972. If the right was an 'asset', then the sum the vendors received on that date was 'derived from' the asset. There was therefore, by virtue of [now TCGA 1992, s 22(1)] a disposal of the asset . . . the sum was paid to satisfy or extinguish the right and not as any part of the consideration for the shareholdings; full consideration had already been given on 15 September 1970.

This decision was followed in *Marson v Marriage*.[2]

Simon's Taxes C2.101.

---

[1] *Marren v Ingles* [1980] STC 500.
[2] [1980] STC 177.

Loss on unascertainable consideration

[16.10] One of the consequences of the decision in *Marren v Ingles* is that the value of the unascertainable consideration which is brought into the computation on the initial disposal may be higher than the actual amount received. This could, for example, be the case where shares are sold in circumstances where at the date of valuation the trading prospects are much better than actually occur over the period for determining the additional amount to be paid. In practice, that situation may not occur that often, by taking care in the valuation at the date of disposal. Where a capital loss did arise before 10 April 2003, it could not be carried back to the earlier years applying the usual principles, such that CGT could be paid on a sum far greater than the true overall proceeds. Carry back relief is available where an allowable loss of this nature arises after 9 April 2003.[1] Even so, the interaction with taper relief should not be ignored because a gain arising on the initial disposal could well be eligible for full business taper relief but the gain arising on the receipt of the right to the unascertainable consideration would not be eligible for business taper relief (only non-business taper and then that right would have to be held for at least three complete years for any relief). High valuations at the date of disposal might be encouraged and especially so if there are other gains arising in the same year on which there is either nil or modest taper relief, as a loss would first be set against the gains eligible for lower taper relief.

The carry back loss relief provisions are complex. Their essence, though, is that a loss arising on the disposal of unascertained consideration (disposal including the actual receipt of that consideration) can be carried back and set against capital gains arising in years when the original assets, from which the unascertained consideration arose, are brought into charge. The loss arising is carried back to the first year in which such a chargeable gain accrues but that cannot be a year earlier than 1992–93. Any loss that cannot be set off in that first year is then brought forward and can be set against later years in which a chargeable gain arises out of the original asset. The detailed rules ensure that allowable losses and taper relief are allowed in the usual way and for the interaction of losses and taper relief where trust gains are assessed on the individual under TCGA 1992, ss 77 and 86, which in turn must take account of the changes in FA 2002. As would be expected, a loss carried back in this way cannot be set against deemed gains arising on overseas settlements under TCGA 1992, s 87 or s 89(2). The provisions also contemplate the possibility of deferral relief under the Enterprise Investment Scheme and Venture Capital Trust provisions, in particular, to permit the offset of this type of loss where a chargeable gain previously deferred is treated as accruing under the EIS and VCT provisions. Moreover, the loss must arise in a year in which the taxpayer is within the charge to capital gains tax, which effectively denies such a claim to a person who is not resident in the UK when the loss arises.

There are detailed provisions to determine whether or not a right is one to unascertainable consideration, broadly being the situation where the amount or value is unascertainable at a time when it is conferred and by reason, in whole or in part, of matters which are uncertain because they have not yet occurred. Moreover, it is specifically provided that consideration is not ascertainable merely because it is postponed or contingent, such that TCGA 1992, s 48 applies. Where TCGA 1992, s 138A applies, the right is also not regarded as unascertainable. Until 9 April 2003, the taxpayer had to elect for s 138A to apply and it is specifically provided that if a loss claim under these provisions is made, the taxpayer is then debarred from making that election where the right was conferred before 10 April 2003.

Various other administrative type provisions are incorporated and in particular that the election for this treatment is irrevocable and that different notices must be given in respect of different losses. The notice to carry back the loss must be given before the first anniversary of 31 January following the year in which the loss actually arises.

[1] FA 2003, s 162.

Apportionment of consideration

[16.11] It may be necessary to apportion consideration between disposals or between income and capital. Statute requires that the method of apportionment adopted be "just and reasonable".[1]

It is to be noted that this provision only empowers apportionment where this is "necessary". Where the vendor and vendee have apportioned consideration in a manner that is not unreasonable, it is considered that TCGA 1992, s 52(4) does not empower the Revenue to impose an alternative apportionment. It would appear, however, that the Revenue do not share this view.

[16.11] Gains and chargeability

As the actual apportionment is a matter of fact and not of law and statute gives the power to apportion to the inspector or, on appeal, to the Commissioners, there has been little supervision of the operation of this section by the courts. In *EV Booth (Holdings) Ltd v Buckwell*,[2] there was an agreement for the sale of shares and also the satisfaction of a debt. The agreement specified separate considerations for the two elements of the agreement. It was held by Browne-Wilkinson J that it was not then open to the taxpayer to reallocate the consideration.

By contrast, the majority in the House of Lords in *Aberdeen Construction Group Ltd v IRC*[3] held that the matter should be remitted to the Commissioners for an appropriate apportionment where the sale agreement required a payment for shares that were being sold and also the waiver of a loan of £250,000. The distinction seems to be between paying one sum for two items (*Aberdeen*) where apportionment follows and two separate sums for two separate items (*Booth v Buckwell*) where it does not. It is not clear whether the Revenue accept this analysis. In correspondence, Revenue officers sometimes refer to seeking "to ascertain hidden consideration". This can be seen as simply an exercise to identify all the terms of a contract—including the terms demonstrated by action or by verbal agreement, as well as the terms that are written. However, there is often not a real practical distinction between the results of such an exercise and a reallocation of consideration declared in a written contract.[4]

Simon's Taxes C2.101.

---

[1] TCGA 1992, s 52(4).
[2] [1980] STC 578.
[3] [1978] STC 127.
[4] TCGA 1992, s 52(4) applies to "necessary apportionment" of either consideration or expenditure. For a further, brief, discussion of the statutory provision as it relates to expenditure see infra, § **16.22**.

Contingent liability

[**16.12**] Where an agreement incorporates a contingent liability, no account is taken of the contingent liability in the initial computation of the gain arising.[1]

However, where "any such contingent liability subsequently becomes enforceable and is being or has been in force, there should be made, on a claim being made to that effect, such adjustment, whether by way of discharge or repayment of tax or otherwise, as is required in consequence".[2]

In *Randall v Plumb*,[3] the taxpayer entered into an agreement whereby a company deposited £25,000 with him in consideration for the grant of an option to purchase land he farmed. If the company exercised the option, this sum was to be treated as part of the purchase price; if planning permission was not obtained by the company for the extraction of sand, etc, the £25,000 was repayable. The court held that the repayment of the deposited sum was not a "contingent liability" within the meaning of TCGA 1992, s 49, but was a more fundamental part of the agreement so that the £25,000 could not be considered fully as sale consideration at that time.

Simon's Taxes C2.107.

---

[1]   TCGA 1992, s 49.
[2]   TCGA 1992, s 49(2)
[3]   [1975] STC 191.

Allowance for liabilities

[16.13] Certain contingent liabilities assumed by the vendor are to be ignored in valuing the consideration received by him. They are:

(1)   in the case of a lease, any liability contingent upon default by the assignee in relation to his obligations under the lease;
(2)   any contingent liability in relation to a covenant for quiet enjoyment or any other obligation assumed as a vendor of land or of any estate or interest in land or as lessor;
(3)   any contingent liability in respect of a warranty or representation made on a disposal by sale or lease of property other than land.[1]

If such a liability has become enforceable, and is in fact enforced, appropriate adjustments are then made to the original assessment.

Any contingent liability other than one referred to above is taken into account in valuing consideration,[2] although practically speaking valuation may be difficult in such cases. Moreover, there is then no statutory basis for the making of subsequent adjustments where the contingent liability becomes enforceable.

Where the vendor assumes an actual liability on the disposal of an asset, it seems clear that the liability must be deducted from any consideration received, although the position in practice will depend upon the terms agreed between the parties. If the transferee assumes any liability of the transferor's as part of the transaction, the value of the liability is to be added to any other consideration given. However, any liability in respect of the asset disposed of which remains with the transferor is not deductible from the consideration received.[3]

Simon's Taxes C2.108; Sumption CGT A4.05.

---

[1]   TCGA 1992, s 49 (CGTA 1979, s 41).
[2]   *Randall v Plumb* [1975] STC 191, 50 TC 392, [1975] 1 All ER 734.
[3]   This seems to follow from the judgment in *Coren v Keighley* [1972] 1 WLR 1556, 48 TC 370.

Consideration liable to income tax

[16.14] In valuing the consideration there is to be excluded any money or money's worth which is chargeable as income of the person making the

[16.14] Gains and chargeability

disposal, whether to income tax or corporation tax, or which enters into the computation of profits for those taxes.[1] There are two exceptions to this general rule. First, where the payment is taken into account for the purposes of a capital allowance balancing charge, the CGT computation is based on original cost, ignoring the balancing charge. Second, the capitalised value of a rentcharge or a right to any other income is expressly included as consideration, notwithstanding that the income receipts will themselves be subject to income tax or corporation tax.[2] In practice, it will sometimes be necessary to determine whether the receipts are in fact income, or instalments of a capital sum.[3] Where there is a disposal for a consideration which includes a rental, the capitalised value of the rental is excluded as consideration although it is relevant in applying the part disposal formula.

Prior to 9 April 2003, this provision lead to the device where an individual purchases an assurance policy which is immediately encashed, thereby triggering a chargeable event.[4] As a chargeable event is an occasion of charge to income tax, the consideration received was not brought into account in computing a capital gain. However, the policy was an asset and the taxpayer had purchased that asset for a capital sum which did not figure in the income tax calculation. Hence, the taxpayer made a capital loss equal to the cost of the insurance policy.

Simon's Taxes C2.102.

---

[1] TCGA 1992, s 37(1). This prevents any CGT liability on payments falling within TA 1988, s 148. In *Drummond v Revenue & Customs Commrs* [2008] EWHC (Ch) 1758, the High Court held that a taxpayer was not entitled to exclude the proceeds of the surrender of second-hand life assurance policies from the consideration for the disposal of the policies under TCGA 1992, s 37(1). He was however, entitled to deduct from what he had received any moneys spent wholly and exclusively for the acquisition of those policies.

[2] TCGA 1992, s 37(2). Note that in such cases the capital element in the annuity which is exempt from income tax under TA 1988, ss 656, 657, is not the same as the capitalised value.

[3] See, for example, *IRC v Adam* (1928) 14 TC 34.

[4] TA 1988, s 541. Now countered by FA 2003, s 157: see infra, § **31.22**.

Life insurance policies and deferred annuity contracts

[16.15] The basic rule is that a gain arising on the disposal of, or interest in, rights conferred by an insurance policy or contract for a deferred annuity do not give rise to a chargeable gain or allowable loss. However, this is not the case if the rights have at any time been acquired for "actual consideration". Thus, there is no actual consideration where there is a total gift (without any sum or other value passing) or, where there is actual consideration for disposals between spouses or in an approved post-marriage disposal. There is no definition of spouse and so this would carry its normal meaning, including transactions up to the decree absolute. A post-marriage disposal arises if the disposal is in consequence of a dissolution or annulment of a marriage under a Court order (or equivalent under other jurisdictions) and the rights disposed of were held immediately before the marriage was dissolved or annulled. Any premiums paid under a policy or lump sum consideration under a deferred annuity contract do not constitute actual consideration. There is a disposal of rights under a policy of insurance on receipt of the sum assured, transfer of assets to the owner of the policy in accordance with its terms or the surrender of the policy. In the case of a deferred annuity contract, there is a disposal on receipt of the first instalment of the annuity at market value of the right to receive further instalments or surrender of the rights.

Prior to 10 April 2003, a market had developed in second hand insurance policies, which exploited a perceived anomaly in the interaction of TCGA 1992, ss 37 and 39 with the special rules for chargeable events on certain life policies. Essentially, someone would pay a lump sum premium in relation to a life policy, which at a later date would be assigned to the taxpayer. The taxpayer would then surrender the policy for an equivalent sum such that there would be no actual loss or a minimal sum. It was claimed that because of ss 37 and 39 there was effectively a capital loss equal to the sum paid on assignment of the policy. Such a claim is prevented in relation to disposals after 9 April 2003 by ensuring that a loss cannot exceed what the loss would be if ss 37 and 39 were disregarded.[1] In most cases, therefore, it is the actual commercial loss that at best can be claimed as a capital loss.

[1] FA 2003, s 157.

Allowable expenditure

[16.16] Acquisition costs that can be deducted from consideration are limited to the categories specifically designated by statute. These are:

(1) Consideration given by the taxpayer, or on behalf of the taxpayer, wholly and exclusively for the acquisition of the asset.
(2) Consideration in money's worth that has been given, wholly and exclusively for the acquisition of the asset.
(3) The incidental cost to the taxpayer of the acquisition.
(4) Expenditure wholly and exclusively incurred by the taxpayer in providing the asset, where the asset was not acquired by the taxpayer.[1]
(5) Costs reasonably occurred in making a valuation required in order to compute the gain.[2]

To this is added "improvement expenditure", which is:

(1) Expenditure wholly and exclusively incurred by the taxpayer for the purpose of enhancing the value of the asset, being expenditure that is reflected in the asset at the time of disposal.
(2) Expenditure incurred in establishing title to the asset. This will include, for example, the Land Registry fee on registering land that has been acquired.

[16.16] Gains and chargeability

(3) Expenditure on preserving or defending the title to the asset. This will include, for example, the cost of a court action to stop the loss of the asset, or damage to an asset, by another person. Such costs are allowable even where the decision of the court is against the taxpayer.[3]

In *Drummond v R & C Comrs*[4], the Special Commissioner held that expenditure incurred on the acquisition of an asset was not wholly and exclusively so incurred when the overall purpose of the purchase was to enter into a tax avoidance scheme (which involved the purchase at an excessive value in the expectation of a corresponding deduction for capital gains tax purposes).

In order to be an allowable cost of improvement, the expenditure must be "reflected in the state or nature of the asset at the time of disposal".[5] In *Trustees of the F D Fenston Will Trusts v R & C Comrs*,[6] the trustees purchased shares for £661 in a company incorporated under the law of Delaware and then made a capital contribution of £1,530,546 to the company. No additional shares were issued for the capital contribution. The Special Commissioners held that the capital contribution payment increased the value of the company, but was not reflected in the shares. The company was, subsequently, wound up and the trustees received only $1. The base cost for computing the capital loss on disposal was $661 only.

Where market value is taken as "acquisition cost", rather than expenditure incurred, the deduction is denied in computing the gain of any incidental expenditure that would have been incurred on an actual acquisition.[7] This does not, however, deny an allowance for the cost of probate.

Simon's Taxes C2.202.

---

[1] TCGA 1992, s 38(1).
[2] TCGA 1992, s 38(2)(*b*): see infra, § **17.30**.
[3] TCGA 1992, s 381(1)(*b*).
[4] (2007) SpC 617.
[5] TCGA 1992, s 28(4).
[6] [2007] SWTI 556, [2007] STC (SCD) 316.
[7] TCGA 1992, s 28(4).

Expenditure not deductible

[16.17] General. Expenditure that would otherwise qualify is not deductible if:

(1) it has been or is to be met out of public money whether of the Crown or any government anywhere or any local authority anywhere;[1]
(2) it consists of premiums or other payments made under a policy of insurance of the risk of any kind of damage or injury to or loss or depreciation of, the asset;[2]
(3) it is a payment of interest.[3]

No deduction may be made more than once.[4] Any allowable expenditure must be incurred. No allowance can be made for the value or purely notional cost of work carried out by the owner himself.[5]

On a deemed disposal and reacquisition only actual expenses may be deducted, but not expenses that would have been incurred had the disposal actually been made.[6] Where legal and other fees were incurred on the preparation of a deed of variation under which funds would be divided between a tenant for life and the remainderman, the variation being a deemed disposal, those expenses were held to be deductible.[7]

Revenue expenditure. In the same way that sums taken into account in computing income are excluded from the consideration for CGT, revenue expenditure is disallowed in computing chargeable gains. First, a sum is not allowable expenditure for CGT if it is allowable as a deduction in computing the profits or losses of a trade, profession or vocation for purposes of income tax, or as a deduction in computing any other income for the purposes of the Income Tax Acts.[8] This exclusion is extended to sums which would be deductible in computing losses but for the fact that there are insufficient profits against which the losses may be offset.

There is a second, more stringent, limitation on the deduction of expenses. Expenditure is not deductible for CGT if, on the hypothesis that the asset were employed as a fixed asset of a trade, the expenditure would be deductible in computing the profits of that trade for income tax purposes.[9]

For assets such as land and buildings, this restriction denies relief for maintenance expenditure, even where the property is not let. It is important to bear in mind that even extensive expenditure on rehabilitating an asset may be deductible for income tax, unless it can be shown that the dilapidations requiring attention depressed the price paid for the asset.[10]

Simon's Taxes C2.215–219; Sumption CGT A4.07.

[1] TCGA 1992, s 50.
[2] TCGA 1992, s 205.
[3] TCGA 1992, s 38(3).
[4] TCGA 1992, s 52(1).
[5] *Oram v Johnson* [1980] STC 222, [1980] 2 All ER 1.
[6] TCGA 1992, s 38(4).
[7] *IRC v Chubb's Settlement Trustees* (1971) 47 TC 353.
[8] TCGA 1992, s 39(1).
[9] TCGA 1992, s 39(2).
[10] *Odeon Associated Theatres Ltd v Jones* [1973] Ch 288, [1972] 1 All ER 681, 48 TC 257, supra, § **8.124**.

Incidental costs of acquisition

[16.18] Incidental costs must have been incurred by the person making the disposal, wholly and exclusively for the purposes of the acquisition. This includes the costs of establishing title. Such costs are expressly limited to fees, commission or remuneration paid for the professional services of any surveyor or valuer, or auctioneer, or accountant or agent or legal adviser and the costs of transfer or conveyance (including stamp duty) together with the costs of advertising to find a seller.[1] Fees for the services on acquisition must be distinguished from the fees payable for investment advice, which are not allowable.

Other costs, such as expenses of travel to inspect property with a view to purchase, are not allowable, even if the property is in fact acquired.

Simon's Taxes C2.208; Sumption CGT A4.06.

[1] TCGA 1992, s 38(2).

Improvement expenditure

[16.19] Expenditure wholly and exclusively incurred on the asset by the person making the disposal or on his behalf is allowable if it is for the purpose of enhancing the value of the asset.[1] Such expenditure must be reflected in the state or nature of the asset at the time of the disposal. If the expenditure is so reflected, no matter in how small a way, it is allowable in full.

It also appears that the expenditure must make an identifiable change in the state or nature of the asset. In *Aberdeen Construction Group Ltd v IRC*,[2] there was expenditure on a waiver but there was no deduction for this expenditure as it did not make an identifiable change in the shares which were sold. It follows that a payment to a valuer to determine the authenticity of a painting or other work of art is not deductible—whatever his verdict. This rule also excludes an advance payment to a builder who goes bankrupt before beginning the work. When the disposal is by contract followed by conveyance it is unclear how far, if at all, the improvements must be reflected in the state or nature of the asset at the time of the conveyance.[3]

A payment may be required in order to make a disposal, but this does not, of itself, permit a deduction for this payment unless the payment makes a change to the asset, or its value. In *Emmerson v Computer Time International Ltd*,[4] rent was owed to a landlord. The landlord agreed to consent to an assignment of the lease on condition that the rent arrears were paid. The rent arrears were not deductible in the CGT computation. Expenditure cannot be "improvement expenditure" if it is simultaneous with the creation of the asset; the asset must be in existence when the expenditure is incurred.[5]

Initial repairs to let property that are not allowable under Schedule A are treated as improvement expenditure allowable in computing a capital gain.[6]

Simon's Taxes C2.206; Sumption CGT A4.06.

[1] TCGA 1992, s 38(1)(b). In *Emmerson v Computer Time International Ltd* the company owed rent to its landlord. The landlord agreed to consent to an assignment of the lease on condition that the rent arrears were paid. The Court of Appeal held that the payments of the arrears were not deductible under this rule;

[1977] STC 170, 50 TC 628, [1977] 2 All ER 545.
[2] [1977] STC 302, Ct of Sess; the point was not raised in the House of Lords.
[3] *Chaney v Watkis* [1986] STC 89.
[4] [1977] STC 170.
[5] *Garner v Pounds* [2000] STC 420, HL per Lord Jauncey at 426j. In that case, the taxpayer needed to pay £90,000 to a third party in order for an option to be granted. The capital gain was the grant of the option (as it was later abandoned); the deduction of £90,000 was denied.
[6] Statement of practice D24.

Expenditure other than by the taxpayer

[16.20] Except for incidental costs of acquisition, expenditure is allowed if incurred on behalf of the disposer, as well as where incurred by him. This phrase is apt to cover expenditure incurred by a person such as a trustee or mortgagee whose acts are treated as those of the owner. If any other person pays for the improvements, eg by way of gift to the owner the position is less clear. It is not necessary that the owner ultimately bears the cost, but it does seem that there should be a contractual relationship between the owner and the person incurring the expenditure, of the nature of an agency.[1]

Particular problems arise in the case of joint tenancies, where one joint tenant incurs expenditure on the asset but the other subsequently becomes solely entitled. Property law suggests that the whole should be allowable since each joint tenant has an interest in the whole property. However, it is unclear that one joint tenant necessarily incurs expenditure on behalf of the other, in the absence of any additional agreement between them. On a death of one of the joint tenants, his severable share will be deemed acquired by the other at its market value,[2] so that any expenditure incurred by the deceased prior to death will no longer be relevant.

Simon's Taxes C2.202, 206.

[1] *Gaspet Ltd v Ellis* [1985] STC 572, [1985] 1 WLR 1214, a case concerning scientific research allowances under CAA 1990, s 137.
[2] TCGA 1992, s 62(10).

Preservation of title

[16.21] A further category of allowable expenditure includes the costs wholly and exclusively incurred by the owner (but not on his behalf), in establishing, preserving or defending his title to, or to a right over, the asset.[1] This category must be distinguished from acquisition costs and operates narrowly. First, the word "establishing" is limited by the words "preserving" and "defending". In a case involving a settlement, a beneficiary secured the agreement of the trustees to vest the trust funds in her absolutely.[2] She was, however, required to take out a single premium policy on her life, written in favour of the trustees, to indemnify them against her predeceasing another beneficiary having a contingent interest. It was held that the payment of the premium was not to establish the beneficiary's defeasible interest in the fund, since that was not in dispute, but to acquire something greater namely the absolute interest. Hence, the costs could only be deducted if they came within the category of acquisition costs.[3]

The main obstacle in the way of claiming allowable expenditure under this heading is the exclusion of expenditure which would be deductible as a revenue expense if the asset were a fixed asset in a trade, and the income tax rule that money spent on defending title to a capital asset is a revenue expense.[4] For example, a sum paid by a liquidator in respect of arrears of rent, even if it had been spent in preserving the asset (a leasehold interest) would not have been deductible.[5] However, the incidental costs of valuing shares and securities for estate duty purposes has been held to be allowable for CGT under this category, on the grounds that the main purpose is to obtain probate of the will, which establishes the title of the executors to the assets.[6] The Revenue allow such expenses in practice on the basis of a fixed scale according to the value of the estate.[7]

If the sum would have been deductible as a trading expense it is not allowable as a CGT deduction: eg *Morgan v Tate & Lyle*.[8]

Simon's Taxes C2.207; Sumption CGT A4.06.

---

[1] TCGA 1992, s 38(1)(*b*). In *Lee v Jewitt* [2000] STC (SCD) 517, the taxpayer successfully claimed a deduction for legal fees in defending an action that established that the payment he had received from his former partners was for his share of goodwill of the partnership. The legal costs of the action were deductible from the capital payment he had received for goodwill on his departure from the partnership.

[2] *Allison v Murray* [1975] STC 524, [1975] 3 All ER 561.

[3] The expense did not come within the first category since it was not consideration for the acquisition of absolute title but to acquire the other beneficiary's contingent interest.

[4] Supra, § **8.115**.

[5] *Emmerson v Computer Time International Ltd* [1976] STC 111, [1976] 2 All ER 131.

[6] *IRC v Richards' Executors* [1971] 1 All ER 785, 46 TC 626; but see also *Passant v Jackson* [1986] STC 164.

[7] See table, infra, § **19.03**.

[8] [1955] AC 21, HL.

Apportionment of expenditure

[16.22] The categories of allowable expenditure all require that the costs be incurred "wholly and exclusively" for acquisition etc, although in practice this phrase is not interpreted as restrictively as for income tax. Expenditure incurred on valuing stocks and shares both for the probate and for estate duty has been held to be allowable notwithstanding the apparent dual purpose.[1] This may, however, simply be because the estate duty payment was incidental to the main purpose of obtaining probate. It is clear that where the main purpose is allowable, expenditure is deductible in full even though there is some subsidiary or incidental purpose which is not allowable. Conversely no sum is deductible at all if the allowable purpose is purely incidental.[2] This leaves open the question whether an apportionment can be made where there are two main purposes only one of which is allowable.[3]

Where a taxpayer carried out a scheme designed to avoid CGT the expenses of the scheme were deductible, even though it could be argued that one of the purposes of the expenditure was to avoid tax.[4]

Where an acquisition has taken place as part of a composite transaction, it is open to the taxpayer (as well as the Crown) to identify the true acquisition cost as a result of a single composite transaction and not merely by looking at its different constituent parts.[5]

TCGA 1992, s 52(4) provides:[6]

> For the purposes of any computation of the gain any necessary apportionments shall be made of any consideration or of any expenditure and the method of apportionment adopted shall, subject to the express provisions of this Chapter, be just and reasonable.

This provision is frequently quoted by the Revenue as justification for allocating consideration to the various items in a contract in a manner other than that in which the contract itself expresses consideration to be allocated. The author considers that, where the parties to a contract have made an allocation of consideration that is not unreasonable, it is not then "necessary" for there to be an apportionment for the purposes of the Taxes Acts. The Revenue appear to reject this reading of the statutory provision.

Simon's Taxes C2.201.

---

[1] *IRC v Richards' Executors* [1971] 1 All ER 785, 46 TC 626.
[2] *Cleveleys Investment Trust v IRC* [1975] STC 457.
[3] The point was not directly faced in *IRC v Richards' Executors* but compare Lord Reid, at 790, 635 with Lord Guest, at 798, 644.
[4] *Eilbeck v Rawling* [1980] STC 192, [1980] 2 All ER 12 not affected by [1981] STC 174, [1981] 1 All ER 865, HL.
[5] *Whittles v Uniholdings Ltd (No 3)* [1996] STC 914, CA, see for example, the judgment of Sir John Balcombe at 932d. TCGA 1992, s 52(4) applies to "necessary apportionment" of either consideration or expenditure. For a further, brief, discussion of the statutory provision as it relates to consideration see supra, § **16.12**.
[6] Quoted are the words of the section, after the amendment made by FA 1996, s 134. Under self-assessment, it is for the taxpayer to make any necessary apportionment. The Revenue can only vary such an apportionment by opening an enquiry into the return and succeeding (by agreement or after appeal) in determining an amendment to the taxpayer's apportionment.

Foreign taxes paid

[16.23] Where tax is charged in an overseas' territory in respect of a capital gain made, double taxation relief may be available against the liability to UK capital gains tax, under the terms of TCGA 1992, s 277.

Foreign tax which arises on the disposal of an asset and which is not relieved under s 277, is allowable as a deduction in the computation of the gain.[1]

Simon's Taxes C2.227.

---

[1] TCGA 1992, s 278.

Inheritance tax treated as a cost

[16.24] Where inheritance tax is chargeable on a transfer which is also a disposal for capital gains tax purposes, holdover relief under TCGA 1992, s 260 is available (see infra, § **18.40**).

Where a transferee pays inheritance tax on a transfer where holdover relief for the capital gain arising was claimed by the transferor under TCGA 1992, s 165, or TCGA 1992, s 260, or FA 1980, s 79, the transferee may claim to treat the inheritance tax or capital transfer tax paid as part of his acquisition cost to be put against the ultimate disposal of the asset.[1]

On deduction of CGT in computing IHT see infra, § 45.28.

Simon's Taxes C1.425.

---

[1] TCGA 1992, ss 67(1), (3), 165(10), (11), 260(7), (8).

Wasting assets

[16.25] No chargeable gain accrues on the disposal of tangible moveable property or an interest in such property, which is also a wasting asset.[1] A wasting asset is defined as an asset having a predictable life of 50 years or less.[2] Plant and machinery is always assumed to have a life of less than 50 years.[3] However, the exemption for wasting chattels does not apply to assets in respect of which capital allowances were or could have been claimed, nor to commodities dealt with on a terminal market.[4]

On the disposal of a wasting asset[1] special rules restrict the allowable expenditure; these rules do not apply to assets in respect of which capital allowances have been or could have been claimed. Any residual or scrap value of the asset is deducted from the costs of acquisition and the resulting figure is written-off on a straight line basis over the life of the asset remaining unexpired at the date of acquisition.[5]

Similarly, where enhancement expenditure is incurred, it is written off on a straight line basis over the life of the asset still unexpired at the time the expenditure is first reflected in the asset.[6] If the enhancement expenditure alters the residual or scrap value, then the writing off of acquisition costs is altered accordingly.

The exemption from CGT of wasting chattels (infra, § **17.18**), and the exclusion for chattels where capital allowances may be claimed, mean that the straight line wasting formula applies primarily to intangible property such as leases, options and life interests in settled property. Straight line wasting does not apply to leases of land.

There is no provision for altering the period taken as the predictable life of the wasting asset, which is to be determined solely on the basis of information ascertainable at the time of acquisition.[7] However, a person acquiring a wasting asset need not take as the predictable life the period assumed by the previous owner, if circumstances have changed in some relevant respect since his acquisition.

The position where a wasting asset ceases to be a wasting asset is not explicitly covered by the legislation. Since the asset will have changed its nature, allowable expenditure on the original asset should be capable of being traced through. In practice, the Revenue appear to require that the expenditure on the original asset be wasted down to the date it ceased to be a wasting asset. The balance is then added to the allowable cost of the new asset in relation to a subsequent disposal. However, the exercise of a wasting option to acquire an asset results simply in the addition of the cost of the option to the cost of the asset.[8]

Simon's Taxes C2.221, Division C2.9; Sumption CGT A4.11.

---

[1] TCGA 1992, s 45(1).
[2] TCGA 1992, s 44.
[3] TCGA 1992, s 44(1)(c). The Revenue consider that the definition of "machinery" includes antique clocks and watches, as well as custom made vehicles such as racing cars, commercial vehicles and locomotives etc: Inland Revenue interpretation RI 88. Such items are consequently exempt if used for private purposes.
[4] TCGA 1992, s 45(2)–(4).
[5] TCGA 1992, s 46.
[6] TCGA 1992, s 46(2)(b).
[7] TCGA 1992, s 44(3).
[8] TCGA 1992, s 144(3).

Losses

[16.26] Losses are computed in the same way as gains. If the disposal can give rise to a chargeable gain, it can also give rise to an allowable loss; whereas if it gives rise to a non-chargeable gain, it cannot give rise to an allowable loss.[1]

There have always been exceptions to mar this symmetry, but, until 1993, these were relatively minor. In 1993[2] the capital gains legislation was changed to restrict indexation allowance by continuing to allow the relief to reduce a

[16.26] Gains and chargeability

gain but not, as previously, to create (or increase) a loss. This change (even though it was a change back to the original version of the relief) took the charge to capital gains tax away from commercial reality. It also had the effect of creating artificial fiscal distinctions between the sale of an asset in one transaction and a sale in two transactions.[3]

From 1998 onwards, there is no taper applied to a loss and a loss is deducted from a gain before taper relief is applied to the net gain.

Where there is more than one gain in the fiscal year, any losses are deducted from the separate gains in the order that gives the lowest charge to tax.[4] The point of this rule is to make it clear that if the taxpayer realises two gains in a year and one had a higher taper relief than the other, losses are to be set first against the gain on the asset with the lower relief. This may happen when one asset has been held for longer than the other or when they have been held for the same length of time but one is a business asset and the other one a non-business asset.

A loss is not an allowable loss and, hence, no relief is available, if it arises as part of arrangements which have a tax advantage as their main purpose, or one of the main purposes.[5] This denial of relief applies to disposals made on or after 5 December 2005[6] where the gain is subject to corporation tax and disposals made on or after 6 December 2006 where the disposal is subject to CGT. See supra, § 4.33 for a discussion of this provision.

Simon's Taxes Division C1.5.

---

[1] TCGA 1992, s 16(2).
[2] TCGA 1992, s 53(2A).
[3] The effect of the treatment that applies where the asset was held between 1993 and 1998 is illustrated in Tiley & Collison: UK Tax Guide 2001–02, § **15.05**. The effect continues for a disposal after 5 April 1998 if the period of ownership commenced before that date. This rule applies both to losses arising in the fiscal year and also to those brought forward from an earlier year.
[4] TCGA 1992, s 2A(2) & (6).
[5] TCGA 1992, s 8(2) amended and TCGA 1992, s 16A inserted by FA 2007, s 27(2) & (3).
[6] FA 2006, s 69 (amended), TCGA 1992, s 8 for corporation tax only. FA 2007, s 27 revokes the FA 2006, s 69 amendments, and substitutes other amendments to TCGA 1992, s 8 in order to disallow tax driven losses for both corporation tax and capital gains tax purposes.

Relief for loss by set-off

[16.27] The charge to capital gains tax is levied on the aggregate of chargeable gains less allowable losses in a year of assessment. Hence, there is automatic relief for an allowable loss against total chargeable gains for the year.[1] This offset is automatic and is made whether or not the effect is to waste the annual exempt amount.

Simon's Taxes C1.502.

[1] TCGA 1992, s 2(2)(a).

Relief for loss by carry forward against gains of later years

[16.28] Any allowable loss that is not relieved by offset against other gains in the year in which it arises is carried forward and set against chargeable gains accruing in the next subsequent year in which they arise.[1] Whereas the offset of an available loss is made before considering the annual exempt amount, losses brought forward from a previous year are only relieved insofar as they bring the net gains down to the amount specified as the annual exempt amount.[2] Where the loss brought forward exceeds the excess of gain over the annual exempt amount, the balance of unrelieved losses are carried forward to a later year (infra, § **16.40**).

Simon's Taxes C1.502.

[1] TCGA 1992, s 2(2)(b).
[2] TCGA 1992, s 3(5)(b).

Losses in the year of death: carry back

[16.29] Where, at death, the market value of an asset is less than the deceased's acquisition cost, no allowable loss arises. The asset is deemed to have been acquired by the personal representatives without the deceased having made a disposal.[1]

However, the deceased may have made disposals prior to his death. Any allowable losses that arise from disposals made by the deceased in the fiscal year in which he dies are first set against chargeable gains for that year and then the excess is put against any chargeable gains in the previous three years, later years being counted before earlier years.[2]

Simon's Taxes C1.501.

[1] TCGA 1992, s 62(1)(b). No chargeable gains arise on death: Chapter 18.
[2] TCGA 1992, s 62(2).

Loss on disposal to a connected person

[16.30] No relief is available where a loss arises on the disposal of an asset to a connected person, other than against a chargeable gain that arises in that fiscal year or any subsequent year from a disposal to the same connected person, whilst he continues to be connected with the taxpayer.[1] (There is a minor relaxation of this rule in relation to a gift of an asset held in trust, the income from which is primarily applicable for educational, cultural or recreational purposes.)[2]

[16.30] Gains and chargeability

Simon's Taxes C1.508.

---

[1] TCGA 1992, s 18(3).
[2] TCGA 1992, s 18(4).

Losses of non-resident: no relief for assets outside charge to CGT

[16.31] A person who is neither resident nor ordinarily resident in the year of assessment is not subject to capital gains tax other than on gains made on assets used for the carrying on of a trade of a branch in the UK.[1] No loss accruing to a person who is neither resident nor ordinarily resident is an allowable loss, unless it is on the disposal of an asset used for such a trade in the UK.[2]

Simon's Taxes C1.602.

---

[1] TCGA 1992, s 10(1).
[2] TCGA 1992, ss 10, 16(3).

Losses suffered by a non-domiciled person; remittance basis

[16.32] An individual who is not domiciled within the UK is subject to capital gains tax only to the extent that gains remitted to the UK from any disposal of any asset situated overseas.[1]

Statute[2] requires assessment to capital gains tax on the basis of remittances when an individual is not domiciled within the UK; in contrast to the statutory formulation of the rule for income tax[3], where the assessment is on remittances if the taxpayer "makes a claim" that he is not domiciled within the UK. It is argued that a taxpayer who is, in fact, domiciled outside the UK is free to choose not to make a claim to that effect and this would have the consequence that he is subject to income tax as if he were a UK-domiciliary. As no claim is required for the CGT treatment to apply, that option is not available for CGT. The effect is that a taxpayer with a non-UK domicile who makes a gain on the disposal of one foreign asset, the proceeds of which he remits to the UK, and, later in the year, suffers a loss on the disposal of another foreign asset, obtains no relief for the loss[4] as the basis of the charge is the remittance of the proceeds of the disposal he makes at a gain. By contrast, a taxpayer with a UK domicile would offset the loss on the second disposal against the gain on the first.

Simon's Taxes C1.603.

---

[1] See infra, § 33.16.
[2] TCGA 1992, s 12(1).
[3] TA 1988, s 65(4)
[4] Relief is specifically prohibited by TCGA 1992, s 16(4).

Assets of negligible value

Negligible value

[16.33] Where a taxpayer has invested money in shares which later become valueless, it is clear that the person has suffered a commercial loss. However, the scheme of the capital gains tax legislation is that a gain or loss is only crystallised when there is a "disposal". Relief is provided in this scenario by allowing the taxpayer to make a negligible value claim, the making of the claim being treated as a disposal for capital gains tax purposes.[1] The claim is not limited to shares; it is available irrespective of the nature of the asset.

A claim can be made following the "entire loss, destruction, dissipation or extinction of an asset", whether or not any capital sum has been received by way of compensation or otherwise. In order to be competent, the value of the asset must have become "negligible" (see supra, § **16.14**).

The effect of a claim is that the asset is treated as having been sold and immediately reacquired at the date of the claim for an amount equal to the value specified in the claim (which is commonly, but not necessarily, £nil).

Normally a claim for negligible value is incorporated in the individual's self-assessment for the year in which the claim is actually made. However, a self-standing claim is possible.[2] The taxpayer computes the amount of tax that is repayable by virtue of the claim. For this purpose, he applies the rates of tax and his personal circumstances for the year to which the claim relates. This gives the quantum of tax for which relief is provided. This relief is, however, not given by amendment of the assessment for that previous year; instead, it is given by a reduction in the tax payable for the year in which the claim is made; it is possible for such a reduction to give rise to a repayment. The effect of this formulation is that the repayment does not attract interest, unless repayment is made after the normal due date for the year in which the claim is made. Thus, if an asset became of negligible value, but the claim is not made until 6 April 2003, no interest is payable on the repayment arising unless that repayment is made after 31 January 2005.

It is not possible to increase the loss arising from a negligible value claim by indexation allowance.[3]

Simon's Taxes C1.321.

[1] TCGA 1992, s 24.
[2] FA 1996, Sch 17, para 2(2) disapplies TMA 1970, s 42(2).
[3] FA 1994, s 93.

'Negligible'

[16.34] The Revenue have expressed the view that 5% of original value is small (infra, § **17.16**) and that negligible "should be considerably less".[1] The Revenue release lists of quoted securities which it accepts have become of negligible value for the purposes of TCGA 1992, s 24.

[16.34] Gains and chargeability

The HMRC Capital Gains Manual instructs inspectors to accept a negligible value claim where the loss is less than £10,000, where the company is registered in the UK, is not a plc and is in liquidation or has ceased trading.[2]

HMRC internal instructions also require inspectors to accept a negligible value claim where an asset is still in existence with its value unchanged, but the owner no longer has an interest in that asset because, for example, the asset has been stolen.[3]

It is possible for an asset to have negligible value at a particular date, but later events lead to the asset regaining a significant value, as occurred, for example, in shares in Rolls Royce.[4] A negligible value claim made then has the effect that the capital gain arising on the ultimate disposal of the asset is calculated as if the asset had been purchased on the date of the claim for the value specified in the negligible value claim (frequently, albeit wrongly, claimed as £nil).[5]

Simon's Taxes C1.321.

---

[1] Letter to CCAB, June 1971. Paul Soper in "*How to avoid paying CGT*" says 2–5%.
[2] HMRC Internal Guidance, Capital Gains Manual, CG 13131.
[3] HMRC Internal Guidance, Capital Gains Manual, CG 13139–13146.
[4] See *Simon's Tax Intelligence* 1975, p 47.
[5] TCGA 1992, s 24(2)(a).

Partnership goodwill written off

[16.35] Since the 1970s it has been common for professional partnerships to resolve that partners shall be admitted without requiring a payment for the partnership goodwill; similarly, retiring partners are not paid for relinquishing their interest in the partnership. A question then arises if a partner has paid for goodwill and then the partnership decides not to require future payments for goodwill and not to make a payment to a retiring partner; does the partner hold an asset with negligible value? Sometimes, but not always, the goodwill has previously been shown in the partnership balance sheet. Its removal is, thus, clear. In other cases, goodwill will have been the subject of off balance sheet sales and purchases between partners. It is considered that nothing hangs on this distinction, which is a matter primarily of presentation rather than substance.

On 1 November 1967, a partnership of chartered accountants decided to value goodwill henceforth at £nil for the purpose of relations between partners. Certain partners then submitted a claim for CGT relief on the basis that an asset for which consideration had been paid had become of negligible value. The claim was refused by the Inland Revenue and the case came before the General Commissioners for London City Division in December 1973. The Commissioners found for the taxpayer. In their decision, they stated that the asset being considered was the individual partner's interest in the goodwill of the firm and not the goodwill of the firm as a whole. The Commissioners considered that the value of the asset held by the individual partner had become negligible by reason of it being unsaleable, as a consequence of the fact that the arrangements between the partners for carrying on the partnership business, for the retirement or death of the partners and the introduction of new partners were made without regard to goodwill.

A slightly different point was taken before the Special Commissioners some ten years later. In that case, J, a partner in a London firm of chartered accountants, claimed a loss equal to the price he paid for goodwill on joining his firm. By virtue of the change in the partnership arrangements, he did not receive a capital sum when he retired from the firm. J did, however, receive an annuity paid by the partnership. In his decision, the Special Commissioner, ruled:

> J's asset, which is the subject of this appeal, was separate and distinct from the goodwill of the practice as a whole . . . Thus, on the facts found, Mr James' asset became of negligible value on (the date of signing the document writing off goodwill) within the meaning of [TCGA 1992, s 24(2)]. Accordingly, I allow the appeal and grant J the relief for losses which he claims.

The instructions given to inspectors by the HMRC Capital Gains Manual show that Revenue practice does not follow the decisions in these cases.[1]

Simon's Taxes Division C3.2.

---

[1] HMRC Guidance, Capital Gains Manual, CG 27700–27733.

Land and buildings: separate assets

[16.36] For the purpose of a negligible value claim, a building may be treated as a separate asset from the land on which it is situated.[1] Where there is a claim that a building has become of negligible value, the effect of the claim is to establish a loss on the building but, at the same time, to treat the site as having been sold and immediately reacquired for an amount equal to its market value.[2]

In principle, this treatment is also applied where the building is unaffected but the land on which it stands becomes of negligible value. But it is difficult to envisage this in practice.

The effect of this treatment can be to restrict severely any benefit for a negligible value claim as is illustrated in the following example.

EXAMPLE

In 1983 barns were built on agricultural land at a cost of £200,000. In September 2009 they are destroyed in an arson attack. They are not insured. The land had been purchased in 1981 and was worth £500 on 31 March 1982.

	CGT computation	£	£
(i)	Value of destroyed barns	nil	
	Cost	(200,000)	
	Loss arising from claim under TCGA 1992, s 24(2)		(200,000)
(ii)	Value of site 2001	100,000	
	MV, 31 March 1982	(500)	

[16.36] Gains and chargeability

CGT computation	£	£
Gain deemed by TCGA 1992, s 24(3)	99,500	99,500
Net loss		(100,500)

Simon's Taxes Division C2.11.

[1] TCGA 1992, s 24(3).
[2] TCGA 1992, s 24(2)(a).

Backdating a negligible value claim

[16.37] A backdating claim[1] can accompany a negligible value claim so that the date of disposal is treated as having been made on any date specified during the period from 24 months before the beginning of the fiscal year in which the claim is actually made. Thus, a claim made on 31 January 2003 can be backdated to 6 April 2000. In order to backdate in this manner, the asset has to be of negligible value at both the date of claim and the earlier date. Indexation can only be claimed in accordance with the legislation in force at the date of claim.

It is not possible to backdate a claim that is made on or after 1 April 2002 if the effect would be to give relief on a disposal of a major shareholding by a company that would be exempt under the legislation that came into effect from that date.[2]

[1] FA 1996, Sch 39, para 4.
[2] TCGA 1992, Sch 7AC, para 33, see infra § **25.09**.

Payment of capital gains tax by instalments

[16.38] Tax may be paid by instalments in three situations:

(a) Where the consideration is payable in instalments,[1] see infra, § **26.06**.
(b) For gifts of assets in the following three categories: (i) land; (ii) shares or securities which are neither quoted or dealt with on the USM;[2] (iii) listed shares or securities that give the donor a controlling interest. This relief is not available if there is a holdover election available under s 165 (gift of business asset) or 260 (gift subject to IHT) see further infra, § **18.38** ff.
(c) The instalment option is also available where an election to hold over the gain is available, but the gain that can be held over under the terms of that election is less than the chargeable gain that arises. This will commonly be the case where shares are given away and the company whose shares are transferred has chargeable assets that are not chargeable business assets.[3]

Under (b) and (c), if the donee sells the asset, all instalments of tax that have not been paid at that date become immediately payable, with interest.[4]

Simon's Taxes C1.108.

---

[1] TCGA 1992, s 280.
[2] TCGA 1992, s 281.
[3] See TCGA 1992, Sch 7, paras 4–7.
[4] TCGA 1992, s 281(1)(b)(ii).

Persons chargeable

[16.39] CGT is charged on chargeable gains accruing to a person in a year of assessment during any part of which he is resident in the UK, or during which he is ordinarily resident in the UK.[1] By concession,[2] an individual who comes to the UK during the course of a fiscal year to take up permanent residence is not charged on gains made prior to the date of his arrival, provided that individual has not been resident or ordinarily resident in the UK at any time during the five years of assessment immediately preceding the tax year of arrival. Similarly, an individual who ceases to reside in the UK during the course of the fiscal year in order to take up permanent residence abroad is not charged on gains made after the date of his departure,[3] although these gains may be brought into charge in a later year if he falls within the provisions for a temporary non-resident, provided that the individual was not resident or ordinarily resident in the UK for the whole of the last four out of the seven years of assessment preceding the tax year of departure.[4] This concessionary treatment is not applied to trustees to change residence during the year. A gain made by an individual or a trustee whilst he is not present in the UK is frequently removed from the charge to UK capital gains tax by the operation of a double taxation agreement with the territory in which he is treated as resident for the purpose of that gain.[5] This is of considerable practical importance in relation to the migration of a settlement.[6]

Non-resident persons are subject to CGT in respect of UK assets used for the purposes of a trade carried on in the UK through a branch, or UK assets held for the purposes of the branch.[7]

Each partner is liable for the tax on his share of the gains realised by the partnership.[8] A European Economic Interest Grouping (EEIG) is treated in broadly the same way as a partnership for the purpose of charging tax on capital gains.[9]

Trustees and personal representatives are chargeable in respect of gains realised on a disposal, whether actual or deemed, in the course of administration.

A body subject to corporation tax has its gains charged to corporation tax and not to CGT. Shareholders are liable to CGT on the disposal of their shares, assuming that they are not corporations. Corporation tax paid by the corporation is not automatically imputed to the shareholder even though it be

[16.39] Gains and chargeability

shown that the latter's gain is attributable entirely to the gain already taxed in the company. This can lead to double taxation of gains—and double relief for losses. However, if the capital gain is distributed by the company to the shareholder, the effect of the tax credit on the dividend and the lower rate of tax applied to dividend income is that a shareholder effectively receives credit for tax paid by the company on a capital gain, as long as the company is subject to corporation tax at small companies rate only (19%). Where the company suffers corporation tax at the full rate of 30%, or at the marginal rate, there is "tax leakage" (infra, § **26.12**). Undistributed capital gains of a non-resident close company may be attributed to the participators.[10]

Authorised unit trusts, unit trusts for exempt unit holders, and investment trusts are exempt from tax on capital gains.[11]

Simon's Taxes C1.102; Sumption CGT A24.03.

[1] TCGA 1992, s 2(1).
[2] Inland Revenue Extra-Statutory Concession D2.
[3] In *R v IRC, ex p Fulford-Dobson* [1987] STC 344 an attempt by a taxpayer to get round this rule by a scheme using extra-statutory concession D2 failed.
[4] TCGA 1992, s 10A.
[5] Such as, for example, Article 13 of the UK/Mauritius Double Taxation Agreement. This is an example of an agreement whereby the right to tax a gain is with the foreign territory, but that foreign territory chooses not to impose a charge on capital gains. The Article does not, however, remove from the charge to UK capital gains tax a gain made on the sale of land in the UK.
[6] Infra, § **34.06**.
[7] TCGA 1992, s 10; infra, § **22.48**.
[8] Infra, § **22.36**.
[9] TA 1988, s 510A(6).
[10] Infra, § **25.27**, § **35.59** and § **36.01**.
[11] TCGA 1992, s 100(1).

Rates of tax and annual exempt amount

[16.40] When originally introduced, the rate of CGT was a flat 30%. This rate applied until 1987–88. From 1988–89 to 1998–99 chargeable gains were taxed at income tax rates. The recasting of the income tax rates in 1999 led to a change to the CGT rate structure: CGT was charged on individuals at the rate of either 20% (the same as the income tax rate from savings) or 40%.[1] The 20% rate applied to the extent that the net chargeable capital gains plus taxable income fell below the basic rate limit. The income tax starting rate of 10% was irrelevant to CGT for 1999–00, but was applied in 2000–01 and subsequent years. It should be noted that the 20% rate applied whatever the nature of the asset; it is irrelevant whether the income from the asset qualifies for the savings rate of 20% or was chargeable at the basic rate of 22%.[2]

From 2008–09 onwards, capital gains tax has reverted to a flat rate, currently 18%.[3]

There is a simple annual exemption for gains accruing to individuals; for 2009–10 the figure is £10,100.[4] This annual exemption is index linked, unless Parliament decides otherwise.[5] Individuals (whether or not part of a couple) are each entitled to the annual exemption. On trusts see infra, § **20.13** and on estates see infra, § **19.03**.

Simon's Taxes C1.107, 401, 402; Sumption CGT A1.01, 14; A5.02, 03A.

[1] TCGA 1992, s 4.
[2] TCGA 1992, s 4(1A), (1B), (3A), (3B) all repealed by FA 1999 having been added in 1992 and 1993.
[3] TCGA 1992, s 4.
[4] Capital Gains Tax (Annual Exempt Amount) Order 2009, SI 2009/824.
[5] TCGA 1992, s 3(3). For 1994–95 onwards the indexation adjustment is by reference to the increase in the retail price index for the year to 30 September in the preceding tax year: TCGA 1992, s 3(3)(*a*), amended by FA 1993, s 83. For 1993–94 and earlier years, the adjustment is by reference to the RPI increase to December.

Spouses and civil partners

[16.41] It has always been the case that the gains and losses arising to one party to a marriage are *computed* separately from those arising to the other party to a marriage. Prior to 1990–91, however, capital gains tax was levied on the husband for gains made both by him and by his wife, unless they were living apart.[1]

Since 6 April 1990, capital gains tax has been charged, as well as computed on each spouse separately. This was extended to civil partnerships when they became formalised in 2005. Each individual has a separate exempt amount which is not transferable to the other partner if not fully used. The allowable losses of one partner are not available for offset against the other's gains. However, the same effect can theoretically be obtained by transferring the asset from one partner to the other but this is subject to rules limiting the perceived abuse of loss relief (see **4.33** and **16.26**).

Simon's Taxes C1.202.

[1] CGTA 1979, s 45; see *Aspden v Hildesley* [1982] STC 206. (There was an election available to charge tax on the wife for her gains, the tax being calculated by splitting the single annual exempt amount between husband and wife.)

Joint property

[16.42] Where there is a disposal of property that has been held jointly by a couple, the split of proceeds and acquisition costs follow the division of the equitable interest between the couple. Where no division is specified, Revenue practice is to regard the split as being into two equal halves.[1] Unless there is

[16.42] Gains and chargeability

evidence of contrary intention, Revenue practice is, thus, to treat a purchase in joint names as being made by way of a gift of cash by one co-owner to the other effected by the purchase, the gift being such as to give equal beneficial interest. This presumption can, however, readily be displaced by evidence (including the evidence of the action of the party) in relation to the purchase. The Revenue statement[2] envisages the possibility of two persons named at the Land Registry as joint tenants of land having, behind the legal title, beneficial ownership that is 100% to one and nil% to the other. This can be analysed as the second individual holding the title on trust for the first. It is, thus, in essence, no different from a single bare trustee, a disposal by whom would be treated as being made by the beneficial owner.[3] The special income tax treatment[4] is not applied, except that where the couple declare an unequal split of income, the Revenue will presume that this also holds for CGT.

Simon's Taxes C1.202.

---

[1] Inland Revenue press release, 21 November 1990, *Simon's Tax Intelligence* 1990, p 985.
[2] Revenue Press Release, 21 October 1990, para 3.
[3] TCGA 1992, s 60.
[4] TA 1988, ss 282, 282B.

Transfers between married couples and civil partners: no gain/no loss

[16.43] Where a couple have lived together at some time during the fiscal year, any transfer of an asset from one to the other is treated on a no gain/no loss basis.[1] Where a disposal is made from one party to the other after the fiscal year in which separation occurs, this treatment is not applied. However, until the couple obtains a decree absolute (or the civil partnership is fully dissolved), they continue to be connected persons and, hence, the connected person rules apply even though they are living apart.[2] This treatment is applied, even where one partner is resident in the UK and the other is not[3] so that the no gain/no loss transfer can lead to a disposal by the non-resident partner who is outside the scope of the charge to UK capital gains tax.[4] Where there is no consideration for the transfer, holdover relief may be available, if the asset is of a nature that attracts holdover relief. Where assets pass on a divorce or dissolution, holdover relief is available if the disposal is made under the terms of a court order, but not otherwise.[5]

Where there is a transfer between a couple living together, any indexation allowance available to the disposer was taken into account in computing the acquirer's cost of acquisition, except where the acquirer disposes of the asset at a loss and the inter-spousal acquisition occurred on or after 30 November 1993.[6] In that case, the indexation allowance assumed to have been given is deducted from the loss, so as to reduce it or to result in no gain/no loss.[7] Further, the acquirer's acquisition was treated as taking place when the other acquired it, where the asset was originally acquired before 1 April 1982.[8] This is technically of no consequence following the abolition of indexation allowance with effect from 6 April 2008. However, where assets were transferred between a couple before that date, any accrued entitlement to indexation allowance would have been reflected in the transferor's base cost. Thus the no gain/no loss calculation which gives rise to the transferee's acquisition cost ensures that the latter is duly enhanced[9].

When considering the five-year minimum period of ownership for CGT treatment on a company purchase of its own shares, the periods of ownership of spouses and civil partners are aggregated.[10]

The no gain/no loss rule does not apply to appropriations to or from trading stock, market value being taken instead to preserve the integrity of the rules concerning the interaction of income and CGT. Nor does it apply to donatio mortis causa, the purpose here being consistency with the exception from CGT of assets passing on death.

When a couple separates or is treated as separated, they are no longer living together, a matter which affects the private residence exemption[11] and the rule relating to transfers between the couple.

Simon's Taxes C1.202.

---

[1] TCGA 1992, s 58(1).
[2] TCGA 1992, ss 286(2), 18(2), 17(1).
[3] *Gubay v Kington* [1984] STC 99, HL.
[4] TCGA 1992, s 2(1).
[5] See infra, § **18.38**.
[6] TCGA 1992, s 56(2).
[7] TCGA 1992, s 56(3).
[8] TCGA 1992, Sch 3, para 1. For disposals by the acquirer on or after 30 November 1993, the indexation allowance due to the disposer on an inter-spousal transfer before 30 November 1993 is preserved: TCGA 1992, s 55(7).
[9] TCGA 1992, s 56(2); technically, this did not apply in cases where the transferor owned the asset before 1 April 1982. However, TCGA 1992, s 35A was introduced specifically to ensure parity of treatment.
[10] TA 1988, s 220(6).
[11] TCGA 1992, s 222(6).

Separation

[16.44] If the couple separates the no gain/no loss rule continues to apply until the end of that tax year. However, they are still connected persons until decree absolute of divorce or the final dissolution of the partnership (and may continue to be connected persons under some other rule eg business partners). A transfer which takes place as part of the financial settlement on divorce or dissolution is normally regarded as being for a consideration which cannot be valued and so takes place at market value.[1] The choice of assets to be transferred is naturally a matter to which thought has to be given. In *Aspden v Hildesley*[2] a husband transferred property to his wife; the property comprised a house which was not his only or main residence; he was held taxable on the increase in value since he had acquired it. The precise timing on transfers is thus a matter of some importance. Where the parties reach agreement on the terms of their settlement and the agreement then becomes part of a court order the usual view is that the transfer takes place at the time of the consent order—and not that of the prior agreement—or, if different, the decree absolute.[3]

Since the couple is no longer living together they may each have an only or main residence for s 222. However, this exemption is tied to ownership. If therefore H owns the property but W occupies it the relief may be lost; in practice this is not a problem if the transfer is made within three years of their separating (not divorcing). While there is a Revenue concession allowing the exemption to continue if W continues to occupy the property as her main residence, its terms are not crystal clear but are very clear in one unfortunate aspect—the concession does not apply if H is living in another property and claiming that as his only or main residence. It is also clear that the concession applies only where H transfers the house to W—and not if the house is sold to a third party. Hence, it may be advantageous for H to transfer his interest to W in the event of the sale by W to a third party.

The courts sometimes order that one party be allowed to occupy the property with the children while they are growing up and then order a sale when the property is no longer so needed with the proceeds being then divided between the parties—the *Mesher* order.[4] The effect of this order is to keep the exemption while the arrangement lasts. There is some uncertainty about the effect of a clause that the occupying party should pay "rent" to the other—if it is truly rent then it will be chargeable income of the recipient (and not deductible by the payer) and will endanger the entitlement to the CGT exemption.[5] Another form of order creates a deferred charge, ie H will receive either a specified sum of money or a specified proportion of the proceeds when the property is sold. Unfortunately, because of the CGT rules about debts, these two forms may produce different results. If H is entitled to a specified proportion of the proceeds H may be treated as realising a gain when the charge is realised.[6] Problems also arise if the couple has joint interests in land and they exchange those interests on separating. There is some relief if the value of the interests exchanged is identical but this will rarely be achieved.[7]

Occasionally courts order what is called secured maintenance. This usually involves the transfer of property by (usually) the husband to trustees; the wife then looks to the trustees and not the husband for payment. When the wife ceases to be entitled to payments the trust ends and the property is transferred back to the husband. The transfer to the trustees will be a disposal for CGT purposes at current market value (since the trustees and the spouses are connected persons). If the trustees dispose of the assets during the trust there will be a CGT charge on them (for which the husband may be made accountable).[8]

Simon's Taxes C1.202.

---

[1] TCGA 1992, s 17(1)(*b*) and Revenue CGT Manual, para 22509. Timing transfers so that they take place after connected party status ceases may be advantageous if TCGA 1992, ss 29 and 30 (value shifting) provisions are potentially applicable.

However, this may not be so simple in practice as the transaction may not be at arm's length.

[2] [1982] STC 206.
[3] See discussion [1996] Taxation vol 138, p 324.
[4] See *Mesher v Mesher and Hall (1973)* [1980] 2 All ER 126n.
[5] See Philip Wylie, ICAEW Tax Digest No 229, May 2002, para 1.8.
[6] Wylie, para 1.9.
[7] Wylie, para 1.10 using s 152 (assets qualifying for business relief) and extra-statutory concession D26.
[8] Wylie, para 1.11.

Charities

Capital gains made by a charity

[16.45] A gain made by a charity is not a chargeable gain and is, hence, not subject to capital gains tax or to corporation tax on a capital gain "if it accrues to a charity and is applicable and applied for charitable purposes".[1] (See infra, § **16.47** for the circumstances where a charity loses this exemption.)

Thus, where a charity sells an asset for cash and applies the proceeds to its charitable endeavours, no charge to tax arises.[2] It may follow that the exemption does not apply where no actual consideration is received—since there is nothing to be "applied", So if a charity, in the course of carrying out charitable work, gives an asset to a beneficiary, any chargeable gain arising is assessable on the charity. There is an argument that the asset and the attached gain are being applied to charitable purposes by being distributed. However, that is not applying the "proceeds" of the gain. In practice, the Revenue is likely to adopt a generous approach where the gift of the asset was clearly made in the pursuance of the charity's objects.

Where there is a deemed disposal, there is no actual consideration and, thus, it cannot be said that the gain is "applied for charitable purposes". In such a case, the charity is subject to capital gains tax on the gain that arises. This has arisen in practice. Charity A owned a freehold which it let for a commercial rent. The tenant was another charity. Charity A decided to help the other charity by altering the lease so that the rent was reduced from a commercial rent to a peppercorn rent. This alteration of the lease caused a deemed disposal under TCGA 1992, Sch 8, para 3(7). As there was no "consideration", there was nothing that could be "applied for the purposes of the charity" and, hence, the charity exemption is not available on this deemed disposal.

There is, potentially, a problem where a charity has set up a wholly-owned subsidiary and passes assets to that subsidiary. Between commercial companies, there would be no doubt that TCGA 1992, s 171 would operate to treat the transfer as at no gain/no loss. However, this is specified in statute as applying only where one company is a subsidiary of another. A charity does not have the equitable interest in assets; instead, it holds those assets on trust for the ultimate beneficiaries.[3] On one interpretation, it follows that no

[16.45] Gains and chargeability

company can be a subsidiary of a charitable corporation. On this reading, the treatment in s 171 does not apply and a chargeable gain arises in the charity. This is not exempt from tax by TCGA 1992, s 256 as the gain cannot be said to have been "applied for charitable purposes" as there is no consideration so to apply. This treatment is not applied by the Revenue. In a letter to the author dated 11 December 1990, Claims Branch (Charities) stated that the Revenue does not take this point and treats a transfer from a charitable corporation to a company, 75% of whose shares are held by the charity, as attracting the treatment afforded by TCGA 1992, s 171.

Simon's Taxes C1.220.

---

[1] TCGA 1992, s 256(1); there is no requirement that the gain be applied for charitable purposes *only*, cf TA 1988, s 505(1), supra, §§ **13.22–13.26**, but note definition of charity in TA 1988, s 506(1). For chargeable periods ending after 11 June 1986, restrictions are placed on the exemption where the charity has non-qualifying expenditure in the period: TA 1988, s 505, supra, § **13.22**.

[2] The exemption is also available where the charity retains the proceeds in its general fund—*IRC v Helen Slater Charitable Trust* [1981] STC 471, CA.

[3] *Von Ernst v IRC* [1980] STC 111.

Definition of a charity

[16.46] "Charity" is not defined for the purpose of CGT. ("Charity" is defined in TA 1988, s 506(1) for the purpose of the corporation tax exemptions as "any body of persons established for charitable purposes only". "Charitable trust" is defined in ITA 2007, s 519 for the purpose of the exemptions available for income tax as "a trust established for charitable purposes only".) It is clear that to be a charity it is not necessary for the body to be registered with the Charity Commissioners, although such a registration is irrefutable evidence that the body is a charity. When a body is correctly regarded as a "charity" the reliefs in TCGA 1992, ss 256, 257 are applicable, whether or not that body is registered with the Charity Commissioners.

The term charity has acquired a highly technical meaning over many years of judicial development and many of the relatively recent cases have arisen in the context of tax.[1]

The exemption from capital gains tax in respect of a gift to charity is also applied where the gift is to:

(a) The National Gallery.
(b) The British Museum.
(c) The National Museum of Scotland.
(d) The National Museum of Wales.
(e) The Ulster Museum.
(f) Any other similar national institution which exists wholly or mainly for the purpose of preserving for the public benefit a collection of scientific, historical or artistic interest and which is approved for the purposes of this Schedule by the Treasury.

(g) Any museum or art gallery in the UK which exists wholly or mainly for that purpose and is maintained by a local authority or university in the UK.
(h) Any library the main function of which is to serve the needs of teaching and research at a university in the UK.
(i) The Historic Buildings and Monuments Commission for England.
(j) The National Trust for Places of Historic Interest or Natural Beauty.
(k) The National Trust for Scotland for Places of Historic Interest or Natural Beauty.
(l) The National Art Collections Fund.
(m) The Trustees of the National Heritage Memorial Fund.
(n) The Friends of the National Libraries.
(o) The Historic Churches Preservation Trust.
(p) Nature Conservancy Council for England.
(q) Scottish Natural Heritage.
(r) Countryside Council for Wales.
(s) Any local authority.
(t) Any Government department (including the National Debt Commissioners).
(u) Any university or university college in the UK.
(v) A health service body, within the meaning of s 519A of the Income and Corporation Taxes Act 1988.[2]

Simon's Taxes C1.220.

---

[1] For the court's approach, see the House of Lords judgments in *IT Special Purposes Comrs v Pemsel* (1891) 3 TC 53 at 94 per Lord McNaughten and, more recently, the decision of the High Court in *IRC v Oldham Training and Enterprise Council* [1996] STC 1218.

[2] TCGA 1992, s 257(1)(*b*) applying IHTA 1984, Sch 3.

Restriction of charitable exemption

[16.47] The restriction on the exemption from income tax where the charity has non-qualifying expenditure (supra, § **13.21**) applies for tax on a charity's capital gains also. Thus, a charity that gives funds for non-charitable purposes loses all or part of its exemption for income tax and CGT, as does a charity which invests in a non-qualifying investment.

Property ceasing to be held on charitable trust

[16.48] There is a deemed disposal of property when it ceases to be held on charitable trust and the gain arising on that deemed disposal is chargeable.[1] There is, thus, no immunity for unrealised capital gains built up behind the screen of charity.[2]

Revenue extra-statutory concession D47 applies where land has been made available to an educational charity subject to it being used for the purposes of that charity. Where such conditions were applied to a gift, often a gift made very many years ago, the closure of the school, or the removal of the school from that site, will normally cause the land to be held on a trust for sale for the benefit of the revertee. Not infrequently, the exact modern identity of the modern revertee is not known at that stage. Where the revertee is known and is itself a charity no problem arises. Where the revertee has not been identified, extra-statutory concession D47 allows the trustees to request that any capital gains tax is not paid until such time as the revertee is identified. If the revertee is then found to be a charity, or if the revertee disclaims his entitlement in favour of a charity, the capital gains tax liability is treated as discharged by the extra-statutory concession.

One situation where property ceases to be held on a charitable trust has arisen from the actions of benefactors in providing a building to be used as a hospital or a school. Frequently, the gift was made subject to the building being used for the stated purpose. In a well-publicised case, the hospital authorities decided to move St George's Hospital from Hyde Park Corner, London SW1 to Tooting, London SW17. The premises at Hyde Park Corner were gifted in 1733 for use as a public hospital. Under the terms of the gift, on the ceasing of the medical use of the premises in 1980, the site reverted to the ownership of the Duke of Westminster. A CGT disposal occurred on the day that the property ceased to be used as a hospital, that being the event that caused the reversion.

A more modest example is afforded by *Fraser v Canterbury Diocesan Board of Finance*.[3] In March 1872 a gift of land was made on which a Church of England primary school was built. Being no longer required for use as a school, the land was sold in April 1992. The Court of Appeal held that the correct interpretation of the terms of the gift made in 1872 was that the change of status of the school that occurred in 1874, when it ceased to be a denominational school, caused a reversion to settlor at that date. Thus the "CGT disposal" took place, albeit unrecognised, ninety-one years before the creation of capital gains tax.

Simon's Taxes C1.220.

---

[1] TCGA 1992, s 256(2).
[2] On one view, a temporary charitable trust is not really a qualifying charity at all, see Whiteman 27–19.
[3] [2001] Ch 669, CA.

Gift to a charity

[16.49] A taxpayer who makes a gift of an asset to a charity is treated as if the asset was sold for a sum such that no gain/no loss arises on the disposal. This treatment is not conditional on the use to which the asset is put by the charity.[1]

This relief exempts a donor from liability to CGT on the gain. Income tax relief (for an individual, but not for a trustee) or corporation tax relief (for a company) is also granted on the market value of the gift, where this consists of an interest in land, listed shares and securities, units in a unit trust, shares in an open-ended investment company or interest in an offshore fund, but not otherwise.[2]

This treatment is also applied where a taxpayer sells an asset to a charity and the sale consideration received does not exceed the acquisition cost plus indexation allowance.[3]

This treatment extends to settled property. Thus, where property has been held in a non-charitable trust and then, under the terms of the trust, a charity becomes absolutely entitled to that property, there is no charge to capital gains tax. This is achieved by the charge on the deemed disposal specified by TCGA 1992, s 71 being treated as if it were a no gain/no loss disposal.[4]

Simon's Taxes C1.220.

---

[1] TCGA 1992, s 257.
[2] TA 1988, s 587B extended by FA 2002, s 97.
[3] TCGA 1992, s 257(2).
[4] TCGA 1992, s 257(3).

17

Assets, exemptions and reliefs

Assets	PARA **17.01**
Exemptions and reliefs	PARA **17.05**
Valuation	PARA **17.25**

Assets

[17.01] All forms of property are assets whether situated in the UK or not.[1] Property is not further defined. Assets are however stated to include (a) options, debts and incorporeal property[2] generally, (b) any currency other than sterling,[3] and (c) any form of property created by the person disposing of it, or otherwise coming to be owned without being acquired. Property owned without being acquired covers items such as generated goodwill.[4] Property created includes not only such items as paintings but also copyrights, patents and crops.

This definition leaves uncertain the scope of incorporeal property. It is not confined to interests in or over other property since the statutory words contain no such limitation. Hence rights under contractual licences or rights of registration under the Matrimonial Homes Act 1983 may equally be "property" and sums received on the redemption of a rentcharge, the release of a covenant and for the release of a right to occupy the matrimonial home may all give rise to CGT.[5] By contrast, a right created by statute[6] or by a court order, such as a divorce,[7] is not an asset.

The meaning of asset was considered by the House of Lords in *O'Brien v Benson's Hosiery (Holdings) Ltd*.[8] It was held that the series of rights of an employer under a service agreement was an asset for CGT so that a sum received to secure the release of the employee was derived from that asset and so liable to CGT. The fact that the rights could not be assigned by the employer was irrelevant. It was sufficient that they could be "turned to account". This may indicate a wide view of the concept; however the right was, like the others already mentioned, legally enforceable in some way or other. It is probably the case that an unenforceable promise is not an asset for the purpose of the CGT legislation. Support for this view is given in *A-G v Murray*[9] where proceeds of an insurance policy were held not to be part of the deceased's estate for the purpose of estate duty and the insurance policy was void. However, the attitude of the court has, in more recent years, been characterised by the maxim "where there is fruit there must be a tree". *Emmet on Title* suggests that a claim is not an asset until it is proved to be well founded. It is, however, the frequent experience of practitioners that a commercial payment is made to dispose of the nuisance value of a claim, even where it is thought that the claim would not succeed before the court. It has been argued by the Revenue in

[17.01] Assets, exemptions and reliefs

correspondence and in court proceedings[10] that such a claim, however unfounded, constitutes an asset. The view taken is that the receipt of money by the claimant is sufficient evidence of his having a right, even though that right may not have been recognised by the court.

Similar obscurity surrounds the position of rights barred by statute. However, it is frequently the case that statute barred rights can be enforced indirectly and the acknowledgement of a claim can revive a right that would otherwise be statute barred[11]. On this analysis, therefore, a receipt arising on a claim that is statute barred attracts a charge to CGT under TCGA 1992, s 22 as "a capital sum derived from an asset".

In order to apply the principles of capital gains tax, the asset, of which the disposal is made, must be correctly identified. In *Burca v Parkinson*[12] a purchase of shares was made using finance provided by the taxpayer's parents, who are not resident in the UK and outside the charge to UK capital gains tax. The agreement was that on the disposal of the shares the parents would receive 60% of the sale proceeds. In the taxpayer's submission, 60% of the company share capital[13] should be identified as an asset held by the taxpayer's parents and, hence, the gain arising on the 60% holding was not charged to UK capital gains tax. The court upheld the Revenue's analysis of the arrangements, that the taxpayer's asset was the entire share capital of the company[14] and the obligation on the taxpayer to pay his parents 60% of the proceeds was an obligation under a loan agreement and did not disturb the charge to CGT levied on the taxpayer on his disposal of the entire shareholding. The right to receive a percentage of the sale consideration was not ownership of the shares.

Simon's Taxes C1.301; Sumption CGT A1.04.

1. TCGA 1992, s 21(1). For the taxation of a gain arising on the disposal of a material interest in an offshore fund, see infra, § **35.45**. For an interesting illustration of the type of analysis favoured by HMRC, see Inland Revenue Tax Bulletin, October 1999, p 699. In this article, the Revenue analyse the status of a bookmaker's pitch following the change in the Pitch Committee rules that, from October 1998 allow pitches to be auctioned. The pitch is an asset for CGT purposes. There is an acquisition cost of £nil, unless the pitch has been purchased at auction or acquired by inheritance after the October 1998 changes. When a pitch is auctioned, the date of disposal is the date on which the purchaser's bid is accepted. A pitch will normally attract 100% business property relief for inheritance tax and CGT taper relief as a "business asset". However, in the Revenue's view, a pitch is not an "interest in land" and, hence, rollover relief is not available.
2. Semble that amateur status is not an asset. See *Jarrold v Boustead*, supra, § **7.28**.
3. Distinguish a holding of foreign currency from a debt expressed in foreign currency which will generally be an exempt asset (for a limited exception, see TCGA 1992, Sch 11, paras 13, 14). On this definition, note also *Greig v Ashton* [1956] 3 All ER 123, 36 TC 581.
4. And know-how: see TA 1988, s 531(2).
5. Under TCGA 1992, s 22.
6. *Davies v Powell* [1977] STC 32.
7. Inland Revenue Tax Bulletin April 2001 page 840.
8. [1979] STC 735, [1980] AC 562, [1979] 3 All ER 652, but cf *Cleveleys Investment Trust Co v IRC* [1975] STC 457 (rights acquired by guarantor against debtor

company on discharge of debt to third party not assets for CGT).
9 [1904] 1 KB 165.
10 See, for example, Revenue submissions in the case stated in *O'Brien v Benson's Hosiery (Holdings) Ltd* [1978] STC 725, HL.
11 See *Emmet on Title* citing *Leroux v Brown* (1852) 12 CB 801 and *Holmes v Cowcher* [1970] 1 All ER 1224.
12 [2001] STC 1298. In this case, £948,226 was received from an investment purchased six years earlier for £50,000.
13 Mr Birca's holding was either 98 or 99 shares out of 100 shares in issue. The documentary evidence was apparently unclear as to which figure was correct.
14 [2001] STC 1298 at 1306f. In this case it was not necessary to identify the nature of the asset (if any) held by the parents, as they were outside the charge to CGT. Although no mention is made in the case stated of *Zim Properties Ltd v Proctor* [1985] STC 90 (see supra, § **16.02**), the case can be analysed in accordance with that decision, the right of the parents to receive part of the consideration being treated as a different asset from the shares.

Link between the receipt and the underlying asset

[17.02] In charging capital gains tax on a disposal, the computation is the consideration received less the cost (or deemed cost) of the asset, the disposal of which causes the receipt of the consideration. Where capital gains tax is charged under TCGA 1992, s 22 on a capital sum derived from an asset, the gain is computed by the reduction from the capital sum received of the cost (in whole or in part) of the asset that has directly caused the receipt of the capital sum. It is, therefore, critical to identify correctly the asset from which the consideration or capital sum is derived.

The most dramatic expression of the judicial view in this field is given in *Zim Properties Ltd v Procter*.[1] In this case a right of action for damages was declared by the court to be an asset separate from any other asset. The taxpayer had contracted to sell property, but the purchaser repudiated the contract as the taxpayer's solicitors failed to demonstrate good title to the property. The taxpayer then sued its solicitors for negligence and claimed damages. The negligence action was settled out of court by the solicitors paying damages to the taxpayer. The question facing the court was, thus, the tax treatment of the sum of £69,000 received by the taxpayer from its solicitors.

The taxpayer company claimed that the sum of £69,000 was received as compensation for the depreciation in value of the property caused by the solicitors' action (or inaction). That argument was rejected by Warner J who said:

> Counsel for the taxpayer company said that the £69,000 was a capital sum received by the taxpayer company by way of compensation for depreciation of the properties, in that, in the events that had happened, the taxpayer company was entitled to receive from the firm compensation for any depreciation in the value of the properties . . . However, assuming . . . that it is proper to describe the £69,000 as 'compensation' for something, it seems to me that it can only be described as compensation for the consequences of the firm's alleged negligence. The depreciation

[17.02] Assets, exemptions and reliefs

in the value of the properties was not a consequence of that negligence. It was something which, if it happened, happened as a result of the forces affecting the property market in Manchester, independently of that negligence.

Simon's Taxes C1.325.

[1] [1985] STC 90.

Revenue concession

[17.03] The effect of this decision would be to deny a deductible acquisition cost in many circumstances. This severe effect is mitigated by extra-statutory concession D33, paras 8 to 10, which state:

> Where a gain arises on the disposal of a right of action, the case may alternatively, by concession, be treated in accordance with the following paragraphs of this statement.
>
> *Underlying assets*
>
> Where the right of action arises by reason of the total or partial loss or destruction of or damage to a form of property which is an asset for capital gains tax purposes, or because the claimant suffered some loss or disadvantage in connection with such a form of property, any gain or loss on the disposal of the right of action may by concession be computed as if the compensation derived from that asset, and not from the right of action. As a result a proportion of the cost of the asset, determined in accordance with normal part-disposal rules, and indexation allowance, may be deducted in computing the gain. For example, if compensation is paid by an estate agent because his negligence led to the sale of a building falling through, an appropriate part of the cost of the building may be deducted in computing any gain on the disposal of the right of action.
>
> The gain may be computed by reference to the original cost of the underlying asset, with time-apportionment if appropriate if the asset was acquired before 6 April 1965, or by reference to its market value at 6 April 1965. For disposals on or after 6 April 1988, the gain may be computed in appropriate cases by reference to the value of the asset on 31 March 1982.
>
> *Other reliefs and exemptions*
>
> If the relief was or would have been available on the disposal of the relevant underlying asset, it will be available on the disposal of the right of action. For example, if compensation is derived from a cause of action in respect of damage to a building suffered by reason of professional negligence, and the compensation is applied in restoring the building, deferment relief under TCGA 1992, s 23 (CGTA 1979, s 21) will be available as if the compensation derives from the building itself and not from the right of action.
>
> Other reliefs which may become available in this way include private residence relief, retirement relief and roll-over relief. The Board of Inland Revenue will be prepared to consider extending time limits in cases where because of a delay in obtaining a capital sum in compensation, the normal time limit allowed for a relief has elapsed. If the right of action relates to an asset which is specifically exempt from capital gains tax, such as a motor car, any gain on the disposal of the right of action may be treated as exempt.

Simon's Taxes C1.325.

Pooling of assets

[17.04] In general each asset is treated as a distinct item so that tax only arises on the disposal of that asset and is then computed in the light of the expenditure on that asset. Shares or securities of a company being of the same class and held by one person in one capacity are regarded as indistinguishable parts of a single asset—a holding—so that the sale of a part of the holding is treated as a part disposal.[1]

Until 5 April 2008, special rules applied to shares acquired before 6 April 1982 and after 5 April 1965. Such shares formed a pool separate from the pool containing shares acquired on or after 6 April 1982.[2] This treatment did not apply to shares held on 6 April 1965, except for quoted shares where an election had been made. However, the general rule for all shares is that they are now held in a single pool. (See infra, § **21.05**.)

Simon's Taxes C2.719; Sumption CGT A12.03.

---

[1] TCGA 1992, s 104(1).
[2] TCGA 1992, s 104(1).

Exemptions and reliefs

[17.05] The following assets are exempt assets so that no charge to capital gains tax arises on the disposal and no relief is given for any loss arising.

(a) Debt other than a debt on a security.[1]
(b) Covenants.[2]
(c) Private residence.[3]
(d) Government stock and qualifying corporate bonds.[4]
(e) Motor car.[5]
(f) Woodlands.[6]
(g) Wasting assets.[7]
(h) A shareholding of 10% or more held by a company.[8]
(i) A non life insurance policy.[9]

The following assets are exempt insofar as no charge to capital gains tax arises on the disposal but relief is given for any loss arising.

(a) EIS shares.[10]
(b) Certain BES shares.

Certain disposals are treated as not giving rise to a chargeable gain:

(a) Death.[11]
(b) Gifts to charity.[12]
(c) Share for share exchange.[13]
(d) Transfers between spouses and civil partners.[14]

[17.05] Assets, exemptions and reliefs

(e) Transfer of assets within a group.[15]
(f) Transfers by certain special taxpayers.[16]
(g) Transfer of shares to an employee share ownership plan.[17]
(h) Transfer to the Treasury in settlement of an inheritance tax liability of a work of art.[18]

Reliefs include:

(a) Loss on a loan to a trader.[19]
(b) Holdover relief.[20]
(c) Entrepreneurs' relief.[21]
(d) Rollover relief.[22]
(e) Deferral relief.[23]

In every capital gains tax computation, taper relief is potentially available: see infra, § **24.01** et seq.

Simon's Taxes Division C1.4.

---

[1] TCGA 1992, s 251. See infra, § **17.06**.
[2] TCGA 1992, s 273. See infra, § **17.11**.
[3] TCGA 1992, s 222. See infra, § **23.06**.
[4] TCGA 1992, s 115. See infra, § **17.12**.
[5] TCGA 1992, s 263.
[6] TCGA 1992, s 250. See infra, § **17.14**.
[7] TCGA 1992, s 45. See infra, § **17.18**.
[8] TCGA 1992 Sch 7AC.
[9] TCGA 1992, s 204 completely rewritten by FA 2006, s 73.
[10] TCGA 1992, s 150A(1) & (2A) with effect in relation to shares issued after 31 December 1993. See infra, § **17.23**. For BES see infra, § **17.24**.
[11] TCGA 1992, s 62. See infra, § **19.01**.
[12] TCGA 1992, s 257. See supra, § **16.49**.
[13] TCGA 1992, s 127. See infra, § **21.12**.
[14] TCGA 1992, s 58. See supra, § **16.43**.
[15] TCGA 1992, s 171. See infra, § **28.21**.
[16] Political Parties, International Organisations, British Museum, Scientific Research Organisations, Reserve Bank of India. TCGA 1992, ss 264, 265, 266, 270, 271(5) to (8).
[17] TCGA 1992, s 236A.
[18] TCGA 1992, s 258(2).
[19] TCGA 1992, s 253. See infra, § **17.07**.
[20] TCGA 1992, ss 165 and 260. See infra, § **18.41**.
[21] TCGA 1992, s 169N.
[22] TCGA 1992, s 142. See infra, § **22.11**.
[23] TCGA 1992, Sch 7C.

Debts

[17.06] No chargeable gain arises on the disposal of a debt, other than a debt on a security.[1]

The rationale of the exemption from capital gains tax in s 251(1) is, no doubt, that an ordinary commercial debt does not normally produce a gain, only the risk of a loss and it would be inappropriate to provide tax relief for losses arising from such risks. Such a simplistic analysis, however, ignores the many varieties of debt and the many circumstances in which they are created. Particularly during the period when a fixed sum debt would always create a loss by virtue of indexation being available, there was considerable activity in attempting to identify a debt as a debt on security[2] and, hence, able to trigger an allowable loss.

It is interesting to note that the exemption for a debt is specifically stated to be applicable to debts in foreign currencies. Thus, if $100,000 is lent when the exchange rate is $1.50 to the pound and then repaid some years later when the exchange rate is $2 to the pound, the gain is not subjected to capital gains tax. This contrasts with the treatment of a bank deposit.[3] If £50,000 is converted at £1 = $2 and put on the dollar denominated bank deposit, and then the $100,000 is withdrawn once the exchange rate has moved to £1 = $1.50, the gain of £16,667 is subject to capital gains tax, unless the deposit is for personal expenditure outside the United Kingdom of the taxpayer or his family or dependants.[4]

The restriction on allowable losses is wider than for the original creditor. No allowable loss can arise on the disposal of a debt (whether or not it is a debt on a security) by a person connected with the original creditor (or with his personal representative or legatee) and they acquired the debt directly from the creditor, or indirectly through other connected persons.[5]

The satisfaction of a debt is treated as a disposal of it by the creditor.[6] This applies to all debts, including debts on a security. The disposal occurs at the time at which the debt is satisfied. If there is satisfaction of part of the debt, this is a part disposal. There is an exception provided for certain company reconstructions and amalgamations.

Where an asset is given by the debtor to the creditor in satisfaction of a debt, other than a debt on a security, the acquisition of the asset is treated as an exempt disposal as far as the debt is concerned.[7] However, the lender is, in principle, subject to capital gains tax on any subsequent disposal of the asset. The effect of s 251(3) is that the lender has a deemed acquisition cost of the asset he acquires, being the higher of (a) the nominal amount of the debt discharged and (b) the market value of the asset acquired. Thus, in effect, where the value of the property acquired exceeds the nominal value of the debt, the debtor is treated as having agreed to sell and the creditor to acquire, the asset at the nominal value of the debt repaid (see *Stanton v Drayton Commercial Investments Ltd*).[8]

Any indexation allowance is calculated on the asset's market value, not on the nominal value of the debt.

Arrangements are sometimes entered into where property is sold and the purchase price is left outstanding by way of a loan and the purchaser defaults so that the vendor takes back the property. Revenue concession D18 operates in such a circumstance to enable the erstwhile vendor to choose to treat the transaction, for capital gains purposes, as if it had not occurred.

[17.06] Assets, exemptions and reliefs

Simon's Taxes C1.408.

[1] TCGA 1992, s 251(1).
[2] eg *Taylor Clark International Ltd v Lewis* [1998] STC 1259, CA.
[3] TCGA 1992, s 252.
[4] TCGA 1992, s 252.
[5] TCGA 1992, s 251(4).
[6] TCGA 1992, s 251(2).
[7] TCGA 1992, s 251(3).
[8] [1982] STC 585.

Loan to a trader

[17.07] Relief is available for a loss on a loan other than a debt on a security made after 11 April 1978 which is:

(a) "the money lent is used by the borrower wholly for the purposes of a trade carried on by him, not being a trade which consists of or includes the lending of money;[1]
(b) the borrower is resident in the UK; and
(c) the borrower's debt is not a debt on a security as defined in section 132."[2]

The relief is only given if:

(a) the loan is wholly or partially irrecoverable;
(b) the lender has not assigned his right to recover the irrecoverable amount; and
(c) the lender and borrower were neither husband or wife nor group companies at the time the loan was made or at any subsequent time. The "subsequent time" is up to the time at which the claim for relief is made even though in practice the relief is backdated. Provisions are incorporated to deny relief where the loss is artificially engendered.

In *Crosby v Broadhurst*[3] a condition for the sale of the company was that loans were released. Hence, the loan was not in existence when the claim for relief on the grounds of irrecoverability was made. It was held that relief was available, even though the loan was no longer in existence. The Special Commissioners preferred a reading of statute that fulfilled the purpose of the provision to that offered by the Revenue, which did not.[4]

In *Robson v Mitchell*[5] the Court of Appeal considered the requirement that the loan must be used by the trader for the purposes of the debtor's trade. In that case, it was not.[6]

As originally enacted, the relief is given on a claim being made and the loss accrues at the date of making the claim, even though the loan may have been irrecoverable at an earlier date. However, from 1996–97, statute provides the ability to specify an earlier time and for the disposal to be treated at that earlier time, in accordance with the provisions of TCGA 1992, s 253(3A), which states:

> For the purposes of subsection (3) above, an earlier time may be specified in the claim if:

(a) the amount to which that subsection applies was also irrecoverable at the earlier time; and either
(b) for capital gains tax purposes the earlier time falls not more than two years before the beginning of the year of assessment in which the claim is made; or
(c) for corporation tax purposes the earlier time falls on or after the first day of the earliest accounting period ending not more than two years before the time of the claim.

This is an enactment of the treatment previously given under extra-statutory concession D36.

No indexation allowance is available to augment the loss.

If the lender subsequently receives any repayment of the loan, or other consideration in respect of it, he is treated as having made a gain equal to "so much of the allowable loss as corresponds to the amount recovered".[7]

Simon's Taxes C1.412.

---

[1] For a case where a loan was held not to be for the purpose of a trade and, hence, no relief is available as it is not a qualifying loan, see *Robson v Mitchell*, [2004] STC 1544.
[2] TCGA 1992, s 253.
[3] [2004] STC (SCD) 348.
[4] [2004] STC (SCD) 348 at [12].
[5] [2005] EWCA Civ 585, [2005] STC 893.
[6] The Court of Appeal relied on a finding of fact by the General Commissioners: see point 8.3.5 of the Case Stated: [2004] STC 1544 at 1549e.
[7] TCGA 1992, s 253(6).

Guarantee

[17.08] Where a payment is made by a guarantor who makes the payment under a guarantee of a loan that qualifies under the terms of TCGA 1992, s 253, the guarantor is able to claim a loss equal to the amount he pays under the guarantee.[1] No indexation allowance is, again, available.

Relief is denied to a guarantor where the borrower and lender are companies in the same group of companies, either when the loan was made or at any subsequent time. It is also denied where the guarantor and lender are both companies in the same group at the time the guarantee was given or at a subsequent time.[2]

Relief is available where the guarantor and the borrower are companies in the same group.

Simon's Taxes C1.412.

---

[1] TCGA 1992, s 253(4).
[2] TCGA 1992, s 253(4)(*b*).

What is a debt?

[17.09] The distinction between a "debt" (which is exempt from CGT) and a "debt on a security" (which is subject to CGT) has been the subject of a number of cases. A preliminary point is, however, the meaning of the word "debt".

In *Marren v Ingles*,[1] Lord Fraser said:

> The meaning of the word debt depends very much on its context. It is capable of including a contingent debt which may never be payable . . . It is also capable of including a sum of which the amount is not ascertained. But . . . does not apply to the obligation of the purchaser under this agreement, which was described by Templeman LJ as 'a possible liability to pay an unidentifiable sum at an unascertainable date'. The words to which I have given emphasis bring out the three factors of this obligation which cumulatively prevent its being a debt in the sense of [TCGA 1992, s 251].

It is to be noted that, in that case, the House of Lords held that the contingent unascertained liability is nevertheless an asset within the scope of the CGT legislation and a gain accordingly arose.

Simon's Taxes C1.408.

---

[1] [1980] STC 500.

Meaning of debt on a security

[17.10] Statute defines "security" as:

> includes any loan stock or similar security whether of the Government of the UK or any other government, or of any public or local authority in the UK or elsewhere, or of any company, whether secured or unsecured.[1]

Judicial opinion on the nature of a debt on a security has varied over the years. However, the current view seems to be that such a debt must be something in the nature of an investment. Lord Cameron said:

> Once the terms of [TCGA 1992, s 132] are examined, it becomes abundantly plain that the word 'security' in [TCGA 1992, s 251(1)] is a substantive and refers to those securities which are or can be subject to a conversion.

In his dissenting judgment, Lord Migdale said:

> I think that the words 'the debt on a security' refer to an obligation to pay or repay embodied in the share or stock certificate issued by a government, local authority or company, which is evidence of the ownership of the share or stock and solves the right to receive payment . . . 'The debt on a security' means a debt evidenced in a document as a security. I cannot see any similarity between the letter of acceptance or the bill of exchange in this case and loan stock or, for that matter, an unsecured debenture.

In *Aberdeen Construction Group Ltd v IRC*,[2] the taxpayer company contracted to sell a subsidiary. The subsidiary's financial state was precarious and the company stood to make a commercial loss of £364,024 on the sale. The terms of the sale were that the share capital in the company was sold for

£250,000 on condition that the company wrote off loans totalling £500,000 that had been made to its subsidiary. Aberdeen Construction Group Ltd contended that the loans it had made constituted a "debt on a security" so that an allowable loss accrued. The Court of Session and the House of Lords rejected the argument that the loans constituted a "debt on a security". Lord Emslie in the Court of Session said:

> What then is 'a security' within the meaning of TCGA 1992, s 251(1)? Reference to s 132(3) shows that it is concerned with 'conversion of securities' and with the word 'security' itself . . . On a proper construction of that subsection, I am persuaded that what is in contemplation is the issue of a document or certificate by the debtor institution which would represent a marketable security, as that expression is commonly understood, the nature and character of which would remain constant in all transmissions.

A different approach was taken by the court in *W T Ramsay Ltd v IRC*.[3] The House of Lords, in that case, considered a complex tax avoidance scheme that for its efficacy relied on a debt being assigned for £393,750 more than its cost. The taxpayer contended that no chargeable gain resulted as it was not a debt on a security. The House of Lords ruled that the loan was a debt on a security and, hence, the tax avoidance scheme failed. Lord Wilberforce said:

> It can be seen, however, in my opinion, that the legislature is endeavouring to distinguish between mere debts, which normally (although there are exceptions) do not increase but may decrease in value and debts with added characteristics such as may enable them to be realised or dealt with at a profit. But this distinction must still be given effect through the words used.

> Of these, some help is gained from a contrast to be drawn between debts simpliciter, which may arise from trading and a multitude of other situations, commercial or private, and loans, certainly a narrower class, and one which presupposes some kind of contractual structure . . .

> With all this lack of certainty as to the statutory words, I do not feel any doubt that in this case the debt was a debt on a security. I have already stated its terms. It was created by contract the terms of which were recorded in writing; it was designed, from the beginning, to be capable of being sold, and, indeed, to be sold at a profit.[4]

In *Tarmac Roadstone Holdings Ltd v Williams*,[5] the Special Commissioner held that the distinguishing feature of a debt on security is that it is in the nature of an investment which can be dealt with as such. The distinction between a debt and a debt on a security is, in the Special Commissioner's judgment, not to be found by looking at TCGA 1992, s 134 alone and must be based on the definition in s 82(3)(*b*).[6] In the case under consideration, Tarmac had made a loss (when measured in sterling) on the encashment of loan notes it held in its US subsidiary. The subsidiary had the power unilaterally to redeem the loan notes and this was held to indicate that the loan notes were not "in the nature of an investment". Hence, the loss arising on the disposal was not relievable. A similar approach was adopted by the court in *Taylor Clark International Ltd v Lewis*,[7] where a loss arose on a promissory note which, the court held, was not a debt on security as "the taxpayer company's loan lacked a 'structure of permanence', because it has no fixed term and repayment could have been demanded by the creditor, or effected

[17.10] Assets, exemptions and reliefs

(without penalty) by the debtor, at any time".[8] The key to the case is that a debt on a security must be marketable in a realistic sense.[9]

Simon's Taxes C1.408.

---

[1] Definition in TCGA, 1992 s 132(2)(*b*) applied by TCGA 1992, s 251(1).
[2] [1978] STC 127.
[3] [1981] STC 174.
[4] [1981] STC 174 at 184b and f.
[5] [1996] STC (SCD) 409.
[6] [1996] STC (SCD) 409 at 418c.
[7] [1998] STC 1259.
[8] Per Robert Walker J at first instance, [1997] STC 499 at 522d.
[9] Per Peter Gibson LJ [1998] STC 1259 at 1272.

Covenants

[17.11] No chargeable gain accrues on the disposal of a right to or to a part of annual payments due under a covenant made by any person and which was not secured on any property.[1]

In *Rank Xerox Ltd v Lane*,[2] the House of Lords held that this rule was confined to situations where there was a gratuitous promise to make the payments and the promise was enforceable only because of its form; in that case the taxpayer was held liable on the gain arising from the disposal to its shareholders of a right to receive royalty payments.

Simon's Taxes C1.410.

---

[1] TCGA 1992, s 237(*c*).
[2] [1979] STC 740.

Government stock and qualifying corporate bonds

[17.12] Any gain or loss on the disposal of gilt edged securities or qualifying corporate bonds is exempt from capital gains tax.[1] The exemption is from CGT only; not from corporation tax. The effect of the loan relationship legislation[2] is that corporation tax is charged on increases in value of Government Stock and qualifying corporate bonds that would be exempt from tax if held by an individual.

Gilt edged securities are defined as those specified in statute,[3] or by Treasury Order made under statutory authority.

It is frequently the case that when a company is sold a shareholder will accept loan stock issued by the purchaser, rather than cash. This will normally delay the disposal for CGT purposes until the loan stock is encashed.[4] If the loan stock fulfils the definition of a qualifying corporate bond,[5] taper relief is frozen and no benefit is gained from the additional period the taxpayer waits to

Exemptions and reliefs [17.12]

receive the cash proceeds of his sale. In addition, the shareholder runs the risk that default by the purchaser will lead to the gain on the shares being taxed but no relief being available for the loss arising from the default.[6] It is, therefore, standard practice for the stock that is issued in these circumstances to be structured so that it does not fulfil the definition of a qualifying corporate bond. A standard approach is to define the redemption process that will arise by reference to foreign currency; that is, shortly before the redemption date the currency of the loan stock converts to, say, US dollars which are then converted back to sterling.[7] Concern has been expressed[8] that the drafting used to ensure that an instrument is not a qualifying corporate bond may make the instrument subject to the deep discount security legislation[9] that imposes an income tax charge.

Simon's Taxes C1.408.

[1] TCGA 1992, s 115(1).
[2] FA 1996, ss 80–89.
[3] Certain gilts are specified as exempt in TCGA 1992, Sch 9, Part 2. TCGA 1992, Sch 9, para 1 authorises The Treasury to specify further issues. Additional issues are listed in nine Capital Gains Tax (Gilt Edged Securities) Orders: SI 1993/950, 1994/2656, 1996/1031, 2001/1122, 2002/2849, 2004/438, 2005/276 and 2006/184. These statutory instruments have a special status in that TCGA 1992, s 287(4) removes from the House of Commons the ability to annul these Treasury Orders. For judicial analysis of the definition of a gilt edged security, vide *Weston v Garnett* [2005] STC 617.
[4] TCGA 1992, s 117 and TA 1988, Sch 18 para 1(5).
[5] TCGA 1992, s 135. See infra, § **21.20**.
[6] TCGA 1992, s 116. See infra, § **21.21**.
[7] Normal practice is to avoid using the euro as the foreign currency out of concern that either the adoption of the euro by the UK would negate the exclusion from QCB status that was sought or, alternatively, an argument under non-discrimination principles would succeed in categorising an instrument in euros as satisfying the QCB requirement for being expressed in sterling. Concern has been expressed that the concessionary treatment given in HMRC Capital Gains Manual para CG 53746 can cause such a loan note to be treated as a QCB. This concession is that the Revenue will not deny QCB treatment where the redemption is not "expressed in sterling" but there is no real likelihood of a gain or loss being made. The concession was introduced to deal with a particular old form of Eurobonds which were designated in sterling but the proceeds were paid in another European currency. The concern is misplaced as the taxpayer can always insist on statutory treatment and avoid being taxed by a purported Revenue concession. Further, the concession is specified as being applicable only in those instances where there is no real exposure to the chance of gain or loss. Where the currency of a loan note converts, there is always a gain or loss on redemption, however short the period may be in the foreign currency.
[8] See, for example, Julian Ghosh "If The Cap Does Not Fit", Taxation, 7 February 2002 p 439.
[9] FA 1996, Sch 13.

Insurance policy

[17.13] The disposal of an interest in a non life policy of insurance is exempt.[1] This exemption does not, however, affect the payment made for a claim under the policy being treated as consideration for a disposal that gives a chargeable gain. It is the disposal of the policy that is exempt; and not the disposal triggered by the receipt of insurance monies.

The exemption is to defeat a widely used scheme whereby a loss arising on the disposal of a capital redemption policy was an allowable loss that was set against a taxpayer's gains, the sum payable on redemption being tax free.

A capital redemption policy is a contract, normally issued by an insurance company, which is made in the course of capital redemption business. Under a capital redemption policy, for consideration of a sum or sums of money, the issuer of the policy guarantees to pay out a larger sum on a specified future date or to make a series of payments. Payment is independent of any contingency. For example, it is not contingent upon a death or the survival of a life. Examples of such contracts include (i) an annuity certain—an annuity payable for a set period not contingent upon the survival of a life, (ii) a leasehold redemption policy—which builds up a fund to be used in some way on the expiry of a lease, and (iii) a sinking fund policy—this accumulates a fund for the eventual replacement of a wasting asset.

[1] TCGA 1992, s 204 completely rewritten by FA 2006, s 73.

Woodlands

[17.14] No CGT charge arises on the disposal of trees or saleable underwood in respect of woodlands managed by the occupier on a commercial basis and with a view to the realisation of profits.[1] With effect from 29 November 1994, land on which short rotation coppice is cultivated is treated as agricultural land, not woodland.[2] Further, on a disposal of any woodland, such part of acquisition cost—or the disposal consideration—as is attributable to the trees and underwood is disregarded for CGT. This exclusion prevents a taxpayer from buying land, cutting the timber and then claiming a loss for the decline in value due to the felling.

Simon's Taxes C2.105.

[1] TCGA 1992, s 250. Before 6 April 1988, the exemption for the disposal of standing timber was applied to woodlands within Schedule B for income tax purposes.
[2] FA 1995, s 154. The provision is deemed to have come into force on 29 November 1994.

Works of art

[17.15] A gain is exempt from the charge to capital gains tax if it arises on the disposal:

(a) of property accepted by the Treasury in satisfaction of a liability to inheritance tax;[1]
(b) to a museum, etc, listed in IHTA 1984, Sch 3, where the disposal is "otherwise than by sale";[2]
(c) of property within IHTA 1984, s 26(2) and a direction has been given by the Revenue in relation to that property (gifts for public benefit).[3]

Simon's Taxes C1.418.

[1] TCGA 1992, s 258(2)(b); IHTA 1984, s 230; FA 1946, ss 50, 51.
[2] TCGA 1992, s 258(2)(a).
[3] TCGA 1992, s 258(1).

Conditional exemption

[17.16] Where IHTA 1984, s 30 gives conditional exemption from inheritance tax on a transfer, there is an equivalent exemption from capital gains tax provided by TCGA 1992, s 258(3). This is, however, confined to gifts and certain deemed disposals by trustees. The conditional exemption takes the form of holdover relief; the disposal is treated as having been made for a consideration such that it is at no gain/no loss.

If there is a subsequent sale of the asset such that inheritance tax becomes chargeable at the time of the sale, TCGA 1992, s 258(5) operates to impose a charge to capital gains tax computed on the basis that the sale has taken place at its then market value, irrespective of any actual consideration that passes.

Anti-avoidance—value shifting

[17.17] The existence of exempt assets enabled tax avoidance schemes to be developed which moved value from chargeable to non-chargeable assets in order to create a loss or remove a gain. Thus in *Eilbeck v Rawling*[1] the taxpayer arranged to shift value from a purchased interest in settled property to an interest in another settlement which had not been purchased and was exempt from CGT. On the sale of the two interests, there arose an allowable loss on the purchased reversionary interest and an equal but non-chargeable gain on the other.[2] The scheme failed because the House of Lords treated the various acts as one whole transaction (supra, § **3.06**).

Nevertheless, specific anti-avoidance legislation[3] was introduced to counter value shifting. It applies where:

(1) there is a disposal other than between spouses or by a personal representative to a legatee;
(2) there is a scheme or arrangements whereby;
(3) the value of an asset has been materially reduced; and
(4) a tax-free benefit has been or will be conferred on any person.

Condition 3 is amplified to ensure that where the disposal precedes the acquisition the reference to reduction includes an increase. Both benefit and

[17.17] Assets, exemptions and reliefs

tax free are defined in the widest possible way for condition 4. There is some minor relief in that if the benefit is conferred on a person other than the disposer or one connected with him, the provision is excluded if it is shown that the avoidance of tax was not a purpose of the scheme or arrangements in question.

Where the provisions apply, the inspector may recalculate any allowable loss or chargeable gain on whatever basis appears to him to be just and reasonable; he may then do whatever is just and reasonable to adjust the base cost of the assets concerned for the following disposal.

The value-shifting rules can apply to transactions far removed in spirit from the artificiality of *Eilbeck v Rawling* and a similar case, *W T Ramsay Ltd v IRC* (supra, § **3.15**), but there is no formal clearance procedure.

The section does not generally apply to a reduction in the value of shares arising from an intra-group dividend or from an intra-group disposal but there are exceptions in relation to disposals on or after 14 March 1989.[4]

Simon's Taxes C1.105, C2.115; Sumption CGT A2.04, A10.13.

[1] [1981] STC 174, [1981] 1 All ER 865.
[2] Infra, § **20.21**.
[3] TCGA 1992, s 30.
[4] TCGA 1992, ss 30–34; infra, §§ **28.30–28.36**.

Tangible movable property—wasting assets

[**17.18**] No chargeable gain accrues on the disposal of tangible movable property or an interest in such property, which is also a wasting asset.[1] A wasting asset is defined as an asset having a predictable life of 50 years or less.[2] Plant and machinery is always assumed to have a life of less than 50 years.[3] However, the exemption for wasting chattels does not apply to assets in respect of which capital allowances were or could have been claimed, nor to commodities dealt with on a terminal market.[4]

Simon's Taxes C1.407; C2.221, 905; Sumption CGT A17.04.

[1] TCGA 1992, s 45(1)
[2] TCGA 1992, s 44 applied by s 45(5).
[3] TCGA 1992, s 44(1)(c). The Revenue consider that the definition of "machinery" includes antique clocks and watches, as well as custom made vehicles such as racing cars, commercial vehicles and locomotives etc: Inland Revenue interpretation RI 88. Such items are consequently exempt if used for private purposes.
[4] TCGA 1992, s 45(2)–(4).

Chattels disposed of for £6,000 or less

[17.19] If an asset which is tangible movable property is disposed of and the amount or value of the consideration does not exceed £6,000, there is no chargeable gain.[1] The consideration taken into account is the gross amount, before any expenses of disposal.

If the asset is sold for more than £6,000 any gain is computed in the normal way. However, there is marginal relief whereby the gain is limited to 5/3rds of the difference between the consideration and £6,000.[2]

EXAMPLE
   M sells a chattel for £6,400, which he had purchased two years before for £800.

Disposal consideration	£6,400
Allowable cost	800
Chargeable gain	£5,600
Gain is limited to 5/3 × (6,400 – 6,000)	£667

Loss relief is restricted where a chattel is disposed of for less than £6,000.[3] The allowable loss is computed on the assumption that the consideration was £6,000.

EXAMPLE
   N acquired an antique object for £7,000 but sells it, in a falling market, for £5,200.

Deemed consideration for disposal	£6,000
Allowable cost	7,000
Allowable loss	£1,000

The relief does not apply to commodities in a terminal market or currency of any description.[4]

Simon's Taxes C1.406; Sumption CGT A17.03.

---

[1] TCGA 1992, s 262(1).
[2] TCGA 1992, s 262(2).
[3] TCGA 1992, s 262(3).
[4] TCGA 1992, s 262(8); the relief being only for tangible movable property means that it is not available for fixtures before severance.

Anti-avoidance provisions—part disposal

[17.20] There are provisions to counter exploitation of the chattel exemption by successive disposals of part-interests in a chattel worth more than £6,000. Where there is a disposal of a right or interest in or over tangible movable property, the consideration for the disposal is treated as the aggregate of the sum received for the interest disposed of *and* the market value of the remainder.[1] Any marginal relief is calculated as already described (supra, § **17.18**) by reference to the deemed consideration for the disposal, and the relief is then allocated pro rata to the actual disposal consideration.

[17.20] Assets, exemptions and reliefs

EXAMPLE

Q sells a one-third share in a watercolour for £2,500. He had bought the watercolour two years before for £900. The value of the remainder is £5,000.

(1) The disposal consideration is deemed to be £7,500, so that the chattel exemption is not available.
(2) The gain is calculated as follows:

Disposal consideration (actual)		£2,500
Allowable cost:	$900 \times \dfrac{2,500}{2,500 + 5,000} =$	300
Gain		£2,200

(3) Marginal relief:

Gain is limited to 5/3 × (7,500 − 6,000) =	£2,500
Allocate pro rata to interest disposed of:	
$2,500 \times \dfrac{2,500}{7,500}$	£833
Relief given: £2,159 − £833 =	£1,326

This principle is applied also to the loss restriction.

EXAMPLE

If, in the preceding example, Q had purchased the picture for £8,400, and had sold a 1/3 share for £1,500 (value of remainder £3,000), the position would be as follows:

Allowable loss without restriction		
Actual proceeds		£1,500
Allowable cost: $£8,400 \times \dfrac{1,500}{1,500 + 3,000}$		£2,800
Allowable loss		£1,300
Deemed disposal proceeds		£6,000
Allowable cost		£8,400
Allowable loss		£2,400
Allowable loss on 1/3 sold restricted to		£800

There may be still an advantage in making a series of part disposals so as to take advantage of the annual exemption.

Simon's Taxes C1.406; Sumption CGT A17.03.

---

[1] TCGA 1992, s 262(5).

Sets of chattels

[17.21] Different provisions apply to a set of articles where the owner can make a disposition of one of the items in the set rather than, in the case of a single object, making a part disposal of it. The disposal of one item of the set is not treated as a part disposal of the set. However, special rules apply if there is a disposal of more than one item either to the same person or to persons who are acting in concert or to persons who are connected with each other (but not necessarily connected with the disposer).

Whether the disposals take place on the same or different occasions the two or more transactions are treated as a single transaction disposing of a single asset with any necessary apportionments of marginal relief and in restriction of losses.[1] The apportionment is made by reference to the consideration received for each of the items concerned. If disposals of parts of a set are made over a period of years, it appears that marginal relief or loss restriction for earlier years may be affected, although there is no extension of the normal six-year time limit for assessment or repayment claims.

EXAMPLE

G purchased a set of six antique dining chairs for £5,400. He sells three of them to a dealer for £4,200. A year later, he sells the remaining three to the same dealer for £4,200.

	£
Disposal proceeds per chair	1,400
Allowable cost	900
Chargeable gain	£500
Marginal relief:	
Deemed transaction value	£8,400
Chargeable gain limited to 5/3 × (£8,400 − £6,000) =	£4,000
Chargeable gain limit per chair: 1/6 × £4,000 =	£667

Marginal relief is therefore inapplicable.

There is no definition of a set although the Revenue seem to take the view that just two items cannot constitute a set. The statute requires that they should all have been owned at one time by one person and that they are disposed of by that person. The provisions do not apply where the set is owned by connected persons.

Simon's Taxes C1.406; Sumption CGT A17.03.

[1] TCGA 1992, s 262(4). Quaere when the recipients must be acting in concert or connected persons; is it the time of the first disposal or the subsequent one or both?

Venture capital trusts

[17.22] CGT reliefs are available for investments in venture capital trusts (infra, § **30.06**). An investment of up to £100,000 in venture capital trusts in any tax year will not give rise to chargeable gains (or allowable losses) on

[17.22] Assets, exemptions and reliefs

disposal of the shares.[1] In addition, investors are entitled to claim a deferral of chargeable gains of up to £100,000 per tax year arising on the disposal of any assets, where the gain is reinvested in shares of venture capital trusts.[2]

The investment must be made within 12 months either before or after the date of the relevant disposal.[3] The gain held over becomes chargeable if the shares are disposed of (other than to the investor's spouse) within five years of the date the investment was made, or on certain other events such as becoming non-resident.[4] Where there is a part disposal of shares in the venture capital trust, the shares disposed of are matched with those acquired on a first-in, first-out basis.[5]

Simon's Taxes Division E3.2.

[1] TCGA 1992, s 151A.
[2] TCGA 1992, Sch 5C, para 2.
[3] TCGA 1992, Sch 5C, para 1(3).
[4] TCGA 1992, Sch 5C, para 3(1).
[5] TCGA 1992, Sch 5C, para 4(2).

Enterprise investment scheme

[17.23] On a disposal of shares which have qualified for income tax relief under the Enterprise Investment Scheme, any gain is exempt from CGT,[1] but any loss is allowable.[2] The exemption for gains is retained if shares which have been held for at least five years are treated the same as a new holding as the result of a merger or reconstruction.[3] In the case of a merger, the other company must be one that has qualified for relief either under the EIS or under the BES.

Simon's Taxes E3.131, 132.

[1] TCGA 1992, s 150A(2).
[2] TCGA 1992, s 150A(2A). The loss is restricted by the income tax relief obtained: s 150A(1).
[3] Simon's Taxes E3.131, 132.
TCGA 1992, s 150A(8A), (8B).

Business Expansion Scheme

[17.24] Shares issued after 18 March 1986 for which business expansion scheme relief has been given and not withdrawn, are exempt assets for CGT purposes. That is, no chargeable gain nor allowable loss arises on disposal.[1]

Where a BES share was issued before 19 March 1986, any gain arising is chargeable. The gain is computed by reference to the amount paid, ignoring the relief.[2] Where, however, a loss arises on disposal, the loss is restricted by the amount of BES relief obtained.[3]

[1] TCGA 1992, s 150(2).
[2] TCGA 1992, s 150(3).
[3] TCGA 1992, s 150(3).

Valuation

The basic rule of valuation

[17.25] In a number of circumstances, the market value of the assets is required to be substituted for any actual consideration passing. Market value means the price which the assets might reasonably be expected to fetch in a sale on the open market at the valuation date.[1] In making that estimate, no reduction is to be made because the whole of the assets are to be hypothetically placed on the market at one time.[2] The legislation seems to assume that the price paid in the open market would be a capital sum. However, it is debatable whether the market consideration for a lease granted at undervalue is the premium otherwise obtainable for a lease at that rent, or instead a rack rent with no premium.

Simon's Taxes C2.120.

[1] TCGA 1992, s 272.
[2] TCGA 1992, s 272(2).

Valuation of quoted securities

[17.26] The value to be taken for quoted shares and securities is taken from the Stock Exchange Official Daily List.[1] It is either the lower of the two prices shown in the quotations plus one-quarter of the difference between the two figures, or halfway between the highest and lowest prices at which bargains, other than bargains done at special prices, were recorded for the relevant date. Where both figures are available it is the lower figure which is used. (Prices in The Times, for example, are at the halfway mark, not quarter-up.)

Statute states that the Daily List price is not taken as market value "if special circumstances exist" to make the market price not a proper measure of market value.[2] This exclusion is of very limited application. The stock market figure is taken even when price sensitive information is known to the directors, but not to the Stock Exchange. In *Crabtree v Hinchcliffe*,[3] negotiations for a takeover were under way. This was known to the director, who was the taxpayer who made the gain, but not to the general public nor to the Stock Exchange. The court held that it was, nevertheless, the Daily List figure that was to be taken, the exclusion not being applicable. In his judgment, Lord Dilhorne suggested that the exclusion would come into play if price sensitive information was known to the directors, but had not been made public, although the nature of the information was such that company law required it to have been placed in the public domain.[4]

Simon's Taxes C2.122.

[1] TCGA 1992, s 272(3).
[2] TCGA 1992, s 272(3).
[3] (1971) 47 TC 419.
[4] (1971) 47 TC 419 at 450.

Valuation of unquoted securities

[17.27] Unquoted shares must be valued in the hypothetical open market. The principles for valuing unquoted shares are discussed with reference to inheritance tax in Chapter 45.

Valuation determined for inheritance tax used for CGT purposes

[17.28] TCGA 1992, s 274 provides that where "on the death of any person inheritance tax is chargeable on the value of his estate . . . and the value of an asset forming part of that estate has been ascertained . . . for the purpose of that tax, the value so ascertained shall be taken (for CGT purposes) to be the market value of that asset at the date of the death".

When valuing for inheritance tax purposes, the value of related property must be taken into account. However, where value is for capital gains tax purposes, related property is not in point. The effect of TCGA 1992, s 274 is that a valuation that has been undertaken under inheritance tax principles automatically applies to determine a valuation for CGT, even though the valuation may be determined by reference to related property.

Consider, for example, a company with an issue shared capital of 100 ordinary shares. Ten shares are owned by the deceased; a further 80 shares are owned by his spouse. After his death, the personal representatives sell the shareholding. If the value of the deceased's shareholding is not "ascertained" for the purposes of inheritance tax, the acquisition cost on the CGT disposal is taken as the value of a 10% shareholding in the company. If, however, the value of that shareholding is "ascertained" for inheritance tax purposes, the effect of TCGA 1992, s 274 is that the "acquisition cost" brought into the CGT computation for the executors is 1/9 of the value of a 90% holding, which is likely to be very substantially higher.

The Revenue view is that acceptance of a taxpayer's valuation, where no inheritance tax is payable, does not constitute the value being "ascertained". Revenue Interpretation RI 110 states:

> If an asset is wholly exempt or relieved from IHT, neither the personal representatives of the deceased nor the Revenue can require the value of that asset to be ascertained for IHT purposes.

Where it is evident that any possible increase or decrease in the value of the chargeable assets of the estate, as included in an Inland Revenue Account, will leave the total value of the estate below the IHT threshold, it will not be necessary to ascertain the value of all the individual assets for IHT purposes. In some cases, particularly where the estate is close to the threshold, values may be considered but not necessarily 'ascertained'.

In *Stonor and anor (exors of Dickinson, decd) v IRC*[1], the executors attempted to make a claim under s 274 to review the values at death to the sale proceeds, when the proceeds were substantially higher than the values at death. In this particular case, the bulk of the estate was left to charity and the legacies chargeable to inheritance tax were less than the IHT nil rate band. By an upward revision of the values for IHT purposes, no IHT would become payable but the CGT liability on the sales would be reduced. The Special Commissioners rejected the claim. The decision was not, however, made on the basis that a claim to increase the value at death is not competent but, rather, that the claim can only be made by what statute refers to as "the appropriate person",[2] being "the person liable for inheritance tax".[3] As there was no inheritance tax payable, there was no person liable to pay it and, in the decision of the Special Commissioner, there was no person competent to make the claim.[4]

1   [2001] STC (SCD) 199.
2   IHTA 1984, s 191(1)(*b*).
3   IHTA 1984, s 190(1).
4   [2001] STC (SCD) 199, para 27 at 205a.

Disposal in a series of transactions

[17.29] In estimating the market value of an asset for CGT, regard is normally had only to that asset in isolation, in contrast to the "loss to estate" principle adopted for IHT. However, the value may be increased where a disposal forms one of a series of linked transactions.

This special rule applies where, by two or more transactions, one person disposes of assets to another person with whom he is connected, or to two or more persons with each of whom he is connected. Connected person status is vital and there must be connection with a common disponor (not necessarily between each disponee).[1] For the special rule to apply to a particular transaction in the series, the original market value[2] of the assets transferred by that transaction must be less than the appropriate portion[3] of the aggregate market value[4] of the assets disposed of by all the transactions in the series. The original market value is simply the market value determined without regard to the linked transactions rule. The aggregate market value used to determine the uplifted transaction value is the value of the transferred assets in aggregate, determined as at the time of the transaction in question.

Transactions are not linked unless they occur within six years of each other. Once a value for a given transaction has been adjusted, it may still be adjusted again if there is a further linked transaction in the series, within the six years time limit.

[17.29] Assets, exemptions and reliefs

The linked transactions rule does not override the normal rule as to valuation on a disposal between spouses living together.[5] There are certain special provisions for assets passed down chains which include intra-group transfers.[6]

In contrast to the rule in *Furniss v Dawson*,[7] it is generally considered that this rule is solely a valuation rule and does not change the timing of the disposal.

Simon's Taxes C2.114.

---

[1] TCGA 1992, s 19(1).
[2] TCGA 1992, s 20(3).
[3] TCGA 1992, s 20(4)(*b*), (6)–(9).
[4] TCGA 1992, s 20(4)(*a*), (6)–(9).
[5] TCGA 1992, s 19(2).
[6] TCGA 1992, s 19(5), (6).
[7] [1982] STC 267.

Costs of valuation

[17.30] "Costs reasonably incurred in making a valuation . . . required for the purposes of the computation of the gain" are allowed, by statute, as a deduction in computing the gain.[1] Revenue Interpretation RI 63, issued February 1994, states the Revenue view as to the extent of the deduction available:

> In our view, the relevant legislation—TCGA 1992, s 38(2)(b)—allows the reasonable costs incurred in making the valuation, so that the gain can be calculated and returned, to be deducted. Any costs subsequently incurred, for example, in negotiating with the District Valuer or of the Shares Valuation Division, or in litigating the matter before any tribunal or in the courts, are not available.

The question was considered in *Caton's Administrators v Couch*.[2] In that case, the administrators sought to deduct not only the costs of negotiating with Shares Valuation Division, but also the costs of the appeal. This deduction was allowed by the Special Commissioner. However, on appeal, the High Court reversed the finding of the Special Commissioners.

The Court of Appeal upheld the judgment of Rimer J in the High Court. In his leading judgment, Morritt LJ said:[3]

> I conclude that the costs and expenses which a taxpayer may deduct pursuant to [TCGA 1992, s 38(2)(b)] in respect of any particular disposal are limited to those which he incurs in complying with his obligations under [TMA 1970, s 12, the obligation to submit a tax return] and do not extend to costs incurred in negotiating over or contesting his liability to capital gains tax arising out of that disposal. The effect, but not the reason for, that conclusion is to preclude the deduction of costs by a taxpayer in conducting a tax controversy with the Revenue.

Simon's Taxes C2.202.

---

[1] TCGA 1992, s 38(2)(*b*).
[2] [1995] STC (SCD) 34.
[3] [1997] STC 970, CA at 979j/980a.

Revenue agreement to valuation

[17.31] With the advent of self-assessment, an individual taxpayer is able to request HMRC to consider his valuation of an asset, where that is required to compute a capital gain. This request can be made any time after the disposal of the asset. The request is made separately from the tax return but is made to the tax district that has responsibility for the return. The request is made on Revenue form CG34, which specifies the information the taxpayer is required to submit in support of his valuation.[1]

---

[1] *Simon's Weekly Tax Intelligence* 1997, p 184. See also Inland Revenue Tax Bulletin April 2001, p 839.

18

Disposal

Meaning of disposal	PARA **18.01**
Time of disposal	PARA **18.05**
Part disposals	PARA **18.13**
Compensation and insurance payments	PARA **18.16**
Use of assets	PARA **18.20**
Mortgages and bankruptcy	PARA **18.21**
Options	PARA **18.23**
Gifts, bargains not at arm's length and other gratuitous transactions	PARA **18.33**
Holdover relief	PARA **18.38**
Gratuitous transfers of value	PARA **18.47**
Connected persons	PARA **18.49**

Meaning of disposal

[18.01] The central concept of disposal is not defined,[1] but nor has it yet caused much reported litigation. In 1980, the Revenue suggested that any form of transfer or alienation of the beneficial title to an asset (whether legal or equitable) from one person to another involves a disposal by the one and an acquisition by the other.[2] This is certainly too wide a definition. Capital gains tax is, fundamentally, concerned with beneficial interest, not legal title.[3] Statute requires[4] you to look through the legal title[5] so that the tax charge arises by reference to the underlying beneficial interest. Hence, transferring ownership to a nominee is not a disposal for CGT purposes. There is, however, a disposal when an asset is transferred to trustees, other than bare trustees. It is well established that an individual who settles his property on trust has made a disposal, even though he may be the only beneficiary entitled to receive capital from that trust.[6] A sale by personal representatives in the course of administration is clearly a disposal on this definition since beneficial title passes to the purchaser and the fact that the disposer is not himself beneficially entitled is quite irrelevant. In principle, a disclaimer is a disposal; however, statute[7] provides that a beneficiary under a will or intestacy can make an election that has the effect that the disclaimer is not treated as a disposal for CGT purposes.

An exchange of assets is a disposal of each asset involved. An example is where a farm is owned by two brothers, each having an undivided share in the whole and they decide that they will construct a boundary so that the first brother has sole ownership of the land north of the boundary, leaving the land to the south in the sole ownership of the second brother. This is a disposal by the first brother of his half interest in the land to the south and a disposal by the second brother of his half interest in the land to the north. Each brother has made a disposal, the consideration for which is the value of the land acquired from the

[18.01] Disposal

other.[8] Another example is the surrender of a lease in exchange for a new one; in order to avoid CGT it is common to grant the new lease subject to the existing lease and perhaps increasing the rent under the existing lease.[9] However, where the new lease and the old lease are identical in the sense of relating to the same property and having the same terms, the Revenue by concession do not treat the surrender as involving any disposal.[10]

There is no general exclusion for involuntary disposals.[11]

The concept of disposal is extended to certain deemed disposals and by treating certain shifts of economic value as disposals even though no asset is disposed of. In *MacNiven v Westmoreland Investments Ltd*, a disposal was held to be a commercial concept and so it was permissible to apply the *Ramsay* principle and look at the effect of the whole scheme in deciding what is disposed of—and to whom.[12]

Disposals may be made either to realise a gain or to realise a loss. On bed and breakfast transactions see infra, § **21.03**.

Simon's Taxes C1.307; Sumption CGT A1.06.

---

[1] Contrast TA 1988, s 776(4) and TA 1988, s 777(2), (3). See *Turner v Follet* [1973] STC 148, 48 TC 614, where the CA made extremely heavy weather of the point if the definition in the text is right. A loan is not a disposal but a loan must be distinguished from a gift, see *Dewar v Dewar* [1975] 2 All ER 728. On switching between different unit trusts in a multi-portfolio see TCGA 1992, s 102 and Inland Revenue press release, 17 March 1987, *Simon's Tax Intelligence* 1987, p 200, for disposals prior to 14 March 1989, and TCGA 1992, s 102 (FA 1989, s 140) for disposals on or after that date.

[2] In the Revenue booklet CG8 published in 1980 it is stated at para 108: 'An asset is disposed of whenever its ownership changes or whenever the owner divests himself of his rights in or interests over that asset, for example, by sale, exchange or gift'. (This booklet has since been withdrawn.)

[3] In *Ingram v IRC* [1997] STC 1234, CA, the Court of Appeal held that the lease created under the tax scheme was imperfect at law but ruled that it was nonetheless effective in equity for the purpose of establishing a charge to CGT. (The House of Lords subsequently held the lease to be valid but this does not reverse the decision of principle made by the lower court.)

[4] TCGA 1992, s 60 requires that, in applying CGT, one looks through a nominee or a bare trustee but only where the beneficial owner is absolutely entitled as against the trustee, or would be so entitled but for being an infant or other person under disability.

[5] TCGA 1992, s 70. In his leading judgment in *Berry v Warnett* [1982] STC 398, HL Lord Wilberforce considered the sale of shares held by nominees for an individual to trustees of a settlement which he created, the terms of which gave him an exclusive life interest. Lord Wilberforce outlined the scheme of the legislation, describing it as "clear and logical" (at 399d). He analysed the facts of the case as: "a disposal in March 1972 of the legal title to the shares [is] . . . to be disregarded . . . as conferring only a nominee interest, but becoming a defective disposal when on 4 April 1972 trusts were declared other than in favour of the settlor, thus making the shares settled property" (at 399j/400a).

[6] TCGA 1992, s 62(6)(a). See *Re Paradise Motor Co Ltd* [1968] 2 All ER 625.

[7] TCGA 1992, s 62(6)(a). See *Re Paradise Motor Co Ltd* [1968] 2 All ER 625.
[8] In this scenario, the Revenue, by concession, allow a roll-over relief claim to avoid payment of tax: extra-statutory concession D26; see infra, § **23.03**. However this does not avoid the exchange being treated as two disposals.
[9] On problems see *Bayley v Rogers* [1980] STC 544.
[10] Extra-statutory concession D39.
[11] But note TCGA 1992, s 66 (bankruptcy not a disposal but acts of trustee treated as acts of bankrupt) and ss 245, 246 (compulsory purchase-disposal).
[12] Per Lord Hoffmann [2001] STC 237 at [41] and [46]; see also *W T Ramsay Ltd v IRC* [1981] STC 174, [1981] 1 All ER 865, particularly so far as it approves dicta of Eveleigh LJ in *Floor v Davis* [1978] STC 436, [1978] 2 All ER 1079.

Hire purchase

[18.02] Where a person acquires an asset under a contract of hire purchase, the transaction is treated as if it amounted to an entire disposal of the asset to that person at the beginning.[1] If the period terminates, but the property in the asset does not pass to him, all necessary adjustments are made. The implication appears to be that the disposal and acquisition deemed to have occurred at the outset are then treated as not having taken place, so that the hirer is not treated as disposing of the asset when his interest terminates. However, he may be treated as having disposed of his rights under the contract, depending upon the circumstances.

The legislation does not say how the disposal consideration is to be valued. However, the Revenue practice in hire purchase cases is to divide the total of the rent and purchase price into capital and interest elements, and tax only the latter as income. If this is followed, the capital element will be the purchase price rather than the sum payable under the option. In practice the asset will probably either be a car (as in *Lyon v Pettigrew*[2] where the vehicle was a taxi but a chargeable gain arose in respect of consideration paid for the licence), a wasting chattel or a chattel whose cost is less than £6,000, so that the problem may not arise often.

Simon's Direct Tax Service C1.310.

[1] TCGA 1992, s 27.
[2] [1985] STC 369.

Disposal without acquisition

[18.03] There may be a disposal of assets by their owner even though no asset is acquired by anyone else, for example, if the owner of the asset receives a capital sum which is derived from the asset.[1] The section applies only to a capital sum; if a receipt is held to be income rather than capital, TCGA 1992, s 22 cannot apply.[2]

The section is stated to apply "in particular" to four types of capital sum. It follows that facts may come within the general words even if not within the

[18.03] Disposal

four categories. However facts apparently within one or other of the four sections cannot be brought within the section if they do not come within the general words; moreover the four examples can be looked at as aids to the interpretation of the general words.[3] The rule does require that the asset should have been owned by the person treated as disposing of them. A mere hope or expectation cannot be owned, and so cannot be an asset.

On a sale of shares for a cash sum plus the right to receive a further sum to be computed by reference to future, unpredictable events, the right to receive the future sum is itself an asset.[4] Such a right is not a debt. When the events occur and the further sum is paid that sum is derived from the right to receive the sum and so there is a disposal of that asset. This is so whether or not the person paying the capital sum acquires any asset.[5]

The requirement that the capital sum must be derived from an asset applies to each of the four types; a sum derived from some other source is not caught by these rules.[6] So sums payable under the Agricultural Holdings Act 1986 to an agricultural tenant for disturbance on the surrender of his tenancy or under the Landlord and Tenant Act 1954 to a business tenant for like loss are not subject to CGT, because the sums are payable under the Acts by way of compensation for various types of loss and expense and are not sums derived from the lease.[7] Compensation under an Order in Council for expropriation of an asset by a foreign government has been held liable to CGT because, inter alia, the right to compensation was an independent property right.[8] By contrast, the right under the Agricultural Holdings Act was a claim against the pocket of the landlord for expense which the tenant was deemed to have suffered.

Where a person received a capital sum in settlement of an action for negligence against solicitors in relation to a conveyancing matter concerning particular properties, it was held that the charge to CGT stemmed from the right to sue and not from the properties concerned and thus was not a part disposal of those properties.[9] A sum received for entering into a restrictive covenant, in connection with the sale of shares in subsidiary companies, has been held not to be as such a capital sum derived from an asset, because the freedom to engage in the activities concerned is not an asset.[10] However, on appeal, it was held that the sum in question was received in part for agreeing not to exploit the goodwill attaching to the group.[11]

Compensation for the release of an option to participate in a development has been held taxable under this head.[12] The fact that another provision[13] states that the abandonment of an option is not the disposal of an asset is irrelevant.

Simon's Taxes C1.319; Sumption CGT A1.09.

---

[1] TCGA 1992, s 22.

[2] *Lang v Rice* [1984] STC 172 where a sum paid as compensation for loss of trading profit was held to be an income receipt and so outside s 22.

[3] *Zim Properties Ltd v Procter* [1985] STC 90 at 106 relying on what, in effect, Lord Wilberforce and Lord Fraser both said in *Marren v Ingles* [1980] STC 500, [1980] 1 WLR 983 to overrule the contrary view expressed by Nourse J in *Davenport v Chilver* [1983] STC 426 at 439.

[4] *Marren v Ingles* [1980] STC 500, [1980] 3 All ER 95.

⁵ Reversing *IRC v Montgomery* [1975] STC 182 at 189. As to "earn-out" sales where the deferred consideration takes the form of shares, see infra, § **21.22**.
⁶ *Davies v Powell* [1977] STC 32, [1977] 1 All ER 471.
⁷ *Drummond v Austin Brown* [1984] STC 321; this distinguished at 325 a sum paid by a landlord in return for the surrender of the "fag end" of a lease. It was also important that the landlord was entitled to possession. Quaere whether the sum was a trading receipt, see supra, § **8.68**.
⁸ *Davenport v Chilver* [1983] STC 426, although in this case liability was virtually escaped because the new right was deemed to have been acquired for market value. The position would now be different as a result of TCGA 1992, s 17, infra, § **18.48**.
⁹ *Zim Properties Ltd v Procter* [1985] STC 90: but see extra-statutory concession D33; infra, § **18.16**. See further, supra, § **17.04**.
¹⁰ *Kirby v Thorn EMI plc* [1986] STC 200.
¹¹ [1987] STC 621.
¹² *Powlson v Welbeck Securities Ltd* [1986] STC 423; affd [1987] STC 468, CA.
¹³ TCGA 1992, s 144(4).

Forfeiture or surrender of rights

[18.04] Capital sums received by a person in return for forfeiture or surrender of rights, eg the surrender of a lease, or for refraining from exercising rights, are taxable. Thus a sum received for the release of a restrictive covenant would be treated as a disposal, as would an agreement not to sue on a contract. It has been said that it is not possible to use TCGA 1992, s 22 to widen the scope of the term "assets".[1] So, according to this view, no charge arises when a sum is received for the surrender of something which is not an asset; for example, the right to play amateur rugby, as in *Jarrold v Boustead*.[2] Nor does a charge arise when the asset surrendered is an exempt asset; eg a life interest under a settlement, or a debt.

If the owner of a right over an asset releases it, there is a disposal even though he receives no consideration.[3]

Simon's Taxes C1.319; Sumption CGT A1.09.

---

[1] *O'Brien v Benson's Hosiery (Holdings) Ltd* [1978] 3 All ER 1057, [1978] STC 549, CA.
[2] (1964) 41 TC 701, CA. Lord Denning MR held that £3,000 paid (in 1958) as a signing on fee for a professional rugby player was not remuneration but a payment for relinquishing amateur status. As the case pre-dates the introduction of CGT, the Court of Appeal did not have to consider whether amateur status is an asset for CGT purposes. However, the comments made in the judgment by Lord Denning to the effect that there was damage to an 's social standing and his ability to compete as an athlete, as well as the prohibition on him ever again performing as an amateur rugby player, would seem to indicate that the payment was, in the eyes of the Court of Appeal, a payment of compensation for damage and, hence, arguably, not capable of being within TCGA 1992, s 22, as there was no asset from which the capital sum could derive.

[18.04] Disposal

[3] The disposal will be treated as taking place at market value if done gratuitously, infra, § **18.47**.

Time of disposal

[18.05] Just as there is no general definition of a disposal so there is no general rule for the timing of a disposal (or acquisition)—although there are some specific rules. These general matters are therefore left as questions of general law. So the gift of a chattel takes effect when there has been delivery of the chattel with the requisite intention. Likewise the transfer of shares requires the signing of a share transfer. Transfers of other types of property such as land or copyright require certain formalities such as a deed in writing.[1]

Sometimes a transfer which falls short of these formalities may nonetheless be effective transfers in equity and so qualify as disposals for CGT. Thus in *Re Rose*[2] a gift of shares was held to be effective in equity when the transferor/settlor had done all in his power to complete the transfer and all that remained was registration by the company. By contrast, in *Re Fry*[3] when the transferor still had to complete certain exchange control forms and so equity could not intervene.

For an example of equity's power to intervene see *Ingram v IRC*[4] where a lease was held by the Court of Appeal to be imperfect at law but the Court ruled it to be, nonetheless, effective in equity.

Where an asset is disposed of and acquired under a contract, the time at which the disposal and acquisition take place is the time the contract is made and not, if different, the date of conveyance.[5] Thus the usual time will be that at which the acceptance reaches the offeror, subject to the rules as to postal acceptance.

Simon's Taxes C1.322.

[1] Law of Property Act 1925, s 52 or Copyright Designs and Patents Act 1983, s 90 (3).
[2] [1949] Ch 78.
[3] [1946] Ch 312.
[4] [1997] STC 1234, CA. The House of Lords subsequently held the lease to be valid. However, the ruling of the Court of Appeal remains that a document may be effective in equity despite being imperfect at law.
[5] TCGA 1992, s 28.

Disposal under contract

When the contract is made: *Jerome v Kelly*

[18.06] This case concerns the meaning of what is now TCGA 1992, s 28, which is a deceptively simple provision. The basic rule is that where there is a disposal under a contract, the date of disposal is deemed to be the date of contract (conditional contracts apart). In *Jerome v Kelly*,[1] there was a binding contract on 16 April 1987 made by the three individuals who owned the land for sale for development but at that time the land did not have planning consent. The purchaser had the right to rescind the contract if planning consent was not granted and it was accepted that this did not amount to a conditional contract within the meaning of s 28. Planning permission was given on 22 February 1990. Between the date of contract and the date when planning was granted, a beneficial interest in the land was assigned on 15 December 1989 to a non-resident trust. The planning gain then accrued to those trustees.

The Revenue argued that [now] TCGA 1992, s. 28(1) operates to determine both the time of the disposal and also the person who is liable to pay the tax (ie the owner of the asset at the time the disposal is treated as having occurred). This argument was accepted by the Special Commissioner.[2]

On appeal Park J took a contrary view.[3] He held that there had to be practical limits to the application of s 28 in this situation to avoid a person being taxed on monies that they could not receive by virtue of the assignment of a contract. Thus, the taxpayer is only assessable on the basis of the proceeds received on the assignment (in this case the market value as the individuals were connected to the trustees of the settlements they created). Thus, there is a distinction between the owner at the time of disposal and the person liable to pay the tax.

The House of Lords upheld the decision of Park J.[4] In the words of Lord Hoffmann:[5]

> In my opinion [TCGA 1992, s. 28(1)] was concerned solely with fixing the time of disposal by a person whose identity is to be ascertained by other means. It follows that the disposal under the conveyance to the purchasers was made by the Bermudian trustees and not by Mr and Mrs Jerome.

Simon's Taxes C1.322.

---

[1] [2004] UKHL 25, [2004] STC 887.
[2] [2001] STC (SCD) 70.
[3] [2002] STC 609.
[4] [2004] UKHL 25, [2004] STC 887. The Court of Appeal [2002] EWCA Civ 1879, [2003] STC 206 had ruled against the judgement of Park J on the following basis:

(a) under the general law laid down in *Lysaght v Edwards* (1876) 2 Ch 499, CA a contracting purchaser acquires an equitable interest in the land;
(b) when part of the beneficial interest in the land was transferred to the Bermudan settlements, it was subject to that contractual obligation;
(c) s 28(1) only applies to disposals' under a contract;
(d) the only contract ever entered into was that of 16 April 1987, for which the actions of the legal owners were attributed to the taxpayers as beneficial owners under s 60(1); but
(e) with regard to the land received by way of gift on 1 May 1987, by reason of *Kirby v Thorn EMI* [1987] STC 621 the taxpayers' ownership could not be backdated before their acquisition of it; and
(f) ss 21(1) and 22(1) could operate where s 28(1) did not.

[5] [2004] UKHL 25, [2004] STC 887. para 12 at 891f. Lord Hoffmann's judgement ends with the words: "I see no elegant solution to the problem posed by [now

Is there a disposal under the contract?

[18.07] The general rule applies only when the disposal takes place under the contract; whether this is so is a question of fact. The question can be particularly difficult if a contract is later varied and the question arises whether the disposal is under the original contract as varied or under a new contract. In *Magnavox Electronics Co Ltd v Hall*[1] X made a contract to sell the property to A in 1978; A later defaulted and a new purchaser, B, was found who was willing to buy but at a lower price. In July 1979 X acquired a company, S; S took an assignment of the contractual rights from A. X and A then varied the original contract so as to reflect the new lower price agreed with B; S made a separate contract to sell the property to B.

The Court of Appeal held that these arrangements did not enable X to argue that the disposal took place under the 1978 contract—and so in 1978. The agreement between X and S did not vary the 1978 contract since A was not a party to it. The Court invoked *Furniss v Dawson*[2] to disregard the interposition of S.

If there is no disposal under a contract, there may, nevertheless, be a capital sum derived from an asset. Such a sum is then a deemed disposal[3] and trigger a charge to capital gains tax. The charge can only apply where an asset can be identified. In *British Telecommunications v R & C Comrs*[4] the Special Commissioner held that a payment of £450,000,000 derived from a right and not from an asset. Hence, there was no deemed disposal and no charge to corporation tax.

Simon's Taxes C1.322.

---

[1] [1986] STC 561, CA.
[2] [1984] STC 153, HL.
[3] TCGA 1992, s 22.
[4] [2006] STC (SCD) 347.

Unenforceable contract

[18.08] However, if the disposal is under the contract it will be treated as made when the contract is made even though the contract itself is unenforceable—*Thompson v Salah*.[1]

Simon's Taxes C1.322.

---

[1] [1972] 47 TC 559 (a case concerning Schedule D, Case VII). Illegality making a contract voidable or unenforceable, does not inhibit its tax ability; *IRC v Aken* [1990] STC 497, CA; *Partridge v Mallandaine* (1886) 2 TC 179 see supra, § **7.08**.

Conditional contract

[18.09] If the contract is conditional then the disposal occurs when the condition is satisfied; condition here means something on which the existence of the contract depends rather than a major contractual term. This will usually be a condition precedent.

In *Hatt v Newman*[1] contracts were exchanged on 21 February 1995, with the date for completion being specified as 20 March 1995, but the contract was subject to planning permission having been granted by the completion date. In fact, the planning committee did not meet until 29 March 1995, permission being granted at that meeting. Completion took place, by agreement, on 6 April 1995. The court held that the agreement of the parties to continue with the contract meant that the disposal took place at the time of the meeting on 29 March 1995 as the condition was then satisfied. The taxpayer's submission that the disposal was in the following fiscal year was rejected.

In *Pym v Campbell*[2] a sale of a patent was subject to the invention being approved by a third party; the third party did not approve and so the purchaser was not liable for refusing to complete the purchase.

As is clear from this case, a contract which is subject to a condition precedent to its formation is not strictly a conditional contract since there can be no contract at all until the condition is satisfied.

The phraseology cannot apply to a condition subsequent. Hence, it is considered that a contract with a condition subsequent would give rise to a disposal only when it is clear that the condition cannot occur.

The fact that a contract to dispose of an asset is expressed to be subject to performance by the transferee of obligations imposed on him by the contract (promissory conditions precedent to performance) does not make the contract a conditional contract. Thus an agreement to grant a lease of land subject to the construction of a building on the land by the intending lessee was held to be unconditional in *Eastham v Leigh London and Provincial Properties Ltd.*[3] Similarly, a condition under which the contract terminates on the failure by one of the parties to perform his obligations under the contract (a promissory condition subsequent) would not make the contract a conditional contract.

Simon's Taxes C1.322.

[1] [2000] STC 113.
[2] (1856) 6 E & B 370.
[3] (1971) 46 TC 687, CA.

Disposals under a matrimonial consent order

[18.10] In matrimonial proceedings, the terms embodied in a consent order derive their effect from the order itself and not from the agreement.[1] In *Aspden v Hildesley*[2] the agreed terms were embodied in an order made before decree absolute. This was not a full consent order, but an order that the agreed terms be filed "and made a rule of court". Nevertheless it was argued that the terms had effect only by virtue of the order and that, as the order was made

[18.10] Disposal

before decree absolute, it was conditional upon the decree nisi being made absolute in due course[3] so that the disposal made under the terms in the order was not effectively made until decree absolute. However, the court held that since the agreement provided for the immediate transfer of the taxpayer's interest in the property and that agreement could not have been set aside if the decree had not been made absolute, it followed that, in these particular circumstances, the disposal was not conditional on decree absolute.

Simon's Taxes C1.322.

[1] *De Lasala v De Lasala* [1979] 2 All ER 1146, PC.
[2] [1982] STC 206.
[3] Matrimonial Causes Act 1973, ss 23(5), 24(3).

Is a contract a disposal?

[18.11] The general rule is that when an asset is transferred under an unconditional contract, the disposal takes place at the time the parties agree to the contract.[1]

This rule, however, does not answer the question whether the contract itself is the disposal. This question can be of importance for three reasons:

(1) The rule applies only when the asset is conveyed or transferred and so does not expressly deal with the contract which is not completed. In such cases there will rarely be a disposal. Two self-cancelling contracts do not, without more, represent two independent disposals; instead they will usually be a cancellation of contractual rights *without* any corresponding disposal.[2] Where a deposit is forfeited the forfeiture is not treated as the disposal of an asset,[3] but the contract itself will be treated as a part disposal of the asset if it creates an interest in or right over the asset,[4] a matter which presumably turns on whether equity could order specific performance of the contract. If, however, the specifically enforceable contract is itself the disposal then the Revenue may be able to ignore the subsequent ending of the contract and so charge CGT both on the original part disposal and the subsequent ending of the equitable interest. This, however, is unlikely.

(2) Reliefs are usually calculated by reference to the period up to the date of disposal.

(3) There is the problem of when the tax is due. Thus if in 2001–02 A made a contract to sell with completion in 2005–06, are the Revenue entitled to demand payment of the CGT on 31 January 2003. If the contract itself is not the disposal then presumably the Revenue may argue that they are entitled to treat the 2001–02 transaction as a part disposal and then when the contract is completed in 2005–06 relate the completion back to 2001–02. This, however, is only partly sound. The postponed completion date does not render the contract conditional so the completed contract will give rise to gains chargeable in 2001–02 but the postponement means that equity could not order specific performance so that there can be no part disposal in 2001–02; the forfeited deposit will be taxed neither on forfeiture nor on the grant of the option. If,

however, the contract is itself the disposal then the Revenue can insist that there is a chargeable disposal in 2001–02 and so demand the tax. Generally it will be the Revenue insisting on the disposal being treated as taking place as early as possible but this will not always be so, eg there might be retirement relief that is available in 2001–02 but not in 2005–06.[5]

In view of the practical difficulties raised it seems preferable to reject the notion that the contract is itself a disposal whether or not the contract is specifically enforceable. It follows that when property is disposed of under an unconditional contract of sale, the disposition takes place under the contract and that when the contract is not followed by a disposal it is not open to anyone to treat the contract itself as a part disposal.[6]

Simon's Taxes C1.307.

[1] TCGA 1992, s 28.
[2] *Underwood v R & C Comrs* [2008] EWHC 108 (Ch).
[3] TCGA 1992, s 144(7).
[4] TCGA 1992, s 21(2).
[5] *Johnson v Edwards* [1981] STC 660. In this case, points 1 and 3 above were important. A further issue arose as, in that case, the taxpayer contended that the rule (introduced by FA 1971, Sch 10, para 10) that a disposal takes place at the time of contract, not completion, had the effect that a sale which was completed in tranches between April 1971 and January 1976 should be treated as having been made in February 1965 and, thus, before the introduction of capital gains tax. Vinelott J rejected this submission.
[6] Cf Forfeiture of a deposit; TCGA 1992, s 144(7).

Time of disposal when loss or destruction

[18.12] Where an asset is deemed to be disposed of by reason of its actual loss or destruction, the time of the deemed disposal is the time at which the loss or destruction occurs.[1] However, where the owner of the asset later receives compensation for the loss, the date of disposal is the date of receipt of the compensation.[2] These statements may be reconciled by treating the right to receive compensation as a separate asset arising at the time of the loss, or at the time the claim is proved, so that the receipt of compensation is the disposal of that right, not the disposal of the original asset. However, the authors consider this conclusion to be inelegant and not consistent with granting rollover relief, for example, in respect of compensation payments received when the underlying asset is within the category specified.[3]

Simon's Taxes C1.322.

[1] TCGA 1992, s 24(1).
[2] TCGA 1992, s 22(2).
[3] The reconciliation of the conflict between dates that is given above could be seen as an identical analysis to the discussion in *Zim Properties Ltd v Procter* [1985] STC 90; see supra, § **17.03**. However, to justify the analysis on this basis, one would have

[18.12] Disposal

to ask why the court decision in 1985 was considered to be such a landmark decision, when statute had predated it by 20 years. In the authors' view, the two different dates are simply a statutory inconsistency that should be corrected.

Part disposals

[18.13] If there is a part disposal, the proportion of the acquisition cost attributable to the part disposal is A/(A+B), where A is the consideration for the disposal and B is the market value of the remainder.[1]

EXAMPLE

X purchased a house and grounds for £20,000 in 1972. He occupied the house as a holiday home but in September 2008, he sold part of the grounds for development, receiving £100,000. The market value of the house and remaining land is then £250,000. The market value of the whole at 31 March 1982 was £95,000.

		£
Disposal consideration		180,000
Allowable cost: $£95,000 \times \dfrac{180,000}{180,000 + 250,000}$		(39,767)
Chargeable gain		140,233

The incidental costs of the part disposal are attributable solely to the part disposed of. It should also be borne in mind that the formula is applied only to those costs common to the part disposed of and the part retained. There is no apportionment of expenditure which, on the facts, is wholly attributable to either the part disposed of or that retained.[2] In practice the formula is not strictly applied on the disposal of shares, whether quoted or unquoted, in a pool, the costs being apportioned simply pro rata to the number of shares disposed of.

In the case of a part disposal before 6 April 1988 of an asset owned on 31 March 1982, the expenditure apportioned under the formula would be the original expenditure or, where relevant the market value at 6 April 1965. If a further disposal or part disposal of the remaining asset occurs on or after 6 April 1988, the expenditure treated as relating to the remainder at the date of the first part disposal is recomputed by reference to the 31 March 1982 market value of the whole asset.[3] This is not necessarily the same result as rebasing the part undisposed of to its separate value at 31 March 1982.

Where the disposal is of land, the cost of the part of the land disposed of can be calculated on an alternative basis to the normal method. Under the alternative basis the part disposed of will be treated as a separate asset and any fair and reasonable method of apportioning part of the total cost to it will be accepted, eg a reasonable valuation of that part at the acquisition date.[4]

Simon's Taxes C1.315.

[1] TCGA 1992, s 42.
[2] TCGA 1992, s 42(4).
[3] TCGA 1992, Sch 3, para 4.
[4] Statement of practice D1.

What is a part disposal?

[18.14] A "disposal" is defined as including a part disposal which is defined as:

> There is a part disposal of an asset where an interest or right in or over the asset is created by the disposal, as well as where it subsists before the disposal, and generally, there is a part disposal of an asset where, on a person making a disposal, any description of property derived from the asset remains undisposed of.[1]

Thus, there is a part disposal when either: (a) there is a disposal of a physical part of an asset or (b) rights are created out of an asset. An example of (b) is the granting of a lease by the freeholder (see infra, § **23.13**).

The definition immediately raises the question as to what is the asset. As discussed at supra, § **17.01**, "an asset" is not defined in statute. The courts have been willing to locate an asset in many situations. The very breadth of what is encompassed in "an asset" makes it difficult to determine whether a disposal is a disposal of an entire asset or a part disposal of a larger asset. The Revenue view was stated in June 1968 to CCAB:

> Our general view is that unless it appears from the facts at the time of acquisition that more than one asset (given its natural meaning) was acquired, a single acquisition of land (with or without buildings) whether obtained by purchase under one contract at an inclusive price or by gift or inheritance as a whole, should be regarded as a single asset (even though it comprises distinguishable elements such as a house and garden, farmhouses, buildings, woodlands, cottages, etc).

> On the other hand, in the case of acquisition by purchase, there may be contemporary evidence showing that the acquisition comprised more than one asset. For example, correspondence etc during negotiations leading up to a purchase may show that the contract price was based upon the sum rounded up or down of a number of valuation units; the land may have been offered for sale by auction in lots: or the rent roll of an estate may show separate tenants paying substantial rents for individual properties such as farms. In such cases it may be possible to make a satisfactory apportionment of the purchase price.

> Where estates of small properties (eg terraced urban dwellinghouses) are acquired, blocks of a size convenient to hold as investments are normally regarded as single assets, but in practice no objection is taken to treating individual dwellinghouses as separate assets and apportioning the cost of the larger unit on the basis of such evidence as is available. As a general rule single buildings in multiple occupation such as blocks of flats or office suites are regarded as single assets, but again no objection is normally taken to treating individual flats, etc as separate assets if it appears that similar flats etc in the same ownership or in the locality have commonly been sold singly as independent dwellings.

There is very little authority to guide one. In *Cottle v Coldicott*[2] the Revenue successfully argued that the sale of a milk quota without any land was the sale

[18.14] Disposal

of a separate asset and not a part disposal of the land, a conclusion which may turn on matters of EC law rather than traditional English law. The Commissioners concluded that the quota was a personal entitlement of the taxpayer, a species of incorporeal property for CGT. In *Anders Utkilens Rederi A/S v O/Y Lovisa Stevedoring Co A/B and Keller Bryant Transport Co Ltd*,[3] the taxpayer was a defendant in litigation. The plaintiff and the taxpayer settled an appeal. Under the terms of the compromise the taxpayer agreed to sell its premises, plant and machinery (the property) and to divide the proceeds with the plaintiff. The taxpayer subsequently went into creditor's voluntary liquidation and a year later the property was sold. In a dispute between the plaintiff and the taxpayer as to the burden of tax, the court held that the compromise was a part disposal by the taxpayer to the plaintiff—and so the taxpayer had to pay the tax then arising. The taxpayer unsuccessfully argued that the terms were merely contractual and that the plaintiff received no proprietary interest until the proceeds were received.

In *Berry v Warnett*[4] S transferred shares to a nominee trustee and a few weeks later assigned his beneficial interest to a Jersey company in return for money and a life interest. The House of Lords held that the sale was a disposal of S's entire beneficial interest in the shares and not a part disposal of the holding. The life interest could not be said to be property that was derived from an asset which remained undisposed of. This case is best seen in the context of the settlement of property; see further infra, § **20.10**. There is also the *Zim*[5] case in which the court held that a sum received on the settlement of a negligence action against solicitors arose from the right to sue which was an asset quite separate from the property to which the claim related.

While robust common sense can solve a number of these problems one also has to reconcile one's conclusions with the words of the statute. Common sense tells one that there are disposals of an entire asset when an asset is transferred to a company in return for new shares issued by the company and where there is a sale of a business for unascertained consideration.[6] On the other hand, part disposals arise from the grant of a lease out of a freehold, the sale of shares where shares of the same category in the vendor's pool remain in his ownership and the sale of land forming part of a larger holding. It has been suggested that a possible test is that in the first two cases the person making the disposal is left with an item of property which did not exist before the disposal; whereas in the last three there is an asset which can be identified as being undisposed of throughout. However, the legislation talks of there being a part disposal when the taxpayer holds "any description of property derived from the asset".[7] This suggests that some disposals are part disposals even where there is not an asset remaining in the vendor's ownership throughout the transaction. Thus, a sale of land subject to a leaseback is generally treated as a part disposal, even though there is an instant during the transaction at which the person making the disposal has no interest in the land at all.

Simon's Taxes C1.315.

[1] TCGA 1992, s 21(2)(*a*).
[2] [1995] STC (SCD) 239.
[3] [1985] STC 301.

[4] [1982] STC 396.
[5] *Zim Properties Ltd v Procter* [1985] STC 90.
[6] *Marren v Ingles* [1980] STC 500.
[7] TCGA 1992, s 22(2)(*b*).

Small disposals

[18.15] The practical disadvantage of the A/(A + B) formula is the need to calculate B, the market value of the part remaining, a process which may be expensive. To solve this, statute provides that in four circumstances, there is no immediate charge to tax in respect of an amount of consideration received that is regarded as "small". Instead, the consideration received is treated as reducing the acquisition cost that is put against the ultimate disposal of the asset concerned. The circumstances where this treatment is adopted are a capital distribution,[1] cash received on a share reorganisation,[2] a premium on conversion of securities[3] and cash received on compulsory acquisition of land.[4]

Statute does not define the word "small" in respect of these provisions. In *O'Rourke v Binks*,[5] the Special Commissioner held that shares to the value of £246,000 could be treated as "small" for the purposes of s 122(2). This sum amounted to 15.58% of the acquisition cost of the original holding, but less than 5% of the value of the original holding immediately before reorganisation. The Court of Appeal reversed this decision saying that what is "small" is a question of fact and degree and has to be considered in the light of the circumstances in any particular case. Judicial comment was made that the purpose of the legislation is to avoid the need for assessments in trivial cases, noting that this was not such a case.

The Revenue subsequently published their interpretation of the meaning of "small".[6] In this the Revenue state that they will continue with their long-standing approach of accepting as "small" 5% or less than the value of the shares/land, but will also accept as "small" any receipt of £3,000 or less. A taxpayer does, however, have the right to argue the particular circumstances of a case to justify an amount in excess of these limits to be regarded as "small" or, alternatively, an amount below these limits should not be so regarded.

Where there is a part disposal of land, this treatment is adopted and the consideration received is treated as reducing the base cost, in the same manner as in the foregoing, if the value of the consideration does not exceed the lower of (1) £20,000 and (2) one fifth of the market value of the landholding immediately prior to the part disposal.[7] For land, it is not necessary to consider whether the amount received is "small".

Where, in any of the four circumstances listed above, the consideration received exceeds allowable expenditure, there is an immediate charge to capital gains tax.[8]

Simon's Taxes C2.1510.

[1] TCGA 1992, s 122(2).
[2] TCGA 1992, s 116(13).
[3] TCGA 1992, s 133(2).

[18.15] Disposal

[4] TCGA 1992, s 243(1)(a).
[5] [1992] STC 703, CA.
[6] Inland Revenue interpretation RI 164; **Simon's Direct Tax Service, Division H5.3**.
[7] TCGA 1992, s 242(1)(a), (3)(a). Other disposals of land in the same year of assessment will prevent the application of s 242 if the total consideration of all land disposals exceeds £20,000.
[8] See, for example, TCGA 1992, s 244 which provides that in these circumstances the "small disposal" treatment does not apply, but allows the taxpayer to elect for the gain that is immediately subject to charge being the excess of consideration over allowable expenditure and for there to be no allowable expenditure to be put against future disposals.

Compensation and insurance payments

[18.16] If capital sums are received by way of compensation for any kind of damage or injury to or loss of or depreciation of assets, there is a disposal of those assets, and so a consequent gain or loss by reference to the acquisition cost of those assets. These words are of wide effect and are not limited to physical damage.[1] A similar rule applies to sums received under a policy of insurance of the risk of any kind of damage or injury to, or the loss or depreciation of, assets. Thus, if a trader loses a capital asset by fire and recovers under his insurance policy, there is a disposal of the asset even though the insurance company does not acquire it.

This rule applies only where the sum is a capital as opposed to an income payment. It is, therefore, important when compensation is received by a trader to dissect the sum received into three elements: (i) the income element (such as compensation for loss of profits); (ii) the capital element (such as compensation for damage or expropriation of land); and (iii) the element of the compensation that is exempt from tax.[2]

Compensation or damages received as the result of a Court action, or by negotiated settlement of such an action, is a disposal of the right of action and is subject to CGT.[3] In most cases, the base cost of the rights will be nil where they came into being on or after 10 March 1981.[4] This is so even if the compensation or damages relates to an underlying asset. However, the Revenue have issued a concession under which compensation or damages will be treated as relating to the underlying asset where the right of action arises because of total or partial loss of or damage to the asset.[5] Thus, the base cost of the asset will be available to compute any chargeable gain, and the various replacement and reinstatement reliefs may be claimed. Where there is no underlying asset, eg in a case involving damages for professional negligence resulting in expense to the plaintiff, any gain is by concession treated as exempt. Payments made under a contractual warranty or indemnity are not regarded as affected by the *Zim Properties* case and will reduce the purchaser's acquisition cost.

Sums obtained by way of compensation or damages for any wrong or injury suffered by an individual in their person or in their profession or vocation are not chargeable gains.[6]

A problem arises if the assets are destroyed, and not just damaged, in that whilst the receipt of the capital sum is treated as a disposal, the destruction of the asset is also treated as a disposal.[7] The logical result is that if the destruction should occur in one year and the receipt in the next year, loss relief should be given immediately and there should be a taxable sum accruing on receipt. The Revenue view is that if no sum is received the disposal occurs at the time of the destruction but that if a payment subsequently accrues the disposal takes place at the time of the receipt.[8]

Simon's Taxes C1.325–327; Sumption CGT A1.09.

---

[1] *Davenport v Chilver* [1983] STC 426.
[2] Such as compensation arising under the Agricultural Holdings Act 1986, or other legislation; see *Davies v Powell* [1977] STC 32, [1977] All ER 471 and *Drummond v Austin Brown* [1984] STC 321. See supra, § **17.03**.
[3] *Zim Properties Ltd v Procter* [1985] STC 90.
[4] TCGA 1992, s 17(2); infra, § **18.48**.
[5] Extra-statutory concession D33.
[6] TCGA 1992, s 23.
[7] TCGA 1992, s 24.
[8] Inland Revenue leaflet CGT 8 (1980), § 230 (now withdrawn).

Insurance receipts

[18.17] When a capital sum is received under an insurance policy, the receipt of the sum is treated as a disposal of assets by their owner, notwithstanding that no asset is acquired by the person paying the capital sum. This treatment is applied to any receipt of a capital sum, whether under a policy of insurance or otherwise.[1]

Where the insurance money is received without being applied to replace or repair the asset, the capital gains tax computation is on the basis of either a complete disposal of the asset or, as appropriate, a part disposal (see infra, § **18.18**). Where the insurance money is used to restore or replace the asset, there is a form of rollover relief (see infra, § **18.19**).

A difficult question often encountered in practice is to determine whether the insurance receipt can truly be regarded as arising from the asset and, hence, the base cost of that asset can be put against the insurance money or, alternatively, the insurance money arises from a right, which has no base cost. The previous importance of taper relief and, hence, the need to determine the length of time an asset has been owned, gave an extra dimension to the need to correctly identify the asset from which the consideration arises. The importance remains (but might prove less crucial in practice) in the context of entrepreneurs' relief.

Simon's Taxes Division C2.5.

---

[1] TCGA 1992, s 22(1).

[18.18] Disposal

Insurance receipt not used to replace or repair asset

[18.18] Where the insurance receipt is not used to replace or repair the asset, the computation may be a disposal or may be a part disposal. This can, perhaps, best be illustrated by means of example.

EXAMPLE—DISPOSAL

In May 1998 Adam bought a Rubens for £5m. He goes down to breakfast one morning in September 2001. He looks on the kitchen wall and sees that the Rubens has been stolen. It is never recovered. The insurance company pays him the current market value of £7m.

He is treated as having made a CGT disposal with the following computation:

	£
Consideration	7,000,000
Acquisition cost	(5,000,000)
Chargeable gain	2,000,000

EXAMPLE—PART DISPOSAL

Alan bought a set of six Chippendale chairs for £60,000. He sits down to breakfast one morning and notices that one chair has been stolen. It is never recovered. A set of five chairs is worth only £40,000. The insurance company pays him £8,000.

He is treated as having made a CGT part disposal with the following computation:

		£
Consideration		8,000
Acquisition cost £60,000×	$\dfrac{8,000}{8,000 + 40,000}$	10,000
Allowable loss		(2,000)

Where an insurance receipt is received for the total loss of tangible movable property, the receipt is treated in the same way as consideration received for the sale of that property. Hence, unless capital allowances could have been claimed for the asset, no charge to capital gains tax arises for insurance receipts of £6,000 or less.[1] For the treatment of an insurance receipt exceeding £6,000 or where the receipt is in respect of damage to property so that the receipt is treated as a part disposal, see infra, § **37.02**.

Simon's Taxes Division C2.5.

---

[1] TCGA 1992, s 262(1).

Insurance receipt used to restore or replace the asset

[18.19] There is no charge to capital gains tax if:

(1) the capital sum is wholly applied in restoring the asset; or

(2) the capital sum is applied in restoring the asset except for a part of the capital sum which is not reasonably required for the purpose and which is small as compared with the whole capital sum; or
(3) the amount of the capital sum is small, as compared with the value of the asset.[1]

The treatment is, then:

(1) the amount of the consideration for the disposal shall be reduced by the amount of the allowable expenditure; and
(2) none of that expenditure shall be allowable as a deduction in computing a gain accruing on the occasion of the disposal or any subsequent occasion.[2]

EXAMPLE

A picture cost Andrew £6,000 in 1977. In 1994 the picture, then worth £120,000 was damaged in a fire and Andrew incurred £20,000 in restoration costs. Andrew received £20,000 under his insurance policy. This can be treated as a disposal of the asset; however, A may instead claim that it should not be so treated, in which case the allowable expenditure on the picture (which includes the cost of restoration) will be reduced by £20,000 if he later sells the picture or otherwise disposes of it. If, however, he recovers £25,000, the part spent in restoration (£20,000) will be treated as just outlined while the balance of £5,000 will be taxed at once.

Where the allowable expenditure is less than the insurance receipt, part of the insurance receipt being used to restore the asset and part not, the taxpayer is entitled under TCGA 1992, s 23(3) to claim that the part used for restoration is not treated for consideration of an immediate disposal but, instead, is deducted from the acquisition costs that would be allowable in computing a gain on any subsequent disposal of the asset.

This relief in effect allows the taxpayer to postpone his tax liability, not escape it, unless perhaps he can later take advantage of an exemption.

These rules are modified for wasting assets.[3]

Where a building is destroyed or irreparably damaged and compensation received is spent on constructing a replacement building on a different site, both the original building and its replacement can be treated as a separate asset from the land on which they stand.

For a consideration of whether the insurance receipt is derived from an asset, see supra, § **17.04**.

Simon's Taxes Division C2.5.

---

[1] TCGA 1992, s 23(1).
[2] TCGA 1992, s 23(2).
[3] TCGA 1992, s 23(8).

Use of assets

[18.20] Capital sums received for the use or exploitation of assets are charged to CGT. Thus a sum received in return for the right to exploit a purchased

[18.20] Disposal

copyright[1] or to use generated (or purchased) goodwill would be caught. This would include, perhaps, the part disposal resulting from a restriction on one's trading activities as in *Higgs v Olivier*.[2]

Simon's Taxes C1.319.

---

[1] However, payments to an author for the use of his writings are income assessed on trading income (*Howson v Monsell* (1950) 31 TC 529).
[2] Supra, § **8.80**.

Mortgages and bankruptcy

[18.21] A mortgage is in essence a security for a debt so neither a conveyance or transfer by way of security nor a retransfer on redemption of the security is treated as involving any acquisition or disposal.[1]

Any dealing with the asset by the mortgagee for the purpose of giving effect to the security is treated as an act by a nominee of the mortgagor. So a sale by him will be a disposal by the mortgagor.[2]

An asset is treated as passing free of the security. When an asset is acquired subject to a security, the value of any liability taken over by the acquirer is treated as part of the consideration; a converse rule applies on disposal.[3] So if X buys an asset for £3,000, subject to a mortgage of £7,000, he is treated as buying it for £10,000 and if he sells it for £5,000 still subject to the mortgage and not having reduced that mortgage, his consideration on disposal will be £12,000—a gain of £2,000.

When a vendor disposes of land, grants a mortgage to the purchaser and later recovers possession on default by the purchaser, the original disposal is, by concession, undone.[4]

Simon's Taxes C1.309; Sumption CGT A1.14.

---

[1] TCGA 1992, s 26(1). On what is a mortgage, see *Beattie v Jenkinson* [1971] 3 All ER 495, 47 TC 121 (a decision on Case VII). Since 1925 a mortgage of freehold land does not end by retransfer but by cesser of the mortgagee's leasehold interest. One must presume that the draftsman's error would be corrected by any court.
[2] TCGA 1992, s 26(2).
[3] TCGA 1992, s 26(3). This rule is stated to apply where the liability is assumed by the acquirer. Emmet, *op cit*, points out that an assignee of a mortgagor does not *assume* the liability, *Waring v Ward* (1802) 7 Ves 332; however, technical arguments have not found great favour with the courts, eg *Pexton v Bell* infra, § **20.20**.
[4] Extra-statutory concession D18.

[18.22] Just as the mortgagee's acts are treated as those of the mortgagor, so the acts of a trustee in bankruptcy are treated as those of the bankrupt.[1] However, the trustee in bankruptcy is assessable for the tax.[2]

Simon's Taxes C1.213; Sumption CGT A8.01.

[1] TCGA 1992, s 66.
[2] Re McMeekin [1974] STC 429, 48 TC 725 (QBD, NI).

Options

[18.23] An option is specifically defined as being an asset for the purposes of capital gains tax.[1]

Special rules are needed to charge any sums paid on the grant of an option (this is achieved by treating the grant of an option as a self standing disposal) and to deal with the effects of both the exercise and the abandonment of an option.

In addition there are a number of special computation rules as well as rules for special types of option. These provisions deal with "call" options ie options under which X has a right to acquire an asset and "put" options where X has a right to sell. It is not necessary that the intended vendor in either of these options should already be the owner of the property.

Statute gives the following definitions.

(a) *Quoted option*
An option which, at the time of the abandonment or other disposal, is quoted on a recognised stock exchange.[2]

(b) *Traded option*
An option which, at the time of the abandonment or other disposal, is quoted on a recognised stock exchange or a recognised futures exchange.[3]

(c) *Financial option*
An option which is not a traded option but which:
(1) relates to currency, shares, securities or an interest rate and is granted (otherwise than as agent) by a member of a recognised stock exchange, by an authorised person within the meaning of the Financial Services Act 1986 or by a listed institution within s 43 of that Act; or
(2) relates to shares or securities which are dealt in on a recognised stock exchange and is granted by a member of such an exchange, acting as agent; or
(3) relates to currency, shares, securities or an interest rate and is granted to such an authorised person or institution as is referred to in point (1) above and concurrently and in association with an option falling within that sub-paragraph which is granted by that authorised person or institution to the grantor of the first-mentioned option; or
(4) relates to shares or securities which are dealt in on a recognised stock exchange and is granted to a member of such an exchange, including such a member acting as agent.[4]

Recognised stock exchanges are London and exchanges designated by statutory order.[5]

[18.23] Disposal

Simon's Taxes Division C2.10.

1   TCGA 1992, s 21(1)(*a*).
2   TCGA 1992, s 144 (8)(*a*).
3   TCGA 1992, s 144(8)(*b*).
4   TCGA 1992, s 144(8)(*c*). The Treasury may expand the categories of financial option by order.
5   For "recognised stock exchange" and "futures exchange" see TA 1988, s 841 applied by TCGA 1992, s 288(1), (6). A full list of foreign stock exchanges currently designated as recognised stock exchanges is given in Inland Revenue Press Release, 8 August 2000: *Simons Weekly Tax Intelligence* 2000, p 1176.

The grant of an option

[18.24] The grant of the option is to be treated as the disposal of an asset, viz. the option.[1]

This treatment is provisional in that later provisions may cause the grant to be charged as part of a larger transaction where the option is exercised.

This treatment is specified as to apply in particular, but not (by inference) exclusively, where grantors bind themselves to sell what they do not own, and, because the option is abandoned, never have occasion to own, and where grantors bind themselves to buy what, because the option is abandoned, they do not acquire.[2]

The part disposal which might otherwise arise if the option was granted over property in which the grantor had an interest and the option were specifically enforceable is excluded.[3]

In *Randall v Plumb*[4] the taxpayer received £25,000 for the grant of the option but this sum was repayable in certain circumstances; the court decided that in the circumstances the contingent obligation to repay had to be taken into account notwithstanding ss 48 and 49. By contrast, in *Garner v Pounds*[5], there was an agreement under which £399,750 was paid to Pounds' solicitors to be held by them as stakeholders until they had procured the release of certain restrictive covenants in favour of a third party, the release of which caused the granting of an option for the purchase of land at a price of £4,490,000. The release of the covenants in question was effected by a payment of £90,000 to a third party. The option granted was never exercised. The House of Lords held that the consideration for the option granted was the full £399,750 and the sum of £90,000 was not available as a deduction as it was not a cost of the option that was granted.[6]

The Revenue appear to view the rule requiring exclusion of the part disposal as being only for the purpose of computing gains on the grant of the options. If, on general principles the option is an interest in the underlying asset (as in the case of an option to acquire an estate in land), the gain is considered to qualify for reliefs available on the disposal of that underlying asset, such as rollover relief, provided that the requisite conditions are satisfied as to the underlying asset.[7] The Revenue practice appears to be confined to rollover relief. It is unclear whether this practice should be extended to other areas. If the principles as stated by the Revenue are correct then this practice should apply for all purposes. Does this conflict with the decision in *Strange v Openshaw*?[8]

Since the grant of an option is considered to be a disposal of a separate asset, and not a part disposal of the grantor's interest in the asset, there is no allowable expenditure other than incidental costs of disposal and the full net amount of any consideration received for the grant of the option is taxable.

The grant of an option to acquire an asset can be a disposal even though the grantor will not dispose of any asset when the option is exercised; for example, if a company issues options to subscribe for its own shares, the exercise of the options would not involve any disposal by the company.

Simon's Taxes C2.1001.

---

[1] TCGA 1992, s 144(1).
[2] TCGA 1992, s 144(1).
[3] TCGA 1992, s 144(1) and *Strange v Openshaw* [1983] STC 416.
[4] [1975] STC 191.
[5] [2000] STC 420, HL.
[6] The £90,000 is treated as a cost of enhancing the value of the land (see the comments of Lord Jauncey at 427D–E). Had the option been exercised, it would have been deductible as a cost put against the receipt of £4,490,000. As the option was abandoned, the cost is carried forward to be put against any disposal there may be of the land at some time in the future.
[7] Inland Revenue interpretation RI 11. Thus, if £20,000 is paid on 1 November 2008 for the grant of an option to buy farmland from a farmer, the option being exercisable 10 years later, the farmer can claim rollover relief against an appropriate purchase made between 1 November 2007 and 21 October 2011. He does not have to wait 10 years until the option is exercised.
[8] [1983] STC 416.

Disposal of option

[18.25] Where a person entitled to exercise an option disposes of it, eg by sale exchange or gift, the gain or loss is computed according to normal CGT principles, including, where appropriate, the wasting asset rules.

Special rules apply only where the disposal is by the abandonment of the option or by its exercise.

The disposal of a traded option by the grantor is disregarded for CGT if it arises because the option is closed out by acquisition of a second traded option of the same description. The costs of closing out, including the cost of the second option plus incidental costs of acquisition, are deducted in computing the gain on grant of the original option.[1]

Simon's Taxes C2.1004.

---

[1] TCGA 1992, s 148.

[18.26] Disposal

Abandonment of option

General rule—no loss

[18.26] The abandonment of the option by the person entitled to exercise is not normally a disposal.[1] The effect is to prevent any argument that any money lost by the grantee should give rise to an allowable loss.

Simon's Taxes C2.1005.

[1] TCGA 1992, s 144(4).

Deemed disposal due to receipt of capital sum

There will however be a disposal by the grantee if a capital sum is received for abandoning the option. However, the disposal arises by virtue of the receipt of the capital sum falling within TCGA 1992, s 22(1) and not the abandonment of the option.[1] This ensures that the sum received on abandonment is charged. The receipt of a sum for the release of an option may give rise to a chargeable gain under TCGA 1992, s 22(1);[2] the agreement to release the option may well also amount to an abandonment.

[1] *Golding v Kaufman* [1985] STC 152.
[2] *Welbeck Securities Ltd v Powlson* [1987] STC 468, CA.

Losses and certain types of option

An allowable loss may however be treated as arising if the option is a quoted option to subscribe for shares, a traded option, a traditional (financial) option or an option to acquire business assets. This is because in relation to these assets TCGA 1992, s 144(4) directs that there is to be a disposal on abandonment. In computing the losses the wasting asset rules in s 46 do not apply.[1]

[1] TCGA 1992, s 146.

Forfeiture of deposit as abandonment of option

The forfeiture of a deposit paid in contemplation of a proposed purchase or in respect of any other transaction is treated as if it were the abandonment of an option binding the grantor to sell.[1] Hence there is no loss relief for the person losing the deposit. However, as under (b) there is a disposal of an asset (the option) by the party who receives the deposit and the amount forfeited is treated as the consideration received by him.

Since the "option" is a chargeable asset in its own right these consequences ensue even though the asset to which it relates may have been exempt, eg a private residence.

[1] TCGA 1992, s 144(7).

Exercise of option

[18.27] Where the option is exercised, the grant and the exercise are treated as one transaction;[1] the disposal is treated as taking place when the option is exercised.[2] One effect of this rule is to prevent a sale from being carried out in two stages by option and exercise so as to take advantage of the annual exemption. However, for the purposes of the indexation allowance, the cost of the option is treated as an expense separate from the price paid for the option.

Simon's Taxes C2.1007, 1008.

[1] TCGA 1992, s 144(2).
[2] TCGA 1992, s 28(2).

Treatment of grantor

(i) **Call option**. In the case of a "call" option, ie one binding the grantor to sell an asset, the consideration received for grant of the option is treated as part of the consideration for the sale.[1] From this one may infer that the single transaction referred to is the sale of the asset. Hence there is no longer any liability under s 144(1) on the grant of the option.

Where the exercise of the option involves a transaction which is not a disposal, eg an option followed by the issue of shares by a company, there would neither be a chargeable gain under s 144(1) on grant of the option nor under s 144(2) on the subsequent transaction. A similar non-chargeable result would ensure if the option was one to purchase an asset where the disposal of the asset would be exempt eg the grantor's principal private residence.

From 30 November 1993, a special rule applies where the grantor pays the option holder cash in full settlement of all obligations under the option. The rule in s 144(2) does not apply; instead the grant and the exercise are treated as a single transaction in which the money paid for the option is the consideration for the option and the sum paid in settlement an item of incidental expenditure incurred.[2] Apportionments are made where a payment is made in partial settlement.

(ii) **Put option**. In the case of a "put" option, ie one binding the grantor to buy, the consideration for the option is deducted from the grantor's allowable costs in respect of the asset when that asset is subsequently disposed of.[3]

Although the allowable costs are reduced, indexation allowance is available in respect of the sum paid for the option, from the time it was paid.[4]

[1] TCGA 1992, s 144(2)(a).
[2] TCGA 1992, s 144A.
[3] TCGA 1992, s 144(2)(b).
[4] TCGA 1992, s 57(2), (3).

[18.27] Disposal

Treatment of grantee

The exercise of the option is not a disposal of any asset by the grantee.[1] Whether the option is exercised as between the original parties or assignees, the acquisition and the exercise of the option are treated as a single transaction.

(i) **Call option.** Where the option binds the grantor to sell, the grantee's costs in acquiring the option are added to the costs of acquiring the asset. Although the option would have been a wasting asset in relation to a disposal of the option, there is no reduction in the cost of the option.

Indexation relief is applied to the two sums separately.[2]

Other rules apply on disposal of an asset acquired by the exercise of an option in situations involving connected persons. Where the grantor and the grantee are connected persons, a loss accruing to the grantee can be an allowable loss only if it accrues on the disposal of the option at arm's length to a person not connected with him.[3] It follows that in the case of a call option, the disposal of any asset acquired by exercise of the option cannot give rise to an allowable loss.

From 30 November 1993, a special rule applies where the grantor pays the option holder cash in full settlement of all obligations under the option. The rule in s 144(3) does not apply; instead the grant and the exercise are treated as a single transaction in which the sum paid is the consideration for the disposal of the option and the settlement money is treated as an item of incidental expenditure incurred.[4] Apportionments are made where a payment is made in partial settlement.

(ii) **Put option.** Where the option binds the grantor to buy, the cost of the option to the grantee (or to his assignees) is treated as an incidental cost in relation to the grantee's disposal of an asset on exercising the option.[5] It follows that there will be no indexation relief in respect of the cost of the option.

If the grantor and the grantee are connected persons, no allowable loss can arise to the grantee on exercise of the option.[6]

---

[1] TCGA 1992, s 144(3).
[2] TCGA 1992, s 145. There are special rules where more shares of the same class, as a pooled holding, are acquired after 5 April 1985 (or after 31 March 1985 when acquired by a company) by the exercise of an option; here the option cost is added to the pool expenditure as part of the acquisition cost of the new shares. The indexed rise will run from the month in which the option cost was incurred. It follows that the pool is increased by an indexed rise calculated by reference to the cost of the option for the period from the month in which the option was acquired until the month in which the option was exercised before the latter costs are added. The formula for the indexed rise is:

(RO − RA)/RA × the cost of the option

where RO is the retail prices index figure for the month in which the option is exercised and RA is the retail prices index figure of the month in which the option was acquired

(or March 1982, if later). If RO is less than or equal to RA, the indexed rise is nil.
[3] TCGA 1992, s 18(4).
[4] TCGA 1992, s 144A.
[5] TCGA 1992, s 144(3)(*b*).
[6] TCGA 1992, s 18(4).

Anti-avoidance provisions

If an option is granted to a connected person, the exercise is assessed to capital gains tax by reference to the market value of the option, when exercised. This has led to avoidance schemes in which an option is sold to an unconnected person before its exercise.[1] From 2 December 2004, statutory provisions[2] seek to defeat the scheme.

[1] Treasury Notes to Finance (No 3) Bill 2005, Schedule 5.
[2] F(No 2)A 2005, Sch 5.

Employee share options

[18.28] In *Mansworth v Jelley*[1] an employee was granted a share option, which he exercised after he ceased to be an employee. Thus, the exercise of the option did not give rise to an income tax charge and the taxpayer claimed that his base cost for the disposal of the shares was the market value at the time of exercise and not the amount paid on exercise. The Court of Appeal agreed with these contentions.[2]

[1] [2002] EWCA Civ 1829, [2003] STC 53. See *Monro v R & C Comrs*, [2007] EWHC 114 (Ch), [2007] SWTI 290, supra, § **2A.69** for denial of relief for a subsequent claimant who has paid tax on the basis that was thought to apply prior to *Mansworth v Jelley*.
[2] For a discussion of the Revenue view following the decision in *Mansworth v Jelley*, prior to the enactment of F(No 2)A 2005, see the 23rd edition of Tiley & Collison's UK Tax Guide at 17.28. It should be noted, however, that on 12 May 2009, HMRC announced a U-turn in their interpretation and published that the decision in *Mansworth v Jelley* was of much narrower scope than previously announced. The consequence was that millions of pounds had been wrongly repaid to taxpayers. Conversely, taxpayers who were expecting a repayment in cases that were still under enquiry or subject to an appealed assessment would suddenly find that the repayment would not be made.

[18.29] Statute[1] provides that the consideration taken into account for capital gains purposes on the acquisition or disposal of an asset is normally the amount of the actual consideration given or received. However, in certain circumstances that actual consideration is ignored and replaced by an amount equal to the market value of the asset. This 'market value rule'[2] applies where the acquisition/disposal is:

(a) not by way of a bargain at arm's length; or

[18.29] Disposal

(b) for a consideration which cannot be valued; or
(c) in consideration for, or in recognition of, a person's service as an employee.

The rule does not, however, apply if the transaction comprises an acquisition but not a disposal for capital gains tax, or when the actual consideration is less than the market value of the asset concerned.

The granting of an option is initially the disposal and acquisition of an asset, ie the rights under the option itself. The consideration for that disposal and acquisition is the amount of the actual consideration given for the grant. If the market value rule applies, the consideration is deemed to be the market value of the rights under the option, (not the underlying asset).

Where the option is exercised and, as a result, the underlying asset is transferred from one person to another, the grant of the option and the transfer of that asset are to be treated as a single transaction. As a result:

(a) the grant of the option itself is no longer the disposal of an asset and any tax originally paid on that event becomes repayable; and
(b) the consideration given or received for the grant is to be part of the consideration given or received for that single transaction.

Where, however, the exercise price of an option is non-commercial, different rules apply.[3] Each party to the transaction is then treated as disposing of (or acquiring, as the case may be) the asset at its market value when the option is exercised. These new rules apply if the relevant option is 'non-commercial.'[4] If an option binds the grantor to buy (a 'put' option), for tax purposes the grantor's acquisition cost of the asset acquired is its market value when the option is exercised. The corresponding disposal consideration is also the asset's market value when the option is exercised. If an option binds the grantor to sell (a 'call' option), for tax purposes the consideration for the asset disposal is its market value when the option is exercised. The corresponding acquisition cost is also the asset's market value when the option is exercised. If all or part of the 'underlying subject matter' (ie the asset falling to be bought or sold) of the option is subject to a right or restriction enforceable by the person selling it or a connected person.[5] The right or restriction is ignored when determining its market value.

---

[1] TCGA 1992, s 144ZA inserted by FA 2003, s 158.
[2] TCGA 1992, s 17.
[3] With effect from 2 December 2004: TCGA 1992, s 144ZB inserted by F(No 2)A 2005, Sch 5.
[4] As defined in TCGA 1992, s 144ZC.
[5] As defined in TCGA 1992, s 286.

Options binding grantor to transactions other than sale or purchase

[18.30] References to options include options binding the grantor to grant a lease for a premium or to enter into any other transaction which is not a sale;

references to buying and selling in pursuance of an option are to be construed accordingly.[1] So if X grants Y a binding option to grant a lease and the option is exercised, the grant of the option plus the grant of the lease for a premium are treated as a single transaction. The consideration received by X for the option will be added to the premium on the lease; the sum will be treated as received by X for the grant of the lease. If the option is not exercised, s 144(1) will treat X as having disposed of the option and so as chargeable.

Since neither the abandonment nor the exercise of the option by Y is a disposal of any asset by Y, a forfeited deposit is not an allowable loss.[2]

Where Y exercises the option, the acquisition of the option and the transaction resulting from its exercise are treated as a single transaction. Y's acquisition costs for the lease will be the sum paid for the option and the premium.

Just as with an option to buy or sell so the option may relate to a transaction which is not a disposal for CGT eg an option binding a company to issue shares to the holder of the option. Where on the exercise of the option the grant of the option and the issue of the shares are treated as a single transaction under s 144(2) no chargeable gain arises. A chargeable gain could, however, arise if the option was abandoned and never exercised, as the grant of the option is treated as a disposal.

Simon's Taxes C2.1009.

[1] TCGA 1992, s 144(6).
[2] TCGA 1992, s 144(7).

Wasting asset rule—options

Application

[18.31] An option having a predictable life of 50 years or less is a wasting asset; the rules in TCGA 1992, s 46 restricting the deduction of expenditure therefore apply. The costs are written off over the life of the option on a straight-line basis.

If there is a transfer of an option to buy or to sell quoted shares or securities, the option is regarded as a wasting asset, the life of which ends when the right to exercise it ends or, if earlier, when it becomes valueless;[1] quoted shares or securities are defined as meaning shares of securities having a quoted market value on a recognised stock exchange in the UK or elsewhere.[2]

If the option is exercised, the full amount paid for the grant is added to (or deducted from) the amount payable on exercise, without writing off any amount up to the date of exercise.

Simon's Taxes C2.1003.

[1] TCGA 1992, s 146(2).
[2] TCGA 1992, s 146(4)(*b*).

[18.31] Disposal

Exceptions

(i) **Traded options** A "traded option" is defined as an option which, at the time of abandonment or other disposal, is quoted on a recognised stock exchange or a recognised futures exchange.[1] The wasting asset rules do not apply to these options.[2]

However, the abandonment of a financial option may give rise to an allowable loss.[3] An allowable loss will not arise if the disposal is exempt, eg gilt-edged securities or qualifying corporate bonds.

Where, after 24 July 1991, the grantor of a traded option closes it out by acquiring a traded option of the same description, the costs of acquiring the latter option (including incidental costs) are allowable as an incidental expense of the grant of the original option and any disposal by the grantor involved in closing out the original option is ignored for capital gains purposes.[4]

(ii) **Financial options** Statute defines a financial option as: "an option which is not a traded option, but which relates to currency, shares, securities or an interest rate and is granted by [or to] a member of a recognised stock exchange . . .".[5]

The wasting asset rules do not apply to financial options.[6]

However, the abandonment of a financial option may give rise to an allowable loss.[7] An allowable loss will not arise if the disposal is exempt, eg the option relates to gilt-edged securities or qualifying corporate bonds.

(iii) **Other exceptions** The wasting rules also do not apply to:

(1)   a quoted option to subscribe for shares in a company; a quoted option is one which is quoted on a recognised stock exchange at the time of disposal or abandonment;[8]

(2)   options to acquire assets to be used if acquired for the purposes of a trade carried on by that person.[9]

---

[1] TCGA 1992, ss 144(8), 287.
[2] TCGA 1992, s 146(1).
[3] TCGA 1992, s 144(4)(*b*).
[4] TCGA 1992, s 148.
[5] The definition extends—with the effect that the term "financial option" encompasses an option over a listed security when it is granted by a stock exchange member or a person authorised under the Financial Services and Market Act 2000 acting as agent (s 144(8)(*c*)(ii) and s 143(8)) or an option over unlisted shares, etc—where the stock exchange member or authorised person acts as principal.
[6] TCGA 1992, s 146(1).
[7] TCGA 1992, s 144(4)(*b*).
[8] TCGA 1992, s 146(4)(*b*).
[9] TCGA 1992, s 146(1)(*c*).

Options over gilt edged securities and qualifying bonds

[18.32] Gains accruing on the disposal by any person of any option or contract to acquire or dispose of gilt-edged securities or qualifying corporate bonds are not chargeable gains.[1]

The concept of disposing of the contract is widened to cover the closing out of the contract by a entering into a contract with reciprocal obligations ie a matched transaction.[2]

Simon's Taxes C2.1013.

---

[1] TCGA 1992, s 115. For treatment of gilt-edged securities issued in exchange for original securities on nationalisation, see TCGA 1992, s 134(2).
[2] TCGA 1992, s 115(3).

Gifts, bargains not at arm's length and other gratuitous transactions

[18.33] TCGA 1992, s 17 directs a market value rule where a person disposes of an asset otherwise than by way of a bargain made at arm's length.[1] This rule applies both to the disposal and to the acquisition and so sets the disposal consideration and the acquisition cost. The market value of an asset gifted is the consideration for the donor and also the acquisition cost for the donee.[2]

This rule applies where the person acquires or disposes of the asset:

(1) by way of gift; or
(2) on a transfer into settlement by a settlor (see infra, § **20.10**); or
(3) by way of a distribution from a company in respect of shares in the company.

The rule does not apply to the acquisition of an asset if there is no corresponding disposal of it and there is no consideration in money or money's worth or the consideration is of an amount or value lower than the market value of the asset. See further infra, § **18.48**.

In *Turner v Follett*[3] a taxpayer gave shares to his children. The Revenue raised an assessment on the basis that a gain was triggered by the gift, being measured by reference to the market value of the shares at the time they were given. The taxpayer claimed that in giving the shares away he had suffered a capital loss and it was contrary to natural justice to treat him as having made a gain. The Court of Appeal rejected the taxpayer's appeal.

A disposal by donatio mortis causa is, however, exempt from capital gains tax.[4]

---

[1] For an examination of one set of facts to see whether there was a bargain at arm's length see *Bullivant Holdings Ltd v IRC* [1998] STC 905.
[2] TCGA 1992, s 17.

[18.33] Disposal

³ [1973] STC 148.
⁴ TCGA 1992, s 62(5).

Date at which a gift was made

[18.34] In *Milroy v Lord*¹ it was held that, under general law, a gift becomes effective if either:

(1) the donor makes an effective transfer of the asset to the donee with the intention of making a gift; or
(2) the donor makes an effective declaration that he is holding the asset in trust for the donee.

Whether a transfer is effective or a declaration effective depends on the law applicable to the particular type of asset that is the subject of the gift. In particular, where the law requires a formality for a transfer to become effective, the law does not recognise the gift until the donor has done all in his power to enable the donee to take the asset. For shares, legal title passes when the shares are registered but CGT is not primarily concerned with legal title; there is a CGT disposal when there is a loss of beneficial ownership. In *Re Rose*² it was held that a gift of shares in a private company was effective when the donor executed the share transfer and handed that and the share certificate to the donee, notwithstanding the fact that the directors did not give the necessary consent for the registration of the transfer until a later date. In that case, the court took the view that the handing over of the documents gave an effective gift of the equitable interests in the shares and that equitable interest would have continued even if the directors had refused to register the transfer.

A different analysis was necessary in *Macedo v Stroud*.³ In that case, the registration was undertaken by the donor himself. As a finding of fact, the commissioner determined that, in that case, the taxpayer donor had the ability to negate the gift until he had performed the act of registration; hence, the disposal was the act of registration and not the earlier date of signing the share transfer form.

In *Berry v Warnett*⁴ the taxpayer settled shares on trust on 4 April 1972 giving himself a life interest. On 6 April 1972 he sold his life interest for £130,753. The House of Lords also held that the act of settlement on 4 April 1972 constituted a disposal for capital gains tax purposes and he was assessed by reference to the market value of the shares on that date. The House of Lords said that the disposal was made on 4 April 1972 as from that time onwards the taxpayer could not have asserted an equitable interest in any of the shares other than under the terms of the settlement.

¹ (1862) 4 De GF & J 264.
² [1952] Ch 499.
³ [1922] 2 AC 330.
⁴ [1982] 2 All ER 630.

Recovery of capital gains tax from the donee

[18.35] The primary liability for capital gains tax payable on a gift lies with the donor. If, however, the donor does not discharge his liability to capital gains tax within 12 months of the date from which it becomes payable, TCGA 1992, s 282(1) empowers the Revenue to raise an assessment on the donee and collect the tax from the donee. The amount of tax, thus, collectable from the donee is computed by reference to the donor's circumstances, irrespective of the circumstances of the donee. Thus, if the donor is a higher rate taxpayer and has used his annual exempt amount on other disposals, the Revenue can collect tax from the donee, even though the donee may be impecunious. TCGA 1992, s 282(2) empowers the donee to require reimbursement from the donor.

Any assessment raised by the Revenue to collect tax from a donee under the authority of TCGA 1992, s 262(1) must be raised within two years of the tax having been due and payable by the donor. Thus, for a gift made in 2001–02, the Revenue is only able to collect tax from the donee by raising an assessment between 1 February 2004 and 31 January 2005.

Payment of tax by instalments

[18.36] Where there is a gift of an asset and holdover relief is not available, the donor can elect to pay capital gains tax in ten equal instalments if the asset concerned is in one of the following categories:

(1) land;
(2) shares and securities of a company in which the donor has a controlling interest;
(3) shares and securities that are neither listed nor dealt with on the Unlisted Securities Market.[1]

Instalments attract interest at the rate used under TMA 1970, s 86.

If the donee sells the asset, all instalments of tax that have not been paid at that date become immediately payable, with interest.[2]

---

[1] TCGA 1992, s 281(3).
[2] TCGA 1992, s 281(7)(*b*).

Gift to housing association

[18.37] TCGA 1992, s 259 provides that where any interest in land is gifted to a housing association registered under the Housing Associations Act 1985 (or its Northern Ireland equivalent) the disposal is treated as no gain/no loss.

This treatment is afforded on a claim being made jointly by the transferor and the housing association.

Simon's Taxes C1.219.

[18.38] Disposal

Holdover relief

[18.38] There are currently two types of holdover relief:

(1) where the capital gains tax disposal is also a chargeable transfer for inheritance tax purposes, a claim can be made under TCGA 1992, s 260;
(2) where the disposal is of an asset within the categories specified in infra, § **18.41**; a claim can be made under TCGA 1992, s 165.

Holdover relief is available not only on gifts; it is available whenever there is "a disposal otherwise than under a bargain at arm's length".[1] For many years, the Revenue took the view that a holdover claim under s 165 was not competent when the transfer took place as part of the division of financial assets on divorce. However, following a decision of the Family Court in 2002, the Revenue have changed their view[2] where there is recourse to the courts and a court order made, including an order that formally ratifies an agreement reached by the divorcing parties dealing with the transfer of assets. In those cases, the Revenue now accept that there is no actual consideration. Previously, they took the view that there was consideration in the form of surrendered rights but now agree that an order made by a court reflects the exercise of its independent statutory jurisdiction. This change of mind is a prime example of the importance of considering the effect of areas of law other than Revenue law. It must be borne in mind, though, that this change only applies in the context of a court order and in other instances a hold-over claim may not be available, in which case the basic principle that transfers should take place in a tax year in which the parties are married and living together could be the more appropriate course to avoid a liability to CGT.

The effect of a claim of holdover relief on a gift is that the gain that would otherwise be chargeable to tax is held over so that the gain crystallised by the donor is reduced to £nil. The amount by which the gain for the donor is reduced, also reduces the acquisition cost that the donee is subsequently able to put against the disposal he ultimately makes on the asset for which the holdover relief election has been made. The gain held over is after taking account of any retirement relief available. The holdover relief claim must be for the whole of the gain (subject only to the statutory reduction given by virtue of actual consideration or by chargeable non-business assets); a partial claim is not possible. The effect of the holdover relief claim on the donee is that indexation allowance is given on the acquisition cost after reduction by the held-over gain.

Taper relief (pre-2008–09) was applied after holdover relief.[3]

EXAMPLE
Gift after 4 years ownership of an asset used for the purposes of a trade.

	£
MV on date of gift	100,000
Cost	(40,000)
	60,000

Holdover relief [18.40]

Gain	60,000
Gain held over	(60,000)
Chargeable gain	Nil

Sale 8 years later and also used for one purpose of a trade

	£	£
Sale proceeds		150,000
MV at acquisition	100,000	
less held over gain	(60,000)	
		(40,000)
		110,000

Simon's Taxes C1.425–428.

1. TCGA 1992, s 165(1)(a).
2. Published in Inland Revenue Tax Bulletin, December 2003, p 1071. Following the obiter of Coleridge J in *G v G* [2002] EWHC 1339 (Fam), [2002] 2 FLR 1143.
3. TCGA 1992, s 2A granted taper relief on the gain that is charged to tax, hence there was no taper relief if the entire gain is covered by a holdover claim.

Claim for holdover relief

[18.39] Holdover relief is only available on a claim. Unless the gain is made on a disposal to trustees, both the donor and donee are required to sign the claim.[1] The claim must be made within five years ten months of the end of the fiscal year in which the disposal is made.[2] The Revenue Staff Manual instructs Revenue officers to require the claim to be signed by the claimants and refuse a claim signed by a tax agent.[3]

A holdover relief claim cannot be made where the recipient is not resident in the United Kingdom or where the recipient is a UK resident company controlled by a person or persons who are neither resident nor ordinarily resident in the United Kingdom and the person who controls the company is connected with the donor.[4]

Simon's Taxes C1.425–428.

1. TCGA 1992, s 165(1).
2. TMA 1970, s 43.
3. Revenue Internal Guidance, Capital Gains Manual, CG 66914.
4. TCGA 1992, s 167.

Transfer subject to inheritance tax

[18.40] A claim can be made under TCGA 1992, s 260 to hold over the gain arising on any transfer to an individual or to trustees which is chargeable to inheritance tax. The 2006 changes made in the inheritance tax code (see infra, § **42.05**) have a consequence that a transfer of property to the vast majority of

[18.40] Disposal

trusts that are created on or after 22 March 2006 is a chargeable transfer for inheritance tax purposes and, hence, the gain arising on the disposal of property to the trust can be held over, as long as the trustees are UK resident (see infra, § **33.40**). A claim under s 260 cannot be made on a transfer to a company.[1] It is not necessary for inheritance tax to be actually payable; the requirement is chargeability and this is satisfied where the size of the transfer is such that either it is covered by the annual exempt amount or by the inheritance tax nil rate band or by agricultural or business property relief. Holdover relief is denied where the transfer is a potentially exempt transfer, even if it becomes chargeable by virtue of the death of the donor within the seven-year period.[2]

Where a claim is competent under s 260, it can be made in respect of any asset, irrespective of its nature.

Holdover relief can also be claimed under s 260 where the disposal would be a chargeable transfer except that it is exempted by one of the following provisions:

(1) IHTA 1994, ss 30 or 78(1) (designated property or work of art).
(2) IHTA 1984, ss 27, 57A or Sch 4 (maintenance funds for historic buildings).
(3) IHTA 1984, s 26 (transfer for public benefit).
(4) IHTA 1984, s 24 (transfer to a political party).
(5) IHTA 1984, s 71 (A & M trust—see below).

A claim for holdover relief under TCGA 1992, s 260 cannot be made in respect of a transfer between spouses or civil partners. Hence, where a couple separates, the transfer of an asset from one to another after the end of the fiscal year in which they separate crystallises a capital gain on which tax is potentially payable, unless the conditions of s 165 are fulfilled.

TCGA 1992, s 260(2)(d) provides that a claim to hold over a gain can be made when the disposal is an occasion on which inheritance tax would be chargeable were it not for the relief given by IHTA 1994, s 71(4). The relief in that section of IHTA is relief against the charge that would otherwise arise when a beneficiary of an accumulation and maintenance trust acquires an interest in possession. However, it is not normally the case that there is a CGT disposal at that particular point in time. If the provisions of Trustee Act 1925, s 31 apply to the settlement, the beneficiary acquires an interest in possession at age 18, although the property remains in the settlement until the date specified in the deed. If those provisions are expressly excluded by the settlement deed, the interest in possession is acquired by the beneficiary at a time specified in the deed which must, however, be by the beneficiary's 25 birthday if the settlement is to qualify as an accumulation and maintenance settlement within the terms of IHTA 1984, s 71. It is common for an accumulation and maintenance settlement to provide for an entitlement to income to arise from age 18, but capital to remain with the trustees until age 25. Another common formulation is for the right to income to arise at age 25 and for capital to remain under the control of the trustees until they choose to make an appointment or until the expiry of 80 years, if later.

Where the vesting of capital has been preceded by the granting of an interest in possession, the conditions for holdover relief under TCGA 1992, s 260(2)(*b*) have not been fulfilled. It is the earlier occasion on which the IHT relief has applied and not the occasion on which the asset passes to the beneficiary. An interesting question arises in a situation such as the following:

> A trust gives an income entitlement at age eighteen and a capital entitlement at age twenty five, with power to the trustees to advance capital earlier at their discretion. The trustees resolve to advance to the beneficiary an asset pregnant with gain, the advancement being deliberately made on the beneficiary's eighteen birthday. Can holdover relief be claimed?

Probably the better view is that holdover relief cannot be claimed as the transfer of the asset is not exempt from a charge to IHT "by virtue of s 71(4)" as that section relates to the granting of the interest in possession, not the transfer of the capital asset. This is, however, perhaps, an over nice distinction and if this distinction is made then TCGA 1992, s 260(2)(*d*) may be robbed of all its meaning. An aspect of this problem was considered in *Begg-MacBrearty v Stilwell*.[3] A discretionary settlement was made in 1959. In 1975 the trustees exercised a power of appointment under the settlement deed. The Family Law Reform Act 1969 reduced the age of majority from 21 to 18 years. Miranda Mary Wilson attained the age of 21 on 27 July 1990. Under the terms of the 1975 appointment, assets from the settlement vested in her on that date. The trustees argued that the holdover election they had submitted in respect of that vesting was competent because it was at age 21 that she acquired the interest in possession (as well as the capital entitlement) and, hence, holdover relief was available under the terms of TCGA 1992, s 260(2)(*b*). The argument for the taxpayer was that the deed was created before the enactment of Family Law Reform Act 1969 and, hence, not only the deed but any appointment made under the deed had to be construed under the terms of statute that applied at the time the deed was created; inter alia, the age of majority is 21 and Trustee Act 1925, s 31 gives an income entitlement at age twenty one, not before. Inland Revenue counsel argued that the deed of appointment was made after the enactment of the Family Law Reform Act 1969 and in full knowledge of that Act and, hence, that deed must be construed on the basis of the age of majority being eighteen years. As, on that construction, the income entitlement arose three years before the asset was transferred to Miranda, the holdover election was not competent. The Court approved the analysis by Revenue counsel, and overturned the decision of the Special Commissioner denying holdover relief.

Simon's Taxes C1.425.

---

[1] TCGA 1992, s 260(1).
[2] TCGA 1992, s 260(2)(*a*).
[3] [1996] STC 413.

Assets qualifying for holdover under TCGA 1992, s 165

[18.41] Holdover relief is only available under this provision if the asset is within one of the following categories:

(1) an asset used for the purposes of a trade carried on by the transferor or by his personal company;[1]

[18.41] Disposal

(2) property that qualifies for agricultural property relief for inheritance tax purposes.[2]

In addition, holdover relief can be claimed on the gift of shares and securities in the categories specified below where the gift is to an individual or a trustee, but not where the recipient is a company.[3]

(3) unquoted shares or securities in a trading company;[4]
(4) shares or securities in a trading company which is the transferor's personal company[5].

An asset used for the purpose of a trade carried on by the donor in partnership is within category (1) above. The size of the individual's interest in the partnership is not relevant.

For the purposes of (3) above, an individual's personal company is one in which the individual is able to exercise not less than 5% of the voting rights in the company.[6]

For property to fall within category (4), it is only necessary that agricultural property relief is available. It is irrelevant whether the relief is at 50% or at 100%. The holdover claim is not limited to the value on which agricultural property relief is available. If farmland is gifted and the majority of the value of the land is a reflection of its potential development value, rather than its agricultural value, holdover relief is nevertheless able to be claimed on the entire gain.

Commercially managed woodlands[7] and furnished holiday lettings are treated as trades for the purpose of holdover relief.[8]

Simon's Taxes C1.425.

[1] TCGA 1992, s 165(2)(*a*).
[2] TCGA 1992, Sch 7, para 1(1).
[3] TCGA 1992, s 165(3), (6A).
[4] TCGA 1992, s 165(2)(*b*)(i).
[5] TCGA 1992, s 165(2)(*b*)(ii).
[6] TCGA 1992, s 165(8)(*a*).
[7] TCGA 1992, s 165(9).
[8] TCGA 1992, s 241(3).

TCGA 1992, s 165: Sale at undervalue

[18.42] Where consideration passes on a transfer, but the consideration is less than the market value of the asset transferred, holdover relief can be claimed as long as the other conditions for relief under either s 260 or s 165 are fulfilled. In such a case, the gain that is held over is reduced by the excess of sale consideration over the sums allowable as acquisition costs.[1]

The effect of claiming holdover relief on the sale at undervalue is to leave in charge the gross gain without any deduction for indexation allowance. The benefit of the indexation allowance is, thus, enjoyed by the donee when he ultimately makes a disposal.

Simon's Taxes C1.425.

[1] TCGA 1992, s 165(7).

TCGA 1992, s 165: Partial relief

[18.43] Quite apart from sales at undervalue, there is partial relief only available in the following circumstances:

(1) where the asset was not used for the purpose of a trade throughout the period of ownership;[1]
(2) where the disposal is of a building and part of the building was not used for the purpose of the trade;[2]
(3) where the disposal is of shares in a company and the company has non-business chargeable assets at the time at which a disposal is made of its shares).[3]

Under statute, holdover relief can only be claimed on the grounds of an asset being used for the purpose of trade, etc, where the asset is so used at the time of disposal. HMRC internal guidance[4] confirms that Revenue officers are instructed to apply this provision strictly, denying a claim for relief where the asset was previously used in a trade, etc, but was not a trading asset immediately prior to the disposal.

Where an asset is used in a trade, etc, at the time of disposal, but earlier during the period in which it was owned by the taxpayer it was not used for the purpose of trade, the held over gain is the gain arising multiplied by the fraction of that period for which the asset was used for the trade bears to the total period of ownership.[5]

Holdover relief is reduced by a fraction "which is just and reasonable" in a situation where part of a building has been used for a trade and part has not.[6] Inland Revenue internal guidance[7] repeats the statutory words in its instructions to Revenue officers, without giving guidance as to how they should be applied. No apportionment is, however, necessary in the case of land and buildings qualifying for agricultural property relief.[8]

Simon's Taxes C1.425.

[1] TCGA 1992, Sch 7, para 5.
[2] TCGA 1992, Sch 7, para 6.
[3] TCGA 1992, Sch 7, para 7.
[4] HMRC Internal Guidance, Capital Gains Manual, CG 66950.
[5] TCGA 1992, Sch 7, para 5(1).
[6] TCGA 1992, Sch 7, para 6(1).
[7] HMRC Internal Guidance, Capital Gains Manual, CG 66952.
[8] TCGA 1992, Sch 7, paras 5(2), 6(2).

[18.44] Disposal

Holdover relief into and out of trust

[18.44] Holdover relief cannot be claimed on a transfer into a settlor-interested trust.[1] This is widely defined to include a potential benefit for the settlor, or his spouse/civil partner, from any arrangements[2] or from any derived property.[3]

As long as the trust is not "settlor-interested", holdover relief can be claimed on the transfer of any property into a discretionary trust[4] and for property within the categories given in supra, § **18.41** when the transfer is into a life interest trust.[5]

An election to hold over a gain that arises on the transfer into trust is made unilaterally by the settlor.[6] An election on the transfer of an asset out of trust is made by the trustees and the recipient beneficiary jointly.

The vesting of property in a beneficiary is a disposal by trustees and is made "otherwise than under a contract at arm's length".[7] Hence, an election for holdover relief can be made where either the transfer is chargeable to inheritance tax (which will always be the case where there is a transfer in or out of a discretionary settlement) or, alternatively, the asset being transferred is within the categories specified in supra, § **18.41**. The settling of property and also the passing of an asset to a beneficiary by virtue of the exercise of trustees' discretion, are both further examples of transfers "otherwise than under a contract at arm's length" and, hence, holdover relief is available, providing the other conditions for the transfer are satisfied.

Holdover relief can be claimed by trustees where an asset is used for the purposes of a trade carried on by a beneficiary who has an interest in possession in the settled property.[8]

Where trustees transfer shares to a beneficiary and wish to claim holdover relief under TCGA 1992, s 165, it is necessary for the shares to be either unquoted shares in a trading company or for the trustees to be entitled to exercise 25% or more of the voting rights in the company immediately prior to the disposal.[9]

Where an election for holdover relief is made on the transfer of an asset into trust, the gain held over is brought into charge at the death of any life tenant of the trust.[10] This charge arises irrespective of which type of holdover was claimed. The gain brought into charge is normally the gain that was held over; however, the gain brought into charge cannot exceed the gain measured by reference to the market value of the asset at the time of the death of the life tenant. This gain may, in turn, be held over under TCGA 1992, s 260 as the death of the life tenant is an occasion of charge to inheritance tax. There is, however, one exception to the availability of the further claim to holdover relief and that is where at the death the property passes to the surviving spouse/civil partner of the deceased life tenant or into trust in which the survivor has a life interest. IHTA 1984, s 18(1) then operates so that the transfer is not chargeable to inheritance tax; hence, the condition for a holdover relief claim under TCGA 1992, s 260 is not satisfied. The gain crystallised, thus, gives rise to an immediate charge to tax in such a circumstance unless it is on an asset specified as being within TCGA 1992, s 165(2), which would enable a holdover relief election to be made under the terms of that section.

Where a holdover election is made under s 260, principal private residence relief is not available on the subsequent disposal.[11]

---

[1] TCGA 1992, s 169B(1) inserted by FA 2004, Sch 21, para 4 with effect from 10 December 2003. Holdover relief is denied on any disposal to a settlor interested trust, including a disposal made by a third party. Thus, the transfer from one trust to another cannot be subject to a holdover relief claim, if the recipient trust is settlor interested. There are also tracing rules whereby holdover relief is denied even if the recipient trust is not settlor interested but the asset was subject to an earlier holdover of disposal into a settlor interested trust. Where a trust is not settlor interested, but becomes settlor interested within six years of the transfer, there is a clawback of the gain held over: TCGA 1992, s 169C.
[2] Defined in TCGA 1992, s 169G inserted by FA 2004, Sch 21, para 4.
[3] TCGA 1992, s 169F(2)(*b*) inserted by FA 2004, Sch 21, para 4.
[4] Under TCGA 1992, s 260: see supra, § **18.40**.
[5] Under TCGA 1992, s 165: see supra, § **18.41**.
[6] TCGA 1992, s 165(1)(*b*).
[7] TCGA 1992, s 165(6).
[8] TCGA 1992, Sch 7, para 2(2)(*a*)(ii).
[9] TCGA 1992, Sch 7, para 2(2)(*b*).
[10] TCGA 1992, s 74.
[11] TCGA 1992, s 226A inserted by FA 2004, Sch 22, para 6 with effect from 10 December 2003. There are transitional provisions where the holdover is pre-10 December 2003 and the subsequent disposal after that date: see infra, § **23.16**.

Holdover relief on assets held at 31 March 1982

[18.45] Where an asset was acquired by means of a holdover election between 1 April 1982 and 31 March 1988 and the person from whom the asset was acquired made his acquisition prior to 1 April 1982, only one half of the gain that was held over is used to reduce the deemed acquisition cost.[1] This treatment is applied only on the making of a claim by the taxpayer. This claim must be made by 31 January two years after the fiscal year in which the disposal occurs.[2] Although statute gives discretion to the Revenue to extend this time limit, internal Revenue instructions, local districts, state that the time limit should only be extended in wholly exceptional circumstances. There is, however, no requirement as to the form a claim should take. A line in the CGT computation that shows one half of the held over gain being used, is sufficient.

---

[1] TCGA 1992, Sch 4, para 5.
[2] TCGA 1992, Sch 4, para 9(1)(*c*). For a company, the time limit is two years after the end of the accounting period: TCGA 1992, Sch 4, para 9(1)(*b*).

[18.46] Disposal

Electing for no formal valuation to be made

[18.46] Revenue Statement of Practice SP 8/92 formalises the procedure to be followed where an election for holdover relief is made without a valuation of the asset being agreed with the Revenue.

In order for the valuation requirement to be waived, SP 8/92 requires that the transferor and transferee both make a request to this effect in writing and provide:

(1) full details of the asset transferred;
(2) its date of acquisition;
(3) its allowable expenditure;
(4) a statement that they have satisfied themselves that the value of the asset at the date of transfer was in excess of the allowable expenditure plus indexation to that date.

Application is normally made on Revenue form IR265. Neither the donor nor the donee is able to withdraw the request once it has been accepted by the Revenue.

Simon's Taxes C1.426.

Gratuitous transfers of value

[18.47] For gratuitous transfers of value[1] generally see **Simon's Taxes** C1.335, 336; Sumption CGT A2.03. The term disposal is widened to catch three types of transaction. In all three, the market value which would be payable by the acquirer under a bargain at arm's length is to be taken as the consideration.

The first of these transactions is where a person has control of a company and exercises that control so that value passes out of shares in the company owned by him, or by a person with whom he is connected, and passes into other shares in or rights over the company. A controlling shareholder using his voting power to pass a resolution increasing the rights of a particular type of share at the expense of his own is clearly shifting value to the other shareholders, although no particular piece of property has been disposed of.[2] Consequently, even where the controlling shareholder's interest in the company is such that he would be entitled to claim holdover relief on a gift of his shares, a deemed disposal under the present provisions would not qualify for relief, as no shares have actually been transferred. Despite the fact that the singular "person" is referred to, it has been held that the section applies where two or more persons control the company.[3] It has also been held that control was exercised when under a pre-arranged scheme a winding up resolution was passed even though the taxpayer himself did not vote on the motion.[4] Outside the context of a scheme the taxpayer must presumably vote in order to exercise control.

The second type of transaction caught is where, after a transaction whereby the owner of any property has become the lessee of the property, there is an adjustment of the rights and liabilities of the lease which, taken as a whole, favour the lessor.

The third is where there is an asset which is subject to a right or restriction and there is a transaction whereby that right or restriction is extinguished or abrogated in whole or in part. Here the figure to be taken is the value accruing to the owner of the property from which the restriction falls.

[1] TCGA 1992, s 29.
[2] The legislation does not, however, limit itself to value shifting into shares held by others and could apply where value is shifted between different classes of shares held by the same person. This is understood to be the Revenue view.
[3] *Floor v Davis* [1979] STC 379, [1979] 2 All ER 677.
[4] In the light of the decision in *W T Ramsay Ltd v IRC* [1981] STC 174, [1981] 1 All ER 865 it would appear that the same result would have been reached if, as part of a scheme, they had voted against the resolution.

Exclusion of market value rule

[18.48] The market value rule does not apply where there is an acquisition of an asset without a disposal and the consideration is either non-existent or is less than the market value.[1] In these circumstances the acquisition consideration will be nil or the actual value as appropriate. The purpose of this rule is to defeat schemes known as "reverse *Nairn Williamson* schemes". Under such schemes, shares were issued to shareholders (so being acquired by them without being disposed of by the issuing company). Although a relatively small amount might be subscribed (especially if the issued share capital was not substantial), the shares acquired were valued at market value thus giving the shareholders a substantial uplift in the base cost of their holding. Such schemes would now probably fall foul of the *Ramsay* principle anyway.[a]

The former exception to the market value rule for disposals by excluded persons, such as non-residents, was withdrawn for disposals after 5 April 1983, subject to transitional rules for disposals before 6 April 1985.

Simon's Taxes C2.109; Sumption CGT A1.12.

[1] TCGA 1992, s 17.
[2] Goldberg (1982) BTR 13 at 16.

Connected persons

[18.49] Where the person making the disposal is connected with the person acquiring the asset, they are treated as parties to a transaction otherwise than at arm's length.[1] This treatment applies irrespective of the motive of the parties or the price paid. The rule does not apply to transactions where there is an acquisition but no disposal eg an issue of shares by a company to a controlling shareholder, or a disposal but no acquisition, eg on the repurchase or redemption of shares by a company.[2] The market value rule could still apply, but on the more general grounds comprised in TCGA 1992, s 17.

1013

[18.49] Disposal

Loss relief is restricted where a loss arises on a disposal to a connected person (see infra, § **18.53**). (In the case of *Kellogg Brown & Root Holdings Ltd v R & C Commrs*[3], the High Court upheld a decision by the Special Commissioners that a company was not entitled to deduct capital loss incurred on the sale of the shares in two of its subsidiaries since the effect of s 286(5)(b) was that the taxpayer company and the purchasing company were connected companies at the time of sale of shares so that the conditions in s 18(3) were satisfied precluding the loss relief sought.)

Where the market value rule imposes deemed consideration in excess of the consideration actually paid, holdover relief may be available (see infra, § **18.52**).

Simon's Taxes C2.110.

[1] TCGA 1992, s 18.
[2] TCGA 1992, s 17(2).
[3] [2009] EWHC 584 (Ch).

Definition of connected persons

[18.50] Connected persons for the purposes of capital gains tax are those within the following five categories:

Relatives

A taxpayer is connected with his/her spouse/civil partner, brother, sister, ancestor or lineal descendant. A taxpayer is also connected with the spouse/civil partner of any one of those individuals. Further, an individual is connected with the relations in the foregoing list of his spouse/civil partner.[1] This definition differs from the definition used for inheritance tax in IHTA 1984, s 272 in that, unlike inheritance tax, an individual's uncle, aunt, nephew and niece, are not connected persons for CGT purposes.

In this definition, a spouse/civil partner means an individual who is married to (or a member of a civil partnership with) the taxpayer, whether or not they are living together. A spouse/civil partner, thus, ceases to be a connected person, and the spouse or civil partner's relatives cease to be connected, only at decree absolute or final dissolution of the partnership.

Simon's Taxes C2.110.

[1] TCGA 1992, s 286(2).

Trustees

A trustee is connected with the settlor of the settlement of which he is trustee and also he is connected with any person who is, himself, connected with the settlor.[1]

For this purpose, the capital gains tax legislation imports the meaning of "settlor" from the settlements provisions in ITTOIA 2005, Pt 5, Ch 5. That is, in addition to the person named on the settlement deed as a settlor, it encompasses any person who has "provided or undertaken to provide funds directly or indirectly for the purpose of the settlement, or has made with any other person a reciprocal arrangement for that other person to make or enter into the settlement".

In addition, a trustee is connected with any close company of which the trustees of the settlement are participators, any company controlled by such a company and any company that fulfils this definition, but is not close solely by virtue of not being resident in the UK.[2]

The network of connections that exist by virtue of a trusteeship operates separately from the network of connections that exist by virtue of an individual, himself. Thus, an individual who is a trustee is treated in the capital gains tax legislation as connected with, for example, the settlor's son in relation to any disposal he makes, as trustee, of trust property. If the same individual sells his personal property to, for example, the son of the settlor of a settlement of which he is trustee, this is not a transaction between connected persons.

A connection can only be made through an individual while he is alive. Thus, after the death of the settlor of a trust, the trustees are not connected under these provisions with any individuals.

[1] TCGA 1992, s 286(3).
[2] TCGA 1992, s 286(3A).

Partners

A person is connected with any person with whom he is in partnership, with the spouse/civil partner of any partner and with the brother, sister, ancestor or lineal descendant of any partner. However, this connection does not apply "in relation to acquisitions or disposals of partnership assets pursuant to bona fide commercial arrangements".[1]

Revenue practice is to treat any transaction between an incoming partner and the existing partners that is a bona fide commercial arrangement as being made otherwise than between connected persons.[2]

The interpretation of the proviso to s 286(4) is difficult. Where the partnership contracts with an individual partner to sell to that partner, for a commercial consideration, an asset that has previously been on the partnership balance sheet, it is clear that the subsection operates so that the transaction is not treated as being made between connected persons. However, it is less clear where the asset in question has not been on the partnership balance sheet. This is commonly the case in partnerships where goodwill is transferred between partners and neither the goodwill nor its transfer is shown in the accounts of the partnership. Probably the better view of such a transaction is that a distinction has to be drawn between: (i) an asset owned by the partnership, which is a "partnership asset" within the meaning of s 286(4) and (ii) an individual's interest in the partnership, which is not a "partnership asset" within the meaning of s 286(4). However, this analysis seems to presuppose

[18.50] Disposal

that one can recognise the partnership as an entity. In English law a partnership is not a legal entity and, furthermore, TCGA 1992, s 59(b) specifies that partnership dealings shall be treated as dealings by the partners and not by the firm as such. Some support for the concept that there is a separation between an individual's interest in the partnership and the proportion of the assets of the partnership that can be attributed to that individual is given by the decision of the Privy Council in *Hadlee v Commissioner of Inland Revenue*.[3] In that case, the court held that a partner's interest in a New Zealand partnership was a chose in action and, as such, settling on another the right to receive partnership income constitutes a settlement of income with the retention of capital such that the income remains assessable on the settlor under the terms of the New Zealand equivalent of TA 1988, s 660A.

[1] TCGA 1992, s 286(4).
[2] Statement of practice D12, para 7; this is clearly extra-statutory.
[3] [1993] STC 294.

Connected companies

TCGA 1992, s 286(5) provides:

> (5) A company is connected with another company:
>
> (a) if the same person has control of both, or a person has control of one and persons connected with him, or he and persons connected with him, have control of the other; or
>
> (b) if a group of two or more persons has control of each company, and the groups either consist of the same persons or could be regarded as consisting of the same persons by treating (in one or more cases) a member of either group as replaced by a person with whom he is connected.

Individual and company connected

A company is connected with an individual if that individual has control of it or where a group of individuals who are connected persons have control of the company.[1] Further, any two or more persons acting together to secure and exercise control of a company are treated in relation to that company as connected with each other.[2]

[1] TCGA 1992, s 286(6).
[2] TCGA 1992, s 286(7).

Holdover election on a transfer between connected persons

[18.51] Where a sale is made between persons who are connected, the sale is always treated as "a transaction otherwise than by way of a bargain made at arm's length".[1] A consequence of this is that an election can be made by the parties under TCGA 1992, s 165 for any gain arising from the market value being in excess of consideration to be held over, where the asset concerned is a business asset within the terms of that section. This can be useful where a commercial bargain is entered into, but the parties cannot be certain that the value placed on the asset by the Revenue will equate to their own view of the value. The availability of a holdover election is also potentially of assistance where there are a number of transactions and one of the transactions, viewed alone, could be held to trigger a gain in excess of the gain computed by reference to the consideration that actually passed.

Simon's Taxes C2.110.

---

[1] As a consequence of the interaction between TCGA 1992, s 286 and TCGA 1992, s 18(1).

Disposals between connected persons: restrictions on loss relief

[18.52] Where the person making the disposal is connected with the person acquiring, the asset, the two persons are treated as parties to a transaction otherwise than at arm's length.[1] Hence the disposal will be deemed to have taken place at market value.[2]

Where a person disposes of an asset to a connected person, and a loss accrues, then, even though the loss occurs after the application of the rule that the consideration for the transaction is deemed to be market value, that loss can *only* be set off against gains accruing from some other disposal to that person.[3] Further, the other disposal must be at a time when they are connected persons.

Special rules apply to the valuation of assets when a connected person has a right over the asset to be valued.[4]

Simon's Taxes C1.508; C2.110; Sumption CGT A2.01.

---

[1] TCGA 1992, s 18. The rule does not seem to apply to transactions where there is an acquisition but no disposal eg an issue of shares by a company to a controlling shareholder, or a disposal but no acquisition, eg on the repurchase or redemption of shares by a company. The market value rule could still apply, but on the more general grounds comprised in TCGA 1992, s 17.
[2] TCGA 1992, s 17.
[3] TCGA 1992, s 18(3).
[4] TCGA 1992, s 18(5), (6).

19

Death

Basic rule: acquisition without disposal	PARA **19.01**
Deed of variation	PARA **19.03**
Inheritance (Provision for Family and Dependants) Act 1975	PARA **19.04**
Disposal to legatee	PARA **19.05**
Death of a life tenant of settled property	PARA **19.07**
Losses	PARA **19.08**
Disposals during period of administration	PARA **19.09**

Basic rule: acquisition without disposal

[19.01] Where the deceased had property of which he was competent to dispose, the personal representatives, or other person on whom it devolves, are deemed to acquire it at market value at the date of death.[1] However, there is no deemed disposal by the deceased. Any potential liability in respect of unrealised gains is extinguished—as are any potential allowable losses.

From 1965 to 1971, both estate duty and capital gains tax were charged at death. Since 1971, the principle underlying the legislation is that the only charge at death is to be the succession tax in force at the time and a disposal occasioned by death is exempt from a charge to capital gains tax.[2] This exemption applies whether its effect is to extinguish a potentially chargeable gain or a potentially chargeable loss. This is effected by TCGA 1992, s 62(1), which provides that personal representatives acquire assets for consideration equal to the market value at the date of death, without there having been a disposal by the deceased (infra, § **19.02**). This provision has effect, whether or not inheritance tax is chargeable on the occasion of death.[3] Thus, for example, a non-UK estate of a non-domiciled individual is acquired by personal representatives at its market value, even though it is outside the charge to UK inheritance tax.

Where personal representatives sell an asset of the estate, CGT is charged on the sale, taking the market value at date of death as the base cost. However, if personal representatives dispose of an asset by passing it to a beneficiary under the will or intestacy, this is not treated as an occasion for the charging of CGT; instead, the scheme of the Act is to treat the beneficiary as if he had acquired the asset at the death of the deceased.[4]

The scheme of death causing a charge to succession tax (currently inheritance tax) and giving an exemption from capital gains tax is carried through to settled property. As would be expected, where a beneficiary is absolutely entitled to the property, there is equivalent treatment.[5] Where an individual has an interest in possession, inheritance tax is charged as if the property from which the income is (or would be) derived is part of the estate of the deceased

1019

[19.01] Death

and the trustees are then treated as having newly acquired the property from which the income entitlement derives at the market value at the date of the beneficiary's death, without there having been a disposal to cause a charge to CGT.[6]

A difference between unsettled property and settled property arises in respect of holdover relief. Where an individual owns an asset at his death which he has acquired as a result of a holdover claim, the effect of the provisions is that the gain that was deferred by holdover is given permanent relief. Where, however, there has been a claim to holdover relief on the gain arising when property is transferred into trust, the death of the beneficiary with an interest in possession causes the held over gain to crystallise, giving a charge to tax payable by the trustees.[7]

Simon's Taxes C1.313.

---

[1] TCGA 1992, s 62(1).
[2] Death is an occasion of charge under the system of taxing offshore income gains, see TA 1988, s 757, infra, § **35.45** and can give rise to tax on a gain held over when property was settled.
[3] However, whether or not there is inheritance tax payable is relevant in identifying the rule to be followed in valuing the property. If the value has been determined for inheritance tax purposes, the IHT value is taken as the market value for CGT purposes also, despite the significant differences between the valuation rules for the two separate taxes: TCGA 1992, s 274. If the asset is passed to the surviving spouse/civil partner, or if the estate is too small to warrant detailed examination by the Capital Taxes Office, the value of an asset will not normally be determined for inheritance tax. In this circumstance, the CGT rules for valuation are applied to determine the base value for the person inheriting the asset.
[4] TCGA 1992, s 62(4). The legislation somewhat confusingly refers to the acquisition "as legatee" but the legatee is defined in s 64(2) as including "any person taking under a testamentary disposition or as intestacy or partial intestacy, whether he takes as beneficiary or as trustee".
[5] TCGA 1992, s 73.
[6] IHTA 1984, s 49; TCGA 1992, s 72.
[7] TCGA 1992, s 74.

Acquisition on death

[19.02] The deceased was competent to dispose of[1] any assets which he could, if of full age and capacity, have disposed of by his will. This includes any severable beneficial share in joint property, but not entailed property nor property over which he had a power of appointment.

Where the value of an asset has been ascertained for IHT that value is taken for CGT;[2] this may not be the same as the value on which IHT is charged. So if farm land is valued at £200,000 the actual value transferred for IHT purposes may be reduced to £100,000 by reason of agricultural relief, infra, § **44.11**; the value for the CGT acquisition will be £200,000.

A donatio mortis causa is not subject to CGT when made; instead the donee takes at the market value at the date of the death.[3] On a gift with reservation, which is treated as remaining part of the donor's estate on death for IHT, the market value for CGT is determined as of the date of the gift if the gift is a disposal for CGT. In the case of a potentially exempt transfer, which becomes a chargeable transfer for IHT if the donor dies within seven years of the date the transfer is made, the CGT treatment of the gift is undisturbed. This is because the gift is not treated as included in the transferor's estate on death.

A potentially interesting issue arises if the deceased made a contract for the sale of land which is completed by the personal representatives. Under the decision of the House of Lords in *Jerome v Kelly* (supra, § **18.06**) this is not treated, retrospectively, as a disposal by the deceased as at the time of the contract. Such land is therefore presumably part of his estate when he dies (and is revalued at its market value, presumably the contract price).

Simon's Taxes C1.206, 313; Sumption CGT A7.01.

[1] TCGA 1992, s 62(10).
[2] TCGA 1992, s 274.
[3] TCGA 1992, ss 62(5) (excluding s 17), 64(2).

Deed of variation

[19.03] If, within a two-year period from the date of death, there is a variation or disclaimer by an instrument in writing, statute provides that the variation or disclaimer is not a disposal (so there can be no CGT) and, the CGT rules apply as if the allocation of the estate specified in the deed of variation had been made by the deceased.[1] This treatment is applied if the claim is made in the instrument that varies the estate (or under which there is disclaimer of an interest arising on an intestacy).[2] The Revenue view is that it is not possible to make the election at a later date if appropriate wording has not been put into the instrument.[3] This view is almost certainly incorrect. As a general principle, where a deed of rectification is made to correct an instrument so that it properly reflects the intentions and actions of the parties, that rectification is read as part of the instrument it rectifies.

It is not always beneficial to elect for a deed of variation to be treated as if it took place at death. If there has been an increase in the value of property between death and the date of the deed of variation, it is beneficial to omit the election where such an increase is less than the annual exempt amount available to the personal representatives. It is also beneficial to omit the election where the variation transfers an interest in the matrimonial home, where an increase in value of the property is covered by principal private residence relief.[4]

The election to treat a variation or disclaimer as taking effect at death cannot be made if consideration is given for the making of the variation.[5] This

[19.03] Death

provision does not stop the diversion of a cash sum, for example, within the estate to another beneficiary; the provision only bites where there is extraneous consideration.

In *Marshall v Kerr* the Court of Appeal held that although the variation is deemed to have been made by the deceased there are limits to the deeming process; the deeming does not necessarily apply in relation to other provisions eg the special rules for settlements made by non-resident, non-domiciled settlors; so it would not deem a settlement made by a non-resident beneficiary to be made by a deceased resident.[6]

A variation may be made whether or not the administration has been completed or the property has been distributed in accordance with the original dispositions.[7]

The admissibility of extrinsic evidence to construe a deed of variation is a matter of some difficulty. In *Schnieder v Mills*[8] a deed of variation suffered from an obvious omission in one clause; if construed literally, that clause would have had the effect of rendering the remaining clauses ineffective for tax purposes. There was no doubt as to what words had been omitted and that the omission had been unintentional. The court held that the deed was effective to vary the terms of the testator's will and made a declaration that it should be construed as if the missing words had been included. However, what was important was that the parties could show both that something had been unintentionally omitted and exactly what correction was needed.

Simon's Taxes C1.206; Sumption CGT A7.06.

---

[1] TCGA 1992, s 62(6). Deeming the variation to have been made by the deceased does not necessarily apply in relation to other provisions eg the special rules for settlements made by non-resident, non-domiciled settlors: *Marshall v Kerr* [1993] STC 360, CA. Capital Taxes Office expresses the view that in order for the IHT deeming provisions of IHTA 1984, s 142 to have effect, it is necessary for the deed of variation to effect events "in the real world". Although no statement has been made to this effect, it is presumably the Revenue's view that the provisions of TCGA 1992, s 62(6) are not effective if the benefit that is varied is one that is incapable of being conferred, such as a benefit accruing under the will to a beneficiary who predeceased the execution of deed of variation.

[2] TCGA 1992, s 62(7) amended by FA 2002, s 52 with effect from 1 August 2002. FA 2002, s 120 gives the same automatic treatment for inheritance tax: see infra, § 40.21.

[3] Inland Revenue Booklet IHT8, para 12.

[4] TCGA 1992, s 222 extended to property held by personal representatives by Inland Revenue Concession D5; see infra, § 23.13.

[5] TCGA 1992, s 62(8).

[6] [1993] STC 360, CA.

[7] TCGA 1992, s 62(9).

[8] [1993] STC 430.

Inheritance (Provision for Family and Dependants) Act 1975

[19.04] Inheritance (Provision for Family and Dependants) Act 1975 enables a court to make an order under s 2 of that Act directing the personal representatives to pass assets or make payments to dependants of the deceased. I(PFD)A 1975, s 19(1) of that Act states:

> For all purposes . . . the order shall have effect, and shall be deemed to have had effect, as from the deceased's death subject to the provisions of the order.

The dependant in whose favour an order is made is expressed in the Act as being treated as if he were a legatee. Hence, for capital gains tax purposes, the person to whom any asset is passed by an order of the court made under I(PFD)A 1975 is treated as if they had acquired that asset for its market value at the date of death. The effect is, thus, the same as if there had been a deed of variation and notice had been given to the Revenue, except that no notice is required and there is no two-year time limit.

Disposal to legatee

Treatment of beneficiary

[19.05] When the estate is administered, the personal representatives will dispose of the property to the specific and residuary legatees. However, on a person acquiring any asset as legatee the legatee is treated as if the personal representatives' acquisition of the asset had been his acquisition of it.[1] Thus if there is a specific legacy of a piece of furniture which cost the deceased £1,500 and which was worth £6,500 when he dies, leaving the piece specifically to A, A will be taken to have acquired it at £6,500, even though when he eventually receives it, it may be worth £8,000 or £5,000. This has the consequence that where some of the assets have accrued gains and other losses and there are two legatees, one resident in the UK and the other non-resident, it will be advantageous to transfer the assets with the losses to the UK resident (so that he may take advantage of them in due course) and the other assets to the non-resident so that they will escape UK CGT.

An asset is acquired by a person "as legatee" if it is taken under a testamentary disposition, or on an intestacy; the phrase is defined as including any asset appropriated by the personal representatives in or towards satisfaction of a pecuniary legacy or any other interest or share in the property devolving under the disposition or intestacy.[2] The effect is that a pecuniary legatee takes as legatee as does a residuary or a specific legatee but that a creditor does not. A person claiming under the Inheritance (Provision for Family and Dependants) Act 1975 takes as legatee.[3] The position of a person entitled to a part of the estate and who buys from the personal representatives an asset in satisfaction of that claim but for a price greater than the value of that claim, by paying the difference, is obscure.[4]

When a beneficiary disposes of property that has been passed to him, whether by assent or by the expiry of the period of administration, the gain is measured

[19.05] Death

by comparing the sale proceeds with the value at the date of death. The general rule is that any relief available is by reference to the period from the date of death to the date of the beneficiary's disposal. Exceptionally, when a dwelling house (or a part interest in a dwelling house) passes on death to the surviving spouse/civil partner, main private residence relief is computed by reference to the period beginning with the date of original acquisition by the deceased spouse/civil partner and ending with the disposal by the surviving spouse/civil partner.[5]

Simon's Taxes C1.206.

---

[1] TCGA 1992, s 62(4).
[2] TCGA 1992, s 64(2).
[3] Under s 19(1) of that Act. See also IHTA 1984, ss 146, 236(2).
[4] In *Passant v Jackson* [1985] STC 133 the reasoning of Vinelott J suggests that such an acquisition is not "as legatee"; appeal dismissed [1986] STC 164, CA.
[5] TCGA 1992, s 222(7)(a). This treatment is also applied where one spouse/civil partner makes an inter vivos gift to the other.

Allowance for cost of probate

[19.06] In *IRC v Richards' Executors*,[1] the House of Lords upheld the decision of the Commissioners that a proportionate part of the cost of obtaining probate of a deceased's estate were correctly regarded as incidental expenses suffered by the executors on their acquisition of the assets at the death of the deceased.

Where there has been actual expenditure on the granting of probate in respect of a specific asset, the amount of that actual expenditure is to be treated as the incidental cost of acquisition. In most cases, however, the expenditure has been on the granting of probate for the whole estate and is not specific to an asset. In order to deal with this, the Revenue will accept a computation with an allowance in accordance with the following table:[2]

	Gross value of estate	Allowable expenditure
A	Up to £50,000	1.8% of the probate value of the assets sold by the personal representatives.
B	Between £50,001 and £90,000	A fixed amount of £900, to be divided between all the assets of the estate in proportion to the probate values and allowed in those proportions on assets sold by the person representatives.
C	Between £90,001 and £400,000	1% of the probate value of the assets sold.
D	Between £400,001 and £500,000	A fixed amount of £4,000, to be divided as at B above.

Disposal to legatee **[19.06]**

	Gross value of estate	Allowable expenditure
E	Between £500,001 and £1,000,000	0.8% of the probate value of the assets sold.
F	Between £500,001 and £5,000,000	A fixed amount of £8,000, to be divided as at B above.
G	Over £5,000,000	0.16% of the probate value of the assets sold, subject to a maximum of £10,000.

The scale does not extend to gross estates exceeding £5,000,000 where the allowable expenditure is to be negotiated between the inspector and the taxpayer according to the facts of the particular case.

Simon's Taxes C2.207.

---

[1] (1971) 46 TC 626.
[2] Statement of Practice SP2/04. There is a separate table for corporate trustees. There are also tables for trustees, covering transfers of assets to beneficiaries, actual disposals and deemed disposals.

Where the death occurred between 6 April 1993 and 5 April 2004, the table is:

	Gross value of estate	Allowable expenditure
A	Up to £40,000	1.75% of the probate value of the assets sold by the personal representatives.
B	Between £40,001 and £70,000	A fixed amount of £700, to be divided between all the assets of the estate in proportion to the probate values and allowed in those proportions on assets sold by the person representatives.
C	Between £70,001 and £300,000	1% of the probate value of the assets sold.
D	Between £300,001 and £400,000	A fixed amount of £3,000, to be divided as at B above.
E	Between £400,001 and £750,000	0.75% of the probate value of the assets sold.

(Statement of practice SP 8/94.)

Death of a life tenant of settled property

[19.07] There is a deemed disposal and reacquisition by the trustees when a life interest in possession terminates on the death of the person beneficially entitled to the interest.[1] To provide the equivalent treatment as afforded in respect of the death of the individual taxpayer, no chargeable gain arises on this deemed disposal.[2]

Unlike the situation for an individual, however, where a gain was held over on the creation of the settlement of the property deemed disposed of, the death of the life tenant may result in a chargeable gain arising to the extent of the gain so held over, where the property remains in the settlement, as well as where it leaves the settlement.[3] Further holding over may be available, given that there will be a deemed chargeable transfer of the trust property on L's death.[4]

Simon's Taxes C4.210.

[1] TCGA 1992, s 72 (1)(*a*).
[2] TCGA 1992, s 72 (1)(*b*).
[3] TCGA 1992, s 74.
[4] TCGA 1992, s 260.

Losses

Losses in year of death: carry back

[19.08] If, in the year of assessment in which he dies, an individual has allowable losses, in excess of chargeable gains, they may be rolled backwards for the preceding three years of assessment, taking later years first.[1] The relief applies to an excess of allowable losses in the year of death only.

Simon's Taxes C1.502; Sumption CGT A7.02.

[1] TCGA 1992, s 62(2).

Disposals during period of administration

Transfer to personal representatives

[19.09] The principle adopted by English law is that all the assets of the deceased devolve upon the personal representatives. The personal representatives are then required to administer the estate and then distribute the estate in accordance with the will of the deceased (or the law of intestacy), taking account of any order made under the Inheritance (Provision for Family and Dependants) Act 1975.

For CGT purposes the assets which the deceased was competent to dispose of at the time of the death pass to the personal representatives; these are assets which, under English law, the deceased could have disposed of by will. For the purposes of this formulation, the assets that pass are those that could have passed under a will made by an adult domiciled in England and Wales. Where the asset is overseas, the effect of foreign law is excluded by deeming the asset to be in England, but only for the purpose of this test.[1]

Assets which are not deemed to have been transferred to the personal representatives for this purpose are:

(1) property over which the deceased had power of appointment;
(2) entailed property which he was empowered by statute to dispose of;
(3) a gift made by the deceased in his lifetime to take effect on his death (*donatio mortis causa*).[2]

In relation to property forming part of the estate of a deceased person, the personal representatives are treated as a single and continuing body of persons, distinct from the persons who may from time to time be the personal representatives, and that body is treated as having the deceased's residence, or ordinary residence, and domicile at the date of death.[3]

While a CGT charge may arise if there is a disposal by the personal representatives the legislation provides that there is to be no chargeable gain on the transfer of an asset by the personal representatives to a legatee; the legatee is deemed to have acquired the asset at the same time and for the same consideration as the personal representatives (see infra, § **21.16**).

Simon's Taxes C4.105.

[1] TCGA 1992, s 62(10).
[2] TCGA 1992, s 62(5), (10).
[3] TCGA 1992, s 62.

Disposals by personal representatives in the course of administration of the estate

[19.10] Disposals may give rise to chargeable gains or allowable losses in the normal way and the personal representatives are assessed accordingly. The assessment may be made in the name of any one of the personal representatives.[1] The personal representative(s) is not an individual and so the tax is charged at special rates, currently 40%.[2]

Chargeable gains on disposals by the personal representatives are calculated in the ordinary way; the full exempt amount is allowed for the year of death and the two following years of assessment.[3] For subsequent years, if the period of administration continues, there is no annual exempt amount. The selection of which assets to sell and which to retain for transmission in specie to the legatees is of great practical importance.

[19.10] Death

The charge arises regardless of the reason for the disposal—whether it is to raise money to pay tax or to pay the proceeds to the beneficiaries. If, however, the beneficiaries are absolutely entitled as against the personal representatives any liability falls on the beneficiaries.[4]

When personal representatives make a disposal of a dwelling house, principal private residence relief is available[5] if both before and after the death of the deceased the house was the principal private residence[6] of an individual who is entitled to 75% or more of the proceeds of disposal.[7] The entitlement can arise under the original will or intestacy, or can be created by deed of variation.

Simon's Taxes C4.108.

---

[1] TCGA 1992, s 65(1).
[2] TCGA 1992, s 4(1AA)(b).
[3] TCGA 1992, s 3(7).
[4] *Prest v Bettinson* [1980] STC 607.
[5] TCGA 1992, s 225A(1).
[6] By virtue of being the only residence of the beneficiary, or his main residence, or the residence for which he has elected under TCGA 1992, s 222(5)(a).
[7] Relief is also available if two or more individuals occupy the house both before or after the death and those two or more individuals are entitled, in aggregate, to 75% or more of the disposal proceeds.

Computation of gain

[19.11] The gain arising on a disposal by personal representatives is measured by comparing the sale proceeds with the value of the asset at death.[1] Where inheritance tax has been paid, the value taken at date of death is the value on which inheritance tax was charged, even where this required a valuation of related property, which would not be brought into account under the normal rules for valuing an asset for capital gains tax.[2] For allowances for the cost of obtaining probate see supra, § **19.06**.

Personal representatives are, in principle, entitled to taper relief. Unless there is a particularly long period of administration, this is not likely to provide a deduction for non-business assets; however, a business asset may well be held for a sufficient period to attract taper relief.

Simon's Taxes C4.106.

---

[1] TCGA 1992, s 62(1)(a).
[2] TCGA 1992, s 274.

Transfer to beneficiaries

[19.12] Where an asset is transferred by personal representatives to a beneficiary, the transfer is treated as giving rise to no chargeable gain.[1] At the subsequent disposal by the beneficiary he is treated as if he had obtained the asset at the date of death of the deceased at the market value at that date, with the appropriate addition for probate expenses.[2]

There are three important effects of this statutory treatment. First, taper relief is applied by reference to the total period from the date of death to the beneficiary's disposal of the asset. Second, the rate of tax on the beneficiary's disposal is not the PRs rate of 34%, but the savings rate of 20% or the higher rate of 40%, according to the circumstances of the beneficiary, alone. Third, each beneficiary has a full, personal annual exempt amount.

Where beneficiaries of an estate are subject to tax at the savings rate of 20% only, it would normally be appropriate for personal representatives to make a declaration that they pass beneficial interest in an asset to one or more beneficiaries in advance of the sale of the asset. Such a sale is then made by the personal representatives acting as bare trustees of the beneficiary. The gain is then subject to tax as a gain made by the beneficiary, taxed at the rate applicable to that particular beneficiary.

Simon's Taxes C2.205.

[1] TCGA 1992, s 62(4)(*a*).
[2] TCGA 1992, s 62(4)(*b*).

20

Settled property

Introduction	PARA **20.01**
Settlor retains an interest	PARA **20.02**
Identifying the settlor	PARA **20.03**
Avoiding the charge on the settlor	PARA **20.04**
Meaning of 'settled property'	PARA **20.05**
Transfer into trust	PARA **20.10**
Disposals during trust period	PARA **20.13**
Deemed disposals	PARA **20.15**
Trust with a vulnerable beneficiary	PARA **20.23**
Non-resident trusts	PARA **20.25**

Introduction

[20.01] A charge to CGT may arise:

(1) on the creation of the settlement;
(2) on gains accruing to trustees during the settlement; and
(3) on the occurrence of certain events which are deemed to be disposals of the trust assets.

In 2 and 3 the general principle is to charge the tax on the trustees, who are treated as a single and continuing body of persons.[1] This is so even if the property is held by different sets of trustees.[2] The charge is not on the trustees where:

(a) the trustee is a bare trustee (infra, § **20.05**);
(b) the settlor has retained an interest in the trust property (infra, § **20.02**);
(c) a trust gain accruing to a non-resident trustee is attributed to a beneficiary (infra, § **35.58**).

The disposal of a beneficial interest in settled property is exempt, thereby avoiding effective double taxation of trust gains. The exemption does not apply if the disposal is by a person who has acquired the interest for a consideration in money or money's worth[3] or if the trustees are not resident in the UK.[4]

Trustees are subject to capital gains tax on gains they make on the disposal of assets. Unless there are any provisions to the contrary, the statutory provisions relating to persons apply to trustees. Trustees are persons and are not individuals; hence, any reliefs, etc, that are expressed to apply to individuals do not apply to trustees unless statute specifically extends the relief to trustees. It is, thus, necessary, for statute to specify the rate of capital gains tax to be paid by trustees and the annual exempt amount to be enjoyed by them. Since 1988, both of these have been different from those that apply for individuals.

[20.01] Settled property

When an asset is put into trust, there is a disposal for capital gains tax purposes. Similarly, when property vests in a beneficiary under the terms of the trust, or when property passes to a beneficiary by the exercise of trustees' discretion, there is capital gains tax disposal by the trustees. Holdover relief may be available on disposals into and out of trust, depending on the nature of the asset and on the type of the trust.

Simon's Taxes C1.401, 402; Sumption CGT A6.01, 11.

[1] TCGA 1992, s 69(1).
[2] TCGA 1992, s 69(3).
[3] TCGA 1992, s 76.
[4] TCGA 1992, s 85(1).

(a) Annual exempt amount for trustees

The basic annual exempt amount[1] for trustees is one-half of the amount available to an individual and so, for 2008–09, is £4,800.

When more than one settlement was made after 6 June 1978 by the same settlor, the annual exempt amount available to each individual trust is the higher of:

(1) the basic annual exempt amount for trustees divided by the number of trusts;
(2) one-tenth of the annual exempt amount available *to an individual*[2]

Where property is held on trust for a mentally disabled person, a person in receipt of an attendance allowance or a person in receipt of a disability allowance,[3] the trustees have available the same annual exempt amount as is available to an individual.[4]

[1] TCGA 1992, Sch 1; TCGA 1992, s 3(3) amended by the Capital Gains Tax (Annual Exempt Amount) Order 2008, SI 2008/708.
[2] TCGA 1992, Sch 1, para 2.
[3] As defined by TCGA 1992, Sch 1, para 1(6).
[4] TCGA 1992, Sch 1, para 1.

(b) Rate of tax for disposals by trustees

	Discretionary Trust, etc	Other trust
1965–66—1987–88	30%	30%
1988–89—1995–96	35%	25%
1996–97	34%	24%
1997–98	34%	23%
1998–99—2003–04	34%	34%

	Discretionary Trust, etc	Other trust
2004-05—2007-08	40%	40%
2008-09	18%	18%

Settlor retains an interest

[20.02] Where the settlor or his spouse retains an interest in the settled property, chargeable gains of the trust are treated as accruing to the settlor and taxed at his marginal rate of income tax.[1] The settlor is entitled to recover from the trustees any CGT paid on trust gains. However, if the trustees have net allowable losses for the year, the benefit of the losses does not pass to the settlor in that year, but they are carried forward for offset against trust gains of the following year.

The settlor retains an interest if the settled property, or income arising to the trustees, may be applied for his benefit or for that of his spouse, or if either of them enjoys any direct or indirect benefit from the property or the income.[2] Thus the settlor has an interest if he is merely a member of a class of discretionary beneficiaries, or if the settled property reverts to him on the happening of certain contingent events. This provision is interpreted strictly. If a trust deed permits the trustees to add a beneficiary and does not specifically exclude a settlor's spouse, then the settlor is treated as having retained an interest in the trust fund and any gain arising to the trustees is assessed on the settlor. Statute[3] excludes the charge on the settlor where the only grounds for such a charge would be that the deed of trust does not exclude a person who the settlor may, at sometime in the future, marry. The charge is also excluded in cases where the settlor can benefit only in the event of the bankruptcy of a beneficiary or on the attempted assignment or mortgaging of trust property by a beneficiary. The settlor is also not treated as having an interest in a marriage settlement if he benefits only after the death of both parties to the marriage and the children of the marriage.[4]

There are provisions excluding trust gains of the year in which the settlor dies, or, if the settlor's spouse has an interest, of the year in which they die or the couple separate.

In respect of income tax and capital gains tax, we now are concerned with three provisions for settlor-interest trusts:

(1) TA 1988, s 660A treats income arising in a settlor-interested trust as if it were the income of the settlor.
(2) TCGA 1992, s 77 treats capital gains on settlement property as if they were capital gains of the settlor.
(3) TCGA 1992, s 169B[5] disapplies gift relief under s 165 or under s 260 where the transfer is to a settlor-interested trust.

All three statutory provisions[6] adopt the same wording for the meaning of "interest in a settlement", viz:

[20.02] Settled property

> An individual is regarded as having an interest in a settlement if . . . any property . . . is, or will, or may become, payable to or applicable for the benefit of the individual or his spouse in any circumstances whatsoever.

A discretionary trust is treated as a settlor-interested trust if there is no default beneficiary (which is usually a charity) and, hence, the death of all the potential beneficiaries would cause the property to revert to the settlor. Exactly the same principle applies to an interest in possession or life interest trust. With such a trust, you ask the question: "Who receives the capital on the death of the life tenant as a consequence of the provisions in the trust?" If there is any possible scenario in which the answer is: "The settlor (or his spouse)", then it is a settlor-interested trust. This could be the case where, for example, father sets up a trust for son James and the trust deed provides that at James' death the capital then goes to James' sister Jill, if she is then living. Clearly, it is possible for Jill to predecease James and the effect would be a failure of beneficiaries with reversion of the property to the settlor.

This must be contrasted with a trust giving James income for life with the capital passing to Jill, absolutely, at James' death. In this case, the capital falls into Jill's estate and passes under Jill's will (or intestacy). It does not revert to father, the settlor.

Should we be concerned if Jill's will leaves property to James' father (or passes to James' father under the rules of intestacy)? In such a case, the capital is not received by father as a consequence of the provisions in the trust; it is received by him as a consequence of the provisions in Jill's will. Hence, the possibility of property being passed to father in such a scenario does not make father's trust a settlor-interested trust. In *Muir v IRC*[7] Pennycuick J said:

> Section 405 is in very wide terms, but it must, I think, be confined to cases where income or property 'will or may become payable to or applicable for the benefit of the settlor' either under the trusts of the settlement itself or under some collateral arrangement having legal force.

It may be necessary to give one caveat to this analysis. If, in our example, Jill knew she was on her death bed and wrote her will deliberately to pass the property back to father, it could be argued that this was the sort of "collateral arrangement" to which Pennycuick J referred and ss 660A, 77 and 169B could then apply.

This treatment does not apply if the settlor dies during the year in which the gain was made, even if the death takes place later than the disposal by the trustees.[8] Where a trust has more than one settlor, the gain arising on the disposal of an asset is imputed to the individual who settled that particular asset, or who settled property from which that asset is derived.[9] This provision can be very difficult to apply in practice, in particular where there is a general investment fund. This difficulty is a powerful argument against allowing a trust to have multiple settlors.

If the settlor has losses that arise on the disposal of assets he has held personally that are in excess of any gains he has made personally, these losses can be set against the trustees' gains that are attributed to him.[10]

Simon's Direct Tax Service C4.206; Sumption CGT A6.02.

[1] TCGA 1992, s 77. The provisions apply to *all* settlements, whenever they were created, unless the settlor and his spouse are both deceased. For an attempt to defeat the rules on non-resident trusts by the use of these provisions, see *de Rothschild v Lawrenson* [1994] STC 8.
[2] TCGA 1992, s 77(3).
[3] TCGA 1992, s 77(3)(*a*). There is an equivalent provision for a future civil partner. This restriction of the charge on the settlor was introduced by FA 1995, Sch 17, para 27. Prior to 1995–96 the failure to exclude a spouse in a deed caused a settlor to be treated as settlor interested, even when the settlor was not married. In *Unmarried Settlor v IRC* [2003] STC (SCD) 274 the settlor was unmarried and a practising homosexual. The Special Commissioner held that there was no need to use this extraneous material to determine whether or not the settlor's spouse can be added as a beneficiary as, under the terms of the trust, anyone in the world could be added as a beneficiary (see para 14 at 278j). The consequence was that a gain of £1,165,000 made in 1991-92 was assessed on Unmarried Settlor and not on the trustees.
[4] TCGA 1992, s 79(4).
[5] FA 2004, Sch 21. See also supra, § **18.44**, footnote 1.
[6] TA 1988, s 660A(2), TCGA 1992, s 77(2) and TCGA 1992, s 169F(1) and (2) inserted by FA 2004, Sch 21, para 4.
[7] (1965) 43 TC 376 at 381.
[8] TCGA 1992, s 77(6).
[9] TCGA 1992, s 79(3).
[10] This treatment is automatic from 6 April 2003: TCGA 1992, s 2(5) & (6) inserted by FA 2002, Sch 11, para 2(2), (3) & (4).

Identifying the settlor

[20.03] A statutory code[1] identifies the person to be treated as settlor. The same code applies for both CGT and income tax purposes.[2] A person is a settlor in relation to a settlement if the settlement was made (or is treated for TCGA purposes as having been made) by that person.[3]

A person is treated for TCGA purposes as having made a settlement if he has made or entered into it, directly or indirectly, or if the settlement arose on his death and any of the settled property is, or is derived from, property of which he was competent to dispose immediately before his death.[4]

A person is treated for TCGA purposes as having made a settlement if he has provided, or has undertaken to provide, property directly or indirectly for the purposes of the settlement,[5] or has provided property under reciprocal arrangements.[6]

[1] TCGA 1992, s 68A inserted by FA 2006, Sch 12, para 1 with effect from 6 April 2006. Prior to 6 April 2006, the definition of "settlor" for CGT differs from that for income tax.
[2] Following the amendments made by FA 2006, Sch 12 para 1, the wording of ITTOIA 2005, s 620 (for income tax) and TCGA 1992, s 68A is identical.

[20.03] Settled property

[3] TCGA 1992, s 68A(1) inserted by FA 2006, Sch 12, para 1.
[4] TCGA 1992, s 68A(2) inserted by FA 2006, Sch 12, para 1.
[5] TCGA 1992, s 68A(3) inserted by FA 2006, Sch 12, para 1.
[6] TCGA 1992, s 68A(4) inserted by FA 2006, Sch 12, para 1.

Avoiding the charge on the settlor

[20.04] Prior to 2000, the charge on the settlor was frequently avoided by the use of a scheme commonly known as "flip flop". This scheme was designed to circumvent the following provisions of TCGA 1992:

(1)   s 77, which attributes the gains of a resident settlement to the settlor if he or his spouse are actual or potential beneficiaries or receive a benefit;
(2)   s 86, which attributes the gains of a non-resident settlement to the settlor if he is resident and domiciled in the UK and he, his children, or his grandchildren (or their respective spouses) are actual or potential beneficiaries or receive a benefit;
(3)   s 87 which attributes the gains of other non-resident settlements to resident and domiciled beneficiaries who receive capital payments.

In essence the scheme involved the following steps:

(1)   in year 1 the trustees borrowed money against the security of the trust assets and advanced it to a new settlement;
(2)   in year 2 the trustees realised gains;
(3)   distributions to the beneficiaries were made from the new settlement.

A flip flop scheme was considered by the House of Lords in *West v Trennery*.[1] The House of Lords, reversing a decision of the Court of Appeal, held that the scheme is not effective as, although the settlor had divested himself of all interest in the first settlement, he is, nevertheless to be regarded as having an interest as the income payable to the settlor derived from the proceeds of the loan.[2] With effect from 21 March 2000, statute[3] deems a disposal of all chargeable assets in the settlement when there is a "transfer of value" in a trust that is within the provisions that charge gains on the settlor.[4]

In order for this deemed disposal to take place, there must be a "transfer of value" which is linked with trustee borrowing.[5] Trustees are treated as making a transfer of value in any of the following circumstances:[6]

(1)   trustees transfer an asset to any person gratuitously or at an undervalue;
(2)   trustees lend money or any other asset to a person;
(3)   trustees issue a security gratuitously or at an undervalue to another person.

"Transfer of value" includes any transfer or loan to another settlement whether of cash or in specie and also includes any distribution or loan to a beneficiary or any loan to an underlying company.

The charge does not arise where the trustees borrow for "normal trust purposes".[7] This includes the acquisition or enhancement of ordinary trust assets or current expenditure incurred by the trustees in administering the settlement or the settled property. The term "ordinary trust assets" means:[8]

(a) shares or securities;
(b) tangible property, whether moveable or immovable;
(c) property used for business purposes by the trustees or any life tenant;
(d) rights or interests over tangible or business property.

To qualify as expenditure on ordinary trust assets, the asset must be held by the trustees immediately after the material time (ie immediately after the transfer of value). There are provisions[9] to deal with sale and reinvestment and where the asset is destroyed or becomes of negligible value.

If the conditions for the application of Sch 4B are met, a deemed disposal takes place at the material time, ie the time of the transfer of value.[10] The deemed disposal is of all the chargeable assets which are in the settlement immediately after the material time. Either there is a complete disposal of all those assets, or each asset suffers a proportionate disposal.

---

[1] [2005] STC 214, HL, reversing the decision of the Court of Appeal [2004] STC 170 and that of the Special Commissioners, sub-nom *Tee v Inspector of Taxes* [2002] STC (SCD) 370.
[2] Per Lord Walker, para 16 at 218f.
[3] TCGA 1992, Sch 4B, para 10(1) inserted by FA 2000, Sch 25 with effect from 21 March 2000. Also see Tax Bulletin August 2003, pp 1048–1051 for a commentary by the Revenue on Schedules 4A and 4B.
[4] TCGA 1992, ss 77, 86 and 87.
[5] TCGA 1992, Sch 4B, para 1(1)(*b*).
[6] TCGA 1992, Sch 4B, para 2.
[7] TCGA 1992, Sch 4B, para 6.
[8] TCGA 1992, Sch 4B, para 7.
[9] TCGA 1992, Sch 4B, para 8.
[10] TCGA 1992, Sch 4B, para 10(1).

Meaning of 'settled property'

[20.05] Property is declared to be settled if it is held in trust and it is not a bare trust, supra, § **19.06**.[1] Property being administered as part of deceased's estate is not settled property,[2] nor is property vested in a trustee in bankruptcy.[3] Since various events cause a deemed disposal of the settled property it is important to know exactly what property is subject to the settlement concerned.[4] Three situations must be considered. First, where trustees exercise a power to subject property to further trusts, it is a question of fact whether the particular new trusts are part of the main settlement or a new one. This is to be decided by invoking practical common sense in the light of established legal doctrine. In a case where a part of the main fund was held by separate trustees on separate trusts, it was held that the property remained subject to one settlement.[5] This had two consequences: (a) there was no deemed disposal just because the power to create new trusts was exercised, and

[20.05] Settled property

(b) less attractively, as the trustees were one continuing body, disposal by the trustees of one part of the fund gave rise to a liability in tax which could be collected from the trustees of the other part.[6] In another case, it was held that property remained part of the first settlement even though appointed on exhaustive trusts because the power under which the appointment was made did not authorise the trustees to remove the property from the trusts altogether.[7] As Slade LJ said, it would be surprising if the CGT rules were different from the general legal rules applying to trusts.[8]

Second, the question may arise whether a single disposition creates two or more settlements. The creation of distinct but undivided shares in one asset gives rise to one settlement even though the shares are held on different trusts.[9] However, a different answer may be reached if there are distinct assets as well as different trusts; this will be especially the case where more than one settlor is involved.

Third, where property is added to an existing settlement, the presumption is that no new settlement is created although special factors such as distinct trustees or an independent trust instrument may lead to a different conclusion.

If there is one settlement and the property is in the hands of different trustees, they are treated as a single body of trustees.[10] An example would be where a part of the land held under the Settled Land Act has been sold so that the proceeds of the sale will be in the hands of the trustees while the remaining land will be in the hands of the tenant for life.

Simon's Taxes C4.206; Sumption CGT A6.02.

---

[1] TCGA 1992, s 68 amended by FA 2006, Sch 12, para 1(1) subject also s 99(1) (s 93) (unit trusts).
[2] Supra, § **18.03**.
[3] TCGA 1992, s 66.
[4] It is also important for other reasons, eg the annual exemption, the residence of trustees and whether trustees of one fund are liable for tax arising as a gain arising from another part.
[5] *Roome v Edwards* [1981] STC 96, [1981] 1 All ER 736; See also *Ewart v Taylor* [1983] STC 721.
[6] The solution seems to be either to ensure that the appointed fund is truly separate and to pay the tax resulting from the deemed disposal of the assets appointed—or to retain control of the subsidiary part by having joint trustees. See also statement of practice SP 7/84 superseding SP 9/81.
[7] *Bond v Pickford* [1983] STC 517.
[8] *Bond v Pickford* [1983] STC 517 at 527.
[9] *Crowe v Appleby* [1976] STC 301, [1976] 2 All ER 914.
[10] TCGA 1992, s 69(3).

Bare trust not settled property

[20.06] Where assets are held by a trustee for another person who is absolutely entitled as against the trustee, or for two or more persons who are so entitled, the property is not settled and the acts of the trustee are treated as the acts of the beneficiary and disposals between them are disregarded.[1] All gains and losses and consequent liability concern the beneficiary and not the trustee.

The beneficiary is absolutely entitled if he has the exclusive right, subject only to satisfying any outstanding charge, lien or other right[2] to direct how an asset shall be dealt with. Other outgoings are construed eiusdem generis with rates and taxes and so do not include an annuity.[3] This definition sits oddly with the trust doctrine that a beneficiary who is absolutely entitled has the right to end the trust but no power to direct the trustee how his discretion shall be exercised.

It appears that a right to call for the conveyance of the trust asset to the beneficiary meets this test even though the beneficiary cannot control the trustee in other ways. If the test is whether the beneficiary can call upon the trustees for the transfer of the trust property, the answer may well turn on the nature of the trust property. Thus, a co-owner of land has no right to call for the land itself because of the trust for sale. Similar problems arise with certain shares in a private company and to mortgage debts.[4] However, it appears likely that such technical points will not be accepted by the courts and that therefore such property is not settled.[5]

Simon's Taxes C4.206; Sumption CGT A6.02, 07.

---

[1] TCGA 1992, s 60(1). The same also applies to Lloyd's Underwriters: TCGA 1992, s 206. So if A transfers property to T to hold on trust for A absolutely there is no chargeable disposal.

[2] These words refer to some personal right of indemnity and are not apt to cover another beneficial interest arising under the same instrument: per Walton J in *Stephenson v Barclays Bank Trust Co Ltd* [1975] 1 All ER 625 at 636. Charges are included in this list because of the estate and powers of the mortgagee to direct how that asset shall be dealt with: TCGA 1992, s 60(2) and per Goff J in *Crowe v Appleby* [1975] STC 502 at 510.

[3] *Stephenson v Barclays Bank Trust Co Ltd* (supra) (the property ceased to be settled property when specific assets were appropriated to satisfy the annuity, that appropriation causing a deemed disposal under TCGA 1992 s 71).

[4] See comments of Walton J in *Stephenson v Barclays Bank Trust Co Ltd* [1975] STC 151 at 163 who said that one of several co-owners would, in these circumstances, have to wait until the property was sold before being entitled to call for the transfer of his or her share. In relation to shares note the special circumstances in *Booth v Ellard* [1980] STC 555, [1980] 3 All ER 569.

[5] See *Jenkins v Brown* [1989] STC 577, where land comprised in a pool held by trustees was conveyed to beneficiaries according to their interests prior to the trust being created.

[20.07] There is a bare trust not only where the person is absolutely entitled as against the trustee, but also where he would be so entitled but for being an infant or other person under a disability. However, this must be the only reason for his not being absolutely entitled. Where property was held "for such of the beneficiaries as shall attain the age of 21 years or marry under that age" (21

[20.07] Settled property

was then the age of majority), the beneficiary, even if he had not been an infant, would not have been absolutely entitled, since his interest was contingent upon attaining his majority (or marrying before that time).[1]

A further reason was that the interests of the beneficiaries might be defeasible pro tanto if other children were born so that it could not be said that these infants had "vested indefeasible interests in possession". The result was that a gain realised by the trustees during the administration[2] was a disposal by the trustees and so chargeable at 30% and could not be attributed to the beneficiaries, in which case the rate would have been nil.

Sumption CGT A6.03.

---

[1] *Tomlinson v Glyn's Executor and Trustee Co* [1970] 1 All ER 381, 45 TC 600. What would have happened if the beneficiary had married and so satisfied the condition precedent while still an infant? Semble that there is a disposal under TCGA 1992, s 71; supra, § **19.10**.
[2] Supra, § **19.08**.

Distinction between settled property and a bare trust

[20.08] The dividing line between CGT being charged on trustees by virtue of property being settled property and CGT being charged on individuals by virtue of the trustees being mere nominees was considered by the court in *Booth v Ellard*.[1] In that case, 12 members of the same family held 72% of the issued share capital of their family company. In 1972 they entered into a written agreement which was expressed to last for 15 years only and which could be brought to an end after ten years by any nine of the family members deciding to terminate the agreement. Under the agreement, the shares held by the 12 individuals were transferred to trustees who were given elaborate instructions as to the way they should exercise their voting rights, deal with bonus and rights issues as well as a pre-emption right being given to the individuals on any disposal by the trustees.

Goulding J held that the shares had not become settled property under the agreement and, instead, fell to be treated as the property of the 12 family members as co-owners. Goulding J held that property held for "a plurality of beneficial owners" is to be treated as nominee property under the terms of (now TCGA 1992, s 60) if two conditions are fulfilled:

(1) the interests of the beneficial owners are concurrent and not successive. This is in contrast to, for example, interest of a life tenant on the one hand and a remainderman on the other;
(2) the interests of co-owners are the same.[2]

The right given to the trustees to deal with the shares did not prevent the arrangement being a bare trust.

---

[1] [1980] STC 555.
[2] [1980] STC 555 at 572.

Co-owners

[20.09] The decision in *Booth v Ellard*[1] was followed in *Jenkins v Brown*.[2] In that case, members of a family had put into a trust various pieces of land. The purpose was to maintain the continuity of the family farming unit. The beneficial interests were expressed as a percentage of the value of the property as a whole, calculated by reference to the values of what was originally put in. One member of the family withdrew the same piece of land that he had put in. The Crown claimed that this was a disposal by trustees and chargeable to capital gains tax.

Knox J held there was no disposal and it was incorrect to treat it as each of the family members having disposed of their interests in that piece of land. The approach adopted by the court was to look at the interests in the mass and not at the individual case. It follows that there would still have been no disposal if the piece of land removed from the co-ownership had been different from that piece put in by that individual, as long as the value of the interest was in the same proportion.

The Revenue Staff Manual instructs inspectors:

> The documentation is to be carefully considered before it is accepted that the decision in *Warrington v Brown* (an alternative for *Jenkins v Brown*) applies.[3]

An unincorporated association is not able to hold land in its own name except, perhaps, where it has been created by statute. Instead, the land is held by trustees on behalf of the unincorporated association. The trustees are then bare trustees for the unincorporated association which is liable to corporation tax on any capital gain arising on the disposal of land.[4]

---

[1] [1980] STC 555.
[2] [1989] STC 577.
[3] Revenue Internal Guidance, Capital Gains Manual, CG 34411.
[4] *Worthing Rugby Football Club Trustees v IRC* [1985] STC 186.

Transfer into trust

[20.10] A transfer into settlement whether revocable or irrevocable is a disposal of the entire property thereby becoming settled property.[1] The provision directs that the disposal shall be total and not partial even though the settlor has some interest under the settlement. (The trust cannot set any of the settlor's losses against trust gains; or vice versa.) This rule is quite different from that for inheritance tax.

The rule applies even where there is consideration.[2] There is, however, a disposal only of the property settled. If, therefore, the settlor has a piece of property but settles only a part of that property there will be a part disposal of the property. If S declares himself trustee of shares for A for life, but does not expressly grant a remainder, the question whether there is a settlement of the shares or of a life interest in the shares must be answered by studying the wording and intention of the settlement.[3]

[20.10] Settled property

The provision probably is superfluous to the extent that it states that there is to be a total disposal even though the settlor is a trustee or the sole trustee of the settlement, since, if this is the only link remaining between settlor and the property settled, it would appear that there has in fact been a total disposal.

Any gain or loss on the disposal is computed by taking the consideration to be the market value of the assets concerned, since the gift is a transaction other than by way of a bargain at arm's length. Since the settlor is connected with the trustees, any allowable loss arising on the gift into settlement will be capable of offset only against chargeable gains arising on subsequent disposals to the trustees.

If the transfer is not a potentially exempt transfer, or if the assets transferred are defined business assets, the settlor may elect that any gain accruing on the transfer should be held over provided that the settlor and the trustees are resident in the UK; the consent of the trustees is not required.[4]

For holdover relief on transfer into trust, see supra, § 18.44.

Simon's Taxes C4.206.

---

[1] TCGA 1992, s 70.
[2] TCGA 1992, s 70.
[3] *Berry v Warnett* [1982] STC 396 (a decision concerned with the earlier formulation of s 70 which spoke of a gift in settlement and where the settlor argued that he had settled the remainder but not the life interest).
[4] TCGA 1992, s 260.

Transfer by trustees within one trust or between two?

[20.11] It is possible for trustees to act so that assets held within a trust are treated as relating to separate funds within that trust. It is also possible for trustees to act so that property held in one trust is thereafter held in two separate trusts. The distinction between the two situations is important for the following reasons:

(1) The annual exempt amount is given to the trustees of a settlement. If one individual is trustee of several settlements then each has its own annual exempt amount.
(2) Losses of one settlement cannot be set against the gains of another.
(3) The charge to capital gains tax arises on the trustees of the settlement, not on the trustees of separate funds within a settlement, even where the trustees have allowed control of assets to pass to "fund holders"
(4) If assets are moved from one fund to another within the settlement, there is no disposal. However, if assets are transferred from one settlement to another, the transfer constitutes a disposal for CGT purposes.

(5) The provision charging a gain on the settlor applies if the settlor or the settlor's spouse can or does benefit from any asset held in the trust. The charge does not apply where the asset from which the benefit arises has been passed out of the trust in question into a separate trust, in which the settlor has not retained an interest.

(6) For the purpose of valuing unquoted shares, the blocks of shares held by trustees of separate settlements are valued separately.

The Revenue Staff Manual instructs Revenue officers:

> In general you should assume that a single deed or will gives rise to a single settlement, even though there may be several distinct trusts. If it is suggested that there is more than one settlement, you should obtain a copy of the instrument and ask the trustees why they think there is more than one settlement . . . You should start by looking at the position at the date of the settlement . . . You should resist any attempt by the trustees to start by analysing the position at the present time.[1]

In *Roome v Edwards*,[2] the House of Lords overturned the finding of the Court of Appeal and held that the actions by the trustees fell short of creating two settlements out of a single settlement.

In that case, a settlement was created in 1944. Eleven years later, in exercise of the power in the original deed, a distinct fund was separated from the other funds held on trust and thereafter held on trusts which were distinct from the trusts of the main fund. At the same time, the life tenant surrendered her life interest in respect of the designated fund. The case concerned a capital gain arising in 1972–73 by which time the separate fund had trustees who were resident in the UK, whereas the trustees for the main fund were resident outside the UK.

In the judgment of Lord Wilberforce,[3] the critical distinction between a single trust and two trusts was stated to lie on the question whether the trusts of the 1955 fund were exhaustive of the beneficial interests. The distinction is, thus, between "a special power of appointment" on one hand and "a power to appoint, appropriate and to settle" on the other.

In *Ewart v Taylor*,[4] this principle was applied to identify a separate trust arising from a particular exercise of a power of appointment. In *Bond v Pickford*,[5] the Court of Appeal considered a trust deed which contained a power given to the trustees to "allocate" assets to a beneficiary and also a power to "settle" funds for the benefit of the beneficiary. The Court of Appeal held that the action of the trustees in question in that case was under the power given to those trustees to "allocate". The Court, thus, held that there was no disposal for CGT purposes. In the judgment of Slade LJ, the distinction was made between "powers in the wider form", the exercise of which would have created a separate settlement and "powers in the narrower form", the exercise of which did not have such an effect.[6]

Simon's Taxes C4.206.

---

[1] Revenue Internal Guidance, Capital Gains Manual, CG 33296, 33301.
[2] [1981] STC 96.
[3] [1981] STC 96 at 100.

[20.11] Settled property

[4] [1983] STC 721.
[5] [1983] STC 517.
[6] [1983] STC 517 at 527.

Transfer to another settlement

[20.12] The property will cease to be settled if it ceases to be subject to the settlement even though it may become subject to another trust. This is because it is necessary only for the person to be entitled absolutely as against the trustee; he need not be entitled beneficially. For example, property may be settled on A for life with remainder to B, and B predeceases A leaving his residuary estate to X and Y on various trusts. If A then releases his life interest, there will be a deemed disposal since X and Y are entitled as against the trustees of the settlement to call for the property. Clearly, the property will not be the subject of a deemed disposal if it remains in the same settlement.[1]

When a trust is varied under the Variation of Trusts Act the variation itself is probably not a disposal but if the terms of the variation provide for any actual or deemed disposal, then there will be such a disposal.[2] Since the better view is that it is the order of the court rather than the arrangement which occasions the variation, the date of the disposal is that of the order.[3] Where some of the beneficiaries are sui juris and the court's consent is sought on behalf of those not sui juris the agreement among the former group is presumably in the nature of a conditional contract, the condition being satisfied by the court order. Where the property reverts to the settlor on the death of a life tenant the disposal and reacquisition takes place not at the value on the death but at the trustee's adjusted base cost.[4]

Simon's Taxes C4.206.

[1] *Roome v Edwards* [1981] STC 96. See Statement of practice SP 7/84. In *Swires v Renton* [1991] STC 490 there was evidence of the trustees' intentions to graft new trusts on to the existing settlement, and thus there was no deemed disposal.
[2] But note TCGA 1992, s 76(2) and *Hoare Trustees v Gardner* [1978] STC 89.
[3] See Lord Reid and Lord Wilberforce in *IRC v Holmden* [1968] AC 685 at 701, 702, 710, 713.
[4] TCGA 1992, s 73(1)(b).

Disposals during trust period

[20.13] Gains or losses will accrue to the trustees when the trustees sell trust investments to buy new ones. The trustees are chargeable on their chargeable gains less allowable losses for the year of assessment in the same way as individuals. The annual exempt amount for 2004–05 is £4,100; £8,200 if the trust is for the benefit of one or more disabled individuals.[1] In cases where the settlor retains an interest in the settled property, the net chargeable gains are his, and not those of the trustees.

A problem not cleared up in the legislation is that of the incidence of the tax as between the beneficiaries. Where the property disposed of forms part of the capital of the trust, any CGT accruing will fall on the capital. If however the trust document or some right were to provide that all the produce of a particular source, even a capital gain, was to be paid to a life tenant it would seem that the tax should fall on the capital enjoyed by that life tenant rather than on the general capital.

For rate of tax, see supra, § **20.03**.

Simon's Taxes C1.206, 402.

---

[1] TCGA 1992, s 3 and Sch 1 as amended by Capital Gains Tax (Annual Exempt Amount) Order 2004 SI 2004/774 *Simon's Weekly Tax Intelligence* 2004, p 944.

CGT exemptions available to trustees

[20.14] An exemption may be claimed by trustees if the dwelling house is owned by them and has been the main private residence of one entitled to occupy it under the terms of the trust, or who is allowed by the trustees to occupy it and would be entitled to the income from the house or from the proceeds of sale.[1] When trustees of a discretionary trust in exercise of their discretion allow a beneficiary of the trust to occupy the house, the beneficiary is entitled to occupy the house under the terms of the trust since he has a right to remain in occupation until asked to leave by the trustees.[2]

By concession the relief applies also to property held by personal representatives but occupied both before and after the death by an individual entitled to an absolute or a limited interest in the proceeds of sale.[3]

Relief is available to trustees on the same basis as for individuals as long as one of two alternative conditions is fulfilled:

(1) the property sold and the property acquired is subject to one or more interests in possession and at least one of the persons is holding the interests in possession is an individual or a charity; or
(2) there is no interest in possession over either the property of which the disposal is made or over the property acquired, but all the interests over that property are held by individuals or a charity.[4]

Simon's Taxes C1.402.

---

[1] TCGA 1992, s 225.
[2] *Sansom v Peay* [1976] STC 494.
[3] Extra-statutory concession D5.
[4] TCGA 1992, Sch 5B, para 17(2), (8).

[20.15] Settled property

Deemed disposals

[20.15] In addition to the actual disposals that arise in the course of the administration of the trust, there are deemed disposals on two principal occasions[1] although only one will give rise to a chargeable gain. These are:

(1) the vesting of trust property in a beneficiary (infra, § **20.16**);
(2) the termination of a life interest in trust property (infra, § **20.18**).

A claim for holdover relief[2] is accepted by the Revenue on deemed disposals where a gain would arise, although strictly it is uncertain that a holdover election is competent.

Sumption CGT A6.07, 08.

---

[1] There is also a deemed disposal where property subject to charitable trusts ceases to be so: TCGA 1992, s 256(2).
[2] TCGA 1992, ss 165, 260: see supra, § **18.41**.

Vesting of trust property in beneficiary

[20.16] When a person becomes absolutely entitled to any settled property as against the trustee, whether because the trust itself ends or the property leaves the settlement through the exercise of a power of advancement, the trustees are deemed to dispose at their market value of all the assets forming part of the settled property to which the beneficiary becomes entitled and immediately to re-acquire them at the same value.[1] The deemed disposal in effect ends the capital gains regime of the trust and commences that of the recipient under a bare trust, even though the assets themselves remain with the trustees. It follows that any gains or losses arising on the deemed disposal will be those of the trust whilst any later gains or losses arising on the assets concerned will be those of the beneficiary. The deemed disposal occurs also if the person would be absolutely entitled as against the trustee but for being an infant or other person under disability.[2]

A trust deed commonly provides that beneficiaries acquire their interest in the trust capital on attaining a specified age. The CGT consequence of this provision varies according to the nature of the asset in trust and whether the class of beneficiaries is closed. Where the division of the asset is known (ie it is to be divided amongst a class of beneficiaries that cannot admit further members) and the asset is an asset that is readily divisible, such as a shareholding, there is a disposal by the trustees as each child attains the specified age, as the child then "becomes absolutely entitled against the trustee".[3] However, this treatment is not applied in the case of a part interest in land (nor in the case of mortgage debts) unless there is a deliberate act by the trustees to advance the property to the beneficiary on the occasion of the beneficiary's birthday. This follows from *Stephenson v Barclays Bank Trust Co Ltd*,[4] where Walton J said:[5]

> When the situation is that a single person who is sui juris has an absolutely vested beneficial interest in a share of the trust fund, his rights are not, I think, quite as

extensive as those of the beneficial interest holders as a body. In general, he is entitled to have transferred to him (subject, of course, always to the same rights of the trustees as I have already mentioned above) an aliquot share of each and every asset of the trust fund which presents no difficulty so far as division is concerned. This will apply to such items as cash, money at the bank or an unsecured loan, stock exchange securities and the like. However, as regards land, certainly, in all cases, as regards shares in a private company in very special circumstances (see *Re Weiner's Will Trusts*) and possibly (although the logic of the addition in fact escapes me) mortgage debts (see *Re Marshall* per Cozens-Hardy MR) the situation is not so simple, and even a person with a vested interest in possession in an aliquot share of the trust fund may have to wait until the land is sold, and so forth, before being able to call on the trustees as of right to account to him for his share of the assets.

In *Crowe v Appleby*,[6] Goff J quoted from the judgement in *Stephenson v Barclays Bank* and ruled that beneficiaries on attaining the specified age in the trust he was considering had not become "absolutely entitled" to property consisting of land in that trust. Hence, there was no capital gain arising on the trustees until the trustees advanced the land or sold the land. The decision of Goff J was subsequently approved by the Court of Appeal.[7]

A trust deed may state that property is to vest in the children of the settlor on the attainment of a specified age by the last child to be born to the settlor. Where the asset is not land nor a mortgage, the effect of such a provision is that there is a CGT disposal when the last child reaches the specified age. For the purpose of the CGT deemed disposal, the test is applied on the assumption that a person is capable of having a child so long as that person is alive. This rule is laid down in *Figg v Clarke*.[8] That case concerned the following facts. In 1963, shares in Liberty & Co had been put into trust. The deed of trust stated that the trust property shall be vested in children of Mr Stewart-Liberty who attained the age of 21. Mr Stewart-Liberty had four children, the last attained the age of 21 in 1977 and Mr Stewart-Liberty died in July 1990. Inland Revenue raised a CGT assessment for 1990–91 in the sum of £1,450,000, being the gain calculated on the vesting of the Liberty & Co shares occasioned by the death of Mr Stewart-Liberty, this being the date on which it could be objectively determined that no further children could be born to Mr Stewart-Liberty and, hence, it was ascertained that each child had an interest of one quarter of the trust property. The trustees appealed on the basis that the capital gains tax charge arose on a deemed disposal in January 1977, being the date on which the last child attained the age of 21, it being impossible for Mr Stewart-Liberty to have any further children as on 17 November 1964 he had suffered an accident as a result of which he was paralysed from the chest down.

The court held that the correct approach for the determination of the date on which a CGT disposal arises is to deem an individual capable of having a child to the end of his or her life. Thus, even though a court has the ability to order that assets be passed to beneficiaries on the basis of evidence of the impossibility of there being any future members of the class of beneficiaries, that is the exercise of the administrative jurisdiction of a court and is not relevant in determining the date of vesting for CGT purposes.

Of course, if the beneficiaries go to court and seek the administrative jurisdiction of the court and obtain an order for distribution there will be a deemed disposal thanks to the order.

[20.16] Settled property

Where the property ceases to be settled on the death of the life tenant there is a deemed disposal but no chargeable gain or allowable loss.[9] However, where a chargeable gain was held over when the settlement was created, the death of the life tenant crystallises a gain which is the lower of:

(1) the gain computed by applying the normal rules, and
(2) the gain that was held over.[10]

The gain can only be crystallised in respect of assets that continue to be held at the date of death. This gain may itself be held over,[11] since there is also a transfer of value subject to IHT. However, if an asset passes to the surviving spouse of the deceased beneficiary (or the surviving spouse becomes the life tenant), the exemption from IHT has the effect that a holdover election is denied. The gain is, then, chargeable, unless the asset is within the categories specified by TCGA 1992, s 165.

Where the life interest extends to only a part of the property, a chargeable gain or allowable loss will arise in respect of the part not represented by the deceased's interest.

The disposal is of those assets to which the person becomes entitled. Where a beneficiary assigned his interest to X who became entitled to a holding in a company but who was then obliged to sell a similar holding to the beneficiary, it was held that the beneficiary became entitled to the shares received from X.[12]

If the trustees and the recipient so elect the gain otherwise accruing may in limited circumstances be held over—provided the recipient is resident in the UK.[13]

Sumption CGT A6.07.

---

[1] TCGA 1992, s 71; on deductible expenditure note s 64(1) (s 47(1)). On hysterectomy and castration as events causing the disposal see [1968] BTR 56 (J.G.M.).
[2] TCGA 1992, s 71(3).
[3] TCGA 1992, s 71(1). The beneficiary is "absolutely entitled" against the trustee, even if the asset is subject to a charge in respect of the payment of "duty, taxes, costs or other outgoings": TCGA 1992, s 60(2).
[4] [1975] STC 151.
[5] At 163g/164a.
[6] [1975] STC 502 at 510c-d.
[7] [1976] STC 301, CA.
[8] [1997] STC 247. The rule applies to a woman in the same way as to a man. In his judgment, Blackburne J quoted, with approval, court decisions where a class of beneficiaries was held not to be closed on the grounds that a women aged 78 could give birth to a further child (*Re Pettifor's Will Trusts, Roberts v Roberts* [1961] Ch 257). The rule was justified by Blackburne J: "it protects the trustees from the possibility . . . of liability or complaint for continuing to manage funds after the class in question has closed . . . to apply TCGA 1992, s 71(1) in such a way as to require an investigation as to the precise date on which a person ceases to be capable of producing children places both the Revenue and taxpayers in the position of having to carry out a virtually impossible task": at 262e.
[9] TCGA 1992, s 73.
[10] TCGA 1992, s 74.

[11] TCGA 1992, s 260.
[12] *Chinn v Collins* [1981] STC 1, [1981] 1 All ER 189.
[13] Supra, § **18.21**. But where the disponee is another trust, a charge will arise if the disponee-trust later becomes non-resident; there is no six-year limit to such a charge.

Losses transferred to beneficiary

[20.17] When a person becomes absolutely entitled to settled property that has formerly been held by trustees, any allowable loss which has accrued to the trustees in respect of that property, or is represented by the property to which the person has become entitled, is transferred to the beneficiary, in so far as it has not been used by the trustee against gains accruing to the trustee.[1]

In addition, expenditure incurred by the trustees in transferring assets to a beneficiary who has become entitled to those assets is treated as expenditure by the beneficiary and can be put against the consideration received on the subsequent disposal of the asset by that beneficiary.[2]

The transfer of losses from the trustees to a beneficiary is mandatory. This can have the effect that the losses are then not used, even though the trustees subsequently make gains against which they could have put the losses had they remained with them.

Where cash is distributed to a beneficiary, it is considered that a loss transfers to the beneficiary from the trustees only where the cash represents the proceeds of the sale of an asset sold at a loss. Where cash comes out of a general pool and is transferred to the beneficiary by an appointment of a specific cash sum, it is considered that no loss is thereby transferred to the beneficiary, even though the trustees may have accumulated losses in that pool. In such an instance, the losses remain and are used against trustees' subsequent gains, with any excess of losses being apportioned to the beneficiaries who become entitled to the fund at the end of the trust period.

The apportionment of losses amongst beneficiaries is not addressed by statute. This causes frequent difficulty in practice, particularly with discretionary trusts where capital is appointed to different beneficiaries on different dates, such as by siblings attaining a specified age. The Revenue Staff Manual instructs Revenue officers:[3]

> Unless specific losses relate to particular funds, they should be allocated on a broad basis according to the share of the capital going to the beneficiary . . . In general, any reasonable basis of apportionment adopted by the trustees should be accepted.

Anti-avoidance rules apply.[4] Where a beneficiary becomes absolutely entitled as against the trustee any loss must first be set off against any "pre-entitlement gains" accruing to the trustee.[5] Pre-entitlement gains are those arising to the trustee on the deemed disposal itself or at any time earlier during the same year of assessment.[6] If the loss cannot be used by the trustee in this way it is transferred to the beneficiary but subject to the very substantial restriction that it can only be set off against a gain arising on the disposal of the same asset. To avoid some problems the loss may be set off against gains arising from an asset derived from that very asset, but this only applies where the asset is land.[7]

[20.17] Settled property

There are rules prescribing when the beneficiary may roll the loss forward.[8] In order to counter an avoidance device, no losses are available to a beneficiary where the transferor of the asset, or a person connected with him, has purchased an interest in the settlement.[9]

Simon's Taxes C4.220.

---

[1] TCGA 1992, s 71(2).
[2] TCGA 1992, s 64(1)(*b*).
[3] Revenue Internal Guidance, Capital Gains Manual, CG 37205.
[4] TCGA 1992, s 71(2I).
[5] TCGA 1992, s 71(2D)(*a*).
[6] TCGA 1992, s 71(2A).
[7] TCGA 1992, s 71(2)(*b*)(ii); the rules are elaborated in sub-s (2B).
[8] TCGA 1992, s 71(2D)(*c*).
[9] TCGA 1992, s 79A.

Termination of a life interest

[20.18] There is a deemed disposal and reacquisition by the trustees when a life interest in possession terminates on the death of the person beneficially entitled to the interest.[1] This deemed disposal will relate to property remaining subject to the settlement; property leaving the settlement will be deemed to be disposed of under the rules already set out, supra, § **20.10**. If, for example, property is settled on A for life or until marriage, with remainder to B for life with remainder to C absolutely, then on A's death there will be a deemed disposal of the settled property at market value. However, consistent with general principles, no chargeable gain or allowable loss arises,[2] except where a chargeable gain was held over on the disposal of the assets to the trustees. Since 5 April 1982 there has been no deemed disposal when the life interest terminates otherwise than on the death of the life tenant; thus the trustees' acquisition cost is unchanged.

The provisions relating to the death of a person having a life interest in possession are extended to other interests in possession not constituting a life interest, eg an interest which terminates on the beneficiary's attaining a specified age.[3] The concession must be claimed and must be applied to all of the assets in which the individual had an interest in possession, except where computations were settled before 17 February 1993 or are subject to a charge under TCGA 1992, ss 67 or 74.[4]

Simon's Taxes C4.210; Sumption CGT A6.01, 08.

---

[1] TCGA 1992, s 72(1)(*a*).
[2] TCGA 1992, s 72(1)(*b*).
[3] TCGA 1992, ss 72 & 73 amended by FA 1996, Sch 29, para 5.
[4] *Simon's Weekly Tax Intelligence* 1996, p 56.

Life interest in possession

[20.19] Life interest as such is not defined so that it must be taken to bear its usual meaning applied in conveyancing law and the distinctions between a lease and a life estate must be observed. However, statute declares that life interest is to include a right under the settlement to the income of, or to the use or occupation of, settled property for the life of a person other than the person entitled to the right so that a life interest pur autre vie is included.[1] The term also includes a right to income under the settlement for lives. A lease for lives does not fall within the provision since settled property is defined as any property held in trust and lease for lives does not operate behind a trust.[2]

There is excluded from the definition of a life interest any right which is contingent on the exercise of the discretion of the trustee or the discretion of some other person.[3] In view of the further requirement that the life interest be in possession, and of the principle that the objects of a discretionary trust do not have any interest in the trust property,[4] this provision may appear superfluous.

An interest in possession is not further defined. Generally, an interest is in possession if it gives an immediate entitlement to the income as it arises. A duty or power to withhold the income negatives possession. Thus, a power to accumulate the income negatives possession save where the accumulation is for the person with the interest.

A power to revoke the entitlement or to appoint another does not affect the immediate entitlement to the income. Until the power is exercised the income belongs to the beneficiary.[5]

Sumption CGT A6.08.

---

[1] TCGA 1992, s 72(3).
[2] LPA 1925, s 149.
[3] TCGA 1992, s 72(3).
[4] *Gartside v IRC* [1968] AC 553, [1968] 1 All ER 121.
[5] Can trustees make a binding decision to appoint income to someone before it has arisen?

Life interest in part of settled property

[20.20] There is a deemed disposal on the death of the life tenant whether the life interest in possession is all or any part of settled property. Where his interest relates only to a part of the property, there is a deemed disposal only of a corresponding part of the property. On the termination of a life interest on an occasion other than death of the life tenant there is now no disposal under these rules.

A life interest which is a right to a part of the income of settled property is treated as an interest in a corresponding part of the property.[1] Thus if property is held on trust for A and B for their lives with remainders over, A's death will cause a deemed disposal of one-half of each of the assets forming part of the settled property. If, however, two settlements had been created the one with life interest to A, the other with life interest to B, there would have been a deemed disposal of all the assets forming part of A's settlement.

If there is a life interest in income from a part of the settled property and no right of recourse to, or to the income of, the remainder of the settled property, that part is treated as a separate settlement. A part in this context means a fraction and not necessarily a separated piece so that four one-quarter shares of the income for life[2] create four separate settlements, hence the termination of one share causes a deemed disposal of that quarter share only and not of the whole settled property.[3]

Normally an annuity is not treated as a life interest notwithstanding that it is payable out of or charged on settled property or the income of settled property.[4] However, it will be so treated if it is created by the settlement *and* some or all of the settled property is appropriated by the trustees as the exclusive fund out of which the annuity is payable.[5] The fund so appropriated is treated as a separate settlement.

Sumption CGT A6.03.

---

[1] TCGA 1992, s 72; see *Pexton v Bell* [1976] STC 301, [1976] 2 All ER 914, noted [1976] BTR 257 (Milne).
[2] Assuming they are not *joint* tenants, yet the wording of s 72(4) stresses that there must be no right of recourse to the income. What of the future right of recourse by virtue of survivorship?
[3] *Pexton v Bell supra*; *Allison v Murray* [1975] STC 524, [1975] 3 All ER 561, hence the termination of one share causes a deemed disposal of that quarter share only and not of the whole settled property.
[4] TCGA 1992, s 72(3).
[5] TCGA 1992, s 72(4).

Disposal of a beneficial interest

[20.21] The interest the beneficiary has in a settlement is an asset for the purposes of capital gains tax. Hence, if a life tenant, for example, sells or gives away his right to receive income, he has made a disposal of an asset, under general principles. Similarly, if the remainderman gives, settles or sells his right to receive capital at, say, the death of the life tenant, he is equally making a disposal of an asset. However, in broad terms, any gain arising on the disposal of an interest under a settlement by a beneficiary as distinct from a purchaser is exempt from a charge to capital gains tax.[1] The way in which the section operates is to recognise the disposal but deem it not to be a chargeable gain.

For this purpose, "an interest under a settlement" includes an annuity, life interest, or reversionary interest. An interest under a bare trust is, however, not an interest under a settlement.[2] Hence, the disposal of an interest under a bare trust is treated as a disposal of the underlying asset.

The exemption from a charge to capital gains tax in respect of the disposal of an interest in settled property does not apply in the following circumstances:

(1) The person disposing of the interest acquired it by purchase and is not the person for whose benefit the interest was created.[3]
(2) The interest on which the disposal is made was acquired by purchase by a previous holder.[4]
(3) The trustees of the settlement concerned are neither resident nor ordinarily resident in the UK.[5]
(4) The disposal took place at a time when the trustees were resident or ordinarily resident in the UK, but the trustees subsequently ceased to be so resident before 19 March 1991.[6]
(5) The settlor had an interest in the settlement at any time in the two fiscal years prior to the disposal of the interest in the settlement.[7]

Where a charge arises on the disposal of an interest under a settlement, the computation is made on the basis that the interest is a wasting asset if the predictable life of the person by reference to whose life the duration of the interest is measured is 50 years or less at the date the interest was acquired.[8]

The form of the charging provision in TCGA 1992, s 76(2) is that a charge arises when a person becomes "absolutely entitled as against the trustee to any settled property". Thus, a charge to capital gains tax arises when assets pass to a beneficiary out of a trust, the interest in which was purchased by the beneficiary. The consideration for such a deemed disposal is the market value of the property received by the beneficiary, less any CGT charge on the trustees under TCGA 1992, s 71(1).

EXAMPLE

Apr 2003 Death of Adam—property with probate value of £10,000 passes into will trust

Sep 2005 Bert purchases the remainder of the will trust for £5,000

Nov 2008 The life tenant surrenders the life interest, causing the property to pass to Bert. The property in trust has a value of £90,000.

Two charges to CGT arise in 2008–09:

(a) a charge on the trustees:

	£
MV on vesting, Nov 2008	90,000
Base cost, 2003	(10,000)
Gain	80,000
Chargeable gain after annual exemption	£75,200
CGT payable by trustees	£13,536

(b) a charge on Bert:

	£
MV on assets received, Nov 2008	90,000
Less: CGT payable	(13,536)
	76,464
Base cost, Sep 2005	(5,000)
Chargeable gain	71,464
CGT payable by Bert[9]	£12,863

[20.21] Settled property

9   In this example, Bert's annual exemption is ignored. The HMRC Capital Gains Manual directs Revenue officers to obtain an estimate of the predictable life of an interest from the specialists in Financial Institutions Division 1 (Life Assurance).

---

1   TCGA 1992, s 76(1).
2   TCGA 1992, ss 60, 68; *Harthan v Mason* [1980] STC 94.
3   TCGA 1992, s 76(2).
4   TCGA 1992, s 76(2).
5   TCGA 1992, s 85(1).
6   TCGA 1992, s 80.
7   TCGA 1992, Sch 4A.
8   TCGA 1992, s 44. Capital Gains Manual, CG 38022.

Sale of a beneficiary's interest

[20.22] Two separate anti-avoidance provisions apply to negate plans to mitigate trust gains by the sale of a beneficiary's interest in the settlement.

There is a disposal of an interest in the settled property for consideration. The settlement is a settlor-interested settlement or includes property derived from a settlor-interested settlement.[1] The trustees of the settlement are deemed to make a disposal[2] of all the trust assets at market value.[3]

The liability falls on trustees, they are entitled to recover it from the person who disposed of the beneficial interest.[4]

The other provision stops trustees relieving a chargeable gain against trust losses.[5] This is designed to counter avoidance schemes involving gifts into trust and purchases of beneficial interests.

The denial of offset for the loss operates if the following conditions are met:

(a)   a chargeable gain accrues to the trustees;
(b)   that gain accrued on the disposal of an asset which the trustees acquired under a gift or other disposal eligible for hold-over relief ("the hold-over disposal");
(c)   the trustees' allowable expenditure is reduced by virtue of the gain on the hold-over disposal having in fact been held over;
(d)   the person who made the hold-over disposal ("the transferor") or any person connected with him, has at some time acquired, or arranged to acquire, a beneficial interest in the settled property;
(e)   a person has received or become entitled to receive consideration in connection with that transaction.[6]

---

1   TCGA 1992, Sch 4A, para 7. See also Tax Bulletin August 2003, pp 1048–1051 for the Revenue interpretation.
2   TCGA 1992, Sch 4A, para 1.
3   TCGA 1992, Sch 4A, para 8 exceptionally, where the interest sold is an interest in a specific fund, the deemed disposal is of the assets in that fund; similarly, if the

interest sold is over a fraction of the income or capital, the deemed disposal of the assets is that fraction of the disposal computed for the entire trust fund: TCGA 1992, Sch 4A, para 8(1) and (2).

[4] TCGA 1992, Sch 4A, para 11.
[5] TCGA 1992, s 79A.
[6] TCGA 1992, s 79A(1).

Trusts with a vulnerable beneficiary

[20.23] Finance Act 2005[1] creates a new tax regime for a trust with a vulnerable beneficiary that satisfies the statutory requirements.[2] The provisions are backdated to have effect from 6 April 2004,[3] but only apply where there is an election.[4]

This regime is introduced in recognition that the rate of 40% applied to capital gains made by trustees is not necessarily appropriate for a trust created to protect a vulnerable person.

The new regime applies to trusts for two types of beneficiary: (a) a disabled person, and (b) a child who has lost a parent.[5]

Where the election is made, the capital gains tax liability on gains made by the trustees is calculated by reference to the circumstances of the vulnerable beneficiary. That is, the tax payable equates to the tax that would have been payable if the beneficiary had enjoyed the gain on the disposal of his own property. The trustees can take account of the vulnerable beneficiary's annual exempt amount and the balance is taxed at any of the beneficiary's starting rate band and basic rate band that is available.[6]

In contrast to the treatment for income tax, this treatment is applied only when the trustees are resident in the UK.[7]

The conditions for a trust to be treated as a trust with a vulnerable beneficiary and the making of the election by the trustees and the beneficiary are discussed at supra, § **13.05–13.07**.

[1] FA 2005, ss 23–45.
[2] The requirements to be fulfilled for the trust: FA 2005, s 24; the requirements to be fulfilled for the beneficiary: FA 2005, ss 34–35.
[3] FA 2005, s 45.
[4] FA 2005, s 37.
[5] Defined in FA 2005, ss 34, 38 & 39.
[6] Defined in FA 2005, s 30.
[7] FA 2005, ss 30(1)(c).

[20.24] The manner in which the trustees' capital gain is taxed on the beneficiary is by treating the beneficiary as if he were the settlor[1] and applying the procedures specified for a settlor interested trust.[2]

[20.24] Settled property

[1] FA 2005, s 31(2)(a).
[2] TCGA 1992, ss 77(1), 78, 79(1)–(5A) & 79(7) & (8).

Non-resident trusts

[20.25] For a discussion of the tax treatment of non-resident trustees as introduced by FA 1991[1] (now TCGA 1992, ss 80–98) see, infra, § 35.58–35.62. Simon's Taxes Division C4.4.

[1] The scope of which is further extended by FA 1998, see infra, § 35.62.

21

Shares and companies

Securities—identification	PARA **21.01**
Capital distribution by a company	PARA **21.11**
Conversion of securities	PARA **21.19**
Company reconstructions and amalgamations	PARA **21.20**
Miscellaneous	PARA **21.28**

Securities—identification

Rules—CGT only

Note: *different rules apply for gains subjected to corporation tax: see TCGA 1992, s 106.*

[21.01] Since 6 April 1998 (the commencement of taper relief for CGT but not for corporation tax), there have been different identification rules for CGT and for corporation tax.

The CGT rules were simplified with effect from 6 April 2008 following the abolition of taper relief and the automatic rebasing of all assets held at 31 March 1982. Consequently, for CGT only, any disposal on or after 6 April 2008 is identified with an acquisition in the following categories. This is a hierarchical list; the identification is carried out in the order listed:

(1) Acquisitions made the same day.[1]
(2) Acquisitions made within the following 30 days.[2]
(3) All acquisitions made on a day prior to the disposal.[3]
(4) Shares acquired more than 30 days after the date of acquisition.[4]

Exceptionally, where an individual acquired shares through an approved employee share scheme and acquired other shares on the same day that were not acquired through the scheme, the individual can elect which shares he matches with any subsequent disposal.[5] This election can be used to match the shares with the higher base cost against shares sold, leaving the larger gain until a subsequent disposal.

Acquisitions in category 4 are only rarely likely to be found. However, this is a possible scenario, for example, where there is an unconditional contract entered into for a private sale of shares that the vendor has the right to acquire at a later date. Another possibility is a mistake, where a taxpayer sells more shares than are owned and there is a delay before the mistake is rectified.

Apart from categories 1 and 2, these rules do not apply to transactions by companies.

[21.01] Shares and companies

For the statutory matching to apply in accordance with the rules outlined above, it is necessary for there to be an actual acquisition and an actual disposal. Where statute deems an acquisition or/and a disposal, this is not matched by the above rules.[6] Hence, the statutory operation of the negligible value claim,[7] which deems there to have been a disposal and an immediate reacquisition of the asset is not affected by these rules. Similarly, where the emigration of assets from the UK creates a deemed disposal,[8] the above matching rules do not operate to nullify the gains that would otherwise arise on emigration.

Simon's Taxes C2.701.

---

[1] TCGA 1992, s 105.
[2] TCGA 1992, s 106A(5), see infra, § **21.05**.
[3] TCGA 1992, s 104(1).
[4] TCGA 1992, s 105(2).
[5] TCGA 1992, s 105A inserted by FA 2002, s 50 with effect for shares acquired after 5 April 2002.
[6] This is in accordance with the Revenue view given in Inland Revenue Tax Bulletin, April 2001, pp 839–840.
[7] TCGA 1992, s 24(2).
[8] TCGA 1992, s 80.

Share identification rules for companies

[21.02] The identifcation rules for shares held by a company[1] are:

First, against acquisitions on the same day,[a]
Second, against acquisitions in the prescribed period which is either one month or six months,[b]
Third, against acquisitions in the previous nine days,[c]
Fourth, against shares in the "section 104 holding",[d]
Fifth, against shares in the "1982 holding",[e]
Sixth, against shares held on 6 April 1965 on a last in first out (LIFO) basis,[f]
Finally against subsequent acquisitions of shares, taking the earliest acquisition first.[g]

[a] TCGA 1992, s 105(1)(*b*).
[b] TCGA 1992, s 106.
[c] TCGA 1992, s 107(3).
[d] TCGA 1992, s 107(7) & (8).
[e] TCGA 1992, s 107(7) & (9).
[f] TCGA 1992, s 107(7) & (9).
[g] TCGA 1992 s 105(2).

From 1 April 2002 gains made by companies on share disposals may, if the necessary conditions are satisfied, be exempt as the disposal of a substantial shareholding.[2] In such cases the shares disposed of are identified in the same way as for disposals giving rise to chargeable gains, so that for any future disposals which do not fall within the Sch 7AC exemption the shares disposed of can be correctly identified.

[1] And also any other concerns within the charge to corporation tax: TCGA 1992, s 106.
[2] TCGA 1992 Sch 7AC see infra, § **28.42**.

Bed and breakfast

[21.03] Where taxpayer sells shares and subsequently purchases an equivalent shareholding in the same company, the sale is identified with the subsequent purchase, if the time between the sale and the subsequent purchase is thirty days or less.[1] Thus, the time honoured simple arrangement known as "bed and breakfasting" no longer has a fiscal effect. If a taxpayer wishes to trigger a gain in order to make use of the annual exempt amount, or wishes to trigger a loss in order to bring net gains within the annual exempt amount, the sale of shares and their repurchase by the same taxpayer the following day will no longer achieve this result.

As with the other identification rules, this rule applies for CGT purposes and not for the purposes of corporation tax paid by a company on its gains.[2]

This rule does not affect a sale of one class of share and the acquisition of a different class of share in the same company. It continues to be effective for one spouse/civil partner to sell a shareholding and the other spouse/civil partner to acquire an equivalent shareholding in the same company. The rule is limited to shares; it remains possible to "bed and breakfast" land or chattels. However, care needs to be taken with such transactions as it is essential for beneficial ownership to pass on the initial sale.[3]

The bed and breakfast rules do not apply[4] in respect of acquisitions made when the person who made the disposal is neither resident nor ordinarily resident in the UK, or when that person is resident or ordinarily resident in the UK but is "Treaty non-resident".[5] This provision was enacted in order to counteract the arrangement used in *Hicks v Davies*.[6]

Simon's Direct Tax Service C2.702.

[1] TCGA 1992, s 106A(5) inserted by FA 1998, s 124(1) with effect from 17 March 1998.
[2] TCGA 1992, s 106A(1). For companies, TCGA 1992, s 106 has the effect that shares purchased are identified with shares previously sold if the shareholding in question is at least 2% of the shares of that class that have been issued and the purchase takes place during a period of one month following the disposal (if the disposal was through a stock exchange) or, a period of six months (if the disposal was off-market). There would appear to be no identification if the sale is by a company and the purchase by another company, even within a 100% group.
[3] The approach taken by the House of Lords in *McNiven v Westmoreland Investments Ltd* [2001] UKHL 6, [2001] STC 237 (see supra, § **3.04**), would seem to

[21.03] Shares and companies

support the proposition that this can be a tax effective scheme. The arrangement could also be justified by reference to the transfer of trust interest among members of the family in the scheme operated in *Countess Fitzwilliam v IRC* [1993] STC 502, HL.

4   With effect from 22 March 2006: FA 2006, s 74(5) & (6).
5   TCGA 1992, s 106A(5A) inserted by FA 2006, s 74.
6   [2005] STC (SCD) 165. In *Hicks v Davies* UK trustees sold shares on 24 October 2000 at 4.24 pm for £1,676,000. At some time prior to 7.20 am on 25 October 2000 the UK trustees retired and a Mauritian trustee was appointed. At 7.21 am on the same day, the new Mauritian trustee purchased £1,676,000 shares. In December 2000 and January 2001, the Mauritian trustee sold all the shares he had bought.

The effect was that:

(a) There was no taxable gain on their emigration of the trust on 25 October 2000 under TCGA 1992, s 80 as the deemed disposal was of sterling cash.
(b) Under the 30-day anti-bed and breakfasting rule in TCGA 1992, s 106A(5), the consideration received for the sale of shares on 24 October 2000 was identified with the subsequent reacquisition cost of the purchase the following day, giving a no gain/no loss on the 24 October 2000 disposal.
(c) No taxable gain arose on the settlor under TCGA 1992, s 86 on the sale on 25 October 2000 because of the terms of the UK/Mauritius double tax treaty.

Matching rules—transfers between spouses and civil partners

[21.04] Where a couple (married or a registered civil partnership) has lived together for at least a part of the fiscal year, any transfer between them is deemed to be made so that no gain and no loss arises on the transfer.[1] This does not, however, negate the normal matching rule,[2] which would have to be applied to determine a consideration that gives the no gain/no loss result. The matching rules do not change the date on which the transferor or transferee is deemed to dispose of or acquire an asset; it simply fixes the disposal and acquisition value at whatever amount results in there being neither gain nor loss on the transfer.

From the point of view of the transferor, this means that the shares transferred are identified with acquisitions under the normal matching rules, and the deemed consideration is determined by those rules. From the transferee's angle, the shares acquired are treated as a single acquisition and are matched with disposals by him/her under the normal rules by reference to the date on which they were acquired on the transfer.

If and when the transferee comes to dispose of the shares and needs to work out what taper relief is available, the transferee was treated for the purposes of taper relief as acquiring the asset at the time when the transferor originally acquired it. This was relevant to determining the transferee's qualifying holding period and the relevant period of ownership.

There was therefore a tension between:

(a)   the basic identification rule, which treats the shares as acquired at the date of the transfer, and

1060

(b) the taper rule, which looks back to the date of original acquisition by the original transferor.

This tension did not matter if all the shares transferred were originally acquired on the same day, nor does it matter if they were acquired on different days but the transferee disposes of them all in one go. In this latter case the different holding periods or relevant periods of ownership are simply applied to the relevant parts of the total holding that is sold. But if the shares transferred were originally acquired on different days, and the transferee disposes of only some of this, it is not immediately clear how to work out the holding period(s) and relevant period(s) of ownership of the shares disposed of on that occasion[3].

Since 6 April 2008, the combination of the rules dealing with transfers between spouses/civil partners and the identification rules still leads to some anomalies. However, these are substantially reduced and will be significant only in extreme cases. For example, suppose Chris were to dispose of shares in X plc on 30 June. Five days later, Chris' civil partner, Alex, acquires some shares in the same company which Alex then transfers to Chris on 12 July. Under the 30-day rule, Chris's disposal on 30 June will be (wholly or partly) identified with the shares transferred by Alex.

[1] TCGA 1992, s 58(1).
[2] TCGA 1992, s 106A.
[3] The Revenue view (set out in Tax Bulletin August 2001, pp 876 to 877) is that in these circumstances:

(a) the transferee is treated as acquiring them as a single asset;
(b) a disposal of some of those shares is therefore a part disposal and the cost of the shares is apportioned under the normal part-disposal formula (under s 42);
(c) the part disposal formula does not attribute to the cost of the holding to any particular shares within it; and
(d) for taper purposes you applied the normal LIFO (last in, first out) rule in working out the period for which the shares disposed of have been held by both members of the couple.

The s 104 pool – companies

[21.05] In determining which securities are disposed of on a particular disposal, special rules apply.[1] These rules applied for all acquisitions up to 5 April 1998 for all taxpayers but since that date only for companies.[2] These rules are relevant not only for indexation relief purposes but whenever allowable expenditure has to be ascertained. In general, all shares or securities of the same class, held by the same person in the same capacity, are pooled. This pooling rule is subject to a number of exceptions and qualifications:

(1) Certain securities are subject to special identification rules linking particular disposals with particular acquisitions.[3] These are:
    (a) shares issued before 19 March 1986 in business expansion schemes, when relief has not been withdrawn;[4]
    (b) loan stock and similar securities subject to the accrued income scheme;[5]

[21.05] Shares and companies

        (c)   deep discount securities;[6]
        (d)   securities comprising a material interest in a non-qualifying offshore fund.[7]

(2)   Certain securities outside the prescribed list in 1 are not pooled. These are securities disposed of on or before the day of acquisition[8] and shares disposed of within ten days after acquisition.[9]

(3)   Other securities of the same class which are held by one person in one capacity are pooled and treated as a single asset.[10] The pooling rule applies notwithstanding that one can or one intends to transfer particular identifiable securities.

The pooling rule is also modified according to the dates on which the securities were acquired:

(4)   *Acquisition before 6 April 1965.* Where no pooling election has been made these remain separate assets. A right to elect for pooling is given.[11] Where an election has been made they form part of the 1982 pool (see 5).

(5)   *Acquisitions before 6 April 1982.*[12] These form a pool of their own[13] distinct from later acquisitions. Where the shares were acquired after 5 April 1981[14] but before 6 April 1982 the rules in force before 6 April 1985 required that to the extent that they represented a net increase in the holding they should be treated as separate assets (infra, § **21.07**). Such segregated shares are added to the 1982 pool with effect from 6 April 1985.[15]

(6)   *Acquisitions since 5 April 1982.*[13] Those which have been acquired since that date and not disposed of before 6 April 1985[11] are now treated as a single asset. The pool will henceforward grow or diminish as shares are acquired or disposed of[16] and anything short of a disposal of all the shares in the pool will be a part disposal.

Shares which are issued on terms restricting the holder's right to dispose, eg to an employee, are pooled separately so long as the restrictions remain.[17] The effects of rebasing CGT to 31 March 1982 are clearly limited only to categories 4 and 5. However, because of the continuing requirement to compare gains or losses computed on the new basis with the result of applying the former rules,[18] categories 4 and 5 still cannot be consolidated in relation to disposals after 5 April 1988 unless the shareholder has elected under TCGA 1992, s 35(5) (FA 1988, s 96(5)).

Rules for the interaction of 4, 5 and 6 are also provided where, as may occur, a holding includes pre-1965 acquisitions, a pre-1982 pool and a current pool. The shares disposed of are treated as coming first from the current pool, then from the pre-1982 pool, then from pre-1965 acquisitions which have not been pooled—such shares are treated as disposed of on a last in, first out basis[19]—and finally from acquisitions after the date of disposal, on a first in first out basis.[20] As with the general pooling rule these rules cannot be overridden by any designation by the parties or the disposal itself. The rules are, however, subject to the special rules for identifying shares bought on the same day or within the previous ten days.[21]

When a taxpayer has entered into a monthly savings scheme to purchase each month a holding in a unit trust, strict application of the statutory rules requires that sale of less than the entire holding is a part disposal of a pool, the calculation of which requires the computation of indexation allowance for each separate month's purchase. A Revenue Statement of Practice allows the 12 purchases made during a year to be treated as if there were one purchase half-way through the year.[22]

Simon's Taxes C2.701, 705–706, 708, 717–718; Sumption CGT A12.04, 13.

---

[1] TCGA 1992, s 108.
[2] For acquisitions after 5 April 1998 by an individual, see infra, § **21.06**.
[3] Rules in CGTA 1979, s 68 apply.
[4] TCGA 1992, s 150 and TA 1988, s 299. The identification rule was that shares disposed of were identified first with shares which qualified for relief under the business start-up scheme, then with shares qualifying under the business expansion scheme, on a first in, first out basis in each case. There was originally a drafting error whereby business start-up scheme shares were to be identified on a LIFO basis under the FA 1985 rules. This was corrected for disposals on or after 19 March 1991: FA 1991, s 99(2).
[5] Defined by TA 1988, s 710; TCGA 1992, s 108 applies. Securities under headings (c)–(e) are covered by the rules (infra, § **21.07**) which applied to securities generally before 6 April 1985.
[6] Defined by TA 1988, Sch 4, para 1; TCGA 1992, s 108 applies. See TA 1988, Sch 4, para 12.
[7] Defined by TA 1988, ss 757–760: TCGA 1992, s 108 applies.
[8] TCGA 1992, s 105.
[9] TCGA 1992, s 107(3)–(6). For companies, see supra, § **21.03**, footnote 2.
[10] TCGA 1992, ss 104, 110, 114.
[11] TCGA 1992, s 109(4).
[12] 1 April for corporation tax.
[13] TCGA 1992, s 109(1).
[14] 31 March for corporation tax.
[15] TCGA 1992, s 109(1).
[16] TCGA 1992, s 104(1).
[17] TCGA 1992, s 104(4).
[18] TCGA 1992, s 35(3). See infra, § **23.03**.
[19] TCGA 1992, s 107(7)–(9).
[20] TCGA 1992, s 105(2).
[21] TCGA 1992, s 107(3), (6). At first sight it would appear that shares acquired after the disposal are identified before pooled shares but s 105(2) makes it clear that shares acquired before the date of disposal must be identified first. It is unfortunate that the opportunity of setting out the order of identification more clearly was not taken on consolidation into TCGA 1992.
[22] Statement of Practice SP2/97. The method of computation in the statement applies to approved investment trusts and open-ended investment companies, as well as authorised unit trusts.

[21.06] Shares and companies

The s 104 pool – capital gains tax

[21.06] Since 6 April 2008, share and securities listed at level 3 in the hierarchy at **21.01** have been treated as allocated to a single pool to the extent that the shares or securities are of the same class, held by the same person in the same capacity. This pooling rule is subject to a number of exceptions and qualifications. In particular:

(a) shares issued under the business expansion scheme or enterprise investment scheme, when relief has not been withdrawn;[1]
(b) loan stock and similar securities subject to the accrued income scheme;[2]
(c) deep discount securities;[3]
(d) securities comprising a material interest in a non-qualifying offshore fund.[4]

Shares which are issued on terms restricting the holder's right to dispose, eg to an employee, are pooled separately so long as the restrictions remain.[5]

Simon's Taxes C2.701, 705–706, 708, 717–718; Sumption CGT A12.04, 13.

[1] TCGA 1992, s 150 and TA 1988, s 299. The identification rule was that shares disposed of were identified first with shares which qualified for relief under the business start-up scheme, then with shares qualifying under the business expansion scheme, on a first in, first out basis in each case. There was originally a drafting error whereby business start-up scheme shares were to be identified on a LIFO basis under the FA 1985 rules. This was corrected for disposals on or after 19 March 1991: FA 1991, s 99(2).
[2] Defined by TA 1988, s 710; TCGA 1992, s 108 applies. Securities under headings (c)–(e) are covered by the rules (infra, § **21.07**) which applied to securities generally before 6 April 1985.
[3] Defined by TA 1988, Sch 4, para 1; TCGA 1992, s 108 applies. See TA 1988, Sch 4, para 12.
[4] Defined by TA 1988, ss 757–760: TCGA 1992, s 108 applies.
[5] TCGA 1992, s 104(4).

Share pooling and indexation

[21.07] The basic principle of pooling under the post 5 April 1985 rules is that, in addition to the allowable cost of the pool, an indexed cost must also be calculated.[1]

Where an event occurs which increases or reduces the qualifying expenditure, an event called an operative event, the "indexed rise" in the value of the pool since the last such event is computed and is added to the indexed cost of the pool.[2] If the operative event is an increase in qualifying expenditure, eg more shares are acquired, the acquisition cost is added to both the unindexed and indexed pools (in the latter case, after computing the indexed rise).[3] If there is a decrease in the qualifying expenditure because there is a disposal, the indexed pool is reduced in the same *proportion* as the unindexed pool.[4] If there is a decrease in the expenditure but no disposal, eg on receipt of a small capital distribution, infra, § **21.17**, the indexed pool is reduced by the same amount as the reduction in qualifying expenditure.[5]

Securities—identification [21.07]

When the holding consists of shares held on 6 April 1985 and acquired since 5 April 1982 the indexed pool consists of the qualifying expenditure plus any indexation allowance due to it down to 6 April 1985.[6]

In the case of any other new holding, ie shares acquired after 5 April 1985, the indexed pool begins when the holding begins[7] and consists of the qualifying expenditure at that time.

The indexed rise is calculated by multiplying the value of the indexed pool immediately before the operative event by the fraction

$$\frac{RE - RL}{RL}$$

expressed as a decimal.[8] RE is the retail prices index for the month in which the operative event occurs and RL is the figure for the month in which the last operative event occurred, or, if there is none, the pool began. If the index drops over this period the indexed rise is nil.[9]

On a disposal of the whole holding, the indexation allowance is simply the difference between the indexed and unindexed pools.[10] Where there is a part disposal the qualifying expenditure in the unindexed pool is attributed to the part disposal in accordance with the part disposal formula,

$$\frac{A}{A+B}$$

(see supra, § **18.14**). For securities which are quoted on the Stock Exchange, the apportionment is made according to the number of shares involved.[11] In practice, the Revenue also allows the apportionment of a pool of unquoted shares by reference to the number of shares. The indexation allowance is then the amount by which the portion of the indexed pool attributed to the part disposal exceeds the portion of qualifying expenditure so attributed.[12]

EXAMPLE

AB made the following transactions in ordinary shares of ER Co plc. He held no such shares before 6 April 1982.

1 June 1983	Bought 1,500: cost £2,750
30 September 1984	Bought 3,500: cost £7,250
15 May 1985	Bought 2,000: cost £4,100
30 September 1985	Sold 1,000: proceeds £2,050
21 March 1986	Sold 6,000: proceeds £10,000

Relevant values of the retail prices index are as follows:

June 1983	334.7
September 1984	355.5
April 1985	373.9
May 1985	375.6
September 1985	376.5
March 1986	381.6

[21.07] Shares and companies

	Shares	Unindexed pool £		Indexed pool £
June 1983 acquisition	1,500	2,750	2,750	
$\dfrac{373.9 - 334.7}{334.7} \times £2,750$			322	3,072
September 1984 acquisition		3,500	7,250	7,250
$\dfrac{373.9 - 355.5}{355.5} \times £7,250$			375	7,625
April 1985 holding	5,000	10,000		10,697
$\dfrac{375.6 - 373.9}{373.9} \times £10,697$				49
May 1985 acquisition	2,000	4,100		4,100
May 1985 holding	7,000	14,100		14,846
$\dfrac{376.5 - 375.6}{375.6} \times £14,846$				36
				14,882
September 1985 disposal	(1,000)	(2,014)		(2,126)
September 1985 holding c/f	6,000	12,086		12,756
September 1985 holding b/f	6,000	12,086		12,756
$\dfrac{381.6 - 376.5}{376.5} \times £12,756$				176
				12,932
March 1986 disposal	(6,000)	(12,086)		(12,932)

		£	Indexed pool £
(a)	September 1985 disposal		£2,050
	Disposal proceeds		
	Allowable cost	£2,014	
	Indexation allowance: £2,126 – £2,014	112	2,126
	Allowable loss		£(76)
(b)	March 1986 disposal		£10,000
	Disposal proceeds		
	Allowable cost	£12,086	
	Indexation allowance: £12,932 – £12,086	846	12,932
	Allowable loss		£(2,932)

Special provisions apply where shares are acquired under an option.[13] The cost of the option is a separate item of expenditure but it is not added to the pool unless and until it is exercised to acquire shares, when the option cost becomes part of the share cost.[14] The indexed rise then takes account of the period during which the option was held prior to exercise.

Simon's Taxes C2.301; C2.719; Sumption CGT A12.04.

---

[1] TCGA 1992, s 110.
[2] TCGA 1992, s 110(8)(a).
[3] TCGA 1992, s 110(8)(b). In the case of an acquisition by way of a no gain, no loss transfer on or after 30 November 1993, the indexation allowance is excluded from the acquisition cost: TCGA 1992, s 110 (6A) inserted by FA 1994, s 93(6).
[4] TCGA 1992, s 110(8)(c).
[5] TCGA 1992, s 110(8)(d).
[6] TCGA 1992, s 110(6).
[7] TCGA 1992, s 110(7).
[8] TCGA 1992, s 110(10), (11). It is unclear why the fraction should be expressed as a decimal, since there is no rounding to a specified number of decimal places; contrast TCGA 1992, s 54(3) in relation to the calculation of indexation factors.
[9] TCGA 1992, s 110(11).
[10] TCGA 1992, s 110(3).
[11] See Revenue booklet CGT 8 (1980) § 152 (now withdrawn).
[12] TCGA 1992, s 110(2).
[13] TCGA 1992, s 114.
[14] TCGA 1992, s 144(3).

Identifying the 6 April 1985 pool

[21.08] In order to calculate which shares are in the pool on 6 April 1985 it may be necessary to consider what has happened to the shares before that date. In particular, the rules as to identification which operated between 1982 and 1985 will have to be taken into account.

For disposals after 5 April 1982 and before 6 April 1985 the rules are as follows: On disposal, shares are to be considered for identification in order of disposal, the earliest disposal being identified first. Shares disposed of must (if quoted) first be identified with any concurrent or later acquisitions in the same Stock Exchange period of account.[1]

Once shares purchased in the same Stock Exchange account have been identified, shares disposed of must be identified first with shares acquired in the previous twelve months, on a first in first out basis, and then with shares acquired more than twelve months before the disposal, on a last in first out basis.[2] Any balance of shares still not identified are then matched with the pre-6 April 1982 pool[3] and then with pre-6 April 1965 acquisitions (if not pooled) on a last in first out basis.

EXAMPLE

A made the following acquisitions and disposals of ordinary shares in PQR plc:

On 6 April 1983   Acquired 2,000

[21.08] Shares and companies

On 6 May 1983	Acquired 1,000
On 6 July 1983	Acquired 1,000
On 6 October 1983	Acquired 3,000
On 6 June 1984	Sold 2,000
On 6 August 1984	Sold 3,000

(1) *Disposal on 6 June 1984*
   (a)   1,000 identified with the 1,000 acquired on 6 July 1983
   (b)   1,000 identified with 1,000 of the 3,000 acquired on 6 October 1983
(2) *Disposal on 6 August 1984*
   (a)   2,000 identified with 2,000 of the 3,000 acquired on 6 October 1983
   (b)   1,000 identified with the 1,000 acquired on 6 May 1983

A's remaining holding therefore consists of the 2,000 shares acquired on 6 April 1983.

Where shares are acquired for delivery on a specified date (or account) and, under the same bargain, are disposed of for delivery on a later date (or account), the acquisition and disposal are identified with each other, notwithstanding the general rules.[4] Such bargains ("contangos") could otherwise have been used to exploit the pre 6 April 1985 indexation rules.

There were rules to prevent indexation allowance being claimed where shares were acquired both within the 12-month period and before it and it is sought to transfer the shares bought within the 12-month period to a spouse or group company so that the indexation allowance could be claimed on the subsequent sale to a third party.[5] This was countered by deeming the order of the transfers to be reversed.

Simon's Taxes C2.718; Sumption CGT A12.05.

[1] TCGA 1992, s 108(4).
[2] TCGA 1992, s 108(5).
[3] Infra, § **21.09**.
[4] TCGA 1992, s 108(7).
[5] FA 1982, s 89.

Pre-6 April 1982 acquisitions

[21.09] Shares held on 6 April 1982 of the same class held by the same person in the same capacity are pooled. Disposals before 6 April 1982 were treated in the same way as disposals from a 1985 pool,[1] but clearly without any special adjustments regarding indexation. However, disposals were identified with shares acquired before 6 April 1965 on a first in, first out basis, not last in, first out as at present.[2] For disposals after 5 April 1982 but before 6 April 1985, special rules applied to adjust the indexation allowance where there was a net addition of shares to the pool during 1981–82, in view of the then 12-month waiting period for indexation.[3] Any acquisitions segregated from the 1982 pool and which remain undisposed of at 6 April 1985 are added back to the 1982 pool for disposals on or after that date,[4] following the abolition of the 12-month waiting period.

For disposals after 5 April 1988, the pool cost is recomputed to include any additions on or before 31 March 1982 at their market value on that date.[5] Additions to the pool on or after 1 April 1982 but before 6 April 1982 are included at cost. It is not clear how to identify these two elements of the 1982 pool where there have been disposals out of the pool before 6 April 1988, since no rules are provided for this purpose.

Simon's Taxes C2.718.

---

1. TCGA 1992, s 109(1)–(3).
2. CGTA 1979, Sch 5, para 2(2) as originally enacted.
3. FA 1982, Sch 13, para 9.
4. TCGA 1992, s 110(4).
5. TCGA 1992, s 35.

Parallel pooling

[21.10] As an alternative to the identification rules described in supra, §§ 21.08–21.09, a modified version of the former pooling provisions,[1] called "parallel pooling" was introduced by FA 1983,[2] and was intended to assist companies with computerised records of large share portfolios subject to rapid turnover. The election for parallel pooling, which was originally irrevocable, was able to be revoked not later than 31 March 1987.[3] In any event, the election ceases to have effect for disposals after 31 March 1985, and the Treasury has issued regulations to facilitate the application of the present rules to holdings still covered by a parallel pooling election.[4]

For an outline of the indexation rules as they applied to disposals before 6 April 1985 to shares held in this way see *Butterworths UK Tax Guide 1984–85*, §§ **19.18–19.19**.

Simon's Taxes C2.718; Sumption CGT A12.10.

---

1. Supra, § **17.04**.
2. FA 1983, s 34, Sch 6.
3. TCGA 1992, s 112. It appears that an election will have effect only from 1 April 1985, so that the holdings concerned will then fall to be treated as part of the 1985 pool. However, the reference to adjustments falling to be made on revocation suggests that the effect might be retroactive.
4. TCGA 1992, s 112; Capital Gains Tax (Parallel Pooling) Regulations 1986, SI 1986/387.

Capital distribution by a company

[21.11] A company makes a capital distribution if it makes any distribution in money or money's worth which would not be treated as income in the hands of the recipient for purposes of income tax.[1] A capital distribution is a disposal or part disposal of the shares held, the consideration being the amount received by the shareholder.[2] However, there is relief from tax where the capital distribution consists of shares or securities issued as part of a capital reorganisation (such as a scrip or rights issue) or, on election, where the capital

[21.11] Shares and companies

distribution is "small".[3] Taxable capital distributions commonly include distributions in liquidation,[4] repayment of share capital,[5] repurchase by a company of its own share capital,[6] and certain capital distributions by foreign companies.[7] For relief on demergers, see infra, § **28.37**.

Simon's Taxes C2.1509; Sumption CGT A10.14.

---

[1] TCGA 1992, s 122(5)(*b*).
[2] TCGA 1992, s 122(1).
[3] Infra, § **21.17**.
[4] Per TA 1988, s 209(1).
[5] Per TA 1988, s 209(2)(*b*).
[6] Per TA 1988, s 219.
[7] Infra, § **35.09**.

Reorganisation

[21.12] A reorganisation is not treated as a disposal of a shareholding.[1] There is a reorganisation if there is a reorganisation or reduction of share capital; this is stated to include (a) the allotment of shares or debentures in proportion to shareholdings and (b) any alteration of share rights—assuming that there are at least two classes.[2] Although a reduction in share capital is a reorganisation, both the paying off of redeemable share capital and the redemption of shares other than by the issue of new shares or debentures are excluded.[3] The reorganisation rules do not apply to the extent that the shareholder receives consideration other than the new holding (such as a cash payment) from the company, or any consideration from the other shareholders.[4]

Simon's Taxes C2.1505, 1506; Sumption CGT A13.02, 03.

---

[1] TCGA 1992, s 127.
[2] TCGA 1992, s 126; an allotment to debenture holders does not qualify. The guiding principle appears to be that there is continued identity of the shareholders, holding their shares in the same proportions: *Dunstan v Young Austen Young Ltd* [1989] STC 69. For a comprehensive review of the requirements for this treatment to apply, see the judgment of Burton J in *Unilever (UK) Holdings v Smith Ltd* [2002] STC 113 and the subsequent judgment of Jonathan Parker LJ in the Court of Appeal [2002] EWCA Civ 1787, [2003] STC 15.
[3] TCGA 1992, s 126(3).
[4] TCGA 1992, s 128(3).

Bonus (scrip) issue

[21.13] Where new shares or securities are allotted to shareholders without consideration, the new shares or debentures are treated as forming one combined asset with the shares previously held, and make a new holding but with the old date of acquisition and acquisition cost.[1] Where the original shares were acquired before 1 April 1982, the rebasing to 31 March 1982 value applies to the whole shareholding, including the bonus shares issued.

There is neither acquisition of the new shares or debentures nor disposal of the original shares. So, on a bonus issue of shares of the same class as the original holding, the bonus shares are simply added to those already held. On any subsequent disposal of a part of the holding, gains or losses are computed by taking the appropriate proportion of the cost of the original shares, supra, § 21.07.

Simon's Taxes C2.1507; Sumption CGT A13.03.

[1] TCGA 1992, s 127. Special rules apply to shares issued as stock dividends (as they are income). They are treated as acquired for the appropriate amount in cash: TCGA 1992, ss 141, 142. Special rules also apply to certain shares acquired as an employee, ITEPA 2003, ss 519–525.

Rights issue

[21.14] If the person provides consideration for the new shares or debentures, as on a rights issue, again the holding forms a single asset but the consideration paid is added to the expenditure incurred on the holding.[1] However, for indexation allowance, the consideration paid is treated as a separate item of relevant expenditure incurred when it is actually incurred and not as having been incurred on the acquisition date of the original shares.[2]

EXAMPLE

V purchased 1,000 ordinary shares in XYZ Ltd in May 1983 for £7,000. In September 1995, there was a rights issue of one ordinary share for every five held, at £9.50 per share. In September 1999, V sold his entire holding of 1,200 shares for £24,000.

	£	£
Disposal consideration		24,000
Allowable cost:		
Original holding	7,000	
Rights issue	1,900	8,900
Gain		15,100
Indexation allowance:		
Original holding	6,370	
Rights issue	139	6,509
Chargeable gain		£8,591

The consideration will not be so added if it originates from the shares themselves rather than from the shareholder, for example if it consists of the surrender, cancellation or alteration of the original shares, nor if the new shares are paid up out of the assets of the company or out of a dividend or any other distribution declared—but not made—out of the company's assets. This is to prevent an uplift in the base cost by the use of the company's assets.

On a reorganisation after 9 March 1981, any new consideration, eg that payable under a rights issue, forms part of the allowable cost of the shares only to the extent that the reorganised shareholding is more valuable than the original.[3] This restriction counters schemes intended to secure relief for losses

[21.14] Shares and companies

on loans.[4] There could be difficulties for a minority shareholder in an unquoted company subscribing for a rights issue since the value of his minority holding is unlikely to increase by as much as the amount subscribed.

Simon's Taxes C2.1508; Sumption CGT A13.03.

[1] TCGA 1992, s 128(1).
[2] TCGA 1992, ss 126, 131, 132.
[3] TCGA 1992, s 128(2), proviso.
[4] See *IRC v Burmah Oil Co Ltd* [1980] STC 731; revsd [1982] STC 30, HL.

Computation

[21.15] Where a reorganisation involves the issue of shares of a different class, or of debentures, the new securities cannot be pooled with the old for computing the allowable cost on a part disposal out of the new holding. Instead, the original consideration and any new consideration are both apportioned between the different classes of securities in the new holding. If any of the classes of shares involved in the reorganisation is listed on a recognised stock exchange the allowable costs are apportioned pro rata to the market values of each element on the first day of market quotation.[1]

Where all classes of shares involved in the reorganisation are unlisted, the apportionment of costs is made pro rata to market values at the date of disposal.[2]

Where there are unpaid calls in respect of any of the shares or securities in the new holding, adjustments may be required when apportioning allowable costs. The amounts unpaid are treated as part of the allowable costs to be apportioned, but the market values used in the apportionment are similarly increased.[3] For indexation purposes, calls paid are treated as expenditure incurred when the shares are acquired, unless payable more than 12 months after that date.[4]

Simon's Taxes C2.1511, 1512; Sumption CGT A12.03.

[1] TCGA 1992, s 130.
[2] TCGA 1992, s 129(1). This provision relates only to the cost of the original shares not to the cost of the rights issue; this is difficult to reconcile with the "one asset" principle of the reorganisation rules.
[3] TCGA 1992, ss 129(1), 130(2). In practice, the Revenue seem usually to accept computations which do not make adjustments for unpaid calls.
[4] TCGA 1992, s 113.

Other capital distributions

Rights issue—sale of rights

[21.16] A sale of rights under a rights issue is an example of a taxable capital distribution. The distribution is not a new holding; instead the shareholder is treated as having disposed of an interest in his holding[1] and as having received consideration equal to the market value of the distribution.[2] The sale of rights under a rights issue will be treated as a part disposal.[3] There will similarly be a part disposal if, on a bonus or rights issue, the company sells fractional entitlements on the market and allocates the cash to shareholders.

Simon's Taxes C2.1508; Sumption CGT A12.23.

[1] TCGA 1992, s 122.
[2] TCGA 1992, s 17(1)(a).
[3] TCGA 1992, s 123. Whether or not company has made a provisional allotment; a relaxed valuation rule applies to disposal of rights.

Small distribution

[21.17] If the amount received is small, it is deducted from the allowable expenditure[1]. The Revenue regard this as a relieving provision, which the taxpayer can choose not to use, if it is more advantageous to treat the disposal as triggering a chargeable gain.[2]

Statute does not define "small". In *O'Rourke v Binks*[3], the Court of Appeal held that what is "small" is a question of fact and degree and has to be considered in the light of the circumstances in any particular case. The Revenue have stated[4] that they will regard a receipt as "small" if it does not exceed 5% of the value of the shares. The Revenue also regard as "small" where the actual sum received is £3,000 or less, however large a percentage this is of the value of the shares.

It is possible for the amount received to exceed the allowable expenditure. If this is the case, the excess is chargeable.[5]

Simon's Taxes C2.1510; Sumption CGT A12.23.

[1] TCGA 1992, s 122(2), (5).
[2] Inland Revenue Interpretation IR34,
[3] [1991] STC 455: see supra, § **18.15**.
[4] Inland Revenue letter to CCAB, June 1965 and Revenue Interpretation IR164
[5] TCGA 1992, s 112(4).

Liquidation

[21.18] If a liquidator makes a distribution of the entire assets of the company to the shareholders, there is a disposition of their shares, for a consideration equal to the value of the assets so distributed.[1] More usually, however, the liquidator will make a number of successive distributions to the shareholders. Since each distribution is a part disposal of the shares, great practical difficulties arise because of the need to find the market value of the shareholding after each such distribution. Where unquoted shares are concerned the Board[2] accept the taxpayer's valuation provided it appears reasonable and the winding-up is expected to be completed within two years, and is in fact completed only shortly beyond that time. There is no need to discount for deferment. If, as will usually be the case, the final distributions are made before the assessments, the market value is ascertained by reference to the sums actually received in the later distributions.

A more fundamental problem is whether there is a notional disposal by the company when winding-up commences. The point here is that the company ceases to be beneficially entitled at that point and a trust arises in favour of creditors and contributories; accordingly it is unclear whether beneficial ownership is in suspense[3] or passes to the shareholders.[4] If the latter view were correct, then the holders would become entitled to receive the assets. This would be a disposal by the company to the shareholders when winding-up commences. The former view seems to be more correct. In practice the Revenue treat the shareholders as making a part disposal as and when cash or other property is received.

Simon's Taxes C2.1509.

[1] This is also a disposal by the liquidator on behalf of the company; infra, § **25.09**.
[2] Inland Revenue press release, 20 January 1972.
[3] *IRC v Olive Mill Ltd* [1963] 2 All ER 130, 41 TC 77.
[4] See Court of Appeal in *Ayerst v C and K (Construction) Ltd* [1975] STC 1, [1975] 1 All ER 162; affd by the House of Lords on other grounds [1975] STC 345, [1975] 2 All ER 537.

Conversion of securities

[21.19] The technique of treating the original and the new holding as the same asset is applied to the conversion of securities. These transactions are dealt with separately in the legislation since securities are distinct from share capital. There is no disposal where debentures are converted into shares or into other securities whether or not the taxpayer could have those securities redeemed for cash as an alternative to conversion.[1] There is, however, a part disposal when the person also receives a premium in addition to new securities—unless the consideration is treated as a small disposal.[2] As to convertible securities which are also deep gain securities, see supra, § **11.24**. Government stock acquired as compensation on nationalisation is not treated as a conversion.[3] The old shares are treated as being sold at a consideration equal to the market value of the government securities at the date of issue. Any chargeable gain or allowable loss crystallises only when the government securities are themselves disposed of. For disposals after 5 April 1988 of government securities acquired as compensation stock before 1 April 1982, no gain or loss crystallises.[4]

Simon's Taxes C2.1515; Sumption CGT A13.04.

[1] TCGA 1992, s 132(1). On the meaning of "securities" see *Cleveleys Investment Trust Co v IRC* (1971) 47 TC 300.
[2] TCGA 1992, s 133. See supra, § **20.16** for a discussion of the meaning of "small". Revenue Interpretation IR164 applies to s 133 in the same way as to s 122.

[3] TCGA 1992, s 134; certain disposals are ignored—sub-s (4) (sub-s (5)).
[4] TCGA 1992, Sch 4, para 4(5).

Company reconstructions and amalgamations

Exchange of securities

[21.20] The issue of shares or debentures in exchange for shares or debentures[1] in another company is treated as if the two companies were the same and the exchange was a reorganisation of the share capital.[2] In other words, the shares in the offeror company are treated as having been acquired by the shareholder at the same time, and for the same consideration, as the shares in the company taken over. If cash forms part of the consideration received by the shareholder, then to that extent there is a part disposal, supra, § **21.10**. The acquiring company must either have or acquire by the exchange more than 25% of the ordinary share capital of the other company[3] or the greater part of the voting power,[4] or the transaction must be part of a general offer seeking control (ie 51%) of that capital (notwithstanding that the offer may subsequently be made unconditional).

Where shares have been exchanged before 1 April 1982, any gains which would otherwise have accrued at that time are now effectively eliminated. This is because the new holding is deemed to have been acquired when the original shares were acquired, so that the holding is rebased to its value at 31 March 1982.[5] A share exchange after that date does not necessarily benefit from the rebasing, and any accrued gain at the time of the takeover remains, subject to subsequent movements in the share value. There is no relief for the deferred gain, in contrast with the position in other rollover or holdovers.

For a corporate shareholder, the reorganisation of a shareholding of more than 10% is normally treated as exempt, being the disposal of a substantial shareholding.[6] The reorganisation provisions are, thus, disapplied.[7]

Simon's Direct Tax Service C2.71521; Sumption CGT A13.06.

[1] This treatment also applies to transactions of units in a unit trust and reorganisations where a company does not have a share capital: TCGA 1992, s 135(4) and (5).
[2] TCGA 1992, s 135. FA 2002, s 45 and Sch 9 amend TCGA 1992, ss 135 and 136 and introduce Sch 5AA to provide the treatment that was generally understood to apply prior to the High Court decision in *Fallon and Kersley v Fellows* [2001] STC 1409.
[3] Defined by TA 1988, s 832(1).
[4] TCGA 1992, s 135(1)(c).
[5] TCGA 1992, s 35.
[6] TCGA 1992, Schs 7A, 7C: see infra, §§ **28.42–28.47**.
[7] TCGA 1992, Sch 7, para 3.

Exchange involving qualifying corporate bonds

[21.21] Where the exchange is in consideration of debentures which are qualifying corporate bonds, any gain (or loss) on the old holding is merely frozen and comes back into charge on the disposal of the bonds.[1] This can result in a considerable burden in cases where the company issuing the bonds becomes insolvent and the bondholders do not recover their investment, since any loss on the bonds themselves is not an allowable loss. A strategy adopted in practice to avoid this unfortunate consequence is to issue bonds containing terms under which the value of the bond automatically translates from sterling into a foreign currency shortly before the bond matures. The currency conversion means that the bonds fail the statutory test for a qualifying corporate bond and, hence, any loss occasioned is an allowable loss.[2] Limited relief is given in the case of bonds issued before 14 March 1989 and still held at that date, where the bonds become qualifying corporate bonds only by virtue of the changes enacted by FA 1989.[3] Relief is given as if the bonds represented a loan to a trader,[4] with clawback if amounts are subsequently recovered.

Where there was an exchange prior to 14 March 1989 and a disposal after that date, the statutory provisions for qualifying corporate bonds do not alter the treatment that was adopted on the reconstruction prior to the date in which the statutory provisions were enacted.[5]

Certain debentures issued on or after 16 March 1993, which are not securities, are treated as corporate bonds where the issue is in exchange for shares or debentures in another company, on a merger.[6]

Simon's Taxes C2.822, 823; Sumption CGT A12.17; A13.02.

---

[1] TCGA 1992, s 116. For judicial analysis of these provisions, in a case where a security is not within the definition of a QCB when acquired, but falls within the definition at the disposal, see *Harding v Revenue and Customs Comrs* [2008] EWHC 99 (Ch). The Court of Appeal in [2008] EWCA Civ 1164 subsequently upheld the decision of the High Court in *Harding* and held that loan notes which contained a currency conversion option did not become QCBs when the option had lapsed.

[2] A "qualifying corporate bond" is defined by TCGA 1992, s 117(1) as a security which, inter alia, "is expressed in sterling and in respect of which no provision is made for conversion, or redemption into, a currency other than sterling". A security can, however, become a qualifying corporate bond merely by the holder failing to exercise the option to convert to the foreign currency and, thereby, cause the proceeds paid at maturity to be payable in sterling.

[3] Extra-statutory concession D38.

[4] TCGA 1992, s 254.

[5] *Jenks v Dickinson* [1996] STC (SCD) 299.

[6] TCGA 1992, s 117(6A).

[21.22] Where a security changes from a chargeable asset to a qualifying corporate bond other than by means of a reorganisation, FA 1997, s 88 provides that the change in status of the security is treated as a conversion of securities within TCGA 1992, s 132. This provision applies to a disposal after 25 November 1996, even if the conversion took place before that date.

Paper issued on an earn-out

[21.23] It is frequently the case that part of the consideration for a company sale is an earn-out. That is, the vendor receives further consideration if the performance of the company he has sold reaches a specified target. If the further consideration is cash, the earn-out is brought into the disposal proceeds and taxed on the sale. If the amount of cash is specified, the full sum receivable is brought into charge;[1] if it varies according to results, the value of the right to receive the further consideration is estimated and that value is brought into charge.[2]

If the further consideration to be received on an earn-out is paper, the basic relief for a paper-for-paper exchange does not apply as what is received at the time of the takeover is not paper, but a contingent right to paper. In these circumstances, an election is available to the taxpayer so that the right to paper is treated as paper and the reorganisation relief applies.[3] The effect of the election is that the right to receive paper is treated as if it were a security in the company making the takeover and is not a QCB.[4] Hence, if the paper to be issued will be a QCB, the date of acquisition of the QCB (and the start of the period for which the asset is exempt from CGT) is the date the profit target is reached, or such other contingency on the basis of which the QCB is issued. It is not the date of sale of the original equity.

The election is available if two main conditions are satisfied:[5]

(a) all or part of the consideration on a takeover is to be satisfied and satisfied only by the issue of shares or debentures; and
(b) the value or quantity of those shares or debentures is unascertainable at the time of the takeover.

The value or quantity of the shares or debentures is treated as unascertainable if and only if it is referable to the future business or assets of the target, the purchasing company, or any member of their respective groups.[6] The reference to future business is perhaps curious in the context of earn-outs, but presumably covers the normal measure of an earn-out, namely the future level of profits.

The value or quantity is not treated as unascertainable if the contingency is merely as to liability, for then TCGA 1992, s 48 applies.[7] A right to choose between shares or debentures does not of itself make their amount or value unascertainable, but nor does it stop s 138A from applying if it would otherwise do so.[8]

A further relief applies if one earn-out is extinguished and replaced by another. In such a case both the old and the new earn-out are treated as securities, the replacement of the old by the new being treated as a conversion of securities.[9] It is to be noted that this treatment applies only if the old and the new earn-out are in the same company.[10]

For rights conferred before 10 April 2003, the deferral benefit of TCGA 1992, s 138A had to be claimed by the taxpayer, within certain time limits. However,

[21.23] Shares and companies

in respect of rights conferred after 9 April 2003, s 138A is applied automatically unless the taxpayer elects for it not to apply.[11]

---

[1] TCGA 1992, s 48. See *Marson v Marriage* [1980] STC 177.
[2] *Marren v Ingles* [1980] STC 500.
[3] TCGA 1992, s 138A(2)(c) inserted by FA 1997, s 89, which gives statutory effect to Extra-statutory concession D27. Section 138A is deemed always to have had effect and so applies to any earn-out whenever conferred (sub-ss (2) and (6)). A claim previously made by the taxpayer under Extra-statutory concession D27 is treated as a claim under s 138A (sub-s (6)(b)).
[4] TCGA 1992, s 138A(3).
[5] TCGA 1992, s 138A(1) & (2).
[6] TCGA 1992, s 138A(7) & (10).
[7] TCGA 1992, s 138A(8).
[8] TCGA 1992, s 138A(9).
[9] TCGA 1992, s 138A(4).
[10] TCGA 1992, s 138A(4)(b).
[11] FA 2003, s 161.

[21.24] The rules relating to reorganisations of capital are also adapted to cover schemes of reconstruction or amalgamation where shares are issued by a company to the shareholders of another, but there is no exchange of shares. Instead, the original shares are either retained, perhaps with altered rights, or cancelled. In this case, the original shares are treated as having been exchanged for the new shares, so that the provisions in supra, § **21.20**, apply.[1] Generally, the new company must carry on substantially the same business as the old, and have substantially the same members. A mere segregation of assets would not be so treated. In practice, the split of a company's business between different sets of shareholders is treated as a reconstruction if it is carried out for bona fide commercial reasons.[2] This treatment was, however, concessionary. In *Fallon (Morgan's Executors) v Fellows*,[3] Park J held that the Revenue's application of its concessionary treatment on an arrangement in 1980 did not prohibit the executors requiring the strict statutory treatment for the computation of the gain that arose seven years later. Statute[4] restores the previous understanding based on Statement of Practice SP 5/85 in respect of shares and debentures issued after 16 April 2002.

Simon's Taxes C2.1521; Sumption CGT A13.06.

---

[1] TCGA 1992, s 136. Debentures are covered as well as shares.
[2] tatement of practice SP 5/85 incorporating statement of practice D14.
[3] [2001] STC 1409.
[4] FA 2002, Sch 9, which amends TCGA 1992, s 136. See also TCGA 1992, Sch 5AA for meaning of "Scheme of Reconstruction".

Anti-avoidance

[21.25] The reliefs outlined in supra, §§ **21.20–21.23**, are available only if two conditions are satisfied:[1]

(1) that the transaction is effected for bona fide commercial reasons; *and*
(2) that it does not form part of a scheme or arrangements of which the main purpose, or one of the main purposes, is avoidance of liability to CGT or corporation tax.

This anti-avoidance provision does not apply—so relief is always available—to a shareholder holding less than 5% of, (and less than 5% of any class of), the shares or debentures of the original company. In calculating this 5%, shares or debentures held by connected persons are treated as held by him.

There is a clearance procedure under which it is possible to establish in advance whether or not conditions 1 and 2 are regarded by the Revenue as satisfied.[2]

Condition 2 does not state which of the parties must have this purpose in mind. Common-sense suggests that the purpose should be that of the disposer since he is the person otherwise liable to an immediate charge to CGT; however, caution suggests that the purpose is to be found in the scheme and so perhaps in the minds of all or any of the parties to it.

In *New Angel Court Ltd v Adam*,[3] the High Court rejected a claim by HMRC that receiving loan notes on a paper for paper exchange constitutes avoidance.

The contrary conclusion was reached in *Snell v Revenue and Customs Comrs*[4] Vincent Snell held 91% of the issued share capital of his family company, for which an offer of £4,600,000 had been made by a third party. At the request of the vendor, the sale was effected by the acquired issuing loan stock, after which Vincent Snell left the UK and cashed in the loan stock while not resident in the UK. The Special Commissioner held[5] "that [Vincent Snell] had the purpose of becoming non-resident before redeeming the loan notes and accordingly that one of his main purposes (indeed the only main purpose) of effecting the arrangements was the avoidance of capital gains tax." The paper-for-paper exchange, thus, constituted a CGT disposal and tax was payable. In the High Court[6] Morritt J stated that it is necessary, first, to identify the arrangement and, then, ascertain its purpose. He commented that for there to be an "arrangement" it must have an ascertainable purpose and that it is the taxpayer's purpose at the date of the exchange that is the determining factor. If he had a purpose of becoming non-resident then an "arrangement" to avoid tax would exist. He then ruled that [TCGA 1992, s 137] provides for a right of deferral to be lost if it is to be used for the purpose not of deferral but of avoidance altogether. If that is a main purpose of the scheme or arrangements it matters not whether the scheme, etc was formed for the purpose of tax mitigation, avoidance or indeed evasion. In his judgement, the word "liability" should not be limited to an actual liability, but must include contingent or prospective liabilities. Sir Andrew Morritt sees "no reason to restrict the ambit of the word 'liability' so as to exclude that which is deferred". Where a charge to tax arises by virtue of this anti-avoidance provision, the charge is primarily on the person who is thereby treated as

[21.25] Shares and companies

making the disposal, being the holder of the original shares. However, there is also provision for the recovery of tax remaining unpaid after six months; tax is recovered from the person holding the shares unless there has been an intervening disposal other than one between spouses or members of a group of companies.[7]

Sumption CGT A13.05, 06.

[1] TCGA 1992, s 137.
[2] TCGA 1992, s 138.
[3] [2004] EWCA Civ 242, [2004] STC 779.
[4] [2007] STI 115 upholding the decision in [2006] STC (SCD) 296.
[5] [2006] STC (SCD) 296 para 16 at 309f.
[6] [2007] STI 115.
[7] TCGA 1992, s 137(4).

Corporate reorganisations—the European Community Directive

[21.26] Under a Directive on mergers and other corporate reorganisations issued in August 1990[1] member states are required to implement rules designed to avoid discrimination in this area.

The Directive on mergers is complex but its purpose is clear. Any tax charge on a capital gain arising on a corporate reorganisation (whether at the company or shareholder level) is to be postponed until the assets or new shares are actually disposed of.

There are limitations on the scope of the Directive. It applies only where the assets or liabilities transferred are "effectively connected with a permanent establishment of the receiving company in the member state of the transferring company"; it does not apply where the assets and liabilities are connected with a permanent establishment in a different state nor where both companies belong to the same state.

Rollover of chargeable gains is permitted where:

(1) an EC company transfers its UK trade to another EC company in exchange for securities issued by the transferee company;[2] or
(2) a UK company transfers its non-UK EC trade to another EC company in exchange for securities issued by the transferee company.[3]

Under 1, the assets are treated as transferred at no gain/no loss; under 2, the net chargeable gain is rolled into the securities acquired.

The Directive further provides that there is to be no charge at the shareholder level on the cancellation of the shares or the allotment of new ones (Articles 7, 8). These ideas are familiar from TCGA 1992, ss 135–138. These provisions have been amended so as to permit rollover whenever a company acquires voting control of another, regardless of whether 25% of the ordinary share capital is acquired.[4]

Two other Articles require mention. The first allows a state to withhold this special tax status when the principal objective of the transaction (or one of the principal objectives) is tax evasion or tax avoidance; if the transaction is not carried out for a valid commercial reason, such as the restructuring or rationalisation of the activities of the company, a presumption may arise that tax avoidance or evasion is intended. The UK implementation of the Directive incorporates the usual anti-avoidance provisions.[5] Relief may also be withheld if the result of the operation is to break any rules for employee-representation (this article will lapse if worker-participation as envisaged under the Social Charter ever reaches the statute book).

The second is Article 10 which deals with third countries. Where there is a transfer by a company of state P to a company of state Q but the assets belong to a permanent establishment in a third state, Z, State Z is to renounce any claim to tax. However where the establishment has incurred losses in Z which have been set against, and so reduced, the profits in state P, P may recapture those profits (Article 10.1). Subject to this both Z and Q must apply the normal rollover rules.[6] Where P taxes on a world-wide basis, as does the UK, it may tax the gains of the permanent establishment on condition that it gives relief for the tax which would have been charged in Z but for this rule (Article 10.2).

Whilst domestic rules insist that qualifying transfers should be wholly in exchange for shares, the Directive will allow up to 10% of the consideration to be in cash, although the cash element is not entitled to the deferral.

The Directive is throughout phrased in terms of capital gains. There is no mention of losses. However, the relevant UK legislation is drafted as an elective procedure in relation to the corporate level, although not at shareholder level, so there is relief for realised losses accruing to companies on a merger.

Simon's Direct Tax Service D1.907-909.

[1] *Simon's Tax Intelligence* 1990, p 749 (with minor corrections in *Simon's Tax Intelligence* 1991, p 92). See Chown *Intertax* 1990 Part 10, at p 409 and Widmann at p 412.
[2] TCGA 1992, s 140A.
[3] TCGA 1992, s 140C.
[4] TCGA 1992, s 135(1)(c), see supra, § **21.20**.
[5] TCGA 1992, ss 140B, 140D.
[6] TA 1988, s 815A.

Shares in building societies

[**21.27**] An investor can place money in a deposit account at a building society or, alternatively, he can open a share account. Although the commercial effect is, in general, identical, in the latter case he is a shareholder in the society with a vote at the annual general meeting. In recent years, a number of building societies have converted from mutual status to become banking companies. Such conversion has often been accompanied by payments to members of the building society. In *Foster v Williams* and *Horan v Williams*[1] the Special Commissioners heard two sample appeals against Revenue assessments to

[21.27] Shares and companies

CGT on sums received by investors in Cheltenham & Gloucester Building Society. In the case of a deposit account, the Special Commissioners held that the deposit account that was then held at Lloyds Bank after the takeover was a novation of the original account and, as such, the sum paid into the account at the time of the takeover is not subject to capital gains tax.

In the case of the building society share account, a charge to capital gains tax arises, but indexation allowance was available against the sum received. The indexation allowance was calculated by multiplying the amount in the share account at 31 March 1982 (or the opening balance, if later)—plus any subsequent deposits and less any withdrawals—by the percentage increase in RPI for the period from 31 March 1982 (or the month of deposit, if later) to the month of the takeover (or 5 April 1998, if earlier). Taper relief was also available. Prior to 29 November 1993 indexation allowance could create an allowable CGT loss, hence a withdrawal from the building society deposit could create an allowable CGT loss. This is no longer the case[2] and the CGT treatment of building society deposits and withdrawals has become academic.

[1] [1997] STC (SCD) 112.
[2] TCGA 1992, s 53(1)(b) amended by FA 1994, s 93(1): see supra, § **16.26**.

Miscellaneous

[21.28] A company does not own its shares so the issue of shares is not a chargeable disposal by the company. The figure at which the shares are issued, a matter of importance in calculating acquisition cost, is governed by TCGA 1992, s 17 (CGTA 1979, s 29A); see supra, § **18.48**.

Alterations in share rights may be chargeable disposals (supra, § **18.47**). On the position of the company's liability to gains, see infra, § **25.09**.

The gain arising on the disposal of a material interest in an offshore fund (an offshore income gain) is charged to income tax or corporation tax under the provisions of TA 1988, ss 757–764 and Sch 27, 28, see infra, § **35.45**.

22

Business and partnerships

Capital allowances	PARA **22.01**
Stock in trade	PARA **22.05**
Trading losses: CGT set-off	PARA **22.09**
Transfer of a business to a company	PARA **22.10**
Rollover relief	PARA **22.11**
Deferral relief	PARA **22.24**
Entrepreneurs' relief	PARA **22.32**
Gifts of business assets—holdover relief	PARA **22.35**
Partnerships	PARA **22.36**
European Economic Interest Grouping (EEIG)	PARA **22.47**
Non-residents trading in the UK	PARA **22.48**

Capital allowances

[22.01] Where assets are sold and a net gain arises on the sale, the fact that capital allowances have been claimed does not prevent the historic cost from being claimed as allowable expenditure;[1] this is because the scheme of allowances is that allowances given are recaptured on a sale by the balancing charge. In order for this treatment to apply, it is not necessary for there actually to be a balancing charge nor any charge. The total cost, before capital allowances, is used as the CGT base cost even if the sale proceeds merely reduce a carried forward capital allowance pool of expenditure on plant and machinery. The total cost, before capital allowances, is also used in computing the capital gain arising on the sale of an industrial building, even where the capital allowance granted will never be clawed back as the industrial building was brought into use more than 25 years before the sale. Where there is a balancing charge, this does not fall to be excluded from the consideration for disposal, notwithstanding the general exclusion for sums chargeable to income tax or corporation tax as income.[2]

Where, however, a loss arises on disposal of an asset on which allowances have been granted, the allowable expenditure is reduced by the amount of the allowance.[3] Allowances include any balancing allowance on disposal, but are net of any balancing charge on disposal. For disposals before 30 November 1993, it was possible for an allowable loss to arise in these circumstances, by virtue of the indexation allowance.[4] Unlike plant and machinery allowances, it is often the case that, on a commercial sale, an election is made so that industrial buildings allowance[5] is not normally clawed back on a transfer. Where the taxpayer has been treated, for capital allowances purposes, as having acquired an industrial building at a written down value, account must be taken in the computation of a capital gain on a subsequent disposal by the transferee of any allowances made to the previous person entitled to them.[6]

[22.01] Business and partnerships

In *Revenue and Customs Comrs v Smallwood*[7] Mr Smallwood invested £10,000 in March 1989 in an Enterprise Zone Property Unit Trust known as PET 8 in the Isle of Dogs Enterprise Zone. The trustees of PET 8 immediately spent the cash subscribed by Mr Smallwood, and the other unitholders, on land and buildings known as No 2 Harbour Exchange. To the extent that the money was spent on buildings, in contrast to the land, 100% first year capital allowances were obtained by Mr Smallwood and the other unitholders. Mr Smallwood's share of those allowances amounted to £9,678. Mr Smallwood claimed this allowance which was set off against his general income for 1988–89.

Nearly ten years later, the trustees realised a gain on the disposal of substantially the whole of their interest in No2 Harbour Exchange. The disposal was structured by the grant of a sub-underlease, designed to avoid balancing charges. In the tax years 1998–99 and 1999–2000, Mr Smallwood received distributions of £5,000 and £125. These fell to be treated for capital gains tax as part disposals by Mr Smallwood of his units.

Warren J ruled that under the statutory provisions[8] that apply to an Enterprise Zone Property Unit Trust the unit holders are treated as having acquired shares in a notional company, that notional company having purchased the property, the acquisition providing the capital allowances that flowed through to Mr Smallwood. On this basis, the capital gain that arises on the disposal of the property is computed without deduction of the capital allowances that were given on the original purchase and are not withdrawn by virtue of the manner in which the disposal was structured.

Simon's Taxes C2.217; Sumption CGT A4.08.

---

[1] TCGA 1992, s 41(1).
[2] TCGA 1992, s 37(2)(*a*). In *Hirsch v Crowthers Cloth Ltd* [1990] STC 174 the court held that the amendments to CGTA 1979, s 31(2) (now TCGA 1992, s 37(2)) made by FA 1980, s 83 merely made explicit what was already implicit in the unamended subsection.
[3] TCGA 1992, s 41—allowances include the renewals allowance (sub-s 4) whether or not the allowance is claimed.
[4] No indexation allowance is given to the extent that it would increase the amount of a loss, or convert a gain into a loss; TCGA 1992, s 53. For special situations, see infra, § **24.05**.
[5] See supra, § **20.17**.
[6] TCGA 1992, s 41(3).
[7] [2006] STC 2050.
[8] TCGA 1992, s 99.

[22.02] Suppose an asset is bought for £8,000; it has capital allowance of £3,000 giving a written down value of £5,000. It is then sold for £8,000. There will be a balancing charge of £3,000. For CGT purposes the asset is treated as bought for £8,000 and sold for £8,000 so giving no gain. If the asset had been sold for £10,000 the balancing charge would still be £3,000 and there would be a raw gain for CGT of £2,000.

Following the rebasing of CGT to 31 March 1982, capital allowances given in respect of the actual expenditure incurred are treated as given in respect of the deemed acquisition cost on 31 March 1982.[1]

Similarly (since 6 April 2008, relevant only for corporation tax), if the asset was acquired before 6 April 1965 and the taxpayer elects to take the value on 6 April 1965 instead of the time apportionment rule, adjustments are made only for allowances after that date.[2]

Simon's Taxes C2.103; Sumption CGT A4.08.

[1] TCGA 1992, Sch 3, para 3.
[2] TCGA 1992, Sch 2, para 20.

Sale proceeds less than £6,000

[22.03] In most cases, plant and machinery on which capital allowances have been claimed are tangible movable property. Where this is the case and the asset is sold for £6,000 or less, the effect of TCGA 1992, s 262 is that no chargeable gain arises. Marginal relief may be available where sale consideration is above this level. Losses are restricted by acquisition being taken as £6,000 where this is greater than the actual acquisition cost.

In most cases plant and machinery on which capital allowances have been claimed are wasting assets. However, the exemption for wasting assets is excluded where since the beginning of the period of ownership, the asset has been used solely for the purposes of a trade, profession or vocation and the taxpayer was entitled to claim capital allowance in respect of the expenditure on the asset.[1] It is not possible for a taxpayer carrying on a trade, etc, to bring himself within the capital gains tax exemption by electing not to claim the capital allowance; the test is whether the allowance could have been claimed under statute. In *Burman v Westminster Press Ltd*[2] the Court confirmed that TCGA 1992, s 45(2) does not have effect where the asset is sold before being brought into use. (A gain arising on the disposal of plant and machinery may, however, be exempt by virtue of it being a chattel sold for £6,000 or less.)[3]

In general, the acquisition cost for a wasting asset is scaled down before the gain is calculated.[4] However, this straight line restriction of allowable expenditure is not applied in the case of a wasting asset that qualified for capital allowances.[5]

Simon's Taxes C1.407, C2.905.

[1] TCGA 1992, s 45(2). Capital allowances are capable of being claimed if the expenditure concerned is of a qualifying kind. Expenditure is not of a qualifying kind if the asset is sold before being brought into use so that no allowances are due: *Burman v Westminster Press Ltd* [1987] STC 669.
[2] [1987] STC 669.
[3] TCGA 1992, s 262(5), see supra, § **17.19**.
[4] TCGA 1992, s 46.
[5] TCGA 1992, s 47(1).

[22.04] Business and partnerships

Renewals allowance

[22.04] Although statute does not specifically authorise the construction of accounts for tax purposes on the basis of "renewals", repeated Revenue statements have confirmed the Revenue's acceptance of this principle.[1] This acceptance is probably based on the concept that profit can properly be measured by the gain made on circulating capital, plus the cost of replacing fixed capital. Such a formulation has little in common with current commercial accountancy, but the courts have frequently expressed 'profit' in these terms.[2]

Where the renewals basis is used, a charge is put into the accounts, being the cost to the taxpayer of replacing an item of plant or machinery when it is in need of renewal.[3]

Where a renewals basis is used, the treatment of capital gains and losses on the disposal of the asset is the same as where a capital allowance has been claimed, except that the amount charged in the accounts for the renewal is treated as if it were a capital allowance.[4]

Simon's Taxes C2.217.

---

1 See, for example, HMRC Guidance, Inspector's Manual, IM 1727a.
2 See, for example, per Swinfen Eady LJ in *Ammonia Soda Co v Chamberlain* [1918] 1 Ch 266 and per Romer LJ in *Golden Horseshoe (New) Ltd v Thurgood* [1934] 1 KB 548, 18 TC 280; *Pattison v Marine Midland Ltd* [1981] STC 540.
3 See further, Chapter 9.
4 TCGA 1992, s 41(5) introduces the concept of a "renewal allowance" and defines it in these terms.

Stock in trade

[22.05] Rules are needed to govern situations in which assets move between the income tax regime and the CGT regime.

Appropriation to trade

[22.06] On the appropriation of capital assets to trading stock of a trade, there is a deemed disposal at market value, unless the nature of the asset is such that the disposal would be exempt from CGT.[1]

Since this disposal does not apply if there would be no chargeable gain, the exemptions for wasting chattels (subject to the capital allowance restriction) and chattels where the consideration does not exceed £6,000 are of particular importance here.

Where the trader is assessable to income or corporation tax in respect of a trade (and the trade is not carried on wholly abroad), the taxpayer can elect that the figure at which the trading stock is entered is reduced by the amount of any gain or increased by the amount of any loss.[2] Where such an election is made no chargeable gain or allowable loss arises on the appropriation to trading stock. Instead the market value of the asset to be included in the computation of trading profit is reduced by the amount of the chargeable gain which would otherwise have arisen (or increased by the amount of the allowable loss which would otherwise have arisen). The effect of this election is to leave income tax to be levied in due course on the profit derived from the disposal in the course of trade.

In order to qualify as an appropriation to trading stock there must be a genuine trading purpose in mind, and not simply a wish to gain a tax advantage.[3] Thus, the asset must not only be of a kind sold in the ordinary course of the trade but also acquired with a view to resale at a profit.[4]

Where the trade is carried on in partnership, all partners must join in the election.[5]

Simon's Taxes C3.801, 802.

[1] TCGA 1992, s 161(1).
[2] TCGA 1992, s 161(3).
[3] Coates v Arndale Properties Ltd [1984] STC 637; Reed v Nova Securities [1984] STC 124, CA; N Ltd v Inspector of Taxes [1996] STC (SCD) 346.
[4] Per Lord Templeman in Reed v Nova Securities Ltd [1985] STC 124 at 130F.
[5] TCGA 1992, s 161(4).

Appropriation from trade

[22.07] Where an asset which has been trading stock is appropriated by the trader for any other purpose or is retained on the ending of the trade, it is deemed to be acquired for CGT at the figure entered in the accounts of the trade.[1] The figure at which the asset is entered in the accounts of the trade will presumably be the amount relevant for income tax purposes. Historically, HMRC have argued that this would be the market value under the rule in *Sharkey v Wernher*[2]. That had been challenged as of late and from 12 March 2008, that rule has been given statutory authority. On a discontinuance, the amount would be that given under ITTOIA 2005, ss 175-178 (or TA 1988, s 100 for corporation tax). On a death ITTOIA 2005 will not apply but market value will be imposed by TCGA 1992, s 62.

Simon's Taxes C3.801, 802.

[1] TCGA 1992, s 161(2).
[2] [1956] AC 58.

Spouses and civil partners

[22.08] In general, there is no chargeable gain or allowable loss on a disposal between spouses or civil partners living together; the asset is treated as disposed of and acquired for a consideration of such amount that neither gain nor loss accrues.[1]

[22.08] Business and partnerships

This treatment does not apply if until the disposal the asset formed part of the trading stock of a trade carried on by the person making the disposal. The transfer is then treated as being made at market value.[2]

The no gain/no loss treatment on a transfer between spouses or civil partners is also excluded where an asset owned by one party is acquired by the other and taken into trading stock. The transfer is, again, treated as being made at market value, but with an election available on the appropriation to trading stock.[3]

Simon's Taxes C1.202, C2.112.

---

[1] TCGA 1992, s 58(1).
[2] TCGA 1992, s 58(2)(a).
[3] TCGA 1992, s 161(3). See supra, § 22.06.

Trading losses: CGT set-off

[22.09] Income losses are not in general a permitted deduction from chargeable gains in the case of persons other than companies. However, a claim may be made to set the trading loss against chargeable gains.[1] The amount of the loss for which relief may be claimed is the trading loss arising, less the amount that has been set-off against income for the year of loss or the preceding year.[2] This amount is then treated as an allowable capital loss for that year and set off against chargeable gains.

For a trading loss suffered in 2004–05, or a later year, the trading loss is set off against the gain. For years before 2008–09 the loss was calculated before applying taper relief.[3] This means that the anomaly that previously arose whereby the loss was restricted to a tapered gain and, hence, part of the gain remained in charge, is then corrected. For a loss arising in 2003–04, the taxpayer can elect for the new treatment to apply.[4]

The setoff is before taking account of the annual exemption. There is no provision for claiming only part of the trading loss that would otherwise be available. If the loss exceeds the chargeable gains for the year, the excess is carried forward as a trading loss, not a capital loss.[5]

Sumption CGT A1.03.

---

[1] FA 1991, s 72.
[2] Under TA 1988, s 380, see supra, § 6.15.
[3] A 1991, s 72(4) amended by FA 2002, s 48(1).
[4] FA 2002, s 48(3).
[5] FA 1991, s 72(3).

Transfer of a business to a company

[22.10] The transfer of a business to a company is a disposal of the assets of the business by the owner and so can give rise to chargeable gains and allowable losses. However, a form of rollover relief applies where shares are received in exchange for the business.[1] This applies where the whole of the business,[2] and not merely the assets of a business, is transferred to a company as a going concern;[3] all the business assets being assigned. In practice, the taxpayer can choose whether or not the company takes on the liabilities of the unincorporated business. In strictness, the assumption of liabilities by the company should be regarded as consideration given for the transfer of the business. By concession, this form of consideration is ignored.[4]

If there is any other form of consideration, the gain allocated to the consideration is chargeable immediately. When the shares are themselves disposed of, the amount by which the gain has been reduced and which escaped tax before must be deducted from the cost of the shares and so becomes chargeable.

Where the transfer of the unincorporated business took place before 6 April 2002, the above treatment is mandatory. Where the transfer takes place on or after 6 April 2002, the taxpayer can elect that the transfer triggers a capital gain and this form of rollover relief is not applied.[5] This election was introduced in the taper relief era because, especially if a sale of the business was imminent, the gain arising on incorporation would have attracted more taper relief than the taper relief arising on the subsequent disposal of the shares.

As in other cases where rollover relief is given, the rebasing of CGT to 31 March 1982 arbitrarily eliminated gains rolled over against shares before 1 April 1982, but not gains rolled over on or after that date. Where the roll-over acquisition was made before 6 April 1988, one-half of the gain rolled over was exempt on a subsequent disposal of the shares.[6] This halving relief was abolished in respect of capital gains tax disposals on or after 6 April 2008 but continues for corporation tax.

Similarly, where a person controls a close company through shares which he acquired before 7 April 1965, there was (and remains for corporation tax) a restriction on the application of time apportionment on disposal of the shares if assets have been transferred to the company by him.[7]

Simon's Taxes Division C3.4; Sumption CGT A14.08.

---

[1] TCGA 1992, s 162. (cf TA 1988, s 386, supra, § **5.13**.)
[2] Quaere the meaning of business as distinct from trade or profession—see *American Leaf Blending Co Sdn Bhd v Director-General of Inland Revenue* [1978] STC 561, [1978] 3 All ER 1185.
[3] There may be no succession to the trade if the company intends to close it down (supra, § **7.51**) but whether there is a continuing business is a question of fact, to be decided on the circumstances at the time of transfer: see *Gordon v IRC* [1991] STC 174, Ct of Sess.
[4] Extra-statutory concession D32.
[5] TCGA 1992, s 162A inserted by FA 2002, s 50(1).

[22.10] Business and partnerships

[6] TCGA 1992, Sch 4, para 2.
[7] TCGA 1992, Sch 2, para 21.

Rollover relief

Outline

[22.11] Rollover relief enables a charge to capital gains tax to be deferred until the subsequent sale of the asset into which the gain has been rolled. Rollover relief is only available for a person carrying on a trade (**22.15** infra) and only for assets within the categories specified by statute (**22.13** infra).

Rollover relief may be complete or partial. Rollover relief is only available where the claimant carries on a trade and both the old and the new assets are used in a trade[1] carried on by the taxpayer.

Where investment is into a depreciating asset, the gain deferred can crystallise before the sale of the new asset.

Rollover relief is also available to an individual in respect of an asset used in the trade of a company, or used in the course of his employment or used by a partnership of which he is a member.

The new asset must be acquired within specified time limits, which can be extended by the exercise of Revenue discretion.

There are special provisions whereby rollover relief can be claimed when there is a disposal by one member of a group of companies and an acquisition by another. However, rollover relief is not available when the reinvestment is into the same asset.[2]

There are also special provisions where a gain is rolled into property that subsequently becomes the taxpayer's main residence.

A taxpayer can choose not to pay capital gains tax on a disposal where he expects to claim rollover relief on that disposal.[3]

Simon's Taxes Division C3.3.

[1] In *Re Loquitar Ltd, IRC v Richmond* [2003] EWHC 999 (Ch), [2003] STC 1394 it was held that there was no real trading activity where there was a failed attempt at tax avoidance.
[2] *Watton v Tippett* [1997] STC 893, CA see infra, § **22.22**.
[3] FA 1996, s 41.

Types of asset

[22.12] The relief is available only for certain types of asset as follows:[1]

(a) any building or part of a building and any permanent or semi-permanent structure in the nature of a building, occupied (as well as used) only for the purposes of the trade;[2]

(b)   any land occupied (as well as used) only for the purposes of the trade;
(c)   fixed plant or machinery which does not form part of a building or of a permanent or semi-permanent structure in the nature of a building;[3]
(d)   ships and aircraft;
(e)   goodwill;
(f)   satellites, space stations and space vehicles (including launch vehicles);[4]
(g)   milk quotas and potato quotas;[5]
(h)   ewe and suckler cow premium quotas;[6]
(i)   fish quota;[7]
(j)   rights of a member of a Lloyd's Syndicate;[8]
(k)   oil licences.[9]

Under (b), land does not qualify if it is occupied for the purposes of a trade of dealing in or developing land, unless the profit on sale of such land would not be a profit of the trade.[10] In order to qualify for rollover relief, land and buildings must be occupied by the taxpayer. The leading case on the nature of occupation is *Northern Ireland Comr of Valuation v Fermanagh Protestant Board of Education*[11] where Lord Upjohn said:[12]

> The result of the authorities on this question of occupation seems to me quite clearly to be as follows. First, if it is essential to the performance of the duties of the occupying servant that he should occupy the particular house, or it may be a house within a closely defined perimeter, then, it being established that this is the mutual understanding of the master and the servant, the occupation for rating and other ancillary purposes is that of the master and not of the servant . . .

A distinction can be drawn between a person who receives from his employer a right to live in the property (which is beneficial occupation by the employee) and an employee who is paid to live in the premises (which is representative occupation). It is only when occupation is in the second category that rollover relief is available.[13] The test here is the general one and not the special test now used in ITEPA 2003, s 99.[14] Occupation of a farmhouse is rarely representative occupation. In *Anderton v Lamb*,[15] rollover relief was claimed for houses occupied by junior partners of a partnership. The claim failed.

Category (e) has caused difficulty in practice. The courts have given the term "goodwill" a wide meaning. In *Balloon Promotions v Wilson*[16] the Special Commissioner held that a payment to a franchisee was a payment for goodwill and qualified for rollover relief. The Commissioner rejected the argument of HMRC Counsel that the only goodwill in a franchise operation belongs to the franchiser. HMRC subsequently published a guidance note[17], in which it is stated: 'As the Commissioner's conclusions were based on findings of fact we do not consider that the decision is of general application to other cases involving the sale of franchised businesses.'

It is not necessary for the old and new assets to be of the same type, provided that both old and new fall within one or other of the classes (a)–(k).

If there was trade use only for a part of the period of ownership an apportionment is made.[18] An asset used only partly for trade purposes does not qualify although this rule is relaxed for buildings.[19] A person carrying on two trades, whether successively or concurrently, is treated as carrying on one trade.[20] Hence relief can be claimed where the old asset belonged to trade A and the new one to trade B. Any artificial discontinuance of a trade for income tax purposes is disregarded.[21] Too long a gap between the end of trade A and the start of trade B will prevent them being treated as being carried on successively.[22]

The requirement that a new asset be acquired is substantially relaxed in practice. The Revenue have stated that the relief applies where a partnership asset, whether land or any other qualifying asset, is partitioned on the dissolution of the partnership.[23] The relief is also available where the disposal proceeds are used to enhance an existing asset used for the purposes of the trade rather than acquiring a new asset,[24] or where the proceeds are spent acquiring a further interest in an asset already used for the trade.[25] The rules are also relaxed where the new asset is not brought immediately into use but work is done on it and it is then brought into use; for example, where land is bought and a building is built or reconstructed. The land must not be used for any non-trade purpose nor let during this period of work.[26] If an unconditional contract for the acquisition has been entered into, provisional rollover relief may be given at once. If the contract is subsequently cancelled, or any other event occurs that changes the tax payable, an adjustment is made later, when the adjusting event occurs.

The new acquisition must take place within a period beginning 12 months before and ending 36 months after the date of disposal or such other time as the Board may by notice in writing allow.[27] The Revenue are prepared to extend the time limit where the new assets acquired are, in broad terms, replacement for the old assets and the taxpayer was prevented by a circumstance beyond his control from investing within the statutory limit, but acted as soon as he reasonably could.[28] The legislation requires that the proceeds be applied in acquiring the new asset; this does not appear to carry too literal an interpretation. In practice, it is sufficient to match disposal proceeds with one or more items of qualifying expenditure, regardless of how that expenditure was in fact financed.

Where the trade is carried on by a family company but the person owning and replacing the asset is an individual, relief may be claimed, provided the company is his family company.[29] This provision does not apply where the asset is held by another company nor if the company owns the asset and the individual carries on the trade. The old and new assets must both be used either for a trade of the individual or for a trade of the company. It is not possible to roll over gains realised by the individual against expenditure incurred by the company, or vice versa.

In *Maclean v Revenue and Customs Comrs*[30] rollover relief was denied on serviced holiday apartments.

Simon's Taxes C3.303.

---

[1] TCGA 1992, ss 152(1), 155.
[2] For an illustration see *Joseph Carter & Sons Ltd v Baird* [1999] STC 120.
[3] *Williams v Evans* [1982] STC 498.
[4] TCGA 1992, s 155.
[5] TCGA 1992, s 155.

6 TCGA 1992, s 155.
7 Finance Act 1993, s 86(2) (Fish Quota) Order 1999, SI 1999/564; see Inland Revenue press release, 2 March 1999, *Simon's Weekly Tax Intelligence* 1999, p 349.
8 FA 1999, s 84.
9 FA 1999, s 103.
10 TCGA 1992, s 156.
11 [1969] 1 WLR 1708.
12 [1969] 1 WLR 1708 at 1772.
13 *Langley v Appleby* [1976] STC 368.
14 See Chapter 7.
15 [1981] STC 43.
16 [2006] STC (SCD) 167.
17 HMRC Tax Bulletin 83, June 2006 pages 1291to 1292. The Revenue confirm that they do not propose to appeal against the decision in *Balloon Promotions v Wilson*.
18 TCGA 1992, s 152(7).
19 TCGA 1992, s 152(6).
20 TCGA 1992, s 152(8).
21 TCGA 1992, s 158(2).
22 *Steibelt v Paling* [1999] STC 594, Ch D.
23 Extra-statutory concession D23.
24 Extra-statutory concession D22. This is one of the concessions at which TCGA 1992, ss 284A and 284B are aimed; see supra, § **16.01**.
25 Extra-statutory concession D25.
26 Extra-statutory concession D24.
27 TCGA 1992, s 152(3), (4).
28 Revenue Manual gives comprehensive guidance to local inspectors on the policy of the Revenue in extending the statutory time limit: see infra § **22.21**.
29 TCGA 1992, s 157.
30 [2007] STC (SCD) 350, [2007] SWTI 1058.

Operation of rollover relief

[22.13] A trader who disposes of assets in the specified categories[1] used for the purposes of his trade throughout the period of ownership may elect to defer any liability to CGT by means of rollover relief.[2] Other qualifying assets must be acquired within a prescribed period before or after the date of the disposal. The deferral is until such time as he disposes of the new assets or interest in the new assets; however, because the deferral simply takes the form of an adjustment of the cost of the new assets the deferred charge does not crystallise just because the trade is discontinued or because the asset ceases to be used for trade purposes.

If the relief is claimed, the disposal is treated as reduced by the lower of: (a) the amount spent on the new asset, and (b) the gain that would otherwise arise on the disposal. The same sum is then deducted from the base cost of the new assets. Full rollover is available provided that the acquisition cost of the new assets equals or exceeds the actual disposal proceeds of the old asset.

[22.13] Business and partnerships

EXAMPLE

K sold for £200,000 a workshop which he had purchased in 1974, realising a chargeable gain of £54,000. Six months later, he exchanges contracts on new business premises which cost £230,000. K claims rollover relief.

(a) Disposal consideration	£200,000
Chargeable gain	54,000
Deemed consideration	£146,000
(b) Cost of new property	£230,000
Chargeable gain rolled over	54,000
Base cost deemed to be	£176,000

A grant obtained is ignored. That is, the gain can be rolled into a new asset where the cost of the new asset equals, or exceeds, the proceeds of sale of the old asset, even if part of the cost of the new asset attracts a grant.[3]

Rollover relief was applied before taper relief.[4]

Where a gain is rolled over against more than one item of qualifying expenditure, there is no prescribed method of apportioning the gain.

Where a chargeable gain was rolled over into an asset acquired after March 1982, the rebasing of CGT to that date has no ameliorating effect. For corporation tax (or, for capital gains tax disposals before 6 April 2008) relief is given by deducting one-half of the rolled over gain when computing gains on a subsequent disposal.[5]

Where a disposal is made after 31 March 1982 and the gain was rolled into an acquisition before that date, the effect of rebasing is to provide a permanent relief for the gain that was rolled over as the base cost for the asset acquired is taken as the value at 31 March 1982, ignoring the reduction occasioned by the rollover.

Relief is available if a person sells a business, or a business asset, and for purely commercial reasons subsequently repurchases the same asset[6] but not for improvement expenditure on an asset following a part disposal out of that asset.[7]

Simon's Taxes C3.301–305.

---

[1] See supra, § **21.16**.
[2] TCGA 1992, s 152.
[3] *Wardhaugh v Penrith Rugby Union Football Club* [2002] EWHC 918 (Ch), [2002] STC 776.
[4] TCGA 1992, s 2A.
[5] TCGA 1992, Sch 4, para 2.
[6] Extra-statutory concession D16. This is one of the concessions at which TCGA 1992, ss 284A and 284B are aimed, see supra, § **16.01**.
[7] *Watton v Tippett* [1997] STC 893, CA. See also infra, § **22.22**.

Partial rollover

[22.14] If the acquisition cost of the new assets is less than the disposal proceeds of the old asset, only partial rollover is available. Relief is available only to the extent that the gain element has to be used in acquiring the new asset.

The chargeable gain is in such a case limited to the difference between the disposal proceeds of the old asset and the acquisition cost of the new assets.[1]

The balance of the chargeable gain is rolled over against the cost of the new assets. Where the gain is only partly chargeable, eg because of time apportionment, the gain rolled over is scaled down rateably.

EXAMPLE 1

N disposes of a qualifying business asset for £75,000, realising a chargeable gain of £25,000. He acquires a replacement asset for £60,000 and claims rollover relief.

Gain remaining chargeable: £75,000 − £60,000 = £15,000
Gain eligible for rollover: £25,000 − £15,000 = £10,000
Adjusted base cost of new asset: £60,000 − £10,000 = £50,000

EXAMPLE 2

J sells a business asset which has been owned since 1960. The sale price is £120,000 and the gain is £90,000. After time apportionment, the chargeable gain is £70,000. J buys a new asset for £100,000 and claims rollover relief.

Gain not reinvested: £120,000 − £100,000		= £20,000
Chargeable gain deemed not reinvested:	$\dfrac{70,000}{90,000} \times £20,000$	= £15,555
Chargeable gain rolled over: £70,000 − £15,555		= £54,445
Adjusted base cost of new asset: £100,000 − £54,445		= £45,555

Relief is also restricted where the old asset was not used for trade purposes throughout the period of ownership,[2] or—in the case of buildings—a distinguishable part was used for non-trade purposes.[3] The restriction in the former case is on a time basis. Only periods after the new base date of 31 March 1982 are relevant in the time apportionment calculation.[4]

Simon's Taxes C3.309, 321.

---

[1] TCGA 1992, s 153.
[2] TCGA 1992, s 152(7).
[3] TCGA 1992, s 152(6).
[4] TCGA 1992, s 152(9).

Trade

[22.15] Rollover relief is available to any person. Thus, a company can claim rollover relief as well as an individual, a trustee or executor. The claimant must be a person who is carrying on a "trade". For this purpose, "trade" is "every trade, manufacture, adventure, or concern in the nature of trade"[1] plus the following that are treated as trades for the purpose of rollover relief only:

(a) the functions of a public authority;[2]
(b) the occupation of woodlands on a commercial basis;[3]
(c) the carrying on of a profession, vocation, office or employment;[4]
(d) non-profit making activities for the protection or promotion of the interests of members who are themselves carrying on a trade;[5]
(e) other non-profit making activities insofar as the assets concerned are used by the non-profit making body;[6]
(f) a company where shares are mostly held for an unincorporated association not established for profit;[7]
(g) a company holding assets used in the trade of another member of the group;[8]
(h) furnished holiday lettings;[9]
(i) the leasing of tied premises (such as by a brewer).[10]

Unless the property is a holiday furnished letting, roll over relief cannot be claimed on the disposal of let property, nor on the acquisition of let property as letting property is not a trade.[11]

Simon's Taxes C3.921.

---

[1] TCGA 1992, ss 152, 158. With effect from 29 November 1994, the cultivation of short rotation coppice is treated as farming, and the land concerned is agricultural land, not woodlands: FA 1995, s 154.
[2] TCGA 1992, s 158(1)(a).
[3] TCGA 1992, s 158(1)(b).
[4] TCGA 1992, s 158(1)(c).
[5] TCGA 1992, s 158(1)(c).
[6] TCGA 1992, s 158(1)(e).
[7] Extra-statutory concession D15. This is one of the concessions at which TCGA 1992, ss 284A and 284B are aimed; see supra, § **16.01**.
[8] TCGA 1992, s 175(2B).
[9] TCGA 1992, s 241.
[10] TCGA 1992, s 156.
[11] *Griffiths v Jackson* [1983] STC 184 applied to CGT by *Hatt v Newman* [2000] STC 113.

Asset used in the trade

[22.16] The new asset[1] must be "taken into use, and used only, for the purposes of the trade".[2] This encompasses expenditure on an asset that is for the trade of a subsidiary.[3]

The new asset must be actually taken into use; intention is not sufficient.[4]

In *Milton v Chivers*[5] John Milton appealed against the rejection of his claim for rollover relief on the basis that the proceeds of disposal were used to purchase premises which were subsequently used for the purpose of an existing launderette trade known as "Bubbles", which was carried on by the taxpayer in partnership with another. The Special Commissioner found, as a fact, that the premises were purchased in August 1991 but the taxpayer did not decide until February 1992 that he would use the premises for this trade and the premises were not opened for business until 24 July 1992. In denying his claim, the Special Commissioner said:

> 'On the acquisition'. . . does not imply immediacy but it does exclude dilatoriness. The taking into use and the acquisition must be reasonably approximate to one another.

The strict statutory requirement is relaxed by extra-statutory concession D24, which states:

> Where a 'new asset' is not, on acquisition, immediately taken into use for the purposes of a trade, it will nevertheless qualify for relief under [ss 152–158] provided that:
>
> (a) the owner proposes to incur capital expenditure for the purposes of enhancing its value;
> (b) any work arising from such capital expenditure begins as soon as possible after acquisition, and is completed within a reasonable time;
> (c) on completion of the work the asset is taken into use for the purpose of trade and for no other purpose; and
> (d) the asset is not let or used for any non-trading purpose in the period between acquisition and the time it is taken into use for the purposes of the trade.

Where a taxpayer carries on more than one trade, rollover relief is available where there is a disposal of an asset used in one trade and an acquisition of a new asset for use in another trade.[6] Revenue practice is to accept a claim for rollover relief where one trade commences after the other has ceased as long as the gap between the two trades does not exceed three years.[7]

Simon's Taxes C3.921.

---

1 On ownership of new asset see *Carter v Baird* [1999] STC 120.
2 TCGA 1992, s 152(1).
3 *Robinson v Scott Bader Co Ltd* [1981] STC 436.
4 *Temperley v Visibell* [1974] STC 64; *Campbell Connelly & Co Ltd v Barnett* [1994] STC 50.
5 [1996] STC (SCD) 36.
6 TCGA 1992, s 152(8).
7 Statement of practice SP8/81.

Investment in a depreciating asset

[22.17] The relief is modified where the new asset is a depreciating asset, that is a wasting asset or one which will become a wasting asset within ten years.[1] The gain is not deductible from the cost of the new asset but instead is held over until:

(a) the new asset is disposed of, or
(b) the new asset ceases to be used for the purposes of the trade, or
(c) ten years have expired,

whichever first occurs. Where the asset ceases to be used for the purposes of the trade by reason of the death of the taxpayer, any gain held over is, by concession, exempted from tax.[2]

If a third asset is acquired, which is not a depreciating asset, the held over gain can be rolled over to the new acquisition and deducted from its acquisition cost in the usual way. The new acquisition need not occur within the usual period beginning on the disposal of the first asset but must occur before one of the events (a)–(c) has occurred. Part of the held over gain may be rolled over if the expenditure on the non depreciating asset is insufficient for full rollover.[3]

Gains arising on disposals prior to 1 April 1982 are not brought back into charge if held over against depreciating assets.[4] In addition, for corporation tax purposes, where a held over gain is attributable to the disposal before 6 April 1988 of an asset acquired before 31 March 1982, one half of the gain is excluded from charge on the occurrence of the relevant event.[5] This was the case for capital gains tax prior to 6 April 2008.

Simon's Taxes C3.311.

[1] TCGA 1992, s 154.
[2] Extra-statutory concession D45.
[3] TCGA 1992, s 154(6).
[4] TCGA 1992, Sch 4, para 4(5).
[5] CGA 1992, Sch 4, para 4.

Asset used in the trade of a company

[22.18] Where an asset is owned by a company that is a member of a group, the rollover relief provisions apply by considering the use of the asset within the group as a whole; that is, the requirement that the asset be "used in the trade" is satisfied if it is used in the trade of another group member.[1] The test of eligibility being applied to a group of companies also allows rollover relief where the disposal is made by one member of the group and the acquisition by another.[2]

It is frequently desirable for land and buildings to be owned by an individual, or a group of individuals, even though the trade is carried on by the family company. Where an asset owned by one or more of the individuals is sold, rollover relief cannot be claimed if the replacement asset is purchased by the company. Where the purchase of the new asset is by the individual who made the disposal, rollover relief is available to that individual where the old asset was used in a trade carried on by a company in which the individual has at least 5% of the voting rights.[3] As capital gains tax is applied to individuals, where an asset is owned jointly by husband and wife or by a group of individuals, whether in partnership or not, the test for the availability of rollover relief is applied by looking at the interest of each individual on whom the gain arises. Thus, for example, if a company carries a retail trade in a shop that is owned equally by husband and wife but all the shares in the company are owned by the husband, he can claim rollover relief on his sale of the shop but she cannot.

It is often desirable for a company to pay rent for the use of a property owned by one or more individuals. This does not necessarily preclude a claim for rollover relief being made by that individual when the property is sold. Section 157 is silent on the question of payment by the company for the use of the asset owned by the individual. Generally, if a property is let, particularly at a full market rent, the nature of the property is that of an investment asset and not a trading asset. However, on examining the structure of s 155, it is apparent that it is the "asset" which must be a qualifying asset, that is, in the case of land or buildings, "occupied (as well as used) only for the purposes of the trade". The disposal and acquisition referred to in s 152(1) may however be of the asset itself or of an interest in such a qualifying asset. Section 157 treats the trade of a personal company as having been carried on by the individual who owned the assets (or an interest in them) so that if in relation to the company the assets are qualifying assets the s 155 test may be satisfied by the individual.

If the company occupies land or buildings under a lease from the individual his reversionary interest is nevertheless an interest in a qualifying asset.

These requirements are not satisfied if the old assets were but the new assets were not used in the trade of his personal company; he is brought within s 152(1) only where both assets were so used. His ownership and the company's use must apply throughout. Similarly, he must have a 5% shareholding on the occasion both of the disposal of the old assets and the acquisition of the new assets, although the company could carry on one trade using the old assets and another trade using the new assets.[4]

The Revenue consider[5] that these provisions apply only to a single company. If the individual has a 5% interest in two companies, the gain he makes on the sale of an asset he owns which has been used in the trade of the first company cannot be rolled into an acquisition of an asset that will be used in the trade of the second company.

Simon's Taxes C3.316.

---

[1] TCGA 1992, s 175: see infra, § **28.28**.
[2] CGA 1992, s 175(2A)(*b*).
[3] TCGA 1992, s 157(*b*); see *Boparan v Revenue and Customs Comrs* [2007] STC (SCD) 297, [2007] SWTI 552.
[4] TCGA 1992, s 152(8).
[5] Inland Revenue Press Release, 10 November 1981.

Asset used in an employment

[22.19] TCGA 1992, s 158(1)(*c*) provides for rollover relief to be available to an employee who disposes of qualifying assets that he has used in his employment and reinvests in further qualifying assets.

Simon's Taxes C3.302.

Partnerships

[22.20] Rollover relief is available to an individual who owns an asset which has been used in the trade he carries on in partnership.

Where an asset is held by a partnership, TCGA 1992, s 59 provides that each individual partner is treated on the basis that he owns a fractional part of the asset. Hence, rollover relief can be claimed by an individual partner in respect of a gain arising on his part of an asset sold by his partnership. The individual partner can then roll the gain into an acquisition by the partnership or, alternatively, an acquisition he makes personally outside the partnership, whether for the purposes of the partnership trade or for some other trade. Each partner is treated separately; it is possible for one partner to claim rollover relief without other partners making a claim.

Simon's Taxes C3.201.

Time limit for new acquisition

[22.21] TCGA 1992, s 152(3) provides that the new asset must be acquired not earlier than 12 months before the date of disposal of the old assets and not later than 36 months after that date. The Revenue are empowered to extend this time limit (in either direction); the General Commissioners have no power to review a Revenue refusal to exercise that discretion.[1] Revenue practice on extending the time limit is given in Revenue Staff Manual which states:

Extension of the time limit in s 152(3) is permitted where:

- the new assets are, in broad terms a replacement for the old assets; and
- the claimants were prevented by some fact or circumstance beyond their control from complying with the time limit; and
- acted as soon as they reasonably could after ceasing to be so prevented.

Where the acquisition preceded the disposal, acceptable reasons might include:

- the threat of compulsory acquisition of the old asset;
- difficulty in disposing of the old asset;
- the acquisition of land with the intention of erecting a building on it;
- the need to have new premises functioning before the old premises can be vacated.

Claimants must satisfy the Board that they had a firm intention to acquire the material qualifying asset within the time limit but were prevented from doing so by circumstances beyond their control. A shortage of funds arising out of inability to sell the newsagent's shop would not be regarded as circumstances beyond the claimant's control.[2]

---

[1] *Steibelt v Paling* [1999] STC 594. But refusal could be the subject of judicial review.
[2] HMRC Guidance, Capital Gains Manual, CG60640–60646.

Reinvestment in the same asset

[22.22] In *Watton v Tippett*[1] the Court of Appeal rejected a claim to rollover relief on the basis that the gain arising on the part disposal of an asset be rolled into the previous acquisition of the same asset.

On 26 July 1988 Mr Tippett purchased freehold land and buildings ("unit 1") for £295,560. These premises he used for the purpose of the trade carried on by him, as the running of an indoor cricket facility. Mr Tippett then incurred a further expenditure on Unit 1 of £131,464 with a view to using the premises as a ten pin bowling alley. Mr Tippett faced funding difficulties and, therefore, sold part of the premises (designated "Unit 1A") on 3 August 1989 for £292,407. Mr Tippett submitted a claim to rollover the gain on the part disposal into the enhancement expenditure that had been incurred less than 12 months before the part disposal and, also, in part, into the original purchase made 373 days before the part disposal. The Board of Inland Revenue agreed to exercise its discretion under TCGA 1992, s 152(3) to extend the period for reinvestment by the eight days necessary to bring it within rollover relief, if rollover relief was available in these circumstances. The Court of Appeal strongly criticised the statutory language used for the rollover relief provisions but ruled, "What is crucial . . . is that there must be an acquisition of assets other than the assets disposed of."[2]

Simon's Taxes C3.304.

---

[1] [1997] STC 893, CA.
[2] er Peter Gibson LJ at 899b.

Deferring payment of tax

[22.23] For any disposal after 5 April 1996, the taxpayer can unilaterally choose not to pay capital gains tax on a disposal where the gain arising is expected to be covered by rollover relief. Thus, a taxpayer is enabled to make his self-assessment without requiring agreement from the Revenue to his provisional rollover relief claim.[1]

In order to avail himself of this provision, the taxpayer is required to make a declaration in his return for the fiscal year in which the disposal takes place. The declaration to be made is:

  (a) that the whole or any specified part of the consideration will be applied in the acquisition of, or of an interest in, other assets ("the new assets") which on the acquisition will be taken into use, and used only, for the purposes of the trade;
  (b) that the acquisition will take place as mentioned in sub-section (3) of section 152; and
  (c) that the new assets will be within the classes listed in s 155.[2]

Tax becomes chargeable if reinvestment does not take place. This is effected by statute suspending the normal time limits for amending self-assessment and imposing such an amendment at any time.[3]

There is an equivalent provision for rollover relief on compulsory purchase of land.[4]

Simon's Taxes C3.306.

---

[1] TCGA 1992, s 153A.
[2] CGA 1992, s 153A(1).

[3] TCGA 1992, s 153A(4).
[4] TCGA 1992, s 247A.

Deferral relief

History

[22.24] Prior to November 1993, when an entrepreneur wished to change the direction of his business activities by selling or liquidating a company he had built up and then investing the proceeds in the establishment of a new company, he normally had to expect that the sum available to invest in the new business was reduced by tax payable on the sale of the old business. With effect from 30 November 1993, reinvestment relief was introduced to facilitate such changes in business activities.[1] The method of relief was novel in a number of respects. First, relief was available not only against gains made on the sale of a business, but could be used to reduce or extinguish the gain arising on the disposal of any asset, as long as actual consideration was received.[2] Second, the taxpayer could choose the amount of the gain to be relieved,[3] this is in sharp contrast to the statutory requirements for rollover relief[4] and means that the taxpayer can arrange to leave in charge an amount of gain that is covered by losses or by annual exempt amount.

Reinvestment relief was widely available. As long as the target company into which reinvestment was made was an unquoted trading company, the restrictions were generally benign. Reinvestment could be made by purchasing shares from another taxpayer and was frequently, in practice, claimed on the purchase of shares from a business associate. There was thus no requirement that the funds used for reinvestment passed to the business acquired.

In 1998, reinvestment relief was discontinued and replaced by deferral relief. Deferral relief has many of the same features of reinvestment relief but has one vital difference. Whereas reinvestment relief reduced the base cost of the new asset, deferral relief has no effect on the base cost of the new asset, but the sale of that asset will trigger the gain that was previously computed. The distinction was critical when taper relief was applied.[5] Deferral relief is designed to give relief to a taxpayer only when funds are reinvested into a new business and the business is of a nature that is encouraged by the legislature. This is put into effect by requiring that the investment is a subscription for new shares[6] and the target company must fulfil the requirements for the enterprise investment scheme.[7] (However, the investor can be connected with the company, unlike the requirements for income tax relief on EIS investment.)[8] The advent of deferral relief gave clarity to what was a grey area for reinvestment relief; deferral relief is specifically stated to be available on any gain, including a gain arising on a deemed disposal.[9] There is provision for deferral relief to be available against the gain that arises when there is a failure of EIS requirements, including a part disposal.[10]

¹ TCGA 1992, ss 164A–164N inserted by FA 1993, Sch 7 and repealed by FA 1998, s 141(1).
² TCGA 1992, s 164A(1). For reinvestment relief, the Revenue view is that a gain arising on the disposal of a qualifying corporate bond that was issued in exchange for shares is potentially eligible for reinvestment relief but the Revenue consider that relief cannot be claimed on an acquisition by inheritance as reinvestment relief requires actual consideration (Inland Revenue Interpretation IR69).
³ CGA 1992, s 164A(2)(a) inserted by FA 1993, Sch 7, para 3 repealed by FA 1998, s 141(1).
⁴ TCGA 1992, s 152(1).
⁵ The qualifying period for taper relief was the period up to the first disposal; the period for which the new asset is held did not increase taper relief.
⁶ CGA 1992, Sch 5B, para 1(2)(a).
⁷ TCGA 1992, Sch 5B, para 1(2)(e); see infra, §§ **31.06–31.15**.
⁸ TA 1988, s 291(1)(b).
⁹ TCGA 1992, Sch 5B, para 1(1)(c).
¹⁰ TCGA 1992, Sch 5B, paras 4 and 19.

Operation of deferral relief

[22.25] Where deferral relief is claimed, the gain arising on disposal is calculated in the usual way. The gain charged on the disposal is then reduced by the amount of the deferral.¹

The amount of the deferral is the lowest of the following three sums:

(a)   the gain that would otherwise be chargeable on the disposal,
(b)   the consideration for the qualifying investment;
(c)   the amount the taxpayer chooses to claim.²

When there is a disposal of the qualifying investment, or another event causing clawback of relief,³ the deferred gain is brought into charge at that date.⁴ The amount brought into charge is the sum that was deferred.

Death does not cause a clawback of deferral relief.⁶

In common with the normal treatment of married couples, there is no clawback of relief on an individual passing shares to his/her spouse while both are living together. Instead, the acquiring spouse is treated as standing in the shoes of the spouse who claimed the deferral relief.⁷

The shares for which the subscription has been made must be issued in the period beginning 12 months before and ending 36 months after the disposal against which relief is claimed.⁸

Statute gives discretion to the Board of HMRC to extend these time limits. However, unlike most other time limit extensions, HMRC internal instructions make it clear that the local District has no power to exercise the Board's discretion. Instead, where a taxpayer applies for the time limit to be extended, the local District is required to refer the matter to HMRC CGT head office (Solihull) for a decision.⁹

Deferral relief can be claimed at any time up to five years after 31 January following the fiscal year in which the shares were issued.[10]

Taper relief was calculated after deferral relief.[11]

---

[1] TCGA 1992, Sch 5B, para 2(1).
[2] TCGA 1992, Sch 5B, para 2(1), (3).
[3] See supra § **20.39**.
[4] TCGA 1992, Sch 5B, para 4(1)(*a*).
[6] TCGA 1992, Sch 5B, para 3(5).
[7] TCGA 1992, Sch 5B, para 3(1)(*a*) and (*d*).
[8] TCGA 1992, Sch 5B, para 1(3).
[9] HMRC Capital Gains Manual, CG62843 and 57485.
[10] TMA 1970, s 43(1) and HMRC Capital Gains Manual, CG62912.
[11] *Daniels v R & C Comrs* [2005] STC (SCD) 684.

Qualifying investor: individuals and trustees

[22.26] In order to claim deferral relief, an individual must be resident or ordinarily resident in the UK both at the time the gain arose and at the time the shares are issued.[1] Relief is denied if the individual is also resident in another country by virtue of double taxation relief arrangements and, hence, would be outside the charge to capital gains tax on the shares were they sold immediately after acquisition.[2]

An individual who is neither resident nor ordinarily resident in the UK is not entitled to claim deferral relief.[3] An individual who is resident in the UK but is treated under the terms of any double taxation agreement as also resident in another territory is, similarly, not entitled to claim deferral relief if, under the terms of the double taxation agreement, UK capital gains tax would not, in principle, be chargeable were there a disposal of the shares immediately after their acquisition.[4]

If the taxpayer ceased to be resident in the UK at any time during the five years following the issue of the eligible shares, the deferred gain is brought back into charge.[5] There is, however, no clawback of deferral relief where the taxpayer becomes non-resident by reason of his/her employment and the following three conditions are satisfied:

(1)   all the duties of the employment are performed outside the UK;
(2)   within three years of the date of becoming non-resident, the taxpayer resumes UK residence; and
(3)   the taxpayer does not sell the shares during the period of non-residence.[6]

In order to claim deferral relief on a gain made from a disposal of trust property, one of two alternative conditions must be satisfied. The first alternative is that the interests in the trust property are held on behalf of individuals who are beneficiaries with interests in possession;[7] the second alternative is that there are no interests in possession and all the potential beneficiaries are individuals.[8] This formulation is designed to exclude the use of deferral relief where the benefit is ultimately enjoyed by a company.

[1] TCGA 1992, Sch 5B, para 1(1)(*a*) and (*d*).
[2] TCGA 1992, Sch 5B, para 1(1) and (4).
[3] TCGA 1992, Sch 5B, para 1(1)(*d*).
[4] TCGA 1992, Sch 5B, para 1(4).
[5] TCGA 1992, Sch 5B, para 3(1)(*c*).
[6] TCGA 1992, Sch 5B, para 3(3).
[7] TCGA 1992, Sch 5B, para 17(2)(*b*).
[8] TCGA 1992, Sch 5B, para 17(2)(*a*).

Qualifying investor: Companies

[22.27] A company can claim investment relief on subscribing for newly-issued shares in an unquoted trading company.[1] When these shares are subsequently sold, the company can claim deferral relief against the gain arising if all or part of the proceeds of sale are applied to subscribe for newly-issued shares in another unquoted trading company,[2] where the subscription fulfils the requirements for investment relief.

Deferral relief is available for a company when the original gain arises on either a qualifying disposal of qualifying shares or a chargeable event and the investor company makes a qualifying investment. The disposal only qualifies if the investor has held the shares without interruption since issue.[3]

To make a qualifying investment the investor must satisfy four conditions:[4] it must subscribe for shares that qualify for investment relief; those shares must not be issued by a prohibited company (as defined below); the shares must be issued at a qualifying time; if the shares were issued before the gain accrued, they must be held at that time and must also then qualify for investment relief.

A prohibited company[5] is one whose shares made up the original holding and any member of its group at the time the gain accrues and/or when the shares were issued. The qualifying time can be any time up to a year before and three years after the time the gain accrued.

The meaning of original holding depends on the circumstances of the original gain. If the gain arose on the disposal of the original shares, it means the shares disposed of. If the gain arose because of a chargeable event, it means the shares involved in that event.

The investor must claim the deferral relief.[6] The maximum amount of relief is the qualifying expenditure on qualifying, replacement shares that has not already been claimed. The relief claimed cannot exceed so much of the original gain as has not already been relieved.

When the first chargeable event occurs relative to qualifying, replacement shares then the investor is treated as making a chargeable gain equal to the deferred gain attributed to those shares.[7] To calculate the gain, the amount of the deferred gain, valued immediately before the event, is apportioned to each share.

The deemed chargeable gain is treated as part of the profits of a non-resident company trading through a branch or agency in the UK.[8]

[22.27] Business and partnerships

A disposal, or the withdrawal or reduction, of all or part of the relief is a chargeable event.[9]

Certain reorganisations exchanges of shares are possible without causing a chargeable event that triggers the deferral relief.

An exchange must satisfy four conditions before it qualifies.[10] First, the only consideration for the acquired shares or securities must be the issue of new shares or securities. Second, the new shares or securities must be issued by a new company that has no issued shares or securities other than subscriber shares and shares or securities previously issued as consideration for the other shares or securities. Third, the new shares or securities must be of the same class, carrying the same rights, as those they replace. Fourth, the replacement shares or securities must be issued in proportion to those they replace.

[1] FA 2000, Sch 15. See infra, § **30.16**: Corporate Venturing Scheme.
[2] FA 2000, Sch 15, para 76.
[3] FA 2000, Sch 15, para 73(3).
[4] FA 2000, Sch 15, para 74(1).
[5] FA 2000, Sch 15, para 74(2).
[6] FA 2000, Sch 15, para 76(1).
[7] FA 2000, Sch 15, para 79(2).
[8] TCGA 1992, s 10(3).
[9] FA 2000, Sch 15, para 78(1).
[10] FA 2000, Sch 15, para 83(2).

The investment

[22.28] For deferral relief to apply, the taxpayer must subscribe for "eligible shares" in a company that fulfils the requirements of the Enterprise Investment Scheme. "Eligible shares" are defined as new ordinary shares, which throughout the period of five years beginning with the date on which they are issued carry no present or future right to be redeemed.[1] Ordinary shares are defined as "shares formerly part of the ordinary share capital of the company".[2] Shares are treated as never having been eligible if the cash raised by the company on the issue of those shares was used for a purpose other than a qualifying business activity.[3]

Eligible shares are treated as ceasing to be eligible if an event occurs after the date of issue which causes the company not to be a qualifying company or, in the case of a group of companies, ceases to be the parent company of a trading group.[4]

Deferral relief is available on investment in eligible shares in an Enterprise Investment Scheme qualifying company, without limit as to the size of the shareholding acquired or the amount invested. However, the company must satisfy all the Enterprise Investment Scheme requirements that relate to a target company.[5] Hence, the company must, throughout the period of deferral, be an unquoted company which exists "wholly for the purpose of carrying on one or more qualifying trades (subject to a *de minimis* exemption) or is the parent company of a trading group".[6]

Qualifying trades are all trades other than:

(1) dealing in land, commodities, shares etc;
(2) dealing in goods other than as a wholesaler or retailer;
(3) banking, insurance or other financial activities;
(4) oil extraction;
(5) leasing;
(6) providing legal or accountancy services;
(7) property development;
(8) farming or market gardening, forestry etc;
(9) managing hotels;
(10) managing nursing homes, etc; or
(11) providing services for any of the foregoing trades, where the service-providing company and the company to which the services are provided are under common ownership.[7]

The balance sheet total of the company must not exceed £7,000,000 before the issue of eligible shares, nor £8,000,000 after the issue of eligible shares.[8]

---

[1] TCGA 1992, Sch 5B, para 19(1) applying TA 1988, s 289(7). For shares issued after 5 April 2000 the period is three years.
[2] TCGA 1992, Sch 5B, para 19(1) applying TA 1988, s 832(1).
[3] TA 1988, 289A(7).
[4] TA 1988, s 289(1A).
[5] TA 1988, ss 289–312.
[6] TA 1988, s 293(2).
[7] TA 1988, s 297.
[8] TA 1988, s 293(6A).

Disposal of EIS shares

[22.29] The basic scheme of deferral relief is that the gain that was deferred is brought into charge on the disposal of the shares into which the deferral is made.[1]

The deferral is triggered by any of the following:

(a) a disposal of the shares at any time;
(b) an event within the company during the three years following the acquisition of the company shares[2] that causes the company to cease to qualify under the EIS rules;
(c) the shareholder ceasing to be UK resident within the three-year period following the date of acquisition of the shares;[3]
(d) during the three year period value (other than insignificant value) is received by the investor.[4]

Provision is made for transfer between husband and wife. As customarily in the scheme of CGT legislation, this is not treated as a disposal, but the acquiring spouse stands in the shoes of the investor, so that a subsequent disposal by the acquiring spouse triggers the gain.[5]

[22.29] Business and partnerships

1   TCGA 1992, Sch 5B, para 4.
2   TCGA 1992, Sch 5B, para 3(1).
3   Where the company issuing the shares under EIS was not carrying on the qualifying trade when the shares were issued, the three-year period commences with the later date on which the qualifying trade commenced: TA 1988, s 312(1) applied to CGT by TCGA 1992, Sch 5B, para 19(1).
4   TCGA 1992, Sch 5B, para 13. Certain receipts are treated as "insignificant" (para 13A) and do not cause the triggering of the deferred gain. These provisions are parallel to those which apply for the clawback of EIS income tax relief: see infra, § **31.14**. In *Wakefield v Inspector of Taxes* [2005] STC (SCD) 439 a gain fell into charge when value was received by a company connected with the investor.
5   TCGA 1992, Sch 5B para 3(1).

Reorganisations and takeovers

[22.30] When a condition of EIS income tax relief requirements from the company is breached, there is a clawback of deferral relief.[1] The gain is treated as arising on the date of the event that causes the company to cease to fulfil the EIS requirements.[2]

Where another company takes over the EIS company, whose shares attracted deferral relief and the shareholders thereby receive cash, there is a clawback of the relief given. Where a company takes over the EIS company and issues shares in exchange for the shares on which deferral relief has been claimed, there is also a clawback of the deferral relief granted,[3] unless the following conditions are satisfied:

(1)   a company, having issued only subscriber shares, acquires all the shares (and any securities) in an EIS qualifying company in exchange for the proportionate issue of its own shares (and securities, if relevant) and the shares issued are of the same class and carry the same rights as the original shares; and
(2)   clearance for the reorganisation has been given by HMRC under TA 1988, s 304A.

1   TCGA 1992, Sch 5B, para 4(1).
2   TCGA 1992, Sch 5B, para 1A(2).
3   TCGA 1992, Sch 5B, para 3(1)(a).

Interaction with exemption for EIS shares

[22.31] Where EIS shares[1] are issued and income tax relief is granted on the subscription, the capital gain arising on the ultimate disposal of those shares is exempt from CGT, unless the income tax relief has been withdrawn.[2]

However, if a loss arises on the disposal, the loss is, nevertheless, allowable and can be relieved against gains, in the normal way.[3] An election can be made under ITA 2007, s 131 so that the capital loss arising can be offset against income and, hence, tax relief is obtained. The loss is after deducting the EIS tax relief.

Where it is necessary to identify shares acquired with shares disposed, the particular share identification rules for the Enterprise Investment Scheme are applied. Thus, where shares have been acquired at different dates, a disposal is identified with earlier dates before later dates.[4] Where shares are all acquired on the same date, the order used for identification is as follows:

(1) against shares for which neither EIS nor deferral relief was attributable;
(2) against shares for which deferral relief was attributable but EIS relief not attributable;
(3) against shares for which EIS relief was attributable but deferral relief was not attributable; and
(4) against shares for which both EIS and deferral relief was attributable.

If an individual subscribes for shares in an EIS company (or several EIS companies) and his subscriptions exceed the EIS income tax limit of £150,000 in the year, capital gains tax arising on the ultimate disposal of the shares is computed as shown below.[5]

EXAMPLE

In May 2004, £250,000 is subscribed for 500,000 ords in an unquoted trading company. £40,000 income tax relief is received. The entire holding is sold in June 2008 for £600,000.

	Income tax relief shares ords 400,000 £	Shares without income tax relief Ords 100,000 £
Sale proceeds, June 08		
Re 400,000 ords	480,000	
Re 100,000 ords		120,000
Cost, May 2004	irrelevant	(50,000)
	exempt	70,000

If capital has been received from the company during the five-year period, a calculation as shown below is required:

EXAMPLE

In May 2000, £150,000 is subscribed for 100,000 ords. EIS income tax relief of £30,000 is obtained. In 2005, £20,000 of value is received from the company. Income tax relief of £4,000 is clawed back by means of an assessment. In June 2008 the shares are sold for £270,000.

CGT computation

	£
Sale proceeds, June 08	270,000
Cost	150,000
	120,000
Gain in charge	$£120,000 \times \dfrac{4,000}{30,000} = 16,000$
Chargeable gain	£16,000

[1] See supra, § **17.23**.
[2] TCGA 1992, s 150A(2).
[3] TCGA 1992, s 150A(2A).
[4] TA 1988, s 299(6).
[5] These examples are based on HMRC CGT Manual, paras 62809–62819.

Entrepreneurs' relief

[22.32] In his first pre-Budget Report, Chancellor Alistair Darling proposed a radical simplification of the capital gains tax rules. At the heart of the simplification was the abolition of taper relief (introduced ten years earlier by his predecessor), the complete withdrawal of indexation allowance (previously frozen as at April1998) and the introduction of a flat rate of tax, 18% (irrespective of the type of asset being disposed of and/or its length of ownership).

Whilst few would criticise plans to make tax simpler, it soon became clear that the Chancellor had not considered the implications for many taxpayers. In particular, the flat rate of 18% would nevertheless represent a significant tax rise for taxpayers who were expecting to pay an effective tax rate of 10% on the disposal of business assets.[1] Particularly hard hit would have been individuals who had hoped to sell their business and retire on the proceeds especially as they might have structured their affairs so as to fit in with the taper relief rules.

Consequently, after a series of leaks and false starts, the Government announced the introduction of a relief ("entrepreneurs' relief") to compensate those worst hit. It is largely based on the rules for retirement relief that were phased out upon the introduction of taper relief. Indeed, some retirement relief cases will once again become relevant again under the new regime.

With hindsight, one can see the irony of the events of Autumn 2007 and Winter 2008. The Government's attempts to simplify the rules have caused confusion and concern amongst taxpayers and 13 pages of new legislation (roughly the same as was repealed by the abolition of taper relief).

[1] With the abolition of indexation allowance as well, increases in tax bills might have been more than 80% between 2007–08 and 2008–09.

The key elements of entrepreneurs' relief

[22.33] Where entrepreneurs' relief is validly claimed, it will have the effect of reducing eligible gains by 4/9.[1] The effect of this is to ensure that gains are taxed at an effective rate of 10%.

Entrepreneurs' relief is available on up to £1m of gains.[2] That amount operates as a lifetime limit.

Claims for relief must be made by the second 31 January following the end of the tax year in which the qualifying disposal was made.³ Therefore, the first claims would be due on 31 January 2011 as the relief applies only to disposals made on or after 6 April 2008.

¹ TCGA 1992, s 169N(2).
² TCGA 1992, s 169N(3).
³ TCGA 1992, s 169M(3).

Qualifying for entrepreneurs' relief

There are, broadly, three types of disposal qualifying for entrepreneurs' relief:

(a) 'material disposals of business assets';
(b) disposals of 'trust business assets'; and
(c) associated disposals.

Relief can be reduced where part of the disposal represents non-business assets.

Material disposals of business assets

A material disposal of business assets is:

(a) a disposal by a individual;
(b) of business assets (as defined); and
(c) which is material (as defined).¹

A disposal is of business assets if it is a disposal of:

(i) the whole or part of a business;
(ii) an asset or assets in use for the purposes of the business at the time at which the business ceases to be carried on;
(iii) an interest or interests in such assets;
(iv) one or more assets consisting of shares in or securities of a company; or
(v) interests in such shares or securities.²

Where the disposal is of the whole or part of the business, the disposal is material if the business had been owned throughout the year ending with the date of the disposal.³

Where the disposal is of assets (or interests in such), the disposal is material if:

(a) the business had been owned throughout the year ending with the date on which the business ceased; and
(b) the disposal takes place within three years of that cessation.⁴

Where the disposal is of shares or securities (or interests in such), the disposal is material if either:

(a) throughout the year ending with the disposal company:
    (i) the company is the individual's personal company;
    (ii) the company is either a trading company or the holding company of a trading group; and
    (iii) the individual is an officer or employee of the company (or, if the company is a member of a trading group) of one or more companies within the group⁵; or

(b) throughout the year ending with the date on which either:
  (i) the company ceases to be a trading company without continuing to be or becoming a member of a trading group; or
  (ii) the company ceases to be a member of a trading group without continuing to be or becoming a trading company,
the following three conditions are met:
  (1) the company is the individual's personal company;
  (2) the company is either a trading company or the holding company of a trading group; and
  (3) the individual is an officer or employee of the company (or, if the company is a member of a trading group) of one or more companies within the group.[6]

[1] TCGA 1992, s 169I(1).
[2] TCGA 1992, s 169I(2).
[3] TCGA 1992, s 169I(3).
[4] TCGA 1992, s 169I(4).
[5] TCGA 1992, s 169I(6).
[6] TCGA 1992, s 169I(7).

Part disposals of business assets

The requirement for there to be a disposal of a business or part of a business is reminiscent of the retirement relief rules. This was an issue that arose in a number of High Court cases – in particular *Purves (HM Inspector of Taxes) v Harrison* (2000); *Barrett (HM Inspector of Taxes) v Powell* (1998); *Wase (HM Inspector of Taxes) v Bourke* (1995); *Jarmin (HM Inspector of Taxes) v Rawlings* (1994); *Pepper (HM Inspector of Taxes) v Daffurn* (1993); *Atkinson (HM Inspector of Taxes) v Dancer* (1988); *Mannion (HM Inspector of Taxes) v Johnson* (1988) and *McGregor (HM Inspector of Taxes) v Adcock* (1977).

The key point is that there is a difference between a business and a mere asset used in the business. In addition, the statute[1] ensures that in the context of partnerships:

(a) disposals of interests in assets used for the purposes of an individual's business on entering into a partnership which will carry on the business is to be treated as a part disposal of the business;
(b) similarly, disposals by individuals of the whole or part of the individual's interest in a partnership's assets will be treated as a disposal of the whole or part of the business carried on by the partnership; and
(c) at any time when a business is carried on by a partnership it is treated as owned by each individual who, at the time, is a member of the partnership.

[1] TCGA 1992, s 169I(8).

Disposals of trust business assets

Trustees are treated as making disposals of trust business assets if:
(a) they make a disposal of assets that are settled property and either:
 (i) consist of shares in or securities of a company; or
 (ii) assets used or previously used for the purposes of a business;
(b) an individual is a qualifying beneficiary (as defined); and
(c) in the case of a disposal of shares or securities, throughout a year ending within three years before the disposal:
 (i) the company is the qualifying beneficiary's personal company;
 (ii) the company is either a trading company or a holding company of a trading group; and
 (iii) the qualifying beneficiary is an officer or employee of the company (or, if the company is a member of a (trading) group of companies, of one or companies within the trading group); and
(d) in the case of a disposal of assets:
 (i) the assets are used for the purposes of the business carried on by the qualifying beneficiary throughout a one-year periods ending during the three years before the disposal; and
 (ii) the qualifying beneficiary ceases to carry on the business on the date of disposal or within the three previous years.[1]

Again the statute provides that businesses carried on by the qualifying beneficiary can include businesses carried on in a partnership of which the qualifying beneficiary is a partner.[2] And cessations of businesses by a qualifying beneficiary include the qualifying beneficiary ceasing to be a member of the partnership or the partnership ceasing to carry on the business.[3]

To be a qualifying beneficiary, an individual must have an interest in possession (other than for a fixed term) in the whole of the settled property or a part of it which consists of or includes the assets disposed of.[4]

[1] TCGA 1992, s 169J(1), (2), (4), (5).
[2] TCGA 1992, s 169J(6)(*a*).
[3] TCGA 1992, s 169J(6)(*b*).
[4] TCGA 1992, s 169J(3).

Associated disposals

The third route to entrepreneurs' relief arises if there is an 'associated' disposal. That arises if:
(a) an individual makes a material disposal of business assets consisting of either:
 (i) the whole or part of the individual's interest in the assets of a partnership;
 (ii) shares in or securities of a company; or
 (iii) interests in such shares or securities;
(b) that disposal is made as part of the individual's withdrawal from participation of the business (which in the case of a disposal of company shares or securities can be carried on by a company which is a member of the same trading group as the company concerned); and

(c) the assets disposed of (in the material disposal of business assets) are in use for the purposes of the business throughout the year ending with the earlier of:
    (i) the date of the material disposal of business assets; and
    (ii) the cessation of the partnership or company's business.[1]

[1] TCGA 1992, s 169K.

Business

Although the statute refers to business assets, as was the case with taper relief, the term "business" is narrowly defined to cover only trades, professions or vocations (as defined in the Income Tax Acts). Furthermore, the activity has to be conducted on a commercial basis *and* with a view to the realisation of profits.[1] Therefore, hobby farms, for example, will not qualify.

[1] TCGA 1992, s 169S(1).

Personal company

For a company to be a personal company, an individual must hold 5% or more of both the ordinary share capital and the voting rights in the company.[1] It is not possible to aggregate shareholdings of connected parties. Thus, suppose a husband and wife owned 4% each of a trading company, neither would qualify for entrepreneurs' relief in respect of that shareholding. One would have to transfer a minimum 1% shareholding to the other at least a year before the earlier of the cessation of the business or the disposal of the shares. For entrepreneurs' relief to available in respect of the combined shareholding then one spouse would have to transfer the entire shareholding to the other at least a year before the earlier of the cessation of the business or the disposal of the shares.

[1] TCGA 1992, s 169S(3).

Payment of rent

The payment of rent will generally preclude an asset qualifying for entrepreneurs' relief. As this was potentially different from the rules that applied under taper relief, a last-minute reprieve means that rents paid in respect of periods before 6 April 2008 will not affect the entitlement to relief.[1]

[1] FA 2008, Sch 3, para 6. For a full discussion of practical issues that arise in this situation, see Kevin Slevin's article in *Taxation*, 'Rent up frustration', 29 May 2008.

Interaction of reliefs

[22.34] The order in which reliefs are applied is:

(1) Rollover relief reduces the consideration to be taken into account in computing the gain on disposal. It comes first.
(2) Deferral relief also reduces consideration. It comes next.
(3) Relief on the transfer of business to a company under s 162 works by reducing the net chargeable gain.
(4) Entrepreneurs' relief.

Holdover relief also works by reducing the chargeable gains. Where an asset is sold at undervalue, rollover relief can be claimed by reference to the sale proceeds and holdover relief claimed for the difference between the market value and the sale proceeds. The interaction between rollover relief and section 162 relief on incorporation is unclear. Section 162 relief is mandatory[1] and the gain on the disposal of assets transferred from an individual's business to a company is automatically rolled into the shares acquired. If those shares are sold within three years of their acquisition, and the proceeds used to purchase a new asset within the categories specified in s 155, it is considered that a claim for rollover relief can be made as the proceeds of the sale of the shares constitute "consideration" for the old asset, within the meaning of s 153(1). A statement by a senior Inland Revenue officer has been made to the effect that such a claim will be admitted if the taxpayer indicated at the outset that it is his intention to make such a rollover relief claim.

It is possible to make a reduced claim for deferral relief and to claim holdover relief for the balance of the gain. This could be advantageous when there is a sale at undervalue particularly when the taxpayer has brought forward losses.

---

[1] Subject to an election made under TCGA 1992, s 162A.

Gifts of business assets—holdover relief

[22.35] For treatment of holdover relief see supra, §§ **18.41** ff.

Partnerships

[22.36] The statutory provision relating to capital gains tax to partnerships is extraordinarily brief. TCGA 1992, s 59 states:

> Where two or more persons carry on a trade or business in partnership—
>
> . . . any partnership dealings shall be treated as dealings by the partners and not by the firm as such

In an attempt to provide a workable regime for capital gains tax relationship to partnerships, on 17 January 1975 the Revenue issued Statement of Practice D 12. This was amplified to take account of indexation allowance by Statement of Practice SP 1/89, reissued on 8 October 2002 as Statement of Practice D12/02 in order to encompass limited liability partnerships. Despite the revisions, the basic regime given in the 1975 Statement of Practice has not been revised. The Statement of Practice is clearly at variance with the true legal position in a number of aspects. It is, therefore, open to any partnership to apply the correct legal position, rather than the treatment specified in a Statement of Practice.

Simon's Taxes C3.201.

Capacity in which a partner holds an asset

[22.37] Where an individual is a beneficial owner of a property and the same individual is also a trustee of a settlement, it is clear that the individual acts in two totally separate capacities. If he made a 31 March 1982 election (no longer relevant in respect of disposals on or after 6 April 2008) in respect of the property he owns beneficially, this election had no effect in respect of the property he owns in his capacity as a trustee of the settlement, and vice versa.

In the Revenue view, the same applies to an individual who is a partner in a partnership. Thus, the Revenue state that an election for rebasing "made in respect of partnership assets is made by a person in the capacity of partner. So a separate election was required for assets held privately. In the same way, an election for assets held privately will not apply to assets held in the capacity of partner."[1] The Revenue view would appear to be in complete contradiction to the statutory direction under which partnership dealings are to be treated as dealings by the partners.[2]

The Revenue statement is of considerable practical importance. Any election for March 1982 value to be taken, ignoring acquisition costs, must be made within two years of the end of the fiscal year of "the first relevant disposal".[3] Where a partnership has not made a disposal, this election continued to be available to the individual partner, even though he had made disposals in this private capacity. Such an election was very attractive where the effect would be to determine a significant deemed acquisition cost for goodwill that has been built up, rather than having been purchased, over the period prior to 1982.

The statement is, furthermore, very interesting as an indication of the degree to which the Revenue regards an individual as operating separately in relation to his partnership as opposed to his actions as an individual. The Revenue statement contrasts the treatment it suggests in relation to a partnership from the position where assets "are held jointly (but without the existence of a partnership)". In such a case, the Revenue's view is that an election made by an individual applies to such assets in addition to assets he holds in his sole name.

Simon's Taxes C3.101.

---

[1] Inland Revenue interpretation RI 9.
[2] TCGA 1992, s 59.
[3] TCGA 1992, s 35(6).

Disposal of assets by a partnership

[22.38] This is, perhaps, the simplest situation and the least controversial. Where an asset is disposed of by a partnership to a third party, each partner is treated as disposing of his fractional share of the asset. In the view of the Revenue, the correct approach is to allocate the gain amongst the partners in "the ratio of their shares in asset surpluses at the time of the disposal".[1] This is, in general, in accordance with the entitlement of the partners to capital profits. However, the gain on a particular disposal of a particular asset may well be allocated differently from that in which is applied to capital profits generally and the specific allocation made is followed in assessing the gain. In terms, where this arises, what has happened is that partners have agreed a change to their capital sharing ratios in relation to that particular disposal and this agreement may be evidenced by the actual allocation of proceeds.

Many partnerships do not specify a particular division of capital profits. Where this is the case, prima facie, the entitlement to capital profits is in the same proportions as the entitlement to income profits. Such entitlement may be shown in a partnership deed or it may be inferred from the action of partners.[2] In the absence of any agreement amongst the partners, capital profits are divided equally amongst the partners (as are income profits).[3]

Simon's Taxes C3.201.

---

[1] Statement of practice D12, para 2.
[2] See, for example, the willingness of the court to identify terms of a purely oral partnership agreement in *Munro v Stamp Duties Comr* [1934] AC 61, [1933] All ER Rep 185, PC.
[3] Partnership Act 1890, s 24(1).

Partnership asset passed to one or more partners

[22.39] Where an asset that has previously been held as "partnership property" is passed to one or more partner, the partner who receives the asset is not regarded as disposing of his fractional share in it.[1]

The Revenue suggest that it is necessary first to make a computation of the gains that would be chargeable on the individual partners if the asset had been disposed of to a third party at its current market value. Gains attributed to partners who do not receive a share in the asset are then chargeable on those partners. Where the gain is allocated to a partner who has received the asset (or a share therein), there is no charge on the distribution. Instead, his allowable cost to be put against a subsequent disposal is the market value of the asset he has received reduced by the amount of the gain that would have been charged on him.

Simon's Taxes C3.203.

---

[1] Statement of practice D12,

Changes in profit sharing ratios—Revenue statement of practice

[22.40] Revenue Statement of Practice D12/02[1] provides a method of dealing with a change in profit sharing ratios. This method is admitted by the Revenue to have little statutory basis, but is advocated by the Revenue as a method that is workable in practice.

The basic rule in the Revenue Statement of Practice is that where there is a change in profit sharing ratio (whether a change amongst existing partners or a change occasioned by the admission of a new partner or the retirement of a partner), the disposals that arise by virtue of that change will be treated as taking place at a consideration that gives rise to neither a gain nor a loss. Where the acquisition was prior to 6 April 1998, the no gain/no loss provision is computed after taking account of indexation allowance and it may be treated for the purposes of TCGA 1992, Sch 3 as if it were in para 1 of that Schedule.

The effect of this treatment is that a partner whose profit share is reduced carries forward a smaller proportion of costs to set against the proceeds of any ultimate disposal. A partner whose share is increased carries forward a larger proportion of such costs. The normal rules for part disposal apportionments are not applied; instead a fractional basis is used.

It is, of course, evident that the use of this approach consistently means that every partner who leaves a partnership for whom the disposal is treated under the terms of Statement of Practice, loses his share of the acquisition costs.

The Statement of Practice requires that this treatment is not applied where one of the following arises:

(a) there is an adjustment through the accounts;
(b) payment is made outside the accounts;
(c) the transfer is between persons who are "connected persons" otherwise than through the partnership.

Simon's Taxes C3.203.

---

[1] Issued on 8 October 2002, *Simons Weekly Tax Intelligence* 2002, p 1372.

Adjustment through the accounts

[22.41] If there is a revaluation of one or more partnership assets at the time of a change of profit share, the change of profit share is treated as a part disposal of the partner's interest in that asset. The consideration for the disposal is the fractional difference between the partner's old and new share applied to the value placed on the revalued asset. This treatment applies where there is a reduction in the value of an asset shown on the balance sheet, as well as where there is an increase. Thus, in a falling property market, a partnership may recognise that the value of its freehold property has reduced and the reduction is shown in the fixed assets on the partnership balance sheet. Any change in profit shares following this reduction gives an allowable loss for some or all partners.

Simon's Taxes C3.201.

Payment outside the accounts

[22.42] Where, on admission, a new partner purchases his share from existing partners, it is normally the case that the purchase is not shown on the face of the partnership accounts. However, the fact that consideration has passed means that there is a disposal for capital gains tax purposes which attracts a charge to capital gains tax, subject to the availability of retirement relief or any other relief.

The base cost may be the actual acquisition cost, or it may be a proportion of part of the value of partnership property and goodwill at 31 March 1982.

Connected persons

[22.43] Partners are connected persons "except in relation to acquisitions or disposals of partnership assets pursuant to bona fide commercial arrangements".[1] Hence, in terms, partners are connected persons in relationship to a disposal of an interest in the partnership, as an interest in the partnership is not a "partnership asset".[2]

The Revenue, however, do not appear to take this point and in the Statement of Practice state that the no gain/no loss treatment "will also be given to transactions between an incoming partner and existing partners". However, where the partners "are connected other than by partnership (for example, father and son) or are otherwise not at arm's length (for example uncle and nephew), the transfer of a share in the partnership assets may fall to be treated as having been made at market value. Market value will not be substituted, however, if nothing would have been paid had the parties been at arm's length".

Simon's Taxes C3.201.

---

[1] TCGA 1992, s 286(4).
[2] See, for example, the discussions on the nature of an interest in partnership in *Hadlee v Commissioner of Inland Revenue* [1993] STC 294, PC.

Changes in profit sharing ratio—analysis based on statute and case law

[22.44] It is normally intrinsic in the change in profit sharing ratios that there is an accompanying change in the relative interests that different partners have in the assets of the firm. Where an asset is potentially chargeable to capital gains tax, there can be little doubt that such a change is a disposal subject to capital gains tax by a partner who reduces his interest in that asset and an acquisition by a partner who increases his interest in the asset. It then becomes necessary to determine what consideration should be brought into the

[22.44] Business and partnerships

computations for capital gains tax purposes. Should this be the actual consideration which passes (which is frequently £nil) or the market value of the asset at that time?

The consideration is taken as the market value of the asset of which the disposal is made where the disposal is "for a consideration that cannot be valued".[1] In particular partnership situations, this may be apt. For example, if a partner's share is decreased because he has given up responsibility for an aspect of the partnership's affairs.

An alternative argument for substituting market value is that statute[2] requires this to be used where a person "disposes of the asset otherwise than by way of a bargain made at arm's length" and s 18 deems all transactions between connected persons to be such.

The definition of connected persons in statute[3], as has already been mentioned, has the effect that partners are connected persons "except in relation to acquisitions or disposals of partnership assets pursuant to bona fide commercial arrangements". It is considered that this definition only has effect in relation to transactions between those who are already partners. Thus, if two individuals are in partnership and decide to admit into partnership a third, the transaction that causes the admission of the third individual is not a transaction between partners and, hence, the first two individuals are not connected with the third, unless there is a totally separate, family, connection.

As to what constitutes a bona fide commercial arrangement, prima facie, the only reason for a commercial partnership to be in existence is for bona fide commercial reasons. If a partner's share increases because of his greater value to the partnership, that increase should be a bona fide commercial transaction. In *A-G v Boden*,[4] a case concerning the estate duty provision[5] it was established that it was a bona fide commercial transaction if younger partners took part of the profit share of the older partner at the time that he was relieved of an appropriate part of the burden of work. By contrast, where the reduction in profit share was, in reality an act of bounty by the older partner, this was not a bona fide commercial transaction.[6]

An area that has caused considerable difficulty in practice is where a partner has retired after the enactment of the provisions in FA 1988. He has not obtained any consideration for goodwill he has surrendered at his retirement, but claims a loss based on the market value of his share of the firm's goodwill at 31 March 1982. In December 1973 the General Commissioners for the City of London held that a partner in a partnership that had chosen to write goodwill out of its accounts had thereby triggered an allowable loss.[7] The Revenue, however, seek to distinguish this case, which was never taken to the courts. The Revenue attack is based on the alternative grounds of (a) the market value of the single partner's share at 31 March 1982 is negligible as he is not able to sell such a share and (b) statute[8] requires the consideration for the disposal at retirement to be taken as the market value of a proportion of the value of the goodwill at that date.

Simon's Taxes C3.203.

---

[1] TCGA 1992, s 17(1)(*b*).

[2] TCGA 1992, s 17(1)(a).
[3] TCGA 1992, s 286(4).
[4] [1912] 1 KB 539.
[5] FA 1894, s 3(1).
[6] *Re Clarke* (1906) 40 ILTR 117.
[7] See supra, § **16.16**.
[8] TCGA 1992, s 17.

Annuity purchased for retiring partner

[22.45] Where an annuity is provided, the capitalised value of that annuity is treated as consideration subject to capital gains tax.[1]

Where this treatment is applied, the sum subjected to capital gains tax in the hands of the retiring partner (whether or not it is covered by retirement relief) is treated as allowable expenditure by the remaining partners on their acquisition of their additional fractional shares in partnership assets.[2]

However, Statement of Practice D12/02, para 8 provides that where a partnership makes annual payments to a retired partner out of its own funds and not by purchase of a life annuity, the capitalised value of the annuity will not be treated as consideration assessable under TCGA 1992, s 37(3) if it is no more than can be regarded as a reasonable recognition of the past contribution of work and effort by the partner to the partnership. Where the former partner had been in the partnership for at least ten years, an annuity is regarded by the Revenue as reasonable recognition if it is no more than two thirds of his average share of the profits for the best three of the last seven years in which he was required to devote substantially the whole of his time to acting as a partner. If he has been a partner for a shorter period, the following fractions are applied:

Complete years in partnership	Fraction for each year
1–5	1/60 for each year
6	8/60
7	16/60
8	24/60
9	32/60

Simon's Taxes C3.225.

[1] TCGA 1992, s 37(3).
[2] Statement of Practice D12/02.

Mergers and demergers of partnerships

[22.46] In principle, a merger or a demerger is treated in the same way as a change of profit share ratio. That is, the same considerations are applied if the treatment in statutory case law is followed as would be the case in a change in profit sharing ratio. It is to be noted, however, that in a merger situation, statute[1] cannot cause a partner in one partnership to be connected with a partner in another partnership simply because the partnerships are about to merge. Where the Revenue Statement of Practice procedure is followed, there being no revaluation in the partnership balance sheets, a merger or demerger is treated as no gain/no loss.

In the more normal situation where the firm is about to merge or the firm is about to demerge and revalues chargeable assets in its balance sheet, rollover relief under TCGA 1992, ss 152–158 can be claimed by a partner insofar as he disposes of part of his share of the assets in the old firm and acquires a share in other assets in the merged firm.[2] Similarly, on a demerger, rollover relief can be claimed, subject to satisfying the normal requirements, where there is a disposal of assets passing to the other part of the demerged firm from that in which the individual remains a partner but, in return, that individual acquires an increased share in the assets of the part of the firm in which he remains.

Simon's Taxes C3.212.

---

[1] TCGA 1992, s 286(4).
[2] Statement of practice D12/02, para 9.

European economic interest grouping (EEIG)

[22.47] The CGT treatment of EEIGs[1] largely follows that of partnerships. Thus, the members of an EEIG are taxed separately on chargeable gains,[2] and disposals are deemed to occur where a person joins or leaves an EEIG, or his share in the EEIG changes.[3]

Simon's Taxes C1.609; Sumption CGT A3.35.

---

[1] That is, groupings formed in pursuance of Council Regulation (EEC) No 2137/85 of 25 July 1985; infra, § 33.30.
[2] TA 1988, s 510A(6) applying TCGA 1992, s 59 (CGTA 1979, s 60).
[3] TA 1988, s 510A(3)(*b*). Note that the Revenue consider that their statement of practice D12 does not apply to non-trading EEIGs: Inland Revenue press release, 19 April 1990; *Simon's Tax Intelligence* 1990, p 382.

Non-residents trading in the UK

[22.48] Non-residents are subject to CGT if they carry on a trade (or from 14 March 1989, a profession or vocation)[1] in the UK through a branch or agency.[2] Gains or losses are within the scope of CGT if they arise in respect of UK assets:

(1) used for the purposes of the branch trade etc; or

(2) held for the purposes of the branch.

The allowable costs of such assets are established in the normal way.[3] If the branch assets are transferred to a UK resident company controlled by the non-resident, they are deemed to have been disposed of at their open market value and a charge to tax may therefore arise.[4] For disposals on or after 20 March 1990, the disposal is treated as made for a consideration giving rise neither to gain nor to loss if the whole or part of the branch trade is transferred and the two companies are members of the same group.[5] No gain, no loss treatment may also be claimed for transfers between companies resident in other EC member states, where the consideration is satisfied by the issue of securities in the transferee company.[6]

There are a number of anti-avoidance provisions to counter the transfer of such assets outside the CGT net, namely:

(1) transfer of assets abroad prior to disposal;[7]
(2) disposal after cessation of UK trade;[8]
(3) rollover of gains against non-UK assets;[9]
(4) use of tax treaty relief by persons resident both in the UK and in another country.[10]

A UK branch or agency of a non-resident is treated as the non-resident's UK representative. For CGT purposes, the UK representative has both reporting and payment obligations in respect of amounts chargeable in respect of assets hold for the UK trade.[11] Agents not carrying on a regular agency for the non-resident are excluded, as are brokers, investment managers and Lloyd's agents for whom the non-resident is not their main principal and who are remunerated at normal commercial rates for their work.[12]

Simon's Taxes C1.602; D4.108; Sumption CGT A3.01.

---

[1] TCGA 1992, s 10(5).
[2] TCGA 1992, s 10.
[3] Even if acquired from another non-resident, but subject to TCGA 1992, s 17 if the non-residents are connected persons. UK branches of non-resident professions or vocations in existence at 14 March 1989 are deemed to have disposed of and reacquired the branch assets at market value on that date.
[4] By TCGA 1992, ss 17(1), 286 or, alternatively, s 25(3).
[5] TCGA 1992, s 172.
[6] TCGA 1992, s 140A, supra, § **21.23**.
[7] TCGA 1992, s 25(1).
[8] TCGA 1992, s 25(3).
[9] TCGA 1992, s 159(1).
[10] TCGA 1992, s 159(3) A company which has dual residency is deemed for all UK tax purposes to be non-UK resident, if it is so treated under the provisions of a double taxation agreement: FA 1994, s 249.
[11] FA 1995, s 126(2)(c), Sch 23.
[12] FA 1995, s 127.

23

Land

Definition of land	PARA 23.01
Capital gain or a trading transaction?	PARA 23.02
Part disposal	PARA 23.03
Exchange of joint interests	PARA 23.04
Furnished holiday lettings	PARA 23.05
Main residence	PARA 23.06
Leases	PARA 23.18
Reverse premiums	PARA 23.26
Mineral royalties	PARA 23.27
ITA 2007, Pt 13, Ch3 / TA 1988, s 776	PARA 23.29

Definition of land

[23.01] The provisions under the Capital Gains Tax Acts do not customarily refer to "land" but to "an interest in land". "Land" includes "messuages, tenements and hereditaments, housings and buildings of any tenure"[1] and any "right in or over land".[2] Hence, any provision in the Capital Gains Tax Acts that refers to "an interest in land" applies to an interest in a building, even though the land underneath may be in separate ownership.

As a result of the wide definition of "land", the Revenue consider that rollover relief is potentially available on the grant of an option over land, despite the treatment in statute[3] where an option is regarded as separate from the asset itself.[4] Freehold land is never a wasting asset, whatever its nature and whatever the nature of the buildings and works on it. A lease with 50 or fewer years to run is a wasting asset.[5] Unsurprisingly, in determining whether an asset is located in the UK or elsewhere, any interest in land is to be treated as situated where the land is situated, except for an interest that is solely in the land acting as security.[6] A debt secured on land is located where the creditor is resident.[7]

---

[1] TCGA 1992, s 288(1).
[2] Interpretation Act 1978, Sch 1.
[3] TCGA 1992, s 144.
[4] Inland Revenue interpretation RI 11.
[5] TCGA 1992, s 44(1)(*a*).
[6] TCGA 1992, s 275(1).
[7] TCGA 1992, s 275(1), (2).

Capital gain or a trading transaction?

[23.02] The sale of land is not always a capital transaction. If a builder buys a piece of land in order to build a house and sell it on completion, his purchase adds to his trading stock and the sale is part of the turnover of his business. He is subject to income tax[1] and there is no question of any capital gains tax liability, nor are any of the CGT reliefs[2] available to him. So, too, a land trader is subject to income tax[3] and not capital gains tax on his trading transactions.

There is a fine dividing line between, on the one hand, making an income profit on a transaction in land and, on the other hand, making a capital gain on a sale of land. The traditional approach to judging which side of the line a particular transaction falls is to consider whether the transaction carries one or more of the "badges of trade".[4] These are:[5]

(1) the subject-matter of the realisation;
(2) the length of period of ownership;
(3) the frequency or number of similar transactions by the same person;
(4) supplementary work on or in connection with the property realised;
(5) the circumstances that were responsible for the realisation; and finally
(6) motive.

Whether a land transaction is a trade, or a venture in the nature of trade, is a question of fact,[6] which, thus, falls to be decided by the Commissioners. In reviewing the correctness, in law, of the approach made by the Commissioners in holding the particular transaction in land was not trading, Sir Nicolas Browne-Wilkinson VC reviewed the way in which the transaction in land was categorised under the badges of trade listed above.[7] He warned against treating these badges as providing a formula:

> I would emphasise that the facts I am going to refer to are in no sense a comprehensive list of all relevant matters, nor is any one of them so far as I can see decisive in all cases. The most they can do is provide common sense guidance to the conclusion which is appropriate.[8]

Having ordered the facts of the particular case into the badges of trade, Sir Nicolas Browne-Wilkinson VC then explained what he was doing:

> I emphasise again that the matters I have mentioned are not a comprehensive list and no single item is in any way decisive. I believe that in order to reach a proper factual assessment in each case it is necessary to stand back, having looked at those matters, and look at the whole picture and ask the question—and for this purpose it is no bad thing to go back to the words of the statute—was this an adventure in the nature of trade? In some cases perhaps more homely language might be appropriate by asking the question, was the taxpayer investing the money or was he doing a deal?[9]

This approach was adopted by Dr Avery Jones, sitting as Special Commissioner, in *Lynch v Edmondson*,[10] where he considered an appeal by a taxpayer against Schedule D, Case I assessments arising from the purchase of land by the taxpayer, who was a self-employed bricklayer, the construction of two flats, the attempt to sell those flats and then the granting of leases for the flats. The Special Commissioner, in holding that the taxpayer was trading, analysed the series of transactions in the following manner:

> Dealing with the badges of trade: (1) this was a one-off transaction, which points away from trading; (2) the building was related to the taxpayer's bricklaying trade,

and he carried out the bricklaying himself, which points towards trading; (3) the subject matter is land which can be the subject of a trading transaction; (4) the way in which the transaction was carried out, being the sale of a lease immediately after building work was complete points towards trading; (5) the source of finance was borrowed from Barclays Bank on terms that it would be repaid out of the proceeds of the first flat to be sold, which points strongly towards trading; (6) building work was carried out on the land, which again points towards trading; (7) the flats were sold separately which is a slight pointer towards trading; (8) the taxpayer had the intention of selling at least one flat at the time of purchase; the terms of the financing required this.

The particular "badges of trade" that tend to give the most productive areas of debate when considering the nature of transactions in land are, first, intention at the time of purchase and, second, frequently of similar transactions.

In *Taylor v Good*,[11] the taxpayer had purchased a large country house at an auction. The house had sentimental value to him, it being the house at which both his parents had been employed. His wife refused to live in the house and it was subsequently sold to a developer for a sum more than ten times that paid on the purchase. The Commissioners held, as a question of fact, that the taxpayer had no intention of onward sale at a profit when he made the purchase at auction. The Court of Appeal upheld the Special Commissioners' decision that there had been no trading as there was no intention to trade. The intention to be considered is intention at the time of purchase; the state of mind of the taxpayer at a later date is not a relevant consideration.[12]

Frequent purchasers and sales indicate trading. As Harman JC said in *J Bolson & Son Ltd v Farrelly*:[13] 'A deal done once is probably not an activity in the nature of trade, though it may be. Done three or four times it usually is. Each case must depend on its own facts.'

Frequency of transactions may have an accumulative effect. In *Hudson v Wrightson*[14] the court considered four property transactions over a seven year period. It was held that the first was correctly regarded as a capital gain and the remaining three as trading transactions.

It is possible for a purchase of a single land holding to be dissected, with part of the purchase being traded as a capital transaction and the remaining part as part of a trading transaction. In *Iswera v Ceylon Commissioners of Inland Revenue*[15] a taxpayer wished to live near the school attended by his children. In order to do so, he bought the only available land on which to build a house. He built a house on part of the land and sold off the surplus as building sites. It was held that he was trading in respect of the land that he purchased with the intention of onward sale.[16]

Where a transaction is held to be part of the trade of dealing in land, the amount subject to tax is the profit of the trade, computed on the principles of commercial accountancy with the necessary adjustments for the purpose of income tax. The particular rules for identifying consideration and acquisition costs that apply for CGT have no application in such a calculation. Interest, for example, can be treated as an expense of the trade, as appropriate. Of particular relevance is the date of the commencement of the trade of land

[23.02] Land

dealing and the date of the permanent discontinuance of that trade. The determination of these two dates follows the principles applicable to income tax.

Quite separate from the treatment of a disposal of an interest in land as part of a trading activity, ITA 2007, Pt 13, Ch3 (income tax) and TA 1988, s 776 (corporation tax) treat as income the profits from certain transactions in land (see infra, § 23.29). It is important to note that a transaction is treated under these rules only if it is, in essence, a capital transaction. Transactions in the course of a trade are not affected by these provisions. One effect of bringing the gain within the scope of income, whether as trading income or by ITA 2007, Pt 13, Ch3 / TA 1988, s 776 is to make a non-resident potentially liable to tax where the land is situated in the UK.

---

[1] Or corporation tax, if the transaction is by a company, etc.

[2] If a transaction is a trading transaction, the principal private residence exemption in TCGA 1992, s 222 is not available. The gain made on the onward sale is fully chargeable to tax, even if the taxpayer has occupied the property as his only residence, see, for example, *MacMahon and MacMahon v IRC* (1951) 32 TC 311.

[3] Or corporation tax, if the transaction is by a company, etc.

[4] The six badges of trade were specified in the royal commission of 1955 Cmd 9474 para 116.

[5] The badges of trade are fully discussed at supra, §§ 8.10–8.25.

[6] In *Rangatira Ltd v IRC* [1997] STC 47, the Privy Council overturned the New Zealand Court of Appeal, which had endeavoured to substitute its own finding of fact as to whether the taxpayer had been trading. The Privy Council restored the decision at the first instance, where the evidence on which the finding of fact was based was given to the hearing.

[7] *Marsor v Morton* [1986] STC 463 at 470j to 471f.

[8] At 470h.

[9] At 471g.

[10] [1998] STC (SCD) 185 at 187g–j.

[11] [1974] STC 148, CA.

[12] At 163h.

[13] (1953) 34 TC 161 at 167.

[14] (1934) 26 TC 55.

[15] [1965] 1 WLR 663, PC.

[16] Cases in which a disposal of land has been held to be part of a trade in land include the following:

Reynolds Executors v Bennett (1943) 25 TC 401—a farm purchased and sold on, in the same year, to a development company followed by a similar transaction two years later.

Broadbridge v Beatty (1944) 26 TC 63—a transaction was carried on by shareholders and directors of a building company held to be trading in land.

Gray and Gillitt v Tiley (1944) 26 TC 80—a builder and a grocer jointly purchased a farm which they sold to estate companies they controlled.

Foulds v Clayton (1953) 34 TC 382—over a six-year period, a former builder sold houses he had built and also others he had bought.

Part disposal

[23.03] For the meaning of "part disposal" and the statutory treatment of a "small disposal", see supra, §§ **18.13–18.15**.

For the issue of a lease, as a part disposal of land, see infra, §§**23.14–23.21**.

Exchange of joint interests

[23.04] Where A and B are joint beneficial owners of a piece of land and they exchange their interests so that each becomes sole owner of part, a strict analysis said that each had made a disposal to the other of his interest in the part, the other now owned solely.[1] By concession the provisions just outlined with regard to rollover or compulsory purchase apply in this situation also. The concession also applies where a number of separate holdings of land are held jointly and each person becomes sole owner of one or more holdings.[2] The concession applies to exchanges after 19 December 1984.

Where the property is a dwelling house and so the only or main residence exemption may apply, the concession will only be given if each individual accepts that he acquires the other person's interest at its original base cost and on the original date of acquisition.

---

[1] Doubt may have been cast on this analysis by the judgment in *Jenkins v Brown* [1989] STC 577, where a disposal was held not to have occurred on a distribution of land holdings out of a pool held by trustees. It was held that the measure of the beneficial interests of the settlors was unaffected by the trust.

[2] Extra-statutory concession D26; the concession extends to exchanges of interests in jointly-owned land by married couples, where each couple becomes the joint owner of a separate part of the land; see further supra, § **16.24**. The calculations are complex.

Furnished holiday lettings

[23.05] Furnished holiday lettings are treated under the Capital Gains Tax Acts as if they were a trade.[1] The 2009 Budget announced that these rules are to be abolished from 2010–11.

The following capital gains tax reliefs are available in respect of furnished holiday lettings:[2]

(a) rollover relief;[3]
(b) holdover relief;[4]
(c) relief for loans to traders;[5]
(d) the business asset rate of taper relief;[6]
(e) exemption for a gain made by a company on the disposal of a substantial shareholding in a company whose main activity is furnished holiday lettings.[7]

[23.05] Land

(f) the business asset rate of taper relief.[8]

The same definition of furnished holiday lettings is used for capital gains as for income tax.[9] TCGA 1992, s 241(2) applies to capital gains tax the definition of furnished holiday lettings given by ITTOIA 2005, s 323. This requires the following conditions to be fulfilled for a property to be regarded as furnished holiday accommodation:

(1) The property is let commercially to the public generally.
(2) The property is available for letting for not less than 140 days in a year.
(3) The property is actually let for at least 70 days in a year.
(4) For any period of seven months it is not normally occupied by the same person for a continuous period exceeding 31 days.

"The year" for which the test is applied is:

(1) Where the property is first let during the fiscal year concerned, a period of 12 months starting with the date of the first letting.
(2) Where the property ceases to be let during the fiscal year concerned, the 12 months ending on the date the property is last let under conditions that fulfil the requirements for a furnished holiday letting.
(3) In any other case, for an individual for the fiscal year; for a company, it is a period of account of 12 months.

The treatment afforded to furnished holiday accommodation is not dependent on profits being made.[10]

ITTOIA 2005, s 326 has the effect of extending the period under which a property can be treated as furnished holiday accommodation and is, thus, of particular relevance to capital gains tax. A claim can be made under s 326 where the days during the fiscal year for which the claim is made and the preceding year on which the accommodation was actually let total at least 140 days and the accommodation was available during that two year period for not less than 280 days. The days do not have to be sequential.

Simon's Taxes C3.319.

---

[1] TCGA 1992, s 241. Individual lettings made by one person (or one partnership) are treated as one single trade: TCGA 1992, s 241(3)(b).
[2] TCGA 1992, s 241(3A).
[3] TCGA 1992, ss 152 157; see supra, §§ **22.11 22.23**.
[4] TCGA 1992, s 165: see supra, § **22.35**.
[5] TCGA 1992, s 253: see supra, § **17.07**.
[6] TCGA 1992, Sch A1.
[7] TCGA 1992, Sch 7AC: see infra, §§ **28.42–28.46**.
[8] TCGA 1992, s 241(3A).
[9] ITTOIA 2005, s 323 applied to CGT by TCGA 1992, s 241(2).
[10] *Walls v Livesey* [1995] STC (SCD) 12.

Main residence

[23.06] Any gain is wholly or partly exempt if it is attributable to the disposal of or of an interest[1] in a dwelling house which is or has been the owner's only or main residence. It is sufficient that the house was the owner's residence at any time during the period of ownership, however long ago the period of owner-occupation ended. For a dwelling house acquired before 1 April 1982, the condtion as to owner-occupation may be satisfied even by residence wholly before that date.[2] Disposals of assets other than interests in the dwelling house are therefore not exempt. Presumably an interest in the proceeds of sale will be exempt. In practice, difficulty is often met when the house is owned through a housing association, the Revenue harshly and probably wrongly denying relief here.

There is no requirement that the residence should be in the UK. It is, however, necessary that it is a dwelling house which has been used as the taxpaye's residence; this is a question of fact—even a caravan has qualified;[3] but a merely transitory occupation of a house does not qualify.[4] It has also been held that a separate bungalow adjacent to but within the curtilage of a dwelling house was part of the dwelling house even though the bungalow was occupied by a part-time caretaker.[5] In *Lewis v Lady Rook*[6], the High Court held that the residence constituted the totality of the parts of the place where the taxpayer lived, which pertained to the whole and were integral to the taxpayer's style of life. However, the Court of Appeal rejected this and considered the dwelling house as an entity, limiting the inclusion of separate buildings only to those within the curtilage of, and appurtenant to, the main house.[7]

The exemption may be applied to the disposal of an interest in the dwelling house. This covers not only a freehold, whether or not held on trust for sale, but also a lease so that a sum paid by a landlord to secure the surrender of a lease of such property would qualify.[8] By concession, the Revenue also extend relief to profits realised by employees who, under relocation arrangements set up by their employer, sell their house to a relocation company (or to the employer) at market value and share in any subsequent profits on the sale of the house.[9]

Simon's Taxes C2.1303.

---

[1] TCGA 1992, s 222. Disposals of assets other than interests in the dwelling house are, therefore, not exempt. Presumably an interest in the proceeds of sale will be exempt. In practice, difficulty is often met when the house is owned through a housing association, the Revenue harshly and probably wrongly denying relief here. The Revenue accept that an "interest" does not extend to a residence occupied under licence, see Inland Revenue interpretation RI 89.

[2] TCGA 1992, s 222.

[3] *Makins v Elson* [1977] STC 46.

[4] *Goodwin v Curtis* [1998] STC 475 where the Court upheld a finding of the Commissioners that one month's stay whilst purchasing a permanent home is not sufficient. See also *Moore v Thompson* [1986] STC 170.

[5] *Batey v Wakefield* [1981] STC 521 distinguished on facts in *Green v IRC* [1982] STC 485; see also *Markey v Sanders* [1987] STC 256 and doubts on analysis used

in that case in *Williams v Merrylees* [1987] STC 445.
6   [1990] STC 23.
7   [1992] STC 171. This analysis was followed in *Honour v Norris* [1992] STC 304, a case involving occupation of flats in separate buildings in a London square. As to the Inland Revenue interpretation of "curtilage", see Inland Revenue interpretation RI 75.
8   Quaere, however if he receives compensation for agreeing not to seek a new lease since the interest is disposed of.
9   Extra-statutory concession D37.

Grounds of the main residence

[23.07] As well as the actual site of the dwelling house, land is included in the exemption if the owner has it as the garden or grounds of the dwelling house, for his own occupation and enjoyment. There is no express requirement that the house and garden be adjacent. If the garden or grounds exceed 0.5 hectare (including the site of the dwelling house), the exemption applies only if the Commissioners are satisfied that the larger area was, having regard to the size and character of the house, required for the reasonable enjoyment as a residence.[1]

To determine what larger area is "required" in any particular case, Evans-Lombe J[2] has adopted the formulation made in the judgment in a 1938 compulsory purchase case:[3]

> 'Required', I think, in this section does not mean merely that the occupiers of the house would like to have it, or that they would miss it if they lost it, or that anyone proposing to buy the house would think less of the house without it than he would if it was preserved to it. 'Required' means, I suppose, that without it there would be such a substantial deprivation of amenities or convenience that a real injury will be done to the property owner, and a question like that is obviously a question of fact. The test is whether the house requires the larger grounds, 'not the wishes, desires or intentions of any particular owner of the house'.

The sale of a garden separate from the rest of the house causes difficulties. To be exempt the garden must be occupied as such, with the house, at the time of the disposal. Where the house is sold with part of the garden and the remainder of the garden is sold later, the subsequent sale is not entitled to the exemption.[4] If the order of sales were reversed both sales would qualify, if, and only if, the area sold is correctly regarded as the grounds of the residence and within the permitted area.[5] The point is taken by the Revenue only where the garden has development value.[6] In *Wakeling v Pearce*,[7] the Special Commissioners granted exemption from capital gains tax on the sale of a plot physically separate from the taxpayer's residence, divided from it by a distance of some 25 to 30 feet. The Commissioners found, as a fact, that the land in question was used as the garden or grounds of the house by the taxpayer for many years and this use continued up to the time of sale. Following this case, the Revenue published its interpretation of the scope of private residence relief.[8] This states:

> In general, the Revenue accept that land surrounding the residence and in the same ownership is in the grounds of the residence, unless it is used for some other purpose. The Revenue would not regard land used for agriculture, commercial woodlands,

trade or business, as part of the garden or grounds. Also, land which has been fenced off from the residence to be sold for development is excluded. Land which has traditionally been part of the grounds of the residence but which, at the date of sale, is unused or overgrown, is not excluded, nor are paddocks or orchards if there is no significant business use. Included in the definition is land which has a building on it, providing the building is not let or in use for a business, and also land which is not used exclusively for recreational purposes. For example, the owner/occupier of a guest house may allow guests to use the garden. The land may still qualify for relief providing the other conditions are satisfied.

A further problem of separate sales is that, where the garden is in excess of 0.5 hectare, it may weaken the plea that the garden was required for the reasonable enjoyment of the house.

The exemption is lost if the acquisition of the house was wholly or partly for the purpose of making a gain from its disposal.[9] Likewise where expenditure is incurred in carrying out improvements or in acquiring additional land with the purpose of gain, then there will be a charge on the proportion of the gain attributable to that expenditure. A mere hope of making a gain is probably insufficient to lose the exemption.[10]

Simon's Taxes C2.1303.

---

[1] 0.5 hectares is approximately 11/4 acres. In relation to disposals before 19 March 1991, the permitted area was one acre.
[2] Per Evans-Lombe J in *Longson v Baker* [2001] STC 6 at 15. This was followed by the Special Commissioner in *Henke v Revenue and Customs Comrs* [2006] STC (SCD) 561, [2006] SWTI 1888.
[3] Per Parcq J in the case of *Re Newhill Compulsory Purchase Order 1937, Payne's Application* [1938] 2 All ER 163, a case decided on 9 March 1938 under the provisions of s 75 of the Housing Act 1936.
[4] *Varty v Lynes* [1976] STC 508.
[5] The line taken by the Revenue when the garden exceeds ½ hectare is that the sale demonstrates that the area sold is not necessary for the enjoyment of the house and, thus is not within the permitted area. Even a small area around a house may fail to attract principal private residence relief unless it can be demonstrated that the area sold was a part of the house grounds, as opposed to an adjoining area.
[6] CCAB, June 1976.
[7] [1995] STC (SCD) 96.
[8] Inland Revenue interpretation RI 119.
[9] TCGA 1992, s 224(3). Semble the onus of proof is on the Revenue. Quaere if the exemption is lost where an intending vendor of a leasehold interest acquires the freehold reversion (under the Leasehold Reform Act 1967) in order to obtain a larger price, see Revenue leaflet CGT 8 (1980), para 76 (now withdrawn).
[10] CP. TA 1988, s 776.

Periods when not used as the main residence

Apportionment

[23.08] Full exemption applies where the dwelling house has been used throughout the period of ownership as the owner's main residence.[1] The last

[23.08] Land

36 months of ownership are treated as a period of owner occupation, whether so occupied or not, provided that the house has at some time been the only or main residence.[2]

Where the house was so used for only a part of the period of ownership, partial exemption applies, and is given by apportionment of the overall gain rateably to the period of owner occupation as a main residence.[3] For disposals on or after 6 April 1988, only periods of ownership after 31 March 1982 are relevant in making the time apportionment,[4] although the last 36 months of ownership are exempt in any case where the taxpayer occupied the property as his principal private residence at some period during the period of ownership, even if his period of occupation was entirely before 31 March 1982.[5] Where the individual has held different interests in the property, the period of ownership is treated as commencing with the acquisition of the first interest in respect of which allowable expenditure was incurred.[6] There is no provision whereby an owner who has used his house as his main private residence, but intends to do so no longer, can have its then value taken and be liable only for any subsequent gain—the apportionment rule is mandatory.

Apportionment will also take place if a part of the house has been used exclusively for business purposes, eg a surgery attached to a doctor's residence.[7]

EXAMPLE

Julius purchased a house as his main residence for £20,000 in March 1973 and occupied it as such until 31 May 1982. From then until its sale in September 2003, the house was occupied rent-free by Julius' son and daughter in law. The net proceeds of sale are £300,000. (Value at 31 March 1982: £80,000.)

	£	£
Disposal consideration, September 2003		300,000
MV, 31 March 1982	80,000	
Indexation allowance:	83,760	163,760
		136,240
Exempt: $\dfrac{3 \text{ years } 2 \text{ months}}{21 \text{ years } 6 \text{ months}} \times £136,240$		(20,709)
		115,531
Gain after taper relief £115,531 × 80%		£92,424

Simon's Taxes C2.1307; Sumption CGT A16.54.

---

[1] TCGA 1992, s 222. The legislation does not say that the ownership must be of the land and it is therefore arguable that the period of ownership is that of the dwelling house, a matter of importance where land is bought and a house later built on it.
[2] TCGA 1992, s 223(1), (2). The period was extended to 36 months in relation to disposals on or after 19 March 1991; previously it was 24 months. The period may, however, be amended again by Treasury order. The length of the period is intended to take account of the prevailing level of activity in the housing market.
[3] TCGA 1992, s 223(2).
[4] TCGA 1992, s 223(7).

Main residence [23.09]

[5] TCGA 1992, s 222 makes no reference to the period of ownership being after 31 March 1982. Hence, occupation before that date provides relief. The phrase "period of ownership" is defined as the period subsequent to 31 March 1982 for the purpose of s 223 only (see s 223(7)) and has no application in construing that phrase for the purpose of s 222. Where occupation was entirely before 31 March 1982, the effect of this definition is to provide relief as a fraction specified by s 223(2) as 36 months divided by the period of ownership since 31 March 1982.
[6] TCGA 1992, s 222(7).
[7] TCGA 1992, s 224(1); no relief is lost if a room is used exclusively for employment purposes or partly for business purposes and partly for personal use. This is confirmed in Inland Revenue interpretation RI 80.

Additional exemption for letting

[23.09] An additional relief arises when a house has been let and, at the same time or another time during the period of ownership, the dwelling house has been the taxpayer's main residence (whether in fact, or by election).[1] This additional relief is available on a letting either of the whole dwelling house or of part of it. The gain which becomes chargeable as a result of the letting is reduced by the smaller of (a) the gain attributable to owner-occupation, and (b) £40,000.[2] It seems that, in a case where chargeable gains arise as a result of letting and also for some other reason, eg house left unoccupied, or partial use for business, the gain resulting from the letting needs to be identified separately. However, there are no provisions setting out how this is to be done.

EXAMPLE

Facts as in the previous example, except that in 1990, Julius' son and daughter-in-law moved out and from 1991 to 2002, Julius let the house commercially.

	£	£
Disposal consideration, September 2003		300,000
MV, 31 March 1982	80,000	
Indexation allowance:	83,760	163,760
		136,240
Exemptions:		
(a) Exemption for occupation by taxpayer		
$\dfrac{3 \text{ years } 2 \text{ months}}{21 \text{ years } 6 \text{ months}} \times £136{,}240$	(20,709)	
(b) Exemption for letting		
lower of: (i) $\dfrac{3 \text{ years } 2 \text{ months}}{21 \text{ years } 6 \text{ months}} \times £136{,}240$		
	(20,709)	
(ii) £40,000		(41,418)
		94,822
Gain after taper relief £94,822 × 80%		£75,857

There is no requirement that the letting be to an unconnected person, nor that the rent must be at a level that would be determined by the Rent Tribunal. Hence, the letting exemption would have been available if Julius's son and daughter-in-law had remained in occupation, but had paid rent. The statutory requirement is for the dwellinghouse to have been "let by" the taxpayer. In *Owen v Elliott*[3] the Court of Appeal held that hotel lettings do not attract the exemption, when the owner lives on the premises, but no decided case has turned on the amount of rent to be charged for the exemption to apply. For the purpose of dependent relative relief,[4] the Revenue apply an extra-statutory concession[5] under which rent paid is ignored it if is less than the costs incurred by the house owner and those costs include capital repayments on any loan to purchase the property. Whilst this is not directly relevant to the letting exemption, it is suggested that a taxpayer proposing to let property for a non-commercial rent would be advised to ensure that the rent receivable exceeds his outgoings, including any capital repayments. This would, it is suggested, defeat any argument that the property was not "let".

Where a house is owned by husband and wife, each is potentially able to have advantage of the additional exemption for letting, without any reduction. This contrasts with the legislation for rent-a-room, where joint ownership leads to a halving of the exemption.[6]

Simon's Taxes C2.1307; Sumption CGT A16.54.

---

[1] TCGA 1992, s 223(4). Distinguish a lodger living as a member of the owner's family, see statement of practice SP 14/80.
[2] TCGA 1992, s 223(4)(*b*). The monetary limit was £20,000 for disposals before 19 March 1991 and £10,000 before 6 April 1983.
[3] [1990] STC 469, CA.
[4] TCGA 1992, s 226.
[5] Extra-statutory concession D20.
[6] F(No.2)A 1992, Sch 10, para 5(4): see supra, § **10.10**.

Periods of deemed residence

[23.10] Certain periods of non-occupation are deemed to be periods of residence. First, the period of 36 months immediately before disposal is treated as a period of owner occupation.[1] This may benefit owners who move elsewhere but experience difficulty in selling the house. In practice a 12-month period before occupation is also treated as owner occupation if the owner cannot take up residence because the house is being built or repaired.[2] Only the excess is then treated as a chargeable gain.[3] Second, certain other periods are treated as periods of residence, provided they are both preceded and followed by periods of occupation[4] and no other residence is eligible for relief during the period of absence. These periods, which may all be claimed in aggregate, are:

(1)　any period of up to three years;
(2)　any period of overseas employment;[5] and

(3) any period not exceeding four years during which the owner could not occupy the house by reason of his place of work or a reasonable condition imposed by his employer that he should reside elsewhere.[6]

Where the period of absence under 1 or 2 is exceeded, only the excess (not the whole period) is treated as giving rise to a chargeable gain.[7]

Third, where a person (either an employee or, from 6 April 1983,[8] a self-employed person) lives in job related accommodation, he may claim another house as his residence, provided he intends in due course to occupy it as his only or main residence.[9]

The deeming provisions in statute apply automatically, no election is required. However, there is a strange statutory definition of "period of absence". Statute[10] states this is a period throughout which the taxpayer had no residence eligible for relief. In the normal case when an individual moves to work in another part of the country, or abroad, the individual will live in a rented house that is, indeed, in principle, eligible for relief. Does that mean that the period away is not a "period of absence". To take such a view is to rob the statutory provisions of any meaning.[11]

Simon's Taxes C2.1304, 1307; Sumption CGT A16.53.

---

1 TCGA 1992, s 223(1).
2 Extra-statutory concession D49.
3 *Simon's Tax Intelligence* 1983, p 116.
4 Periods of occupation need not *immediately* precede and follow the period of absence, but they must be periods of *actual* occupation, not other qualifying periods of absence. Where on a person's return he is not able to resume occupation because the terms of his employment require him to live elsewhere this condition is treated as satisfied, extra-statutory concession D4.
5 Where the house belongs to one spouse and the other is required to go overseas, the condition is treated as satisfied, extra-statutory concession D3 (1994).
6 TCGA 1992, s 223(3), (7).
7 *Simon's Tax Intelligence* 1983, p 116, para 13, and confirmed by the Inland Revenue Technical Division.
8 TCGA 1992, s 222(9).
9 TCGA 1992, s 222(8) amended by FA 1984, s 25. For earlier periods see less generous Revenue press release, 27 September 1973 but note interest deduction case of *Frost v Feltham* [1981] STC 115.
10 TCGA 1992, s 223(7).
11 The Revenue Capital Gains Manual at para CG 65046 suggests that an election to treat the permanent dwelling house as the principal private residence is to be advised.

Election for main residence

[23.11] An individual may only have one exempt residence. If he has more than one residence, he may elect[1] which is to be exempt. It is, however, necessary for each dwelling house to be a residence of the taxpayer. Thus he

[23.11] Land

could not select a house which he always lets to tenants, although an occasional letting is probably not inconsistent with his residence. Any such election can take effect for a period beginning up to two years before the election is made.[2] In *Griffin v Craig-Harvey*[3], Vinelott J held that the election must be made within two years of the taxpayer's first coming to have more than one residence. The basis of this decision was that s 222(5)(b) must be read before s 222(5)(a).[4] However, as the former sub-sub-section is now revoked, it would be interesting to see whether a court felt itself bound by this precedent or whether what the author considers to be the more natural reading of the statutory provision should apply, which would have the consequence that an election could be made at any time.[5] Strangely, in the same case, Vinelott J held that, once an election has been made within the two-year period, it can be altered at any time, even after the two years has expired.[6]

If a taxpayer has more than one residence then if his interest in each of them, except one, is such as to have no more than a negligible capital value on the open market (eg a weekly rented flat or accommodation provided by an employer), the two year time limit for nominating one of those residences as the individual's main residence for capital gains purposes will be extended where the individual was unaware that such a nomination could be made. The late election will be deemed effective from the date on which the individual first had more than one residence.[7]

Where a husband and wife live together they are entitled to only one private residence exemption between them and they must jointly make any election.[8] The effect of TCGA 1992, s 222(6) is that, for the purpose of this election, husband and wife are treated as if they were one single person. The election must be made jointly by them for one of the properties only.

The wording in statute states that this provision applies "in the case of a man and his wife living with him". The meaning of this phrase is given by TA 1988, s 282 (which is applied to capital gains tax by TCGA 1992, s 288(3)) as:

> A husband and wife shall be treated for income tax purposes as living together unless—
>
> (a) they are separated under an order of a court of competent jurisdiction, or by deed of separation or
> (b) they are in fact separated in such circumstances that the separation is likely to be permanent.

This provision was considered by the House of Lords in *Gubay v Kington* [1984] STC 99, HL. Mr Gubay lived in the UK and was treated for tax purposes as UK resident; Mrs Gubay lived mainly in the Isle of Man and was treated for tax purposes as not resident in the UK and was, hence, not subject to capital gains tax. The House of Lords held that Mr and Mrs Gubay were correctly regarded for CGT purposes as "living together". The effect of the decision was that tax on a gain of £1.4m was avoided.

Whether or not the spouses have more than one house, a spouse may in determining liability, take advantage of any period during which the house was the main residence of the other.[9] Consider the situation where husband and wife jointly own a property in the country and they then jointly purchase a flat in London. The husband lives continuously in the country home but the wife lives in the London flat during the week to be near her work. The husband and wife can elect, if they wish, for the London flat to be treated as the principal private residence of both of them, even though the husband never resides in the flat. The gain arising on the ultimate disposal of the flat will then be exempt, even for the husband. If the house in the country was their sole residence before they bought the London flat, a sale of the house in the country will attract the private residence exemption for the last 36 months of ownership, even if they own the London flat during that period and they have elected for the flat to be treated as the principal private residence.

Simon's Taxes C2.1303, 1305; Sumption CGT A16.52.

[1] TCGA 1992, s 222(5).
[2] TCGA 1992, s 222(5)(*a*).
[3] [1994] STC 54.
[4] At 59j.
[5] See also Keith Gordon's articles, 'Main residence relief – the two year time limit revisited' (2005) *Personal Tax Planning Review*, 10(1), pp27–38 and 'Private Residence Relief: the true status of the two-year rule' (2008), *Private Client Briefing*, 4, pp184–191.
[6] "Mr Ewart who appeared for the taxpayer before the commissioner and before me pointed out that if the Crown's construction is correct a taxpayer who prudently gives notice before the end of two years from the period when he first owns two or more residences can later vary that notice with retrospective effect **at any time**. He does not have that right if he does not give notice and he loses it notwithstanding that he might by the notice have done no more than state the obvious, namely that the residence which the inspector would inevitably conclude was his main residence was his main residence. I accept that that conclusion follows . . ."
[7] Extra-statutory concession D21.
[8] TCGA 1992, s 222(6). As to the position where one spouse has interests in more than one residence, and the other spouse has none, see Inland Revenue interpretation RI 75. The position is unaffected by the independent taxation of married couples. On separated couples, see extra-statutory concession D6 (1994)—disposal by one spouse of interest in former matrimonial home is treated as falling within TCGA 1992, s 222 (CGTA 1979, s 101) provided the other has continued to live in the house *and* the one has not elected that some other house should be treated as his main residence for this period. The concession is very narrow, and since it encourages the spouses to rearrange their property interests before separation (so that the husband may make an election for some other house) also encourages the taking of hostile acts. This runs counter to much recent family law legislation and contrasts with the IHT exemption for transfers between spouses.
[9] TCGA 1992, s 222(7).

Pre-1988 residence of dependent relative

[23.12] An individual or married couple living together may also claim exemption in respect of one private residence which has been provided continuously since a date prior to 6 April 1988 for a dependent relative rent-free and without any consideration of any sort.[1] The strictness of the last condition is considerably relaxed by an extra-statutory concession[2] under

[23.12] Land

which rent paid is ignored it if is less than the costs (taking one year with another) incurred by the house owner. Those costs include capital repayments on any loan to purchase the property.

For disposals on or after 6 April 1988, the exemption is withdrawn except where the property was the sole residence of a dependent relative on 5 April 1988 or at some earlier time.[3] Where a dependent relative has ceased to occupy the residence, but it is later reoccupied (after 5 April 1988) by that or another dependent relative of the owner, the subsequent period of occupation is ignored in computing the exempt gain.

A dependent relative is:

(a) any relative of his or his wife who is incapacitated by old age or infirmity from maintaining himself; or
(b) his or his wife's mother who, whether or not incapacitated, is either widowed, or living apart from her husband, or a single woman in consequence of dissolution or annulment of marriage.[4]

Simon's Taxes C2.1311.

[1] TCGA 1992, s 226.
[2] Extra-statutory concession D20.
[3] TCGA 1992, s 226.
[4] TCGA 1992, s 226.

Dwelling house held by trustees

[23.13] An exemption may be claimed by trustees if the dwelling house is owned by them and has been the main private residence of one entitled to occupy it under the terms of the trust[1], which includes a beneficiary who is allowed by the trustees to occupy it and would be entitled to the income from the house or from the proceeds of sale.[2] When trustees of a discretionary trust in exercise of their discretion allow a beneficiary of the trust to occupy the house, the beneficiary is entitled to occupy the house under the terms of the trust since he has a right to remain in occupation until asked to leave by the trustees.[3] In *Sansom v Peay*[4] Brightman J said:[5]

> Counsel for the Crown has made the very fair concession, and I think correct concession, that the expression 'under the terms of the settlement' is capable of including 'under the exercise of a power conferred by the settlement'. That concession is in accordance with the general principles which will be found in

> In this case the beneficiaries were in occupation of Wickwoods throughout the relevant period as their only or main residence. They were in occupation pursuant to the exercise by the trustees of a power expressly conferred by the settlement to permit those beneficiaries to go into occupation and remain in occupation. The trustees exercised that power, and the beneficiaries thereupon became entitled to go into occupation and to continue in occupation until the permission was withdrawn. The trustees never did withdraw permission until they required vacant possession in order to complete the exchange. Therefore, looking at the matter at the date of the disposal, the beneficiaries were persons who, in the events which happened, were entitled to occupy the house and did occupy it under the terms of the settlement. That, in my view, is the correct approach to the subsection in dealing with the type

of case which is before me, and in those circumstances I reach the view that the terms of [now TCGA 1992, s 225] have been satisfied and that the gain is exempt from capital gains tax.

Simon's Taxes C2.1306.

---

1. TCGA 1992, s 225.
2. In *Sansom v Peay* [1976] STC 494, [1976] 3 All ER 375, Brightman J said (at 497j) that this is "the obvious case to which [now s 225] applies".
3. Care must be taken by trustees in this situation. Giving right of occupation to a beneficiary will often be construed as giving that beneficiary a lease for life, so that the value of the house is treated as part of the estate of the beneficiary for IHT purposes: see infra, § **42.10**.
4. [1976] STC 494.
5. At 497h.

Transfer of dwelling house between spouses

[23.14] Statute[1] requires that principal private residence relief is computed by aggregating the periods for which a dwelling house has been the main residence of either of the spouses. This can arise in two different forms. First, an inter vivos transfer between spouses. Second, a transfer at death to the surviving spouse.

Where there is an inter vivos transfer, the acquiring spouse takes the base cost of the spouse who made the original acquisition.[2] Taper relief is calculated for the period from the date on which the first spouse made the acquisition.[3] The exemption for the main residence is then calculated by reference to this total period. This treatment applies even if the original acquisition was made prior to the marriage. Thus, it is possible for part, indeed most, of the period treated as period of ownership to be a time when the two individuals, as unmarried persons at the time, had separate properties on which the main residence exemption applied.

Statute specifically applies this provision when a house (or a part interest in a house) passes from one spouse to the other at a death.[4] The computation of main residence relief on the subsequent disposal by the surviving spouse can produce surprising results. Consider the following situation:

"Homeland" purchased by Alan (alone) in October 1997 for £100,000.

Alan and his wife, Betty, have two houses and have elected for PPR on the other house.

The other house is sold in April 2004, leaving "Homeland" as the only residence, which, thus, attracts PPR from that date.

Alan dies October 2004. The probate value of "Homeland" is £200,000.

Homeland is inherited by Betty.

Betty sells Homeland in October 2007 for £300,000.

One would expect the gain to be fully exempt as the house has been Betty's main residence throughout her period of ownership. Indeed, if the disposal had been made by a legatee other than the surviving spouse, the entire gain would have been exempt.

As the wife inherited the house from her husband, statute requires us to compute the exemption by reference to the period October 1997 to October 2007 to give the following chargeable gain:

	£
Sale proceeds, October 2007	300,000
Value at death, October 2004	(200,000)
	100,000
PPR £100,000 × 3.5/10	(35,000)
Chargeable gain	65,000

This unsatisfactory position can be corrected by the sale of the house being made, not by the surviving spouse, but by the personal representative (see infra, § **23.15**). This will, however, only be a possibility if the period of administration has not expired and if the property has not been transferred to the surviving spouse during the period of administration.

---

[1] TCGA 1992, s 222(7)(*a*). See supra, § **16.43**.
[2] TCGA 1992, s 58(1).
[3] TCGA 1992, Sch A1, para 15. Indexation allowance for the period prior to 6 April 1998 is, similarly, computed by reference to the entire period: TCGA 1992, s 56(2).
[4] TCGA 1992, s 222(7)(*a*).

Sale by personal representatives

[23.15] Principal private residence relief can be claimed by personal representatives.[1] Relief is available if one or more legatees are entitled under the will or intestacy to at least 75% of the net proceeds of the house and the residence was the only or main residence of the individual or individuals concerned both immediately before and immediately after the death. In computing the 75% entitlement[2] it is assumed none of the proceeds are required to meet liabilities of the estate, including inheritance tax. The 75% entitlement can either be outright or by way of interest in possession.[3]

A claim by the personal representatives is required.[4]

If it is necessary to elect for the residence to be treated as the occupier's main residence, the election must be given by a joint notice from the personal representative and the individual who occupies the dwelling house.[5]

---

[1] TCGA 1992, s 225A inserted by FA 2004, Sch 22, para 5 with effect from 10 December 2003. This statutory provision replaces extra statutory concession D5. The previous extra-statutory concession required 100% of the interest passing to go to the beneficiary occupying the property.
[2] TCGA 1992, s 225A(4).
[3] TCGA 1992, s 225A(3).
[4] TCGA 1992, s 225A(6).
[5] TCGA 1992, s 225A(5)(*b*).

Principal private residence relief after holdover relief

[23.16] For a disposal after 9 December 2003, principal private residence relief is not available if there was a claim for holdover relief on the acquisition of the property.[1]

Prior to 10 December 2003, it was possible to make a gift of a dwelling house into, say, a discretionary trust, avoiding the charge to tax by making a hold-over claim. The trustees would then permit a beneficiary to live in the house and on disposal the gain would be claimed as wholly exempt.[2] The broad effect of the restriction[3] is to deny private residence relief where there has been a prior hold over claim under s 260, such that the base cost in computing the gain is reduced by the held-over gain (but subject to transitional provisions mentioned below). Private residence relief is denied whether the relevant disposal is made by the trustees or by an individual, the latter being relevant where, for example, the trustees have made a disposal to an individual. The only exception[4] is where trustees have elected that the provisions for a maintenance fund for a historic building shall apply.[5]

There are transitional provisions, which apply where the disposal that would otherwise give rise to private residence relief is made after 9 December 2003 but the earlier disposal or disposals, as the case may be, occurred before then. In that situation, relief is given for the period from acquisition to 9 December 2003 but denied for subsequent periods (and also ignoring the rule whereby the last 36 months is treated as occupation to the extent that the period falls after 9 December 2003).

Notwithstanding the changes made by FA 2004, there could still be circumstances where it is beneficial to make a disposal into a trust and benefit from the relief for trustees' disposals under s 225. For example, suppose a house with 0.5 hectare of land is currently worth £250,000 but not a residence of the owner. There is scope for increasing the value with planning for redevelopment, the expected value then being £1 million. The house could be transferred to an interest in possession settlement and capital gains tax paid on the basis of the value at that date. Any future gain should be eligible for private residence relief if a beneficiary lives in the house meeting the requirements of s 225 so that the gain in excess of the market value at the date of transfer can be wholly relieved. Another approach would be to use a discretionary trust to receive the house on the basis that if planning consent does not seem likely, a hold-over claim could then be made as this can be within five years ten months of the end of the tax year in which the disposal to the trustees takes place. Clearly, there will be a chargeable transfer for inheritance tax purposes and so the value at the date of transfer is important. Moreover, capital gains tax would have to be paid if a hold-over claim has not been made by the due date for payment. This does provide some flexibility, bearing in mind that there may, in the event, be no tax saving if, in this example, planning consent is never obtained and the house continues to be owned within the same family group. The loss of non-business asset taper relief for the period before transfer to trustees should also be taken into account.

---

[1] TCGA 1992, s 226A inserted by FA 2004, Sch 22, para 6.
[2] Under TCGA 1992, s 225.

[23.16] Land

[3] TCGA 1992, s 226A inserted by FA 2004, Sch 22, para 6.
[4] Under TCGA 1992, s 226B inserted by FA 2004, Sch 22, para 6.
[5] TA 1988, s 691(2).

[23.17] Moreover, in some cases it might be appropriate to seek to revoke a hold-over claim if the eventual sale proceeds are such that greater tax would be saved by having private residence relief on the sale rather than denied by the FA 2004 changes. The question is whether or not a hold-over claim can be revoked within the same time limit for actually making the claim. There is no doubt that a claim can be amended within 12 months from the date it is made, or if made in the return, in the 12 months after the filing date. Although not stated explicitly in the legislation, it would seem that once these relevant time limits have passed, a hold over claim could not be revoked even if still within 5 years 10 months of the end of the tax year in which the relevant disposal was made. Even where it is possible to revoke a claim, the trustees could be in an invidious position. A hold-over claim where there is a transfer into a settlement can be made by the transferor alone but on a disposal by trustees, the claim must be made by both the trustees and the transferee. It could be the case that the trustees have held a property for some time where not eligible for private residence relief but could be transferred to an individual who would then live in the property. There could again be circumstances depending upon values where it is better to pay the tax because greater relief would be obtained on the eventual sale. Before acceding to a revocation request the trustees would need to ensure that they are not in breach of trust or, if nothing else, perhaps seek some form of indemnity from the beneficiary to whom the property is transferred.

Leases

[23.18] The rules governing leases are complex. In part this simply reflects the complexity of the transactions with which the law is dealing; however, it reflects also the complexity of neighbouring areas of tax law, especially income tax.

The provisions deal with two main issues:

(a) the determination of gains or losses on the disposal of the lease by the lessee;
(b) the circumstances in which the grant of a lease is a disposal or part disposal by the landlord—and how any gains should be computed.

There are special rules for computing the capital gain or loss which accrues on the disposal of a lease which has 50 years or less to run at the time of the disposal. Such a lease is a wasting asset.[1]

The wasting asset writing down rules apply as soon as the lease becomes a wasting asset;[2] but then they apply regardless of the original length of the lease.

Simon's Taxes Division C2.12.

[1]   TCGA 1992, s 44.
[2]   TCGA 1992, Sch 8, para 1(5).

Duration of a lease

[23.19] There are three rules for the duration of a lease; they are similar to but not identical with the Schedule A rules in TA 1988, s 38.[1] The duration of a lease is decided in relation to the grant or any disposal of the lease by reference to the facts which were known or ascertainable at the time when the lease was created or acquired.[2]

These rules are designed to prevent taxpayers from presenting short leases as long leases. They are as follows:

Simon's Taxes C2.1202.

[1]   TCGA 1992, Sch 8, para 8.
[2]   TCGA 1992, Sch 8, para 8(6).

Notice to end

A lease is treated as ending at the earliest date on which it could be determined by notice given by the landlord.[1] So a lease for 50 years which the landlord may terminate by notice after five years is treated as a five-year lease (because of para 8(6) this will be so even after the five-year period has passed).

[1]   TCGA 1992, Sch 8, para 8(2).

Commercial reality

Where any of the terms of the lease render it unlikely that the lease will continue beyond a certain date, the lease is treated as ending on that date.[1] A lease that specifies a date on which rent is to be increased is treated as a lease expiring on that date.[2]

[1]   TCGA 1992, Sch 8, para 8(3).
[2]   TCGA 1992, Sch 8, para 8(4).

Extension

Where the terms of the lease include provision for the extension of the lease beyond a given date by notice given by the tenant, these provisions apply as if the term of the lease extended for as long as it could be extended by the tenant, but subject to any right of the landlord by notice to determine the lease.[1] However, rights under the Leasehold Reform Act 1967 do not cause a lease to be treated as extended as the Act gives a right to acquire a new tenancy in substitution for the existing tenancy not a right to extension of the lease.[2]

A lease of movable property which is a wasting asset is deemed to terminate not later than the end of the life of the wasting asset.[3]

[23.19] Land

1. TCGA 1992, Sch 8, para 8(5).
2. *Lewis v Walters* [1992] STC 97.
3. TCGA 1992, Sch 8, para 9(3).

Writing down the expenditure

[23.20] A lease of land becomes a wasting asset until the time when its duration does not exceed 50 years.[1] When a lease has no more than 50 years to run, the expenditure attributable to its acquisition is deemed to waste away over the balance of its duration. For a lease other than a lease of land, the expenditure is written off on a straight line basis; a special curved basis applies to a lease of land.

Where applicable, indexation relief is given only on the expenditure not yet written off.[2]

The fraction of the acquisition cost that is taken into the CGT calculation is given in a statutory table.[3] This table gives a geometric progression so that there is less depreciation in the early years of the lease, depreciation accelerating the closer the lease is to the end of its term. It is interesting that the time apportionment provisions that are applied to a pre-1965 acquisition[4] require a straight line calculation and not a geometric calculation. Both the lease provisions of Schedule 8 and the pre-1965 acquisition provisions of Schedule 2 were introduced in FA 1965. In *Smith v Schofield*,[5] counsel for the Revenue stated in court that the way in which a gain should be apportioned to give a true commercial measure, was by adopting a geometric division, such as used for leases. This is not, however, the method determined by Parliament for assets generally and, as far as we are aware, the Revenue in 1965 did not suggest the adoption of a geometric division for assets other than leases.

Simon's Taxes C2.1203.

1. TCGA 1992, Sch 8, para 1(1).
2. TCGA 1992, s 53(3).
3. TCGA 1992, Sch 8, para 1.
4. TCGA 1992, Sch 2, para 16.
5. [1993] STC 268, HL.

Two interests: extensions of leases and mergers of leases

[23.21] A new lease granted as the result of an application under the Landlord and Tenant Act 1954 was held to be an asset separate from the original lease and so not derived from it.[1] This issue was addressed in connection with time apportionment for assets held since before 1965. This is because the new tenancy may differ significantly from the old and because the old lease will have expired leaving no asset from which the new one can be said to be derived. Where this occurs none of the expenditure in respect of the original lease is available for being taken into account in relation to a disposal of the new lease.

A new lease under the Leasehold Reform Act is not an extension of the old lease.[2] The question was whether the lease was a wasting asset and the court decided that it was and that one could not take into account the fact that there were rights to an extension under the Leasehold Reform Act 1967.

By concession, no CGT charge is treated as arising if the old lease is surrendered in return for the grant of a new, longer lease of the same property to the same lessee.[3] This concessionary treatment applies where the terms of new lease, other than its duration and the rent payable, are not materially different from those of the old and that the surrender and re-grant are either between unconnected parties or, if the parties are connected, the terms of the transaction are equivalent to those that would have been made between unconnected parties bargaining at arms length.[4]

Where the lessee acquires a superior lease or the freehold reversion, the interests are merged and the original lease extinguished and the two assets are merged.[5]

In these circumstances the expenditure allowable on a disposal of the merged interest will include not only the cost of the superior interest but also the cost of the first lease written down, if the duration was less than 50 years, to the date of the acquisition of the superior interest. If the superior interest is itself a lease with a duration of less than 50 years, the total of these amounts is written down to the date of disposal of the merged lease.[6]

Indexation relief is available on the cost attributable to the inferior lease by reference to the date of its acquisition. For disposals before 30 June 1992, Revenue practice was even more generous and computed the indexation allowance on both the inferior and the superior interests by reference to the date of acquisition of the inferior interest. The Revenue view is that in strictness, indexation allowance on the total of these two amounts is calculated by reference to the date of acquisition of the superior interest.

[1] *Bayley v Rogers* [1980] STC 544.
[2] *Lewis v Walters* [1992] STC 97.
[3] Extra-statutory concession D39. This is one of the concessions targeted by TCGA 1992, ss 286A and 286B (added by FA 1999, s 76), see supra, § **15.01**.
[4] Amendment to extra-statutory concession D39 published as part of the Revenue interpretation RI 205, June 1999.
[5] TCGA 1992, s 43.
[6] Extra-statutory concession D42.

Exceptions

[23.22] Leases with less than 50 years to run are not treated as wasting assets in two situations.

(1) Where at the beginning of the ownership of a lease it is subject to a sublease not at a rack rent and it is estimated at that time that the value of the lease, when the sublease falls in, will exceed the lessee's acquisition cost; such a lease is not a wasting asset until the sublease falls in.

This is in accord with common sense. It is not clear whether when the lease does become a wasting asset P(1) is 100.00 (the normal rule for leases which become wasting assets through passing the 50-year point) or the percentage applicable to the actual duration left—the latter seems more sensible.

(2) Where the lease qualifies for capital allowances, eg on a lease of an industrial building; this is the normal rule for all assets qualifying for capital allowances.[1]

Simon's Taxes C2.1203.

[1] TCGA 1992, Sch 8, para 1(6).

Grant of a lease—definition of a premium

[23.23] The CGT rules on the grant of a lease refer frequently to the concept of a premium. A "premium" is defined by TCGA 1992, Sch 8, para 10(2) as including "any like sum, whether payable to an intermediate or a superior landlord"; presumably this means any sum like a premium, a term usually meaning a sum paid by the tenant to the landlord for the lease.

A "premium" includes any sum (other than rent) paid on or in connection with the granting of a tenancy, except in so far as other sufficient consideration for the payment is shown to have been given.[1]

In *Clarke v United Real (Moorgate) Ltd*[2] Walton J said:

Now what is a premium? Having in mind the dictum of Lord Goddard CJ in *R v Birmingham (West) Rent Tribunal* [1951] 2 KB 54 at 57, [1951] 1 All ER 198 at 201, that 'The whole conception of the term is a sum of money paid to a landlord as consideration for the grant of a lease', I ventured to define a premium as any sum paid by the tenant to the landlord in consideration of the grant of the lease. Counsel for Moorgate made one addition to that definition—an addition which he saw as vital—but subject thereto accepted it as a definition. The addition which he made to the definition was the words 'as landlord': the payment has to be to the landlord in that capacity. It would not do, said counsel for Moorgate, if, for example, the landlord were a plumber and the tenant paid the landlord some sum for plumbing work done by him on behalf of the tenant. That sum would fall to be excluded. I do not wish in any way to quarrel with the thought behind counsel for Moorgate's addition, although in my view it is an otiose addition, because the cost of the plumbing work would not be paid to the landlord 'in consideration of the grant of the lease', and so would not fall within the definition I have given in any event . . .

'Premium' may convey different things to different minds, and a businessman may well have a definition in his mind which is miles removed from the legal one . . .

Counsel for the Crown submitted that if the total sum here in question was not a premium it was certainly a 'like sum' . . . Hence, 'like sums' are only relevant in connection with the granting of a tenancy . . . 'Key money' was a premium, and hence, in any event, available to be caught as such under that description.

The following payments are treated as lease premiums:

(1) Payment in lieu of rent.

(2) Consideration for the surrender of a lease.
(3) Consideration for the variation of a lease.³

In addition, where there is a variation or waiver of any of the terms of a lease and, had the transaction been at arm's length a sum would have been expected to have been paid as consideration for the variation or waiver, this sum is treated as a lease premium if the landlord and tenant are connected persons, or the transaction was entered into gratuitously.⁴

The time at which the lease premium is deemed to have arisen depends on the event. The main rules are:

(1) Where an actual premium is paid, the time is the date of the grant of the lease.⁵
(2) A payment in lieu of rent or a variation or waiver is treated as arising when the sum is payable.⁶
(3) Where the premium is imputed by the relationship between the parties, the operative date is the date on which the sum would have been payable had the parties acted at arm's length.

In relation to Scotland, a premium includes in particular a grassum payable to any landlord or intermediate landlord on the creation of a sublease.⁷

The definition of a premium applies to leases generally, not just to leases of land.

Simon's Taxes C2.1216.

---

1   TCGA 1992, Sch 8, para 10(2).
2   [1988] STC 273 at 299–300.
3   TCGA 1992, Sch 8, para 3.
4   TCGA 1992, Sch 8, para 3(7).
5   TCGA 1992, s 28(1) and Sch 8, para 3.
6   TCGA 1992, Sch 8, para 3(2)(*a*), (3)(*a*).
7   TCGA 1992, Sch 8, para 10(3).

Grant of a lease—out of freehold or long lease

[23.24] Where the payment of a premium is required under a lease there is a part disposal of the freehold or other asset out of which the lease is granted.¹ Less obviously, the grant of a lease for a full rent without a premium is also a part disposal. However, no gain will actually arise since the only consideration received is the right to the rent and that is prevented from being relevant consideration by TCGA 1992, s 37(1).

In applying the A/A + B formula in TCGA 1992, s 42, the property remaining undisposed of, (B), includes the right to the rent or other payment and that right should be valued at the time of the disposal.²

The part disposal formula does not apply in the case of a lease granted out of a lease which is a wasting asset.³

If the lease granted is a bargain at arm's length or if the lessee is a person connected with the lessor, the amount of the premium deemed to have been given is the market value of the lease.⁴

[23.24] Land

EXAMPLE

BC purchased a freehold factory for £180,000 in May 1994. After occupying it for the purposes of his own business, he grants a 15-year lease to a company for £50,000 with effect from 1 December 2003. The capitalised value of rentals under the lease is £150,000 and the freehold reversion is worth £200,000.

	£	£
Disposal consideration		50,000
Allowable expenditure		
£180,000 × [50,000/(50,000 + 200,000 + 150,000)]	22,500	
Indexation allowance:	2,633	(25,133)
		24,867
Gain after taper relief £24,887 × 25%		£6,221

Simon's Taxes C2.1216.

---

1. TCGA 1992, Sch 8, para 2(11).
2. TCGA 1992, Sch 8, para 2(2) applying s 42.
3. TCGA 1992, Sch 8, para 4.
4. TCGA 1992, s 17(1).

Grant of lease out of a wasting lease

[23.25] Where a lease is granted out of a lease which is a wasting asset, the part disposal formula is not used to govern the allowable expenditure.[1] Instead only that part of the expenditure on the head lease which will be written off over the period of the sublease may be deducted from the premium for the sublease. The writing off rules are the familiar ones of the curved line basis for land and the straight line basis for other assets.[2]

If the lease is granted out of a short lease, the allowable expenditure is the amount which will have wasted over the term of the sublease, given by the fraction [(P(4)–P(5))/P(1)], where:

P(1) = percentage applicable to unexpired term of head lease at date of acquisition;

P(4) = percentage applicable to unexpired term of head lease at date sublease is granted;

P(5) = percentage applicable to unexpired term of head lease at date sublease expires.

These rules apply not only to acquisition costs but also to expenditure on improvements.

A further rule does apply if the premium is less than what would be obtainable if the rent receivable under the sublease were the same as the rent payable under the head lease. This will arise if for example the rent charged on the sublease is higher than that charged under the lease out of which the sublease is created. If, say, the premium is one half of the amount so obtainable only one half of the expenditure attributable to the sublease is taken.³

There are also provisions dealing with the grant of a sublease of part of the land comprised in the head lease.⁴ The proportion of the expenditure is taken by comparing the value of the property covered by the sublease with the value of all the property comprised in the head lease; the remainder of the expenditure is apportioned to the part not disposed of.

Where income tax has been paid by the sub-lessor further rules are needed to prevent double charging.

On the grant of a lease for a term of less than 50 years, any premium may be subject in part to income tax. If the lease has been granted out of a freehold or long lease, the premium subject to CGT is reduced by the amount subject to income tax.⁵ However, the reduced premium is substituted only in the numerator, not in the denominator, of the A/A + B formula for apportioning allowable expenditure. In the case of a short lease granted out of a short lease, the CGT computation follows the normal format and the amount of the premium subject to income tax is then deducted from the chargeable gain.⁶ This deduction may reduce a gain but may not create an allowable loss.

Simon's Taxes C2.1217.

1   TCGA 1992, Sch 8, para 4.
2   TCGA 1992, Sch 8, para 4(2)(*a*).
3   TCGA 1992, Sch 8, para 4(2)(*b*).
4   TCGA 1992, Sch 8, para 4(3).
5   TCGA 1992, Sch 8, para 5(1).
6   TCGA 1992, Sch 8, para 5(2).

Reverse premiums

[23.26] Reverse premiums are better described as lease inducement payments since they are paid by the landlord to the tenant to persuade the tenant to take up the lease on the terms offered. Such premiums received on or after 9 March 1999 are treated as revenue receipts,¹ and so cannot give rise to CGT for the landlord. Before 1999 there were no CGT implications for the tenant since the tenant was not disposing of an asset.

Simon's Taxes C2.1233.

1   FA 1999, s 54 and Sch 6. The Revenue view of the practical effect of these provisions is given in Inland Revenue Tax Bulletin, December 1999, pp 711–713, see supra, § **8.135**.

Mineral royalties

Basic treatment

[23.27] Where mineral royalties are received under a mineral lease or agreement, one half of the royalties received are treated as income and one half as capital.[1] The capital element is then a capital sum derived from an asset.[2]

If the royalty received relates both to the winning and working of minerals and to other matters,[3] there is an apportionment between:

(1) the amount which it could be expected would have been paid if the agreement had only related to the winning and working of minerals, and
(2) the amount which it could be expected would have been paid for the other matters.

Simon's Taxes C2.1111.

---

[1] TCGA 1992, s 201(1).
[2] TCGA 1992, s 22(1)(d). See Revenue Internal Guidance, Capital Gains Manual, CG12960–12966.
[3] The Mineral Royalties (Tax) Regulations 1971, SI 1971/1035.

Set-off of income tax deducted

[23.28] For individuals or trustees, the income tax deducted from the gross royalties is treated as follows.

(1) It is set off against the recipient's liability to income tax on the one-half of the royalties treated as income.
(2) The remainder, if any, is set off against the recipient's liability to CGT on the one-half of the royalties treated as capital.
(3) The remainder, if any, is to be repaid.[1]

---

[1] TA 1988, s 122(4).

ITA 2007, Pt 13, Ch3 / TA 1988, s 776

[23.29] These provisions were introduced in 1969[1] to charge to income tax certain gains of a capital nature arising from the disposal of land. The purpose is to charge profits that escape taxation as trading income and to charge the prime mover in schemes such as *Ransom v Higgs*, supra, § **8.06** rather than the person making the trading profit.

TA 1988, s 776(2) says that the section applies wherever:

(a) land, or any property deriving its value from land, is acquired with the sole or main object of realising a gain from disposing of the land, or

(b) land is held as trading stock, or
(c) land is developed with the sole or main object of realising a gain from disposing of the land when developed,

and any gain of a capital nature is obtained from the disposal of the land—

(i) by the person acquiring, holding or developing the land, or by any connected person, or
(ii) where any arrangement or scheme is effected as respects the land which enables a gain to be realised by any indirect method, or by any series of transactions, by any person who is a party to, or concerned in, the arrangement or scheme;

and this subsection applies whether any such person obtains the gain for himself or for any other person.

A similar wording is found for income tax purposes in ITA 2007, s 756.

Thus the rules apply only to the gain arising on an actual disposal of the land which had been so acquired, held or developed. It has, however, been observed that the rule that the gain of a capital nature must be derived *from* the disposal of land may have to be treated differently when paragraph (c) is involved from situations where paragraphs (a) and (b) are involved. Differently probably means more widely. So in *Page v Lowther*[2] X granted a lease of land to Y and, in accordance with an arrangement between X and Y, Y arranged for payments due on the grants of subleases to be made to X by the sub-lessee. Y having developed the land, the court held that X was liable under s 776(2)(c) as X had arranged for a gain to be realised by X by an indirect method—getting Y to make the sub-lessee make the payments to X.

It should be noted that the section is not confined to "artificial transactions" in land, ie to transactions entered into for the purpose of tax avoidance.[3]

The charge for corporation tax arises under Schedule D, Case VI and is generally made under s 776(3)(b) on the person realising the gain. However, s 776(8) provides that:

if all or any part of the gain accruing to any person is derived from value, or an opportunity of realising a gain, provided directly or indirectly by some other person, whether or not put at the disposal of the first-mentioned person, subsection (3)(b) of this section shall apply to the gain, or that part of it, with the substitution of that other person for the person by whom the gain was realised.

So when A provides B with an opportunity of realising a gain the gain which B makes can be taxed as the income of A: A is given an indemnity against B.[4]

The charge is on the whole of the gain and is made for the year in which the gain is obtained but TA 1988, s 777(13) provides that an amount in money or money's worth shall not be regarded as receivable by some person until that person can effectively enjoy or dispose of it. So A's liability does not arise until B can effectively enjoy or dispose of the gain.

The charge arises regardless of the residence of the taxpayer if all or any part of the land is situated in the UK.[5] However s 776 is backed up by various powers, one of which allows the Revenue to require a payment to be made under deduction of tax at basic rate if the payee is non-resident.[6] Since this power arises only once the non-resident is entitled to the money, this power is of little use if completion follows closely on the contract.[7]

Simon's Taxes B5.236.

[23.29] Land

1   FA 1969, s 32; it does not apply to gains realised before 15 April 1969. On validity of alternative assessments see *Lord Advocate v McKenna* [1989] STC 485; and on whether assessments are cumulative or alternative see *IRC v Wilkinson* [1992] STC 454, CA.
2   [1983] STC 799, CA.
3   *Page v Lowther* [1983] STC 799, CA. The taxpayer argued unsuccessfully that the heading of TA 1988, Part XVII (in which s 776 occurs), "Tax avoidance", and the side heading of TA 1988, s 776, "Artificial transactions in land" restricted the scope of the section.
4   TA 1988, s 777(8); B is treated as having paid income tax for the purposes of CGT, TA 1988, s 777(12).
5   TA 1988, s 776(14); in the case of a non-resident the Board may direct the deduction of income tax at basic rate—TA 1988, s 777(9).
6   TA 1988, s 777(9).
7   As in *Pardoe v Entergy Power Development Corpn* [2000] STC 286.

The three situations

Where land or property deriving its value from land, is acquired with the sole or main object of realising a gain from disposing of the land

[23.30] **Land or property.** Land includes references to all or any part of the land and includes buildings and any estate or interest in land or buildings.[1] So a disposal of the benefit of a contract to buy land or the grant of a lease are covered. The interest may be legal or equitable.[2] Property deriving its value from land includes any shareholding in a company or any partnership or interest or any interest in settled property deriving its value directly or indirectly from land and any option consent or embargo affecting the disposition of land; so the right to insist that a sale should take place only with A's consent gives A the necessary property deriving its value from the land.

Simon's Taxes B5.236, 237.

1   TA 1988, s 776(13), see also TA 1988, s 777(5).
2   *Winterton v Edwards* [1980] STC 206, [1980] 2 All ER 56.

[23.31] **Disposal.** The property is disposed of if (a) the property in the land, or (b) the property deriving its value from the land, or (c) control over the land is effectually disposed of.[1]

The word effectually prevents too much legalism. Thus the grant of a long lease for a premium will not permanently dispose of control of the land but presumably a suitably long lease with wide powers in the tenant would deprive the nominal landlord of effectual control. In appropriate circumstances the Revenue might argue that that portion of a premium on a lease which escaped tax as property income (or, for corporation tax, under Schedule A) by reason of the fractional reduction would fall within this charge. Disposal of a majority shareholding in a company holding land would come within (c); on the other hand the disposal of a minority shareholding does not come within (c) but instead comes within (b).

These words are widened still further by TA 1988, s 777 which provides:

(2) . . . account shall be taken of any method, however indirect, by which—

    (a)   any property or right is transferred or transmitted, or

    (b)   the value of any property or right is enhanced or diminished, and accordingly the occasion of the transfer or transmission of any property or right, however indirect, and the occasion when the value of any property or right is enhanced, may be an occasion when, under the principal sections, tax becomes chargeable.

(3) Subsection (2) above applies in particular—

    (a)   to sales, contracts and other transactions made otherwise than for full consideration or for more than full consideration, and

    (b)   to any method by which any property or right, or the control of any property or right, is transferred or transmitted by assigning share capital or other rights in a company or any partnership or interest in settled property and

    (c)   to the creation of any option or consent or embargo affecting the disposition of any property or right, and to the consideration given for the option, or for the giving of the consent or the release of the embargo, and

    (d)   to the disposal of any property or right on the winding up, dissolution or termination of any company, partnership or trust.

Further, TA 1988, s 776(5) allows any number of transactions to be treated as one disposal.

Simon's Taxes B5.236.

---

[1]   TA 1988, s 776(4).

[23.32] Object. The principal practical problems concern the requirements that the sole or main object should be the realising of a gain from disposing of the land and that this should be the object at the time of acquisition.[1] In choosing the word object rather than intention or purpose the legislature has presumably left it for the courts to infer as a matter of fact regardless of any document stating the powers and objects of any company partnership or trust. An intention to hold the land as a source of income will not prevent a charge from arising if there was also the object of making a gain from disposing of the land, provided that object was the main one. If the two objects were equal it would appear to follow that TA 1988, s 776 cannot apply. If land is acquired with this object, a subsequent change of mind is irrelevant.

Objects other than making a gain include deriving income from it, preservation of visual or other amenity value of existing land, the provision of accommodation for a relative and in the case of a company retention of family control. One must not forget that for TA 1988, s 776 to apply the object of gain must relate to the property acquired and not some other land.

The rule that the property must be acquired with the object of making a gain has on the not dissimilar Australian legislation been held not to include property acquired under a testamentary gift;[2] however, buying the land from executors in satisfaction of a pecuniary legacy is clearly distinguishable.

Simon's Taxes B5.236.

[23.32] Land

[1] eg *Sugarwhite v Budd* [1988] STC 533, CA.
[2] *McClelland v Taxation Comr of Australian Commonwealth* [1971] 1 All ER 969.

Where land is held as trading stock

[23.33] When land held as a trading stock is disposed of the profits would normally enter a computation under Schedule D, Case I and as such would be outside TA 1988, s 776. The purpose of s 776(3)(*b*) in conjunction with s 776(8) is to catch the indirect disposals which might otherwise give rise to income accruing to others. This charge does not extend to property deriving its value from land.

Simon's Taxes B5.236.

Where land is developed with the sole or main object of realising a gain from disposing of land when developed

[23.34] If land is acquired without the object of realising a gain from disposing of the land TA 1988, s 776(2)(*a*) does not apply. Where, however, land is developed with that object a charge arises under this provision. Development is not defined. The object of realising a gain on disposal must presumably exist at the moment of development but it is unclear whether it is necessary that the object should be to dispose of the land immediately the land is developed. The fact that it is envisaged that the land should be used as a source of, say, rental income for a few years before its final effectual disposal should be only one factor in deciding whether the sole or main object of the development was to realise the gain. Conversely if the object is to use the property developed as a source of rental income but, after development, a change of mind occurs, no charge under TA 1988, s 776 can arise. What happens when the change of mind occurs during the development is less clear since s 776(2)(*c*) simply states that the land is to be developed with the object of realising a gain. Such words would appear apt to cover any development in the course of which there was at any time such a sole or main object.

Where s 776(2)(*c*) applies so much of the gain as is attributable to the period before the intention to develop is formed is excluded.[1]

This provision was successfully invoked by the Revenue in *Page v Lowther*.[2]

Simon's Taxes B5.236.

[1] TA 1988, s 776(7) makes the facts satisfy (*a*) or (*b*) although in such circumstances the charge is apparently made under (*c*). This slice is chargeable to CGT. Presumably the existing use value is taken as the figure at which the charge for capital gain to taxable income occurs.
[2] [1983] STC 799; see supra, § **23.25**.

Exceptions

[23.35] The charge does not apply to a gain accruing on the disposal of the taxpayer's principal private residence, as defined for CGT purposes. However, such a residence which was bought partly with a view to gain while not exempt from CGT is not liable to a charge under ITA 2007, s 755.[1]

The charge does not apply where there is a disposal of shares in a company which holds land as trading stock or in a company that is a dealing company not an investment company which owns directly or indirectly 90% or more of the ordinary share capital of another company which holds land as trading stock provided that all the land so held is disposed of in the normal course of trade, and so that all opportunity of profit accrues to the company.[2] This exclusion applies to the straightforward disposition of the shares but does not apply to a scheme or arrangement enabling a gain to be achieved by indirect means.

When the land is held by a company it may be in the company's interest to escape TA 1988, s 776 since not only will the tax paid be lower but also the company may be able to use rollover relief.[3]

Simon's Taxes B5.236.

---

[1] TA 1988, s 776(9).
[2] TA 1988, s 776(10); in practice the Revenue confine this provision to companies already dealing in land.
[3] Infra, § **28.25**.

Computation and clearance—and losses

[23.36] The computation of the gain is defined in very broad terms, the statute merely directing that there shall be used such method as is just and reasonable in the circumstances, taking into account the value obtained for the land, but allowing only such expenses as are attributable to the land disposed of. This broadness may assist the taxpayer. If he submits a computation based on Schedule D, Case I principles it appears that in practice it will be for the Revenue to show that the computation is not just and reasonable, it is not enough for them to show that another method is also just and reasonable.

Because of the vague and broad nature of the charge there is a clearance procedure. However, taxpayers seldom apply for clearance and when they do they are usually refused.

TA 1988, s 776 makes no mention of losses. It appears therefore that other Schedule D, Case VI losses can be set off against TA 1988, s 776 income and vice versa.[1] For income tax, the position is made explicit by ITA 2007, s 152 which provides for loss relief in respect of what the statute refers to as 'section 1016 income'.

Simon's Taxes B5.236, 238–246.

---

[1] TA 1988, s 392 is sub silentio authority for this: it puts an express ban on TA 1988, ss 34–36 but does not mention TA 1988, s 776.

An example—Yuill v Wilson

[23.37] In *Yuill v Wilson*[1] the taxpayer and connected settlements controlled company X which owned two pieces of land. He set up a non-resident trust

[23.37] Land

which controlled two other non-resident companies C and M which proceeded each to buy a property from X for full market value. The trust then disposed of its shares in C and M to an overseas company in which neither the taxpayer nor his family had any interest, the consideration due to C and M was to be paid in instalments on the happening of certain contingencies.

The House of Lords held that TA 1988, s 776(2) applies to the gains realised by C and M. The gains had been obtained for the companies either directly or through his companies and with the aid of the trustees and the taxpayer remained liable notwithstanding his subsequent sale of his shares in C and M to the overseas company. The House also held that a right to money which could not be said to be effectively enjoyed was not yet taxable; it followed that as yet there was no liability in respect of the unpaid conditional instalments.[2]

Simon's Taxes B5.236.

---

[1] [1980] STC 460, [1980] 3 All ER 7. For another recent example see *Chilcott v IRC* [1982] stc 1.
[2] The taxpayer unsuccessfully appealed again on the grounds that the contingent rights of the companies to the instalments were "money's worth", capable of being valued and sold within a year of the contract. Following *Yuill v Wilson*, however, the gains were realised only when the instalments were received and ceased to be subject to restriction: *Yuill v Fletcher* [1984] STC 401.

Compulsory purchase

[23.38] Where there is a disposal of land to an authority exercising or having compulsory powers rollover relief is available to put against the gain arising.[1] The computation of rollover relief and its method of application are the same for rollover relief to replace an asset of a trader[2] (see supra, §§ **22.13–22.14**). However, rollover relief on compulsory acquisition of land can be claimed by any person and the gain rolled into any land that is acquired,[3] other than a dwelling house.[4] The relief is available if the "new land" is acquired at any time during the period commencing 12 months before the disposal and 36 months after this disposal.[5]

In order to qualify for rollover relief, statute[6] requires that the landowner did not take any steps, by advertising or otherwise, to dispose of the land or to make his willingness to dispose of it known to the authority or others.[7] HMRC take a generous view of this provision and state[8] that any attempt to market the land is to be disregarded if it took place more than three years "before the compulsory acquisition in question".

The statutory requirement for both disposal and acquisition to be of "land", is satisfied by any interest in land[9] and, under HMRC practice, the relief is applied where the rollover is into buildings, whether owned with the land or not.[10]

It is not necessary that the land be acquired under a compulsory purchase order. The statutory requirement is that it must be acquired by an "authority exercising or having compulsory powers",[11] which is defined as a body who "has or have been, or could be, authorised to acquire it compulsorily for the purposes for which it is acquired, whether or not the purchase was made under a compulsory purchase order".[12]

Many "official" bodies, including central government and public and local authorities, have powers of compulsory purchase—for example, the Secretary of State for Defence has powers under the Military Lands Act 1892 and regional development agencies have powers under the Regional Development Agencies Act 1989. The possession of such powers is not confined to "official" bodies. Some commercial organisations possess compulsory purchase powers—for example utility companies and railway companies. Their powers are usually granted by private Acts of Parliament, for example the Channel Tunnel Rail Link Act 1996. A purchase by any one of these bodies has the potential for rollover relief for the vendor, even if the purchase is made for a purpose totally unconnected with the activity for which compulsory purchase powers have been granted by Parliament.

HMRC accept that a tenant exercising a right to buy a freehold reversion under the Leasehold Reform Act 1967 can be an "authority" for this purpose.

---

[1] TCGA 1992, s 247(2).
[2] TCGA 1992, ss 152 & 153.
[3] TCGA 1992, s 247(2)(b).
[4] TCGA 1992, s 248(1).
[5] TCGA 1992, s 247(5)(b), see *Watton v Tippett* [1997] STC 893.
[6] TCGA 1992, s 247(1).
[7] HMRC CG Manual para 72202.
[8] HMRC CG Manual para 72202.
[9] Interpretation Act 1987, Sch 1.
[10] HMRC Statement of Practice SP 13/93.
[11] TCGA 1992, s 247(8).
[12] TCGA 1992, s 243(5).

24

Taper relief, indexation allowance and rebasing

Introduction	PARA **24.01**
Taper relief	PARA **24.02**
Indexation allowance	PARA **24.02**
Rebasing to 31 March 1982	PARA **24.10**
Time apportionment—assets held at 6 April 1965	PARA **24.13**

Introduction

[24.01] The contents of this Chapter were made more or less redundant for capital gains tax purposes with effect 6 April 2008 following the Chancellor's decision to 'simplify' the rules from 2008-09. That simplification exercise, however, was a perfect illustration how not to effect changes to the tax system, especially in an area where decisions are often made by taxpayers with the long term in view. As the then President of the Chartered Institute of Taxation commented, 'In taxation, the only time that change should come before consultation is in the dictionary'[1].

---

[1] Reported widely but no longer available from the CIOT website.

Taper relief

[24.02] Taper relief was introduced for capital gains tax in respect of disposals after 5 April 1998. It was withdrawn in respect of disposals after 5 April 2008. The aim of taper relief was to reduce the chargeable gain (after deducting all other reliefs) by reference to the period of ownership – the longer that an asset had been held, the greater the reduction. Different rates of reduction applied depending on whether or not the asset disposed of qualified as a business asset.[1]

Although the underlying concept was broadly welcomed, the rules (which were inserted as TCGA 1992 Sch A1) were widely criticised. The principal criticism was that the tapering of gains stopped after two years for business assets and after ten years for non-business assets. Thus any argument that the rules encouraged long-term ownership of assets was clearly misleading. The consequence of this was that detailed records continued to need to be kept whereas the initial hope was that taper relief would signal the end of such record-keeping for assets held for long periods.

[24.02] Taper relief, indexation allowance and rebasing

Other criticisms were based upon the underlying complexity of the rules, the fact that they were regularly tinkered with causing additional complexity and anomalous results and the fact that the rules were rather crudely bolted onto the rest of the CGT legislation leaving many questions as to the actual effect of the legislation in certain situations.

Although it was initially thought that the corporation tax rules would also adopt the taper relief rules, this idea was fairly swiftly dismissed. This led to a clear divergence in the two codes dealing with capital gains. Whilst the 2008 abolition of taper relief could have brought the codes closer together, if anything, they are now further apart than ever.

For a detailed commentary on the taper relief rules as they applied before 2008-09, see Chapter 24 of the 25th edition of this work.

---

[1] The term 'business asset' was actually a misnomer as business asset status depended, broadly, on the asset being used for the purposes of a trade (or profession or vocation). Property businesses generally fell outside this definition.

Indexation allowance

[24.03] Indexation allowance was first introduced in the early 1980s to compensate taxpayers for the effects of inflation that were rendering the gains made in theory (paper gains, being the difference between the proceeds and cost) meaningless. The allowance was 'frozen' for capital gains tax purposes in April 1998 upon the adoption of taper relief and abolished altogether with effect from 6 April 2008. However, the changes did not affect its application for corporation tax.

For a disposal by a company, indexation allowance is computed up to the month of disposal. On the disposal of an asset, an indexation allowance is given, equal to the allowable expenditure multiplied by the fraction

$$\frac{RD - RI}{RI}$$

where RD is the retail prices index figure for the month in which the disposal occurs and RI that for the month in which the expenditure is incurred.[1] If RI exceeds RD, the indexation allowance is nil.[2]

The fraction has to be expressed as a decimal, taken to the nearest three decimal places.[3] Where there are several items of allowable expenditure incurred at different times, the indexed rise is calculated separately for each, and the aggregate is then the indexation allowance. However, indexation applies only to items of relevant allowable expenditure, broadly the cost of acquisition and any expenditure on enhancement or preservation of title (supra, §§ **16.19–16.21**).[4] It does not apply to other deductions eg for IHT on a gift (infra, § **45.26**) or foreign tax which is not creditable (supra, § **16.23**). The indexation allowance is treated as a deduction from the gain computed under general CGT rules. It may reduce the gain to produce either a smaller gain or neither a gain nor a loss, but cannot turn the gain into a loss or increase a loss. The gain prior to deduction of indexation allowance is termed the "unindexed gain".[5]

EXAMPLE

C purchased shares in D plc for £10,000 in July 1987 which are sold for £12,000 in September 2001.

Disposal consideration	£12,000
Deduct Allowable costs	10,000
	2,000
Indexation allowance (0.552 × 10,000)	5,870
Restricted to	2,000
Chargeable gain/allowable loss	nil

Where an asset was acquired before 1 April 1982 and is disposed of after 5 April 1988 the allowance is calculated by reference to the market value on 31 March 1982 rather than the various items of expenditure incurred before that date, if this gives a result favourable to the taxpayer.[6] However, the 31 March 1982 value must be used to compute the indexation allowance if the taxpayer has elected under TCGA 1992, s 35(5) (FA 1988, s 96(5)) (infra, § **24.09**). Provision is made for changes in the state of the asset since 31 March 1982.[7] For disposals before 6 April 1988, but after 5 April 1985, the use of the 31 March 1982 value for indexation purposes was elective.

Simon's Taxes C2.301–303; Sumption CGT A4B.01.

---

[1] TCGA 1992, s 54(2).
[2] TCGA 1992, s 54(8).
[3] TCGA 1992, s 54(4).
[4] TCGA 1992, s 53(2)(*b*).
[5] TCGA 1992, s 53(2)(*a*).
[6] TCGA 1992, s 55(1), (2).
[7] TCGA 1992, s 55(4).

Part disposal

[24.04] On a part disposal the deductible expenditure in respect of the whole asset must be apportioned before the indexation allowance is calculated. The indexation allowance on the part disposal applies only to that part of each item of expenditure which is to be taken into account on the disposal.[1]

Where an element of expenditure falls to be reduced (the most obvious example concerns the reduction of expenditure on leased property), increased or excluded, the indexed rise is to apply only to the expenditure as reduced, increased or excluded.[2]

Simon's Taxes C2.303, 404; Sumption CGT A4.09.

---

[1] TCGA 1992, s 56(1).

[24.04] Taper relief, indexation allowance and rebasing

2   TCGA 1992, s 53(3). On a merger of a lease into a superior interest, the indexation allowance on disposal of the merged interest will be based on the expenditure on the original lease, wasted down to the date of the merger where appropriate: extra-statutory concession D42.

Special situations

[24.05] Certain CGT provisions apply a no gain/no loss rule on certain types of disposal, for example on a transfer of an asset between member companies in groups (see infra, § **28.29**) and (when relevant for capital gains tax, on a gift between husband and wife living together). For a disposal of this kind after 5 April 1985, the consideration for the disposal takes account of any indexation allowance due to the transferor, by treating the disposal as giving rise to an indexation allowance equal to the indexed gain.[1]

However, for assets transferred under such a disposal before 6 April 1985 but after 5 April 1982, the rules were somewhat different.[2]

Where a person acquired an asset after 31 March 1982 by a no gain/no loss disposal and any earlier disposal of the asset after that date was also such a disposal,[3] he is treated as having held the asset on 31 March 1982 and so is eligible to take 31 March 1982 as the base date value for indexation relief. Any indexation relief already taken into account in the no gain/no loss disposal must be deducted in arriving at the 31 March 1982 base cost.[4]

This rule was modified with effect from 6 April 2008 for capital gains tax purposes. When the plan to abolish indexation allowance was announced, it became apparent that spouses and civil partners could generally preserve any accrued indexation allowance by effecting a no gain/no loss transfer between themselves before 6 April 2008. That transfer, under the provisions of TCGA 1992, ss 56 and 58, would increase any base cost of the acquiring spouse by reference to any indexation allowance that had accrued between the original acquisition date and April 1998. However, the legislation would not have permitted this result if the original acquisition had taken place before 1 April 1982. Consequently, FA 2008 contained a provision to extend the preservation of indexation allowance to all pre-1998 assets, provided that the transfer between spouses or civil partners took place before 6 April 2008.[5]

If there is a no gain/no loss disposal on or after 30 November 1993, and the acquirer disposes of the assets at a loss, the indexation allowance assumed to be given on the no gain/no loss transaction is deducted from the loss.[6] The adjustment cannot result in a gain but can reduce the loss to nil.

In relation to an asset acquired after 31 March 1982 by way of a no gain/no loss transaction, the acquirer's base cost includes any indexation assumed to be given on that transaction, so that a loss on a disposal of the asset after 30 November 1993 will be increased by the "rolled-up" indexation.[7]

Although this might be corrected, it appears that the abolition of indexation allowance provisions might have inadvertently overridden this rule, allowing full loss relief in cases where there was a transfer between spouses or civil partners before 6 April 2008 and a disposal on or after that date either at a loss or where the indexation allowance exceeds the gain.

Simon's Taxes C2.301, 304; Sumption CGT A4A.01; A12.10.

[1] TCGA 1992, s 56(2).
[2] FA 1982, Sch 13, para 3 repealed by FA 1985, Sch 19, para 5(3). See *Butterworths UK Tax Guide 1985-86*, § **24.12** for an explanation of the earlier rules.
[3] Defined in TCGA 1992, s 55(5).
[4] TCGA 1992, s 55(6). TCGA 1992, Sch 3, para 1; see supra, § **22.25**. This special rule for indexation purposes is now mirrored by the general rule for computing gains or losses on assets held on 31 March 1982.
[5] TCGA 1992, s 35A.
[6] TCGA 1992, s 56(3).
[7] TCGA 1992, s 55(8).

Relevant receipts

[24.06] The receipts of certain sums are treated as not giving rise to a disposal, but rather as reducing the base cost of the asset. For example, on a rights issue if the shareholder sells his "rights", the amount received is not treated as a chargeable disposal if the proceeds amount to less than 5% of the value of his shareholding ex-rights.[1] The proceeds are instead deducted from the acquisition cost of the shares. Here, the indexation allowance on a disposal of the shares takes account of the reduction in allowable expenditure but only from the date of the receipt.[2]

Simon's Taxes C2.302; Sumption CGT A4.17.

[1] Supra, § **21.17**.
[2] TCGA 1992, s 57.

Reorganisations etc

[24.07] Where, on a reorganisation of a company or an amalgamation, new shares are acquired, they are generally treated as if the original acquisition were still in existence. If new consideration is provided, it is treated as new relevant allowable expenditure.[1] The indexed rise on the expenditure is therefore calculated by reference to the date the new consideration was provided, not by reference to the date the allowable expenditure on the original shareholding was incurred.

Simon's Taxes C2.1505.

[1] TCGA 1992, s 131 (FA 1982, Sch 13, para 5).

Calls on shares etc

[24.08] Unpaid calls due in respect of the shares are treated as having been paid when the shares were acquired provided they are paid within 12 months

[24.08] Taper relief, indexation allowance and rebasing

of that date.[1] Calls paid outside the 12-month period are treated as separate items of expenditure incurred when paid, and the indexation allowance on disposal of shares is calculated accordingly.

Where the subscription agreement gives the shareholder the right to pay by instalments, it is arguable that the whole of the consideration is given at the time of issue, so that the 12-month limitation does not apply.[2] In a number of so-called "privatisation issues", the 12-month rule is also inapplicable in relation to payment of the purchase consideration, as there is no issue of shares, merely a transfer of existing shares by the Secretary of State.

Simon's Taxes C2.717.

[1] TCGA 1992, s 113(1)(*b*).
[2] Cf under TCGA 1992, s 48, there is no adjustment for postponement of the right to receive consideration.

Options

[24.09] Special rules apply to options. The acquisition of property under an option is treated as an acquisition when the option is exercised but, in computing the indexed rise, the sums paid for the option are treated as separate items of expenditure incurred when the option was acquired.[1]

Simon's Taxes C2.302; Sumption CGT A12.10; A20.07.

[1] TCGA 1992, s 145 (FA 1982, Sch 13, para 7). On treatment of sums paid for shares under the 1985 rules see TCGA 1992, s 114 (FA 1985, Sch 19, para 15).

Rebasing to March 1982

Capital gains tax

[24.10] From 6 April 2008 the following rules apply. Prior to that date, the capital gains tax rules followed those applicable now to corporation tax.

If an asset was acquired before 31 March 1982, the base cost used in computing the capital gain is the value of the asset on 31 March 1982.[1] Statute requires that it 'shall be assumed that the asset was on 31 March 1982 sold by the person making the disposal, and immediately reacquired by him, at its market value on that date'. Thus, the condition of the asset on that date and the market conditions on that date must be considered. There is no scope for saying that, in the commercial world, a taxpayer would not have made a sale on that date. If a property had sitting tenants in occupation on 31 March 1982, the valuation that is used is the value as depreciated by the actual occupation.

[1] TCGA 1992, s 35 as amended by FA 2008.

Corporation tax

[24.11] If an asset was acquired before 31 March 1982, the base cost used in computing the capital gain is the value of the asset on 31 March 1982 (unless the actual cost is higher).[1] Statute requires that it "shall be assumed that the asset was on 31 March 1982 sold by the person making the disposal, and immediately reacquired by him, at its market value on that date".[2] Thus, the condition of the asset on that date and the market conditions on that date must be considered. There is no scope for saying that, in the commercial world, a taxpayer would not have made a sale on that date. If a property had sitting tenants in occupation on 31 March 1982, the valuation that is used is the value as depreciated by the actual occupation.

Where the asset consists of a shareholding in an unquoted company, the size of the holding that is to be valued is normally the number of shares held in that company by that taxpayer on 31 March 1982.

TCGA 1992, s 35 requires that a gain be computed by reference to the value of the asset at 31 March 1982. Where the asset consists of shares, TCGA 1992, s 104 provides that the shares of the same class in the same company constitute a single asset. The nature of that asset is given by TCGA 1992, s 109(1) which has the effect that the asset which is taken into the rebased computation is the shareholding as determined by FA 1985, Sch 19, Pt. II. Where there has been a disposal of shares between 1982 and 1985, the shares sold are clearly not part of the holding in 1985. Hence, in the Revenue's view, the 1982 holding to be valued for a capital gain computation under the rebasing rules is:

> The share pool that was frozen when FA 1982 came into force, less any disposals between 1982 and 1985".[3]

> "Although a 1982 holding represents a share pool which was frozen in 1982, it was not created until 1985 . . . Any disposal of shares held in 1982 made between 1982 and 1985 would not be included in the 1982 holding and should not be included in the valuation.[4]

The principles of valuation are considered more fully at infra, § **45.02**.

Simon's Taxes C2.601.

---

[1] Where the computation produces a loss, the allowable loss is the lower of the loss computed by reference to the March 1982 value and the loss computed by reference to actual expenditure prior to that date. If a valid election has been made under TCGA 1992, s 35(5) (see Tiley & Collison: UK Tax Guide 2001–02 § **35.38**), the historic cost is ignored and the March 1982 value is used, even if this gives a larger loss.
[2] TCGA 1992, s 35(1).
[3] Revenue Internal Guidance, Capital Gains Manual, CG50874.
[4] Revenue Internal Guidance, Capital Gains Manual, CG50902.

Relief for gains rolled over

[24.12] This commentary applies only for the purposes of corporation tax after 5 April 2008.

[24.12] Taper relief, indexation allowance and rebasing

If a gain was rolled into an asset acquired prior to 31 March 1982, the effect of rebasing at that date is to give permanent relief for the gain that was rolled over.

If an asset was held at 31 March 1982 and sold prior to the rebasing provisions being brought into effect in 1988, a rollover relief claim on that sale would, in the absence of any relieving provision, bring into charge the heldover gain, even if it mainly arose prior to the rebasing date.

In order to provide a measure of relief in this circumstance, where a gain arising on an asset held on 31 March 1982 has been the subject of a rollover claim, the reduction in the base cost of the "new asset" acquired is reduced by one-half.[1] The deduction must have been wholly or partly attributable, directly or indirectly, to gains accruing on the disposal before 6 April 1988 of assets acquired before 31 March 1982. The reduction can apply only once, which leaves it unclear whether a part disposal has the effect of denying relief on a subsequent disposal of the asset retained. The roll-over provisions that qualify for this treatment are:

(1)   replacement of assets lost or destroyed (TCGA 1992, s 23(4), (5));
(2)   compulsory acquisition of land (TCGA 1992, s 247);
(3)   replacement of business assets (TCGA 1992, s 152);
(4)   incorporation of business (TCGA 1992, s 162);
(5)   gifts of business assets (TCGA 1992, s 165);
(6)   gifts (FA 1980, s 79).

In cases where gains are held over without being deducted from allowable expenditure, the deferred gain is reduced by one-half.[2] The deferral provisions that qualify for this relief are:

(1)   domestication of foreign branch (TCGA 1992, s 140);
(2)   degrouping (TCGA 1992, s 178(3));
(3)   compensation stock on nationalisation (TCGA 1992, s 134);
(4)   compulsory acquisition of land—depreciating asset acquired (TCGA 1992, s 248(3));
(5)   replacement of business assets—depreciating asset acquired (TCGA 1992, s 154(2));
(6)   emigration of donee after gifts holdover (TCGA 1992, s 168);
(7)   reorganisation involving qualifying corporate bonds (TCGA 1992, s 116(10), (11)).

Where an asset was not owned at 31 March 1982, it may still be traced back to that date for the purposes of rebasing. This is done if the asset was acquired by means of a defined no gain/no loss transaction and either the transferor held it at 31 March 1982 or it was acquired through one or more disposals after that date which were all no gain/no loss transactions.[3] The main types of no gain/no loss disposals covered are:

(1)   between spouses living together (TCGA 1992, s 58);
(2)   settled property passing on the death of the life tenant (TCGA 1992, s 73);
(3)   between members of a group of companies (TCGA 1992, s 171).

Where the asset concerned consists of shares, and the transferee held shares of the same class in his own right at 31 March 1982, the value of the combined holding must be determined at that date. The allowable cost on a disposal is determined on a simple pro rata basis.[4]

There is also provision for rebasing where an asset is derived from another asset held on 31 March 1982,[5] eg an undivided interest in land formerly held as joint tenant.

Where an asset was held at 31 March 1982 and there was then a part disposal before 6 April 1988, the allowable expenditure attributable to the part remaining is the amount relating to the whole asset less the fraction allocated to the part disposed of.[6] The effect of rebasing is not to value the retained part separately at 31 March 1982 but to recompute the allowable expenditure taking the cost of the whole asset as its value at that date.[7]

Relief for pre-6 April 1988 charges is due only if claimed within two years of the end of the year of assessment in which the asset concerned is disposed of after 5 April 1988.[8]

Simon's Taxes C2.605.

---

[1] TCGA 1992, Sch 4, para 1. This relief was incorporated in FA 1988 during the committee stage, to give a rough and ready measure of equity in comparison to the relief arising from rebasing which would have been given had the gift not been made.
[2] TCGA 1992, Sch 4, paras 1–4, 9. The original legislation was defective in permitting relief to extend to certain post 5 April 1988 gains, eg by rolling such gains into assets subject to relief or, in the case of holdover under TCGA 1992, s 154 (CGTA 1979, s 117), where the pre-6 April 1988 holdover gain was rolled permanently into non-depreciating assets. These loopholes were blocked with effect from 19 March 1991.
[3] TCGA 1992, Sch 3, para 1. As to adjustments where losses arise on disposal, see supra, § **24.04**.
[4] Statement of practice SP 5/89.
[5] TCGA 1992, Sch 3, para 5.
[6] TCGA 1992, s 42; see supra, § **18.14**.
[7] TCGA 1992, Sch 3, para 4.
[8] TCGA 1992, Sch 4, para 9.

Time apportionment—assets held at 6 April 1965

[24.13] This commentary applies only for the purposes of corporation tax after 5 April 2008.

FA 1965 introduced capital gains tax with effect from 6 April 1965. The legislation operates so as to exclude from the charge to capital gains tax any part of a gain that is treated as arising before 6 April 1965. For some assets, or where the taxpayer elects, this is achieved by valuing the asset at 6 April 1965 and calculating the gain as if the taxpayer had acquired the asset at that date for its then market value (subject, of course, to rebasing to 31 March 1982). Valuation is costly, time consuming and imprecise for many types of

[24.13] Taper relief, indexation allowance and rebasing

asset; hence, FA 1965 introduced a method of excluding part of the gain by apportioning the gain on a straight line basis over the length of the period the asset had been owned.

Any gain to be treated as arising before 6 April 1965 is calculated by time apportionment in respect of all assets other than the following:

(1) shares and securities which were quoted on a recognised stock exchange at any time before 7 April 1959 and 6 April 1965 (TCGA 1992, Sch 2, para 1(1)(*a*));
(2) units in a unit trust where the unit trust managers regularly publish prices (TCGA 1992, Sch 2, para 1(1)(*b*));
(3) land reflecting development value (TCGA 1992, Sch 2, para 9);
(4) any asset for which the taxpayer elects under TCGA 1992, Sch 2, para 17(1) that the base cost be taken as the value of the asset at 6 April 1965;
(5) unquoted shares that were subject to reorganisation before 6 April 1965 (TCGA 1992, Sch 2, para 19(1)).

Simon's Taxes C2.610–614.

Method of calculation

[24.14] The gain is presumed to grow evenly from the date of acquisition or the 6 April 1945 whichever is the later.[1] However, expenditure incurred before 6 April 1945 is taken into account in computing the gain. Where expenditure is incurred after the asset is acquired (but before 6 April 1965), the gain attributable to that expenditure is treated as accruing at an even rate from the date when the expenditure was first reflected in the value of the asset, and not from the date of acquisition. The total gain is allocated between the original acquisition expenditure and the subsequent expenditure according to the amounts of each.[2] Each element is then time apportioned as appropriate, but gains attributable to expenditure incurred after 5 April 1965 are not adjusted. However, the gain will be divided according to the value actually attributable to each and not the costs incurred if there is no expenditure on acquisition, or if that initial expenditure was disproportionately small compared with any item of subsequent expenditure, having regard to the value of the asset immediately before that subsequent expenditure.[3]

Special provisions apply to part disposals; in essence, the whole of the remainder is deemed disposed of at open market value.[4] On a part disposal before 6 April 1965, the effect is that time apportionment on subsequent disposals on or after that date runs from the date of the earlier part disposal. On a part disposal after 5 April 1965, the time apportionment ends on the date of the part disposal and subsequent gains on the remainder are brought in without reduction.

Where part of a gain arising from a dwelling-house acquired before 6 April 1965 is chargeable, the time apportionment rule is applied first and then the appropriate fraction.[5]

Where one asset is derived from another the new asset is treated as if it had been acquired at the same time as the other.[6]

Simon's Taxes C2.611.

1 TCGA 1992, Sch 2, para 16(6).
2 TCGA 1992, Sch 2, para 16(4).
3 TCGA 1992, Sch 2, para 16(5).
4 TCGA 1992, Sch 2, para 16(7).
5 TCGA 1992, Sch 2, para 16(10).
6 TCGA 1992, Sch 2, para 16(9).

Time apportionment and indexation allowance

[24.15] In *Smith v Schofield*,[1] the House of Lords held that any indexation allowance is deducted from the gain before the time apportionment fraction is applied. The effect of this is, of course, that part of the allowance for inflation after 1982 is allocated against the gain that arose prior to April 1965. Lord Jauncey commented:

> My Lords, I reach this decision with regret because its effect is that an allowance which was given to offset the effect of inflation on gains accruing from and after 1982 is in part being attributed to notional non-chargeable gains accruing prior to 6 April 1965, a situation which cannot occur where an election of valuation on that date is made. In the present case the effective value of the indexation allowance will be reduced by more that one-third. The decision will have the same effect on losses. I should be surprised if Parliament had intended such a result.

Simon's Taxes C2.303.

1 [1993] STC 268.

Part IV

Corporation tax

For payment of corporation tax, returns, enquiries, appeals and other administrative matters, see Chapter 2 and Chapter 2A.

Part IV

Corporation tax

25

Profits and chargeability
The charge to tax
Taxable profits
Transfer pricing
Tonnage tax
Capital gains
Charges on income and capital
Losses
Accounting period
Small companies rate
Associated companies
International aspects
Incorporation of a business
Corporate acquisitions and disposals
The currency used for accounts

26

Distributions
Distributions
Tax on distributions
Post-1999 shadow ACT
Stock dividends
Purchase by a company of its own shares and treasury shares

27

Loan relationships, foreign exchange and intellectual property
Loan relationships
Foreign exchange gains and losses
Derivative contacts
Intellectual property
Islamic finance

28

Groups, consortia and substantial shareholdings
A group
A consortium
One company or a group?
Distributions
Restriction on group finance costs
Group relief (75% subsidiaries and consortia)

1175

Surrender of reliefs
Other rules
Transfer of company tax refunds
Intra-group transfers of capital assets (75% subsidiaries)
Transfer of trading stock
Rollover relief and a group
Anti-avoidance provisions for groups
Demergers
Exemption on the disposal of substantial shareholdings

29

Close companies
Definition of a close company
Deemed distribution for a close company
Loans to a participator
Close investment holding company—full rate of tax
Can a company carry on a profession?

30

Investment companies
Management expenses
Revenue view
The relief
Investment trusts
Unit trusts
Open-ended investment companies

25

Profits and chargeability

The charge to tax	PARA **25.01**
Taxable profits	PARA **25.04**
Transfer pricing	PARA **25.07**
Tonnage tax	PARA **25.16**
Capital gains	PARA **25.17**
Charges on income and capital	PARA **25.21**
Losses	PARA **25.23**
Accounting period	PARA **25.34**
Small companies rate	PARA **25.40**
Associated companies	PARA **25.42**
International aspects	PARA **25.45**
Incorporation of a business	PARA **25.51**
Corporate acquisitions and disposals	PARA **25.52**
The currency used for accounts	PARA **25.54**

For payment of corporation tax, see supra, §§ 2A.20–2A.22.

The charge to tax

[25.01] Corporation tax was introduced in 1965. Companies resident in the UK are subject to corporation tax, not income tax, on their profits, the term profits covering both income and capital gains.[1] Companies in this context include unincorporated associations, such as sports clubs, and permanent establishments of overseas companies (see infra, § **25.03**). Corporation tax is charged on the profits of a company for its accounting period; the rate of corporation tax is set for each financial year.[2] The general rate of corporation tax is 28%,[3] a lower rate (misleadingly termed "the small companies rate") of 21%[4] and an effective rate of 29.75% on profits in the taper between the two rates. These rates are charged on the company whether it distributes or retains its profits.

In 2006–07 corporation tax was paid by 881,143 entities. For that year, corporation tax of £45,648,000,000 was collected. Of this, £24,963,000,000 (55% of the total) was paid by just 1,035 companies.[5]

Shareholders are liable to income tax on dividends (and other distributions) received from the company.[6] A dividend comes with a tax credit attached to it; this tax credit is currently 1/9th of the dividend, so a dividend of £90 comes with a credit of £10. Many, but not all, shareholders will be able to use this credit. Where the shareholder is entitled to use the credit, the taxable income is the sum of the dividend (£90) and the credit (£10) or £100. Basic rate and starting rate shareholders pay tax at the special dividend income tax rate of 10% so that there is no further tax to pay. Higher rate taxpayers pay at the special dividend higher rate of 32.5% which means that after the £10 credit the

[25.01] Profits and chargeability

taxpayer will have to pay another £22.50. It is a fundamental feature of the current system that the shareholder cannot claim any repayment of tax credit from the Revenue—or from the company.

From 1973 until 1997 the traditional imputation system was in force. This system emphasised the close relationship between the shareholder and the corporation by allowing the shareholder to use a part of the corporation tax paid by the company to offset his own liability to income tax. Technically it was a "partial imputation" system since only a part of the corporation tax paid by the company was imputed to the shareholder. In order to ensure that the tax used as a credit by the shareholder represented tax actually paid by the company, the company when paying the dividend (or any other qualifying distribution) had to pay advance corporation tax (ACT) to the Inland Revenue. Liability to pay ACT arose whether or not the company was liable to pay corporation tax, eg through lack of profits. ACT paid was, then, set against the company's liability to corporation tax.

The Labour government, when it came to power in 1997, made two major changes. First, it abolished the right to recover the tax credit paid in respect of the dividend or other qualifying distributions. Second, after a certain amount of hesitation, it abolished the obligation of the company to pay ACT when making a qualifying distribution. In order to maintain the government's cash flow it replaced ACT with an obligation on larger companies to pay corporation tax in advance by a system of quarterly payments.[7] Despite these changes the structure of the UK tax is still based, at least in form, on the imputation system: a part of the corporation tax paid by the company is imputed through to the shareholder who, if a basic rate taxpayer or another UK company, has no further tax to pay.

Simon's Taxes D1.101, 102.

[1] CTA 2009, s 2(2).
[2] See infra, § **25.37**.
[3] FA 2008, s 6.
[4] FA 2009, s 8.
[5] Calculated from HMRC corporation tax statistics published on the HMRC website, Table 11.6.
[6] ITTOIA 2005, ss 382–401.
[7] See supra, § **2A.21**.

[25.02] Corporation tax is chargeable on the profits of companies, less any deduction due for brought forward capital losses, management expenses and charges on income.[1] "Profits" means the aggregate of income and chargeable capital gains.[2] The same rate of tax is now charged on all profits, whether income or capital gain.

The charge to corporation tax excludes any charge to income tax and capital gains tax.[3] Where profits accrue in the course of winding up, corporation tax is payable notwithstanding the fact that fiduciary obligations are owed to the shareholders.[4] Where profits accrue to the company from its membership of a partnership the company is chargeable to corporation tax.[5] The liability of the

The charge to tax [25.02]

company is the corporation tax on the company share of the partnership's profits as allocated to the company's accounting periods, even though other members of the partnership may be individuals who are subject to income tax on their shares of the partnership's profit, as allocated to fiscal years. Similarly, if a company is a beneficiary of a trust, the income it enjoys from the trust attracts a charge to corporation tax.

The rate of corporation tax is imposed for a "financial year",[6] which is the twelve months beginning on 1 April.[7] Thus, for the period 1 April 2008 to 31 March 2009, a rate of 28% is levied.

There is no charge to corporation tax where profits are received by a company in a representative or fiduciary capacity[8] or on a distribution received from a company resident in the UK. A company that is under a legal duty to hold funds in trust on behalf of others, is not subject to corporation tax on the income arising from that trust fund.[9] A flat management company is required by statute[10] to put any sinking funds in respect of residential property into a trust fund. This may be a sinking fund or it may be a service charge fund. In either case, where the fund is created by a statutory requirement, with a direction to accumulate income arising, the income from the trust fund is subject to tax at the rate applicable to trusts, the company acting as trustee and, thus, liable to pay the income tax charge arising.[11]

Where a fund in a company is created by a voluntary decision of the freeholders or tenants of a property (or others having a direct interest in the operation of a flat management company), and not by a legal requirement, the tax treatment depends on the terms under which the company holds the funds. If a company holds the funds under a contractual arrangement to supply services, the company includes the income arising from those funds in its profits that are subject to corporation tax.[12] Alternatively, where the company acts as a trustee for the beneficiaries, income arising to the funds is assessed to income tax, the assessment being on the company, as trustee.[13]

Simon's Taxes D1.106–108.

---

[1] Brought forward capital losses are deductible against gains; not against other profits: TCGA 1992, s 8(1)(b). In *Taylor v MEPC Holdings Ltd* [2003] UKHL 70, [2004] STC 123, a case concerning group relief, the House of Lords, agreeing with the Special Commissioner and overruling the Court of Appeal and High Court held that "total profits" of the claimant company meant a sum computed after the deduction of capital losses and other deductions allowed by statute. This reverses the decision of the Court of Appeal [2002] EWCA Civ 883, [2002] STC 997 but restores the decision of the Special Commissioner [2000] STC (SCD) 504: see infra, § **28.12**.

[2] CTA 2009, s 2(2).

[3] CTA 2009, ss 3, 4. But a company may be accountable for income tax of another: TA 1988, Sch 16, infra, § **25.22**.

[4] CTA 2009, s 6(2).

[5] CTA 2009, s 2(1).

[6] CTA 2009, s 2(1).

[7] TA 1988, s 834(1). The rate of corporation tax for a financial year was traditionally imposed in arrears by the Finance Act after the end of the financial year. In recent

years, this tradition has been swept aside and the rate of corporation tax has often been announced in a Budget more than one year before the start of a financial year. Thus, the rate for financial year 2009 is specified in FA 2008, s 6; for small company rate and starting rate; see infra, § **25.44**.

[8] CTA 2009, s 7.
[9] CTA 2009, s 6(2).
[10] Landlord and Tenant Act 1987, s 42.
[11] TA 1988, s 686: dividends are subject to the dividend trust rate of 32.5%; all other income is subject to the rate applicable to trusts of 40%. See supra, § **13.11**.
[12] Inland Revenue Tax Bulletin August 2000, p 772.
[13] Inland Revenue Tax Bulletins October 1998, p 598 and August 2000, pp 770–774 give considerable detail of the Revenue's view of the treatment of funds created by the Landlord and Tenant Act 1987, s 42 and for other purposes in connection with the management of a block of flats.

A company

[25.03] A company means[1] any body corporate or unincorporated association,[2] but does not include a partnership, a limited liability partnership,[3] a local authority[4] or a local authority association. Individuals who invest in a joint account; eg as members of an investment club, are not treated as a company.[5]

In *Conservative and Unionist Central Office v Burrell*[6] Lawton LJ defined an unincorporated association as meaning (a) two or more persons bound together for one or more common purposes, not being business purposes, by mutual undertakings, (b) each having mutual duties and obligations, (c) in an organisation which had rules which identified in whom control of it and its funds rested and on what terms, and (d) which can be joined or left at will. He went on to hold that the structure of the Conservative Party was such that it lacked elements (b) and (c); rather it was, as it described itself, an amorphous combination of elements, with the result that the party was not liable to corporation tax on its investment income. The Revenue had accepted that the party's "Central Office" was not an unincorporated association but argued that the party was such an association and comprised all the individual members of the local constituency associations and the parliamentary party. This finding does not stop each individual constituency association being an unincorporated association and, hence, subject to corporation tax.

Authorised unit trusts are treated as if they were companies.[7] A charitable company will be entitled to exemption on so much of its profits as satisfy the income tax or capital gains tax rules for charities.[8] There are also exemptions for registered and unregistered friendly societies, for trade unions, for scientific research associations and for some more esoteric bodies.[9]

This definition of a company applies for the purposes of corporation tax.[10] Special rules apply to miscellaneous housing bodies,[11] and various marketing boards.[12]

Simon's Taxes D1.104.

1   TA 1988, s 832(1), (2). Contrast the much more detailed definition in TCGA 1992, s 170. On charitable bazaars, see extra-statutory concession C4 (1994). Simon's Taxes, Division G2.2
2   See *Frampton (Trustees of the Worthing Rugby Football Club) v IRC* [1987] STC 273 and *Blackpool Marton Rotary Club v Martin* [1988] STC 823. On liability of officers, see TMA 1970, s 108(2), (3). In practice, HMRC will not issue a notice and not pursue a liability for corporation tax on a club or an unincorporated association where the liability is not expected to exceed £100. See supra, § **2A.06**.
3   For international problems see infra, § **35.10**.
4   A local authority is defined in TA 1988, s 842A as amended by FA 1995, s 144.
5   Example given in Inland Revenue Guide to Corporation Tax Self-Assessment (1999). Presumably, the point being made is that investment in a joint account giving joint ownership of investments purchased does not have the characteristics of "persons bound together for common purposes", which is required for an unincorporated association.
6   [1982] STC 317, CA. See also *Re Koeppler's Will Trusts* [1985] 2 All ER 869 at 874, where Slade LJ described an unincorporated association as an association of persons bound together by identifiable rules and having an identifiable membership.
7   TA 1988, s 468.
8   CTA 2009, s 979(2)(*b*).
9   TA 1988, ss 459, 460, 467, 508, 516, 517.
10 And for income tax.
11 TA 1988, s 488.
12 CTA 2009, s 153.

Taxable profits

[25.04] The statutory premise is that the profits of a company subject to corporation tax (CT) are computed according to the principles used for income tax and CGT. However, there has been a trend during the 1990s and subsequently to legislate separately for companies. Hence, the loan relationship regime (infra, §§ **27.01–27.12**) applies solely to corporation tax; the equivalent for individuals, trustees, etc is provided by the income tax charge on savings income (supra, §§ **11.05–11.06**), the accrued income regime (supra, §§ **11.07–11.11**) and the CGT regime (see supra, § **17.12** for exemptions). Other rules confined to corporation tax include those for foreign exchange transactions and financial instruments. No less significantly the 1998 changes to CGT do not apply to CT; so indexation relief still applies and the tapering charge does not. The CT share pooling rules are likewise different.

Profits accruing for the benefit of the company that arise under a trust or by virtue of it being a partner in a partnership are taxable as if they had accrued directly to the company.[1] The company is also chargeable on profits accruing during winding up but "not *otherwise* on profits accruing to it in a fiduciary or representative capacity except as respects its own beneficial interest (if any) in those profits". This could be made to suggest that both corporation tax (CT) and income tax could be chargeable on income arising to the company as

[25.04] Profits and chargeability

trustee during the period of winding up.[2] Income arising to a company as trustee is chargeable to income tax even though the beneficiary is a company.

Self-assessment for companies means that a claim by a company is made unilaterally; it does not require acceptance by HMRC. An example is rollover relief for capital gains. The taxpayer company unilaterally defers the payment of tax on a capital gain, where the company intends to roll the gain into the future acquisition of an asset.[3] If a replacement asset has not been acquired, a tax charge arises 48 months after the end of the accounting period.[4]

Simon's Taxes D1.106, 1301.

---

[1] CTA 2009, s 6(1), 7. On overseas profits, see CTA 2009, s 5(1) and on overseas income from land, see CTA 2009, s 209; on profits in course of winding-up see CTA 2009, s 6(2); on profits from building societies, see CTA 2009, s 498; on profits where the company is trustee, see supra, § 25.02.
[2] On the liability of the liquidator see *Re Mesco Properties Ltd* [1979] STC 788.
[3] TCGA 1992, ss 153A, 247A.
[4] TCGA 1992, s 153A(3)(*b*), (5)(*b*).

Income

[25.05] The amount of income is computed according to the principles in the Corporation Taxes Act.[1] Where the accounting period spans two fiscal years, the profits for the accounting period must be apportioned between those fiscal years and tax calculated accordingly.[2] A company is not entitled to any personal reliefs since it is not an individual and because those reliefs apply to income tax and not to corporation tax.[3]

Some minor qualifications should be noted. First, the company which begins or ceases to be within the charge to CT in respect of a trade, is treated for the purposes of computing its income as if it in fact began or ceased to trade.[4] Second, the remittance basis of taxation does not apply for CT.[5] Third, not surprisingly, there are no deductions for payments in respect of dividends or other distributions.[6] Fourth, CT has it own code for calculating interest paid and received—see infra, § **27.01**. These provisions, introduced by FA 1996, known as "loan relationships", give a treatment for gains and losses on a very wide variety of financial instruments, which differs substantially from the treatment applied for income tax purposes. Rules unique to CT also apply to intangible fixed assets and some financial instruments. Special arrangements are also made for companies with an investment business. There are minor differences for capital allowances and for trading losses.

One virtually automatic adjustment in any corporation tax computation is to add back depreciation/amortisation. The amount to be added back might seem obvious but it has taken a pair of cases going to the House of Lords to show that the add back should be the amount actually charged to the profit and loss account. HMRC had argued (but lost) that the 'gross' depreciation, before any amount carried forward in closing stock, was the correct figure.[7]

Simon's Taxes D1.302–309.

1   CTA 2009, s 2(4).
2   CTA 2009, s 8(2), (5).
3   CTA 2009, s 3.
4   CTA 2009, ss 9(1)(a), 10(1)(d).
5   CTA 2009, s 5(1),(3) and infra, § **35.12**.
6   CTA 2009, s 1305.
7   *Revenue and Customs Comrs v William Grant* and *Small v Mars UK Ltd* heard together by the House of Lords: [2007] STC 680, HL, [2007] UKHL 15.

Allowable deductions

General

[25.06] The profits computation for corporation tax purposes follows generally accepted accounting practice, subject to any adjustment required or authorised by law.[1]

1   CTA 2009, s 46.

Gifts of medical supplies

In addition to the allowable deductions outlined in supra, §§ **8.139–8.141**, companies may also obtain relief for gifts of medical supplies and equipment, including transportation, delivery and distribution costs.[1]

1   CTA 2009, s 107.

Employee share schemes

A statutory corporation tax deduction is available for the "costs" incurred—in particular the costs incurred in providing shares—in the running of employee share schemes for accounting periods starting on or after 1 January 2003. The deduction is basically equal to the amount taxable (either as income or capital gains) on the employee, or for an approved scheme, the gain the employee makes.[1]

There are various requirements relating to the company's business being within the charge to corporation tax.[2]

The eligible shares must be:

(a)   shares of a class listed on a recognised stock exchange, or
(b)   shares in a company which is not under the control of another company, or
(c)   shares in a company that is under the control of a company (other than a close company or a company that if resident in the United Kingdom would be a close company) whose shares are listed on a recognised stock exchange.

The shares must also be fully paid up, non redeemable ordinary shares.[3]

[25.06] Profits and chargeability

The shares must be in:

(a) the employing company, or
(b) a company that at the time of the award, is a parent company of the employing company, or
(c) a company that, at the time of the award, is a member of a consortium that owns the employing company or a company within (b) above, or
(d) where at the time of the award the employing company or a company within paragraph (b) is a member of a consortium that owns another company, a company that at that time:
    (i) is a member of the consortium or a parent in relation to a member of the consortium, and
    (ii) is also a member of the same commercial association of companies as that company.[4]

There are also conditions relating to the income tax position of the employee.[5] There is no requirement that the share scheme or share option scheme be approved by HMRC. Costs of running the scheme that are eligible for relief are outlined[6] as are those that are excluded[7] such as establishing and administering the scheme, borrowing costs and commissions (although note that these may still be deductible under the general computation rules). There are similar rules when there is the grant of an option to acquire shares[8] and when the shares are subject to restriction.[9]

Measures have also been introduced from the same date to prevent the avoidance of corporation tax and National Insurance by using employee benefit trusts (EBTs) The deduction that is allowed in respect of such payments is limited to the extent that the EBT or other relevant third party uses the employer's contribution to provide qualifying benefits or to pay qualifying expenses. A deduction is available only if the payment is made during the company's accounting period or within nine months of the end of that period.[10]

Prior to 1 January 2003, corporation tax relief was available for contribution into a qualifying employee share ownership trust (QUEST).[11]

---

[1] CTA 2009, Part 12, Ch 2 (ss 1006–1013).
[2] CTA 2009, s 1007(2).
[3] CTA 2009, s 1008.
[4] CTA 2009, s 1008.
[5] CTA 2009, s 1009.
[6] CTA 2009, s 1038(2).
[7] CTA 2009, s 1038(5).
[8] CTA 2009, Part 12, Ch 3 (ss 1014–1024).
[9] CTA 2009, Part 12, Ch 4 (ss 1025–1029).
[10] CTA 2009, s 1290.
[11] FA 2003, s 142.

Transfer pricing

Transactions between connected parties not at arm's length

[25.07] For transactions taking place between related parties on or after 1 April 2004 the transfer pricing regime, which previously applied only to cross-border transactions, is extended to apply also to transactions within the UK[1]. On the same date the separate rules regarding thinly capitalised companies were abolished and subsumed within the new transfer-pricing regime.[2]

Small– and medium-sized enterprises are exempt from the new transfer pricing regime, except in relation to transactions with a related business in a territory with which the UK does not have a double taxation treaty containing a suitable non-discrimination article, and except where the Inland Revenue requires, in exceptional circumstances, a medium-sized enterprise to apply the rules. Dormant companies are also exempt from the new regime so long as they remain dormant.[3] Whilst a penalty regime is incorporated in the regime there was a temporary relaxation of certain penalties until 31 March 2006 in respect of the failure to keep evidence to demonstrate that transactions with related parties have been carried out at an arms length.[4]

The transfer pricing regime requires a business to calculate its taxable income by reference to an arm's length result for transactions with connected businesses.

The purpose of the transfer pricing legislation is to ensure that the taxable profits of an enterprise are not understated as a result of using prices between connected parties, which are higher or lower than the price that would have applied between unrelated parties. If prices between connected parties cannot be considered to be determined on an arm's length basis the profits of the enterprise are adjusted to what they would have been had arm's length prices been used. In practice the determination of whether prices established between related parties are on an arm's length basis may be highly subjective.

It should be noted that if a UK taxpayer has no related parties or there are no "transactions" with any related parties the transfer pricing rules cannot apply in such circumstances.

---

[1] This is achieved by FA 2004, ss 30–37 making numerous amendments to TA 1988, Sch 28AA. From 1 April 2004, there is no distinction between UK and non-UK companies in respect of the transfer pricing provisions. This has the effect that a small company in the UK is within these provisions in respect of its overseas trade for transactions before 1 April 2004, but is not subject to this transfer pricing legislation for transactions on and after that date. From 4 March 2005, the provisions were further amended by F(No 2)A 2005, Sch 8.
[2] FA 2004, s 34.
[3] FA 2004, s 31.
[4] FA 2004, s 33.

[25.08] Profits and chargeability

Related parties

[25.08] The transfer pricing rules apply to "persons" and accordingly the rules can apply not only to companies and partnerships but also individuals and trusts if they are related to a company or partnership. Consequently an individual will be connected with a company which he owns and the transfer-pricing regime will apply potentially to transactions between the shareholder and the company. The rules do not apply to transactions between spouses or between an individual and a trust.

A company is related to another company if one controls the other or they are both under common control. A company is related to any other legal person where that person controls it. Control of a company arises from voting power of more than 50%. Control for these purposes can be exercised indirectly. Control can also be attributed where more than 40% of the voting power is held by one person and between them two persons own 80% or more of a company.

To decide whether a person controls a company that person is attributed with certain rights and powers including those of any persons that are connected with him. For this purpose individuals are connected with their spouses, civil partners, brother, sister, ancestor and lineal descendants. Trusts are connected with the settlor of the trust and any persons connected with him.

In relation to financing arrangements, the rules have been extended to catch persons who "act together" in providing finance to a company but do not individually control the borrower. This is mainly aimed at private equity funds thinly capitalising their acquisitions.[1]

---

[1] TA 1988, Sch 28AA, para 5B(5).

Relevant transactions

[25.09] The transfer pricing rules do apply to any transaction (or "provisions") where one party has derived a benefit from the connected party. Such provisions obviously include the sales of goods and services, the provision of finance, the transfer of tangible and intangible assets. However also included is the provision of indirect benefits such as the use of property or personnel without an arm's length charge being made for the benefit provided. Previously companies within a group may not have recharged all such benefits where both companies had profits which were within the charge to UK tax.

The definition of "provision" within the legislation is sufficiently widely drawn to apply to almost all financial interaction between connected parties.

Small-sized enterprise exemption

[25.10] The new transfer-pricing regime does not apply to enterprises which are defined as "small".

For these purposes an enterprise is small if it has fewer than 50 employees and either (or both) its turnover or assets are no more than Euro 10 million.

These limits are applied on an annual basis and on the basis of consolidated accounts, which includes the accounts of linked businesses. The definition of a linked business is similar to the definition of control outlined above. As mentioned above the exemption does not apply with respect to transactions with non-UK affiliates in territories without a UK double tax treaty with a suitable non-discrimination clause.[1]

[1] TA 1988, Sch 28AA, paras 5B(4) and 5E.

Medium-sized enterprise exemption

[25.11] The exemption also applies to medium-sized enterprises which are defined as those with fewer than 250 employees. Either its turnover must be no more than Euro 50 million or its assets must be no more than euro 43 million.

However HMRC has the right to notify such an enterprise that the exemption has been withdrawn. Such a notice will be made retrospectively after a tax return has been submitted and a significant amount of tax is at stake.[1]

[1] FA 2004, s 31.

Penalties

[25.12] Under existing legislation introduced in 1998 there are two types of penalty relating to transfer pricing. A penalty of £3,000 per tax return arises in respect of the failure to keep proper records recording the basis of transfer pricing with affiliates. A further penalty applies if an understatement of UK profits is found to have been caused by negligent tax compliance, or fraud, on behalf of the taxpayer. In these cases a penalty of up to 100% of the tax arising can be made. Under the new regime penalties under the former category did not come into effect until 31 March 2006.[1]

The Revenue has the power to mitigate penalties.

[1] FA 2004, s 33.

Returns, balancing payments and compensating adjustments

[25.13] Companies affected by the transfer pricing regime will be required to deal with this issue in their CTSA returns in one of two ways. A company can either confirm that arm's length prices have been applied to relevant transactions or an appropriate adjustment to rectify the position can be made in the corporation tax computations.

If pricing of a transaction is adjusted under the transfer pricing rules, the other party to the transaction may be eligible for a "corresponding adjustment". Corresponding adjustments may be available on UK-to-UK transactions by statute or under treaty relief in respect of cross border transactions.[1]

The legislation also provides for balancing payments to restore the cash position to the arm's length position when a transfer pricing adjustment is

[25.13] Profits and chargeability

made. As a result the party whose profit is reduced can make a payment (up to the amount of the adjustment) to the party whose profit is increased.[2]

---

[1] TA 1988, Sch 28AA, para 6.
[2] TA 1988, Sch 28AA, para 7A.

Thin capitalisation

[25.14] From 1 April 2004, thin capitalisation is included within TA 1988, Sch 28AA as an aspect of transfer pricing. As a result, loans between UK companies under common control are subject to thin capitalisation rules for the first time.[1] The exemption which previously applied within TA 1988, s 212(1) is withdrawn. Where a loan between connected parties exceeds the amount that would have been made available by an unconnected lender the interest on the excessive part is disallowed as a tax deduction for the borrower. A compensating adjustment will also be made so that the lender is taxed only as if it had received only the arm's length amount of interest.

Under "severance" rules the assets and income of the borrower and its direct and indirect subsidiaries should be taken into account to determine its borrowing capacity. However assets within other group companies are disregarded.

A company may be thinly capitalised not only because of the connection between the borrower and lender but because a debt is guaranteed by a connected person. The term guarantee includes any case where the lender has a real expectation that he will receive payment from the guarantor under the terms of a written or unwritten agreement.[2] As with connected party loans the thin capitalisation regime will have the effect of disallowing the deduction for interest in excess of that which would have been allowable to the borrower on a stand-alone basis.[3]

Where interest has been disallowed because of a guarantee a compensating adjustment can be made in respect of the guarantor. The guarantor is treated as if the guarantor has obtained the loan and paid the interest rather than the actual borrower. This interest deduction is in turn subject to the thin capitalisation regime.[4]

The Revenue have published their view of the way in which the provisions work in the form of a guidance note[5] but have declined to give details of any "safe harbour" which can be used to establish an acceptable debt to equity ratio, saying that each case must be judged on its own merits. However, for some guidelines see infra, § **26.07**.

---

[1] The exemption which previously applied in TA 1988, s 212(1) was withdrawn by FA 2004 for chargeable periods beginning on or after 1 April 2004.
[2] TA 1988, Sch 28AA para 1B (6) and para 1A(7).
[3] TA 1988, Sch 28AA, para 1B.
[4] TA 1988, Sch 28AA, para 6C.

[5] Inland Revenue Press Release, 30 March 2004: *Simon's Weekly Tax Intelligence* 2004, pp 974–978.

Transactions between a dealing company and an associated non-dealing company

[25.15] The rule that an expense may be a revenue expense of the payer but a capital receipt of the payee, with consequent leakage of tax, is modified where one company is a dealing company and the other an associated[1] non-dealing company. A dealing company is one dealing in securities, land or buildings. Special rules[2] apply if the dealing company becomes entitled to a deduction on account of the depreciation of any right against the other company or makes any deductible payment to the other and the depreciation or payment is not brought into account in computing the profits or gains of the other. These special rules make the latter chargeable on an amount equal to the deduction[3] either under the charge to corporation tax on income or, if it carries on a trade, as a trading receipt of such of its trades as it selects. A purchaser of the non-dealing company may thus find an unexpected liability.

An example[4] of a device at which these rules were aimed was where a dealing company A waived a loan which it had made to the non-dealing company B; A might get relief for the loan and, but for these rules, B would have kept the money tax-free; these rules made B liable to tax on the amount waived.

Simon's Taxes D7.401.

[1] See *IRC v Lithgows Ltd* (1960) 39 TC 270.
[2] TA 1988, s 774.
[3] TA 1988, s774(3) excludes the application of TA 1988, s 774 if the non-dealing company has incurred a non-allowable capital loss as a result of the loan or payment being used as abortive expenditure.
[4] See also *Alherma Investments Ltd v Tomlinson* [1970] 2 All ER 436, 48 TC 81.

Tonnage tax

[25.16] From 1 January 2000, the liability to corporation tax of a shipping company can be measured by reference to the tonnage of its fleet, ignoring the profits actually generated.[1] For "tonnage tax" to apply, the company must elect during the accounting period for which it is to apply.[2] Existing shipping companies had to elect by 28 July 2001.[3] If a company elects for corporation tax to be computed on the tonnage tax basis, capital allowances are not available. Further restrictions on capital allowances available on ships used for leasing falling within tonnage tax were introduced in respect of leases entered into on or after 19 December 2002. Prior to that date only ships leased under finance leases were affected.[4]

[1] FA 2000, Sch 22, para 4.

[25.16] Profits and chargeability

[2] FA 2000, Sch 22, paras 7–14.
[3] FA 2000, Sch 22, para 10.
[4] FA 2003, Sch 32.

Capital gains

[25.17] Corporation tax is levied on the "profits" of companies and "profits" include chargeable gains.[1] Corporations are not subject to CGT but only to CT—the distinction between CT and CGT is of importance and has been further emphasised since FA 2008:

(1) Indexation relief[2] continues to apply for corporation tax.
(2) If a company ceases to be resident in the UK there may be a deemed disposal of its assets.[3] There is no deemed disposal by an individual who ceases to be resident.
(3) The share identification rules are different for the two taxes.
(4) The rules for assets acquired before 31 March 1982 has been radically simplified for CGT.

The distinction between capital and income is also important, thus:

(1) Where a trading loss is carried forward to a later accounting period under s 393 it may be set off only against trading income—and not capital gains—of that trade of that period.
(2) A capital loss cannot be set off against ordinary income—even income of the same accounting period.
(3) A capital loss, unlike a trading loss, cannot be passed to other members of a group under the group relief rules.

For a company, gains and losses arising from differences in foreign exchange are treated within the loan relationship rules (see infra, § **27.11**). They are not treated within the capital gains regime.

For companies, an asset may be transferred at a tax neutral value between group members.[4] Notional transfers may be made.[5]

Simon's Taxes D1.901.

[1] CTA 2009, s 2(2) and TCGA 1992, s 8 amended by FA 2007, s 27 (see **CHAPTER 24**).
[2] TCGA 1992, s 53(1A).
[3] TCGA 1992, s 185.
[4] TCGA 1992, s 171. See para **28.21**.
[5] TCGA 1992, s 171A. See para **28.22**.

The company and the shareholder—general

[25.18] A double charge to tax can arise if the company realises a gain but for some reason the profits are not distributed to the shareholders. In such circumstances there will have been a full charge to tax on the gain in the hands of the company and a further charge on the shareholder when the shares are sold. This leads to double taxation where there is a profit and double relief where there is a loss. The problem can be exaggerated—it arises also when the company makes a trading profit, retains some or all of that profit and the shareholder later sells the shares.

Simon's Taxes D1.121, 6.658.

Transfer of business on company reconstruction

[25.19] If a company's business is transferred to another company,[1] the transfer will normally involve the transfer, and so the disposal, of chargeable assets. This result will be mitigated for assets other than trading stock[2] in that neither gain nor loss accrues to the company making the disposal provided:

(1) the scheme involves the transfer of the *business* in whole or in part, as opposed simply to the transfer of assets;[3]
(2) relevant assets remain subject to UK tax on subsequent capital gains;[4] and
(3) the transferor receives no consideration other than the transferee taking over any liabilities from the transferor.

This provision is mandatory, not a matter of election. It is similar in intent to those which apply on the incorporation or takeover of a business; where the rule applies the disponee takes over the base cost of the disponor.

If the main purpose, or one of the main purposes, is the avoidance of liability to CT, CGT or income tax, the section does not apply and the normal rules applicable to a disposal will apply;[5] any CT due can be recovered from the disponee if the disponor has not paid within six months of the tax becoming payable.[6]

The term "scheme of reconstruction" is now defined by statute[7] as "a scheme of merger, division or other reconstructing" that involves the issue of ordinary share capital[8] to those holding, directly or indirectly, shares in the company, the entitlement[9] being in proportion to the size of the shareholding and *either* (a) the effect is to create a successor company[10] (or companies) to carry on the business of the company being reconstructed *or* (b) to infect a statutory[11] compromise or arrangement without the transfer of business."[12]

Prior to the statutory enactment of the definition, the term reconstruction had been construed by the courts[13] to require a degree of continuity of common ownership. On this view the paper for paper treatment would not apply when a business is split between two different groups of shareholders but the Revenue took a more generous position.[14]

Simon's Taxes C2.1521.

---

[1] But not to a unit trust or an investment trust. See TCGA 1992, s 139(4).
[2] TCGA 1992, s 139(2). Trading stock of the transferor will be valued under TA 1988, s 100 for computing income and so is excluded.
[3] Cf *McGregor v Adcock* [1977] STC 206 and similar cases.

[25.19] Profits and chargeability

4   TCGA 1992, s 139(1A). The treatment is also applied where a non-resident company carries on a trade in the UK through a PE: TCGA 1992, s 25(3A).
5   TCGA 1992, s 139(5).
6   TCGA 1992, s 139(7): tax can also be recovered from certain subsequent holders. There is no need for a formal assessment to tax now that pay and file has taken effect.
7   TCGA 1992, Sch 5AA, para 1.
8   TCGA 1992, Sch 5AA, para 2.
9   TCGA 1992, Sch 5AA, para 3.
10 TCGA 1992, Sch 5AA, para 4.
11 Under Companies Act 1985, s 425 or Companies (Northern Ireland) Order 1966, art 418.
12 TCGA 1992, Sch 5AA, para 5.
13 *Brooklands Selangor Holdings Ltd v IRC* [1970] 2 All ER 76.
14 Originally in statement of practice SP 5/85. Simon's Taxes, Division G1.2. The statement of practice has been incorporated into legislation in what is now TCGA 1992, Sch 5AA which defines a "scheme of reconstruction", primarily for the relief under TCGA 1992, s 136. This follows the case of *Fallon v Fellows* [2001] STC 1409, that showed that the Revenue treatment given in SP5/85 was not in accordance with the law.

Postponement of charge on transfer of assets to non-resident company

[25.20] The charge arising on the disposal of an overseas trade plus its assets[1] to a non-resident company[2] in return for shares may be deferred provided the transferor company ends up with at least 25% of the ordinary share capital of the transferee company.[3] It is postponed until (a) the transferor company disposes of all or any of the shares, or (b) the transferee company disposes of all or some of the assets; however the charge under (b) arises only if the disposal is within six years.[4] Where only a part of the consideration received is in the form of shares or loan stock then only a proportionate part of the charge is postponed. The purpose of the rule is to acknowledge that the gain is primarily a paper gain and to give the company time to find the cash; the technique used is a form of rollover. This is a matter of taxpayer election; it has the effect of deferring losses as well as gains and so the alternative of electing for TCGA 1992, s 152 rollover should be considered. The fact that foreign tax may have been paid and so is available for credit relief may make both of these elections superfluous or inadvisable.

Simon's Taxes D4.811.

1   But not if the assets consist wholly of cash.
2   Treasury consent was needed for the transfers prior to the enactment of FA 2009 if it involves shares or debentures were transferred: TA 1988, s 765 (though the transaction was often be covered by the Treasury General Consents 1988).
3   TCGA 1992, s 140; a claim under s 140C excludes a claim under s 140 and vice versa. See ss 140(6A), 140C(4). Ordinary share capital is defined in TA 1988, s 832(1).

[4] Other than by a group transfer within TCGA 1992, s 171; the non-residence bars in s 170 are ignored for (b).

Charges on income and capital

[25.21] Following the changes made in 2005,[1] the only charges on income that arise to a company are payments to a charity. These are of two types: (i) qualifying donations,[2] and (ii) gifts of assets.[3]

Relief that was formerly given as a charge, in particular annuities and other annual payments, is now given as an expense of management.

Simon's Taxes D1.315.

[1] F(No 2)A 2005, s 38 amends the definition of "charges" in TA 1988, s 338A.
[2] TA 1988, s 339.
[3] TA 1988, s 587B, see supra, §§ **6.38**, **8.141** and **16.49**.

[25.22] A donation by a company to a charity made under the gift aid scheme[1] is treated as a charge on the income of the company. It is made without deduction of tax by the company.[2] In all other respects, the gift aid scheme for a company follows the scheme available to individuals.[3]

Where the donor company is a wholly-owned subsidiary of the recipient charity, the subsidiary company can treat a donation it makes to a charity during the nine months following the end of its accounting period as if it were made during the accounting period. It is therefore treated as a charge on income against the profits of that accounting period, thereby reducing (or eliminating) its liability to corporation tax.[4]

Simon's Taxes D1.321.

[1] TA 1988, s 339.
[2] Amendments to TA 1988, s 339 effected by FA 2000, s 40.
[3] FA 1990, s 25, see supra, §§ **6.36–6.37**.
[4] TA 1988, s 339(7AA).

Losses

Trading loss

Set-off against future trading income from the trade

[25.23] Where a company incurs a trading loss various forms of relief are permitted. First, and most simply, the company may roll the loss forward and

[25.23] Profits and chargeability

set it off against the trading income of the trade of succeeding accounting periods, so long as the trade continues,[1] the loss being set off against the earliest available profits first.[2]

The boundary between trading income and other income can be a fine one. In one case income generated by investments financed by funds set aside for the eventual replacement of the company's fixed assets was held to be investment income and so unavailable for this relief.[3]

Where a loss has been so rolled forward but the trading profits of that period are insufficient to absorb it, account may be taken of any interest or dividends which would have been taken into account as trading receipts in computing that income but for the fact that they have been subjected to tax under other provisions.[4] The test used in deciding the hypothetical trading nature of the income is whether the interest or dividends were the fruit derived from a fund employed in and risked in the business.[5] Whether this extends to UK dividends which are excluded from CT.[6] is doubtful.

Under self-assessment trading losses automatically enter the calculation of profits for which the company has to make a return. As a result it is not necessary to make a claim for trading losses carried forward under TA 1988, s 393.

Simon's Taxes D1.1106.

[1] In *Netlogic Consulting Ltd v R & C Comrs* [2005] STC (SCD) 524, the Special Commissioners held that the change in the activities of the company was sufficiently fundamental to constitute a change in the trade. Thus, the losses could not be put against profits generated after the change in activities.
[2] TA 1988, s 393.
[3] *Bank Line Ltd v IRC* [1974] STC 342. In *Nuclear Energy plc v Bradley* [1996] STC 405, HL, the House of Lords held that, in the particular circumstances of that case, interest received on long loans could not be regarded as trading income against which brought forward losses could be put.
[4] TA 1988, s 393(8).
[5] *Nuclear Electric plc v Bradley* [1995] STC 285.
[6] CTA 2009, Part 9A (exemption for dividends, including foreign dividends – being inserted by FA 2009).

Set-off against general profits of the same accounting period and the preceding one year (ordinary loss) or three years (terminal loss)

[25.24] A trading loss is computed to include capital allowances, being treated as an expense. The loss can then be relieved as follows:

(1) The company may set the loss against its profits of whatever description, ie covering both non-trading income and capital gains, of the same accounting period.[1]

(2) The company may carry the loss back and set it against its profits of whatever description of preceding accounting periods falling wholly or partly within the period of one year immediately preceding the period in which the loss occurs; to qualify for this carry back the company

must have been carrying on the trade and been within the charge to CT in that prior accounting period;[2] where there is an accounting period straddling the anniversary the loss may be set only against that part of the profits attributable to the period falling within the year.

(3) The period of one year is extended to three in the case of a terminal loss, ie any loss incurred in the trade in the last 12 months of trading[3] apportioning the profits of any period straddling that anniversary.[4] Thus a terminal loss may be set against profits of whatever description and not just trading income.

The general rule is that losses must be set against profits of later periods first.[5]

Any repayment supplement due in respect of a repayment of tax already paid will be calculated by reference to (a) the period against which the loss is relieved, if this is within 12 months preceding the loss making period,[6] or (b) by reference to the loss making period, in any other case.[7]

Losses arising in accounting periods ending between 24 November 2008 and 23 November 2009 may be carried back for up to three years, with losses set off first against profits of the most recent year. A maximum of £50,000 of losses may be set-off against profits of the previous second and third years (pro-rata for shorter accounting periods); there is no restriction on the standard carry back against the preceding accounting period.[8]

Simon's Taxes D1.1105.

---

[1] TA 1988, s 393A(1)(a).
[2] TA 1988, s 393A(1)(*b*), (2), (9).
[3] Terminal loss relief is only available if there is a termination of the trade. Cessation of manufacturing was held not to be termination of trading in *Flectronics Ltd v Inspector of Taxes* [2005] STC (SCD) 512.
[4] TA 1988, s 393(2A)–(2B).
[5] TA 1988, s 393A(1).
[6] TA 1988, s 825(4)(*c*)(i).
[7] TA 1988, s 826(4)(*c*)(ii).
[8] FA 2009, s 23 and Sch 6.

Non-allowable trading losses

[25.25] Loss relief under the rule in supra, § 25.24 does not apply to trades carried on wholly outside the United Kingdom.[1]

The restrictions on loss relief applied to persons in respect of farming and market gardening where there has been a loss in each of the previous five years apply here also.[2] Further, the trade whether or not connected with farming must either have been carried on (a) under some enactment, or (b) on a commercial basis and with a view to the relation to gain whether in itself or as part of a larger undertaking of which the trade formed part.[3] A reasonable expectation of gain at the end of the period will satisfy this test.[4]

Simon's Taxes D1.1110.

---

[1] TA 1988, s 393A(3).

[25.25] Profits and chargeability

² TA 1988, s 397; supra, § **6.29**: note the relaxation allowed by concession for 2001–02. This is available for incorporated farming trades, as well as unincorporated trades.
³ TA 1988, s 393A(3).
⁴ TA 1988, s 393A(4).

Charges on income as losses

[25.26] Where charges on income consisting of payments made wholly and exclusively for the purposes of a trade carried on by the company, and those and other charges on income exceed the profits of that period against which they are deductible, then whichever is the smaller of those payments or the excess, added to a trading loss[1] and so becomes entitled to loss relief but only by carry forward and terminal carry-back. Where the company carries on two trades, the excess charge which falls to be treated as an allowable loss may be set off only against future income of the trade for which the charge was raised; the fact that there are individual (beneficial) side effects for the other trade is irrelevant.[2]

Simon's Taxes D1.316.

¹ TA 1988, s 393(9); on management expenses of an investment company see TA 1988, s 75(3) or deducted from a trading profit to produce a loss.
² *Olin Energy Systems Ltd v Scorer* [1982] STC 800.

Expansion

Company reconstruction without change of ownership

[25.27] Where a company transfers a trade or part of a trade to another company, and there is no change of ownership, the change is ignored for the granting of allowances under CAA 2001[1] and any trading loss may be rolled forward[2] to be set off against the subsequent trading income subject only to the first company's right to set the loss against other profits,[3] and the possibility of 'streaming' being required in the transferee company.[4] Assets qualifying for capital allowances will be transferred at the written down value;[5] there will therefore be no balancing charges (or allowances) nor any first year allowance. Where a company ceases to trade or to carry on a part of a trade restrictions apply if the transferring company is insolvent.[6] The amount of the loss that may be taken over is reduced by the amount by which the transferor company's "relevant liabilities"[7] exceed its "relevant assets".[8]

If a company wishes to separate a particular business and place it in a subsidiary, often called a hive-down, this rule with regard to accrued trading losses will be invoked; TCGA 1992, s 171 (infra, § **28.20**) will be used for assets with potential capital gains liability. The Revenue has indicated that where a receiver intending to sell off a company, trade, or part of it effects a hivedown, the *Ramsay* approach will not normally be considered relevant provided the entire trade (or part) and its assets are transferred with a view to its being carried on in other hands.[9]

These are the only purposes for which the change is ignored. Therefore the successor company cannot use any miscellaneous income losses or capital losses of its predecessor. This is scarcely unreasonable since, for this rule to apply, it is necessary only that the predecessor company cease to trade. It is not necessary that the company should cease to exist; such losses will be relieved by being set against subsequent miscellaneous income gains or capital gains of the predecessor company.

There is regarded as being no change of ownership if on, or at any time within two years of, the ending of the trade by the predecessor, the trade or an interest amounting to not less than 75% of it should belong to the same persons as the trade or such interest belonged to within a year before the event. It is also necessary that the trade should be carried on by companies which are within the charge to CT.[10]

If the successor company itself ceases to carry on the trade within four years and is entitled to more terminal loss relief than it can use the question may arise as to whether the relief may be carried back to the original transferor. Under the old legislation[11] this was specifically provided for. The revised legislation for terminal losses does not make this point explicitly although it is thought that the effect of TA 1988, s 393A and the wording in s 343 should achieve this.[12] Provision is also made for the situation in which the successor company transfers its trade to a new owner[13] and for that in which the successor company treats the trade as part of its trade.[14] Where the first successor company does not satisfy the common control test but the second one does (in comparison with the original transferor) the losses may be used by the second successor—provided it is within the four-year period.

Simon's Taxes D1.1113.

[1] TA 1988, s 343(2).
[2] Under TA 1988, s 393(1).
[3] Under TA 1988, s 393A(1).
[4] TA 1988, s 343(8).
[5] TA 1988, s 343(2).
[6] TA 1988, s 343(4).
[7] A liability assumed by the transferee company cannot be a relevant liability; TA 1988, s 344(6).
[8] TA 1988, s 343(4) proviso. "Relevant assets" are defined in TA 1988, s 344(5) and "relevant liabilities" in TA 1988, s 344(6).
[9] See a letter sent by the Revenue to the Institute of Chartered Accountants for England and Wales, *Simon's Tax Intelligence* 1985, p 568; but the Revenue would not give an assurance that the new approach would never be relevant.
[10] TA 1988, s 343(1).
[11] TA 1988, s 343(6) repealed by FA 1991.
[12] TA 1988, s 343(3).
[13] TA 1988, s 343(7).

[25.27] Profits and chargeability

[14] TA 1988, s 343(8), (9); as to whether enough trading activities have been taken over, see *Falmer Jeans Ltd v Rodin* [1990] STC 270.

[25.28] In determining whether the trade belongs to the same persons, the law pierces not only the veil of any company but also that of any trust identifying shareholders and beneficiaries as the people with the interest in each case.[1] Persons who are relatives or who are entitled to the income of the trust are treated as being one person.[2] If shares in company A Ltd are held on trust for L, M, N and P, and the company transfers the trade to a company whose shares are held on trust for L, M, N, P and Q it would appear that there has been a change in ownership since although less than 3/4 of the interest has been changed, each body of beneficiaries is treated as a single person. In determining the extent of a person's interest in a trade one looks to the extent of his entitlement to share in the profits.[3]

Simon's Taxes D1.1113.

---

[1] TA 1988, s 344(1). On ownership where there is a conditional contract of sale, see *Wood Preservation Ltd v Prior* [1969] 1 All ER 364, 45 TC 112; because the controlling company had accepted the conditional offer, it was no longer the beneficial owner of the shares needed to entitle it to set off the loss, but if the condition had then failed, would the failure have been retroactive?
[2] TA 1988, s 344(4).
[3] TA 1988, s 344(1).

Restriction

Change in ownership of company and change in trade

[25.29] The converse case arises when the control of the trade passes to other people but the identity of the person trading remains the same. The right to roll losses forward under TA 1988, s 393 is excluded if either:

(1) within any period of three years there is *both* a change in the ownership of the company *and* (either earlier or later or simultaneously) a major change in the nature or conduct of a trade carried on by the company; or

(2) there is a change in the ownership of the company at any time—and not just within a three-year period—after the scale of the activities in a trade carried on by a company has become small or negligible, and before any considerable revival of the trade.

Where these conditions are satisfied, losses accruing up to date of the change in ownership are not capable of being carried forward. These provisions were introduced in 1969 to stop the sale of companies simply for their tax losses. The going rate was then 10p for £1 of loss. Some companies were kept in existence only for their losses—hence 2. This provision does not apply to capital losses.[1]

A similar rule applies to prevent the carry back of losses under TA 1988, s 393A to accounting periods beginning before the change in ownership.[2] This applies to changes in ownership on or after 14 June 1991.[3]

The rules for ascertaining the change in ownership are complex.[4] A change of ownership is to be disregarded if before and after the change the company is a 75% subsidiary of another company. This provision is aimed at the situation in which the company ceases to be the directly owned 75% subsidiary of another company but remains within the same ultimate ownership. The definition of 75% ownership includes not only ordinary share capital but also entitlement to profits and to assets on winding up. These rules are already in place for group loss relief and so it is not surprising to find that TA 1988, Sch 18 also applies.[5]

A change in the ownership of a company which has a 75% subsidiary (whether owned directly or indirectly) automatically brings about a change in the ownership of the 75% subsidiary (unless, of course, the rule in the previous paragraph applies). There may also be a deemed change of ownership where a subsidiary is a 60% subsidiary of one company within a group and the 40% subsidiary of another such company—or the 50% subsidiary of each; the sale of the 60% holding and of the 40% holding to the same purchaser brings about a change in the ownership of the subsidiary for the purpose of s 769.[6]

The concept of a major change in the trade is amplified by "including" a major change in the property dealt in, services or facilities provided or in the customers, outlets or markets.[7] Moreover where the change has been a gradual process it may be treated as a change even though it took more than three years. Since it is almost inevitable that a person taking over a loss-making business will want to make some changes the courts will have some nice questions to decide. However, in *Willis v Peeters Picture Frames Ltd*[8] it was emphasised that these are essentially matters of fact. There the taxpayer company was taken over by a group and its sales to its former customers were thereafter made through distribution companies in the same group; this reorganisation was held by the Commissioners to be not a major change and the court declined to interfere with that decision. In *Purchase v Tesco Stores Ltd* it was said that the word "major" imported something more than significant but less than fundamental; the effects of the change should be considered.[9] Revenue practice is not to treat a change as major if a company rationalises its product range by withdrawing unprofitable items and, possibly, replacing them with new items of a kind already being produced, or if the company makes changes to increase its efficiency or to keep pace with changing technology or management techniques.[10]

There are technical provisions to treat a company reconstruction without a change in ownership as concerning only one company and for allowing for intra group transfers to take place without raising TA 1988, s 768.[11]

Where the loss is due to an unused capital allowance, provisions ensure that no balancing charge[12] applies to the extent that the charge reflects the unallowable loss.

Simon's Taxes D1.1113.

[25.29] Profits and chargeability

1   But see rules on pre-entry losses and gains in TCGA 1992, Sch 7A and ss 184A–184I.
2   TA 1988, s 768A; s 768(2)–(4), (8)–(9) are applied by s 768A(2).
3   TA 1988, s 768A(3).
4   TA 1988, s 769.
5   TA 1988, s 769.
6   TA 1988, s 769(6)–(6C).
7   TA 1988, s 768(4). Of course if the change in trade was sufficiently great, losses could not be carried forward, whether the trader was an individual or a company, by virtue of the rules as to discontinuance of a trade, supra, § **8.51**.
8   [1983] STC 453.
9   [1984] STC 304; see also *Pobjoy Mint Ltd v Lane* [1985] STC 314, CA (both cases on stock relief under FA 1976, Sch 5, para 23).
10   Statement of practice SP 10/91. Simon's Taxes, Division G1.2.
11   TA 1988, s 768(5).
12   TA 1988, s 768(6).

Successor companies: groups—leasing contracts

[25.30] A further restriction applies where two companies are concerned and where either they are connected companies,[1] or there is a company reconstruction without change of ownership as defined by TA 1988, s 343. If a company incurs expenditure on machinery and plant which it leases to another person and there are arrangements[2] whereby a successor company will be able to carry on any part of that company's trade which includes that lease, the first company can set that loss off only against the profits of the leasing contract, the contract being thus treated in effect as a separate trade.[3] But for this special provision, the first company would be able to create a loss to set off against its profits while giving the successor company profits to set off against its losses, and thus in effect permit the assignment of the generous capital allowances provided for machinery and plant.

A similar rule applies where a company is a member of a partnership and arrangements exist whereby the company's share of profits or losses is adjusted for a consideration in money or money's worth. Here too, in broad terms, the company's shares in the partnership loss may be set off against the profits of the firm.[4]

Simon's Taxes D1.1112.

1   Under TA 1988, s 839.
2   Arrangements may be of any kind, whether in writing or not, TA 1988, s 395(5); see also *Pilkington Bros Ltd v IRC* [1982] STC 103.
3   TA 1988, s 395(4).
4   TA 1988, s 116.

Transfers of trade: balancing allowances

[25.31] FA 2008 introduced TA 1988, s 343ZA which is designed to prevent schemes in which a transfer of trade was effected in order to give rise to a balancing allowance in the predecessor company. Where such an allowance is the or a main purpose of the arrangement then TA 1988, s 343 will apply so as to ensure that the successor takes over the historical allowances calculation from the predecessor.

Other losses

[25.32] A property income loss under CTA 2009, Part 4 may be set against total profits for the period of the loss[1] and then rolled forward to be set against the total profits of a later period so long as the property business is carried on.[2] Losses from overseas property business can be set only against profits of that business for later years.[3]

Losses from miscellaneous income under CTA 2009, Part 10 may be set off against other miscellaneous losses for that or any subsequent accounting periods.[4]

Another problem arises when a company has ceased trading but receives investment income. Reliefs for the incidental expenses will not be available since it is not a trading company any longer and was not set up as an investment company. Unrelieved trading losses from its trading days cannot be used since the company is no longer trading. TA 1988, s 109A does not apply for the purposes of CT.[5]

Simon's Taxes D1.1115.

[1] TA 1988, s 392A(1).
[2] TA 1988, s 392A(2).
[3] TA 1988, s 392B.
[4] TA 1988, s 396.
[5] TA 1988, s 109A(7).

Capital losses

[25.33] Allowable capital losses may be set off against chargeable gains of that or any later accounting period[1] but not against income. Such losses are not affected by TA 1988, s 768 (above). Group relief does not extend to capital losses.[2]

Simon's Taxes D1.1119.

[1] TCGA 1992, s 8(1).
[2] But see TCGA 1992, s 171A for the ability to reallocate capital gains and losses within groups.

[25.34] Profits and chargeability

Accounting period

Financial years—accounting periods and periods of account

[25.34] Corporation tax is charged on the profits of the corporation during the financial year.[1] The"" "financial year" is the year starting on 1 April.[2] Hence "financial year 2009" is 1 April 2009 to 31 March 2010.[3] However, assessments are made by reference to accounting periods.[4] Where the accounting period does not correspond with the financial year the profits of the period are apportioned to compute the tax liability. The apportionment is on a strict pro rata basis, irrespective of the date in the accounting period on which profit arose.[5] Where the rate changes from one financial year to the next, each rate is applied to that portion of the accounting period falling within it.

EXAMPLE

In financial year 1 the rate is 40%; in financial year 2, 35%. The company makes up its accounts to 30 June and the total profit for the accounting period ending on 30 June year 2 amounts to £612,000. Corporation tax will be (using months for simplicity but in practice days should be used):

9/12 × £612,000 × 40% = £183,600
3/12 × £612,000 × 35% = 53,550
Total £237,150

The financial year is relevant only to the rate of tax. If the method of computing income or capital gains and so corporate profits changes from one year to the next, the accounting period is treated as if it were a year of assessment,[6] although various provisions (eg change of ownership) require an accounting period to be split for specific purposes.

When a company is to be dissolved after it has been in administration, then the corporation tax rates to be used are those in force for the previous financial year. This helps in an early settlement of the tax bill before the administrator has disposed of all of the company's assets[7]

Simon's Taxes D1.106–108.

[1] CTA 2009, s 2(1).
[2] Interpretation Act 1978, Sch 1.
[3] TA 1988, s 834(1).
[4] CTA 2009, s 8(2).
[5] CTA 2009, s 1311
[6] CTA 2009, s 8(2).
[7] TA 1988, s 342A(2) introduced by FA 2003, s 196, Sch 41 to accommodate the regime for companies in administration introduced by the Enterprise Act 2002.

[25.35] Accounting periods will usually be the successive periods for which the company makes up its accounts. An accounting period cannot exceed

12 months. A period of account is simply the period taken by the company in computing its accounts.¹ Where the period of account exceeds 12 months one accounting period ends after 12 months and a new one begins. Thus if the period of account is 16 months there will be an accounting period of 12 months followed by one of four months the profits will be allocated 3/4 to the first period and 1/4 to the second.

Where one set of accounts covers more than one period, an apportionment may be made on a time basis unless a more accurate method can be established.² This apportionment is carried out on the basis of days.³

When a company draws up accounts, the accounting date to which the accounts are drawn determines the accounting period(s) for assessment of the company's profits. The Revenue have no power to substitute an accounting period which they would prefer. Once an assessment is raised for an accounting period, that assessment cannot be revised by virtue of the inspector wishing to use a different period as the accounting period.⁴

Where, however, at the time of making an assessment, the date that an accounting period begins or ends is uncertain, the inspector is empowered to make an assessment for such period "as appears to him appropriate".⁵ This is not an area where the inspector uses his subjective judgment; the inspector is required only to identify an "appropriate" period if the statutory rules fail to identify a period.⁶ An administrator may make an assumption about when the date of dissolution is likely to be under the new administration rules. If this later proves to be incorrect then a new accounting period will commence at that date and the administrator may subsequently make a further assumption about the likely date of dissolution. While a company is in administration, a corporation tax assessment may be made before the end of the period to which it relates.⁷

Simon's Taxes D1.108, D1.309.

---

1   On the position where a company makes its accounts up both yearly and six-monthly, see *Jenkins Productions Ltd v IRC* [1943] 2 All ER 786, 29 TC 142 and extra-statutory concession C12 for retail co-operative societies; see Simon's Taxes, Division G2.2. On accounts for an unauthorised period, see *BFP Holdings Ltd v IRC* (1942) 24 TC 483.
2   CTA 2009, ss 52, 1307; *Marshall Hus & Partners Ltd v Bolton* [1981] STC 18. In *Camcrown Ltd v McDonald* [1999] STC (SCD) 255, the Special Commissioners held that, in the facts of that particular case, time apportionment did not give a just and reasonable result. In order to avoid injustice and unreasonableness, the losses represented by first year allowances had to be allocated to the period in which the expenditure was incurred. This case was, however, decided by reference to different statutory provisions.
3   CTA 2009, s 52(3), 1307(4).
4   *Kelsall v Stipplechoice Ltd* [1995] STC 681, CA.
5   TA 1988, s 12(8).
6   See the judgment of Peter Gibson LJ in *Kelsall v Stipplechoice Ltd* [1995] STC 681 at 683c–e.

[25.35] Profits and chargeability

[7] TA 1988, s 342A(6) introduced by FA 2003, Sch 41, para 3 to accommodate the regime for companies in administration introduced by the Enterprise Act 2002).

[25.36] An accounting period begins because the previous accounting period has ended and the company remains subject to charge or if the company, not then being within the charge to corporation tax, comes within it, whether by the company becoming resident or acquiring a source of income.[1] A new accounting period begins immediately before a company goes into administration.[2] A UK resident company which has not yet commenced business is not yet within the charge to corporation tax. So a company which simply receives dividend income will not be treated as coming into charge until it commences a business of some sort.[3]

Simon's Taxes D1.108.

[1] CTA 2009, s 9(1).
[2] CTA 2009, s 12(2).
[3] CTA 2009, s 9(2).

[25.37] An accounting period ends[1] on the expiration of 12 months from its beginning or, if earlier, any of the following:

(1) the end of the company's period of account;
(2) if there is a period during which no accounts have been taken at the end of that period;
(3) the company begins or ceases to trade or to be within the charge to corporation tax in respect of the trade, as where a non-resident company continues to trade but no longer through a permanent establishment here; if the company carries on more than one trade the charge to tax must cease in respect of all of them if the period is to end;
(4) the company begins or ceases to be resident; or
(5) when a company ceases to be in administration[2] in which case the company's final accounting period is the last period before an application for dissolution under the administration rules;[3] or
(6) the company ceases to be within the charge to corporation tax.

Simon's Taxes D1.108.

[1] CTA 2009, s 10.
[2] CTA 2009, s 10(1)(j)
[3] TA 1988, s 342A(5).

[25.38] The scheme of tax is designed so that the period of account will usually coincide with the accounting period and is designed to interfere as little as possible with the freedom of the company to take whatever period of account it likes. If the company has two trades and each trade has a separate period of account and the company does not make up accounts for the company as a whole, an officer of HMRC can determine which accounting date to take for tax purposes if the officer has reasonable grounds for thinking that the date chosen by the company is inappropriate. If an officer of HMRC determines the accounting date, profits of the other trade will have to be apportioned.[1] This emphasises the point that the taxable person is the corporation and not the trade.

An accounting period ends and a new one begins when the winding up of a company commences.[2] Thereafter the accounting period will end every 12 months until the winding-up is complete.

Simon's Taxes D1.108.

---

[1] CTA 2009, s 11(3).
[2] CTA 2009, s 12(2); on effect of an uncertain date, see TA 1988, s 12(8).

[25.39] It is perfectly possible for there to be gaps between accounting periods as when the company ceases to trade and then starts again. This gives rise to a problem should a capital gain accrue during this period of quiescence. It is therefore provided that an accounting period is to commence when the chargeable gain or allowable loss accrues to the company.[1] Should the company subsequently begin to trade again the deemed period will end and a new one begin.

If despite these rules the beginning or end of a period is uncertain the inspector may make an assessment for such periods not exceeding 12 months as seems to him appropriate.[2]

If the company is a member of a partnership, its share of the profits is ascertained as an ordinary person and then allocated to its corresponding accounting period making any apportionments that may be necessary.[3]

Simon's Taxes D1.108.

---

[1] CTA 2009, s 9(3).
[2] TA 1988, s 12(8).
[3] CTA 2009, ss 1262, 1265.

Small companies rate

Small profits relief: the 21% rate

[25.40] A special rate of 21% is applied to the first band of a company's total profits.[1] Profits above a defined level are charged at the full rate of corporation tax, 28%. In order to avoid a sudden change from each rate to the next, a form of marginal relief by taper applies between the two rates. Although this gives a graduation from one rate to the other, the effect of the formula is to charge profits generated in the taper at a rate higher than the full rate.

Thus, the effective rates for financial year 2009 are (but see below for the strict calculation of marginal relief):

[25.40] Profits and chargeability

Profits:
£1–£300,000   21%
£300,001–£1,500,000 29¾%
over £1,500,000   28%

These rates[2] apply to companies resident in the UK (other than close-investment-holding companies; see infra, § **29.13–29.15**) but not to non-resident companies with a UK permanent establishment.[3] The Revenue, however, interpret a non-discrimination clause in an applicable double tax agreement as entitling the non-resident company to this rate. The *Commerzbank* decision of the European Court seems to give permanent establishments of companies of another member state a right to use that rate.[4]

The 21% rate is known in statute as "small companies relief". For the purposes of this relief "profits" includes income, capital gains and franked investment income (FII) but not group income or FII received from a subsidiary.[5]

Although the rate of tax for such "small companies" has generally fallen, in line with headline tax rates more generally, the Government has expressed concern that it has encouraged some businesses to incorporate merely for the tax advantages that incorporation can give.[6] Consequently, since 2007, the rate has started to creep up, whilst the main rate of corporation tax has fallen. It is widely expected that the two rates will merge in the relatively near future.

Simon's Taxes D1.1202.

[1] FA 2009, s 8(1)(a).
[2] The full rate for financial year 2009 is specified in FA 2008, s 6.
[3] However, a non-resident company may be an associated company; see infra, § **25.46**.
[4] *R v IRC, ex p Commerzbank AG (Case C-330/91)* [1993] STC 605, ECJ.
[5] TA 1988, s 13(7). FII is also excluded if it would have been group income if an election under TA 1988, s 247 had been made.
[6] Of course, such concerns can, at least partly, be blamed on the Government itself. In 2003, it foolishly introduced a nil% corporation tax starting rate and announced in Parliament that taxpayers who failed to take advantage of it would be looking a gift horse in the mouth.

Marginal relief

[25.41] Marginal relief applies when the profits exceed £300,000 but not £1.5m. The corporation tax due at the full rate of 28% is calculated and then reduced by a sum determined by the formula:[1]

$$\frac{\text{Appropriate fraction} \times (\text{UL} - \text{NP}) \times \text{PCTCT}}{\text{NP}}$$

Where: UL = Upper limit (currently £1,500,000)

Small companies rate [25.41]

NP = Notional profits
PCTCT = Profits chargeable to corporation tax

The effect of the reduction given by this formula is to cause the reduction from the full rate of 28% to decline until the figure reaches £1.5m at which point it vanishes; it provides a smooth graduation of liability from the lower rate to the full rate of CT; this gives a marginal tax rate higher than full rate.[2] The figures of £300,000 and £1.5m are not index-linked and were last increased in 1994.[3]

EXAMPLE

A Ltd has for the financial year 2009 trading income of £372,000, capital gains of £30,000 (realised in June 2009) and franked investment income of £25,000.

Profits are
Income   372,000
Capital gain   30,000
Franked investment income   25,000
                              427,000

As franked investment income is exempt from CT, normal corporation tax at 28% would be £402,000 @ 28% = £112,560. The reduction is:

$$(\pounds 1.5m - \pounds 427{,}000) \times \frac{402{,}000}{427{,}000} \times \frac{1}{400} = \pounds 25{,}254$$

which makes final corporation tax of £94,882.

This relief is described in statute as mitigation of corporation tax liability for small companies. This is a complete misnomer since the relief is available wherever there are small profits regardless of the size of the company and regardless of the size of profits retained in previous years.

If the accountancy period straddles the end of the financial year and rates change, a new period is treated as starting on the first day of the new year. The new rates and bands apply only to the profits (appropriately calculated) of the new year.[4] The limits of £300,000 and £1.5m are proportionately reduced for periods of less than 12 months.[5]

Simon's Taxes D1.1202.

---

[1] For financial year 2009 the fraction is 7/400, which gives a marginal rate of 29.75%.
[2] FA 2009, s 8(2)(a).
[3] TA 1988, s 13(3); when the company's accounting period straddles the financial year, apportionments are to be made.
[4] This is a consequence of the rates and fraction being fixed separately for each financial year.
[5] TA 1988, s 13(6).

Associated companies

[25.42] But for express provision, it would be easy to exploit these benefits by dividing a business between many companies. It is therefore provided that when the company has one or more associated companies in the accounting period the figures of £300,000 and £1.5m shall be divided by the total number of companies which are associated with each other.[1] This technique of crude division by the number of companies rather than division according to the size of profits, has the effect that two associated companies each with a profit of £300,000 will together pay less tax than if one had profits of £599,000 and the other of £1,000. It arises, however, because company A may be associated with companies B and C without B being associated with C. For this purpose, overseas companies under common control are treated as "associated companies", even if the overseas company has no liability to UK tax.

Particular problems may arise where a person with substantial interests in one company joins in a new venture under the enterprise investment scheme (see infra, § **30.10**). If the two companies are associated the limits for the relief will have to be divided between the two companies, something the other members of the new venture may not have expected.

Simon's Taxes D1.1203.

---

[1] TA 1988, s 13(3). On associated status see supra, § **25.43**. By Extra-statutory concession C9, for the purpose of small companies' rate, the Revenue treats as a relative only a husband or a wife or a minor child. There is some evidence that the Revenue are more active than formerly in pursuing an argument that companies are associated, see Mark Morton "A + B = Control?", *Taxation* 12 May 2005, pp 160–161.

[25.43] Companies are associated[1] if at the relevant time, or at any time within one year previously, one has control of the other or both are under the control of the same person or persons.[2] A person has control if he exercises or is able to exercise or is entitled to acquire control over the company's affairs, a phrase which could mean:

(1) the power to carry a resolution at a general meeting, including the power to elect the board of directors; or
(2) more narrowly, the power to run the company's affairs, that is power at the director level, the point being that the general meeting cannot usually tell its directors how to manage the day-to-day affairs of the company.

In *Steele v EVC International NV*[3] the Court of Appeal preferred 1 to 2. Control of the affairs of a company meant control at the level of general meetings of shareholders, as control at that level carried with it the power to make the ultimate decisions as to the business of a company and in that sense to control its affairs.

Control is, however, declared[4] to exist in defined circumstances although these are without prejudice to the broad principle. These circumstances are where one possesses or is entitled to acquire:

(1)   the greater part of the share capital or issued share capital of the company or of the voting power of the company; or
(2)   such part of the share capital as would entitle him to the greater part of the income of the company were it all distributed ignoring any loan capital; or
(3)   such rights as would entitle him in the event of the winding up of the company to the greater part of the assets of the company.

Where two persons together satisfy any of these tests they are taken to have control of the company.[5]

EXAMPLE

So if L and M each have 50% of the shares of A Ltd, they have control of A Ltd. If they also have control of B Ltd, then A Ltd and B Ltd are associated.

If L and M each have 50% of the shares of A Ltd but each has 25% of the shares in C Ltd, these two companies are not associated since L and M do not have control of C Ltd.

If the remaining 50% are divided equally between N and P and N transfers his 25% to L, the companies now become associated since L and M together have 75% of the shares in C Ltd. The fact that M might vote with P and block L is irrelevant. If, however, M then transferred his 25% holding in C Ltd to P the companies would cease to be associated since while L and M control A Ltd, they do not have control of C Ltd.

A nice question arises if L and M still have 50% of the shares in A Ltd and L obtains 75% of the shares in C Ltd. If the remaining 25% of the shares in C Ltd are held by M the companies will be associated. If however the remaining 25% are held by P the companies would appear not to be associated since although L had control of C Ltd he does not have control of A Ltd for in regard to this company he must rely on M's holding.

An associated company is not brought into the calculation of the small companies rate limits if it "has not carried on any trade or business at any time in that accounting period".[6] In *Revenue and Customs Comrs v Salaried Persons*,[7] a company that was not dormant was excluded as an associated company for this purpose. By contrast in *Land Management v Fox*,[8] a holding company that made a loan to its subsidiary, received interest, paid administrative expenses and declared a dividend was held to be carrying on a business and was brought into account when calculating the limits for small companies rate in assessing the profits of its subsidiary. By contrast, a company formed to hold a house in France, for use by the family who paid no rent, was held not to be carrying on a business.[9] Park J held in *Jowett v O'Neill and Brennan Construction Ltd*[10] that it is possible for a company not to be carrying on a business, although it receives interest in the accounting period. Park J stressed in his judgment, which upheld the finding of fact by the Special Commissioner, that it is only in a exceptional case that a company can receive income but be held not to be carrying on a business.[11]

For the purposes of small profits relief the Revenue, by concession[12] disregard common control arising when companies are controlled by a common trustee, such as a trustee company of a clearing bank, by a common commercial loan creditor or by a common shareholder by virtue of fixed rate preference shares. This means that the companies are associated neither with each other nor with the company with control.

Simon's Taxes D1.1205.

---

[1]   A matter relevant to TA 1988, ss 13 and 774.

[25.43] Profits and chargeability

2   TA 1988, s 13(4). On shareholdings by different trusts with common trustees, see *IRC v Lithgows* (1960) 39 TC 270. Simon's Taxes, Division H3.4.
3   [1996] STC 785.
4   TA 1988, s 416(2).
5   TA 1988, s 416(3).
6   TA 1988, s 13(4).
7   [2006] STC 1315. The High Court upheld the decision of the Special Commissoner, as a finding of fact: *Salaried Persons Postal Loans Ltd v Revenue and Customs Comrs* [2005] STC (SCD) 851. The Special Commissioner was applying the decision in *American Leaf Blending Co Sdn Bhd v Director General of Inland Revenue* [1978] STC 561.
8   [2002] STC (SCD) 152.
9   *John M Harris (Design Partnership) Ltd v Lee* [1997] STC (SCD) 240.
10 [1998] STC 482.
11 At 490a.
12 Extra-statutory concession C9 para 4. Simon's Taxes, Division H4.2.

[25.44] In applying these rules there is to be attributed to a person any rights held by a nominee for him[1] and also the rights held by any associate[2] of his, a wide term[3] including any relative[4] or partner (see below) or any trust of which the individual is the settlor.[5]

However, by concession,[6] for the purpose of identifying an associated company only, the only relatives who are treated as associates are spouses and minor children, unless there is substantial commercial interdependence between the two companies. There may also be attributed to him all the powers of any company of which he has control whether by himself or with associates.[7] The House of Lords has determined that the attribution of rights by the Revenue is mandatory.[8] There is no underlying policy restricting the concept of control to those who might actually benefit from companies over which they were deemed to have control.

Despite these attributions it is possible for companies not to be associated. Thus if L controls A Ltd and M controls B Ltd the companies are not, without more, associated and in practice this is so even if L controls A Ltd and L and M together control B Ltd. If the companies agree to pool their profits or a percentage of them they will still not be associated unless the Revenue succeed in arguing that they have become partners. Yet if they were to put themselves under a holding company they would become associated since they would each be controlled by the holding company.

In computing the reduced relief it is immaterial that the other company was associated for only a part of the accounting period or that it was not resident.

It became apparent in 2006 that the strict application of the rules led to an anomaly and an administrative nightmare. The problem arose when HMRC were investigating schemes, often known as film schemes, in which unrelated investors subscribe to a scheme which takes advantage of the former rules intended to encourage investment in British films so as to create income losses. The standard schemes would involve the investors becoming partners in a film "business". However, that also meant that one investor's portfolio of companies would automatically become associated with any companies controlled by any of the other partners.

FA 2008 has partially remedied this by modifying the control test in TA 1988, s 416, but only for the purposes of ascertaining the number of associated companies. Another partner's companies are to be counted only if:

(1) the individual and the partner are both involved in arrangements that have effect in relation to the company whose corporation tax is in issue; and

(2) those arrangement secure a reduction in the company's corporation tax liability as a result of the small companies' relief.[9]

Simon's Taxes D1.1205.

[1] TA 1988, s 416(5).
[2] TA 1988, s 416(6).
[3] *R v IRC, ex p Newfields Developments Ltd* [2001] UKHL 27, [2001] STC 901.
[4] TA 1988, s 417(3)(*a*)
[5] TA 1988, s 417(3)(*b*). It is on this ground that companies were held to be associated in *Gascoines Group Ltd v Inspector of Taxes* [2004] EWHC 640 (Ch), [2004] STC 844.
[6] Extra-statutory concession C9 para 5. Simon's Taxes, Division H4.2.
[7] TA 1988, s 417(3).
[8] *R v IRC, ex p Newfields Developments Ltd* [2001] UKHL 27, [2001] STC 901.
[9] TA 1988, s 13(4A)—(4C)

International aspects

Non-resident companies

[25.45] For accounting periods beginning on or after 1 January 2003, non-resident companies[1] are subject to corporation tax if they are carrying on a trade in the UK through a permanent establishment. Before this date, such companies were subject to corporation tax only if they operated in the UK through a branch or agency. So some non-resident companies may now become taxable for the first time under the new broader rules. "Permanent establishment" is an internationally recognised term that is generally used in the UK's double tax agreements. However, the definition in FA 2003 differs slightly from that used in the OECD model treaty and may not necessarily be identical to the definition of "permanent establishment" contained in existing double tax treaties.

A non resident company has a permanent establishment in the UK in two situations: if there is a fixed place of business in the UK through which the company's business is wholly or partly carried out or if the company's business in the UK is carried out by an agent who has the authority to do business on the company's behalf.[2] This does not include an independent agent acting in

[25.45] Profits and chargeability

the ordinary course of his (ie the agent's) business.[3] Preparatory or auxiliary activities, in relation to the activities of the company as a whole, are specifically excluded.[4]

A few examples (but not an exhaustive list) of what constitutes a fixed place of business includes:

(a) a place of management;
(b) a branch;
(c) an office;
(d) a factory;
(e) a workshop;
(f) an installation or structure for the exploration of natural resources;
(g) a mine, an oil or gas well, a quarry or other place of extraction of mineral resources;
(h) a building site or construction or installation project.[5]

When a non-resident company, as a consequence of this rule, is subject to UK corporation tax, statute states that corporation tax is then charged on "all profits, wherever arising".[6] This is a deceptively wide statement since the profits attributable to a permanent establishment are then defined[7] as:

(1) trading income from the permanent establishment;
(2) income from property or rights held by the permanent establishment eg royalties on a patent held by the permanent establishment and profits on the realisation of assets held on a short-term basis and funded by an insurance company's surpluses;[8] and
(3) chargeable gains accruing from the disposal of assets used in or for the purpose of the trade carried on through the permanent establishment or used or held by the permanent establishment.[9]

EXAMPLE

X Ltd, a non-resident company, carries on a trade in the UK through a permanent establishment. The permanent establishment has a UK trading income of £17,500,000 and sells UK property from its trade realising a capital gain of £600,000; it also sells overseas property realising a gain of £750,000. The charge to UK corporation tax is:

Trading income	£17,500,000
Chargeable gains (infra, § 25.17)	£600,000
Chargeable profits	£18,100,000
Corporation tax at 28%	£5,068,000

If the company carries on a trade here otherwise than through a permanent establishment, it can be liable to income tax on its yearly interest income and other items that payers have to deduct income tax from.

Companies not resident in the UK but carrying on a trade through a permanent establishment here, hence subject to corporation tax, will have to submit both the profit and loss accounts of the UK PE and of the company itself for the relevant period. Additionally, the balance sheet of the company at the end of the period, and if available, the balance sheet of the permanent establishment must also be submitted. The good news is that where there is more than one permanent establishment only one corporation tax return is required.

International aspects [25.45]

The profits attributable to the permanent establishment are "the profits it would have made if it were a distinct and separate enterprise, engaged in the same or similar activities under the same or similar conditions, dealing wholly independently with the non resident company".[10] Two assumptions are made about the permanent establishment: it has the same credit rating as the non-resident company and the amount of equity and loan capital attributed to it is the same that an independent enterprise would have. These assumptions are basically additional thin capitalisation rules for permanent establishments that may be overridden only if the relevant treaty makes specific mention of capital attributions to permanent establishments. However, this new legislation may be in breach of EU law.[11] Branches of foreign banks are the most likely entities to be affected by these new thin capitalisation rules. These rules apply for accounting periods beginning on or after 1 January 2003.

Deductions are allowed for "allowable expenses" in the UK or elsewhere, ie those expenses that would be deductible if incurred by a company resident in the UK.[12] Rules are outlined for the assessment, collection and recovery of tax from non-resident companies.[13] If the permanent establishment ceases to trade in the UK, it is regarded as being the company's representative in the UK, ie a distinct and separate person. In these situations the permanent establishment is not liable to be prosecuted for a criminal offence committed by the overseas company unless the permanent establishment actually committed (or was a party to) the offence.[14]

Interest is paid without deduction of tax if it is paid to a company that is within the charge to UK corporation tax. Hence, a non-resident company that trades through a permanent establishment is entitled to receive interest gross.[15]

Simon's Taxes D4.117, 118.

1. On company residence see, infra, § 33.25.
2. FA 2003, s 148(1).
3. FA 2003, s 148(3).
4. FA 2003, s 148(4), (5).
5. FA 2003, s 148(2).
6. CTA 2009, s 5(2); on mode of assessment, see FA 2003, s 150; for permanent establishment refer also to infra, § 36.07. On place of trade see infra, § 36.03, for an example see *IRC v Brackett* [1986] STC 521.
7. CTA 2009, s 19(2),(3).
8. *General Reinsurance Co Ltd v Tomlinson* (1970) 48 TC 81.
9. TCGA 1992, s 10B(1) and infra, § 35.46.
10. CTA 2009, s 21.
11. *Compagnie de Saint-Gobain, Zweigniederlassung Deutschland v Finanzant Aachen-Innenstadt (Case C-307/97)* [2000] STC 854, 2 ITLR 146, ECJ; *Lankhorst-Hohorst Gmbh v Finanzant Steinfurt (Case C-324/00)* [2003] STC 607; ECJ.
12. CTA 2009, s 29.
13. FA 2003, s 150.
14. FA 2003, s 150(6).
15. TA 1988, s 349B(2) inserted by FA 2001, s 85.

[25.46] Profits and chargeability

Change of residence

[25.46] If a resident company ceases to be resident or ceases to be liable to UK tax there is a deemed disposal of its capital assets.[1] However, there is no deemed disposal of assets which remain in the permanent establishment in the UK and so within the charge to CT.[2] If the company fails to pay the tax within six months from its becoming payable, the unpaid tax may be collected from:

(a) any company in the same group as the non-resident company (51% common ownership);
(b) any member of a consortium (consortium relief definition) which owns the non-resident company; or
(c) a member of the same group (group relief definition) as the member of that consortium.[3]

HMRC may serve notice on any of the above companies to pay the unpaid tax, or, in a consortium case, the appropriate proportion of the unpaid tax, together with interest from the due and payable date. The notice is treated as if it were a notice of assessment.[4]

The notice may be served up to three years after the date when the non-resident company's liability is finally determined.[5]

A company which pays tax under the above rules may recover it from the company originally liable.[6]

Schemes to avoid this charge by leaving the assets within the scope of corporation tax by leaving them with a permanent establishment in the UK at the time of migration but then leasing them to another UK resident company were stopped by the creation of another deemed disposal.[7]

Where a permanent establishment is converted into a UK company, the UK company is treated as acquiring the assets of the permanent establishment at such a figure that neither gain nor loss accrues; this defers the charge otherwise arising.[8]

Corporation tax is levied on the profits of a company that arise during liquidation. The corporation tax liability arising on profits made after the commencement of a winding up is an expense in the winding up and is payable in priority to the claims of creditors.[9]

Simon's Taxes D4.131; STP [30.6].

---

[1] TCGA 1992, s 185; there are special rules when the migrating company is a 75% subsidiary of a company which is not migrating: s 187; a company can cease to be liable to UK tax through the application of a double tax treaty. On change of residence see infra, § 33.36.
[2] TCGA 1992, s 185(4).
[3] FA 2000, Sch 28, para 2.
[4] FA 2000, Sch 28, para 3.
[5] FA 2000, Sch 28, para 4.
[6] FA 2000, Sch 28, para 3.
[7] Now in TCGA 1992, s 25(3); see infra, § **35.46**.
[8] TCGA 1992, s 171(1A).

⁹   Re *Toshoku Finance UK* [2002] UKHL 6, [2002] STC 368. In his judgment, Lord Hoffman noted that the order of priority for payments by liquidators was codified by the Companies (Winding Up) Rules 1890 Rule 31 and no subsequent statute has changed its effect in this respect.

The EC Mergers Directive

[25.47] A Directive, generally known as the "Mergers Directive", was published in August 1990 and took effect on 1 January 1992.¹

The normal corporation tax rules are modified in a number of situations involving a qualifying company,² company A, making a transfer to another qualifying company, company B, resident in another member state. A company is resident in a member state if it is subject to a charge to tax under the law of that state because it is regarded as resident there for the purposes of the charge; this is subject to any overrule by a double taxation agreement giving a different residence for treaty purposes.³

In *Leur-Bloem v Inspecteur der Belastingdienst*⁴ the European Court considered the application of the Directive to the creation of a holding company and an exchange of shares of the holding company for shares in two trading companies. Having held that it had jurisdiction under a reference under Art 177 to give an opinion on the interpretation of legislation designed to implement a Directive (the Mergers Directive) even though the facts were all in one country (the Netherlands) and so purely domestic it then held that, although the Directive allowed a member state to prevent its use by taxpayers for avoidance purposes, this did not permit the member state to prohibit whole categories of transactions whether or not there was actual tax avoidance or evasion. The court also held that the Directive could apply even if (a) the acquiring company did not carry on a business itself; (b) there was no merger of two companies into a single unit from the financial or economic viewpoint; or (c) the same person was sole shareholder and director of both companies.

A complete code⁵ has been incorporated into the Taxes Acts to specify the taxation treatment of a Societas Europaea, the European company, usually created by cross-border merger.⁶

Simon's Taxes D4.128.

¹   Directive 90/434/EEC.
²   Defined as a body incorporated under the law of a member state; see TCGA 1992, ss 140A(7), 140C(9).
³   TCGA 1992, ss 140A(5), (6), 140C(6), (7).
⁴   Case C-28/95: [1997] STC 1205.
⁵   F(No 2)A 2005, ss 51–65
⁶   The Treasury Notes to Finance (No 3) Bill 2005 clauses 51–65 state:

> European Company Statute (ECS) Regulation was adopted by the EU Council of Ministers on 8 October 2001. The Regulation brought into existence the European Company (Societas Europaea or SE) and provides rules governing SEs. Tax is not explicitly covered within the regulation so the tax law of the member state in which the SE is based applies to SEs. The addition of SEs to other EU legislation (the Mergers Directive) means that UK tax measures

[25.47] Profits and chargeability

are needed to ensure that a UK company's decision to merge with a company in another member State to form an SE is not disadvantaged (or driven) by tax considerations. Implementation of the legislation has been held back by agreement on the Mergers Directive.

Transfer of a UK trade

[25.48] Where there is a transfer of the whole or part of a trade carried on by A in the UK to B, that transfer is wholly in exchange for shares or debentures and both A and B so elect,[1] the two companies, subject to further conditions, are treated so that the assets are transferred at such figure that neither gain nor loss accrues.[2] Similarly the legislation excludes the deemed disposal otherwise arising under TCGA 1992, s 25(3) where the owner of an asset ceases to carry on a trade in the UK through a permanent establishment here.[3] Although the transfer must be wholly in exchange of shares or debentures the fact that the buyer takes over liabilities does not disqualify it.[4]

It is not necessary that A should be resident in the UK; it is sufficient that A is carrying on the trade in the UK. However, if A and B are resident[5] in the same EC country this provision does not apply.

There are two alternative conditions which B must satisfy. If immediately after the transfer B is not resident in the UK the condition is that any disposal of the asset would give rise to a charge to CT.[6] If B is resident in the UK the condition is that the company is not able to escape a charge to UK corporation tax in relation to any of the assets by reference to a double taxation agreement.[7] The effect is to allow deferral only when B will be fully exposed to UK tax in due course.

Finally, there is an anti-avoidance rule. The section does not apply unless the transfer of the trade is effected for bona fide commercial reasons and does not form part of a scheme or arrangements of which the main purpose, or one of the main purposes, is the avoidance of liability to income tax, corporation tax or CGT.[8] There is a clearance procedure on an application by A and B.[9]

Simon's Taxes D4.127.

[1] TCGA 1992, s 140A.
[2] TCGA 1992, s 140A(4).
[3] TCGA 1992, s 140A(4)(b).
[4] HMRC Capital Gains Manual, para 45709.
[5] On the meaning of residence see TCGA 1992, s 140A(5) and (6) stating that a company is resident where it is taxable on the basis of residence (as opposed to source) provided it is not treated as resident elsewhere for treaty purposes.
[6] ie under TCGA 1992, s 10(3); TCGA 1992, s 140A(2).
[7] TCGA 1992, s 140A(3).
[8] TCGA 1992, s 140B.
[9] TCGA 1992, s 140B(2); TCGA 1992, s 138(2)–(5) also applies s 140B(3).

Transfer of non-UK trade and double taxation relief

[25.49] To illustrate transfer of non-UK trade and double taxation relief[1], A, resident in the UK, makes a transfer of a trade in whole or in part to B and, immediately before the transfer, the trade is carried on by A in a member state other than the UK through a permanent establishment. The same no-gain/no-loss treatment of the aggregate of gains and losses arising is directed if the transfer includes the whole of the assets of company A used for the purposes of the trade (although cash, a term which is not defined, can be excluded), the transfer is wholly or partly in exchange for shares or debentures issued by B to A and the aggregate of the chargeable gains exceeds the aggregate of allowable losses.[2] A claim must be made by A (not A and B).[3] The special double taxation relief rule (see below) applies.[4]

There is an anti-avoidance provision similar to that for TCGA 1992, s 140A (supra, § 25.52) although here only A applies for clearance.[5] Relief under this rule is excluded if the more general deferral for the transfer by a UK company of a trade to a non-UK resident company (TCGA 1992, s 140) applies.[6]

Simon's Taxes D4.811.

[1] TA 1988, s 815A.
[2] TCGA 1992, s 140C(1), (3); in relation to insurance companies one should note the exclusion of TA 1988, s 442(3); see TCGA 1992, s 140C(8).
[3] TCGA 1992, s 140C(1)(e).
[4] ie TA 1988, s 815A; see TCGA 1992, s 140C(5).
[5] TCGA 1992, s 140D(2); ss 138(2)–(5) apply.
[6] TCGA 1992, s 140C(4).

Capital allowances on transfer of a trade

[25.50] Where there is a no-gain/no-loss rollover on the transfer of a UK trade in circumstances satisfying TCGA 1992, s 140A, the transfer is not to be treated as giving rise to any allowances or charges and everything done by company A is treated as done by company B.[1] There is no provision requiring capital allowance rollover also on a transfer within s 140C—presumably because this is now a matter for the law of the other member state. However, this means that a balancing charge or allowance may have to be calculated.

Simon's Taxes D4.128.

[1] CAA 2001, s 561(1), (2); any apportionment of expenditure between assets included in the transfer and other assets to be carried out in such manner as is just and reasonable; s 561(3).

Incorporation of a business

[25.51] The consequences of incorporation are varied. The first and obvious difference is that the profits of the trade will now be charged to corporation tax instead of income tax; and capital gains will be charged to corporation tax instead of to CGT. In this connection the widening differences between the tax bases are significant. The rate of corporation tax will depend on the level of

[25.51] Profits and chargeability

profits; directors remuneration is deductible[1] so that although the company is not entitled to personal allowances enough can be paid out to ensure that the personal allowances of the incorporators and their bands of income liable to basic rate income tax are all used up.

Assuming that the company's profit was substantial and that the director's marginal rate of income tax exceeds 28%, the company appears to be a tax shelter in that 28% is the maximum rate of tax on the company's profits. This appears to be a significant advantage over an unincorporated business if the business is looking to internal sources of finance for growth. However, the taxpayer will, presumably, eventually wish to get his capital out of the company and this means selling shares, so incurring CGT or taking dividends and paying income tax.

From the director's point of view there are advantages and disadvantages. First, he becomes liable to income tax on employment income and so to the PAYE system and Class I National Insurance contributions, and, second, he becomes liable to the stringent rules surrounding benefits derived from the company, supra, § 7.102. Against this he may find that the benefit rules are not as strict as may appear at first sight. Further, he will be substantially better off as far as pensions are concerned. As a director he can have a pension of up to 2/3 of final salary; as a self-employed person he funds his own pension and the contributions he can make to his fund are limited by reference to his age. Unless the taxpayer is young and has taken maximum advantage of this entitlement throughout his working life he could not hope to build up so large a fund at least until the recent stock market records. Income distributed as salary to the employee/director is fully deductible by the company; income distributed as dividend is not deductible.

It should also be noted that the company is a separate legal person so that its trading or capital losses cannot be set off against the shareholder's income or gains—or vice versa. Other matters are that gains made by the company are in effect subject to double taxation, infra, § 27.02; that TA 1988, s 703 hangs over the problem of extracting reserves from the company otherwise than by dividend or straightforward liquidation, supra, § 4.18.

Once a company is established it is possible to use the annual £3,000 exemption for IHT to make gifts of shares to trusts for children or others. More generally it is easier to pass a share in an incorporated business to a child than a portion of an unincorporated business. The exemption of many business assets and shareholdings from IHT may reduce the scope of this point. (See infra, §§ **44.01, 44.04**.)

On the other hand individuals exporting a business to a non-resident may run into TA 1988, s 739, infra, § 35.26 and as self-employed persons they have to pay Class 2 and Class 4 National Insurance contributions.

When the business is incorporated, the shift from income tax to corporation tax is made by discontinuing the trade for income tax with an assessment for a long period, perhaps with only a little overlap profit relief. However, loss relief may be preserved (supra, § **6.20**) and rollover relief is granted for CGT, supra, § **22.10** provided *all* the assets are transferred to the company if in return for shares.

These issues apply whether the business being incorporated is run by a sole person or a partnership.[2]

One factor that gave a significant boost to incorporation was the introduction of a 0% rate of corporation tax on profits below £10,000. Predictably, this led to a rush of incorporations from small businesses seeking to take advantage of the tax saving opportunities. This in turn seemed to surprise the Government who responded by levying a tax charge of 19% on 'non-corporate distributions' and, then, from April 2006, the abolition of the 0% rate (and the abolition of the tax charge on 'non-corporate distributions'). The Government justified its move by citing the need to control 'tax motivated incorporations'.[3]

This list has concentrated on the tax aspects of incorporation. However, the non-tax aspects are of great importance. These include the costs of running the paperwork of a company; the fact of limited liability, although this is likely to be qualified by the bank's insistence of collateral personal liability at least in the early stages and the significant change in status, when more than one person is involved, on moving from equal partner to minority shareholder. Further, company law requirements seem to be becoming more stringent and some professions do not allow incorporation. One should also note that a company may find it easier to raise finance since, unlike an individual, it can create a floating charge.[4] In the United States certain closely-held corporations can be taxed as if they were partnerships—an election that lies with the relevant taxpayers.

---

[1] There can be disallowance of excessive remuneration, but this is rare for a trading company.
[2] On incorporation of professional partnership see ICAEW Guidance Note, TAX 7/95; *Simon's Weekly Tax Intelligence* 1995, p 362.
[3] FA 2006, s 26 abolished the 0% corporation tax rate and the charge on non-corporate distributions.
[4] For a comparison with partnerships see Simon's Taxes D1.121.

Corporate acquisition and disposals

[25.52] The acquisition of a company's business can be achieved in one of two alternative ways. First, the acquirer can purchase the share capital and thereby take over ownership of the business; second, the acquirer can purchase the assets (including the goodwill) that comprise the business from the vendor company.

After acquisition, there are, similarly, two alternative strategies that may be adopted. First, the acquired business may constitute a separate company within the acquirer's group. This can be achieved when those assets are purchased by a newly created company formed for this purpose. In the second alternative, the business that has been acquired is assimilated into a pre-existing company, perhaps one that already carries on a comparable business, so that a complete merger is effected.

[25.52] Profits and chargeability

The choice of mechanism for the acquisition, as well as the choice of structure for the continuation of the business after acquisition, are primarily a matter of commercial decision. It may be undesirable to purchase a company's share capital if it is thought that there could be contingent liabilities within the company. By contrast, it may be easier to retain customers and suppliers if the business is demonstrably carried on by the same, continuing company, even though the company is part of a corporate group rather than having previously been in private ownership. Commercial considerations can relate to the employment contracts of employees who are to be taken over (and the status of individuals whose services are not acquired by the acquirer) and, also, whether the acquirer wishes to take some and not all the assets of the business. Financial considerations are also relevant. If the acquirer wishes to limit cash expenditure, a share issue in the acquiring company may be made to the vendors as all or part of the consideration. It will usually be the case that a share issue can more easily be effected where this is a paper for paper exchange for shares of the target company. Other financial arrangements can include the distribution of cash reserves out of the target company before its acquisition or, even, the acquisition being effected by means of a dividend in specie, being the trade that the acquirer wishes to acquire.

When the purchase is of the assets of the target company, tax implications include a consideration of what capital allowances are available on the acquisition of those particular assets and the purchase price for individual assets being a base cost for the future calculation of a capital gain arising. VAT can also be an important consideration on the acquisition of a business. Unless the transfer is of a going concern, assets sold attract a charge to VAT.

Where losses have arisen in the target company, relief is not available for those losses after the sale of the business, if the sale is effected by a sale of assets. By contrast, loss relief continues to be available after the sale, if this is effected by a sale of shares in the target company. However, the continuation of loss relief is, even then, restricted. Losses brought forward can be relieved only against future trading profits of the same trade.[1] Where, within a period of three years of change of ownership in the company, there is a major change in the nature or contract of the trading carried on by the company, relief for previous trading losses is denied.[2] Relief for surplus ACT is lost where there is a major change in the nature of conduct of trade within the three year period and where there is a change of ownership.

Where there is a sale of assets, various provisions affect the change in ownership. Balancing allowances and charges arise if capital allowances have been claimed on the assets. The sale of assets triggers a capital gain for the selling company. Although there is, in practice, a degree of freedom available to the parties for the allocation of the price amongst the assets, that allocation will determine both the gain made by the vendor and the base cost for the acquirer and may be disregarded if the Revenue can demonstrate that it is "necessary" to reallocate the declared division of the consideration.

---

[1] TA 1988, s 393(1).
[2] TA 1988, s 768, see *Willis v Peeters Picture Frames Ltd* [1983] STC 453.

[25.53] The tax treatment of the sale of a business by a company requires consideration of the status and consequences of transfer of each individual asset. The effect of the Taxes Act on some of the more common assets transferred on the sale by the company of a business on an asset basis can be summarised as follows:

Land and buildings

For the vendor the capital gain arising attracts corporation tax although rollover relief may be available. If industrial buildings allowances have been claimed, a balancing charge arises which is taxed as a trading receipt under CTA 2009, Pt 3.

For the purchaser the price paid is the purchaser's base cost. A gain qualifying for rollover relief can be rolled into this cost. If the buildings qualify for industrial building allowance, this is available over the remaining tax life of the building.

Plant and machinery

For the vendor a balancing allowance or a balancing charge arises by reference to the capital allowance pool. If the proceeds exceed index cost, a capital gain arises.

For the purchaser, capital allowances are available based on the price paid.

Goodwill

For the vendor a capital gain arises, which is eligible for rollover relief. The tax treatment of any acquisition made after 1 April 2002 will follow the accounting treatment and will not fall under the capital gains regime. There is a modified rollover relief available (see infra, § **27.24**).

For the purchaser the price paid is the purchaser's base cost. A gain qualifying for rollover relief can be rolled into this cost. Any acquisitions made after 1 April 2002 fall under the new regime for intangibles whereby the tax treatment basically follows the accounting treatment (see infra, § **27.21**). A modified rollover relief is available.

Know-how

For the vendor, a capital gain arises, the know-how being treated as goodwill. Alternatively, the vendor and purchaser can jointly elect for the excess to be treated as an income receipt (chargeable under CTA 2009, Pt 10), instead of a capital gain. Disposals of know-how acquired after 1 April 2002 follow the new regime for intangibles whereby tax treatment follows accounting treatment (see infra, § **27.21**).

For the purchaser the price paid is the purchaser's base cost. A gain qualifying for rollover relief can be rolled into this cost. Alternatively, if an election has been made a writing-down capital allowance is available on the expenditure at

20% on the reducing balance. Acquisitions made after 1 April 2002 fall under the new regime for intangibles whereby the tax treatment follows the accounting treatment. The 25% allowance is no longer available (see infra, § 27.23).

Patents

For the vendor, if capital allowances have been claimed, there is a balancing allowance or a balancing charge. Disposals of patents acquired after 1 April 2002 fall under the intangibles regime whereby tax treatment follows accounting treatment (see infra, § 27.21).

For the purchaser, a writing-down capital allowance is available at the rate of 20% on the reducing balance. Acquisitions made after 1 April 2002 fall under the new regime for intangibles whereby the tax treatment follows the accounting treatment. The 25% allowance is no longer available (see infra, § 27.23).

Trading investments

For the vendor, the capital gain arising attracts corporation tax although rollover relief may be available. Specific share pooling rules apply for shares owned by a company.

For the purchaser, the price paid is the purchaser's base cost.

Stock

For the vendor, the sale proceeds are part of turnover, which leads to a profit attracting a charge as trading income under CTA 200, Pt 3.

For the purchaser the price paid is part of the purchase cost and, hence, expenditure in the computation of profit.

Tax losses

For the vendor, trading losses brought forward are put against trading profits of final period. Losses made during the final 12 months of trading are set against the total profits of the final accounting period with a loss in excess of those profits being carried back against the profits of the 36 months preceding the final 12 months. Capital losses are set against capital gains in the final accounting period.

The purchaser cannot inherit any unused losses of the vendor.

VAT Treatment

If the assets, taken together, comprise the entire business, the sale can be treated as a transfer of a business as a going concern and, hence, no VAT is charged on the transfer. If, however, the assets do not comprise the entire business, VAT is levied on each individual asset.

The currency used for accounts

[25.54] The general premise of UK tax legislation, is that, in order to calculate a tax liability, the profits or losses of a trade are computed and expressed in sterling. However, there is no requirement in UK company law for a company to produce its statutory accounts in sterling. A UK-registered company may be controlled from abroad and it may be appropriate for it to draw up its accounts in the foreign currency.

Where accounts are drawn up in a foreign currency, statute[1] requires that the profits be translated into sterling for the purpose of computing the liability to corporation tax.

---

[1] FA 1993, s 92; FA 1998, s 163 amended by FA 2002, s 80 and Sch 24 to provide for the modification of the law if the euro is adopted by the UK.

26

Distributions

Distributions	PARA **26.01**
Tax on distributions	PARA **26.12**
Post-1999 Shadow ACT	PARA **26.17**
Stock dividends	PARA **26.18**
Purchase by a company of its own shares	PARA **26.20**

Distributions

[26.01] A dividend paid by a UK company carries a tax credit of one-ninth of the dividend for the recipient.

When a distribution is made by a company resident in the UK to another UK resident company, there is no charge to tax on the receipt of the dividend.[1] When the distribution is received by any other person, the recipient is assessable to income tax.[2] Distributions are classified as qualifying or non-qualifying distributions. Distributions are not deductible in computing the profits of the company.

There are special rules for stock dividends, infra, § **26.19**, for purchase by a company of its own shares, infra, § **26.21** and for demergers, infra, § **28.37**.

These rules are applicable to the payment of income and capital distributions except that distributions in respect of share capital in a winding up,[3] including surplus assets distributed, are not income distributions.[4] They are simply treated as the return of capital[5] and give rise to chargeable capital gains or allowable losses. This is so even if the payments represent arrears of undeclared cumulative preference dividends.[6]

Other payments which are not distributions are donations to charity,[7] and certain payments by an industrial provident society,[8] or a mutual trading society.[9]

Distribution income that also forms part of a taxpayer's trading profits or property income is taxed as part of those profits.[10] Dividends, etc received by a company otherwise than as part of trading profits are termed "franked investment income" of that company. Franked investment income is not brought into the calculation of total profits on which corporation tax is charged, but it is brought into the calculation to determine the application of small company's rate of corporation tax.[11] Hence, although a company's receipt of a dividend does not give rise directly to income tax charge, the effect of the receipt may be to increase the corporation tax rate on the company's profits.

[26.01] Distributions

The dividend charging provisions have priority over other savings and investment income except for building society dividends and industrial and provident society payments.[12]

Simon's Taxes D5.101–102.

---

[1] CTA 2009, s 1285(1)–(4).
[2] ITTOIA 2005, s 383. Distributions by industrial and provident societies are not treated as such: TA 1988, s 486 and ITTOIA 2005, s 379.
[3] By concession this includes dissolution under the Companies Act 1985, s 652, or the Companies Act 2006, s 1000, where the Registrar strikes off a defunct company provided certain assurances are given to the inspector before the event: extra-statutory concession C16; **Simon's Taxes Division G2.2**.
[4] TA 1988, s 209(1); *IRC v Burrell* [1924] 2 KB 52, 9 TC 27. This exclusion applies, by concession, to the winding up of social or recreational unincorporated associations, provided that the distributions are not large: extra-statutory concession C15; **Simon's Taxes, Division G2.2**.
[5] TCGA 1992, s 122, supra, § **21.11**.
[6] *Re Dominion Tar and Chemical Co Ltd* [1929] 2 Ch 387.
[7] TA 1988, s 339(7AA), (4).
[8] CTA 2009, s 132 and Sch 1, para 100. On shellfish and other agricultural and fishing co-operatives, see TA 1988, s 486(9) and ITTOIA 2005, s 379.
[9] TA 1988, s 490.
[10] ITTOIA 2005, s 366 and CTA 2009, s 130.
[11] ITTOIA 2005, s 367.
[12] See supra, § **25.44**.

[26.02] Since the abolition of advanced corporation tax (ACT) with effect from 6 April 1999, the distinction between a qualifying distribution made by a company and a non-qualifying distribution is largely academic. However, statute retains the distinction.

There are three categories of qualifying distribution. It is of the essence of a qualifying distribution that it is made in respect of the shareholding of the company. That is, the receipt is in respect of the shares held and not for some other reason, such as by virtue of employment with the company, whether as a director or otherwise. Qualifying distributions are not, however, limited to sums that are paid to all shareholders. Statute treats a payment by a close company to a single shareholder as a distribution, even though other shareholders in the company may not have receipt.[1] The first category of qualifying distribution is a dividend. Any dividend paid by a company prior to the winding up of the company, is a qualifying distribution.[2] This includes a dividend paid out of capital profits.

The second category of qualifying distribution is a transfer of an asset to a shareholder for less than the market value of the distribution.[3] The amount of the qualifying distribution is then the market value of the asset transferred less any consideration paid, directly or indirectly, by the shareholder to the company and less any amount which represents a repayment of capital on the shares. Thus, under basic principles, a reorganisation scheme that involved the transfer of a company's assets is a distribution. However, if such distribution is made under the terms of the demerger legislation,[4] the distribution of the reorganisation is treated as an exempt distribution. Assets transferred at an undervalue to a UK resident company are not treated as a qualifying distribution.[5] This includes the transfer of an asset, such as a trade, to the company's parent, to a fellow subsidiary,[6] or a company not in the group; however, this treatment does not apply where the distribution is of cash to a company not in the group.[7]

Third, a purchase by a company of its own shares is a qualifying distribution, unless the purchase satisfies the conditions for treatment as a capital gain.[8]

---

[1] TA 1988, s 418. See infra, § **29.09**.
[2] TA 1988, s 209(1).
[3] TA 1988, s 209(2)(*b*) and (4).
[4] TA 1988, s 213.
[5] TA 1988, s 209(6).
[6] TA 1988, s 209(6).
[7] TA 1988, s 209(6). See infra, §§ **26.20–26.29**.
[8] TA 1988, ss 219–224.

Non-qualifying distributions

[26.03] The right to receive assets in the future is a non-qualifying distribution. A non-qualifying distribution is, in essence, the right to receive assets, which may include cash, at a future date. There are two categories of non-qualifying distribution.

First, a bonus issue by a company of redeemable share capital or securities in that company is a non-qualifying distribution.[1] This may entitle the recipient shareholder to receive future dividends declared on the bonus shares issued; such dividends will then be qualifying distributions at the time that the dividend is paid.

Second, a distribution made by a company of a bonus issue of shares in another company, is a non-qualifying distribution.[2]

---

[1] TA 1988, s 14(2)(*a*).
[2] TA 1988, s 14(2)(*b*).

Definition

[26.04] (1) **Section 209(2)(a). Dividends, including a capital dividend.** A dividend is regarded as paid when it becomes due and payable,[1] that is when it becomes an enforceable debt, not necessarily the date of the resolution. The directors have power to stipulate the date of payment of a final dividend and a dividend is treated as paid on the date thus stipulated. If no date is given in the Directors' Resolution, payment of the dividend is, prima facie, due when declared and so creates an immediate debt. An interim dividend resolved upon

[26.04] Distributions

by the directors may be reviewed by them and so does not create an immediate debt.[2] A dividend which has been waived in advance of its date of payment will be effective to prevent the income from accruing to the shareholder.[3]

The amount on which the recipient will be taxed depends on whether he is entitled to a tax credit; if he is so entitled his income will be the sum of the dividend and the credit and, if not so entitled, the amount of the dividend.

The reference to a capital dividend is probably otiose. A dividend paid out of capital is still a dividend but the matter had given rise to problems before the introduction of corporation tax in 1965.[4]

Simon's Taxes D5.110.

---

[1] TA 1988, s 834(3).
[2] *Potel v IRC* [1971] 2 All ER 504, 46 TC 658.
[3] On IHT consequences see infra, § **39.20** (4).
[4] Wilson *Tax-efficient extraction of cash from companies* § **2A.24**.

[26.05] (2) Section 209(2)(b). **Any other distribution out of the assets of the company,** in cash or otherwise.

A payment will not be within this category if it represents a repayment of capital on the share nor if, and to the extent that, new consideration is received by the company for the distribution.[1] Consideration is new if it is external to the company, that is, it is not provided directly or indirectly by the company itself.[2] So a bonus issue is not a distribution since there is no cost to the company; nor is a rights issue since the consideration is new.

The issue of a bonus issue of *redeemable* shares may give rise to other consequences.[3]

The purchase by a company of its own shares from its shareholders will give rise to distribution treatment under head (2) unless special rules otherwise direct.[4] The amount of the distribution must allow for the deduction of the consideration originally paid for them but there is no indexation provision.

Simon's Taxes D5.130.

---

[1] TA 1988, s 209(2)(*b*), but note TA 1988, s 209(5) and (6).
[2] TA 1988, s 254(1).
[3] Infra, § **26.10**.
[4] Infra, § **26.20**.

[26.06] (3) Section 209(2)(c). The issue of any *redeemable* share capital or any security issued by the company in respect of shares or securities is a distribution unless it is wholly or in part for new consideration.[1] Where part of the amount issued is not referable to the new consideration the excess is treated as a distribution. Thus the issue of bonus redeemable preference shares, or debentures or loan stock in A Ltd by A Ltd are all treated as distributions. This definition[2] does not cover the non-redeemable bonus share; the mere prospect of an eventual return of capital on a winding up does not make an ordinary share redeemable. Bonus securities on the other hand are in their nature redeemable and therefore fall within the term distribution.

The redemption of bonus securities or bonus redeemable share capital is a distribution.[3]

Simon's Taxes D5.131.

[1] Defined in TA 1988, s 254(1).
[2] TA 1988, s 254(1).
[3] TA 1988, ss 210, 211; infra, §§ **26.10–26.11**.

Interest payments

[26.07] (4) **Section 209(2)(d) and (2)(da).** By s 209(2)(*d*) any interest (or other distribution out of the assets of the company in respect of its securities) will be a distribution if the consideration given by the company represents more than a reasonable commercial return. This rule only applies to the amount of interest which exceeds that reasonable commercial return.[1]

In determining what is a reasonable commercial return, any premium paid on issue is taken into account.[2] If the amount repaid exceeds the amount paid on issue, the determination is to be made by reference only to the amount paid on issue.[3] This last rule is subject to two exceptions; the first is if the amount repaid is linked to the issuer's shares (or those of an associated company).[4] The second is if there are hedging arrangements relating to the securities which will result in a mismatch between the deduction for the interest and the taxation of the return on the hedge.[5]

The general rule is that interest paid on a security where the interest is to any extent dependent on the results of the company business is treated as a distribution.[6] However, some companies have issued "ratchet loans", which have the provision that interest falls as results improve (and interest increases as the results deteriorate). Any payment of interest under such a ratchet loan, when made after 20 March 2001, is treated as interest (that is, TA 1988, s 209(2)(*e*)(iii) is disapplied) and not as a dividend.[7]

Simon's Taxes D5.120.

[1] TA 1988, s 209(2)(*d*).
[2] TA 1988, s 209(3A).
[3] TA 1988, s 209(3AA).
[4] TA 1988, s 290(A).
[5] TA 1988, s 209(B).
[6] TA 1988, s 209(2)(*e*)(iii).
[7] FA 2000, s 86.

[26.08] (5) **Section 209(2)(e).** Certain interest payments are treated as distributions in full. Although interest payments on debentures are not within

[26.08] Distributions

the term distribution, and therefore are deductible in computing profits, there are rules designed to equate debenture interest payments with dividends where the debenture is more like a share than a genuine debenture.[1] So if the debentures had themselves been distributions, any interest or other distribution of assets in respect of those securities are treated as distributions. Also, payments of interest on securities which are convertible directly or indirectly into shares of the company or carry a right to receive shares in or securities of the company are distributions unless the initial securities are quoted on the Stock Exchange or are on terms comparable with those of quoted securities. Interest payments in respect of securities under which the consideration given by the company for the use of the principal secured is to any extent dependent on the result of the company's business are treated as distributions where the return is at more than a reasonable commercial rate.[2] Finally interest on certain securities "connected with" shares of the company is caught.

(6) **Section 209(4).** Also within the definition is any excess in the market value of an asset transferred by a company to its members[3] or of a liability transferred to a company over any new consideration given. Consideration is new if it is external to the company, that is, it is not provided directly or indirectly by the company.[4] Special rules apply to transfers by subsidiary companies to parents or between truly independent companies.[5]

Section 212 provides an override to the distribution treatment imposed by s 209(2).[6] The payment falls to being treated as interest provided it is paid to another company that is within the charge to corporation tax. However, any excess caught by s 209(2)(d) is treated as a distribution. There is an override for some pre-1982 loans which serves to retain distribution treatment.

Simon's Taxes D5.121, D5.123–125.

---

[1] TA 1988, s 209(2)(e).
[2] TA 1988, s 209(2)(e) applying s 209(2)(d).
[3] On the definition of member of company see Companies Act 2006, s 112.
[4] TA 1988, s 209(4).
[5] TA 1988, s 209(5) and (6).
[6] TA 1988, s 212(1).

[26.09] (7) **Section 209(2)(e)(vii).** The boundary between distribution and debt has been further highlighted by the phenomenon of the perpetual debt instrument under which a loan is not repaid, commonly known as equity notes. A decision of the Special Commissioners held that payments of interest under such instruments were interest rather than dividends for the purpose of the relevant double tax treaty and that they were not distributions under the present definition. This led to a tax asymmetry between the US and the UK. Money would be borrowed in the US where interest would be deductible; the payment would then be moved to an associated company in the UK as a debt; the repatriation of that money to the US as interest meant that no tax was charged or withheld by the UK tax authorities.[1] In consequence payments made on or after 15 May 1992[2] are distributions if the equity notes are issued by one company and held by a company which is associated with the issuing company or is a funded company. An equity note is elaborately defined but broadly means one which is not redeemable within 50 years from the date of issue; redeemability is defined in terms of the real world.[3] Companies are associated if one is a 75% subsidiary of the other or they are both 75% subsidiaries of a third company.[4] A company is a funded company if there are arrangements involving the company being put in funds (directly or indirectly) by the issuing company or by a company associated with the issuing company.[5] Although the Revenue contemplated an appeal[6] none was ever taken.

[1] HC Official Report, Standing Committee B, 30 June 1992, col 439, 440.
[2] TA 1988, s 209(2)(e)(vii); see also Inland Revenue press release, 15 May 1992, *Simon's Tax Intelligence* 1992, p 519; for history from Revenue standpoint see HMRC International Tax Handbook, para 1249.
[3] TA 1988, s 209(9).
[4] TA 1988, s 209(10).
[5] TA 1988, s 209 (11); on association see F(No 2)A 1992, s 209(10), supra.
[6] HC Official Report, 14 May 1992, cols 779, 780.

Certain repayments of share capital

[26.10] The rule that a distribution out of the assets of the company in respect of shares is a distribution expressly excludes a repayment of capital. TA 1988 goes on to provide two important qualifications of this rule. The first is TA 1988, s 211 which applies where a company has issued (after 6 April 1965), or paid up (after 6 April 1973) any share capital otherwise than for new consideration, and the amount so paid up was not a qualifying distribution at that time. In such circumstances a subsequent distribution in respect of the capital is not to be treated as a repayment of capital; it will therefore be treated as a distribution with the usual consequences for the receipt.

Since neither a bonus issue of paid up irredeemable shares nor the repayment of share capital are distributions avoidance could be rife. Thus, if a company had £10,000 to distribute it would be unwise for the Revenue—from their point of view—to allow the company to capitalise the reserve and distribute it by way of bonus shares and then repay the bonus capital without at any stage falling foul of the distribution rules. The effect of TA 1988, s 211 is that if a company has made a bonus issue which was not treated as a distribution, repayments of such share capital are so treated to the extent to which those repayments of capital exceed the amount paid up on the share.[1] So if the company had an issued share capital of 20,000 £1 shares and it distributed by way of bonus 10,000 fully paid up £1 shares and it then made a reduction of capital of 50p per share on all 30,000 issued shares, the payments to shareholders would amount to £15,000 of which £10,000 would be treated as distribution and £5,000 as repayment of capital. So one can say that to the extent that value has been distributed by way of non-distributions, subsequent repayments of capital will be treated as distributions. In applying this rule any previous repayments are brought into account.[2]

There are special rules for premiums. A premium paid on the redemption is not treated as a return of capital.[3] If the share was issued at a premium which represented new consideration, the amount of the premium is to be treated as

[26.10] Distributions

part of the share capital and so the repayment of the premium will fall outside TA 1988, s 211.[4] This exception does not apply where the premium has been applied in paying up share capital.[5]

The ambit of TA 1988, s 211 is subject to a time limit. A distribution in respect of an irredeemable share originally issued as a bonus which is made more than ten years after the issue will escape s 211 provided the company is not closely controlled.[6]

Simon's Taxes D5.141.

---

[1] TA 1988, s 211.
[2] TA 1988, s 211(3).
[3] TA 1988, s 211(7).
[4] TA 1988, s 211(5).
[5] TA 1988, s 211(6); the share capital may have been paid up under Companies Act 1985, s 130.
[6] TA 1988, s 211(2). The definition of control is by reference to TA 1988, s 704 (supra, § **4.25**) which refers to TA 1988, s 416; infra, § **29.03**.

Repayment of share capital followed by bonus issue

[26.11] The second provision is TA 1988, s 210 which deals with the situation in which the repayment of share capital is followed by a bonus issue. The amount treated as a distribution is the amount paid up on the new shares or the amount repaid on the old shares whichever is the lower.

EXAMPLE

A Ltd repaid 50p per £ on its £20,000 ordinary stock; the nominal value of the stock is reduced to £10,000. This stock was originally issued wholly for new consideration so no distribution arose on the repayment. Two years later A Ltd capitalises its reserves and makes a distribution of stock on the basis of 1 for every £5 stock held. The amount paid up is £2,000. As this is less than the amount repaid (£10,000), the whole £2,000 will be a qualifying distribution.

This rule is modified in two important ways. First there is an exception for preference shares issued before 6 April 1965 or issued after that time but for new consideration.[1] Secondly, as with TA 1988, s 211, there is a time limit. Where the new shares are irredeemable bonus shares issued more than ten years after the reduction in share capital, TA 1988, s 210 applies only where the company is closely controlled.[2]

Simon's Taxes D6.221.

---

[1] TA 1988, s 210(2).
[2] TA 1988, s 210(3); control is defined by reference to TA 1988, s 704, on which see supra, § **4.26** which in turn refers to TA 1988, s 416; infra, § **29.03**.

Tax on distributions

UK resident individuals

[26.12] The amount charged to tax is the amount of the distribution plus the amount of the credit.[1] An individual can set the credit against his total income. This income is treated for higher rate purposes as the highest part of his income.[2]

There is no tax credit in respect of a distribution by a non-resident company.

Simon's Taxes E1.412–414.

---

[1] Since 6 April 1999, the credit has been one-ninth (that is, 10% of the gross), TA 1988, ss 20(2), 231(1A).
[2] ITA 2007, s 16(3).

Non-resident individuals

[26.13] Statute[1] limits the liability of a non-resident to UK taxation. Unless there is a chargeable UK representative of the foreign taxpayer, the effect of these provisions is to remove any liability to UK income tax on a dividend received by an individual not resident in the UK (see infra § **36.02**).

Where there is a chargeable UK representative[2] of the non-resident taxpayer, it is necessary to consider the availability of the tax credit attached to a dividend declared by a company within the charge to UK corporation tax. A tax credit is, in general, available only to UK residents.[3] However, credit may be claimed by an individual who is not resident if that individual is entitled to personal allowances[4] or has an entitlement to the tax credit under the terms of Double Taxation Agreement.

Simon's Taxes E6.127.

---

[1] FA 1995, s 128(1), (2) and (3)(*a*).
[2] FA 1995, s 126(2) states that a branch or agency through which the non-resident carries on a trade, etc, alone or in partnership is a "UK representative" in relation to income connected with the branch or agency. FA 1995, s 127 specifies persons who are not treated as UK representatives for this purpose, which exempts most independent investment managers.
[3] ITTOIA 2005, s 397(1).
[4] Under TA 1988, s 232(1) referring to TA 1988, s 278; supra, § **6.10**.

[26.14] When a company makes a distribution to a non-resident with a UK representative who is not entitled to a tax credit, the non-resident is liable to income tax. There is no liability at the dividend ordinary rate (10%). If there is liability at the dividend upper rate (32.5%) the distribution is grossed up by the dividend ordinary rate and the non-resident is then treated as having

[26.14] Distributions

already paid tax at the dividend ordinary rate leaving a residual liability of 25% of the net dividend. Such a distribution cannot cover an annual payment within TA 1988, s 348[1].

[1] TA 1988, s 348.

Companies resident in the UK

[26.15] When the recipient is another company resident in the UK the qualifying distribution plus the credit is franked investment income and not subject to CT.[1] Likewise a non-qualifying distribution is not liable to CT.[2]

When a UK resident company received a dividend from a foreign company prior to 1 July 2009, the dividend received was charged to corporation tax.[3] FA 2009 introduced an exemption[4] from corporation tax for dividends and other distributions received by companies on or after 1 July 2009 from foreign companies. This change in policy was prompted, at least in part, by the Government's defeat in the FII Group Litigation case.[5]

For small groups (less than 50 employees and less than €10m turnover or less than €10m balance sheet assets), the exemption from corporation tax is available if the distribution is received from a company located in a country with which the UK has a double tax agreement containing a non-discrimination provision.[6] The payment of the distribution must also not be tax-deductible by the payer, and the payment must not be part of a tax avoidance scheme.

For groups which are not small, the exemption is available if the distribution is not a payment of interest that is treated as a distribution (under thin capitalisation rules), and is within an exempt class, and is not tax-deductible by the payer. The exempt classes[7] are:

- distributions from controlled companies;
- distributions in respect of non-redeemable ordinary shares;
- distributions from portfolio holdings;
- distributions from shares accounted for as liabilities under the loan relationships rules; and
- distributions derived from transactions which are not intended to avoid UK tax.

A controlled company is one which is either:

- a 51% subsidiary, controlled by the recipient of the distribution alone; or
- a joint venture, controlled by the recipient and another person, each of whom holds at least 40% of the shares.

A portfolio holding is one in which the recipient of the distribution holds less than 10% of the issued share capital of the payer, and is entitled to less than 10% of the profits for distribution and also less than 10% of the assets of the payer available for distribution on a winding up.

There are various anti-avoidance provisions primarily targeting schemes intended to obtain a tax advantage by manipulating the exempt classes. In particular, distributions will not be exempt if they are connected with a payment for goods or services,[8] or if the distribution is disguised trading income.[9]

A company can elect that a distribution received from a foreign company not be treated as exempt.[10] This is principally likely to be useful where withholding tax will be imposed by the payer if the distribution is not taxable in the UK and deductions are available in the UK to reduce the taxable amount.

Simon's Taxes D5.101, D1.106.

[1] CTA 2009, s 1285.
[2] CTA 2009, s 1285.
[3] CTA 2009, 1305.
[4] FA 2009, s 34 and Sch 14, inserting CTA 2009, Part 9A
[5] *Test Claimants in the FII Group Litigation v HMRC* [2008] EWHC 2893 (Ch).
[6] CTA 2009, ss 931B, 931C, inserted by FA 2009, Sch 14.
[7] CTA 2009, ss 931E–931I, inserted by FA 2009, Sch 14.
[8] CTA 2009, s 931P, inserted by FA 2009, Sch 14.
[9] CTA 2009, s 931Q, inserted by FA 2009, Sch 14.
[10] CTA 2009, s 931R, inserted by FA 2009, Sch 14.

Non-resident companies

[26.16] Statute[1] limits the liability of a non-resident company to UK taxation; the effect of these provisions is to remove any liability to UK tax on a dividend received by a company not resident in the UK (see infra § **36.02**).

It is possible for double tax treaty to provide for repayment of part of the tax credit, even though there would be no repayment if the dividend had been received by a UK-resident company. So when the recipient is a Dutch corporation which holds at least 10% of the voting shares of the paying UK company, the Dutch corporation is entitled to a repayment of one-half of the tax credit but with a withholding tax of 5% of the sum of the dividend and the half-credit. So if £9,000 was paid and the ordinary tax credit was £1,000, the Dutch corporation is entitled to repayment of £500 but with a withholding tax of 5% of £9,450, ie £470, the net repayment is only £25.[2]

The compatibility of this double taxation treaty rule with the principles of EC law where the shareholder company is resident in another member state was considered in *Océ van Grinten NV v IRC*.[3] The ECJ considered the application of arts 5(1) and 7(2) of the Parent and Subsidiary Directive[4] to UK tax treaties. The Directive required dividends between such companies free of withholding tax.

The ECJ separated the payment into the charge on the dividend and the charge on the credit. They held that the first part came within art 5 of the Directive, since it was a direct charge on the dividend, the charge was proportional to the amount of the dividends, and the taxable person was the parent company. They then held that the second part did not come within art 5; the tax credit was a fiscal instrument designed to avoid double taxation, in economic terms,

[26.16] Distributions

in the hands, first, of the subsidiary and then of the parent receiving dividends, of the profits distributed as dividends. It did not constitute income from shares. That was borne out, inter alia, by the fact that the counterpart of the 5% charge was the obligation of deduction in the Netherlands under art 22 of the treaty. However they went on to hold that the first part was saved by art 7(2); the article had been drawn up to take account of the UK system under which the distribution of dividends was accompanied by a right to payment of a partial tax credit where a double taxation agreement so provided. Regard being had to all the circumstances, the withholding tax at issue could be considered as falling within a body of agreement-based provisions relating to the payment of tax credits to dividend recipients and thereby designed to mitigate double taxation.

[1] FA 2003, s 151, which rewrites FA 1995, 128 to reflect the change from "branch or agency" to "permanent establishment".
[2] UK/Netherlands Double Taxation Treaty, SI 1980/1961, art 10(3)(c).
[3] (case C-58/01) [2003] STC 1248.
[4] EC Council Directive 90/435.

Post-1999 Shadow ACT

[26.17] The concept of shadow ACT was introduced with the abolition of advanced corporation tax with effect from 6 April 1999 to give a measure of relief for any surplus ACT which had built up by that date and had not been relieved. For a discussion of shadow ACT, see the 2005–06 and earlier editions of this book.

Stock dividends

[26.18] When a person has an option[1] to receive either a dividend or additional share capital, special rules treat the share capital so issued as giving rise to a charge to tax on the recipient. The recipient may be liable to the upper rate of tax.

A higher-rate taxpayer selling a non-trading company was previously in a better position receiving a qualifying distribution, rather than suffering a charge to capital gains tax on a sale of shares in the company. However, that higher-rate taxpayer pays an effective rate of 25% income tax on the dividend received, compared to a rate now of 18% on the element of the receipt that will constitute a capital gain and so will generally prefer to pay capital gains tax. A basic rate taxpayer, however, will pay no additional income tax by virtue of the qualifying distribution received and so will continue to be in a better position.

Prior to the changes to capital gains tax, a higher-rate taxpayer would pay an effective tax rate of 25% on the stock dividend, but would have paid 40% capital gains tax on the sale of shares in a non-trading company (assuming business asset taper relief was not available). A planning technique was to issue a stock dividend prior to a sale of a company with the stock dividend calculated to absorb the charge which would otherwise be treated as a capital gain,[2] leaving the balance of the consideration to be received on the sale equal to the index-based cost of the individual shareholding. There was no liability to ordinary rate income tax. These rules also apply if the shareholder has shares which carry the right to receive bonus share capital[3] and that right is conferred by the terms on which the shares were issued (or later varied if bonus share capital is then issued). It is inherent in every share that it carries the right to any scrip issue, the right arising from the articles of association, but it seems likely that the provision will not be given so wide a scope.[4]

These rules apply only to stock dividends paid by companies resident in the UK.

A stock dividend received by trustees of a discretionary trust is treated as income available for accumulation and the additional tax charge under TA 1988, s 686 is applied.[5]

---

[1] Defined in TA 1988, s 251(1)(c). The failure to exercise a right is taken to be the exercise of the option.
[2] When taper relief was available against a gain this approach was unattractive as the charge to capital gains tax was on only 50% or 25% of the gain arising and, hence, the capital gain attracted an effective rate of tax of 20% or 10% when enjoyed by a higher rate taxpayer. For a company, a stock dividend could be attractive, as the company itself is not required to make a cash payment to the individual shareholders.
[3] Meaning share capital issued otherwise than wholly for new consideration: TA 1988, s 251(1)(a).
[4] C Official Report, 18 July 1975, Vol 895, col 1881.
[5] *Howell v Trippier* [2004] EWCA Civ 885, [2004] STC 1245; see supra, § **13.10**.

[26.19] Liability is based on "the cash equivalent of the share capital," usually the cash dividend alternative.[1] The market value of the shares is substituted where the dividend is greater or smaller by 15% or more[2] than that.

The "cash equivalent of the share capital" is grossed up at the dividend ordinary rate and forms part of his income.

---

[1] ITTOIA 2005, s 412(1). On trusts and estates see ITTOIA 2005, s 410(3) and (4).
[2] On tax treatment where an enhanced stock dividend is received by a trust see statement of practice SP 4/94; **Simon's Taxes Division G1.2**.

Purchase by a company of its own shares and treasury shares

[26.20] Provision was made in the Companies Act 1981, ss 45, 46[1] for a company to issue redeemable equity shares and to purchase its own shares,

[26.20] Distributions

subject to authorisation in the company's memorandum and articles of association and to various conditions imposed by the Act.

Any excess of the redemption proceeds over the amount subscribed for the shares would constitute a qualifying distribution under TA 1988, s 209(2)(b) and so be treated in the same way as a dividend. In such circumstances there is also a disposal for capital gains purposes. There may be advantages to the individual to take the receipt by way of capital gain rather than income, depending on their personal CGT or income tax position.

Prior to November 1996, it was common practice for a company to purchase its own shares in such a way as to deny CGT treatment where the shares being purchased were from a second company. The second company then used the tax credit to frank its own dividend, or elected under TA 1988, s 242 for the tax credit to be set off against franked investment income, leading to repayment, see infra. The Revenue estimate that up to £400,000,000 of tax was lost by use of this strategem. Today with the abolition of ACT and the franking system the income is simply a qualifying distribution complete with tax credit for the vendor.[2] However, the vendor company would have an advantage if the receipt were treated as franked investment income. The Revenue argue[3] that such a receipt, being exempt from corporation tax on income, should none the less be subject to corporation tax as a capital gain. The Revenue's argument was upheld by the Court of Appeal.[4]

Under company law, a listed company is able to hold its own shares that it has purchased[5] until the company subsequently sells the shares, transfers them to an employee share scheme or cancels them. Such shares are commonly called "Treasury shares". For tax purposes, the shares are treated as cancelled immediately on purchase, whether or not the company actually cancels the shares.[6] If the purchased shares are subsequently sold to another person, the shares sold are treated as newly-issued shares.[7]

A company's holding in its own shares can be taken into account when, generally speaking, the company reorganises its share capital.[8]

Simon's Taxes C2.1513.

---

[1] Now Companies Act 1985, ss 159–162 and Companies Act 2006, ss 684–686, and Part 18, Chapter 4.
[2] From 1996 until 1999 the distribution fell under the foreign income dividend scheme so that any ACT was recoverable but there was no tax credit. FA 1997, Sch 7, para 2, amending TA 1988, s 246A but repealed by F(No 2)A 1997, s 36(3).
[3] In SP 4/89
[4] *Strand Futures and Options Ltd v Vojak* [2004] STC 64, CA.
[5] Under Companies (Acquisition of Own Shares) (Treasury Shares) Regulations 2003, SI 2003/1116.
[6] FA 2003, s 195(2).
[7] FA 2003, s 195(8)(a).
[8] FA 2003, s 195(11).

Purchase of own and treasury shares [26.23]

Conditions for disposal by the shareholder to be treated as a capital gain

[26.21] This sections and those which follow (§§ 26.23–26.31) outline the circumstances in which CGT treatment is applied. If any of these conditions are not satisfied, the company purchase of its own shares is treated as a distribution by the company and tax is applied accordingly.

The company buying its own shares must be an unquoted company;[1] the exclusion of quoted companies is based on the belief that a ready market exists for the disposal of shares in such companies. The company is unquoted if its shares are not listed on the official list of a stock exchange; shares dealt in on the Alternative Investment Market (AIM) qualify as unquoted shares.[2] A company which is a 51% subsidiary of a quoted company is a quoted company.[3]

Simon's Taxes D6.610–618.

---

[1] TA 1988, s 229(1)(*a*).

[2] TA 1988, s 219(1) gives the requirement that the company is "an unquoted trading company" (or the unquoted holding company of a trading group). "Unquoted company" is defined in s 229(1) as "a company which is neither a quoted company nor a 51% subsidiary of a quoted company", "quoted company" being defined in the same section as "a company whose shares (or any class of shares) are listed in the official list of a stock exchange". This is interpreted by HMRC as meaning a "recognised stock exchange", which is defined by TA 1988, s 841(1) as "(a) the stock exchange; and (b) any such stock exchange outside the United Kingdom . . . designated . . . as a recognised stock exchange by order made by the board". A series of statutory instruments designate foreign stock exchanges that are recognised stock exchanges. The full list is given on www.hmrc.gov.uk/fid/rse.htm. Shares on the Alternative Investment Market are not listed on the London exchange and, hence, are "unquoted shares" within the meaning of this definition, except for the rare situation where a company has shares on AIM but has another class of shares dealt with in a recognised stock exchange.

[3] TA 1988, s 229.

[26.22] The company must be a trading company or a holding company of a trading group. For these purposes a holding company is one whose main business (apart from any trading activities of its own) is to hold shares in one or more 75% subsidiaries.[1] A trading group will consist of a holding company or one or more 75% subsidiaries where the main business of the members taken together is the carrying on of the trade or trades. For these purposes dealing in shares, securities, land or futures does not qualify.[2]

Simon's Taxes D6.610–618.

---

[1] TA 1988, s 229.
[2] TA 1988, s 229.

[26.23] Unless the sale is needed to pay IHT on a death (see **26.28**), the purchase of shares must be made wholly or mainly to benefit the trade of the

[26.23] Distributions

company concerned or of any of its 75% subsidiaries.[1] Clearly, a company purchase of its own shares is likely to be of benefit to the individual shareholder making the sale. The benefit may be that the gain is a small part of the proceeds, or that CGT taper relief gives a lower effective rate of tax[2] or it may be that there is not an easy market for the sale of the shares, other than purchase of the company. The fact that the shareholder benefits does not mean that the test that the main benefit of the company buying the shares is the benefit to the trade of the company cannot be satisfied. Typically, the rationale is presented (and, typically, accepted in the Revenue Clearance) as concentrating the ownership of the company after the sale in the hands of those who have direction and management of the company. This is recognised in the Revenue statement:[3]

> If the purpose is to ensure that an unwilling shareholder who wishes to end his association with the company does not sell his shares to someone who might not be acceptable to the other shareholders, the purchase will normally be regarded as benefiting the company's trade.

Frequently, the vendor of shares purchased by the company has been a director as well as a shareholder and received a substantial part of his income from the company. The Revenue view[4] is:

> if although the vendor is selling all his shares he is retaining some other connection with the company—for example, a directorship or an appointment as consultant—it would seem unlikely that the transaction could benefit the company's trade, so the trade benefit test will probably not be satisfied.

Revenue practice is to deny clearance where there is not a substantial reduction. It is difficult to see any justification in statute for the Revenue's position. The statutory requirement focuses solely on the company. It could be argued that failure to employ an individual with particular skills that are necessary for the continuing trade of the company would be a denial of a benefit to the trade, rather than the converse.[5]

In addition to directing that the purchase must be to benefit a trade of the company, the legislation provides that the purchase must not form part of a scheme or arrangement, a main purpose of which is either to avoid tax or to enable the shareholder to share in the company's profits otherwise than by receiving a dividend.[6]

Simon's Taxes D2.504–509A.

---

[1] TA 1988, s 219(1); on purchase to pay IHT see infra, § **26.28**. The purpose of benefiting the trade will not of itself make legal and other expenses associated with the purchase deductible—see Inland Revenue interpretation RI 4, **Simon's Taxes Division G3.**

[2] There are occasions when the tax payable on an income distribution is less than CGT payable. This can arise when the recipient has available the larger part of his/her basic rate band (and, hence, a income distribution attracts no additional charge to tax), or where the business asset rate of taper relief was not, or was only partially, available (such as, when shares were held before 6 April 2000). Where this is the case, it is usual to structure the transactions so that it fails the test for CGT treatment. It must be noted that CGT treatment does not require a claim; CGT

treatment is applied whenever the statutory tests are satisfied. Hence, to obtain income tax treatment, the arrangement must be structured so that the arrangement fails the tests for CGT treatment. The customary approach is to pass the shares to a nominee, so that the test for five years ownership is not satisfied: vide TA 1988, s 220(5).

[3] See statement of practice SP 2/82, para 2. The Revenue statement gives examples of unwilling shareholders as:

- an outside shareholder who has provided equity finance (whether or not with the expectation of redemption or sale to the company) and who now wishes to withdraw that finance;
- a controlling shareholder who is retiring as a director and wishes to make way for new management;
- personal representatives of a deceased shareholder, where they wish to realise the value of the shares;
- a legatee of a deceased shareholder, where he does not wish to hold shares in the company.

[4] See Statement of Practice SP 2/82, para 3. The Revenue statement says that: "the Board do not raise any objection if for sentimental reasons it is desired that a retiring director of a company should retain a small shareholding in it, not exceeding 5% of the issued share capital".

[5] The matter has not been satisfactorily tested in the courts. Only one case has been heard on the legislation relating to company purchase of own shares: in *Moody v Tyler* [2000] STC 296, the court declared that it could not interfere with the finding of facts made by the General Commissioners that a particular purchase by a company of its own shares was not made wholly or mainly for the purpose of benefiting a trade carried on by the company.

[6] TA 1988, s 219(1)(*a*).

[26.24] The vendor must meet certain residence requirements.[1] A shareholder whose shares are purchased must be resident and ordinarily resident in the UK in the year of assessment in which the shares are purchased. In the case of a company it is not necessary to be ordinarily resident. If the shares are held by a nominee both the nominee and the beneficial owner must be resident and ordinarily resident. The residence status of a personal representative is taken to be that of the deceased immediately before his death. The residence and ordinary residence of trustees is determined as for CGT.[2]

Simon's Taxes D6.610–618.

[1] TA 1988, s 220.
[2] The reference to CGT is now TCGA 1992, s 69.

[26.25] There are minimum holding period requirements for the vendor.[1] First, he must have owned the shares for at least five years at the time they are purchased by the company; however, if the shareholder acquired the shares from his spouse or civil partner, their period of ownership will be counted towards the five year condition—provided the transferor was then living with the vendor and was then the vendor's spouse or civil partner.[2] Where different shares are acquired at different times, a first in first out rule is applied.[3]

[26.25] Distributions

If the vendor became entitled to the shares on an intestacy or under the will of the previous owner, he may bring in both the period of ownership of the testator or intestate and that of the personal representatives; moreover the period is reduced to three years.[4] Where the vendor is the personal representative of a deceased owner, he may bring in the deceased's period of ownership; again the period is reduced to three years.[5]

Bonus share and other shares acquired on a company reconstruction, reorganisation or amalgamation are treated as acquired at the same time as the original holding in respect of which they are issued. However, this favourable treatment is not extended to rights issues or stock dividends.[6]

Simon's Taxes D6.610–618.

---

[1] TA 1988, s 220(5).
[2] TA 1988, s 220(6); however the period may not be added if the spouse or civil partner is still alive at the date of the purchase but no longer the vendor's spouse or civil partner living with him, ie they are divorced or separated.
[3] TA 1988, s 220(8).
[4] TA 1988, s 220(7).
[5] TA 1988, s 220(7).
[6] TA 1988, s 220(9).

[26.26] The vendor's interest in the company must either be completely eliminated or be substantially reduced as a result of the purchase of the shares by the company.[1] A reduction is not substantial if it is less than 25%.[2] If the company is a member of a 51% group it is the shareholder's interest in the group that must be reduced by at least 25%.[3] For these purposes the holdings of associates can be taken into account.[4] It is also necessary that there should be a corresponding reduction in shareholders' entitlement to profits.[5] If the shareholder sells all his shares to the company and does not retain shares in any company which is a member of the same group the 25% condition does not have to be fulfilled.[6] These rules are of great importance where the vendor retains shares of another class.

Where the vendor's holding is not eliminated he may be in difficulty meeting the requirement that the purchase must be for the sole or main purpose of benefiting the company's trade. Where his continuing presence is regarded as a danger to the trade the interest ought to be eliminated completely and the Revenue have indicated a firm line on this; their view is that the requirement will only[7] be satisfied if the interest retained was minimal or for sentimental reasons or, where the intention is to terminate the interest but this has to be achieved by more than one transaction (eg because the company cannot afford to buy all his shares at one time).[8] This last example is interesting since it raises the question whether a series of purchases by the company can be linked together so as to achieve the 25% reduction where no individual purchase meets that condition; such a linkage is allowed in the US under their step transaction doctrine but the doctrine has also had this effect where the taxpayer sells some shares and gives others away provided it is all part of the one plan; at this stage it is thought unlikely that the UK courts would accede to such an argument.

Simon's Taxes D6.610–618.

1. TA 1988, s 221.
2. TA 1988, s 221(4).
3. TA 1988, s 222(6).
4. TA 1988, s 221(2). The combined holdings of the vendor and the associate have to be reduced by at least 25% (TA 1988, s 222(3) which extends the rule in TA 1988, s 222(2) to the situation in which groups are involved) and TA 1988, s 224 (which provides that where the conditions are satisfied as to the combined holdings of the vendor and the associate and the vendor joined in to help the associate meet those conditions in all the conditions in TA 1988, ss 221–223 are to be treated as satisfied for both of them); for the definition of associate, see TA 1988, s 227.
5. TA 1988, s 221(5)–(8).
6. TA 1988, s 221.
7. There is some evidence that a more lenient attitude is adopted where the shares were acquired under an approved share option scheme since here the Revenue do not insist that the vendor should cease to be an employee; Simon's Taxes D6.610–618.
8. Statement of practice SP 2/82, para 3; Simon's Taxes Division G1.2.

[26.27] The purchase must not be part of a scheme or arrangement which is designed or likely to result in the vendor or any associate having an interest in the company such that if he had that interest immediately after the purchase any of the previous conditions would not be satisfied.[1] There is a conclusive presumption that transactions within one year of each other are part of such a scheme.[2]

The vendor must not immediately after the purchase be connected with the company or any other member of the group.[3]

Simon's Taxes D6.610–618.

1. TA 1988, s 223(2).
2. However succession to property on death is not regarded as a "transaction" for this purpose; see statement of practice SP 2/82, para 8; Simon's Taxes Division G1.2.
3. TA 1988, s 223(1); on the definition of "connected", see TA 1988, s 228.

[26.28] This special treatment is also available if the purchase is not for the benefit of the trade but the vendor needs the funds to discharge a liability to IHT arising on death. In these circumstances it is not necessary for conditions in supra, §§ **26.21–26.27**, to be met. The whole or substantially the whole of the payment must be paid in respect of the liability to IHT falling on the shareholder as a result of a death; this rule is applied after taking out the funds needed to pay any CGT liability consequent upon the purchase.[1]

The IHT payment must be made within two years of death and it must be shown that the liability could not have been met without undue hardship otherwise than through the purchase.[2] The attitude of the Revenue to the test of "undue hardship" was given in a statement in the House of Lords:[3]

[26.28] Distributions

Where the company has surplus funds sufficient to discharge the inheritance tax liability, the Revenue take the view that there would be no hardship since the liability could be met by dividend payments from the company.

Simon's Taxes D6.610–618.

[1] TA 1988, s 219(1)(b).
[2] TA 1988, s 219(2).
[3] House of Lords Written Answer by Lord Brabazon of Tara, Government spokesman in the Lords for the Treasury, 17 March 1988, Hansard Vol. 494, col 1349.

[26.29] If the conditions outlined above are complied with the transaction will be treated as a disposal by the shareholder for CGT purposes and not as a distribution. If the shareholder is a dealer in securities the transaction will be treated as a trading transaction not a distribution.[1]

The company may apply to the Revenue for advance clearance as to the treatment of any payment made by it for the purchase of shares. The procedure is available whether the purchase is for the benefit of the trade or is needed to pay IHT. The application must be made in writing to the Board giving full particulars of the transactions proposed. Within 30 days the Board must either request further particulars or give a decision on the application.[2]

Simon's Taxes D6.610–618.

[1] CTA 2009, s 130 and ITTOIA 2005, s 366(1).
[2] TA 1988, s 225.

[26.30] The method of taxing a company purchase of own shares is not as attractive for a corporate shareholder as may at first appear. When a company receives a dividend, the dividend is not counted as income of the company in computing the charge to corporation tax.[1] This does not, however, mean that the sum paid by a company to a corporate shareholder for a non-qualifying purchase of its own shares is a tax-free receipt. The Taxation of Chargeable Gains Act 1992 removes from the computation of a chargeable gain any sum that is taxed as income.[2] However, in *Strand Options and Futures v Vojak*[3] it was held that the effect of the rule that a distribution received by a company is not part of the company's income is that the sum received by a corporate shareholder on a company's purchase of its own shares is consideration in calculating the capital gain arising to that company on its disposal of the shareholding.[4]

[1] CTA 2009, s 1285.
[2] TCGA 1992, s 37(1) applied to corporation tax on capital gains by TCGA 1992, s 8(1).
[3] [2002] STC (SCD) 398.
[4] Having previously treated a distribution on a non-qualifying purchase by a company of its own shares as being non-taxable income in the hands of a recipient corporate shareholder, the Revenue changed its view by the issue on 19 April 1989 of statement of practice SP4/89. The analysis expounded in that statement of

practice was unsuccessfully challenged in *Strand Options and Futures Ltd v Vojak* [2004] STC 64, where the Court of Appeal held that TA 1988, s 208 does not exempt a charge to corporation tax on the distribution received in so far as the distribution was an element in the consideration received on the disposal of the shares for chargeable gains purposes.

27

Loan relationships, foreign exchange, intellectual property and Islamic finance

Loan relationships	PARA **27.01**
Foreign exchange gains and losses	PARA **27.11**
Derivative contracts	PARA **27.13**
Intellectual property	PARA **27.21**
Islamic finance	PARA **27.28**

Loan relationships

[27.01] Since 1 April 1996, corporate and government debt have been subject to a single regime called "loan relationships".[1] The provisions apply for corporation tax but not for income tax. The regime brings together interest and exchange movements arising on debt and the gain or loss arising from the holding of a financial instrument. All profits and gains arising from a loan relationship are assessed to corporation tax even if there is a foreign element. The scheme of the legislation is to bring together all loan relationships of the company. Where a loan is shared between companies, the appropriate part of the loan is treated separately in the separate companies. Thus, where a company is in partnership with other companies, or with individuals, each company partner computes separately loan relationship debits and credits arising on the money debt.[2]

The basic concept behind the loan relationship regime is that tax is to follow the accounting treatment adopted by the particular company. On this basis, in *HSBC Life (UK) Ltd v Stubbs*[3] it was held that transactions that are not treated as loans in the accounts of a finance company are not within the loan relationship provisions.

Provided a generally accepted accounting practice is used to prepre the company's accounts, the tax treatment follows the accounts treatment.[4]

The scheme of the loan relationships provisions was described by the Financial Secretary to the Treasury in the following terms:

> The basic rules are, first, that the tax system should recognise all debit and credit that arises from borrowing and lending . . . Second, these should be calculated according to authorised accounting methods . . . Third, the figures should follow those that are produced for non-tax purposes wherever they are acceptable . . . We are moving to a more simplified method of ensuring that debits, credits and taxation follow accounts . . . The clause simplifies our tax code, repeals some existing legislation and allows the strip gilt market to proceed. These matters are of great importance to us all . . . This reform is not about raising additional tax revenue. The estimated overall effect will be broadly neutral. It will undoubtedly benefit

[27.01] Loan relationships, etc.

everyone in the long run in that it is more coherent. But one group of people who will certainly lose will be the people who set up tax driven arrangements designed to profit at the Exchequer's expense from the weakness of the currency.

Under the loan relationship legislation, the old distinctions between income and capital are swept away. Many special statutory schemes were abolished for taxpayers subject to corporation tax: the accrued income scheme, the statutory provisions for deep gain securities, and deep discount securities. While most of these schemes remain in place for income tax some were simplified (see supra, § **11.17**).

In the loan relationship regime the distinction between yearly interest and short interest remains of importance only in respect of withholding tax[5] (infra, § **27.07**), the distinction is abolished for the purpose of establishing deductibility.

The legislation introduces the concepts of "trade interest" and "non-trade interest". The former is interest payable on a loan for the purpose of a trade. Relief for both is obtained by bringing the expense into the calculation of trading income subject to corporation tax.[6]

The manner in which loan relationship credits are calculated is considered in *Greene King No 1 Ltd v Adie*.[7]

Simon's Taxes D1.702.

---

[1] CTA 2009, Part 5 – originally introduced by FA 1996, ss 80–105 and Schs 8–11, with substantial elaboration of the provisions by subsequent Finance Acts, notably F(No 2)A 2005, Sch 8.
[2] CTA 2009, Pt 5, Ch 9. The Revenue view as to the manner in which this provision operates is given in Inland Revenue Tax Bulletin December 2002, pp 987–989.
[3] [2002] STC (SCD) 9.
[4] CTA 2009, s 307.
[5] The loan relationship legislation does not alter the obligation to withhold tax on payments, even where the interest received is taxed as part of the Case I profit of a company, Inland Revenue Tax Bulletin, August 1999, pp 685–686.
[6] CTA 2009, ss 297 and 301.
[7] [2005] STC (SCD) 398.

Definition

[27.02] The statutory provisions apply to a "loan relationship". This is defined in statute in one of two separate ways. First, a loan relationship arises where a company is a debtor or a creditor in respect of a money debt which arose as a result of a transaction for the lending of money,[1] so finance leases and hire purchase contracts are not loan relationships.[2] Second, it also arises where an instrument is issued for the purpose of representing security for, or the rights of a creditor or in respect of, a debt.[3] One of the critical words here is "security"; the issue of an invoice is not the issue of a security,[4] nor is the issue of a share.[5]

For the first alternative definition, a money debt is defined as one which is, or has at any time been, one that falls, or may at the option of the debtor or creditor fall to be settled by the payment of money or the transfer of a right to settlement, such as by the issue of a security,[6] or the issue or transfer of any shares and disregarding any other option exercisable by either party.

The second definition is provided to bring loan notes and promissory notes within the legislation. If there is no instrument issued, a debt does not fall within the second definition. In particular, "it does not extend to invoices or payments under guarantee . . . If there is a loan of money, the promissory note is covered; if there is not, then it is not".[7]

To stop the use of schemes in which an interest-like return on shares was generated in the form of a capital gain, certain shares are treated as if they were creditor loan relationships. These are of three kinds:

(a) shares subject to outstanding third party obligations to meet unpaid calls or contribute capital whose fair value is likely to increase at a rate which represents a return on an investment of money;
(b) shares whose fair value is likely to increase at a rate which represents a return on an investment of money but the increase in value is attributable to the assets of the company, or a scheme involving the shares and associated transactions;
(c) the shares increase in value, and the shares are redeemable at a sum above the issue price.[8]

A guarantee is outside the scope of the provisions since, in order for a loan relationship to exist the company must be a creditor or a debtor[9] and a guarantor is not, itself, in that relationship. This does not stop relief as a trading expense for a loss on a guarantee being called where the company carries on a trade of providing guarantees.

Simon's Taxes D1.703–705.

[1] CTA 2009, s 302.
[2] HMRC Corporate Finance Manual, para 5057a.
[3] CTA 2009, s 303(3).
[4] HMRC Corporate Finance Manual, para 5058a.
[5] CTA 2009, s 303(4).
[6] CTA 2009, s 303(1),(2).
[7] Statement by the Economic Secretary to the Treasury, HC Official Report, 28 February 1996, col 613.
[8] CTA 2009, ss 522–533 and Sch 1, para 367.
[9] CTA 2009, s 302.

Recognising credits and debits

[27.03] Income and expenditure is within the regime when it is credited or debited to the company's financial statements drawn up in accordance with generally accepted accounting practice.[1] If the financial statements for that year (or an earlier year) are not correct, then the amounts taken are those that would have been recognised if the statements had been correct.[2] Provision is also made for changes in accounting policy.[3]

[27.03] Loan relationships, etc.

Generally accepted accounting practice is defined to include accounts prepared in accordance with UK generally accepted accounting practice and accounts prepared in accordance with international financial report standards.[4] Gains and losses arising from intangible fixed assets are specifically excluded.[5]

Where interest paid is capitalised by the payer, the interest is, nevertheless, brought into the calculation for tax purposes and relief is obtained.

The expenses for which relief is available are restricted to those incurred in bringing the loan relationship into existence, making payments under that relationship, expenses incurred in ensuring that payments are received or expenses in relation to a "related transaction".[6]

A "related transaction" is defined as any disposal or acquisition of rights and liabilities under a loan relationship.[7] The concept of a related transaction is important because all profits or gains or losses arising from such transactions have to be brought into account. It covers not only sale or gift but also the surrender, redemption or release of a debt.[8]

Abortive expenditure, including the costs of setting up a loan relationship that is not subsequently proceeded with, is specifically allowed, as long as it falls within the categories of expenditure that are permitted where a transaction is taken to its anticipated conclusion.[9]

So, within the calculation of the tax charge, there will be brought interest payable, interest receivable, exchange gains, exchange losses, any discount, premiums gains and losses arising from the disposal of the instrument, any reimbursement required to a lender, the costs of obtaining loan finance such as bank fees, abortive expenditure in respect of loan finance that is not drawn down, early redemption penalties and costs in pursuing debtors.[10]

Simon's Taxes D1.716–717.

---

[1] These are defined in CTA 2009, s 308(1) as the profit and loss account, income statement, statement of recognised gains and losses, statement of changes in equity or any other statement of items brought into account in computing the company's profit and loss for the period. Amounts recognised in equity or shareholders' funds are also brought into account: CTA 2009, s 321.

[2] CTA 2009, ss 307, 309.

[3] CTA 2009, s 315–318.

[4] CTA 2009, s 509–510.

[5] CTA 2009, s 906.

[6] CTA 2009, s 307(4) and see Inland Revenue, Tax Bulletin, October 1996, p 336.

[7] CTA 2009, s 304.

[8] HMRC Corporate Finance Manual, para 5067; on repos and stock lending see CTA 2009, s 332.

[9] CTA 2009, s 329.

[10] HMRC Corporate Finance Manual, paras 5200–5300.

[27.04] There are a number of anti-avoidance rules. Thus one deals with the importing of a loan relationship where a loss arose at a time when the relationship was not subject to UK tax[1] and another imposes an exit charge on a company ceasing to be UK resident.[2]

A more wide ranging one bars relief for debits where or to the extent that the loan relationship was incurred for an unallowable purpose.[3] Furthermore, for accounting periods beginning after 30 September 2002 such payments are not allowable under any other provisions.[4] This tainting purpose may arise from the loan relationship itself or from a related transaction. Although a business or commercial purpose is normally an allowable purpose this will not be so if the purpose relates to an activity not within the charge to corporation tax eg the purposes of an overseas subsidiary (as opposed to an overseas branch none of whose profits are charged to corporation tax because any UK tax liability is wiped out by the overseas tax credit). Another example would be a company which is not carrying on any activity.[5] A Revenue example suggests a golf club raising a loan to finance construction of a new club house; here the interest paid would have to be apportioned into allowable (for non-members) and non-allowable (for members) because of the mutuality principle.[6]

FA 2009 introduces further anti-avoidance rules relating to disguised interest[7] and shares accounted for as liabilities.[8]

A tax avoidance purpose is not a business purpose, the concept of tax avoidance taking its familiar meaning in terms of a tax advantage under TA 1988, s 709. The Revenue will not give advice on the meaning of the term beyond the recitation of a ministerial mantra.[9]

Where a creditor loan relationship and debtor loan relationship are "matched" any amounts not fully recognised are to be brought into account in respect of the creditor loan relationship.[10]

Schemes involving securities where the terms changed significantly after issue in a way designed to create a tax advantage are also dealt with.[11] Transfers of income streams are also taxed as loan relationships.[12]

The debits and credits on transfers of loan relationships on non-arm's length terms are determined on the assumption that the transaction was entered into on arm's length terms.[13]

Simon's Taxes D1.725, D1.735, D1.787.

---

[1] CTA 2009, s 327.
[2] CTA 2009, s 321.
[3] CTA 2009, s 441; a similar rule applies for financial instruments generally, with effect from 26 July 2001: FA 2002, s 69.
[4] CTA 2009, s 441(4),(5).
[5] For Revenue views see Corporation Tax Manual para 12670 et seq.
[6] Note Revenue's opposite interest in this point in context of associated companies and small profits relief and cases cited at supra, § **25.34**, notes 7 and 8.
[7] CTA 2009, Pt 6, Ch 2A, inserted by FA 2009, s 48 and Sch 24.
[8] CTA 2009, Pt 6, Ch 6A, inserted by FA 2009, s 48 and Sch 24.
[9] For terms of mantra see Hansard, 28 March 1996, Finance Bill Report Stage, Columns 1192–1193 reprinted in Corporation Tax Manual, para 12673. The section is not to be applied without reference to CD(SIS1), see COT12681.
[10] CTA 2009, s 311.
[11] CTA 2009, s 454.
[12] FA 2009, s 49, Sch 25 and CTA 2009, Pt 6, Ch 2B.

[27.04] Loan relationships, etc.

[13] CTA 2009, ss 444–445 unless the parties are connected in which case the provision of TA 1988, Sch 28AA have precedence or the grouping provisions apply, infra, § 28.26

Deficits on loan relationships

[27.05] The legislation introduces the concepts of "trade interest" and "non-trade interest". The former covers a relationship to which it is a party for the purposes of a trade carried on by it and interest payable on a loan to purchase a trading asset. Relief is obtained by bringing the expense into the calculation of profit subject to tax as trading income.[1] Where the company is the creditor rather than the debtor a stricter test applies—the loan must be an integral part of the trade.[2] Interest incurred on pre-trading loans is the subject of a special provision.[3] Where a deficit arises from such trading loan relationships, relief is given by the rules applying to trading income.[4]

Non-trade interest is brought into the calculation of the sum subject to corporation tax on income.[5] A company with a non-trading deficit on its loan relationships can claim for the whole or part of the deficit to be set against any of its profits of the deficit period;[6] or to be eligible for group relief;[7] or to be carried back against profits for loan relationships of earlier accounting periods;[8] or to be carried forward against non-trading profits of the next accounting period.[9] FA 2002 provides for an automatic carry forward of a non-trading deficit that has not already been surrendered or set off. A claim may be made to utilise any part of the deficit (ie it does not have to be for the total amount) in the following (or any subsequent) accounting periods, eg because of the availability of double taxation credit relief which would otherwise be wasted.[10] The claim must be made within two years of the end of the period into which the loss is carried.[11]

Relief for losses can be obtained by carrying back on a last in first out basis against the company's previous 12 months' profits arising from its non-trading loan relationships.[12]

Different claims may be made for different parts of the deficit for any period.[13]

All claims must be made within two years of the end of the accounting period, with discretion given to the Board of HMRC to allow an extension of this period.[14]

Where a charitable company suffers a deficit in loan relationships, no relief can be obtained for that deficit, neither within the charitable company nor by group relief.[15] This does not, however, restrict the relief available to a company that is a subsidiary of a charitable company, when it is the non-charitable subsidiary that has suffered the deficit.

Simon's Taxes D1.730, D1.776.

[1] CTA 2009, s 297.
[2] CTA 2009, s 298(1) and HMRC Corporation Tax Manual, para 12221 (see also *Nuclear Electric Ltd v Bradley* [1996] STC 405, HL).

[3] CTA 2009, s 330(3)–(5).
[4] CTA 2009, s 297.
[5] CTA 2009, s 301.
[6] CTA 2009, s 461.
[7] TA 1988, ss 403(1)(a) and 403ZC.
[8] CTA 2009, s 457.
[9] CTA 2009, s 457.
[10] CTA 2009, s 457.
[11] CTA 2009, s 460.
[12] CTA 2009, ss 459, 463(5).
[13] CTA 2009, s 460.
[14] CTA 2009, s 460(1)
[15] CTA 2009, s 459(3).

Carry back of losses

[27.06] Priority is given for relief against profits of the current accounting period. Losses to be carried back are restricted to those that exceed the income of the current period against which such losses could be relieved.[1] Subject to this, a loss can be carried back, whether it is a deficit on a trading relationship or on a non-trading relationship. The mechanism, however, differs.[2]

The carry back of a non-trading loss is against non-trading loan relationship profits of the preceding 12 months, with relief being applied in a later year before an earlier year. In no case can relief be obtained against a period before 1 April 1996.[3] The following reliefs are given before relief is obtained for a carry back loss:

(1) Relief under TA 1988, s 338 for charges on income that are made exclusively for the purposes of a trade.[4]
(2) Relief under TA 1988, s 392A for property business or s 393A for trading losses.[5]
(3) A claim under CTA 2009, s 457 for the surrender of non-trading loan relationship losses within a group.[6]
(4) In the case of an investment company, any capital allowance for machinery and plant, any management expenses and any charges on income.[7]

Simon's Taxes D1.775.

[1] CTA 2009, s 462(2).
[2] Relief for a trading relationship deficit is obtained as part of a loss relief claim under TA 1988, s 393A. Relief for a deficit on a non-trading relationship is obtained under CTA 2009, s 462.
[3] CTA 2009, s 463(1)–(3).
[4] CTA 2009, s 463(5)
[5] CTA 2009, s 463(5).
[6] CTA 2009, s 463(5).

[27.06] Loan relationships, etc.

[7] CTA 2009, s 463(5) in respect of reliefs under CAA 1990, s 28, TA 1988, s 75 and TA 1988, s 338.

Connected party transactions

[27.07] Any loan relationship with a connected person is required to be dealt with under an amortised cost basis of accounting and not under a fair value basis of accounting.[1] An amortised cost basis of accounting is one under which an asset or liability is shown in the accounts at cost adjusted for amortisation and any impairment, repayment or release; fair value accounting means a basis under which assets or liabilities are shown at their fair value.[2]

Where the interest is paid more than 12 months late and the lender does not take credits into account (usually because the lender is a non-UK group member), the borrower (on a connected party loan relationship) is unable to get relief for the corresponding debit during the period in which it accrues.[3] Any relief is deferred to the period in which it is paid. There is an equivalent provision in respect of relief for a discount; this only being available if the full amount of the discount is brought into account for each period by the creditor and is thus taxable. If this is not the case then the discount may only be recognised at redemption.[4] For a close company, no relief is available on a discount held by a participator or his associate until the discounted security is redeemed.[5]

Two companies are treated as connected if, at any time in the accounting period one company has control of the other or the two companies are under common control.[6] Additionally, (for this purpose of late interest only) two companies are also considered connected in certain other circumstances. Broadly, these are when the debtor is a close company and the creditor is one of the participators in the close company, the debtor (or creditor) has a major interest[7] in the other company or when the loan is made by the trustees of an occupational pension scheme.[8] The Revenue have indicated that where the only link between the parties is a loan relationship they will not treat the parties as connected persons even where the relationships would give the lender the greater part of the assets on a winding-up.[9]

Losses suffered on a connected party debt generally do not attract relief, even when they arise on the sale of the debt to an unconnected third party[10] or the connection has ceased.[11] Moreover, a charge is imposed on a debtor where a connected company acquires the debtor's impaired debt from an unconnected third party.[12] However, from 1 October 2002 it is possible to obtain relief if the creditor company goes into insolvent liquidation. The quid pro quo for the denial of relief to the creditor is that a connected debtor is not charged on any release whereas an unconnected debtor generally would be. The Revenue consider the possibility of a purchase discount where the parties are connected but the loan is repayable on demand; the likelihood of the payment being demanded at once is to be considered.[13]

A specific rule brings into account credits or debits arising on a change of accounting basis following the creation or cessation of a connection between the creditor and debtor[14] and schemes which diverted some of the return on a creditor loan relationship to a connected party have now been blocked.[15]

Simon's Taxes C1.740.

1. CTA 2009, s 349–351.
2. CTA 2009, s 313.
3. CTA 2009, s 372–373.
4. CTA 2009, ss 406–407.
5. CTA 2009, s 409.
6. CTA 2009, s 348. There are, however, exceptions to this general rule; see s 468-470.
7. CTA 2009, s 473.
8. CTA 2009, s 378; on changes of status see HMRC Corporation Tax Manual, paras 12520 et seq.
9. Inland Revenue interpretation RI 176; by contrast, if the loan is with a shareholder, the loan will be taken into account. Simon's Taxes, Division G3.1.
10. CTA 2009, s 352. See *Trend Properties Ltd v Crutchfield* [2005] STC (SCD) 534.
11. CTA 2009, s 355.
12. CTA 2009, s 361.
13. See Inland Revenue interpretation RI 172; **Simon's Taxes, Division G3.1**.
14. CTA 2009, ss 250–351.
15. CTA 2009, s 453.

Restriction on group finance costs

[27.08] FA 2009, s 25 and Sch 15 introduced a restriction on the ability of UK companies to deduct interest on debts owed to group companies in certain circumstances – see infra § **28.05**.

Excluded securities

[27.09] If generally accepted accounting practice divides a loan relationship into a host (debt) contract and an embedded derivative, the profits and losses on the embedded derivative are dealt with under the rules for derivatives contracts.[1]

Two specific gilts (31/2% Funding 1999–2004 and 51/2% Treasury 2008–12) are excluded from the loan relationship treatment, unless they are held as trading stock by the company.[2] Interest arising on these stocks is, however, included in the normal calculation. The uplift enjoyed by the holder of indexed gilts is, similarly, excluded from charge.[3]

Simon's Taxes D1.758.

1. CTA 2009, s 415.
2. CTA 2009, Sch 2, para 69.
3. CTA 2009, s 399–400.

[27.10] Loan relationships, etc.

Gilt strips

[27.10] The stripping of a gilt causes the entitlement to interest to be held separately from the entitlement to capital repayment. This helps companies to closely mark their cashflow. The two separate entitlements in such a stripped gilt can be reconstituted into its original form.

Where a gilt is stripped, the gilt is treated as if it had been redeemed for its market value.[1] Where the two separate interests are amalgamated into a single holding, the treatment is repeated, each separate interest being subjected to the loan relationship regime as if there had been a disposal of each of the separate interests, each for its market value.[2]

Simon's Taxes D1.758.

---

[1] CTA 2009, s 401(2)–(4).
[2] CTA 2009, s 401(5)–(7).

Foreign exchange gains and losses

General rule

[27.11] The general rule is that profits, gains and losses from a company's loan relationship (and related transactions) include exchange gains and losses.[1]

This general rule is subject to a number of exceptions:

(a) An exchange gain or loss is excluded to the extent that it is recognised in the company's statement of recognised gains and losses or statement of changes in equity.[2]
(b) An exchange gain or loss on a security issued by a company is excluded to the extent that it arises on a loan hedging shares, ships and aircraft.[3]
(c) All or part of interest paid by a company on a security is treated as a distribution[4] (interest paid to an associated company); or
(d) The transfer pricing provisions[5] apply as if all or part of the loan had not been made.[6]
(e) Where a company makes a loan which would not have been made on an arm's length basis (or would have been made in a smaller amount), exchange gains and losses on the loan (or on the excess of the loan over one at arm's length) are left out of account, unless exchange gains or losses of the same amount are brought into account by a company to whom the loan is made.[7]

---

[1] CTA 2009, s 328.
[2] CTA 2009, s 328.
[3] CTA 2009, s 328.
[4] CTA 2009, s 447.
[5] CTA 2009, s 447.

[6] CTA 2009, s 447; FA 1996, Sch 9, para 11A(1); FA 2002, Sch 23(4),(5), para 11(1),(2).
[7] FA 2002, Sch 23, para 11(4)–(6).

Money debts not loan relationships

[27.12] Interest, exchange gains and losses and certain discounts on money debts are brought within the new regime, even where the money debt itself is not within the definition of "loan relationship" because there is no transaction for the lending of money. Thus, for example, any interest arising on a trade creditor is aggregated with other interest, as is interest computed under judgment debts, transfer pricing legislation, interest on building society accounts and dividends on industrial and provident society shares. Any profit (not loss) arising on the sale of the right to receive the interest is also brought into account.[1]

The debits and credits are to be brought into account as trading or non-trading debits and credits according to whether the company is party to the money debt for the purposes of the company's trade or received in the course of trading activities. Interest paid to or by HMRC is always a non-trading debit or credit.[2]

Exchange gains and losses are not taken into account if they relate to UK or foreign taxation (unless allowed as a deduction in the absence of allowance for tax credit). Nor are they taken into account where, but for a prohibition, they would be treated as a trade expense or as management expenses; the prohibition does not extend to items charged to capital.[3]

So far as exchange gains and losses are concerned, the following items are treated as money debts:

(a) currency;
(b) the balance of deferred acquisition costs relating to non-life insurance business;
(c) provision for future trading or property business liabilities;
(d) unearned premium reserves and unexpired risks of insurance companies.[4]

The discounts included are those arising on the sale of an asset on deferred payment terms; this is intended to prevent interest being disguised as sale price and taxed as capital gain rather than income.[5]

Impairment provisions in respect of trading and property payments are also brought into account in accordance with the loan relationships rules.[6]

[1] CTA 2009, s 481.
[2] CTA 2009, s 482(1).
[3] CTA 2009, s 486(1)–(4).
[4] CTA 2009, s 483.
[5] CTA 2009, s 481.
[6] CTA 2009, s 486.

[27.13] Loan relationships, etc.

Derivative contracts

[27.13] Derivative contracts are taxed by reference to the treatment adopted by accounting standards.

A derivative contract is (a) an option, (b) a future, or (c) a contract for differences (CD).[1]

An "option" is stated to include a warrant which is then defined as an instrument which entitles the holder to subscribe for shares in a company or assets representing a loan relationship of a company; for these purposes it is immaterial whether the shares or assets to which the warrant relates exist or are identifiable.[2]

A future is a contract to sell property with delivery at a later date but agreed at the time of the contract and at a price agreed then too. A contract which includes a term not for the delivery of property but for the payment of a cash sum is not within (a) or (b)[3] but may come within (c). However, a future or option whose underlying subject matter is currency is included as a future or option.

The term CD is defined at some length.[4] It is a contract the purpose or pretended purpose of which is to make a profit or avoid a loss by reference to fluctuations in (a) the value or price of property described in the contract, or (b) an index or other factor designated in the contract.[5] For the purposes of sub-paragraph (b) an index or factor may be determined by reference to any matter and, for those purposes, a numerical value may be attributed to any variation in a matter. Certain matters are excluded from being a contract for differences. These are (a) a future; (b) an option; (c) a contract of insurance; (d) a capital redemption policy; (e) a contract of indemnity; (f) a guarantee; (g) a warranty; (h) a loan relationship.

[1] The model for many of these definitions is the Financial Services and Markets Act 2000 (Regulated Activities) Order 2001, SI 2001/544.
[2] CTA 2009, s 580(1).
[3] CTA 2009, s 580(3),(4) and s 581(3),(4).
[4] For an example of when it matters whether a contract is a CD or some other type of derivative see CTA 2009, s 593 allowing apportionment for futures and options but not for CDs.
[5] CTA 2009, s 582(3),(4).

Subject matter

[27.14] The contract must either be a derivative financial instrument[1] or the underlying subject matter[2] of the contract must be commodities. If the contract is a contract for difference (a "CD"), the subject matter can also be land, tangible moveable property, intangible fixed assets, weather conditions or creditworthiness.[3]

The presence of certain underlying subject matters, in whole or in part, will prevent CTA 2009, Pt 7 from applying in relation to an option or future. Thus,

Pt 7 is disapplied when the underlying subject matter is intangible fixed assets, shares[4] (other than shares treated as loan relationships)[5] and rights of a unit holder in a unit trust scheme (also apart from rights treated as a loan relationship) if the circumstances are, as follows:[6]

(a) where the company is carrying on life assurance business—Pt 7 is disapplied when the contract is approved for the purposes of the Integrated Prudential Sourcebook;
(b) where the contract is hedging shares or units—Pt 7 is disapplied when the company owns, or has issued, the shares;
(c) where the contract is a quoted option over shares held for non-trading purposes or for the purposes of a life assurance business—Pt 7 is disapplied when the contract is hedging a loan relationship which is bifurcated in the company's accounts.

There is also a de minimis rule.[7] The Treasury may amend any of these rules by order.[8]

---

[1] CTA 2009, s 579(1).
[2] Defined in CTA 2009, s 583.
[3] CTA 2009, s 579(2).
[4] Defined in CTA 2009, s 710 as giving rise to an entitlement to distributions.
[5] CTA 2009, s 589(3).
[6] CTA 2009, ss 589, 591.
[7] CTA 2009, s 590.
[8] CTA 2009, s 701.

Tax treatment

[27.15] To the extent that the contract is one to which the company is party for the purposes of a trade the relevant credits and debits are treated as receipts or expenses of the trade- and TA 1988 s 734 is excluded.[1] Non-trading credits and debits are treated as if they arise under the loan relationship rules.[2]

Which debits and credits are to be brought into account when and at what value are determined by reference to the company's accounts as drawn up in accordance with generally accepted accounting practice, the relevant provision being an adaptation of the loan relationship rules.[3] The discharge of the contract by performance is a related transaction.[4]

The profits and losses on certain derivative contracts are treated as chargeable gains or allowable losses even though the recognition follows the accounts. These include contracts relating to land or tangible moveable property, options over specified shares and property based total return swaps.[5] Provision is made for the carry-back of losses against earlier profits.

The rules exclude exchange gains and losses arising in relation to contracts whose subject matter is currency if the exchange movements are taken to a company's statement of recognised gains and losses or statement of changes in equity.[6] The rules also include matching rules, which exclude exchange gains and losses if they relate to contracts hedging shares, ships or aircraft.[7]

[27.15] Loan relationships, etc.

The rules on bad debt relief are the same as for loan relationships.[8]

An exit charge is imposed on a company ceasing to be UK resident.[9]

Where debits and credits are capitalised as allowed under a generally accepted accounting practice they are treated as giving rise to debits and credits at the time of capitalisation.[10]

The anti-avoidance rules dealing with provision not at arm's length, ie the transfer pricing rules in TA 1988, Sch 28AA, apply to derivative contracts, with a separate application to any exchange element.[11] For this reason there is no simple re-enactment of FA 1994, s 165. However, there is a specific rule to deal with a situation involving the expiry of an option for which a sum was paid.[12] The amount of the sum is treated as a transfer of value and so as a credit accruing to the transferor.

[1] CTA 2009, s 573.
[2] CTA 2009, 574.
[3] FA 2004, Sch 10 paras 1–45.
[4] CTA 2009, s 596.
[5] CTA 2009, Pt 7, Ch 7.
[6] CTA 2009, s 701(3).
[7] CTA 2009, s 328.
[8] CTA 2009, s 611.
[9] CTA 2009, ss 609–610.
[10] CTA 2009, s 604.
[11] CTA 2009, s 694.
[12] CTA 2009, s 695.

Unallowable purposes

[27.16] There are also rules about derivative contracts which have an unallowable purpose.[1] A purpose is unallowable if it is not amongst the business or other commercial purposes of the company; a tax avoidance purpose is a business or other commercial purpose only where it is not a main purpose for entering into a transaction.[2]

Where the company has activities outside the charge to UK corporation tax the purposes relating to those activities are not business and other commercial purposes; so transactions for those purposes are unallowable.[3]

The effects of an unallowable purpose[4] depend on whether there is an exchange credit or gain. One first hives off any exchange credit. The amount by which the debits for unallowable purposes exceed the exchange credits just hived off is treated as net loss.[5] A net loss can be set off against credits. There is a concept of a credit for an unallowable purpose.

[1] CTA 2009, ss 690–691.
[2] CTA 2009, s 691(1),(3)–(6).
[3] CTA 2009, s 691(2).

⁴ CTA 2009, ss 690, 692.
⁵ CTA 2009, s 692.

Groups

[27.17] When one group company replaces another as party to the contract the matter is treated as simply that and so giving rise to no relevant event, although there is an exception in respect of any discount arising. There are also special rules excluding this neutral approach for certain insurance company transactions involving the transfer of long term insurance contracts.[1] It is also excluded if the transferor company uses fair value accounting; such a company must bring in the transfer at the fair value of the contract.[2] If the transferee company leaves the group less than six years after the transaction, a "de-grouping" charge arises in the same way as it does on chargeable gains transfers.[3]

A similar relief is provided in relation to the formation of a Societas Europaea.[4]

[1] CTA 2009, s 636, referring to TA 1988 s 440(4).
[2] This is analogous to CTA 2009, s 341.
[3] CTA 2009, ss 630–632 (infra, § **28.24**).
[4] CTA 2009, s 684.

Derivative contracts with non-residents

[27.18] There are separate statutory[1] provisions where the derivative is entered into by the qualifying company with a person who is not resident in the UK. It applies whether they are parties from the outset or become parties to the contract later.

Where debits and credits arise, eg payments under an interest or currency rate swap any "relevant debits" is excluded. A relevant debits arises if the contract makes provision for notional interest payments. This exclusion is limited to the amounts arising while they are both parties to the contract.[2] Notional interest payments arise when a payment is:

> any payment the amount of which falls to be determined (wholly or mainly) by applying to a notional principal amount specified in a derivative contract, for a period so specified, a rate the value of which at all times is the same as that of a rate of interest so specified.[3]

The relevant debit is the amount (if any) by which the notional interest payments made exceeds notional interest payments received.

This exclusion does not apply in three sets of circumstances. The first is where the qualifying company is a bank, building society or financial trader and it holds the qualifying contract solely for the purposes of a trade or part of a trade carried on by it in the UK, provided it is not party to the contract as agent or nominee of another person.[4] The second is where the non-resident holds the qualifying contract solely for the purposes of a trade or part of a trade carried

[27.18] Loan relationships, etc.

on by him in the UK through a permanent establishment; again he must not be an agent or nominee of another person.[5] The third is where the non-resident is resident in a territory with which the UK has a double tax treaty which makes provision, whether for relief or otherwise, in relation to interest (as defined in the arrangements). In this situation the non-resident may be an agent or nominee of another person, but the rule has effect as if the reference to the territory in which the non-resident is resident were a reference to the territory in which the real beneficiary is resident.[6]

[1] CTA 2009, s 696.
[2] CTA 2009, s 696(1)–(3).
[3] CTA 2009, s 696(4).
[4] CTA 2009, s 697(1).
[5] CTA 2009, s 697(1).
[6] CTA 2009, s 697(2)–(4).

Special savings vehicles

[27.19] Further rules relate to contracts relating to holdings in unit trusts, OEICs and offshore funds. These contracts start by not being derivative contracts but the rules treat them as if they were and require them to use fair value accounting.[1] Further provisions set out how the transition to the derivative regime applies to an existing contract which changes its character so as to become subject to the rules.[2]

Other rules apply to Venture Capital Trusts and Investment Trusts. So carrying debts and credits to reserve does not give rise to a debit or credit.[3] Also, such income is treated as income from shares and securities for the purpose of the relevant approvals.[4] Yet further rules apply to insurance and mutual trading companies.[5]

[1] CTA 2009, ss 587, 601.
[2] CTA 2009, s 602.
[3] CTA 2009, ss 637–638.
[4] CTA 2009, Sch 1, para 277.
[5] CTA 2009, ss 633, 634.

Special situations

[27.20] Change of status When a derivative contract whose underlying subject matter consists of shares and units ceases to be held for trading purposes but the company is still party to the relevant contract, there is a deemed disposal at market value now renamed fair value.[1] Conversely when such a contract becomes held for trading purposes and so comes within these new rules, the rules in TCGA 1992, s 161 apply—but without the option of an election under s 161 (3).[2]

Apportionments The next rule applies only to options and futures and not to CD. Where the contract would be excluded as relating to a prohibited underlying subject matter of an excluded type, an apportionment can be made between the part qualifying for derivative treatment, eg shares, and the non-qualifying part.[3] The apportionment is on a just and reasonable basis.

[1]   CTA 2009, s 662.
[2]   CTA 2009, s 661.
[3]   CTA 2009, s 593.

Intellectual property

[27.21] Intellectual property includes goodwill, registered designs, copyrights, design rights, trademarks, patents and know how as well as licences for any of these, which are known, collectively as "intangibles".[1] Any information or technique not protected by a right but having industrial, commercial or other economic value[2] falls within this. A specific regime,[3] setting out a comprehensive set of rules so that the tax treatment follows the accounts treatment, was introduced for all companies acquiring, or creating, intellectual property was introduced in 2002 where that intellectual property is acquired or created by the company for use on a continuing basis in the course of the company's activities.[4] The treatment outlined in the following sections does not, therefore, apply to intellectual property purchased by a dealer for resale,[5] although the definition would appear to include intellectual property purchased as an investment, such as a royalty purchased for the continuing royalty income receivable.

The intangible assets tax rules in CTA 2009, Part 8 apply only to companies. They have no application for an unincorporated business.

All intellectual property existing before 1 April 2002 continues to be taxed under the old regime as long as it remains with the existing owner. On disposal the vendor will be taxed according to the old regimes: the Part 8 regime applying for the corporate purchaser. The old system, which developed in a piecemeal fashion is briefly outlined below.

[1]   Known in statute as "intangible fixed assets". This phrase is defined by CTA 2009, ss 712–713 as: "'Intangible asset' has the meaning it has for accounting purposes". Statute then states that this phrase includes "intellectual property": para 712(2). An asset that is not specifically defined may still be classified as intellectual property if accounting practice classifies it as such, eg agricultural quotas are classified as intangible assets under FRS 10.
[2]   CTA 2009, s 712(3)(c).
[3]   CTA 2009, Pt 8 (formerly FA 2002, Schs 29 and 30).
[4]   CTA 2009, s 713.
[5]   Such as by a company carrying on the trade of buying and selling businesses. In *Leach v Pogson* (1962) 40 TC 585, the court held that the taxpayer was carrying on the trade of establishing driving schools, disposing of each after it was established.

[27.22] Loan relationships, etc.

Intellectual property acquired or created before 1 April 2002

[27.22] Purchases of know how[1] and patents[2] were eligible for capital allowances at 25% on a reducing balance basis (note that these allowances continue to be available at 25%, regardless of the reduction in plant and machinery allowances to 20%). Balancing charges and allowances arose on subsequent disposal (see supra, § **8.76** for further details of the disposal receipts. The cost of an application for a patent and the registration of a design or trademark is specifically allowable as a deduction.[3] Royalties recognised for accounting purposes on or after 1 April 2002 fall within the new provisions even if the underlying asset was in existence before 1 April 2002.[4]

Goodwill, although not actually defined by statute, fell under the CGT rules. Any gain arising on disposal was eligible for rollover relief.[5] A company's internally generated goodwill will only treated be treated as a new regime asset if neither the company nor a related party held the asset before 1 April 2002.[6]

The rollover relief introduced by the new, post 1 April 2002 regime, is also available for the capital gain arising on the disposal of any of these old regime intangibles. It is also available when there is a degrouping charge.[7] The category of assets that this rollover relief applies to is wider than that for normal rollover relief. It does not include part realisations between related parties.

---

[1] CAA 2001, s 458.
[2] CAA 2001, s 472.
[3] CTA 2009, s 89.
[4] CTA 2009, s 896.
[5] TCGA 1992, s 155.
[6] CTA 2009, s 884.
[7] CTA 2009, ss 898–900.

Intellectual property acquired or created from 1 April 2002

[27.23] The new corporation tax regime follows the generally accepted accounting treatment (specified by FRS10). So there have to be tax adjustments if the company itself deviates from the accepted accounting principles. Tax relief is based on the expenditure written off in the accounts as it is incurred.[1] Even royalties payable in respect of intellectual property may be deducted (although this does not affect the rules concerning deduction of tax at source). Any amortisation in respect of a capitalised intangible fixed asset is also allowed.[2] Alternatively an irrevocable election may be made for a fixed allowance of 4% per annum[3] of the cost recognised for tax purposes. This would be applicable for a well-known brand name that is either not amortised or amortised over more than 25 years because it must not necessarily have been capitalised in order to fall within these provisions.[4] These allowable expenses are referred to as "debits" in the legislation. Debits representing reversals of earlier taxable credits may also be brought into account.[5]

Receipts are recognised as they accrue[6] and credits are allowed on revaluation but are restricted to debits previously deducted.[7] Negative goodwill, on the acquisition of a business and attributable to intangible assets, gives a tax charge.[8] This occurs in the rare case where negative goodwill is recognised under FRS 7 on the acquisition of a business, the negative goodwill arising from when the price of the business is less than the fair value of assets and liabilities. Accounting debits and credits[9] arising from an asset held for trade purposes are treated as expenses or receipts of the trade.[10] Any net non-trading gains are chargeable to tax as miscellaneous income.[11] Non-trading losses may be offset against total profits on a claim being made,[12] or surrendered to other group companies in the accounting period in which they arise. Any non-trading loss balance is automatically carried forward as a non-trading debit.[13] Insurance companies have special provisions.[14] There are specific rules for the treatment of the part/whole realisation of an intangible fixed asset[15] and the calculation of any tax written down value.[16] New rules have been inserted to cover the impact of a change in accounting policy and, in particular, where a company moves from preparing its accounts following UK generally accepted accounting practice ("GAAP") to preparing its accounts in accordance with International Accounting Standards ("IAS").[17]

---

[1] CTA 2009, s 728.
[2] CTA 2009, s 729.
[3] CTA 2009, ss 730–731.
[4] CTA 2009, s 713(3),(4).
[5] CTA 2009, s 732.
[6] CTA 2009, s 721.
[7] CTA 2009. s 723.
[8] CTA 2009, s 724.
[9] CTA 2009, Pt 8, Ch 2–3.
[10] CTA 2009, s 747.
[11] CTA 2009, s 751.
[12] CTA 2009, s 753.
[13] CTA 2009, s 753(3).
[14] CTA 2009, s 901.
[15] CTA 2009, Pt 8, Ch 4.
[16] CTA 2009, Pt 8, Ch 5.
[17] CTA 2009, Pt 8, Ch 15.

Rollover relief

[27.24] Rollover relief may be claimed[1] where the proceeds from a chargeable intangible asset,[2] including those from a partial realisation,[3] are reinvested in chargeable intangible assets. These assets must be capitalised in the accounts and the reinvestment must take place within 12 months before or three years after the date of realisation.[4] The effect of the claim is to reduce the realisation proceeds of the old asset and the cost of the new asset by the same amount.[5] It is possible to make a declaration of provisional entitlement to relief before formally making the claim.[6] Partial relief is available where only part of the proceeds is reinvested.[7] Generally deemed acquisition and disposals are disregarded for this rollover relief with the exception to the charge arising on degrouping[8] see below. Capital gains arising on the disposal of intellectual property acquired or created before 1 April 2002, and so under the old regime, are also eligible for this rollover relief.[9] This also includes circumstances when there is a degrouping charge on an old regime intangible asset.[10] It should be noted that this rollover relief may not be particularly beneficial because the amortisation subsequently allowed each year will be based on a lower cost figure.

There are special provisions for groups of companies.[11] A group for these purposes follows the definition used for capital gains purposes,[12] expanded by the irritating approach adopted by the Tax Law Rewrite project. Chargeable intangible assets[13] may be transferred at book value on a tax-neutral basis in a similar way to chargeable assets covered by the capital gains rules.[14] When a chargeable intangible asset potentially falls within both the reconstruction provisions in the new regime, and the grouping provision; the latter takes priority.[15] Upon the transferee company leaving the group within six years of the transfer, a degrouping charge similar to TCGA 1992, s 179 arises,[16] although there are specific exemptions to the degrouping provisions.[17] These provisions[18] are parallel provisions to those found in the capital gains tax legislation. Rollover relief is available for this degrouping charge[19] and an election may be made to reallocate the degrouping charge within the group[20] or alternatively it is possible to recover it from another group company[21] or a controlling director. When there is a disposal of a chargeable intangible asset, rollover relief is available to other group members.[22] The acquisition of a group company may be treated as the acquisition of the underlying intangible assets for rollover relief purposes.[23] Payments between group members for reinvestment relief or the reallocation of a degrouping charge are tax-neutral, subject to certain conditions.[24]

---

[1] CTA 2009, ss 754, 757.
[2] CTA 2009, s 741.
[3] CTA 2009, s 755.
[4] CTA 2009, s 756.
[5] CTA 2009, s 758.
[6] CTA 2009, s 761.
[7] CTA 2009, ss 758–759.
[8] CTA 2009, ss 791 and 794.
[9] CTA 2009, s 898.
[10] CTA 2009, s 899.
[11] CTA 2009, Part 8, Ch 8.
[12] CTA 2009, ss 764–773, which is modelled on the definition in TCGA 1992, s 170.
[13] CTA 2009, s 741.
[14] CTA 2009, s 775.
[15] CTA 2009, s 818(3).
[16] CTA 2009, s 780.
[17] CTA 2009, ss 783–787.
[18] CTA 2009, Pt 8, Ch 9.
[19] CTA 2009, s 791.

[20] CTA 2009, ss 792–794.
[21] CTA 2009, ss 795–798.
[22] CTA 2009, s 777.
[23] CTA 2009, ss 778–779.
[24] CTA 2009, s 799.

Assets excluded from these provisions

[27.25] Assets excluded from this regime are rights over land and tangible movable property,[1] oil licences,[2] financial assets[3] and shares/rights/interests in companies, trusts and partnerships.[4] These assets would mostly be considered outside the scope of FRS 10. Any intangibles that are held either for non-business purposes or for activities not falling within the corporation tax net are likewise excluded.[5] Further assets are excluded but the royalties arising from them are included: life assurance business[6] (though exceptionally, transactions by a life assurance business are within the scheme when they relate to computer software),[7] mutual trade or business,[8] film and sound recordings.[9] Computer software is treated as part of the related hardware.[10] Although expenditure on R & D is excluded, because it is relieved elsewhere, proceeds derived from the exploitation of intellectual property resulting from that R & D fall within these provisions. The definition of R &D in this instance includes oil and gas exploration and appraisal.[11]

It is possible to elect[12] to exclude capital expenditure on computer software so as to be able to claim first year allowances.[13] This is election is irrevocable.[14] On the subsequent realisation of the software, any receipts in excess of those that fall within the capital allowances regime fall within this regime.

Where there is a scheme of reconstruction or amalgamation involving the transfer of the whole or part of a business from one company to another, the transfer of any chargeable intangible asset is tax-neutral. This is as long as the assets remain in charge to corporation tax both before and after the reconstruction.[15] The definition of a scheme or amalgamation is the same as used in the capital gains legislation.[16] The provisions are the same.[17] Where a transfer is made within a group, the treatment given for intra-group transfers[18] take precedence over these provisions. Tax neutrality is also possible when there is transfer of UK trade between companies resident in different EU member states which mirrors provisions in TCGA 1992, ss 140A and 140B[19] and on the formation of a Societas Europaea.[20] There are also provisions to postpone the charge on the transfer of intangible fixed assets to non-resident companies[21] and the transfer of non UK trade from a EU company resident in another EU state.[22] For these, there are statutory clearance procedures.[23]

Transfers of life assurance business,[24] transfers from a building society to a company[25] and amalgamation of certain societies (or the transfer of engagements from one society to another)[26] is treated as taking place at a tax-neutral value.

[1] CTA 2009, s 805.
[2] CTA 2009, s 809.

[27.25] Loan relationships, etc.

3 CTA 2009, s 806: but see CTA 2009, s 854 and below.
4 CTA 2009, s 807.
5 CTA 2009, s 803.
6 CTA 2009, s 902.
7 CTA 2009, s 902(3).
8 CTA 2009, s 810.
9 CTA 2009, ss 811–812.
10 CTA 2009, s 813.
11 CTA 2009, s 814.
12 In writing within two years.
13 CTA 2009, ss 815–816.
14 CTA 2009, s 816(4).
15 CTA 2009, s 818.
16 TCGA 1992, s 136.
17 TCGA 1992, s 137.
18 CTA 2009, s 775.
19 CTA 2009, s 819.
20 CTA 2009, ss 820 and 822.
21 CTA 2009, ss 827–829.
22 CTA 2009, Sch 1, paras 257–259.
23 CTA 2009, s 832.
24 CTA 2009, s 904.
25 CTA 2009, s 824–825.
26 CTA 2009, s 826.

Related party transactions

[27.26] Any transfers of chargeable intangible assets between related parties are deemed to take place at market value[1] although transfer-pricing rules[2] take precedence over the market value rule as does any rule under Part 8 that treats the transfer as tax neutral.[3] There are now two further exceptions for transfers chargeable to tax as a distribution or as employment income and transfers where the transferee claims holdover relief.[4] Rollover relief is denied for part realisations involving related parties.[5] There are also other provisions for related party transactions[6] as well as the various definitions such as "related party", "control" and "major interest".[7]

From 5 December 2005 avoidance schemes which sought to artificially generate tax relief by moving rights in existing intangible assets around a group were blocked.[8]

1 CTA 2009, ss 845–846.
2 TA 1988, Sch 28AA.
3 CTA 2009, s 845.
4 CTA 2009, s 847.
5 CTA 2009, s 850.
6 CTA 2009, Pt 8, Ch 12.

[7] CTA 2009, ss 835–837.
[8] FA 2006, s 77.

Miscellaneous points

[27.27] Grants,[1] other then exempt grants,[2] and contributions may either be classified as incomings or netted off against expenditure. Although financial assets (including loans) are outside this legislation,[3] the Treasury has the power to make regulations for finance lessors of intangible assets so as to bring them within these provisions. This is to prevent any finance leasing of intangible assets being at a commercial disadvantage.[4]

There are also provisions for fungible intangible assets (a fungible asset is an asset that, when split, has indistinguishable parts, such as a dairy farmer's milk quota).[5]

Under certain circumstances, there is a deemed realisation and acquisition at market value when an intangible ceases to be a "chargeable intangible asset".[6] The circumstances are:

(1) when the company ceases to be resident in the UK;
(2) the asset is held by a company resident outside the UK that stops using it for its UK trade; or
(3) the asset begins to be used for the purposes of a mutual business.

It may be possible to postpone the gain arising which parallels provisions in TCGA 1992, s 187.[7]

There are also provisions dealing with the converse circumstances when the asset becomes a chargeable intangible asset[8] and also some tax avoidance rules.[9]

If there is a delayed payment of staff emoluments[10] or pension contributions[11] that are associated with the intangible asset (eg where staff are employed in promoting the company's brand names) then the corresponding debit is not deductible until such payments are actually made.[12]

Bad debt treatment is outlined[13] as well as assumptions that need to be made when dealing with controlled foreign companies.[14] Commencement and transitional provisions are outlined.[15]

[1] CTA 2009, s 852.
[2] CTA 2009, s 853.
[3] CTA 2009, s 806.
[4] CTA 2009, ss 854–855.
[5] CTA 2009, s 858.
[6] CTA 2009, s 859.
[7] CTA 2009, ss 860–862.
[8] CTA 2009, s 863.
[9] CTA 2009, s 864.
[10] CTA 2009, ss 866–867.
[11] CTA 2009, s 868.

[27.27] Loan relationships, etc.

[12] Note that there is a nine month period after the end of the accounting period when emoluments may be paid but this extra length of time does not apply to pension payments.
[13] CTA 2009, s 869.
[14] CTA 2009, s 870.
[15] CTA 2009, Pt 8, Ch 16.

Islamic finance

Overview

[27.28] Part of the success of London's financial centre is attributed to the way in which it has adapted its procedures and products to fit the changing economic environment and the different demands from different parts of the world. The London stock market has been described[1] as the stock market for the world, by comparison the New York stock exchange being the stock market for the US. It is, therefore, perhaps, not surprising that the UK is the first western government to provide a framework for financing in accordance with Islamic rules and the UK government is issuing alternative financial products that will enable those who follow strict Muslim lines on investment to obtain the equivalent benefits to those who hold Government Stock and National Savings products.

The Koran prohibits Muslims from the practice of "riba" which is generally understood in Islamic law (Sharia) to mean the receipt or payment of interest. As a result, Muslims have devised other financial structures such as "morabaha" (sale on deferred payment terms—infra, § **27.30**), "modaraba" (providing finance to a venture in exchange for a share of the profits—infra, § **27.31**), "wakala" (a profit share agency—infra, § **27.32**) and "diminishing musharaka" (an arrangement of diminishing shared ownership—infra, § **27.33**) to facilitate commercial transactions. Statute[2] provides a code for the taxation of all financing arrangements which fall into these four statutory definitions, regardless of whether they are or are not "morabaha", "modaraba", "wakala" or "diminishing musharaka".

The code only applies where one of the parties to the contract is a financial institution. The general approach taken is to identify the nearest equivalent in tradition, Western business practice. Thus, the difference between the purchase price and the sale price on a deferred sale contract is treated as interest. Similarly, a profit sharing return paid by a financial institution, if it equates to interest, is taxed as interest.

Statute[3] empowers the Treasury to issue statutory instruments to make future changes to deal with alternative finance arrangements. The power only applies to arrangements which, in the opinion of the Treasury, equate in substance to transactions of a kind that generally involve the payment of interest. Accordingly, if someone designs a sharia compliant credit card, regulations could be made, but the power could not be used to legislate for, say, takaful (Islamic insurance).

[1] Financial Times, April 2007.
[2] CTA 2009, Pt 6, Ch 6.
[3] FA 2006, s 98.

Financial institution

[27.29] The tax code for alternative finance arrangements only applies where the contract is with a "financial institution".[1] The customary statutory definition[2] for "a bank" is widened for this purpose[3] to include a building society, a wholly-owned subsidiary of a bank or a building society, a person authorised by a licence under the Consumer Credit Act 1974 or a person authorised in a jurisdiction outside the UK to receive deposits or other repayable funds from the public and to grant credits for its own account.

An equity capitalised company set up to provide Islamic finance not licensed to take deposits fails to meet the definition of a financial institution, and this may be a problem for some foreign Islamic financiers. The requirement for bank or building society subsidiaries to be wholly-owned makes it relatively straightforward for bank groups to avoid these rules, if they so desire.

[1] FA 2005, s 47(2)(a) (unincorporated), CTA 2009, s 503 (companies)..
[2] TA 1988, s 840A.
[3] By FA 2005, s 46(2) (unincorporated), CTA 2009, s 502 (companies).

Morabaha

[27.30] For the purpose of the statutory provisions, Morabaha is regarded as[1] an arrangement entered into between two persons under which:

(a) a person ("X") purchases an asset and sells it, either immediately or in circumstances in which the conditions in subsection (2) are met, to the other person ("Y");
(b) the amount payable by Y in respect of the sale ("the sale price") is greater than the amount paid by X in respect of the purchase ("the purchase price");
(c) all or part of the sale price is not required to be paid until a date later than that of the sale; and
(d) the difference between the sale price and the purchase price equates, in substance, to the return on an investment of money at interest.

(Note: The word "Morabaha" does not appear in the statutory provisions. The approach adopted in statute is to describe an arrangement and then specify a tax treatment to be applied to it. Hence, it is perfectly possible for an Islamic Bank, for example, to produce a financial product that it labels as "Morabaha", but it is outside the provisions of the UK tax code; equally, a financial product that is not so labelled, may fulfil the UK statutory definition and, hence, have the tax treatment applied to it.)

[27.30] Loan relationships, etc.

Where this arrangement is entered into, the difference between the sale price and the purchase price is allocated to the period in the arrangement, the amount being allocated to each period is then taxed as if it were interest received by the "lender".[2] Statute requires the lender to apportion the effective return in accordance with generally accepted accounting practice. This means that a straight-line apportionment is probably unacceptable. A strict actuarial apportionment is clearly acceptable, and in most cases also an apportionment using the "rule of 78".

There are special provisions for arrangements in a foreign company,[3] with non-residence[4] and arrangements giving a return based on a share of profit.[5]

[1] FA 2005, s 47(1) (unincorporated), CTA 2009, s 503 (companies).
[2] FA 2005, s 47(8) (unincorporated), CTA 2009, s 511 (companies).
[3] FA 2005, s 48(1).
[4] FA 2003, s 148(5A).
[5] FA 2005, s 49 (unincorporated), CTA 2009, s 505 (companies).

Modaraba

[27.31] A Modaraba arrangement is described in statute[1] as an arrangement under which:

(a) a person "("the depositor") deposits money with a financial institution;
(b) the money, together with money deposited with the institution by other persons, is used by the institution with a view to producing a profit;
(c) from time to time the institution makes or credits a payment to the depositor, in proportion to the amount deposited by him, out of any profit resulting from the use of the money; and
(d) the payments so made or credited by the institution equate, in substance, to the return on an investment of money at interest.

(Note: As with a Morabaha, see supra, § 27.30, the word "Modaraba" does not appear in the statutory provisions. Hence, it is perfectly for an Islamic Bank, for example, to produce a financial product that it labels as "Modaraba", but it is outside the provisions of the UK tax code; equally, a financial product that is not so labelled, may fulfil the UK statutory definition and, hence, have the tax treatment applied to it.)

Where a company is a party to Modaraba, statute[2] applies the loan relationship provision[3] as if:

(a) the arrangements were a loan relationship to which the company is a party;
(b) any amount which is the purchase price were the amount of the loan made (as the case requires) to the company by, or by the company to, the other party to the arrangements; and
(c) alternative finance return payable to or by the company under the arrangements were interest payable under that loan relationship.

For a person other than a company alternative finance return or profit share return is treated for the purposes of ITTOIA 2005 as if it were interest.[4]

[1] FA 2005, s 49(1) (unincorporated), CTA 2009, s 505(1) (companies).
[2] CTA 2009, s 510(3).
[3] In particular CTA 2009, s 479(2).
[4] FA 2005, s 51(1).

Wakala

[27.32] Wakala is a profit share agency under which the principal incurs much less credit risk in relation to the financial institution, ie the contract is that of principal and agent and does not entail the investor making a loan to the financial institution.

The tax code applies where the payments to the principal equate, in substance, to the return on an investment of the money at interest,[1] but only where one party to the transaction is a financial institution.[2]

Where a company is a party to arrangements the loan relationship provisions have effect in relation to the arrangements as if:[3]

(a) the arrangements were a loan relationship to which the company is a party;
(b) the amount provided under the arrangements were:
 (i) in relation to a company which is the principal under the arrangements, the amount of a loan made by the company to the agent; and
 (ii) in relation to a company which is the agent under the arrangements, the amount of a loan made to it by the principal; and
(c) profit share return payable to or by the company under the arrangements were interest payable under that loan relationship.

[1] FA 2005, s 49A inserted by FA 2006, s 95(3) (unincorporated), CTA 2009, s 506 (companies).
[2] FA 2005, s 49A(1)(a) inserted by FA 2006, s 95(3) (unincorporated), CTA 2009, s 506(1)(a) (companies).
[3] CTA 2009, s 510(4).

Diminishing Musharaka

[27.33] "Diminishing musharaka" is an arrangement of diminishing shared ownership under which an eventual owner pays a higher rate of rent (and sometimes other payments) to a financial institution in return for which a small share of the asset held by the eventual owner is increased over time, until the eventual owner owns 100% of the property.

Statute[1] treats the payments to the "lender" as if they were interest, in so far as they exceed the original purchase price apportioned to the interest that is transferred (normally, each year).

[27.33] Loan relationships, etc.

An employee who is within a diminishing musharaka arrangement, is treated as receiving a beneficial loan for his employer computed as if the "alternative finance return" were interest.[2]

[1] FA 2005, s 47A inserted by FA 2006, s 96(3) (unincorporated), CTA 2009, s 504 (companies).
[2] FA 2006, s 97.

Provisions not at arm's length

[27.34] Where there is sufficient connection between the payer and the recipient for the transfer pricing rules in TA 1988, Sch 28AA to be applicable, and the recipient is not subject to tax in the UK or elsewhere, then a UK deduction is denied[1] even if the financial arrangements are on arm's length terms. This draconian provision is part of the Revenue's new approach to international tax arbitrage.

[1] FA 2005, s 52 (unincorporated), CTA 2009, s 508 (companies).

28

Groups, consortia and substantial shareholdings

A group	PARA **28.01**
A consortium	PARA **28.02**
One company or a group?	PARA **28.03**
Distributions	PARA **28.04**
Restriction on group finance costs	PARA **28.05**
Group relief (75% subsidiaries and consortia)	PARA **28.06**
Surrender of reliefs	PARA **28.13**
Other rules	PARA **28.19**
Transfer of company tax refunds	PARA **28.20**
Intra-group transfers of capital assets (75% subsidiaries)	PARA **28.21**
Transfer of trading stock	PARA **28.27**
Rollover relief and a group	PARA **28.28**
Anti-avoidance provisions for groups	PARA **28.29**
Demergers	PARA **28.37**
Exemption on the disposal of substantial shareholdings	PARA **28.42**

A group

[28.01] A group consists of a parent company and its subsidiaries which may in turn have subsidiaries. Broadly, a company is a subsidiary if the other company owns the relevant percentage of its issued ordinary capital[1]—more than 50% (commonly called a 51% subsidiary), 75% or more, 90% or more and even 100%. It is probably axiomatic that a group can only exist if there is more than one company. So if all but one of the members of a group leave that group the group ceases to exist and the survivor is no longer a member of a group.[2]

If a company does not have an issued share capital, it cannot be a member of a group.[3]

Ordinary share capital means "all issued share capital (by whatever name called) of the company, other than capital the holders of which have a right to a dividend at a fixed rate but have no other right to share in the profits of the company".[4] So loan stock and non-participating preference shares are not treated as ordinary share capital. Conversely, however, shares can be ordinary share capital even if they carry no voting rights.

Ownership must be beneficial.[5] Beneficial ownership has nothing to do with value or the economic attributes of ownership and may therefore exist even though another person has an option to buy the shares.[6] Where, however, that other person has a specifically enforceable right to acquire the shares the original owner's ownership ceases to be beneficial.[7] Where the rights of the

1275

other person fall short of this it would appear that the beneficial ownership remains in the first person unless the rights of ownership are reduced to the state of a mere shell.[8] It follows that when shares are subject to a contract beneficial ownership will usually be in some person and is not to be in a state of suspense.[9] The beneficial ownership of shares will however be in suspense if the company in question goes into liquidation or if the owner goes bankrupt or is an enemy alien so that property vests in a custodian of the enemy or if the owner of the property dies and the shares are held as part of that person's unadministered estate.[10] The courts have struggled to disentangle the notion of beneficial ownership from that of legal or equitable ownership but their comments have not always been helpful.[11]

Ownership may be direct or indirect. It will be seen that the parent must be a company. If an individual, P, owns all the shares in X Ltd and all the shares in Y Ltd, X Ltd and Y Ltd do not form a group. If a company buys shares in return for £1 the purchaser becomes beneficially entitled to the shares; it is not necessary to prove that the £1 was paid as failure to pay entitles only the vendor (not the Revenue) to set the transfer aside for failure of consideration.[12]

In most instances the share capital owned directly must be held as an investment (not as a trading asset);[13] if the shares are held indirectly the intermediate companies must hold the assets as investments.

In applying group relief, there is no requirement that a company be resident in the UK.[14] If a non-resident company is subject to UK corporation tax, by virtue of a permanent establishment in the UK, a loss arising in another member of the group can be offset against the liability arising on the profits of that permanent establishment; conversely, a loss arising on the permanent establishment's trade can be put against profits of other companies of the group that attract a charge to UK corporation tax. Similarly, group relief is available between two UK resident companies that are both subsidiaries of a non-resident holding company.

For accounting periods ending before 1 April 2000, group relief was only available where the group could be traced through UK resident companies. In *ICI v Colmer*,[15] the taxpayer company argued that UK legislation was contrary to the non-discrimination provisions of European Community law and, hence, should be struck out. The attempt failed but only because 13 out of 23 of the subsidiaries of ICI were not resident in EU countries.[16] Then, in *Marks & Spencer Plc v Halsey*[17] the ECJ held that the UK breaches European law by not allowing a UK parent company to claim relief for the losses of a foreign subsidiary, where the foreign subsidiary cannot relieve the losses under the taxation system of the EC state in which it operates. Statute[18] was then enacted to enable the taxpayer to trace group membership and obtain the benefit of group relief, irrespective of the residence of the individual companies in the group.

Simon's Taxes D2.105, 106.

---

[1] TA 1988, s 838(1).
[2] *Lion Ltd v Inspector of Taxes* [1997] STC (SCD) 133.
[3] *South Shore Mutual Insurance Co Ltd v Blair* [1999] STC (SCD) 296.

4   TA 1988, s 832(1); quaere whether a preference share with a fixed rate of dividend but a right to share in surplus assets as a winding up is ordinary share capital as the surplus assets are from profits of the company; see also *Tilcon Ltd v Holland* [1981] STC 365.
5   TA 1988, s 838(3); see also statement of practice SP 3/93; **Simon's Taxes, Division G1.2.**
6   *J Sainsbury plc v O'Connor* [1991] STC 318, CA.
7   Per Nourse LJ in *J Sainsbury plc v O'Connor* [1991] STC 318 at 330.
8   Per Lloyd LJ at 328. The decision of the Court of Appeal in *Wood Preservation Ltd v Prior* (1968) 45 TC 112 must be seen in this light; the comments of some of the members of the 1968 Court must be read in the light of the 1991 decision.
9   Per Nourse LJ at 331.
10 Per Lloyd LJ at 325, 326.
11 *J Sainsbury plc v O'Connor* [1991] STC 318.
12 *Irving v Tesco Stores (Holdings) Ltd* [1982] STC 881.
13 Note *Cooper v C & J Clark Ltd* [1982] STC 335.
14 FA 2000, s 97 and Sch 27.
15 [1999] STC 1089, HL; [1998] STC 874, ECJ.
16 See the judgment of Lord Nolan at 1095f.
17 (Case C-446/03) [2006] STC 237, ECJ.
18 TA 1988, s 402(2A) & (2B) inserted by FA 2006, Sch 1, para 1

A consortium

[28.02] Consortia are particularly common in advanced technology projects and the extension of group income and group relief concepts to them allows for the pooling of resources and of risks. The definition of a consortium varies (infra, § **28.11**).

Consortium relief is available to a UK resident company with a shareholding in a loss making company even where all other shareholders in the loss making company are not resident in the UK.

One company or a group?

[28.03] If a company's trading activities are divided up between different companies, the premise of UK tax law is that each company is a separate entity with separate profits and therefore separate corporation tax liability. There is no simple charging of the group as a whole on its group profits.[1]

The advent of self-assessment has made a number of procedural changes but the return must still be made by each company separately.[2] There are detailed rules for claiming group relief[3] and including joint amended returns.[4] There is also the possibility of paying corporation tax on a group basis.[5]

Simon's Taxes Divisions D2.2.

1   Although instalments of corporation tax can be paid on a group basis.

[2] FA 1998, Sch 18, paras 2 and 7.
[3] FA 1998, Sch 18, paras 66–77A.
[4] FA 1998, Sch 18, para 77.
[5] FA 1998, s 36.

Distributions

[28.04] The transfer of an asset at an undervalue is normally to be treated as a distribution. However, this does not apply when both transferor and recipient are resident in the UK and one is a 51% subsidiary of the other or both are 51% subsidiaries of another resident company.[1] In determining whether the company is a 51% subsidiary of the other, holdings, whether direct or indirect, do not qualify if a profit on the sale would be a trading receipt or if the company is non-resident.[2]

In other respects the definition of distribution is unchanged save that a distribution made by one company out of its assets but in respect of shares or securities of another company in the same 90% group is treated as a distribution if all other conditions are satisfied.[3] This is primarily concerned to extend to groups another provision dealing with distribution by two or more companies to each other's members; such avoidance schemes do not work.[4]

Simon's Taxes D1.102.

[1] TA 1988, s 209(5).
[2] TA 1988, s 209(7).
[3] TA 1988, s 254(1)–(4).
[4] TA 1988, s 254(8).

Restriction on group finance costs

[28.05] FA 2009 introduced a restriction[1] on the ability of UK members of multinational groups to deduct interest costs on debts owed to other group companies; the restriction is, in effect, the cost of the exemption from corporation tax for dividends from foreign companies.[2] The restriction applies for accounting periods beginning on or after 1 January 2010.

The restrictions apply only to groups with non-UK companies; broadly, the restriction limits the tax deduction available for interest and finance expenses payable by UK companies to the consolidated worldwide interest and finance expenses of the group as a whole. This will impact UK companies within multinational groups that have substantial borrowing from other cash-rich group companies, where the group as a whole has little or no external debt.

There are exclusions for financial services companies, group treasury functions and certain short-term debt.

1   FA 2009, s 35 and Sch 15.
2   Sees supra, § **26.15**.

Group relief (75% subsidiaries and consortia)

[28.06] Group relief enables current trading losses, capital allowances, a non-trading deficit on loan relationships, excess management expenses, excess property business losses, excess non-trading losses on intangible fixed and excess charges on income to be surrendered by one company (the surrendering company) to another (the claimant company) enabling the latter to put the other company's loss etc against its total profits. Both companies must satisfy the group or consortium tests throughout their respective accounting period but need not be members of the same group or consortium when the claim is made.[1]

If Company A makes a loss and surrenders that relief to Company B, Company A may insist upon receiving some payment. This will be particularly so if it is not a wholly owned subsidiary so that there will be different minority interests as well as different creditors. If the amount paid is due under a legally enforceable[2] agreement and does not exceed the amount surrendered the payment is ignored in computing the profits and losses of either company and is treated neither as a distribution nor as a charge on income.

This device is of particular use when for example a company with (say) trade losses and foreign income is relieved from CT by the foreign tax credit or where the surrendering company is entitled to the reduced rate of 21% and the claimant is not.

Where the loss arises in a group member that is not resident in the UK, group relief is only available if the surrendering company is resident in another member state of the EEA[3] and the loss is not relievable in that other member state.[4]

Simon's Taxes D2.201, 243.

1   *A W Chapman Ltd v Hennessey* [1982] STC 214.
2   TA 1988, s 403(7).
3   Or has a permanent establishment in another EEC member state.
4   TA 1988, Sch 18A, paras 5–7.

Group relief and self-assessment

[28.07] The claim must be made in the claimant company's company tax return whether in the return originally made or by amendment.[1] The claim must specify the amount of relief claimed; this amount need not be for as much as the amount available for surrender.[2] If the claim is for an amount greater than the amount available for surrender the whole claim is ineffective.[3]

[28.07] Groups, consortia and substantial shareholdings

The return must include the name of the surrendering company,[4] and must be accompanied by a notice of consent from the surrendering company.[5] A consortium claim must also be accompanied by copies of the notices of consent given by each member of the consortium.[6] The consent cannot be amended but it may be withdrawn and replaced by a fresh consent.[7]

The notice of consent may mean that the surrendering company has to amend its tax return—eg if it has already made one and has claimed relief under TA 1988, s 393.[8] If the return is not amended when it should be, the notice of consent is ineffective.

The claim itself cannot be amended once it has been made. However, it may be withdrawn and replaced by a fresh claim.[9]

There are time limits for these claims.[10] The claim for group relief may be made or withdrawn at any time up to the first anniversary of the filing date for the company tax return of the claimant company for the accounting period for which the claim is made. However, when a HMRC issues notice of enquiry into a tax return, the issuing of the notice automatically extends the time limit to the latest[11] of: (a) 12 months after the filing date; (b) 30 days after the enquiry is completed; (c) 30 days after notice of amendment is issued by the Revenue; and (d) 30 days after the date on which the appeal against an amendment is finally determined. These limits may be extended by the Revenue.[12]

The legislation has to provide for the possibility that the amount available for surrender is later reduced.[13] The surrendering company must, within 30 days, withdraw sufficient notices so as to bring the total of the notices within the revised amount available for surrender and, if needed, give new notices of consent. The withdrawals and any new notices must be given in writing to the claimant companies and the Revenue. The Revenue have powers to act if the surrendering company does not. The claimant companies must amend their returns as necessary. Where the amount available for group relief has been reduced in this way the tax charged may in certain circumstances be recovered from another group member.[14]

The Revenue have power to recover excessive group relief by assessment.[15] They may also make a discovery assessment under para 41 or amend the returns of the claimant and surrendering companies.

Simon's Taxes D2.240–245.

---

[1] FA 1998, Sch 18, para 67. HMRC provides a form for the purpose, but this is not a statutory form.
[2] FA 1998, Sch 18, para 69.
[3] FA 1998, Sch 18, para 69(2).
[4] FA 1998, Sch 18, para 68.
[5] FA 1998, Sch 18, para 70. On contents see para 71.
[6] FA 1998, Sch 18, para 70(5).
[7] FA 1998, Sch 18, para 71.
[8] FA 1998, Sch 18, para 72; the normal time limit in para 15 does not apply.
[9] FA 1998, Sch 18, para 73; a withdrawal has to be done by the claimant company amending its return.

[10] FA 1998, Sch 18, para 74.
[11] FA 1998, Sch 18, para 74(1).
[12] FA 1998, Sch 18, para 74(2).
[13] FA 1998, Sch 18, para 75.
[14] FA 1998, Sch 18, para 75A.
[15] FA 1998, Sch 18, para 76.

The group

[28.08] Two companies are members of the same group for group relief purposes if one is a 75% subsidiary of the other or both are 75% subsidiaries of a third company[1]. For this purpose any bodies corporate can form a group, irrespective of whether the individual member companies are resident.[2]

Whilst the group can be traced through non-resident companies, the actual claimant and surrendering companies have always been required to be UK resident[3] (or a UK branch of a non-resident company). However, this was challenged by *Marks and Spencer v Halsey*[4] under the principle in European Law of Freedom of Establishment (see supra, § **1.11**). The company had incurred losses in France, for which it could not get relief (in fact it had sold its French operations). The company's claim for group relief against its UK profits was finally upheld by the ECJ to a limited extent.

This led to amendments to the group relief rules in FA 2006,[5] bringing in entitlement to claim group relief in the UK for EU losses provided:

(1)   the losses are of a kind relievable in the UK (eg not capital losses);
(2)   the losses existed if calculated under UK tax rules;
(3)   no relief was possible in any other period for the loss;
(4)   no other company could get relief for the loss.

The test for the availability of other relief for the losses must be tested for "immediately after the end of the current period", ie the loss making period. This makes claiming the relief in practice most unlikely and has been criticised as not being in keeping with the ECJ decision.

Simon's Taxes D2.105–108.

[1] TA 1988, s 413(3)–(5).
[2] With effect from 1 April 2000: FA 2000, Sch 27, see supra, § **28.01**.
[3] TA 1988, s 402(3B) introduced by FA 2000.
[4] (Case C-446/03) [2003] STC (SCD) 70; (Case C-446/03) [2006] STC 237, ECJ.
[5] FA 2006, s 27, Sch 1, inserting TA 1988, Sch 18A.

[28.09] In addition, the parent must be entitled to not less than 75% of any profits available for distribution to equity holders of the subsidiary company and to not less than 75% of any of its assets available for distribution to its equity holders on a winding up.[1] In determining this percentage certain loans of a non-commercial nature are treated as equity[2] and the court must have regard to any arrangements which could affect those rights.[3] These provisions have received a narrow but purposive construction.[4] The purpose of these rules is to confine the passing of the reliefs, especially capital allowance, to parents who were such in commercial as well as legal terms at some time during the accounting period in which the loss arises. It is also necessary, for similar reasons, to show that there are no arrangements in existence for transfer of control of the surrendering company without also transferring control of the claimant company.[5] Here the term "arrangements" is broadly construed.[6] Without some such rule an outside company could buy participation preference shares to establish 75% control and later the shares would be redeemed or sold back to the parent; in this way the loss could be sold to an outsider. Where arrangements are in force the effect of these provisions is to bar relief for those losses attributable to the period during which the arrangements subsisted.[7]

Where an option is granted, in order to calculate the extent of the equity holder's entitlement to profits or assets one must calculate the entitlements on the assumption that the option has been exercised. The equity holder is then treated as being entitled only to the lower of the percentage entitlement before the option is exercised and the percentage entitlement after the option is exercised.[8]

Simon's Taxes D2.106.

---

[1] TA 1988, s 413(7),(10), Sch 18.
[2] TA 1988, Sch 18, para 1(5E)–(5I) refine the notion of a normal commercial loan by treating as commercial loans, and so not as equity, loans where the interest rate reduces when the results of the company improve (to assist management buy-outs) and loans which are limited or non-recourse in nature and the security for the payment of principal or interest is restricted to land other than dealing property.
[3] TA 1988, Sch 18, para 5.
[4] *J Sainsbury plc v O'Connor* [1991] STC 318, CA.
[5] TA 1988, s 410(1)–(6). For this purpose, members of a consortium are not held to be "acting together" to control a company (TA 1988, s 410(5)) and Revenue Interpretation RI 160; Simon's Taxes, Division G3). Further, where an arrangement is conditional on the consent of the Office of Fair Trading, that arrangement cannot be held to be in existence until such consent has been obtained, *Scottish and Universal Newspapers Ltd v Fisher* [1996] STC (SCD) 311.
[6] *Pilkington Bros Ltd v IRC* [1982] STC 103; *Irving v Tesco Stores (Holdings) Ltd* [1982] STC 881.
[7] *Shepherd v Law Land plc* [1990] STC 795 rejecting the Revenue view that relief was barred for all the losses arising in the accounting period during part of which the arrangements subsisted.
[8] TA 1988, Sch 18, para 5B(9), reversing the effect of the decision in *J Sainsbury plc v O'Connor* [1991] STC 318, CA.

Overlapping periods

[28.10] The relief allows one company to use the losses sustained by the other in the overlapping accounting period.[1] If both companies have the same accounting period the whole loss is available for offset, assuming of course that they fulfil all the other conditions for group membership at that time.[2] Conversely when the company joins or leaves the group the profits of the relevant accounting periods must be apportioned to ensure that only losses of post-entry or pre-departure periods are used.

To carry out this process the legislation creates the concepts of the "surrenderable amount" of the loss and the unrelieved part of the profits. The amount of the loss which can be set off against the profits of the claimant is the lesser of two sums—(a) is the unused part of the surrenderable amount for the overlapping period and (b) is the unrelieved part of the claimant's profits for the period. A time basis is used in allocating these amounts to different parts of an accounting period, unless that would be unjust or unreasonable in relation to any person in which case a just and reasonable basis is used, but only to the extent necessary to avoid injustice and unreasonableness.[3] The last formulation is a considerable tightening in comparison with the old law and creates its own problems, eg if what would be required to be just to one party would create injustice for another. The balance of the loss may be carried forward and put against future trading profits of the company where the loss arose.[4]

Where there are several companies in the group with different accounting periods, the profit of the overlap period is allocated according to strict rules which place great emphasis on the order in which claims take effect.[5] These rules will have effect unless the companies choose a different order (though of course a claim may be withdrawn with consequential adjustments under these rules).[6]

These rules were introduced because of defects in the previous rules which used the concept of the "corresponding accounting period". The defects arose where more than two companies were involved.[7]

Simon's Taxes D2.216.

[1] TA 1988, s 403A.
[2] TA 1988, s 403(1), (8)–(10).
[3] TA 1988, s 403B.
[4] TA 1988, s 393, see supra, § **25.23**.
[5] TA 1988, s 403B.
[6] TA 1988, s 403B.
[7] Inland Revenue press release, 2 July 1997, para 6, *Simon's Weekly Tax Intelligence* 1997, p 912.

Consortium

[**28.11**] Group relief may also be claimed by members of a consortium in respect of losses and other debit items incurred by companies which the consortium owns.[1] A consortium owns a company if 75% of the ordinary share capital of that company is directly and beneficially owned between the consortium members, each owning at least 5%.[2] There is no requirement that any of the companies be resident apart from the restriction that only UK companies are allowed to benefit from group/consortium relief. Consortia may

[28.11] Groups, consortia and substantial shareholdings

therefore be traced through companies anywhere in the world.[3] The requirements of entitlement to divisible income and to assets on a winding up applied to groups apply also to consortia.[4] Consortium relief is restricted in the case of overlapping accounting periods.[5]

The group relief may be claimed by members of the consortium in three situations:

(1) if the surrendering company
    (a) is owned by the consortium,
    (b) is not a 75% subsidiary of any company, but
    (c) is a trading company;
(2) if the surrendering company
    (a) is a 90% subsidiary of a holding company which is owned by the consortium,
    (b) is not a 75% subsidiary of any other company, but
    (c) is a trading company; and
(3) if the surrendering company
    (a) is a holding company which is owned by the consortium, but
    (b) is not a 75% subsidiary of any company.

A trading company is defined as one the business of which consists wholly or mainly in the carrying on of a trade or trades.[6] A holding company is defined as one the business of which consists wholly or mainly in the holding of shares or securities of companies which are its 90% subsidiaries and which are trading companies.[7]

The relief may be claimed by the member of the consortium, not necessarily by the holding company. A consortium claim may not be made if the member company's share holding is of such a nature that a profit on the sale of that shareholding in the other company would be a trading receipt.[8] The amount of relief available in a consortium claim is the lowest of three percentages:

(a) the ordinary share capital held;
(b) the profit entitlement on a notional distribution;
(c) the asset entitlement of a notional winding up.

If the percentages have fluctuated during the period an average is used.[9] Where relevant, the overlapping period concept is used.

Group relief within a consortium may pass in either direction.[10] Each member may claim only that part of the loss which is proportionate to its share in the consortium. Where a member surrenders downwards to a trading company that amount can only be set against a similar proportion of the trading company's profits. There is no surrender to the intermediate holding company but that company may claim group relief proper. There is no objection to finding a group within a group or a group within a consortium.

Simon's Taxes D2.230.

---

[1] TA 1988, s 402(3); on FA 1997, s 68 see supra, § **28.09** footnote 5.
[2] TA 1988, s 413(6).
[3] TA 1988, s 413(5), amended with effect from 1 April 2000.

[4] TA 1988, s 413(10).
[5] TA 1988, s 403C.
[6] TA 1988, s 413(3)(c).
[7] TA 1988, s 413(3)(b).
[8] TA 1988, s 402(4); this provision also applies in the context of holding companies.
[9] TA 1988, s 403C(2) and (3).
[10] TA 1988, s 402(3); a surrender downwards may affect that company's ability to surrender further losses within its group.

Groups and consortia

[28.12] Consortium relief may "flow through" a consortium member to and from other companies in the same group.[1] The maximum relief which may be claimed through a consortium member is restricted, in essence to the claim the consortium member could itself make.[2] If overlapping period calculations are required, they are made by reference to the actual group and consortium members.[3]

It is also possible to surrender part of the available relief to a group company and part to a consortium company.[4]

Simon's Taxes D2.231.

[1] TA 1988, s 406.
[2] TA 1988, s 406(4), (8).
[3] TA 1988, s 406(4), (7).
[4] TA 1988, s 405(6).

Surrender of reliefs

[28.13] Seven reliefs may be surrendered to the claimant company:

(1) Trading losses may be set off against the total profits of the claimant company for its overlapping accounting period.[1] The trading loss of a consortium-owned company must, as far as possible, be set off against the company's other profits of the same accounting period and only the balance is available for set-off against the profits of consortium member companies.[2]

(2) Minor capital allowances in excess of income of the relevant class arising in that accounting period;[3] these are allowances which attract relief through the discharge of tax rather than being treated as a trading expense (supra, § **9.07**). These can be surrendered to the extent that they exceed income of the relevant class. Again the set-off is against total profits of the claimant company for its corresponding accounting period.

[28.13] Groups, consortia and substantial shareholdings

(3) Management expenses[4] in excess of the company's profits may be set off against the total profits of the claimant company for the overlapping accounting period of the claimant company.[5] The total profits of the surrendering company means profits before deduction of any losses or allowances of other periods and before deduction of all reliefs.[6]

(4) The amount paid by way of charges on income of the surrendering company and exceeding the profits of that company for that period may be surrendered to be set off against the total profits of the claimant company for the corresponding accounting period.[7] This means that if charges are carried forward from a previous period they cannot be used to free current reliefs for grouping; such charges can therefore become locked into the company.

(5) Any non-trading deficit on loan relationships.[8]

(6) Property business losses.[9]

(7) Non-trading deficits on post–1 April 2002 "intangible fixed assets".[10]

Reliefs 3, 4, 6 and 7, unlike 1, 2 or 5, must be set off against other profits of the company for the accounting period concerned and only the resulting balance surrendered.[11]

The surrendering company is not of course obliged to give up its loss relief and it may, if it wishes, surrender only part of the loss. Further the relief may be claimed by more than one company in the group or member of the consortium.

Group relief is given against the "profits" of the recipient company. In *MEPC Holdings v Taylor*,[12] the House of Lords, agreeing with the Special Commissioner and overruling the Court of Appeal and High Court held that "total profits" of the claimant company meant a sum computed after the deduction of capital losses and other deductions allowed by statute. Group relief is applied *before* any reliefs that may be brought back into the accounting period from future periods.[13]

Simon's Taxes D2.217.

---

1 TA 1988, s 403(1).
2 TA 1988, s 403(ZA)(3).
3 TA 1988, ss 403(1)(*a*), 403ZB.
4 Infra, § **30.01**.
5 TA 1988, s 403(1)(*b*).
6 TA 1988, s 403ZE.
7 TA 1988, s 403(1)(*b*).
8 CTA 2009, s 459, TA 1988, s 403ZC.
9 TA 1988, s 403(1).
10 CTA 2009, s 753.
11 TA 1988, s 403(3).
12 [2003] UKHL 70, [2004] STC 123, HL.
13 TA 1988, s 407. Terminal loss relief can also now be given against total profits: s 393.

Pre-entry losses and gains

[28.14] Schemes to use capital losses incurred before the company entered the group, are now governed by legislation restricting the use of such losses.[1] The effect is to ring fence capital losses available to a company at the time it joins the group. Such losses enjoy unrestricted rights of set off only against gains arising in respect of assets held by the company at the date of its entry into the group, or acquired by that company from outside the new group and used in a trade carried on by the company before it joined the new group.[2]

The rules apply where there is a company which is or has been a member of a group, called the relevant group, and that company has pre-entry losses.[3] The key concept of pre-entry loss is defined as covering first any allowable loss that accrued to that company at a time before it became a member of the relevant group. This is reasonably easy to grasp.[4] However, the concept also covers the pre-entry proportion of any allowable loss accruing to that company on the disposal of any pre-entry asset.[5] The purpose here is to ring fence the asset only in relation to the period before it joins the group. An asset is a pre-entry asset if it was held by any group member immediately before that group member joined the group or, broadly, derives its value from such an asset.[6] An asset is not a pre-entry asset if it has been transferred within the group in circumstances not covered by TCGA 1992, s 171.[7] There are provisions to deal with the situations in which the company has joined the group more than once or assets have been issued more than once.

The meaning of relevant group came under consideration in the combined appeals of *R & C Comrs v Prizedome Ltd and Limitgood Ltd*.[8] In that case, a loss-making company was acquired by a group of companies (the first group) which was then acquired by a second group of companies (the second group). The intention was for the closing words of para 1(6) to apply so that the members of the first group are deemed to have joined the relevant group when they joined the second group. Blackburne J held that para 1(6) applied on a loss-by-loss basis and, in particular, not to losses that precede the company's acquisition by the first group.

Simon's Taxes D2.401.

---

[1] TCGA 1992, s 177A, Sch 7A.
[2] Inland Revenue press release, 16 March 1993, *Simon's Tax Intelligence* 1993, p 474.
[3] TCGA 1992, Sch 7A, para 1(1).
[4] TCGA 1992, Sch 7A, para 1(2)(*a*).
[5] TCGA 1992, Sch 7A, para 1(2)(*b*).
[6] TCGA 1992, Sch 7A, para 1(3), (6).
[7] TCGA 1992, Sch 7A, para 1(4).
[8] [2008] EWHC 19 (Ch).

[28.15] There are elaborate provisions for calculating the pre-entry proportions of any loss. These provisions provide a basic time apportionment rule, an alternative method of calculation based on a deemed disposal at market value

[28.15] Groups, consortia and substantial shareholdings

when the asset came into the group, and further rules for pooled assets. The purpose is to ensure that it is only the pre-entry proportion of the loss which is restricted.

The basic rule apportions a segment of the "total indexed rise" to each of the various items of allowable expenditure separately. Each segment is then time apportioned on a straight-line basis between the periods before and after the company joined the group. The sum of the pre-entry segments is the pre-entry loss.[1] An asset acquired on a no gain, no loss disposal is treated as acquired on the last occasion which was not such a disposal.[2] There is also a provision dealing with the effect of reorganisation relief.[3] In applying the basic formula where an asset has been derived from another under a corporate reorganisation the asset treated as acquired when the original asset was acquired—except for indexation purposes.[4] As originally drafted these provisions failed to deal with two situations. The first was where a company made an intra-group transfer of an asset carrying an unrealised loss. Where an asset was transferred to another group member before there was a disposal of the asset outside the group the time apportionment formula is to treat the asset as having been acquired at the date of the transfer within the group; this meant that the loss attributable to the period before the asset was brought into the group was nil. In relation to gains and losses realised after 10 March 1994 the formula is applied by reference to the time of the asset by the company for which it is a pre-entry asset ie the original acquisition of the asset and not the intra-group transfer.[5] The second situation arose where a group wishing to shelter a gain acquired a company with an unrealised loss. The gain would be realised while the company was in the group but would then be sold on before the loss was realised.[6] This too is stopped as from the same date.

The alternative basis is the lesser of the actual indexed loss and the indexed loss which would have accrued on a market value disposal of the pre-entry asset when the initial company joined the group.[7] The taxpayer must elect for this basis and do so within two years beginning with the end of the accounting period of that company in which the disposal is made on which the loss accrues or such longer period as the Board may by notice allow.[8]

Simon's Taxes D2.421–424.

---

[1] TCGA 1992, Sch 7A, para 2(1)–(3).
[2] TCGA 1992, Sch 7A, para 2(5)–(7).
[3] TCGA 1992, Sch 7A, para 2(8).
[4] TCGA 1992, Sch 7A, para 2(4); this applies also to para 3.
[5] TCGA 1992, Sch 7A, para 2(6A), (6B); see also Inland Revenue press release, 11 March 1994, *Simon's Tax Intelligence* 1994, p 341.
[6] TCGA 1992, Sch 7A, para 2(7); see also Inland Revenue press release cited in previous note.
[7] TCGA 1992, Sch 7A, para 5.
[8] TCGA 1992, Sch 7A, para 5(8).

[28.16] Once the losses have been calculated one can turn to the specifics of the provision. Pre-entry losses are only to be set against certain specified gains.[1] These are later defined as those accruing from:

(1) disposals made before the company joined the group;
(2) assets held at the time of joining; and
(3) assets acquired from persons outside the group after joining and which have been used only for the purposes of a trade which had been carried on before the company joined the group.[2]

Where one is dealing with the pre-entry proportion of a loss accruing on the disposal of a pre-entry asset one naturally finds a different set of rules.[3] These losses can only be set against:

(1) a gain arising from a disposal made by the company before it joined the group provided that that company (called the initial company) is the one by reference to which the asset on the disposal of which the loss accrues is a pre-entry asset;
(2) the pre-entry asset and the asset on the disposal of which the gain arises were each held by the same company immediately before it joined the relevant group; or
(3) the gain accrues on an asset which was acquired by the initial company from outside the group and has since been used only for the purposes of a trade carried on by that company and which was being carried on when it joined the group.

Further rules apply if the initial company was a member of another group when it joined the group and other companies joined at the same time.[4]

Naturally, the legislation contains rules for the order in which the reliefs are to be given. Broadly where pre-entry losses can be set against a gain those of the current or a previous accounting period are offset before other losses of such periods[5] and pre-entry losses of the current period are used before those brought forward from an earlier one. Where there is more than one pre-entry loss the company may elect the order in which they are to be set off, but must do so within two years of the end of the accounting period in which the gain offset accrues; in the absence of an election older losses are used first.

Simon's Taxes D2.425, 431.

---

[1] TCGA 1992, Sch 7A, para 6.
[2] TCGA 1992, Sch 7A, para 7(1).
[3] TCGA 1992, Sch 7A, para 7(2).
[4] TCGA 1992, Sch 7A, para 7(3).
[5] TCGA 1992, Sch 7A, para 6(1).

[28.17] Clearly HMRC felt the pre-entry loss rules were not working as effectively as they would wish. In the 2005 Pre-Budget Report, three "Targeted Anti-Avoidance Rules" (TAARs) were announced; these were duly effected in FA 2006.[1] They attack:

(1) contrived creation of capital losses;[2]
(2) loss buying and gain buying;[3]
(3) conversion of income to capital and using capital losses to create a deduction against income.[4]

The hub of the loss buying provisions is that they prevent an offset of losses acquired where the change of ownership of the company in question occurs "directly or indirectly . . . in connection with any arrangements the main purpose, or one of the main purposes of which, is to secure a tax advantage".[5] The existing pre-entry tax loss rules are left in place; accordingly any purchase of a company with existing capital losses will have two hurdles to overcome:

(1) the old rules to be applied to all situations on a mechanical basis
(2) the new rules to be applied to situations where tax avoidance was part of the motiviation behind the transaction.

The new rules provide for some careful identification of 'pre-change assets' to identify tainted losses.

There are then parallel provisions which target pre-entry gain buying.[6] These replace the pre-existing provisions.

---

[1] FA 2006, ss 69–71.
[2] FA 2006, s 69 amending TCGA 1992, s 8.
[3] FA 2006, s 70 inserting TCGA 1992, s 184A–184F.
[4] FA 2006, s 71 inserting TCGA 1992, s 184G–184I.
[5] TCGA 1992, s184A(1)(c).
[6] TCGA 1992, s 184B.

Pre-entry gains

[28.18] Further rules deal with the opposite case—where a company with realised gains (G) is imported into a group with unrealised losses.[1] The rules only affect the accounting period in which G realises a gain and then joins a group; this is because losses realised later cannot be carried back to be set against the realised gains.[2] There are no provisions equivalent to the TCGA 1992, Sch 7A, para 2 rules requiring apportionment of latent losses in the gains rules. The gains for the accounting period are then split between pre- and post-entry gains, the former group being subject to the new rules; the splitting is done by the date of realisation.[3] Pre-entry gains may only be set against losses which are sufficiently connected with G; these are losses arising before or at the same time as the gain, or at some later time provided it is before G joins the group and losses arising after the joining but in respect of assets which G owned at that time.[4]

Where G has acquired assets at different times there are further identification rules depending on whether they are treated as pooled assets or not. Pooled assets become a notional separate pool with subsequent disposals being identified with the pre-entry pool rather than with any post-entry acquisitions. Other assets are the subject of a special rule where a loss arises after G joins the group so as to determine what part of the loss should be treated as a qualifying loss; an apportionment procedure may be used.[5]

Special rules apply to companies carrying on life assurance business.[6] It is also made for certain unit trusts and to offshore funds; here provision has to be made for certain gains or losses which are spread forward; the effect of the rules being to ensure that they are treated as pre-entry gains or losses.[7]

Simon's Taxes D2.505.

1   TCGA 1992, Sch 7AA.
2   TCGA 1992, Sch 7AA, para 1.
3   TCGA 1992, Sch 7AA, para 2; this does not apply to companies joining a group before 17 March 1998—s 135(5) on gains.
4   TCGA 1992, Sch 7AA, paras 3 and 4.
5   TCGA 1992, Sch 7AA, paras 5 and 6.
6   FA 1998, s 135(3) and (4) amending TCGA 1992, s 213—on commencement see s 135(3B).
7   TCGA 1992, Sch 7AA, para 7.

Other rules

[28.19] There are yet further provisions. There are restrictions if within a three-year period there is both a major change in the nature of the company's trade and the company joins the group.[1] There are rules to cover the situation in which the company belongs to more than one group and to determine which is the relevant group and how the loss should be apportioned.[2] These rules are strengthened for accounting periods ending on or after 17 March 1998. In identifying the groups to which the pre-entry loss rules apply specific attention is now given to more than one move being made in the same accounting period. The pre-entry loss rules are to apply on the basis that each group is taken separately whenever in the same period a company becomes a member of a group which is then taken over by a second group.[3] There are rules for appropriations to trading stock[4] and for looking through various changes of company form.[5]

Simon's Taxes D2.410–420.

1   TCGA 1992, Sch 7A, para 8.
2   TCGA 1992, Sch 7A, para 9.
3   TCGA 1992, Sch 7A, para 9(6).
4   TCGA 1992, Sch 7A, para 10.
5   TCGA 1992, Sch 7A. paras 11, 12.

Transfer of company tax refunds

[28.20] Where one company in a group has a duty to pay unpaid tax and another has a right to a tax repayment the companies may merge the duty and the right and so avoid letting the Revenue get the benefit of the difference in interest rates.[1] To qualify for this surrender the two companies must make a joint surrender notice, they must have the same accounting period for the period in respect of which the repayment claim is being surrendered and they must be members of the same group throughout the relevant period, ie from the start of the accounting period for which the claim is made until the date of the surrender notice.[2] The definition of "group" is the same as "group" relief (supra, §§ **28.08** ff).[3]

The refunds which may be surrendered are repayments of corporation tax for the accounting period and repayment of income tax on unfranked investment income, eg interest.[4] The effect of the surrender is that the recipient company will be treated as having paid corporation tax of that amount in the relevant date and the surrendering company as having received a repayment of tax on the same date. The relevant date is the date on which the corporation tax was actually paid by the surrendering company or, if later, the date on which the corporation tax became payable, ie the end of the company's nine-month period.[5] This timing rule does not apply to any sum which is due as a tax-geared penalty.[6] Any sums paid in exchange for the surrender are ignored—they are neither taxable receipt of the surrendering company nor deductible items for the claimant company provided they do not exceed the amount of the refund in question.[7]

The system extends to the situation in which a "large" company has made instalment payments under the regulations[8] and is now entitled to a refund.[9] A company which does not wish to claim a refund, but wishes to transfer the benefit of that overpayment to another group company may do so.[10]

Simon's Taxes D1.1321.

[1] FA 1989, s 102.
[2] FA 1989, s 102(1), (2), (4).
[3] FA 1989, s 102(8).
[4] FA 1989, s 102(3).
[5] FA 1989, s 102(5).
[6] FA 1989, s 102(6)—ie penalty under TMA 1970, s 94(6).
[7] FA 1989, s 102(7); this is similar to payments for group relief, TA 1988, s 402(6).
[8] See Corporation Tax (Instalment Payments) Regulations, SI 1998/3175.
[9] Under SI 1998/3175, para 6.
[10] Under SI 1998/3175, para 9.

Intra-group transfers of capital assets (75% subsidiaries)

Tax neutrality

[28.21] The transfer of a chargeable asset between two members of a group takes place at such figure as ensures there is neither chargeable gain nor allowable loss.[1] The effect is to postpone any capital gains liability until the asset is disposed of outside the group. This is a matter of law, not of election and overrides the normal rule that bargains otherwise than at arm's length are to be treated as taking place at market value.[2] An interesting question arises if one company surrenders a lease of land to another group member since it can be argued that what happens is that the lease ends and the landlord company acquires no asset at all.[3]

The general rule is excluded in certain situations; what these have in common is that value is being received by one company but the capital gains structure, for reasons of its own, treats the receipt as being in exchange for an asset. The first situation is where a debt is disposed of by one group member to another and the debt is disposed of by being satisfied in whole or in part. This rule contains the interesting idea that there is a disposal of a debt when it is satisfied—as distinct from the disposal of the property being transferred to satisfy the debt. There is also the point that except for a debt on a security no chargeable gain can arise on the disposal of a debt. One is therefore left with the idea that s 171 is excluded where a debt on a security is satisfied—as where one member company pays off a debenture and another member company receives a payment in respect of it; the overall effect being presumably to allow the claim of a loss or, occasionally, to tax a gain—as where a debt is acquired for less than face value and afterwards settled in full.[4]

The second is where redeemable shares are disposed of on redemption. So a gain on redemption will be taxable notwithstanding that there is a disposal of the shares in exchange for the consideration received on redemption.

The third is a disposal by or to an investment trust.[5] Further rules restrict relief if assets are transferred to a group company which is or will become exempt from tax on its gains such as an Enterprise Investment Trust or a Venture Capital Trust.[6]

The fourth is the deemed disposal which arises on a capital distribution by a member company in which it holds shares; there will still be a disposal by the company making the capital distribution and this *will* fall within s 171.[7]

The fifth is where the asset consists of shares which are regarded as a loan relationship, by virtue of FA 1996, s 91A, in the hands of one of the member companies party to the disposal but is not so treated in the hands of the other.

Where the asset is disposed of by destruction and compensation is payable, the disposal is deemed to be to the person who ultimately bears the burden of paying the compensation money, eg an insurance company.[8]

The principle applies whether there is an actual disposal or a deemed disposal and acquisition. However, it is now provided that the principle does not apply where the statute directs that there is neither a disposal nor an acquisition.[9]

These postponement provisions do not apply to transfers between subsidiary and a parent in liquidation since, once liquidation of the parent has begun, the shares in the subsidiary are not held by the parent beneficially but on trust for its own members.[10] The effect of a voluntary winding up is less clear.[11] Distributions by a subsidiary in liquidation are likewise taxed immediately. These problems can be overcome by arranging for transfers and distributions by or to the parent before liquidation.

Simon's Taxes D2.310–317.

---

[1] TCGA 1992, s 171. For an unsuccessful attempt to obtain relief see *Johnston Publishing (North) v R & C Comrs* [2008] EWCA Civ 858 where the Court of Appeal held that both the Special Commissioner and the High Court had been

[28.21] Groups, consortia and substantial shareholdings

correct in holding that TCGA 1992, s 179(2) requires that not only should the companies leaving the group be associated companies at the time they leave but also at the time of the acquisition of the relevant asset in a previous intra-group transfer.
[2] TCGA 1992, s 17. Section 171 applies "notwithstanding any provision in [TCGA] fixing the amount of the consideration deemed to be received".
[3] See Law Society Revenue Law Reform proposals, *Simon's Tax Intelligence* 1991, p 1069.
[4] As in the example of a loan account; see **Simon's Taxes D2.314**.
[5] TCGA 1992, s 171(2)(*c*).
[6] TCGA 1992, s 171(2)(*cc*), (*cd*), (*da*).
[7] *Innocent v Whaddon Estates Ltd* [1982] STC 115.
[8] TCGA 1992, s 171(4).
[9] TCGA 1992, s 171(3): the corporate reorganisation provisions are TCGA 1992, ss 127, 135, and Sch 5AA supra, § **21.11** ff. This provision reverses *Westcott v Woolcombers Ltd* [1986] STC 182; see also *NAP Holdings UK Ltd v Whittles* [1994] STC 979, HL.
[10] *Ayerst v C & K (Construction) Ltd* [1975] STC 345, [1975] 2 All ER 537. The House of Lords decided only that the company ceased to be beneficial owner of its assets. The Court of Appeal had held that the ownership was in suspense [1975] STC 1, [1975] 1 All ER 162.
[11] *Wadsworth Morton Ltd v Jenkinson* [1966] 3 All ER 702, 43 TC 479.

Notional transfer of assets

[28.22] The ability to transfer an asset within a group without a tax charge makes it beneficial for an asset to be transferred to a group member with brought forward losses prior to the sale of the assets to a third party, where the sale triggers a gain. The actual transfer of the asset can, however, create three types of problem. First, stamp duty land tax may be payable on any land transferred unless a certificate can properly be given that the asset is not subject to an agreement for an onward sale (see infra, § **60.04**). Second, where there are minority shareholdings in the group, some compensation for the loss of value to the minority shareholders is necessary and agreement to this may not be forthcoming. Third, there may be contingent liability relating to the assets, particularly if it is a trade that is to be sold, and the purchasers will wish to bind the company that has used the asset and not solely the company making the sale.

Where the sale is made on or after 1 April 2000, the liabilities of the parties to tax on the capital gain arising can be computed as if there were an inter-group transfer prior to a sale to a third party. This novel concept[1] gives a hypothetical element to the computation of a tax liability greater than has ever previously been enacted in a deeming provision.

Let us say that an asset is sold by company A to a third party, outside the group. In the same 75% group, company B has brought forward capital losses. If the disposal to the third party that is actually made by company A is after 31 March 2000, companies A and B can jointly elect[2] to compute their respective total profits for corporation tax purposes as if the asset had been transferred from company A to company B immediately and then sold to the third party by company B. This treatment applies so long as had the actual physical transfer been made it would have fallen within s 171(1).[3] The expenses actually incurred by company A that would be deductible as costs of sale are relieved in computing the gain that is deemed to have been made by company B. In this scenario, company A has obtained a commercial advantage by a reduction of its overall tax liability. Hence, if there are minority shareholders in one or both of the companies, it is likely that a payment will be required from A to B to reflect the benefit of a reduced tax charge (and also, the cost to B of using up capital losses that would otherwise be available to put against future gains). Any such payment is ignored for corporation tax purposes as long as it does not exceed the amount of the chargeable gain or allowable loss.[4]

The joint election must be made within two years of the end of the accounting period of company A.[5]

Once the asset is disposed of to a person outside the group the normal liability to corporation tax in respect of the capital gain follows.[6] If an asset has been acquired under an intra-group transfer or on the transfer of an asset from the permanent establishment of a non-resident company to a UK company and is later disposed of outside the group, provision has to be made to reflect the group's ownership of the asset. So the disposing company is treated as having acquired the asset, at a consideration giving no gain/no loss to the disposing company, when it was originally acquired by a group member. Provision is made for recognising the previous ownership by another group member for pre-1965 acquisitions.[7] The tax may be recovered from the principal member at the time the gain accrues and from any previous owner.[8]

Simon's Taxes D2.329.

[1] TCGA 1992, s 171A.
[2] TCGA 1992, s 171A(2).
[3] If A is UK-resident and B is a non-resident company with a UK branch, the asset deemed to pass is deemed not to change its locus: F(No 2)A 2005, s 36.
[4] TCGA 1992, s 171A(5).
[5] TCGA 1992, s 171A(4).
[6] TCGA 1992, s 8.
[7] TCGA 1992, s 174(4).
[8] TCGA 1992, s 190.

The group

[28.23] In order for a transfer to be made at no gain/no loss the two companies concerned must be members of a 75% group[1], consisting of a principal company and all its 75% subsidiaries. The 75% is applied to the beneficial ownership of shares; unlike group income this relief is available even though the shares are held otherwise than as investments. A company owns shares beneficially if it is free to dispose of them as it wishes; it is irrelevant that the shares may not be owned very long.[2]

[28.23] Groups, consortia and substantial shareholdings

Further, the group remains the same group so long as the same company remains the principal company. If the principal company becomes a 75% subsidiary of another company the group is regarded as expanded rather than ended and refounded. Similarly if the principal company becomes a Societas Europaea or a subsidiary of a Societa Europaea, the group identity is unaffected.[3]

There are further rules on the definition of a group to counter the use of "bridge" companies.[4] These are arrangements which use a company with special classes of share; in turn these enable the commercial control of companies to pass to a company outside the group while allowing the company to remain within the group structure for tax purposes and so avoiding the triggering of charges that would otherwise arise on the company ceasing to be a member of the group. This led to the avoidance of tax on the capital gains that would otherwise arise on the sale of a subsidiary or the sale of an asset.[5]

The group is still made up of the principal company and its 75% subsidiaries, including 75% subsidiaries of those subsidiaries and so on. However, a subsidiary which is not an effective 51% subsidiary is excluded.[6] A company is an effective 51% subsidiary only if the parent is beneficially entitled to more than 50% of any profits available for distribution or of any assets on a winding-up.[7]

Further, a company can only be a principal company if it is at the head of the corporate chain. So a company cannot be a principal company if it is a 75% subsidiary of another company.[8] There is an exception if the company does not form part of a group because it is not an effective 51% subsidiary.[9] To reinforce this policy it is provided that a company may not be a member of more than one group; to carry this policy through the legislation contains a descending order of tests.[10] To prevent a charge from arising unexpectedly as a result of this change where a principal company subsequently becomes a 75% subsidiary of another company, thereby bringing two groups together, the two are regarded as being the same group for the purposes of determining whether there has been a transfer of an asset within the group (TCGA 1992, s 171) and whether a company has ceased to be a member of another group (TCGA 1992, s 179).[11] Thus a charge under TCGA 1992, s 179 is not triggered simply by such an event. It is also provided that the winding up of a company in the group does not result in either that company or any other company in the group being treated as ceasing to be a member of the group.[12]

There is no requirement that a company should be UK resident.

Simon's Taxes D2.305.

---

[1] TCGA 1992, s 170(2).
[2] *Burman v Hedges & Butler Ltd* [1979] STC 136.
[3] TCGA 1992, s 170(10A).
[4] There is also a consequential change for IHT—IHTA 1984, s 97. These rules are further backed up by a cross reference to TA 1988, Sch 18.
[5] *Simon's Tax Intelligence* 1989, p 222. HC Official Report, Standing Committee G, col 597.

[6] TCGA 1992, s 170(3).
[7] TCGA 1992, s 170(7).
[8] TCGA 1992, s 170(4).
[9] TCGA 1992, s 170(5).
[10] TCGA 1992, s 170(6).
[11] TCGA 1992, s 170(10).
[12] TCGA 1992, s 170(11).

Company leaving the group after intra-group transfer

[28.24] The privilege of postponing tax liability on transfers within the group was in addition to the basic rule that there could be no charge without a disposal of the asset. So an asset would be transferred to another company within the group in exchange for shares which would then be sold to a stranger company without giving rise to a chargeable gain.

If a company leaves a group[1] (the departing company) and it then holds a chargeable asset which it has acquired from another member of the group within the previous six years, the departing member is treated as having disposed of the asset and reacquired it at its market value at the time of that intra-group acquisition.[2] Historically, this has been a stumbling block to company reorganisations but provisions in recent Finance Acts have largely begun to redress this.[3]

The gain or loss accruing to the company is treated as arising immediately after the beginning (or end) of the accounting period in which the company ceases to be a member of the group or, if later, when it acquired the asset from the other member of the group; although the calculation of the gain is based on the transfer taking place at the time of the intra-group transfer.[4] The effect of this is to remove retrospectively the immunity enjoyed by the intra-group acquisition, but to impose the charge primarily on the company then acquiring the asset. There is power to recover the unpaid tax from the principal member of the group and any other company that owned the asset in the 12 months prior to the gain accruing.[5] The company assessed has the right to recover tax from the chargeable company—including the right to recover any interest it has to pay.[6] HMRC must serve notice on the company within three years of the date on which the company's tax liability is finally determined.

An election can be made jointly by two companies in a group for the gain to be re-allocated within the group.[7] The election must be within two years from the end of the transferee company's accounting period in which the gain/loss crystallises and must be for all or part of this gain to be reallocated to another group member in the old group. The group company at the time of the accrual must be resident in the UK or own assets falling within the UK corporation tax net and it cannot be either a qualifying friendly society or an investment trust. Any payment made for the reallocation of the gain/lose is disregarded for tax purposes as long as it does not exceed the reallocated gain or loss.[8] Two or more elections may be made provided that the total amount of the reallocated gain or loss is not greater than that crystallising. A non-resident company, trading in the UK through a permanent establishment, is also within these provisions as long as any resulting chargeable gain forms part of its chargeable profits for UK tax.

[28.24] Groups, consortia and substantial shareholdings

Rollover relief can be claimed on the degrouping charge.[9] The provisions echo those for rollover relief on reinvestment in qualifying assets.

---

[1]   TCGA 1992, s 170(10).
[2]   TCGA 1992, s 179(1), (3). Note. On extension of time limit for election in respect of pre 1965 assets, see statement of practice D21; **Simon's Taxes, Division G1.2.**
[3]   See notes 4, 11 and 12 below.
[4]   TCGA 1992, s 179(4) as amended by FA 1993, s 89.
[5]   TCGA 1992, ss 190(3), (4) & (7).
[6]   TCGA 1992, s 190(11).
[7]   TCGA 1992, s 179A(3).
[8]   TCGA 1992, s 179A(11).
[9]   TCGA 1992, s 179B and Sch 7AB introduced by FA 2002, s 43 and Sch 7 with effect from 1 April 2002. The reinvestment period, of up to 12 months before and three years after, operates from the date the company leaves the group. Reduced rollover is available where only part of the deemed sale consideration is reinvested. This may happen when an election has been made under s 179A for part of the gain to be reallocated or when another company, within the original group, makes a partial roll over relief claim.

[28.25] Where a principal company subsequently becomes a 75% subsidiary of another company, thereby bringing two groups together, the two are regarded as being the same group so that this event will not of itself cause a company to cease to be a member of the group.[1] The passing of a resolution for the winding up of a company is not to have such an effect either.[2]

Where s 179(3) would be triggered in respect of a company deemed to leave the group but only by reason of the principal company becoming a member of another group, a deemed sale of assets previously transferred under s 171 to the company leaving the group, will be deemed to occur if, within six years of the company leaving the group, the company ceases to satisfy certain conditions.[3] Those conditions are:[4]

(1)   that it remain a 75% subsidiary of one of the members of the group; and
(2)   that it remain an effective 51% subsidiary. The chargeable gain or allowable loss arises at the time the conditions cease to be satisfied.[5]

These rules are to apply whether the company on leaving the group owns the original asset or another in respect of which replacement rollover relief has been obtained under TCGA 1992, ss 152–158.[6] Rollover relief could not be claimed when the new company leaves the group since it applies only when a new asset is acquired. An asset owned by the chargeable company when it leaves the group is also treated as being the same as the asset acquired from the other group member if it derives its value in whole or in part from the first asset;[7] this rather delphic rule is stated to apply specifically where the first asset was a leasehold interest and the second asset is the freehold the lessee having in the meantime acquired the reversionary interest.

Where two or more companies leave the group at the same time and together they form a group the rules do not apply to acquisitions which had taken place between companies within the newly independent group.[8] As originally drafted this meant that the two companies concerned with the transfer of the asset could then leave the new group without incurring the charge under s 179(1). There was no degrouping charge on the break up of the first group because of s 179(1) while there was none on the second either since the asset was acquired before the second group was established. Restrictions, however, now apply where the company ceases to be a member of the second group[9] but only if there has been what the legislation calls a connection between the two groups; the connection is elaborately defined but basically means the companies being under common control.[10] Under these circumstances the charge in s 179(1) is to apply after all; the section has effect as if it had been the second group of which both companies had been members at the time of the acquisition. These changes are not the end of the story. As originally defined they made the deferred charge only where the common control was exercised by a company; where the company leaves the second of the two groups on or after 17 March 1998 there will be a charge whether the common control is by any person or persons (ie companies) or other bodies.[11]

Also outside the rules are certain types of merger, provided that they do not have the avoidance of tax as one of their main objects.[12] The relevant provision on mergers was enacted to assist with the Dunlop Pirelli merger some years ago. The essence is that cross holdings of at least 25% are established for full value. Demergers are also outside s 179.[13]

The section is also excluded if the company ceases to be a member of the group in consequence of another member of the group ceasing to exist.[14] The reference to the other company "ceasing to exist" is a relatively limited exemption from the s 179 charge. At one time the wording allowed schemes such as that successfully used in *Burman v Hedges & Butler Ltd*[15] but the wording now allows only for s 179 where (in effect) a subsidiary moves within a group by virtue of a subholding company being wound up.

EXAMPLE

A has a subsidiary, B. In 2003 it transferred to B an asset with a base cost of £10,000 but with a current value of £15,000. TCGA 1992, s 171 ensures that the base cost to B is £10,000 and that no chargeable gain arises in 2003.

If, in September 2007, A sold its shareholding in B, B will be treated as receiving a chargeable gain of £5,000. This will be calculated by reference to values in 2003 but taxed as profit arising in 2007.

If in 2005 B had sold the asset to an independent purchaser for £18,000 and replaced it with another asset which cost £18,000 the rollover relief in TCGA 1992, s 152 will then have treated the disposal as being for £10,000. When s 179 is applied in 1999 B will be treated as notionally disposing of the replacement asset at £15,000 with consequent adjustment to its cost base. If rollover relief had not been claimed s 179 will not apply—because the capital gains liability would have been discharged in 2005.

Simon's Taxes D2.307, 333–334.

1 TCGA 1992, s 179(1).
2 TCGA 1992, s 179(6).
3 TCGA 1992, s 179(7).
4 TCGA 1992, s 179(8).
5 TCGA 1992, s 179(9).

[28.25] Groups, consortia and substantial shareholdings

6   TCGA 1992, s 179(10)(b).
7   TCGA 1992, s 179(10)(c).
8   TCGA 1992, s 179(2A); see Inland Revenue press release, 29 November 1994, Simon's Tax Intelligence 1994, p 1485.
9   Defined in TCGA 1992, s 179(2B); control is defined by reference to TA 1988, s 416.
10 TCGA 1992, s 179(2B)(b) and (c); Inland Revenue press release, 17 March 1998, Simon's Weekly Tax Intelligence 1998, p 455, para 9. For exception for investments trusts see s 179(2C).
11 TCGA 1992, s 181.
12 TCGA 1992, s 192(3).
13 TCGA 1992, s 179(1).
14 F(No 2)A 1992, s 25(2).
15 [1979] STC 136.

Transfer of loans

[28.26] Where a loan is transferred between companies that fall within the corporation tax net in respect of that transaction in a 75% group, the basic provision is that the transfer is not treated as giving rise to any charge or allowance on either the transferor or the transferee.[1] The transferee company, after the transfer, becomes entitled to any debits and credits that arise thereafter which are not related to the transfer. This treatment extends to a "related transaction"[2] between two group companies and to any series of transactions, where two companies were members of the same group at some time during the course of the series of transactions. The treatment applies where there is an effective transfer by novation. Thus, the release of the former borrower does not cause a taxable receipt in the hands of that company. The provision does not apply if the transferor accounts for the loan on a fair value basis[3] and any discount arising on the transaction is also excepted.[4] A charge also now applies on the transferee company leaving the group within six years of the transfer similar to the capital gains charge on such an occasion.[5]

1   FA 1996, Sch 9, para 12.
2   CTA 2009, s 304.
3   CTA 2009, s 341.
4   CTA 2009, s 341.
5   CTA 2009, ss 344–345.

Transfer of trading stock

[28.27] Where one company transfers a capital asset to another company in the group and the recipient company appropriates the asset to trading stock, the rule that the disposal should be at such a figure that neither gain nor loss accrues collides with the principle that the asset should enter the trading stock at market value.[1] The legislation therefore provides that the recipient company should receive the asset as a capital asset and then transfer the asset to trading stock at market value. This gives the recipient the right to choose between an immediate chargeable gain and a later trading profit because of the available election under s 161(3). When deciding whether a company received an asset from another group member as trading stock or as a capital asset it was held that the circumstances as a whole should be examined to determine the motive for the realisation of the asset.[2]

Where the asset transferred was trading stock of the transferring company, but is received as a capital asset by the recipient, it is treated as having ceased to be trading stock before the transfer; the consequence is that for capital gains purposes the transferor is treated as having disposed of the asset to himself at whatever figure is entered in the books of the trade in respect of the asset.[3] For a person to appropriate an asset as trading stock there must be a genuine intention to trade and not simply a wish to gain a tax advantage.[4] The asset must not only be of a kind sold in the ordinary course of the trade but must be acquired with a view to resale at a profit.[5]

Simon's Taxes D2.656.

[1] TCGA 1992, s 173, referring to TCGA 1992, s 161; supra, § **22.06**.
[2] *New Angel Court Ltd v Adam* [2003] EWHC 1876 (Ch), [2003] STC 1172.
[3] TCGA 1992, s 173(2) refers to TCGA 1992, s 161 which treats the disposal as being at such figure as is entered in the computation of trading profit; this will usually be current market value because of *Sharkey v Wernher*.
[4] *Coates v Arndale Properties Ltd* [1984] STC 637, HL; *Reed v Nova Securities Ltd* [1985] STC 124, HL.
[5] Per Lord Templeman in *Reed v Nova Securities Ltd* [1985] STC 124 and 130, HL.

Rollover relief and a group

[28.28] Another way in which the group is recognised as the relevant owner concerns the rollover provisions for business assets.[1] These rules are of concern for us. First, all the trades of the member companies are treated as being one trade so that if X Co sells an asset and buys another for use by Y Co, its subsidiary, rollover relief may be claimed.

This relief does not apply if the acquisition by Y is itself a transfer within the group.[2] Without such a rule X could make a disposal outside the group and realise a gain which could then be rolled over by a shuffling of assets within the group. The rule is also excluded if X's disposal is a transfer at no gain/no loss.[3]

Second, rollover relief also applies where the disposal is by a company which, at the time of the disposal, is a member of a group of companies and the acquisition is by another company which, at the time of the acquisition is a member of the same group. The claim must be made by both companies, as if both companies were the same person.[4] This provision enacts previous Revenue practice; this stated that it was not necessary for the acquiring company to satisfy the group requirements when the other company made the disposal provided that it did so when the asset was acquired.[5]

Third, rollover relief applies where, a non-trading member of the group disposes of assets (or an interest in assets) used, and used only, for the purposes of the trade deemed to be carried on by the other trading members of the group.[6] The same applies to acquisitions by the non-trading member.

For the purposes of the rule restricting rollover relief where the replacement asset is a depreciating asset, not only are all the trades treated as one but that trade is deemed to be carried on by one person.[7] Where an event occurs giving rise to a chargeable gain that gain accrues to the member holding the replacement asset at that time.

For an international group of companies, rollover relief is available amongst the members of a group that are resident in the UK and also the non-resident companies in the group insofar as the asset is used (or is brought into use) for the purpose of a trade of the permanent establishment in the UK.[8] Rollover relief does not, however, apply when the investment in the new asset is made by a dual resident investment company.[9]

Simon's Taxes D2.341.

---

[1] TCGA 1992, s 175(1). On position of a non-trading member, see [1971] BTR 268.
[2] TCGA 1992, s 175(2C); this a natural consequence of treating the activities of the group as a single trade.
[3] The list of no gain, no loss provisions that disapply rollover relief is given in TCGA 1992, s 35(3)(d).
[4] TCGA 1992, s 175(2A).
[5] This is the Revenue view. See statement of practice SP 8/81; **Simon's Taxes, Division G1.2.**
[6] TCGA 1992, s 175(2B) enacting extra-statutory concession D30 and added by FA 1995, s 48.
[7] TCGA 1992, s 175(3).
[8] TCGA 1992, s 175(1A) & (2AA).
[9] TCGA 1992, s 175(2) as amended by FA 1994, s 251(8). On dual resident investment companies see infra, § **33.30**.

Anti-avoidance provisions for groups

[28.29] If there is a disposal[1] by one group member to another of an asset at a nominal figure, neither gain nor loss arises (TCGA 1992, s 171); this may cause a decline in the value of the former company. Losses resulting from such depreciatory transactions within a group[2] and realised on a subsequent disposal of the shares or securities are disallowed by s 176. The disallowance is limited to the under-value of the transaction.[3] If there is a later disposal of the shares in the acquiring company the previously disallowed loss can reduce the gain.[4] Section 176 restricts losses; it does not create or increase gains.[5] Section 177 deals with dividend stripping. The payment of accumulated profits by means of an intra-group dividend can be treated as giving rise to a depreciatory transaction and any resulting capital loss disallowed by s 176.

This was introduced in 1969 as a companion [now TA 1988] (s 736 (supra, § **4.17**) which deals with share-dealing companies.

EXAMPLE

X buys the share capital of Y for £100,000. A dividend of £60,000 is then declared by Y which is then liquidated. The distribution to X on the liquidation of Y is £40,000. Although X has a capital loss of £60,000 on its investment in Y, s 177 empowers the inspector to disallow that loss to the extent of the dividend received (£60,000).

This section deals only with the disallowance of losses it does not apply to the reduction of gains. It follows that the common practice of a subsidiary making a distribution shortly before it is sold—so reducing the gain on the sale of those shares—is not caught by this provision.

Statute[6] disallows a loss where, after the loss arising, the company in which the loss occurs is transferred from one company to another by means of a "change of ownership directly or indirectly in consequence of . . . any arrangements the main purposes, or one of the main purposes, of which is to secure a tax advantage". This provision seeks to put a stop to schemes which have been created to deliberately avoid the existing capital gain and loss buying rules on a change of company ownership.[7]

Similar rules are targeted at denying the use of an intermediary's capital losses to shelter gains.[8]

With effect from 5 December 2005 statute[9] aims to stop relief for capital losses against income arising from a scheme to convert income to capital by using two types of scheme that secure tax deductions in this area:

(1) conversion of income to capital arrangements in which the converted income is then sheltered by existing capital losses;
(2) creating a capital gain which is covered by existing capital losses, and as a consequence of the arrangements, an income deduction is created.

The new rules will apply where the obtaining of a tax advantage was the main or one of the main purposes of the arrangements and HMRC has issued a notice to counteract the avoidance. The purpose of the legislation is to capture tax avoidance schemes and not commercial transactions, such as sale and leaseback arrangements which are specifically excluded from the new anti-avoidance rules. Informal clearance procedures are available in respect of these arrangements.

Further provisions are aimed at stopping arrangements where a company is purchased for its capital losses[9] (or gains[10]) and arrangements where income is converted to capital.[11]

Simon's Taxes D2.350–352.

---

[1] TCGA 1992, s 176(8) includes a claim under TCGA 1992, s 24(2), that the value of shares or securities has become negligible.
[2] Defined by TCGA 1992, s 176(3) as including the cancellation of securities under Companies Act 1985, s 135; it is perhaps odd that there should be no mention of the Companies Act 1985, s 425.

[28.29] Groups, consortia and substantial shareholdings

3   But includes disallowance of indexation allowance; *X plc v Roe* [1996] STC (SCD) 139.
4   TCGA 1992, s 176(6).
5   Defined by TCGA 1992, s 176(4).
6   TCGA 1992, s 184A inserted by FA 2006, s 70(2).
7   The new rules apply to tax advantages arising on or after 5 December 2005.
8   TCGA 1992, s 184B inserted by FA 2006, s 70(2).
9   TCGA 1992, s 184A inserted by FA 2006, s 70(2).
9   TCGA 1992, s 184A inserted by FA 2006, s 70(2).
10 TCGA 1992, s 184B inserted by FA 2006, s 70(2).
11 TCGA 1992, s 184G inserted by FA 2006, s 71. Guidance on the manner in which HMRC intends these provisions to operate is given in Treasury Notes to Finance Bill 2006.

Value shifting transactions

[28.30] By 1989 the practice of reducing the value of subsidiary companies prior to disposal of those companies outside the group was in danger of becoming a standard feature of UK tax practice. The basic scheme, according to the government, involved stripping out of a subsidiary unrealised gains in the value of its chargeable assets by means of a tax-free intra-group dividend out of artificially created profits. In this way the group would shelter from tax that would otherwise be, and effectively were, realised gains in the sale of the subsidiary. That could even mean a group lending money to one subsidiary to buy an asset from another.[1]

At first sight one might have thought that this was precisely the sort of value shifting at which TCGA 1992, s 30 (supra, § **17.17**) was directed. However, that provision in its original version, specifically excluded the shifting of value arising from the payment of dividends between members of a group of companies within the meaning of TCGA 1992, s 170 and the disposal of assets between them.

Closure of this loophole was enacted as FA 1989, ss 135–138 which amended the original version of what became TCGA 1992, s 30 and gave us ss 31–34. Section 30 enables the Revenue to get at the reduction in the value of the asset; sections 31–34 define certain circumstances in which there is such a reduction in value and its extent. So s 30 has a life independent of ss 31–34 but we are here concerned with the circumstances in which ss 31–34 add to the scope of s 30. Section 31A (infra § **28.33**) was added in 1999. Section 33A was added in 2002 to deal with the application of these rules to chargeable intangible assets.[2]

In attacking those devices the legislation safeguards ordinary dividend payments within a group and tries not to penalise a group for extracting profits from a subsidiary before sale by a dividend payment where the profits supporting that dividend have borne tax. The target is the extraction of gains from profits that have not borne tax.[3] Not surprisingly, in seeking to target a specific type of abuse the provisions are extremely detailed and complex. Where the new rules apply, the chargeable gains on the sale of the subsidiary are increased (or the allowable losses reduced) by an amount which appears to the inspector or on appeal the Commissioners, to be just and reasonable.[4] The legislation refers to associated companies but this means simply that they are members of the same group.[5]

Simon's Taxes D2.353–358; STP [36.224]–[36.260].

[1] HC Official Report, Standing Committee G, col 598 (Mr Lamont).
[2] See supra §§ **27.31** ff.
[3] HC Official Report, Standing Committee G, col 598 (Mr Lamont).
[4] TCGA 1992, s 30(5).
[5] TCGA 1992, s 33(9); groups are defined by reference to ss 170, 33(10).

[28.31] TCGA 1992, s 30 applies, as respects the disposal of an asset if a scheme has been effected, or arrangements have been made, (whether before or after the disposal) whereby the value of the asset has been materially reduced and a tax-free benefit results. Section 30 applies to a reduction in the value of an asset where the asset consists of shares owned by a company (the first company) in another company (the second company) and the sale of shares owned by one company in another company in the circumstances set out in ss 31–33.[1] Of these s 31 deals with distributions within a group followed by a disposal of shares and s 32 deals with disposals within a group followed by a disposal of shares. Section 33 contains supplementary provisions. In addition s 34 modifies the normal reorganisation rules.

There is much useful material on these sections in HMRC Capital Gains Manual, paras 46800 ff.

[1] TCGA 1992, s 30(8).

Distributions within a group followed by a disposal of shares

[28.32] TCGA 1992, s 31 brings within s 30 a reduction in the value of the subsidiary to be sold arising from the payment of dividends generated by the chargeable profits, the so-called drain out dividend. The disposal of the shares is the disposal for s 30 purposes and the distribution is the related reduction in value. That distribution must be at a time when the two companies are associated, ie within the same group.

For example X Co holds shares in its subsidiary, A. Company A sells an asset on which there are unrealised capital gains to company B another member of the group; the section proceeds to describe such an asset as the asset with enhanced value. The sale is at market value so giving company A the cash which will be used to pay the dividend but, because of TCGA 1992, s 171, the transaction is taken for tax purposes to be at such an amount that neither a gain nor loss accrues. The value of A is then reduced by A declaring a dividend of the realised but untaxed capital gain.

Section 30 will apply to the extent (if any) that the dividend is attributable to "chargeable" profits of the company. Chargeable here means not chargeable under ordinary rules and therefore specially chargeable for this section or, as the legislation puts it, distributable profits are chargeable profits to the extent that they are profits arising on a transaction caught by the section.[1] Since the sale to B is within the list of situations which can give rise to chargeable profits, s 30 will apply to the extent that the distribution is paid out of the chargeable profits.

Turning to the more formal structure of the legislation one finds that s 31 makes s 30 apply if each of three conditions with regard to the transaction is met.[2]

First the transaction (from which chargeable profits can arise) must be:

(1) the disposal of an asset by one group company to another in circumstances such that neither a gain nor a loss is deemed to arise (ie TCGA 1992, s 171); or
(2) an exchange of shares or debentures held by a company for shares in or debentures of another company which becomes associated with it immediately after the exchange, where the exchange is not treated as a disposal thanks to TCGA 1992, s 132(3); or
(3) a revaluation of the asset in the company's accounting records.[3]

As seen in the example above the asset passing out of company A with an unrealised and untaxed gain is referred to as an asset with enhanced value.

The second condition is also complex and consists of exclusions. During the period beginning with the transaction described in the previous condition and ending immediately before the distribution the asset with enhanced value must not have been subsequently the subject of a CGT disposal.[4]

The third condition is that the asset must, immediately after the s 30 disposal (ie the disposal of the shares in A) be owned by a person other than the distributing company or by any company associated with it.[5] Where company A disposed of the asset to B and X then disposed of the shares in A, this condition is obviously satisfied.

Chargeable profits are attributed to any person in receipt of a distribution in the same proportion as chargeable gains bears to total distributions.[6]

In calculating whether distributions are paid out of chargeable profits one begins with the determination of the total amount of the company's distributable profits.[7] Any distributions already made are then deducted as are later distributions in respect of other classes of share.[8] The actual distribution is then treated as coming out of any remaining distributable profits other than chargeable profits.[9] Any losses (or other sums deductible in computing the distributable profits) are to be set first against profits other than chargeable profits.[10]

Section 31 is excluded if, at the time of the disposal, share exchange or revaluation, company A carries on a trade and a profit on the disposal would form part of the trading profits; there is a similar exclusion if it is company B which is carrying on the trade.[11] Section 31 is also excluded if by reason of the nature of the asset neither chargeable gain nor allowable loss can arise on the disposal; since the asset is not subject to CGT provisions no abuse occurs.[12]

Allowance is made for any dividend paid out of the chargeable profits by B.[13]

Provision is made for part disposals of an asset with enhanced value and for situations in which an asset comes into existence with a value which is derived from the asset with enhanced value.[14]

One other complexity is anticipated by the section. So far we have assumed that the subsidiary which is sold is the subsidiary which carried out the transaction. It may however be that the disposal of shares is preceded by a distribution by a subsidiary of the company now being disposed of. It is therefore provided that where a company, M, makes a distribution attributable (in whole or in part) to chargeable profits of another company, N, the distributable profits of N so far as they represent that distribution or so much as was attributable to chargeable profits are chargeable profits of N.[15]

Simon's Taxes D2.355.

[1] TCGA 1992, s 31(3)(a). This is widened by s 31(3)(b).
[2] TCGA 1992, s 31(5).
[3] TCGA 1992, s 31(3)(a), (5), (6). These were outlined as targets in Inland Revenue press release, 14 March 1989, *Simon's Tax Intelligence* 1989, p 220, para 2.
[4] Other than a disposal under TCGA 1992, s 171 (no gain/no loss transfer within a group): TCGA 1992, s 31(7); on disposal and other terms see s 31.
[5] TCGA 1992, s 31(8); Inland Revenue press release, 14 March 1989, *Simon's Tax Intelligence* 1989, p 220, para 3; on the meaning of disposal and other terms used in s 31 see s 33.
[6] TCGA 1992, s 31(11).
[7] Computed on a commercial basis and after allowing any proper provision for tax; TCGA 1992, s 31(4).
[8] TCGA 1992, s 31(10)(a).
[9] TCGA 1992, s 31(10)(b).
[10] TCGA 1992, s 31(3).
[11] TCGA 1992, s 31(9)(a), (c).
[12] TCGA 1992, s 31(9)(b); on the meaning of disposal see s 33.
[13] TCGA 1992, s 33(8).
[14] TCGA 1992, s 33(2)–(4), (8).
[15] TCGA 1992, s 31(3)(b).

Pre sale transfers to non-resident companies

[28.33] Section 31A is aimed at this mischief. Section 31 had addressed the situation in which value had been stripped out of the subsidiary before its sale and that stripping had taken a non-taxable form; it did so by allowing the Revenue to adjust the capital gain arising on the sale of the subsidiary itself. Safeguards in the original legislation[1] meant that no adjustment could be made by the Revenue if the subsidiary, having been part of a world-wide group, after the stripping but before the sale, had been transferred to a non-resident member of the group. The adjustment power in s 30 can be used if either of two events occurs. The first is if within six years of the stripping disposal within s 30 the subsidiary leaves the group.[2] The charge is not triggered if the group of which it is a member is taken over by another group. This is achieved by saying that the charge does not arise if the principal member of the group

[28.33] Groups, consortia and substantial shareholdings

becomes a member of another group. The second is if the group of which it is a member has been taken over by another group (and so is excluded from the first event) but the company holding the asset is then disposed of outside the original group.[3] This is achieved by saying that there is a charge if it ceases to be a 75% subsidiary or an effective 51% subsidiary of any member of the group.

There are provisions to prevent double charges,[4] to specify the amount of the adjustment,[5] to indicate whether the company to be charged is the company which made the disposal or the principal member of the group[6] and to deal with losses from sale to connected persons which might otherwise be lost.[7]

Simon's Taxes D2.356.

---

[1] TCGA 1992, s 31(8).
[2] TCGA 1992, s 31A(4).
[3] TCGA 1992, s 31A(5).
[4] TCGA 1992, s 31A(6).
[5] TCGA 1992, s 31A(7), (8).
[6] TCGA 1992, s 31A(9).
[7] TCGA 1992, s 31A(10).

Transfer within a group followed by a disposal of shares

[28.34] TCGA 1992, s 32 tackles the avoidance of capital gains on the sale of a subsidiary by transferring assets from the subsidiary to other members of the group at a price below market value and cost price so reducing the value of the shares subsequently disposed of. The policy behind TCGA 1992, s 171 does not require a deferral in such circumstances. Section 32 can therefore be seen as a logical extension of TCGA 1992, s 176 (supra, § **28.29**).

The provision is excluded if the asset is disposed of for bona fide commercial reasons and the disposal does not form part of any scheme or arrangement of which the main purpose—or one of the main purposes—is the avoidance of tax.[1] It is also excluded where the subsequent disposal of shares in the subsidiary is a capital distribution in the course of a winding up.[2]

The effect is that s 30 will apply if there is a reduction attributable to a s 171 disposal of an asset ("the underlying asset") by company A at a time when it and company B are associated, the actual consideration for the underlying asset is, as already stated, less than the market value and the cost.[3] Cost is defined as any capital expenditure incurred in acquiring or providing the asset and any other capital expenditure incurred during the transferor's ownership of the asset; it makes no allowance for any indexation relief.[4]

Provision is made for part disposals.[5]

Simon's Taxes D2.357.

---

[1] TCGA 1992, s 32(2).
[2] TCGA 1992, s 32(5).
[3] TCGA 1992, s 32(2).

⁴ TCGA 1992, s 32(3).
⁵ TCGA 1992, s 32(4).

Reorganisations

[28.35] Because of TCGA 1992, s 34, a charge may arise under s 30 if a company disposes of shares or debentures in exchange for shares in or debentures of another company and that exchange would fall within the reorganisation provisions in TCGA 1992, ss 127, 135(3). In such circumstances the company selling the shares in the subsidiary is to be treated for the purposes of s 128(3) as receiving an amount in cash, as opposed to shares or securities, that would have been calculated by applying s 30. This withholds the normal deferral on a reorganisation to the extent that s 30 would apply. This is made to apply also to the situation in which s 30 applies by virtue of the new s 31A (supra, § **28.33**).

Reduction in value of relevant asset followed by disposal of shares in a subsidiary

[28.36] TCGA 1992, s 30 applies where there has been a material reduction in the value of a relevant asset. Where there is a disposal by a company, "the disposing company", A, of shares in, or securities of, another company, B, another asset is relevant if, at the time of the disposal, it is owned by a company associated with company A. This is a wide definition but the scope of the provision is immediately narrowed by the direction that account is only to be taken of the reduction in value of the relevant asset in certain prescribed circumstances, these being situations two of which are also excluded from s 31.[1] These two are (a) that during the period beginning with the reduction in value and ending immediately before the disposal of shares there is no disposal of the relevant asset other than one falling within TCGA 1992, s 171(1), and (b) that during the same period there has been no deemed disposal of the asset under TCGA 1992, s 179 (company ceasing to be member of the group). In addition it is provided[2] that the reduction is to be taken into account if, on certain assumptions the value of the shares would have been materially greater had the relevant asset not been reduced in value. Those assumptions are that the reduction had not taken place and that there was no change in any consideration given for the relevant asset and in any other material circumstances (including, specifically, consideration given before the disposal but for the asset concerned).

This rule, which was part of the original 1989 package is designed to counter variations of a technique for avoiding TCGA 1992, s 30 whereby the asset that is reduced in value is subsequently transferred to another company and it is the shares in the company which are disposed of.[3]

Simon's Taxes D2.354; STP [36.262]–[36.270].

[1] TCGA 1992, s 30(2)(*a*) and (*b*).
[2] TCGA 1992, s 30(2)(*c*).
[3] Inland Revenue press release, 14 March 1989, *Simon's Tax Intelligence* 1989, p 221, para 10.

Demergers

[28.37] Until 1980 it was difficult to split a group up. The difficulty was that the transfer of the piece being split off would cause the value received by the shareholder to be treated as a qualifying distribution supra, § **26.02**; in addition there were capital gains and stamp duty problems when a company or assets left the group. As part of a campaign to free British industry from unnecessary constraints Parliament included certain provisions—now TA 1988, ss 213–218—to encourage the process of "demerging" by removing some of the obstacles.[1]

There are three types of demerger provided by the Act. These are:

(1) where a company spins off a subsidiary directly to its shareholders ie where it distributes shares in a subsidiary to its shareholders so that those shareholders control the former subsidiary directly and no longer through the distributing company—the conditions are discussed at infra, § **28.38**;

(2) where a company spins off a trade to its shareholders but indirectly ie where it transfers a trade to another company in exchange for shares and those shares are not held by the parent but distributed to its shareholders—see infra, § **28.39**; and

(3) where a company spins off a subsidiary indirectly to its shareholders, ie where it transfers shares in a subsidiary to another company in exchange for shares but the shares are not held by the subsidiary but distributed to the shareholders of the parent—see infra, § **28.40**.

One situation not covered by these alternatives arises when the company has a trade which it wishes to transfer to its shareholders directly, ie by transferring ownership of the trade itself rather than having to use a company to hold the trade and transferring shares in the company. It is presumably thought that such a situation would involve the trade leaving the corporate sector entirely and should not therefore be an occasion for relief.

Certain conditions are common to all of them. First, there must be a transaction which would otherwise be a distribution of income under TA 1988, s 209.[2] This means amongst other things that the new reliefs cannot apply to a demerger in the course of a liquidation. Also, under TA 1988, s 209, a distribution other than a dividend, eg a distribution of shares, is not a distribution if it represents a repayment of capital.[3]

Second, the company making the distribution must, at the time of the distribution, be a trading company[4] (or a member of a trading group—a phrase which will not be repeated); certain trades notably those dealing in shares, land and commodity futures are excluded.[5]

Third, the transaction must be wholly or mainly to benefit some or all of the trading activities involved in the demerger.[6] This test is a narrow one. A demerger will not qualify simply because there are bona fide commercial reasons for it. It is probably sufficient that the benefit should be either to the retained or the transferred trade and not to both but this is not absolutely clear.

The combination of these two conditions means that relief is available only where trade is being demerged from trade and so not, for example, to the demerger of trade from investment. In many instances the exact status of the secondary business of an unlisted company may be in doubt; such doubts need to be resolved before a demerger is embarked upon.

Fourth, it is intended that the newly demerged trade should be left free to operate under its new independent management—quite separate from the former parent. To this end it is provided that where the company distributes shares in its subsidiary to its members (type 1 above) those shares must not be redeemable and must represent the whole or substantially the whole of the distributing company's interest.[7] If the transfer is of a trade to another company (type 2) the distributing company is not to retain anything more than a minor interest in the trade[8] while if it is of shares in a subsidiary (type 3) the shares must not be redeemable and must represent the whole or substantially the whole of the distributing company's interest.[9]

Fifth, all the companies involved must be resident in the UK at the time of the distribution.[10]

Finally, one should note that there are elaborate anti-avoidance provisions which may disqualify the scheme altogether. Thus the demerger must not be part of a scheme or arrangement for the avoidance of tax, for the making of a chargeable payment,[11] for the acquisition of control of any company involved by a third person nor for the cessation of a trade or its sale after demerger. The purpose of the demerger provisions is to encourage the hiving off of active businesses so that they may thrive on their own; so the provisions are designed to ensure that assets remain within the corporate sector and not used to get tax advantages on what is really the sale of a business; hence a passing of control to another company in return for shares which flow back to the shareholders in the previous owners is essential. Intra-group transfers cannot qualify for this treatment.

These rules are not designed to assist intra-group demergers. Where therefore there is a chain of companies it will be necessary to demerge the group from the bottom up.

Simon's Taxes D6.420–429.

---

[1] See *Simon's Tax Intelligence* 1980, pp 171, 418 and statement of practice SP 13/80; **Simon's Taxes, Division G1.2.** In practice, it is often preferable to split a company by using a reconstruction rather than the statutory demerger provisions. For a useful case study on this, see Peter Rayney's article "Breaking Up Is Hard To Do", *Taxation* 27 May 2004 pp 217-221.

[2] Statement of practice SP 13/80; **Simon's Taxes, Division G1.2.**

[3] Supra, § **26.01**.

[4] TA 1988, s 213(5); the terms are defined in TA 1988, s 21.

[5] TA 1988, s 218(1)—"trading".

[6] TA 1988, s 213(10).

[7] TA 1988, s 213(6).

[8] TA 1988, s 213(8)(*a*).

[9] TA 1988, s 213(8)(*b*).

[10] TA 1988, s 213(4).

[11] TA 1988, s 213(11).

Demerger of subsidiaries

[28.38] The first type of demerger allowed arises where one company, X, transfers to all or any of its members, ie ordinary shareholders[1] shares in a directly owned 75% subsidiary, Z.[2] This allows a simple spinning off of the distinct business run by Z which is already a separate entity and takes the form of a simple distribution in specie. The insistence on a 75% holding in Z is to be noted. The transfer must be to X's shareholders and not simply to another conglomerate.

The conditions for the relief require, inter alia, that Z must be a trading company[3], that its shares must not be redeemable[4] and that the shares distributed must constitute substantially the whole of X's holding in Z and also confer on them substantially the whole of X's voting rights.[5] The Revenue view is that "substantially the whole" represents at least 90%. These demerger provisions are intended to operate only where the control passes from X to the shareholders. It will also be noted that the conditions insist that the transfer should be of the *ordinary* shares in Z and to the *ordinary* shareholders of X.[6] It follows that preference shareholders of X may not benefit from these distributions although, of course, they may be in a position, by virtue of their voting rights, to exact a high price for their concurrence in any demerger scheme.

There are also conditions to ensure that X should not only have been a trading company before the spin off[7] but continues as a trading entity after the demerger[8] save where it is disposing of all its net assets and at least two companies such as Z are involved.[9] This is to prevent the use of the demerger rules on what is really a simple cessation.

A transfer of shares by X of this sort would normally cause a number of tax consequences; some of these are modified. First, the distribution is to be exempt.[10] It follows that there will be no income tax. Neither will there be a capital distribution to the shareholders which might otherwise cause capital gains consequences under TCGA 1992, s 122[11] (capital gains liability is thus deferred until the shares are disposed of). Further as Z is leaving the group, there might be a charge under TCGA 1992, s 178 on assets acquired from other members of the group within the last six years;[12] however, the receipt of a chargeable payment within five years will revive such a charge.[13]

Yet some tax consequences remain. Since Z ceases to be a member of the group it will not in future be entitled to group privileges such as, for example, group less relief. Second, the change in control of Z will mean that the restrictions on loss relief in TA 1988, s 768 and potential liability for postponed corporation tax under s 767AA may have to be noted should a change in Z's trade be contemplated; however, the Revenue have indicated sympathetic treatment here by treating the underlying ownership as remaining unchanged. Third, where close companies are involved there may be IHT implications.

Another very important tax consequence is that X will be disposing of its holding in Z, a disposal that may give rise to substantial liability on the gains involved. This cost may be reduced if either the gains are minimal or X has unrelieved capital losses. Where this is not so it may be possible to reduce the value of the shares in Z by paying a dividend. However, the more unusual the steps taken the greater the risk that the scheme will fall into the anti-avoidance provisions on the ground that it forms part of a scheme one of the main purposes of which is the avoidance of tax. This very high tax cost may inhibit many schemes of demerger under these rules. However, in many cases the FA 2002 substantial shareholding exemption will solve this problem.[14]

To assist the process in some respects it is possible to apply to the Revenue for clearance and thus obtain their binding agreement that the proposed distribution is indeed within these rules. Details of the information required are set out in the Revenue statement of practice SP 13/80.[15]

Simon's Taxes D6.421–424.

[1] A consequence of the definition of "member" in TA 1988, s 218(1).
[2] TA 1988, s 213(3)(a).
[3] TA 1988, s 213(6)(b).
[4] TA 1988, s 213(6)(a).
[5] TA 1988, s 213(8)(a) and (b). The Revenue view is given in Statement of practice SP 13/80; **Simon's Taxes, Division G1.2**.
[6] TA 1988, s 218(1).
[7] TA 1988, s 213(5).
[8] TA 1988, s 213(6)(b); this rule does not apply when the distributing company is the 75% subsidiary of another company—TA 1988, s 213(12).
[9] TA 1988, s 213(7) and see extra-statutory concession C11; **Simon's Taxes, Division G2.2** (company may return funds to meet costs of liquidation provided excess is negligible).
[10] TA 1988, s 213(2).
[11] TCGA 1992, s 192.
[12] TCGA 1992, s 192(3).
[13] TCGA 1992, s 192(4).
[14] TCGA 1992, Sch 7AC.
[15] See **Simon's Taxes, Division G1.2**.

Three party demergers

[28.39] The second type of demerger arises when X disposes of a trade to Y and, in exchange, Y issues shares not to X but to the ordinary shareholders of X. In this way the trade is hived off from the rest of X's activities and thus demerged and X's ordinary shareholders receive shares in Y.[1] The legislation refers simply to the transfer of a trade. The Revenue take a broad view of this requirement and will regard it as satisfied when what is received by Y is a trade. Hence what is transferred may be only a part of X's trade eg the retail end of a combined manufacturing/retailing trade. Or the assets transferred may be being assembled for the first time from one or more trades carried on by X—or by other members of the group. It may even be that some of the assets have not previously been used in any trade, eg land held by an investment company. What matters, according to the Revenue, is that there should be a division of trading activities and that the assets transferred should be transferred to be used in a trade carried on by Y and should be so used.

Relief is not denied solely because some minor asset is transferred which is linked with a trading asset, eg a flat over a shop.[2]

The conditions for relief here require that X itself should after the demerger hold only a minor interest in the transferred trade.[3] The term interest is not defined but in the Revenue's view it must be given a wide meaning; it therefore covers not only an interest in the trade giving rise to a right to profits or an asset of the trade but also less obvious rights such as an entitlement to be a main supplier or customer.[4] The Revenue view is that common management may "possibly" amount to such a right. In these less obvious cases the Revenue would normally concede that the interest was a minor one unless the interest gave control of the trade or its assets or a material influence on the profits or their destination. In general the term "minor" is regarded as the corollary of "substantial", and therefore as being, in those circumstances where quantification is possible, 10% or less.[5]

It is also necessary that Y's only or main activity is to be the transferred trade.[6] Further, control must be shifted to X's ordinary shareholders from X, so Y's shares must not be redeemable[7] and must constitute in the Revenue's view at least 90% of the issued ordinary share capital and carry 90% of the voting rights.[8]

Other provisions relate to X. So there are also provisions to ensure that X continues as a trading entity[9] save where it is transferring all its net assets and at least two companies in Y's position are involved.[10]

Normally such a distribution by X of its assets would be treated as a distribution but as with the first type of demerger it is provided that the distribution is to be exempt so there is no income tax charge.[11] In addition, TCGA 1992, s 179 is excluded.[12] The legislature has not thought it necessary to exclude any charge as a capital distribution under TCGA 1992, s 122 in these circumstances, presumably because in these circumstances it is Y rather than X that is making the distribution to X's shareholders; in the light of the new approach this assumption becomes debatable. However, the rules make no provision for other consequences. Thus X is disposing of the trade, one of its capital assets, and its shareholders are receiving an amount with capital gains implications; these consequences can be avoided by ensuring that the scheme is a company reconstruction and so making use of the provisions of TCGA 1992, ss 136, 139. Another set of consequences will flow from the fact that X ceases to carry on this trade and that Y begins to carry it on; this will give rise to all the usual problems of discontinuance and commencement with restrictions on losses, unused capital allowances and possible changes of accounting date.

Simon's Taxes D6.421–424.

---

[1] TA 1988, s 213(3)(b). On consequences where trusts are involved see Law Society press release, 22 July 1992, *Simon's Tax Intelligence* 1992, p 762.

[2] This is taken almost verbatim from statement of practice SP 13/80; although the UK demerger provisions are very different in some ways from the US provision (see Internal Revenue Code § 355), this passage in statement of practice SP 13/80 shows clear signs of having been written in the light of the US experience; **Simon's Taxes, Division G1.2.**

[3] TA 1988, s 213(8)(*a*).
[4] Here the emphasis must be on the word "entitlement".
[5] Statement of practice SP 13/80; **Simon's Taxes, Division G1.2**.
[6] TA 1988, s 213(8)(*c*); this condition must be met both at the time of the distribution and thereafter, a phrase which is interpreted by the Revenue as meaning not forever thereafter but simply sufficient to show a bona fide trade by Y; see statement of practice SP 13/80.
[7] TA 1988, s 213(8)(*d*).
[8] TA 1988, s 213(8)(*d*) and HMRC Statement of practice SP 13/80; **Simon's Taxes, Division G1.2**.
[9] TA 1988, s 213(8)(*b*).
[10] TA 1988, s 213(9); as in note 6 this does not mean forever thereafter.
[11] TA 1988, s 213(2).
[12] TCGA 1992, s 192(3); however the receipt of a chargeable payment within five years will revive the liability under these rules, TCGA 1992, s 192(4).

[28.40] The third type of demerger is a mixture of the first two. Here X transfers shares in its 75% subsidiary Z to Y and Y in turn issues shares in Y to the ordinary shareholders of X.

The conditions for relief are similar to those for the first two. So Z must be a trading company[1] and the shares transferred by X to Y must be at least 90% of X's holding of the ordinary shares capital and voting power of Z[2] and Z must be a 75% subsidiary of X.[3] Y's only or main activity must be to hold the shares in Z.[4] The shares issued by Y must not be redeemable and must constitute at least 90% of its issued share capital[5] and a similar percentage of its voting power. Again after the demerger X must continue to be a trading company or dispose of all its net assets with two or more X companies being transferred to two or more Y companies.[6]

The tax consequences are a similar mixture of the first and the second. As with the first the distribution of the shares in Y is to be an exempt distribution[7] with the result that there is no income tax nor franked investment income. Z leaves the group controlled by X but there is exemption from TCGA 1992, s 179[8] as in the first type of demerger. X's disposal of the shares in Z may give rise to chargeable gains (subject to substantial shareholdings relief) but those can be avoided by using a reconstruction; and the same device will save the shareholders in X from liability. As the control of Z passes from X there will be matters to be noted with regard to losses and loss of group benefits as already set out under the first type. Where this type of demerger scores over the first is in the matter of the tax cost arising from the realisation of any gains on the disposal of the shares in Z.

Simon's Taxes D6.421–424.

[1] TA 1988, s 213(5) as must X.
[2] TA 1988, s 213(8)(*b*).
[3] TA 1988, s 213(8)(*b*).
[4] TA 1988, s 213(8)(*c*).
[5] TA 1988, s 213(8)(*d*).
[6] TA 1988, s 213(8)(*e*).

[7] TA 1988, s 213(2).
[8] TCGA 1992, s 192(3); this is subject to the receipt of a chargeable payment in the next five years (TCGA 1992, s 192(4)).

Subsequent chargeable payments as income

[28.41] Although a demerger under these rules may have been successfully carried through, a subsequent "chargeable payment" during any of the next five years may have serious consequences.

A chargeable payment is any payment which is not itself a distribution (or an exempt distribution) made otherwise than for a bona fide commercial reason, or forming part of a scheme or arrangement for the avoidance of tax and made between companies or between a company and a shareholder in a company in the demerger; the payment must have been made in connection with the shares of the company.[1] Only intra-group payments are saved from the ambit of this definition[2] which is widened yet further when dealing with unquoted companies.[3]

The effect of such a payment within the five year period is that it will itself be treated as income of the recipient and so is liable to tax.[4] No deduction for the payment can be made in computing profits chargeable to CT.[5] Further the exclusion of TCGA 1992, s 179 is withdrawn.[6]

An example of a situation in which this will arise is where a company demerges a subsidiary by transferring shares to its members and then buys them back. The repurchase price would normally be a capital receipt but is instead to be taxed as income of the shareholder. This device has been preferred by Parliament to the alternative of retrospectively withdrawing exemption from the distribution.

Simon's Taxes D6.423.

[1] TA 1988, s 214(2).
[2] TA 1988, s 214(2)(c).
[3] TA 1988, s 214(3).
[4] TA 1988, s 214(1)(a); TA 1988, s 349(1) applies unless the payment is a transfer of money's worth—TA 1988, s 214(1)(a), TA 1988, s 214(1)(b).
[5] TA 1988, s 214(1)(c); nor is it a repayment of capital within TA 1988, ss 210, 211, see TA 1988, s 214(1)(d).
[6] TCGA 1992, s 192(4).

Exemption on the disposal of substantial shareholdings

[28.42] This relief,[1] following extensive consultation beginning in June 2000, is designed to facilitate corporate restructuring by preventing a large tax charge arising. It is probably one of the most valuable reliefs available.

From 1 April 2002, companies are exempt from tax on any gains arising from the disposal of substantial (10% or more) shareholdings in certain companies.

This has brought the UK tax treatment more into line with other countries such as the Netherlands that has been a favourite location for many sub-holding companies within international groups. Unlike the simple participation exemption generally found elsewhere, there are strict qualifying conditions; however, interest on borrowings to fund acquisitions is still deductible which is often not the case in other countries. Because this legislation is also applicable to losses, any loss made on the disposal of a substantial shareholding will not give rise to an allowable capital loss.

A substantial shareholding remains a chargeable asset, despite the exemption arising on its disposal. Shares are still classified as "chargeable assets" for the capital venturing and other schemes.[2]

[1] TCGA 1992, Sch 7AC, inserted by FA 2002, s 44 and Sch 8.
[2] TCGA 1992, Sch 7AC, para 32.

The three exemptions

[28.43] Three exemptions from corporation tax on the gain are available.

The main exemption[1] covers a disposal by a trading company (or a member of a trading group) of all or part of a substantial shareholding in another trading company (or the holding company of a trading group or subgroup) as long as certain conditions are met. This substantial shareholding may include shares or an interest in shares and they must have been held for at least a continuous 12 month period during the two years immediately before the disposal.

An appropriation of an asset to trading stock is deemed to be a disposal and immediate acquisition at market value. However, if it would fall under these provisions if it had actually been a disposal, there is no chargeable gain or loss.[2] A deemed disposal under the TCGA 1992, s 179 degrouping provisions is similarly exempt if it relates to a substantial shareholding.[3]

The first subsidiary exemption extends this to an asset related to shares,[4] eg options over or securities convertible into shares, provided that the conditions are met.

The second subsidiary exemption covers situations where although the conditions were not satisfied at the actual time of disposal, if the disposal had been made during the previous two years it would have satisfied the conditions for the main exemption[5].

A disposal of shares under a conditional contract is not straightforward. The date of disposal is the date that the condition is satisfied[6] but the contract date is used for determining the two year period.[7]

The various "stand in shoes" provisions (eg share exchanges) are disapplied if any gain/loss arising in the absence of those provisions would fall under the three exemptions.[8] If this causes the investing company to lose investment relief under the Corporate Venturing Scheme, though, the "stand in shoes" provisions are not disapplied. This means that companies will not lose out because of the share exchanges where there is a deferred gain on the original shares.

[28.43] Groups, consortia and substantial shareholdings

A "no gain/no loss" transfer is not affected by these provisions,[9] nor is a transfer of an asset between different categories of business within a life insurance company.[10]

These provisions do not apply to held over gains from the gifts relief provisions of TCGA 1992, s 165.[11]

There are also anti-avoidance measures to prevent companies from using any of the exemptions to indirectly realise untaxed income,[12] or if arrangements exist such that the sole or main benefit that might be expected would be the exemption.[13] The sole or main benefit test has subsequently been clarified[14] and although the Revenue expect cases where such arrangements exist to be "unusual and infrequent" reference should be made to this statement of practice.

---

[1] TCGA 1992, Sch 7AC, para 1; for a discussion of the availability of the relief where either the investor company carries on a profession or the investee company carries on a profession, see infra, § **29.15**.
[2] TCGA 1992, Sch 7AC, para 36.
[3] TCGA 1992, Sch 7AC, para 38.
[4] TCGA 1992, Sch 7AC, paras 2 & 30.
[5] TCGA 1992, Sch 7AC, para 3.
[6] TCGA 1992, s 28.
[7] TCGA 1992, Sch 7AC, para 3(7).
[8] TCGA 1992, Sch 7AC, para 4.
[9] TCGA 1992, Sch 7AC, para 6.
[10] TCGA 1992, Sch 7AC, para 6.
[11] TCGA 1992, Sch 7AC, para 37.
[12] TCGA 1992, Sch 7AC, para 5.
[13] TCGA 1992, Sch 7AC, para 5(2). The way in which the Revenue intends to apply these anti-avoidance provisions is given in Inland Revenue statement of practice SP5/02, 29 October 2002, Simons Weekly Tax Intelligence 2002, p 1423. The statement includes the comment: "we expect cases where the anti-avoidance rule is in point to be unusual and infrequent" (at para 3).
[14] Statement of practice SP 5/02, **Simon's Taxes, Division G1.2.**

Definition of substantial shareholding

[28.44] A substantial shareholding is defined as one where the company holds at least 10% of the company's ordinary share capital and is entitled to at least 10% of the profits available for distribution to equity holders and is entitled to at least 10% of the company's assets available for distribution on winding up.[1] The various tests in TA 1988, Sch 18 are also imported.

If a part disposal takes the substantial shareholding below the 10% threshold, further disposals may continue to qualify, subject to the other provisions being met for a further 12 month period, within the two years immediately prior to disposal (see infra § **28.45**).

Requirement as to period of ownership

[28.45] The substantial shareholding must be owned[1] throughout a twelve month qualifying period beginning not more than two years before the disposal.[2]

Group companies[3] aggregate the holdings of all companies in the group to achieve the 10% level[4] and can "look through" an intra-group transfer, including share exchanges, to achieve the qualifying period.[5]

A company is treated as not having held the shares throughout a period if there is a deemed disposal and reacquisition[6] hence, if the substantial shareholder is held by a company that leaves its group, the departure from the group within two years of acquisition of the substantial shareholder could trigger a charge that would otherwise be exempt. Share transfers under repurchase agreements are also excluded,[7] the original beneficial owner being treated as continuing to be the present beneficial owner. Stock loans are also excluded in a similar way.[8] Special provisions, providing transparency, are provided for share exchanges (deemed and otherwise).[9] Specific treatment is also outlined for the demerger of a subsidiary.[10] A company in liquidation does not lose beneficial ownership of its assets if those assets are vested in a liquidator.[11] There are special rules for an insurance company's long term insurance fund.[12]

---

[1] ie it must be held continuously.
[2] TCGA 1992, Sch 7AC, para 7.
[3] A group for these purposes is a "51% group" TCGA 1992, Sch 7AC, para 26(4), (5).
[4] TCGA 1992, Sch 7AC, para 9.
[5] TCGA 1992, Sch 7AC, para 10.
[6] TCGA 1992, Sch 7AC, para 11.
[7] TCGA 1992, Sch 7AC, para 12.
[8] TCGA 1992, Sch 7AC, para 13.
[9] TCGA 1992, Sch 7AC, para 14. Applies when there has been a share for share exchange under TCGA 1992, ss 127, 135 and 136.
[10] TCGA 1992, Sch 7AC, para 15.
[11] TCGA 1992, Sch 7AC, para 16.
[12] TCGA 1992, Sch 7AC, para 17.

Requirement to be a trading company

[28.46] Both during the qualifying period (see supra, § 28.45) and immediately after the disposal the investing company must have been either a sole trading company[1] or have been a member of a trading group.[2] Essentially this means that the company/group is a trader, with no "substantial" non-trading activities. In this context there is no formal definition of substantial, but the Revenue have indicated[3] that they will follow the guidance given for the similar legislation on CGT taper relief where substantial is taken to be more than 20%. Trading activities include those carried on when the company is preparing to trade.[4] Any intra group activities (such as letting property to another group member) are to be disregarded when determining whether the group is a trading group but this does not extend to transactions with non-group joint venture companies.[5]

Both during the qualifying period and immediately after the disposal the company invested in must have been either a trading company[6] or the holding company of a trading group[7] or trading subgroup.[8] Relief is extended to companies intending to trade.[9]

An investment in a joint venture company[10] is treated as being an investment in the underlying activities of the joint venture company.[11] A qualifying share holding in a joint venture company is again 10%.[12]

[1] TCGA 1992, Sch 7AC, paras 18 & 20.
[2] TCGA 1992, Sch 7AC, paras 18, 20 & 21.
[3] SP 5/02, 29 October 2002, *Simons Weekly Tax Intelligence* 2002, p 1423.
[4] TCGA 1992, Sch 7AC, para 20(2).
[5] TCGA 1992, Sch 7AC, para 21.
[6] TCGA 1992, Sch 7AC, para 19.
[7] TCGA 1992, Sch 7AC, para 19.
[8] TCGA 1992, Sch 7AC, paras 20 & 22.
[9] TCGA 1992, Sch 7AC, para 20(2)(c).
[10] Defined in TCGA 1992, Sch 7AC, para 24(1).
[11] TCGA 1992, Sch 7AC, para 23.
[12] TCGA 1992, Sch 7AC, para 24.

Earlier reorganisations, negligible value claims and other events before 1 April 2002

[28.47] Any deemed accrual of a chargeable gain or an allowable loss held over from earlier reorganisations, conversions and reconstructions is not exempt.[1] Any losses from negligible value claims[2] cannot be backdated.[3] Postponed gains arising from assets being transferred to a non-resident company, do not fall under these exemptions, and are brought into charge.[4]

[1] TCGA 1992, Sch 7AC, para 34.
[2] Under TCGA 1992, s 24(2).
[3] TCGA 1992, Sch 7AC, para 33.
[4] TCGA 1992, Sch 7AC, para 35.

29

Close companies

Definition of a close company	PARA **29.02**
Deemed distribution for a close company	PARA **29.09**
Loan to a participator	PARA **29.10**
Close investment holding company—full rate of tax	PARA **29.13**
Can a company carry on a profession?	PARA **29.15**

[**29.01**] The taxation of close companies differs from that of other companies in three major respects. First, the law takes a wider view of what[1] amounts to a distribution, with the result that not only are such payments not deductible in computing profits of the close company, but also taxable in the hands of the recipients as dividend income. Second, where the company makes a loan to a participator it must make a payment equivalent to tax at 25% to the Revenue. Third, a close company which is a close investment holding company must pay CT at the full rate of 28% on all its profits and not the reduced rate of 21%.

In so far as the shareholders envisage an eventual sale of the company they may find that their expected CGT liability is turned into an income tax liability by TA 1988, s 703,[2] a provision which has acquired a new impact by the introduction of highly favourable rates of taper relief for CGT, which are not available when computing a liability to income tax.

The definition of close company is used in a number of other contexts in the tax legislation.

Simon's Taxes D3.101.

---

[1] See TA 1988, ss 210(3), 211(2).
[2] Especially TA 1988, s 704 D; supra, § **4.26**.

Definition of a close company

The tests

[**29.02**] A company is designated a close company if it satisfies any of three tests. There are exceptions discussed below. The tests are (a) that it is controlled by five or fewer participators, (b) that it is controlled by its directors,[1] and (c) if five or fewer participators, or participators who are directors, together possess or are entitled to acquire such rights as would, in the event of the winding-up of the company entitle them to receive the greater part of the assets of the relevant company which would then be available for distribution among the participators. The company will also be a close

[29.02] Close companies

company if these persons could obtain such rights as would in that event so entitle them if any rights which any of them or any other person has as a loan creditor (in relation to this or any other company) were disregarded.[2] There are elaborate rules setting out the basis upon which the hypothetical winding-up is to be carried out. The part of the assets available for distribution among the participators which any person is entitled to receive is the aggregate of (a) any part of those assets which he would be entitled to receive in the event of the winding-up of the company, and (b) any part of those assets which he would be entitled to receive if (i) any other company which is a participator in the relevant company and is entitled to receive any assets in the notional winding-up were also wound up on the basis set out in this subsection, and (ii) the part of the assets of the relevant company to which the other company is entitled were distributed among the participators in the other company in proportion to their respective entitlement to the assets of the other company available for distribution among the participators.[3] In the application of this rule to the notional winding-up of the other company and to any further notional winding-up required by (b) (or by any further application of that paragraph), references to "the relevant company" have effect as references to the company concerned.[4]

A non-resident company, even if controlled by a resident company, cannot be a close company. However, it is sometimes necessary to apply the statutory test to a non-resident company to determine whether a UK resident subsidiary is close company.[5]

EXAMPLES

(1) The share capital of X Ltd (a private company) is owned as to 25% by three directors and the 75% balance by ten individuals, no five of which own over 50%. X Ltd is not a close company.

(2) The directors of X Ltd, numbering 12, own 51% of the ordinary share capital. X Ltd is a close company.

(3) The directors of Z Ltd, numbering 3, own 45% of the ordinary share capital. Two other unconnected individuals own 8%. Since five persons own 53% of the share capital of Z Ltd, it is a close company.

The Revenue have extensive information gathering powers.[6]

Simon's Taxes D3.102–110.

---

[1] TA 1988, s 414(1).

[2] TA 1988, s 414(2).

[3] TA 1988, s 414(2A).

[4] TA 1988, s 414(2B). In ascertaining above whether five or fewer participators, or participators who are directors, together possess or are entitled to acquire the rights mentioned, (a) a person shall be treated as a participator in or director of the relevant company if he is a participator in or director of any other company which would be entitled to receive assets in the notional winding-up of the relevant company on the basis set out in sub-s (2A) above, and (b) except in the application of sub-s (2A) above, no account shall be taken of a participator which is a company unless the company possesses or is entitled to acquire the rights in a fiduciary or representative capacity; TA 1988, s 414(2C). TA 1988, s 416(4)–(6) apply; TA 1988, s 414(2D) for the purposes of sub-ss (2), (2A) above as they apply for the purposes of sub-s (2) of that section.

⁵   TA 1988, s 414(6): see infra, § **29.07**.
⁶   FA 1989, Sch 12, paras 1–4.

Control

[29.03] Control¹ is central to the first two tests but it can be satisfied in many, sometimes overlapping ways. A person is taken to control a company if he exercises or is able to exercise now or as of right in the future, or is entitled to acquire (now or as of right in the future) control over the company's affairs. "Control over the company's affairs" is not defined and may mean control at a general meeting or control of those matters which are within the discretion of the directors. Precise analysis is probably unnecessary since the statute gives certain instances which are, however, not to detract from the generality of the principle:

(1)   the greater part of the share capital or of the issued share capital; or
(2)   the greater part of the voting power of the company; or
(3)   such part of the share capital as would entitle him to receive the greater part of the income of the company if, ignoring the rights of loan creditors, it were all distributed among the participators; or
(4)   such rights as would enable him to receive the greater part of the assets of the company in the event of a winding up or in any other circumstances.

Simon's Taxes D3.107–109.

¹   TA 1988, s 416(2).

Who has control?

[29.04] Having ascertained the meaning of control one then looks to see who, and how many, have got it. If two or more persons together satisfy the test of control they are taken together to control it.¹

In assessing the extent of a person's control all rights and powers held by him or by nominees are included.² Less obviously but equally crucial in establishing the extent of a person's control is the attribution to a person of all the rights and powers held by an associate.³ An associate means⁴ any relative—which means spouse, civil partner, direct ancestor or issue, or brother or sister⁵—or partner and any trustee of a settlement⁶ of which he, or any relative, as previously defined, is the settlor.

The definition of associate depends on the type of participator.⁷ Where the participator is interested in any shares or obligations of a company which are subject to any trust, the trust or trustees of the settlement concerned are associates.⁸ Likewise if the participator is a company and is interested in shares held on trust, any other company interested in those shares or obligations is an associate.⁹ These rules apply also where shares are held as part of the estate of a deceased person. The effect is to make the trustees associates rather than the beneficiaries, as had previously been the case, save where the beneficiary is another company. The term "interested" is not defined; it is unclear whether being an object of a discretion is sufficient to make one "interested".

If our participator has control of another company, the power of that company and of any other he may control are attributed to him as are powers of companies controlled by him and his associates.[10] While the powers of nominees of associates are to be attributed to the participator, those of associates of associates are not so the rights of a sister-in-law would be ignored.

Simon's Taxes D3.103–107, 110.

[1] TA 1988, s 416(3).
[2] TA 1988, s 416(5). The Revenue have no really effective means of discovering whether a shareholder is a nominee. TMA 1970, s 26 is in practice insufficient.
[3] TA 1988, s 416(6).
[4] TA 1988, s 417(3).
[5] TA 1988, s 417(4). Simon's Taxes, Division H3.4.
[6] TA 1988, s 417(3)(*b*); supra, § **15.02**. There are exceptions for certain funds for employees. TA 1988, s 417(3). A will is not a settlement: *Willingale v Islington Green Investment Co* [1972] 1 All ER 199, 48 TC 547.
[7] By TA 1988, s 417(3)(*c*). This provision was changed in 1986. The previous provision went on to exclude individuals who were interested in trusts which were exempt approved pension schemes or for the benefit of employees; with the shift to the trustees as the associated persons this part of the section becomes redundant and is repealed; trustees of such schemes are now associates as are corporate beneficiaries.
[8] TA 1988, s 417(3)(*c*)(i).
[9] TA 1988, s 417(3)(*c*)(ii). The term was part of the previous TA 1970, s 303(3)(*c*); it was then held that an executor was interested in shares held as part of an incompletely administered estate—*Willingale v Islington Green Investment Co* [1972] 1 All ER 199, 48 TC 547.
[10] TA 1988, s 417(6).

Test 1—control by directors

[29.05] A company controlled by its directors[1] is a close company no matter how many directors there are. Persons listed as directors are any persons occupying the position of director by whatsoever name called, and any person in accordance with whose wishes the directors are accustomed to act. Also qualifying as a director is any person who is a manager or otherwise concerned with the management of the company's trade or business and who controls (or is able to control) 20% of the ordinary share capital of the company. There is the customary attribution of the control of associates and intermediate companies even if the manager himself has no shares at all.

Simon's Taxes D3.106.

[1] TA 1988, s 417(5).

Test 2—control by participators

[29.06] If control does not rest in the directors, the company will still be close if control rests in five or fewer participators.[1]

A participator is defined as any person with a share or interest in the capital or income of the company and in particular (a) one with or who is entitled to acquire share capital or voting rights, or (b) entitled to secure that income or assets (present or future) will be applied directly or indirectly for his benefit, or (c) entitled to receive or participate in distributions of the company or entitled to any amounts payable by the company in cash or in kind by way of premium on redemption, or (d) certain loan creditors,[2] a term defined to include one who has a beneficial interest in the debt. A creditor of a nearly insolvent company might well be entitled to the greater part of the company's assets and thus could find himself to be a participator with the result that the company would be a close company. To avoid such complications bona fide commercial loans, salvage operations and business loans made by a person carrying on a banking business are ignored. A person may be a director although not a participator.

Simon's Taxes D3.103, 108.

[1] TA 1988, s 417(1).
[2] Defined in TA 1988, s 417(7)–(9). This is omitted for IHT, infra, § **39.21**. Recognised money brokers lending to stock jobbers are excluded. extra-statutory concession C8; **Simon's Taxes, Division G2.2**.

Exceptions

[29.07] Certain companies cannot be close companies even though they satisfy one or other of these tests.

A company is not a close company if it is controlled by one (or more) open companies and it cannot be treated as close except by taking an open company as one of its five or fewer participators.[1] Thus the subsidiary of a non-close company is not close any more than a company set up by two or three such companies. However, if another test of control would result in its being a close company, the company would be close.

Also excluded and therefore not close is a company which is only close because it has one or more open companies as loan creditors with control[2] under that rule which gives control to one entitled to the greater share of the assets on a winding-up.

In looking at these cases of control by non-close companies, a non-resident company which would be a close company if it were resident is treated as if it were close.[3]

[29.07] Close companies

A company controlled by the Crown is never a close company.[4]

A company that is not resident in the UK, is not a close company.[5] However, a non-resident company is treated as if it were a close company in order to apply the test to a resident company;[6] for example, to test that a resident company is controlled by five or fewer participators, the participation being traced through the non-resident company.

Simon's Taxes D3.113.

[1] TA 1988, s 414(5)(*a*).
[2] TA 1988, s 414(5)(*b*).
[3] TA 1988, s 416(2)(*c*).
[4] TA 1988, s 414(4).
[5] TA 1988, s 414(1).
[6] TA 1988, s 414(6).

The 35% rule

[29.08] A quoted company is not a close company if shares carrying 35% or more of the voting power[1] of the company have been allotted unconditionally to or acquired unconditionally by and are at the time beneficially held by members of the public.[2]

Shares entitled to a fixed rate of dividend do not count towards the 35%. This applies even though they carry voting rights and participate in profits.

Shares are not treated as held by the public if they are owned by (a) a principal member (ie the top five[3] of those with more than 5% of the voting power other than an approved pension scheme or a non-close company), (b) any director or his associate, (c) any company controlled by (b), (d) any associated company, and (e) any fund (eg a pension fund) for the benefit of any employee or director of the company or of a company within (c) or (d).

This exception does not apply if the voting power possessed by all its principal members is more than 85%.[4] At first sight, since shares held in a principal member's holding cannot be held by the public, it is hard to see how a company with 35% of its shares held by the public could have 85% of its shares held by principal members. However, shares held by open companies or approved superannuation funds are treated as owned by the public even if the company or fund is a principal member. Therefore, where one of the principal members is an open company with, say, 25% of the voting power and together the principal members control 80% of the voting power, the company so controlled is an open company under the 35% rule. If, however, the principal members had controlled 86%, it would have been a close company.

Simon's Taxes D3.114.

[1] Thus the surrender of voting shares for non-voting shares may enable a company to come within this rule.
[2] TA 1988, s 415.

[3] TA 1988, s 415(6)(a): if there are two or more with equal percentages five may be increased to six or more.
[4] TA 1988, s 415(2).

Deemed distribution for a close company

Expenses of participators or their associates

[29.09] The definition of distribution is widened in the case of a close company to cover expenses incurred by the company for the benefit of a participator. When a company has incurred expenses in providing a participator, including one who is a participator in a controlling company or who is an associate of a participator,[1] with the provision of living or other accommodation, of entertainment, of domestic or other services, or other benefits or facilities of whatsoever nature, statute directs that expense so incurred is to be treated as a distribution. In valuing the expense,[2] there is no grossing up and there is a deduction for sums made good by the participator. Curiously, whereas a deemed distribution from a close company, there is no statutory exemption for expenses that are excluded from the benefit charge.[3] It is understood that, in practice, the Revenue would not seek to charge an expense that would not be an employment income benefit.

The section does not apply to expenses incurred in the provision of living accommodation provided by reason of the employment or of benefits on death or retirement for the participator or his dependants.[4] It is also excluded if the participator is another close company and one is the subsidiary of the other or both are subsidiaries of a third company and the benefit arises on the transfer of assets or liabilities by or to the company.[5]

Attempts might be made to avoid TA 1988, s 418 where one has a participator in one close company but not in another close company by the companies agreeing that the other pays or should provide the facilities for that person. In such circumstances the payment is treated as coming from the company in which he is a participator.[6]

The payment is declared to be a distribution and income tax is due as if it were a dividend.

Simon's Taxes D3.301.

[1] TA 1988, s 418(8).
[2] TA 1988, s 418(4).
[3] By ITEPA 2003, s 202.
[4] TA 1988, s 418(3).
[5] TA 1988, s 418(5). Subsidiary is defined in sub-s (6).
[6] TA 1988, s 418(7).

Loan to a participator

[29.10] Where a loan is made to a participator a sum equal to corporation tax at 25% is due from the company to the Revenue by way of corporation tax when the loan is made.[1] This advance payment cannot be set off against the company's own liability to CT on its profits. This payment is additional to any other liability. The reason for this non-deduction may be the rule that as the loan is repaid the tax is refunded to the company.[2] Thus the rule requires in effect the payment of a special refundable deposit. Without some rule governing loans to participators and their associates, it would be easy for the company to avoid the widened definition of distribution and still enable the participators to enjoy the untaxed capital reserves of the company.[3] The section does not apply if the loan is made in the ordinary course of a business carried on by the company which includes the lending of money.[4]

If the loan is at a low rate of interest, the borrower may incur liability under ITEPA 2003, ss 7, 174, see supra, § **7.111**.

When the loan is made neither by the close company, A, nor by another close company which A controls but by a non-close company which A controls,[5] TA 1988, s 422 makes s 419 apply. To catch obvious avoidance devices, loans existing when A acquires control are treated as being made after that control was acquired thus falling within TA 1988, s 422.

The section is aimed at schemes to avoid s 419 and therefore provides an exception when

> ... it is shown that no person has made any arrangements (otherwise than in the ordinary course of a business carried on by him) as a result of which there is a connection
>
> (a) between the making of the loan and the acquisition of control; or
> (b) between the making of the loan and the provision by the close company of funds for the company making the loan;
>
> and the close company shall be regarded as providing funds as aforesaid if it directly or indirectly makes any payment or transfers any property to or realises or satisfies (in whole or in part) a liability of, the company making the loan.[6]

The onus of establishing that the loan was in the ordinary course of business or that there was no arrangement is thus placed on the taxpayer. In *Brennan v Deanby Investment Co*[7] the Court of Appeal denied an application by the company that the loan was made as part of the business which included the lending of the money, holding that the test to be applied is that in the Moneylenders Acts[8], where the word "business" "imports the notion of system, repetition and continuity".[9]

Unless the company is a "large" company and so liable to pay the charge as part of its quarterly self-assessment payment, it is not required to pay the quasi-CT to the Revenue until nine months after the end of the accounting period in which the loan has been extended to the participator.[10] Where the payment is not made by the company, interest runs from this date. A consequence of this provision is that no sum is payable and no interest charge arises, if the participator has repaid the loan by that date.[11] However, if the repayment is made after that date the due date for refund of tax in respect of the repayment of the loan is nine months after the end of the accounting period in which repayment is made.[12]

A repayment of the tax may arise not only when the loan is repaid but also, as from 6 April 1999, when the loan is written off or released.[13] Interest may also be due.[14]

Simon's Taxes D3.402–404.

---

[1] TA 1988, s 419(1). Under self-assessment, the company has the obligation to make the payment: FA 1998, Sch 18, para 8.
[2] TA 1988, s 419(4).
[3] See *Jacobs v IRC* (1925) 10 TC 1.
[4] TA 1988, s 419(1); and see Inland Revenue interpretation RI 16; **Simon's Taxes, Division G3.**
[5] TA 1988, s 422(2). When two or more companies control the lender the company is treated as controlled by each—but the loan is apportioned between them: TA 1988, s 422(3).
[6] TA 1988, s 422(4).
[7] [2001] STC 536, NI CA.
[8] [2001] STC 536 at 548c.
[9] Per McCardie J in *Edgelow v MacElwee* [1918] 1 KB 205 at 206, following *Newton v Pyke* (1908) 25 TLR 127. The Court noted a New Zealand judgment *Calkin v Commissioner of Inland Revenue* [1984] 1 NZLR 440 that underlying the word "business" "was the fundamental notion of the exercise of an activity in an organised and coherent way which is direct to an end result".
[10] TA 1988, s 419(3).
[11] TA 1988, s 826(4).
[12] TA 1988, s 419(4A).
[13] FA 1998, Sch 3, para 24.
[14] TA 1988, s 826(4).

[29.11] Statute[1] includes within the definition "loan", for this purpose, (a) a participator incurs a debt to the close company; or (b) a debt due from a participator to a third party is assigned to the close company. It has been suggested that this extended meaning of the term brings a tax charge on the company under TA 1988, s 419 where the company issues partly paid shares on which calls are subsequently made or where the company issues shares on terms that the issue price is to be paid by fixed instalments. It is suggested that this view is incorrect. Under Companies Act 1985, s 14, the shareholder's liability on a call is to the specialty debt. But liability does not mature into a debt until the call is made: vide *Whittaker v Kershaw*.[2] Where the company issues shares on terms that the issue price is to be paid by fixed instalments, it cannot call up the instalments before they are due in reliance on a general power to make calls conferred by the Articles: vide *Re Cordova Union Gold Company*.[3]

It has been held that there has to be some consensual element so that money due to a company by way of restitution of sums misappropriated by a director did not give rise to a liability on the company by virtue of TA 1988, s 419 as the director had no intention of repaying the company; hence, it was incorrect under general law to regard the relationship as that of extending and receiving a loan, nor could it properly be regarded as a debt within the statutory extension of the term loan.[4] Section 419 applies when a debt to the company is "incurred" by the participator. It has been held that a debt is incurred for this purpose when the fact of liability is established even though the payment will become due at some future time and is for an indefinite amount. An estate agent ran his business as an unincorporated business but formed a personal service company of which he was a participator. The sums due from business to the company were held to fall within s 419.[5]

If the borrower is a full-time worker for, and does not have a material interest in the company or an associated company, the charge is excluded if the total loan outstanding does not exceed £15,000.[6] In computing the amount of the loan there are to be included loans made to the spouse (or associate) of the director or employee. Provision is made for the possibility of acquiring a material interest after the date of the loan by deeming a new loan on that happy occasion. A participator who is neither a director nor an employee is not entitled to those exceptions.

Exceptions are also made for ordinary trade credit (subject to a six month maximum period).[7]

Simon's Taxes D3.401, 402.

---

[1] TA 1988, s 419(2).
[2] (1890) 45 ChD 320 at 326.
[3] [1891] 2 Ch 580.
[4] *Stephens v T Pittas Ltd* [1983] STC 576.
[5] *Andrew Grant Services Ltd v Watton* [1999] STC 330, Ch D.
[6] A special rule applies for pre-1971 housing loans—TA 1988, s 420(2).
[7] TA 1988, s 420(1).

Loan release

[29.12] Should a loan falling within s 419 later be released or written off in whole or in part, the person to whom it was made is treated as if he/she has received a dividend of the amount of the loan. Thus, the amount of the loan is grossed up by the dividend ordinary rate (10%) and any higher rate tax is charged at the higher rate for dividends, with a tax credit for the lower rate used in the grossing up. No liability, thus, arises on a loan written off where the statutory total income of the individual who receives the loan plus the amount of the loan falls within the basic rate band. No repayment of income tax can be claimed and the income is not treated as having been taxed for the purposes of TA 1988, ss 348, 349.[1]

The term "release" is not defined and is therefore to be given its plain and ordinary meaning. It is not necessary that the release should be voluntary or for inadequate consideration; the substitution of a new debtor for the original borrower is therefore a release.[2] The only question is whether the taxpayer has been released from his obligation to pay otherwise than by performance or satisfaction. A covenant not to sue will, on this broad interpretation, be treated as a release.

When a loan is released any tax paid by the company under s 419 is repaid to the company.[3]

For repayment supplement purposes, the repayment is treated as being of CT paid in the repayment period[4]—ie the supplement, if any, is not calculated by reference to the date of the original payment to the Revenue under s 419.

Simon's Taxes D3.406, 407.

[1] ITTOIA, ss 415–421.
[2] *Collins v Addies* [1991] STC 445. This interpretation causes difficulties and has recently been reviewed in the context of loan relationships (see supra, § **27.01**) in *Greene King No 1 Ltd v Adie* [2005] STC (SCD) 398.
[3] Since 5 April 1999, statute has made no distinction between a repayment made to a company on a loan being released and the repayment made to the company when a loan is repaid to the company: TA 1998, s 419(4).
[4] TA 1988, s 825(4)(*b*).

Close investment holding company—full rate of tax

[29.13] A close investment holding company cannot use the reduced rates of corporation tax. All profits are taxed at the full corporation tax rate of 28%.[1]

Simon's Taxes D3.201.

[1] TA 1988, ss 13 and 13A added by FA 1989, s 105.

Defining a close investment-holding company

[29.14] A close investment holding company is defined by exception.[1] Every close company is a close investment holding company, and hence, does not have the lower rates of tax available,[2] unless the company exists "wholly or mainly" for any one or more of six specified purposes.

The first qualifying purpose is carrying on a trade or trades on a commercial basis.[3] Statute makes no reference to professions.[4] The second purpose is that of making investments in land where the land is, or is intended to be, let to unconnected persons.[5]

The remaining qualifying purposes embroider the first two. Thus a company will escape close investment company status if its purpose is to hold shares in and securities of or making loans to a qualifying company[6] or to co-ordinate the administration of two or more qualifying companies.[7] It may also exist for the purposes either (a) of a trade carried on, on a commercial basis, by a

[29.14] Close companies

company which controls it or by a qualifying company, or (b) of making investments by a company which controls it or by another qualifying company. There is a special provision for companies in the course of a winding-up.[8]

This statutory provision has not been the subject of a reported case. However, the phrase "wholly or mainly" is used elsewhere in the Taxes Act, such as one of the qualifying terms for a company purchase of its own shares to be treated under CGT,[9] the dividing between zero rating and exemption for VAT treatment of a new building[10] and in the test for inheritance tax business property relief.[11] The last of these provisions is directed at consideration of the purpose of the company and, hence, it is in the reported cases considering the IHT provision that one may expect to find the best guidance on the approach to be taken in deciding whether or not a company is a close investment holding company.[12] In *Phillips v Revenue and Customs Comrs*[13] the Special Commissioner, Nuala Brice, states that she gains most assistance on the manner in which the question should be approached from the judgment of Carnwarth LJ in the Court of Appeal in *IRC v George*:[14] "that the business should be considered in the round and that there was no decisive factor which would indicate whether a business consisted 'wholly or mainly' of the making or holding of investments".

The HMRC Manual[15] follows the approach of "looking at matters in the round" in deciding whether a company is a close investment holding company, stating:

> In order to be excluded from close investment holding company status, the relevant company must exist throughout the accounting period **wholly or mainly** for the excluded purpose. Where, for example, a company has substantial income from sources other than (or as well as) trading or property investment, its purpose may not be clear cut. There will also be cases where the amount and source of income is inconclusive as a test of purpose. In such cases, a common sense approach is needed, and a review of all the facts should enable you to make a decision, for example:
>
> - What are the relative levels, and sources, of income?
> - What activities has the company undertaken?
> - What do minutes of meetings and other documents reveal about the company's business?
> - What are the assets (nature and amount) and to what uses have they been put?

Simon's Taxes D3.202.

---

[1] TA 1988, s 13A(1).
[2] TA 1988, s 13(1)(*b*).
[3] TA 1988, s 13A(2)(*a*).
[4] See infra, § **29.15**.
[5] TA 1988, s 13A(2)(*b*).
[6] TA 1988, s 13A(2)(*c*), on definition of qualifying company, see TA 1988, s 13A(3).
[7] TA 1988, s 13A(2)(*d*).
[8] TA 1988, s 13A(4).
[9] TA 1988, s 219(1)(*a*) see *Allum v Marsh* [2004] STC 147, para [12], [2005] STC (SCD) 191.
[10] VATA 1994, Sch 10, para 3A(7) see *Principal and Fellows of Newnham College in the University of Cambridge v Revenue and Customs Comrs* [2006] STC 1010, CA.
[11] IHTA 1984, s 105(3).

¹² But note should be taken the warning by Carnwath LJ that cases relating to different taxes and different subject matter are unlikely to be helpful: [2004] STC 147, para [12] at 151d.
¹³ [2006] STC (SCD) 639.
¹⁴ [2004] STC 147.
¹⁵ [2006] STC (SCD) 639, para 31 at 647a referring to [2004] STC 147, para [13], CA.

Can a company carry on a profession?

[29.15] Every close company pays tax at the full rate of 28% on all its profits, without the benefit of the small companies rate of 21%, unless it is a company within the statutory list of exceptions,[1] by which a close company is declared not to be a CIC. The main exception is for a close company that carries on a trade. Statute makes no mention of a close company that carries on a profession hence, prima facie, any company controlled by five or fewer participants[2] is denied the benefit of the lower tax rates if the main activity of the company is the carrying on of a profession. The question is of importance in other connections also. EIS relief is available to an investor in a company carrying on a qualifying trade but no provision is made in statute for EIS investment relief to be granted where the company carries on a profession.[3] The exemption of gains on the disposal of substantial shareholdings is expressed as applying to a disposal by a trading company of shares in another trading company.[4] There is no provision in statute for the substantial shareholding exemption to apply where either the business of the company making the disposal or the business of the company of whom the shares are disposed is the carrying on of a profession.

The traditional approach to a question that is posed is to say that the concept of a profession connotes activity by an individual, or a group of individuals, and no company, being an artificial person, can carry on a profession. This view is based on the judgment of Rowlatt J in *William Esplen, Son and Swainson v IRC*[5] when he said:

> The question is whether the company is carrying on a profession within the meaning of s 39, para (c) of the Finance (No 2) Act, 1915. In my opinion the company is not carrying on the profession of naval architects within the meaning of the section, because for this purpose it is of the essence of a profession that the profits should be dependent mainly upon the personal qualifications of the person by whom it is carried on, and that can only be an individual. There can be no professional qualifications except in an individual. A company such as this can only do a naval architect's work by sending a naval architect to its customers to do what they want done.

The UK Institutes of Chartered Accountants[6] accept registration of a company as carrying on the profession of an accountant as long as the individuals who are its directors[7] are qualified accountants. The Chartered Institute of Taxation accepts that a company in its own right can carry on the professional business of tax consultancy. The Law Society also accepts that qualified individuals can form a limited company in order to practise as solicitors. For many years it has been possible for a company secretary to be a limited company. The traditional approach is to say that a company is not an accountant, for example, but carries on the trade of supplying the professional services of accountants. In *Newstead v Frost*,[8] Browne-Wilkinson J refused to express a view as to whether a limited company can carry on a profession, but stated that there is no legal reason why the offshore company whose affairs he was considering could not be correctly regarded as being in partnership with David Frost, the television personality, the business of that partnership being the exploiting of David Frost's talents. On the traditional view, the transfer of a profession from a natural person to an artificial person automatically changes the profession into a trade.

It is necessary to recognise the authority that case law has as a binding precedent. A court case is a judgment of the court on a particular question in relation to the matter in front of it. In 1919, no professional institute recognised a company as being competent to carry on the activities of the profession it regulated. In 2003, professional institutes readily accept a company. Is the correct view of the decision in *Esplen* that a company cannot carry on a profession if professional institutes do not accept the company? In *Castleton Management Services v Kirkwood* [2001] STC (SCD) 95, T H K Everett said of a company (at 100c): '[Revenue Counsel] has submitted that the distinction between the provision of services of accountants and the provision of accountancy services is in fact a distinction without a difference and having heard all the evidence I am driven to the conclusion that I must agree with him.' On this view, a company can correctly be regarded as carrying on a profession. If such a company is controlled by five or fewer participants, as is often the case, statute provides that all its profits are taxed at the full corporation tax rate of 28%, without the benefit of the lower rates. In practice, the Revenue do not reject a corporation tax computation for a professional company that applies the lower rates.

The basis for the Revenue treatment is unclear. It may be that the Revenue consider, on the authority of *Esplen*, that no company can carry on a profession and the transfer of a profession from a natural person to an artificial person automatically changes the profession into a trade. Alternatively, this may be a Revenue concession.

---

[1] In TA 1988, s 13A(1): see supra, § **29.14**.
[2] Or which falls to be treated as a close company by applying way of the other tests: see supra, §§ **29.02–29.08**.
[3] TA 1988, s 289(2)(a): see infra, § **31.12**.
[4] TCGA 1992, Sch 7AC, para 18(1)(a) and 19(2): see supra, § **28.43**.
[5] [1919] 2 KB 731 at 734.
[6] The Institute of Chartered Accountants in England and Wales and the Institute of Chartered Accountants of Scotland.
[7] Or a specified percentage of them; there are also requirements relating to the percentage of the issued shares being held by qualified individuals.
[8] [1978] STC 239 at 249g–250a.

30

Investment companies

Management expenses	PARA **30.01**
Revenue view	PARA **30.05**
The relief	PARA **30.07**
Investment trusts	PARA **30.12**
Unit trusts	PARA **30.13**
Open-ended investment companies	PARA **30.18**

Management expenses

[30.01] Most revenue expenses incurred in earning profits assessable as trading income, or assessable as income from a property business, are deductible from gross receipts in arriving at the net income assessable. No relief is normally given, however, for expenses incurred in earning investment income, such as company dividends, and interest. Companies with investment business[1] are entitled to set their expenses of management against total profits, thus reducing the profits assessable, or entitling the company to a repayment of tax deducted at source from income received.

For accounting periods commencing on or after 1 April 2004 relief is available for management expenses of any company that carries on investment business, whether or not this is the main business of the company.[2]

Prior to 1 April 2004, this relief was restricted to investment companies and life assurance companies.[3]

Simon's Taxes D7.301; STP [23.94]–[23.99a].

---

[1] CTA 2009, s 1218.
[2] CTA 2009, Part 16, Ch 2.
[3] For the provisions applying to investment companies for periods prior to 1 April 2004 see Tiley & Collison *UK Tax Guide 2003–04* and earlier editions. A list of relevant cases on the meaning of "investment companies" is given in Tiley & Collison *UK Tax Guide 2006–07 edition*, § 30.01, note 1.

[30.02] Statute[1] states that expenses of management are "expenses of management of the company's investment business" to the extent that: (a) the expenses are in respect of so much of the company's business as consists in the making investments, and (b) the investments concerned are not held by the company for an unallowable purpose during the accounting period.

---

[1] CTA 2009, s 1219.

[30.03] Investment companies

[30.03] Viscount Simonds said in *Sun Life Assurance Society v Davidson*[1] that the term "expenses of management" is "insusceptible of precise definition". It is clearly wider than the expenses to which the managers are put, but does not extend to all expenses incurred by the company. In *Sun Life*, the House of Lords held that all revenue expenses incurred by a company in managing its business qualify for relief. By contrast, the cost of acquisition is not an expense of management and is not deductible.[2]

Relief is given for revenue expenses incurred in managing the investment business.[3] These expenses will include:

(1) staff costs, including wages, salaries, pension contributions, and the cost of staff training and welfare;
(2) other indirect costs, including stationery, printing, advertising, repairs to equipment, legal and other professional fees, and unrelieved VAT; and
(3) property maintenance costs, including rents, rates, maintenance and repairs of premises occupied for business purposes.

In addition, certain expenses qualify for relief by statute. The cost of maintaining let property is not a management expense, but is deductible from property business income.[4] Sums paid to purchase investments are not management expenses, and, moreover, in *Sun Life*, it was held that expenses necessarily incurred in acquiring investments were part of the costs of the investments, and not management expenses. Thus stamp duty and brokerage on the acquisition or sale of investments are not management expenses, and likewise legal expenses incurred in the acquisition of heritable property in an investment are not deductible. Relief is available, however, for expenditure incurred in evaluating an investment, such as the legal costs of investigating title, as well as for expenditure on an abortive investment. Relief is given for expenses incurred but not paid at the end of an accounting period, although wages and salaries accrued at the end of the accounting period do not qualify for relief unless paid within nine months of the end of the accounting period.[5]

Simon's Taxes D7.305.

---

[1] [1958] AC 184 at 196, 37 TC 330 at 354.
[2] Per Lord Reed in *Sun Life Assurance Society v Davidson* (1958) 37 TC 330 at 360. See also *Camas plc v Atkinson* [2004] EWCA Civ 541, [2004] STC 860.
[3] *Holdings Ltd v IRC* [1997] STC (SCD) 144, where relief was allowed for fees levied by accountants and solicitors in respect of any company investigation and enforceability of letters of assurance, respectively.
[4] CTA 2009, ss 1219(3), 1232.
[5] CTA 2009, ss 1249–1250.

[30.04] Among the expenses which do not qualify for relief are:

(1) capital expenditure on plant and equipment, vehicles, fixtures and fittings;
(2) entertainment expenditure;

(3) losses on the disposal of investments, except that relief may be given for certain losses on the disposal of shares in unquoted trading companies by investment companies;[1]
(4) exchange losses in some circumstances.[2]

In *Hoechst Finance Ltd v Gumbrell*,[3] however, commissions paid by a company to its parent company for guaranteeing of loans to other subsidiaries of the parent were held not to be deductible; although the taxpayer's business was the provision of finance to those companies, the costs of the commission could not be severed from the other costs of raising capital.[4]

Simon's Taxes D7.305.

---

[1] TA 1988, s 573.
[2] Bennet v Underground Electric Railways Co of London [1923] 2 KB 535, 8 TC 475; but see the FX rules in the loan relationship legislation.
[3] [1983] STC 150.
[4] But see CTA 2009, s 307(4).

Revenue view

Investment business

[30.05] The view of HMRC is that a trading company that happens to be left with income yielding assets after the cessation of its trade does not automatically become an investment company (or "company with investment business").[1] It will only become "a company with investment business" if there is evidence that (all or) part of its business will be the making of investments.

Inspectors will argue that where trading ceases and funds are held on deposit pending the liquidation of the company, or in the period between trades, that the company is not an investment company or "company with investment business". The comments of Lord Denning in *EYL Trading Co Ltd v IRC*[2] are used to support a restrictive view of an "investment" business. He said "the mere provision of cash at the bank pending its subsequent use is not the 'holding' of investments . . . something much more in the nature of a business activity is needed".

It is noted that what a company may intend is not always clear cut. If a company can demonstrate an intention to make investments and, for example, holds money on deposit for some time it may be conceded that it comes within the definition of "a company with investment business".[3]

Where a company is in liquidation HMRC consider that the liquidator's main objective is to realise a company's assets and wind up its affairs. It is not the liquidators purpose to make a profit by continuing to hold investments and as a consequence is therefore unlikely to have an investment business and satisfy the requirements of CTA 2009, s 1218.

[30.05] Investment companies

Generally authorised unit trusts and housing associations will qualify as companies with investment business. The issue of whether Development Corporations have an investment business will be decided on the facts of the particular case.

In the case of a holding company where there is some intermingling of the management of the business of the holding company and the businesses of the subsidiary companies inspectors are advised not to disallow expenditure if the expenses would have been allowable for UK tax purposes if incurred by the subsidiary, and, if the holding company arranges to charge out future expenses to the subsidiary.

---

[1] *Carpet Agencies Ltd v IRC* (1958) 38 TC 223.
[2] (1962) 40 TC 386 at 399, CA.
[3] CTA 2009, s 1218.

Management expenses generally

[30.06] Advice is given to Inspectors[1] regarding qualifying management expenses generally. It is considered that the direct costs of changing investments do not qualify as management expenses. The direct costs of changing investments are considered to include:

(1) brokerages, and
(2) stamp duties.

These costs are not admissible on the authority of:

(1) *Capital and National Trust Ltd v Golder*,[2] and
(2) *Sun Life Assurance Society v Davidson*.[3]

It is noted that companies can incur a substantial amount of expenditure on less direct costs relating to acquisitions and disposals. When considering whether this expenditure qualifies for relief as an expense of management Inspectors are advised to consider two arguments:

(1) Is the expenditure an expense of managing the investment business?
(2) Is the expenditure capital in nature?

Statute[4] disallows relief for expenses of management that are of a capital nature, other than through the capital allowance system, or other provisions, such as venture capital relief.[5] When considering case law, it must be noted that this provision did not apply prior to 1 April 2004; hence, the courts have not previously been required to make the same distinction between revenue and capital as was the case for the computation of, for example, trading income.

They considered the earlier management expenses cases and in particular the 'severability' test which had formed the basis of the decision in Sun Life.

Using that test the Revenue had contended that expenditure could not be severed from the costs of acquisition of an investment once a particular target had been identified. This view had been supported by the Irish Supreme Court case, *Hibernian v Macuimis*.[6]

This argument was rejected. The Courts concluded that expenditure does not form part of the acquisition costs until, at the earliest, the date of the decision to acquire the investment. Prior to that date the expenditure is generally preparatory to a decision to acquire and as such is not closely enough linked to the acquisition to form part of the acquisition costs. Expenditure does not cease to be on management simply because a target has been identified.

It is conceded that even after there has been a decision to acquire, expenditure could still qualify for relief as expenses of management (see below).

Expenditure preparatory to making a decision to purchase will generally be an expense of management. Once the decision to acquire has been made then the expenditure is likely to fall into the category of "costs of implementation of a purchase already decided upon" and will therefore not be an expense of management.

It is further noted that the date of the decision to acquire does not necessarily provide an absolute cut-off point in deciding whether expenditure of this nature is or is not an expense of management. In this context HMRC seek to differentiate between decision making expenditure and costs of implementation of a purchase already decided upon, the former being expenses of management and the latter not.

In each case the detailed facts are to be considered as they are crucial. If expenditure relates to managerial decision making then even if the expenditure occurs after the date of the decision to acquire/dispose, it could be expenses of management. Only costs of implementation of a purchase already decided upon will not be expenses of management. The principles established apply equally to acquisitions and disposals and to abortive as well as to successful expenditure.

Success fees/Contingency fees

As far as success fees or contingency fees are concerned HMRC consider that these expenses can only become due once a decision to acquire has been made and therefore they fall on the side of "costs of implementation of a purchase already decided upon". Such fees are also likely to be capital in nature and would therefore fall within the capital exclusion after 1 April 2004.

Bid defence costs

Inspectors are advised to undertake a detailed and comprehensive review of the purpose and circumstances surrounding bid defence costs claimed as management expenses.

Public Quotation Cost

HMRC considers that cost in connection with a stock exchange quotation can never be claimed as a management expense.

Valuation Costs

It is considered that valuation costs which are required for Companies Act purposes are allowable management expenses but that valuations connected with acquisitions and disposals are not.

[30.06] Investment companies

[1] Published as Inland Revenue Guidance Note 15 June 2004: *Simon's Weekly Tax Intelligence* 2004, pp 1472–1475.
[2] (1949) 31 TC 265, CA.
[3] (1957) 37 TC 330, HL.
[4] CTA 2009, ss 1219(3), 1221(1).
[5] FA 2000, s 63 and Schs 15 and 16, see infra, § **31.16**.
[6] [2000] ITR 75.

The relief

Timing of deduction

[30.07] Expenses are deductible under CTA 2009 for the accounting period in which they are charged against profit in accordance with generally accepted accounting practice as defined by statute.[1]

Simon's Taxes D7.307.

[1] FA 2004, s 50 amplified by FA 2005, ss 80–84, see supra, § **8.65**.

Depreciation

[30.08] Prior to 1 April 2004, no relief was available for depreciation, since that was an accounting allowance, and not a disbursement. However, since 1953 investment companies had been entitled to claim capital allowances. Allowances for expenditure on qualifying assets, in so far as they could not be set against income from any other source, could be added to the expenses of management for the year, with any balancing charges being brought in as income. Alternatively, allowance for expenditure on plant, etc could be claimed on a renewals basis.

Capital allowances are now allowed as management expenses under CTA 2009, s 1221(3).[1]

Simon's Taxes D7.308.

[1] CTA 2009, s 1221(2).

Method of giving relief

[30.09] Relief is given by deducting expenses of management from total profits.[1] "Total income" includes chargeable gains. Expenses of management are deducted before charges on income.[2] Expenditure still unrelieved can be carried forward, without time limit, against future income, from whatever source, of the company,[3] or it can be relieved by way of group relief.[4] Excess management expenses, unlike trading losses, cannot be carried back to previous accounting periods.

Simon's Taxes D7.311.

[1] CTA 2009, s 1219(1).
[2] TA 1988, s 338(2).
[3] CTA 2009, s 1221(2).
[4] TA 1988, s 403(4), (5).

[30.10] Statute[1] restricts the carry forward of excess management expenses where there has been a change in the ownership of an investment company. The legislation comes into effect where there has been a change in the ownership of an investment company and:

(1) after the change there is a "significant increase" in the amount of the company's capital; or
(2) within the period of six years beginning three years before the change there is a major change in the nature or conduct of the business carried on by the company; or
(3) the change in the ownership of the company has occurred at any time after the scale of the business activities of the company has become small or negligible and before there has been any considerable revival.

[1] TA 1988, ss 768B, 768C inserted by FA 1995, Sch 26, para 2 and amended by F(No 2)A 2005, Sch 7, para 3.

[30.11] There is a "significant increase" in the amount of an investment company's capital if, in the three years after the change of ownership, the company's capital is either at least double, or greater by £1m than, the amount of capital before the change. There are rules in TA 1988, Sch 28A to prevent avoidance by the manipulation of capital at or around the time of the change of ownership. A company's capital is the aggregate of its paid-up share capital, its redeemable loan capital, the amount of debts incurred by the company otherwise than from a bank in the ordinary course of its banking business, and the amount of any share premium account. Interest due but unpaid on a debt is added to the amount of the debt.

There is a major change in the nature or conduct of a business where there is a major change in the nature of the investments held by the company, even as a result of a gradual process which began before the six-year period.

Where the section applies, the accounting period of the company in which the change of ownership occurs is divided into two parts by reference to the date of the change. The expenses of management for that accounting period, including charges paid during the period and excess expenses brought forward from earlier periods are then apportioned between the two parts. Capital allowances which form part of management expenses are apportioned rateably. Expenses brought forward are apportioned to the first part of the

[30.11] Investment companies

accounting period. Other expenses and charges are apportioned according to the time when they were due to be paid. Interest is assumed to become due on a daily basis; special provisions apply when a payment of interest was being delayed. There is power to use any other method of apportionment where it would give a more just and reasonable result.

A further restriction applies where, on the change of ownership of an investment company, there is no circumstance in TA 1988, s 768B requiring an apportionment of expenses of management, but after the change, the investment company acquires an asset from another member of the same group on a no gain/no loss basis. If that asset is disposed of within three years of the change of the ownership of the company, and a chargeable gain arises, then management expenses apportioned to the period before the change in ownership cannot be carried beyond it.

Simon's Taxes D7.320.

Investment trusts

[30.12] An investment trust is a company which by complying with TA 1988, s 842 is exempt from tax on its chargeable gains.[1] This exemption enables the company to switch investments tax-free. All other income of the company, however, is taxed in the usual way. The exemption for CGT does not extend to shareholders. To obtain relief, the company must comply with the conditions in TA 1988, s 842 for, that is throughout, its accounting period although there are extra-statutory concessions for the first accounting period of a new investment trust and for the accounting period in which an investment trust is wound up. The conditions in TA 1988, s 842 are as follows:

(1) The company must be UK resident; it must not be a "close" company; and every class of its ordinary share capital must be quoted on a recognised stock exchange.

(2) The company's income must be derived wholly or mainly from shares or securities. The Revenue regard this condition as satisfied if 70% of gross income, before expenses, is so derived.[2]

(3) The company's Memorandum and Articles of Association must prohibit the distribution by way of dividend of surpluses arising on the realisation of investments.

(4) The company must not retain, for any accounting period, more than 15% of the income it derives from shares and securities. With effect from 26 July 1990, this rule does not apply to income which cannot be distributed because of a legal restriction. Where the retention exceeds 15% of income, or, if greater, the amounts which cannot be distributed because of a legal restriction, s 842(1)(e) will not be regarded as infringed if the excess does not exceed £10,000.[3]

(5) No holding of shares and securities in a company must represent more than 15% by value of the investing company's investments. This condition does not apply:

    (a) where a holding, when it was acquired, was worth no more than 15% of the then value of the investing company's investments; and

(b) to shares held in a company which is itself an investment trust, or would be an investment trust if its ordinary share capital was quoted on a stock exchange.

Simon's Taxes D7.335–339; STP [7.359]–[7.362].

[1] TCGA 1992, s 100(1).
[2] By agreement with the Association of Investment Trust Companies.
[3] TA 1988, s 842(2A)–(2C).

Unit trusts

[30.13] Unit trusts are trusts in the strict legal sense of the word, and operate in accordance with the terms of their trust deed. The trustee is usually a bank or insurance company, but the management of the trust is carried on by a separate management company. The unit holders are simply beneficiaries under the trust whose rights are regulated by the trust deed. A unit holder disposes of his units by selling them to the trust manager at a price equal to asset value, less a small discount. The manager may either hold the units for sale to an investor, or it may sell them back to the trustee, when they are cancelled.

Simon's Taxes D8.101; STP [7.224]–[7.226].

Unit trusts

[30.14] The taxation treatment of a unit trust scheme depends on whether the trust is an authorised unit trust. A "unit trust scheme" takes its meaning from the Financial Services and Markets Act 2000,[1] and a trust is an authorised unit trust if an order under the Financial Services and Markets Act 2000, s 243 is in force for, or for any part of, an accounting period.[2]

A unit trust scheme which is not an authorised unit trust is taxed as a trust. In the first instance, income received is taxed as the income of the trustees, who are liable to pay income tax on it in the usual way. Income distributed to unit holders is deemed to have been paid under deduction of income tax at the basic rate.

The trustees are also liable to CGT on trust capital gains, except where, throughout the year of assessment, all the unit holders are themselves exempt from tax from capital gains (otherwise than by reason of residence) when trust capital gains are not chargeable to tax.[3]

Simon's Taxes D8.130.

[1] TA 1988, s 469.
[2] TA 1988, s 468(6).
[3] TCGA 1992, s 100(2).

[30.15] Investment companies

Authorised unit trusts

[30.15] An authorised unit trust is treated, in relation to income received by the trustees, as though it were a UK resident company, and as if the units were shares in the company.[1] Profits consist of income less expenses of management. Capital profits on loan relationships and derivative contracts are not taxable.[2] Capital gains are also not chargeable to tax.[3] Corporation tax on the profits of an authorised unit trust is charged at a rate equal to the lower rate of income tax, ie 20%.[4]

Simon's Taxes D8.111.

[1]   TA 1988, s 468(2).
[2]   Authorised Investments Funds (Tax) Regulations 2006, SI 2006/964, reg 10(2) and regs 10(2) and 11(2), *Simon's Weekly Tax Intelligence* 2006, p 1275.
[3]   TCGA 1992, s 100(1).
[4]   TA 1988, s 468E(2).

[30.16] When an authorised unit trust makes a distribution, the trust is able to designate[1] income distributed to its unit holders as *either* a franked payment *or* as an interest distribution, that is, as yearly interest subject to deduction of basic rate income tax at source.

The treatment of a distribution as an interest distribution is only possible if the trust satisfies the "qualifying investments test". Essentially, this means that at least 60% of the market value of the trust's investments must be interest-bearing assets, eg money placed at interest, securities and building society shares.

Where the trust makes an income distribution, it must deduct income tax at the lower rate from the amount distributed, and remit the income tax so deducted to the Revenue, except where the interest distribution is paid to companies, or to individuals not ordinarily resident in the UK, where the interest distribution can be paid gross. The amount of the income distribution is then deducted by the trust from its total profits for the accounting period after any other tax relief to which the trust is entitled. If the interest distribution exceeds profits liable to corporation tax, the excess would be carried forward.

Where all or part of a distribution is treated as a franked payment the tax treatment of the amount received by a corporate unit holder depends on the source from which the franked payment was made. Broadly, to the extent to which the franked payment has come from franked investment income received by the authorised unit trust, it will be treated as franked investment income in the hands of the corporate unit holder. To the extent that it has come from unfranked income, it is liable to corporation tax in the hands of the unit holder, with a credit for tax suffered at source on the income. The legislation contains rules to determine how this allocation should be made.

Simon's Taxes D8.156–157.

[1]   Authorised Investments Funds (Tax) Regulations 2006, SI 2006/964, reg 17, *Simon's Weekly Tax Intelligence* 2006, p 1275.

CGT computation

[30.17] In principle, the computation of a gain arising on the disposal of a unit in an authorised unit trust follows the normal rules, it being necessary to identify each acquisition now that shares are no longer pooled.[1] However, many taxpayers have contracts with unit trust suppliers whereby they pay a monthly subscription and are allotted a number of units each month. The strict statutory calculation in such an arrangement is onerous. A Revenue statement of practice allows the capital gain on disposal of a unit trust to be computed as if all units acquired during a fiscal year had been acquired on 7 July during that year.[2]

[1] TCGA 1992, s 104(2)(*aa*).
[2] Inland Revenue Statement of Practice SP2/99, **Simon's Taxes, Division G1.2.**

Open-ended investment companies

[30.18] Open-ended investment companies (OEICs) are investment companies with variable share capital, being a hybrid form of company with many of the features of a unit trust. The tax treatment[1] follows the principles which apply to authorised unit trusts.[2]

OEICs are often constituted so that the share capital of the company, available to be issued to investors, consists of participating redeemable shares. Essentially, the value of the issued share capital of the company will at all times equal its net assets. The investor realises his investment either by selling the shares to another potential investor or by asking the company to redeem them. Both kinds of transactions will be substantially at the investor's proportionate share of the net asset value of the underlying investments of the company, adjusted for expenses.

The company can issue separate classes of redeemable participating shares, each class representing a different type of investment, eg in different currencies or different types of shares or securities. The investor may switch from one share class to another usually at nil or low cost, the share capital of the fund being reorganised to reflect the new position. This type of OEIC is generally referred to as an "umbrella fund".

The profits of an OEIC are subject to corporation tax at the income tax lower rate (20%).[3] The normal rate of corporation tax does not apply to an OEIC.

An OEIC is excluded from the loan relationship provisions that otherwise apply for corporation tax,[4] and from the provisions for derivative contracts.[5]

An OEIC is required to prepare accounts under UK general accepted accounting practice[6] and, specifically, the distinction between capital and income is required to be made in accordance with general accepted accounting practice.

Distributions made by an OEIC fall in to one of two categories:[7] (a) yearly interest (b) dividends. Yearly interest (which can include alternative finance

[30.18] Investment companies

arrangements in relation to "Islamic finance")[8] is taxed as interest received in the hands of the unit holder.[9] Dividends are taxed as dividends received in the hands of the unit holder.[10] Interest is paid after deduction of tax at the lower rate, unless the unit holder has made a declaration that he is not resident in the UK,[11] in which case the distribution is made without deduction of tax.[12]

No tax is charged on capital gains made within the OEIC.[13] Instead, the charge is on the unit holder.

Simon's Taxes D8.141.

---

[1] FA 1995, s 152, F(No 2)A 2005, ss 17–22 and Authorised Investment Funds (Tax) Regulations 2006, SI 2006/964, *Simon's Weekly Tax Intelligence* 2006, p 1275.
[2] TA 1988, s 468
[3] TA 1988, s 468A.
[4] SI 2006/964, reg 10(2).
[5] SI 2006/964, reg 11(2).
[6] SI 2006/964, reg 12.
[7] SI 2006/964, reg 20, Category 8.
[8] SI 2006/964, reg 18(2). See supra, §§ **27.28–27.34**.
[9] SI 2006/964, reg 22(2).
[10] SI 2006/964, reg 26.
[11] SI 2006/964, reg 47(1).
[12] SI 2006/964, reg 26(4)(*d*).
[13] SI 2006/964, regs 98–100.

Part V

Savings

31

Savings products with tax exemptions or reliefs
Individual Savings Account
National Savings
Friendly societies
Enterprise investment scheme
Corporate venturing scheme
Venture capital trust
Life assurance policies
Purchased annuities
Child Trust Fund
Real Estate Investment Trust

32

Pensions
Pensions taxation reform
Sharing of pensions on divorce
Earlier developments
Occupational schemes
Additional voluntary contributions
Money purchase scheme
Personal pensions
Retirement age
Secured and unsecured Income
Transitional protection for members of schemes before 6 April 2006
Unauthorised payments

31

Savings products with tax exemptions or reliefs

Individual Savings Account	PARA **31.01**
National Savings	PARA **31.04**
Friendly societies	PARA **31.05**
Enterprise investment scheme	PARA **31.06**
Corporate venturing scheme	PARA **31.16**
Venture capital trust	PARA **31.17**
Life assurance policies	PARA **31.19**
Purchased annuities	PARA **31.30**
Child Trust Fund	PARA **31.32**
Real Estate Investment Trust	PARA **31.33**

This chapter considers savings products that attract specific tax reliefs. For a discussion of the taxation of savings income, see **Chapter 11**.

Individual savings account

[31.01] Since 6 April 1999 the Individual Savings Account[1] (ISA) has been available. Investment in ISAs is substantial. £2,500,000,000 was invested during the tax year 2005–06 (although this nearly halved in the tax year 2006—07)[2] Unlike the predecessor schemes, the ISA includes a number of voluntary standards designed to make some schemes attractive to savers as distinct from fund managers; these are the CAT standards[3] which set levels for charges, access and terms.

The ISA is a scheme of investment which can be used by a qualifying individual.[4] A qualifying individual must be an individual who is 16 or over[5] and is both resident and ordinarily resident in the UK, or, alternatively, is a Crown employee serving overseas subject to UK tax under ITEPA 2003, s 28[6], or is a spouse or civil partner of such a Crown employee.[7] The individual must not break the rules for the number of ISA investments in the year.[8] There are provisions about ceasing to qualify.[9]

The ISA allows an individual to hold various investments free of income tax and CGT.[10] However, there is no repayment of the tax credit on a dividend.[11] An ISA account may be made up of one or more of the following components only:

(1) stocks and shares;
(2) cash;
(3) (until 5 April 2005) life assurance.[12]

Until 5 April 2008, the ISA language referred also to accounts being designated as a maxi-account or a mini-account or a TESSA only account; this designation was made by the account manager.[13] From 6 April 2008, the terminology changed to refer to stocks and shares accounts and cash accounts.[14]

A stocks and shares account may contain other components but it must be the only account to which the individual subscribes that year.[15]

The limit that any one individual investor can invest in an ISA in any one fiscal year is £7,200 (before 6 April 2008: £7,000), of which a maximum of £3,600[16] may be a cash account.[17]

Alternatively, an investor can open two different accounts – a stocks and shares account and a a cash account. The latter is subject to a maximum investment of £3,600; the former is capped at £7,200 less the amount invested into a cash account.[18]

The TESSA-only account was one which accepted a transfer of funds from a matured TESSA.[19] On the maturity of a TESSA, the investor could transfer the balance in the TESSA account into a cash only ISA and enjoy the tax exemption benefits that a cash ISA attracts.[20] There is no limit to the sum that can be transferred in this way, other than the limit being the balance in the TESSA at its maturity. The "TESSA-only ISA" is separate from the cash mini-ISA or the cash element of a maxi-ISA. Thus, an investor could contribute the full £3,000 permitted each year into a cash ISA and was still able to transfer his or her TESSA on maturity as well. Interest that had been generated in the TESSA had to be paid to the investor, it could not form part of the sum transferred into the TESSA-only ISA.[21]

The investor is free to choose any ISA provider. The investor does not have to choose the institution with which he or she held the TESSA. In order to facilitate transfer from one institution to another, the investor had six months from the date the TESSA matured in which to deposit the proceeds into a TESSA-only ISA.[22]

An individual not resident in the UK is not permitted to open an ISA,[23] unless the individual is deemed to perform the duties of a Crown appointment within the UK. However, a UK resident who goes abroad can continue to hold the ISA whilst not resident in the UK, without time limit, although he is not permitted to make further subscriptions to the ISA after ceasing to be resident in the UK.[24]

When an investor dies, the ISA is treated as ceasing at the time of the investor's death and all income arising from the fund after the investor's death is subject to income tax in the usual way. During the period of administration, this is income of the personal representatives and tax liabilities are assessable on the personal representatives.

There are many rules for accounts managers,[25] and for transfer of accounts to other managers.[26] There are also many administrative and information rules.[27] Another provision adapts the CGT rules, eg by directing a disposal and acquisition at market value when the administrator transfers assets to the investor.[28]

There are separate regulations for insurance companies[29] and the overseas life assurance business of such companies.[30] The effect of these regulations is to provide a scheme that is in some respects akin to PAYE in that commercial organisations administer the tax system in relation to ISAs. The control exercised by HMRC is, to a substantial extent the spot examination of a very small sample of returns made by commercial organisations approved under the regulations.

The ISA, by abolishing the PEP distinction between qualifying and non-qualifying funds, has a slightly wider geographical spread than the PEP and permits investments in gilts. Like the PEP[31] but unlike the TESSA the ISA has no lock-in period to qualify for tax relief. An ISA may be opened by someone on behalf of the qualifying individual.

There are, however, disadvantages when the ISA is compared with the TESSA and PEP. The maximum sums which may be invested each year are lower than under the old regimes. Other disadvantages are that cash held as part of the investment or insurance component of an ISA attracts tax at 20% on interest arising[32] and that the tax credit repaid in respect of dividends is limited to 10% and lasted only until 2004.

Simon's Taxes Division E3.3.

---

[1] Regulations are made under ITTOIA 2005, ss 694 and 697, TCGA 1992, s 151. The principal regulations are the Individual Savings Account Regulations 1998, SI 1998/1870.

[2] Figures from the Investment Management Association reported at www.myfinances.co.uk.

[3] The concept of a capital CAT standard is an interesting use of public relations by the Government. The standards are not set by statutory instrument but are simply declared by the Treasury. Plan managers who wish to adhere to the Treasury specification on access and level of charges, can then advertise an ISA as satisfying the CAT standard.

[4] Individual Savings Account Regulations 1998, SI 1998/1870, reg 4(1).

[5] With effect from 6 April 2001 Individual Savings Account Regulations 1998, SI 1998/1870, reg 10(2) amended and new regs 4(1)(f)(ia) and 4 (2A) were inserted by Individual Savings Account (Amendment) Regulations 2001, SI 2001/908, regs 3(4), 3(6) and 5(a). These amendments have the effect that a person aged between 16 and 18 can invest up to £3,600 (before 6 April 2008: £3,000) per year in the cash element of an ISA, but is not able to invest in the other elements of an ISA until attaining the age of 18.

[6] SI 1998/1870, reg 10; ie falling within the former TA 1988, s 132(4)(a), so that services were *treated* as being performed in the UK.

[7] Individual Savings Account Regulations 1998, SI 1988/1870, reg 10(2)(d)(iii) added by Individual Savings Account (Amendment) Regulations 2001, SI 2001/908, reg 5(b), with effect from 6 April 2001.

[8] Only one maxi-account is allowed and only one mini-account: SI 1998/1870, reg 10(2)(*b*) and (*c*).

[9] SI 1998/1870, reg 11.

[10] SI 1998/1870, reg 22.

[11] Prior to 6 April 2004, the manager of an ISA could obtain repayment of the tax credit: FA 1998, s 76(1)(*a*).

[12] SI 1998/1870, reg 4(1); the various components are defined in paras 7, 8 and 9 subject to the general rules in reg 6.

[31.01] Savings products with tax exemptions or reliefs

[13] SI 1998/1870, reg 4(1)(a).
[14] SI 2007/2119.
[15] An investor could in addition invest in a TESSA only account to reinvest the cash arising from a matured TESSA investment.
[16] Before 6 April 2008: £3,000.
[17] Individual Savings Account (Amendment) Regulations 2000, SI 2000/809, reg 2. The former limit for insurance products was £1,000.
[18] SI 1998/1870, reg 4(3) (as substituted by SI 2007/2119, reg 6).
[19] SI 1998/1870, reg 4(1)(e) and reg 5. A TESSA is a cash account offered by a building society or an institution authorised under the Banking Act 1987 (or a relevant European institution) where interest and any bonus credited to the account is exempt from income tax.

No TESSA can be opened after 5 April 1999. However, existing TESSAs at that date are allowed to run the full five-year term and continue to enjoy tax relief until the account matures. When a TESSA matures, the capital in the TESSA, being the sums invested (but not the interest that has been generated) can be invested in a cash mini-ISA or the cash element of a maxi-ISA. This deposit is in addition to the £3,000 limit for the year.

For further details on a TESSA (including a follow-up TESSA) see *Tiley & Collison's UK Tax Guide* 1998–99 edn.

[20] SI 1998/1870, reg 5.
[21] SI 1998/1870, reg 5(1).
[22] SI 1998/1870 reg 5(1).
[23] SI 1998/1870, reg 10(2)(d).
[24] SI 1998/1870, reg 11.
[25] SI 1998/1870, regs 14–20.
[26] SI 1998/1870, reg 21.
[27] SI 1998/1870, regs 24–33 and 35.
[28] SI 1998/1870, reg 34.
[29] Individual Savings Account (Insurance Companies) Regulations 1998, SI 1998/1871, *Simon's Weekly Tax Intelligence* 1998, p 1230 and Individual Savings Account (Amendment) Regulations 1999, SI 1998/3174, reg 13, *Simon's Weekly Tax Intelligence* 1999, p 97.
[30] Insurance Companies (Overseas Life Assurance Business) Regulations 1998, SI 1998/1872, *Simon's Weekly Tax Intelligence* 1998, p 1235.
[31] A personal equity plan (PEP) is a portfolio of shares held by an approved plan manager on behalf of an individual investor. Provided the conditions of the scheme are satisfied, gains from the sale of shares within a plan, and withdrawal of capital from a plan are free of CGT. Dividends, and interest from cash holdings in the plan, are exempt from income tax if they are reinvested in the plan. However, there is no repayment of the tax credit on a dividend.

A plan cannot be opened after 5 April 1999, nor can further funds be added to the plan after that date. However, a plan that is in existence at that date continues to enjoy the tax advantages offered.

For further details on personal equity plans, see *Tiley & Collison's UK Tax Guide* 1998/99 edn.

[32] SI 1998/1870, reg 23, Inland Revenue press release, 1 April 1999, *Simon's Weekly Tax Intelligence* 1999, p 733.

Stocks and share component

[31.02] The stocks and shares component can include the following:[1]

(1) Shares issued by companies listed on a recognised stock exchange anywhere in the world.
(2) Corporate bonds issued by companies listed on a recognised stock exchange anywhere in the world.
(3) Securities issued by a company that is a 75 per cent subsidiary of a company listed on a recognised stock exchange anywhere in the world.
(4) UK government stock ("gilts").
(5) Securities equivalent to gilts issued by governments and central banks of all countries in the European Community and other members of the European Economic Area (EEA).
(6) Strips of gilts and of their foreign EEC equivalents.
(7) Units in UK authorised unit trusts which invest in shares and securities (securities funds, warrant funds and "funds of funds" that invest in them).
(8) Shares in UK open-ended investment companies (OEICs).
(9) Shares and securities in approved investment trusts (other than property trusts).
(10) Units or shares in Undertakings for Collective Investment in Transferable Securities (UCITS) funds based in a member state of the European Community (ie the mainland EC equivalent of a UK unit trust or OEIC).
(11) Crest depository interests representing shares that would, themselves, qualify under the conditions stated above.

The cash sum paid by the investor into the stocks and shares component (which can be the whole £7,200 invested in the year, if there is neither a cash element to the account, nor a life assurance element) is invested by the account manager who purchases stocks and shares, which are held by the account manager and registered in the account manager's name (not the name of the investor) but held as the individual's ISA fund.

An individual can transfer stocks and shares in his or her personal portfolio into his or her ISA account. The transfer is treated as taking place at the market value of the holding on the day of transfer.[2] Thus, it is a CGT disposal for the individual and potentially creates a liability to pay CGT as the CGT exemption is on gains made by the approved ISA account manager within the ISA account; there is no exemption on disposals made by the individual investor. Exceptionally, an employee who has obtained shares under the Employee Share Ownership Plan[3] scheme is entitled to transfer those shares directly into the stocks and shares component of an ISA, without the transfer being treated as a CGT disposal.[4]

The investments in the stocks and shares component produce cash by means of dividends, interest and other payments. This cash can be paid to the investor or can be collected and held by the account manager in the stocks and shares component as a temporary fund. Cash from dividends, etc is not part of the cash component of the ISA. This cash will, itself, produce an interest payment. This "secondary interest" does not attract the full tax exemption for the

[31.02] Savings products with tax exemptions or reliefs

component of an ISA. Instead, a statutory instrument[5] gives a special tax regime, whereby the ISA account manager is required to withhold tax at the basic rate (20 per cent) on the "secondary interest" and the account manager pays the tax withheld to HMRC. No entry is required on the tax return of the investor and there is no tax liability on the investor, even if the investor is a higher rate taxpayer.[6]

Employees who acquire shares from an approved all-employee share scheme (ie Approved Profit Sharing scheme, Savings-Related Share Option Scheme, or Share Incentive Plan) may transfer them directly into a stocks and shares component of an Individual Savings Account (ISA). In 2001–02,[7] around 35,000 people transferred in around £180 million of shares in this way. ISA managers cannot accept shares acquired via tax-advantaged discretionary share option schemes (ie Discretionary and Company Share Options and Enterprise Management Incentives).

Employees' shares must be transferred into an ISA within 90 days of emerging from the scheme. The aggregate market value of the shares when transferred must be within the normal annual ISA subscription limits. There is no charge to capital gains tax on shares transferred. Prior to the introduction of ISAs, from 1992, shares acquired via approved all-employee schemes could similarly be transferred into a single company Personal Equity Plan.

---

[1] Individual Savings Account Regulations 1998, SI 1998/1870, reg 7 and the Individual Savings Account (Amendment No 3) Regulations 2000, SI 2000/3112, reg 3.
[2] SI 1998/1870, reg 6(2).
[3] FA 2000, s 47 and Sch 8.
[4] SI 2000/2079, reg 4(2).
[5] SI 1998/1870, reg 23).
[6] SI 1998/1870, reg 23.
[7] The material on share schemes that are no longer available to be established is based substantially on Inland Revenue Guidance Note, 2 August 2004; Employee Share Schemes, *Simon's Weekly Tax Intelligence* 2004, pp 1808–1810.

Life assurance component

[31.03] The life assurance component can include:

(1) with profits' policies;
(2) unit linked policies;
(3) investment linked policies.

Unlike the other two components, this component consists of investments that are only available to the investor who chooses to hold them in an ISA. Life policies available in this component of an ISA are designed and approved specifically for ISAs. Policies that are generally available in the market are unlikely to be approved for an ISA account manager to hold. If there is cash in the life assurance component of an ISA, interest arising on this cash is subject to tax at the basic rate,[1] the same system of assessment being applied as is outlined above for the stocks and shares component.[2]

[1] Prior to 6 April 2008: the lower rate of 20%.
[2] SI 1998/1870, reg 23.

National savings

[31.04] Income and gains arising on the following products issued by National Savings and Investments is exempt from income tax and capital gains tax:

(1) Premium Bonds.
(2) Fixed Interest Savings Certificates.
(3) Index Linked Savings Certificates.
(4) Children's Bonus Bonds.[1]
(5) Ulster Savings Certificates[2].
(6) The first £70 of interest credited to a National Savings and Investment ordinary account is exempt from income tax.[3]

[1] ITTOIA 2005, s 692. Ulster Savings Certificates are similarly exempt.
[2] ITTOIA 2005, s 693.
[3] ITTOIA 2005, s 691

Friendly societies

[31.05] Friendly societies (other than unregistered societies) are exempt on the profits of certain life and annuity business. The conditions under which policies and contracts constitute exempt business of friendly societies have been the subject of frequent changes in recent years. Life policies and contracts issued after 30 April 1995 are exempt policies if the premiums or premiums payable in any 12 month period do not exceed £270.[1] Annuity contracts are exempt if the annual sum payable does not exceed £156.

The policy may be tax-exempt as well as being a qualifying policy for terms longer than ten years; if the policy is a non-qualifying policy any gain will attract a basic rate charge and the policy will not be tax-exempt. The surrender of an annuity contract is a chargeable event,[2] unless it is an assignment on divorce.[3] Breach of the limits by a policy invalidates the policy.[4]

A friendly society is taxed as a mutual life assurance company in respect of its taxable insurance business.[5]

Simon's Taxes D7.601, 604; STP [7.183]–[7.189].

[1] FA 1995, s 54, Sch 10.
[2] TA 1988, s 539(3) but only if the contract was made after 31 May 1984.
[3] TA 1988, s 462(1) and (1A) substituted and inserted by FA 2007, s 44 with effect from 1 January 2007. This provision also exempts any consequence of breaching of

    the exempt premium limit when a tax exempt policy is assigned without the receipt of consideration, whether the assignment is on divorce or otherwise.
4   TA 1988, Sch 15, paras 3–6.
5   That is, insurance business which is not tax exempt under TA 1988, s 461. Regulations modify the way in which the legislation on life assurance taxation, in TA 1988, Part XII, is applied: TA 1988, s 463(1) and Friendly Societies (Modification of the Corporation Tax Acts) Regulations 1992, SI 1992/1655. F(No 2)A 1992 introduced a number of amendments to the 1988 Act provisions, including three sections 461A–461C after TA 1988, s 461. The aim of these sections is to regulate the taxation of a friendly society on income and gains, other than from exempt life and endowment business. The tax exemption does not extend to income derived from subsidiary companies. Where, however, the other activities, or gains from them, become excessive, there is power under s 461C to remove the tax exempt status altogether.

TA 1988, s 461D (introduced by FA 2008) ensures that exemption is maintained when one friendly society acquires an exempt business from another society. FA 1993 has enabled the Treasury to regulate the repayment of tax suffered by deduction on the investment income of friendly societies carrying on tax-exempt business: Friendly Societies (Provisional Repayments for Exempt Business) Regulations 1993, SI 1993/3112.

Enterprise investment scheme

Overview

[31.06] From 1983 until December 1993 the UK tax system included a business expansion scheme (BES). This was a development of an earlier but far briefer relief, called the business start-up scheme.[1] The BES gave tax relief at the marginal rate of tax, ie as high as 40%, on investments in unquoted companies carrying on qualifying trades. This relief became the subject of much planning and loss of revenue. Although designed to encourage investment in risky business the risk element was largely removed by devices such as loan back schemes[2] and by the decision of Parliament to extend the ambit of the scheme to the provision of housing to be let on assured tenancies.

The basic idea behind the legislation was to encourage equity investment and, since the raising of equity finance for new and small companies is seen as a major problem of the economy, it came as no surprise that the business expansion scheme was stopped[3] and replaced by a more closely targeted scheme, the enterprise investment scheme (EIS). EIS applies to investment on or after 1 January 1994. The legislation takes the form of a resurrection and adaptation of the earlier provisions.

Simon's Taxes Division E3.1.

[1] ITA 2007, Pt 5; on the start-up scheme see FA 1981, s 53.

[2] Stopped by what is now ITA 2007, s 164 added by FA 1993, s 111 for shares issued on or after 16 March 1993.
[3] F(No 2)A 1992, s 38.

[31.07] An individual is eligible for enterprise investment scheme relief if eligible shares in a qualifying company for which he has subscribed are issued to him.[1] The shares must be issued in order to raise money for the purpose of a qualifying business activity,[2] and the money raised must be used for the purpose of that activity, 80% being used within 12 months of the issue and the remaining 20% within 24 months.[3]

The shares must be eligible shares. Shares are eligible if they are new ordinary shares which, throughout the period of five years beginning with the date on which they are issued, carry no present or future preferential right to dividends or to a company's assets on its winding up and no present or future preferential right to be redeemed.[4]

A taxpayer can elect that when shares are issued before 6 October in a year of assessment up to one half (subject to a maximum of £50,000) may be deducted for the preceding year; it is a matter of taxpayer choice—there is no obligation to carry an investment back.[5] The minimum investment for shares issued in one year by one company is £500[6] (unless an approved investment fund is used[7]) and the maximum is £500,000 a year.[8] The limit is applied to a spouses and civil partners separately. Investment can be through an approved investment fund.[9]

The relief has its own anti-avoidance rule. An individual is not eligible for relief in respect of any shares unless the shares are subscribed, and issued, for bona fide commercial purposes and not as part of a scheme or arrangement the main purpose or one of the main purposes of which is the avoidance of tax.[10] Statute seeks to give a very wide meaning to the word "arrangements" for the purpose of EIS relief, by defining the word as including "any scheme, agreement or understanding, whether or not legally enforceable". However, the exact scope of this restriction remains debatable. It is almost certainly the case that there has to be some connection between the withdrawal from the loan account and the subsequent investment for EIS relief to be denied by virtue of the anti-avoidance provision. The courts have interpreted the word "arrangements" in various ways, according to its context. In *J Sainsbury plc v O'Connor*,[11] the word was given a restricted meaning, which could be of benefit if it is necessary to argue that EIS relief is available (usually, this will be CGT deferral relief) on a subscription in a company that has previously had a loan from the investor.

Simon's Taxes Division E3.1; STP Ch 21.

[1] FA 1994, s 137. The shares must be issued in exchange for cash: ITA 2007, s 173(3)(*a*). In *Thompson v Hart* [2000] STC 381 EIS relief was denied as the shares were issued in exchange for the transfer of properties. On date of issue of shares see *National Westminster Bank Ltd v IRC* [1994] STC 184, CA.
[2] The payment of dividends to investors is not a qualifying business activity: *Forthright (Wales) Ltd v Davies* [2004] EWHC 524 (Ch), [2004] STC 875. In his

[31.07] Savings products with tax exemptions or reliefs

judgement, Lightman J expressed doubt whether payment to employees by way of dividends is any different from payment of dividends to investors (para 21 at 886d), but did not rule on the point as EIS relief was denied on other grounds.

3 ITA 2007, s 175. Statute requires that the money "is employed wholly for the purpose of the activity". One commentator has stated that this "means something like 'irrevocably designated for business purposes'. This is not the same as 'spent'. The Revenue may need reminding of this."

In *GC Trading Ltd v R & C Comrs*(2007) Sp C 630, G subscribed for two issues of shares in the taxpayer, an advertising company, and simultaneously loaned monies to other companies. The Special Commissioner held that, on the evidence before him, the loans were equivalent to a bank deposit and therefore the two share issues had been employed wholly for the purpose of acquiring the taxpayer's qualifying trade notwithstanding that as part of that enterprise they had raised money from the share issue and had preserved it by loaning out to other companies.

4 ITA 2007, s 173(2).
5 ITA 2007, s 158(5).
6 ITA 2007, s 157(2).
7 ITA 2007, s 251(3). An investment fund must be approved by HMRC. The revised criteria for approval were published by the Revenue in 1990; see *Simon's Tax Intelligence* 1991, p 34.
8 ITA 2007, s 158(2); between 2006–07 and 2007–08 the limit was £400,000; prior to 2006–07 the limit was £200,000.
9 ITA 2007, s 251(3) and supra, note 6.
10 FA 2000, Sch 17, para 4(1).
11 [1991] STC 318 at 332a.

[31.08] Where a person has made a chargeable gain on the disposal of any asset, and at any time in the period beginning 12 months before and ending three years after the date of the disposal, he subscribes for shares in a company that qualifies under the EIS, then the amount of the chargeable gain equal to the amount of the EIS investment is treated as postponed.

For details of this relief, called deferral relief, see supra, §§ **22.25** ff. A condition for deferral relief is that the shares are issued by a company that fulfils the EIS requirement but it is not necessary for the shares issued to qualify for income tax relief under the EIS provisions. Thus, for example, CGT relief (but not income tax relief) is available to an individual who is already connected with the company before the issue of shares and is also available where the individual subscribes for shares in excess of the £200,000 limit for the income tax relief.[1]

Simon's Taxes Division E3.1.

1 Deferral relief is governed by TCGA 1992, Sch 5B. Relief is provided to an individual or trustee who makes "a qualifying investment", para 1(1)(*c*), which is defined as subscribing for "eligible shares" in "a qualifying company", para 1(2)(*a*) and (*b*). "Eligible shares" and "qualifying company" are defined by para 19(1), as those that fulfil the EIS conditions of TA 1988, s 289(7) and ss 289–312 respectively.

1360

Form of relief

[31.09] Where the individual eligible for relief in respect of any amount subscribed for eligible shares makes a claim, then relief is given by way of a reduction in tax. The reduction is calculated at 20% of the sum invested, up to a maximum of £500,000,[1] invested by one individual.[2] Where the amount is greater than that which would reduce his liability to nil only the latter (smaller) amount is due for relief.[3]

In calculating the amount of tax against which the relief is to be set, no account is taken of other tax reductions ie deductions for qualifying maintenance payments, mortgage interest, medical insurance, foreign tax credit or income subject only to basic rate tax which can be charged to someone else.

There are also conditions which must be satisfied by the company both with regard to itself and with regard to the trade (infra, §**31.12**).

In order that the rules for the relief may work it is necessary to attribute the relief (ie the reduction in tax) to the shares for which the taxpayer subscribed. So a reduction for a single issue[4] of shares in a year is given in a straightforward way; where more than one issue occurred the relief is given in proportion to the amounts subscribed for each issue.[5] Further rules apply to bonus shares with the relief being spread over the entire new holding.[6] Where part of the relief is claimed by being taken back to the previous year the relief is attributed to two separate holdings.[7] Where relief is withdrawn the relief attributable to each share in question is reduced to nil; there are reduced attributions for reductions in relief.[8]

Simon's Taxes E3.103.

[1] Prior to FA 2008: £400,000.
[2] ITA 2007, s 158(1).
[3] ITA 2007, s 158(2).
[4] On meaning see ITA 2007, s 255.
[5] ITA 2007, s 201(2).
[6] ITA 2007, s 201(3).
[7] ITA 2007, s 201(4), (5).
[8] ITA 2007, s 201(7).

Prohibition of loan backs

[31.10] Relief under the EIS scheme is not available if there is a loan during what was previously known as 'the relevant period'[1] to that individual investor or an associate.[2]

The concept of a loan is widely defined.[3] In order to prevent an ordinary loan disqualifying an investor it is also provided that the loan will not have this drastic effect if it would have been made on these terms if there had been no EIS investment.[4]

[1] The period begins with whichever is the earlier of the incorporation of the company and two years before the issue of the shares; it ends five years later: ITA 2007, s 159.

[31.10] Savings products with tax exemptions or reliefs

² Defined by ITA 2007, s 253.
³ ITA 2007, s 164(3).
⁴ ITA 2007, s 164(2).

Conditions to be satisfied by the individual

[31.11] For the enterprise investment scheme it is not necessary that the individual should be resident and ordinarily resident in the UK when the shares are issued. However, he must subscribe for shares on his own behalf.[1]

The investor must not be connected with the company at any time within the designated period. This period begins with the incorporation of the company (or two years before the issue of the shares, if later) and ends three years after the issue of the shares.[2]

The tests used for determining whether a person is a connected person are that a person is connected with a company if he controls it, if he owns, with his associates,[3] more than 30% of the voting power of the company,[4] or owns any of its loan capital, or if he or an associate is an employee or a partner of the company. However, an overdraft from a bank is not treated as loan capital if it arose in the ordinary course of the bank's business.[5] An individual is also treated as connected with a company with which he would not otherwise be connected if he subscribes for shares as part of an arrangement under which another person subscribes for shares in a different company with which any party to the arrangement is connected.[6]

Directors are not treated as connected with the company if they are unpaid. This is widely defined as not receiving or becoming entitled to payments from the company or from a related person during the period of three years beginning with the date on which the shares are issued.[7]

The investor can be a director of the company into which he makes the EIS investment if one of two alternative conditions are fulfilled. First, he can be an unpaid director. For the purpose of this rule, certain payments are disregarded.[8] Disregarded payments include not only the reimbursement of expenses wholly, exclusively and necessarily incurred in the performance of his duties as a director, but also reasonable returns by way of interest and dividends on investments in the company and rent on property occupied by the company and reasonable charges for services provided to it.[9] Second, he can be a paid director receiving remuneration that is reasonable for the services rendered to the company as director.

The directorship must be the only reason for being connected with the company. He must not have been connected with the company before the share issue nor employed by the company's predecessor in trade.[10]

Simon's Taxes E3.106–111.

[1] ITA 2007, s 157(1).
[2] ITA 2007, ss 159(2), (3) and 163.
[3] ITA 2007, s 170(9): see *Cook v Billings* [2001] STC 16, CA.

[4] ITA 2007, s 170. On the situation where a taxpayer holds one of two subscriber shares following incorporation, see extra-statutory concession A76.
[5] ITA 2007, s 170(10).
[6] ITA 2007, s 171.
[7] ITA 2007, s 168(1). For definition of related person see s 168(4)—the term covers (a) any company of which the individual or his associate is a director and which is a subsidiary or a partner of the issuing company or of a subsidiary, and (b) any person connected with the issuing company or with a company falling within (a).
[8] ITA 2007, s 168(2).
[9] ITA 2007, s 168(3).
[10] ITA 2007, s 169.

Conditions to be satisfied by the company—its activity and its trade

[31.12] Three sets of rules have to be considered. First, the company must be carrying on a qualifying business activity at the relevant time. Second, the company must be a qualifying company. Third, the company must carry on a qualifying trade, or be a holding company of one or more subsidiaries carrying on a qualifying trade. Fourth, there is a limit to the size of the company, or the group.

The enterprise investment scheme requires that the company should carry on a qualifying business activity.[1] In relation to the company this means that the company should either carry on a qualifying trade on the date the shares are issued or, at the time of the shares issue be preparing to carry on a qualifying trade and actually begin to carry on the qualifying trade within two years after that date. It is also necessary that the trade be carried on wholly or mainly in the UK. An alternative way in which a company can qualify is that it is a holding company with a 90% subsidiary and the subsidiary fulfils the requirement of carrying on a qualifying trade.[2]

There is a second head of qualifying business activity to cover research and development. Either it must be carrying on the research and development at the time of issue or begins to carry it on immediately afterwards or it must intend that a qualifying trade will be derived from the research and development which the company or any subsidiary will carry on wholly or mainly in the UK. There is a further constraint in that at any time in the relevant period when the research and development or the qualifying trade derived from it is carried on, it must be carried on wholly or mainly in the UK.

A third head of qualifying business activity applying until 7 March 2001 related to oil exploration.[3]

A company is a qualifying company if for three years from the issue of the shares (or from the time it begins a qualifying trade, if later) it meets certain conditions.[4] It is immaterial where the company was incorporated or is resident or ordinarily resident—as distinct from where it carries on its qualifying activity.[5] However, it must be unquoted, ie a company none of whose shares, stocks, debentures or other securities are marketed to the general public.[6]

1363

[31.12] Savings products with tax exemptions or reliefs

The company must exist wholly for the purpose of carrying on one or more qualifying trades; the effect of the word wholly is softened by a rule that one may ignore purposes capable of having no significant effect (other than in relation to incidental matters) on the extent of the company's activities.[7] A holding company may also qualify since the rule includes a company whose business consists wholly of holding shares or securities in, or making loans to, one or more qualifying subsidiaries. A company also qualifies if its business consists wholly of carrying on one or more qualifying trades in the UK and of holding shares or securities, or making loans to, qualifying subsidiaries. A subsidiary is a qualifying subsidiary if it meets a similar test.[8]

The share capital must be fully paid up and subscribed for wholly in cash.[9] The company must not be controlled by, or control, alone or together with connected persons, another company, nor must it be, or own, a 51% subsidiary[10]—unless it is a qualifying subsidiary. A qualifying subsidiary is a wholly owned subsidiary which carries on a qualifying trade and is a 90% subsidiary.[11]

A trade is a qualifying trade if it meets certain conditions.[12] These mostly relate to disqualifying trades—so the company may not at any time carry on one of these trades, whether or not it carries on other trades as well. The list[13] includes dealing in land, in commodities or futures, or in shares, securities or other financial instruments; others featured include the provision of legal and accounting services,[14] banking, insurance and leasing.[15] The list has been extended by the FA 2008 to include shipbuilding, producing coal or producing steel. There then follow a number of provisions designed to ease the disqualification in certain narrowly defined circumstances.[16] In any event hobby trades do not qualify; the trade must be conducted on a commercial basis with a view to the realisation of profit.[17] In comparison with BES some trades are no longer disqualified—these are farming, property development and the supply of services by a subsidiary to a parent where the parent carries on a non-qualifying trade.[18]

The procedures for granting tax relief for the investor necessitate the company issuing a certificate certifying that the requirements on the recipient company are fulfilled. The company (or its 90% subsidiary) must carry on the trade for four months before it is permitted to issue a certificate.[19]

The company's assets (before deducting liabilities) must not exceed £7,000,000 immediately before the issue of EIS shares and must not exceed £8,000,000 immediately after the issue.[20]

Simon's Taxes E3.115, 119–122.

---

[1] ITA 2007, s 179. The conditions are discussed in *4Cast v Mitchell* [2005] STC (SCD) 287 and, comprehensively, in *Optos v Revenue and Customs Comrs* [2006] STC (SCD) 687.
[2] ITA 2007, s 190.
[3] Former TA 1988, s 289(2)(c).
[4] ITA 2007, s 181(2). Unless within that time it is wound up or dissolved for bona fide commercial reasons and assets distributed to shareholders; ITA 2007, s 182(4); on scope see Inland Revenue interpretation RI 14.

5   ITA 2007, s 179.
6   ITA 2007, s 184.
7   ITA 2007, s 181.
8   ITA 2007, s 181.
9   ITA 2007, s 173(3).
10 ITA 2007, s 185.
11 As defined in ITA 2007, s 190.
12 ITA 2007, s 189.
13 ITA 2007, s 192(1).
14 In *Castleton Management Services v Kirkwood* [2001] STC (SCD) 95, the Special Commissioners held that a company created to employ the staff of a partnership of chartered accountants was not carrying on a qualifying trade and, hence, EIS relief for the investors in the company was denied. In the decision, the Commissioners stated: '[Revenue Counsel] has submitted that the distinction between the provision of the services of accountants and the provision of accountancy services is in fact a distinction without a difference and having heard all the evidence I am driven to the conclusion that I must agree with him.' (At 100c).
15 The Revenue view of what constitutes leasing, receiving royalties and licence fees is given in Inland Revenue Tax Bulletin August 2001, p 877.
16 ITA 2007, ss 193–199.
17 ITA 2007, s 189(1)(a).
18 Former TA 1988, s 297(2)(h) and (j).
19 ITA 2007, s 176(7)(2).
20 ITA 2007, s 186 (the limits as amended by FA 2006, Sch 14, para 1(1)).

Disposal of EIS shares

[31.13] Two provisions fall to be considered here. The first relates to the possible loss of relief by reason of a disposal of the shares; the second to relief for losses on such shares.

The first provision was recast for the change from the Business Expansion Scheme to the enterprise investment scheme but the changes were not substantial. Where the individual disposes of eligible shares before the end of the relevant period, and the disposal is not by way of a bargain at arm's length, any relief attributable to those shares is withdrawn.[1] Otherwise one compares the relief given with the amount of basic rate tax[2] on the value received; if the relief is less than that amount it is withdrawn; otherwise it is simply reduced by that amount.[3] Naturally the recapture is reduced if the relief originally given was less than the tax on the amount subscribed.[4] An option the exercise of which would bind the grantor to sell the shares within the relevant period also causes a loss of relief.[5] Disposals stemming from corporate reorganisations[6] and those between spouses or civil partners who are living together are not treated as disposals for this purpose.[7]

Where the disposal is of shares on which relief has not been withdrawn, there is no charge to CGT on a gain,[8] but a capital loss is not denied relief.[9]

Special loss relief is available where the disposal is of shares on which relief has not been withdrawn and is either for full consideration or on a winding-up or

[31.13] Savings products with tax exemptions or reliefs

because the shares have become of negligible value. Where such a disposal results in a loss, relief can be given by treating the loss as falling within ITA 2007, Pt 4 and so giving rise to an income loss rather than a loss for CGT.[10]

Simon's Taxes E3.146.

---

[1] ITA 2007, s 209 (2).
[2] Prior to 6 April 2008: the 20% lower rate.
[3] ITA 2007, s 209(3).
[4] ITA 2007, s 210.
[5] ITA 2007, s 212.
[6] ITA 2007, s 246(6).
[7] ITA 2007, s 299(4).
[8] TCGA 1992, s 150A(2).
[9] TCGA 1992, s 150A(2A).
[10] ITA 2007, Pt 5 Ch 6; the relief is provided for by s 131.

Other events causing loss of relief

[31.14] Related to this provision are rules also causing a withdrawal of relief, this time where value is received from the company; each such receipt from the company during the relevant period causes the loss of a proportionate part of the relief.[1] The types of value received are specified in the legislation. They include the repayment, repurchase or redemption of the shares or securities, cancellation of debts and making of a loan, the provision of a benefit or facility, the transfer of an asset from the company for a figure below market value or by the company at an overvalue and the winding up of the company as a result of which the shareholder receives value for his ordinary shares.[2] This extends also to the receipt of value from a 51% subsidiary of the company, whether it becomes such a subsidiary before or after the individual concerned receives any value from it.[3]

A "receipt of insignificant value"[4] does not cause withdrawal of relief.[5] Also, relief is preserved if there is full restitution of the value,[6] whether in cash or in specie.[7] For shares issued on or after 17 March 2004[8] the repayment of a loan made to the company does not cause loss of relief, unless the loan was part of an arrangement for the share subscription.[9] In *Blackburn & Anor v R & C Commrs* [2008] EWHC 266 (Ch), there were payments to the company in advance of the issue of shares. The High Court held that those shares were to be treated as capital contributions and not loan arrangements and therefore not caught by the 'value received' provisions. The Court added that the purpose of the scheme was to encourage investment by drawing in new money and that any device or scheme which did not draw in new money would be disallowed. There are also rules reducing or withdrawing the relief where the company repays, redeems or repurchases share capital from someone else, ie a member who is not an individual whose relief is reduced under the rule in the previous paragraph.[10] On appeal by the Revenue, the Court of Appeal reviewed the nature of the payments and share allotments once again and allowed the appeal in part. The Court unanimously held that only payments for shares (in the sum of £149,998) which had been made by the appellant by paying for a property bought in the company's name would be disallowed. The Court held that these payments appeared to be either a gift or a loan to the company and that in either case the requirements of para 1 of Sch 5B would not be satisfied and as a consequence EIS relief would be lost. In *Optos v Revenue and Customs Comrs*[11] there was an arrangement involving conversion shares and loan notes. This was held to be a return of value[12] as the conversion shares were not issued wholly for cash.[13]

Further rules deal with replacement capital.[14] Relief is withdrawn if at any time in the relevant period, the company or any subsidiary begins to carry on as its trade or as part of its trade a trade which was previously carried on at any time in that period[15] and the individual had an interest amounting in aggregate to more than half the trade;[16] for this purpose it suffices that the individual was one of a group of persons who had such an interest. Withdrawal also occurs if the company acquires not the trade itself but the whole or the greater part of the assets of a trade in which the taxpayer had such an interest.[17] It also applies where the individual controlled or is part of a group which controlled the company and also controlled the other company which carried on the trade.[18]

Simon's Taxes E3.145.

[1] ITA 2007, s 213ff.
[2] ITA 2007, s 216. For an illustration of the wide scope of these provisions see *Fletcher v Thompson* [2002] EWHC 1552 (Admin), [2002] STC 1149, where the court approved the Revenue's withdrawal of BES relief on the grounds that a receipt by a company controlled by the taxpayer constituted the value received by the taxpayer.
[3] ITA 2007, s 221.
[4] As defined in ITA 2007, s 215(2).
[5] ITA 2007, s 214.
[6] ITA 2007, ss 222 and 223.
[7] ITA 2007, s 222(4).
[8] There is a transitional provision whereby a debt may be repaid if the subscription was before 17 March 2004 but the issue of shares after that date and the debt incurred after that date: FA 2004, Sch 18, para 6(3).
[9] ITA 2007, s 216(2)(*b*).
[10] ITA 2007, ss 224—231.
[11] [2006] STC (SCD) 687.
[12] Within TCGA 1992, Sch 5B, para 13(2).
[13] As required by former TA 1988, s 289(1)(*a*) applied by TCGA 1992, Sch 5B, para 1(2)(*a*).
[14] ITA 2007, s 232.
[15] ITA 2007, s 232(1).
[16] ITA 2007, s 232(2).
[17] ITA 2007, s 232(1)(*a*)(ii).
[18] ITA 2007, s 232(3).

[31.15] Savings products with tax exemptions or reliefs

Claims for relief—and withdrawal of relief

[31.15] To obtain relief, a claim must be made.[1] A claim cannot be made until the qualifying trade has been carried on for four months and must be made before 31 January in the sixth year after the year in which investment is made.[2] Once a claim has been accepted, the relief may be given by the self-assessment process through the individual's PAYE coding. There is also a time limit for the company to inform the inspector of the issue of shares—generally two years.[3] Similarly, a person making a claim must have received from the company a certificate issued by the company in the form prescribed, certifying that the conditions for relief are satisfied in relation to those shares.[4] Where relief is withdrawn the recaptured relief is taxed as income. Tax is charged back to the year in which the relief was given but, for interest purposes, the reckonable date is the date of the event causing the withdrawal.[5]

Where relief is to be withdrawn on the ground that the company is not a qualifying company,[6] the inspector must give notice of this fact to the company—unless the company has already provided information under s 241.[7]

There are also information requirements.[8]

Simon's Taxes E3.140, 145.

---

[1] ITA 2007, s 158(1)(*b*).
[2] ITA 2007, s 202(1)(*a*). Where the trade does not commence until a year later than the year of investment, the time limit is the 31 January in the sixth year following the fiscal year in which the trade commenced (ITA 2007, s 202(1)(*b*)).
[3] ITA 2007, s 205(4).
[4] In the case of *Ashley v R & C Comrs* (2007) Sp C 633, it was held that the lack of a valid certificate with regards to certain shares negated a claim for EIS relief.
[5] ITA 2007, s 239.
[6] Or that the requirements of s 174 or 175 are not met.
[7] Or TCGA 1992, Sch 5B, para 16(2) or (4)) ITA 2007, s 234(2). The giving of such notice is treated as a decision refusing a claim made by the company.
[8] ITA 2007, ss 240-244.

Corporate venturing scheme

[31.16] From 1 April 2000, for a ten-year period, the corporate venturing scheme provides an equivalent investment arrangement for companies to that which is available to individuals under the enterprise investment scheme. A company can invest by subscribing for new shares in an unquoted trading company and obtain a reduction in corporation tax at 20% as long as the shares are retained for at least three years. On any disposal of the shares thereafter, the chargeable gain arising can be rolled into a further investment that qualifies under the scheme. Where the disposal of shares gives rise to a loss, this is allowable against capital gains subject to corporation tax. The loss is computed as net of the investment relief obtained on the original investment.[1]

As with the EIS, there are three reliefs available to the corporate investor. These are relief against corporation tax[2], relief against company profits for losses incurred on disposal of shares to which investment relief is attributable[3] and the deferment of a chargeable gain where there is reinvestment into shares qualifying under the corporate venturing scheme.[4]

Relief under the corporate venturing scheme is restricted to companies that carry on a trade, other than in financial services.[5] Alternatively, a holding company can qualify if the trade is carried on by 90% subsidiaries.[6]

The intention behind the corporate venturing scheme is that investment is made in an unconnected company. Relief is not available for investment in a subsidiary or an associated company; the investor company must not own more than 30% of the ordinary share capital of the target company, nor must there be arrangements in place under which it is entitled to acquire more than that percentage.[7]

---

[1] FA 2000, s 63 and Schs 15 and 16. For detailed provisions relating to subsidiaries of the issuing company, see the amendments made by FA 2004, Sch 20.
[2] FA 2000, Sch 15, paras 1–6.
[3] FA 2000, Sch 15, paras 67–72.
[4] FA 2000, Sch 15, paras 73–79.
[5] FA 2000, Sch 15, paras 10 and 11. The FA 2008 has extended this restriction to companies that carry on a trade in shipbuilding, production of coal or production of steel.
[6] FA 2000, Sch 15, para 23 amended by FA 2004, Sch 20, para 7.
[7] FA 2000, Schs 15 and 16 contain lengthy provisions that parallel the statutory requirements for the EIS.

Venture capital trust

[31.17] Although the aim of the enterprise investment scheme (EIS) (see supra, § 31.06) is to encourage individuals to subscribe for shares in unquoted trading companies, it was recognised that there would be difficulties for individuals in finding suitable unquoted companies, in evaluating the investment opportunities, and in monitoring the progress of the companies after investments had been made. A venture capital trust is a form of collective investment scheme managed by professional managers where the investments made by the managers are in two companies which fulfil the EIS requirements.

An individual who subscribes for shares in a venture capital trust is entitled to income tax relief of 30%[1] of the amount subscribed, up to a maximum subscription of £200,000[2] in any year. In contrast to the provisions for EIS and CVS, a chargeable gain cannot[3] be deferred by subscription in a venture capital trust.

VCT shares must be retained for five years in order for the relief to be granted and not withdrawn.[4] If the conditions are satisfied throughout a period of ownership of at least five years, any gain arising on the disposal of shares in the

[31.17] Savings products with tax exemptions or reliefs

VCT is exempt from capital gains tax.[5] A venture capital trust is an investment company which, throughout its accounting period, meets the following conditions:[6]

(1) Its income must be derived wholly or mainly from shares or securities.
(2) Its ordinary share capital (and each class, if more than one) must be quoted on the Stock Exchange.
(3) It must not retain, for any accounting period, more than 15% of the income it derives from shares or securities.
(4) At least 70% of its investments must be represented throughout its accounting period by "qualifying holdings" of shares or securities.
(5) At least 50% by value of those "qualifying holdings" must be represented by "eligible shares", that is, ordinary shares carrying no present or future preferential rights to dividends or to assets on a winding up, and no present or future preferential right to be redeemed.
(6) The gross assets of the investee companies must not exceed £7,000,000 before the investment and £8,000,0000 after the investment.

Most of the legislation on venture capital trusts has been taken from the legislation on investment trusts in TA 1988, s 842, and many of the provisions of s 842 apply to them. But there are two important exceptions:

(1) a venture capital trust is not prevented from distributing, by way of dividend, surpluses arising on the disposal of investments; and
(2) the word "security" includes any loan, whether secured or not, which is made on terms that it is not to be repaid, repurchased or redeemed, within the period of five years from the making of the loan, or the issue of the security.

The term "qualifying holding" is defined in ITA 2007, s 286. The definition is long and complicated. Only shares or securities which are subscribed for by the venture capital trust can form qualifying holdings. The issuing company must be an unquoted company, that is, none of its shares or debentures or other securities may be marketed to the general public through any Stock Exchange in the UK or abroad, or on the unlisted securities market or a foreign equivalent. In addition, shipbuilding, producing coal and producing steel are expressly excluded activities by the FA 2008 from the "qualifying holdings" definition. However, there are provisions that permit a venture capital trust to receive and retain shares issued in preparation for a stock market flotation (for example)[7] or to exercise conversion rights.[8] But a listing on the Alternative Investment Market is acceptable. Where a venture capital trust acquires a qualifying holding and, subsequently, the issuing company ceases to be an unquoted company, the holding continues to qualify for a further five years.

There are conditions as to the activities of the issuing company, referred to, in the VCT legislation, as the "relevant company". It must exist only for the purpose of carrying on one or more "qualifying trades" although it may carry on other activities provided that they are insignificant in relation to the main purpose. Alternatively, its business must consist of the holding of shares in, or securities of, or making loans to, one or more qualifying subsidiaries whether or not it also carries on a qualifying trade or trades. Trades must be carried on wholly or mainly in the UK. The term "qualifying trade" is defined, broadly, as for the EIS, and extends to trades of research and development. The EIS anti-avoidance legislation has been largely replicated. The money raised by the qualifying company from the venture capital trust must be employed for the purposes of a trade carried on by it or by a qualifying subsidiary. But the fact that part of the amount subscribed has been used for some other purpose will be ignored if that amount is insignificant.

Money subscribed by a venture capital trust can only count towards a "qualifying" holding, if it does not exceed the maximum qualifying investment for the period. The maximum qualifying investment for any accounting period is £1m in shares in, or securities of the relevant company, and a company is not a relevant company if the value of its assets as a whole, immediately before the issue of the shares or securities within the relevant holding, exceeded £7m (or £8m afterwards).[9]

There are detailed provisions under which relief is not withdrawn if a VCT is wound up but the investments pass to another VCT.[10]

Simon's Taxes Division E3.2.

---

[1] ITA 2007, s 263(2). For shares issued between 6 April 2004 and 5 April 2006 relief is provided at 40%.
[2] ITA 2007, s 262(3)
[3] FA 2004, Sch 19, paras 4–7 repeals TCGA 1992, Sch 5C (which provided for deferral relief), in respect of VCT shares issued on or after 6 April 2004.
[4] TCGA 1992, Sch 5C, para 3(2).
[5] See supra, § **17.22**.
[6] ITA 2007, Pt 6, Ch 3. The detailed provisions controlling the nature of the holdings allowed to a Venture Capital Trust are given in Ch 4 and regulations made under s 330, such as the Venture Capital Trust (Exchange of Shares and Securities) Regulations 2002, SI 2002/2661, *Simons Weekly Tax Intelligence* 2002, p 1401.
[7] ITA 2007, s 326.
[8] ITA 2007, s 329.
[9] ITA 2007, s 297 (prior to 6 April 2006, the limits were £15m and £16m).
[10] FA 2002, Sch 33.

Exclusion of 'guaranteed VCTs'

[31.18] VCTs are required to ensure that at least 10% of the total investment from the VCT in any one company is in ordinary, non-preferential shares.[1] Guaranteed loans and securities do not count towards the fixed proportion of qualifying investments which a VCT must hold.[2]

The following are some of the excluded activities:

— Farming and market gardening.
— Forestry and timber production.
— Property development.
— Operating or managing hotels or guest houses.
— Operating or managing nursing or residential care homes.[3]

[31.18] Savings products with tax exemptions or reliefs

These activities are subject to additional qualifications.[4] In respect of investments made on or after 6 April 2008, the following activities were included in the list of excluded activities.

— Shipbuilding.
— Producing coal.
— Producing steel.[5]

Simon's Taxes E3.201.

[1] ITA 2007, s 289.
[2] ITA 2007, s 288.
[3] ITA 2007, s 303.
[4] ITA 2007, ss 304-313.
[5] FA 2008 inserting ITA 2007, s 303(1)(ia)—(ic).

Life assurance policies

Qualifying assurance policies

[31.19] The UK tax system accords special treatment to the life insurance industry. Until 1984 there was income tax relief on premiums;[1] a special system of taxing income and gains applies to insurance companies;[2] in addition the proceeds of a policy are exempt from CGT unless the policy was not owned by the original owner and was acquired for money or money's worth.[3] These privileges and reliefs were granted to encourage savings so that people would be encouraged to provide for their old age and for their dependants. However, in recent years these advantages have been used to promote tax avoidance schemes which probably push the concessions to or even beyond the reasonable limit; many restrictions applied to policies qualifying for relief. These culminated in the decision embodied in FA 1984, to withhold relief from premiums on insurance policies taken out after 13 March 1984. However, the relief remains intact for policies taken out before that date; hence the following exposition retains the present tense.

Simon's Taxes E1.1300.

[1] Infra, § **31.21**.
[2] Supra, §§ **30.18**.
[3] TCGA 1992, s 210.

Non-qualifying policies—excess liability charge

[31.20] If the policy is a non-qualifying policy a special charge to income tax may arise on the occurrence of a chargeable event. The familiar top slicing process is used.[1] Examples of such policies are single premium property bonds and policies. These rules do not apply to mortgage protection policies, retirement annuity policies, policies forming part of pension schemes, nor group life policies.[2]

With effect from 6 April 2004, the notional tax credit used in calculating any tax due on a chargeable event is at the basic rate of tax (ie 20%).[3] This cancels a tax liability arises to a basic rate taxpayer, as a chargeable event is treated as savings income.[4]

---

[1] ITTOIA 2005, Pt 4 Ch 9.
[2] ITTOIA 2005, s 481 with effect from 9 April 2003. The Revenue note states that the changes were introduced in order to exclude charges that would otherwise arise to members of trade unions, professional associations, partnerships, credit unions and life insurers.
[3] ITTOIA 2005, s 530. Before 6 April 2008, the lower rate (also 20%) was used.
[4] ITTOIA 2005, s 530(1). The charge arising on a charitable trust is effectively removed by the deemed tax credit being equal to the charge that is limited to basic income rate by ITTOIA 2005, s 467. Between 2003 and 2008, the charge was limited to the savings rate.

[31.21] Where a policy has been issued by a non-UK resident life assurance company the policy is non-qualifying, and the income tax charge on a "chargeable event" is not limited to the higher rate of tax. In consequence, in the right circumstances, tax may be imposed at 40%. Two categories of life assurance companies are not affected by this rule. They are:

(1) Companies carrying on life assurance business in the UK through branches, and resident in a country with which Britain has a double taxation treaty which allows the UK domestic law on life assurance taxation to apply provided that the policy has been issued by the branch. The countries affected are most Commonwealth and former Commonwealth countries and the Republic of Ireland.
(2) Companies resident within the European Economic Area (the EU and EFTA); which compute profits by reference to investment income and gains; and which impose tax at at least 20% on profits.[1]

Where a non-resident individual who owns a non-resident policy becomes resident in the UK, any tax charge arising, subsequently, on the non-resident policy will be limited, proportionally, to the period of UK residence.

Simon's Taxes B8.645.

---

[1] ITTOIA 2005, s 532.

[31.22] Chargeable events. The events are[1]:

(1) death giving rise to benefits under the policy;
(2) the maturity of the policy;
(3) the total surrender[2] of the rights under the policy including bonus;[3] and
(4) the assignment of the rights for money or money's worth; and
(5) a loan taken by trustees who would be subject to the chargeable event if capital were paid to them.[4]

[31.22] Savings products with tax exemptions or reliefs

When an insurance policy is transferred from one spouse to another as part of a divorce settlement under a court order, this is not a chargeable event.[5]

Simon's Taxes B8.645.

---

[1] ITTOIA 2005, s 484.
[2] On partial surrender, see ITTOIA 2005, s 507.
[3] Payment of a bonus may be treated as a part surrender: ITTOIA 2005, s 500—and so may loans (infra, § **31.34**).
[4] ITTOIA 2005, s 501 in respect of chargeable events on or after 9 April 2003.
[5] Inland Revenue Tax Bulletin December 2003, p 1071. This Revenue statement is a change to the previous view that had been held, consequent upon the judgment of Coleridge J in *G v G* [2002] EWHC 1339 (Fam), [2002] 2 FLR 1143, [2003] Fam Law 14, who held that transfer on a divorce is not the receipt of money or money's worth. It is presumed that a similar approach would apply on the dissolution of a civil partnership.

[31.23] The gain. On death the gain is the amount by which the surrender value immediately before the death plus the "relevant capital payments", such as bonuses, exceeds the total amount paid by way of premiums, plus any sums already treated as gains on partial surrender or assignment.

On maturity or surrender in whole, the gain is the excess of the proceeds including bonuses over the premiums paid with adjustments for sums treated as gains on earlier partial surrender or assignment.

On assignment the gain is the excess of the consideration received (except for connected persons when market value is substituted[1]) plus the amount or value of any relevant capital payments over the total amount of premiums paid with adjustments for the assignment.[2]

Partial surrenders and partial assignments are also chargeable events. Many modern policies allow partial surrenders at frequent intervals and such surrenders gave rise to complex calculations. In an attempt to reduce the work involved, both for life offices and the Revenue, a different system of determining both whether there has been a gain and its extent applies.[3]

The chargeable amount is defined as an excess of "net total value of rights" over "net total allowable payments".[4] The former term is calculated in s 507(4), the latter in s 507(5). In certain circumstances, it is necessary to deduct commission that has been rebated or reinvested from the premium paid.[5] The deduction of commission is required where the premium paid exceeds £100,000.[6] In considering this limit, it is necessary to look at the tax year of the payment and any payments made in the preceding three tax years. There is provision for aggregating policies in testing the £100,000 limit.[7]

Each year there is an allowance of (a) 5% of any premium paid up to the end of the year, and (b) 5% of any premiums on which an allowance has been due in previous years, up to a maximum of 20/20th. So a premium payment only gets a full allowance 20 years after payment. Allowances not used will be carried forward accumulatively. The effect of this is to allow withdrawals of up to 5% of premiums paid without attracting any charge.

If the gain arises in respect of a new non-resident policy or a new offshore capital redemption policy, it is reduced to take account of periods of residence outside the UK.[8] The gain is reduced by the fraction:

$$\frac{\text{number of days for which the policy ran (up to the chargeable event) in which the holder was UK resident}}{\text{total number of days for which the policy ran up to the chargeable event}}$$

Simon's Taxes B8.653.

[1] ITTOIA 2005, s 493(6).
[2] ITTOIA 2005, s 491.
[3] Inland Revenue press release, 10 December 1974, see *Simon's Tax Intelligence* 1974, p 518.
[4] ITTOIA 2005, s 507(2). Prior to ITTOIA 2005, the legislation referred to the excess of "reckonable aggregate value" over "allowable aggregate amount" (TA 1988 s 540(1)(a)(v)).
[5] ITTOIA 2005, s 541A(2) inserted by FA 2007, s 28(3) with effect for policies made on or after 21 March 2007, or policies before that date whose terms are varied, or rights are exercised on or after that date, so as to increase the benefits under it. This provision is designed to defeat a scheme whereby substantial commission was paid by the insurer out of the premium and this commission was passed on to the policy holder. The policy was cashed in just before the value had grown to the initial premium (ignoring the payback of commission). Hence, there was no gain to be charged on the policyholder.
[6] ITTOIA 2005, s 541A(3) inserted by FA 2007, s 28(3).
[7] ITTOIA 2005, s 541A(4) inserted by FA 2007, s 28(4).
[8] TA 1988, s 553(3).

[31.24] The slice of the gain. Individuals may claim top-slicing relief, a process which requires first the calculation of the slice of the gain.[1] To do this one spreads the gain back over a number of years by multiplying it by one over the number of complete years (a) on the first chargeable event—back to the start of the policy, (b) on any later chargeable event other than final termination—back to the previous chargeable event, (c) on final termination—the number of whole years from the start of the policy. In calculating the top-slicing relief for a gain on a new non-resident policy or a new offshore capital redemption policy, the number of complete years is, in each case, reduced by the number of complete years during which the holder was non-resident.[2]

The slice of the gain is then added to the taxpayer's other income to discover the amount of extra tax payable by reason of its addition. If the addition of that sum does not give rise to anything but tax at the basic rate, no tax is payable.[3] If, however, extra tax is payable, the amount of that tax is then calculated. The average of that tax rate is then ascertained, the basic rate deducted and the resulting rate applied to the whole gain.[4] Although a policy gain is not liable to basic rate income tax, the amount is income for age relief purposes and may restrict the amount of that relief. This relief is not affected by the abolition of top-slicing relief by FA 1988, s 75.

When there is a chargeable event through death or maturity and there is a loss, an individual may deduct that loss from total income so far as it does not

[31.24] Savings products with tax exemptions or reliefs

exceed gains taxed in earlier partial surrender or assignments.[5] Thus the tax on gains made earlier may be recovered. The relief does not apply to losses on assignments nor does it make any allowance for inflation.

Simon's Taxes B8.653.

[1] ITTOIA 2005, s 535.
[2] ITTOIA 2005, s 536(7).
[3] However, if the effect is to cause the withdrawal of age relief some liability may arise.
[4] ITTOIA 2005, s 36.
[5] ITTOIA 2005, s 539.

Qualifying policies

[31.25] It would be easy to create a qualifying policy, to convert it and then to realise it in an attempt to avoid these rules. Hence the charge applies also to qualifying policies if any of these events occur provided that the policy is dealt with within its first ten years or first three-quarters of its term if this is shorter. Thus if the policy is converted into a paid up policy and then the death occurs or the policy matures before the expiry of ten years from the making of the insurance or, if sooner, 75% of the term of the policy, or if it is surrendered or assigned for money or money's worth within that time, a charge accrues.[1] No charge would have arisen for a qualifying policy simply because the death occurred within ten years—a dealing is also needed.

Simon's Taxes E1.1311.

[1] TA 1988, s 340(1)(*b*).

[31.26] Trusts and companies. Where a non-qualifying policy is held by trustees, the charge to tax falls on the settlor, if he is alive, although there is an indemnity against the trustees.[1] With effect from 6 April 1998, if the settlor is dead, the charge arises on the trustees.[2] A close investment company must treat as income, any gain arising on a non-qualifying policy,[3] or if the policy was issued before 14 March 1989, and has not been varied or extended since that date on a qualifying policy where the gain is of a kind described in supra, § **31.31**. For policies issued to a company, close or otherwise, after 13 March 1989, or existing policies which are varied or extended after that date, the entire gain, that is, the excess of the surrender value of the policy over premiums paid, is treated as income. A company is similarly liable in respect of a policy which secures a debt owed by the company, as well as a policy settled by the company on trust. Special rules apply to the calculation of a policy gain where the policy secures a debt.[4]

[1] TA 1988, s 551, but see TA 1988, s 547(1)(*a*).
[2] TA 1988, s 547(1)(*d*).
[3] TA 1988, s 547(1)(*b*).
[4] TA 1988, s 541(4A), (4B).

Personal portfolio bonds

[31.27] A personal portfolio bond is one where benefits are due under a life assurance policy, the value of which is linked to assets which are personal to the policyholder. Such bonds have normally been marketed by insurance companies operating outside the UK. The policyholder is, thereby, able to directly influence the timing of both disposals within the bond and withdrawals from the bond. It has, thus, been possible for some taxpayers to avoid a charge to UK tax by deferring a chargeable event until the taxpayer is not resident in the UK.

A taxpayer who holds a personal portfolio bond is treated as subject to a chargeable event each fiscal year, whether or not there is a withdrawal from the bond. The event is calculated as 15% of the total premiums paid into the bond since it was first taken out, less taxable amounts withdrawn in earlier years.[1]

---

[1] ITTOIA 2005, s 522. No charge arises in respect of any personal portfolio bond that was taken out before 17 March 1998, unless additions have been made to the bond since that date: (ITTOIA 2005, Sch 2, para 112.

Loans

[31.28] If money were withdrawn in the form of loans instead of by the normal surrender of policy rights, these rules might be frustrated. It is therefore provided that loans are in general equivalent to surrender of rights[1] but with exceptions for loans at a commercial rate on qualifying policies.[2] Any repayment of the loan is treated as a premium.[3] This counters the common borrow-all arrangement under which the policyholder paid the first few premiums out of his own resources and then borrowed from the insurance company—at interest—to pay subsequent premiums.

Special rules once restricted the deductibility of interest on loans used to pay premiums. In view of the general restrictions on the deduction of interest these have been repealed.[4]

More importantly, TA 1988, s 554 treated certain borrowings against life policies as income taxable under Schedule D, Case III unless the Revenue are satisfied that the borrowings do not amount to disguised annuity payments.[5] This provision was not rewritten into ITTOIA 2005 which deemed it unnecessary.

Simon's Taxes B8.303.

---

[1] For determining any excess charge and any clawback.
[2] ITTOIA 2005, s 503(2). There was also an exception for house loans to full time employees of the body issuing the policy: ITTOIA 2005, s 503(3) (replacing extra-statutory concession A47 to employees of certain insurance associations; and for certain loan annuity contracts made by the elderly: TA 1988, s 271(2)(*b*).
[3] TA 1988, s 548(2).
[4] TA 1970, ss 403, 404 (repealed by FA 1987, Sch 16, Part VII).

1377

[31.28] Savings products with tax exemptions or reliefs

[5] Reversing *IRC v Wesleyan and General Assurance Society* [1948] 1 All ER 555, 30 TC 11.

Life annuity contracts

[31.29] The rules prescribing excess liability on chargeable events in relation to endowment policies are adapted to the surrender of life annuity contracts.[1] Special rules apply to guaranteed income bonds; a charge to basic rate income tax is made.

Simon's Taxes B8.647.

---

[1] See for example ITTOIA 2005, s 531(1), (3).

Purchased annuities

[31.30] The investment of one's capital in the purchase of an annuity meant that one was buying income with capital and that income tax was therefore due on the whole of each payment received, even though in commercial reality one was receiving back each year a part of one's capital together with interest. A number of ways around this rule were devised. The first, which lasted until 1949, provided for an advance by way of interest-free loan each month which was to be extinguished by set off against a capital sum due under the contract on his death.[1] The Revenue's argument that these were in substance annual payments was rejected. Such loans are now treated as income. A second way, which still survives, applies to an annuity certain, that is an annuity payable for a stated number of years, not depending on the survival of the annuitant. Here the Court of Appeal held that tax was chargeable only on so much of the payment as represented interest and not on the whole sum.[2] This split treatment was not accorded to normal annuities which terminated on the death of the annuitant and so companies would issue "split annuities", meaning an annuity certain for a stated number of years to be followed by a deferred annuity. The payments under the former annuity would be divided into capital and interest and while the latter would be taxable in full it was arranged that the sum payable under the contract would be higher and in any case the cost of it would be lower in view of the more advanced age.

Simon's Taxes B8.433.

---

[1] *IRC v Wesleyan and General Assurance Society* (1946) 30 TC 11, supra, § **31.35**.
[2] *Perrin v Dickson* [1930] 1 KB 107, 14 TC 608; but doubted in *Sothern-Smith v Clancy* [1941] 1 All ER 111, 24 TC 1.

[31.31] A purchased annuity,[1] but not any other type of annuity, is divided into two elements, the division being made actuarily. The capital element is exempt from tax: the income element attracts income tax. An annuity is not split if, apart from TA 1988, s 656, it is treated as having a capital element, or if it qualifies for relief in respect of the premiums paid under TA 1988, ss 266, 273 or 623. Also taxable in full are annuities purchased or provided for under a will or settlement, out of income of property disposed of by the will or settlement (whether with or without resort to capital) or provided under a sponsored superannuation scheme.[2] Tax is deducted in respect of the income element by the payer.

The method of apportionment between income and capital is carried out by dividing the sum spent by the normal expectation of life according to Government mortality tables, regardless of the individual.[3] The sum so ascertained is the capital element and this remains constant and is not revised to take account of the length of time the annuitant actually survived. The actuarial value is computed as at the date when the first payment begins to accrue.[4] If there are contingencies other than the ending of a human life, the capital element is such as may be just having regard to the contingency.[5] Annuities may be geared to inflation; the Revenue practice is to fix the capital content at the start of the annuity so making all increases wholly taxable.

Simon's Taxes B8.433.

[1] A "purchased life annuity" is given a special definition by ITTOIA 2005, s 423; that is, an annuity granted by (broadly) a life company for money or money's worth. Where a life company gives an annuity to compensate for mis-selling, there is consideration in money's worth (the compensation) for the grant of the annuity. On this basis, ITTOIA 2005, Pt 6, Ch 7 operates to split each monthly receipt between a taxed sum and a tax-free sum.
[2] ITTOIA 2005, s 718.
[3] The tables are authorised under ITTOIA 2005, s 724. They must be obeyed: *Rose v Trigg* (1963) 41 TC 365. This is hard since a person with lower than average life expectancy may get special terms from a company.
[4] ITTOIA 2005, ss 720(3) and 721(3). It is usually paid half yearly in arrears.
[5] ITTOIA 2005, s 719(3), (4). Where the amount (and not just the term) is to vary, see ITTOIA 2005, s 719(8).

Child trust fund

[31.32] A child trust fund[1] is available to a child born on or after 1 September 2004. In order to qualify the child must be settled in the United Kingdom and have a right of abode in the UK.

The Child Trust Fund Account is operated by commercial providers, with competition between providers being encouraged. The account is opened by the parent (or guardian), but contributions into the account can be made by anyone, including the child himself.

There are three types of Child Trust Fund account: (a) a savings account for a cash deposit; (b) a shares account; (c) a stakeholder account. The third type of account invests in company shares until the child's 13th birthday, when equities are sold and the proceeds are held as cash, or government stock.

[31.32] Savings products with tax exemptions or reliefs

Any account can be moved from one category to another. Until the child is aged 16 the transfer is made by the parent. Once the child is aged 16, he or she controls the account but cannot make withdrawals until age 18.

The maximum amount that can be invested in a child's Trust Account is £1,200 each year (excluding the government contribution). For this purpose, a year starts as commencing on the child's birthday.

The Government contributes £250 for each Child Trust Fund account that is opened. For the household is £13,480 or less, the Government contribution is increased to £500. (The income limit is given for £2004–05; the limit is that which applies for qualification for Income Support.)

At age seven a further Government contribution is made: the amount will announced before the first of such contributions becomes due in 2009.

The Child Trust Fund is exempt from income tax and capital gains tax.

[1] A useful non-technical leaflet on Child Trust Funds can be printed from HMRC website.

Real estate investment trust

[31.33] Real estate investment trusts and similar structures have become a global trade, trading successfully in North America (USA and Canada), Australia, Asia-Pacific (Japan, Singapore, Hong Kong, Malaysia, Thailand, South Korea and Taiwan) and Europe (The Netherlands, Belgium, Greece and France). From 1 January 2007, the UK provides[1] a special regime that shifts the burden of taxation of property rental business from the company that carries on the business to the shareholders that invest in the company.

By converting to a UK-REIT, a company will no longer pay UK direct tax on the profits and gains from its qualifying property rental businesses in the UK, and elsewhere, provided that certain conditions are met. This will effectively reduce the burden of taxation for most shareholders in respect of the company's tax-exempt business and enable them to gain access to more flexible indirect property investments for their portfolios. Non-qualifying profits will continue to be subject to corporation tax as normal.

The entry cost of conversion to UK-REIT status has been set[2] by the UK Treasury at 2% of the market value of the assets within the company's tax-exempt business immediately prior to entry into the UK-REIT regime.

The special regime is available to companies whose business is at least 75% property rental. The property can be in the UK or overseas. The regime can apply also to a group of companies that have 75% of their aggregated business as property rental.

The rental income from the properties is exempt from corporation tax, as are capital gains on disposal of rental properties. The Real Estate Investment Trust must distribute 90% of the rental profits from its tax-exempt property rental business, and pay these distributions under deduction of basic rate income tax. For UK tax purposes, these property income distributions are treated in the same way as UK property income in the hands of the investors.

To opt for this treatment, the company has to carry on a 'property rental business'[3] which can include profits from interests in UK and foreign property.

The statutory conditions include six relating to the company itself, four to its 'property rental business' and two to the amount of property rental business it carries on in comparison with other types of activity undertaken by the company.

The six company conditions are:[4]

(1) The company must be UK resident.
(2) Its shares must be listed on a recognised stock exchange.
(3) The company is not an open-ended investment company.
(4) It is not a 'close' company (that is, controlled by five or fewer people).
(5) The company can issue only one class of ordinary shares and fixed-rate non-voting preference shares.
(6) It cannot borrow money on terms that effectively entitle the lender to a share of the profits.

The company conditions are designed to restrict the regime to publicly listed companies with their equity and debt finance arranged in such a way as to ensure that tax-exempt profits are paid out to shareholders as income taxable under Schedule A.

The four conditions relating to the property rental business are:[5]

(1) The business must have at least three rental properties.
(2) No one property can represent more than 40% by value of the rental portfolio.
(3) Properties occupied by the company are excluded from the property rental business.
(4) The company must distribute 90% of rental profits (calculated on a tax basis) as dividends.

The two conditions relating to the balance of business[6] carried on by the company are that the property rental business accounts for 75% of the company's business, measured by assets and by income.

The balance of business conditions[7] are designed to ensure that the main activity of the company is property investment. The 25% of other activities are allowed to provide sufficient margin for activities that may be closely related to property investment, such as small-scale development for resale, to take place without affecting the tax-exempt status of the property investment business although there is no restriction on the nature of these activities.

The exemption from corporation tax applies to profits[8] (income and gains) of the property rental business.

There is a ring fence around the tax-exempt business at the point of entry to the regime.[9] The purpose is to separate profits and losses of the pre-entry property rental business from the property rental business once the company has joined the regime, and to re-base assets of the property rental business to market value as they enter the regime.

[31.33] Savings products with tax exemptions or reliefs

Schedule A and Schedule D, Case V losses that arose in pre-entry periods are extinguished[10] but allowable capital losses continue to be available to carry forward for use against future chargeable gains in the non tax-exempt part of the post-entry business of company.[11]

A ring fence is set[12] around the tax-exempt business carried on by a company to which the Real Estate Investment Trust legislation applies. The ring fence is there to isolate the profits, losses and gains of the tax-exempt business from those arising from other activities carried on by the company.

Basic rate income tax is deducted[13] from distributions of profits of the tax-exempt business of a Real Estate Investment Trust.

A group of companies can join the regime to become a Group Real Estate Investment Trust,[14] which is broadly a group as defined for taxation of chargeable gains purposes.[15]

---

[1] FA 2006, ss 103–145 and Schs 16 & 17 amended by FA 2007, Sch 17. Details are given in statutory instruments: Real Estate Investment Trusts (Assessment and Recovery of Tax) Regulations 2006, SI 2006/2867, Real Estate Investment Trust (Joint Ventures) Regulations 2006, SI 2006/2866, Real Estate Investment Trusts (Financial Statements of Group Real Investment Trusts) Regulations 2006, SI 2006/2865, Real Estate Investment Trusts (Breach of Conditions) Regulations 2006, SI 2006/2864. *Simon's Weekly Tax Intelligence* 2006, p 2404. The scheme is available to a company for an accounting period commencing on or after 1 January 2007: FA 2006, s 145(1).
[2] FA 2006, s 112(3).
[3] FA 2006, s 104.
[4] FA 2006, s 106.
[5] FA 2006, s 107.
[6] FA 2006, s 108.
[7] Set out in FA 2006, s 108.
[8] As defined in FA 2006, s 104.
[9] FA 2006, s 111.
[10] FA 2006, s 111(1).
[11] FA 2006, s 111(4).
[12] FA 2006, s 113.
[13] FA 2006, s 122(2)(*a*).
[14] FA 2006, s 134.
[15] FA 2006, s 134(2).

32

Pensions

Pensions taxation reform	PARA **32.01**
Sharing of pensions on divorce	PARA **32.02**
Earlier developments	PARA **32.03**
Occupational schemes	PARA **32.08**
Additional voluntary contributions	PARA **32.30**
Money purchase scheme	PARA **32.31**
Personal pensions	PARA **32.32**
Retirement age	PARA **32.34**
Secured and unsecured income	PARA **32.35**
Transitional protection for members of schemes before 6 April 2006	PARA **32.37**
Unauthorised payments	PARA **32.42**

Pensions taxation reform

[32.01] The taxation of pensions schemes was radically overhauled with effect from 6 April 2006, often referred to as 'A-Day'. The key elements are as follows:

(a) Anyone can pay up to £3,600 a year into a registered pension scheme regardless of their earnings. This means that individuals without earnings can contribute up to £3,600 a year. There is no minimum age; hence, a child can, from birth, contribute £3,600 a year into a pension. Other groups of individuals for whom this provision may be relevant include non-earning spouses, individuals taking career breaks, carers and those working abroad who are not in a UK registered pension scheme.

(b) Contributions over £3,600 can be made based on earnings—up to 100% of earned income subject to an annual allowance of £235,000.[1]

(c) All contributions are generally paid net of basic rate tax. The pension provider will reclaim that tax from HMRC. The only exceptions relate to retirement annuity policies and to occupational pension schemes where members make contributions and receive tax relief through the net pay agreement. Shares from an approved employee share scheme can be put into a pension arrangement within the contribution limits and attract tax relief.

(d) There is a lifetime allowance limit of £1.65 million[2] on tax-privileged pension savings. Pension rights valued over this figure when benefits are crystallised are subject to the lifetime allowance charge. The excess fund is thus subject to tax at 25%. If the remaining fund after the lifetime allowance charge is to be taken as a lump sum then a further 40% tax liability results in an overall effective tax charge of 55%.

(e) The compulsion to buy an annuity by age 75 applicable to all forms of defined contribution arrangements has been abolished.
(f) New concepts of secured and unsecured income as the means of taking pension benefits have been introduced.
(g) Employer contributions to registered pension schemes become unlimited but tax relief relies on satisfying the wholly and exclusively test.

The reform of pensions taxation resulted in the eight different tax regimes governing pensions prior to 6 April 2006 being replaced with one single regime covering all forms of pension schemes. The concept of pension arrangements being approved by HMRC is replaced by scheme registration.

[1] Rising to £245,000 and £255,000 in 2009/10 and 2010/11 respectively.
[2] Rising to £1.75m and £1.8m in 2009/10 and 2010/11 respectively.

Sharing of pensions on divorce

[32.02] The Welfare Reform and Pensions Act 1999 gives the court the power to divide a taxpayer's entitlement to a pension fund between the taxpayer and his/her ex-spouse. Finance Act 1999[1] contains the provisions necessary to deal with the fiscal consequences of such a court order.[2] In order to have the benefit of this new legislation, a court order is necessary.[3] This concept of pensions division is generally referred to as Pensions sharing.

For those who have "pension debits" and "credits" at 5 April 2006 there are important changes. Anyone who has a pension sharing order effected before 6 April 2006 will be able to apply for an increase in their lifetime allowance to offset any "pension credit" entitlement. However, this will not be available for anyone who wishes to opt for primary protection.

Any 'pension debit' from a pension sharing order effected before 6 April 2006 can be ignored. This means that anyone who may need to apply for transitional protection can exclude the value of any "pension debit".

For pension sharing orders effected after 5 April 2006 the concept of "debits" and "credits" remains. A "pension credit" will count towards the lifetime allowance of the ex-spouse. A "pension debit" will not count when testing benefits against the lifetime allowance. This creates a much fairer system than that which applied before 6 April 2006.[4]

Simon's Taxes, Division E7.1.

[1] FA 1999, s 7 and Sch 10.
[2] The intention is that the provisions of FA 1999, Sch 10 will be brought into effect at the same time as a pension-splitting court order is permitted under the Welfare Reform and Pensions Act 1999: see FA 1999, Sch 10, para 18 and HMRC press release, 31 March 1999, *Simon's Weekly Tax Intelligence* 1999, p 777.
[3] TA 1988, s 590(4C).
[4] FA 2004, s 220.

Earlier developments

[32.03] The reforms introduced from 6 April 2006 represent the largest set of reforms since 1970. The earlier tax regimes had built up progressively over many years. For example fundamental changes were made by F(No 2)A 1987 as follows:

(1)   Introduction of new approved personal pension schemes in place of approved retirement annuity contracts.
(2)   Provision for new "freestanding" AVC schemes in which the employee can invest additional contributions in a scheme of his own choice.
(3)   Introduction of new controls to prevent abuse of the tax privileges enjoyed by approved occupational pension schemes. One of the main changes was to increase the minimum number of years service required to generate a maximum pension of two thirds final remuneration from 10 to 20 years.
(4)   Provisions to allow free transfer from one kind of approved pension arrangement to another and to end an employer's right to insist on compulsory membership of an occupational pension scheme.
(5)   Provisions to allow and encourage individuals to contract out of the State Earnings Related Pension Scheme (SERPS) by having the relevant part of national insurance contributions paid directly into appropriate personal pensions.

After considerable consultation with the pensions industry, the Pensions Act 1995 obtained Royal Assent on 19 July 1995. The Act contains 181 sections and 7 Schedules, much of it being enabling legislation with the detail being the subject of subsequent regulations. The main provisions of the Act include:

(1)   The requirement from 6 April 1997 for occupational pension schemes to include member nominated trustees. At least one third of a scheme's trustees should be member nominated.
(2)   The Act clearly sets out the responsibilities of employers, trustees, professional advisors and members. The Act includes provisions headed "Blowing the whistle" the effect of which is to place an obligation on the pension scheme auditor or actuary to give a written report to the pension schemes regulator (The Occupational Pensions Regulatory Authority) of any failure in the administration of the scheme to comply with prescribed duties.
(3)   The minimum funding requirement (MFR). The Pensions Bill originally included a provision for a statutory minimum solvency requirement but during the Bill's committee stage and report stage in the House of Lords, it was agreed that the minimum solvency requirement could have had far reaching consequences for the future of defined benefit schemes. An alternative mechanism—the minimum funding requirement—was therefore accepted and is the subject of comprehensive regulations. The MFR will not necessarily guarantee a scheme's solvency on a wind-up.

[32.03] Pensions

(4) A new occupational pension schemes regulator has been established in the form of the Occupational Pensions Regulatory Authority (OPRA) and replaces the old Occupational Pensions Board. OPRA (now the pensions regulator) is the main authority for the regulation and supervision of occupational pension schemes in the UK.

(5) The establishment of a compensation scheme, financed by a levy on all occupational schemes to be introduced to protect members against the dishonest removal of assets.

(6) Fundamental changes were made to the way in which employers have been able to contract out of the State Earnings Related Pensions Scheme. With effect from 6 April 1997 defined benefit schemes did not have to provide guaranteed minimum pensions in respect of service after that date.

Simon's Taxes Division E7.1.

Preservation

[32.04] When an employee leaves an occupational pension scheme the retirement benefits earned by pensionable service to date must be preserved. This may be achieved in various ways. SSA 1985 introduced a new alternative: the cash equivalent of the accrued pension entitlement may be applied towards "other types of pension arrangements that meet prescribed conditions". As an alternative to leaving the deferred pension rights with the old employer's scheme, the options available to the individual are:

(1) Transfer into the new employer's pension scheme.

(2) Transfer to a deferred annuity buy-out contract, commonly referred to as a section 32 policy after FA 1981, s 32 (later, TA 1988, s 591(2)(g)).[1]

(3) Transfer to a personal pension scheme set up by the employee.

Simon's Taxes E7.103–106, 215.

---

[1] FA 1994, s 107.

Early leavers—options and effects

[32.05] The preservation requirements only secure pension entitlement earned by service up to the point of leaving the scheme. Thus in a typical final salary scheme providing a pension of 40/60ths of final salary an employer who leaves after 20 years service is entitled to a deferred pension of 20/60ths of final salary at the date of leaving the scheme, not final salary prior to eventual retirement.

An employee whose career development may entail several job changes is thus at a particular disadvantage when pension is provided by final salary schemes.

Some alleviation for those at the start of their careers was made by a provision in SSA 1985 requiring an early leaver's accrued pension entitlement to be revalued by cost of living increases (up to a maximum increase of 5% per year) for pensionable service from 1 January 1985. SSA 1990 extended this revaluation to pensionable service before that date for those who terminate their employment after 1 January 1991.

But the main response by government to this problem has been to encourage adoption of money purchase schemes. A money purchase scheme is one where the employee or employer (or both) make defined contributions to a fund and the ultimate pension depends on the size of the fund when the employee retires. With such an arrangement the employee on changing jobs takes with him the part of the fund that represents contributions made by or for him and the income and gains thereon.

A personal pension scheme is a money purchase arrangement set up by the employee which is not dependent on a particular employment. The employer may, however, contribute to such a scheme.

A significant change made in SSA 1986 makes it unlawful for a contract of employment to require compulsory membership of the employer's occupational scheme. An employee is free to elect not to belong to the employer's scheme and to have a personal pension scheme instead.

In December 1993 the Securities and Investment Board (SIB) published the results of a report it had commissioned on practices within the life assurance industry relating to individuals who had transferred their deferred pension rights from the previous employer's scheme into individual pension policy arrangements. It was found that the evidence on why such recommendations were made was inadequate. More worrying, however, was the finding that many individuals had been persuaded to leave their existing employer's pension scheme in favour of a personal pension scheme. Only in a minority of cases could such advice be justified. The SIB findings raised questions about the adequacy of regulation and competence within the industry, resulting in the publication by the SIB of a statement of policy and specification of standards and procedures. This is concerned with personal pension transfers and opt outs (where an employee opts out of the employer's occupational scheme in favour of a personal pension). The personal pension scheme member may be entitled to financial redress if:

(1) The sale of the personal pension policy did not comply with four main criteria:
    (a) the requirement to "know your customer" and suitability of the policy;
    (b) the accuracy of the information provided;
    (c) an explanation of the risks associated with a personal pension and the member's understanding of these risks;
    (d) there must have been no misleading information or statements made in connection with the sale of the policy;
(2) where the personal pension member has suffered a loss either actual or prospective; and
(3) it would have to be shown that the sale of the policy did not comply with the criteria listed in 1 above.

In cases where the compliance criteria were properly carried out, and that those were fully understood by the policy holder, it is considered unlikely that any financial redress would be due.

[32.05] Pensions

If financial redress is obtained in the form of a capital sum by way of compensation relating to pension mis-selling, income tax is not chargeable on the capital sum.[1]

[1] FA 1996, s 148.

Increasing cost of the state scheme

[32.06] It has been calculated that by the year 2035 each pensioner will be supported by only 1.6 persons in employment as against 2.3 persons in 1985.[1] This is the result of changes in the birth rate and an increased life expectancy of those now coming up to pensionable age.

This anticipated trend has serious implications for the financing of the state pension scheme especially the second tier previously known as the state earnings related pensions scheme (SERPS). SERPS provides for a supplementary earnings-related component to be added to the basic flat-rate pension provided increased graduated national insurance contributions have been paid by the employer and employee. SERPS has been replaced by the State Second Pension (S2P).

Because the state scheme including SERPS/S2P is not funded and benefits are paid out of current contributions, the increasing number of pensioners will cause heavy costs to fall on those in employment in the coming decades.

Introduced by the Child Support, Pensions and Social Security Act 2000, the State Second Pension (S2P) is the successor to SERPS and was effective from 6 April 2002. S2P gives a higher level of second tier State pension than SERPS for the lower paid.[2]

Initially S2P is based on an earnings-related system similar to SERPS but with different accrual rates. The Government have proposed that in the future S2P will be a flat-rate additional state pension.

[1] Green Paper "Reform of Social Security" Cmnd. 9517 para 5.4.
[2] Child Support, Pensions and Social Security Act 2000, Pt II, Ch 1.

The types of pensions schemes available

[32.07] The main tax-favoured pension arrangements available are summarised below:

(1) *Occupational pension schemes*. This refers to the typical "company" scheme sponsored by an employer where the pension entitlement may be on either a defined benefit or defined contribution basis. This is explained further at infra, § **32.08**. Separate provisions exist for a special type of occupational scheme, known as a "small self-administered scheme". These rules are explained further at infra, § **32.17**.

(2) *AVC arrangements.* Under these an employee covered by an occupational scheme makes additional provision within the overall limits allowed. The additional contribution may be made to the employer's scheme or as from 26 October 1987 to a "freestanding" scheme established by the employee. From 6 April 2006 additional contributions may be paid to a personal pension and the extent to which additional contributions may be made becomes much more generous.

(3) *Retirement annuity contracts.* These were issued by life companies up until 1 July 1988. Contributions of 17.5% of net relevant earnings were permitted for individuals up to age 50 increasing to 27.5% for contributors over the age of 60. The earnings cap introduced in FA 1989 did not apply where retirement annuity contributions are paid. The age and earnings related contribution limits were abolished as a part of the reforms introduced at 6 April 2006. Retirement annuities are explained further at infra, § **32.32**.

(4) *Personal pension schemes.* These schemes took the place of retirement annuity contracts and are widely available. They came into operation on 1 July 1988. The earnings cap applied to contributors to personal pension schemes but the percentage contribution rate varied from 17.5% of net relevant earnings for those under age 36 to 40% to those aged 61 or over. The age and earnings related contribution limits were abolished as a part of the reforms introduced at 6 April 2006. These are explained further at infra, § **32.33**.

(5) *Flexible benefits (income drawdown – or unsecured income).* An additional way of taking pension benefits was introduced in FA 1995. This gives members the right to elect to defer the purchase of an annuity and to take income withdrawals from their pension fund in the meantime. The extension of this facility beyond age 75 is a radical change introduced from 6 April 2006 through the alternatively secured pension. This is explained further at infra, § **32.35** and **32.36**.

(6) Unapproved "top-up" schemes. These were schemes made possible by FA 1989. They were intended to be used in cases where the earnings cap of £105,600 (for 2005–06) restricted maximum pension and the maximum lump sum commutation payment and the employer wished to make additional pension provision on an unapproved basis. With effect from 6 April 2006 these have been replaced by Employer Financed Retirement Benefits Schemes

Unless they choose to register, and meet the conditions required, current Unapproved "top-up" schemes will not be treated as registered schemes. If they are not registered they will be treated as "employer-financed retirement benefit schemes". There will be no tax advantages associated with these schemes. (See infra, § **32.19**.)

These various arrangements are discussed in more detail in the following paragraphs.

Simon's Taxes Part E7.

Occupational schemes

[32.08] The modern approved occupational scheme owes a great deal to the Civil Service schemes which were established during the 19th century. This is in part because the railway companies and certain other large commercial concerns of the time modelled their own arrangements on those of the Civil Service. More importantly, however, it was also because when the "old code" of approval was brought in by FA 1921 the former Inland Revenue, in exercising their discretionary power to approve schemes, looked to the rules of the state schemes in deciding what could be accepted: hence such rules as the maximum pension payable being 40/60 of final salary became part of the code.

The "old code" remained in being until 1970 but did not cover all forms of occupational scheme. As a result there were inconsistencies between the tax treatments applying to different kinds of scheme. Certain staff assurance schemes, for example, did not qualify for tax exemption of the income generated by the amounts subscribed. Again under "old code" approved schemes it was not possible for the member to commute part of his pension into a tax-free lump sum whereas this had long been allowed under statutory schemes and certain other arrangements requiring a more limited form of approval.

The "new code" of approval was established in 1970 to replace the "old code": it provided a uniform framework of rules and practices applying to all occupational pension schemes. The relevant legislation became ITEPA 2003, ss 386 ff.

Under the transitional arrangements occupational schemes approved under the old code had to be re-approved under the new code by 5 April 1980 in order to retain their privileges.[1]

The main consequences of obtaining exempt approval under the new code were:

(1) employer contributions are allowable tax deductions to the extent that they are ordinary annual contributions;
(2) employee contributions are deductible from earnings subject to an overall limit of 15% of annual remuneration;
(3) the employer's contributions are not taxable emoluments of the employee;
(4) the income and capital gains arising on fund investments are exempt from tax;
(5) pensions paid during retirement are taxable on the members as employment income under ITEPA 2003.

They only apply to schemes which obtained full approval and were thus "exempt approved schemes") see infra, § **32.18**). A more limited form of "bare" approval only secured the advantage in 3, ie avoidance of the employer's contributions being taxed on the employee.

Many different kinds of scheme could qualify as exempt approved schemes. They included:

Occupational schemes **[32.08]**

(1) Employer-sponsored schemes which provide for defined benefits, ie a pension payable by reference to final salary. The employee's contributions, if the scheme is contributory, will normally be fixed (as for example a percentage of annual earnings) and the employer must bear the responsibility for seeing that the fund is sufficient to meet the pension benefits which must eventually be provided. The vast majority of occupational schemes (in terms of value and number of members) are of this kind. But they are in decline because of financial and legal pressures associated with the operation of such schemes.

(2) Employer-sponsored schemes under which defined contributions by both employer and employee are made, ie "money purchase" schemes. Here the pension benefits ultimately made available depend on the build-up of the fund representing the contributions made.

(3) Hitherto such an arrangement has been uncommon in occupational schemes but as explained in supra, § **32.06**, nearly all new schemes are now established on a money purchase basis. Many employers, particularly smaller employers, have closed their existing defined benefit schemes either completely or to new members, to be replaced by money purchase arrangements.

(4) Indeed many employers, particularly those with a small number of employees have opted for a group personal pension approach to employee pension funding as an alternative to a final salary or money purchase based occupational scheme. Amongst the advantages claimed for the group personal pension approach is the virtual non-application of the Pensions Act 1995.

(5) The majority of small self-administered schemes, which tend to be the preserve of director controlled companies, are established on a money purchase basis (see infra, § **32.17**).

(6) Schemes which until the 1980s were known as "top hat" schemes where the employer has some discretion over the amount of benefit provided. These are either "stand alone" or are used to supplement benefits for senior and key employees. They are now generally referred to as individual pension arrangements (IPAs) or as executive pension plans (EPPs).

(7) The trustees of registered schemes may secure pensions through insurance contracts or through making direct investments. In practice most small occupational schemes are run through insurers unless they qualify under the special regime for small self-administered schemes.

(8) The statutory schemes for public sector employees were strictly outside the scope of the "new code" but their tax rules have been brought closely into line with those of exempt approved schemes.[2]

Occupational pension schemes like all forms of previously approved schemes become registered pension schemes with effect from 6 April 2006. They are thus subject to the single framework of tax rules associated with all forms of registered scheme,

Simon's Taxes E7.102, E7.211.

[1] For the position of frozen s 208 schemes which did not apply for approval under the new code, see **Simon's Taxes E7.271**.
[2] TA 1988, s 594.

Meaning of 'retirement benefits scheme' and 'registered scheme'

[32.09] Approval could (before 6 April 2006) be given to "any retirement benefits scheme". Such a scheme is one which provides for "relevant benefits". These are very widely defined.[1] HMRC regarded a single ex-gratia lump sum given on retirement or death, or in anticipation of retirement as constituting a retirement benefits scheme unless the lump sum is paid by reason of redundancy or loss of office.[2] Benefits provided solely for disablement or death by accident during though not necessarily arising out of service are specifically excluded.

Schemes providing relevant benefits may relate to only a small number of employees or even one and they may provide for the pension to start immediately. Provision of relevant benefits includes provision by means of a contract with a third party, eg an insurance contract.

A retirement benefits scheme may be divided into two or more schemes relating to different classes of employee such as employees of different group companies. This procedure is commonly followed for a world-wide scheme set up by a multinational group.

HMRC automatically treats approved pension schemes as registered under the new tax regime for pension schemes from 6 April 2006. Certain other tax-privileged schemes or contracts are automatically treated as registered.

HMRC recognises as a **registered pension scheme** any **pension scheme** that on 5 April 2006 fell within any of the following categories.

(1) A retirement benefit scheme approved under TA 1988, Part 14, Chapter 1 (commonly known as an approved occupational pension scheme). This includes Additional Voluntary Contribution (AVC) schemes.
(2) A personal pension scheme approved under TA 1988, Part 14, Chapter 4 (commonly known as an approved personal pension scheme—including an approved stakeholder pension scheme—or an approved group personal pension scheme (GPP).
(3) A retirement annuity contract or retirement annuity trust scheme approved before 1 July 1988 under TA 1988, Part 14, Chapter 3.
(4) Relevant statutory schemes—more commonly known as public sector pension schemes—which are not approved schemes. Examples include schemes for employees of the NHS, civil service, police, fire, armed forces, teachers, Parliament and National Assemblies, and also schemes not established by statute but which have been treated as statutory schemes.

(5) Former approved superannuation funds (more commonly called "old code" schemes). These are schemes which were approved before 1970, but have not been re- approved as "new code" occupational pension schemes. However, they have retained their former approved status if no contributions have been made to the scheme since 5 April 1980).

For a scheme to be newly registered on or after 6 April 2006, the **scheme administrator** must submit to HMRC:

(a) a fully completed application in the form specified by HMRC (this is an on-line application), and
(b) a declaration that the person making the application understands that they are responsible for discharging the functions conferred or imposed on the scheme administrator of the **pension scheme** by the tax legislation for **registered pension schemes** and intends to discharge those functions at all times.

Only the scheme administrator can make the application for registration of the pension scheme. Once the scheme administrator has gone through the application process and all the data given has been validated, the on-line service will automatically register the **pension scheme**.

Simon's Taxes E7.202.

[1] TA 1988, s 612(1).
[2] Joint Office Memorandum 111 and HMRC statement of practice SP 13/91.

Consequences of non-approval/non registration

[32.10] If a scheme or arrangement is a retirement benefits scheme but (before 6 April 2006) was not an approved scheme, the main consequence was that any sum paid by the employer with a view to the provision of relevant benefits is treated as income of the employee.[1]

This is a severe sanction: it derives from an anti-avoidance provision in FA 1947, s 19 to counter the practice of an employer making pension provision for an employee out of all proportion to his current salary, part of which could be commuted into a tax-free lump sum.

In an unfunded scheme the employee is not taxed on the employer's notional cost but any benefit received from the scheme, including a lump sum payment, is taxed as pension income.[2] If the benefit is received by a person other than an individual, the scheme administrator is to be charged to tax on the amount received or the cash equivalent of the benefit.[3] In the case of a funded unapproved scheme, lump sum payments (but not pension payments) to the employee are tax-free so long as the payments can be attributed to employer contributions which have been taxed on the employee.

If the scheme was not approved, neither may it be an exempt approved scheme (see infra, § **32.18**) and hence the tax privileges enjoyed by such schemes, eg exemption for income and gains on investments held by the fund, are not available.

[32.10] Pensions

The various tax exemptions afforded to exempt-approved pension schemes, coupled with the special rules available to small self-administered pension schemes led to arrangements being effected under which the trustees of some small self-administered schemes exploited the tax approval system. To counteract such practices, there are anti-avoidance measures: see infra, § **32.17**.

Those who set up a **pension scheme** on or after 6 April 2006 may not wish it to be registered. HMRC does not need to know about such a scheme, as it will not be governed by the tax regime for **registered pension schemes**. However, other parts of HMRC may need to be informed of the existence of such a pension scheme.

A pension scheme that is not a registered scheme does not qualify for the tax reliefs relevant to registered schemes. If a pension scheme which is not registered is an **occupational pension scheme**, it is likely to be an 'employer-financed retirement benefits scheme' for the purposes of tax legislation.

Simon's Taxes E7.212.

---

[1] ITEPA 2003, ss 7, 10 and 386.
[2] ITEPA 2003, ss 393, 394 and 400. In *Venables v Hornby* [2003] UKHL 65, [2004] STC 84 the House of Lords held that the provisions did not apply where the individual retired as an employee, even though he continued as a director. See infra, § **32.26**.
[3] ITEPA 2003, ss 394 and 398, 415 and 718.

Conditions for approval pre 6 April 2006

[32.11] Approval of a scheme rests with HMRC[1] although this must be given if the scheme satisfies all the "prescribed conditions" in TA 1988, s 590(2), (3): this is known as mandatory approval. However, the Board is empowered to approve schemes which do not satisfy these prescribed conditions on a discretionary basis: this is normally referred to as discretionary approval.

Approval has to be applied for by the scheme administrator. During its monitoring of pension schemes, the HMRC Pension Schemes Office (formerly known as the Superannuation Funds Office) found that it was not always clear who was responsible for a scheme's tax affairs. Statutory rules identify the administrator of a pension scheme.[2] Primarily, the trustees (or sponsors) are responsible but they may appoint another person in their place. There are now time limits for the submission of new scheme documents for approval. Essentially, if the scheme is established between 6 October to the following 5 April the application must be made within six months from the end of the tax month in which the scheme is established. If the scheme is established in the six months to 5 October, the application must be made by the following 5 April.[3]

Unless these time limits are met, HMRC approval, if obtained, will not be backdated to when the scheme was established and the scheme will therefore be unapproved for the period before the approval is granted.

There are prescribed forms for submitting applications for multi-employer, single employer and "Hancock" annuities respectively. For the application to be accepted as valid, it must be completed fully: entries such as "not known" or "to follow" are not generally accepted. One copy of the scheme instrument, eg trust deed, and one copy of the scheme rules have to accompany the application.[4]

Simon's Taxes E7.214, 215.

---

[1] In fact with the Pension Schemes Office.
[2] TA 1988, s 611AA amended by FA 1999, s 48 and Sch 5, para 5.
[3] HMRC publication IR 12 (1991) § **18.5**.
[4] HMRC publication IR 12 (1991) § **18.4**.

Mandatory approval pre 6 April 2006

[32.12] The prescribed conditions (applicable only before 6 April 2006) to qualify for mandatory approvalare in TA 1988, s 590(2) and were that:

(1) the scheme is bona fide established for the sole purpose of providing relevant benefits in respect of service as an employee. These may be paid to the employee, his personal representative, his widow, children or dependants;
(2) the scheme is recognised by employer and employee and that written particulars are given to every employee eligible to belong;
(3) there must be a person resident in the UK to fulfil the duties of an administrator, in particular to make the necessary returns to HMRC;
(4) the employer must be a contributor;
(5) the scheme must be in connection with some trade or undertaking carried on in (not with) the UK by a person resident in the UK; and
(6) in no circumstances can any repayment of contributions be made to the employee.

These conditions simply lay down a framework. To be assured of automatic approval a scheme must further satisfy the conditions in TA 1988, s 590(3) (as amended by FA 1991) which are:

(1) the benefit is a pension on retirement at an age between 60 and 75 (this applies to both men and women), and that the pension must not exceed $x/60$ of the employee's final remuneration, meaning the average annual remuneration over the previous three years where x is the number of years of service but may not exceed 40, a maximum of 2/3rds;
(2) any pension to the employee's widow is to commence on the employee's death after retirement and must not exceed 2/3rds of the employee's pension;
(3) no other benefits are payable under the scheme; and
(4) no pension can be surrendered, commuted or assigned save that the scheme may allow a lump sum of up to $3x/80$ of the final remuneration, where x is the number of years of service but may not exceed 40—a maximum lump sum of $1 1/2$ times the final remuneration. This has an impact on 1 in that it must be converted into a pension equivalent and added to the figure in 1 in calculating the maximum benefit.

Final remuneration is limited to an "earnings cap" for the purpose of determining both pension benefit and the maximum lump sum commutation payment.[1] The cap is increased by Treasury order under a formula which reflects price inflation per the retail price index.[2] There are special rules which apply the restriction on an aggregated basis in cases where the employee belongs to a scheme through having "relevant associated employments" or the scheme to which the employee belongs is "connected with" another approved scheme.[3]

Very few schemes satisfied all these conditions.

Simon's Taxes E7.214.

---

[1]   TA 1988, s 590C(1).
[2]   TA 1988, s 590C(2)–(6).
[3]   TA 1988, ss 590A, 590B.

Discretionary approval pre 6 April 2006

[32.13] HMRC were allowed (pre 6 April 2006) to approve schemes that did not meet these conditions, a process known as discretionary approval.[1] They were in particular empowered to approve schemes providing for higher pensions, death in service pensions for widows, pensions for children and dependants, lump sum death-in-service benefits of up to four times the final remuneration exclusive of any refund of contributions, pensions within ten years of retirement age, or earlier incapacity, the refund of contributions and pensions which relate to a trade carried on only partly in the UK and by a non-resident.[2]

HMRC published detailed practice notes (IR12) applied in exercising their discretion. Within the parameters indicated in IR12 schemes could be approved even though they fell substantially short of the conditions laid down for mandatory approval. HMRC practice was to refuse to approve (or to withdraw approval) where the view is taken that the conditions of the scheme, or its manner of operation, constitute what is considered by HMRC as unacceptable tax avoidance. In *R v IRC, ex p Roux Waterside Inn*,[3] a judicial review case, the Court refused an application to overturn the withdrawal of approval. HMRC is entitled to look at the broad facts and the purpose for which the pension scheme was designed to be used.[4] In that case, Tucker J held[5] that the principle in *W T Ramsay Ltd v IRC*[6] required that in considering discretionary approval of a pension scheme, HMRC is required to look, not just at the pension scheme itself, but at any series or combination of transactions, of which the establishment of the pension scheme was a part.[7]

Simon's Taxes E7.215.

---

[1]   TA 1988, s 591(1).
[2]   TA 1988, s 591(2).
[3]   [1997] STC 781.
[4]   At 786g: 'It is in my opinion unrealistic to suggest that Mr Roux was not the controlling influence in the setting up of both schemes . . . In my view . . . the Pension Schemes Office was entirely justified in concluding that Mr Roux was the prime mover behind the scheme, and that he procured the taking of the action

necessary to implement it . . . . It is artificial and inaccurate to suggest that the new scheme was either approved or seeking approval. The very reverse was the reality of the situation.'

5   At 786h.
6   [1981] STC 174.
7   This decision was followed by Sullivan J in R *(on the application of Mander) v IRC* [2001] EWCA 358 (admin) [2002] STC 631 in refusing an application for judicial review of HMRC withdrawing approval from a pension scheme.

Discretionary approval subject to F(No 2)A 1987 changes

[32.14] For schemes which obtained discretionary approval before 23 July 1987 F(No 2)A 1987 introduced the following new rules which if necessary override the scheme's own rules. These rules, which are now in TA 1988, Sch 23, are in summary as follows:

(1) Where a late entrant joins the approved scheme after 16 March 1987, a new "accelerated accrual" scale applied in relation to pension entitlement. The maximum rate of accrual allowed is 1/30th of the "relevant annual remuneration", ie normally final remuneration, for each year of service up to a maximum of 20.

(2) If the employee becomes a member of the approved scheme after 16 March 1987, the provisions of the scheme allowing for commutation of part of the pension into a lump sum were modified as follows:

   (a) If the pension before commutation is not subject to accelerated accrual, eg it is calculated at the rate of 1/60th of relevant annual remuneration for each year of service up to a maximum of 40, no accelerated accrual can be applied to the lump sum commutation payment allowed, ie that payment is limited to 3/80ths of relevant annual remuneration for each year of service up to a maximum of 40. This rule counteracts the practice that was previously possible of applying accelerated accrual to the lump sum when the pension itself was not subject to accelerated accrual, so enabling a disproportionately high tax-free lump sum to be obtained.

   (b) If the pension before commutation results from application of the new accelerated accrual scale for pension entitlement (1/30th for each year of service up to a maximum of 20), the existing uplifted 80ths scale of accelerated accrual (which permits a maximum lump sum of 11/2 times final salary to be obtained after 20 years service) can still be applied to the calculation of the lump sum commutation payment.

   (c) If the pension before commutation reflects some measure of accelerated accrual but is less than one produced by the new scale of 1/30th of relevant annual remuneration for each year of service up to a maximum of 20, accelerated accrual based on the uplifted 80ths scale can still be applied to the lump sum to be taken in commutation but only to the extent to which accelerated accrual is applied to the calculation of pension benefit.

[32.14] Pensions

For schemes set up after 13 March 1989 and, in relation to schemes set up before that day, for members who join after 31 May 1989, the foregoing provisions were replaced by a simpler and often more favourable rule (see infra, § 32.15).

For schemes set up after 13 March 1989 and, in relation to schemes set up before that day, for members who join after 31 May 1989, this restriction is displaced by the earnings cap originally set at £60,000 (but price inflation-linked) which is relevant to all benefits, not simply the maximum lump sum commutation payment (see infra, § 32.15).

Simon's Taxes E7.216.

Discretionary approval subject to FA 1989 changes

[32.15] As with the changes made by F(No 2)A 1987, FA 1989 applied certain statutory overriding provisions to the rules of certain schemes. In general these provisions only apply to schemes which come into existence on or after 14 March 1989 and, in the case of schemes which were already in existence before that day, to employees who join the schemes after 31 May 1989.[1] The main changes made are in summary:

(1) For the purpose of calculating maximum benefits, eg pension benefit, lump sum commutation payment, death-in-service benefit etc, final remuneration is limited to the earnings cap.[2] The earnings cap for 2005–06 was £105,600.

(2) A simpler rule was applied for calculating accelerated accrual of the lump sum commutation payment. Under the new rule the maximum lump sum commutation payment is to be the greater of:
    (a) 3/80ths of final remuneration for each year of service up to a maximum of 40; and
    (b) the pension (before commutation) for the first year in which it is payable multiplied by 2.25.[3]

(3) Because the new rule on accelerated accrual of the lump sum benefit will often be more favourable than the corresponding statutory override made by F(No 2)A 1987 (see above), a member who joined the scheme on or after 17 March 1987 but before 1 June 1989 was given the right to elect to be treated as if he became a member on 1 June 1989.[4]

(4) In applying the 15% of remuneration limit on permitted employee contributions (see infra, § 32.23), remuneration is limited to the earnings cap as periodically revised (see 1 above).

It was now possible in discretionary approved schemes to provide early retirement benefits of 1/30th for each year of service but as a corollary increases for late retirement must then be limited to N/30ths or by taking final salary at actual retirement.[5]

Simon's Taxes E7.216.

---

[1] FA 1989, Sch 6, para 28.
[2] FA 1989, Sch 6, para 20.
[3] FA 1989, Sch 6, para 23.

[4] FA 1989, Sch 6, para 29.
[5] Memorandum 100, Appendix; practice notes 9.12, 9.13 and 13.2A.

Registered pension schemes

[32.16] It will be seen that both F(No 2)A 1987 and FA 1989 introduced a number of sweeping changes to the regimes governing approval of occupational schemes.

But the three tax regimes associated with occupational pensions (generally referred to as the pre-1987, 1987 to 1989, and post-1989 regimes) have with effect from 6 April 2006 been replaced by the single tax regime that governs all form of pension arrangements. The information covered in the previous sections relating to the earlier tax regimes is retained because it forms a legacy that has influenced the design of occupational pension schemes over many years.

The introduction of the new single tax regime has not in most instances immediately caused a change in scheme design. This is because the existing scheme designs in the overwhelming majority of cases fit within the new tax framework.

The legislation[1] allows any of the following to set up a registered pension scheme.

(1) An employer or more than one employer—if the membership of the scheme is open to its own, or any other employees. Such a scheme is an **occupational pension scheme**. The employer will be recognised as a '**sponsoring employer**' under FA 2004, s 150(6) where one or more of its employees are members and the scheme benefits for those members are directly related to their employment with the employers in question.
(2) Government Departments or Ministers and UK Parliamentary bodies. Such a scheme is a "**public service pension scheme**".
(3) An **insurance company**.
(4) A **unit trust scheme manager**.
(5) An operator, trustee or depositary of a **recognised European Economic Area (EEA) collective investment scheme**.
(6) An **authorised open-ended investment company (OEIC)**.
(7) A **building society**.
(8) A **bank**.

Tax law does not specify any particular legal form for a **registered pension scheme**. A **pension scheme** may be established by different methods, for example, by a trust, a contract, a board resolution, or a deed poll.

Any scheme applying for registration on or after 6 April 2006 must have appointed a person or persons to be responsible for carrying out the duties imposed on the **scheme administrator**. This person or persons must have made statutory declarations to HMRC. The person(s) appointed in accordance with the **pension scheme** rules are responsible for the discharge of the functions conferred or imposed on the scheme administrator of the pension scheme by FA 2004, Part 4. This person must be resident in an **EU member state** or in Norway, Liechtenstein or Iceland. The person must have made the declarations to HMRC required by FA 2004, s 270(3).[2]

[32.16] Pensions

A **registered pension scheme** qualifies for relief and exemption from various taxes. In summary:

(1) Contributions by members and payments made on behalf of members (except payments by employers) up to the higher of £3,600 and 100% of earnings are tax-relieved. The tax relief in respect of member contributions is subject to the annual allowance.[3]

(2) Increase in pension benefits promised in **defined benefit arrangements** within the **annual allowance**.

(3) Employer contributions. Tax relief on employer contributions to a **registered pension scheme** is given by allowing contributions to be deducted as an expense in computing the profits of a trade, profession or investment business, and so reducing the amount of an employer's taxable profit.

(4) Investment income—free of income tax—excepting the reclaim of the tax credit on UK dividends.

(5) Investment gains—free of capital gains tax.

(6) Lump sum benefits, in specified circumstances are paid free of income tax.

(7) Pension business—such of a life assurance company's business as relates to contracts entered into for the purposes of a registered pension scheme.

Simon's Taxes E7.217.

---

[1] FA 2004, ss 154 & 150(5).
[2] FA 2004, ss 154 & 150(5).
[3] FA 2004, s 270.

Small self-administered schemes

[32.17] Until 5 April 2006 there was a special regime for small self-administered pension schemes. But this type of scheme now is a form of occupational pension scheme that comes under the single tax regime that governs pension arrangements from 6 April 2006. Thus a scheme of this nature is now a form of registered pension scheme. However, there do remain some specific features associated with such arrangements arising from their being employer sponsored schemes that are regarded as being "member directed".

Although from 6 April 2006 the rules governing small self-administered schemes are almost the same as those governing self-invested personal pension schemes, the employer sponsored nature of the former does lead to a small number of features that apply only to a small self-administered scheme.

A small self-administered scheme is defined as one where:

(1) some or all of the income and other assets are invested otherwise than in insurance policies; and

(2) one of the members is connected with another member, or with a trustee of the scheme, or with a person who is an employer in relation to the scheme; and
(3) the scheme has less than 12 members.

The connection required in 2 will be met if the two persons are husband and wife or the one is a relative of the other, or the other's spouse, or the husband or wife of a relative. "Relative" for this purpose means brother, sister, ancestor or lineal descendent.[1] where the employer is a partnership, a member who is connected with a partner is treated as connected with the employer.[2] Where the employer is a company the member is treated as connected with the employer if he or a person connected with him has been a controlling director of the company during the preceding ten years.[3]

The principal attraction (usually to controlling directors) of a small self-administered scheme is the degree of permitted self-investment. SSA 1990 introduced restrictions to prohibit self-investment beyond 5% of a pension scheme's resources. Small self-administered schemes are exempt from the 5% limit provided:

(1) there are less than 12 members;
(2) all members are trustees; and
(3) all members agree in writing to the self-investment.

These rules were introduced by the Occupational Pension Schemes (Investment of Scheme's Resources) Regulations 1992, SI 1992/246.

The introduction of the tax simplification of pensions with effect from 6 April 2006 has led to a new set of investment related rules if a small self-administered scheme is to operate correctly as a registered pension scheme.

(1) Borrowing by the scheme is restricted to 50% of the market value of the scheme investments.
(2) Investment by way of loans to the sponsoring employer company must not exceed 5% of the market value of the scheme assets. This rule may extend to up to four sponsoring employers.
(3) Investment in personal chattels other than choses in action is effectively prohibited. This rules out investment in such "pride of possession" assets as works of art, jewellery, vintage cars, yachts, gold bullion etc. Although it was originally intended that such assets would become permitted investments, the taxation consequences for the member and for the scheme of investing in such assets has the same effect as outright prohibition.
(4) Investment in residential property is effectively prohibited unless it is for occupation by an unconnected employee as a condition of employment, eg a caretaker, or it is for occupation by an unconnected person in connection with his or her occupation of business premises which are held by the trustees as a scheme asset, eg a flat above a shop where both premises are scheme assets.

[32.17] Pensions

(5) Investment in shares in an unlisted company is permitted but if used for the purpose of investing in personal chattels and residential property the corporate structure is "see through" and the taxation consequences on the scheme member and the scheme are the same as if those assets were in directly.

(6) The direct or indirect purchase, sale or lease of any asset by the trustees to a scheme member or a connected person is permitted under the new pensions taxation regime.

(7) But where assets are bought from or sold to a connected party the price must be in accordance with a professional valuation.

(8) Loans to members or persons connected with members (other than the employer) are prohibited.

(9) Loans to the employer or an associated company must be for the purpose of the borrower's business and be for a fixed term of no more than five years, at a commercial rate of interest (specified as 1% over bank base rate) and secured by way a first charge on assets of at least equivalent value.[4]

(10) The requirement that of the trustees has to be a "pensioneer trustee", ie a reputable professional person with pensions experience approved by HMRC was abolished from 6 April 2006.

The regulations contain transitional rules to permit certain transactions entered into before the enactment of the new rules, to continue.

When a member of a small self-administered scheme retires, the purchase of the member's pension annuity could be deferred for a period of five years during which time the pension could be paid directly out of the fund. HMRC agreed that with effect from 2 February 1994, the purchase of an annuity could be deferred for retiring members until they reach age 75.

This change was agreed by HMRC after pressure from the industry that it would have disadvantaged certain members to buy an annuity during a period of prevailing low annuity rates.

The ability to defer the purchase of an annuity also extended to personal pensions (see infra, § **32.35**) and the practice of annuity deferral can be exercised in executive type pension schemes—typically insured arrangements for the benefit of individual directors and executives.

Annuity deferral is now a form of "unsecured income" with an amended basis by reference to a "relevant annuity". (See infra, § **32.35**.)

Simon's Taxes E7.217.

---

[1] SI 1991/1614, reg 2(4).
[2] SI 1991/1614, reg 2(5)(*a*).
[3] SI 1991/1614, reg 2(5)(*b*).
[4] Registered Pension Schemes (Prescribed Interest Rates for Authorised Employer Loans) Regulations, SI 2006/3449, *Simons Weekly Tax Intelligence 2006*, page 169.

Exempt approved schemes—pre 6 April 2006

[32.18] Obtaining HMRC approval of a pension scheme, whether on a mandatory or discretionary basis, only secured exemption from the charge to tax on the employee in respect of employer contributions (see supra, § **32.10**).

For the full range of tax privileges to apply, the scheme had not only to have been approved but also had to be an "exempt approved scheme". An exempt approved scheme was defined as:

(1) any approved scheme which is shown to the satisfaction of HMRC to be established under irrevocable trusts; or
(2) any other approved scheme which HMRC, having regard to any special circumstances directs shall be an exempt approved scheme.[1]

In practice HMRC did not insist on a formal trust deed provided that the fund or policy is held in a fiduciary capacity and that the disposal of assets is governed by the approved terms of the scheme.[2]

Simon's Taxes E7.203.

---

[1] TA 1988, s 592(1).
[2] HMRC publication IR 12 (1991) § **2.3**.

Unapproved schemes and unregistered schemes

[32.19] Before the introduction of the "earnings cap" by FA 1989, unapproved schemes not only did not enjoy the tax privileges accorded to exempt approved schemes but in addition were subject to certain anomalies. In particular, if the scheme was unfunded, the employee would be taxed year by year on notional employer contributions made for his benefit and in addition would also be taxed on the pension when it came into payment.

However, to facilitate the making of unapproved "top-up" schemes, the former Schedule E charge on notional employer contributions was removed from 1988–89 onwards.[1] The position until 5 April 2006 with unapproved schemes depended on whether they are funded or unfunded. In a funded scheme the employer typically secures future benefits by means of an insurance policy or establishes a separate trust fund. In an unfunded scheme the employer simply gives an undertaking to provide pension or other retirement benefits. The respective tax rules are summarised as follows.

With a funded unapproved scheme, payments by the employer to a third party, eg the trustees in the case of a trust arrangement, to provide relevant benefits are assessable as employment income on the employee.[2] The definition of relevant benefits[3] is extended to include benefits payable to the employee's wife or widow, children, dependants and personal representatives.[4] Where the payment covers more than one employee, an apportionment is required.[5]

When pension payments are made, they are chargeable to tax under ITEPA 2003 in the ordinary way;[6] lump sum commutation payments, however, are not taxable so long as the lump sum is attributable to an employer's contribution (or contributions) on which the employee has been subject to tax.[7] There is a special charge to tax on non-cash benefits provided by the scheme except to the extent that the benefit is attributable to employer payments on which the employee has already been taxed.[8]

With unfunded schemes, pension payments are charged to tax under ITEPA 2003 in the ordinary way but lump sum benefits are also charged to tax, in this case because of necessity they will not be attributable to payments by the employers on which the employee has already been taxed.

Unless they choose to register, and meet the conditions required, current FURBS and UURBS will not be treated as registered schemes. If they are not registered they will be treated as "employer-financed retirement benefit schemes". There will be no tax advantages associated with the schemes. But transitional protection means that the pre 6 April 2006 benefit taxation basis associated with these arrangements will be maintained if only in respect of contributions made and benefits accrued by 5 April 2006.

Simon's Taxes E7.256–258.

[1] FA 1989, Sch 6, para 7.
[2] ITEPA 2003, ss 7, 10 and 386.
[3] TA 1988, s 612(1).
[4] ITEPA 2003, s 386.
[5] ITEPA 2003, s 388.
[6] ITEPA 2003, s 569.
[7] ITEPA 2003, ss 395–397, 401 and 637.
[8] ITEPA 2003, ss 393, 394, 398, 400, 415 and 718.

FURBS

[32.20] A particular attraction of a funded unapproved scheme under trust (commonly known as a FURBS—ie a funded unapproved retirement benefit scheme) is that income on investments held by the trustees may be subject to income tax at only the basic rate of 23%. However, as a result of the changes for trust taxation, from 6 April 1998 capital gains within a FURBS attract tax at 34%.[1] This will depend on whether the scheme has been established for the sole purpose of providing relevant benefits within the meaning of TA 1988, s 612 since in that event the additional rate of income tax normally charged on trustees of discretionary settlements will not apply.[2] This position (ie tax at basic rate only) has been preserved following the introduction of the combined basic and additional tax rate for trustees.[3]

A number of FURBS were established with non-resident trustees with the view of securing complete freedom from UK tax on investment income and gains. Further, if the trust was located in a suitable jurisdiction, local taxes might also be avoided. In appropriate circumstances, HMRC can invoke anti-avoidance provisions, in particular:

(1) the "transfer of assets abroad" provisions (TA 1988, ss 739, 749);
(2) the CGT anti-avoidance provisions (TCGA 1992, Sch 5);

(3) the rules on off-shore roll-up funds (TA 1988, s 757 ff).

As regards 1, HMRC confirmed that these provisions would not be invoked where the trustees are obliged under the trust deed to invest solely in pooled investments and the employee has absolutely no control over the investments or investment policy. As regards 2 HMRC had confirmed that these provisions would not be applied "if the arrangement forms part of ordinary commercial arrangements made by an employer for the purpose of remunerating his employees".[3]

A lump sum benefit received by the relevant member is taxed to the extent that the benefit exceeds the aggregate of contributions paid by the employer and employee.

The assets held in trust will not form part of the member's estate for IHT purposes so long as the scheme is regarded as a "sponsored superannuation scheme"[4] (this can normally be achieved by suitable drafting of the scheme rules), the member is barred from exercising rights in advance of retirement, and in the event of a member dying before retirement, benefits can only be paid to family members etc at the trustees' absolute discretion.

Transitional protection available to FURBS means that:

(1) Contributions can continue to be made—but those made after 5 April 2006 will be treated as contributions to an Employer Financed Retirement Benefit Scheme.
(2) Where the employer has not paid into the scheme after 5 April 2006 any lump sum benefit paid will, as a consequence, be tax-free.
(3) Where the employer has not paid into the scheme after 5 April 2006 any lump sum benefit paid will, as a consequence, be tax-free.
(4) Where no contributions are paid after 5 April 2006, pre 6 April 2006 inheritance tax treatment will apply to the 5 April 2006 value of the fund.
(5) Where additional contributions are made to a FURBS on or after 6 April 2006 there will be special provisions applied in respect of the "protected portion" (ie the pre 6 April 2006 fund).

Simon's Taxes E7.257.

---

[1] TCGA 1992, s 4(1AA).
[2] TA 1988, s 686(2)(c)(i).
[3] Confirmation given to the Law Society (see *Law Society's Gazette*, 29 January 1992).
[3] Confirmation given to the Law Society (see *Law Society's Gazette*, 29 January 1992).
[4] TA 1988, s 624(1); IHTA 1984, s 151.

Employer Financed Retirement Benefits Schemes

[32.21] The rules applicable to Employer Financed Retirement Benefits Schemes are:

(1) Employer payments to employer financed retirement benefits schemes will not be taxable or liable to National Insurance contributions.
(2) The employer will not get any tax relief on contributions until benefits start to be paid and taxed on the employee.
(3) All investment income and capital gains received by trust based employer financed retirement benefits schemes will be liable at the rate applicable to trusts generally. This means a tax rate of 40% (32.5% on dividends).
(4) Employer financed retirement benefits schemes which are discretionary trusts will be subject to the normal IHT charging rules.
(5) Subject to transitional provisions all benefits paid from an employer financed retirement benefits scheme after A Day will be liable to tax.
(6) Where an unfunded employer financed retirement benefits scheme is concerned, employers will be allowed to continue to provide suitable security and/or underwriting for the promised benefits subject to the individual paying a benefit in kind charge on the cost to the employer of providing the security.

Employer's contribution—deduction as an allowable expense

[32.22] If the scheme is a registered scheme a specific provision gives allowance for employer contributions either as an expense of the trade or as a management expense.[1]

Tax relief on employer contributions to a **registered pension scheme** is given by allowing contributions to be deducted as an expense in computing the profits of a trade, profession or investment business, and so reducing the amount of an employer's taxable profit.

The contributions will only be deductible if they are brought into account in the profit and loss account of the employer. And in the case of a trade or profession, employer contributions will be deductible as an expense provided that they are incurred wholly and exclusively for the purposes of the employer's trade or profession.[1]

The HMRC officer dealing with the income tax/corporation tax return of the employer will consider questions as to whether the contribution is an allowable expense.

As a contribution needs to meet the 'wholly and exclusively' rule if tax relief is to be given in computing the profits of a trade or profession for tax purposes, special consideration needs to be given in making any risk assessment to schemes with multiple employers and contributions paid in respect of members who are controlling directors or are connected to a controlling director

Tax relief can only be given on contributions that have actually been paid. The amount shown in the profit and loss account in respect of obligations in respect of defined benefit schemes may be substantially different from the amount of contributions paid to the scheme. But it is only the amount actually paid that can be considered for tax relief. It is not possible to carry the contribution back or forward to other periods.

Under the rules for spreading[2] special contributions relief has to be spread if the employer contribution exceeds certain limits. Broadly if the employer contribution has increased between one year and the next by more than 210% and exceeds £500,000 then the following table will be used to determine the length of time over which tax relief on the excess contribution will be spread.

Size of special contribution	Period of spread
Less that £500,000	No spreading
£500,000 to £999,999	2 years
£1 million to £1,999,999	3 years
£2 million and over	4 years

For chargeable periods of less than one year the limits are pro-rated.

Simon's Taxes E7.231.

[1] TA 1988, s 74(1)(a)—corporation tax; and ITTOIA 2005, s 34—income tax.
[2] For the main rules on spreading see HMRC Registered pension schemes manual (RPSM05102070) and FA 2004, s 197(1)–(3) & s 197(6)–(10).

Employee's contribution—deduction for income tax

[32.23] Up until 5 April 2006 the maximum deduction for contributions paid by an employee in a year of assessment could not exceed 15% of his remuneration for that year.[1] This limit applied to all contributions to exempt approved schemes including AVC schemes whether set up by the employer or the employee (see infra, § 32.29).

The annual remuneration subject to the 15% limit was restricted to the earnings cap (£105,600 for 2005–06).

From 6 April 2006 members of registered pension schemes which include occupational pension schemes may pay unlimited contributions but those that are tax privileged and thus will enjoy income tax relief are "restricted" to the greater of £3,600 or 100% of earned income. Any contributions over the tax relief limit may still be paid into the pension scheme, but the member will not receive any tax relief on them.

An individual can have tax relief in respect of any relievable pension contributions provided the individual is:

(a) an **active member** of a **registered pension scheme**, and
(b) a **relevant UK individual**,

in the tax year in which the contribution is paid. Tax relief can only be claimed for a contribution in the tax year that the contribution is actually made.

The one remaining constraint is that the pension input amount should not exceed the annual allowance. If the annual allowance is exceeded (£215,000 for the 2006–07 tax year) then they will be an annual allowance charge on the excess. This being a charge at the rate of 40% in respect of the amount by

[32.23] Pensions

which the **total pension input amount** for a tax year in the case of an individual who is a member of one or more **registered pension schemes** exceeds the amount of the **annual allowance** for the tax year.

Measuring the pension input amount in respect of a defined contribution scheme member is straightforward, being simply the contributions made in aggregate by employer and by or on behalf of the employee. Measurement of the pension input value for a defined benefit scheme member is based upon the increase in the accrued defined benefit between one year and the next, this being multiplied by 10 to show the pension input value of the increased benefits earned.[2]

Although contributions can be paid after a member has reached the age of 75, they are not **relievable pension contributions** and do not qualify for tax relief.

Simon's Taxes E7.232.

---

[1] TA 1988, s 592(8).
[2] See HMRC Registered pension schemes manual (RPSM06103000).

Taxation of the fund

[32.24] A registered pension scheme enjoys certain specific tax exemptions. The basic exemption is that income from the investments and deposits held for the purposes of the scheme is exempt from income tax.[1] Gains from disposals of investments (but not deposits) held for the purposes of the scheme are exempt from CGT.[2]

However, there is an exception to this normal rule in relation to income derived from investments or deposits held by a registered pension scheme as a member of a property investment limited liability partnership. A gain arising from the acquisition or disposal of assets held as a member of a property investment LLP is a chargeable gain liable to capital gains tax.

Income from a trading activity undertaken by a registered pension scheme is not investment income and so does not qualify for this tax exemption.

Stock lending fees and income derived from futures and option contracts might normally be considered trading income. However, subject to special rules, such income in relation to registered pension schemes can qualify for tax relief.

Underwriting commissions, to the extent that they are applied for the purposes of the scheme and would otherwise be chargeable to tax are also exempt from income tax.

In the case of an insured scheme, the insurance company is granted exemption from corporation tax on income and capital gains in respect of investments and deposits referrable to its "pension business". Such business includes contracts with persons having the management of an exempt approved scheme.

Where investment income falls within the above exemption and that income includes income subject to deduction of tax at source or dividends from UK resident companies carrying tax credits in respect of the ACT payable by the distributing company, the pension fund trustees periodically claim repayment of the tax deductions and tax credits.

A pension fund is not able to obtain repayment of the tax credit on any dividend paid on or after 2 July 1997.[3]

Simon's Taxes E7.233.

---

[1] TA 1988, s 592(2). An interest rate swap contract or a currency swap contract can be an investment of an approved pension scheme, as can credit derivatives: HMRC Tax Bulletin August 2003, p 1056, para 18. In HMRC's view, these swaps are correctly regarded as investments of a pension scheme when they are held to hedge risks inherent in the existing investment portfolio or as part of an investment strategy to enhance return of the pension fund's investment portfolio or to create a synthetic exposure to investments of a particular type or in a particular market in line with the fund's normal policies of investing directly in such instruments.
[2] TA 1988, Sch 29, para 26.
[3] TA 1988, s 231A.

Taxation of pensions

[32.25] Pension payments are charged to tax under ITEPA 2003 whether or not paid by a registered pension scheme. The charge under ITEPA 2003, ss 566 and 567 is on "taxable pension income" less "the total amount of any deductions". The term pension is not defined but ITEPA 2003, s 570 states that "'pension' includes a pension which is paid voluntarily".

The term "pension" has not been defined by statute or judicially; indeed judges have refused to attempt such a definition. In *McMann v Shaw*[1] a series of payments was held to be compensation for loss of office as opposed to pension, the deciding factor being that they were not payments for services past or present—they were in fact payments to the former Borough Treasurer of Southall whose position was abolished under the London Government reorganisation in 1963 and the payments were made from the time he became redundant until he became entitled to a pension in respect of his previous service. In *Johnson v Holleran*[2] it was held that retirement was not an essential condition for certain payments to be a pension but that the former employment must have ceased.

However, where the payment is a pension payable from a registered pension scheme there is a specific statutory rule that the pensions shall be charged to tax under ITEPA 2003[3] and PAYE is applied. From 6 April 2007, retirement annuities are also brought within the PAYE regime.[4]

In the case of foreign pensions chargeable, the remittance basis is not to apply but the income to be charged is reduced by 10%. The same reduction also applies to certain Commonwealth Government pensions.

Simon's Taxes E4.802, E7.205, 416.

---

[1] [1972] 3 All ER 732, 48 TC 330.

[32.25] Pensions

2   [1989] STC 1.
3   ITEPA 2003, s 580.
4   HMRC Press Release 10 January 2007, *Simon's Weekly Tax Intelligence* 2007, p 155.

Lump sums

[32.26] The lump sum which may be paid when benefits are taken from a registered pension scheme is called a pension commencement lump sum[1] and is free of income tax in the hands of the recipient.

The scheme member's lump sum entitlement is connected to an arising entitlement to a 'relevant pension' benefit under the same **registered pension scheme**. This is also known as a "benefit crystallisation event".[2]

A **pension commencement lump sum** cannot be paid once the registered scheme member has gone beyond the age of 75. The permitted maximum amount of the pension commencement lump sum is defined in the legislation as being the lower of two measures. These are:

(a) 25% of the available portion of the member's lump sum allowance—this is a measure of the member's **lifetime allowance** available at that time, and is calculated on the basis that the member is entitled only to the **standard lifetime allowance;** and

(b) the applicable amount—this represents a 25% measure of the capital value of the benefits coming into payment under the relevant arrangements under the scheme generating the lump sum payment.

With regard to a defined contribution arrangement then the 25% measure is straightforward, being 25% of the fund value. Under a defined benefit scheme then the defined pension benefit is multiplied by 20 in order to give it a value. The permitted tax-free cash pension commencement lump sum is restricted to 25% of this figure.

Since 6 April 2006 types of pension arrangement which did not allow for the payment on a tax-free lump sum now permit such an entitlement. These include benefits from all forms of additional voluntary contribution arrangements, including those that are free standing, and also from protected rights funds.

Other types of lump sum are subject to special rules of taxation. Thus the consideration paid for a restrictive covenant given in connection with an office or employment past or present or future is liable to income tax as employment income. Second, sums payable for termination of the office are chargeable to tax under ITEPA 2003, ss 401, 403 and 404 to the extent that they exceed £30,000.[3] Third, an ex-gratia lump sum payment given on retirement will now be regarded as a benefit provided by an unfunded unapproved pension scheme and so be taxable in full.[4] This is subject to exceptions in the case of redundancy and compensation for loss of office, including the case of forced voluntary resignation,[5] unless the employee does not belong to a registered pension scheme. In such a case a lump sum ex-gratia payment can be made on retirement but subject to normal HMRC limits and subject to a day minimis limit for which prior approval is not required (see supra, §§ **32.07–32.10**).

Simon's Taxes E7.234.

[1]   FA 2004, Sch 29, **para 1** and see HMRC Registered pension schemes manual (RPSM09104110).
[2]   FA 2004, s **216(1) and Sch 32**.
[3]   Supra, § **7.36**.
[4]   This follows from the change in HMRC practice indicated in supra, § **32.09**; see also § **32.19**.
[5]   Statement of practice SP 13/91.

Refunds of employee contributions and special commutation payments

[32.27] Where an employee's contributions are refunded as a consequence of leaving the scheme there is a special tax of 20% levied on the trustees.[1] This will then be reclaimed from the member's refund.

From 6 April 2006 a refund of member's contributions can be taken from an occupational pension scheme if the member leaves the scheme within two years, but once a member has been in the pension scheme for three months or more they must also be offered a transfer of their benefit entitlement to another scheme.

If a member is suffering from serious ill-health then, provided certain conditions are met,[?] the registered pension scheme **administrator** may commute any pension entitlement that member holds under the scheme and pay the member their entire benefit entitlement under an **arrangement** as a lump sum. This is referred to as a **serious ill-health lump sum.** Before making the payment the registered pension scheme scheme administrator must receive written evidence from a registered medical practitioner confirming that the member is expected to live for less than one year.

The serious ill-health lump sum is not subject to tax so long as it falls within the scheme member's remaining lifetime allowance. Otherwise a lifetime allowance charge would be triggered at the rate of 55%.

Where a registered pension scheme member has paid **relievable pension contributions** in a tax year of more than the maximum amount that can receive tax relief the amount of contributions that cannot receive tax relief (the excess) may be repaid to the member. The payment of a refund of excess contributions must be made before the end of the period of six years following the end of the tax year in which the excess contribution was paid.

If when benefits are to be taken the amount of the member's total pension rights are worth less than £15,000 (1% of the lifetime allowance as it changes from year-to-year) then these trivial rights may be commuted for a lump sum. This is permitted once the registered pension scheme member has reached the age of 60 but has not reached age 75. Of this trivial compensation lump sum

[32.27] Pensions

75% is treated as taxable pension income of the member for the tax year in which the payment is made, accountable through PAYE.

Simon's Taxes E7.234–240.

---

[1] TA 1988, s 598(2). The rate of tax was increased from 10% to 20% for payments made on or after 6 April 1988; Occupational Pension Schemes (Rate of Tax under Paragraph 2(2) of Part II of Schedule 5 to the Finance Act 1970) Order 1988, SI 1988/504. This may be deducted from the payment made. On effect of deduction of tax, see *Lord Advocate v Hay* (1924) 21 ATC 146 and *Bridges v Watterson* [1952] 2 All ER 910, 34 TC 47. FA 2004 Sch 29, **para 5.**

[2] FA 2004, Sch 29, **para 4**, s 216(1), Sch 32, para 15.

Correction of surpluses

[32.28] As a result of a sustained appreciation in stock market prices over a number of years up to and including 1986 it was not unusual for a pension scheme to hold assets of a value beyond that required to meet future obligations. The precise position depended on the method of actuarial valuation which was consistently followed.

The problem of overfunding received Government attention when certain schemes applied for permission to make refunds to employers of past contributions. Hitherto when an approved scheme became overfunded HMRC only permitted a refund of employer contributions as a last resort after all other steps to deal with the surplus, eg providing for a contribution holiday for up to five years, had been taken.

The Government took the view that it was no longer appropriate for such a question to be determined by HMRC practice and in FA 1986, now TA 1988, ss 601–603, Sch 22, introduced "clear and objective rules" for identifying and remedying pension scheme surpluses. Subject to transitional provisions covering the period 19 March 1986 to 5 April 1987, these rules took full effect from 6 April 1987. Many of the substantive rules are in supporting regulations dealing with valuation and administration respectively.[1]

The key feature of these rules was that an actuarial valuation on a prescribed basis be periodically submitted to HMRC.[2] The prescribed basis of actuarial valuation is "the projected accrued benefit method"; this takes account of accrued service to the date of valuation and projected salary increases to retirement attributable both to inflation and career progression. The various assumptions to be made in applying this method are set out in the regulations dealing with valuation.[3]

An actuarial valuation on this basis must be provided whenever a valuation of the scheme assets and liabilities is made. Such a valuation will therefore be an additional valuation where the valuation for the purpose of the scheme rules is on a different basis. The interval between successive valuations on the prescribed basis must not exceed three years and six months (five years in the case of public service schemes) as measured by reference to the dates taken for the purposes of such valuations.[4]

As an alternative to submitting an actuarial valuation on the prescribed basis, the scheme administrator may submit a certificate indicating whether on the prescribed basis a surplus does or does not exceed the permitted limit but where such a certificate is given HMRC is entitled to call for a valuation on the prescribed basis in support.

If the valuation on the prescribed basis shows a surplus of scheme assets in excess of liabilities by more than 5%, the scheme administrator is required to submit proposals for reducing the surplus to that level by one or more of certain "permitted ways".[5] These are:

(1) returning contributions to the employer;
(2) suspending or reducing employer's contributions for up to five years;
(3) suspending or reducing employees' contributions for up to five years;
(4) improving scheme benefits;
(5) providing additional benefits;
(6) other methods that may be prescribed by regulations.

These methods may be used singly or in combination. Unlike HMRC practice which previously regulated the correction of surpluses, no order of priority is laid down. The Pensions Act 1995 introduced, with effect from 6 April 1997, a requirement for pensions in payment to be increased in line with the retail price index up to a maximum of 5% per year, in relation to pensionable service on or after that date. This is called Limited Price indexation.

Prior to 6 April 1997, there was no legal requirement for pensions in payment to be subject to annual increases (apart from the element relating to the guaranteed minimum pension, broadly the SERPS substitute). For schemes that do not provide annual increases to pensions in payment, there is a particular disincentive to making a surplus refund back to the employer. SSA 1990 provided that a refund could not be made to an employer unless annual increases to pensions for all past service had first been provided. Only after past service pension increases have been provided, can a surplus be refunded to the employer. In that case the new charge to tax on payments to employers will apply, as explained below. If this particular course is chosen the surplus must not be reduced to below 5% of the scheme liabilities.[6]

If the scheme administrator does not submit proposals, or the proposals are not approved by HMRC, or the proposals are approved but not carried out in the time allowed, HMRC may restrict the tax exemptions enjoyed by the scheme to the proportion A/B where A is HMRC's estimate of the scheme liabilities as increased by a specified percentage (set at 5%[7]) and B is its estimate of the scheme assets.[8]

If one of the permitted ways used to reduce the surplus is to return contributions to the employer, a freestanding tax charge of 35% applies.[9] The tax payable cannot be reduced by loss reliefs or set-offs and is not available for set-off of other tax.[10] The charge applies to all payments by the scheme to the employer except for certain "excluded payments" which include reimbursements of expenditure incurred by the employer relating to the administration of the scheme and loans to the employer provided the interest produced is a reasonable commercial return.[11]

[32.28] Pensions

Where the freestanding tax charge of 35% applies, the scheme administrator is required to deduct the tax at source when making the payment to the employer and to file a return within 14 days of making the payment.[12] The tax deducted has to be paid to HMRC when the return is made.[13] If this procedure is not followed, HMRC may recover the tax due in respect of the payment by an assessment on the administrator in the name of the employer and where the administrator then pays the tax he is entitled to recover it from the employer.[14]

If a surplus arises the first call on the surplus will be to provide guaranteed cost of living increases for pensions in payment (limited to the greater of the increase in the retail price index or 5%) in respect of pension rights built up before that date. Only after that can any remaining surplus be used, for example, to let employers have a contribution holiday.[15]

Finance Act 2004 repeals HMRC provisions relating to the calculation and reduction of pension funds surpluses in prescribed pension schemes. From 6 April 2006, any payments of 'surplus' funds from a registered occupational pension scheme to an employer sponsoring the scheme will simply be taxed at 35% provided such a payment is allowed under DWP and corresponding HMRC legislation.

Section 37 of the Pensions Act 1995 allows payments of an actuarial surplus to be made to an employer provided HMRC's conditions on the calculation of the surplus are met. Section 250 of the Pensions Act 2004 substitutes a new s 37 of the 1995 Act which allows trustees to make a payment to the employer out of funds held for the purposes of the scheme if certain conditions are met.

Draft regulations specify the prescribed requirements which must be satisfied. These provide that a payment cannot be made unless the assets of the scheme are more than the cost of 'full buy-out'.

See **Simon's Taxes** E7.249.

---

[1] Pension Scheme Surpluses (Valuation) Regulations 1987, SI 1987/412 and Pension Scheme Surpluses (Administration) Regulations 1987, SI 1987/352.
[2] TA 1988, Sch 22, para 2.
[3] SI 1987/412, regs 5–8.
[4] SI 1987/412, reg 4.
[5] TA 1988, Sch 22, para 3.
[6] TA 1988, Sch 22, para 3(2)(*b*).
[7] Pension Scheme Surpluses (Valuation) (Amendment) Regulations 1989, SI 1989/2290, reg 6.
[8] TA 1988, Sch 22, para 7.
[9] TA 1988, s 601, amended by FA 2001, s 74(3). Prior to 11 May 2001, tax was charged at 40%.
[10] TA 1988, s 602(4).
[11] SI 1987/352, reg 4.
[12] SI 1987/352, reg 3.
[13] SI 1987/352, reg 5.
[14] SI 1987/352, reg 6.
[15] Pensions Act 1995, s 37 (previously Pension Schemes Act 1993, s 104).

Equality of treatment between men and women

[32.29] On 17 May 1990, the European Court of Justice gave its judgment in *Barber v Guardian Royal Exchange Assurance Group*.[1] That case, on which the European Court of Justice gave its judgment on 17 May 1990, concerned the equality of treatment between men and women in relation to pension benefits, and could cause severe funding problems if it applies to benefits based on service up to, as well as after, 17 May 1990. In fact a protocol to the Treaty of Maastricht limits the application of the *Barber* judgment to benefits based on service as from 17 May 1990. In *Coloroll Pension Trustees Ltd v Russell*,[2] the European Court of Justice was concerned with further questions arising from the *Barber* case as to when and in what manner sex equality rulings should take effect. The *Barber* case only concerned equality within a contracted out defined benefit pension scheme. The *Coloroll* case raised questions concerning some 16 pension schemes operated by the Coloroll group of companies including defined benefit and defined contribution (money-purchase schemes, some of which were contracted out of SERPS and others not). The uncertainties raised in the *Coloroll* case are the subject of an EC Directive, the main rulings of which are as follows:

(1) Pensions in respect of service before 17 May 1990, the date of the *Barber* judgment may be unequal as between men and women.

(2) Pensions in respect of service after 17 May 1990 must be on an equal basis. Those schemes which have subsequently equalised pension rights between men and women or which still have to do so, will therefore have to provide benefits on the following basis:

    (a) Pensions in respect of service before 17 May 1990 may be unequal.

    (b) Pensions in respect of service between 17 May 1990 and the date of equalisation will have to be provided on the higher of the two bases as between men and women.

    (c) Pensions in respect of service after the date of equalisation must be on an equal footing. Whether equalisation is achieved upwards or downwards is of secondary importance as far as pure pension rights are concerned, but either way could impact on the terms and conditions of employment contracts which may have to be revised.

(3) It would not be illegal for bridging pensions to be paid. In the UK, the State retirement age for women is currently 60 and 65 for men. If a man is retired early either voluntarily or through redundancy, he may be paid a bridging pension up to age 65 when his normal State pension scheme would commence. As a women's pension would start at age 60 it was originally thought that bridging pensions would be considered illegal.

(4) Another consideration of the equal treatment debate was whether the normal practice of applying different actuarial annuity factors, arising out of different life expectancy, would be allowed to continue. It has been held that different actuarial factors can continue to be used.

The question of the equality of treatment between men and women in relation to pension benefits has largely been resolved with the Government proposing

[32.29] Pensions

that State pension age for women will be changed from 60 to 65 with full effect from the year 2020. Women born before April 1950 will still get their State pension at age 60, but those born after March 1955 will have to wait until age 65, with gradual phasing in for women born between those two dates.

SSA 1990 also introduced a specific prohibition against the scheme making a refund to the employer unless limited cost of living increases (as described in the previous paragraph) are first provided.[3] This provision came into effect on 17 August 1990, in order to prevent employers from taking refunds in advance to pre-empt the new surplus rules.

The Act also provides for mandatory cost of living increases for pensions in payment as from the appointed day (again limited to the greater of the RPI increase or 5%) in respect of pension rights built up after the appointed day: this provision is not dependent on the fund being otherwise in surplus. Pensions Act 1995 includes a provision for annual increases to pensions in payment relating to pensionable service after 5 April 1997[4] (see supra, § 32.03).

Simon's Taxes E7.238, 239, 248, 249.

---

[1] C-262/88: [1990] 2 All ER 660. See HC Official Report, 26 June 1991, Vol 193 cols 997–999.
[2] C-200/91: [1995] All ER (EC) 23.
[3] SSA 1990, s 11(3).
[4] Pensions Act 1995, s 51.

Additional voluntary contributions

[32.30] The maximum contribution to an exempt approved scheme which an employee can make and obtain deduction was until 5 April 2006 limited to 15% of annual remuneration. Such remuneration was limited for 1989–90 onwards to the earnings cap (£105,600 for 2005–06) for members of schemes set up on or after 14 March 1989 or in the case of schemes already in existence before that day, for members who joined after 31 May 1989.

All employees were able to make additional contributions to those required under the scheme rules without exceeding the 15% of remuneration limit. Such contributions are termed "additional voluntary contributions" or AVCs.[1]

From 6 April 2006 member contributions to registered pension schemes are only constrained as described supra, § **32.23**.

The employee can choose between an additional voluntary contribution into his employer's scheme and an additional voluntary contribution into a scheme he establishes separate from the employer's fund, known as "a freestanding AVC". A freestanding AVC scheme is one which is established by the employee and is completely separate from the employer's scheme.

But the need to use a freestanding AVC to receive such additional contributions where investment is required outside of the employer's fund has been removed by the ability to make such contributions to a personal pension. Thus freestanding AVC plans so far as new contracts are concerned will become redundant from 6 April 2006.

Simon's Taxes E7.221.

---

[1] Social Security Act 1986, s 12.

Money purchase scheme

[32.31] The "money purchase" occupational scheme is with effect from 6 April 2006 identical in terms of its tax rules to a personal pension schemes (see infra, § **32.34**) except that this is an employer-sponsored scheme.

Personal pensions

Main features

[32.32] (1) A personal pension plan is available to any UK resident, who is not a member of his employer's pension scheme. He can be employed, self-employed or unemployed. Indeed, a UK resident who goes abroad can continue to make contributions after ceasing to be resident in the UK, the contributions being £3,600 per annum, less tax at basic rate.[1]

(2) All contributions to a personal pension plan by an individual are made net of basic rate tax. (A contribution paid by an employer into an employee's personal pension plan is, however, made gross.) The scheme of net payments applies whether the individual is employed or self-employed. Contributions made by an individual with no taxable income are, similarly made net of basic rate tax. There is no clawback of this deduction. It operates as a Government subsidy to encourage the individual to fund his own retirement.

(3) For the higher rate taxpayer, relief against higher rate is given by extending the basic rate.[2]

(4) Where an individual has relevant UK earnings, the amount that can be paid into a personal pension scheme can be increased from £3,600 per annum (see 1 above) to the amount representing up to 100% of earned income. **Relevant UK earnings** means:

(a)   employment income such as salary, wages, bonus, overtime, commission providing it is chargeable to tax under ITEPA 2003, s 7(2);
(b)   income chargeable under ITTOIA 2005, Part 2, that is income derived from the carrying on or exercise of a trade, profession or vocation (whether individually or as a partner acting personally in a partnership);
(c)   income arising from patent rights and treated as earned income under TA 1988, s 833(5B);

(d) general earnings from an overseas Crown employment which are subject to tax in accordance with ITEPA 2003, s 28.

If the individual does not participate in an occupational pension scheme related to his employment the earnings are not treated as arising from a pensionable employment and may therefore be included in relevant earnings.

Participating in a an employer sponsored scheme no longer prevents separate participation in a personal pension scheme. One constraint is that contributions may not exceed 100% of relevant earnings. The other constraint is the annual allowance (£215,000 for 2006–07 rising to £255,000 by 2010–11). The annual allowance[3] limits the extent to which an individual's tax privileged pension rights are allowed to accrue between one year and the next.

A personal pension scheme is a form of registered pension scheme. A registered pension scheme may be established by any of the following:

(1) An employer, who may establish a scheme in respect of their employees.
(2) An insurance company.
(3) A unit trust scheme manager.
(4) An operator, trustee or depository of a recognised EEA collective investment scheme.
(5) An authorised open-ended investment company.
(6) A building society.
(7) A bank.
(8) An EEA investment portfolio manager.

Contributions to a registered scheme are treated as in respect of "pension business" carried on by the insurance company, bank, building society or other qualifying institution to which they are paid. Income from investments and deposits held for the purposes of the scheme is exempt from income tax;[4] likewise gains from the disposal of investments held for that purpose are exempt from CGT.

The fund created by the personal pension plan contributions is used to provide an income paid for the life of the member commencing after an age between 50 and 75, the age being chosen by the member. Payment of the pension can begin earlier if it is payable on the individual becoming incapable through infirmity of body or mind of doing his job or a similar one, or if the occupation is one in which it is customary to retire at an earlier age. HMRC have published a list of occupations where an earlier retirement age is accepted.

Contributions may be paid by the personal pension scheme member, a third party on behalf of the member, or a member's employer or former employer. Where a third party pays a contribution, such contributions are treated as if they had been paid by the member.

No income tax liability will apply in respect of an employee whose employer has contributed on their behalf to a registered pension scheme. Provision can also be made for the payment of an income after the individual's death to a surviving spouse or to other dependants. Any provision of an income for a surviving spouse or dependants has to be part of the personal pension scheme, not a separate arrangement, and accordingly there is no separate limit relating to this benefit.

Any provision for payment of a lump sum on death before the age of 75 must also be part of the personal pension scheme but the lump sum payment from all registered schemes on death, if exceeding £1.5 million (2006–07) will attract a lifetime allowance charge of 55%. Income benefits payable to a surviving spouse or other dependants are not taken account of in terms of valuing benefits for the purposes of the lifetime allowance.

The pension income payable from a retirement annuity contract or personal pension scheme is treated as earned income.

A part of the pension to be provided by the arrangement may be exchanged for a tax-free lump sum. The maximum lump sum must not exceed 25% of the total value of the benefits provided by the scheme at the time the commutation is made. This, with effect from April 2006, includes that value of the fund that may have been accumulated from rebates of national insurance contributions arising because of the member having at some stage been contracted out. This is known as the protected rights fund.

Simon's Taxes Division E7.3.

---

[1] An individual who is a member of a **registered pension scheme** and is no longer resident in the UK is a **relevant UK individual** for a tax year if they were resident in the UK both:

(a) in the year in which they became a member of the registered pension scheme, and
(b) in any of the five tax years previous to the tax year in which a contribution is paid.

These individuals may also qualify for tax relief on contributions up to the 'basic amount' of £3,600.

[2] TA 1988, s 639(5A). The calculation specified in statute is modified by extra-statutory concession A101: *Simons Weekly Tax Intelligence* 2001, p 1142.
[3] FA 2004, s 228(1) & (2).
[4] FA 2004, s 186.

[32.33] "Appropriate" personal pension schemes can be contracted out of the State Second Pension (S2P), previously SERPS. In this case the employer and employee continue to pay national insurance contributions on the same basis as if the employee was contracted in but the DWP will pay the contracted-out rebate directly into the personal pension scheme. The part of the contracted-out rebate attributable to the employee's contributions will be grossed up at the basic rate of income tax[1] and the DWP will recover the grossing up addition from HMRC under a deficiency claims procedure.[2]

The amounts paid by the DWP into a personal pension scheme (together termed "minimum contributions") do not have to be taken into account in measuring the extent to which the individual has used their annual allowance.

An employee who belongs to an employer's contracted-in scheme can set up a personal pension scheme to contract out of S2P without having to leave the employer's scheme. The employee's share of the contracted-out rebate will be grossed up as described above, so effectively giving the employee income tax relief. With this arrangement, the fund secured by the minimum contributions is the "protected rights fund".

[32.33] Pensions

There is free transferability into a personal pension scheme from the other kinds of pension scheme. In particular the regulations[1] require a personal pension scheme to accept a transfer payment from an approved occupational scheme, a statutory scheme, another personal pension scheme or a retirement annuity contract or trust scheme.[2] Some types of transfers, however, are not permissible, eg a personal pension into a retirement annuity contract.

Simon's Taxes, Division E7.4.

---

[1] Memorandum 104, paras 3, 4.
[2] TA 1988, s 646(6A).

Retirement age

[32.34] The concept of a Normal Retirement Date (NRD) as was previously necessary in the context of an occupational pension scheme is no longer required. Registered pension schemes may choose to keep the concept in place, however, if they wish to do so.[1]

Subject to the scheme rules permitting, scheme members may take benefit from the scheme whilst continuing to work. This applies to all forms of registered schemes. This contrasts with the previous situation whereby to take benefit from an occupational pension scheme it was necessary to retire from that employment. Thus occupational schemes and personal pension schemes have been brought into line in terms of the circumstances in which benefits may be taken. It is also not necessary to take all the benefits at the same time.

The minimum age from which benefits may be drawn in normal health will increase from age 50 to 55. This change will apply from 6 April 2010.

There are, however, two circumstances where benefits may continue to be taken whilst the member is in normal health before age 55.

(1) Where members of occupational schemes have a contractual right to draw benefits prior to the "normal minimum pension age" (ie age 50 before 6 April 2010 and age 55 thereafter). This right will be honoured where it was in force before 10 December 2003—and where it continued to apply to 6 April 2006. This right must be capable of being exercised by the employee or ex-employee unilaterally. There must not be the operation of any trustee's discretion to enable this provision to apply.
All the benefits from the scheme in question must be taken when this right is used and the individual must no longer be employed by the employer when benefits commence. Thus if the member of the occupational scheme has not already left they must retire from the service of that employer.
(2) Where individuals are members of a personal pension/stakeholder scheme, or a retirement annuity policy at 6 April 2006 from which they are able to draw benefits before age 50 because they are in a "special

occupation" (eg professional footballer). So long as benefits are taken in full from the scheme at the permitted lower age, then this facility will remain.

In each of the above cases the member's lifetime allowance will be reduced by 2.5% for each complete year before the "normal minimum pension age" that the benefit is taken. For example, if a benefit is taken at age 35 for a professional footballer in 2011, the reduction in his/her lifetime allowance would be 50% (ie 20 × 2.5%).

Further pension rights may accrue. However, the individual in this example would only be able to use the remaining 50% of their lifetime allowance for the purpose of accumulating further tax privileged savings.

No such reduction will be applied to the lifetime allowance for members of the armed forces, police or fire services who take benefits prior before 55 under their current schemes. New schemes will be introduced for these groups of individuals before 2010 which will not allow benefits to be taken before age 55.

Benefits from the registered scheme may be taken before age 55 where the member is in ill health. To pay benefits in these circumstances the scheme will need a written opinion from a registered medical practitioner that the member is incapable of continuing their current occupation because of ill-health.

Simon's Taxes E7.418.

---

[1] FA 2004, ss 165(1) & 279(1) and see Registered pension schemes manual (RPSM08100000).

Secured and unsecured income

[32.35] Before 1 May 1995 personal pension scheme members who wished to commence drawing benefits from their fund had to buy an annuity with the balance of the fund, after having drawn out the permitted tax free lump sum. Low interest rates in recent years have had a depressing effect on annuity rates available from insurance companies.

Instead of being locked into a poor annuity rate for life when an annuity is purchased, some insurance companies attempted to launch a form of flexible or managed annuity but met HMRC resistance. After some pressure from the pensions industry, HMRC accepted the argument in favour of a flexible annuity, and which extended the practice of deferring the purchase of an annuity in small self-administered schemes (see supra, § 32.17) to personal pensions. It enabled the individual to elect to defer the purchase of an annuity to age 75 and in the meantime to draw an income, taxable and within defined limits, from the pension fund. This facility was until 5 April 2006 known as "income drawdown". The tax-free lump sum (now called a pension commencement lump sum) can be drawn in full at the outset.

To prevent the untimely depletion of the fund from which income withdrawals are being taken, there is a stipulated limit on the maximum permitted income

[32.35] Pensions

withdrawal. This is on the basis of a single life, level rate annuity income in accordance with tables of rates published by the Government Actuaries Department (GAD). Revised GAD rates alongside the transition from the pre 6 April 2006 income withdrawal basis to unsecured income have been introduced from 6 April 2006. These revised tables primarily take account of increased life expectancy since the original tables were first introduced.

There is no maximum pension that can be paid from a registered scheme. However, pensions must be paid at least annually and PAYE operated. In line with the commitment made by the Financial Secretary to the Treasury during the passage of Finance Act 2004, pension annuity contracts, including retirement annuity contracts, were brought within PAYE from 6 April 2007.

Pension benefits may be taken initially in one of four ways:

(1) *Scheme pension.* The pension is provided from the registered scheme, or from an insurance company selected by the scheme administrator. This is the only option available to members of defined benefit schemes. This is a form of secured income.

(2) *Lifetime annuity.* This is an annuity payable as a consequence of the annuity being secured through an insurance company which the scheme member has the opportunity to choose. This is another form of secured income.

(3) *Unsecured income.* This option is available before and until age 75. Unsecured income may be provided in the form of a short-term temporary annuity (ie up to five years) or through income withdrawal from the fund.

(4) *Alternatively Secured Pension (ASP).* This is a new concept and is a restricted form of income withdrawal, only available from age 75.

Pensions paid direct from the scheme (a scheme pension) and through the purchase of a lifetime annuity are collectively referred as a 'secured pension'. This is because both forms of pension are guaranteed for the life of the member. It is not a phrase that appears in the legislation.

A scheme pension may be guaranteed for a certain term not exceeding ten years. So if the member dies before that term has ended the scheme pension will continue to be paid regardless to the end of the guarantee period, but to another person. The ten year maximum term-certain period runs from the date the member first becomes entitled to that scheme pension.

Alternatively a registered pension scheme may provide a member with 'pension protection' with their scheme pension. This means that they guarantee that if the member dies before their 75th birthday, and has not received a certain total level of scheme pension by that time, they will pay the balance as a lump sum on the member's death. No such benefit can be paid if the member dies on or after reaching their 75th birthday. This lump sum paid in this circumstance is referred to as a pension protection lump sum death benefit.

Members of a defined contribution scheme (occupational scheme or personal pension etc) may take benefits in the form of a scheme pension, lifetime annuity or unsecured income up to age 75. From age 75 onwards benefits may not continue to be provided on an unsecured basis, although the option of an alternatively secured pension will then become available for those who do not wish to secure an annuity.

To allow maximum flexibility over when and how benefits are finally secured, pension benefits from a money purchase arrangement may be taken before the member attains age 75 in a more flexible and unsecured form, direct from the scheme within certain limits (an 'unsecured pension').

Pension income must be taken annually or more frequently. Finance Act 2004 does not specify a minimum level of required income. The maximum income will be 120% of a "relevant annuity". The definition of "relevant annuity" is set out in Regulations and is the members fund multiplied by the GAD rate[1]. The original intention was to calculate the relevant annuity by reference to the FSA comparative annuity tables but HMRC eventually bowed to pressure not least from the FSA and have reverted to the GAD rates.

Maximum income must be reviewed at least every five years, based on the then value of the fund and the level of the then "relevant annuity". There is no minimum level of required income.

In addition to the five year review mechanism certain events trigger an additional review. Where part of the fund value is lost, with part of the **unsecured pension fund** being used to purchase a **lifetime annuity** (or surrendered to provide a **scheme pension**), there needs to be a reduction in the maximum to reflect the reduced **unsecured pension fund**. Alternatively, where the **unsecured pension fund** is boosted with the member "designating" that **unvested funds** held in the **arrangement** are brought in to the **unsecured pension fund**, the maximum needs to be reset at a higher level to reflect the increased fund size.

A registered pension scheme member may choose to secure part (or all) of their unsecured pension through the purchase of a short-term annuity contract from an insurance company. The unsecured pension secured through that contract will be paid direct by an insurance company (rather than the scheme administrator), as dictated by the annuity contract, and a proportion of the unsecured pension funds held in the arrangement will therefore be lost when the contract is purchased.

The term of the short-term annuity contract cannot be more than five years, and is bound by exactly the same rules as income withdrawal payments. So the income provided by that annuity is bound by the same limits, and the term of that annuity must not extend beyond the member's/annuitant's 75th birthday.

After the death of the individual, the surviving spouse or other financial dependant may also elect to defer the purchase of an annuity and make income withdrawals as unsecured income.

Income withdrawals by a surviving spouse or other financial dependant cannot continue beyond age 75 or if earlier, after the person concerned attains age 75. This is called a **dependants' unsecured pension**. The income withdrawals are calculated in exactly the same way as described above in relation to the registered scheme member. But the relevant annuity associated with the surviving spouse or other dependant is calculated by reference to the GAD rate relevant to the income recipient.

[32.35] Pensions

After the death of the member, and before an annuity has been purchased (ie the deceased member had been taking income withdrawals) the options available to the surviving spouse or financial dependants are:

(1) Elect to take income withdrawals through unsecured income as detailed above.
(2) Purchase an annuity.
(3) The balance of the fund can be paid out as a lump sum subject to income tax.

In the case of the third option the scheme administrator will be charged income tax at the rate of 35% on the payment.[2] The payment of the lump sum (net of 35% income tax) to the surviving spouse or financial dependant would normally be exempt from inheritance tax.

After the pension date has been determined (the date on which the member elects to defer the purchase of an annuity and commences to make income withdrawals), no further contributions can be made into that arrangement nor can any further transfer payments be transferred in.[3]

The scheme member who wishes to take income withdrawals while continuing to make pension contributions from a source of relevant earnings, would therefore have to have a minimum of two pension arrangements, one to receive the contributions and the other to provide the income withdrawals.

Income withdrawals from a flexible annuity will be treated as earned income of the recipient assessable to tax under ITEPA 2003 and subject to PAYE.[4]

Simon's Taxes E7.406, 417.

---

[1] FA 2004, Sch 29, **para 10.**
[2] TA 1988, s 648B(1)–(4).
[3] TA 1988, s 638(7A).
[4] ITEPA 2003, ss 684 and 308.

Alternatively secured pension

[32.36] Once the member reaches the age of 75 there are stricter rules on how a pension can be provided. HMRC expect any pension paid on or after this date to be provided for in a more secure manner, with a guarantee that pension income will last for the individual's lifetime, no matter how long that may be (so a 'secured pension'). Thus the pension for life must be provided in a secure and guaranteed manner from age 75 onwards, either through the purchase of a guaranteed lifetime annuity from an insurance company or direct from the scheme as a guaranteed scheme pension.

However, for money purchase schemes HMRC will allow that pension to be provided beyond age 75 through a restricted form of income withdrawal (an "alternatively secured pension"). However, given the lack of pension guarantee here, the rules provide for a more conservative annual maximum payment than before age 75 (for "unsecured pensions"), and a yearly review of that limit, to ensure that the individual does not exhaust their pension fund before death.

Alternatively secured pensions were developed in recognition of the fact that some religious groups object to annuities due to their concerns about insurance and the pooling of mortality risk. They are an alternative way of providing income for life[1].

This option is only available from age 75 and pension income using this option must again be taken annually or more frequently.

From 6 April 2007, any individual aged 75 or more is obliged to withdraw an annual sum from his alternatively secured pension fund.[2] The amount of the withdrawal depends on the age of the individual, being calculated as 55% of a "basis amount",[3] which is the annuity which could have been purchased from the pension fund.

The maximum level of the alternatively secured pension is calculated in exactly the same manner as with unsecured pension limits, with the scheme administrator calculating a basis amount by reference to the GAD tables the "relevant annuity"—to be based on the assumption that the member is aged 75. This gives a measure of the annual level of lifetime annuity the alternatively secured pension fund could generate at that point, based upon the member's sex, age and gilt yields.

The maximum alternatively secured pension is 70% of the "relevant annuity". The maximum income will be reviewed annually. The scheme member using ASP can at any time choose to purchase an annuity.

The maximum level of alternatively secured pension is recalculated automatically every year at the beginning of each pension year based on the level of alternatively secured pension fund held in the arrangement at that point.

It is possible for an alternatively secured pension to be guaranteed for up to ten years from the point "entitlement" to that pension arises. For example, where "entitlement" arises at age 75, up until the member's 85th birthday, at the end of the tenth (alternatively secured) pension year. This means that if the member dies during this ten year term then those income withdrawal payments the member would have received may continue until the end of that period.

Where a member or dependant dies while taking ASP the residual fund will revert to the scheme and must in the first instance be used to provide a dependant's pension for any other surviving dependant of the original member. Where there are no dependants of the member the scheme may use the remaining fund to:

(1) Augment benefits of any remaining scheme members nominated by the deceased member (or by the scheme administrator if the deceased member or the member's dependants had not made a nomination). This is referred to as a "transfer lump sum death benefit".[4] This opens up the possibility of intergenerational transfers of pension funds but following an announcement in the 2006 budget will be subject to inheritance tax.

(2) Be paid to a charity nominated by the member (or by the scheme administrator if the deceased member or the member's dependants had not made a nomination). This is referred to as a "charity lump sum death benefit". This will be free from IHT.

[32.36] Pensions

[1] FA 2004, s 165(1) (pension rules 6 and 7) and Sch 28, paras 11 to 14 amended by FA 2007, Sch 19, para 2 with effect from 6 April 2007.
[2] FA 2004, s 181A(1) inserted by FA 2007, Sch 19, para 14.
[3] Defined in FA 2004, Sch 28, para 10(6).
[4] FA 2004, ss 166, 167(1) (pension death benefit rules 1, 5 and 6), Sch 28, paras 12(2), (3), and 15–27 and Sch 29, paras 18, 19.

Transitional protection for members of schemes before 6 April 2006

[32.37] Individuals should be able to protect their pre 6 April 2006 pension rights from the lifetime allowance charge, provided these are not excessive by reference to pre 6 April 2006 limits.[1]

There are two options for transitional protection from the lifetime allowance charge:

(1) Primary protection—the member's pre 6 April 2006 will be registered and protected to the extent that the lifetime allowance increases over time.

(2) Enhanced protection—this will be available to pension scheme members who ceased active membership of approved pension schemes before A Day. So long as they do not resume membership of a registered scheme after 5 April 2006 all of their benefits when they come into payment will be exempt from the lifetime allowance charge. This form of protection is available to those with pre 6 April 2006 benefits irrespective of whether or not the accumulated pension value then exceeds the applicable lifetime allowance of £1.5m.

[1] See the Registered pension schemes manual (RPSM03100010).

Primary protection

[32.38] Individuals with accrued rights in excess of £1.5 million 'as at' 5 April 2006 are entitled to apply for 'primary protection'.[1]

The operation of primary protection is straightforward. If an individual for example has pension rights at 5 April 2006 that are valued at £3m—then registering for primary protection will mean that their lifetime allowance is twice the standard lifetime allowance.

If when benefits are taken (crystallised), the standard lifetime allowance is for example £1.8m then no lifetime allowance charge will apply so long as the then value of the benefits does not exceed £3.6m.

This factor is referred to in the legislation as the 'primary protection factor'. Where an individual believes they are entitled to a 'lifetime allowance enhancement factor' they must obtain a certificate confirming this entitlement from HMRC. This is required by the Pension Schemes (Enhanced Lifetime Allowance) Regulations, SI 2006/131[2]. Once the enhancement is registered and accepted, HMRC will provide the individual with a certificate confirming the level of 'lifetime allowance enhancement factor'.

This factor is referred to in the legislation as the 'primary protection factor'. Where an individual believes they are entitled to a 'lifetime allowance enhancement factor' they must obtain a certificate confirming this entitlement from HMRC. This is required by the Pension Schemes (Enhanced Lifetime Allowance) Regulations, SI 2006/131[2]. Once the enhancement is registered and accepted, HMRC will provide the individual with a certificate confirming the level of 'lifetime allowance enhancement factor'.

To claim primary protection, an individual must notify HMRC of their intention to rely on this protection. The notification must be made on the "Protection of Existing Rights" form which must reach HMRC on or before 5 April 2009. The form can be completed and sent online.

[1] See the Registered pension schemes manual (RPSM03100050).
[2] *Simon's Weekly Tax Intelligence 2006*, page 258

Enhanced protection

[32.39] Where an individual elects for enhanced protection[1] this means:

(1) For a member of a defined contribution scheme, all post 5 April 2006 fund growth will be exempt from the lifetime allowance charge. There must be no further contributions but contracted out rebates of National Insurance Contributions received after A Day will not count as contributions for this purpose unless contracting-out commenced for the first time after 6 April 2006.

(2) For a member of a defined benefit scheme, pre A Day pension rights may be based on earnings when benefits are first taken, rather than on historic earnings. It will be the date when benefit is first taken from the defined benefit scheme that sets the maximum final pensionable salary for the member concerned. Final pensionable salary for this purpose must then be no greater than that determined using prescribed rules. The individual must become an "inactive member" under the defined benefit scheme.

An individual can revoke their election for enhanced protection at any time before they reach age 75 by resuming active membership of a registered scheme.

If enhanced protection ceases, the individual will revert to primary protection if they had a fund at 5 April 2006 at least equivalent to the lifetime allowance of £1.5m, and if they made a primary protection election as well as an enhanced protection election.

[1] See the Registered pension schemes manual (RPSM03100040).

Transitional protection for pre 6 April 2006 rights to tax-free lump sums

[32.40] There are three kinds of tax-free cash sum rights that can be given transitional protection[1]. These are:

(1) Where a member has elected for primary protection and has a fund value in excess of £1.5 million at A Day it is possible to protect any tax free cash sum entitlement of more than £375,000. The member's tax free cash sum entitlement is calculated at 6 April 2006 and this amount is then increased each year in line with increases in the lifetime allowance.

(2) Where an individual has elected for enhanced protection their maximum tax free cash sum will be a percentage of the pension fund value when benefits are taken. This will be the same percentage as applied to the members unvested pre A Day pension rights.

(3) Where a member had not registered for any transitional protection of their pension benefits but has tax free cash sum rights at A Day that exceed 25% of the value of his pension benefits the tax free cash is protected. Here when the individual vests their pension fund they can take the tax free cash sum to which they were entitled at A Day increased in line with the increase in the lifetime allowance. Where contributions to a registered scheme continue beyond A Day the maximum tax-free cash will be the pre A Day tax free cash sum duly increased, plus 25% of the capital value of the pension fund that has accrued after A Day.

All pension and tax free cash sum rights for which transitional protection is sought must be valued at 5 April 2006, as follows:

(1) Defined contribution rights will be valued as the market value of the member's fund.

(2) Defined benefit scheme rights will be valued as 20 times the accrued pension. Where the scheme provides for a separate tax free cash sum the actual amount will be added to the figure so calculated.

All rights to pensions and lump sums from occupational pension schemes are subject to the pre A Day limits permitted by HMRC.

Where an individual has occupational pension scheme rights that exceed HMRC limits on 5 April 2006 these amounts must be excluded from the valuation for the purpose of protection from the lifetime allowance charge. Excess benefits prior to registering for enhanced protection can be surrendered.

Where a member has unvested occupational pension benefits and wishes to take advantage of the transitional protection they must arrange for the scheme administrator to undertake a benefit check. Where the member has a section 32 buyout policy they must arrange for the buyout provider to check that the market value of the policy (divided by 20) does not exceed the maximum permitted pension benefit—plus any tax-free cash written into the policy.

---

[1] See the Registered pension schemes manual (RPSM03105000).

Registering pre 6 April 2006 rights to obtain transitional protection

[32.41] In order to benefit from transitional protection unvested pre 6 April 2006 rights must be registered with HMRC by 6 April 2009.[1]

Where a pension scheme member needs to protect their pre 6 April 2006 tax-free cash sum rights but is not registering for transitional protection of pension benefits, the tax-free cash sum benefits do not need to be registered, but these benefits must be recorded by the scheme.

Before an existing occupational scheme member can elect for primary or enhanced protection of their pre 6 April 2006 benefits they must test these benefits against the maximum benefit limits under the existing tax regime.

The Finance Act 2004 introduced a new calculation formula applicable in respect of members of defined benefit schemes.

[1] See the Registered pension schemes manual (RPSM03105010).

Unauthorised payments

[32.42] Four tax charges can be applied on funds held by, or payments made out of, registered pension schemes:[1]

(1) *Unauthorised payments charge.* This is a tax charge of 40% of the payment applicable to any scheme member or sponsoring employer who receives an unauthorised scheme payment.
(2) *Unauthorised payment surcharge.* This 15% additional charge will be levied in addition to the 40% charge above, making a total tax charge of 55%. This can be imposed where the value of the unauthorised payment was 25% or more of the pension fund value.
(3) *Scheme sanction charge.* This charge may be imposed on a scheme administrator if in any one year the scheme has made one or more unauthorised payment. The maximum scheme sanction charge is 40% of the fund.
(4) *De-registration charge.* This charge of 40% of the fund value applies where HMRC withdraws a scheme's registration.

[1] See FA 2004, Part 4, Ch 5.

Part VI

The international dimension

Part VI

The international dimension

33

Connecting factors
Overview
Individuals
Corporations
Partnership
Trustees
Personal representatives
European economic interest groupings

34

Enforcement of foreign revenue laws
Taxes of other EC states
General principle
Consequences in the UK
Consequences in a foreign jurisdiction
Double taxation treaties
Exchange of information

35

Foreign income and capital gains of residents
Place of trade
The remittance basis
Relief for unremittable foreign income
Transfers of assets abroad—attribution of income
Offshore funds
Capital gains tax
Overseas trusts
Controlled foreign companies resident in low tax areas

36

The foreign taxpayer and the united kingdom tax system
Limits on income chargeable to tax
Place of trade
Collecting the tax from a non-resident
Non-resident landlords' scheme
Foreign entertainers and sportsmen
Foreign trustees

37

Double taxation relief
Introduction
Treaty relief by credit
Capital gains
Relief by exemption
Employment income exempted: 'the 60 day' rule
Interpretation of UK treaties
Changes to double tax treaties
Treaty shopping
Reform and planning

33

Connecting factors

Overview	PARA **33.01**
Individuals	PARA **33.02**
Corporations	PARA **33.25**
Partnership	PARA **33.38**
Trustees	PARA **33.39**
Personal representatives	PARA **33.42**
European Economic Interest Groupings	PARA **33.43**

Overview

[33.01] In general a UK resident is taxable in respect of all income no matter where it arises; a non-resident is taxable on income arising from sources within the UK.[1] The former is taxed because, whether he be a British subject or not, he enjoys the benefit of our laws for the protection of his property; the latter because in respect of his property in the UK he enjoys the benefit of our law for the protection of that property.[2]

The UK regards citizenship[3] as providing jurisdiction to prosecute a man for child offences but not jurisdiction to tax him.[4]

Even if all foreign systems of taxation accepted these principles there would be occasions on which a particular piece of income would be taxed in two countries—a non-resident with a source of income in the UK would be taxed both here and at home while a UK resident with a foreign source would be taxed both in the country of source and in this country. These problems are exacerbated by the different bases used by different countries; thus one country may tax by residence, another by domicile and a third by citizenship.

Simon's Taxes E6.101, 401.

---

[1] On definition of United Kingdom, see supra, § **1.01**; for an example of this fundamental principle see *Becker v Wright*, supra, § **15.20**.
[2] Per Lord Wrenbury in *Whitney v IRC* [1926] AC 37, 10 TC 88 at 112.
[3] A company incorporated abroad is a subject of that country—*Janson v Driefontein Consolidated Mines* [1902] AC 484.
[4] Citizenship entitles a non-resident to personal allowances. The entitlement has always been enjoyed by a citizen of any Commonwealth country; since 6 April 1996 this has been extended to citizenship of any EC country: TA 1988, s 278.

[33.02] Connecting factors

Individuals

Residence

[33.02] There is no statutory definition of residence. Hence, to determine residence it is necessary to consider the case law that has built up since the introduction of income tax.

There are three difficulties inherent in determining residence by reference to case law. First, the job of a judge is to decide a particular case, not to lay down a code that can be applied generally. This is particularly evident on the question of residence, where the court has frequently declared that an individual's residence is to be decided by looking at all facts relating to that individual and not by the application of a formula. Second, whilst there could be some criticism of the courts for a lack of consistency in their approach on residence matters in some respects, in a very important respect there is total consistency. The court has always declared that a person's residence is a question of fact and not of law. It is, thus, for the commissioners to make the finding of fact, which will only be overturned by the court on appeal if it can be demonstrated that the finding is perverse.[1]

The third difficulty is that the tax practitioner needs to determine the residence of his client and it is most unlikely that the precise facts relating to his client will exactly reproduce those in a decided case. Given the necessity of determining residence of individuals routinely and in many cases each year, the Revenue have published a code of practice.[2] The basis for this code is uncertain since the cases on which they rest are for the most part illustrations of the principle that since residence is a question of fact the courts cannot reverse a finding by the Commissioners simply because they would not reach the same conclusion. The Revenue practice is based on decisions in favour of the Revenue and conveniently ignores those in favour of the taxpayer.

Residence is distinct from domicile in its legal nature and purpose. The tax system asks whether a person is resident in the UK not whether he is resident in this country or another; conflict of laws asks where a person has his domicile. Hence a person may have two residences but not two domiciles.[3] Equally he may have no residence but must have a domicile.[4]

In the one context where it is important to determine whether an individual is resident in this country or that country, namely that of double tax treaties, each treaty will generally contain its own code for determining residence, which code has nothing to do with common law residence.[5]

Simon's Taxes E6.101, 301.

---

[1] That is, the court applies the principle in *Edwards v Bairstow* (1955) 36 TC 207, HL. This is well illustrated by comparing the finding of fact in *IRC v Lysaght* (1928) 13 TC 511, HL with the decision of fact in *IRC v Brown* (1926) 11 TC 292: see infra, § **33.06**. In both cases, the court held that it could not interfere with the decision of the Commissioners although, if one looks at the two cases side by side, it is difficult to imagine that the same tribunal looking at both sets of facts would have declared Lysaght to have been resident and Brown to be not resident.

2   Inland Revenue leaflet IR20 (1999).
3   *A-G v Coote* (1817) 4 Price 183, 2 TC 385; *Lloyd v Sulley* (1885) 2 TC 37.
4   *Bell v Kennedy* (1868) LR 1 Sc & Div 307 at 320.
5   Infra, § **36.12**.

[33.03] Certain rules may be laid down:

(1) Residence is a question of fact (and, therefore, falls to be decided by the Commissioners).[1]

(2) In considering whether an individual (or any other person) is resident in the UK, the court looks at the relevant factors, in the round. In *Shepherd v Revenue and Customs Comrs*,[2] Lewison J approved the methodology adopted by the Special Commissioner, Dr A N Brice, saying:[3] 'I can detect no error of law in [her] conclusion'. The conclusion approved by the High Court was:[4]

> Taking into consideration all the evidence before me, and the facts I have found, especially having regard to the appellant's past and present habits of life, the regularity and length of his visits here, his ties with this country, and the somewhat temporary nature of his attachments abroad, I have come to the conclusion that a least until 5 April 2000 he continued to be resident and ordinarily resident in the United Kingdom. He dwelt permanently here and this was where he had his settled or usual abode and so he was resident here. He resided here continuously as part of his everyday life; his residence here was part of the regular and habitual pattern of his mode of life and it persisted despite temporary voluntary absences to fly in the course of his employment, or to go to Cyprus, or to go sailing, or to visit Europe; his residence here also had a settled purpose and so I also conclude that the appellant was ordinarily resident here.

(3) A person need not be physically present during the tax year to be resident. This was decided by Nicholls J in *Reed v Clark*;[5] the question is one of fact and the issue is not beyond doubt[6]. For some persons a clear rule is laid down by ITA 2007, s 829 which applies to a person whose ordinary residence has been in the UK.[7] Such a person is taxed as if he were actually resident if he has left the UK for the purpose only of occasional residence[8] abroad. So a master mariner whose wife and family lived in the UK throughout the tax year while he was absent, was taxed as if still resident in the UK.[9] However, in *Reed v Clark* it was held that a person who was absent from the UK for the whole of a tax year and who set himself up in another country in such a way as to acquire residence there was not within what is now ITA 2007, s 829, as he was not in the other country for the purpose of "occasional" residence. A person can thus escape s 829 even though his time abroad is limited and he always intends to return.[10]

(4) A place of residence is not essential. In the normal case residence means the place where one dwells permanently or for a considerable time, where one has one's settled or usual abode or the particular place at which one lives,[11] but "resident" indicates a quality of the person to be charged not of his property.[12] A vagrant is not the less resident in the

[33.03] Connecting factors

UK for preferring a different hedgerow or doss house each night nor is a person with a place of abode abroad incapable of being also resident in the UK,[13] even though he should lack such a place here.

(5) A person may be resident here notwithstanding the absence of any element of intention or desire. An intention to depart at any moment is no hindrance to residence.[14] Thus a person may be resident here if his presence is compelled by reasons of business,[15] military service,[16] attendance at school[17] or even ill health.[18] A foreigner compelled to spend time in a UK prison[19] is presumably also resident here.

Among the factors that the courts look at are past[20] and present habits of life,[21] the frequency, regularity and duration of visits to the UK,[22] possibly the purpose of such visits,[23] ties with this country,[24] nationality[25] and whether or not a place of abode is maintained in this country.[26] In considering this test, however, it is essential to bear in mind that "residence is not a term of invariable elements, all of which must be satisfied in each instance. It is quite impossible to give it a precise and inclusive definition. It is highly flexible and its many shades of meaning vary not only in the contexts of different matters but also in different aspects of the same matter."[27]

Simon's Taxes E6.102, 110–112.

---

[1] *IRC v Zorab* (1926) 11 TC 289, *Shepherd v Revenue and Customs Comrs* [2006] EWHC 1512 (Ch), [2006] STC 1821 per Lewison J, para [21] at 1840f. Compare with the case of *Grace v R & C Comrs* (2008) SpC 663. Upon appeal in *Grace v R & C Comrs* [2008] EWHC 2708 (Ch), Lewsion J having identified an error of law in the Special Commissioner's decision nevertheless felt that the facts could only justify a finding that the taxpayer was resident and ordinarily resident and allowed HMRC's appeal. This case is scheduled to be heard by the Court of Appeal in October 2009.

[2] [2006] STC 1821. Also see *R & C Comrs v Grace* [2008] EWHC 2708 (Ch) where a list of relevant factors was given by the Judge (see paragraph 3).

[3] [2006] STC 1821, para [23] at 1841a.

[4] [2005] STC (SCD) 644, para [72] at 660a/b.

[5] [1986] Ch 1, [1985] STC 323.

[6] *Iveagh v IRC* [1930] IR 386 is to the contrary and most of the (few) cases relied on could be, and maybe were, decided on the basis of the rule now in ITA 2007, s 829.

[7] Before 6 April 2007 this rule, then in TA 1988, s 334, applied only to Commonwealth citizens or citizens of the Republic of Ireland but it was thought that the extension, by removing the limitation, would have had no effect in practice.

[8] See per Lord President Clyde in *IRC v Combe* (1932) 17 TC 405.

[9] *Rogers v IRC* (1879) 1 TC 225. Contrast *Turnbull v Foster* (1904) 6 TC 206 where the merchant had not previously been ordinarily resident in the UK and so was held not resident.

[10] *Reed v Clark* [1986] Ch 1, [1985] STC 323.

[11] Per Viscount Cave LC in *Levene v IRC* [1928] AC 217 at 222, 13 TC 486 at 505.

[12] Per Lord Sumner in *IRC v Lysaght* [1928] AC 234, 13 TC 511.

[13] *IRC v Lysaght* [1928] AC 234, 13 TC 511.

[14] *Brown v Burt* (1911) 5 TC 667 (yacht in tidal water—resident).

[15] *IRC v Lysaght* [1928] AC 234 at 248.

[16] *Inchiquin v IRC* (1948) 31 TC 125.

17 *Miesagaes v IRC* (1957) 37 TC 493.
18 *Re MacKenzie* [1941] Ch 69, [1940] 4 All ER 310.
19 Viscount Sumner in *Egyptian Delta Land and Investment Co Ltd v Todd* [1929] AC 1 at 12, 14 TC 119 at 140.
20 *Levene v IRC* [1928] AC 217 at 227, 13 TC 486 at 501, Viscount Sumner.
21 *Levene v IRC* [1928] AC 217, 13 TC 486.
22 *Levene v IRC* [1928] AC 217, 13 TC 486; *IRC v Brown* (1926) 11 TC 292 and *IRC v Zorab* (1926) 11 TC 289.
23 In *Lysaght v IRC*, it was stressed that volition was not necessary. Intention is relevant for ITA 2007, ss 829 et seq.
24 *IRC v Lysaght* [1928] AC 234; *Kinloch v IRC* (1929) 14 TC 736.
25 *Levene v IRC* [1928] AC 217 at 224, 13 TC 486 at 506, and ITA 2007, s 829.
26 *Cooper v Cadwalader* (1904) 5 TC 101.
27 Per Rand J in *Thomson v Minister of National Revenue* [1946] SCR 209 at 224.

Revenue rule 1: 183 days actual residence

[33.04] One who has actually resided in the UK, a confusing statutory phrase, for a period equal to or in excess of 183 days in any year of assessment is treated as resident.[1]

The phrase "actually resides" causes some difficulty since it may simply mean "is physically present" or it may be wider so that a visitor with a short lease on a house might be treated as "actually resident" even during a week's visit to France if he left his wife and family in the house. The former meaning seems preferable and is accepted by the Revenue,[2] yet it means that, while he may be a non-resident, his wife and children may be residents.

The 183-day test replaced the more ambiguous six-months test that existed previously but reflected the widespread practice. Under the code six months was equated with 183 days ignoring the days of arrival and departure, and whether or not it is a leap year.[3] It appears that no-one took the point that it was open to one who was present for six of the months of 31 days (with intervals abroad during the short months) to argue that he was present for only six months even though his actual presence was 186 days. This overcame one of the difficulties in *Wilkie v IRC*[4]. In that case, the respondent arrived in the UK at 2 pm on 2 June 1947 intending to leave at the end of November. Events conspired against him and not only did he have to undergo an operation which compelled him to select a flight out of the UK at the last possible moment, but his arrangement to fly on 30 November was cancelled by the airline. He finally left at 10 am on 2 December, 182 days and 20 hours after his arrival. The court rejected the idea that "months" meant lunar months[5] not calendar months, and the respondent escaped a tax charge of £6,000. The court held that the correct approach was to add up the total number of hours that Mr Wilkie had spent in the UK during the fiscal year. As this was four hours less than six months, he was held not to have satisfied this first test of residence.

The period spent in the UK need not be continuous. The test focuses only on the year of assessment. Therefore one who arrives on 6 April can, on the view taken in the code, only stay 183 days in the next 12 months whereas one who arrives on 5 October may stay all but 12 months and still not be resident.

[33.04] Connecting factors

ITA 2007, s 832 contains the corollary that one who has not actually resided in the UK for 183 days is not treated as resident if he is in the UK for some temporary purpose only and not with any view or intent of establishing residence.[6] "The meaning of it is this, if a foreigner comes here for merely temporary purposes connected with business or pleasure, or something else, and does not remain for a period altogether within the year of 183 days, he shall not be liable for a certain portion of taxation . . . He would have been liable but for this exemption."[7] This rule applies to exempt from tax non-UK source income chargeable under the provisions specified in ITTOIA 2005, s 830(2), foreign pension income and foreign benefits income[8] and to state a special residence rule for employment income[9] (see supra, § **7.02**). It does not affect other aspects of residence. In applying those provisions one is to ignore any accommodation which may be available in the UK for the person's use.[10]

The statement of practice allowing some relaxation of time limits where a person's stay is prolonged because of exceptional circumstances beyond that person's control, eg illness, does not apply to this rule.[11]

Simon's Taxes E6.102, 120–122.

---

[1] ITA 2007, s 831(1).
[2] Inland Revenue leaflet IR20 (1999) § **1.2**.
[3] Inland Revenue leaflet IR20 (1999) § **1.2**.
[4] [1952] 1 All ER 92, 32 TC 495.
[5] Such a contention was not as obscure as it might seem; previous practice was to interpret statutory references to months in such a fashion.
[6] ITA 2007, s 831(1).
[7] Per Lord Inglis in *Lloyd v Sulley* (1884) 2 TC 37 at 42.
[8] TA 1988, s 831(2).
[9] TA 1988, s 832(1).
[10] TA 1988, ss 831(1), 832(1) added by FA 1993, s 208(1) as from 1993–94.
[11] Statement of practice SP 2/91 (especially para 3).

Revenue rule 2—new residents and visitors—the role of habitual and substantial visits

[33.05] A person intending to live in the UK permanently or to come and remain for three years or more is treated as resident and ordinarily resident from the date of arrival.[1]

A visitor is normally regarded as resident here if he visits the UK regularly, ie his visits after four years average 91 days or more in the tax year; such a visitor becomes resident as from the fifth year.[2] If he intends to follow this pattern from the beginning he is treated as resident from the beginning. Equally a decision say in year 3 that the visits will follow this pattern will cause him to be resident as from 6 April of year 3. The role of intention is of great importance in such cases. In calculating the periods of 91 days over four years HMRC will not take into account days spent in the UK because of exceptional circumstances, eg illness.[3]

The bases for this rule are the decisions of the House of Lords in *Levene v IRC*[4] and *IRC v Lysaght*,[5] each of which concerns a claim by a resident to have given up residence and the Special Commissioner decision in *Shepherd v R & C Commrs*.[6]

In *Levene v IRC* the taxpayer had been resident in this country in previous years but had left the country in 1919. He did not set up a place of abode overseas. From 1919 to 1925 he spent about five months in each year in the UK but had no fixed abode in this country. He was "a bird of passage of almost mechanical regularity".[7] The reasons for his visits were the obtaining of medical advice, visiting his relatives, taking part in certain religious observances and dealing with his income tax affairs. The Commissioners held that he was resident here, a decision not reversed by the House of Lords.

Simon's Taxes E6.112.

[1] Inland Revenue leaflet IR20, (1999) § 3.1.
[2] Inland Revenue leaflet IR20, (1999) § 3.3 and see Statement of Practice SP 3/81.
[3] Statement of practice SP 2/91 and Inland Revenue leaflet IR20 (1999) § 3.3 point (i); see also Inland Revenue Interpretation RI 72.
[4] [1928] AC 217, 13 TC 486.
[5] [1928] AC 234, 13 TC 511.
[6] SpC 484 [2005] STC (SCD) 644 but see most recently the case of *Grace v R & C Comrs* [2008] EWHC 2708 (Ch) (overturning a finding of non-residence by the Special Commissioner at (2008) SpC 663.
[7] [1928] AC 217, per Viscount Sumner, at 226, 501.

[33.06] In *IRC v Lysaght* the taxpayer had resided in England where he lived with his family and was managing director of the family business. In 1919 he went to live permanently in Ireland and set up a home there. He retained a seat on the board of the company, visited England once a month for meetings but for no other purposes. On such visits he was not accompanied by his wife and he usually stayed at a hotel. The Commissioners held that he was still resident in the UK. The House of Lords could find no reason for holding that there was no evidence to support that finding and therefore dismissed the appeal. For Viscount Sumner the crucial point appeared to be that the taxpayer was obliged to come to this country, that that obligation was continuous and the sequence of the visits excluded the element of chance and occasion.[1] For Lord Buckmaster with whom Lord Atkinson agreed the matter was one of fact and degree and so pre-eminently one of fact.[2] Lord Warrington was not sure that he would have taken the same view as the Commissioners.[3] Viscount Cave dissented, arguing that the matter was one of mixed fact and law and so could be interfered with and, if it was a matter of fact, that there was no evidence to support the conclusion reached by the Commissioners.[4]

IRC v Lysaght has generally been looked upon as marking the most extreme frontier of residence. However, the case concerned the two years immediately after the move to Ireland. The court considered that significant weight should be given to the way in which the taxpayer carried on his business, which was in England:

[33.06] Connecting factors

> Here is the great business . . . of Lysaght and Co. He is the advisory director of it, at £1,500 a year, and he comes here every month for an average of a week. He sleeps here and he has to be here doing the business of the company for about a week a month . . . As things are . . . he came this month; he will have to come next month . . . and he will have to come the month after. He will have to come perfectly regularly and unless he gives up his position he could not alter it . . . Under the circumstances—I do not decide more than this particular case—the ordinary course of his life made him resident in this country.[5]

The taxpayer was still involved in the running of the English business and he had no business interests in Ireland. He remained a member of a London club and had a bank account in Bristol. Moreover his visits, although only for company meetings once a month, lasted on average a week and meant that he was physically present in England for 100 days in the one year, 94 days in the second and 84 days in the third, giving an average of 93 days a year. The fact that he had found a permanent home outside the jurisdiction is only one factor to be weighed against these.

The importance of recognising that in *IRC v Lysaght* the House of Lords merely declined to interfere with a finding of fact by the Commissioners is shown by a comparison of that case with *IRC v Brown*[6] where the taxpayer's usual habit was to spend seven months in Mentone, two months in Switzerland or at the Italian lakes and three months in the UK.[7] The Special Commissioners held that he was not resident. Rowlatt J held that he could not interfere with that finding. The same judge later held that he could not interfere with the finding of fact by the Commissioners in *IRC v Lysaght*. Yet it is the *Lysaght* case, despite the doubts on the facts expressed in the House of Lords, which is taken as the basis of current Revenue practice under the code.

In *Gaines-Cooper v R & C Comrs*[8] not only did the Special Commissioner ignore the 90 day formulation suggested in HMRC Booklet IR20 but counsel for HMRC submitted that the normal Revenue practice of ignoring days of arrival and departure (as stated in IR20) should not be followed.[9] The Special Commissioner commented: "in this appeal we must apply the law rather than the provisions of IR20". The Special Commissioner's decision in ruling that the taxpayer was resident in the UK throughout the period under appeal was based on the taxpayer's purpose:

> we find that the appellant's purpose in visiting the United Kingdom was not a purpose which lasted for a limited time; the purpose was to visit his wife and son, his mother and, to a lesser extent, his other friends. This was a permanent and not a transient purpose nor was it simply a passing need. Neither was it a casual purpose but rather it was in pursuance of the regular habits of the appellant's life. A decision to visit the United Kingdom on a large number of days each year to be with one's wife and child is not a temporary purpose.

Statute excludes foreign income from the UK income tax charge when it arises to an individual who "is in the United Kingdom for some temporary purpose only and with no view to establishing the individual residence in the United Kingdom". In *Gaines-Cooper v R & C Comrs* the Special Commissioner rejected the submission that the taxpayer came within this provision, stating:

> The appellant relied upon the fact that from 1996–97 onwards most of the visits to the United Kingdom were for two days or less and that pointed to the conclusion

that each of the visits was for a temporary purpose only within the meaning of [now ITA 2007, s 831(1)]. The appellant's evidence was that some of his visits to the United Kingdom were short because London was a convenient hub for international flights and sometimes he would be in the United Kingdom while in transit . . . We conclude that the presence of the appellant in the United Kingdom for the years under appeal was not for a temporary purpose.

The High Court[10] upheld this decision but exclusively dealing with the question of domicile. The taxpayer chose not to appeal the decision on residence but instead pursued a judicial review of the Revenue's failure to apply its own IR20 guidance. This was heard initially by the Administrative Court in the Queen's Bench Division of the High Court. However, another similar case (*R (on the application of Davies & Anor) v Revenue & Customs Commrs*) had also been considered by that Court. Initially, the Court held that the matter ought to be considered first by what was then the Special Commissioners, so that facts could be established. However, on appeal, the Court of Appeal felt that a decision of the Special Commissioners would inevitably lead to a ruling on the law which would have had to have been enforced by HMRC so that the Court of Appeal was minded to allow the case to proceed.[11] With that the Court of Appeal remitted the case to the High Court for further consideration. In the meantime, the Court heard the application in Mr Gaines-Cooper's case: having considered the Court of Appeal's decision in *Davies*, the High Court considered that the prior decision of the Special Commissioners in that case precluded any further consideration of the matters by way of judicial review. A couple of weeks later, however, the *Davies* case was reheard by the High Court which then held that the matter should be first heard by the Special Commissioners. Both decisions were then appealed again to the Court of Appeal which concluded that the judicial reviews in both cases should be permitted to proceed and would be heard by the Court of Appeal, probably early in 2010.

In both cases, the taxpayers are arguing that they had a legitimate expectation that their arrangements were not liable to UK tax, because they were not resident within the United Kingdom for the relevant tax year. Their contention that they had such an expectation was based on their reliance upon IR20. The claim for judicial review was that the Revenue in those guidance notes set out very clear criteria (90-day test) for non-residence that the claimants complied with, therefore it would be wrong for the Revenue to depart from the test and the apparent satisfaction of the test set out in the guidance notes.

Simon's Taxes E6.112, 120–122.

---

[1] [1928] AC 234, 13 TC 511, per Viscount Sumner, at 245, 529.
[2] [1928] AC 247, 534.
[3] [1928] AC 251, 537.
[4] [1928] AC 241, 533.
[5] 13 TC 511 per Rowlatt J at 517.
[6] (1926) 11 TC 292.
[7] Case stated, para 3(4). One difference from *Levene* is that *Brown* had no business interests here. This difference is not reflected in the code.
[8] [2007] STC (SCD) 23.

[9] [2007] STC (SCD) 23 para [10] at 44j/45a. Following this case, HMRC issued, on 5 January 2007, HMRC Brief 01/2007—Residence: *Simon's Weekly Tax Intelligence* 2007 p 132. In this brief, HMRC confirms that there has been no change to its practice in relation to residence and the "91 day test", stating:

The guidance provided by booklet IR20 is general in nature. If, on the facts of the matter, a dispute arises over the application of this general guidance and the parties cannot resolve their dispute by agreement, the Commissioners will determine any appeals. The Commissioners are bound to decide the legal issues by reference to statute and case law principles rather than HMRC guidance. Where a dispute relates to particular facts the Commissioners will consider the evidence and make findings of fact to which they will apply the law.

[10] [2007] EWHC 2617 (Ch).
[11] [2008] EWCA Civ 933.

Revenue rule 3—coming to the UK

[33.07] A person coming to the UK for a purpose, eg employment, and intending to stay for at least two years will be treated as resident from the day of arrival until the date of departure.[1] A person coming for a purpose lasting less than two years or not knowing how long the stay will be will only be treated as resident here if he spends 183 days or more in the UK in the tax year (ie he comes within rule 1). A person coming to the UK for purposes other than work may also now be treated as resident as from the date of his arrival.

For tax years before 1993–94 there was a further rule giving rise to residence if there was accommodation available to that person in the UK. That rule has probably now been abolished (see infra, § **33.08**).

Simon's Taxes E6.121.

[1] Inland Revenue leaflet IR20, (1999) § **3.7**; this was wider than the pre 1996 practice—see Inland Revenue press release, 29 January 1996, *Simon's Weekly Tax Intelligence* 1996, pp 214, 265.

Relevance of available accommodation

[33.08] At one time the Revenue took the view that if a person had accommodation available to him, any visit to the UK would suffice to make that person a UK resident for the fiscal year in which the visit took place. FA 1993, s 208 inserted what is now the proviso to ITA 2007, ss 831(1) and 832(1) which abolishes the "available accommodation" rule for the purpose of that section, which is entitled "temporary residence in the United Kingdom".[1] This leaves open the question as to whether the available accommodation rule was abolished for other tax purposes.

The view is taken that new ss 831 and 832 have the effect of abolishing the available accommodation rule for all tax purposes. This is not evident from the wording for statute, but was clearly stated by the Chief Secretary to the Treasury in Parliamentary debate. On the basis that statute is ambiguous, the Government statement would be admitted by the court under the rule in *Pepper v Hart*.[2] The contrary view has been given by Dr A N Brice, sitting as

Special Commissioner in *Shepherd v R & C Comrs*.³ Dr Brice stated that, in her view, the words are not ambiguous and do not lead to absurdity.⁴

Inland Revenue Booklet IR20 (last published in December 1999) and the notes to the self-assessment tax return, treat the FA 1993 amendment as applying for all purposes of income tax and capital gains tax. However, the IR Booklet makes the availability of accommodation relevant in other ways. Thus it may undermine an argument that the taxpayer has left the UK permanently (para 2.8) and is taken into account in deciding whether a person coming to the UK is treated as resident or ordinarily resident as from the date of arrival (paras 3.7–3.13). For these latter purposes the Revenue look to ownership and to leases for three years or more.⁵

Simon's Taxes E6.120.

---

1. Inland Revenue press release, 16 March 1993, *Simon's Tax Intelligence* 1993, p 468. Change of residence during tax year: concession A11.
2. Official Report (Hansard) of the proceedings in Standing Committee A on the Finance (No 2) Bill 1993 on 24 June 1993 at Cols 590–592.
3. [2005] STC (SCD) 644, para 71 at 659J. For a later discussion of ss 831 and 832 and its application see the case of *Grace v R & C Comrs* [2008] EWHC 2708 (Ch), where it was held that regular visits to the UK for the reasons of employment do not amount to "temporary purpose".
4. However, Dr Brice had already ruled that the taxpayer was not "a temporary or occasional visitor to the United Kingdom" and, hence, what is now ss 831 and 832 did not apply and, thus, the words of Mr Dorell do not address the question of residence in this particular case.
5. In April 2008, the booklet was brought up to date to reflect HMRC's view of the law as at 5 April 2008. A formal revision is expected later in 2008 to reflect the changes made in FA 2008.

Days of arrival and departure

[33.09] The *Wilkie* case led to the practice of HMRC ignoring days of arrival and departure when counting days present in the UK. From 6 April 2008, however, statute now provides that as a general rule days of arrival will count towards the 183-day total, provided that the individual does not leave the country on the same day. Provision is made for taxpayers in transit through the UK who do not engage in activities "that are to a substantial unrelated to the individual's passage through the United Kingdom" so that such days do not count, provided that they do in fact leave the UK on the following day.¹

The statutory test is unsatisfactory as it would undoubtedly lead to anomalies.² For example, an individual could arrive in the UK at 9am, spend the day in meetings and leave at 6pm. That day would not count as a day spent in the UK. However, an individual who arrives at 9pm and leaves at 6am the following morning would be so caught if the individual pre-arranges a dinner with a client during the stay.

HMRC guidance suggests that the 91-day rule is to be similarly interpreted. However, since the 91-day rule has no statutory effect, the rule cannot be modified by statute. On the other hand, the practice of counting days of arrival was reflected by the Special Commissioners in the *Shepherd* and *Gaines-Cooper* cases that brought the issue to the fore. It should still be remembered that there is nothing sacred about the 91-day rule and it is open to a taxpayer who has regularly spent say 93 days in the UK to argue that, on the facts, he was not resident in the country.

[1] ITA 2007, ss 831(1B) and 832(6).
[2] This is one of the reasons why many professional bodies have called for a straightforward day counting test as is applied in other jurisdictions, notably the United States.

Split year treatment

[33.10] Not all persons acquiring residence do so on 6 April and the Tax Acts make no provision for splitting a tax year so as to tax the new resident only for that part of the year which he was resident.[1] By concession, however, a split is carried out where an individual, who has not prior to his arrival been ordinarily resident in the UK, comes to the UK to take up permanent residence, or to stay at least two years regardless of the purpose[2], or ceases to reside by leaving for permanent residence abroad. This concession is extended to the years of departure and return where, subject to conditions, an individual goes abroad under a contract of employment. The conditions for the extension are:

(1) the absence and the contract of employment extend over a period covering a complete tax year; and
(2) any interim visits do not amount to 183 days or more in any tax year or an average of 91 days or more in a tax year (the average is taken over a maximum of four years);[3]

The time of departure or arrival can make a significant difference to total tax liability since personal reliefs are not apportioned by reference to the duration of residence. As with all concessions, the benefit is withheld if the taxpayer is using it for tax avoidance.[4] There is also a concession for CGT.[5]

Simon's Taxes E6.123.

[1] See *Neubergh v IRC* [1978] STC 181.
[2] This applies as from 1995–96; previously the period was three years but was reduced to two if the person was coming to the UK for purposes of employment.
[3] Extra-statutory concession A11. Concession A11 does not apply to FA 1995, s 128, IHT or CTT, nor to trusts. See also Inland Revenue leaflet IR20 (2000) §§ **1.5–1.7**.
[4] *R v IRC, ex p Fulford-Dobson* [1987] STC 344.
[5] Extra-statutory concession D2 revised to reflect FA 1998 s 127.

Giving up residence—working abroad

[33.11] Under the Revenue Code a person who leaves the UK to work full-time abroad under a contract of employment is treated as not resident and not ordinarily resident if both the absence from the UK and the employment last for at least a whole tax year. Analogous treatment is provided for trades' professions and vocations.[1] The code also mentions visits back to the UK. These are ignored if they total less than 183 days in any tax year, and average less than 91 days a tax year. In the Revenue view, a mobile worker with a home in the UK retains UK residence, despite the number of days spent abroad. This situation would arise, for example, for a lorry driver, a sales person or other employee who goes abroad most weeks but usually returns to the UK for the weekend.[2]

---

[1]   IR20 (1999) §§ 2.2–2.5.
[2]   Inland Revenue Tax Bulletin, April 2001, p 836.

Giving up residence—the role of return visits

[33.12] Under the code if a person has accommodation available to him in the UK, he is regarded as resident here if he pays a visit to the UK during the tax year and as ordinarily resident if he comes here in most years. If he has no such accommodation here, he is regarded as remaining both resident and ordinarily resident if he returns for periods which amount to an average of three months a year. If he claims that he has ceased to be resident and ordinarily resident here and can produce some evidence for this (eg that he has sold his house here and set up a permanent home abroad) his claim is usually admitted provisionally with effect from the date following his departure. Normally this provisional ruling is confirmed after he has remained abroad for a period which includes a complete tax year and during which his visits to this country have not amounted to an annual average of three months.

If, in the event, the visits to the UK have exceeded the annual average of three months, Revenue practice is to treat the individual as never having ceased to be resident in the UK.

Where residence is given up during a tax year in order to take up permanent residence abroad, an individual by concession may be charged only by reference to the actual period of residence.[1]

On 1998 rules for capital gains disposals by individuals temporarily non-resident, see infra, § **35.46**.

Simon's Taxes E6.122.

---

[1]   Extra-statutory concessions A11, D2. See also Inland Revenue leaflet IR20 (1999) § **1.5**.

Concessionary relief for accompanying spouses

[33.13] Where a taxpayer, T, has a spouse, S, the status of each is to be determined independently. However, where T goes abroad for purposes of whole time employment and S goes either at the same time or afterwards but for a different purpose, T may cease to be resident and ordinarily resident as from the day after the date of departure to the date of return while S may find residence and ordinary residence persisting.[1] A concession therefore applies[2] where S, the accompanying spouse, is abroad for a complete tax year and

[33.13] Connecting factors

interim visits to the UK do not amount to 183 days or more in any one tax year or an average of 91 days or more in a tax year. In these circumstances the residence of S for tax liability for the years of departure and return will be determined by reference to actual residence during the year. An early return home because T's employment ends unexpectedly will not prevent ordinary residence from having ceased provided it includes a complete tax year of absence and any visits to the UK average less than 91 days a tax year.

Simon's Taxes E6.130.

---

[1] ITA 2007, s 830 and extra-statutory concession A78. See also Inland Revenue leaflet IR20, (1999) § **2.6.** For years before 1993–94 there were further rules relating to accommodation available to the spouse.

[2] Extra-statutory concession A78.

Ordinary residence

[33.14] The concept of ordinary residence separate from residence[1] appears in two disparate parts of the Taxes Act. First, a charge to capital gains tax[2] arises when the person is *either* resident *or* ordinarily resident in the UK.[3] Second, in order to claim tax credits, the claimant must be ordinarily resident in the UK.[4]

Some commentators[5] have equated ordinary residence with habitual residence. Whilst this may have a degree of validity for the second use of the concept in the Taxes Act, it is clearly incorrect when considering the basis of the charge to capital gains tax. It is not possible to be habitually resident in more than one country at the same time[6] but it is well established that it is possible to be ordinarily resident in more than one country at the same time.[7]

The clearest judgment on the nature of ordinary residence is that of Lord Scarman in *Shah v Barnet London Borough Council*:[8]

> I unhesitatingly subscribe to the view that 'ordinarily resident' refers to a man's abode in a particular place or country which he has adopted voluntarily and for settled purposes as part of the regular order of his life for the time being, whether of short or of long duration.

The Revenue not infrequently alleged that an individual is within the charge to capital gains tax by virtue of being ordinarily resident for the fiscal year, although he/she is not resident. On the basis of the judicial comment above, this position is rarely likely to occur. An individual imprisoned in a foreign jail may, perhaps, be ordinarily resident in the UK whilst not present in the UK, as may a backpacker during the gap year between school and university, for example. However, the more common situation where an individual makes substantial capital gains having left the UK to live abroad would appear to permit no effective distinction between that individual's residence and that individual's ordinary residence. If he has moved to another country then his residence in that other country is likely to be ordinary and not extra-ordinary,[9] however short the stay in the foreign country.

Non-tax cases would seem to establish that ordinary residence does not connote continuous physical presence, but it does connote physical presence with some degree of continuity, notwithstanding occasional temporary absences.[10] There must be some physical presence. Intention to reside is not, alone, sufficient.[11]

In *Levene v IRC* [12] Viscount Cave said:

> The expression 'ordinary residence' . . . is contrasted with usual or occasional or temporary residence; and I think that it connotes residence in a place with some degree of continuity and apart from accidental or temporary absences. So understood the expression differs little in meaning from the word 'residence' . . . and I find it difficult to imagine a case in which a man while not resident here is yet ordinarily resident here.

In *Lysaght v IRC* Viscount Sumner said:[13]

> My Lords, the word 'ordinarily' may be taken first. The Act on the one hand does not say 'usually' or 'most of the time' or 'exclusively' or 'principally' nor does it say on the other hand 'occasionally' or 'exceptionally' or 'now and then', . . . I think the converse to 'ordinarily' is 'extraordinarily' and that part of the regular order of a man's life, adopted voluntarily and for settled purposes, is not 'extraordinarily'. Having regard to the times and duration, the objects and the obligations of Mr Lysaght's visits to England, there was in my opinion evidence to support . . . a finding, that he was ordinarily resident . . .
>
> Grammatically the word 'resident' indicates a quality of the person charged and is not descriptive of his property, real or personal. To ask where he has his residence is often a convenient form of inquiry but only as leading to the question: 'Then where is he resident himself'

In *Gaines-Cooper v Revenue and Customs Comrs*[14] the Special Commissioner considered a claim of non-residence by a taxpayer who sent considerable time in the Seychelles but whose wife lived in England for half each year and he visited the marital home frequently, but normally for only one or two days each visit. The Special Commissioner said:[15]

> Applying those principles to the facts of the present appeal we conclude that the appellant was resident in the United Kingdom in the years of assessment under appeal and that his residence here was continuous in the sense that it continued from year to year. It was ordinary and part of his everyday life bearing in mind that his everyday life was far from ordinary. We are also of the view that the appellant would still be ordinarily resident in the United Kingdom even if there were an occasional year when he was not resident here.

The High Court[16] as per Lewison J upheld the General Commissioner's decision in this case but did not consider the question of ordinary residence.

In *Genovese v HMRC*[17] the Special Commissioner held that an employee would (subject to the facts) often become ordinarily resident three years after first arriving in the country. It is suggested that this was not a correct interpretation of the legal tests.[18]

---

1 "Ordinary residence" combined with "residence" is used to provide the charge to income tax which forms the subject of ITEPA 2003, Chapter 4: rules applying to employee residence, ordinary residence and domiciled in UK (formerly Case I of Schedule E: TA 1988, s 19). The concept of ordinary residence was discussed by Dr A N Brice in *Shepherd v R & C Comrs* [2005] STC (SCD) 644, para 71 at 659J in

[33.14] Connecting factors

this context. The taxpayer was held to be resident in the UK. The finding that he was ordinarily resident was a priori a logical consequence. Although other commentators have taken a different view, the view of the authors is that this case is not a helpful discussion of the concept of ordinary residence when separated from the concept of residence. Compare with the case of *Grace v R & C Comrs* (2008) SpC 663.
2   And corporation tax on capital gains made by corporations.
3   TCGA 1992, s 2(1).
4   Tax Credits (Residence) Regulations 2003, SI 2003/654, reg 3(1).
5   Including North and Fawcett in *Private International Law*, where decisions in a number of abduction cases are cited.
6   *Re V (Abduction: Habitual Residence)* [1995] 2 FLR 992; *Dickson v Dickson* 1990 SCLR 692 at 703; *Findlay v Findlay* 1994 SLT 709; *Cameron v Cameron* 1996 SLT 306.
7   *IRC v Lysaght* [1928] AC 234; *Hopkins v Hopkins* [1951] P 116, [1950] 2 All ER 1035; *Shah v Barnet London Borough Council* [1983] 2 AC 309, at 342; *Britto v Secretary of State for the Home Department* [1984] Imm AR 93; *R v Secretary of State for the Home Department, ex p Zahir Chugtai* [1995] Imm AR 559.
8   [1983] 2 AC 309, HL. This was adopted for tax purposes by Nicholls J in *Reed v Clark* [1985] STC 323 at 345e.
9   See comments interpreting "ordinary" as the contrary of "extraordinary" in *Shah v Barnet London Borough Council* [1983] 2 AC 309.
10 *Levene v IRC* [1928] AC 217 at 232; *Shah v Barnet London Borough Council* [1983] 2 AC 309, at 341–342; *R v Immigration Appeal Tribunal, ex p Siggins* [1985] Imm AR 14; *Re Vassis* (1986) 64 ALR 407.
11 National Insurance Decision No R(P) 1/72.
12 [1928] AC 217 at 225, 13 TC 486 at 507.
13 [1928] AC 234 at 243–244, 13 TC 511 at 527.
14 [2007] STC (SCD) 23.
15 [2007] STC (SCD) 23, para 190 at 61c.
16 [2007] EWHC 2617 (Ch).
17 (2009) Sp C 741.
18 See the analysis of this case in *Tax Adviser*, July 2009, pp 27-29.

Domicile

The difficulty and importance of the concept

[33.15] Arguably, domicile is the most difficult of the concepts on which the charge to tax is based. It is, also arguably, the concept most frequently overlooked by the tax adviser in failing to identify an opportunity for tax mitigation by his client.

Every tax system has to define the population on which it is imposed. The formulation most commonly found is that a tax on income is imposed on persons resident within the territory of the taxation authority and those not resident are subject to tax only on income arising within that territory. This gives a class of person who are resident in the territory for the year but whose focus is not with that territory but with another. Most advanced countries limit the tax charge imposed on those in this class of persons. In some countries it is by exemption of foreign source income; in some countries it is by charging foreign source income only in so far as it is brought into the country. The UK follows the second alternative and taxes foreign income of such persons, and capital gains arising on the disposal of foreign assets, as, and only if, it is remitted to the UK.

Different countries adopt different approaches to defining the class of persons who do not have their primary links with the country in which they happen to be resident for the year and to whom this more preferable tax regime is to apply. Some countries adopt a test of citizenship; the United States, indeed, applies citizenship to give the liability to federal income tax irrespective of residence. Many civil law jurisdictions apply a concept of habitual residence, exempting or limiting the tax charge on those resident in the country in the year but whose habitual residence is elsewhere. The UK adopts the common law principle of domicile.

Domicile is a concept unique to common law jurisdictions. It is not known in civil law jurisdictions; the correct translation of the French concept "domicile fiscale", for example, is, "habitual residence", not the English concept "domicile". The concept of domicile arose through common law and was a particularly important, and useful, concept during the heyday of the British Empire, when it was used to identify those who the law should treat as English (or Scottish or Northern Irish), wherever in the Empire they may have been born, have lived their lives, or, indeed, died. The concept of domicile is one that England exported to its colonies and now forms part of the law of those common law jurisdictions. In England, the concept of domicile has been largely unaffected by statute, other than a restriction in the concept of domicile of dependency.[1] In New Zealand and Australia, the basic English law concept of domicile has been retained but statute has abolished the English law principle of reversion to domicile of origin (see infra, § **33.19**).[2]

It is important for the tax lawyer to recognise that domicile is a concept that tax law has taken from the law of family relations and family property. Domicile is a vital, basic principle in English personal law, which addresses questions relating to the essential validity of a marriage; the effect of marriage on the proprietary rights of husband and wife; jurisdiction in divorce and nullity of marriage; legitimacy, legitimation and adoption; and wills and intestate succession to movables.

The fact that domicile is, almost only incidentally, a basic concept of tax law means that there is a wealth of case law that needs to be considered in the determination of domicile, much of it addressing questions that are totally different from those to be addressed in tax matters. As a matter of legal theory, the test which determines the place of a person's domicile must remain constant, no matter what the nature of the issue may be before the court. However, the reality may be different. The role of the court is to decide the case in front of it and English courts have striven to apply a decision that is equitable and just for the parties in the instant case. One commentator[3] concludes, after analysing judicial decisions on domicile applied to a variety of circumstances, that courts apply a different test for domicile according to the nature of the issue. Another commentator[4] states that there is evidence that the courts wish to achieve a number of differing policy objectives; the court will endeavour to validate a will rather than leave an estate to intestate succession and will endeavour to take jurisdiction to grant a divorce whenever possible. The apparent variation in judicial approach has itself been the subject of judicial comment in *Re Fuld's Estate (No 3)*.[5] In that case, Scarman J stated that the difficulty of reconciling the numerous statements arises not from lack of clarity of judicial thought, but from the nature of the subject. The cases involve a detailed examination of the facts and it is not surprising that different judicial minds concerned with different factual situations have chosen different language to describe the law. Scarman J regards the difference between the statements of judges as showing a difference of emphasis and therefore as being of no great moment.[6]

A person's domicile is a question of fact. It is decided by considering everything that the court considers to be a relevant fact relating to the individual's life. In taxation, decisions on fact are exclusively the province of the Commissioners.[7] Courts, on appeal, have shown enthusiasm to adjudge whether the Commissioners have applied the correct test. This does not, however, change the fundamental point that any decision on domicile by the High Court, Court of Appeal or House of Lords in a tax matter is a review of the findings of fact made by the Special Commissioners. The court does not engage in a fact-finding expedition; it relies on the Commissioner's decision to identify the facts which may be relevant. These facts may be many. In *Drevon v Drevon*,[8] it was said that no fact is too trifling to merit consideration. In *Casdagli v Casdagli*,[9] that judgment states: His aspirations, whims, amours, prejudices, health, religion, financial expectations—all are taken into account. Faced with this brief, it is often difficult to ascertain what points led to a judgment in a particular case and which were rejected by the judge as of little moment. This makes analysis of decided cases difficult[10] and the application of principle unclear. As Sir Peter North says:

> One of the defects of English law is that the evidence adduced in a disputed case of domicile is often both voluminous and difficult to assess. This is due to the over-scrupulous manner in which the courts attempt to discover a man's exact intention. The tendency is to investigate his actual state of mind, rather than to rest content with the natural inference of his long-continued residence in a given country. This, indeed, is to set sail on an uncharted sea.[11]

The Inland Revenue have reported[12] that 60,000 individuals currently state on their self-assessment tax return that they are domiciled outside the UK. Only one or two of these statements each year will ever be considered by the Special Commissioners. All the rest are considered, if at all, by HMRC officers only. The resources allocated by the Revenue to the determination of domicile are finite and do not permit widespread application of the "roving commission" favoured by the courts in decided cases. The procedure adopted by the Revenue is for the local district to accept a claim for a foreign domicile in those cases where a foreign individual has come to take up employment in the UK for a fixed period only and then to request all other claimants to complete a HMRC form,[13] on the basis of which HMRC Foreign Division makes a "determination" of domicile, normally without any further information being requested from the taxpayer. This process means that the Revenue's view of an individual's domicile status is effectively determined by the information presented on behalf of the individual. A competent tax adviser will ensure that relevant information is presented on the Revenue form in a manner that most readily assists a proper determination of domicile by the Revenue officer.

1. The common law rule that a wife automatically takes her husband's domicile is abolished where the marriage took place on or after 1 January 1974, by Domicile and Matrimonial Proceedings Act 1973, s 1.
2. The common law rule of the automatic revival of the domicile of origin is abolished in Australia by Domicile Acts 1982, s 7 and in New Zealand by Domicile Act 1976, s 11.
3. WW Cook *Logical and Legal Bases of the Conflict of Laws,* pp 194 et seq.
4. Fawcett (1985) 5 OJLS 378.
5. [1968] P 675 at 682–683.
6. [1968] P 675 at 684. The potential for a drama in the recounting of a life history in domicile proceeds is well illustrated by the recounting of events in the life of Errol Flynn in *Re Flynn, Flynn v Flynn* [1968] 1 All ER 49, (1968) 1 WLR 103. This case also demonstrates the potential for repeated litigation that is not infrequent in domicile matters. *Re Flynn, Flynn v Flynn* was followed the same year by *Re Flynn, Flynn v Flynn (No 2)* [1968] 112 Sol Jo 804, and, a year later by *Re Flynn, Flynn v Flynn (No 3)* [1969] 2 All ER 557.
7. Under TA 1988, the taxation of foreign income on a remittance basis was achieved by making a claim to the Board that the taxpayer was not domiciled within the UK (TA 1988, s 65(4)). In the consolidation, under the tax law rewrite procedure, of this provision, ITTOIA 2005, s 832(1) merely provides that the remittance basis is applied by a non domiciliary making a claim, without specifying that the claim is to the Board. The effect of this change is that the General Commissioners are now competent to hear a case that turns on the determination of the taxpayer's domicile. Previously, this question was the exclusive concern of the Special Commissioners, who have solid jurisdiction where statute provides that a claim is made "to the Board": TMA 1970, s 46C(1)(*a*).
8. (1864) 34 LJ Ch 129
9. [1919] AC 145 at 178. Hearsay evidence is admissible: *Scappaticci v A-G* [1955] P 47, [1955] 1 All ER 193n.
10. Consider the case of *Winans v A-G* [1904] AC 287. Winans was born in the US in 1823. He lived in the US until 1850, when he moved to Russia, never again to set foot in the USA. In 1859 his doctor advised him to spend the winter in England and not in Russia. Between 1860 and 1893 his year was divided between Russia, England, Scotland and Germany. From 1893 until his death in 1897 he lived entirely in England. His estate at death was over £2,000,000 (at 1897 prices) and the UK Revenue claimed estate duty on the basis that he had acquired an English domicile. Faced with those facts, Kennedy J in the court of first instance had no hesitation in deciding that Winans had taken an English domicile of choice. All the judges in the Court of Appeal came to the same conclusion, again without hesitation. In the House of Lords, Lord Macnaughton said that 'up to the very last he had an expectation or hope of returning to America' and held that he had retained his domicile of origin. Lord Halsbury found it impossible to decide what had been the intention of Winans. Lord Lindley vigorously dissented and decided that Winans had given up any serious idea of returning to America. All eight judges had been given the same evidence. Which pieces of evidence persuaded which judge? Each judge's judgement refers to facts that the individual judge considered

[33.15] Connecting factors

supported the judgement he made but we cannot tell from the judgements what any individual judge thought of the facts other members of the judiciary thought important.

[11] Cheshire and North's *Private International Law* (13th edn), p 143.
[12] Statement made during a public consultation meeting following the publication of the HM Treasury discussion paper: "Reviewing the residence and domicile rules as they affect the taxation of individuals: a background paper", April 2003.
[13] DOM 1.

The importance of domicile for tax purposes

[33.16] An individual who is domiciled within the UK[1] is subject to income tax on income arising worldwide.[2] He is subject to capital gains on the disposal of assets anywhere in the world.[3] At his death, inheritance tax is charged on his worldwide estate[4] plus the capital in any settlement in which he has a current right to income.[5]

By contrast, an individual who is domiciled outside the UK is subject to income tax on foreign income only in so far as that income is brought into the UK.[6] He is, similarly, outside the charge to UK capital gains tax on the disposal of an asset located outside the UK, unless he brings into the UK the proceeds of disposal.[7] At his death, inheritance tax is charged on his estate within the UK only,[8] unless his period of residence in the UK is sufficient to trigger the special IHT deemed domiciled rule.[9] The special provisions for inheritance tax may give rise to a charge on the worldwide estate of the deceased; however, any foreign assets that were put into a settlement by the non-domiciled individual before he had spent 17 years resident in the UK are "excluded property"[10] and do not attract a charge to IHT. In addition, the gift with reservation provisions do not apply. Such "excluded property" is outside the charge to inheritance tax even for an individual with UK domicile who subsequently acquires an interest in possession in the settlement.[11]

There is a distinction between the statutory formulation for, on the one hand, income tax and that, on the other hand, for both capital gains tax and inheritance tax. For income tax[12], the assessment is on remittances if the taxpayer "makes a claim" that he is not domiciled within the UK. The inheritance tax charge on foreign-situs assets owned by an individual not domiciled within the UK is removed by declaring them "excluded assets";[13] statute[14] requires assessment to capital gains tax on the basis of remittances when an individual is not domiciled within the UK. It is argued that a taxpayer who is, in fact, domiciled outside the UK is free to choose not to make a claim to that effect and this would have the consequence that he is subject to income tax as if he were a UK-domiciliary. As no claim is required for the CGT treatment to apply, that option is not available for CGT.

The effect of the formulation for CGT is that a taxpayer with a non-UK domicile who makes a gain on the disposal of one foreign asset, the proceeds of which he remits to the UK, and, later in the year, suffers a loss on the disposal of another foreign asset, obtains no relief for the loss,[15] as the basis of the charge is the remittance of the proceeds of the disposal he makes at a gain.

The tax treatment may influence the case the taxpayer may wish to make. Where it is a question of taxation of income, the taxpayer will usually wish to

Individuals [33.16]

claim that he/she is domiciled outside the UK, so that he can establish a portfolio of non-UK investments and enjoy the income arising therefrom without a UK income tax charge. Exceptionally, a basic rate taxpayer may wish to establish a domicile within the UK if he has remitted foreign dividends. An individual with a domicile within the UK is subject to tax at the rate of 10% on foreign dividends arising but an individual with a foreign domicile is subject to tax at 22% on the same dividend income.

Where the tax in question is capital gains tax, the individual will usually seek to obtain Revenue agreement that he is domiciled outside the UK as he will then be able to sell investments, or any other assets, without exposure to UK capital gains tax. Exceptionally, a domicile within the UK will be advantageous if the sale of a foreign asset is at a loss.[16]

For inheritance tax, there are two contrasting situations. During the first 16 years of his/her residence in the UK, the taxpayer will usually wish to put the case that he/she has retained the domicile of origin outside the UK as this then keeps foreign assets outside the charge to inheritance tax in the event of death. It also enables the taxpayer to create an accepted asset settlement by settling assets before acquiring the IHT deemed domicile at the end of the sixteenth year of residence.[17] However, a foreign born spouse of a UK domiciliary may wish to put the case that he/she has acquired a domicile within the UK in the event of being widowed during the first 16 years of residence in the UK. If the domicile of the widow/widower has changed to a UK domicile, the inheritance from the deceased spouse is then free of IHT by virtue of the interspouse exemption; if the domicile of the surviving spouse is a foreign domicile, only a £55,000 exemption is available.[18]

---

[1] The concept of domicile attaches to a single legal system. Hence "a domicile in the UK" is a domicile in England and Wales, or a domicile in Scotland or a domicile in Northern Ireland.
[2] ITTOIA 2005, ss 6,2 69, 368, & 577.
[3] TCGA 1992, s 1(1).
[4] IHTA 1984, s 5(1). Other than settled assets which are excepted assets: IHTA 1984, s 48(3) see infra, § **47.13**.
[5] IHTA 1984, s 49(1).
[6] ITTOIA 2005, s 832. See infra, §§ **35.12–35.22**.
[7] TCGA 1992, s 12(1).
[8] IHTA 1984, s 6(1).
[9] IHTA 1984, s 267.
[10] IHTA 1984, ss 3(2) & 48(3).
[11] The definition of "excluded property" in section 48(3) is made by reference solely to the domicile of the settlor, irrespective of the domicile of the beneficiary.
[12] ITTOIA 2005, s 831.
[13] IHTA 1984, s 6(1).
[14] TCGA 1992, s 12(1).
[15] Relief is specifically prohibited by TCGA 1992, s 16(4).
[16] TCGA 1992, s 16(4).
[17] IHTA 1984, s 267.
[18] IHTA 1984, s 18(2).

[33.17] Connecting factors

The five rules of domicile

[33.17] The concept of domicile is characterised by five rules.

First, every individual has a domicile. In this respect, domicile is in complete contrast to residence (and ordinary residence). This first rule means that if an individual leaves the country of his origin with a clear intention of never returning to it again he, nevertheless, retains his domicile of origin in that country until he settles in the country of his choice and has—viewed objectively—both established permanent links with the country of his choice and abandoned his links with his country of origin.[1] Similarly, if an individual has acquired a domicile of choice but then leaves that territory, this first rule means that his domicile of origin revives until such time (if ever) that he acquires a domicile of choice in another territory.[2]

Second, a person cannot have more than one domicile at any one time.[3] This rule follows from the basic concept of domicile, which is to establish the legal system that provides the personal law for that individual.[4]

Third, an individual's domicile is always in a territory subject to a single system of law. Thus, in a federal state, the domicile is in the individual state, not in the federation. No one is domiciled in the United States of America, each individual with a US domicile is domiciled in one of the 50 individual states.[5]

Fourth, there is a presumption in favour of the continuance of an existing domicile. Therefore the burden of proving a change lies in all cases on those who allege that a change has occurred.[6] This presumption may have a decisive effect, for if the evidence is so conflicting or indeterminate that it is impossible to elicit with certainty what the resident's intention is, the court will decide in favour of the existing domicile.[7]

Fifth, the domicile of a person is to be determined according to the English concept of domicile.[8]

---

[1] *Munro v Munro* (1840) 7 Cl & Fin 842 at 876.
[2] *Udny v Udny* (1869) LR 1 Sc & Div 441 at 457.
[3] *IRC v Bullock* [1976] 1 WLR 1178 at 1184; *Lawrence v Lawrence* [1985] Fam 106 at 132.
[4] See supra, § **33.15**.
[5] In India, one set of legal rules applies to inheritance for Hindus and another set of rules applies for inheritance for Muslims. Nevertheless the domicile is with the territory unit of India, not with the religious grouping.
[6] *Winans v A-G* [1904] AC 287 at 289; *Re Lloyd Evans* [1947] Ch 695; *Messina v Smith* [1971] P 322 at 330; *Puttick v A-G* [1980] Fam 1 at 17; *Spence v Spence* 1995 SLT 335.
[7] *Winans v A-G* [1904] AC 287. Lord Halsbury held that the Crown had not discharged its duty of proving a change of domicile. (For the author's comments on the judgements in this case, see supra, § **33.14** footnote 10.) In *Henderson v Henderson* [1967] P 77 at 80, Sir Jocelyn Simon P said that, when the displacement of a domicile of origin by a domicile of choice is alleged, "the standard of proof goes beyond a mere balance of probabilities". See also *Steadman v Steadman* [1976] AC 536 at 563.

[8] *Lawrence v Lawrence* [1985] Fam 106 at 132; *Rowan v Rowan* [1988] ILRM 65 at 67.

Domicile of origin

[33.18] At birth a person acquires a domicile of origin. This will be the domicile of his father if he is legitimate. It is the domicile of his mother if he is a posthumous or illegitimate child.[1] If his mother is living apart from his father at the time of birth, his domicile of origin will be that of his father although his domicile of dependency (see infra, § **33.20**) will be that of his mother. A foundling has a domicile of origin in the place where he is found.

If a child is born illegitimate, but is later legitimated, he acquires his father's domicile from the date of legitimation, but it is probable that this is a domicile of dependency and his domicile of origin remains that of his mother, presuming that at his birth his parents were domiciled in different countries. It is important to note that, with one exception, a domicile of origin once acquired remains constant throughout life. The one exception is the case of adoption. The effect of the Adoption Act 1976, s 39(1) & (5) would appear to be that, at the date of adoption, an individual is given the domicile of his adoptive father as a domicile of origin.[2]

[1] *Udny v Udny* (1869) LR 1 Sc & Div 441 at 457, HL.
[2] In the exceptional case of an adoption that is not by a couple but is by an unmarried woman, acting alone, the individual acquires, at the date of adoption, his adoptive mother's domicile as a domicile of origin.

Reversion to domicile of origin

[33.19] A domicile of choice is extinguished by leaving the territory of choice with an intention not to return.[1] Change of intention, without a departure from the country, does not, however, cause an abandonment of a domicile of choice.[2]

By contrast, a domicile of origin is not extinguished by a change of residence with an intention not to return. It is not lost by mere abandonment. A domicile of origin endures until supplanted by a fresh domicile of choice. In *Bell v Kennedy*[3] Bell was born in Jamaica, of Scottish parents. He was educated in Scotland and then returned to Jamaica. In 1837, he left the island without any intention of returning, resided with his mother-in-law in Scotland, and looked for an estate in Scotland on which to settle down. He had not found an estate to buy when his wife died in 1838.

It was held that his domicile at his wife's death was in Jamaica. Although he had abandoned the island for good in 1837 and was resident in Scotland, he had not at that time decided to make his permanent residence there. The evidence showed that in 1838 his mind was vacillating with regard to his future home. Therefore, since he had not acquired a Scottish domicile of choice, he retained his domicile of origin, even though he gave clear evidence that he had determined not to return to Jamaica.

[33.19] Connecting factors

If the domicile of origin is displaced as a result of the acquisition of a domicile of choice, the rule of English law is that it is merely placed in abeyance for the time being. It remains in the background and is revived immediately an individual abandons his domicile of choice.[4]

---

[1] In *Re Flynn* [1968] 1 WLR 103 at 113, Megarry J said it is unnecessary to prove a positive intention not to return, since the "merely negative absence of any intention" to resume the residence will suffice to effect an abandonment of the domicile.

[2] In *Re Raffenel's Goods* (1863) 3 Sw & Tr 49; *Faye v IRC* (1961) 40 TC 103; *Re Adams* [1967] IR 424 at 452; *IRC v Duchess of Portland* [1982] STC 149; *Rowan v Rowan* [1988] ILRM 65.

[3] (1868) LR 1 Sc & Div 307. This was followed in *Brown v Brown* (1981) 3 FLR 212, CA.

[4] *Udny v Udny* (1869) LR 1 Sc & Div 441; *Tee v Tee* [1974] 1 WLR 213, at 215–216, CA; see also Wade (1983) 32 ICLQ 1 at 12 et seq.

Domicile of dependency

[33.20] There are two separate types of domicile of dependency:

(1) the domicile of dependency for child under age 16,
(2) the domicile of dependency of a woman married before 1 January 1974.

Until he reaches the age of sixteen years or marries under that age,[1] a child's domicile follows that of his parent, a dependent domicile. This will be that of his father if he is legitimate or legitimated and of his mother if he is illegitimate. If a legitimate child's father and mother live apart, whether divorced or not, his domicile will follow that of his mother if he has his home with her and not with his father.[2] This will remain his domicile if she should then die and he has not since had a home with his father. On his father's death a child who until that time has had his father's domicile will acquire his mother's domicile of dependency.[3]

A woman marrying before 1974 automatically acquired her husband's domicile by virtue of the marriage; a woman married after 1973 does not.[4] A woman married before that date and who therefore acquired his domicile, retains it unless or until it is changed by acquisition or revival on or after that date.[5]

Where, immediately before 1 January 1974, a married woman had her husband's domicile by dependence, she is treated as retaining that domicile until such time as the married woman actually returns to reside in the country of her domicile of origin and her acts are such that she has clearly abandoned her domicile of dependence.[6] The Domicile and Matrimonial Proceedings Act 1973, of itself, does not cause a woman to revert to her domicile of origin. Exceptionally, where a woman is a US citizen, the domicile of dependency arising from a pre-1974 marriage is ignored for the purposes of income tax and capital gains tax. This is a consequence of the UK/USA double tax agreement which disapplies the concept of a domicile of dependency for the purposes of those taxes only.[7] Article 4(4) of the double tax treaty states:

A marriage before 1 January 1974 between a woman who is a United States national and a man domiciled within the United Kingdom shall be deemed to have taken place on 1 January 1974 for the purpose of determining her domicile on or after 6 April 1976 for United Kingdom tax purposes.

[1] Domicile and Matrimonial Proceedings Act 1973, s 3(1).
[2] Domicile and Matrimonial Proceedings Act 1973, s 4(1).
[3] See supra, § **33.18**.
[4] Domicile and Matrimonial Proceedings Act 1973, s 1(1).
[5] Domicile and Matrimonial Proceedings Act 1973, s 1(2).
[6] IRC v Duchess of Portland [1982] STC 149.
[7] Note that the domicile of dependency applies for the purposes of inheritance tax, which is not subject to the UK/USA Double Taxation Agreement, and also for purposes of general law (so that English courts have jurisdiction in divorce matters, for example).

Domicile of choice

[33.21] The question that causes the most difficulty in practice for the tax practitioner is to determine whether an individual has abandoned his/her domicile of origin and acquired a domicile of choice. It is important for the practitioner to note that this is neither a purely technical matter, nor is it primarily a tax matter.

The use of the word "abandon" is particularly apt. The acquisition of the domicile of choice is a fundamental change in the status of the individual. Someone who has acquired a domicile of choice has changed from one legal system to another to determine how his/her will is to be interpreted, how property passes in the case of death without a will, as well as the other basic family questions (see supra, § **33.15**). In an important sense, the use of the concept of taxation purposes is a mere ancillary to the determination of the personal law governing the status of the individual.

The manner in which the question of alleged change of domicile is to be approached is given by Scarman J:[1]

> Two things are clear – first that unless the judicial conscience is satisfied by evidence of change, the domicile of origin persists; and secondly, that the acquisition of a domicile of choice is a serious matter not be lightly inferred from slight indications or casual words.

In order to abandon the domicile of origin and acquire a domicile of choice[2] there are two requirements to be satisfied: (1) residence and (2) intention.

(1) It must be proved that the person in question established his *residence* in a certain country;[3] and
(2) there must be an *intention* to remain permanently in the territory in which he resides.[4]

Both requirements must be satisfied, but the intention may either precede or succeed the establishment of the residence. An emigrant forms an intention before he leaves England for Australia; the émigré who flees from persecution may not form it until years later.

[33.21] Connecting factors

The strength of the presumption that the domicile of origin is retained is illustrated in *Bowie (or Ramsay)v Liverpool Royal Infirmary*.[5] George Bowie left a will that was only valid if he was domiciled in Scotland at his death. Bowie was born with a Scottish domicile of origin and lived in Glasgow until he gave up work at age 37. Thereafter, for the remaining 45 years he lived in Liverpool as his brother and sister lived there and were prepared to support him financially. He remained living in Liverpool for seven years after both of them had died. During those 45 years he did not even visit Scotland, even for his mother's funeral. The House of Lords held unanimously that George had not acquired a domicile of choice in England & Wales, but died domiciled in Scotland, his domicile of origin.

Another case in which the domicile of origin was retained despite long residence in England is *Cyganik v Agulian*.[6] Andreas Nathanael was born in Cyprus in 1939. He fled to England in 1958 after breaking off an arranged marriage. In 1972 he returned to his home village, a Greek Cypriot village in the north of the island, but left in 1974 when his village was bombed during the invasion of the northern part of the island by Turkish troops. Thereafter, he lived and ran a hotel in England, but made frequent visits to his daughter in Cyprus. He died with an estate in excess of £6,000,000. Of this, only £50,000 was left to Renata Cyganik, the woman with whom he had lived. Ms Cyganik claimed against the estate under the Inheritance (Provision for Family & Dependents) Act 1975. In order to claim under IPFDA 1975, the deceased must have been domiciled in England & Wales at death. The claim succeeded in the High Court, but failed in the Court of Appeal. The Court of Appeal reiterated the doctrine that the burden of proof lies on the person who claims that a domicile of origin has been abandoned. And that is a heavy burden of proof. Although away from home for 43 years and having his business interests in England, Andreas Nathanael's links with his home country were deep and it cannot be said that he abandoned his domicile of origin in Cyprus.

The necessity for intention means that a child under age 16 or an individual who does not have legal capacity by virtue of a mental disorder cannot acquire a domicile of choice.[7] It is possible for an individual to abandon a domicile of choice. Unless there is a new domicile of choice, this will cause the individual's domicile of origin to revive. In *Allen v R & C Comrs*[8] the Special Commissioners held that, on the facts of that case, the taxpayer living with family members in England for the last six years of her life did not constitute an abandonment of her long established domicile of choice in Spain.

---

[1] *Re Fuld's Estate (No 3)* [1968] P 675 at 686. This was followed in *Gaines-Cooper v Revenue and Customs Comrs* [2007] STC (SCD) 23, where the claim that the taxpayer had abandoned his domicile of origin in England and Wales and acquired a domicile of choice in the Seychelles was rejected. The Special Commissioner said: 'We . . . find that in fact the appellant never did wholly reject England nor, indeed, that small part of it located in Berkshire and Oxfordshire where he had so many ties and connections; on the contrary he felt its pull upon his affections and interests all his days.' Para 146 at 53d. This decision was later affirmed in the High Court ([2007] EWHC 2617 (Ch)) by Lewison J.
[2] Or change from one domicile of choice to another domicile of choice.
[3] *Harrison v Harrison* [1953] 1 WLR 865.

[4] *Re Fuld's Estate (No 3)* [1968] P 675 at 684.
[5] [1930] AC 588, HL, 99 LJPC 134.
[6] [2006] EWCA Civ 129, [2006] 1 FCR 406.
[7] Although a person without legal capacity may change domicile by virtue of a change in the domicile of dependency: see supra, § **33.20**. It would appear that the Court of Protection has the capacity to change the domicile of a mentally disordered individual under its care.
[8] [2005] STC (SCD) 614.

Actual residence

[33.22] For the acquisition of a domicile of choice, there must be actual residence in the territory of choice. Residence, for this purpose, has been defined by the court as:

> Residence in a country for the purposes of the law of domicile is physical presence in that country as an inhabitant of it."[1]

In that case a taxpayer who spent ten to twelve weeks each year in Quebec for the purpose of maintaining her links with that Province with a view ultimately to returning to live there was held not to be a resident of Quebec during her presence there since she was not there as an inhabitant.

The courts[2] have attached little weight to the length of residence, and have taken the view that, although a material consideration, it is rarely decisive. It is the fact of residence that is necessary, not its duration. The duration may (or may not) give an indication of intention. That is the second, and separate, consideration.

In *Jopp v Wood*[3] it was held that a residence of 25 years in India did not suffice to give John Smith an Indian domicile because of his alleged intention ultimately to return to Scotland, the land of his birth. Again, in *IRC v Bullock*[4] a Canadian who had a domicile of origin in Nova Scotia was held not to have become domiciled in England, despite the fact that he had either served in the RAF or lived in England for over forty years. He retained his domicile in Nova Scotia because he intended to return there should his wife predecease him.

---

[1] *IRC v Duchess of Portland* [1982] STC 149.
[2] For example, *Puttick v A-G* [1980] Fam 1 at 17 and the decision of the House of Lords in *Winans v A-G* [1904] AC 287 at 297–298.
[3] (1865) 4 De GJ & Sm 616, 99 LJ Ch 228.
[4] [1976] 3 All ER 353.

Intention

[33.23] The acquisition of a domicile of choice requires an intention to remain permanently in the territory in which he resides. The definition of "permanent" in the Shorter Oxford English Dictionary is "lasting or designed to last indefinitely without change". This is the definition that most of the judges have recognised when required to consider the nature of the intention necessary for a change of domicile. In *Udny v Udny*[1] Lord Westbury described the intention as being one to reside "for an unlimited time". Scarman J[2] referred to an intention to reside "indefinitely".

A conditional intention does not create a domicile of choice. In *Cramer v Cramer*[3] a woman with a French domicile of origin came to England intending to remain here and marry an Englishman, who was already married. Her intention to remain was conditional on both herself and her proposed husband obtaining divorces and on their relationship continuing; she was held not to have acquired a domicile of choice in England.

In *IRC v Bullock*[4] a husband intended to return to Canada if his wife predeceased him. It was held that the husband had not acquired an English domicile of choice, since there was a real possibility, in view of their ages, of this happening.

As stated in 1869 by Lord Westbury:[5]

> Domicile of choice is a conclusion or inference which the law derives from the fact of a man fixing voluntarily his sole or chief residence in a particular place, with an intention of continuing to reside there for an unlimited time. This is a description of the circumstances which create or constitute a domicile, and not a definition of the term. There must be a residence freely chosen, and not prescribed or dictated by any external necessity, such as the duties of office, the demands of creditors, or the relief from illness; and it must be residence fixed not for a limited period or particular purpose, but general and indefinite in its future contemplation.

This was followed 99 years later in *Re Fuld's Estate (No. 3), Hartley v Fuld*[6] where Scarman J said:[7]

> In *Udny v Udny* Lord Westbury emphasised that the intention must be formed free of external constraining factors, eg the demands of creditors.

Later[8] he continued:

> . . . a domicile of choice is acquired only if it be affirmatively shown that the person is resident within a territory subject to a distinctive legal system with the intention, formed independently of external pressures, of residing there indefinitely.

In *F v IRC*[9] the Special Commissioner ruled that the Revenue failed to demonstrate that an Iranian who came to England in 1949 at the age of 19 and spent the larger part of his time thereafter in the UK until his death in 1992 had made such a fundamental change in his way of life as to demonstrate the acquisition of a domicile of choice in England and Wales. In that case, the Special Commissioner commented:[10]

> There is virtually no evidence of such integration by the deceased. The evidence is almost entirely to the effect that he did not so integrate and that he did not wish to do so, except in relation to the world of classic cars. He disliked the English weather, English fruit and the English class system, and he thought that England and its economy were on a downward spiral. Although his house in England adjoined the local church, his relationship with the vicar was poor and it seems that he took no part in village life.

In *Civil Engineer v IRC*[11] the taxpayer had spent 30 years living and working Hong Kong. He gave the Special Commissioner a 196 page document supporting his intention that he had acquired a domicile of choice in Hong Kong. The Special Commissioner stated:[12]

I am unable to find that he had ever established a domicile of choice in Hong Kong.

By contrast, in *Surveyor v IRC*,[13] the Commissioners held that the appellant's residence in Hong Kong was not solely for a commercial reason; his family, social, business and financial ties were there. On that basis, he was held to have abandoned his domicile of birth in England and Wales and acquired a domicile of choice in Hong Kong.

In *Moore's Executors v IRC*,[14] the deceased had a domicile of origin in Missouri but died in London. The Special Commissioner said: 'I am left with the impression of a cultured person who is obviously fully at home in Europe, . . . who used England as a base for travel to Europe.'[15] The Special Commissioner held that he had not demonstrated the necessary intention to acquire a domicile in England and, hence, had retained his domicile of origin in Missouri, despite having ceased residing in that state 55 years earlier.

---

[1] (1869) LR 1 Sc & Div 441 at 458.
[2] *Re Fuld's Estate (No 3)* [1968] P 675 at 684.
[3] [1987] 1 LFR 116.
[4] [1976] 1 WLR 1178.
[5] *Bell v Kennedy* (1868) LR 1 Sc & Div 307, HL.
[6] [1968] P 675.
[7] At 684.
[8] At 684. A recent illustration of a decision based on evidence of intention is *Morgan v Cliento* [2004] EWHC 188 (Ch), [2004] All ER (D) 122 (Feb).
[9] [2000] STC (SCD) 1. This case, which arises in the context of CGT, gives a very useful review of the law on domicile.
[10] At 15e.
[11] [2002] STC (SCD) 72.
[12] At 76d.
[13] [2002] STC (SCD) 501.
[14] [2002] STC (SCD) 463.
[15] At 466h.

Evidence of intention

[33.24] The burden of proof which lies on the party who alleges an abandonment of a domicile of origin and the acquisition of a domicile of choice is a heavy one.[1] In *Winans v A-G* Lord Macnaghten said:[2]

> [How] heavy is the burden cast upon those who seek to shew that the domicile of origin has been superseded by a domicile of choice!

In *Henderson v Henderson*,[3] Sir Jocelyn Simon P stated[4] that:

> . . . to displace the domicile of origin in favour of the domicile of choice, the standard of proof goes beyond a mere balance of probabilities.

One of the difficulties of analysing case law on domicile is that it is not always clear what evidence was put to the court and which items of evidence the court considered carried weight and which did not. It is not particularly helpful to have judicial comments such as: "Nothing must be neglected that can possibly indicate the bent of the resident's mind".[5]

[33.24] Connecting factors

The common law rule, that expressions of intention by a living person cannot be received in evidence is not applicable when the issue is domicile[6] and it is common for witnesses to report declarations made by the person whose domicile is in question. The weight given to such a statement is, however, generally, not great, as, it is commented, such evidence is suspect, for witnesses may lie or forget.[7] Thus, for example, if a widower testifies that at the time of his wife's death he and she regarded Scotland as their permanent home, the fact that by Scots law he is entitled to one-half of his wife's property may make his testimony a little suspect.[8]

In *Hodgeson v De Beauchesne*[9], it was said that undue stress must not be laid on any single fact however impressive it may appear when viewed out of its context, for its importance as a determining factor may well be minimised when considered in the light of other qualifying events. Again, no one fact is of constant value, for every case varies in its circumstances, and what is of decisive importance in one may be of little weight in another.

---

[1] A useful discussion of case law on the evidence to be given in determining domicile questions is in Cheshire and North's *Private International Law* th edn) pp 143–146.(13
[2] [1904] AC 287 at 291.
[3] [1967] P 77.
[4] At 80.
[5] *Casdagli v Casdagli* [1919] AC 145 at 178. The judge went on to state: 'His aspirations, whims, amours, prejudices, health, religion, financial expectations—all are taken into account.'
[6] *McMullen v Wadsworth* (1889) 14 App Cas 631 at 636, PC.
[7] For example *Hodgson v De Beauchesne* (1858) 12 Moo PCC 285.
[8] *Re Craignish* [1892] 3 Ch 180 see also *Spence v Spence* 1995 SLT 335—here the dominant reason for a couple's departure from Spain had been to avoid tax liability. It was held that the husband had not acquired a domicile of choice in Spain, where he had lived for nine years. The court was wary of his statement of an intention to remain in Spain in the future.
[9] *Hodgson v De Beauchesne* (1858) 12 Moo PCC 285.

Corporations

Residence

The case law test

[33.25] Since income tax originally applied both to individuals and to companies it was perhaps inevitable that residence would be taken as the basis of taxation of companies. The first two recorded cases considering the residence of a company were both decided in 1876. *Calcutta Jute Mills Co Ltd v Nicholson*[1] and *Cesena Sulphur Co v Nicholson*[2] established the principle that the residence of a company is where the directors meet and where they transact their business and exercise the powers conferred on them. The long-established case law test of residence was laid down by Lord Loreburn in *De Beers Consolidated Mines Ltd v Howe*[3] "... a company resides, for the purpose of income tax, where its real business is carried on ... and the real business is carried on where central management and control actually abides". As Lord Radcliffe has remarked, "this judgment must be treated today as if the test which it laid down was as precise and unequivocal as a positive statutory injunction".[4] Under this test a company is resident where its controlling board meets rather than where its directors are resident.[5]

In the *De Beers* case the company was registered in South Africa as were the mines whose diamonds the company marketed, its head office, and the venue of its shareholders meetings. The diamonds were sold through a London syndicate. Directors meetings were held both in South Africa and London but it was in London that the majority of the directors resided. The Commissioners held that London was the place from which the directors controlled and managed the chief operations of the company. In challenging this conclusion, the company took as a point of law the proposition that being incorporated and registered in South Africa it must be resident in South Africa. That proposition was rejected by the House of Lords.

The word "actually" in the formulation in *De Beers* is crucial. In *Unit Construction Co Ltd v Bullock*[6] the boards of the subsidiaries did not meet at all, as the parent company usurped their powers. In that case, Lord Simonds said:[7] 'it is the actual place of management, not the place in which it ought to be managed, which fixes the residence of a company'. In *Wood v Holden*[8] a company with a limited number of transactions executed all legal documentation in Amsterdam.[9] The company was held to be resident in the Netherlands.[10]

In *Wood v Holden*, Counsel for the Revenue argued that the professional advisor who was the architect of the scheme could be the person exercising central management and control of the company Eulalia. This was rejected by Park J:[11] "Advisers are in no position to give orders to major banks and trust companies. It is inherently unlikely that [the professional adviser] did anything of the sort, and all the evidence of the communications with [the sole director of Eulalia] showed that he did not".

Influence is not the same thing as control; a Board of Directors may act under the influence of another person or persons but that does not necessarily mean that the Board of Directors has ceased to exercise central management and control.[12]

The tests formulated in *De Beers* and *Wood v Holden* were applied by the Special Commissioner in *News Datacom Ltd v Atkinson*[13] where a Hong Kong company had appointed an "Executive Committee" in the UK which had significant measure of control over its activities. As far as the Commissioner was concerned there were two limbs to the residence test:

(1) Was central management and control exercised through the company's 'constituent organs' (normally its Board of Directors)?
(2) If the function of the Board was usurped, where was that usurping body resident?

[33.25] Connecting factors

In that case, there was a finding of fact that the Board still had control and exercised overall control outside the UK.

This rule was modified as from 30 November 1993. Where a company would be treated as resident in the UK under this rule but as non-resident under the terms of an applicable double taxation agreement it is now to be treated as non-resident for all UK tax purposes. This means that the treaty provision prevents dual residence.[14]

The Revenue have issued a statement of practice on the residence of companies under the case law test.[15]

Simon's Taxes D4.101–104, 108.

[1] (1876) 1 TC 83.
[2] (1876) 1 TC 88.
[3] [1906] AC 455 at 458, 5 TC 198 at 212.
[4] In *Unit Construction Co Ltd v Bullock* [1960] AC 351 at 366, 38 TC 712 at 738. The test was adopted by the legislature in TA 1988, s 769(1) repealed by FA 1988, Sch 14, and was approved by RC 1st Report § 11, and is present in eg the UK–USA Double Tax Treaty, art 4(1)(*a*)(ii). The UK–Netherlands Treaty uses the phrase "effective management", art 4(3); on effective management in relation to trusts see *Wensleydale's Settlement Trustees v IRC* [1996] STC (SCD) 241.
[5] *John Hood & Co Ltd v Magee* (1918) 7 TC 327.
[6] (1960) 38 TC 712.
[7] At 729.
[8] [2005] EWHC 547 (Ch), [2005] STC 789.
[9] [2005] EWHC 547 (Ch), [2005] STC 789 at [43].
[10] In *Wood v Holden* [2005] EWHC 547 (Ch), [2005] STC 789 Park J considered the residence of two companies which were both incorporated outside the UK and created to give effect to a scheme for the avoidance of UK tax on a large capital gain. In his judgment, Park J gives a useful summary of the case law on company residence: paras 21–27 at 824d to 829b. Upholding the decision of Park J, in his leading judgment in the Court of Appeal, Chadwick LJ said: 'For my part I find the judge's analysis compelling': *Wood v Holden* [2006] EWCA Civ 26, [2006] STC 443, CA, para 35 at 463g.
[11] [2005] STC 789 para 42 at 834g to 834h.
[12] *Re Little Olympian Each Ways Ltd* [1995] 1 WLR 560, *New Zealand Forest Products* (1995) 17 NZTC 12, 073, *Esquire Nominees* (1971) 129 CLR 173 and *Untelrab v McGregor* [1996] STC (SCD) 1.
[13] (SpC 561) [2006] STC (SCD) 732.
[14] FA 1994, s 249.
[15] Statement of Practice SP1/90.

[33.26] It was not clear whether Lord Loreburn's test meant that a company could have only one residence. This was discussed in the difficult and unfortunate decision of *Swedish Central Rly Co Ltd v Thompson*.[1] The company had been set up in England to obtain the concession for and then build a railway line in Sweden. The company had in 1900 leased the railway to a Swedish company in return for an annual rent of £33,500. In 1920 the articles of the company were altered to remove the central management and control of the company to Stockholm and the Revenue admitted that the company was now controlled and managed from Sweden, so as to cease being liable to tax under Schedule D, Case I. If, however, the company was still resident in England it would be liable to tax under Schedule D, Case V.[2] The Special Commissioners observed that Lord Loreburn's test was laid down in a case concerning a foreign company,[3] and concluded that the company was resident in the UK. The conclusion that a company could have two residences was upheld by Rowlatt J by the Court of Appeal[4] (Atkin LJ dissenting) and by the House of Lords (Lord Atkinson dissenting); what is less clear is the reasoning on which that conclusion was applied to the facts.

Simon's Taxes D4.109.

[1] [1925] AC 495, 9 TC 342. The Swedish Central Railway opened up the Bergslagen Region—a remote forested area. The track was 621/4 miles long with, in 1920, four passenger trains a day taking an average of five hours for the journey. (Bradshaw's Continental Railway Guide 1920.)
[2] This minimal activity was still a business—see *IRC v South Behar Rly Co Ltd* (1925) 12 TC 657.
[3] Case stated, para 17. 9 TC 342 at 347.
[4] [1924] 2 KB 255, 9 TC 342.

[33.27] The major difficulty lies in reconciling the case with the decision of the House of Lords four years later in *Todd v Egyptian Delta Land and Investment Co Ltd*.[1] The company was incorporated in 1904 in England for the purpose of dealing in and developing land in Egypt; in 1907 most of its functions were transferred to Egypt. All that remained in London was required by the Companies Act—a registered office, which meant simply an address rather than a specific amount of floor area, a register of members and a register of bearer warrants. There was a London secretary of the company who dealt with occasional correspondence and filed the annual returns, a job he did for many other companies.

The company contended, that the mere satisfaction of the requirements of the Companies' Acts could not constitute residence.[2] The Revenue on the other hand contended that if management and control were not the sole test of residence there were carried on in the UK acts of sufficient importance to justify a finding of residence.[3] The Special Commissioners decided that the *Swedish Railway* case was distinguishable on its facts.[4] Rowlatt J reversing the Commissioners held that the duties which the law imposed on the company fulfilled the idea of residence. The Court of Appeal decided unanimously for the Crown. The company's appeal to the House of Lords was allowed unanimously. The mere satisfaction of the requirements of the Companies Acts could not be sufficient residence otherwise all English companies would be resident here while foreign companies might also be held to be resident here on the *De Beers* principle. The Crown could not have it both ways. In reliance on the *De Beers* principle many English companies had shifted their management overseas to escape UK taxation.[5] Moreover Parliament in F(No 2)A 1915 had adopted a form of words[6] that displays an assumption that a British company could be a non-resident person, a point not

[33.27] Connecting factors

taken in *Swedish Central Rly Co*, but repeated by the two other members of the House to deliver reasoned speeches.[7]

Simon's Taxes D4.104, 108.

---

[1] [1929] AC 1, 14 TC 119.
[2] [1929] AC 1, 14 TC 119, case stated § 8.
[3] [1929] AC 1, 14 TC 119, case stated § 9.
[4] [1929] AC 1, 14 TC 119, case stated § 10.
[5] [1929] AC 1 at 34, 14 TC 119 at 157.
[6] F(No 2)A 1915 consolidated in Income Tax Act 1918, Sch 1, General Rule 7: "Where a non-resident person . . . not being a British company. . ." Vide the judgement of Lord Warrington 14 TC 119 at 163.
[7] Lord Buckmaster, at 37, 159 and Lord Warrington at 40, 162.

[33.28] The reconciliation of these two cases is not easy[1] but, however the cases are reconciled, one can take them as authority for three propositions:

(1) that the test of residence laid down in the *De Beers* case applies to all corporations regardless of the place of registration or incorporation;
(2) that a company may be resident in two places; and
(3) that a finding of dual residence is not to be made unless the control of the general affairs of the company is not centrally placed in one country but is divided among two or more.

It is also clear that residence may be in one country and the company's sole trade carried on in another,[2] and conversely that the mere carrying on of trade in the UK is not sufficient to establish residence here.[3]

Where the 1988 rules apply and a company is resident here through incorporation a dual residence problem cannot arise, since incorporation is the only test.[4] However, dual residence problems will arise when this test does not apply.

Simon's Taxes D4.109.

---

[1] See, amongst others, Dixon J. in *Koitaki Para Rubber Estates Ltd v Federal Comr of Taxation* (1940) 64 CLR 15.
[2] eg *San Paulo (Brazilian) Rly Co v Carter* [1896] AC 31, 3 TC 407. *New Zealand Shipping Co Ltd v Thew* (1922) 8 TC 208, HL.
[3] *A-G v Alexander* (1874) LR 10 Exch 20.
[4] FA 1988, s 66(1).

Relevant control

[33.29] The control which is important, at least for a company under an English type of company law, is that of the directors rather than the shareholders.[1] The shareholders can by virtue of their votes control the corporation; they can compel the directors to do their will[2] but it does not follow that the corporators are managing the corporation. However, the mere fact that English company law takes this view is not conclusive. The question is one of the control of the business and under a foreign system of company law a different conclusion might be justified.

The place of control and management means that of actual control and not the place where control should be exercised. In *Unit Construction Co Ltd v Bullock*[3] three subsidiary companies had been incorporated and registered in Kenya. Their articles of association placed the management and control of the business in the hands of directors and stated that meetings must be held anywhere outside the UK. However, all decisions of major importance and many of minor importance were taken by the parent company in the UK.

The House of Lords held that the three subsidiaries were resident in the UK. As Viscount Simonds put it, "The business is not the less managed in London because it ought to be managed in Kenya."[4]

Simon's Taxes D4.104, 107.

[1] *American Thread Co v Joyce* (1911) 6 TC 1 at 32–3 cf *John Hood & Co Ltd v Magee* (1918) 7 TC 327 at 351, 353, 358.
[2] But only by dismissal—*Automatic Self Cleansing Filter Syndicate Co Ltd v Cunninghame* [1906] 2 Ch 34.
[3] [1960] AC 351, 38 TC 712.
[4] [1960] AC 363, 736.

The statutory test of incorporation in the UK

[33.30] There is a second test. A company which is incorporated in the UK is resident in the UK for tax purposes; such a company is not also resident where its central management and control exists.[1] The introduction of this incorporation test in 1988 was a major change which brought the UK tax system into line with the tax system of the majority of developed countries.

This rule is, however, frequently overridden by specific provision in a double taxation agreement.

Where a company would be treated as resident in the UK under this rule but as non-resident under the terms of an applicable double taxation agreement it is now to be treated as non-resident for all UK tax purposes.[2]

The introduction of the test based on incorporation does not mean the abolition of the old case law test that a company is resident where its central management and control are to be found. The test of residence at the place of central management and control remains particularly important where the company is incorporated abroad.

Simon's Taxes D4.101, 103, 108.

[1] FA 1988, s 66(1).
[2] FA 1994, s 249.

Connecting factors

Dual resident investing companies

[33.31] Certain reliefs are restricted where a company is resident under the domestic tax systems of the UK and another country.[1] The problem may be illustrated simply.

When a company is incorporated in the USA, but has its central management and control in the UK, it will be treated as resident in the USA under US rules and in the UK under UK rules. Such a company is able to use many UK reliefs, such as loss relief and capital allowances on the basis that it is a UK resident company and will be able to pass the benefit of those reliefs to other companies within its group notwithstanding that it is also resident in the USA and so able to claim reliefs under that tax system as well. Particular problems arise from the payment of interest. The dual resident company can pass the benefit of such a payment to other companies in the US and UK groups and so get relief twice. Where the borrowing is from another company within the multinational's structure the recipient of the interest will perhaps pay tax once but this will be more than off set by the double relief.

Restrictions now apply where the company is a "dual resident investment company".[2] The process of defining an investment company is tortuous; it begins with a rule of exclusion—an investment company is one which is not a trading company; however, the term trading company is itself defined so as to exclude a company whose main function is to carry on all or any of various activities such as acquiring and holding shares in dual resident companies or raising finance; this is backed up by the exclusion of other companies carrying on such activities to an extent which does not appear to be justified by any trade it does carry on or for a purpose which does not appear to be appropriate to any such trade.[3]

The reliefs restricted are those relevant to group relief, ie losses, excess capital allowances, expenses of management and charges on income.[4] However, there are further provisions dealing with certain intra group transactions for capital allowances purposes.[5] There are also restrictions on the operation of TA 1988, s 343 (see supra, § **25.27**), TCGA 1992, s 171 (see supra, § **28.21**) and TCGA 1992, s 175.[6]

These rules are seen as complementary to the US 1986 provisions.[7] The effect is to ban relief under the rules of both systems where a dual resident company makes the payment and so to encourage the group to ensure that deductible payments are in future made only by companies which are resident in only one jurisdiction.

Simon's Taxes D4.109.

---

[1] The proposal to restrict these reliefs goes back to a consultative document issued by the Revenue in November 1984; the provisions in F(No 2)A 1987 are based on draft clauses published in December 1986. On capital gains position note repeal of TCGA 1992, s 188 by FA 1994, s 251(10).
[2] TA 1988, s 404(1) adapted for the 1996 loan relationship rules by FA 1996, Sch 14, para 21.
[3] TA 1988, s 404(6).
[4] TA 1988, s 404(2).

⁵ CAA 2001, ss 266, 267, 570(2), 577(1); all these provisions are concerned with a right to take a price other than market value as the basis for capital allowances.
⁶ TA 1988, s 343(2), TCGA 1992, ss 171(2), 175(2).
⁷ IRC § 1503(d) introduced by Tax Reform Act 1986, § 1249; for a comparison of the two sets of rules see *Law Society's Gazette*, 11 March 1987, pp 713, 714.

Ordinary residence

[33.32] No point in Revenue law seems to turn now on the distinction between residence and ordinary residence of corporations. In *Re Little Olympian Each Ways Ltd*[1] the ordinary residence of a company was equated with its residence and, accordingly, it was necessary to ascertain the location of its central control management. However, it is more difficult for a company to be ordinarily resident in more than one place than it is for it to have dual residence.[2] It was apparently admitted in *Union Corpn v IRC*[3] that residence and ordinary residence of companies were coextensive.

Simon's Taxes D4.104, 107.

¹ [1995] 1 WLR 560.
² *Re Little Olympian Each Ways Ltd* [1994] 4 All ER 561, [1995] 1 WLR 560 at 565.
³ This case arose in the context of a claimant giving security for the defendant's costs of an action, which is by reference to ordinary residence.

Domicile

[33.33] When one refers to the domicile of a person, one is stating the law that governs the status of that person. If the person is a corporation, it can be so only by virtue of the law by which it was incorporated. It is to this law alone that all questions concerning the creation and dissolution of the corporate status are referred.[1] The domicile of a corporation cannot be changed. It cannot be converted into a domicile of choice.[2]

¹ *Lazard Bros & Co v Midland Bank Ltd* [1933] AC 289 at 297.
² *Gasque v IRC* [1940] 2 KB 80.

Tax presence

[33.34] In *Clark v Oceanic Contractors Inc*[1] the House of Lords invented a new connecting factor-tax presence. This is a presence sufficient to make the PAYE system applicable; see supra, § **7.148**.

Simon's Taxes E4.122.

¹ [1983] STC 35.

Certification of residence

[33.35] For the purpose of claiming relief under the terms of a double taxation agreement, it is often necessary to obtain a certificate from HMRC

[33.35] Connecting factors

that a company is regarded as resident in the UK. HMRC practice is to certify residence on a form designed for use for the specific double taxation agreement, if there is one. The test of residence then applied is the test under UK law, as amended by the specific provisions of the specific double tax agreement. It is only when the double tax agreement does not specify a form that the Revenue is prepared to issue a letter certifying residence. Before issuing such a letter the Revenue require details of the nature of the proposed transaction and any resulting income, in connection with which the letter of certification is to be presented to the foreign Revenue authority.[1]

---

[1] Details of the Revenue's approach and the information required are given in Inland Revenue Tax Bulletin December 2002, pp 989–991.

Change of corporate residence—TA 1988, ss 765–767

[33.36] In the absence of any targeted legislation, it would be possible for a UK resident company with foreign subsidiaries to move value out of the UK and outside the scope of UK taxation by making changes in the structure of the overseas subsidiaries, where these are not resident in the UK and not subject to UK tax.

If a body corporate which is resident in the UK wishes to cause or permit its non-resident subsidiary to create or issue any shares or debentures, statute requires the company to obtain the consent of the UK Treasury.[1] Free movement of capital is, however, required within the European Community. If the change of capital is intra-EC, then there is simply a duty to report.[2]

The sanction for failure to obtain Treasury consent for the creation of shares in a non-resident subsidiary, etc, is a criminal sanction, under which each director of the UK company can be imprisoned for up to two years;[3] apparently no prosecution has ever been brought.

On deemed disposals see supra, §§ **25.46** ff.

Simon's Taxes D4.132.

---

[1] TA 1988, s 765(1)(c). On history see HMRC International Taxation Handbook, Chapter 13.

[2] TA 1988, s 765A added by FA 1990, s 68(2), (4); amendments to TMA 1970, s 98 are made by s 68(3). See also the Movements of Capital (Required Information) Regulations 1990, SI 1990/1671. HMRC views on the boundary between the duty to report and the need to obtain consent are explained in a Revenue document (SP 2/92). A similar consent or duty to report is needed if the resident body corporate wishes to transfer shares or debentures of its non-resident subsidiary; this consent is only needed if the resident body owns or has an interest in the shares or debentures and is not needed if the transfer is for the purpose of enabling a person to be qualified to act as a director (TA 1988, s 765(1)(d)). This is all that remains of a wider power (Sub-ss 1(a), (b) were repealed by FA 1988, Sch 14, Part IV); under that provision Treasury consent was needed for a company to cease to be resident in the UK (the validity of this control was upheld by the European Court—*R v HM Treasury, ex p Daily Mail and General Trust plc* [1988] STC

787—neither art 52 nor art 58 were breached).
3. TA 1988, s 766. Sub-s (2) provides a statutory presumption that each director of the company was a party to the act of the company and was aware that he was performing an unlawful act.

Treasury General Consents

[33.37] The requirement to obtain Treasury consent for a wide variety of corporate restructuring when there is an overseas subsidiary has, in practice, been made considerably less onerous by the issue of "Treasury General Consents".[1]

Where the creation, issue or transfer of shares or debentures is within the parameters specified in the Treasury General Consents, no application to the Treasury is required.

Treasury General Consents apply to the creation or issue of shares or debentures within the following parameters:[2]

(a) the creation of shares by the non-resident company;
(b) the issue of shares by the non-resident company;
   (i) to another member of the overseas group, or
   (ii) subject to the conditions prescribed by para 4, to the resident company or to another member of the resident group, or
   (iii) subject to the conditions prescribed by para 5, to a person not connected with the resident company, or
   (iv) subject to the conditions prescribed by para 6, to all persons who are its shareholders at the time of the issue;
(c) the creation of debentures by the non-resident company and their issue:
   (i) to another member of the overseas group, or
   (ii) subject to the condition prescribed by para 7, to the resident company or to another member of the resident group, or
   (iii) subject to the conditions prescribed by para 5, to persons not connected with the resident company;
(d) transactions of any kind described in sub-s (1)(c) where the non-resident company:
   (i) was incorporated after 31 December 1951,
   (ii) is liable to tax in a Commonwealth territory other than the UK by reason of domicile, residence or place of management, and
   (iii) was incorporated for the purpose of starting and carrying on a new industrial activity in that Commonwealth territory,
   and in this sub-paragraph "industrial activity" means any productive, extractive or manufacturing industry, any public utility, fisheries or any form of husbandry.

Treasury General Consents apply to the transfer or issue of shares or debentures within the following parameters:

(a) the transfer by the resident company of shares or debentures of the non-resident company to another member of the resident group;

(b) subject to the conditions prescribed by para 9, the transfer by the resident company or by a company which is not resident in the UK (in para 9 referred to in either case as "the transferor company") of shares or debentures of the non-resident company to a person not connected with the resident company;

(c) the transfer by a company which is not resident in the UK of shares or debentures of the non-resident company to a company which is a member of a territorial group of which the first mentioned company is also a member.

---

[1] The Treasury General Consents were issued in 1988 and amended on 28 July 2000 to reflect the amendments to the statutory definition of a "group". The full wording of the consent, with information on the procedures to be adopted and Treasury guidance notes are given in Butterworths Yellow Tax Handbook, Part II, Misc VI.

[2] The categories of action listed here are subject to detailed provisions that are specified in the Treasury General Consents.

Partnership

Residence

[33.38] In order to apply the provisions of a double taxation agreement, it is sometimes necessary to determine where a partnership is resident. In *Padmore v IRC*,[1] the Court of Appeal held that a trading partnership is resident where the control and management of the trade is situated regardless of the residence of the partners.[2]

The liability to UK income tax is, however, not determined by the residence of a partner but by the residence of each individual partner, whether or not the partnership is carrying on a trade.

There is no reported case on other unincorporated bodies.

---

[1] [1989] STC 493, CA. ITTOIA 2005, s 857.

[2] The exemption from tax gained by the individual partner in *Padmore v IRC* is excluded for subsequent years by the enactment of FA 1995, s 125(3), which amends TA 1988, s 112(4) & (5) (now ITTOIA 2005, s 858). This forms the subject matter of an unsuccessful claim for tax exemption brought by an individual partner in *Padmore v IRC (No 2)* [2001] STC 280.

Trustees

Residence

Income tax

[33.39] The position with regard to trustees is now governed by legislation. For CGT it has long been established that the trust is non-resident if the majority of the trustees are non-resident and the trust is ordinarily administered overseas.[1] However, there was no direct provision for income tax. The Revenue view was that the residence of one trustee within the UK was enough to make the whole trust liable to UK income tax on the basis of residence. However, this view was rejected by the House of Lords in *Dawson v IRC*.[2] Parliament responded by passing FA 1989, s 110.

FA 1989, s 110 applies only where one of the trustees is resident in the UK and another is not. It has no application where all the trustees are resident or non-resident. Where trustees have mixed residence they will be treated as UK residents if the settlor was resident, ordinarily resident or domiciled in the UK at any time when he put funds into the settlement.[3] In the case of a testamentary trust the critical time is the date of death. The effect of these rules is that a settlement with a UK settlor will be taxed on its foreign income so long as there is at least one UK resident trustee. Conversely a foreign settlor will be able to appoint UK trustees and preserve non-resident status for the trust by ensuring that he retains at least one non-resident trustee.[4] As a non-resident body the provisions of ITA 2007, Pt 13, Ch 2 (Transfer of assets abroad) may fall to be considered.

Simon's Taxes D4.808, E6.135.

---

1. TCGA 1992, s 69(1), (2) (infra, § **35.55**). For a decision on the different question of where a trust is effectively managed, a question which arises in the context of double taxation treaties, see *Wensleydale's Settlement Trustees v IRC* [1996] STC (SCD) 241.
2. [1989] STC 473.
3. FA 1989, s 110(2), (3); there is a wide definition of settlor in sub-s (4).
4. Hansard Standing Committee G, 22 June 1989, cols 609, 610. Quaere whether any action could lie against the non-resident trustee if he were to become a UK resident, eg by staying in the UK for more than six months in a year of assessment.

Capital gains tax

[33.40] Trustees do not take over the residence of their settlor; they are treated as resident and ordinarily resident in the UK unless the majority of them are not so resident and the general administration of the trust is ordinarily carried on overseas.[1] The assessment may be made on all the trustees or on those resident in the UK.[2] In *Roome v Edwards*[3] an assessment on UK trustees of a part of the fund was upheld even though the gain accrued to the trustees of another part, all those trustees being non-resident.

When some of the trustees are UK-resident and some are not, the test of residence is applied by treating any professional trustee as if he were not

[33.40] Connecting factors

resident in the UK. Thus, in *Green v Cobham*[4] there were ten trustees of the trust, being five individuals not resident in the UK plus four UK-resident individuals plus Mr Mellowes. The administration of the trust was carried out in the British Virgin Islands. Mr Mellowes was a solicitor in practice, resident in the UK. As Mr Mellowes was a professional trustee, he was counted as if he were not resident and, hence, the trust was a non-resident trust. On 31 December 1990, Mr Mellowes retired from practice but remained a trustee. This had the effect that, from 1 January 1991 onwards, he is treated as having his actual residence status and, thus, his retirement caused the trust to be a UK resident trust from that date onwards, as the majority of the trustees was no longer not resident in the UK. The trustees were not aware of the true position. They made an appointment which, if it were made by a UK trust, would give a substantial tax liability[5] but no liability if it were made by a non-resident trust. The Court granted an application that the appointment was made by mistake, in ignorance of its true effect and, under the doctrine in *Hastings-Bass v IRC*[6] should be declared void.

Trustees may cease to be resident in the UK but they remain subject to UK capital gains tax on disposals made during the remainder of the tax year.[7] A migration within six years of the creation of the settlement may cause the tax held over on the creation of the settlement to fall due.[8]

Simon's Taxes Division C4.4; Sumption CGT A3.08.

[1] TCGA 1992, s 69(1) amended, with effect from 6 April 2007 by FA 2006, Sch 12, paras 30–41. The rule is relaxed for professional trustees of a trust created by a person resident and domiciled outside the UK; TCGA 1992, s 69(2). On Revenue practice see statement of practice SP 5/92, paras 2, 3.

[2] TCGA 1992, s 65.

[3] [1981] STC 96, [1981] 1 All ER 736, HL.

[4] [2002] STC 820.

[5] TCGA 1992, s 13 applied to a UK-resident trust, with the effect that accumulated gains of £35,000,000 in the underlying company would be charged on the UK resident trustees.

[6] *Re Hastings-Bass, Hastings-Bass v IRC* [1974] STC 211, CA. In that case, Buckley LJ said (at 221f):

In our judgement, where by the terms of a trust (as under s 32) a trustee is given a discretion as to some matter under which he acts in good faith, the court should not interfere with his action notwithstanding that it does not have the full effect which he intended, unless (1) what he has achieved is unauthorised by the power conferred on him, or (2) it is clear that he would not have acted as he did (a) had he not taken into account considerations which he should not have taken into account, or (b) had he not failed to take into considerations which he ought to have taken into account.

[7] The (restricted) concession allowing individuals who have been resident for a short period then to be treated as non-resident for the remainder of the year in which they migrate does not apply to trustees in their capacity as trustees: extra-statutory concession A11.

[8] TCGA 1992, s 168.

Domicile

[33.41] Every individual has a domicile and the concept of domicile extends to partnerships and (with difficulty) to companies. The concept of domicile does not, however, extend to a trust. ITTOIA 2005, s 832 applies the remittance basis for income arising to a non-domiciled "person". A trust is not a "person", hence it is not necessary to attribute a domicile to a body of trustees.

Personal representatives

Residence

[33.42] When the estate of a deceased person has appointed personal representatives, some of whom are resident in the UK and some not, statute[1] applies the same test for income tax as for mixed resident trustees.

[1] FA 1989, s 111.

European economic interest groupings

[33.43] A European Economic Interest Grouping (EEIG) is a form of business entity set up by enterprises of two or more member states.[1] It is intended to be an attractive vehicle for international co-operation within the EC among enterprises which may include companies and other bodies subject to corporation tax or partnerships or sole traders, which are subject to income tax. The purposes for which the EEIG may be formed include such activities as packaging, processing, marketing or research which are ancillary to the business of and which are for the common benefit of members of the EEIG. A EEIG may not be formed in order to make profits for itself.[2] The scope for using EEIGs is therefore very limited.

The principle to be applied in charging a EEIG to tax is fiscal transparency; the grouping is simply an agent for its members.[3] Any profits of the EEIG are to be taxed in the hands of the members only and not at the level of the EEIG. Subject to any contractual arrangements, shares are governed by the share of profits to which the members are entitled under the contract.[4] Where, however, no trade or profession is carried on, a member joining a EEIG is treated as acquiring a proportionate share in the assets of the EEIG; likewise on disposal there is a disposal of a share in the assets then held; a disposal of the assets by the EEIG is treated as a disposal by the members of their shares in the assets.[5] Contributions towards running expenses and capital allowances for contributions towards capital expenditure are determined according to the normal rules.[6] However, this principle of fiscal transparency does not apply to machinery provisions. Thus where the EEIG is a UK registered company it may have to deduct tax at source of making a payment of interest or other charge on income.[7]

[33.43] Connecting factors

This simple outline of the legislation masks many conceptual and practical problems.[8] These entities are the subject of their own HMRC manual.
Simon's Taxes D4.501.

[1] TA 1988, s 510A; the grouping is in pursuance of Council Regulation (EEC) No. 2137/85 of 25 July 1985. There are information gathering powers in TMA 1970, s 12A, penalty provisions in s 98B.
[2] Inland Revenue press release, 19 April 1990, *Simon's Tax Intelligence* 1990, p 382 citing Article 3.1. of the Council Regulation No. 2137/85.
[3] TA 1988, s 510A(2).
[4] TA 1988, s 510A(4), (5); if the contract makes no provision equal shares are presumed—sub-s (5).
[5] TA 1988, s 510A(3)(*b*).
[6] Inland Revenue press release, 19 April 1990, *Simon's Tax Intelligence* 1990, p 382, para 2.
[7] Under ITA 2007, Pt 15.
[8] See Anderson *European Economic Interest Groupings* (1990) Chs 4, 8; Wales (1990) BTR p 335 and *Tax Review* pp 86, 90.

34

Enforcement of foreign revenue laws

Taxes of other EC states	PARA 34.01
General principle	PARA 34.02
Consequences in the UK	PARA 34.04
Consequences in a foreign jurisdiction	PARA 34.06
Double taxation treaties	PARA 34.07
Exchange of information	PARA 34.08

Taxes of other EC states

[34.01] In a fundamental change to previously generally accepted international practice, FA 2002 authorises courts in the UK to take proceedings in respect of claims for taxation levied in other EC states,[1] by providing that the law relating to claims for the payment of UK tax shall apply "with any necessary adaptations" in relation to the claim for the foreign tax. Proceedings in the UK are taken by the appropriate Revenue department, acting on behalf of its foreign counterpart.[2] Proceedings are taken by HMRC for the taxes that are the subject of this book.

The background to the UK legislation is the EC Mutual Assistance Recovery Directive.[3] FA 2002 has the effect that any tax charge imposed by any EC public authority that is declared to be within the Mutual Assistance Recovery Directive can be collected in the UK,[4] irrespective as to whether the foreign tax has a UK equivalent. Thus, proceedings before a court in the UK would be taken by the UK HMRC for the collection of church tax that is imposed in Denmark on income and capital.[5]

A member of the HMRC is prohibited from passing information on a taxpayer to another UK Government department.[6] However, this prohibition is disapplied by statute when action is taken in relation to the EC Directive on exchange of information.[7] In such a case, a member of the UK Revenue can pass any information within the EC Mutual Assistance Directive to the relevant tax authority in the other EC state.[8]

The detailed operation of the administrative cooperation is the subject of regulations in a statutory instrument.

---

1   FA 2002, Sch 39, para 2(1)(*a*).
2   FA 2002, Sch 39, para 2(2) and (1)(*a*).
3   Council Directive 76/308/EEC supplemented by Directive 2002/94/EC, as amended by Directive 2004/79/EC: FA 2002, s 134(2) and the Act of Accession 2003.
4   The Treasury is empowered to make regulations for the application, non-application or adaption of any statutory provision or rule of law to enable the collection of a foreign tax, but any statutory instrument made by the Treasury is

subject to annulment by a resolution of the House of Commons: FA 2002, Sch 39, paras 3(4) & (5). Statute permits the Treasury to make regulations in the future to give effect to future amendments of the Mutual Assistance Recovery Directive: FA 2002, s 134(6).

[5] The example is taken from *Explanatory notes, Finance Bill 2002*, published by HM Treasury, 24 April 2002, Clause 131, Note 15. It would be interesting to see the Court's approach to the Human Rights argument that Church Tax is discriminatory in that Danish Law provides that the tax be levied on those who declared themselves to be members of the Catholic Church or the Lutheran Church but is not levied on those who are members of a non-Danish church, for example, the Church of England.

[6] Prior to 18 April 2005, the prohibition arose from the statutory declaration made by each HM Inspector of Taxes on appointment, under the terms of TMA 1970, Sch 1, Part III. This statutory declaration is repealed for all Revenue officers being appointed on or after 18 April 2005: CRCA 2005, Sch 4, para 13.

[7] Directive 77/799/EEC; see, in particular, the preamble.

[8] FA 2003, s 197 (as amended by SI 2003/3092) and SI 2004/674 (as amended by SI 2004/800) gives effect to Directive 77/799/EEC (as amended by Directives 2003/93/EC and 2004/56/EC) in respect of "taxes on income and capital", insurance premium tax and excise duties. These provisions previously applied also to VAT; VAT was removed from the scope of these provisions by SI 2003/3092 as regards the UK and by the 2003 Directive as regards the EC generally. The provisions for exchange of information on VAT are Reg (EC) No 1798/2003. As this regulation has direct effect, it does not require to be mentioned in UK legislation: see also infra, § **63.03**.

General principle

[34.02] Apart from proceedings under the EC Mutual Assistance Recovery Directive (see supra, § **34.01**), UK courts decline to exercise jurisdiction to entertain a suit for the enforcement of the revenue law of another country;[1] nor can a foreign judgment for a sum payable in respect of taxes be registered under the Foreign Judgments (Reciprocal Enforcement) Act 1933.[2] Following the same approach it has been held that such a judgment is not a civil matter within art 1 of the Brussels Convention.[3] Where a foreign government had successfully sued in its own courts for tax due to it and recovered the tax but not the costs, it was not able to sue for the costs in the UK since no separate claim lies for costs under English or Scottish law.[4] What is a revenue law is a matter for the lex fori. It has extended to compulsory contributions to a state insurance scheme since a compulsory contribution levied by a state organisation is a revenue matter.[5] A payment for services supplied by the state would, however, seem to fall outside this definition, at least where there is some choice over whether to accept the services.

Current UK insolvency legislation provides for assistance between courts in territories designated by the Secretary of State. The matter arises where X is insolvent in one state, owing tax there, but has assets in another state. The legislation as interpreted by the courts in other countries allows the trustee in bankruptcy or receiver to get at the assets in the other country; however it should be noted that none of these cases concerns the situation in which the only creditor is the tax authority.[6] In *QRS 1 Aps v Frandsen*[7] the court declined an invitation to allow the Brussels convention to be used when the only creditor was a foreign tax authority.

---

[1] *Government of India v Taylor* [1955] AC 491, [1955] 1 All ER 292; noted 3 ICLQ 161 & 465; 4 ICLQ 564. See also *Re State of Norway's Application* [1990] 1 AC 723, [1989] 1 All ER 745, HL and the curious case of *Re Tucker* [1990] Ch 148, CA. See generally Carter, 1989 CLJ, 417.

[2] Section 1(2)(*b*).

[3] The Convention on Jurisdiction and Enforcement of Judgment in Civil and Commercial matters; see *QRS 1 Aps v Frandsen* [1999] STC 616, CA.

[4] *A-G for Canada v William Schulze & Co* 1901 9 SLT 4.

[5] *Metal Industries (Salvage) Ltd v ST Harle (Owners)* 1962 SLT 114 (employer's contribution); however issues which have been held not to be revenue matters include exchange control (*Kahler v Midland Bank Ltd* [1950] AC 24, [1949] 2 All ER 621) and a legal aid contribution (*Connor v Connor* [1974] 1 NZLR 632).

[6] See Baker in *Tolley's International Tax Planning*, para 33.4 and note JFAJ [1991] BTR 109 on an unsatisfactory case from Florida.

[7] [1999] 3 All ER 289.

[34.03] The general principle given above probably originates in a dictum of Lord Mansfield in 1775[1] when, upholding a vendor's claim for the purchase money due on goods sold in France and which the purchaser intended, to the vendor's knowledge, to smuggle into England, he said that 'no country ever takes notice of the revenue laws of another'. The proper law of the contract being French, English law was irrelevant.

The principle extends to an indirect attempt to enforce a foreign revenue law as is shown by the Irish decision in *Peter Buchanan Ltd and MacHarg v McVey*.[2] The taxpayer, a director of a Scottish company, had disposed of his shares in two other companies and, after full disclosure to the UK Inland Revenue, was assured that the deal did not involve excess profits levy. Subsequently the levy was retrospectively applied to the taxpayer. He therefore arranged to transfer his stock of whisky and his private assets to safe hands in Ireland, followed his wealth to Ireland and thought that "he might safely snap his hands in the face of the disgruntled Scottish Revenue". The liquidator of Peter Buchanan Ltd, a man admittedly chosen by the Revenue because of his potentialities as a financial Sherlock Holmes, then sued in the Irish courts on the ground that the stripping of the company's assets was ultra vires the company and a breach of his duty as director. The action was dismissed on the ground that it was in substance an indirect attempt to enforce the revenue laws of another country. At first instance Kingsmill Moore J placed some weight on the fact that the Inland Revenue was the only unpaid creditor but this point was not touched on by the Supreme Court of Eire.

[1] *Holman v Johnson* (1775) 1 Cowp 341.
[2] [1954] IR 89.

Consequences in the UK

[34.04] The result of the rule is to permit a person to avoid his tax liability to a foreign country by bringing himself and his wealth within the UK. However, the rule is that UK courts will not enforce a foreign revenue law not that they will not recognise it. Thus in *Regazzoni v KC Sethia (1944) Ltd* Viscount Simonds said: 'It does not follow from the fact that today the court will not enforce a revenue law at the suit of a foreign state that today it will enforce a contract which requires the doing of an act in a foreign country which violates the revenue laws of that country'[1], a statement which may limit the initial decision of Lord Mansfield.

More recently the courts have distinguished enforcing the foreign revenue law from enforcing the consequences of that revenue law.[2]

In *Brokaw v Seatrain UK Ltd*[3] household goods were on the high seas on a US ship sailing from Baltimore to England when the US Treasury served a notice of levy on the shipowner and demanded the surrender of all property in their possession. When the ship reached England the US Government claimed possession and the consignees of the goods sued the shipowners in detinue. It was held that the service of the notice of levy was insufficient to reduce the goods into the possession of the US Government and therefore that Government has to rely upon its revenue law to support its claim to possession.

If, however, the notice of the levy had been sufficient, under English conflict of law rules, to reduce goods into the possession of the US Government, that claim would have been enforced because the English courts would then be enforcing an actual possessory title and not a revenue law.[4] How this can be reconciled with those cases in which the courts have refused indirectly to enforce a revenue law is a difficult matter.[5] Perhaps a proprietary claim cannot be an indirect enforcement whereas a personal claim may be.[6]

The English courts have also held that a person can be extradited for an offence of fraud falling within the relevant treaty even though the fraud relates to a tax matter.[7]

[1] [1957] 3 All ER 286 at 292.
[2] The line is not easy to draw. See Dicey and Morris, *Conflict of Laws* Rule 3, p 102.
[3] [1971] 2 QB 476, [1971] 2 All ER 98.
[4] *Brokaw v Seatrain UK Ltd* 100, 482. Cf *Singh v Ali* [1960] AC 167, [1960] 1 All ER 269.
[5] *Peter Buchanan Ltd v McVey* (infra, § **35.02**); see also *Jones v Borland* (1969) 4 SA 29 and *Rossano v Manufacturer's Life Insurance Co Ltd* [1962] 2 All ER 214, [1963] 2 QB 352. If a foreign court made a person bankrupt for non-payment of tax, how far would the UK courts go in deciding the consequences of that status?

6   Thus if a foreign country holds X liable for Y's tax (cf TMA 1970, s 78) can X bring an action on an indemnity against Y in the UK courts? Such a claim succeeded in *Re Reid* (1970) 17 DLR (3d) 199.
7   *R v Chief Metropolitan Stipendiary Magistrate, ex p Secretary of State for the Home Department* [1989] 1 All ER 151, [1988] 1 WLR 1204, DC.

[34.05] Since a foreign tax law cannot be enforced in the UK courts it follows that it cannot give rise to a legal obligation enforceable here; it might in turn follow that for a trustee to pay such a tax would be a breach of trust. However, in deciding such issues the court must pay attention to the consequences for the trust of non-payment. These points emerge from *Re Lord Cable's Will Trusts, Garret v Waters*.[1] The issue was whether the court should grant an injunction to prevent the passing of money from the UK to trustees in India given that the primary purpose of the payment was to enable the trustees to make payments due under the Indian exchange control legislation. If the payment was not made the trustees were liable to imprisonment and to a penalty of up to five times the sum involved. Slade J refused to grant an injunction.

This leaves various questions open. First, would the position be the same for a tax as for exchange control? The answer appears to be yes, since Slade J went on to consider obiter the position of payments of Indian estate duty.[2] Second, would it be a breach of trust for the trustees to pay? The refusal of an injunction to prevent the trustees from paying is not conclusive of this issue; however, Slade J said that the reimbursement of the trustees from the trust funds in respect of estate duty so paid would be a proper payment.[3] Third, would it be a breach of trust not to pay? The effects for the trust fund would be so drastic that it would appear that the trustee's general duty to preserve the trust fund would require him to pay and so would make it a breach of trust not to pay. However, both in relation to this and the second point it must be remembered that this was a case of an Indian trust with funds and trustees in India; had there been no such connection with the country asserting a claim against the trust funds, a different result might have followed as indeed might have been the case if the consequences of non-payment had been minimal.

1   [1976] 3 All ER 417.
2   [1976] 3 All ER 417 at 435, 436.
3   [1976] 3 All ER 417 at 435, 436, citing *Re Reid* (1970) 17 DLR (3d) 199 (Canada) and explaining dicta of Lord Robertson in *Scottish National Orchestra Society Ltd v Thomson's Executors* 1969 SLT 325 at 330. This would distinguish the payment of a foreign tax from the payment of a statute barred debt.

Consequences in a foreign jurisdiction

[34.06] Other problems arise when a foreign country will regard payment of UK tax as a breach of trust where it is not specifically permitted under the deed establishing the trust.[1] There is considerable variation between different countries on these issues.[2]

[34.06] Enforcement of foreign revenue laws

The general principle that proceedings cannot be taken in one jurisdiction that arise from a tax liability arising in another jurisdiction can cause a severe problem for UK-resident trustees who resign on the appointment of trustees overseas. It is commonplace for a deed of resignation to incorporate an indemnity under which the resigning trustees will seek to be reimbursed by their successors for any tax charge levied on them, whether anticipated or not. If the successor trustees in another jurisdiction fail to reimburse their UK-resident predecessors, it is likely that the overseas jurisdiction will refuse to order the new trustees to pay under the indemnity as such an order would be the indirect enforcement of a foreign Revenue law. This is of little comfort to the UK-resident former trustees, for whom the tax liability is a personal liability.[3]

[1] In *Re T's Settlement* (6 February 2002, unreported), an application to vary the trust deed under the trust (Jersey law 1984 Articles 43 and 47), the Jersey court held (at para 27) that it would be a breach of trust for the Jersey trustees to reimburse the UK resident settlor with the UK capital gains tax charge that was levied on the settlor by TCGA 1992, s 86 for gains made by the Jersey trustees, such reimbursement being a statutory right under UK law by virtue of TCGA 1992, Sch 5, para 6. The statement of the court is, however, obiter and the point was not argued before the court as both counsel proceeded on the assumption that this would be a breach of trust.
[2] Baker, *Tolley's International Tax Planning*, para 33.6.
[3] TMA 1970 s 71(1).

Double taxation treaties

[34.07] Most double tax treaties attempt to counter some evasion techniques by providing for the exchange of information.[1] Some treaties, although none involving the UK, actually make provision for the mutual enforcement of tax claims.[2] Some treaties require mutual assistance in recovering tax due to ensure that treaty benefits are not given to people who are not entitled to them.[3]

On obligations to exchange information with other EC Member states see supra, § **34.01**.

[1] The experience has not been happy—see 50 Col LR 490. There is no such clause in the UK–US Treaty.
[2] OECD Model, art 26. On whether the treaty requires the UK tax authorities to provide information to a foreign tax authority if there is no UK tax in issue.
[3] OECD Model Agreement Art 26.

Exchange of information

[34.08] The declaration made by each Inspector of Taxes appointed prior to 18 April 2005[1] is that no information will be disclosed "except for the purposes of my duties . . . or in such other cases as made as required by law".

The Council of the European Union has issued a directive ("the Mutual Assistance Directive") which provides for information to pass between the Revenue departments of member states. UK statute[2] now provides that the obligation of secrecy imposed on an Inspector does not prevent him from disclosing information required under the Mutual Assistance Directive to the authority of another member state.

Under the Mutual Assistance Directive, the UK Revenue may obtain information from the Revenue authority of another EC member state. Statute[3] requires that the UK Revenue may not then use the information to obtain information for any purpose other than taxation.

Double taxation agreements entered into between the UK and other territories commonly contain powers to exchange information. When there is no double taxation agreement with a particular territory, statute[4] authorises the UK to enter into a tax information exchange agreement with the tax authorities of the other territory. The information exchanged must be "foreseeably relevant to the administration or enforcement" of tax legislation.[5]

Statutory provision has been made[6] for the exchange of information between the UK Revenue and the Revenue authorities of other EU member states in relation to EU directives on savings income.

---

[1] TMA 1970, Sch 1, Part III. Prior to 18 April 2005, the prohibition arose from the statutory declaration made by each HM Inspector of Taxes on appointment, under the terms of TMA 1970, Sch 1, Part III. This statutory declaration is repealed for all Revenue officers being appointed on or after 18 April 2005: CRCA 2005, Sch 4, para 13.

[2] F(No 2)A 2005, s 68. This replaces the procedure in FA 2003, s 197, the major difference being that, with effect from requests received on or after 1 January 2005, there is no longer a statutory obligation on the person providing the information to be satisfied that the Revenue authority in the other state is bound by rules of confidentiality that are at least as strict as those applying in the UK.

[3] FA 2003, s 197(3).

[4] TA 1988, ss 788(2) and 815C(1) for income tax, capital gains tax and corporation tax and IHTA 1984, s 158(1A) for inheritance tax.

[5] Amended by FA 2003, s 198(3).

[6] FA 2003, s 199.

35

Foreign income and capital gains of residents

Place of trade	PARA 35.02
The remittance basis	PARA 35.12
Relief for unremittable foreign income	PARA 35.24
Transfers of assets abroad—attribution of income	PARA 35.26
Offshore funds	PARA 35.40
Capital gains tax	PARA 35.46
Overseas trusts	PARA 35.55
Controlled foreign companies resident in low tax areas	PARA 35.64

[35.01] A person resident in the UK, whether an individual, a body of trustees or a company is, in principle, subject to UK tax on overseas income, but the extent of the liability may be affected by the status of the person. Thus, for example, an individual who is domiciled within the UK is subject to overseas income as it arises: whereas an individual whose domicile is outside the UK might be subject to overseas income when it is remitted to the UK (see supra, § **33.16**). The significance of place of trade is now largely a question of the application of the relevant double tax agreement, if any. For income tax, the abolition of the Schedular system for trading income[1] gives the same computational rules irrespective of the location of the trade. However, for corporation tax, the location of a trade continues to determine the Schedule under which the trading profit is taxed.[2]

---

[1] See supra, § **5.03**.

[2] ITTOIA 2005 has no application for corporation tax. TA 1988, s 6(1) continues to impose a charge to corporation tax on "the profits" of a company. TA 1988, s 9(1) then states that the amount of any income is to be computed "in accordance with income tax principles". Post-ITTOIA 2005, this is a strange provision. The hybrid nature is apparent from the wording of TA 1988, s 9, as now amended by ITTOIA 2005, Sch 1, para 7:

  (2) For the purposes of this section 'income tax law' means, in relation to any accounting period, the law applying, for the year of assessment in which the period ends, to the charge on individuals of income tax, except that it does not include such of the enactments of the Income Tax Acts as make special provision for individuals in relation to matters referred to in subsection (1) above.

  (2A) But no income shall be computed, and no assessment shall be made, for purposes of corporation tax under ITTOIA 2005.

  (2B) Instead, income shall continue to be computed, and the assessment shall continue to be made, for purposes of corporation tax under Schedules A and D and the Cases of Schedule D.

  (2C) For (but only for) the purposes of continuing to apply for purposes of corporation tax, those Schedules and Cases are treated as if they were still part of income tax law (and therefore applied in accordance with subsection (1) above for purposes of corporation tax).

(3) Accordingly, for purposes of corporation tax, income shall be computed, and the assessment shall be made, under—

    (a) Schedules A and D, and the Cases of Schedule D, and
    (b) the following provisions of ITEPA 2003 (which impose charges to income tax)—
        (i) Part 2 (employment income),
        (ii) Part 9 (pension income), and
        (iii) Part 10 (social security income),

and in accordance with the provisions applicable to those Schedules and Cases and those Parts, but (subject to the provisions of the Corporation Tax Acts) the amounts so computed for the several sources of income, if more than one, together with any amount to be included in respect of chargeable gains, shall be aggregated to arrive at the total profits.

Place of trade

[35.02] ITTOIA 2005, designates a category of income as "trading income", without differentiation as to whether it is an overseas trade or a UK trade. However, if the income arises to an individual subject to the remittance basis, it is necessary to make the distinction between an overseas trade and a UK trade in order to decide whether profits are taxed as they arise, or as they are remitted. For corporation tax, a trade carried on wholly overseas is assessable under Schedule D, Case V, whereas a trade carried on wholly or partly in the UK is assessable under Schedule D, Case 1.[1]

It is difficult for a sole trader to establish that his trade is carried on wholly overseas. In *Ogilvie v Kitton*[2] the taxpayer who was resident in Aberdeen was the sole owner of a business of woollen warehousemen carried on by his employees in Toronto. He had the sole right to manage and control his business and although that right was not exercised, it could have been. The trade was therefore not wholly overseas.

By contrast where a trade is carried on in partnership, it may be easier to establish that the trade is carried on wholly overseas, as was the finding in *Sulley v A-G*.[3] The taxpayer bought goods in the UK for export to America where they were resold by his partners; the trade was carried on wholly overseas, and so was within Case V, not Case I.

Where a company wishes to trade overseas, it may do so by direct exporting, by a licensing system or by establishing a branch in the foreign country, or by establishing a foreign subsidiary company. In such instances, the profits will flow back to the UK in the form of dividends, interest, royalty payments and in other forms such as payments for services. The flow can be reversed by loans. The company can thus become an overseas incorporated piggy bank—subject to any possible application of the CFC rules (see infra, §§ **35.67** ff).

Simon's Taxes D4.115.

1   Cases that turn on the distinction include: *Colquhoun v Brooks* (1889) 14 App Cas 493, 2 TC 490, but note explanation by Lord Watson in *San Paulo (Brazilian) Rly Co v Carter* (1895) 3 TC 407 at 411. See also *Comr of Inland Revenue v Hang Seng Bank Ltd* [1990] STC 733, PC.
2   (1908) 5 TC 338.
3   (1860) 5 H & N 711, 2 TC 149, n.

[35.03] Where the resident company sets up a wholly owned subsidiary in the foreign country to carry on a trade there, it is a question of fact whether that subsidiary is carrying on its own trade or is simply acting as agent for its parent's trade.[1] The question is, however, not concluded by saying that the overseas company is a wholly owned subsidiary[2] and one may not argue that "in substance" the trade is for the parent and so is the parent's trade.[3] The question depends on who manages the trade and not on who owns the shares.[4]

Simon's Taxes B3.106.

1   *Apthorpe v Peter Schoenhofen Brewing Co Ltd* (1899) 4 TC 41.
2   *Gramophone and Typewriter Ltd v Stanley* [1908] 2 KB 89, 5 TC 358; and see *Watson v Sandie and Hull* [1898] 1 QB 326, 3 TC 611.
3   *IRC v Duke of Westminster* [1936] AC 1, 19 TC 490 (supra, § **3.12**).
4   *Kodak Ltd v Clark* [1903] 1 KB 505, 4 TC 549.

[35.04] A corporation is resident in the UK because its central management and control is in the UK from which it might appear to follow that it cannot trade wholly overseas.[1] Thus, in *San Paulo (Brazilian) Rly Co v Carter*,[2] Lord Halsbury said that the place of trade was not the place where the subject matter of the trade was, in that case a railway in Brazil, but where the conduct and management, "the head and the brain of the trading adventure" was to be found.[3] Despite this the House of Lords held in *Egyptian Hotels Ltd v Mitchell*[4] that a company resident in the UK could be trading wholly abroad. The company was resident in England and carried on the business of hotel proprietors. They so amended their articles of association as to provide for the carrying on of their Egyptian business by a local board[5] in that country which was to be wholly independent of the London board or any other part of the company. The only way in which the London board could have influenced their activities was by controlling the remuneration of the directors in Egypt. The Court of Appeal held that the company was carrying on a trade wholly outside the UK and an evenly divided House of Lords could not reverse that decision.[6] This case must be confined to its special facts.

Other cases[7] have shown that regular oversight of the foreign trade will prevent it from being one carried on wholly overseas. It is important that in the facts of the case there was no power directly to control the Egyptian trade. In *Mitchell v B W Noble Ltd*[8] control was shared between London and Paris, and it was held that the trade did not fall within Case V.

Where the trade is carried on partly in the UK and partly overseas so that Case DI applies, concessionary relief is available for certain unremittable debts.[9]

[35.04] Foreign income and capital gains of residents

Simon's Taxes B3.103, 105; B8.513.

---

[1] eg per Hamilton J in *American Thread Co v Joyce* (1911) 6 TC 1 at 18.
[2] [1896] AC 31, 3 TC 407.
[3] [1896] AC at 38, 410.
[4] [1915] AC 1022, 6 TC 542. For a similar result in relation to a trust see *Ferguson v Donovan* [1929] IR 489. HMRC International Tax Manual, para 343 suggests that the Revenue would now view the company as non-resident.
[5] The Egyptian Board controlled only the Egyptian business per Viscount Cave LC in *Swedish Central Rly Co Ltd v Thompson* [1925] AC 495 at 523, 524.
[6] Mere oversight regularly exercised is sufficient control but merely to have the right to intervene and not to exercise that right is not—per Lord Sumner in *Mitchell v Egyptian Hotels Ltd* [1915] AC 1022 at 1040, 6 TC 542 at 551.
[7] *San Paulo Brazilian Rly Co v Carter*, supra.
[8] [1927] 1 KB 719, 11 TC 372.
[9] Extra-statutory concession B38.

Basis of assessment—trading income

[35.05] When an individual enjoys income arising from an overseas trade, profession or vocation, the basis period is determined by the rules applicable to trading income.[1] The opening and closing year provisions apply to overseas trades, etc, as they apply to UK trades, etc. There is, thus, overlap profit relief for an overseas trade income.

All other foreign income is assessed on a strict fiscal year basis. Thus, the basis period for 2005–06 is income arising from 6 April 2005 to 5 April 2006.[2]

Where an individual is subject to UK income tax on the remittance basis, the charge in respect of overseas income is on income remitted to the UK during the fiscal year. This applies irrespective of the nature of the overseas income. Thus, for a non-domiciled individual taxable on a remittance basis, the basis period for an overseas trade is the fiscal year and not the accounting period.[3]

---

[1] See supra, §§ **8.43** and **8.46**.
[2] TA 1988, s 7. Instructions have been issued by HMRC Policy Division to local tax offices that any local agreement between a tax office and a taxpayer that provided for a basis period to be used that was not in accordance with statute, should now be brought to an end.
[3] ITTOIA, s 832.

Basis of assessment—investment income

[35.06] Where a UK partnership has investment income arising to the partnership, the basis period that applies for the trading income (normally, the income of the accounting period that has been chosen) is also applied for the assessment of investment income.[1]

This has a curious effect for the individual partner. Let us say the partnership makes up accounts to 31 December each year. Investment income he receives in his personal capacity during the period 1 January 2007 to 5 April 2007 is subject to tax for 2006–07; however, his share of the partnership's investment income that arises during that period is subject to tax for fiscal year 2007–08.

[1] ITTOIA 2005, ss 854 and 855.

Income from overseas property

[35.07] Rental and similar income from property overseas is the subject of the same statutory regime as that for income from property in the UK;[1] this regime does not apply for corporation tax.[2] Capital allowances and the treatment of premiums for CGT applies as for UK property income.[3] It follows that interest payable on a loan to buy the property is available as an expense.[4]

Expenses on travelling to the foreign property (which statute specifically allows in the computation of profits from a foreign trade[5]) are excluded.[6]

A potential trap existed for UK residents who had purchased holiday homes overseas through a corporate vehicle – generally in order to avoid local succession rules or (in some cases) to comply with local laws. In many cases, taxpayers by doing so could have unwittingly found themselves taxed under the employment income rules as having the benefit of accommodation provided by reason of their employment.[7] In the 2007 Budget it was announced that legislation would be introduced to remove this anomaly. That legislation was introduced by FA 2008 and is considered in more detail at 7.50 supra.

Simon's Taxes B9.101.

[1] ITTOIA 2005, ss 263–321, except that rental from overseas property is not subject to UK tax when it arises to a person not resident in the UK (ITTOIA 2005, s 269(2)) and is assessable on a remittance basis when it is income of a UK resident who is not domiciled within the UK (ITTOIA 2005, s 269(3)), for which special rules apply ss 357–360; exceptionally, income arising from letting of land in the Republic of Ireland is taxable on an arising basis even if the taxpayer is not domiciled within the UK (ITTOIA 2005, s 269(3)).
[2] TA 1988, s 70A.
[3] CAA 2001, s 250 and TCGA 1992, Sch 8, para 7A.
[4] Inland Revenue press release, 29 November 1994, *Simon's Tax Intelligence* 1994, p 1463, para 5.
[5] ITTOIA 2005, s 92(3)(a).
[6] See the table in ITTOIA 2005, s 272(2).
[7] The directorship of the corporate vehicle being deemed to be an employment.

Foreign dividends, distributions and interest

[35.08] Domestic dividends and distributions chargeable on an individual now attract rates of 10% and 32.5%. This applies also to similar distributions by foreign companies. This does not apply if the receipt is income under a foreign law but does not fit within the Taxes Act definition of distribution (see infra, § **35.10**), nor does it apply if the income is taxable on a remittance basis (see infra, § **35.12**), nor if the income is income paid to a beneficiary in respect of a foreign estate. From 6 April 2008, UK residents and other individuals who qualify for personal allowances under ITA 2007, s 56(3) are entitled to a non-repayable tax credit in respect of overseas dividends. This tax credit (calculated on the same basis as with domestic dividends) correspondingly increases the taxable income.[1] The purpose of this is to ensure that EU dividends are treated no less fairly than UK dividends although the provisions are not limited to dividends from EU companies. The rules also limit the credit to taxpayers with shareholdings of less than 10%.[2] However, it is proposed that other shareholders will be covered by legislation to be enacted in 2009.

The regime for UK interest applies also to interest from foreign sources—with the same exceptions for income, the remittance basis and foreign estates. Such income will therefore be taxed at the basic or higher rates, or the starting rate if applicable.[3]

When (prior to 2008/09) savings income was generally taxed at a lower rate than the basic rate, this expressly excluded from annuities, and other annual payments which are not interest; these exclusions presumably applied to analogous foreign income, also.

[1] ITTOIA 2005, s 92.
[2] ITTOIA 2005, s 92(2).
[3] Supra, § **7.133** but not identical, eg there is no need for separate reimbursement (there is no one to do the reimbursing).

Travel expenses

[35.09] An individual who carries on a trade, profession or vocation wholly outside the UK and who is not taxable on a remittance basis may claim the deduction of certain travel costs.[1] The allowable expenses are those for travel by the businessman from any place in the UK to any place where the business is carried on or from any such place to any place in the UK and for board and lodging.[2] These rules are similar to those introduced for the assessment of employment income.[3] The similarity is taken further in that the rules allow also for the deduction of the costs of travel for a spouse/civil partner and child under 18.[4] In these cases the taxpayer's absence from the UK must be wholly and exclusively for the purpose of performing the function of the trade, profession or vocation or those of some other business, with apportionment between the different businesses.

Where there are two or more overseas locations the taxpayer may deduct the cost of travel from one to the other; of the two at least one must satisfy the rules, ie be an overseas source in respect of which an arising basis of assessment is used.⁵ The absence from the UK must still be wholly and exclusively for the purpose of performing the functions of both activities and he must actually perform those functions at each location. The deduction is put against the trade carried on at the destination unless it is outside these rules in which case the place of departure is taken instead. Where there are two businesses at the place of destination or departure apportionment is carried out.

¹ ITTOIA 2005, s 92.
² ITTOIA 2005, s 92(2).
³ Supra, § **7.133** but not identical, eg there is no need for separate reimbursement (there is no one to do the reimbursing).
⁴ ITTOIA 2005, s 92.
⁵ ITTOIA 2005, s 93.

Is it income? Is it a taxpayer?—the role of foreign law

[35.10] The question whether a particular payment is income arising from security or possession is a question for UK tax law but that question must be determined according to the legal nature of the rights arising from the security or possession under the foreign law. In *Garland v Archer-Shee*¹ a tenant for life was entitled under a New York trust and the issue was whether money to which the taxpayer was entitled, was income "from stock and securities",² the alternative view being that a tenant for life had only a right to see that the property was correctly administered by the trustees. By English law the former had already been held to be correct³ but, on evidence being presented that by New York law the latter was correct, the House of Lords held that the rights of the beneficiary could not be said to be income arising "from stocks and shares". Since the UK tax liability turned on the nature of that foreign right, foreign law was relevant in determining that right.

The quality of the receipt must be determined according to the legal rights of the taxpayer, in respect of that income, but UK tax rules must then be applied to those rights. So in *Rae v Lazard Investment Co Ltd*⁴ a distribution in partial liquidation, a process known to Maryland law but not to UK company laws was a payment of capital.⁵ By contrast in *Inchyra v Jennings*⁶ a direction in an American trust that a beneficiary should receive 1% of the trust capital each year was held to create annual payments⁷ and so income for UK tax law.

Slightly different policies may present themselves in connection with double tax treaties. In *Memec plc v IRC*⁸ the court had to consider whether a receipt from a foreign silent partnership was a dividend for the purposes of double taxation relief. As the case involved a double tax treaty the court held that it should adopt a purposive construction and try to achieve symmetry between the two systems. However, the case also illustrates the fact that the starting point is the UK court's analysis of the rights arising under the foreign law.

Matters become murkier yet when UK tax rule and the treaty meaning diverge. So the UK tax system with its divisions, taken from domestic law, between partnerships and companies has to classify a number of foreign entities.

[35.10] Foreign income and capital gains of residents

Simon's Taxes B8.505, 510; E1.480.

1. [1931] AC 212, 15 TC 693.
2. See Income Tax Act 1918, Schedule D, Case IV, Rule 1.
3. *Archer-Shee v Baker* [1927] AC 844, 11 TC 749 (supra, § **13.15**).
4. (1963) 41 TC 1, noted [1963] BTR 121 (JGM).
5. To the same effect *Courtaulds Investments Ltd v Fleming* [1969] 3 All ER 1281, 46 TC 111.
6. [1965] 2 All ER 714, 42 TC 388.
7. Supra, § **13.21**. Cf *Lawson v Rolfe* [1970] 1 All ER 761, 46 TC 199, [1970] BTR 142 (JGM).
8. [1996] STC 1336 upheld [1998] STC 754, CA.

[35.11] HMRC has published a list showing those overseas business entities that, in their view, are transparent (that is a UK resident individual is treated as if he were a partner and in receipt of a proportionate part of profits as they arise) or that, in their view, are opaque (that is the UK resident is treated as if he were a shareholder receiving distributions from a company).[1]

Country and name of entity	UK tax treatment	Date last considered
ANGUILLA Partnership	Transparent	10/1991
ARGENTINA Sociedad de responsibilidad limitada	Opaque	6/1958
AUSTRIA Kommanditgesellschaft (KG)	Transparent	8/1971
Kommand Erwerbsgesellschaft (KEG)	Transparent	11/2003
GmbH & Co KG	Transparent	5/2002
Gesellschaft mit Beschrankter Haftung (GmbH)	Opaque	11/2005
Aktiengesellschaft (AG)	Opaque	11/2005
BELGIUM Société de privée à responsabilité limitée (SPRL)	Opaque	8/1994
Société en nom collectif (SNC)	Transparent	5/1992
Société Anonyme (SA)	Opaque	11/2005
Naamloze Vennootschap (NV)	Opaque	11/2005
Société en commanditaire par actions (SCA)	Opaque	11/2005
Commanditaire venootschap op aandelen (CVA)	Opaque	11/2005
BRAZIL Sociedade por quotas de responsabilidade limitada	Opaque	1/1977

Place of trade [**35.11**]

Country and name of entity	UK tax treatment	Date last considered
CANADA Partnership and Limited Partnership	Transparent	11/2005
CAYMAN ISLANDS Limited Partnership	Transparent	11/1993
CHILE Sociedad de responsibilidad limitada (S.R.L)	Transparent	9/2003
CHINA Wholly Foreign Owned Entity (WFOE)	Opaque	10/2005
CZECH REPUBLIC Akciova spolecnost (as)	Opaque	11/2005
Spolecnost s rucenim omezenym (sro)	Opaque	11/2005
European Union Societas Europeas (SE)	Opaque	7/2005
FINLAND Kommandiittiyhtiö, Ky	Transparent	5/1991
Osakeyhtio (Oy)	Opaque	11/2005
Aktiebolag (Ab)	Opaque	11/2005
FRANCE Groupement d'Intérêt economique (GIE)	Transparent	5/1988
Société en nom collectif (SNC)	Transparent	8/2000
Société civile immobiliére (SCI)	Opaque	11/2005
Société civile agricole (SCA)	Opaque	2/1998
Société anonyme (SA)	Opaque	4/2004
Société en commandite simple (SCS)	Transparent	9/1997
Société en participation (SP)	Transparent	1/1997
Société à responsabilité Iimitée (SARL)	Opaque	
Fonds Commun de Placement à risques (FCPR)	Transparent	1/1997
Société par Actions Simplifiee (SAS)	Opaque	4/2004
Groupement Foncier d'Agricole (GFA)	Opaque	5/2001
Société Civile (SC)	Opaque	11/2005
GERMANY Stille Gesellschaft	Opaque	6/1998
Kommanditgesellschaft (KG)	Transparent	2/1997
Offene Handelsgesellschaft (OHG)	Transparent	9/1996
Gesellschaft mit Beschränkter Haftung (GmbH)	Opaque	2/1997
GMBH & Co. KG	Transparent	2/1997

[35.11] Foreign income and capital gains of residents

Country and name of entity	UK tax treatment	Date last considered
Gesellschaft des Bürgerlichen Rechts (GBR)	Transparent	4/1994
Aktiengesellschaft (AG)	Opaque	11/2005
GUERNSEY Limited Partnership (LP)	Transparent	1/2005
Protected Cell Company (PCC)	Opaque	11/2004
Open Ended Investment Company with Limited Liability	Opaque	11/2004
HUNGARY Korlatolt feleossegu tarsasag (Kft)	Opaque	11/2005
Reszvenytarsasag (Rt)	Opaque	11/2005
ICELAND Hlutafelag	Opaque	11/2005
IRELAND Limited Partnership	Transparent	
Irish Investment Limited Partnership	Transparent	
Common Contractual Fund (CCF)	Transparent	1/2004
ITALY Societa per Azioni (SpA)	Opaque	11/2005
JAPAN Goshi-Kaisha	Transparent	2/1997
Gomei Kaisha	Transparent	
Tokumei Kumiai (T.K.)	Transparent	11/2005
Kabushikikaisha	Opaque	11/2005
Yugen-kaisha	Opaque	11/2005
JERSEY Limited Liability Partnership (LLP)	Opaque	2/2001
KAZAKHSTAN Limited Liability Company (LLC)	Opaque	9/2005
LIECHTENSTEIN Anstalt	Opaque	3/2004
LUXEMBOURG Société en commandite par-actions (SCA)	Opaque	7/1992
Fonds commun de placement (FCP)	Transparent	5/2005
Societe anonyme (SA)	Opaque	11/2005
Societe a responsabilite limitee (SARL)	Opaque	11/2005
Societe d'investment a capitale variable (SJCAV)	Opaque	3/2006
NETHERLANDS Vennootschap Onder Firma (VOF)	Transparent	2/1995

Place of trade [35.11]

Country and name of entity	UK tax treatment	Date last considered
Commanditaire Vennootschap both "open" and "closed" (CV)	Transparent	8/2000
Naamloze Vennootschap (NV)	Opaque	10/1981
Besloten Vennootschap Met Beperkte Aansprakelijheid (BV)	Opaque	10/1981
Maatschap	Transparent	10/1993
Stichting	Transparent	7/2005
Cooperatie (Co-op)	Transparent	7/2004
NEW CALEDONIA Societe en nom collectif (SNC)	Transparent	7/2005
NORWAY Alkjeselskap (AS)	Opaque	
Kommandittselkap (K/S)	Transparent	1/1981
POLAND Spolkaz ograniczonaodpowiedzialno-scia (SP.zo.o)	Opaque	3/1996
PORTUGAL Sociedade por quotas (Lda)	Opaque	4/1993
Sociedade Anónima (SA)	Opaque	4/1993
RUSSIA Joint Venture under "Decree No.49"	Opaque	1/1993
Limited Liability Company (LLC)	Opaque	11/2003
SLOVAK REPUBLIC Spolocnost's rucenim obmedzenim (sro)	Opaque	11/2005
SPAIN Sociedad Civila SC)	Opaque	12/1980
Sociedad Anonima (SA)	Opaque	11/2005
Comunidad de bienes	Transparent	6/2001
Sociedad de Responsabilidad Limitada (Srl)	Opaque	11/2005
SWEDEN Aktiebolag (AB)	Opaque	11/2005
Kommanditbolag (KB)	Transparent	10/2005
SWITZERLAND Société Simple (SS)	Transparent	12/1990
Gesellschaft mit beschrankter Haftung (GmbH)	Opaque	11/2005
TURKEY Attorney Partnership (AP)	Transparent	4/2004
Anonim Sirket (AS)	Opaque	11/2005

Country and name of entity	UK tax treatment	Date last considered
Limited Sirket (Ltd/S)	Opaque	11/2005
USA Partnership set up under the Uniform Partnership Act	Transparent	9/1983
Limited Partnership set up under the Uniform Limited Partnership Act	Transparent	8/2000
Limited Liability Company (LLC)	Opaque	6/1997
Limited Liability Partnership (LLP)	Transparent	12/1999
Massachusetts Business Trust (MBT)	Transparent	2/1980
S. Corporation (S.Corp)	Opaque	7/2005

[1] HMRC Tax Bulletin, June 2006, pp 1296-1298. This is a revision and extension of the list first published in Inland Revenue Tax Bulletin December 2000, pp 810–812.

The remittance basis

When the remittance basis applies

[35.12] Income tax is charged on the remittance basis if one of two conditions is fulfilled: (a) the taxpayer is not domiciled in the UK or, (b) the taxpayer is not ordinarily resident in the UK.[1] For the remittance basis to apply, the person was historically required to make a claim (which was normally made within the tax return). Despite the changes introduced with effect from 2008–09 onwards, a claim is still required in many cases.[2] However, no claim is required if:

(a) the individual's unremitted foreign income and gains for a particular year is less than £2,000[3]; or
(b) the individual:
 (i) has no UK income or gains for the year; and
 (ii) either:
  (A) is aged under 18 throughout the tax year; or
  (B) has been resident in the UK for six or fewer of the nine immediately previous tax years.[4]

Such an individual is also subject to capital gains tax on a remittance basis when the gain arises from disposal of property located overseas.[5]

The remittance basis does not apply to trading income of corporations.[6] However, if a foreign trade is run through a subsidiary company resident in that other country, the profits will not generally be taxed in the UK until they are transferred to this country as dividends, interest or royalty payments.[7]

Where the remittance basis applies, dividends are taxed at the full rates (20% and 40%) rather than the dividend ordinary and dividend upper rates of 10% and 32 1/2%.[8] The effect is, thus, that a basic rate taxpayer domiciled within the UK pays tax at 10% on overseas dividends and at the basic rate on overseas bank interest, for example; by contrast, a basic rate taxpayer resident in the UK but not domiciled within the UK who chooses to bring to the UK the whole of his overseas income pays tax at 20% on his overseas bank interest and also his overseas dividends. Statute[9] applies the remittance basis to overseas income where the taxpayer makes a claim that he is not domiciled in the UK. It would appear to be the case, therefore, that an individual can choose not to make such a claim and, thereby, obtain the benefit of the lower rates of tax, even though he is, in fact, not domiciled within the UK.

The remittance basis applies only to certain types of person and to certain types of income. It applies to overseas income generally[10] and, in restricted circumstances, to employment income[11]. Prior to 6 April 2008, it did not apply to sources in Eire.[12] However, this rule was removed as it was susceptible to a challenged under European law.[13]

For capital gains tax, the remittance basis is available only to taxpayers who are not domiciled in the UK; the remittance basis will apply only in situations in which it is available also to income.[14]

If a claim is made under ITA 2007, s 809B, the taxpayer will lose entitlement to personal allowances, reductions for married couples and civil partners and relief under ITA 2007, ss 457-459 (payments for life assurance etc). For reasons that are inexplicable, the tax reductions for qualifying maintenance payments[15] are not similarly affected. The capital gains tax annual exemption will also be forgone in such cases.

Simon's Taxes E1.478.

[1] ITTOIA 2005, s 831.
[2] ITA 2007, s 809B.
[3] ITA 2007, s 809C.
[4] ITA 2007, s 809D.
[5] TCGA 1992, s 12.
[6] TA 1988, s 70(2).
[7] Debt is usually easier to repatriate than equity. On controlled foreign company legislation see infra, § **35.67**.
[8] ITA 2007, s 13; between 2005-06 and 2007-08 (inclusive) a drafting anomaly meant that higher rate taxpayers on the remittance basis were liable only to the dividend upper rate. This was corrected in FA 2008.
[9] ITTOIA 2005, s 227. By contrast, TCGA 1992, s 12(1) directs that CGT is not charged on unremitted gains of an individual with a non-UK domicile; there is no claim required for CGT and, hence, no facility for deciding to be taxed as if a UK-domicile had been obtained.
[10] ITTOIA 2005, s 832.
[11] ITEPA 2003, s 22.
[12] Former ITTOIA 2005, s 831(5).
[13] An option that remains open to taxpayers in relation to earlier years.

[35.12] Foreign income and capital gains of residents

[14] ITA 2007, ss 453-456.
[15] ITA 2007, ss 453-456.

Remittance claims

[35.13] For taxpayers who claim to be subject to the remittance basis, who are 18 or over and have been UK resident in at least seven of the previous nine tax years, the claim must also nominate that income and those gains for which tax is to be paid on the arising basis.[1]

The taxpayer must then ascertain the "relevant tax increase". This is:

(a) the taxpayer's liability to income tax and capital gains tax for the year; minus
(b) the total liability that there would have been but for the nomination of the income to be taxed on the arising basis.[2]

This figure is then compared with the figure of £30,000. If the relevant tax increase is less than £30,000 then the individual's tax liability is charged separately by the difference.[3]

EXAMPLE

An individual who makes a claim for the remittance basis has overseas unremitted income of £1m. In his claim under ITA 2007, s 809B, he nominates income of £65,000 to be taxed on an arising basis.

Assume that that nomination gives rise to a tax increase of £26,000. The individual must therefore pay additional income tax of £4,000.

This provision ensures that:

(i) there is a minimum cost of £30,000 to claim the remittance basis; and
(ii) the £30,000 is a tax (rather than a voluntary charge). This can be important when considering double taxation agreements.

A claim made under ITA 2007, s 809B may be amended within the limited time permitted to correct a return.[4] However, it is explicitly excluded from the rules permitting taxpayers to correct errors or mistakes outside this period.[5] Thus, taxpayers must be careful to ensure that:

(a) they wish to elect for the remittance basis; and
(b) they are required to make a claim for the remittance basis to apply.

[1] ITA 2007, ss 809B(3), 809G(2).
[2] ITA 2007, s 809G(5).
[3] ITA 2007, s 809G(4).
[4] TMA 1970, s 9ZA.
[5] TMA 1970, s 33(2A)(c).

Remittances of nominated income

[35.14] ITA 2007, ss 809H and 809I provide additional complexity in cases where an individual actually remits some of the nominated income or gains but also has (either for that year or a previous year) income that is subject to the remittance basis but which has not been remitted. The purpose of these provisions is to ensure that (whilst keeping the £30,000 charge as an imposition of tax) the £30,000 charge is imposed in addition to any tax payable as a result of the remittance of income or capital gains.

ITA 2007, s 809I provides, where necessary, a priority of types of income or gain that are deemed to be remitted in preference to other sources. That priority is:

(a) relevant foreign earnings (not subject to a foreign tax);
(b) foreign specific employment income (not being income subject to a foreign tax);
(c) relevant foreign income (other than income subject to a foreign tax);
(d) foreign chargeable gains (other than gains subject to a foreign tax);
(e) relevant foreign earnings (subject to a foreign tax);
(f) foreign specific employment income (being income subject to a foreign tax);
(g) relevant foreign income (subject to a foreign tax); and
(h) foreign chargeable gains (subject to a foreign tax).

Employment income

[35.15] An individual resident and ordinarily resident in the UK is assessed on employment income as it arises, irrespective of the domicile of the employee, where either the employer is a UK employer or the duties of the employment are performed within the UK.[1]

Where the employee is not domiciled within the UK, the employee is entitled to the remittance basis and the employment is with a foreign employer the emoluments received for duties of employment which are performed wholly outside the United Kingdom are assessed to income tax on the remittance basis.[2] The amount remitted can, however, be relieved by employment expenses,[3] pension contributions[4] and employees' capital allowances.[5]

For employment income, there was a statutory definition of a remittance.[6] This is now replaced by a consistent set of rules in ITA (see below). Earnings were treated as remitted to the UK if they are "paid, used, or enjoyed in the United Kingdom, or transmitted or brought into the United Kingdom in any manner or form". In addition, sums are treated as being remitted to UK if they are applied outside the UK to satisfy "a UK linked debt", which is elaborately defined.[7]

From 2008–09, remittances of income deriving from employment-related securities (as dealt with by ITEPA 2003, Pt 7, Ch 2, 3, and 3C to 5) are considered in ITEPA 2003, Pt 2, Ch 5A.

[1] ITEPA 2003, s 15.
[2] ITEPA 2003, s 22.
[3] ITEPA 2003, s 23(3).
[4] ITEPA 2003, s 23(3).
[5] ITEPA 2003, s 23(3).

[35.15] Foreign income and capital gains of residents

[6] Former ITEPA 2003, s 33.
[7] Former ITEPA 2003, ss 33(4) & 34.

What is a remittance?

[35.16] Where the remittance basis applies, income tax is levied on the full amount of relevant foreign income received in the UK.[1]

In general, a transfer of money cannot be a remittance unless there is a source of that remittance in existence in the tax year in which the money is transferred.[2] For employment income, however, statute[3] provides that a remittance is assessable as employment income, even if the employment has ceased.

[1] ITTOIA 2005, s 832. On valuation and the time at which the exchange rate should be applied see *Magraw v Lewis* (1933) 18 TC 222 and *Payne v Deputy Federal Comr of Taxation* [1936] AC 497, [1936] 2 All ER 793. On negligence liability of intermediaries see *Schioler v Westminster Bank Ltd* [1970] 2 QB 719, [1970] 3 All ER 177.
[2] See supra, § **5.05**.
[3] ITEPA 2003, s 22(3).

Rules before 2008-09

Statute[1] treats repayment of UK linked debts as a remittance. Thus, the taxpayer is treated as having made a remittance by virtue of having received in the UK the value of the reduction in the debt.

If foreign income were converted into a car which was then brought into the UK, no liability would arise under the remittance basis. If, however, the car were then sold, the proceeds might be taxable.[2] If by that time the source has been extinguished, or he had given the car to someone else, the proceeds will not be taxable.[3]

[1] Former ITTOIA 2005, s 833.
[2] In the year in which the car was sold. *Scottish Provident Institution v Farmer* (1912), 6 TC 34.
[3] *Bray v Best* [1989] 1 All ER 969, [1989] STC 159, HL. This was a decision under Schedule E, Case I and involved no international element. It has since been reversed by legislation—FA 1989 s 36(3).

Rules from 2008-09

A uniform statutory code applies with effect from 6 April 2008. There will be a remittance if any of the following situations arises.

Situation 1

Money or other property is brought to the UK. This covers money or property received or used in the UK. The money or other property must be brought to the UK by or for the benefit of a relevant person (see below). Alternatively, a service must be provided in the UK to or for the benefit of a relevant person.[1]

In addition:

(a) the property or consideration for the service must be (wholly or partly) income or chargeable gains;
(b) the property or consideration for the service must be property of a relevant person or consideration given by a relevant person that derives (wholly or partly, directly or indirectly from income or chargeable gains);
(c) the income or chargeable gains is used outside the UK in respect of a relevant debt; or
(d) anything deriving from such income income or gains is so used.[2]

[1] ITA 2007, s 809K(2).
[2] ITA 2007, s 809K(3).

Situation 2

This situation covers gifts of income or gains made by the individual to a person other than a relevant person and the subject matter of the gift is then brought to the UK for or by a relevant person (as per situation 1).[1]

[1] ITA 2007, s 809K(4).

Situation 3

This situation is similar to situation 2 but covers third parties who bring money to the the UK with reference to (or with a view to enabling or facilitating) a disposition that is:

(a) made by a relevant person;
(b) made to or for the benefit of the third party;
(c) derives from the inidividual's income or chargeable gains; and
(d) does not represent full consideration for the transaction in which the money is brought to the UK.[1]

[1] ITA 2007, s 809K(5) and s 809N.

Relevant persons

The following are relevant persons in respect of an individual:

(a) the individual;
(b) the individual's spouse or civil partner (or cohabitee);
(c) any child or grandchild of the individual (if aged under 18);
(d) any company that is close and by reference to which the individual (or any other relevant person) is a participator;
(e) any company that would fall within the above if the company were resident in the UK;

(f) the trustees of any settlement to which a relevant person is the settlor or trustee;
(g) a body connected (as per ITA 2007, s 993) with such a settlement.

(ITA 2007, s 809L).

Amount remitted

ITA 2007, ss 809O-809R determine how much is treated as remitted and deal specifically with cases where the amount is transferred from a mixed fund, ie a fund with:

(a) a mixture of different types of income or capital; or
(b) income or capital from different tax years.

Exceptions

The following do not count as remittances to the UK:

(a) *direct* payments to HMRC:
   (i) provided that they are in relation to the payment of the £30,000 charge; and
   (ii) (or to the extent that) the payments are £30,000 or less.[1]
(b) personal chattels that meet the personal use rule;
(c) other property if either:
   (i) it meets the public access rule;
   (ii) the notional remitted amount is less than £1,000 (small personal chattels);
   (iii) it meets the temporary importation rule; or
   (iv) it meets the repair rule.[2]

For this category of 'other property' the exception will apply to income and capital gains so far as the public access rule is concerned. For the other exceptions (eg temporary importation, repairs and the small personal chattels), the exception applies only to income.

---

[1] ITA 2007, s 809S.
[2] ITA 2007, s 809T.

Direct payments

The first exception above is a complete exemption provided that the payment is not received by HMRC from a UK source. However, it will cease to apply if to the extent that the money is repaid by HMRC.[1]

Therefore, it gives rise to the situation in which an individual wishes to be taxed on the remittance basis and pays £30,000 to achieve this. However, it transpires that the taxpayer had not been resident in six of the previous nine tax years and, therefore, the claim under ITA 2007, s 809B was unnecessary.

If HMRC then repay the £30,000, the payment is retrospectively reclassified as a remittance. Consequently, the repayment by HMRC of the £30,000 could actually give rise to a tax liability on the individual. Arguably, the remittance is treated as taking place when HMRC make the repayment. However, in the authors' view, the better interpretation of the legislation is that the time of the original remittance is the time that counts.

[1] ITA 2007, s 809S(2).

The other exemptions

The other exemptions are more provisional. Where an exemption ceases to apply, the property is then treated as remitted to the UK. That deemed remittance is statutorily deemed to take place at the time when it ceases to be exempt.[1]

These exemptions will cease to apply if either:

(a) the property is sold whilst it is in the UK[2]; or
(b) the rule affording the exemption ceases to apply whilst the property is in the UK and no other rule applies.[3]

[1] ITA 2007, s 809U(1).
[2] ITA 2007, s 809U(3).
[3] ITA 2007, s 809U(4).

Those other exemptions in more detail

Public access rule

This rule covers artwork and collectors' pieces. It requires the following conditions to be met:

(A) The property must be imported under Schedule 2, Group 9 to the Value Added Tax (Imported Goods) Relief Order 1984[1]; that applies to works of art and collectors' pieces imported by approved museums, galleries or other institutions provided that:
 (i) the property is of an educational, scientific or cultural character; and
 (ii) imported free of charge or, if for a consideration, are not supplied to the importer in the course or furtherance of any business,
 or would apply if one overlooked the VAT requirement that the goods come from outside the EU.[2]
(B) The property must be either:
 (i) in transit between a place outside the UK and premises in the UK at which the property is to be (or has been) available for public access;
 (ii) in transit between a place outside the UK and other premises in the UK used by the approved museum, gallery or other institution for storage before or after its availability for public access;

(iii)   in transit between such premises; and
(iv)   available for public access at an approved museum, gallery or other institution (as per the VAT rules).[3]

(C)   The property may not normally be in the UK for a single visit of more than two years unless HMRC specify a longer period.[4]

[1] ITA 2007, s 809V(3)(a).
[2] The VAT rules also require that the purpose of the importation to be other than for sale. That requirement is lifted in the present context (ITA 2007, s 809V(3)(b)(ii)).
[3] This is defined to mean:

(a)   on public display there;
(b)   held by the establishment and made available to the public on request for viewing or for educational use; or
(c)   held for public exhibition in connection with the sale of the property (ITA 2007, s 809V(9)).

(ITA 2007, s 809V(4).)
[4] ITA 2007, s 809V(5).

Personal use rule

This rule governs clothing, footwear, jewellery and watches. The property must belong to a relevant person (as per ITA 2007, s 809L – see supra) and for the personal use of an individual who is also a relevant person.[1]

Thus it should be noted that aunts and uncles or great-grandparents or godparents may not use this rule to lend clothing to their favoured nephews, nieces, great-grandchildren or godchildren.

[1] ITA 2007, s 809W(2)(3).

Repair rule

This rule exempts property that is brought to the UK for repair or restoration. Property is exempted under this rule whilst it is:

(a)   in transit between the UK and the place at which the repair is (or was) to be undertaken;
(b)   in transit between the UK and a place at the repairer or restorer uses for the storage of property before or after the repair is undertaken; or
(c)   actually under repair or restoration.[1]

[1] ITA 2007, s 809W(4)(5).

Temporary importation rule

This rule exempts property that is in the UK on or throughout 275 or fewer days.[1]

This includes days spent in the UK which are covered by the personal use, public access or repair rules.[2]

The 275 day limit applies on an aggregate basis with previous importations of the property.[3]

[1] ITA 2007, s 809W(6).
[2] ITA 2007, s 809W(8).
[3] ITA 2007, s 809W(7).

Notional remittances

Finally, property is exempted if it would otherwise amount to *less than* £1,000. Where only part of a collection is brought to the UK, it is valued as a proportion of the whole set.[1]

Simon's Taxes E1.479, 480.

[1] ITA 2007, s 809X(3)(4).

Income of the taxpayer

[35.17] To be taxable the money must have the character of income of the taxpayer when it is remitted to this country. The mere arrival of the money will not be sufficient if it has been the subject of a complete and irrevocable gift to someone else before it arrives. In *Carter v Sharon*,[1] the taxpayer arranged for a banker's draft to be sent to her daughter from California. It was shown that by Californian law the gift was complete not later than when the draft was posted; the money therefore was not a remittance of income to the taxpayer. Had the mother simply sent her daughter a cheque drawn on her California bank account the money when it arrived in England would still have been the taxpayer's since she could have revoked the cheque.[2] The question of the effectiveness of the gift is judged according to the foreign law.

Simon's Taxes E6.111.

[1] [1936] 1 All ER 720, 20 TC 229. Cf *Thomson v Bensted* (1918) 7 TC 137.
[2] As in *Timpson's Executors v Yerbury* [1936] 1 All ER 186, 20 TC 155.

[35.18] Another situation in which income altered its character before it arrived in this country was *Timbrell v Lord Aldenham's Executors*[1] where a London firm was a partner in a firm in Australia and in another firm in Chile. The Australian firm had made a profit and the Chilean firm a loss which the London firm had to meet. Money due to the London firm from the Australian profits was transmitted to Chile to discharge the debt of the Chilean firm to the London firm, a process involving the eventual arrival of the money in London. It was held that what arrived was not income from Australia but the payment of a debt from Chile.

[35.18] Foreign income and capital gains of residents

Simon's Taxes E1.480.

[1] (1947) 28 TC 293.

[35.19] If the taxpayer has both capital and income abroad and remits only capital, there will be no charge to tax.[1] The same result follows if he has both taxed and untaxed income abroad[2] (taxed meaning either that the income is taxed on an arising basis or that in some other way UK tax has been paid) and only the taxed income is remitted. One major problem is that of proof. There is no rule that if there is foreign income and remittances from abroad then the Revenue can tax the foreign income by assuming that the remittances are of income.[3] It is a question of fact in every case. The mere fact that the taxpayer's foreign bank account is overdrawn is not sufficient to show that money remitted from the account is capital.[4] In *Walsh v Randall*[5] it was held that a taxpayer could not convert what was undoubtedly income into capital simply by investing it. If he sells his investment and then remits the proceeds to this country he is treated as remitting income[6] even though by the tax law of the foreign country he is taxable in respect of a capital gain.

Simon's Taxes E1.480.

[1] *Kneen v Martin* [1935] 1 KB 499, 19 TC 33 (separate accounts in USA for income and capital).
[2] *Walsh v Randall* (1940) 23 TC 55 at 56, para 3; p 57, para 7 of the Case Stated. For another example but in a different context see *IRC v McNaught's Executors* (1964) 42 TC 71.
[3] *Kneen v Martin* supra, per Finlay J at 43. The point was not even argued in the Court of Appeal. For Revenue practice, see Inspectors Manual, para 25401.
[4] *Fellowes-Gordon v IRC* (1935) 19 TC 683.
[5] *Walsh v Randall* (1940) 23 TC 55 at 56, para 3; p 57, para 7 of the Case Stated. For another example but in a different context see *IRC v McNaught's Executors* (1964) 42 TC 71.
[6] *Patuck v Lloyd* (1944) 26 TC 284.

Remittance of money

[35.20] Considerable difficulty has been experienced in deciding what is a remittance of money. Clearly it is not necessary to have a receipt of coins; equally the mere entry of a sum of money in a balance sheet is not generally a remittance if the actual funds remain outside the UK.[1]

If sums received here are derived from the application of income overseas which is taxable on a remittance basis, there is a remittance.[2] This may take the form of a loan. So there was a remittance in *Harmel v Wright*[3] where the taxpayer had funds overseas with which he bought shares in a company which he controlled, that company made an interest-free loan to an independent company which in turn made a loan to the taxpayer in the UK. It was important in that case that the sums could be quite clearly traced through the different transactions.

For the treatment of remittances from a fund in which there is a mixture of income, capital gains and original capital, see infra, § 35.50.

Simon's Taxes E1.479.

1   *Gresham Life Assurance Society v Bishop* [1902] AC 287, 4 TC 464.
2   Per Lord Radcliffe in *Thomson v Moyse* [1960] 3 All ER 684 at 688 and 39 TC 291 at 331.
3   [1974] STC 88, [1974] 1 All ER 945.

[35.21] Particular difficulty was experienced when a taxpayer with funds overseas taxable on a remittance basis borrowed money in the UK and the loan was then repaid from the fund overseas. The problem is whether the economic value accruing to the taxpayer results from the receipt of income in the UK or the export of a debt from the UK. There was statutory intervention to widen or render certain the scope of remittance when the taxpayer was ordinarily resident in the UK,[1] but taxpayers who are not ordinarily resident had to rely on the old case law.[2] This is now rendered academic following the introduction of ITA 2007, s 809K with effect from 2008–09.

Simon's Taxes E1.479.

1   Former ITTOIA 2005, ss 833 & 834.
2   The cause of the difficulty was a confusion of two distinct questions, has there been a remittance and has there been a remittance of income, but this has been compounded by a basic uncertainty in applying the physical notion of a receipt to the metaphysical notion of money.

Avoiding remittance liability

[35.22] Avoidance methods were many. Most were closed down as part of the raft of changes introduced by FA 2008. Obviously, the simplest avoidance technique remains using the money, for example to finance overseas holidays.

A loan taken out before arrival in the UK will escape a charge under ITTOIA 2005, s 833 if paid off after leaving this country. An employer may perhaps guarantee the loan.[1]

For a fuller discussion of the pre-2008 legislation (and, in particular, the cases of *IRC v Gordon*[2] and *Thomson v Moyse*[3]) and how it was possible to circumvent the remittance rules, see the 25th edition of this work at 35.20, 35.21 and 35.22.

1   See *Newstead v Frost* [1980] STC 123, [1980] 1 All ER 363.
2   [1952] 1 All ER 866, 33 TC 226 and see *Hall v Marians* (1935) 19 TC 582.
3   [1960] 3 All ER 688, 39 TC 339.

[35.23] ITTOIA 2005, s 832A (introduced with effect from 6 April 2008) ensures that liability cannot be avoided simply by taxpayers remitting income or gains in a tax year in which they are not UK resident. It operates in a similar way to TCGA 1992, s 10A (see 35.47 infra) and catches cases where:

(a) a taxpayer is resident in one tax tear;
(b) a taxpayer was resident in a previous tax year but not the tax year immediately before the tax year in question;
(c) there were fewer than five tax years intervening; and
(d) the taxpayer had been resident in at least four of the previous seven tax years.

Where those conditions are met, any remittances made in the intervening years, but relating to previous years of residence, are treated as remitted to the UK in the year of return.

Unlike the capital gains tax rule, however, this rule will not catch income arising in the years of non-residence.

In addition, it should be noted that, whilst remittances cannot be effected through a third party (such as a spouse or civil partner), couples (say) can make a decision to keep one member on the remittance basis (with, if necessary, a £30,000 charge being paid) and the other coming onto the arising basis.

Simon's Taxes E1.479.

Relief for unremittable foreign income

[35.24] Tax is postponed where income taxed on an arising basis, whether in full or on a reduced sum, cannot be remitted, whether because of laws, executive action or a barrier placed on converting the local currency to sterling, and the taxpayer has not realised the income outside the territory for a consideration either in sterling or in a currency which could be converted into sterling.[1] The export to this country of an object paid for with the foreign currency will not end the relief at least until it is sold; nor apparently will the spending of the income within the foreign country. The taxpayer must make a claim for relief.

Simon's Taxes E1.477.

[1] ITTOIA 2005, ss 841–845.

[35.25] A similar rule applied if the unremittable foreign income was taxable on a remittance basis. That has been repealed with effect for the 2008-09 tax year.[1]

Simon's Taxes E1.481.

[1] Former ITEPA 2003, ss 35–37; former ITTOIA 2005, ss 835–837. For a discussion of the previous rules see 35.24 of the 25th edition of this work.

Transfers of assets abroad—attribution of income

[35.26] The taxation of residents coupled with the non-taxation of non-residents might encourage residents to arrange for income which would otherwise come to them to be held by non-residents and especially by such artificial entities as trusts[1] and companies. As income is assessable on the beneficial owner,[2] the appointment of a bare trustee overseas does not remove the assessment on a beneficial owner resident in the UK. However, a further provision was introduced in 1936 (now ITA 2007, s 721) to counter devices whereby assets would be transferred to persons resident or domiciled outside the UK in whose hands the income would either not be taxed at all by the UK or would be taxed only on a remittance basis, and some benefit of that income would or might accrue to the original resident. Where income accrues to a non-UK resident that income can be attributed to the individual who transferred the assets to the non-resident that now generate the income, if that transferor continues to have a power to enjoy the income[3] or if he/she receives a capital sum.[4] It is not necessary for the transferor to receive the income.[5] The question whether a transfer has been made by a particular person is one of fact.[6] The provision applies only to individuals.

The House of Lords held that these provisions[7] only applied if the transferor was ordinarily resident in the UK at the time of the transfer.[8] However, this has been reversed by statute.[9] The reversal applies to income arising on or after 26 November 1996 regardless of when the transfer or associated operations took place.[10]

Where the person with the power to enjoy or in receipt of the capital sum is not the transferor or his spouse/civil partner these provisions do not apply. This was held by the House of Lords in *Vestey v IRC*[11] the primary reason being the absence of any provision in the section whereby the income of the foreign entity could be appropriately attributed to the beneficiaries and a reluctance on the part of the court to allow that attribution to be carried out simply by Revenue discretion. So in *IRC v Pratt*[12] the court held that what is now ITA 2007, s 721 did not apply to multiple transfers if the respective interests of the assets transferred could not be separated and clearly identified.

Separate statutory provisions[13] are (see infra, § **35.39**) designed to fill the resulting gap by making persons other than the transferor or his spouse/civil partner liable when and to the extent that they receive a benefit which is not otherwise chargeable to income tax. In applying these rules a body incorporated outside the UK, is treated as if resident outside the UK.[14] Moreover it should be remembered that a company treated as resident outside the UK for tax treaty purposes is now treated as not resident in the UK for all purposes.[15]

Where ITA 2007, s 728 operates to treat the profits of a company as being income of a UK resident taxpayer, the charge on the taxpayer does not exclude a charge to corporation tax on the company.[16]

Simon's Taxes D4.108.

---

[1] eg *Astor v Perry* [1935] AC 398, 19 TC 255.
[2] See, for example, ITTOIA 2005, ss 371 and 385(1)(*b*).

[35.26] Foreign income and capital gains of residents

[3] ITA 2007, s 721. For the Revenue view on the interpretation (of ss 739–741) [now ITA 2007, ss 714-751] see Inland Revenue Tax Bulletin, Issue 40, *Simon's Weekly Tax Intelligence* 1999, p 829. For an extended decision on the scope of what is now ITA 2007, s 721, and a rejection of the Revenue's attempt to apply the situation in relation to the particular facts of the case, see *Carvill v IRC* [2000] STC (SCD) 143, the subsequent High Court action for restitution *Carvill v IRC* [2002] EWHC 1488 (Ch), (No 2) [2002] STC 1167 and an unsuccessful application for judicial review *R (Carvill) v IRC (No 2)* [2003] EWHC 1852 (Admin), [2003] STC 1539.

[4] ITA 2007, s 728.

[5] See Carswell LJ in *IRC v McGuckian* [1994] STC 888, CA (NI) at 916. The point was conceded by taxpayer's counsel in the subsequent hearing in the House of Lords: [1997] STC 908, HL at 912c.

[6] *IRC v Pratt* [1982] STC 756, 57 TC 1.

[7] *IRC v Willoughby* [1997] STC 995, HL. For Professor Willoughby's account of the litigation see *The Offshore Taxation Review* Vol 8, pp 17–36.

[8] TA 1988, s 739(1A)(*a*), inserted by FA 1997, s 81(1). On unusual Revenue practice giving effect to the decision not only to open assessments but also to others in certain circumstances see Inland Revenue press release, 18 December 1997, **Simon's Weekly Tax Intelligence** 1998, p 10.

[9] FA 1997, s 81(2).

[10] [1980] AC 1148, [1980] STC 10, reversing the earlier House of Lords decision in *Congreve v IRC* [1948] 1 All ER 948, 30 TC 163. On the scope of the *Vestey* decision see Venables, *The Offshore Tax Planning Review* Vol 1, p 19.

[11] [1980] STC 10, 54 TC 503 HL.

[12] [1982] STC 756.

[13] ITA 2007, ss 731–735.

[14] ITA 2007, s 718(2)(*a*).

[15] FA 1994, s 249 (supra, § **33.30**).

[16] In *R v Dimsey* [2001] STC 1520, HL, Lord Scott said (at 1534a): '[now ITA 2007, s 218(2)] on its true construction does not, in my opinion, relieve transferees of their normal liability to pay tax on their income.' The House of Lords ruled that the legislation did not contravene the European Convention on Human Rights as it "is well within the margin of appreciation allowed to member states in respect of tax legislation. The public interest requires that legislation designed to combat tax avoidance should be effective. That public interest outweighs, in my opinion, the objections." (At 1535j.)

[35.27] ITA 2007, s 721 applies where any individual[1] has power to enjoy income of a person abroad as a result of a "relevant transfer" and that income would be chargeable to income tax if it were received by the individual in the UK. "Relevant transfer" is defined[2] as a transfer of assets as a result of which (or as a result of associated operations) income becomes payable to a person abroad. Statute[3] extends the concept of "transfer" to include the creation of rights. "Assets" are, then, defined[4] to include "property or rights of any kind" and "specifically, obligations of any company . . . or of any other person to whom the assets, income or accumulations are or have been transferred". Such income is deemed to be that of the person with the power to enjoy and is taxed as if the individual had received the income directly. The concept of income becoming payable to a non-resident is wide enough to include the profits of a non-resident trader.[5]

---

[1] ITA 2007, s 714(4); but not a widow: *Vestey's Executors v IRC* [1949] 1 All ER 1108, 31 TC 1.
[2] ITA 2007, s 716(2).
[3] ITA 2007, s 716(2).
[4] ITA 2007, s 717.
[5] *IRC v Brackett* [1986] STC 521.

[35.28] ITA 2007, s 728 applies where income has become the income from a person abroad as a result of a relevant transfer (or by associated operations) and the individual receives or is entitled to receive any capital sum.[1] The charge applies even if the capital sum was paid in an earlier tax year to that in which the transfer of assets occurs,[2] but not if it was a loan which was wholly repaid before the start of the tax year in which the transfer occurred.[3] In order for the charge to apply, the payment of the capital sum must be "connected with the relevant transactions;.[4] "Capital sum" is widely defined as "any sum paid or payable otherwise than as income and not for full consideration in monies worth,[5] and specifically includes "any sum paid or payable by way of a loan or a repayment of a loan".[6] The transferor is assessable if a capital sum falling within this definition is received by another person, either at the transferor's direction, or as a result of an assignment of a right by the transferor.[7]

It will be noticed that tax under this section is not limited to the capital sum[8] but goes on for ever—or at least for the duration of the life of the individual or so long as income accrues to the non-resident.

---

[1] ITA 2007, s 729(3).
[2] ITA 2007, s 729(1)(*a*)(ii).
[3] ITA 2007, s 729(2). Leaving money outstanding on a purchase is not a loan: *Ramsden v IRC* (1957) 37 TC 619.
[4] ITA 2007, s 729(1)(*b*).
[5] ITA 2007, s 729(3)(*b*).
[6] ITA 2007, s 729(3)(*a*).
[7] ITA 2007, s 729(4).
[8] *Vestey v IRC* [1980] AC 1148, [1980] STC 10.

Defences

[35.29] The provisions of ITA 2007, ss 765–767 do not apply if the individual "satisfies an officer of Revenue & Customs"[1] that *either* (a) "it would not be reasonable to draw the conclusion, from all the circumstances of the case, that the purpose of avoiding liability to taxation was the purpose, or one of the purposes, of which the relevant transactions or any of them were affected"[2] *or* (b) "all the relevant transactions were genuine commercial transactions and it would not be reasonable to draw the conclusion, from all the circumstances of the case, that any one or more of those transactions was more than incidentally designed for the purpose of avoiding liability to taxation".[3]

Where the transfer of the asset abroad took place before 5 December 2005 (and any associated operations also took place before that date) a different test is applied.[4] In this case in order to exclude the income tax charge on the UK resident individual, that individual must satisfy the officer of Revenue & Customs that *either* (a) the purpose of avoiding liability to taxation was not the purpose, or one of the purposes, for which the relevant transactions or any of them were effected[5] *or* (b) the transfers in any associated operations were genuine commercial transactions and were not designed for the purpose of avoiding liability to taxation.[6]

There are provisions[7] for partial exemption, by reference to considering the circumstances as to how far any of the associated operations directly or indirectly affect the nature or amount of any persons income or any person to enjoy any income.[8] The manner in which partial exemption is to work is specified in an interesting demonstration of the new style in which statute is written. Partial exemption "is so much of the income as appears to an officer of Revenue & Customs to be justly and reasonably attributable to the operations . . . in all the circumstances of the case."[9]

This was one of the first legislative attempts at an anti-avoidance clause. The test of purpose was held to be subjective in *Beneficiary v IRC* (1999).[10] Subsequent legislation designed to counter tax avoidance has tended to test commerciality by reference to the object of the action; that is, the test is designed to be objective, not subjective.[11]

At one time it was said that the defence in (a) did not apply if one among many purposes was the saving of tax.[12] Today this seems very hard to satisfy as judges have come to expect taxpayers to take tax matters into account (see supra, § **32.33**); moreover where someone other than the transferor is involved it may be very difficult to establish what the purposes of the perhaps now deceased transferor were.[13] In *IRC v Willoughby* Lord Nolan said that it would be absurd to describe as tax avoidance the acceptance of an offer of freedom from tax which Parliament had deliberately made. A UK resident might opt not to own investments directly but to profit from the investments through the medium of the personal portfolio bond. The former would be liable to income tax at both basic and higher rates on the income from the investments, and also to capital gains tax on chargeable gains realised on disposal. The latter, under the tax regime applicable to overseas life policies, would pay no tax on the income or capital gains until the maturity of the bond or the occurrence of one of the other specified chargeable events. Taking the option so offered was not tax avoidance.[14] The test of purpose is to be applied only to the transfer in question; it is not clear whether a subsequent tax-induced associated operation may infect the initial transfer.[15] Taxation includes taxes other than income tax, eg death duties,[16] but, it appears, not foreign taxes.[17] The burden is on the taxpayer to bring himself within the defence. There is no formal clearance procedure. Under self-assessment the taxpayer must disclose any income or benefit assessable under these rules and whether reliance is placed on the exemptions.[18]

Some points can be noted: (i) the intentions of advisers have to be taken into account in determining whether there was a tax avoidance purpose; (ii) "commercial transaction" (in relation to Condition B for exemption) does not include either transactions made other than on arm's length terms; or making/managing of investments, except where the activity is carried out between independent persons dealing at arm's length; (iii) "taxation" includes NIC.

---

[1] ITA 2007, s 737(2). Prior to the enactment of ITA 2007, the individual had to "show" his purpose. On importance of burden of proof on the taxpayer, see *Philippi v IRC* [1971] 3 All ER 61, 47 TC 75.
[2] ITA 2007, s 737(3).
[3] ITA 2007, s 737(4)(a). "Commercial transaction" is then defined: ITA 2007, s 778.
[4] ITA 2007, s 739(1).
[5] ITA 2007, s 739(3).
[6] ITA 2007, s 739(4).
[7] ITA 2007, s 742.
[8] ITA 2007, s 742(3).
[9] ITA 2007, s 742(2).
[10] [1999] STC (SCD) 134. However, HMRC attempt to give an objective interpretation of the statutory provision: Inland Revenue Tax Bulletin, Issue 40.
[11] ITA 2007, ss 765–767.
[12] *Cottinghams's Executors v IRC* [1938] 3 All ER 560, 22 TC 344.
[13] *MacDonald v IRC* [1940] 1 KB 802, 23 TC 449.
[14] [1997] STC 993 at 1004; the question whether the transaction came within (b) as a bona fide commercial transaction was deliberately left open.
[15] But, semble, not—*IRC v Herdman* [1969] 1 All ER 495, 45 TC 394. On the other hand note Salmon LJ in *Philippi v IRC* (1971) 47 TC 75 at 113–114.
[16] *Sassoon v IRC* (1943) 25 TC 154.
[17] *IRC v Herdman* [1969] 1 All ER 495, 45 TC 394.
[18] Inland Revenue interpretation, 27 April 1999, *Simon's Weekly Tax Intelligence* 1999, p 832.

Elements

[35.30] (1) For both provisions there must be a transfer of assets or operations associated with the transfer. Further the income accruing to the non-resident must accrue by virtue of or in consequence of that transfer or those operations.[1] It is not necessary that the income should come from the transferred assets. The situs of the assets is unimportant. The term asset is defined to include property or rights of any kind[2] and has been construed in a way similar to that for CGT (see supra, § **17.01**). It therefore includes rights under a contract of employment.[3] The term transfer is defined to include the creation of rights or property.[4]

---

[1] See *Vestey's Executors v IRC* [1949] 1 All ER 1108, 31 TC 1.
[2] ITA 2007, s 717(a).

[35.30] Foreign income and capital gains of residents

3   *IRC v Brackett* [1986] STC 521.
4   ITA 2007, s 716(2).

[35.31] (2) For both provisions the transferee must be either not resident or not domiciled in the UK when the income accrues, regardless of his residence when the transfer is made.[1] Whether they apply if the transferor becomes ordinarily resident only after the transfer is not completely clear, but it is unlikely that they apply.[2]

1   *Congreve v IRC* [1946] 2 All ER 170, 30 TC 163.
2   But in pre-*Vestey* days a person within s 739(2) who acquired UK ordinary residence after the transfer was caught. *IRC v Herdman* [1969] 1 All ER 495, 45 TC 394. For discussion see Venables, *The Offshore Tax Planning Review*, Vol 1, p 19.

[35.32] (3) For both provisions the associated operations may be by the transferor or the transferee or any other person.[1] The scope of an "associated operation" is very widely defined. Thus the transfer of shares or a partnership to a company,[2] taking up residence or domicile overseas,[3] an exchange of debentures[4] and the making of a will have all been held to be associated operations, but not the death of a testator.[5] Whether debentures are associated is a question of fact.[6]

1   eg *Lord Chetwode v IRC* [1977] STC 64, [1977] 1 All ER 638.
2   *Latilla v IRC* [1943] 1 All ER 265, 25 TC 107.
3   *Congreve v IRC* [1946] 2 All ER 170, 30 TC 163.
4   *Earl Beatty's Executors v IRC* (1940) 23 TC 574.
5   *Bambridge v IRC* [1955] 3 All ER 812, 36 TC 313 (intestate succession).
6   *Corbett's Executrices v IRC* [1943] 2 All ER 218, 25 TC 305.

[35.33] (4) For income to be charged on the transferor, the transferor has to retain a power to enjoy income. This requirement is satisfied if any of the following sets of circumstances exist:[1]

(A)   The income is in fact so dealt with by any person as to be calculated, at some point of time and whether in the form of income or not, to enure for the benefit of the individual.
      Although there is a House of Lords dictum that "So dealt with" denotes activity,[2] there is now Court of Appeal authority that a dealing does not require a positive act and that the mere retention and investment of income will be enough.[3]
(B)   The receipt or accrual of the income operates to increase the value to the individual of assets held by him or for his benefit.
      The income need not be received by the transferor; but it must increase the value of his assets, as where an individual resident transferred assets to a non-resident company in return for promissory notes, income subsequently accruing to the company increased the value of the notes.[4] Moreover where a vendor transferred shares to a company but left the purchase money outstanding it was held that he had the power to enjoy

the income accruing to the company in the form of dividends since the income of the company increased the value of the right to recover the debt.⁵ This seems open to question at least where the company could always meet its obligations—but ITA 2007, s 721 directs attention to substance not form.

(C) The individual receives or is entitled to receive, at any time any benefit provided or to be provided out of that income or out of moneys that are or will be available for the purpose by reason of the effect or successive effects of the associated operations on that income and on any assets which directly or indirectly represent that income.

This turns on actual receipt or entitlement to receipt by the transferor. The possession of shares in a company gives a right to any dividends that may be declared.⁶ There is some doubt whether loans fall within 3.⁷ In *IRC v Brackett*⁸ the benefits provided included the provision of liquidity through the purchase of assets he could not otherwise dispose of easily, the provision of money for repairs he could not otherwise afford and the payment of money in discharge of his moral obligations. These were held sufficient for C. ITA 2007, s 721 is widened by ss 722 & 723 but not widened so far as to make a person liable for benefits which have not been received.⁹

(D) The individual may, in the event of the exercise or successive exercise of one or more powers by whomsoever exercisable and whether with or without the consent of any other persons, become entitled to the beneficial enjoyment of the income.

This provision is designed to apply where foreign trustees of a discretionary trust own shares in an overseas company controlled by persons other than the trustees. The term "power" is undefined—and therefore unlimited.

(E) The individual is able in any manner whatsoever, and whether directly or indirectly, to control the application of the income.

For this, it will be noted, he need not control the application for his own benefit! A right to control investments is not a right to control the application of the income. Control of a company gives control over income through control over the directors.¹⁰ However, the donee of a special power of appointment among a defined and ascertainable group of persons does not have the power required for this head,¹¹ a decision since extended to the donee of an intermediate power, that is a power to appoint among the whole world subject to the exclusion of a defined class of persons which included the donee.¹² Where a settlor has a power to appoint and remove trustees it should not be assumed that the trustees will disregard their fiduciary duties and simply act as the settlor directs.

In determining whether a person has this power the terms of any relevant instrument must be construed to ascertain their true legal effect; so if a person apparently able to exercise a power in his own favour would find that appointment barred by the doctrine of fraud on a power, there is no power to enjoy under this head.¹³ In *IRC v Botnar*¹⁴, the taxpayer was an "excluded person" under the terms of the trust deed that he made. However, the deed permitted the trustees, acting in the light of counsel's advice, to transfer capital to another

[35.33] Foreign income and capital gains of residents

settlement, the terms of which could allow a benefit to pass to the taxpayer. The Court of Appeal held that the taxpayer had "power to enjoy", within section 739, income from the original settlement he created.

As if these provisions (1)–(5) were not wide enough it is further provided that, when these tests are applied, regard is to be had to the substantial results and effects of the transfer or the operations and all benefits accruing as a result of the transfer are to be taken into account regardless of the nature or form of the benefits and whether or not he had any rights.[15] This clause was intended to counteract the Cayman Islands legislation[16] reducing the legal character of interests of beneficiaries under trusts subject to Cayman Island law to that of mere spes.

[1] ITA 2007, s 723.
[2] Per Lord Simonds in *Lord Vestey's Executors v IRC* [1949] 1 All ER 1108, 31 TC 1 at 86.
[3] *IRC v Botnar* [1999] STC 711, CA.
[4] See *Lord Howard de Walden v IRC* [1942] 1 KB 389, 25 TC 121.
[5] *Ramsden v IRC* (1957) 37 TC 619; *Earl Beatty's Executors v IRC* (1940) 23 TC 574.
[6] *Lee v IRC* (1941) 24 TC 207.
[7] Obiter of Lord Normand in *Lord Vestey's Executors v IRC* (1949) 31 TC 1 at 90.
[8] [1986] STC 521.
[9] *IRC v Botnar* [1999] STC 711 paras 48–53, CA.
[10] *Lee v IRC* (1941) 24 TC 207.
[11] *Vestey's Executors v IRC* [1949] 1 All ER 1108.
[12] *IRC v Schroder* [1983] STC 480.
[13] Case stated of the Special Commissioners in *IRC v Botnar* [1998] STC 38 paras 155 and 156 at 60b–e. The decision of the Special Commissioners was reversed by the High Court, but on the basis of the court constructing the cross terms in a different manner; no reference was made to the assertion that a fraudulent appointment is void. (See also 36 *Halbury's Laws* (4th edition) para 962.)
[14] *IRC v Botnar* [1999] STC 711, CA.
[15] ITA 2007, s 722(4)(*b*).
[16] Cayman Islands Trust Act 1967, s 75(3)—all rights were vested in the Registrar of Trusts.

[35.34] (5) The fact that the resident has no power to enjoy the income of the transferee is not conclusive; the section asks whether he has the power to enjoy any income of any person; so control over the transferee is sufficient.[1]

[1] *Earl Beatty's Executors v IRC* (1940) 23 TC 574 at 590.

[35.35] (6) The Board has the most extensive power to demand information[1] in applying this section both from the transferor and any other person. There is some protection for solicitors[2] and bankers.[3]

[1] ITA 2007, s 748—eg *Clinch v IRC* [1973] 1 All ER 977, 49 TC 52.

² ITA 2007, s 748(4) & 749.
³ ITA 2007, s 750. Strictly construed in *Royal Bank of Canada v IRC* [1972] 1 All ER 225, 47 TC 565.

The charge

[35.36] Under these provisions the whole of the income of the non-resident person may be treated as that of the transferor, and this even though the "power to enjoy" does not extend so far. In logic this should extend to all income, whether or not from the assets transferred but in practice the HMRC appear to take a less exacting line. HMRC treat only the income of the non-resident derived from the transfer or associated operations as taxable.¹

Where the individual is not domiciled in the UK a remittance basis is used.²

¹ The Revenue approach derives some support from *Congreve v IRC* [1948] 1 All ER 948, 30 TC 163; at 954 and 199 per Cohen LJ.
² ITA 2007, ss 726 & 730; see Brandon, *Offshore and International Taxation Review*, vol 9 p 225.

[35.37] The income caught is that "which becomes payable" to the non-resident, and the House of Lords has held that deduction may not be made for the non-resident's management charges.¹ Expenses of collection are allowable as are deductions and reliefs that would be allowed if the income belonged to the individual.²

When the income of the non-resident is in the form of a dividend from a UK company that person will, as a non-resident,³ not be entitled to the tax credit. However, the resident whose income it is deemed to be is presumably so entitled. In the heyday of offshore funds it appears that the UK tax authorities were not very active in using TA 1988, s 739 even to charge a UK resident on his proportionate share of the income, apparently because these funds had a favourable effect on the UK balance of payments.

¹ *Lord Chetwode v IRC* [1977] STC 64, [1977] 1 All ER 638; on the meaning of payable see also *Latilla v IRC* [1943] 1 All ER 265, 25 TC 107.
² ITA 2007, s 746(2).
³ ITTOIA 2005, s 397(1).

Limitations

[35.38] These provisions are not completely unlimited. First, they apply only where the power to enjoy income or the receipt of a capital sum rests in or accrues to an individual. Intermediaries such as UK trusts and companies are not individuals although of course transfers by such bodies may be associated with earlier or later transfers by individuals.

Second, the income must accrue to the non-resident person *in consequence* of the transfer or the associated operations. In *Fynn v IRC*¹ an individual had a right to demand repayment of a loan from a foreign company which he had set up. He also had a charge on the company's assets. It was held that he had no power to enjoy the income accruing to the company in consequence of the charging of the assets of the company.

Third, the section applies only where the individual is ordinarily resident in the UK

Fourth, the provisions are limited to situations where income accrues to the non-resident person. Investment of assets transferred abroad so that no income is produced therefore avoids.[2] The question whether a particular receipt is income is presumably to be decided by UK tax law in the light of the rights and duties arising under the foreign law.[3]

---

[1] [1958] 1 All ER 270, 37 TC 629.
[2] For CGT anti-avoidance provisions, see infra, §§ **35.53–35.56**.
[3] Supra, § **35.10**. On inclusion of guaranteed returns on transactions in futures and options see ITTOIA 2005, s 569; TA 1988, Sch 5AA, para 8 inserted by FA 1997, Sch 11, extended to options by FA 1998, s 99.

Charge on non-transferor

[35.39] This provision[1] is designed to charge a person other than the transferor who receives a benefit (see supra, § **35.26**). As with the charge on the transferor, there must be an initial transfer of assets either alone or in conjunction with associated operations and as a result income must become payable to a person resident or domiciled outside the UK; further the person chargeable must be an individual ordinarily resident in the UK. Various supporting provisions, including those on information powers are made expressly applicable. In addition, the general defences, (see supra, § **35.29**) apply to s 740. The payment may also include a capital gains element.

When the charge is not on the transferor, the income tax charge is calculated by reference to the benefit received to the extent that it falls within relevant income.[2] Relevant income is income accruing in that year or in any previous tax year to a person resident or domiciled outside the UK and which can by virtue or in consequence of the transfer or associated operations be used directly or indirectly for providing a benefit for the individual or enabling a benefit to be provided for him.[3]

To the extent that the benefit falls within the amount of relevant income up to and including that year it is taxable as income of the individual. If the benefit should exceed that income it is carried forward and can be made liable to tax in later years by reason of the existence of relevant income in those later years.[4]

Where the person is not domiciled in the UK a remittance basis is applied.[5] There is no charge if the benefit is not received in the UK. On a literal interpretation a benefit received abroad and later brought to the UK escapes charge as it is not received in the UK.

To prevent double charges, no amount of income may be charged more than once. It may happen that the transferor has a power to enjoy or has received a benefit. In such circumstances the Revenue are to attribute the income as appears to them just and reasonable, a decision made reviewable by the Special Commissioners.

1   ITA 2007, s 731.
2   ITA 2007, s 733.
3   ITA 2007, s 733(1) Step 3(b).
4   ITA 2007, s 733(1) Step 6.
5   ITA 2007, s 735.

Offshore funds

[35.40] Statute[1] imposes a charge to income tax (or corporation tax under Schedule D Case VI) on the offshore income gain which arises to an investor disposing of material interests[2] in any offshore fund which is, or has at any material time been, a non-qualifying offshore fund.[3]

1   TA 1988, ss 757–764 and Schs 27, 28 amended by FA 2007, s 56.
2   TA 1988, ss 757(1), 759.
3   TA 1988, ss 757(1), 760, Sch 27.

Disposals

[35.41] The capital gains tax definition of disposal[1] applies, with two amendments. First, death is an occasion of charge, the gain being calculated by reference to the market value of the deceased's interest in the fund,[2] and second, the provisions covering exchange of securities (on take-overs, reconstructions and amalgamations, for instance)[3] are modified.[4]

1   TA 1988, s 757(2).
2   TA 1988, s 757(3).
3   TCGA 1992, ss 135, 136.
4   TA 1988, s 757(5), (6).

Material interests

[35.42] On or after 29 November 1994 interests caught by the rules are interests in a collective investment scheme as defined by FSMA 2000, constituted by non-resident companies or in unit trusts with non-resident trustees or arrangements which, under the laws of a foreign territory, create rights in the nature of co-ownership in a collective investment scheme.[1] Non-collective investment schemes are now outside these rules, but with the threat that they will be brought back if used for abuse.[2]

An interest is a material interest if, when it was acquired, it was reasonable to suppose that the value of the interest could be realised within the next seven years.³ A person is deemed to be able to realise the value of his interest if he can realise an amount which is approximately equal to the proportion of the underlying assets of the company (or assets subject to the unit trust scheme or arrangements) which his interest represents.⁴ Realisation of the amount can be in money or in assets of that value.⁵

Certain interests are excluded from the definition of material interests.⁶ They include an interest in respect of loan capital or other debt incurred for money lent in the ordinary course of a banking business,⁷ and rights under an insurance policy. Special rules apply to exclude shares in overseas companies,⁸ provided that four conditions are met:

(1) the shares are held by the company because it is necessary or desirable for the maintenance and development of the trade carried on by that company or an associated company;

(2) the shares must confer at least 10% of the voting rights in the overseas company and also a right, in winding up, to at least 10% of the residual assets after all prior liabilities have been discharged;⁹

(3) the maximum number of persons holding shares in the company is ten and all the shares must confer both voting rights and a right to participate in the assets in the event of a winding up;

(4) at the time the shares were acquired, the company must have reasonably expected that the holder would be able to realise their value in only one, or both, of the following circumstances:

    (a) under an arrangement whereby, at some time within seven years, the company could require other participators to purchase the shares; or

    (b) because of an agreement between the participators under which the company will be wound up within a period which is or is reasonably expected to be, less than seven years.

Simon's Taxes C1.620.

---

[1] TA 1988, s 759(1).
[2] HC Official Report, Standing Committee D (Eighteenth Sitting), cols 563–571.
[3] TA 1988, s 759(2); see also statement of practice SP 2/86, para 2.
[4] TA 1988, s 759(3); see also statement of practice SP 2/86, para 4.
[5] TA 1988, s 759(4).
[6] TA 1988, s 759(5), (6).
[7] See statement of practice SP 2/86, para 3.
[8] TA 1988, s 759(6).
[9] TA 1988, s 759(6).

Distributing funds and non-qualifying offshore funds

[35.43] The legislation charges realisations from an offshore fund to tax as income rather than as chargeable gains, unless the offshore fund is certified by the Revenue as having "distributor status" throughout the time that the investor held the relevant shares or units. In order to obtain distributor status an offshore fund must distribute annually at least 85% of its income and must meet certain other conditions.

If an offshore fund has distributor status, investors are within the chargeable gains rules in respect of their disposal of units or shares in the fund. This reflects the fact that the bulk of the fund's income will have been distributed and charged to income tax annually, and that the fund will therefore have been operating in more or less the same way as a UK-based fund.

If the fund does not have distributor status, disposals of shares/units are charged to tax as income to reflect the fact that the increased value of the holding will derive to a significant extent from accumulated income.

A fund must apply annually for distributor status and it is considered separately for each account period of the fund. In respect of an individual investor, the fund must have had distributor status throughout the period that the investor held the shares/units that are the subject of the relevant disposal. It is quite possible for different investors to be in a different position in relation to the same fund, or indeed for the same investor to be in a different position in relation to different holdings of shares/units in the same fund.

United Kingdom equivalent profits ("UKEP") is important for the purpose of distributor status as a fund has to distribute annually at least 85% of its income as measured by UKEP (as well as 85% of its income as measured by the fund's accounts).[1]

UKEP used in deciding whether a fund is a qualifying fund, is computed by applying to the profits of the offshore fund the rules that apply for UK corporation tax. Thus, interest income is computed using the same "loan relationship" rules[2] as for UK companies. Income from derivative contracts is computed using the same corporation tax rules[3] as for UK companies.

A fund will only be so certified if it has a full distribution policy during the period.[4] The conditions are set out in detail in TA 1988, Sch 27, but in general the following must be met:[5]

(1) a distribution must be made for the account period or for some other period which falls, in whole or in part, within the account period;
(2) the amount of the distribution made to holders of material and other interests in the fund must equal at least 85% of the fund's income for the period, and be not less than 85% of the fund's UK equivalent profits for the period;
(3) the distribution must be made during the account period, or within the following six months or such longer periods as the Board may allow.[6]

In 2 above, one-half of any income of an offshore fund which is derived from dealing in commodities is left out of account in determining the distributable income of an offshore fund, or in calculating the fund's UK equivalent profits.[7] The fund's UK equivalent profits are the total profits of the fund upon which, after deductions, corporation tax would be chargeable, but for this purpose profits *exclude* chargeable gains.[8]

A fund is treated as following a full distribution policy if there is no income of the fund and there are no UK equivalent profits of the fund.[9] For account periods ending after 28 November 1994 the same result applies if the amount of the gross income of the fund does not exceed 1% of the average value of the fund's assets held during the account period.[10]

Simon's Taxes C1.620.

[1] TA 1988, Sch 27, para 1(1).
[2] FA 1996, ss 80–105, Sch 8–11. See supra, §§ **27.01–27.10**.
[3] FA 2002, Sch 26.
[4] TA 1988, s 760(2).
[5] TA 1988, Sch 27, para 1; changes to the detailed requirements are made by FA 2004, Sch 26.
[6] TA 1988, Sch 27, para 14; this applies for accounting periods ending after the passing of F(No 2)A 1987.
[7] TA 1988, Sch 27, para 4.
[8] TA 1988, Sch 27, para 5(2).
[9] TA 1988, Sch 27, para 1(2).
[10] TA 1988, Sch 27, para1(2)(*b*).

Exchanges within an offshore fund

[35.44] Statute[1] treats an exchange as not being a disposal, and hence, no income tax charge arises on the exchange, where the exchange is within an offshore fund that has distributor status. There are consequential changes for capital gains tax purposes. The situation is illustrated by a Revenue example: An offshore fund has different classes of interest that are treated as separate offshore funds. An investor acquires a class of interest (A) in the offshore fund for £100. (A) does not have "distributor status" so any gain on disposal is chargeable to tax as income.

Subsequently the investor exchanges (A) for another class of interest (B) that does have "distributor status". The exchange is such that, for chargeable gains purposes, it would be treated as involving no disposal of (A). At that time the market value of (A) was £120. Finally the investor disposes of (B) for £150 making an overall profit from the investment of £50.

Although the exchange of (A) for (B) does not involve any disposal of (A) under the chargeable gains rules, TA 1988, s 762A operates so that a gain of £20 (£120 market value less £100 cost) chargeable to income tax under the offshore fund rules arises at the time of the exchange.

For chargeable gains purposes (B) is treated as if the consideration the investor gave to acquire it was the £100 given to acquire (A). TA 1988, s 763(6A) results in the £20 charged to income tax being treated as additional consideration given for the investment. So the chargeable gain (before any reliefs or allowances due) on the disposal of (B) is £30 (disposal proceeds £150, less deemed original cost £100, less amount charged as income £20).

[1] TA 1988, s 762A, inserted by FA 2004, Sch 26, para 15.

The charge to tax

[35.45] If a disposal gives rise to an offshore income gain, the gain is treated as arising at the time of the disposal.[1]

The rules for calculating the gain are set out in TA 1988, Sch 28. Except where the disposal involves an equalisation element,[2] it is necessary to calculate the unindexed gain on the disposal, ignoring the charge to income tax or corporation tax. If the gain or loss has to be calculated in a way which takes account of the indexation allowance on an earlier no gain/no loss disposal (eg transfers between spouses/civil partners) the unindexed gain is calculated on the basis that no indexation allowance was available on the earlier disposal. The general relief for gifts, and rollover relief on the transfer of a business, are not available. If the computation produces a loss, the unindexed gain is deemed to be nil and there is no material disposal.

If the interest disposed of was acquired, or is deemed to have been acquired, before 1 January 1984, the interest is deemed to have been sold and immediately reacquired on 1 January 1984 at its then market value. The unindexed gain is calculated using that value, unless that method produces a larger gain. An interest acquired after 1 January 1984 on a no gain/no loss basis must be traced back to its original acquisition, the last no gain/no loss disposal before 1 January 1984, or to the last material disposal.[3]

If the material disposal also gives rise to a charge to CGT, the consideration taken into account for CGT is reduced by the offshore income gain.[4]

Special rules apply to persons resident and domiciled abroad,[5] insurance companies[6] and trustees.[7] Charities are exempt.[8]

Simon's Taxes C1.621.

[1] TA 1988, s 761(1).
[2] See TA 1988, Sch 28, Part II.
[3] TA 1988, Sch 28, paras 2–5.
[4] TA 1988, s 763.
[5] TA 1988, s 762.
[6] TA 1988, s 441(8).
[7] TA 1988, s 764. See also TA 1988, ss 663(2), 687(3).
[8] TA 1988, s 761(6).

Capital gains tax

[35.46] A person is chargeable to CGT if he is resident or ordinarily resident in the UK for at least a part of the year of assessment.[1] If he is not resident in the UK he is chargeable only if he is carrying on a trade through a branch or agency or in the case of a non-resident company a permanent establishment and the asset was both situated in the UK and either used in or for the trade when or before the gain accrued or used by or for the branch or agency or permanent establishment at or before the gain accrued.[2] This potential charge has now been extended from trades to professions.[3] These rules preserve the basic premise that a person is taxable either because he is resident or because the source is here, but curiously restricts the source to the one type—through a branch or agency or permanent establishment. Thus a non-resident without such a trade or profession bears no capital gains tax even though he buys an asset in the UK. Equally, a resident with a substantial liability to CGT could, until 1998, go overseas, lose both his UK residence and ordinary residence, and then dispose of his assets free of all UK tax, at least if he waited until the next year of assessment.[4]

However, in some respects the system is gradually being tightened up. 1998 saw the introduction of rules for temporary non-resident individuals (see infra, § **35.47**). Earlier, 1988 had seen the introduction of a general deemed disposal rule for companies (see supra, § **25.46**). 1989 saw legislation directing that a non-resident who has chargeable assets in the UK, as with a trade or profession, will be treated as making a disposal of them when the assets cease to be chargeable assets by being removed from the UK.[5] Curiously, as if to underline the timidity of the approach, this charge does not apply if the non-resident is also ceasing, contemporaneously, to carry on the trade or profession through a permanent establishment here or if the asset is an exploration or exploitation asset.[6] There is a similar charge if the asset ceases to be a chargeable asset because he ceases, after 13 March 1989, to carry on his trade or profession in the UK through a permanent establishment.[7] There is no deemed disposal if the asset remains a chargeable asset. The transfer of a permanent establishment within a group of companies is made without triggering a gain if, but if only if, the transferor and transferee companies are both UK resident.[8] Residence and ordinary residence have the same meanings as for income tax,[9] and one who is in the UK for some temporary purpose and not with a view to establishing his residence here, is treated as resident only if his period of residence in the UK exceeds six months.[10]

Where an asset is acquired and disposed of in foreign currency, acquisition cost and disposal proceeds are calculated at the exchange rates prevailing at the acquisition and disposal.[11] On foreign currency as a chargeable or exempt asset see supra, § **17.06**.

The extended scope of the charge in 1988 and 1989 has led to the introduction of special rules with regard to rollover relief for non-residents. The general rule, applicable to disposals and acquisitions after 13 March 1989, is that rollover relief is not permitted if the old assets are "chargeable assets in relation to a person" at the time of the disposal unless the new assets are similarly related immediately after the time of acquisition.[12] The expression "chargeable assets in relation to a person" is defined as referring to assets in relation to which a non-resident would be subject to tax under TCGA 1992, s 10B in the case of a non-resident company and s 10(1) in relation to a non-resident with a branch or agency.[13]

This exclusion of rollover relief does not apply if the person acquiring the new asset had come within the UK tax net by reason of his personal status, ie by becoming resident or ordinarily resident in the UK, when the asset was acquired.[14] However, this (logical) generosity is withheld (logically) from dual residents in whose hands the assets are safe from the UK tax charge by reason of a double tax agreement.[15]

Simon's Taxes C1.102, 201, 602, 604; D2.917; Sumption CGT A3.01.

1. TCGA 1992, s 2(1). On the concessionary split year treatment see supra, § **33.10**. If the individual is resident in the UK but is not domiciled within the UK the charge is limited in the case of a disposal of a foreign asset to sums remitted to the UK: see supra, § **35.12** and infra, § **35.48**.
2. TCGA 1992, s 10; he may also be exempt by treaty, see s 10 (infra, § **37.04**). On post-cessation disposals see TCGA 1992, s 10(2). The term "permanent establishment" is used for a company. The older term "branch or agency" continues to be used for unincorporated business.
3. TCGA 1992, s 10(5). This deemed disposal began in 1989—on deemed acquisition of assets see s 10(5).
4. If he tried to dispose of the asset in the same year as he acquired non-residence, relying on extra-statutory concession D2, he would run foul of *R v IRC, ex p Fulford-Dobson* [1987] STC 344.
5. TCGA 1992, s 25(1), (7).
6. TCGA 1992, s 25(2). Exploration and exploitation assets are defined by s 25(6); the relevant deemed disposal is governed by s 199.
7. TCGA 1992, s 25(3).
8. TCGA 1992, s 171(1A) inserted by FA 2000, Sch 29, para 2.
9. On residence of partners see TCGA 1992, s 59 and ITTOIA, ss 857 & 858.
10. TCGA 1992, s 9(3).
11. *Capcount Trading v Evans* [1993] STC 11, CA, reaffirming *Bentley v Pike* [1981] STC 360, 53 TC 590.
12. TCGA 1992, s 159(1).
13. TCGA 1992, s 159(4).
14. TCGA 1992, s 159(2).
15. TCGA 1992, s 159(3).

Temporary non-residence and capital gains

[35.47] The rule which excluded a non-resident from UK tax on gains made even on UK assets, combined with the absence of a deemed disposal on emigration and the relative ease with which properly advised taxpayers with mobile lifestyles could achieve non-resident status,[1] gave rise to Revenue worries. The resulting legislation, TCGA 1992, s 10A,[2] does not, however, impose a general deemed disposal at market value charge on assets on emigration (or an equivalent deemed acquisition on immigration). The target is much more specific.

Section 10A applies if B, an individual and one-time resident of some duration, having become a non-resident, then reacquires resident status; the charge arises only in the year of return.[3] The rules apply to individuals becoming non-resident on or after 17 March 1998.[4]

Section 10A only applies where B returns to the UK after having been non-resident for less than five complete tax years of assessment and, further, B was, prior to his departure, resident in the UK for at least four of the seven years immediately before the non-residence; for this purpose residence for any part of the year suffices.[5]

[35.47] Foreign income and capital gains of residents

Section 10A charges gains realised during the period of non-residence including any liability in respect of s 13 (see infra, § **35.53**), s 86 and s 87 (see infra, § **35.63**) which would have arisen if B had been resident.[6] Relief is given for any losses.[7] Gains and losses on assets acquired after becoming non-resident or Treaty non-resident are in general excluded but there are substantial rules denying relief where the new asset exploits a deferral of or exemption from UK tax, eg the acquisition was one on which neither gain nor loss accrued to the disposer or rollover relief reduced the cost of the asset, was acquired from a spouse/civil partner or consists of an interest in the settlement.[8] Provision is made to ensure that the tax position of a non-resident carrying on a trade or profession in the UK through a branch or agency is not affected.[9]

In practice, the temporary non-residence provisions could easily be avoided by a footloose individual by locating himself in a country which has taxing rights that exclude a UK charge by virtue of a double taxation agreement. When the asset is acquired after 15 March 2005, statute[10] excludes the tax exemption that would otherwise arise under the terms of the double taxation agreement.

Simon's Taxes C1.601.

---

[1] eg *Reed v Clark* [1985] STC 323, 58 TC 528.
[2] Introduced by FA 1998, s 127.
[3] On period during which assessment may be made see TCGA 1992, s 10A(7).
[4] FA 1998, s 127(4).
[5] TCGA 1992, s 10A(1), (8) and (9).
[6] TCGA 1992, s 10A(2).
[7] TCGA 1992, s 10A(2).
[8] TCGA 1992, s 10A(3) and (4). The no gain no loss disposals are those in ss 58 (spouses and civil partners), 73 (death) and 258(4) (works of art); the reductions are those under ss 23 (reinvestment of compensation money), 152 (acquisition of business asset), 162 (transfer of business) and 247 (compulsory acquisition). There are further rules for reorganisations of bonds and gilts (s 116), for acquisition of compensation stock (s 134) and rollover relief where the new assets are depreciating assets (s 154).
[9] TCGA 1992, s 10A(5).
[10] F(No 2)A 2005, s 32.

Remittance basis

[35.48] If the person is an individual resident or ordinarily resident, but not domiciled, in the UK then, in accordance with the rules set out at 35.12 supra, the charge to tax on gains accruing from the disposal of an asset outside the UK may be limited to the amount received in this country in respect of those gains.[1] In computing the amount of the gain any liability to foreign tax is deductible in full.[2] Where the proceeds of the disposal are remitted to the UK and exceed the gain, the Revenue adopt an apportionment principle when deciding how much of the remittance is in respect of the gain.

The availability of the remittance basis is thus dependent on the status of the person and the location of the asset. One consequence of the rule is that a gift does not give a UK CGT liability as there are no proceeds to be remitted.

Simon's Taxes C1.102; Sumption CGT A3.05.

[1] TCGA 1992, s 12. Since the remittance basis applies only to individuals why does s 62(3) treat the personal representatives as domiciled where the deceased was domiciled? See the discussion by Brandon in *Offshore and International Taxation Review*, vol 9 p 211.
[2] TCGA 1992, s 278, unless relief is given under s 277.

Losses and the remittance basis

[35.49] Until the reforms of the remittance basis with effect from 6 April 2008, non-domiciled individuals were given no relief for overseas losses (former TCGA 1992, s 16(4)) although the shrewd operator might have been able to bring the asset standing at a loss into the UK before disposal. Now that the remittance basis will not always be attractive to taxpayers, a new set of provisions has been introduced.

Elections regarding losses

TCGA 1992, s 16ZA provides that an election may be made by taxpayers in respect of the first year in which they are not domiciled in the UK and claim to be taxed on the remittance basis.[1]

Where an election is made, it is irrevocable.

If an election is made:

(a) gains which:
 (i) arise in a tax year on or after the first in which the remittance basis is claimed under ITA 2007, s 809B (and the taxpayer is not UK-domiciled); but
 (ii) are remitted in a subsequent year (and are so taxed in that later year),
 do not qualify for loss relief and (assuming that the remittance basis is not claimed in that later tax year under ITA 2007, s 809B) cannot be offset by the annual exemption.[2] This applies whether or not the taxpayer is subject to the remittance basis in this later year.
(b) in years for which the remittance basis applies (whether or not claimed), loss relief is available but such losses must be set off against:
 (i) first, foreign gains of that tax year to the extent that they are remitted to the UK in that year;
 (ii) next, foreign gains of that tax year to the extent that they are not remitted to the UK tax year; and
 (iii) finally, UK gains of that year.[3]

When setting off losses against unremitted foreign gains special rules apply if the losses are not sufficient to exhaust all such gains:

(a) first, losses are deducted from the latest such gains before any earlier gains;
(b) however, where the gains of a particular day exceed any remaining loss relief available, the losses are apportioned.[4]

[35.49] Foreign income and capital gains of residents

[1] Under ITA 2007, s 809B.
[2] TCGA 1992, s 16ZB.
[3] TCGA 1992, s 16ZC.
[4] TCGA 1992, s 16ZC(2).

Consequences of not making an election

Where no election is made, the taxpayer will not be entitled to loss relief in respect of any overseas assets for that year or any subsequent tax year.[1]. The legislation appears to prevent such loss relief in respect of overseas assets even if the taxpayer were subsequently to acquire a UK domicile. That must be susceptible to challenge under European law if it is not subsequently revised.

[1] TCGA 1992, s 16ZA(3).

Mixed fund

[35.50] ITA 2007, s 809P determines how to ascertain whether or not a remittance is made and, if so, the amount remitted. This replaces the practice that existed beforehand. For a commentary of the previous practice, see para 35.48 of the 25th edition of this work.
Simon's Taxes C1.605; Sumption CGT A3.05.

[35.51] The remittance basis applies *only* to foreign assets. The rules as to the location of assets are:[1]

(1) the situation of rights or interests (otherwise than by way of security) in or over immovable property is that of the immovable property;
(2) subject to the following provisions of this subsection, the situation of rights or interests (otherwise than by way of security) in or over tangible movable property is that of the tangible movable property;
(3) subject to the following provisions of this subsection, a debt, secured or unsecured, is situated in the UK if and only if the creditor is resident in the UK;
(4) shares in or debentures of a company incorporated in the UK have UK situs. This rule extends to interest in a company with no share capital;[2]
(5) shares or securities issued by any municipal or governmental authority, or by any body created by such an authority, are situated in the country of that authority;
(6) a ship or aircraft is situated in the UK if and only if the owner is then resident in the UK, and an interest or right in or over a ship or aircraft is situated in the UK and if and only if the person entitled to the interest or right is resident in the UK;
(7) intangible assets are located in the UK if subject to UK law; that is, the right to the asset is enforceable in the UK, or governed by or, otherwise subject to UK law;[3]
(8) a judgment debt is situated where the judgment is recorded;
(9) a non-sterling bank account is situated outside the UK unless the branch at which it is maintained is in the UK.

Simon's Taxes C1.604; Sumption CGT A3.10.

1 TCGA 1992, s 275 amended by F(No 2)A 2005, Sch 4, para 4.
2 TCGA 1992, s 275(2) amended by F(No 2)A 2005, Sch 4, para 4.
3 TCGA 1992, s 175 inserted by F(No 2)A 2005, Sch 4, para 5.

Delayed remittances

[35.52] If a person is chargeable to tax on a gain accruing from the disposal of an asset situated overseas, but is unable to remit that gain to the UK then, if he makes a claim and is not chargeable on a remittance basis, he, or his personal representative,[1] is not assessed to tax on those gains as they arise, on conditions analogous to income tax relief (see supra, § **35.24**). The inability to remit gains to the UK must arise from the laws of the territory where the asset was situated or from the executive action of its government or from the impossibility of obtaining foreign currency there. Since tax is levied as soon as the conditions cease it may happen that gains accruing over several years will come into charge at one time. In such circumstances, unlike income tax, there is no charge by reference to the years in which the gain accrued. This may mean the loss of the annual exemption for the years in which the gains actually arose. Similar Revenue reasoning means that this relief does not apply where the taxpayer is chargeable on a remittance basis.

The relief for a delayed remittance is only available where the claimant is "unable to transfer the qualifying gains to the United Kingdom".[2] Thus, the relief is not available where there is a deemed disposal, such as the attribution of gains made by the non-resident company to its members resident in the UK.[3] This can create problems in practice, where the non-resident company is in a jurisdiction that does not allow repatriation of capital. The UK resident shareholder is, thus, assessable on gains he can never enjoy, so long as he remains within the UK.

Simon's Taxes C1.605; Sumption CGT A3.05.

1 TCGA 1992, s 279.
2 TCGA 1992, s 279(3)(*a*).
3 TCGA 1992, s 13.

Attribution of gains made by a non-resident company

[35.53] Gains accruing to a company are not usually attributable to their shareholders, but an exception is made by TCGA 1992, s 13 where the company would be a close company but for being non-resident. The gain will be attributed to a shareholder who is either resident or ordinarily resident and, if an individual, is domiciled in the UK. Further he must have a shareholding of at least 10%[1] in the company, his portion being ascertained by reference to his share of the assets on a hypothetical liquidation. The charge cannot be avoided by placing another non-resident company between the shareholder

[35.53] Foreign income and capital gains of residents

and the company to which the gain accrues since the Revenue are given power to attribute the gain down through any number of intervening companies to the real shareholders.[2]

EXAMPLE

X Ltd is a non-resident company. Smith buys 25% of the share capital in X Ltd. X Ltd realises a gain of £10,000; £2,500 is attributed to Smith making a tax liability (but for any exemption) of £750. If Smith later sells his shares realising, say, a gain of £1,000 that gain will be reduced by the £750 to £250.

It was found that s 13 could be circumvented where offshore assets were held by an offshore company owned by a trust and a double tax treaty gave an exemption for such gains. The treaty would give exemption even though the settlor and/or the beneficiaries and/or the trustees were resident in the UK. FA 2000 therefore provides that for gains of non-resident companies arising on or after 21 March 2000, s 13 is to be applied without regard to such a treaty.[3]

Simon's Taxes C1.606; Sumption CGT A3.20.

---

[1] TCGA 1992, s 13(4).
[2] TCGA 1992, s 13(9).
[3] TCGA 1992 s 79B added by FA 2000, s 94.

[35.54] The section only applies where "chargeable gains accrue to the company". This means that all the provisions of TCGA 1992 potentially apply. For example, the no gain/no loss rule applies on an intra-group transfer even though the companies are non-resident.[1] On this construction the purpose of the section is simply to prevent abuse of the exemption of non-resident companies.

If before three years after the end of the company's accounting period, the company makes a distribution, any income tax paid by the recipient of the distribution is treated as a credit against the CGT charge.[2] Further the amount of CGT paid by the shareholder is deductible in computing any later gain accruing on the disposal of the shares, unless that tax is reimbursed by the company,[3] always assuming, however, that there is a chargeable gain on such disposal.[4] Losses can be attributed only to cover attributable gains.[5] The company gains are calculated as if it was subject to corporation tax, ie indexation still applies.[6]

The section carries the very real risk that a taxpayer will be liable to CGT without being able to secure the payment or get his hands on any of the gain. Relief for unremittable gains[7] does not extend to gains which he cannot get out simply because of his status as a minority as opposed to a majority shareholder.[8]

The section applies only when the company is, or would, if resident, be, a close company. It does not apply to individuals domiciled abroad nor when the part to be attributed is less than 10% of the whole.[9] Further losses accruing to the company can be brought in.[10]

Special provision is made for non-resident groups.[11]

Simon's Taxes C1.606; Sumption CGT A3.20, A3.21.

1   Inland Revenue interpretation RI 43.
2   TCGA 1992, s 13(5A). The period given by statute is, as stated above, or, earlier, 48 months from the date of the chargeable gain: TCGA 1992, s 13(5B)(*b*).
3   Such a reimbursement is exempt from tax; TCGA 1992, s 13(11).
4   TCGA 1992, s 13(7).
5   TCGA 1992, s 13(8).
6   FA 1998, s 120(4).
7   TCGA 1992, s 279 (supra, § **35.52**).
8   One solution may be to sell the shares in the non-resident company before the company disposes of the asset.
9   TCGA 1992, s 13(4).
10 TCGA 1992, s 13(8).
11 TCGA 1992, s 14.

Overseas trusts

CGT charge when overseas trustees appointed

[35.55] There is a deemed disposal where trustees cease to be resident in the UK. For CGT, trustees are resident in the UK unless the general administration of the trust is ordinarily carried on outside the UK and the trustees or a majority of them are not resident or not ordinarily resident in the UK.[1] It follows that a trust can migrate if the trust administration shifts abroad, if a change in the trustees alters the territorial balance or if a particular trustee decides to migrate.

Where trustees cease to be resident in the UK there is a deemed disposal of all defined assets;[2] assets are defined assets unless they are going to stay within the UK CGT net[3] or if they were already outside that net by reason of a double tax treaty.[4] No chargeable gain arises in respect of assets used by the trustees to carry on a trade in the UK.[5]

Special rules apply where the migration is caused by the death of a trustee. If the trust resumes its UK residence within six months from the death the deemed disposal is excluded save for assets which have been the subject of an actual disposal in the meantime,[6] or which would have been protected by a double tax treaty anyway.[7] Conversely a trust which has become UK resident by reason of such a death will not be the subject of a deemed disposal (save for assets which have been the subject of holdover relief) if it resumes its non-resident status within six months.[8]

Tax due under a deemed disposal can be collected from any person who ceased to be a trustee within the period of 12 months ending with the migration; the ex-trustee has a right of indemnity in such circumstances.[9] This potential liability does not apply to a trustee who establishes that he ceased to be a trustee before the end of the relevant period and that at that time there was no proposal that the trustees might become non-resident.[10]

[35.55] Foreign income and capital gains of residents

There is a similar deemed disposal if the trust while remaining resident under UK ordinary tax rules ceases to be so thanks to the application of a double tax treaty.[11] There is also a restriction on rollover relief where the new asset is acquired by such trustees.[12]

In *Hicks v Davies*[13] it was held that this emigration charge is calculated on the assets actually held in the trust at the time of emigration. In that case, UK trustees sold shares, then resigned in favour of trustees in Mauritius, who then repurchased shares of the same class in the same company. The identification rule[14] treated the sale by the UK trustees as being of the shares purchased by the Mauritian trustees. Although the shares were deemed to be held by the trustees on the date that emigration occurred for the purpose of calculating the gain on the disposal, it was held that they were not to be treated as assets of the trust for the purpose of calculating the capital gain arising on emigration.

Simon's Taxes, C4.435.

[1] TCGA 1992, s 69(1); FA 1989, s 110 reversing the decision in *IRC v Dawson* has no application to CGT.
[2] TCGA 1992, s 80(1), (2). On practice under ss 80–85, see statement of practice SP 5/92, paras 4–6.
[3] TCGA 1992, s 80(3), (4) referring to assets remaining in a UK branch or agency.
[4] TCGA 1992, s 80(3), (5).
[5] TCGA 1992, s 80(6), (7).
[6] TCGA 1992, s 81(1), (3).
[7] TCGA 1992, s 81(4).
[8] TCGA 1992, ss 81(5)–(7), 84.
[9] TCGA 1992, s 82.
[10] TCGA 1992, s 82(3).
[11] TCGA 1992, s 83. See *Smallwood & Anor (trustees of Trevor Smallwood Settlement) v R & C Commrs* [2009] EWHC 777 (Ch).
[12] TCGA 1992, s 84.
[13] [2005] STC (SCD) 165.
[14] TCGA 1992, s 106A.

Capital gains charged on beneficiaries

[35.56] Gains realised by overseas trustees are attributed to beneficiaries. This treatment is applied irrespective of the domicile and residence of the settlor when the trust was created.[1] These provisions also apply to trusts which are resident in the UK for domestic purposes but which are treated as non-resident by a double tax treaty; in such circumstances the trust gains giving rise to potential attribution to the settlor will be the lesser of (a) the actual gains, and (b) the gains protected by the treaty.[2]

As gains accrue to non-resident trustees they are cumulated as "trust gains".[3] Capital payments[4] received by the beneficiaries are then attributed to the trust gains which become chargeable gains in the hand of the beneficiaries.[5] This applies only to beneficiaries who are domiciled in the UK, at some time during the year.[6] When a capital payment is made to a beneficiary in one year and a trust gain arises in a later year, a charge may arise in that later year. Relief may be claimed for trust losses.[7]

The gains are attributed to beneficiaries in proportion to the capital payment received by them, but are not to exceed those payments.[8] This obscure provision seems to mean that if the only payments made to the beneficiaries are made to A, then A can be assessed for all the gains accruing to the non-resident trustees up to the amount he has received; he is thus at risk for up to 40% of the entire sum received.

For this purpose the term settlement receives not its narrow CGT meaning but the wide income tax meaning of arrangement.[9]

A capital payment includes the transfer of an asset, a loan, and various indirect payments.[10] It does not cover a payment by way of bargain at arm's length.[11] The Court of Appeal has held that an interest free loan, payable on demand, is to be treated as a capital payment. The charge under s 97 is the interest that would have been charged on a loan at a commercial rate of interest for the period for which the loan actually extended, even though the loan was repayable on demand.[12]

In an effort to discourage the use of settlements as devices to retain gains rather than distribute them this charge is supplemented.[13] The tax is increased by 10%[14] from the year in which the gain arose to the trustees up to the year in which the capital payment is made to the beneficiary. This is subject to a maximum of 60%.[15] The manner of calculating the period is odd as it relates to the payment date that applied to CGT before 1996–97. The period for which the 10% charge is calculated is the whole number of years in the period from (a) 1 December following the year in which the capital gain was made by the trustees; to (b) 30 November in the tax year following that in which the beneficiary receives the capital payment.[16] So if a capital payment is made in 2007–08 and the payment is matched with trust gains accruing in 2005–06 there will be 20% supplementary charge for the period 1 December 2006 to 30 November 2008. This charge applies regardless of when in 2005–06 the capital payment is made.

The 10% rate of interest can be varied by Treasury Order,[17] but no order has been made since the enactment of this provision in 1992.

It will be seen that if a beneficiary is a 40% taxpayer and the payment has been made out of the oldest possible trust gains, the combination of the normal CGT charge and the present increased charge leads to a charge of 64% of the capital payment (40% + 60% × 40% = 64%).

There are rules for the matching of payments with trust gains; generally a first-in, first-out approach is adopted.[18] There are also rules to cover situations in which a payment is matched with trust gains from more than one year, ie there is more than one qualifying amount,[19] where the payment falls to be matched with trust gains falling partly within and partly without the last two years,[20] and where part of a capital payment has to be matched with part of a qualifying amount.[21]

The definition of a chargeable payment includes a payment by a company controlled by the trustees, a payment received from a qualifying company

[35.56] Foreign income and capital gains of residents

controlled by the trustees being treated as if it had been received direct from the trustees. A company is a qualifying company if it is a close company or if it would be close if it were resident in the UK.[22] The definition of beneficiary includes people who receive capital payments from the settlement. However, the trustees of a settlement are not to be treated as beneficiaries, a rule which prevents appointments or advances to sub-trusts being capital payments.[23]

Not infrequently, the sum received by a beneficiary (or by beneficiaries, in aggregate) exceeds the relevant income that has arisen to the trustees. When this is the case, any relevant income arising to the trustees in a later year can be charged on the beneficiary, by virtue of his earlier receipt.[24] This treatment does not apply insofar as the excess of the distribution over the relevant income has been charged as a capital gain on the recipient.[25]

The replacement of overseas trustees by UK resident trustees does not stop further payments to beneficiaries being matched with gains made by the overseas trustees, and the consequential CGT charge, augmented by the supplement, as appropriate.[26]

Simon's Taxes C4.404; Sumption CGT A3.08.

---

[1] TCGA 1992, ss 87(1), 88(1).
[2] TCGA 1992, s 88.
[3] ie such gains as would have been chargeable if they had been resident or ordinarily resident in the UK.
[4] Which can include hypothetical receipts, such as the notional interest arising on an interest-free loan: *Billingham v Cooper* [2001] EWCA Civ 1041, [2001] STC 1177.
[5] TCGA 1992, s 87(4).
[6] TCGA 1992, s 87(7).
[7] TCGA 1992, s 97(6).
[8] TCGA 1992, s 87(5).
[9] TCGA 1992, s 97(7).
[10] TCGA 1992, s 97(1), (2); on valuation see s 97(4).
[11] TCGA 1992, s 97(1)(b).
[12] *Billingham v Cooper* [2001] EWCA Civ 1041, [2001] STC 1177.
[13] TCGA 1992, s 91.
[14] TCGA 1992, s 91(3).
[15] TCGA 1992, s 91(5)(b).
[16] TCGA 1992, s 91(4) & (5).
[17] TCGA 1992, s 91(6).
[18] TCGA 1992, s 92(4); special rules apply when part only of a payment is taxable; s 92(5).
[19] TCGA 1992, s 93(2).
[20] TCGA 1992, s 93(3).
[21] TCGA 1992, s 93(4).
[22] TCGA 1992, s 96 (but only for payments received on or after 19 March 1991; s 96(11)). On practice see statement of practice SP 5/92, paras 38–40.
[23] TCGA 1992, s 97(8)–(10).
[24] TA 1988, s 740(2)(a).

[25] That is, a CGT charge under TCGA 1992, s 87 or s 89(2) or Sch 4C, para 8: TA 1988, s 740(6)(a).
[26] TCGA 1992, s 89(2).

Overseas gains charged on trustees

[35.57] Where trustees are resident outside the UK for the entire fiscal year, no CGT liability can be imposed on the trustees.[1] Where trustees change during the course of a fiscal year, so that UK resident trustees are acting for a part of the year, the trustees are treated as a single and continuing body of persons[2] and the gains made throughout the year are charged on UK residents who act as trustees for a part of the year.[3] The charge on a beneficiary receiving a capital payment from an overseas trust is specifically supplied where trustees have been UK resident at any time during the tax year.[4]

This lead to an arrangement whereby gains were triggered by trustees in a territory that had sole taxing rights by virtue of a double taxation agreement. The gain could not be taxed on the trustees, nor on the beneficiaries. Where a disposal is made by overseas trustees after 15 March 2005, the gain is taxed on the UK-resident trustees appointed later in the year, irrespective of any provisions in a double taxation agreement.[5]

[1] See TCGA 1992, s 2(1) unless the gain is on assets of a UK branch, etc (s 10).
[2] TCGA 1992, s 69(1).
[3] See TCGA 1992, s 2(1).
[4] TCGA 1992, s 87(1).
[5] F(No 2)A 2005, s 33

Borrowing by trustees

[35.58] In order to avoid the CGT charge on a beneficiary (which can be at an effective rate of 64%[1]) a scheme was devised, which is known as the "flip flop" scheme.[2] In a year before any gains have been realised, the trustees of an overseas settlement borrowed money secured on the current value of the trust property and settled the borrowed money into a new settlement ("settlement 2"). In the following year, the old settlement would realise the gains in the trust fund and use the proceeds to repay the borrowing from settlement 2. A distribution to beneficiaries would then be made from settlement 2. As this new settlement had not realised any gains itself, there was no charge on the beneficiaries.

The legislation in FA 2000 was intended to stop this scheme. However, a new version of the flip flop scheme was then introduced.

This time the scheme involved a settlement which had already realised gains but which had not made any capital payments to its beneficiaries. If the trustees made a transfer of value linked to trustees borrowing, to a second settlement so that Sch 4B applied, the resulting gain on the deemed disposal and reacquisition would be minimal as all the chargeable assets held at that time would have been realised (or if the proceeds had been reinvested in other chargeable assets, those replacement assets would not have a market value above cost).

Because Sch 4B applied, s 90 was excluded and could not, therefore, be used to attribute the actual ss 87/89 gains of the first settlement to beneficiaries who received capital payments from the second settlement.

To counter this new scheme, statute[3] provides, from 21 March 2002, that Sch 4B trust gains are attributed to a beneficiary if the following conditions are met:

(1) The beneficiary is a beneficiary of either the transferor or any transferee settlement. The transferor settlement is the settlement suffering the deemed disposal. The term transferee settlement does not mean any settlement whose funds are derived from the transferor settlement. Instead it is defined by reference to the transfer of value and means any settlement which is the recipient of the transfer of value.[4]

(2) The beneficiary has received a capital payment from either trust in the year in which the Sch 4B trust gains accrue or in the immediately preceding year.[5]

(3) The capital payment has not been taxed by reference to actual trust gains under TCGA 1992, s 87 in either the current or a previous year or by reference to Sch 4B trust gains in a previous year.

---

[1] See supra, § **35.56**.
[2] The House of Lords held that the flip flop scheme is not effective: *West v Trennery* [2005] UKHL 5, [2005] STC 214. A "Mark II" flip flop scheme was held not to be effective in a decision of the Special Commissioner in *Herman v Revenue and Customs Comrs* [2007] SWTI 1441, SCD.
[3] TCGA 1992, Sch 4C inserted by FA 2000, Sch 26.
[4] TCGA 1992, Sch 4C, para 14.
[5] TCGA 1992, Sch 4C, para 9(3)(*b*).

A transfer of value—the Revenue view

[35.59] TCGA 1992, Sch 4B is concerned with the situations where trustees make "a transfer of value" which is treated as linked with trustee borrowing. The Revenue have published[1] their view as to what is, and is not, a transfer of value.

In contrast to the definition for inheritance tax,[2] the Revenue consider that any distribution made by overseas trustees which is treated as income of the recipient for UK tax purposes is not a transfer of value, within the meaning of Sch 4B.

Difficulty in interpreting the scope of the provision frequently arises in connection with occupation of property. The Revenue consider that "a transfer of value" arises when the occupation is a consequence of the exercise by the trustees of a power of appointment or advancement. By contrast, where the occupation arises from rights personal to the beneficiary under Trusts of Land and Appointment of Trustees Act 1996, s 12, such occupation does not give rise to a transfer of value.

The Revenue look at the entire trust fund when considering whether there has been a transfer of value. Thus, if the trustees borrow money from a non-resident company which they control, there is no change in the aggregate fund and, in the Revenue view, there has been no transfer of value, even though if the company were UK resident a charge[3] would arise.

[1] Inland Revenue Tax Bulletin, August 2003, p 1049.
[2] IHTA 1984, s 3.
[3] TA 1988, s 419.

Disposal of a beneficial interest

[35.60] The disposal of a beneficial interest does not usually give rise to a charge to CGT, the charge on disposals by the trustees being thought sufficient.[1] However, the disposal of a beneficial interest by a UK resident beneficiary under a non-resident trust is expressly made chargeable since in such cases there will be no charge at the trustee level.[2] With effect from 6 March 1998, the disposal of a beneficial interest is chargeable where the trust is treated as resident in the UK, but had been an offshore trust at any time during its history.[3] Where there is a charge on the migration of the trust under the rules just outlined and that migration was after the beneficiary had acquired the interest, whether by purchase or having the interest conferred, the gain accruing on a subsequent disposal of that interest is calculated on the assumption that it was acquired for market value at the time of the migration, the so-called uplift.[4] The effect will be to give relief for those gains charged at the trustee level when the trust migrates, assuming that there are gains; where there are losses the same rules apply so the real function of the rule is simply to mark the boundary between trustee taxation and beneficiary taxation. There is no provision allowing the beneficiary to use losses sustained by the trust.

This approach has to be modified where the trust continues to be resident under normal CGT rules but is treated as non-resident by a double tax treaty. Where this occurred before the beneficial interest was acquired by the beneficiary no relief applies; otherwise there is a deemed acquisition when the treaty migration occurs.[5]

There is no uplift for "relevant gains", a phrase preferred by the legislation to the more common "stockpiled gains".[6] The relevant gains are those which would have been available to become chargeable if there had been capital payments to UK resident beneficiaries.[7] The avoidance scheme at which the charge is aimed arose where the non-resident trust had such gains but had not made any chargeable payments; the gains remain "stockpiled". The trust became resident in the UK but was then taken offshore again taking advantage of the uplift as it left the UK. This change applies to trusts becoming non-resident on or after 21 March 2000.[8]

[35.60] Foreign income and capital gains of residents

Simon's Taxes, C4.436.

[1] TCGA 1992, s 76.
[2] TCGA 1992, s 85(1). On practice see statement of practice SP 5/92, paras 4–6.
[3] TCGA 1992, s 76 amended by FA 1998, s 128.
[4] TCGA 1992, s 85(3).
[5] TCGA 1992, s 85(4)–(8).
[6] TCGA 1992, s 85(10) added by FA 2000, s 95(4).
[7] ie those within TCGA 1992, s 89(2) and Sch 4C, para 8(3)–s 85 (11).
[8] FA 2000, s 95(5).

Revenue practice

[35.61] The Revenue has published[1] its interpretation of the way in which the CGT charge is computed and applied where there is a disposal of a beneficial interest in a non-resident trust and there is a period between the beginning of the disposal of the interest in question and the "effective completion" of it. In this situation the deemed disposal[2] of the relevant trust assets occurs at the moment of effective completion of the disposal of the interest. This is required for testing the conditions relating to the residence status of the trustees and settlor[3] and the interest of the settlor in the settlement.[4]

The charge applies if the following conditions as to the residence of the settlor and the trustees are met:

(a) the tax year in which the disposal of the interest began, or
(b) the tax year in which it was effectively complete, or
(c) any tax year in between.

The condition as to the interest of the settlor is met if it applied at any time between:

(1) The beginning of the tax year two years before the tax year in which the disposal of the interest began and
(2) The date of the effective completion of the disposal.

These two dates are inclusive.

The beginning of the disposal is defined[5] as, in the case of a disposal involving the exercise of an option, the date of the grant of the option, and in any other case involving a contract, the date the contract was entered into.

The effective completion is defined[6] as "the point at which the person acquiring the interest becomes for practical purposes unconditionally entitled to the whole of the intended subject matter of the disposal". The main purpose of the words "for practical purposes" is to cover cases where the buyer has the power to compel the trustees to transfer the property to him on giving due notice. Another example would be where the buyer has a right to enjoy the property now, but is not entitled to it until a particular contingency is fulfilled, and there is no real likelihood of its not being fulfilled.

[1] Inland Revenue Tax Bulletin August 2003, p 1049.

² TCGA 1992, Sch 4A, para 4(1).
³ TCGA 1992, Sch 4A, paras 5 & 6.
⁴ TCGA 1992, Sch 4A, para 7.
⁵ TCGA 1992, Sch 4A, para 13(2)(*a*).
⁶ TCGA 1992, Sch 4A, para 13(2)(*b*).

Attribution of gains to settlor with an interest

[35.62] Where a UK resident trust realises a gain at a time when the settlor has an interest under it, the gain will be attributed to the settlor.[1] Gains of a non-resident trust are attributed to the settlor who is domiciled in the UK at some time in the year and is either resident in the UK during part of the year or ordinarily resident during the year in which the gain arises.[2] The term settlement is defined as for income tax legislation; it thus covers a whole variety of situations in which property originates from the settlor.[3]

The general scheme of the provision is to treat the settlor as having an interest in a settlement when the beneficiaries, or potential beneficiaries, include any child of the settlor, any child of the settlor's spouse/civil partner and any spouse/civil partner of such a child.[4]

Where the settlement is made on or after 19 March 1991, the charge applies if a settlor's grandchild is amongst the beneficiaries or potential beneficiaries.

When the settlement was created before 19 March 1991 and (broadly) no further property has been added to the settlement since that date, unborn children and future spouses/civil partners of the settlor or of his children being within the class of potential beneficiaries are also ignored in applying this test.[5] The presence of the settlor's grandchildren among the beneficiaries is not fatal to the trust's claim to be a protected settlement and so outside these rules.[6]

The Revenue are given extensive information powers.[7]

Losses arising on disposals made by the settlor, personally, can be offset against trustees' gains assessed on him.[8]

In *Trevor Smallwood and Mary Caroline Smallwood (Trustees of the Trevor Smallwood Trust) v R & C Comrs*[9], the Special Commissioners held that liability could not be avoided by reference to the former terms of the UK-Mauritius double taxation agreement in a scheme widely known as the 'round the world scheme'. On appeal, the High Court (*Smallwood & Anor (Trustees of Trevor Smallwood Settlement) v R & C Commrs*)[10] held that the Mauritius double tax treaty gave the right to tax capital gains to the state in which there was residence at the time of the disposal. In that case it was Mauritius and the Special Commissioners were said to have made an error in creating a simultaneous residence for the trustees during that period.

¹ TCGA 1992, s 77 (supra, § **20.01**).
² TCGA 1992, s 86(1), (3); details of the charge are set out in s 86(4), (5). On practice see statement of practice SP 5/92, paras 7–10.
³ TCGA 1992, Sch 5, paras 7, 8.

1541

4   The settlor is taken to have an interest in a very wide variety of circumstances. The definition covers circumstances in which income or property is or will or may become applicable, in any circumstances whatsoever, for the benefit of or payable to defined persons. The list of defined persons includes the settlor and a long list of persons—the settlor's spouse and children, the spouse of any such child, any company controlled by such persons and any company associated with such a company (TCGA 1992, Sch 5, para 9; para 2(1)–(3)). There is an exclusion for certain types of interest (TCGA 1992, Sch 5, para 2(4)–(6)). The charge is avoided if the settlor dies during the year or if the only listed person giving rise to such an interest (or all such persons) die in the year (TCGA 1992, Sch 5, paras 3–5).
5   Inland Revenue interpretation RI 198; in addition, a child under the age of 18 does not have the legal capacity to exclude itself as a beneficiary without consent of the court. Hence, the charge on the settlor does not apply where the only members of the settlor's immediate family who can benefit are children who are under the age of 18 as at 5 April 1999.
6   TCGA 1992, Sch 5, para 9(10A)(b)–(d) inserted by FA 1998, s 132.
7   TCGA 1992, Sch 5, paras 10 & 14.
8   TCGA 1992, s 2(5) as amended by FA 2002, Sch 11, para 2.
9   (2008) SpC 669.
10 [2009] EWHC 777 (Ch).

Settlor's right to reimbursement

[35.63] Statute[1] provides a statutory right of indemnity for the settlor in relation to capital gains tax which the settlor has to pay under s 86(4). It is commonplace for a trust deed to incorporate a direction to the trustees such as: "No capital under any circumstances whatsoever be payable to or applicable for the direct or indirect benefit of any the settlor". The statutory right of indemnity overrides any terms to the contrary in any settlement. In any event, there is no "benefit" where the settlor has paid tax due as a result of gains realised by the trustees and then enforces his right to be reimbursed.[2] Indeed, the statutory right itself is not a benefit as it merely ensures that the settlor can recover the tax which he has had to pay in respect of the gains of the settlement. This is the view taken by HMRC.[3] Trustees are able to pay any tax properly due directly to the Revenue.[4] The rule of construction for the interpretation of the provisions of a private deed where that deed declares the proper law to be applied is that all the law, including statute, of the jurisdiction is applied in interpreting the provisions of the deed. Hence, if the trust deed is governed by the law of England and Wales, the UK statutory right of reimbursement is automatically read into the deed, irrespective of the location of the trustees.

Commonly, however, an offshore trust is established under the proper law of the location of the trustees. It is likely that foreign jurisdictions will follow the 1775 dictum of Lord Mansfield:[5] "No country ever takes notice of the Revenue laws of another". This would appear to be the case where the proper law of a trust is the law of the Island of Jersey. But not, it would appear where the proper law of a trust is the law of the island of Guernsey.[6] In the Jersey case *Re T's Settlement*, an application to vary the trust deed,[7] the Jersey court held[8] that it would be a breach of trust for the Jersey trustees to reimburse to the UK resident settlor, the UK capital gains tax charge that was levied on the settlor by TCGA 1992, s 86 for gains made by the Jersey trustees, such reimbursement being a statutory right under UK law.[9] The statement of the court is, however, obiter and the point was not argued before the court as both counsel proceeded in that case on the assumption that this would be a breach of trust.[10]

There are two alternative routes that can be followed to seek a solution to this problem. First, change the proper law governing the settlement to the law of a part of the UK, so that the statutory right of reimbursement automatically applies. Second, arrange for the foreign law to allow reimbursement. The first course has been followed where the proper law is the law of the Cayman Islands. However, this was refused where the proper law was the law of Jersey, the view being expressed that a change in the proper law would give an indirect benefit to the settlor being a UK statutory right which is inapplicable in Jersey, such action being described under Jersey law as not only a breach of trust but also a potential fraud on the power.

Perhaps surprisingly, the second course of action has proved successful in Jersey. In *Re T's Settlement*, the Jersey court approved an application[11] to write into the settlor exclusion clause: 'for the avoidance of doubt, no provision herein shall prevent any payment being made to the settlor . . . by way of reimbursement of any tax liabilities.'[12] In a muddled judgement, the Jersey court justified the addition to the trust deed as it benefited the family, other than the settlor, by fulfilling the "moral obligation to Mrs T"[13] as expressed unanimously by seventeen adult members of the family. It is difficult to see how a court can regard a proposed reimbursement as a breach of trust but then authorise the same reimbursement using the words "for the avoidance of doubt . . .". The effect of this insertion is to allow reimbursement of CGT paid by an ageing settlor who did not have the financial means to pay large CGT liabilities.

The lesson may be that when creating offshore trusts, there can be an advantage in retaining the proper law as the law of England and Wales, this may more particularly be the case if the law of perpetuities in England and Wales is changed in accordance with the recommendation of the Law Commission so that accumulation of income can take place over 100 years, as is currently the case under Jersey law, rather than the 21 year period that is imposed at present.

---

[1] TCGA 1992, Sch 5, para 6(2).

[2] Support for this view is given in *Fuller v Evans* [2000] 1 All ER 636, in which Lightman J declared that trustees were entitled to pay the school fees of the settlor's son when a divorce order required the father to pay the fees not otherwise discharged. The expenditure of the settlor was, thereby, reduced in a case where the trust deed expressly excluded the provision of any benefit to the settlor. Lightman J declared the deed to exclude direct benefit and declared the payment of the school fees to be an indirect benefit only.

[3] Inland Revenue statement of practice SP5/92 para 9 states: 'this statutory right is not regarded as a reservation of benefit.'

[4] The settlor could borrow the money, pay the tax, receive the indemnity payment from the trustees and repay the borrowing; equity does not require circuitous

transactions of that sort: *Re Collard's Will Trusts* [1961] Ch 293.
5   *Holman v Johnson* (1775) 1 Cowp 341.
6   The author has received an opinion from a Guernsey advocate that Guernsey law recognises the right in UK statute for a settlor to be reimbursed and that such reimbursement, by contrast to the view taken in Guernsey, would not be considered to be outlawed by a clause in the trust deed prohibiting benefit passing to the settlor.
7   *Re T's Settlement*, Royal Court of Jersey (Samedi Division), 6 February 2002 (unreported). The application was made under Trusts (Jersey) Law 1984, Articles 43 and 47.
8   *Re T's Settlement at para 27.*
9   TCGA 1992, Sch 5 para 6.
10 It appears that neither Counsel had been instructed on the decision in *Fuller v Evans* [2000] 1 All ER 636.
11 *Re T's Settlement para 37.*
12 *Re T's Settlement para 14.*
13 *Re T's Settlement para 33.* The court found support for this approach in the judgment of Pennycuick J, in the English court, in *Re Clore's Settlement Trusts* [1966] 1 WLR 955 at 958: 'The improvement of the material situation of a beneficiary is not confined to his direct financial advantage . . . It includes the discharge of certain moral or social obligations on the part of the beneficiary' (quoted in *Re T's Settlement para 31*).

Controlled foreign companies resident in low tax areas

[35.64] If in any accounting period a company is "resident" outside the UK but is controlled by persons resident in the UK and the company is subject to a lower level of taxation in that country of residence, special rules, known as Controlled Foreign Company (CFC) rules apply.[1] These rules apportion the total *income* profits of the foreign company computed as for UK corporation tax (its chargeable profits) and any creditable tax among all the persons who had an *interest* in the company during the accounting period.

A charge can only be made on a company resident in the UK which has a minimum 25% interest in the CFC.[2] It is for this UK company to include the amount chargeable under these rules in its self-assessment return.[3]

The CFC rules only allow attribution to a UK company but they require that the CFC be controlled by persons (not just companies) resident in the UK. So if a company is resident outside the UK but has 30% non-UK shareholders, 40% UK corporate shareholders and 30% UK individual shareholders, the company is controlled by persons resident in the UK, and these rules can apply to the 40% UK corporate shareholders. Control is also extended to situations where a UK company controls 40% or more of the shares in the non-resident company and between 40% and 55% is controlled by a non-UK resident.[4]

There are a number of major exceptions to these rules:

(1)   no charge is made unless the amounts apportioned to the entity (or any associates) equals or exceeds 25% of the total chargeable profits of the foreign company;[5]

(2) no charge is made unless the chargeable profits of the foreign company exceed £50,000;[6]
(3) no charge is made unless the foreign company is resident in a country in which there is a lower level of taxation;
(4) no charge is made if the foreign company follows an acceptable distribution policy;
(5) no charge is made if the company fulfils the public quotation condition (repealed from 6 December 2006);
(6) no charge is made if the foreign company's activities are exempt.

Tax on the amount apportioned to, and chargeable on, a UK company is attributed to the accounting period of the UK company in which the relevant accounting period of the controlled foreign company ends.[7]

In some circumstances there may be an overlap with other rules. Where profits are apportioned to a UK company in this way it may happen that a charge may also appear to arise under TA 1988, s 739. When TA 1988, s 739 applies to treat the profits of the controlled foreign company attributed to the UK resident shareholders as the profits of an individual, the s 739 charge is excluded.[8] In order to prevent the avoidance of the 25% minimum by fragmentation of share ownership, it is provided that shares held by connected or associated persons are to be taken into account in calculating the extent of the interest.[9] This does not mean that the connected or associated persons are liable to tax under these rules, nor that the amounts apportioned to them are taxable in the hands of the UK resident taxpayer. These rules allow the Board to charge a UK resident company to a sum equal to UK corporation tax. They do not allow the Board to go further and to attribute the UK resident company profits amongst those with interests in the UK company.

Simon's Taxes Division D4.3.

---

[1] TA 1988, ss 747–756 amended by FA 2007, Sch 15. See generally Arnold, *The Taxation of Foreign Controlled Companies: An International Comparison*, Canadian Tax Foundation (1986). There is useful updating material in Sandler, *Pushing the Boundaries*, IFS, London 1994. For Revenue views see Inland Revenue Controlled Foreign Companies Self Assessment Book June 1999.
[2] TA 1988, s 747(5).
[3] TA 1988, s 747(4)(a) and FA 1998, Sch 18, para 8 third step. The inspector may not issue a closure notice nor make a discovery assessment without Board approval (TA 1988, s 754B). This means that the company's return may not be amended by an inspector without Board approval—or without the company's written agreement.
[4] TA 1988, s 747 (1A)
[5] TA 1988, s 747(5).
[6] TA 1988, s 748(1)(d).
[7] TA 1988, s 754(2).
[8] TA 1988, s 747(4)(b).
[9] TA 1988, s 747(5)(b).

EU Subsidiary

[35.65] In *Cadbury Schweppes Plc v Revenue and Customs Comrs*[1] the ECJ considered the argument that the UK controlled foreign company legislation was contrary to the freedom of establishment under Article 43 of the EC Treaty. The Court ruled that a restriction of the freedom of establishment could be justified in the case of wholly artificial arrangements aimed at circumventing the state's legislation.[2] For that to be so, the restriction had to have the specific aim of preventing artificial arrangements not reflecting economic reality which were set up in order to escape tax. The legislation would not comply with Community law if, despite the existence of tax motives, the establishment of the CFC reflected economic reality—a matter that had to be determined on the basis of objective factors which were ascertainable by third parties, as, for example, the existence of premises, staff and equipment in the country in which the CFC is resident. The CFC could be a fictitious establishment (in particular if it was a "letterbox" or "front" subsidiary) but the fact that the subsidiary's activities could equally well have been carried out in the parent's state did not necessarily mean that the creation of the subsidiary was a wholly artificial arrangement.

The ECJ stated that it is acceptable for the UK CFC legislation to charge UK tax on the profits of a foreign subsidiary created by a wholly artificial arrangement. By contrast, UK legislation would not be compatible with Articles 43 and 48 of the European Convention if the UK CFC legislation charges UK tax on the profits of a foreign subsidiary created by an arrangement that was not artificial, even if the central intention in incorporating the foreign subsidiary was to reduce the liability to UK tax.

In response to this ruling, the controlled foreign company legislation is amended[3] with effect from 5 December 2006. Where a UK resident company can demonstrate that a CFC has a business establishment in another EU member state (or another EEA state with which the UK has International Tax Enforcement Arrangements), and that the CFC is undertaking genuine economic activities at that business establishment, the UK parent can then exclude the profits arising from those genuine economic activities of that CFC from the profits subject to UK corporation tax.

In order to obtain this exemption, the UK parent company is required to submit an application to HMRC for the chargeable profits of the controlled foreign company to be eliminated, or reduced,[4] in computing the profits to be assessed on the UK parent.

There is an attempt in the legislation to deny the exemption to a subsidiary company incorporated in another EC state where the activities of the company are primarily outside the EC. Statute[5] disapplies the exemption "unless there are sufficient individuals working for a company in the [EU state, etc] who have the competence and authority to undertake all, or substantially all, of the company's business." The position of a subsidiary company established in, say Germany, whose workers are mainly in another EU state, such as Poland, is unclear.

---

[1] Case C-196/04, [2006] STC 1908, [2006] SWTI 2201.

² TA 1988, ss 751A and 751B inserted by FA 2007, Sch 15, which also makes a large number of small amendments to existing legislation.
³ TA 1988, ss 751A and 751B inserted by FA 2007, Sch 15, para 5, and consequential amendments made by FA 2007, Sch 15 para 1–4 & 6–10.
⁴ TA 1988, s 751A(2) inserted by FA 2007, Sch 15, para 5.
⁵ TA 1988, Sch 25, para 8(5) inserted by FA 2007, Sch 15, para 7(4). Para 8(6) then states that 'individuals are not to be regarded as working for a company in any territory unless (a) they are employed by the company in the territory or (b) they are otherwise directed by the company to perform duties on its behalf in the territory.'

Motive test

[**35.66**] Even if none of the exemptions given at supra, § 35.64 applies, the profits of the controlled foreign company are not assessed on the UK parent if it meets the requirements of the motive test. It must be demonstrated that a reduction in UK tax by diversion of profits from the UK was not the main reason, or one of the main reasons, for the company's existence in that accounting period and, also, one of the two alternative conditions is satisfied:

(1)   the reduction in UK tax is minimal; or
(2)   the reduction in UK tax liability was not the main purpose or, one of the main purposes, of the transactions which gives rise to the profits of the CFC in the accounting period.[1]

This motive test has been part of the CFC legislation since its introduction in 1984.[2] It has been a source of continuing difficulty for the practitioners in this area but, surprisingly, has not been the subject of any judicial analysis, other than a Special Commissioners' decision.[3] The approach taken by statute is to consider all the transactions of (and with) the CFC during each separate accounting period. It is, thus, perfectly possible for a foreign company to satisfy the motive test during one accounting period but not for either of the adjacent periods.[4] However, the decision of the ECJ in *Cadbury Schweppes plc v Revenue and Customs Comrs*[5] has an impact on the workings of the rule where EEA territories are concerned.

The precise consequence of that decision was the centre of the discussion in the further hearing by the Special Commissioners of *Vodafone 2 v Revenue and Customs Comrs*[6]. One Special Commissioner[7] reached the view that the CFC legislation could apply only in cases where the arrangements were wholly artificial. The other[8] concluded that the rules can have a broader effect, subject to the national legislation implementing them. That difference of opinion did not affect the final outcome in that particular case.

¹ TA 1988, s 748(3). These provisions are augmented by TA 1988, Sch 26, paras 16–19, but the augmentation does little to aid interpretation.
² TA 1988 Sch 25 para 16(2)(*b*) amended by FA 1996 s182 and Sch 36 para 4 (6)(*b*) make it clear that, in judging whether there is a reduction of UK tax, one can take account of the combined effect of two separate transactions.
³ *Association of British Travel Agents v IRC* [2003] STC (SCD) 194.

⁴   This was the finding in *Association of British Travel Agents v IRC* [2003] STC (SCD) 194, para 112 at 231h. It is interesting to note the Special Commissioners final comment that the hearing lasted for 17 days, of which 11 days were spent hearing oral evidence, little of which assisted the Special Commissioners.
⁵   Case C-196/04, [2006] STC 1908.
⁶   (2007) SpC 622.
⁷   John Walters QC.
⁸   Theodore Wallace.

Where the CFC is resident

[35.67] The legislation only applies where the company is not resident in the UK but is resident in a country with a lower rate of tax.[1] This is one of the unusual situations in which the UK tax system, having decided that a company is not resident in the UK, has to determine exactly where the company is resident. The basic rule is that a company is regarded as resident in any territory in which throughout the relevant accounting period it is liable to tax (whether or not it actually pays any) by reason of its domicile, residence or place of management.[2] These phrases are designed to distinguish taxation on the basis of residence from tax on the basis of source. Presumably this question is determined by reference to the UK tax system's assessment of the foreign tax law; the question whether the entity is a company is, again presumably, to be decided by UK tax law.

The basic rule may provide more than one country. Where the company is liable to tax in more than one country those with more than 50% of the interests which are chargeable under s 747 may select the territory.[3] This test is not straightforward because of the reference to those chargeable under s 747. If all those with interests in the CFC are companies resident in the UK, those with 51% will be able to elect. If only 60% of those with interests in the company are companies resident in the UK, one looks to find a majority in that 60%. The selected majority are very accurately described as those with "the majority assessable interest".[4] In order to prevent overnice (and expensive) arguments, the question whether one has an assessable interest is framed in terms of whether it is "likely" that the company would be chargeable.[5] Failing such an election one looks first to the place of effective management, failing which the situs of the majority of the assets; as a last resort the Revenue officer may designate the country.[6] These elections and designations are irrevocable.[7]

If no territory of residence can be found under these rules then the company is presumed to be resident in a territory with a lower rate of tax.[8]

There is an override which provides that if a company does not fall to be taxed by virtue of its domicile, residence or place of management in the territory where it is incorporated, it will only be treated as resident there if it is also liable to tax there.[9]

Simon's Taxes D4.307.

---

[1]   TA 1988, s 747(1)(c).

2   TA 1988, s 749(1).
3   TA 1988, ss 749(4) and 749A(1); for procedures see s 749A generally.
4   TA 1988, s 749(8).
5   TA 1988, s 749(9).
6   TA 1988, s 749(2), (3) and (6).
7   TA 1988, s 749A(1)(*b*).
8   TA 1988, s 749(5).
9   SI 2005/185 amending SI 1998/3081 (the Excluded Countries Regulations).

A lower level of taxation

[35.68] A company is regarded as subject to a lower level of taxation if the local tax paid is less than three-quarters of the corresponding UK tax on its profits.[1]

The calculations of chargeable profits, the creditable tax and the corresponding UK tax are based on the following assumptions:

(1)   [2] The controlled foreign company is to be deemed resident in the UK.
(2)   [3] It is assumed that the company has claimed or is to be given the maximum amount available of those reliefs which have to be claimed and allowances which are given automatically but which can be disclaimed in whole or part, unless any UK company or companies holding a majority interest disclaim any such relief or claim a smaller amount.[4]
(3)   [5] The full range of capital allowances, including research and development allowances, are treated as available.
(4)   [6] Relief may be given for unremittable foreign income under TA 1988, s 584 (see supra, § **35.24**).

Expenditure for which tax relief is given in the foreign territory, but which is not recognised in the CFC's accounting profits is not deductible.[7]

Attempts to circumvent the rules by using 'booster' structures (typically bringing UK dividend income into the subsidiary company) were blocked in 2005.[8] If the CFC has income which would not be taxed in the UK (such as UK dividends) then that is ignored in working out the comparable UK tax on the CFC's profits.

When profits are apportioned to a UK company, there are further rules indicating the reliefs available to it. These include excess relevant allowances[9] (eg loss relief).

Where the CFC is not a 100% subsidiary, its profits are apportioned in proportion to the number of shares held by each shareholder.

Simon's Taxes D4.316.

1   TA 1988, s 750(1).
2   TA 1988, Sch 24, paras 1–4.
3   TA 1988, Sch 24, paras 5–9.
4   The time limit is 20 months from the end of the accounting period but may be extended: TA 1988, Sch 24, paras 4(2), 9(4).

5   TA 1988, Sch 24, para 10.
6   TA 1988, Sch 24, para 12.
7   TA 1988, ss 750 amended by F(No 2)A 2005, s 44.
8   TA 1988, s 750(1A) inserted by F(No 2)A 2005, s 44.
9   TA 1988, Sch 26, para 1.

Classification by territory

Territories with an 'acceptable' level of taxation

[35.69] If a company is resident in an "excluded country", being one that has been declared to have an acceptable level of taxation, the controlled foreign company provisions do not apply. Those countries which are regarded as either wholly or completely outside these rules and listed in a statutory instrument.[1] A company which is resident in and carrying on business in a country in Part I of the list is outside these rules while a similar relief is given for a country in Part II of the list only if it does not benefit from one of the reliefs specified. A company is regarded as carrying on a business in a country if 90% of its commercially quantified income is local source income.

This is not a list of countries which are regarded as not having a low level of taxation. The basis for the exclusion of the rules must be sought in the motive test. The point is explained by Arnold thus, "the reason . . . appears to be that low taxation is determined only for the country in which the company is resident. By adding the requirement that a company derive at least 90% of its income from the country, the list permits inclusion of high tax countries (such as France) that exempt foreign income."[2]

As much CFC planning has revolved around the excluded countries list, the rules have been tightened and now include what is effectively a general anti-avoidance rule.[3] This denies the ECL exclusion if the CFC has been involved in a scheme or arrangement the main purpose of which is to obtain a reduction in UK tax.

Simon's Taxes D4.344.

1   Controlled Foreign Companies (Excluded Countries) Regulations 1998, SI 1998/3081, *Simon's Weekly Tax Intelligence* 1999, p 85.
2   [1985] BTR 302; see also *Taxation of Controlled Foreign Corporations: an International Comparison* (1986) p 321.
3   SI 2005/186, effective from 31 March 2005.

Territories with an 'unacceptable' level of taxation

[35.70] If a company is resident in a country specified in a statutory instrument[1] as a country with an "unacceptably low" level of taxation, the controlled foreign company provisions apply automatically.[2]

[1] Authority to issue the statutory instrument is given by FA 2002, s 89. At the time of writing, no statutory instrument has yet been issued.
[2] TA 1988, s 748A inserted by FA 2002, s 89.

[35.71] The CFC rules do not apply if the foreign company follows an acceptable distribution policy.

The conditions which must be met to satisfy this test are:[1]

(1) a dividend, which is not paid out of specified profits, is paid for the accounting period in question;

(2) it is paid during or within 18 months after that period (the Revenue may extend the time allowed for this); and

(3) a company distributes by way of dividend an amount not less than 90% of its available profits for the accounting period to UK residents. Where there is only one class of shares and all the interests are share interests held by UK residents,[2] only 90% of profits attributable to the UK shareholders must be distributed.[3] There is a similar relief if one class is voting shares and the other is non-voting fixed rate preference shares.

(4) the dividend is subject to UK tax in the hands of the company; certain schemes to get round this requirement were stopped by FA 2001 (see below).

A payment of dividend to a company is not relevant unless it is taken into account in computing the company's income for corporation tax.[4] It should be remembered, of course, that TA 1988, s 208 does not apply to foreign dividends. Further rules apply to dividends paid by a CFC on or after 7 March 2001.[5] These rules counter a scheme whereby the acceptable distribution test was met by way of the issue of CFC shares to a UK bank followed by a dividend payment and share repurchase.

Since 1990 it has not been possible to avoid a UK tax charge arising on an apportionment by making the CFC UK resident before payment of the dividend required to satisfy an acceptable distribution policy. In these circumstances the dividend has to be taken into account in computing the company's income for corporation tax.[6]

Where the ownership of a profitable UK resident subsidiary of a group is transferred to the CFC and the profits of that subsidiary passed to the CFC and in turn are paid as a dividend to the UK resident shareholders such dividends will represent part of an acceptable distribution to the extent that the CFC's relevant profits comprise dividends exempt from UK tax under TA 1988, s 208 or which would have been exempt if the company had been resident at the time. This rule applies for dividends paid by a CFC on or after 9 March 1999 for accounting periods ending on or after that date.[7] Any profits which are subject to UK tax may still be brought in.

Dividends paid by a CFC which escape the CFC legislation because, and only because, of the acceptable distribution test, cannot be mixed with other dividends for the purposes of DTR credit relief (see infra, § **36.20**). In the language of the Act, these dividends must be separately streamed.[8]

Simon's Taxes D4.330–336.

1. TA 1988, Sch 25, paras 1–4; see also Inland Revenue decision RD 2.
2. TA 1988, Sch 25, para 2(4) does not apply as 2(4)(b) is not satisfied.
3. At one time a trading company need only distribute 50% of its profits but this was changed by FA 1995, Sch 36, para 4.
4. TA 1988, Sch 25, paras 2(1A), 4(1A).
5. TA 1988, Sch 25, para 2.
6. TA 1988, Sch 25, para 2(1A).
7. TA 1988, Sch 25, para 2(1B).
8. TA 1988, s 801C.

The public quotation condition (abolished)

[35.72] The legislation had provided that an apportionment was not to be made if the CFC fulfilled a public quotation condition closely modelled on TA 1988, s 415 (see supra, § **29.08**). However, this exemption was abolished from 6 December 2006.[1]

The test required that not less than 35% of the voting power must be held by "the public" and there was a bar if more than 85% of that power was at any time within the period possessed by all the company's principal members. The shares must have been the subject of dealings on a recognised stock exchange situated in the territory in which the company was resident, these dealings must have taken place within the 12 month period ending with the end of the accounting period and the shares must have been quoted on the official list of that stock exchange.[2]

Simon's Taxes D4.360.

1. FA 2007, Sch 25 para 8.
2. TA 1988, Sch 25, Part III.

Exempt activities

[35.73] Some companies operate in low tax jurisdictions to exploit the market in that location, or for some other normal commercial purpose. A foreign company is excluded from the CFC provisions if it satisfies four conditions.[1] These are:

(1) that it has a real presence, ie a business establishment with an effective management[2] in its territory of residence, sufficient and local staff, not merely a formal presence such as just a registered address in the territory;

(2) that its main activity is not leasing, dealing in securities or the receipt of income such as dividends, interest, or royalties and is not such that the company may be used as an invoicing route;

(3) that its business is not primarily with associates in those trades which frequently involve cross-frontier transactions;

(4) that the company does not receive a significant amount of dividends from controlled foreign companies except where the exemption for holding companies applies.[3]

CFCs in low tax areas [**35.74**]

Simon's Taxes D4.340–347.

1   TA 1988, Sch 25, paras 5–12.
2   TA 1988, Sch 25, paras 7, 8.
3   TA 1988, Sch 25, paras 6(4), 12.

[**35.74**] Arbitrage is the exploitation of differences between or within national tax systems. This can result, for example, in a tax deduction being given by both the UK and another country for the same expense (a double dip) or a deduction being given for a payment when tax on the corresponding receipt has been avoided.

A significant number of statutory disclosures[1] are stated by the Revenue to involve arbitrage. From 16 March 2005, the Revenue is empowered to issue a notice to require a company to increase its self-assessment of corporation tax payable if the company has used a scheme involving certain types of hybrid entities.

In order for the statutory provisions to apply four conditions must be satisfied:

(1)   There is a "qualifying scheme".[2]
(2)   There is or will be a tax deductible expense or other set-off.[3]
(3)   The purpose or one of the main purposes of the schemes is to achieve a "UK tax advantage".[4]
(4)   The tax advantage is not minimal.[5]

The anti-arbitrage rules overlap and in some ways complement a number of changes to the loan relationshiprules also introduced in 2005[6] attacking 'avoidance involving financial arrangements'

1   Under FA 2004, ss 306–319 (the disclosure rules).
2   "Scheme" and "qualifying scheme" are exhaustively defined in F(No 2)A 2005, Sch 3, paras 1–11.
3   F(No 2)A 2005, s 24(4).
4   F(No 2)A 2005, s 24(5). "UK tax advantage" is defined in F(No 2)A 2005, s 30(2).
5   F(No 2)A 2005, s 24(6).
6   F(No 2)A 2005, Sch 7, in particular para 10 introducing FA 1996, ss 91A–91E.

36

The foreign taxpayer and the United Kingdom tax system

Limits on income chargeable to tax	PARA **36.02**
Place of trade	PARA **36.03**
Collecting the tax from a non-resident	PARA **36.07**
Non-resident landlords' scheme	PARA **36.10**
Foreign entertainers and sportsmen	PARA **36.11**
Foreign trustees	PARA **36.12**

[36.01] Income tax is charged on persons not resident in the UK from sources within the UK.

Corporation tax is charged on non-resident companies trading through a permanent establishment in the UK[1] (see supra, § **25.38**).

On limit on liability for certain investment income see infra, § **36.02**.

CGT is charged on the trade assets situated in the UK of non-residents trading through a branch or agency; supra, § **35.46**.

---

[1] TA 1988, s 6 and 11.

Limits on income chargeable to tax

[36.02] A non-resident is liable to UK income tax in full on profits arising from a trade, profession or vocation carried on in the UK and from land in the UK. The same is true of other sources of income if the non-resident has a UK representative under the rules discussed above.

However, if there is no chargeable UK representative, the liability of an individual who is not resident in the UK is limited to the tax deducted at source on the income listed below.[1] Equivalent provisions apply to a company that is not resident.[2]

The limit applies to income under:

(a) interest[3] and dividends;[4]
(b) transactions and deposits;[5]
(c) social security benefits etc;[6]
(d) income arising from a business carried out through a broker or investment manager.[7]

1555

The effect of limiting the tax liability to tax deducted at source is to exclude any liability at higher rate. Hence, there is never a tax liability on a dividend paid by a UK company to a non-resident shareholder, however large the dividend may be.

Many non-resident individuals are entitled to personal allowances (see supra, § **6.10**). A personal allowance is, however, first put against any income where the liability is limited to tax deducted at source. Thus, if, for example, the non-resident has received a UK dividend of a size which at least equals the personal allowance, that allowance is then wasted as the tax credit on the dividend is not repayable. Any other income, such as rental income, arising to the non-resident is then subject to tax without the benefit of the personal allowance.

[1] FA 1995, s 128.
[2] FA 2003, s 151.
[3] Income within ITTOIA 2005, s 369 (income tax); Schedule D, Case III (corporation tax).
[4] Income within ITTOIA 2005, s 383 (income tax); Schedule F (corporation tax).
[5] Income within ITTOIA 2005, s 552 (income tax); TA 1988, s 56 (corporation tax).
[6] Income within ITTOIA 2005, s 53.
[7] FA 1995, s 127 (2)(e). However, the limitation is not provided for profits of the underwriting business for a member of Lloyds: FA 1993, s 171(2).

Place of trade

[36.03] A non-resident is taxable on his profits from a trade *in* as opposed to one *with* the UK.[1] On the other hand, the presence of an administrative office or perhaps a representative office supplying information in London will not give rise to tax so long as the office does not trade. United Kingdom practice appears to be generous, especially in the banking and finance fields. A company may of course have both a representative office and a separate trading branch. The UK has traditionally used two tests: either the place where the contract is made or, where that test is inappropriate, the place where the operations take place from which the profits in substance arise (see infra, § **36.05**). Both tests place the source in one, and only one, place. This all-or-nothing approach means that profits cannot be apportioned. Such an approach may be seen as increasingly unreal in the new global market place.

It was decided early on that the mere purchase of goods in this country for export and resale abroad was not enough to amount to trading here.[2] Trading here was defined by Brett LJ in *Erichsen v Last*:[3]

> Wherever profitable contracts are habitually made in England by or for a foreigner with persons in England because those persons are in England, to do something for or to supply something to those persons, such foreigners are exercising a profitable trade in England even though everything done or supplied by those persons in order to fulfil the contract is done abroad.

Hence the running of a cabled message service sending messages overseas and the running of a shipping company[4] are trades within the UK.

Simon's Taxes B3.308, 309.

---

[1] ITTOIA 2005, s 6(2).
[2] *Sulley v AG* (1860) 5 H & N 711, 2 TC 149n; cf *Greenwood v F L Smidth & Co* [1922] 1 AC 417, 8 TC 193 where the goods were sold in England and *Taxation Comrs v Kirk* [1900] AC 588, PC where the goods were manufactured here for export and not simply bought. The danger in the rule in *Sulley v AG* is that a foreigner may employ an agent here to buy goods and yet the agent may have an undisclosed interest in the business. This may lead to evasion especially when the agent is a relative of the principal.
[3] (1881) 8 QBD 414, 4 TC 422 at 425.
[4] *Nielsen, Andersen & Co v Collins* [1928] AC 34, 13 TC 91.

[36.04] Most of the cases have been concerned with the sale of goods by a non-resident to someone in the UK, and the basic test has been that the trade is carried on where the contracts of sale are made.[1] The place of a contract is determined according to English domestic law and this is the place at which the acceptance of an offer is communicated. It follows that an acceptance by post completes the contract at the place of posting whereas an acceptance by telex completes the contract at the place of receipt. This principle is comparatively simple to apply when the foreigner deals directly with the customer but difficult questions of fact arise when an intermediary is employed. The fact that the foreigner uses an agent or stations an employee[2] in England is not sufficient to create a trade in as distinct from with the UK. Here too great attention is paid to the place of the contract.[3]

Where a contract is made through an agent, the normal principles of offer and acceptance must be applied to determine where the contract is made. Where an agent merely has to consult his foreign principal before accepting contracts the trade is carried on here. If, however, his sole function is to pass the offer to head office which communicates directly with the customer, the foreigner is trading with and not within the UK.

In *Grainger & Son v Gough*[4] Louis Roederer canvassed orders for champagne in the UK through the firm of Grainger and Son, who would pass on all orders and money received from the customers in the UK to Rheims from where Roederer would despatch the champagne. The contracts for the sale of wine being made in France and both the property and the risk passing to the purchasers in France, the House of Lords held, reversing the Commissioners, that Roederer was not trading in but with the UK. There being no liability on Roederer, Grainger and Son were not accountable for tax as agents of Roederer.

The place of the contract distinguished *Grainger v Gough* from the earlier cases in which the courts had held that a trade was carried on in the UK. In *Pommery and Greno v Apthorpe*,[5] the London agents of Pommery held stocks of wine in London which were used for all save orders for "considerable quantities" and paid moneys received into Pommery's London bank account.

[36.04] Foreign taxpayers and the UK system

The court had little difficulty upholding the Commissioners' finding that the trade was carried on in England. The fact that Pommery had a principal establishment outside the UK and that their sales in the UK amounted to only a small part of their total trade was irrelevant.

Simon's Taxes B3.309, 310.

---

1   eg *Maclaine & Co v Eccott* [1926] AC 424, 10 TC 481. On importance of place of delivery see Wills J in *Thomas Turner (Leicester) Ltd v Rickman* (1898) 4 TC 25 at 34, but cf Lord Cave in *Maclaine & Co v Eccott* at 432, 575.
2   As in *Greenwood v F L Smidth & Co* [1922] 1 AC 417, 8 TC 205.
3   eg per Will J in *Thomas Turner (Leicester) Ltd v Rickman* (1898) 4 TC 25 at 34.
4   [1896] AC 325, 3 TC 462.
5   (1886) 2 TC 182; cf *Werle & Co v Colquhoun* (1888) 20 QBD 753, 2 TC 402.

[36.05] The notion that the place of the contract determines the place of the trade is a very English notion since it combines the obsession with sale as the paradigm contract with the doctrine of the source. As Esher MR, put it in *Werle & Co v Colquhoun,* "the contract is the very foundation of the trade. It is the trade really"[1] or, as Rowlatt J, put it, until the sale is effected the trade is incomplete.[2] There has to be some practical limit saying how far the courts are to go back in locating profits. The question is where the profits are made and not why. So the courts do not go beyond the business operations from which the profits derive.

The cases also show that the place of the contract is not a touchstone. In *Maclaine & Co v Eccott* while describing the place of the contract as the most important and indeed the crucial question, Lord Cave listed other factors such as the place where payment is to be made for the goods sold, and the place where the goods are to be delivered, and disclaimed any exhaustive test.[3] The place of contract has been further downgraded by Lord Radcliffe[4]—"It cannot mean more than that the law requires that great importance should be attached to the place of sale. It follows that the place of sale will not be the determining factor if there are other circumstances present that outweigh its importance." The formulation generally preferred is that of Atkin LJ—"Where do the operations take place from which the profits in substance arise?"[5] So in *IRC v Brackett*[6] a non-resident company was held to be trading in the UK where its agent carried on its activities in the UK, these being the essential operations of the company's trade.

Simon's Taxes B3.308–317.

---

1   2 TC 402 at 410 and [1908] AC 46 PC.
2   *F L Smidth & Co v Greenwood* (1920) 8 TC 193 at 199.
3   [1926] AC 424 at 432. To the same effect Scrutton LJ in *Belfour v Mace* (1928) 13 TC 539 at 558.
4   *Firestone Tyre and Rubber Co v Lewellin* [1957] 1 All ER 561, 37 TC 111 at 142.
5   *F L Smidth & Co v Greenwood* [1921] 3 KB 583 at 593, 8 TC 193.
6   [1986] STC 521 the case concerned the services of a property consultant working for a Jersey company created by a settlement of which he was the settlor. The settlor

was held assessable under TA 1988, s 739 (supra, § **35.26**) on his own account and on behalf of the company under TMA 1970, s 79 (infra, § **36.10**).

[36.06] The place of contract, although useful as a test in the area of a single sale, is less happy in the manufacturing sphere.[1] It is perfectly possible for a manufacturing business to be carried on in the UK even though the contracts for the sale of goods are made abroad. This was the situation in *Grainger & Son v Gough*, where Lord Esher said:[2] 'The contracts in this case were made abroad. But I am not prepared to hold that this test is decisive. I can imagine cases where the contract of resale is made abroad and yet the manufacture of the goods, some negotiation of the terms and complete execution of the contract take place here under such circumstances that the trade was in truth exercised here. I think the question is where do the operations take place from which the profits in substance arise.'

In *Firestone Tyre and Rubber Co Ltd v Lewellin*[3] the UK subsidiary—Brentford—of a US parent—Akron—made tyres in the UK and supplied them to foreign subsidiaries at cost plus 5%. The court held that the US parent was trading in the UK—as was the UK subsidiary and that the location of the master agreement governing the trade between the parent and its subsidiaries was not conclusive.

The operations, the supply of the tyres and delivery alongside ship in a UK port, took place in England, constituted the carrying on of a trade in England and that trade, the Commissioners had correctly held, was the trade of Akron not Brentford.[4] The obligation on Brentford to account to Akron for any profit in excess of 5% was of crucial importance here. It followed that Brentford as the regular agents of Akron could be assessed to the tax due from Akron.

Simon's Taxes B3.118.

[1] Lord Salvesen in *Crookston Bros v Furtado* (1910) 5 TC 602 at 623.
[2] (1896) 3 TC 311 at 317.
[3] [1957] 1 All ER 561, 37 TC 111.
[4] Per Lord Radcliffe at 143.

Collecting tax from a non-resident

Non-resident company

[36.07] Where a non-resident company carries on a trade, profession or vocation in the UK through a permanent establishment the Revenue can collect tax on the profits from that permanent establishment. Statute deems the permanent establishment to be the agent of the non-resident and liable to discharge the fiscal obligations of the non-resident company.[1] This responsibility continues even after the permanent establishment ceases.[2]

Simon's Taxes B1.210.

[1] FA 2003, s 150(1), (2)(a).
[2] FA 2003, s 150(2)(b).

Non-resident individual

[36.08] In principle, tax can be collected from a non-resident in the same way as from a resident.[1] In practice, the mechanism for collecting tax is more difficult for the Revenue to apply in its relations with a uncooperative non-resident than will often be the case with an individual resident in the UK. Statute[2], thus, imposes obligations on the UK representative of a non-resident.

The obligations of the non-UK resident to make returns, self-assess and pay the tax, interest and penalties, if any, apply as if they were also the joint obligations of the UK representative.[3] These obligations may be discharged either by the non-resident's UK representative or by the non-resident himself and any acts or omissions of the UK representative are treated as acts or omissions of the non-resident.[4]

The responsibilities of the independent agent in acting as the non-resident's UK representative is to discharge his obligations so far as it is practicable to do so by acting to the best of his knowledge and belief, after having taken all reasonable steps to obtain the necessary information. The agent would therefore be exonerated where the non-resident withheld information. The obligation of the non-resident to supply any additional information is confirmed and the non-resident is able to correct any error or mistake made by his UK representative which was not an act or omission of the non-resident himself, one to which he consented or in which he connived.

Information includes anything contained in a return, self-assessment account, statement or report required by the Revenue.[5]

An independent agent of the non-resident is entitled to be indemnified in respect of any tax obligation of the non-resident and to retain such amounts from any sums otherwise due to the non-resident.[6]

[1] See supra, §§ 2.7–2.28, 2A.14–2A.20 and 2A.90–2A.91.
[2] FA 1995, s 126.
[3] FA 1995, Sch 23, para 1.
[4] FA 1995, Sch 23, para 2.
[5] FA 1995, Sch 23, para 4.
[6] FA 1995, Sch 23, para 6.

Persons not treated as UK representatives of non-resident's trade

[36.09] There are three principal categories of excluded agents. The first is the occasional agent, ie a person carrying out transactions as agent for the non-resident but not doing so in the course of carrying on a regular agency for that non-resident. This repeats words found in earlier legislation where they were described by one judge as "apparently very vague".[1]

The second category is the defined broker.[2] A broker, unlike an agent, acts for both sides.[3] The broker must have been carrying on the business of a broker, must have carried out the transaction in the ordinary course of that business and at a rate of remuneration not less than that which would have been customary for the transaction. If these conditions are satisfied, the broker is not liable even though he acts regularly for the non-resident. There is no definition of the term "broker".[4]

The third category is the investment manager carrying out investment transactions for the non-resident.[5] The manager must be carrying on a business of providing investment management services, have carried out the transaction in the ordinary course of business and have received not less than the customary charge for the service. Further the manager must have acted in an independent capacity. In deciding whether the manager has acted independently the courts are to have regard to the legal, financial and commercial characteristics of the relationship between the manager and the client.[6]

In addition, the manager (and any connected person) must not, in broad terms, be beneficially entitled to more than 20% of the taxable income of the non-resident from transactions carried out through brokers and investment managers. This 20% test may be applied to any period up to five years. Where the 20% limit is exceeded it is only the income of the non-resident which accrues to the manager or connected persons beneficially which is caught.[7] The 20% rule is softened to exclude situations where this percentage is exceeded owing to matters outside the manager's control (assuming the manager takes reasonable mitigating steps); this is primarily to prevent the agent from becoming liable just because of a sudden swing in the market. These rules are modified for collective investment schemes.[8] The reasoning behind these 20% rules is apparently to permit managers to put "seed money" into such investment schemes.

Investment transactions are defined[9] as transactions in shares, stocks, futures contracts, opinions contracts or securities of any description not otherwise mentioned; however, an exception is made for futures contracts and option contracts relating to land. It extends also to foreign currency transactions. The category may be extended by statutory instrument to include other transactions. If the investment business is part of a larger business it is treated as a separate trade.

There is also a special non-liability agency rule for Lloyd's.[10]

Simon's Taxes B1.210.

---

1 FA 1995, s 127(1)(*a*). Per Rowlatt J. in *T L Boyd & Sons Ltd v Stephen* (1926) 10 TC 698 at 747. For a more recent example see *Willson v Hooker* [1995] STC 1142.
2 FA 1995, s 127(1)(*b*), (2).
3 Per Bankes L.J. in *Wilcock v Pinto & Co* [1925] 1 KB 30 at 42, 9 TC 111 at 130.
4 In general the words of s 127 re-enact TMA 1970, s 82(1); however, s 82 defined a broker as including a "general commission agent". In *Fleming v London Produce Co Ltd* [1968] 2 All ER 975 at 985–6 Megarry J. said that this term must

be construed eiusdem generis with broker; such an agent held himself out as willing to act for others. Rowlatt J. once said that a general commission agent generally negotiates for commission; in that case the agent was held not to be a general commission agent when he paid for the goods as soon as he received them instead of waiting to pay the principal out of the proceeds of the sale (*T L Boyd & Sons Ltd v Stephen* (1926) 10 TC 698 at 746).

[5] FA 1995, s 127(1)(*c*), (3).
[6] FA 1995, s 127(18).
[7] FA 1995, s 127(4)–(8).
[8] FA 1995, s 127(9)–(11).
[9] FA 1995, s 127(12).
[10] FA 1995, s 127(1)(*d*).

Non-resident landlords' scheme

[36.10] When a payment of rent arises from occupation of land in the UK and that payment is made to any person who is not resident in the UK, the payer is obliged to withhold tax at basic rate in making the payment.[1] This requirement is imposed on the person who makes the payments to the non-resident. This may be a tenant, if payment is made direct, including payment into an account at a UK bank held in the name of the non-resident. Alternatively, the requirement may fall on an agent who has received rent from a tenant and who passes payments to the non-resident. The identity of the non-resident does not affect the requirement: tax is required to be withheld on payments to an individual, to trustees, to a partnership or to a company of any nature. The tax withheld is retained by the Revenue and put against the liability declared by, or on behalf of, the non-resident. This may lead to a further liability, if the non-resident recipient is subject to higher rate, or a repayment, as is more frequently the case where expenses are deductible from the gross rent received by the non-resident.

A non-resident can apply to the Revenue for a certificate. Production of this certificate exempts the UK resident payer from the obligation to deduct tax. A certificate is issued[2] where the non-resident makes a commitment to comply fully with the requirements of self-assessment, following the necessary self-assessment procedures and either (i) the non-resident has a history of compliance with UK tax procedures or (ii) the non-resident has not previously had a liability to UK tax.

[1] Taxation of Income from Land (Non-Residence) Regulations 1995, SI 1995/2902 reg 8, made under the authority of TA 1988, s 42A(1).
[2] The certificate is issued by HMRC Financial Intermediaries and Claims Office (NRLS Section). The current practice of FICO is to issue a certificate on receipt of an application. This certificate is then withdrawn if investigation indicates that the non-resident has not previously complied with the requirements of UK self-assessment. Application can be made by, or on behalf of, any person who has an interest in land in the UK; it is not necessary to wait until rent arises from that land. The way in which the Revenue operate the scheme is given in Revenue Booklet

IR140, Non-Resident Landlord, their agents and tenants. Application is made on form NRL2 (for a company) or NRL1 (for an individual or any other person).

Foreign entertainers and sportsmen

[36.11] A scheme[1] of withholding tax at source applies to any payment made for an activity[2] performed in the UK by an entertainer or sportsman[3] who is not resident in the UK.

Requirement to deduct tax arises where the payment (or payment in kind) is for an activity in the year of assessment in which the individual was not resident in the UK. There is, thus, no requirement to deduct tax if the entertainer or sportsman was resident in the year in which the activity was performed, even if he is non-resident in the year of assessment in which the payment is actually made.[4]

The requirement is to deduct tax at the basic rate of income tax on any payment relating to the activity. The tax as collected is then held to the credit of the entertainer or sportsman. In *Agassi v Robinson*,[5] the House of Lords held that the scheme requires the deduction of UK withholding tax on payments made by foreign companies to a US company controlled by the international tennis player, who was ordinarily resident and domiciled outside the UK, where the payments arose from sporting activity within the UK (the Wimbledon lawn tennis championships).

The scheme works by requiring the profits of this deemed trade to be computed and the income tax liability calculated. (The basis period is always the tax year; there is no provision for choosing an accounting date other than 5 April.[6]

[1] TA 1988, ss 555–558.
[2] "Relevant activity" is very widely defined: Income Tax (Entertainers and Sportsmen) Regulations 1987, SI 1987/530, reg 6.
[3] "Entertainer" is defined very widely, a sportsman being defined as a type of entertainer: Income Tax (Entertainers and Sportsmen) Regulations 1987, SI 1987/530, reg 2.
[4] TA 1988, s 555(1).
[5] [2006] UKHL 23, [2006] STC 1056, HL, reversing the decision of the Court of Appeal [2005] STC 303, CA.
[6] Income Tax (Entertainers and Sportsmen) Regulations 1987, SI 1987/530, reg 13.

Foreign trustees

[36.12] In principle, trustees resident outside the UK are subject to UK tax on UK source income. This includes tax charged at the trust rate and the dividend trust rate.[1] When computing the income to be charged at these trust rates, allowable expenses that are deducted in the computation are restricted by the proportion that the UK income bears to the total income of the trustees.[2]

[36.12] Foreign taxpayers and the UK system

When UK resident trustees make a discretionary payment to a beneficiary, the discretionary payment is treated as being grossed up by the trust rate.[3] This enables a basic rate taxpayer receiving such a payment to obtain repayment. The requirement is that the trustees are obliged to make a payment of tax sufficient to "frank" the discretionary payment, unless they have made sufficient payments of tax on the income they have received.

The regime of "franking" discretionary payments does not apply where the trustees are not resident in the UK.[4] Instead, HMRC operate an extra statutory regime to give to a recipient beneficiary the benefit of tax paid by the foreign trustee.

Trustees of an overseas trust are never entitled to issue form R185, even when the trustees have paid UK tax at the trust rate on trust income with a UK source. Instead, HMRC advise that the net sum received should be reported on the recipient's tax return Foreign Supplementary Pages in box 6.5 and in the white space below should be written: "I apply for relief under ESC 18 for tax paid by the trustees of xxxx trust (UTR: xxx) on this income." The procedure within HMRC is, then, that the recipient's district contacts the ESC 18 specialist at HMRC Centre for Non-Residents for him to advise the district of the amount of UK tax (plus overseas tax, if appropriate) that is to be given as a credit.

---

[1] ITA 2007, s 9 charged under ITA 2007, s 479, see supra, § **13.11**.
[2] ITA 2007, s 487.
[3] ITA 2007, s 494(2).
[4] vide ITA 2007, s 493(1)(*b*).

37

Double taxation relief

Introduction	PARA **37.01**
Treaty relief by credit	PARA **37.09**
Capital gains	PARA **37.29**
Relief by exemption	PARA **37.30**
Employment income exempted: 'the 60 day' rule	PARA **37.31**
Interpretation of UK treaties	PARA **37.33**
Changes to double tax treaties	PARA **37.35**
Treaty shopping	PARA **37.36**
Reform and planning	PARA **37.37**

Introduction

[**37.01**] The UK taxes income if it arises here or if the person entitled to it is resident here. This leaves untaxed only foreign income[1] arising to a non-resident. Since other countries too adopt a generous view of their own taxing powers it is inevitable that some income will be taxed twice.

Such double taxation is thought to be objectionable since, by making overseas profits more expensive than domestic profits, it discourages a person from trading overseas and so interferes with international trade. The ideal situation would be one in which there was neutrality both between the tax burdens of a person trading at home and abroad and between a resident and a non-resident trading in the same country. Until, however, there is one tax system common to all countries it will be impossible to achieve both these objectives.

According to the European Commission, EC law does not yet oblige a member state automatically to grant the withholding tax rate of its most favourable bilateral agreement to taxpayers of another member state which is not covered by the agreement.[2] The European Court of Justice also appears to take this view.[3] The Commission has expressed an interest in co-ordinating the work of individual governments in treaty matters by looking at major issues and especially limitation of benefit clauses.[4]

While much effort has been spent over the last few decades to try and remove discrimination against non-residents the attention of the OECD is now turning to the opposite problem—tax discrimination in favour of non-residents. This practice has developed as states scramble for inward investment. Where this goes too far it is referred to as "fiscal dumping"; the use of the term dumping, which is also used for practices banned under GATT and now the World Trade Organisation, is deliberate. The OECD is considering rules which would prevent harmful tax competition; the EC Commission has also endorsed these ideas for discussion.[5]

[37.01] Double taxation relief

Simon's Taxes E5.112; Divisions E6, F1.

[1] On concessionary double taxation relief for two types of UK income see extra-statutory concession A12 (1996)—maintenance payable under UK court order—and B8 (1996)—royalties due under UK patent etc.
[2] Written Answer, 9 November 1992, Question No. 647/92; *Simon's Tax Intelligence* 1993, p 302.
[3] *Gilly v Directeur des Services Fiscaux du Bas-Rhin* (Case C-336/96) [1998] STC 1014, ECJ.
[4] Institute of Taxation TR 6/93, *Simon's Tax Intelligence* 1993, p 350.
[5] Information is available on the OECD website. See also Liebman and Leventhal *European Taxation* 1998, p 96.

Methods of avoiding a double charge to tax

[37.02] A tax system could achieve the avoidance of double taxation in a number of ways. Thus it could simply decide not to tax overseas income, either generally or of a particular sort. Such was in effect the case when the remittance basis was at its height, before 1914,[1] and until 1974 when the remittance basis was available to UK residents in respect of income earned overseas. Many countries give substantial exemptions for overseas trade in an attempt to assist their own balance of trade and general level of economic activity.[2] Today France practices an extensive but not universal exemption system for foreign income. Germany and Australia operate an exemption system if income comes from a country which is a treaty country (Germany) or is a listed country (Australia).[3] The Netherlands is closer to France on this matter but applies a principle of exemption with progression.

[1] FA 1914, s 5. For history see RC (1953) 1st Report Cmd 8761, §§ 15–20.
[2] See RC (1953) 1st Report, § 23 and Final Report 1955, App III, and see supra, § 35.13.
[3] See Arnold et al Working Paper 96–1 for the Technical Committee on Business Taxation, Department of Finance, Ottawa—available on the Internet at www.fin.gc.ca/

[37.03] Short therefore of abandoning the taxation of overseas income, the government has three options. First, the UK has comprehensive double taxation agreements with 109 other territories,[1] a process authorised by TA 1988, s 788. Treaty relief may exempt some income from tax in one country and give[2] credit for foreign taxes on other income. Section 788 only allows the Revenue to propose Orders in Council if they are consistent with the purposes there spelt out. For this reason it is thought that the UK treaties may only relieve from tax and not increase it; however, the Revenue were known to be interested in the question whether use of the associated enterprises could increase the burden of tax on companies as compared with the application of the UK statutory transfer pricing rules.[3]

Second, it can unilaterally allow the foreign tax paid as a credit against the UK tax liability. This is permitted by TA 1988, s 790. The rules which the foreign tax must satisfy in order to qualify as a tax credit are the same whether the credit arises under treaty or unilaterally.[4]

Third, it can decide that the foreign tax shall be deductible in computing the profits of the business, thus treating the foreign tax like any other business expense. This is permitted by TA 1988, s 811; such foreign tax may not be deducted in respect of income charged on a remittance basis. The time limits for making a claim under s 811 where there has been an adjustment to the foreign tax are set by FA 2000 at six years from the date of the adjustment. However, there is also an obligation to give notice to the Revenue within one year of the adjustment; the obligation carries a tax-related penalty.[5]

If the foreign tax is available as a credit at a rate which wipes out any UK tax liability it might appear that there is very little difference between a credit system and an exemption system. However under a credit system the foreign income will still be relevant in calculating the person's total income and so the marginal rate of tax. However, this distinction is itself blurred since some countries which operate an exemption system, eg the Netherlands, still take account of the foreign income in computing taxable income; this system is called exemption with progression.

A person may elect not to take the credit relief.[6] This he will usually do if to treat the foreign tax as a deduction in computing income from that source will yield tax advantages. An unusable tax credit may be useful if it forms part of a loss allowable against general income of that year. Taxpayers may not elect to treat a part of the foreign tax as a credit and the balance as a deduction. However they may treat one foreign tax as a credit and another as a deduction.

Conversely as country of source, the UK may wish to levy income tax on income accruing to a non-resident. Here it may either not tax at all (eg certain government securities held by non-residents) or may give credit for tax paid in the country of residence (not a feature of the UK tax system) or it may under treaty levy a reduced rate of tax, often called a withholding tax, leaving the other country to give credit if it wishes.

Similar provisions apply to CGT[7] and to corporation tax[8] on capital gains.

The basic pattern is for UK treaties to follow that laid down in successive model treaties devised by the OECD in 1946, 1963, 1977 and 1992. This pattern has been criticised for its bias in favour of the country of residence over the country of source. This bias may have been acceptable to West European governments anxious for foreign, particularly American, involvement but has caused great difficulties for less developedcountries.[9] In 1988 the UN published a model treaty for the benefit of developing countries.[10] The US[11] and the Netherlands[12] have published their own model treaties. Multilateral treaties are relatively rare.[13]

Simon's Taxes E6.401–404.

---

[1] As at 31 December 2005, listed in Inland Revenue Tax Bulletin, August 2004, pp 1140–1144. FA 2002, s 88(2)(b), (3) permit the making of an agreement between the UK government and a territory that is not recognised as a foreign government. This change was necessary to bring into force the double tax agreement with

[37.03] Double taxation relief

Taiwan. On treaty law and practice see *Vogel on Double Taxation Conventions*, English edn, and Baker, *Double Taxation Agreements and International Tax Law*.
2. This provision does not allow a treaty to grant entitlement to repayment supplement since repayment supplement does not come within s 788(3); *R v IRC, ex p Commerzbank AG* [1991] STC 271 see JFAJ [1991] BTR 405. However, the European Court has ruled in this case that TA 1988, s 825 does not entitle the Revenue to withhold repayment from a German bank with a UK branch since this amounts to discrimination on grounds of nationality and would be in breach of Community rules, *R v IRC, ex p Commerzbank AG*: C-330/91 [1993] STC 605, ECJ. On process of implementation see Bartlett [1991] BTR 76.
3. See Edwardes Ker Tax Treaty Interpretation, Chapter 44 especially 44.04.
4. ie rules in TA 1988, ss 792–806.
5. FA 2000, Sch 30, para 19 adding TA 1988, sub-ss (4)–(10).
6. TA 1988, s 805.
7. TCGA 1992, ss 277, 278, on which see statement of practice SP 6/88; and [1989] BTR 105 (JOBO).
8. TA 1988, ss 788(1) and 790(1).
9. See Irish, 1974 ICLQ p 292; Atchabahian, 1971 JBIFD p 451 and Caroll, *International Lawyer*, vol. 2, p 692. Other models have been drawn up in Mexico (1943) and by the Andean States.
10. Surrey 19, Harvard International Law Journal, 1 and 4, IFA Congress Seminar Services (1979).
11. For texts see 31 BIFD, p 313 and 36 BIFD, p 15 (1982).
12. *Vogel on Double Taxation Conventions*, p 10.
13. They are to be found in Africa and in the Nordic countries. See *Vogel on Double Taxation Conventions*, p 11.

Double taxation relief available to a UK resident

[37.04] A UK resident subject to UK tax on income or gains that have suffered foreign tax can have the following alternative mechanisms for relief available:

(a) The foreign tax can be treated as an expense (see infra, § **37.05**).
(b) The foreign tax may be a credit against the UK tax liability (see infra, § **37.06** for unilateral relief and infra, § **37.09** for relief under a double tax agreement).
(c) A double tax agreement may exempt from UK tax the foreign income (see infra, § **37.30**).

Foreign tax as an expense

[37.05] Any taxpayer can choose to treat foreign tax levied on an item of income as if it were an expense.[1] This treatment is not confined to trading income; investment income can similarly be reduced under this election. Where there is a double taxation agreement between the UK and the territory in which the income originates, the taxpayer can elect not to take the credit arising under the double agreement but, instead, treat the foreign tax as an expense.[2]

This treatment is advantageous where the taxpayer is treated under UK rules as having a loss. The effect is, thus, to increase the loss rather than to provide a credit that cannot be used. This treatment can also be attractive to a private individual who has a small amount of foreign tax deducted at source, for example on interest arising in a foreign bank account. Frequently, the cost of reclaiming the foreign tax under the terms of a double tax agreement is significantly greater than the tax levied in the UK.

[1] TA 1988, s 811.
[2] TA 1988, s 805.

Unilateral tax relief

[37.06] The unilateral tax credit was introduced into the UK in 1950. At first the credit was to be for 3/4 of Commonwealth taxes and 1/2 of foreign taxes. This may have been because of the notion of imperial preference or because to give full credit unilaterally would weaken the hand of the UK negotiators as they worked towards a full set of bilateral arrangements. The pace of negotiation was slow and in 1953 these limits on credit were abolished.[1]

The credit is of use today in four main situations, first where there is no double tax treaty with the country of source[2] and second where there is but it does not cover this particular tax.[3] Third, it may also be used for taxes on income levied by municipalities or other constituent parts of the state. Fourth, it can relieve (and repay) the "special withholding tax" to be levied by Austria, Belgium and Luxembourg from the date the EU Savings Directive takes effect.[4]

Treaty relief takes precedence because it is to apply "notwithstanding anything in any enactment".[5] However, the legislation goes on to limit the extent to which the treaty applies to the extent that it provides relief. It may therefore be argued that where a less generous treaty relief appears to supersede a unilateral relief, the latter relief may still be claimed.

The interaction of unilateral and treaty relief was changed fundamentally by FA 2000. TA 1988, s 793A introduced by FA 2000, provides that treaty rules will exclude unilateral relief in two situations. If invoked this power will provide an interesting example of a treaty imposing a charge to tax which would not otherwise arise. The situations are:

(1) Where the treaty (or the law of the foreign country implementing the treaty) expressly grants a credit for foreign tax paid.
(2) Where the treaty expressly denies a credit. In each case unilateral relief will not be available.

This new relationship is confined to credit relief and only applies to future treaties. It is not clear that these changes are justified in principle.

Simon's Taxes E6.414.

[1] FA 1950, s 36.
[2] As recommended by RC (1953) 1st Report §§ **40–42**.

[37.06] Double taxation relief

3   TA 1988, s 790(12). On application to dividend income see statement of practice SP 12/93.
4   FA 2004, ss 107–115, which enact the requirement to give credit imposed on EU member states by Article 14 of EU Savings Directive (Directive 2003/48/EC).
5   TA 1988, s 788(3).

[37.07] The credit is for the amount of taxes paid under the foreign law and computed by reference to income arising within the foreign territory.[1] That sum is allowed by way of credit against any UK tax computed by reference to that income. This means that foreign income taxes on the income from the foreign source are allowed against the UK tax charged on the income from that source. In *George Wimpey International Ltd v Rolfe*[2] the taxpayer company made profits in three countries and paid local tax on them but made an overall trading profit of nil. However, the company had other sources of income which gave rise to profits chargeable to UK tax. Hoffmann J, upholding the decision of the Special Commissioner, held that the taxpayer company was not entitled to double taxation relief. He reached this decision in reliance on the doctrine of the source and the Schedular system.

The question of whether the income arises in the foreign territory is determined according to English law.[3] In order for foreign tax to be allowable for offset against UK income tax it must be a tax which is "charged on income and which corresponds to United Kingdom income tax".[4] The test is that profits arise where the operations take place from which those profits in substance arise;[5] the overall effect of these rules may be that there are substantial unusable foreign tax credits.

Simon's Taxes E6.414.

1   TA 1988, s 790(4).
2   [1989] STC 609.
3   *GCA International Ltd v Yates* [1991] STC 157.
4   TA 1988, s 790(12)(*a*). The equivalent provision for relief against UK corporation tax is that the foreign tax is required to be "charged on income or chargeable gains and which corresponds to United Kingdom corporation tax": TA 1988, s 790(12)(*b*).
5   *FL Smidth & Co v Greenwood* (1921) 8 TC 193 and *IRC v Hang Seng Bank Ltd* [1990] STC 733, PC.

[37.08] Unilateral relief differs from treaty relief in three ways, all related to the obvious general difference that in treaty relief one looks first to the terms of the treaty:

(1)   Although treaty relief was, until FA 2000, available only to one resident in the UK throughout the year, unilateral relief was given:
    (a)   for tax paid under the law of the Isle of Man or the Channel Islands if the person is resident in the UK *or* the Isle of Man or the Channel Islands; and

(b) for tax paid under a foreign law computed by reference to income from an office or employment the duties of which are performed wholly or mainly in that territory, against UK income tax chargeable under Schedule E, whether the person is resident here or in that country.[1]

(2) In deciding whether the tax paid in this country is related to tax paid in the foreign country the formula is that the foreign tax is a credit against UK tax if the latter is computed "by reference to" that income.[2]

(3) Relief for underlying tax is governed by TA 1988, s 801 which states the rules now sought when treaties are renegotiated. The relief is as stated infra, § 37.25.[3]

Simon's Taxes E6.414.

[1] TA 1988, s 794.
[2] TA 1988, s 790(4).
[3] TA 1988, s 790(5)(c).

Treaty relief by credit

[37.09] Where a treaty provides for relief by way of credit for the foreign tax paid, the way of giving relief is a matter for UK law.[1] The UK Treasury has power to deny tax credit refund under a treaty to companies which have, or are associated with companies which have a qualifying presence in a state which practises unitary taxation (called a unitary state).[2] This power would have been exercised in relation to California,[3] but, happily the dispute with California has been resolved.

Relief must be claimed by the date six years after the end of the accounting period to which it relates, or, if later, one year after the foreign tax is paid.[4]

[1] The methodology is in TA 1988, ss 792–806.
[2] TA 1988, ss 812–815.
[3] Treasury Press Releases, 13 May 1993 and 15 September 1993, *Simon's Tax Intelligence* 1993, pp 858, 1250.
[4] TA 1988, s 806(1).

Limitation on tax credit for foreign tax paid

[37.10] The credit against UK tax is given for what statute refers to as "foreign tax", which is defined in statute[1] as tax chargeable by a foreign territory. HMRC have always interpreted this provision by applying the "minimum foreign tax rule".[2] This interpretation distinguishes between "chargeable" and "paid". In the Revenue view, the provision has always been that the word "chargeable" restricts the amount to the tax that falls due if all relief available under the double tax agreement is obtained. Hence, if a greater amount of tax has been actually paid, this greater sum is ignored in favour of

[37.10] Double taxation relief

the lesser sum that is "chargeable". Curiously, the Revenue argued against its own interpretation before the Special Commissioners in *Sportsman v IRC*.[3]

In that case, a sportsman was chargeable to French tax but did not actually pay it. He failed in his attempt to obtain a credit for the French tax chargeable (but unpaid) against his UK tax liability. Statute[4] now specifies that the credit for foreign tax "shall not exceed the credit which would be allowed had all reasonable steps been taken . . . to minimise the amount of [foreign] tax payable". The section specifically requires the taxpayer to be treated as having made all reasonable steps under both the domestic law of the foreign territory and under the double tax agreement.

This provision gives rise to two very practicable and, usually insoluble, problems.

First, there is the problem faced by the private investor who has a relatively small amount of foreign source income and for whom the foreign tax repayable is exceeded by the cost of obtaining that repayment. This is an all too familiar problem and has lead some commentators to comment that the UK's proud boast of having over 100 double tax agreements works against the interests of private investors in the UK. The problem becomes extreme when there is a question of claiming back tax for undeclared income. HMRC practice is to compute the UK liability calculated on the assumption that the taxpayer has made all claims available for repayment of tax in excess of the limits specified in the relevant double tax agreement. A contract settlement is drawn up on that basis. As the income in the circumstances has not, in fact, been declared no claim will have been made and double taxation results.

The second problem arises from the statutory requirement that the taxpayer shall "be treated as having made all reasonable steps". This is given statutory elaboration by being expressed as the steps which it would have been reasonable for a person in the UK to have taken.[5] We are, here, however, looking at foreign tax, not UK tax. Whereas it might be totally reasonable for a UK resident to complete a UK tax claim, the circumstances in the foreign territory may well make a claim from repayment extremely onerous. There is also the problem as to whether a certain claim under the provisions for the foreign tax would have given an overall position (perhaps for the group of companies, taken as a whole) which would be detrimental. The UK statutory provision appears to restrict the UK double tax relief to the foreign tax which would have been payable by the individual company in the group had action been taken by that individual company to obtain all possible repayment (or mitigation) of the foreign tax, even though the consequence of the claim would have been detrimental to the group of companies taken as a whole.

---

[1] TA 1988, s 792.
[2] See HMRC Double Taxation Relief Manual para DT675.
[3] [1998] STC (SCD) 289.
[4] FA 2000, Sch 30, para 6 introduces TA 1988, s 795A with effect to claims for double taxation credit made after that date.
[5] TA 1988, s 795A(3).

Residence

[37.11] The taxpayer must have been resident in the UK—whether or not also resident in another country—for the chargeable period.[1] This requires that he has been a resident throughout the period. Residence is defined by UK law—not by the code in the treaty.

A non-resident company that trades in the UK through a permanent establishment can claim double taxation relief in respect of the permanent establishment's activities.[2] The relief is granted on the same basis as is available to a UK company. The total relief is not to exceed what would have been available if the permanent establishment had been a person resident in the UK.

---

[1] TA 1988, s 794. For unilateral relief in two cases where taxpayer not resident. See also TA 1988, s 794 which extends relief to UK branches of non-resident banks.
[2] TA 1988, ss 790 and 794.

The foreign tax relievable

[37.12] The foreign tax is defined as the tax chargeable under the laws of the foreign territory.[1] The treaty making power is limited to relief for income tax or corporation tax and any taxes of a similar character imposed by the laws of that territory.[2] It is usual for the treaty to state precisely the taxes which may be claimed for credit. The Revenue publish a list of admissible and inadmissible taxes.[3]

The foreign tax is that chargeable rather than that paid so that credit is given only to the extent of the tax properly payable to the foreign country.[4] So if a claim had to be made in due time under the foreign tax system and was not so made the UK will grant relief only on the basis that the claim had been made in time.

When there is a transfer of a non-UK trade by a person resident in the UK to a person resident in another EC member state, double tax relief may be given for tax which has not been actually paid.[5]

The problem of calculating the correct amount of tax in California has been the subject of Revenue guidance.[6] If the amount of the foreign tax liability changes so that relief given becomes excessive there is now an obligation on the taxpayer to inform the Revenue.[7]

The exchange rate to be used is that in force at the time of payment.[8]

Taxpayers must be able to show that they have taken all reasonable steps to minimise their liabilities to the foreign tax whether by reason of the laws of the other territory or the treaty itself.[9] This is to encourage taxpayers to take such steps rather than just sitting back in the confident expectation that any reduction of the foreign tax would simply mean more UK tax and so would make no difference overall.

It is also axiomatic that the foreign tax must have been paid by the taxpayer. This axiom is softened at the edges eg where foreign groups or certain foreign

[37.12] Double taxation relief

entities are concerned, if tax is paid by the taxpayer company for all the companies in the group as a single taxable entity and one of the subsidiary companies then pays a dividend to a related company.[10]

---

[1] TA 1988, s 792(1). On adjustments to foreign tax by reason of change in exchange rate, see *Greig v Ashton* (1956) 36 TC 581. In some treaties, although none involving the UK, the credit may exceed the local tax charged, eg Argentine–West Germany 1966, which allowed a 15% credit although the Argentine tax was then 8%.

[2] TA 1988, s 788(1). The Revenue often declares that taxes are similar, eg [1980] BTR 606. A Venezuelan tax charging 90% of the gross receipts was held to be a similar tax for unilateral relief in *Yates v GCA International Ltd* [1991] STC 157. More recently, the methodology was explored in *Legal and General Assurance Society v Thomas* [2005] STC (SCD) 350.

[3] See Inland Revenue booklet IR 146; see Inland Revenue press release, 27 March 1995, *Simon's Weekly Tax Intelligence* 1995, p 518.

[4] On method of calculation see Inland Revenue press release [1979] BTR 459. See also the curious case of *Sportsman v IRC* [1998] STC (SCD) 289, supra § **37.10**.

[5] TA 1988, s 815A; supra, § **25.20**.

[6] Inland Revenue interpretation RI 102.

[7] TA 1988, s 806(3)–(6). See Inland Revenue press release, 17 March 1998, *Simon's Weekly Tax Intelligence* 1998, p 466 on timing.

[8] *Grieg v Ashton* (1956) 36 TC 581.

[9] TA 1988, s 795A.

[10] TA 1988, s 803A.

Pioneer relief or tax sparing

[37.13] The logic of the tax credit scheme of relief means that concessions whereby the country of source lowers its tax rates are cancelled out since it results simply in a lower credit to set against the tax liability in the country of residence. Treaties with Barbados, Israel, Malaysia, Malta, Jamaica, Pakistan, Portugal, Singapore and Trinidad and Tobago contained clauses under which the amount of the relief in the foreign country can be treated as if it were tax paid.[1] This is only effective in providing a credit for UK tax where the relief sought is unilateral and either both the overseas company and the subsidiary are resident in the same country or the sparing relief is provided by the treaty between the UK and the territory from which the profits arose.[2]

The device of tax-sparing has been heavily criticised in and scarcely used by the US. The main objection to it is that by giving a positive advantage to the citizen trading overseas it breaks the fundamental principle underlying the notion of the tax credit which is neutrality between citizens trading abroad and those trading at home. Other objections are that it gives the largest tax benefits to the countries with the highest nominal tax rates[3] without any necessary relationship to the fundamental economic needs of the country. It should not, however, be inferred that the US ignores the problem; it gives relief in a different way by in effect granting capital allowances in respect of expenditure outside the US, something permitted only under the UK capital allowance system.

[1] The UK's 100% tax allowances for machinery and plant (supra, § **9.15**) placed the UK in a similar position *vis à vis* foreign countries whose capital this country is anxious to attract.
[2] TA 1988, ss 788(5), 790(10A)–(10C).
[3] Counter-measures taken by developing countries include conditional withholding tax (Jamaica) and the raising of the tax level (Panama).

Income taxed under UK rules

[37.14] In order to calculate the UK tax against which the foreign tax is to be set as a credit, one must first calculate the income to be taxed under UK law.[1]

Income which is taxed on a remittance basis is grossed up to include the foreign tax payable. One cannot remit a sum net of tax and ask to have the foreign credit set against the UK tax on the net sum.

Income taxed on an arising basis is taken gross, that is without any deduction for the foreign tax. Where the income is a dividend and credit relief is due for the corporation tax underlying it, the sum must be grossed up to take account of the underlying tax.

Naturally the UK tax is calculated in accordance with UK tax rules.[2]

[1] See TA 1988, s 795; on loan relationships see TA 1988, s 795(4) overriding FA 1996, s 80(5).
[2] TA 1988, s 810 contained a special rule allowing taxpayers to postpone claims for certain UK allowances; as this only applied to expenditure incurred on or after 27 October 1970, it was repealed with effect from 1 April 2000 by FA 2000, Sch 30, para 18 on grounds of obsolescence.

The credit given

[37.15] Where credit is to be allowed against any of the UK taxes chargeable in respect of any income, the amount of the UK taxes so chargeable shall be reduced by the amount of the credit.[1] This simple rule masks many problems.

[1] TA 1988, s 793(1). On credit for banks see TA 1988, s 794.

Different basis periods

[37.16] Problems arise where the profits arise over a period (eg business profits) and the foreign tax system and the UK have different basis periods, as where the UK operates on its year of assessment for income tax, or financial year for corporation tax while the foreign system operates on a calendar year basis. Here an apportionment of the foreign tax must be made. So if X has foreign income for the year ended 31 March 2003, relief will be given against UK tax for 3/4 of the foreign tax paid in the calendar year 2002 and 1/4 of that paid for 2003; the fact that X may not know the amount of foreign tax paid in 2003 when making the return for year ended 31 March 2003 is immaterial save at the practical level.[1] This problem does not arise where a withholding tax is levied at source since here it will be the withholding tax that is the tax on the income.

---

[1] For practice, see HMRC Double Taxation Relief Manual, para 651.

[37.17] Overlap profit relief for a sole trader or a partnership leads to difficulty in the application of double taxation relief.

The double taxation relief credit is used in respect of the overlap profit notwithstanding that it has been allowed as a credit against income taxed in a previous year of assessment.[1] An overlap profit is defined as profit which, by virtue of Chapter 15 of Part 2 of ITTOIA 2005, is included in the computations for two successive years of assessment.[2]

Under the opening year provisions for a sole trader or a partnership (see supra, § 8.44) income forming part of the first and second year of business will often be taxed twice to the extent that the first year's profits fall short of the first 12 months and that credit for the double amount of UK tax is given only where the business eventually ends, or if the period of account exceeds 12 months in the meantime.[3] So if credit has been given for the foreign tax more than once in respect of the income which is the overlap profit (the original income) and in a later year that original income becomes deductible under TA 1988, s 63A, a set-off is to be given against that deductible income. The first step is to ascertain the total amount of credit that was set off over the two years of assessment when the original income was taxed twice and deduct from it the amount that would have been set off if that income had been taxed only once.[4] This original excess is now used to reduce any double tax credit that would have been allowed in respect of that source in the final period under s 63A and only the balance, if any, is available for set-off as a foreign tax credit.[5] If the original excess exceeds the credit for the final period a special charge to income tax is made—the person chargeable is treated as having received in that year a payment chargeable under Schedule D, Case VI of an amount such that income tax on it at the basic rate is equal to that excess.[6]

Where there is an overlap period and a deduction under TA 1988, s 63A(1), ie not on the discontinuance of the trade, the double tax credit in relation to each element of the overlap is treated in that proportion which that overlap profit bears to that aggregate of taxable profits.[7]

---

[1] TA 1988, s 804(1).
[2] FA 1994, s 217(3).
[3] TA 1988, s 63A.
[4] TA 1988, s 804(5A).
[5] TA 1988, s 804(5B)(*b*).
[6] TA 1988, s 804(5B)(*a*).
[7] TA 1988, s 804(5C).

The relief
Income tax and capital gains tax

[37.18] Once the amount of the credit has been ascertained, it is set against the UK tax chargeable and the latter is reduced by the amount of the credit. However, the amount of the credit is not to exceed the difference between (a) the amount of income tax which would be borne by the taxpayer if he were charged to income tax on his total income from all sources, including the foreign income grossed up as necessary, and (b) the tax borne by him on his total income but minus the foreign income as computed.[1] The effect of this rather inelegant formula is to treat the income as the top slice of his income thus treating the UK tax against which the foreign tax is to be credited as his top slice rate and not his average rate. Although the foreign tax has to be paid in respect of the same source it does not have to be paid by the same taxpayer. Thus if state A taxes the income of a child as income of the child and the UK taxes it as income of the parent, the parent can use the foreign tax paid.

Where more than one foreign source is involved, each is treated separately but in order, the order being at the taxpayer's option.[2] In such circumstances it obviously pays to take the income taxed at the highest foreign rates first. In any event the total tax credit is not to exceed the total income tax payable.[3]

Equivalent relief is given for CGT.[4] It may happen that the UK allows a deferral of CGT when the foreign system does not. A Revenue Statement of Practice provides that they will allow the foreign tax as a credit on the occasion of the subsequent disposal which gives rise to UK CGT.[5] The Statement does not cover the converse situation where the UK tax becomes due before the foreign.

Relief for foreign income tax may not be set against Class 4 National Insurance contributions.[6]

Simon's Taxes E6.410.

---

[1] TA 1988, s 796(1).
[2] TA 1988, s 796(2).
[3] TA 1988, s 796(3).
[4] TCGA 1992, s 277 and see statement of practice SP 6/88.
[5] Statement of practice SP 6/88.
[6] HMRC Double Taxation Relief Manual, para 601.

Corporation tax

[37.19] Where the income is subject to corporation tax, the amount of credit is not to exceed the corporation tax attributable to that income.[1] This leads to companies with high overseas income from countries with high rates of tax deciding to expand their UK operations. In *George Wimpey International Ltd v Rolfe*[2] the company had paid foreign tax in respect of foreign profits but made an overall trading loss. It argued that it should be entitled to set off the foreign tax against the UK corporation tax in respect of its non-trading income. It argued that the UK tax was computed "by reference to" the foreign income because that income had been taken into account in computing its overall income.

[37.19] Double taxation relief

Hoffmann J rejected this argument. He referred to the scheme of the legislation and said that that led to the need to identify exactly the fund charged to overseas tax with a fund chargeable also to UK tax.

> The reference in s [790(4)] to United Kingdom tax being computed by reference to income on which the foreign tax had been computed was introduced in consequence of the decision in *Duckering v Gollan* 42 TC 333, and was intended to ensure that the identity was not between funds which might notionally be regarded as taxable income in that foreign territory and the UK but between the actual funds by reference to which the computation of tax was made. This identification of the income subject to UK corporation tax can, in my judgment, only be made in accordance with income tax principles. On this basis it seems to me the income in respect of which the taxpayer company became liable to corporation tax was its non-trading income notwithstanding that the computation of that income was made subject to deduction for losses which took into account the company's trading in the three territories. The company was not chargeable to any tax in respect of the income which had been subject to foreign tax and accordingly no credit can be allowed.[3]

Where a company has overseas income and domestic income it is necessary to allocate such items as non-trading deficits on loan relationships and charges on income among the different sources so as to calculate the amount of UK corporation tax attributable to that foreign income. TA 1988, s 797A provides first that non-trading credits are calculated on their own, ie without any deduction for non-trading debits. The non-trading debits have to be calculated by taking the debits for the period and then deducting any which have been relieved in other ways or which have been carried forward from an earlier period. In accordance with the general 1996 scheme those carried forward can only be set against non-trading profits. Provision is made to exclude deficits which have been set off against general profits of the same or the preceding period. FA 2000 widens s 797A significantly by changing the reference to interest to cover any other non-trading credit; this applies to any accounting period ending on or after 21 March 2000.[4] The purpose of s 797A is to permit the operation of s 797 even though the foreign interest is no longer separately distinguished. Where s 797A does not apply s 797(3) still allows the company to allocate these deficits as it thinks fit subject to three qualifications. First, any decision by the company to set off a non-trading deficit against trading profits of the same period must be respected here also.[5] Second, if the deficit is carried forward from an earlier period it may only be set against non-trading profits.[6] Third, it is not open to a company to allocate excess charges to UK income greater than the amount of that income so as to set up a loss which could be carried forward.[7]

It remains the case that when loss relief is available it will be applied first, thus cancelling the tax credit for any double tax relief; as unused double tax relief may not be carried forward as double tax relief but only, when relevant, as a deduction and so perhaps a trading loss, the point is one of some importance.

Simon's Taxes E6.410; STP [35.101]–[35.120].

---

[1] TA 1988, s 797.
[2] [1989] STC 609.
[3] [1989] STC 616.

[4] FA 2000, Sch 30, para 7.
[5] TA 1988, s 797(3A).
[6] TA 1988, s 797(3B).
[7] *Commercial Union Assurance Co plc v Shaw* [1999] STC 109, CA.

Dividends and underlying tax: basic rules

[37.20] Where a UK resident receives a dividend from a non-resident company, he is liable to income tax under or, if a company, to corporation tax.[1] The tax deducted in the country of source will have been a withholding tax, probably at the rate of 5 or 15%[2] if there is a treaty and the full local income tax rate if there is none. These taxes may be taken as credits against the UK tax due, whether income tax or corporation tax. Where, however, the foreign tax system has charged a separate tax on the profits of the company, it would be equitable to allow credit not only for the income tax charged on the dividend but also for at least a proportion of the tax levied on the profits of the company which underlie the dividend.

Although the UK refers to this by the formula "relief for the underlying tax" most other countries refer to it as an "indirect tax credit"; the UK formula may be long-winded but it is precise and avoids problems of confusion with relief for indirect taxes.

Recent treaties provide[3] that relief for the underlying tax is to be given only if the UK resident is a *company* which either (a) controls directly or indirectly, or (b) is a subsidiary of a company which so controls at least 10% of the voting power in the overseas company.

A company is a subsidiary of another if that other controls directly or indirectly not less than 50% of the voting power in the first company.[4] So where a parent has such control over the foreign dividend paying company, relief for the underlying tax may be claimed by the parent *and* by any of its 51% subsidiaries receiving dividends.

These restrictions apply also to unilateral relief[5] but provision is made for the preservation of this relief where a 10% holding is reduced by dilution.[6]

The question whether a particular receipt is a dividend is a question of law. In considering the nature of the right under the foreign law the court should adopt a purposive construction and try to achieve symmetry between the two systems.[7]

---

[1] The payment is not franked investment income (and so exempt from corporation tax) as the payer is a non-resident, and the payment therefore falls outside the scheme. The words of the treaty may produce some surprises.
[2] Or whatever rate is specified in the double tax treaty.
[3] See Inland Revenue leaflet IR 6 § **1**. The problem with wider relief is one of proof—see RC (1955) § **708**. Formerly relief could be claimed without such control and this survives in some treaties. The change in policy occurred in FA 1966, s 40.
[4] TA 1988, s 792.
[5] TA 1988, s 790(3), (4); s 800 has been repealed.
[6] TA 1988, s 790(6)–(10).

[37.20] Double taxation relief

[7] *Memec plc v IRC* [1996] STC 1336. Taxpayer's appeal dismissed [1998] STC 754, CA.

Relevant profits

[37.21] Where relief for the underlying tax is given, the next step is to ascertain the profits underlying the dividend, the rate of tax available for credit depending on a comparison of the tax paid with the profits.

The amount of underlying tax available for relief is computed by reference to the "relevant profits" out of which the dividend is paid.[1] The relevant profits are the profits available for distribution, determined for accounting purposes and not for tax purposes in the territory concerned.[2]

[1] TA 1988 s 799 amended by FA 2000, Sch 30, para 9.
[2] *Bowater Paper Corp v Murgatroyd* (1969) 3 All ER 111; 46 TC 37. This is now made explicit in statute: FA 2000, s 103

Foreign tax paid on the basis of a group

[37.22] In some countries the law may provide that one company may pay tax in respect of the aggregated profits of itself and others as if they were a single entity.[1]

UK statute provides that, for the purpose of calculating UK double taxation relief:

(1) the relevant profits of these companies are regarded as a single aggregate figure in respect of a single company; and
(2) the foreign tax paid by the responsible company as having been paid by that single company.[2]

There is, thus, an actual dividend received in the UK, which may be treated, under these rules, as having been paid by a notional foreign company. The identity of the group of companies is determined according to the foreign law but cannot, for UK purposes contain companies where the shareholding is less than 10% of the voting power.[3]

In some countries a consolidated group may own more than 10% of the shares of a second consolidated group, but an insufficient amount to permit consolidation of the second group with the first under local law. In these circumstances, the legislation does not permit the first and second groups to be treated as a "single taxable entity".

The legislation does not extend to "quasi-consolidations", where countries do not permit the filing of consolidated tax returns, even if they arrive at the same result by allowing the surrender of tax attributes among companies.

Section 803A applies where "tax is payable by any one company . . .." In the US, for example, tax may be paid by any or several members in a single year, and not necessarily by the company which is the common parent. The legislation covers any type of consolidation that falls within the stated criteria.

There may be more than one consolidated group in a country, and the legislation is framed so that each tax-filing group will be treated as a "single taxable entity".

The foreign tax consolidated group may consist of a number of companies and a partnership. The pre-conditions of s 803A are satisfied for the companies, but the partnership is not, by definition, a company and so it cannot be included. As for a branch of a foreign company, the appropriate amounts of relevant profits and foreign tax need to be excluded from the calculation of underlying tax for the s 803A entity.

Countries that provide for the aggregation of profits within a group include the Netherlands (99% ownership is required), the USA (80% ownership is required), Germany (an "Organschaft" for which 50% shareholding is required), France (an "Integration Fiscale", for which 95% shareholding is required), Luxembourg (95% ownership is required), New Zealand (100% ownership is required) and Spain (90% ownership is required).[4]

[1] TA 1988, s 803A inserted by FA 2000, Sch 20, para 15.
[2] TA 1988, s 803A(2). Considerable detail of the way in which the Revenue interprets these provisions is given in Inland Revenue Tax Bulletin August 2001, pp 870–874, which include worked examples.
[3] TA 1988, s 803A(3).
[4] Detail on the grouping arrangements in these countries is given in Inland Revenue Tax Bulletin February 2002, pp 911–913. HMRC is prepared to examine the circumstances of any particular foreign group and give guidance as to its view of the operation of the double taxation relief provisions in relation to that particular group. Application should be made to: International (External Relations Group), (Underlying Tax Group), Fitzroy House, PO Box 46, Castle Meadow Road, Nottingham, NG2 1BD.

Capping the underlying tax

[37.23] Where there is a chain of companies including a UK company, any dividends paid by companies in the chain below the UK company have the foreign tax credit capped by reference to the normal CT rate, currently 30%. The formula used is (D+U) × M%. D is the amount of the dividend, U is the underlying tax and M is the maximum relievable rate; M is defined as the rate of corporation tax in force when the dividend is paid.[1] So the effect of this rule is to cap by reference to the current UK corporation tax rate of 30%. The formula applies to any dividend paid to the UK resident company, ie whether it is from the company which is at the top of the chain, usually the mixer itself, or one lower down. Companies can exclude any amount of the underlying tax if they wish; they might wish to do so if this will bring the amount of tax down below the cap level and so avoid "tainting" the dividend.[2] Although sometimes referred to as a disclaimer it must be understood that this is a disclaimer for UK tax purposes only. The foreign tax has been paid and does not cease to be paid—and cannot be used as a deduction.[3]

Some tax avoidance schemes, which came to the attention of HMRC under the new disclosure regime, sought to make use of the fact that certain payments

[37.23] Double taxation relief

may be characterised as interest for tax in other jurisdictions but as a dividend under UK tax law. As a consequence the payer obtained a deduction for payment in the other jurisdiction but claimed credit for underlying relief in the UK. From 16 March 2005 no underlying relief will be given if a tax deduction is given in another jurisdiction calculated by reference to the amount of such a dividend.[4]

[1] TA 1988, s 799(1A).
[2] TA 1988, s 799(1B).
[3] TA 1988, s 811.
[4] FA 2005, s 85 inserting TA 1988, s 799(2A).

Relievable tax: relief for capped tax from 30% to 45%

[37.24] Relief is given for foreign tax, whether underlying or on the dividend itself, which is above the 30% cap but below a maximum of 45%.[1] The upper percentage is allowed against the UK tax payable on certain other foreign dividends; these other dividends must not themselves have been subject to the cap or to another form of limitation on relief, such as being trading income and so able to make use of trading deductions or losses.

The 45% figure is referred to in the legislation as the "upper percentage" and must of course be distinguished from the "maximum relievable rate" referred to in the general rule above and which is currently 30%. In following these rules it is necessary to distinguish "relievable" tax which means tax above the 30% cap rate but below the 45% upper percentage from what has been called "actual" tax, ie tax which is below the 30% and is given effect under the general credit rules.[2] Another way of putting this is that the ceiling rate of 45% is 1.5 times the mixer cap rate.

The purpose of this pooling is to avoid the need for mixer companies by allowing to happen within the UK what previously had to happen offshore through the mixer company. The 45% rate is applied to dividends from any company in the chain; and not, as was at one time proposed, only at the highest point in the chain at which the cap has been applied. As the Revenue note to these amendments made clear:

> The effect of those and of other changes will be to allow onshore pooling of dividends without allowing companies to obtain excessive amounts of relief by artificially boosting the rates of foreign tax that they pay.

Since, as the same note points out, mainstream corporate tax rates on distributed profits in other EC member states, the USA and Japan for example, are below 45%, there should not be any difficulty with EC law, especially with regard to free movement of capital.

[1] TA 1988 s 806B; on upper percentage see s 806J.
[2] The dividends are listed in TA 1988, s 806A(2); trading income is defined by reference to s 393, including s 393(8).

Mechanics

[37.25] In order to carry this out the legislation directs a pooling of various elements which are spelt out. Element 1, unrelated qualifying dividends, are dividends received from a company which is not related to the recipient (ie the company controls less than 10% of the voting power).[1] Element 2, related qualifying dividends, arise when the recipient company has this degree of control. 1 and 2 differ in that there will be relief for underlying tax in 2 but not in 1. Elements 3 and 4 comprise the underlying tax and the other tax (usually withholding tax). Each element is aggregated and credit relief is applied to the resulting combined facts.[2]

The statutory language used to achieve these goals is self-contained. The foreign tax which is above the 30% rate and so is capped but which is below the 45% rate and which is available for credit relief is called "eligible unrelieved foreign tax on dividends",[3] which was quickly reduced to EUFT. Presumably this could not be called excess credit since the 30% cap prevented it from being allowable credit at all.

The statute divides the situations with which it is going to deal into two. What the statute calls "Case A" is the normal situation which arises where:

(1) the capped credit for all the foreign tax, ie direct and underlying, allowable against corporation tax on the dividend, exceeds
(2) the amount of the credit for foreign tax which, under the arrangements, is allowed against corporation tax in respect of the dividend.[4]

Case B involves situations in which there is excess underlying tax which has to be capped. When the statute moves on to calculate the amount of EUFT, it distinguishes situations in which the underlying tax has been paid by the company paying the dividend from those in which the underlying tax has been paid lower down the chain.[5] FA 2001 tries to ensure that dividends arising in the UK cannot give rise to EUFT.[6]

For the purposes of these pooling rules the dividends must meet the criteria already set out in supra, § **37.26** and not be either (a) a dividend paid by a CFC which escapes the CFC legislation because, and only because, of the acceptable distribution test or which represents such a dividend; or (b) a dividend in respect of which there is EUFT.[7] Such dividends must be separately streamed.[8]

EXAMPLE: CALCULATING EUFT

Where Case A applies, the first step in determining the amount of EUFT is to find the amount of all allowable relevant foreign tax, ie direct withholding tax on the dividend and underlying taxes but restricted by the 30% cap. The second step is to determine the amount of tax that would be allowable for credit—ie under the general rules in s 797 if the 45% rate applied. The difference is the EUFT.[9]

UK company has shares in a company based in Ruritania. UK receives a dividend of £90 net of Ruritanian tax of £10. UK has Case V income of £100 and a tax credit of £10 against the United Kingdom corporation tax liability of £30. Now suppose that UK is entitled to credit for underlying Ruritanian tax of £65. Although the total foreign tax paid is now £75, the 30% cap will restrict relief to 30% of £165, ie £49.50. One then has to recalculate using the upper rate of 45% so making the maximum allowable relief 45% of £165 ie £74.25. The EUFT is the difference between £65 and £49.50; ie £15.50. Suppose the underlying tax is £100; so income taxed under Schedule D Case V is £200. The 30% cap restricts relief to £60: the 45% cap gives a figure of £90. EUFT will be the difference between £90 and £60 ie £30 but foreign tax of £20 will be wasted.

[37.25] Double taxation relief

Where case B is involved there is one set of calculations where the 30% mixer applies to the dividend and another where it applies at a lower level.[10]

---

[1] TA 1988, s 806C(2); the definition of related company in s 806J refers back to s 801(5).
[2] TA 1988, s 806C.
[3] EUFT is defined in TA 1988, s 806A; the calculation rules are in s 806B.
[4] TA 1988 s 806A(4); for calculations see s 806B(2).
[5] TA 1988 s 806A(5); for calculations see s 806B(3)–(7) as amended by FA 2001, Sch 27, para 5.
[6] TA 1988, ss 801 and 806A. TA 1988, s 801 is amended by F(No 2)A 2005, s 43 with effect from 1 January 2005 in order to enact the amended EU Parent/Subsidiary Directive.
[7] TA 1988, ss 806A(2) and 806C(1).
[8] TA 1988, s 801C.
[9] TA 1988, s 806B(2).
[10] TA 1988, s 806B(3), (4). There are some helpful examples in Simon's Finance Act Handbooks for 2000 and 2001.

Other set-off rules

[37.26] Any foreign tax which cannot be used in this way may be rolled backwards for three years[1] or carried forward indefinitely[2] or surrendered to another company in the same group.[3]

The carry back rules require the company to use the corporation tax of a later accounting period before an earlier one. Within the same accounting period the order of priority is given first to the aggregated foreign tax in respect of the single dividend arising in that accounting period, so far as not consisting of relievable tax arising in another accounting period; and then for relievable tax arising in any accounting period before that in which the relievable tax in question arises.

Credit must be given for any underlying tax before other foreign tax.[4] More fully, actual underlying tax is relieved before actual withholding tax; actual withholding tax relieved before "relievable" underlying tax and relievable underlying tax before relievable withholding tax. The reason for this order is that underlying tax cannot be set off against UK tax on unrelated dividends.

The group relief rules are implemented by statutory instrument.[5]

The carry forward rules apply to underlying tax only if the companies are related. A foreseeable problem—with a foreseeable solution—arises with the right to carry forward on underlying tax if the company no longer meets the 10% minimum required for underlying relief. Under such circumstances the right to carry forward is lost; it is not revived if the test is met in a later year.

---

[1] TA 1988, ss 806D and 806E.
[2] TA 1988, s 806D.
[3] TA 1988, s 806H.
[4] TA 1988, s 806F.

5 Double Taxation (Taxes on Income) (Underlying Tax on Dividends and Dual Resident Companies) Regulations 2001, SI 2001/1156, *Simons Weekly Tax Intelligence* 2001, p 635.

Further restrictions

[37.27] Dividends received by a foreign company from subsidiaries resident in the same territory can be pooled; the reason given by the Revenue for this is that the tax rules and rates will be the same; this assumption may be misplaced especially within a federal jurisdiction but the different companies may have different levels of relevant profits and so the point is of practical importance. The rule is stated (negatively).[1] That provision also allows the Treasury to make regulations for other cases to which the cap is to apply; regulations have been enacted for dual resident companies.[2]

There are some possible adjustments to DTR calculations where CFCs are involved. If UK plc owns a CFC which in turn owns another subsidiary, the mixer cap is modified to be:

$$\frac{D}{(1-X)} \times X\%$$

where X% is the rate of corporation tax.[3]

If the UK company has trading income which derives from outside the UK and which carries DTR, the question will arise as to what expenses if any should be set against the overseas income for the purposes of calculating any DTR cap. In *Legal & General Assurance Society v Thomas*[4] it was held that no expenses out of any general trading expenses needed to be so offset. This went against HMRC's contention and so the law was changed to require expenses to be allocated between those deducted in the Schedule D Case I calculation and those deducted in the Schedule D Case V calculation.[5]

In a clear sign that HMRC were fed up with DTR planning, in 2005 introduced what is, in effect, a mini-GAAR for DTR. Conditions are set out which, on a Board direction, will negate DTR planning.[6]

[1] TA 1988, s 801(2A).
[2] Double Taxation (Taxes on Income) (Underlying Tax on Dividends and Dual Resident Companies) Regulations 2001, SI 2001/1156, *Simons Weekly Tax Intelligence* 2001, p 635.
[3] TA 1988, s 801(2B).
[4] [2005] STC (SCD) 350, SpC 461.
[5] FA 2005 s 86 introducing a new TA 1988, ss 798, 798A, 798B and 798C.
[6] TA 1988, ss 804ZA–804ZC inserted by FA 2005, s 87(1).

Permanent establishments

[37.28] These rules are adapted to apply to UK permanent establishments of companies resident elsewhere.[1]

These rules are also adapted to overseas permanent establishments of companies resident in the UK.[2] Excess foreign tax can be carried forward without limit, or backwards to the accounting periods over the three previous years. The principle of the source is maintained by saying that the excess can only be set against UK tax chargeable on income from the same qualifying source. Such UK income is referred to as the company's qualifying income.[3]

[1] TA 1988, s 806K.
[2] TA 1988 s 806L and 806M.
[3] TA 1988 s 826(7B).

Capital gains

[37.29] The provisions in TA 1988, ss 788–806 are extended to CGT[1] including the unilateral tax credit and the power to make treaties to give relief for foreign tax charged on the same disposal. Where credit relief is not available, or not available in full, the unused foreign tax may be treated as an allowable deduction.

Owing to the variety of systems of taxing gains this relief may be lost. Thus, different events may give rise to a tax liability in respect of what is in substance the same gain. For example, a capital asset in a foreign permanent establishment may incur a tax charge in that country if, without being sold, it is written up in the books, and the foreign country charges tax on the unrealised gain. If, in a later year, the asset is sold and UK CGT liability arises it seems that DTR should not be available in respect of the earlier foreign disposal; however, in practice a generous approach is adopted.[2]

A problem arises in practice with wealth tax. Many foreign jurisdictions take the approach that capital is primarily to be taxed by means of an annual levy expressed as a percentage of the individual's net assets. In this way, many foreign jurisdictions do not charge tax on the disposal of an asset or on the gain arising on that disposal. Where an asset has been held for many years, a significant amount of wealth tax may have been paid over the years. That tax is, however, not relievable against UK capital gains tax as it is neither tax on the disposal nor tax on the gain.[3]

Simon's Taxes C1.615, 616.

[1] TCGA 1992, s 277.
[2] See statement of practice SP 6/88.
[3] Statement of practice SP 6/88.

Relief by exemption

[37.30] This simply provides that income of the type stated shall be exempt in one country.[1] Whether and to what extent it will be taxable in the other country is a matter for the revenue law of that other country. For example income earned overseas by a visiting teacher there for temporary purposes, is sometimes exempt from tax in the country of service but is taxed in the country of residence.[2] If, until 1998, that employment lasted more than 365 days and the teacher was continuously absent from the UK for that period, no UK tax would be payable either.[3] A more common form of exemption will exempt a person from tax in the country where the income arises if he is subject to tax in respect of the income in the other country. It appears to be the generous practice of some foreign countries to regard income taxed in the UK on preferential reduced or remittance bases as being "subject to tax" in the UK and so not liable to the foreign tax.

Examples of income which is often given exemption in either of these forms include trading profits arising otherwise than through a permanent establishment and pensions and salaries paid by governments.

The effect of the exemption is that these receipts are not included in the receipts of the taxpayer's business. This could in turn mean that the business had a loss rather than a profit. A further rule applies therefore where the person is not resident in the UK but is carrying on a business in the UK. Receipts of interest, dividends or royalties are not excluded.[4]

[1] Receipts by a non-resident carrying on a banking, insurance or share-dealing business in the UK, although exempt from UK tax, are not to be excluded in computing the profits of that business so as to give rise to a loss under TA 1988, ss 393, 393A or 436: TA 1988, s 808. This ends a "fascinating anomaly" by which UK branches of US banks and insurance companies could claim treaty exemption on US source interest without restriction on the right to offset interest paid on the corresponding borrowing against their other UK income.
[2] eg 1975 UK–US Treaty, art 20. For a curious interpretation of the equivalent clause in the UK-Hungary treaty see *IRC v Vas* [1990] STC 137; see also the more straightforward case of *Devai v IRC* [1997] STC (SCD) 31.
[3] TA 1988, s 193, Sch 12, para 3.
[4] TA 1988, s 808.

Employment income exempted: 'the 60 day' rule

[37.31] Most of the United Kingdom's double taxation agreements contain a provision by which an employee who comes to work in the UK on a short-term basis is taxed only in his home country. An employee must show that he or she fulfils a series of conditions specified in the agreement to make a valid claim to exemption from UK tax. One of those conditions will be that the employee's remuneration must be "paid by or on behalf of an employer" who is not resident in the United Kingdom.

In many cases, it is clear that the employer is the non-resident company for whom the taxpayer was working before he or she came to the UK. In other cases, the employee may have been seconded by his or her overseas employer to work for a UK company, or the overseas employer may carry on a business of hiring out staff to other companies. A formal contract of employment

[37.31] Double taxation relief

remains with the overseas employer, but the employee works in the business of the UK company, which obtains the benefits and bears any risks in relation to the work undertaken by the employee. In economic terms, this state of affairs is recognised by the overseas employer recharging the cost of the employee's earnings to the UK and the UK company might be described as the "economic employer".

In such a case, the exemption from UK tax for short-term visitors is not available.

HMRC practice[1] is to treat as exempt under an irrelevant double tax agreement income of a foreign employee seconded to a UK company or where:

(1) the employee concerned is in the UK for less than 60 days in a tax year; and
(2) that period does not form part of a more substantial period when the taxpayer is present in the UK.[2]

---

[1] Inland Revenue Tax Bulletin October 1996.
[2] Details are given of the Revenue approach, with examples, in Inland Revenue Tax Bulletin December 2003, pages 1069–1071.

Share options granted to internationally mobile employees

[37.32] Granting share options to senior staff in multinational corporations is commonplace. It is said that 92% of middle managers and 96% of senior executives in United States companies are granted share options.[1] An individual may be granted a share option while working overseas and exercise it after coming to the UK, or he may exercise an option granted during work in the UK after he has become non-resident or may be granted an option for a period of employment during part of which he was resident in the UK and part he was not. In all three circumstances, there is a potential interaction between a UK tax liability and tax liability in another jurisdiction and double taxation relief is in point.

In *Abbott v Philbin*,[2] Mr Abbott was given an option to purchase 2,000 shares in his employer company. Although the reason for the option being given to Mr Abbott was his employment with that company, it was held that his exercise of the option and the value he released by that exercise was not an emolument of his employment. At that time, there was no capital gains tax and, hence, the benefit of the option was enjoyed by Mr Abbott tax free. In order to impose a tax charge, statute[3] was enacted to deem the benefit of the share option to be charged as employment income. This charge is, however, separate from the charge on emoluments; statute does not deem a share option to be part of emoluments.

Under UK legislation, an income tax charge can arise if the individual is resident in the UK at the date of the grant of the share option or if the option was granted in respect of duties carried out in the UK. The income tax charge may arise at the date the option is granted, the date the option is exercised and also at the date of disposal of the shares acquired by the exercise of the option.

Further, capital gains tax may be levied where the ultimate sale price exceeds the exercise price. The UK tax charge may be triggered by other events, such as assessment or release of an option to acquire shares or the conversion of shares acquired by reason of employment from one class of share to other.

The first difficulty to be faced in applying double taxation relief to tax charges arising on share options arises from the way which the legislation imposes an income tax charge without deeming the option to be part of emoluments. Article 15 of the OECD model tax convention is typical of provisions to deal with "wages, salaries and similar remunerations" in that it provides for emoluments to be charged by the territory in which the employment is carried on. By contrast, the provision for income does not fall into any of the categories specified in the double tax agreement that such "other income" is taxable only in the country of the taxpayer's residence. In the Revenue's view[4] the charge as employment income that arises on a share option comes within the double taxation agreement provisions for "wages, salaries and similar remunerations".

Where an employee:

(1) was granted a share option in the United Kingdom during the course of an employment;
(2) exercised that employment in the other country during the period between grant and exercise of the option;
(3) remains in that employment at the date of the exercise;
(4) would be taxed by both of them in respect of the option gain; and
(5) is not resident in the United Kingdom at the date of exercise;

then the United Kingdom will give relief in calculating the tax charge of the proportion of the option gain which relates to the period or periods between grant and exercise of the option during which the employee exercised the employment in the other country.[5]

Revenue practice where the employment has been carried on in different territories is to time apportion on a straight-line basis the benefits of the share option between the time spent employed in the UK and the time elsewhere. There seems little authority for this approach, which is not even applied consistently in the Revenue's own examples. An alternative reading of Article 15(1) of the OECD model agreement could be to apportion in accordance with the quantum of the emoluments or, even, consider the changes in the price of the shares over which the option is granted.

An additional level of complexity is given where the employment for which the share option is granted has, in part, been exercised in a third country that does not seek to tax the benefit from the share option. In the Revenue worked examples, no part of the gain is allocated to such periods in the third country as the gain is treated as purely a matter between the two contracting states of the double tax agreement. It seems difficult to substantiate such an approach if it is accepted that apportionment of the gain by reference to the periods of employment in different territories is appropriate.

By extra-statutory concession[6], the amount of PAYE[7] that is levied on the exercise of a share option where this is within an employment to which PAYE applies can be reduced by excluding the part of the share option gain that will not be chargeable to UK income tax by application of the preceding provisions.

If an individual is resident in the UK when he sells shares obtained under a share option arising from an employment overseas, a charge to UK capital gains tax will arise.

Even though exercise will not normally trigger a UK income tax liability in this case, it may well give rise to a tax charge in another country. Strictly, the exercise of the option and the subsequent disposal of the shares are two distinct events and the UK is not obliged to allow a foreign tax credit for any foreign tax paid on exercise against any UK capital gains tax payable on disposal. Nevertheless, where tax has been paid in a treaty partner country, the Revenue will treat all or part of the gain as falling within the provisions of the employment income Article of the relevant double taxation agreement and allow the relevant proportion of the foreign tax paid as a credit against the UK capital gains tax:

(1) If the options are exercised and the shares sold on the same day, the whole gain is treated as falling within the provisions of the employment income Article of the relevant DTA.
(2) If the shares are disposed of at a later date, part of the gain may be treated as falling within the employment income Article of the agreement.
(3) The Revenue will allow a proportion of the foreign tax paid as a credit against UK capital gains tax normally calculated on a time apportionment basis by reference to periods of employment abroad.

---

[1] US National Centre for Employee Ownership.
[2] (1960) 39 TC 82.
[3] Inland Revenue Tax Bulletin October 2001, p 883. This Bulletin contains five worked examples.
[4] In Taxation, 28 February 2002, Peter Morrats reports that a letter dated 11 June 2001 from Inland Revenue Personal Tax Division stated: 'The United Kingdom's view [on the amount of relief due under a double taxation agreement] is not dependent on the domestic treatment of share/stock options in the other state.'
[5] Inland Revenue Tax Bulletin October 2001, p 884.
[6] Published in Inland Revenue Tax Bulletin October 2001, p 885.
[7] The exercise of the option gives a charge to PAYE if the shares are readily convertible assets: TA 1998, s 203FB; the measure of the PAYE is given by TA 1988, s 203F(3). The Revenue interpretation of these provisions is given in Inland Revenue Tax Bulletin October 2001, p 885.

Interpretation of United Kingdom treaties

[37.33] A double taxation treaty provision being made under statutory authority and so becoming part of municipal law[1] may override the normal rules of UK tax law, but whether it does so or not is a matter of construction.[2] So in *Padmore v IRC (No 2)* the court held that the UK had successfully amended its rules so as to override the interpretation reached in *Padmore v IRC* itself (see supra, § **33.38** and infra, § **37.35**).[3] Where a treaty assigns a tax exclusively to the UK this is not a direction that the UK shall tax, but rather the recognition of a power to tax. An appropriately drafted treaty might be interpreted as a direction to tax, but it is unclear whether this would override the normal domestic tax law.[4]

The correct approach to the interpretation of a treaty is unsettled.[5] The Vienna Convention on the Law of Treaties 1969 requires that the treaty be interpreted in good faith in accordance with the ordinary meaning to be given to the terms of the treaty in their context and in the light of their object and purpose.[6] It then defines "context" as including any associated agreements and instruments and goes on to permit reference to subsequent agreements and practices between the parties directed to interpretation and also to travaux preparatoires. Where the treaty is authenticated in two languages each is of equal weight unless the agreement states otherwise.[7] In other areas of law reference to decisions in other jurisdictions is permitted.[8] The English courts have authorised reference to travaux preparatoires and to the commentaries to the OECD treaty[9] and have acknowledged that tax treaties are not necessarily to be interpreted as if they were domestic UK legislation.[10] However, the actual results reached can reflect a more traditional English approach of strict interpretation.[11]

Some of the problems thrown up are familiar to students of private international law. Thus art 3(2) of the Model Treaty provides that any term which is not defined is to have the meanings assigned to it under the domestic law of the State concerned, unless the context otherwise requires. It is anything but clear what is meant by "context" in this context or what meaning is to be assigned to the term if the context excludes the domestic meaning.[12] However, this simply leads to the next problem which is which interpretation is to apply if the two domestic systems give different meanings; in the absence of a common meaning double taxation may ensue. There is also the problem of choosing the right interpretation if the domestic meaning is A when the treaty is signed, but B by the time the relevant year had been reached. Canadian courts have favoured the static approach over the ambulatory but have been almost instantly reversed by the legislature.[13] The UK position is undecided.[14] The ambulatory position is to be preferred as a matter of theory.[15]

The Special Commissioners have invoked the Vienna Convention concept of "good faith", giving it its ordinary meaning and purpose and thus have held that the purpose of the treaty was not only to prevent double taxation but also to prevent illegitimate tax evasion. This was concluded despite the absence of the second phrase from the list of statutory purposes in TA 1988, s 788(3). They then held that the treaty should not be interpreted so as to allow a taxpayer to pay no tax in either country and so concluded that the taxpayer was not entitled to credit for tax which had not been paid in the other country; the taxpayer had argued that credit relief should be given on the basis that the tax was payable in the foreign country.[16] This conclusion is at odds with the wider definition in TA 1988, s 792(1) which refers to tax "chargeable" in the foreign country but may best be treated as a case in which the taxpayer had failed to establish that the foreign tax was chargeable.

In general, relief under a double tax agreement is available to the person with the beneficial entitlement to income, etc. The term "beneficial owner" has been used in tax treaties since the 1940s; it is in the OECD and UN and US Models; it is found in virtually every UK tax treaty, usually being found in the dividend, interest and, sometimes, the royalties articles. These articles generally provide for a reduced level of withholding tax on the relevant category of income: however, the reduced tax is only available if the "beneficial owner" of the dividends, interest or royalties is a resident of the state which is a party to the treaty. In *Indofood International Ltd v JP Morgan*,[17] an action between two financial institutions, the case concerned an obligation under the contract between the two parties that the borrower had the option to repay the loan early if there were no reasonable steps it could take to revert to the reduced withholding tax. The simple solution proposed was to interpose a Dutch entity between the Indonesian borrower and the Mauritius entity and obtain the benefit of the Indonesia/Netherlands Tax Treaty, which also had a 10% reduced withholding tax (or even the possibility of a zero withholding tax). If the proposed Dutch company would not be the "beneficial owner" of the interest, then the proposed Dutch company would simply not achieve the reduced withholding tax. A measure which was doomed to failure could not be a reasonable measure to take, thus, the borrower could repay the loan early, which is what he wanted to do in the light of reduced interest rates in the market. The Court of Appeal held the term "beneficial owner" should not take a meaning according to the domestic law of the UK, but that it should have an "international fiscal meaning". On this basis, the Court of Appeal held that the proposed intermediary company would not be the "beneficial owner" of the loan interest and, hence, would not have been able to claim the lower rate of withholding tax given under the double taxation agreement. In his leading judgment in the Court of Appeal, Sir Andrew Morritt quoted,[18] with approval, the commentary by Professor Philip Baker[19] on the OECD model convention:

> The essence of this Commentary is to explain that the 'beneficial ownership' limitation is intended to exclude:
>
> (a) mere nominees or agents, who are not treated as owners of the income in their country of residence;
> (b) any other conduit who though the formal owner of the income, has very narrow powers over the income which render the conduit a mere fiduciary or administrator of the income on behalf of the beneficial owner.
>
> It is worth making the point that, as seems clear from this amended Commentary, the mere fact that the recipient may be viewed as a conduit does not mean that it is not beneficial owner.

Professor Baker suggests[20] that, as a practical approach, one can ask whose income the dividends (interests/royalties) are in reality. One way to test this is to ask: what would happen if the recipient went bankrupt before paying over the income to the intended, ultimate recipient? If the ultimate recipient could claim the funds as its own, then the funds are properly regarded as already belonging to the ultimate recipient. If, however, the ultimate recipient would simply be one of the creditors of the actual recipient (if even that), then the funds properly belong to the actual recipient.

Some double tax agreements contain a non-discrimination clause. The courts have tended to interpret this restrictively.[21]

1. It follows that where the text of the order in council does not agree with that of the treaty, the former prevails. See [1970] BTR 388 (Oliver), at 398–400.
2. *IRC v Collco Dealings Ltd* [1961] 1 All ER 762, 39 TC 509, and see *Ostime v Australian Mutual Provident Society* [1960] AC 459, 38 TC 492 (TA 1988, s 445 excluded by treaty).
3. [2001] STC 280; the court rejected an argument that the overriding legislation had to be incorporated into TA 1988 Part XVIII itself.
4. On the present UK position see supra, § **37.03**, note 3.
5. See generally Avery Jones [1984] BTR 14, 90.
6. Art 31.
7. Arts 31–33, reprinted Baker, *Double Taxation Agreements and International Tax Law* (1991), pp 15, 16.
8. Munday (1978) ICLQ 450.
9. *Sun Life Assurance Co of Canada v Pearson* [1986] STC 335, CA.
10. eg Harman J in *Union Texas Petroleum Corpn v Critchley* [1988] STC 691 at 707c.
11. eg *IRC v Commerzbank AG* (Mummery J). See also the divergence of view on the materials which may be considered shown in *Memec plc v IRC* [1998] STC 754, CA.
12. See Baker, *Double Taxation Agreements and International Tax Law* (1991), p 23.
13. Income Tax Conventions Interpretation Act 1984, reversing *R v Melford Developments Inc* (1982) 82 DTC 6281.
14. However Baker, *Double Taxation Agreements and International Tax Law* (1991), p 27 points out that the Canadian Supreme Court in the *Melfort* case placed some reliance on dicta in *IRC v Collco Dealings Ltd* [1962] AC 1 and *Woodend (KV Ceylon) Rubber and Tea Co Ltd v Comr of Inland Revenue* [1971] AC 321, PC.
15. See Baker, *Double Taxation Agreements and International Tax Law* (1991), pp 29–31.
16. See *Sportsman v IRC* [1998] STC (SCD) 289.
17. [2006] EWCA Civ 158, [2006] STC 1195, CA.
18. [2006] STC 1195, paras 27 and 38 at 1208c-j.
19. Philip Baker QC, *Double Taxation Conventions*, para 10B-10.4, of his commentary on the OECD model convention.
20. In *Double Taxation Conventions*, para 10B-15. See also Philip Baker, *Beneficial Ownership After Indofood*, GITC Review vol VI No 1 p 15.
21. See, for example, *UBS V R&C Comrs* [2005] STC (SCD) 589.

Is the payment dividend or interest?

[37.34] Where a business is carried on through a permanent establishment in a foreign country business profits earned by that permanent establishment are taxable in the country of source.[1] Profits earned otherwise than by the establishment are taxable in the country of residence. If the trader decides to set up a subsidiary company in the country of source, the profits of that company will be taxable in that country and there will be no immediate double tax problem. It is however possible to make sure, for example by fixing the prices at which goods are sold between different subsidiaries of the same multinational group, that the profits made in particular countries are not spectacular.[2] Moreover charges can be made for interest. Double tax problems arise when interest payments are made to the parent company and when the profits earned by the subsidiary leave that country in the form of dividends.

The model agreement provides for a withholding tax of a maximum of 10% on payments of interest[3] and of 15% on dividends save where the recipient is a company holding at least 25% of the shares in the paying company when the rate is 5%.[4] Royalty payments are taxable only in the country of residence save where there is an effective connection between the permanent establishment in the source country and the property giving rise to royalties.[5] By contrast the Mexico model gave the taxation of dividends to the place where the capital was invested,[6] of interest to the place of indebtedness[7] and of royalties to the place of exploitation[8]—that is the country of source. Many of these provisions in the OECD model, particularly those relating to dividends are simply unacceptable to less developed countries.

The definition of interest is a matter for the UK courts but statute now provides special rules.[9] Treaties often provide that where owing to a special relationship the amount of the interest paid exceeds the amount that would have been paid in the absence of the relationship only that hypothetical amount is to be treated as interest. Where such a clause is relevant the special relationship is to take account of all factors, but express mention is made of whether the loan would have been made at all, the amount of the loan and the rate of interest and other terms that would have been made. The burden is then on the taxpayer to establish that there is no such special relationship. The section further provides that where the company making the loan does not have a business of making loans generally, that fact is to be disregarded.[10] It also provides that the direction to regard all the factors does not apply where the relationship expressly requires regard to be had to the amount of the debt on which the interest is paid and it limits the factors to be taken into account.[11]

References to "special relationships" are found not only in articles on interest but also in those on royalties. The factors to be taken into account are now set down in statutory form; they are equivalent to those for interest.[12] The new rule applies to payments on the day of the Royal Assent or later.

Where relief from UK tax in respect of interest is in issue, it is essential that a claim is made as soon as possible in order that tax is not deducted at source. Notice of exemption from such deduction may have retroactive effect but only to the date that the certified treaty claim is received by the proper officer of Revenue.[13]

Some payments that are regarded as dividends under UK rules are treated by foreign jurisdictions as payments of interest and, hence, deductible in computing profits. Statute[14] provides that no deduction is made for such a payment when calculating double tax relief.

Simon's Taxes F1.512, 515–523.

---

[1] 1992 Model Treaty, art 7(1).
[2] Note Model Treaty, art 7(2).
[3] Model Treaty, art 11. Uruguay levies a withholding rate of 44%. Some treaties exempt interest on normal intra-group loans. On practice see supra, § **37.06**.
[4] Model Treaty, art 10. On practice see supra, § **37.06**.

[5] Model Treaty, art 12.
[6] Article IX.
[7] Article II.
[8] Article X (copyright royalties were excluded).
[9] TA 1988, s 808A. See the important correspondence between the Law Society and the Inland Revenue reported in *Simon's Tax Intelligence* 1993, p 307.
[10] TA 1988, s 808A(4).
[11] TA 1988, s 808A(5). See also Inland Revenue press release, 15 May 1992, *Simon's Tax Intelligence* 1992, p 519.
[12] TA 1988, s 808B.
[13] Revenue interpretation RI 79; that officer is now the Financial Intermediaries and Claims Office (FICO) (International) formerly the Inspector of Foreign Dividends.
[14] TA 1988, s 799(2A) inserted by FA 2005, s 85.

Changes to double tax treaties

[37.35] Double tax treaties are not immutable. The usual method of change adopted is renegotiation, a process which may be accelerated by announcing that a particular country will no longer be bound by its present treaties after a certain date.[1] Changes in the domestic tax law are not inhibited by the presence of a treaty[2] and some changes may have the effect of altering completely the basis of a treaty, eg the adoption of the imputation system of corporate taxation. These are of course only UK rules; other countries, especially those which incorporate treaties into domestic law directly, may well take a different view. One may also note that the 1998 changes which extend the CGT charge to temporary non residents make express provision to ensure that it does not override treaties.[3]

An interesting example of this process is TA 1988, s 112(4), (5) which was designed to reverse the decision in *Padmore v IRC*.[4] That case held that where a partnership was resident in Jersey the effect of the UK–Jersey treaty was that not only was the Jersey Partnership as such exempt from UK tax on its profits but, more surprisingly, that a UK resident individual partner was exempt from UK income tax on his share of the profits. The new provision reverses this decision by amending TA 1988, s 112 with retroactive effect[5] and states that the treaty is not to affect any liability to tax in respect of the resident partner's share of any income or capital gains of the partnership.[6]

A change to one provision of a treaty made be made by the signing of a protocol. The UK Revenue had noted the increase in use of a scheme to "wash out" gains in an overseas trust, known as the "round the world scheme". Trustees in another overseas jurisdiction resigned in favour of trustees resident in Mauritius who then made the disposal triggering the large gain that was to be sheltered. The effect of the UK/Mauritius double tax agreement Article 13 was that the right to levy tax on the gain was with Mauritius and not with the UK. Mauritius chooses not to levy tax on capital gains. The final part of the arrangement was the resignation of the Mauritius trustees and the appointment of UK resident trustees during the same tax year in which the gain was made, thereby excluding a charge under TCGA 1992, s 87. On 27 March

2003, the UK government and the government of Mauritius issued a protocol to the double taxation agreement deleting the operative part of Article 13 and replacing it with a provision that enables the UK to tax such gains.[7]

Butterworths Tax Treaties; Simon's Taxes E6.402.

---

[1] eg Dominica in 1986, or the UK ending the agreement with the Netherlands Antilles in 1989.
[2] Whether the new domestic law is excluded by the treaty is a question of construction—*IRC v Collco Dealings Ltd* [1961] 1 All ER 762, 39 TC 509.
[3] TCGA 1992, s 10A(1). On s 10A, see supra, § **35.47**.
[4] [1989] STC 493, CA.
[5] The new provision is deemed always to have been made save that it is not to affect any court decision before 17 March 1987 or the law to be applied by an appellate court where the judgment of the High Court or Court of Session was given before that date—one infers that no litigation was concluded in Northern Ireland. FA 1989, s 115 purports to affect the construction of a treaty, an altogether different matter, but also retrospectively.
[6] Such a formula had been employed in other treaties, eg Art II(3) of the UK–Switzerland Treaty of 1955.
[7] *Simons Weekly's Tax Intelligence* 2003, page 521.

Treaty shopping

[37.36] No chapter on treaties would be complete without a reference to the practice of treaty shopping. This practice consists in a resident of a state which is not a party to the convention establishing an entity within a state which is party to the treaty in order to take advantage of its provisions.[1] An OECD report concludes that the practice is consistent with treaty law but should be countered by express provisions in the treaties themselves or by the extension of domestic anti-avoidance legislation.[2] It would seem unlikely that the New Approach can be used to strike down such devices, especially after *Craven v White*.[3]

The general attitude of the UK has been to avoid over-hasty provisions of wide ambit.[4]

---

[1] Baker, *Double Taxation Agreements and International Tax Law* (1991), p 52; see also Edwardes Ker, chapters 58–60.
[2] OECD International Tax Avoidance and Evasion—Four Related Studies. For literature and discussion see Baker, *Double Taxation Agreements and International Tax Law* (1991), pp 52–63.
[3] Contrast the US position in *Johansson v US* 336 F 2d 809 (1964) and *Aiken Industries v Comr* 56 TC (US) 925 (1971).
[4] Beighton (1994) FT World Tax Report, p 2.

Reform and planning

General

[37.37] Despite all the changes made by FA 2000 various issues remain. The first is the role of the credit itself. The foreign tax credit—whether by treaty or unilateral—at first sight appears fair and reasonable. If the foreign tax is lower than the domestic tax, as will usually be the case (since the domestic tax rate reflects the person's total income from all sources as opposed to his income from one country where he is not resident) the effect is to deprive the country of residence of a part of its tax but to enable it to preserve equality of tax rates between the person with foreign income and his fellow resident with only domestic income (unless the foreign rate exceeds the UK rate). However, the tax credit has some increasingly debated consequences particularly where the profits of incorporated business are concerned. Historically the extensive use of the tax credit by the US has had two consequences. First, it has encouraged other countries to put a tax on the profits of companies, at a time when in the US the wisdom of taxing such profits was coming increasingly into question. Second, it encouraged the countries of source to pitch their corporate tax rates as high as the US since this would simply increase their share of the tax which the company had to pay anyway thus causing a loss to the US Revenue without any disincentive for the company.[1]

One alternative would be to extend the relief to indirect taxes—a course which has some attractions for those who believe that an indirect tax on the turnover of companies is to be preferred to a direct tax on their profits. Other courses of action would be simply to abolish the credit, thereby penalising the resident with foreign income, or at the other extreme, to abolish the taxation of foreign income, thereby penalising the stay-at-home. Another possibility would be differential tax rates. Other devices include deferment of tax in the country of residence until the income has been repatriated (an extension of the remittance basis) and the use of investment credits.

---

[1] eg Panama.

Particular

[37.38] (1) The band of taxes[1] against which the tax credit works, income and corporation taxes[2] and CGT and foreign taxes similar in character,[3] is narrow. Indirect taxes are regarded traditionally as deductible in computing the profits[4] and so as a part of the costs of the enterprise. A different explanation for the restriction may be that historically the demand was for relief against the double taxation of income. This causes trouble where the country of source, seeing that it can only levy low withholding rates of tax on dividends and interest, decides to levy taxation by means of royalties, or devices such as the famous Middle Eastern posted prices for oil[5] which charge local tax on an inflated price. The argument against this extension would be that to allow relief now would simply encourage the source countries to raise their rates of indirect tax.

[37.38] Double taxation relief

Following a High Court decision[6] the Revenue have decided to resolve this problem by examining the foreign tax in its legislation context in the foreign territory and deciding whether it serves the same function as income and corporation tax serves in the UK in relation to the profit of a business.[7] Turnover taxes as such are still excluded but taxes on gross receipts or on a percentage of gross receipts are not necessarily excluded.[8]

[1] See Shelburne (1957) BTR 48, 143—still astonishingly relevant.
[2] TA 1988, s 790(6).
[3] TCGA 1992, s 277.
[4] Supra, § **8.108**.
[5] See Public Accounts Committee 1972–73. First Report §§ 14, 57. There are no full double tax treaties with these countries.
[6] *Yates v GCA International Ltd* [1991] STC 157.
[7] Statement of practice SP 7/91.
[8] *Yates v GCA International Ltd* [1991] STC 157.

[37.39] (2) The credit itself is narrow. It may be used only against the UK tax on that source. If the foreign tax is higher, that excess may not be set off against other income, not even against UK tax on other foreign income. There is thus no pooling of foreign income for credit-relief[1]—a rule reinforced by the anti-dividend mixer company legislation in FA 2000. Even the FA 2000 relaxation of the rules forbidding the carry forward or back of an unused credit is very restricted in that it applies only to the tax on dividends. The general restriction to tax on income from the same or any other source remains. These rules make the credit quite distinct from an expense item or a trading loss. There is of course no reason why the UK Revenue should refund tax collected by another country, unless it be to encourage exports and for this there may be more efficient methods. The UK does recognise the excess as a deduction in computing the extent of foreign income for such purposes as determining the profits of a close company for distribution, but some further relaxation of the present rules may seem desirable.

[1] Criticised by CBI—Select Committee on Corporation Tax (1971) p 149, § **11**; see also RC (1955), § 732; contrast US Internal Revenue Code, s 904(*a*)(2). One avoidance device is to interpose an overseas holding company from which alone the foreign profits (and credits) are channelled to the UK.

[37.40] (3) There are problems over differences between the fiscal concepts used in different systems. One example is that under Australian law that part of a director's fees in excess of reasonable remuneration may be treated as dividend. The tax paid on this notional dividend would be ineligible for relief in the UK where, if tax were levied, the whole of the director's fees would be taxable as such.[1]

[1] Shelburne (1957) BTR 53.

[37.41] (4) There are problems where a third country enters the scene since treaties are bilateral arrangements and very few lay down how each party is to give credit for taxes paid in a third country. While the UK may give unilateral relief or even treaty relief under an arrangement between this country and the third country,[1] such rules do not solve the interaction of the relief with the third country and the relief with the second.[2]

---

[1] eg the 1955 UK–Denmark Treaty, Art XVII, para 4 and RC 1955, § 759. The 1980 Treaty with Denmark does not contain this provision.
[2] For a recent example see *IRC v Commerzbank* [1990] STC 285.

[37.42] (5) The present tax treaties often frustrate the domestic purposes of the source country. Thus if a UK company operated a mine in the USA before 1963 it found that its American depletion allowances were cancelled out by the UK tax, the USA not being one of the underdeveloped countries with which we have treaties allowing for pioneer relief. The obvious tax planning answer in such circumstances is that a separate company should be formed in the USA.

[37.43] (6) There were the complications and nonsenses which surrounded the preceding[1] year of assessment and still arise from the new rules with their overlap profit and the inequities surrounding the operation of TA 1988, s 804.

---

[1] Supra, § **37.22**. RC (1955), § 789 recommended a current year basis.

Part VII

Inheritance tax

For payment of inheritance tax, returns, enquiries, appeals and other administrative matters, see Chapter 2 and Chapter 2A.

38

Introduction
Charge to IHT
An outline of IHT
Calculation of tax

39

Transfers of value by disposition
Transfer of value
Potentially exempt transfers
Disposition
Time
Value transferred
Omission to exercise a right
Future payments
Disposition of excluded property
Voidable transfers
Matters which are not transfers of value
Close companies
Disposition by associated operations

40

Death
Transfer at death
Valuation of estate on death
Life policies in the estate at death
Effect on lifetime transfers
Events after death
Quick succession relief
Reliefs for earlier transfers of the same property by the same transferor
Abatement of exemptions on death
Pension fund

41

Gifts with reservation
What is a gift with reservation?
Gift of an interest in land
Excluded property
Inter-spouse transfer
Consequences
Income tax charge on pre-owned assets

42

Settled property
IHT and settled property
What is a settlement?
Categories of trust
Interest in possession created prior to 22 March 2006
Estates in administration and survivorship clauses
Transfers of settled property
Depreciatory transactions
Exceptions
Reversionary interests
Potentially exempt transfers—special rate of charge
Estate duty trusts
Charge on trustees
The charge at the ten-year anniversary
The exit charge
Accumulation and maintenance trusts
Special trusts

43

Exempt transfers
Exempt lifetime transfers
Transfers between spouses
Gifts for public purposes
Other exempt transfers
Partly exempt transfers—allocation of relief
Matters which are not transfers of value

44

Business property relief and other reliefs
Business property relief
Agricultural property relief
Interactions between business property relief and agricultural property belief
Relief for works of art and other heritage property
Relief for timber

45

Valuation
Introduction
A fiscal valuation and a commercial valuation

Chattels
The special purchaser
Restrictions on sale
Related property
Relief for loss after death
Land
Debts due to the transferor
Accrued income to date of transfer
Liabilities

46

Liability for payment of IHT
Liability for tax
Transfers reported late
Position of accounting parties
Position of beneficiaries

47

Foreign element
Territorial limits
Location of assets
Property in the United Kingdom
Excluded property
Double taxation relief
Debts and liability

38

Introduction

Charge to inheritance tax	PARA **38.01**
An outline of IHT	PARA **38.06**
Calculation of tax	PARA **38.13**

For *payment of inheritance tax*, see **2A.23–2A.25**

Charge to inheritance tax

[38.01] Inheritance tax (IHT) is a tax on transfers of capital. Unlike capital transfer tax (CTT) which preceded it for transfers between 27 March 1974 and 17 March 1986, IHT is designed to operate primarily as a tax on transfers which occur on death. Inheritance tax is imposed by amendments made to the CTT legislation which had been consolidated in 1984.[1] In order to limit avoidance the tax also charges retrospectively gifts made within the previous seven years, (see infra, § **39.02**) and property used by the deceased despite having been gifted to another, (see infra, § **41.01** ff).

Gifts are taken into account in calculating the tax at death if the transferor dies within seven years of the gift. A gift is given the awkward statutory term: "a potentially exempt transfer", (see infra, § **39.02**). There is no tax on a potentially exempt transfer, when it is made but if the donor dies within seven years the exemption is lost. Most gifts to an individual are potentially exempt; but most gifts into trust are chargeable immediately.[1]

Unlike the old estate duty it otherwise so greatly resembles, IHT charges certain transfers inter vivos immediately. However, unlike CTT, there is no immediate charge to tax on most types of inter vivos transfer and IHT has an unfortunate willingness to determine the tax payable by looking at the moment of the death of the donor, not only to see whether a potentially exempt transfer has become chargeable but also whether certain conditions for relief are still satisfied. Unlike a true succession duty, and despite its name, it is charged by reference to the circumstances of the transferor and not those of the transferee. IHT is a charge on the reduction in the estate of the transferor. In this, it is in sharp contrast to CGT which is computed on the value of the property disposed of.[2] Some transfers will give rise to both taxes with the liability to IHT only becoming clear on the deceased's death.

---

[1] Formerly the Capital Transfer Tax Act 1984. FA 1986, s 100(1)(*a*) states that CTTA 1984 "may be known as the Inheritance Tax Act 1984".

[2] This means that, when computing the value for IHT purposes, it is necessary to look at property that remains with the transferor; see infra, § **41.07**.

[38.02] Introduction

[38.02] Thought is sometimes given, though not recently, it would appear, in government circles, to the question whether it would be sensible to move from the present donor-based tax to a donee-based tax, such as the tax imposed in the Irish Republic, capital acquisition tax.[1] In 1972 the Conservative government published a Green Paper on whether an inheritance tax should replace the then estate duty.[2] Criticisms of the estate duty were grouped under three main heads. First it was pointed out that since that tax simply reduced the overall size of the estate the duty was not related to the relative size of the legacy received nor to the taxable capacity of the recipient. Second, the tax did not lend itself to variation of the burden by reference to the relationship of the deceased to the beneficiary or some other circumstance. Third, the tax did not take account of the expense incurred in administration.

Estate duty was criticised on other grounds: its general burden; it caused problems for the passing on of a business; it was not sufficiently comprehensive; it was readily avoided.

The Green Paper also said there were a number of real advantages in estate duty. Compared with a tax which had to take account of the circumstances of individual beneficiaries the duty was comparatively simple, both for the Inland Revenue and for executors. It was easily collectable and was certain as soon as the value of the total property passing on death had been ascertained. It was also less affected than alternative taxes by the intricacies of wills and settlements. The values in these advantages are typical of the Revenue. Thus they did not bother to make the point that a donor-based tax makes an advantage of something its critics think wrong—by not shaping the tax according to the circumstances of the beneficiary the tax enabled the person to distribute property on death free of any pressures from the taxman, an example of fiscal neutrality

---

[1] The basis of the tax charged in the Irish Republic is the value of the asset received by the donee. It is interesting to note that, despite the fundamental difference between the UK donor based charge and the Irish donee based charge, the Irish Statute Capital Acquisitions Consolidation Act 2003 borrows many of its terms from the UK Inheritance Tax Act 1984 and, also, from the UK statute imposing stamp duty, Finance Act 1894. A leading Irish practitioner has stated that it is common practice in the Irish Republic to quote UK case law to support arguments on the correct interpretation of the Irish statute, despite the complete contrast in the basis of the charge.

[2] Cmnd 4930 (March 1972).

[38.03] Many of these points in defence of a donor-based tax such as estate duty remain valid, just as many of the criticisms of the estate duty still hold good in relation to inheritance tax; even though the rates are much lower at 40% rather than 75%, they are still significant. Would-be reformers have a bewildering range of choice before them but also many difficult policy decisions to make.

If one views the tax as part of the redistribution of wealth to other sectors of society, one may well arrive at a system of confiscation on death or its modern equivalent of high rates of tax on death levied by reference to the circumstances of the deceased. If on the other hand one opts for a system of family protection, one may well opt for a system under which transfers within the family are exempt or taxed only at low rates, while charging transfers outside the family net at quite high rates. This basis lends itself to some sort of compromise if it is felt that the purpose of family protection is to exempt transfers within the same generation eg to a spouse, rather than to allow the passing of fortunes to one's children.

While an integrated gift and estate tax looks like the logical answer there are social facts to observe; people are much less inclined to give away money during their lifetimes and lifetime giving has a different pattern from death giving—lifetime giving tends to be unequal between the next generation; giving at death tends to give greater equality amongst the children.[1] The failure to give away more in life is not tax driven; indeed, people would give away far more if that were their object.

If one opts for a transferor-based system one has many further choices. Thus should one system apply to both lifetime and death transfers, should there be separate taxes or should there be just tax on death? IHT with its limit lifetime cumulation to a period of seven years seems to make the tax on lifetime transfers voluntary. Thus a married couple (or the members of a civil partnership) could, by using the £3,000 exemption each year for seven years and the £312,000 threshold, transfer £666,000 between them every seven years and pay no IHT.[2] Those who are caught are the foolish or the unlucky, or poorly advised, or perhaps simply parents who do not sufficiently trust (or like) their children. It is also highly questionable whether there should be such a marked absence of tax neutrality as to the timing of gifts.

---

[1] See NBER Research Papers No 6345 by McGarry and No 6337 by Poterba reviewed in the Economist, 28 February 1998, p 101.
[2] This amount is increased if the couple makes use of the small gift exemption, for example, to give £250 to each grandchild each year.

[38.04] A donee-based tax is quite different; it charges by reference to the circumstances of the donee. This may be called an accessions tax or an inheritance tax; it is quite different from our current IHT; old UK taxes such as succession duty and legacy duty are examples. Donee-based taxes may be progressive or flat rate. They may charge different rates according to the relationship between the deceased and the legatee as in many continental European countries.[1] Such a tax may even take account of the existing wealth of the legatee or other legacies or gifts already received by the legatee. Ireland has an interesting lifetime cumulative accessions tax.

Some say that a donee-based tax would encourage the wider distribution of wealth since a lower amount of tax will be payable if wealth is dispersed among a number of beneficiaries than if it is given only to one. This assumes that the actions of individuals in this area are influenced by taxation to a greater extent than is likely to be the case. Further, those who talk of the distribution of wealth as one of the objectives of a tax system generally advocate redistribution from the (very) rich to the very poor rather than the distribution of wealth among four children of a wealthy person—such a distribution is likely to occur anyway.

[1] Messere *Tax Policy in OECD Countries*, IBFD Amsterdam (1993) 11.6 lists 17 such OECD countries.

[38.05] Alternatives that have been canvassed include taxing gifts as income and abandoning transfer taxes in favour of a wealth tax. A wealth tax taxes static wealth; it was last suggested officially in the UK in the 1970s; a select committee examined the question in 1976 but were unable to agree.[1] A variant form of wealth tax would include an element of differentiation: this would charge inherited wealth at a higher rate than earned wealth; moreover, the more distant the relative from whom the wealth was inherited the higher the rate, so a transmission of property inherited from one's parents might be taxed at 20% while that of property from one's grandparents might attract a tax of 50%. All these ideas are very unfashionable and today's theorists think in terms of abolition not extension. Such transfer taxes are not inevitable—neither Australia nor Canada has such taxes having opted for a charge to CGT on death instead.

Further ideas were explored by the Meade Committee, which developed an ingenious set of ideas based ultimately on a merger of wealth and accessions taxes. The core element was called AWAT: an annual wealth and transfer tax.[2]

[1] Select Committee on a Wealth Tax Cmnd 5704 (1975). The Chancellor of the Exchequer of the time, Denis Healey, wrote in his memoirs: "Another lesson was that you should never commit yourself in Opposition to new taxes unless you had a very good idea how they will operate in practice. We had committed ourselves to a Wealth Tax; but in five years I found it impossible to draft one which would yield enough revenue to be worth the administrative cost and the political hassle . . . I suspect the Conservative Party is even more unhappy that Mrs Thatcher promised to abolish the rates without having the slightest idea what to put in their place" (p. 404). Much useful material on wealth taxes is gathered in Smith, *Personal Wealth Taxation*, Canadian Tax Foundation Tax Paper (1993).
[2] Chapter 13 of the *Structure and Reform of Direct Tax*, IFS George Allen and Unwin (1978)); see review by Bracewell Milnes [19679] BTR 25.

An outline of IHT

Charge to inheritance tax

[38.06] Inheritance tax is payable when there is a chargeable transfer. The rate of tax is that applicable at the time of the transfer (see infra, § **38.13**). The person liable to pay the tax depends on the nature of the transfer of value (see infra, §§ **46.01–46.07**). A transfer of value is a chargeable transfer if it is made

An outline of IHT **[38.07]**

by an individual and is not an exempt transfer.[1] Whenever there is a disposition that causes a diminution in the value of a person's estate, there is a transfer of value (see infra, § **38.07**).[2]

Simon's Taxes I3.102; Foster's Inheritance Tax C1.02.

---

[1] IHTA 1984, s 2(1). There are certain other situations where the legislation provides that an event is a transfer of value, although there is no disposition (see infra, §§ **38.08–38.10**).

[2] IHTA 1984, s 3(4).

A disposition

[38.07] IHT is payable on a transfer of value. A transfer of value is any disposition by which the value of a person's estate is reduced. In the case of a lifetime chargeable transfer, the tax is levied at one of two rates: either 0% or 20%. In the case of the transfer at death, the tax is levied at one of two rates: either 0% or 40%.[1] The effect is a mixture of proportional and progressive features, ie the more transfers of value made the higher the average tax liability is likely to be.[2] A transfer is cumulated with all chargeable transfers made in the previous seven years.

A transfer inter vivos (eg a gift) will be a transfer of value unless the transfer is exempt or potentially exempt. Where the transfer is for consideration the consideration received will enter into the computation of the value transferred, only the balance being chargeable. However, transactions intended by the parties to be commercial before and after that are not treated as transfers of value, nor are certain other dispositions.[3]

It is necessary to divide transfers of value into those which are immediately chargeable and those which are only potentially chargeable, which the Act chooses to call potentially exempt. Chargeable transfers enter the cumulative total of transfers made by the transferors at once and, if the total goes over the nil rate band, will give a charge to tax straight away. Potentially exempt transfers by contrast do not give rise to a charge straight away and do not enter the transferor's cumulative total of transfers unless and until the donor dies within a period of seven years from the date of the transfer, whereupon they become chargeable as lifetime transfers but at death rates, with reductions if the donor dies more than three years after the gift. Most types of gift are potentially exempt transfers.

Simon's Taxes I3.102.

---

[1] IHTA 1984, s 7(2), Sch 1. From 5 April 2008, tax at 0% is chargeable on the first £312,000 of a chargeable transfer and at 20%/40% for the value in excess of £312,000. The nil rate band for future years has been announced: £325,000 for 2009–10 and £350,000 for 2010–11, vide Finance Act 2006, s 155(3) & (4) and FA 2007, s 4.

[2] Infra, §§ **38.13** ff.

[3] Infra, § **40.01**.

[38.08] Introduction

Events treated as transfers of value

[38.08] On a person's death statute[1] deems there to be a transfer of all the property to which he was beneficially entitled immediately before his death; the transfer on death is accumulated with inter vivos transfers whether originally chargeable or having become chargeable by reason of the loss of their potentially exempt status made up to seven years before, see Chapter 40.

The death charge differs from the inter vivos in four ways. First, the rate is higher on death than on chargeable inter vivos transfers.[2] The higher rate is applied retrospectively to inter vivos transfers made within seven years of death although there is some tapering relief for transfers between four and seven years before the death.

Second, some of the exemptions are confined to inter vivos transfers and others are confined to transfers on death.

Third, while chargeable inter vivos transfers must be grossed up to ascertain the loss to the transferor's estate where the burden of IHT falls on the transferor, there is usually no need to gross up on death for the simple reason that the benefits eventually distributed out of the estate will necessarily be net of IHT. For similar reasons there is no grossing up of potentially exempt transfers should tax become payable.

Fourth, events after death may sometimes affect IHT charged on the death but these do not affect lifetime transfers, even those which were potentially exempt and which only became chargeable because of the death of the transferor within seven years.

Simon's Taxes I3.102, I4.101.

---

[1] IHTA 1984, s 4(1).
[2] Value in excess of the nil rate band attracts tax at 40% at death, but at 20% inter vivos. IHTA 1984, s 7(2).

[38.09] There is a transfer of value not only where the transferor makes a chargeable transfer, but also where he is treated as making one. This may occur if a person is beneficially entitled to an interest in possession in property settled before 22 March 2006, as such entitlement is treated for IHT purposes as extending not to the value of the life interest but to the value of the settled property underlying it. For example, if X is entitled to the whole of the income of a fund worth £50,000, X is subject to the IHT regime as if he were beneficially entitled to £50,000.[1] X is, therefore, treated as making a transfer of value of £50,000 if X dies, or disposes of the interest, or if the interest ends. This is accumulated and, where appropriate, aggregated with X's own property, see Chapter 42. If X gives away his life interest more than seven years before X dies the gift can qualify as a potentially exempt transfer.[2]

Simon's Taxes I3.102.

---

[1] However, the value of the settled estate is computed separately from the value of the free estate: a point that is of significance if there are unquoted shares in both the

settled estate and the free estate: this follows from the wording of IHTA 1984, s 19(1) and the fact that the definition of "related property" in s 161 does not include property in trust: see infra, § **42.07**.

[2] IHTA 1984, s 3A.

[38.10] Where property is held in the settlement there is, in general, a deemed transfer of value every ten years of the property held in the settlement on such trusts. If property ceases to be subject to the trust, because, for example, it is advanced to a beneficiary, there is a deemed transfer of value at that time. Certain trusts[1] are exempt from the ten year charge, notably trusts where an interest in possession is given at age 18 or where the trust was created before 22 March 2006 and the interest in possession in existence on that date continues to be held by the same person.

Tax is charged on a deemed transfer of value in such settled property at a special rate. The theory behind the regime of tax in trusts is that over a 30-year period (approximately a generation) the IHT paid approximates to that which would be paid on the transfer of free estate from one generation to the next. In practice, however, there is not such a neat equation and the 2006 changes have done nothing to advance the conceptual purity of the notion.

Simon's Taxes I5.101.

[1] For a detailed discussion of the settlements within this charge see Chapter 42.

[38.11] IHT is charged on a chargeable transfer. A transfer of value is not a chargeable transfer unless it is made by an individual.[1] Hence, a company is, not liable to IHT, even if it acts so that its assets are reduced. Exceptionally, a company may be entitled to a beneficial interest in possession in settled property but, unless the company's business consists of the acquisition of interests in settled property, the settlement will be taxed as if there were no interest in possession.[2]

Where a *close* company makes a transfer of value the transfer of value may however be attributed to its individual participators and be treated as having been made by them.[3] There may also be a charge on the trustee participators, depending upon the type of trust. There is also a deemed transfer of value by an individual when that individual's rights in the company are reduced in value as a result of an alteration in the rights of his shares.

Simon's Taxes I3.113.

[1] IHTA 1984, s 2(1).
[2] IHTA 1984, s 59(1).
[3] Infra, § **39.21**.

Exemptions and reliefs

[38.12] Exemptions and reliefs take various forms. Some direct that a particular transfer shall be exempt up to a certain limit. Others direct that a

[38.12] Introduction

transfer shall be exempt in full. Others give relief by a special basis for valuation, or a reduction in the value transferred. Yet others take the form of a reduction in the tax otherwise payable so that the value transferred must be cumulated in full and the tax normally payable ascertained before relief can be given. Reliefs may also take the form of an exemption in whole or in part from aggregation. In addition some dispositions are not "transfers of value"; this means that they have no effect for IHT if made inter vivos. Such a transfer may, however, be chargeable if made on death.[1]

Simon's Taxes Division I3.03.

[1] See Chapters 43 and 44.

Calculation of tax

Rates

[38.13] Inheritance tax is charged on death at 40% (and on a lifetime transfer, at 20%) on the amount by which the diminution of the estate exceeds the inheritance tax nil rate band for the year. In applying the rate of tax, the payment of tax is, itself, treated as a diminution of the estate. Hence, if the transferor pays the tax on the lifetime transfer, the sum gifted has to be grossed up in order to calculate the tax liability arising.

The IHT nil rate band has been announced for the following periods:[1]

| 2009–10 | £325,000 |
| 2010–11 | £350,000 |

Grossing up applies to inter vivos transfers which are chargeable and to the exit charge on property leaving a discretionary trust.[2] Grossing up does not apply to an inter vivos transfer that is a potentially exempt transfer.[3] Grossing up applies, also, where there is a transfer of an exempt, or partially exempt, residue on death.[4]

Foster's Inheritance Tax Division T2.

[1] FA 2006, s 156. The nil rate band for 2010–11 is given by FA 2007, s 4(1) & (2).
[2] See infra, § **42.39**.
[3] See infra, § **39.08**.
[4] See infra, § **46.16**.

Transfer of nil rate band

[38.14] The Pre-Budget Report of 9 October 2007 announced an innovation designed, principally for short-term political gain[1] but also to ensure that married taxpayers (and civil partners) could be more flexible about the use of the nil rate band without being required to enter into more complex arrangements, such as a nil-rate band discretionary trust.

The basic problem was that many spouses and civil partners leave their estate in the entirety to the surviving spouse or civil partner. Such a transfer would inevitably waste the transferor's nil rate band except where the transferor is, and the survivor is not, UK-domiciled.[2] Thus upon the second death and the transfer of the remainder of the combined estate to the next generation, only one nil rate band would be available.

For properly advised couples, the alternative strategy was relatively straightforward, at least in theory. A trust would be written into the will so as to absorb the unused element of the deceased's nil rate band.[3] The surviving spouse or civil partner would be a beneficiary of the trust and, to the average client, the trust would often not be noticed. However, as there would have to be some effective trust management, this solution was not without some practical obstacles.

So that some of these possibilities would be made more available, FA 2008, Sch 4 provides that unused nil rate bands may be transferred between spouses and civil partners. The new rules[4] apply in respect of deaths on or after 9 October 2007 where the deceased had previously been widowed (or whose civil partner had died). It does not matter how long ago the first death took place as long as there was an unused element of the nil rate band (or its equivalent under previous legislation). To assist taxpayers, tables have been published of the nil rate band going back to the start of the First World War although ascertaining how much of the band had not been used on such early deaths might prove rather tricky.

The transfer works in proportions. Therefore, if the first of a couple used none of the nil rate band then the survivor would be entitled to the equivalent of an additional nil rate band at whatever width it is on the second death. Therefore, a widow (whose husband left his entire estate to his wife), dying on 10 October 2008, would have a nil rate band of £624,000. And, if the husband had used half of his nil rate band, then the widow's nil rate band on her death would be only 150% × £312,000 = £468,000.

It should be noted the the transfer applies only on the second party's death. Therefore chargeable lifetime transfers will not benefit from an enhanced nil rate band. Additionally, whilst surviving spouses and civil partners can accumulate unused nil rate bands from more than one previous relationship, the amount that may be transferred is capped at one full nil rate band. Consequently, there will still be situations in which the nil rate band discretionary trust arrangement will prove a useful device.

Some might note (especially in the light of the failed attempts by the Burden sisters[5] to secure the same rights to inheritance tax savings as civil partners) that it is regrettable that the transfer of nil rate bands is not extended to other couples. Alternatively, the timing of the announcement was not without irony because the Government was promoting one area in which couples could share allowances but at the same time the Government was proposing to clamp down on what it considered to be unacceptable income shifting.[6]

[38.14] Introduction

[1] A snap General Election was widely expected to follow that Autumn.
[2] IHTA 1984, s 18.
[3] For clients who had not written the appropriate wills, the same effect could be achieved by using a deed of variation – see **40.22**.
[4] Inserted as IHTA 1984, s 8A.
[5] *Burden v Burden v United Kingdom* (2008).
[6] The latter legislation was subsequently deferred.

Aggregation

[38.15] Where more than one piece of property is the subject of a single chargeable transfer, the tax chargeable on the total or aggregate value transferred is attributed to the properties in the proportion which they bear to the aggregate.[1] The most obvious example is a transfer on death. Here there will be a transfer of all the pieces of property which form part of the deceased's estate, as defined.

The principle of aggregation is also be relevant to inter vivos transfers. Thus if S settles property which includes some land and some shares the burden of the tax is shared rateably between the different pieces of property transferred, and thus affect the extent of the HMRC charge on each piece.

When different funds pass to different persons, the rate of tax which has to be borne by each fund is increased by reason of the existence of other funds passing elsewhere. Thus if the deceased had a free estate of £100,000 and a life interest in the settlement with a capital value of £300,000, the liability to inheritance tax, if he had made a lifetime transfer, would be as follows:

	£
Free estate	100,000
Settled estate	400,000
	500,000

Inheritance tax payable:
£312,000 @ 0%	—
£188,000 @ 40%	75,200
	75,200

Liabilities:
IHT payable by executors as a charge on free estate:

$$£75,200 \times \frac{100,000}{500,000} = £15,040$$

IHT payable by trustees as a charge on trust capital:

$$£75,200 \times \frac{400,000}{500,000} = £60,160$$

Simon's Taxes I3.524; Foster's Inheritance Tax C5.24.

[1] IHTA 1984, s 265 but for a minor qualification see infra, § **42.24**, note 5.

Exemptions from aggregation

[38.16] Transfers which are exempt from liability are exempt also from aggregation. For the same reason transfers which are conditionally exempt, such as works of art, (see infra, § **40.05**) and, but only on death, timber, (see infra, § **40.05**), are also exempt from aggregation and so do not affect the tax paid by the rest of the property transferred.

Transfers on same day

[38.17] All chargeable transfers, including potentially exempt transfers which have become chargeable, made on the same day are aggregated regardless of the actual order in which they are made, save that an inter vivos gift made on the day of death is treated as taking place before that on death.[1]

However, in calculating the amount of tax they are assumed to be made in the order which results in the lowest value chargeable, a matter of importance where one gift bears its own tax while another does not; the lower the figure at which grossing up is to be carried out the less the tax. As potentially exempt transfers always bear their own tax this rule has little importance for them.

EXAMPLE

A whose cumulative total stands at £262,000 settles £50,000 (after using the annual exempt amount) into discretionary trust X. On the same day, he settles a further £60,000 into discretionary trust Y. The gift to trust X is to bear its own tax; that for trust Y is to be borne by A.

If the gift to trust X is made first the tax on it will be nil; this will exhaust the zero lifetime rate band so that trust Y will have its tax assessed on the basis that £60,000 has to be grossed up at 20% making tax of £15,000. A's cumulative total will be £375,000.

If, however, the gift to trust Y is made first, tax on it will be £2,500 and tax on trust X will be £10,000 making total tax of £12,500. A's cumulative total is then £372,000.

It follows that the second method should be used.

Simon's Taxes I3.525; Foster's Inheritance Tax C5.25.

[1] IHTA 1984, s 266(1).

Cumulation

[38.18] Cumulation requires that the tax on the present transfer must take account of chargeable transfers already made by the transferor and which remain chargeable. Chargeable transfers made more than seven years previously cease to be cumulated.[1] It is important to grasp that when a transfer ceases to be cumulated that is all that happens; there is no question of repaying the tax charged. Also, cumulation over a preceding seven year period means

[38.18] Introduction

that IHT payable on a potentially exempt transfer that becomes a chargeable transfer is calculated by reference to any chargeable transfers during the preceding seven year period including those more than seven years before the date of death (see infra, § **38.19**).

Simon's Taxes I3.521; Foster's Inheritance Tax C5.21.

---

[1] IHTA 1984, s 7(1); FA 1986, s 101, Sch 19.

[38.19] The transfers which are cumulated are those which are the chargeable transfers of this transferor. Exempt transfers are not cumulated; nor are conditionally exempt transfers until a chargeable event has occurred; nor are potentially exempt transfers unless and until the donor dies within the seven year period[1] nor are the transfers which are made by others. Transfers which are of settled property but which are treated as made by this transferor, eg the termination of this person's beneficial life interest in possession are cumulated if death follows within seven years.

The values to be cumulated are those transferred by chargeable transfers. Where a particular relief takes the form of a reduction in the value of the property and so in the value transferred, such as agricultural relief or relief for business assets, it is the value so reduced which is cumulated. Where, however, the relief takes the form of a reduction in tax, such as quick succession relief or double taxation relief by credit, the whole value transferred must be cumulated both to ascertain the amount of tax which is to be reduced and to ascertain the value transferred for subsequent transfers.

---

[1] IHTA 1984, s 3A(5) but then with retroactive effect.

Estate

[38.20] The notion of an estate is important because a disposition only gives rise to IHT if it causes a reduction in the value of the transferor's estate[1] and also because on death a person is treated as having made a transfer of value equal to the value of his estate immediately before death.[2]

An estate is the aggregate of all the property to which the person is beneficially entitled. Allowable deductions are made in calculating the value of the estate.[3] Property held in a fiduciary capacity is not included,[4] nor is property to which a person is entitled as a corporation sole.[5] Property is widely defined as "including rights and interests of any description". It will therefore cover not only tangible property, but also equitable rights, debts and other choses in action, and indeed any rights capable of being reduced to a money value. However, statute provides that the value of a right held by the settlor of a settlement, that is created by the act of settling property, such as a right for assets to be passed back to the settlor, is ignored.[6] So on death a person's estate will include a share of property held in common and a severable share of property held on joint tenancy. It would not include damages obtainable under the Fatal Accidents Act in respect of a wrongful act causing death since these belong to the deceased's dependants and not to him.

A mere spes is presumably not a "right" even "of any description"; however, a completed payment stemming from such a spes is not a mere spes. Gratuities payable as of right do form part of an estate even though no precise amount can be placed upon them.[7] Sums paid by trustees of a superannuation scheme in the exercise of a discretion to pay a lump sum death benefit to a member's dependant do not form part of the member's estate but will of course become part of the estate of the dependant.

A concept of great importance is that of "excluded property", which is elaborately defined in statute. Such property does not form part of a person's estate immediately before death (see infra, § **38.20**; see infra, § **39.12** for other transfers).

A person beneficially entitled to an interest in possession in property settled before 22 March 2006 is treated as beneficially entitled to the property in which the interest subsists and not to the interest itself.[8] Thus the tenant for life of a fund worth £300,000 whose free estate is worth £100,000 will on death make a chargeable transfer of £400,000.

A person's estate will include property (other than settled property) over which he has a general power which enables him, or would if he were sui iuris enable him, to dispose of it;[9] he is treated as beneficially entitled to the property. If he has a general power to charge money on such unsettled property he is treated as beneficially entitled to the money. "General power" is defined as "a power or authority enabling the person by whom it is exercisable to appoint or dispose of property as he thinks fit".[10] The scope of this rule is not completely certain. Where a person makes an incomplete gift there will be no disposition since the title has not passed and so there is no reduction in the value of the transferor's estate. This will still be so even though the title is eventually perfected under the rule in *Strong v Bird* (1874) since here the title is not perfected until death and the transfer on death is treated as taking place immediately before death. If the true nature of a joint bank account is that the parties have placed the funds in the account so that each can withdraw whatever sum is needed by that party, the entire balance in the account is in the estate of each of the two parties.[11]

There is no rule which prevents an asset from being in two estates at the same time. This is a common situation, as a result of the rules treating a gift subject to reservation as remaining chargeable on the donor's death. Where A makes a revocable gift of personalty to B, the property appears to form part of the estate of both of them. It forms part of the estate of A since there are no restrictions on the right to revoke; A can therefore revoke the gift and dispose of the property as he thinks fit. It forms part of the estate of B since B gets good title subject to A's right to revoke.[12] A power of appointment will not fall within this rule since such a power will only form part of a settlement and the present rule is restricted to unsettled property.

Where a person has a general but fiduciary[13] power over property, eg an agent duly authorised to sell on behalf of the owner, it would appear that the property ought not to form part of his estate. It is however arguable that the rule could be used to reverse this conclusion. The rule defines a general power as one to dispose of the property as he thinks fit and is not expressly confined

[38.20] Introduction

to one which carries with it the beneficial right to the proceeds of sale. Such a conclusion would have the odd result that the property will at once form part of the estate of the vendor and of the agent and so is most unlikely.[14] One answer to this is to say that the agent has a power to sell, not a power to give and so no power to dispose as he thinks fit; this leaves open the case of a power of attorney.

Simon's Taxes I3.211–213; I4.111; Foster's Inheritance Tax C2.11–13; D1.11.

[1] IHTA 1984, s 3(1).
[2] IHTA 1984, s 4(1).
[3] IHTA 1984, s 5(1). See infra, § **39.08** and § **45.25**.
[4] Winnings on a football pool accruing to the members of a syndicate accrue to the members even though the winnings are initially received by a person as stakeholder for the syndicate. Statement of practice E14; **Foster's Inheritance Tax, Division W2**.
[5] IHTA 1984, ss 47A & 55A inserted by FA 2002, s 119 with effect from 17 April 2002 when calculating a lifetime chargeable transfer and with retrospective effect for the estate at death and potentially exempt transfers that are chargeable by virtue of the death. This provision reverses the decision in *Melville v IRC* [2001] EWCA Civ 1247, [2001] STC 1271; see also infra, § **39.06, 39.07**.
[6] *A-G v Quixley* (1929) 98 LJKB 652, CA.
[7] IHTA 1984, s 271.
[8] IHTA 1984, s 49(1).
[9] In *O'Neill v IRC* [1998] STC (SCD) 110 the entire value of a joint account at an Isle of Man bank was treated as being comprised in the estate of the deceased. The Commissioners found that the motive of the deceased in setting up the joint bank account was concealment, both from the UK Revenue and from his estranged wife. During his lifetime he, and he alone, had operated the account even though it had been set up jointly with his daughter.
[10] IHTA 1984, s 5(2).
[11] *Sillars v IRC* [2004] STC (SCD) 180. The conclusion that the bank balance is in both estates can be reached by two separate routes. First, each party has "a general power which enables him to dispose of the property" and, thus, the effect of IHTA 1984, s 5(2) is that the bank balance is in the estate, Second, the party depositing the capital has made a gift to the other but reserving the ability to withdraw the cash; it is a gift with reservation. See supra, § **40.04**.
[12] Semble that A's right to revoke will be taken into account in valuing B's right.
[13] IHTA 1984, s 5(2) declares that the person with a general power is to be treated as beneficially entitled to it so that the fiduciary quality of the power is irrelevant.
[14] See Standing Committee A, 4 February 1975, col 629, 630.

Excluded property

[38.21] The following is excluded property:[1]

(1) property, other than settled property, situate outside the UK provided the person beneficially entitled to it is an individual domiciled outside the UK;[2]
(2) settled property situate outside the UK if the settlor was domiciled outside the UK when the settlement was made;[3]

(3) a reversionary interest in settled property provided the person beneficially entitled to it is not domiciled in the UK;[4]
(4) certain other reversionary interests[5] in settled property.
(5) certain types of property situated in the UK owned by persons domiciled elsewhere—infra, § 47.08.

Simon's Taxes I9.311; Foster's Inheritance Tax J3.11; STP [12.42].

---

[1] On effects see IHTA 1984, ss 3(2), 5(1); infra, § **39.12** and IHTA 1984, ss 53(1), 82; infra, § **42.17**.
[2] IHTA 1984, s 6(1); infra, § **47.12**.
[3] IHTA 1984, s 48(3); infra, § **47.13**.
[4] IHTA 1984, s 6(1); infra, § **47.16**.
[5] IHTA 1984, s 48(1) as amended.

Exempt persons

[38.22] Although not excluded property, property of the following persons is exempt from the charge to IHT:

(1) foreign diplomats (Diplomatic Privileges Act 1964);
(2) members of International Organisations (International Organisations Act 1968); and
(3) consular officers (Consular Relations Act 1968).

Simon's Taxes I9.327; Foster's Inheritance Tax J3.27.

39

Transfers of value by disposition

Transfer of value	PARA **39.01**
Potentially exempt transfers	PARA **39.02**
Disposition	PARA **39.04**
Time	PARA **39.05**
Value transferred	PARA **39.06**
Omission to exercise a right	PARA **39.10**
Future payments	PARA **39.11**
Disposition of excluded property	PARA **39.12**
Voidable transfers	PARA **39.13**
Matters which are not transfers of value	PARA **39.14**
Close companies	PARA **39.21**
Disposition by associated operations	PARA **39.28**

Transfer of value

[39.01] Whether one is dealing with a transfer which has been chargeable ab initio or one which was originally potentially exempt but which has become chargeable by reason of the death of the donor within seven years, the central concept is the transfer of value; IHT is charged on the value transferred by a chargeable transfer.[1]

A transfer of value is any disposition made by a person (the transferor) as a result of which the value of his estate immediately after the disposition is less than it would be but for the disposition.[2] The amount of the transfer of value is the amount by which the estate has been reduced by the disposition.

If it is shown that the transfer was not intended to confer any gratuitous benefit on any person and, either it was made in a transaction at arm's length between persons not connected with each other or was such as might be expected to be made in such a transaction, statute declares the reduction in the estate not to be a transfer of value.[3]

A chargeable transfer is any transfer of value made by an individual after 26 March 1974 that is not an exempt transfer[4] nor a potentially exempt transfer.[5]

At a technical level it is necessary to distinguish (a) the value transferred by a transfer of value from (b) the value transferred by a chargeable transfer. This is because (a) is calculated ignoring the exempt transfer rules and without regard to grossing up (on which see infra, § **39.09**). The technical niceties are important when considering the application of reliefs such as business relief.

Where a gift is made by means of a cheque, the transfer of value is when the cheque is cleared; until that date there is no completed gift.[6]

[39.01] Transfers of value by disposition

Simon's Taxes I3.101–114; Foster's Inheritance Tax C1.01–14.

[1] IHTA 1984, s 1.
[2] IHTA 1984, s 3(2).
[3] IHTA 1984, s 10; infra, § **39.14**.
[4] IHTA 1984, s 2(1). On partly exempt transfers see IHTA 1984, s 2(2); see also infra, § **43.17** ff for rules on allocation of reliefs.
[5] IHTA 1984, s 3A(1).
[6] In *Curnock v IRC* [2003] STC (SCD) 283, a cheque for £6,000 designed to utilise the annual exemption was drawn before death but cleared after death. It was held not to be a transfer of value, the bank balance at death being the amount without the £6,000 deduction. This case applies for IHT principles established for estate duty in *Re Swinburne, Sutton v Featherley* [1926] Ch 38, CA, *Re Owen, Owen v IRC* [1949] 1 All ER 901 and *Hewitt v Kaye* (1868) LR 6 Eq 198.

Potentially exempt transfers

[39.02] A key concept in IHT is the concept of the potentially exempt transfer. There are three elements.[1] First, the transfer must be a transfer of value made by an individual.[2] Second, it must (apart from this provision) be a chargeable transfer, and not an exempt transfer. Third, it must, in broad terms, be either a gift to another individual or a gift of property settled on or after 22 March 2006 over which the individual has an interest in possession.[3]

The second is what weight to put on the meaning of the word 'gift', as used in the statutory requirement that a transfer of value is a potentially exempt transfer 'to the extent that it constitutes . . . a gift'.

Where the value is not attributable to property becoming comprised in the estate of another person it is treated as being to an individual to the extent that, by virtue of the transfer, the estate of that person is increased; again it does not matter that the increase is in the value of settled property comprised in his estate. This rule is designed to cover indirect transfers, ie situations in which there is a transfer of value but no property becomes part of the transferee's estate as where the donor pays off some debts of the donee or pays a premium on a life policy belonging to him or allows an option to buy on advantageous terms to lapse. However, it contains something of a trap since the opening words[4] refer to the situation where the value is not attributable to property becoming comprised in the estate of another *person* (not individual). So a gift to a company which has the incidental effect of increasing the value of the estates of its participators cannot be a potentially exempt transfer.[5]

What both rules have in common is a requirement that there should be an increase in the value of the estate of an individual; from this it follows that if there is no such increase the transfer cannot be a potentially exempt transfer. One situation in which this would seem to occur is where a grandparent pays the school fees of a grandchild; here there is no increase in the value of the grandchild's estate. The result is that there may be a chargeable, rather than a potentially exempt, transfer. This unfortunate result may be avoided by making the gift directly to the child or, if the parents are the contracting parties, to the parents. Similar problems (and solutions) arise if A buys B a holiday. The payment of a premium on a life assurance policy kept up for the benefit of an accumulation and maintenance or disabled trust is not a potentially exempt transfer.

Where under the provisions of the Act tax is charged 'as if' a transfer of value had been made, the transfer cannot be a potentially exempt transfer.

In addition various situations have been specifically excluded from being potentially exempt transfers. So where there is an alteration in the rights in a close company falling within s 98 the transfer of value cannot be potentially exempt.[6] There are special provisions dealing with timber which have their origins in estate duty.[7]

The effect of the seven year cumulation period applied to a potentially exempt transfer is that the calculation of the tax charge can be affected by chargeable transfers made up to 14 years before the death. If a chargeable transfer occurred less than seven years before a potentially exempt transfer which proves to be chargeable by virtue of a subsequent death, the value of the chargeable transfer is brought into the calculation of the tax payable on the potentially exempt transfer, even though there will be no further tax payable on a chargeable transfer made more than seven years before the death.

When a chargeable transfer and a potentially exempt transfer take place during the same fiscal year, the annual exemption for that year is put against the chargeable transfer. If death occurs within seven years, the annual exemption continues to be put against the immediately chargeable transfer, even if the potentially exempt transfer was earlier in the fiscal year.[8] The potentially exempt transfer, thus, is subject to IHT without a deduction for the annual exemption, if this has been fully utilised on an immediately chargeable transfer.

By contrast, if there is no immediate chargeable transfer in a particular fiscal year and the annual exemption is carried forward to the following year and put against a chargeable transfer in that second year, a death within seven years of any potentially exempt transfer in the first of the years will displace the annual exemption so that it is put first against that potentially exempt transfer that has become chargeable.[9] The effect of this treatment is, thus, that the annual exemption is no longer available against the transfer that was immediately chargeable in the second year.

Where property is transferred on a potentially exempt transfer and part, or all, of that property is transferred back to the donor, who then dies within seven years of the potentially exempt transfer, making it, thereby, chargeable, a measure of relief is given.[10]

Simon's Taxes I3.311–319; Foster's Inheritance Tax C3.11–19; STP [9.4], [9.71]–[9.100]; [11.9].

[1] IHTA 1984, s 3A(1).
[2] On or after 18 March 1986.
[3] As defined in IHTA 1984, s 71; see infra, §§ **42.49** ff.
[4] IHTA 1984, s 3A(2)(*b*).

[39.02] Transfers of value by disposition

[5] Venables *Inheritance Tax Planning*, 2.1.4 who however points out that where the donor simply allows an option to lapse which has the effect of increasing the value of the company's assets and so the estates of the participators, the gift *can* be a potentially exempt transfer since the words at the start of this rule exclude it only where no *property* becomes part of the estate of another person.
[6] IHTA 1984, s 98(3)
[7] FA 1986, Sch 19, para 46; infra, § **44.33**.
[8] IHTA 1984, s 19(3A).
[9] Section 19(3A)(*b*) deems a potentially exempt transfer that becomes chargeable to have been made later during the fiscal year than any chargeable transfer in that year. The deeming provision cannot treat a potentially exempt transfer as being made in the later year.
[10] See infra, § **40.30**.

Taxation of potentially exempt transfers

[39.03] A potentially exempt transfer is exempt after the passage of seven years without the transferor dying;[1] if the transferor dies in that period, it becomes chargeable. It is to be assumed that the transfer will reach total exemption until this is disproved by the transferor dying within seven years,[2] hence no tax is due at the time of the gift. If the transferor dies within the seven year period, the transfer has its potentially exempt status retrospectively removed and it falls to be taxed as a chargeable transfer on the date when it was made. This will have consequences where the donor makes a potentially exempt transfer within the seven-year period but later makes a chargeable transfer; here the tax on the chargeable transfer will have been calculated on the basis that the previous transfer was exempt; this has to be corrected. The amount of tax will be determined by reference to the cumulative total of chargeable transfers in the previous seven years prior to the date of the potentially exempt transfer. The removal of the exempt status is, however, not completely retrospective since the rates to be applied will be those in force at the date of death with a reduction if the transfer was made more than three years before the death. The rate of tax is reduced by a tapering relief if the donor dies more than three years after making the potentially exempt transfer.

EXAMPLE

D dies in year 20.

In year 11, D settled £400,000 on discretionary trusts, tax (of £40,000, say) to be paid by the trust; this is a chargeable transfer.

In year 16 D gave A £163,000; this is a potentially exempt transfer.

On the death of D in year 20, the gift to A will cease to be potentially exempt and will become chargeable. The rates used will be those in force at the death of D but there will be a 20% reduction in the tax because D died four years after the gift. In calculating the tax D will be assumed to have a cumulative total of £400,000.

Using the 2008–09 rates, tax payable on the gift in year 16 will therefore be:

Tax on £563,000 (£100,400) less tax on £400,000 (£40,000) = £60,400 reduced by 20% = £48,320.

On D's death he is treated as making a transfer of his remaining estate. This will be charged on the basis that his cumulative total for lifetime transfers will be £163,000. This is because the gift in year 16 is relevant as it is now chargeable but that in year 11 is not relevant as it was made more than seven years before the death and therefore ceases to be cumulated.

If the transfer in year 11 had been an outright gift to B, it would have been a potentially exempt transfer which would have achieved exempt status in year 18. It would have been ignored in calculating the tax on the gift in year 16 and the tax due in respect of the gift in year 16 would have been £nil.

It might seem that where a transferor has made no previous transfers but proposes to dispose of a large amount of wealth, it would usually be advantageous for the chargeable transfer to precede the potentially exempt one so as to enable the former to use the transferor's nil rate band. However, whereas the tax payable on the death in respect of a potentially exempt transfer is always determined de novo, this is not true of the chargeable transfer. So where the tax paid in respect of the chargeable transfer on that occasion is higher than that which would be payable on such a transfer on the death, there is no refund of the tax already paid and this gives rise to a greater total burden of tax.

Simon's Taxes I3.501, 511, 521, 531, 705; Foster's Inheritance Tax C5.01, 11, 21, 31; C7.05.

[1] IHTA 1984, s 3A(4).
[2] IHTA 1984, s 3A(5).

Disposition

[39.04] although it is stated to include a disposition effected by associated operations. The word 'disposition' is not the same as the word disposal used in CGT nor is it the same as a 'gift' in the IHT legislation dealing with a gift with reservation. A disposition need not be of any existing property

If one wishes to say that the destruction of a picture is not a transfer of value[1] whereas the surrender of a lease is, there are several ways of justifying one's distinction. The first is to say that in the case of a surrender there may be a scintilla temporis during which the landlord holds the tenant's interest before it is destroyed by merger; the picture case is therefore distinguishable. The second is to say that the loss must be to the transferor's estate and an estate consists of *rights*; the surrender of the lease is a loss of the tenant's rights whereas the destruction of the asset is not. A third is to say that, whether or not the estate consists of rights, there is a transfer of property by an act of the lessee in surrendering his lease; one difficulty here is that an act whereby the lessee forfeits his lease cannot be treated in the same way.[2]

The incurring of a liability will result in a reduction of a person's estate and so be a disposition provided the liability is deductible in computing the value of his estate under the relevant rules (infra, § **45.20**). Where the liability is not deductible there is no reduction in the transferor's estate and so no value is transferred. Thus if I agree to guarantee my son's overdraft, there will be no reduction in the value of my estate since a liability incurred otherwise than for consideration is only deductible if and to the extent that it is incurred for

[39.04] Transfers of value by disposition

consideration in money or money's worth.[3] Should I have to pay sums under the guarantee such payments will be transfers of value at that time.

On the discharge of a non-deductible liability in respect of a loan as a transfer of value see infra, § 45.25.

The voluntary waiver of a loan is a transfer of value by the creditor: in practice the Revenue insist upon a deed in such cases.[4]

---

[1] But suppose that A has a valuable stamp and his son B has another copy of the same stamp and that these are the only two copies known to exist in private hands; each stamp is worth £20,000 but if A destroys his stamp B's will be worth £60,000. A destroys his stamp.

[2] Does the forfeiture count as an omission under IHTA 1984, s 3(3)—probably not; see infra, § **39.10**.

[3] One must distinguish a liability from a contract with proprietary effect. Thus if A contracts to sell land to B, B acquires an estate contract—an incumbrance against that land; the loss to A's estate therefore arises at the time of the contract.

[4] *Law Society's Gazette*, 18 December 1991, *Simon's Tax Intelligence* 1992, p 30. The Revenue rely on *Pinnel's Case (1602) 5 Co Rep 117a*, and *Edwards v Walters* [1896] 2 Ch 157, CA.

Time

[39.05] The concept that a disposition is the loss to the estate means that where a person transfers shares to his son by way of gift, there is a transfer of value as soon as the estate suffers loss, ie when the transferor has done all in his power to effect the transfer, not the later time when the transfer is entered in the books of the company.[1] Similarly, where there is a sale at an undervalue the transfer of value will take place when the contract is made.

It also follows that subsequent changes in the value of the thing disposed of are ignored. So it is advantageous to retain things whose value will remain static or even fall and to give away things which will appreciate. This can be a powerful argument in favour of transferring shares that are expected to increase in value into a discretionary trust, even if the settlor is unlikely to survive the seven year period.

Simon's Taxes I3.131–134; Foster's Inheritance Tax C1.31–34.

---

[1] *Re Rose, Midland Bank Executor and Trustee Co Ltd v Rose* [1949] Ch 78, [1948] 2 All ER 971.

Value transferred

[39.06] The value transferred is the amount by which the value of the transferor's estate is reduced no regard is taken of the increase (or lack of it) in the estate of transferee.[1] If A agrees to lend B an asset for a specified period without charge it will be possible, under general principles, to calculate the loss to A's estate, by reference to income foregone, and other matters reducing A's estates. However, where the property can be recalled at will, the loss appears to be negligible.

The concept of diminution in value of the estate is an essential concept in inheritance tax. There are three aspects.

[1] IHTA 1984, s 3(1).

[39.07] (1) In order to measure the value transferred, it is necessary to look at all property in the transferor's estate before and after the transfer, other than property that statute directs you to ignore, such as the value of a power over settled property.[1]

Any consideration provided in return for the property is automatically taken into account. Thus if A sells a piece of property worth £1,000 to his son B for £400, there will be a transfer of value of £600. Where the consideration provided in return is full but is paid to someone other than the vendor there will also be a transfer of value, being the diminution in the estate. Thus, A owns a 10% shareholding valued at £20,000. B, who has a 45% shareholding offers to pay £20,000 for A's shares. A directs B to pay the £20,000 to his son. The transfer of value is £10,000, being the diminution in the estate; not £20,000, the price paid by B and received by A's son.

Simon's Taxes I3.201; Foster's Inheritance Tax C2.01.

[1] In the Court of Appeal, Peter Gibson LJ rejected the submission by Revenue Counsel that the power created in this clause is not 'property', saying:

the basis scheme of the 1984 Act to charge tax on chargeable transfers made, or deemed to be made, by individuals . . . A right to dispose of value assets as one thinks fit is plainly a valuable right. . . .. Section 272 extends the original meaning of "property" by an inclusive definition, providing . . . "In this Act . . . 'property' includes rights and interests of any description". (at 1281a, 1278g and 1276b)

Thus, in this case, the value transferred was less than the IHT nil rate band and, hence, no IHT was payable but a CGT holdover election could be made under TCGA 1992, s 260.

The provisions of ss 47A and 55A have effect from 17 April 2002 when calculating a lifetime chargeable transfers and are deemed always to have had effect when calculating the IHT liability on an estate at death and potentially exempt transfers that are chargeable by virtue of the death.

[39.08] (2) The estate concerned is that of the transferor; that of the transferee is not relevant in determining whether there is a transfer of value, although there must be an increase in the transferee's estate if the transfer is to be potentially exempt. So if a particular disposition results in a greater loss to the transferor than benefit to the transferee it is that greater loss which is taken into account for tax. For example if A has 60% of the shares in a company[1]

[39.08] Transfers of value by disposition

and B has 40%, the transfer by A to C of one-third of his holding (20% of the shares of the company) will give C simply a minority holding in the company. On the other hand A will have lost control of the company so that the loss he sustains will be greater than the value of the benefit received by C; it is A's loss which is used to measure the value of the transfer for tax. Again, suppose that G pays the school fees of his grandson J; the value transferred is the loss to G, the amount spent by him, and the issue of how to value the benefit received by J does not arise;[2] however, as no property passes to J and it is impossible to see that J's estate is increased, it follows that the transfer cannot be potentially exempt. The converse of this consequence is equally true. Where a particular disposition results in a greater benefit to the transferee than loss to the transferor only that loss is taxed.[3] So, to revert to the earlier example, if B now gives her 40% holding to C it is the loss of a 40% holding which will be taxed even though the benefit to C, through now having a 60% holding, is much greater.

The loss to the transferor's estate will depend on the extent of his estate. Where A gives B a fur coat or a painting it is clear that there is a transfer of the coat or the painting and the value of that object grossed up as necessary will be the measure of the transferor's loss and so the chargeable amount. More complicated questions may however arise where A buys the object for B. Suppose that A sees a picture for sale in an antique shop for £50 but knows that it is really by a famous artist and worth £50,000. If A buys the picture and takes it home where he gives it to B, that will be a net chargeable transfer by A of £50,000. If, however, he is in the shop with B and pays £50 to B with which to buy the picture or perhaps himself pays over the £50 instructing the antique dealer to deliver the picture to B, then so long as neither the picture nor any right to the picture becomes part of A's estate there will be a net chargeable transfer of only £50.[4] The question of the precise subject-matter of the gift is also relevant to gifts with reservation since the rules as to tracing property do not apply if the property given is a sum of money in sterling or any other currency.

Where A's transfer to B is void, there is no loss to A's estate and so no chargeable transfer. Where the transfer is voidable the same result should follow since A's right to rescind the transfer and recover the property is part of his estate; there may be a transfer when the right to rescind is lost. However, IHTA 1984, s 150, is premised on the assumption that a voidable transfer is effective despite the existence of the right to rescind; see infra § **39.13**. Similarly a gift subject to a condition precedent causes no loss to the estate until the condition occurs; a gift subject to a condition subsequent is analogous to a voidable transfer when the right to rescind has not yet become exercisable.

Simon's Taxes I3.251; Foster's Inheritance Tax C2.51.

---

[1] If A had 80% and he gave 20% to C he would still have voting control of the company but would have lost the power to wind up the company (which requires 75%).

[2] Under the estate duty rules it was Revenue practice that education could not be valued and so its value was nil.

[3] IHTA 1984, s 3(3); see also IHTA 1984, ss 148(2)(*a*), 149(5)(*a*).

[4] Cf Goff J in *Ralli Bros Trustee Co Ltd v IRC* [1967] 3 All ER 811 at 820.

[39.09] (3) *Grossing up*. Suppose that A has made chargeable transfers of £300,000 when he makes an immediately chargeable transfer of £10,000 to a discretionary trust. If A bears the burden of the tax the amount of the gift must be grossed up at 20% to take account of the tax due; the loss sustained by him will be the amount transferred by him plus the tax due (a total of £12,500) since this is the total amount of the loss to his estate. A is thus taken now to have made transfers of £312,500. If on the other hand the trust bears the burden of the tax there is no grossing up and the total loss to A's estate is only £10,000. Grossing up has no role in potentially exempt transfers since the primary liability rests on the donee.

This strengthens rather than weakens the logical structure of the tax as IHT charges the reduction in the value of the estate. The grossing up rule has the further strength that it avoids differences of principle between chargeable transfers inter vivos and those on death. On death it will only be the sums net of tax that reach the beneficiaries. One is used to thinking of transfers on death in gross terms. There is no reason why this should not apply to transfers inter vivos as well.

Where A settles shares on trust there may also be incidental costs and even CGT. Where these costs are borne by A they are not grossed up; where they are borne by the trust they reduce the value transferred; infra, § **45.28**.

Simon's Taxes I3.258, 523; Foster's Inheritance Tax C2.58; C5.23.

Omission to exercise a right

[39.10] states: '. . . Where the value of a person's estate is diminished and that of another person's estate is increased by the first-mentioned person's omission to exercise a right he shall be treated as having made a disposition at the time, or the latest time, when he could have exercised the right, unless it is shown that the omission was not deliberate.'

This is one of the rare instances in which an increase in the other person's estate is relevant; however, the measure of value is still the loss to the transferor not the benefit to the transferee. It follows that if the omission does not increase another person's estate, no tax is due. Where a benefit to the other person's estate occurs, the transfer may be potentially exempt since statute treats the omission as a disposition and not simply as an event to be taxed as if it were a transfer of value.

The failure of a landlord to exercise a rent review clause, thus increasing the value of the lessee's interest, would fall within this provision; as would the failure on the part of a shareholder to exercise rights under a rights issue, a course of action which might increase the value of shares taken up, especially where control of a company is involved, or allowing an option to purchase a property at a favourable price to lapse. The Revenue have invoked IHTA 1984, s 3(3) where a settlor, chargeable to income tax on income of a settlement under the rules considered in Chapter 15, supra, failed to exercise his right of indemnity against the trust.

It must not, however, be forgotten that this rule only declares that the omission will be treated as a disposition and it is therefore open to the person to bring

[39.10] Transfers of value by disposition

the transaction within one of the rules excluding liability, particularly that for bona fide deals without donative intent in IHTA 1984, s 10.

IHTA 1984, s 3(3) applies only on the omission to exercise a right. 'Right' is not defined but presumably means a legal right. Thus if a tenant commits an act as a result of which his lease is forfeited, it may well be that the section cannot be used to charge him on the ground that he omitted to exercise his 'right' not to commit the act.

Future payments

[39.11] Where there is a transfer of value by disposition and payments are to be made or assets transferred by the transferor more than 12 months after the disposition, each payment or transfer is taxed separately. However, tax is charged on that fraction of the payment or transfer represented by the fraction A/B where A is the original value transferred (the gift element) and B the total value of the payments made or assets transferred calculated at the time of the disposition.[1]

This provision is more complex than at first appears since it applies only where the assets are transferred by the transferor more than one year after the disposition. Thus it does not apply simply because A sells an asset to B at a figure below market value and B is to pay by instalments—in such a case B may be paying by instalments but B is not making a transfer of value—A is. So the section does apply where A agrees to transfer an asset in stages to B.

EXAMPLE

A agrees to sell B 10,000 shares worth £60,000 for £18,000,[2] the shares to be transferred in tranches of 2,000 shares over five years.

Tax will be charged on fraction

$$\frac{(60,000 - 18,000)}{60,000} = \frac{7}{10}$$

making the transfer in the first year

$$\frac{7}{10} \times £12,000$$

or £8,400.

The importance of this fraction is considerable. By spreading the value over the five years s 40 may enable A to use his annual £3,000 exemption. On the other hand there may have been intervening transfers having the effect of increasing the rates of tax. However the important point is that this fraction is applied to the value of the shares at the time each transfer is made. So if the shares double in value the chargeable transfer of the next tranche will be 7/10 × £24,000 or £16,800.[3]

The section applies only where the disposition is for a consideration in money or money's worth. It would therefore not apply if A simply made a covenant to transfer the shares over five years.

Simon's Taxes I3.256; Foster's Inheritance Tax C2.56.

---

[1] IHTA 1984, s 262.
[2] It is assumed that the £18,000 is a single cash payment. However, if B agreed to pay £25,000 over five years it would be necessary to discount this figure of £25,000 and

one might again have £18,000 as the present value of the sums to be paid.
3   Note that the fraction does not increase to 8.5/10.

Disposition of excluded property

[39.12] A person's estate is the aggregate of all the property to which he is beneficially entitled, except that the estate of a person immediately before his death does not include excluded property.[1] It follows from this that excluded property does form part of a person's estate at other times. From this it follows that there is no charge to tax if a person sells non-excluded property and invests the proceeds in excluded property—or vice versa.

It is further provided that no account is to be taken of the value of excluded property which ceases to form part of a person's estate as a result of a disposition.[2] It follows from this that while a transfer of excluded property will not give rise to liability in respect of the property transferred, liability will accrue if the transfer of non-excluded property causes a loss to the excluded property.

EXAMPLE

A, a person domiciled outside the UK, owns 40% of the shares in X Ltd, an English company. Another 30% of the shares are held by Y Ltd, a foreign company. A owns 75% of the shares in Y Ltd so that he has control of X Ltd by virtue of the two holdings of 40% and 30%. If A makes a transfer of his 40% holding in X Ltd, there will be a transfer of value, whether chargeable or potentially exempt. There is a chargeable transfer since those shares are not excluded property.

The value transferred is the loss to A's estate and this will therefore take account of the loss of control notwithstanding that control is achieved only by the inclusion of excluded property.

Liability may also arise if the transfer of excluded property causes a loss to other property forming part of the estate. So if A had transferred the holding in Y Ltd first there would again have been a loss to his estate, perhaps a loss of control. It might be argued that since no account is taken of the value of the excluded property transferred and since that property gave A control it ought to follow that the loss of control will escape tax. However, it may be replied that the 'value of the excluded property' is to be valued on its own and so without reference to the power it gave A over X Ltd, so that the difference between the loss of control and the value of the excluded property on its own is taxable; the position is not completely clear but on balance liability seems to arise.

A yet more absurd situation is where A has control of a company through shares which are all excluded property, eg a 55% holding, and he then gives a 10% holding to B. It cannot be supposed that a charge to tax arises here and yet the gift of the 10% causes a loss to A's estate reflecting the loss of control.

Simon's Taxes I3.217, 254; Foster's Inheritance Tax C2.17, 54.

1   IHTA 1984, s 5(1).
2   IHTA 1984, s 3(2).

Voidable transfers

[39.13] Where by virtue of any enactment or rule of law the whole or any part of a transfer has been set aside as voidable or otherwise defeasible, a claim may be made[1] and

(1) any tax[2] due shall cease to be due;
(2) any tax[2] already paid in respect of that or any other chargeable transfer[3] made before the claim that would not have been payable if the transfer had been void ab initio can be reclaimed;
(3) where the transferor has subsequently made other transfers, the rates of tax are determined as if the first transfer had been void.[4]

Examples include bankruptcy[5] and gifts made under undue influence.

The provision, although well intentioned, is not without its difficulties. First, it applies not just where the transfer is voidable but also where it is otherwise defeasible. Hence perhaps a subsequent condition which defeats the grant of an interest may come within this rule. However, a transfer subject to a condition precedent which has not yet occurred would appear to be ineffective and so not to fall within this rule even though it should come about that the condition can never occur.

Second, it applies only where the transfer has been set aside and so not where the parties elect or the court directs that the transferor shall receive damages in lieu of the setting aside. Such matters ought technically to be treated as mutual transfers.

Third, it assumes that a voidable transfer is an effective transfer yet, in theory, the reduction in the value of the estate should be exactly offset by the value of the right to recover the property.

Simon's Taxes I3.562; Foster's Inheritance Tax C5.62.

---

[1] IHTA 1984, s 150.
[2] And any interest due, IHTA 1984, s 150(2); interest paid to the taxpayer is tax-free: IHTA 1984, s 236(3).
[2] And any interest due, IHTA 1984, s 150(2); interest paid to the taxpayer is tax-free: IHTA 1984, s 236(3).
[3] As when the voidable transfer was exempt under IHTA 1984, s 19 and the second would have been if the first had not been made.
[4] IHTA 1984, s 150(1).
[5] Insolvency Act 1986, ss 339, 340, 423.

Matters which are not transfers of value

Transactions with no intent to give

[39.14] IHT is intended to be a tax on gratuitous transfers of value. If the transferor shows:

(1) that the transfer was made:
  (a) in a transaction at arm's length between persons not connected with each other;[1] or
  (b) if they are so connected, that the transfer was such as might be expected to be made in a transaction at arm's length; and
(2) that the transfer was not intended and was not made in a transaction intended to confer a gratuitous benefit on *any* person,

then it is not a transfer of value.[2]

Not only is intention to be judged according to the normal legal rule that a person is taken to intend the natural and probable consequences of his acts[3] (or omissions) but there is the further point that the onus is placed on the transferor to show that he had no intention to confer gratuitous benefit. However, it is perfectly possible for a taxpayer to discharge this burden even though the sale is at a figure below that ultimately determined to be the fair market value of the property, such as where the taxpayer is acting under a mistake.[4]

EXAMPLES

(1) G, a grandfather, pays £20,000 to a school fees scheme for his grandson. This does not escape tax since although the purchase is an arm's length transaction, G intends to confer a gratuitous benefit on his grandson. Moreover it may well be an immediate chargeable transfer rather than a potentially exempt one; supra, § **39.02**.

(2) G sells a picture for £10,000; unknown to him the picture is worth £100,000. Assuming that these facts are established, IHTA 1984, s 10 prevents there being a transfer of value despite the loss to G's estate.

(3) F grants his son S the protected tenancy of a dwelling house. Although S pays the maximum fair rent the Revenue may treat the grant of the lease as subject to tax, as it is clearly a disposal causing loss to F's estate, and deny the availability of IHTA 1984, s 10 on the ground that persons dealing at arm's length do not usually grant protected tenancies. A similar argument arose out of the grant of tenancies of agricultural land but there special legislation now applies, infra, § **39.20** (6). Returning to the grant of a protected tenancy one may perhaps distinguish the parent who grants a tenancy of the only property he has other than his own home from one who regularly lets property to protected tenants and who treats his son in the same way as any other tenant. As always the question is one of fact. Since the lease is an asset of S's estate, the grant would seem to be capable of being a potentially exempt transfer rather than an immediately chargeable one.

(4) F takes his two children into partnership with him on terms which provide that the children must devote such time as the business may require, that F need only devote such time as he sees fit and that F's share will accrue to the children on F's death without further payment.[5]

This provision does not apply to:

(1) a sale of unquoted shares or debentures[6] unless it is shown that the sale was at a price freely negotiated at the time of the sale (so that for example a sale at a price fixed under the provisions of the company's articles of association can trigger liability to IHT);[7]
(2) certain reversionary interests.[8]

For this purpose the expression 'transaction' is expressly stated to include a series of transactions and any associated operations.

Aspinall (executors of Postlethwaite, dec'd) v Revenue and Customs Comrs[9] gives an interesting illustration of the judicial approach to this exemption.

[39.14] Transfers of value by disposition

Dr Postlethwaite was a skilled engineer. In 1991 he created a company, incorporated in Jersey, of which he was sole employee and sole shareholder. The company contracted with a third party to provide Dr Postlethwaite's services for a fee of £600,000 a year. Dr Postlethwaite took a salary from the Jersey company of £75,000 a year, plus a possible bonus to be paid at the discretion of the trustees. In 1993 the Jersey company made a payment of £700,000 to a pension fund to provide pension benefits for Dr Postlethwaite and his family. Dr Postlethwaite died on 13 April 1999, aged 55, before drawing a pension. The Revenue issued a determination that the £700,000 payment by the company was a transfer of value to be apportioned entirely to Dr Postlethwaite as the sole participant in this close company.[10] The executors appealed. The Special Commissioner, HM Nowlan ruled:[11]

> Relevant intention under s 10(1) is that of the transferor, here the company. The intentions of Dr Postlethwaite are relevant only to the extent that they can be imputed to the directors through whom the company acted . . . . The word 'gratuitous' is not statutorily defined. When linked with benefit it clearly connotes bounty. It is used in the first sense given in the

> In the present case the contract between Dr Postlethwaite and Pintacorze specifically contemplated a bonus in addition to a salary and pension arrangements to be agreed. A surplus in excess of £800,000 had accrued by the end of July 1993 generated entirely from income earned for the company by Dr Postlethwaite. In those circumstances we do not consider a payment of £700,000 to a pension arrangement for him can properly be described as 'given' for nothing' or 'not earned' to use the meaning given in the

> The service agreement provided for the pension arrangements to be agreed. If the sum had been paid as a bonus it would not have been apt to describe it as given for nothing. We do not see that the fact that a large FURBS payment was made instead of a bonus affects the position. If the payment had been excessive in comparison with what Dr Postlethwaite had earned for the company, the position might well have been very different. That was not however the case. We conclude that it has been shown that payment of £700,000 was not intended to confer a gratuitous benefit on Dr Postlethwaite or anyone else.

Simon's Taxes I3.141–148; Foster's Inheritance Tax C1.41–48.

---

[1] IHTA 1984, s 10.
[2] An example would be employers making ex-gratia payments to their employees.
[3] See *Cunliffe v Goodman* **[1950] 2 KB 237 AT 253**.
[4] *IRC v Spencer-Nairn* [1991] STC 60, Ct of Sess, dismissing Crown's appeal against decision of Special Commissioners.
[5] The inspiration for this example is *A-G v Boden* [1912] 1 KB 539 but it must be stressed that each case will turn on its own facts.
[6] On meaning of quoted and unquoted shares see IHTA 1984, s 272 as amended by FA 1987, Sch 8, para 1; shares listed on the USM are quoted securities, although they are treated as unquoted for purposes of business relief and payment by instalments.
[7] The requirements of IHTA 1984, s 10(1) must presumably, also be met. However, the Revenue may argue that when the vendor has a 75% holding, the sale of a 33%

holding is only freely negotiated if the purchaser pays a price equal to 33/75ths of the value of the 75% holding.

[8] IHTA 1984, s 55, infra, § **42.23**.
[9] [2007] SWTI 346, [2007] STC (SCD) 83.
[10] Under ITA 1984, s 94(1), see infra, § **39.21**.
[11] [2007] STC (SCD) 83, paras 88, 90, 91 and 97 at 97d, 97f-j and 98g.

Dispositions for maintenance of family

[39.15] Certain dispositions for the maintenance of one's family are not transfers of value.[1]

A disposition made by one party to a marriage in favour of the other party is not a transfer of value if it is for the maintenance of the other party. Further, 'marriage' is defined in relation to a disposition made on the occasion of the dissolution or annulment of a marriage, and in relation to a disposition varying a disposition so made, as including a former marriage.

The exemption is necessary because the general exemption for transfers between spouses (infra, § **43.01**) is limited to £55,000[3] where the transferor is, but the transferee is not, domiciled in the UK, and does not apply to former spouses. However, the Revenue have indicated that transfers of money or property pursuant to an order of the court in consequence of a decree of divorce or nullity will in general be regarded as exempt as being given for full consideration, the consideration being the divorce, and not a voluntary disposition.[4]

The scope of this relief is uncertain in a number of respects. First, there is the problem of the precise meaning of the word disposition. This is apt to cover a transfer within IHTA 1984, s 2 and is expressly stated to cover the termination of an interest in possession in settled property under IHTA 1984, s 51(1).[5] This leaves open those matters which are treated as transfers of value. Thus a deemed transfer by participators in a close company under IHTA 1984, s 98(1); infra, § **39.30**, is treated as being a disposition by them; when a person dies he is treated as having made a transfer of value; infra, § **40.01**, but this is not expressly stated to be by way of disposition although other provisions assume that he does make a disposition.[6]

The Revenue view is that a transfer on death cannot be a disposition for maintenance of the family. This view is probably correct but is harsh,[7] hard to justify and in need of reform. One should also recall that a deemed transfer of value otherwise than by disposition cannot be a potentially exempt transfer.

The second difficulty is that the transfer must be 'in favour of' the other spouse. This is sufficient to cover payments direct to the other spouse or to trustees for the spouse absolutely and probably also a transfer to a trust to hold on trust for the spouse for life but may not extend to the creation of a discretionary trust of which the spouse is to be one of the objects. If a transfer to a trust under which the spouse takes a life interest is completely exempt it may follow that a transfer to a trust under which the spouse takes a reversionary interest is taxable in full.

1637

[39.15] Transfers of value by disposition

Certain practical problems arise over the implementation of agreements or court orders on divorce or annulment. If the carrying out of the agreement or order is deferred until after decree absolute the transfer is presumably made 'on the occasion of' the dissolution or annulment and so qualifies for relief; moreover a transfer is defined in terms of the date of the loss to the transferor's estate and so presumably the date of the transfer is that on which the agreement or order was made. Such transfers ought therefore to be safe whether carried out before or after decree absolute. Subsequent transfers in favour of the ex-spouse will, however, only be exempt if they vary the disposition made on the divorce or annulment; such transfers should therefore be expressed to be by way of such variation. Whether a completely new agreement can be by way of variation of the old is unclear.

It is unclear whether transfers which simply implement orders made by the court can ever have any tax consequences. It can be argued that these are not 'dispositions' so long as there is no consensual element in them. Alternatively, it can be argued that they are protected from tax as they are transactions with no intent to give.

Simon's Taxes I3.151; Foster's Inheritance Tax C1.51; STP [9.76].

[1] IHTA 1984, s 11
[3] IHTA 1984, s 51(2).
[4] Statement of practice E12; **Foster's Inheritance Tax, Division W2.**
[5] IHTA 1984, s 18(1).
[6] IHTA 1984, ss 18(1), 147 also Administration of Estates Act 1925, s 1.
[7] On this view transfers under IHTA 1984, s 98 could fall within IHTA 1984, s 11 but those on death or under IHTA 1984, s 94 and payments ceasing to be relevant property under IHTA 1984, s 65 cannot.

[39.16] (2) *A child of either party to a marriage.* A disposition by one party to a marriage in favour of a child of either party for the maintenance, education or training of the child for a period ending in the year in which the child attains the age of 18 or, if later, ceases to undergo full-time education or training is not a transfer of value. Child includes a stepchild and an adopted child. The word training is undefined; presumably solicitors' articles provide training.

The rule enables a parent, but not a grandparent, to make transfers free of tax. The transfer may be in favour of the child. The provision is presumably designed to exempt a parent from liability to tax in respect of private school fees.

Where a child resumes full-time education or training after attaining 18, a literal reading suggests that later transfers may not come within the provision.

Another problem is that where a husband covenants to pay his wife annual sums for a child until he reaches 21 the payments will presumably be treated as made year by year, each year being a period. If, however, he hands over a lump sum for the maintenance of the child until he reaches 21 regardless of whether or not the child receives full time education after reaching the age of 18 the transfer would appear to fall outside the relief.

[39.17] (3) *A child not in the care of his parent.* Where the child is not in the care of a parent a disposition—by anyone—for his maintenance, education or training is not a transfer of value if (a) it is for a period ending not later than the year in which he attains the age of 18 or, (b) if the child has for substantial periods been in the custody of the transferor, the year in which he ceases to undergo full time education or training.

[39.18] (4) *Illegitimate child of the transferor.* A disposition in favour of an illegitimate child of the transferor is not a transfer of value. The disposition must be for the maintenance, education or benefit of the child and for the same period as for other children.

[39.19]–[39.20] (5) *Dependent relative.* A disposition in favour of a dependent relative is not a transfer of value provided it is a reasonable provision for his care or maintenance. The notion of a dependent relative is narrowly defined as (a) any relative[1] of the transferor or his spouse who is incapacitated by old age or infirmity from maintaining himself, and (b) the mother of the transferor or his spouse if widowed or living apart from her husband or, in consequence of dissolution or annulment of the marriage, a single woman.[2] By concession this extends to a gift by a child to his unmarried mother, but only if the mother is genuinely financially dependent on the child making the disposition; this restriction forms no part of the statutory provision which applies if the mother does get married (and for which marriage to anyone will do).[3]

Simon's Taxes I3.152, 153; Foster's Inheritance Tax C1.52, 53; STP [9.76].

---

[1] The term 'relative' is not specifically defined for the purposes of this section. However, in the definition of 'connected persons' (IHTA 1984, s 270) the word 'relative' means brother, sister, ancestor, lineal descendant, uncle, aunt, nephew and niece; definition in TCGA 1992, s 286(8) extended by IHTA 1984, s 270.

[2] The same as TA 1988, s 263, now repealed by FA 1988, s 25 and TCGA 1992, s 225; supra, § **23.11**.

[3] Extra-statutory concession F12; **Foster's Inheritance Tax, Division U2**.

Other transfers not transfers of value

(1) A disposition which is allowable in computing the transferor's profits or gains for income tax or corporation tax is not a transfer of value. The same applies where the sum would be so allowable if the profits or gains were sufficient and fell to be so computed.[1]

(2) A disposition which is a contribution to an approved retirement benefits scheme or personal pension plan and provides benefits in respect of service with the transferor is not a transfer of value.[2] The same applies to one made so as to provide benefits on or after retirement for an employee who is not connected with the transferor or for the widow or dependants of such a person if the benefits do not exceed those that would have been provided under an approved scheme. For this purpose the right to occupy a dwelling rent free or at a rent below market value is treated as a pension equal to the amount of rent forgone.

[39.19] Transfers of value by disposition

(3) A waiver or repayment of remuneration is not a transfer of value if:
  (a) it would have been chargeable to income tax under Schedule E; and
  (b) the sum, if not waived, would have been deductible in computing the profits of the payer and, by reason of repayment or the waiver, is not allowed or is brought back into charge.[3]

(4) A waiver of any dividend on shares of a company within 12 months before—but not after—any right to dividend has accrued is not a transfer of value;[4] the right accrues when the dividend is declared, not when it becomes enforceable.[5] It will be noted that there is no provision dealing with the waiver of interest or rent.

(5) Transfer to an employee share ownership trust[6] by a close company; a similar transfer by an individual is an exempt transfer[7] and qualifies for exemption only if the trust has control.

(6) The grant of an agricultural tenancy is declared not to be a transfer of value if it is made for full consideration in money or money's worth.[8] The reason for this is that the grant of such a lease inevitably reduces the value of an estate owing to the different values of freehold and tenanted land and the system of control of agricultural rents. But for such a provision a landlord would find himself liable to tax on granting a lease to his son even though the terms were the best he could obtain from any third party.[9] This provision does not address the quite separate problem of the lifetime transfer of a Scottish agricultural tenancy.[10]

Simon's Taxes I3.154–159; Foster's Inheritance Tax C1.54–59.

---

[1] IHTA 1984, s 12. The wording is wide enough to cover a trade which in fact makes a loss or which is not within the charge to UK tax, eg a foreign trade.
[2] IHTA 1984, s 12(2).
[3] IHTA 1984, s 14. Remuneration is not defined—quaere whether it extends to any payment falling within Schedule E. An example of a payment falling within (b) is *White v Franklin*; supra, § **4.17**.
[4] IHTA 1984, s 15.
[5] Long-term waiver may cause liability to tax under IHTA 1984, s 98; infra, § **39.30** and to tax under TCGA 1992, s 29.
[6] IHTA 1984, s 13.
[7] IHTA 1984, s 28.
[8] IHTA 1984, s 16.
[9] IHTA 1984, s 10 would not apply as, in the Revenue view, no-one in his right mind would grant a lease of such land anyway and therefore there must have been an intention to confer a gratuitous benefit.
[10] See *Baird's Executors v IRC* [1991] 1 EGLR 201 and infra, § **44.25**.

Close companies

[39.21] Although transfers by companies do not generally give rise to IHT an exception is made for a transfer by a close company;[1] otherwise property could be transferred to a tame company in return for shares only for the company then to give the property to the intended donee.

The value transferred is charged as if each participant had made a transfer of value, an expression which ensures that it cannot be a potentially exempt transfer.[2] The value transferred is apportioned among the participators in the company by reference to their rights immediately before the transfer. The transfer is treated as made by each participator; where that amount is less than 5% of the value transferred it is not cumulated. When the participator is itself a close company sub-apportionments are made until the individual participators are discovered.

The amount apportioned is reduced by the amount by which the value of the participator's estate is increased. In making this calculation the value of his rights in the company is ignored; so the Revenue cannot use any loss in the value of the shares to reduce the increase to his estate.

EXAMPLE

X Ltd is valued at £150,000 and is owned equally by A and B. X Ltd gives A £18,000 and B's daughter £24,000. The values transferred are apportioned to A and B equally. Of the £18,000, £9,000 is attributed to B and none to A (as the increase in his estate is set off against it). The £24,000 is attributed equally to A and B and must be grossed up at their respective rates.

For this purpose the corporation tax definition of a close company is adopted supra, § **28.02** save that it is extended to cover non-resident companies. The definition of participator is also adopted save that loan creditors are ignored.

Simon's Taxes Division I6.1; Foster's Inheritance Tax Part F1.

---

[1] IHTA 1984, s 94(1). For a case that seeks to attribute a transfer made a close company on its sole shareholder, see *Aspinall (executors of Postlethwaite, dec'd) v Revenue and Customs Comrs* [200] SWTI 346, [2007] STC (SCD) 83, see supra, § **39.14**. However, in this case, it was held that the transaction by the close company was not a transfer of value.

[2] IHTA 1984, ss 3A(6), 94(1).

Liability

[39.22] The primary liability rests on the company but those liable to apportionment or to whom the transfer is made are also liable;[1] this secondary liability is limited to the amount apportioned or the increase in value as appropriate. An exception is made in that a person to whom not more than 5% of the value transferred is apportioned is not liable, leaving the company solely liable.

Simon's Taxes I6.129; I10.114; Foster's Inheritance Tax F1.29; K1.14.

[39.22] Transfers of value by disposition

[1] IHTA 1984, s 202(1).

Exemptions

[39.23] If there is a transfer of value to a participator's spouse the spouse exemption will apply. Other exemptions available are the participator's annual £3,000 exemption and those for charities, political parties and other public benefit. The small gifts and marriage gifts rules do not apply and potential exemption treatment is not available.

There is also a specific exception for payments that fall to be taken into account in computing the recipient's profits or gains or losses for income or corporation tax[1]—eg a dividend.[2] There is also an exception where the person to whom the transfer would be apportioned is domiciled outside the UK and the apportionment is attributable to property situated outside the UK. Further exceptions apply to the surrender of ACT or group relief.

It is possible for companies in a group to elect for a capital gain to be calculated and taxed, as if an intra group transfer were made prior to the onward sale to a third party.[3] The application of this election changes the burden of the corporation tax charge between members of a 75% group. The effect can be the utilisation of brought forward capital losses in Company A to reduce the tax charge suffered by Company B. This could, under general principles, be a transfer of value between the shareholders of Company A and the shareholders of Company B. This transfer of value is exempt.[4] Statute provides that any consideration paid by Company A to Company B for use of its losses shall be ignored for corporation tax purposes.[5] The effect of the IHT exemption when consideration is paid is obscure. The exemption is on the deemed transfer, no mention is made of an exemption for the consideration. However, the true construction may be that the consideration operates simply to reduce the transfer of value and s 106 exempts that reduced transfer of value.[6]

[1] Or would do so but for TA 1988, s 208.
[2] Another example would be where the transfer is caught by TCGA 1992, s 29 as a transfer at an under-value causing a reduction in the acquisition value of the shares for CGT.
[3] TCGA 1992, s 171A.
[4] IHTA 1984, s 97(1).
[5] TCGA 1992, s 171A(5).
[6] The contrary view is taken by the author of the relevant note in Butterworths Annotated Finance Act 2001. The author of that note considers that the payment of consideration is not exempt as it is separate from the transfer of value occasioned by the making of the election.

[39.24] In order to prevent overnice calculation there are further rules where the transfer of value has only a small effect on the value of preference shares;

provision is also made for transfers between members of a group or between close companies in both of which the participators has an interest, the purpose here being to get the right value.[1]

Simon's Taxes I6.126; Foster's Inheritance Tax F1.26.

---

[1] IHTA 1984, ss 95–97.

Alteration in share rights

[39.25] There is a deemed disposition when there is an alteration to the company's unquoted share or loan capital or any alteration in the rights attached to the unquoted shares or unquoted debentures of the company.[1] Alteration includes extinguishment. The effect is to charge the participators on the value shifted even though nothing emerges from the company; without some such rule wealth could be shifted by juggling share rights. Although IHTA treats this as a disposition, it also makes it clear that this cannot be a potentially exempt transfer.[2] This provision does not apply to alterations in the rights of quoted securities.[3]

The transfer is deemed to be made by the participators and they are liable for any tax payable; there is no liability on the company.[4]

EXAMPLE

Y Ltd has an issued share capital of 100 ordinary shares of £1 owned equally by C and D; the value of each holding is £40,000. If the company now issues 75 such shares each at par to C's son (CS) and D's daughter (DD) the parents' holdings will drop in value. Suppose the value of each parent's holding after the issue of the new shares is £13,000.

Hence, after the new shares are issued, the position is as follows:

	Holding	Value
C	50	£13,000
D	50	13,000
CS	75	27,000
DD	75	27,000
		£80,000

C and D have each made a transfer of value of £40,000 − £13,000 = £27,000.

In order to prevent schemes to reduce tax by removing rights from shares on death it is provided that a decrease in value occurring on death and resulting from an alteration within these provisions does not affect the valuation of the shares for the purposes of the transfer on death.[5]

Simon's Taxes I6.111; Foster's Inheritance Tax F1.11.

---

[1] IHTA 1984, s 98(1).
[2] IHTA 1984, s 98(3) added by FA 1986, Sch 19, para 20. For this purpose, 'transfers within a group' are defined as those to which the no gains/no loss treatment of TCGA 1992, s 171 is applied. With effect from 1 April 2000, FA 2001, s 106

retrospectively brings within the definition a disposal where relief against the capital gain is claimed under TCGA 1992, s 171A(2) as this had been a transfer within a group: see supra, §

[3] On meaning of unquoted see IHTA 1984, s 272 as amended by FA 1987, Sch 8, para 17; securities listed on the USM are now treated as quoted.

[4] IHTA 1984, s 98(1) deems the alteration in the close company share or loan capital, or rights therein, as being a disposition by the participators.

[5] IHTA 1984, s 98(1).

Settled property trustees as participators

[39.26] A transfer by a close company[1] can be apportioned to trustee-participators. In such an event there is a deemed coming to an end of a qualifying interest in possession: the value concerned is that apportioned to the participators less any increase in the value of the settled property (other than the value of rights in the company). Any person who is beneficially entitled to a qualifying interest in possession under the settlement is treated as the participator in place of the trustees.[2]

If there is no qualifying interest in possession, as with a discretionary trust, the trustees are treated as having made a disposition reducing the value of the settled property by a similar amount and so giving rise to an exit charge under IHTA 1984, s 65.

Simon's Taxes I6.112, 127; Foster's Inheritance Tax F1.12, 27.

[1] Under either IHTA 1984, s 94 or under s 98.
[2] IHTA 1984, ss 99, 100.

Close company as beneficiary

[39.27] Where a close company is entitled to an interest in possession those who are participators in relation to the company are treated as entitled to the interest for all purposes other than in relation to acquired reversions and IHTA 1984, s 10.[1]

This deeming provision must be carried right through. When the interest in possession ends there is a transfer of value by the participators.[2] The company is not to be treated as having an interest in the settled property; in consequence any rights the company may have to the income are to be disregarded.[3]

Simon's Taxes I6.131; Foster's Inheritance Tax F1.31.

[1] IHTA 1984, s 101(1).
[2] *Powell Cotton v IRC* [1992] STC 625 which considered a transfer of value charged under IHTA 1984, s 52(1).
[3] *Powell Cotton v IRC* [1992] STC 625.

Disposition by associated operations

[39.28] A disposition is defined[1] as including one made by associated operations.[2] Further, statute[3] provides that a transaction includes a series of transactions and any associated operations.[4] Operations that are associated are treated as a single transaction; all are treated as made at the time of the last. Associated operations are defined[5] as:

> any two or more operations of any kind whether effected by the same person or by different persons and whether or not simultaneous being (a) operations which affect the same property or one of which affects some property and the other or others affect property which represents, directly or indirectly, that property or income arising from that property or any property representing accumulations of such income or (b) any two operations of which one is effected with reference to the other or with a view to enabling the other to be effected or facilitating its being effected and any further operations having a like relation to any of those two and so on . . ..

The word 'operation' is not defined save that it is to include omission.

Simon's Taxes I2.212, I3.115, 116, 132, 261–267; Foster's Inheritance Tax B2.12; C1.15, 16, 32; C2.61–67.

---

[1] IHTA 1984, s 268.
[2] IHTA 1984, s 272.
[3] IHTA 1984, s 10.
[4] *Macpherson v IRC* [1988] STC 362, [1988] 2 All ER 753, HL.
[5] IHTA 1984, s 268(1).

Rysaffe Trustee Co (CI) v IRC

[39.29] The meaning of 'associated operations' was explored and given its clearest judicial definition to date in

> I agree with, and find it impossible to improve upon, the judge's concise and clear statement of his reasoning in his excellent judgement.

Rysaffe Trustee Co (CI) v IRC was concerned with the calculation of the ten year charge on a discretionary settlement.[1] On each of the five days, 7, 10 and 13 February, 1 and 12 March 1984 Richard John Warburton Utley signed a settlement deed. Each settlement was in exactly the same form except for the date. Mr John Utley gave deeds on 16 March 1984 and his signature was witnessed by a solicitor. He drew one cheque for £50 being the £10 for each of his five settlements. A representative of the firm of solicitors then inserted five separate dates on the deeds being 16, 19, 21, 23 and 26 March 1984. The deeds were executed by the trustee on 27 March 1984. They were then returned to the solicitors and stamped in the same way as Mr Richard Utley's deeds.

On 15 November 1984 at an extraordinary general meeting of Richard Utley Limited, the company redesignated the larger part of its share capital to deferred shares.

Thereafter Mr Richard Utley transferred 6,900 A deferred shares to the trustee for each of his settlements (making a total of 34,500 A deferred shares

[39.29] Transfers of value by disposition

transferred) and Mr John Utley transferred 6,900 B deferred shares to the trustee for each of his five settlements (also making a total of 34,500 B deferred shares transferred). On 3 May 1994 the deferred shares were re-designated as ordinary shares. All the deferred shares then ranked pari passu with the ordinary shares. The Revenue argued that the effect of the associated operations rule was that the dispositions in creating the five Richard Utley settlements are correctly viewed as a single disposition, with the consequence that the 10 year IHT charge is computed by treating the shares in all five settlements as if they were contained in a single settlement.

In the judgment that was held in such high esteem by the Court of Appeal, Park J said:[2]

> A helpful way to approach the matter is to begin with one of the transfers of a parcel of shares, say the transfer of 'parcel 1' to settlement no 1. That transfer was certainly an 'operation'. The question is: with what other operations was it associated within the meaning of para (a) or (b) of s 268(1)? The question can be covered by asking it in detail of three other operations, as follows:
>
> (i) The answer to this question is: yes. The conclusion can be reached in either of two ways. First, the transfer of parcel 1 to settlement 1 was effected 'with reference to' the earlier payment of £10 to settlement 1 because the shares were transferred to be held on the trusts of the settlement created by the payment of the initial sum of £10. Second, the initial payment of £10 was effected with a view to enabling the later transfer of shares to be effected.
>
> (ii) Was the operation of the transfer of parcel 1 to settlement 1 associated with the operation of transferring other parcels of shares to other settlements, say the transfer of parcel 2 to settlement 2? This seems to me to be the critical question. Neither transfer was effected with a view to enabling the other transfer to be effected. Nor was either transfer effected with a view to facilitating the other transfer being effected. My answer to this question (ii) is: no.
>
> (iii) Was the operation of the transfer of parcel 1 to settlement 1 associated with the operation of paying £10 to any of the other settlements, say to settlement 2? If I am right in my answer to (ii) above, the answer to this question must also be: no.

---

[1] IHTA 1984, s 64.
[2] [2002] EWHC 1114 (Ch), [2002] STC 872 para 37 at 898b to 899f.

Consequences of operations being associated

Timing

[39.30] Where a transfer of value is carried out by associated operations at different times, it is treated as made at the time of the last one. This may increase the rate of tax payable on earlier transfers not only because there may have been other transfers in the interval raising the rate of tax but also because the last happens within three years of the transferor's death thus triggering the higher rates of tax. So the grant of the lease and the gift of the reversion may be treated as a transfer of the fee simple made at the time of the gift of the reversion. Likewise where A gave £250 to X and another £250 to Y for transmission to X, the scheme will be treated as being a disposal by A to X of £500 and so chargeable in full, infra, § **43.02**. It also affects the date for valuing the property involved.

Taking account of earlier transfers

[39.31] Where two transactions are carried out by the same person the value transferred by the earlier operation is treated as reducing the value transferred by all the operations taken together. This is to prevent a double charge to tax. Presumably, however, this could lead to a repayment of tax if the effect of the first rule is to bring the earlier transfer into a period of lower (or even nil) rates.

So if in the example infra, § **39.35** A had granted the lease at a nominal rent so that there was a reduction in the value of A's estate of, say £10,000, and a consequent charge in 1994, this in turn would have reduced the later transfer from £70,000 to £60,000.

This affects not only the value of the property transferred but also the rate at which any grossing up is carried out. It also seems to follow that where there have been intermediate transfers the tax on those transfers may have to be reopened; this is because the first transfer is now treated as taking place at the time of the last of the associated transfers.[1]

---

[1] IHTA 1984, ss 268(1)(*b*), 272.

If prior transfer is exempt

[39.32] The rule that value transfer by the earlier operation reduces the value by the operations taken together does not apply to the extent that the transfer constituted by the earlier operations, but not that made by the operations taken together, is exempt as a transfer between spouses. So where A transferred £3,000 to his son and another £2,500 to his wife for transmission to the son the transfer will be treated as one of £5,500 to the son.

It will be noticed that there is no prohibition on the reduction where the earlier transfer is exempt by reason of some other provision. So if C gives his daughter D shares worth £10,000 in five equal instalments and makes no other transfers each year, the transfers will be associated operations and so will be treated as being of £10,000 in year 5 but reduced by the aggregate of the annual exemptions for each of years 1–4. Lest potential Cs should be carried away it should be remembered that if in year 5 the value of the shares rises sharply to £20,000, that increase will determine the value transferred.

Simon's Taxes I3.261–267; Foster's Inheritance Tax C2.61–67.

Further points

[39.33] A consequence of the transactions being associated is that IHTA 1984, s 10 must be applied to the single transaction. So if A grants B a lease at full rent and then sells him the reversion for full market value there may still be a chargeable transfer if the grant of the lease caused a drop in market value.[1]

One matter which IHTA 1984, s 268 does not resolve is just who is to be treated as making the reconstructed transfer. Thus if A uses the spouse exemption to channel a controlling interest to his son is the whole transfer to be treated as made by A or is the value to be allocated between A and Mrs A? The latter will at first sight avoid problems if A has died before the associated

[39.33] Transfers of value by disposition

transfer is made by Mrs A but this will not avoid the problem of reopening the transfer by A to give it a different value.

Where parents sell property to children but leave the purchase price outstanding to be released year by year using the annual exemption, the Revenue regard the operations as associated. However, the gift of an asset to a child, the child to pay the IHT, followed by gifts within the annual exemption limit to fund the IHT are not so regarded.[2]

It has previously been thought that the associated operations rule was capable of being applied where H, having a 60% holding, transfers 35% to his son, having previously transferred 25% to his wife who later transfers that holding to the son. However, the decision in *Rysaffe Trustee Co (CI) v IRC*[3] would seem to indicate that associated operations are not in point here, unless one disposition depends on another.[4]

---

[1] But on agricultural land see IHTA 1984, s 16.
[2] *Law Society's Gazette*, 1 March 1978; **Foster's Inheritance Tax X6.09**.
[3] [2002] EWHC 1114 (Ch), [2002] STC 872.
[4] Even without the associated operations rule, the loss of control will be taxed, thanks to the related property rules; infra, § **45.07**; however, the later transfer by the wife will not be caught by those rules.

Associated operations by spouses

[39.34] in the House of Commons that the Revenue will not invoke the associated operations rules where the spouse receives property and then makes a gift of that property 'of his own volition':

> There are ordinary, perfectly innocent transfers between husband and wife. For example, where a husband has the money and the wife has no money—or the other way round, which happens from time to time—and the one with the money gives something to the other to enable the spouse to make a gift to a son or a daughter on marriage, that transaction would not be caught by the clause. It would be a reasonable thing to do. I have made that clear in Committee upstairs, and I make it clear again now.

This analysis has been criticised by commentators as, in a scenario such as this, a charge arises on H without invoking the associated operations rules: on the facts given, W is acting under the instruction given by H, her transfer is not of her own volition.

Associated operations and Ramsay

[39.35] Although the effect of the decisions of the House of Lords on the new approach has been at times bewildering, it is now established that since the new approach is based on a principle of statutory construction or, probably, more correctly, statutory application, there is no reason why it should not apply in the IHT context where this is appropriate, and cases decided before the decision in *MacNiven v Westmoreland Investments Ltd* confirm that view.[1] As the courts have emphasised, it is important in such cases that when the Revenue invoke this approach they should make it clear what fiscal consequences they attach to what is said to be a single composite transaction and

Disposition by associated operations [39.35]

under which provision of the taxing statutes a charge to tax arises or a claim for exemption or relief fails.[2] Case law requires the courts to explore the relationship between the general anti-avoidance rule of construction (if that is what the new approach now is) and IHTA 1984, s 268, which is a specific but wide ranging anti-avoidance provision.[3]

A number of distinct problems arise from that relationship. First, if the operations are associated under IHTA 1984, s 268, will the courts allow the Revenue to use the new approach? This issue is still open.[4] Logically, the new approach, if it applies at all, should be applied before s 268 so as to assemble the facts to which s 268 will apply. This will have the advantage that the courts can then allow the detailed provisions in IHTA 1984, s 268(3) as to the effects of operations being associated to apply. This is of particular importance where IHTA 1984, s 268(3) determines the timing of a transaction, the more so since it has been said that under the new approach a taxable transaction taken in steps is to be treated as taking place when the first step is taken.[5]

Second, if the only reason why the operations are not associated is the applicability of the exclusion in IHTA 1984, s 268(2) will the courts allow the Revenue to use the new approach?[6] The exclusion from IHTA 1984, s 268 is an implied direction that the matters must be treated as separate transactions for tax purposes.

Third, if IHTA 1984, s 268 does not apply because the operations do not fall within the definition in IHTA 1984, s 268(1) will the courts allow the Revenue to use the new approach? The answer is now a clear yes.[7]

Fourth, if the answer to the previous question is yes, will the courts require the Revenue to proceed by analogy with IHTA 1984, s 268(3) in reconstructing the transaction? There would seem to be good sense in such a requirement but the Revenue may find the timing rule in particular to be unnecessarily constraining and again, it would appear that there is nothing in the reasoning in the cases to limit the applicability of the new approach in this way.

These detailed but compelling issues only become relevant if *Ramsay* is still applicable to IHT. It has been suggested in Chapter 3, supra, that Lord Hoffmann's distinction between commercial and juristic meanings makes a false contrast in a non-commercial area such as IHT and that a better contrast is between concepts which are to be interpreted broadly and those which are to be interpreted technically. It has to be said that in IHT there are many concepts which are to be interpreted technically; however we shall just have to wait and see how the courts develop this area. Meanwhile, we should note that the leading House of Lords IHT case—*Fitzwilliam v IRC* was cited in argument in *MacNiven* but was not mentioned in any of the speeches; no other IHT case was even cited in argument.

Simon's Taxes I2.212; Foster's Inheritance Tax B2.12.

---

1. The decisions in *Fitzwilliam v IRC* [1993] STC 502, HL, *Hatton v IRC* [1992] STC 140 and *Ingram v IRC* [1997] STC 1234, CA are all expressed in terms of there being a rule of statutory construction that is applicable to all cases. It must follow that the rule of construction declared by Lord Hoffman in the House of Lords in his decision in *McNiven v Westmoreland Investments Ltd* [2001] UKHL 6, [2001] STC

[39.35] Transfers of value by disposition

237 must, similarly, be of general application.

2   *Fitzwilliam v IRC* [1990] STC 65 at 120, approved by Nourse LJ in [1992] STC 185 at 189, CA. Here Vinelott J concluded, as has since the House of Lords, that the transaction could not be treated as a single composite transaction and so it was unnecessary for him to consider how the single transaction could be treated for IHT purposes but he did say that he did not think the Crown had been able to show how it should have been treated. In the Court of Appeal the Revenue submitted an amended notice of determination. Of this Nourse LJ said simply 'It has to my mind clarified both the essentials of the Crown's claim and its inability to sustain them': [1992] STC 185 at 189.
3   Cf *Commissioner of Inland Revenue v Challenge Corpn Ltd* [1986] STC 548, PC.
4   Per Lord Browne-Wilkinson in *Fitzwilliam v IRC* [1993] STC 502, HL, at 536 g.
5   Vinelott J in *Shepherd v Lyntress Ltd* [1989] STC 617 at 650.
6   See also *IRC v McGuckian* [1997] STC 908, HL.

Fitzwilliam v IRC

[39.36] *Fitzwilliam v IRC*[1] is a House of Lords decision on the application of the *Ramsay* principle to a capital transfer tax saving scheme. The facts of the case are complicated as the following explanation will underline; however, the lessons to be drawn from the case are relatively simple. The first is that the Revenue cannot alter the nature of a particular transaction in a series; secondly the Revenue cannot pick some bits and reject others; and thirdly the fact that a series of transactions is preordained is not of itself enough to enable the Revenue to undo a scheme—where the scheme involves the use of a particular exemption they must also be able to show that the reconstruction of the transaction which they are able to substantiate is inconsistent with the application of that exemption. These points are drawn principally from the speech of Lord Keith who drew them together in the proposition that in order to treat a series of transactions as one composite whole the Revenue had to show that it was realistically and intellectually possible to do so.

Simon's Taxes I2.207, 212; I5.132; Foster's Inheritance Tax B2.07, 12; E1.32.

1   [1993] STC 502, HL.

[39.37] Lord Fitzwilliam (LF) had died unexpectedly in September 1979 at the age of 75 leaving no issue. He was survived by his widow, Lady Fitzwilliam (F) and her daughter by a previous marriage, soon to be Lady Hastings (H). Under the terms of his will LF had created a 23-month discretionary trust at the end of which the property was to be held on trust for F for life with an ultimate trust over in favour of H provided she survived LF by one month.

If nothing had been done then on the expiry of the 23-month period the property would have passed to F. The exemption for property transferred to a spouse would have applied on that transfer and another provision would have prevented a charge on the death of LF. Unhappily there was some risk that F would not survive the 23-month period; she was in a state of shock at the death of her husband and at the death of her sister two weeks later. If she had died then the whole estate of some £11m would have been subject to CTT at 75%. In fact, F was in good health at the time of the hearing in 1993, when she was 95, but the risk of her early death was sufficiently substantial for the trustees of the estate to seek advice. F ultimately died in July 1997, aged 98 and her daughter, H, died within 12 months of her mother's death.

[39.38] The scheme involved five steps.

(1) 20 December 1979: the trustees appointed £4m in favour of F; no tax due—spouse exemption.

(2) 7 January 1980: F gave H £2m; she funded this out of the £4m received. This was found by the Commissioners to be a genuine gift. The fiscal effect would be that there would be a charge to CTT on this lifetime gift but this effect was to be undone at step 4.

(3) 14 January 1980: The trustees appointed £3.8m in trust to pay the income to F until 15 February 1980 or her death if earlier; subject to this one half (the vested half) was to go to H absolutely and the other half to her contingently on surviving until the ending of F's income interest. H thus had two interests in the trust, each worth 1.9m, but one vested and the other contingent. Fiscal effect—the appointment in favour of F was exempt as a transfer to a spouse.

(4) 31 January 1980: F sold the income interest just created at step 3 in the contingent half to H for £2m. Fiscal effect—the ending of F's interest would normally have given rise to CTT but that was not so if the amount paid by H matched or exceeded the £1.9m in the settlement; as H paid £2m there was no charge. We left F with a potential charge to tax on the gift of £2m at step 2; however, the mutual transfer provisions (which were repealed in 1986 and do not form part of IHT) meant that the F–H transfer at step 2 was cancelled and that the H–F payment at step 4 was not a transfer of value. It can be seen that the single H–F payment of £2m operated to prevent two heads of charge.

(5) 5 February 1980: H established a nominal settlement to pay income to F until 15 March 1980 or her earlier death and subject thereto for H absolutely; two days later H assigned to this trust her interest in the vested half of the trust created at step 3. The financial effect was to prolong F's income interest created at step 3 by a further month. Fiscal effect—there was a potential charge to CTT on the establishment of the nominal settlement but it was hoped that there would be none on its termination by reason of the reverter to settlor exemption; this depended on H being regarded as the settlor.

[39.39] Before the House of Lords the Revenue argued that while step 1 was not part of a preordained series of transactions steps 2–5 were. The House of Lords, by a majority of 4–1, with Lord Templeman as the dissenting voice held that steps 2–5 did not constitute associated operations that fell to be taxed under the principles in s 268. The principal speech for the majority was delivered by Lord Keith with whom Lords Ackner and Mustill agreed. He said that the correct approach was to ask whether realistically steps 2–5 constituted a single and indivisible whole in which one or more of them was simply an element without independent effect and whether it was intellectually possible so to treat them.[1] This test was drawn from words used by Lord Oliver in his speech in *Craven v White*[2] but it has to be said that those words were used in a descriptive rather than a prescriptive mode.

Taking his test as established Lord Keith then pointed to certain real fiscal consequences of each step—eg whether F was liable to pay tax on the income during the short period of her entitlement. One reads this with some anxiety since Lord Keith fails to address the question whether income tax would have been due if the *Ramsay* case was correctly applied; later he pointed to the risk that there would have been a charge to CTT if H or F had died while entitled to an interest in possession—again this assumes the answer.

He then said that the Revenue reconstruction would have charged CTT on the £3.8m passing to H on the basis that there was a termination of F's interest in possession; however in order to substantiate that basis they had to admit that step 3, creating the two income interests in F, and steps 4 and 5, making the assignments, were effective. This, said Lord Keith, was simply not possible either realistically or intellectually. The Revenue could not both accept that step 2 was a genuine unconditional gift and then seek to recast it as a conditional gift; nor could they pick bits out of steps 3, 4 and 5 and treat them as effective in order to say that they were not effective. The fact of preordainment did not negative the application of the exemption which the transactions were seeking to create unless the series was capable of being construed in a manner inconsistent with that exemption. There was no rational basis under which steps 2–4 could be treated as effective for the purpose of creating a charge to tax on the ending of F's interest in possession, but ineffective for the purpose of attracting the exemptions for the purchase of the interest or the reverter to the settlor. Lord Keith regarded it as important that Lady Hastings was given separate advice before steps 4 and 5 were undertaken.

The other member of the majority, Lord Browne-Wilkinson, used a very different approach. For him part of that real transaction was a transfer out of the estate of LF of £3.8m to H and he would have treated it in that way if the elements of the *Ramsay* test had been satisfied so as to treat steps 1–5 as one transaction. The Crown had not sought to argue that and therefore could not have steps 2–5 treated as a "mini-*Ramsay*".

Lord Templeman gave the minority opinion. In Lord Templeman's view[3] the associated operations rule[4] operated to defeat the scheme.

Simon's Taxes I2.207, 212; I5.132; Foster's Inheritance Tax B2.07, 12; E1.32.

---

[1] [1993] STC 502, at 513.

[2] [1988] STC 476, HL.

[3] For those who admire Lord Templeman's approach to these matters, attention may be drawn particularly to the six points where he disagrees with Lord Keith's decision, [1993] STC 502, HL, at 532–534. Lord Templeman's six criticisms can be summarised as:

(1) People should be judged by the results of their actions not by the language of documents intending to mislead

(2) Lord Keith dismisses the findings of the Special Commissioners on the grounds that they did not enjoy the benefit of the speeches in *Craven v White*. But in *Craven v White* the

(3) A client who adopts, ratifies and claims the benefit of the actions of his solicitors cannot deny the real consequences or avoid the fiscal consequences on the grounds of personal ignorance.
(4) The 'separate advice', was planned as part of the scheme. This advice was a foregone conclusion.
(5) The Special Commissioners found that, after step 3, there was no practical possibility that Lady Hasting would not take steps 4 and 5 which could not do her any harm.
(6) The scheme 'trembled on the brink of a sham' and employed the same devices which proved ineffective in

4   IHTA 1984, s 268.

Associated operations and life assurance

[39.40] A relaxed approach in the application of the associated operations rules is given in the context of life assurance policies and annuities. In Statement of Practice E4, HMRC provide:

> Life assurance policies and annuities are regarded as not being affected by the associated operations rule if, first, the policy was issued on full medical evidence and, secondly, it would have been issued on the same terms if the annuity had not been bought.

HMRC consider themselves bound by the statement but do not consider a medical questionnaire to constitute full medical evidence. The High Court held that the meaning of the phrase would depend on the facts of the case and it was suggested that "in the great majority of cases a report from the applicant's medical practitioner familiar with his health record will be called for (and, on occasion,) there may be need for a specialist". It was also suggested that in exceptional cases, there might be no need for medical evidence although it is hard to understand how this could be consistent with the wording of the statement.[1]

1   *Smith & Ors v Revenue and Customs Commissioners* [2007] EWHC 2304 (Ch). It is understood that the taxpayers are appealing this decision.

40

Death

Transfer at death	PARA **40.01**
Valuation of estate on death	PARA **40.07**
Life policies in the estate at death	PARA **40.10**
Effect on lifetime transfers	PARA **40.15**
Events after death	PARA **40.22**
Quick succession relief	PARA **40.29**
Reliefs for earlier transfers of the same property by the same transferor	PARA **40.30**
Abatement of exemptions on death	PARA **40.35**
Pension fund	PARA **40.36**

Transfer at death

[40.01] The statutory scheme[1] is that, on the death of any person, tax is charged as if, immediately before his death, he had made a transfer of value and the value transferred by it had been equal to the value of his estate immediately before his death; this includes the current value of any property of which the deceased made gift with reservation, if the reservation exists at the donor's death.

The rate(s) at which IHT is charged is determined by adding the value of the deemed transfer at death to the deceased's cumulative total of chargeable transfers (including potentially exempt transfers which have become chargeable by reason of the donor's death) over the last seven years. The value transferred is simply that of the estate; there is no need to gross up since after distribution there will be no estate left—the transfer on death is necessarily gross. The amount of tax, but not the chargeable value, may be reduced by the availability of quick succession relief see, infra, § **40.27**. On liability for tax see infra, § **45.05**.

Simon's Taxes I4.101; Foster's Inheritance Tax D1.01.

---

[1] IHTA 1984, s 4

Joint assets in the estate at death

[40.02] The legal title does not determine the beneficial owner's interest, which is the subject matter for the imposition of the IHT charge. For IHT, what is critical is the interest over which the deceased had the power of disposition.[1]

[1] IHTA 1984, s 5(2).

Joint property other than bank account

[40.03] For property other than money accounts, the approach usually adopted is for the value of the entirety to be allocated amongst co-owners, in accordance with the interests displayed during the lifetime of the deceased.

Joint bank account

[40.04] To ascertain the IHT treatment of a bank account in joint names, it is necessary first to ascertain the true nature of the bank account. In *O'Neill v IRC*[1] the Special Commissioner stated, in construing the statutory provision for the imposition of inheritance tax:

> There can, to my mind, be no doubt that a person's 'estate' comprises only property to which he is beneficially . . . entitled, and does not include property over which he may have merely de facto control.

In *Young v Sealey*[2] the funds in the account were regarded by the parties as being the funds of the party who made the deposits, the reason for the two signatures on the bank mandate being to obtain use of the funds after death. The transfer of value, thus, took place at death and not before. The joint account in *O'Neill v IRC*[3] was of a similar nature. The reason for the account in the name of father and daughter was concealment from the Revenue of the father's funds. The entire fund was correctly regarded as the father's property.

This is in sharp contrast to the situation in *Anand v IRC*,[4] where the Commissioner found that a bank account in the sole name of the deceased was a fund (or, perhaps more correctly, funds) divided equally amongst the members of the family. The named account holder acted as family treasurer. The estate of the deceased included only one-quarter of the bank balance.

A common situation is intermediate between these two extremes. The analysis of such an account was suggested by Megarry J[5] in the following terms:

> It may be that the correct analysis is that there is an immediate gift of a fluctuating and defeasible asset consisting of the chose in action for the time being constituting the balance in the bank account.

In *Sillars v IRC*[6] there was a joint bank account in the joint names of the deceased and her two daughters. Dr John Avery Jones, sitting as Special Commissioner, held that the nature of this account was of this intermediate nature described by Megarry J. The understanding between the deceased and her daughters was that any one of the three named account holders could draw funds, when funds were required. It was, thus, neither an account regarded by the family as exclusively for one account holder, nor was it an account that could correctly be analysed as consisting of separate discrete funds.

The basis of the inheritance tax charge at death is a charge on what is specified in statute as constituting the estate of the deceased. Statute[7] states:

Meaning of estate

> A person who has a general power which enables him . . . to dispose of any property . . . shall be treated as beneficially entitled to the property or money; and for this purpose 'general power' means a power or authority enabling the person by whom it is exercisable to appoint or dispose of property as he thinks fit.

Adopting the analysis of Megarry J to a bank account of this nature, the deceased clearly has "general power" as defined to dispose of the whole of the bank balance. Hence, for inheritance tax purposes, the entire balance in the joint bank account was in the estate of the deceased. (It is also, of course, in the estate of the survivor.)

Dr Avery Jones suggested that a second analysis is also possible. Each deposit that had been made by the deceased into this joint bank account was, in essence, a gift as the daughter was able to withdraw funds from the account at will. However, the deceased retained the power to withdraw the deposits he made and hence, each deposit was a gift with reservation.[8] On this analysis, also, the entire balance on the joint bank account was chargeable to inheritance tax at the death of the deceased.

[1] [1998] STC (SCD) 110 per B M F O'Brien at 113, construing "general power" in IHTA 1984, s 5(2).
[2] [1949] Ch 278, [1949] 1 All ER 92.
[3] [1998] STC (SCD) 110.
[4] [1997] STC (SCD) 58.
[5] In *Re Figgis, Roberts v MacLaren* [1969] 1 Ch 123 at 149.
[6] [2004] STC (SCD) 180. The decision was followed in *Perry v IRC* [2005] STC (SCD) 474.
[7] IHTA 1984, s 5(2).
[8] FA 1986, s 102: see Chapter 41.

Posthumous acquisition

[40.05] The general rule in IHTA 1984, s 4 means that property added to the estate after the death will not be subject to tax. This is of importance where it cannot be known which of two or more deceased persons survived the other or others. For IHT purposes they are assumed to have died at the same instant.[1]

EXAMPLE

Suppose A left his residuary estate to his son B and they are both killed outright in a road accident, tax will be chargeable on the transfers made on their deaths by A and B. However, since A and B are deemed to have died simultaneously the property passing from A to B will be taxed on A's death as property forming part of his estate immediately before his death, but not on B's since the property did not form part of his estate at that time but only later.

This rule applies only where it cannot be known which of A and B died first. Where the order of deaths is known and B survives A there will be a transfer by A to B and then one by B, although the latter may qualify for quick succession relief.

[40.05] Death

This rule does not change the general principle but that what is in the estate at death is computed on the accruals basis. Hence, any interest earned on a bank account or any dividend on a shareholding is included in the value of the estate where it accrued during the period up to the date of death. The interest, or dividend, received at a date after the date of death is apportioned to the period before the date of death (which is part of the estate at death) and the period after the date of death (on which interest tax is not charged).[2] This rule is in contrast to the rule that applies for income tax. Income tax is charged by reference to the date on which interest is paid (or credited to an account) or a dividend becomes payable. The mismatch between the treatment of inheritance tax and the treatment for income tax is mitigated by relief for inheritance tax paid being applied against the personal representative's income tax liability.[3]

Simon's Taxes I4.101, 102; Foster's Inheritance Tax D1.01, 02.

[1] IHTA 1984, s 4(2).
[2] IRC v Henderson's Executors (1931) 16 TC 282. See supra, § **14.01**.
[3] TA 1988, s 699.

Exemption—members of armed forces

[40.06] IHT is not chargeable on the death of a person dying from a wound inflicted, an accident occurring or a disease contracted or aggravated while a member of the armed forces of the Crown, if the deceased was on active service or on service of a warlike nature or involving the same risks.[1] Service in Northern Ireland is currently regarded as coming within this exemption[2] as was active service in the Falkland Islands.[3]

A person dies "from" a wound if he dies earlier than he otherwise would have done. In *Barty-King v Ministry of Deffence*,[4] the executors of the late fourth Duke of Westminster were successful in obtaining a court order requiring the Ministry of Defence to certify that the death of the Duke on 25 February 1967 was as a consequence of a wound he sustained on 18 July 1944 when he was a Lieutenant Colonel in command of a cavalry regiment in action against the enemy. The estate of the fourth Duke of Westminster was, thus, exempt from inheritance tax.

The exemption applies only on death but covers all property transferred on death under IHTA 1984, s 4 including settled property in which he had a life interest.

[1] IHTA 1984, s 154(1).
[2] See also extra-statutory concession F5; **Foster's Inheritance Tax Division U2**.
[3] *Simon's Tax Intelligence* 1982, p 271.
[4] [1979] STC 218, [1979] 2 All ER 80.

Valuation of estate on death

[40.07] The rule that on death a person is deemed to make a transfer of all the value of his estate immediately before the death[1] is substantially modified when it comes to valuation. Changes in the value of the estate which have occurred by reason of the death are taken into account as if they had occurred before the death.[2] Such changes are (a) additions to the property comprised in the estate, such as lump sums payable to the estate under pension schemes, and (b) any increase or decrease of the value of the property in the estate. Thus the death of a proprietor of or a partner in a business frequently causes loss of goodwill, and this reduces the value of his business or his partnership share. If life assurance results in a sum being payable to the estate (as opposed to the beneficiaries), this payment forms part of the estate for valuation purposes. Similarly, if a company has taken out key man assurance and thereby receives a sum of money by virtue of the death of the deceased, this receipt is taken into account in assessing the value of any shares in the company that are in the estate of the deceased.

However, it is provided that "the termination on the death of any interest or the passing of any interest by survivorship" does not fall within this special valuation rule. On the death of a joint tenant his interest passes to the surviving joint tenants; in valuing the right of the deceased joint tenant the fact of his death is to be ignored since otherwise the value would be nil.[3] This provision may also be meant to ensure that life interests in settled property are valued in full.

Simon's Taxes I4.114; Foster's Inheritance Tax D1.14.

---

[1] IHTA 1984, s 4. For the general valuation rules see infra, Chapter 46. For deduction of liabilities see infra, §§ **45.20** et seq.
[2] IHTA 1984, s 171. For the effect on the value of life policies, see infra, § **40.08**.
[3] Problems arise if an option expires on the death of an option holder.

Property excluded from estate at death

[40.08] The general notion of an estate is modified on death in the following ways:

(1) *Excluded property.* Excluded property does not form part of the estate immediately before the death.[1]

(2) *Cash options under approved annuity schemes.* Where on a person's death a pension becomes payable to his widow or dependant and, under the terms of the contract or scheme, a sum of money might at his option be payable instead to his personal representatives, the mere fact that the sum could be so paid—so that he could be said to have a general power over it—is not sufficient to cause it to form part of his estate.[2] However, where the option is exercised and the sum is paid it will form part of the estate. This exception is stated to apply only where the scheme is approved or is an approved personal pension plan;[3] where the scheme is not so approved therefore the sum of money will form part of the estate whether or not the option is exercised.[4]

[40.08] Death

(3) *Overseas pensions.* In valuing a person's estate there is to be left out of account any pensions payable under a fund falling within the Government of India Act 1935, s 273 or the Overseas Pensions Act 1973, s 2. Sums payable to his estate on his death are exempt from tax.[5]

(4) Further, pensions payable under certain schemes, including sums payable on death and returned contributions, are to be treated as paid by the government of the country in which the colonial service was performed even though the obligation to pay them has been assumed by a fund in this country.[6] The effect is simply to alter the situs of the pensions and so, where the deceased was not domiciled here, to bring them into the category of excluded property under IHTA 1984, s 6(1).[7]

(5) *Reverter to settlor.* Settled property in which the deceased had a life interest is not taken into account if it thereby reverts to the settlor and the settlor is still alive[8] unless the settlor acquired the reversion for money or money's worth;[9] infra, §§ **42.17–42.18**. The exclusion does not apply, so tax will be due, if the reversionary interest has itself been settled after[10] March 1981 and this is how it comes to revert to the settlor.

(6) *Reverter to settlor's spouse.* Settled property in which the deceased had a life interest is not taken into account if it thereby reverts to the spouse of the settlor, unless the spouse was not domiciled in the UK at the time of death. The spouse must become beneficially entitled to the property on the death, a requirement which is satisfied whether the entitlement is absolute or to a beneficial interest in possession in property remaining settled. Spouse includes widow or widower if the settlor died less than two years before the deceased; infra, §§ **42.17–42.18**. The special restrictions on settled and purchased reversionary interests apply here also.[11]

(7) *Trustee's annuity.* An interest in possession which the deceased had in settled property and to which he was entitled as remuneration for his services as trustee is not taken into account to the extent that it represents a reasonable amount of remuneration:[12] infra, § **42.21**.

(8) *Pension and annuity.* If the deceased had an interest in various types of superannuation or under funds or schemes, that interest is left out of account provided it does not result from the application of any benefit provided otherwise than by way of a pension or an annuity (eg a lump sum[13]).

(9) *Conditional exemption.* Works of art, any other objects and land may enjoy conditional exemption on a transfer on death; if they qualify they are left out of account; infra, § **44.27**.

(10) *Timber.* The value of timber may be left out of account until such time as the timber is sold; it is then restored to the estate unless there has been another transfer on death in the meantime; infra, § **44.35**.

(11) *Surviving spouse trust charged to estate duty.* Under estate duty law if property was left on trust with a life interest to the surviving spouse, as for example where she had only a life interest, the property was exempt from estate duty on the death of the surviving spouse. Where the first death occurred before 13 November 1974, the settled property is exempt from IHT on the death of the surviving spouse.[14]

(12) *Exempt transfers.* Transfers to a surviving spouse, to certain heritage bodies, to charity and to political parties, are exempt transfers on death; infra, Chapter 43. Values which are the subject of exempt transfers do not form part of the estate on death. Other exempt transfers, most notably £3,000 of value transferred in one year, do not apply on death.

(13) *Survivorship clauses.* Property left to a person contingently upon his surviving a period of time may be treated as not forming part of his estate if he fails to survive that period—see infra, § **42.13**. This avoids the second charge that would arise on the death of the beneficiary, a form of complete quick succession relief built in by the testator.

(14) *Not transfers of value.* Certain transfers by way of disposition are declared not to be transfers of value. As the transfer on death is not deemed to be a disposition these exclusions do not apply,[15] supra, § **39.14** ff.

Cross references to other works:

(1) Excluded property—**Simon's Taxes I4.121; Foster's Inheritance Tax D1.21.**
(2) Cash options under approved annuity schemes—**Simon's Taxes I4.125; Foster's Inheritance Tax D1.25.**
(3) Overseas pensions—**Simon's Taxes I4.126; Foster's Inheritance Tax D1.26.**
(4) Reverter to settlor—**Simon's Taxes I5.252, 734; Foster's Inheritance Tax E2.52; E7.34.**
(5) Reverter to settlor's spouse—**Simon's Taxes I5.253, 734; Foster's Inheritance Tax E2.53; E7.34.**
(6) Trustee's annuity—**Simon's Taxes I5.256; Foster's Inheritance Tax E2.56.**
(7) Pension and annuity—**Simon's Taxes I4.125; Foster's Inheritance Tax D1.25.**
(8) Conditional exemption—**Simon's Taxes I7.511–515; I10.122; Foster's Inheritance Tax G5.11–15; K1.22.**
(9) Timber—**Simon's Taxes Division I7.4; Foster's Inheritance Tax Division G4.**
(10) Surviving spouse trust charged to estate duty—**Simon's Taxes I5.921–926; Foster's Inheritance Tax E9.21–26.**
(11) Exempt transfers—**Simon's Taxes I4.111; Foster's Inheritance Tax D1.11.**
(12) Survivorship clauses—**Simon's Taxes I4.453; I5.264, 340; I12.905; Foster's Inheritance Tax D4.53; E2.64; E3.40; M9.05.**

---

[1] IHTA 1984, s 5(1). This rule does not mean that the value of excluded property is always ignored. If a UK domiciled husband has a non-UK domiciled wife and each has shares in an unquoted foreign company, the wife's holding is treated as related property to that of the husband in assessing the value of the husband's shares at death, even though the wife's shareholding is excluded property.
[2] IHTA 1984, s 152.
[3] Approval is given under TA 1988, ss 619–621. Personal pension plans are authorised by TA 1988, ss 630–655, ITEPA 2003, ss 7, 224, 308, 601.
[4] See supra, § **38.20**.

[40.08] Death

5   IHTA 1984, s 153.
6   IHTA 1984, s 153(2).
7   Infra, § **49.14**.
8   IHTA 1984, s 54(1).
9   IHTA 1984, s 53(3).
10 IHTA 1984, s 54(2).
11 IHTA 1984, ss 54(3), 53(5).
12 IHTA 1984, s 90.
13 IHTA 1984, s 151(2); see also F(No 2)A 1987, s 98(4). Inland Revenue Pension Schemes Office model rule 11.17 provides that a lump sum death benefit arising under that rule does not attract a charge to inheritance tax (*Simon's Weekly Tax Intelligence* 1995, p 1361).
14 IHTA 1984, Sch 6, para 2 applying FA 1994, s 5(2). See also extra-statutory concession F13 when the first death was before 12 March 1952 and the estate was exempt as the property of a common seaman, marine or soldier who died in the service of the Crown; **Foster's Inheritance Tax Division U2**.
15 However, a waiver of remuneration or dividends (supra, § **39.20**) does not have to be by disposition; quaere whether these are therefore exempt on death if effected by will.

Loss on sale of property after death

[40.09] Although property is valued at the date of death, relief is available where the property is realised for a lower value within a certain period from the death; the lower value being substituted. This relief applies only to certain securities—where the loss arises on a sale within one year, infra, § **45.12**; and interests in land—where the loss arises on a sale within three years, infra, § **45.15**. Relief is also available where property is valued by reference to related property and is later sold; here the related property valuation may be undone if the sale is within three years; infra, § **45.09**.

Simon's Taxes I8.102.

Life policies in the estate at death

[40.10] On the death of the life assured, the proceeds of the policy will be payable to the person owning the policy. If that person is the life assured, the proceeds will be paid to his personal representatives, will form part of his estate and so will be the subject of the transfer of value he is deemed to have made immediately before death. If that person is not the life assured the proceeds do not form part of the estate of the life assured.

If the beneficial owner of the policy is not the life assured, the policy is not part of the estate of the life assured but of the beneficial owner. On the occasion of the death of that beneficial owner, the value of the policy is part of his estate subject to inheritance tax, under the usual rules.

On an inter vivos transfer of the policy the special valuation rule infra, § **40.10** may apply.

Modern practice is to write a life assurance policy in trust. This practice is routine in modern contracts for personal pension plans. Where a policy is written in trust, the proceeds of the policy are paid to the trustee and not to the estate. Hence, the proceeds payable at death do not form part of the estate of the deceased for inheritance tax purposes.

A further provision is aimed at insurance based IHT unification schemes. In determining the value of a person's estate immediately before his death no account is taken of any liability under or in connection with a life insurance policy made after 30 June 1986 unless the whole of the sum assured is part of the estate.[1] So if the deceased made a contract with the company that on his death the company would pay out a sum to a named person in return for a premium to be paid out of his estate on his death, the liability to the company is not deductible.

Simon's Taxes I4.147; Foster's Inheritance Tax D1.47.

---

[1] FA 1986, s 103(7).

Premiums as transfers of value

[40.11] Where a life policy has been taken out by the life assured who assigns the policy but pays the premiums, each premium payment will be a transfer of value, being the amount paid in respect of the premiums, grossed up as necessary. There is no provision deeming the transferor to have transferred a proportion of the policy proceeds as opposed to the amount of the premium.

Where a person pays a premium on a policy owned by another, that payment, although a transfer of value, may fall within one of the exemptions, in particular the exemption for normal and reasonable expenditure out of income; see infra, § **43.03**.[1] However, the rules relating to gifts with reservation and deduction of debts are designed to ensure that the policy proceeds will be included in the donor's estate if any interest is retained in the policy or any benefit enjoyed from it and that if they are not included in the donor's estate any borrowing in connection with the policy is not deductible.

Simon's Taxes I3.325; Foster's Inheritance Tax C3.25.

---

[1] IHTA 1984, s 21.

Associated operations in relation to life policies

[40.12] Annuities on wealthy persons' lives coupled with life assurance policies on those lives in the hands of relatives were long useful in avoiding estate duty. Such devices may fall foul of IHTA 1984, s 263.[1] This applies in the following terms:

Where:

(a) a policy of life insurance is issued in respect of an insurance made on or after 27 March 1974 or is on or after that date varied or substituted for an earlier policy; and

[40.12] Death

(b) at the time the insurance is made or at any earlier or later date an annuity on the life of the insured is purchased; and

(c) the benefit of the policy is vested in a person other than the person who purchased the annuity;

then, unless it can be shown that the purchase of the annuity and the making of the insurance (or, as the case may be, the substitution or variation) were not associated operations, the person who purchased the annuity shall be treated as having made a transfer of value by a disposition made at the time the benefit of the policy became so vested (to the exclusion of any transfer of value which, apart from this section, he might have made as a result of the vesting or of the purchase and the vesting being associated operations).

In practice operations will only be regarded as associated if the life policy has been issued on terms different from those which would have applied if the annuity had not been taken out or if there are exceptional circumstances, such as a very short life expectancy whether due to bad health or advanced age or the payer is very old and dies before the second payment is made. In essence the life policy must be issued on normal underwriting terms.

[1] See supra, §§ 39.28 et seq.

[40.13] When the life policy and the annuity are regarded as associated operations, not only will the exemption for normal and reasonable gifts be lost, but the two transfers will be elided and treated as a transfer of the total sums spent by the person purchasing the annuity.

EXAMPLE

M, an elderly millionaire on his death-bed, spends his £1m (without having a medical examination) with the L Assurance Co Ltd of the Bahamas on an annuity of £100,000 pa for the rest of his life. M could give this annuity to his only son, S, who could then assure M's life (without a medical examination) with the L Assurance Co Ltd for £960,000 with a first premium payable of £101,000; this could virtually be paid for out of the first annuity payment. If M then died, his estate shortly before his death will have been diminished by the value of the annuity given to S: but this diminution would have been small since the value of the annuity lost by him would have been small in view of his terminal state of health. S would receive £960,000 under the life assurance policy.

M is regarded as making a transfer of value to S. The transfer is treated as taking place when the benefit is so vested, so that the rule cannot be avoided by vesting the benefit of the policy in M who later assigns the policy. It will be seen that the rule does not require that benefit to be vested in that person beneficially.

The value thus transferred is whichever is the lesser of (a) the consideration given for the annuity *and* any premium paid or other consideration given for the policy on or before but not after, the transfer (£1,101,000) and (b) the value of the greatest benefit capable of being conferred at any time by the policy, calculated as if that time were the date of the transfer (£960,000); by taking the lower figure the legislation recognises the cost to M.

[40.14] The value of the benefit of the policy is that of the greatest benefit capable of being conferred *at any time* by the policy, so that if the benefit should vary under the terms of the policy, only the highest benefit will be taken; great practical problems arise over the valuation of with profits policies and unit-linked policies. There would appear to be no discounting of that value even though the sum is not payable until a future event, the death of the life assured.

Effect on lifetime transfers

[40.15] The death may affect lifetime transfers in four ways (infra, §§ 40.14–40.20):

Death within seven years—additional tax on chargeable transfers

[40.16] If the transferor has made a chargeable transfer of value, tax will have been paid at that time. However, if he dies within seven years additional tax may become due since the transfer falls to be taxed at death rates instead of lifetime rates.[1] The transferee is primarily liable,[2] a rule which avoids the problem of re-grossing up. The donor may provide that the additional liability is to be met from his estate or the donee may take out an insurance policy to cover the risk. Where the death was due to some tort, the additional tax may be recoverable by way of damages.[3]

When the death is not more than three years after the transfer, the full death rates will apply but with credit for the tax already paid. When the death is more than three but not more than four years later, there is a 20% reduction in the tax given by the death rate figure and a further 20% reduction for each of the next three years.[4] When the death rate figure would be less than the lifetime rate tax already charged, the lifetime tax is left to stand—there is no repayment of the lifetime tax.[5]

Where the rates of tax have changed between the date of the transfer and that of the death, the additional tax is calculated on the rates prevailing at the time of death but with full credit for the lifetime tax actually paid.[6]

EXAMPLE

In September 2005, A, whose cumulative total already exceeded the then nil-rate band, then settled on discretionary trusts shares worth £80,000, A agreeing to pay the tax. This would be grossed up at 20% to make a gross chargeable transfer of £100,000 and tax of £20,000.

(a) If A died in October 2005 the additional tax would be calculated using death rates on a transfer of £100,000, ie at 40% giving tax of £40,000 making the additional tax payable £20,000 (ie after allowing for the £20,000 already payable).
(b) If A died in May 2008, the additional tax would be calculated using the 2008–09 death rates.
(c) If A died in August 2009 the additional tax would be calculated using the 2009–10 rates but with a 20% reduction.

The effect of taper relief and the increase each year of the nil rate band means that the tax computed at death on a lifetime transfer is frequently less than the tax actually paid. Where this is the case, no further tax is charged but there is no repayment of tax.

By contrast, there are three circumstances under which death causes an increase of tax payable on a previous lifetime transfer. First, where the transfer was a potentially exempt transfer and becomes chargeable by virtue of the death and, with other transfers, exceeds the nil rate band. Second, where tapering relief is insufficient to reduce the tax charge below the lifetime rate of 20%. Third, where the property qualified for business or agricultural relief at the time of the lifetime transfer but does not qualify at the time of the death transfer.[7]

[40.16] Death

Simon's Taxes I3.511, 531–534, 705; Foster's Inheritance Tax C5.11, 31–34; C7.05.

1   IHTA 1984, s 7(2).
2   IHTA 1984, s 199(2).
3   *Davies v Whiteways Cyder Co Ltd* [1975] QB 262.
4   IHTA 1984, s 7(4).
5   IHTA 1984, s 7(5).
6   IHTA 1984, Sch 2, para 2.
7   See infra, §§ **45.11** and **45.19**. A fourth possibility is that the rates in force at the time of the death may be higher than those in force at the lifetime transfer.

Death within seven years—loss of potential exemption

[40.17] Transfers which are potentially exempt will become chargeable if the donor dies within seven years. The amount of tax will be determined by using the death rates prevailing at the time of the death, although the transfer is for most purposes treated as having taken place when it actually occurred.

Where the donor dies more than three years after the transfer the amount of tax, as distinct from the amount of value transferred, is reduced by 20% for each complete year survived.[1] Thus if the donor died five and a half years after the transfer, having made a potentially exempt transfer of £50,000 the death rate of, one assumes, 40%, ie tax of £20,000 is to be reduced to 40% of that rate, ie 16% or £8,000. Naturally if the donor's cumulative total does not pass the top of the nil rate band these problems are of no practical importance.

The tax due under this rule is due from the donee and so there is no grossing up to be carried out.

Where a potentially exempt transfer becomes chargeable in this way it is treated as a chargeable transfer as of the date at which it actually took place. This may mean that tax in respect of the later chargeable transfer will have been understated. It may also mean an adjustment in the total of chargeable transfers made by the deceased in the seven years before he established a trust without an interest in possession, (see infra, § **42.36**).

The concept of potentially exempt transfer is discussed at supra, § **39.02**. The nature of the charge to inheritance tax that arises when death occurs within seven years of the potentially exempt transfer is discussed at supra, **39.03**.

Simon's Taxes I3.531–534; Foster's Inheritance Tax C5.31–34.

1   IHTA 1984, s 7(4).

Relief for decline in value between transfer and death

[40.18] Where tax (under § **40.15** on potentially exempt transfers) and additional tax (under § **40.14** on chargeable transfers) becomes due because the transferor dies within seven years, that tax is generally calculated by reference to the value actually transferred so that the extent of liability (potential or actual) crystallises at the date of the transfer and later changes in value are normally ignored. There is no provision requiring a higher value to be taken when the asset has increased in value since the transfer. However, relief is available in limited circumstances if the property has declined in value since the death. This relief is only available when the property was the subject of a potentially exempt transfer. There is no relief when property transferred by a chargeable transfer reduces in value. In order to qualify for this relief, one of two conditions must be satisfied:

(1) since the transfer, the property has been held continuously by the transferee or his spouse; or
(2) the property has been sold by a "qualifying sale".

In 1 if the market value at the time of death is less than the market value at the time of the transfer, the value transferred is reduced by the decline in value for the tax or additional tax.[1] For property attracting agricultural or business relief the reduction is that remaining after applying these reliefs.[2] In 2 the same applies save that the market value at the date of the qualifying sale is taken rather than that at the time of death.[3] A sale is a qualifying sale if:

(a) it is at arm's length for a price freely negotiated at the time of the sale; and
(b) no person concerned as vendor (or having an interest in the proceeds of the sale) is the same as or connected with any person concerned as purchaser (or as having an interest in the purchase); and
(c) no provision is made, in, or in connection with the agreement for the sale, that the vendor (or any person having an interest in the proceeds of sale) is to have any right to acquire some or all of the property sold or some interest in or created out of it. This relief does not apply to tangible movable property which is a wasting asset.[4]

EXAMPLE

If the shares, originally worth £80,000 (see example supra, § **40.14**) had declined in value to £60,000 when A died in October 2004, the additional tax is calculated as if the value transferred (£100,000) were reduced by £20,000 to £80,000. This would make the tax due only £32,000 so that additional tax would be £12,000.

It will be noted that there is no recalculation of the original value transferred by the lifetime transfer so as to gross up from a figure of £60,000 rather than £80,000. This seems to follow from the form of the legislation.

Where there is a change in the property between the lifetime transfer and the death, there are special rules for the application of this relief. The rules differ for shares (infra, § **40.22**), for land (infra, § **40.23**) and for other property (infra, § **40.24**).

Relief under IHTA 1984, s 131 only applies where a failed PET exceeds the IHT nil rate band at death. If the failed PET is less than the IHT nil rate band, there is no relief for the loss of value of the PET even though the PET is taken into account in computing IHT payable at death. This can be illustrated by comparing Example 1 with Example 2:

[40.18] Death

EXAMPLE 1

Alan dies on 16 February 2008 with an estate of £860,000.

Alan had made a gift of £240,000 on 25 April 2006. The donee invested this unwisely and the investments purchased were worth £140,000 on 16 February 2008.

IHT computation:

		£
Estate at death		860,000
Failed PET (ignoring AE)		240,000
		1,100,000

IHT payable thereon:

£300,000 @ 0%	–
£800,000 @ 40%	320,000

No relief under IHTA 1984, s 131 as tax on failed PET is £nil.

EXAMPLE 2

Alan dies on 16 February 2008 with an estate of £240,000. Alan had made a gift of £860,000 on 25 April 2006. The donee invested this unwisely and the investments purchased were worth £760,000 on 16 February 2008.

IHT computation:	£
Estate at death	240,000
Failed PET (ignoring AE)	860,000
	1,100,000
IHT payable on estate at death	
£240,000 @ 40%	96,000
IHT payable on failed PET	
£300,000 @ 0%	–
£560,000 @ 40%	224,000
Less: relief under IHTA 1984, s 131	
£100,000 @ 40%	(40,000)
	184,000
IHT payable	280,000

Simon's Taxes I3.361–364; Foster's Inheritance Tax C3.61–64.

[1] IHTA 1984, s 131. This does not affect the value for tax on the original transfer. Market value is defined by IHTA 1984, s 140(2).
[2] IHTA 1984, s 131(2A).
[3] IHTA 1984, s 131(3). These restrictions are the same as IHTA 1984, s 176; infra, § 45.09.
[4] IHTA 1984, s 132.

[40.19] Relief when property altered: shares.

Capital payments to which the transferee or his spouse becomes entitled in respect of the shares, for example bonus issues, have to be brought into account and are added to the market value at the date of the death or sale;[1] conversely, a reduction is to be made if any calls have been made.[2] The transferee or his spouse are treated as retaining their shares notwithstanding certain alterations such as reorganisation or amalgamation or takeover.[3]

Effect on lifetime transfers [40.20]

Where there has been a transfer of value by a close company under s 94(1) or an alteration in the rights attached to any unquoted shares or unquoted debentures and so a deemed transfer by the company and a transfer of value by the participators under IHTA 1984, s 98(1) the market value at the relevant date is treated as increased;[4] the amount of the increase is the reduction in value attributable to the transfer under IHTA 1984, s 94(1) or s 98(1) assuming it had occurred *before* the transfer now subject to additional tax.[5] So if A gave B shares and later value flows out of these shares to C, that decrease must be added back. This hypothetically timed increase is to be reduced by any increase in the value of the estate of the transferor or his spouse[6] and is not to affect the value of the shares at the time of the chargeable transfer.[7]

Simon's Taxes I3.365, 366; Foster's Inheritance Tax C3.65, 66.

---

[1] IHTA 1984, s 133(1).
[2] IHTA 1984, s 134.
[3] IHTA 1984, s 135; see now TCGA 1992, s 127 and associated provisions, supra, Chapter 21. Allowance is made where value is paid or received on the changeover.
[4] IHTA 1984, s 136; on meaning of quoted and unquoted see IHTA 1984, s 272.
[5] IHTA 1984, s 136(2).
[6] IHTA 1984, s 136(3).
[7] IHTA 1984, s 136(4).

[40.20] Relief when property altered: land

If the interest in land is not at both critical dates the same in all respects and with the same incidents and/or the land is not in the same state and with the same incidents, the market value is increased or reduced to take account of what its value would have been if it had remained unaltered.[1]

If the interest was worth £12,000 but has become subject to a restrictive covenant which reduces its value to £10,000 and, at the relevant time, the land freed from the covenant would be worth £13,000 but subject to it is worth £10,500, then the market value for this relief is £13,000 and since that exceeds the original market value of £12,000 the relief does not apply.

If compensation is received under some enactment for a reduction in the value of the interest, that sum is added to the market value at the relevant time just as bonus issues are added in the case of shares.[2]

Leases which, at the time of the chargeable transfer had no more than 50 years to run are subject to a special rule to offset the inevitable reduction in value due to the passing of time. The market value is increased by the amount by which the value of the lease is treated as having wasted between the two dates, the percentage table from CGT being used.[3]

Relief when property altered: other property

Where the property is not in all respects the same at the time of the chargeable transfer and the relevant date the market value is ascertained as if the change had not occurred.[4] Where benefits in money or money's worth have been derived from the property and those benefits are in excess of a reasonable

1669

[40.20] Death

return on its value at the time of the chargeable transfer, the excess is added back and any effect of those benefits on the transferred property is ignored.[5]

Simon's Taxes I3.367, 368; Foster's Inheritance Tax C3.67, 68.

[1] IHTA 1984, s 137.
[2] IHTA 1984, s 137(2).
[3] IHTA 1984, s 138, TCGA 1992, Sch 8, para 1.
[4] IHTA 1984, s 139.
[5] IHTA 1984, s 139(4).

Transfer undone by court order

[40.21] Where a transfer of value is undone by an order made under Inheritance (Provision for Family and Dependants) Act 1975, s 10 the transfer of value is treated as if it had never taken place. Hence, any tax paid is to be repaid or, if unpaid, to cease to be payable; the transfer on death is charged as if the previous transfer had not been made but the money or property recovered does form part of the estate for the purpose of the transfer on death. No time limit applies.[1]

Simon's Taxes I4.441–443; Foster's Inheritance Tax D4.41–43, 47.

[1] IHTA 1984, s 146.

Events after death

Disclaimers and rearrangements

[40.22] Where within two years of a death the disposition on death is varied or a benefit disclaimed, neither the variation nor the disclaimer is a transfer of value. The variation is treated as if made by the deceased, as though the benefit had never been conferred.[1] For the inheritance tax exemption to apply, a variation must be within two years of the death and must be carried out by an instrument in writing made by the beneficiaries affected. From 1 August 2002, the deed must incorporate an election[2] that the variation is to have effect for inheritance tax purposes. (Alternatively the parties can choose to omit the election and thereby make the deed a transfer of value, without its effect being backdated to death for the purpose of computing IHT liabilities.) The election (and, hence, normally the deed) must be signed by the personal representatives if the variation results in additional tax being payable.[3] However, statute[4] forces the personal representatives to sign the deed when required to do so by the parties to the deed, unless the assets they hold are insufficient to pay the additional tax. An election for CGT,[5] if made, must also be incorporated within the deed. It is possible to elect for IHT but choose not to elect CGT; such an arrangement is frequently advantageous if the increase in value of the assets diverted since the date of death is less than the CGT annual exempt amount available to the personal representatives.

In principle, it is possible that the conduct of the beneficiary is such as to constitute a disclaimer.[6] As the statutory provisions requiring a written election refer consistently to a deed, it would appear that a disclaimer made within 24 months of the death has IHT effect without a written election.

The provision that IHT is calculated as if the deed of variation had been effected at death is applied, notwithstanding that benefit has arisen under the succession. However, this will not be so if consideration other than another right in the succession is provided.[7] So a variation in return for £15,000 would not be within these rules whereas a variation in return for an interest under the will worth £15,000 would be. A transfer to the deceased's widow in return for property already owned by her would not be within these rules and it is at this arrangement that the provision is aimed.

If a beneficiary of a will dies before a variation is made, the legal personal representatives of the beneficiary (the second deceased) may enter into a variation of the disposition of the estate of the first deceased. Where this variation reduces the entitlement of any beneficiary of the second deceased, then the Revenue requires evidence of the consent of the beneficiary of the second deceased to the variation. This can be given by being a party to the variation, or by producing other written evidence of consent.[8]

The statutory provision[9] refers to a variation of a disposition "whether effected by will, under the law relating to intestacy or otherwise". In the Revenue view, the words "or otherwise" bring within the rules the automatic inheritance of a deceased owner's interest in jointly held assets by the surviving joint owner(s).

Where a variation results in property being held in trust for a person for a period ending within two years of the death that person's interest is disregarded,[10] except that the variation does not have the intended IHT effect if made in the three months after the date of death.[11] So if property is held under the variation of D's will for A for life with remainder to B and A dies or releases his interest within two years of D's death the property is treated as if it had passed direct from D to B. This result applies only where the parties have elected to treat the variation as made by D.

The exemption in s 142 applies to all property in the deceased's estate immediately before his death, including property in which the deceased had a joint interest[12] and also excluded property. Settled property in which the deceased had an interest in possession and gifts subject to a reservation where the reservation still exists at the death are, however, not included.

In *Russell v IRC* it was held that a further deed varying a prior deed was not entitled to even though expressed to be supplemental to the prior deed and fulfilling the other requirements of this section.[13] Knox J stressed that the second deed substantially altered the beneficiaries' rights under the first and did not merely increase them.[14] The result would have been different if the first deed could be construed in the way the parties hoped or[15] had contained an error which could be the subject of a claim for rectification, in which case there would have been no second deed.[16]

[40.22] Death

A Special Commissioner in *Glowacki (dec'd) v R & C Comrs*[17] held that s 142 did not have effect so as to convert a testamentary into a lifetime gift.[18]

When a deed of variation (or a disclaimer) is made, the deed operates similarly for capital gains tax;[19] that is, those who receive assets under the terms of the variation have the value at the date of death as the base value for subsequent disposals. Curiously, there is no provision for a deed of variation to have any particular income tax effect. Hence, income arising between the date of death and the date of the deed of variation arises to the personal representatives during the period of administration (for distribution in accordance with the treatment that arises under the will or intestacy) and to the beneficiaries under the original will or intestacy until the date of the deed of variation is entered into. There is no provision in relation to TA 1988, s 660B; so if a parent varies the grandparent's will in favour of the parent's infant children, the variation will be effective for IHT and CGT but does not defeat the charge to income levied on the parent in respect of income arising to his minor unmarried children by virtue of the deed of variation of which he has been a party.[20]

The effect of the CGT provisions dealing with variation of an inheritance is limited. The House of Lords held that a trust created by deed of variation was a settlor interested trust for CGT purposes in *Marshall v Kerr*.[21] The Revenue consider that the IHT provisions are separate and are not affected by this decision.[22] Hence, a trust created by a deed of variation is not treated for inheritance tax purposes as a gift with reservation by the party to the deed of variation. A stamp duty Category M exemption certificate is required where a deed of variation alters the destination of stock, shares or marketable securities; in all other cases, no stamp duty exemption certificate is required.[23]

Simon's Taxes I3.134; I4.411–419; Foster's Inheritance Tax C1.34; D4.11–19, 24; STP [9.229]–[9.250]; [11.307]–[11.309].

---

[1] IHTA 1984, ss 17, 142. The Revenue accept that IHTA 1984, s 142 applies where a residuary legatee makes a partial disclaimer under Scots Law: Inland Revenue statement of practice E18.
[2] IHTA 1984, s 142(2).
[3] IHTA 1984, s 142(2A)(b).
[4] IHTA 1984, s 142(2A) extenso.
[5] TCGA 1992, s 62.
[6] For a case in which conduct was considered, but held not to constitute a disclaimer see *Cook v IRC* [2002] STC (SCD) 318.
[7] IHTA 1984, s 142(3). On dangers of this trap where a testamentary gift to children is routed back through a surviving spouse see *Capital Taxes and Estate Planning Quarterly* 1991, p 1.
[8] Revenue Interpretation RI 127, Inland Revenue Tax Bulletin, December 2004, p 1170.
[9] IHTA 1984, s 142(1).
[10] IHTA 1984, s 142(4).
[11] *Frankland v IRC* [1997] STC 1450, CA.
[12] *Law Society's Gazette*, 22 May 1985, p 1454, *Simon's Tax Intelligence* 1985, p 298; **Foster's Inheritance Tax X6.30.**
[13] *Russell v IRC* [1988] STC 195, [1988] 2 All ER 405.

[14] [1988] STC 195.
[15] As in *Schnieder v Mills* [1993] STC 430.
[16] On rectification see *Lake v Lake* [1989] STC 565, *Matthews v Martin* [1991] STI 418 and *Racal Group Services Ltd v Ashmore* [1994] STC 416. The Revenue accepts that the document does not have to be expressed to be by way of variation of the will provided it identifies the disposition to be varied and varies it. A variation is treated as irrevocable so that a variation of a variation is not entitled to the protection of IHTA 1984, s 142. Law Society's Gazette, 22 May 1985, p 1454, *Simon's Tax Intelligence 1985*, p 298; **Foster's Inheritance Tax X6.30**.
[17] (2007) SpC 631.
[18] That case was taken because the timing of the gifts affected how the inheritance tax liability fell on the beneficiaries.
[19] TCGA 1992, s 62(6). FA 2002, s 52 mirrors s 115 by providing that post-31 July 2002 deeds have effect for CGT without the necessity for an election.
[20] TA 1988, ss 660B(1)(*a*) and 660C(1).
[21] [1994] STC 638.
[22] Revenue Interpretation RI 101 *Simon's Weekly Tax Intelligence* 1995, p 303. Revised version: Inland Revenue Tax Bulletin, December 2004, p 1169.
[23] Inland Revenue IHT Newsletter April 2004, p 4.

Soutter's Executry v IRC

[40.23] In 1995, the Revenue published its view[1] that if a beneficiary dies during the period of administration of the deceased under whose will (or intestacy) he benefits, the legal personal representatives of that beneficiary may enter into a variation and sign the form. If the variation reduces the rights of any beneficiary of the second deceased, the Revenue will require written evidence of that beneficiary's consent. However, in 2001 the Revenue changed its view stating:[2] that a deed of variation, to be valid, "must be implemented in the real world." The Revenue newsletter gives the following example:

> Under the will of A, B has an interest in possession in settled property, and on its cesser the beneficial interest in possession passes to C. In other words A leaves a life interest in property to B, with remainder to C. Following B's death within two years of A, C makes a deed of variation—still within that two-year period, which purports to vary the will of A by redirecting B's interest to C or to extinguish it totally. In the real world B's interest does not exist, there is nothing for the deed to bite upon, and so section 142 simply cannot apply. If the situation had been that it was possible for B's executors to disclaim his life interest as a matter of general law, then that should fall within the protection of section 142.

It is suggested that the Revenue's view as stated in this 2001 article is incorrect. The provision of s 142 is a deeming provision; a declaration that inheritance tax is levied as if the deceased had made certain provisions in his will. On this view, there is no scope for any requirement of perceived "reality" in judging whether effect is given to those provisions, which are written into the deed of variation.[3]

The Revenue's view appears to have been upheld by the Special Commissioner in *Soutter's Executry v IRC*.[4]

[40.23] Death

Miss Soutter died on 11 November 1999. At the time of her death Miss Soutter was the sole proprietor of a house, where she resided with her friend Miss Mabel Elizabeth Greenlees. In the terms of a trust disposition and settlement by Miss Soutter, dated 11 August 1993, and registered in the Books of Council and Session on 12 November 1999, the day after Miss Soutter's death, Miss Greenlees was allowed, in the event of Miss Soutter predeceasing her, a free liferent and useful occupation of the house as long as Miss Greenlees wished to reside there.

Miss Greenlees survived Miss Soutter and continued to live at the house following Miss Soutter's death. Several months after Miss Soutter's death Miss Greenlees was diagnosed as being seriously ill and was taken to hospital, Carluke, where she died on 6 November 2000. Her personal possessions and furniture were still at the house on her death. The administration of Miss Soutter's estate had not been completed prior to Miss Greenlees' death.

As Miss Greenlees died within two years of Miss Soutter the executors and beneficiaries in Miss Soutter's estate and the executors and beneficiary in Miss Greenlees' estate agreed to enter into a deed of variation in Miss Soutter's estate in terms of IHTA 1984, s 142 removing the liferent provision in Miss Soutter's trust disposition and settlement. The deed of variation was submitted to the Revenue on 3 April 2001 and was acknowledged by the Revenue on 5 April 2001.

The Revenue refused to accept the deed of variation on the grounds that there was no interest that could be varied at the date the deed was made. The will of the deceased left a life interest to Miss Greenlee. That life interest came to an end at Miss Greenlee's death and did not exist when the deed of variation was made after her death. The Special Commissioner dismissed the executor's appeal, saying:

> The executors of a liferentrix have nothing they can vary. That situation is wholly different from an outright gift because the estate of the second deceased has received benefit and can refund it, presumably if the beneficiary who had received the funds agreed. But Miss Greenlees' executors did not succeed to anything. They had neither right, title or interest to any liferent. The liferent could only come into existence if the liferentrix survived the deceased. Miss Greenlees' executors could not have continued to receive the liferent so they had nothing to give up or vary. The liferent was not and could not be assigned to them. It is in that sense that a purported assignation of an expired liferent has no reality.[5]

---

[1] Revenue Interpretation RI 101.
[2] Inland Revenue Capital Taxes Office Newsletter, December 2001.
[3] See further Ralph Ray "Out of This World", Taxation 21 March 2002, p 594.
[4] [2002] STC (SCD) 385.
[5] At 388f.

Election by surviving spouse to redeem life interest on intestacy

[40.24] Where a surviving spouse elects to redeem the life interest given him under the intestacy legislation and the election is under those rules, the

Events after death [40.27]

consequent ending of that life interest is not treated as a transfer of value.[1] The normal effect of the termination of the interest is that there is a transfer of value equal to the value of the settled property save and to the extent that the person entitled to the interest in possession now becomes entitled to the capital.[2] This exception makes sure that there is no transfer of value even though the surviving spouse does not become entitled to the whole of the settled property.

Simon's Taxes I4.452; Foster's Inheritance Tax D4.52.

[1] IHTA 1984, ss 17, 145.
[2] IHTA 1984, s 53(2), infra, § **42.16**.

Payment out of property settled by will on trusts with no interest in possession

[**40.25**] Where the property was settled by the will and no interest in possession has yet vested in the property, tax is not chargeable. Instead tax applies as if the payment out of the trust had been made by the testator in his will.[1] When the death is on or after 22 March 2006, statute[2] provides that the "favoured treatment" (see Chapter 42) is applied where funds are passed to a trust for a bereaved minor or a disabled person within two years of death. This can be effected by a deed of variation.

Simon's Taxes I4.431–433.

[1] IHTA 1984, s 144.
[2] IHTA 1984, s 144(3) inserted by FA 2006, Sch 20 para 27.

Carrying out the testator's wishes

[**40.26**] A testator may express a wish that the legatee should transfer the property to someone else. If that wish is legally binding the transfer to that other is a transfer by the testator; if, however, it is not legally binding there would be a transfer by the testator followed by a transfer by the legatee. To avoid a double charge to tax the transfer is treated as made by the testator provided the transfer by the legatee is within two years of the death.[1]

Simon's Taxes I4.451; Foster's Inheritance Tax D4.51.

[1] IHTA 1984, ss 17, 143.

Inheritance (Provision for Family and Dependants) Act 1975

[**40.27**] Where an order is made by a court under this Act, IHT is charged as if the property had devolved on the death in accordance with the order.[1] In contrast to a situation where a deed of variation is made by the parties without

[40.27] Death

involvement of the court, the effect of a Court Order under I(PFB)A 1975 is that the amount and burden of IHT is altered automatically. No election is required and there is no time limit.[2] It is necessary for any Court Order so made to be endorsed on or annexed to the Grant of Probate or Letters of Administration.[3] Where the effect of the court order is to change the quantum of IHT payable, interest on the overpayment or underpayment runs from the date of the order.[4]

Simon's Taxes I4.441–447; Foster's Inheritance Tax D4.41–47.

[1] IHTA 1984, s 146; see also IHTA 1984, s 236(2), (3).
[2] I(PFD)A 1975, s 19(1).
[3] Section 19(2)(c).
[4] IHTA 1984, s 236(2).

Legitim

[40.28] Under Scots law a child is entitled to certain fixed rights in his parent's estate even against the surviving spouse, but cannot renounce those rights while still a minor. When the bequest to the spouse reduces the child's rights the executors may assume either that full rights of legitim will be claimed thus reducing the spouse's share (and increasing the IHT) or that the will will be allowed to stand. Any adjustments due when the child reaches 18 must be made.[1] If the person renounces his or her claim to legitim, tax is repaid to the estate with (non-taxable) interest.[2]

Simon's Taxes I4.464; Foster's Inheritance Tax D4.64.

[1] IHTA 1984, s 147.
[2] IHTA 1984, s 236(4).

Quick succession relief

[40.29] Where a person's estate is increased by a chargeable transfer—the first transfer—and the recipient dies within five years, the tax chargeable on his death—the second transfer—is reduced by a percentage of the tax paid in respect of the first.[1] The percentage is 100% for death within the first year and then drops by 20% a year.

The tax paid on the first transfer only qualifies for use later if, and to the extent that, it relates to the amount of increase in the estate.

EXAMPLE

In year 1 A dies. B inherits an asset worth £24,000; suppose tax is payable by A at a rate of 40% making a gross transfer of £40,000 including tax of £16,000.

If B then dies two and a half years later the amount available by way of credit on B's death will be 60% of tax at 40% on £24,000 (the increase in B's estate) ie £5,760.[2]

1676

This credit is available regardless of any change in the value of the asset given. It applies whenever there is an increase in B's estate and so whether what is given is an identifiable asset or cash.

In determining whether a person's estate has been increased, excluded property is to be left out of account. So if D died leaving property to A for life with remainder to B and then B predeceased A, no quick succession relief would be available on B's death for any IHT paid on D's death since B's reversion is excluded property.

Simon's Taxes I5.283, 292; Foster's Inheritance Tax E2.83, 92.

[1] IHTA 1984, s 141.
[2] There is no case for relief on the tax on the grossed-up value of £40,000 since B's estate was only increased by £24,000 and that is what he is now paying tax on.

Reliefs for earlier transfers of the same property by the same transferor

[40.30] With IHT reaching back to catch events that happened before death there was the risk of a dual charge to tax in certain circumstances. HMRC have made regulations[1] to cover three defined situations—and any similar ones. For a list of situations not covered see **Simon's Taxes I3.502; Foster's Inheritance Tax C5.02**.

The new regulations differ from the old capital transfer tax (CTT) rules for mutual transfers which had been part of that tax code from its early days.[2] The old CTT rules for mutual transfers were repealed for deaths and other transfers after 17 March 1986 in order to avoid the possibility of using the rules to convert a pre-1986 chargeable transfer into a potentially exempt transfer.[3] The IHT rules apply only where the second of the two transfers comes about on the death of the transferor (A). They require two sets of calculations and a comparison of the outcome. One set disregards the lifetime transfer; the other disregards the death transfer. The calculation giving the higher overall liability is preferred. When the two calculations give the same figure the first calculation is preferred.[4]

Simon's Taxes I3.502, 513, 534, 543–545; Foster's Inheritance Tax C5.02, 13, 34, 43–45.

[1] Inheritance Tax (Double Charges Relief) Regulations 1987, SI 1987/1130; Foster's Inheritance Tax, Division T2. See *Simon's Tax Intelligence* 1987, pp 506, 602.
[2] FA 1976, ss 87, 88.
[3] The old rules were CTTA 1984, ss 148, 149.
[4] SI 1987/1130, reg 8.

[40.31] Death

Potentially exempt transfers and death transfers of same property (reg 4)

[40.31] The first situation is where A makes a potentially exempt transfer[1] which proves to be a chargeable transfer by reason of A's death within seven years and, immediately before his death, A's estate includes property acquired by A from B after the A–B transfer and otherwise than for full consideration in money or money's worth.[2] A's death within seven years makes the A–B transfer chargeable instead of potentially exempt while the property returned forms part of A's estate and so is chargeable on A's death.

The property transferred by B may be the original property given or property which directly or indirectly represents that property.[3] It is hard to know whether to insist on giving these words meaning;[4] if A gives B a painting, must B give the identical one back? If A gives B money, must B give A money or will any property do—and must B be able to show that the money could in some way have been channelled into the property given to A? What is clear is that once the relevant property restored to A has been identified reg 4 requires that very property to be in A's estate on A's death and that it should be chargeable property on that death (and so not, for example, excluded property).

The rules then demand that two calculations of the total tax chargeable as a consequence of the death of A should be made. The first requires that in calculating the tax on the potentially exempt transfer one should disregard the value of the property given by A to B and then restored, so leaving it to be part of the death transfer. The second requires that one should disregard the same value in calculating the tax on the transfer on death, so leaving it to be taxed as an originally potentially exempt but now chargeable transfer.[5] Put more simply, one calculates the tax assuming that the value restored forms part of one transfer only. Where this results in two different figures the lower one is reduced to nil and the higher is taken; if the two figures are the same the transfer is treated as being part of the death transfer and not a potentially exempt transfer.[6]

EXAMPLE

This example is based on that issued by the Revenue as part of the Regulations but the material is rearranged.

The facts:

- July 1987: A makes a potentially exempt transfer of £100,000 to B.
- January 1988: A makes a chargeable transfer of £95,000—and pays IHT of £750.
- February 1988: A makes a further chargeable transfer of £45,000 and pays tax of £6,750.
- January 1990: B dies and the property transferred by the 1987 potentially exempt transfer returns to A.
- December 1992: A dies. His estate (value £300,000) includes the property restored to him in 1990 (still worth £100,000).

The first calculation assumes that the £100,000 forms part of A's death estate and is not chargeable as a potentially exempt transfer. A therefore has an estate on death of £300,000 but a lifetime cumulative total of £140,000. Tax on the death estate (ignoring quick succession relief under IHTA 1984, s 141) will be £116,000 which, when added to the additional tax due on the two chargeable transfers, because A dies within seven years, become liable to tax at death rates for 1992–93 (nil and nil), making a total of £116,000.

Reliefs for transfers of the same property [40.32]

The second calculation charges the £100,000 as a potentially exempt transfer (but with taper relief[7]) and reduces the estate on death to £200,000. Tax on the potentially exempt transfer will be nil. Tax at 1992–93 death rates on an estate of £200,000 with a lifetime cumulative total of £240,000 will give tax on the death of £80,000 but when the additional tax on the chargeable transfers is included, £10,050 and £4,050 (after taking account of the reduction in tax by reason of the number of years since the transfers and the higher cumulative total to take account of the £100,000 potentially exempt but actually chargeable transfer) gives a total for tax on death of £94,100.

As the first calculation gives the greater amount of tax it is preferred and tax is calculated for all purposes as if the potentially exempt transfer were reduced to nil. This has the curious consequence that no additional tax is due on the two chargeable lifetime transfers.

Simon's Taxes I3.513; Foster's Inheritance Tax C5.13.

---

[1] By definition therefore, but also expressly, the transfer must be on or after 18 March 1986.
[2] FA 1986, s 104(1)(a); Inheritance Tax (Double Charges Relief) Regulations 1987, SI 1987/1130, reg 4; **Foster's Inheritance Tax Division T2**.
[3] The term 'property' is defined as including part of any property; SI 1987/1130, reg 4.
[4] Contrast the care lying behind the formulation in FA 1986, s 103.
[5] SI 1987/1130, reg 4(4).
[6] SI 1987/1130, reg 8.
[7] Although the potentially exempt transfer qualifies for taper relief of 60% this does not affect the calculations since (a) the tax is nil anyway and (b) the reduction would be a reduction in tax and not in the value transferred.

Chargeable transfer and death transfer of same property (reg 7)

[40.32] The second situation is that in which A makes a chargeable transfer to B but dies within seven years and the property forms part of A's estate on his death having been returned by B.[1] The difference from the first situation is that the A–B transfer is a chargeable transfer not a potentially exempt transfer. As the A–B transfer must be made after 17 March 1986[2] the scope of this rule is not great. With the expansion of the concept of a potentially exempt transfer in 1987 the scope of this regulation is further reduced. Today its principal application will be where A sets up a discretionary trust of which he is an object and the trustees later advance property to him; however, this situation also falls within the gift with reservation rules dealt with in reg 5 and one might conclude that reg 5 would apply in priority.

Here the same principles are applied as in supra, § **40.30** with credit being given for the tax already paid in respect of the A–B transfer. One first disregards the lifetime transfer. Then one disregards the death transfer and one then compares the results. If the second calculation gives the higher figure that is that. If the first calculation gives the higher figure it is taken. If this leads to

1679

[40.32] Death

a reduction in the value transferred by the A–B chargeable transfer, there is nonetheless to be no change to A's cumulative total for the purpose of any discretionary trust charges under the rules outlined at infra, § **42.34** ff. In making these calculations credit is to be given for tax paid before the death.[3]

EXAMPLE

Again this uses the Revenue example which forms part of the regulations but sets the material out differently and follows rather than reproduces that example. The example assumes that the 1987–88 rates apply rather than any later actual ones; this is in order to facilitate checking against the Revenue text which is not easy to understand.

The facts:

- May 1986: S makes a gross transfer of £150,000 on discretionary trusts; tax at 1986–87 rates £13,750.
- October 1986: S settles shares worth £85,000 on T for life; under the rules then in force this is a chargeable transfer (would have been a potentially exempt transfer if made a year later); tax due under 1986–87 rates £19,500.
- January 1991: S makes a potentially exempt transfer to R of £20,000.
- December 1992: T dies; shares revert to S—no charge to tax; supra, § **40.06** (4).
- August 1993: S dies. His estate includes the shares (now worth £75,000); his other property is worth £144,000.

The first calculation treats the shares as part of the death estate. More than seven years have passed since May 1986, and so there is no additional tax. October 1986 gift is ignored[4]—no adjustment to tax already paid. January 1991 potentially exempt transfer attracts tax of £8,000.[5] The estate at death is £219,000.[6] The cumulative total of chargeable transfers in last seven years is £20,000 so tax would be £56,500, but this is reduced for the purpose of this calculation by £19,350 to £37,150 to take account of the lifetime tax already paid in respect of the shares.[7] This makes the total tax on death £45,150.

The second calculation treats the shares as settled on T in October 1986 and not part of the estate on death. May 1986 transfer is treated as in the first calculation. October 1986 chargeable transfer is followed by death within seven years but there is no additional tax.[8] January 1991 potentially exempt transfer attracts tax of £10,000 (potentially exempt transfer of £20,000 by person with pre-potentially exempt cumulative total of £235,000). Death estate is now £144,000 by person with cumulative lifetime total over last seven years of £105,000 (£85,000 and £20,000); this makes tax of £57,000 and so total tax of £65,000 due on death. In this instance no credit can be given for the inter vivos tax since it is restricted to the amount of tax paid on the death and as that amount is nil there is no credit.

The second calculation gives the higher figure and so is taken.

Simon's Taxes I3.513, 534; Foster's Inheritance Tax C5.13, 34.

---

[1] This is treated in the regulations as the fourth situation as it is not expressly listed in FA 1986, s 104 but relies on the "similar situations" power in s 104(1)(*d*).

[2] The position of A–B transfers made before 18 March 1986 is obscure. They are, by definition, chargeable rather than potentially exempt transfers. They are unable to use IHTA 1984, ss 147, 148 if the B–A transfer is on or after that date and yet are not covered by these Regulations.

Reliefs for transfers of the same property [40.33]

3 The credit is authorised by reg 7(5)(b); the example which follows assumes that the credit rules are relevant in determining the amounts under reg 7(4) since this is what the Revenue example assumes also. However, a case can be made for saying that the credit is not relevant to the calculations under para (4) and only comes into play when applying reg 7(5).
4 It will be noted that although A gave B shares worth £85,000 and the value of the property on return is only £75,000 one ignores the whole of the A–B transfer and does not seek to treat £10,000 of it as still chargeable. Presumably this is because what was restored by B was the entire holding.
5 Tax at 1987–88 rates on transfer of £20,000 by person with cumulative total of £150,000.
6 ie (£144,000 + £75,000).
7 The figure of £19,350 is the amount of the death tax which is attributable to the shares, ie £75,000/£219,000 × £56,500. The amount of lifetime tax was £19,500 but as the proportion of death tax attributable to the shares is less, that lesser figure is taken by way of credit.
8 Tax, after taper relief, would be £7,100 but as this is less than the tax already paid (£19,500), no additional tax is due.

Transfer and gift with reservation of same property (reg 5)

[40.33] The third situation covered by the regulations[1] is that in which there is a transfer of value which is also a gift with reservation under FA 1986, s 102 (infra, § **41.01**) but the property also forms part of the estate of the donor on death; an example is where A makes a gift to a discretionary trust of which he is a potential beneficiary and dies within seven years.[2] Here A's rights (or hopes) under the trust will bring him within s 102, as the property does not otherwise form part of his estate immediately before his death; the property was also the subject of a (chargeable) transfer when it was settled; the risk of a dual charge is therefore present. This situation is illustrated by the example in the regulations. The regulation also embraces the situation in which the gift with reservation ceases to be subject to a reservation in circumstances amounting to a potentially exempt transfer but the donor dies within seven years.[3]

As in the other regulations, calculations are made on the alternative assumptions that the s 102 charge applies or the charge on the original property applies and whichever assumption gives the higher tax is taken as the basis of liability. Where this leads to a reduction of the original inter vivos transfer the reduction is not to affect any discretionary trust charges arising before A's death if the transfer was chargeable when made.[4] Provision is also made for credit to be given for tax already paid on the original transfer to be set against the tax now charged on the assumption that the earlier transfer is to be ignored (or reduced).[5]

Simon's Taxes I3.543; Foster's Inheritance Tax C5.43.

1 Regulation 5 stemming from FA 1986, s 104(1)(b).
2 eg A gives a house to B but takes a life interest in it in circumstances which do not permit A to argue that A only gave B the reversion. This is not a situation in which

a double charge can arise since s 102 only applies if the property which is the subject of the gift with reservation would not otherwise be chargeable on death.
3   And so a charge arises under FA 1986, s 102(4).
4   Inheritance Tax (Double Charges Relief) Regulations 1987, SI 1987/1130, reg 5(4)(*b*); **Foster's Inheritance Tax, Division T2.**
5   SI 1987/1130, reg 5(4)(*a*).

Loanbacks

[40.34] Finally, the regulations provide for the situation in which A's estate is subject to a liability in favour of B but A's estate is unable to deduct that liability because of FA 1986, s 103 (see infra, §§ **45.23** ff). Broadly this rule applies where A makes a gift to B but B later lends the property (or equivalent wealth) back to A; the liability to repay is clearly for money's worth but s 102 bars the deduction.[1] This could lead to a double charge if the original gift is also chargeable, whether because it was a chargeable transfer all along or has become one because A dies within seven years. The usual alternative calculations are made—the one on the basis of disallowing the debt and ignoring the transfer, the other on the basis of charging the transfer but allowing the debt. Section 102 only applies where the loan is made after 17 March 1986;[2] the regulation only applies where the original transfer occurs after the same date.[3]

Simon's Taxes I3.545; Foster's Inheritance Tax C5.45.

1   Inheritance Tax (Double Charges Relief) Regulations 1987, SI 1987/1130, reg 6; **Foster's Inheritance Tax, Division T2.**
2   FA 1986, s 103(6).
3   SI 1987/1130, reg 6(2); this therefore leaves without any relief against dual charges any case where the loan is after 17 March 1986 but the gift was a chargeable transfer made before 18 March 1986. There is also no relief in any case where the loan is repaid within seven years of death and there is a charge under s 103(5).

Abatement of exemptions on death

[40.35] The exemptions in ss 18 and 23–28[1] are subject to a rule of abatement. The abatement applies where a transfer of value would be exempt but the beneficiary under the exempt transfer, known as the exempt beneficiary,[2] disposes of property not derived from the exempt transfer of value to settle the whole or part of a claim against the estate.[3] The abatement does not apply if the claim being settled is a liability which would be deductible in computing the value of the estate.[4]

Thus suppose that D leaves an estate worth £200,000 to his widow and that he has made chargeable lifetime transfers equal to the nil rate band. Suppose also that the son makes a claim under the Inheritance (Provision for Family and Dependants) Act 1975 which is settled at £50,000. Under the normal rules of administration of estates a payment would be made out of the estate to the son in satisfaction of his claim; this sum would not be deductible in computing the value of D's estate for IHT. The property remaining in the estate after satisfying the son's claim and the tax in respect of it would pass to the widow and be exempt but, as just seen, IHT would have been paid on the value needed to finance the payment to the son.

This result would, but for the abatement rule, be avoided if the widow were to pay the £50,000 out of her own money. The whole £200,000 would pass to her free of tax and her payment of £50,000 would be a PET.

To counter this choice of tax liabilities, IHTA 1984, s 29A provides that the reduction in the value of the exempt beneficiary's estate by the payment or, if less, the legacy to her,[5] is to be treated as a chargeable specific gift[6] (thus perhaps giving rise to grossing-up, infra: § **43.22** ff); to this extent the exemption is abated.

In determining the value of the exempt beneficiary's estate for this purpose, no deduction is to be made for the claim.[7] Moreover neither agricultural nor business reliefs are to be available for the property she transfers and no deduction is to be made for any tax borne by her.[8]

The term "claim" is not defined.

It will be noticed that this provision does not apply when the widow pays the son out of property derived from D's estate but the payment falls outside IHTA 1984, s 146 etc. The rationale for this is obscure.

Simon's Taxes I4.445, 446; Foster's Inheritance Tax D4.45, 46.

[1] IHTA 1984, s 29A(10) defines exempt gift; where the exemption extends up to a certain figure these rules apply only to the extent that the transfer is exempt.
[2] Defined in IHTA 1984, s 29A(10).
[3] IHTA 1984, s 29A(1).
[4] IHTA 1984, s 168(5).
[5] IHTA 1984, s 29A(2).
[6] IHTA 1984, s 29A(3).
[7] IHTA 1984, s 29A(4)(*b*)(i).
[8] IHTA 1984, s 29A(4)(*b*)(ii).

Pension fund

[**40.36**] When a person dies before age 75, any pension fund that passes at his death is exempt from inheritance tax.[1]

Commonly, a pension fund is used to purchase an annuity, on or before the pensioner's 75th birthday. Under the pension regime that applies from 6 April 2006[2] it is possible to retain a pension fund, even after attaining the age of 75. Periodic payments are then made by withdrawals from the fund, rather than the purchase of an annuity. Such a pension arrangement is known as "an alternatively secured pension". When a member of a pension scheme dies after age 75 whilst receiving an alternatively secured pension the value of the funds supporting the alternatively secured pension are liable to IHT.[3] In calculating the liability to IHT at the death, any part of the fund that is used to pay a pension to a dependent is excluded.[4] IHT is, then, chargeable on the value of the alternatively secured pension fund at the time the dependants' pension ceases.[5] (If there are no dependants, the whole fund is charged at the date of death of the member.)[6] The fund charged at the cessation of the pension to the dependant is taxed at the rates that would have applied on death of the member, calculated as if that amount had been a chargeable transfer on the death of the member and formed the highest part of the value of the member's chargeable estate.[7] Provision is also made for the situation where a dependant of the scheme member himself dies whilst receiving an alternatively secured pension after age 75.[8]

An omission to exercise a right under a pension scheme is treated as not being a transfer of value, and, hence, no charge to inheritance tax arises, in two circumstances. The first circumstance is when a member of a pension scheme omits to take his pension at a time when his life expectancy is seriously impaired resulting in enhanced benefits being paid on their death.[9] The second circumstance is when a member of a pension scheme omits to take his pension at the time that his life expectancy is seriously impaired and death benefits are paid to a dependant or charity.[10]

---

[1] IHTA 1984, s 151.
[2] See Chapter 32.
[3] IHTA 1984, s 151A inserted by FA 2006, Sch 26, para 4.
[4] IHTA 1984, s 151A(3)(b) & (4).
[5] IHTA 1984, s 151B(3).
[6] IHTA 1984, s 151A(3)(a) inserted by FA 2006, Sch 15, para 14. Note: in this case, the deduction given by s 151A(3)(b) is £nil.
[7] IHTA 1984, s 151B(5) inserted by FA 2006, Sch 15, para 14.
[8] IHTA 1984, s 151C.
[9] IHTA 1984, s 12(2B) inserted by FA 2006, Sch 22, para 2.
[10] IHTA 1984, s 12(2D) inserted by FA 2006, Sch 22, para 2.

41

Gifts with reservation

What is a gift with reservation?	PARA 41.02
Gift of an interest in land	PARA 41.08
Excluded property	PARA 41.11
Inter-spouse transfer	PARA 41.12
Consequences	PARA 41.13
Income tax charge on pre-owned assets	PARA 41.14

[41.01] Statute[1] directs that property which the transferor has given[2] away in his lifetime shall be treated as forming part of his estate immediately before his death, if the transferor has reserved a benefit out of the property given, no matter how long previously the gift was made (subject to the important proviso that the rule applies only to gifts on or after 18 March 1986). The object of the provision is to counter avoidance devices that might otherwise escape the potentially exempt transfer rules and, in particular, to charge inheritance trusts and similar devices which had proliferated since the advent of CTT and which enabled a person to give property away while deriving benefit from it for the remainder of his or her lifetime.[3] While the rule treats the property as forming part of the estate on death—and is therefore valued at that time—the initial gift remains a transfer of value. Where the transfer is, for example, into a discretionary trust in which there is a reservation of benefit, an immediate charge to IHT arises on the transfer of property into trust. Other transfers may also be subject to a charge to inheritance tax as potentially exempt transfers which become chargeable by virtue of the transferor's death within seven years. There is, thus, a double charge to tax. The effect of regulations[4] is to levy tax equal to the higher of the two charges.

The gift with reservation provisions do not apply where the gift is an exempt transfer within the following categories:[5]

(a) transfers between spouses[6] (exempt under IHTA 1984, s 18);
(b) small gifts (exempt under IHTA 1984, s 20);
(c) gifts in consideration of marriage (exempt under IHTA 1984, s 22);
(d) gifts to charities (exempt under IHTA 1984, s 23);
(e) gifts to political parties (exempt under IHTA 1984, s 24);
(f) gifts to housing associations (exempt under IHTA 1984, s 24A);
(g) gifts for national purposes (exempt under IHTA 1984, s 26);
(h) maintenance funds for historic buildings (exempt under IHTA 1984, s 27);
(i) employee trusts (exempt under IHTA 1984, s 28).

For consideration of a reservation of benefit relating to excluded property, see infra, § **41.12**.

Simon's Taxes Division I3.4 especially I3.401, 402, I3.441–454; Foster's Inheritance Tax Division C4 especially C4.01, 02, C4.41–54; STP [10.232].

[41.01] Gifts with reservation

[1] FA 1986, s 102.
[2] A sale at an undervalue, is analysed as, in part, a sale and, in part, a gift. Hence, a sale at undervalue is within the scope of the gift with reservation provisions.
[3] Inland Revenue press release, 18 March 1986, *Simon's Tax Intelligence* 1986, p 193. On Revenue practice, note *Law Society's Gazette*, 10 December 1986, reproduced in **Foster's Inheritance Tax X6.36**, correspondence with the Country Landowner's Association reproduced in **Foster's Inheritance Tax X6.37** and *Law Society's Gazette*, 1 June 1988, reproduced in **Foster's Inheritance Tax X6.40**.
[4] This is achieved by tax being levied on the lifetime charge and then treating the sum paid as a credit against the charge on the same property that arises at death: IHT (Double Charges Relief) Regulations 1987, SI 1987/1130, reg 5(4)(*a*) made under the authority of FA 1986, s 104(2).
[5] FA 1986, s 102(5).
[6] See *IRC v Eversden* [2002] EWHC 1360 (Ch), [2002] STC 1109 discussed at infra, § 41.12.

What is a gift with reservation?

[41.02] FA 1986, s 102, following the old estate duty definition,[1] applies where an individual disposes of property and either (a) possession and enjoyment of the property is not bona fide assumed by the donee at or before the beginning of the relevant period, or (b) at any time in the relevant period, the property is not enjoyed to the entire exclusion, or virtually the entire exclusion,[2] of the donor and of any benefit to him by contract or otherwise. The relevant period is the seven year period ending with the donor's death.[3] The section expressly contemplates the possibility that a gift may be made subject to a reservation and the reservation itself may end at a later time but before the death.

If the gift is to escape IHT on the ground that it was made outside the statutory period, the first essential is that possession or enjoyment must have been assumed to the exclusion of the donor before the start of the period of seven years up to the donor's death. The donee's possession and enjoyment must then satisfy rule (b) which contains two distinct limbs, there must be both (i) the entire exclusion of the donor and (ii) the entire exclusion of any benefit to him by contract or otherwise.

Statute[4] deems the termination of an interest in possession, on or after 22 March 2006, to be a gift for the purpose of gift with reservation provisions, even if made during the 24 months after death. Thus, if the will of the deceased establishes an interest in possession trust in favour of the surviving spouse, or civil partner, with the terms of the trust giving the trustees an overriding power of appointment, an exercise of that power of appointment shortly after death to create a discretionary trust with the surviving spouse as a potential beneficiary is treated as gift with reservation by the surviving spouse.

Simon's Taxes I3.402, 411–416; Foster's Inheritance Tax C4.02, 11–16.

[1] FA 1984, s 2(1)(c), incorporating Customs and Inland Revenue Act 1881, s 38(2) and Customs and Inland Revenue Act 1889, s 11.
[2] Not part of the estate duty legislation; for a practice favourable to tax approved pension schemes see statement of practice SP 10/86.
[3] FA 1986, s 102(1).
[4] FA 1986, s 102ZA inserted by FA 2006, Sch 20 para 33.

[41.03] The first limb of rule (b) requires the total exclusion of the donor both in law and in fact; however, this is subject to three statutory qualifications; see infra, § 41.04. Two cases taken from equivalent provisions for estate duty illustrate the severity of this rule. In *Stamp Duties Comr of New South Wales v Permanent Trustee Co of New South Wales*[1] the donor had settled property on his daughter contingently on her attaining the age of 30; he retained no benefit and was entirely excluded. Fourteen years later, shortly before the daughter reached 30, he arranged with the daughter to borrow some of the income of the trust fund. He later died within the relevant period beginning with the date of the loan. The property was included in his estate as he had not been entirely excluded from it. So the rule may apply not only where the donee is obliged to allow the donor to continue to use the property, but also where there is an "honourable understanding" to this effect and even where there is no such understanding but simply an application of the property for the benefit of the donor at some later time.[2]

Chick v Stamp Duties Comr[3] is similar. In 1934, a father made an absolute gift of grazing land to his son. A year later the son brought the land into a farming partnership with his father and another brother. The partnership was an arm's length arrangement and yet the Privy Council held that the son had not retained possession and enjoyment of the land to the entire exclusion of the donor, so that when the father died some 18 years after the original gift, the land was charged with estate duty.

Simon's Taxes I3.402, 411–416; Foster's Inheritance Tax C4.02, 11–16.

[1] [1956] AC 512, [1956] 2 All ER 512, PC.
[2] Taken from Beattie's *Elements of Estate Duty*, 8th edn, p 99.
[3] [1958] AC 435, [1958] 2 All ER 623, PC.

[41.04] This severe rule is subject to three statutory qualifications apart from the important transitional rule that gifts before 18 March 1986 are ignored. These qualifications apply to both limbs of rule (b). The first is the de minimis qualification, not to be found in the estate duty rule, which requires entire or "virtually" the entire exclusion of the donor. The precise ambit of these words is inevitably obscure; one wonders why the legislation retains the words "entire exclusion" if "virtually entire exclusion" will do. The Revenue view is that these words exclude very small benefits as where a father gives his son a painting and the father enjoys looking at the painting hanging on the wall of his son's house, when he pays the occasional visit.[1]

The second was introduced for estate duty as a result of the *Chick* case. In the case of property which is an interest in land or a chattel, retention or

[41.04] Gifts with reservation

assumption by the donor of actual occupation of the land or actual enjoyment of an incorporeal right over the land, or actual possession of the chattel shall be disregarded if it is for full consideration in money or money's worth.[2] So where a donor makes a gift of a house to a donee and continues to reside in it under a lease providing for payment of a full rent, presumably the maximum allowed by law, there is no gift with reservation. One must also note that this qualification applies only to land and chattels and that the only types of enjoyment ignored are actual occupation and enjoyment. Thus the rule has no mitigating effect in a situation such as the *New South Wales* case or trusts of insurance policies. The taxpayer will have to prove that full consideration was given, as where both sides have bargained at arm's length and have been separately advised and the lease follows normal commercial criteria in force at the time it is negotiated.[3]

This was the subject of elaboration in the course of the debate on the 1986 Finance Bill, when the Financial Secretary to the Treasury said: 'Elderly parents make unconditional gifts of undivided shares in their house to their children and the parents and the children occupy the property as their family home, each owner bearing his or her share of the running costs. In these circumstances, the parents' occupation or enjoyment of the part of the house they have given away is in return for similar enjoyment of the children of the other part of the property. Thus the donor's occupation is for full consideration.'[4] When relying on this ministerial statement, note must be taken of the stress placed by the Financial Secretary in his adjacent comments as to the fullness of the consideration he would expect to be given by the children. It would, thus, be open to the Revenue to argue that a gift with reservation arises where mother gives daughter an undivided half share in the house they jointly occupy but mother continues to pay all household bills. It should also be noted that this parliamentary statement was made in 1986 in respect of the legislation introduced at that time. In any arrangement entered into now, it is also necessary to consider the effect of extension of the gift with reservation legislation made by FA 1999.[5]

The third qualification is a new provision[6] which says that where the property is an interest in land, any occupation by the donor can be ignored if it was unforeseen, was not brought about by the donor to receive the benefit of the rule, occurs when the donor is unable to maintain himself through old age, infirmity or otherwise and it represents a reasonable provision for the care and maintenance of the donor. The donee must also be a relative of the donor or his spouse.

Simon's Taxes I3.433, 434; Foster's Inheritance Tax C4.33, 34.

---

[1] IHT1, para 3.4; see also Inland Revenue interpretation RI 55.
[2] FA 1986, Sch 20, para 6(1)(*a*); see also Inland Revenue interpretation RI 55.
[3] IHT1, para 3.5; this is simply an illustration. See *IRC v Spencer-Nairn* [1991] STC 60, Ct of Sess.
[4] 3 HC Official Report, Finance Act 1986, Standing Committee G, 10 June 1986, col 425. Emphasis was placed on the fullness of the consideration.
[5] Now FA 1986, s 102A; see infra, § **41.08**.
[6] FA 1986, Sch 20, para 6(1)(*b*).

[41.05] The first limb of rule (b) refers to the property being enjoyed to the exclusion of the donor. In this context care is needed in order to determine the exact extent of the property given: only enjoyment which affects the property given can cause the rule to apply. It will have been noted that the two cases mentioned above in § 41.03 concern situations in which the donor first gave away the property and then received some benefit from it. Thus suppose that in the *Chick* case the formation of the partnership and the transfer of the land to the son had occurred at the same time. Could not one argue that the gift to the son was not a complete gift of the grazing land, but rather a gift of the land subject to the rights of the partnership, with the result that there would have been no gift with reservation? This matter has been discussed in connection with the second limb, the entire exclusion of the donor from any benefit by contract or otherwise but it is equally applicable to the first. The current view is as stated by Lord Simonds in *St Aubyn v AG*.[1] By retaining "something which he has never given, a donor does not bring himself within the mischief of [the statutory provisions] . . . In the simplest analysis, if A gives to B all his estates in Wiltshire except Blackacre, he does not except Blackacre out of what he has given; he just does not give Blackacre."[2]

In *Munro v Stamp Duties Comr*[3] a father, the donor, owned freehold land which was farmed by a partnership of himself and his six children. In 1913 he gave the land to the children but he continued as a partner in the business until his death in 1929. The Privy Council held that the property given was not the land but his interest in the land subject to the rights of the partnership. There seems little justification for the different result reached in *Chick* and the distinction that in *Chick* the father's interest was taken back out of property that had already been given has been described as "so fine as to be almost beyond perception".[4] The distinction gives rise to much planning, known as "shearing", and is apparently accepted by the Revenue.[5]

More recently in *Nichols v IRC*[6] the Court of Appeal held that where a donor made a gift of property subject to an obligation on the donee to grant a lease back to the donor the property given was the land subject to the obligation and not the land unfettered. However, the charge to estate duty was not escaped in that case since certain benefits were then reserved to the donor.

---

[1] [1952] AC 15, [1951] 2 All ER 473, HL.
[2] [1952] AC 15 at 29, [1951] 2 All ER 473 at 483, HL.
[3] [1934] AC 61, 103 LJPC 18.
[4] Beattie's *Elements of Estate Duty*, 8th edn, p 101.
[5] *Law Society's Gazette*, 1988, Vol 21, p 50.
[6] [1975] STC 278, [1975] 2 All ER 120, CA.

[41.06] The second limb of rule (b) requires the property to be enjoyed to the exclusion of any benefit to the donor by contract or otherwise. One falls foul of this rule where the benefit impinges on the possession and enjoyment of the property, even though it may not have been reserved out of the property itself.[1] Thus, a covenant by the donee to pay the donor an annuity, even though not charged on the property given, has been held sufficient,[2] as has a right to remuneration as a trustee.[3] Similarly where an annuity is charged on the whole

[41.06] Gifts with reservation

of the property given, the whole property given will be a gift with reservation, however small a percentage of the property's income the annuity may represent.[4] These points are reinforced by the rule that a benefit obtained by virtue of any associated operations, as defined in IHTA 1984, s 268, of which the disposal by way of gift is one shall be treated as property comprised in the gift.[5]

The meaning of "or otherwise" in the expression "by contract or otherwise" has not been definitively settled by the courts. In *A-G v Seccombe*[6] the donor made a gift of a farm to his great nephew who resided with him and who had taken over the management of the farm the previous year. Until his death the donor continued to reside in the farmhouse and was, from the date of the gift, maintained by the donee. The donor no longer sat at the head of the table but at the side. There was no enforceable agreement, nor any arrangement, that the donor should continue to reside there. It was held that the donee had assumed possession and enjoyment of the property to the entire exclusion of the donor and of any benefit to him by contract or otherwise. The court said that 'or otherwise' should be construed eiusdem generis with contract and so required an enforceable obligation. If it is correct to conclude that the presence or absence of a legal right is irrelevant to the first limb, ie in determining whether the donor has been entirely excluded from the property, one wonders why a different rule should apply for the second limb. One wonders why *A-G v Seccombe* did not fall within the first limb anyway. Today it can hardly be contended that the extensive privileges enjoyed by the donor were such as to amount to his virtual exclusion from the property and there must be some doubt about the correctness of the decision.

In the *Ingram* case,[7] although the Court of Appeal held that the transfer of an interest in the property was a gift with a reservation, all the judges in the Court of Appeal were agreed that the landlord's covenant for quiet enjoyment did not come within this limb.

Simon's Taxes I3.414, 415; Foster's Inheritance Tax C4.14, 15.

1 See the discussion in Beattie's *Elements of Estate Duty*, 8th edn, p 100.
2 *A-G v Worrall* [1895] 1 QB 99, 64 LJQB 141, CA.
3 *Oakes v Stamp Duties Comr of New South Wales* [1954] AC 57, [1953] 2 All ER 1563, PC.
4 *Earl Grey v A-G* [1900] AC 124, 69 LJQB 308, HL.
5 FA 1986, Sch 20, para 6(1)(c).
6 [1911] 2 KB 688.
7 [1997] STC 1234, CA. See supra, § **41.05**.

[41.07] Two cases have concerned settled property. In *Stamp Duties Comr of New South Wales v Perpetual Trustee Co Ltd*[1] a father settled property on his infant son but failed to direct what should happen to the property in the event that the son should fail to reach 21. The Privy Council held that the property given was not the entire settled property but rather that property minus the settlor's remainder interest. In this way, the charge to estate duty was avoided. In *Oakes v Stamp Duties Comr of New South Wales*[2] the deceased had been a trustee of the settlement and, as such, entitled to remuneration as trustee; this right was held to constitute a benefit. Today the right to remuneration as trustee might be held to be like the remainder in the previous case, at least where he was a trustee from the time the settlement was created, or it might come within the de minimis exception.

Simon's Taxes I3.416; Foster's Inheritance Tax C4.16

[1] [1943] AC 425, [1943] 1 All ER 525, PC.
[2] [1954] AC 57, [1953] 2 All ER 1563, PC.

Gift of an interest in land

Ingram v IRC

[41.08] The distinction between giving something subject to a reservation and giving only a part of a thing is at the centre of the decision of the House of Lords in *Ingram v IRC*.[1] Lady Ingram (I) was the absolute owner of the family home. She wanted to settle this on her family while wanting to continue to live in it—just the sort of thing s 102 is designed to stop. She therefore transferred the fee simple to a nominee (her solicitor); the next day the solicitor granted her two leases of the property which gave her rent-free occupation for 20 years. The following day the solicitor transferred the reversion on the lease to trustees. The purpose of the scheme was to try to make a potentially exempt transfer of the freehold reversion; she would have had to pay tax on the lease itself as part of the death transfer. The scheme failed before the Special Commissioner, succeeded in the Chancery Division, failed by 2–1 in the Court of Appeal but succeeded in the House of Lords.

In his leading judgment, Lord Hoffmann gave his views as to the general policy of the gift with reservation legislation:

> It is in one sense a penal section. Not only may you not have your cake and eat it, but if you eat more than a few de minimis crumbs of what was given, you are deemed for tax purposes to have eaten the lot . . .

> What, then, is the policy of section 102? It requires people to define precisely the interest which they are giving away and the interest, if any, which they are retaining. Once they have given away an interest they may not receive back any benefits from that interest . . . It laid down a rule that if the donor continued to derive any benefit from the property in which an interest had been given, it would be treated as a pretended gift unless the benefit could be shown to be referable to a specific proprietary interest which he had retained.[2]

In his judgment, Lord Hoffmann states that he has no doubt that the interest retained by Lady Ingram was a proprietary interest defined with the necessary precision.[3] The trustees and beneficiaries never at any time acquired the land free of Lady Ingram's leasehold interest and the need for a conveyance to be followed by a leaseback was merely a matter of conveyancing form. In his judgment, the leases were valid and, as a matter of land law, a nominee can grant a lease to his principal.[4]

[41.08] Gifts with reservation

Despite the subsequent statute that treats a gift followed by a leaseback as a gift with reservation, statute has not changed the nature of the analysis in the House of Lords that is at the heart of this decision. A lease is one asset; the freehold interest is another. This analysis can be applied in other situations. It is not infrequently the case that an individual is a major shareholder in a private company and also has a service contract to work as a director of that company. Concern has been expressed that a gift of shares in the company could be treated as a gift with reservation if the conditions of the director's service contract are subsequently changed so that an increased remuneration is paid to the director which would reduce the distributable profit and, hence, the value of the shares that had been gifted. It would appear that adopting the analysis of the House of Lords in *Ingram v IRC*, a distinction must be made between the asset that is gifted, the shares, and the asset from which the donor receives subsequent enjoyment, his service contract. Hence, a benefit received from the service contract is not a reservation of the shares that have been gifted.

Simon's Taxes I3.416; Foster's Inheritance Tax C4.16.

---

[1] [1995] STC 564; on appeal [1997] STC 1234, CA; revsd [1999] STC 37, HL.
[2] [1999] STC 37 at 45c and h, HL.
[3] [1999] STC 37 at 44j, HL.
[4] [1999] STC 37 at 46a–d, HL.

[41.09] With effect from 9 March 1999, where there is a gift of land and the donor subsequently enjoys "a significant right or interest . . . in relation to the land" the subject matter of the gift is treated as a gift with reservation.[1] In this way, Parliament has legislated to rob the arrangement followed in the *Ingram* case of its fiscal effect where the original gift is made on or after Budget Day 1999. The legislation does not, however, affect gifts made before that date.

In the legislation, a "significant right or interest" is one that either gives entitlement to occupy the land or, more generally, enables the donor to occupy the land or to enjoy some right in relation to the land other than for full consideration.[2] The de minimis provision that exists in the original legislation is carried through into these new provisions.[3]

There is also a gift with reservation where the donor is party to "a significant arrangement", after which the donor enjoys a right over the land. This is, presumably, intended to stop reciprocal arrangements. The principle is extended to the situation where one of a number of co-owners makes a gift of his interest in the land but subsequently occupies, or is one of the occupiers of, that land.[4]

In accordance with the general scheme of the gift with reservation legislation, the provisions only have effect where the benefit is enjoyed during the period of seven years prior to the donor's death.[5]

For the statutory provisions to apply, there has to be a gift.[6] If a taxpayer sells, for its full market value, a freehold out of which he has carved a lease to himself for a peppercorn rent, the gift with reservation provisions do not operate. By contrast, if the sale of the encumbered freehold is for £1 less than its full market value, there is a gift, which attracts the same consequences as if the transferor received no consideration for the freehold. The de minimis provisions do not save the arrangement.[7]

Other arrangements are made to avoid the effect of s 102A. These include the sale of the property under a contract which provides that a long lease to a children's trust commences some years after the sale and, hence, the value at which the property is sold is depressed by the onerous lease. Another arrangement is sale of unencumbered property at its full market value, with the consideration being satisfied by an IOU which the donor then gives to a life interest trust for his children.[8]

Simon's Taxes I3.416.

---

[1]   FA 1986, s 102A(2).
[2]   FA 1986, s 102A(3).
[3]   FA 1986, s 102A(4).
[4]   FA 1986, s 102B.
[5]   Referred to in the legislation as "the relevant period": FA 1996, s 102A(2).
[6]   FA 1986, s 102A(1).
[7]   The de minimis exclusion applies only when deciding whether the donor has, after the gift, a "significant interest" in the land concerned: FA 1986, s 102A(4)(*a*).
[8]   A short analysis of these schemes is given by Elizabeth Wilson in (2001) 8 Personal Tax Planning Review 99–101.

[41.10] The provisions in FA 1986, s 102A only apply when no charge arises under the gift with reservation provisions as originally enacted.[1] Hence it is, in principle, necessary to look at any situation in the light of the decision in *Ingram v IRC* (see supra, § 41.09). Section 102A only applies where, on the basis of the judgment in that case, there would not otherwise be a gift with reservation.

Under these provisions, a gift of an interest in land made on or after 9 March 1999 is deemed to be property subject to a reservation where the donor or his spouse has, during the relevant period, a significant right or interest or is party to a significant arrangement.[2] A right, interest or arrangement is "significant" for these purposes if and only if it entitles or enables the donor to occupy all or part of the land, or to enjoy some right in relation to all or part of the land, other than for full consideration in money or money's worth.[3] The use of the word "enables" presumably means that an arrangement under which the new owner allows use of the land is caught, even if the donor has no entitlement enforceable in law.

It is considered that a lease which carves out sporting rights, which are retained by the donor, would be caught by these provisions as enabling the donor to "enjoy some right in relation to . . . the land". It can be that the continuing enjoyment of a piece of land that is retained is only possible if there is an easement (such as for access) over land that is gifted. The strict statutory position when such an easement is created on a gift is not clear. However, it is likely that the Revenue will continue their existing practice of treating as not

[41.10] Gifts with reservation

a reservation of benefit the retention or creation of an easement of a kind that would be retained on a commercial sale.[4]

The tracing provisions[5] apply for this purpose, only in so far as the property into which the gift with reservation is traced is an interest in land.[6] Business property relief or agricultural property relief is given to land subject to gift with reservation, where the conditions for the relief are satisfied.[7]

Where there is a gift of an undivided share of land, the new provisions provide a separate code.[8] Under this, where a gift of an undivided share of land is made on or after 9 March 1999, this is treated as property subject to reservation unless one of four alternative conditions is fulfilled. The first is that the donor does not occupy the land.[9] The second is that occupation is for full consideration.[10] The third is that no benefit is received, other than one within the de minimis exemption.[11] The fourth is that occupation of the land is a result of a change in circumstances such that the donor cannot maintain himself and this was unforeseen at the time of the gift.[12] In addition, an exempt transfer to a spouse or a charity is excluded from the new provisions.

Where a gift of a part share has been made to a co-occupier and the property is then occupied by its co-owners, the gift is not treated as a reservation of benefit[13] if the following conditions are satisfied:

(1) the donor has made the gift of the undivided share in an interest on or after 9 March 1999,
(2) the donor and the donee occupy the land, *and*
(3) the donor does not receive any benefit other than a negligible benefit provided by or at the expense of the donee for some reason connected with the gift.

An equivalent exemption applies to exclude an income tax charge under the pre-owned asset regime.[14]

Simon's Taxes I3.416.

---

[1] FA 1986, s 102C(7).
[2] FA 1986, s 102A(2).
[3] FA 1986, s 102A(3).
[4] Capital Taxes Office Advanced Instruction Manual, para D45, example 9.
[5] FA 1986, Sch 20, para 2.
[6] FA 1986, s 102C(5).
[7] FA 1986, s 102C(4).
[8] FA 1986, s 102C.
[9] FA 1986, s 102C(3)(*a*).
[10] FA 1986, s 102C(3)(*b*).
[11] FA 1986, s 102C(4).
[12] FA 1986, s 102C(2), (3) applying Sch 20, para 6(1)(*b*).
[13] FA 1986, s 102B(4). This section was inserted by FA 1999, s 104 to enact the practice specified in the House of Commons by Peter Brook, Secretary to the Treasury, on 10 June 1986:

> It may be that my Honourable Friend's intention concerns the common case where someone gives away an individual share in land, typically a house, which is then occupied by all the joint owners including the donor. For example, an elderly parent may make unconditional

gifts of undivided shares in their house to their children and the parents and the children occupy the property as their family home, each owner bearing his or her share of the running costs. In those circumstances, the parent's occupation or enjoyment of the part of the house that they have given away is in return for similar enjoyment of the children of the other part of the property. Thus the donor's occupation is for full consideration.

Accordingly, I assure my honourable friend that the gift with reservation rules will not be applied to an unconditional gift of an undivided share in land merely because the property is occupied by all the joint owners or tenants in common, including the donor. (Hansard, Treasury Standing Committee G, 10 June 1986, Col 425.)

[14] See supra, § **12.20**.

Excluded property

[41.11] It has generally been considered that a gift of excluded property[1] cannot be subject to the gift with reservations provisions. This follows from the scheme of the Act, whereby inheritance tax is charged when there is a transfer of value.[2] The Act gives a direction that in measuring a transfer of value "no account should be taken of the value of excluded property".[3]

Foreign property in a settlement is excluded property if the property was settled by an individual who was not domiciled within the UK at the time of settlement.[4] The effect of the rule is not only to exclude the property at the death of the settlor but also to exclude the property at the death of any beneficiary (wherever domiciled) who has a life interest in the settlement. Where a settlement is a discretionary settlement, the 10 year charge and periodic charge are similarly excluded. The test is applied at the date at which there would be a charge. Hence, if a non-domiciliary creates a settlement with UK situs property, there is no charge to inheritance tax at the death of the life tenant, if the UK situs property has been sold and the proceeds reinvested in foreign situs property before the death of the life tenant.

The tax advantages available have been so substantial that it has become standard practice for an non-domiciled individual to create a settlement in the 16th year of residence in the UK, in advance of acquiring a deemed UK domicile the following year.[5]

An extension of this tax planning manoeuvre has been for the settlement created by the non-domiciliary to name the settlor as a potential beneficiary, or even as the life tenant with entitlement to income. UK situs assets, such as land in the UK, have frequently been, in effect, converted to foreign situs assets to be held by the trustees of such a settlement by interposing a company incorporated outside the UK to hold the assets, so that the asset held by the trustees have been the shares in a foreign company. The definition of excluded property makes no mention of the residence of the trustees; the structure can be created with UK resident trustees, if that is thought appropriate.

The Revenue are challenging the generally accepted interpretation of the interaction between the excepted property provisions and the gift with reservation provisions. In updating the CTO internal manual in 2001, it is stated:[6]

[41.11] Gifts with reservation

D.8 Excluded Property The donor, who is domiciled in Australia, puts foreign property into a discretionary trust under which he is a potential beneficiary. He dies some years later domiciled in England and without having released the reservation.

"The property is property subject to a reservation and is therefore deemed to be part of the donor's death estate. Any cases where this is the situation must be referred to the Litigation Team.

"D.9 Reservation ceasing Had the donor in Example 2 in D.8 attained a UK domicile after the gift and in donor's lifetime then released the reservation during his lifetime, it is arguable that the release would have been a PET which became a chargeable transfer on the death within seven years. The release would thus have triggered a charge which would not have arisen had the release not been made. Any case in which such a charge is thought to arise, or any enquiry about the possibility of such a charge arising, should be referred to the Litigation Team.

---

[1] Defined in IHTA 1984, s 6 and 48(3). See infra, §§ **47.11** and **47.12**.
[2] IHTA 1984, ss 1 and 2(1). It is also specified that in order to be a chargeable transfer, the transfer of value must not be an exempt transfer.
[3] IHTA 1984, s 3(2).
[4] IHTA 1984, s 48(3)(a).
[5] IHTA 1984, s 267. See infra, § **47.07**. IHTA 1984 s 48 states that all foreign property in a settlement is excluded property "unless the settlor was domiciled in the United Kingdom at the time the settlement was made". An imaginative construction of this provision has lead to the suggestion that foreign property in a trust created by a deed of variation is always excluded property, as the settlor of a deed of variation is deemed to be the deceased who is clearly no longer domiciled in the UK, or anywhere else in the world, at the time the settlement is made. This construction is almost certainly incorrect as the provision in s 142(1) that deems the disposition made by a deed of variation to have been made by the settlor should be read in the light of s 4 that deems the transfer by the deceased to have been made, not at his death, but immediately before his death.
[6] Capital Taxes Office Advanced Instruction Manual, paras D.8 and D.9.

Inter-spouse transfer

[41.12] Statute[1] provides that the gift with reservation provisions do not apply "to the extent that the disposal of property by way of gift is an exempt transfer by virtue of . . . s 18, transfers between spouses". The exemption for an inter-spouse transfer extends to a transfer from an individual to a settlement in which his spouse has an interest in possession.[2]

This statutory exclusion of the gift with reservation provisions has led to the following arrangements: a settlor passes property to trustees. The trust deed states that the settlor's spouse has an immediate interest in possession; if that interest in possession comes to an end, the trustees then have discretionary powers to apply income or capital for the benefit of any of a list of beneficiaries, which includes the settlor. The trustees are empowered to bring the spouse's interest in possession to an end at a time of their choosing. The settlement created is treated as an interest in possession settlement, notwithstanding the overriding powers of appointment[3] and forms part of the spouse's estate.[4] Hence, the exemption operates so that the disposition is not treated as a gift with reservation. After six months or so, the trustees exercise their powers to bring the spouse's interest in possession to an end, whereafter income and/or capital can be paid to the settlor. As the trustees' act in bringing the settlement to an end is not, at that time, a disposition by the settlor (who has no power to require the trustees to take this act) there is not a gift with reservation created at that point.

A scheme of this nature is that considered in *IRC v Eversden*.[5] In that case, the settlor appointed herself and two others to be the trustees of the settlement. The settlement provided that the income of the trust fund should be paid to the settlor's husband during his life, after his death, for a specified period of 80 years on discretionary trusts for a class of beneficiaries including the settlor, and at the end of the 80 years on trust for the settlor's daughter Mrs Eversden (or her issue) absolutely. The settlor conveyed Beechwood Cottage to the trustees to hold on trust as to 5% for the settlor absolutely and as to 95% on the trusts of the settlement. The husband thereafter as life tenant occupied Beechwood (together with the settlor) until he died on 6 February 1992. The trustees then sold Beechwood and purchased 6 Barn Meadows and an investment bond. Thereafter the settlor had a 5% interest in 6 Barn Meadows and the bond. From the date of its purchase until her death on 27 October 1998 the settlor was in sole occupation of 6 Barn Meadows and paid all the expenses relating to it. On the death of the settlor the trust fund comprised the 95% interest in 6 Barn Meadows (valued at £171,000) and the 95 % interest in the bond (valued at £149,213.43).

The Revenue contended that s 102(3) deems the trust fund to form part of the settlor's estate because at the time of her death the trust fund was held upon discretionary trusts which included the settlor among the class of beneficiaries and because she had occupied 6 Barn Meadows.

Before the Special Commissioner[6] the Revenue argued that, at the creation of the settlement, there were three gifts: one was the life interest to the spouse; the second was the gift to the beneficiaries at the discretion of the trustee after the death of the spouse; and the third was the value given by the default provisions in the settlement deed (which were effectively valueless at the time of the settlor's death) and that it was necessary to consider the separate beneficial interests. On this analysis, the second gift was a gift with reservation and was not exempted by s 104(5)(1) and, thus, the £320,000 trust fund (or a substantial proportion of it) fell to be taxed as part of the estate of the settlor at his death. The Special Commissioner held that there was a single gift. The court accepted this finding of fact by the Special Commissioner. In rejecting the Revenue's contention that the gift with reservation provisions applied, Lightman J said:[7]

> The language of s 102(5) looks at the disposal at the date on which it is made and its character (as a transfer between spouses) must, as it seems to me, be determined as at that date. If the gift answers that character at that date, the provisions of s 102 relating to property subject to a reservation have no application. For the purposes of s 18 of the 1984 Act the duration of the proprietary interest gifted to the spouse

[41.12] Gifts with reservation

is irrelevant even as it is irrelevant how long the spouse retains the proprietary interest and whether the spouse gifts the proprietary interest on to someone else eg the children of the donor and donee. Likewise the duration of the proprietary interest is irrelevant for the purposes of s 102(5).

This case provides authority for a widely used arrangement whereby a husband creates a discretionary trust with a widely defined class of potential beneficiaries, including himself and his wife. The trust deed provides, however, that there is, from the commencement of the trust, a revocable life interest in favour of the wife, revocation being possible by the trustees unilaterally. Husband passes investments into the trust. After a decent interval, the trustees exercise their power and revoke the wife's interest, from when the trust fund is held in a discretionary settlement from which the trustees can from time to time resolve to pass income and/or capital back to the settlor. No charge to IHT arises on the settlor passing funds into this settlement.[8] When the trustees revoke the wife's interest in possession, this is a chargeable transfer by the wife, which will commonly be covered by her nil rate band.[9] This scheme was presented to the Court of Appeal[10] by Revenue Counsel, in response to which, Carnwath LJ said[11]: 'If that is of concern to the Revenue, they must look for correction to Parliament, not to the courts.'

It has not taken long for the Revenue to take note of the comments of Carnwath LJ. Statute[12] now provides that if the transfer into trust takes place on or after 20 June 2003, a transfer of value is made at the later date when the spouse's interest in possession comes to an end. The effect of this is that a transfer by husband to a trust in which his wife has an interest in possession is exempt from the gift with reservation provisions as long as the wife's interest in possession continues. If the interest in possession ceases, the earlier transfer by the husband is treated for the purpose of the GWR provisions only as taking place at the date the wife's interest in possession has ceased. This treatment does not apply when the transfer into trust took place before 20 June 2003[13], even if the cessation of the wife's interest in possession is after that date. If the arrangement outlined above is made post-20 June 2003 and the wife's interest in possession is retained until after the husband dies, the cancellation by the trustees of the wife's interest in possession post-death does not cause the GWR provisions to apply.

---

[1] FA 1986, s 102(5)(*a*).
[2] IHTA 1984, s 49(1).
[3] See Inland Revenue press release, 12 February 1976 following the decision in *Pearson v IRC* [1980] STC 318, HL. A beneficiary has an interest in possession by virtue of the beneficiary's rights under the terms of the settlement; the investment of the trust fund in property that, by its nature, cannot produce income does not inhibit the interest in possession: *Gartside v IRC* (1968) 41 TC 92, HL.
[4] IHTA 1984, s 49(1).
[5] [2002] STC 1109 and [2003] EWCA Civ 668, [2003] STC 822. The Court of Appeal unanimously upheld both the decision and the ratio decidendii of the judgment of Lightman J.
[6] [2002] STC (SCD) 39 at 46d.
[7] At 113h [para 34].
[8] Exempt as a transfer between spouses: IHTA 1994, s 18.

[9] A variant of the arrangement is that a capital payment is made back to the settlor at this point, with the trust fund being placed on life interest trusts for the children or accumulation and maintenance trusts for children/grandchildren.
[10] [2003] EWCA Civ 668, [2003] STC 822 at [24], at 831a–b.
[11] Para 25 at 831d.
[12] FA 1986, s 102(5A)–(5C) inserted by FA 2003, s 185.
[13] FA 2003, s 185(4).

Consequences

[41.13] Where a gift with reservation is made and the reservation continues until the time of the donor's death the property is treated as property to which he was still beneficially entitled immediately before his death and so as part of his estate for IHT.[1] Where at some time before the end of the relevant period, which is at the donor's death, the property ceases to be subject to a reservation, the donor is treated as if he had at that time made a disposition of property by a disposition which is a potentially exempt transfer,[2] and so one waits a further seven years to see whether it becomes an exempt transfer; the annual exemption is not available on this occasion.[3]

However, it may be that the original gift with reservation is itself a fully chargeable transfer, as where it is a settlement. In such circumstances regulations prevent a double charge to tax.[4] Where a settlor settles property but is not entirely excluded from it and he later releases his rights there will, it is assumed, be a chargeable transfer on the occasion of the settlement and it is hard to see why there should also be a potentially chargeable transfer on the occasion of the release.

Further rules are intended to prevent any use being made of IHTA 1984, s 142 to undo the gift with reservation (alteration of disposition within two years of the death)[5] and direct that the donee is primarily liable for the tax.[6]

This complex of rules does not apply where the transfer would be an exempt transfer (save for the annual exemption and the small expenditure out of income exemption).[7] Gifts made after 17 March 1986 under the terms of regular premium insurance policies made before 18 March 1986 and not altered since then are excluded from these rules by FA 1986, s 102(6), (7).

The rules are designed to bring into the estate the value of the property immediately before the donor's death and not its original value at the time of the gift. Where the reservation ceases at an earlier time but still within the relevant period it is the value at that time which is taken. Rules therefore have to be provided to determine how far one may trace the property between the date of the gift and the subsequent cesser of the reservation or death. These are less sweeping than the estate duty rules of 1957.[8] The first set of rules is designed to trace the value of the gift made with reservation into property substituted for the gift and into all accretions to the property.[9] Where an accretion involves expenditure by the donee, eg rights issues, any consideration provided for the accretion is deductible.[10] Where the donee dies before the donor it is the donee's personal representatives that take over and tracing continues into their acts.[11]

[41.13] Gifts with reservation

The tracing rules do not apply where the property is settled (there are separate rules for these) or where the property given is a sum of money in sterling or any other currency.[12]

Where the donee gives the property away, other than to the donor, or otherwise than for consideration in money or money's worth not less than the value of the property at that time, he is treated as continuing to have the possession or enjoyment of the property.[13] This is presumably because the basic rule is defined in terms of the donee assuming possession and enjoyment of the property to the exclusion of the donee.

The rules as to settled property[14] require that the property in the settlement should be taken as representing the original property. If the settlement comes to an end, in whole or in part, before the reservation ends then the property ceasing to be settled is treated as the given property but with a deduction for property becoming property of the donor and with an addition of any money the donor pays at that time. Where the property is not originally settled but is settled by the donee these rules apply. Although income which is accumulated becomes part of the settled property this is not to apply to income accumulated after the date of the ending of the reservation.

Simon's Taxes I3.421–429; Foster's Inheritance Tax C4.21–29.

---

[1] FA 1986, s 102(3).
[2] FA 1986, s 102(4).
[3] This is also now the Revenue view—see Inland Revenue interpretation, *Simon's Tax Intelligence* 1993, p 1409 repudiating IHT1, para 3.4.
[4] The Inheritance Tax (Double Charges Relief) Regulations 1987, SI 1987/1130 made under the authority of FA 1986, s 102(1)(b).
[5] By providing that the property does not form part of his estate on death—see IHTA 1984, s 142(5).
[6] IHTA 1984, s 204(9).
[7] FA 1986, s 102(5); gifts to charities are subject to their own reservation of benefit rules—see IHTA 1984, s 23(4). On the position of death benefits under the tax-approved superannuation schemes note statement of practice SP 10/86; Foster's Inheritance Tax, Division W3.
[8] FA 1957, s 38.
[9] FA 1986, Sch 20, para 2.
[10] FA 1986, Sch 20, para 3.
[11] FA 1986, Sch 20, para 4.
[12] FA 1986, Sch 20, para 2(2).
[13] FA 1986, Sch 20, para 2(4); on "voluntary" see para 2(5).
[14] FA 1986, Sch 20, para 4.

Income tax charge on pre-owned assets

[41.14] From 6 April 2005, an income tax charge can arise where there has been a disposal of land at any time after 17 March 1986 and the donor occupies the land after 5 April 2005 but the disposal of the land was not

Income tax charge on pre-owned assets [41.14]

treated as a gift with reservation. Equivalent provisions apply where there has been a disposal of a chattel or a disposal of intellectual property[1] into a trust.

The rationale behind the income tax charge is that it penalises those who have entered into schemes to avoid inheritance tax. As stated in the 2004 budget press release:[2]

> The Government is aware that various schemes designed to avoid inheritance tax have been marketed in recent years. These use artificial structures to avoid the existing rules and gifts made with reservations. As a result, people have been removing assets from their taxable estate but continuing to enjoy all the benefits of ownership. The Government is determined to block this sort of avoidance and announced in the pre-budget report that people who benefit from these sorts of schemes will be subject to an income tax charge from April 2005, to reflect their additional taxable capacity from receiving these benefits at low or no cost.

These provisions are considered at supra, §§ **12.15–12.22**.

---

[1] Which is bizarrely defined to mean any property that is not land or a chattel: FA 2004, Sch 15, para 1. Hence, stocks and shares are "intellectual property" for the purpose of the pre-owned asset regime.

[2] REVBN, 40: "Tax treatment of pre-owned assets", *Simon's Weekly Tax Intelligence* 2004, p 812.

42

Settled property

IHT and settled property	PARA **42.01**
What is a settlement?	PARA **42.02**
Categories of trust	PARA **42.05**
Interest in possession created prior to 22 March 2006	PARA **42.07**
Estates in administration and survivorship clauses	PARA **42.11**
Transfers of settled property	PARA **42.12**
Depreciatory transactions	PARA **42.15**
Exceptions	PARA **42.16**
Reversionary interests	PARA **42.23**
Potentially exempt transfers—special rate of charge	PARA **42.24**
Estate duty trusts	PARA **42.25**
Charge on trustees	PARA **42.28**
The charge at the ten year anniversary	PARA **42.33**
The exit charge	PARA **42.41**
Accumulation and maintenance trusts	PARA **42.49**
Special trusts	PARA **42.54**

IHT and settled property

[42.01] From 1974 to 2006 a basic and simple concept was applied in charging IHT (and formerly CTT) to settled property. Where a beneficiary is entitled to the income that arises, the trust property that generates the income has been treated as if he were the beneficial owner.[1] Where there is no beneficiary entitled to income arising on trust property, an inheritance tax charge has been levied on the trust fund.[2] (Exemption has been given for certain favoured trusts.)

From 22 March 2006,[3] the goal posts have moved and this neat concept has been discarded. For most new trusts, the creation of the trust is a chargeable transfer, and, thereafter, a charge to IHT is levied on the trustees, for both interest in possession trusts and for discretionary settlements, the trust fund being treated as a separate entity and not as part of the beneficiary's estate. However, there are certain favoured trusts (notably a trust that passes capital at age 25, and satisfy certain conditions, and a trust for a disabled beneficiary) for which the pre-2006 treatment is retained.[4] There are awkward transitional provisions,[5] under which the fund of a trust created prior to 22 March 2006 is treated as the estate of a beneficiary who enjoys the interest in possession, but only so long as the individual who has that interest at 22 March 2006 continues to have the interest. When his interest ceases (or, in some circumstances, is amended) the trust is, thereafter, treated as if it were a post March 2006 trust. There is an IHT charge (often a PET) on the beneficiary at the time

[42.01] Settled property

of change and a charge on the trustees on each ten year anniversary of the original creation of the trust, where the date falls after the cessation of the interest in possession.

The so-called favourable treatment that puts the trust fund into the estate of the beneficiary and excludes the IHT charge in the trustees could lead to a higher tax charge. This favourable treatment is available when the terms of the trust give entitlement to capital at age 25, but not when property remains in trusts after that age.[6] How many readers consider that every 25 year old should be given unfettered control of a substantial inheritance? It is unfettered control at age 25 that is encouraged by the tax regime introduced in 2006. One is led to ask whether the Government thinks that it is wrong for the young to be protected.

[1] IHTA 1984, s 49.
[2] IHTA 1984, ss 58–69; see infra, § **42.58**.
[3] One previous legislative change can be criticised similarly. The introduction on 18 March 1986 of the gift with reservation provisions created a similar duplication of deemed ownership. Where property is gifted subject to a reservation, the property gifted is treated as remaining in the estate of the donor but is, nevertheless, also chargeable in the estate of the donee.
[4] FA 2006, Sch 20.
[5] FA 2006, Sch 20, paras 2–4.
[6] Unless the beneficiary is a disabled person: see IHTA 1984, s 49(1A)(b) inserted by FA 2006, Sch 20, para 4(1) and the amendments made to IHTA 1984, s 89 by FA 2006, Sch 20, para 6.

What is a settlement?

[42.02] For IHT purposes only, statute[1] defines a settlement as:

Any disposition or dispositions of property, whether effected by instrument, by parol or by operation of law, or partly in one way and partly in another, whereby the property is for the time being:

(a) held in trust for persons in succession or for any person subject to a contingency; or
(b) held by trustees on trust to accumulate the whole or any part of any income of the property or with power to make payments out of that income at the discretion of the trustees or some other person, with or without power to accumulate surplus income; or
(c) charged or burdened (otherwise than for full consideration in money or money's worth paid for his own use or benefit to the person making the disposition), with the payment of an annuity or other periodical payment payable for a life or any other limited or terminable period;

or would be so held charged or burdened if the disposition or dispositions were regulated by the law of any part of the UK; or whereby, under the law of any other country, the administration of the property is for the time being governed by provisions equivalent in effect to those which would apply if the property were so held, charged or burdened.

Property is settled whether or not the settlement was created for value[2]—except for head (c).

What is a settlement? [42.03]

Head (a) is sufficient to cover entailed interests, life interests and contingent interests, but not purely concurrent interests, while head (b) catches discretionary and accumulation trusts.

Head (c) deals only with annuities or other periodical payments which are charged on property. Annuities payable under a personal obligation only do not create settlements. The phrase "or other periodical payments" is presumably to be construed eiusdem generis with annuity and so does not cover instalments of capital.[3] The obligation must be for life or any other limited or terminable period so that while a rent charge for a limited period will give rise to a settlement unless for full consideration, a perpetual rentcharge will not. When full consideration is in issue, it does not matter who provides it.[4]

The concluding words of the section are aimed at foreign devices such as a *Stiftung*. They had no counterpart in estate duty legislation. The words are also needed because these rules extend to property outside the UK if the settlor was domiciled in the UK at the time the settlement was made.[5]

The definition is adapted for Northern Ireland;[6] for Scotland there is an extended definition.[7]

Partnership assurance schemes were often arranged on the basis that each partner effected a policy on his own life in trust for the other partners. Such arrangements usually create settlements. However by concession policies effected before 15 September 1976 are not treated as settlements provided (a) there is no variation after that date, (b) the premium payments fall within IHTA 1984, s 10 and (c) the trusts are governed by English or Scots law—and, in the latter case, the partnership itself is not involved as a separate persona.[8]

Simon's Taxes I5.111–122; Foster's Inheritance Tax E1.11–22.

[1] IHTA 1984, s 43(1).
[2] The question whether the creation of the trust is a chargeable transfer is quite distinct.
[3] Supra, § **13.21**.
[4] *A-G v Boden* [1912] 1 KB 539.
[5] IHTA 1984, s 48(3), infra, § **47.13**.
[6] IHTA 1984, s 43(5).
[7] IHTA 1984, s 43(4) states:

In relation to Scotland 'settlement' also includes-

(a) an entail,
(b) any deed by virtue of which an annuity is charged on, or on the rents of, any property (the property being treated as the property comprised in the settlement), and
(c) any deed creating or reserving a proper liferent of any property whether heritable or moveable (the property from time to time subject to the proper liferent being treated as the property comprised in the settlement);

and for the purposes of this subsection 'deed' includes any disposition, arrangement, contract resolution, instrument and writing.

[8] Extra-statutory concession F10; **Foster's Inheritance Tax, Division U2.**

[42.03] As for CGT supra, § **20.05** it is often important to know whether property is part of an existing settlement or subject to a separate settlement.

[42.03] Settled property

Where two documents create one compound settlement there is just one settlement; equally, however, one document may create two settlements as where a will creates a trust of a specific legacy and separate trusts or residue. what is not so clear is whether the addition of property by someone other than the original settlor creates a new settlement or merely adds to an existing one;[1] trust law distinguishes an accretion to a settlement from a new referential settlement.[2] The Revenue view seems obscure.

Where a power of appointment over property is exercised so that the property does not vest in an object absolutely the question whether the property remains subject to the original settlement is one of construction, supra, § **20.05**. However, for the purposes of the ten year charge (see 42.33 infra), it is provided that the property is to be treated as remaining subject to the first settlement.[3]

Simon's Taxes I5.118; Foster's Inheritance Tax E1.18.

---

[1] IHTA 1984, s 44(2) says that they may be treated as separate settlements where the circumstances so require subject to exceptions in IHTA 1984, s 48(4)–(6).
[2] eg *Re Rydon's Settlement* [1955] Ch 1. *Re Gooch* [1929] 1 Ch 740.
[3] IHTA 1984, s 81.

Settlor and trustees

[42.04] The "settlor" is not exhaustively defined but the term is stated to include any person by whom the settlement was made directly or indirectly and, in particular, (but without prejudice to the generality of the preceding words) includes any person who has provided funds directly or indirectly for the purpose of, or in connection with, the settlement or has made with any other person a reciprocal arrangement for that other person to make the settlement.[1] As with the similar test of income tax and settlements this test is only satisfied if there is some conscious association of the provider of funds with the settlement in question. It is not enough that the settled funds happen historically to have come from a person; otherwise anyone who gave funds unconditionally to another person who then, of their own volition, settled them would fall to be treated as a settlor.[2] In *Hatton v IRC* Chadwick J invoked this rule to hold that each of two persons was, as a result of the associated operations rule, treated as a settlor in relation to the composite settlement.[3]

Where more than one person is settlor in relation to a settlement it is provided that this Part of the Act is to apply as if the settled property were comprised in separate settlements, where the circumstances require.[4] In *Hatton v IRC* Chadwick J said that where other provisions required there to be a single settlor, eg the reverter to settlor exemption,[5] the separate settlement rule should be applied if this was practicable. He then said:[6]

> Circumstances in which [s 44(2)] is commonly found to apply include those in which two or more persons have separately provided funds from their own independent resources to be held on the trust of the same settlement. In such a case the effect of [s 44(2)] is, I suspect, generally thought to be that the settled property is treated as if a proportionate or identifiable part were held in one settlement and other

proportionate or identifiable parts were held in other, separate settlements; each notionally separate settlement having its own single settlor. But, examination of [s 44(1)] shows that there may well be more than one person who is a settlor in relation to a settlement in circumstances in which the settled property cannot sensibly be apportioned or partitioned amongst a series of notionally separate settlements. In such a case, as it seems to me, [s 44(2] requires that [this Part of the Act is] to apply as if there were a number of separate settlements each with its own single settlor and each comprising the whole of the settled property . . .

Suppose that under an arrangement between A and B, A settles his own property on X for a term say, the duration of his schooling—with remainder to himself; and B settles his own property on Y for a similar term, with remainder to himself. X is a person whom B wishes to benefit, and Y is a person whom A wishes to benefit. The settlements are made under an arrangement (not having contractual effect) between A and B; each perhaps hoping to obtain some advantage by conferring benefits indirectly on the object of the other's settlement.

In those circumstances it seems to me impossible to avoid the conclusion that each of A and B is a settlor, in accordance with the provisions of [s 44(1)], in relation to each of the settlements. In particular, it is impossible to avoid the conclusion that in relation to the settlement (settlement A), made by A out of his own property, each of A and B is a settlor; and neither can be regarded as the dominant settlor to the exclusion of the other.

How then, in circumstances posed by the example, is tax to be charged under [this Part of the Act] in relation to settlement A on the death of X during the life of A? If A is to be treated as the settlor, the provisions of [s 53(3)] will be satisfied, and no tax is chargeable under [s 52(1)]. If B is to be treated as settlor as [s 44(2)] requires [s 53(3)] has no application and there is no relief from the charge imposed by [s 52(1)]. If the status of B as a settlor of settlement A is to be disregarded in applying the provisions of para 4 of the Schedule, then it is difficult to see what was the purpose in the express reference in [s 44(1)] to settlements made under reciprocal arrangements.

I was told by Mr McCall QC for the Crown in the course of argument that in the circumstances posed by the example the Revenue would seek to tax settlement A on the basis that B was the real or dominant settlor. This appears to me to be a correct tax treatment; although not, perhaps, for the reason given. I think that the correct approach is that required by [s 44(2)]; that is to say, where the circumstances so require, to apply the provisions of [this part of the Act] to settlement A as if the property comprised in that settlement were comprised in two separate settlements say, settlement A1 of which A is settlor, and settlement A2 of which B is settlor. On that basis, when applied to settlement A1, the provisions of [s 53(3)] will be satisfied; but when applied to settlement A2 those provisions will not be satisfied. Accordingly, by treating the settled property as comprised in separate settlements one of which is settlement A2 of which B is the settlor tax will be chargeable under the provisions of [s 52(1)]. This, as it appears to me, gives effect to the legislative intention which is to be derived from the extended meaning given to the concept 'settlor' by [s 44(1)].

In a settlement under English law, the identity of the trustees will normally be easily ascertained. This may not be so clear in the case of certain arrangements under foreign law that fall within the IHT definition of "settlement". Statute[7] therefore defines "trustees" as any persons in whom the settled property or its

[42.04] Settled property

management is for the time being vested. This ensures that there will always be some trustee as an accounting party liable for payment of IHT in respect of settled property.[8]

Simon's Taxes I5.131–133; Foster's Inheritance Tax E1.31–33.

[1] IHTA 1984, s 44(1); this is very different to the definition of settlor for income tax in ITTOIA 2005, s 620 and in ITA 2007, s 467 and is also different to the definition for capital gains tax in TCGA 1992, s 68A.
[2] *Fitzwilliam v IRC* [1993] STC 502, HL, at 516 per Lord Keith.
[3] [1992] STC 140.
[4] IHTA 1984, s 44(2).
[5] IHTA 1984, s 53(3); he also instanced s 48(3)(a) (excluded property), s 53(4) (reverter to settlor's spouse) and s 89(2) (trusts for disabled persons).
[6] [1992] STC 140 at 159–160.
[7] IHTA 1984, s 45. This may affect the settlor's liability to pay the tax under IHTA 1984, s 201(1)(d).
[8] IHTA 1984, ss 199(4), 200(4), 201(1), 204(2), 216(1)(b).

Categories of trust

[42.05] The general rule is that the transfer, on or after 22 March 2006, of property into a settlement at its creation (or later) is a chargeable transfer.[1] Thereafter, the trust is treated as a separate entity, with a charge to IHT each 10 years[2] and whenever the property leaves the trust.[3]

These rules do not apply for five "favoured" types of trust:

(a) *A transitional serial interest*[4]
This is an interest in a settlement that commenced before 22 March 2006, with an interest in possession subsisting prior to that date, when the prior interest came to an end on or after 22 March 2006 and before 6 October 2008. The transfer from the existing beneficiary to the next is a potentially exempt transfer, and there are no ten-year anniversary charges during the remainder of the lifetime of the second beneficiary. If the second beneficiary is the wife, husband or civil partner of the first, then the transfer is exempt.

(b) *A second type of transitional serial interest*[5]
This is an interest in a settlement that commenced before 22 March 2006, with a person enjoying an interest in possession prior to that date. The beneficiary died on or after 22 March 2006 and is succeeded by his/her spouse or civil partner. The transfer from the first beneficiary to the second is exempt. This treatment is available for such a transfer at any date, not only before 6 October 2008. This treatment applies only on the death of a spouse/civil partner and not on a lifetime termination of an interest in possession.

(c) *An immediate post-death interest*[6]

This is an interest in possession taking immediate effect under the will of a testator, or under intestacy.[7] The trust does not have to be in favour of the surviving spouse/civil partner and so could be an alternative way to provide for young people. The value of the fund forms part of the young person's estate and is not "relevant property" for the purpose of the regime charging IHT on property in trust. There can be an overriding power of appointment, or a power to advance capital, or both, and there is no restriction on the trusts in reversion.

(d) *A trust for bereaved minors*[8]

This is a trust under a will or intestacy giving capital to a child of the deceased parent at age 18. This includes statutory trusts under an intestacy. A "bereaved minor" is a person under age 18 at least one of whose parents had died. The meaning of "parent" is extended to include a step-parent and a person with parental responsibility under the respective laws of England and Wales, Scotland, and Northern Ireland. This treatment applies to settled property held on statutory trusts for a bereaved minor under the intestacy rules or trusts under the will of a parent or established under the Criminal Injuries Compensation Scheme, provided the bereaved minor would become absolutely entitled to the settled property and any income arising no later than age 18 and provided no other beneficiary can benefit in the interim. Such a trust could arise on the intestate death of a grandparent of the bereaved minor but could not arise under the will of a grandparent unless the grandparent had parental responsibility.

(e) *An age 18 to 25 trust*[9]

This is a will trust giving capital to a child of the testator at age 25, or before. It applies to settled property, whenever settled, held for the benefit of a person under age 25 at least one of whose parents has died. The trust must be established under the will of a deceased parent or under the Criminal Injuries Compensation Scheme. The terms of the trust must provide that the beneficiary will become absolutely entitled to the capital and income no later than age 25. Note that the beneficiary must take the capital at age 25, not just the income, and the income must be paid to the beneficiary in the interim or accumulated for his benefit. Accumulation of income is allowed but only for the child in question.

For these five types of trust the IHT treatment is the same as that given in infra, § **42.07** for interest in possession trusts created prior to 22 March 2006. The creation of the trust, if during lifetime, is a potentially exempt transfer. The property in trust is treated, for IHT purposes, as if it were part of the estate of the beneficiary with the interest in possession. There is no 10 year charge and, apart from the exception below, no IHT charge on property leaving the trust.

Exceptionally, there is an exit charge applied to an age 18 to 25 trust when property leaves the trust and is passed to a beneficiary who is aged over 18. There is no charge when property passes on the 18th birthday.

The exit charge for property passing out of a 18 to 25 trust is calculated as:[10]

chargeable amount × relevant fraction × settlement rate.

The chargeable amount = (broadly) the value of the fund.

[42.05] Settled property

The relevant fraction = 3/10 × quarters elapsed since beneficiary attained age 18 or date when fell within IHTA 1984, s 71D.

Settlement rate = (broadly) calculated as under present discretionary trust regime.

Applying this formula where a testator's will provides for his minor children to inherit outright at age 25 (the most common provision for children) there will be a maximum IHT charge on their attainment of that age of 4.2 per cent of the value of the trust fund in excess of the nil rate band. This is calculated by reference to the 28 quarters that had elapsed between ages 18 and 25. In most cases the effective rate would be less, and frequently £nil, as the trust has its own nil rate band.

Simon's Taxes I5.131, 132; Foster's Inheritance Tax E1.31, 32. On interaction with income tax see statement of practice SP1/82.

[1] FA 2006, Sch 20, para 9 amending IHTA 1984, s 3A.
[2] IHTA 1984, s 64, see infra, §§ **42.35–42.41**.
[3] IHTA 1984, s 65(1)(*a*), see infra, § **42.42**.
[4] IHTA 1984, s 49C inserted by FA 2006, Sch 20, para 5(1). The 6 October 2008 deadline was an extension of the original deadline of 6 April 2008 (made by FA 2008).
[5] IHTA 1984, s 49D. The 6 October 2008 deadline was an extension of the original deadline of 6 April 2008 (made by FA 2008).
[6] IHTA 1984, s 49A.
[7] For this treatment to apply, IHTA 1985, s 49A requires that four conditions are satisfied. Condition 1 is that the settlement "was effected by will [or intestacy]". Where there is a deed of variation, IHTA 1984, s 143(1) declares that IHTA 1984 "shall apply as if the variation had been affected by the deceased". Quaere—is a settlement created by a variation of will that is deemed to have been effected by the deceased within the statutory definition of a "settlement effected by will"? The answer is probably yes, but there must be doubt until the question has been decided by a court.
[8] IHTA 1984, s 71A inserted by FA 2006, Sch 20, para 1(1).
[9] IHTA 1984, s 71D.
[10] IHTA 1984, s 71F inserted by FA 2006, Sch 20, para 1(1).

CGT holdover relief

[42.06] A direct consequence of the IHT regime that applies to an interest in possession trust created on or after 22 March 2006 is that an election to hold over a gain arising on property moving into the settlement at its creation is now available for any type of property. An election to holdover a gain is not, however, available where the transfer is into a "settlor-interested" settlement; this includes any settlement where the spouse, or civil partner, of the settlor is a potential beneficiary.

As the passing of property to any settlement (other than one in the small number of "favoured" categories)triggers an immediate charge to IHT, an election[1] can be made to hold over the gain (see supra, § **18.40**).

The transfer of property out of such a trust triggers an IHT exit charge. Hence, an election[2] can, similarly, be made to hold over the gain arising to the trustees on an asset being advanced to a beneficiary, or vesting in a beneficiary. Where the beneficiary has an interest in possession over the income arising on the asset being advanced, there is, thus, a distinction between a trust that continues under the pre-March 2006 regime and a trust that is under the post-March 2006 regime. An advancement from a pre-March 2006 interest in possession trust triggers a capital gain that cannot be held over (unless the asset is a business, etc asset[3]). An advancement that is from a trust that is within the post 21 March 2006 regime, gives the opportunity for holding over the capital gain arising. Consideration may, therefore, be given, in appropriate cases, to the deliberate triggering of a change into the new regime if the advantage of obtaining holdover relief is greater than any potential inheritance tax charge. (This will, particularly, be the case where the value of the trust fund is less than the IHT nil rate band available.)

---

[1] TCGA 1992, s 260. Note, this election is not available if the trustees are not resident in the UK.
[2] Again, an election is available under TCGA 1992, s 260.
[3] TCGA 1992, s 165; see supra, §§ **18.41–18.43**.

Interest in possession created prior to 22 March 2006

[42.07] The tax statutes do not give a definition for "interest in possession", however, it has been described by the House of Lords as: "a present right of present enjoyment".[1] Where there is an interest in possession created prior to 22 March 2006, the property to which the interest in possession extends is charged to IHT as if it were in the estate of the beneficiary who has the interest in possession. This is not the same as treating the trust property as owned by the beneficiary in two important respects:

(1) the value of property in a settlement is ascertained without reference to any property held beneficially: a matter of considerable importance in valuing a minority shareholding in an unquoted company;
(2) the obligation to pay IHT calculated on the trust fund falls on the trustees, not on the beneficiary. The expression "interest in possession" is also crucial in that a transfer to a trust with such an interest is a potentially exempt transfer but a transfer to a trust without an interest in possession is a chargeable transfer. In ordinary property law the term is used to distinguish present interests from future interests, such as remainders or reversions. Thus a gift to A for life but with power to pay the income over to someone else is an interest in possession notwithstanding its defeasibility.[2]

In *Pearson v IRC*[3] property was held on trust for specified beneficiaries subject to a power in the trustees to accumulate income for 21 years. The House of Lords held that this power prevented the beneficiaries from having an interest in possession. The basis for the view of the (bare) majority was that an interest in possession was one which gave a present right to present enjoyment.[4] The

[42.07] Settled property

beneficiaries had agreed that if there had been a *duty* to accumulate they would not have had a right to present enjoyment. The Revenue argued—successfully—that there was no difference between a duty to accumulate and a power, since the exercise of that power by the trustees would prevent the beneficiaries from having anything to enjoy.

The case is authority for two other propositions. The first is that a power to advance capital to a remainderman would not have prevented the beneficiaries from having an interest in possession. This turns not, as one might have thought, on the need for the life tenant to give his consent to the exercise of the power, but on the distinction between a power to terminate a present right to present enjoyment (eg the power of advancement) and a power to prevent a present right of present enjoyment from arising (eg the power to accumulate).

The second proposition is that a power in the trustees to apply income to meet trust expenses etc does not prevent the life tenant from having an interest in possession. Although that power could be said to prevent a present right to present enjoyment it does not have that effect since it is an administrative power as distinct from a dispositive power. This distinction is stated rather than explored in the speeches. More recently the Court of Session, in holding that a power to make a payment out of income in order to meet the depreciation of capital value was an administrative power, said that this was because it was not a power to increase the capital value of the estate by diverting the income to those in right of capital.[5]

If A has a life interest and there is no power to withhold income from him short of depriving him of capital, he has an interest in possession notwithstanding that the trust fund is invested in a form such that no income, in fact, can arise.[6]

Where there is a duty to distribute the income amongst a class and, at the relevant time, there is only one person in the class but there is a chance that others may be added to it as the class is not closed, the one person does not have an interest in possession.[7] When trustees appoint property to a beneficiary but resolve to make the payment only after receiving an indemnity from the appointee, it is a question of construction whether the interest in possession arises at the time of the resolution or on receipt of the indemnity.[8]

Where, by virtue of an interest in possession, settled property is subjected to inheritance tax at the death of the beneficiary, the inheritance tax liability arising is calculated by measuring the capital value of the settled estate and adding this to the free estate, then calculating inheritance tax on the aggregate. Thus, the settled estate and the free estate are two separate entities. In *St Barbe Green v IRC*[9] the court held that the excess of liabilities over assets in the free estate of the deceased gave a value of the estate of £0. It was not possible for the excess liabilities to be put against the value of the settled estate.

Simon's Taxes I5.141–152; Foster's Inheritance Tax E1.41–52; STP [9.134]–[9.137].

---

[1] *Pearson v IRC* [1980] STC 318 per Viscount Dilhorn at 326b. In respect of Scotland "any reference to an interest in possession in settled property is a reference to an interest of any kind under a settlement actually being enjoyed by the person in right of that interest and the person in right of such an interest at any time shall

be deemed to be entitled to a corresponding interest in the whole or any part of the property comprised in the settlement": IHTA 1984, s 46.
2. He has a right to the income once the period for the trustees to exercise their discretion has expired—*Re Allen-Meyrick's Will Trusts, Mangnall v Allen-Meyrick* [1966] 1 All ER 740.
3. [1980] STC 318, [1980] 2 All ER 479.
4. So a right to income under the Trustee Act 1925, s 31(1)(ii) suffices for there to be an interest in possession, *Swales v IRC* [1984] STC 413.
5. *Miller v IRC* [1987] STC 108.
6. On effect of a power to allow a beneficiary to occupy a dwelling house see statement of practice SP 10/79; **Foster's Inheritance Tax Division W3.**
7. *Moore and Osborne v IRC* [1984] STC 236.
8. *Stenhouse's Trustees v Lord Advocate* [1984] STC 195.
9. [2005] EWHC 14 (Ch), [2005] STC 288.

Surviving spouse

[42.08] An arrangement frequently entered into, and not always solely with a view to mitigating inheritance tax, is that husband and wife hold the matrimonial home as tenants in common. At the first death, the interest of the deceased passes direct to the children, with the survivor continuing to occupy the entire property. Such an arrangement would appear to be effective.[1] Some practitioners have wished to strengthen the interest of the surviving spouse vis-è-vis the children by drafting a will so that the deceased leaves the surviving spouse a right under the will to occupy the property, in addition to any established right of occupation that arises under the rule in *Bull v Bull*.[2] It was such a provision that was considered by the court in *IRC v Lloyds Private Banking Ltd*.[3] In that case, the will left the beneficial share of the deceased to a trustee, on terms that so long as her husband wished to live in the house during his lifetime, then the trustee was obliged neither to enforce the trust for sale nor charge the husband a rent. The terms of trust on which the half share of the house was held provided that at the husband's death that share of the house should pass to the daughter. In fact, the husband did live in the house for the rest of his life. The court ruled that the correct construction of the will was that it made a disposition of an interest to the surviving spouse and was not merely an administrative direction, as was contended by the executors. On this basis, there was a determinable life interest which created a settlement.[4] The effect was that, on the death of the surviving spouse, the trustee of the settlement that had been created was liable to IHT.

1. See *Woodhall v IRC* [2000] STC (SCD) 558.
2. [1955] 1 QB 234, CA.
3. [1998] STC 559, reversing the decision of the Special Commissioner [1997] STC (SCD) 259.
4. IHTA 1984, s 49(1), see *Pearson v IRC* [1980] STC 318.

[42.09] Settled property

Extent of entitlement

[42.09] A person beneficially entitled[1] to an interest in possession in property settled before 22 March 2006 is treated as beneficially entitled to the property in which the interest subsists.[2] It follows that if B dies leaving a free estate of £50,000 and was also life tenant of a fund whose value was £30,000, he is treated as beneficially entitled to the whole of the property comprised in the settlement at his death, making a total transfer of property worth £80,000. A special rule may sometimes direct that the transfer is taxed as if made by the settlor, infra § **42.25** but this is ignored for present purposes.

Where a person is entitled to part only of the income his interest is treated as subsisting in that part of the property comprised in the settlement which corresponds with his share of the income.[3] So a half share in the income gives rise to a half share in the capital.

Where the part of the income is a specified amount, eg an annuity of £100, or the whole income less a specified amount, eg to B for life subject to the payment of an annuity of £100 to A, the interest corresponds with that part of the property which produces that income.[4]

Where the annuity is fixed and the income of the fund is constant, no difficulty will be encountered in discovering the shares of capital. However, where the income fluctuates the shares of A and B will vary from time to time.

If A were old or critically ill it would be in the interests of the trust to increase the income of the trust substantially so as to reduce the proportion of trust income needed to pay A's annuity; the opposite would arise if B were old or critically ill. In order to counter such arrangements, the Treasury prescribe higher and lower rates by statutory instrument.[5] The higher or maximum rate is applied in relation to A and IHT is charged as if the rate of return were that maximum rate.

EXAMPLE 1

Under a settlement worth £200,000 A receives an annuity of £2,000 pa whilst B receives the balance of income. Out of the £40,000 income A receives £2,000 and B £38,000. If A's interest terminates when the higher rate is 15% A's share will not be taken as 2,000/40,000 of £200,000 = £10,000. The higher rate of 15% only allows a notional income of £30,000 instead of the actual £40,000 income. So A's share is taken as 2,000/30,000 of £200,000 = £13,333.

It is expressly provided that the value taken as a result of this rule is not to exceed 100% of the settled property.

EXAMPLE 2

Under a settlement worth £200,000 A receives an annuity of £32,000 pa whilst B receives the balance of income. Out of the £40,000 income A receives his £32,000 and B £8,000. If A's interest terminates when the higher rate is 15% A's share will not be taken as 32,000/40,000 of £200,000 = £160,000. On applying the higher rate of 15% as the maximum allowable yield a notional £30,000 income only is allowed, but 32,000/30,000 of £200,000 would result in a chargeable value of £213,333 which is £13,333 more than the whole capital value. Accordingly A's share is treated as no greater than the whole capital value of £200,000.

The lower or minimum rate is applied in relation to B.

EXAMPLE 3

Under a settlement worth £200,000 A receives an annuity of £2,000 pa and B receives the balance of income. Out of the £6,000 income B thus receives £4,000. If B's interest terminates when the lower rate is 5% B's share will not be taken as 4,000/6,000 of £200,000 = £133,333. The lower rate of 5% treats a notional income of £10,000 to have arisen instead of the actual £6,000 income. So B's share is taken as 8,000/10,000 of £200,000 = £160,000.

However, neither of these rates is to apply where the chargeable transfers are made simultaneously and the tax is chargeable by reference to the interests of both A and B as where both interests end on the death of X and the property then vests in C. In such circumstances the Revenue will collect tax on 100% anyway.

The upper limit is the yield compiled on the FT share index for irredeemable gilts; the lower limit is the actual dividend yield compiled for the FT-SE All Share Index.[6] The rate is that which applies at the date of the transfer.

Concessionary relief is available when the annuitant dies or disposes of his interest and the annuity is charged in whole or in part on land. Where the capital valuation reflects an anticipated increase in rents available for use after the date of the transfer, "appropriate" relief is given in calculating the proportion of the property on which tax is chargeable.[7]

Although the legislation does not define how income is to be computed, one presumably looks at the income of the trust after the deduction of trust expenses but ignoring income tax and one compares this with the rights of A and B again before income tax. However, there are other possibilities.

Where the person entitled to the interest in possession in a pre-22 March 2006 settlement is not entitled to any income but is entitled jointly or in common with one or more others to the use and enjoyment of the property, his interest is that proportion which the annual value of his interest bears to the aggregate of all their interests.[8] This applies only where the person is not entitled to the income; this is presumably because if he could turn his enjoyment into income, as by selling the asset and taking income from the proceeds of sale or by leasing it,[9] the matter would fall within previous rules. For the same reason someone solely entitled to the use of property is not within this rule. Where the rule applies, annual value is presumably to be determined by reference to actual enjoyment of the property but this is unclear.[10]

Simon's Taxes I5.201, 202, 211–213; Foster's Inheritance Tax E2.01, 02, 11–13.

[1] If property is settled on X for life remainder to Y and X declares himself trustee of his interest for P and Q, P and Q are beneficially entitled to the interest in the settled property.
[2] IHTA 1984, s 49(1).
[3] IHTA 1984, s 50(1).
[4] IHTA 1984, s 50(2).
[5] IHTA 1984, s 50(3).
[6] Inheritance Tax (Settled Property Income Yield) Order 2000, SI 2000/174, see *Simons Weekly Tax Intelligence* 2000, p 129.
[7] Extra-statutory concession F11; **Simon's Taxes I5.213; Foster's Inheritance Tax, E2.13; Division U2.**
[8] IHTA 1984, s 50(5).

[42.09] Settled property

[9] eg by virtue of the powers conferred on the tenant for life under a strict settlement within SLA 1925.

[10] If A and B are entitled to a picture and B allows A to have the whole use of it, does A have a 100% interest or do A and B each have 50%?

Lease for life

[42.10] A lease[1] for life does not usually create a settlement under general law since LPA 1925, s 149(6) provides that the lease falls outside the Settled Land Act if it is in consideration of a fine or at a rent. However, a lease of property for life, or for a period ascertainable only by reference to a death—for example, a lease to end ten days after A's death—is to be treated as a settlement for IHT unless granted for full consideration in money or money's worth.[2] In *Faulkner (Adams'Trustee) v IRC*[3], the will of the deceased stated that the Mr and Mrs Harrison 'or the survivor for the time being still living may live in the house and have the use of the furniture as long as he/she or they so wish'.[4] Mr Harrison occupied the house shortly after the death of the deceased and lived there for 18 years until he died. The Special Commissioner held that, at his death, he held a lease for life which fell to be taxed as an interest in possession.[5] The same applies where the lease is for a term of years but is terminable on or at a date ascertainable by reference to a death. A lease for life is to be contrasted with a lease for a specified term: if the lessee is expected to live for 10 years, a lease for 10 or 15 years is not a lease for life.

Where a lease for life is a settlement, it is not the lease which is the settled property but the interest out of which the lease was created. The landlord has a reversion.[6]

By LPA 1925 a lease terminable on marriage is likewise converted into a 90 year lease if granted in consideration of a fine or at a rent. Such a lease does not create a settlement for the purpose of inheritance tax.

Deciding whether full value has been given depends upon the facts. Where a vendor retains a lease for life the reduction in price because of the reservation of the leasehold interest is taken into account.[7]

Where a lease for life is treated as a settlement, the lessor is treated as retaining a beneficial interest in part of the leased property, such interest being the proportion of the value of the consideration at the time the lease was granted bears to the then value of the full consideration: the tenant is treated as having a beneficial interest in the rest.[8] Thus, if property is let to T for life at one-tenth of the then full market rent, the lessor is treated as owning one tenth of the property and T is treated as owning nine tenths of the property. When a vendor wishes to retain a lease for life at full rent, it makes no difference whether the lease is reserved out of the interest conveyed or is the subject of a separate grant.[9]

Simon's Taxes I5.119, 120; Foster's Inheritance Tax E1.19, 20.

[1] Quaere whether an agreement for a lease is a lease—semble not, see *City Permanent Building Society v Miller* [1952] 2 All ER 621, [1952] Ch 840. In respect of

Northern Ireland references to property held in trust for persons are to include references to property standing limited to persons and as if the lease treated as a settlement under IHTA 1984, s 43(3) above did not include a lease in perpetuity within s 1 of the renewable Leasehold Conversion Act 1849 or a lease to which s 37 of that Act applies: IHTA 1984, s 43(5).

2 IHTA 1984, s 43(3).
3 [2001] STC (SCD) 112.
4 At 115b.
5 At 117e/118a.
6 On valuation see IHTA 1984, s 170; the rules for reversionary interests, infra, §§ 42.24 ff, do not apply: IHTA 1984, s 48(1)(c).
7 Statement of practice E10; **Foster's Inheritance Tax, Division W2**.
8 IHTA 1984, ss 50(6), 150.
9 Statement of Practice E10; **Foster's Inheritance Tax, Division W2**.

Estates in administration and survivorship clauses

[42.11] A person having an interest in possession in the residuary estate of a testator which is still being administered does not have an interest in the property but only a right of action against the executor to ensure due administration.[1] However, for the purposes of inheritance tax the residuary estate is to be treated as if it had been administered. The interest is deemed to exist from the date when he became entitled to income from the residue which will usually be the date of death.[2] To ascertain the residue allowance has to be made for specific dispositions,[3] annuities,[4] general and demonstrative legacies, statutory legacies on an intestacy, funeral, testamentary and administration expenses, debts and liabilities, and any apportionment required between capital and income.[5]

The position of one entitled to an interest in a specific or pecuniary legacy is unclear in theory;[6] there is no special IHT provision.

Where property is held for a person conditional upon his surviving the testator for a certain period, a settlement might be created by reason of the condition.[7] It is therefore provided that if the period does not exceed six months, the resulting disposition which takes effect, whether on his surviving the six months or his prior death, is treated as having had effect from the beginning of the period.[8] However, this is not to affect the application of tax to any distribution or application of property before the disposition takes effect.

Simon's Taxes I4.453; I5.161–164; Foster's Inheritance Tax D4.53; E1.61–64.

1 *Stamp Duties Comr (Queensland) v Livingston* [1965] AC 694, [1964] 3 All ER 692.
2 IHTA 1984, s 91.
3 TA 1988, s 701(5).
4 TA 1988, s 701(6).
5 eg *Allhusen v Whittell* (1867) LR 4 Eq 295 (apportionments).
6 See *Re Leigh's Will Trusts, Handyside v Durbridge* [1970] Ch 277, [1969] 3 All ER 432, 86 LQR 20 (PVB).

[42.11] Settled property

⁷ Because the arrangement comes within (*a*) at supra, § **42.02**.
⁸ IHTA 1984, s 92.

Transfers of settled property

[42.12] Certain events are treated as lifetime transfers of value by the person beneficially entitled to the interest in possession.¹ If he dies within seven years his circumstances therefore determine the rate of tax payable and whether any exemptions or reliefs apply. If the transfer is immediately chargeable the total transferred is added to his lifetime total of chargeable transfers for the purpose of determining liability on any subsequent transfer. However, there is no grossing up. The title by which he has become entitled is quite irrelevant: he may be the designated life tenant or have acquired it by assignment: all that matters is that he is entitled to that interest and that his entitlement is beneficial.²

Simon's Taxes I5.221, 222; Foster's Inheritance Tax E2.21, 22.

---

¹ IHTA 1984, ss 51, 52.
² Property is held on trust for A for life with remainder to B. A settles his life interest on X to hold on trust for C for life with remainder to D. Semble C's entitlement is beneficial and X's is not.

Termination

[42.13] Where at any time during the life of a person beneficially entitled to an interest in possession the interest comes to an end, he is treated as if he had then made a transfer of an amount corresponding to the value of the property in which his interest subsisted;¹ the transfer will be a potentially exempt transfer if the property becomes part of the estate of another person.²

EXAMPLES

(1) Property is held on trust for C for the life of X with remainder to B. C dies; X dies. On C's death there is a transfer by C under IHTA 1984, s 4. On X's death there is a transfer under IHTA 1984, s 52 by the person then entitled to the interest in possession but it will be a potentially exempt transfer as it goes into the estate of B.
(2) Property is held on trust for A for life with remainder to B for life with remainder to C. B dies; A dies. On B's death there is no charge on the settled property since B was not entitled in possession; on A's death there is a charge under IHTA 1984, s 4.
(3) Property is held on trust for A for life or until remarriage, with remainder on discretionary trusts. A remarries. There is a charge under s 52 and it cannot be a potentially exempt transfer.

Where the interest is an annuity charged on real or leasehold property, concessionary relief may be given to exclude such part of the capital value as is attributable to an anticipated increase in rents obtainable for the same use after that date.³

When the termination of an interest in possession in a pre 22 March 2006 trust causes property to transfer into the free estate of an individual, that transfer is a potentially exempt transfer.[4] By contrast, when the termination of an interest in possession in a pre 22 March 2006 trust has the effect that property remains in trust, the transfer is an immediately chargeable transfer that is deemed to be made by the individual who held the interest in possession.[5]

Simon's Taxes I5.222, 224; Foster's Inheritance Tax E2.22, 24.

---

[1] IHTA 1984, s 152. The settled property is valued in isolation without reference to any similar property; Inland Revenue press release, May 1990, *Simon's Tax Intelligence* 1990, p 446; **Foster's Inheritance Tax X6.43**.
[2] Unless before 17 March 1987 IHTA 1984, s 3A(6).
[3] Extra-statutory concession F11; **Foster's Inheritance Tax, Division U2**.
[4] IHTA 1984, s 3A as amended by FA 2006, Sch 20, para 9.
[5] IHTA 1984, s 51(1B) inserted by FA 2006, Sch 20, para 11.

Disposal

[42.14] Where the person beneficially entitled to an interest in possession in a pre 22 March 2006 trust disposes of his interest, the disposal is treated[1] as the termination of the interest thus causing a transfer[2] equal to the value of the property in which his interest subsisted. The disposal of the interest may be by assignment or, perhaps by surrender, it may be voluntary or involuntary.

Where the disposal is for a consideration in money or money's worth, tax is charged as if the value transferred were reduced by the amount of the consideration.[3] However, in determining the value of that consideration the value of any reversionary interest in the property or of any interest[4] in any other property comprised in the same settlement is left out of account. So if property is settled on A for life with remainder to B and there is a partition of the property, the value of B's interest is not treated as consideration for the disposal of the life interest; hence there is a deemed transfer of value of the property allotted to B but not that allotted to A because of the rule in infra, § 42.16.

If B provides A not with an interest under the settlement but with full market value in cash, there will inevitably be a charge since the market value of A's life interest must be less than the full value of the settled property. However, B is also treated as making a transfer of value if he pays a sum equal to the value of the underlying settled property.[5] Such a purchase can now be a potentially exempt transfer.[6]

Simon's Taxes I5.225, 226; Foster's Inheritance Tax E2.25, 26.

---

[1] By IHTA 1984, s 51.
[2] IHTA 1984, s 3A(2).
[3] IHTA 1984, s 52(2).
[4] Presumably not just reversionary interests but also, eg a life interest in another part of the settlement.
[5] IHTA 1984, s 49(2).

[42.14] Settled property

⁶ IHTA 1984, s 49(3) added by FA 1986, Sch 19, para 14 but repealed by F(No 2)A 1987, s 96(4).

Depreciatory transactions

[42.15] A charge arises where a depreciatory transaction is entered into between (a) the trustees and (b) any beneficiary or potential beneficiary or any person connected therewith. For example, under an express authorisation in the trust instrument trustees might sell property at an undervalue or lease at a low rent, eg by allowing a beneficiary to occupy a house under a lease at less than the rack rent, or lend money for a fixed period at well below market rates without being in breach of trust. To the extent that such a transaction reduces the value of the settled property which will be chargeable to tax at some future date, partial termination of the interest in possession in the property is deemed by IHTA 1984, s 52(3), the beneficiary with such interest being the transferor in respect of this transfer of value.[1] However, the transaction will not constitute a notional termination where it would not constitute a transfer of value if the trustees were beneficially entitled, eg where the transaction was not intended to confer any gratuitous benefit and was such as might be expected to be made in a transaction at arm's length between persons not connected with each other.[2]

Simon's Taxes I5.227; Foster's Inheritance Tax E2.27.

[1] IHTA 1984, s 3(4).
[2] IHTA 1984, ss 52(3), 10.

Exceptions

Where the beneficiary becomes entitled to the property or to another interest in possession in the property

[42.16] This exception[1] is dictated by the logic of the charge on interests in possession. If property is held on trust for A for life, he is treated as beneficially entitled to the whole property; if the settlement adds, "but to A absolutely if he reaches the age of 25", it would be contrary to all sense to direct a transfer by A on his 25th birthday when the property then becomes part of his free estate. It is not necessary that the new interest should arise under the terms of the settlement so no charge arises whether the property is appointed to A under a power in the settlement or he partitions the property with the remainderman and becomes entitled to a capital sum absolutely. Equally the exercise of a power to augment the tenant for life's income from capital causes no charge to this tax.[2]

The section also applies where the person with the interest in possession becomes entitled not absolutely but to another interest in possession. So when a tenant in tail's interest is reduced to a life interest on a resettlement this exception applies.

A restriction applies in that if the value of the property to which he becomes entitled is less than the value on which tax would otherwise be chargeable, tax is chargeable on the difference.[3] Thus if A is entitled to a life interest in the whole of the property until marriage but that interest is to be reduced to two-thirds on marriage, there will, in the event of marriage, be a transfer of one-third of the settled property. Likewise when A, the life tenant, partitions the property with B, the remainderman, there will be a charge on that part of the property which becomes the property of B.

EXAMPLE

S, who has made chargeable transfers of £50,000 settled £10,000 on A for life with remainder to B, and directed the trustees to pay the tax on the transfer. Five years later the fund is worth £10,000. A and B agree to divide it equally. A has made previous transfers of £20,000, B of £1 million. When S created the settlement he made a chargeable transfer of £10,000; his total then rose to £60,000. When A and B divide the fund there is a termination of A's interest in £10,000 (IHTA 1984, s 52) but tax is not chargeable on the half which he takes; he therefore makes a potentially exempt transfer of the other half, ie £5,000, so that his total remains at £20,000. IHT will become due if A dies within seven years.

The exception was modified for cases where a person becomes beneficially entitled to an interest in possession on or after 22 March 2006. Provided that the interest is not a disabled person's interest the exception will no longer apply if the person whose interest came to an end becomes beneficially entitled to another interest in possession in the property on that occasion.[4]

For persons becoming beneficially entitled to the interest in possession on or after 12 March 2008, the exception applies only if the other interest is a disabled person's interest or a transitional serial interest. That applies irrespective of when the previous interest in possession that came to an end began.[5]

Simon's Taxes I5.521; Foster's Inheritance Tax E2.51.

[1] IHTA 1984, s 53(2).
[2] Statement of practice E6; Foster's Inheritance Tax, Division W2.
[3] IHTA 1984, s 52(4)(*b*).
[4] IHTA 1984, s 53(2A) (as inserted by FA 2006, Sch 20, para 14(3)).
[5] IHTA 1984, s 53(2A) (as substituted by FA 2008).

Where the property reverts to the settlor

[42.17] If in a pre 2006 trust an individual has an interest in possession, a termination of the life interest that causes the property to revert to the settlor is exempt[1] if, and only if, the trust was either: (i) for a disabled person;[2] or (ii) the interest terminates before 6 April 2008.[3]

If these conditions are satisfied, tax is not chargeable[4] on the occasion of the reversion to the settlor. The purpose of this relief is to enable persons to

[42.17] Settled property

provide life interests for relatives without charge to tax; however, this relief is not confined to such transfers and does not preclude a charge on the creation of the settlement.

The exception applies only where the reverter is during the life of the settlor; however, it applies even though the settlor takes a beneficial life interest in possession.[5]

The exception is lost if the settlor acquired a reversionary interest in the property for money or money's worth.[6] Thus if the property was settled on B for life with remainder to C absolutely, the exception would not apply on the ending of B's interest in possession if S, the settlor, had bought C's remainder. However if S had acquired the remainder by way of gift from C, the exception would apply. It appears that the purchase of any reversionary interest is fatal. If B's life interest had been preceded by a life interest to A and S had then bought B's interest and been given C's interest, the exception would have been lost even though B predeceased A without his interest ever vesting in possession.

The exception is also lost if the reversionary interest has itself been settled after 9 March 1981.[7] Property could be settled on A for life, remainder to B. B would then settle the remainder on C for life with remainder to B. While there would be a charge when A died there would not be when B created the settlement as the subject matter was excluded property (rule (10) below), nor when C died, thus leaving C free to enjoy the income after A; death without risk of IHT after the creation of the settlement. The 1981 charge creates a charge on C's death.

Simon's Taxes I5.252, 734; Foster's Inheritance Tax E2.52; E7.34.

[1] IHTA 1984, s 54 amended by FA 2006, Sch 20, para 15.
[2] As defined in IHTA 1984, s 89 amended by FA 2006, Sch 20, para 6.
[3] Defined as a "transitional serial interest" by IHTA 1984, s 49C inserted by FA 2006, Sch 20, para 5.
[4] IHTA 1984, s 53(3).
[5] This was not so under the old estate duty exemption and is not obvious but appears to be the Revenue view.
[6] IHTA 1984, s 53(5)(a).
[7] IHTA 1984, s 53(5)(b).

Pre 2006 trust reversion: transfer on termination to the settlor's spouse

[42.18] Since a reversion to the settlor is the subject of one exception and a transfer between spouses is exempt, the legislation also provides that tax is not chargeable if when the interest comes to an end and on the same occasion the settlor's spouse becomes beneficially entitled to the settled property.[1]

This exception does not apply if the settlor or the spouse acquired a reversionary interest for consideration in money or money's worth; nor does it apply if the spouse was not at the relevant time domiciled in the UK. However, it applies for a limited period after the death of the settlor in that the term spouse is to include widow or widower if the settlor has died less than two years before the interest ends.

The restriction on settled reversionary interests applicable to the rule in supra, § **42.17** applies here also.[2]

Simon's Taxes I5.253, 734; Foster's Inheritance Tax E2.53; E7.34.

---

[1] IHTA 1984, s 53(4).
[2] IHTA 1984, s 53(5).

Pre 2006 trust reversion: disposition to provide family maintenance

[42.19] Where a disposition for the maintenance of one's family satisfied the conditions of IHTA 1984, s 11 but amounts to the disposal of an interest in possession, and so would be treated as a termination, the interest is not to be treated as coming to an end.[1] This applies to partial terminations as well as to total terminations as where a father tenant for life consents to an advance of capital to enable the outright purchase of an annuity to cover his son's future public school fees.

Simon's Taxes I5.263; Foster's Inheritance Tax E2.63.

---

[1] IHTA 1984, s 51(2); supra, § **42.16**.

Disclaimer

[42.20] On a disclaimer made otherwise than for consideration in money or money's worth, the person disclaiming is treated as never having become entitled to the interest.[1] A disclaimer cannot be made once the gift has been accepted; a surrender is not a disclaimer.[2]

Simon's Taxes I5.254; Foster's Inheritance Tax E2.54.

---

[1] IHTA 1984, s 93; *Re Sharman's Will Trusts, Public Trustee v Sharman* [1942] Ch 311, [1942] 2 All ER 74. Variation relating to settled property are excluded from IHTA 1984, s 142 by s 142(5).
[2] See, however, supra, § **40.21** for the special provisions relating to a disclaimer of an inheritance. IHTA 1984, s 142 operates to treat a disclaimer as if it were made at the date of death for IHT purposes, even when the individual has received, and retained, income arising between the date of death and the date of the disclaimer.

Trustees' annuities

[42.21] Where a person is entitled to an interest in settled property as remuneration for his services as trustee, tax is not charged on the termination

[42.21] Settled property

of that interest to the extent that it represents a reasonable amount of remuneration.[1] This exclusion does not apply if the trustee disposes of the right. In valuing the interest of the beneficiary it is presumably possible to make allowance for that proportion of the trust income needed for the annuity.

Simon's Taxes I5.256; Foster's Inheritance Tax E2.56.

---

[1] IHTA 1984, s 90.

Redemption of life interest on intestacy

[42.22] Where the surviving spouse of an intestate has a life interest in possession and exercises her statutory right to redeem her life interest for a capital sum she is to be treated as always having been entitled to the capital sum and so not as having been entitled to the interest in possession.[1]

Simon's Taxes I4.452.

---

[1] IHTA 1984, s 145. The right arises under the Administration of Estates Act 1925, s 47A; presumably this exemption applies only if the redemption takes place under this Act so that a simple partition will be exempt only if it comes within the previous exception.

Reversionary interests

[42.23] A reversionary interest[1] is a future interest under a settlement, whether vested or contingent (including an interest expectant on the termination of a lease treated as a settlement, eg a lease for life at a nominal rent).[2] A future interest must be distinguished from a mere spes. So where property is settled on A for life with remainder to Y, but with overriding power for the trustees to appoint capital to such of B to X as they see fit, then B merely has a spes whilst Y has a reversionary interest.

In general, a reversionary interest is excluded property.[3] Thus, if property was settled on A for life with remainder to B and B died before A there would be no transfer on B's death of the interest in the settled property, the Revenue being content to wait and to tax the transfer of the property on the termination of A's interest. This prevents overcharging to IHT.

Since the general immunity of reversionary interests is open to exploitation IHTA 1984, s 48(1) provides that a reversionary interest in settled property in the UK is not excluded property:

(1) if it has *at any time* been acquired (whether by the person entitled to it or by a person previously entitled to it) for a consideration in money or money's worth; or

(2) it is one to which either the settlor or his spouse is or has been entitled under a settlement; or

(3) if it is the interest expectant on the termination of a lease treated as a settlement, ie a lease for life at a nominal rent.[4]

Further IHTA 1984, s 55(1) provides that where a person entitled to an interest (whether in possession or not) in any settled property acquires a reversionary interest expectant (whether immediately or not) on that interest, the reversionary interest is not treated as part of that person's estate.

The effect of these rules is not immediately obvious but is to be discerned from the avoidance of tax. If property worth £130,000 is held on trust for A for life, with remainder to B, and A has free estate worth £50,000 there will on A's death be a transfer of £180,000. If A buys B's remainder for £40,000 the property will cease to be settled but there will be no transfer of value in that event because although A's life interest in the property terminates he becomes on the same occasion absolutely entitled to it. When A dies the formerly settled property will pass as his free estate. The avoidance consists in the fact that A purchases B's remainder for full consideration of £40,000. This has the effect of reducing the value of A's free estate by £40,000 so that on A's death the total value of the property transferred will only be £140,000 and not £180,000. Thus A has depleted his free estate by a payment which is not itself a transfer of value and has replaced it with property which would have been chargeable in any event.

The legislative solution is to treat A's purchase of B's remainder as a transfer of value by A of the amount of the purchase price notwithstanding that full value has been given for the remainder. This is achieved by IHTA 1984, s 55(1) which directs that A's estate is not increased by the reversion with the result that the money passing to B is pure loss to A's estate and so chargeable (s 55 also specifically excludes IHTA 1984, s 10). If the purchase is effected after 16 March 1987 it is a potentially exempt transfer.[5]

IHTA 1984, s 55(1) is also useful where A has both a life interest and a purchased remainder. Thus suppose that property is settled on A for life, remainder to X for life, remainder to Y absolutely. On a purchase by A of Y's remainder A will be deemed to make a gift to Y of the consideration he gives Y. However, owing to the purchase, the reversionary interest no longer ranks as excluded property and so forms part of A's estate in which the value of the settled property is already represented owing to A's life interest in possession. Since A has already been charged with IHT in respect of the value of the reversionary interest, IHTA 1984, s 55(1) excludes the reversion from A's estates. A is thus deemed to have acquired nothing, so on a subsequent transfer of the reversion by A, eg on A's death no transfer of value can arise since there can be no loss in the value of A's estate.

Rule 2 has the effect of treating a reversion falling within it as non-excluded property. If S settles property, say £100,000, on X for life with remainder to himself, the transfer by S is not of £100,000 but only of that sum *less* the then actuarial value of the reversion. It follows that if S then gives away the reversion there may be a charge to IHT; equally it follows that if S sells it for full market value there will not.

In 1981 the rule was extended to cover the situation in which S, or his spouse, had at any time been entitled to the reversionary interest. Under the previous

[42.23] Settled property

rule the interest would, as now, not be excluded property while S was alive; he could then leave the interest to his spouse free of CTT. However, as a widow is not a spouse the interest became excluded property on reaching her. The new rule makes sure that the reversion remains chargeable.

Simon's Taxes, Division 15.7; Foster's Inheritance Tax Division E7.

[1] IHTA 1984, s 47.
[2] IHTA 1984, s 43(3), see, supra, § **42.10**.
[3] IHTA 1984, s 48(1).
[4] IHTA 1984, s 48(1). On reversionary interests belonging to a person domiciled abroad see infra, § **47.16**.
[5] IHTA 1984, s 55(2).

Potentially exempt transfers—special rate of charge

Special rate of charge on chargeable transfer of settled property following potentially exempt transfer creating settlement

[42.24] As a consequence of the introduction of the potentially exempt transfer rule into the area of settled property, a special rate of charge may apply where a chargeable transfer of settled property follows a potentially exempt transfer creating the settlement.[1] This will apply where an interest in possession comes to an end on its termination under s 52 or the person beneficially entitled dies;[2] this formulation is presumably wide enough to cover deemed terminations of interest such as a disposition of the interest in possession or a depreciatory transaction.

The reason behind the rule is apparently to prevent a settlor (S) from gaining an advantage by creating a discretionary trust subject to an initial life interest in favour, say, of A as distinct from creating one immediately. The advantage would be that S could avoid his personal cumulative total being used to calculate the tax on the chargeable (not potentially exempt) transfer arising on the creation of the discretionary trusts. This could be achieved by settling the property on trusts such that, before the discretionary trusts arise, there is a short interest in possession in favour of A, a person who, it is hoped, will have a cumulative total of zero by the time that the interest in possession terminates and the discretionary trusts arise. Tax will be due if S dies within seven years as the potentially exempt status of the transfer to A will be lost; there is the further risk of a charge to tax when A's interest ends if A's cumulative total is not then sufficiently low.

The five conditions which trigger this charge are cumulative.[3] First the creation of the settlement must have been a potentially exempt transfer—as distinct from a chargeable or exempt one. So the settlement of property on a spouse for life with a discretionary trust over will not cause this charge to apply. Equally it cannot apply unless the trust is created after 16 March 1987.[4] Provision is made for the situation in which only a part of the transfer was potentially exempt.[5] Second, the ending of the interest in possession or death of the life tenant must occur within seven years of the potentially exempt transfer by which the settlement was made. Third, the settlor must be alive at the time of the ending of the interest or the death of the life tenant.

Fourth, on that termination or death the property must become settled property in which no qualifying interest in possession[6] subsists (other than an accumulation and maintenance settlement). So the charge applies where property is settled by S on A for life with remainder over on discretionary trusts and A dies within seven years or releases the life interest. There will be a chargeable transfer in either of these events; it cannot be a potentially exempt transfer by A since the property does not become part of the estate of any other person.

Fifth, the property must not have become settled property in which an interest in possession subsists or which is an accumulation and maintenance settlement or become property to which an individual is beneficially entitled within six months of the termination. This rule, added late in the legislative process, gives the trust six months to escape from the special rate.

Tax would apart from these special rules be chargeable by reference to the circumstances of A in these events, and as S is still alive and the creation of the settlement was potentially exempt there would not be any charge on S. The alternative charge under the special rules is by reference to S's personal circumstances, and applies if—and only if—it results in more tax being chargeable. There is assumed a hypothetical transfer by a person with a cumulative total of chargeable transfers equal to that of S's cumulative total at the time the settlement was created; this total is to include any sums already caught by these rules,[7] and lifetime rates are applied.[8] Thus one calculates the amount of tax that would have been due if the original transfer in trust had been chargeable and not potentially exempt, although using the current and not the original value of the settled property. If this tax would be greater the greater amount is due now[9]—it is primarily due from the trustees of the settlement.[10]

The charge applies only where S is still alive. If S should die later but within seven years of the settlement extra tax may be due from the settlement.[11] Conversely if A's interest ends but A dies within seven years additional tax may also be due.[12] These deaths are to be ignored in determining the sum initially due under these rules.

Simon's Taxes I3.526, 527; Foster's Inheritance Tax C5.26, 27; STP [10.67].

---

1 IHTA 1984, s 54A.
2 IHTA 1984, s 54A(1).
3 IHTA 1984, s 54A(2).
4 The rules cannot apply where there was a settlement before that date on a disabled person as s 54(2)(a) is specific as to the date; moreover the charge cannot apply where the trust is initially an accumulation and maintenance settlement since there is no initial interest in possession—this raises questions as to the policy behind the rule.
5 By use of the concept of "special rate property"—IHTA 1984, s 54B(3). The burden of the tax falls exclusively on this part of the settled property: IHTA 1984, s 265.

[42.24] Settled property

6   See infra, § 42.03.
7   IHTA 1984, s 54B(4)–(6).
8   IHTA 1984, s 54A(6).
9   IHTA 1984, s 54A(5).
10 IHTA 1984, s 54B(3).
11 IHTA 1984, s 54B(1).
12 IHTA 1984, s 54B(2).

Estate duty trusts

Surviving spouse relief

[42.25] Prior to the introduction of CTT in 1974, estate duty was charged on the estate passed to the surviving spouse. There would, therefore, be a double charge to tax if inheritance tax were now charged on the property left in trust for the surviving spouse. Relief is provided by the interest in possession being treated as excluded property. Where a person died before 13 November 1974 and left property in trust in possession for his/her surviving spouse, the value of that property is left out of account in calculating the estate of the surviving spouse when that interest in possession comes to an end, whether at death of the surviving spouse, or otherwise.[1]

1   IHTA 1984, Sch 6, para 2. The exemption is provided by importing the exclusion that was applicable by estate duty by virtue of Finance Act 1894, s 5(2).

Purchasers

[42.26] Special provision was made to prevent purchasers or mortgagees of reversionary interests before 27 March 1974 being caught out by the then new CTT provisions. The tax payable by such persons when the reversionary interest falls into possession is not to exceed the amount of estate duty that would have been payable: any tax which thereby becomes payable by the mortgagor instead of the mortgagee is to rank as a charge subsequent to that of the mortgagee.[1] This applies also to IHT.

Simon's Taxes I5.285; Foster's Inheritance Tax E2.85.

1   IHTA 1984, Sch 6, para 3.

Pre-1975 election to defer estate duty

[42.27] Between 1895 and 1975 estate duty was chargeable on the value of a reversionary interest.[1] However, the personal representatives had available to them an election[2] to defer the payment of the estate duty until the reversionary interest crystallised formally on the death of the existing life tenant. In the

Revenue view, estate duty remains collectible if the death of the life tenant now causes the reversionary interest to crystallise. Although FA 1975, s 49 is headed "Abolition of estate duty" this heading is, in the Revenue view, misleading and the effect of that section is to abolish the charge to estate duty solely for the events on or after 13 March 1975. Estate duty, in these circumstances, is calculated on the value of the settled property, valued at the date of the death of the life tenant, to which estate duty rates current at the date for which the election was made (ie the death of the holder of the reversionary interest) are applied.[3] The charge is, thus, potentially significant.

The alternative view is based on the treatment afforded to an interest in possession by IHTA 1984, s 49(1). This states: "A person beneficially entitled to an interest in possession in settled property shall be treated for the purposes of this act as beneficially entitled to the property in which the interest subsists". Inheritance tax is charged on the occasion of a person's death on that person's estate, being "the aggregate of all the property to which he is beneficially entitled".[4] Hence, in this view, the effect of the Inheritance Tax Act is to make the settled property on which estate duty would be charged part of the "principal value" of the estate of the person who dies in the IHT era. On this view, FA 1975, s 49(1), thus acts to abolish the estate duty charge on this settled property.

---

[1] FA 1894, s 6(1).
[2] FA 1894, s 7(6).
[3] FA 1894, s 7(5). This interpretation of the statutory provision was determined in *Re Eyre* [1907] 1 KB 331 and approved by the Court of Appeal in *Astley v IRC* [1975] STC 557, CA.
[4] IHTA 1984, s 5(1).

Charge on trustees

[42.28] A specific IHT regime applies to settled property which is defined in the legislation as "relevant property".[1] For a trust created on or after 22 March 2006 (other than a specially favoured trust which terminates at age 18, or is for a disabled person), this term is used for all settled property other than property specifically excluded (see infra, § **42.32**).

For a trust created before 22 March 2006, "relevant property" is property over which there is no interest in possession.

Simon's Taxes I5.311; Foster's Inheritance Tax E3.11; STP [9.138]–[9.140]; [10.132]–[10.134].

---

[1] IHTA 1984, s 58(1).

[42.29] Settled property

Related settlements

[42.29] When computing a charge arising under this special IHT regime, it is necessary to bring into the calculation the value of property in a related settlement. Settlements are related if they are made by the same settlor on the same day; a settlement which would be related by this rule is not related if immediately after the settlement commenced the property was held for charitable purposes only and without limit of time.[1]

Simon's Taxes I5.314; Foster's Inheritance Tax E3.14.

---

[1] IHTA 1984, s 62; when part of the income is to be applied to such purposes a corresponding part is treated as held for charitable purposes; IHTA 1984, s 84.

Settlements—property moving between settlements

[42.30] The definition of settlement and who is a settlor are the same as for the rules described above (see supra, §§ **42.02** and **42.04**).

Where property moves between settlements it is provided that the property is to be treated as remaining in the first settlement.[1] This rule applies even if the original settlement has come to an end. However, this rule does not apply if in the meantime any person becomes beneficially entitled to the property (as distinct from becoming entitled to an interest in possession in the property). This strange rule can have unexpected consequences. The author advises trustees who hold property that was originally settled in 1937. In 1984 each of the three children of the settlor settled his reversionary interest onto new trusts. Following the death of the 1937 settlor, the assets came to be held in the three separate 1984 trusts. The children are treated as the settlors of the 1984 trust funds; the gains made by the overseas trustees of each of the three settlements is assessed on the 1984 settlor of that settlement. However, the ten-year charge to IHT arises on the tenth anniversary of the original settlement in 1937. Had the fund been distributed in 1984 and then resettled, the ten-year charges would be on the anniversaries of the date in 1984. (Had the arrangement been that the 1937 trust had been divided in 1984, there would now be no CGT charge on the children.)

This rule applies only if the property ceases to be subject to one settlement after 10 December 1981 but a similar rule applies where the cesser occurred after 26 March 1974 but before 11 December 1981.[2] As originally drafted this rule, which is wider than its predecessor[3], had the effect that if a reversionary interest arising under a settlement was itself settled on trusts of another settlement and then fell into possession, the property would have to be treated as remaining in the first settlement. This is not to apply to events occurring after 14 March 1983 if the reversion was settled before 11 December 1981 and the reversion is expectant on the termination of a qualifying interest in possession. The purpose of the change is to restore the law to the position which was expected when the reversion was settled.[4]

Simon's Taxes I5.453; Foster's Inheritance Tax E4.53.

1   IHTA 1984, s 81; on conditions for status as excluded property see IHTA 1984, ss 48(3), 82.
2   IHTA 1984, s 81(2).
3   FA 1975, Sch 5, para 11(4).
4   IHTA 1984, s 81(3).

Commencement of settlement

[42.31] In deciding when a settlement commences the rule is that one looks to the time when property first becomes comprised in it.[1]

Simon's Taxes I5.313; Foster's Inheritance Tax E3.13.

1   IHTA 1984, s 60.

Relevant property—the exclusions

[42.32] The property is not relevant property—and so these rules do not apply—if the property is held on certain special trusts.[1] These are:

(1) property held for charitable purposes only, whether for a limited time or otherwise;
(2) property held as maintenance funds for historic buildings, etc;
(3) property held on accumulation and maintenance settlements created before 22 March 2006;
(4) property held on approved superannuation schemes;
(5) property held on trusts for employees or the special newspaper trusts;
(6) property held on the discretionary trusts arising under a protective trust and arising before 12 April 1978;
(7) property held on trusts for disabled persons and settled before 10 March 1981;
(8) property held on a trade or professional compensation fund;
(9) excluded property;
(10) sums received by trustees and any assets representing them (but not any income or gains arising from them) if held by trustees as a result of the reduction in pool betting duty intended for football ground improvements[2] or to support games, etc[3]; and
(11) property forming part of a premium trusts fund or ancillary trust fund of a corporate member of Lloyd's.[4]

A charge to tax may, nonetheless, arise in relation to these trusts; see infra, §§ **42.49** ff.

On charges relating to works of art, see infra, § **44.27**.

Simon's Taxes I5.312; Foster's Inheritance Tax E3.12.

1   IHTA 1984, s 58.
2   FA 1990, s 126.

[42.32] Settled property

³ FA 1991, s 121.
⁴ FA 1994, s 248(2); for definitions see FA 1994, ss 222, 223.

The charge at the ten-year anniversary

The principal occasion of charge

[42.33] Tax is charged on the value of that relevant property at a ten-year anniversary.[1] The Revenue view is that the relevant property does not include undistributable income which has not been accumulated.[2] As it is the value of this relevant property that is taken there is no grossing up. After the 1986 changes the periodic charge continues to arise at ten-yearly intervals notwithstanding the reduction in the general accumulation period from ten years to seven; but the hypothetical cumulative total used in calculating the charge assumes a cumulative period of seven years, see infra, § **42.36**.

It is first necessary to define the ten-year anniversary. Generally this means the tenth anniversary of the date on which the settlement commenced and subsequent ten-year anniversaries.[3]

It will be noted that the ten-year period runs from the date of the creation of the settlement (or its predecessor settlement). This is not necessarily the same as that on which the property became relevant property. So if the settlement created on 1 May 1976 began with a life interest in possession, the first ten-year anniversary would still be 1 May 1986, although no charge would then arise unless the property had then become relevant property, ie no qualifying interest in possession then subsisted in it.

Special rules apply if the settlement begins with an interest in possession in the settlor or his spouse.[4]

The value of the property will be reduced if the property is entitled to agricultural or business relief.

The severity of this charge is mitigated where the property, although relevant property on the anniversary, has not been so throughout the period. This may be because it was not "relevant" or because it was not comprised in the settlement at all. The mitigation takes the form of a reduction in the rate at which the tax is to be charged.[5] (By contrast, there is no reduction when computing the exit charge for property that has been introduced since the last ten-year anniversary.)[6]

Simon's Taxes I5.321; Foster's Inheritance Tax E3.21.

[1] IHTA 1984, s 64.
[2] Statement of practice SP 8/86; Foster's Inheritance Tax Division W3.
[3] IHTA 1984, s 61.
[4] IHTA 1984, s 80; infra, § **42.47**.
[5] IHTA 1984, s 66(2).
[6] See infra, § **42.41**.

Rate of tax on the principal occasion of charge—IHTA 1984, s 66

Trusts created after 26 March 1974

[42.34] The rate at which tax is charged is to be 30% of "the effective rate". In making these calculations only the lifetime rates of tax are used. With the top applicable rate of tax reduced to 20% this makes the maximum rate on a ten-year charge 30% × 20% = 6%.

The effective rate is the tax chargeable, using lifetime rates, expressed as a percentage of the amount on which it is charged. The tax chargeable depends on a calculation of a hypothetical value to be taxed and a hypothetical point from which that value is to start. It is inherent in these rules that a particular figure should not enter both hypothetical parts.

These rules give rise to the important planning points that where a settlor proposes to make a "discretionary trust" and another "fixed trust" (a) they should be created on different days, and (b) the discretionary trust should be created first; (a) avoids the related property rules infra, § **42.35**, while (b) ensures a lower starting point by reducing figure 1 infra, § **42.36**.

The hypothetical value transferred

[42.35] The value deemed to be transferred for this purpose is the aggregate of:

(1) the value charged under IHTA 1984, s 66(4);
(2) the value, immediately after the settlement was created, of any part of the property then comprised in the settlement which has not then and has not since become relevant property (eg a life interest which still subsists); and
(3) the value immediately after a related settlement commenced of the property then comprised in it.

EXAMPLE

On 4 April 1992 S, whose cumulative total of transfers stood at £100,000 made two settlements. No 1 was of £100,000 and was to be held on discretionary trusts subject to a life interest in half the income in favour of A. No 2 was of £70,000 and was to be held only on discretionary trusts. On the ten-year anniversary on 4 April 2002 the value of No 1 is £320,000 and that of No 2 is £90,000; A is still alive; £10,000 was advanced to a beneficiary from No 2 on 1 May 1998.

In calculating the 2002 charge one begins with the hypothetical value transferred. For settlement No 1 that is:

(a) £160,000, ie the half of the £320,000 that is relevant property,
(b) £50,000, ie the initial value of the property in which A has a life interest, and
(c) £70,000 ie the initial value of the related property settlement = £280,000.

The hypothetical value transferred for Settlement No 2 is:

(a) £90,000, (b) nil, and (c) £100,000 = £190,000.

It will be noted that the sum charged under s 64 on a previous ten-year anniversary is ignored. On the second ten-year anniversary in 2012 the hypothetical value of settlement No 1 will, assuming the value of fund No 1 to be £500,000 and that A is still alive, be the sum of (a) £250,000, (b) £50,000 and (c) £70,000, ie £370,000.

[42.36] Settled property

The starting point: the hypothetical cumulative total

[42.36] The rules suppose a transferor who has made aggregate total transfers of:

(1) all chargeable transfers made by the settlor in the seven-year period ending with the date the settlement was made, but disregarding transfers made on that day; plus
(2) all property that has been the subject of an exit charge since the last ten-year charge, valued at the time the exit charge arose, see infra, § 42.46. (If it is the first ten-year charge, it is the aggregate of the property that has left the settlement since its creation.)

EXAMPLE (FACTS AS SUPRA, § 42.35)
Settlement No 1
On 4 April 2002 the hypothetical starting point is:

(a)   £100,000 + (b) nil = £100,000

So, putting (a) and (b) together one calculates the IHT at lifetime rates of a transfer of £280,000 by a person with a cumulative total of £100,000.

The tax will be:

Tax at lifetime rates on £(100,000 + 280,000)	£27,600
less tax at lifetime rates on £100,000	Nil
	£27,600

Tax of £27,600 on £280,000 would give an effective rate of 9.857% so the rate of charge is 30% of that, ie 2.957% and this is applied to £160,000 to give total tax of £4,731.

Settlement No 2
The hypothetical starting point is:

(a)   £100,000 + (b) £10,000 (the sum advanced to A) = £110,000

so one calculates IHT at lifetime rates of a transfer of £190,000 by a person with a cumulative total of £110,000.

Tax at lifetime rates on (110,000 + 190,000)	£11,600
less tax at lifetime rates on £110,000	Nil
	£11,600

Tax of £11,600 on £190,000 would give an effective rate of 6.105% so the rate of charge is 30% of that, ie 1.832% and this is applied to £90,000 to give total tax of £1,648.

One effect of IHTA 1984, s 66(4), (5) is that any tax paid by the settlor on the creation of the settlement is ignored.

On effect of purchase of a work of art, see infra, § **44.19**.

A potentially exempt transfer becomes chargeable if the donor dies within seven years but is treated as having taken place at the time of the transfer not the time of death. If the settlor has made such a transfer, then settles this property on discretionary trusts, and then dies within seven years of the potentially exempt transfer, there may be additional tax to pay on the creation of the settlement by virtue of an increase in the total of chargeable transfers in the seven years ending with the date of the settlement.[1]

The effect of bringing into the calculation the value of capital advances made since the last ten-year charge (or since the commencement of the settlement, if it is the first ten-year charge) is normally to use part of the nil rate band and, thereby, increase the effective rate of tax applied at the ten-year anniversary. However, this increase in the tax burden is never as great as the increase in the tax payable that would have arisen had the value of the trust property been increased by the amount that was distributed. Hence, unless values fall, distributing never increases the tax charge. This can be illustrated:

EXAMPLE

(Assume:

(i) no BPR;
(ii) the settlor has no cumulative total;
(iii) the nil rate band in 2012–13 is £500,000).

On 20 May 2002 shares valued at £250,000 are settled.

By early May 2012 the value of the shares has risen to £2,500,000.

1st scenario: No distribution is made.
10 year charge on 20 May 2012:
£2,500,000–£500,000 × 20% × 30%
= IHT payable   £120,000

2nd scenario: On 19 May 2012 half the shares are distributed.
Exit charge on 19 May 2012
£1,250,000–£500,000 × effective rate of 0%   nil
10 year charge on 20 May 2012:
£1,250,000 [nil rate band used by capital distribution] × 20% × 30%
= IHT payable   £75,000

---

[1] Simon's Taxes I5.431–436; Foster's Inheritance Tax E4.31–36.

The extra tax is due six months from the death of the settlor; IHTA 1984, s 226(3B). Instalment relief may be available; IHTA 1984, s 236(1A).

Trusts created before 27 March 1974

[42.37] For settlements created before 27 March 1974 a simpler regime applies. The hypothetical value transferred consists simply of the value charged under IHTA 1984, s 64, ie the value of the relevant property on the anniversary. For second and subsequent anniversaries the hypothetical cumulative total consists simply of sums charged under IHTA 1984, s 65.[1] As one is dealing with a pre-1974 settlement, there will be no chargeable transfer made by the settlor before the settlement.

[42.37] Settled property

Simon's Taxes I5.411, 412; Foster's Inheritance Tax E4.11, 12.

[1] IHTA 1984, s 66(6).

Property relevant property for only part of the period

[42.38] Where the property to be charged under IHTA 1984, s 66, although relevant property on the anniversary, has not been so throughout the period a reduced rate applies.[1] The reduction is 1/40th for each quarter in that period which expired before the property became or last became relevant property comprised in the settlement.

This provision would appear to apply whenever a ten year charge arises on a pre 22 March 2006 interest in possession trust. At the first ten year anniversary after March 2006, it is necessary, first, to identify the date on which, by applying the transitional provisions, the property in trust first became relevant property and then to compute the ten year charge by reference to the period between that date and the date of the ten year anniversary.

EXAMPLE

On the tenth anniversary the fund is worth £600,000. A died half-way through the ten-year period. For the first five years one-half of the income of the fund was paid to A by reason of a life interest. A's one half of the property was not relevant property throughout the ten-year period; the rate otherwise due on that part, £300,000, is therefore reduced by 20/40ths. There will have been an occasion of charge on the ending of A's life interest but under the rules discussed in the previous chapter.

While the principle behind the mitigation is clear, it is anything but clear how the rules should be applied where the property was not relevant property by reason of some annuity since it is difficult to see exactly what part of the property is to be reduced by the 40ths formula.

This reduction is only applied when calculating the tax arising on the ten year charge. There is no reduction in calculating the effective rate for the charging of tax on property that leaves a settlement before the first 10 year charge or between 10 year charges (the exit charge: infra, § **42.41**).

Simon's Taxes I5.422; Foster's Inheritance Tax E4.22.

[1] IHTA 1984, s 66(2).

Added property etc

[42.39] Special provision has to be made for the situation in which value is added to the settlement during the ten years before the anniversary on which the principal charge arises.[1] The risk of an increase in the hypothetical cumulative total stemming from even the slightest addition to the settlement is a major point in tax planning for such trusts. These rules apply whenever the settlor makes a chargeable[2] transfer in that time as a result of which the property in the settlement is increased in value; it is not necessary that there

The charge at the ten-year anniversary [42.39]

should have been any increase in the property in the settlement. Thus these rules will apply when the settlor makes an omission which results in an increase in the value of the settlement and so is a chargeable transfer by him; however, an exception is made when the transfer was not primarily intended to increase the value of the settled property and the increase in the value of the settled property was not more than 5%.[3]

Where value is added in this way these rules provide for an adjustment of the starting point, ie the hypothetical cumulative total from which to begin the calculation of the effective rate. The rule is that instead of the values transferred by chargeable transfers by the settlor in the period, as from 18 March 1986, of seven (previously ten) years before the day on which the settlement was made there shall, if greater, be taken the aggregate of values transferred by chargeable transfers by the settlor in the ten years ending with the day on which the addition occurred, but disregarding the transfers made on that day.[4]

If the settlor has made more than one addition the highest figure is taken. If, as is likely, the seven-year period brings in the sum originally settled that sum is excluded. This is because it will be brought into account in other parts of the IHTA 1984, s 66 calculation. For similar reasons property which has ceased to be settled and on that account is part of the hypothetical starting point is also excluded.[5]

EXAMPLE

In 1987 S made a chargeable transfer of £300,000.

In 1992 S made two settlements on discretionary trusts on the same day; No 1 of £550,000 and No 2 of £450,000.

In 1993 S made a chargeable transfer of £200,000.

In 1999 S adds £250,000 to settlement No 1 and £100,000 to settlement No 2.

In 2002 the first ten-year anniversary comes round. The cumulative total will be the greater of (a) £300,000 and (b) £300,000 + 200,000—ie (b). If the chargeable transfer of £200,000 had taken place in 1993 not 1988 (and so more than ten years after 1982), the figures would have been (a) £300,000 and (b) £200,000 so (a) would have been taken.

It will be noticed that for settlement No 1 the £100,000 is ignored—as being a transfer made on the same day as the value added to settlement No 1—as are the sums of £450,000—taken in as the initial value of a related settlement in calculating the amount to be used in calculating the value used to find the effective rate—and the £250,000 itself.

Where the settlement was made before 27 March 1974 but an addition is made after 8 March 1982 the hypothetical cumulative total (or starting point) is the aggregate of the settlor's chargeable transfers made in the seven years before the addition.[6]

Simon's Taxes I5.431–436; Foster's Inheritance Tax E4.31–36.

---

[1] IHTA 1984, s 67. Settled property which is sold and the proceeds of which are reinvested is not "added to" the settlement: statement of practice E9; Foster's Inheritance Tax Division W2.

[2] An exempt transfer is not a chargeable transfer nor is a potentially exempt transfer unless the donor dies within seven years.

[3] IHTA 1984, s 67(2).

[4] IHTA 1984, s 67(3).

[5] IHTA 1984, s 67(5).
[6] IHTA 1984, s 67(4).

[42.40] If property ceases to be relevant property through, say, being appointed to A for life, and is then subject to a charge under IHTA 1984, s 65, but the property later comes back into the category of relevant property (because, say, A dies) also within the ten-year period, the sum charged under IHTA 1984, s 65 would feature in both hypothetical parts. A reduction in the hypothetical cumulative total is therefore directed. The reduction is by the lesser of (a) the amount on which the tax was charged (ignoring the fractions and any grossing up), and (b) the hypothetical value chargeable.[1] Where only part of the property is involved, apportionments are made. It will be noted that only sums subject to the exit charge are taken into account—not capital distributions under the pre-1982 rules.[2]

Simon's Taxes I5.431–436.

[1] IHTA 1984, s 67(6).
[2] IHTA 1984, s 67(4).

The exit charge

Property ceasing to be relevant property

[42.41] A charge to tax arises when property is advanced to a beneficiary, or otherwise where the property ceases to be relevant property.[1] In accordance with the general scheme adopted for inheritance tax, the exit charge is based on the diminution in value of the trust fund; this means that where the IHT charge is paid out of the remaining trust fund, the charge is computed by grossing up the transfer of value made to the beneficiary.[2] Compared with the 1975 rules three points stand out. First, the rate of charge is reduced; second, a number of exceptions in the 1975 rules (eg reverter to settlor) are not part of the 1982 scheme. The reason for these is the same—the 1982 exit charge is a proportionate ten-year anniversary charge designed to compensate the Revenue for the fact that this property will not be relevant property when the next ten year anniversary comes round. The third difference is the change to basing liability on loss to the trust.

The first situation covered by this rule is that in which the property ceases to be comprised in the settlement. In this connection the rule treating property moving to a different settlement as remaining comprised in the first settlement[3] must not be overlooked. Property transferred to a beneficiary under a power of appointment or of advancement or simply distributed from the discretionary settlement could give rise to a charge under this rule. Where the property is transferred to an individual absolutely it is to be presumed that the transfer is chargeable and cannot be potentially exempt.

The second situation is that in which the property remains comprised in the settlement but ceases to be relevant property, as where the beneficiary is given a life interest in a fund. There will be a charge under the present rule. If the property is still held for the beneficiary when the ten-year anniversary comes round, that part cannot be charged under the principal charge as it is not then relevant property—hence the present charge.

Another way in which the property ceases to be relevant property is where there is still no qualifying interest in possession but the trust falls within the list of excluded trusts—above. One example would be when an accumulation and maintenance settlement arises.

Exceptions are made where the property (a) is a payment of costs and expenses properly attributable to the relevant property, and (b) if the payment is income of any person for the purposes of UK income tax (or would be if he were resident in the UK).[4]

The amount to be taxed under IHTA 1984, s 65 is the reduction in the value of the property in the settlement. So if the trust had a 60% shareholding in a company and the trustees granted A a 15% holding, the loss of control would be taken into account.

If the tax is paid out of other relevant property remaining comprised in the settlement, the sum otherwise chargeable must be grossed up.

In contrast with the calculation of the ten year charge, when calculating an exit charge, there is no reduction made for property added after the creation of the settlement by the first property transfer.[5] The effect of this rule can be to create, or increase, a tax charge disproportionately where a property is added to a discretionary settlement that is in excess of the nil rate band and then advanced to beneficiaries after a relatively short period.

Simon's Taxes I5.322, 323; Foster's Inheritance Tax E3.22, 23.

[1] IHTA 1984, s 65(1)(*a*).
[2] IHTA 1984, s 65(2)(*a*).
[3] IHTA 1984, s 81.
[4] IHTA 1984, s 65(5).
[5] The reduction in the rate of tax for computing the 10 year charge is given in IHTA 1984, s 66(2) and is applicable solely for the purpose of that section. The calculation of the rate that is applied for the exit charge is specified by s 65(3) as that computed under ss 68 or 69.

Disposition by the trustees—loss to the trust

[42.42] There is also a charge under IHTA 1984, s 65 if the case does not fall within the previous rule but the trustees make a disposition as a result of which the value of the relevant property comprised in the settlement is less than it would be but for the disposition.[1]

As with the previous rule no charge arises if it occurs within three months of the creation of the settlement or a ten year anniversary.[2] Equally there is no charge if the disposition is a payment by way of expenses or costs fairly

[42.42] Settled property

attributable to the relevant property or the payment would be income of the recipient (or would be if he were resident in the UK).[3]

This head of charge is similar in formulation to the general rule applying to dispositions by individuals[4] and the rules relating to transfers by omissions[5] are therefore adapted as is the defence in IHTA 1984, s 10 where no gratuitous benefit is intended.[6]

Simon's Taxes I5.324; Foster's Inheritance Tax E3.24.

---

[1] IHTA 1984, s 65(1)(b).
[2] IHTA 1984, s 65(4).
[3] IHTA 1984, s 65(5).
[4] IHTA 1984, s 3(1).
[5] IHTA 1984, s 3(3).
[6] IHTA 1984, s 65(6).

Foreign element

[42.43] Where the settlement was created by a settlor who was not then domiciled in the UK, there will be no charge where the property becomes excluded property (and so ceases to be relevant property—thus causing a drop in the value of the relevant property)[1] or, if the beneficiaries are also foreign, where the trustees acquire gilt edged securities (which qualifies as excluded property).[2]

Simon's Taxes I5.335; Foster's Inheritance Tax E3.35.

---

[1] IHTA 1984, s 65(7).
[2] IHTA 1984, ss 65(8), 267.

Other exclusions

[42.44] No charge arises if the property becomes settled on certain favoured trusts or by certain bodies; these are permanent trusts for charitable purposes, a qualifying political party, a qualifying national body or a registered housing association.[1] There are also exceptions where property becomes the property of maintenance funds for heritage property[2], and for shares or securities of a company becoming held on employee trusts.[3] If the amount chargeable but for the exception exceeds the value of the property subject to most of these favoured trusts or bodies, the excess is chargeable.[4]

Simon's Taxes I5.336–338; Foster's Inheritance Tax E3.36–38.

---

[1] IHTA 1984, s 76; for qualifying parties and bodies, see IHTA 1984, ss 24, 24A, 25.
[2] IHTA 1984, s 77, Sch 4.
[3] IHTA 1984, s 75.
[4] IHTA 1984, s 76(3), Sch 4.

Exit charge before the first ten-year anniversary

[42.45] An exit charge before the first ten-year anniversary, is at a special rate, which is the "appropriate fraction" of the effective rate on a hypothetical transfer.[1]

The "appropriate fraction" is 3/10 multiplied by so many fortieths as there are complete successive quarters in the period beginning with the day on which the settlement commenced and ending with the day before the occasion of charge—so the greater the number of quarters, the higher the appropriate fraction.[2] The effect of this rule is that no exit charge arises when property leaves a trust within 91 days of the creation of the settlement or within 91 days of a 10 year charge.

EXAMPLE (SUPRA, § 42.35 CONT)

In relation to the £10,000 advanced on 1 May 1998 from settlement No 2 the number of completed quarters would be 24 and the fraction therefore 3/10 × 24/40.

Adjustments are made to the number of quarters for chargeable property which was either not comprised in the settlement at all throughout these quarters—as when it was added later—or was not relevant property throughout these quarters—as where there was a life interest in possession which ended before the charge under IHTA 1984, s 65 arose. Quarters expiring before the property became (or last became) relevant property are excluded; conversely the quarter then in progress is included.[3]

The hypothetical value[4] to be transferred is the sum of (a) the value immediately after the settlement commenced of the property then comprised in it, (b) the similar value of any related settlement, and (c) the initial value of any property later added to the settlement (whether or not it remained in the settlement). There is no grossing up at this point.

The hypothetical starting point[5] is the sum of any chargeable transfers made by this settlor in the period of seven years ending with the day on which the settlement commenced, disregarding transfers made on that day.

EXAMPLE (SUPRA, § 42.35 CONT)

Settlement No 2. When £10,000 leaves the settlement on 1 May 1998 the hypothetical starting point is £100,000 and the hypothetical value to be transferred is (a) £70,000, (b) £100,000, (c) nil = £170,000.

Tax at lifetime rates on 170,000 + 100,000	£5,600
less tax at 1995–96 lifetime rates on £100,000	Nil
	£5,600

The charge is therefore

The tax is therefore:

$$\frac{5,600}{170,000} \times \frac{3}{10} \times \frac{24}{40} \times 10,000 = £59.29.$$

As £10,000 is the gross sum, the beneficiary received £9,940.71.

[42.45] Settled property

The gearing of the rate of tax charged to the initial value of the settled property has led to the creation of nil rate band discretionary trusts. So long as the settlor's cumulative total means that the rate of tax charged on the initial value is nil, any distribution out of the capital of the trust before the tenth anniversary will be free of IHT. It is of course necessary to take any related settlements into account.

Simon's Taxes I5.421–424; Foster's Inheritance Tax E4.21–24.

[1] IHTA 1984, s 68(1).
[2] IHTA 1984, s 68(2).
[3] IHTA 1984, s 68(3).
[4] IHTA 1984, s 68(5).
[5] IHTA 1984, s 68(4).

Between the ten-year anniversaries

[42.46] When the exit charge arises between ten-year anniversaries the rate is the appropriate fraction of the rate used for the ten year charge on the previous anniversary. Where this rate was further reduced for certain property which was not relevant property throughout the previous ten years, those further reductions are ignored.[1] The rate used on the most recent anniversary is recalculated if there has been a reduction in the rates of tax since the anniversary.[2] Further, if the anniversary was before 18 March 1986, and the exit charge arises on or after that date, the rate may have to be recalculated to take account of the reduction from ten years to seven in the period during which chargeable transfers by the settlor before the creation of the settlement are relevant.[3]

The appropriate fraction is determined as for IHTA 1984, s 65 save that the quarters begin with the last ten-year anniversary.[4]

EXAMPLE (SUPRA, § 42.35 CONT)

From Settlement No 1 (supra, § **42.36**) the trustees advance £25,000 to a beneficiary, the beneficiary to pay the tax. The advance is made on 4 April 2004, two years and two months after the first ten-year anniversary.

The amount to be charged is £25,000.

The appropriate fraction is 8/40.

The tax is:

$$\frac{8}{40} \times \frac{3}{10} \times \frac{27,600}{280,000} \times 25,000 = £147.86$$

Adjustments are made to the rate to take account of property becoming relevant property since the last ten-year anniversary and so not taken into account in computing the last ten-year charge. Property which has become comprised in this settlement and which either (a) became relevant property straight away, or (b) was not and has not become relevant property is taken at its value when joining the settlement; ie its central value.[5] The rate is that which would have been charged on the anniversary if the property had been relevant property at that time; it will be noted that this applies whether or not the property has ever become relevant property. Other added property is taken at the value when it became (or last became) relevant property.

Property which was comprised in the settlement at the anniversary but was not then relevant property is likewise taken into account if it has since become relevant property by being added to the sum to be charged at the last ten-year anniversary; for this purpose then it is valued as at the date it became (or last became) relevant property.[6]

EXAMPLE

Suppose that in settlement No 1 (supra, § **42.35**) A had died one year after the anniversary and that the value of the fund at that time was £400,000. The effect of A's death would be that half the fund, £200,000, would become relevant property but that figure of £200,000, would be reduced by the tax payable on A's death to, say, £120,000. Suppose again that £25,000 is advanced two years and two months after the anniversary.

This leads to a recalculation of the rate charged under IHTA 1984, s 66 (supra, § **42.36**). The hypothetical value is now (a) £160,000 + £120,000 + (b) £nil + (c) £70,000 = £350,000; the hypothetical starting point is unchanged at £100,000.

The tax would be:

Tax at lifetime rates on £(100,000 + 350,000)	£41,600
less tax at lifetime rates on £100,000	Nil
	£41,600

The effective rate is therefore:

$$\frac{59,200}{350,000} = 16.91\%$$

of which 30% is taken, ie 3.566%.

The £25,000 is advanced to a beneficiary one year and two months after A's death, ie two years and two months after the ten-year anniversary, the appropriate fraction is 8/40 so the tax is:

$$\frac{8}{40} \times \frac{3}{10} \times \frac{59,200}{350,000} \times £25,000 = £253.71.$$

This applies unless the property to be charged under IHTA 1984, s 69 is the property coming in on A's death. In that event the rate of tax is further reduced. This may mean some difficulty in trust administration since it may not be clear where B's money comes from.

If the rate of tax has been reduced by legislation since the last ten-year anniversary, these figures are calculated as if the lower rates now applying had been in force at the time of the anniversary.[7]

Simon's Taxes I5.441; Foster's Inheritance Tax E4.41.

---

[1] IHTA 1984, s 69(1).
[2] IHTA 1984, Sch 2, para 3.
[3] FA 1986, Sch 19, para 43.
[4] IHTA 1984, s 69(4).
[5] IHTA 1984, s 69(2), (3).
[6] IHTA 1984, s 69(2)(b), (3).
[7] IHTA 1984, Sch 2, para 3.

[42.47] Settled property

Initial interest of settlor or spouse

[42.47] A special provision applies where the settlor or his spouse, a term which includes widow or widower, is beneficially entitled to an interest in possession in the settled property immediately after the settlement is set up.[1] For the purpose of calculating a ten-year charge or an exit charge, the property is treated as if it were added to the settlement on the date on which the interest in possession ended. However, the ten-year anniversaries are determined by reference to the date of the original settlement.[2]

EXAMPLE

H settled property on trust for W for life with remainder on discretionary trusts under s 120. Such property does not become comprised in a settlement until W dies (or for some other reason her interest ends); on such occasion the settlement is treated as made by W at that time with consequent results in calculating the effective rate.

If W had been entitled to a life interest in one third of the settled property, two-thirds is treated as subject to the rules set out above on the basis that H is the settlor, while the remaining third will become subject to those rules when W's interest ends, but as a settlement made by W.

These rules do not apply if the property became settled before 27 March 1974.

Simon's Taxes I5.452; Foster's Inheritance Tax E4.52.

---

[1] IHTA 1984, s 80; on conditions for status as excluded property see IHTA 1984, s 82.
[2] IHTA 1984, s 6(2).

Planning

[42.48] The 2006 changes have the effect that many of the points that previously were relevant for a discretionary trust are now relevant for all trusts. Among the points to bear in mind are the following:

(1)   No IHT is payable on the creation of a trust if the sum settled is within the settlor's cumulative INT nil rate band.
(2)   If there is a disabled person as one of the class of persons to benefit, it is probably better to create a separate trust for the "favoured beneficiary".
(3)   If the settlor wishes to make both a "favoured trust" and a "non-favoured trust", the "non-favoured trust" should be made first.
(4)   The settlor should avoid making two settlements on the same day.
(5)   It is better to make several small trusts rather than one big one.
(6)   It is better to create a new trust than to add to an existing one.
(7)   If a trust has been set up since March 1974 it is usually better to make any distribution before rather than after the ten-year anniversary.

Foster's Inheritance Tax Division M5.

Accumulation and maintenance trusts

IHT reliefs for pre-22 March 2006 trusts

[42.49] The transfer of property prior to 22 March 2006 to an accumulation and maintenance trust was a potential exempt transfer.[1] From 22 March 2006, the transfer of property to an accumulation and maintenance trust is a chargeable transfer, unless the terms of the trust provide that the trust property vests in the beneficiaries at age 25.[2]

The property in an accumulation and maintenance trust that gives absolute entitlement at age 18 is exempt from the ten year anniversary charge and the exit charge.[3] In addition the legislation provides that there is to be no charge where the beneficiary becomes beneficially entitled to, or to an interest in possession in, settled property on or before attaining the specified age; similarly there is to be no charge on the death of a beneficiary before attaining the specified age.[4] In the event of death between 18 and attaining the specified age there may be a charge under IHTA 1984, s 4 if he has an interest in possession thanks to Trustee Act 1925, s 31.[5] The result is similar where such a beneficiary has such an interest and another member of the class comes into existence thus causing a reduction in the first beneficiary's share; in this case the charge arises under IHTA 1984, s 52.

However, subject to the previous paragraph, there is a charge, using the tapered charge basis, if the property ceases to satisfy the conditions entitling it to this special treatment or if the trustees make a disposition reducing the value of the settled property.[6]

The conditions entitling these trusts to special treatment are given at infra, § 42.50.

Simon's Taxes Division I5.5; Foster's Inheritance Tax Division E5; STP [10.27]–[10.60], [10.94]–[10.98].

[1] IHTA 1984, s 3A(1)(c) before FA 2006 amendment.
[2] IHTA 1984, s 71(1)(a) amended by FA 2006, Sch 20, para 3(1).
[3] IHTA 1984, s 58.
[4] IHTA 1984, s 71(4).
[5] eg *Swales v IRC* [1984] STC 413.
[6] IHTA 1984, s 71(3).

[42.50] Accumulation and maintenance trusts are narrowly defined as settlements where:

(1) one or more persons (in this paragraph referred to as beneficiaries) will, on or before attaining a specified age not exceeding 25, become entitled to, or to an interest in possession in, the settled property or part of it;
(2) no interest in possession subsists in the settled property or part and the income from it is to be accumulated so far as not applied for the maintenance, education or benefit of a beneficiary; and
(3) either[1]

[42.50] Settled property

(a) not more than 25 years have elapsed since the day on which the settlement was made or, if it was later, since the time (or latest time) when the conditions stated in paragraphs 1 and 2 above became satisfied with respect to the property[2] (ie 25 years since the settlement was created or it became an accumulation and maintenance settlement); or

(b) all the persons who are or have been beneficiaries are or were either grandchildren of a common grandparent or children,[3] widows or widowers of such grandchildren who were themselves beneficiaries but died before the time when, had they survived, they would have become entitled as mentioned in paragraph 1 above.

Condition 1 is applied strictly. In *Inglewood v IRC*[4] property was settled on trust for the children of Lord Barnard conditional on their attaining the age of 21 (or marrying, if earlier). However, a clause in the trust deed empowered the trustees to make a new appointment, as long as this was made before the children attained the age of 21. In fact, the trustees did not exercise this power. In the Court of Appeal, Fox LJ held that the use of the word "will" in IHTA 1984, s 71(2) involves a degree of certainty which is inconsistent with the trustees having a power that, if exercised, would result in a beneficiary not having an interest in possession.[5] Hence, the settlement in this case was declared not to fulfil the requirements of s 71 and, thus, to be subject to inheritance tax as on the basis that applies to a discretionary trust.

Now that transfers to such settlements can be potentially exempt transfers it is possible to settle property on A for life and get potentially exempt treatment if A is 24 but not if he is 25.

Condition 2 demands a duty to accumulate surplus income rather than a mere power.

The reasoning behind condition 3 is the wish to prevent relief from being rolled forward from one generation to the next under settlements containing a power to substitute successive generations for the present one. Condition 3(b)—known as the common grandparent condition—is needed as an alternative to 3(a) since the class may include unborn children, in which case the 25-year rule cannot easily be satisfied. This definition is apt to cover the simple case where income is accumulated and the capital plus accumulations are to pass to beneficiaries contingent upon them attaining the age of 21 or 25 as the case may be. Where the condition is attaining an age greater than 25, the trust will still satisfy these conditions if Trustee Act 1925, s 31 gives the contingent beneficiary a right to intermediate income and so an interest in possession. In general it is not necessary that a particular age is specified in the trust instrument, provided it is clear that a beneficiary will in fact become entitled to the property or an interest in it by the age of 25.[6] The definition is, however, a narrow one as the following examples issued by HMRC will show:

> The examples set out below are used on a settlement for the children of X contingently on attaining 25, the trustees being required to accumulate the income so far as it is not applied for the maintenance of X's children.

Accumulation and maintenance trusts [42.50]

A. The settlement was made on X's marriage and he has yet no children.	[IHTA 1984, s 71] will not apply until a child is born and that event will give rise to a charge for tax under [IHTA 1984, s 65(1)(*a*)].
B. The trustees have power to apply income for the benefit of X's unmarried sister.	[IHTA 1984, s 71] does not apply because the condition of [IHTA 1984, s 71(1)(*b*)] is not met.
C. The trustees have power to apply capital for the benefit of X's unmarried sister.	[IHTA 1984, s 71] does not apply because the condition of [IHTA 1984, s 71(1)(*a*)] is not met.
D. X has power to appoint the capital not only among his children but also among his remoter issue.	
E. The trustees have an over-riding power of appointment in favour of other persons.	[IHTA 1984, s 71] does not apply (unless the power can be exercised only in the favour of persons who would thereby acquire interests in possession on or before attaining 25). A release of the disqualifying power would give rise to a charge for tax under [IHTA 1984, s 65(1)(*a*)]. Its exercise would also give rise to a charge under [IHTA 1984, s 65(1)(*a*)].
F. The settled property has been revocably appointed to one of the children contingently on his attaining 25 and the appointment is now made irrevocable.	If the power to revoke prevents [IHTA 1984, s 71] from applying (as it would, for example, if the property thereby became subject to a power of appointment as at D or E) tax will be chargeable under [IHTA 1984, s 65(1)(*a*)] when the appointment is made irrevocable.
G. The trust to accumulate income is expressed to be during the life of the settlor.	As the settlor may live beyond the 25th birthday of any of his children, the trust does not satisfy the condition in [IHTA 1984, s 71(1)(*a*)] and the paragraph does not apply.

Simon's Taxes I5.511–524; Foster's Inheritance Tax E5.11–24.

[1] IHTA 1984, s 71(2). Settlements in existence on 15 April 1976 are subject to transitional rules.
[2] This will have caused a charge under FA 1975, Sch 5, para 15(3) if after 12 March 1975 and under IHTA 1984, s 65 if after 8 March 1982.
[3] Defined IHTA 1984, s 76(8) as including illegitimate children, adopted children and stepchildren.
[4] [1983] STC 133.
[5] At 141h. Inland Revenue statement of practice E1 states that, in the Revenue's view, a trust deed that provided for a member of a class of potential beneficiaries to be granted an interest in possession before that individual attains the age of 25 is potentially capable of satisfying the terms of s 71, if neither the exercise nor the release of the power could break the condition that the interest in possession is granted. By contrast, in the Revenue's view, the benefit of s 71 is excluded if the power given to the trustees could allow the trustees to prevent an interest in possession in the settled property from commencing before the beneficiary concerned attained the age specified. The benefit of s 71 is then excluded by the existence of the power; it is irrelevant whether or not the trustees actually exercised this power.
[6] Extra-statutory concession F8.

Some problems

[42.51] Condition 1. Where S settles property to be accumulated with the capital and accumulations to pass to such of his grandchildren as attain 25 but with an overriding power in the trustees to appoint the income and capital to such of his children and grandchildren as they think fit, the settlement is outside IHTA 1984, s 71. The children are not the beneficiaries in 1 and their presence means that it cannot be said that 'the income is to be accumulated so far as not applied for the maintenance, education or benefit of a beneficiary', ie a grandchild.

Even if the children are deleted from the overriding power of appointment it would seem that the trust still does not come within IHTA 1984, s 71 since the overriding power of appointment could be exercised so as to enable one of the older grandchildren to become entitled to, or to an interest in possession in, the settled property or part of it well after attaining the age of 25 so preventing requirement 1 from being satisfied, since it will not be the case that the beneficiaries between them will, on or before attaining 25, become entitled to the settled property or to an interest therein. IHTA 1984, s 71, it seems, will only be satisfied if the overriding power is exercisable only in favour of grandchildren who have not attained 25 and only so as to confer an absolute interest or an interest in possession in such grandchildren. If the power could be exercised so as to appoint the capital to trustees upon discretionary trusts for the grandchildren or to trustees for the grandchildren upon attaining 30 it could not be said that the grandchildren *will* before attaining 25 become *entitled* to, or to an interest in possession in, the property.

Condition 2. First, a literal interpretation might require that the income be capable of being applied for the maintenance, education or benefit of the beneficiary.[1] On such a construction a trust from which the statutory powers of maintenance and advancement were excluded would not satisfy IHTA 1984, s 71. This result might be avoided where the court has an inherent power to order maintenance even in the face of an express clause.

Second, problems arise if the settlement, although for grandchildren contingent upon their attaining the age of 25, contains an express[2] power of advancement on discretionary trusts for the grandchildren since this power might be exercised so as to give the grandchild an interest contingent upon reaching an age greater than 25.[3]

Third, the requirement in IHTA 1984, s 71(1) that income "is to be accumulated so far as not applied for the maintenance education or benefit of a beneficiary" raises particular dangers where the accumulation period expires before the attainment of a specified age such as 25. This will be the case where no express accumulation period exists so that accumulation is only under the trust contained in the Trustee Act 1925, s 31(2) so that accumulation must cease when the beneficiary in question attains 18 in a post-1969 settlement or 21 in a pre-1970 settlement. Thus, if property is settled on A and B upon attaining 25 the trust to accumulate will cease when the younger attains 18 or 21 as the case may be and the favoured treatment accorded to the settlement will then cease although the tax consequences of this will depend on what trusts of income then follow. In many cases A and B will then have interests in possession under Trustee Act 1925, s 31(1)(ii).

Simon's Taxes I5.512; Foster's Inheritance Tax E5.12.

[1] On which point see Pettit, *Equity and the Law of Trusts*, (7th edn) p 447.
[2] This would be ultra vires the statutory power—*Pilkington v IRC* [1962] 3 All ER 622, 40 TC 416.
[3] Perhaps the reasoning in *Blausten v IRC* [1972] 1 All ER 41, 47 TC 542 could be used to limit the power so as not to fall outside IHTA 1984, s 71(1)(b).

[42.52] Condition 3, IHTA 1984, s 71(2). This too has its dangers. Alternative (a) requires that the beneficiaries must actually become entitled in the 25-year period. This may well be difficult in the case of a settlement on a class which is not yet closed. It may therefore be necessary for the trustees to use their powers of advancement or appointment over the whole trust fund; they should also be given the power to accelerate interests in possession in favour of minors.

Alternative (b) requires particular care where substitutional clauses are involved. It appears that if the clause comes into operation after the testator's death condition 3 is satisfied but if before that death it will not be; this anomaly appears to be quite nonsensical.

Care should also be taken to ensure that the clause is restricted to situations in which the beneficiary dies before attaining an interest in possession rather than attaining a specified age, say of 25. While the mere possibility that such a clause might operate in this way may not prevent (b) from being satisfied, it appears that the actual operation of that clause in that way will.

One may note that condition 3 was added in 1976, and that where the trust existed on 1 April 1976 and satisfied conditions 1 and 2 condition 3(a) needs only 25 years from that date and 3(b) is also relaxed.

The tapered charge

[42.53] The exemption from the ten year charge for a favoured accumulation and maintenance trust is not absolute. The exemption applies when either (a) all beneficiaries are grandchildren of a common grandparent (or a surviving spouse of such a grandchild);[1] or (b) not more than 25 years have elapsed since 15 April 1976[2] or, if later, the creation of the settlement.[3]

When these conditions fail to be satisfied, there is a tapered charge. By virtue of (b) the first of these taper charges arose on 15 April 2001. The amount on which the tapered charge is levied is the amount of the reduction in the value of the settled property as a result of the event. If the tax is paid out of the settled property subject to the charge, the value has to be grossed up.[4]

The rate at which the tax is charged reflects the length of time the property has been in the favoured settlement. The rate for the first 40 successive quarters in the relevant period is 0.25% each quarter, ie 10% after the first ten years. The figures for subsequent decades are 0.20% each quarter (8%), 0.15% (6%), 0.10% (4%) and 0.05% (2%).[5] The relevant period begins with the date on which the property first fulfilled the conditions entitling it to special treatment subject to the important proviso that the start cannot be taken back beyond 13 March 1975.[6] Years during which the property was excluded property are to be ignored[7] (eg property situated abroad by a settlor not domiciled in the UK) for events occurring after 8 March 1982.

Simon's Taxes I5.601–614; Foster's Inheritance Tax E6.01–14.

---

[1] IHTA 1984, s 71(2)(*b*).
[2] This was the date on which the rules for accumulation and maintenance were finalised: IHTA 1984, s 71(6)(*a*). There are special provisions dealing with the transitional period between 15 April 1976 and 1 April 1977: vide s 71(6)(*b*), (*c*).
[3] IHTA 1984, s 71(2)(*a*).
[4] IHTA 1984, s 70(5)(*b*).
[5] IHTA 1984, s 70(6).
[6] IHTA 1984, s 70(8).
[7] IHTA 1984, s 70(2).

Special trusts

Temporary charitable trusts

[42.54] A charitable trust is exempt from the ten year charge and the exit charge.[1] However, it is possible to create a trust that has charitable purposes for a specified length of time.[2] Such a temporary charitable trust attracts a tapered charge that is computed in the same way as the tapered charge for an accumulation and maintenance settlement. The tapered charge would be levied if settled property ceases to be held for charitable purposes and is not distributed for charitable purposes, or if the trustees make a disposition reducing the value of the settled property.[3] One should note that while a temporary charitable trust is favoured in this way, a gift to such a trust will not be an exempt transfer (see infra, § **43.12**).

---

[1] IHTA 1984, s 76(1).
[2] It has been argued that a temporary charitable trust is not, in general law, a charitable trust at all. The Charity Commissioners will refuse to register such a trust as a condition of registration is that the funds held in trust will always be held for charitable purposes, until they are dispensed in the performance of the charitable purpose of the trust.
[3] IHTA 1984, s 70(2).

Employee trusts and newspaper trusts

[42.55] Settled property satisfying the rules in IHTA 1984, ss 86 and 87 are also favoured. Property held on such trusts is not relevant property. Further, property becoming comprised in such trusts but coming from a discretionary trust and so ceasing to be relevant property is exempt from a charge under

IHTA 1984, s 65.[1] There may, however, be a tapered charge on property when property leaves the trust.[2] In addition, any interest in possession is disregarded if it is less than 5% of the whole.[3]

Simon's Taxes I5.631, 632, 648; Foster's Inheritance Tax E6.31, 32, 48.

[1]   IHTA 1984, s 75.
[2]   IHTA 1984, s 72.
[3]   IHTA 1984, s 86(4)(*b*).

Funds for maintenance of heritage property

[42.56] These are favoured trusts and there is a charge when property leaves such trusts other than for its favoured purposes: IHTA 1984, Sch 4, para 8. The calculation of the rate of tax is not always the same as that outlined in supra, § 42.53. The rules distinguish situations in which the property extends the maintenance fund from a discretionary trust from other situations. In the former the relevant period begins on the latest of (a) the last five-year anniversary of the discretionary trust, (b) the day on which the property became relevant property (ie entered the discretionary trust), and (c) 13 March 1975. The rules at § 42.53 are then applied. However, in other situations one takes the higher of two rates. The first rate is similar to that in § 42.53, taking the period the property was held on approved maintenance trusts, while the second is the rate that would be charged on the settlor (if he is still alive) or would be charged if it were added to his estate (if he is dead). If the settlor has died lifetime rates are used unless the settlement was made on death. When more than one settlor is involved the Revenue can pick the relevant settlor. There is also provision when the second rate is used and another charge has arisen in the previous ten years.[1]

Where the property went into the maintenance fund on the death of a person entitled to an interest in possession (or is treated as doing so through being so placed within two years of the death of such a person) the rules are now modified.[2] In particular the charge will be based on the cumulated lifetime chargeable transfers of the life tenant rather than the settlor.

Simon's Taxes I5.651, 652; Foster's Inheritance Tax E6.51, 52.

[1]   IHTA 1984, Sch 4, paras 11–13.
[2]   IHTA 1984, Sch 4, para 15A.

Protective trusts

[42.57] Although under Trustee Act 1925, s 33 a discretionary trust will arise on the bankruptcy of the principal beneficiary and will endure for the remainder of his life, this trust is ignored and his original interest is treated as still subsisting. It follows that sums paid to other objects to the discretionary trust will be treated as transfers by him, but that there will be no charge on the

[42.57] Settled property

arising of the discretionary trust, even though his interest ceases under s 33. Another consequence is that if on his death, the property devolves on his widow the spouse exemption may apply.[1]

To achieve these results the statute says that "the failure or determination" of the life interests is to be disregarded.[2] This was given a restrictive interpretation in *Cholmondley v IRC*[3] so that one could not disregard property which left the settlement under the exercise of an overriding power and which did not bring about the forfeiture of the life interest.

Simon's Taxes I5.621–623; Foster's Inheritance Tax E6.21–23.

---

[1] IHTA 1984, s 88; see *Egerton v IRC* [1982] STC 520.
[2] On the scope of protective trusts see statement of practice E7; Foster's Inheritance Tax, Division W2.
[3] [1986] STC 384; this case is also important as a scheme case. Property was appointed on protective trusts which were ended within 24 hours by the use of the overriding power. Scott J said that there never had been intention to hold the property on protective trusts.

Trust for a disabled person

[42.58] A special regime applies to a discretionary trust where the beneficiary is a disabled person and certain conditions are fulfilled. Strangely, the inheritance tax treatment that flows from this provision is often less attractive than the treatment applied to discretionary trusts. Hence, many practitioners, in creating trusts for a disabled person, would ensure that the conditions are not fulfilled.

For the special treatment to apply, there must be no interest in possession in the settled property and the terms of trust must provide that not less than half of the settled property applied during the lifetime of a disabled person is applied for his benefit.[1]

For this purpose, a disabled person is defined[2] as: (a) a person incapable by reason of mental disorder of administering his property; or (b) a person in receipt of an attendance allowance; or (c) a person in receipt of disability living allowance.

When these conditions are fulfilled, the disabled person is treated as if he had an interest in possession in the property in trust.[3] Payments from the trust to the disabled person are free of tax;[4] and a gift by an individual to such a trust is a potentially exempt transfer.[5] At the death of the beneficiary a charge to inheritance tax arises on the value of the settled property.[6]

Simon's Taxes I5.626–628; Foster's Inheritance Tax E6.26–28.

---

[1] IHTA 1984, s 89(1).
[2] IHTA 1984, s 89(4).
[3] IHTA 1984, s 89(2).
[4] IHTA 1984, s 89.

[5] IHTA 1984, s 3A.
[6] IHTA 1984, s 49(1), 5(1) and 4(1).

43

Exempt transfers

Exempt lifetime transfers	PARA **43.01**
Transfers between spouses	PARA **43.06**
Gifts for public purposes	PARA **43.14**
Other exempt transfers	PARA **43.20**
Partly exempt transfers—allocation of relief	PARA **43.22**
Matters which are not transfers of value	PARA **43.34**

Exempt lifetime transfers

Annual exemption

[43.01] Each tax year a person may make transfers of value that total up to £3,000 without incurring any liability to tax. Such transfers are exempt—not potentially exempt.

Where several transfers are made in one year, the exemption is given according to the date of the transfer, the earlier transfers enjoying the exemption. Where two transfers are made on the same day, the exemption is apportioned between them in proportion to the values transferred; this is so even though one knows the order in which the transfers were made.[1]

To the extent that transfers in one year fall short of £3,000 the amount by which they fall short may be rolled forward to the next year and used to exempt gifts in that year.[2] Any shortfall still unused at the end of the second year is lost.

This exemption applies to all dispositions inter vivos to the termination of a life interest in possession[3] and to sums apportioned under IHTA 1984, s 94 (close companies).[4] However, it does not apply on death.

EXAMPLE

On 10 June year 1 A transfers £2,826 to B. He makes no other transfers in that year. In year 2 A makes the following transfers:

10 May   1,400 (C)
11 May   £1,000 (D) and £1,500 (E)
12 May   £3,000 (F)

A can roll forward £174 of the £3,000 exemption from year 1 to year 2.

In year 2, transfer C is exempt. Transfers D and E are partly exempt, the remaining exemption (£1,600 + £174) being apportioned 2/5 to D (£710) and 3/5 to E (£1,064), ie £290 of transfer D and £436 of transfer E are chargeable. The whole of transfer F is chargeable.

[43.01] Exempt transfers

Where there is a potentially exempt transfer in the year, the annual exemption is set first against any chargeable transfers even if made after the potentially exempt transfer.[5] If it later becomes a chargeable transfer the better view is that it is treated, for this purpose only, as made after the other transfers in that year.[6]

EXAMPLE

In year 1, D makes a potentially exempt transfer of £3,000. In year 2, D makes a chargeable transfer of £6,000. Originally the whole of the transfer in year 2 would be exempt. However, if D dies within seven years of the transfer of £3,000 the year 1 exemption will be switched from year 2 to year 1.[7]

The annual exemption is put against transfers of value actually made and cannot be put against a deemed disposition. Hence, if property has been subject to the provisions for a gift with reservations,[8] the cessation of the reservation of benefit is deemed to be a potentially exempt transfer,[9] against which the annual exemption cannot be put.[10]

Simon's Taxes I3.321–323; Foster's Inheritance Tax C3.21–23; STP [20.191].

---

[1] IHTA 1984, s 19(3).
[2] IHTA 1984, s 19(2).
[3] IHTA 1984, s 19(5).
[4] IHTA 1984, s 94(5).
[5] IHTA 1984, s 19(3A)(a).
[6] IHTA 1984, s 19(3A)(b). For debate see **Simon's Taxes I3.322; Foster's Inheritance Tax C3.22**.
[7] IHTA 1984, s 19(3A) allows the potentially exempt transfer to be left out of account only for the year in which it was made.
[8] See infra, Chapter 41.
[9] FA 1986, s 102(4).
[10] Revenue Interpretation RI55.

Small gifts to the same person

[43.02] Transfers of value made by a transferor in any one year by outright gifts to any one person are exempt to the extent that the values transferred, without grossing up, do not exceed £250. There is no rollover of any unused portion of £250. This is intended as a de minimis exception and so cannot be used to exempt the first £250 of a larger transfer.

The restriction to "outright gifts" bars inter alia a transfer to trustees to hold on trusts unless perhaps to hold on bare trusts for one or more of full age and capacity.[1] The phrase would appear to exclude a transfer at an undervalue, and sums apportioned under IHTA 1984, s 94 (close companies).[2]

A gift with reservation cannot qualify for this exemption.[3]

---

[1] In practice the reservation of an interest is ignored.

² Compare IHTA 1984, s 20(3) with IHTA 1984, s 79(5).
³ FA 1986, s 102(5).

Normal expenditure out of income

[43.03] A transfer is exempt to the extent[1] that it is shown that:

(1) it was made as part of the normal expenditure of the transferor; and
(2) that taking one year with another it was made out of income; and
(3) that after allowing for all transfers forming part of his normal expenditure, the transferor was left with sufficient income (after tax) to maintain his usual standard of living.[2]

The capital repayment element in a purchased life annuity is declared not to form part of the transferor's income for this purpose unless purchased before 13 November 1974.[3]

Whether a gift forms part of the deceased's normal expenditure is a question of fact.[4] A single transfer is unlikely to qualify unless presumably it is part of his normal pattern of expenditure to make isolated gifts. A single first payment when there is a continuing obligation will qualify, eg an assurance premium[5] or a payment under a deed of covenant unless death was imminent.[6]

This exemption applies to any disposition inter vivos, including payments to a settlement but not to a gift with reservation.[7]

In *McDowall v IRC*[8], the person holding the enduring power of attorney for William McDowall made lifetime gifts that had all the characteristics of normal expenditure of the deceased out of his income, apart from the fact that the power of attorney did not authorise such gifts. The Special Commissioners found[9] that the making of unauthorised gifts gave William McDowall the right to recover the gifts. This right was in his estate immediately before his death and forms part of the property to which he was beneficially entitled. The value of the right was equal to the gifts made. Hence, there was no effective relief given by the exemption for normal expenditure out of income.

The Revenue has a standard form that can be used for a claim.[10]

Simon's Taxes I3.325; Foster's Inheritance Tax C3.25; STP [20.191].

---

[1] Where the transfer exceeds this limit, only the excess is chargeable.
[2] IHTA 1984, s 21(1).
[3] IHTA 1984, s 21(3).
[4] *A-G for Northern Ireland v Heron* [1959] TR 1. See also **Foster's Inheritance Tax**, X6.06.
[5] Provided it was capable of continuing for at least three years.
[6] IHTA 1984, s 21 does not use the phrase outright gift but does exclude IHTA 1984, s 3(4). The usefulness of deeds of covenant is greatly restricted by TA 1988, s 347A.
[7] FA 1986, s 102(5).
[8] [2004] STC (SCD) 22.
[9] at 34.

[43.03] Exempt transfers

[10] Inland Revenue IHT Newsletter, April 2004 p 1. The form is not a statutory return; its use is optional.

Application: the Bennett decision

[43.04] In *Bennett*[1] A testator had left property on trust to pay the income to his widow, B, for her life and then to his three sons (T). Trust shares in the family company were sold in return for shares in another company and cash, a sale which meant a substantial increase in trust income. B felt she had been adequately provided for even before the sale. The clear evidence was that she had a modest lifestyle, which was unlikely to, and in the event did not, change during the remainder of her life.

B decided that surplus income should go to T and authorised the trustees to distribute equally between the taxpayers "all or any of the income arising in each accounting year as is surplus to my financial requirements of which you are already aware". In February 1989, a payment of £9,300 was made to each of the sons and in February 1990 a further payment of £60,000 was made to each son. This did not, in fact, exhaust the income in the relevant accounting years, as there were delays in determining the surplus available for distribution. Mrs B died unexpectedly on 20 February 1990.

T argued that the payments in 1989 and 1990 were exempt transfers under IHTA 1988, s 21 as being part of B's normal expenditure. On the substantive point Lightman J. said that it was necessary and sufficient that the evidence should manifest the substantial conformity of each payment with an established pattern of expenditure by the individual concerned—a pattern established by proof of the existence of a prior commitment or resolution or by reference only to a sequence of payments (at p 59d).

Elaborating on issues raised he made a number of points. It followed from his formulation that there was no minimum period. A single payment might suffice if the pattern was there; equally in the absence of such a pattern a substantial number of payments would fail to achieve exemption. The pattern must have been intended to remain in place for more than a nominal period and indeed for a sufficient period (barring unforeseen circumstances) in order for any payment fairly to be regarded as a regular feature of the transferor's annual expenditure. It followed that a "death bed" resolution to make periodic payments "for life" and a payment made in accordance with such a determination would not suffice. It was not necessary for the amount of the expenditure to be fixed in amount or for each payment to be made to the same person. If the transferor had not adopted a fixed sum it would have to be shown that a formula or standard had been adopted which could be quantified, eg the costs of a sick or elderly dependant's residence at a nursing home. As regards the payees, it is sufficient that their general character or the qualification for benefit is established, eg members of the family or needy friends. There was no requirement for the expenditure to be reasonable. The fact that the objective behind the expenditure is tax planning, eg to prevent an accumulation of income in the hands of the transferor liable to inheritance tax on his death, was no impediment.

Simon's Taxes I3.325; Foster's Inheritance Tax C3.25.

[1] *Bennett v IRC* [1995] STC 54. The judgment of Lightman J. in this case was applied by the Special Commissioner in *Nadin v IRC* [1997] STC (SCD) 107 to deny a claim by the executors that gifts totalling £271,770 be treated as normal expenditure out of income. The gifts were all made during 1993–94, when the deceased had gross income of £18,625.

Gifts at marriage

[43.05] Three rules apply:

(1) The first £5,000 of a transfer of value made by gift made in consideration of marriage by the parent of either party to the marriage is exempt from tax.[1]

(2) Where the transferor is a remoter ancestor or is a party to the marriage, the first £2,500 is exempt.[2]
For 1 and 2 the gift may be an outright gift or the property settled by the gift—subject to further rules set out below.

(3) The first £1,000 of a marriage gift made by a person other than a party to the marriage or his or her parent or remoter ancestor, is also exempt.

The net effect is that the four parents can between them make exempt transfers of £20,000 to the couple—but not to each of them. If a single donor makes more than one gift in consideration of the same marriage, the exemption is applied to the gifts rateably according to their respective values.[3] An event causing a charge on settled property when there is a beneficial interest in possession, as where a power of appointment or advancement is exercised, can come within these rules provided notice is given to the trustees of the availability of this exemption;[4] a gift with reservation is also eligible.[5] Property which ceases to be settled property is treated as an outright gift; property remaining settled is treated as property becoming settled.

There is no qualification to these exemptions where the gift is an outright gift to one or other of the parties to the marriage,[6] but where the gift is by way of settlement, exemption will be given only if the settlement is primarily for the benefit of the parties to the marriage, their issue (including legitimated and adopted issue) and the spouses of their issue.

It must also be shown that the gift, including its extended sense relating to settled property, is in consideration of marriage. Neither a gift made on the occasion of a marriage, nor one made conditional upon the marriage taking place, is necessarily made in consideration of marriage. The question is one of fact, and where the gift is in settlement the solution may lie in the terms of the settlement in the light of the surrounding circumstances.[7] If therefore the settlor's prime motive was to save IHT and so benefit his family as a whole rather than the individual who was getting married, the gift is not in consideration of marriage; but it appears that an absolute disposition in favour of a party to their marriage cannot be attacked on this ground.[8] Subject to this it is irrelevant to the question whether a gift is made for such consideration that there are beneficiaries outside the marriage consideration.

Simon's Taxes I3.326, 327; Foster's Inheritance Tax C3.26, 27; STP [20.191].

[43.05] Exempt transfers

[1]   IHTA 1984, s 21(1)(a). Where the gift is to a child, child includes an illegitimate child, an adopted child and a step child, IHTA 1984, s 22(2).
[2]   IHTA 1984, s 22(1)(b).
[3]   IHTA 1984, s 22(1).
[4]   IHTA 1984, ss 22(6), 57(2).
[5]   FA 1986, s 102(5).
[6]   IHTA 1984, s 22(4). Free loans are treated as outright gifts—IHTA 1984, s 29(3).
[7]   Per Lord Guest in *Rennell v IRC* [1964] AC 173 at 209, [1963] 1 All ER 803 at 817.
[8]   *Re Park, IRC v Park (No 2)* [1972] Ch 385, [1972] 1 All ER 394.

Transfers between spouses

Both spouses domiciled within the UK

[43.06] A transfer of value by one spouse is an exempt transfer (a) to the extent that the value transferred is attributable to[1] property which becomes comprised in the estate of the other spouse, or (b) so far as the value transferred is not so attributable, to the extent that that estate is increased.[2] The reason for this formulation lies in the wide range of chargeable transfers. (a) makes it clear that the transfer is exempt in full even though the loss to the transferor is greater than the benefit to the transferee, as might happen when a husband gave his wife a chair which broke up a set belonging to the husband. (b) is designed to deal with situations in which there would otherwise be a chargeable transfer but no asset becomes the property of the other spouse as where a husband pays his wife's debts or he pays a premium on a life policy belonging to her.

From 22 March 2006, a transfer into a settlement in which the spouse has an interest in possession does not benefit from the IHT inter-spouse exemption, see infra, § **43.42**.[3]

The Special Commissioners have ruled that the exemption being given to married persons but not being available to a cohabiting couple does not infringe the provisions of the Human Rights Act 1998.[4]

Simon's Taxes I3.332; I4.212–214; Foster's Inheritance Tax C3.32; D2.12–14; STP [9.31]–[9.32], [9.75]; [11.3]–[11.5].

[1]   This means that the relief is not confined to the value received by the transferee.
[2]   IHTA 1984, s 18; this formula is also used in IHTA 1984, s 3A(1).
[3]   Unless the interest in possession is (a) an immediate post-death interest, (b) a disabled person's interest, or (c) a transitional serial interest: IHTA 1984, s 49(1A) inserted by FA 2006, Sch 20, para 4.
[4]   *Holland v IRC* [2003] STC (SCD) 43. See also supra, § **1.20**.

Conditions

[43.07] The transfer will only be exempt if it satisfies certain rules.

(1) *Intervening transfer*—The disposition by which the transfer of value takes effect must not take effect on the termination after the transfer of any interest or period.[1] The phrase "takes effect" is not defined but presumably means takes effect in possession. So if D left his property to his widow for life with remainder to A, the transfer on D's death to his widow would be free of tax; however, if he had left his property to A for life with the remainder to his (D's) widow, the transfer on D's death would not be exempt unless A predeceased D.

Simon's Taxes I3.339; I4.214; Foster's Inheritance Tax C3.39; D2.14.

[1] IHTA 1984, s 18(3)(*a*).

[43.08] (2) *Survivorship clause*—The exemption is available on death where the will of the deceased provides that this spouse will inherit only if he/she survives the deceased by a short period. The exemption does not apply if the disposition by which the property is given depends on a condition which is not satisfied within 12 months after the transfer.[1] A legacy to a surviving spouse conditional on surviving nine months will be exempt under this rule if she survives.

Simon's Taxes I4.214.

[1] IHTA 1984, s 18(3)(*b*).

[43.09] (3) *Reversionary interests.* While the exemption will apply when, on the termination of an interest, the property passes to the previous life tenant's spouse, this is not so if that spouse purchased the reversionary interest for a consideration in money or money's worth.[1] This is to prevent abuse of the relief. For example if A wishes to benefit his son B, he could settle property on himself for life with remainder to B. On A's death there would be a transfer of value under IHTA 1984, s 52; however, if on A's death the property passed to A's widow the transfer would be exempt. If therefore A's widow bought B's remainder, the exemption on A's death would arise. It is true that the sum paid might well be a chargeable transfer but this would be a transfer by the spouse and not by A, and the sum paid by the spouse would reflect the fact that the transfer by A would become exempt. If the life interest ends after 16 March 1987, the exemption will, after all, apply if B *gives* the remainder to A's spouse.[2]

A similar restriction applies in relation to property given in return for a purchased reversionary interest.[3]

Simon's Taxes I4.214; Foster's Inheritance Tax D2.14.

[1] IHTA 1984, s 56(2).
[2] F(No 2)A 1987, Sch 7, para 2.
[3] IHTA 1984, s 56(1); a reversionary interest is also excluded from the inter-spouse exemption if it is acquired by the beneficiary who has an interest in possession, or

[43.09] Exempt transfers

any other interest on which the reversionary interest is expectant, and thus falls within IHTA 1984, s 55(1).

Spouses with separate domiciles

Transferee spouse domiciled outside the UK

[43.10] Where, immediately before the transfer, the transferor was domiciled in the UK but the spouse was not, the exemption on an inter-spouse transfer is limited. The policy behind the limited inter-spouse transfer exemption is that foreign property will be excluded property in the hands of the non-domiciled transferee—infra, § 47.11. Such a transfer is exempt to the extent only that it does not exceed £55,000 less any amount previously taken into account for the purposes of the section.[1] The limit is cumulative throughout life, the seven year rule does not apply. Once the £55,000 total has been exceeded, the exemption is lost. (However, the PET regime applies in the normal way. Hence, a transfer may not be chargeable to tax as it is a PET made more than seven years before death.)

For the "non-domiciled inter-spouse exemption", an amount is taken into account for the purpose of the relief for spouses even though it later transpires that it would have been exempt on different grounds such as because the donor died more than seven years after the gift so achieving actual, as opposed to potential, exemption; by exhausting the £55,000 limit this may cause a gift within the seven-year period to be chargeable. Originally the value of this exemption moved in line with the threshold for tax, but it has not been increased since 1982.[2]

EXAMPLE

H, who is domiciled in England and Wales gives W, his wife who is domiciled in a state of the USA, a gift of £10,000. The gift is exempt.

Two years later, H makes a further gift of £20,000. The cumulative total for this exemption is £30,000 and the exemption was then £25,000 so that there is a chargeable transfer of £5,000.

If H makes a further gift of £40,000 in December 2008 the amount of the transfer would be £10,000; this would be a potentially exempt transfer because although the cumulative total for this exemption stood at £70,000 only £25,000 had previously been taken into account for the exemption leaving £30,000 free to exempt this transfer under this rule leaving the balance of £10,000 as potentially exempt.

Where a transfer of property from a UK domiciled individual to a non-domiciled spouse is being considered, it is important to recognise that a charge to inheritance tax does not arise if the disposition is not intended to confer gratuitous benefit.[3] This is the situation, for example, on a divorce, if one party to the marriage transfers property in satisfaction of the liabilities created by their relationship (or, perhaps, recognised by the divorce settlement). Clearly, a transfer of property that is required by a court order is not one that confers gratuitous benefit and is, thus, outside the charge to IHT. Arguably, a transfer on a separation, even if not followed by divorce, is similarly outside the charge to tax unless it is disproportionate.

Simon's Taxes I4.213; Foster's Inheritance Tax D2.13.

[1] IHTA 1984, s 18(2)—ie for s 18(1) or 18(2).
[2] FA 1982, s 92(1), (3) substituted £55,000 with effect for transfers of value made after 8 March 1982. On 14 March 1995 the Secretary of State undertook to review the limit in the light of obligations under the EC treaty not to discriminate between nationals of member states (HC Official Report, Standing Committee D, col 726, 14 March 1995, *Simon's Weekly Tax Intelligence* 1995, p 501). No change has been made.
[3] IHTA 1984, s 10(1).

Transferee spouse domiciled within the UK

[43.11] The effect of a transfer from a non-domiciled spouse to a spouse domiciled within the UK is potentially to bring within the charge to UK inheritance tax foreign situs assets that would have been outside the charge to tax if they had remained in the ownership of the non-domiciled spouse. Hence, there is no limit to the exemption available on such a transfer.[1]

[1] IHTA 1984, s 18(1) applies and is not disapplied by s 18(2).

Both spouses domiciled outside the UK

[43.12] The inter-spouse exemption is fully available.[1]

[1] IHTA 1984, s 18(1) applies and is not disapplied by s 18(2).

Spouse

[43.13] The legislation does not find it necessary to define spouse. A polygamous marriage will presumably be recognised. On the other hand a void marriage, however innocent the parties, is not a marriage. It is however important to remember that a decree of divorce does not become effective until it is made absolute and that a decree of nullity in relation to a voidable marriage has the same effect as a decree of divorce.[1] Hence, the inter-spouse exemption operates on transfers between separated spouses and continues until the divorce is absolute. This is in contrast to the rule for capital gains tax[2] where the exemption ceases at the end of the fiscal year of separation, even though the parties are still married.

An ex-spouse is not a spouse, and the inter-spouse exemption has no relevance to a transfer after the decree absolute. Fiancés are not spouses; however, when a man wishes to buy a house before his marriage and give his future wife a half share he can achieve his object by making her a loan with which she buys her half share and then releasing the debt after marriage.

Simon's Taxes I4.212.

[1] Matrimonial Causes Act 1973, s 16.
[2] TCGA 1992, s 58.

Gifts for public purposes

[43.14] This group of exempt transfers covers gifts to charities,[1] to political parties,[2] to housing associations[3] and for national and similar purposes.[4]

Simon's Taxes I4.215–219.

---

[1] IHTA 1984, s 23.
[2] IHTA 1984, s 24.
[3] IHTA 1984, s 24A.
[4] IHTA 1984, s 25.

Conditions

[43.15] Such gifts must all satisfy certain conditions[1] designed to prevent abuse of the exemptions given. The first two are the same as for transfers to a spouse:

(1) The disposition must not take effect on the termination after the transfer of value of any interest or period. Unlike the transfer to spouse but for self-evident reasons, there is no relaxation of this condition for a period of survivorship.[2]

(2) The disposition must not depend on a condition which is not satisfied within 12 months of the transfer.[3]

(3) A transfer to these bodies or for these purposes will not be exempt if the disposition is defeasible.[4] Any sdisposition which has not been defeated 12 months after the transfer and is not defeasible thereafter is treated as indefeasible even though it was defeasible when made or at some time during the 12-month period.[5]

(4) The transfer will not be exempt if the property or any part of it may become applicable for purposes other than charitable purposes or those of a body mentioned in the exemptions; this is to prevent finite charitable trusts.[6]

(5) The transfer will not be exempt if the disposition is of an interest in property and that interest is less than the donor's or the property is given for a limited period.[7] This question is to be decided as at a time 12 months after the transfer of value. This rule is relaxed to allow the donor to give the benefit of an agreement restricting the use of land which he retains to bodies specified in IHTA 1984, Sch 3, see infra, § **43.19**.

EXAMPLE

If D leaves property by will to A for life with remainder to charity and A dies two years after D, the property will not be exempt from tax on D's death since it breaks both the rules 1 and 5. If A had died after six months the gift would have broken 1 but not 5. Therefore whether A died two years or six months after D's death there is a chargeable transfer on D's death. However, there will be an exempt transfer on A's death.

Simon's Taxes I3.331; I4.201; Foster's Inheritance Tax C3.31; D2.01.

---

[1] IHTA 1984, s 23(2)(*a*).

² IHTA 1984, s 23(2)(*b*).
³ IHTA 1984, s 23(2).
⁴ IHTA 1984, s 23(2)(*c*).
⁵ IHTA 1984, s 23(2).
⁶ IHTA 1984, s 23(5).
⁷ IHTA 1984, s 23(3).

Settled property, and reserved rights

[43.16] Further rules apply to prevent the avoidance of tax through these reliefs. The transfer is not exempt if:

(1) the property is an interest in possession in settled property and the settlement does not come to an end in relation to that settled property on the making of the transfer;¹
(2) the property is land or a building but subject to an interest reserved or created by the donor which entitles him, his spouse or any person connected with him to possession of, or to occupy, the whole or part of the land or building rent free or at a rent less than might be expected to be obtained in a transaction at arm's length between persons not connected with each other;
(3) the property is not land or building and is given subject to an interest reserved or created by the donor other than:
  (a) an interest created by him for full consideration in money or money's worth; or
  (b) an interest which does not substantially affect the enjoyment of the property by the person or body by whom it is given.²

Further a special rule applies to reversionary interests. Where a person or body acquires a reversionary interest in any settled property for a consideration in money or money's worth, this relief does not apply to the property when it becomes the property of that person or body on the termination of the interest to which the reversionary interest is expectant.³

The purpose of rule 1 is to prevent avoidance through the gift of a life interest in possession. A would create a settlement on himself for life with remainder to his son B and would then assign the life interest to a charity; the charity would then be used as an intermediary and the benefit would pass to B.

Rule 1 prevents the transfer to charity from enjoying relief. However, if the settlement had been on A for life with remainder to charity the transfer to charity occurring on the ending of A's interest would be exempt. Here, however, the special rule comes in. If the settlement had originally been on A for life with remainder to B and the charity had bought B's interest, the price naturally reflecting the immunity from IHT that would result on the termination of A's interest, then the exemption is not to apply on that termination.

Rules 2 and 3 are designed to deal with arrangements similar to this covered by 1 but which are not technically settlements.

Simon's Taxes I3.340; I4.221; Foster's Inheritance Tax C3.40; D2.21.

¹ IHTA 1984, s 56(3).

[43.16] Exempt transfers

[2] IHTA 1984, s 23(4). These apply to transfers of value made after 15 April 1976 but not to certain payments out of discretionary trusts.
[3] IHTA 1984, s 56(2).

Charities

[43.17] Transfers to charities are exempt transfers. The Revenue view is that s 23 exempts the whole of the diminution in the value of the transferor's estate, even if this is greater than the value of the property received by the transferee.[1] A transfer is to charity if it becomes the property of charities or is held on trust for charitable purposes only.[2] For this purpose a gift of residue for charitable purposes only is a gift to charity even though it could not be said that the residue was capable of being applied for such purposes *immediately* after the death of the testator by reason of an application for cy-près.[3]

Simon's Taxes I3.333; I4.215; Foster's Inheritance Tax C3.33; D2.15.

[1] Such as, for example, where a private company has 100 shares in issue and a shareholder gives a charity two shares out of the 51 shares he holds. Statement of practice E13; **Foster's Inheritance Tax, Division W2**.
[2] IHTA 1984, s 23(1), (6). On the position of Roman Catholic religious communities when there is no trust note extra-statutory concession F2; **Foster's Inheritance Tax Division U2**.
[3] *Guild v IRC* [1991] STC 281, Ct of Sess; this point was not pursued in the House of Lords: [1992] STC 162.

Political parties

[43.18] Gifts to political parties are wholly exempt from IHT.[1]

A political party qualifies only if at the general election preceding the transfer the party secured two seats in the House of Commons or, alternatively, only one MP was elected but not fewer than 150,000 votes were cast in favour of the candidates from that party.[2]

Simon's Taxes I3.334; I4.216; Foster's Inheritance Tax C3.34; D2.16.

[1] FA 1988, s 137 amending IHTA 1984, s 24.
[2] For a list of qualifying parties see **Simon's Taxes I4.216; Foster's Inheritance Tax D2.16**.

Specified bodies

[43.19] Gifts to certain bodies are exempt whether on death or inter vivos. The bodies listed[1] include the National Gallery, the British Museum, the Historic Buildings and Monuments Commission for England, any local authority, any government department and any university or university college in the UK. Oxford and Cambridge colleges are regarded as being on the list.[2] Gifts of land to a registered housing association are also exempt.[3]

Simon's Taxes I3.335, 336; I4.217, 218; Foster's Inheritance Tax C3.35, 36; D2.17, 18.

[1] IHTA 1984, Sch 3.
[2] As well as being charities, by virtue of the terms of the Royal Charter given to each college.
[3] IHTA 1984, s 24A. For a death prior to 17 March 1998, any land, buildings, contents of buildings, maintenance funds and any work of art or scientific collection given for the public benefit to a body not established or conducted for profit is exempt from tax if the Treasury so directs: IHTA 1984, s 26. This provision is repealed by FA 1998, s 143(1) in respect of deaths after 16 March 1998 as it was found to be effectively redundant. In practice, the Treasury were not prepared to grant an exemption unless the recipient was a charity or a "specified body".

Other exempt transfers

[43.20] A transfer by an individual to an employee trust[1] is an exempt transfer if it meets the full requirements of IHTA 1984, s 28, in particular that the trustees have, then or within one year, control of the company.[2] A transfer to a maintenance fund for heritage property is an exempt transfer.[3]

Simon's Taxes I3.341–343; Foster's Inheritance Tax C3.41–43.

[1] As defined by IHTA 1984, s 86.
[2] IHTA 1984, s 28(2); contrast IHTA 1984, s 13.
[3] IHTA 1984, s 27, Sch 4.

Decoration awarded for valour

[43.21] Under extra-statutory concession F19,[1] the transfer of a decoration awarded for valour or gallant conduct is treated as excluded property if it can be shown that it was never previously transferred for consideration in money or money's worth.

[1] Extra-statutory concession F19, *Simons Weekly Tax Intelligence 2000, p 1224*.

Partly exempt transfers—allocation of relief

[43.22] Special rules apply where a transfer includes a gift to a spouse and the transfer is exempt only as to a part of the value whether because the recipient's spouse is not domiciled in the UK and the limit of £55,000 is

[43.22] Exempt transfers

exceeded, or because the gifts do not meet the conditions at supra, § **43.15** in relation to all the property, or because the transfer also contains gifts to others. The purpose of these rules is to ensure that the benefit of the exemption accrues primarily to the gifts which are exempt. These rules do not apply where the transfer is wholly chargeable nor where it is wholly exempt.

These problems will usually arise on death, but may arise on transfers inter vivos. Moreover the gifts may be made separately out of separate funds as where A holds free estate of which he is to leave a substantial part to a political party and also holds a life interest in possession in settled property which on his death is to pass at least in part to a political party. Where this occurs the rules which follow are to be applied separately to the gifts taking effect out of each fund, with the necessary adjustments of values and amounts referred to in those provisions.[1] This provision is particularly obscure.[2]

The practical (ie arithmetical) difficulties in this area have been greatly reduced by the advent of a single rate of IHT. However, problems still arise.

Simon's Taxes I4.231; Foster's Inheritance Tax D2.31, 40.

---

[1] IHTA 1984, s 40. On change in Revenue practice see *Simon's Tax Intelligence* 1990, p 446; **Foster's Inheritance Tax X6.43**.
[2] See **Simon's Taxes I4.240; Foster's Inheritance Tax D2.40**.

Definitions

[43.23] Gift. This is widely defined and means the benefit of any disposition or any rule of law by which, on the making of a transfer, any property becomes the property of any person or applicable for any purpose or would do so if it were not abated.[1] So the benefit of a disposition inter vivos, or by will or on an intestacy all qualify as a gift. A surviving joint tenant obtains the benefit of the rule of law known as the ius accrescendi whereby the interest of the deceased joint tenant is extinguished; however, the interest of the deceased joint tenant does not "become" the property of the survivor so it is doubtful whether such a transfer comes technically within this definition.

Although these rules use the word gift and require these gifts to be valued they do not state how this valuation is to be carried out. Presumably all must be valued as at the time of the transfer; since the transfer on death is treated as occurring immediately before death any expenses of administration must be left out in valuing the estate as must any gains or losses realised in the course of administration save perhaps in so far as they are the subject of later relief.[2]

Simon's Taxes I4.233; Foster's Inheritance Tax D2.33.

---

[1] IHTA 1984, s 42(1).
[2] Supra, § **40.05**.

[43.24] Specific gift. These rules distinguish gifts of residue, which must necessarily bear their own tax, from other gifts. Gifts which are not of residue

Partly exempt transfers—allocation of relief [43.27]

or of a share in residue are specific gifts.[1] A liability which is not deductible in computing the value of the estate is treated as a specific gift for this purpose[2] including one not deductible by FA 1986, s 103. Legal rights in Scotland are also treated as specific gifts.[3]

Simon's Taxes I4.233; Foster's Inheritance Tax D2.33.

[1] IHTA 1984, s 42(1) see also *Russell v IRC* [1988] STC 195, [1988] 2 All ER 405.
[2] IHTA 1984, s 38(6).
[3] IHTA 1984, s 42(4).

[43.25] Bearing its own tax. A gift bears its own tax if the tax attributable to it falls on the person who becomes entitled to the property given or if the tax is payable out of property applicable for the purposes for which the property given becomes applicable.[1] The direction that the tax must fall on the person suggests that the mere presence of an HMRC charge will not be sufficient to make the gift bear its own tax. The same direction also suggests that if the tax is in fact paid by someone else the gift does not bear its own tax; presumably the draftsman intended to indicate that the tax should fall on the beneficiary rather than on some other part of the estate but this is not what he has said.

Simon's Taxes I4.233; Foster's Inheritance Tax D2.33.

[1] IHTA 1984, s 42(2).

[43.26] Where the value transferred or part of it is attributable to property which is the subject of two or more gifts and the aggregate value of the property so given is less than the value transferred, the value of each gift is the proportion of the value transferred or part of it which the value of the property given by it bears to the aggregate.[1] So if a 90% share holding is left to two people equally, each is treated as obtaining half the value of a 90% holding—not that of a 45% holding.

Simon's Taxes I4.233; Foster's Inheritance Tax D2.33.

[1] IHTA 1984, s 42(3).

[43.27] First one must calculate the values which are exempt and so discover both the value of residue and the tax due on the transfer. The major problem is the calculation of the value of specific gifts (IHTA 1984, s 38). The residue is whatever is left after the valuation of the specific gifts (IHTA 1984, s 39).

Situation 1. Where the only gifts are specific gifts which bear their own tax or which are wholly exempt: here a simple rule applies—the face value is taken.

EXAMPLE

D, who has made chargeable lifetime transfers of £380,000, dies in February 2008 leaving an estate of £150,000 consisting of a legacy of £40,000 to his son on condition that he pays the tax and the residue to his widow.

Tax due will be £16,000 being the tax due on a gross transfer on death of £40,000 by one who has already made transfers of more than the nil rate band. This tax will fall on the son. In

[43.27] Exempt transfers

addition, tax of £32,000 is payable in respect of the lifetime transfers; this is charged on the donees of the lifetime transfers, less any tax paid inter vivos.

Situation 2. Where there are specific gifts bearing their own tax and only a *part* of the residue is exempt. Here again life is relatively simple; there is no grossing up.

EXAMPLE

D, who has made chargeable lifetime transfers of £380,000, dies in February 2008 leaving an estate of £150,000. He leaves a legacy of £40,000 to his son on condition that he pays the tax and the residue to be divided between his widow and his sister.

The value attributable to the legacy to the son is £40,000, the residue is therefore £110,000 and the 1/2 share in the residue is worth £55,000. Tax is therefore due on £95,000 at death rates for one who has already transferred more than the nil rate band, ie £38,000. The son will therefore pay 40/95 × £38,000 = £16,000 and the sister will pay 55/95 × £38,000 = £22,000. In addition, tax of £32,000 is payable in respect of the lifetime transfers; this is charged on the donees of the lifetime transfers, less any tax paid inter vivos.

Situation 3. Where the only gifts with respect to which the transfer might be chargeable are specific gifts which do *not* bear their own tax a grossing up process is carried out. The amount to be attributed to the specific gifts is the aggregate of (a) the sum of the value of those gifts, and (b) the amount of tax chargeable if the value transferred equalled that aggregate.[1] The grossing up process is thus geared to the tax applicable if the transfer consisted only of these free-of-tax gifts. This grossing up process tends to induce numbing terror; however it is really quite logical once one remembers that one does not usually have to gross up on death and realises that that is what is unusual about it. The purpose of this rule is to ensure that the tax should be the same whether the legacy is at the grossed up figure bearing its own tax or at the net figure but not bearing its own tax.

EXAMPLE

D, who has made chargeable lifetime transfers of £380,000, dies in February 2008 leaving an estate of £150,000 bequeathing a legacy of £40,000 net of tax to his son and the residue to his widow.

The calculation requires care since one must gross up from a net figure when all the previous calculations have involved gross figures.

The grossed up value of the legacy is £66,667 and the tax borne by the estate is £26,667. In addition, tax of £32,000 is payable in respect of the lifetime transfers; this is charged on the donees of the lifetime transfers, less any tax paid inter vivos.

When it is necessary to gross up separate gifts made out of different funds, the Revenue now accept that the rate of tax to be used is found by looking at each fund separately.[2]

Simon's Taxes I4.233–237; Foster's Inheritance Tax D2.33–37.

---

[1] IHTA 1984, s 38(3).
[2] Inland Revenue press release, May 1990, *Simon's Tax Intelligence* 1990, p 446.

[43.28] Situation 4. Where the specific gifts not bearing their own tax are not the only gifts with respect to which the transfer is or might be chargeable. This will arise if there is a specific legacy not bearing its own tax and a division of residue between exempt and non-exempt transferees; there may also be other

Partly exempt transfers—allocation of relief [43.28]

specific gifts, some exempt, others not. Here the non-exempt specific gifts are grossed up at "the assumed rate" which is[1]:

(a) the rate found by dividing the assumed amount of tax by that part of the value transferred with respect to which the transfer would be chargeable on the hypothesis that
  (i) the amount corresponding to the value of specific gifts not bearing their own tax [grossed up as in situation 3 above], and
  (ii) the parts of the value transferred attributable to specific gifts and to gifts of residue and shares in residue are determined accordingly; and
(b) the assumed amount of tax is the amount that would be charged on the value transferred on the hypothesis mentioned in (a).

EXAMPLE

The facts are as in the previous example save that D leaves one half of the residue to his daughter. If there had been no other taxable gift the grossed up legacy to the son would be £66,667.

This is taken as the initial gross value of the legacy in order to determine the value of the non-exempt share of residue which will be 1/2 × (£150,000 − £66,667) = £41,667. The total chargeable transfer based on these initial values would be:

Gross legacy	£66,667	(a(i))
Non-exempt residue	41,667	(a(ii))
	£108,334	

The tax which would be chargeable on a transfer of this amount is calculated, to give the assumed rate for the purposes of the revised grossing up of the legacy.

	Gross	Tax
	£	£
Previous cumulative total	380,000	0
Gross transfer on death	108,334	43,334
	483,334	43,334

(The tax on the previous cumulative total is calculated at the rate applying at the date of death, for the purpose of this calculation only.)

The assumed rate is 43,334/101,666.

The net legacy of £40,000 is now grossed up at the assumed rate:

$$£40,000 \times \frac{101,666}{101,666 - 32,666} = £58,936$$

The revised gross value of the legacy is higher than the earlier gross value as it reflects the fact that one-half of the residue is also chargeable to tax.

The total chargeable transfer on death is recalculated using the revised gross value of the legacy:

Gross legacy	£66,667	
Non-exempt residue		
1/2 × (£150,000 − £66,667)	41,667	
	£108,334	

[43.28] Exempt transfers

The actual tax borne by the estate is charged on this amount.

	Gross £	Tax £
Previous cumulative total	380,000	32,000
Gross transfer on death	108,334	43,334
	238,468	75,334

The tax on the estate is £33,787.

It is possible to create more complex examples where there are (a) exempt specific gifts, (b) non-exempt specific gifts bearing their own tax, (c) non-exempt specific gifts not bearing their own tax, (d) exempt shares in residue, and (e) non-exempt shares in residue. In such instances the gifts in (c) are first grossed up using the calculation in situation 3, and then all the non-exempt gifts in (b) at probate value, (c) at probate value but as just grossed up, and (e), are aggregated to discover the assumed rate. This assumed rate is then again applied to (c) to give the revised grossed up value. It will be seen that both in this example and the worked example the only gift requiring to be grossed up is the non-exempt gift not bearing its own duty and this is done at the assumed rate, which, however, takes account of the previous grossing up. There are therefore two grossing up steps to be taken. The purpose of the calculation is simply to put a value on the specific gift not bearing its own duty. The assumed rate is not the rate applied to the chargeable portion of the estate.

Simon's Taxes I4.238; Foster's Inheritance Tax D2.38.

---

[1] IHTA 1984, s 38(4), (5).

[43.29] Where two or more specific gifts are exempt but exempt only up to a limit, two rules apply: (a) the excess is attributed to gifts not bearing their own tax before gifts which do bear their own tax, and (b) subject to rule (a) the excess is attributed to the gifts in proportion to their value.[1] The removal of all but one of the pecuniary limits for exemptions makes the application of this rule a rarity.[2]

Simon's Taxes I4.235; Foster's Inheritance Tax D2.35.

---

[1] IHTA 1984, s 38(2).
[2] The remaining pecuniary limit is the £55,000 ceiling on a transfer by a UK domiciled spouse to a non-UK domiciled spouse; supra, § **43.10**.

Abatement

[43.30] Where a gift would be abated owing to an insufficiency of assets but ignoring tax, the gift must be abated before the rules for valuation of specific gifts are applied.[1] Those rules are then applied.

A separate problem arises where the grossing up process in paragraph 19 leads to the value exceeding the total value transferred. Here the gift is to be treated as reduced to the extent necessary to reduce their value to that of the value transferred. The reduction is made in the order in which under the terms of the relevant disposition or any rule of law, it would fall on a distribution of assets.[2]

Simon's Taxes I4.234, 241; Foster's Inheritance Tax D2.34.

[1] IHTA 1984, s 37(1).
[2] IHTA 1984, s 37(2).

Burden of tax

[43.31] The burden of tax is given[1] as:

Notwithstanding the terms of any disposition—

(a) none of the tax on the value transferred shall fall on any specific gift if or to the extent that the transfer is exempt with regard to the gift; and
(b) none of the tax attributable to the value of the property comprised in residue shall fall on any gift of a share of residue if or to the extent that the transfer is exempt with regard to the gift.

This is a significant restriction on the testator's freedom of testamentary disposition. The most common situation when this arises is when part of the residue is left to a charity. The intention behind the legislation is to enable the charity to gain the full benefit of IHT exemption. Its practical effect is to increase the tax burden on non-exempt beneficiaries, typically family members.

Where therefore there is a non-exempt specific legacy not bearing its own tax, the tax due will not fall on an exempt specific legacy but on residue; it will fall on residue whether the residue is exempt or not. However, tax in respect of non-exempt shares in residue must fall on the non-exempt parts.

While s 41 states these restrictions, the application of s 41 will depend on the construction of the document. In *Re Ratcliffe, Holmes v McMullan*,[2] the will provided that one-half of the estate was to pass to two individuals and one-half to four charities. The executors applied to the court for a direction as to how the parts were to be calculated. Blackburne J held that the residue of the estate included the inheritance tax payable. The fact that the executors were liable for the tax[3] and were entitled to repayment from the estate[4] as a testamentary expense did not alter the fact that the inheritance tax attributable to the share to be enjoyed by the individuals was part of the testator's gift to them. Hence, in the direction given by the court, the correct approach was to divide the gross and for the inheritance tax payable to be borne by the half share enjoyed by the individuals; there was, thus, no deduction of the inheritance tax in calculating the share that passed to the charities.

By contrast, in *Re Benham's Will Trusts*,[5] T left the residue of her estate on terms that beneficiaries named in list A were to receive 3.2 times as much as beneficiaries named in list B. It was held that the words meant that the list A beneficiaries were entitled to a fund 3.2 times the size of the fund shared by list

[43.31] Exempt transfers

B beneficiaries. The next problem was that in each list there were some charitable and some non-charitable beneficiaries. The alternative consequences were spelt out as follows: (1) that the non-charitable beneficiaries receive their respective share, subject to inheritance tax, which would mean they would receive less than the charitable beneficiaries; (2) that the non-charitable beneficiaries are entitled to have their respective shares "grossed up" so the net result is that equality is achieved between charitable and non-charitable beneficiaries; (3) that the executors should pay the inheritance tax as part of the testamentary expenses . . . of the will and distribute the balance equally between the exempt and non-exempt beneficiaries. The judge rejected (3) as being precluded by s 41 and preferred (2) to (1). It was the plain intention of the testatrix that each beneficiary of the respective lists, whether charitable or non-charitable, should receive the same amount as other beneficiaries in the same list.

Simon's Taxes I4.243; Foster's Inheritance Tax D2.43.

[1] IHTA 1984, s 41.
[2] [1999] STC 262.
[3] IHTA 1984, s 200(1).
[4] IHTA 1984, s 211(1).
[5] [1995] STC 210.

Planning

[43.32] Particular care is needed when a part of the property is entitled to a relief such as business or agricultural relief. If such property is left to the exempt person and other property to a chargeable person the benefit of the relief is lost; if the gifts were reversed, the property going to the exempt person would attract no tax while the other gift would be reduced in chargeable value.

Agricultural and business reliefs

[43.33] Rules are provided for the interaction of the reliefs for agricultural and business property and the rules for partly exempt transfers.[1] The purpose of these rules is to protect the Revenue. Before these rules it was common to avoid CTT by leaving to the surviving spouse a pecuniary legacy of a value equal to the estate as reduced by these reliefs. This attributed the whole of the value transferred on the death to the spouse's legacy, the residue passing to the other beneficiaries free of tax—thanks to the reliefs.

The first rule is that the value of specific gifts of business or agricultural property are to be taken to be their value as reduced by the relevant reliefs.[2] The second rule is more complex and directs that the value of any other specific gifts shall be "the appropriate fraction" of their value.[3] The numerator of the appropriate fraction is the difference between the value transferred and the value of any specific gifts of business or agricultural property as reduced after the application of the first rule and the denominator is the difference between the unreduced value transferred and the value, before the reduction, of property falling within the first rule.[4] The rule is of more significance where the relief is at less than 100%, as can arise on shares in an unquoted trading company with excepted property (see infra, § **44.08**), or is in the categories for which 50% business property relief is granted, such as a factory occupied by a partnership (see infra, § **44.01**). A, perhaps greater, problem that is now frequently faced is where a will provides for a (chargeable) transfer at death "of the maximum sum that can be passed without the payment of inheritance tax". Where the estate includes business assets or agricultural property attracting relief at 100%, a natural reading of this provision passes the entire business and agricultural property to the named individual, or into trust, *plus* the unused part of the £300,000 nil rate band. This may not have been what the testator had intended.

In essence what the rule is trying to do is to provide a formula whereby a part of the benefit of the agricultural and business reliefs is attributed to the exempt transfer even though the effect is that the estate loses the value of part of the relief. It will thus no longer be possible to have the chargeable part of the estate reduced by the full amount of the reliefs even though the property goes, or is treated as going, in part, to an exempt beneficiary.

It is further provided that in calculating the value of the specific gift of agricultural or business property any pecuniary legacy which is charged on that property must be deducted before these rules are applied.[5] The pecuniary legacy will then come within the second rule.

Simon's Taxes I4.240; Foster's Inheritance Tax D2.40.

[1] IHTA 1984, s 39A.
[2] IHTA 1984, s 39A(2).
[3] IHTA 1984, s 39A(3).
[4] IHTA 1984, s 39A(4).
[5] IHTA 1984, s 39A(5).

Matters which are not transfers of value

[43.34] In addition to declaring certain transfers as exempt transfers, statute declares some transactions as not being transfers of value. These are:

(1) Transactions with no intent to give.[1]
(2) Dispositions from maintenance of the family.[2]
(3) A disposition which is allowable in computing profits for income tax or corporation tax.[3]
(4) A contribution to an approved retirement benefit scheme, etc[4]
(5) Certain waivers.[5]
(6) A transfer to a employee share ownership trust.[6]
(7) The grant of an agricultural tenancy charging a full market rent.[7]

[1] IHTA 1984, s 10, see supra, § **39.14**.
[2] IHTA 1984, s 11, see supra, § **39.15**.

[43.34] Exempt transfers

[3] IHTA 1984, s 12, see supra, § **39.20**.
[4] IHTA 1984, s 12(2), see supra, § **39.20**.
[5] IHTA 1984, ss 14 and 15, see supra, § **39.20**.
[6] IHTA 1984, s 13, see supra, § **39.20**.
[7] IHTA 1984, s 20.

44

Business property relief and other reliefs

Business property relief	PARA 44.01
Agricultural property relief	PARA 44.11
Interaction between business property relief and agricultural property relief	PARA 44.26
Relief for works of art and other heritage property	PARA 44.27
Relief for timber	PARA 44.33

Business property relief

[44.01] Relief of either 100% or 50% is applied to transfers of certain business property provided (a) the asset is relevant business property, (b) the business is a qualifying business, (c) the asset has been held for the minimum period of ownership, and (d) the asset is not an excepted asset. A legacy that can only be satisfied by resort to an identified asset which is subject to business property relief is entitled to this relief.[1] The relief is applied to the value transferred, not the chargeable transfer and not the property.[2] It is therefore applied before other relief, such as annual exemption. Where the property is the subject of a chargeable transfer but the donor dies within seven years (so that additional tax may be due) or is the subject of a potentially exempt transfer (so that tax may become due) the benefit of the relief may, in those terms, be clawed back unless further conditions (set out infra, § **44.10**) are satisfied at the time of the death.

There are six categories of relevant business property: three qualify for 100% relief; three qualify for 50% relief.[3]

The categories of property that attract 100% relief are:

(1) A business or an interest in a business, other than an excluded business (see infra, § **44.04**);[4]
(2) *unquoted* shares (but not securities) in any company, unless the company carries on an excluded business (see infra, § **44.04**);[5]
(3) *quoted* shares or securities which give the transferor *control* of the company either by themselves or with other shares or securities owned by the transferor;[6]

A 50% shareholding has been held to be control where the shareholder was chairman of the company with a casting vote.[7]

The categories of property which attract 50% relief are:

(1) *unquoted* securities of a company in which the transferor had a controlling interest before the transfer;[8]

[44.01] Business property relief and other reliefs

(2) any land or building, machinery or plant which, immediately before the transfer, was used wholly or mainly for the purposes of a business carried on by a company of which the transferor then had *control* or by a partnership of which he was then a partner;[9]

(3) land or buildings used for the purposes of a business carried on by the transferor where the property is settled but the transferor had a beneficial interest in possession at the time of the transfer.[10]

Business property relief is deducted from the value of the business. The value transferred by the transfer of value has to be attributable to the net value of the business; there is no requirement that the transfer has to be of a "whole" business rather than merely business assets.[11]

The value of the business is defined in statute as "the value of the assets used in the business (including goodwill) reduced by the aggregate amount of any liabilities incurred for the purposes of the business".[12]

The relief is designed to alleviate the tax consequences of the transfer of a business. For this reason the transfer of property subject to a binding contract for sale is not relevant business property save where the property is a business or an interest in a business and the sale is to a company which is to carry on that business and is made in consideration wholly or mainly of shares or securities in that company.[13] For similar reasons a sale of shares or securities for the purpose of reconstruction or amalgamation is ignored.

Private use may not necessarily restrict business property relief. In *Ninth Marquess of Hertford (Executors of the Eighth Marquess of Hertford) v IRC*[14] a lifetime transfer was made of Ragley Hall, a historic Grade 1 listed house. The donor died less than seven years later. 78% of the floor area of the house was open to the public, in the pursuance of a business that attracted business property relief. The executors claimed that 100% of the value of the building should attract 100% business property relief as the public could see the whole of the exterior. The claim was accepted by the Special Commissioners.

Simon's Taxes I7.101–111, 135; Foster's Inheritance Tax G1.01–11; 35; STP [9.102]–[9.103d], [9.272].

---

[1] *Russell v IRC* [1988] STC 195, [1988] 2 All ER 405.
[2] IHTA 1984, ss 103, 104.
[3] IHTA 1984, s 104(1). Prior to 9 March 1992, the percentages were 50% and 30%.
[4] IHTA 1984, s 105(1)(*a*).
[5] IHTA 1984, s 105(1)(*bb*).
[6] IHTA 1984, s 105(1)(*cc*). As with the other categories, business property relief is excluded if the company carries on an excluded business (see infra, § **44.04**).
[7] *Walker's Executors v IRC* [2001] STC (SCD) 86.
[8] IHTA 1984, s 105(1)(*b*). As with the other categories, business property relief is excluded if the company carries on an excluded business (see infra, § **44.04**). The definition of the term "security" in TCGA 1992, s 132(2)(b) is considered at supra, § **17.10**. However, it is of limited use. First, it is not, in truth, a definition but merely a declaration that the term encompasses certain items. Second, there is no statement, explicit nor implicit, that this "definition" applies for the purpose of inheritance tax business property relief.

[9] IHTA 1984, s 105(1)(d). In order for the property to be within this category, the shares in the company concerned must be capable of satisfying the conditions in 2 or 3 and the partnership the conditions applicable to 1.
[10] IHTA 1984, s 105(1)(e). The business must not be an excluded business (see infra § **44.04**).
[11] *Nelson Dance Family Settlement, Re; Trustees of Nelson Dance Family Settlement v Revenue & Customs Comrs* (2008) SpC 682.
[12] IHTA 1984, s 105(12A) overriding the general definition in IHTA 1984, s 272.
[13] IHTA 1984, s 113; property subject to certain "buy and sell" agreements is therefore not eligible for this relief; see statement of practice SP 12/80; **Foster's Inheritance Tax, Division W3** and, on background, ICAEW Memorandum TR 557, reproduced in **Foster's Inheritance Tax X6.27**.
[14] [2005] STC (SCD) 177.

A business

[44.02] Statute gives no definition of "business"[1] except to state that it includes a profession or vocation "but does not include a business carried on otherwise than for gain".[2]

The word "business" must, thus, be given its general meaning, which is very wide. As Lord Diplock said:[3]

> The carrying on of 'business' no doubt, usually calls for some activity on the part of whoever carries it on, though, depending on the nature of the business, the activity may be intermittent with long intervals of quiescence in between . . . Business is a wider concept than trade . . . In the case of a private individual it may well be that the mere receipt of rents from property that he owns raises no presumption that he is carrying on a business. In contrast, in their Lordships' view, in the case of a company incorporated for the purpose of making profits for its shareholders any gainful use to which it puts any of its assets prima facie amounts to the carrying on of a business. Where the gainful use to which a company's property is put is letting it out for rent, their Lordships do not find it easy to envisage circumstances that are likely to arise in practice which would displace the prima facie inference that in doing so it was carrying on a business.

For inheritance tax business property relief to apply, however, it is necessary that the business is not an excluded business.[4]

Furnished holiday lettings attract the income tax advantages afforded to trades and a property used for a furnished holiday let is treated as if it were an asset used in a trade for the purposes of the capital gains tax reliefs (see supra, § **23.05**), and the income tax reliefs (supra, § **10.15**). There is no specific entitlement to business property relief for furnished holiday letting. The activity of letting the furnished property has to be judged, on a case by case basis, to determine whether the activity is correctly regarded as a business (and not an excluded business) or whether it is, in essence, obtaining income from an investment property. HMRC practice is stated[5] as:

> In some instances the distinction between a business of furnished holiday lettings and, say, a business running a hotel or a motel may be so minimal that the Courts would not regard such a business as one of 'wholly or mainly holding investments' for the purposes of s 105(3).

[44.02] Business property relief and other reliefs

You may therefore normally allow relief where:

- The lettings are short-term (for example, weekly or fortnightly); and
- The owner – either himself or through an agent such as a relative or housekeeper – was substantially involved with the holidaymaker(s) in terms of their activities on and from the premises even if the lettings were for part of the year only.

---

[1] This is in contrast to the provisions for value added tax, where a definition of "business" can be read into directive 77/388/EEC Article 4. See infra, § **62.13**. Hence, it is suggested, that the case law on the meaning of the word "business" for value added tax is not correctly applicable when considering direct taxes.

[2] IHTA 1984, s 103(3). The words within inverted commas are almost certainly redundant. Although the concept of "business" is very wide, it, surely, must connote the pursuit of profit in some form. This concept appears to be behind the decision of the Special Commissioner in *Grimwood-Taylor v IRC* [2000] STC (SCD) 39, who ruled that a company, NHF Limited, was not carrying on a business as "there is no evidence that the directors were concerned with profit: they were content to allow a loss making situation to continue for many years" (at 46b).

[3] *American Leaf Blending Co Sdn Bhd v Director General of Inland Revenue* [1978] STC 561, PC at 565f.

[4] IHTA 1984, s 105(3). See infra, § **44.04**.

[5] HMRC Share Valuation Manual SVM 27600.

Shares or securities

[44.03] A "share" is not defined and the word is given the widest possible meaning. The inheritance tax relief is potentially available on voting or non-voting shares, on ordinary or preference shares. For relief to be granted within category 3[1] the shares must be unquoted. In deciding whether shares are quoted or unquoted for the purpose of this relief one asks whether they are quoted on a recognised stock exchange. For the purposes of this relief a USM or AIM company is treated as unquoted so enabling the holding to qualify for 100% relief under category 2 or category 4.

Where an individual has lent money to finance an unquoted trading company, 100% business property relief can be available in respect of that loan, where the company has issued a debenture and the investor has a 51% shareholding in the company (that is, he is able to cast more than half of the votes at any general meeting).[2] If, however, the investor does not have control of the company, no business property relief is available on the debenture. This is a matter of considerable significance when considering passing the family company to the next generation; it is often desirable for the debentures to be passed before transferring a tranche of shares that would cause a loss of control.

The word "securities" is, similarly, not defined. It is clearly more than a simple debt. Although for the particular purpose of the capital gains tax exemption, it has been held that "loan on a security" does not require a document,[3] it is likely that any property on which IHT business property relief can be claimed is represented by a document.

[1] See supra, § **44.01** above.
[2] IHTA 1984, ss 105(1)(b), 169(1).
[3] In *WT Ramsay Ltd v IRC* [1979] STC 582, CA at 590g Lord Scarman said: 'In simple English (not of course appropriate to the complications of a taxing statute) the distinction [between a debt and a security] is between a loan and an investment' . . . This case, in its various hearings, gives very extensive judicial comment on the word "security"; however, it is of little direct guidance to inheritance tax as the courts were construing the phrase in CGT legislation "debt on a security"; which is not necessarily the same as construing the single word "security". In the House of Lords Lord Wilberforce said: 'I think it no overstatement to say that many learned judges have found [the distinction] baffling, both on the statutory wording and as to the underlying policy . . . Some help is gained from a contrast to be drawn between debts simpliciter, which may arise from trading in a multitude of other situations, commercial or private, and loans, certainly a narrow class, and one which presupposes some kind of contractual structure': [1981] STC 174, HL at 184a-g.

Excluded business

[44.04] Business property relief is not available where the business carried on by the individual, the trustees, in partnership or by the company whose shares are under consideration "consists wholly or mainly of one or more of the following, that is to say, dealing in securities, stocks or shares, land or buildings or making or holding investments".[1]

The denial of business property relief when there is an excepted business, is a matter of considerable practical importance and has been the subject of a number of reported cases. The question as to whether the unincorporated business or the business of the company is "wholly or mainly" the non-trading activities specified in the legislation is a question of fact and, hence, is a matter for the Special Commissioners.[2] In *Weston v IRC*[3] the Special Commissioner considered the activities of a company that owned a caravan park and received rents from the owners of residential caravans. The activities of the company also included the purchase and the sale of caravans and the maintenance and administration of the park. The previous year, the same Special Commissioner, in *Furness v IRC*[4] had considered the business known as Riverside Caravan Park on which there were 218 static caravans and 8 touring ones, the business including running a fishing club, bowling club and other recreations, as well as the buying and selling of caravans. In the *Weston* case, the Commissioner held that business property relief was not due as the business of the company was substantially that of letting, with the caravan sales being ancillary to pitch fees at the park. In the *Furness* case, the Commissioner held that this was a business that did not consist wholly or mainly of holding investments; hence, business property relief was granted. The *Weston* case was the subject of appeal to the High Court, where the court reviewed the approach taken by the Commissioner, who had described the process he undertook as: "standing back and looking at the matter in the round". Of this approach, Lawrence J commented:[5]

the approach of the decision is wholly correct in law and cannot be faulted . . . He applied the right test . . . He took all of the relevant matters into account, and reached a conclusion which was justified by the evidence.

This approach has also been approved by the Court of Appeal. In *IRC v George*,[6] another caravan park case, the Special Commissioner had looked at the total activity of the company and declared that business property relief was available.[7] In the High Court[8] this decision was overturned as the Court considered that the terms of the leases and licences under which caravans had use of the caravan park were definitive in establishing the activity of the company as being that of mainly holding investments.[9] In the Court of Appeal, restoring the Special Commissioner's decision, Carnwath AJ said:[10]

> The holding of the property as investment was only one component of the business, and on the findings of the commissioner it was not the main component. In my view, the commissioner's overall approach was correct in law, and he reached a view which was open to him on the facts.
>
> I would add that I am happy to be able to arrive at this conclusion. I find it difficult to see any reason why an active family business of this kind should be excluded from business property relief, merely because a necessary component of its profit-making activity is the use of land.

This was fully supported by Hale LJ:[11]

> I agree. This was essentially a question of fact for the Special Commissioner who asked himself the questions which the statute requires him to ask. The Special Commissioners are the experts here . . . The court should resist any attempt to dress up a question of fact as if it involved a question of law.

Where an estate consists of shares in a number of different companies, it is necessary to consider the business of each company separate from any other. This can have unfortunate results. In *Grimwood-Taylor v IRC*,[12] there appears to have been a reorganisation of the family's farming business, with the result that, at his death, Robin Richard Mallander held shares in four separate companies that were all involved in land around the family home in Derbyshire, one company owning land, one company providing finance and another company undertaking some farming. Taken separately, the activity of each company could not be taken to be a business qualifying for business property relief although, if the activities of all four companies could be considered together, relief may have been due.

A Special Commissioner has held that a business is disqualified whether its holding and making of investments is active or passive.[13] A Special Commissioner has denied relief where trading income is ancillary to the main business of receiving rents.[14] In *Farmer v IRC*, the profit from letting buildings on the farm varied between 50 1/2% and 100% of the total net profit from the farm business.[15] The Special Commissioner found that "taking the whole business in the round, and without giving predominance to any one factor, the conclusion is that the business consisted mainly of farming and not of making or holding investments".[16] Hence, 100% relief was available against the value of the entire business.

A distinction has been made between the business of running a holiday park with caravans and the business of running a residential caravan park. The former, was held to be trade[17]; the latter was held to be investment.[18]

It is necessary to look at the nature of the business over a period and not solely at the date of death. Relief was granted in respect of shares in a company which, at the date of death, consisted substantially only of cash arising from the sale of a night club. It was accepted by the Special Commissioner that this was merely an interval in the company's continuing trade and there was an intention to purchase a further night club.[19]

The question as to whether inheritance tax business property relief is available, is to be decided quite separately from the way in which income has been subjected to income tax or corporation tax. The correct approach is specified by T H K Everett, sitting as Special Commissioner:[20]

> In my judgement, the income tax status of the income of the business is irrelevant in the context of inheritance tax. The district inspector may or may not have been correct in his assessment but his decision can have no relevance to the question which I have to decide.

Where a business holds cash, it is a question of fact whether the cash is a business asset or an investment. In *Barclays Bank Trust Co Ltd v IRC*,[21] a company held cash of some £450,000. The Special Commissioners ruled that £150,000 of this sum was required for the business of the company and attracted business property relief, but £300,000 did not attract business property relief.

The capital account of a former partner is not business property; the former partner is merely a creditor of the partnership.[22]

For relief under category 5 or 6, you must, first, identify the property and, second, find that the property concerned is "used in" the business. In *IRC v Mallender*[23] the executors made a claim for business property relief on the value of commercially let land, on the basis that the deceased was carrying on business as a Lloyds Underwriter and the bank guarantee that enabled him to carry on that business was secured on that land. In the High Court, Jacob J, reversing the decision of the Special Commissioner, held that the property "used in the business" was the guarantee and not the land on which it was secured.[24]

"An interest in the business" includes the interest held by a partner in a partnership, whether a traditional partnership or a limited liability partnership.[25]

In *Phillips v Revenue and Customs Comrs*[26] business property relief was granted with a shareholding in a company whose business was the business of making loans. Starting in the 1950s, Philip Phillips established and acquired companies to pursue his business as a valuer and estate agent. By the time of the death of his widow, on 27 June 2001, there were eight companies, seven of which were controlled by his widow. The companies were held by means of parallel shareholdings and were not in a group. The function of one company, P P Investments Ltd, in which the deceased had a 89.09% shareholding, was to lend to the other seven companies to enable those companies to purchase property. The Special Commissioner held[27] that the business of P P Investments Ltd was not "wholly or mainly" of the making or holding of investments, saying:[28]

> In my view P P Investments Ltd was in the business of making loans and not in the business of investing in loans. The loans were not assets acquired or held by the company for the purpose of making profits for division among the shareholders but were rather made for the purpose of providing a benefit to the other companies. The loans were not investments for their own sake but the provision of a finance facility to the other companies . . . The business carried on by P P Investments Ltd at the date of the death of the deceased did not consist wholly or mainly of making or holding investments.

Business property relief was, thus, granted.

In making her decision, Dr Nuala Brice, the Special Commissioner, adopted the five principles laid down by Carnwarth LJ in the Court of Appeal in *IRC v George*,[29] which can be summarised as:

(1) The decision is a matter of fact for the Special Commissioners.[30]
(2) Cases relating to different taxes and different subject matter are unlikely to be helpful.[31]
(3) There can be a spectrum (in that case of the exploitation of land), at one end of which the business of a company could be that of investment but at the other end of which the business is not investment.[32]
(4) Previous decisions are generally distinguishable either on the facts or because the arguments were different.[33]
(5) The business should be considered in the round; there is no one decisive factor to determine whether the business of a company consists of making or holding investments.[34]

It is interesting to note the factors that the Special Commissioner records as not being of importance in the decision she has to make on the nature of the company's business:[35]

> In reaching my view I have not been influenced by the description of the activities of the company in the directors' reports but rather have had regard to the facts I have found on the evidence before me. Neither have I been influenced by the treatment of the company for the purposes of corporation tax, bearing in mind the view of Carnwarth LJ in George that cases relating to different taxes and different subject matter are unlikely to be helpful. Neither have I found comparisons with banks to be helpful. Although P P Investments Ltd made loans it could not be said to act in that respect like a bank because it did not take security for the repayment of the loans and it did not act in other respects like a bank. Finally, although I accept the argument of the appellant that if P P Investments Ltd were investing in loans it would have been better to invest directly in property where the return was much greater, in my view this does not assist in determining whether the business of P P Investments Ltd consisted wholly or mainly of making or holding investments.

In *McCall & Ors (PRs of McClean deceased) v Revenue and Customs Comrs*[36], a Northern Ireland case, business property relief was denied in respect of agricultural land let under conacre. Although the work performed on the land was sufficient to constitute a business, the income arose mainly from making the land available to third parties for payment. As there was no substantial separate provision of other goods and services, the Special Commissioner held that the business was one of holding investments.

---

[1] IHTA 1984, s 105(3). Exceptionally, business property relief is available if the business concerned is wholly that of a market maker or a discount house and is

carried on in the UK: IHTA 1984, s 105(4)(a). "Market maker", which included jobber, is defined in IHTA 1984, s 105(7) modified by the Inheritance Tax (Market Makers) Regulations 1992, SI 1992/3181, to reflect the stock exchange rule that was introduced on 27 October 1986 which prohibited a person from carrying on a business both as broker and jobber.

2   All appeals on inheritance tax are to the Special Commissioners; the General Commissioners have no jurisdiction for inheritance tax: IHTA 1984, s 222(2). (There is a procedure to "leap frog" an appeal direct to the High Court: IHTA 1984 s 222(3). The procedure is rarely used and would not be available for this question as the decision required is on the question of fact.)
3   [2000] STC (SCD) 30.
4   [1999] STC (SCD) 232.
5   Weston v IRC [2000] STC 1064 at 1078g.
6   [2003] EWCA Civ 1763, [2004] STC 147.
7   [2002] STC (SCD) 358, sub nom *Stedman's Executors v IRC*.
8   [2003] EWHC 318 (Ch), [2003] STC 468.
9   IHTA 1984, s 105(3).
10 [2003] EWCA Civ 1763, [2004] STC 147, paras 60 and 61 at 163a/b.
11 [2003] EWCA Civ 1763, [2004] STC 147, para 63 at 163c.
12 [2000] STC (SCD) 39.
13 *Martin v IRC* [1995] STC (SCD) 5; see also *Burkinyoung v IRC* [1995] STC (SCD) 29.
14 *Hall v IRC* [1997] STC (SCD) 126 and, again, in *Clark and anor (exors of Clark dec'd) v R & C Comrs* [2005] STC (SCD) 823.
15 [1999] STC (SCD) 321 at 332d.
16 [1999] STC (SCD) 321 at 333d.
17 In *Furness v IRC* [1999] STC (SCD) 232 the deceased managed a residential caravan park, which he also used as a site for the business of purchasing and selling caravans. Having considered the level of business activity, the Special Commissioner granted 100% business property relief against the value of the entire business.
18 *Weston v IRC* [2000] STC 1064.
19 *Brown's Executors v IRC* [1996] STC (SCD) 277.
20 In *Powell v IRC* [1997] STC (SCD) 181 at 185.
21 [1998] STC (SCD) 125.
22 *Beckman v IRC* [2000] STC (SCD) 59.
23 *IRC v Mallender* [2001] STC 514. In this case, the taxpayer unsuccessfully attempted to argue that the words "assets used in the business" in IHTA 1984, s 110(b) can bring within business property relief any property that is thus used, even if it is not "used wholly or mainly for the purposes of a business", as required by s 105(6).
24 *IRC v Mallender* [2001] STC 514 at 521b-d. In part, this decision is a purposive construction of statute: see 521e.
25 Inland Revenue Tax Bulletin December 2000, p 805.
26 [2006] SWTI 2094, [2006] STC (SCD) 639.
27 [2006] STC (SCD) 639, para 38 at 648h.
28 [2006] STC (SCD) 639, para 35 at 647g.
29 [2004] STC 147, CA.
30 per Carnwarth LJ para [5] at 150c applied by Dr A Nuala Brice [2006] STC (SCD) 638, para 31 at 646j.

[44.04] Business property relief and other reliefs

[31] per Carnwarth LJ para [12] at 151d applied by Dr A Nuala Brice [2006] STC (SCD) 638, para 31 at 646j.
[32] per Carnwarth LJ para [12] at 151d applied by Dr A Nuala Brice [2006] STC (SCD) 638, para 31 at 646j.
[33] per Carnwarth LJ para [13] at 151g applied by Dr A Nuala Brice [2006] STC (SCD) 638, para 31 at 647a.
[34] per Carnwarth LJ para [5] at 152c applied by Dr A Nuala Brice [2006] STC (SCD) 638, para 31 at 647a.
[35] [2006] STC (SCD) 648, para 39 at 648e–g.
[36] (2008) SpC 678.

Period of ownership

[44.05] The property must have been owned by the transferor throughout the two years immediately preceding the transfer.[1] Alternatively it must have replaced other property and it, the other property and any property directly or indirectly replaced by the other property must have been owned by the transferor for periods which together comprised at least two years falling within the five years immediately preceding the transfer of value.[2] For the alternative rule it is further necessary that any replaced property should have fulfilled all the conditions of relevant business property other than the minimum period of ownership. The number of replacements is not limited; nor is there any need when one business replaces another for the two businesses to be related in any way. The requirement is on the length of the period of ownership, not on the period for which the property has been a business asset. Hence, if an individual has, for many years, owned a shop which he has let to his son for the purpose of the son's trade, the creation of a partnership between father and son to carry on the trade will lead to business property relief on the shop, even if father dies only a few weeks after the partnership is created.

Where the transferor became entitled to the property on the death of another person, the period of his ownership is taken back to the date of death and if the deceased was his spouse he may also use any of the spouse's periods of ownership.[3]

Where property has been replaced and the new property has not been owned for two years, the relief is not to exceed what it would have been had the replacement not been made. This is designed to prevent a person from obtaining relief through death-bed purchases of extra business property. This purpose is achieved by comparing the values at the time the property is replaced, but this is difficult to reconcile with a literal interpretation of the rule. Changes resulting from the formation, alteration or dissolution of a partnership and from the incorporation of a business into a close company are to be ignored for this rule.

Where there is an IHT charge under the gift with reservation rules, on the death of the donor or the cesser of the reservation within seven years of his death, there are special provisions directing that the question whether the property qualifies for business relief is to be determined as if the transfer were one by the donee so far as it is attributable to property comprised in the gift.

However, in determining whether the property qualifies for the 100% relief under 2 or 3, the transfer is to be treated as if it were by the donor—so enabling the donor's other holdings (including related and settled property) to be taken into account.[4]

Simon's Taxes I7.113; Foster's Inheritance Tax G1.13.

[1] IHTA 1984, s 106.
[2] IHTA 1984, s 107. This includes shares obtained on a reorganisation (FA 1996, s 184(3) inserting IHTA 1984, s 107(4)).
[3] IHTA 1984, s 108.
[4] FA 1986, Sch 20, para 8.

Succession

[44.06] Where A transfers the property to B (T1) and within two years B transfers the property to C (T2) the minimum period of ownership cannot be complied with. However the relief can still be obtained provided:

(a) either T1 or T2 was a transfer on death;
(b) the property fulfilled the conditions for relief at T1—including the minimum period of ownership;
(c) the property transferred under T1 had become the property of B or B's spouse;
(d) the property would have been relevant business property but for the minimum period of ownership rule.[1]

Where only a part of the property under T1 qualified for relief whether because some of the assets were excepted assets (infra, § **44.08**) or there was some replacement element in the T1 transfer only that same part qualifies for relief on T2.

EXAMPLE

In year 5 A who had owned the relevant business property for 5 years sold it to B; the property was then worth £60,000 but the sale was for £20,000. In year 6 B died leaving the property to C, the property then being worth £75,000. Both A and B fulfilled all the conditions for relief apart from the period of B's ownership. The relief is available on B's death.

Simon's Taxes I7.116, 127.

[1] IHTA 1984, s 109.

Replacement property

[44.07] The period of ownership requirement can be satisfied by the property concerned being a replacement for property that would have qualified for business property relief.[1] The test that is applied is whether business property relief would have been available on the property previously owned, if there had been a transfer of value immediately before it was replaced.[2] There can, in principle, be any number of replacements that together make up the two-year qualifying period of ownership.

[44.07] Business property relief and other reliefs

The requirement that business property relief would have been available on the property that has been replaced, necessitates a two-year period of ownership for that original property,[3] unless it would, itself, qualify as replacement property for the property transferred on an earlier disposal.

This rule also automatically imports the excepted assets provisions, so that business property relief is restricted if the relief is claimed by reference to the property being replacement property and the property that it replaced was shares in a company that had excepted assets.

---

[1] IHTA 1984, s 107.
[2] IHTA 1984, s 107(1)(*b*).
[3] IHTA 1984, s 107(2).

Excepted assets

[44.08] A totally separate concept from that of an "excluded business", is the concept of "excepted assets". The first step is to consider whether the business that is carried on by the individual, by the individual's partnership or by the company of which shares are held is an excluded business. If it is, no business property relief is available. If it is not, the next step is to consider whether any asset held in the business (or on the balance sheet of the trading company) is an excepted asset. If so, the quantum of relief is reduced.

Any value attributable to an excepted asset is to be left out of account.[1] This is to prevent private assets from being disguised as business assets. An asset is excepted if it fails both of the following two tests:

(a) it was not used wholly or mainly for the purposes of the business concerned;[2]
(b) it is required at the time of the transfer for future use for the purposes of the business concerned.

It should be noted that the criterion is whether or not the asset is used for the purpose of the company's business (or as required for such future use). An asset may not be used for the company's trade, but this does not give that asset the status of an excepted asset if the asset is held for the business of the company. Holding investments is a business (see IHTA 1984, s 105(3)). HMRC internal instructions for corporation tax purposes[3] give the Revenue view that a company starts business (and, hence, comes within the charge to corporation tax) "on the date when it first holds shares in another non-dormant company". As support for this, the manual quotes from *American Leaf Blending Co v Director General of Inland Revenue*[4] where it was said:

> In the case of a private individual it may well be that the mere receipt of rents from property that he owns raises no presumption that he is carrying on a business. In contrast, in their Lordships' view, in the case of a company incorporated for the purpose of making profits for its shareholders any gainful use to which it puts any form of its assets prima facie amounts to the carrying on of a business

...

The carrying on of 'business', no doubt, usually calls for some activity on the part of whoever carries it on, though, depending on the nature of the business, the activity may be intermittent with long intervals of quiescence in between.

It is difficult to see, from the wording of statute, how there is a distinction between the tests applied for corporation tax and the tests applied for inheritance tax.

Under this approach, activities such as stock market investment by a company can correctly be regarded as a business. Hence, the assets used in that business are not excepted assets.[5] However, this appears not to be the Revenue view. Where a part of any land or building is used exclusively for business purposes but the land or building would be an excepted asset, the two parts may be treated as separate assets and the value of the part used exclusively for business will qualify for relief; so a surgery attached to a doctor's home will qualify for relief. However, the benefit of this rule does not extend to machinery or plant.

Simon's Taxes I7.119; Foster's Inheritance Tax G1.19.

---

[1] IHTA 1984, s 112. The rule as given applies unless the property is relevant business property by virtue of category 4 only, Where the asset is relevant business property by virtue of category 3 only, the rule is adjusted to take account of replacements. In order that the property be treated as relevant business property it must be shown that the asset was used wholly or mainly for the purposes of the business concerned throughout the two years immediately preceding the transfer or it replaced another asset so used and the periods of such use together with those of any other assets replaced comprised at least two of the last five years immediately preceding the transfer. It will be seen that assets not so used are not technically excepted assets but rather do not qualify as relevant business property.

[2] The test is applied to the whole or the last two years of the "relevant period". The relevant period is that immediately preceding the transfer during which the asset was owned by the transferor or his company. An asset which is used wholly or mainly for the personal benefit of the transferor or of any person connected with him is deemed not to be used wholly or mainly for the purposes of the business and so is an excepted asset.

[3] HMRC Company Taxation Manual, para 42.

[4] [1978] STC 561.

[5] An interesting discussion of the scope of the concept of excepted assets is given in Malcolm Gunn's article "A Business Proposal" in *Taxation* 1 July 2004, pp 358–360.

Companies—special rules

[44.09] With regard to excepted assets, where the company is a member of a group, use by another company within the group is treated as use for the purposes of the business provided the other company was a member of the group both at the time of the use and immediately before the transfer and the other company was not excluded by the next rule.[1] Although there is no statutory definition of "group" for inheritance tax purposes, it would appear that the relationship of one company to another must be that of voting control.² A collection of companies created to hold property in connection with a family farming business, where the shares were owned by different members of the family in different proportions, was held not to be a group.³

Where the company is a member of a group and another company in the group has a non-qualifying business, the shares and securities in the company are to be valued as if the non-qualifying company was not a member of the group.⁴ An exception is made where the business consists wholly or mainly in the holding of land or buildings wholly or mainly occupied by members of the group with qualifying businesses.

No relief can be given if the company is in liquidation.⁵

Simon's Taxes I7.121–131; Foster's Inheritance Tax G1.21–32.

---

1. IHTA 1984, s 112(2), (5).
2. "Control" is defined in IHTA 1984, s 249.
3. *Grimwood-Taylor v IRC* [2000] STC (SCD) 39.
4. IHTA 1984, s 111.
5. IHTA 1984, s 105(5).

Business property relief on a potentially exempt transfer

[44.10] Where a donor makes a potentially exempt transfer and dies within seven years, tax will not have been due at the time of the transfer but may become due on the death. Business relief is available on that death only if further conditions are fulfilled as at the date of that death.¹ Similarly, where a chargeable transfer has taken place, additional tax may become due by reason of the transferor's death within seven years; here nothing affects the tax due on the original transfer but the additional tax now due² may be calculated on the basis that business property relief is not available this time.³ Although it is convenient to refer to this as clawing back the earlier relief, the rule does not take that form. The original tax, if any, remains unaffected; only the additional tax falling due on death may have to be calculated on the basis that the business relief does not apply.

The first condition is that the original property must have been owned by the transferee from the time of the original transfer down to the death of the transferor or, if earlier, that of the transferee.⁴ It will be noted that this condition is framed in terms of ownership rather than beneficial entitlement. As expressed, this condition is absolute so that even a transfer by way of gift to a spouse, something which in terms of the theory of IHT is meant to be a tax-free event, will bring about the loss of the relief. The legislation provides that where the property is settled on trusts with no interest in possession the trustees are to be treated as the owners and transferees.⁵ This leaves open the situation in which the property is settled on trusts with an interest in possession although it is thought that the person with the interest in possession will, under the general principles of IHT, be treated as the transferee. Where the property is settled on discretionary trusts and the trustees then appoint that property to someone absolutely, the condition is presumably not satisfied. In determining what is the original property a change of shares on a reorganisation of a company is ignored as is a transfer of a business in exchange for shares.[6]

The second condition supposes a hypothetical transfer by the transferee on the death of the transferor (or, if earlier, the death of the transferee). In order for business property relief to be granted in respect of the potentially exempt transfer that has become chargeable, the conditions for business property relief must be satisfied at the date of the death.[7] This strict rule is subject to relaxation in three respects:

(1) if the property is unquoted shares in a trading company, the cessation of the trade between the date of the PET and the death does not deny relief, as long as the shares remain unquoted;[8]
(2) if the property consisted of a controlling interest in a quoted trading company, relief is not denied if the holding at the date of the death is less than a controlling interest;[9]
(3) there is no requirement for a two-year ownership period at the date of death;[10]
(4) there are provisions for replacement property (see below).[11]

Unless the property is within one of these limited exceptions, no business property relief is available if the property has changed its nature by the date of death. Thus, if unquoted shares are gifted and the company prior to the death of the donor becomes listed, business property relief is denied.

Since the transferee may legitimately (ie for business reasons) wish to replace the actual property given provision is made for the wider problem of replacement property.[12] In essence the property given and the property replacing it must be the subject of arm's length transactions, the whole of the proceeds must be applied in acquiring the replacement property and the replacement must occur within an allowed period after the disposal.[13] For transfers of value made on or after 30 November 1993 that period is three years or such longer period as the Board may allow.[14] The conditions are then adapted for the two properties. Provision is also made for the situation in which the transferor dies before the transferee but the transferee has disposed of the property by that time; he is allowed to replace it within 12 months of his disposal.[15] The rules are adapted for the situation in which the transferee predeceases the transferor.[16] They also apply where only part of the property is replaced.

Simon's Taxes I7.191; Foster's Inheritance Tax G1.91.

[1] IHTA 1984, s 113A.
[2] This presumably means the additional tax in respect of the transfer of the business property. However, since the effect of withdrawing the benefit of the relief is that the original value has to be increased there may be a knock-on effect on later chargeable transfers so that more tax may be due from them by reason of a higher cumulative total—see Venables *Inheritance Tax Planning*, p 31.
[3] This explains why the additional tax can be greater than the original tax even though the original tax was calculated at lifetime rates whereas the additional tax is charged at 40% or 20% of the death rates in force at the time of the death.

4   IHTA 1984, s 113A(3)(a), (4).
5   IHTA 1984, s 113A(8).
6   IHTA 1984, s 113A(6); the reorganisation rules are defined by reference to TCGA 1992, ss 126–130 and ss 132–136.
7   IHTA 1984, s 113A(3)(b), (4).
8   IHTA 1984, s 113A(3)(b) *proviso*.
9   IHTA 1984, s 113A(3)(a).
10 IHTA 1984, s 113A(b) *proviso*.
11 IHTA 1984, s 113B.
12 IHTA 1984, s 113B.
13 These rules are much stricter than for rollover relief under TCGA 1992, s 152; thus no provision is made for the situation in which the replacement property is acquired before the disposal.
14 IHTA 1984, s 113B(2)(a), (5)(b).
15 IHTA 1984, s 113B(5).
16 IHTA 1984, s 113B(4).

Agricultural property relief

[44.11] A special reduction applies to the agricultural value element in transfers of agricultural property in the UK,[1] the Channel Islands or the Isle of Man or within a state of the EEA at the time that the transfer of value in question is made.[2] The relief applies also to controlling interests in farming companies.[3] It applies whether the transfer is inter vivos, on death or relates to settled property. The relief is against the agricultural value of the land, not against its full market value, which may be greater. The agricultural value is specified by statute as being "the value of the property if the property were subject to a perpetual covenant prohibiting its use otherwise than as agricultural property".[4]

The reduction applies to the agricultural value of the land so there is no reduction for the value attributable to non-agricultural purposes, eg the development value of agricultural land. Where the farming business is carried on by the transferor, it is likely that any value of the land used for farming that is in excess of the agricultural value (such as hope value) will satisfy the test for business property relief (see supra, § **44.01**).

Agricultural property is defined as meaning agricultural land or pasture and as including the woodlands (as distinct from the timber) and buildings for intensive fish-farming or livestock-rearing if occupied with such land or pasture. Whether property is agricultural property is a question of fact and decided by looking at the matter "in the round".[5] In *Dixon v IRC*[6] a claim for agricultural property relief was made for a land holding of 0.6 acres on which damson trees were planted and where the house in which the deceased lived was situated. The Special Commissioner said:[7]

> I first apply the elephant test and conclude that Nook Cottage is not of a character appropriate to agricultural land or pasture but rather the converse. That is, that the orchard and garden are of a character appropriate to Nook Cottage which is a private residence in a rural area. Applying the second test in my view the educated

rural layman would regard the property as residential cottage with land. Finally, there is no history of agricultural production but rather a history of the use of a property as a private residence in a rural area . . . That means that the property is not agricultural property.

Short rotational coppice is agricultural land for this purpose.[8] Stud farms qualify,[9] but a meadow used for horses to graze does not qualify, where the horses are not used to pull the plough or otherwise in connection with agriculture.[10] Sport is not agriculture[11] but land in habitat schemes qualifies.[12]

Relief is lost if the transferor has entered into a binding contract of sale at the time of the transfer. An exception is made where this property is being sold to a company which the transferor controls.[13]

The form of the relief is a reduction in the "transfer of value" and not as previously the chargeable transfer. It does not have to be claimed. The relief is now very similar to that for business property. The Revenue have issued guidance on the interaction with business relief, as where agricultural property is sold and the proceeds reinvested in business property—and vice versa.[14]

Simon's Taxes I7.301; Foster's Inheritance Tax G3.01; STP [9.102]–[9.103d], [9.272].

---

[1] IHTA 1984, s 115(1) & (5).
[2] Retrospective amendment made by FA 2009.
[3] IHTA 1984, s 122.
[4] IHTA 1984, s 115(3).
[5] This is consistent with the approach used in judging the nature of a business for business property relief: see *Weston v IRC* [2000] STC 1064 at 1078g to 1079a.
[6] [2002] STC (SCD) 53.
[7] At 59j to 60a. The Special Commissioner was responding to the submission of taxpayer's Counsel in which he had quoted from McCutcheon *Inheritance Tax* § 14.72, where the author describes the "character test" as: "The present position is that the "character test" is considered against three main tests: (i) the elephant test: although you cannot describe a farmhouse which satisfies the character test you will know one when you see it! (ii) man on the (rural) Clapham omnibus: would the educated rural layman regard the property as a house with land or a farm? (iii) historical dimension: how long has the house in question been associated with the agricultural property and is there a history of agricultural production?"
[8] FA 1995, s 154(2).
[9] IHTA 1984, s 115(4).
[10] *Wheatley v IRC* [1998] STC (SCD) 60.
[11] *Earl of Normanton v Giles* [1980] 1 WLR 28.
[12] IHTA 1984, s 124C.
[13] IHTA 1984, s 124.
[14] Inland Revenue interpretation RI 95.

Dwelling house

[44.12] A dwelling house can qualify for agricultural relief under one of two alternative provisions:[1]

(1) a dwelling house that is occupied "with agricultural land or pasture and the occupation is ancillary to that of the agricultural land or pasture";
(2) the dwelling house fits the description of "cottages, farm buildings and farmhouses, together with the land occupied with them, as are of a character appropriate to the property".

[1] IHTA 1984, s 115(2).

Dwelling house occupied 'with agricultural land'

[44.13] To say that the building is occupied "with agricultural land or pasture and the occupation is ancillary to that of the agricultural land or pasture", the occupation of the building must be representative occupation. That is, the person occupies as a representative of the farmer. Some farm workers are in representative occupation and, hence, the house occupied by such a worker attracts agricultural property relief under this heading.

The leading case on the nature of representative occupation is *Northern Ireland Commr of Valuation v Fermanagh Protestant Board of Education*[1], where Lord Upjohn said:[2]

> The result of the authorities on this question of occupation seems to me quite clearly to be as follows. First, if it is essential to the performance of the duties of the occupying servant that he should occupy the particular house, or it may be a house within a closely defined perimeter, then, it being established that this is the mutual understanding of the master and the servant, the occupation for rating and other ancillary purposes is that of the master and not of the servant.

A distinction can be drawn between a person who receives from his employer a right to live in the property (which is beneficial occupation by the employee) and an employee who is paid to live in the premises (which is representative occupation). It is only when occupation is representative occupation[3] that agricultural property relief under the first alternative is available.

Occupation of a farmhouse is rarely representative occupation. In *Anderton v Lamb*,[4] a rollover relief case, it was claimed that occupation of several houses by junior partners of a partnership was representative occupation. The claim failed. A better argument can, perhaps, be put where the farmhouse is owned by a farming company. However, it is considered that agricultural property relief will be available only if occupation of that particular dwelling is essential to the proper carrying on of the trade of the company.

[1] [1969] 1 WLR 1708.
[2] At 1772.
[3] *Langley v Appleby* [1976] STC 368.
[4] [1981] STC 43, a rollover relief case.

The farmhouse

[44.14] The second, alternative, ground for claiming agricultural property relief on a building is that the relief is granted for "such cottages, farm

Agricultural property relief [44.14]

buildings and farmhouses, together with the land occupied with them, as are of a character appropriate to the property."

In order to obtain relief under this provision, it is, first, necessary to determine that the house is correctly described as a "farmhouse". When considering income tax legislation, Lord Upjohn in the House of Lords[1] said:

> I would think that to be 'the farmhouse' for the purposes of the section it must be judged in accordance with ordinary ideas of what is appropriate in size, content and layout taken in conjunction with the farm buildings, and the particular area of farm land being farmed, and not part of a rich man's considerable residence.

In *Higginson's Executors v IRC*[2] the Special Commissioner rejected the claim for agricultural property relief on the basis that Ballyward Lodge was not a "farmhouse". The deceased did not need the farm, although he used the land for farming, He enjoyed living at the lodge which was of considerable size: the farmland was limited in extent. By any ordinary standard, Ballyward Lodge was never a "farmhouse".[3] In the opinion of the Special Commissioner:

> while I accept [Counsel's] view that the land and the house in the present case formed a unit, the house being integral thereto, I am of the clear opinion that for the purposes of s 115(2) the unit must be an agricultural unit; that is to say, that within the unit the land must predominate. As Morritt LJ said in *Starke v IRC*,[4] 'It is as though the draftsman had started with the land then dealt with what should be treated as going with it.' For present purposes any qualifying cottages, farm buildings or farmhouses must be ancillary to the land[5]

Once a house has been correctly identified as a farmhouse, it is then necessary to decide whether it is "of a character appropriate to the" agricultural property.[6]

In *Lloyds TSB (personal representative of Antrobus) v IRC*[7] the Special Commissioner said:[8]

> Thus the principles which have been established for deciding whether a farmhouse is of a character appropriate to the property may be summarised as: first, one should consider whether the house is appropriate by reference to its size, content and layout, with the farm buildings and the particular area of farmland being farmed (see *IRC v Korner*); secondly, one should consider whether the house is proportionate in size and nature to the requirements of the farming activities conducted on the agricultural land or pasture in question (see *Starke v IRC*);[9] thirdly that although one cannot describe a farmhouse which satisfies the 'character appropriate' test one knows one when one sees it (see *Dixon v IRC*;)[10] fourthly, one should ask whether the educated rural layman would regard the property as a house with land or a farm (see *Dixon*); and, finally, one should consider the historical dimension and ask how long the house in question has been associated with the agricultural property and whether there was a history of agricultural production (see *Dixon*).

Lloyds TSB (personal representative of Antrobus) v IRC[11] concerned Cook Hill Priory, a substantial house in Warwickshire with a recorded history dating from 1188 for much of its history. Certainly continuously since 1907, the house had been occupied in conjunction with farmland which, at the date of the death of the deceased, amounted to 126 acres. The Special Commissioner adopted the approach that, elsewhere, has been described as "I can recognise an elephant when I see one":[12]

In asking what the man or woman on the rural omnibus would think, and whether the educated rural layman would regard the property as a house with land or a farm, I rely upon the evidence of both Mr Beer and Mr Humphries and also the evidence of the photographs which I saw. That leads to the conclusion that the house in this appeal was, at the date of the death of Miss Antrobus, a farmhouse with a farm and definitely not a house with land. The whole use and visual presentation of the property, in particular the siting of the modern agricultural buildings within the line of view of the west front, and the concrete apron and the other farm buildings surrounding it which cluster round the east front, support that view.

Finally, turning to the historical dimension it is necessary to ask how long the house in question has been associated with the agricultural property and whether there was a history of agricultural production. Here the answer is that the house has been associated with the agricultural property since at least 30 May 1902, namely 100 years, and since at least 1907 there has been a history of agricultural production within the same family.[13]

The Special Commissioner determined that the character of Cook Hill Priory was appropriate to the agricultural holding. Agricultural property relief was applied without restriction.

For a farmhouse to attract agricultural property relief, it is crucial that it is occupied, at the date of death, with the agricultural land. Different ownership is fatal.

In *Starke v IRC*.[14] Wilfred Brown died in 1988. In 1946 he bought a farm of 171 acres with a six bedroom property built some ten years earlier. As a part, it would appear, of a misconceived tax planning exercise, some 169 acres of farmland were transferred to a company that carried on the farming activity; the shares of the company being held by members of the family other than the deceased. The deceased retained ownership of the six bedroom farmhouse and its grounds of two and a half acres. Inland Revenue refused agricultural property relief on the basis that a six bedroom farmhouse is not "of a character appropriate to" any agricultural use there may have been on the two and a half acres. By agreement, the case was not heard by the Special Commissioners but went straight to the High Court and thence to the Court of Appeal. Both the High Court and the Court of Appeal upheld the denial of agricultural property relief.

The analysis of a set of circumstances is taken further in *Rosser v IRC*.[15] As in *Starke v IRC*, there had been a gift of the substantial area of the farm prior to the death of the deceased. In a careful judgment, the Special Commissioner analyses the statutory provision for agricultural property relief in a farmhouse as requiring a nexus between the house and the agricultural land and that the nexus must be derived from common ownership rather than common occupation.[16] This meant that the land in the estate extended to two acres only. However, in contrast to *Starke v IRC*,[17] the Revenue accepted that this two acres was agricultural land. It was, therefore, necessary to determine whether the house was a farmhouse in relation to this agricultural land and, if so, whether it was of a character appropriate to the property. The Revenue contended that in order for the house to qualify as the farmhouse it must be the centre of operations or the headquarters for the farming activities on the two acres of agricultural land. To this, the Commissioner stated: 'The ordinary and natural meaning that I would attach to the word "farmhouse" in s 115(2) is that it must be a dwelling for the farmer from which the farm is managed.';[18]

In evidence, it had been stated that two activities associated with farming carried on at the material time at the house on Cwm Farm, namely, provision of early morning refreshments and the midday meal and the storage of agricultural equipment and pesticides. The Special Commissioner concluded that those activities were incidental to the prime function of the house as a retirement home and not sufficient to characterise the house as a farmhouse. Agricultural property relief was, thus denied.

As with business property relief, the relief is denied if the property is subject to a binding contract of sale at the time of transfer,[19] however, the contract does not deny relief if it is for the acquisition by the property of a company which the transferor controls.[20]

In *Arnander (executors of McKenna, decd) v Revenue and Customs Comrs*[21] Dr Nuala Brice, Special Commissioner, held that no agricultural property relief was available for a value of Rosteague House in the estate of Lady Cecilia Elizabeth McKenna. Rosteague House was a house of 865 square metres that sold, after Lady Cecilia's death, for £2,030,000 (plus a further £1,020,000 for the accompanying land). From 1984 until Lady Cecilia's death at age 91, on 29 January 2003, the land was farmed under a series of contract farming arrangements. The Special Commissioner noted the decision in *Rosser v IRC*[22] used, for deciding on the availability of APR, that the definition of "farmhouse" in dictionaries "gives an ordinary and natural meaning of the word 'farmhouse' as a dwelling for the farmer from which the farm is managed". The meaning of the phrase "a dwelling for the farmer from which the farm is managed" was, itself, amplified in the decision of the Lands Tribunal in *Lloyds TSB Private Banking Plc v Twiddy*[23] which states:

> . . . A farmhouse is the chief dwelling-house attached to a farm, the house in which the farmer of the land lives. There is, we think, no dispute about the definition when it is expressed in this way.

Dr Brice ruled that Rosteague House was not "a farmhouse" as the contract farming arrangements meant that Lady Cecilia did not manage the farm from that house. Hence, agricultural property relief was not available.

1   *IRC v Korner* (1969) 45 TC 287, HL at 249C.
2   [2002] STC (SCD) 483.
3   At 486d.
4   [1995] STC 689, CA at 694.
5   At 486g.
6   IHTA 1984, s 115(2).
7   [2002] STC (SCD) 468.
8   At 480 d–f.
9   [1994] STC 295, [1994] 1 WLR 888.
10   [2002] STC (SCD) 53.
11   [2002] STC (SCD) 468.
12   See supra, § **44.11** footnote 6.

[13] At 482 a–c.
[14] [1995] STC 689, CA.
[15] [2003] STC (SCD) 311.
[16] Paras 47 to 49 at 321d to h.
[17] [1994] STC 295 at 298d.
[18] [2003] STC (SCD) 311, para 53 at 322h.
[19] IHTA 1984, s 124.
[20] IHTA 1984, s 124(1).
[21] [2006] STC (SCD) 800.
[22] [2003] STC (SCD) 311, para 53 at 322h.
[23] [2006] 1 EGLR 157 *(Antrobus 2)*, para 49, see infra, § **44.16**.

Other buildings

[44.15] A building can attract agricultural relief if it satisfies one of two alternative sets of conditions:

(1)　it is a cottage or a farm building[1], or
(2)　it is a building "used in connection with the intensive rearing of livestock . . . if the . . . building is occupied with agricultural land or pasture and the occupation is ancillary to that of the agricultural land or pasture".[2]

In each alternative the conditions are restrictive. For a "farm building" statute requires that the building, and the land occupied with it, is of a character appropriate to the property.

To satisfy the conditions of the second alternative, the occupation of the building is required by statute to be "ancillary" to the agricultural land and to be "occupied with" the agricultural land. In *Williams (personal representative of Williams, dec'd) v R&C Comrs*[3], the Special Commissioner held that neither condition was fulfilled in respect of a broiler house for the intensive rearing of chickens. As the Special Commissioner stated:

> The broiler houses were occupied by SPL together with the blue land. The purpose for which the broiler houses were used did not serve to help or assist the purposes of the occupation of any of the blue land other than that on which they were situated . . . .. Thus in my judgement the broiler houses would qualify only if they were occupied as an 'add-on' to or as a subsidiary part of the purposes of a larger agricultural enterprise carried out on the other land with which they were occupied. The purposes for the occupation of the remainder of the blue land do not enable that condition to be satisfied because the use of the broiler houses dominated the use of the blue land. There was no evidence that SPL conducted a wider agricultural enterprise on other land it occupied.

[1] IHTA 1984, s 115(2).
[2] IHTA 1984, s 115(2).
[3] [2005] STC (SCD) 782.

Value qualifying for APR

[44.16] Agricultural property relief is 100% of the "agricultural value of agricultural property".[1] Statute[2] provides that "agricultural value" is the value that the property would have if it "were subject to a perpetual covenant prohibiting its use otherwise than as agricultural property". Thus, if farmland has the potential for development, APR is given only on its value as farmland: the hope value of the land does not attract APR.

The manner in which the statutory valuation provision operates in relation to a farmhouse was considered by the Lands Tribunal in *Lloyds TSB Private Banking Plc v Inland Revenue Capital Taxes*.[3] The property had, already, in separate proceedings,[4] been declared to be agricultural property and attract agricultural property relief. The issue before the Land Tribunal was the effect on valuation of the statutory provision[5] requiring APR to be granted only on the value of the property as agricultural property. The particular property in question would be expected to attract what the tribunal described as "a life style farmer" who commutes each day to the City of London and may spend 95% of his working life in the city. Such a potential purchaser would always outbid the professional farmer who would look to the profits of the farm to derive his living. The tribunal ruled[6]:

> In our judgement a farmhouse for the purposes of s 115(2) is the house of the person who lives in it in order to farm the land comprised in the farm and who farms the land on a day to day basis. The agricultural value of the house in the present case therefore falls to be determined on the assumption that the perpetual covenant to be implied by virtue of s 115(3) would have prevented its use other than in this way. This would have excluded, therefore, the lifestyle purchaser whose principal reason for living in the house was the amenity afforded by it and by the land.

---

[1] IHTA 1984, s 116(1).
[2] IHTA 1984, s 116(3).
[3] DET/47/2004.
[4] *Lloyds TSB (personal representative of Antrobus, dec'd) v IRC* [2002] STC (SCD) 468.
[5] IHTA 1984, s 115(3).
[6] DET/47/2004 Para 71.

Shares of a company owning agricultural land

[44.17] Agricultural property relief can be available against the value of shares or securities in a company where the property of the company fulfils the conditions for agricultural property relief but only if the transferor had over 50 per cent of the voting rights in the whole company immediately before the transfer.[1]

Where the transferor has such a controlling interest, agricultural property relief is deducted in so far as the value of the shares is attributable to the agricultural value of agricultural property which forms part of the company's assets.[2]

[44.17] Business property relief and other reliefs

There are the usual provisions for replacement of agricultural property or replacement of shares.

[1] IHTA 1984, ss 122(1) and 269(1).
[2] IHTA 1984, s 122(1)(a).

Rate of relief

[44.18] The rate of relief for transfers and other events on or after 10 March 1992 is 100% in three situations. The first is where the transferor has vacant possession of the property or the right to obtain it within 12 months.[1] By concession, this is extended to 24 months.[2] (The same concession extends 100% relief to land subject to a tenancy, where the valuation of the land is at an amount broadly equivalent to the vacant possession value of the property, notwithstanding the tenancy.) Joint tenants and tenants in common satisfy this requirement if the aggregate of their interests carry the right to vacant possession.[3] The second applies to transfers and events on or after 1 September 1995 and arises where the transferor's interest fails to meet the first test because the property is let on a tenancy beginning on or after 1 September 1995.[4] The third applies as from 1992 and arises where the transferor has been beneficially entitled to the interest since before 10 March 1981 and he would have been entitled to the relief under the pre-1981 rules but has no right to vacant possession, eg the transferor was a "working farmer" but the tenant was an employer or a relative who had occupied the farm since the transferor retired or a transfer to a company which the taxpayer controlled or a partnership of which he was a member.[5] Such a person not only preserves his 100% relief but has previously been able to reduce the value of his estate, without liability, by creating the lease. 100% relief is also available, but by concession, where the transferor's interest carries a right to vacant possession within 24 months (as distinct from the statutory 12 months) or the value of that interest was, despite the tenancy, broadly equivalent to vacant possession value.[6]

In most other instances, eg where the transferor is the landlord of tenanted land under a tenancy begun before September 1995, the reduction as from 10 March 1992 is 50%.[7] The 100% relief for land let on or after 1 September 1995 is available when the taxpayer became tenant of the land on or after that date by statutory succession.[8] Where a tenancy is acquired by succession, succession is treated as taking place at the death of the tenant from whom the succession occurs.[9]

The reduction applies to the value before the exemptions but before any grossing up;[10] it is excluded by business relief where that applies.

Simon's Taxes I7.302, 304; Foster's Inheritance Tax G3.02, 04.

[1] IHTA 1984, s 116(2)(a).
[2] Extra-statutory concession F17.
[3] IHTA 1984, s 116(6).
[4] IHTA 1984, s 116(2)(c).

⁵ There is a restriction to £250,000 or 1,000 acres for this transitional relief.
⁶ Extra-statutory concession F17.
⁷ IHTA 1984, s 116(2)(*b*), (4).
⁸ Inland Revenue interpretation RI 121.
⁹ FA 1996, s 185(5), (6).
¹⁰ IHTA 1984, s 116(7).

[44.19] Generally a person can claim the 50% transitional relief only if he has held the interest since before 10 March 1981. However, he can also make the claim if he succeeded to the property on the death of his spouse after 8 March 1981 and that spouse would have been entitled to the relief. He is deemed to have been beneficially entitled to the interest to which his spouse was so entitled. The condition barring the relief if the taxpayer could have obtained vacant possession is applied to both spouses.[1]

Simon's Taxes I7.323; Foster's Inheritance Tax G3.23.

¹ IHTA 1984, s 120(2).

Two conditions

[44.20] To qualify for the relief, whether 100% or 50%, the transferor must either (a) have occupied the property for agricultural purposes throughout the last two years, or (b) have owned the land throughout the last seven years provided in this instance that the land has been occupied by himself or another for agricultural purposes.[1] The purpose behind (b) is to prevent short term investment in land simply for tax purposes. The requirement of occupation has been relaxed for cases of representative occupation.[2]

Simon's Taxes I7.311, 321; Foster's Inheritance Tax G3.11, 21.

¹ IHTA 1984, s 117.
² Extra-statutory concession F16.

[44.21] Various rules apply to determine the period in special cases. Thus if he became entitled to the property on a death his ownership or occupation run from the date of death.[1] If the death was that of a spouse that spouse's ownership or occupation may be taken over.[2] Occupation by a controlled company or by a Scottish partnership is attributed to the controller or partners.[3] It is not necessary that the main business of the company should be farming in the UK.[4]

Where there is an IHT charge under the gift with reservation rules there are special provisions enabling the donee's ownership and occupation to be taken into account for the purposes of agricultural relief on the property subject to the charge.[5] The donor's ownership and occupation are included as if it were the donee's to see if this two year minimum ownership rule is satisfied.

Simon's Taxes I7.311, 321; Foster's Inheritance Tax G3.11, 21.

¹ IHTA 1984, s 120(1).

[44.21] Business property relief and other reliefs

[2] IHTA 1984, s 120(2).
[3] IHTA 1984, s 119.
[4] On valuation, see IHTA 1984, s 122.
[5] FA 1986, Sch 20, para 8.

[44.22] Provision is also made for replacement farms so that the ownership or occupation of the previous farm can be counted. Thus the period of occupation is satisfied by including the occupation of a previous farm within the last five years and that of ownership by seven of the last ten years.[1] Where these farms differ in value only the lowest agricultural value qualifies, although special rules apply to partnership changes.

Simon's Taxes I7.313, 322; Foster's Inheritance Tax G3.13, 22.

[1] IHTA 1984, s 118(1).

[44.23] Provision is also made for relief where the conditions as to length of occupation or ownership are not satisfied but the farm was acquired on a previous transfer which did qualify for relief. It is further necessary that it should be only these conditions which prevent relief on this occasion and that one of the transfers should be on death.[1] Provision is made for the replacement of property between the two transfers; as with the general replacement rule relief is restricted to the lower of the agricultural values of the replaced and present farms.[2] Where on the previous transfer only a part of the value qualified for relief as where the earlier transfer was a part purchase, only a like part can be reduced on the present transfer.[3]

Simon's Taxes I7.314, 315, 323, 324; Foster's Inheritance Tax G3.14, 15, 23, 24.

[1] IHTA 1984, s 121.
[2] IHTA 1984, s 121(2).
[3] IHTA 1984, s 121(3).

Agricultural property relief on a failed potentially exempt transfer

[44.24] Where a donor makes a potentially exempt transfer and dies within seven years, tax may become due; similarly where a chargeable transfer takes place, additional tax may become due by reason of a prior potentially exempt transfer which has become chargeable. The problem is the same as that for business relief, and the legislative solution parallels that for BPR, see supra, § **44.10**.

As with business relief the first condition is that the original property transferred must be owned by the transferee from the time of the transfer down to the death of the transferor or the earlier death of the transferee.[1] There is a similar definition of transferee which provides that where property is settled on trusts in which there is no interest in possession the trustees are to be treated as the transferee.² One presumes that where the property is settled on trusts which give a person a beneficial interest in possession that person is the transferee. The condition means that a gift to a spouse results in loss of relief.

The second condition is that the original property should be agricultural property immediately before the death (of the transferor or, if earlier, that of the transferee) and should have been occupied by the transferee (or another) for the purpose of agriculture throughout the relevant period.³ This condition is obviously inapplicable where the original property consists of shares in a farming company and so in this instance it will suffice that the company owned the land and the farm was occupied for the purposes of agriculture throughout the period.⁴

The insistence on the property being the original property is relaxed where there has been a reorganisation of share capital or where the property held at the date of the death consists of shares for which the original property was exchanged.⁵ In the 1986 version the shares were to be treated as if they were the original property; this was not effective and so in 1987 the wording was amended to provide that ownership of the shares is deemed to be that of the original agricultural land—as from 17 March 1987.

As with business relief there is a further section to cover the situation in which the agricultural property is replaced.⁶ As with the other relief the rule can apply only where both the disposal of the original property and the acquisition of the replacement are made in a bargain at arm's length or on such terms as would be contained in such a bargain.⁷ The current time limit of three years or such longer period as the Board may allow is also the same.⁸ The conditions for the relief are then applied to the original and replacement property so that the transferee must have owned the original property down to the date of the disposal and the replacement as from the date of the acquisition. The properties must have been occupied for purposes of agriculture during these times and the replacement property must be agricultural property immediately before the death.⁹ The rules are also adapted where the transferor dies before the transferee but the replacement process is not then complete as the new property has not yet been acquired by the transferee.¹⁰

Simon's Taxes I7.381A–381C; Foster's Inheritance Tax G3.81A–81C.

1   IHTA 1984, s 124A(3)(*a*), (4).
2   IHTA 1984, s 124A(8).
3   IHTA 1984, s 124A(3)(*b*).
4   IHTA 1984, s 124A(3)(*c*).
5   IHTA 1984, s 124A(6).
6   IHTA 1984, s 124B.
7   IHTA 1984, s 124B(2).
8   IHTA 1984, s 124B(2)(*a*), (5)(*b*).
9   IHTA 1984, s 124B(3).
10 IHTA 1984, s 124B(5).

Scottish agricultural tenancies

[44.25] Under Scots law if neither party gives notice of termination to end the lease when it expires the tenant can stay on by virtue of a doctrine called tacit relocation. It is expressly provided that in valuing a person's estate immediately before death this prospect of renewal by tacit relocation, which is in effect a right to extend a lease, is not to be taken into account when valuing a tenant's existing rights—whether those rights arise under a lease[1] or already by tacit relocation.[2] This is subject to the condition that the deceased had been a tenant for at least two years before his death or had acquired the tenancy by succession.[3] The value left out of account is not to include any rights in respect of compensation for tenants' improvements.[4] However, this rule does not extend to life-time transfers of such property.[5]

This distinction between a lifetime transfer and one on death seems anomalous; amending legislation has not so far been introduced.

Simon's Taxes I7.361–369; Foster's Inheritance Tax G3.61–69.

[1] IHTA 1984, s 177(1), (3).
[2] IHTA 1984, s 177(2), (3).
[3] IHTA 1984, s 177.
[4] IHTA 1984, s 177(4).
[5] See comments by Scottish ICA, *Simon's Tax Intelligence* 1991, p 1143 and *Baird's Executors v IRC* [1991] 1 EGLR 201.

Interaction between business property relief and agricultural property relief

[44.26] It is possible for one property to qualify for both agricultural property relief and business property relief, such as when the deceased has farmed land, as a sole trader or in partnership. Agricultural property relief takes precedence and provides relief against the agricultural value of the land.[1] If there is potential for development, the market value of the land at death may be substantially higher than its agricultural value; business property relief in these circumstances provides relief against this additional hope value.

[1] IHTA 1984, s 116(1). See supra, § **44.11**.

Relief for works of art and other heritage property

[44.27] There are two quite distinct exemptions from IHT for works of art and heritage property:

(1)   transfers of certain objects or land to the Revenue in satisfaction of tax are exempt transfers;[1]

Relief for works of art [44.27]

(2) when the transfer of value is of a "designated" object and certain undertakings are given to the Treasury, the transfer may be treated as conditionally exempt.[2]

Conditional exemption is given to:

(a) any transfer on death; and
(b) any other transfer of value provided
- (i) the transferor or his spouse, or the transferor and his spouse between them, have been beneficially entitled to the property throughout the six years ending with the transfer; or
- (ii) the transferor acquired the property on death and the property was then the subject of a conditionally exempt transfer.[3]

In the case of a potentially exempt transfer of heritage property, no claim for conditional exemption can be made until the death of the transferor, and no claim at all can be made if the property has been sold before then.[4] However, if the property has, between the transfer and the death, been sold by private treaty or given to an exempt public body,[5] or transferred to the Government in satisfaction of IHT,[6] the transfer becomes exempt.[7]

A similar exemption applies where there is an occasion giving rise to tax in relation to property held on discretionary trusts.[8] Exemption may be claimed both in respect of the ten-year charge[9] and the exit charge. Exemption from the ten-year charge is complete if there was a conditionally exempt transfer of the asset or a capital gains tax rollover on or before the occasion on which it became settled. In other situations a subsequent chargeable event gives rise to a charge to tax similar to that outlined at supra, § **42.49** where privileged tax treatment of a favoured discretionary trust ceases.[10] If the trustees buy a "designated object" it enters the cumulative hypothetical total for the calculation of the tax.[11]

Simon's Taxes I7.511; I10.122; Foster's Inheritance Tax G5.11; K1.22.

---

[1] IHTA 1984, s 230. On present practice see statement of practice SP 6/87; **Foster's Inheritance Tax, Division W3.**
[2] For post-1976 transfers see IHTA 1984, s 30; on transitional rules see IHTA 1984, s 35. The conditional exemption will yield to the general spousal exemption where applicable.
[3] IHTA 1984, s 30(3).
[4] IHTA 1984, ss 3A–3C.
[5] Specified in IHTA 1984, Sch 3.
[6] Under IHTA 1984, s 230.
[7] IHTA 1984, s 26A.
[8] IHTA 1984, s 78.
[9] IHTA 1984, s 79.
[10] IHTA 1984, s 79(3)–(8).
[11] Under IHTA 1984, s 66(5); see IHTA 1984, s 79(9), (10).

Designated objects

[44.28] The exemption from IHT is conferred in respect of pictures, prints, books, manuscripts, works of art or scientific collections or other things not yielding income appearing to the Treasury to be of national, scientific, historic or artistic interest.[1] National interest includes interest within any part of the UK.[2] The exemption is only available if the property has been designated under this provision by the Treasury.[3] When the thing so appears to the Treasury it is designated by the Treasury. The exemption must be claimed within two years of the relevant transfer or event.[4]

Undertakings must be given to keep the object permanently in the UK (save for a purpose and a period approved by the Treasury), and to take reasonable steps for its preservation and to give reasonable facilities for its examination to make sure that it is being preserved, or for purposes of research, by persons approved by the Treasury. The Treasury will only designate property where there is public access, which must be available without prior appointment,[5] although the Treasury may here allow a reasonable degree of confidentiality.[6] The Revenue keep a register of the relevant objects which it publishes on a regularly updated basis and in computer readable format.[7]

From 17 March 1998, there are stricter provisions requiring public access to items on which the IHT exemption has been granted.[8] Previous arrangements can be revised.[9] If agreement for greater access cannot be agreed between HMRC and the owner, the Special Commissioners are given the power to direct the variation to a previously given undertaking if this appears to the Commissioner to be just and reasonable in all the circumstances.[10] In *Re an application to vary the undertakings of A*[11] the first such case to be heard, the Special Commissioner rejected the Revenue's application.

The exemption is conditional in that tax is payable if the Treasury are satisfied that the undertakings are broken in a material respect,[12] or if the object is disposed of, whether by sale or otherwise or on death. Presumably the word disposal receives its ordinary meaning and does not extend to situations where there is a deemed disposal for CGT, as where the object is accidentally destroyed by fire and insurance proceeds are received.[13] The case of deliberate destruction seems less clear.

A disposal will not cause a liability to pay IHT if the object is disposed of otherwise than by sale and fresh undertakings are accepted.[14] Acceptance of the object by way of payment of tax likewise causes no charge.[15]

Simon's Taxes I7.512; Foster's Inheritance Tax G5.12.

---

[1] IHTA 1984, s 31. On foreign owned works of art see extra-statutory concession F7 (1994); **Foster's Inheritance Tax, Division W2**.
[2] IHTA 1984, s 31(5).
[3] IHTA 1984, s 31(1).
[4] IHTA 1984, ss 30(3BA), 78(1A).
[5] IHTA 1984, ss 31(4FA).
[6] See Inland Revenue press release, 17 December 1992 announcing improvements to a list maintained by the Victoria and Albert Museum and other institutions to

enable access to take place; *Simon's Tax Intelligence* 1992, p 1098.
[7] The register can be viewed on the Internet at www.cto.eds.co.uk. The register lists over 18,000 items. For full details of viewing arrangements, see *Simon's Weekly Tax Intelligence* 1996, p 2096 and the Inland Revenue Guidance Note issued 11 February 1999: *Simon's Weekly Tax Intelligence* 1999, p 251.
[8] IHTA 1984, s 32; the burden of the tax is governed by IHTA 1984, s 207. HMRC has a charge for unpaid tax over the object itself, or proceeds from its sale or property received in substitution: IHTA 1984, s 237(3C).
[9] IHTA 1984, s 35A, inserted by FA 1998, Sch 25, para 8.
[10] IHTA 1984, s 35A(2)(c).
[11] [2005] STC (SCD) 103.
[12] TCGA 1992, ss 22–24.
[13] IHTA 1984, s 32(5).
[14] IHTA 1984, s 32(4).
[15] IHTA 1984, s 230.

Land

[44.29] Conditional exemption can be provided for land.[1] The land must be of outstanding scenic or historic interest, or adjoin a building of outstanding historic or architectural interest. In relation to events after 19 March 1985 the latter category is widened to include land which, although not adjoining the building, is nonetheless essential for the protection of the character and amenities of the building.[2] The exemption is conditional on undertakings being given.[3] The conditions relate to the maintenance of the land, the preservation of its character, the repair and preservation of other property and keeping objects associated with a building with the building concerned and to reasonable access for the public. The only significant difference seems to be that a chargeable event with regard to a part of the property is treated as a chargeable event relating to the whole and any associated property unless the Treasury otherwise directs.

Where there is a disposal of property which is conditionally exempt, the conditional exemption is reviewed. Current practice is that if the disposal does not materially affect the heritage entity, the designation remains in force and the charge is limited to the part disposal.[4] Where the part disposal results from leasehold enfranchisement under the Leasehold Reform, Housing and Urban Development Act 1993, or the Leasehold Reform Act 1967, and there is no breach of the undertakings in respect of the retained property, this practice was to have been made statutory in 1993 but this was not done.

Simon's Taxes I7.511, 512; I10.122; Foster's Inheritance Tax G5.11, 12; K1.22.

[1] IHTA 1984, s 31(1)(b)–(e). See statements on practice made in the House of Commons by relevant ministers and recorded in *Simon's Tax Intelligence* 1992, pp 699–700.
[2] FA 1985, s 94, Sch 26.

[44.29] Business property relief and other reliefs

[3] IHTA 1984, s 31(4).
[4] Inland Revenue press release, 7 May 1993, *Simon's Tax Intelligence* 1993, p 760.

The charge

[44.30] When a chargeable event occurs and the conditional exemption ceases, tax is charged on an amount equal to the value of the property at the time of the chargeable event.[1] The value will be measured by the sale proceeds or market value as appropriate.[2]

The tax is calculated by reference to the circumstances of the "relevant person". This will be the person who made the last conditionally exempt transfer, save that where there have been two or more such transfers within the last thirty years, the Revenue may select whichever of the transferors they choose.[3] For these purposes the Revenue may not go back beyond a chargeable event.[4]

EXAMPLE

A makes a conditionally exempt transfer to B in 1984.

B makes a conditionally exempt transfer to Y (A's son) in 1989.

Y gives the property to Z, his son. At the time of the transfer, A has a cumulative total of £130,000 and B has a cumulative total of £40,000. The Revenue are entitled to select A as the relevant person and charge tax at the rate appropriate to his cumulative total of chargeable transfers.

The rate of tax is, if the relevant person is still alive, the lifetime rate. The tax is calculated as on a transfer made by the relevant person at the time of the chargeable event.[5] If the relevant person has died, tax is charged as if it had been added to the value transferred on his death and had formed the highest part of that value.[6] The lifetime rate is used even where the transfer was within three years of the death; the death rates are used if the transfer was on death.[7]

EXAMPLE

C makes conditionally exempt lifetime transfers to P and Q.

P makes a conditionally exempt lifetime transfer to V.

C dies; his cumulative total of chargeable transfers (including the value of his estate immediately before his death) is £300,000.

Q sells his property for £65,000 and this is a chargeable event (event 1). The rate of tax is 20% (the lifetime rate on the top £65,000 slice of an estate of £365,000 (£300,000 + £65,000)).

V then sells his property for £30,000 and this is a chargeable event (event 2). C is nominated as relevant person. The rate of tax is 20% (the lifetime rate on the top £30,000 slice of an estate of £395,000.

It should be emphasised that the only function of the relevant person is the calculation of tax. The relevant person is not liable for the tax.

Where the asset is transferred in circumstances which do not qualify for conditional exemption, it may well happen that not only will tax be due but also that the conditional exemption on the previous transfer will be lost so that two lots of tax are due. In such cases the tax on the present transfer is available as a credit against the tax due in respect of the earlier transfer; this is a credit of tax against tax. If the chargeable transfer is not a chargeable event, the tax paid will be available as a credit against liability when the conditional exemption is lost.[8]

There are similar arrangements for crediting the tax on a chargeable event against the tax on a potentially exempt transfer which becomes chargeable and which was made after the conditionally exempt transfer to which the chargeable event relates.[9]

Simon's Taxes I7.513, 514; I10.122; Foster's Inheritance Tax G5.13, 14; K1.22.

---

[1] IHTA 1984, s 33(1)(*a*) on calculation of *estate duty* clawback charge see statement of practice 11/84; Inland Revenue press release, 3 May 1984, *Simon's Tax Intelligence* 1984, p 359 and 1987, p 815.
[2] IHTA 1984, s 33(3).
[3] IHTA 1984, s 33(5); the object is to prevent the use of a man of straw to make the fateful transfer.
[4] IHTA 1984, s 33(6).
[5] IHTA 1984, s 33(1)(*b*)(i).
[6] IHTA 1984, s 33(1)(*b*)(ii).
[7] IHTA 1984, s 33(2).
[8] IHTA 1984, s 33(7).
[9] IHTA 1984, s 33(8).

The transferor's cumulative total

[44.31] Where there has been a chargeable event so that the conditional exemption is lost, the cumulative total of the person making that conditionally exempt disposal is adjusted; this is done whether or not he is the relevant transferor. If he is still alive the amount chargeable is added to his total as at the time of the chargeable event and so affects rates of tax on chargeable transfers made after that event.[1]

If, however, he has died and he is the relevant transferor and is so in relation to more than one chargeable event, the amounts liable to IHT are added to the value of the estate in chronological order.[2]

A special rule applies to settlements. If within the previous five years the property was comprised in a settlement made within the previous 30 years, and the person who made the last conditionally exempt transfer is not the relevant transferor, the previous rules are applied to the estate of the *settlor* if he made a conditionally exempt transfer of the property within the thirty years.[3] Thus suppose that in year 1 S settled property on A for life, remainder to B and that the transfer was conditionally exempt as was the transfer on A's death in year 21. If in year 25 a chargeable event occurs, the Revenue may select S as the relevant transferor and can alter *his* total. The total of the person who made the last conditionally exempt transfer is not affected where this rule applies. For this rule any conditionally exempt transfer by the settlor prior to a chargeable event relating to the property is ignored as are transfers prior to an

[44.31] Business property relief and other reliefs

event which is declared not to be a chargeable event because it is a disposal to an approved body or in payment of tax.[4]

If a chargeable event follows "a conditionally exempt occasion", the relevant person is the settlor or, if more than one, whichever the Board selects.[5] The rule assumes a further transfer by that person; the sum is added to his cumulative total if he is still alive; otherwise it is added to his estate. Death rates are used only if the trust was established by his will. The rate is then reduced to 30% of that death rate if there have been no ten-year anniversaries while the asset was comprised in the settlement and to 60% if there had been just one.

Simon's Taxes I7.515; Foster's Inheritance Tax G5.15.

[1] IHTA 1984, s 34(1).
[2] IHTA 1984, s 34(2).
[3] IHTA 1984, s 34(3).
[4] IHTA 1984, s 34(4).
[5] IHTA 1984, s 78(4).

Maintenance funds for historic buildings, etc

[44.32] Special rules apply also to funds set up for the maintenance of these types of property. Broadly such funds are exempt from income tax, CGT and IHT. Transfers to such funds are exempt transfers.[1] After an initial six year period the asset may be returned to the settlor or applied for non approved purposes but should this occur there will be a charge to income tax and CGT designed to put the settlor back in the tax position he would have been in if he had simply maintained the property out of his new post tax income.[2] There is also a charge to IHT[3] see supra, § **42.59**.

For deaths of a person with an interest in possession in settled property relief is available for any property going into a maintenance fund within two years of the death; this period is extended to three years if a court order is needed, eg under the Variation of Trusts Act 1958.[4]

Simon's Taxes I7.541–543; Foster's Inheritance Tax G5.41–43.

[1] IHTA 1984, s 27.
[2] IHTA 1984, s 77, Sch 4, FA 1980 s 82 (CGT) and FA 1977, s 38 and TA 1988, s 694 (income tax).
[3] IHTA 1984, Sch 4, paras 16–18.
[4] IHTA 1984, s 57A.

Relief for timber

[44.33] A special relief is available in respect of growing timber[1] if certain conditions are satisfied, the person liable so elects[2] and the value is transferred on death. Tax may be deferred until the timber is disposed of or until the value is transferred on another death. In the former case the tax becomes due on the net proceeds or value. In the latter case no IHT will ever become due in respect of the first death. It does not apply to inter vivos transfers. Historically, it did not apply to land outside the UK, but this was realised to be in breach of EC law and this restriction was removed with retrospective effect by FA 2009 so as to cover any land in the EEA at the time of the person's death. The relief applies to the timber and not to the land; the 1995 changes in the income tax treatment of short rotation coppice do not extend to IHT. The effect of the relief is to reduce the overall inheritance tax due on the death; however, the relief is one of postponement not exemption.

The deceased must have been beneficially entitled to the land or to an interest in possession in the land[3] throughout the five years immediately preceding his death *or* became beneficially entitled to it otherwise than for consideration in money or money's worth. Hence, one who inherits timber land and dies after only three years of beneficial entitlement may use the relief, but one who buys may not. This condition is aimed at deathbed purchases of timber. Beneficial ownership of shares in a company which is entitled to possession of the land does not suffice.[4]

The refusal to extend this treatment to inter vivos transfers or to discretionary trusts seems odd.

Simon's Taxes I7.401–403, 407; Foster's Inheritance Tax G4.01–03, 07.

[1] IHTA 1984, s 125.
[2] Semble that he can elect for different areas of woodland.
[3] IHTA 1984, s 49(1).
[4] However, this may qualify for agricultural or business relief IHTA 1984, ss 115(2), 103, see also IHTA 1984, s 127(2).

The relief

[44.34] The relief provided is that the value of the timber may be left out of account in determining the value transferred on death if the person liable so elects within two years of death or such longer period as the Board may allow.[1] The relief applies only to the trees or underwood; it does not apply to the value of the land itself which however may qualify for agricultural or business relief. Land used for short rotational coppice may qualify for agricultural relief.[2]

Where the person liable has elected to take the relief, the tax will nonetheless become payable if the timber should be disposed of before the next death, whether by sale for full consideration or not. Since the tax has merely been deferred since death, the tax will become payable on a subsequent disposal whether or not that disposal is itself a chargeable transfer. The only exception is that a disposal by a person to his spouse will not cause the provisional exemption to be lost.[3]

Where the disposal is itself a chargeable transfer so that two sets of liability to tax will arise, the first by reference to the previous death, the second by reference to the disposal, it is provided that in computing the value transferred on the second transfer a deduction is made for the tax chargeable on the first.[4] The deduction is simply in valuing the transfer. It is not a credit of tax against tax. Where the second transfer is an occasion for business relief, the reduction under that relief is applied to the value as reduced by the tax paid in respect of the first death.[5]

This regime for timber is still highly favourable but not as favourable as that under estate duty. Under that tax the value of the timber was excluded from the estate and the proceeds of sale of the timber were taxed at the rate which had applied to the estate; this was the basis upon which the proceeds were charged until the next death when the process would be resumed using the new deceased person's estate rate. Where a person died under the estate duty regime this option was preserved notwithstanding the introduction of CTT; however, it was provided that the period during which this potential charge to tax was calculated on this basis should end not only on the death of that person but on any prior chargeable transfer.[6] This remains the case with the rider that such a transfer after 30 June 1986 is not to be treated as a potentially exempt transfer so far as concerns that part of the value transferred which is attributable to the woodlands which are subject to a deferred estate duty charge.[7]

Simon's Taxes I7.402; Foster's Inheritance Tax G4.02.

---

[1] IHTA 1984, s 125(1).
[2] FA 1995, s 154(2).
[3] IHTA 1984, s 126.
[4] IHTA 1984, s 127.
[5] IHTA 1984, s 114(2).
[6] FA 1975, s 49(4).
[7] FA 1986, Sch 19, para 46, modified by extra-statutory concession F15; Foster's Inheritance Tax, Division U2.

The charge on later disposal

[44.35] If the timber is sold for full consideration in money or money's worth, tax becomes payable on the net proceeds of sale. The person exclusively liable is the person who is or would be entitled to the proceeds. In any case other than sale for full consideration in money or money's worth, tax is payable on the net value of the trees or underwood valued at the time of the chargeable event, not the date of death;[1] however, plantings since the death are ignored.[2] The proceeds are therefore aggregated with the rest of the property transferred on the previous death. There is, however, no retrospective increase in the amount of tax payable in respect of all the other items in the estate, the whole burden of the marginal rate of tax thus falling on the timber. It will also be seen that the proceeds caught are the *net* proceeds of sale or the *net* value. For the net proceeds of sale one must deduct from the proceeds certain expenses, namely those incurred in the disposal, in replanting within three years or such longer time as the Board may allow,[3] and in replanting to replace earlier disposals so far as not allowable on those previous disposals.[4] These deductions, however, are not allowed if they are allowable for income tax, a phrase which presumably means theoretically allowable, and so excludes deduction for IHT whether or not there is sufficient income to absorb its expense. The net value is the value of the timber after allowing for these deductions.

When rates of IHT change the tax is charged at the death rates prevailing at the time of the sale;[5] it may be inferred that this is because it is presumed that the increase in rates simply reflects the change in values due to inflation, a presumption that is usually quite untrue.

EXAMPLE

D made inter vivos chargeable transfers of £90,000 and left E his entire estate which, after omitting the timber, came to £300,000. After D's death E sold one parcel for £5,000 and another for £15,000, these being the net proceeds of sale.

IHT is due at 40% on the disposals, so that the tax will be £2,000 and £6,000 respectively.

If E had given the second parcel, still worth £15,000 to his son, F, this would again trigger IHT liability of £6,000 as regards D's death. However the tax is deducted to leave £9,000 as the value of the property in calculating such tax as might arise on the potentially exempt transfer to F if E should die within seven years.

Simon's Taxes I7.404, 406; Foster's Inheritance Tax G4.04, 06.

[1] IHTA 1984, s 130.
[2] IHTA 1984, s 126(1).
[3] This power is needed because planning permission can take substantially more than three years.
[4] IHTA 1984, s 128.
[5] IHTA 1984, Sch 2, para 4.

45

Valuation

Introduction	PARA **45.01**
A fiscal valuation and a commercial valuation	PARA **45.03**
Chattels	PARA **45.04**
The special purchaser	PARA **45.05**
Restrictions on sale	PARA **45.06**
Related property	PARA **45.07**
Relief for loss after death	PARA **45.11**
Land	PARA **45.16**
Debts due to the transferor	PARA **45.18**
Accrued income to date of transfer	PARA **45.19**
Liabilities	PARA **45.20**

Introduction

[45.01] Where property has to be valued for IHT the general rule is that the value is the price which it might reasonably be expected to fetch if sold on the open market[1] at the relevant time; the costs of such a sale are ignored. The price is not to be reduced on the ground that the whole property is placed on the market at the same time. While this exercise presupposes a hypothetical value of hypothetical property between hypothetical parties, evidence of actual transactions is admissible, the question of what weight should be attached to those transactions is one of fact.[2]

The whole process has been summarised by Hoffmann LJ as follows:[3]

> Certain things are necessarily entailed by the statutory hypothesis [of sale at market value]. The property must be assumed to have been capable of sale in the open market, even if in fact it was inherently unassignable or held subject to restrictions on sale. The question is what a purchaser in the open market would have paid to enjoy whatever rights attached to the property at the relevant date (see *IRC v Crossman*[4]). Furthermore, the hypothesis must be applied to the property as it actually existed and not to some other property, even if in real life a vendor would have been likely to make some changes or improvements before putting it on the market (see *Duke of Buccleuch v IRC*[5]). To this extent, but only to this extent, the express terms of the statute may introduce an element of artificiality into the hypothesis.
>
> In all other respects, the theme which runs through the authorities is that one assumes that the hypothetical vendor and purchaser did whatever reasonable people buying and selling such property would be likely to have done in real life. The hypothetical vendor is an anonymous but reasonable vendor, who goes about the sale as a prudent man of business, negotiating seriously without giving the impression of being either over-anxious or unduly reluctant. The hypothetical buyer is slightly less anonymous. He too is assumed to have behaved reasonably, making proper inquiries about the property and not appearing too eager to buy. But he also

[45.01] Valuation

reflects reality in that he embodies whatever was actually the demand for that property at the relevant time. It cannot be too strongly emphasised that although the sale is hypothetical, there is nothing hypothetical about the open market in which is it supposed to have taken place. The concept of the open market involves assuming that the whole world was free to bid, and then forming a view about what in those circumstances would in real life have been the best price reasonably obtainable. The practical nature of this exercise will usually mean that although in principle no one is excluded from consideration, most of the world will usually play no part in the calculation. The inquiry will often focus on what a relatively small number of people would be likely to have paid. It may have to arrive at a figure within a range of prices which the evidence shows that various people would have been likely to pay, reflecting, for example, the fact that one person had a particular reason for paying a higher price than others, but taking into account, if appropriate, the possibility that through accident or whim he might not actually have bought. The valuation is thus a retrospective exercise in probabilities, wholly derived from the real world but rarely committed to the proposition that a sale to a particular purchaser would definitely have happened.

It is often said that the hypothetical vendor and purchaser must be assumed to have been 'willing', but I doubt whether this adds anything to the assumption that they must have behaved as one would reasonably expect of prudent parties who had in fact agreed a sale on the relevant date. It certainly does not mean that having calculated the price which the property might reasonably have been expected to fetch in the way I have described, one then asks whether the hypothetical parties would have been pleased or disappointed with the result; for example, by reference to what the property might have been worth at a different time or in different circumstances. Such considerations are irrelevant.

Simon's Direct Tax Service I8.201; Foster's Inheritance Tax H2.01.

---

[1] IHTA 1984, s 160; this rule is identical to TCGA 1992, s 272(2) and enacts the estate duty view, eg *Duke of Buccleuch v IRC* [1967] 1 AC 506, HL.
[2] *IRC v Stenhouses's Trustees* [1992] STC 103, Ct of Sess.
[3] *IRC v Gray* [1994] STC 360 at 371–2, CA.
[4] [1937] AC 26.
[5] [1967] 1 AC 506 at 525.

Case law and valuation

[45.02] To perform a fiscal valuation is to follow statutory fiction. In *IRC v Crossman*,[1] Lord Russell said:

> It is not a question of ascertaining their actual value, or their true value, or their intrinsic value, or their value in some particular person's ownership, the value to be ascertained is their statutory value.

On which, in *Holt v IRC*,[2] Danckwerts J commented:

> The result is that I must enter into a dim world peopled by the indeterminate spirits of fictitious or unborn sales.

In the real world, there may be restrictions on a sale taking place. These restrictions may be legal, administrative, or purely practical. In judging the market value for statutory purposes, all restrictions must be assumed to be removed. Any person who would have to give consent to a sale is assumed to have given that consent. In *Re Aschrott, Clifton v Strauss*,[3] the shares were held by an enemy alien in time of war. Any sale would have been illegal. The court ruled that the illegality of a sale was to be ignored in judging the market value of the shares.

All possible purchasers must be considered. In *A-G v Jameson*,[4] Fitzgibbon LJ said:

> . . . that means the price which would be obtainable upon a sale where it was open to everyone, who had the will and the money, to offer the price which the property of Henry Jameson in the shares was worth as he held them.

In *Re Lynall*,[5] Harman LJ said 'All likely purchasers are deemed to be in the market' and held that special purchasers must be considered when valuing.

In *IRC v Clay*,[6] Cozens-Hardy J said:

> To say that a small farm in the middle of a wealthy landowner's estate is to be valued without reference to the fact that he will probably be willing to pay a large price, but solely with reference to its ordinary agricultural value, seems to me absurd. If the landowner does not at the moment buy, landbrokers or speculators will give more than its purely agricultural value with a view to reselling it at a profit to the landowner.

If a higher price is to be obtained by dividing up an asset, such as a shareholding, it is this higher price that is to be taken. In *Smyth v Revenue Comrs*,[7] Hanna J said:

> In my judgment, you must take into consideration the possibility of the shares being divided up among several purchasers, either members of the family or the public.

The position regarding amalgamating different assets in order to get a higher price is less clear. In *A-G of Ceylon v Mackie*,[8] Lord Reid approved a valuation obtained by such an amalgamation:

> It was admitted for the appellant that no purchaser would have paid anything like Rs. 250 per share for the management shares in face of the company's articles unless he could buy at the same time a large block of the preference shares and so have a majority of the votes.

The same approach was followed by the Court of Appeal in *IRC v Gray*,[9] where the value of the freehold of agricultural land encumbered by a lease was adjudged on the assumption that the sale of the land would take place along with the sale of the deceased's 98% interest in the partnership which was entitled to the tenancy under the lease.

Events after valuation date are ignored, except insofar as they could have been foreseen.

The valuation must be as at the actual date. In *Duke of Buccleuch v IRC*,[10] Lord Morris of Borth-y-Gest said:

> 'At the time of the death' must not be paraphrased or altered so as to read 'within a reasonably short time of the death'.

Again, in *Duke of Buccleuch v IRC*,[11] Lord Reid said:

Here, however what must be envisaged is sale in the open market on a particular day. So there is no room for supposing that the owner would do as many prudent owners do—withdraw the property if he does not get a sufficient offer and wait until a time when he can get a better offer.

In making a valuation, no regard is had to the expenses that would arise on an actual sale. In *Duke of Buccleuch v IRC*,[12] Lord Reid said:

> I am confirmed in my opinion by the fact that the Act of 1894 permits no deduction from the price fetched of the expenses involved in the sale (except in the case of property abroad under section 7(3)) . . . I find it impossible to suppose that they can have contemplated that the kinds of hypothetical sale which they envisaged would involve heavy expenses.

Where the value is of shares in a private company, the statutory fiction is that the hypothetical purchaser will be entered onto the company register, but he has then acquired shares which are subject to the restrictions in the articles on any subsequent sale he wishes to make.

In *A-G v Jameson*,[13] Holmes LJ said:

> the principal value of the shares is to be estimated at the price which, in the opinion of the Commissioners, they would fetch if sold in the open market, on the terms that the purchaser should be entitled to be registered as holder of the shares, and should take and hold them subject to the provisions of the articles of association, including the articles relating to alienation and transfer of the shares of the Company.

The courts have recognised that many family companies are run on the basis that it is only members of the family that are allowed to hold shares and only members of the family that are, in reality, allowed to decide on the conduct of the company.

In *Re Thornley*,[14] Rowlatt J said:

> the imagined purchaser in this case (having regard to the circumstances of the particular family business) would find himself a detested intruder with a minority interest and under articles already summarised (containing very stringent restrictions and pre-emption rights), and I wonder very much whether anyone could be found to take the position on lucrative terms to the seller of the shares.

Equivalent comments were made in *Salvesen's Trustees v IRC*,[15] by Lord Fleming and in *Dean v Prince*,[16] by Sir Raymond Evershed MR.

If an actual sale from an estate would trigger a liability, the valuation is, first, undertaken without regard to the consequence of this deemed disposal. The liability thus triggered is, then, treated as a liability of the estate.[17]

A prospective purchaser is expected to be prudent. In *Holt v IRC*, Danckwerts J said:

> He would, in my view, be the kind of investor who would not rush hurriedly into the transaction, but would consider carefully the prudence of the course, and would seek to get the fullest possible information about the past history of the company, the particular trade in which it was engaged and the future prospects of the company.

The same principles were applied in *Bower & Anor (Exors of Bower dec'd) v R & C Comrs*.[18] That case concerned the value of an annuity taken out by a 90-year old woman.

Introduction [45.02]

In looking to see how an actual value is attributed to an asset, and particularly to a shareholding, it is important to recognise that a valuation is a finding of fact; it is for the Special Commissioners to make the findings of fact. The role of the court on appeal is limited to considering points of law that arise. It is clear from reported judgments that a valuation must be undertaken by bringing together all the various matters that affect the value of a shareholding. The value finally determined is a matter of balancing the different considerations that affect the value of a shareholding. Valuation is an art not a science; no valuation is merely an automatic numerical exercise. For an illustration of the Special Commissioners' approach to the valuation of a shareholding, it is instructive to read the lengthy consideration of the various different matters involved in determining the value of shares considered in *Caton's Administrators v Couch*.[19]

In *Caton*, the Special Commissioners also considered the application of the "information provision".[20] A valuation for capital gains tax purposes was required as at 7 September 1987, the date of death. The deceased held 14.02% of the issued share capital of the company, the largest single holding. Some seven months later, the administrators sold the shareholding, the purchaser acquiring at the same time all other shares in the company. In the period prior to the date of death, a number of approaches had been made to the company by those wishing to acquire its entire business. However, no information on this had been made public. Moreover, there had been a substantial increase in profits for the year ended 31 August 1987, but the profit figures had not been published at the date of death. The Special Commissioner held[21] that in determining the value of this holding "it should be assumed that unpublished information about the profits and budget forecasts of the company, and unpublished information about a possible sale of the company, would be available to the purchaser." The Special Commissioner held that the value of the shares on the date of death for CGT purposes was 56p each. The expert witness called by the taxpayer had put the value at 88p per share on the basis that the "secret information" was available; the Revenue had proposed 35p per share.

In *Clark v Green*,[22] the same Special Commissioner made a comparable decision in a case where the valuation dispute represented 3% of the company's issued share capital and the published information was more than a year out of date.

In recent years, much has been made of the rights of a participant in the type of company known as a "quasi partnership".[23] In cases involving an oppressed minority, or where a court has, on other grounds, ordered compensation or damages to be paid, judgment is commonly given for a proportionate part of the total value of a company, without discount, where the relationship between the shareholders is the equivalent of partnership. Such considerations are largely irrelevant[24] for valuation for inheritance tax purposes. For IHT, we are not looking to see how much compensation would be given to a known individual; we are looking to see what an unconnected third party purchaser would pay to step into the shoes of the shareholder, in his role as shareholder only. *Irvine v Irvine*,[25] although not an IHT case, is a useful corrective to any mistaken belief on valuation of a minority shareholding. The shareholder to be valued was 49.96% of the total issued share capital, all the remaining shares

[45.02] Valuation

being held by Patricia Irvine's brother-in-law. The court ruled that the correct basis for valuing Patricia Irvine's shareholding was by applying the discount that is appropriate for a minority holding.

Simon's Direct Tax Service I8.203, 203A; Foster's Inheritance Tax H2.03, 03A.

---

[1] [1937] AC 26.
[2] [1953] 2 All ER 1499.
[3] [1927] 1 Ch 313.
[4] [1905] 2 IR 218.
[5] [1969] 1 Ch 421.
[6] [1914] 3 KB 466.
[7] [1931] IR 643.
[8] [1952] 2 All ER 775.
[9] [1994] STC 360.
[10] [1966] 1 QB 851.
[11] [1966] 1 QB 851.
[12] [1966] 1 QB 851.
[13] [1905] 2 IR 218.
[14] (1928) 7 ATC 178.
[15] (1930) 9 ATC 43.
[16] [1953] Ch 590.
[17] In *Alexander v IRC* [1991] STC 112, CA, a long leasehold interest in a flat was acquired by the deceased at large discount under the "right to buy" legislation. It was a condition of the purchase that, if the tenant sold the property within five years, a sum equal to the discount was payable to the vendor public authority. In valuing the long lease in the estate at his death shortly after the purchase, it was held that the value of the lease on death had to take account of the tenant's obligation to repay the discount if he sold within five years of his acquisition. However, this was to be done by recognising the liability to repay as a liability of the estate and the valuation of the house was on the basis that the hypothetical purchaser's hypothetical acquisition did not give rise to the obligation to repay the discount.
[18] (2008) SpC 665.
[19] [1995] STC (SCD) 34. Other cases in recent years that illustrate the way in which the Special Commissioners gather together facts relating to the company, its industry and the demands for its shares before determining a value for inheritance tax, or any other purpose are: *Hawkings-Byass v Sassen* [1996] STC (SCD) 319, *Denekamp v Pearce* [1998] STC 1120, *Billows v Hammond* [2000] STC (SCD) 430. In each of these cases the Commissioner's decision can be used as a model for a share valuer's report.
[20] TCGA 1992, s 273(3).
[21] [1995] STC (SCD) 34 at 56e.
[22] [1995] STC (SCD) 99.
[23] Cases such as *Re Yenidje Tobacco Co Ltd* [1916–17] All ER Rep 1050, *Ebrahimi v Westbourne Galleries Ltd* [1972] 2 All ER 492, *Re Bird Precision Bellows Ltd* [1985] 3 All ER 523, CA and *Strahan v Wilcock* [2006] EWCA Civ 13, [2006] 2 BCLC 555.
[24] Exceptionally, the fact that a company is a quasi-partnership may mean that there is another shareholder who is willing to pay a higher price as he is a special

purchaser, who would obtain full value in the event of disagreement with his fellow shareholders. For a fuller discussion of the effect of a quasi-partnership, and also of a special purchaser, on share valuation see David Collison *Share Valuation Handbook* (third edn, 2007), section 4.6 and the commentaries on cases 10, 31, 35 and 49.

25   [2006] EWHC 583 (Ch), [2006] 4 All ER 102.

A fiscal valuation and a commercial valuation

[45.03] Statute requires a market value for the purpose of inheritance tax (as for capital gains tax) to be determined as "the price at which the property might reasonably be expected to fetch if sold on the open market".[1] This is, thus, not an artificial price but an actual price which, in the view of the appropriate expert valuer, would actually be offered by a purchaser on the valuation date. However, it is important to recognise that the value that is required for inheritance tax is the value of the asset actually in the estate of the deceased (with any related property) and is the value that could be obtained on the date of death. There is no scope for applying the normal commercial judgement on a sale that it would be worthwhile retaining the asset longer until a better offer is obtained. Equally, unless it is related property as defined in statute, there is no scope for assuming that other individuals would sell at the same time. This is particularly important when considering the value of unquoted shares. In the commercial world, an incorporated business is usually sold by all shareholders jointly selling their shares in the company. The value that can be obtained for 100% interest in a company is the value that is required for some statutory purposes, such as proceedings for a professional, minority or another order on winding up of a company.[2] Decided cases where a valuation is required for this purpose are of limited use in considering a value to be taken for inheritance tax purposes, although there may be circumstances where the increased financial remedy available to a minority shareholder in such a "quasi partnership" could have a positive effect on the value of the minority shareholding.

The price realised on a sale of property in the open market after a transfer may provide some evidence of the value of that property at the time of the transfer but hindsight is not permitted.[3]

Simon's Direct Tax Service I4.311–313; I8.101.

1   IHTA 1984, s 160.
2   A recent example of a valuation of a shareholding in such a "quasi partnership" is *CVC v Demarco Almeida* [2002] UKPC 16, [2002] 2 BCLC 108. Older examples are *Re Yenidje Tobacco Co Ltd* [1916] 2 Ch 426, [1916–17] All ER Rep 1050 and *Ebrahimi v Westbourne Galleries Ltd* [1972] 2 All ER 492, HL.
3   eg per Dankwerts J in *Holt v IRC* [1953] 2 All ER 1499. See also *IRC v Marr's Trustees* (1906) 44 SLR 647 and *Re Lynall* [1972] AC 680, HL.

Chattels

[45.04] In principle, the valuation of chattels follows the same rules as the valuation of a landholding, of a shareholding, and of any other asset. The case law on the valuation of landholdings and of shareholdings is, in principle, equally applicable to chattels. In practice, the valuation of chattels is made difficult by the facts that (a) many valuable chattels, particular works of art, are unique and direct comparisons of price cannot be made as readily as in the case of, say, houses, and (b) the market for chattels is often an auction and auctions are notorious for widely varying prices being obtained.

The HMRC division dealing with valuation has, in 2007, changed its name to "HMRC Shares and Assets Valuation" in order to reflect the recognition of HMRC of the importance of chattel valuations. The division has a team of eight valuers dealing with valuations of chattels and bloodstock. All of the work of this division arises from referrals from either CTO (for IHT matters) or from a local district (for capital gains matters). Referral is at the discretion of the office to whom the return is made, following an assessment by that office of the tax likely to be at stake. HMRC report that 87% of chattel valuations referred to HMRC Shares and Assets Valuation are accepted without contact being made with the taxpayer or agent. Of the 13% that are challenged, the total adjustment on values finally agreed amounted to £4,000,000 over a six month period.[1]

When a valuation is required for IHT at death, the Revenue frequently request a list of prices obtained if chattels are subsequently sold at auction. Two points arise.

First, the statutory provisions require tax to be levied on the sum which a prospective purchaser would pay. This is not the same as the sum which would be received by a vendor. Hence, the auctioneer's commission is not deductible (*Duke of Buccleuch v IRC*[2]).

Second, the valuation of a chattel, as any other asset, under the statutory provisions, is the highest price that one would be reasonably certain to obtain at the date of death. This may be very different from the price subsequently obtained at auction. As Danckwerts J said in *Holt v IRC*:[3]

> It is necessary to assume the prophetic vision of a prospective purchaser at the moment of the death of the deceased, and firmly to reject the wisdom which might be provided by the knowledge of subsequent events.

In *IRC v Marr's Trustees*,[4] William Smith Marr died on 7 June 1904 and in his estate was a herd of prize shorthorn cattle. This herd was valued at £9,031. Four months later on 11 October 1904, the herd was sold for £17,722 17s. The Inland Revenue attempted to assess estate duty on the basis of the sale price achieved four months after the death. This was rejected by Lord Johnston, giving his judgment in the High Court, saying:[5]

> I am of opinion that the position taken by the Commissioners of Inland Revenue is not well founded . . . .. Notwithstanding these differences the value of estate duty is to be taken at the price which the property would fetch in open market at the time of the deceased's death. I think that the sale which actually did take place in October was accompanied by certain adventitious circumstances which, though they re-

dounded very much to the advantage of the estate, render the sale price obtained a misleading criterion of the true market value of the herd at the date of the death, or indeed at any other date.

As a side note, the comment of the judge on the expert witness who appeared by the taxpayer is interesting:[6]

> Great exception was taken by counsel for the Commissioners to the manner of Mr Ritchie's valuation . . . . I think it right to state that I was much impressed by Mr Ritchie's appearance in the witness box. He was not a voluble witness, and did not always find it easy to put in words a reason for the faith that was in him but he had lived for years with the herd under his eye . . . I would infinitely rather trust his trained and practical intuition, though it may appear on paper to produce somewhat of a rule of thumb result, than many a more apparently scientific valuation by classification. And I am persuaded that Mr Ritchie's valuation of June is a fair valuation, against which the Commissioners of Inland Revenue have no just cause of complaint.

In connection with the income tax charge on pre-owned assets (see supra, § **12.18**) it is sometimes necessary to determine the market rent that would be paid for the use of a chattel. This is difficult as there are rarely convincing comparatives availably commercially. HMRC Shares and Assets Valuation have stated:[7]

> If a meaningful rental market exists there is not usually a problem as all concerned will be guided by the prices achieved in that market. The issue becomes problematical when the assets in question are items such as country house chattels or valuable works of art where there may be no meaningful rental market. In these cases HMRC advice has been that the rental rate is unlikely to be challenged if the taxpayer can demonstrate that it resulted from:
>
> (1) a bargain negotiated at arms length
> (2) by parties who were independently advised
> (3) which followed the normal commercial criteria in force at the time it was negotiated.

The facts of individual cases will vary but, against this background, HMRC experience is that an accepted norm of 1% of capital value has arisen. This rate has no robust basis but is regularly accepted by HMRC, on a without prejudice basis, as an informal way of resolving a difficult issue.

---

1 Minutes of meeting on 22 November 2006 of HMRC Chattels Valuation Fiscal Forum, available at www.hmrc.gov.uk/cto/cvminutes-221106.htm
2 [1966] 1 QB 851.
3 [1953] 2 All ER 1499.
4 (1906) 44 SLR 647.
5 (1906) 44 SLR, para 13 at 648.
6 (1906) 44 SLR, para 12 at 648.
7 HMRC Chattels Valuation Fiscal Forum 22 November 2006, Minutes, para 5.

The special purchaser

[45.05] In computing market value it would seem that account is to be taken of the possibility of an offer from any person who may be specially interested in the purchase of the property.[1] The true value lies somewhere between normal market value and the highest price which the special purchaser would pay.

The problem of the special purchaser frequently arises in the case of shares in a private company. The other shareholders may be particularly anxious to acquire the deceased's shares, in order to prevent them going to the public or to strangers.

In one case of shares in a private company decided by the House of Lords,[2] the argument that a higher valuation should be put on the shares because they were a kind of investment which was particularly attractive to a trust corporation was rejected by at least one of the law lords. But this decision cannot be treated as a binding authority for the view that the existence of a special purchaser should be disregarded, because in that particular case restrictions in the company's articles would have discouraged an acquisition by a trust corporation.

The area of law relating to the role of the special purchaser is one of some subtlety. As an example one may take the following comments of Harman LJ in *Re Lynall*:

> It was the taxpayer's argument that directors must be excluded from amongst possible purchasers because they would be special purchasers. I do not accept this . . . In Crossman's case it was decided that the fact that a 'special' purchaser, namely a trust company, would have offered a special price must be ignored, but this was because that particular purchaser had a reason special to him for so doing. So here a director who would give an enhanced price because he would thus obtain control of the company would be left out of account. But that is not to say that directors as such are to be ignored. All likely purchasers are deemed to be in the market.[3]

It is for the Commissioners, as the tribunal of fact, to consider who are the special purchasers at a valuation date. The statutory valuation provisions do not require that the landlord should be hypothetical; they assume a sale in the real world.[4]

Simon's Direct Tax Service I8.204, 208; Foster's Inheritance Tax H2.04, 08.

---

1. *IRC v Clay*, *IRC v Buchanan* [1914] 3 KB 466 (an increment duty case); and note the comment of Lord Pearson in *Re Lynall* that in the Clay case the fact enhancing the price was assumed to be a matter of local knowledge: [1971] 3 All ER 914 at 920. See also *Glass v IRC* 1915 SC 449.
2. *IRC v Crossman*, *IRC v Mann* [1937] AC 26, [1936] 1 All ER 762.
3. [1969] 3 All ER 984 at 990; note that the decision of the Court of Appeal was reversed by the House of Lords [1971] 3 All ER 914.
4. *Walton v IRC* [1996] STC 68, CA.

Restrictions on sale

[45.06] The fact that the property cannot be sold, or can be sold only to certain persons or at a certain price, or otherwise subject to restrictions, does not preclude the requirement to value on an open market value. The value has

Restrictions on sale [45.06]

to be found on the assumption that the property can be offered freely in the market. Nevertheless, the effect of any restrictions on sale, if they will persist when the property reaches other hands, is not nugatory. The value is to be found on the assumption that the purchaser, buying freely in the market, will be subject, after he has become the purchaser, to the same restrictions on sale as those affecting the vendor[1]. Accordingly, the market price, although found on the assumption of a free market, will be lower than it would have been had no restrictions existed. Although this view has been widely held, it has been denied recently by the Revenue where the property concerned was a lease containing a covenant against assignment. The Revenue position, which requires the covenant to be disregarded and the asset to be treated as simply any other assignable leasehold, seems to be wrong.[2]

The rule that one must take account of a restriction on the right to dispose of the property could provide an easy way of saving tax. A restriction would be created by contract, the value of the property would fall and on a subsequent transfer only the reduced value would be transferred. To counter this it is provided that where a restriction or exclusion has been placed upon the right to dispose, then on the occasion of the next relevant event, ie chargeable transfer of the property, that restriction or exclusion is to be taken into account only to the extent that consideration in money or money's worth was given for it.[3]

EXAMPLE

A grants B an option to buy Blackacre for £40,000 at any time in the next three years, its then market value. After two years when Blackacre's value ignoring the option is £80,000 A gives the land to B. A then dies so making the transfers chargeable rather than potentially exempt.

In calculating the value transferred when A gives the land to B the option is to be taken into account only to the value of the consideration given. If B paid £4,000, the then market value of the option, the value of Blackacre would be reduced to £76,000.

It will be seen that the option is ignored only on the next chargeable transfer, so if A had given the land to C the option would have been taken into account only to this limited extent. If C later gave the land to D the option would now be taken into account in full.

If the next transfer is not a chargeable one, eg because A gives the land to Mrs A, the rule would still apply to the next chargeable transfer of the land by Mrs A.

It will be seen that this rule applies even though the option is granted for full consideration. In effect the issue of whether or not there is a chargeable transfer and if so its extent is left in suspense until the next chargeable transfer.

Where the grant of the option is itself a chargeable transfer of value, a different rule applies—to avoid a double charge. An allowance is to be made on the next chargeable transfer for the value already transferred, ignoring any grossing up, or for so much of it as is attributable to the restriction.

EXAMPLE

P grants Q an option to buy Whiteacre at any time in the next three years for £50,000, its current market value. If Q paid nothing for the option which had a value of £5,000 that sum perhaps grossed up would have been chargeable on that occasion. If P later gave the land to Q when it was worth £90,000 there would be a deduction for the £5,000, making the value of the property £85,000. This would be so whether the original £5,000 were grossed up or were reduced by the annual exemption.

Simon's Direct Tax Service I8.231; Foster's Inheritance Tax H2.31.

[1] IRC v Crossman, IRC v Mann [1937] AC 26, [1936] 1 All ER 762; Lynall v IRC [1972] AC 680, [1971] 3 All ER 914, 47 TC 375.
[2] There is no question of IHTA 1984, s 163 applying. The case relied on by the Revenue is A-G (Ireland) v Jameson [1905] 2 IR 218.
[3] IHTA 1984, s 163.

Related property

[45.07] Where (a) there is a transfer of property, and (b) other property is related to it, and (c) the value of the property transferred is less than the value of the "appropriate portion" of that plus the related property, the value of the property transferred is that portion.[1] In determining the appropriate portion, the general rule is that the value of each property is taken as if it did not form part of the aggregate; however, this rule does not affect the calculation of the aggregate value.[2] Where shares of the same class are concerned, the appropriate proportion will be found by taking simply the number of shares.[3]

[1] IHTA 1984, s 161.
[2] IHTA 1984, s 161(3); this is not crystal clear, but is (undoubtedly) the official view.
[3] IHTA 1984, s 161(4). On definition of the same class see IHTA 1984, s 161(5).

[45.08] Property is related if (a) it forms part of the estate[1] of his spouse, or (b) it is property which has within the preceding five years been the property of a charity or other exempt body under an exempt transfer made by the transferor or his spouse. Under (b) the property remains related property, despite being disposed of by the trust or body, for a period of five years after that disposal.

The purpose of this rule is to prevent the avoidance of IHT through the use of exempt transfers. Thus if A holds 800 of the 1,000 shares of a family company and he transfers 350 of them to his son, there will be a transfer of value which will take account of the loss of control of the company.[2] However, if he transfers them to his wife the transfer will be exempt.[3] If he then gives a further 350 to his son he will be reducing a 45% holding to a 10% holding and so there will be no loss of control. This rule therefore provides that as the value of the property transferred—35%—is less than the appropriate portion of the aggregate of the holdings of A and Mrs A—35/80ths of an 80% holding, the value of the property transferred[4] will be 35/80ths of the value of their combined holdings. It will be seen that this rule applies whether it is A or Mrs A who makes the transfer to the son. However a subsequent transfer of her 35% holding by Mrs A to make the son's total up to 70% will only be a transfer of 35/45ths of a 45% holding so that IHT may be reduced by this procedure.

The purpose of group (b) is to prevent the loss of IHT arising on an exempt transfer which results in a loss of control. Thus if A holds 51% of the shares in a company and gives 2% to charity, he will have lost control of the company and perhaps reduced the value of the holding by 50%.

Although shares in a family company are the most likely objects of these rules, other assets caught will be collections and sets of valuable objects, property held jointly or by a partnership. It has been suggested that if a wife holds a lease and her husband the reversion, these rules do not apply. This seems to be doubtful.

Simon's Direct Tax Service I8.241; Foster's Inheritance Tax H2.41.

---

[1] Simon's Direct Tax Service I8.242; Foster's Inheritance Tax H2.42.
IHTA 1984, s 161. Note the wide definition of estate—excluded property is included. It should be noted that the settled estate is not related property. Inheritance tax is charged on the settled estates because IHTA 1984, s 49(1) deems the settled estate to be part of the estate at death.
[2] Supra, § **39.29**.
[3] Supra, § **43.06**.
[4] The actual value transferred will depend on who bears the tax.

Undoing related property valuation after death

[45.09] Where within three years of the death the executors or beneficiaries sell property which has been valued as related property, the value for IHT purposes can be recalculated as if the related property rules did not apply. This is needed to achieve fairness where for example shares are left to beneficiaries who are not related to the spouse.[1]

Thus if A had 80% of the shares in a company and transferred 35% to his wife, the transfer would be exempt and no IHT would be payable notwithstanding that A had lost control of the company. If A died his 45% holding would be valued as the appropriate portion (45/80ths) of the 80% holding. If, however, A's executors sold the 45% for the market value of a 45% holding the related property rule would be excluded; this does not necessarily mean taking the sale proceeds instead but rather the recalculation of the value at death.

To qualify for this relief the sale must be an arm's length sale for a price freely negotiated and not in conjunction with a sale of any of the related or other property to which the relief applies; there must be no provision for reacquisition and no person concerned as vendor (or having an interest in the proceeds of sale) may be the same as or connected with any person concerned as purchaser (or having an interest in the purchase). Further the vendors must be the deceased's personal representatives or those in whom the property vested immediately after the death.

An alteration in the company's share or loan capital or rights attached to shares or securities of a close company will disqualify the property from this relief if the effect of that alteration is to reduce the value of the property by more than 5%.

This relief applies also whenever property falls to be valued in conjunction with property which was also comprised in the deceased's estate but has not at any time since the death been vested in the vendors,[2] as where D held a 60% holding in a company and left half to A and half to B and A now sells his half.

[45.09] Valuation

Simon's Direct Tax Service I4.321–324.

[1] IHTA 1984, s 176(1)(a).
[2] IHTA 1984, s 176(1)(b).

Valuation of jointly owned property

[45.10] Husband and wife have lived in the marital home for many years, which they hold as tenants in common. Husband dies and, by his will[1], leaves his undivided half share to the next generation. Wife remains living in the house and is expected to do so for many years to come. What is the value of the husband's interest in the house for the purpose of computing inheritance tax at his death?

This was the question addressed by Dr Nuala Brice sitting as Special Commissioner in *Arkwright (Personal Representatives of Williams) v IRC*.[2]

On 20 June 1979 Bernard Everall Williams and his wife, Mrs Margaret Patricia Williams, purchased Ash Lane Farm as their matrimonial home. Mr and Mrs Williams held Ash Lane Farm as tenants in common in equal shares and occupied it together until the death of Mr Williams. Mr Williams died on 18 February 2001; Mrs Williams was then 79 years of age and in good health. The open market value of Ash Lane Farm immediately before the death of Mr Williams was £550,000. The Revenue were of the view that inheritance tax was due on one-half of that value, namely £275,000.

The Trusts of Land and Appointment of Trustees Act 1996, s 12[3] provides that a beneficiary who is beneficially entitled to an interest in land subject to a trust of land is entitled to occupy the land at any time if, at that time, the purposes of the trust include making the land available for his occupation or the land is held by the trustees so as to be so available; s 13(7) provides that the trustees may not prevent any person who is in occupation of land from continuing to occupy the land. As a result of these provisions, on the death of Mr Williams, Mrs Williams remained entitled to occupy Ash Lane Farm.

The valuation provision in the Inheritance Tax Act[4] states:

> On the death of any person tax shall be charged as if, immediately before his death, he had made a transfer of value and the value transferred by it had been equal to the value of his estate immediately before his death.

Immediately before his death Mr Williams owned a half share in the property which he could dispose of subject to the rights of Mrs Williams to occupy the property until she died.

Lynall v IRC[5] established the principle that the Inheritance Tax Act 1984 assumes an open market hypothetical sale to a hypothetical willing purchaser who has informed himself of all the available facts relating to the property. Applying this principle to the facts of the present case, the Special Commissioner accepted the argument of taxpayer's counsel that the hypothetical willing purchaser would discount the value of Mr Williams' interest to take account of the fact that the purchaser of that interest would be unable to

Related property [45.10]

benefit from his investment until Mrs Williams died. In valuing Mrs Williams' share the hypothetical purchaser would know that Mr Williams was older than she was and not in good health and that, after his death, Mrs Williams would have a right of continuing occupation. It followed that the value which a hypothetical willing purchaser would place on Mr Williams' share immediately before his death would be less than the value that the same hypothetical willing purchaser would place on the value of Mrs Williams' share immediately before the death of Mr Williams. The values of the two shares were not identical.

The Special Commissioner then considered the statutory provisions[6] for changes in value occurring on death:

(1) In determining the value of a person's estate immediately before his death changes in the value of his estate which have occurred by reason of the death and fall within subsection (2) below shall be taken into account as if they had occurred before the death.
(2) A change falls within this subsection if it is an addition to the property comprised in the estate or an increase or decrease of the value of any property so comprised . . . but the termination on the death of any interest or the passing of any interest by survivorship does not fall within this subsection.

In this case, the deceased's interest did not terminate on his death (as it passed to his two daughters) and as his interest did not pass by survivorship (but by his will, as amended by the deed of variation) the proviso cannot apply. Hence, the decrease in value of Mr Williams' interest in Ash Lane Farm which occurred by reason of his death has to be taken into account when determining the value of his interest immediately before his death.

The Special Commissioner then turned to the statutory provisions[7] for related property:

(1) Where the value of any property comprised in a person's estate would be less than the appropriate portion of the value of the aggregate of that and any related property, it shall be the appropriate portion of the value of that aggregate.
(2) For the purposes of this section, property is related to the property comprised in a person's estate if –
 (a) it is comprised in the estate of his spouse . . .

In this case Mrs Williams' interest as tenant in common of Ash Lane Farm was related property within the meaning of s 161(2)(a) as it was property related to Mr Williams' interest.

The effect of s 161(1) and (3) is that, where there is related property, it is first necessary to determine the value of the aggregate of the deceased's property and the related property taken together (the aggregate). It is then necessary to value the deceased's property and the related property separately as if they did not form part of the aggregate and, from those two values, to establish a ratio. That ratio is then applied to the aggregate and, if the value of the deceased's part of the aggregate is greater than the value of his property taken separately, it is his part of the aggregate which is taken as the value of his property.

The conclusion[8] of the Special Commissioner was stated succinctly:[9]

[I conclude] that the value of Mr Williams' interest in Ash Lane Farm was less than a mathematical one-half of the vacant possession value and that it should be valued

[45.10] Valuation

taking into account: (a) the rights of occupation given to Mrs Williams by the 1996 Act; (b) the decrease in the value of Mr Williams' interest which occurred by reason of his death; and (c) the related property provisions, namely the value of the aggregate; the value of each share separately and the ratio; and the application of the ratio to the aggregate.

In the High Court[10] Gloster J held that the Special Commissioner was correct in deciding the point of law but exceeded her jurisdiction in reaching a conclusion on the valuation issue:[11]

> Whilst in my judgment the Special Commissioner was clearly entitled to conclude that, because s 161(4) did not apply, the value of the deceased's interest in the property was not inevitably a mathematical one-half of the vacant possession value, it was not for her to go on to determine . . . as a matter of fact, the value of his interest was indeed less than a mathematical one-half of the vacant possession value. That was properly an issue that should have been referred to the Lands Tribunal[12] for determination by it. . . . The Revenue does not criticise the proposition that a purchaser might take into account the fact that Mrs Williams had rights under the 1996 Act and that, accordingly, the valuation of the deceased's half-share might be adversely affected by the existence of such rights. What it says, however, is that this was not a matter for the Special Commissioner to decide; that there was no evidence before her that such rights were a matter (let alone the only matter) which a purchaser would take into account in valuing a beneficial half-share in land; and that accordingly, whether such rights did impact on the valuation of the deceased's half-share should have been left to the Lands Tribunal to decide.
>
> In my judgment, the Revenue's criticism in this respect is also well founded. Whether a notional purchaser of the deceased's half-share might take the existence of Mrs Williams' rights under the 1996 Act into account and, if so, how this would affect the value, was a valuation issue that should have been referred to the Lands Tribunal to decide on appropriate evidence.

The case was subsequently compromised by the parties before a decision could be reached by the Lands Tribunal.[13]

---

1. In fact, in this case, the passing of the half interest was a consequence of a deed of variation which was accepted by the Special Commissioner as having effect in the same way as if it had been made in the original will. Clause 2(a)(1) of his will gave to Mrs Williams a life interest in that 50% share with the remainder to his daughters. By Deed of Variation of 6 January 2002 Mrs Williams and her two daughters deleted clause 2(a)(1) of the will so that Mr Williams interest in Ash Lane Farm vested in his daughters.
2. [2004] STC (SCD) 89.
3. Trusts of Land and Appointment of Trustees Act 1996 ss 12 & 13 state:

   Section 12: The right to occupy

   (1) A beneficiary who is beneficially entitled to an interest in possession in land subject to a trust of land is entitled by reason of his interest to occupy the land at any time if . . .
   (b) the land is held by the trustees so as to be so available.
   (2) Subsection (1) does not confer on a beneficiary a right to occupy land if it is either unavailable or unsuitable for occupation by him.
   (3) This section is subject to section 13.

   Section 13: Exclusion and restriction of right to occupy

(1) Where two or more beneficiaries are (or apart from this subsection would be) entitled under section 12 to occupy land, the trustees of land may exclude or restrict the entitlement of any one or more (but not all) of them.
(2) Trustees may not under subsection (1) –
　(a) unreasonably exclude any beneficiary's entitlement to occupy land, or
　(b) restrict any such entitlement to an unreasonable extent. . . .
(3) The powers conferred on trustees by this section may not be exercised –
　(a) so as to prevent any person who is in occupation of land (whether or not by reason of an entitlement under section 12) from continuing to occupy the land, or
　(b) in a manner likely to result in any such person ceasing to occupy the land, unless he consents or the court has given approval.

[4] IHTA 1984, s 4(1).
[5] (1971) 47 TC 375, HL.
[6] IHTA 1984, s 171.
[7] IHTA 1984, s 161.
[8] This appeal also considered the separate question of jurisdiction on questions of valuation. The Revenue submitted that the appeal should be struck out as the question for determination was a question of the value of land, which could only be determined by the Lands Tribunal. Dr Nuala Brice held that Special Commissioners (Jurisdiction and Procedure) Regulations 1994, SI 1994/1811, reg 23(2)(a) requires the Special Commissioners to determine all questions other than questions as to the value of land and the questions raised by the instant case are not questions as to the value of any land but rather questions as to the interpretation of the legislation. She then gave a ruling that the parties should first attempt to agree the value of Mr Williams' interest on the above basis. If they cannot agree then they should apply to the Special Commissioners for a reference to be made to the Lands Tribunal.
[9] Para 72 at 102j/103a. A fuller version of the conclusion is given also at paras 47 and 48, 98g/j.
[10] [2004] STC 1323.
[11] ITHA 1984, s 222(4A) gives the Lands Tribunal jurisdiction "if and so far as the question in dispute on any appeal . . . is a question as to the value of land in the United Kingdom".
[12] Paras 12, 14 and 15 at 1139b/1139j–1340b.
[13] See also Revenue & Customs Brief 71/07.

Relief for loss after death

[45.11] For two types of property only there is relief available where the property is sold after death for a price that is lower than at the date of death. This relief only applies to sales of shares (more strictly a "qualifying investment") and sales of land. In each case there are strict conditions that have to be fulfilled for the relief to be available.

Relief for sales of shares at a loss following transfer on death

[45.12] Where investments are the subject of a transfer on death[1] the general rule is that for IHT they carry the value they bore immediately before the

[45.12] Valuation

death. If, however, qualifying investments are sold at a lower value within 12 months of the death, the lower value may be used instead.[2]

Where the sale is preceded by a contract, the date of sale is that of the contract.[3] If it results from the exercise of an option, the critical date is that of the grant of the option.

The relief applies to any shares forming part of his estate on death, whether free estate or settled property, save for shares held by a company in which the deceased had a controlling interest.

The relief applies only to qualifying investments,[4] ie broadly, quoted shares and securities and units in authorised unit trusts.

Qualifying investments which are in the estate immediately before the death but which were cancelled within the next 12 months without being replaced are to be treated as sold for a nominal consideration immediately before the cancellation.[5] The shares must have been held by the appropriate person at the cancellation. When shares are suspended within 12 months of the death and are still suspended on the first anniversary of the death the value that is taken for the purpose of computing this relief is the market value on that anniversary.[6]

Simon's Direct Tax Service I4.301–309; Foster's Inheritance Tax D3.01–09.

[1] IHTA 1984, Part VI, Chapter III.
[2] IHTA 1984, s 179(1).
[3] IHTA 1984, s 189.
[4] IHTA 1984, s 178; on suspended shares, see IHTA 1984, ss 178(2), 186B; on meaning of quoted and unquoted see IHTA 1984, s 272 as amended by FA 1987, Sch 8, para 17; securities listed on the USM are now treated as quoted.
[5] IHTA 1984, s 186A.
[6] IHTA 1984, s 186B.

[45.13] Where more than one sale of qualifying investments takes place within the 12-month period, all such sums received must be aggregated to determine the relief. If the sum is less than the principal value at the date of death, the difference, called the loss on sale, is deducted from the value at death.[1] So if an estate includes eight blocks of shares, each worth £1,000 at the date of death, and in the next 12 months three blocks are sold at £700, £900 and £1,050 respectively, the loss on sale is £3,000 − £2,650 = £350 and the value will be reduced to £7,650.

In making these calculations the Revenue may substitute for the actual sale price the best consideration which could reasonably have been obtained.[2] Any commission or stamp duty[3] and, in accordance with general principles,[4] any expenses of sale and any capital gains liability are all ignored. There are rules for bringing into account both capital sums received[5] and calls made[6] in respect of the investments between the death and the sale.

Under no circumstances can any investment be treated as being sold at a loss greater than its basic value at the date of death.[7] This might occur if calls were made and the shares then sold for a low price.

Relief for loss after death [45.15]

Simon's Direct Tax Service I4.302, 303; Foster's Inheritance Tax D3.02, 03.

[1] IHTA 1984, s 179; on effect of sale of part of a holding, see IHTA 1984, s 186.
[2] IHTA 1984, s 179(1): this rule is to be ignored for cancelled and suspended shares; ss 186A(2), 186B(3) inserted by FA 1993, s 198.
[3] IHTA 1984, s 178(5).
[4] See infra, § **45.21**.
[5] IHTA 1984, s 181.
[6] IHTA 1984, s 182.
[7] IHTA 1984, s 188.

[45.14] To claim relief, the sale must have been carried out by the appropriate person.[1] This is the person liable for the tax in respect of the investments,[2] that is the executors, trustees or the beneficiary. If only one of them is paying the tax he is the appropriate person. For this purpose the personal representatives of the estate and the trustees of a settlement are each treated as a single and continuing body of persons.[3] The very fact that a person holds property subject to a charge for the tax is sufficient to make him—as well as the property—liable and so he is an appropriate person.[4]

Simon's Direct Tax Service I4.301; Foster's Inheritance Tax D3.01.

[1] IHTA 1984, s 179(1).
[2] IHTA 1984, s 178.
[3] IHTA 1984, s 178(4).
[4] IHTA 1984, s 200(1)(c).

[45.15] The primary reason for the relief was to provide for the case where securities having been valued at death had then to be sold in order to pay the tax and were sold at a loss. The relief is not confined to such sales. Relief may be claimed simply because of a change in investments. However, where new shares or securities are bought the relief may be extinguished or reduced.[1] This will occur if the purchases take place within the period beginning at the date of death and ending two months after the last sale within the 12-month period. Where the purchase is by a personal representative or trustee then all the purchases of qualifying investments are aggregated. This forms the numerator of a fraction whose denominator is the total sales figure for the qualifying investments sold since the death, taking actual price obtained or the best consideration that could have been obtained as above. This fraction is then applied to the loss on sale and only the proportion of that loss remaining after taking away the fraction is eligible for relief. Thus suppose that the proceeds of sale come to £3,000 giving a loss on sale of £600 and that £1,000 is then reinvested. The fraction will be 1,000/3,000. The relief will therefore be reduced by one-third to £400.

If the reinvestment is carried out by someone other than a trustee or personal representative, the loss claim will be reduced only if the purchase is of the same description as the investments sold.[2] Investments are not of the same description if they are quoted separately on a recognised stock exchange or dealt in

[45.15] Valuation

separately on the Unlisted Securities Market or Alternative Investment Market, nor if they are different authorised unit trusts.[3] A person selling Lloyds Bank shares could therefore purchase Midland Bank shares the next day without imperilling his claim for relief.

Where shares or securities are exchanged for other property and the market value of the investments at the time of the exchange is greater than their value on death, that market value is taken into account.[4]

Special rules apply to ignore certain transactions which relate more to the form than the substance of an investment, for example a reorganisation or reduction of the share capital or the conversion of securities.[5] These transactions are only partly ignored if the appropriate person has to give new consideration for the new holding. If the new holding is itself sold within 12 months of the death, the sale is treated in the normal way.

Simon's Direct Tax Service I4.304–309; Foster's Inheritance Tax D3.04–09.

[1] IHTA 1984, s 180(1) distinguish subscribing for new shares *Re VGM Holdings Ltd* [1942] Ch 235, [1942] 1 All ER 224.
[2] IHTA 1984, s 180(1).
[3] IHTA 1984, s 180(3). Shares on the USM and AIM are treated as unquoted for the purpose of business property relief (see supra, § **44.01**, note 12) but this does not change the basis of valuation.
[4] IHTA 1984, s 184.
[5] IHTA 1984, s 183.

Land

Relief for sales at a loss following transfer on death

[45.16] For deaths on or after 16 March 1990 where an interest in land was included in a person's estate immediately before his death and was later sold within four[1] years of the death and the sale price was less than the value at the date of death, the sale price can be substituted if the "appropriate person" so claims.[2] The costs of sale are ignored.[3] The effect is, thus, that whenever this relief is claimed for IHT, a loss arises for CGT equal to the costs of sale. This recognition of a decline in value after the death applies only where the sale is by the appropriate person, is not to a beneficiary of the estate or one of his near relatives and the vendor has no right to repurchase the interest sold or any other interest in the same land.[4] The sale price is not necessarily conclusive since the Revenue will substitute the best consideration that could reasonably have been obtained for it at the time of the sale, if this would be greater. This relief is not to apply if the decline in the value of the interest is £1,000 or 5% of the value at death, whichever is the lower; however a drop of £1,001 will be recognised in full.

EXAMPLE

A's estate included four pieces of land, two of which were sold in the months following his death.

Land [45.16]

	Value at date of death £	Sale value £	Profit or loss £
Property 1	10,500	7,750	(2,750)
Property 2	16,000	16,200	200
Property 3	18,000	17,850	(150)
Property 4	23,000	23,900	900
	67,500	65,700	(1,800)

Although the total loss is £1,800, the gain on property 2 (£200) and the loss on property 3 (£150) are ignored because they are neither £1,000 nor 5% of the value of the properties at death. The adjusted overall loss is therefore increased to £1,850.

An interest in land is not defined. While an interest in the proceeds of sale is in practice treated as an interest in land, neither an interest in a company owning land nor an interest in unadministered residue appear to qualify.

In deciding whether the sale is within four years of the death the critical date is that of the contract to sell; if the sale results from the exercise of an option to sell, the date will be the exercise of the option unless the exercise was within six months of the grant in which case the date of grant is preferred.[5]

If land in an estate at date of death is subject to the compulsory purchase order, under which the value receivable is less than the valuation at death, a claim can be made to reduce the valuation of the land to the sum payable under the compulsory purchase order as long as the order is made within three years of the date of death (although the eventual conveyance may be at a later time).[6]

All sales within the period must be brought into account to determine the overall loss.

In order for the relief to be claimed, there must be an actual sale. An abortive sale will not do.[7]

Particularly where an IHT relief is available, it may be advantageous to increase the value used for IHT to equal the higher subsequent sale proceeds and, thus, cancel a CGT charge. Statute does not permit an increase; the essence of the provision is that it is a relief, not an adjustment.[8]

Simon's Direct Tax Service I4.311–313; Foster's Inheritance Tax D3.11–13.

---

[1] The time limit of four years has some exceptions: see IHTA 1984, s 197A.
[2] IHTA 1984, ss 191, 197A. IHTA 1984, s 190(4).
[3] IHTA 1984, s 191(1) directs that the value for IHT when this claim is made "shall ... be its sale value". IHTA 1984, s 190(1) then, unhelpfully, states that "sale value" means "sale price" and defines "sale price" as "the price for which it is sold". The denial of relief for the costs of sale is consistent with the approach taken in ascertaining market value for IHT purposes. In *Duke of Buccluch v IRC* [1967] 1 AC 506, [1967] 1 All ER 129, HL, Lord Guest said (at para 56): 'The words "price the property would fetch" mean in s 7(5) [FA 1894] that it is not the price which the vendor would have received but what the purchaser would have paid to be put into the shoes of the deceased. This means that the costs of realisation do not

[45.16] Valuation

form a legitimate deduction in arriving at the valuation.'
4   IHTA 1984, s 191.
5   IHTA 1984, s 198.
6   IHTA 1984, s 197; FA 1993 s 199(1)(b).
7   *Jones v IRC* [1997] STC 358.
8   *Stoner and anor (exors of Dickinson, dec'd) v IRC* [2001] STC (SCD) 199.

Adjustments and restrictions

[45.17] In comparing the sale price with the value at date of death a number of adjustments may have to be made:

(1) Any change in the interest in land arising between the death and the sale must be taken into account;[1] likewise, if the interest is a lease with less than 50 years to run, the value is increased to take account of the inevitable loss due to the passage of time.[2] This is to ensure that the two values are compared on the same basis.

(2) Where on the death other interests, whether in the same or other land, were taken into account, eg where the other interest is related property, the excess attributable to that other value must be brought into account again by being added to the sale price.[3]

(3) Where other interests in land in the estate are sold by the claimant in the same capacity, that is as personal representative or as beneficiary, any gains on such sales must be set off against the loss. If the claim relates to more than one interest, the gains are apportioned between the interests. The same applies to a sale to a connected person.[4]

(4) If the claimant reinvests in land, that is if he buys other land within the period beginning with the death and ending four months after the last sale in respect of which relief is claimed, then, if the aggregate of the purchase prices (A) exceeds the aggregate of the sales (B) no relief may be claimed. If A does not exceed B the fraction A/B is applied to the sale price and the resulting sum is added to it.[5] In applying this rule no account is to be taken of a sale in the fourth year.[6] When a claim relates only to sales in the fourth year, rule 4 is not to apply.[7]

If in consequence of all or any of these rules the sale price should be reduced, that reduction must be carried out.[8]

Simon's Direct Tax Service I4.314–319; Foster's Inheritance Tax D3.14–19.

1   IHTA 1984, s 193.
2   IHTA 1984, s 194.
3   IHTA 1984, s 195.
4   IHTA 1984, s 196.
5   IHTA 1984, s 192.
6   IHTA 1984, s 197A(3).
7   IHTA 1984, s 197A(3).
8   IHTA 1984, s 192(4).

Debts due to the transferor

[45.18] In valuing the debt it is assumed that the debt will be paid in full unless and to the extent that recovery of the sum is impossible or not reasonably practicable. Even then recovery will be assumed if the non-recoverability is due to any act or omission on his part.[1]

Where a debt thought at the death of the creditor to be irrecoverable is subsequently paid, the debt will on payment become part of the deceased's estate and so will be added to it.

Simon's Direct Tax Service I8.372; Foster's Inheritance Tax H3.72.

---

[1] IHTA 1984, s 166.

Accrued income to date of transfer

[45.19] Included in the valuation of an estate is income upon the property included therein that has accrued up to the relevant date, usually the death of the transferor.[1]

In the case of quoted securities, which are not ex-dividend, the accrued income is included in the valuation and does not have to be accounted for separately. In all other cases, such as land producing rents, income which is accruing due at the date of transfer must be apportioned, and the proportion (less income tax, if deductible) up to the relevant date included in the estate.

Simon's Direct Tax Service I8.373.

---

[1] There is no express provision similar to FA 1894, s 6(5) which applied for estate duty; however if this income were not included there would have been no need for FA 1975, Sch 12, para 16(2) amending TA 1970, s 430 (now TA 1988, s 699); supra, § **14.01**.

Liabilities

[45.20] Liabilities fall to be taken into account[1] and valued either to determine the overall value of an estate, whether of the transferor or someone else, or to determine the loss to that estate when a liability is incurred.

In *Hardcastle v IRC*,[2] an underwriting member of Lloyd's had accrued losses of £301,311 at the date of his death. He held an estate protection plan policy but the maximum payable under this was some £50,000 less than the losses. The Revenue contended that the £50,000 excess was a reduction in the value of the Lloyds underwriting business which, therefore, reduced the value on which 100% business property relief was claimed.[3] The Special Commissioner determined that the £50,000 excess liability was a liability of the total estate

[45.20] Valuation

and deductible from the aggregates of assets chargeable to inheritance tax; it was not a reduction in the value of the asset that attracted relief.

Where the estate had free estate and settled estate, the liabilities can only be set against the category of estate to which they relate. In *St Barbe Green v IRC*[4] the 12th Duke of Manchester died with assets of £4,600 and liabilities of around £49,000. He was life tenant of two settlements in which there were assets of some £340,000. In the High Court, Mann J held that the correct calculation was to put the personal liabilities against the personal assets and determine the free estate at £0 and then add to it the settled estate of £340,000, in order to calculate the inheritance tax arising as a consequence of the death of the 12th Duke of Manchester. There was no provision allowing for excess liabilities to be transferred from the free estate to the settled estate.

It should be noted that the settled estate is not related property. Inheritance tax is charged on the settled estate because statute[5] deems the settled estate to be part of the estate at death.

Simon's Direct Tax Service I3.231–239; Foster's Inheritance Tax C2.31–39.

[1] IHTA 1984, s 5(3).
[2] [2000] STC (SCD) 532.
[3] See supra, § **43.06**.
[4] [2005] EWHC 14 (Ch), [2005] STC 288.
[5] IHTA 1984, s 49(1).

Liabilities incurred by the transferor

[45.21] These are in general allowable deductions provided that, and then only to the extent that, they were incurred for a consideration in money or money's worth.[1] This proviso does not apply to liabilities imposed by law.

It is not sufficient to show that payment is made under a legal obligation of the transferor, eg by reason of the covenant being under seal; the subsequent discharge of the obligation will be the chargeable transfer. Deduction is excluded, because the consideration was not money or money's worth.

Payments by a husband to his wife under a valid deed of separation may continue during the life of the wife, whether or not the husband predeceases her. On the death of the husband, the wife being still alive, future covenanted payments are a debt of his estate. The payments are for full consideration in money or money's worth, since he would have had to pay larger amounts during his lifetime had he not entered into a covenant binding on his executors.

Where the liability is incurred for a consideration in money or money's worth it is not necessary that that consideration should move to the transferor. Thus if A agrees to sell a chair worth £500 for that sum on condition that the proceeds of sale are paid to B, but dies before making delivery, the liability to transfer the chair is an allowable deduction in valuing A's estate. Equally of course the direction to pay £500 to B would, if discharged before A's death, itself have been a separate transfer of value.

In these instances, however, deduction is allowed only to the extent of the consideration in money or money's worth. Suppose therefore that A has agreed to buy a chair worth £500 from B for £800. The liability to pay £800 is deductible only to the extent of £500 and so not allowable as to £300.

Simon's Direct Tax Service I3.231; Foster's Inheritance Tax C2.31.

---

[1] IHTA 1984, s 5(5).

Incumbrances created by the transferor

[45.22] A liability which is an incumbrance[1] on any property is as far as possible taken to reduce the value of that property.[2] If a husband leaves the matrimonial home to his widow subject to a mortgage, the transfer to the widow is exempt and the debt to the lender is taken as reducing the value of the property transferred to the widow and so will be ignored in computing the value of the rest of the estate unless the debt is greater than the value of the house. It will be seen that the rule talks of a liability which is an incumbrance. The husband in our example is liable to the building society for the sum owed and this liability is personal as well as being an incumbrance on the house itself. It is not open to him to deduct his personal debt as distinct from the sum secured by the incumbrance since there is only one liability and that is an incumbrance on the property.

The rule is also important when one comes to liability for the tax. Property bearing its own tax may find the burden greatly reduced and the Inland Revenue charge will be for a lower sum.

It is to be assumed that where the debt is properly payable out of more than one item of property, the person liable to pay the debt must apportion the liability.

Simon's Direct Tax Service I3.232; Foster's Inheritance Tax C2.32.

---

[1] Defined in IHTA 1984, s 272.
[2] IHTA 1984, s 162(4).

The estate immediately before death

[45.23] With the introduction of IHT it became necessary to revive certain estate duty rules for determining the value of a person's estate immediately before death. A debt or incumbrance incurred or made after 17 March 1986[1] is to be disallowed to the extent to which the consideration given for it is property derived from the transferor.[2] This rule is widened to cover the situation in which the consideration is given not for the very property derived from the deceased but from the economic value which that property represents. So the provision also applies to disallow the deduction where there is consideration given by any person who was at any time entitled to property derived from the deceased or among whose resources such property was at any time to be found.[3]

[45.23] Valuation

This rule is aimed at the simple device of a loanback.[4] Two examples may be given. First a father gives money to his son; some time later the son lends it back to his father; when the father dies the loan would, but for this rule, be an allowable deduction. Second, the same father wishes to give his son some property but wishes at the same time to keep control of it and retain the income from it. If he makes a gift of the property on these terms there will be a gift with reservation. If, however, he gives the property to his son and then buys it back and leaves the purchase price outstanding, the value of the property, which would still form part of his estate as property to which he is beneficially entitled would, but for this rule, be reduced by the amount of the debt. The prohibition on the deduction of debts incurred otherwise than for full consideration (supra, § 45.21) would not apply as there would be full consideration. In these two examples, therefore, deduction of the debt is disallowed by this rule.

The expression "property derived from the deceased" is defined widely to cover property which was the subject matter of a disposition by the deceased whether by him alone or in concert with others whether directly or indirectly and including any property which represented the subject matter of such a disposition.[5] The term disposition includes disposition by associated operations.[6]

This wide definition of property derived from the deceased is not without its difficulties. Thus if the father gives his son a house which the son sells and the son then uses the proceeds to buy shares[7] it appears that there are three sets of property ready to trigger this rule should the father buy them and not have paid the debt before he dies viz the house, the price and the shares. There is nothing in the legislation to state that only the house is to be taken as the property derived from the father or that it is replaced by the shares.

This very wide definition is then narrowed by a provision that it cannot apply to a disposition which is not a transfer of value.[8]

So if the father gives the property to the son as in the previous example the deduction will be disallowed but if he sells the property for full value and later buys it back and the price is left outstanding, the debt will be an allowable deduction. It will be seen that if the initial sale by the father is at an undervalue the rule will apply.

Simon's Direct Tax Service I4.151–154; Foster's Inheritance Tax D1.51–54.

---

[1] FA 1986, s 103(6).
[2] FA 1986, s 103(1)(*a*); the provision re-enacts FA 1939, s 31. The provision is explored by the Special Commissioner in *Phizackerley v Revenue and Customs Comrs* [2007] STC (SCD) 328 where the deduction of the debts was denied. In that case, a joint tenancy was severed four years before death.
[3] FA 1986, s 103(1)(*b*); it is most unclear what is added by the idea of property "found" amongst his resources.
[4] See McCutcheon *Inheritance Tax* (3rd edn) §§ 13.56 ff; the so called "inheritance trust" is a further example popular in the days of CTT. F would lend money to trustees of a trust for his children; the trustees would buy a single premium insurance bond; they would withdraw 5% pa as allowed as tax-free return of

capital (see supra, § 31.29) and pay this to the father; thus the capital would enure to the children with no CTT other than that (if any) due on the creation of the trust and the father would enjoy a tax free 5% return until the debt was paid off.

[5] FA 1986, s 103(3); the term "subject matter" is defined in s 103(6) to include annual or periodical payments due under the disposition.
[6] IHTA 1984, s 272.
[7] The problem is raised by Venables *Inheritance Tax Planning* § 2.4.4.6. Presumably the problem will arise whether the father buys back the house from the son or buys it from someone else.
[8] FA 1986, s 103(4); it is also necessary that the disposition should not be part of associated operations designed to circumvent this rule.

[45.24] It will be recalled that the liability is also disallowed if the consideration for the debt was given by any person who was then entitled to any property derived from the deceased or among whose resources the property was at any time to be found. The formula for determining the disallowance involves an abatement of the liability otherwise deductible to an extent proportionate to the value of any consideration given which consists of the property derived directly or indirectly from the transferor.[1] This is needed for situations in which the amount of the debt and that of the consideration do not correspond.

So if the father gives the son a house and the son does not sell the house but lends the father money this rule applies to the extent that the father's liability to repay falls within the value of the house;[2] so if the house is worth £50,000 and the son lends the father £40,000 there is no deduction for the liability to repay in calculating the value of the father's estate; if the loan is for £60,000 there is a disallowance to the extent of £50,000.

One matter not addressed in the legislation is the problem of timing. Where the property in respect of which the liability arises is the same as that received under the original transfer of value, ie when the first rule applies, there is no problem and the change in the value of the property will have to be taken into account. What is not clear is how matters will be treated under the second rule. Thus in the example just considered what is to happen if the house was worth £50,000 at the time of the transfer but is worth £60,000 when the son makes the loan back? In applying this rule one is to exclude such property which is not derived from the deceased (but only brought in under the wider formula) "as to which it is shown that the disposition of which it, or the property which it represented, was the subject matter was not made with reference to, or with a view to enabling or facilitating, the giving of the consideration or the recoupment in any manner of the cost thereof."[3] So, to continue with the same generous father, let us suppose that the father gives his son a house and some shares and the son later sells his father the shares and some other property and the sums due have not been paid at the time the father dies. The general rule will apply in relation to the debt due in respect of the shares[4] but in relation to the other property the present exclusion rule will exclude the liability (ie permit its deduction after all) if it can be shown that the gift of the house was not made to enable the other property to be sold to the father; if this cannot be shown then the liability in respect of the other property will be non-deductible subject to an upper limit equal to the value of the house.

[45.24] Valuation

This rule will also be relevant if the son should sell the house to a stranger and the father should subsequently buy property from that stranger and die with the liability still outstanding. However, it appears that this rule has no relevance if the father should buy the house from the stranger and leave the liability outstanding when he dies.[5]

Simon's Direct Tax Service I4.151–154; Foster's Inheritance Tax D1.51–54.

[1] FA 1986, s 103(2); no "abatement", ie disallowance is made to the extent that the father's liability to repay exceeds the value of the property.
[2] It will be noted that what is at issue is the value of the property derived by the son from the father; this may be a quite different value from that of the loss of the father's estate.
[3] FA 1986, s 103(2)(*b*).
[4] FA 1986, s 103(2)(*a*).
[5] Because of FA 1986, s 103(2)(*a*).

[45.25] To reinforce this legislative strategy it is provided that the *repayment* of a loan which is non-deductible by reason of the rules just outlined is to be treated as a transfer of value; the only relief is that the transfer is to be treated as potentially exempt and so will not cause a charge if the payment occurs more than seven years before the payer's death.[1] To continue the example of father and son, suppose that the father gives the property to the son and buys it back leaving the purchase price outstanding but later pays off the debt. The son is better off to the extent of the payment of the debt and the father has reduced his estate by a similar amount. If the father dies within seven years IHT may become due.

This rule causes some surprises. Thus if the father gives a house to his son who sells it to a stranger and the father later buys it from the stranger and dies without paying the debt there will, as already seen, be no deduction for the liability. What this rule seems to say is that if the liability is paid off there will be a chargeable transfer if the father should die within seven years.[2]

This rule is also difficult in that it fails to define when there is a liability, a matter of some importance as it applies only where there is a liability which is discharged. The intention is to reinforce the rule barring the deduction of a liability remaining unpaid at the date of death. If therefore no liability is created the rule cannot apply. So if the father buys the property back from the son and does not leave the money outstanding but pays the price at the same time as—or before—the date of performance it appears that this rule cannot apply. One wonders whether a few days delay in settling the debt will be enough to trigger the present rule or whether some clear intention to allow time to pay will be required.

Simon's Direct Tax Service I4.151–154; Foster's Inheritance Tax D1.51–54.

[1] FA 1986, s 103(5).
[2] See Venables, *Inheritance Tax Planning*, § 2.4.4.10.

Other debts and incumbrances

[45.26] In the case of debts which were not incurred, and incumbrances which were not created, by the transferor himself, but for which he or the property is liable, allowance is made whether or not the debts were incurred or the incumbrances created for consideration. Thus, if the deceased had acquired property subject to a mortgage, the mortgage money would be deductible even if the mortgagee received his mortgage as a gift from the previous owner of the property. Future liabilities must be discounted.[1]

Simon's Direct Tax Service I3.237; Foster's Inheritance Tax C2.37.

[1] IHTA 1984, s 162(3).

Unenforceable debts

[45.27] If neither the executor nor anyone else is liable to pay the debt, nor is it charged on any property, then no deduction is allowed.

In *Re Barnes*,[1] the deceased had made gifts inter vivos within the statutory period before death rendering them liable to estate duty, amounting to £185,000. He died leaving assets worth £12 and debts and funeral expenses amounting to £90,000. It was held that estate duty was payable on the value of the gifts inter vivos without deduction of the debts and funeral expenses, because those liabilities were neither chargeable on the gifts nor payable by the donees. It was immaterial that the donees in fact paid the debts.

For the same reason, debts which are unenforceable, such as gaming debts, debts under illegal contracts, and debts of which evidence in writing required by statute is absent, are not allowable. Statute-barred debts, which an executor may pay if he chooses, are not apparently allowable if actually paid.[2]

No allowance is to be made for any debt in respect whereof there is a right to reimbursement from any other estate or person, unless such reimbursement cannot reasonably be expected to be obtained.[3]

Debts incurred or incumbrances created by the executor, such as administration expenses, not being debts of the deceased, are not deductible.

Simon's Direct Tax Service I3.235; Foster's Inheritance Tax C2.35.

[1] [1939] 1 KB 316, [1938] 4 All ER 870.
[2] *Norton v Frecker* (1737) 1 Atk 524.
[3] IHTA 1984, s 162(1).

Interaction with other taxes

[45.28] Where A makes a chargeable transfer of property to B both IHT and CGT may arise. The following rules should be borne in mind. In deciding whether the IHT should be borne by A or by B one should also note that IHT may be paid by instalments if B pays this tax, infra, § **46.14**.

[45.28] Valuation

(1) Where the IHT is borne by A it may have to be grossed up. This is because the transferor's liability to tax resulting from the transfer is to be taken into account in determining the value of his estate immediately after the transfer.[1] Where the tax is borne by B there is no grossing up. In potentially exempt transfers there is no grossing up.

(2) Where CGT falls due, and is borne by A, no deduction can be made on account of the CGT in calculating the value for IHT.[2] So where the transfer gives rise to a liability to CGT (a) the value transferred is the value of the asset grossed up as necessary to take account of the IHT but not the CGT, but (b) equally the amount payable by way of CGT is not deductible in computing the value transferred. The reason for (a) is self-evident. The reason for (b) is to prevent anomalies. If A transfers an asset worth £5,000 on which there is a capital gains liability of £1,000, his liability to CGT and IHT should be the same as where he sells the asset for £5,000 and then transfers the proceeds of sale. It should be noticed that the liability to CGT is ignored only in determining the value of the estate immediately after the transfer. So if A should die the day after making the transfer his liability to CGT on the previous transfer would be deductible in computing the value of his estate.

Quite different rules apply when the tax is borne by B; there the tax paid by B is deductible in computing the value transferred. It should be noted that this is deductible whether it is A or B who actually pays the IHT.

Similar rules apply to the payment of incidental expenses; they are deductible only if borne by B.[3]

(3) Where CGT arises but an election to defer the CGT liability was made under the now repealed FA 1980, s 79[4] and IHT also arises, the IHT will be deductible in computing the chargeable gain on a subsequent disposal by B but only to the extent of wiping out a chargeable gain; the IHT cannot be used to create a loss. This applies even though the IHT is borne by A; in this instance the IHT is that due after the grossing up rules have been applied. If the IHT is subsequently increased through A dying within seven (in practice not more than five) years of the gift adjustments are made to the CGT to give effect to the extra deduction now due. A similar rule applies where the transfer is potentially exempt but tax becomes due because the donor dies within seven years.

Where a value is "ascertained" for IHT, that value is used in a CGT computation on a sale by the person taking the property, see supra, § **19.02**.

Income and other taxes due from and repayments of such taxes due to the estate must be taken into account.[5]

An outstanding liability to pay tax on an earlier transfer tax (whether CTT or IHT) is deductible on death only if actually paid out of the estate.[6]

Foreign taxes are generally allowed only as deductions from foreign property.[7]

Simon's Direct Tax Service I3.252, 253; Foster's Inheritance Tax C2.52, 53.

---

[1] IHTA 1984, s 5(4) On settled property, see IHTA 1984, s 165.
[2] IHTA 1984, s 165.

3   IHTA 1984, s 164.
4   Repealed by FA 1989, Sch 17, Part VII but effect preserved for disposals before 14 March 1989.
5   On complications of repayments to a married man see *Re Ward, Harrison v Ward* [1922] 1 Ch 517.
6   IHTA 1984, s 174(2).
7   Because not enforceable in the UK; infra, § **47.21**.

Valuation of debts due from the estate

[45.29] There is no statutory provision stating how debts owing by the transferor are to be valued. It is, therefore, a matter of finding how much money was really owing at the date of transfer, or, in the case of liabilities of uncertain amounts and contingent liabilities, of estimating the value of the debt as at the date of transfer in the light of circumstances which then exist.[1] In the case of a certain liability which is not to mature until a future date, the amount will have to be discounted according to the time which is to elapse before maturity.[2]

Any payments in advance, which fell due before the transfer, but are unpaid at the transfer, are proper deductions. The value obtained by advance payment is not taxable as an asset of the estate, unless it is capable of being turned into money. For example, if council tax had been payable in advance before the date of death, the amount (if not paid) would be a proper deduction from his estate. The value to the estate of the rates paid in advance would not be included unless the executors were reasonably able to obtain a cash advantage therefrom by arrangements with an incoming occupier.

Simon's Direct Tax Service I4.114; Foster's Inheritance Tax D1.14.

1   IHTA 1984, s 162(2).
2   IHTA 1984, s 162(2).

Funeral expenses

[45.30] In determining the value of the estate immediately before death allowance is made for reasonable funeral expenses.[1]

The cost of mourning is not part of the funeral expenses but under a concession a reasonable amount for mourning for the family and servants is allowed.[2] The cost of a tombstone or gravestone is now allowed.[3]

Simon's Direct Tax Service I4.142; Foster's Inheritance Tax D1.42.

1   IHTA 1984, s 172.
2   Extra-statutory concession F1; **Simon's Direct Tax Service, Division H4.2;** Foster's Inheritance Tax, Division U2. This concession is operated restrictively. Revenue practice is to allow a deduction for a modest meal after the funeral service but to deny a deduction for the cost of the family travelling to the funeral.

[45.30] Valuation

[3] Statement of practice SP 7/87; Simon's Direct Tax Service, Division H3.2; Foster's Inheritance Tax, Division W3.

46

Liability for payment of IHT

Liability for tax	PARA **46.01**
Transfers reported late	PARA **46.08**
Position of accounting parties	PARA **46.09**
Position of beneficiaries	PARA **46.15**

For the procedures for the payment of inheritance tax, see supra, §§ 2A.23–2A.25.

Liability for tax

Lifetime transfers

[46.01] Those liable to account to the Revenue for tax are:

(1) the transferor;
(2) the transferee;
(3) any person in whom the property is vested whether beneficially or not;
(4) any person beneficially entitled to an interest in possession in the property;
(5) where the property has become settled property as a result of the transfer any person for whose benefit the property or income is applied;[1]
(6) the transferor's spouse who has been the recipient of a transfer of value from 1 since 26 March 1974 and was his spouse at the time of each transfer;[2] and
(7) in the case of a potentially exempt transfer the transferor's personal representatives (this rule also applies to any additional tax due in respect of other chargeable transfers[3] including tax due in respect of a gift with reservation).

Liability under 6 may not exceed the market value of the property at the time of the transfer to the spouse.[4] If the property was transferred to the spouse before the chargeable transfer and the property has since that time declined in value, the spouse's liability does not exceed the market value of the property at the time of the chargeable transfer or, if sold by the spouse under a qualifying sale, at the time of that sale; this relief does not apply to tangible moveable property.[5] References to property in these rules 1–5 include references to property directly or indirectly representing that property.[6]

For the tax due in respect of chargeable transfers the primary liability rests on 1[7] and the others become liable only if the tax remains unpaid after the due date; they have the further advantage that they are not to be liable to a greater extent than if the transfer had been gross rather than net, ie for no more than the tax due if the transfer had not been grossed up.[8] If a transferee bears the tax in this way it is presumably not open to the Revenue to collect the balance of tax due to the grossing up from the transferor unless perhaps the transferor reimburses the transferee.

Making anyone other than the transferee liable for the additional tax due in respect of a chargeable transfer where the transferor dies within seven years is a major change from the days of CTT. Presumably this was to bring matters into line with the rules of potentially exempt transfers. In both these instances the primary liability remains that of the transferee and the liability of the personal representatives is limited. For potentially exempt transfers it appears[9] that personal representatives are liable only after all other possible candidates or if the tax remains unpaid 12 months after the end of the month in which the death occurred and then subject to the limit of the assets.[10] A similar rule applies to gifts with reservation.[11] For all these transfers and gifts the primary liability is on the donees.

Simon's Direct Tax Service I10.111; Foster's Inheritance Tax K1.11.

[1] IHTA 1984, s 199(1).
[2] IHTA 1984, s 203(1).
[3] IHTA 1984, s 199(2).
[4] IHTA 1984, s 203(1).
[5] IHTA 1984, s 203(2).
[6] IHTA 1984, s 199(5).
[7] IHTA 1984, s 204(6).
[8] IHTA 1984, s 204(5).
[9] The wording of IHTA 1984, s 204(7), (8) is extremely obscure—see Venables *Inheritance Tax Planning* p 22.
[10] IHTA 1984, s 204(8).
[11] IHTA 1984, s 204(9).

Settled property

[46.02] Those primarily liable are the trustees.[1] In addition tax can be collected from:

(1) any person entitled to an interest in possession in the settled property whether beneficially or not, eg the trustees of a subsequent settlement;
(2) any person for whose benefit the property or income is applied, eg a discretionary beneficiary; and
(3) the settlor, provided
    (a) the settlement was made in his lifetime; and
    (b) the trustees are not for the time being resident in the UK.

Point 3 does not apply if the settlement was made before 11 December 1974 and the trustees having been resident in the UK when the settlement was made have been non-resident from 10 December 1974 to the date of the transfer.[2] Point 3 is also excluded in relation to any additional tax that becomes due by reason of the settlor's death within seven years.³ Similar rules apply to potentially exempt transfers. Point 3 is further restricted where there is a potentially exempt transfer on the termination of an interest in possession. Here the trustees are primarily liable but the settlor will be liable under point 3 unless the settlement was made before 17 March 1987, the trustees were initially resident in the UK but had become non-resident by that day and remained so until the death of the transferor.⁴

Simon's Direct Tax Service I10.113, 114; Foster's Inheritance Tax K1.13, 14.

1   IHTA 1984, s 201 defined by IHTA 1984, s 199(4) and see *IRC v Stype Investments (Jersey) Ltd* [1981] STC 310 and subsequently [1982] STC 625.
2   IHTA 1984, s 201(3)
3   IHTA 1984, s 201(2).
4   IHTA 1984, s 201(3A).

Death

[46.03] Here liability is on:

(1) the personal representatives—so far as the property[1] is not settled unless it is settled land in the UK which devolves on them;
(2) the trustees—so far as concerns property settled immediately before death;
(3) the beneficiaries, or any other person in whom the property is vested after the death, eg the trustees of a settlement created by the will; and
(4) where property was settled at the time of the death—any person for whose benefit property or income is applied, eg a person benefiting under a trust which became discretionary on the death of the life tenant.

As far as the personal representatives are concerned it should be noted that there is no immunity from liability simply because the person is not resident in the UK and that the liability is personal (not simply representative).[2]

Personal representatives are required to calculate the inheritance tax arising on the basis of the figures they enter on the HMRC return. This tax liability is then divided between property on which there is an instalment option[3] and property on which there is no instalment option. Personal representatives are required to send payment of the tax calculated as relating to the non instalment option property when they submit the HMRC account at death. The grant of probate is not made unless payment of inheritance tax so computed has been made. As the effect of death is normally to freeze the bank account of the deceased, it is usually necessary to borrow the sum required to discharge the immediate inheritance tax liability and then repay the loan once probate has been granted. Since 31 March 2003, an arrangement has been available under which a UK bank or building society will make a payment in respect of inheritance tax direct to HMRC from an account held in the name of the deceased, prior to the grant of probate.[4]

[46.03] Liability for payment of IHT

If any tax that is not paid carries interest from the due date, see infra, § **46.12**. Penalties are levied if the account is not delivered within 12 months, see supra, § **2A.48**.

Where the personal representatives have distributed the estate and obtained a certificate of discharge but a lifetime transfer then comes to light, they are liable for any extra tax. However, the Revenue will not usually make any claim against them if they have made the fullest possible enquiries that were reasonably practicable in the circumstances and have done all in their power to make full disclosure.[5]

Simon's Direct Tax Service I10.112; Foster's Inheritance Tax K1.12.

---

[1] Defined IHTA 1984, s 200 and see *IRC v Stype Investments (Jersey) Ltd* [1981] STC 310, **[1981] 2 ALL ER 394** and subsequently **[1982] STC 625**; liability on foreign assets may be deferred if the foreign government imposes restrictions—extra-statutory concession F6; **Simon's Direct Tax Service, Division H4.2; Foster's Inheritance Tax, Division U2.**

[2] *IRC v Stannard* [1984] STC 245.

[3] IHTA 1984, s 227(1).

[4] Full details of the operation of the scheme are given in Inland Revenue IHT Newsletter, April 2003. The scheme is operated by those banks and building societies that have chosen to join the scheme; there is no obligation on a bank so to do.

[5] **Simon's Tax Intelligence** 1991, p 238; **Foster's Inheritance Tax X6.44**; this is without prejudice to any claim under s 199(2).

Limitations of liability

[46.04] A purchaser is liable if and to the extent that the property is subject to an HMRC charge (infra, § **46.06**).[1] So if F gives property to S who sells it to X, X may escape liability notwithstanding that he is a person in whom the property is vested (supra, §§ **46.01–46.03**, group 3).

Personal representatives are liable only to the extent of the assets they received or would have received but for their own neglect or default.[2] A similar rule applies to limit their liability to tax on UK settled land devolving on them. Trustees are only liable to the extent of the property available to them as trustee or which they have actually received or disposed of or they have become liable to account for to the beneficiaries;[3] the property here means the property in relation to which the charge arises.

Those liable as having possession of or a beneficial interest in property have their liability limited to the extent of that property.[4] This limitation does not mean that they are liable only to the extent that the tax is attributable to that property; the value of the whole property can be taken.

Those liable as receiving benefits under a discretionary trust cannot be made liable beyond the amount received (less any liability to income tax).[5]

On limits of liability of personal representatives in relation to potentially exempt transfers and gifts with reservation, see, supra, § **46.01**.

Simon's Direct Tax Service I10.111, 112, 125; Foster's Inheritance Tax K1.11, 12, 25.

1   IHTA 1984, s 200.
2   IHTA 1984, s 204(1).
3   IHTA 1984, s 204(2).
4   IHTA 1984, s 204(3).
5   IHTA 1984, s 204(5).

Special cases

[46.05] Special rules apply to limit those accountable as follows:

(1)   Transfers within seven years of death. Any tax or additional tax may be collected from any of those set out above at supra, §§ **46.01–46.02** and settled property with the exception of the transferor, the transferor's spouse and if the property was settled the settlor.[1] This is not a charge on the transferor's estate. Liability is limited where the person liable is not entitled to the property beneficially; his liability is limited to the value of the property still vested in him at the death or which he handled as trustee after the death.[2]

(2)   Designated objects—loss of conditional exemption. Those liable are:
     (a)   those who disposed of the object; and
     (b)   those for whose benefit the object was disposed.[3]

(3)   Timber. Those liable for tax deferred from death are those entitled to the proceeds of sale or who would be if there were a sale.[4]

(4)   Close companies—see supra, § **39.22**.[5]

Simon's Direct Tax Service I10.112, 125; Foster's Inheritance Tax K1.12, 25.

1   IHTA 1984, ss 199(2), 201(2).
2   IHTA 1984, s 204(4).
3   IHTA 1984, s 207.
4   IHTA 1984, s 208.
5   IHTA 1984, s 202(3).

HMRC charge

[46.06] Where tax is not paid on the due date in respect of a transfer of property, a charge for the unpaid tax arises;[1] in the case of settled property this extends to all the property comprised in the settlement.

The charge does not apply to personal property in the UK which was beneficially owned by the deceased immediately before his death and which vests in his personal representatives; however, this charge does apply to land, including leases.[2] The charge does not apply to heritable property in Scotland.

The charge covers property, moveable or immoveable, outside the UK, real property, joint personal property which has accrued to a surviving joint owner

[46.06] Liability for payment of IHT

and personal property nominated under a general power to dispose (eg under a power to nominate benefits under a superannuation fund[3]) unless the general power is contained in a settlement (when the trustees are liable for the tax, though it is a charge on the settled property).[4] In all these instances the personal representatives, even though they have transferred the property to the beneficiary, can still recover from him the tax that they have paid, though there will be obvious practical difficulties in the case of property situated outside the UK if the foreign executors and the beneficiary are out of the jurisdiction.

The charge takes effect subject to existing incumbrances. If the property is land in England, Wales or Northern Ireland and the charge is not registered a purchaser takes clear of the charge, which is transferred to the proceeds of sale. In other cases a purchaser will take clear of the charge if he had no notice of it. He will also escape the charge if the Revenue have issued a certificate of discharge and he is not aware of any grounds that would invalidate it or by the effluxion of time—six years from the date the tax became due or the delivery of the account whichever is the later.

The charge applies to property subject to a potentially exempt transfer when that property is still retained by the transferee at the transferor's death.[5] However, when that property is sold before the transferor's death the charge is placed instead on the proceeds or the property received in its place.[6] Property which is disposed of by the donee, otherwise than by sale, is subject to the charge.[7]

Simon's Direct Tax Service Division I11.6; Foster's Inheritance Tax Division L6.

---

[1] IHTA 1984, ss 237, 238.
[2] The charge extends to leases where the death was after 9 March 1999; IHTA 1984, s 237(3) amended by FA 1999, s 107(1).
[3] IHTA 1984, s 151(4); *O'Grady v Wilmot* [1916] 2 AC 231.
[4] IHTA 1984, s 237.
[5] IHTA 1984, s 237(3A)(*a*).
[6] IHTA 1984, s 237(3C).
[7] IHTA 1984, s 237(3A)(*b*).

Certification of settlement of liabilities

[46.07] Statute[1] provides for a certificate of discharge. However, HMRC have now instituted a procedure[2] of certification without the statutory certificate of discharge. The letter from Capital Taxes Office provides the necessary confirmation that our enquiries are settled and that *either*:

(a) no tax is due, *or*
(b) all the tax has been paid, *or*
(c) all the tax has been paid except for any tax being deferred (eg on timber) or otherwise being paid later (by instalments).

The letter will be signed and stamped and HMRC state that it will treat that letter as having exactly the same effect as a formal certificate. So, for example, if HMRC have sent such a closure letter both to the executors and to the trustees of a Will trust and the executors subsequently notify HMRC of an increase in value of the free estate, HMRC will regard the trustees as protected by the letter and HMRC will not seek to collect any additional tax that is attributable to the trust.

Simon's Direct Tax Service I11.413, 414; Foster's Inheritance Tax L4.13, 14.

---

[1] IHTA 1984, s 239.
[2] From 30 April 2007. The HMRC statement is made in IHT Newsletter, April 2007, p 4.

Transfers reported late

[46.08] The cumulative principle requires that transfers be correctly and promptly reported. Where a transfer is reported late and in the meantime a later transfer has been taxed, that tax may not have been correctly calculated. Where there is a seven-year gap between the transfers there is no problem owing to the rule that gifts cease to be cumulated after seven years; tax (plus interest) will be due on the unreported transfer at the rates prevailing at the date of the transfer and not at later (and, most probably, lower) rates. Where the gap is less than seven years the earlier transfer used to be treated as taking place after the later one thus putting the extra tax on the earlier transfer. Now a different rule applies; the tax on the earlier transfer is charged as at the rates appropriate to its actual date; the extra tax which should have been collected from the second transfer is then added to the tax charged on the earlier one; interest is charged on the tax which should have been paid on the earlier transfer in the normal way, but interest on the additional tax relating to the later transfer (but charged on the earlier transfer) runs only from six months from discovery of the earlier transfer.[1]

Where there are two unreported transfers the extra tax is apportioned by reference to the values transferred.[2] This rule is modified if tax has been settled in respect of one of the earlier transfers; no further tax is due in respect of the settled transfer but this does not reduce the liability of the unsettled transfer.[3] Provision is also made for the situation in which the transfer is itself an earlier transfer in relation to another later transfer.[4]

EXAMPLE

In November 2006 A made a chargeable gift of £30,000 having used his annual exemptions earlier in the year. His cumulative total before making the gift was £288,000 and consisted of chargeable transfers made in August 2004. He failed to report the November 2006 gift.

In June 2008 A made a chargeable transfer of £100,000 gross.

IHT paid on the 2008 gift was	
Tax at lifetime rates on £388,000	£15,200
Less tax at lifetime rates on £288,000	nil
	£15,200

[46.08] Liability for payment of IHT

Subsequently the November 2006 transfer is discovered. A must pay:

(a) the IHT that should have been paid on the earlier transfer using 2006–07 rates   £1,200
(b) the additional IHT on the June 2008 transfer using 2008–09 rates   £6,000

If, instead of making one transfer of £30,000 in 2006, A had made one of £12,000 in May 2006 and one of £18,000 in June 2006, the additional tax of £6,000 would be divided between them in the proportion 12/30 (£2,400) and 18/30 (£3,600).

If the later transfer were in June 2012 instead of June 2006 more than seven years would have elapsed since the 2004 gift. This would not affect A's liability to pay IHT at the 2006–07 rates on the transfer in November 2006.

Simon's Direct Tax Service I3.551–554; Foster's Inheritance Tax C5.51–54.

[1]   IHTA 1984, s 264(6).
[2]   IHTA 1984, s 264(3).
[3]   IHTA 1984, s 264(4).
[4]   IHTA 1984, s 264(5).

Position of accounting parties

Transferors

[46.09] If the transferor has accounted for the tax, he has no right to raise the tax out of the property under IHTA 1984, s 212(1) nor to recover it from the transferee unless the transferee has expressly agreed to pay it.[1] In such a case it would seem that since the transferor has an enforceable right to reimbursement in respect of liability to tax this liability should be ignored in determining the loss in value of the transferor's estate so that the transferor should pay tax on the net and not the gross value of the transfer.

[1]   Simon's Direct Tax Service I10.111; I11.211; Foster's Inheritance Tax K1.11; L2.11. IHTA 1984, s 162(3).

Transferees

[46.10] If the beneficial transferee pays the tax, he has no right to recover it from the transferor unless by deed under seal[1] the transferor has expressly agreed to pay it. The transferee will pay tax on the net value of the transfer; any transfer of the amount of this tax to him later on by the transferor will be a further transfer of value.[2] The tax may be raised out of the property.[3]

Simon's Direct Tax Service I10.111; I11.211; Foster's Inheritance Tax K1.11; L2.11

[1] Or by contract outside IHTA 1984, s 10.
[2] IHTA 1984, s 5(5); but taxable only if not exempt.
[3] IHTA 1984, s 212(1).

Trustees

[46.11] If trustees pay the tax they may recover the amount out of any money in the settlement held on the same trusts as the property in respect of which the tax was payable.[1] Whether or not the property in respect of which they have paid tax is vested in them (as will usually be the case), they have power to raise the amount of the tax by sale or mortgage of the property.[2]

Simon's Direct Tax Service I10.116; I11.213, 221; Foster's Inheritance Tax K1.16; L2.13, 21.

[1] IHTA 1984, s 212(1).
[2] IHTA 1984, s 212(1).

Limited owners

[46.12] A person having a limited interest in property (eg a life tenant or an annuitant or a remainderman) who pays the tax in respect of the property is entitled to the same charge as if the money had been raised by a mortgage to him.[1] This charge arises automatically[2] and, being equitable, is registrable as a Class C (ii) land charge, if the land is unregistered, or protectible by entry of a notice or caution, if the land is registered, assuming the land is in England or Wales.

Simon's Direct Tax Service I10.116; Foster's Inheritance Tax K1.16.

[1] IHTA 1984, s 212(2). Presumably, the fact of reimbursing personal representatives tax paid by them should enable a person to fall within IHTA 1984, s 212(2) as a person who "pays the tax attributable to" the property.
[2] *Lord Advocate v Countess of Moray* [1905] AC 531 at 539.

Discretionary beneficiaries

[46.13] A beneficiary under a discretionary trust or the object of a power of appointment who pays the tax has power, even though the property in respect of which he has paid the tax is not vested in him, to raise the amount of the tax by sale or mortgage of the property under IHTA 1984, s 212(1). The power may be used for the purpose of paying the tax in the first place. The power, is indeed, available for any person liable to pay the tax except a transferor or a spouse of his who is accountable under IHTA 1984, s 203 to the extent of property received from him.

Simon's Direct Tax Service I10.116; Foster's Inheritance Tax K1.16.

[46.14] Liability for payment of IHT

Personal representatives

[46.14] Where personal representatives have paid IHT in respect of a chargeable transfer on death and the tax is not a testamentary expense (see infra, § 46.23) the personal representatives have a right to repayment by the person in whom the property is vested, property including any property directly or indirectly representing the original property.[1]

They also have an indemnity where settled land[2] or formerly settled land[3] vests in them.[4] A similar rule exists for heritable property in Scotland.[5]

An official certificate, specifying the tax paid, can be obtained from the Revenue.[6] Repayments are made to the person producing the certificate.

If the person who has paid the tax could have paid it by instalments, the other persons can insist upon reimbursing him by instalments.[7]

Simon's Direct Tax Service I10.116; I11.212; Foster's Inheritance Tax K1.16; L2.12

---

[1] IHTA 1984, s 211(3).
[2] Administration of Estates Act 1925, s 22(1); Supreme Court Act 1981, s 116.
[3] Re Bridgett and Hayes Contract [1928] Ch 163.
[4] IHTA 1984, ss 211(1), 237.
[5] IHTA 1984, ss 237(4), 211(1)(b).
[6] IHTA 1984, s 214.
[7] IHTA 1984, s 213.

Position of beneficiaries

Estates of deceased persons

[46.15] Where, under the rules outlined at supra, §§ 46.05–46.06, personal representatives are liable for tax, the tax is treated as part of the general testamentary and administration expenses of the estate.[1] The effect is to cause the incidence of the tax to fall on the assets of the estate in the order set out in the Administration of Estates Act 1925, Sch 1, Part II or as varied by the testator.[2]

This broad rule does not apply to all types of property which are treated as disposed of on the death, but only to property in the UK which vests in the personal representatives and was not immediately before the death comprised in a settlement. The rule is further narrowed by the right of the testator to express a contrary intention in his will.[3]

The broad rule draws no distinction between real and personal property. This marks a change not only from the old law of estate duty but also from the original CTT provision as it was thought it should be construed. However in Re Dougal[4] what is now the broad rule was accepted by a Scottish court; the rule was made statutory in 1983.[5]

When property does not fall under this general rule, whether because the rule does not, in terms, apply or because it is excluded by the testator, it bears its own tax. If, nonetheless, the personal representatives have paid tax, as may have been necessary in order to obtain probate, the amount of tax is to be repaid by the person in whom the property is vested.

Simon's Direct Tax Service I10.201; Foster's Inheritance Tax K2.01.

---

1   IHTA 1984, s 211(1).
2   Administration of Estates Act 1925, s 34(3), Sch 1, para 8.
3   IHTA 1984, s 211(2).
4   [1981] STC 514.
5   But only for deaths after 25 July 1983.

Works of art and heritage property

[46.16] The burden of deferred tax on works of art etc falls on those entitled to the proceeds of sale[1] not the estate; for other special cases see supra, § **46.05**.

Simon's Direct Tax Service I10.111; Foster's Inheritance Tax K1.11.

---

1   IHTA 1984, s 207.

Apportionment of tax

[46.17] Where tax is payable as a testamentary expense, the general rule is that the tax exhausts each category of property available for payment of testamentary expenses and, to the extent that a particular category of property is only partially reduced, the partial reduction is borne rateably by all those interested in that particular category of property.

Where personal representatives have a right to recover the tax under IHTA 1984, s 212 no problems arise if the beneficiaries are absolutely entitled between them to the property: the tax is simply divided between them according to their appropriate interests in the property.

If property is left on trust for A for life with remainder to B the tax charged in respect of it comes out of the capital of the settled property, though interest should come out of income.[1] A bears his proportion of IHT by suffering a reduction of income through diminution of the capital.

A pecuniary legacy will always bear the tax when it has to be paid out of property in respect of which personal representatives have a right of recovery, as where T bequeaths foreign property subject to payment of legacies thereout or where legacies have to be paid thereout in due cause of administration.

Simon's Direct Tax Service I10.112; Foster's Inheritance Tax K1.12.

---

1   IHTA 1984, s 212.

[46.18] If there is *no* express direction for payment of legacies out of property but in due course of administration it is necessary to pay legacies, for example, out of foreign property then to the extent that they are so paid they must bear the tax.

Annuitant and remainderman

[46.19] If real property is left on trust for A for life and after his death on trust to pay an annuity to X for life and subject thereto to hold the property on trust for B absolutely the tax is payable out of the capital of the settled property.[1] However, when A dies, thereby causing IHT to fall on the settled property even if it is personal property, X, the annuitant, and B, the residuary legatee, bear the tax on the property in respect of A's death rateably according to the value of their respective interests.[2] X will bear his share by way of a reduction in the amount of his annuity and not by a lump sum payment of a part of the tax. The tax will be paid out of the capital of the property, being raised by way of sale, mortgage or otherwise.

Simon's Direct Tax Service I10.205; I11.406; Foster's Inheritance Tax K2.05; L4.06.

[1] IHTA 1984, s 212.
[2] IHTA 1984, s 212; *Re McNeill, Royal Bank of Scotland v Macpherson* [1958] Ch 259, [1957] 3 All ER 508.

[46.20] The difficulty lies in determining the amount by which the annuity is to be reduced. In simple cases it will no doubt be a sufficient approximation to reduce the annuity by the percentage equal to the over-all effective rate of capital transfer tax. But if greater accuracy is necessary, the method laid down in *Re Parker–Jervis, Salt v Locker*[1] may perhaps be followed. Calculate the "slice" of capital supporting the annuity according to the income yield of the estate; notionally apportion the tax between this "slice" of capital and the rest of the estate; and charge the annuitant, in reduction of the annuity, with interest on the tax so apportioned to the "slice" of capital. The interest should be charged at the rate at which interest is payable on tax until payment of the tax, and thereafter at the rate at which the amount of the tax can be raised by mortgage of the property.

This method is not satisfactory when the yield is abnormally high or low.[2] In such cases the "slice" of capital should perhaps be found by reference to the mean between the gross dividend yield appearing in the Financial Times Actuaries Share Index and the yield obtained from irredeemable gifts as revealed by the same Index.[3]

[1] [1898] 2 Ch 643.
[2] *Re Viscount Portman, Portman v Portman* [1924] 2 Ch 6.
[3] These are the low and high yields used etc, see supra, § **42.09**.

[46.21] These problems of valuation arise also on the death of the annuitant,[1] as where property is settled on trust to pay an annuity of £2,000 a year to X and on X's death a similar annuity to A and subject to these for B absolutely. On X's death the burden must be shared between A and B on the basis of one of the methods just outlined.

Simon's Direct Tax Service I8.375; Foster's Inheritance Tax H3.75.

---

[1] Cf *Re Palmer, Palmer v Palmer* [1916] 2 Ch 391; *Re Weigall's Will Trusts, Midland Bank Executor and Trustee Co Ltd v Weigall* [1956] Ch 424, [1956] 2 All ER 312.

Death of life tenant of part

[46.22] If a life tenant of part of settled property dies the loss of income arising from the payment of the tax is to be borne solely by those who become entitled to the income of the deceased's share and the loss of capital by those who eventually take the deceased's share, and not at all by the other beneficiaries.[1] This will arise if T leaves property on trust to pay the income equally between X, Y and Z during their respective lives and on the death of each of them to pay his share of income to his children during their lives and X dies. The distinctive feature of this kind of case is that what is charged to tax on the death of X is an aliquot share of the property to which X's children succeed. The reduction of income to be suffered by the children can be calculated at current mortgage interest rates on the amount of IHT payable as in *Re Parker-Jervis* unless the fund is physically divided following the death.

Simon's Direct Tax Service I10.112.

---

[1] Cf *Betts Brown's Trustees v Whately Smith* 1941 SC 69.

Person exercising option

[46.23] If T by his will gives B an option to purchase foreign property at a price below its probate value and B exercises the option, B must bear the proportion of tax attributable to the excess of the value of the property above the option price. Essentially, B is obtaining a pecuniary legacy of the excess value and to the extent that it is paid out of property in respect of which personal representatives have a right or recovery of tax it will bear a proportion of that tax.[1] Thus if foreign property worth £21,000 is purchased under an option for £14,000 then B will have to bear one-third of the tax payable in respect of the foreign property. The position is otherwise if the option were to purchase some of the deceased's property in the UK for in such a case the personal representatives have no right of recovery: the tax in respect of such property is a testamentary expense and such property subject to an option at an undervalue is the last category of property available for payment of testamentary expenses, debts and liabilities.[2]

Simon's Direct Tax Service I8.231; Foster's Inheritance Tax H2.31.

[46.23] Liability for payment of IHT

1   Cf *Re Lander, Lander v Lander* [1951] Ch 546, [1951] 1 All ER 622.
2   *Re Eve, National Provincial Bank Ltd v Eve* [1956] Ch 479, [1956] 2 All ER 321.

Variation of incidence by will or other document

[46.24] A clause in a will or settlement varying the ordinary rules of incidence must be interpreted in accordance with the precise words of the will or settlement. The only case law concerns estate duty.[1] The general approach of the courts where there has been any ambiguity has been to presume that "free of estate duty" clauses have altered the ordinary rules of incidence as little as possible. It seems that such a clause in a will should be interpreted as conferring only freedom from tax payable in respect of a testator's death.[2] Thus if a testator gives foreign property free of tax to A for life, with remainder to B it will be presumed (rebuttably)[3] that the clause refers only to IHT payable in respect of the testator's death and not A's death or on an earlier disposal of A's interest, so that B will bear the tax on A's death or on the earlier disposal of A's interest. This facilitates the administration of the testator's estate for it is most inconvenient if the executors have to retain a significant part of the residuary estate to meet the tax claim that will arise if A disposes of his life interest or when A dies.

1   Free of estate duty includes free of CTT or IHT; free of CTT includes free of IHT: IHTA 1984, Sch 6, para 1 and FA 1986, s 100(1)(*b*), the use of expressions like "clear of all deductions" or "net sum" will probably be regarded as importing freedom from CTT and IHT: *Re Sebright, Public Trustee v Sebright* [1944] Ch 287, [1944] 2 All ER 547; *Re Saunders, Saunders v Gore* [1898] 1 Ch 17.
2   *Re Shepherd, Public Trustee v Henderson* [1949] Ch 116, [1948] 2 All ER 932; *Re Embleton's Will Trusts, Sodeau v Nelson* [1965] 1 All ER 771.
3   *Re Paterson's Will Trusts, Lawson v Payn* [1963] 1 All ER 114.

[46.25] It is likely that a similar approach will prevail in respect of "free of inheritance tax" clauses in a settlement though not quite so severely since the executor's convenience rationale is absent.

It would seem that a direction to pay "testamentary expenses" out of residue would be construed as a direction to pay thereout only such IHT which ranks as a testamentary expense,[1] and so not tax on foreign property.

Where a testator directs the payment of tax out of residue this will usually be construed as freeing from tax any property in respect of which IHT does not rank as a testamentary expense.[2] But if in such a case the will contains not only a general clause for payment of tax out of residue but also clauses specially freeing certain devises and bequests from IHT, the general provisions for payment of tax out of residue will not necessarily be construed as referring to tax on gifts of foreign property which are not specially freed from IHT[3] although in some cases it may be, depending upon the context of the particular will.[4]

A bequest free of IHT of designated works of art etc on which tax is not payable until they are sold or until certain conditions are broken will relieve only the beneficiary under the will. If such a beneficiary gives the articles away, and the donee sells them, thereby attracting IHT the donee will not be able to take advantage of the clause, and will have to bear the tax himself.[5]

Simon's Direct Tax Service I10.211–216; Foster's Inheritance Tax K2.11–16.

[1] *Re Owers* [1941] Ch 17, [1940] 4 All ER 225.
[2] *Re Pimm, Sharpe v Hodgson* [1904] 2 Ch 345.
[3] *Re King, Barclays Bank Ltd v King* [1942] Ch 413, [1942] 2 All ER 182.
[4] *Re Neeld, Carpenter v Inigo-Jones* [1964] 2 All ER 952n at 953.
[5] *Re Oppenheimer, Tyser v Oppenheimer* [1948] Ch 721.

47

Foreign element

Territorial limits	PARA **47.01**
Location of assets	PARA **47.02**
Property in the United Kingdom	PARA **47.08**
Excluded property	PARA **47.11**
Double taxation relief	PARA **47.17**
Debts and liability	PARA **47.21**

Territorial limits

[47.01] The provisions of IHTA 1984 relating to IHT operate in England, Wales, Scotland and Northern Ireland. They do not extend to the Channel Islands nor to the Isle of Man. Transfers of foreign property may be subject to IHT. Broadly, where the transferor is domiciled, or treated for IHT purposes as domiciled, in the UK, a charge to IHT arises regardless of the location of the asset; if he is not so domiciled the charge arises only if the asset is located in the UK. The rules are thus very different from those for CGT. The rules may be overridden by double tax agreement.[1]

When a charge is imposed on foreign property it does not follow that the Revenue will be able to collect the tax. The Revenue may find themselves unable to sue in the foreign court.[2] In such circumstances the liability of persons within this country for tax on property outside the UK assumes great importance.[3]

Simon's Direct Tax Service I9.101; Foster's Inheritance Tax J1.01.

---

[1] IHTA 1984, s 158; and see extra-statutory concession F6; **Simon's Direct Tax Service, Division H4.2; Foster's Inheritance Tax, Division U2.**
[2] Supra, § **34.02**. Proceedings can be brought before the courts of other EC countries by the Revenue department in that country, acting on behalf of HMRC; EC Mutual Assistance Recovery Directive 76/308/EEC, see supra, § **34.01**.
[3] Infra, § **47.22**, supra, Chapter 46.

Location of assets

[47.02] The location of an asset is determined by reference to English, Scottish or Northern Ireland laws (see infra, §§ **47.03–47.06**). Foreign law rules of situs are irrelevant. However, it is foreign law that will determine the rights in an asset, in particular where the asset is either land or a shareholding

[47.02] Foreign element

in a foreign company. Capital Taxes Office has published a leaflet detailing some of the information it may require to be satisfied that the location of assets is correctly determined.[1]

Simon's Direct Tax Service I9.401; Foster's Inheritance Tax J4.01.

---

[1] *Simon's Tax Intelligence* 1994, p 736.

Land

[47.03] Land is located in the country in which it is physically situated.

Mortgages of land are not treated as land but as debts, except in the one case where they are a charge on land only, not accompanied by any personal obligation of the mortgagor to repay.

Exceptionally, a Scottish heritable bond is treated in the same way as land.

Simon's Direct Tax Service I9.461; Foster's Inheritance Tax J4.61.

Debts

[47.04] A simple contract debt is in general situated in the country where the debtor resides, that being the country where the debt can be recovered.

A specialty debt, eg one payable by virtue of a document under seal, is located in the country where the document evidencing the debt is physically situated. Different rules apply under Scottish law.

A judgment debt is located in the country where the judgment is recorded.

Simon's Direct Tax Service I9.421–425; Foster's Inheritance Tax J4.21–25.

Stocks, shares and other securities

[47.05] A bearer security is located in the country where the document of title is physically situated.

Registered or inscribed securities are located in the country in which the register is required to be kept. This rule extends to debenture stock, but not apparently to a debenture, which, if under seal, is to be regarded as a specialty debt.

Stocks and shares in a company registered under UK Companies Acts are therefore generally situated in the UK, even though the entire business of the company, and even its residence, may be abroad. So while dividends may be treated as income from a foreign source, the shares themselves may be treated as located in the UK for IHT. Rights under renounceable letters of allotment have been held to be situated where the company resides or is registered since this is where the rights are enforceable. For an instrument to be treated as analogous to a chattel more is required than mere transferability of title by delivery. What is required is a market for these rights.[1]

Companies incorporated abroad cause problems, especially when securities are entered on two principal registers, one in the UK and one abroad. The rational approach is to ask where the transferor dealt, or, for a transfer on death, would have dealt, with the shares in the ordinary course of affairs.[2] Physical presence of the share certificate in the one country[3] may be sufficient to turn the scales in favour of that country.

Simon's Direct Tax Service I9.411, 412; Foster's Inheritance Tax J4.11, 12.

[1] *Young v Phillips* [1984] STC 520.
[2] *Standard Chartered Bank Ltd v IRC* [1978] STC 272, [1978] 3 All ER 644.
[3] *R v Williams* [1942] AC 541, [1942] 2 All ER 95.

Miscellaneous

[47.06] Tangible property, such as furniture, coins or bank notes, is located in the country of physical situation, so a yacht berthed in an English harbour was situated in the UK even though it was registered in Jersey.[1]

Business assets, including goodwill, or a share in a partnership firm, are located in the country where the business is carried on. This does not, however, determine the situs of the beneficiary's interest save where a beneficiary with a valid interest in possession is treated as having a right in rem in the trust assets. A reversionary interest under a trust for sale has been treated as a chose in action and so as located where the trustees are resident.[2] In the confused state of the authorities it is safe to say only that the chose in action treatment is given where there is a trust for sale *and* more than one beneficiary, or the trust may be varied.[3]

A share in the unadministered estate of a deceased person giving rise to an interest in possession is located in the country where the assets are to be found.[4]

The location of property held in trust is found according to the rules applying to the particular property, without regard to the proper law of the trust or the residence of the trustees.

Currency is located in the country of physical situation, without regard to the country by which the currency was issued.

A bank account is located in the country in which the branch of the bank at which the money is payable is situated.[5]

Certain pensions in respect of service overseas are treated as payable outside the UK even though the UK government may have become liable to pay them. Life assurance policies are regarded simply as debts.

A cause of action in tort is probably located where it arose.

Simon's Direct Tax Service I9.471, 481, 491; Foster's Inheritance Tax J4.71, 81, 91.

[1] *Trustees Executors and Agency Co Ltd v IRC* [1973] Ch 254, [1973] 1 All ER 562.

[47.06] Foreign element

² *Re Smyth, Leach v Leach* [1898] 1 Ch 89.
³ IHTA 1984, s 91.
⁴ Simon's Direct Tax Service I9.431; Foster's Inheritance Tax J4.31.
⁵ *R v Lovitt* [1912] AC 212, PC, subject to IHTA 1984, s 135 for foreign currency accounts.

Deemed domicile

[47.07] The notion of domicile, supra, § 33.13 is extended by IHTA 1984, s 267 in two ways. (The extension does not, however, apply for provisions under a double tax agreement,[1] nor for the designation of certain government securities as excluded property when held by a non-UK domiciled individual.)[2]

(1) A person is treated for IHT purposes only as domiciled in the UK and not elsewhere[3] if he was so domiciled after 9 December 1974 and within three years immediately preceding the relevant time. The three-year period begins to run only from the date on which the new domicile is acquired. So where a person previously domiciled in the UK establishes a domicile overseas, any transfer he makes within the succeeding three years is potentially within the charge to UK inheritance tax, regardless of the situs of the asset.

(2) A person is treated for IHT purposes only as domiciled in the UK and not elsewhere[4] if he was *resident* in the UK on or after 10 December 1974 and in not less than 17 of the 20 years of assessment ending with the year of assessment in which the relevant time falls. In deciding whether a person is resident income tax rules are used; no regard is had to any dwelling-house available in the UK for his use.[5]

Simon's Direct Tax Service I9.206, 211; Foster's Inheritance Tax J2.06, 211; STP [12.43]–[12.60].

¹ IHTA 1984, s 267(2).
² IHTA 1984, ss 6(2), (3), 48(4).
³ IHTA 1984, s 267(1).
⁴ IHTA 1984, s 267(1)(*b*).
⁵ IHTA 1984, s 267(4).

Property in the United Kingdom

[47.08] As a general rule property in the UK, whether real or personal, which is the subject of a chargeable transfer is liable to tax whatever foreign elements may be concerned in the passing. For example, if an Arab sheikh, four years before his death, gifts his son a house in London and some shares on the register of a company incorporated in England, IHT is payable on the gift, even though the sheikh and his son may have never been resident in the UK, are not domiciled in the UK and the gift is made by the sheikh handing his son transfer documents as they sit under a Middle Eastern sun. The value of these gifts will be aggregated with any previous chargeable transfers to ascertain the rate of tax and will thus raise the rate of tax payable on subsequent transfers.[1] For obvious reasons it is common for the sheikh to have established a non-resident company to buy the house.[2]

There are, however, some exceptions to this general rule:

(1) Property may be deemed to be located abroad under a double tax treaty; such property is therefore foreign property.[3]

(2) Certain pensions payable in respect of colonial service do not form part of a person's estate for the purposes of the transfer on death.[4]

(3) National Savings and other "small" savings held by persons actually (as opposed to deemed) domiciled in the Channel Islands or Isle of Man are treated as excluded property.[5]

(4) Property of members of visiting forces or of staff of allied headquarters is also excluded property.[6]

(5) Certain international securities are exempt.[7]

(6) Certain British government securities are excluded property if owned by persons neither domiciled[8] nor ordinarily resident in the UK.[9] A transfer of such stock by such a person is therefore a transfer of excluded property. The power to issue securities on such terms was granted in 1915.[10]

(7) Where the securities are settled property, the securities are excluded property so long as the person beneficially entitled to an interest in possession in them is neither domiciled nor ordinarily resident.[11] On the other hand there is some doubt as to the position where there are two or more persons entitled to interests in possession, eg joint life tenants, only some of whom are ordinarily resident and domiciled outside the UK. In such a situation it would appear that since there is a deemed transfer of only a part of the settled property and the legislation speaks only of "an interest" as opposed to "the interest" in possession, it will be sufficient that the conditions are fulfilled with regard to the one person who is making the deemed transfer and the property will not be excluded on the occasion of a deemed transfer by one who did not fulfil those conditions.

(8) Foreign-owned works of art which are chargeable to IHT solely by reason of their presence in the UK at the relevant date will by concession be excluded from tax if their presence here was solely for public exhibition, cleaning or restoration.[12]

Simon's Direct Tax Service I9.321–328; Foster's Inheritance Tax J3.21–28.

---

[1] On the other hand transfers by the same person of property situated outside the UK will be transfers of excluded property and so will not be aggregated.

[2] The difficulty with this arrangement is that any periods that the house is available to the sheikh for his occupation are likely to give rise to an income tax charge under ITEPA 2003, ss 105 and 106 as these charges apply to occupation by individuals under whose instruction the directors of the company are accustomed to act: see *R v Allen* [2001] UKHL 45, [2001] STC 1537. See supra, §§ **7.47** and **7.89**.

[3] IHTA 1984, s 158; infra, § **47.18**.

[4] IHTA 1984, s 153.

[5] IHTA 1984, s 6(3); deemed domicile is excluded by IHTA 1984, s 267(2).

[47.08] Foreign element

[6] IHTA 1984, s 155.
[7] eg FA 1976, s 131.
[8] Deemed domicile is ignored, IHTA 1984, s 267(2).
[9] IHTA 1984, s 6(2).
[10] Because of the sharp increase in tax rates due to war; F(No 2)A 1915, s 47; the power lapsed in 1922 but was revived by FA 1931, s 22; see also TA 1988, s 47 and supra, § **10.27**.
[11] IHTA 1984, s 48(4).
[12] Extra-statutory concession F7; **Simon's Direct Tax Service, Division H4.2; I9.324**; **Foster's Inheritance Tax, Division U2; J3.24**. This concession extends also to works of art held by discretionary trusts.

[47.09] Where the securities are settled property and no qualifying interest in possession subsists in them, IHTA 1984, s 48(4)(*b*) provides that they are excluded property only if it can be shown that all known persons for whose benefit the settled property or the income from it has been or might be applied or who might become beneficially entitled to an interest in possession in it are persons neither domiciled nor ordinarily resident in the UK. This extraordinarily wide list was narrowed slightly by the decision of the Court of Appeal in *Von Ernst & Cie SA v IRC*[1] that an unincorporated association or company established only for charitable purposes cannot become beneficially entitled nor have property or income applied for it. It followed that where the beneficiaries comprised UK resident charities and non-resident non-domiciled individuals the relief applied.

This case also held that the test as to the list of beneficiaries and their residence must be answered on the facts as they are immediately before the relevant event. In *Minden Trust (Cayman) Ltd v IRC*[2], government securities were bought by trustees of the A settlement; they resolved to advance these to be held on trust for the B settlement; the trustees of the B settlement then appointed the property in favour of X, a non-resident. The court held that in applying para 3 the expression "the settled property" referred to the property which had been in the A settlement and which was advanced to the B settlement; it followed that that property was excluded property.

[1] [1980] STC 111, [1980] 1 All ER 677.
[2] [1985] STC 758.

[47.10] A non-resident's foreign currency bank account does not form part of his estate for the purpose of the transfer immediately before death, even when the account is at a UK bank. The person must not be domiciled in the UK nor may he be resident or ordinarily resident here at the time of death. The account must not be denominated in Sterling.[1]

Similar rules apply to bank accounts held by trustees of settled property in which the deceased had a beneficial interest in possession, although the exclusion will be lost if the settlor was domiciled in the UK when he made the settlement or if the trustees were domiciled resident or ordinarily resident in the UK immediately before the beneficiary's death.[2]

Simon's Direct Tax Service I9.321C; Foster's Inheritance Tax J3.21C.

[1] Simon's Direct Tax Service Division 19.3; Foster's Inheritance Tax Division J3. IHTA 1984, s 157(1)(a).
[2] IHTA 1984, s 157(1)(b).

Excluded property

Property owned by an individual

[47.11] When owned by an individual who is not domiciled within the UK, the following categories of property constitute excluded property[1] so that a transfer of value of the property does not give rise to a charge to inheritance tax:[2]

(1) foreign property held in an individual's free estate where the individual is not domiciled within the UK;[3]
(2) "exempt" government stock;[4]
(3) a holding in a UK authorised Unit Trust;[5]
(4) a holding in a UK open ended investment company.[6]

Where the individual is domiciled in the Channel Islands or the Isle of Man, the following additional categories of properties are excluded property:[7]

(1) war savings certificate;
(2) national savings certificates (including Ulster savings certificates);
(3) premium savings bonds;
(4) deposit with the National Savings Bank;
(5) deposit with a trustee savings bank;
(6) a certified contractual savings scheme.[8]

It has generally been considered that the gift with reservation provisions cannot apply to excluded property in either of the above categories. However it appears that this view is being challenged by the Revenue.[9]

[1] IHTA 1984, s 6 as extended by FA 2003, s 186.
[2] IHTA 1984, s 3(2).
[3] IHTA 1984, s 6. See infra, § **47.12**.
[4] IHTA 1984, s 6(2).
[5] IHTA 1984, s 6(1A) inserted by FA 2003, s 186(2). In the 2003 Budget bulletin, issued by HM Government, it is stated that the rationale for keeping Unit Trusts and OEICs as excluded property when held by an individual not domiciled within the UK is that these measures "will remove barriers to sales of UK authorised investment funds abroad".
[6] IHTA 1984, s 6(1A) inserted by FA 2003, s 186(2).
[7] IHTA 1984, s 6(3).
[8] Within the meaning of TA 1988, s 326.
[9] Capital Taxes Office Advance Instruction Manual paras D.8 and D.9. See supra, § **41.12**.

[47.12] Foreign element

[47.12] Property other than settled property situated outside the UK is excluded property if the person beneficially entitled to it is an individual domiciled outside the UK.[1] The individual in question is the transferor not the transferee and generally the question must be answered by reference to the facts at the time of the transfer. It follows that a person who is not domiciled here can avoid IHT by converting UK property into foreign property—even as a death bed transaction.

Simon's Direct Tax Service I9.301; Foster's Inheritance Tax J3.01.

---

[1] IHTA 1984, s 6.

Settled property

[47.13] Where property is settled a very different approach prevails. The key elements are the domicile of the settlor at the time of the settlement and the situs of the asset. The status of the trustees and even of the beneficiaries is ignored. The rule is that where property is situated outside the UK, the property (but not a reversionary interest in that property) is excluded property unless the settlor was domiciled in the UK at the time the settlement was made.[1] This rule applies whether or not there is an interest in possession. The settlor's domicile at the time of the settlement fixes liability to the tax on the settlement regardless of his subsequent changes of domicile. If the property became comprised in a settlement before 10 December 1974 domicile has its ordinary and not its extended meaning.

Excluded property held on discretionary trusts is not relevant property and so is not subject to the ten year or intermediate charges—supra, Chapter 42. Where the property is situated in the UK it will not be excluded property and so can be relevant property; however, no charge arises under IHTA 1984, s 65 simply because the property ceases to be situate in the UK or is invested in government securities and so becomes, in either case, excluded property.[2]

Collection of the tax will be a separate matter but it must not be forgotten that the settlor will be liable for the tax on a chargeable transfer, for example the death of a life tenant, occurs during his life and the trustees are not resident in the UK.[3]

Where a settlement was made by an individual not domiciled within the UK, a holding in a UK unit trust or OEIC is excluded property, even though located in the UK.[4] In addition, if *either* an interest in possession is held by an individual not ordinarily resident in the UK *or* potential beneficiaries of a discretionary trust are not ordinarily resident in the UK, "exempt" government stock is excluded property.[5]

Simon's Direct Tax Service I9.326, 332, 333; Foster's Inheritance Tax J3.26, 32, 33.

---

[1] IHTA 1984, s 48(3). The rule is framed in terms of exemption for the property comprised in the settlement; however changes of investments by the trustees after the settlor has become domiciled in the UK do not deprive the settled property of

its status as excluded property: *Law Society's Gazette*, 3 December 1975.
2   IHTA 1984, ss 65(7), (8), 267(3).
3   IHTA 1984, s 201(1)(*d*), supra, § **46.02**.
4   IHTA 1984, s 48(3A) inserted by FA 2003, s 186(3).
5   IHTA 1984, s 48(4).

Settlement consisting of a mixture of excluded property and non-excluded property

[47.14] When a periodic charge or exit charge arises in respect of trust property, the charge is not levied on excluded property in the settlement (see supra, § **47.13**). Thus, when it is necessary to calculate a periodic charge in respect of a discretionary trust created by an individual not domiciled within the UK at the time of creation, the charge will be calculated by reference to assets within the UK at that time and not assets outside the UK ("excluded property"). However, an "excluded asset" is not always completely irrelevant in this calculation. In considering the value of a shareholding located in the UK under the situs rules, it is necessary to have regard to any "excluded property" held by the trustees that affects the value of that shareholding. Hence, in an extreme example, if trustees hold a majority shareholding in a holding company whose share register is kept outside the UK, that controlling interest must be taken into account in valuing a minority interest in a subsidiary of the group which has its share register within the UK.[1] Similar considerations apply in valuing a UK situs asset at the time it is settled on discretionary trust by a non-domiciled individual.

Simon's Direct Tax Service I9 311; Foster's Inheritance Tax J3.11.

[1] Revenue Interpretation RI 166, *Simon's Weekly Tax Intelligence* 1997, p 304.

Adding property to an excluded property settlement

[47.15] IHTA 1984, s 43(2) defines as a "settlement", inter alia, "any . . . disposition of property". The Revenue view is that this has the effect, for IHT purposes, that an addition to an existing settlement is, by itself, to be treated as a settlement in its own right. A common arrangement for IHT mitigation is for a non-domiciled individual to create a settlement in the sixteenth year of residence in the UK. Overseas property that is in the settlement thus created is then "excluded property" at any time during the life of the settlement, even though the settlor may have acquired a UK deemed domicile the following year. UK situs property settled in this way can be converted to excluded property by encashment and reinvestment or deposit of the proceeds outside the UK.

A consequence of the Revenue interpretation of IHTA 1984, s 43 is, however, that property added to such a settlement by the settlor at any time after he has acquired deemed UK domicile cannot be excluded property, nor can property derived from such an addition. The Revenue consider that if assets added

[47.15] Foreign element

before and after the date of the acquisition of the deemed domicile have become mixed, any dealings in the settlement property have to be traced in order to calculate a periodic charge or exit charge.

As in § **47.14** supra, excluded property in such a settlement is relevant in determining the value of chargeable property. Thus, following the Revenue's published view, if a non-domiciled individual settles a 45% holding in an overseas company in the sixteenth year of residence in the UK and then adds a further 10% holding to the settlement the following year, the periodic charge that arises on that 10% is calculated by valuing the 10% holding on the basis of a controlling interest.[1]

Where a single settlement is created by dispositions made by more than one person, inheritance tax is charged as if each individual had created a separate settlement.[2] Where it is not feasible to identify separately the property attributed to the different dispositions by the different individuals, the Revenue consider that any charge to IHT arises on the basis that each individual who has contributed to the single settlement is the settlor for the whole of the property in that settlement. On this analysis, where one individual was not domiciled at the time of settlement and another individual was so domiciled, a periodic charge arises over the whole of the property in the settlement.[3]

Simon's Direct Tax Service I9.311; Foster's Inheritance Tax J3.11.

[1] Revenue interpretation RI 166, *Simon's Weekly Tax Intelligence* 1997, p 304.
[2] IHTA 1984, s 44(2).
[3] *Hatton v IRC* [1992] STC 140; Revenue interpretation RI 166, *Simon's Weekly Tax Intelligence* 1997, p 304.

Reversionary interests in foreign property

[47.16] A reversionary interest in settled property does not come under the settled property[1] rule but under the general rule: so it is excluded property if the person beneficially entitled to it is an individual domiciled outside the UK and it is situated outside the UK; the situs of the reversionary interest is not necessarily that of the settled property.[2] Where the settled property is itself a reversionary interest the settled property rule applies to it.

EXAMPLES

(1) X dies domiciled in England, leaving land abroad and shares in companies whose registers of shareholders are abroad. The land abroad and the shares are liable to IHT.

(2) X dies domiciled abroad, leaving land abroad and shares in companies whose registers of shareholders are abroad. The land and shares are excluded property and so not liable to IHT.

(3) X, domiciled in Canada, gives Y domiciled in the UK £1,000 in Toronto; the gift is of excluded property.

(4) X, domiciled in Canada wishes to give Y, domiciled in the UK, £1,000 and does so by sending Y a cheque drawn on X's account in London; the gift is not of excluded property.

(5) In 1984 A, domiciled in the UK, settled English property on B for life with remainder to C, both of whom were domiciled in the UK. In 1987 B emigrated to Canada and established domicile there. C remained in the UK and died in 1994. B died of frostbite in 1995. On B's death there will be a charge by reason of the location of the property in the UK and A's domicile in 1984. There will be no charge on the reversionary interest on C's death in 1994.

(6) In 1984 X domiciled in Canada settled Canadian property on Y for life with remainder to Z, both of whom were then domiciled in Canada. In 1987 Y and Z migrated to and established domicile in the UK. Z died of sunstroke in 1993. Y died in 1994. On Y's death there will be no charge since the property was situated outside the UK and the settlor was not domiciled here when the settlement was made. There will be a charge on the reversionary interest on Z's death.

(7) A testator dies domiciled in England, leaving foreign land and shares on trust for X for life. X dies domiciled abroad. The shares and the land are liable to IHT on the death of the testator and in theory on the later death of X but the testator's estate is not liable for the IHT on X's death.

(8) A testator dies domiciled abroad, leaving foreign property on trust for X for life. X dies domiciled in England, and at his death the trust fund consists of foreign land and shares. There is no charge to IHT on the death of the testator, nor on that of X.

Simon's Direct Tax Service I9.341; Foster's Inheritance Tax J3.41.

1 IHTA 1984, s 48(3) applying IHTA 1984, s 6(1).
2 IHTA 1984, s 6(1).

Double taxation relief

[47.17] Where tax is payable in two countries it is generally on the basis of the location of the property being in one country and the domicile of the transferor in the other. The law of the UK (and of many foreign countries) makes provision for relief in respect of such double taxation in certain circumstances. What follows is concerned with relief granted by the law of the UK; for relief granted by the laws of a foreign country, reference must be made to those laws.

Double taxation conventions that apply for IHT have been signed with ten countries.[1] Of these, the only agreements that can be regarded as having significant effect are those with France,[2] Ireland,[3] Italy,[4] Netherlands,[5] South Africa,[6] Sweden.[7] For various reasons[8] the others are of limited, and some are of no effect. The provisions of these treaties apply for IHT payable in respect of a death but not for any IHT lifetime charge.[9]

Simon's Direct Tax Service Part F7; Foster's Inheritance Tax Division J5; Part R.

1 India (SI 1956/998), Pakistan (SI 1957/1522), Switzerland (SI 1957/426,1994/3214), USA (SI 1979/1454): **Simon's Direct Tax Service, Division F7.5; Foster's Inheritance Tax, Division R4.**
2 SI 1963/1319.
3 SI 1978/1107.
4 SI 1968/304.
5 SI 1980/706, 1996/730.
6 SI 1979/576.
7 SI 1981/840, 1989/986.
8 An agreement was signed with India on 3 April 1956 (SI 1956/998). It is of limited effect, following the abolition of estate duty in India. Discussions about a protocol began in November 1980 and continued to October 1984 but talks were later

discontinued. Talks with Germany were held in 1996 but were discontinued. The agreement with Canada (SI 1946/1884) was terminated in relation to deaths after 30 September 1978. The convention was of limited effect after the abolition of estate duty in Canada. An agreement with Pakistan (SI 1957/1522) was signed on 8 June 1957 but was of limited effect, following the abolition of estate duty in Pakistan.

[9] IHTA 1984, s 158(6).

[47.18] Two sorts of arrangement were made for estate duty. One type applies now to IHT on death. These are arrangements under F (No 2) A 1945, s 54. These contain codes for determining the situs of certain kinds of property, which may in certain cases lead to property which is situate in the UK being treated as situate in the other country, and so excluded property. In other situations one tax can be used as a credit against the other; the effect is that the transfer will not bear tax in excess of the larger amount due to each country separately. The difference between the two reliefs is substantial. Not only will transfer within the first relief escape UK tax completely and usually only partly under the latter, but the transfer under the former relief will be of excluded property and so exempt from aggregation whereas under the latter the value transferred must be aggregated with any other value transferred and cumulated. These treaties often also contain tests for the resolution of dual domicile problems. The OECD has produced a model convention. The pattern of the new treaties, and this model, is to allow states the primary right to tax on the basis of situs if the property is immovable or is a business based there and otherwise to grant the (primary) right to tax to the country of fiscal domicile, a concept loosely defined as almost any connecting factor on which a state may wish to tax but with a tie breaker clause like the dual residence provision mentioned at supra, § **37.09**.[1]

Simon's Direct Tax Service F7.102; Foster's Inheritance Tax J5.04.

[1] See [1995] BTR 1, p 12.

Unilateral relief

[47.19]–[47.20] Unilateral relief is available[1] against any amount of tax chargeable by reason of any disposition or event provided (a) the tax is similar in character to IHT or is chargeable on or by reference to death or gifts inter vivos and (b) the IHT chargeable is attributable to the value of that property. This relief is by way of credit so that the transfer remains nonetheless a chargeable transfer and must be cumulated in the usual way. Unilateral relief may be claimed even if there is a double tax agreement provided it exceeds the relief under the agreement.[2]

Simon's Direct Tax Service F7.104; Foster's Inheritance Tax J5.02.

[1] IHTA 1984, s 159.
[2] IHTA 1984, s 159(7).

The credit

(1) *Single situs:* Where the asset is situated in the foreign country the credit is for the full amount of the foreign tax on the property.[1] This credit concedes priority of taxation to the country of situs.

(2) *Dual situs:* Where the property is situate in both (or neither) of the UK[2] and the foreign country, credit is determined by the formula

$$\frac{A}{A+B} \times C$$

where A is the IHT, B is the overseas tax and C is whichever is the smaller of A and B.[3] This form of relief is used in some double tax agreements[4] and is often more advantageous than that in other agreements. The relief has the curious effect that the greater the foreign tax the less credit is available; this is understandable where, as in a treaty, the other country uses the same formula but is very odd in unilateral relief.

(3) *A third country taxes:* Where three countries are involved B becomes the aggregate of the foreign taxes and C the aggregate of A and B minus the largest single charge.[5]

(4) *Effect of foreign credit:* Where relief by credit is available, whether by convention or unilaterally, and rule 2 or 3 applies, any credit under the

$$\frac{A}{A+B} \times C$$

formula is calculated by treating A as the tax as reduced by any credit relief due in respect of tax in another country; equally B is to be reduced by any credit available under the foreign law.[6]

EXAMPLES

(1) A dies domiciled in the UK but some of the assets are in another country, Q. Suppose that the charge to tax is £5,000 and Q charges tax of £3,000. Assuming that under UK rules the assets are in Q, the IHT liability will be £2,000.

(2) If, however, Q says the assets are in Q and the UK says the assets are in the UK, the formula will be applied:

$$\frac{5,000}{5,000 \times 3,000} \times 3,000 = £1,875$$

so IHT liability would be £5,000 − 1,875 = £3,125.

The same would result if both the UK and Q regarded the property as located in a third country, R, assuming that R charged no tax.

Assuming that Q uses the same formula the credit there will be

$$\frac{3,000}{8,000} \times 3,000 = £1,125,$$

making a tax liability in Q of £1,875. The aggregate of the liabilities in the UK and Q will be £5,000. If, however, Q has no treaty the total tax liability may be as much as £(3,000 + 3,125).

[47.19] Foreign element

(3) If R also charged tax on the property say of £1,000 the credit against tax would for the tax charged in Q and R be

$$\frac{5,000}{5,000 + (3,000 + 1,000)} \times (3,000 + 1,000) = £2,222.$$

(4) If, however, UK and Q gave credit for the tax of £1,000 in R the credit against IHT is adjusted and the formula gives the following credit for the tax levied in Q

$$\frac{5,000 - 1,000}{(5,000 - 1,000) + (3,000 + 1,000 - 1,000)} \times (3,000 - 1,000) = £1,143.$$

Simon's Direct Tax Service F7.104; Foster's Inheritance Tax J5.02.

---

[1] IHTA 1984, s 159(2).
[2] Presumably situs is determined according to the law of each country and not just by the law of the UK; this is the official view—thus if UK law says the situs is X and X says the situs is the UK, or vice versa, relief is available. However there appears to be a gap if UK law says that the situs is X while X says the situs is Y.
[3] IHTA 1984, s 159(3).
[4] USA, South Africa, India and Pakistan.
[5] IHTA 1984, s 159(4).
[6] IHTA 1984, s 159(5).

Debts and liability

Foreign debts

[47.21] A liability to a person resident outside the UK is allowable as a deduction in computing the value of the estate provided it satisfies the general rules at supra, § 45.21. However, where the liability falls to be discharged outside the UK and is not an incumbrance on property inside the UK, the liability is, so far as possible, taken to reduce the value of property outside the UK.[1] One reason for this rule is that a person not domiciled in the UK is liable to IHT only on property in the UK and it would be giving him an undue advantage to allow him to deduct all his overseas liabilities while taxing him only on some of his property. Such a person can avoid the problem by making his creditors reside in the UK or creating an incumbrance on his UK property. Another reason for the rule concerns persons domiciled in the UK. Such persons pay tax on their foreign property but there may be double tax relief by way of allowing a credit for the foreign tax payable in respect of the property. Foreign liabilities must be set off against the value of overseas property so far as possible. If therefore the particular asset is exempt from tax under the double tax treaty the benefit of that exemption may be cancelled by the disallowance of the liability.

Additional expenses of administering foreign property, incurred by reason of its being situate abroad, may be allowed as a deduction from the value of the property for the purpose of capital transfer tax, but not exceeding 5% of the value of the property.[2]

Simon's Direct Tax Service I9.122; Foster's Inheritance Tax J1.22.

[1] IHTA 1984, s 162(5).
[2] IHTA 1984, s 173.

Liability

[47.22] A foreign resident may become liable for tax or liable to indemnify English executors or others who have paid tax which falls to be borne by him.[1] However, personal liability of a foreign resident cannot be enforced by legal process in the UK unless he is personally present in, or has assets situate in the UK or unless the foreign courts permit enforcement. A charge of duty on foreign property cannot be enforced, unless the property, or the proceeds of sale thereof, is brought to this country or unless the foreign courts permit enforcement. The reason for these difficulties is that, by international law, the courts of one country will not usually enforce the revenue laws of another (see supra, Chapter 34).

Where, because of restrictions imposed by the foreign government, executors cannot immediately transfer to the UK sufficient of the foreign assets to pay the IHT attributable to them, concessionary relief allows them to defer payment. If the amount brought in is less than the tax deferred this balance is waived.[2]

Simon's Direct Tax Service I9.121–123.

[1] As the property is outside the UK, IHTA 1984, s 211(1) (supra, § **46.23**) does not apply and IHTA 1984, s 211(3) preserves the personal liability of the holder of the property to indemnify the personal representatives.
[2] Extra-statutory concession F6; Simon's Direct Tax Service Division H4.2; Foster's Inheritance Tax Division U2.

Part VIII

National Insurance Contributions

Part VIII
National Insurance Contributions

48

The contributory scheme
Introduction
The National Insurance Fund
The contribution classes
Relevant law

49

The employed earner
Categorisation
Employee or self-employed?
Categorisation by regulations
Personal service companies and other intermediaries

50

Employment earnings
Meaning of earnings
Gratuities; employee trusts
Pension payments
Reimbursement of expenses
Petrol allowances
Termination payments etc
Other special cases
Payments in kind; securities
Retrospective liability on earnings
Harmonisation with PAYE

51

Employer and employee contributions
Class 1 contributions
Earnings limits, thresholds and rates
Earnings periods
Company directors
Anti-avoidance rules
More than one employment
Annual maximum contributions
Collection of Class 1 contributions
Class 1A contributions
Class 1B contributions

52

The self-employed earner
Class 2 contributions
Class 4 contributions

53

Interaction with benefits
Earnings factors
Credits
Voluntary contributions
Late paid contributions

54

The international dimension
Territorial scope
Reciprocal agreements and double contribution conventions
EC law
Planning considerations

55

Administration
HM Revenue & Customs and the Department for Work and Pensions
Powers to introduce secondary legislation
Disclosure of avoidance schemes

48

The contributory scheme

Introduction	PARA **48.01**
The National Insurance Fund	PARA **48.06**
The contribution classes	PARA **48.07**
Relevant law	PARA **48.14**

Introduction

[48.01] The inclusion of National Insurance among the subjects covered in a publication dealing with UK taxation may call for some explanation.

Contributions under the National Insurance scheme go into a separate fund used solely to pay for contribution-based benefits; strictly such contributions do not form part of the central government's revenue. Moreover, on the face of it there would seem to be no choice but to pay the contributions due and no opportunity to control the amounts required and if there are no opportunities for planning is there any point in studying a multitude of detailed rules?

For the reasons explained below, it will be found that National Insurance has some of the characteristics of a tax system and requires consideration as such. From the detailed treatment of the subject, it will become apparent that choices are available and that substantial sums can be involved. For this reason, throughout this part, attention is drawn to the relevant planning considerations.

Certainly, as originally conceived, the British National Insurance scheme was intended to be wholly different from a tax regime. Beveridge sharply distinguished taxation from insurance contributions in the following words:

> The distinction between taxation and insurance contribution is that taxation is or should be related to assumed capacity to pay rather than to the value of what the payer may expect to receive, while insurance contributions are or should be related to the value of the benefits and not to the capacity to pay.[1]

The current National Insurance system, which was set up in 1946[2] to implement the proposals of the Beveridge Report, was based on a view of social security which enjoyed widespread support at the time. Beveridge expressed this view thus:

> The plan is not for giving to everybody something for nothing and without trouble or something that will free the recipients for ever thereafter from personal responsibilities. The plan is to secure income for subsistence on condition of service and contribution and in order to make and keep men fit for service.[3]

The means adopted was to apply, on a unified and comprehensive basis, the form of National Insurance first introduced in this country by Lloyd George to

[48.01] The contributory scheme

provide sickness benefit and, in some industries, unemployment benefit and which was administered through approved friendly societies.[4] This scheme was inspired by the system of social security which was well established in Germany by the end of the 19th century. It involved a tripartite system of contributions under which the employee, the employer and the state respectively made contributions into a designated fund at prescribed rates.

At the heart of the Beveridge plan was what is known as the contributory principle. That this principle is still alive is evident from a comment made by the Chancellor of the Exchequer in his 1989 Budget Statement. In describing why a low-paid employee earning just slightly above the then threshold for starting to pay National Insurance contributions should pay 86p per week on the first £43 of his earnings, the Chancellor explained:

> The step which has always existed at the lower earnings limit, where people first come into the national insurance system, is the entry ticket to the full array of contributory benefits. As such it is an essential feature of the contributory principle.[5]

Nonetheless, this "entry ticket" was abolished with effect from 6 April 1999 as regards employers' contributions and from 6 April 2000 as regards employees' contributions.

What is the contributory principle and why is it so important? When a senior official gave a sober and reasoned explanation of this principle to a House of Commons subcommittee he was asked:

> Do you agree that it is mumbo-jumbo?[6]

But for Beveridge the contributory principle was quite clear and entirely appropriate. It was the principle "that a material part of the total cost of maintaining income under the plan should be met from monies contributed by citizens as insured persons".[7] It was only by adopting this principle that Beveridge considered benefits could be made available without a means test, against which then, as probably now, there was strong popular objection on the ground that those who had put by savings against a rainy day were penalised.[8] Hence, the Beveridge plan was intended to be "first and foremost a plan of insurance—of giving in return for contributions, benefits up to subsistence level, as of right and without means test".[9]

But despite the theory, the connection between contributions and benefits has always been tenuous and in recent years, certainly in relation to retirement pensions, there has been an increasing awareness that "the working generation today basically pays for the pensions of the generation that has now retired".[10] It is, however, worth restating what is meant by the contributory principle and the motivation behind it, particularly since social security continues to be a topic of public debate and there have been two recent studies proposing a replacement of the present arrangements by a system of true tax credits for all those whose income is below a basic standard.[11]

Moreover, in the General Election of 1992 the National Insurance system for the first time in many years became a major issue in British politics, although it cannot be said that the contributory principle as such was widely debated. In fact the programmes of the opposition parties entailed abolition of the contributory principle completely: Labour by its proposed removal of the upper earnings limit for employee contributions and the Liberal Democrats by their proposed assimilation of National Insurance contributions to the income tax system.

In the General Election of 1997 "New" Labour's manifesto made no reference to the abolition of the contributory principle or the removal of the upper earnings limit for employee contributions. On the contrary, a number of comments were made during the election campaign that the Labour party had no plans to remove the "cap" on employee contributions, a promise broken in the 2002 Budget which announced the changes that took effect in April 2003.[12] However, the manifesto did contain a commitment to review the interaction of the tax and benefit systems and, separately, undertake a fundamental review of the benefit system. Many of the new government's plans were included in the Social Security Act 1998, which received Royal Assent in May 1998. The Budget on 17 March 1998 contained reports by Martin Taylor, of which "*The Modernisation of Britain's Tax and Benefit System*" was one.[13] Its recommendations on contributions were all accepted, although some were not fully implemented until 6 April 2001.

During the latter part of 1999, the Social Security Select Committee heard evidence from a number of parties on "the contributory principle". Future attitudes to the contributory principle will depend on whether a wholly collectivist view of social security is espoused or whether the view is taken that the self-worth of the individual who becomes unemployed or otherwise in need of support from the public purse is more affirmed if he or she can be said to have already paid for the benefit claimed. But in any event it has to be accepted that the National Insurance system which we have at present has departed from Beveridge's principle in a number of important respects. Particular examples are set out in the following paragraphs.

---

[1] Social Insurances and Allied Services (Cmd 6404 (Beveridge Report) para 272).
[2] By the National Insurance Act 1946. This came into effect in 1948.
[3] Beveridge Report, para 455.
[4] The arrangement established by the National Insurance Act 1907.
[5] Hansard, 14 March 1989, Vol 149, col 308.
[6] Minutes of evidence, Subcommittee of the House of Commons Treasury and Civil Service Committee, (Session 1982–83) "The Structure of Personal Income Taxation and Income Support", para 840.
[7] Beveridge Report, para 273.
[8] Beveridge Report, para 21.
[9] Beveridge Report, para 10.
[10] The structure of Personal Income Taxation and Income Support, supra, para 841.
[11] Institute of Fiscal Studies Report 1984 *The Reform of Social Security* (authors A W Dilnot, J A Kay and C N Morris; *Stepping Stones to Independence; national insurance after 1990*, Brandon Rhys Williams (ed Hermione Parker, Aberdeen University Press).
[12] That promise was seen as less politically-sensitive than that not to increase the headline income tax rates. The consequence was not only the introduction of new complexities but also the confirmation that earned income was to be subject to more taxation and contributions than equivalent levels of unearned income.

[48.01] The contributory scheme

[13] Report by Martin Taylor, Chief Executive of Barclays plc, which looks at the options for reform. Chapter 2 of *"The Modernisation of Britain's Tax and Benefit System"* refers to National Insurance contributions.

[48.02] (1) For Beveridge, the plan of insurance proposed involved a pooling of risks on a community-wide basis as opposed to adjusting premiums according to the level of risk for different categories of insured persons.[1] On this basis contributions were to be at a flat rate and likewise benefits, "each individual paying the same contribution for the same rate of benefit".[2]

However, in 1959 the graduated pension scheme was superimposed on the 1946 arrangements. This required employees to pay additional contributions at 4% of their earnings between £9 and £18 a week in return for a very small increase in retirement pension related to the additional contributions paid. The graduated system was introduced simply because the flat-rate scheme generated insufficient income to finance the benefits fully. The contributory principle followed here was a different one; enhanced benefits in return for additional contributions, though in fact the extra pension secured was not commensurate with the additional contributions.

With all party agreement the graduated pension scheme was replaced in 1975[3] by the system of National Insurance which is still in operation today. The principle of graduated contributions dependent on the level of earnings between the lower earnings limit (later the earnings threshold) and the upper earnings limit was now incorporated into the basic scheme. A supplement to the basic retirement pension was provided by the State Earnings Related Pension Scheme (SERPS) from 1978 and for those many employees who were contracted out[4] of this scheme (as well as for those contracted in), both employee and employer contributions (after deduction of the contracted-out rebate) varied according to the level of the employee's earnings. However, the state pension for contracted-out employees does not vary according to earnings and thus the direct relationship between contributions and benefits was breached in this situation. From 6 April 2002, SERPS was "replaced" by the State Second Pension (S2P), although S2P is arguably little more than SERPS with a change of rules to benefit the lower paid.

[1] Beveridge Report, para 25.
[2] Beveridge Report, para 273.
[3] As a result of the Social Security Act 1975 (SSA 1975) and the Social Security Pensions Act 1975 (SSPA 1975).
[4] For contracting-out, see further supra, § **32.06**.

[48.03] (2) Self-employed persons were not included in SERPS, nor are they currently included in S2P, but the introduction of graduated contributions in respect of employed persons into the main contributory scheme meant that a wide divergence opened up between the contributions required from an employed person with earnings at or above the upper earnings limit and those payable by a self-employed person with the same level of earnings: these were still at a flat rate. This was considered inequitable notwithstanding that the self-employed person could expect only the basic state pension and was not (and still is not) entitled to what is now contribution-based jobseeker's allowance (once 'unemployment benefit'). In order to correct the divergence, a new class of contributions—Class 4—was imposed on those carrying on a trade, profession or vocation on their own account. Class 4 contributions are payable on the contributor's business profits as assessed for income tax but secure no additional benefits. They therefore represent a further departure from the Beveridge principle of "benefit in return for contributions".[1]

[1] Beveridge Report, para 21.

[48.04] (3) Until 1985 both employee and employer contributions reached a maximum where the employee's earnings passed above the upper earnings limit. But in October 1985 this ceiling was removed for employer contributions and in April 2003 for employee contributions. Accordingly, once earnings are above a certain lower threshold (for 2009–10 £5,715 pa) employer contributions are payable at 12.8% on the employee's earnings without any upper limit. From the outset the employer contributions could be seen as "a direct tax on employment"[1] since the employer gains little from the payment of the contributions. However, since 1985 the employer contributions have borne no relationship at all to benefits provided by the scheme and represent nothing more than a payroll tax, as is the case also as regards the employee surcharge of 1% on earnings above the upper earnings limit from 6 April 2003.

[1] Beveridge Report, para 276.

[48.05] (4) In the social security scheme envisaged by Beveridge, virtually all benefits were to be contributory, non-means tested benefits. Only for "the limited number of cases of need not covered by social insurance" would "national assistance subject to a uniform means test" be made available.[1]

But the last 61 years have seen a continuous growth in the range of non-contributory benefits, many of which such as child benefit and the disability benefits are not means tested. As a result, many who are entitled only to limited contributory benefits have their income supplemented by non-contributory benefits and the so-called "tax credits" introduced in April 1999 and revised in April 2003. This tends to reduce the distinctiveness of the contributory scheme and the practical importance of the contributory principle.

The introduction of graduated contributions, the removal of the upper limit on first employer contributions and then employee contributions also, the introduction of Class 1A (at first only on cars and fuel, but from 6 April 2000 charged on all taxable benefits) and Class 1B employer-only contributions and, for self-employed persons, the introduction of Class 4 contributions have all considerably eroded the contributory principle and made National Insurance progressively more like a tax.

Considered as a tax, National Insurance is the second largest source of revenue after income tax: in 2008–09 the yield is likely to be around £104,600m,[2] of

[48.05] The contributory scheme

which well over half represents employer contributions based on the earnings of their employees. Value added tax now comes in some way behind with projected receipts of £83,800m in 2008–09.[3]

In view of the character of the contributory system and the size of the figures involved, it will now be clear why treatment of this subject is appropriate in a comprehensive account of UK taxation.

It will also be evident from the comments already made that there are a number of features that distinguish the UK system of National Insurance from the taxation system. These were usefully summarised in a 1991 harmonisation report[4] which set out the following as the important and distinctive features of NICs:

(1) they are compulsory insurance premiums to fund state benefits;
(2) they are payable by both employers and employees;
(3) an employee's NICs are credited to that employee's National Insurance account to establish entitlement to contributory state benefits;
(4) they are charged on "earnings" defined as "any profit or remuneration derived from employment";
(5) they are non-cumulative and calculated on a strict pay period basis (ie the liability arises when the earnings are paid and is final);
(6) there is no provision for assessment at the end of the financial year of employers' or employees' NICs.

In contrast, tax deducted under PAYE:

(1) does not fund a particular type of expenditure;
(2) is a liability of the employee only;
(3) does not confer entitlement to benefit;
(4) is charged on payments of emoluments defined as "salaries, fee wages, perquisites and profits whatsoever";
(5) represents a provisional payment (calculated cumulatively) on account of an annual liability;
(6) is credited against the annual tax assessed to be due at the end of the tax year (where such an assessment is necessary).

---

[1] Beveridge Report, para 11.
[2] Government Actuary's report (Cm 7021) on the Social Security Benefits Up-rating Order 2007, SI 2007/688, and the Social Security (Contributions) (Re-rating and National Insurance Funds Payments) Order 2007, SI 2007/1052.
[3] Economic and Fiscal Strategy Report and Financial Statement and Budget Report, Budget 2008 (formerly "Red Book").
[4] The report was distributed to employers' representatives on the DSS regulation panel.

The National Insurance Fund

[48.06] Because the National Insurance system is founded on the conception that the members of the community provide against risks on a community-wide basis, an essential feature is that all contributions should be held in a separate fund and that benefits or claims should be met out of that fund. That separate fund is the National Insurance Fund, which was first set up in 1948. Originally there were in addition two other separate funds, the National Insurance (Reserve) Fund and the Industrial Injuries Fund, but these funds were absorbed into the National Insurance Fund in 1975.

The following statement shows the estimated income and outgoings of the Fund for 2009–10:[1]

	£m
	Income
Balance brought forward	52,717
Contributions	100,275
Consolidated Fund	1,988
State scheme premiums	78
Investment income	2,495
	£157,553
Outgoings	
Benefits	74,887
Allocation to National Health Service	21,239
Transfer to Northern Ireland	395
Administration	1,301
Statutory pay recoveries and compensation	1,996
Personal pension contracted-out rebates	2,541
Other net outgoings	16
Redundancy fund payments (net)	349
Balance carried forward	54,829
	£157,553

As will be seen, the main source of income is the contributions. From 2003–04 onwards a much greater allocation is made to the National Health Service and this is because the entire revenue from the extra 1% charge imposed from April 2003 is allocated to the NHS and is not retained by the National Insurance Fund. The major part of the contribution income comes from Class 1 contributions as shown in the following analysis:

Contributions		£m
Class 1—primary	40,028	
Class 1—secondary	55,928	
		95,956
Class 1A and Class 1B		1,126
Class 2		365

[48.06] The contributory scheme

Class 3	105
Class 4	2,723
	£100,275

As may be expected, the main outgoings are the contributory benefits met out of the Fund. These are shown in the following analysis:

Contributory benefits	£m
Retirement pension	66,330
Bereavement (formerly widow's) benefits	630
Contribution based jobseeker's allowance	765
Incapacity benefit (previously invalidity and sickness benefits)	6,665
Maternity allowance	354
Guardian's allowance	2
Christmas bonus to pensioners	131
	£74,877

The contributory system is not funded on insurance principles at all, ie there is no attempt to relate contributions to future obligations nor are contributions invested to any appreciable extent, so producing investment income and capital appreciation to go towards meeting the liabilities as they mature. Instead the National Insurance Fund is run on the "pay as you go" principle, ie receipts are required to cover outgoings by a reasonable margin year by year.

The recession of the early 1990s resulted in less contribution revenue (because of fewer people at work) and more benefits being paid out (because of more people claiming contribution-based jobseeker's allowance and a rise in the long-term sick claiming incapacity benefit). As a result it became necessary for a time to restore the practice of the Treasury making a grant to ensure that the estimated balance of the National Insurance Fund is equal to one-sixth of the benefit expenditure. The Social Security Act 1993 authorised a transfer of up to 20% of benefit expenditure for 1994–95 to be transferred to the Fund. For 2008–09 the estimated transfer required is, however, Nil—as has been the case since 1997–98.

Because the Fund operates on a finely balanced basis, the Secretary of State for Work and Pensions (formerly the Secretary of State for Social Security) and the Treasury have to carry out a yearly review of the general level of earnings and other matters considered relevant in order to make any changes required to contribution rates and earnings limits and thresholds for the following tax year.[2] These changes are made under the statutory order procedure and the draft order laid before Parliament has to be supported by a report from the Government Actuary (or Deputy Government Actuary) on the state of the fund and the effect of the proposed changes.[3] Such changes are normally announced in November or December and take effect from the following 6 April or, in the case of benefits, very shortly thereafter.

The Government Actuary is also required to review and report on the state of the Fund at every fifth anniversary after 6 April 1975. The object of this quinquennial review is to assess whether the Fund can meet from year to year demands likely to be placed on it, having regard to current and expected contribution rates and other matters considered relevant, eg demographic trends, expected levels of unemployment, trends in earnings levels etc.

Simon's NIC [1.21]–[1.40].

---

[1] These and the following estimates are taken from the Government Actuary's Report on the drafts of the Social Security Benefits Up-rating Order 2009 and the Social Security (Contributions) (Re-rating) Order 2009 presented in January 2009 (Cm 7537).

[2] SSAA 1992, s 141. Properly, the purpose of the annual review is solely to consider possible revision of the Class 2, 3 and 4 contributions, but advantage is usually taken of the annual review to consider Class 1 contribution rates and earnings brackets at the same time.

[3] SSAA 1992, s 142.

The contribution classes

[48.07] Contributions to the contributory scheme fall into six classes.

Class 1

[48.08] These are due in respect of the earnings of "employed earners" as defined[1] which are broadly employees and office holders:

(1) *Primary contributions.* These are due (normally by deduction under the PAYE system) from the employed earner. From 6 April 2003, these are due on all earnings above the earnings threshold, but at only 1% on those earnings above the upper earnings limit. From 6 April 2000, they were payable only on earnings between the primary earnings threshold and the upper earnings limit. From 6 April 2001, the primary threshold is the same as the secondary threshold, and both are the same (within the odd pound or two) as the personal tax allowance. For 1999–2000, they were payable on earnings between the lower and upper earnings limits and were not due on the excess. Prior to that, they were payable on total earnings if they reached the lower earnings limit but only on earnings up to the upper earnings limit and were not due on the excess.

(2) *Secondary contributions.* These are due from the "secondary contributor", ie the employer or government department, public authority etc paying the office holder.[2] They are payable on all those earnings of the employed earner which exceed the secondary earnings threshold. Prior to 6 April 1999 they were payable at a multiplicity of rates on all earnings, if earnings exceeded the lower earnings limit. Since 6 October 1985 there has been no ceiling on secondary contributions.

Simon's NIC [1.51]–[1.55].

[48.08] The contributory scheme

[1] SSCBA 1992, s 2(1)(a).
[2] SSCBA 1992, s 7.

Class 1A

[48.09] These are yearly contributions payable by employers in respect of taxable benefits in kind provided to their employees. They are payable at a rate equivalent to the not contracted-out rate for Class 1 secondary contributions and are calculated on amounts parallel to those used under the income tax rules for taxing benefits provided to directors and those employees with annual remuneration of £8,500 or more.[1] Until 6 April 2000, Class 1A contributions were payable only in respect of the provision of cars and private use petrol.

Class 1A contributions secure no benefits for employees under the contributory scheme.

[1] SSCBA 1992, s 10.

Class 1B

[48.10] These are yearly contributions payable by employers in respect of PAYE Settlement Agreements. They are also payable at a rate equivalent to the not contracted-out rate for Class 1 secondary contributions.[1]

Like Class 1A contributions, the Class 1B charge also secures no benefits for employees under the contributory scheme.

[1] SSCBA 1992, s 10A.

Class 2

[48.11] These are modest flat rate contributions payable by all self-employed earners.[1] They secure incapacity, maternity and long-term benefits, mainly retirement pension and bereavement benefits.

[1] SSCBA 1992, s 11.

Class 3

[48.12] These are voluntary contributions which can be paid only by those not otherwise securing benefits through contributions and secure only the long-term benefits, ie mainly retirement pension and bereavement benefits.[1]

[1] SSCBA 1992, s 13.

Class 4

[48.13] These are payable on business profits above a lower threshold, but at only 1% above an upper threshold, which are immediately derived by an individual from carrying on a trade, profession or vocation.[1] They are thus payable by the majority of self-employed earners who also pay Class 2 contributions. Until 6 April 2003, they were payable only on profits between a lower and upper threshold.

Business profits for this purpose are ascertained as for income tax and collection is through the income tax system, ie the Class 4 contributions are treated as amounts payable under the self-assessment for income tax purposes.

Contribution liability under all of these classes is described in detail in the succeeding sections.

---

[1] SSCBA 1992, s 15.

Relevant law

[48.14] The primary legislation relating to contribution liability is contained in the Social Security Contributions and Benefits Act 1992 (SSCBA 1992) and the Social Security Administration Act 1992 (SSAA 1992). These Acts, however, are a consolidation of various social security Acts going back to 1975. There is in addition a vast body of secondary legislation including regulations dealing with categorisation, contributions, credits, earnings factors, adjudication and certain other specific issues. Many of these were consolidated with effect from 6 April 2001 by The Social Security (Contributions) Regulations 2001 (SI 2001/1004), although these regulations have been subject to much amendment since that time already. Matters in the previous regulations relating to things such as credits—which remain the policy responsibility of the Department for Work and Pensions (formerly the Department of Social Security)—are in the separate consolidated regulations The Social Security (Crediting and Treatment of Contributions, and National Insurance Numbers) Regulations 2001 (SI 2001/769). The secondary legislation also includes a number of reciprocal social security agreements which the UK has made with certain other countries. Finally, it should be borne in mind that certain EC legislation touches social security questions and is binding on the UK.

This publication does not deal with the law relating to social security benefits except in general terms but it should be appreciated that each benefit has its own regime (normally found in regulations) dealing with conditions of entitlement, calculation of the benefit, claims and manner of payment.

49

The employed earner

Categorisation	PARA **49.01**
Employee or self-employed?	PARA **49.02**
Categorisation by regulations	PARA **49.04**
Personal service companies and other intermediaries	PARA **49.24**

Categorisation

[49.01] One of Beveridge's six principles of social insurance was that there should be different insurance classes corresponding to different sections of the community and their needs;[1] in particular a sharp distinction has always been made between employees (Class 1) and self-employed persons (Class 2).

The process by which persons were allocated to different classes was originally called "classification" but in the scheme at present in operation the term used is "categorisation". However, more than a change of name has occurred. In the original scheme persons had to be classified either as employed or self-employed whereas now it is particular kinds of employment that are categorised and give rise to appropriate contribution liability. So, for example, an individual may have one employment in which he is an employee and so pays Class 1 contributions and at the same time be in business on his own account and be liable as a self-employed person to Class 2 contributions and, since 1975, Class 4 contributions.

The two kinds of employment are termed in the National Insurance legislation as those of an "employed earner" and of a "self-employed earner" respectively. An employed earner is defined as "a person who is gainfully employed in Great Britain either under a contract of service or in an office (including elective office) with general earnings chargeable to income tax".[2] By contrast, a self-employed earner is "a person who is gainfully employed in Great Britain otherwise than in employed earner's employment (whether or not he is also employed in such employment)".[3] The qualifying adverb "gainfully" is significant in relation to the definition of self-employed earner (see infra, § **52.01**) but is redundant in the definition of employed earner since contribution liability depends on there being earnings which reach the earnings threshold (although benefit entitlement depends on earnings reaching the lower earnings limit).

It will be noted that an employed earner either has a contract of service or holds an office. An office involves "a degree of continuance (not necessarily continuity) and of independent existence; it must connote a post to which a person can be appointed, which he can vacate and to which a successor can be appointed".[4] Common examples of office holders are company directors, Members of Parliament and Trade Union officials. So a person appointed to

[49.01] The employed earner

hold a public inquiry on a temporary ad hoc basis was held not to hold an office. Salaries, fees etc arising from an office fall within the charge to tax as "general earnings" (formerly under Schedule E).[5]

A contract of service has to be distinguished from a contract for services; an individual having a contract of service is an employed earner but not one performing a contract for services. This important distinction is considered further below (see infra, § **49.03**).

Simon's NIC [3.1], [11.1], [12.11], [12.12].

---

[1] Beveridge Report, para 309.
[2] SSCBA 1992, s 2(1)(*a*), as amended by ITEPA 2003, s 722, Sch 6, paras 169, 171.
[3] SSCBA 1992, s 2(1)(*b*).
[4] *Edwards v Clinch* [1981] STC 617, [1981] 3 All ER 543, HL.
[5] ITEPA 2003, ss 6–8.

Employee or self-employed?

[49.02] There is a substantial divergence between the contributions payable by a self-employed person and those payable on the earnings of an employee.

EXAMPLE

Both A and B are public relations consultants with annual earnings of £50,000: A is employed by a company but B works on a freelance basis.

Contributions in 2009–10:

A
Primary Class 1 contributions
—on earnings from primary earnings threshold (£110 × 52 = £5,720) to upper earnings limit (£884 × 52 = £43,888) at 11%   4,198.48
—on earnings above upper earnings limit (£50,000 − £43,888 = £6,112) at 1%   61.12
Secondary Class 1 contributions on earnings from secondary earnings threshold (£110 × 52 = £5,720) − £44,280 at 12.8%   5,667.84
                                                                                   £9,927.54

B
Class 2 contributions: 52 at £2.40   124.80
Class 4 contributions:
—on profits from lower profits limit (£5,715) to upper profits limit (£43,875) at 8%   3,052.80
—on profits above the upper profits limit (ie £50,000 − £43,875 = £6,125) at 1%   61.25
                                                                                   £30,238.85

Consequently self-employed status holds out attractions so far as contribution liability is concerned and for more than 60 years, ie since the introduction of the post-war National Insurance scheme, many who might otherwise be employees have attempted to become self-employed and the authorities have constantly challenged such attempts.

How are such questions resolved and on what grounds?

Prior to 1 April 1999, the matter could be resolved only by a "determination" by the Secretary of State for Social Security acting in his judicial capacity. Only the contributor could appeal against an unsatisfactory decision, and then only to the High Court on a question of law.

Following the transfer of responsibilities for National Insurance contributions to what was then the Inland Revenue (now HM Revenue & Customs (HMRC)) with effect from 1 April 1999 (see supra, § **2A.51**), disputes with regard to contributions liabilities are, from the same date, generally to be heard by the General and Special Commissioners. In the event of a dispute, a formal decision will be issued by an officer of the Board of HMRC and an appeal must be made within 30 days of its issue.[1] The exception is that decisions relating to contracting-out and contribution credits and related matters are heard through the benefit appeals route.[2]

Certain determinations made by the Secretary of State in the 1950s under the previous procedure were once published[3] and the decisions reported still provide useful guidance. However, on the supposed grounds of confidentiality, publication subsequently ceased.

---

[1] Social Security Contributions (Transfer of Functions, etc) Act 1999, ss 8, 11 and 12.
[2] First to a social security tribunal, from there to the Social Security Commissioners with any further appeals heard by the Court of Appeal.
[3] "Selected Decisions of the Minister on Questions of Classification and Insurability"; each decision is given a reference beginning with M and followed by a number.

The case law

[49.03] In applying the statutory definitions to the particular facts, regard must be had to the case law bearing on the terms. One of the key terms in the definition of an employed earner is "contract of service". The distinction between a contract of service and a contract for services is often difficult to draw and has given rise to a substantial body of case law. It should be appreciated that the question also has to be considered in contexts other than contribution liability. For example, it determines in employment law whether employer obligations to the employee and to third parties arise and in relation to income tax whether income is assessed as general earnings (formerly Schedule E) or, on the other hand, what was formerly Schedule D, Case I or Case II. The general consensus now is that cases decided in these other areas of law are equally relevant to the meaning of the term in relation to contribution liability. Moreover, the courts will expect a position taken by the parties in, for example, an employment law context to be followed for income tax and National Insurance.[1]

The test which originally was regarded as decisive was whether the individual was placed under the control and supervision of the person to whom service was rendered as in a master and servant relationship: "a servant is a person subject to the command of his master as to the manner in which he shall do his work".[2] In many instances this test can be applied easily and settles the matter. Thus "a ship's master, a chauffeur, and a reporter on the staff of a newspaper are all employed under a contract of service; but a ship's pilot, a taxi-man and a newspaper contributor are employed under a contract for services".[3]

But there are many situations where the control test alone is inadequate to determine the position. For example, professional and highly skilled people use their own judgement as to how they perform their tasks whether they are employees or in business on their own account. For this reason, a further test has been developed alongside the control test which is known as the integration test. This was introduced by Lord Denning who declared: 'In this connection I would observe the test of being a servant does not nowadays rest on submission to orders. It depends on whether the person is part and parcel of the organisation'.[4] In another case he expressed the test as whether the individual was "employed as part of the business and his work is done as an integral part of the business".[5] Thus in *Cassidy v Ministry of Health*[6] a consultant surgeon appointed by a hospital board was held to be a servant of the board because the operations he performed were an integral part of the work of the hospital.

A still further supplementary test which has been adopted by the courts, here taking a lead from the US Supreme Court, is the economic reality test—essentially whether the individual is in business on his own account. This test was first applied in *Market Investigations Ltd v Minister of Social Security*.[7] It is decided by such factors as whether the individual is at financial risk, or responsible for the management of the work and stands to gain or lose according to how well the work is managed, whether he can directly employ others to assist and whether he provides substantial equipment.

In certain recent cases an increased emphasis has been placed on the control test. Thus in a Privy Council decision on an appeal from Australia it was held that "in most cases the decisive criterion is the extent to which the person, whose status as employee or independent contractor is at issue, is under the direction and control of the other party to the contract with regard to the manner in which he does his work under it".[8] Again in a Court of Appeal case in 1984, the view that the economic reality test was "the fundamental test" was rejected, it being regarded as "no more than a useful test".[9]

In certain of the cases a further test has been debated. This addresses the preliminary question of whether there are sufficient mutual obligations on each side to create a contract of service. However, while it has been held that there has to be "an irreducible minimum of obligation"[10] to create such a contract, little more is required than the payment of remuneration in return for work:

> There must be a wage or other remuneration. Otherwise there will be no consideration, and without consideration no contract of any kind. The servant must be obliged to provide his own work and skill.[11]

In two cases concerning outworkers[12] the finding that the employer had no obligation to supply any work and that employees were under no obligation to accept any work was not regarded as precluding the existence of a contract of service which could be inferred from a course of dealing extending over several years. This test is therefore not normally decisive, though in one case concerning casual workers at a hotel it was found that there was no mutuality of obligation and the casual workers were not working under any overall contract of employment.[13]

In the judicial review in 2001 relating to contractors in the IT industry, the judge criticised the HMRC Employment Status Manual in its conclusion at ESM0514 (in the version as it existed at that time) that "mutuality of obligation" is not a relevant issue.[14]

A recent tendency has been to pay increased attention to the actual contractual terms to determine the nature of the contract, particularly if the relationship is ambiguous, though the court will not accept a written contract which deliberately sets out a contractor/client relationship because that is what the parties want, when in reality there is a master/servant relationship.[15]

Since several different tests may be applied and none in particular can be regarded as fundamental, it may be wondered whether a decision on an individual's employment status can be reached only in a somewhat arbitrary manner. The approach taken by the industrial tribunal in one of the relevant cases was to:

> consider all aspects of the relationship, no single factor being in itself decisive and each of which may vary in weight and direction, and having given such balance to the factors as seems appropriate, to determine whether the person was carrying on business on his own account.[16]

The Court of Appeal approved this procedure as wholly correct in law and considered that it could interfere only if the determination made on the basis of such evaluation of the factors was "perverse", ie one which a person acting judicially and properly instructed in the law could not have reached from the primary facts found—the principle established in *Edwards v Bairstow and Harrison*.[17]

HMRC issues a leaflet setting out certain practical tests applied in distinguishing employment from self-employment.[18] The leaflet does not purport to represent a comprehensive summary of the relevant case law and in fact is too influenced by the economic reality test as expounded in the *Market Investigations Ltd* case.

For certain industries HMRC has drawn up lists of types of worker whose working arrangements justify self-employed status and hence taxation under what was formerly Schedule D. For some time the former DSS was reluctant to accept such lists as a basis for contribution liability but in December 1992 issued a Note confirming that henceforth it would recognise the lists used by what was then the Inland Revenue for behind the camera/microphone workers in the television, radio, film and video industries. However, the validity of the lists was somewhat undermined by the *Hall v Lorimer*[19] case in which it was held that a vision mixer was self-employed.

The lists will be used as a basis for identifying employment status but where an individual has agreed special terms, ie outside the normal working arrangements, the then DSS reserved the right to consider the issue according to the particular circumstances. Moreover, it now remains open to both the company and the individual to appeal to the General or Special Commissioners (see supra, § 2A.51) if dissatisfied with the status accorded as a result of using the industry list.

More recently, the construction industry came under the scrutiny of the former Inland Revenue and the former DSS. At the time, the DSS stated that although normally it would accept a certificate issued by the Inland Revenue under the construction industry tax deduction scheme as prima facie evidence of self-employment, it reserved the right to recategorise an individual's status if the facts revealed that a contract of service was in existence. In a press release issued in November 1996 the Inland Revenue and DSS warned employers in the industry to review the status of workers and set up PAYE arrangements where these were necessary by 5 April 1997 at the latest. The former Contributions Agency subsequently issued a leaflet to address construction workers' most common National Insurance concerns.[20]

In March 2004, the Inland Revenue announced that a review was being undertaken whereby at a future time all labour-only contractors might be deemed to be employed persons for both tax and NIC purposes. Whilst it was said that the Inland Revenue would report to the Chancellor before the 2004 Pre Budget Report no further announcement has been made either then or in subsequent Budgets.[21]

Simon's NIC Chapter 3.

---

[1] *Young & Woods Ltd v West* [1980] IRLR 201, CA.
[2] *Yewens v Noakes* (1880) 6 QBD 530, 1 TC 260, CA.
[3] *Stevenson, Jordan and Harrison Ltd v Macdonald and Evans* [1952] 1 TLR 101, CA.
[4] *Bank voor Handel en Scheepvaart NV v Administrator of Hungarian Property* [1954] AC 584, 35 TC 311, HL.
[5] *Stevenson, Jordan and Harrison Ltd v Macdonald and Evans* [1952] 1 TLR 101, CA.
[6] [1951] 1 All ER 574, [1952] 2 KB 343.
[7] [1969] 2 QB 173, [1969] 3 All ER 732.
[8] *Narich Pty Ltd v Pay-roll Tax Comr* [1983] ICR 286, PC.
[9] *Nethermere (St Neots) Ltd v Gardiner* [1984] ICR 612, CA.
[10] *Nethermere (St Neots) Ltd v Gardiner* [1984] ICR 612.
[11] *Ready-Mixed Concrete (South East) Ltd v Ministry of Pensions* [1968] 2 QB 497, [1968] 1 All ER 433.
[12] *Airfix Footwear Ltd v Cope* [1978] ICR 1210; *Nethermere (St Neots) Ltd v Gardiner* [1984] ICR 612.
[13] *O'Kelly v Trusthouse Forte plc* [1984] QB 90, [1983] 3 All ER 456, CA.
[14] *R v IRC, ex p Professional Contractors Group Ltd* [2001] EWHC Admin 236, [2001] STC 629.
[15] *BSM (1257) Ltd v Secretary of State for Social Services* [1978] ICR 894; *Narich Pty Ltd v Pay-roll Tax Comr* [1983] ICR 286, PC; *Davies v Presbyterian Church of Wales* [1986] 1 All ER 705, [1986] 1 WLR 323, HL.
[16] *O'Kelly v Trusthouse Forte plc* [1984] QB 90, [1983] 3 All ER 456, CA.
[17] [1956] AC 14, 36 TC 207, HL (see supra, § 49.02).
[18] H M Revenue & Customs leaflet IR 56.

[19] *Hall v Lorimer* [1992] STC 599.
[20] CA leaflet CA 80, now withdrawn. The new practice was not to be applied retrospectively without agreement between the workers and the employer/client concerned. If there is such agreement and an individual previously treated as an employee is reclassified as self-employed, claims will be accepted for refund of overpaid contributions. Benefits such as statutory sick pay, statutory maternity pay and contribution based jobseekers' allowance paid on the basis of Class 1 contributions were deducted from any refund.
[21] Inland Revenue press release 23 March 2004.

Categorisation by regulations

[49.04] There are certain occupations where it is often difficult to determine whether the individual is an employee or self-employed, eg actors, musicians, part-time lecturers and teachers, and because the arrangements differ according to the particular case there can be—indeed have been—many disputed rulings often resulting in determinations by the Secretary of State for Social Security and appeals to the court. For this reason the Secretary of State was authorised to introduce regulations which treat persons in prescribed occupations as either employed earners or self-employed earners as the case may be, whether or not they would be so categorised on the basis of the particular facts and relevant law, and since the transfer of functions in 1999 these powers now lie with the Treasury.[1] Such regulations may also provide for persons in prescribed occupations to be treated as non-earners and so free from any contribution liability.[2] Regulations have been made under these provisions; these are usually known as the "Categorisation Regulations".[3]

The Categorisation Regulations require individuals in the following employments to be categorised as employed earners notwithstanding that they may not have contracts of service or hold offices with general earnings chargeable to income tax.

Simon's NIC [4.1], [4.21]–[4.439].

[1] SSCBA 1992, s 2(2)(*b*).
[2] SSCBA 1992, s 2(2)(*b*).
[3] Social Security (Categorisation of Earners) Regulations 1978, SI 1978/1689.

Employed earners

[49.05] Office cleaners etc. This head includes an operative acting in a similar capacity to an office cleaner in any premises other than a private dwellinghouse: it will therefore cover cleaners at airports, theme parks, shops and shopping precincts etc[1] By an amendment made in 1990, cleaners of telephones and associated fixtures, eg telephone kiosks, in non-domestic premises have been included in this head.[2]

Simon's NIC [4.31]–[4.50].

[49.05] The employed earner

[1] SI 1978, No. 1689, Sch 1, Part I, para 1.
[2] Social Security (Categorisation of Earners) (Amendment) Regulations 1990, SI 1990/1894, reg 2.

[49.06] Agency workers. The rules defining agency workers are framed in similar language to that in the corresponding rules for income tax purposes.[1] An agency worker is defined as a person who is required to render personal service and is subject to supervision, direction or control (or to the right of supervision, direction or control) as to the manner of rendering the service. The agency worker must be supplied by a third person (the agency) and the earnings for the service either have to be paid for on the basis of accounts submitted by the agency or other arrangements made with the agency or there must be payments (other than to the agency worker) made by way of fees, commission etc which relate to the agency worker's continued employment. The wording is deliberately wide; eg it appears not to matter whether it is the agency or the person receiving the personal service (the client) which exercises the supervision, direction or control. However, it should be noted that the supervision, direction or control has to be exercised over *the manner of rendering* the service. This implies a substantial degree of day-by-day supervision such as might be appropriate where a temporary secretary is supplied but would not be appropriate to senior executives or professional persons who can be expected to know how best to perform their job, being accountable primarily for achieving objectives or applying their skills to particular projects. It has been held that head-chefs supplied on a temporary basis to a restaurant were akin to such professional persons and not subject to such supervision as would apply to ordinary employees. The test applied in this case was: "Did management have the right to tell Mr G and Mr A not only what job to do, but how they should do it?"[2] This decision could remove many high level staff from the scope of the agency workers rules.

Certain kinds of agency workers are excepted from this categorisation rule and may therefore still be treated as self-employed depending on the particular facts; they are certain homeworkers, fashion, photographic and artist's models, and those who are merely introduced to the client and as a result become employees of the client and the agency has no direct financial interest in the continuation of the employment[3] and, until 17 July 1998, actors, musicians and other entertainers (see also infra, § **49.10**).[4]

Where an agency provides the services of a worker in the construction industry, and there is no contract of employment between the agency and the worker or between the contractor and the worker there was no obligation to account for PAYE until 6 April 1998.[5] However, agencies have always been obliged to account for NICs, including both primary and secondary Class 1 contributions, in respect of payments they make to construction workers.[6]

Simon's NIC [4.51]–[4.120].

[1] ITEPA 2003, ss 44–47; Social Security (Categorisation of Earners) Regulations 1978, SI 1978/1689, Sch 1, Part I, para 2, Col (A).
[2] *Staples v Secretary of State for Social Services* (15 March 1985, unreported), QBD.

3   SI 1978/1689, Sch 1, Part I, para 2, Col (B).
4   SI 1998/1728 and SI 1999/3.
5   FA 1998, s 55, amending former TA 1988, s 134(5)(c).
6   See CA National Insurance News, Issue 8, Summer 1997.

[49.07] Employment by spouse or by civil partner. The employment of a person by their spouse or civil partner, for the purpose of the partner's employment (which for this purpose includes self-employment) has to be treated as employed earners' employment.[1] The extension to include civil partners in this rule was effective from 5 December 2005.[2]

Simon's NIC [4.121]–[4.130].

1   Social Security (Categorisation of Earners) Regulations 1978, SI 1978/1689, Sch 1, Part I, para 3.
2   Amendment made by Social Security (Categorisation of Earners) (Amendment) Regulations 2005, SI 2005/3133, reg 3.

[49.08] Lecturers, teachers, instructors etc. This head applies only if the lecturers etc are not already treated as employed earners under the agency workers rules. To fall within this head, the individual has to be employed as a lecturer, teacher, instructor or in any similar capacity at an educational establishment.[1] An educational establishment is defined as including a place where instruction is provided in any course or part of a course designed to lead to a certificate, diploma, degree or professional qualification. It can also include a place where similar instruction is given but which is not designed to lead to a certificate etc; this renders the definition very wide.[2] It is also necessary for the earnings to be paid by or on behalf of the provider of the education and for the individual to give the instruction in the presence of the persons to whom the instruction is given, except in the case of the Open University where such presence is not a condition.[3]

Exception is made for lecturers etc who have agreed in advance to give the instruction on not more than three days in three consecutive months and for those who deliver public lectures.[4]

Simon's NIC [4.131]–[4.150].

1   Social Security (Categorisation of Earners) Regulations 1978, SI 1978/1689, Sch 1, Part I, para 4, Col (A).
2   SI 1978/1689, reg 1(2).
3   SI 1978/1689, Sch 1, Part I, para 4, Col (A)(b), (c).
4   SI 1978/1689, Sch 1, Part I, para 4, Col (B)(a), (b).

[49.09] Ministers of religion. Many ministers will be employed earners by virtue of holding an office, as is the case generally with Church of England clergy, or as employees under contracts of service, the position in many of the non-conformist churches. Ministers not holding an office or having a contract

[49.09] The employed earner

of service might otherwise fall to be treated as self-employed but the Categorisation Regulations render such persons as employed earners regardless.[1]

An exception is made for a minister whose remuneration does not consist wholly or mainly of stipend or salary.[2] Remuneration for this purpose excludes any payment in kind,[3] such as the provision of free living accommodation, and other exclusions from earnings made under the Contribution Regulations and any specific and distinct payment made towards the maintenance or education of the minister's dependants.[4]

The term "minister of religion" is not defined but it has been held that it implies a "differentiation between the clergy on the one hand and the laity on the other", the minister belonging to the former category.[5] Where the religious grouping makes no such differentiation, there will be no minister of religion in this sense.

Simon's NIC [4.151]–[4.179].

[1] Social Security (Categorisation of Earners) Regulations 1978, SI 1978/1689, Sch 1, Part I, para 5, Col (A).
[2] SI 1978/1689, Sch 1, Part I, para 5, Col (B).
[3] SI 1978/1689, Sch 1, Part I, para 5, Col (B) (parenthesis).
[4] SI 1978/1689, reg 1(2).
[5] *Walsh v Lord Advocate* [1956] 3 All ER 129, HL.

[49.10] Actors, musicians and other performers. Certain actors, musicians and other performers are categorised as employed earners with effect from 17 July 1998.[1] This provision does not, however, apply in the case of those whose remuneration "does not consist wholly or mainly of salary".[2] Whilst "entertainer" is defined in the legislation, "salary", until April 2003, was not. Case law suggested to HMRC that a sum will be salary if it is paid in respect of services rendered or to be rendered, and is payable under the terms of a contract, and is computed by time and payable at a fixed time, and is in respect of services which have an element of continuity or recurrence. The Revenue says that specific advice should be sought from them in all cases of dispute or difficulty but that, as a general rule of thumb, sums payable under most contracts which import Equity conditions in relation to hours of work, etc are likely to be regarded as salary. Because of the need for an element of recurrence "it seems unlikely that remuneration for a one-off engagement for one day or less could reasonably be described as salary". The Revenue stresses that the special categorisation rules apply if the entertainer is remunerated "wholly or mainly" by salary. Where that is the case, all payments from the engagement are liable to Class 1 National Insurance contributions and not just the salary element.[3] From 6 April 2003, "salary" is specifically defined.[4] The definition was introduced due to the law not having previously operated as the authorities had intended since the 1998 change. A by-product of this is that some actors, etc and their engagers were able to obtain refunds of Class 1 contributions paid from July 1998 to 5 April 2003[5] provided applications were made by 5 April 2005.[6]

Simon's NIC [4.180]–[4.190].

[1] Social Security (Categorisation of Earners) Regulations 1978, SI 1978/1689, Sch 1, Part I, para 5A, Col (A), inserted by SI 1998/1728, reg 3(b).
[2] Social Security (Categorisation of Earners) Regulations 1978, SI 1978/1689, Sch 1, Part I, para 5A, Col (B), inserted by SI 1998/1728, reg 3(b).
[3] Inland Revenue Film and TV Industry notes.
[4] Social Security (Categorisation of Earnings) Amendment Regulations 2003, SI 2003/736.
[5] Inland Revenue Tax Bulletin, June 2003, p 1033.
[6] Updated Inland Revenue guidance notes, placed on its website, Autumn 2004.

[49.11] In one case only, the Categorisation Regulations require the occupation to be treated as self-employed: this is that of examiners, moderators, invigilators etc and those engaged to set examination questions so long as the contract for the whole of the work has to be performed in less than 12 months.[1] An exception would be where the examiner etc is supplied by an agency and the agency workers rules apply.[2]
Simon's NIC [4.271]–[4.290].

[1] Social Security (Categorisation of Earners) Regulations 1978, SI 1978/1689, Sch 1, Part II, para 6, Col (A).
[2] SI 1978/1689, Sch 1, Part II, para 6, Col (A) (parenthesis).

[49.12] In the following cases the Categorisation Regulations require the employment to be regarded as non-earner's employment and so disregarded for contribution purposes:

(1) employment by spouse or civil partner otherwise than for the purpose of the partner's employment (which for this purpose includes self-employment);[1]
(2) employment by certain close relatives for domestic purposes;[2]
(3) employment as a self-employed earner where the earner is not ordinarily so employed (see infra, § **52.02**);[3]
(4) employment as a returning officer or counting officer;[4]
(5) employment as a member of a visiting force or (unless ordinarily resident in the UK) as a civilian employee of such force;[5]
(6) employment as a member of an international headquarters or defence organisation.[6] This is subject to exceptions for serving members of the regular armed forces of the Crown based in the UK and for civilians ordinarily resident in the UK who do not belong to a scheme providing retirement benefits established by the international headquarters or defence organisation;[7]
(7) from 6 April 1994 to 5 July 2006, employment as a Queen's Gurkha officer or as a member of the Brigade of Gurkhas of a person who was recruited for that Brigade in Nepal.[8]

Simon's NIC [4.341]–[4.410].

[1] Social Security (Categorisation of Earners) Regulations 1978, SI 1978/1689, Sch 1, Part III, para 8, Col (A), as amended by Social Security (Categorisation of Earners)

[49.12] The employed earner

(Amendment) Regulations 2005, SI 2005/3133, reg 4.
2. SI 1978/1689, Sch 1, Part III, para 7, Col (A).
3. SI 1978/1689, Sch 1, Part III, para 9, Col (A).
4. SI 1978/1689, Sch 1, Part III, para 10, Col (A).
5. SI 1978/1689, Sch 1, Part III, para 11, Cols (A), (B).
6. SI 1978/1689, Sch 1, Part III, para 12, Col (A).
7. SI 1978/1689, Sch 1, Part III, para 12, Col (B)(*a*), (*b*).
8. SI 1978/1689, Sch 1, Part III, para 13, Col (A), removed by SI 2006/1530.

[49.13] Where the Secretary of State for Social Security made a determination before 1 April 1999 on a categorisation question from which there was an appeal to the High Court and the determination was overruled, the Secretary of State could direct that the employment status which he determined should apply up to the date of the decision of the High Court if it appeared to him that this would be in the interests of the contributor or any person claiming benefit on the basis of the contributions.[1] This power was normally exercised only where the individual was categorised as an employed earner under the Secretary of State's determination and the High Court decided that he was self-employed.

This provision is effectively spent in view of the replacement of that 'appeals' system from 1 April 1999, and the revocation of SSAA 1992, s 19 to which the regulation still notionally refers.

Simon's NIC [4.1].

1. Social Security (Categorisation of Earners) Regulations 1978, SI 1978/1689, reg 4.

Secondary contributors

[49.14] If a person is categorised as an employed earner, a corollary is that there must be an employer or equivalent, called in the legislation the "secondary contributor". Where the employed earner is employed under a contract of service, the secondary contributor is the employer.[1] Where the employed earner holds an office with general earnings chargeable to income tax, the secondary contributor is either the government department, public authority or body responsible for paying those earnings or a person specifically prescribed by regulations.[2]

The Categorisation Regulations set out various situations where a prescribed person is to be treated as the secondary contributor.[3] They are as follows.

Simon's NIC [4.31]–[4.260].

1. SSCBA 1992, s 7(1)(*a*).
2. SSCBA 1992, s 7(1)(*b*).
3. Social Security (Categorisation of Earners) Regulations 1978, SI 1978/1689, Sch 3.

[49.15] **Office cleaners etc.** In the case of office cleaners (for definition see supra, § **49.05**), the supply agency is to be treated as the secondary contributor if the cleaner is remunerated by the agency but where there is no agency or the agency does not remunerate the cleaner, the client is to be the secondary contributor (unless the cleaner is employed by a company in voluntary liquidation when the rule set out below applies).[1]

[1] SI 1978/1689, Sch 3, Col (B), para 1(a), (b).

[49.16] **Agency workers.** In the case of agency workers (for definition see supra, § **49.06**) it is the agency, eg the third person by whom or through whose agency the worker is supplied, who is to be treated as the secondary contributor.[1] Where, in England and Wales, a person is supplied by an unincorporated body of persons and that person is a member of that body, the other members of that body are to be regarded as the secondary contributor.[2] However, where the agency, ie the third person or other members of the unincorporated body, does not meet the residence or presence conditions for contribution liability to arise, the client, ie the person to whom the agency worker is supplied, is to be treated as the secondary contributor[3] (see infra, § **54.05** particularly for periods before 6 April 1994 for the non-applicability of these rules in relation to UK host companies in cases where certain overseas companies send expatriate staff to work in this country).

[1] SI 1978/1689, Sch 3, Col (B), para 2(a), (b).
[2] SI 1978/1689, Sch 3, Col (B), para 2(a).
[3] SI 1978/1689, Sch 3, Col (B), para 2(c).

[49.17] **Employment by spouse or by civil partner.** Where a person is employed by their spouse or civil partner for the purpose of the spouse's employment, the spouse or civil partner is to be treated as the secondary contributor.[1]

[1] SI 1978/1689, Sch 3, Col (B), para 3; Social Security (Categorisation of Earners) (Amendment) Regulations 2005, SI 2005/3133, reg 4.

[49.18] **Company in voluntary liquidation.** Where a person is employed by a company in voluntary liquidation (and providing the agency workers rules do not apply), the liquidator is to be treated as the secondary contributor.[1]

[1] SI 1978/1689, Sch 3, Col (B), para 4.

[49.19] **Barrister's clerk.** Where a person is employed as an employee in chambers as a barrister's clerk, the head of chambers is to be treated as the secondary contributor.[1]

[1] SI 1978/1689, Sch 3, Col (B), para 5. For the circumstances where a barrister's clerk may be self-employed, see *McMenamin v Diggles* [1991] STC 419.

[49.20] The employed earner

[49.20] Lecturers, teachers, instructors etc. Where lecturers, teachers or instructors are treated as employed earners under the Categorisation Regulations (see supra, § **49.08**), the person providing the education is to be treated as the secondary contributor.[1]

---

[1] SI 1978/1689, Sch 3, Col (B), para 6.

[49.21] Ministers of religion. Where the minister is a minister in the Church of England and his employment is not under a contract of service (as would be the case where, for example, the minister is employed as a hospital chaplain), the Church Commissioners are to be treated as the secondary contributor.[1] In other cases, unless the employment is under a contract of service or is not remunerated wholly or mainly by way of salary or stipend, the secondary contributor is to be the person responsible for the administration of the fund from which the remuneration is paid.[2] Where the remuneration is paid by more than one fund, the relevant fund is either that which also pays other ministers, or if there is more than one such fund, the fund which pays the greatest number of ministers carrying out their duties in Great Britain or if neither rule identifies a particular fund, the relevant fund is that from which the minister first receives a payment of remuneration in the tax year.[3]

---

[1] SI 1978/1689, Sch 3, Col (B), para 7.
[2] SI 1978/1689, Sch 3, Col (B), para 8(*a*).
[3] SI 1978/1689, Sch 3, Col (B), para 8(*b*).

[49.22] Where payments to an entertainer fall within the definition of salary, etc (see supra, § **49.10**) the producer of the entertainment is to be treated as the secondary contributor.[1]

---

[1] SI 1978/1689, Sch 3, Col (B), para 10, as amended by SI 2003/736, reg 4 with effect from 6 April 2003.

[49.23] Where an employed earner works under the general control or management of a person other than the immediate employer the Treasury may introduce regulations which prescribe which person is to be treated as the secondary contributor.[1] This power now lies with the Treasury, following the transfer of responsibility for policy issues, etc from the former DSS with effect from 1 April 1999. The Categorisation Regulations are made in part on the basis of this enabling power.[2] Schedule 4 of the 2001 Contributions Regulations deals with the collection of contributions under PAYE and incorporates relevant parts of the PAYE Regulations: this might suggest that the principal employer, eg a UK subsidiary to which expatriate staff have been assigned by an overseas employee, is made the secondary contributor but the better view would seem to be that the provision makes the principal employer the secondary contributor only for collection purposes and so the provision operates only where the immediate employer is already liable for secondary contributions.[3]

[1] SSCBA 1992, s 7(2).
[2] SI 1978/1689, foreword and reg 5.
[3] Social Security (Contributions) Regulations 2001, SI 2001/1004, Sch 4, para 3.

Personal service companies and other intermediaries

[49.24] In certain fields of activity, including amongst computer software programmers, it is common for the individuals concerned to provide their services not as self-employed persons but through personal service companies. With such an arrangement the individual owns the majority of the shares in the personal service company but is also an employee of the company; the personal service company makes the services of the individual available in consideration for a fee or time charge. Until 6 April 2000, this was attractive so far as contribution liability was concerned because although primary and secondary Class 1 contributions will be payable in respect of the individual's remuneration from employment with the personal service company, such remuneration can be kept fairly low, in which case a net profit may result so allowing a dividend to be paid to the individual in his capacity as majority shareholder. A dividend is not earnings from the employment and does not require contributions to be paid. By this means contribution liability could previously be held to a modest level.

For a long time, the former DSS appeared to be happy to accept the arrangement in cases where, as in the computer service industry, work assignments tend to be fairly short-term, eg not usually exceeding six months and the client does not wish to assume the employer obligations which would arise from having a contract of employment. It should be appreciated that the personal service company arrangement has a variety of implications in other areas, eg the overall level of tax on income derived in the form of dividend—this will not be greater than that applying to equivalent salary so long as corporation tax is payable only at the small companies rate—the build-up of value in the company and hence capital gains and inheritance tax implications and possible restriction of pension entitlement because of salary being kept at a low level. It should also be appreciated that the fees charged by the personal service company to the client company for the services of the individual in question would generally be subject to VAT at the standard rate and therefore recovery of the input tax may be restricted where the client company is a partially exempt trader.

However, it was announced in the 1999 Budget that further restrictions would apply to personal service companies with effect from 6 April 2000. The National Insurance legislation is contained in SI 2000 No 727, *The Social Security Contributions (Intermediaries) Regulations 2000* (made under powers contained in the *Welfare Reform and Pensions Act 1999).*

These rules rely on the pre-existing tests to distinguish employment and self-employment. Therefore, if it can be established that, were the intermediary not in existence, the individual would be self-employed then the new rules will not apply to that contract.[1]

[49.24] The employed earner

The beauty of the proposals from the government's point of view is that they apply automatically, under pain of penalties, and will no longer exclude—as had been the practice previously—those cases where the arrangements have been properly and legally executed. Any intermediary is potentially affected, and will be affected if:

(1) a worker is supplied by an intermediary to a customer (end-user); and
(2) that worker controls* the intermediary; and
(3) had the contract been between the worker and the customer direct, the relationship would have been that of employment, rather than self-employment.[2]

(*Subject to provisions affecting certain associated companies (as defined by ICTA 1988, s 416), the rules apply to income generated by workers who have a material interest in a company. A material interest is where the worker or an associate, either alone or with (other) associates have beneficial ownership, or the ability to control—directly or indirectly—more than 5% of the ordinary share capital of the company, or possession of or entitlement to acquire rights entitling the holder to receive more than 5% of any company distributions or, if a close company, entitlement to receive more than 5% of the assets in a winding up.)[3]

Engagements which fall into the above categories are termed "relevant engagements" and all earnings from them fall within the scheme. Note that some intermediaries will have both "relevant engagements" and other engagements. The latter are not affected by the legislation. Similarly, the engagements of some employees of a company or a partner in a partnership will be "relevant engagements" and those of others may not.

"Associate" in relation to an individual is as defined by TA 1988, s 417(3) and (4) and in relation to a company is as defined by ICTA 1988, s 839. In relation to a partnership it means any associate of a member of the partnership.[4]

For all purposes of these NIC Regulations a man and a woman living together as husband and wife are treated as if they were married to each other. This extension of the definition did not, though, extend to couples of the same sex living together until 5 December 2005.[5]

Engagements where services are provided in domestic circumstances, eg a plumber fixing the kitchen sink, were specifically excluded until 1 September 2003[6] (the equivalent income tax exclusion ceased to apply from April 2003).

As regards partnerships, these rules—as already suggested—apply only to engagements which would fall within the definition of employment if the contract were between the client and the individual instead of the partnership. But, in addition, these provisions apply only to partnerships where:

(1) an individual, or persons connected with him or her, is entitled to 60% or more of the profits; or
(2) all or most of the partnership's income in the relevant tax year is derived from the provision of services, in a form which would fall within the definition of relevant engagements, to a single client or associate of that client; or

(3) the profit sharing arrangements in the partnership provide for the income of any of the partners to be based on the amount of income generated by those partners through relevant engagements.

If none of the above tests applies to a partnership, the rules will not affect it.[7] If the rules do apply, then since there is no employment of a partner by his partnership, there will not be any deduction in the calculation of deemed payment for salary already paid and Class 1 thereon.

Intermediaries will be responsible for applying PAYE and National Insurance contributions to all earnings from relevant engagements, whether paid to the worker or not.[8] Such calculation is to be made as at 5 April each year and after deducting:[9]

(1) all expenses paid in the tax year that would be allowable under the normal tax rules for general earnings (ie ITEPA 2003, s 336—including travelling, subscriptions, professional indemnity insurance, etc);
(2) employer pension contributions paid in the tax year to a registered scheme (together with levies under the Pensions Act 2004);
(3) 5% of the gross relevant payments, to cover other miscellaneous running expenses of the intermediary;
(4) any salary actually paid in the tax year and benefits in kind provided;
(5) the amount of employer's National Insurance contributions payable for the year, plus any Class 1 due on the deemed payment, plus any Class 1A due in respect of the year, payable on the succeeding 19 July.

The following points should be noted.

(1) The operation of the usual self-employment test has resulted in a number of appeals to the Commissioners, a number of which have had outcomes beneficial to the taxpayer.
(2) The fact that the end-user is relieved of any obligation and exposure under the new arrangements creates added pressure for such contacts to come into existence.
(3) The rules apply to all intermediaries—not just limited companies.
(4) The rules apply to all "relevant" engagements—not just to those of directors, although, in practice, it is likely that many of the individuals affected will indeed be company directors.
(5) There is an additional administrative burden for those affected by the scheme if they do not have a financial year end coinciding with 5 April.
(6) It is necessary to operate the rules on income received, so if accounts are prepared on a normal, accruals basis then a different set of figures will need to be compiled.
(7) The limited expenses allowed apply, it seems, only on a payments, rather an accounting accruals, basis. Section 336 refers to the obligation "to incur and pay". But the deduction for employers National Insurance contributions is clearly stated to be "for the year", ie, "accruals basis".
(8) There is no special relief for training expenses (which may be high in some industries, eg IT), which will be allowable from the deemed payment only if falling within the categories mentioned above—in particular the 5% general allowance.

[49.24] The employed earner

(9) Debts unpaid as at 5 April 2000 were excluded from the rules. Prepayments made before 6 April 2000, for work to be carried out subsequently, are caught by the provisions.

These provisions have been commonly avoided by a number of 'providers' who have marketed managed service and composite companies enabling a wide variety of workers to operate through the medium of a limited company where they would not ordinarily have done so. Whilst a few of these might arguably have been self-employed but for the existence of the corporate structure the overwhelming majority would be employees. The effectiveness of the marketed schemes seems to be reliance on HMRC lack of available resources in policing the personal service companies rules coupled with the ability to wind up companies leaving unpaid tax/NIC debts under those rules and then form a completely different entity to carry on the same activities. The Government announced in the December 2006 Pre Budget Report that such companies would be brought into a scheme similar to the 2000 one—yet with subtle differences—from 6 April 2007 for PAYE and from 6 August 2007 for National Insurance. There are also arrangements to enable debts unpaid by the 'scheme provider' to be transferred and then enforced against the directors, scheme provider and a wide range of third parties.

Finance Act 2007 inserts a new Chapter 9 into ITEPA 2003 which defines a 'managed service company' (MSC) as an additional enforcement measure of IR35 type schemes and subjects payments received by persons relating to services provided through such companies ie body corporate or partnership, as employment income. This applies even if the worker would, but for the corporate structure, be self-employed—such persons will need to operate through their own company doing as much management as possible themselves in order to fall within the 2000 rules to the exclusion of the 2007 rules.[10]

In defining a 'managed service company' there are four requirements to be met:

(I) the business of the company consists wholly or mainly of providing, directly or indirectly, the services of an individual(s) to other persons;
(II) payments, directly or indirectly, to the individual providing their services or those of their associates, are made which equate to the majority (or all) of the company is paid for the provision of the individual's services;
(III) the way in which the individual or their associates is paid results in them receiving more money than they would have received, after PAYE and NICs have been deducted, if all the payments had been employment income; and
(IV) the person termed as 'MSC provider', whose business is that of promoting and facilitating the use of companies to provide the service of individuals, is involved in the company.

In the case of IV above there are three points:

(a) the MSC provider's business is that of promotion and facilitation of companies;
(b) the business is not simply that of promoting or facilitating companies, but specifically promoting or facilitating companies to provide the services of individuals; and

(c) the MSC provider is 'involved with' the company.

For these purposes *involved with* is defined as being any associate or associate of the MSC provider who benefits financially, influences or controls those services or payments, influences or controls the company's finances or any activities, and, gives or promotes an undertaking to make good any tax loss.[11]

As regards debts incurred for directors or office holders of MSCs and MSC providers (and associates of those persons), the debt transfer provisions also took effect from 6 August 2007 but will not take effect before 6 January 2008 in the case of other persons (such as agencies).

A major difference between the MSC rules and the IR35 legislation is that those who fall within IR35 can claim comparatively generous travel and subsistence allowances and a general expenses deduction of 5%. This is not the case under the MSC rules. They remove the tax/NICs advantage in respect of travel altogether.[12]

---

[1] Social Security Contributions (Intermediaries) Regulations 2000, SI 2000/727, reg 6.
[2] SI 2000/727, reg 6(1)(c).
[3] SI 2000/727, reg 5.
[4] SI 2000/727, reg 3.
[5] SI 2000/727, reg 2(5), (6). Regulation 2(6) amended by Social Security Contributions (Intermediaries) (Amendment) Regulations 2005, SI 2005/3131, reg 4.
[6] Social Security Contributions (Intermediaries) (Amendment) Regulations 2003, SI 2003/2079.
[7] SI 2000/727, reg 5(5), (6), as amended by Social Security Contributions (Intermediaries) (Amendment) Regulations 2005, SI 2005/3131, reg 5.
[8] SI 2000/727, reg 7.
[9] SI 2000/727, reg 7, as amended by Social Security Contributions (Intermediaries) (Amendment) Regulations 2005, SI 2005/3131, reg 6.
[10] FA 2007, s 25, Sch 3.
[11] ITEPA 2003, s 61B(2).
[12] ITEPA 2003, s 61G(3).

50

Employment earnings

Meaning of earnings	PARA **50.01**
Gratuities; employee trusts	PARA **50.04**
Pension payments	PARA **50.05**
Reimbursement of expenses	PARA **50.06**
Petrol allowances	PARA **50.07**
Termination payments etc	PARA **50.09**
Other special cases	PARA **50.17**
Payments in kind; securities	PARA **50.21**
Retrospective liability on earnings	PARA **50.36**
Harmonisation with PAYE	PARA **50.37**

Meaning of earnings

[**50.01**] The basic definition of earnings for contribution purposes is that "earnings includes any remuneration or profit derived from an employment".[1] The expression "an employment" refers both to employment as an "employed earner" and to employment as a "self-employed earner".[2] "Remuneration" is a term appropriate to the wages, salaries, fees etc earned by an employee, whereas "profit" is appropriate to the business profits of a self-employed person. Nevertheless an employee's earnings can also include "profit" as is apparent from the provisions dealing with the collection of Class 1 contributions through the PAYE system. There "general earnings"—in this context the earnings on which contributions have to be paid through the PAYE system—are as defined in ITEPA 2003, s 7(3).[3]

It is on the basis that an employee's earnings include profit that the authorities consider that such items as benefits in kind (in so far as not subject to the payment in kind exclusion) and round sum allowances give rise to Class 1 contribution liability (see further infra, § **50.06** and § **50.21**).

However, before the profit can be included in the employee's earnings, it must be derived from the employment and therefore the income tax cases which consider whether or not a payment to the employee arises out of the employment are highly relevant. In the leading case of *Hochstrasser v Mayes*, Upjohn J in the High Court summarised the authorities thus: 'in my judgment not every payment made to an employee is necessarily made to him as a profit arising from his employment. Indeed in my judgment the authorities show that to be a profit arising from the employment, the payment must be made in reference to the services the employee renders by virtue of his office and it must be in the nature of a reward for services past, present or future.'[4] When the case came before the House of Lords, Viscount Simonds considered the summary could not be improved upon, except for the reference to past services which was open to question.

In another House of Lords judgment Lord Radcliffe laid down the following test for determining whether the payment arises from the office or employment: 'while it is not sufficient to render a payment assessable that an employee would not have received it unless he had been an employee, it is assessable if it has been paid to him in return for acting or being an employee'.[5]

The latter passage has frequently been cited as the main ground for the decision and was relied on in the more recent case of *Hamblett v Godfrey*.[6] Here attention was focused on the final phrase "or being an employee" and it was held that because a payment to an employee at the Cheltenham GCHQ in recompense for withdrawing her right to belong to a trade union could have been made only because she was an employee, the source of the payment was the employment and the payment must be a profit arising from the employment. The former DSS was known to have considered this decision and taken legal advice on its implications in relation to contribution liability.

The application of this principle is illustrated in several of the specific situations considered in the following paragraphs. It will often result in a payment having to be treated as earnings which would not otherwise be so treated, eg as where a payment in lieu of notice is provided for under the terms of the employment contract. But this will not always be the case: eg relocation payments such as were the subject of *Hochstrasser v Mayes* were held in that case not to be "a profit arising from the employment". However, the conventional approach now is to accept the validity of the new policy and legislation effective from 6 April 1998 which gives Class 1 NIC relief on all relocation expenses which qualify for tax relief.

Certain payments are specifically required to be included in "remuneration" and so are within the definition of earnings for contribution purposes. They are:

(1) statutory sick pay, statutory maternity pay, statutory paternity pay and statutory adoption pay;[7]
(2) sickness payments under arrangements made by the employer where the employer has made or is liable to make contributions to fund such payments;[8]
(3) payments for restrictive covenants where a tax liability arises under ITEPA 2003, ss 225–226.[9] Until 10 July 1997, a payment taxable under what is now s 226 was not subject to National Insurance contributions;[10]
(4) any gain arising from securities and securities options (shares and share options, until 1 September 2003) on which the earner is chargeable to income tax under ITEPA 2003, s 476, reduced by amounts deducted under ITEPA 2003, s 480(1)–(6).[11]

The result of including "profits" in the employee's earnings and including the above payments in "remuneration" will be to bring closer what are earnings for contribution purposes with what are earnings for tax purposes. But the two expressions do not in fact converge and therefore do not always have precisely the same scope.

The main reasons for a divergence occurring are:

(1) certain income tax rules allowing specific deductions have no application to contribution liability; and
(2) there are certain specific exclusions from earnings for contribution purposes that do not necessarily apply for tax purposes.

These matters are considered further at infra, §§ 50.02–50.03.

Simon's NIC [5.2], [5.21]–[5.30].

---

[1] SSCBA 1992, s 3(1).
[2] SSCBA 1992, s 2(1)(a), (b).
[3] Social Security (Contributions) Regulations 2001, SI 2001/1004, Sch 4, para 1.
[4] (1957) 38 TC 673 at 705.
[5] (1959) 38 TC 673 at 707.
[6] [1987] STC 60.
[7] SSCBA 1992, s 4(1)(a).
[8] SSCBA 1992, s 4(1)(b).
[9] SSCBA 1992, s 4(4)(b).
[10] SSA 1998, s 50(1) and (3).
[11] SSCBA 1992, s 4(4)(a).

Deductions not allowed

[50.02] The following deductions which can be made from income for tax purposes have no application to earnings for contribution purposes:

(1) Employee's expenses wholly exclusively and necessarily incurred in the performance of the duties (ITEPA 2003, ss 228, 292, 294, 328–330, 336, 359, 368). There is, however, a special rule covering reimbursement of identified expenses of the employment (see infra, § **50.06**).
(2) Charitable donations under the payroll deduction scheme (ITEPA 2003, ss 713–715).
(3) Employee contributions to registered pension schemes (FA 2004, Pt 4, Ch 4).
(4) The 100% deduction from earnings where there are overseas duties and a qualifying period of absence of at least 365 days up to and including 17 March 1998, but only "seafarers" thereafter (ITEPA 2003, ss 328, 329, 342, replacing former TA 1988, s 193 as amended by FA 1998, s 63).

Payments excluded from earnings

[50.03] The contribution regulations require many payments to be excluded from earnings for Class 1 contribution purposes, although in some instances a Class 1A charge may arise from 6 April 2000.[1] The following are the most important exclusions:

(1) Payments in kind subject to certain specified exceptions; provision of board or lodging or of services or other facilities.[2]

[50.03] Employment earnings

(2) Specific reimbursement of expenses actually incurred by the employee in carrying out the employment.[3]

(3) Employer contributions to a registered pension scheme providing they are within the permitted maximum and so do not fall to be treated as general earnings of the employee.[4]

(4) Payments from registered pension schemes[5] and some similar payments from unregistered schemes (but not payments of a kind which would not have been permitted had the scheme been a registered scheme).[6]

(5) A payment by way of shares or options over shares in an employing company or in a company controlling the employing company under schemes approved by HM Revenue & Customs.[7]

(6) Options to acquire shares in 13 above.[8]

(7) Payments of amounts previously included in earnings.[9]

(8) Holiday pay paid directly or indirectly from a centralised fund operated by a number of employers and not under the management and control of those employers, or where the person making the payment is entitled to be reimbursed by such a fund.[10]

(9) Gratuities or offerings, subject to certain conditions (see below).[11]

(10) Home to work travelling expenses paid to disabled persons under the Disabled Persons (Employment) Act 1944.[12]

(11) Sickness payments out of a fund representing contributions by the employee.[13]

(12) VAT chargeable on goods or services supplied by an employed earner which is included in the earnings paid to or for the benefit of the employee,[14] eg where an office is accepted and services are supplied by the employed earner as the holder of the office.[15]

(13) Redundancy payments.[16]

(14) Payments in respect of employee liabilities and indemnity insurance which are allowable for income tax under ITEPA 2003, s 346.[17]

(15) Payments in respect of "incidental overnight expenses" (formerly "personal incidental expenses") where the employee is required to stay away overnight for the purposes of the employment.[18]

(16) Various training costs and course expenses.[19]

(17) Relocation expenses where income tax relief is available or would have been available had the £8,000 limit not been exceeded.[20]

(18) Professional, etc subscriptions that are tax allowable under ITEPA 2003, ss 343 and 344.[21]

(19) From 6 April 2005, childcare vouchers (currently) up to £55 per week.[22]

(20) Fees paid to ministers of religion not forming part of their stipend or salary.[23]

Holiday pay normally falls to be included in earnings when paid unless it represents sums previously set aside with the earner's consent and which were treated as earnings at that time: in that case when the holiday pay is paid it will be excluded by virtue of 1 above.

The kind of holiday pay scheme which would fall within 2 are those found in the construction and allied industries, eg the building and civil engineers industries holiday pay scheme. In such schemes the employer purchases special stamps to build up holiday pay entitlement for the employees and the amounts spent on these stamps do not have to be included in earnings.[24] Thus, provision of holiday pay in this way completely escapes contribution liability. It was possible to apply those rules more widely, leading to abuse. Consequently, the rules were changed with only workers in the construction sector qualifying with effect from 30 October 2007. The relief will be fully withdrawn with effect from 30 October 2012.

Certain of the other items are considered in more detail in the following sections.

Simon's NIC [5.399]–[5.437].

[1] The exclusions are set out in the Social Security (Contributions) Regulations 2001, SI 2001/1004, regs 26, 26, and Sch 3.
[2] SI 2001/1004, Sch 3, Part II, para 1 subject to Sch 3, Part II, para 2.
[3] SI 2001/1004, Sch 3, Part VIII, para 9.
[4] SI 2001/1004, Sch 3, Part VI, para 2, as amended by Social Security (Contributions) (Amendment No. 2) Regulations 2006, SI 2006/576, reg 8.
[5] SI 2001/1004, Sch 3, Part VI, para 2, as amended by Social Security (Contributions) (Amendment No. 2) Regulations 2006, SI 2006/576, reg 8.
[6] SI 2001/1004, Sch 3, Part VI, para 10, as inserted by Social Security (Contributions) (Amendment No. 2) Regulations 2006, SI 2006/576, reg 8.
[7] SI 2001/1004, Sch 3, Part IX.
[8] SI 2001/1004, Sch 3, Part IX.
[9] SI 2001/1004, Sch 3, Part X, para 2.
[10] SI 2001/1004, Sch 3, Part X, para 12.
[11] SI 2001/1004, Sch 3, Part X, para 5.
[12] SI 2001/1004, Sch 3, Part X, para 8(c).
[13] SI 2001/1004, Sch 3, Part X, para 7.
[14] SI 2001/1004, Sch 3, Part X, para 9.
[15] VATA 1994, s 94.
[16] SI 2001/1004, Sch 3, Part X, para 6.
[17] SI 2001/1004, Sch 3, Part X, para 10.
[18] SI 2001/1004, Sch 3, Part X, para 4.
[19] SI 2001/1004, Sch 3, Part VII.
[20] SI 2001/1004, Sch 3, Part VIII, para 2.
[21] SI 2001/1004, Sch 3, Part X, para 11.
[22] SI 2001/1004, Sch 3, Part V, para 7, as amended by Social Security (Contributions) (Amendment No. 3) Regulations 2006, SI 2006/883, reg 2.
[23] SI 2001/1004, Sch 3, Part X, para 13.
[24] HM Revenue & Customs CWG 2 (2007) pp 28–31.

Gratuities; Employee trusts

[50.04] For gratuities or offerings to fall within the exclusion from earnings one of two alternative conditions needs to be met:[1] either

[50.04] Employment earnings

(1) the payment is not made directly or indirectly by the secondary contributor and the sum paid does not comprise or represent a sum previously paid to the secondary contributor;[2] or

(2) the payment is not directly or indirectly allocated by the secondary contributor to the earner.[3]

In relation to tips, these rules mean that the exclusion will apply when customers pay the employees directly or if the tips are paid to the employer in the first instance, eg by additions included in cheque, credit card or debit card payments etc, the pool then being shared without the employer's involvement, eg a tronc master or committee decides the allocation. Such a procedure will not be effective in relation to service charges made in the bills because these are legally due to the employer and any allocation must necessarily involve the employer. In the case *Nerva v United Kingdom*, the European Court of Human Rights ruled as regards the National Minimum Wage that tips paid by cheque or credit card are the property of the employer and can be used to pay the basic staff wage. Some commentators and Inland Revenue compliance officers did suggest up to early 2005 that there could therefore be a Class 1 liability on such tips paid by a 'troncmaster' where none had existed previously. Initial Inland Revenue guidance was that contributions were due in many cases where tips are distributed by troncs, but this was based on incorrect reading of the legislation set out above. The Inland Revenue said that contributions were due where the employer has "interfered" in the allocation of the tips. This is not a feature of the legislation and the interpretation of the word "interfere" was also, of itself, arguably excessive. However, the 2005 edition of the guidance now accepts that credit card commission may now be deducted by the employer when passing over tips to the troncmaster without that, unless there are other undesirable features present, creating an NIC liability on the distributions from the tronc.[4] The 2005 guidance, however, did continue to say that if an employment contract states that an employee has a right to participate in a tronc then all payments from the tronc are liable for NIC. This was incorrect and HMRC finally relented early in 2006. Further, those who had made settlements on the basis of the previous, incorrect interpretation can claim a refund if this had not already been offered by 31 May 2006.[5]

It has been suggested that the exclusion for gratuities can be exploited to provide discretionary bonuses to employees. The procedure would be for the employer to set up a discretionary employee trust and for the trustees to make discretionary payments to employees out of funds provided by the employer. Prior to 6 October 1987 there were specific exclusions from earnings for payments to and from such a trust which were repealed from that date.[6] However, if the payments to the employees can be regarded as "gratuities" the separate exclusion discussed above would apply. This interpretation was a feature of the Channel Five case[7] and in what was seemingly a direct response to that, this part of the legislation on gratuities was tightened with effect from 23 February 2004.[8]

Simon's NIC [5.45]–[5.49].

---

[1] Social Security (Contributions) Regulations 2001, SI 2001/1004, Sch 3, Part X, para 5.

2   SI 2001/1004, Sch 3, Part X, para 5(2).
3   SI 2001/1004, Sch 3, Part X, para 5(3).
4   HMRC booklet E24.
5   HMRC *Tax Bulletin*, Issue 82, April 2006.
6   Formerly SI 1979/591, reg 19(1)(e).
7   *Channel 5 TV Group Ltd v Morehead* [2003] STC (SCD) 327.
8   SI 2001/1004, Sch 3, Part X, para 5(4)–(6), inserted by Social Security (Contributions) (Amendment) Regulations 2004, SI 2004/173.

Pension payments

[50.05] From 6 April 2006, payments out of pension funds are excepted from a National Insurance charge only if they are:

(a)   from a registered pension scheme;[1]
(b)   benefits deriving from contributions made under FA 2004, Sch 33, para 2 or Taxation of Pension Schemes (Transitional Order) 2006, SI 2006/572, art 15(2);[2]
(c)   from a FURBS where the contributions were put in before 6 April 1998;[3]
(d)   from a FURBS where the contributions were put in on or after 6 April 1998, but before 6 April 2006, and NIC (Class 1) have been paid on the contributions made;[4]
(e)   certain schemes exempt under double taxation agreements;[5]
(f)   certain payments from employer financed retirement benefit schemes and from employer financed pension only schemes;[6]
(g)   certain payments from unregistered schemes which would have been allowed had they been from a registered scheme.[7]

As regards (c), the exemption is arguably of no application because the exemption as it is now written is given by reference to 'relevant benefits' as defined in ICTA 1988, s 612. However, that provision was withdrawn as a result of the changed tax regime from 6 April 2006. HM Revenue and Customs has however confirmed to the Tax Faculty of the Institute of Chartered Accountants in England and Wales that it was not the intention to withdraw that exemption and that they will continue to apply it as if s 612 were still a current tax provision. But they have no plans to amend the NIC legislation formally.[8]

Prior to 6 April 2006, there was a specific exception from earnings for NIC purposes for "any payment made by way of pension".[9] The term "pension" has not been defined by statute and judges have refused to attempt such a definition. Generally, for payments to be "pension" they will need to be in respect of past service as opposed, for example, to compensation for loss of office, a question considered in *McMann v Shaw*.[10] However, it was decided in *Johnson v Holleran*[11] that it is not necessary for the employee to have retired for the payments to be pension—ill-health or disability could be the reason—but it is essential that the employment in respect of which the payments are made has ceased. So, for example, if on ceasing to be employed by one employer, an individual enters employment with another employer, payments made following the end of the first employment may still be regarded as pension notwithstanding that the individual is concurrently still employed but with a different employer.

Past guidance from the former DSS on the scope of the exception passed through successive changes. The guidance in the 1993 edition of the Employer's Manual read:

> Any payment made by way of pension for long service, retirement or ill health or widowhood should not be included in gross pay. If payments which are not in the form of a pension are made under a trust arrangement during the course of employment, these must be included in gross pay.[12]

This omitted the sentence included in the previous version:

> For payment to be regarded as a pension, the employment must have ceased.[13]

The reason for this change was that the former DSS recognised that in the case of exempt approved schemes subject to discretionary approval by the Commissioners for HMRCs, it is possible in certain circumstances for a pension to be paid while the member is still in service. One case is where the pension is taken at normal retirement date but the member continues to work for the employer company beyond that date, although this practice is still the subject of continuing attacks by HMRC Pension Schemes Office. Nonetheless, the former DSS did not wish to treat pension paid during service in these particular circumstances as earnings for NIC purposes.

More problematic were lump sum payments. One of the characteristics of a pension is regularity of payment. This is clearly lacking in the case of a lump sum payment. Nevertheless, the former DSS did not take such a strict line and previously confirmed that there is no problem where a lump sum is paid as part of the benefits of the scheme in addition to subsequent regular payments of pension (as is the case with civil service schemes).

The former DSS also confirmed that a lump sum commutation payment will be accepted as within the exception so long as what is commuted is a true pension but declined to elaborate on what constitutes a true pension. This means that the case law discussed above will be relevant, except that the requirement for the individual to have ceased employment with the employer in question will in certain circumstances be disregarded.

All of these issues have been, and in some instances, still remain, especially pertinent in relation to funded unapproved retirement benefit schemes (FURBS) where for tax reasons it was desirable that a lump sum as opposed to ongoing pension was paid.[14] The anticipated freedom from NIC liability on the employer contributions and on the lump sum payment was one of the attractions of such an arrangement. The reference in the guidance of the former DSS cited above to "payments which are not in the form of a pension . . . made under a trust arrangement" may have been relevant in this connection. In general, where the FURBS has a normal retirement age broadly corresponding to what the former Inland Revenue would require in an approved scheme, it was thought that there would be little difficulty over the former DSS accepting the arrangement as a genuine pension scheme and hence there being no NIC liability on the employer contributions or the lump sum. But where the retirement age for the purpose of the FURBS is only a short time after the payment of an employer contribution and the employee remains in service after such age because, for example, the normal retirement date under an approved scheme to which he belongs is many years hence, the matter may be entirely different. It was therefore announced on 22 July 1997 that clauses would be included in the Social Security Bill to bring FURBS payments into charge to contribution liability from 6 April 1999, but then the Contributions Agency confirmed in a press release[15] on 17 November 1997 that in their view FURBS had always, technically, been liable to contributions and that the CA expected employers to comply by 6 April 1998. The CA also stated that they would look at earlier FURBS transactions where payments have been made out of the scheme very quickly after its set up. The views set out in the CA press release of 17 November 1997 are highly questionable but the then Inland Revenue reiterated its previous position in the *Tax Bulletin*, June 2003. The only legal challenge to reach judgment was the Special Commissioner's case in *Telent plc v HMRC*;[16] the company's appeal in that case was dismissed. However, the significant changes from April 2006 make this issue less relevant as, now, benefits out cannot be free of liability unless Class 1 NIC were paid on contributions to the FURBS made from 6 April 1998 up to 5 April 2006.

This potential difficulty should not arise with approved pension schemes which provide primarily a lump sum benefit, eg money-purchase schemes, executive pension plans and add-ons to company pension schemes for specific individuals. However, in the case of a FURBS, the terms of which are such that the authorities ought to have little difficulty in accepting as a genuine pension arrangement, it was nevertheless advisable that the entitlement should be expressed as the payment of such pension as will result from the purchase of an annuity with the whole of the trust fund held for the benefit of the member. This would have ensured that the lump sum is essentially a payment in commutation of pension, and will be vital if the assertion of liability in the CA press release of November 1997 is to be questioned even now.

Regulations,[17] effective from 6 April 1999 up to and including 5 April 2006, provided for the apportionment of payments into a FURBS which related to two or more earners, confirmed that employer contributions to HMRC approved schemes are not "earnings" and provided exceptions from liability as regards payments of benefits from a FURBS. However, these exceptions were of course of no relevance if the assertion that liability exists, made in 1997 and propounded by the former Inland Revenue, was incorrect.

Simon's NIC [5.462]–[5.475].

---

1. Social Security (Contributions) Regulations 2001, SI 2001/1004, Sch 3, Part VI, para 2, as amended by Social Security (Contributions) (Amendment No 3) Regulations 2006, SI 2006/883, reg 8.
2. Social Security (Contributions) Regulations 2001, SI 2001/1004, Sch 3, Part VI, para 3, as amended by Social Security (Contributions) (Amendment No 3) Regulations 2006, SI 2006/883, reg 8 and by Social Security (Contributions) (Amendment No 5) Regulations 2006, SI 2006/2829, reg 3.

[50.05] Employment earnings

[3] Social Security (Contributions) Regulations 2001, SI 2001/1004, Sch 3, Part VI, para 4.
[4] Social Security (Contributions) Regulations 2001, SI 2001/1004, Sch 3, Part VI, para 5, as amended by Social Security (Contributions) (Amendment No 3) Regulations 2006, SI 2006/883, reg 8.
[5] Social Security (Contributions) Regulations 2001, SI 2001/1004, Sch 3, Part VI, para 7, as amended by Social Security (Contributions) (Amendment No 3) Regulations 2006, SI 2006/883, reg 8.
[6] Social Security (Contributions) Regulations 2001, SI 2001/1004, Sch 3, Part VI, paras 8, 9, both as amended by Social Security (Contributions) (Amendment No 3) Regulations 2006, SI 2006/883, reg 8.
[7] Social Security (Contributions) Regulations 2001, SI 2001/1004, Sch 3, Part VI, para 10, as amended by Social Security (Contributions) (Amendment No 3) Regulations 2006, SI 2006/883, reg 8.
[8] TAXline, March 2007.
[9] Social Security (Contributions) Regulations 2001, SI 2001/1004, Sch 3, Part VI, para 1, but amended from 6 April 2006 by Social Security (Contributions) (Amendment No 3) Regulations 2006, SI 2006/883, reg 8.
[10] [1972] 3 All ER 732, 48 TC 330.
[11] [1989] STC 1.
[12] DSS leaflet NI 269, (1993 edn) p 58, para (41).
[13] DSS leaflet NI 269, (1991 edn) p 57, para (38), p 61, para (84).
[14] See §§ 31.19–31.20.
[15] CA Press Release CA47/97, 17 November 1997; Social Security Act 1998, s 48.
[16] (2007) SpC 632.
[17] Social Security (Contributions) Regulations 2001, SI 2001/1004, Sch 2, para 13.

Reimbursement of expenses

[50.06] The Contribution Regulations require a person's earnings for Class 1 purposes to "be calculated on the basis of that person's gross earnings from the employment".[1] This rule is subject to the specific exclusions from earnings made by regulation 25 and Sch 3 but the only provision dealing with expenses is one which "for the avoidance of doubt" states that in calculating the earnings paid to or for the benefit of the employee "there shall be disregarded . . . any specific or distinct payment of, or contribution towards expenses actually incurred by an employee in carrying out his employment".[2]

This rule is not giving an allowance for business expenses as such: there is in fact no equivalent to the income tax rule which permits deduction for expenses only where "the employee must be obliged to expend the money wholly, exclusively and necessarily in the performance of the duties of the employment".[3] Even if the employee incurs expenditure which meets this severe test but is not reimbursed for the expenditure, no deduction can be made from the gross earnings which are subject to contribution liability.

Rather, the rule is dealing with whether the reimbursement of expenses has to be treated as a profit of the employment and hence to be included in earnings for contribution purposes[4] and the statement "for the avoidance of doubt" confirms that a reimbursement of the kind indicated is not such a profit. Whether or not a reimbursement is a "profit derived from an employment"[5] will be largely dependent on the principles established in the income tax cases dealing with whether certain payments are profits arising from the employment.[6] It has been held that not included in this category are, for example, reimbursement of the home to work travel expenses of a hospital consultant who was held to be "on duty" from the moment he received a telephone call from the hospital.[7]

By contrast, the reimbursement of ordinary home to work travel expenses will be regarded as earnings for contribution purposes. This view previously rested on the relevant income tax case on this issue—*Ricketts v Colquhoun*[8]—though properly that case dealt with whether expenses incurred personally could be deducted from the emoluments of the employment and not with whether a reimbursement of expenses was a profit of the employment. The matter was put beyond doubt upon the introduction of the changed travel expenses rules from 1998.[9]

A round sum allowance does not meet the test of being a "specific or distinct business expense" and should therefore be included in earnings. In practice specific business expenses which are subsequently identified or paid out of the allowance can be excluded so that only the balance, referred to as the "profit element", is treated as earnings.[10]

The kinds of round sum allowance which have caused particular difficulty in the past include:

(1) reimbursement of telephone bills where no records are maintained of business and private calls respectively;[11]
(2) reimbursement of petrol etc costs before 6 April 1991 where no detailed mileage logging was maintained.[12]

In such cases the former DSS required contributions to be paid on the full amount of the reimbursements. Arrears of contributions on this basis were normally sought for the previous six tax years.

In February 1995, the then DSS announced the conclusions of a review of its policy regarding evidence to substantiate expenses for NIC purposes.[13] The legal advice it received indicated that its policy may have been incorrect, particularly with regard to petrol and telephone expenses. The new policy was set out in the revised edition of the Employer's Manual, as follows:

> To prove that they are expenses actually incurred by employees in carrying out their work you must be able to identify the business expense. Evidence of the business expense is required to establish:
>
> (1) the amount of the business expense;
> (2) that the employee incurred the expense while carrying out their work.
>
> The type of evidence will depend on the item of business expenditure. For example, evidence could include:
>
> - a log of business phone calls or visits; or
> - credit card bills;
> - receipts;
> - work diaries showing the employee's engagements;

[50.06] Employment earnings

- [Inland Revenue] dispensation;
- a representative survey of the costs involved (that is a scale rate).

This list is not a complete list and any evidence will be considered.

The former DSS invited employers[14] to apply for refunds of contributions paid under its former policy or in cases where expenses, which were treated as earnings for NICs purposes, were covered by a P11D dispensation (see below). The latest guidance is set out in similar terms to the above in the Employer Further Guide to PAYE and NICs.[15]

Following the 1994 Budget Speech the Secretary of State for Social Security announced on 30 November 1994 some limited initiatives to reduce the burdens on business and align more closely the NIC and income tax rules. Employers are allowed to take account of HMRC dispensations in deciding whether NICs should be paid on expenses payments to employees. The new arrangements were confirmed in the 1995 edition of the Employer's Manual and applied with retrospective effect.[16] Refunds were available where contributions were incorrectly paid in the past.[17]

Realising the inequity of a simplistic differentiation between specific reimbursements on the one hand and all other reimbursements on the other, the former DSS, beginning with the edition of the Employer's Manual, which took effect from 6 April 1989, recognised a third class of reimbursement. This is where the reimbursement represents a reasonable estimate of the expenses likely to be incurred but the employee is not required to list and claim specific items. Subsistence allowances often follow this basis, as did relocation allowances before the new legislation effective from 6 April 1998. For the authorities to accept such an arrangement it must satisfy the following conditions:

(1) the scheme must not have an overall profit element;
(2) the payments must be based on an accurate survey of the costs involved;
(3) the scheme must allow for a movement in prices;
(4) the payments must be reasonable in relation to the employment involved; and
(5) the employee must make a claim for each payment made (to them).[18]

It is important to note that where exclusion for specific reimbursements is sought, it is necessary only to show that the expenses covered were actually incurred by the employee in carrying out the employment. This is a less restrictive test than that which applies for deduction of expenses from income chargeable to income tax where the expense must be incurred "wholly, exclusively and necessarily" in the performance of duties in the employment. This means that where duality of purpose lies behind the expenditure and deduction from general earnings chargeable to income tax would not be possible, the expense reimbursement may nevertheless be excluded from earnings for contribution purposes; thus in the case of an overseas visit combining both sight-seeing and business duties, it seems clear that specific reimbursements of expenses should be excluded from earnings for contribution purposes, even though—strictly—no deduction can be made from the income assessable to tax.[19]

In the past employers had to recognise that the former Inland Revenue concessionary treatments had no relevance to contribution liability in general.

This cut both ways. If the conditions of the then DSS regarding estimated allowances were not met, the allowances had to be included in earnings except in so far as specific items could be identified. On the other hand if the reimbursement was entirely in respect of specific items, it could be excluded for contribution purposes even if the total reimbursement exceeded any then current Inland Revenue limits.

A programme of matching NIC law with certain extra-statutory tax concessions was completed in 1998 but some disparities still remain.

Simon's NIC [5.311]–[5.398].

1   Social Security (Contributions) Regulations 2001, SI 2001/1004, reg 24 and Sch 2.
2   SI 2001/1004, Sch 3, Part VIII, para 9.
3   ITEPA 2003, s 336.
4   SSCBA 1992, s 3(1)(*a*).
5   SSCBA 1992, s 3(1)(*a*).
6   See discussion supra, § **50.01**.
7   *Pook v Owen* (1969) 45 TC 571, HL.
8   (1925) 10 TC 118, HL.
9   Social Security (Contributions) Regulations 2001, SI 2001/1004, Part VIII, para 3 and ITEPA 2003, ss 338 et seq.
10 HM Revenue & Customs leaflet CWG 2 (2007) p 87.
11 DSS leaflet NI 269, (1993 edn) p 62, para (77).
12 DSS leaflet NI 269, (1993 edn) p 65, Table A.
13 DSS *National Insurance News* 1995, No 3, p 6.
14 DSS leaflet CA 28 (NI 269), (1995 edn) p 84, para (163).
15 HM Revenue & Customs leaflet CWG 2 (2008) p 84.
16 HM Revenue & Customs leaflet CWG 2 (2008) p 84, para 137
17 DSS leaflet CA 28 (NI 269), (1995 edn) p 84, para (163).
18 HM Revenue & Customs leaflet CWG 2 (2007) p 86.
19 *Thomson v White* (1966) 43 TC 256.

Petrol allowances

[50.07] The Employer's Manual which was issued in March 1989 and the supplement issued in October 1989 caused some controversy by the comments made on the provision of petrol. The guidance given required the purchase of petrol by use of a company credit card to be included in earnings unless business use could be identified.[1] The unstated basis for this guidance was that in *Richardson v Worrall*[2] it was held that a contract for the purchase of petrol was made at the pump when the tank is filled up and that the employee did not enter into the contract as agent of the employer. Hence use of the company credit card discharged the employee's liability.

The pre-existence of this oral contract, "the forecourt arrangement" was recognised in *Re Charge Card Services Ltd*,[3] where the legal consequences of the service station subsequently accepting payment by credit card were considered. The former DSS therefore appeared to have strong grounds for claiming that where an employee purchases petrol using a company credit card or agency card, he incurs a personal liability which is discharged by the credit card arrangement. On the other hand certain counsel disputed this interpretation of the relevant law.

[1] DSS leaflet NI 269 (April 1989 edn), p 61, para (68): October 1989 supplement p 7, para (68).
[2] [1985] STC 693.
[3] [1989] Ch 497, [1988] 3 All ER 702, CA.

The effect of the Overdrive decision

[50.08] Because of their interest in the question, the fuel card companies represented by Overdrive Credit Card Ltd applied to the court, under the judicial review procedure, for the following declarations:

(1) That payment of an employee's petrol purchases by use of a company credit card does not give rise to contribution liability.
(2) That no distinction as regards contribution liability is to be drawn between:
 (a) use of a company credit card or agency card;
 (b) production of vouchers which cannot be exchanged for cash; and
 (c) charging the petrol purchased to an employer's garage account.
(3) That contribution liability under each method of payment depends entirely upon whether the employee as principal incurred personal liability for the price of the petrol in the first instance.

The court refused to grant the declaration under 1 on the grounds that it was too wide but did grant the declarations under 2 and 3. In the course of the judgment, the judges established the following points of law:

(a) The discharge of an employee's personal liability by the employer represents payment of earnings for contribution purposes. This confirmed that the principle established in *Hartland v Diggines* [1926] AC 289, [1926] All ER Rep 573 in relation to income tax applied equally to NICs.
(b) When petrol is purchased at a self-service station, the normal position is that the employee incurs a personal liability for the petrol purchased at the point when the tank is filled up. This followed from the decision in *Richardson v Worrall* (supra). In this situation, therefore, the discharge of the employee's personal liability by any of the means indicated in 2 above will constitute earnings for contribution purposes.
(c) But where, contrary to the normal practice in the UK, the employee before filling the tank makes it clear to the service station staff that he is buying as agent for the employer, eg by producing the company credit card at that stage, he does not incur a personal liability to pay for the fuel. Accordingly in this situation the purchase does not become earnings for contribution purposes. If reliance is placed on this exception, it is understood that the authorities will require to be satisfied that

employees were instructed to go through the necessary process each time a purchase was made and that the employer made regular checks to ensure that the procedure was followed.

The *Overdrive* case was the first case to consider specifically the scope of the payment in kind exception for contribution purposes. Certain of the points established are of enduring importance. However, in relation to the provision of petrol for private use where the car is made available by the employer, the decision was overtaken by events. The judgment[1] was delivered on 8 February 1991 but in his Budget Statement, on 19 March 1991, the Chancellor of the Exchequer announced that there would be a new scale charge for NIC purposes to cover petrol provided in company cars wholly or partly for private use as well as on the taxable benefit in respect of the provision of the car itself.[2] The primary legislation dealing with this charge was set out in the Social Security (Contributions) Act 1991.[3]

Simon's NIC [5.258]–[5.270].

---

[1] *R v Department of Social Security, ex p Overdrive Credit Card Ltd* [1991] STC 129, DC.
[2] See *Simon's Tax Intelligence* 1991, p 248.
[3] See further infra, § **51.13**.

Termination payments etc

[50.09] Various kinds of payments may be made when an employment is terminated. If the payments are made after the employment has ceased, there had in the past been some doubt whether the primary legislation imposed contribution liability assuming that the payments are treated as earnings from the employment. The doubt arose because of the manner in which the main charging provision is now phrased following consolidation of the contributions legislation. The provision now covers the situation "where in any tax week earnings are paid to or for the benefit of an earner in respect of any one employment of his *which is* employed earner's employment".[1] The words in italics were previously "being"[2] and it was previously argued that the change implied that the employment must still be carried on at the time the payment is made for contributions to become payable.[3] The change, however, appears in the 1992 Act which is a consolidation Act and the former DSS always argued that any disputes regarding definitions will be determined by looking at the original Act. Nevertheless, the Contributions Regulations assume that contribution liability can arise in certain circumstances after the employment has ceased and there is a specific rule which deals with the case where "the employment in respect of which the earnings are paid has ended" and "after the end of the employment" there is "a payment . . . by way of addition to a payment [of earnings] made before the end of the employment".[4] In *RCI (Europe) Ltd v Woods*,[5] Dr John Avery Jones held that the word was not used in the temporal sense described above but to distinguish employees from the self-employed. Whilst there was a further appeal in this case, the decision remained unchanged.[6]

[50.09] Employment earnings

Assuming therefore that payments post cessation of employment do indeed give rise to contribution liability as the unchallenged *RCI (Europe) Ltd* case confirms, then the appropriate treatment of termination payments for contribution purposes depends on a correct analysis of the nature of the payment in question. The actual words used by the parties concerned, eg "ex-gratia payment", "pay in lieu of notice" etc do not necessarily convey their true nature. Guidance on these payments was first brought together in one place in the 1995 edition of the Employer's Manual.[7] The principles which govern whether or not a payment on termination is subject to contribution liability are now examined. A summary of the authorities' current view of the correct PAYE and NIC treatment is set out in the Employer Further Guide to PAYE and NICs.[8]

Simon's NIC [5.107]–[5.112].

---

[1] SSCBA 1992, s 6(1).
[2] SSA 1975, s 4(2).
[3] See further Booth's NIC Brief, April 1993, p 7.
[4] Social Security (Contributions) Regulations 2001, SI 2001/1004, reg 3(5).
[5] [2003] STC (SCD) 128.
[6] [2003] EWHC 3129 (Ch); [2004] STC 315.
[7] DSS leaflet CA 28 (1995 edn) p 90, paras (93)–(99).
[8] HM Revenue & Customs leaflet CWG 2 (2007) pp 90–93.

Redundancy pay

[50.10] "For the avoidance of doubt . . . there shall be disregarded . . . any payment by way of redundancy payment."[1] This provision is not strictly making a deduction from earnings but simply confirming that redundancy payments do not come within the expression "remuneration or profit derived from an employment"[2] in the first instance and therefore do not need a specific exclusion: hence the introducing words "for the avoidance of doubt".

The term "redundancy payment" is not defined for this purpose and the question therefore arises whether it is confined to statutory redundancy pay under the employment protection legislation or can include additional payments on account of redundancy. This issue was considered in *Mairs v Haughey*[3] where the view was upheld that so far as taxability is concerned there is "no difference in principle between statutory redundancy payments and payments of the same character made in genuine redundancy circumstances under consensual arrangement".[4] According to Lord Hutton CJ, the enhanced redundancy payment would not have been made to the employee "in return for acting as or being an employee" (alluding to the test in *Hochstrasser v Mayes*) but "because he was ceasing to be an employee and to cushion him against the hardship of losing his employment".[5]

Certainly in practice the former DSS did not distinguish between statutory and additional redundancy pay but it is essential that the ground of the payment should be genuine redundancy.

For this purpose the definition of redundancy in the employment protection legislation is certainly illustrative although being a definition confined to that legislation is not directly relevant to contribution law. This defines redundancy as follows:

> For the purposes of this Act an employee who is dismissed shall be taken to be dismissed by reason of redundancy if the dismissal is wholly or mainly attributable to:
>
> (a) the fact that his employer has ceased, or intends to cease—
>   (i) to carry on the business for the purposes of which the employee was employed by him, or
>   (ii) to carry on that business in the place where the employee was so employed; or
> (b) the fact that the requirements of that business—
>   (i) for employees to carry out work of a particular kind, or
>   (ii) for employees to carry out work of a particular kind in the place where the employee was employed by the employer, have ceased or diminished or are expected to cease or diminish.[6]

It will be noted that the essence of redundancy as so defined is that the job is no longer required, not that the job holder is no longer wanted.

Following the transfer of the functions of the Contributions Agency to what is now HMRC on 1 April 1999, some employer compliance officers equate the NIC term "redundancy pay" with "statutory redundancy pay". This is incorrect and such interpretation should be resisted.

Simon's NIC [5.119]–[5.121]; Simon's Taxes E4.327.

---

[1] Social Security (Contributions) Regulations 2001, SI 2001/1004, Sch 3, Part X, para 6.
[2] SSCBA 1992, s 3(1)(a).
[3] [1992] STC 495; the House of Lords subsequently upheld the decision of the Court of Appeal in a judgment given on 22 July 1993.
[4] [1992] STC 495 at 542.
[5] [1992] STC 495 at 519.
[6] Employment Rights Act 1996, s 139(1).

Compensation for loss of employment

[50.11] Such compensation will not be earnings for contribution purposes if it represents compensation for breach by the employer of the terms of the employment contract.[1] Compensation in this sense implies that either the employee is in a position to seek redress before the employment tribunal (or the court) or is actually doing so. In either case the compensation is to satisfy an actual or potential claim against the employer. It is not necessary that the employee should threaten to take legal action, or even that he should be aware that he could bring a claim against the employer: what is required is that there should be at the least a potential claim. Former DSS guidance referred to the compensation payment being "made voluntarily".[2] The guidance is correct if what is meant is making a payment to discharge a potential claim before the employee has considered making such a claim.

[50.11] Employment earnings

Compensation of this kind must be distinguished from that which arises under the terms of the employment contract, eg where the contract provides for an amount payable on premature termination. Because compensation of this kind is contractual, it is a profit derived from the employment and is therefore rightly to be included in earnings for contributions purposes.[3]

Guidance indicates that where it is the normal practice to make non-contractual compensation payments on termination of the employment, they should be "treated as earnings".[4] This is because it is considered that such payments will have become part of the contractual arrangements if there is such a normal practice but this is not necessarily the case: one test is whether the employee could sue for the payment if it was not made in his or her own case.

Simon's NIC [5.81], [5.113].

---

[1] The principle established for income tax purposes by *Du Cros v Ryall* (1935) 19 TC 444.
[2] DSS leaflet CA 28 (NI 269), (1995 edn) p 90, para (95).
[3] This follows the distinction made in the employment law case, *Delaney v Staples* [1991] 2 QB 47, [1991] 1 All ER 609, CA. However, the House of Lords' judgment in *Mairs v Haughey* [1993] STC 569, HL, brings that point into question.
[4] HMRC leaflet CWG 2 (2007) p 90, item 1.

Ex-gratia payments

[50.12] An ex-gratia payment is quite simply a payment which the employer is under no legal obligation to make. It will therefore cover the bounty element in a compensation for loss of employment payment, ie the amount by which the payment exceeds any potential claim the employee could make.

Such a payment will not be earnings for contributions purposes so long as it does not represent a reward for services under the employment.[1] For this reason it is unwise to make or agree to make the ex-gratia payment until after the employment has ceased.

As with compensation for loss of employment, HMRC has said that ex-gratia payments should be treated as earnings where "it is your normal practice to make a payment on termination". Again it appears that such a practice is regarded as having become part of the contractual arrangements but this is not necessarily the case, especially if employees are not generally aware of the terms given to previously departing colleagues.

---

[1] See Simon's Direct Tax Service E4.404.

Pay in lieu of notice

[50.13] Pay in lieu of notice may either be a particular form of compensation for breach of contract by the employer or it may be compensation provided under the terms of the employment. In order to distinguish between the two, the former DSS described the latter as "pay in lieu of remuneration".

When under the contract of employment the employer is required to give say three months' notice but does not do so, the employee could claim for breach of contract. Accordingly "pay in lieu of notice" in this situation falls into the former category and is not earnings for contribution purposes. But where the contract allows the employer either to give three months' notice or to give pay in lieu, or where under a fixed term contract the balance of remuneration becomes payable on premature termination these payments are contractual and so earnings for contribution purposes. Likewise, the pay in lieu of notice will be contractual if the employer gives the required period of notice but does not require the employee to work during the notice period or if the contract provides for this possibility. The principles followed are those discussed above, in relation to "Compensation for loss of employment". In particular, HMRC says that pay in lieu of notice should be treated as earnings where "it is your normal practice to make a payment on termination".[1]

It will be apparent that this is an area where much turns on fine distinctions; accordingly, great care should be taken over the drafting of employment contracts and letters of dismissal if pay in lieu of notice is to be free of contribution liability. Similar considerations affect whether income tax liability will arise and HM Revenue & Customs employer compliance officers will inquire closely into this matter. Where a contract provides the employer with the discretion to make a payment of pay in lieu of notice this too will be taxable and, by inference for the same reasons, subject to National Insurance contributions.[2] Whilst this treatment might be called into question by the decision in *Cerberus Software Ltd v Rowley*[3] HM Revenue & Customs continues to deny that this is the case.[4]

Simon's NIC [5.107]–[5.112].

[1] HMRC leaflet CWG 2 (2007) p 90, item 1.
[2] *EMI Group Electronics Ltd v Coldicott* [1999] STC 803, [2000] 1 WLR 540.
[3] [2001] EWCA Civ 78, [2001] IRLR 160.
[4] Inland Revenue Tax Bulletin, Issue 63, February 2003.

Employment Rights Act payments

[50.14] Where the former employee successfully brings a claim for unfair dismissal or constructive dismissal, the award will be in the nature of compensation for infringement of the employee's statutory rights and will not be earnings for contributions purposes. This will apply equally to any payment made in return for withdrawing the claim.

There are, however, certain payments which can be made under the employment protection legislation which are specifically required to be treated as earnings for contributions purposes. They include guarantee payments, medical supervision payments and awards by an industrial tribunal for arrears of pay under an order for reinstatement, pay due on an order for continuation of employment or following a protective award.[1]

[50.14] Employment earnings

Simon's NIC [5.84]–[5.95].

[1] SSCBA 1992, s 112, HMRC leaflet CWG 2 (2007) pp 93–94.

Back pay

[50.15] Backdated pay awards received after termination are earnings from the employment and should be subject to contributions; likewise arrears of holiday pay (unless treated as earnings when first set aside). These are simply elements of the employee's remuneration and are still earnings notwithstanding that the source has ceased—they are clearly within the ambit of the regulation dealing with post-employment additional payments discussed above.[1]

Simon's NIC [7.82]–[7.100], [7.174].

[1] Social Security (Contributions) Regulations 2001, SI 2001/1004, reg 3(5), (6).

Inducement payments

[50.16] Sometimes payments are made on the termination of one employment as inducements to enter a new employment. These are sometimes called golden handshakes, golden hellos or golden goodbyes. Guidance requires all such payments to be treated as earnings "as they stem from, or are a result of the employment".[1]

However, this will not always be the case. A payment for a permanent loss of status, eg on giving up professional practice was held not to be emoluments of the employment.[2] The same should apply for contribution purposes.

But it is not necessary that the payment should be made by the new employer. A payment to the employee by the existing employer in return for his agreeing to become an employee of another employer was held to be an emolument for income tax purposes.[3] On the same reasoning it will be earnings for contribution purposes.

Simon's NIC [5.99]–[5.106].

[1] HMRC leaflet CWG 2 (2007) p 75.
[2] *Pritchard v Arundale* [1972] Ch 229, 47 TC 680 but contrast *Glantre Engineering Ltd v Goodhand* [1983] STC 1.
[3] *Shilton v Wilmshurst* [1990] STC 55, CA; revsd [1991] 1 AC 684, [1991] STC 88, HL.

Other special cases

[50.17] In the Employer Further Guide to PAYE and NICs (CWG 2), in a section headed "What to include in gross pay", HMRC gives guidance on the appropriate treatment of a number of specific items set out over five pages.[1] In general, what is attempted is to apply the relevant law to particular cases. In some cases there is an element of concession, eg in those cases where the extra-statutory concessions for tax purposes were adopted for NIC purposes too.[2] In certain cases the guidance does not appear to be well founded in law and should not be accepted: some examples have already been given. The position regarding PAYE and NIC status is summarised in the Employer Further Guide to PAYE and NICs.[3]

The following are further items where the guidance is or has been controversial.

[1] HMRC leaflet CWG 2 (2007) pp 74 ff.
[2] See infra, § **50.19**.
[3] HMRC leaflet CWG 2 (2007) pp 74–78.

Payment of bills charged to directors' current account

[**50.18**] Former guidance originally read: "If you pay, for example, a director's personal bill and you then transfer the transaction to the director's loan or current account, liability for NICs arises when you pay the bill".[1] The former DSS originally appeared to consider that where the director's account was already in credit, eg as a result of undrawn fees previously voted, the debit in respect of the personal bill was nevertheless a payment of earnings.

This matter was taken up by representative bodies and on 13 November 1992 the then DSS issued a letter confirming that provided the loan or current account was already in credit and the transaction does not take the account into debit, debiting the personal bill to the account does not give rise to NIC liability.[2] This guidance is confirmed in the Employer Further Guide to PAYE and NICs.[3] The practical outworking of this rule in a series of examples involving both debiting drawings and payments of bills was subsequently considered by the former DSS in response to questions put by the ICAEW.[4] Further clarification of the rules was obtained by the ICAEW in an exchange of correspondence with the former DSS.[5] The correspondence confirms a change in the view of the DSS in relation to overdrawn directors' loan accounts. The former DSS accepted that NIC liability can arise only where payments charged to a directors' loan account and cause it to become overdrawn; where it can be shown that they are not, there is no liability to NICs. This is undoubtedly correct.

Notwithstanding the large measure of agreement now reached on this issue, there is still one respect in which the present guidance is controversial. It appears that in 1990, under the question for determination procedure that then applied, the Secretary of State for Social Security held that drawings made in anticipation of fees which had not been voted at the time of the drawings should not be treated as earnings under the rule which deals with payments on account or advances of earnings.[6] If this decision is applied generally, the debiting of a personal bill to a director's current account which is already in debit or thereby put into debit, will not give rise to NIC liability in cases where the debiting is made in anticipation of fees still to be voted.

In a letter dated 24 February 1994 the then DSS seemed to be confirming that where a director's loan account is overdrawn and it was the clear intention to remove the debt by introducing funds which would not attract NIC liabilities, eg from a dividend payment, then no NIC liability would arise.[7] This guidance was subsequently confirmed in official publications.[8]

[1] DSS leaflet NI 269 (April 1991 edn) p 57, para (35).
[2] The letter is reproduced in Annex B of Technical Release Tax 21/92 issued by the ICAEW.
[3] HMRC leaflet CWG 2 (2007) p 75.
[4] See Technical Release Tax 21/92, paras (6)–(38) issued by the ICAEW.
[5] See Technical Release Tax 5/94, paras (8)–(10), Annex B issued by the ICAEW, *Simon's Tax Intelligence* 1994, p 560.
[6] The determination is not published but has been disclosed to the Tax Faculty.
[7] Letter to the Tax Faculty, 24 February 1994.
[8] HMRC leaflet CA 44, (2007) pp 11 and 12, para 29.

Loans written off

[50.19] There is no equivalent in the contribution legislation to the provisions in ITEPA 2003, ss 184, 187–188 which require the write-off of a loan to the employee to be treated as general earnings for income tax purposes.

However, the guidance for contribution purposes is that if a loan or part of a loan which an employee owes is written off the loan should be included in the gross pay when it is written off.[1] However, in English law the right of the employer to be repaid is not extinguished by merely writing off the loan. The debt can be abandoned only by a release under seal or in return for some consideration. If, in law, the employer can still require repayment even though in fact this is not being pursued, it is hard to see how the write-off can be a "profit derived from the employment"[2] such as has to be included in earnings for contribution purposes.

[1] HMRC leaflet CWG 2 (2007) p 75.
[2] SSCBA 1992, s 3(1)(*a*).

Staff suggestion schemes

[50.20] Previous guidance on this topic reflected the inhibition of the former DSS from making a concession as such. The various conditions required to be met for awards not to be earnings for contribution purposes are intended to establish that the awards are not contractual and not derived from the employment, ie are akin to ex-gratia payments. These conditions were:

(1) the making of staff suggestions is outside the scope of an employee's normal duties;
(2) there is no contractual entitlement to awards;

(3) there is no expectation that an award will be made in any particular case; and
(4) the awards are discretionary as to eligibility of the suggestion, acceptance or rejection of the suggestion and as to the award made.[1]

However, the corresponding income tax concession was legislated for National Insurance purposes from 6 April 2001.[2] The income tax concession was enshrined into legislation in ITEPA 2003, s 321.

Simon's NIC [5.55]–[5.56].

[1] DSS leaflet CA 28 (NI 269), (1995 edn) p 80, para (58).
[2] SI 2001/1004, Sch 3, Part X, para 8(*a*); see also HM Revenue & Customs leaflet CWG 2 (2007) p 77.

Payments in kind; Securities

Status of the exclusion

[50.21] There is a specific exclusion from earnings for Class 1 contribution purposes in respect of "any payment in kind"—certain exceptions are then indicated—"or by way of the provision of board and lodging or services or other facilities".[1] This provision which is part of the secondary legislation dealing with contribution liability assumes that but for the exclusion benefits in kind would fall within the definition of earnings in the primary legislation as being covered by the expression "profit derived from the employment".[2]

Several leading Tax Counsel dispute this assumption.[3] In their view, since the contributory scheme is modelled on the PAYE system and requires contributions to be paid only when there is a payment of earnings,[4] the term earnings must be confined to cash payments or at most what are called "money benefits" or "pecuniary benefits". If this is so, the exclusion for payments in kind is redundant or at best a "for the avoidance of doubt" provision and any exceptions made from the exclusion in the secondary legislation are at variance with the charging provisions in the primary legislation and so invalid.

Since this reasoning would frustrate the successive amendments made to the secondary legislation to narrow the scope of the "payment in kind" exclusion, it is reasonable to assume that recourse to the court will be necessary to establish the true legal position. In fact in the only case so far considered by the court on the general payment in kind exclusion,[5] it was taken for granted that the issues turned on the application of the provision in question (Sch 3, Part II). It was not argued that this provision was redundant and therefore the issues should be considered solely on the basis of the charging provisions in the primary legislation.

Moreover, it should be appreciated that the money benefits or pecuniary benefits which it is accepted are within the scope of earnings subject to contribution liability are not confined to cash payments to the employees concerned.[6] In the first place, the basic charging provision deals with "earnings which are paid to or for the benefit of the earner":[7] therefore a payment to a third party for the benefit of the earner is covered. Second, payments which discharge a personal liability of the employee have been held to be payments of earnings for contribution purposes.[8] Third, it should be remembered that the term "payment" has in other areas of law been very widely construed; in one case where a couple who were persuaded to sell the house which they owned for £500 less than its market value, the House of Lords held that this was the payment of a premium to obtain a tenancy subject to rent control.[9]

In the following discussion, it will be assumed that the payment in kind exclusion is a valid provision and that the amendments made to narrow its scope are effective.

Simon's NIC [5.141]–[5.245R].

[1] Social Security (Contributions) Regulations 2001, SI 2001/1004, Sch 3, Part II, para 1.
[2] SSCBA 1992, s 3(1)(a).
[3] See *Tax Journal*, 28 June 1990, p 8.
[4] SSCBA 1992, s 6(1).
[5] *R v Department of Social Security, ex p Overdrive Credit Card Ltd* [1991] STC 129, DC.
[6] See *Tax Journal*, 27 September 1990, p 13.
[7] SSCBA 1992, s 6(1).
[8] *R v Department of Social Security, ex p Overdrive Credit Card Ltd* [1991] STC 129, DC, following *Hartland v Diggines* [1926] AC 289, 10 TC 247, HL.
[9] *Elmdene Estates Ltd v White* [1960] AC 528, [1960] 1 All ER 306, HL.

Scope

[50.22] In general, so long as certain precautions are taken (see below), taxable benefits in kind will constitute payments in kind and so not be earnings for Class 1 contribution purposes, although in the case of directors and employees paid more than £8,500 annually they will be charged to income tax under special provisions.[1] Such benefits include the fringe benefits frequently provided with a job, eg private medical insurance, club membership, magazine subscriptions etc. It should, however, be appreciated that most such items do instead, from 6 April 2000, attract a Class 1A charge.

Before 6 April 1991, a company car was a benefit that could be provided without giving rise to liability for NICs. But this very common fringe benefit resulted in a substantial loss of contribution revenue—an estimated £550m for 1991–92.[2] The government therefore introduced a special charge to contributions on the provision of company cars (and fuel, if provided also) which is based on the same scale amounts used for assessing the taxable benefit for directors and employees earning £8,500 or more a year.[3]

Until 6 April 2000, remunerating employees through provision of benefits other than cars was attractive from a National Insurance point of view, particularly in the case of employees already earning above the upper earnings limit since in their case maximum employee contributions were being paid and it was only employer contributions which were being reduced so that benefit entitlement was not impaired in any way. For this reason there was a tendency to provide more than the customary fringe benefits, particularly as a means of paying bonuses or other special awards. So, for example, expensive holidays, kitchen or bathroom refurbishments, suites of furniture, the use of yachts or overseas apartments may all be encountered. From 6 April 2000, such provision is beneficial only to the extent that earnings fall short of the upper earnings limit and the particular asset in question is not a "readily convertible asset" so that a more worthwhile saving of the employee Class 1 contributions is made. As far as the employer is concerned, however, a Class 1 charge at 12.8% is merely replaced with a Class 1A charge—also at 12.8% (although payable after the end of the year, rather than on a monthly basis). Since the introduction of the "additional rate" of 1% for employees on 6 April 2003, there is a fresh tendency for payments in kind to find favour as there is, of course, no employee charge where the contributions liability is to Class 1A only.

Formerly, particularly where a number of employees were involved, employers wished to provide the kind of asset that is stable in value and capable of being readily sold for cash. That led to the government introducing amending regulations to take specified assets out of the scope of the payment in kind exclusion. Until May 1988 many employers awarded bonuses in the form of short-dated gilt-edged securities. With this type of security price fluctuations are minimal and there is a narrow bid/offer spread; the asset provided was thus almost equivalent to cash. A substantial amount of contribution revenue was being lost to the National Insurance Fund as a result of widespread use of this device and in May 1988 a statutory instrument was laid[4] which introduced a new regulation into the Contributions Regulations.

This blocking measure was remarkably specific; it simply laid down that securities (as defined) and derivative instruments (also as defined) were not to be treated as payments in kind for the purpose of exclusion from earnings. The securities indicated were debentures, loan stock, certificates of deposit—in fact all instruments evidencing indebtedness—whether issued by a government (not necessarily the British Government), local authority or a company or an individual. Derivative instruments were widely defined but there had to be a security in the first place; they included options over securities and warrants to subscribe for securities.

The then regulation 19C indicated two exceptions which were outside its scope and therefore continued to be used for payments in kind. These were:

(1) shares in a company;
(2) certificates for units in an authorised unit trust.

Naturally payment in such forms received considerable attention, though if payment took the form of shares (but not units in a unit trust[5]) these had to be excluded from relevant earnings for pension purposes and also contributions to a personal pension scheme had to be restricted.[6]

The widespread use of unit trusts as a means of providing bonuses led to a succession of further blocking measures being introduced.

[50.22] Employment earnings

Simon's NIC [5.141]–[5.245R].

1   ITEPA 2003, Part 3, Ch 2–11.
2   HC Written Answer, 30 April 1991, Vol 190, col 163.
3   See infra, § 51.13.
4   Social Security (Contributions) Amendment (No 3) Regulations 1988, SI 1988/860.
5   *Taxation*, 27 September 1990, p 716.
6   TA 1988, s 644(4)(*a*).

The November 1991 blocking measures

[50.23] On 6 November 1991 amending regulations were laid before Parliament which narrowed still further the scope of the payments in kind exclusion.[1] Their effect can be briefly described as follows:

(1) The previous blocking measure which prevented "securities" and "derivative instruments" from being payments in kind that can be excluded from earnings was removed,[2] with it was also removed the exception for shares and certificates in an authorised unit trust.

(2) There was substituted a much wider restriction of the payments in kind exclusion. From midnight on 6 November 1991 (when the amending regulations took effect), the following are not to be treated as payments in kind such as to be excluded from earnings for contribution purposes:

(1)   Payments under specified kinds of insurance policies which confer on the employee a beneficial interest in the policy. The insurance policies affected are life and annuity policies, linked long-term policies and capital redemption policies, as well as policies which partly fall within any one of these categories.[3]

(2)   The provision of any asset falling within what was then Schedule 1A to the Contributions Regulations.[4] Schedule 1A listed the following as assets to be disregarded under the payment in kind exclusion and these were incorporated in 2001 into the current Sch 3, Part IV:
  (a)   Shares and stock in the share capital of a company (securities and securities options generally from 1 September 2003).
  (b)   Debentures, loan stock, bonds, certificates of deposit etc*.
  (c)   Loan stocks, bonds and other debt instruments issued by a government local authority or public authority*.
  (d)   Warrants or other instruments entitling the holder to subscribe for assets within (a), (b) or (c) above*.
  (e)   Certificates or other instruments which confer:
     (i)   property rights in respect of any asset within (a), (b), (c) or (d) above;
     (ii) "any right to acquire, dispose of, or convert an asset, being a right to which the holder would be entitled if he held any such asset to which the certificate or instrument relates";
     (iii) a contractual right other than an option to acquire "any such asset" (this appears to refer to assets within (a), (b), (c) or (d) above) other than by subscription.

Payments in kind; Securities [50.23]

It should be noted that unlike the position in (i) or (iii) the asset in view in (ii) is not specifically indicated as one falling within (a), (b), (c) or (d). However, certain counsel, on the basis of the parallel provisions in the Financial Services Act 1986, consider that only such assets are meant*.

(f) Units in a collective instrument scheme, including shares or securities of an open-ended investment company. The definitions of collective investment scheme and open-ended investment company in Financial Services Act 1986 are adopted for this purpose*.

(g) Options to acquire or dispose of:
 (i) an asset falling within any head in the Schedule;
 (ii) currency of the UK or any other country or territory;
 (iii) gold, silver, palladium or platinum;
 (iv) an option over any asset within the foregoing (i), (ii) or (iii).

The above items marked * were removed from the regulations with effect from 1 September 2003. No specific reference is now required to these items as they are embraced by the charge on securities and securities options generally – see infra, § **50.29**.

(3) However, a new exclusion from earnings was made for the provision of shares or options to acquire shares where the shares form part of the ordinary share capital of the secondary contributor or a company which has control of the secondary contributor or where a consortium owns either the secondary contributor or a body corporate which controls the secondary contributor, a company which is a member of the consortium or has control over such a member. This has been further restricted subsequently.

These provisions mean that the majority of approved share schemes will be unaffected by the restrictions.[5] It is also provided that any benefit derived from priority share allocations for directors and employees is to be excluded from earnings for contribution purposes.[6] Unapproved arrangements are, however, affected by subsequent changes (see infra, § **50.27** and **50.29**).

(4) In those cases where the regulations cause the provision of a benefit to be included in earnings for contribution purposes, there are provisions for arriving at the value of the benefit which is to be treated as a payment of earnings. The basic rule is that the value should be the price which the beneficial interest might reasonably be expected to fetch if sold on the open market on the day on which it is conferred.[7] If the asset is not quoted on a recognised stock exchange, it has to be assumed that the prospective purchaser has all the information which a prudent prospective purchase might reasonably require.[8]

---

[1] Social Security (Contributions) Amendment (No 6) Regulations 1991, SI 1991/2505 and Social Security (Contributions) Regulations 2001, SI 2001/1004, Sch 3, Part IV.
[2] SI 2001/1004, Sch 3, Part II, para 1.
[3] SI 2001/1004, Sch 3, Part II, para 2(1)(*a*)(ii) & (3).

[50.23] Employment earnings

4   SI 2001/1004, Sch 3, Part II, para 2(1)(a)(i) & Parts III, IV.
5   SI 2001/1004, Sch 3, Part IX, paras 6, 7.
6   SI 2001/1004, Sch 3, Part IX, para 5.
7   SI 2001/1004, Sch 2, para 2(1).
8   SI 2001/1004, Sch 2, para 2(2).

The December 1993 blocking measures

[50.24] Whilst the November 1991 measures closed many of the straightforward avoidance schemes it was still possible to avoid NIC liabilities by transferring assets to employees. The most favoured scheme involved gold bullion although in practice many other commodities were used.

Further regulations were introduced from 1 December 1993[1] making liable for contributions any commodity or other property that did not fall under specific paragraphs within what is now Sch 3, Part IV to the Contributions Regulations provided that commodity or other property is capable of being sold on a recognised investment exchange. In addition any voucher capable of being exchanged for any asset included in the then Schedule was also made liable for contributions.

It will be seen from this outline that these regulations close many avenues besides the use of unit trusts and gold bullion. Nevertheless, with a view to circumventing the regulations, schemes based on diamonds and fine wines were developed.

Other schemes involved the employer directly or indirectly making an additional payment under an insurance policy previously taken out by the employee. Such a payment will not confer any beneficial interest in the policy on the employee but there is a danger that even though the new regulations do not bite, the payment by the employer will simply be a payment of earnings "for the benefit of the earner"[2] and so not a payment in kind at all. During 1994 the then DSS commenced enquiries into the life insurance schemes and was understood to have identified a number of employers for investigation. In summer 2000, despite the reservations just mentioned, a Secretary of State's decision confirmed no liability.[3]

1   SI 2001/1004, Sch 3, Part II, para 2 (a)(i).
2   SSCBA 1992, s 6(1).
3   *Tullet and Tokyo Forex International Ltd v Secretary of State for Social Security* (25 May 2000, CO/2038/1999).

The August 1994 blocking measures

[50.25] On 23 August 1994 amending regulations[1] were laid before Parliament with the intention of blocking the loopholes left by the December 1993 measures. In announcing the measures the Secretary of State for Social Security said:

> Companies and their accountant advisers who devise ways of paying earnings which avoid their liability for national insurance contributions will find it increasingly

unattractive to produce and operate such schemes. These regulations are clear evidence of the Government's intention to act speedily to close national insurance loopholes if they come to light.[2]

The amending regulations apply to schemes involving gemstones and certain alcoholic liquors. The definition of "gemstone" includes "stones such as diamond, emerald, ruby, sapphire, amethyst, jade, opal or topaz and organic gemstones such as amber or pearl, whether cut or uncut and whether or not having an industrial use". The definition of "alcoholic liquor" is "any alcoholic liquor within the meaning of s 1 of the Alcoholic Liquor Duties Act 1979 in respect of which no duty has been paid under that Act".

The amending regulations did not entirely eliminate the scope for scheme-based avoidance and the focus of attention turned to "strategic metals" such as cobalt, chromium, titanium, cadmium, manganese and arsenic. These metals are not traded on "recognised investments exchanges".[3] Prices are negotiated between merchants or between suppliers and industrial users. The prices are reported in US dollars in a publication called *The Metal Bulletin* and, on a weekly basis, in the *Financial Times*.

[1] Social Security (Contributions) Amendment (No 3) Regulations 1994, SI 1994/2194 and SI 2001/1004, Sch 3, Part IV, paras 9, 10.
[2] DSS press release, 23 August 1994, *Simon's Tax Intelligence* 1994, p 1107.
[3] SI 2001/1004, Sch 3, Part III, paras 1, 2.

The April 1995 blocking measures

[50.26] On 5 April 1995 amending regulations were laid before Parliament with the intention of eliminating the loophole left by the August 1994 measures. In announcing the measures the Secretary of State for Social Security reiterated his resolve to stamp out any further schemes designed to avoid contribution liability.[1]

The amending regulations applied to schemes involving assets for which "trading arrangements" exist enabling the employee to exchange the assets for cash of a similar amount to that of providing the asset, without the creation of a contribution liability. The regulations also apply to vouchers for such assets and vouchers which are themselves subject to trading arrangements.

These provisions were superseded by the "readily convertible assets" provisions (see the October 1998 blocking measures, infra, § **50.28**).

[1] HC Written Answer, 5 April 1995, Vol 257, col 1228.

The December 1996 blocking measures

[50.27] On 5 December 1996 amending regulations were laid before Parliament with the intention of blocking the loophole involving company shares and share options which remained following the 1991 measures. In announcing the measures the Pensions Minister said:[1]

[50.27] Employment earnings

We are committed to acting against exploitation of the national insurance system by employers who undermine the contributory principle by avoiding paying their proper share of contributions on the earnings they pay to their employees.

I have today laid regulations (SI 1996/3031)[2] which tighten the rules for contributions where employers pay their staff in shares and share options.

Earnings paid in the form of shares provided under schemes not approved by the Revenue and using shares or options for shares which are capable of being traded on a recognised investment exchange as defined in the Financial Services Act 1986, or which are provided in circumstances where 'trading arrangements' exist within the meaning of FA 1994, will be subject to national insurance contributions.

They will be treated in the same way as income provided in cash or in the form of other non-cash assets such as gold bullion and diamonds.

The regulations will come into effect from midnight tonight. Shares acquired under options granted before midnight today will not be affected.

Simon's NIC [5.236].

[1] DSS press release, 4 December 1996, *Simon's Weekly Tax Intelligence* 1996, p 2059.
[2] Social Security (Contributions) Amendment (No 6) Regulations 1996, and SI 2001/1004, Sch 3, Part III, Part IV and Part IX, para 2.

The October 1998 blocking measures

[50.28] Because employers continued to attempt to avoid NICs, arguing that the "trading arrangements" provisions did not catch their particular arrangements, further measures were announced in the 1998 Budget and took effect from 6 April 1998 for PAYE purposes and 1 October 1998 for NIC purposes.[1]

In the main, the changes extend the "trading arrangements" rules to situations where "trading arrangements" may yet come into being and also include the assignment of debts, both trading and others, these being collectively known as "readily convertible assets".

See also § **50.35**.

[1] Social Security (Contributions) Amendment (No 3) Regulations 1998, SI 1998/2211, reg 5 and SI 2001/1004, Sch 3, Part III, para 1.

Subsequent changes in respect of shares, securities and options

[50.29] The position as regards shares (see supra, § **50.27**) was further amended from 6 April 1999[1] in that a charge to NICs will arise on the exercise of options (if granted on or after that date) instead of on the occasion of the grant itself. Exceptionally, but in line with income tax, a charge still arose on grant prior to 1 September 2003 (as well as on exercise) if the option is a "long" option. Further, following changes announced in the Budget on 17 March 1998, a "long" option then became one capable of being exercised after more than ten years, rather than seven as previously applied for income tax purposes, although no charge arises from 1 September 2003—see below.

It should be appreciated that these rules still do not apply in the case of options provided under a HMRC approved scheme. Nor do they apply where the options provided and the underlying shares are not "readily convertible assets" (see infra, § **50.28**), eg in the case of shares or options in an unquoted company where no trading facility, such as an employee trust, has been set up.

After the 1999 change, concern was expressed, particularly on behalf of e-commerce and high-tech companies, at the charging of the employer's national insurance contribution on gains arising on the exercise of unapproved schemes. Following the 2000 Budget, the Government legislated to allow all or part of the employer's NIC liability being met by the employee by mutual agreement. Alternatively, liability may be formally transferred to the employee. From 1 September 2004, these opportunities extend not just to share options, but to all securities options.[2]

Where options were granted on or after 6 April 1999 but before 19 May 2000, that legislative change was of no help. A further measure enabled companies to elect to "freeze" the Class 1 liability to the 7 November 2000 value of the shares if an election is made, and payment also made, within 92 days of the Act having received Royal Assent.[3] This 92-day period expired on 10 August 2001. If however, there would have been no liability as at 7 November 2000 either because the shares and options were not "readily convertible assets" or because the market value was at that time less than the exercise price then no formal election is required. Instead, the Act provides that, in these circumstances, an election is deemed to have been made.[4]

The introduction by FA 2003, Sch 22 of the new employment related securities regime also applies for contributions purposes from 1 September 2003. It has also created some new uncertainties. ITEPA 2003, s 421B(3) provides that where a right or opportunity to acquire securities or an interest in securities is made available by a person's employer (or a person connected with the employer) that right is to be treated as made available by reason of the employment unless the right or opportunity is made available by an individual and it is made available in the course of the domestic, family or personal relationships of that person. This may clearly cause concern in relation to the treatment of earn-outs in a company sale where these are satisfied by loan notes in the acquirer, shares in the acquirer, or a mixture. HM Revenue & Customs considers that a right of this kind falls within the definition of a securities option.[5] Thus in the appropriate circumstances a Class 1 National Insurance charge would arise. However, the former Inland Revenue did confirm that where an earn out fully represents the consideration for the sale of the (target) company's shares (as will usually be the case), the potential National Insurance charges will not be applied. Conversely, where all or part of an earn out relates to value provided to an employee as a reward for services over a performance period, the remuneration element will constitute taxable earnings under the new ITEPA 2003 regime, with potential Class 1 liability accordingly.

In addition, from 1 September 2003 a security which is not a readily convertible asset, but in respect of which a corporation tax deduction is not available is nonetheless to be treated as a readily convertible asset.[6]

[50.29] Employment earnings

Finally from 1 September 2003, the charge on the grant of a long option was removed, this now being covered within the new restricted securities regime.[7]

---

[1] Social Security Act 1998, s 50 and FA 1998, s 49; see also CA Press Release CA 12/98, 1 April 1998.
[2] SSCBA 1992, Sch 1, paras 3A, 3B, as amended by National Insurance Contributions and Statutory Payments Act 2004, ss 3, 4, Social Security (Contributions) (Amendment No 10) Regulations 2000, SI 2000/2744, Social Security (Contributions) (Amendment No 4) Regulations 2004, SI 2004/2096.
[3] Social Security Contributions (Share Options) Act 2001, Social Security (Contributions) Regulations 2001, SI 2001/1004, Sch 4, para 23, Sch 5, paras 1–3.
[4] Social Security Contributions (Share Options) Act 2001, s 1(6).
[5] ITEPA 2003, s 420(8).
[6] Social Security (Contributions) Regulations 2001, SI 2001/1004, Sch 3, Part III, para 1, as amended by Social Security (Contributions) (Amendment No 5) Regulations 2003, SI 2003/2085, reg 10(2) and ITEPA 2003, s 702(5A), inserted by FA 2003, s 140, Sch 22.
[7] Social Security (Contributions) Regulations 2001, SI 2001/1004, Sch 3, Part IX, para 3A, removed by Social Security (Contributions) (Amendment No 5) Regulations 2003, SI 2003/2085, reg 12.

Traps for the unwary

[50.30] Even though an asset provided might be outside the scope of the blocking measures mentioned at supra §§ **50.23** et seq, it will not necessarily constitute an effective payment in kind such as to avoid contribution liability. In the following cases in particular, and the list is not exhaustive, there will not be a payment in kind such as to be excluded from earnings for contribution purposes.

[50.31] If the asset can be surrendered and exchanged for cash. In this case the former DSS considered that the employee is in effect being provided with cash, whether or not an actual surrender takes place. Guidance continues to distinguish items which can be turned into cash if sold from those which can be turned into cash by surrender and instances premium bonds and national savings certificates as examples of the latter kind.[1]

The precise legal grounds for this rule are unclear; very likely the possibility of obtaining cash by surrender of the asset is seen to give the benefit a monetary character.

---

[1] HM Revenue & Customs leaflet CWG 2 (2007) p 76.

[50.32] If the employee already has an entitlement to a cash sum. In this situation the remuneration is treated as paid at the point the entitlement arises and the asset provided merely discharges the cash sum due.

This follows from the principle established in *Garforth v Newsmith Stainless Ltd*,[1] in which it was held in the case of directors that payment of remuneration is made at the time sums are placed unreservedly at their disposal. Thus, if the resolution or other form of consent of the shareholders authorising the directors' remuneration[2] does not refer expressly and exclusively to the provision of assets, the directors may be treated as having a cash entitlement which is subsequently satisfied by the transfer of the assets.

If the company does not already own the asset which it is purporting to award to the director or employee, there is a danger that the resolution could be construed as giving a cash entitlement, ie because the director or employee can then require the company to buy the asset for him.

[1] [1979] STC 129.
[2] For other forms of shareholders' consent, see *Re Duomatic Ltd* [1969] 2 Ch 365, [1969] 1 All ER 161.

[50.33] If a liability of the employee is discharged by the employer. In *Hartland v Diggines*,[1] an income tax case, it was held that payment by the employer of a liability due from the employee—in that case income tax due on his salary—constituted an emolument of the employment. On similar reasoning such a payment is regarded as earnings for contribution purposes. This means that if the employee himself makes the contract for the supply of the goods or services in question and is reimbursed by the employer, the reimbursement becomes a payment of remuneration in cash. The point is well known in connection with telephone charges; the employer must be the subscriber if payment for private telephone use is to be excluded from earnings,[2] and even if it is so excluded from earnings it does, from 6 April 2000, attract a Class 1A charge.

Simon's NIC [5.246]–[5.253].

[1] [1926] AC 289, 10 TC 247, HL.
[2] HMRC leaflet CWG 2 (2007) p 78.

[50.34] If a cash equivalent is stated in the documentation supporting the provision of the asset. In some old cases, under arrangements to provide remuneration in the form of, for example, units in a unit trust, the board resolution or notification of the award was on the following lines: 'It was decided to award X a bonus of £10,000 payable only in units in the ABC unit trust'. Such wording does not give the individual a right to obtain £10,000 in cash but the Revenue have argued that the wording increases the individual's gross remuneration by £10,000 notwithstanding that he can take the increase in units only; on this view he has in effect consented to the increase being payable in units. So far as the general charge to income tax is concerned, this is supported by the old case of *Smyth v Stretton*[1] which is customarily cited in this connection. There a pay increase given to masters at Dulwich College which was required to be placed in a provident fund was held to be an addition to the gross remuneration for income tax purposes. However, the former Inland Revenue went on from there to argue that the provision of the units in such a case constitutes a *payment* of emoluments for PAYE purposes. If this is conceded, it would almost certainly have to be accepted as likewise a payment of earnings for contribution purposes.

This extension of the application of *Smyth v Stretton* is controversial. It is understood that in an appeal brought before the General Commissioners, the Revenue position was upheld. There were at one time, however, understood to be other appeals pending, but no outcomes are in the public domain. Seemingly now established, the principle involved has far-reaching consequences.

[1] *Smyth v Stretton* (1904) 5 TC 36.

The 'Ramsay' principle

[50.35] It had been thought for many years that the "*Ramsay*" approach to tax avoidance could not be applied to NICs, given the contributory nature, rather than tax-raising purpose, of the charge (see supra, § **48.01**).

However, some cases determined by the Secretary of State for Social Security under the pre-April 1999 regime have been decided, without explanation, on the basis that the *Ramsay* principle is applicable. The *Ramsay* principle was also in point, but not finally concluded because "trading arrangements" were held to be applicable, in a High Court tax case[1] concerning the provision of a reversionary interest in an offshore trust to company directors and in a High Court National Insurance case.[2]

Amongst other arguments, a purposive approach and the *Ramsay* principle were successful for HMRC in a case involving the payment of directors' bonuses by way of antique gold coins during the mid 1990s.[3]

The same issues were reinforced later in 2006 in a case involving the transfer of trade debts to employees—a technique that had been conceded as successful for the employer by the Secretary of State for Social Security. However, following the 1999 transfer of the Contributions Agency, the issue was revived by the then Inland Revenue.[4]

[1] *DTE Financial Services Ltd v Wilson* [1999] STC 1061.
[2] *NMB Holdings Ltd v Secretary of State for Social Security* (2000) 73 TC 85.
[3] *EDI Services Ltd v Revenue and Customs Comrs* SpC 539, [2006] STC (SCD) 392.
[4] *Spectrum Computer Supplies Ltd & Kirkstall Timber Ltd v Revenue and Customs Comrs* SpC 559.

Retrospective liability on earnings

[50.36] The National Insurance Contributions Act 2006 provided the power to make regulations in respect of retrospective National Insurance liability where a Finance Act has similarly imposed retrospective tax liability in respect of what the government sees as abusive schemes involving securities. Various Regulations came into force on 6 April 2007 with effect from 2 December 2004. The latter date was the date of the 2004 Pre Budget Report when the Paymaster General gave notice that employment income tax and NIC avoidance schemes would be closed down with retrospective effect.

The National Insurance legislation is amended to mirror tax changes.[1] The latter introduce the concept of a special return P35(RL) to cover retrospective tax and National Insurance liability. Those returns cannot be made electronically and electronic payment is also not possible. In case it might apply, there is also provision to exclude the tax and National Insurance on retrospective payments being counted when determining whether the employer is small enough to qualify for quarterly remittances to HMRC. Payment of the retrospective National Insurance is due 14 days after the end of the tax month following the tax month in which the relevant contributions regulations came into force. The first such payments of retrospective liability were therefore due by 19 June 2007, and the first returns were due by 19 May 2008.[2]

Retrospective National Insurance contribution liability applies to employment income arising by virtue of F(No 2)A 2005, Sch 2 from 2 December 2004 and before 20 July 2005 and to similar income arising by virtue of FA 2006, s 92 from 2 December 2004 and before 19 July 2006.[3]

Further regulations ensure that the retrospective earnings are taken into account for statutory payments, maternity allowance and other benefit purposes and enable occupational pension contributions to be deducted from the retrospective earnings.[4]

The good faith error rules which permit recovery of employees contributions in certain circumstances (see infra, § 51.09) are replicated in respect of retrospective earnings and employers may well face situations where the employee liability on retrospective earnings cannot be recovered from the employee.[5]

Extra-stautory concession B46 does not apply to the submission of Forms P35(RL) and associated P14s.

Employers will not have to recompute student loan deductions where retrospective liability applies as Education (Student Loans) (Repayments) Regs 2000 SI 2000/944, reg 39 already states that no recalculation is required where NIC-able earnings increase for any reason.

---

[1] Income Tax (Pay As You Earn)) (Amendment) Regulations 2007, SI 2007/1077.
[2] SSCBA 1992, Sch 1, para 3 and various provisions of Contributions Regs 2001 as amended by the Social Security Contributions (Consequential Provisions) Regulations 2007, SI 2007/1056.
[3] Contributions Regs 2001, reg 22(9) and (10) inserted by the Social Security (Contributions) (Amendment No. 2) Regulations 2007, SI 2007/1057.
[4] Social Security, Occupational Pension Schemes and Statutory Payments (Consequential Provisions) Regulations 2007, SI 2007/1154.
[5] SI 2007/1154.

Harmonisation with PAYE

[50.37] Because PAYE is operated on payments of general earnings (previously called "emoluments") and Class 1 contributions are due on payments of earnings, it will be readily apparent that the two regimes share a largely overlapping base. There are, however, divergences, in particular because certain deductions allowed for income tax have no National Insurance equivalent, because the extra-statutory concessions made for tax purposes are not entirely matched. Further, in some cases the earnings are arrived at on different principles, eg because under contribution law there is no rule allowing a deduction for business expenses.

Nevertheless it is administratively inconvenient to employers, particularly in the case of small businesses, for differences between the two regimes to have to be observed when operating PAYE and accounting for PAYE deductions and NICs.

For this reason, in December 1990 the government announced that a number of reviews were to be undertaken as part of the government's deregulation initiative. One of these reviews was to be conducted by the former DSS with assistance from the then Inland Revenue and was to consider the definition of earnings and expenses for PAYE and contribution purposes respectively. The aim was "to explore the scope for eliminating some of the differences in definitions of earnings for PAYE and NIC purposes first by reviewing administrative solutions".

The first stage of the review involved identifying the differences between the definitions under the two systems. The second stage involved consultation with employers: a consultation paper was issued to employers' representatives on the DSS deregulation panel and their views were invited.

Finally the then DSS prepared a "Final Report" making specific recommendations made in the light of responses received from the employers' representatives. The report was issued in December 1991.[1]

The report acknowledged that certain fundamental differences between the two regimes prevent full harmonisation (see supra, § **48.05**), but notwithstanding these fundamental distinctions, it recommended changes falling into three categories: those which could be made through "administrative action", those which are possible by "improved guidance" to employers and those which require amendments to the secondary legislation.

The harmonisation process was carried a stage further in early 1993 with the setting up of a joint working group with members drawn from the Confederation of British Industry, Institute of Directors, Association of British Chambers of Commerce, the Federation of Small Businesses, the accountancy and payroll management professions as well as the DSS and Inland Revenue.

Its terms of reference were to "review how employees' earnings and expenses are defined for NIC and tax purposes and, having regard to the contributory principle for National Insurance, and the importance of a broad tax and NIC base in order to make further progress towards lower tax rates, *to identify* changes which would reduce burdens on employers".

In connection with the words in italics, members canvassed which divergences between the NIC and tax treatments are most troublesome to employers and should therefore receive top priority.

The working group was asked to report its findings and make recommendations by the end of September 1993 and this they duly did although as well as making a series of recommendations[2] they also highlighted a number of options.

The main recommendation was that there should be a common definition of earnings for both income tax and NIC assessment but there were a number of other recommendations including:

(1) Inland Revenue extra-statutory concessions should be extended to cover NICs.
(2) Inland Revenue "care and management" powers should be extended to the DSS.
(3) The aligned definitions of earnings and emoluments should be contained in a single body of law.
(4) The Inland Revenue and the DSS should carry out joint audits or, at least, exchange details of intended audits.
(5) There should be a significant improvement in communications with more seminars and helplines, quick guides and earlier joint guidance.
(6) The DSS should wholly administer reduced rate elections.

In publishing the report the Secretary of State for Social Security indicated the need for the wider community to have the opportunity to consider the recommendations of the working group, and stated that he was attracted to the suggestion of aligning the definitions of earnings for NIC and tax purposes.

After the publication of the report, a joint DSS/Inland Revenue team, with the assistance of the DTI, investigated the potential for alignment. The team identified many difficulties. In an effort to shorten the time scale in which solutions could be found, the team arranged a series of meetings, commencing in September 1994, for the purpose of informal discussions with individuals drawn from the professions, industry and other interested groups. The team sought solutions within the present NIC system, and without major changes in employer's and government's systems and procedures. At the conclusion of these discussions the team made recommendations for changes which were for consideration by Ministers. A memorandum issued by the ICAEW set out the developments.[3]

The transfer of the administrative functions of the Contributions Agency and the policy responsibilities of the DSS to the Inland Revenue and the Treasury respectively, with effect from 1 April 1999,[4] aids the process of harmonisation between contributions and PAYE. Indeed, this is one of the specific objectives of the transfer.[5] (On 18 April 2005, the Inland Revenue merged again, this time with HM Customs and Excise to become HM Revenue & Customs).

The former Inland Revenue issued the first ever extra-statutory concession in respect of NICs on 18 May 1999, relating to interest on appeal cases to be heard by the Commissioners of the Inland Revenue.[6]

Some further small divergences were removed immediately prior to the consolidation of the main Regulations.[7]

[50.37] Employment earnings

A consultation document was issued in summer 2000 "Simplifying National Insurance contributions". The Inland Revenue did not publish its summary of responses until summer 2001, by which time some minor changes to bring the contributions treatment of some further items of earnings into line with income tax had already been made from 6 April 2001. Nonetheless, there remain many differences still. It had been proposed to transfer supposed Class 1 liability on FURBS (see above) to Class 1A but this was not proceeded with on the grounds of the wider pensions consultation that commenced in December 2002 and culminated in "A-day" on 6 April 2006. Other changes were in the National Insurance Contributions and Statutory Payments Act 2004, namely:

(1) Aligning procedures and periods of notice for distraint and summary action with tax (effective date – 1 September 2004).
(2) Aligning the tax and contributions powers of inspection (effective date – 6 April 2005).
(3) Decriminalising statutory sick pay and statutory maternity pay offences to bring their treatment into line with statutory paternity pay and statutory adoption pay (effective date – 1 January 2005). [8]

In the 2007 Budget, early announcement was made of higher than indexation increases to the upper earnings limit in both 2008 and 2009, reaching parity with the starting point for 40% income tax by the latter date. This is said to "harmonise" that aspect of the two regimes but will do no such thing as many affected employees will be of the kind who will have one or more benefits in kind liable to Class 1A contributions. Accordingly, such persons will attract a 40% PAYE liability before the point at which the additional Class 1 rate of 1% will apply and will thus face a 51% rate of combined duty on an element of their pay. In addition, harmonization is merely a euphemism to disguise the fact that the increase in the upper earnings limit simply brings employees, who were previously paying 1% NICs, back into the 11% bracket.

[1] The report was distributed to employers' representatives on the DSS regulation panel.
[2] Deregulation Review—Report of the Tax/NICs Working Group—September 1993.
[3] National Insurance Contributions: TAX 5/97, issued by the Tax Faculty.
[4] Social Security Contributions (Transfer of Functions, etc) Act 1999.
[5] Budget day press release IR 44, 17 March 1998.
[6] Inland Revenue press release 1999/100, 18 May 1999, *Simon's Weekly Tax Intelligence* 1999, p 943.
[7] Social Security (Contributions) (Amendment No 3) Regulations, SI 2001/596; now superseded by SI 2001/1004.
[8] National Insurance Contributions and Statutory Payments Act 2004 (Commencement) Order 2004, SI 2004/1943.

51

Employer and employee contributions

Class 1 contributions	PARA **51.01**
Earnings limits, thresholds and rates	PARA **51.02**
Earnings periods	PARA **51.03**
Company directors	PARA **51.04**
Anti-avoidance rules	PARA **51.06**
More than one employment	PARA **51.07**
Annual maximum contributions	PARA **51.08**
Collection of Class 1 contributions	PARA **51.09**
Class 1A contributions	PARA **51.13**
Class 1B contributions	PARA **51.19**

Class 1 contributions

[51.01] Where an employment is categorised as an employed earner's employment, both the employee, ie the employed earner (the primary contributor), and the employer (the secondary contributor), are normally required to pay respectively primary and secondary Class 1 contributions. If the employee is under 16, neither employee nor employer has this obligation until the employee reaches the age of 16[1] after which earnings paid to him may become liable to both primary and secondary contributions. Where the employee reaches pensionable age (currently 65 for a man and 60 for a woman) liability for primary contributions on earnings paid to him or her after that date ceases, unless the earnings would normally fall to be paid before that date.[2] Conversely, if earnings are paid before the date but in the tax year in which pensionable age is reached and those earnings would normally be paid in a following tax year those earnings do not give rise to primary contributions.[3] The employer is still required to pay secondary contributions in respect of the employee's earnings after pensionable age is reached.[4]

From 6 April 2000, no primary contribution liability arises until the employee's weekly earnings reach the primary earnings threshold[5] and no secondary contribution liability arises until the employee's earnings reach the secondary earnings threshold.[6] From 6 April 2001, the primary and secondary thresholds are the same.

Since 6 October 1985 there has been no upper limit to the earnings on which the employer must pay secondary contributions, and unlike primary contributions, they are payable at the full rate above the upper earnings limit.

In the case of primary contributions until 6 April 2003, the maximum liability was reached when earnings were at or above a further threshold, the upper earnings limit; earnings above that limit did not attract primary contributions.[7] From 6 April 2003, primary contributions are payable at 1% on all earnings above the upper earnings limit.

1953

[51.01] Employer and employee contributions

For 1999–2000, primary contributions were payable only on the earnings which exceeded the lower earnings limit and secondary contributions were payable on the earnings which exceeded the secondary earnings threshold. Prior to 6 April 1999, contributions were payable on all earnings once the lower earnings limit was reached.

Simon's NIC Chapter 8.

---

[1] SSCBA 1992, s 6(1)(*a*).
[2] SSCBA 1992, s 6(3); Social Security (Contributions) Regulations 2001, SI 2001/1004, reg 29.
[3] SI 2001/1004, reg 28.
[4] SSCBA 1992, s 6(3).
[5] SSCBA 1992, s 6(1)(*a*).
[6] SSCBA 1992, s 6(1)(*b*) and s 9.
[7] SSCBA 1992, ss 6(1)(*a*) and 8(1)(*b*).

Earnings limits, thresholds and rates

[51.02] The lower earnings limit is tied to the basic Category A retirement pension. It must be a figure very close to the Category A retirement pension, the margin allowed being up to 99p. The retirement pension is revalued each year by reference to price inflation: the revised amounts which are payable from the following April are usually announced in the autumn, based on retail price index movements measured from September to September. Increases made by any Act or more usually statutory instrument before the beginning of a tax year must be taken into account in fixing the lower earnings limit for that year so long as the increases take effect before 6 May in that year.[1] In this way the lower earnings limit is revised annually in tandem with the basic retirement pension. Since employee contributions are now payable only from a higher level (the earnings threshold—£110 per week for 2009–10) the lower earnings limit is relevant in entitling individuals to contributory benefits only where their earnings have equalled or exceeded that lower limit, even though no contributions may be payable. It is partly for this reason that employers therefore still have to record earnings at this level in their payroll records even though no contributions are actually due until the earnings threshold is reached. The Pensions Act 2007 will disassociate the lower earnings limit and the rate of state pension from 2010.

The upper earnings limit formerly had to be a figure approximately equal to seven times the basic retirement pension but subject to a margin of half the amount of the basic pension but it is now geared to the same multiples of the primary earnings threshold.[2] Increases to the upper earnings limit in 2008 and—particularly—2009, announced in the 2007 Budget, will fall outside these parameters and this was effected by the National Insurance Contributions Act 2008 which introduced the new concept of the "upper accrual point", which is seven times the primary threshold (but allowing the upper earnings limit to exceed this level, so as to bring more earnings within the 11% NICs bracket).

Earnings limits, thresholds and rates [51.02]

Whereas fixing the earnings limits and thresholds determines the level of earnings at which contribution liability begins and for employees the level of earnings at which maximum liability—of a kind—is reached, the rates at which contributions are payable have to be reviewed annually and must be set so as to result in contributions paid into and benefits paid out of the National Insurance Fund being approximately in balance in each tax year. The changes which result from the review will apply as from the following 6 April.

The earnings threshold from which secondary contributions become payable is, in practice, left in line with the personal tax allowance. From 6 April 2001, the primary earnings threshold is also set at that same level.

The amended structure in place for 1999–2000 onwards whereby contributions are due only on the excess of earnings over the appropriate threshold or limit rather than, as before, on all earnings if that limit was equalled or exceeded means that neither employee nor employer will see their share of contributions rise, as could be the case previously, by an amount greater than any increase in earnings.

For 2009–10 the lower earnings limit has been set at £95 per week and the upper earnings limit at £844 per week. The earnings threshold is set at £110 per week, £476 per month and £5,715 pa. The standard rates for primary and secondary Class 1 contributions in 2009–10 are as follows:

Standard rates for the year from 6 April 2009

Primary contributions	*Percentage*
On earnings from £110 to £844 per week	11%
On earnings above £844 per week	1%

Secondary contributions	*Percentage*
On earnings from £110 per week, without limit	12.8%

The above tables show the rates for standard contributions. There are two other sets of rates—contracted-out rates and the reduced rate.

The contracted-out rates apply where the employee belongs to an occupational pension scheme which has received a contracting out certificate. For the conditions which need to be fulfilled to obtain such a certificate see supra, § **32.06**. Because the employee, as a result of being contracted-out, will not be entitled to the additional pension based on earnings related contributions provided by the State Second Pension (S2P) and previously SERPS, both employee and employer contributions are payable at a reduced rate on earnings between the lower and upper earnings limit. The reduction in rate results from the application of a rebate to compensate for the loss of entitlement to additional pension. The rebate is fixed following reviews generally made every five years by the Controller and Auditor General. The total rebate is allocated between employer and employee contributions as the Secretary of State decides.

[51.02] Employer and employee contributions

Until 1996–97 employees who were members of either contracted-out salary related schemes (COSR) or contracted-out money purchase schemes (COMPS) received the same rebate irrespective of age. For 1997–98 and 1998–99, the contracted-out rebate for COSR was 1.6% for the employee, 3.0% for the employer; and for COMPS was 1.6% for the employee, 1.5% for the employer. The position is the same for 1999–2000, 2000–01 and 2001–02 except that the employer's rebate for a COMPS scheme was further reduced to 0.6%.[3] The contracted-out rebates from 6 April 2002 to 5 April 2007 were 3.5% (employer) and 1.6% (employee) for COSR schemes and 1.0% (employer) and 1.6% (employee) for COMP schemes.[4] The contracted-out rebates from 6 April 2007, notionally for a five year period but subject to review as other Pensions Act 2007 changes come nearer, are 3.7% (employer) and 1.6% (employee) for COSR schemes and 1.4% (employer) and 1.6% (employee) for COMP schemes.[5] In the case of COMPS schemes and holders of appropriate personal pensions, additional age-related rebates are paid by HM Revenue & Customs on behalf of the DWP. The employer's contracted-out rebate for 1999–2000 onwards still applies to earnings between the lower earnings limit and the upper earnings limit, notwithstanding that actual contribution liability arises only from higher levels. Contracting out rebates for COMP schemes will cease in or after 2010.

As a result of applying the rebate the contracted-out primary and secondary Class 1 contributions in 2009–10 are as follows:

Contracted-out rates for the year from 6 April 2009

Primary contributions	Percentage (COSR and COMP)
On earnings from:	
£95 to £109.99 per week	(1.6%)
£110 to £844 per week	9.4%
On earnings above £844 per week	1%

Secondary contributions	COSR Percentage	COMP Percentage
On earnings from:		
£95 to £109.99 per week	(3.7%)	(1.4%)
£110 to £844 per week	9.1%	11.4%
On earnings above £844 per week	12.8%	12.8%

The reduced rate applies in the case of certain married women and widows who prior to 12 May 1977 had elected to pay reduced contributions[6] into the scheme and have not subsequently revoked the election[7] or lost the right to pay reduced contributions. The woman will lose this right if her marriage ceases otherwise than through the death of her husband, if on becoming a widow she subsequently remarries or otherwise ceases to be a qualifying widow, if there is a consecutive period of two tax years in which she has no earnings on which

Earnings limits, thresholds and rates [51.02]

any primary Class 1 contributions would be payable and in which she was not at any time a self-employed earner and in certain other circumstances.[8] The rate of secondary contributions payable by the employer is not affected by the employee's entitlement to pay the reduced rate of primary contribution.

The reduced rate contributions secure no entitlement to benefits and in consequence are very low—for 2009–10 they are payable at the rate of 4.85% on earnings from £110 per week to £844 per week and at 1% thereafter.

It will be noted that the earnings limits and the earnings brackets are expressed in terms of earnings per week. This is because the legislation assumes that normally the earnings period, ie the interval at which earnings are regularly paid (see infra, § **51.03**) will be one week. But earnings periods can be for longer periods and in such cases there are rules for converting the weekly figures to equivalent amounts for the longer period. For the lower earnings limit and the upper earnings limit the rules are the same as one another, as follows:

(a) where the earnings period is a multiple of a week, multiply the weekly amount by the multiple in question;
(b) where the earnings period is a month, multiply the weekly amount by 4 1/3;
(c) where the earnings period is a multiple of a month, multiply the weekly amount by 4 1/3 and then multiply the result by the multiple;
(d) in any other case divide the weekly amount by 7 and multiply the result by the number of days in the earnings period.[9]

In the case of the earnings thresholds, the corresponding amounts are specified for the year 2008–09 by regulation as:

(1) £4/6 per month, where the earnings period is a month;
(2) £5,715 pa, where the earnings period is a year;
(3) where the earnings period is a multiple of weeks or months, the annual threshold divided by 52 or 12 (as the case may be), multiplied by the number of weeks or months in the earnings period and then rounded up to the next whole pound;
(4) in any other case, the annual threshold divided by 365 and multiplied by the number of days in the earnings period, rounded to the nearest penny (1/2p rounded down).[10]

Simon's NIC [8.71]–[8.86].

---

[1] SSCBA 1992, s 5(2).
[2] SSCBA 1992, s 5(3).
[3] SI 1996/1054, SI 1998/945 and Occupational and Personal Pension Schemes: Review of Certain Contracting-out Terms (Cm 3221).
[4] Social Security (Reduced Rates of Class 1 Contributions) (Salary Related Contracted-out Schemes) Order 2001, SI 2001/1356 and Social Security (Reduced Rates of Class 1 Contributions, and Rebates) (Money Purchase Contracted-out Schemes) Order 2001, SI 2001/1355.
[5] Social Security (Reduced Rates of Class 1 Contributions, Rebates and Minimum Contributions) Order 2006, SI 2006/1009.
[6] Social Security (Contributions) Regulations 1979, SI 1979/591, reg 127(1), (4).

[51.02] Employer and employee contributions

[7] SI 2001/1004, reg 127(5), (6).
[8] SI 2001/1004, reg 128(1).
[9] SI 2001/1004, reg 11(2), (4), (5).
[10] SI 2001/1004, reg 11(3), (4), (5).

Earnings periods

[51.03] The earnings period is the period taken for the purpose of calculating contribution liability. Where earnings are normally paid at regular intervals, the earnings period will normally be the length of the period between each pay date, eg if earnings are paid weekly, one week, if they are paid monthly, one month.[1] A regular interval in this connection means the interval at which under the express or implied agreement between the employer and the employee the earnings are normally paid, each interval being of substantially equal length.[2] Where earnings are normally paid at a regular interval, eg every Friday but occasionally a payment is made at another time, eg because of public holidays, such a payment is to be treated as made at the regular interval.[3]

There are certain other circumstances in which earnings are to be treated as paid at regular intervals:

(1) Where there is a succession of periods of equal length, ie consisting of the same number of days, weeks or calendar months, and one and only one payment is made in each period, the payments are to be treated as made at the end of such period.[4] This covers such cases as where weekly pay is paid on either Thursday or Friday depending on the time taken to prepare the payroll or where monthly pay is paid on the last Friday in each month.

(2) Where the earnings are payable at regular intervals but the payments are not in fact made at such regular intervals the payments are to be treated as made at the end of each such interval.[5]

However, these deeming provisions are not to have the effect of causing a payment of earnings made in one tax year to fall in another tax year.[6] Despite this, HMRC instructed employers due to make wage and salary payments on 6 April 2007 (Good Friday) or later over the holiday weekend to treat the payments as made at the normal time, even though a new tax year had commenced. The same approach may be adopted on future occasions where payment is made early due to bank holidays.[7] The next time Good Friday will coincide with the start of the tax year is 2012—the last time having been 1928, before earnings-related national insurance contributions, or indeed PAYE, had been invented.

Where a payment of earnings (but not on termination of the employment) includes holiday pay which under the deeming provisions would be treated as paid at a regular interval of a week or a multiple of weeks, the earnings period may be the length of the period in respect of which the payment is made.[8] This is optional; otherwise the holiday pay is treated as pay in the week or weeks in question.

Earnings periods [51.03]

The following rules cover further cases where earnings are paid or treated as paid at regular intervals:

(1) The employee may have earnings payable at one regular interval and other earnings payable at different regular intervals, eg basic pay paid weekly, overtime paid monthly and commissions paid quarterly. In this situation the earnings period is based on the shortest interval,[9] in this case one week, subject to a possible exception indicated below.

(2) If the regular interval at which earnings are paid is less than seven days, the earnings period will be one week. This will also be the case where earnings are payable at different regular intervals, each of which is less than seven days.[10]

(3) Where earnings are being paid at different regular intervals and some intervals are seven days or more and others are less than seven days, the earnings period will be one week.[11]

The importance of the earnings period can be seen from the following example.

EXAMPLE

Alice is a shop manager. She receives basic pay of £300 per week and in addition is entitled to a bonus related to sales targets which is paid at the end of the following month. She was awarded a bonus of £900 for March.

Her primary contributions in April are as follows:

Week ending	Basic pay	Bonus		Primary Contributions
6 April	300			22.00
13 April	300			22.00
20 April	300			22.00
27 April	300	900	(to £770 only)	73.15
			(remainder at 1%)	4.30
	£1,200	£900		£143.45

If Alice's employer decides to pay all her earnings monthly by bank transfer the position becomes:

Month ending	Earnings		
30 April	£2,100		£181.17
		Increase	£37.72

The reason for the increase is that when an earnings period of one month is applicable the excess of earnings over the upper earnings limit (chargeable at only 1%) is reduced or (as in the above example) eliminated.

Where different elements of earnings are paid at differing regular intervals it is often possible to reduce contributions liability by increasing earnings payable at longer intervals at the expense of earnings paid at the shortest interval. Consequently there is an anti-avoidance rule which applies if HM Revenue & Customs gives notice to that effect. If the greater part of the total earnings is normally (ie this implies a regular practice) paid at intervals of greater length

[51.03] Employer and employee contributions

than the shorter or shortest interval as the case may be, the earnings period is to be the longer or longest interval.[12] This provision is brought into operation by HM Revenue & Customs (formerly the Secretary of State for Social Security) giving notice to the employer and the employee, indicating the date from which the new earnings period is to be adopted.

Thus, if in the above example Alice's bonuses normally exceeded her basic pay, a notice could be issued making the earnings period one month. If the longer or longest interval is one year and the notice under this provision makes the earnings period one year, the change takes effect only so as to make the remainder of the tax year after the change the earnings period.[13]

Earnings periods, whether a week, month or other period, must always begin on the first day of the tax year and follow in succession from that date.[14] Earnings periods of one week and one month respectively will therefore correspond to the tax weeks and months used for operating PAYE. Where, however, the earnings period is of some other length, there may be a gap between the end of the last full earnings period in the tax year and the end of that year: in that case the period covering the gap is to be treated as an earnings period of normal length.[15]

Where the earnings are paid at irregular intervals and the rules for deeming the payments to be made at regular intervals do not apply, the earnings period is to be the length of the period for which the earnings are paid or a week whichever is the longer.[16] If it is not reasonably practicable to determine that period, the earnings period is the period from the last payment of earnings (or if none, the commencement of the employment) until the date of the payment but in any case no less than a week.[17] If the payment is made before the employment begins or after it ends, the earnings period is to be one week.[18]

There are special rules for determining the earnings period in the case of payments under the employment protection legislation.[19]

If there is a change in the regular intervals at which earnings are paid and the new earnings period is longer than the old, a payment of earnings made at the old interval may fall within the first new earnings period. In that case the contributions payable on payments made after the date of change are limited to those which would be payable if all payments made during the first new earnings period had been paid at the new interval.[20]

There is a special rule dealing with additional payments of earnings made after the employment has ceased. If the additional payment is not in respect of a regular interval at which earnings were paid during the continuance of the employment, eg a discretionary bonus, the earnings period for the additional payment is the week in which the payment is made.[21]

Simon's NIC Chapter 7.

[1] Social Security (Contributions) Regulations 2001, SI 2001/1004, reg 3(1)(a)(i).
[2] SI 2001/1004, reg 1(2).
[3] SI 2001/1004, reg 7(1)(a).
[4] SI 2001/1004, reg 7(1)(b), (2).
[5] SI 2001/1004, reg 7(1)(c), (2).

[6] SI 2001/1004, reg 7(3).
[7] CWG 2 (2007), page 12.
[8] SI 2001/1004, reg 19.
[9] SI 2001/1004, reg 3(1), as amended by Social Security (Contributions) (Amendment No 3) Regulations 2002, SI 2002/2366, reg 4.
[10] SI 2001/1004, reg 3(1), as amended by SI 2002/2366, reg 4.
[11] SI 2001/1004, reg 3(1), as amended by SI 2002/2366, reg 4.
[12] SI 2001/1004, reg 3(2B), as amended by SI 2002/2366, reg 4.
[13] SI 2001/1004, reg 3(3).
[14] SI 2001/1004, reg 3(2), as amended by SI 2002/2366, reg 4.
[15] SI 2001/1004, reg 3(2), as amended by SI 2002/2366, reg 4.
[16] SI 2001/1004, reg 4(*a*).
[17] SI 2001/1004, reg 4(*b*)(i).
[18] SI 2001/1004, reg 4(*b*)(ii).
[19] SI 2001/1004, reg 5.
[20] SI 2001/1004, reg 18.
[21] SI 2001/1004, reg 3(5).

Company directors

[51.04] The term "director" was not originally defined for the purpose of these rules (although the term "company" now means in the Contribution Regulations a company within the meaning of Companies Act 1985, s 735(1) or a body corporate to which any provision of that Act applies by virtue of s 718).[1] However, with effect from 6 April 1997 the definition of a director in ITEPA 2003, ss 18, 31 and 686 has been adopted for NIC purposes.[2] The authorities continue to make it clear that a director of a building society (other than a demutualised society) is not a company director.[3]

Where the employed earner is a company director there are special rules for determining the earnings period and for defining what constitutes a payment of earnings. These rules were introduced in 1983 to frustrate widespread exploitation of the earnings period rules on the part of directors. As to earnings periods, if the individual was a company director at the beginning of the tax year, the earnings period is that year, even if he does not remain a director for the rest of the year.[4] If the person is appointed a director during the course of a tax year, the earnings period is the remainder of the tax year beginning with the week in which he is appointed.[5]

The effect of a company director having an annual earnings period will normally be that the total Class 1 contributions for the tax year have to be paid in the early months of that year instead of being paid evenly during the course of the year. This is because each time earnings are paid contributions have to be calculated on the cumulative earnings to date and on the basis of the primary threshold and the upper earnings limit applicable to an annual earnings period. The contributions paid on previous payments of earnings are then deducted from the result and the balance becomes the further contributions due. Subject to adopting alternative procedures (see below) this places the

[51.04] Employer and employee contributions

company director at an initial disadvantage compared with a non-director employee having the same earnings. This can be seen from the following example:

EXAMPLE

Director paid £11,000 per month in 2009–10:

	Primary Class Contributions due for month £	Cumulative Primary Class 1 Contributions £
Month 1		
Earnings to date (£11,000)	581.35	581.35
Month 2		
Earnings to date (£22,000)	1,210.00	1,791.35
Month 3		
Earnings to date (£33,000)	1,210.00	3,001.35
Month 4		
Earnings to date (£44,000)	1,917.50	4,198.85
Month 5 (etc)		
Earnings to date (£55,000)	110.00	4,308.85
Month 12		
Earnings to date (£132,000)	110.00	5,078.55

Note

If the director were an ordinary employee earning the same salary, employee NICs would be paid at £423.24 per month, the cumulative total for the year (of £5,078.88) being reached in Month 12.

To illustrate the principles involved in the example above, the modified exact percentage method has been used. In practice the modified tables method is likely to be used but the results produced are virtually the same.

From 6 April 1999, employers may in most cases but only with the consent of the director, apply normal earnings periods during the course of the tax year (so that the effect illustrated in the above example would not then be encountered) with a final calculation then being made in the final week or month of the year re-calculating liability using the correct annual earnings period and adjusting any under or overpayments. This adjustment would recover any underpayment arising through what the authorities see as "abuse" of the earnings periods rules.[6]

There is also a special rule as to the earnings which are to be treated as paid to a company director; any payment to or for the benefit of a director which is made on account of or by way of an advance of remuneration is to be treated as a payment of earnings for contribution purposes, if it would not otherwise be so treated.[7] However, it has come to light that, on a "question for determination" heard in 1990, the Secretary of State for Social Security decided that an advance in respect of directors' fees which at the time of the advance had not been voted on should not be treated as a payment of earnings under this rule.[8] This decision if applied generally would severely limit the application of the rule but the former DSS was always of the view that the determination is not of general application and is dependent on the particular facts of the case submitted for adjudication.

In certain professions it is common for members of partnerships to hold directorships in client companies; likewise it is common for companies which have substantial shareholdings in other companies to nominate directors to those companies. As from 6 January 1988, fees and other payments received by such directors can be excluded from their earnings from such offices if the individual has to account for such fees to the partnership or company appointing him and the fees are brought into the accounts of the partnership or company and charged to tax. Where a partnership is concerned, this rule applies only if the director is a partner in the firm concerned and the payment received forms an insubstantial part of the gross income of the firm.[9] No similar relief is available for a sole practitioner in similar circumstances.

[1] Social Security (Contributions) Regulations 2001, SI 2001/1004, reg 1(2).
[2] SI 2001/1004, reg 1(2).
[3] Leaflet CA 44 (2007) p 3, para 4.
[4] SI 2001/1004, reg 8(3).
[5] SI 2001/1004, reg 8(2).
[6] SI 2001/1004, reg 8(6).
[7] SI 2001/1004, reg 22.
[8] Disclosed to the National Insurance Committee of the Tax Faculty of the ICAEW, see the Tax Faculty's Technical Release Tax 21/92 para 8.
[9] SI 2001/1004, reg 27.

Director's liability for company's contribution arrears

[51.05] Social Security Act 1998, s 64 effective from 6 April 1999 inserted a new offence[1] where a company's failure to pay contributions "appears" to HMRC to be attributable to fraud or neglect on the part of one or more individuals who were officers of the body corporate. This therefore allows culpable directors to be personally liable for corporate NIC debts. As well as being liable for their proportion of debt applicable to their culpability they are also liable for accrued and future interest and penalties thereon as well.[2]

In the first appeal involving s 121C[3] a director's appeal against the issue of a personal liability notice was dismissed. The company had never had a bank account and had only one customer. That customer paid net wages to the employees of the directors 100% owned company, but PAYE/NIC was not accounted for. The company was subsequently liquidated and the NIC due remained unpaid. The director withdrew two of his three grounds of appeal just before the appeal hearing, but the Commissioner felt unable to award costs to HMRC.

Directors, as well as others, might also fall foul of the separate offence where *any* person 'is knowingly concerned in the fraudulent evasion of any contributions which he or any other person is liable to pay"[4]. A person guilty of this offence shall be liable to imprisonment for a term not exceeding seven years, or a fine, or both.[5]

---

[1] SSAA 1992, s 121C; Social Security Act 1998 (Commencement No 4) Order 1999, reg 2.
[2] See also DSS Press Release 98/020, 5 February 1998.
[3] *Inzani v Revenue and Customs Comrs* (SpC 529) [2006] STC (SCD) 279.
[4] SSAA 1992, s 114, as amended by Social Security Act 1998, s 61, effective from 6 April 1999; Social Security Act 1998 (Commencement No 4) Order 1999, reg 2.
[5] SSAA 1992, s 114(2).

Anti-avoidance rules

[51.06] There are regulations which enable HMRC (previously the Secretary of State for Social Security) to counter practices which avoid or reduce the payment of Class 1 contributions. One deals with abnormal pay practices;[1] the other with irregular or unequal payments of earnings.[2]

An abnormal pay practice is described as one which is followed in the payment of earnings and is abnormal for the employment in question.[3] If HMRC have reason to believe that such a practice has been or is being followed, they may make a determination on any question regarding contribution liability on the basis that the abnormal practice is ignored and that the practices normal for the employment in question apply.[4] The determination can apply retrospectively to the tax year before that in which the decision is given.[5] This particular power is rarely, if ever, invoked. If additional primary contributions become payable for the previous year HMRC may enter into a direct collection arrangement with the employee, but if they do not the employer may not be able to recover all of them from the employee.[6]

A possible limitation on the scope of the power lies in the fact that it can be exercised only where the secondary contributor has followed the abnormal pay practice in the payment of earnings. So it could be argued that where the payment falls within one of the specific exclusions from earnings, eg it is a payment kind, the power cannot be used. This is, however, open to question: a practice of, for example, paying some remuneration in kind leaving cash earnings reduced could well be seen as a practice followed in paying the latter earnings. Although the former DSS never in fact sought to use this provision to counter unusual payments in kind, the provision, it would seem, gives a reserve power which might be invoked in certain circumstances.

Alternatively, a simple direction may be given to counter a practice involving irregular or unequal payments of earnings.[7] The practice in this case is one involving the payment of earnings under which the incidence of contributions is avoided or reduced. The provision clearly has in view the manipulation of earnings periods; where a direction is made it is to the effect that contribution liability is to be calculated as if the practice in question was not being followed. Such a direction shall not have any retrospective effect.[8]

With regard to the attitude towards anti-avoidance of National Insurance contributions and also income tax, the statement made by Dawn Primarolo on 2 December 2004 gives an insight into the Government's current views.[9]

Latterly the former DSS also countered avoidance by the introduction of new regulations, eg those dealing with company directors in 1983, those dealing with discretionary employee trusts in 1987 and those dealing with certain securities or commodities used for payments in kind in 1988, 1991, 1993, 1995 and 1998—see, for example, supra, § **50.23** ff.

Simon's NIC [8.466]–[8.500].

---

[1] Social Security (Contributions) Regulations 2001, SI 2001/1004, reg 30, as amended by Social Security (Contributions) (Amendment No 3) Regulations 2002, SI 2002/2366, reg 5.
[2] SI 2001/1004, reg 31, as amended by SI 2002/2366, reg 6.
[3] SI 2001/1004, reg 30(2), as amended by SI 2002/2366, reg 5.
[4] SI 2001/1004, reg 30(2), as amended by SI 2002/2366, reg 5.
[5] SI 2001/1004, reg 30(3), as amended by SI 2002/2366, reg 5.
[6] SI 2001/1004, Sch 4, para 7(3).
[7] SI 2001/1004, reg 31, as amended by SI 2002/2366, reg 6.
[8] SI 2001/1004, reg 31(2)(a), as amended by SI 2002/2366, reg 6.
[9] Written Statement by the Paymaster General, Pre Budget Report 2004.

More than one employment

[51.07] If an individual is an employee under more than one employment with the same employer, the primary rule is that the earnings paid in the week or other earnings period in respect of each employment have to be aggregated and treated as a single payment of earnings in respect of one employment only.[1] The former DSS confirmed to the ICAEW that associated companies in the same group do not represent the same employer but divisions of a company do. This rule is necessary to prevent a fragmentation of an essentially single employment with the earnings under some of the resulting employments being below the earnings thresholds or, previously, the lower earnings limits and so escaping contribution liability.

An exception from this rule is made to cover the case where the aggregation is "not reasonably practicable because the earnings in the respective employments are separately calculated".[2] The former DSS once indicated that it regarded this condition as met if the employer worked out earnings at different paying points, eg where employees are paid locally at different branches.[3] Where the employments were dealt with under separate PAYE schemes, the test was once also likely to be met. These factors alone will no longer be sufficient reason not to aggregate and subsequent guidance makes no reference to these points, simply stating: 'If exceptionally you find that it is not practicable to add all the earnings together, work out NI contributions on each set of earnings separately.'[4] The present guidance gives an example of when it might not be practicable, where the payroll program used is unable to perform the calculations and these would have to be done manually. But employers may nonetheless be required to show why it has not been reasonably practicable to aggregate the earnings.[5]

There is another primary rule that concerns the case where the individual has more than one employment but with different employers. Again in this case also the earnings paid in the week or other earnings period from each of the employments have to be aggregated and treated as a single payment of earnings from one employment but in this case only in prescribed circumstances.[6]

The circumstances where aggregation is required are where:

(1) the different employers carry on business in association with each other; or
(2) there are different employers but one of them is treated as the secondary contributor under the categorisation rules (see supra, §§ **49.15–49.23**) in respect of each of the employments; or
(3) the earnings are paid by various persons for whom the work is performed and some other person is treated as the secondary contributor under the categorisation rules.[7]

In these cases there is also an exception for the case where it is not reasonably practicable to aggregate the earnings: but there is no condition in this case that the earnings should be separately calculated.[8]

No indication is given in the regulations as to what is meant by employers carrying on business in association with each other but the guidance once stated 'their respective businesses serve a common purpose and to a significant degree, they share such things as accommodation, personnel, equipment or customers'. More recently the then Inland Revenue suggested a tighter test including the employers alleged need to take into account the employee's likely contributory benefit record.[9] Whether employer companies belong to the same group is not of itself decisive, though ordinarily in such a case the required degree of interdependence will be found.

Where earnings from two or more employments (whether with the same or different employers) have to be aggregated and the earnings periods for the various employments when considered separately are of different lengths, special rules determine the earnings period to be taken for the combined earnings:

(1) if there are both contracted-out and not contracted-out employments, the earnings period is that for the contracted-out employment or if there is more than one such employment that for the one having the shorter or shortest earnings period and, if both types of contracted-out employment exist, the COMPS employment takes priority;[10]
(2) otherwise, the earnings period is the shorter or shortest period for all the employments;[11]
(3) but if in the case of any of the employments the earnings period rules for directors have been applied, the earnings period so found or the longer or longest such period must be taken as the earnings period for the combined earnings.[12]

Where earnings from contracted-out and not contracted-out employments are aggregated, the calculation of the Class 1 contributions is subject to special rules.[13] These require that the calculation of both primary and secondary contributions is on the basis that the earnings from the contracted-out employment or employments form the first part of total earnings and therefore not contracted-out rates apply to the remainder.

All the above rules that give priority to the contracted-out employments are, however, reversed where the employee is also a member of an appropriate personal pension as regards a further employment.

Simon's NIC [6.01]–[6.60].

[1] SSCBA 1992, Sch 1, para 1(1)(a).
[2] Social Security (Contributions) Regulations 2001, SI 2001/1004, reg 14.
[3] DSS leaflet NI 269, (1991 edn) p 34, para 91.
[4] DSS leaflet NI 269, (1993 edn) p 27, para 73.
[5] HMRC leaflet CWG 2 (2007) p 38, para 67; HM Revenue & Customs National Insurance Manual 10009.
[6] SSCBA 1992, Sch 1, para 1(1)(b).
[7] SI 2001/1004, reg 15(1).
[8] SI 2001/1004, reg 15(1) proviso.
[9] HMRC leaflet CWG 2 (2007) p 38, para 65; *Tax Bulletin*, Issue 48 August 2000, p 767; HM Revenue & Customs National Insurance Manual 10009.
[10] SI 2001/1004, reg 6(3)(a), (b), (c).
[11] SI 2001/1004, reg 6(3)(d).
[12] SI 2001/1004, reg 8(4).
[13] SSCBA 1992, Sch 1, para 1.

Annual maximum contributions

[51.08] There may be cases where an individual has employments with different employers which are not required to be aggregated, eg because the different employers do not carry on business in association with each other. In such cases contribution liability will be calculated separately for each employment, and the upper earnings limit applied in each case without reference to the other employments. So, for example, if Dizzy has earnings for 2009–10 of £600 per week from employment with Roller Ltd and £400 per week from employment with Coaster Ltd, a wholly independent company, earnings of £(490 plus 290), ie £780 will be subject to primary contributions all at 11% as opposed to only £734 (844 − 110) if the earnings had been aggregated (together with the balance at 1%).

Similarly where an individual in the same tax year has earnings both as a self-employed person and as an employee, his total contributions could be much higher than if all his earnings arose from being an employee.

For these reasons annual limits have been placed on the total contributions payable. There are two rules to consider. The first rule limits the total primary

[51.08] Employer and employee contributions

Class 1 and Class 2 contributions payable at the main rate to 53 primary Class 1 contributions at the maximum weekly standard rate,[1] ie for 2009–10:

53 × 11% × (£8440 – £110) = £4,279.22, plus whatever adjustment is required to this figure for the 1% additional rate according to the individual's own earnings profile, ie, in principle, 1% × £156 (1,000 – 844) in the case of Dizzy above (these are approximate figures as the precise method of calculation specified in the legislation treats weekly and annual equivalents in different ways at different stages of the calculation. Small differences result in practice).

The maximum is set in terms of contributions at not contracted-out rates, so if the individual has actually paid contributions in respect of a contracted-out employment or where the reduced rate is paid by certain married women these have to be converted to contributions at the standard rate for the purpose of seeing whether the maximum has been exceeded. But if it has been exceeded and a repayment is therefore due, the amount to be repaid is based on the actual contributions paid, ie overpaid standard rate contributions are converted back to the contracted-out, etc rates at which they were paid. Contributions paid at the reduced rate are similarly converted to standard rate contributions in applying the maximum but any repayment is based on the actual contributions paid.

It should be noted that the maximum applies only where an individual has more than one job or to employee and self-employed contributions. Because the upper earnings limit is not relevant to secondary Class 1 contributions, non-aggregation of earnings does not result in excess employer contributions being paid.

The other rule applies in the case where Class 4 contributions are payable in addition to primary Class 1 and Class 2 contributions. In this situation the Class 4 contributions at the full 8% rate are not to exceed A–B, where A is:

53 Class 2 contributions, ie in 2009–10 53 × £2.40	£127.20
Plus the maximum Class 4 contributions at the full rate, ie in 2009–10 8% × £(43,875 – 5,715)	£3,052.80
	£3,180.00

and B is the aggregate of the primary Class 1 (other than at the additional 1% rate) and Class 2 contributions paid.[2] For this purpose also Class 1 contributions paid at contracted-out rates or at the reduced rate are converted to standard rate contributions.[3] In relation to A the Class 2 contributions are to be taken as such higher rate as that which is required by reason of any late payment (see infra, § **53.13**).

EXAMPLE

Ruby works as a cook in a restaurant at £360 per week; in 2009–10 she earned £18,200 from this employment. She is also in business on her own account, providing catering at wedding receptions, business functions etc; in 2009–10 she earns £28,280 after expenses from this business.

Her contribution liabilities for 2009–10 before application of the annual maxima will be:

Annual maximum contributions [51.08]

	£
Class 1	
52 weeks at £(360 − 110) × 11%	1,430.00
Class 2	
52 weeks at £2.40	124.80
	1,554.80
Class 4	
£(28,280 − 5,715) × 8%	1,805.20
	£3,360.00

Restrictions

The total Class 1 and Class 2 contributions (£1,554.80) are less than 53 Class 1 contributions at the maximum weekly standard rate (ie £4,279.22—see above). The Class 1 and Class 2 contributions are therefore not restricted.

But the Class 4 contributions at the main rate (currently 8%) are restricted to:

	A (see above)	3,180.00
Less:	B (the total Class 1 and Class 2 contributions paid)	1,554.80
		£1,625.20

The balance of Class 4 not due at 8% is £180.00, which represents profits of £2,250 (£180.00 × 100/8). This amount is subject to the 1% additional rate, ie £22.50. Thus the total Class 4 due is £1,647.70 (£1,625.20 + £22.50).

Where through application of these limits, contributions have been overpaid, or where contributions have been paid in error, there are complex rules for dealing with a return of contributions: these establish an order of priority for refunding different kinds of contribution.[4] Broadly, any overpaid Class 4 contributions are repayable first, then primary Class 1 contributions at the reduced rate, followed by Class 2 contributions and then primary Class 1 contributions at the standard rate on not contracted-out employments. Last to be repaid are primary Class 1 contributions in respect of contracted-out employments where there are further rules governing the repayment of amounts paid at not contracted-out rates and contracted-out rates respectively.[5]

Where it is anticipated that the annual maximum limits will be exceeded, it is advisable to apply for deferment of contributions before the start of the tax year for which deferment of liability is sought. There are two kinds of deferment available. One covers the case where the individual in a tax year will have earnings from two or more employments and is expected to pay, in respect of one of the employments, contributions equal to 52 primary Class 1 contributions at the rate applicable to earnings at the upper earnings limit. In such a case deferment will be granted in respect of the other employments.[6] The other kind of deferment covers the case where the individual is both an employee and self-employed in a tax year. It is necessary to show that the annual maximum which limits the total primary Class 1 and Class 2 contributions to 53 primary Class 1 contributions at the maximum standard rate (see above) is likely to apply. In that case a deferment arrangement in respect of the Class 2 contributions may be made.[7] Similarly if it can be shown that the annual maximum restricting Class 4 contributions described above is likely to apply, a deferment of liability for Class 4 contributions may also be granted.[8] In all cases of deferment, the position is reviewed after the end of the tax year and any unpaid contributions are then payable by means of direct collection. Where deferment of primary contributions is granted and the maximum amount is not paid for any reason all contributions due will be collected from the employee. Where, however, employers operate unofficial deferment procedures, ie not approved by HM Revenue & Customs, any arrears due will be sought from the employer.

Simon's NIC [8.161]–[8.250].

---

[1] Social Security (Contributions) Regulations 2001, SI 2001/1004, reg 21, as amended by Social Security (Contributions) (Amendment) Regulations 2003, SI 2003/193, reg 6.
[2] SI 2001/1004, reg 100(1), (2), (3), as amended by SI 2003/193, reg 14.
[3] SI 2001/1004, reg 100(4), as amended by SI 2003/193, reg 14.
[4] SI 2001/1004, reg 52A.
[5] SI 2001/1004, reg 54.
[6] SI 2001/1004, reg 84.
[7] SI 2001/1004, reg 90(4).
[8] SI 2001/1004, regs 95–97.

Collection of Class 1 contributions

Collection through PAYE

[51.09] Class 1 contributions are normally payable under the PAYE system, ie the employer must account for the primary contributions deducted from pay and for the secondary contributions for which he is liable to the Receivables Management Service. This must be done within 14 days from the end of each tax month (or 17 days where payment is made electronically from May 2004, whether compulsorily or otherwise). HM Revenue & Customs in due course surrenders the contributions collected for payment into the National Insurance Fund.

To enable this procedure to operate, the PAYE regulations (subject to some modification) have been incorporated into the Contributions Regulations.[1] The following points should be noted.

(1) The employer, ie the secondary contributor, is liable both for his own contributions and for the employee's primary contributions[2] but he is entitled to recover the primary contributions by deduction from the employee's earnings.[3] Where an under-deduction occurs, the right to recover the shortfall is restricted to earnings subsequently paid in the same tax year and/or the following tax year[4] but with the further

(2) Under the present arrangements for statutory sick pay, statutory maternity pay, statutory paternity pay and statutory adoption pay, the employer is required to pay these benefits to employees entitled to them but currently he has the right to recover only 92% of the payment of statutory maternity pay, statutory paternity pay and statutory adoption pay unless the employer is a small employer. For this purpose, a small employer is defined as one whose contribution payments (including primary contributions) in the tax year preceding that in which the days of absence fall do not exceed £45,000[6] where the employer is a small employer recovery at the rate of 104.5% of the payment of statutory maternity pay, statutory paternity pay and statutory adoption pay is allowable.[7] In the case of statutory sick pay, reimbursement for all employers is the amount by which the statutory sick pay payments in a particular month exceed 13% of the NIC liability for that month.[8]

restriction that any additional deduction must not exceed the amount deductible from the payment of earnings in the ordinary way, ie the normal deduction can be doubled but no more.[5]

With effect from 6 April 1997 there is no longer a requirement to operate the statutory sick pay rules or keep statutory sick pay records for any day of incapacity for work where, for the same day, the employer pays contractual remuneration at or above the current rate of statutory sick pay. Employers are required to keep records only of all sickness absence and remuneration paid during those absences. This "easement" of the rules is voluntary and can be adopted whenever the employer chooses; there is no requirement to give notice to the authorities. Furthermore, the easement does not have to be applied to all employees or throughout an individual employee's period of incapacity for work although flexibility may be limited by the contractual arrangements. Operation of the easement will not disentitle recovery of statutory sick pay under the percentage threshold scheme although the amount recovered may reduce in the case of employers habitually making recoveries under the scheme. The reimbursement and compensation referred to above is to be deducted from contributions which the secondary contributor is liable to pay to the Receivables Management Service.

---

[1] Social Security (Contributions) Regulations 2001, SI 2001/1004, Sch 4.
[2] SSCBA 1992, Sch 1, para 3(1).
[3] SSCBA 1992, Sch 1, para 3(3) and SI 2001/1004, Sch 4, para 7(1).
[4] SI 2001/1004, Sch 4, para 7(3).
[5] SI 2001/1004, Sch 4, para 7(5).
[6] Statutory Maternity Pay (Compensation of Employers) and Miscellaneous Amendment Regulations 1994, SI 1994/1882. The previous thresholds were £16,000, £20,000 and then from 6 April 2002 £40,000.
[7] Statutory Maternity Pay (Compensation of Employers) and Miscellaneous Amendment Regulations 1994, SI 1994/1882, as amended by Statutory Maternity Pay (Compensation of Employers) Amendment Regulations 2004, SI 2004/698.
[8] Statutory Sick Pay Percentage Threshold Order 1995, SI 1995/512.

Penalties and interest

[51.10] As from 6 April 1990 a change in PAYE compliance rules for employers was introduced following the recommendations of the Keith Committee. Previously the year-end returns giving details of pay, PAYE and NIC deductions (on forms P14, P35 and P38/P38A) were due on 19 April following the end of the tax year. The due date (for returns covering 1989–90 and subsequent years) was put forward to 19 May but tax penalty proceedings could be taken for late submission of returns.

Penalties may also be applied for where submission of the year end returns is delayed by more than 12 months and where due to negligence or fraud an incorrect return results in loss of tax; in these cases the penalties may be up to 100% of the tax underpaid or paid late.[1]

SSA 1990 provided that the penalties in these latter cases may also be up to 100% of the contributions underpaid or paid late.[2] This means, for example, that a failure to return an item which should be treated as pay for contributions purposes (but not for PAYE purposes) could result in a penalty of 100% of the contributions underpaid.

Beginning with the tax year 1992–93, PAYE deductions and Class 1 NICs which remain unpaid 14 days after the end of the tax year (17 days from 2004–05 onwards, if the payment is made electronically) automatically carry interest from that day (termed "the reckonable date") until payment.[3] The rate of interest charged is the rate prescribed under FA 1989, s 178, ie the rate (as periodically revised) which is charged on overdue tax.[4]

Where contributions for any tax year (beginning with 1992–93) are repaid, eg as a result of a repayment claim being agreed, the repaid contributions carry interest as from the last day of the tax year after the tax year in respect of which contributions were paid. If, however, the overpayment remains unsettled more than 12 months after the end of the tax year to which the payment related, interest runs from the last day of the tax year in which the overpayment was made.[5]

Where the employer has paid interest on contributions and it is found that interest should not have been paid although the contributions were due, the interest is repayable.[6] Likewise, interest is repayable where the contributions in respect of which the interest was paid are refunded under repayment claims.[7]

There are three circumstances in which interest will be remitted:

(1) Where the liability to pay the interest arises as a result of "an official error".[8] An official error is defined as a mistake or omission by an official or employee of HMRC or predecessor bodies (ie, the Inland Revenue or the Contributions Agency) acting in their official capacity. But the employer or any person acting on his behalf must not have caused or materially contributed to that mistake or omission.[9]

(2) A question relating to the employer's liability to pay the contributions was, before 1 April 1999, put to the Secretary of State for Social Security for determination. There is no equivalent "freezing" of interest under the current appeals procedure for National Insurance contributions.

(3) A question of law arising in connection with the Secretary of State's determination is referred to the High Court or in Scotland to the Court of Session. It is noteworthy that putting a question of law to the High Court under the judicial review process is not a circumstance for which remission of interest is provided.

Where interest is to be remitted, the period of remission is to be in the case of an official error from the reckonable date (see above) or if later, the day when the official error occurred until 14 days after the official error is rectified and the employer is advised in writing.[10] In the case of a question being put for determination, the period is to be from the date of submission until the determination of the question and in the case of a referral to the High Court or Court of Session, the period is to be from the referral to the court until the disposal of the case. If the question was not determined by the Secretary of State before 1 April 1999, remission of interest will cease from the time that an HMRC officer makes a decision or 1 August 1999, whichever is the earlier.[11]

In respect of monthly remittances that relate to 2004–05 tax and Class 1 NIC onwards there are an extra three days available where the payment is made electronically (whether compulsorily or otherwise). However, the payment must reach HMRC on or before the 22nd of the month so such payments will need to allow for both bank non-working days and transmission time.

---

[1] TMA 1970, s 98A(4).
[2] SSA 1990, s 17(7), Sch 5 introducing para 5A, SSA 1975, Sch 1, Social Security (Contributions) Amendment (No 4) Regulations 1990, SI 1990/1935, reg 2(2): this provision came into force on 22 October 1990.
[3] Social Security (Contributions) Regulations 2001, SI 2001/1004, Sch 4, para 17, as amended by Social Security (Contributions, Categorisation of Earners and Intermediaries) (Amendment) Regulations 2004, SI 2004/770.
[4] SI 2001/1004, Sch 4, para 17(1).
[5] SI 2001/1004, Sch 4, para 18.
[6] SI 2001/1004, Sch 4, para 19(a).
[7] SI 2001/1004, Sch 4, para 19(b).
[8] SI 2001/1004, Sch 4, para 20.
[9] SI 2001/1004, Sch 4, para 20(3)(a).
[10] SI 2001/1004, Sch 4, para 20(3)(c).
[11] Inland Revenue press release 1999/100, 18 May 1999, *Simon's Weekly Tax Intelligence* 1999, p 943.

Direct collection

[51.11] Although collection of contributions through the PAYE machinery is the normal procedure, there is also provision for arrangements to be made to recover Class 1 contributions by means of direct collection.[1] This can occur in the following circumstances:

[51.11] Employer and employee contributions

(1) a deferment of Class 1 contributions has been granted (see supra, § **51.08**) and the employee has agreed to pay any primary Class 1 contributions that may ultimately become due;[2]
(2) the secondary contributor has failed to account for primary Class 1 contributions and the failure is due to an act or default on the part of the employee and not to any negligence on the part of the secondary contributor;[3]
(3) the collection provisions cannot be enforced against the secondary contributor because protection is afforded by an international treaty or convention and the secondary contributor is unwilling to pay primary contributions on behalf of the employee;[4]
(4) the employer does not fulfil the conditions as to residence, presence or having a place of business in Great Britain so as to become liable as the secondary contributor to account for primary contributions.[5]

---

[1] Social Security (Contributions) Regulations 2001, SI 2001/1004, reg 68.
[2] SI 2001/1004, reg 84(1).
[3] SI 2001/1004, reg 86(1)(a), as amended by Social Security (Contributions, Categorisation of Earners and Intermediaries) (Amendment) Regulations 2004, SI 2004/770.
[4] SI 2001/1004, reg 86(1)(b).
[5] SI 2001/1004, reg 145(1)(b); Sch 4, para 30(1).

Repayment claims; interest

[51.12] Overpayments of contributions can arise in a variety of circumstances. The most common situation is where the contributions paid exceed the annual maxima.[1] In such cases there is no longer any time limit within which an application for refund must be made. There are also cases where the authorities accept that its former practice was incorrect in law and contributions paid on that basis are therefore refundable. One instance of this was where the former DSS withdrew from its original position on payments of personal bills charged to directors' current accounts;[2] another was the former DSS' acceptance that the agency workers' rules did not enable secondary contributions to be collected from a UK host company to which employees of overseas companies were seconded;[3] and another in 2006 was in respect of the authorities' further change of view regarding tips and gratuities.[4]

A claim for repayment of contributions paid in error has to be made within six years of the end of the tax year for which the contributions were paid.[5] An extension is allowed where the applicant has a reasonable excuse for not making the claim within the six-year period allowed.[6]

Until the provisions for charging interest on overdue contributions were introduced (see under "Collection", § **51.09** supra), there were no statutory provisions under which interest would be paid on refunded contributions. Interest is added to repayments for 1993–94 onwards.[7] However, as a matter of practice, the former DSS was prepared to pay "compensation for delay in payment" where there was a delay in making a repayment which was due to a clear and unambiguous error on the part of the authorities and the delay in making the refund exceeded 12 months. No compensation was paid if the delay was in part attributable to unreasonable inactivity on the part of the contributor or his or her agent.

In those cases where the overpaid contributions have been paid on the basis of advice given by the DSS, Inland Revenue or HMRC which the respective Department subsequently accepted was incorrect in law, there may be grounds for claiming interest on the overpaid contributions on the basis of general law, in particular under the principles established in *Woolwich Equitable Building Society v IRC*.[8]

[1] See supra, § **51.08**.
[2] See supra, § **51.11**.
[3] See infra, § **54.17**.
[4] See supra, § **50.04**.
[5] Social Security (Contributions) Regulations 2001, SI 2001/1004, reg 52(8), as amended by Social Security (Contributions, Categorisation of Earners and Intermediaries) (Amendment) Regulations 2004, SI 2004/770, reg 12.
[6] SI 2001/1004, reg 52(8), (9), as amended by Social Security (Contributions, Categorisation of Earners and Intermediaries) (Amendment) Regulations 2004, SI 2004/770, reg 12.
[7] SI 2001/1004, Sch 4, paras 18, 19.
[8] [1991] STC 364.

Class 1A contributions

[**51.13**] A new class of national insurance contributions was introduced as from 6 April 1991—Class 1A. These contributions are payable by employers only and were originally charged only on company cars and fuel provided partly or wholly for private use. However, from 6 April 2000, Class 1A contributions are payable on most taxable benefits in kind. No benefit entitlement is derived from the payment of Class 1A contributions.

No benefit entitlement is derived from the payment of Class 1A contributions.

The charge on fuel, when introduced, was intended to replace the charge under Class 1 under which as a result of the *Overdrive* decision fuel provided partly or wholly for private use will generally have to be treated as earnings of the employment (see supra, § **50.07**). In this respect the introduction of Class 1A contributions was intended to avoid the administrative complications of employers having to account month by month for contributions on petrol purchases or allowances involving some element of private use, although it has subsequently become another "hidden tax". To prevent the charge under Class 1 overlapping that under Class 1A, it was intended that the Contributions Regulations should be amended to that effect. After considerable delay, this was eventually done.[1] For the future Class 1 liability in respect of fuel purchases is likely to be confined mainly to the following cases:

(1) where the employee provides his own car and is paid a mileage allowance in excess of the HM Revenue & Customs approved rate;

(2) where a round sum allowance is paid which "bears no relation to the actual expenses incurred".[2]

Simon's NIC Chapter 9.

[1] SI 1996/700.
[2] CWG 2 (2007), p 87 and DSS leaflet NI 269 (April 1992 supplement), pp 7, 12.

The basic scheme

[51.14] The primary legislation was introduced in the Social Security (Contributions) Act 1991: the provisions have now been consolidated in SSCBA 1992, s 10. Regulations have been introduced under enabling provisions[1] which contain many of the detailed rules required. The original legislation was amended by the Child Support Pensions and Social Security Act 2000, further regulations made thereafter and then subsequently consolidated.

The contributions are based on the taxable benefit in kind in respect of all such items (but only on company cars and fuel until 6 April 2000). For Class 1A contributions to become payable, two basic conditions must be met.[2]

(1) For the tax year under consideration, there must be a charge to income tax as "employment income".
(2) This will therefore apply only to directors and higher-paid employees to whom benefits have been made available by reason of the employment and, in the case of a car, it is available in the tax year in question for private use.[3] Benefits which arise on lower paid employees ("P9D cases") do not attract the extended Class 1A liability.
(3) The employment by reason of which the benefits are made available is employed earner's employment. This requires the employee concerned to be gainfully employed in Great Britain under a contract of service or in an office with income chargeable to tax as 'employment income'.[4] This provision will therefore remove from the charge those employees whose employment is wholly carried out abroad.

Where these conditions are met, an annual Class 1A contribution is payable in respect of the taxable benefits.

The liability is on benefits and not reimbursed expenses. Reimbursed business expenses are not liable to national insurance contributions of any Class. Reimbursed personal expenses have always been liable to Class 1 contributions (ie, monthly/quarterly remittances) and will remain so for the foreseeable future. The form P11D was redesigned for 2000–01 onwards to take into account the reporting needs of the new, extended Class 1A charge.

Where there is mixed business use of an item, either there will be a Class 1A charge on all of it or else there will be no Class 1A charge at all. Where the non-business use is "insignificant" the item will be treated as being entirely for business purposes and so no NIC charge will arise. Where the non-business use is not "insignificant", then the extended ITEPA 2003, s 336 relief in respect of benefits will not be available for Class 1A purposes and NIC will be due on the

Class 1A contributions [51.14]

entire amount.⁵ This will affect various types of benefit, including the provision of a chauffeur or a home telephone through an employer's contract. In the latter case, reversion to an employees contract may be beneficial since the Class 1 charge can usually still be apportioned.

The Chancellor announced in the March 2000 Budget that the extended Class 1A charge would not—as a temporary measure—be levied on childcare provision. This related to employers contracts, whether they were such as to qualify for exception from the tax benefits in kind charge or not. Reimbursement to an employee, or settlement of their personal bills for childcare, continues to attract Class 1 contributions—as had always been the case. From 6 April 2005, the national insurance treatment fell fully into line with the new tax regime that also commenced at that time. Workplace nurseries remain tax and NIC-free. Other provision is now subject to a limit of £55 per week per employee (£50 per week 2005–06). Excess childcare payments where there is an employer's contract direct with the childcare provider is subject to Class 1A. In the case of vouchers, the excess is liable to Class 1 and so needs entering into the payroll for that purpose, even though the tax liability is not through PAYE.

In addition, Class 1A contributions are not due where benefits are:

(1) Exempt from income tax, eg certain living accommodation, employer provided mobile phones but only one such mobile phone per employee from 6 April 2006.⁶ Reimbursement of the employee's own costs of providing his own mobile phone is, as it has always been, subject to Class 1 on the non-business element.
(2) Returnable only on Form P9D.⁷
(3) Covered by an Extra-Statutory Concession (although tax concessions do not have the force of law, Class 1A exemption for the same items is enshrined in regulations). Where an ESC is applicable for income tax purposes, then—by law, notwithstanding that the tax position is only a concession—there is no Class 1A liability.⁸
(4) Covered by a dispensation for tax purposes.⁹
(5) Included in PAYE Settlement Agreement (PSA), in which case Class 1B contributions (see infra, § **51.19**) may be due on the expense/benefit and will most certainly be due on all the tax accounted for under the PSA.¹⁰
(6) Already liable for Class 1 National Insurance contributions.¹¹
(7) Exempt from Class 1 National Insurance contributions, eg redundancy and certain pension payments, specific and distinct business expenditure.¹²
(8) Provided entirely for business use.¹³

It was possible to avoid Class 1A contributions on cars where the benefit of the vehicle was freely convertible into cash as the benefit was then taxable under the general income tax rules (rather than under what was TA 1988, s 157) under the rule established in *Heaton v Bell*.¹⁴ However, the loophole was closed with effect from 5 April 1995 by FA 1995, s 43. This section provides that where an employee would otherwise be within the special income tax rules for calculating the benefit of the private use of a company car, and an alternative to the car is offered, the mere fact that an alternative is offered will not make the benefit chargeable instead under the general income tax rules.

[51.14] Employer and employee contributions

Class 1A contributions are payable at the same rate as that for secondary Class 1 contributions,[15] ie for 2009–10, 12.8%.

Class 1A contributions are payable only by the person who is liable to pay the secondary Class 1 contributions on the last or only relevant payment of earnings in the tax year.[16] A relevant payment of earnings is a payment made to or for the benefit of the earner in respect of the employment by reason of which the benefit is made available.[17] Where no secondary contributions are payable in respect of a relevant payment of earnings because the earnings of the employee do not reach the earnings threshold or, previously, the lower earnings limit, Class 1A contributions are payable by the person who would be the secondary contributor if any earnings had exceeded that limit.[18] (This latter provision will mainly affect directors with very modest earnings from a particular directorship but who are provided with a company car and/or other benefits.)

The need for there to be a secondary contributor (or potential secondary contributor) in effect forms a third basic condition for Class 1A liability to arise. So, for example, when an expatriate employee is sent to work in the UK, in certain circumstances (see infra, § **54.08**) the overseas employer will not be liable to pay secondary Class 1 contributions even though the employee is liable to pay primary contributions: in such a case there will be no Class 1A contribution liability.

Simon's NIC Chapter 9.

---

[1] SSCBA 1992, s 10(8), (9), Sch 1, paras 5, 8(1)(*b*).
[2] SSCBA 1992, s 10(1).
[3] SSCBA 1992, s 10(1)(*b*)(ii).
[4] SSCBA 1992, s 2(1)(*a*) and s 10(1)(*b*)(i).
[5] SSCBA 1992, s 10(7).
[6] SSCBA 1992, s 10(1)(*a*).
[7] SSCBA 1992, s 10(1)(*b*).
[8] SI 2001/1004, reg 40(7).
[9] SSCBA 1992, s 10(1)(*a*).
[10] SSCBA 1992, s 10(6).
[11] SSCBA 1992, s 10(1)(*c*).
[12] SI 2001/1004, reg 40(2), Sch 3.
[13] SSCBA 1992, s 10(1)(*a*).
[14] *Heaton v Bell* (1969) 46 TC 211.
[15] SSCBA 1992, s 10(5).
[16] SSCBA 1992, s 10(2)(*a*).
[17] SSCBA 1992, s 10(3).
[18] SSCBA 1992, s 10(2)(*b*).

Cars and fuel

[51.15] As regards cars and fuel and as under the corresponding provisions dealing with the income tax scale charges, for 1994–95 to 2001–02 the car benefit was determined as for income tax under the regime under which the charge was to be 35% of the list price of the car at first registration plus the price of extras provided with or subsequently added to the car. A reduction of one-third was to be made where the employee drove at least 2,500 business miles in the tax year or two-thirds if the employee drove at least 18,000 business miles in a tax year. For 1999–2000 to 2001–02 inclusive, the reduction for business mileage of 2,500 to 17,990 was 25% of the list price and, in respect of business mileage of 18,000 or more 15% of the list price.

For 2002–03 onwards, the car benefit percentage is determined according to the CO_2 emission factor of the car—as for income tax—and the business mileage undertaken is no longer of any relevance.

For 2003–04 onwards the car fuel benefit scale charge was replaced also by the same CO_2 emission-based percentage, based on an amount of £16,900 (£14,400 until 2007–08).

As for income tax, the scale charge on the car is reduced by any contribution made by the employee for private use whereas the scale charge for fuel cannot be reduced by a partial reimbursement by the employee: only if the employee reimburses the full cost of the private fuel will the charge be reduced to nil. For this reason it will generally be more effective for the employee to make a contribution towards private use of the car than towards the cost of private fuel.

Mileage thresholds—evidence needed

[51.16] In the case of the Class 1A charge for car benefits, the onus was on the employer to be able to show that the business mileage up to 5 April 2002 exceeded the 2,500 or 18,000 mile threshold, that the car was unavailable for a particular period or that a particular car, where more than one was made available to an employee, was the one used to the greatest extent for business travel.[1]

In fact, as regards business mileage it had to be assumed that the business miles travelled were less than 18,000 miles or 2,500 miles as the case may be unless the employer "has information to show to the contrary".[2] This raised the question of what kind of records the employer was to maintain if Class 1A contributions were not to be based on the highest levels of cash equivalents. Initially, it was feared that detailed mileage logging of both business and private mileage would be necessary but in moving the second reading of the Social Security (Contributions) Bill,[3] the Government Minister stated:

> There will be no requirement to maintain comprehensive business mileage records in every case and, generally speaking, we shall be adopting precisely the same approach to this as the Inland Revenue does at the moment in assessing individual liability; and after consulting employers, we shall be providing them with detailed guidance about what information will be required to comply with the requirements of the system.[4]

In another part of the Minister's speech, he said 'we believe that in the majority of cases the information will already be available from the employer's records. First, it will generally be clear from the nature of the employee's job whether a discount for business use over 2,500 or 18,000 miles is appropriate'.[5] On this point the former DSS appeared to be satisfied if the specific business travel requirements of the job were identified. For example, if the employee had to make a regular weekly journey of 70 return miles, it would be accepted that his annual business travel exceeded 2,500 miles. Again, a salesperson who was on the road all week covering say, the North of England would be treated as having a business mileage of more than 18,000 miles.[6]

These points were also made in the mailshot sent to all employers in October 1991. That mailshot also said: 'You can rely on any records which employees may keep for income tax purposes.' For the first year of operation (1991–92) only, the mailshot indicated that employers would be allowed to arrive at the business mileage on an estimated basis by carrying out a sampling exercise for each employee over the last three months of the tax year and extrapolating the result to arrive at the annual average.

Latter guidance indicated that where the expected business mileage was less than 2,500 in the tax year no record-keeping was needed; where the expected business mileage was between 2,500 and 17,999 miles in the tax year, it was simply necessary to be able to show that the business mileage exceeded 2,499 miles, the nature of the employment being taken as a good guide. Where the business mileage was 18,000 miles or more the authorities expected sufficient information to be kept.[7]

Simon's NIC [9.121]–[9.240].

---

[1] Former SSCBA 1992, s 10(6)—see references to "the person liable to pay the contribution".
[2] Former SSCBA 1992, s 10(6)(*b*).
[3] Enacted as SS(C)A 1991.
[4] HC Official Debate, 9 May 1991, Vol 190, col 853.
[5] HC Official Debate, 9 May 1991, Vol 190, col 853.
[6] This was confirmed in a letter from the DSS to the Tax Faculty of the ICAEW.
[7] Inland Revenue leaflet CA 33 (2002) p 24, para 103.

Cars—special cases

[51.17] Because the rules covering Class 1A contribution liability are dependent on the tax rules, power is given to make regulations carrying through for Class 1A purposes any alterations made to the tax legislation.[1] Because, unlike the then Inland Revenue, the former DSS had only a limited power to make concessions, power was given to introduce regulations excepting persons from Class 1A liability or reducing such liability.[2] Accordingly provisions similar to the former extra-statutory concession A59 and the former extra-statutory concession A71 (both these having been enshrined into ITEPA 2003) were introduced: the former prevents scale charges being made where a severely disabled employee is given assistance with home to work travel; the latter prevents a double charge where the same car is shared by two or more directors or higher-paid employees or where a car is made available to a member of the director's or employee's family or household and the family member is charged to tax on the benefit in his or her own right.[3]

These special cases dealt with by regulation are as follows:

(1) Where a car (or other benefit) is made available to an employee (A) who is a member of the family of another employee (B).
Ordinarily there would be a car benefit charge in respect of (B) but this is not to arise if there is a car benefit charge in respect of (A) as an employee. If there is no car benefit charge in respect of (A) because his general earnings including benefits are less than £8,500, there will still be no car benefit charge in respect of (B) so long as either the provision of the car follows the normal commercial practice for the kind of employment in question or equivalent cars are made available on the same terms to other employees in similar employments to (A) with the same employer and who are not related to directors or higher paid employees of that employer.

(2) Where two or more cars were made available concurrently to one employee.
The previous increases to the car benefit charges in this situation were to be made only where the cars were made available by reason of one or more employments with the same employer or with different but associated employers.[4]

(3) Where one car is made available to an employee by reason of two or more employments or to two or more employees concurrently under the same employer.
In these cases:
(a) in considering whether the former 2,500 or 18,000 mile thresholds (ie, up to 5 April 2002) were exceeded, the business mileage in each employment was aggregated;[5]
(b) where there is more than one employment, the scale charge in respect of each employment is reduced by

$$\frac{X-1}{X}$$

where X is the total number of employments. This results in the aggregate reduced scale charges equalling a single scale charge.[6]

(4) Where a car was made available to a disabled employee partly to assist his travelling between home and work.
In such a case the home to work travel is treated as business mileage in considering whether the former 2,500 or 18,000 miles thresholds were exceeded.[7]

(5) Where a car is made available to a disabled employee but only for business and home to work travel.
In this case, the provision of the car is exempted from Class 1A contribution liability.[8]

The provisions in 2, 3(a) and 4 above are of no practical application after 5 April 2002 because regard is no longer had to business mileage.

Simon's NIC [9.91]–[9.95].

---

[1] SSCBA 1992, s 10(8)(*b*).
[2] SSCBA 1992, s 10(9).

[51.17] Employer and employee contributions

3 Social Security (Contributions) Regulations 2001, SI 2001/1004, reg 36.
4 Former SI 2001/1004, reg 34.
5 Former SI 2001/1004, reg 35.
6 SI 2001/1004, reg 36.
7 Former SI 2001/1004, reg 37.
8 SI 2001/1004, reg 38.

Collection

[51.18] The power to collect Class 1 contributions with tax deducted under PAYE was extended to Class 1A contributions in respect of the liability for years up to and including 1999–2000.[1] The general regulation-making powers conferred by the SSCBA 1992[2] are extended to cover the keeping of records to enable Class 1A contribution liability to be determined.[3] Such powers are also extended to cover the treatment of Class 1A contributions as payment of secondary Class 1, Class 1B or Class 2 contributions and vice versa,[4] and to deal with the repayment of Class 1A contributions.[5] These provisions enable overpayments of Class 1A contributions to be rectified. An overpayment will occur where, for example, following submission of the year-end return (see below) the employer obtains information that the car was unavailable for a period of 30 days or more or, in the past, that an employee's business mileage was higher than that assumed when making the return.

The detailed collection procedures were first set out in amending regulations introduced in January 1992.[6] At that time, they required the Class 1A contributions to be recorded on each employee's PAYE deductions working sheet (P11) with a category letter as instructed by the former DSS (letter "Y" being used). This had to be done no later than (originally) 19 June following the end of the tax year in question and it was on that date that the Class 1A contributions for all the employees had to be paid to the then Collector of Taxes (unless PAYE was being paid on a quarterly basis when 19 July was the relevant date).[7] The time limit for the payment of Class 1A contributions in respect of 1996–97 and subsequent years was extended to 19 July because of the self-assessment/P11D timetable. From July 2005 (ie, payment for 2004–05 onwards), whilst there is no compulsion on employers of any size (unlike Class 1), payments made electronically are due to be received by HM Revenue & Customs by the extended date of 22 July. Where that day is not a bank working day, value must be received on the last such day before the 22 July.

Because many employers preferred to account for the Class 1A contributions outside the PAYE system—it will often be the staff responsible for completing forms P11D rather than the payroll administration staff who will calculate the Class 1A contributions due—the then DSS introduced a pilot scheme (the "Alternative Payment Method") under which employers who provide ten cars or more were given the opportunity to pay the Class 1A contributions due for 1991–92 direct to the DSS via the bank giro credit system. To take advantage of this opportunity employers had to respond to the DSS originally by 2 December 1991[8] but the closing date was later extended to 13 March 1992. The scheme was extended further to cover Class 1A contributions due for 1992–93 and later years, and from the 1993–94 year to all employers irrespective of the number of cars provided.[9] Employers who used the alternative method of payment provided by the scheme in respect of earlier years did not have to re-apply to use that method in respect of future years. Other employers who wished to use the alternative method for 1999–2000 had to submit applications by 20 May 2000.

This "Alternative Payment Method", suitably amended, forms the basis for the only method of collection available in respect of the liability for 2000–01 onwards but the calculation is now included in a revised version of form P11D(b).

Where the business is transferred, under employment law (assuming the Transfer of Undertakings Regulations applies[10]) the employments continue with the successor. In this case, the successor business becomes liable for the Class 1A contributions if it pays earnings in the last tax month of the year in which the benefits are provided and in that case must account for them at the normal payment date (the following 19 July, currently).[11] But where employees leave before the transfer of the business the predecessor employer is liable to account for the Class 1A contributions[12] as in the situation where the business ceases altogether.[13]

The provisions dealing with penalties are extended to cover Class 1A contributions.[14]

The provisions relating to interest charges always caused great confusion, given the two different accounting methods. However, under the single system relating to 2000–01 onwards the position is clear. Interest is charged the day after the due date, ie from 20 July after the end of the tax year in question (22 July if payment is made electronically in respect of 2004–05 or a later year).[15] Interest is paid where Class 1A contributions are refunded[16] and can also be remitted in the case of official error.[17]

[1] SSCBA 1992, Sch 1, para 6.
[2] SSCBA 1992, Sch 1, para 8(1).
[3] SSCBA 1992, Sch 1, para 8(1)(*a*).
[4] SSCBA 1992, Sch 1, para 8(1)(*l*).
[5] SSCBA 1992, Sch 1, para 8(1)(*m*); see also Social Security (Contributions) Amendment Regulations 1992, SI 1992/97, reg 4.
[6] SI 1992/97, reg 13.
[7] SI 1992/97, reg 14.
[8] The invitation to participate took the form of a business reply card inserted in the October 1991 mailshot.
[9] DSS leaflet NI 280 (April 1994), para (7).
[10] Transfer of Undertakings (Protection of Employment) Regulations 2006, SI 2006/246.
[11] Social Security (Contributions) Regulations 2001, SI 2001/1004, reg 72.
[12] SI 2001/1004, reg 71(1).
[13] SI 2001/1004, reg 73.
[14] SSCBA 1992, Sch 1, para 7(11)(*a*) (see supra, § **51.10**).
[15] SI 2001/1004, reg 76.

[51.18] Employer and employee contributions

[16] SI 2001/1004, reg 77.
[17] SI 2001/1004, reg 79.

Class 1B contributions

[51.19] A further class of contribution is payable in respect of 1999–2000 and subsequent years where an employer has entered into a PAYE Settlement Agreement (PSA). For 2006–07 the rate at which the contribution is to be paid is 12.8%; there is no employee contribution and, also like Class 1A, no benefit entitlement is derived from such contributions. Whilst the Class 1A contribution rate is automatically linked to the secondary not contracted-out Class 1 rate, the rate of Class 1B contributions could initially be increased by up to 2 percentage points pa, but this is now also maintained at the same rate as the secondary Class 1 rate.[1]

Class 1B is payable on all those items included in the PSA which, were that not the case, would be liable to Class 1 or Class 1A contributions together with all the tax due under the PSA (whether the tax relates to items potentially liable to Class 1/1A or not).[2]

Payment is due on 19 October following the end of the year to which the liability relates and so the first payment of Class 1B was due on 19 October 2000. Payments under PSAs made on 19 October 1999 were of tax only, there being no Class 1B liability for 1998–99 or earlier years. From October 2005 (ie, payment for 2004–05 onwards), whilst there is no compulsion on employers of any size (unlike Class 1 contributions), payments made electronically are due to be received by HM Revenue & Customs by the extended date of 22 October. Where that day is not a bank working day, value must be received on the last such day before the 22 October (eg in 2005, 21 October, as 22 October was a Saturday).

Simon's NIC Chapter 9A.

[1] SSCBA 1999, s 10A(6), amended by the Welfare Reform and Pensions Act 1999, s 77.
[2] SSCBA 1992, s 10A(2), inserted by Social Security Act 1998, s 53.

52

The self-employed earner

| Class 2 contributions | PARA **52.01** |
| Class 4 contributions | PARA **52.05** |

Class 2 contributions

[52.01] Every self-employed earner[1] is required to pay Class 2 contributions from age 16 onward until reaching pensionable age.[2] Liability, however, is confined to such contribution weeks during any part of which he is treated as such a self-employed earner in Great Britain.[3]

Whether a person is a self-employed earner or an employed earner[4] is a matter of categorisation which is often difficult to determine.[5] Whether a person falls into the category of self-employed earner depends, inter alia, on whether or not he is ordinarily employed in employment as a self-employed earner,[6] and where he has been treated as falling into that category, he will continue to be so treated unless and until he is no longer ordinarily employed.[7]

The effect of these rules is that if a person is treated as ordinarily so employed in self-employed earner's employment,[8] liability for Class 2 contributions will continue during weeks of holiday or other inactivity. When, however, the individual ceases to be so ordinarily employed there is to be no such liability even if the previous activity produces a continuing source of income, eg licence-royalties from devices which an inventor has patented.

Because to be a self-employed earner, a person must be "gainfully employed",[9] certain activities by themselves will not give rise to Class 2 contribution liability, eg the receipt of investment income, the letting of property in some circumstances, the receipt by a sleeping partner of a share of a firm's profits.

Class 2 contributions, where payable, are at a small flat rate (for 2009–10 £2.40 a week). The rate used to be slightly above that for Class 3 contributions as in addition to securing entitlement to long-term benefits (as do Class 3 contributions) Class 2 contributions also enable sickness and invalidity benefits to be claimed. Class 2 contributions do not create rights to contribution-based jobseeker's allowance. However, from 6 April 2000, the Class 2 rate was cut by nearly 70% but the Class 3 rate was not reduced at the same time and has since continued to increase annually. There is now therefore a disparity in that the cheaper contribution of the two (ie Class 2) actually earns a greater contributory benefit entitlement.

Class 2 contributions cannot be deducted as an allowable business expense for income tax purposes.[10]

Class 2 contributions originally were payable by purchase of special stamps available from the Post Office which were then affixed to a contribution card.

[52.01] The self-employed earner

From April 1993, payment has to be made direct either on receipt of a quarterly statement[11] or under a direct debit arrangement with a bank or through a giro system under which payments are made monthly in arrears.[12]

There is a requirement for a person, who becomes, or ceases to be liable, to pay Class 2 contributions or who, although not liable to do so, becomes or ceases to be entitled to pay such contributions, to give written notice to HM Revenue & Customs immediately.[13] In practice, "immediately" now means within three complete calendar months—see below. Likewise, any person, who is liable to pay Class 2 contributions or who pays such contributions although not liable to do so, must give written notice of any change of address immediately.[14]

The latest date for payment of Class 2 contributions where a quarterly statement has been issued is 28 days after the date of notification of the amount due.[15] There is as yet no interest charge on overdue Class 2 contributions but contributions paid later than the end of the year following that in which they were due will be payable at the highest rate in force between the due date and payment date.[16]

Until 5 April 2009 there was, in addition, a penalty for late notification of liability to pay Class 2 contributions. Where notification of liability to Class 2 took place more than three complete calendar months after commencement of that liability, a fixed penalty of £100 was due. The first penalties could not be imposed until 1 May 2001.[17] For example:

> liability first arose at any time on or before 31 January 2001—penalty if not notified by 30 April 2001
> business commenced 2 February 2001—penalty if not notified by 31 May 2001
> business commenced 28 February 2001—penalty if not notified by 31 May 2001
> business commenced 1 March 2001—penalty if not notified by 30 June 2001
> business commenced 12 February 2008—penalty if not notified by 31 May 2008.

From 6 April 2009, these provisions were replaced. Notification must now be made by 31 January following the end of the tax year in which the liability to make contributions first arose. The maximum penalty is 100% of the contributions paid late (capped at the contributions payable for the first six years). That 100% penalty is payable, however, only in cases where the omission was deliberate and concealed; other deliberate failures are subject to a 70% penalty. In all other cases a 30% penalty is payable, but the penalty is removed altogether in cases where the trader has a reasonable excuse for not notifying the liability to HMRC.[18] All penalties are reduced in cases where the taxpayer makes a disclosure of the omission, a larger discount in cases where there is an unprompted disclosure.[19]

Simon's NIC Chapter 13.

---

1   SSCBA 1992, s 2(1)(*b*).
2   SSCBA 1992, s 11(1); SSCBA 1992, s 11(2).
3   SSCBA 1992, s 2(1)(*b*).

4   SSCBA 1992, s 2(1).
5   See supra, § **49.02**.
6   Social Security (Categorisation of Earners) Regulations 1978, SI 1978/1689, Sch 1, para 9.
7   SI 1978/1689, Sch 2.
8   SSCBA 1992, s 2(1)(*b*).
9   SSCBA 1992, s 2(1)(*b*).
10 ITTOIA 2005, s 53(1).
11 Social Security (Contributions) Regulations 2001, SI 2001/1004, reg 89.
12 SI 2001/1004, reg 90(1), (6).
13 SI 2001/1004, reg 87(1).
14 SI 2001/1004, reg 88.
15 SI 2001/1004, reg 89(2).
16 SSCBA 1992, s 12(3).
17 SI 2001/1004, reg 87(4), (5).
18 SI 2001/1004, reg 87B.
19 SI 2001/1004, regs 87C, 87D.

Exceptions from Class 2 liability

[52.02] There are a number of exceptions from liability to pay Class 2 contributions. The most important of these is normally referred to as "the small earnings exception".

It applies where the self-employed earner can show that his earnings do not exceed a specified figure for the tax year for which application for the exception to operate is made.[1] This can be met best by showing either that for that year the earnings are likely to be less than the specified amount or that for the preceding year the earnings were less than the amount specified for that year and that since then there has been no material change of circumstances.[2]

The specified figure for 2009–10 is £5,075; for 2008–09 it was £4,825. The figure is revised each year and is maintained at a small margin above the lower earnings limit for Class 1 contribution purposes.

The exception does not apply unless the self-employed earner makes an application for a certificate of exception.[3] This has to be in a prescribed form;[4] HMRC require form CF 10 to be used. The applicant has to provide such information and evidence relating to his earnings as HMRC may require, either at the time of application and/or subsequently.[5] HMRC may require accounts or tax computations for a recent tax year together with estimates for the tax year for which the application is made or the preceding year.

The earnings to take into account are the applicant's net earnings from employment as a self-employed earner.[6] No detailed rules are laid down as to how such earnings are to be computed. However, if employment earnings are included in the self-employed earners business accounts, such earnings are disregarded when establishing the person's net earnings from self-employment for the purpose of a certificate of exception from Class 2 liability by reason of small earnings.[7]

[52.02] The self-employed earner

The certificate when granted relates to such period as may be specified:[8] normally this is for the whole of at least one complete tax year and for part or all of the current tax year. The authorities are allowed discretion to backdate the certificate for no more than 13 weeks before the date on which the application was filed.[9]

SSA 1990 enabled regulations to be made to provide for repayment on application of Class 2 contributions for a tax year in which the self-employed earner has earnings below the small earnings exception.[10] The regulations[11] which were subsequently introduced allow repayment claims to be made in respect of periods beginning not earlier than 6 April 1988 in which the self-employed earner's earnings were less than the amount specified.[12] A claim has to be made no earlier than 6 April and no later than 31 January immediately following the tax year for which the claim is made.[13] The claim has to be supported by evidence of the claimant's earnings in the period for which the claim is made[14] and when the authorities are satisfied that the earnings were within the small earnings exception, they have to make the repayment[15] and issue a certificate of exception from Class 2 liability.[16] But where the claimant has obtained benefits which would not have been paid to him but for making the Class 2 contributions, which are the subject of the claim, these must be deducted from the contributions to be repaid.[17]

Frequently those starting a new business will find it difficult to provide evidence that their expected earnings will be below the specified limit. Accordingly, a new procedure was introduced enabling new traders who apply for certificates of exception to no longer be required to provide evidence and this now extends to all such claimants, although established traders should possess the requisite evidence in case HM Revenue & Customs subsequently require it.[18] Where the trader has failed to notify HMRC of the liability to register for Class 2 contributions (and consequently failed to apply for the small earnings exception), the penalty payable for the late notification is reduced to reflect any relief available for small earnings.[19]

Where a certificate is issued, the self-employed earner is relieved of the obligation to pay Class 2 contributions for the period covered, but is entitled to pay such contributions if he wishes.[20] This would improve his contribution record in relation to claims for long-term benefits and has the advantage over paying Class 3 contributions of also securing entitlement to sickness, incapacity and maternity benefits as well as, from 6 April 2000, being less expensive.

Simon's NIC [13.161]–[13.199].

---

[1] SSCBA 1992, s 11(4).
[2] Social Security (Contributions) Regulations 2001, SI 2001/1004, reg 45(1).
[3] SI 2001/1004, reg 44(1).
[4] SI 2001/1004, reg 44(2).
[5] SI 2001/1004, reg 44(3).
[6] SI 2001/1004, reg 45 (2)(*a*).
[7] SI 2001/1004, reg 45 (2)(*b*).
[8] SI 2001/1004, reg 44(4).
[9] SI 2001/1004, reg 44(5)(*b*).
[10] SSCBA 1992, Sch 1, para 8.

[11] SI 2001/1004, reg 47.
[12] SI 2001/1004, reg 47(1).
[13] SI 2001/1004, reg 47(2), as amended by Social Security (Contributions) (Amendment No 7) Regulations, SI 2003/2958, reg 3.
[14] SI 2001/1004, reg 47(1).
[15] SI 2001/1004, reg 47(3).
[16] SI 2001/1004, reg 47(4).
[17] SI 2001/1004, reg 47(5).
[18] Leaflet CA 02 (April 2004) p 14. (Since withdrawn).
[19] SI 2001/1004, reg 87B(5)(b).
[20] SI 2001/1004, reg 46.

[52.03] There are other exceptions from liability to pay Class 2 contributions, including:

The spare time employment exception

This applies where the individual has a substantial regular job as an employed earner and the income from the self-employed activity may be disregarded.

The basis of this exception is that in these circumstances the individual will not be regarded as ordinarily employed in a self-employed earner's employment (see supra, § **52.01**).

Exceptions for receipt of benefits etc

[52.04] If in any contribution week, the self-employed earner is in receipt of incapacity benefit, or maternity allowance, or is incapable of work or in prison or legal custody, or in receipt of unemployability supplement or carer's allowance, he or she will be excepted from liability to pay Class 2 contributions.[1] Such a person is nevertheless entitled to pay such contributions if he or she so wishes.[2]

Simon's NIC [13.211].

[1] SI 2001/1004, reg 43(1).
[2] SI 2001/1004, reg 43(3).

Class 4 contributions

[52.05] Prior to 1975 the flat-rate principle favoured by Beveridge[1] was still much in evidence in the contributory system: both the self-employed person and the employee paid flat-rate contributions although the latter also paid additional graduated contributions in exchange for additional pension entitlement under the graduated pension scheme introduced in 1959. With the replacement of the scheme by SERPS (initially) and then State Second Pension (from April 2002) and the introduction of graduated rates for primary and secondary Class 1 contributions with effect from 6 April 1975, a substantial difference opened up between the still flat-rate contributions payable by a

[52.05] The self-employed earner

self-employed person with earnings at or above the upper earnings limit and those payable by an employee with the same earnings.

Unlike the employee, the self-employed person had no entitlement to the additional pension provided by SERPS but the differential was considered inequitable. One solution would have been to increase sharply the level of flat-rate contributions for all self-employed persons but this would have borne hardly on those with modest earnings but not covered by the small earnings exception. Instead, the solution adopted was to impose a new class of contribution, Class 4, payable on business profits as assessed for income tax under what is now Chapter 2 of Part 2 of ITTOIA 2005. In this way the self-employed were subjected to an additional separate contribution dependent on the level of business profits.

Because no additional benefit entitlement is obtained by payment of Class 4 contributions many saw the introduction of the new class as no more than a tax which discriminated against the self-employed. There was fierce opposition at the time and an architect even challenged Parliament's right to introduce such a measure on the ground that during the second reading of the Social Security Act 1975 all MPs had changed their status from being self-employed to employees and this, he argued made them employees holding offices for profit under the Crown and so disqualified them from passing any Act of Parliament, including the Social Security Act 1975. The attempt failed.[2]

Nowadays, the Class 4 contributions are accepted without demur even though no S2P coverage is nor can be purchased by the self-employed and because employer contributions do not attach to the earnings of a self-employed earner, self-employed status is still very advantageous.[3]

Class 4 contributions are payable at a prescribed main rate on a band of profits between a lower profits limit and an upper profits limit, with a 1% charge from 6 April 2003 on all profits above the upper limit.[4] The lower limit is, from 6 April 2000, set at the level of the personal tax allowance and the upper limit is generally set at the same level as the upper earnings limit for Class 1 contribution purposes. Both upper and lower limits are revised annually: for 2009–10 the lower limit is £5,715[5] and the upper limit is £43,875[6]. The prescribed main rate is intended to be maintained year by year—each tax year since 1983–84 up to 1993–94 the rate was 6.3%—but the authorities have an enabling power to alter the main rate but not to more than 8.25%.[7] For the 1994–95 and 1995–96 years the rate was increased to 7.3%, but was then reduced to 6% for 1996–97, 1997–98, 1998–99 and 1999–2000, to adjust for the fact that tax relief is not available for 50% of all contributions with effect from 6 April 1996. From 6 April 2000 it again increased—to 7%—as part of the shift in emphasis between Class 2 and Class 4 liabilities—and that rate was maintained also for 2001–02 and 2002–03. From 6 April 2003, the main rate rose to 8% on profits up to the upper limit, with a charge on all higher profits at an additional rate—currently 1%.

Although the intention behind the introduction of Class 4 contributions was to put the self-employed person with high earnings on a similar footing to an employed person with similar earnings, there is in fact still a differential.

Class 4 contributions [52.05]

EXAMPLE

Employed earner with earnings in 2009–10 at the upper earnings limit (£43,875):

Primary Class 1 contributions in 2009–10
52 × £(844 − 110) × 11%   £4,198.48

Self-employed earner with earnings at the upper profits limit (£43,875):

Class 2
52 × £2.40   124.80
Class 4
8% × £(43,875 − 5,715)   3,052.80
                                                      £3,177.60

Class 4 contributions are collected through inclusion in the self assessment for income tax purposes and payment is made to the Receivables Management Service with the usual self-assessment payments on account and balancing payments. The income tax appeal provisions have always applied to the determination of Class 4 contribution liability. When the assessment becomes final and conclusive for income tax purposes, it also becomes final and conclusive as regards the Class 4 contribution liability.[8] As from 19 April 1993, interest is chargeable on overdue Class 4 contributions and the repayment supplement is available in respect of overpaid Class 4 contributions.[9] Previously, interest could be charged on overdue Class 4 contributions only in the case of an assessment to make good a loss due to the taxpayer's fault and the repayment supplement was not available.[10]

It is possible to recover overpaid Class 4 contributions either through the income tax provisions under which a self-assessment can be adjusted[11] or through direct application for repayment to the National Insurance Contributions Office at Newcastle.[12]

Class 4 contributions are payable with a few exceptions by all self-employed persons below pensionable age[13] whose business income reaches the lower limit. However, the charging provision[14] bases liability not on persons but on "all annual profits immediately derived from the carrying on" of a trade profession, or vocation. Because the profits have to be immediately derived from carrying on the profession etc, the share of profits allocated to a sleeping partner will not give rise to Class 4 contributions. There are also exceptions from liability for:

(1) persons not resident in the UK in the tax year in question;[15]
(2) divers and diving supervisors;[16]
(3) persons under the age of 16 (but an application has to be made for this exception to apply);[17]
(4) trustees, guardians etc of incapacitated persons;[18]
(5) trustees who are charged to tax under ITTOIA 2005, s 8 on the income of others.[19]

For the position of persons who are treated as employed earners but who receive income taxed under Chapter 2 of Part 2 of ITTOIA 2005 see infra, § **52.07**.

[52.05] The self-employed earner

Simon's NIC Chapter 14.

1. See supra, § **48.02**.
2. *Martin v O'Sullivan* [1984] STC 258n, CA.
3. See supra, § **49.02**.
4. SSCBA 1992, s 15(3ZA).
5. SSCBA 1992, s 15(3)(*a*).
6. SSCBA 1992, s 15(3)(*b*).
7. SSCBA 1992, s 15(3); SSAA 1992, s 143(4)(*b*).
8. SSCBA 1992, Sch 2, para 7
9. SSCBA 1992, Sch 2, para 6 substituted by SS(CP)A 1992, Sch 4, para 8.
10. SSCBA 1992, Sch 2, para 6, brought into effect as from 19 April 1993 by Social Security (Consequential Provisions) Act 1992 Appointed Day Order 1993, SI 1993/1025.
11. SSCBA 1992, Sch 2, para 8.
12. Social Security (Contributions) Regulations 2001, SI 2001/1004, reg 102, as amended by Social Security (Contributions) (Amendment No 3) Regulations 2002, SI 2002/2366, reg 15.
13. SI 2001/1004, reg 91(*a*).
14. SSCBA 1992, s 15(1), (2), (5).
15. SI 2001/1004, reg 91(*b*).
16. SI 2001/1004, reg 92.
17. SI 2001/1004, reg 93.
18. SSCBA 1992, Sch 2, para 5(*a*).
19. SSCBA 1992, Sch 2, para 5(*b*).

Computation of profits for Class 4 contributions

[52.06] The charging provision[1] requires the annual profits on which Class 4 contributions are payable to be those which are "chargeable to income tax under Chapter 2 of Part 2 of ITTOIA 2005" but "as computed in accordance with Schedule 2" of SSCBA 1992 which makes certain specific adjustments.[2] This means that the profits as adjusted for Chapter 2 of Part 2 of ITTOIA 2005 purposes form the starting point of the amount on which Class 4 contributions are payable, ie the same adjustments for entertaining and other disallowable expenses etc are made.

There are, however, certain special rules which enable certain losses and similar items which are not deductible as expenses in arriving at the profits for Chapter 2 of Part 2 of ITTOIA 2005 purposes to be deducted from the profits for Class 4 contribution purposes.

These items are:

(1) interest, annuities and other annual payments deductible from total income for income tax purposes so far as incurred exclusively for the purpose of the trade, profession or vocation;[3]

(2) trading losses brought forward from an earlier year under ITA 2007, s 83[4] or in the case of terminal losses carried back under ITA 2007, s 89;[5]

(3) trading losses and excess capital allowances over trading income which can be set off against general income under ITA, ss 64, 74.[6]

The losses in 3, being available against general income for the current or succeeding tax year, normally reduce taxable income from sources other than the trade or profession in which they arise. The fact that such losses thereby become used up against other source income for income tax purposes is irrelevant in relation to Class 4 contributions: in calculating contributions such losses continue to be regarded as unused and can therefore be carried forward for deduction from Chapter 2 of Part 2 of ITTOIA 2005 profits for a later period for national insurance purposes even though all tax losses have been utilised already.[7] This means that in the subsequent period the profits for Class 4 purposes will be lower than for income tax purposes. It is very easy to overlook this point when considering the position for the subsequent year.

The following items, however, are not deductible from the profits on which Class 4 contributions are payable:

(1) personal reliefs;[8]
(2) interest payments for which relief is given under ITA 2007, s 383;[9]
(3) interest treated as a loss for the purposes of carry forward or carry back under ITA 2007, ss 88, 94,[10]
(4) the relief formerly given for income tax purposes for Class 4 contributions;[11]
(5) retirement annuity contract premiums;[12]
(6) contributions to personal pension schemes.[13]

There was some debate as to whether contributions made to a personal pension were deductible from the profits on which Class 4 contributions were collected. The matter has been put beyond doubt by SSCA 1994[11] which specifically states no relief is available backdated to the coming into force of F(No 2)A 1987, s 31.

As to 5, it should be appreciated that in computing total income for income tax purposes one-half of the Class 4 contributions was deductible for years up to and including 1995–96.[15]

Simon's NIC [14.11]–[14.50].

---

[1] SSCBA 1992, s 15(1).
[2] SSCBA 1992, s 15(1)(*b*), (3)(*a*).
[3] SSCBA 1992, Sch 2, para 3(5).
[4] SSCBA 1992, Sch 2, para 3(1)(*c*).
[5] SSCBA 1992, Sch 2, para 3(1)(*d*).
[6] SSCBA 1992, Sch 2, para 3(1)(*a*).
[7] SSCBA 1992, Sch 2, para 3(3).
[8] SSCBA 1992, Sch 2, para 3(2)(*a*).
[9] SSCBA 1992, Sch 2, para 3(2)(*b*).
[10] SSCBA 1992, Sch 2, para 3(2)(*d*).
[11] SSCBA 1992, Sch 2, former para 3(2)(*e*).
[12] SSCBA 1992, Sch 2, para 3(2)(*f*).
[13] SSCBA 1992, Sch 2, para 3(2)(*g*).

[14] SSCA 1994, s 3 and SSCBA 1992, Sch 2, para 3(2)(g).
[15] TA 1988, s 617(5).

Differing employment status for tax and National Insurance purposes

[52.07] It will sometimes be the case that a person is categorised as an employed earner for contribution purposes (as will be the case for, eg office cleaners, and certain lecturers, teachers and instructors), and so has to pay Class 1 contributions for contribution purposes despite earnings being taxed under Chapter 2 of Part 2 of ITTOIA 2005 for income tax purposes. Again it is common in certain professions, eg solicitors and accountants, for practitioners to hold offices such as directorships where the fees are brought into their accounts and assessed to income tax under Chapter 2 of Part 2 of ITTOIA 2005 but the earnings are subject to Class 1 contributions.

Where the earnings are properly chargeable to income tax under Chapter 2 of Part 2 of ITTOIA 2005, those earnings will also clearly have to be included in the profits taken into account for Class 2 and Class 4 contribution purposes. In these cases, in the absence of a special rule, the earnings on which Class 1 contributions have been paid could give rise to an additional Class 4 contribution liability. It is, however, possible to apply in such cases for exception from Class 4 contribution liability.[1] The exception will in effect cover the amount of the earner's profits which have been subject to Class 1 contributions.

EXAMPLE

In 2009–10 M, a chartered accountant practising in partnership with S, is assessed under Chapter 2 of Part 2 of ITTOIA 2005 on £37,490 being the share of adjusted profits for the year to 31 December 2009. In December 2009, M receives a gross fee of £6,000 as a director of Omicron Ltd under deduction of standard rate Class 1 contributions. In addition, £10,000 was added to the profit and loss account for the year ended 31 December 2005 in respect of a UITF40 adjustment.

	£
Business profits otherwise subject to Class 4 contributions £37,490–£5,715	31,775
Earnings in respect of which Class 1 contributions payable (there is an annual earnings period but the fee is above the earnings threshold and below the upper earnings limit for 2009–10)	6,000
Profits liable to 8% main rate after exception	25,775

Note that in the above example the £10,000 of UITF40 profits is "adjustment income" and whilst taxable is not taxable under Chapter 2 of Part 2 of ITTOIA 2005. Accordingly, there is no Class 4 liability on that adjustment income, whether spread over three years, or a longer period, or an election is made to accelerate the tax charge.

This exception illustrated in the above example will not be available unless the individual makes an application for it. The application should be made before the tax year to which the exception is to apply or such later date as may be allowed.[2] Because it is not possible to know in advance the Class 1 contributions which the individual will pay or the level of his business profits, the amount to be excepted cannot normally be calculated until after the end of that tax year and consequently in practice a certificate of deferment of Class 4 contribution liability is issued in response to such an application.[3]

Where the individual has to account for the director's fees to the company appointing him or to the partnership in which he is a partner—this possibility does not apply to a sole practitioner—and the fees are brought into the accounts of the company or partnership and are subject to tax, the fees may be excluded (subject to certain conditions) from the earnings from the directorship and so will not be subject to Class 1 contributions.[4] This is an alternative means of avoiding the same earnings giving rise to both Class 1 and Class 4 contributions.

The National Insurance Contributions Office also formerly considered that where the salary etc is in fact assessable as "employment income" but is brought into the business accounts of the individual concerned, it was correct in law to include the salary in the profits for Class 4 purposes such that the relief illustrated in the above example was not then available: this is an issue that is of concern to sub-postmasters in particular[5] and in one such instance in late 2000 a sub-postmaster overturned the National Insurance Contributions Office view before the General Commissioners. However, National Insurance Contributions Office said that the decision relates only to the particular case in question—a doubtful view—and did not change its guidance.

Nonetheless, the additional 1% charge for both Class 1 and Class 4 prompted a change effective only from 6 April 2003. A new provision purports to allow the Class 1 earnings to be deducted from the Class 4 profits and this is the practice that HMRC clearly adopted for 2003–04 onwards. Nonetheless, the legislation is arguably little different from that which caused the supposed difficulty for many previous years.[6] The effect of this new provision is that where cases involving the payment of Class 1 contributions are correctly treated as self-employed income for tax purposes the deferment procedure mentioned above will need to be followed. However, where the earnings are also strictly employment income for tax purposes (eg subpostmasters—even where an "NT" tax code is in use) then from 6 April 2003 the amount of "salary", etc included in the accounting profit is simply deducted in box 101 on the self employment pages of the Tax Return, preferably with a suitable explanation in the 'white space'. Only the remaining balance is then subject to Class 4 at the main and/or additional rate, as the case may be.

Where a person whose earnings are taxed as "employment income" is, under the categorisation regulations, treated as a self-employed earner and the earnings in the tax year exceed the lower profit limit for Class 4 purposes, special Class 4 contributions are payable at the main rate (currently 8%) on the earnings in excess of the lower profit limit but not exceeding the upper profit limit for Class 4 purposes, together with the additional rate (currently 1%) on income above the upper profits limit.[7] The earnings are arrived at for this purpose as if earnings-related Class 1 contributions were payable.[8]

Simon's NIC [14.205]–[14.240].

[52.07] The self-employed earner

1. Social Security (Contributions) Regulations 2001, SI 2001/1004, reg 94(1).
2. SI 2001/1004, reg 94(2).
3. SI 2001/1004, reg 94(4).
4. SI 2001/1004, reg 27 (see supra, § **51.04**).
5. The anomalies that result from this treatment were discussed with the former DSS by the ICAEW. See the Tax Faculty's Technical Release Tax 21/92 paras 42–50, *Simon's Tax Intelligence* 1993, p 171.
6. SI 2001/1004, reg 94A, as inserted by Social Security (Contributions) (Amendment No 7) Regulations 2003, SI 2003/2958, reg 4.
7. SI 2001/1004, reg 103.
8. SI 2001/1004, reg 105.

53

Interaction with benefits

Earnings factors	PARA 53.01
Credits	PARA 53.02
Voluntary contributions	PARA 53.08
Late paid contributions	PARA 53.09

Earnings factors

[53.01] This publication does not attempt to deal with the circumstances in which the various contributory and non-contributory benefits can be claimed and the conditions which have to be fulfilled. However, it should not be forgotten that under the contributory scheme there is an essential link between contributions paid and some benefits claimable and therefore a brief review of this link is appropriate.

It is difficult to summarise the contribution requirements for the different kinds of contributory benefits since each has its own set of rules. But at the risk of oversimplification, it is useful to draw a distinction between short-term and long-term benefits. Examples of short-term benefits are contribution-based jobseeker's allowance and benefits in respect of illness. The main long-term benefits are retirement pensions and bereavement benefits (the latter having replaced widow's pension etc from April 2001).

With both short-term and long-term benefits, entitlement depends on both an entrance fee requirement, ie the payment of sufficient contributions to be regarded as eligible for benefit, and also a continuing membership record. The terms used in the relevant regulations are the first and second contribution requirements respectively. In both cases contributions are deemed to be paid where there are post 6 April 2000 earnings at or above the lower earnings limit but below the earnings threshold so that no contributions are, in fact, paid. Throughout this chapter, references to the payment of actual contributions (as opposed to credits) should be taken to include the deemed contributions on those earnings below the earnings threshold provided that the lower earnings limit is equalled or has been exceeded.

In the case of the entrance fee, only contributions which are actually paid count but in the case of the membership record, credits (see below) can usually be taken into account. So, for example, to be eligible for contribution-based jobseeker's allowance, the employee first must have actually paid Class 1 contributions on earnings of at least 25 times the weekly lower earnings limit in one of the last two complete tax years before the calendar year in which the benefit is claimed *and* secondly the employee must have paid or been credited

1997

[53.01] Interaction with benefits

with Class 1 contributions on earnings of at least 50 times the weekly lower earnings limit in each of the last two complete tax years before the calendar year in which the benefit is claimed.

The main distinction between the two classes of benefit is that for the long-term benefits, the membership record or, more precisely, the extent to which contributions have been maintained over the claimant's working life is the critical test and directly affects the level at which the benefit is payable, whereas for short-term benefits only the recent contribution record counts. Thus, to qualify for the maximum basic rate retirement pension, the claimant must have paid or been credited with contributions for broadly nine out of every ten years from age 16 until pensionable age (currently 65 for a man or 60 for a woman). The rule more precisely is that over the duration of the individual's working life there must be a specified number of qualifying years, ie years in which sufficient contributions have been paid or credited. An individual's working life begins with the tax year in which the 16th birthday falls and ends with the year before that in which he or she reaches pensionable age or dies before reaching that age. The required number of qualifying years is found from the following table:

Length of working life	Qualifying years required
10 years or under	Length of working life minus 1 year
11–20 years	Length of working life minus 2 years
21–30 years	Length of working life minus 3 years
31–40 years	Length of working life minus 4 years
41 years or over	Length of working life minus 5 years

If the number of qualifying years is not sufficient to give entitlement to the maximum basic rate pension, a reduced pension is payable based on the proportion that the number of actual qualifying years bears to the number of qualifying years required. However, that proportion must be at least one-quarter for a reduced pension to be payable. In all cases the first contribution requirement must also be met but this is not difficult since contributions need be actually paid for only one tax year to meet this requirement.

In the form of the contributory system that was in force before 1975 contributions were at a flat rate and the contribution requirement could be expressed simply in terms of the number of weekly contributions that had to be paid in a year. Because since 1975 Class 1 contributions have been payable at graduated rates, depending on the level of earnings, it has become necessary to use a mechanism which gives due weight to contributions payable at higher rates when considering whether the contribution requirement has been satisfied. This mechanism consists of expressing contribution requirements and contributions paid or credited in terms of "earnings factors". An earnings factor is a notional amount of earnings derived from the contributions paid or, from 6 April 2000, from a notional amount of earnings where actual earnings have equalled or exceeded in any earnings period the lower earnings limit but fallen short of the earnings threshold so that no contributions have actually been paid. Only the lower earnings limit is of any application to the derivation of earnings factors—the earnings threshold is of no relevance. Thus, so far as entitlement to retirement pension is concerned, an individual is treated as having paid contributions for a particular tax year only if the contributions paid or credited are equivalent to 52 weeks' contributions at the lowest rate, ie as if his earnings were continuously at the lower earnings limit. The qualifying earnings factor in this case is thus 52 weeks of earnings at the lower earnings limit.

The individual's earnings factor is then compared with this requirement. For years before 1987–88 very complicated calculations are required to arrive at an individual's earnings factor but from 1987–88 onwards all that is necessary is to take the earnings on which Class 1 contributions have been paid (or treated as paid), ie ignoring earnings in earnings periods which were below the lower earnings limit or if they were above the upper earnings limit, ignoring the excess (and this is still the case for 2003–04 onwards, notwithstanding the 1% additional rate above the upper earnings limit introduced with effect from 6 April 2003), and to add in earnings credited, eg in relation to periods of unemployment or sickness (see below).[1]

If the individual was self-employed for part or all of the year in question or has paid Class 3 contributions in respect of that year, each Class 2 and Class 3 contribution paid produces an earnings factor at a weekly rate equivalent to the lower earnings limit.[2]

The earnings factors produced by Class 1 contributions and credits and by Class 2 and Class 3 contributions are aggregated. In a case where the total of the earnings factors falls short of the required sum (qualifying earnings factor) or the "standard level" (50 weeks at the lower earnings limit) by a relatively small amount (not exceeding £50) the shortfall is added to the total earnings factors. Where the total earnings fall short of one-half of the standard level by an amount not exceeding £25, that amount is added to the total earnings factors.[3]

[1] Social Security (Earnings Factor) Regulations 1979, SI 1979/676.
[2] SI 1979/676, Sch 1, para 8.
[3] SI 1979/676, Sch 1, para 4.

Credits

[53.02] Reference has already been made to credits. A credit is an amount of deemed earnings which an individual is allowed to bring into the calculation of his total earnings factors (see supra, § **53.01**). Credits are given in certain, but not all, situations where the individual will not normally be able to pay contributions. In the following situations credits are given for the purpose of claiming any benefit:

[53.03] Contribution-based jobseeker's allowance or short-term incapacity benefit. An earnings credit is given for each complete week of unemployment or incapacity. Where the benefit being claimed is itself jobseeker's allowance or sickness benefit, the credit is dependent on fulfilment of certain other conditions.[1]

Simon's NIC [15.21]–[15.100].

---

[1] Social Security (Credits) Regulations 1975, SI 1975/556, regs 8A, 8B.

[53.04] Other non-working periods. Credits are also given for weeks in respect of which an individual receives a carer's allowance,[1] or for which maternity or adoption pay was paid[2] or for which the individual's earnings fall below the lower earnings limit as a result of jury service[3] in part or all of the week in question.

---

[1] SI 1975/556, reg 7A.
[2] SI 1975/556, reg 9C.
[3] SI 1975/556, reg 9B.

[53.05] Education and training. Earnings credits are given to those who already have a contribution record and who, after reaching the age of 18 undertake an approved full-time course not intended to last for more than 12 months and not related to the individual's employment.[1]

---

[1] SI 1975/556, reg 7.

[53.06] Working tax credit. Persons in receipt of the disability element or severe disability element of working tax credit can receive a general credit for each week that the tax credit is paid. Others in receipt of working tax credit can also receive a credit but for long term-benefit purposes only. In either case the credit can be awarded only to a self-employed person with a small earnings exception or to any employed person, but not if credits are already being awarded by reason of unemployment or incapacity.[1]

---

[1] SI 1975/556, reg 7B, 7C.

[53.07] Retirement at 60. Pensionable age for a man under the state scheme is currently 65. Whether or not he has retired, he is entitled to earnings credits (if needed) for contribution years in which he is not working beginning with the year in which he reaches 60 provided he is neither self-employed nor out of the country for more than half the year.[1]

If the individual is nonetheless actually employed or self-employed all contributions due under normal rules still apply notwithstanding the availability of a credit. This does, though, enable a Class 2 contributor to claim small earnings exception if the business profits are below the limit, without the need to consider whether such a claim is prejudicial to state pension entitlement in due course.

For the purpose of claiming certain benefits, credits are also given in other circumstances. For example, in the case of claims to contribution-based jobseeker's allowance and short-term incapacity benefit, termination credits are given to women whose marriage has terminated and to an individual who has completed an approved course of full-time education begun before reaching the age of 21.[2]

For the purpose of entitlement to long-term benefits only, ie principally retirement pension, persons under 18 are credited with Class 3 contributions for the years in which their 16th, 17th and 18th birthdays fall.[3]

[1] SI 1975/556, reg 9A.
[2] SI 1975/556, reg 8.
[3] SI 1975/556, reg 4.

Voluntary contributions

[53.08] To enable individuals to improve deficient contribution records, the possibility of paying Class 3 contributions has been provided. These are voluntary contributions (for 2009–10, £12.05 a week) which produce an earnings factor at a rate per week equal to the lower earnings limit. They count for the purpose of the long-term benefits, eg Category A and Category B retirement pensions, bereavement benefits (formerly widow's pension etc) but not for short-term benefits such as contribution-based jobseeker's allowance, short-term incapacity benefit or invalidity benefit.

Class 3 contributions can be paid only if the total of contributions already paid for the year in question plus any earnings credits fall short of the qualifying earnings factor, ie 52 times the weekly lower earnings limit for the year in question.[1] There are a number of situations set out in the contribution regulations[2] where the individual is debarred from paying Class 3 contributions. The purpose of these rules is, in the main, to prevent an individual from paying Class 3 contributions in circumstances where no advantage would result.

The normal rule is that Class 3 contributions can be paid in respect of a particular tax year so long as the payment is made within the following six years.[3] (See below, however, regarding contribution years 1996–97 to 2001–02 inclusive). There may be a further extension if the tax year for which the Class 3 contributions are to be paid includes a period of at least six months (or the preceding or following year included such a period and part of the period falls in the year in question), during which the contributor was undergoing full-time education or full-time apprenticeship or training for which any earnings fell below the lower earnings limit, or was undergoing imprisonment or detention in legal custody. In these cases Class 3 contributions can be paid within the six years following that in which the education, apprenticeship, training, imprisonment or detention terminated.[4] Special time limits apply to contributions for the years 1996–97 to 2001–02 inclusive because of delays in the then Inland Revenue issuing "deficiency notices" for these years following computer

[53.08] Interaction with benefits

delays. The time limits for all six years stated are 5 April 2009 (ordinarily) or, if the individual reached state pensionable age before 24 October 2004, the time limit is 5 April 2010.[5] In some instances the 5 April 2009 limit is an extension of a year to that stated in legislation, but is confirmed by the HMRC National Insurance Manual.[6]

In order to be able to pay Class 3 contributions, certain residence conditions have to be met. These are described in infra, § **54.05**.

Since 11 April 1993 anyone who is entitled to pay Class 3 contributions and wishes to do so or to cease to do so must immediately notify the authorities of the date from which he wishes to begin or cease to pay such contributions.[7] Anyone paying Class 3 contributions must immediately notify HMRC of any change of address.[8] The collection arrangements in respect of Class 2 contributions, ie by payment on a quarterly statement or by bank direct debit or giro transfer monthly in arrears were intended to be applied to the payment of Class 3 contributions but in practice it is accepted that in certain circumstances, eg where the contributor is abroad, the contributions can be paid on an annual basis as before.[9]

Whether or not it is desirable to pay Class 3 contributions depends on the particular circumstances, but the following points should be noted.

(1) Most young people who go on to higher education after leaving school at about age 18 will have up to a three-year gap in their contribution record for long-term benefit purposes. This means that if any further break occurs during their working lives (which is not covered by credits) their retirement pension may well be at a reduced rate unless either the earlier or subsequent gap is made good by voluntary contributions. The current Pensions Bill will replace this rule, assuming that it is enacted as proposed, with a simpler requirement to contribute in any 30 years. This particular difficulty will therefore be of less importance for current and future students, though the remaining points remain fully relevant, including (2) as the 30 year rule for state pension will not apply to bereavement benefits.

(2) It is particularly important for married people to maintain a good contribution record. This is because if they die, bereavement benefits will be based on that record, although, dependent on the normal time limits, it will be possible for the widow/widower to make good missing years. If the husband or wife dies at a very early age, any contribution gap (such as, for example, of a kind mentioned in (1) above) will have a disproportionate effect on the entitlement to such benefits.

(3) In relation to retirement pension, it is necessary to consider whether the man's or the wife's contribution record is the more important. For example if the wife has been in paid work for only, say, 15 years before reaching pensionable age, she would have to pay Class 3 contributions for about nine further years before the pension she could claim in her own right would equal the additional pension payable on the husband's contribution record (60% of the pension for an unmarried person) assuming that record is sound. If, however, there are substantial gaps in the husband's contribution record, it would be better in such a case for the husband to pay Class 3 contributions to improve his record.

However, if the wife has held a job for 24 years or more and thus will be able to claim a substantial pension on her own contribution record, it may be considered worthwhile for her to pay Class 3 contributions to cover missing years and bring her pension entitlement up to the maximum so that both husband and wife can each then have full retirement pensions (as is payable for unmarried persons).

(4) If an individual spends part of his working life abroad and as a result fails to pay British contribution for a period, it may be worthwhile to pay Class 3 contributions to make good the gap. This will depend on whether while abroad he was required to pay contributions in the other country and in consequence qualifies for a state pension from that country related to the contributions paid. In some cases an employed person working abroad can pay Class 2 contributions voluntarily. This has always provided greater contributory benefit coverage and, from 6 April 2000, is cheaper than the payment of Class 3 contributions. Where the UK has made a reciprocal social security agreement with the other country this will normally contain a "totalisation" provision which is intended to prevent a reduction in entitlement because the normal qualifying period in either country has not been fulfilled.

Where there is a totalisation provision, each country generally pays a state pension arrived at on the following basis:

(1) calculate the theoretical pension the country would pay if the periods of coverage in both countries had been completed in the country in question;
(2) apply to the theoretical pension so found the proportion that the actual periods of coverage in the country in question bear to the total periods of coverage.

A similar arrangement applies where the individual has worked and paid contributions in another EEA member state.

A period of coverage is a period in which the individual is subject to the contribution law of the country concerned and for which stipulated minimum contributions have been paid.

Even where there is such a totalisation provision, the payment of Class 3 contributions will often enhance the individual's entitlement to UK state pension without prejudicing the pension to be provided by the other state.

Where there is a reciprocal agreement with the other country or the other country is an EEA member state and the assignment does not exceed a specified maximum period, it may be possible subject to certain conditions for contribution liability to be maintained in the home country (see infra, § **54.08**). In that event there will be no break in the UK contribution record while the individual is abroad and hence no need to pay Class 3 contributions to avoid a shortfall caused by the assignment.

Simon's NIC [15.1].

---

[1] SSCBA 1992, s 14.
[2] Social Security (Contributions) Regulations 2001, SI 2001/1004, regs 49(1), 132.

[53.08] Interaction with benefits

3   SI 2001/1004, reg 48(3)(*b*)(i). For any tax year up to 5 April 1982 the payment had to be made within the following two years.
4   SI 2001/1004, reg 48(3)(*b*)(ii), (iii).
5   Inland Revenue Press Release 5 April 2003; Social Security (Crediting and Treatment of Contributions, and National Insurance Numbers) Amendment Regulations 2004, SI 2004/1361; Social Security (Contributions) (Amendment No 3) Regulations 2004, SI 2004/1362.
6   HMRC National Insurance Manual, NIM25043.
7   SI 2001/1004, reg 87(1) and (2).
8   SI 2001/1004, reg 88.
9   SI 2001/1004, regs 89, 90 (see supra, § 52.01).

Late paid contributions

[53.09] Contributions may be paid after the normal due date in a variety of circumstances, in particular where:

(1)   a deferment of liability has been granted (see supra, § 51.08);
(2)   the employer has failed to account for Class 1 contributions under the PAYE procedure;
(3)   Class 2 contributions are being paid in arrears;
(4)   Class 3 contributions are paid after the tax year to which they relate but within the period allowed (see supra, § 53.07).

A still further case is where as a result of ignorance or error the contributor has failed to pay within the time allowed voluntary Class 3 contributions or Class 2 contributions which he is entitled but not obliged to pay: so long as there was no failure on the contributor's part to exercise due care and diligence H M Revenue & Customs may grant an extension of the time allowed for payment.[1]

In April 2003, the then Inland Revenue announced that the time limit for payment of Class 3 contributions would be extended for the years 1996–97 to 2000–01 inclusive to 5 April 2008 (the same as that for 2001–02) and this date was subsequently further extended to at least 5 April 2009—see supra, § 53.07. This follows the failings of the NIRS2 computer in earlier years, as "deficiency notices" were not sent out promptly by the new computer. The process resumed late in 2003 and continued throughout 2004. In addition, those making payment as a result of being contacted about gaps in their National Insurance records for 1996–97 to 2001–02 will not have to pay the "penalty rate" that would otherwise apply where payment is made more than two years after the end of the year to which Class 3 contributions relate.[2] Single year deficiency notices commenced to be issued in respect of 2002–03 late in 2004 and this pattern has continued subsequently.

In all cases of late payment it is necessary to determine both the rate at which the late paid contributions should be paid and the time at which they are deemed to be paid for the purpose of the contribution conditions for entitlement to benefit. The relevant rules are set out infra, §§ 53.11–53.13.

Simon's NIC [33.111]–[33.117].

[1] Social Security (Contributions) Regulations 2001, SI 2001/1004, regs 50, 61.
[2] Inland Revenue press release 5 April 2003; Social Security (Crediting and Treatment of Contributions, and National Insurance Numbers) Amendment Regulations 2004, SI 2004/1361; Social Security (Contributions) (Amendment No 3) Regulations 2004, SI 2004/1362.

General rules regarding contribution conditions

[53.10] For the purpose of the contribution conditions for benefit entitlement the general rule is that any contribution paid after the year to which it relates but within the following six years is treated as paid on the date when it is actually paid and if paid after the end of those six years is treated as not paid at all.[1] But this general rule is modified or displaced in certain of the situations discussed below.

There is in addition a special rule relating to the contribution requirements for short-term benefits. For the purpose of the second contribution requirement, the continuing membership record (see supra, § **53.01**), a late paid Class 1 or Class 2 contribution is treated as paid on the due date for contribution-based jobseeker's allowance or incapacity benefit only if it is paid before the start of the benefit year or if paid after the start of that year, it is treated as not paid until a period of 42 days (including Sundays) has elapsed from and including the date on which the contribution is paid.[2]

For the purpose of entitlement to maternity allowance, a late paid contribution is taken into account only if it is paid before the beginning of the period for which the allowance is claimed.[3]

[1] Social Security (Crediting and Treatment of Contributions, and National Insurance Numbers) Regulations 2001, SI 2001/769, reg 4. For Class 2 contributions payable in respect of a contribution week before 6 April 1983 and for Class 3 contributions payable in respect of a year before 6 April 1982, for six years read two years.
[2] SI 2001/769, reg 4(8).
[3] SI 2001/769, reg 4(7).

Deferment

[53.11] Where Class 1 or Class 2 and/or Class 4 deferment certificates have been issued and after the end of the tax year it is found that further contributions are due, these will be payable within 28 days from demand. The rates at which the contributions are payable are those applying for the year for which the deferment was granted and in this situation for the purpose of the contribution conditions for benefit entitlement, the deferred contributions will be treated as paid on the dates when they would have been due but for the deferment.[1]

[53.11] Interaction with benefits

[1] Social Security (Crediting and Treatment of Contributions, and National Insurance Numbers) Regulations 2001, SI 2001/769, reg 8.

Late payment by employer of Class 1 contributions

[53.12] Where the employer fails to account for primary and secondary Class 1 contributions at the due time, the employer will remain liable to pay those contributions but at the rates when they were originally due. The employer's right to recover the primary contributions from the employee may be lost or subject to restriction (see supra, § **51.09**) and the employer may be exposed to penalties for late payment.

But so long as the employee did not consent to or connive at the non-payment by the employer and such non-payment was not attributable to any negligence on the part of the employee, the primary contributions will be treated as paid on the due dates for the purpose of the contribution conditions for benefit entitlement.[1] As regards the first contribution condition, the entrance fee requirement (see supra, § **53.01**), the contributions will be treated for jobseeker's allowance, incapacity benefit or maternity allowance, as paid on the day on which the earnings on which the contributions are based were paid.

[1] Social Security (Contributions) Regulations 2001, SI 2001/1004, reg 60, Social Security (Crediting and Treatment of Contributions, and National Insurance Numbers) Regulations 2001, SI 2001/769, reg 5.

Class 2 contributions

[53.13] In certain circumstances the rate at which late paid Class 2 contributions are to be paid will be higher than the rate applying when they were originally due. For the purpose of the contribution conditions for benefit entitlement, the general rules set out above will operate.

Where a Class 2 contribution is paid late but within the tax year in which the related contribution week falls due, ie "the contribution year" or within the following tax year the rate applicable will be that for the contribution year.[1] But if the Class 2 contribution is made after the end of that following tax year, the rate applicable will be the highest weekly rate applying from the related contribution week until the day on which the contribution is paid.[2]

There are special rules for the following circumstances. Where an undertaking has been entered into to pay arrears of Class 2 contributions by instalments and the undertaking is entered into in the contribution year or the following year, the Class 2 contributions remain payable at the rate for the contribution year.[3] But where the undertaking was entered into after the end of that following year, the Class 2 contributions are payable at the weekly rate applying at the time when the undertaking is given.[4] If the contributions are paid other than in accordance with the undertaking, eg the instalments are paid late, the contributions are payable at the rate applying when a further undertaking is entered into, or otherwise at the weekly rate applying when the contributions are actually paid.[5]

There are also special rules dealing with a notification of arrears. If in the last month of a tax year the authorities issue a notification of arrears of Class 2 contributions and the contributor pays the contributions within one calendar month of the notification being given but during the following tax year, the contributions remain payable at the rate applying in the previous tax year.[6]

---

[1] SSCBA 1992, s 12(2).
[2] SSCBA 1992, s 12(3).
[3] Social Security (Contributions) Regulations 2001, SI 2001/1004, reg 63(2)(*a*).
[4] SI 2001/1004, reg 63(2)(*b*).
[5] SI 2001/1004, reg 63(2)(*c*).
[6] SI 2001/1004, reg 64.

Class 3 contributions

[53.14] Where a Class 3 contribution is paid in one tax year but in respect of an earlier tax year, the rate at which it is payable depends on the length of the intervening period. If the Class 3 contribution is paid within the two tax years following the contribution year, the rate for the contribution year applies.[1] If the Class 3 contribution is paid more than two years after the contribution year, the rate applicable will be the highest weekly rate applying from the relevant contribution week until the day on which the contribution is paid.[2]

The general rules as regards the contribution conditions for benefit entitlement (see above) apply to late paid Class 3 contributions but with the following modifications. Where a Class 3 contribution is paid in respect of a year which includes a period of education apprenticeship, training, imprisonment or detention in legal custody, the contribution counts for the purpose of retirement benefits, or bereavement benefits only if paid within six years of the year preceding the date on which the person concerned reached pensionable age or died under that age or other relevant time for the purpose of the contribution conditions.[3]

There are also special rules dealing with a notification of arrears. If in the last month of a tax year the authorities issue a notification of arrears of Class 3 contributions and the contributor pays the contributions within one calendar month of the notification being given but during the following tax year, the contributions remain payable at the rate applying in the previous tax year.[4]

All these rules are subject to the extensions mentioned in supra, §§ **53.08, 53.09** for the years 1996–97 to 2001–02 inclusive.[5]

---

[1] SSCBA 1992, s 13(4).
[2] SSCBA 1992, s 13(6), (7).
[3] Social Security (Crediting and Treatment of Contributions and National Insurance Numbers) Regulations 2001, SI 2001/769, reg 4(4).

[53.14] Interaction with benefits

⁴ SI 2001/1004, reg 64.
⁵ SI 2001/769, reg 6A, inserted by SI 2004/1361, reg 2(b).

Class 2 and Class 3 contributions paid late through ignorance or error

[53.15] So long as H M Revenue & Customs is satisfied that a failure to pay a Class 2 or Class 3 contribution by the due date was the result of ignorance or error on the part of the contributor but not due to failure to exercise due care and diligence, the contribution when paid is payable at the weekly rate for the period for which it is payable.[1] There is a parallel rule covering the case where a Class 3 contribution is paid through ignorance or error after the end of the two years following the contribution year: the contributions are payable at the rate applicable to the period for which they are paid.[2] There is a further rule covering Class 3 contributions where the contributions remain unpaid by reason of ignorance or error for a period commencing at any time after the end of the two years following the contribution year: here the contributions are payable at the rate applicable at the beginning of such period of non-payment.[3] As the contributor is never under an obligation to pay a Class 3 contribution, it may be difficult to establish that non-payment is the result of ignorance or error. The last provision is particularly curious since it applies only where "during the relevant period only", ie of non-payment after the two years, the contributor has not paid the contribution by reason of ignorance or error: must he therefore have been free of such ignorance or error before the said period began?

In *Clements v R & C Comrs*[4], a Special Commissioner[5] refused to allow the contributor to make late payments of Class 3 contributions 40 years after he ceased to be obliged to make compulsory contributions.

[1] Social Security (Contributions) Regulations 2001, SI 2001/1004, reg 65(2).
[2] SI 2001/1004, reg 65(3).
[3] SI 2001/1004, reg 65(4).
[4] (2008) SpC 677.
[5] And one with particular expertise in Social Security law.

54

The international dimension

Territorial scope	PARA 54.01
Reciprocal agreements and double contribution conventions	PARA 54.11
EC law	PARA 54.12
Planning considerations	PARA 54.17

Territorial scope

[54.01] The National Insurance system described in this chapter is of application only to Great Britain. There is a virtually identical system for Northern Ireland. Great Britain comprises mainland England, Wales and Scotland and off lying islands such as the Isle of Wight and the Hebrides, but not the Isle of Man or the Channel Islands which though having the same Sovereign are separate jurisdictions. For this reason the social security legislation when referring to the home territory frequently indicates Great Britain. In a few provisions the term UK is used: this expression covers both Great Britain and Northern Ireland. The territorial scope of the legislation is important in relation to contribution liability. A person is not liable to pay Class 1 or Class 2 contributions unless prescribed conditions of residence or presence in Great Britain are fulfilled.[1] Similarly a person is not entitled to pay Class 3 contributions unless such conditions are fulfilled although in the case of Class 3 contributions the residence test does not have to be satisfied over a recent period of time.[2]

The prescribed conditions are set out in the contributions regulations.[3] The conditions make use of a number of terms, the meaning of which must be considered before proceeding further. They are described below.

Simon's NIC Chapter 23.

[1] SSCBA 1992, s 1(6)(a).
[2] SSCBA 1992, s 1(6)(b).
[3] Social Security (Contributions) Regulations 2001, SI 2001/1004, reg 145.

Definitions

Residence

[54.02] The question of what constitutes residence has been considered in a number of decided cases, including such leading cases as *Lloyd v Sulley*,[1] *Reid v IRC*[2] and *Lysaght v IRC*.[3] These cases were decided in the context of potential income tax liabilities, but they were concerned with the term "reside"

[54.02] The international dimension

as used "in its common sense"[4] and the decisions are therefore relevant to the interpretation of the Contributions Regulations.

The decided cases establish that the question of residence is "a matter of degree" and therefore "a question of fact";[5] accordingly the courts will not overturn a determination made by the Special Commissioners on this issue unless "the facts found are such that no person acting judicially and properly instructed as to the relevant law could have come to the determination under appeal".[6] It has been held that it is not necessary to maintain a settled residence or home in the UK to be resident here: in one case spending part of each year in various hotels in the UK was found to constitute residence.[7] It has also been held that visits of quite short duration if sufficiently repeated to form part of a person's regular habits of life can constitute residence, as where for example, an individual came to England every month to attend directors' meetings and the aggregate visits were less than three months a year.[8]

The former Inland Revenue developed certain practices for settling questions of residence and these are set out in leaflet IR 20 (last formally released in December 1999 but provisionally updated in an internet-only version in April 2008). These practices were intended to give practical effect to the decided cases and in so far as they properly reflect the position, those authorities also in practice generally determined the position for National Insurance purposes, though it must be emphasised that these practices were not binding on the former DSS. However, HMRC were noted to have reinterpreted the guidance in IR 20 and formally withdrew it from 6 April 2009. Its replacement (HMRC6) covers much of the same ground but makes fewer statements that could be relied upon by individuals.

[1] (1884) 2 TC 37.
[2] (1926) 10 TC 673.
[3] (1928) 13 TC 511; see also **Simon's Direct Tax Service** E6.101–102, 110–112.
[4] IRC v Lysaght (1928) 13 TC 511 at 533–544, HL.
[5] IRC v Lysaght (1928) 13 TC 511, HL.
[6] Edwards v Bairstow and Harrison (1955) 36 TC 207 at 229, HL.
[7] Levene v IRC (1928) 13 TC 486 at 500, HL.
[8] IRC v Lysaght (1928) 13 TC at 534, HL.

Presence

[54.03] This term usually occasions no difficulty; it is normally simply a question of fact whether or not a person is present in Great Britain.

Directors of British registered companies who live abroad may be present in Great Britain through attending board meetings. The authorities may, by concession, ignore such visits if the visits are only to attend board meetings in this country and no more than ten board meetings are attended in a year so long as no single attendance lasts for more than two days, or, if there is only one board meeting in a tax year, that meeting lasts for no more than two weeks.[1] It is also sometimes possible to persuade the authorities to agree to ignore time spent in the UK which does not fit exactly the published concession. The test seems to be whether or not the time is inconsiderable.

It is not possible to use this concession where the director comes from another EEA member state or country with which the UK has a social security agreement. In the case of the EEA, liability arises in the EEA member state in which the director is habitually resident. In such cases there will be an NIC liability. In the case of a country with which there is a reciprocal agreement, the terms of that agreement will apply.

[1] HM Revenue and Customs leaflet CA 44 (2009 edn) p 35, para 69.

Ordinary residence

[54.04] There is similarly a body of case law concerning the meaning of ordinary residence. This term is encountered in certain income tax legislation and again HMRC has developed certain practices for determining the question. However, here the former DSS, having regard to a Benefits Tribunal decision on the meaning of the term, took a different approach and their practice was once to regard an individual as continuing to be ordinarily resident in Great Britain where he is absent from Great Britain for up to five years but during that time has not abandoned the intention to return. That approach is no longer followed.[1] Nonetheless, it follows that it is very difficult to shake off ordinary residence for National Insurance purposes. The comments made at § **54.02** about "residence" are equally applicable.[2]

[1] Leaflet NI 38 (October 2004 edn) pp 11–13.
[2] Leaflet IR 20 (December 1999 edn), para 11.2.

Place of business

[54.05] The question of where the employer has a place of business is important in several provisions. A place of business is regarded as being any place from which a person can, as of right, conduct his business, or from which his agent has power to conduct business on his behalf. A company incorporated under the Companies Act 1985 is normally regarded as having a place of business in Great Britain although in one piece of written guidance from the former DSS, a registration without activity did not create a place of business. Whether an overseas company has such a place of business depends on the particular facts. In this connection the case law on whether an overseas company is required to file particulars under what is now Companies Act 1985, s 691(1) will be relevant: that question turns on whether the company has established a place of business in the UK.

A UK resident subsidiary of an overseas company will not be regarded as a fixed place of business of such a company but an overseas company which carries on business through a branch in Great Britain will without question have a place of business here.

In response to questions raised by practitioners the former DSS issued a guidance note on what it regarded as constituting a place of business in Great Britain.[1] Generally, two basic conditions must be met:

[54.05] The international dimension

(1)   the employer must have a fixed address in Great Britain where he has the right to be; and
(2)   salaried employees undertake an activity there which is not necessarily remunerative in itself, but is in furtherance of the purpose for which the business exists. In correspondence the Contributions Agency replaced "salaried employees" with servants.

As to whether there is a fixed address the former DSS looked to the following pointers, and these are still used by HMRC:

(1)   name plate on the door;
(2)   headed letter paper and use of business cards;
(3)   an entry in a telephone or trade directory;
(4)   a lease or rent agreement as some sort of financial transaction for the use of the premises;
(5)   a registered office in the UK;
(6)   registration as a company incorporated outside the UK but with a place of business in the UK for the purpose of the Companies Act 1985;
(7)   if the employer has any other premises in the UK.[2]

In deciding whether there is a business activity carried out at the fixed address, the former DSS considered whether the servants are carrying out the business of the employer. It is not necessary for the staff in this country to be carrying out the main activity of the company: an ancillary role is sufficient. The DSS instanced a foreign bank having a branch in this country which is not actually banking and a foreign building firm having an office here which is not actually building as cases where a business activity is carried out. Similarly, if orders are collected and passed on to the foreign company to accept and execute, this will amount to a business activity. Whether the overseas company has salaried staff under a contract of service working in Great Britain is taken as a strong pointer to the existence of a place of business, but is not a necessary condition. So, for example, there could be a place of business where no one has a contract of service, eg one manned by self-employed partners or directors without a contract of service but working from a base in Great Britain and having employees abroad.

The former DSS confirmed that the premises of a British subsidiary cannot as such be treated as a place of business of its overseas parent but the position will be different if there is tangible evidence that the overseas company has the legal right to occupy part of the British subsidiary's premises.

The DSS did not regard registration under the Companies Act 1985, s 691(1) as conclusive proof of having a place of business in Great Britain but it will be taken as a strong indication. On the other hand the fact that the overseas company has not registered in this way does not necessarily mean that it does not have a place of business in Great Britain.

Simon's NIC [24.41]–[24.80].

---

[1]   The guidance note is reproduced in Annex F of Technical Release Tax 21/92 issued by the ICAEW.
[2]   CWG 2 (2009), p 72.

Liability

[54.06] It is now possible to state the residence conditions for contribution liability for the respective classes of contribution as follows:

(1) *Primary Class 1.* The employed earner must be resident or, subject to any temporary absence, present in Great Britain at the time of the employment or be ordinarily resident in Great Britain at such time.[1]

(2) *Secondary Class 1.* The secondary contributor must be resident or present in Great Britain when the secondary contributions become payable or must have a place of business in Great Britain at that time.[2] See infra, § **54.17** for details of the secondary contributor where the employer is neither resident nor present in the UK. Where there is secondary Class 1 liability, there will also be Class 1A and Class 1B liability (if liable benefits etc are provided).

(3) *Class 2.* The self-employed earner must be ordinarily resident in Great Britain in the period for which the contributions are due, or if not so ordinarily resident, then before that period he must have been resident in Great Britain for a period at least 26 out of the immediately preceding 52 contribution weeks.[3]

There are also residence rules as regards entitlement to pay contributions which are not obligatory. Thus the secondary Class 1 contributor is permitted to pay the secondary contributions even though the normal residence conditions are not met.[4] A self-employed person covered by the small earnings exemption is entitled to pay Class 2 contributions for any contribution week in which he is present in Great Britain.[5] Class 3 contributions, which are always voluntary, can normally be paid only if the following residence conditions apply:

(1) the individual was resident in Great Britain throughout the tax year in question; or

(2) the individual arrived in Great Britain in that tax year and was liable to pay Class 1 or Class 2 contributions in respect of an earlier period during that year; or

(3) the individual arrived in Great Britain in that year and was either ordinarily resident in Great Britain throughout the whole of the tax year or became so ordinarily resident during the course of it; or

(4) the individual not being ordinarily resident in Great Britain, arrived in the tax year or the previous tax year and has been continuously present for 26 complete contribution weeks. (Where the arrival was in the previous tax year entitlement is from the next year only.)[6]

However, where the individual goes abroad, these "normal" conditions are displaced and Class 3 contributions can be paid where either:

(1) the individual was resident in the UK for a continuous period of not less than three years at any time before the period for which Class 3 contributions are to be paid; or

(2) contributions of the "appropriate amount" have been paid for each of the three years ending at any time before the period for which the Class 3 contributions are to be paid. The appropriate amount means contri-

[54.06] The international dimension

butions, the earnings factor (see supra, § **53.01**) derived from which is not less than 52 times the lower earnings limit for Class 1 contributions.[7]

Where this extension applies, the normal time limit for paying Class 3 contributions still operates.[8]

There is a parallel extension of entitlement to pay Class 2 contributions where either of these conditions is met. Here, however, the individual must be gainfully employed outside Great Britain and immediately before he left Great Britain he must have been ordinarily an employed earner or a self-employed earner.[9] A temporary return visit to Great Britain does not remove this entitlement.[10]

Where an individual takes up employment overseas with an overseas employer not having a place of business in Great Britain, it may be preferable for him to pay Class 2 as opposed to Class 3 voluntary contributions, since the former as opposed to the latter contributions will safeguard his entitlement to incapacity benefit on return to the UK. From 6 April 2000, Class 2 contributions are much cheaper than Class 3 (see supra § **53.09**).The rules for entitlement to incapacity benefit (and some others) are different where an employee is sent abroad by an employer who has a place of business in Great Britain. In this situation entitlement to incapacity benefit is preserved so long as Class 1 contributions are paid during the first 52 weeks abroad, and the employee remains ordinarily resident in Great Britain for social security purposes while working abroad. For the general considerations determining whether it is advisable to pay Class 3 (or Class 2) contributions when working abroad, see supra, § **53.09**.

Simon's NIC [24.41]–[24.80].

---

1   Social Security (Contributions) Regulations 2001, SI 2001/1004, reg 145(1)(*a*).
2   SI 2001/1004, reg 145(1)(*b*).
3   SI 2001/1004, reg 145(1)(*d*).
4   SI 2001/1004, reg 145(1)(*b*).
5   SI 2001/1004, reg 145(1)(*c*).
6   SI 2001/1004, reg 145(1)(*e*).
7   SI 2001/1004, reg 147(3).
8   SI 2001/1004, reg 148(*a*).
9   SI 2001/1004, reg 147(3).
10 SI 2001/1004, reg 147(2).

Special rules for continental shelf workers, airmen and mariners

[54.07] Certain kinds of workers have activities which take them physically outside Great Britain for most of their working time. In the absence of special rules such workers might escape contribution liability and hence be denied entitlement to state benefits through not being gainfully employed in Great Britain[1] or through not meeting the conditions as to residence or presence in Great Britain.[2] However, special rules have been laid down to cover the cases of continental shelf workers, airmen and mariners.[3]

Territorial scope [54.07]

The special rules which deal with airmen and mariners apply only to those having a contract of service, ie employees. The rules for continental shelf workers apply whether the person is employed under a contract of service or not, ie they apply equally to self-employed persons as to employees.[4] The workers subject to these rules are those whose employment relates to any of certain specified exploration and exploitation activities,[5] and who carry out their employment in any designated area of the continental shelf, ie specific areas outside the three mile limit but within the areas of the continental shelf over which the UK has jurisdiction under international agreement.[6] Where the rules operate, the designated area is treated as being in Great Britain and thus the continental shelf worker is made subject to contribution liability, notwithstanding that he may not otherwise satisfy the residence or presence conditions.[7]

An airman for the purposes of the special rules is a person employed under a contract of service on board an aircraft as a pilot, commander, navigator or other crew member or in any other capacity related to the aircraft, its crew, passengers, cargo or mail, where the contract has been entered into in the UK with a view to its performance (in whole or in part) while the aircraft is in flight.[8]

In the following situations an airman as so defined, is to be treated as an employed earner and so subject to contribution liability notwithstanding that he is not gainfully employed in Great Britain or does not fulfil the residence or presence requirements. The situations are where the employer or the person who pays the airman his earnings (whether or not as agent for the employer) or the person (if different from the employer) under whose directions the terms of the employment (this suggests the fixing of duty rosters etc) and the calculation of the earnings to be paid are determined, has:

(1) in the case of an aircraft being a British aircraft, a place of business in Great Britain;[9] or
(2) where the aircraft is not a British aircraft, his principal place of business in Great Britain.[10]

A British aircraft in this context means an aircraft belonging to the Crown or an aircraft registered in the UK and having an owner or managing owner (if more than one owner) who resides or has his principal place of business in Great Britain. Where an aircraft has been leased, the owner for this purpose is the person having possession and control over the aircraft.[11]

But the foregoing rule will not apply if the airman in question is neither domiciled nor has a place of residence (a more concrete test than that of being resident) in Great Britain.[12] In such a case unless a reciprocal social security agreement (see infra, § **54.11**) provides otherwise the airman will not be treated as an employed earner subject to British contribution liability.[13]

A mariner for the purpose of the special rules is a person employed under a contract of service either as a master or member of the crew of any ship or vessel or in any other capacity on board any ship or vessel for the purpose of the ship or vessel or crew or passengers or cargo or mails where the contract is entered into in the UK with a view to its performance (in whole or in part) while the ship or vessel is on her voyage.[14] Those who serve "in any other

2015

[54.07] The international dimension

capacity" would include supernumeraries such as hairdressers, shopkeepers etc. The term does not include members of the forces.

The special rules for mariners displace the normal conditions as to residence or presence in Great Britain but, subject to any reciprocal social security agreement, for contribution liability to arise the mariner must be domiciled or resident in Great Britain and for secondary contributions to be payable the secondary contributor must be resident or have a place of business in the United Kingdom.[15]

Under these rules a mariner is treated as an employed earner subject to UK contribution liability in the following situations:

(1) the employment is on board a British ship;
(2) the employment is under a contract entered into in the UK with a view to its performance (in whole or in part) while the vessel is on her voyage and the person paying the mariner's earnings has a place of business in Great Britain, or if the mariner is employed as the master or member of the crew and the person by whom the mariner's earnings are paid or the owner (or the managing owner) has a place of business in Great Britain;
(3) neither 1 nor 2 applies but the mariner is employed as a master, member of the crew or radio officer (but not as a supernumerary) on board any ship or vessel, the contract is not entered in the UK but the employer or the person paying the earnings has his principal place of business in Great Britain;
(4) neither 1 nor 2 applies but the mariner is employed as a radio officer, the contract in this case is entered into in the UK and the employer or person paying the radio officer his earnings has a place of business in Great Britain.[16]

A British ship for this purpose means a ship or vessel belonging to the Crown or registered in the United Kingdom, or any hovercraft registered in the United Kingdom.[17]

In these provisions, very wide interpretation is placed on such expressions as "the person by whom the mariner's earnings are paid" and "the person paying the earnings". While the authorities will not generally regard the bank which makes bank transfers to the employees concerned as such a person, they may treat the company handling the payroll function as such a person, particularly if the instructions to effect wage increases or to make special deductions from pay emanate from that company.

In the case of mariners there are special rules for the ascertainment of earnings,[18] the determination of earnings periods[19] and calculation of contributions;[20] there are also provisions for treating the person paying the earnings as the secondary contributor[21] and allowing for a small reduction in secondary contributions in some instances.[22] Share fishermen are subject to a separate regime under which they are treated as self-employed for contribution purposes but because they are entitled to contribution-based jobseeker's allowance they must pay Class 2 contributions at a higher rate.[23]

Simon's NIC [11.71]–[11.180], [27.1]–[27.70].

---

[1] SSCBA 1992, s 2(1)(*a*).

² Social Security (Contributions) Regulations 2001, SI 2001/1004, reg 145(1)(*a*).
³ SI 2001/1004, Part 9, Cases A, B, C.
⁴ SI 2001/1004, reg 114(1).
⁵ As set out Petroleum Act 1998, s 11(2).
⁶ Continental Shelf Act 1964, s 1(7) provides for such designation.
⁷ SI 2001/1004, reg 114(2).
⁸ SI 2001/1004, reg 111.
⁹ SI 2001/1004, reg 112(1)(*a*).
¹⁰ SI 2001/1004, reg 112(1)(*b*).
¹¹ SI 2001/1004, reg 111.
¹² SI 2001/1004, reg 112(2).
¹³ SI 2001/1004, reg 112(3).
¹⁴ SI 2001/1004, reg 115.
¹⁵ SI 2001/1004, reg 117.
¹⁶ SI 2001/1004, reg 118.
¹⁷ SI 2001/1004, reg 115.
¹⁸ SI 2001/1004, reg 123.
¹⁹ SI 2001/1004, reg 120.
²⁰ SI 2001/1004, reg 121.
²¹ SI 2001/1004, reg 122.
²² SI 2001/1004, reg 119.
²³ SI 2001/1004, reg 125.

Coming to and going from United Kingdom

[54.08] There are special rules to cover respectively the case where a non-UK resident is temporarily employed in the UK and the case where a person previously resident in the UK is posted abroad. These rules, however, do not apply where the individual is coming from or moving to a country with which the UK has signed a social security agreement (see infra, § **54.11**) or to which EC law is applicable (see infra, § **54.12**). Each of these rules is hedged round by a multitude of conditions but where they apply they respectively provide a 52-week contribution holiday for the employee sent to the United Kingdom and impose a 52-week continuation of contribution liability on the employee sent overseas. The rule for incoming employees is an unbroken sentence of 255 words.[1] Unsurprisingly, the rule is in many respects obscure and has given rise to difficulties of interpretation. It may be summarised as follows:

Where the employee:

(1) is not ordinarily resident in the UK; and
(2) is not ordinarily employed in the UK, ie apart from the temporary posting; and
(3) the posting is in the course of an employment mainly outside the UK

and the employer sending him has his place of business outside the UK (if there is more than one place of business the authorities consider that the principal place of business must be outside the UK), and the employment is "for a time" in Great Britain, then no primary or secondary contributions will be payable

[54.08] The international dimension

on the employee's earnings from the date of the employee's "last entry into Great Britain" until "he has been resident in Great Britain . . . for a continuous period of 52 contribution weeks", starting with the beginning of the contribution week following that in which his "last entry" fell.

The former DSS always took the view that the date of last entry for this purpose is the date of last entry for the purpose of taking up employment as an employed earner for his employer. On this view (which is not necessarily correct) a subsequent temporary visit abroad does not cause a further 52-week contribution holiday to run from the date of returning to the UK. If that were the case, UK contribution liability might be delayed indefinitely through the simple expedient of taking a day trip to the continent just before each 52-week contribution holiday expired. However, another reason why this expedient may not succeed is that the contribution holiday ends not when the employee has been "continuously present" in Great Britain for 52 weeks but rather when he has been "resident for a continuous period" of 52 weeks: a period of absence abroad would have to be quite substantial to cause "residence" in Great Britain to cease before subsequently being resumed. This assumes that the term "residence" is given its "common meaning" as established in the income tax cases but the concept of being resident for a continuous period of contribution weeks as is found in this provision is unusual and perhaps inconsistent with the common meaning of residence (see supra, § **54.02**). At one time the former DSS is understood to have taken the view that an absence of at least 28 days is required to break the period of continuous residence in Great Britain and to allow a further 52-week contribution holiday to run but that in any event the Department would have regard to the particular circumstances, eg whether a home was maintained etc, in order to see whether the residence in Great Britain continued during a period of temporary absence abroad. Although this view is not provided by legislation the former DSS regarded residence as continuing if there are any ties such as accommodation, bank accounts, family or even a motor vehicle left in the UK.

It will be noticed that this is one of the provisions where there are references to UK (because it is intended that a truly foreign connection should be established) as well as to Great Britain (which is relevant to contribution liability).

The provision gives some temporary relief from British contribution liability in a case where a foreign employer sends a foreign employee to Great Britain on a temporary assignment. What is meant by a temporary assignment is simply indicated by the expression "for a time" and no limitation is specified for the duration of this period. However, if it became too long, the condition that the employment should be mainly outside the UK would not be fulfilled. The former DSS used to take the view that a maximum period of five years was appropriate but latterly ceased to follow this approach. It should be noted that the relief is not given where the foreign employee takes up a new employment in Great Britain, eg with a UK subsidiary under a new contract of employment such that the UK employer becomes the legal employer. A secondment arrangement, under which the employer is still employed by the overseas employer but his services are made available to the UK subsidiary, may, however, enable the contribution holiday to be obtained.

The practice of extending the 52-week period by, as mentioned above, ensuring a short absence abroad in each complete 52-week period, became widespread. It is understood that a Secretary of State for Social Security decision upheld the former DSS view, but no details are publicly available nor did the DSS announce whether the decision is of general application or limited to the facts of the case.

HMRC believes that in some cases where workers are seconded into the UK from a country outside the EU and with which there is not a reciprocal agreement or double contributions convention, earnings (which will not in any event usually attract UK liability during the first 52 weeks) may be apportioned in some cases. This will result in some part of the earnings not attracting liability to UK contributions. This announcement in autumn 2005 came about due to the interaction between regs 145 and 146 where the employee, having been seconded to the UK, returns to the home country for a time to perform duties for the purpose of that foreign employer. The following conditions must be met for apportionment to apply:

(a) the employee is not ordinarily resident in the UK;
(b) the employee works in the UK under contract to their foreign employer and returns overseas to perform duties overseas for that same foreign employer;
(c) a salary is paid in respect of the UK employment and the employment with the sending employer; and
(d) the employment costs were met by the overseas employer for the purposes of that foreign business.

Tax Bulletin 79[2] contains details of the information required to make a refund claim for past in-date periods, the address to which to make it and also some worked examples.

Simon's NIC [24.191]–[24.230].

---

[1] Social Security (Contributions) Regulations 2001, SI 2001/1004, reg 145(2).
[2] HMRC *Tax Bulletin*, Issue 79, October 2005.

[54.09] The converse rule which imposes a continuation of contribution liability for 52 weeks is easier to state. Where the employee is gainfully employed outside the United Kingdom and that employment, if it had been in Great Britain or Northern Ireland, would have been employed earner's employment, that employment is to be treated as employed earner's employment for the period specified below, provided that:

(1) the employer has a place of business in Great Britain or Northern Ireland (as the case may be); and
(2) the employee is ordinarily resident in Great Britain or Northern Ireland (as the case may be); and
(3) immediately before the overseas employment began, the employee was resident in Great Britain or Northern Ireland (as the case may be).[1]

The period for which the employment outside the United Kingdom is to be treated as an employed earner's employment is the "period of 52 contribution weeks from the beginning the contribution week in which that employment begins". The result of the employment being treated as an employed earner's employment is that primary and secondary Class 1 contributions become payable on "any payment of earnings for the employment outside Great Britain"[2] as well as, in the appropriate circumstances, Class 1A and Class 1B.[3]

This rule too is not without its difficulties. At first sight it appears to cover only the situation where a new employment is taken up which from the start is carried out wholly abroad. In practice the rule is applied to the case where during a continuing employment an employee is sent by his UK employer to work abroad for a temporary period, the overseas posting being regarded as a separate employment for the purpose of the rule. In spite of some ambiguity in the wording, the legitimacy of this application will normally have to be accepted. On that basis, the period of 52 contribution weeks will be that which runs from the contribution week in which the overseas posting begins, although it would obviously be attractive to argue that the period began with the commencement of the employment as a whole since in many cases 52 weeks of contribution liability will have already elapsed before the commencement of the overseas posting.

It is questionable whether an employee actually needs to be sent abroad by a UK employer for the 52-week contribution liability to arise. The three conditions outlined above make no reference to a posting from the UK and so an employee making his own arrangements to take up a position abroad could, in practice, create a contribution liability for an employer in the UK who knows nothing about the employee. This in turn raises all sorts of problems for deducting and collecting contributions.

This continuation of contribution liability can be avoided if the overseas employment is with a separate, albeit affiliated, employer which does not have a place of business in Great Britain. However, this course has a number of other implications (see supra, § **54.08**).

Where contribution liability continues for a further 52 weeks, certain rules are operated in practice to cover the case of an employee returning to the UK in that period on paid leave or paid sick leave or unpaid leave or for a period of temporary duty in the UK and in certain other special circumstances.[4]

If before the end of the 52-week period the employee returns to the UK on paid leave, Class 1 contributions continue to be payable until the end of the 52-week period; after that Class 1 contributions again became payable only if and when the employee takes up further UK duties.[5] The position is similar where the employee returns during the 52 weeks for a period of temporary duty in the UK. But where the 52 weeks of continued contribution liability has already been completed, Class 1 contributions are not payable for the first six weeks of the period of temporary duty. Where the period of temporary duty in the UK exceeds six weeks, a further 52 weeks of contribution liability is likely to start to run when the employee returns to work abroad.[6]

Simon's NIC [23.191]–[23.230].

---

[1] Social Security (Contributions) Regulations 2001, SI 2001/1004, reg 146.
[2] SI 2001/1004, reg 146(2)(*a*).

³ SI 2001/1004, reg 146(2)(c).
⁴ Leaflet NI 132 (April 2002 edn), p 8. (Now withdrawn).
⁵ Leaflet NI 132 (2002 edn) p 8. (Now withdrawn).
⁶ Leaflet NI 132 (2002 edn) p 9. (Now withdrawn).

[54.10] There are two further rules that concern certain types of student working temporarily in the United Kingdom. So long as the student is not ordinarily resident in the UK, he or she will be exempt from contribution liability in spite of being resident or present in the United Kingdom in the following situations:

(1) the student is pursuing a course of full-time studies outside the UK but during the vacation during that course, he or she takes up a temporary employment in Great Britain which is of a nature similar to or related to the course of studies;[1]
(2) the student has a master/apprentice relationship with some person outside the UK and has entered into an employment in Great Britain which began before he or she attained the age of 25 and which is similar to or related to employment under the master/apprentice relationship outside the UK.[2]

Both provisions are construed somewhat narrowly by the authorities. In the first case, the former DSS never accepted the vacation period following completion of the course as occurring in the course of studies. In the second case, where typically there is a training contract in the UK, the master/apprentice relationship is primarily between the student and the UK principal. It is difficult to show that there is an equivalent relationship with the overseas sponsor.

Simon's NIC [23.218]–[23.230].

[1] Social Security (Contributions) Regulations 2001, SI 2001/1004, reg 145(3)(a).
[2] SI 2001/1004, reg 145(3)(b).

Reciprocal agreements and double contribution conventions

[54.11] As explained above, when an employee previously resident in Great Britain takes up an overseas employment and the employer has a place of business in Great Britain, British contribution liability will normally continue for 52 weeks. But for part or all of that period the employee may also be required to pay social security contributions in the overseas country where he is employed. The employee and probably the employer will therefore be obliged to pay contributions in two countries at the same time.

Some countries, eg the USA, have a social security system which requires contributions to be maintained indefinitely during periods of working abroad. So, for example, if an American is sent by his employer for a tour of duty in the UK for three years, he would be liable to pay British National Insurance contributions as well as FICA payments after the first 52 weeks of his employment in the UK but for there being some special arrangement. It is to prevent such cases of dual liability that the UK has made reciprocal social security agreements with certain countries which contain rules which fix contribution liability in only one of the two countries and, according to the circumstances, determine which country that should be.

The countries with which the UK has concluded reciprocal agreements containing contribution liability provisions are as follows: Barbados, Bermuda, Canada, Israel, Jamaica, Japan, Korea (Republic of), Mauritius, Philippines, Switzerland, Turkey, the USA and the various countries previously making up Yugoslavia. There are also agreements between the UK and Gibraltar, Guernsey (including Alderney, Herm and Jethou), Jersey and the Isle of Man. Additionally, the UK has agreements with many of the other 29 countries which form the European Economic Area (EEA).

The UK also made reciprocal social security agreements with Australia and New Zealand which deal with only the reciprocation of benefits. That with Australia came to an end on 28 February 2001, but that with New Zealand remains in force. A social security contributions only agreement (called a "Double Contributions Convention"—(DCC)) between the UK and Canada was signed on 1 January 1997 and came into effect from 1 April 1998, the previous position being that only benefits were covered by the reciprocal arrangements.

The agreements with Korea and Japan came into effect on 1 August 2000 and 1 February 2001 respectively and are also DCCs.

The general pattern of a reciprocal agreement containing contribution liability provisions is that there is a primary rule that an employee is liable only to pay contributions in the country in which he is actually employed but this may be over-ridden by an important exception covering a temporary assignment from the employee's home country to the other country. The exception applies where the employee is employed by an employer based in his home country who sends him to work in the other country for not longer than a specified maximum period. Where the exception applies, the employee continues to be subject only to contribution liability in the home country.

A necessary condition is that prior to the temporary assignment the employee was already subject to contribution liability in the home country. It is essential that during the temporary assignment the legal employer of the employee remains an employer based in the home country whether or not the employee is seconded to a company in the host country. The maximum period allowed for a temporary assignment varies from agreement to agreement. In the majority of the agreements it is one year; with Austria two years is the specified period; in the case of Israel the period is three years. More modern agreements, eg those with the USA, Canada, Korea and Japan specify five years as the limit for a temporary assignment. A period of five years is likely to become standard in future agreements that may be concluded from time to time. Should the actual assignment last longer than originally expected, the agreement normally allows for an application to be made for an extension of the time allowed: this would require mutual agreement by the social security authorities in both countries.

The majority of the reciprocal agreements treat each contract of employment separately. So, for example, where a US company sends one of its employees to work in the UK, either at a UK branch or under a secondment agreement with a UK subsidiary, the US FICA contributions will continue to be payable for the duration of the posting so long as the posting is not expected to continue for more than five years. But if the same employee is also appointed a director of the UK subsidiary, that will be a separate employment which of necessity is with a UK employer and the earnings from that employment will be subject to UK National Insurance contributions. On the other hand, some of the older agreements which the UK has made, eg that with Jersey, are drafted on the basis that there is one overall employment (or self-employment) which is carried on in the territory concerned.

Reciprocal social security agreements dealing with contribution liability normally also contain provisions dealing with the self-employed and with mariners, air crews, government employees, and members of the armed forces.

With some but not all of the reciprocal social security agreements, the employee must be a citizen or national of one of the respective countries for the provisions to apply. In many of the reciprocal agreements, the UK is defined as including the Isle of Man; in some Guernsey and Jersey are also included. Where the reciprocal agreement was made before 1 January 1983, the term British citizen will include not only British citizens as defined by the British Nationality Act 1981 but also citizens of the British dependent territories and British overseas citizens.[1]

Written confirmation of where the contribution liability arises is controlled via a series of certificates issued by the appropriate social security administrators.

Simon's NIC Chapter 28.

---

[1] British Nationality Act 1981, s 51(2).

EC law

[54.12] Prior to the UK's accession to the Treaty of Rome in 1973 by which it became a member of the European Economic Communities (EEC) (now the European Union (EU)), the UK had already concluded reciprocal social security agreements with the countries which then constituted the Community, though not all covered contribution liability. All these agreements have been superseded by a Regulation made by the European Council in 1971 which is binding on all the member states. This Regulation,[1] which is supplemented by a further Regulation which deals only with implementation,[2] is in effect a reciprocal agreement covering not two countries, but all the countries of the Community. However, unlike the normal reciprocal agreement which forms part of the secondary social security legislation of the UK, the European Council Regulation takes precedence over the national law of member states and where necessary overrides inconsistent provisions in that law.

[54.12] The international dimension

The Regulation applied only to EC nationals until 1 June 2003, ie those who qualify as citizens of any one of the member states of the EC under the national legislation of the member state in question and certain refugees or stateless persons. Thereafter the provisions apply to persons of any nationality moving between member states (other than Denmark, Switzerland and EEA member states). The member states of the EC comprised Belgium, Denmark, France, Germany, Greece, Ireland, Italy, Luxembourg, Netherlands, Portugal, Spain and the UK but as explained below from 1 January 1994, for social security purposes, these states were joined by Austria, Finland, Iceland, Norway and Sweden, from 1 May 1995 by Liechtenstein, from 1 June 2002 by Switzerland from 1 May 2004 by Cyprus, Czech Republic, Estonia, Hungary, Latvia, Lithuania, Malta, Poland, Slovakia and Slovenia and from 1 January 2007 by Bulgaria and Romania.

In the case of the UK, the following are its citizens for the purpose of the Regulation:

(1)   British citizens;
(2)   British subjects with the right of abode in the UK;
(3)   citizens of the dependent British territory of Gibraltar.

Until 1 June 2003, where a person who was not an EC national and was assigned from one EC member state to another, the Regulation did not normally apply. However, in this situation the reciprocal agreements which the UK had previously made with individual countries which are now part of the EC may well have been relevant. Furthermore, for periods before 1 January 1994 under certain social security agreements made by the UK under the auspices of the Council of Europe, citizens of certain European countries not belonging to the EC, eg Norway, Sweden etc, who are working in the UK on a long-term basis were entitled to be treated as UK nationals in relation to any reciprocal agreements which the UK has made.

Regulation 1408/71/EC will be replaced in due course by Regulation 883/2004. At the time of writing this is expected to take place later in 2009.

Simon's NIC Chapter 29.

[1]   Regulation 1408/71/EC.
[2]   Regulation 574/72/EC.

[54.13] On 2 May 1992 the EC member states made a treaty with the member states of the European Free Trade Association (EFTA) establishing the European Economic Area (EEA). The member states of EFTA are Austria, Finland, Iceland, Liechtenstein, Norway, Sweden and Switzerland. The intention was that following ratification by all the states involved and the European Parliament, the treaty would take effect on 1 January 1993. However, as a result of a referendum Switzerland decided not to ratify the treaty and Liechtenstein also decided not to join until it was able to disentangle its financial and other arrangements with Switzerland. An amended treaty excluding Switzerland and Liechtenstein was agreed from 1 January 1994. One of the effects of the ratification of the EEA treaty by all the countries concerned is that the EC Regulation on social security applies to all the countries in the EEA, including former EFTA countries, and existing reciprocal social agreements between EC member states and EFTA member states are superseded by that Regulation. Liechtenstein subsequently joined on 1 May 1995. From 1 June 2002, the EC Regulations also apply to Switzerland as it entered into a bi-lateral agreement with the EC on social security matters—the agreement, however, extends only to EC nationals and not those of the EEA states. In addition, further countries were admitted to full EC membership in 2004 and 2007—see supra, § **54.12**.

The Regulation covers both social security benefits[1] and contribution liability. Articles 13–17 contain the rules for determining which country's contribution law shall apply. The principle on which these rules are based is that a person shall be subject to the legislation of a single member state only.[2] For a person who is an employee, this principle is given effect by a primary rule that if the employee is employed in the territory of one member state he is to be subject to that state's contribution legislation even though he may be resident in another member state or the employer may have its registered office or place of business in another member state.[3] But, as with reciprocal agreements generally, this rule is displaced where an employee is sent to work in another member state on a temporary posting. In this case contribution liability continues in the home country for the duration of the assignment. The conditions to be met for this rule to apply are:

(1) the person must immediately prior to the assignment be employed in the home country by an undertaking to which he is normally attached;
(2) the posting to the other member state must be made by that undertaking;
(3) the employee must perform work in the other member state for that undertaking;
(4) the anticipated duration of the assignment must not exceed 12 months; and
(5) the assignment must not be a replacement posting, ie the employee must not be sent to replace another person who has completed his posting.[4]

In order to operate this provision, the employer should apply to the social security authority of the home country for a certificate of coverage to be issued on form E101. The certificate will satisfy the authority in the country where the employer is posted that contributions in that country are not required.

HMRC Centre for Non-Residents (formerly International Services) at the National Insurance Contributions Office in Newcastle, in considering such applications, will not issue a certificate if the employee is not already paying British contributions. The employee does not have to be already working for the UK employer which posts him to the other member state but in a case where a person is recruited in the UK for an immediate posting in the other country the UK employer must directly employ the individual in activities which the employee would normally carry out in the UK. These restrictions are intended to prevent the UK being used as a social security haven—both the contribution levels and benefits are lower in the UK than most other EC/EEA countries.

If, owing to unforeseen circumstances, the duration of the work extends beyond that originally anticipated and as a result exceeds 12 months, there is provision for home country contribution liability to be extended but this requires the agreement of the social security authority in the member state where the employee is posted. An application for an extension must be made by completing form E102 and sending it to the social security administrators in the country where the work is undertaken, before the expiry of the 12 month period and under this provision the extension cannot be given for more than a further 12 months.[5]

One effect of the new Regulation 883/2004 (see supra, § **54.12**) when it eventually comes into force will be that the period of temporary posting of up to 12 months which retains home country liability automatically will rise to 24 months, and the current E102 procedure will cease to exist.

Simon's NIC Chapter 29.

[1] Regulation 1408/71/EC Art 4.
[2] Art 13(1).
[3] Art 13(2)(*a*).
[4] Art 14(1)(*a*).
[5] Art 14(1)(*b*).

[54.14] However, in some cases it is possible to obtain an agreement from the two authorities that home country contribution liability should be continued for a longer period, eg up to five years. This is because there is provision[1] for the authorities of the two member states concerned to make by common agreement exceptions from the strict application of the rules. A specific application setting out the circumstances will need to be made to the social security authority in the home country who will, if they agree to support the application, contact the social security administrators where the work is undertaken and seek their confirmation that home country contribution liability should continue. Following a recommendation by the Administrative Commission of the European Communities on Social Security for Migrant Workers, the then DSS issued certain guidance on the circumstances in which applications for extended periods of home country contribution liability will be accepted. This will be the case where:

(1) the employee has special skills or knowledge in the job in question; or
(2) the employer has specific objectives in the other country for which the employee's services are required.

In the case of 1 it will be necessary to show that the knowledge or skills are not available on the local labour market in the other EC/EEA member state and that the job cannot be done without such knowledge or skills. In the case of 2 it is necessary to show that the employee is familiar with the employer's specific objectives in the other EC/EEA member state.

Where neither of these circumstances applies it may still be possible for the employee to remain subject to home country contribution liability even though the assignment is for more than 12 months but it will be necessary to show that this will be in the employee's own best interests and the social security authorities in both the EC/EEA member states will have to agree to this course.[2] Such an agreement if obtained will be for a stated fixed period.

Where home country contribution liability no longer continues, eg because of expiry of the period allowed for a temporary posting, the employee will become liable to contributions in the member state where the employment is carried out. However, the employer, ie the secondary contributor, often in such a case will not be resident in that country and consequently that country may find it difficult to collect secondary contributions. In the UK, for example, the claim of a foreign government to payment of contributions due under its own law will not be recognised.[3] The Regulation accordingly allows member states to make agreements for the mutual recovery of contributions.[4] The UK, however, has not so far made such an agreement with any member state and therefore the other member states will not be able to recover secondary contributions from UK resident employers in a UK court. Likewise the authorities will normally be unable to recover secondary contributions from employers in the other member states in the courts of such states. In some countries, however, the employee is made responsible for paying over the total contribution and he then needs to reclaim the money from his employer.

Simon's NIC Chapter 29.

[1] Regulation 1408/71/EC Art 17.
[2] Leaflet SA 29 (2006) para 8.
[3] *Metal Industries (Salvage) Ltd v Owners of the ST Harle* 1962 SLT 114.
[4] Regulation 1408/71/EC Art 92.

[54.15] There may be situations where a person is employed in more than one member state at the same time with the same or different employers. The current Regulation deals with these situations by fixing contribution liability in the territory where the individual resides if he pursues his employment activity partly in that territory or if he is attached to several undertakings or several employers with registered offices or places of business in different member states.[1] If the individual does not reside in any of the member states where he works, he is to be subject to contribution liability of the member state in which the employer has its registered office or place of business.[2] For the purposes of the Regulation the country where a person resides is that in which he habitually resides:[3] this has been interpreted as meaning the country where the habitual centre of his interests lies.[4] As long as it is possible to demonstrate continuing strong ties with a home country it is possible to pay contributions in that country—this means that reliance on the five-year rule may not be necessary. There are special rules for the situation where the employer is an undertaking which straddles a frontier between two member states.[5]

There are also special rules for diplomatic staff.[6]

Workers engaged in international transport undertakings are subject to the following rules. An international transport undertaking is one which operates services for passengers or goods by rail, road, air or inland waterway. A person who belongs to the travelling or flying personnel of such an undertaking is liable for contributions in the member state where the undertaking has its registered office or place of business but subject to the following exceptions:

[54.15] The international dimension

(1) if the undertaking has a branch or permanent representation in another member state any person employed by such branch or permanent representation is liable for contributions in that other state; and

(2) if a person is employed principally in the member state in which he resides he is liable for contributions in that state even if the undertaking has no registered office, place of business, branch or permanent representation in that state.[7]

Mariners are subject to the following rules. The primary rule is that a person who is employed on board a vessel flying the flag of a member state is to be liable to contributions in that state.[8] But this is subject to the following exceptions:

(1) if a person is normally employed on board a vessel flying the flag of one member state or otherwise employed in the territory of that state and the undertaking to which he is normally attached posts him to work on board a vessel flying the flag of another member state, he is to remain subject to contribution liability in the former member state;[9]

(2) if a person is not normally employed at sea but performs work in the territorial waters or in a port of one member state on a vessel flying the flag of another member state but is not a member of the crew of that vessel, he is to be subject to contribution liability in the former member state;[10]

(3) if a person is employed on board a vessel flying the flag of one member state but is remunerated by an undertaking having a registered office or place of business in another member state and the person is resident in the territory of that state, he is to be subject to contribution liability in the latter state.[11]

Simon's NIC Chapter 29.

---

[1] Regulation 1408/71/EC art 14(2)(b)(i).
[2] Art 14(2)(b)(ii).
[3] Art 1(h).
[4] Case 76/76: *Di Paolo v Office National de l'Emploi* [1977] ECR 315, [1977] 2 CMLR 59, ECJ.
[5] Art 14(3).
[6] Art 16.
[7] Art 14(2)(a).
[8] Art 13(2)(c).
[9] Art 14b(1).
[10] Art 14b(3).
[11] Art 14b(4).

[54.16] The Regulation deals with self-employed persons in the following way. A person who is normally self-employed in one member state and who performs work in another member state will continue to be subject to contribution liability in the member state where he normally works provided the anticipated duration of the work in the other state does not exceed 12 months.[1] There is provision for an extension of home country contribution liability for a further 12 months in a case where due to unforeseen circumstances the work in the other state extends beyond the duration originally anticipated.[2] If a person is normally self-employed in two or more member states he is to be subject to contribution liability in the member state where he resides if that is one of the states where he pursues any part of his activity.[3] Again, in this context a person will be regarded as residing in the country where he habitually resides and where the habitual centre of his interests lies.[4] If he does not pursue any activity in the member state where he resides, he is to be subject to contribution liability in the member state where he pursues his main activity.[5] However, these last two rules will be overruled if the result would be that the individual could not even on a voluntary basis join a (state) pension scheme: in that event the position apart from these provisions will apply and if the legislation of two or more member states would then apply, the member states concerned will have to decide on which should apply by mutual agreement.[6]

There may be cases where a person is at one and the same time self-employed in one member state and working as an employee in another member state. In such a case he will be subject to contribution liability in the member state where he works as an employee in paid employment[7] except in certain specified instances where he will be simultaneously subject to contribution liability in two member states.[8]

Simon's NIC Chapter 29.

[1] Art 14a(1)(*a*).
[2] Art 14a(1)(*b*).
[3] Art 14a(2).
[4] The decision in *Di Paolo* (see supra, note 4) is also likely to apply to the interpretation of this provision.
[5] Art 14a(2).
[6] Art 14a(4).
[7] Art 14c(*a*).
[8] Art 14c(*b*) and Annex VII.

Planning considerations

[54.17] It will be evident that whether the Contributions Regulations, a reciprocal agreement or the European Council Regulation is relevant, a number of planning opportunities open up wherever an expatriate is assigned to the UK or a British resident is posted abroad. There are choices available as to duration of the assignment and the form of the employment arrangements. For example, if the posting is made the subject of a new contract of employment such that the former employer ceases to be the legal employer, continuation of home country liability will not normally apply and the employer will become liable for contributions in the country where he is assigned.

It is difficult to give general guidance as to the best course to follow since the objectives of different employees and their employers will vary. For example

[54.17] The international dimension

the minimisation of contribution liabilities will not always be the aim since in some countries benefits, such as retirement pension, may be very significant and preservation of entitlement to full benefits may be the prime concern. What should not be ignored in such circumstances is the possibility of maintaining benefit rights by paying voluntary contributions.

There are, however, certain common planning areas where comment is appropriate:

(1) Where a UK company sends British employees to countries which are members of the EC/EEA, it will be generally preferable to retain UK contribution liability for as long as possible. Since UK contributions are generally lower than in other such countries, this may require an application for a certificate of coverage form E101 for an extended period under the provisions of Regulation 1408/71/EC Art 17 (see supra, § **54.14**). Where the posting to the other country is expected to last indefinitely, consideration should be given to making use of the multi-state employments rule (see supra, § **54.14**), eg by having some duties performed in the UK which are the subject of a separate, genuine contract of employment. In such circumstances the five-year rule need not be used.

(2) When a UK company sends British employees to countries which are not members of the EC/EEA and with which there is no reciprocal agreement having contribution provisions, liability for both primary and secondary contributions will normally continue for a further 52 weeks (see supra, § **54.08**). This liability could be avoided by the assignment overseas being made the subject of a new contract of employment with a company which does not have a place of business in Great Britain. It will, however, be necessary to consider all the other implications, including those affecting the corporation tax position, the individual's personal tax position and their occupational, etc the pension arrangements. Where the situation is not, for whatever reason, avoided in this way and a discretionary bonus is to be paid, it will clearly be preferable for this to be paid after the 52 week period has ended. The same point should also be borne in mind if varying a contract of employment that specifies due dates for non-discretionary bonuses.

(3) If an employer in a non-EC/EEA country which has no reciprocal agreement with the UK sends employees to the UK, primary Class 1 contributions will become payable after the first 52 weeks (see supra, § **54.08**). There will also be a secondary liability if the foreign employer has a place of business in Great Britain or if there is a "host employer" (see below), such as a fellow subsidiary or other associate. Where a discretionary bonus is to be paid, it will clearly be preferable for this to be paid before the 52 week period has ended. The same point should also be borne in mind if varying a contract of employment that specifies due dates for non-discretionary bonuses.

Because a substantial amount of secondary contributions may be irrecoverable if overseas employers ensure that they do not have a place of business in Great Britain, HMRC Centre for Non-Residents in Newcastle attempts to establish where it can that there is such a place of business despite precautions being taken to avoid this. Where there is a place of business in Great Britain, this will enable secondary contributions to be collected in respect of all employees of the overseas company working in Great Britain and not simply those attached to the place of business or the UK affiliate most closely associated with the place of business.

As a second line of attack, the former DSS for many years sought to apply to secondment situations the part of the Categorisation Regulations which relate to agency workers, the overseas employer being treated as the agency and the UK resident host company to which the employee was seconded as the client. If these rules could properly apply to this situation, the UK resident host company would be treated as the secondary contributor and secondary contributions could then be collected without difficulty. However, advisers disputed whether the conditions for the rules to apply were met, particularly in the case of high-level executives accountable primarily for the results of their work not the manner of its performance.[1]

Ultimately, in February 1993 the then DSS issued a note in which it accepted that the rules were not appropriate to non-UK employees of overseas companies seconded to the UK to work temporarily for a subsidiary or independent company.[2] Moreover, where previously secondary contributions had in fact been paid on the basis of the former view, the note indicated that refunds would be made on application.[3]

Because of the lost revenue the former DSS amended the law from 6 April 1994[4] to ensure that where an employee liability arises in such situations, then an employer liability will follow. In the case of seconded workers the host employer in the UK becomes liable to pay such secondary contributions. The only relief was that seconded workers already in the UK before 6 April 1994 were not affected by these new rules.[5]

As regards 1 above, HMRC can be expected to look closely at dual-contract arrangements in order to argue that in reality there is only one employment contract. In many cases, this would then create arrears of the National Insurance contributions which the planning sought to escape.[6]

---

[1] See supra, § **49.06**; also the article "Second thoughts on seconded employees" in *Tolley's Practical NIC*, January 1993.
[2] Undated Note issued by the Contributions Agency in February 1993, para 3.
[3] Para 5 of the undated Note.
[4] Social Security (Categorisation of Earners) Amendment Regulations 1994, SI 1994/726, reg 2, inserting SI 1978/1689, Sch 3, para 9.
[5] SI 1994/726, reg 4, inserting SI 1978/1689, Sch 3, para 9(c).
[6] HMRC Tax Bulletin, Issue 76, April 2005, pp 1201–1204.

55

Administration

HM Revenue & Customs and the Department for Work and Pensions	PARA **55.01**
Powers to introduce secondary legislation	PARA **55.03**
Disclosure of avoidance schemes	PARA **55.04**

HM Revenue & Customs and the Department for Work and Pensions

[55.01] Until 1 April 1999, the National Insurance system was overseen by the then Department of Social Security (DSS)—see below. It was also responsible for policy matters related to the contributory scheme, both as regards contributions and benefits, and also the payment of non-contributory benefits made available under social security legislation.

Prior to 26 July 1988 the DSS was part of a larger department, the Department of Health and Social Security, which in addition administered the National Health Service.

As part of the Government's "Next Steps" initiative, the Contributions Agency came into being in April 1991.

On 1 April 1999, the administrative functions carried on by the Contributions Agency and the policy functions carried on by the DSS were transferred to the Inland Revenue and the Treasury respectively.[1]

In June 2001, the DSS became the Department for Work and Pensions (DWP), also incorporating the Employment Service of the Department for Trade and Industry.

Agencies of the DWP include the Pensions Service, Jobcentre Plus and the Child Support Agency.

On 18 April 2005, the Inland Revenue and HM Customs and Excise were merged to become HM Revenue & Customs (HMRC).[2]

Whilst HMRC is now therefore responsible for the income side of the National Insurance Fund, the DWP continues to handle benefits.

The old Contributions Agency site at Newcastle is retained as HM Revenue & Customs' National Insurance Contributions Office (NICO).

NICO at Newcastle continues to deal with over 1.3m annual returns from employers, covering some 47m individual P14s. It also handles the contributions made by about 3m self-employed persons and the voluntary contributions made by some 93,000 contributors.

[55.01] Administration

HMRC is also responsible for providing information to employers and other contributors about their obligations. In this connection they operate a telephone line service for employers on 08457 143 143 or in the case of the deaf or hard of hearing on 08456 021380 (calls in either case are charged at local rates).

Simon's NIC Chapter 30.

---

[1] Social Security Contributions (Transfer of Functions, etc) Act 1999, ss 1 and 2.
[2] Commissioners for Revenue and Customs Act 2005, s 4.

The Employer Guides and other publications

[55.02] HMRC publishes a number of free leaflets giving guidance on contribution matters. They deal with specific topics and most are quite short, eg CA 04 Direct debit the easier way to pay, NI 38 Social Security Abroad. However, many such leaflets were withdrawn in 2005 and 2006—whilst some have been replaced with guidance on the HMRC website, others contain guidance which has not yet been replaced in any format.

A particularly important publication is the Employer's Further Guide to PAYE and NICs, now published by HMRC (CWG 2 (2009)). The current version is sufficiently large for a supporting set of booklets (E10–E18) to be produced: these set out the general rules and the Manual gives detailed guidance. Both CWG 2 and the supporting booklets have appeared in various different guises. While no departmental publication purports to represent an authoritative statement of the law on the subject covered, the Manual for employers (and its predecessors) does set out the authorities' interpretation of the relevant provisions and in cases of doubt the employer is asked to consult the Employer's Helpline.[1] With the passing of the years, the guidance has become increasingly detailed and focused on specific topics. So, for example, the edition of NP 15 which applied for 1987–88 and 1988–89 gave for the first time detailed guidance on the contribution liability under the various possible ways in which the employer can deal with home telephone charges. The Employer's Manual (CA 28/NI 269) gave similar detailed guidance for the first time on a variety of topics including essential car users allowances, use of credit cards and provision of petrol. Although it has not always been the case, currently the guide is fully republished each year.

The significance of such detailed guidance is that it puts the employer on notice of how the authorities consider the item in question should be treated. If the employer has treated the item differently in the past, HMRC does not usually in practice require adjustments to be made retrospectively, ie for periods which have elapsed before the new guidance is issued. Thereafter if the employer disagrees with the guidance, eg because there are special circumstances or there is reason to question the legal basis of the guidance, it is generally desirable to take up the issue as soon as possible. If the employer fails to account for National Insurance contributions on the basis of the guidance given and the matter subsequently comes to light in the course of an employer compliance visit, the employer's negotiating position is weakened. In the event of the employer and HMRC not being able to come to an agreement on the treatment to be followed, the employer must either concede or appeal to the General or Special Commissioners.

[1] See for example leaflet CWG 2 (2009) p 31, para 45.

Powers to introduce secondary legislation

[55.03] The social security legislation as amended in April 1999[1] gives the Treasury and what is now HM Revenue & Customs very wide powers to introduce regulations by means of the statutory instrument procedure. In practice, changes which impose extra charges on employers and/or individual contributors will be made by Statutory Instrument handled by the Treasury. HM Revenue & Customs itself will usually be able to instigate only secondary legislation which provides the administrative framework to a change already legislated for.

In appropriate circumstances, and because of the link with benefit entitlement through the National Insurance Fund, the Treasury or HMRC, as the case may be, are required to liaise with what is now the DWP and the Secretary of State for Work and Pensions before new legislation can be put forward.

The DWP alone retains policy responsibility in respect of statutory sick pay, statutory maternity pay and contracting out matters (rather inconsistently, that for statutory paternity pay and statutory adoption pay rests with the Department for Trade and Industry). The powers of the Treasury and HMRC to make subordinate legislation do not therefore extend to these areas.[2]

Contributions are brought under the care and management of HMRC but it is placed under a duty to collect contributions.[3]

[1] Social Security Contributions (Transfer of Functions, etc) Act 1999, s 2 and Sch 3.
[2] SSC(TF)A 1999, s 2.
[3] SSC(TF)A 1999, s 3.

Disclosure of avoidance schemes

[55.04] Consultation on draft regulations under NCA 2006, s 7 closed in November 2006 and the National Insurance Contributions (Application of Part 7 of the Finance Act 2004) Regulations 2007 (SI 2007/785) finally came into force on 1 May 2007. This follows the statement made at Pre Budget Report 2004.[1] The regulations require disclosure of an arrangement where:

(1) it will, or might be expected to, enable any person to obtain a National Insurance contribution advantage;
(2) that advantage is, or might be expected to be, the main benefit or one of the main benefits of the arrangement; and

[55.04] Administration

(3) it is a National Insurance contribution arrangement that falls within any description (the 'hallmarks'—see infra, § **55.05**) prescribed in the relevant regulations.

The duty to make disclosure of a National Insurance contribution scheme is the same as for income tax, corporation tax and capital gains tax and normally falls on the scheme promoter.

Broadly, where the scheme "promoter" is required to make the disclosure it must be made within five days of the earlier of the date on which the promoter:

(1) makes the scheme available for implementation by another person; or
(2) becomes aware that the scheme has been implemented by a transaction taking place that forms part of it.

Where the scheme user is required to make the disclosure as a result of the scheme being marketed by an offshore promoter or by a lawyer who is unable to make a disclosure because of legal professional privilege it must be made within five days of entering into the first transaction forming part of the scheme.

Where there is no promoter, such as with 'in-house' schemes, the scheme user must disclose within 30 days of entering into the first transaction forming part of the scheme.

---

[1] Written Statement by the Paymaster General, Pre Budget Report 2004.

Tests and hallmarks

[55.05] The definition of "arrangements" is widely defined in the primary legislation to include any scheme, transaction or series of transactions.[1]

"National Insurance contribution advantage" means:

(1) the avoidance or reduction of a liability for that contribution, or
(2) the deferral of the payment of that contribution.[2]

This definition is widely drawn and potentially applies to all classes of National Insurance. However, in practice, HMRC acknowledges that it is likely that disclosed schemes will arise only in respect of Class 1 primary (employees) and secondary (employers), and Class 1A contributions.

With regard to whether the advantage is a main benefit of the arrangements or whether there is a promoter, the general guidance dated August 2006 (http://www.hmrc.gov.uk/aiu/index.htm#guidance) applies.

In essence the existing tax hallmarks apply equally to National Insurance save for the loss scheme hallmark and the leasing of plant and machinery hallmark.

A single arrangement may provide both a National Insurance contribution advantage and a tax advantage. In such cases each advantage is legally subject to its own disclosure considerations. Where both advantages are required to be disclosed, HMRC anticipates that the timing rules will always require them to be disclosed at the same time. For administrative ease, HMRC will accept combined disclosure. However, the scheme description must make it clear that there is both a National Insurance contribution and a tax advantage and explain how both of those advantages arise. Only one scheme reference number (infra, § **55.06**) will be issued.

[1] SSAA 1992, s 132A(7)
[2] SSAA 1992, s 132A(7).

Scheme reference numbers

[55.06] The Anti-Avoidance Group in HMRC will issue a unique scheme reference number for each disclosure of a National Insurance contribution scheme it receives. The number is issued within 30 days of the Anti-Avoidance Group receiving the disclosure.

The reference numbers are eight digits in length and are issued to either scheme promoters or, where they have the liability to make disclosure, the scheme user.

Promoters are required to provide the reference numbers allocated by the Anti-Avoidance Group to clients who use their schemes.[1] Promoters may find it more convenient to issue the number to their clients when it is received although the strict statutory requirement does not require this. Promoters should ensure that they inform their clients of their obligation to include the reference number on form AAG 4 (see below).

Employers using NI contribution schemes are required to notify HMRC that they have used or are using it.[2] As it is most likely that users of these schemes will be employers, the employer should make a disclosure on form AAG 4 within the following time limits:

(1)   Arrangements relating to Class 1 contributions—by the filing date of the PAYE return that relates to the earnings period in which the advantage is first expected to arise (ie by 19 May);
(2)   Arrangements relating to Class 1A contributions—by the filing date of the P11D(b) return that relates to the tax year in which the advantage is first expected to arise (ie by 6 July).

If a scheme involves both Class 1 and 1A contributions, the employer should submit the disclosure by 19 May. Employees are not required to disclose use of NIC schemes where this is done by the employer.

[1] National Insurance Contributions (Application of Part 7 of the Finance Act 2004) Regulations 2007, SI 2007/785, reg 11.
[2] National Insurance Contributions (Application of Part 7 of the Finance Act 2004) Regulations 2007, SI 2007/785, reg 12.

[55.07] Administration

Penalties

[55.07] Promoters and scheme users are liable to a penalty if they fail to comply with their obligations.[1]

No penalty will charged for a failure to disclose a NI contribution arrangement if the arrangement, or substantially the same arrangement, is also a disclosable tax arrangement and a penalty has been imposed for failing to disclose that arrangement.[2]

The same principle applies for failures to declare a scheme reference number.

---

[1] National Insurance Contributions (Application of Part 7 of the Finance Act 2004) Regulations 2007, SI 2007/785, regs 14 and 15). The penalties are as set out in TMA 1970, ss 98C(1) (promoters) and 98C(3) (scheme users).

[2] National Insurance Contributions (Application of Part 7 of the Finance Act 2004) Regulations 2007, SI 2007/785, reg 14(6).

Part IX

Stamp taxes

Part IX

Stamp taxes

56

Stamp duty—general
Introduction and history
Basic principles
Administration
Instruments not properly stamped
Exemptions

57

Heads of charge
Introduction
Conveyance or transfer on sale
Miscellaneous fixed transfer duty
Lease
Other heads of charge
Abolished heads of charge

58

Stamp duty in specific situations
Sale of a business
Land
Trusts and settlements
Wills and intestacies—variations
Matrimonial arrangements
Intellectual property

59

Companies—stamp duty (and stamp duty reserve tax)
Share transactions
Capital duty—abolition
Bearer instruments
Unit trusts—transfer of units

60

Companies—reliefs
Relief from conveyance on sale and lease duty—transfers and leases between associated bodies corporate
Relief from conveyance on sale duty—company reconstructions
Relief from conveyance on sale duty—marketable securities

Relief from duty—demutualisation of insurance companies

61

Stamp duty reserve tax
Introduction
The charge
The higher rate charge
Chargeable securities
Exceptions
Liability, accountability and time for payment
Administration, determination and recovery

62

Stamp duty land tax
Introduction
Scope of the charge
Chargeable consideration
Amount of tax chargeable
Leases and agreements for lease
Reliefs and exemptions
Returns, liability and compliance
Special situations
Transitional provisions

56

Stamp duty—general

Introduction and history	PARA **56.01**
Basic principles	PARA **56.09**
Administration	PARA **56.20**
Instruments not properly stamped	PARA **56.29**
Exemptions	PARA **56.34**

Introduction and history

Introduction

[56.01] Stamp duties are one of the oldest taxes. They were originally introduced in 1694.[1] Strictly, they are taxes on documents and not on transactions or persons and are now governed by the Stamp Act 1891 and the Stamp Duties Management Act 1891 as amended by numerous Finance Acts and by various Revenue Acts. In addition, a number of regulations have been made. The basic structure had changed little over the years and although there were plans for the stamp duties legislation to be consolidated, no date was ever announced.[2] FA 1999 significantly altered the structure of the stamp duties legislation in relation to sales and it also attempted to modernise some of the statutory language and procedure relating to penalties and appeals, for example. Stamp duties bring in a modest but not insignificant amount of revenue and they are relatively cheap to administer and collect. In the year ended 31 March 2008 stamp taxes in total raised approximately £14 billion, which was more than the combined take from capital gains tax, inheritance tax and petroleum revenue tax; however, in the year ended 31 March 2009 this fell to £8 billion.

As stated above, stamp duty is a tax on documents. There are a number of separate duties, under different heads of charge. The main stamp duty is a percentage charge of the price paid (ad valorem) on a conveyance or transfer on sale of various types of property by means of a document. The amount of the percentage varies according to the type of property being conveyed or transferred and the amount of the price paid. The threshold below which no stamp duty is payable on land and buildings and certain other property is currently £125,000. Fixed (previously 50p but increased to £5 for documents executed on or after 1 October 1999) duties which arose on certain documents not on sale, eg on declarations of trust were abolished with effect from 13 March, 2008 except for instruments effecting land transactions.[3]

FA 1990, ss 107, 108 included provisions for the future abolition of all the stamp duty charges (including stamp duty reserve tax) on transactions in shares, from a date to be fixed by Treasury order. FA 1991, ss 110–114 included provisions to limit stamp duty to instruments embodying transactions concerning interests in land and buildings. However, the outcome of the General Election in May 1997 affected the implementation of these provisions: the Labour government indicated that it would retain stamp duty (and stamp duty reserve tax) on transactions in securities. In July 2001, the re-elected Labour government stated that it would retain stamp duty (and stamp duty reserve tax) on shares despite calls by share traders for its abolition or reduction. In April 2002 the Government issued a Consultative Document entitled "Modernising Stamp Duty on land and buildings in the UK". The intention was to effect a major reform of stamp duty in relation to UK land and buildings in order to cope with the introduction of digital signatures, e-conveyancing and the ease with which the existing duties could be avoided. As a consequence, FA 2003 abolished stamp duty on land and buildings and in its place created stamp duty land tax, from 1 December 2003 (see infra, Chapter 62).

The introduction of an electronic system for holding and transferring title to securities ("CREST") in July 1996 had a significant impact on the way in which stamp duty (and stamp duty reserve tax) are charged in respect of transactions involving changes in title or ownership of securities.[4] Because CREST is a paperless system, there is no instrument of transfer on which stamp duty can be paid. Instead, stamp duty reserve tax is charged on agreements to transfer securities within CREST. In consequence, stamp duty reserve tax has become the principal tax on transactions in securities.

Sergeant and Sims A1.4.

---

[1] See Stamp Duty Act 1694 Will & Mary c 21.
[2] The Law Commission's 26th Annual Report 1991 (Law Com No 206) para 2.53. See eg Lord Mishcon's plea in the course of the second reading of the Taxation of Chargeable Gains Bill, Hansard, HL, 14 January 1992, Vol 534, col 118.
[3] FA 2008, Sch 32, para 22.
[4] See generally **Sergeant and Sims A1.2 [41]**.

Form of stamp duties

[56.02] The law of stamp duties is governed solely by statute and no document can be charged with stamp duty unless it comes within the clear words of an Act of Parliament.[1] The general rules for the construction of taxing statutes apply (see supra, §§ **1.22–1.28**) and there is a special rule to deal with the situation where a document would have been taxable under a particular head of charge which has been repealed.[2] In these cases the instrument will not be charged under an unrepealed general head.

SA 1891 is divided into three parts. Part I consists of a number of general provisions and which until 1 October 1999 contained the charging section[3] which imposed the stamp duties specified in the first schedule to the Act on the documents set out in that schedule. These were arranged in alphabetical order and were called the *heads of charge*. Part II consists of a number of explanatory sections which relate to and supplement the various heads of charge. Part III contains supplementary provisions relating to stamp duties. The duties specified in the First Schedule were of two kinds, fixed and ad valorem. Fixed duties do not vary with the consideration for the document whereas the ad valorem duties vary with the amount of the consideration and in accordance with the scales stated in the schedule as amended by subsequent Finance Acts.

With effect from 1 October 1999, FA 1999 significantly altered the structure of stamp duty law by repealing the charging section[4] and the First Schedule and replacing it with three new charging provisions dealing with sales, leases and other instruments in FA 1999, Sch 13, Parts I to III respectively. FA 2003 abolished stamp duty on land and buildings and in its place created stamp duty land tax from 1 December 2003 (see infra, Chapter 62). Stamp duties continue to apply to instruments relating to shares and securities, acquisitions of an interest in a partnership and on bearer instruments (see infra, § 62.33) and this chapter plus Chapters 57–61 remain relevant to such transactions.

Sergeant and Sims A2.1.

[1] *Morley v Hall* (1834) 2 Dowl 494 per Taunton J at 497.
[2] *A-G v Lamplough* (1878) 3 Ex D 214.
[3] SA 1891, s 1.
[4] SA 1891, s 1.

Rates of ad valorem duty

[56.03] The current ad valorem stamp duties are:

Bearer instrument § 59.33

Transfer on sale § 59.02

Certain contracts, transfers in contemplation of sale, and exchanges are chargeable under this head: see infra, §§ 57.02 ff.

The current rates can be found in the table of tax rates and reliefs (pp. xvi–xxiv).

Sergeant and Sims A2.1.

Fixed duties

[56.04] The current fixed duties are:

	Amount
Transfer otherwise than on sale (unless certified as exempt)— § 57.24	£5
Declaration of trust § 57.36	£5
Duplicate or counterpart § 57.37[a]	£5

[56.04] Stamp duty—general

	Amount
Partition § 57.38[b]	£5
Leases—small furnished lettings § 57.25	£5
Leases—miscellaneous § 57.25	£5
Release or renunciation § 57.40	£5
Surrender § 57.41	£5

[a]   Or less: SA 1891, Sch 1; FA 1974, Sch 11, para 9.

[b]   Unless relating to an estate or interest in land and the value of the equalisation payment exceeds £100: see infra, § 57.38.

These fixed duties were increased to £5 for documents executed on or after 1 October 1999.[1] However with effect from 13 March, 2008 these duties apply only to instruments effecting land transactions.

Sergeant and Sims A2.1.

---

[1]   FA 1999, s 112 and Sch 13.

Exempt instruments—fixed duty

[56.05] FA 1985, s 87 contains an enabling power under which the Board of HMRC is able to provide that documents remaining liable to a fixed duty shall be certified in a form prescribed by the Board. The Stamp Duty (Exempt Instruments) Regulations 1987, SI 1987/516, which came into force on 1 May 1987, were made under this power.

Under the regulations, a number of instruments liable to a £5 fixed duty under certain heads of charge[1] are now exempt from duty under those heads if executed after 30 April 1987 and certified in accordance with the regulations. The instruments remaining liable to fixed duty are those relating to land transactions. The instruments exempted under the regulations are listed in the Schedule to the Order which is reproduced below. Furthermore, an instrument which is certified in accordance with the regulations and executed after 30 April 1987 is no longer required under FA 1985, s 82 (which abolished ad valorem duty on gifts inter vivos) or s 84 (which exempted variations on death and appropriations) to be adjudicated.

When certified, exempted instruments should not be sent to Stamp Offices but to the company registrar or other person who needs to act upon them.

    Schedule

    An instrument which effects any one or more of the following transactions only is an instrument specified for the purposes of regulation 2:

    (A)   The vesting of property subject to a trust in the trustees of the trust on the appointment of a new trustee, or in the continuing trustees on the retirement of a trustee.

    (B)   The transfer of property the subject of a specific devise or legacy to the beneficiary named in the will (or his nominee).

    (C)   The transfer of property which forms part of an intestate's estate to the person entitled on intestacy (or his nominee).

(D) The appropriation of property within section 84(4) of the Finance Act 1985 (death: appropriation in satisfaction of a general legacy of money) or section 84(5) or (7) of that Act (death: appropriation in satisfaction of any interest of surviving spouse and in Scotland also of any interest of issue).
(E) The transfer of property which forms part of the residuary estate of a testator to a beneficiary (or his nominee) entitled solely by virtue of his entitlement under the will.
(F) The transfer of property out of a settlement in or towards satisfaction of a beneficiary's interest, not being an interest acquired for money or money's worth, being a conveyance or transfer constituting a distribution of property in accordance with the provisions of the settlement.
(G) The transfer of property on and in consideration only of marriage to a party to the marriage (or his nominee) or to trustees to be held on the terms of a settlement made in consideration only of the marriage.
(H) The transfer of property within section 83(1) of the Finance Act 1985 (transfers in connection with divorce etc).
(I) The transfer by the liquidator of property which formed part of the assets of the company in liquidation to a shareholder of that company (or his nominee) in or towards satisfaction of the shareholder's rights on a winding-up.
(J) The grant in fee simple of an easement in or over land for no consideration in money or money's worth.
(K) The grant of a servitude for no consideration in money or money's worth.
(L) The transfer of property operating as a voluntary disposition inter vivos for no consideration in money or money's worth nor any consideration referred to in section 57 of the Stamp Act 1891 (conveyance in consideration of a debt etc).
(M) The transfer of property by an instrument within section 84(1) of the Finance Act 1985 (death: varying disposition).
(N) Declarations of trust within life insurance policies.[2]

The certificate

The certificate should:

be—

— included as part of the document or—
— endorsed upon the document or—
— firmly attached to the document (if prepared separately);

include—

— the category into which the document falls and—
— a sufficient description of the document where the certificate is separate but physically attached.

be signed by the transferor or grantor, or by a solicitor on his behalf. (An authorised agent of the transferor or grantor who is not a solicitor may also sign provided he states the capacity in which he signs, confirms that he is authorised and that he has knowledge of the facts of the transaction.)

A suggested form of words[3] is:

I/We hereby certify that this instrument falls within category . . . in the Schedule to the Stamp Duty (Exempt Instruments) Regulations 1987

Insert the letter opposite the category concerned.

---

[1] **Sergeant and Sims A17, A15.2, A15.3.**

ie under the headings "Transfer of any kind not herein before described" and "Disposition in Scotland of any property or any right or interest therein not described"

[56.05] Stamp duty—general

in SA 1891, Sch 1 and under FA 1985, s 83(2) (divorce etc) or 84(8) (varying testamentary dispositions etc).

[2] Such instruments have been brought within the exempt categories from 1 October 1999 by SI 1999/2539 as announced by IR Press Release 112/99.

[3] See Stamp Office Technical Note (April 1987), obtainable from any Stamp Office.

[56.06] Although the regulations seem clear and straightforward, it is apparent that they may lead to practical difficulties and some uncertainty in relation to the stamping of settlements and declarations of trust[1] and the instruments required for the vesting of settled property in the trustees. Broadly, the position seems to be as follows. Since 13 March 2008 only instruments effecting a land transaction are within the scope of these requirements. The basic principle is that an instrument which effects a gift qualifies for the appropriate certificate under the regulations and, if certified, is exempt from duty and need not be sent to the Stamp Office for adjudication; but an instrument which serves merely to transfer the legal interest in settled property does not qualify for a certificate and must be stamped £5.

It seems to follow that:

(1) if the settlement is stated to be executed before the transfers (so that it is the latter which effect the gift), the settlement must be stamped £5 and must not be certified, and the transfers require to be certified and then attract no duty (but if not certified attract £5 and require adjudication); and

(2) if the settlement is stated to be executed after the transfers (or if there is no evidence as to the order of execution, in which case this will be presumed to be the position); then
    (a) subject to (b) below, the settlement has to be certified and then attracts no duty (but if not certified attracts £5 duty and requires adjudication), and the transfers attract £5 duty;
    (b) but if the settlement "contains provision for future additions to the Trust Fund" it too requires a £5 stamp whether or not it contains a certificate (but then would not require to be adjudicated).

As regards this type of case the official view seems to be:

(1) that if a settlement makes no provision for further additions, the trustees have no power to accept them;

(2) that the charge to £5 duty in respect of such a provision is justified by *Ansell v IRC* [1929] 1 KB 608 and by the Stamp Act 1891, s 4.

[1] Sergeant and Sims A17, A15.2, A15.3.

As to declarations of trust in relation to settlements, see infra, §§ 58.06–58.07.

The administration of stamp duty

[56.07] Stamp duty is managed by the Commissioners for Her Majesty's Revenue and Customs.[1] The Provisional Collection of Taxes Act 1968 (see supra, § **1.20**) does not apply but similar legislation was introduced by FA 1973, s 50 and this has now been supplemented by a power to vary an existing stamp duty by regulation.[2] The Stamp Act 1891, s 1 charged the duties specified in the First Schedule on the instruments specified in the said Schedule; this was the only section of the Act which imposed directly any obligation to stamp any instrument.[3] With effect from 1 October 1999, FA 1999 repealed this old charging section and introduced three new charging provisions dealing with sales, leases and other instruments in FA 1999, Sch 13, Parts I to III respectively. FA 2003 abolished stamp duty on land and buildings and in its place created stamp duty land tax from 1 December 2003 (see infra, Chapter 62). Stamp duties continue to apply to transactions in shares and securities, bearer instruments and acquisitions of a partnership interest (see infra, § **62.23**). The process of determining formally the correct duty is by adjudication. An instrument must be sent to the Commissioners of Revenue & Customs for adjudication. For the procedure and requirements generally, see infra, § **56.20**. Except where the appeal relates only to the penalty payable upon late stamping, an appeal lies from their decision by way of case stated to the Chancery Division in England and Wales, in Scotland to the Court of Session, in Northern Ireland to the High Court, with further rights of appeal as for ordinary tax cases. In England and Wales, by virtue of para 23.2 of Practice Direction 52 made under the Civil Procedure Rules 1998, revenue appeals are assigned to the Chancery Division and heard and determined by a single judge of the High Court. The necessary case stated must be lodged in Chancery Chambers. Where the appeal relates only to the penalty payable upon late stamping on documents executed on or after 1 October 1999, the appeal is to the First-tier Tribunal (under SA 1891, new s 13A) who will determine the amount of the penalty. An appeal against a determination by the First-tier Tribunal lies to the Upper Tribunal.

The provisions in FA 1989, s 182 forbidding disclosure of information apply to stamp duty.

Sergeant and Sims A18.1, A20.1, A20.2.

[1] SDMA 1891 and Inland Revenue Regulation Act 1890 as altered by Commissioners for Revenue and Customs Act 2005, s 5.
[2] The legislation in FA 1973, s 50 is not identical since the duty must be final—income tax can be adjusted later; for this reason the rate approved in the resolution is binding for the period stated. The power to vary by regulation was added by FA 2000, s 117 and Sch 33.
[3] Fletcher Moulton LJ in *Maple & Co (Paris) Ltd v IRC* [1906] 1 KB 834 at 843; this judgment contains a useful analysis of the Stamp Act 1891.

Territorial limits

[**56.08**] Stamp duty is levied on a world-wide basis. The territorial limits of stamp duty are defined incidentally in SA 1891, s 14(4) which lays down the rules of inadmissibility of unstamped documents. Such documents are barred if the instrument is executed in the UK or relates to property in the UK.[1] Stamp duty applies in Scotland and Northern Ireland, as well as England and Wales.

[56.08] Stamp duty—general

An instrument chargeable both in Great Britain and in Northern Ireland which has been stamped in either of those parts of the UK is deemed to be stamped in the other part of the UK unless the stamp duty chargeable in that other part of the UK exceeds the stamp duty chargeable in the part of the UK in which it has been stamped.[2]

Sergeant and Sims A1.3, A1.4.

---

[1] See generally *Parinv (Hatfield) Ltd v IRC* [1998] STC 305, CA.
[2] FA 1998, s 150.

Basic principles

Stamp duties are duties on documents

[56.09] Stamp duties are duties basically on instruments[1] and for the purposes of stamp duty an instrument is defined to include every written document.[2] If a transaction is effected orally or arises solely from the conduct of the parties so that there is no document to stamp, then, generally there can be no duty. So on a transfer of ownership of chattels by delivery no duty arises but if the ownership is transferred by bill of sale duty must be paid on that instrument.[3]

It is sometimes possible to structure transactions so that they are not effected by documents and this may be done in one of three main ways; by delivery or conduct, by operation of law or orally. Delivery or conduct can be used to make gifts or to accept contracts. Operation of law will apply where by statute or common law an event or act gives rise to a particular legal consequence without any, or any further, documentation, eg:

(1) where property vests in a trustee on his appointment as a trustee;[4] or
(2) a donatio mortis causa;[5] or
(3) an oral declaration of trust.[6]

The Stamp Office are also sometimes prepared to accept that a company merger occurring under the laws of a foreign jurisdiction where the two corporate entities literally merge or are absorbed by a successor entity, can be treated in relation to the transfer of any UK assets as a transfer by operation of law otherwise than on sale and hence the relevant instruments are stampable with a fixed £5 duty rather than ad valorem. However, where all the normal attributes of a sale are present such as the issue of consideration shares and the assumption of liabilities, the public merger deed and any transfers of UK assets may be liable to ad valorem duty as documents effecting a sale.

For stamp duty saving purposes advantage has been taken of this rule wherever it is possible to effect a transaction without using an instrument, but in the case of securities this method is severely restricted by the imposition of stamp duty reserve tax introduced in FA 1986, Part IV (see infra, § **61.01**).

A contract need not be in writing, so one of the issues in the well known case of *Carlill v Carbolic Smoke Ball Co*[7] was whether evidence could be given of

Basic principles [56.09]

the contract because the document issued by the defendants was not stamped. It was held that the contract was made by acceptance and, as that was not in writing, no stamp was needed. It should, however, be borne in mind that some transactions must be in writing if they are to be valid. Examples of such transactions include the creation or disposition of a legal estate in land for which a deed is required[8] and the disposition of an existing equitable interest by the beneficial owner,[9] while a declaration of trust relating to land may be made orally but must be evidenced in writing.[10]

Problems of evidence may arise where there is no document to act as evidence of a transaction and there are other risks inherent in disposing of the need for a document, in particular where assignments are involved because an oral assignment will, in most cases, be an equitable assignment and not the more favourable legal assignment. In some cases this will not matter, where for example the two parties are connected as where a debt owed by a subsidiary company is assigned to the parent company. Here the parent company can enforce payment by its subsidiary so it is possible to ensure that the debt is paid to the assignee.

Situations where it might be possible to save stamp duty by regard to the fact that the transaction does not have to be in writing or evidenced in writing include severing fixtures when land is sold so that they pass by delivery rather than conveyance of the land itself and allowing title to chattels to pass by delivery when a business is sold. It is difficult to create oral trusts for this purpose because a prior oral transaction and its subsequent written record can be treated as one transaction[11] but as there is no exemption for stamp duty in relation to transactions between spouses (other than on a separation or divorce) an oral declaration of trust could be used to pass property between spouses. There could be a problem where the property was land because such a trust must be evidenced in writing signed by the settlor[12] but it seems that the statutory declaration, which is merely a formal record of evidence, is not stampable at all as it does not create or dispose of rights or interests in property.

Sergeant and Sims A3.1.

---

[1] FA 1999, s 112(3), Sch 13 setting out the instruments chargeable to stamp duty and the rates of duty—the old charging section, SA 1891, s 1 has been repealed in relation to instruments executed on or after 1 October 1999.
[2] SA 1891, s 122(1).
[3] FA 1999, Sch 13 and SA 1891, s 41.
[4] Trustee Act 1925, s 40.
[5] *Birch v Treasury Solicitor* [1951] Ch 298.
[6] Law of Property Act 1925, s 53 sets out the instruments for which writing is required.
[7] [1892] 2 QB 484.
[8] Law of Property Act 1925, s 52(1).
[9] Law of Property Act 1925, s 53(1)(c).
[10] Law of Property Act, 1925, s 53(1)(b).
[11] *Cohen and Moore v IRC* [1933] 2 KB 126.
[12] Law of Property Act 1925, s 53(1)(b).

Documents are stamped according to their legal effect

[56.10] If because of a misapprehension an appointment of new trustees is made by the wrong person, the document has no legal effect and does not attract stamp duty.[1] The legal effect of an instrument depends on its substance so in *Eastern National Omnibus Co Ltd v IRC*[2] an agreement to discontinue business in a specified area, to assist their successors to obtain the necessary licences and not to compete, made by a public motor service company was held to be an agreement for the sale of goodwill even though it was not recorded in that manner.

As to the doctrine of form and substance in tax matters generally see now supra, §§ 2.03, 2A.10, 2A.12, 2A.27 and 3.17 following the decision in *Furniss v Dawson* [1984] STC 153, HL. It has been decided that the principle of that case is applicable to stamp duty[3] and although it initially appeared that the principle may be more limited in its application to stamp duty than in relation to other taxes this is no longer the case.[4]

Duty paid on an instrument which fails to carry out a transaction may be recovered.[5]

Sergeant and Sims A3.3.

---

[1] See *Oughtred v IRC* [1958] Ch 678 per Lord Evershed MR at 688; affd on appeal [1960] AC 206.
[2] [1939] 1 KB 161.
[3] See *Ingram v IRC* [1985] STC 835.
[4] See *MacNiven v Westmoreland Investment Ltd* [2001] UKHL 6, [2001] STC 237; *Collector of Stamp Revenue v Arrowtown Assets Ltd* [2003] FACV no 4 of 2003 Court of Final Appeal Hong Kong; *Stamp Comr v Carreras Group Ltd* [2004] UKPC 16, [2004] SWTI 990.
[5] SDMA 1891, s 9(7).

Time of execution governs (complete and incomplete documents)

[56.11] The original theory of the Stamp Act was that liability was determined as the instrument was prepared and before it was executed;[1] hence the practice of preparing an instrument on stamped paper. This can still be seen in SA 1891, s 15(1) (as substituted by FA 1999, s 109(1)) which imposes certain penalties on instruments stamped after execution (infra, § 56.30) and in the provisions relating to wasted stamps (infra, § 56.27). Today this theory bears little relation to practice since it is clear that there is no obligation to stamp an instrument at all, although the consequences of not stamping it may compel one to do so, and that, in practice, the Revenue do not insist on the strict interpretation of s 15(1), there being a general period of grace of 30 days following the date of execution. It is, however, a common practice for solicitors and stockbrokers to keep a stock of share transfer forms pre-stamped with the fixed £5 duty purely for convenience.

The principle that the time of execution governs means, as the House of Lords held in *Wm Cory & Son Ltd v IRC*,[2] that the liability of an instrument to

Basic principles [56.11]

stamp duty arises when it is executed and that the character of an instrument is ascertained by reference to its legal effect at that date and not by what use was made of it later. This does not prevent the courts from looking at later events to discover the true position when the instrument was executed.

An incomplete document does not need a stamp. It follows that it can be produced in evidence unstamped[3] but it also follows that if the rate of stamp duty changes before the document is complete it will be the later rate of duty that applies.[4]

The true test is probably that a document is complete when it has been executed by the last party to execute whose execution is necessary to make it an effective document, and this is the date which should be inserted in the document. So a transfer by way of gift is complete in equity when the donor has done all in his power to perfect the gift;[5] if, however, the transfer requires registration before it is complete the instrument is not complete until executed by all the parties necessary for registration.[6]

A deed normally takes effect, ie is complete, on delivery. A deed which has been signed and sealed but not delivered, is not yet complete and so not yet liable to stamp duty. The same rule now applies to a deed delivered in escrow, ie one that has been delivered but which is to take effect only on the satisfaction of some condition. The execution of deeds and escrow are now regulated by the Law of Property (Miscellaneous Provisions) Act 1989.

In *Terrapin International Ltd v IRC*[7] a deed of exchange was delivered in escrow and stated that, subject to satisfactory land searches being obtained by one party, the exchange would take place on 30 April 1974. Owing to delay in the Land Registry, completion did not take place until 8 May 1974. It was held that the deed was complete only when the conditions were satisfied and the rate of stamp duty was therefore that applying on 8 May; the rate had been doubled for documents executed after 30 April 1974.

It had been suggested that this approach was inapplicable in Scotland and that execution meant only signed, and not unconditional delivery. To put the position beyond doubt in all parts of the UK, s 122 of the Stamp Act 1891 and s 27 of the Stamp Duties Management Act 1891 have been amended so as to provide that a deed shall be treated as executed when it is delivered or, if delivered subject to conditions, when the conditions are fulfilled.[8]

Sergeant and Sims A3.1.

---

1 Per Dixon J in *Stamp Duties Comr (Queensland) v Hopkins* (1945) 71 CLR 351 at 379.
2 [1965] AC 1088 especially per Lord Reid at 1105; this particular loophole has now been closed (FA 1965, s 90). For a case when this principle operated against the taxpayer see *Western United Investment Co Ltd v IRC* [1958] Ch 392.
3 *Sinclair v IRC* (1942) 24 TC 432 at 442.
4 *Terrapin International Ltd v IRC* [1976] 2 All ER 461; see also *Crane Fruehauf Ltd v IRC* [1975] 1 All ER 429 (document not under seal but subject to condition; date of instrument was date condition satisfied). Cf now the Law of Property (Miscellaneous Provisions) Act 1989, s 1.
5 See *Re Rose* [1952] Ch 499 at 515.

[56.11] Stamp duty—general

[6] *Sinclair v IRC* (1942) 24 TC 432 at 444.
[7] [1976] 2 All ER 461.
[8] FA 1994, s 239.

Overlapping heads of charge

[56.12] If an instrument is chargeable under more than one head, the Crown may choose the head but may not charge under both heads.[1] This situation should be distinguished from that in which one instrument carries out separate transactions and is therefore liable to duty as separate instruments.
Sergeant and Sims A3.5.

[1] *Speyer Bros v IRC* [1908] AC 92; *Anderson v IRC* [1939] 1 KB 341.

Leading and principal object

[56.13] The leading and principal object rule directs that the liability of an instrument to duty is determined by its leading and principal object. If that object does not give rise to duty, no duty is due merely because there is a subsidiary clause with a different object; and vice versa.[1] If an instrument is stamped in respect of the leading and principal object there is no need to stamp it for matters which are merely accessory,[2] but the problem is deciding when the second matter is merely accessory and when it is not. The test appears to be whether the second contract can "stand on its own feet".[3]

This point arises in connection with the conveyance of land where covenants in the conveyance do not give rise to further duty unless they clearly amount to further consideration.
Sergeant and Sims A3.6, A3.7, A3.8.

[1] *Deddington Steamship Co Ltd v IRC* [1911] 2 KB 1001.
[2] *Limmer Asphalte Paving Co Ltd v IRC* (1872) LR 7 Exch 211 per Martin B at 217.
[3] *General Accident Assurance Corpn Ltd v IRC* 1906 8F (Ct of Sess) 477 per Lord Dunedin at 482.

One instrument—two instruments (alterations)

[56.14] If more than one instrument is written on the same piece of paper each instrument must be stamped separately, eg an endorsement postponing the completion of a contract of sale, the contract being a chargeable instrument.[1] Hence, if an instrument is executed and subsequently altered to a substantial degree, further stamp duty may be required.[2] This does not apply if the first document was only a draft and so not executed; so a stamp on an incomplete document will cover a subsequent alteration.[3] The alteration of an instrument after execution may make a new stamp necessary either because it is a new instrument or because it increases the amount of duty payable on the other instrument.[4]

Sergeant and Sims A3.6.

1. SA 1891, s 3(2); *Bacon v Simpson* (1837) 3 M & W 78.
2. *Prudential Assurance Co Ltd v IRC* [1935] 1 KB 101.
3. *Matson v Booth* (1816) 5 M & S 223.
4. *London and Brighton Rly Co v Fairclough* (1841) 2 Man & G 674; *Bambro (No 2) Pty Ltd v Stamp Duties Comr* (1964) 8 WN (NSW) 1142.

One instrument—two or more matters

[56.15] Where one matter is ancillary to the other, the general principle of the leading and principal object ensures that only one stamp is required.

SA 1891, s 4 provides that, subject to the provisions of the Stamp Acts,[1] an instrument containing or relating to several distinct matters is to be separately and distinctly charged as if it were a separate instrument with duty in respect of each of the matters.

It follows that an instrument passing property of two different classes for stamp duty must be stamped in respect of each.[2] So an instrument which both appointed new trustees and vested property in them was liable both to appointment duty and to deed duty prior to the abolition of these heads of charge.[3] An instrument vesting property in separate persons requires a stamp for the transfer to each person;[4] so also an instrument effecting both a sale and a sub-sale of shares requires more than one stamp.[5] However, it is possible for persons to transfer interests by one instrument when they act jointly. So in *Wills v Bridge*[6] several shareholders transferred their holdings to a common purchaser by one instrument and the single *ad valorem* stamp was held sufficient. So also a lease to joint tenants requires only one stamp.[7]

The word "matters" is not defined in s 4. Matters would appear to be distinct when each falls within a different classification created by the Act for the purpose of specifying the nature (fixed or ad valorem) and amount or rate of the duty chargeable.[8]

Sergeant and Sims A3.6, A3.8.

1. eg SA 1891, s 77 (leases).
2. *Ansell v IRC* [1929] 1 KB 608.
3. *Hadgett v IRC* (1877) 3 Ex D 46; see now supra, § **56.03**.
4. *Freeman v IRC* (1871) LR 6 Exch 101, 40 LJ Ex 85.
5. *Fitch Lovell Ltd v IRC* [1962] 3 All ER 685.
6. (1849) 4 Exch 193.
7. *Cooper v Flynn* (1841) 3 ILR 472.
8. *Stamp Duties Comr of New South Wales v Pendal Nominees Pty Ltd* (1989) 167 CLR 1 at 10–12.

One instrument—two or more considerations

[56.16] Section 4 then provides that an instrument made for any consideration in respect whereof it is chargeable with ad valorem duty, and also for any further or other valuable consideration or considerations, is to be separately and distinctly charged, as if it were a separate instrument, with duty in respect of each of the considerations.[1]

An example would be a lease made in consideration of a premium and a rent but this must be distinguished from the situation in which the lessee promises to pay rent and to look after the property, the latter promise being clearly ancillary to the leading object and so not separately chargeable.

Sergeant and Sims A3.6, A3.8.

---

[1] SA 1891, s 4(b).

Two instruments—one transaction

[56.17] A transaction may require more than one instrument to complete it. It is a general rule that ad valorem duty is not paid more than once. So where there are several conveyances for completing title to property sold, the principal conveyance only is charged with ad valorem stamp duty. This is in accordance with Revenue practice and statutory provision as regards conveyances.[1]

Sergeant and Sims A3.8.

---

[1] eg SA 1891, s 58(3).

The contingency principle—consideration uncertain

[56.18] On a transfer on sale, ad valorem duty is chargeable on the amount or value of the consideration.[1] If, at the time the instrument is executed, the amount or value of the consideration is uncertain because the obligation to pay is to arise, or the amount payable is to be quantified, by reference to an event after execution, the authorities suggest that the contingency is to be ignored and duty is chargeable by reference to any maximum, minimum or basic sum agreed upon by the parties.[2] The consideration is ascertained for the purposes of the charge provided such a sum is specified in the instrument or can otherwise be identified at the time the instrument is executed.[3] Accordingly:

(1)   a figure that may be varied up or down may be taken;[4]
(2)   if a definite minimum figure can be set, ad valorem duty is charged on that figure;[5]
(3)   if a definite maximum figure can be set, ad valorem duty is charged on that figure notwithstanding that the actual consideration finally paid may be less;[6]
(4)   if both a maximum and a minimum figure can be set, duty is chargeable on the maximum.

If no sum is specified by the parties, so that the consideration is not quantified in any respect, eg is expressed simply as a percentage of future profits, rents or royalties, and the transaction does not relate to the transfer or vesting of any estate or interest in land or the grant of a lease (as to which, see below), then there is nothing by reference to which ad valorem duty may be assessed and no such duty is payable on the instrument.

The effect of uncertainty as to amount is illustrated by the decision of the House of Lords in *Independent Television Authority and Associated Rediffusion Ltd v IRC*[7] where a series of payments was due but the sum would be varied (up or down) by reference to the retail prices index. It was held that the sum dutiable was that stated in the agreement notwithstanding the possibility of later variation.

The principle was most recently applied in *L M Tenancies 1 plc v IRC*.[8] In that case, premiums payable under leases were to be calculated by reference to a formula, one element of which was the closing price of a particular stock on a specified date after the execution of the leases. The Court of Appeal held that the leases were chargeable by reference to the premiums calculated by taking the last closing price of the stock prior to execution. Any variation upwards or downwards by virtue of a change in the closing price of the stock in the period between execution and the date after execution specified in the leases was a contingency which fell to be disregarded.

Following *L M Tenancies 1 plc v IRC*, and until a change of practice was announced in Press Release 98/99, 14 May 1999, the Stamp Office had applied the contingency principle to rent reviews under leases calculated on the rate of change in the Retail Price Index by ascertaining the annual average rent by reference to the increase over the 12 months prior to the date of execution.[9]

The Stamp Office have taken fresh legal advice and Press Release 98/99 is the result. Although not relevant to lease transactions within stamp duty land tax, this states that:

> In future, where there is a formula expressed in the lease for rent reviews based on the RPI, only any change in the RPI up to the date of its execution will be taken into account for Stamp Duty purposes. This is expected to result, in most cases, in the average rent being little more than the initial rent.

Although this represents a welcome change of practice, the Press Release itself does not make it clear what will be the date from which changes in the RPI will be taken into account before the date of execution of the lease in question. It seems obvious, however, that changes in the RPI before the date of execution will now only be taken into account for the purposes of the stamp duty calculation where the lease in question specifies a period of time during which any RPI change is to be used in calculating the first rent review and that period of time commences before the date of execution of the lease. The Stamp Office have subsequently confirmed that this is the case and they have provided the following examples:

(1) A lease is executed on 1 January 1999. The term is specified as 99 years from 1 January 1998. There is no prior agreement for lease and the rent reviews are upward only. The first rent review is on 1 January 2000 by reference to the increase in RPI between the date of execution of the lease and the rent review date. In a document such as this, where the base date for the RPI calculation is on or after the date of execution of the lease we would not apply any RPI increase. Since the rent review is upward only we would calculate the average annual rent for the period from 1 January 1999 to the end of the term, 31 December 2096 and apply the appropriate rate of stamp duty to that rent. The calculation would not include any RPI element.

[56.18] Stamp duty—general

(2) Let us say now that the same lease had a rent review clause which specified the base date for the RPI calculation as 1 January 1998. It follows that the increase in RPI between 1 January 1998 and 1 January 1999 is known as at the date of execution of the lease. We will therefore apply the stamp duty contingency principle to the rent and assume that at the first review date the initial rent as at 1 January 1999 will increase on 1 January 2000 by the percentage change in RPI between 1 January 1998 and 1 January 1999. We will, of course, apply that increase by reference to the rent review formula used in the lease but if it was a straightforward increase in line with RPI and RPI had increased, say, 3% in the period 1 January 1998 to 1 January 1999 we would say the contingency is that the rent at the first review will be the rent at 1 January 1999 increased by 3%. We will not apply any subsequent contingent increase in such a case.

Although the Press Release does not mention agreements for lease in this context it seems that each document will be treated separately for these purposes. This means that where there is an agreement for lease followed by a lease in conformity with it, the stamp duty calculations for each may differ. This could arise where, at the date of execution of the agreement for lease, the relevant RPI period had not yet commenced (or only commenced upon execution) but that when the lease came to be executed the RPI period had already begun resulting in a higher amount of stamp duty on the lease.

The simple message following this change of practice is that, where commercially possible, the base rate for calculating RPI changes should be on or after the date of execution of the lease so that no RPI changes will then be taken into account for the purposes of calculating stamp duty.

Sergeant and Sims A6.5.

---

[1] A sum payable only on breach of a term of the contract is not consideration—*Western United Investment Co Ltd v IRC* [1958] Ch 392.
[2] See *Coventry City Council v IRC* [1979] 1 Ch 142 at 145, 150 and the cases there cited; for transactions in land see now FA 1994, s 242.
[3] *Underground Electric Railways Ltd v IRC* [1906] AC 21, HL.
[4] *Independent Television Authority and Associated Rediffusion Ltd v IRC* [1961] AC 427, HL.
[5] *Underground Electric Railways v IRC* [1916] 1 KB 306, CA; *Jones v IRC* [1895] 1 QB 484; SA 1891, s 4(b).
[6] *Underground Electric Railways Ltd v IRC* [1906] AC 21, HL.
[7] [1961] AC 427. Contrast *Clifford v IRC* [1896] 2 QB 187. The particular charging provision in the former case (bond covenant duty) was repealed by FA 1971, s 64.
[8] [1998] STC 326.
[9] See Sergeant and Sims Division EB, Hansard extract for 6 November 1996.

Unascertainable consideration

[56.19] In relation to instruments executed after 7 December 1993, where, for the purposes of stamp duty chargeable under or by reference to the heading "Conveyance or transfer on sale", the consideration or any part of the consideration for the transfer or vesting of any estate or interest in land or the grant of a lease cannot be ascertained at the time the instrument is executed, the consideration shall be taken to be the market value of the estate or interest immediately before the instrument is executed.[1] Care should therefore be taken to avoid stating a sum in the instrument, payable subject to contingencies, which exceeds the market value of the property.

The manner in which this provision operates in practice has been the subject of an article in the August 1995 edition of the Inland Revenue Tax Bulletin,[2] the main effects of which appear to be as follows:

(1) The provision does not apply if, by the application of the contingency principle, the consideration is ascertainable, ie a maximum, minimum or basic sum is agreed upon and specified by the parties as the subject of payment, in which case duty is charged by reference to the specified sum. Accordingly, the provision will not be applied where the total consideration is subject to a minimum payment specified in the instrument, so that duty is chargeable by reference to the specified minimum, rather than by reference to the value of the property sold. However, the Revenue do not accept that the consideration is ascertained for the purposes of the provision where a nominal sum is specified as such sum does not represent the agreed consideration.

(2) The provision does apply where either all or a distinct part of the consideration is unascertainable, ie the consideration is not quantified and cannot be quantified by the application of the contingency principle, eg where no sum is set or a fixed sum is payable plus a percentage of profits in respect of which no maximum, minimum or basic sum is specified. In these circumstances, duty is chargeable by reference to the market value of the property sold.

(3) A promise to pay a sum to be quantified in the future is itself property, ie a chose in action. It is therefore possible that there may be some cases which could fall also within the scope of the exchange provisions (see infra, § **57.26**). In the event that there is any difference between the amounts of duty chargeable under the two sets of provisions, duty will be charged under the provisions producing the higher amount of duty (see infra, § **56.12**).

Where the provision applies, the value of the property should be set out in the instrument[3] and the Stamp Office may require the parties to provide evidence of value to support the statement of value in the instrument.[4]

Sergeant and Sims A6.7, Division E.

[1] FA 1994, s 242.
[2] Set out in **Sergeant and Sims Division E**.
[3] SA 1891, s 5.
[4] SA 1891, s 12(2) (as substituted by FA 1999, Sch 12, para 1).

Administration

Methods of stamping

[56.20] Instruments are presented at one of the Stamp Offices. There is a duty to set out in an instrument all the facts and circumstances affecting its liability to duty.[1]

The stamp duty legislation provides for stamp duty to be recorded on a document by means of an impressed stamp. Postage stamps are no longer acceptable.[2] The machines currently employed emboss the stamp or stamps on the document by means of a die.

FA 1993, s 204 enables the Treasury to make regulations governing the method by which the payment of stamp duty is denoted on documents and the Stamp Office is thus able to consider alternative stamping methods for the future, for example, the use of electronic equipment.

For addresses see **Sergeant and Sims Division G**.

[1] SA 1891, s 5.
[2] Formerly acceptable for heads of charge which have been repealed.

Adjudication and adjudication stamp

[56.21] The special nature of stamp duties is illustrated by the adjudication process which enables the correct amount of duty to be determined—usually conclusively—by the Revenue. Any person may require the Commissioners to express their opinion on the liability to duty or the amount due. Following such an opinion the instrument *may* be stamped with the amount of duty determined and a further stamp—the adjudication stamp—denoting that it is duly stamped or with a stamp to show that it is not chargeable. There is in general no statutory obligation to pay the duty assessed subject, however, to a fine of £300 if the duty assessed following an adjudication has not been paid within 30 days, under SA 1891, new s 12A(2) for documents executed on or after 1 October 1999. Since 24 April 2002 however, where group relief under FA 1930, s 42 (or relief under FA 1986, s 76) has been given in relation to a transfer of land but is then withdrawn because the relevant company or it and a relevant associated company leave the group (or in the case of relief given under s 76, control of the acquiring company or of it and a relevant associated company changes) within three years, the stamp duty that would have been payable but for the relief becomes payable and IR Stamp Taxes may determine and recover the amount payable with interest.[1] The absence of a stamp may, however, give rise to difficulty where a party needs to rely upon or register the instrument: for the consequences of not stamping an instrument liable to duty, see infra, § **56.28**. The instrument for adjudication may be delivered to any Stamp Office together with any information required, accompanied by Form Adj 467.[2]

In some instances adjudication is compulsory:

(1) conveyance in contemplation of sale;[3]
(2) orders made under the Variation of Trusts Act 1958;[4] and
(3) orders made under the Companies Act 2006, s 900.[5]

It is also required when relief or exemption is claimed under:

(1) FA 1930, s 42 (transfer between associated companies);
(2) FA 1980, s 98 (maintenance funds for historic buildings);
(3) FA 1980, s 102 (conveyances in consideration of a debt);
(4) FA 1982, s 129 and FA 1983, s 46 (for conveyances, transfers or leases to charities or the National Heritage Memorial Fund or the Historic Buildings and Monuments Commission for England);
(5) FA 1986, ss 75–77 (reconstruction of companies and acquisition of share capital);
(6) FA 1995, s 151 (lease or tack or agreement for lease or tack between associated bodies);
(7) FA 1997, s 96 (demutualisation of insurance companies).

Under the Stamp Duty (Exempt Instruments) Regulations 1987, SI 1987/516 adjudication is no longer required for instruments under FA 1985, s 82 or s 84 if duly certified (supra, § **56.05**).

Apart from satisfying statutory requirements the main advantages in requesting adjudication is that the instrument is—if duly stamped under the adjudication process—admissible for all purposes notwithstanding any objection relating to duty;[6] thus it is the most that can be done to convince third parties. The process is also the first step in disputing the Stamp Office's view of the correct amount of duty.

The adjudication process is normally conclusive of the amount of duty but here too there are exceptions:

(1) some instruments also require a produced stamp (infra, § **56.24**);
(2) if the document requires two stamps, adjudication of one is not conclusive of duty on the other;[7]
(3) bearer instruments require a stamp under FA 1999, Sch 15, para 21 (replacing FA 1963, s 60(3));
(4) the court can probably go behind the adjudication stamp if it was obtained by misrepresentation or without full disclosure of the material facts.[8]

Sergeant and Sims A18.

---

[1] FA 2002, ss 111 and 113. as amended by FA 2003, ss 126 and 127) increasing the clawback period from two to three years for instruments executed after 14 April 2003 and see infra, 62.15 for transactions after 30 November 2003.
[2] SA 1891, s 12(2) (as substituted by FA 1999, Sch 12, para 1) and see Official Notes indicating information required in certain common situations which is reproduced in **Sergeant and Sims Division F.**
[3] FA 1965, s 90.
[4] For practice, see **Sergeant and Sims A18.**
[5] **Sergeant and Sims A18.**
[6] SA 1891, s 12(6) as substituted by FA 1999, Sch 12, para 1 for old s 12(5).

[7] *Fitch Lovell Ltd v IRC* [1962] 1 WLR 1325 at 1363.
[8] SA 1891, ss 5, 12(2) (as substituted by FA 1999, Sch 12, para 1).

Limits of adjudication

[56.22] The process of adjudication is not without its limits. Thus the process cannot authorise the stamping after the execution thereof of any instrument which by law cannot be stamped after execution.[1] Moreover if a court has ruled that an instrument is not duly stamped, subsequent adjudication cannot retrospectively make it duly stamped;[2] for the same reason the process cannot prejudice rights that have been established and relied upon prior to adjudication. As Brightman J (as he then was) has said:

> Suppose a vendor of land requires the purchaser to accept a title deed which is not properly stamped. The purchaser declines. The vendor serves a notice to complete. The purchaser does not complete. The vendor forfeits his deposit. Suppose that this purchaser was right in law in his assessment of the stamp duty liability. It would be absurd to suppose in that case that the purchaser loses his deposit merely because the vendor between rescission and trial succeeds in getting the instrument in question erroneously adjudicated as not liable to duty.[3]

Sergeant and Sims A18, A20.2.

[1] SA 1891, s 12(6)(*b*) (repealed by FA 1999, s 109(3) and Sch 12 for documents executed on or after 1 October 1999).
[2] *Prudential Mutual Assurance Investment and Loan Association v Curzon* (1852) 8 Ex 97.
[3] *Marx v Estates and General Investments Ltd* [1976] 1 WLR 380 at 387 per Brightman J.

Denoting stamp

[56.23] The amount of ad valorem duty due may depend on whether another instrument has been duly stamped. So no ad valorem duty will be due on a conveyance on sale if it carries out an agreement for sale which has itself borne ad valorem duty.[1] In such an instance the conveyance will carry a stamp showing—or denoting—the amount of duty paid on the agreement.

Such a stamp does not guarantee that the stamp on the agreement is sufficient; such a guarantee requires adjudication. The denoting stamp is usually impressed only when both the original and the new instruments are presented at the same time.[2]

On the transfer or conveyance of a freehold or leasehold interest or the grant of a lease for a term exceeding 35 years (which is not directly enforceable against any intermediate interest in the land) the duty paid on the agreement must be denoted on the conveyance, transfer or lease.[3]

An agreement for a lease executed on or after 1 October 1999 may be produced for stamping with the lease, without interest and penalty notwithstanding that the period of 30 days specified in s 15A(1)(*b*) of the Stamp Act 1891 has passed since the execution of the agreement.[4] However, no lease shall be treated as duty stamped unless:

(1) it contains a certificate that there is no agreement to which it gives effect;[5] or
(2) it is stamped with a stamp denoting:
    (a) that the agreement is not chargeable; or
    (b) the duty paid on the agreement.[6]

Other instances of denoting stamps are:

(1) bearer instruments chargeable upon issue—these require a stamp denoting that the instrument has been produced to the Commissioners prior to issue although such a stamp does not denote duty paid on another instrument;[7] and
(2) on duplicates or counterparts.[8]

Sergeant and Sims A18.2, A20.2.

---

[1] FA 1999, Sch 13, para 7(3) and (4) replacing SA 1891, s 59(3), and see also FA 2002, s 115(4) where a sale contract for more than £10m has been stamped under s 115(2).
[2] SA 1891, s 11.
[3] FA 1984, s 111(2), (3).
[4] FA 1994, s 240 (as substituted by FA 1999, Sch 12, para 4) for the duty chargeable on the agreement, see infra, § **57.30**, and see infra, § **62.33** for where the lease is granted after 31 December 2003.
[5] As to which, see FA 1994, s 240(4) (as substituted by FA 1999, Sch 12, para 4).
[6] FA 1994, s 240A (as substituted by FA 1999, Sch 12, para 4)
[7] FA 1999, Sch 15, para 21(2), infra, § **59.11**.
[8] FA 1999, Sch 13, Part III, para 19 replacing SA 1891, s 72.

Produced stamp—Particulars Delivered form

[56.24] On the occasion of:

(1) any transfer on sale of the fee simple of land;
(2) the grant of any lease of land for a term of seven or more years (in Northern Ireland, any lease); or
(3) any transfer on sale of any such lease;

it is the duty of the transferee or lessee to produce to the Stamp Office, whether or not duty is payable, the conveyancing document together with a form (known as Particulars Delivered form) which summarises the details of the transaction.[1] A lease need not be produced if the agreement for lease has been produced and the required particulars were supplied with the agreement. The document is stamped with a "produced stamp" in addition to any ad valorem duty stamp. Without the produced stamp the document is not duly stamped. Failure to produce the document within 30 days attracts a fine.

Sergeant and Sims A17.5, A18.2, Division D.

[56.24] Stamp duty—general

[1] FA 1931, s 28. The particulars are to be found in FA 1931, Sch 2 as amended and FA 1985, s 89 and the Stamp Duty (Exempt Instruments) Regulations 1985, SI 1985/1688. For Northern Ireland, see FA 1994, ss 244, 245 and the Stamp Duty (Production of Documents) (Northern Ireland) Regulations 1996, SI 1996/2348. In Scotland, Form LV(A) is used for leases.

Exempt instruments—produced stamp

[56.25] FA 1985, s 89 contains an enabling power under which the Treasury is able to exempt specified documents from the requirements of a produced stamp. The Stamp Duty (Exempt Instruments) Regulations 1985, SI 1985/1688 were made under this power.

Under the regulations, in England and Wales the majority of conveyances of registered land where the sale price is below the stamp duty threshold (currently £125,000) go direct to the Land Registry together with the Particulars Delivered form. The documents to which the regulations apply are:

(1) transfers on sale of commercial premises as well as land and houses; and
(2) assignments or surrenders of an existing lease.

They do not, however, apply to:

(1) transfers on sale of property which attract stamp duty;
(2) transfers on sale which do not fall to be registered with the Land Registry;
(3) grants of new leases;
(4) documents which require adjudication (even if it is thought that no duty is due);
(5) documents which do not contain a certificate that the consideration does not exceed the stamp duty threshold.[1]

In Scotland arrangements exist for non-dutiable dispositions of property to be sent direct to the Keeper of the Registers of Scotland. Similar arrangements have been introduced in Northern Ireland.[2]

It will be seen that, for stamp duty purposes, there is no obligation to produce a voluntary conveyance; there is also no need to produce an instrument relating solely to incorporeal hereditaments, a grave, a right of burial or the transfer of a mining lease.

Sergeant and Sims A17.4, A18.2, Division D.

[1] See infra, §§ 57.15–57.16.
[2] FA 1994, ss 244, 245 and the Stamp Duty (Production of Documents) (Northern Ireland) Regulations 1996, SI 1996/2348.

Appeals following adjudication and judicial review

[56.26] Except where the appeal relates only to the penalty payable upon late stamping, an appeal in a stamp duty matter lies to the High Court (or in

Scotland to the Court of Session) by way of case stated but only after an adjudication and payment of the duty.[1] The appeal must be made within 30 days of notice of the adjudication decision being given. The Commissioners of Revenue & Customs must, if required by the appellant, state a case and deliver it to the appellant who may then within 30 days set it down for hearing. The legislation, remarkably, gives the Commissioners the right to state the case and thus to determine the facts on the basis of which the appeal will be heard in the first instance. However, not only is oral or affidavit evidence admissible to supplement the case stated,[2] but, in practice, the case is submitted to the appellant in draft form.[3]

If the appeal is successful, overpaid duty is repaid with interest. For instruments executed on or after 1 October 1999 the general right to a payment of interest on a repayment of stamp duty applies from the later of 30 days after the instrument was executed or the date on which the duty was paid.[4] The Revenue may not sue to recover the excess of any higher duty the court may determine; in such circumstances the instrument is simply not duly stamped unless the excess is paid.

It is to be observed that, except where the appeal relates only to the penalty payable for late stamping, stamp duty appeals cannot be made to the First-tier Tribunal. Therefore they are expensive. It is an unsatisfactory system and in need of reform.

Where the appeal relates only to the penalty payable upon late stamping on documents executed on or after 1 October 1999, the appeal is to the First-tier Tribunal under SA 1891, new s 13A who will determine the amount of the penalty. An appeal against a determination by the First-tier Tribunal lies to the Upper Tribunal.

An application for judicial review is open to a taxpayer in appropriate circumstances, but for an unsuccessful application, see *J Rothschild Holdings plc v IRC*.[5]

Sergeant and Sims A20.3.

---

[1] SA 1891, s 13 (as substituted by FA 1999, Sch 12, para 2).
[2] Eg *Holmleigh (Holdings) Ltd v IRC* (1958) 46 TC 435 where oral evidence was admitted; *Peter Bone Ltd v IRC* [1995] STC 921 and *L M Tenancies 1 plc v IRC* [1996] STC 880 where affidavit evidence was admitted.
[3] Sergeant and Sims A20.3.
[4] FA 1999, s 110 and see infra, § **56.30**.
[5] [1989] STC 435, CA.

Spoiled stamps

[56.27] By SDMA 1891, s 9 an allowance is made for spoiled stamps in certain defined circumstances, including an instrument if executed but:

(1) found to be void ab initio; or
(2) found to be unfit, by reason of error or mistake therein, for the purpose originally intended; or

(3) which fails by reason of the inability or refusal or some other person to sign it or complete the transaction; or
(4) which fails by reason of the inability or refusal of some other person to act under it or for want of enrolment or registration within a time limit; or
(5) which has become useless in consequence of another instrument being executed (and duly stamped) effecting the same transaction.

This relief is limited in that there is a two year time limit for claiming the allowance and no legal proceeding must have been commenced in which the instrument could be offered in evidence. It is also limited in that the conditions do not cover instruments failing for non-fulfilment of a condition precedent or relating to transactions which are voidable. This point is less troublesome if one considers that the transaction was initially valid and therefore the document should have been stamped; this, however, must be balanced by the fact that if the instrument had not been stamped no-one could be any the worse off and that these restrictions do not apply to the wider relief for duty on a conveyance on sale in FA 1999, Sch 13, Part I, para 9. It is also a condition of the relief that the instrument must be given up to be cancelled.

There is also relief where a person has inadvertently used a stamp of greater value than was necessary.[1]

Claims should be made in writing to the Stamp Office which stamped the original instrument.

Sergeant and Sims A18.3.

---

[1] SDMA 1891, s 10.

Lost or spoiled instruments

[56.28] When an instrument is lost there is a presumption that it was duly stamped; however if it can be shown that the instrument had not been stamped the presumption is that it remained unstamped.[1] An instrument which is not lost can be presented for stamping out of time on payment of penalties: a lost instrument obviously cannot be so presented nor—if it was unstamped—can secondary evidence of its contents be given.

SDMA 1891, s 12A,[2] provides for free stamping of a replacement instrument where a duly stamped original instrument has been accidentally lost or spoiled. In the case of a lost instrument, the applicant must undertake to deliver it up for cancellation if it is subsequently found. In the case of a spoiled instrument, the application must be made within a two year time limit for the claim, no legal proceedings must have been commenced in which the original could be offered in evidence and the original must be delivered up for cancellation. Where the section applies, the replacement instrument is not chargeable with duty but is stamped as if it were and is deemed duly stamped. If any duty was paid in respect of the replacement before the application was made, it is repaid. The Commissioners of Revenue & Customs may require such evidence by statutory declaration or otherwise in support of an application as they think fit.

Sergeant and Sims A19 [1444].

---

[1] *Marine Investment Co v Haviside* (1872) LR 5 HL 624.
[2] Inserted by FA 1996, s 201, Sch 39, Part III, para 10(3) and enacting existing extra-statutory concessions.

Instruments not properly stamped

Admissibility

[56.29] The failure to stamp a document (unlike a failure to pay income tax) is not an offence and, in general, the Crown cannot sue for duty on an unstamped instrument. However, the Stamp Act 1891 imposes a number of restrictions in respect of unstamped or insufficiently stamped instruments.[1] Furthermore, the offences of cheating the public revenue and of conspiring to cheat the public revenue would seem to be relevant in relation to the misuse of certificates and false statements in stamp duty matters.[2]

It is expressly provided that an instrument which is not duly stamped in accordance with the law in force at the time when it was first executed "shall not, except in criminal proceedings, be given in evidence, or be available for any purpose whatsoever . . ." (SA 1891, s 14(4)). This cannot be remedied by the consent of the parties.[3] The instrument is not admissible whether directly or for a collateral purpose;[4] nor is secondary evidence of the instrument admissible;[5] cross-examination upon an unstamped document is not allowed[6] but unstamped instruments are admissible to refresh a witness's memory[7] and to prove fraud[8] or an act of bankruptcy.[9] It has been held that a claimant for capital allowances who is unable to prove that he has legal title to equipment due to the inadmissibility of an unstamped bill for sale could nevertheless prove the necessary ownership in equity by showing that it became the beneficial owner of the equipment under the terms of the relevant acquisition agreement and by reference to the conduct and intention of the parties.[10] It is considered that this decision is questionable in that the court did not appear to consider the best evidence rule under which the claimant should have been required to produce the best evidence, namely the bill of sale proving legal title in order to prove ownership. This may have been on the basis that the appeal was from the Commissioners where formal rules of evidence do not apply. Nevertheless, had the court taken notice of this rule of evidence the claimant would not have been allowed to rely on lesser evidence in the form of the non-stampable agreement and the parties' conduct to prove ownership. In failing to apply this rule the Court undermined the statutory policy enshrined in SA 1891, s 14(4) which is the principal means by which the payment of stamp duty is enforced. It has also been held that a plaintiff need not stamp an instrument when he was trying to prevent the transaction from being implemented and was arguing that the agreement was void.[11] The prohibition on admissibility does not extend to criminal proceedings, nor apparently, to rent tribunals[12] since these are not courts of law. This reasoning could be

[56.29] Stamp duty—general

extended to proceedings before the Commissioners[13] but not to the High Court on appeal by way of case stated. The words "available for any purpose whatever" mean that one party cannot compel another to rely on and accept as having legal effect an instrument which is not duly stamped.[14] In practice, HMRC will refuse to give effect to unstamped instruments. For example, the Stamp Office will not accept that fixed duty is payable on a transfer of land on the basis that the beneficial interest in the land has been conveyed by an unstamped instrument held overseas: if the assignment of the beneficial interest is on sale, the transfer will be assessed with ad valorem duty calculated by reference to the consideration for the sale. This view has been confirmed as correct by the Court of Appeal.[15] The effect of the general rule as to late stamping on payment of a penalty (infra, § **56.30**) is that the defect of non-stamping is inherently remediable. One consequence of this was that it was considered unprofessional for counsel to object to the admissibility of the document for non-stamping unless the case was a revenue case or the defect went to the validity of the document.[16] Counsel could, however, take the stamp point if this would unfairly prejudice his client after the trial; so counsel for a purchaser of land could take the point that a document of title was not stamped. However, since August 2001 the Bar Council apparently intends that it no longer be unprofessional for counsel to take a stamping objection. This has potentially far reaching consequences and is likely to mean that it is now incumbent on counsel to review the stamp duty liability of instruments relevant to his client's case with a view to taking or preparing for a stamping objection to be taken by the other side.

However, it has always been the duty of the court, arbitrator or referee to take the stamp objection itself;[17] when this is done the legislation prescribes the method to be adopted but in practice the unstamped instrument is admitted subject to an undertaking by the conducting solicitor to have the instrument stamped.[18] The court's decision is final.[19]

Sergeant and Sims A19.1, A19.2.

[1] SA 1891, ss 14, 17.
[2] *R v Mavji* [1986] STC 508, CA; *R v Mulligan* [1990] STC 220, CA, applying *R v Hudson* [1956] 2 QB 252, CA and *R v Redford* [1988] STC 845, CA. See also **Simon's Taxes, A6.1107**.
[3] *Nixon v Albion Marine Insurance Co* (1867) LR 2 Exch 338.
[4] *Fengl v Fengl* [1914] P 274 although the position in Scotland seems unsettled—*Watson v Watson* 1934 SC 374 at 379 but the Privy Council in deciding on a comparable provision of the Indian Stamp Act took the view that collateral matters were not admissible: *Ram Rattan v Parma Nand* (1945) LR 173 Ind App 28.
[5] *Hamilton Finance Co Ltd v Coverley Westray Waltaum & Toseti Ltd* [1969] 1 Lloyd's Rep 53; *Re Brown & Root McDermott Fabricators Ltd's Application* [1996] STC 483.
[6] *Baker v Dale* (1858) 1 F & F 271.
[7] *Birchall v Bullough* [1896] 1 QB 325.
[8] *Re Shaw* (1920) 90 LJ KB 204.
[9] *Re Gunsbourg* (1919) 88 LJ KB 562.
[10] *BMBF (No 24) Ltd v IRC* [2002] EWHC 2466 (Ch), [2002] STC 1450.

¹¹ *Mason v Motor Traction Co* [1905] 1 Ch 419.
¹² See *R v Fulham etc Rent Tribunal* [1951] 2 KB 1 at 7–8.
¹³ See *Sinclair v IRC* (1942) 24 TC 432 at 444 and Vaisey J in *Lamport and Holt Line Ltd v Langwell* (1958) 38 TC 193 at 198. However this is unlikely.
¹⁴ *Marx v Estates and General Investments* [1975] 3 All ER 1064 at 1072; *Dent v Moore* (1919) 26 CLR 316 at 324; cf *Re Indo China Steam Navigation Co* [1917] 2 Ch 100 at 106.
¹⁵ *Parinv (Hatfield) Ltd v IRC* [1998] STC 305.
¹⁶ Boulton, *Conduct and Etiquette at the Bar* (6th edn) p 70; see also *Skandinavia Reinsurance Co of Copenhagen v Da Costa* [1911] 1 KB 137 when the successful objector was deprived of costs.
¹⁷ SA 1891, s 14(1) but only when the point is clear—*Don Francesco v De Meo 1908 SC 7*; in practice doubtful points are covered by requiring an undertaking that the instrument will be submitted for adjudication. If the form of the undertaking cannot be agreed upon it would appear that the document will not be admitted.
¹⁸ eg *Parkfield Trust Ltd v Dent* [1931] 2 KB 579 at 582; this seems to rest on the status of the solicitor as an officer of this court—an undertaking by a barrister would therefore not suffice.
¹⁹ Old RSC Ord 59, R 11(5) but curiously this has not been included in Schedule 1 to the Civil Procedure Rules 1998—an appeal is possible; see *The Belfort (1884) 9 PD 215*.

Penalties for late stamping

[56.30] The failure to stamp an instrument is not a criminal offence although a £300 penalty is payable if the duty is not paid within 30 days after notice of an assessment is issued following an adjudication, under SA 1891, new s 12A(2). However, SA 1891, new ss 15, 15A and 15B provide a new simplified tariff of interest and penalties for late stamping in relation to instruments executed on or after 1 October 1999[1] (see § **58.30** of the previous edition of this work for the position regarding penalties for instruments executed before 1 October 1999). Any interest or penalty is to be denoted on the instrument in question.[2]

Interest is payable under SA 1891, new s 15A if an instrument chargeable with ad valorem duty is not duly stamped within 30 days of execution and is charged on the unpaid duty from the end of the 30-day period until the duty is paid. Under SA 1891, old s 15(3) if an instrument was executed outside the UK, interest and penalties only began to run if the stamp duty was not paid within 30 days of the instrument being first received in the UK. Under SA 1891, old s 15(2)(*a*), even when the instrument had been executed in the UK, no interest and penalties arose if the instrument was submitted for adjudication within 30 days of execution.

However, under SA 1891, new s 15A interest is chargeable from 30 days after execution in relation to any unpaid ad valorem duty regardless of where the instrument was executed and whether it has been submitted for adjudication within 30 days of execution. Hence, it is necessary in practice when submitting a document which is or may be liable to ad valorem duty for adjudication, to lodge an estimate of the duty payable in order to forestall an interest charge and SA 1891, new s 15A(2) gives statutory recognition to the concept of lodging an estimate of the amount of duty with the Commissioners.[3] Where payable, interest is calculated at the usual rate under FA 1989, s 178 and is rounded down to the nearest multiple of £5 and is not payable if less than £25.

A penalty is payable under SA 1891, new s 15B [4] on an instrument which is not presented for stamping within 30 days after:

(1) if the instrument is executed in the UK or relates to land in the UK, the day on which it is executed;
(2) if the instrument is executed outside the UK and does not relate to land in the UK, the day on which it is first received in the UK.

The maximum penalty is £300 (or the amount of unpaid duty if less) if the instrument is presented for stamping within one year of the 30-day period in 1 or 2 above. If the instrument is not presented for stamping until after the end of one year from the 30-day period mentioned in 1 or 2 above, the maximum penalty is the greater of £300 or the unpaid duty. The Commissioners may mitigate or remit any penalty and no penalty is payable if there is a reasonable excuse for the delay in presenting the instrument for stamping.[5]

An appeal against the penalty payable on late stamping lies to the First-tier Tribunal rather than the High Court.[6]

Sergeant and Sims A18.5, A19.9.

---

[1] Substituted by FA 1999, s 109.
[2] SA 1891, s 15(2).
[3] Interest is payable by the Commissioners not only on overpaid stamp duty but also on the repayment by the Commissioners of the balance of any amount lodged with them in excess of the stamp duty actually paid: FA 1999, s 110.
[4] As amended by FA 2002, s 114.
[5] SA 1891, new s 15B(4) and (5) and see The Stamp Office Manual para 3.30 et seq and the SO Customer Newsletter of February 2001 for details of their mitigation policy.
[6] SA 1891, new ss 13(4) and 13A.

Money received for duty and not appropriated

[56.31] Anyone who receives money as or for any duty is accountable for that duty to the Crown and may be sued.[1] This is an exception to the general principle that the Crown cannot sue for stamp duty. This covers not only public officials but also a solicitor who has charged his client for the duty.[2]

Sergeant and Sims A19.7.

---

[1] SDMA 1891, s 2(1).
[2] *Lord Advocate v Gordon* (1901) 8 SLT 439.

Penalties other than on late stamping

[56.32] From 1 October 1999, administrative fines were replaced by penalties. The general level of penalties (other than on late stamping) was increased and a modern collection and appeals structure was introduced.[1] These penalties relate to various administrative offences including a failure to provide information, refusal to allow the inspection of documents and fraudulent acts or omissions. In most cases the penalty is £300 but this is increased to £3,000 where fraud is involved. All penalties may be mitigated by the Commissioners. An appeal against a penalty determination lies to the First-tier Tribunal.

Perhaps the two most important penalties in practice are those of £3,000 in relation to SA 1891, s 5 (failure to disclose the facts and circumstances affecting liability to duty) and of £300 in relation to SA 1891, s 17 (registrar enrolling instrument not duly stamped).

The Treasury are empowered to make regulations under FA 1999, Sch 17, Part III applying the Taxes Management Act 1970 in relation to the collection and recovery of penalties.[2]

Sergeant and Sims A18.5.

---

[1] FA 1999, s 114 and Sch 17.
[2] The Stamp Duty (Collection and Recovery of Penalties) Regulations SI 1999/2537.

Miscellaneous

[56.33] The rights of a party acquiring property under a transaction are obviously affected by the proper stamping of any document. For this reason it has been held that a purchaser may have the instrument properly stamped and charge the amount to the vendor; this extends to all documents on which the purchaser's title depends,[1] but not to others.[2] Likewise he is entitled to repudiate the contract if the vendor refuses to stamp an unstamped instrument.[3] The onus is on the purchaser to prove improper stamping.[4] If the land is registered the title will not be registered if the documents are insufficiently stamped.[5]

These rights depend on contract; once the transaction has been completed or the purchase money has been paid, the purchaser has lost his power over the vendor.

Sergeant and Sims A19.2 [1448].

---

[1] *Whiting to Loomes* (1881) 17 Ch D 10 on specific performance see *Glessing v Green* [1975] 2 All ER 696 at 702.
[2] *Ex p Birkbeck Freehold Land Society* (1883) 24 Ch D 119.
[3] SA 1891, s 117 invalidates conditions and agreements designed to get around this rule.
[4] *Re Weir & Pitt's Contract* (1911) 55 Sol Jo 536.
[5] Land Registration Act 1925, s 14(3) and rules 94, 95; SA 1891, s 17.

Exemptions

General exemptions under FA 1999, Sch 13, Part IV

[56.34] Some instruments are exempt under FA 1999, Sch 13, Part IV; others have been removed from charge by earlier Acts. These exemptions may be from all stamp duties, a general exemption, or from a particular stamp duty—a particular exemption. A general exemption will not apply if the matter for which it is exempt is not the primary purpose of the instrument.[1] The exemptions which follow are general exemptions (FA 1999, Sch 13, Part IV):

(1) transfers of shares in the government or parliamentary stocks or funds or strips of such stocks or funds;
(2) instruments for the transfer of ships;[2]
(3) testaments, testamentary instruments and dispositions mortis causa in Scotland;
(4) renounceable letters of allotment, letters of rights or other similar instruments where the rights under the letter or other instrument are renounceable not later than six months after its issue.

Sergeant and Sims A17.3.

---

[1] See *Deddington Steamship Co Ltd v IRC* [1911] 2 KB 1001.
[2] See *Deddington Steamship Co Ltd v IRC* [1911] 2 KB 1001.

Exemptions under Finance and other Acts and Orders

[56.35] A number of other enactments grant exemptions from stamp duty. For example:[1]

(1) Land Registration Act 1925, s 130—various documents;
(2) Agricultural Credits Act 1928, s 8—agricultural charges;
(3) FA 1930, s 42 and FA 1995, s 151—conveyances, leases and agreements for lease between associated bodies corporate;[2]
(4) FA 1946, s 52 and various specific later Acts, eg Atomic Energy Authority Act 1971, s 22—nationalisation schemes;[3]
(5) FA 1947, s 57—certain documents relating to local authority loans and Treasury guaranteed stock;
(6) FA 1963, s 65(3)—forms relating to Legal Aid;
(7) FA 1964, s 23—contracts of employment and memoranda thereof;
(8) Sharing of Church Buildings Measure 1970, s 2 and Consecration of Churchyards Act 1867, s 6—certain documents relating to church lands;
(9) FA 1976, s 127 and FA 1986, s 114, Sch 23, Part IX—transfers to a stock exchange nominee and other transactions;
(10) Civil Aviation Act 1982, s 59—certain conveyances and transfers of land;
(11) F(No 2)A 1983, s 15 (as amended by FA 1985, s 82)—conveyances and transfers between local constituency associations of political parties on reorganisation of constituencies;

(12) County Courts Act 1984, s 79—agreement to treat county court decisions as final;
(13) FA 1985, s 96 and European Communities (Tax Exempt Securities) Order 1985, SI 1985/1172—the European Economic Community, the European Coal and Steel Community; the European Atomic Energy Community, the European Investment Bank and the European Bank for Reconstruction and Development;
(14) Building Societies Act 1986, s 109 and FA 1988, s 145, Sch 12, para 8—transfers of shares in a building society;
(15) Insolvency Act 1986, s 190—various documents on winding-up;
(16) Insolvency Act 1986, s 378—various instruments relating to bankruptcy;
(17) FA 1986, ss 75-77—various instruments relating to the acquisition of a corporate undertaking on reconstruction etc;[4]
(18) FA 1986, ss 80A, 80B inserted by FA 1997, s 97—transfers of stock to intermediaries;[5]
(19) FA 1986, s 80C inserted by FA 1997, s 98—instruments relating to repurchases and stock lending;[6]
(20) FA 1986, s 79—transfers of loan capital;[7]
(21) FA 1987, s 50 as amended by F(No 2)A 1987, s 99—extends stamp duty exemptions that apply to gilt edged securities and to most categories of loan stock to options to acquire or dispose of such stock;
(22) FA 1988, s 143—paired shares;[8]
(23) FA 1996, s 186—transfers of securities to members of electronic transfer systems etc;[9]
(24) FA 1997, s 96—certain transfers of property of a mutual insurance company to a company with share capital.[10]
(25) FA 2000, s 129—transfers of intellectual property.[11]
(26) FA 2001, ss 92, 92A and 92B and Sch 30—land in disadvantaged areas.[12]
(27) FA 2001, ss 92 and 94—unit trusts and open ended investment companies exemption for individual pension accounts.[13]
(28) FA 2001, s 95—employee share ownership plans.
(29) FA 2002, s 116—abolition of duty on goodwill.
(30) FA 2003, s 125 – abolition of duty except on instruments relating to stock or marketable securities and acquisitions of partnership interests and on bearer instruments.

Sergeant and Sims A17.

---

[1] The examples given are by way of illustration only and do not purport to constitute an exhaustive list. For a fuller treatment, see **Sergeant and Sims A17**. FA 2003 abolished stamp duty on land and buildings and in its place created stamp duty land tax from 1 December 2003 (see infra, Chapter 62). Stamp duties continue to apply to transactions in shares and securities, bearer instruments, transfers of land into and out of partnerships and acquisitions of a partnership interest (see infra, § 62.33).

[2] See infra, §§ **60.01** ff.

[3] Note that there is no general exemption for conveyances on the compulsory purchase of land and that, where property is purchased under a statutory power, FA

1895, s 12 specifies the document to be stamped.
4   See infra, §§ **60.06** ff.
5   See infra, § **60.10**.
6   See infra, § **60.11**.
7   See infra, § **59.05**.
8   See infra, § **59.13**.
9   See infra, § **59.04**.
10 See infra, § **59.15**.
11 See infra, § **58.16**.
12 See also the Stamp Duty (Disadvantaged Areas) (Application of Exemptions) Regulations 2003, SI 2003/1056 effective from 10 April 2003, and Statement of Practice SP1/2003.
13 See infra, § **59.21**.

Crown and departmental exemptions

[56.36] FA 1987, s 55 replaces exemptions from stamp duties granted to the Secretaries of State for the Environment and Transport with a general exemption in respect of any conveyance, transfer or lease to a Minister of the Crown or the Treasury Solicitor. Also exempt are various documents connected with the workings of government, eg instruments:

(1) relating to the business of the Social Security Administration Act 1992, s 188(1), (2) or Industrial Injuries Acts or War Pensions (War Pensions Act 1920, s 10);
(2) relating to and under the Diplomatic and other Privileges Act 1971;
(3) relating to various international banking bodies;
(4) relating to barracks and camps and other needs and facilities of visiting forces: FA 1960, s 74; or
(5) relating to a conveyance to reduce the National Debt or in satisfaction of IHT (FA 1946, s 50) or relating to National Savings.

Sergeant and Sims A17.5.

Charities

[56.37] No duty is charged on transfers on sale, voluntary dispositions and leases, made to bodies of persons or trusts established for charitable purposes only. It is thought that this exemption applies to charities formed or established under UK law only and not to non-UK charities.[1] The instrument must be adjudicated.[2] The Historic Buildings and Monuments Commission for England established under the National Heritage Act 1983 is now treated as a charity for stamp duty exemption purposes.[3] The Stamp Office has issued a detailed statement on stamp duty relating to charities and procedures in England and Scotland.[4]

Sergeant and Sims A17.5.

1   *Camille and Henry Dreyfus Foundation Inc v IRC* [1956] AC 39, [1955] 3 All ER 97, HL.

² FA 1982, s 129.
³ FA 1983, s 46(3).
⁴ See Stamp Office leaflet SO 11 (1997).

Registered social landlords

[56.38] No duty is charged on transfers or leases of land to registered social landlords. The instrument must be adjudicated.[1] No duty is charged on certain leases of dwellings by registered social landlords to individuals under arrangements with a housing authority for the provision of temporary accommodation.[2]

¹ FA 2000, s 130.
² FA 2003, ss 128–130.

Registered social landlords

12s.28J No duty is placed on a PRP or HA to lend to registered social landlords.[?] No investment must or should be made. No duty is charged on extra-leases of dwellings by registered social landlords to individuals under arrangements with a housing authority for the provision of temporary accommodation.[?]

[?] HA 2000, s10.
[?] HA 2003, ss.125-130.

57
Heads of charge

Introduction	PARA 57.01
Conveyance or transfer on sale	PARA 57.02
Miscellaneous fixed transfer duty	PARA 57.24
Lease	PARA 57.25
Other heads of charge	PARA 57.33
Abolished heads of charge	PARA 57.42

Introduction

[57.01] Stamp duty was charged on the specific categories of instruments referred to in FA 1999, Sch 13 and bearer instruments referred to in FA 1999, Sch 15. FA 2003 abolished stamp duty chargeable under FA 1999, Sch 13 except in relation to instruments relating to stock or marketable securities and acquisitions of partnership interests from 1 December 2003.[1] Stamp duty land tax applies to sales and other acquisitions of UK land from this date and the discussion in this chapter relating to land should be read on this basis.

In this chapter the provisions of the more important categories of stampable instrument are dealt with; this is followed by a chapter dealing with stamp duty in specific types of transaction. Bearer instruments are dealt with infra, § **59.08**.

---
[1] See supra, § **56.02**. FA 2003, s 125 and Sch 15, Part 3 (as amended).

Conveyance or transfer on sale

The rates and thresholds

Introduction and previous rates

[57.02] The first type of instrument mentioned in FA 1999, Sch 13 is the conveyance or transfer on sale.[1]

Since 23 March 2006, no ad valorem duty has been charged on such transfers (other than stock or marketable securities) if the consideration does not exceed £125,000 (previously £120,000 since 16 March 2005 and £60,000 since 16 March 1993).[2] Before 8 July 1997, where the consideration exceeded £60,000, transfers were charged at a uniform rate of 1% of the consideration.[3] Transfers made on or after 8 July 1997 were charged at 1.5% where the

[57.02] Heads of charge

consideration was more than £250,000 and 2% where the consideration was more than £500,000 save where executed in pursuance of a contract already made on or before 2 July 1997.[4] For transfers executed on or after 24 March 1998 (save those executed in pursuance of a contract made on or before 17 March 1998), the rates were increased to 2% where the consideration was more than £250,000 and 3% where the consideration exceeded £500,000.[5] On 9 March 1999, the Chancellor announced that the rates of duty would be further increased to 2.5% where the consideration was more than £250,000 and to 3.5% where the consideration was more than £500,000. These rates applied to transfers executed on or after 16 March 1999 save where executed in pursuance of a contract already made on or before 9 March 1999.[6]

[1] FA 2005, s 95 amending FA 1999, Sch 13, Part 1, para 4. For transfers on sale of stocks and shares and the relevant rate of duty, see infra, §§ **59.01** ff. FA 2003, Sch 20, Part 2, para 3 substituted "transfer" for the previous expression "conveyance or transfer" and related expressions.
[2] FA 1963, s 55 amended by FA 1993, s 201.
[3] FA 1963, s 55 as amended by FA 1984, s 109.
[4] FA 1963, s 55 as amended by F(No 2)A 1997, s 49.
[5] FA 1963, s 55 as amended by FA 1998, s 149.
[6] FA 1963, s 55 as amended by FA 1999, s 111.

Present rates

[57.03] On 21 March 2000, the Chancellor announced that the rates of duty would be further increased to 3.0% where the consideration is more than £250,000 and to 4.0% where the consideration is more than £500,000. These rates apply to transfers executed on or after 28 March 2000 save where executed in pursuance of a contract made on or before 21 March 2000 unless the transfer results from the exercise of an option, assignment or further contract made after 21 March 2000.[1]

In summary, the current position is that duty is charged on conveyances or transfers on sale of any property (other than stocks and shares):

(1) at nil if the consideration is £125,000 or less;
(2) at 1% if the consideration is more than £125,000 but not more than £250,000;
(3) at 3.0% if the consideration is more than £250,000 but not more than £500,000;
(4) at 4.0% if the consideration is more than £500,000.

It should be noted that instruments must contain an appropriate certificate of value in order to qualify for the nil, 1% or 3.0% rates rather than the 4.0% rate.[2]

For the current rate of duty on transfers of stocks and shares see 59.04.

In relation to instruments executed on or after 1 October 1999 the current rates of duty are set out in FA 1999, Sch 13, Part I, para 4 and FA 1963, s 55 has been repealed.

[1] FA 1999 Sch 13, Part I, para 4 as amended by FA 2000, s 114.
[2] See infra, §§ **57.15–57.16**.

Transfer

[57.04] FA 1999, Sch 13, Part I, para 1(2) defines a transfer on sale as including "every instrument, and every decree or order of a court or Commissioners, by which any property, or any estate or interest in property, is, on being sold transferred to or vested in the purchaser, or another person on behalf of or at the direction of the purchaser". If therefore the instrument transfers property[1] and does so on sale, duty will be chargeable.

This definition has to be broken down into its constituent elements but three general points should be noted. First, in conformity with general principle, a transfer of property on sale which does not take the form of an instrument cannot give rise to duty under this head—eg a sale of goods by delivery. Second, it is not necessary that any beneficial interest should pass under the instrument, although this may be reflected in the consideration, by reference to which duty is calculated. Third, it is necessary that property be transferred by the instrument; so a letter of renunciation is not a transfer of shares[2] nor is an ineffective transfer.[3] Subject to the special provisions mentioned below, the instrument must effect a transfer of property when the instrument is executed.[4] Where property of a partnership was transferred to a company it was held that there was a transfer in return for the shares in the company so that duty was due and the fact that the partners were also the shareholders was quite irrelevant.[5]

An executory agreement is not a transfer, notwithstanding that, in the case of land, the purchaser may have a beneficial interest in the land by reason of the doctrine of specific performance.[6] However, special provisions apply to contracts for the sale of certain property, including an equitable estate or interest in land (see infra, § **57.18**), and agreements for the surrender of a lease which is not effected by deed (see infra, § **57.23**), by which the agreement is charged as a transfer.

Sergeant and Sims A5.2, A5.4, A7, A8.2.

[1] eg the direction to a company to allot shares to persons nominated by the partner in *Letts v IRC* [1956] 3 All ER 588 (an assignment of a chose in action).
[2] *Re Pool Shipping Co Ltd* [1920] 1 Ch 251.
[3] *R v Ridgwell* (1827) 6 B & C 665.
[4] *Wm Cory & Son Ltd v IRC* [1965] AC 1088 at 1105, HL; revsg [1964] 3 All ER 66 at 74, CA, per Diplock LJ. See supra, § **56.11**.
[5] *John Foster & Sons Ltd v IRC* [1894] 1 QB 516.
[6] See infra, § **57.23**.

[57.05] Heads of charge

Instrument—meaning of

[57.05] The word "instrument" includes every written document.[1] A court order was also included in SA 1891, s 54 being the predecessor to FA 1999, Sch 13, Part I, para 1(2) and will doubtless continue to be capable of constituting a stampable conveyance or transfer on sale provided it satisfies the other elements of that definition, eg an order sanctioning a scheme of arrangement under Companies Act 2006, s 899[2] and a foreclosure order.[3] An order is executed when it is drawn up, passed and entered.[4]

Where a statute vests property by way of sale in a person, that person has to present a copy of the Act for stamping.[5]

Sergeant and Sims A7.

---

[1] SA 1891, s 122.
[2] *Sun Alliance Insurance Ltd v IRC* [1972] Ch 133.
[3] FA 1898, s 6.
[4] *Sun Alliance Insurance Ltd v IRC* [1972] Ch 133.
[5] FA 1895, s 12.

Property

[57.06] The term "property" is not defined.[1] It has been held that property does not include the grant of a mere permission—or licence—to do something on property remaining vested in the owners.[2] It has been said that property is something which belonged to a person exclusive of others and which can be the subject of bargain and sale to another; it followed that an assignment of goodwill was a transfer of property.[3] The status of know-how is uncertain; there are dicta for and against the view that know-how is property[4] but it can clearly be the subject of bargain and sale and can, by agreement, be enjoyed to the exclusion of others; know-how has been treated as part of goodwill for bankruptcy purposes.[5] A mere covenant to pay money is not a conveyance since no property passes under the covenant.[6]

Items which have been held to be property include goodwill,[7] copyrights,[8] debts,[9] the benefit of a contract,[10] an option[11] and a contingent interest.[12] On the other hand a right to property which in a business sense is almost certain to arise but has not yet arisen is not property.[13]

When the property to be transferred consists partly of property for which an instrument is necessary, eg shares or land, and partly of other property, duty may be saved by ensuring that the other property is not transferred by the instrument.[14]

Sergeant and Sims A2.1 [104], A4.1.

---

[1] Cf IHT supra, § **38.22**.
[2] *Conservators of the River Thames v IRC* (1886) 18 QBD 279; it was, however, liable to duty as an agreement.
[3] *Potter v IRC* (1854) 10 Exch 147 at 156 (Pollock CB).

4   eg *Phipps v Boardman* [1967] 2 AC 46 per Lord Hodson at 107 but contra Lord Upjohn at 127–8: see also *Handley-Page v Butterworth* (1935) 19 TC 328 per Lord Tomlin at 372 and Lord Radcliffe in *Musker v English Electric Co Ltd* (1964) 41 TC at 585.
5   *Re Keene* [1922] 2 Ch 475.
6   *Ashby v Comr of Succession Duties* (1942) 67 CLR 284.
7   *Eastern National Omnibus Co Ltd v IRC* [1939] 1 KB 161.
8   *Leather Cloth Co v American Leather Cloth Co* (1865) 11 HL Cas 523.
9   *Measures Bros Ltd v IRC* (1900) 82 LT 689.
10 *Western Abyssinian Mining Syndicate v IRC* (1935) 16 ATC 286.
11 *George Wimpey & Co Ltd v IRC* [1975] 2 All ER 45.
12 *Onslow v IRC* [1891] 1 QB 239; even an equitable interest—see *Grey v IRC* [1958] Ch 690 per Lord Evershed at 707.
13 *Re Duffy* [1949] Ch 28.
14 Supra, § **56.09**; cf *Stamps Comrs v Queensland Meat Export Co Ltd* [1917] AC 624.

On sale

[57.07] In order for the transfer to be "on sale" it requires a vendor, a purchaser, property sold and a price. It is satisfied if there is a contract in existence at the time of the transfer,[1] but a separate preceding contract is not required. A transfer at a time where no such contract exists, even though in contemplation of a sale to a particular person, is not a conveyance on sale but is now the subject of special legislation.[2] It is not necessary that the transfer should correspond exactly with the contract;[3] it suffices that it gives effect to that contract.

In this context, a sale ordinarily requires a price in money paid or payable.[4] However, there are certain special provisions pursuant to which transfers of property for things other than money are treated as sales and duty is charged by reference to the value of the consideration. SA 1891, ss 55, 57 provide that a transfer of property in return for stocks or securities[5] or in satisfaction of a debt[6] is to be treated as a transfer on sale. Similarly, in relation to documents executed on or after 8 December 1993, the transfer of an estate or interest in land or the grant of a lease in return for any property is treated as a transfer on sale, with the result that an exchange of land for land gives rise to two chargeable transfers.[7] However, in the absence of a special provision, a transfer of property in exchange for property will not be a sale.

It is necessary that the transfer be on sale but this does not mean an outright sale of the vendor's entire interest. So to grant a lease may be a transfer on sale[8] as may a declaration of trust.[9]

Some element of consensus is needed for a sale, although the cases do not draw a very clear line. Thus some early stamp duty cases suggest that a compulsory acquisition is a sale[10] and more recently it has been held that the compulsory transfer of shares following a take-over under the Companies Act 2006, ss 974, 981 is a sale, the consent of the statutory agent supplying the necessary consent.[11] However, the Revenue do not treat as a sale an election by a

[57.07] Heads of charge

surviving spouse of an intestate to have the matrimonial home appropriated in satisfaction of his or her claims under the intestacy legislation.

The term sale covers a multitude of transactions. Thus on the foreclosure of a mortgage the court held that there was a conveyance by sale by reason of the original agreement of mortgage.[12] Likewise there is a transfer on sale if there is an exchange of property with a cash equalisation payment,[13] or a cash payment under a deed of family arrangement.[14] In the context of a partnership it has been held to cover the transfer of a share in the partnership in return for cash[15] but not, in practice, when the new partner brings cash into the partnership and no other partner withdraws capital on that occasion. A withdrawal of capital by a partner under the terms of the partnership agreement generally operates as a partition carrying fixed duty of £5 and not as a transfer on sale.[16] Stamp duty is also avoided by taking the amount due to the retiring partner and then giving a receipt absolving the other partners from all liability.[17]

On the liability of a conveyance in contemplation of a sale see infra, § **57.17**.

Sergeant and Sims A5.1.

---

1. *Ridge Nominees v IRC* [1962] Ch 376.
2. FA 1965, s 90 nullifying *Wm Cory & Son Ltd v IRC* [1965] AC 1088; see infra, § **57.17**.
3. *A-G v Brown* (1849) 3 Exch 662.
4. *Littlewoods Mail Order Stores Ltd v IRC* [1963] AC 135 at 152 per Viscount Simonds.
5. Including a future contingent issue of stocks or marketable securities: SA 1891, s 55 as amended by FA 2000, s 126; for an attempt to depreciate the value of shares between agreement and conveyance see *Fitch Lovell Ltd v IRC* [1962] 3 All ER 685; on valuation see *Hatrick v IRC* [1963] NZLR 641. An exchange of shares has been held to come within this category of sale by reason of s 55—*J & P Coats Ltd v IRC* [1897] 2 QB 423.
6. SA 1891, s 57. The position as to conveyances in consideration of a debt is now often regulated by FA 1980, s 102.
7. See infra, § **57.19**.
8. *Littlewoods Mail Order Stores Ltd v IRC* (supra).
9. Such a declaration will, if oral, escape s 54 (see *West London Syndicate Ltd v IRC* [1898] 2 QB 507 at 520)—but may be caught by s 59; infra, § **57.18**.
10. eg *IRC v Glasgow and South Western Rly* (1887) 12 App Cas 315, but cf *Kirkness v John Hudson & Co* [1955] AC 696. See **Sergeant and Sims A6.15**.
11. *Ridge Nominees v IRC* [1962] Ch 376. See also *Sun Alliance Insurance Ltd v IRC* [1972] Ch 133 (s 306).
12. *Huntington v IRC* [1896] 1 QB 422 since affirmed by FA 1898, s 6.
13. *Littlewoods Mail Order Stores Ltd v IRC* [1963] AC 135 at 151 per Viscount Simonds.
14. *Bristol v IRC* [1901] 2 KB 336.
15. *Christie v IRC* (1866) LR 2 Exch 46; see also **Sergeant and Sims A4.9 [313]**.
16. *Macleod v IRC* (1885) 12 R (Ct of Sess) 105.
17. *Garnett v IRC* (1899) 81 LT 633.

Consideration

Generally

[57.08] The duty on a transfer on sale is charged ad valorem on the amount or value of the consideration.[1] The amount of cash consideration is straightforward. It has been held that interest on the sum due is to be ignored.[2] Foreign currency is valued at the current rate of exchange at the date of the instrument.[3] Quoted stocks and securities are meant to be valued at the average price on the relevant date but, in practice, the CGT rule is used. Unquoted shares are valued by whatever means may be appropriate.[4] If the consideration consists of unmarketable securities it is taken to be the amount due at the date of the conveyance for principal and interest.[5] Where property is given for a transfer of an estate or interest in land, duty is charged by reference to the market value of the property: infra, § **57.19**. A sum payable only on breach of a term of the agreement is not consideration.[6]

There are special provisions for reducing the consideration on the sale of houses at discount by local authorities.[7]

The consideration in respect of which an instrument is chargeable with ad valorem duty is the consideration ascertainable at the time the instrument is executed, though not necessarily appearing in the instrument itself.[8] As to consideration which is uncertain or unascertainable when the instrument is executed, or is payable subject to contingencies, see supra, §§ **56.18–56.19**. As to periodical payments, see infra, § **57.10**.

Sergeant and Sims A6.2, A6.11.

---

[1] On inclusion of an offer made to the vendors by a third party see *Central and District Properties Ltd v IRC* [1966] 2 All ER 433.
[2] *Hotung v Collector of Stamp Revenue* [1965] AC 766.
[3] SA 1891, s 6 and FA 1985, s 88.
[4] SA 1891, s 6: The IHT provisions in IHTA 1984, s 168 (supra, § **45.10**) do not apply.
[5] SA 1891, s 6.
[6] *Western United Investment Co Ltd v IRC* [1958] Ch 392.
[7] FA 1981, s 107 as amended by FA 1984, s 110.
[8] See eg *Parry v Deere* (1836) 5 Ad & El.551; *Ulverstone and Lancaster Rly Co v IRC* (1864) 2 H & C 855, 10 Jur NS 1133; *Underground Electric Railways Ltd v IRC* [1906] AC 21; and the observations of Scrutton J in *Underground Electric Railways Ltd v IRC* [1914] 3 KB 210; affd [1916] 1 KB 306.

Value added tax

[57.09] As regards VAT on supplies relating to buildings and land, the question arises as to the treatment of VAT in determining consideration for the purpose of stamp duty on a transfer of land. It affects the stamp duty on leases also. The position appears to be as follows. It is, of course, subject to the important proviso that it is essential to consider the terms of any particular instrument before determining the stamp duty position. The official view is that stamp duty is chargeable in law on any VAT element in either the sale price

[57.09] Heads of charge

of a new—or used—non-domestic building, or the rent charged therefor. In other words consideration for stamp duty is inclusive of VAT.

This view has received the sanction of the court in a Scottish case relating to the sale of land, where it was held that the consideration for the sale was the total amount which the purchaser had to pay to obtain title, including VAT.[1]

The position may be further explained thus. To take sales first, it is implicit in VATA 1994, s 19 that the consideration for the "supply" is the gross amount of the consideration inclusive of VAT. So where VAT is payable, the stamp duty charge falls on the total consideration. This is the position already with sales of businesses or business assets subject to VAT. It follows that the effect of these changes on non-domestic construction, sales of non-domestic buildings is that they fall also into this category.

As to rent, there are two separate situations to be considered and distinguished.

The first is where the VAT actually forms part of the rental consideration. This would be the case where the rent is reserved by reference to a net amount plus VAT, producing a gross rental figure, on which it seems that stamp duty is chargeable. Alternatively, where the VAT does not form part of the rent, it will be regarded as a separate item of consideration—but still within the charge to stamp duty. The landlord is able to add VAT to the rent (or any increase in the rate of VAT) unless the terms of the lease or tenancy specifically prevent him from passing on VAT to the lessee or tenant. The Revenue have issued a detailed statement of practice on this difficult subject.[2] In March 1996, the Stamp Office issued an information leaflet SO12 "Stamp Duty on Commercial Leases and Agreements for Leases" which further sets out its view as to the circumstances in which duty will be calculated by reference to rent which includes VAT which is or may be payable under a lease.

Sergeant and Sims A6.9, Division E.

[1] *Glenrothes Development Corpn v IRC* [1994] STC 74.
[2] See statement of practice SP 11/91, set out at **Sergeant and Sims Division E.** Following the publication of this statement, the Law Society issued a statement of its Revenue Law Committee on 4 March 1992, see **Sergeant and Sims Division E.** The Faculty of Taxation (the Institute of Chartered Accountants) has also issued a guidance note, Tax 19/92 dated 25 November 1992.

Periodical payments as consideration

[57.10] When the consideration consists of periodical payments, SA 1891, s 56 provides a special set of rules. A covenant to pay a balance of purchase money in instalments comes within these rules.[1]

(1) where there is a definite period of payment not exceeding 20 years so that the total can be ascertained, that total is the consideration;
(2) where the period is definite but will exceed 20 years, or is in perpetuity or indefinite (but not terminable with life) the total payable during the next 20 years is taken;[2]

(3) where the period is for life or lives, the amount payable for the next 12 years is taken.

It appears that a period for a certain number of years but terminable on earlier events is to be treated as being for the definite period of that number of years[3] with the result that payments for the life of A will come within rule 3 but payments for 20 years or until A dies whichever shall first happen will come within rule 1. It has also been held that money is payable periodically even though payments may be contingent.[4] In determining the amount of the consideration, the contingency principle must be borne in mind.[5] It is the amount of consideration calculated under these rules which is relevant for determining whether the reduced rates apply.

It has been held that where a sum of money only becomes due at a particular time if the contract is broken, one should ignore that possibility.[6] So when the sums were payable in 125 annual instalments but the sums remaining would become due immediately in the event of default it was held that the chargeable amount of the consideration was the total of the first 20 scheduled payments—rule 2 being applied.

Sergeant and Sims A6.4.

[1] *Limmer Asphalte Paving Co Ltd v IRC* (1872) LR 7 Exch 211.
[2] *Blendett v IRC, Quietlece v IRC* [1984] STC 95, CA.
[3] *Earl Mount Edgecumbe v IRC* [1911] 2 KB 24.
[4] *Underground Electric Railways Ltd v IRC* [1906] AC 21; this is similar to the element of recurrence in Schedule D, Case III, § **11.24**.
[5] See supra, § **56.18–56.19**.
[6] *Western United Investment Co Ltd v IRC* [1958] Ch 392.

Conveyances and transfers of property subject to a debt

SA 1891, s 57

[57.11] Where property is conveyed or transferred subject to a debt (eg a house or flat on which there is a mortgage), the stamp duty payable on the sale reflects any part of the debt taken over by the transferee. If there is no cash element, the debt taken over will account for the whole of the chargeable consideration on which the duty is calculated.

Since the abolition of the duty on voluntary dispositions in 1985 there has been some uncertainty about the stamp duty chargeable on conveyances etc, subject to a debt where *no* chargeable consideration (eg money or stock) unrelated to the debt is given by the transferee.[1] A statement of practice[2] has been issued which sets out the Revenue's view of the correct stamp duty treatment of such conveyances. The statement relates to conveyances or transfers where:

(1) the transferee takes over liability for the whole or part of the debt; *and*
(2) there is no other consideration for the transfer (in particular, no monetary payment).

Where a purchaser agrees to pay the vendor's legal costs, the rule that it is the amount of the debt that is taken into account—not its value (so a bad debt is

[57.11] Heads of charge

included at face value)[3] gave rise to uncertainty. The position, however, is now largely regulated by FA 1980, s 102. Where property is conveyed wholly or in part in consideration of a debt due to the transferee the duty chargeable is now limited by reference to the value of the property conveyed if this is less than the amount of the debt. However, that rule is somewhat limited in its application; see further **Sergeant and Sims A6.12**.

Not all liabilities increase the chargeable value. On an assignment of a lease one does not take into account the liability of the assignee to pay the rent. This is because the liability to pay rent is inherent in the property, like the liability to pay a call on shares.[4] Likewise the future interest element on an assignment of a mortgage is to be ignored.

Sergeant and Sims A6.12, Division E.

---

[1] Where chargeable consideration unrelated to a debt *is* given by the transferee, SA 1891, s 57 renders the conveyance liable to ad valorem duty on the aggregate of that consideration and the debt whether the transferee assumes liability for the debt or not: *IRC v Liquidators of City of Glasgow Bank* (1881) 8 R 389, 18 SLR 242.
[2] Statement of practice SP 6/90, see **Sergeant and Sims Division E**.
[3] *IRC v North British Rly Co* (1901) 4 F (Ct of Sess) 27 but in *Huntington v IRC* [1896] 1 QB 422, it was held that the consideration is not to exceed the value of the property.
[4] *Swayne v IRC* [1900] 1 QB 172.

Apportionment of consideration

[57.12] If there are separate conveyances for separate parts of the property, the consideration is to be apportioned among the conveyances as the parties may see fit.[1] When the different parts go to different people, as where A buys for A, B and C, the consideration must be specified in each conveyance.[2] For instruments executed on or after 1 December 2003 where part of the property consists of stock or marketable securities, the consideration is apportioned on a just and reasonable basis rather than as the parties think fit. Where different parts go to different people and part of the property consists of stock or marketable securities and the transferees are connected with one another the consideration is to be apportioned on a just and reasonable basis.[3]

Where several instruments are required to complete the purchaser's title, only the principal instrument is chargeable with ad valorem duty, the others bear such duty as may be appropriate, eg as miscellaneous transfers, but not so as to exceed the duty on the principal instrument.[4] It is for the parties to determine which is to be the principal instrument.[5]

Sergeant and Sims A6.3, A6.4.

---

[1] SA 1891, s 58(1).
[2] SA 1891, s 58(2).
[3] FA 2003, Sch 20, Part 1. Whether the transferees are connected with one another is determined in accordance with ICTA 1988, s 839.

[4] SA 1891, s 58(3).
[5] SA 1891, s 61.

Sub-sales

[57.13] A common problem of sub-sale is dealt with by SA 1891, s 58 which, as amended by FA 1984, s 112, provides that in specified circumstances ad valorem duty need not be paid twice. So where P has contracted to purchase property from V but has not yet obtained a conveyance and he contracts to sell it to R, the conveyance from V to R is charged on the consideration due from R to P, not that due from P to V;[1] originally this applied whether the R-P consideration was more or less than the P–V consideration but now if the sub-sale was agreed after 19 March 1984 this does not apply when the consideration for the sub-sale is less than the value of the property immediately before the sub-sale was agreed (except where the sub-sale falls within FA 1981, s 107 and FA 1984, s 110—certain sales at a discount). For this relief to operate P must not have taken a conveyance from V. Further the property conveyed to R must be the property which P had agreed to purchase from V. It was observed in *Fitch-Lovell v IRC*,[2] that the point is, in a sense, of a metaphysical character, rather like the familiar dilemma whether a river is still the same river at different points, it was concluded that where the agreement related to shares the rights of which had changed before the transfer to R, the relief in s 58(4) should not apply notwithstanding the fact that both contract and transfer related to ordinary shares in the company. The same case seems to exclude the relief under s 58(4) where P's contract to sell to R precedes the contract to buy from V.

In *Keston v IRC* [2004] EWHC 59 (Ch); [2004] STC 902, it was held that a conveyance by a vendor to a sub-purchaser is, in the absence of sub-sale relief, chargeable to stamp duty by reference to both the consideration moving from the purchaser to vendor and from sub-purchaser to purchaser. It was also held that because in that case the sub-sale consideration has been structured so that only £10,000 of the sub-sale consideration moving from the sub-purchaser was chargeable with stamp duty and this was less that the £1.3m value of the property at the date of the sub-sale, sub-sale relief did not apply.

When the sub-sale is to several persons the duty is on the value of the consideration moving from the sub-purchasers subject to exceptions.[3] When there is a sub-sale of part of the property to R, the remainder being transferred to P, *Maples v IRC*[4] decides that the duty is charged on the consideration moving from R together with an apportioned part of consideration from P to V; it is *not* charged on the whole of the consideration from P to V less the sum recouped from R.

When it is intended to utilise sub-sale relief in relation to contracts for the sale of an interest in UK land where the consideration exceeds £10m, the effect of FA 2002, s 115 and Sch 36 should be considered. This section imposes a stamp duty charge on the contract unless a conveyance in conformity with the contract is presented for stamping within 90 days of the contract or such longer period as IR Stamp Taxes think is reasonable in the circumstances. The

[57.13] Heads of charge

scheme of sub-sale relief described above is effectively reversed in the case of a conveyance where there has been a prior contract for the sale of UK land where the consideration exceeds £10m (approximately £8.5m plus VAT where VAT could be chargeable) and ad valorem duty is paid on the contract under s 115 (see infra, § **57.18**). In such a case duty on the sub-sale contract or subsequent sub-sale contracts is chargeable only in respect of the amount (if any) by which the chargeable consideration for the sub-sale exceeds that on the earlier sub-sale or, if there has been more than one sale, on the highest amount of chargeable consideration on which duty has been paid. Where there are sub-sales of part an appropriate proportion determined on a just and reasonable basis is taken for this purpose.[5]

The sub-sale treatment of the conveyance itself is reversed in the sense that with duty having now been paid on the original sale contract (and in respect of any intermediate sub-sale contracts, on any additional consideration), the conveyance from the original seller to a sub-purchaser will be chargeable with duty only to the extent that the duty that would have been chargeable on it exceeds the duty already paid on the original sale contract and on any intervening sub-sale contracts.[6] There is provision for repayment of duty to the extent that the duty that would have been chargeable on the conveyance would be less than the duty paid on the original sale and any intervening sub-sales.[7]

Sergeant and Sims A5.6, A7.1.

[1] SA 1891, s 58(4) as amended by FA 1984, s 112(1); but distinguish the case when duty has been charged on the V–P contract as an agreement to sell—infra, § **57.18**.
[2] [1962] 1 WLR 1325 at 1341–1344. There the change flowed from the creation of a class of preferred shareholders which effectively took all the distributable profit. The device of omitting to insert the transferee's name is now unlawful; FA 1963, s 67.
[3] SA 1891, s 58(5) as amended by FA 1984, s 112(1).
[4] [1914] 3 KB 303.
[5] FA 2002, s 115 and Sch 36, para 3 and see Stamp Taxes Customer Newsletter "Contracts for the Sale of an Estate or Interest in Land—Section 115 and Schedule 36 Finance Act 2002", July 2002.
[6] FA 2002, Sch 36, para 5.
[7] FA 2002, Sch 36, para 6.

Sale of an annuity

[57.14] The creation of an annuity by grant or conveyance in return for consideration in money or shares will attract duty as a transfer on sale. The narrow scope of this rule is extended by SA 1891, s 60 which provides that "where upon the sale of an annuity or other right not before in existence, such annuity or other right is not created by actual grant or conveyance, but is only secured by bond, warrant of attorney, covenant, contract or otherwise, the bond or other instrument, or some one of such instruments, if there be more than one, is to be charged with the same duty as an actual grant or conveyance on sale . . .".

For this rule to apply there must be a sale (as to which, see supra, § **57.07**). The words "other right not before in existence" are vague but it has been held that the right must be one the sale of which can be completed by grant or conveyance.[1]

Sergeant and Sims A4.2 [233].

---

[1] See Collins LJ in *Great Northern Rly v IRC* [1901] 1 KB 416 at 426.

Certificate of value

[57.15] For transfers of property other than stock or marketable securities where the consideration does not exceed £125,000 the duty is nil. The nil rate of duty operates only if the instrument is certified as being for a consideration not exceeding the sum of £125,000.[1] Certification requires that the instruments contain a statement certifying that the transaction does not form part of a larger transaction or series of transactions in respect of which the amount or value, or aggregate amount or value of the consideration exceeds the relevant figure. The provision against abuse of this rule is SA 1891, s 5; supra, § **56.32**.[2]

Freedom from ad valorem duty also ensures freedom from miscellaneous transfer duty.[3]

Similar certificates certifying that the consideration does not exceed £250,000 or £500,000 are required for the 3% and 4% rates respectively to operate.

Transfers of stock or marketable securities executed on or after 13 March 2008 where the amount or value of the consideration does not exceed £1,000 are not chargeable with duty if they are certified at £1,000.[4]

Sergeant and Sims A2.3.

---

[1] FA 1999, Sch 13, Part I, para 6; the certification should be in the instrument although the Revenue allow this to be added later.
[2] See Stamp Taxes Bulletin Issue 3, October 2002 for the view of IR Stamp Taxes on the use of certain options to reduce the stamp duty payable.
[3] *A-G v Lamplough* (1878) 3 Ex D 214.
[4] FA 1999, Sch 13, Part 1, para 1(3A).

One transaction

[57.16] The question whether the transaction forms part of a larger transaction is a complicated one and one on which there is little guidance from the cases. Some guidelines based on decisions have been suggested:[1]

(1) Purchases between the same parties at public auctions in separate lots are not one transaction;[2] the reasoning that there is no contractual linkage may apply equally to purchases by private treaty but the Revenue would require strong evidence.
(2) A simultaneous related transaction which is not a sale, may be disregarded.[3]

(3) Transactions between different and non-associated persons should be disregarded even if part of one transaction.
(4) However, all property transferred by sale should be included, whether or not by the instrument, unless statute directs otherwise. So a sum paid for fixtures should be included,[4] but on the sale of a business, goods, wares and merchandise not actually conveyed by the instrument may be omitted.[5] Intellectual property and goodwill which is exempt from stamp duty is disregarded,[6] as is property situated in a disadvantaged area.[7]
(5) A succession of sales governed by a single master agreement constitutes a series of transactions and so each forms part of a larger transaction.

[1] Sergeant and Sims A2.3.
[2] A-G v Cohen [1937] 1 KB 478 and [1937] 1 KB 478.
[3] Kimbers & Co v IRC [1937] 1 KB 132 and Paul v Paul 1936 SC 443.
[4] See further infra, § **58.02**.
[5] Because FA 1999, Sch 13, Part I, para 6(2) says so.
[6] FA 2000, Sch 34, para 4, infra, § **58.16** and FA 2002, Sch 37 para 3.
[7] FA 2001, Sch 30, para 3.

Conveyance or transfer in contemplation of a sale

[57.17] A conveyance or transfer in contemplation of a sale is charged as if it were on a sale (FA 1965, s 90 as amended by FA 1985, s 82, Sch 27, Part IX), the consideration being the value of the property. It must be submitted for adjudication.[1]

The valuation of the property should ignore any power (in any person) to cause the property to reinvest in the seller or in any person on his behalf; the same applies to forfeitable annuities and life or other interests reserved out of the property.[2]

If the contemplated sale does not materialise and the property is transferred back to the transferor (or his successor in title on death or bankruptcy) and a claim is submitted within two years of the transfer, the duty will be repaid. If the price on the sale is less than that assessed on the original transfer, excess duty is repaid.

Sergeant and Sims A5.4.

[1] FA 1965, s 90(3) see Stamp Taxes Customer Newsletter "Split Title Schemes and Section 90 FA 1965", July 2002 explaining the views of IR Stamp Taxes on the application of this provision to transfers to nominees where there is an intention to sell the property.
[2] FA 1965, s 90(5).

Agreements for sale

[57.18] A contract or agreement for the sale of:

(1)　　any equitable interest in any property; or
(2)　　any estate or interest in property other than:
　　　(a)　　land;[1]
　　　(b)　　foreign property;
　　　(c)　　goods,[2] wares or merchandise;
　　　(d)　　stock or marketable securities; or
　　　(e)　　ships;

is charged with the same ad valorem duty as if it were an actual conveyance on sale under FA 1999, Sch 13, Part I, para 7(1). FA 2003 abolished stamp duty on land and buildings from 1 December 2003 (see infra, Chapter 62). However, stamp duties continue to apply to transactions in shares and securities, bearer instruments and acquisitions of an interest in a partnership (see infra, § **62.33**). This provision applies only if the agreement is written or under seal; oral contracts are outside its scope. If an instrument in fact conveys an equitable interest on its execution, duty will be payable under FA 1999, Sch 13, Part I, para 1 rather than under para 7(1) as a conveyance on sale of an equitable interest.[3]

This provision was designed to counter *IRC v Angus*[4] where it was held that an agreement for the sale of goodwill, although specifically enforceable in equity, was not a conveyance on sale, a contract to convey being different from a conveyance. The provision provides that the subsequent conveyance shall bear no duty although a sub-sale gives rise to ad valorem duty if the consideration is greater than that under the contract;[5] the conveyance carries a stamp denoting the duty paid on the agreement.[6] Any apportionment of consideration in the event of sub-sale must be bona fide.[7]

An example of the section in operation is an agreement to hold property on trust for another in return for money or stock.[8] Where the contract was to transfer a legal estate but with an option in the vendor to declare himself a trustee for the purchaser instead it was held that this was not an agreement for the sale of an equitable interest.[9] It has also been held that an option to buy is a mere offer to sell and so not an agreement for sale under FA 1999, Sch 13, Part I, para 7(1); likewise, the acquisition of an option is not the same as an agreement for the sale of an equitable interest but rather a transfer of the option and so a transfer of property which, if for consideration, is a transfer on sale.[10] An agreement for the sale of an estate or interest in UK land where the amount or value of the consideration exceeds £10m (approximately £8.5m plus VAT where VAT has or could be charged) becomes chargeable with ad valorem duty payable by the purchaser unless a conveyance conforming to the agreement is presented to IR Stamp Taxes within 90 days of the execution of the agreement or such longer period as IR Stamp Taxes think is reasonable in the circumstances. The rules as to inadmissibility of unstamped instruments and interest and penalties for late stamping do not apply until after the end of the 90-day period (or such longer period as has been allowed). If the agreement is later rescinded or not substantially performed any duty paid is repayable.[11] A subsequent conveyance to the purchaser is only chargeable with duty to the

[57.18] Heads of charge

extent that the ad valorem duty that would be chargeable on it exceeds the duty paid on the agreement. If the ad valorem duty on the conveyance turns out to be less than the duty on the agreement the difference is repayable to the person who paid the duty on the sale agreement.[12] It seems that duty paid on the agreement is available as a credit against duty on the conveyance but the reverse is not true. For the position regarding sub-sales see supra, § 57.13.

Sergeant and Sims A4.2, A8.

---

[1] But note the effect of FA 2002, s 115 in relation to land contracts for more than £10m, see above and supra, § 57.13.
[2] Electrical energy is deemed to be goods (Electricity Act 1989, s 4(4)); in Northern Ireland, see Electricity (Northern Ireland Consequential Amendments) Order 1992, SI 1992/232, *Simon's Tax Intelligence* 1992, p 349.
[3] *Peter Bone Ltd v IRC* [1995] STC 921.
[4] (1889) 23 QBD 579.
[5] FA 1999, Sch 13, Part I, para 7(3); there is no reduction if the consideration on the sub-sale is less.
[6] FA 1999, Sch 13, Part I, para 7(4).
[7] *West London Syndicate v IRC* [1898] 2 QB 507 at 526.
[8] *Chesterfield Brewery Co v IRC* [1899] 2 QB 7 at 12 per Wills J: it was also held that this was a conveyance on sale.
[9] [1898] 2 QB 507 at 512 but it was an agreement for the sale of property other than land and so chargeable under the section.
[10] *Wm Cory & Son Ltd v IRC* [1965] AC 1088 at 1107–1110.
[11] FA 2002, s 115.
[12] FA 2002, Sch 36, paras 5 and 6.

Exchanges deemed to be sales

[57.19] Ad valorem transfer on sale duty has been extended to:

(1) the transfer of one interest in land or the grant of a lease in exchange for another transfer or grant; and
(2) the transfer of land or the grant of a lease where the consideration for the transfer consists of or includes other property.[1]

This provision applies to documents executed on or after 8 December 1993, unless the document implements a contract made before 30 November 1993. Where the consideration for the transfer of an estate or interest in land or the grant of any lease includes any property, conveyance on sale duty is chargeable by reference to the market value of the property immediately before the instrument was executed. The head of charge "Exchange or Excambion" in SA 1891, Sch 1 has been repealed and so has s 73 of that Act. Exchanges of land are therefore treated as two conveyances on sale, both of which are chargeable with ad valorem duty calculated by reference to the market value of the other property. Any property received for land is now chargeable consideration.

The provision is intended to place exchanges involving land and leases on the same basis as sales for stamp duty purposes.[2] The manner in which the provision operates in practice has been the subject of statements by the Government in the parliamentary debates on the 1994 Finance Bill which introduced it[3] and an article in the Inland Revenue Tax Bulletin in August 1995[4] (see infra, § **57.20**).

Sergeant and Sims A6.11.

---

[1] FA 1994, s 241.
[2] HC Official Report, 17 March 1994, cols 713, 718 set out in **Sergeant and Sims** Division E.
[3] HC Official Report, 17 March 1994, cols 709ff, set out in **Sergeant and Sims** Division E.
[4] Set out in **Sergeant and Sims Division E**.

Transactions structured as sales

[57.20] Where an interest in land is transferred or a lease is granted in return for the transfer or grant of a similar interest, the question of whether both instruments are liable to ad valorem duty will depend on the form of the transaction.[1]

Where the transaction is structured as an exchange, eg the contract states that property A is given in exchange for property B, both transfers are liable to ad valorem duty on the value of the other property. Note: the examples below assume that the nil rate threshold has remained at £60,000.

EXAMPLE 1
Property A valued at £100,000 is exchanged for property B of the same value. Ad valorem duty of 1%, ie £1,000, is chargeable on both transfers of property A and property B. The total stamp duty payable in respect of the transaction is therefore £2,000.

EXAMPLE 2
Property A valued at £100,000 is exchanged for property B valued at £80,000 plus £20,000 to be paid as equality money. Ad valorem duty of 1%, ie £1,000 is chargeable on the transfer of property A and, provided that a notional part of the value of property A (ie £80,000) is attributed to the transfer of property B or it is clear from the contract that the cheaper property is to be transferred for the more expensive property less the equality money, ad valorem duty of 1%, ie £800, is chargeable on the transfer of property B. The total stamp duty payable in respect of the transaction is therefore £1,800.

EXAMPLE 3
Property A valued at £100,000 is exchanged for more than one property, eg property B and property C, each valued at £50,000. Ad valorem duty of 1%, ie £500 will be chargeable on each of the transfers of property B and property C, provided that a notional part of the value of property A (ie £50,000) is attributed to each transfer.

However, where the transaction is structured as a sale, eg the contract states that property is sold to the purchaser for a price which may be satisfied in part by the transfer of property B,[2] the transfer of property A will be chargeable with ad valorem duty calculated on the value of property B plus any other chargeable consideration (eg money or shares) and the transfer of property B will be chargeable only with fixed duty of £5 as a conveyance of any other kind. The stamp duty threshold of £60,000 is not relevant to the transfer of property B as it is not a conveyance on sale.

[57.20] Heads of charge

EXAMPLE 4

Property A is sold for a price of £100,000 which may be satisfied by the transfer of property B valued at £80,000 plus £20,000 to be paid in cash. Ad valorem duty of 1%, ie £1,000, is chargeable on the transfer of property A and the transfer of property B is chargeable with fixed duty of £5, The total stamp duty payable in respect of the transaction is therefore £1,005.

Anti-avoidance provisions were enacted in FA 2000 to counter attempts to exploit the position illustrated in Example 4 by substituting property which is exempt from stamp duty as Property A in that example, such as a government gilt security, with the objective of achieving a sale of Property B without attracting ad valorem stamp duty. The instrument transferring Property B is deemed to be a sale and ad valorem duty is chargeable accordingly subject to a reduction for any ad valorem duty chargeable on the other property but only to the extent that it consists of land.[3]

Separate anti-avoidance provisions were also enacted in FA 2000 in relation to the transfer of land to a company connected with the transferor or where the consideration includes an issue of shares in a company connected with the transferor.[4] Although the drafting of these provisions is problematic their broad effect is to deem such a transfer to be a sale and to charge ad valorem stamp duty on the market value but reduced by any actual consideration which does not consist of property. These provisions only apply if they lead to a greater amount of stamp duty than would otherwise arise and specifically exclude:

(1) transfers to or from a nominee or bare trustee;
(2) transfers to or from a settlement which could fall to be exempt under category F of the Stamp Duty (Exempt Instruments) Regulations 1987;
(3) transfers to an independent corporate trustee; and
(4) transfers forming part of a distribution including distribution on liquidation where the asset was acquired by the company by virtue of a duly stamped instrument.

Sergeant and Sims A6.11, A6.13.

---

[1] See the Inland Revenue Tax Bulletin of August 1995 and the parliamentary statements referred to supra, § **57.19**. These now need to be read subject to FA 2000, ss 118 to 121 as mentioned below.
[2] It would seem that a cash element that is not merely nominal is necessary if a transaction is to be structured as a sale: *Connell Estate Agents v Begej* [1993] 2 EGLR 35 at 38 per Hirst LJ.
[3] FA 2000, s 118.
[4] FA 2000, ss 119 to 121.

Thresholds and certification

[57.21] The stamp duty threshold and the thresholds for the 1% and 3.0% rates apply independently to each side of the exchange. Each side of the exchange is considered to be a separate transaction for the purpose of a certificate of value under FA 1999, Sch 13, Part I, para 6 (see supra, §§ **57.15–57.16**), so that, where property A is exchanged for properties B and C, the threshold is applied to the transfer of property A without regard to the transfers of properties B and C, but the transfers of properties B and C are each regarded as part of a larger transaction and stamp duty is chargeable if the total consideration for both exceeds £60,000.

EXAMPLE 1

Property A valued at £60,000 is exchanged for property B valued at £40,000: a certificate that the consideration does not exceed £60,000 may be made for each transfer.

EXAMPLE 2

Property A valued at £70,000 is exchanged for property B valued at £50,000 plus property C valued at £20,000: no certificate may be made in respect of any of the transfers.

Sub-sales

[57.22] SA 1891, s 58(4) applies to a sub-sale following an exchange in the same way as it applies following a sale for a price expressed in money (as to which, see supra, § 57.13).

Agreements to surrender leases

[57.23] The surrender of a lease which is effected by deed may be chargeable as a conveyance on sale where there is chargeable consideration for the surrender. However, a lease may be surrendered by operation of law where the actions of the parties demonstrate unequivocally that the lease has come to an end (eg where the lessee ceases to occupy the premises and delivers the keys and the lease to the landlord). It was therefore possible to avoid conveyance on sale duty on the surrender by providing in the agreement for surrender that the parties would engage in conduct which amounted to the surrender of the lease by operation of law on the date of completion, thereby avoiding the need for a deed. The agreement was not chargeable as no property was transferred or vested upon its execution. This method could also be used to minimise the duty payable on a sale of land (company A would grant a long lease to its subsidiary, B; A would then agree to sell its freehold reversion to the purchaser for a nominal sum; at the same time company B would agree to surrender its lease by operation of law to the purchaser for an amount representing the market value of the freehold—the only chargeable instrument created was the transfer of the land from company A which attracted a small amount of duty calculated solely on the nominal sum paid for the freehold reversion).

To counter this practice, it is provided that where, pursuant to an agreement, any lease is surrendered otherwise than by deed, the agreement shall be treated as if it were a deed effecting the surrender.[1] This provision applies to agreements to surrender leases made after 7 December 1993. The views of the Stamp Office in respects of what will be regarded as an "agreement" have been published.[2]

This provision only caught written agreements and in practice it was relatively easy to avoid such an agreement. As a result it is now provided that any document evidencing the lease surrender is to be treated as if it were a deed effecting the surrender. Such documents are deemed to include an application to HM Land Registry for making or removing an entry relating to the lease and a statutory declaration made under the Land Registration Rules 1925 is specifically chargeable with stamp duty despite rule 316(1) thereof.[3]

[57.23] Heads of charge

Sergeant and Sims A9.7, Division E [5547].

[1] FA 1994, s 243. As to what constitutes an "agreement" in this context, cf *Fleetwood-Hesketh v IRC* [1936] 1 KB 351 and note the requirements of the Law of Property (Miscellaneous Provisions) Act 1989, s 2 in relation to dispositions of land.
[2] In an article in the August 1995 Inland Revenue Tax Bulletin, see **Sergeant and Sims** Division E [5547].
[3] FA 2000, s 128.

Miscellaneous fixed transfer duty

[57.24] A fixed stamp duty of £5 is charged on a "transfer of property otherwise than on sale". A voluntary disposition would now be chargeable under this head unless appropriately certified as exempt (see supra, § **56.05**).

The exclusion of sales is because ad valorem duty is charged on such transfers by other provisions; mortgage duty and voluntary disposition duty were also separate charges until their abolition in 1971 and 1985 respectively. Although sale is excluded, the structure of this charge includes the requirements of an instrument and a transfer of property like the sale charge; so, as with that charge, there is no need for a transfer of any beneficial interest in the property.

Examples are numerous.[1] A conveyance in consideration of service is not a sale, since there is no price in money and nothing which is to be treated as equivalent to a money price by virtue of any special provision (as to which see supra § **57.07**). However, many instruments which would have attracted the fixed duty under this charge are now exempt if appropriately certified (see supra, § **56.05**). A conveyance to a residuary legatee, to a beneficiary under a settlement or under the exercise of a power of advancement or by a liquidator to a shareholder in the course of a winding-up[2] are all examples of such.

Sergeant and Sims A2.1.

[1] On construction see the observations of Lord Evershed in *Littlewoods Mail Order Stores Ltd v IRC* [1961] Ch 597 at 624. See also *GHR Co Ltd v IRC* [1943] KB 303.
[2] *Henty & Constable (Brewers) Ltd v IRC* [1961] 3 All ER 1146.

Lease

The charge

[57.25] The principal charge under the heading "Lease" in Part II of Sch 13 to FA 1999 is in para 12 which charges stamp duty when the lease is for a definite term of one year or more or for any indefinite term. FA 2003 abolished stamp duty on land and buildings including lease duty from 1 December 2003 (see infra, Chapter 62). The charge to lease duty is ad valorem duty on the rent or the premium or both if both are paid. As to what constitutes rent or premium, see infra, §§ 57.28–57.29. The lease must be of lands, tenements or heritable subjects so that leases of chattels are excluded. The word lease, which is not defined, is construed as excluding licences so a licence of real property is not chargeable.[1] A written acknowledgement of an existing lease is not a lease[2] but an instrument withdrawing a valid notice to determine a lease is treated as a new lease.[3]

An agreement for lease is chargeable as if it were the actual lease: see infra, § 57.30. However, an agreement for lease executed on or after 6 May 1994 may be presented for stamping with the lease without incurring interest and a penalty;[4] supra, § **56.18**.

The charge arises on the grant of a lease; the assignment or surrender of a lease will give rise to conveyance on sale duty if in return for chargeable consideration. As to the surrender of a lease, see supra, § **57.23**.

The other heads of charge are:

(11) In the case of a lease for a definite term less than a year the duty is as follows—

1. Lease of furnished dwelling house or apartments where the rent for the term exceeds £5,000	£5
2. Lease of any lands, tenements or heritable subjects not as described above	The same duty as for a lease for a year at the rent reserved for the definite term

(13) Stamp duty of £5 is chargeable on a lease not within paragraph 11 or 12 above.

The £5,000 threshold in 1. above was increased from £500 for leases executed on or after 28 March 2000 by FA 2000, s 115.

Duty on the lease of a furnished dwelling-house when the rent is £5,000 or less, and so outside (11), will be nil because para 12(3)1 of Sch 13, Part II as applied by para 11.2 so provides.

The fixed £5 charge under para 13 is confined to leases of land although this is not explicitly stated. Strictly speaking, the word "lease" is not apt to describe the hire of chattels.

For some purposes of the Stamp Act a lease may be treated as a conveyance, eg for the purpose of deciding in connection with FA 1930, s 42 (as amended) (see infra, § **60.01**) whether an interest was previously conveyed or transferred by an unassociated body corporate; see *IRC v Littlewoods Mail Order Stores Ltd* [1962] 2 All ER 279. Although the Law of Property Act 1925, s 72(3) and (4) provides that a person may convey land to or vest land in himself, or that two or more persons may convey property vested in them to any one or more of themselves, and although under s 205(1)(ii), "conveyance" includes a lease, it was held by the House of Lords in *Rye v Rye* [1962] 1 All ER 146 that a person cannot grant a lease of property to himself. It has been held, however, that in English law a lease can be granted to a nominee.[5]

In certain cases of shared ownership transactions the lease is chargeable not under the head "Lease" but under the head "Conveyance or transfer on sale".[6]

[57.25] Heads of charge

As to stamping conveyances in connection with rent to mortgage schemes, see FA 1993, s 109, infra, § **57.31**. As to the interaction of VAT and stamp duty following the changes to VAT on supplies relating to buildings and land under FA 1989, s 18, Sch 3 see supra, § **57.09**.

Sergeant and Sims A9.2.

---

1 See the test in *Addiscombe Garden Estates Ltd v Crabbe* [1958] 1 QB 513 (CA).
2 *Eagleton v Gutteridge* (1843) 11 M & W 465.
3 *Freeman v Evans* [1922] 1 Ch 36, CA.
4 FA 1999, Sch 12, para 4 substituting new FA 1994, s 240(2).
5 *Ingram v IRC* [1999] STC 37, HL, holding that the reasoning of the Court of Session in *Kildrummy (Jersey) Ltd v IRC* [1990] STC 657 was not applicable in England because a trustee in English law is not an agent for his beneficiary. As to proprietors pro indivisio in Scotland, see *Bell's Executors v IRC* 1987 SLT 625.
6 FA 1980, s 97.

Leases—duration and commencement

[57.26] The question of duration is important for determining both the head of charge and the amount of duty. In deciding whether a lease is for a definite term statute provides that a lease for a fixed term and thereafter until determined should be treated as a lease for a definite term equal to the fixed term together with such further period as must elapse before the earliest date at which the lease can be determined.[1]

A lease for a certain period but terminable on some event is not within this rule but, it has been held, is to be treated as a definite term for the certain period.[2] As a lease for an indefinite term, eg until the end of the war,[3] is void, it appears that the phrase "indefinite term" refers to periodic tenancies like weekly and monthly tenancies and tenancies at will. A lease for x years with an option to renew for y years is treated as a lease for x years and not one for x + y years.[4]

A lease expressed to commence on a date prior to the instrument is regarded as starting on the date of execution.[5]

Sergeant and Sims A9.4.

---

1 FA 1999, Sch 13, Part II, para 15.
2 *Earl Mount Edgecumbe v IRC* [1911] 2 KB 24.
3 *Lace v Chandler* [1944] KB 368.
4 *Hand v Hall* (1877) 2 Ex D 355.
5 (1963) 60 *Law Society's Gazette* pp 175, 176.

Duty charged on rent

[57.27] The duty is charged ad valorem on the rent charged. The table reproduced in the table of rates and reliefs, supra, shows that the rate increases with the length of the lease and has an initial sliding scale.[1] (As to the impact of VAT see supra, § **57.09**.)

It will be seen from that that the rate of duty rises sharply with the duration of the lease so that a lease of 60 years will carry duty of 12% of the rent, whereas one of 30 years will carry duty of only 2%. One method of reducing the duty on a long lease is to grant an initial lease for 20 years and then a lease of the reversion for the balance of 40 years.[2] There is no rule aggregating the leases in such circumstances.[3] The first lease will carry duty at 2% and the reversionary lease will carry fixed duty of £5 under para 13, Sch 13, Part II, FA 1999.

Where the consideration is payable for a definite period exceeding 20 years the charge is limited to the amount payable during the 20-year period. This relief, however, applies only to sums "payable periodically for" the period; such sums must be payable within the period.[4]

Sergeant and Sims A9.3.

---

[1] A defect in Schedule 13 to the Finance Act 1999 meant that from 1 October 1999 the 1% charge on the rental element of leases not exceeding seven years ceased to apply to leases of exactly seven years. This defect was corrected by FA 2000, s 116 and Sch 32.

[2] It should be noted that the initial lease should not be for 21 years or more because of LPA 1925, s 149(3), and that the lease can be registered voluntarily under the Land Registration Rules 1925, R 47.

[3] Cf TA 1988, s 38.

[4] *Blendett v IRC, Quietlece v IRC* [1984] STC 95, CA.

Rents

[57.28] The expression rent is not defined for stamp duty.[1] It has been defined generally as the recompense paid by the tenant to the landlord for the exclusive possession of the land; this payment must be reserved out of the land.[2]

The charge refers to the rate "or average rate" of the rent without stating expressly what the rate is; however, it is obvious that a yearly rate is to be taken. These words refer to the possibility of a varying rent level. So if a lease is at a rent of £3,000 pa for the first 30 years and a peppercorn for the next 15 it will be treated as a lease for 45 years at a rent of £2,000 pa[3]

When the rent is variable the contingency principle (supra, § **56.18**) may apply. In *Coventry City Council v IRC*[4] rent was due under a sublease from the council to a developer; that rent was expressed to be 8.142% of the total expenditure up to a maximum of £130,000. Brightman J held that stamp duty was due on a rent equal to 8.142% of £130,000 even though the actual rent might not be that percentage of that figure. If the maximum figure had not

[57.28] Heads of charge

been inserted, no duty would have been payable by reason of the uncertainty of the consideration; the same reason prevented any duty from being claimed by the Crown on rent in the form of sums equal to a share of the annual rents received by the corporation from occupants of the building in excess of a certain minimum. However, rent due in the form of a sum equal to that paid by the developer under the headlease was taken into account.

Where, in relation to an instrument executed after 7 December 1993, the rent or any part of the rent cannot be ascertained at the time the lease is executed, the rent is taken to be the market rent at that time.[5] This does not include cases where the rent could be ascertained on the assumption that any future event mentioned in the instrument were or were not to occur.[6] Accordingly, it would seem that the contingency principle still applies: supra, § **56.18**.

Any penal rent, or increased rent in the nature of a penal rent, is ignored for stamp duty.[7] A penal rent is an additional rent becoming payable if the lessee breaks a covenant in the lease.[8] However, if the lessee has a choice between paying an increased rent and doing—or not doing—some act, the increased rent is not penal.[9]

If a lease is granted for consideration, whether rent or premium, in respect of which it is chargeable with ad valorem duty and in further consideration of a covenant to improve the property, no duty is chargeable on the further consideration.[10] However, this section does not apply if this covenant would be subject to ad valorem stamp duty if it were in a conveyance by itself.[11]

Duty may be chargeable on the surrender of a lease either as a surrender-fixed duty of £5—or as a sale should the landlord pay money for the surrender. As to the surrender of a lease, see supra, § **57.23**. A lease or agreement for a lease is not chargeable with duty by reason of being made in consideration of the surrender of an existing lease or agreement relating to the same subject matter.[12]

Service charges are not dutiable as part of the consideration unless they are reserved as rent; how they will then be charged depends on whether they are ascertainable.

An instrument increasing the rent under the term of the lease does not cause a surrender and regrant of the lease and so is the subject of a special rule: the instrument increasing the rent is chargeable with duty as if it were a lease in consideration of the additional rent made payable by it.[13]

Sergeant and Sims A9.3 [657].

---

[1] See *Gable Construction Co Ltd v IRC* [1968] 1 WLR 1426 at 1435.
[2] For the distinction between a rent and a premium see *Hill v Booth* [1930] 1 KB 381 and *Samuel v Salmon & Gluckstein* [1946] Ch 8; on that between rent and royalties see *T and E Homes Ltd v Robinson* [1976] STC 462.
[3] The head of charge thus nullifies *Pearson v IRC* (1868) LR 3 Exch 242.
[4] [1979] Ch142, [1978] 1 All ER 1107.
[5] FA 1994, s 242(2).
[6] FA 1994, s 242(3)(*a*).
[7] SA 1891, s 77(1).

[8] eg he fails to follow a stipulated system of cultivation—*Fuller v Fenwick* (1846) 3 CB 705.
[9] *French v Macale* (1842) 2 Dr & War 269.
[10] SA 1891, s 77(2), this is similar to FA 1900, s 10 (which relates to conveyances on sale).
[11] FA 1909, s 8 enacted to nullify *British Electric Traction v IRC* [1902] 1 KB 441, CA—the covenant would have been liable to bond covenant duty but the charge was repealed for electricity by FA 1958, s 35(1) and the remaining heads were almost all abolished by FA 1971, s 64 (see infra, § **57.35**).
[12] SA 1891, s 77(1).
[13] FA 1999, Sch 13, Part III, para 20 (replacing SA 1891, s 77(5)).

Duty on premium

[57.29] When the consideration or part of the consideration for the lease moves to the lessor, or some other person, and consists of money, stock or securities, duty is charged ad valorem in the same way as would be charged on a conveyance or sale. So there is a nil rate if the premium does not exceed £125,000 and the rent does not exceed £600 pa. Otherwise, duty is charged at 1%, 3.0% or 4.0% as appropriate.[1] Payment by the lessee of the lessor's legal fees on the grant of the lease is ignored;[2] however, if the landlord incurs expenses before the lease at the lessor's request and the lessee reimburses the landlord those payments are taken into account as a premium.[3] A premium payable periodically is chargeable on the basis laid down by SA 1891, s 56.[4]

Where, in relation to an instrument executed after 7 December 1993 (not being an instrument executed pursuant to a contract made before 30 November 1993), the consideration for the grant of a lease consists of or includes any property, the instrument is chargeable with ad valorem duty as a conveyance on sale calculated on the market value of the property given in consideration for the grant.[5]

Where, in relation to an instrument executed after 7 December 1993, the consideration, or any part of the consideration, for the grant of a lease cannot be ascertained at the time the lease is executed, the consideration for the grant is taken to be the market value of the lease immediately before the lease is executed.[6] However, the cases where consideration cannot be ascertained do not include cases where the consideration could be ascertained on the assumption that any future event mentioned in the instrument were or were not to occur. Accordingly, it would seem that the contingency principle still applies: supra, § **56.18**.

The relief from conveyance on sale duty under FA 1930, s 42 (transfers between associated companies) does not apply to this head of duty; however, an almost identical relief applies under FA 1995, s 151.[7]

An anti-avoidance provision was enacted in FA 2000 in relation to the grant of a lease to a company connected with the grantor or where the consideration includes an issue of shares by a company connected with the grantor.[8] Although the drafting of this provision is problematic the broad effect is to deem a market value consideration to have been given for the grant but

[57.29] Heads of charge

reduced by any actual consideration which does not consist of property. This provision only applies if it leads to a greater amount of stamp duty than would otherwise arise.

Sergeant and Sims A9.5.

---

1. See supra, § **57.03**.
2. (1959) *Law Society's Gazette*, p 95.
3. Sergeant and Sims A9.5 [692].
4. FA 1994, s 241. See supra, § **57.10**; *Blendett v IRC, Quietlece v IRC* [1984] STC 95, CA.
5. FA 1994, s 242. See supra, § **57.19**.
6. FA 1994, s 242(3)(*a*). See supra, § **56.18**.
7. As amended by FA 2000, s 125, which considerably tightened up the scope of the relief by aligning the definition of a stamp duty group of companies with the corporation tax group definition. See infra, § **60.02**.
8. FA 2000, s 121.

Agreement for a lease

[57.30] An agreement for a lease is chargeable as if it were the actual lease irrespective of the length of the term.[1] Unlike the analogous provision for sale agreements there is no provision for repayment of duty if the agreement is cancelled.[2] However, an agreement for lease executed on or after 6 May 1994 may be presented for stamping with the lease without incurring interest or a penalty, see supra, § **56.23**.

Where the duty has been paid on an agreement for a lease, the duty payable on a lease granted pursuant to such agreement is reduced by the amount of duty already paid.[3]

Where a freehold or leasehold interest is conveyed or transferred or a lease is granted subject to an agreement for a lease for a term exceeding 35 years (which is not directly enforceable against any intermediate interest in the land) the duty paid on the agreement must be denoted on the conveyance, transfer or lease.[4]

An agreement for a lease for a term of seven years or more also requires a produced stamp; there is no need to produce the subsequent lease.[5]

Sergeant and Sims A9.6 [698].

---

1. FA 1999, Sch 13, Part II, para 14. In Scotland a concluded contract is a lease.
2. FA 1999, Sch 13, Part II, para 14.
3. FA 1999, Sch 13, Part II, para 14(2).
4. FA 1984, s 111(2).
5. FA 1931, s 28.

The rents to mortgages scheme

[57.31] The rents to mortgages scheme was introduced by the Leasehold Reform, Housing and Urban Development Act 1993 to enable public sector tenants wishing to purchase their homes to pay for them over a period. The scheme operates in England and Wales and there is a similar scheme in Scotland—"rent to loan".[1] The scheme works by giving tenants the option of buying their homes for an initial payment (which can be financed by a mortgage and repaid in place of rent) plus a balance to be met by an interest-free loan from the landlords. The loan is expressed as a percentage of the value of the property rather than as a cash sum. In consequence, the amount needed to redeem the loan depends on the value of the property at that time (and on any further discount available) and this means that the total purchase price of the property is not known at the outset.

There are special stamp duty rules in FA 1993, s 202 (England and Wales) and s 203 (Scotland) to deal with the difficulty of the total purchase price of the property not being known. Stamp duty is charged on the market value of the property less any discount that may be due under the "right to buy" provisions.[2] This means that the duty is the same as if the property was paid for all at once. Those buying under rents to mortgages whose property is valued at £60,000 or less after discount will have no stamp duty to pay. If the value after discount is more than £60,000, duty will be charged on that figure. The object of the legislation appears to be to ensure that purchasers under the scheme pay the same amount of duty as if they were buying their homes in the ordinary way.

Except in Scotland, tenants may take a long lease under the scheme rather than buying the freehold of their property. The stamp duty rules are the same.

Sergeant and Sims A4.10 [318].

---

[1] Housing Act (Scotland) Act 1987, Part III.
[2] Under the Housing Act 1985, Part V.

Shared ownership transactions

[57.32] Shared ownership leases granted by local housing authorities or certain specified bodies (such as housing associations and housing action trusts) or granted by persons against whom the preserved right to buy under the Housing Act 1985 is exercisable or to a qualifying person for the purposes of the reserved right to buy are charged as conveyances or transfers on sale.[1] The consideration on which duty is charged is the market value of the property or a sum calculated by reference to that value provided that certain specified conditions are satisfied.[2] Where duty is paid on a lease in this way, no duty is charged on an instrument by which the reversion is transferred to the lessee provided that it contains a statement to the effect that it has been executed in pursuance of the lease.[3]

Sergeant and Sims A4.10 [318].

---

[1] FA 1980, s 97 and FA 1981, s 108 as amended by FA 1987, s 54.

[57.32] Heads of charge

² FA 1980, s 97(2).
³ FA 1980, s 97(4).

Other heads of charge

Bearer instruments

[57.33] This charge which was introduced by FA 1963, s 59 and is now contained in FA 1999, Sch 15 is dealt with in the section dealing with companies at infra, §§ 59.08–59.13.

Bills of sale

[57.34] An absolute bill of sale is liable to ad valorem duty as a conveyance on sale; a bill of sale cannot be registered unless a duly stamped original is produced.[1]

Sergeant and Sims A4.3 [237].

[1] SA 1891, s 41.

Bonds, covenants or instruments of any kind whatsoever

[57.35] The remaining charge under this head was on instruments increasing the rent reserved by a lease which was not duly stamped.[1] In cases where the lease to which the instrument relates is duly stamped, SA 1891, s 77(5) appeared to substitute lease duty for bond duty.[2] However, for instruments executed on or after 1 October 1999 this remaining charge has been repealed and replaced by FA 1999, Sch 13, Part III, para 20 which charges duty on the instrument increasing the rent.

Sergeant and Sims A9.3 [674].

[1] FA 1971, s 64(1)(*a*)(i); SA 1891, s 77(5).
[2] See *Gable Construction Co Ltd v IRC* [1968] 2 All ER 968.

Declaration of trust

[57.36] Under FA 1999, Sch 13, Part III, para 17 a declaration of trust by any writing not being a will or instrument liable to ad valorem duty is liable to duty of £5, see infra, § 58.07. For instruments executed on or after 1 October 1999 this fixed duty of £5 does not apply to declarations of trust contained within life insurance policies as these have been brought within the scope of the Stamp Duty (Exempt Instruments) Regulations 1987, SI 1987/516, see supra, § **56.05**.

Duplicate or counterpart

[57.37] The duplicate or counterpart of any instrument chargeable with any duty is chargeable with duty of £5. So the duplicate of a conveyance where the consideration does not exceed £60,000 will not be chargeable to duty either.

A duplicate or counterpart of an instrument chargeable to duty is duly stamped if it is stamped as an original or, if as a duplicate, it indicates by a denoting stamp that duty has been paid on the original.[1]

An exception provides that the counterpart of a lease does not require a denoting stamp if it is not executed by the lessor or grantor.[2]

Sergeant and Sims A10.5.

---

[1] FA 1999, Sch 13, Part III, para 19(2).
[2] FA 1999, Sch 13, Part III, para 19(3).

Partition or division of land

[57.38] If there is a division or partition of any estate or interest in land and the equality money exceeds £100, FA 1999, Sch 13, Part III, para 21 provides that ad valorem duty be paid on the equality money at a rate equal to that for a transfer on sale; the same reduced and nil rates apply. This duty is charged on the principal instrument. If the equality money is less than £100 a fixed duty of £5 is charged. As to an exchange of land, see supra, § **57.19**.

Sergeant and Sims A10.6.

Transfer of units in unit trusts

[57.39] The transfer of units in unit trusts has from 6 February 2000 been subject to a new stamp duty reserve tax regime.[1] These matters are dealt with infra, §§ **59.17–59.18**.

---

[1] FA 1999, s 122 and Sch 19.

Release or renunciation

[57.40] A release or renunciation of any property or of any interest in property (eg an interest under a partnership) is liable to fixed duty of £5 unless it is upon a sale in which case it attracts ad valorem duty as a conveyance on sale.[1] For instruments executed on or after 13 March 2008 this fixed duty applies to instruments effecting a land transaction.[2]

Sergeant and Sims A10.7.

---

[1] FA 1999, Sch 13, Part III, para 22.
[2] FA 2008, Sch 32, para 22.

[57.41] Heads of charge

Surrender

[57.41] A surrender of any kind whatsoever, not chargeable with duty as a conveyance on sale, attracts duty of £5.[1] As to the surrender of a lease, see supra, § 57.23.

Sergeant and Sims A10.7.

---

[1] FA 1999, Sch 13, Part III, para 23.

Abolished heads of charge

[57.42] Among the stamp duties which have been abolished are:[1]
(1) duty on voluntary dispositions inter vivos;[2]
(2) fixed duty on an instrument appointing a new trustee or one, not being a will, in execution of a power of any property, or for any use, shares or interest in any property;[3]
(3) duty on contract notes for the sale or purchase of any stock or marketable security;[4]
(4) fixed duty on deeds;[5]
(5) duty on assignments of life policies, along with the duty on superannuation and purchased life annuities;[6]
(6) duty on the grants of a mortgage, or equitable mortgage, a collateral or substituted mortgage, the assignment of a mortgage or a security, the reconveyance of a mortgage and the release of a debt.[7]
(7) the remaining fixed duties for instruments executed on or after 13 March 2008 except in relation to instruments effecting a land transaction.[8]

Sergeant and Sims A1.2 [28].

---

[1] The examples given are by way of illustration only and do not purport to constitute an exhaustive list. For a fuller treatment, see **Sergeant and Sims A1.2 [28]**.
[2] FA 1985, s 82, Sch 27. For the position in respect of fixed duty, see supra, § **56.05**.
[3] FA 1985, s 85, Sch 24; FA 1987, s 49.
[4] FA 1985, s 86. However, note that stamp duty reserve tax is imposed on agreements to transfer securities for consideration: see infra, § **61.01**.
[5] FA 1985, s 85, Schs 24, 27.
[6] FA 1989, s 173. However, note that a declaration of trust continues to be chargeable with fixed duty (£5) although it is anticipated that declarations of trust within life policies will be brought within the Stamp Duty (Exempt Instruments) Regulations from 1 October 1999: see supra, § **56.05**.
[7] FA 1971, s 64.
[8] FA 2008, Sch 32, para 22.

Potential abolition of stamp duties on shares and securities

[57.43] FA 1990, ss 107, 108 provide for the abolition of all stamp duty charges (including stamp duty reserve tax) on transactions in securities, from a date to be fixed by Treasury Order. FA 1991, ss 110–114 include provisions to limit stamp duty to instruments embodying transactions concerning interests in land and buildings although these provisions seem redundant in view of the introduction of stamp duty land tax (see infra, Chapter 62). However, the implementation of the provisions relating to shares and securities was affected by the result of the General Election in May 1997: the Labour Government has indicated that it intends to retain stamp duty (and stamp duty reserve tax) on transactions in securities. As a result abolition is now unlikely to occur.

Sergeant and Sims A17.1 [1244].

58

Stamp duty in specific situations

Sale of a business	PARA **58.01**
Land	PARA **58.02**
Trusts and settlements	PARA **58.06**
Wills and intestacies—variations	PARA **58.13**
Matrimonial arrangements	PARA **58.15**
Intellectual property	PARA **58.16**

Sale of a business

[58.01] With the abolition of stamp duty on land and buildings from 1 December 2003, stamp duty is restricted to transactions in shares and securities, bearer instruments and acquisitions of partnership interests (see infra, § **62.33**). Accordingly, the few remaining assets vulnerable to stamp duty on the sale of a business such as tenant's fixtures, the benefit of contracts and trade debts ceased to be liable to stamp duty from 1 December 2003. Sales and certain other transfers of land and buildings will be liable to stamp duty land tax and stamp duty will apply only to the extent that the consideration is apportioned to shares and securities, bearer instruments and partnership interests.

Sergeant and Sims A6.12 [504].

Land

Sale of land

[58.02] FA 2003 abolished stamp duty on land and buildings and in its place created stamp duty land tax from 1 December 2003, see infra, Chapter 62. The following describes the application of stamp duty to land transactions, prior to abolition.

A contract for the sale of a legal estate or interest in land is not liable to stamp duty.[1] However, a contract for the sale of an equitable interest in land is chargeable with ad valorem duty as if it were a conveyance on sale.[2] A contract for the sale of an option to purchase land may be chargeable as a contract for the sale of an equitable interest in the land, whereas an agreement creating the option may be chargeable as a conveyance on sale of the option.[3]

In *George Wimpey & Co Ltd v IRC*[4] the Court of Appeal held that a contract creating an option to buy a legal interest in land was chargeable as a conveyance on sale of the option, ie that the option was acquired for a money

[58.02] Stamp duty in specific situations

price and nothing further needed to be done to vest the option in the purchaser. In option cases close attention is needed to determine what is sold.[5]

The conveyance of the land on sale will attract ad valorem duty under FA 1999, Sch 13, Part I, para 1. The usual practical problem is to ensure that the value is kept to a level low enough to be duty free; certification of value is required.[6] It is common for a vendor to sever any severable chattels before the sale in the hope that a part of the consideration can be attributed to those chattels; this method will be successful only where the transfer of those chattels is not effected by the conveyance but by a separate transaction not involving an instrument and only when severance has taken place; fixtures which have not been severed must normally be included as they are part of the land.[7]

Sergeant and Sims A7.3.

---

[1] FA 1999, Sch 13, Part I, para 7(1) except where the contract relates to UK land, the consideration exceeds £10m and a conveyance in conformity with the contract is not presented to IR Stamp Taxes within 90 days of the contract. FA 2002, s 115, see supra, § **57.18**.
[2] FA 1999, Sch 13, Part I, para 7(1).
[3] FA 1999, Sch 13, Part I, para 1.
[4] [1975] 2 All ER 45, [1975] STC 248.
[5] eg *Muller & Co's Margarine Ltd v IRC* [1900] 1 QB 310 as explained by Collins LJ in *Danubian Sugar Factories Ltd v IRC* [1901] 1 KB 245 at 251.
[6] Supra, §§ **57.15–57.16**.
[7] See *Law Society Gazette*, November 1963, p. 782 and Stamp Taxes Bulletin No 1, August 2001.

Covenant to improve property

[58.03] Where a purchaser covenants to improve property or where the conveyance is in consideration of his having previously improved the property, or of any covenant relating to the subject matter, the value of the covenant is ignored in calculating the duty.[1] So where V sells land to P in consideration of a sum of money and a covenant—in a separate contract—by V to build a house for P, ad valorem duty is chargeable only on the price paid by P.[2] This must be distinguished from the case where V has already built the house and then sells both the land and the house to P. This has given rise to considerable difficulty when there is a conveyance of land and a separate contract to build.[3]

Sergeant and Sims A6.2 [464].

---

[1] FA 1900, s 10.
[2] *Kimbers & Co v IRC* [1936] 1 KB 132.
[3] See infra, § **58.04**.

Conveyances and leases of building plots with contracts to build

[58.04] In *Prudential Assurance Co Ltd v IRC* [1992] STC 863, the appellant entered into a sale agreement with two companies (the developers) whereby the appellant agreed to buy a freehold property from the developers. On the same day, the appellant and the developers entered into a development agreement. The terms of that agreement provided for the development of the property by the developers in return for which the appellant agreed to pay the developers certain building costs. By a transfer of the same date the developers transferred to the appellant the land agreed to be sold. At the date of the transfer, a substantial part of the construction work had already been carried out on the property. The transfer was assessed to stamp duty by reference to the total amount of consideration payable for the sale of the land and all the building works on the basis that there was a single contract of sale contained in two instruments (the sale agreement and the development agreement) by which the appellant agreed to buy from the developers the land together with the completed buildings. The appellant contended that there were two separate contracts, one relating to the sale of land and the other to the building works, and that stamp duty was payable only in respect of the consideration for the sale of the land and the building works completed thereon as at the date of the transfer.

The appeal was allowed. It was held that the transaction entered into by the taxpayer could not be characterised as a sale of land with finished buildings thereon. That was not the legal shape of the transaction. The sale agreement was completed independently of the due execution of the building works under the development agreement. The sale agreed and completed was of the land and the buildings as they then were and the consideration for that sale, for the purposes of stamp duty, was the price due for the land and the building works already completed as at the date of the transfer.

The Board of HMRC have issued statement of practice SP 8/93 which sets out their view of how stamp duty is charged on certain transactions involving new buildings in view of the *Prudential* case.[1] The statement says that where there are two separate transactions embodied in two independent contracts, one for the site and one for the building works, the transfer or lease will be assessed solely by reference to the consideration or rent paid for the site. However, if there is one transaction relating to land and building works, the Stamp Office will approach the matter as follows:

(i) If the two contracts are so interlocked that they cannot be said to be genuinely capable of independent completion (and in particular where if default occurs on either contract, the other is then not enforceable) ad valorem duty will be charged on the total consideration for the land and buildings, whether completed or not, as if the parties had entered into only one contract.

(ii) If the two contracts are shown to be genuinely independent of each other, ad valorem duty will be charged by reference to the consideration paid or payable for the land and any building works on that land at the date of execution of the instrument. It follows that, where the instrument is executed after the building works are completed, ad valorem duty will be charged on the consideration for the land and the completed building(s).

The fact that the contracts are part of the same transaction may mean that the transfer cannot be certified for the purposes of obtaining the benefit of the stamp duty threshold: see supra, §§ **57.15–57.16**.

Sergeant and Sims A6.2 [464].

[1] See Sergeant and Sims Division E [5504].

Leases—a way of reducing duty

[58.05] On creating a leasehold interest duty may be reduced by granting a lease for not more than 35 years with options for one or more renewals. The existence of the option is not considered to make the lease one of more than 35 years[1] although further stamp duty will be payable when the options are exercised. Alternatively a 21-year lease with a 35-year reversionary lease with options can be used, in which case duty will be paid on both the 21-year lease and the reversionary lease immediately even though the reversionary lease is not a lease in possession. This allows a long lease to be granted at a more advantageous rate.

Sergeant and Sims Division B [3048]–[3187].

[1] *Hand v Hall* (1877) 2 Ex Div 355.

Trusts and settlements

Declaration of trust

[58.06] A declaration of trust by any writing not being a will or instrument liable to ad valorem duty, is liable to duty of £5. Following the abolition of stamp duty on land and buildings from 1 December 2003, stamp duty is restricted to instruments relating to stock or marketable securities, acquisitions of partnership interests and bearer instruments and the liability of declarations of trust to stamp duty is limited accordingly.[1] An ineffective transfer to trustees is not construed as a declaration of trust and therefore is not liable to this duty.

If a person declares himself trustee of personal property the trust is effective and binding save only perhaps where his interest in the property is equitable.[2] It follows that since a subsequent transfer to trustees is not a sale it will bear only miscellaneous transfer duty of £5 since no beneficial interest passes; here the decision in *Cohen & Moore v IRC* must be borne in mind.[3] A transfer direct from vendor to trustees at the direction of the purchaser/settlor attracts conveyance on sale duty and an additional £5 duty.[4]

Where a settlor agrees to sell his property to the trust the subsequent instrument of transfer will be chargeable as a disposition on sale or the agreement may be chargeable as an agreement to convey.[5]

It is the view of the Stamp Office that the inclusion of a certificate under the Exempt Instrument Regulations 1987 (see supra, § **56.05**) cannot be allowed and the inclusion of such a certificate does not remove this charge.

Sergeant and Sims A10.4 [734].

1 The fixed £5 duty is abolished for instruments executed on or after 13 March 2008 except for instruments effecting a land transaction. See FA 2008, Sch 32, para.22.
2 See infra, § **58.11**.
3 [1933] 2 KB 126 and **Sergeant and Sims A3.3 [188]**.
4 See **Sergeant and Sims A3.3 [188]**.
5 FA 1999, Sch 13, Part I, para 7, supra. § **57.18**.

Change of trustees

[58.07] Duty (formerly 50p fixed duty) is no longer charged on the appointment of a new trustee,[1] and a transfer effecting a land transaction from the old to the new trustee is exempt if appropriately certified (see supra, § **56.05**).

1 FA 1985, s 85, Sch 24(*b*).

Distributions

[58.08] Distributions by the trustees in the course of administering the trust are not transfers on sale. Instruments effecting such distributions which effect a land transaction will be exempt if appropriately certified (see supra, § **56.05**).

Revocation of a trust—repeal of duty

[58.09] The revocation of a trust no longer attracts fixed duty of 50p.[1]

1 For its repeal, see FA 1985, s 85, Sch 24(*k*).

Assignment of interests under trusts

[58.10] The assignment of a beneficial interest under a trust[1] must be in writing to satisfy the requirements of LPA 1925, s 53(1)(*c*); it follows that there must be an instrument and so something chargeable, whether as a sale or a gift. The same conclusion is reached if the beneficiary directs the trustees to hold his interest on trust for someone else in view of the decision of the House of Lords in *Grey v IRC*.[2] The House rejected the argument that the word "disposition" in s 53(1)(*c*) should be equated with the words "grant" or "assignment" formerly found in the Statute of Frauds and did so because the LPA 1925 consolidated not the Statute of Frauds but subsequent amending Acts[3] so that one could not assume that no change of scope was intended; it followed that the word "disposition" should receive its natural meaning. What is not clear is whether a declaration of trust by a beneficiary of his beneficial interest is now a disposition and so void under LPA 1925, s 53(1)(*c*). What is clear is that if such a declaration—or instruction as in *Grey v IRC*—falls

[58.10] Stamp duty in specific situations

within s 53(1)(c), and is not in writing, it is void and so a subsequent document confirming the transfer is itself the conveyance and so liable to duty if such a conveyance attracts duty.

If the beneficiary instructs the trustee to transfer both his equitable and the trustee's legal interest to a third person the instruction does not require writing under s 53(1)(c)[4] but the transfer to the third person may have to be by instrument anyway.

In *Oughtred v IRC*[5] a trust held shares for A for life with remainder to B. B agreed to surrender his remainder in exchange for certain shares held by A absolutely; the effect would be to change A's life interest in the settled shares into an absolute one. The parties executed a deed of release whereby A and B released the trustees, the deed reciting that the trust shares were now held for A absolutely and that it was intended to transfer them in return for the release. A deed between A and the trustees transferred the shares to A on the same day.

The question was whether the transfer of the shares to A was subject to ad valorem duty as a transfer on sale,[6] the sale being of B's equitable interest. It was argued that the effect of the contract was that A became the beneficiary under a constructive trust so that the deed simply vested A with legal title to what was already hers. By a bare majority the House of Lords rejected the argument and held that ad valorem stamp duty was chargeable. Of the majority Lord Jenkins, with whom Lord Keith agreed, held that the prior constructive trust did not prevent the subsequent transfer from being a transfer on sale. He said:

> The parties to a transaction of sale and purchase may no doubt choose to let the matter rest in contract. But if the subject matter of a sale is such that the full title to it can only be transferred by an instrument, then any instrument they executed by way of transfer of the property sold ranks for stamp duty purposes as a conveyance on sale notwithstanding the constructive trust which arose on the conclusion of the contract.[7]

Lord Denning expressed it in wider terms. He said:

> In my opinion, every conveyance or transfer by which an agreement for sale is implemented is liable to stamp duty on the value of the consideration . . . the instrument is the means by which the parties choose to implement the bargains they have made. It is then a conveyance on transfer consequent upon the sale of the property and in implementation of it.[8]

The dicta of Lord Jenkins and Lord Denning in *Oughtred v IRC* were referred to with approval by Millett LJ in *Parinv (Hatfield) Ltd v IRC*.[9] In that case, the Court of Appeal held that ad valorem duty was chargeable on a conveyance of registered land notwithstanding that the parties had purported to vest the equitable title in the purchaser by means of an earlier offshore declaration of trust.

Where an instrument transfers both an equitable interest and the related legal interest, Revenue practice does not require an additional £5 duty on the transfer of the latter.

Sergeant and Sims A10.4 [734].

¹ For the application of stamp duty land tax to transfers of interest under trusts owning land see infra, § **62.29**.
² [1960] AC 1.
³ See now also the Law of Property (Miscellaneous Provisions) Act 1989.
⁴ *Vandervell v IRC* [1967] AC 291.
⁵ [1960] AC 206.
⁶ The fact that the consideration was shares not money is irrelevant—see SA 1891, s 55.
⁷ At 241.
⁸ At 237; see also Wills J in *Chesterfield Brewery Co v IRC* [1899] 2 QB 7 at 12 and Wilberforce J in *Fitch Lovell Ltd v IRC* [1962] 3 All ER 685.
⁹ [1998] STC 305.

Variation of trusts

[58.11] If one beneficiary buys another beneficiary's interest for cash or shares there will be a conveyance on sale liable to ad valorem duty. If, however, the beneficiaries divide the funds according to an actuarial valuation of their interests, stamp duty will not be payable ad valorem since no interest passes and hence there is no sale.

If there is a danger that the transaction will be treated as one of sale and the value of the interest transferred is not above £60,000, certification is desirable to ensure freedom from duty: supra, § **57.16**.

Where the interest of one beneficiary is bought out by the others, the disposal of parts of his share to each of the others may with advantage be done by separate instruments if this would enable the nil duty rate to apply where it otherwise would not. It is felt that these would be separate transactions.

[58.12] The stamp duty on the creation of a trust or settlement inter vivos depends on the nature of the instrument effecting it and the nature of the assets. Where there is more than one instrument effecting it, the duty in practice is charged on what is regarded as the final instrument in the transaction. If the instrument is a declaration of trust it will attract duty of £5 under FA 1999, Sch 13, Part III, para 17 if it effects a land transaction.¹

Where there is more than one instrument involved it will be necessary for ascertaining which instrument requires to be stamped to determine either by reference to the date of the instrument(s) which one of the instrument(s) was first executed to accept whether a certificate is appropriate. In the absence of any such indication the instrument creating the settlement or trust will be treated as the final instrument for stamping.

Sergeant and Sims A20.2 [1544].

¹ FA 2008, Sch 32, para 22.

[58.13] Stamp duty in specific situations

Wills and intestacies—variations

General

[58.13] A will or testamentary instrument is exempt from stamp duty. An assent under Administration of Estates Act 1925, s 36 is not liable to duty. Where property is appropriated by a personal representative in or towards satisfaction of a general legacy of money no duty is now chargeable on an instrument giving effect to the appropriation.[1]

Sergeant and Sims A17.3 [1261].

---

[1] FA 1985, s 84(4).

Deeds of variation

[58.14] No ad valorem conveyance or transfer on sale duty is chargeable where, within two years of a person's death, any of the dispositions (whether effected by will, under the law relating to intestacy or otherwise) of the property of which he was competent to dispose are varied by an instrument executed by the persons or any of the persons who benefit or would benefit under the dispositions.[1]

However, this provision does not apply where the variation is made for monetary consideration other than consideration consisting of the making of a variation in respect of another of the dispositions.[2] This provision applies whether or not the administration of the estate is complete or the property has been distributed in accordance with the original dispositions.[3] All qualifying deeds of variation and similar instruments are exempt also from £5 fixed duty unless they effect a land transaction in which case they may be appropriately certified (see supra, § **56.05**).

Sergeant and Sims A17.3 [1261].

---

[1] FA 1985, s 84(1).
[2] FA 1985, s 84(2).
[3] FA 1985, s 84(3).

Matrimonial arrangements

Transfer of property on the break-up of a marriage

[58.15] There is an exemption from transfer on sale duty in respect of an instrument executed on or after 26 March 1985 which transfers property from one party to a marriage to the other if:

(1) it is executed in pursuance of a court order made on the granting of a decree of divorce, nullity of marriage or judicial separation;[1] or

(2) it is executed in pursuance of a court order made in connection with the dissolution or annulment of the marriage or judicial separation and is made at any time after the granting of such a decree;[2] or
(3) it is executed at any time in pursuance of an agreement made in contemplation of or otherwise in connection with the dissolution or annulment of the marriage or judicial separation.[3]

Such instruments are exempt also from £5 fixed duty unless they effect a land transaction in which case they may be appropriately certified (see supra, § **56.05**).[4]

As to the position where a share in the matrimonial home or part of it is transferred subject to a mortgage, see supra, § **57.11**.

Sergeant and Sims A17.5 [1285].

[1] FA 1985, s 83(1)(*a*).
[2] FA 1985, s 83(1)(*b*).
[3] FA 1985, s 83(1)(*c*).
[4] FA 1985, s 83(2).

Intellectual property

[58.16] No stamp duty is chargeable on any contract or transfer relating to the sale or other disposition of intellectual property. This exemption was introduced for documents executed on or after 28 March 2000.[1] For the purposes of this exemption "intellectual property" means patents, trade marks, registered designs, copyrights or design rights, plant breeders' rights and licences or other rights relating to such matters. The sale consideration must be apportioned on a just and reasonable basis where part of the property sold consists of intellectual property.[2] Intellectual property is not taken into account for the purposes of a certificate of value.[3] In practice it is understood that the Stamp Office are willing to treat certain types of intellectual property which do not fall within the statutory definition as also exempt and to accept that any goodwill inherent in an item of exempt intellectual property is also exempt.

[1] FA 2000, s 129.
[2] FA 2000, Sch 34, paras 2 and 3.
[3] FA 2000, Sch 34, para 4 and see supra, § **57.15**.

59

Companies—stamp duty (and stamp duty reserve tax)

Share transactions	PARA **59.01**
Capital duty—abolition	PARA **59.07**
Bearer instruments	PARA **59.08**
Unit trusts—transfer of units	PARA **59.14**

Share transactions

Company formation and issue of shares for cash

[59.01] On the formation of a company incorporated in the UK no stamp duty is payable, as the memorandum of association and articles of association do not require duty.

The issue of shares on the formation of a company for cash no longer attracts duty as a result of the abolition of capital duty.[1]

If the shares issued are bearer shares they are liable to bearer instrument duty, infra, §§ **59.08–59.13**.

Sergeant and Sims A13.6 [954]–[990].

---

[1] FA 1988, s 141. See infra, § **59.07**.

Issue of shares for consideration other than cash

[59.02] Where the issue of shares is in return for assets, there may be an agreement or conveyance on sale of the assets and liability to duty.[1] Where the shares issued are bearer shares, there may be conveyance on sale duty and also bearer instrument duty.

In addition, where shares are issued for consideration other than money, Companies Act 1985, s 88 requires the return of allotment filed at Companies House (Form 88(2)) to be accompanied by either a duly stamped contract or particulars of the contract (Form 88(3)) under which the consideration was provided.[2] Such a contract or Form 88(3) may be stampable under FA 1999, Sch 13, Part I, para 7. Under new arrangements introduced from 1 April 1997, the Form 88(2) and the contract or Form 88(3) in such cases should be sent to the Stamp Office for stamping within 30 days of the date of execution before they are forwarded to Companies House.[3]

2119

[59.02] Companies—stamp duty (and stamp duty reserve tax)

There is no similar requirement to produce a duly stamped contract or particulars of the contract under Companies Act 2006, s 555 which replaced Companies Act 1985, s 88 on 1 October 2006. Details of non-cash consideration need to be entered on form SH01.

---

[1] SA 1891, s 55, as amended by FA 2000, s 126 to include future issues of stock.
[2] Companies Act 1985, s 88(3).
[3] See generally *Bristol Stamp Office Customer Newsletter* dated February 1997 and Companies House Notice to Customers.

Other issues of capital

[59.03] Loan capital duty was repealed in 1973. The only stamp duty now is conveyance or transfer on sale duty if the loan capital is issued in consideration for the transfer of assets.

Transfer of shares

[59.04] A contract for the sale of shares does not attract stamp duty,[1] but gives rise to a charge to stamp duty reserve tax.[2] A transfer of shares on sale will, subject to certain exemptions,[3] be chargeable with stamp duty as a conveyance on sale at a rate of 0.5%.[4] For instruments executed on or after 13th March 2008 sale duty is not chargeable if the amount or value of the consideration for the sale is £1,000 or less and the instrument is certified at £1,000 (FA 2008, s 98 adding para 1(3A) to FA 1999, Sch 13, and see **56.05**). However, payment of stamp duty on a share transfer usually cancels the stamp duty reserve tax charge provided that this is done before the expiry of the period of six years from the date on which the stamp duty reserve tax charge arises.[5] A duly stamped instrument of transfer is necessary to complete the sale to the purchaser unless the transfer is within CREST or another system of electronic settlement.[6]

If the sale is of a bearer instrument no duty will be due unless it is the first transfer in the UK of an overseas instrument; infra, § **59.09**.

An exchange of shares may give rise to conveyance or transfer on sale duty.[7] An exchange of marketable securities for debt, stock or securities which are not chargeable securities for the purposes of stamp duty reserve tax where the transfer of the marketable securities would not otherwise be on sale, is treated as a sale of the marketable securities.[8]

For reliefs for companies, see §§ **60.01–60.05**.

Particular note should be taken of the fact that, in cases where securities are transferred under CREST, stamp duty reserve tax will be charged on the agreement to transfer the securities. There will be no instrument of transfer on which stamp duty may be paid. For this reason, it has now been provided that transfers of securities, executed on or after 1 July 1996, to a member of an electronic transfer system in a form which will ensure that the shares are changed from being held in certificated form to being held in uncertificated form so that title may become transferable by means of that electronic system, are not chargeable with stamp duty.[9]

[1] FA 1999, Sch 13, Part I, para 7; see supra, § **57.18**.
[2] See infra, §§ **61.01–61.02**.
[3] See supra, §§ **56.34–56.37**; infra, §§ **60.10** ff.
[4] FA 1999, Sch 13, Part I, para 3; see the table of ad valorem stamp duties on page xxiii.
[5] See infra, §§ **61.01–61.02**.
[6] SA 1891, s 17 makes a person liable to a penalty if he registers an improperly stamped transfer.
[7] SA 1891, s 55; *J & P Coats Ltd v IRC* [1897] 2 QB 423.
[8] FA 2000, s 122.
[9] FA 1996, s 186; see generally infra, §§ **61.01** ff.

Loan capital

[59.05] FA 1986, s 79 provides a regime for loan capital and for a number of exemptions. These are as follows:

(1) There is an exemption from duty for issues and transfers of loan capital in bearer form.[1]
(2) There is an exemption for transfers of loan capital issued by certain named organisations and by "designated international organisations" for which the UK is under a treaty obligation to provide an exemption.[2] The loans covered by this provision are loans raised by:
   (a) the Organisation for Economic Co-operation and Development;
   (b) the Inter-American Development Bank;
   (c) the Asian Development Bank;
   (d) the African Development Bank; and
   (e) the European Bank for Reconstruction and Development (SI 1991/1202).
   The following bodies in respect of which the UK has a similar obligation to provide an exemption retain exemptions under other legislation:
   (i) the International Bank of Reconstruction and Development;
   (ii) the European Economic Community;
   (iii) the European Coal & Steel Community;
   (iv) the European Atomic Energy Authority;
   (v) the European Investment Bank.
(3) There is an exemption for transfers of any other loan capital[3] subject to the following exceptions:
   (a) There is an exception from the exemption for transfers of loan capital which is convertible into equity.[4]
   (b) There is an exception from the exemption for transfers of loan capital which carry, or have carried:
      (i) interest rights which significantly exceed what is normally expected in a commercial loan;

(ii) interest rights which are geared to such factors as production achieved by the borrower, his trading results or the price of commodities; and
(iii) an entitlement to a premium on maturity which is unusually large by ordinary commercial standards.[5]

(4) There is a provision which prevents the provisions referred to in paragraphs 3(b)(i) and (iii) above being triggered simply because the terms of the loan link either the interest return or the amount ultimately repayable to movements in a general domestic prices index.[6]

(5) Paragraph 3(b)(ii) above is not triggered simply because the loan capital carries a right to interest which reduces if the results of the business or the value of the property improves or if the right to interest increases in the event that the business results or property value deteriorates.[7]

(6) Paragraph 3(b)(ii) above is also not triggered by reason only that the instrument carries or had carried a right to interest which ceases or reduces if, or to the extent that the issuer, after meeting or providing for other obligations specified in the arrangements, had insufficient funds available from that arrangement to pay all or part of the interest otherwise due.[8]

(7) Stamp duty at the rate of 0.5% is charged on transfers of loan capital.[9]

Sergeant and Sims A17.4 [1267].

---

[1] FA 1986, s 79(2).
[2] FA 1986, s 79(3).
[3] FA 1986, s 79(4).
[4] FA 1986, s 79(5).
[5] FA 1986, s 79(6).
[6] FA 1986, s 79(7).
[7] FA 1986, s 79(7A) inserted by FA 2000, s 133.
[8] FA 2008, s 101 amending FA 1986, s 79 inserting new FA 1986, s 79(7B).
[9] FA 1986, s 79(8).

Purchase by a company of its own shares

[59.06] A company is required to file a return with the Registrar of Companies whenever it purchases its own shares, either for cancellation under Companies Act 2006, s 707, or for those shares to be held in treasury under Companies Act 2006, s 707. Each return is chargeable with stamp duty at the 0.5% rate.[1] It is considered that the provisions do not apply to a redemption by a company of its own redeemable shares. If once held in treasury, ie registered in the name of the company, the shares are subsequently cancelled or disposed of to an employee share scheme then a further return must be filed with the Registrar of Companies under Companies Act 2006, ss 728, 730 and this return is no longer liable to stamp duty of £5.[2]

If treasury shares are subsequently sold or transferred the sale or transfer instrument is no longer liable to a fixed £5 duty as a transfer otherwise than on sale unless the transfer is to a person whose business is issuing depositary receipts or who provides clearance services when the 1.5% rate will apply.[3]

HMRC consider that a company's purchase of its own shares held on an overseas branch register is relieved from stamp duty by Companies Act 2006, s 133 (HMRC website announcement, 7 September 2009).

1   FA 1986, s 66 as amended.
2   FA 2008, Sch 32, para 5.
3   FA 1999, Sch 13, paras 1(3)–(6) added by FA 2003, Sch 40, para 5 and amended by FA 2008, Sch 32, para 10(2).

Capital duty—abolition

[59.07] Capital duty which was imposed by FA 1973, ss 47, 48, Sch 19 (all repealed) and was introduced in conformity with an EEC Directive was abolished by FA 1988, s 141.

Sergeant and Sims A1.2 [28].

Bearer instruments

The charge

[59.08] This charge, introduced by FA 1963, s 59, has been restated and is now contained in FA 1999, Sch 15 and applies to bearer instruments. Stamp duty is charged:

(1)   on the issue of a bearer instrument in the UK; and
(2)   on the issue of a bearer instrument outside the UK by or on behalf of a UK company.[1]

Stamp duty is also charged on the transfer in the UK of stock constituted by a bearer instrument if duty was not charged on the issue of the instrument,[2] provided either that stamp duty would be charged if the instrument was not in bearer form or the stock consists of units in a unit trust.[3]

Sergeant and Sims A13.5 [938].

1   FA 1999, Sch 15, para 1.
2   As to meaning of place of issue see *Grenfell v IRC* (1876) 1 Ex D 242; *Chicago Railway Terminal Elevator Co v IRC* (1891) 75 LT 157; *Brown v IRC* (1900) 84 LT 71; *Revelstoke v IRC* [1898] AC 565 and *Canada Permanent Mortgage Corpn v IRC* 1932 SC 123.
3   FA 1999, Sch 15, para 2.

Rates of duty

[59.09] The rate of stamp duty charged on bearer instruments is 1.5% of the market value of the stock constituted or transferred by the bearer instrument.[1]

[59.09] Companies—stamp duty (and stamp duty reserve tax)

This rate is three times the normal sale duty charged on transfers of shares and securities and is intended to reflect the fact that with the 1.5% duty having been paid on issue the bearer instrument can then be transferred on sale by delivery without attracting any further stamp duty.

The 1.5% rate is reduced, however, in the following instances:

(1) the rate is 0.2% of the market value in respect of deposit certificates in a single non-UK company and bearer instruments by usage issued by a non-UK company;[2] and
(2) a fixed duty of £5 was charged in respect of bearer instruments given in substitution for similar instruments stamped ad valorem but this duty has been abolished for instruments executed on or after 13 March 2008 although to be duly stamped the substitute instrument must bear a stamp denoting that full and proper duty was paid on the original.[3]

Sergeant and Sims A13.5 [939].

[1] FA 1999, Sch 15, para 4.
[2] FA 1999, Sch 15, para 5.
[3] FA 1999, Sch 15, para 6 omitted by FA 2008, Sch 32, para 11 and replaced by FA 1999, Sch 15, para 12A.

Amount of duty

[59.10] The amount of duty charged on the issue of the bearer instrument at either the 1.5% or the 0.2% rate is based on the market value of the stock constituted by the bearer instrument in question. The market value is ascertained according to three different situations:

(1) in the case of stock offered for public subscription within 12 months before the issue of the bearer instrument, the market value is taken to be equal to the amount subscribed for the stock;
(2) in other cases, the market value is the value of the stock on the first day that such stock is traded on a UK stock exchange if this happens within one month of the issue of the bearer instrument; and
(3) otherwise it is the value of the stock immediately after issue of the bearer instrument.[1]

On the transfer of a bearer instrument the market value, in the case of a transfer pursuant to a contract of sale, is that on the day of the contract. Otherwise, it is the value of the stock on the day before the instrument is presented for stamping or on the transfer date if not so presented.[2]

Sergeant and Sims A13.5 [939].

[1] FA 1999, Sch 15, Part I, para 7.
[2] FA 1999, Sch 15, Part I, para 8.

Procedures and penalties

[59.11] On issue of a bearer instrument, duty is chargeable if it is (a) issued in the UK,[1] or (b) issued—anywhere—by or on behalf of a company or a body of persons, corporate or unincorporated, formed or established in the UK. A Societas Europaea ("SE") which has its registered office in the UK following a transfer is within (b) but an SE which has transferred its registered office out of the UK is not within (b).[2] An exception is made to (b) if the instrument is a foreign loan security.[3] An exception is made to (a) *and* (b) if it is expressed in any currency other than sterling or in any units of account defined by reference to more than one currency (whether or not including sterling).[4]

The duty is technically due on issue but the instrument should be lodged before issue; the instruments are then stamped with a denoting stamp and returned. The duty is actually payable within six weeks of the issue, or such longer time as the Commissioners may allow.[5] Failure to lodge or pay at the right time carries a penalty of the duty plus £300—apart from liability to pay the duty;[6] this liability (including the unpaid duty plus interest) is imposed on the person by whom or on whose behalf the instrument is issued as well as on the agent of these persons.

On the *transfer* of a bearer instrument the instrument must be presented for stamping. Again there are fines on the transferor and any broker or agent concerned in the transfer if the instrument is not duly stamped. However, the charge on transfer arises only in respect of those instruments which were not charged on issue.

Sergeant and Sims A13.5 [942]–[951].

[1] Ie this includes Northern Ireland.
[2] F(No 2)A 2005, s 58(3)(a).
[3] FA 1999, Sch 15, Part II, para 13.
[4] FA 1999, Sch 15, Part II, para 17.
[5] FA 1999, Sch 15, Part III, para 21.
[6] FA 1999, Sch 15, Part III, para 22.

Bearer instruments not chargeable to duty

[59.12] Certain instruments are not chargeable to duty as bearer instruments.[1] These are:

(1) Instruments relating to stock (except for unit trust units) which are exempt from all stamp duties under the general exemption in FA 1999, Sch 13, Part IV, para 24(*a*) or any other enactment.
(2) Instruments issued by certain designated international organisations or transfers of stock constituted or transferable by means of any instrument issued by the organisation.[1]
(3) Renounceable letters of allotment and related instruments where the rights are renounceable within six months after issue.[2]

[59.12] Companies—stamp duty (and stamp duty reserve tax)

(4) Instruments issued for stock expressed in a currency other than sterling or in European Currency Units (ECUs).[3] This exemption is disapplied where the instruments in question are issued by an open-ended investment company.[4]

(5) Paired shares, see FA 1988, s 143 (as amended by FA 1990, s 112); infra, § **59.13**.

It should be noted that provisions have now been introduced in respect of agreements to transfer securities constituted by or transferable by means of certain UK bearer instruments not chargeable to stamp duty so as to make such agreements chargeable to stamp duty reserve tax.[5]

Sergeant and Sims A13.6 [953].

[1] TCGA 1992, s 265 and FA 1985, s 96.
[2] FA 1999, Sch 15, Part II, para 16.
[3] FA 1999, Sch 15, Part II, para 17.
[4] Stamp Duty and Stamp Duty Reserve Tax (Open-ended Investment Companies) Regulations 1997, SI 1997/1156, reg 5; see infra, § **59.20**.
[5] FA 1997, s 105 repealing FA 1986, s 90(3)(*b*) and inserting FA 1986, ss 90(3A)–(3F), (8) and (9); and FA 1999, ss 116 and 117; see infra, § **61.13**.

Paired shares

[59.13] FA 1988, s 143 (as amended by FA 1990, s 112) and s 144 are designed to deal with matters of stamp duty and stamp duty reserve tax respectively in relation to what are described as paired shares.

FA 1988, s 143 as amended by FA 1990, s 112, applies only where:

(1) a UK company's Articles of Association and the equivalent constitutional documents of a foreign incorporated company each provide that a share in one company can only be transferred as part of a unit involving a share in the other company; and

(2) other units are to be, or have been, offered for sale to the public both in the UK and in the country in which the foreign company is incorporated at a broadly equivalent price. The offers are required to be made at the same time.[1]

There is an exemption from bearer instrument duty[2] which applies to any bearer instrument representing shares in a UK company, or to a right of allotment of such shares or subscription therefore if issued:

(1) for sale (as part of units) pursuant to either the simultaneous public offerings at broadly equivalent prices referred to above or in a country other than the UK or the country of incorporation of the foreign company; or

(2) to effect an allotment of such shares (as components of such units) as fully or partly paid bonus shares.[3]

It is provided that where bearer shares in, or bearer warrants over shares of, the foreign company are issued otherwise than pursuant to any of the public offers referred to above, bearer instrument duty will be payable as if the foreign company was formed or established in Great Britain (and the exemption from duty relating to stock in foreign currencies will not apply (FA 1999, Sch 15, Part II, para 17)).[4]

Stamp duty is payable at the rate of 1.5% on transfers of relevant securities in UK companies to certain transferees under FA 1986, ss 67, 68 (depositary receipts) and ss 70, 71 (clearance services). It is provided that where a foreign company's shares are paired with those of the UK company, the foreign company will be treated as incorporated in the UK so that duty will be charged on the consideration for the unit and not just for the UK component.[5]

There is provision to eliminate the need for any bearer instrument representing shares or a right to allotment of, or to subscribe for, shares in either the UK or the foreign company, to be separately stamped as regards each security represented thereby.[6]

Sergeant and Sims A13.5 [954]–[990].

[1] FA 1988, s 143(1) as amended by FA 1990, s 112.
[2] FA 1988, s 143(2) as amended by FA 1999, Sch 16, para 11.
[3] FA 1988, s 143(3) as amended by FA 1999, Sch 16, para 11.
[4] FA 1988, s 143(4) as amended by FA 1999, Sch 16, para 11(4).
[5] FA 1988, s 143(5), (6).
[6] FA 1988, s 143(7).

Unit trusts—transfer of units

History

[59.14] Unit trusts were previously subjected to stamp duty in two principal ways. The first was unit trust instrument duty, which was charged by FA 1946 and later by FA 1962, s 30(1), when the trust was created or added to by contribution of capital: this head of charge was abolished by FA 1988, s 140. The second was the appropriate head of duty applicable on the transfer of units in the trust which could have been a conveyance on sale or a conveyance by voluntary disposition (unless certified as exempt).

It is provided that any references to stock in stamp duty legislation includes a reference to unit trust units[1] (and sub-units);[2] among the consequences of this were that a transfer of property to trustees in exchange for units was a conveyance on sale[3] and that the nil rate of conveyance on sale duty did not apply.[4] It also followed that an agreement for sale of units was not liable to duty as a conveyance under SA 1891, s 59.

However, no stamp duty is chargeable on transfers of units in a unit trust scheme that take place on or after 6 February 2000. From this date a new stamp duty reserve tax regime applies for the transfer of units.[5]

Sergeant and Sims A12.1 [831].

[59.14] Companies—stamp duty (and stamp duty reserve tax)

1   FA 1946, s 54(1).
2   FA 1946, s 57(1) "unit".
3   SA 1891, s 55; supra, § 57.07.
4   FA 1984, s 109. See supra, §§ 57.02–57.03.
5   FA 1999, s 122 and Sch 19 and the Stamp Duty Reserve Tax (Amendment No 2) Regulations 1999, SI 1999/3264 which provide for the administration and enforcement of the SDRT regime; for stamp duty reserve tax generally, see infra, Chapter 61.

Unit trust instrument duty—abolition

[59.15] As indicated unit trust instrument was abolished by FA 1988, s 140.

There is now a fixed stamp duty of £5 (as a declaration of trust) on a trust deed or other instrument creating or recording a unit trust.

Stamp duty reserve tax on surrenders of units

[59.16] Stamp duty reserve tax is charged where a unit holder under a unit trust scheme on or after 6 February 2000 transfers a unit to the scheme managers or authorities or requires the managers to treat him as no longer interested in a unit under the scheme.[1] The tax charge is at 0.5% of the market value of the unit surrendered at the time it is surrendered.[2] The trustees of the unit trust are liable for the tax. The tax charge applies whether or not the transfer takes place in, or any of the parties are resident or situated in, the UK at the time of the surrender.

Where the unit trust is growing and there are at least as many sales to new investors (including the resale of existing units and the issue of new ones) as there are surrenders, this 0.5% charge will be the final liability. However, where the unit trust is shrinking and there are more surrenders of units than sales of units to new investors during a two-week period starting at the beginning of the week in which the surrender occurred (and for this purpose a week is seven days beginning with a Sunday), the tax charge is reduced by applying the following fraction:

$$\frac{\text{Number of sales to new investors}}{\text{Number of surrenders}}$$

See FA 1999, Sch 19, para 4.

This reduction in the tax charge is only available to surrenders for which the unit holder only receives money. This prevents a double charge when the trust's underlying assets are sold because these normally attract stamp duty in their own right. The overall effect of these rules is that where a unit is surrendered and then that unit is resold or a new unit is sold to another investor so there is in effect a transfer between two investors, there will be one 0.5% tax charge just as when company shares are transferred between two investors. However, when the surrender is not matched by a sale to a new investor there will be no tax charge as there is no effective transfer between two investors.

[1] FA 1999, Sch 19, para 2
[2] FA 1999, Sch 19, para 3.

Transfer on sale duty

[59.17] The abolition of unit trust instrument duty does not affect stamp duty and stamp duty reserve tax on the transfer of property to a unit trust.

Unit trust schemes

[59.18] "Unit Trust Scheme" has the same meaning as in the Financial Services and Markets Act 2000, s 237.

An employee share ownership plan approved under FA 2000, Sch 8 is not a "unit trust scheme".[1] Unit trust schemes and open ended investment companies where the units or shares can only be held within individual pension accounts and a limited partnership formed under the Limited Partnerships Act 1907 are not treated as unit trust schemes for the purposes of stamp duty and stamp duty reserve tax.[2]

Sergeant and Sims A2.1, A6.11 [487].

[1] Stamp Duty and Stamp Duty Reserve Tax (Definition of Unit Trust Scheme) (Amendment) Regulations 2000, SI 2000/2549.
[2] Stamp Duty and Stamp Duty Reserve Tax (Definition of Unit Trust Scheme and Open Ended Investment Company) Regulations 2001, SI 2001/964 and Stamp Duty and Stamp Duty Reserve Tax (Definition of Unit Trust Scheme) Regulations 1988, SI 1988/268.

Mergers of authorised unit trusts

[59.19] From 19 March 1997 to 1 July 1999, there was an exemption from charges to stamp duty in respect of instruments which were executed to transfer property on the merger of authorised unit trusts.[1]

The conditions for exemption were as follows:

(1) the transfer forms part of an arrangement under which the whole of the available property of the transferring unit trust is transferred;
(2) all of the units in the transferring unit trust are extinguished;
(3) part or all of the consideration provided to the persons who held extinguished units is the issue of units in the acquiring unit trust issued in proportion to their holdings of the extinguished units; and
(4) the consideration does not include anything else other than the assumption or discharge by the acquiring unit trust of the liabilities of the trustees of the transferring unit trust.[2]

Provision was made so that each of the parts of an "umbrella scheme" (within the meaning of TA 1988, s 468) was regarded as an authorised unit trust for this purpose.[3]

[59.19] Companies—stamp duty (and stamp duty reserve tax)

Instruments which were not chargeable to stamp duty by virtue of this exemption had to be adjudicated pursuant to SA 1891, s 12, and stamped with a stamp denoting that they were not chargeable with any duty.[4]

It has been held by a Special Commissioner that a scheme of amalgamation under which the units in the discontinuing scheme were cancelled and new units in the continuing scheme would be created and issued to unit holders in the discontinuing scheme, took effect by operation of law and did not involve an agreement to transfer chargeable securities so that no stamp duty reserve tax liability arose.[5]

Sergeant and Sims Division B [3786]–[3820].

[1] FA 1997, s 95(1), (4) and (6); an authorised unit trust is defined as a unit trust scheme in the case of which an order under Financial Services and Markets Act 2000, s 243 is in force. See also infra, § **59.20** note 6.
[2] FA 1997, s 95(2).
[3] FA 1997, s 95(5).
[4] FA 1997, s 95(3).
[5] *Save and Prosper Securities Ltd v IRC* [2000] STC (SCD) 408. See also SDRT Customer Newsletter no 7 issued 24 May 2004, dealing with amalgamations and mergers and other transactions relating to unit trusts and open-ended investment companies and outlining the circumstances in which it is accepted that stamp duty and stamp duty reserve tax will not arise.

Open-ended investment companies

[59.20] The Treasury have by regulations made provision in order that special stamp duty and stamp duty reserve tax rules apply to open-ended investment companies.[1] Where the shares of an open-ended investment company are repurchased by its authorised corporate director, these rules mirror the stamp duty and stamp duty reserve tax rules for repurchases of units in authorised unit trusts.[2] The regulations also introduced an exemption from stamp duty when the whole of an authorised unit trust (or sub-fund of an umbrella authorised unit trust) converts to an open-ended investment company or a sub-fund of an umbrella company.[3] There was also a temporary exemption until 30 June 1999 where the whole of an authorised unit trust (or sub-fund of an umbrella authorised unit trust) merged with a continuing open-ended investment company or a continuing sub-fund of an umbrella company.[4] It is also provided that neither FA 1930, s 42 nor FA 1986, ss 75–77 apply in relation to open-ended investment companies.[5]

Regulations made under FA 1995, s 152 apply the stamp duty reserve tax regime for transfers of units in a unit trust contained in FA 1999, Sch 19 to dealings in shares in open-ended investment companies with appropriate modifications.[6]

Sergeant and Sims Division D [5100]–[5101].

[1] See Stamp Duty and Stamp Duty Reserve Tax (Open-ended Investment Companies) Regulations 1997, SI 1997/1156, which were made under FA 1995, s 152 and came

into force on 28 April 1997. See also Inland Revenue Press Releases dated 7 April 1997.
2   SI 1997/1156, reg 4.
3   SI 1997/1156, reg 7.
4   SI 1997/1156, reg 9. This exemption was first extended until such time as Treasury regulations were made to allow the formation of a wider range of open-ended investment companies when the exemption was to end one year after the coming into force of such regulations: Inland Revenue press release 105/99 and SI 1999/1467. Such regulations were made under the Financial Services and Markets Act 2000 with effect from 1 December 2001. However, the exemption has now been extended indefinitely.
5   SI 1997/1156, regs 11, 12.
6   The Stamp Duty and Stamp Duty Reserve Tax (Opened-ended Investment Companies) (Amendment No 2) Regulations 1999, SI 1999/3261 and see FA 1999, Sch 19, para 13 giving a more comprehensive definition of stamp duty reserve tax in FA 1995, s 152 to enable the regulations to be made.

Individual Pension Accounts (IPAs)

[59.21] FA 2001, ss 93 and 94 together with SI 2001/964 create an exemption from stamp duty reserve tax for units in unit trusts and shares in open-ended investment companies held within IPAs. Surrenders of units held in IPAs are exempt from stamp duty reserve tax and are left out of account for the purpose of calculating the tax payable under FA 1999, Sch 19. Surrenders of shares within IPA classes are also exempt and are similarly left out of account when calculating the tax payable. A Stamp Office Newsletter dated 15 May 2001 explains the three methods available to investment fund managers to operate these exemptions.

60

Companies—reliefs

Relief from conveyance on sale and lease duty—transfers and
leases between associated bodies corporate — PARA **60.01**
Relief from conveyance on sale duty—company reconstructions — PARA **60.06**
Relief from conveyance on sale duty—marketable securities — PARA **60.10**
Relief from duty—demutualisation of insurance companies — PARA **60.16**

Relief from conveyance on sale and lease duty—transfers and leases between Associated Bodies Corporate

The relief

[60.01] FA 1930, s 42 provides relief from conveyance on sale duty[1] for an instrument which transfers a beneficial interest in property from one associated company to another. Section 42 was amended by FA 1995 so as to relax the conditions to which the relief is subject (the requirement of 90% of beneficial share ownership for associated status being reduced to 75%) and the relief was also extended to instruments chargeable under the lease charge. However, FA 2000, s 123 has considerably tightened up the scope of the relief by aligning the definition of a stamp duty group of companies with the corporation tax definition.

For the relief to apply, both parties must be bodies corporate which are associated at the time the instrument is executed.[2] The relief is not available if the instrument is executed in pursuance of or in connection with an arrangement whereby:

(1) the consideration was to be provided or received by a person other than an associated body corporate; or
(2) the parties were to cease to be associated; or
(3) in relation to conveyance on sale relief, the beneficial interest conveyed was previously conveyed by a person other than an associated body corporate.[3]

The relief is disapplied in relation to open-ended investment companies.[4]

The relief will be withdrawn in relation to transfers of UK land where in certain circumstances the transferee company leaves the group within two years holding an interest in the land.[5]

As with other reliefs the claim must be adjudicated.[6] The Stamp Office has issued explanatory notes about the procedural requirements.[7]

[60.01] Companies—reliefs

Sergeant and Sims A14.1, Division B [3224]–[3225].

[1] It is considered to apply to purchases by companies of own shares (see supra, § 59.06).
[2] FA 1930, s 42(2) (conveyances); FA 1995, s 151(2) (leases). See infra, § 60.02.
[3] See infra, §§ 60.03–60.04.
[4] Stamp Duty and Stamp Duty Reserve Tax (Open-ended Investment Companies) Regulations 1997, SI 1997/1156, reg 11; see supra, § 59.20.
[5] FA 2002, s 111; see infra, § 60.05.
[6] FA 1930, s 42(1) (conveyances); FA 1995, s 151(5) (leases).
[7] The notes are reproduced in **Sergeant and Sims Division B [3225]**. The Stamp Office no longer routinely requires a formal statutory declaration in support of such a claim, see Budget Press Release REV5, 21 March 2000.

Conditions for relief—associate status

[60.02] Companies are treated as associated if (a) one is the beneficial owner of at least 75% of the ordinary share capital of the other, or (b) a third body corporate is the beneficial owner of at least 75% of the ordinary share capital of both bodies corporate.[1] So if X Ltd owns all the shares of Y Ltd and Z Ltd, X is associated with Y and with Z under rule (a) and Y and Z are associated with each other under rule (b). Ordinary share capital means all the issued share capital (by whatever name called), other than capital the holders of which have a right to a dividend at a fixed rate but have no other right to share in the profits of the body corporate.[2] Prior to FA 1995, FA 1930 s 42 referred to "issued share capital" and it was held that the amount of issued share capital is calculated by adding up the nominal value of the shares issued without regard either to market value or to different classes of shares.[3] Shares which have not yet been registered are not regarded as issued for this purpose.[4]

In this context, beneficial ownership is ownership either directly or through another body corporate or other bodies corporate, or partly directly and partly through another body corporate or other bodies corporate, and FA 1938, Sch 4, Part I (determination of amount of capital held through other bodies corporate), applies for the purposes of the relief.[5] Indirect holdings are taken into account using a multiplication formula; so if P Ltd owns 80% of the shares in Q Ltd which holds 50% of the shares in R Ltd, P owns 40% of the shares in R Ltd.

In addition, FA 2000, s 123 (amending FA 1930, s 42) imposed the following additional tests:

(1) the parent must be beneficially entitled to not less than 75% of any profits available for distribution to equity holders of the other company; and
(2) the parent would be beneficially entitled to not less than 75% of any assets of the other company available for distribution to its equity holders on a winding-up; and

(3) the relief will not apply if at the time the instrument is executed arrangements are in existence by virtue of which at that or some later time any person has or could obtain, or any persons together have or could obtain, control of the transferee company but not of the transferor.[6]

TA 1988, Sch 18 applies for the purposes of 1 and 2 above as it applies for the purposes of corporation tax (with the exception of paragraphs 5(3) and 5B to 5E in relation to the transferor company only) and in 3 above "control" is construed in accordance with TA 1988, s 840.[7]

The beneficial ownership of property will normally pass from a vendor to a purchaser upon their entering into an unconditional contract of sale. Accordingly, once a body corporate has entered into an unconditional contract to sell shares in its subsidiary to a person other than an associated body corporate it will cease to be the beneficial owner of those shares and a conveyance of property from that subsidiary to its parent or to another subsidiary of the parent will not qualify for relief unless the 75% condition can be satisfied by reference to shares not comprised in the contract.[8] As to beneficial ownership, see the cases noted infra, § **60.03**.

Sergeant and Sims A14.1, Division B [3224]–[3225], [3229]–[3240], [3322]–[3745].

[1] FA 1930, s 42(2A), (2B) inserted by FA 1995, s 149 (conveyances); FA 1995, s 151(7) (leases).
[2] FA 1930, s 42(4) inserted by FA 1995, s 149 (conveyances); FA 1995, s 151(9) (leases).
[3] *Canada Safeway Ltd v IRC* [1972] 1 All ER 666.
[4] *Holmleigh (Holdings) Ltd v IRC (1958) 46 TC 435*; *National Westminster Bank plc v IRC* [1994] STC 580, HL; 3 All ER 1.
[5] FA 1930, s 42(3) (conveyances); FA 1995 s 151(10) (leases).
[6] FA 1930, s 42(2), (2B) amended and inserted by FA 2000, s 123.
[7] FA 1930, s 42(5), (6) inserted by FA 2000, s 123.
[8] *Parway Estates Ltd v IRC* (1958) 45 TC 135.

Conveyances—transfer of beneficial interest

[60.03] Where the instrument of transfer has been preceded by an agreement for sale between associated bodies corporate the beneficial interest will in most cases have passed to the transferee by virtue of the agreement. Nevertheless, the instrument will qualify for relief as it is to be stamped in respect of the consideration for the beneficial interest which passed under the agreement.[1] However, where the beneficial interest has previously passed to the transferee from a person who is not an associated body corporate, a subsequent transfer of the legal estate to the transferee by an associated body corporate will not qualify for relief.

There was a divergence of opinion in the House of Lords in *Escoigne Properties Ltd v IRC*[2] as to whether an instrument could qualify for relief if the transfer of the beneficial interest was not the sole effect of the instrument. In that case the instrument operated not only to transfer the beneficial interest from a purchaser to a sub-purchaser but, in addition, to complete a sale agreed on some years before between the purchaser and his vendor. Lord Simonds and Lord Reid expressed the view that an instrument would not be deprived of relief because it had a dual effect whereas Lord Keith thought that it would. Lord Denning arrived at the same conclusion as Lord Simonds and Lord Reid but for different reasons. Lord Somervell did not express any view on the matter being of the opinion that the instrument was chargeable "in respect of the equitable interest as passing from the original vendor to the sub-purchaser" and therefore did not satisfy the requirements for relief.

A company which has entered into an unconditional contract of sale is not the beneficial owner of the property.[3] Even a conditional contract has had this effect if the purchaser can waive the conditions[4] or where the vendor is otherwise unable to sell.[5] The courts have even held that when a company is controlled by persons who have bound themselves to procure a sale by the company, the company is not the beneficial owner.[6] A company ceases to be a beneficial owner when it is placed in liquidation.[7] In a case involving an option to purchase shares, it has been held that although beneficial ownership could not exist without equitable ownership, it involved more than ownership of an empty shell bereft of those rights of beneficial enjoyment which normally attached to equitable ownership.[8]

Sergeant and Sims A14.1, Division B [3224].

---

[1] FA 1930, s 42(2)(*a*).
[2] *Escoigne Properties Ltd v IRC* [1958] AC 549.
[3] *Parway Estates Ltd v IRC (1958) 45 TC 135*; *Baytrust Holdings Ltd v IRC* [1971] 3 All ER 76.
[4] *Wood Preservation Ltd v Prior* [1968] 2 All ER 849.
[5] *Brooklands Selangor Holdings Ltd v IRC* [1970] 2 All ER 76.
[6] *Holmleigh (Holdings) Ltd v IRC (1958) 46 TC 435*.
[7] *Ayerst v C & K (Construction) Ltd* [1976] AC 167.
[8] *J Sainsbury plc v O'Connor* [1991] STC 318, CA, involving a group relief claim under TA 1970, s 258 (now split between TA 1988, ss 402 and 413)—F(No 2)A 1992, s 24, Sch 6, para 2 alter the tax law on this point—(*Wood Preservation Ltd v Prior* [1969] 1 All ER 164, [1969] 1 WLR 1077, CA, was distinguished).

Restriction of relief

[60.04] It is also necessary to show[1] that the conveyance, lease or agreement for lease was not effected in pursuance or in connection with any arrangement under which:

(1) the consideration—or any part of it—was to be provided or received, directly or indirectly, by a person other than a body corporate which was then an associated body corporate; or

(2) the transferor and transferee or the lessor and lessee were to cease to be associated by reason of the transferor/lessor or a third party corporate ceasing to be the transferee's/lessee's parent; or
(3) in relation to a conveyance, the beneficial interest was previously conveyed or transferred, directly or indirectly, by such a third party.

Under the previous legislation it had been held that a third party "provided consideration" if the amount due was left unpaid and that person guaranteed it or otherwise intends to provide for payment,[2] or if the money is to be raised by a sale of the assets to that person.[3]

The words "conveyed or transferred" referred to in paragraph 3 above have been construed widely to include the grant of a lease by the third party.[4]

These conditions were enacted to counter avoidance schemes.[5] The general words "in connection with" and "arrangement" are presumably to be construed widely.[6]

It is not necessary that the company seeking the relief be an English or Scottish company.

An example of the device at which these rules are aimed is the "dummy bridge company". It was explained by Lord Denning in *Escoigne Properties Ltd v IRC*[7] as follows:

> They took advantage of s 42 by forming a small company which was a puppet in their hands. It was done in this way: If company A. wished to sell property to company B. for £100,000 and avoid stamp duty, company A. would form a small 'bridge' company of 100 £1 shares in which it held all the shares. Company A. would convey the property to the 'bridge' company for £100,000 but the price would be left owing. By reason of s 42 that conveyance would be exempt from stamp duty. Then company A. would sell the 100 shares in the 'bridge' company to company B. for £100: and stamp duty of a trifling amount would be paid on the transfer. The 'bridge' company would then convey the property to company B. for £100,000 on the terms that the £100,000 should be paid direct to company A. By reason of s 42 no stamp duty would be payable on that conveyance. So the sale from company A. to company B. was completed without paying any stamp duty on the £100,000. . . . The object of s 50 was to put a stop to that device: and it succeeded. If any one were to resort to it after 1938 both conveyances would be liable to stamp duty. The first conveyance would be caught by subsection (1)(

It has been suggested that relief should not be excluded by reason only of a previous transfer having been made which was duly stamped.[8]

The then Inland Revenue issued Statement of Practice 3/98 on 13 October 1998 outlining the way the Stamp Office approach the application of the above anti-avoidance rules.

Sergeant and Sims A14.1, Division B [3225].

---

[1] Pursuant to FA 1967, s 27(3) (conveyances); FA 1995, s 151(2)(*d*), (3), (4) (leases).
[2] *Curzon Offices Ltd v IRC* [1944] 1 All ER 163 and 606.
[3] *Metropolitan Boot Co Ltd v IRC* (1958) 46 TC 435.
[4] *IRC v Littlewoods Mail Order Stores Ltd* [1963] AC 135.
[5] See *Shop and Store Developments Ltd v IRC* [1967] 1 AC 472 and *Times Newspapers Ltd v IRC* [1973] Ch 155.

[60.04] Companies—reliefs

[6] See *Clarke Chapman-John Thompson Ltd v IRC* [1976] Ch 91.
[7] [1958] AC 549.
[8] See Law Society's Revenue Law Committee Memorandum "Revenue Law Reform 1990–91", *Simon's Tax Intelligence* 1991, p 39.

Withdrawal of relief

[60.05] Where the relief has been applied to a transfer of UK land and within three years of the date of the transfer the transferee company cease to be a member of the same group as the transferor company and at that time the transferee (or a relevant associated company) holds an interest in the land that was transferred to it or that is derived from the land transferred, the group relief is withdrawn. The stamp duty that would have been payable but for the relief had the land been transferred at market value becomes payable within 30 days of the transferee leaving the group. To be subject to withdrawal the relevant transfer instrument must have been executed after 23 April 2002.[1] There are detailed rules relating to the scope and operation of the withdrawal of the relief.[2] In particular the relief will not be withdrawn if the transferor company leaves the group. Where the relief is withdrawn interest is charged from 30 days after the transferee leaves the group, the transferee company is required to notify IR Stamp Taxes and the unpaid duty can be recovered from the transferor, another group company that is above the transferee in the group structure or a controlling director of either the transferee or of a company having control of the transferee, if the transferee company fails to pay it within six months.

[1] FA 2002, s 111 amended by FA 2003, s 126 increasing the clawback period from two to three years for instruments executed after 14 April 2003; see infra, § **62.15** or transactions after 30 November 2003.
[2] FA 2002, Sch 34 amended by FA 2003, s 126.

Relief from conveyance on sale duty—company reconstructions

Acquisition reliefs

Schemes of reconstruction

[60.06] There is an exemption for schemes of reconstruction where there is no real change of ownership.[1]

The provision applies where a company acquires the whole or part of an undertaking of another company (the target company) as part of a scheme of reconstruction.[2] The exemption from stamp duty applies provided that two conditions are met.[3] Broadly these ensure that the undertaking continues to be owned by the same shareholders before and after the acquisition.

Relief from conveyance on sale duty, etc. [60.07]

There is a requirement of adjudication where the instrument transferring the undertaking or part of an undertaking is claimed to be exempt from duty under these provisions.[4]

As regards the first of the conditions[5] to be satisfied in order to qualify for the exemption, the consideration for the transfer[6] of the undertaking must be the issue of shares in the acquiring company to all the shareholders of the target company. The shares issued as consideration for the undertaking must be non-redeemable shares.[7] There must be no other consideration apart from the assumption or discharge by the acquiring company of the target company's liabilities.

As regards the second condition[8] the undertaking must be acquired for bona fide commercial reasons and the acquisition must not form part of a scheme which has as its main purpose, or one of its main purposes, the avoidance of tax. There is also a requirement that the shares must be issued on a pro rata basis so that each shareholder holds the same, or as nearly as may be the same, proportion of shares in both companies both before and after the acquisition.

As regards both the first and second conditions, any shares held by either the target company or the acquiring company in itself immediately before the acquisition are treated as if they had been cancelled so that the company concerned is treated as if it were not a shareholder in itself.[9]

The relief is disapplied in relation to open-ended investment companies.[10]

Sergeant and Sims A15.2, Division B [3442]–[3539].

---

[1] FA 1986, s 75. As to the meaning of "reconstruction", see *Swithland Investments Ltd v IRC* [1990] STC 448. For precedent letter of claim, see infra, § **60.09**.
[2] FA 1986, s 75(1).
[3] FA 1986, s 75(2).
[4] FA 1986, s 75(3).
[5] FA 1986, s 75(4) as amended by FA 2006, s 169(2)(a).
[6] See *IRC v Kent Process Control Ltd* [1989] STC 245.
[7] FA 1986, s 75(4), as amended by FA 2000, s 127.
[8] FA 1986, s 75(5) as amended by FA 2006, s 169(2)(b).
[9] FA 1986, s 75(5A) added by FA 2007, s 74(1).
[10] Stamp Duty and Stamp Duty Reserve Tax (Open-ended Investment Companies) Regulations 1997, SI 1997/1156, reg 12; see supra, § **59.20**.

Acquisition of target company's share capital

[60.07] During the debate at the report stage of the 1986 Finance Bill, attention was drawn to a problem which seemed to emerge from the wording of the Bill enacted as FA 1986, s 75 outlined above. Whilst it was clear that the relief thereunder would apply where the reorganisation involved a transfer of a trading subsidiary from one group member to another, provided the consideration consisted of shares and the shares were issued to the shareholders of the target company, it appeared that they could not be issued to the target company itself. On that basis, therefore, there would have been no relief where a group wished to restructure itself and put a new holding company on

[60.07] Companies—reliefs

top of the existing group.[1] In such a situation the acquiring company would have needed to issue shares to the target company and not to the shareholders of the target company. The problem was recognised and accepted by the Government and a new clause to the Finance Bill was introduced. The provisions are now contained in FA 1986, s 77 to take into account the possibility of placing a holding company over the top of an existing group and to grant the relief in such circumstances provided the conditions laid down therein are satisfied.

The conditions[2] are that:

(1) the transfer forms part of an arrangement by which the acquiring company acquires the whole of the issued share capital of the target company;

(2) acquisition is effected for bona fide commercial reasons and does not form part of a scheme or arrangement of which the main purpose, or one of the main purposes, is avoidance of liability to stamp duty, stamp duty reserve tax, income tax, corporation tax or CGT;

(3) the consideration for the acquisition consists only of the issue of shares in the acquiring company to the shareholders of the target company;

(4) after the acquisition has been made, each person who immediately before it was made was a shareholder of the target company is a shareholder of the acquiring company;

(5) after the acquisition has been made, the shares in the acquiring company are of the same classes as were the shares in the target company immediately before the acquisition was made;

(6) after the acquisition has been made, the number of shares of any particular class in the acquiring company bears to all the shares in that company the same proportion, or as nearly as may be the same proportion, as the number of shares of that class in the target company bore to all the shares in that company immediately before the acquisition was made; and

(7) after the acquisition has been made, the proportion of shares of any particular class in the acquiring company held by any particular shareholder is the same, or as nearly as may be the same, as the proportion of shares of that class in the target company held by him immediately before the acquisition was made.

The references to shares and to share capital in the provisions include references to stock.[3]

The relief applies to any instrument executed after 31 July 1986[4] but is disapplied in relation to open-ended investment companies.[5]

Any shares held by either the target company or the acquiring company in itself immediately before the acquisition are treated as if they had been cancelled so that the company concerned is treated as if it was not a shareholder in itself.[6]

Sergeant and Sims A15.2, Division B [3442]–[3539].

---

[1] FA 1986, s 75(6), (7).
[2] FA 1986, s 77(3) as amended by FA 2006, s 169(4).

³ FA 1986, s 77(4).
⁴ FA 1986, s 77(5).
⁵ Stamp Duty and Stamp Duty Reserve Tax (Open-ended Investment Companies) Regulations 1997, SI 1997/1156, reg 12; see supra, § **59.20**.
⁶ FA 1986, s 77(3A) added by FA 2007 s 74(2).

Further relief provisions

[60.08] FA 1986, s 76 is designed to ensure that transfers of property (other than shares) previously exempt under the provisions repealed from 27 October 1986 are charged to no more than the 0.5% rate on or after 27 October 1986.

The relief applies where a company (the acquiring company) acquires the whole or part of the undertaking of another company (the target company).[1]

(1) There is provision for a special rate of duty (as set out) where an instrument is executed for the purposes of transferring an undertaking or for the transfer to the acquiring company by a creditor of "relevant debts" (as defined and explained below) by a creditor of the target company.[2]

(2) There is then set out the conditions to be satisfied for the 0.5% rate of duty to apply. The consideration must include the issue of shares to the target company itself or some or all of its shareholders.[3] The shares issued must be non-redeemable shares.[4]

In relation to an instrument transferring UK land, a further condition applies. This is that the acquiring company must not be associated with another company that has entered into arrangements with the target company relating to the consideration shares issued by the acquiring company ie for the other company to acquire the consideration shares from the target company.[5]

The only other consideration allowed is:

(1) cash (not exceeding 10% of the nominal value of the shares issued); and
(2) the assumption or discharge by the acquiring company of the liabilities of the target company.

A duty at a rate of 0.5% is imposed where the instrument is within the terms of paragraph 1 and satisfies the condition in paragraph 2.[6]

There is a requirement of adjudication where an instrument is liable to the 0.5% rate under this provision.[7]

The expression "relevant debts" is defined as debts owed by the target company to a bank or a trade creditor or any other debt incurred not less than two years before the transfer takes place.[8]

The provisions in FA 1986, s 76 apply to instruments executed after 26 October 1986. Instruments executed earlier are covered by FA 1986, s 73.[9]

The relief is disapplied in relation to open-ended investment companies.[10]

The relief is subject to withdrawal in the case of a transfer of UK land where within three years of the transfer, control of the acquiring company changes

[60.08] Companies—reliefs

and at that time the company (or a relevant associated company) holds an interest in the land that was transferred to it by the transfer or is derived from it. "Control" is as defined in TA 1988, s 416.[11] There are detailed rules providing for the scope and operation of the withdrawal of the relief.[12] In particular, the relief will not be withdrawn if control of the acquiring company changes as a result of a transfer of shares to which either group relief applies or relief under FA 1986, s 77 applies: see supra, §§ **60.01** and **60.07**. Where the relief is withdrawn interest is charged from 30 days after control of the acquiring company changes, the acquiring company is required to notify IR Stamp Taxes and the unpaid duty can be recovered from another group company that is above the acquiring company in the group structure or a controlling director of the acquiring company or of a company having control of the acquiring company, if the acquiring company fails to pay it within six months.

Sergeant and Sims A15.3, Division B [3442]–[3539].

[1] FA 1986, s 76(1). For explanatory notes and precedent letter of claim, see infra, § **60.09**.
[2] FA 1986, s 76(2).
[3] FA 1986, s 76(3) as amended by FA 2006, s 169(3).
[4] FA 1986, s 76(3) as amended by FA 2000, s 127.
[5] FA 1986, s 76(3A) inserted by FA 2002, s 112.
[6] FA 1986, s 76(4).
[7] FA 1986, s 76(5).
[8] FA 1986, s 76(6).
[9] FA 1986, s 76(7).
[10] Stamp Duty and Stamp Duty Reserve Tax (Open-ended Investment Companies) Regulations 1997, SI 1997/1156, reg 12; see supra, § **59.20**.
[11] FA 2002, s 113 amended by FA 2003, s 127 increasing the clawback period from two to three years for instruments executed after 14 April 2003; see infra, § **62.19** for transactions after 30 November 2003.
[12] FA 2002, Sch 35 amended by FA 2003, s 127.

Procedure

[60.09] The Stamp Office has issued a set of explanatory notes and precedent letters of claim for relief under FA 1986, ss 75–77.[1] Comparable precedent letters are available from the Stamp Offices in Edinburgh and Belfast.

[1] The notes are reproduced in **Sergeant and Sims Division F [5709]** and the precedent letters are reproduced on **Division F [5721]**.

Relief from conveyance on sale duty—marketable securities

Sales to intermediaries

[60.10] For instruments executed before 20 October 1997, FA 1986, s 81 provided an exemption from stamp duty for purchases of shares, etc by market makers. For instruments executed on or after that date, this exemption was replaced by an exemption for such purchases by intermediaries. The exemption was contained in FA 1986, s 80A.[1] A number of supplementary definitions are contained in FA 1986, s 80B.[2]

The scope of this exemption was widened significantly for instruments executed on or after 1 November, 2007 following the implementation of the Markets in Financial Instruments Directive (2004/39/EC) on that date.[3]

An instrument qualifying for this exemption must be stamped with a stamp denoting that the instrument is not chargeable with any duty.[4]

---

[1] Inserted by FA 1997, s 97(1) which was brought into force on 20 October 1997 by the Finance Act 1997 (Stamp Duty and Stamp Duty Reserve Tax) (Appointed Day) Order 1997, SI 1997/2428. FA 1997, s 97(2) repealed FA 1986, s 81 with effect from the same date.
[2] Inserted also by FA 1997, s 97(1).
[3] FA 2007 s 73, Sch 21. A detailed explanation of the relief is contained in a note entitled "Intermediary and Stock Landing Reliefs – FA 2007 Changes" published by HMRC.
[4] FA 1986, s 80A(7)

Repurchases and stock lending

[60.11] Repurchases ("repos") and stock lending arrangements are arrangements for the sale and return, or lending and return, of securities. Under FA 1986, s 80C these transactions are exempt from stamp duty (and from stamp duty reserve tax under FA 1986, s 89AA) provided that securities of the same kind and amount are returned to the seller or lender under the terms of the arrangement. The instruments of transfer must be stamped with a stamp denoting that the instrument is not chargeable with any duty. At least one of the parties must be authorised under the law of a state of the European Economic Area to provide investment services or execution of orders, etc in stock of the kind concerned and stock of that kind must be regularly traded on a regulated market. There are also other conditions stipulated in FA 1986, s 80C. With effect from 1 September 2008 the new FA 1986, s 80D[1] has provided that where the securities are not returned to the seller or lender because one of the parties has become insolvent, stamp duty is not chargeable on any instrument transferring to the solvent party replacement stock or any further replacement stock.

Sergeant and Sims Division B [3442]–[3539], Division D [5102].

[60.11] Companies—reliefs

---

[1] Inserted by FA 2009, s 82 and Sch 37.

Composition agreements

[60.12] The Revenue are enabled to enter into composition arrangements for the payment of stamp duty with recognised clearing houses.[1] FA 1970, s 33 already provides for this in relation to the Stock Exchange. Section 33 is amended to enable similar arrangements to be made with other clearing houses established under the regulatory regime now being provided by the Financial Services Act 1986.[2] The terms of the composition arrangement are to be such as to ensure that there is no loss of duty.

The provision comes into force on a date appointed by the Board of HMRC by statutory instrument.[3]

Sergeant and Sims A18.1 [1321]–[1322], Division B [3442]–[3539].

---

[1] FA 1986, s 83.
[2] FA 1986, s 83(2).
[3] FA 1986, s 83(3).

Transfers to clearing houses

[60.13] There is an exemption for transfers of shares to a clearing house which has entered into a composition arrangement.[1]

There are detailed arrangements for the starting date of these provisions pursuant to an order to be made by the Revenue.[2]

Sergeant and Sims A18.1 [1322].

---

[1] FA 1986, s 84, and see also FA 1991, ss 116 and 117 and the Stamp Duty Reserve Tax (Investment Exchanges and Clearing Houses) (The London Stock Exchange) Regulations 2001, SI 2001/255.
[2] FA 1986, s 84(4)–(6).

Depositary receipts

[60.14] Stamp duty at 1.5% is imposed on the consideration paid when UK shares are transferred against the issue of depositary receipts.[1] Transfers to which the 1.5% stamp duty applies are transfers to nominees which only hold shares for depositary receipt purposes. It is, however, provided that the Treasury shall have the power to extend stamp duty to other nominees if this should prove necessary to prevent avoidance of the charge.[2] There is provision to enable the Revenue to obtain relevant information. It requires persons who issue depositary receipts, or who hold shares as nominees to a person who issues such receipts, or companies which find their shares are being held as depositary receipts, to notify the Revenue of the fact.[3] There are detailed definitions of the terms used.[4] There are equivalent provisions for stamp duty on shares put into duty free clearance systems.[5] In the latter case, it is now possible for an operator of such a clearance system to elect for a charge to stamp duty reserve tax of 0.5% on agreements to transfer chargeable securities within the system rather than the once and for all charge of 1.5% to stamp duty or stamp duty reserve tax on issue or transfer into that system.[6] The existing relief for transfers of shares from one depositary to another, and from one clearance service to another, has been extended to include transfers between the two types of system.[7]

Sergeant and Sims A13.3 [917]–[930], Division B [3442]–[3539].

[1] FA 1986, s 67.
[2] FA 1986, s 69.
[3] FA 1986, s 68.
[4] FA 1986, s 69.
[5] FA 1986, ss 70–72 and FA 1987, s 52.
[6] See infra, § **61.04**.
[7] FA 1986, s 72A inserted by FA 2000, s 134.

Futures markets

[60.15] FA 1991, s 116 provides for powers to make regulations to deal with any stamp duty consequences of the merger between the London Traded Options Market and the London International Financial Futures Exchange ("LIFFE"). Prior to 20 October 1997, the relevant regulations were the Stamp Duty and Stamp Duty Reserve Tax (Investment Exchanges and Clearing Houses) Regulations 1992, SI 1992/570. With effect from that date, these regulations were repealed and replaced by FA 1986, ss 80A, 80B[1] and 80C[2] and by the Stamp Duty and Stamp Duty Reserve Tax (Investment Exchanges and Clearing Houses) Regulations 1997, SI 1997/2429 which together introduce new rules conferring relief from stamp duty for intermediaries dealing in UK securities and in connection with stock borrowing and sale and repurchase agreements.[3]

Sergeant and Sims Division B [3700]–[3708], Division D [5103].

[1] See supra, § **60.10**.
[2] See supra, § **60.11**.
[3] See Inland Revenue press release dated 9 October 1997.

Relief from duty—demutualisation of insurance companies

[60.16] For instruments executed on or after 19 March 1997, there is a limited exemption from stamp duty where they are executed for the purposes

[60.16] Companies—reliefs

of or in connection with the transfer of part or all of the business carried on by a mutual insurance company ("mutual") to a company with a share capital.[1] A mutual is defined as an insurance company carrying on business without having any share capital.[2]

The exemption is conditional upon the satisfaction of the following requirements in relation to the shares of the acquiring company or a company which is a wholly-owned subsidiary of that company:

(1) the shares must be offered to at least 90% of the persons who are members of the mutual immediately prior to the transfer; and
(2) all the shares in the acquiring company which will be in issue immediately after the transfer, other than shares which are to be or have been the subject of a public offer, must be offered to persons who are, at the time of the offer, members of the mutual or persons entitled to become members or employees, former employees or pensioners of the mutual or of a company which is a wholly-owned subsidiary of the mutual.[3]

The transfer must also be one to which the Insurance Companies Act 1982, Sch 2C applies or would apply but for s 151(1A) of that Act.[4]

Instruments which are not chargeable to stamp duty by virtue of this exemption must be adjudicated pursuant to SA 1891, s 12 and stamped with a stamp denoting that they are not chargeable with any duty.[5]

The Treasury may by regulations alter the percentage of members in a mutual to which shares must be offered[6] and prescribe different classes of members to be taken into account in different cases.[7]

Sergeant and Sims Division B [3786].

---

[1] FA 1997, s 96(1).
[2] FA 1997, s 96(8).
[3] FA 1997, s 96(3), (4).
[4] FA 1997, s 96(7).
[5] FA 1997, s 96(5).
[6] FA 1997, s 96(9).
[7] FA 1997, s 96(10).

61

Stamp duty reserve tax

Introduction	PARA **61.01**
The charge	PARA **61.02**
The higher rate charge	PARA **61.04**
Chargeable securities	PARA **61.05**
Exceptions	PARA **61.06**
Liability, accountability and time for payment	PARA **61.16**
Administration, determination and recovery	PARA **61.25**

Introduction

[61.01] Stamp duty reserve tax[1] is charged in respect of agreements to transfer[2] chargeable securities[3] for money or money's worth. For unconditional agreements made before 1 July 1996 or agreements becoming unconditional before that date, the charge was deferred. A liability to tax was imposed after two months except where, within that period, an agreement to transfer securities to a purchaser or a nominee was completed by an instrument of transfer which, if chargeable with stamp duty or otherwise required to be stamped, was duly stamped. Where those conditions were fulfilled within six years of the charge to stamp duty reserve tax arising, there was provision for the repayment of the tax or the cancellation of the charge. There was also an immediate and unconditional charge in respect of agreements to transfer chargeable securities constituted by or transferable by means of certain renounceable instruments as soon as they were made to which the conditions for relief from the charge did not apply.

Under the paperless securities transfer system, CREST, which was introduced in July 1996, changes in title or ownership are made electronically. Accordingly, stamp duty is not paid on an instrument where a transfer is made within the CREST system. For this reason, the two-month period has been removed in relation to agreements made on or after 1 July 1996 or becoming unconditional on or after that date so that the charge to stamp duty reserve tax is now immediate in all cases.[4] Where a transaction is completed by a duly stamped instrument within six years from the date on which the charge is imposed, there is, as before, a provision for the repayment of the tax or the cancellation of the charge.[5] The provisions for repayment or cancellation do not apply in a number of cases.[6]

In each case tax is imposed at the rate of 0.5% of the amount or value of the consideration rounded to the nearest penny. A higher rate charge of 1.5% is imposed in respect of certain transactions involving depositary receipts and clearance services, although it is possible for the operator of a clearance service to elect for a 0.5% charge on agreements to transfer chargeable securities

[61.01] Stamp duty reserve tax

within the system.[7] The value of consideration other than money is the price it might reasonably be expected to fetch in the open market at the time the agreement is made.[8] The rates for stamp duty reserve tax are therefore the same as those for stamp duty on share transfers, but the tax base is broader. Stamp duty reserve tax applies to transactions which are not effected by means of an instrument of transfer and the tax is imposed irrespective of the nature of the consideration. It is for this reason that the introduction of CREST has had a significant impact on stamp duty reserve tax.

Liability for stamp duty reserve tax is imposed on the purchaser,[9] but the tax is usually collected and paid by intermediaries in the securities market or, where transfers are effected on CREST, by the system operator, CRESTCo.[10]

The tax applies whether or not the relevant transaction is made or effected in the UK and whether or not any of the parties are resident or situate in any part of the UK.[11]

As with stamp duty, the tax is under the care and management of the Commissioners of Revenue & Customs.[12] Unlike stamp duty, the tax is directly enforceable and may be recovered by the Commissioners.[13] Appeals are heard in the first instance by the Special Commissioners, rather than upon a case stated to the High Court.[14]

The provisions of PCTA 1968 apply to the tax, thereby allowing future charges and changes to take effect provisionally from the Budget. The provisions of FA 1989, s 182, forbidding the disclosure of information, also apply to the tax.

The administrative scheme for stamp duty reserve tax is set out in the Stamp Duty Reserve Tax Regulations 1986.[15] In order to put beyond doubt the power of the Treasury to make regulations for the administration of the tax, FA 1999, s 121 provides specifically that the power conferred on the Treasury for that purpose by FA 1986, s 98(1) includes power to apply the provisions of the Taxes Management Act 1970 about interest and penalties, to require information to be provided and to require specified persons to account for and pay the tax. A booklet entitled *Stamp Duty Reserve Tax—Notes for Guidance* was reissued by the Stamp Office in February 1998 and this has now been superseded by Chapters 10 to 15 of the Stamp Office Manual published on 20 March 2000.

Sergeant and Sims A19.1 [1421].

---

[1] Introduced by FA 1986, Part IV (ss 86–99). Provision has been made for the abolition of the tax from a date to be appointed by statutory instrument: FA 1990, ss 100, 111.

[2] An issue is not a "transfer". The extent that the stamp duty reserve tax provisions address the issue of securities they do so in express terms: cf FA 1986, ss 89A(2), 93(1)(*b*), 96(1)(*b*). For the difference between the transfer of shares and the issue of shares, see *Re VGM Holdings Ltd* [1942] Ch 235 at 240, 241.

[3] For the meaning of chargeable securities, see infra, § **61.05**.

[4] FA 1996, s 188 amending FA 1986.

[5] See infra, § **61.21**.

[6] See infra, § **61.24**.

[7] See infra, § **61.04**.

[8] See FA 1986, s 87(7).
[9] See infra, § **61.16**.
[10] See infra, § **61.18**.
[11] FA 1986, s 86(4), inserted by FA 1996, s 187. However, the Treasury may make regulations to exempt from the tax UK depositary interests (see infra, § **61.04**) in foreign securities to allow the operator of an electronic settlement service such as CREST to offer a settlement service for deals in foreign shares without incurring a tax liability: FA 1999, s 119.
[12] FA 1986, s 86(2).
[13] See infra, § **61.31**.
[14] See infra, § **61.29**.
[15] SI 1986/1711 as amended by the Stamp Duty Reserve Tax (Amendment) Regulations 1988, SI 1988/835; the Stamp Duty Reserve Tax (Amendment) Regulations 1989, SI 1989/1301; the Stamp Duty Reserve Tax (Amendment) Regulations 1992, SI 1992/3287; the Stamp Duty Reserve Tax (Amendment) Regulations 1993, SI 1993/3110; the Stamp Duty Reserve Tax (Amendment) Regulations 1997, SI 1997/2430.

The charge

Agreements to transfer chargeable securities

[**61.02**] Subject to certain exceptions,[1] where a person (A) agrees with another person (B) to transfer[2] to B or another person chargeable securities[3] for consideration in money or money's worth, there is a charge to stamp duty reserve tax on the day on which the agreement is made (or, where the agreement is conditional, the day on which the condition is satisfied).

Tax is charged at the rate of 0.5% of the amount or value of the consideration.[4] The purchaser, B, is liable for the tax.[5] However, provision is made for collection and payment of the tax by intermediaries in the securities market or operations of systems such as CREST.[6]

Sergeant and Sims A11.1 [771], Division B [3442].

[1] See infra, §§ **61.06** ff.
[2] The word "transfer" does not mean "issue": see supra, § **61.01** note 2.
[3] For the meaning of "chargeable securities", see infra, § **61.05**.
[4] FA 1986, s 87(6).
[5] FA 1986, s 91.
[6] See infra, § **61.18**.

Sub-sales

[**61.03**] FA 1986, s 87(7A)[1] applies where shares (or other chargeable securities) are subsold and the number of shares bought exceeds the number of shares subsold. The subsection provides for FA 1986, ss 87, 88(5) and 92 to have effect as if there were separate agreements in respect of each parcel of

[61.03] Stamp duty reserve tax

shares. The effect of this is that where stamp duty is paid on the share transfers, stamp duty reserve tax is only paid in respect of the shares subsold. The following example shows how this provision operates:

    A   sells to B 1,000 shares in X plc for £1,500;
    B   resells 750 of these shares to C;
    A   transfers 750 shares to C and 250 shares to B.

Subsection (7A) deems the agreement between A and B to be two separate agreements, one in respect of 750 shares and one in respect of 250 shares with the result that B incurs a stamp duty reserve tax liability on the agreement to purchase 750 shares, ie on £1,125 (75% of £1,500). The stamp duty payable on the transfer to B of the 250 shares cancels the stamp duty reserve tax liability on that agreement.

On a strict construction of s 87 as originally enacted there seemed to be a stamp duty reserve tax charge on the whole of the consideration paid by B to A. The original *Stamp Duty Reserve Tax—Notes for Guidance* issued by the Stamp Office in 1986 indicated that tax would only be sought in respect of that part of the consideration which related to the shares subsold. The introduction of s 87(7A) provided a statutory basis for the practice.

Sergeant and Sims A11.4 [794], Division B [3442].

---

[1]   As substituted by FA 1997, s 106(2).

The higher rate charge

Depositary receipts and clearance services

[61.04] Subject to certain exceptions[1] stamp duty reserve tax at 1.5% is imposed where chargeable securities are issued or transferred in exchange for a depositary receipt or appropriated towards satisfaction of a depositary receipt holder's right to obtain chargeable securities under a depositary receipt arrangement.[2] Stamp duty reserve tax at 1.5% is also imposed where chargeable securities are transferred or issued to a clearance house.[3] In each case, the stamp duty reserve tax charge is disapplied to the extent that ad valorem stamp duty is chargeable on an instrument effecting the transfer.[4] There are supplementary provisions to ensure that where securities are purchased in instalments only the instalments will be liable for the stamp duty reserve tax.[5] Where the depositary bank or clearance house which would be chargeable is not resident in the UK and has no branch or agency therein the stamp duty reserve tax may be recovered from the person to whom the shares are transferred.[6]

A clearance service is an arrangement for trading transactions in securities. Securities within the system are held in the name of a nominee company acting for the clearance system. Once in the system, securities can be traded *without* the need for a transfer document hence the higher rate stamp duty reserve tax charge *on the transfer into the settlement system*. However, an operator of a clearance service may elect, with the approval of the Revenue, for a stamp duty reserve tax charge of 0.5% on agreements to transfer chargeable securities within the system rather than the higher rate charge of 1.5%, either as stamp duty or stamp duty reserve tax, payable when the chargeable securities enter the system.[7]

Sergeant and Sims A13.3 [920]–[930].

[1] See infra, § **61.15**.
[2] FA 1986, ss 93, 94.
[3] FA 1986, s 96.
[4] FA 1986, ss 93(7), 96(5).
[5] FA 1986, ss 93(10), 94(1), 96(4).
[6] FA 1986, ss 93(9), 96(7).
[7] FA 1986, s 97A inserted by FA 1996, ss 196(3)(*b*) with effect from 1 July 1996.

Chargeable securities

[**61.05**] Subject to the exceptions mentioned below, "chargeable securities" means:[1]

(1) stocks, shares or loan capital;
(2) interests in, or in dividends or other rights arising out of, stocks, shares or loan capital;
(3) rights to allotments of or to subscribe for, or options to acquire, stocks, shares or loan capital; and
(4) units under a unit trust scheme.[2]

"Chargeable securities" does not include:

(1) securities falling within 1, 2 or 3 above which are issued or raised by a body corporate not incorporated in the UK unless:
    (a) they are registered in a register kept in the UK by or on behalf of the body corporate; or
    (b) in the case of shares, they are paired with shares issued by a body corporate incorporated in the UK;[3] or
    (c) in the case of securities falling within paragraph 2 or 3 above, paragraph (a) or (b) above applies to the stocks, shares or loan capital to which they relate;[4] or
    (d) they are issued or raised by a Societas Europaea with its registered office in the UK.[5]
(2) Securities falling within 1, 2 or 3 above if they are issued or raised by a Societas Europaea with its registered office outside the UK.[6]
(3)
    (a) securities the transfer of which is exempt from all stamp duties; or
    (b) securities falling within 2 or 3 above and which relate to stocks, shares or loan capital the transfer of which is exempt from all stamp duties (eg government stock: see supra, § **56.34**).[7]
(4) Interests in depositary receipts for stocks or shares.[8]

[61.05] Stamp duty reserve tax

A depositary receipt for stocks or shares is an instrument acknowledging:
(a) the deposit of stocks or shares or of an instrument evidencing the right to receive them; and
(b) the entitlement of a person to rights, whether expressed as units or otherwise, in or in relation to stocks or shares of the same kind.[9]

The conditions for excluding the exception referred to in paragraph (1) above are modified in respect of clearance and depositary receipts.

An amendment to FA 1986, s 99 by way of substitution has the effect that paragraph (1)(a) above and the reference to sub-paragraph (a) in sub-paragraph (c) is to be ignored for the purposes of the stamp duty reserve tax charge in relation to clearance services and depositary receipts.[10] In interpreting "chargeable securities" in FA 1986, ss 93 or 96 (depositary receipts and clearance services: see supra, § **61.04**) in a case where:

(a) newly subscribed shares; or
(b) securities falling within 2 or 3 above which relate to newly subscribed shares;

are issued in pursuance of an arrangement such as is mentioned in that section (or an arrangement which would be such an arrangement if the securities issued were chargeable securities), in paragraph 1(b) above and the reference to that paragraph in paragraph 1(c) is to be ignored for the purposes of the higher rate stamp duty reserve tax charge.[11] For the purpose of these provisions "newly subscribed shares" means shares issued wholly for new consideration in pursuance of an offer for sale to the public.[12]

Sergeant and Sims Division F [5702], Division E [5516]–[5519].

---

[1] See FA 1986, s 99(3) substituted by FA 1988, s 144(2).
[2] "Unit" and "unit trust scheme" have the same meanings as in the Financial Services and Market Act 2000, ss 236, 237 but do not include arrangements falling within FA 2005, s 48A (alternative finance bonds): FA 1999, s 99(9)(9A).
[3] As to when shares of a foreign company are paired with those of a UK company, see FA 1986, s 99(6A) substituted by FA 1988, s 144(2); FA 1986, s 99(6B) added by FA 1990, s 113; Inland Revenue press release, 15 June 1990, *Simon's Tax Intelligence* 1990, p 540.
[4] FA 1986, s 99(4) substituted by FA 1988, s 144(2).
[5] FA 1986, s 99(4)(d) inserted by F(No 2)A 2005, s 57(1).
[6] FA 1986, s 99(4A) inserted by F(No 2)A 2005, 57(1).
[7] FA 1986, s 99(5) substituted by FA 1988, s 144(2).
[8] FA 1986, s 99(6) substituted by FA 1988, s 144(2).
[9] FA 1986, s 99(7).
[10] FA 1986, s 99(10) substituted by FA 1988, s 144(4) and amended by FA 1996, s 196(5), (6).
[11] FA 1986, s 99(11) inserted by FA 1988, s 144(5).
[12] FA 1986, s 99(12) inserted by FA 1988, s 144(5). As to what constitutes an offer to the public, see infra, § **61.11**.

Exceptions

Intermediaries

[61.06] The charge to stamp duty reserve tax in respect of agreements executed or becoming unconditional before 20 October 1997 between A and B to transfer chargeable securities[1] did not apply in certain circumstances if B was a broker and dealer or a market maker.[2] In respect of agreements executed on or after that date, the charge to stamp duty reserve tax does not apply where B is an intermediary.[3] The details of the relief, in particular the conditions for exemption, was similar to those for the corresponding relief from stamp duty in the case of transfers of stock to intermediaries.[4] The scope of this exemption was widened significantly from 1 November, 2007 following the implementation of the Markets in Financial Instruments Directive (2004/39/EC) on that date.[5]

Sergeant and Sims Division D [5102], Division B [3442]–[3539]. [3786]–[3820].

[1] See supra, § **61.02**.
[2] FA 1986, s 89.
[3] FA 1986, ss 88A, 88B inserted by FA 1997, s 102(1) which was brought into force on 20 October 1997 by the Finance Act 1997 (Stamp Duty and Stamp Duty Reserve Tax) (Appointed Day) Order 1997, SI 1997/2428. FA 1997, s 102(2) repealed FA 1986, s 89 with effect from the same date.
[4] See supra, § **60.10**.
[5] FA 1986, s 88A(2). By FA 2007, s 73 and Sch 21. A detailed explanation of the relief is contained in a note entitled 'Intermediary and Stock Lending Reliefs – FA 2007 Changes' published by HMRC.

Repurchases and stock lending

[61.07] Repurchases ('repos') and stock lending arrangements are arrangements for the sale and return or lending and return, of securities. Under FA 1986, s 89AA these transactions are exempt from stamp duty reserve tax (and from stamp duty under FA 1986, s 80C) provided that securities of the same kind and amount are returned to the seller or lender under the terms of the arrangement. At least one of the parties must be authorised under the law of a state of the European Economic Area to provide investment services or execution of orders, etc in stock of the kind concerned and stock of that kind must be regularly traded on a regulated market. There are also other conditions stipulated in FA 1986, s 89AA. With effect from 1 September 2008 the new FA 1986, s 89AB[1] has provided that where the securities were not returned to the seller or lender because one of the parties has become insolvent, no stamp duty reserve tax will be charged on the purchaser or borrower nor will stamp duty reserve tax be charged on an insolvent lender who fails to return collateral securities to a borrower. Stamp duty reserve tax will also not be charged where a party acquires replacement securities because of the insolvency of the borrower or the lender.

[61.07] Stamp duty reserve tax

Sergeant and Sims Division D [5102], Division B [3442]–[3539], [3786]–[3820].

[1] Inserted by FA 2009, s 82 and Sch 37.

Unit trusts

[61.08] A new stamp duty reserve tax regime[1] has applied to transfers of units in a unit trust scheme[2] on or after 6 February 2000 and the stamp duty regime applying up until then has been abolished. Under the new regime there is a general tax charge of 0.5% on all surrenders of units to the trust managers. Where the unit trust is growing and there are at least as many sales to new investors (including the resale of existing units and the issue of new ones) as there are surrenders, this 0.5% is the maximum liability. Where the trust is shrinking but there are both surrenders of units and sales to new investors, the tax charge is proportionately reduced: see supra, §§ **59.14–59.19**.

Sergeant and Sims A16.1 [1161].

[1] FA 1999, s 122 and Sch 19.
[2] FA 1986, s 90(1). For the meaning of "unit" and "unit trust scheme", see supra, §§ **61.05** and **59.18**.

Mergers of authorised unit trusts

[61.09] From 19 March 1997 to 1 July 1999, the charge to stamp duty reserve tax in respect of agreements between A and B to transfer chargeable securities[1] which constitute property which is subject to the trusts of an authorised unit trust[2] did not apply where that property was transferred to the trustees of another authorised unit trust provided that certain conditions were satisfied.[3] The details of the relief, in particular, the conditions for exemption, were the same as those for the corresponding relief from stamp duty in respect of instruments executed to transfer property on a merger of authorised unit trusts.[4]

There was a similar relief where a merger of authorised unit trusts was effected by a direction by the holders of units to the trustees of one authorised unit trust that the property of that trust be held on the trusts of another authorised unit trust,[5] provided that the trustees of both trusts were the same persons.[6] Where this relief was available, there was also an exemption from stamp duty reserve tax in respect of any agreement, actual or deemed, to transfer units to the managers of the transferor trust for cancellation.[7] Following their defeat in *Save and Prosper Securities Ltd v IRC*[8] IR Stamp Taxes issued SDRT Customer Newsletter no 7 on 24 May 2004, dealing with amalgamations, mergers and other transactions relating to unit trusts and open-ended investment companies and outlining the circumstances in which they accept that stamp duty and stamp duty reserve tax will not arise.

Sergeant and Sims Division B [3786].

1. See supra, § **61.02**.
2. An authorised unit trust is defined as a unit trust scheme in the case of which an order under Financial Services Act 1986, s 78 is in force.
3. FA 1997, s 100(1) and see infra, § **61.10**, note 4.
4. FA 1997, s 100(2) and see supra, § **59.19**.
5. FA 1997, s 101(1) and see also *Save and Prosper Securities Ltd v IRC* [2000] STC (SCD) 408 where the Special Commissioner held that a scheme of amalgamation took effect by operation of law and that therefore there was no agreement to transfer chargeable securities.
6. FA 1997, s 101(2)(*a*).
7. FA 1997, s 101(3).
8. [2000] STC (SCD) 408.

Open-ended investment companies

[61.10] The Treasury have by regulations made provision in order that special stamp duty and stamp duty reserve tax rules apply to open-ended investment companies.[1] Where the shares of an open-ended investment company are repurchased by its authorised corporate director, these rules mirror the stamp duty and stamp duty reserve tax rules for repurchases of units in authorised unit trusts.[2] The regulations also introduced an exemption from stamp duty reserve tax when the whole of an authorised unit trust (or sub-fund of an umbrella authorised unit trust) converts to an open-ended investment company or the sub-fund of an umbrella company.[3] There was also a temporary exemption until 30 June 1999 where the whole of an authorised unit trust (or sub-fund of an umbrella authorised unit trust) merged with a continuing open-ended investment company or a continuing sub-fund of an umbrella company.[4]

Regulations made under FA 1995, s 152 apply the new stamp duty reserve tax regime for transfers of units in a unit trust contained in FA 1999, Sch 19 to dealings in shares in open-ended instrument companies with appropriate modifications.[5] Following their defeat in *Save and Prosper Securities Ltd v IRC*[6] IR Stamp Taxes issued SDRT Customer Newsletter no 7 on 24 May 2004, dealing with amalgamations, mergers and other transactions relating to unit trusts and open-ended investment companies and outlining the circumstances in which they accept that stamp duty and stamp duty reserve tax will not arise.

Sergeant and Sims Division D [5100]–[5101].

1. See Stamp Duty and Stamp Duty Reserve Tax (Open-ended Investment Companies) Regulations 1997, SI 1997/1156, which were made under FA 1995, s 152 and came into force on 28 April 1997. See also Inland Revenue press release dated 7 April 1997.
2. SI 1997/1156, reg 4.
3. SI 1997/1156, reg 8.
4. SI 1997/1156, reg 10. This exemption was first extended until one year after the coming into force of Treasury regulations allowing the formation of a wider range of open-ended investment companies: Inland Revenue press release 105/99. Such

[61.10] Stamp duty reserve tax

regulations were made under the Financial Services and Markets Act 2000 with effect from 1 December 2001. However, the exemption has now been extended indefinitely.
[5] The Stamp Duty and Stamp Duty Reserve Tax (Open-ended Investment Companies) (Amendment No 2) Regulations 1999, SI 1999/3261, and see FA 1999, Sch 19, Part III, para 13 giving a more comprehensive definition of stamp duty reserve tax in FA 1995, s 152 to enable the regulations to be made.
[6] [2000] STC (SCD) 408.

Public issues

[61.11] The charge to stamp duty reserve tax in respect of agreements between A and B to transfer chargeable securities[1] does not apply in the following circumstances:

(1) The charge does not apply as regards an agreement to transfer securities other than units under a unit trust scheme to B or B's nominee if:
    (a) the agreement is part of an arrangement, entered into by B in the ordinary course of B's business as an issuing house, under which B (as principal) is to offer the securities for sale to the public;
    (b) the agreement is conditional upon the admission of the securities to the Official List of the Stock Exchange;
    (c) the consideration under the agreement for each security is the same as the price at which B is to offer the security for sale; and
    (d) B sells the securities in accordance with the arrangement referred to in paragraph 1 above.[2]

(2) The charge does not apply as regards an agreement if the securities to which the agreement relates are newly subscribed securities other than units under a unit trust scheme and:
    (a) the agreement is made in pursuance of an offer to the public made by A (as principal) under an arrangement entered into in the ordinary course of A's business as an issuing house;
    (b) a right of allotment in respect of, or to subscribe for, the securities has been acquired by A under an agreement which is part of the arrangement;
    (c) both those agreements are conditional upon the admission of the securities to the Official List of the Stock Exchange; and
    (d) the consideration for each security is the same under both agreements;
and for these purposes "newly subscribed securities", are securities which, in pursuance of the arrangements referred to in paragraph (a) above, are issued wholly for new consideration.[3]

(3) The charge does not apply as regards an agreement if the securities to which the agreement relates are registered securities other than units under a unit trust scheme and:
    (a) the agreement is made in pursuance of an offer to the public made by A;
    (b) the agreement is conditional upon the admission of the securities to the Official List of the Stock Exchange; and

(c) under the agreement A issues to B or his nominee a renounceable letter of acceptance, or similar instrument, in respect of the securities.[4]

The exemptions in paragraphs 1 and 2 above were inserted to enable public offerings to be structured with merchant banks acting as principals without creating additional stamp duty reserve tax liabilities. The exemption in paragraph 3 above was inserted so as to preclude a charge to both stamp duty reserve tax and stamp duty arising.

The meaning of the phrase "offer to the public" is that in common financial parlance, ie an invitation made to the public generally.[5] However, it seems likely that the courts would have regard to the extended definition of this phrase in the Companies Act 1985, ss 59, 60 (previously CA 1948, s 55), notwithstanding the repeal of these provisions.[6] Accordingly, it would seem that there will be an offer to the public where there is either an offer to the public generally or an offer to any section thereof, whether selected as members of the company or clients of the issuing house or otherwise,[7] which is "calculated to result, directly or indirectly, in the shares becoming available" to persons other than those receiving the offer.[8]

In *Governments Stock and Other Securities Investment Co Ltd v Christopher*,[9] Wynn Parry J considered the question of whether an offer was made to the public in circumstances where the offer was made to all the share holders of two companies. The offer was subject to quotation on the Stock Exchange. Those who accepted the offer received non-renounceable letters of allotment. Wynn Parry J said that the test is not who receives the circular containing the offer, but who can accept the offer put forward.[10] As non-renounceable letters of allotment were to be issued, so that only the shareholders could accept the offer, he concluded that the offer was not calculated to result in the shares becoming available to persons other than those receiving the offer and, therefore, that the offer was not an offer to the public. It would seem to follow, and appears to be accepted by the Stamp Office, that an offer to a section of the public involving the issue of renounceable letters of allotment is an offer to the public within the meaning of FA 1986, s 89A.

In *National Westminster Bank plc v IRC*,[11] the House of Lords held, by majority, that shares are issued for the purposes of TA 1988 when an application has been followed by allotment and notification and completed by entry on the register. In the view of the majority, the term "issue" in relation to shares meant something distinct from allotment and required some subsequent act whereby the title of the allottee is completed. The Companies Act 1985 preserved the distinction in English law between an enforceable contract for the issue of shares (constituted by an allotment) and the issue of shares, which was completed by registration. Accordingly, the word "issue" was appropriate to indicate the whole process whereby new shares were applied for, allotted and finally registered. There would appear to be no reason why the word "issued" should be given a different meaning in the context of FA 1986, s 89A.

It should be noted that, although rights to the allotment of shares constituted by a renounceable letter of allotment are chargeable securities,[12] an agreement to issue a renounceable letter of allotment between the company and the allottee is not chargeable under FA 1986, s 87. An agreement to "issue" chargeable securities is not an agreement to "transfer" chargeable securities within the meaning of that provision.[13] Accordingly, the relief in FA 1986, s 89A is only required in respect of agreements to renounce a right to an allotment of shares in favour of a purchaser, which will ordinarily attract an immediate charge to stamp duty reserve tax.[14]

The Treasury is empowered to make regulations which amend the condition relating to the listing of securities in each case.[15]

Sergeant and Sims A16.4 [1185]–[1187], Division B [3442].

[1] See supra, § **61.02**.
[2] FA 1986, s 89A(1).
[3] FA 1986, s 89A(2).
[4] FA 1986, s 89A(3).
[5] *Cheatle v IRC* (1982) 56 TC 111 at 126.
[6] Cf *Burrows v Matabele Gold Reefs and Estates Co Ltd* [1901] 2 Ch 23 at 27, CA.
[7] Companies Act 1985, s 59(1), now repealed.
[8] Companies Act 1985, s 60(1), now repealed.
[9] [1956] 1 WLR 237.
[10] [1956] 1 All ER 490 at 493, [1956] 1 WLR 237 at 242.
[11] [1994] STC 580, [1994] 3 All ER 1, HL.
[12] See supra, § **61.05**.
[13] See supra, § **61.01**, note 2.
[14] See supra, § **61.02**.
[15] FA 1986, s 89A(4).

Charities and institutions

[**61.12**] The charge to stamp duty reserve tax in respect of agreements between A and B to transfer chargeable securities[1] does not apply to an agreement to transfer securities to:

(1) a body of persons established for charitable purposes only;[2]
(2) the trustees of a trust so established;[3]
(3) the trustees of the National Heritage Memorial Fund; or
(4) the Historic Buildings and Monuments Commission for England.[4]

Sergeant and Sims A17.5 [1283], Division B [3442]–[3539], [3549].

[1] See supra, § **61.02**.
[2] It is thought that this exemption applies to charities formed or established under UK law only and not to non-UK charities: see supra, § **56.37**.
[3] It is thought that this exemption applies to charities formed or established under UK law only and not to non-UK charities: see supra, § **56.37**.
[4] FA 1986, s 90(7); FA 1987, Sch 7, para 6.

Bearer instruments

[61.13] The charge to stamp duty reserve tax in respect of agreements between A and B to transfer chargeable securities[1] does not apply to an agreement to transfer securities constituted by or transferable by means of a UK bearer instrument[2] unless:

(1) the instrument falls within the exemption from stamp duty in FA 1999, Sch 15, Part II, para 16 (renounceable letter of allotment etc where rights are renounceable not later than six months after issue);[3] or

(2) the instrument was issued by a body corporate incorporated in the UK (other than a Societas Europaea with its registered office outside the UK) and stamp duty under FA 1999, Sch 15 was not chargeable on the issue of the instrument by virtue only of the exemption for bearer instruments relating to foreign currencies in FA 1999, Sch 15, Part II, para 17, save where the chargeable securities in question are, or a depositary receipt for them is, listed on a recognised stock exchange and the agreement to transfer those securities was not made in contemplation of, or as part of an arrangement for, a takeover of the body corporate which issued the instrument;[4] or

(3) the instrument was issued by a body corporate incorporated in the UK (other than a Societas Europaea with its registered office outside the UK) and the following requirements are satisfied:

   (a) on the issue of the instrument, stamp duty FA 1999, Sch 15 was not chargeable by virtue only of FA 1986, s 79(2) (exemption for bearer instruments relating to loan capital) or that subsection and FA 1999, Sch 15, Part II, para 17; and

   (b) stamp duty would be chargeable on an instrument transferring the loan capital to which the instrument relates by virtue of FA 1986, s 79(5) (convertible loan capital) or FA 1986, s 79(6) (loan capital carrying special rights)

   save where the chargeable securities in question are, or a depositary receipt for them is, listed on a recognised stock exchange; the agreement to transfer those securities is not made in contemplation of, or as part of an arrangement for, a takeover of the body corporate which issued the instrument and those securities do not carry any right of the kind described in FA 1986, s 79(5) (right of conversion into, or acquisition of, shares or other securities) by the exercise of which securities which are not listed on a recognised stock exchange may be obtained.[5]

The charge to stamp duty reserve tax in respect of agreements between A and B to transfer chargeable securities[6] does not apply to an agreement to transfer securities constituted by or transferable by means of non-UK bearer instrument.[7]

Sergeant and Sims Division B [3442]–[3539], [3786]–[3820].

---

[1] See supra, § **61.02**.

[2] FA 1986, s 90(3), (3A)–(3F), the latter inserted by FA 1997, s 105 in respect of agreements executed or becoming unconditional on or after 26 November 1996 if the inland bearer instrument in question was issued on or after that date and

[61.13] Stamp duty reserve tax

amended by FA 1999, Sch 16 to reflect the restating of the stamp duty bearer instrument charge in FA 1999, Sch 15. See also FA 1999, Sch 15, Bearer Instrument: supra, § **59.10**.

[3] FA 1986, s 90(3B) as amended by FA 1999, Sch 16 to reflect the restating of the stamp duty bearer instrument charge in FA 1999, Sch 15.

[4] FA 1986, s 90(3C), (3D) as amended by FA 1999, Sch 16 to reflect the restating of the stamp duty bearer instrument charge in FA 1999, Sch 15.

[5] FA 1986, s 90(3E), (3F) as amended by FA 1999, Sch 16 to reflect the restating of the stamp duty bearer instrument charge in FA 1999, Sch 15.

[6] See supra, § **61.02**.

[7] FA 1986, s 90(3)(a) as amended by FA 1999, Sch 16, para 6, Bearer Instrument: supra, § **59.08**.

Miscellaneous exceptions

[61.14] The charge to stamp duty reserve tax in respect of agreements between A and B to transfer chargeable securities[1] does not apply to:

(1) an agreement which forms part of an arrangement falling within the provisions in relation to depositary receipts and clearance services (subject to the operator of a clearance service electing for the alternative system of charge at 0.5%—see supra, § **61.04**);[2]

(2) an agreement to transfer securities which the Board is satisfied are held, when the agreement is made, by a person whose business is exclusively that of holding shares, stock or other marketable securities (a) as nominee or agent for a person whose business is or includes the provision of clearance services for the purchase and sale of marketable securities and (b) (in a case where the business does not consist exclusively of clearance services) for the purposes of such part of that business as consists of the provision of such services;[3] or

(3) certain transactions with the London Clearing House Limited and clearing members in relation to transactions on the London International Financial Futures Exchange (LIFFE);[4] or

(4) certain agreements to transfer securities in the course of trading on Tradepoint;[5] or

(5) an agreement to transfer any shares in a company which are held by the company whether in accordance with Companies Act 2006, s 724 (treasury shares) or otherwise.[6]

Sergeant and Sims A17.6 [1289]–[1320], Division B [3442]–[3539], [3700]–[3708].

[1] See supra, § **61.02**.

[2] FA 1986, s 90(4). Such arrangements attract the higher rate charge of 1.5%: see supra, § **61.04**.

[3] FA 1986, s 90(5), (6); FA 1987, Sch 7, para 5. As to the meaning of "marketable securities", see Stamp Act 1891, s 122(1).

[4] FA 1991, ss 116, 117; Stamp Duty and Stamp Duty Reserve Tax (Investment Exchanges and Clearing Houses) Regulations 1997, SI 1997/2429 set out in **Division D [5103]**.

[5] FA 1991, s 117; Stamp Duty Reserve Tax (Tradepoint) Regulations 1995, SI 1995/2051, reg 4, set out in Sergeant and Sims Division D [5103].
[6] FA 1986, s 90(7A), see supra, § **59.06**.

Miscellaneous exceptions from the higher rate charge

[61.15] There is no charge to stamp duty reserve tax at the higher 1.5% rate under the provisions relating to depositary receipts[1] in respect of the following:

(1) a transfer of securities to a company which at the time of the transfer falls within FA 1986, s 67(6) (stamp duty on transfers to depositories) from such a company (ie transfers between depositories);[2]

(2) a transfer, issue or appropriation of a UK bearer instrument[3] except in the case of an instrument within the exemption from stamp duty under FA 1999, Sch 15, para 16 (ie renounceable letters of allotment and similar instruments where the rights are renounceable not later than six months after the issue of the letter); or an instrument within the exemption conferred by FA 1999, Sch 15, Part II, para 17 (non-sterling instruments)[4] which does not raise new capital; or[5]

(3) an issue by a company (A) of securities in exchange for shares in another company (B) where A has control of B[6] or will have such control in consequence of the exchange or of an offer as a result of which the exchange is made and the shares in B are held under a depositary receipt scheme;[7]

(4) the transfer, issue or appropriation of new securities into a depositary receipt system in place of old securities which are already held in the system and which bore the 1.5% tax charge on entry;[8]

(5) the Treasury also has the power by regulation to exclude from the definition of chargeable securities[9] exempt UK depositary interests in foreign securities.[10] Such regulations have been made and provide a relief for the settlement of trades in non-UK shares held in depositary receipts;[11]

(6) the existing relief for transfers of shares from one depositary to another (see point 1) and from one clearance service to another, has been extended to include transfers between the two types of system.[12]

The exceptions from the higher rate charge in respect of clearance services broadly correspond to those in respect of depositary receipts.[13]

Sergeant and Sims A13.4 [931]–[937], Division B [3442]–[3539].

[1] See supra, § **61.04**.
[2] FA 1986, s 95(1) as amended by FA 2000, s 134(3).
[3] As to the meaning of "UK bearer instrument", see FA 1986, s 99(1A) inserted by FA 1999, Sch 16, para 9.
[4] FA 1986, s 95(2)(a) and (b) as amended for instruments issued on or after 30 January 1999 by FA 1999, s 116, for instruments issued on or after 9 March 1999 by FA 1999, s 117 and for instruments issued on or after 1 October 1999 by FA 1999, Sch 16, para 7.

[61.15] Stamp duty reserve tax

5. Such a UK bearer instrument "raises new capital" and is therefore exempt from the 1.5% charge only if the instrument is issued in conjunction with the issue of securities for which only cash is subscribed and those securities either fall within the definition of loan capital for stamp duty purposes or carry a dividend at a fixed rate: FA 1999, s 117 inserting new FA 1986, s 95(2A)–(2D). The 1.5% rate charge on the transfer of a UK bearer instrument denominated in a non-sterling currency into a depositary receipt form does not apply if the instrument gives effect to an agreement for a company merger or take-over entered into in writing by the companies involved before 30 January 1999.
6. Company A has control of company B if A has power to control B's affairs by virtue of holding shares in, or possessing voting power in relation to, B or any other body corporate: FA 1986, s 95(4).
7. FA 1986, s 95(3), as amended by FA 1998, s 15(1). The meaning of "shares held under a depositary receipt scheme" and "an issue by A in exchange for shares in B" is clarified by FA 1986, s 95(5), (6), added by FA 1998, s 151(2).
8. FA 1986, s 95A inserted by FA 1999, s 118(1).
9. See supra, § **61.05**.
10. FA 1999, s 119.
11. The Stamp Duty Reserve Tax (UK Depositary Interests in Foreign Securities) Regulations 1999 and the Amendment Regulations 2000, SI 1999/2383 and SI 2000/1871.
12. FA 1986, s 97B inserted by FA 2000, s 134.
13. FA 1986, s 97 as amended by FA 1999, s 118(3).

Liability, accountability and time for payment

Persons liable to stamp duty reserve tax

[61.16] Liability to the tax ordinarily falls on the purchaser, whether or not the purchaser is the transferee.[1] However, where an accountable person is involved in the transaction (ie a securities market intermediary) that person is required to give notice of the transaction to the Stamp Office and pay the tax.[2] Liability in respect of a charge under the provisions relating to depositary receipts and clearance services[3] ordinarily falls on the person issuing the depositary receipt or providing the clearance service as the case may be.[4] Where transactions are effected which involve a relevant system,[5] such as CREST, it is the operator, such as CRESTCo, which is required to give notice of the transaction to the Stamp Office and pay the tax.[6]

Sergeant and Sims A2.6 [134]–[139], Division B [3442]–[3539], Division D [5023]–[5044].

1. FA 1986, ss 87(1), 91.
2. Stamp Duty Reserve Tax Regulations 1986, SI 1986/1711, reg 4. See infra, § **61.18**.
3. See supra, § **61.04**.
4. FA 1986, ss 93(8)–(10); 96(6)–(8); SI 1986/1711, reg 2.
5. See the Uncertificated Securities Regulations 1995, SI 1995/3272, reg 2(1).

[6] SI 1986/1711, reg 4A, inserted by the Stamp Duty Reserve Tax (Amendment) Regulations 1997, SI 1997/2430, reg 5.

Time for payment

[61.17] Stamp duty reserve tax is due and payable on the accountable date.[1]

The 0.5% charge on agreements to transfer chargeable securities is no longer deferred until the expiration of two months beginning with the day on which the agreement is made (or, where the agreement is conditional, the day on which the condition is satisfied). Instead, there is now an immediate 0.5% charge in respect of agreements to transfer chargeable securities (see supra, § 61.02) which may be cancelled where the transaction is completed by a duly stamped transfer within six years of the agreement being made or becoming unconditional (see infra, §§ 61.21 ff). The accountable date is the fourteenth day following the transaction where it is effected by means of a relevant system[2] (such as CREST) or where it is reported to an exchange or recognised body unless another date has been agreed between the Commissioners of Revenue & Customs and the operator of such a system. If the transaction could have been so reported but was not, the accountable date is the fourteenth day following the transaction. In any other case, the accountable date is the seventh day of the month following the month in which the charge to tax occurred.[3]

EXAMPLE
A agrees to transfer registered shares to B on 1 February. The charge arises on 1 February. Stamp duty reserve tax is due and payable on 15 February or other agreed date if the transaction is effected by means of a relevant system (such as CREST) or if it is reported to an exchange or recognised body. If the transaction could have been so reported but was not, stamp duty reserve tax is due and payable on 15 February. In any other case, stamp duty reserve tax is due and payable on 7 March.

Interest charged on tax paid late but in their "Notes for Guidance" (February 1998) the Stamp Office state that they will not seek interest in relation to transfers of securities held outside CREST if a duly stamped instrument or transfer is produced by the later of seven days after the end of the month in which the charge arises or 30 days after the agreement. This has now been extended to 60 days from the date on which the charge arises by concession as explained in the Inland Revenue Tax Bulletin of October 1998 and confirmed by section 13.18 of the Stamp Office Manual published on 20 March 2000 and updated in March 2002.

Sergeant and Sims A2.6 [134]–[139], Division D [5023]–[5044].

[1] Stamp Duty Reserve Tax Regulations 1986, SI 1986/1711, regs 2, 3.
[2] See the Uncertificated Securities Regulations 1995, SI 1995/2372, reg 2(1).
[3] SI 1986/1711, reg 2 as amended by the Stamp Duty Reserve Tax (Amendment) Regulations 1997, SI 1997/2430, reg 3.

[61.18] Stamp duty reserve tax

Accountability for stamp duty reserve tax

[61.18] To facilitate collection, stamp duty reserve tax has separate rules about liability and accountability. Where a member of the Stock Exchange is party to a deal, whether as principal or agent, the Stamp Office will look to the member for any tax that arises. In other circumstances either a "qualified dealer" or the purchaser is accountable.

An accountable person must, on or before the accountable date, give written notice in the prescribed form to the Board of each charge to tax and pay the tax due.[1]

The rules for ascertaining the accountable person for the purposes of the stamp duty reserve tax charge in respect of agreements to transfer chargeable securities[2] are as follows. Where the buyer is a market maker or broker and dealer,[3] or if a broker and dealer is acting as an agent for the buyer, that market maker or broker and dealer is accountable. Failing that, if the seller is a market maker or broker and dealer, or if a broker and dealer is acting as an agent for the seller, that market maker or broker and dealer is accountable. Failing that, if the buyer is a qualified dealer, or if a qualified dealer is acting as agent for the buyer, that qualified dealer is accountable. Failing that, if the seller is a qualified dealer, or if a qualified dealer is acting as an agent for the seller, that qualified dealer is accountable. Failing that, the buyer, that is, the person referred to as B in FA 1986, s 87(1) is accountable.[4]

The accountable person in respect of the higher rate charge imposed under the provisions relating to depositary receipts and clearance services will ordinarily be the person issuing the depositary receipt or providing the clearance services as the case may be.[5]

Where transactions are effected which involve a relevant system,[6] such as CREST, it is the operator, such as CRESTCo, which is required to give notice of the transaction to the Stamp Office and pay the tax.[7]

Investors normally have to account for the tax themselves only when they purchase shares privately without the involvement of a member of an exchange or a relevant system such as CREST.

Sergeant and Sims A2.6 [134]–[139], Division D [5023]–[5044].

---

[1] Stamp Duty Reserve Tax Regulations 1986, SI 1986/1711, regs 2, 4. Provision is made for the imposition of penalties for failure to give a notice of charge and for fraudulently or negligently giving an incorrect notice or failing to correct an error which is identified after notice was given: reg 20. See TMA 1970, ss 93, 95, 97, 99, 100–105 and 118(2) as modified, applied and restated in SI 1986/1711, Sch, Part II.

[2] See supra, § **61.02**.

[3] For the definitions of "market maker" and "broker and dealer", see FA 1986, s 89 as substituted by the Stamp Duty Reserve Tax (Amendment) Regulations 1992, SI 1992/3286: Stamp Duty Reserve Tax Regulations 1986, SI 1986/1711, reg 2.

[4] SI 1986/1711, reg 2 as amended by the Stamp Duty Reserve Tax (Amendment) Regulations 1988, SI 1988/835.

[5] SI 1986/1711, reg 2.

[6] See the Uncertificated Securities Regulations 1995, SI 1995/3272, reg 2(1).

[7] SI 1986/1711, reg 4A, inserted by the Stamp Duty Reserve Tax (Amendment) Regulations 1997, SI 1997/2430, reg 5.

Relief from accountability

[61.19] If on a claim in relation to a charge under FA 1986, s 87[1] to stamp duty reserve tax an accountable person or operator[2] other than the person[3] liable to the tax, proves to the satisfaction of the Board that he has taken without success all reasonable steps, both before and after the date of the agreement, to recover from the person liable tax for which he is accountable,[4] he is relieved of his liability to account for and pay that tax and any interest on that tax.[5]

Sergeant and Sims A2.6 [134]–[139], Division D [5023]–[5044].

[1] See supra, § **61.02**.
[2] As to the meaning of "accountable person" and "operator", see supra, § **61.18**.
[3] ie the purchaser: see supra, § **61.16**.
[4] ie accountable under the Stamp Duty Reserve Tax Regulations 1986, SI 1986/1711, regs 4, 4A; see supra, § **61.18**.
[5] SI 1986/1711, reg 7.

Payment

[61.20] Stamp duty reserve tax is administered by the Stamp Office, Bush House, London. Notification of charges to stamp duty reserve tax and payment should be made to the Shares Unit, Ground Floor, East Block, Barrington Road, Worthing, West Sussex, BN12 4SE; tel. 01903 509467/509471; fax 01903 509462.

Repayment or cancellation of stamp duty reserve tax

[61.21] FA 1986, s 92 provides for repayment or cancellation of the tax where stamp duty is also paid. It ensures that stamp duty and stamp duty reserve tax should not both be paid in respect of a transaction.

Section 92 applies where it is proved to the Board's satisfaction that the conditions for the relief of the charge in respect of agreements to transfer chargeable securities to B or his nominee which is charged to tax under FA 1986, s 87, have been fulfilled within the period of six years from the date on which the charge arose.[1] The conditions are that:

(1) an instrument is (or instruments are) executed in pursuance of the agreement and the instrument transfers (or the instruments between them transfer) to B or his nominee all the chargeable securities to which the agreement relates; and

(2) if the instrument is chargeable with stamp duty or is otherwise required to be stamped, it is duly stamped in accordance with the enactments relating to stamp duty.[2]

[61.21] Stamp duty reserve tax

There is also provision for repayment or cancellation of the tax in relation to agreements to transfer shares in a company to that company where, within six years of the tax charge arising, a return required under Companies Act 1985, s 169(1) or (1B) has been duly stamped under FA 1986, s 66 (see supra, § **59.06**).[3]

Where the charge applies and a claim is made within six years of the agreement (the relevant day as mentioned in s 87(3)) there is a provision for the tax (not the stamp duty) to be repaid with interest if the tax is not less than £25.[4] To the extent that the tax charged has not been paid, provision is made for the tax charge to be cancelled.[5]

The rate of interest on repayments is set by regulations made under FA 1989, s 178.[6] The Treasury is given power to vary the rate of interest. It is provided that the Treasury order making power under the above provision is exercisable by statutory instrument and subject to a negative resolution procedure in the House of Commons.[7]

Sergeant and Sims A2.6 [134]–[139], Division B [3442]–[3539].

[1] FA 1986, s 92(1).
[2] FA 1986, s 92(1A), (1B), inserted by FA 1996, s 192(4) with effect in relation to agreements made or becoming unconditional on or after 1 July 1996.
[3] FA 1986, s 92(1C), (1D), inserted by FA 2003, Sch 40, para 4.
[4] FA 1986, s 92(2).
[5] FA 1986, s 92(3).
[6] FA 1986, s 92(2).
[7] See the Taxes (Interest Rate) Regulations 1989, SI 1989/1297.

Interest on repayments exempt from income tax

[61.22] FA 1987, Sch 7, para 7 exempts from income tax interest paid on repayments of reserve tax. This brings the stamp duty reserve tax repayment provisions into line with similar provisions for other taxes. The exemption is deemed always to have applied.

Purchase with loan

[61.23] FA 1986, s 92(7)[1] applies where there is a transfer of chargeable securities to a person (eg a bank) who is providing a loan for the purchase and who is to hold the chargeable securities as security for the loan. On a strict construction of FA 1986, s 87 as originally enacted the transaction gave rise to a double charge—stamp duty reserve tax on the purchase agreement and ad valorem stamp duty on the transfer of chargeable securities to the person who is to hold them. The transaction would not fall within the repayment and cancellation provisions in FA 1986, s 92, as the transfer to the bank would not be to the person who had agreed to purchase the chargeable securities or to his nominee. The subsection brings the transaction within the terms of these provisions with the result that the stamp duty reserve tax charge may be cancelled.

Sergeant and Sims A11.4 [795].

[1] Inserted by FA 1997, s 106(8); in relation to agreements made or becoming unconditional before 4 July 1997, FA 1986, s 87(7B) had similar effect.

Cases in which the execution and stamping of an instrument will not cancel the charge to stamp duty reserve tax

[61.24] The conditions in FA 1986, s 92 for the cancellation of stamp duty reserve tax do not apply in respect of the following instruments:

(1) renounceable letters of allotment and similar instruments where the rights are renounceable not later than six months after issue;[1]
(2) transfers to a stock exchange nominee, ie SEPON;[2]
(3) transfers to a recognised investment exchange or recognised clearing house, or a nominee of either, and a composition agreement is in force at the time of the transfer;[3]
(4) transfers to members of electronic transfer systems, ie CREST, whereby the securities are placed within the system unless the transfer is made by a stock exchange nominee, ie SEPON, and the maximum stamp duty chargeable, apart from FA 1996, s 186, would be £5;[4]
(5) transfers between associated bodies corporate where[5] any of the chargeable securities were acquired within two years of the transfer and the transferor acquired any of them:
    (a) in a transaction effected by an instrument of transfer which was exempt from stamp duty under the exemption for sales to intermediaries;[6]
    (b) under an agreement to transfer securities which was exempt from stamp duty reserve tax under the exemption for agreements to transfer securities to intermediaries;[7]
    (c) under an agreement to transfer securities which was exempt from stamp duty reserve tax under the exemption for agreements to transfer securities in the course of repurchases and stock lending;[8]
    (d) in circumstances where a charge to stamp duty or stamp duty reserve tax is treated as not arising by regulations made under FA 1991, ss 116, 117;[9] and
(6) transfers which were exempt from stamp duty by reason of being made in accordance with certain arrangements between A and B for repurchases and stock lending[10] where:
    (a) it subsequently becomes apparent that stock will not be transferred to B or his nominee by A or his nominee in accordance with the arrangement;[11] or
    (b) relief from stamp duty has been granted on such a transfer but it subsequently becomes apparent that either the arrangement for repurchase and lending is not on arms length terms or that any of the benefits or risks arising from fluctuations in the relevant value of the stock before the transfer to B or his nominee takes place accrue to or fall on A.[12]

[61.24] Stamp duty reserve tax

[1] FA 1986, s 88(1)(*aa*), (*ab*) inserted by FA 1996, s 188(2) with effect in relation to agreements made or becoming unconditional on or after 1 July 1996.
[2] FA 1986, s 88(1)(*a*).
[3] FA 1986, s 88(1)(*b*).
[4] FA 1986, s 88(1A), inserted by FA 1996, s 189 with effect in relation to an instrument executed on or after 1 July 1996 and amended by FA 1999, Sch 14, para 20(3).
[5] FA 1986, s 88(1B), inserted by FA 1996, s 190(1), (3) and amended by FA 1997; see also FA 1986, s 88(4), (5), (5A) and (6).
[6] See supra, § **60.10**.
[7] See supra, § **61.06**.
[8] See supra, § **61.07**.
[9] See supra, §§ **60.15** and **61.14**.
[10] See supra, § **60.11**.
[11] FA 1986, s 88(1C), inserted by FA 1997, s 103(4).
[12] FA 1986, s 88(1D), inserted by FA 1997, s 103(4).

Administration, determination and recovery

Power to require information

[61.25] The Board may by notice in writing require any person to furnish them within such time, not being less than 30 days, as may be specified in the notice with such information (including documents or records) as the Board may reasonably require for the purposes of stamp duty reserve tax.[1] A barrister or solicitor is not obliged in pursuance of such a notice to disclose, without his client's consent, any information with respect to which a claim to professional privilege could be maintained.[2]

Sergeant and Sims A18.1 [1321]–[1340], Division D [5023]–[5044].

[1] Stamp Duty Reserve Tax Regulations 1986, SI 1986/1711, regs 2, 5(1). By virtue of reg 20, the following provisions of TMA 1970 apply, with certain modifications, to stamp duty reserve tax: ss 23 (power to obtain copies of registers); 25 (power to require returns by issuing houses, stockbrokers etc); 26 (information from nominee shareholders); 98, 100–105 (penalties for non-compliance); 108 (responsibility of company officers); 111 (valuation and power to inspect); 114 (want of form not to invalidate documents); and 118(2) (no failure if reasonable excuse). These provisions as modified and applied are restated in SI 1986/1711, Sch, Part II. See supra, § **61.01**.
[2] SI 1986/1711, reg 5(2).

Inspection of records

[61.26] Every accountable person or operator[1] must, whenever required to do so, make available for inspection by an officer of the Board authorised for that purpose all books, documents and other records in his possession or under his control containing information relating to any relevant transaction[2] to which he was a party or in connection with which he acted.[3] Where records are maintained by computer, the person required to make them available for inspection must provide the officer making the inspection with all facilities necessary for obtaining information from them.[4]

Sergeant and Sims A18.1 [1321]–[1340], Division D [5023]–[5044].

[1] As to the meaning of "accountable person" and "operator", see supra, § **61.18**.
[2] "Relevant transaction" means an agreement to transfer chargeable securities falling within FA 1986, s 87 (see supra, § **61.02**) or a transaction caught by the provisions relating to clearance services or depositary receipts (see supra, § **61.04**): Stamp Duty Reserve Tax Regulations 1986, SI 1986/1711, reg 2.
[3] SI 1986/1711, reg 15(1).
[4] SI 1986/1711, reg 15(2).

Notice of determination

[61.27] Where it appears to the Board that a relevant transaction[1] has taken place or where a claim is made to the Board in connection with a relevant transaction, they may give notice[2] to any person who appears to them in relation to that transaction to be the accountable person or operator,[3] or the person liable for any of the stamp duty reserve tax charged or to the claimant, stating that they have determined the matters specified in the notice.[4] If it appears to the Board that any such matter specified in a notice of determination is, or may be, material as respects any liability to stamp duty reserve tax of two or more persons, they may give notice[5] of the determination to each of those persons. Any matter that appears to the Board to be relevant for the purposes of the 1986 Act, Part IV may be determined and specified in the notice.

A determination for the purposes of a notice of any fact relating to a relevant transaction[6] (a) must, if that fact has been stated in a notice of charge given by an accountable person[7] and the Board are satisfied that the notice is correct, be made by the Board in accordance with that notice, but (b) may, in any other case, be made by the Board to the best of their judgment.[8]

Subject to any variation by agreement in writing or on appeal,[9] a determination in a notice under these provisions is conclusive for the purposes of the tax against a person on whom the notice is served.[10] As to recovery of the tax, see infra, § **61.33**.

Sergeant and Sims A18.1 [1321]–[1340], Division D [5023]–[5044].

[1] "Relevant transaction" means an agreement to transfer chargeable securities falling within the FA 1986, s 87(1) (see supra, § **61.02**) or a transaction caught by the provisions relating to clearance services or depositary receipts (see supra, § **61.04**): Stamp Duty Reserve Tax Regulations 1986, SI 1986/1711, reg 2.

[61.27] Stamp duty reserve tax

2   Such a notice must be in writing and must state the time within which and the manner in which an appeal against any determination in it may be made: SI 1986/1711, regs 2, 6(5).
3   As to the meaning of "accountable person" and "operator", see supra, § **61.18**.
4   SI 1986/1711, reg 6(1).
5   SI 1986/1711, reg 6(2).
6   "Relevant transaction" means an agreement to transfer chargeable securities falling within the FA 1986, s 87(1) (see supra, § **61.02**) or a transaction caught by the provisions relating to clearance services or depositary receipts (see supra, § **61.04**): Stamp Duty Reserve Tax Regulations 1986, SI 1986/1711, reg 2.
7   As to the meaning of "accountable person" and "operator", see supra, § **61.18**.
8   SI 1986/1711, reg 6(4).
9   As to appeals, see infra, § **61.29**.
10 SI 1986/1711, reg 6(6).

Service of documents

[61.28] A notice or other document which is to be served on or given to a person under the Stamp Duty Reserve Tax Regulation 1986[1] may be delivered to him or left at his usual or last known place of residence or served by post, addressed to him at his usual or last known place of residence or place of business or employment.[2]

Sergeant and Sims A 18.1 [1321]–[1340], Division D [5023]–[5044].

1   SI 1986/1711.
2   SI 1986/1711, reg 19.

Appeals against determination

[61.29] A person on whom a notice of determination[1] has been served may, within 30 days of the date of the notice, appeal against any determination specified in it by notice in writing given to the Board specifying the grounds of appeal.[2] The appeal is to the First-tier Tribunal[3] unless (a) the appellant and the Board agree that it should be to the High Court or (b) the High Court, on an application made by the appellant, is satisfied that the matters to be decided on the appeal are likely to be substantially confined to questions of law and gives leave for that purpose.[4] Neither the First-tier Tribunal nor the High Court may determine any question as to the value of land in the UK on any appeal under these provisions. On any such question the appeal must be to the Upper Tribunal in England or Wales, or the Lands Tribunal for Scotland or Northern Ireland.

An appeal under the above provisions may be brought out of time with the consent of the Board or the Tribunal. The Board (a) must give their consent if satisfied, on an application for that purpose, that there was a reasonable excuse for not bringing the appeal within the time limited and that the application was made after that time without unreasonable delay.[5]

On appeal, the Special Commissioners must confirm the determination appealed against unless satisfied that it ought to be varied or quashed.[6] The onus on appeal is therefore upon the appellant.

As with tax appeals generally, the procedure before the Special Commissioners on appeal from a notice of determination of stamp duty reserve tax is now governed by the Special Commissioners (Jurisdiction and Procedure) Regulations 1994.[7]

As with tax appeals generally, the procedure before the Special Commissioners on appeal from a notice of determination of stamp duty reserve tax is now governed by the Special Commissioners (Jurisdiction and Procedure) Regulations 1994.[8]

Any party to an appeal, if dissatisfied in point of law with the decision of the Special Commissioners, may appeal to the High Court.[9] On any such appeal, the High Court may reverse, affirm or vary the decision, or remit the matter to the Special Commissioners with the opinion of the court, or make such other order as the court thinks fit.

Sergeant and Sims Division D [5023]–[5044].

[1] See supra, § **61.27**.
[2] Stamp Duty Reserve Tax Regulations 1986, SI 1986/1711, reg 8(1).
[3] SI 1986/1711, reg 8(2).
[4] SI 1986/1711, reg 8(3). For the procedure governing appeals and applications for leave to appeal to the High Court under reg 8(3), see RSC Ord 91, R 2.
[5] SI 1986/1711, reg 9.
[6] SI 1986/1711, reg 8(4B); inserted by the General and Special Commissioners (Amendment of Enactments) Regulations 1994, SI 1994/1813, reg 28.
[7] SI 1994/1811.
[8] SI 1994/1811.
[9] SI 1986/1711, reg 10; substituted by the General and Special Commissioners (Amendment of Enactments) Regulations 1994, SI 1994/1813, reg 29. For the procedure governing stamp duty reserve tax appeals from the Special Commissioners to the High Court, see RSC Ord 91, R 5A.

Underpayments and overpayments

[61.30] Where too little stamp duty reserve tax has been paid in respect of a relevant transaction,[1] the tax underpaid is payable with interest, whether or not the amount that has been paid was that stated as payable in a notice of charge given by an accountable person or operator.[2] However, where any payment has been made and accepted in satisfaction of any liability for tax and on a view of the law then generally received or adopted in practice, any question whether too little or too much has been paid or what was the right amount of tax payable is determined on the same view, notwithstanding that it appears from a subsequent legal decision or otherwise that the view was or may have been wrong.[3]

Where tax is paid in accordance with a notice of charge given to the Board and the payment is made and accepted in full satisfaction of the tax, no additional

[61.30] Stamp duty reserve tax

amount of tax may be determined and specified in a notice of determination after the end of the period of six years beginning with the later of (a) the date on which the payment was made and accepted and (b) the relevant accountable date;[4] and at the end of that period, any liability for the additional tax is extinguished.[5]

If on a claim made within a period of six years beginning with the later of (a) the date on which the payment was made and (b) the relevant accountable date it is proved to the Board's satisfaction that too much tax has been paid in respect of any relevant transaction, the excess (and any interest paid on it) must be repaid by the Board.[6] Where tax repaid under the previous provision is not less than £25 it must be repaid with interest on it at the appropriate rate from the time it was paid.[7]

Where an amount of tax has been repaid, or interest has been paid, to any person which ought not to have been repaid or paid to him, that amount may be determined and recovered as if it were tax due from him.[8] Such a determination may be made before the expiration of six years from the date on which the amount was repaid or paid.[9]

Sergeant and Sims A2.7 [151]–[153].

---

[1] "Relevant transaction" means an agreement to transfer chargeable securities falling within FA 1986, s 87 (see supra, § **61.02**) or a transaction caught by the provisions relating to clearance services or depositary receipts (see supra, § **61.04**): Stamp Duty Reserve Tax Regulations 1986, SI 1986/1711, reg 2.

[2] SI 1986/1711, reg 4; 13(1). As to the meaning of "accountable person" and "operator", see supra, § **61.18**.

[3] SI 1986/1711, reg 17.

[4] As to the meaning of "accountable date", see supra, § **61.17**.

[5] SI 1986/1711, reg 13(2). In any case of fraud, wilful default or neglect by or on behalf of any person in connection with or in relation to tax, the period mentioned in reg 13(2) is the period of six years beginning when the fraud, default or neglect comes to the knowledge of the Board: reg 13(3).

[6] SI 1986/1711, reg 14; see also, reg 17.

[7] SI 1986/1711, regs 11, 14. The rate is the same as that under FA 1986, s 92, as to which see supra, § **61.21**.

[8] SI 1986/1711, reg 18(1). In reg 18, an amount repaid or paid includes an amount allowed by way of set off: reg 18(4).

[9] SI 1981/1711, reg 18(2). In any case of fraud, wilful default or neglect, the period mentioned in reg 18(2) is six years from the date on which the fraud, wilful default or neglect comes to the knowledge of the Board: reg 18(3).

Recovery of tax

[61.31] The Board must not exercise any remedy or take any proceedings for the recovery of any amount of stamp duty reserve tax which is due from any person unless the amount has been agreed in writing between that person and the Board or has been determined and specified in a notice of determination.[1] Where an amount has been so determined and specified, but an appeal[2] is

Administration, determination and recovery [61.31]

pending against the determination, the Board must not exercise any remedy or take any legal proceedings to recover the amount determined except such part of it as may be agreed in writing or determined and specified in a further notice of determination to be a part not in dispute.[3]

For the purposes of the Stamp Duty Reserve Tax Regulations 1986,[4] a notice[5] specifying any determination which can no longer be varied or quashed on appeal is sufficient evidence of the matters specified.[6] In any proceedings for the recovery of tax or interest on tax, a certificate by an officer of the Board (a) that the tax or interest is due or (b) that, to the best of his knowledge and belief, it has not been paid, is sufficient evidence that the sum mentioned in the certificate is due, or, as the case may be, unpaid.[7]

The collection and recovery provisions of TMA 1970 apply, with certain modifications, to stamp duty reserve tax.[8]

Sergeant and Sims A19.12 [1504]–[1540].

1   ie under the Stamp Duty Reserve Tax Regulations 1986, SI 1986/1711, reg 12(1); see supra, § **61.27**.
2   ie any appeal under SI 1986/1711, reg 8 (see supra, § **61.29**) but not any further appeal: reg 12(3). Regulation 8 applies to a determination made under reg 12(2) as if reg 8(4) were omitted: reg 12(3). As to appeals, see supra, § **61.29**.
3   SI 1986/1711, reg 12(2).
4   SI 1986/1711.
5   ie a notice under SI 1986/1711, reg 6, see supra, § **61.27**.
6   SI 1986/1711, reg 16(1).
7   SI 1986/1711, reg 16(2). A document purporting to be a certificate within reg 16(2) is deemed to be such a certificate unless the contrary is proved: reg 16(2).
8   SI 1986/1711, reg 20; see TMA 1970, ss 60, 61, 65, 66, 68, 69, 71–74, 78, 83, 86 and 90 as modified, applied and restated in SI 1986/1711, Sch, Part II.

62

Stamp duty land tax

Introduction	PARA **62.01**
Scope of the charge	PARA **62.02**
Chargeable consideration	PARA **62.05**
Amount of tax chargeable	PARA **62.09**
Leases and agreements for lease	PARA **62.10**
Reliefs and exemptions	PARA **62.13**
Returns, liability and compliance	PARA **62.23**
Special situations	PARA **62.27**
Transitional provisions	PARA **62.33**

Introduction

[62.01] Stamp duty land tax or "SDLT" replaced stamp duty on land in the UK from 1 December 2003.[1] After more than 300 years stamp duty on land was perceived by HM Treasury as outdated, not suited to the development of e-conveyancing and relatively easy to avoid. HMRC initially concluded in 2001 that the existing stamp duty simply required surgical alteration in the manner of a provision deeming an electronic conveyance to be an "instrument" for stamp duty purposes and triggering an obligation to pay the duty, to cope with the fact that under e-conveyancing there would not be a paper instrument on which to apply the stamp.[2] However, during the latter half of 2001 HM Treasury became aware of the scale of stamp duty avoidance in relation to land transactions caused by the quadrupling in rates since 1997 and instead of proposing further suitable amendments to stamp duty to counter the avoidance, chose the more complex task of replacing stamp duty on land with a new tax modelled along the lines of a compulsory self-assessed transaction tax.[3] The desire on the part of Government to prevent avoidance of a tax that raises up to about £14 billion annually became the driving force behind the new tax just as it became apparent that the original reason for replacing stamp duty ie e-conveyancing, would not begin in England even on a voluntary trial basis until at least 2007. The legislation in the Finance Bill 2003 that followed the abrupt suspension of the consultation process on the new tax in January 2003[4] created the impression of having been rushed out under pressure from Treasury Ministers anxious to abide by the statement in the foreword to the April 2002 Consultative Document that legislation would occur in 2003. The provisions themselves are in parts hard to follow, ill thought through and leave large gaps intended to be filled by copious amounts of regulations.[5] Further guidance in the form of bulletins and "customer" (sic) newsletters have also been promised. During the debates in Parliament on these provisions MP's were given to protest that at the same time as they were scrutinising the provisions in committee under pressure of the guillotine, the Chief Secretary to the Treasury was continuing to consult widely outside Parliament with a view to introducing further amendments subsequently at the report stage.[6] The unsatisfactory state of the legislation was demonstrated by the need to issue detailed changes correcting mistakes, plugging gaps and in some cases recasting charging provisions by way of statutory instruments prior to December 2003.[7] These were followed by the further detailed changes in subsequent Finance Acts as described in this chapter. SDLT avoidance schemes involving commercial property worth £5m or more have also been brought within the scope of the rules relating to disclosure of tax avoidance schemes in Finance Act 2004, Part 7 with effect from 1 August 2005.[8] A statutory general anti-avoidance rule for SDLT was introduced by FA 2007.[9]

Sergeant and Sims AA1.

[1] See infra, § **62.33** for the transitional provisions which in some cases bring contracts entered into before this date within SDLT. Stamp duty has been retained for transactions in shares and securities, bearer instruments and acquisitions of partnership interests: FA 2003, s 125 and Sch 15.
[2] Proceedings of the Tax Advisory Group set up by Inland Revenue Capital and Savings Division with the approval of a Treasury Minister (unpublished).
[3] See "A Consultative Document April 2002: Modernising Stamp Duty on land and buildings in the UK" issued by Inland Revenue.
[4] See "The Finance Bill 2003", Select Committee on Economic Affairs, 3rd report, session 2002–03, HL vol 1 paras 4.4 and 4.9.
[5] Without sight of the briefs sent to Parliamentary Counsel it is not possible to determine the reason for this.
[6] For example HC Official Report, Standing Committee Debates, Finance Bill, Tuesday 3 June 2003, col 360.
[7] For example the Stamp Duty and Stamp Duty Land Tax (Variation of the Finance Act 2003) (No 2) Regulations 2003, SI 2003/2760.
[8] The Stamp Duty Land Tax Avoidance Schemes (Prescribed Description of Arrangements) Regulations SI 2005/1868 and the Tax Avoidance Schemes (Information) (Amendment) Regulations SI 2005/1869.
[9] FA 2003, ss 75A, 75B and 75C, as added by FA 2007 s 71 and see infra, § **62.34**.

Scope of the charge

Introduction

[62.02] Stamp duty land tax is charged in accordance with Part 4 of the Finance Act 2003 on "land transactions" (see infra, § **62.03**). SDLT is also charged on the consideration paid for non-land transactions where the conditions for the operation of the statutory general anti-avoidance rule in FA 2003, s 75A are satisfied (see infra, § **62.34**). The tax is under the care of the Commissioners of Revenue & Customs and is administered by HMRC Stamp Taxes. In contrast with the tax it replaced, SDLT is chargeable whether or not there is an instrument. It is also expressed to be chargeable whether or not any party to the transaction is present or resident in the UK although this was never a requirement for stamp duty to apply.[1] The purchaser must deliver a land transaction return for every "notifiable transaction" (see infra, § **62.23**) within 30 days of the "effective date" of the transaction (see infra, § **62.04**) containing a self-assessment of the tax chargeable. Payment of the SDLT chargeable is also due within 30 days of the "effective date" of the transaction and need not accompany the tax return.[2]

Sergeant and Sims AA2.

[1]   FA 2003, s 42.
[2]   FA 2003, s 76 as amended by FA 2007, s 80.

Land transactions

[62.03] A "land transaction" is any acquisition of a "chargeable interest" and stamp duty land tax applies however the acquisition is effected whether by an act of the parties, an order of a court or other authority, by or under any statutory provision or by operation of law.[1] A "chargeable interest" is defined widely as:

(1)   an estate, interest, right or power in or over land in the UK, or
(2)   the benefit of an obligation, restriction or condition affecting the value of any such estate, interest, right or power,

other than an exempt interest.

Exempt interests are any security interest, a licence to use or occupy land and (in England, Wales or Northern Ireland) a tenancy at will, advowson, franchise or manor.[2] Chargeable interests therefore include freeholds and leasehold interests and their Scottish and Northern Irish equivalents, rights over another's land and powers of appointment exercisable over trusts of land. Both legal and equitable interests are included and the exclusion of licences is for the avoidance of doubt because a licence being a mere personal right is not an estate, interest or right over land. An assignment of the right to receive rents is undoubtedly a transfer of an interest in land.[3]

The "purchaser" and "vendor" in relation to a land transaction are defined as the person acquiring and the person disposing of the subject matter of the transaction (which will be the chargeable interest acquired together with any interest or right attached to it that is acquired with it).[4] However, a person cannot be a "purchaser" unless he has given consideration for or is a party to the transaction.[5] This is subject to the special tax charge arising on a contract under which A is to convey a chargeable interest at the direction or request of B to a person C who is not a party to the contract. B is deemed to have acquired a chargeable interest when the contract is substantially performed.[6]

The purchaser is the person who is required to file a land tax return and pay any tax due. The following illustrates who will be regarded as the purchaser in a variety of transactions:

Transaction	Purchaser
Conveyance, assignment or assignation	Transferee or assignee
Grant of lease	Lessee
Grant of easement etc	Person entitled to the right
Surrender of lease	Landlord
Certain variations of lease	Person whose estate interest or right is enlarged or benefits
Making or release of a covenant or condition	Person whose estate interest or right is enlarged or benefits

Having defined "chargeable interest" in wide terms the legislation then defines the concept of an "acquisition" of such an interest in equally wide terms by providing that the creation, surrender, release or variation of a chargeable interest is an "acquisition".[7] The variation of a lease is treated as an acquisition and disposal of a chargeable interest only where it is treated as the grant of a new lease or if there is a reduction in the rent or term or where the lessee gives consideration for a lease variation other than a variation of the rent or the term of the lease.[8]

Sergeant and Sims AA3.

---

[1] FA 2003, s 43(1), (2).
[2] FA 2003, s 48. A "security interest" means an interest or right (other than a rent charge) held for the purpose of securing the payment of money or the performance of any other obligation.
[3] See *IRC v John Lewis Properties plc* [2001] STC 1118, Ch D, which considered the issue in detail and was confirmed by the Court of Appeal at [2002] EWCA Civ 1869, [2003] STC 117, and Law of Property Act 1925, s 205.
[4] FA 2003, s 43 (4), (6).
[5] FA 2003, s 43(5).
[6] FA 2003, s 44A and see infra, § **62.30**.
[7] FA 2003, s 43(3).
[8] FA 2003, s 43(3)(d) and Sch 17A, para 15A as amended by F(No 2)A 2005, Sch 10, para 13.

Contracts, conveyances and 'effective date'

[62.04] A contract for a land transaction that contemplates completion by conveyance of the legal estate will have an "effective date" for stamp duty land tax of the earlier of "substantial performance" of the contract or the conveyance. The mere entry into such a contract itself is ignored and is not regarded as entering into a land transaction.[1] The occurrence of the "effective date" triggers the duty to deliver the land tax return and pay the SDLT within 30 days of such date.[2] It appears that in England contracts for equitable interests only[3] that will not be completed by conveyance are brought within the tax indirectly as being the acquisition of a chargeable interest[4] that is a

Scope of the charge [62.04]

notifiable transaction[5] giving rise to the obligation to deliver a land tax return.[6] "Substantial performance" occurs when either:

(1) the purchaser (or a person connected with the purchaser) takes possession of the whole or substantially the whole of the chargeable interest (by receiving or becoming entitled to receive rents and profits whether under the contract or a separate licence or lease of a temporary character), or

(2) a substantial amount of the consideration is paid or provided (in the case of rent or both rent and other consideration this means the first payment of rent or in the case of other consideration substantially the whole of the other consideration).[7]

A "substantial amount" of the consideration is an amount that is equal to or greater than 90% of the consideration payable.[8] In the majority of cases substantial performance will occur at completion and therefore the effective date will arise on the date of the conveyance as it did with stamp duty. However, if substantial performance of the contract occurs earlier then so will the effective date, thus preventing the purchaser from deferring the SDLT indefinitely by "resting on contract" and putting off taking a conveyance as could be done for contracts for a consideration of £10m or less under stamp duty.[9]

This rule also affects how sub-sales are charged under SDLT, as to which see infra, § **62.30**.

If the contract is substantially performed before completion and there is a subsequent conveyance both the contract and the conveyance are notifiable transactions[10] and additional SDLT is payable on the conveyance to the extent that the SDLT on the conveyance exceeds the SDLT on the contract.[11] If the contract is rescinded or annulled or not carried into effect, any SDLT paid on the contract can be reclaimed by submitting an amended land tax return.[12]

---

[1] FA 2003, s 44(1)–(3).
[2] FA 2003, ss 76 and 119, and is also the date on which the conditions for any available relief must be met, see for example infra, § **62.15** (group relief).
[3] See *Peter Bone Ltd v IRC* [1995] STC 921 and supra, §§ **57.18** and **58.02**.
[4] FA 2003, ss 43 and 48.
[5] FA 2003, s 77.
[6] FA 2003, s 76.
[7] FA 2003, s 44(4)–(6).
[8] See HC Official Report, Standing Committee Debate, Finance Bill, Tuesday 3 June 2003, col 315.
[9] See supra, § **57.18**.
[10] FA 2003, s 77.
[11] FA 2003, s 44(8); the wording of s 44(8)(*b*) appears odd because one is required to compare the same amount with itself ie the tax chargeable on the conveyance, and pay the difference and logically there can be no difference. It is thought that a court would interpret the first "chargeable" as meaning "payable" to make sense of the sub-section.
[12] FA 2003, s 44(8).

[62.05] Stamp duty land tax

Chargeable consideration

General

[62.05] Stamp duty land tax is charged as a percentage of the "chargeable consideration" for the land transaction.[1] The chargeable consideration is any consideration in money or money's worth given for the acquisition of the chargeable interest, whether given directly or indirectly by the purchaser or a person connected with him.[2] The chargeable consideration may also include consideration given or received in respect of a non-land transaction where that transaction is "involved in connection with" a land transaction and the conditions for the operation of the statutory general anti-avoidance rule in FA 2003, s 75A are met.[3]

The use of money or money's worth as the criterion means that a wider class of consideration is recognised for SDLT than for stamp duty on land where broadly only money, shares, the release or assumption of a debt and other property count as sale consideration.[4] The expression money or money's worth is not defined for SDLT although it must be something that is capable of being sold. This is the general principle and is reinforced by FA 2003, Sch 4, para 7 which requires that the value of any chargeable consideration other than money or debt shall be taken to be its market value. In *Secretan v Hart*[5] Buckley J thought that the expression included, "services or other property, where the price or consideration which the acquirer gives for the property has got to be turned into money before it can be expressed in terms of money".[6] The main difference between SDLT and stamp duty is that the latter did not include the carrying out of building works or the provision of services as consideration.[7]

The carrying out of building works is however specifically excluded from constituting chargeable consideration to the extent that:

(1) the works are carried out after the effective date of the transaction;
(2) the works are carried out on land acquired or to be acquired under the transaction or on other land held by the purchaser or a person connected with him; and
(3) it is not a condition of the transaction that the works are carried out by the vendor or a person connected with him.[8]

In relation to the rule that where a contract is substantially performed before completion both the contract and the conveyance are notifiable transactions (see supra, § **62.04**), the condition in 1 above is treated as met in relation to the conveyance if it is met in relation to the contract.[9]

Where the value of works is included in the chargeable consideration the value is taken to be the amount that would have to be paid in the open market for the carrying out of the works in question.[10]

On 2 April 2004 IR Stamp Taxes issued a statement in relation to when the vendor agrees to sell land to a purchaser and also agrees to carry out building works on the land sold. The statement concedes that the decision in *Prudential Assurance Co Ltd v IRC*[11] applies for SDLT as it applied for stamp duty

Chargeable consideration [62.05]

because the basis of the decision was the identification of the subject matter of the transaction and this was as relevant to SDLT as it was for stamp duty. It was also confirmed that SP8/93 will be applied to SDLT.[12] However, where the land contract and the building contract are "in substance" one bargain then the requirement to apportion the aggregate consideration on a just and reasonable basis will apply.

Where the consideration consists of the provision of services (other than the carrying out of works referred to above) the value of the consideration is taken to be the amount that would have to be paid in the open market for the works in question.[13]

In determining the amount or value of the consideration no discount is allowed for postponement of the right to receive any of the consideration.[14] Any value added tax chargeable is included in the consideration liable to SDLT except any value added tax chargeable because of an option to tax made after the effective date of the transaction.[15] Consideration attributable to two or more land transactions or in part to a land transaction and in part another matter or in part to matters making it chargeable consideration and in part to other matters, is to be apportioned on a just and reasonable basis.[16] It is provided that for these purposes any consideration given for:

what is in substance one bargain shall be treated as attributable to all the elements of the bargain, even though:

(a) separate consideration is, or purports to be, given for different elements of the bargain, or

(b) there are, or purport to be, separate transactions in respect of different elements of the bargain.[17]

It is difficult to understand how there can "in substance be one bargain", even though in the words of the provision: "there are separate transactions in respect of different elements of the bargain" given that SDLT is a tax on "land transactions" and not on "land bargains".[18] It is also difficult to understand how a court faced with having to apply this provision can avoid in effect being forced into rewriting the commercial bargain reached at arm's length by the parties and in effect substituting its own subjective opinion of how it would have apportioned if it were vendor and purchaser respectively. A court would normally take strenuous steps to avoid any such exercise precisely because it would be forced to substitute its own subjective views for those of the parties reached during actual commercial negotiations. This would be a tortuous exercise particularly where it was clear that the parties had different priorities in terms of how the consideration was allocated as regards for example capital allowances and capital gains tax.[19]

The amount or value of consideration is measured in sterling and the sterling equivalent of an amount expressed in another currency is taken by reference to the London closing exchange rate on the effective date, unless the parties have used a different rate for the transaction.[20] For exchanges of chargeable interests see infra, § **62.12**. In the case of a partition or division of a chargeable interest, the share held by the purchaser immediately before the partition or division does not count as chargeable consideration.[21]

Where the chargeable consideration consists wholly or partly of:

[62.05] Stamp duty land tax

(1) the satisfaction or release of debt due to the purchaser or owed by the vendor, or
(2) the assumption of existing debt by the purchaser,

the amount of the debt is taken as chargeable consideration up to a maximum of the market value of the chargeable interest acquired.[22]

There is a deemed assumption of debt by the purchaser constituting chargeable consideration where debt is secured on the property immediately before and immediately after the land transaction and the rights or liabilities in relation to that debt of any party are changed as a result of or in connection with the transaction.[23]

Where accommodation is provided to an employee, the chargeable consideration for SDLT is the higher of a market value rent or the amount treated as employment income unless the provision of the accommodation is treated as exempt from income tax. In that case there is no chargeable consideration for SDLT except to the extent of any actual consideration given. In any other case the consideration is to be not less than market value of the chargeable interest at the effective date of the transaction.[24]

The following matters do not count as chargeable consideration in relation to both the grant of a lease and the assumption or release of such obligations on the assignment of a lease:

(1) tenant's repairing, maintaining or insuring obligations;
(2) service charges and similar items;
(3) other obligations not affecting the rent that a tenant would be prepared to pay;
(4) guarantees of payment or performance;
(5) penal rent payable for breach of tenants' obligations;
(6) costs borne by a tenant exercising a statutory right to be granted a new lease;
(7) any other obligation by a tenant to bear the landlord's reasonable costs incidental on the grant of a lease;
(8) an obligation under a lease, on its termination, to transfer to the landlord payment entitlements under the scheme of income support for farmers in respect of land subject to the lease.[25]

There are also exemptions relating to arrangements involving public or educational bodies.[26]

For surrenders of existing leases in return for new lease and reverse premiums see infra, § **62.12**.

Where the purchaser indemnifies the vendor in respect of a liability to a third party arising from a breach of an obligation owed by the vendor in relation to the land transferred, neither the agreement nor any payment pursuant to it counts as chargeable consideration.[27]

Where a purchaser becomes liable to pay, agrees to pay or does in fact pay any inheritance tax due, that does not count as a chargeable transaction. Where land is acquired otherwise than by way of a bargain made at arm's length or is treated as so acquired by TCGA 1992, s 18 and the purchaser is or becomes liable to pay or does pay any capital gains tax due in respect of the corresponding disposal, his liability or payment does not count as chargeable consideration as long as there is no other chargeable consideration given.[28]

[1] FA 2003, s 55.
[2] FA 2003, s 50 and Sch 4, para 1.
[3] See infra 62.34.
[4] See supra, § **57.07**.
[5] (1969] 45 TC 701.
[6] *Secretan v Hart* (1969) 45 TC 701 at p 705.
[7] See for example Inland Revenue Tax Bulletin 43, October 1999, "PFI projects—stamp duty": "a contract to carry out works is not 'consideration [which] consists of property' for the purposes of FA 1994, s 241".
[8] FA 2003, Sch 4, para 10. This exclusion was originally misinterpreted by IR Stamp Taxes as a charging provision in relation to sales of land where the vendor agrees to carry out building works for the purchaser.
[9] FA 2003, Sch 4, para 10(2A).
[10] FA 2003, Sch 4, para 10(3)(*b*).
[11] [1992] STC 863.
[12] See supra, § **58.04** for the stamp duty position.
[13] FA 2003, Sch 4, para 11.
[14] FA 2003, Sch 4, para 3.
[15] FA 2003, Sch 4, para 2 and see VATA 1994, Sch 10, para 2 for the option to tax, and infra, § **62.10** for the position regarding leases.
[16] FA 2003, Sch 4, para 4.
[17] FA 2003, Sch 4, para 4(3).
[18] For example see *Kimbers v IRC* [1936] 1 KB 132 and supra, §§ **58.03** and **58.04**. This provision may be yet a further attempt by IR Stamp Taxes to sidestep the consequences of there being in substance two or more legally separate transactions.
[19] For the previous position under stamp duty where the parties were able to apportion consideration as they thought fit, provided they did not intend to defraud the Inland Revenue, see *Re Brown and Root McDermott Fabricators Ltd's Application* [1996] STC 483.
[20] FA 2003, Sch 4, para 9.
[21] FA 2003, Sch 4, para 6.
[22] FA 2003, Sch 4, para 8.
[23] FA 2003, Sch 4, para 8(1A). The amount of the debt treated or assumed is limited to the person's share of the property where it is jointly owned: para 8(1B).
[24] FA 2003, Sch 4, para 12.
[25] FA 2003, Sch 17A, para 10 as amended by SI 2006/875.
[26] FA 2003, Sch 4, para 17.
[27] FA 2003, Sch 4, para 16.
[28] FA 2003, Sch 4, para 16A.

Contingent, uncertain or unascertained consideration

[62.06] Stamp duty dealt with contingent consideration in a blunt manner. If the consideration was uncertain because the obligation to pay or the amount

[62.06] Stamp duty land tax

payable was linked to an event after execution, the contingency was ignored and stamp duty was charged by reference to any maximum, minimum or basic amount ascertainable at the date of execution. This resulted in stamp duty being payable by reference to an amount of consideration that might never be paid and there was no provision for a refund of the "overpaid" stamp duty.[1] In relation to land where the contingent consideration was truly unascertainable such that no maximum, minimum or basic sum could be ascertained the consideration was taken to be the market value of the estate or interest.[2]

Stamp duty land tax adopts a more flexible approach to contingent consideration by not automatically requiring tax to be paid on any maximum ascertainable sum and by providing for the possibility of deferral of tax and the repayment of any tax paid on a greater amount of consideration than is eventually payable.

Where the whole or part of the chargeable consideration is payable only if an uncertain future event occurs the amount or value of the consideration is to be determined on the assumption that the consideration is payable (or does not cease to be payable as the case may be).[3] Where the chargeable consideration is uncertain (because its amount or value depends on uncertain future events) or is unascertained, its amount or value is to be taken on the basis of a reasonable estimate.[4]

Several possibilities are therefore included within these provisions from simple situations where the consideration is neither contingent nor uncertain but simply unascertained (because a set of accounts has not yet been drawn up) through to more complex situations where the consideration is contingent (assume therefore it is payable) and uncertain (amount depends on an uncertain future event) when a reasonable estimate at the effective date of the transaction will be required.[5] See infra, § 62.23 for the obligation to file a further land tax return and make a payment of any further tax due when the outcome of the contingency or any uncertain or unascertained consideration becomes known.

An application to defer payment of tax may be made to IR Stamp Taxes where the amount of tax payable depends on the amount or value of chargeable consideration that at the effective date is contingent or uncertain and falls to be paid on one or more future dates, of which at least one falls or may fall more than six months after the effective date of the transaction.[6] Where the tax is deferred interest will only run on any such tax after 30 days from the date the deferred payment is due.[7]

Sergeant and Sims AA54.

---

[1] See supra, § **56.18**.
[2] See supra, § **56.19**.
[3] FA 2003, s 51(1).
[4] FA 2003, s 51(2) and (3).
[5] See supra, § **62.04** for "effective date" and also HC Official Report, Standing Committee B, Thursday 5 June 2003, col 386.
[6] FA 2003, s 90 and see infra, § **62.25**. See Stamp Duty Land Tax (Administration) Regulations 2003, SI 2837/2003 for the regulations relating to deferred payment of SDLT.

[7] FA 2003, s 87(3)(b). In respect of contingent or uncertain consideration on which tax is not deferred, interest runs on tax unpaid more than 30 days after the effective date of the transaction although lodgement of the tax reduces interest accordingly: FA 2003, s 87(5) and (6).

Consideration consisting of an annuity

[62.07] Where the chargeable consideration consists of annuity payments whether for life, in perpetuity, for an indefinite period or for a definite period exceeding 12 years, the consideration taken into account is limited to 12 years' annual payments.[1] This contrasts with stamp duty which used a 20 year period for payments lasting more than 20 years or in perpetuity, and a 12 year period for payments lasting for life.[2] Where the amount payable varies or may vary from year to year the twelve highest annual payments are taken. No account is taken of any provision in the annuity for adjustment of the amount payable in line with the retail price index and no discount is given for the fact that the amounts are payable in the future.[3]

The rules relating to contingent and uncertain consideration discussed in supra, § **62.06** above apply to determine the value of any annuity payment where necessary and an "annuity" means any consideration other than rent that falls to be paid or provided periodically.[4] No application can be made to defer the tax payable nor is there any facility to file a further land tax return and make an adjusting tax payment or receive a repayment when a contingency or any uncertain consideration becomes known.[5]

Sergeant and Sims AA55.

[1] FA 2003, s 52(1) and (2), and see infra, § **62.10** for the application of this provision in relation to VAT payable under a lease that is not reserved as rent.
[2] See supra, § **57.10**.
[3] FA 2003, s 52(3).
[4] FA 2003, s 52(5) and (6).
[5] FA 2003, s 52(7) and see supra, § **62.06**.

Connected companies

[62.08] When a company purchases a chargeable interest and the vendor is connected with the company or some or all of the consideration consists of the issue or transfer of shares in any company with which the vendor is connected, the chargeable consideration is to be taken to be not less than the market value of the interest acquired at the effective date of the transaction plus any rent payable if the acquisition is the grant of a lease.[1]

The fact that there may be no chargeable consideration actually given for the transfer does not affect the application of the market value rule. However, any other available exemption from SDLT overrides the market value rule.[2]

This provision means that tax is charged when a business is incorporated and land is transferred to the proprietors' company. Despite doubts about the

[62.08] Stamp duty land tax

equivalent market value rule in stamp duty, it has been confirmed that under SDLT the market value is based on the nature of the interest transferred and that if a legal but not a beneficial interest is transferred then the market value will be taken to be the nominal value of the legal interest and not the full value of the beneficial interest.[3] However, in the cases of a grant of a lease to a bare trustee and a grant of a lease by a bare trustee, tax is charged as if the whole of the interest in the lease was acquired or disposed of accordingly.[4]

The market value rule does not apply in the following cases:

(1) Case 1 is where the company is to hold the property as trustee in the course of a business carried on by it that consists of or includes the management of trusts.[5]

(2) Case 2 is where the company is to hold the property as trustee and the vendor is connected with the company only because of TA 1988, s 839(3) (trustee connected with any individual who is a settlor in relation to the settlement etc) and is not otherwise connected.[6]

(3) Case 3 is where the vendor is a company and the transaction is, or is part of, a distribution of assets of that company (whether or not in connection with its winding up) and there has not been a claim for group relief[7] by the vendor in respect of the chargeable interest transferred in the previous three years.[8]

The equivalent market value rule in stamp duty also had additional exemptions relating to transfers to and from nominees and bare trustees and transfers from one nominee or bare trustee to another. These exceptions are not required in stamp duty land tax because no SDLT arises on a transfer of a bare legal estate from a nominee to its principal and on a transfer to a nominee or bare trustee of bare legal title, due to the market value of such an interest being nominal at most.[9]

However, a further exception from the stamp duty market value rule relating to the transfer out of a settlement to a beneficiary who did not acquire his interest for money or money's worth being a distribution in accordance with the settlement, has not been carried over into SDLT.[10] Under SDLT there is a market value charge if the beneficiary who receives the land is a company, to avoid the possibility of land being passed through a settlement to avoid SDLT.

Sergeant and Sims AA58.

---

[1] FA 2003, s 53(1) and (1A). TA 1988, s 839 applies to determine whether the company and the vendor are connected. Instances where the vendor is not connected with the purchasing company and the consideration includes the issue of shares must surely be rare. For SDLT the "market value" is determined as for capital gains tax: see TCGA 1992, ss 272–274: FA 2003, s 118.

[2] FA 2003, s 53(4) disapplying FA 2003, Sch 3, para 1 (no chargeable consideration).

[3] HC Official Report, Standing Committee B, Thursday 5 June 2003, col 389.

[4] FA 2003, Sch 16, para 3 as amended by F(No 2)A 2005, Sch 10, para 11.

[5] FA 2003, s 54(2). It is thought that this case relates to companies that carry on an actual business of managing trusts and that a company that acts as nominee or bare trustee for a particular principal or beneficiary or partnership and has been incorporated or acquired simply to hold legal title for such persons cannot take advantage of this case.

[6] FA 2003, s 54(3).
[7] See infra, § **62.15** (group relief).
[8] FA 2003, s 54(4).
[9] HC Official Report, Standing Committee B, Thursday 5 June 2003, col 390, but see above for dealings in leases and bare trustees.
[10] FA 2000, s 120(5) and see HC Official Report, Standing Committee B, Thursday 5 June 2003, col 390.

Amount of tax chargeable

General

[62.09] Stamp duty land tax is charged as a percentage of the chargeable consideration for the transaction. Where the relevant land consists entirely of residential property, the percentages in Table A apply:[1]

TABLE A: RESIDENTIAL

Relevant consideration	Percentage
Not more than £125,000	0%
More than £125,000 but not more than £250,000	1%
More than £250,000 but not more than £500,000	3%
More than £500,000	4%

In the September 2008 Pre-Budget Report the Chancellor announced that "relevant" residential property would be exempted under regulations from the tax where the chargeable consideration was no more than £175,000 for transactions having an effective date between 3 September 2008 and 2 September 2009. "Relevant" residential property means an acquisition of a freehold or a leasehold interest (but not other interests in or over land) other than the grant of a lease for less than 21 years or the assignment of a lease with less than 21 years to run.[2] Under FA 2009, s 10 the regulations were revoked for transactions with an effective date on or after 22 April 2009 and the threshold on residential property in the table above was kept at £175,000 until 31 December 2009.

Where the relevant land consists of or includes land that is not residential property, the percentages in Table B apply:

TABLE B: NON-RESIDENTIAL OR MIXED

Relevant consideration	Percentage
Not more than £150,000	0%

[62.09] Stamp duty land tax

Relevant consideration	Percentage
More than £150,000 but not more than £250,000	1%
More than £250,000 but not more than £500,000	3%
More than £500,000	4%

In the above tables the "relevant consideration" is the chargeable consideration and when the amount of the chargeable consideration exceeds a rate threshold the higher rate applies to the total consideration and hence the system is known as the "slab system".

If the transaction forms part of a number of linked transactions the relevant consideration for the purpose of the tables above is the total of the chargeable consideration for all the linked transactions.[3] Transactions are "linked" if they form part of a single scheme, arrangement or series of transactions between the same vendor and purchaser or persons connected with them. While it seems that the stamp duty cases on certificates of value will remain relevant in determining whether a transaction forms part of a series of transactions it is clear that the criteria for "linked" transactions are much wider than the criteria for certificates of value since they also refer to "single scheme" or "arrangement" terms which did not feature in the "larger transaction or series of transactions" criteria for certificates of value.[4] There are exceptions for transactions carried out in pursuance of a right of collective enfranchisement or of a crofting community right to buy where the tax is determined by reference to a fraction of the relevant consideration.[5]

Where the whole or part of the chargeable consideration consists of rent, the tax on the rent is calculated separately under different rules and although the tables above apply to compute the tax on any premium paid for the grant of the lease, the nil rate band is not available if the land is non-residential property and annual rent exceeds £1,000[6] in order to prevent advantage being taken of the nil rate band twice in respect of the same lease.

Sergeant and Sims AA7.

---

[1] FA 2003, s 55(1) and (2) as amended by FA 2006, s 162 for transactions after 22 March 2006. For the definition of "residential" and "non-residential" property see FA 2003, s 116 and infra, § **62.14**.

[2] SDLT (Exception of Certain Acquisitions of Residential Property) Regs, SI 2008/2339 and the SDLT (Variation of Part 4 of the Finance Act 2003) Regs, SI 2008/2338.

[3] FA 2003, s 55(4).

[4] FA 2003, s 108. TA 1988, s 839 is applied to determine whether persons are connected for these purposes. For the equivalent stamp duty position and cases see supra, §§ **57.15** and **57.16**.

[5] FA 2003, ss 55(5), 74 and 75.

[6] FA 2003, s 56 and Sch 5, para 9A and see infra, § **62.10**.

Leases and agreements for lease

General

[62.10] Stamp duty land tax is charged in respect of leases on any premiums paid for the grant of a lease and also on any rent. Lease premiums are taxed in accordance with either Table A or Table B in supra, § **62.09** and SDLT on the rent is calculated according to the special formula described in infra, § **62.11**. As was the case with stamp duty, the distinction between a lease and a licence continues to be important because under SDLT a licence to use or occupy land and a tenancy at will are exempt interests and are not liable to the tax.[1]

Although there was originally no express charge in relation to agreements for lease, such agreements were liable to SDLT anyway by implication as contracts for a land transaction under which the transaction is to be completed by a "conveyance" and the usual rules as to the timing of the tax charge applied according to whether or not substantial performance of the contract has occurred prior to completion in the form of the grant of the lease.[2] Accordingly under an agreement for a lease where both a premium and rent were payable on the grant of the lease, the grant of the lease would be the effective date of the transaction giving rise to the obligation to file a land tax return and pay the SDLT chargeable.[3] However, substantial performance of the agreement for lease was possible giving rise to a tax charge for SDLT purposes in respect of the agreement for lease itself despite no lease having been granted, where substantially the whole of the premium was paid.[4] In such cases where the lease was granted following substantial performance of the agreement the term of the lease was taken to be the period from substantial performance of the agreement until the end of the lease period.[5]

However, for transactions with an effective date after 17 March 2004 a new para 12A of FA 2003, Sch 17A specifically addresses the grant of an agreement for lease which is substantially performed prior to the grant of the actual lease. The agreement is treated as if it were the grant of a lease on the date of substantial performance. This notional lease is treated as if it were surrendered on the grant of the actual lease and the actual lease is treated as granted in consideration of the surrender of the notional leases. "Overlap" relief will apply so that the rent payable under the actual lease for the same period as the notional lease will be reduced by the amount of rent that would have been payable for that period under the notional lease in assessing SDLT on the rent under the actual lease.[6] The notional lease and the actual lease are not treated as a single lease under FA 2003, Sch 17A, para 5 so that the rent under both is not aggregated: see infra § **62.11**. There is also a provision dealing with the assignment of an agreement for lease prior to substantial performance: see infra, § **62.30**.

Leases granted to a company connected with the lessor or where some or all of the consideration consists of the issue or transfer of shares in a company with which the lessor is connected, fall within the scope of the market value rule for SDLT; see supra, § **62.08**.

Any VAT chargeable in respect of the lease other than value added tax chargeable by virtue of an election to tax the property made after the effective date of the transaction is taken to be part of the chargeable consideration.[7] It seems that any VAT payable in respect of the rent that is not reserved as rent under the lease will not be rent for SDLT purposes and as for stamp duty will be taxed as consideration other than rent. Accordingly, the total VAT payable over the term of the lease will be chargeable except where the lease exceeds 12 years when the amount chargeable will be limited to the total of the 12 highest annual payments; see supra, § 62.07.

None of the following counts as chargeable consideration on the grant of a lease:

(1) an undertaking by the tenant to repair, maintain or insure the let premises;
(2) a tenant's undertaking to pay in respect of services, repairs, maintenance, insurance or management costs;
(3) any other tenant's obligation that does not affect the open market rent;
(4) any rent or performance guarantee;
(5) penal rent;
(6) costs borne by a tenant exercising a statutory right to be granted a new lease;
(7) any other obligation by a tenant to bear the landlord's reasonable costs incidental on the grant of a lease;
(8) an obligation under a lease, on its termination, to transfer to the landlord payment entitlements under the scheme of income support for farmers in respect of land subject to the lease.

A payment made under any of the above obligations is also ignored. The assumption or release of any obligation above on the assignment or surrender of the lease is also ignored.[8]

Where on the grant or assignment of a lease the lessee or assignee makes a loan or pays a deposit to any person and the repayment of the loan or deposit is contingent on anything done or omitted to be done by the lessee or assignee or on the death of the lessee or assignee, the amount is treated as chargeable consideration other than rent. This will not apply where the amount of the deposit does not exceed twice the rent determined under FA 2003, Sch 17A, para 7(3) (the "relevant maximum rent"). In case of the grant of a lease, the relevant maximum rent is the highest amount of rent payable in respect of any consecutive 12-month period in the first five years of the term. In the case of a lease assignment, the relevant maximum rent is the highest amount of rent payable in respect of any consecutive 12-month period in the first five years of the term remaining outstanding as at the date of the assignment.[9] No tax repayment claim may be made in respect of any such loan or deposit treated as chargeable consideration which is later repaid or in respect of the refund of any consideration given where the refund is made under arrangements made in connection with the transaction and is contingent on the determination or assignment of the lease or on the grant of a chargeable interest out of the lease.[10]

Sergeant and Sims AA81, AA82.

[1] FA 2003, s 48(2), and see supra, § **57.25**. See FA 2003, Sch 17A, para 1 for the definition of a "lease".
[2] FA 2003, s 44 and see supra, § **62.04**. It seems that for SDLT a "conveyance" includes the grant of a lease: FA 2003, s 44(9).
[3] FA 2003, s 44(2).
[4] FA 2003, s 44(6) or the lessee has taken possession or been granted a licence to occupy in the meantime.
[5] FA 2003, Sch 5, para 6(3).
[6] FA 2004, Sch 17A, paras 12A and 9.
[7] FA 2003, Sch 4, para 2. HMRC issued a guidance note dated 3 December 2008 stating their view of how the temporary reduction in the standard rate of VAT from 17.5% to 15% announced in the 2008 Pre-Budget Report should be dealt with for SDLT purposes. If the effective date of the grant of the lease is on or after 1 December 2008 the VAT chargeable in respect of the rent should be estimated using 15% for payments of rent with a tax point until 31 December 2009 and 17.5% from 1 January 2010.
[8] FA 2003, Sch 4, para 13.
[9] FA 2003, Sch 17A, para 18A.
[10] See supra, § **62.06**; FA 2003, s 80(4A).

Rent

[62.11] Stamp duty land tax is charged on any chargeable consideration consisting of rent as a percentage of the net present value of the rent payable over the term of the lease.[1]

In other words, the total rent payable over the term of the lease is charged to tax at a flat percentage (after discounting each annual rent by 3.5% per annum to arrive at its present value). This contrasts with stamp duty on rent that was charged on only one year's average rent at varying percentages according to the term of the lease. On average, the SDLT charge on rent represents an increase of four times the stamp duty charge on a ten year lease.

The net present value (V) of the rent payable over the term of the lease is calculated by applying the formula:[2]

$$V = \sum_{i=1}^{n} \frac{r_i}{(1+T)^i}$$

r_i is the rent payable in respect of year i

i is the particular year of the term for which the calculation is performed (a calculation being required for each year)

n is the term of the lease

T is the temporal discount rate (currently 3.5%).

Having calculated the net present value of the rent (referred to as the "relevant rental value") the tax is charged as a percentage of so much of that value as falls within each rate band according to the following two tables.[3] Table A

[62.11] Stamp duty land tax

applies where the relevant land consists entirely of residential property and Table B applies where the relevant land consists of or includes land that is not residential property. Hence tax is charged on each "slice" of the rental value at either the nil or the 1% rate as appropriate thus ensuring that credit is given for the first £125,000 or £150,000 as appropriate where the rental value exceeds this figure.

TABLE A: RESIDENTIAL

Rate bands	Percentage
£0 to £125,000	0%
Over £125,000	1%

In the September 2008 Pre-Budget Report the Chancellor announced that "relevant" residential property would be exempted under regulations where the chargeable consideration was no more than £175,000 for transactions having an effective date between 3 September 2008 and 2 September 2009. "Relevant" residential property means an acquisition of a freehold or a leasehold interest (but not other interests in other land) other than the grant of a lease for less than 21 years or the assignment of a lease with less than 21 years to run.[4] Under FA 2009, s 10 the regulations were revoked for transactions with an effective date on or after 22 April 2009 and the threshold on residential property in the table above kept at £175,000 until 31 December 2009.

TABLE B: NON-RESIDENTIAL OR MIXED

Rate bands	Percentage
£0 to £150,000	0%
Over £150,000	1%

If the lease is one of a number of linked transactions for which the chargeable consideration includes rent then the net present values of the rents payable under all the linked leases are aggregated for the purpose of applying the percentages in the above tables.[5]

Where successive linked leases are granted or treated as granted (at the same or different times) of substantially the same premises and the grants are linked transactions then the series of leases is treated as a single lease granted at the time of the first lease for the aggregate term and rent of the series of leases and a return is required under FA 2003, s 81A on the grant of each successive lease with the tax payable adjusted accordingly.[6]

A single sum expressed to be payable in respect of rent or expressed to be payable in respect of rent and other matters such as a service charge, but not apportioned is treated as entirely rent. This is expressly without prejudice to a just and reasonable apportionment where separate sums are expressed to be payable in respect of rent and other matters.[7]

Penal rent or increased rent in the nature of a penal rent payable in respect of the breach of any obligation of the tenant does not count as chargeable consideration.[8]

Contingent, uncertain or unascertained rent is taken into account and dealt with under the usual rules for SDLT; see supra, § **62.06** subject to the following modifications. No application may be made to defer payment of the tax on contingent or uncertain rent.[9] No account is taken of any provision for the rent to be adjusted in line with the retail price index and the starting rent is used for calculating the tax.[10] This apparently generous concession is counter-balanced by the relatively low temporal discount rate of 3.5% used for the purposes of discounting future rent payments in the formula above which does not take into account price inflation.

Where the lease provides for the rent to be reviewed or varied or the rent is contingent, uncertain or unascertained the actual rent payable in the first five years of the term is taken into account for the purposes of the tax computation. However, the rent payable for any period after the end of the fifth year of the term is assumed to be at an annual amount equal to the highest amount of rent payable for any consecutive period of 12 months in the first five years (including any contingent, uncertain or unascertained rent).[11] Where the first rent review occurs in the final quarter of the fifth year that is ignored for these purposes.[12] Where the end of the fifth year is reached or the amount of rent payable in the first five years ceases to be uncertain at an earlier date, the tenant must make a return to HMRC within 30 days and pay any tax due if as a result the transaction becomes notifiable or tax or additional tax becomes payable. If less tax turns out to be payable than has already been paid then a claim for repayment can be made.[13]

If after the end of the fifth year of the term the amount of rent increases either in accordance with the provisions of the lease or otherwise and the increase is treated as "abnormal" then the increase in the rent is treated as if it were the grant of a new lease in consideration of the excess rent and tax is payable accordingly.[14]

In computing the tax payable on a lease for a fixed term no account is taken of any contingency which may cause the lease to end before the expiry of the fixed term or the existence of a break or renewal clause.[15]

When a lease continues after a fixed term it is treated as a single lease growing by one year at a time and tax is payable accordingly at each interval.[16] A lease for an indefinite term is treated in the first instance as if it were a lease for a fixed term of one year and if it continues in existence it is treated as a single lease growing by one year at a time and tax is payable accordingly at each interval.[17]

Where a tenant continues in occupation after the end of the contractual term and is subsequently granted a new lease of the premises with a term expressed to begin from the end of the old contractual term, the term of the new lease is treated for SDLT as beginning on the date it is expressed to begin. This is despite the rule in *Bradshaw v Pawley*[18] that the lease term commences on the later of the contractual term start date and the actual date of grant. However, any rent payable under the new lease in respect of any period after the old

[62.11] Stamp duty land tax

contractual term and before the actual date on which the new lease is granted is for SDLT purposes to be reduced by the amount of taxable rent that is payable in respect of that period otherwise than under the new lease. This means that a credit is given for SDLT payable in respect of that period under the notional lease which is treated as growing one year at a time following the end of the old lease. However, a credit will not be available to the extent that the actual date of grant of the new lease occurs before the next anniversary of the notional growing lease. Where possible therefore the new lease should not require rent to be payable in respect of any period prior to the next anniversary of the notional growing lease.

Where a lease is varied so as to increase the rent as from a date before the end of the fifth year of the term, the variation is treated as if it were the grant of a lease for the additional rent payable and tax is chargeable. However, an increase in rent under the existing terms of a lease such as on a scheduled rent review is not chargeable unless it is an "abnormal" rent increase after the fifth year of the term.[19]

---

[1] FA 2003, s 56 and Sch 5, para 2.
[2] FA 2003, Sch 5, para 3.
[3] FA 2003, Sch 5, para 2(3).
[4] SDLT (Exception of Certain Acquisitions of Residential Property) Regulations, SI 2008/2339 and the SDLT (Variation of Part 4 of the Finance Act 2003) Regulations, SI 2008/2338.
[5] FA 2003, Sch 5, para 2(5) and see supra, § **62.09** for 'linked transactions'.
[6] FA 2003, Sch 17A, para 5.
[7] FA 2003, Sch 17A, para 6.
[8] FA 2003, Sch 17A, para 10(1)(e).
[9] FA 2003, s 90(7).
[10] FA 2003, Sch 17A, para 7(5).
[11] FA 2003, Sch 17A, para 7.
[12] FA 2003, Sch 17A, para 7A although the reference in that provision to 'ending with the review date' needs to be read as 'ending the day before the review date' in order to make the provisions work.
[13] FA 2003, Sch 17A, para 8.
[14] FA 2003, Sch 17A, paras 14 and 15 as amended by FA 2006, Sch 25, paras 7 and 8 replacing the previous criterion of 5% + RPI compound with a flat rate increase of 20% per year. It is understood that HMRC accept that the SDLT return for the rent increase should be filed within 30 days of the date when the rent increase is agreed and not, if earlier, the date from which the increased rent became payable.
[15] FA 2003, Sch 17A, para 2.
[16] FA 2003, Sch 17A, para 3.
[17] FA 2003, Sch 17A, paras 1 and 9A.
[18] [1979] 3 All ER 273.
[19] FA 2003, Sch 17A, para 13 and amended by FA 2006, Sch 25, para 6.

Surrender and regrant, sale and leaseback

[62.12] Where a lease is granted in consideration of the surrender of an existing lease between the same parties the grant of the new lease does not count as chargeable consideration for the surrender and the surrender does not count as chargeable consideration for the grant of the new lease so that FA 2003, Sch 4, para 5 (exchanges—see infra, § **62.31**) is disapplied.[1] In the case of the grant, assignment or surrender of a lease a reverse premium does not count as chargeable consideration.[2]

The leaseback element of a sale and leaseback arrangement is exempt where the leaseback is granted out of the sale of a major interest in land by way of transfer or grant if:

(1)　the sale is entered into wholly or partly in consideration of the leaseback;
(2)　the only other consideration for the sale is cash or debt;
(3)　the sale is not by way of sub-sale, and
(4)　the parties are not members of a group of companies for the purposes of group relief.[3]

Sergeant and Sims AA86.

[1]　FA 2003, Sch 17A, para 16.
[2]　FA 2003, Sch 17A, para 18.
[3]　FA 2003, s 57A.

Reliefs and exemptions

General

[62.13] A number of reliefs are available from stamp duty land tax including the following:

(1)　Disadvantaged areas relief—FA 2003, s 57.[1]
(2)　Sales and leasebacks—FA 2003, s 57A.[2]
(3)　Certain acquisitions of residential property by house builders and property traders—FA 2003, s 58A and Sch 6A.
(4)　First acquisition of zero-carbon homes – FA 2003, ss 58B, 58C.
(5)　Compulsory purchase facilitating development—FA 2003, s 60.
(6)　Purchases by public authorities in connection with planning agreements—FA 2003, s 61.
(7)　Group relief, reconstruction and acquisition reliefs—FA 2003, s 62 and Sch 7.[3]
(8)　Demutualisation of insurance company—FA 2003, s 63.
(9)　Demutualisation of building society—FA 2003, s 64.
(10)　Initial transfer of assets to a unit trust scheme—FA 2003, s 64A (withdrawn from 22 March 2006).
(11)　Incorporation of limited liability partnership—FA 2003, s 65.

(12) Transfers between public bodies on a reorganisation—FA 2003, s 66.
(13) Transfers in consequence of reorganisation of parliamentary constituencies—FA 2003, s 67.
(14) Acquisitions by charities—FA 2003, s 68 and Sch 8.[4]
(15) Acquisitions by bodies established for national purposes—FA 2003, s 69.
(16) Right to buy and shared ownership transactions—FA 2003, s 70 and Sch 9 as amended by FA 2009, s 81.
(17) Acquisitions by registered social landlords—FA 2003, s 71 as amended by FA 2009, s 80.
(18) Alternative property finance—FA 2003, ss 71A, 72, 72A, 73, 73A, 73AB, 73B and FA 2009, s 122 and Sch 61.
(19) Collective enfranchisement by lease holders—FA 2003, s 74 as amended by FA 2009, s 79, removing the requirement that a "Right to enfranchise" or RTE company be used.
(20) Crofting community right to buy—FA 2003, s 75.
(21) Restricted sub-sale relief—FA 2003, s 45.[5]

The following transactions are exempt from SDLT:[6]

(1) A transaction for no chargeable consideration—FA 2003, Sch 3, para 1.[7]
(2) Grant of leases by registered social landlords—FA 2003, Sch 3, para 2.
(3) Transfers between spouses on divorce—FA 2003, Sch 3, para 3.
(4) Assents and appropriations by personal representatives—FA 2003, Sch 3, para 3A.
(5) Variation of testamentary dispositions—FA 2003, Sch 3, para 4.

Where the purchaser is a public office or department of the Crown no payment of SDLT is required if that would ultimately be borne by the Crown. This includes ministers of the Crown but not local authorities or similar bodies and does not apply to the acquisition of private property for the Sovereign.[8]

Sergeant and Sims AA86–AA213.

---

[1] See infra, § 62.14.
[2] See supra, § 62.12.
[3] See infra, §§ 62.15–62.21.
[4] See infra, § 62.22.
[5] See infra, § 62.30.
[6] And are therefore not chargeable transactions for SDLT: FA 2003, s 49.
[7] But this exemption is overridden by the market value rule for transfers to connected companies, see supra, § 62.08.
[8] FA 2003, s 107.

Disadvantaged areas relief

[62.14] Relief for acquisitions of land in designated disadvantaged areas was introduced for stamp duty purposes with effect from 30 November 2001 and initially was available only for transfers on sale and lease premiums where the consideration did not exceed £150,000.[1]

Note: the temporary increase in the threshold for residential property to £175,000 referred to at 62.09 above trumps the £150,000 relief for acquisitions of residential property in designated disadvantaged areas.

An area is disadvantaged for the purposes of the relief if it is designated as such in the Stamp Duty (Disadvantaged Areas) Regulations 2001, SI 2001/3747.[2] The designation is based on wards listed in the various indices of multiple deprivation maintained by central and regional government. The £150,000 cap was removed from non-residential property in disadvantaged areas after 9 April 2003 and transfers on sale and grants of leases for a premium or rent or both became absolutely exempt after this date and the £150,000 cap applied to residential property only.[3] An equivalent relief for acquisitions of chargeable interests in designated disadvantaged areas was carried over into stamp duty land tax and the regulations mentioned above designating areas as disadvantaged areas have continuous effect for SDLT.[4] Disadvantaged areas relief for non-residential property was removed for transactions with an effective date after 16 March 2005.[5]

The term "residential property" is defined and is used in the SDLT legislation for the purpose of distinguishing between residential and non-residential property in the application of the disadvantaged areas relief and also generally for determining which set of tables of rates apply to the chargeable consideration.[6] Broadly, "residential property" is a building or part of a building which is in use as a dwelling, or is suitable for use as a dwelling, or is in the process of being constructed or adapted as a dwelling, including any land forming part of the garden or grounds of such a building and any outbuilding on that land. A single transaction involving the acquisition of a major interest in or the grant of a lease over six or more separate dwellings is treated as relating to non-residential property. "Non-residential" property is defined as any property that is not "residential property".

The relief operates according to whether the land in question is wholly or partly situated in a disadvantaged area. If the land is wholly situated in a disadvantaged area and all the land is non-residential property then since 16 March 2005 the transaction is no longer exempt from SDLT. If the land is wholly within a disadvantaged area but all the land is residential then the transaction is exempt from SDLT if either:

(1) the consideration does not include rent and the "relevant consideration" does not exceed £150,000, or
(2) the consideration consists only of rent and the "relevant rental value" does not exceed £150,000.

"Relevant consideration" is the consideration that would be taken into account in applying the tables of rates in supra, § **62.09** were it not for disadvantaged areas relief, and "relevant rental value" is the amount that would be taken for the purpose of applying the table of rates for the lease rentals in supra, § **62.11** were it not for the relief.

If the consideration includes rent and other consideration and the "relevant rental value" does not exceed £150,000, the rent does not count as chargeable consideration. The other consideration is also ignored if it does not exceed £150,000. Where the land is partly non-residential and partly residential the consideration is to be apportioned on a just and reasonable basis. The consideration attributable to the non-residential property counts as chargeable consideration and the consideration attributable to the residential property is dealt with as above.[7]

If the land is partly in a disadvantaged area and partly outside such an area, the consideration is to be apportioned on a just and reasonable basis.

Where the land situated in a disadvantaged area is either all residential property or partly residential and partly non-residential the rules similar to those set out above relating to residential or mixed property wholly situated in a disadvantaged area apply to determine the extent to which the consideration including rent counts as chargeable consideration.[8]

Sergeant and Sims AA212.

---

[1] FA 2001, s 92 and Sch 30, prior to its amendment by FA 2002, s 110(1) and see generally statement of practice 1/03 and 1/04.
[2] Made by the Treasury under FA 2001, s 92 (4) and (9).
[3] FA 2001, s 92A and the Stamp Duty (Disadvantaged Areas) (Application of Exemption) Regulations 2003, SI 2003/1056 made by the Treasury under FA 2001, ss 92A, 92B and FA 2002, s 110(6) following the grant of European Union state aid approval (due to expire in 2006) and revoking the Variation of Stamp Duties Regulations 2001, SI 2001/3746.
[4] FA 2003, s 57 and Sch 6, paras 1 and 2.
[5] FA 2005, s 96 and Sch 9.
[6] FA 2003, s 116 and see supra, §§ **62.09** and **62.11**.
[7] FA 2003, Sch 6, Part 2.
[8] FA 2003, Sch 6, Part 3.

Group relief: introduction

[62.15] A land transaction is exempt from stamp duty land tax if the vendor and purchaser are companies that at the effective date of the transaction are members of the same group.[1] The equivalent stamp duty group relief concentrated on relieving specific instruments from stamp duty and therefore expressly required that the relevant instrument transferred a beneficial interest in the property and that the companies in question were members of the same group at the time the instrument (normally, the conveyance) was executed even though the beneficial interest could pass on earlier exchange of contract and payment. Although in practice these factors will often be present they are not strict conditions for the SDLT group relief to be available. Accordingly, for SDLT group relief the acquisition of a chargeable interest will be exempt if at the "effective date" the companies are grouped together. This will normally be the date of the conveyance but may be earlier when a substantial amount of the consideration is paid or provided before possession or a conveyance is taken; see supra, § **62.04**.

The relief must be claimed in the land tax return and is subject to detailed anti-avoidance rules and to clawback if the acquiring company leaves the group pursuant to arrangements made within three years of the acquisition.[2]

For the purposes of group relief a "company" means any body corporate (wherever incorporated or resident) and companies are members of the same group if one is the 75% subsidiary of the other or both are 75% subsidiaries of a third company.[3] A company ("A") is the 75% subsidiary of another company ("B") if B:

(1) is beneficial owner of not less than 75% of the ordinary share capital of A;
(2) is beneficially entitled to not less than 75% of any profits available for distribution to equity holders of A; and
(3) would be beneficially entitled to not less than 75% of any assets of A available for distribution to its equity holders on a winding-up.[4]

The ownership referred to in 1 above is ownership either directly or through another company or companies and TA 1988, s 838 (5)–(10) applies to determine the amount of shares of A owned by B through another company or companies.[5] Indirect holdings are taken into account using a multiplication formula so if P Ltd owns 80% of the shares in Q Ltd which owns 50% of the shares in R Ltd, P Ltd is taken to own 40% of the shares in R Ltd.[6] "Ordinary share capital" means all the issued share capital of the company other than capital the holders of which have a right to a dividend at a fixed rate but have no other right to share in the profits of the company.[7] The corporation tax group relief tests relating to equity holders and profits and assets available for distribution in TA 1998, Sch 18 apply for the purposes of 2 and 3 above save that paras 5(3) and 5B to 5E are "switched-off" for SDLT purposes in respect of both the transferor and the transferee (the equivalent stamp duty group relief switched these provisions off only in respect of the transferor).[8] Given that corporation tax is an annual tax assessed retrospectively by reference to accounting periods, the tests in TA 1988, Sch 18 are applied over the accounting period current at the time in question and are only finally judged when the accounting period has ended. It is apparent therefore that the direct application of these provisions to a transaction tax such as SDLT gives rise to the question of how does one judge that the various tests for group relief to be available have been met at any point during the accounting period in which the land transaction occurs. It seems that logically this is not possible and one must wait for the end of the accounting period before deciding. Under the equivalent stamp duty provisions a pragmatic view of the position seems to have been adopted by taxpayers and HMRC and applications for group relief that certified that the requirements of TA 1988, Sch 18 were met at the date of the relevant instrument were not challenged on the basis that one strictly should "wait and see" until the end of the accounting period. It may be, however, that because of the nature of SDLT as a mandatory transaction tax where in some circumstances the tax can be adjusted subsequently and corrective returns filed, the stamp duty practice may change. It is unclear how this situation would be resolved under the existing SDLT provisions other than by initially paying the SDLT and then submitting a retrospective claim for the relief once the accounting period had ended.

Sergeant and Sims AA162.

[62.15] Stamp duty land tax

1. FA 2003, s 62 and Sch 7, para 1(1) and see supra, § **60.01** et seq for the equivalent stamp duty group relief which differs in significant respects from the SDLT group relief as discussed below.
2. FA 2003, s 62(3) and Sch 7, para 3; the equivalent stamp duty group relief clawback was restricted to where the acquiring company actually left the group within three years; see supra, § **60.05**.
3. FA 2003, Sch 7, para 1(2).
4. FA 2003, Sch 7, para 1(3).
5. FA 2003, Sch 7, para 1(4).
6. TA 1988, s 838(9).
7. FA 2003, Sch 7, para 1(5).
8. FA 2003, Sch 7, para 1(6).

Group relief: restriction on availability of relief

[62.16] There are four types of arrangements which can prevent group relief from applying. These relate to control of the purchasing company, the provision of consideration by someone outside the group, where the purchaser is to cease to be a member of the same group as the vendor or where the transaction is not effected for bona fide commercial reasons or forms part of tax avoidance.

First, group relief is not available if at the effective date[1] of the transaction there are arrangements in existence by virtue of which at that or some later time a person has or could obtain control of the purchaser but not of the vendor.[2]

"Arrangements" is defined to include any scheme, agreement or understanding, whether or not legally enforceable.[3] "Control" for this purpose is the test contained in TA 1988, s 840.[4] In stamp duty, IR Stamp Taxes accepted that the equivalent anti-avoidance provision relating to arrangements for loss of control of the transferee[5] was to be interpreted in the light of statement of practice 3/93 "Groups of companies—arrangements", which gives general guidance on how HMRC interpret "arrangements" for corporation tax group relief purposes, and extra-statutory concession C10 which excludes certain types of arrangements including mortgages of shares. Although the stamp duty group relief provisions did not include a definition of arrangements and the SDLT provisions do include such a definition, it is submitted that statement of practice 3/93 and extra-statutory concession C10 should apply to the interpretation of "arrangements" for SDLT purposes given that the corporation tax group relief provisions include a similar although truncated definition of arrangements[6] and there can be no logical grounds for discriminating between the group relief provisions for corporation tax and those for SDLT by having a wider meaning of "arrangements" for the latter tax. Inland Revenue Tax Bulletin April 2004 contains an article entitled "Stamp Duty Land Tax: Group Relief" which in effect confirms that the principles and practice arising out of statement of practice 3/98 will be applied to SDLT with any necessary adaptation.

Reliefs and exemptions [62.16]

This first type of restriction on group relief does not apply to arrangements entered into with a view to an acquisition of shares to which exemption from stamp duty under FA 1986, s 75[7] will apply and as a result of which the purchaser will be a member of the same group as the acquiring company.[8] It is not clear how this exception will be policed in terms of what degree of likelihood is required at the time of the intra-group transfer so that the subsequent loss of control of the purchaser will indeed take the form of an acquisition of shares to which FA 1986, s 75 applies (and what if anything will be done if exemption under that provision turns out not to be available). It is also unclear as to whether this exception will operate where the arrangements for subsequent loss of control of the purchaser could take the form of a FA 1986, s 75 reconstruction but might alternatively take the form of some other transaction not qualifying for relief.

Second, group relief is not available if the transaction is effected in pursuance of, or in connection with, arrangements under which the consideration (or any part of it) is to be provided or received directly or indirectly by a person other than a group company.[9]

Third, group relief is not available if the transaction is effected in pursuance of, or in connection with, arrangements under which the vendor and the purchaser are to cease to be members of the same group by reason of the purchaser ceasing to be a 75% subsidiary of the vendor or a third company.[10]

Fourth, SDLT group relief will be denied if the transaction is:

(a) not effected for bona fide commercial reasons, or
(b) forms part of arrangements of which the main purpose, or one of the main purposes, is the avoidance of liability to tax.[11]

The thrust of judicial decisions on very similar anti-avoidance wording in TA 1988, s 703 and its predecessors, TA 1970, s 460 and FA 1960, s 28, suggest that this measure may not have a great impact on transactions that when looked at in the round are carried out for commercial reasons but happen to have tax planning measures built into them. On the other hand purely tax driven transactions will be at risk. The leading cases[12] show that HMRC are not entitled to isolate particular steps in a transaction that were admittedly inserted to give tax efficiency and apply the above tests to that step only. Assuming that the courts follow precedent in this area then a reading of the cases leads to the tentative conclusion that intra-group property transfers that are carried out as a preparatory step to a larger commercial restructuring or sale out of the group should continue to qualify for group relief (subject of course to the existing anti-avoidance rules) as long as the wider transaction is not tax driven. It is noteworthy that the existing statutory provisions on which the wording of this provision is based have specific written clearance procedures whereas the new SDLT provision has none.[13] HMRC published guidance on FA 2003, Sch 7, para 2(4A) on 10 February 2006 setting out a list of examples where they accept that group relief is not denied by this provision. The list is as follows:

(1) The transfer of a property to a group company having in mind the possibility that shares in that company might be sold more than three years after the date of transfer.

(2) The transfer of a property to a group company having in mind the possibility that shares in that company might be sold within three years of the date of transfer, with a consequent claw back of group relief, in order that any increase in value of the property after the intra-group transfer might be sheltered from SDLT.

(3) The transfer of property to a group company having in mind the possibility that either 1 or 2 might occur.

(4) The transfer of a property to a group company prior to the sale of shares in the transferor company, in order that the property should not pass to the purchaser of the shares.

(5) The transfer of property to a group company in order that commercially generated rental income may be matched with commercially generated losses from a Schedule A business.

(6) The transfer of property to a group company in order that commercially generated chargeable gains may be matched with commercially generated allowable losses.

(7) The transfer of property to a non-resident group company in the knowledge that future appreciation or depreciation in value will be outside the scope of corporation tax on chargeable gains.

(8) Transactions undertaken as part of a normal commercial securitisation.

(9) The transfer of the freehold reversion in a property to a group lessee in order to merge the freehold and the lease, and thus prevent the lease being subject to the wasting assets rules as respects corporation tax on chargeable gains.

'Transfer' means the transfer of a freehold (in Scotland, ownership of land) or the assignment (in Scotland, assignment) of a lease. Cases involving the grant of a lease will be considered by HMRC on their facts.

Sergeant and Sims AA163.

---

[1] See supra, § **62.04**.
[2] FA 2003, Sch 7, para 2(1); this restriction does not apply to transfers in connection with the demutualisation of insurance companies: FA 2003, Sch 7, para 2(3A).
[3] FA 2003, Sch 7, para 2(5).
[4] FA 2003, Sch 7, para 2(5).
[5] FA 1930, s 42(2).
[6] TA 1988, s 410(5).
[7] See supra, § **60.06**.
[8] FA 2003, Sch 7, para 2(1).
[9] FA 2003, Sch 7, para 2(2)(a).
[10] FA 2003, Sch 7, para 2 (2)(b); this restriction does not apply to transfers in connection with the demutualisation of insurance companies: FA 2003, Sch 7, para 2(3A).
[11] FA 2003, Sch 7, para 2(4A) inserted by F(No 2)A 2005, Sch 10, para 19.
[12] See for example (1967) *IRC v Brebner* 43 TC 705, HL.
[13] See TA 1988, s 707 and TCGA 1992, s 137.

Reliefs and exemptions [62.17]

Group relief: withdrawal and claw-back of relief

[62.17] Where a land transaction is exempt from SDLT because of group relief and the purchaser ceases to be a member of the same group of companies as the vendor within the three years beginning with the effective date[1] of the transaction (or at any time in pursuance of arrangements made before the end of that period), the group relief is withdrawn if at the time the purchaser leaves the group, it or a "relevant associated company" holds the chargeable interest that was originally acquired (or is derived from it).[2] The relief is not withdrawn if the chargeable interest was subsequently reacquired at market value under a chargeable transaction for which group relief was available but was not claimed.

A "relevant associated company" means a company that is a member of the same group as the purchaser immediately before the purchaser leaves the vendor's group and ceases to be a member of the vendor's group *in consequence of the purchaser so ceasing*.[3]

The inclusion of relevant associated companies is to prevent the initial intra-group property transfer on which group relief was claimed escaping claw-back by the simple device of subsequently transferring the property to a third group company which would then leave the group with the purchaser (in a sub-group by themselves), a technique known as the "double drop-down". However, for the third company to be a "relevant associated company" it must cease to be a member of the same group as the vendor *in consequence of the purchaser so ceasing*. It is arguable that in the following situations the third company (B Ltd) does not cease to be a member of the vendor's group *in consequence of the purchaser so ceasing* and so claw-back does not arise:

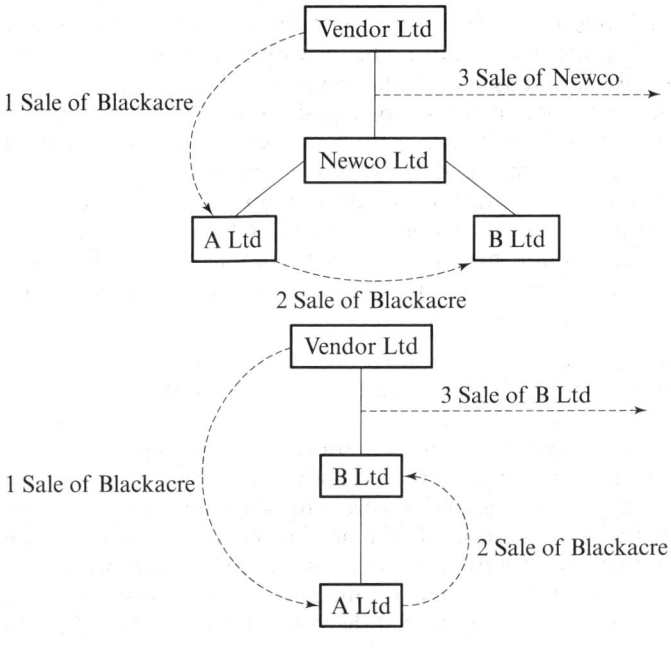

2203

[62.17] Stamp duty land tax

It is possible however that if a court were required to decide the matter policy considerations might dictate that the expression "in consequence of" was given a wide meaning equivalent to "in concurrence with" sufficient to bring the first and possibly the second examples above within the scope of the claw-back provisions. Although such an interpretation would stretch the language of the provision a court may be prepared to do so in order to achieve what it perceives to be the intention of Parliament in the face of what is pure tax avoidance and because there appears to be no compelling policy reason not to, other than the general concern about courts rewriting statutory wording.

However, rather than risk-testing the matter in the courts HMRC have sought to reinforce the claw-back charge with a further anti-avoidance provision that concentrates on a change in control of the purchaser.[4] This provision applies where:

(1) the purchaser claims group relief for a transaction ("the relevant transaction") and within three years beginning with the effective date of the relevant transaction (or at any time in pursuance of arrangements made before the end of that period),
(2) there is a change in control of the purchaser (within TA 1988, s 416) and,
(3) group relief is not otherwise withdrawn.

In such a case it is then necessary to identify the earliest "previous transaction". A previous transaction is one where:

(1) group relief, reconstruction relief or acquisition relief was claimed,
(2) the effective date of that transaction was within the last three years, and
(3) the chargeable interest acquired under the relevant transaction is essentially the same as that acquired under the previous transaction.

The claw-back provisions then have effect as if the vendor in the earliest previous transaction was also the vendor in the relevant transaction. In the two situations illustrated above and assuming that the events all occur within three years of each other, the change in control of B Ltd out of Vendor Ltd would result in the vendor in the sale of Blackacre to B Ltd being taken to have been Vendor Ltd rather than A Ltd thus giving rise to the claw-back of group relief on the transfer of Blackacre to B Ltd. Unfortunately this provision is capable of giving rise to multiple claw-back charges where there have been more than two successive transfers within three years. It appears that this possibility is unintended but it is not yet known whether HMRC understand that this is the case and if so what their approach will be.

Group relief is not withdrawn in four situations. First, where the purchaser leaves the vendor's group because the vendor itself leaves the group. The vendor is regarded as leaving the group if the purchaser and the vendor cease to be members of the same group because of a transaction relating to shares in either the vendor or another company that is above the vendor in the group structure and as a result of the transaction ceases to be a member of the same group as the purchaser.[5] The question of whether the purchaser could then be sold out of the original group within three years of the transaction free of claw-back once the vendor company had left the group had not been tested in the courts. However, since 13 March 2008 if there is a change in control of the purchaser after the vendor leaves the group the claw-back provisions have effect as if the purchaser had then ceased to be a member of the same group as the vendor.[6] It is not clear if this deeming provision also operates in the context of a winding-up of the vendor although it is thought that it does not and HMRC have confirmed that "paragraph 4ZA will not normally apply" in this situation in an article published on 26 November 2008 entitled "Stamp Duty Land Tax: Group Relief – Paragraph 4ZA of Schedule 7 FA 2003". Second, where the purchaser ceases to be a member of the same group as the vendor by reason of the winding up of the vendor or another company that is above the vendor in the group structure.[7] There seems to be no reason why the purchaser cannot be "another company that is above the vendor in the group structure" for this purpose and hence the winding up of the purchaser pursuant to a scheme under Insolvency Act 1986, s 110 and the distribution of its assets qualifying for exemption under reconstruction relief in FA 2003, Sch 7, para 7(1) should not give rise to a withdrawal of group relief. It appears that HMRC may now agree with this interpretation of the legislation because in the article referred to HMRC state that "A company above the vendor in the group structure can be the purchaser". The third case is where there is an acquisition of shares by another company to which the exemption in FA 1986, s 75 applies.[8] However, in such cases claw-back can still apply if the purchaser leaves the same group as the acquiring company within three years of the original land transaction (or at any time in pursuance of arrangements made before the end of that period) and it or a "relevant associated company" own the chargeable interest.[9] The fourth case is where the purchaser ceases to be a member of the vendor's group in connection with the demutualisation of insurance companies and the purchaser is immediately after the transfer of the vendor's business to another company, a member of the same group as the acquiring company.[10]

Where the tax is chargeable because group relief has been withdrawn as above and the tax having been finally determined is not paid within six months after it became payable, it may be recovered from the vendor, any company that at any "relevant time" was a member of the same group as the purchaser and above it in the group structure, or any person who at any "relevant time" was a controlling director of the purchaser or of a company having control of the purchaser.[11] "Relevant time" means any time between the "effective date"[12] of the land transaction and the purchaser ceasing to be a member of the same group as the vendor.[13] In order to recover the tax HMRC must serve a notice on the relevant person stating the amount of tax to be paid and the notice must be served before the end of three years from the date of the final determination of the tax payable.[14] The notice is treated as if it were a notice of assessment of SDLT[15] and interest runs accordingly on any tax remaining unpaid following the issue of the notice. A person who has paid tax pursuant to such a notice has a statutory right to recovery from the purchaser although this is likely to be worth little in the circumstances of the purchaser having originally failed to pay.[16]

Where the tax is chargeable the amount will be the tax that would have been originally chargeable if the chargeable consideration had been equal to the market value of the chargeable interest transferred or if the acquisition was the grant of a lease at a rent, that rent.[17]

[62.17] Stamp duty land tax

Sergeant and Sims AA164.

[1] See supra, § **62.04**.
[2] FA 2003, Sch 7, para 3(1).
[3] FA 2003, Sch 7, para 3(4).
[4] FA 2003, Sch 7, para 4A inserted by F(No 2)A 2005, Sch 10, para 6.
[5] FA 2003, Sch 7, para 4ZA(1)–(3).
[6] FA 2003, Sch 7, para 4(2), (3).
[7] FA 2003, Sch 7, para 4(4).
[8] FA 2003, Sch 7, para 4(5) and see supra, § 60.06.
[9] FA 2003, Sch 7, para 4(6), (7).
[10] See FA 1997, s 96 and FA 2003, Sch 7, para 4(6A).
[11] FA 2003, Sch 7, para, 5(1), (2).
[12] See supra, § **62.04**.
[13] FA 2003, Sch 7, para 5(3)(*a*).
[14] FA 2003, Sch 7, para 6(1), (2).
[15] See infra, § **62.23**.
[16] FA 2003, Sch 7, para 6(5).
[17] FA 2003, Sch 7, para 3(2).

Reconstruction relief

[62.18] An exemption from SDLT is available for land transactions entered into in connection with the acquisition by a company ("the acquiring company") of the whole or part of the undertaking of another company ("the target company") on a reconstruction of the target company.[1]

In stamp duty, IR Stamp Taxes did not accept the wider interpretation of "reconstruction" used for other taxes such as in statement of practice 5/85 which included a partition and its statutory enactment in TCGA 1992, Sch 5AA. It was, however, stated by the Government during the debates on the Finance Bill 2002 that this restrictive interpretation would be reconsidered for the new SDLT legislation.[2] In the absence of any HMRC announcement, however, it would be prudent to assume that the existing practice of HMRC Stamp Taxes in operating a restrictive interpretation of "reconstruction" based on case law will continue in SDLT for the time being. Consequently a "scheme for the reconstruction of the target company" requires that there is a transfer of an undertaking or part from an existing company to a new company with substantially the same membership as the old company and that undertaking continues substantially unaltered.[3] The liquidation of the target company is not essential. A scheme of amalgamation connotes the merging of two or more businesses with ownership through shareholdings remaining substantially the same and is therefore quite different from a scheme of reconstruction and relief under FA 2003, Sch 7, para 1 is limited to schemes of reconstruction.[4]

It is noteworthy, however, that the requirement in the equivalent stamp duty reconstruction relief in FA 1986, s 75(4) that the registered office of the acquiring company is in the UK is not a requirement for the availability of the SDLT exemption.

The availability of the exemption is subject to meeting each of three conditions. The first condition is that the consideration for the acquisition consists wholly or partly of the issue of non-redeemable shares in the acquiring company to all the shareholders of the target company. The only other permitted consideration is the assumption or discharge by the acquiring company of the liabilities of the target company.[5]

The second condition is that after the acquisition has been made:

(1) each shareholder of each of the companies is a shareholder of the other, and
(2) the proportion of shares of one of the companies held by any shareholder is the same, or is nearly as may be the same, as the proportion of shares of the other company held by that shareholder.[6]

If, immediately before the acquisition, either the target company or the acquiring company holds any of their own shares, such shares are treated as cancelled so that either company is not to be treated as a shareholder in itself.[7]

The third condition is that the acquisition is effected for bona fide commercial reasons and does not form part of a scheme or arrangement of which the main purpose, or one of the main purposes, is the avoidance of liability to stamp duty, income tax, corporation tax, capital gains tax or SDLT.[8]

The fact that a transaction has been structured in order to claim this exemption is not of itself evidence of such a scheme or arrangement since one is taking advantage of a statutory exemption from tax.

Sergeant and Sims AA165.

[1] FA 2003, Sch 7, para 7(1).
[2] House of Commons Official Report, Standing Committee F, Tuesday 21 May 2002 (Morning) cols 163 and 164.
[3] See *Brooklands Selangor Holdings Ltd v IRC* [1970] 2 All ER 76; *Baytrust Holdings Ltd v IRC* [1971] 3 All ER 76; *IRC v Kent Process Control Ltd* [1989] STC 245; *Swithland Investments Ltd v IRC* [1990] STC 448.
[4] See *Crane Frueharf Ltd v IRC* [1975] 1 All ER 429, CA; *IRC v Ufitec Group Ltd* [1977] STC 363.
[5] FA 2003, Sch 7, para 7(2), (3).
[6] FA 2003, Sch 7, para 7(4).
[7] FA 2003, Sch 7, para 7(5A).
[8] FA 2003, Sch 7, para 5.

Acquisition relief

[62.19] There is also relief known as "acquisition relief" for a land transaction entered into as part of the acquisition of an undertaking or part of an undertaking of another company in exchange for the issue of shares.[1] This relief reduces the rate of stamp duty land tax to 0.5%. The availability of this relief is subject to four conditions. First, the consideration for the acquisition must consist wholly or partly of the issue of non-redeemable shares in the

[62.19] Stamp duty land tax

acquiring company to the target company or to all or any of the target company's shareholders. Where the consideration does not consist wholly of the issue of shares as above, the rest of the consideration must consist wholly of either or both of cash not exceeding 10% of the nominal value of the shares issued or the assumption or discharge by the acquiring company of liabilities of the target company.[2]

The second condition is that the acquiring company is not "associated" with another company that is party to "arrangements" with the target company relating to the shares of the acquiring company issued in connection with the transfer of the undertaking or part.[3] For this purpose companies are "associated" if one has control of the other or both are controlled by the same person or persons, with control construed in accordance with TA 1988, s 416.[4] "Arrangements" includes any scheme, agreement or understanding, whether or not legally enforceable.[5] Unlike the equivalent stamp duty relief in FA 1986, s 76,[6] it is not a requirement that the registered office of the acquiring company be in the UK.

Acquisition relief is subject to withdrawal as described in infra, § **62.20**.

The third condition is that the undertaking has as its main activity the carrying on of a trade that does not consist wholly or mainly of dealing in chargeable interests.[7]

The fourth condition is that the acquisition is effected for bona fide commercial reasons and does not form part of arrangements of which the main purpose or one of the main purposes is the avoidance of tax.[8]

Sergeant and Sims AA166.

---

[1] FA 2003, Sch 7, para 8(1).
[2] FA 2003, Sch 7, para 8(2), (3).
[3] FA 2003, Sch 7, para 8(4). This is intended to prevent the parties setting up a new company which acquires the undertaking for shares which are issued to the target company (or its shareholders) which shares are then sold to the purchaser for cash and then claiming acquisition relief to reduce the SDLT from 4% to 0.5% on the transfer of the undertaking, with the subsequent sale of the issued shares to the purchaser giving rise to stamp duty (or stamp duty reserve tax) of 0.5% or nil if a non-UK incorporated company was used.
[4] FA 2003, Sch 7, para 8(5)(*a*).
[5] FA 2003, Sch 7, para 8(5C).
[6] See supra, § **60.08**.
[7] FA 2003, Sch 7, para 8(5A).
[8] FA 2003, Sch 7, para 8(5B).

Withdrawal of reconstruction or acquisition relief

[62.20] Except in the cases mentioned in infra, § **62.21**, where a land transaction is exempt because of reconstruction relief (see supra, § **62.18**) or has taken advantage of the 0.5% rate of SDLT because of acquisition relief (see supra, **62.19**) but control of the acquiring company changes within three years of the effective date[1] of the transaction (or at any time if pursuant to arrangements made within that time) the reconstruction or acquisition relief is withdrawn and tax is chargeable if at the time control of the acquiring company changes, it or a "relevant associated company" holds the chargeable interest that was acquired (or an interest that is derived from it). The amount chargeable is the tax that would have been chargeable if the consideration had been equal to the market value of the property concerned and, if the acquisition was the grant of a lease at a rent, that rent.[2] The relief if not withdrawn where the interest has been subsequently acquired at market value under a chargeable transaction for which reconstruction or acquisition relief was available but was not claimed.[3] A "relevant associated company" means a company that is controlled by the acquiring company immediately before control of the acquiring company changes and of which control changes in consequence of the change of control of the acquiring company.[4] "Arrangements" includes any scheme, agreement or understanding whether or not legally enforceable and "control" is construed in accordance with TA 1988, s 416.[5]

References to control of the acquiring company changing are to the company becoming controlled:

(1) by a different person;
(2) by a different number of persons; or
(3) by two or more persons at least one of whom is not a person, or one or more persons, by whom the company was previously controlled.[6]

It therefore seems that where the acquiring company is not under the control of any person at the time of the land transactions qualifying for the relief and only becomes controlled by a person or persons after the transaction, there will not be a change of control for these purposes because a change of control implies that the company was previously controlled by a person or persons.

Where reconstruction or acquisition relief is withdrawn and the amount of tax chargeable has been finally determined and remains unpaid six months after the date it became payable, the following persons may be required to pay the unpaid tax:

(1) any company that at any "relevant time" was a member of the same group as the acquiring company and was above it in the group structure;
(2) any person who at any "relevant time" was a controlling director of the acquiring company or a company having control of the acquiring company.[7]

"Relevant time" means any time between the effective date[8] of the transaction and the change of control causing the tax to become chargeable.[9]

HMRC must serve a notice on a person within 1 or 2 above requiring him to pay within 30 days of service and such a notice must be served with three years of the final determination of the tax chargeable.[10]

Sergeant and Sims AA167.

---

[1] See supra, § **62.04**.

[62.20] Stamp duty land tax

[2] FA 2003, Sch 7, para 9(2) as substituted by F(No 2)A 2005, Sch 10, para 9.
[3] FA 2003, Sch 7, para 9(1).
[4] FA 2003, Sch, 7, para 9(4).
[5] FA 2003, Sch 7, para 9(5)(a), (b).
[6] FA 2003, Sch 7, para 9(5)(c).
[7] FA 2003, Sch 7, para 12(1), (2).
[8] See supra, § 62.04.
[9] FA 2003, Sch 7, para 12(3).
[10] FA 2003, Sch 7, para 3.

Reconstruction and acquisition relief not withdrawn

[62.21] There are five cases in which reconstruction and acquisition relief is not withdrawn despite a change of control of the acquiring company. These are where control changes:[1]

(1) as a result of transactions in connection with divorce;[2]
(2) as a result of the variation of a testamentary disposition;[3]
(3) as a result of a transfer of shares that is exempt from stamp duty under stamp duty group relief[4] (but see below);
(4) as a result of a transfer of shares to another company that is exempt from stamp duty under FA 1986, s 77[5] (but see below); or
(5) as a result of a loan creditor becoming, or ceasing to be, treated as having control of the company and the other persons who were previously treated as controlling the company continue to be so treated.[6]

Where 3 above applies, if a company holding the shares in the acquiring company that were subject to stamp duty group relief ceases to be a member of the same group of companies as the target company within three years of the relevant land transaction (or at any time if pursuant to arrangements made within that period) and the acquiring company or a "relevant associated company"[7] holds the chargeable interest acquired, the reconstruction or acquisition relief is withdrawn and tax is chargeable.[8]

Where 4 above applies, if control of the other company changes within three years of the relevant land transaction (or at any time if pursuant to arrangements made within that period) at a time when that other company holds any of the shares transferred to it and the acquiring company or a "relevant associated company"[9] holds the chargeable interest acquired, the reconstruction or acquisition relief is withdrawn and tax is chargeable.[10]

In both cases the tax chargeable is the amount that would have been chargeable if the chargeable consideration for the relevant land transaction had been equal to the market value of the chargeable interest transferred.[11]

Sergeant and Sims AA167.

[1] FA 2003, Sch 7, para 10.
[2] FA 2003, Sch 3, para 3(a)–(d).
[3] FA 2003, Sch 3, para 4.

4   See supra, § **60.01**.
5   See supra, § **60.07**.
6   See TA 1988, s 417(7) to (9) for the meaning of "loan creditor".
7   See FA 2003, Sch 7, para 11(5).
8   FA 2003, Sch 7, para 11(1).
9   FA 2003, Sch 7, para 11(5).
10 FA 2003, Sch 7, para 11(2).
11 FA 2003, Sch 7, para 11(3).

Acquisitions by charities

[62.22] A land transaction is exempt from stamp duty land tax if the purchaser is a charity provided two conditions are met.[1] First, the purchaser must intend to hold the subject matter of the transaction for qualifying charitable purposes which are defined as either:

(1) for use in furtherance of the charitable purposes of the purchaser or another charity, or
(2) as an investment from which the profits are applied to the charitable purposes of the purchaser.[2]

Where the land transaction would not be exempt because the condition above is not met, exemption is still available if the charity intends to hold the greater part of the land for qualifying charitable purposes.[3]

The second condition is that the transaction must not have been entered into for the purpose of avoiding SDLT whether by the purchaser or any other person.[4] It has been confirmed by the Government that this condition does not relate to the claiming of the exemption from SDLT by the charity itself.[5]

"Charity" means any body or trust established for charitable purposes only.[6] This definition has been extended to include "charitable trusts" that is trusts of which all the beneficiaries are charities or unit trust schemes in which all the unit holders are charities.[7] It is thought that this exemption applies to charities formed or established under UK law only and not to non-UK charities.[8]

The exemption must be claimed in a land transaction return.[9]

The exemption will be withdrawn and tax become chargeable if within three years of the land transaction (or at any time if pursuant to arrangements made within that time), the purchaser holds the land and ceases to be established for charitable purposes only or the land is used or held by the purchaser otherwise than for qualifying charitable purposes (as defined above).[10] Where the exemption was claimed because the charity intended to hold the greater part of the land for qualifying charitable purposes, the withdrawal of relief will also occur on any transfer of a major interest in the whole or part of the land or any grant out of the land of a lease at a premium with a low rent within the same time frame, that is not made for charitable purposes.[11] The tax that becomes chargeable is the tax that would have been chargeable in respect of the land transaction had the exemption not been claimed. The exemption is only withdrawn if the charity still holds the land at the time of the disqualifying event and so the withdrawal of relief will not apply to a disposal of the land itself within the three year period or if the land falls vacant within such period. A disposal to a non-charity for less than market value consideration within that period might however raise the question of whether the charity originally intended to hold the land for qualifying charitable purposes and therefore satisfied the first condition above on the acquisition of the land by the charity.

Sergeant and Sims AA211.

[1] FA 2003, s 68 and Sch 8, para 1(1).
[2] FA 2003, Sch 8, para 1(2).
[3] FA 2003, Sch 8, para 3.
[4] FA 2003, Sch 8, para 1(3).
[5] HC Official Report, Standing Committee B, Tuesday 10 June 2003, col 439.
[6] FA 2003, Sch 8, para 1(4).
[7] FA 2003, Sch 8, para 3.
[8] *Camille and Henry Dreyfus Foundation Inc v IRC* [1956] AC 39, [1955] 3 All ER 97.
[9] FA 2003, Sch 8, para 1(2).
[10] FA 2003, Sch 8, para 1(2).
[11] FA 2003, Sch 8, para 3.

Returns, liability and compliance

Returns

[62.23] A major difference between stamp duty on land and SDLT is the requirement in the latter tax to deliver a tax return to HMRC. Every "notifiable transaction" must be reported by delivery of a land transaction return to HMRC before the end of 30 days after the "effective date"[1] of the transaction.[2] A land transaction return must include a self-assessment of the tax chargeable. However the return need not be accompanied by payment of the amount of tax due, although the tax is payable before the and of 30 days after the "effective date".[3]

A "notifiable transaction" is:

(1) an acquisition of a major interest in land that does not fall within one or more of the exceptions listed in (A) to (F) below;
(2) an acquisition of a chargeable interest other than a major interest in land where SDLT is chargeable at the rate of 1% or higher or would be so chargeable but for a relief;
(3) a land transaction that a person is deemed to have entered into under FA 2003, s 44A(3) see infra **62.30**;
(4) a notional land transaction under FA 2003 s 75A see infra **62.34**.[4]

References to a "relief" above do not include any exemption under FA 2003, Sch 3.[5]

The exceptions referred to in (1) above are:

(A) an acquisition which is exempt under FA 2003, Sch.3;
(B) an acquisition (other than the grant, assignment or surrender of a lease) where the chargeable consideration for that acquisition, together with any linked transaction, is less than £40,000;
(C) the grant of a lease for a term of 7 years or more where any chargeable consideration other than rent is less than £40,000 and the relevant rent is less than £1,000;
(D) the assignment or surrender of a lease where the lease was originally granted for a term of 7 years or more and the chargeable consideration for the assignment or surrender is less than £40,000;
(E) the grant of a lease for a term of less than 7 years where the chargeable consideration does not exceed the "zero-rate threshold"; and
(F) the assignment or surrender of a lease where the lease was originally granted for a term of less than 7 years and the chargeable consideration does not exceed the "zero-rate threshold".

Chargeable consideration does not exceed the "zero-rate threshold" if it does not consist of or include any amount in respect of which tax is chargeable at a rate of 1% or higher or any amount in respect of which tax would be so chargeable but for a relief (excluding any exemption under FA 2003, Sch 3).[6]

No account is to be taken for the purpose of the requirement to notify of the provisions of FA 2003, Sch 6 to the effect that consideration is not "chargeable consideration" in relation to acquisitions of land qualifying for disadvantaged areas relief.[7]

In general, therefore, acquisitions of major interests in land including the grant of leases which are not exempt are notifiable where the chargeable consideration is £40,000 or more. Interests other than major interests are notifiable only if the tax is charged at the 1% rate or higher or would be chargeable but for a relief.

A "major interest" in land is defined as:

(1) (in England and Wales) an estate in fee simple absolute (freehold) or a term of years absolute (leasehold) whether in law or in equity;
(2) (in Scotland) the interest of an owner of land or the tenant's right over or interest in a property subject to a lease; and
(3) (in Northern Ireland) any freehold or leasehold estate whether in law or in equity.[8]

There are detailed rules relating to returns, enquiries, assessments and appeals in FA 2003, Sch 10 and the following is a summary of the main provisions:

(1) a land transaction return must be in the prescribed form;[9]
(2) failure to deliver a land transaction return by the filing date gives rise to a flat rate penalty of £100 (if the return is delivered within three months after the filing date) and £200 in any other case plus (in the case of a "chargeable transaction") where the return is not delivered within 12 months of the filing date, a tax-related penalty not exceeding the tax chargeable (the filing date is the last day of the period within which the return must be delivered);[10]
(3) a purchaser may amend a land transaction return given by him by notice to HMRC normally within 12 months of the filing date;[11]

(4) HMRC may by notice to the purchaser amend a land transaction return so as to correct obvious errors or omissions whether errors of principle, arithmetical mistakes or otherwise within nine months of the day the return was delivered or the amended return was made; the purchaser may reject the correction by amending the return or if after the period during which he may amend the return but within three months of the notice of correction, give notice rejecting the correction;[12]

(5) a penalty not exceeding the tax understated arises in the case of a purchaser who fraudulently or negligently delivers an incorrect return in respect of a chargeable transaction or who discovers that a return delivered by him in respect of a chargeable transaction (neither fraudulently or negligently) is incorrect and does not remedy the error without unreasonable delay;[13]

(6) a purchaser required to deliver a return must keep sufficient records preserved for six years after the effective date of the transaction and until any later date on which any enquiry into the return is completed or HMRC no longer have power to enquire into the return;[14]

(7) there are detailed powers for HMRC to conduct an enquiry into a return generally within nine months of the filing date;[15]

(8) HMRC have the power to make a determination of the tax payable if no return is delivered by the filing date, within six years of the effective date of the transaction;[16]

(9) HMRC have the power to issue a discovery assessment for any tax that ought to have been assessed, or for an assessment that is or has become insufficient, where a relief given is or has become excessive or where tax has been repaid that ought not to have been repaid; generally such an assessment may not be made more than six years after the effective date of the transaction but this is increased to 21 years in the case of fraud or negligence;[17]

(10) a mistake in a return leading to excessive tax may be corrected by giving notice of such a claim to HMRC within six years of the effective date of the transaction and such repayment will be made as is reasonable and just but no repayment shall be given if the return was made on the basis of or in accordance with the practice generally prevailing at the time it was made or in respect of a mistake in a claim or election included in the return;[18]

(11) there are detailed rules governing the right to bring an appeal relating to an assessment before the First-tier Tribunal and internal review of the matter by HMRC including a facility to apply for postponement of payment of tax;[19]

(12) where a later transaction that is linked to an earlier transaction results in the earlier transaction becoming notifiable or liable to tax or additional tax, a return must be delivered within 30 days of the later transaction. Payment of the tax due must also be made within 30 days of the later transaction. A return must be made in respect of the later transaction and tax paid in respect of that also;[20]

(13) detailed provision has been made for the making of claims that are not made in a return.[21]

Where the chargeable consideration for a land transaction was contingent, uncertain or unascertained and the contingency occurs (or it becomes clear that it will not occur) or any amount or instalment of uncertain or unascertained consideration becomes ascertained, a further return must be made within 30 days. Payment of the tax (or any further tax) payable is also due within the 30 days. If the effect of the new information is that less tax is payable than has already been paid, a purchaser may claim repayment of the overpaid tax together with interest as from the date of payment of the tax by the purchaser.[22]

Where either group relief, reconstruction or acquisition relief or charities relief is withdrawn the purchaser must deliver a further return within 30 days after the occurrence of the disqualifying event. Payment of the tax chargeable must also be made within the 30 days.[23]

HMRC may treat a return as not having been delivered or a document as not having been provided where it has been lost or destroyed or been so defaced or destroyed as to be illegible or otherwise useless. In such cases HMRC may proceed as if the return or document had not been made or delivered but any tax paid in respect of the transaction will reduce any further tax charged or give rise to a repayment as appropriate.[24]

Although any assessment, determination or notice must be in the prescribed form it will not be ineffective for want of form or by reason of any mistake, defect or omission in it if it substantially conforms with the specified requirements and its intended effect is reasonably ascertainable by the person to whom it is directed. Any mistake as to the name of the person liable or the amount of tax charged will not affect the validity of the assessment or determination nor will any variance between the notice of assessment or determination and the assessment or determination itself.[25] Delivery and service of documents is regulated by FA 2003, s 84.

The return must be signed by the purchaser (or each of them) or by someone holding a written power of attorney signed by an individual purchaser or by the authorised agent of an individual.[26]

Sergeant and Sims AA233.

---

[1] See supra, § **62.04**.
[2] FA 2003, s 76(1).
[3] FA 2003, s 76(3) as amended by FA 2007, s 80.
[4] FA 2003, s 77(5).
[5] FA 2003, s 77(3).
[6] FA 2003, s 77A inserted by FA 2008, s 94.
[7] FA 2003, Sch 6, para 13.
[8] FA 2003, s 117.
[9] FA 2003, Sch 10, para 1(1), (2) as amended by FA 2007, s 80.
[10] FA 2003, Sch 10, paras 1(2), (3), (4), and "chargeable transaction" is a transaction that is not exempt from SDLT: FA 2003, s 49.
[11] FA 2003, Sch 10, para 6.
[12] FA 2003, Sch 10, para 7.
[13] FA 2003, Sch 10, para 8.

[62.23] Stamp duty land tax

[14] FA 2003, Sch 10, para 9 and see infra, § **62.24**.
[15] FA 2003, Sch 10, Part 3.
[16] FA 2003, Sch 10, Part 4.
[17] FA 2003, Sch 10, Part 5.
[18] FA 2003, Sch 10, Part 6.
[19] FA 2003, Sch 10, Part 7 as amended.
[20] FA 2003, s 81A as amended by FA 2007, s 80.
[21] FA 2003, s 82A and Sch 11A.
[22] FA 2003, s 80 and see supra, § **62.06**.
[23] FA 2003, s 81 as amended by FA 2007, s 80 and see supra, § **62.17, 62.20** and **62.22**.
[24] FA 2003, s 82.
[25] FA 2003, s 83.
[26] FA 2003, s 81B and Sch 10, paras 1(1)(c), 1A.

Registration of land transactions and certificates

[62:24] Except for sub-sales, assignments of agreements for lease, agreements for lease which are substantially performed prior to grant of the lease, certain lease variations and contracts caught by FA 2003, s 44A—see supra, § **62:03**, a land transaction must not be registered at the Land Registry unless there is produced with the application to register a certificate of compliance. The certificate must be a certificate by HMRC that a land transaction return has been delivered in respect of the transaction (a "Revenue certificate" known as an "SDLT 5"). The certificate by the purchaser or by the authorised agent of an individual purchaser that no land transaction return was required in respect of the transaction (a "self-certificate" known as an "SDLT 60") was abolished for transactions with an effective date on or after 12th March 2008.

Liability and payment

[62.25] Except in the case of bearer instruments where the person issuing the instrument is specifically made liable to pay the duty chargeable, stamp duty has not specified the person who is liable to pay the duty ever since the changes introduced by FA 1999.[1] For SDLT however, FA 2003, s 85 provides that the purchaser is liable to pay the SDLT in respect of a chargeable transaction. Joint purchasers are jointly and severally liable to pay the SDLT.[2] Partners who are partners at the effective date of the transaction (but not any person who becomes a partner afterwards) are jointly and severally liable to pay the SDLT in respect of purchases of chargeable interests by the partnership.[3] SDLT may be recovered from any one or more of the trustees of a settlement who were trustees at the effective date of the transaction or who subsequently became a trustee.[4]

SDLT payable in respect of a land transaction must be paid no later than the filing date of the relevant return.[5] Any tax payable as the result of the withdrawal of either group relief, reconstruction or acquisition relief and charities relief must be paid no later than the filing date of the return made in respect of the withdrawal.[6]

Returns, liability and compliance [62.25]

These provisions are subject to any application to defer payment of tax in the case of contingent or uncertain consideration under FA 2003, s 90[7] or to postpone payment of tax pending an appeal under FA 2003, Sch 10, paras 39, 40.

Interest is payable on the amount of any unpaid SDLT after 30 days from the effective date[8] of the transaction. In the case of the withdrawal of group relief, reconstruction or acquisition relief or charities relief giving rise to tax, interest is charged after 30 days following the disqualifying event.[9] In the case of tax deferred under FA 2003, s 90[10] interest is charged after 30 days from when the deferred payment is due.[11] However, where contingent, uncertain or unascertained consideration is not deferred under FA 2003, s 90 interest on any tax that becomes payable under FA 2003, s 80 (adjustment where the contingency ceases or consideration becomes ascertained) runs from the effective date of the transaction.[12] An amount of tax lodged with HMRC in respect of the tax will reduce the interest payable accordingly.[13]

Penalties carry interest from the date they are determined until payment.[14] A repayment of SDLT (including an amount lodged under FA 2003, s 87(6)) carries interest at the rate applicable under FA 1989, s 178 between the payment of the tax and the repayment (unless it is a payment made in consequence of a court order or judgment of a court having power to allow interest on the payment). Any such interest paid is not income for tax purposes.[15]

FA 2003, s 91 and Sch 12 govern the collection and recovery of SDLT including any penalties and interest. Under FA 2003, s 92 where payment to HMRC is made by cheque and the cheque is paid on its first presentation to the bank on which it is drawn the payment is treated as made on the day the cheque was received by HMRC.

---

1 FA 1999, s 109(1) replaced the old SA 1891, s 15 which had specified which person was liable to a penalty for late stamping and by implication who was principally liable to pay the stamp duty, normally the purchaser.
2 FA 2003, s 103(2)(c).
3 FA 2003, Sch 15, para 6(2) and 7(1) and (1A).
4 FA 2003, Sch 16, para 5(1), (3).
5 FA 2003, s 86(1) as amended by FA 2007, s 80.
6 FA 2003, s 86(2) as amended by FA 2007, s 80 and see supra, §§ **62.17**, **62.20** and **62.22**.
7 See supra, § **62.06**.
8 See supra, § **62.04**.
9 See supra, §§ **62.17** and **62.20**.
10 See supra, § **62.06**.
11 FA 2003, s 87.
12 FA 2003, s 87(5) and see supra, § **62.04** for "effective date".
13 FA 2003, s 87(6).
14 FA 2003, s 88. Interest is charged at the rate applicable under FA 1989, s 178.
15 FA 2003, s 89.

Compliance and offences

[62:26] FA 2003, s 93 and Sch 13 govern the powers of HMRC to call for documents and information for the purposes of stamp duty land tax. The Board of HMRC may authorise an officer of theirs to inspect any property in order to ascertain its market value or for any other relevant matter.[1]

FA 2003, s 95 creates the statutory criminal offence of a person being knowingly concerned in the fraudulent evasion of SDLT by him or any other person. If found guilty the person is liable on summary conviction to imprisonment for a term not exceeding six months or a fine not exceeding the statutory maximum (or both) and on conviction on indictment to imprisonment for a term not exceeding seven years or a fine (or both). This section is based on and largely copies FA 2000, s 144 which was introduced to make prosecution of PAYE and NIC fraud involving payment of wages by cash in hand without deducting tax more effective. When that provision was introduced into the Finance Bill 2000 at a late stage unease was expressed about the imprecision inherent in the phrases "knowingly concerned" and "fraudulent evasion". In response the Paymaster General explained the use of these phrases as follows:

> I will deal with the important point about the words 'knowingly' and fraudulent evasion'. . . . My officials will smile when they hear this, but initially I said to them, 'Surely evasion is fraud', and asked why it needed to be qualified as 'fraudulent evasion'. I have received assurances which I will pass on to the Committee. The juxtaposition of the words 'knowingly' and 'fraudulent evasion' reinforces exactly which offences the provision is aimed at.

Let us take the question of someone who is knowingly concerned in the evasion of income tax. I want to make it clear that it is not enough for this purpose to show that a person should have suspected that someone was evading tax. The person must have knowledge and involvement in the fraud. For example, he could help someone evade tax by helping to produce false business records.

People may ask why we have put the words 'fraudulent' and 'evasion' together. I am reliably informed by people who know better than I do that, in English usage, 'to evade' can mean to dodge, without any dishonest intent. Although 'evasion' has come to imply dishonesty in the context of tax, the Bill needs to be drafted tightly. 'Fraudulent' may not appear to add much to 'evasion', but the expression 'fraudulent evasion' is well precedented and subject to interpretation by the courts."[2]

Therefore the phrase "knowingly concerned" requires knowledge of (rather than mere suspicion) and involvement in the evasion of tax and the phrase "fraudulent evasion" requires proof of dishonest intent. In relation to tax planning, assurances were sought as to the meaning of "evasion" and in particular whether those involved in tax avoidance schemes might be charged with the commission of this offence where the scheme was adjudged to have failed on technical grounds. In this respect the Paymaster General said:

> No one could be convicted as a matter of general law unless it was proved that he or she had a dishonest intention. . .

The Right Hon. Member for Wells asked about tax advisers who gave advice on avoidance schemes that failed. A failed scheme whose details are not hidden from the Revenue amounts not to tax evasion, but to tax planning . . . The Government may not like some of that planning and may legislate against it, but, as it is not hidden, it does not fall within the remit of the measure . . .

. . . avoidance is not evasion; there are separate laws to deal with the latter. The Right Hon. Gentleman asked when avoidance became evasion. Unless he can give an example, I cannot think of such an eventuality".[3]

Further guidance has been issued in Inland Revenue Tax Bulletin, Issue 49 (October 2000) to the effect that those persons who advise on what turn out to be fiscally ineffective tax avoidance schemes are only likely to be charged with the offence where dishonesty is involved. In the opinion of the then Inland Revenue such dishonesty may be evident where those involved in a scheme "are not merely relying on the intrinsic technical soundness of the arrangements actually put in place to reduce their liability, but also on concealment of the true facts from the inspector". The Inland Revenue would not expect a criminal offence to have been committed where there is no concealment of the facts and there is a "respectable technical case". Thus a critical question in determining whether a prosecution will occur is likely to be whether there has been "concealment of the true facts". However, this phrase gives rise to its own uncertainty given that "concealment" can occur in different ways ranging from deliberate covering up of facts through partial disclosure of accurate information which conveys a misleading impression to failure to appreciate (and therefore disclose) that certain information would be considered relevant by the Inland Revenue. Given the guidance available, however, it seems that in any case where the technical merits of a tax mitigation structure involving SDLT are open to different interpretations the safest course of action will be to disclose all material facts to HMRC Stamp Taxes and argue the case on technical merit rather than risk an allegation that facts were concealed if a prosecution under FA 2003, s 95 is to be safely ruled out.

A person who assists in or induces the preparation or delivery of any information, return or other document that he knows will be, or is likely to be used for any purpose of SDLT and he knows to be incorrect is liable to a penalty not exceeding £3,000.[4]

FA 2003, Sch 14 governs the determination of penalties and related appeals.

---

[1] Sergeant and Sims AA273. FA 2003, s 94.
[2] HC Official Report, Standing Committee H, 29 June 2000, col 1010.
[3] HC Official Report, Standing Committee H, 29 June 2000, cols 1012 and 1013.
[4] FA 2003, s 96.

[62.27] Stamp duty land tax

Special situations

Partnerships

[62.27] A "partnership" for SDLT is defined as a partnership under any of the Partnership Act 1890, the Limited Partnerships Act 1907, the Limited Liability Partnerships Act 2000 or a firm or entity of a similar character to any of these formed under the law of a foreign jurisdiction.[1] For SDLT purposes a chargeable interest held by or on behalf of a partnership is treated as held by or on behalf of the partners and a land transaction entered into for the purposes of a partnership is treated as entered into by or on behalf of the partners and not by the partnership as such despite the partnership being regarded as a legal person or body corporate by the law under which it was formed.[2]

A partnership is treated as the same person despite a change in the partners as long as at least one person who was a partner before the change remains a partner after the change.[3] A partnership is not treated for SDLT as a unit trust scheme or open-ended investment company.[4] See supra, § **62.25** for the liability of partners to pay SDLT.

SDLT applies in the usual way to what are referred to as "ordinary partnership transactions" which are transactions entered into as purchaser by or on behalf of the members of a partnership other than transactions to which the special partnership provisions apply.[5] The special partnership provisions apply where:

(1) land is transferred to a partnership by a partner (or a person who becomes a partner in return for the land or land is transferred by a person connected with either person);
(2) there is a transfer of an interest in a partnership; or
(3) land is transferred from a partnership to a partner (or a person who has been a partner or a person connected with either person).[6]

Stamp duty continues to apply to any instrument by which the transfer of an interest in a partnership is effected. The manner in which this has been achieved has descended into farce. It was intended by the Government that a stamp duty charge would only apply to the extent that the partnership held shares. This would deal with concerns that partnerships might be used as a stamp duty free wrapper for share deals. The stamp duty charge was therefore supposed to be restricted to that which would arise on a direct sale of the shares themselves held by the partnership and if the partnership held no shares then no stamp duty would arise. Paragraphs 31 to 33 of Schedule 15 as originally enacted however did not achieve this. Rather they applied a full stamp duty charge at up to 4% on transfers of partnership interests even by reference to assets held such as goodwill and intellectual property which were exempt from stamp duty before. Paragraph 33 was intended to restrict the overall stamp duty charge as mentioned above but the drafting failed to achieve this and there was a further error which resulted in the stamp duty charge relating to the share of the partnership that is not transferred. As amended by F(No 2)A 2005, Sch 10, para 21, para 33 now provides that there is no stamp duty charge unless the partnership property includes stock or marketable securities, in which case the stamp duty charge is on an amount of consideration equal to the net market value of the stock and marketable securities attributable to the interest of the incoming partner or increase in an existing partner's share. There is still a slightly redundant provision that where the partnership owns land the consideration liable to stamp duty is reduced by a proportion of the market value of the land less any loan secured solely on the land, representing the proportionate interest acquired by the purchaser of the interest in the partnership. The intention is to give a credit against the stamp duty charge for the SDLT payable in relation to the land under 2 above.[7] It is understood that prior to the amendment to para 33 the then Inland Revenue dealt with this disgraceful mess by only charging stamp duty by reference to the shares held if any. It is interesting to note that the instrument will not be duly stamped unless it is adjudicated.

The transfer of an interest in land to a partnership by a partner or a person who becomes a partner (or someone connected with either) is a chargeable transaction. The chargeable consideration is taken to be the proportion of the market value of the land equal to the total of the other partners' shares immediately after the transfer. The shares of partners who are individuals and who are connected with the transferor are ignored for this purpose.[8] Where there is such a transfer of land into a partnership and within three years of the transfer there is a withdrawal of money or money's worth other than income profit or a loan is repaid (in relation to the transferor or a person connected with him), the withdrawal or repayment is treated as a chargeable transaction and the chargeable consideration is taken to be the withdrawal or repayment up to the market value of the chargeable interest transferred, less any tax previously chargeable.[9] There is also special provision for partnerships consisting of bodies corporate who are members of the same group of companies.[10]

The transfer of a partnership interest in a property investment partnership (a "PIP") but not in any other form of partnership, is a chargeable transaction when the partnership property includes land. A PIP means a partnership whose sole or main activity is investing or dealing in land whether or not that involves carrying out construction operations on the land. The chargeable consideration is taken to be equal to a proportion of the market value of the land where there is consideration. Where there is no consideration for the transfer the market value of the land owned by the partnership is still used as the basis of the tax calculation. However, in such a case the value of land is excluded for the purposes of the calculation to the extent that the partnership made an election on acquisition of the land to disapply the special partnership provision and instead pay SDLT by reference to the market value of the land.[11] There is a transfer of a partnership interest where a person acquires or increases a partnership share. That proportion is equal to the partnership interest acquired.

The transfer of an interest in land from a partnership to a partner or former partner (or a person connected with either) is a chargeable transaction. The chargeable consideration is taken to be a proportion of the market value of the land.[12]

[62.27] Stamp duty land tax

Where the acquisition of the underlying land would qualify for the disadvantaged areas relief, the transfer of the partnership interest will to that extent also be exempt.[13] Other reliefs are also available.[14]

Sergeant and Sims AA40.

[1] FA 2003, Sch 15, para 1.
[2] FA 2003, Sch 15, para 2.
[3] FA 2003, Sch 15, para 3.
[4] FA 2003, Sch 15, para 4.
[5] FA 2003, Sch 15, para 5.
[6] FA 2003, Sch 15, Part 3.
[7] FA 2003, Sch 15, paras 31, 32 and 33.
[8] FA 2003, Sch 15, paras 10–12 as amended by FA 2006, Sch 24, paras 2, 3 and 4 and FA 2007, s 72.
[9] FA 2003, Sch 15, para 17A inserted by F(No 2)A 2005, Sch 10, para 10.
[10] FA 2003, Sch 15, para 27A.
[11] FA 2003, Sch 15, paras 14 and 36 as amended by FA 2007, s 72 and FA 2008, Sch 31.
[12] FA 2003, Sch 15, paras 16, 17, 18 and 19 as amended by FA 2006, Sch 24, paras 5, 6 and 7 and FA 7007, s 72.
[13] FA 2003, Sch 15, para 26.
[14] FA 2003, Sch 15, paras 25, 27 and 28.

Unit trusts and open-ended investment companies

[62:28] A unit trust scheme is treated generally for SDLT as if the trustees were a company and the units in it were shares and each part of an umbrella unit trust scheme is treated as a separate unit trust.[1] However, a unit trust scheme is not treated as a company for the purposes of group relief, reconstruction relief or acquisition relief (see supra, § **62.15** et seq).[2]

Open-ended investment companies are intended to be treated in a similar fashion to unit trusts for SDLT purposes and regulations are to be made accordingly.[3]

Prior to 22 March 2006 the acquisition of an interest in land by the trustees of a unit trust scheme was exempt from SDLT if:

(1) immediately before the acquisition there were no assets held by the trustees and no units were in issue;
(2) the only consideration for the acquisition is the issue of units; and
(3) immediately after the acquisition the vendor is the only unit holder of the scheme.[4]

Sergeant and Sims AA39.

[1] FA 2003, s 101(1), (2), (3) and (4); "unit trust scheme" has the same meaning as in the Financial Services and Markets Act 2000.
[2] FA 2003, s 101(7) as amended by FA 2006, s 166(3).

[3] FA 2003, s 102; "open-ended investment company" has the meaning in the Financial Services and Markets Act 2000, s 236.
[4] FA 2003, s 64A now withdrawn for transactions after this date by FA 2006, s 166.

Trusts

[62:29] Where a chargeable interest (or an interest in a partnership) is acquired by a bare trustee or a nominee, SDLT applies as if the interest had been acquired by the person for whom the bare trustee or nominee acts, except in relation to the grant of a lease, where the bare trustee is treated as the purchaser of the whole of the interest acquired.[1] Where the trustee or trustees of any other type of trust acquire a chargeable interest (or an interest in a partnership) as trustees they are treated for SDLT purposes as purchasers of the entire interest acquired including the beneficial interest.[2]

Beneficiaries of trusts formed under Scottish or non-UK laws are treated for SDLT as having an equitable interest in trust property if that would be the case had the trust been formed under English law. The acquisition of the interest of such a beneficiary under the trust is treated expressly as the acquisition of an interest in the trust property for SDLT purposes.[3]

However, there is no equivalent provision for English trusts expressly providing that the acquisition of the equitable interest of a beneficiary under a trust formed under English law is to be treated as the acquisition of an interest in the trust property for SDLT purposes. Instead, the SDLT legislation assumes that under the principles of equity and trust law the interest of a beneficiary is an interest in the underlying trust property. Does the beneficiary merely have a right in *personam* against the trustee to see that the trust is administered properly or does he have a right *in rem* or a proprietary interest as owner of the beneficial interest? It seems that English law has not been capable of supplying a conclusive answer to this question and has been content to adopt a pragmatic approach to the issue, usually in tax cases where the language of the statute will determine the answer.[4] There has been a series of cases in which the courts have had to decide whether a beneficiary under a trust for sale of land had an interest in land for the purposes of a particular statute and the courts have usually held that an interest in land existed.[5] *The Trusts of Land and Appointment of Trustees Act 1996* provides that where land is held by trustees on a trust for sale, the land is not to be regarded as personal property. This abolishes the doctrine of conversion in the case of express trusts for sale. In SDLT a "chargeable interest" is defined in FA 2003, s 48(1)(*a*) to include an interest, right or power in or over land in the UK. If, as is likely, a similar pragmatic approach is adopted, it seems that for SDLT purposes the life tenant of a trust formed under English law has an equitable interest in the trust property. The purchase of a life interest in possession, or an interest in an accumulation and maintenance trust or a reversionary interest in a trust formed under English law whose assets include land in the UK will be a land transaction for SDLT purposes (as will be the purchase of an equivalent type of interest under a Scottish or foreign trust).[6] However, a discretionary

[62:29] Stamp duty land tax

beneficiary does not have an equitable interest or any other interest in the assets of the trust under English law and so the interest of such a person is not a "chargeable interest" for SDLT.[7]

Where an equitable interest in a trust holding land in the UK is acquired by the exercise of a power of appointment or the exercise of a discretion vested in the trustees, any consideration given for the exercise is treated as chargeable consideration for SDLT purposes.[8] During the debates on the Finance Bill 2003, the Chief Secretary to the Treasury declined to give an assurance that the exercise of a power of appointment or the surrender of a life interest to a remainderman for no consideration did not give rise to stamp duty or SDLT.[9] See supra, § **62.25** for the liability of trustees to pay SDLT and FA 2003, s 106 for the rules governing persons acting in a representative capacity.

It is specifically provided that where the trustees of a settlement reallocate trust property in such a way that a beneficiary acquires an interest in certain trust property and ceases to have an interest in other trust property and the beneficiary consents, the fact that he consents does not mean that there is chargeable consideration for his acquisition.[10]

Sergeant and Sims AA33.

[1] FA 2003, s 195 and Sch 16, paras (1) and (3) as amended by F(No 2)A 2005, Sch 10, para 11 and FA 2007, s 72.
[2] FA 2003, Sch 16, para 4 as amended by FA 2007, s 72.
[3] FA 2003, Sch 16, para 2.
[4] See Hanbury and Martin, *Modern Equity* 17th edn at 1–019 which suggests that the interest of a beneficiary may actually be *sui generis* and see *Baker v Archer-Shee* [1927] AC 844 and *Archer-Shee v Garland* [1931] AC 212.
[5] See Megarry & Wade, *The Law of Real Property* 6th edn at 8–121 and the cases referred to in footnote 13 on p 434.
[6] See footnote 3 above.
[7] See footnote 5 above.
[8] FA 2003, Sch 16, para 7.
[9] HC Official Report, Standing Committee B, Tuesday 3 June 2003, cols 344 and 345.
[10] FA 2006, s 165.

Sub-sales

[62:30] Stamp duty land tax does not contain any general equivalent of stamp duty sub-sale relief under Stamp Act 1891, s 58(4); see supra, § **57.13**. Instead, where there is an assignment, sub-sale or other transaction relating to a contract for a land transaction that is to be completed by a conveyance ("the 'original' contract") the assignee or sub-purchaser is treated as the purchaser under a hypothetical contract (called the "secondary contract") and the chargeable consideration for the secondary contract is that which remains to be paid by the assignee or sub-purchaser under the original contract (or by a person connected with him) if any, plus any consideration given to the original purchaser for the assignment or sub-sale.

The substantial performance or completion of the original contract is ignored if it occurs at the same time as and in connection with the substantial performance or completion of the secondary contract (except where the secondary contract is itself exempt from tax under the exemption for alternative property finance arrangements in FA 2003, s 73).[1]

Thus where there is an assignment or a sub-sale any consideration paid by the purchaser under the original contract to the vendor will be ignored if the purchaser has not substantially performed the contract or completed it except at the same time as the substantial performance or completion of the secondary contract.. Normally of course the purchaser will pay all the consideration under the original contract to the vendor and on a sub-sale the sub-purchaser will pay an uplifted price to the original purchaser and thus SDLT will be payable in respect of each contract on the effective date of each transaction[2] unless that contract is not substantially performed or completed by the original purchaser until the substantial performance or completion of the sub-sale contract.

For the purposes of group relief (see supra, § **62.15**) the vendor under the hypothetical secondary contract is expressly stated to be the vendor under the original contract. This is to prevent an attempt to claim group relief by treating the original purchaser as the vendor when it acquires property from a third party and sells it on to a fellow group company thus eliminating SDLT on the entire acquisition.[3] This was probably not needed because it seems reasonably clear that the vendor under the "secondary contract" was the original vendor and the sub-purchaser was the purchaser and thus there was no sale contract between the original purchaser and the sub-purchaser for the purposes of SDLT which was capable of being relieved by group relief. However, it is also now provided that in all other contexts references to the vendor are to either the vendor under the original contract or the original purchaser as the context permits.[4]

There are provisions relating to the assignment or novation of a contract providing for a conveyance to a third party where, under FA 2003, s 44A, a deemed acquisition of a chargeable interest arises under the original contract.[5]

Where a person assigns his interest as lessee under an agreement for a lease and the assignment occurs before the agreement has been substantially performed, the agreement is treated as if it were with the assignee and the consideration given included any given by the assignee for the assignment. If the assignment occurs after substantial performance the assignment is a separate land transaction.[6]

Sergeant and Sims AA35.

---

1 FA 2003, s 45(1), (2) and (3) as amended by F(No 2)A 2005, Sch 10, para 2.
2 See supra, § **62.04**.
3 FA 2003, s 45(5A)(b).
4 FA 2003, s 45(5A)(b).
5 FA 2003, s 45A and see supra, § **62.03**.
6 FA 2003, Sch 17A, para 12B.

Exchanges

[62:31] Where there is an exchange of chargeable interests each leg of the exchange is treated for stamp duty land tax as a separate land transaction.[1] Each such transaction is charged to SDLT separately from the other and the "single-sale" route previously available under stamp duty is not available in SDLT (see supra, § **57.20**). If either leg of an exchange involves a "major interest" in land then chargeable consideration for each acquisition is the market value of the interest acquired plus any rent payable if the acquisition is the grant of a lease.[2]

Where neither leg of an exchange involves a "major interest" in land, SDLT is charged on each acquisition to the extent that any chargeable consideration is given for the acquisition separate from the interest given for the acquisition ie only on the equality money or equivalent.[3] Where a house building company or a property trader acquires a dwelling from an individual in exchange for a new dwelling supplied to the individual, the acquisition by the company is treated as if it were for nil chargeable consideration if the conditions in FA 2003, Sch 6A, para 1 are satisfied.

Exchanges between connected persons are expressly excluded from the linked transactions rule.[4]

Sergeant and Sims AA34.

---

[1] FA 2003, s 47(1) and see supra, § **62.12** for surrenders and regrant of leases.
[2] FA 2003, s 47(2) and (3) and see FA 2003, s 117 for the definition of a "major interest" being broadly a freehold or leasehold interest.
[3] FA 2003, s 47(4).
[4] See supra, § **62.09** and FA 2003, s 47 as amended by FA 2007, s 76.

Options

[62:32] The acquisition of an option binding the grantor to enter into a land transaction and the acquisition of a right of pre-emption restricting or preventing the grantor from entering into a land transaction (ie a right of first refusal) are each land transactions in their own right for stamp duty land tax purposes. They are separate from any land transactions that result from the exercise of the option or right.[1] The effective date of the land transaction is when the option or right is acquired and not when it is exercisable.[2]

Sergeant and Sims AA36.

---

[1] FA 2003, s 46(1), but see infra, § **62.33** for options and rights granted after 16 April 2003 and before 1 December 2003 which are excised on or after the latter date.
[2] FA 2003, s 46(3).

Transitional provisions

[62:33] The provisions of FA 2003 governing the transition from stamp duty on land to stamp duty land tax are confusing and hard to follow. The relevant provisions are contained in FA 2003, s 125 and Schs 15, 19 and 20 and their effect can be summarised as follows.

A transaction is not an SDLT transaction unless:

(1)   "the effective date" of the transaction is on or after 1 December 2003;[1] and
(2)   it is pursuant to a contract entered into after 10 July 2003[2] (or it is pursuant to a contract entered into on or before 10 July 2003 if subsequently that contract was varied or assigned, or an option, right of pre-emption or similar right has been exercised or where the purchaser is a person other than the purchaser under that contract because of an assignment, sub-sale or other transaction made after that date[3]).

The "effective date" of the transaction is normally the date of completion by conveyance unless the contract is "substantially performed" before completion when the effective date is when the contract is substantially performed.[4] However, in the transitional provisions "effective date" has a special meaning. Where 2 above applies and the contract is substantially performed after 10 July 2003 but before 1 December 2003 and is not completed until on or after the latter date, the effective date of the transaction is the date of completion (regardless of the fact that substantial performance occurred before 1 December 2003).[5]

From 1 December 2003 ("the implementation date")[6] stamp duty is chargeable only on:

(1)   instruments relating to stock or marketable securities (this includes shares and non-exempt loan capital);[7]
(2)   bearer instruments;[8]
(3)   acquisitions of partnership interests;[9] and
(4)   any dealing in land that is not an "SDLT transaction".[10]

Therefore, contracts that are completed before 1 December 2003 will not be SDLT transactions and contracts that were entered into on or before 10 July 2003 and have not been varied, novated or sub-sold etc since that date but do not complete until on or after 1 December 2003 will give rise to stamp duty only and not SDLT.[11]

Where a transaction chargeable to SDLT is effected pursuant to a contract entered into before 1 December 2003, any ad valorem stamp duty paid on the contract is available as a credit against the SDLT payable (but no refund is available should the stamp duty exceed the SDLT).[12]

In relation to the stamping of agreements for lease entered into before 1 December 2003 where the lease is granted on or after that date and the transaction is an SDLT transaction, the protection against interest and penalties under FA 1994, s 240[13] on the presentation of the agreement for stamping is continued by FA 2003, Sch 19, para 8. If the agreement is presented for stamping together with a Revenue certificate in relation to the grant of the lease then the payment of SDLT (or the fact that no SDLT was payable) on the grant of the lease is to be denoted on the agreement and the agreement shall be deemed to have been duly stamped.

Where an option to enter into a land transaction or a right of pre-emption relating to a land transaction was acquired after 16 April 2003 but before 1 December 2003 and exercised on or after the latter date, any consideration given for the grant of the option or right is treated as part of the chargeable consideration for the land transaction resulting from the exercise of the option or right.[14]

Sergeant and Sims AA21.

1. FA 2003, Sch 19, para 2(1).
2. FA 2003, Sch 19, para 3(1).
3. FA 2003, Sch 19, para 3(3).
4. FA 2003, s 44 and see supra, § 62.04.
5. FA 2003, Sch 19, para 4.
6. To be appointed by Treasury order under FA 2003, Sch 19, para 2(2).
7. FA 2003, s 125(1).
8. FA 1999, Sch 15 remains in full force and effect.
9. FA 2003, s 125(8) and Sch 15, para 13(2).
10. FA 2003, s 125(5)(*b*); this ensures that stamp duty continues to apply where a contract relating to land was entered into on or before 10 July 2003 (Royal Assent to FA 2003) but was not completed by instrument until on or after 1 December 2003. Under the original terms of clause 125 such instruments would not have been SDLT transactions and stamp duty would not have applied so the transaction would have escaped both SDLT and stamp duty.
11. Where there is a sub-sale after 10 July 2003 that is not completed until on or after 1 December 2003 and the original contract was substantially performed on or before 10 July 2003 it is thought that the sub-sale does not make the first contract an SDLT transaction given that the policy is to exclude from SDLT any contract substantially performed on or before 10 July 2003 it is understood that HMRC accept that is the position. However, where the original contract was not substantially performed on or before 10 July 2003 a sub-sale occurring after that date will cause the original contract to be chargeable with SDLT if it was substantially performed on or after 17 March 2004 because it will be an SDLT transaction as a result of the substitution of FA 2003, Sch 19, para 3(3)(*c*) by FA 2004, Sch 39, para 12.
12. FA 2003, Sch 19, para 5(1).
13. See supra, § 57.30.
14. FA 2003, Sch 19, para 9(1), (2).

Statutory general anti-avoidance rule

[62:34] A general anti-avoidance rule for SDLT was introduced with effect from 6 December, 2006 by regulations in the form of FA 2003, s 75A.[1] This provision was replaced by FA 2003, new s 75A, s 75B and s 75C with effect from the same date by FA 2007, s 71. The rule is intended to block the creation of SDLT avoidance schemes which exploit particular provisions in the SDLT code without the need for HMRC to continually enact targeted anti-avoidance provisions. The rule applies where:

(1)   there is a disposal and acquisition of a chargeable interest (or a derivative interest);
(2)   a number of transactions are involved in connection with the disposal and acquisition (referred to as "scheme transactions"); and
(3)   the total SDLT payable in respect of the scheme transactions is less than the SDLT that would be payable on a notional land transaction between the disponer and acquiror of the chargeable interest.[2]

When the anti-avoidance rule applies the actual land transactions are ignored and the chargeable consideration for the notional land transaction is the largest amount given by or on behalf of any one person for the scheme transactions or received by or on behalf of the vendor or a person connected with the vendor as consideration for the scheme transactions.

Transactions which are merely "incidental" to the transfer of the chargeable interest are ignored.[3] A number of exclusions also apply.[4]

The "scheme transactions" can include a non-land transaction; an agreement, offer or undertaking not to take a specified action; any kind of arrangement; and a transaction taking place after the acquisition of the chargeable interest.[5] Therefore consideration paid in respect of a non-land transaction can nevertheless be taxed as if it were consideration for a notional land transaction.

The drafting of the general anti-avoidance rule is problematic and the rule may not operate in the way intended by HMRC. One difficulty that is emerging is the question of whether the relevant disposal and acquisition of the chargeable interest must be between persons dealing direct with each other or whether the relevant disposal and acquisition can be separated by one or more intermediate disposals and acquisitions. Although HMRC take the latter view this is disputed in the absence of express statutory wording authorising such an approach. Such an approach hints at discretionary taxation and may not be supported by the courts.

Another area of difficulty relates to sub-sales. Although the technical guidance issued by HMRC assumes that a sub-sale was caught by the new rule when the consideration given for the sub-sale was less than the consideration given for the original sale so that the higher amount was taken to be chargeable, this appears to be incorrect. FA 2003, s 45(3) provides that the substantial performance or completion of the original contract at the same time as, and in connection with, the substantial performance or completion of the so-called secondary contract shall be disregarded except in the case of a transaction which is exempt under FA 2003, s 73(3) (alternative property finance). This statutory disregard is absolute and no exception from it has been made for FA 2003, s 75A. On this basis the completion of the original sale contract and the consideration paid under it falls to be disregarded and so is not a "scheme transaction" for the purposes of FA 2003, s 75A. Therefore the relevant disposal for the purposes of the general statutory anti-avoidance rule is that between the original purchaser and the sub-purchaser and the consideration payable under the original sale is not to be taken into account. Although this interpretation is contrary to HMRC's technical guidance, where official guidance as to the interpretation of a statutory provision differs from the plain meaning of the words enacted, the plain meaning is likely to prevail: see Lord Steyn's speech in *R (Westminster City Council) v National Asylum Support Service*[6]. Notwithstanding that HMRC's interpretation is thought to be wrong it would be prudent to make a disclosure to HMRC when carrying out a transaction and relying on the plain meaning of the legislation, in order to avoid any suggestion that the tax planning was hidden and to gain certainty from a subsequent 'discovery' assessment issued beyond the statutory enquiry period of nine months from the effective date of the land transaction.

[1] SI 2006/3237.
[2] FA 2003, s 75A.
[3] FA 2003, s 75B.
[4] FA 2003, s 75C.
[5] FA 2003, s 75A(2).
[6] [2002] UKHL 38, [2002] 4 All ER 654 at 658.

Disclosure of SDLT avoidance schemes

[62.35] Since 1 August 2005 disclosure has been required of certain stamp duty land tax ("SDLT") schemes. The rules have been built onto and incorporate most of the direct tax scheme disclosure rules that were already in existence on 1 August 2005, referred to here as "the basic rules". The basic rules contain a lot of definitions and other matters relating to tax scheme disclosure generally.

Detailed guidance on the basic rules, including the definitions of key terms, is published by LexisNexis in **Simon's Taxes Division A7.2**. The relevant statutory instruments are:

(1)   the Stamp Duty Land Tax Avoidance Schemes (Prescribed Descriptions of Arrangements) Regulations 2005, SI 2005/1868); and
(2)   the Tax Avoidance Schemes (Information) (Amendment) Regulations 2005, SI 2005/1869.

Copies of the relevant official forms are available on the Anti Avoidance Group section of HMRC's website at: www.hmrc.gov.uk/ai/index.htm.

Note: In PNO3 issued on 20 March 2008, the Government announced that the SDLT disclosure rules will be extended to residential property worth at least £1 million by regulations to be made later in 2008. No regulations were made; however on 22 April 2009 HMRC issued a consultation document entitled "Disclosure of Tax Avoidance Schemes (DOTAS): Stamp Duty and Land Tax" containing draft regulations for residential property schemes and also proposals to identify users of such schemes.

Part X

Value added tax

Part X

Value added tax

63

Introduction
Liability to registration
Taxable persons
Business
Supplies
Acquisitions
Imported goods
Simplification schemes

64

Registration
Liability to registration
Entitlement to registration
Exemption from registration
VAT groups

65

The charge to tax
Introduction
Charge I—Supplies of goods and services
Charge II—Events treated as supplies of goods or services
Charge III—Goods acquired from another EU member state
Charge IV—Goods imported from a third country

66

Tax credits, repayments and refunds
Introduction
Nature of input tax
Input tax credit
Input tax excluded from credit
Deduction and variation of input tax credit
Repayments of tax
Refunds

67

Accounting and payment
VAT returns
Other accounting systems

Correction of errors

68

Exemption
Introduction
The option to tax
Exempt supplies

69

The zero rate
Introduction
Specific provisions
Common provisions

70

The reduced rate
Introduction
Common provisions

63

Introduction

Administration	PARA **63.01**
Taxable persons	PARA **63.10**
Business	PARA **63.14**
Supplies	PARA **63.18**
Acquisitions	PARA **63.34**
Imported goods	PARA **63.39**
Simplification schemes	PARA **63.41**

Administration

History

[63.01] Member states of what is now the European Union (EU) seek to achieve their treaty aims by establishing a common market and progressively harmonising their economic policies.[1] The common (or "internal") market was to be established by 31 December 1992 so as to comprise an area without internal frontiers in which the free movement of goods, persons, services and capital is ensured.[2]

The original text of EC Treaty Article 99 required the EC Commission to consider how the legislation of the various member states concerning turnover taxes could be harmonised in the interest of the common market. The proposals submitted by the Commission under this provision ultimately led to the adoption of value added tax (VAT) as the common turnover tax of the member states from 1 January 1972.[3] The broad framework of VAT adopted at the same time[4] required further consideration both to fulfil the harmonising aims of Article 99 and to enable the system of "own resources" adopted by the member states[5] to be fully implemented. These requirements ultimately led to the adoption of a common system of VAT from 1 January 1978.[6]

In practice, this system was far from common due to the number of derogations made available to the member states in relation to specific provisions,[7] for a transitional period,[8] or subject to notification to the Commission before 1 January 1978.[9] Moreover, member states were permitted to introduce special measures to simplify procedures or counter avoidance and evasion when so authorised by the Council.[10] Furthermore, with each successive enlargement, the Accession Treaties have granted new derogations to new member states.[11] On the other hand, some progress has been made in reducing the number of derogations available.[12] Nevertheless, there remain significant differences between the VAT systems applied by the 27 member states. This

[63.01] Introduction

clearly creates compliance problems for traders making supplies in other member states. It has also given rise to litigation in connection with double taxation[13] and non-taxation.[14]

A number of matters were held over in 1977 for further consideration[15] and further measures have been adopted from time to time when member states reached a common position.[16] The Single European Act (1986) injected a sense of urgency into these deliberations by inserting a new Article 99. This required provisions for the harmonisation of legislation concerning turnover taxes to be adopted by 31 December 1992 "to the extent that such harmonisation is necessary to ensure the establishment and functioning of the internal market". The necessary legislation was adopted and came into operation on 1 January 1993.[17]

The First and Sixth Directives were repealed and replaced by Directive 2006/112/EC with effect from 1 January 2007. Although the effect of the repealed directives is largely unchanged, the text has been redrafted to achieve greater clarity and eliminate discrepancies between the different language versions. Individual articles have been sub-divided and the arrangement improved. The new directive incorporates a number of amendments. It also incorporates provisions relating to new member states derived from the Third, Fourth and Fifth Accession Treaties.

The United Kingdom (UK) became an EC member state on 1 January 1973 and was obliged to introduce VAT in accordance with its Treaty obligations. In fact, the necessary legislation had already been enacted and came into force on 1 April 1973.[18] This legislation was substantially amended to comply with the EC harmonising provisions effective from 1 January 1978[19] and was consolidated with effect from 26 October 1983.[20] It was further amended to comply with the single market provisions effective from 1 January 1993[21] and consolidated with effect from 1 September 1994.[22]

De Voil Indirect Tax Service V1.202–209, 226–227.

[1] EC Treaty, art 2.
[2] EC Treaty, art 8A (inserted by the Single European Act).
[3] Directives 67/227/EEC (the First Directive) (repealed) and 69/463/EEC (the Third Directive) (spent). This time limit was deferred until 1 July 1972 and 1 January 1973 respectively in relation to Italy by Directives 71/401/EEC (the Fourth Directive) (spent) and 72/250/EEC (the Fifth Directive) (spent).
[4] Directive 67/228/EEC (the Second Directive) (repealed).
[5] Decision 70/243/ECSC, EEC, Euratom.
[6] Directive 77/388/EEC (the Sixth Directive) (repealed). This time limit was deferred until 1 January 1979 in relation to Denmark, France, Germany, Ireland, Italy, Luxembourg and the Netherlands by Directive 78/583/EEC (the Ninth Directive) (spent).
[7] For examples, see Directive 77/388/EEC, arts 4(4) (where the member state is required to consult the VAT Committee before acting) and 5(3), (5), (6), (8) (where it is not) (repealed). For the consequences of failing to make the required notification to the VAT Committee, see *Stradasfalti Srl v Agenzia delle Entrate – Ufficio di Trento* (case C-228/05) [2006] ECR I-8391, [2006] SWTI 2207, ECJ. For a simplification scheme requiring notification which went beyond what was

permitted, see *Commission v Austria* (case C-128/05) [2006] ECR I-9265, [2006] SWTI 2259, ECJ.
[8] See Directive 77/388/EEC, art 28(3) (repealed). It was visualised that the transitional period should expire on 1 January 1983.
[9] Directive 77/388/EEC, art 27(5) (repealed). For the notification made by the UK, see infra, § **63.02**.
[10] Directive 77/388/EEC, art 27(1)–(4) (repealed). For authorisations made in respect of the UK, see infra, § **63.02**.
[11] See, for example, the Act of Accession (2003), Annexes V–XIV in relation to the enlargement on 1 May 2004.
[12] The scope of Directive 77/388/EEC art 28(3)(e) (repealed) and Annexes E, F (repealed) was reduced by Directives 89/465/EEC (repealed), 94/5/EEC (repealed) and 98/80/EEC (repealed). More recently, Directive 2006/69/EC (repealed) repealed a number of derogations granted to individual member states under amended Directive 77/388/EEC art 27(1)–(4) (repealed) and amended the text of the directive to make them generally available to all member states.
[13] For an example, see *ARO Lease BV v Inspecteur der Belastingdienst Grote Ondernemingen, Amsterdam* (case C-190/95) [1997] ECR I-4383, [1997] STC 1272, ECJ.
[14] For an example, see *Revenue and Customs Comrs v IDT Card Services Ireland Ltd* [2006] EWCA Civ 29, [2006] STC 1252, CA.
[15] See Directive 77/388/EEC arts 14(2), 16(3), 17(4), 17(6), 24(2), 24(9), 25(11), 28(2), 28(4), 28(5), 32 and 35 (repealed).
[16] For early examples, see Directives 79/1072/EEC (the Eighth Directive); 83/181/EEC (regarding exemption from VAT on imported goods); 85/362/EEC (Seventeenth Directive); 86/560/EEC (Thirteenth Directive).
[17] Directives 91/680/EEC (repealed), 92/77/EEC (repealed) and 92/111/EEC (repealed), which principally amended Directive 77/388/EEC (repealed).
[18] FA 1972, Part I and Schs 1–5 (repealed).
[19] FA 1977, s 14, Sch 6.
[20] VATA 1983 (repealed).
[21] F(No 2) A 1992, s 14, Sch 3.
[22] VATA 1994.

EU directives

[63.02] A directive is a legislative instrument which creates an obligation on member states to enact national legislation giving effect to a stated policy.[1] Although addressed to member states, the provisions of a directive are capable of having direct effect,[2] ie they can create rights which are enforceable in national courts. In order to have direct effect, a provision must meet three tests: (a) it must be clear and precise; (b) it must be clear and unconditional; and (c) it must not allow member states any substantial latitude or discretion in implementing it.[3]

From 1 January 2007, the broad framework of the common system of VAT adopted by the EU is set out in Directive 2006/112/EC.[4] It is supplemented by the directives on repayment of VAT to EC and third country traders,[5] the directives on mutual assistance for the recovery of claims,[6] the directives concerning reliefs on imported goods[7] and the regulations on administrative cooperation.[8] These directives are given effect in the UK by means of the national legislation described in infra, § **63.03**. The regulations are binding in their entirety and are directly applicable in the member states.[9]

Although VAT is primarily administered in accordance with UK legislation giving effect to directives, the principle of direct effect cannot be ignored. The directives can be invoked in the following circumstances.

First, the courts are entitled to resort to the relevant provisions[10] and certain travaux preparatoire[11] where the UK legislation is unclear or ambiguous. A meaning which accords with a Directive is to be preferred to one which does not.[12] Where the relevant EC provision is unclear, the court may decide the matter itself in accordance with principles laid down by, and relevant decisions of, the European Court of Justice,[13] or it may apply to the European Court of Justice for a preliminary ruling.[14] The courts have sometimes overcome a difficulty[15] in construing the UK legislation by concentrating on the directive.[16] The legislative history of UK legislation is relevant when interpreting the descriptions of supplies charged to tax at the zero rate.[17]

Second, there may a conflict between the clear meanings of the directive and the national legislation. National courts are required to interpret domestic legislation, so far as possible, in the light of the wording and purpose of a directive in order to achieve the result pursued by the directive.[18] However, there is clearly some limit on what the national courts can do.[19] National courts must disapply national legislation infringing directly enforceable Community rights if a conforming construction is not possible.[20] The Court of Appeal has taken a robust approach to what is possible as a matter of statutory interpretation in cases where something can be done: the courts may depart from the unambiguous meaning of a statute, read the legislation expansively or restrictively, and read words into the legislation. However, the courts may not adopt a meaning that conflicts with a fundamental or cardinal feature of the legislation.[21]

Third, there may be a gap or overlap in the application of the directive by the member states which results in double taxation or non-taxation. The Court of Appeal has recognised the existence of three general principles of the Sixth Directive: the avoidance of non-taxation, the avoidance of double taxation and the prevention of the distortion of competition. It has applied these principles to defeat a case of non-taxation resulting from differing treatments adopted by Ireland and the UK in relation to phone cards.[22]

Fourth, where an EC provision having direct effect has not been enacted in national legislation, the EC provision should prevail. This is a principle of EC law[23] which is recognised by European Communities Act 1972, s 2(1) and applied by the courts.[24]

Fifth, where a member state has made an authorised derogation from a Directive, national courts have a duty to determine whether the national legislation falls outside the margin of discretion allowed by the Directive and to take this into account when giving effect to the taxpayer's claim.[25] Derogations are authorised partly under rules which allow member states to apply special measures to simplify procedures or prevent avoidance[26] and partly under the specific terms of individual provisions.[27] Derogations are construed strictly.[28] Although national provisions may be amended to reduce or remove their divergence from the object of the directive, they cannot be restored once removed or varied so as to increase the extent of that divergence.[29]

As a general principle, the Commissioners cannot invoke direct effect[30] for to do so would result in a charge to tax which has not been approved by Parliament. Thus, although certain supplies have been exempt from tax[31] or zero-rated[32] under UK law in breach of the Sixth Directive, traders could continue to exempt or zero rate those supplies until such time as the UK legislation was amended.

It is settled law that the incompatibility of national legislation with Community provisions can be finally remedied only by means of national provisions having the same legal force as the provisions in need of amendment. Mere administrative practice cannot do this.[33] Nor can judges.[34]

A member state may incur liability for loss and damage caused to individuals by virtue of a breach of Community law for which it is responsible. Three conditions must be met: (a) the rule of law infringed must be intended to confer rights on individuals; (b) the breach must be sufficiently serious; and (c) there must be a direct causal link between the breach concerned and the damage sustained. It is for the national court to determine whether these conditions have been met. A breach meets the test in point (b) if the member state has manifestly and gravely disregarded the limits on the exercise of its powers. Factors taken into account in determining this include the clarity and precision of the rule breached.[35]

De Voil Indirect Tax Service V1.226–227, 235.

---

[1] EC Treaty, art 249 (ex art 189).

[2] *Van Duyn v Home Office* (case 41/74) [1975] Ch 358, [1975] 3 All ER 190, ECJ.

[3] *Becker v Finanzamt Münster-Innenstadt* (case 8/81) [1982] ECR 53, ECJ; *Verbond van Nederlandse Ondernemingen v Inspecteur der Invoerrechten en Accijnzen* (case 51/76) [1977] ECR 113, ECJ. See also *Naturally Yours Cosmetics Ltd v Customs and Excise Comrs* [1987] VATTR 45.

[4] Directive 2006/112/EC (as last amended by Directive 2009/69/EC) is prospectively amended from varying dates between 1 January 2009 and 1 January 2015 by Directive 2008/8/EC. For a brief overview of the changes coming into force on 1 January 2010 in relation to the place of supply of services and the reverse charge, see infra, §§ **63.31** and **65.34** respectively. The directive is interpreted in accordance with Regulation (EC) No 1777/2005.

[5] Directives 79/1072/EEC (the Eighth Directive) and 86/560/EEC (the Thirteenth Directive). Directive 79/1072/EEC is repealed and replaced by Directive 2008/9/EC with effect from 1 January 2010.

[6] Directives 2008/55/EC (which repealed and replaced Directive 76/308/EEC with effect from 30 June 2008) as implemented by Regulation (EC) No 1179/2008 (which repealed Directive 202/94/EC with effect from 1 January 2009).

[7] For small non-commercial consignments, see Directive 2006/79/EC (which replaced Directive 78/1035/EEC with effect from 6 November 2006). For goods imported by persons travelling from third countries, see Directive 2007/74/EC (which repealed

[63.02] Introduction

and replaced Directive 69/169/EEC with effect from 1 December 2008).
8   Regulation (EC) Nos 1798/2003 and 1925/2004.
9   EC Treaty, art 249 (ex art 189).
10 *English-speaking Union of the Commonwealth v Customs and Excise Comrs* [1980] VATTR 184. All foreign language texts should be referred to: see *British Tenpin Bowling Association v Customs and Excise Comrs* [1989] 1 CMLR 561, [1989] VATTR 101.
11 *Open University v Customs and Excise Comrs* [1982] VATTR 29. The material concerned must: (a) be public and accessible, and (b) clearly and indisputably point to a definite legislative intention.
12 *UFD Ltd v Customs and Excise Comrs* [1981] VATTR 199.
13 European Communities Act 1972, s 3(1). For the principles of construction, see Lord Denning MR in *H P Bulmer Ltd v J Bollinger SA* [1974] 2 All ER 1226 at 1237, CA.
14 EC Treaty, art 234 (ex art 177).
15 For a criticism of the practice of rewriting treaties, conventions and directives, see Jacob J in *Beliot Technologies Inc v Valmet Paper Machinery Inc* [1995] RPC 705 at 737. In relation to VAT, see more recently *Scottish Exhibition Centre Ltd v R & C Comrs* [2006] CSIH 42, [2008] STC 967 at para 4.
16 This was done, for example, in *Customs and Excise Comrs v Chinese Channel (Hong Kong) Ltd* [1998] STC 347, *Century Life plc v Customs and Excise Comrs* [2001] STC 38, CA and *Bookit Ltd v Revenue and Customs Comrs* [2006] EWCA Civ 550, [2006] STC 1367, CA, where, in each case, the UK legislation was intended to give effect to provisions having direct effect. It may be significant that the taxpayers were not disadvantaged by this procedure.
17 For the relevance of legislative history and its consequences in relation to zero-rating, see infra, § **69.12**.
18 *Marleasing SA v La Comercial Internacional de Alimentacion SA* (case C-106/89) [1990] ECR I–4135, ECJ.
19 In *Customs and Excise Comrs v Isle of Wight Council* [2004] EWHC 2541 (Ch), [2005] STC 257, Pumfrey J was "inclined to the view" that VATA 1994 could not be "coerced by any process of interpretation into a state of consistency with [art 4(5) of] the Sixth Directive", although he did not need to come to a concluded view on the matter.
20 See Lord Walker of Gestingthorpe in *Fleming (trading as Bodycraft) v Revenue and Customs Comrs, Condé Nast Publications Ltd v Revenue and Customs Comrs* [2008] UKHL 2, [2008] STC 324, HL at paras 24, 25, where the Court held that a transitional period could not be read into VAT Regulations, SI 1995/2518, reg 29(1A) where none had been provided.
21 *Revenue and Customs Comrs v IDT Card Services Ireland Ltd* [2006] EWCA Civ 29, [2006] STC 1252, CA.
22 *Revenue and Customs Comrs v Card Services Ireland Ltd* [2006] EWCA Civ 29, [2006] STC 1252, CA.
23 *Becker v Finanzamt Münster-Innenstadt* (case 8/81) [1982] ECR 53, ECJ.
24 For examples, see *Yoga for Health Foundation v Customs and Excise Comrs* [1984] STC 630; *Parkinson v Customs and Excise Comrs* [1985] VATTR 219; *Merseyside Cablevision Ltd v Customs and Excise Comrs* [1987] VATTR 134.
25 *Verbond van Nederlandse Ondernemingen v Inspecteur der Invoerrechten en Accijnzen* (case 51/76) [1977] ECR 113, ECJ.

Administration [63.03]

[26] For derogations applicable in the UK under Directive 2006/112/EC art 394, see the letter to the EC Commission dated 28 December 1977 reproduced in *Direct Cosmetics Ltd v Customs and Excise Comrs* [1983] VATTR 194 at 203, and subsequent proceedings [1985] STC 479, ECJ. These derogations continue to have effect in relation to retailers, registration and terminal markets. For derogations under Directive 2006/112/EC art 395, see Decisions 89/466/EEC, 89/534/EEC (cf *Direct Cosmetics Ltd and Laughtons Photographs Ltd v Customs and Excise Comrs (joined cases 138 and 139/86)* [1988] STC 540, ECJ), 2006/659/EC, 2006/774/EC, 2007/133/EC, 2007/250/EC (as amended by Decision 2009/439/EC), 2007/884/EC and an unnumbered Authorisation dated 10 December 1986.

[27] In particular, Directive 2006/112/EC art 110 authorises the UK to apply "exemption with refund" (ie zero-rating) until definitive arrangements have been adopted by the EC. For the extent to which VATA 1994, Sch 8 derives its authority from this provision, see infra, § **69.12**.

[28] See *Finanzamt Bergisch Gladbach v Skripalle* (case C-63/96) [1997] STC 1035, ECJ.

[29] See *Norbury Developments Ltd v Customs and Excise Comrs* (case C-136/97) [1999] STC 511, ECJ; *EC Commission v French Republic (United Kingdom intervening)* (case C-345/99) [2003] STC 372, ECJ; *EC Commission v French Republic* (case C-40/00) [2003] STC 390, ECJ.

[30] *National Smokeless Fuels Ltd v IRC* [1986] STC 300. But see *Arts Council of Great Britain v Customs and Excise Comrs* [1994] VATTR 313 where the trader was an "organ of the state".

[31] *EC Commission v United Kingdom* (case 353/85) [1988] STC 251, ECJ.

[32] *EC Commission v United Kingdom* (case 416/85) [1988] STC 456, ECJ.

[33] *EC Commission v United Kingdom* (case C-C-33/03) [2005] ECR I-1865, [2005] STC 582, ECJ

[34] Per Lord Scott of Foscote in *Fleming (trading as Bodycraft) v Revenue and Customs Comrs, Condé Nast Publications Ltd v Revenue and Customs Comrs* [2008] UKHL 2, [2008] STC 324, HL at para 22. Lord Walker of Gestingthorpe (at para 61) took the view that the principle was inapplicable in this case because the point at issue was the duration of an adequate transitional period rather than the continuing non-transposition or incorrect transposition of the Sixth Directive (now Directive 2006/112/EC).

[35] *Sweden v Stockholm Lindöpark AB* (case C-150/99) [2001] STC 103, ECJ, where Sweden's failure to implement an exemption from tax was held to be a serious breach of Community law.

UK VAT legislation

[63.03] The basic framework of VAT is enacted in VATA 1994, which came into effect on 1 September 1994. This framework is supplemented by primary and secondary legislation derived from a number of sources:

[63.03] Introduction

(1) Many of the detailed provisions are set out in orders, rules and regulations made by statutory instrument.[1] The Treasury is given wide powers to make orders, usually of a policy nature, and the Commissioners are given similarly wide powers to make regulations, usually on matters of an administrative nature.

(2) Some of the information set out in the Commissioners' public notices has the force of law.[2] The modern practice is to box this information and clearly label it as such in the notices concerned.[3]

(3) The Customs and Excise Acts[4] and regulations relating to postal packets[5] apply in a modified form to goods imported from third countries.[6] Offences specifically applied to assigned matters also apply to VAT.[7] Orders made under Customs and Excise Duties (General Reliefs) Act 1979, ss 7, 13 and 13A apply to VAT by virtue of the specific provisions contained therein.[8] Civil penalties for dishonest conduct and contravention of a statutory requirement apply in relation to VAT chargeable on imported goods.[9]

(4) Isle of Man Act 1979, which gives effect to the customs union between the UK and the Isle of Man, largely applies to VAT.[10] The two countries form a single area for VAT purposes, and the textual modifications to the VAT legislation required to give effect to this concept are contained in orders[11] made under Isle of Man Act 1979, s 6.

(5) FA 2002, s 134[12] and Sch 39 and regulations[13] made thereunder give effect to the mutual assistance directives concerning the recovery of VAT due in other EU member states.[14] FA 2003, s 197, which deals with the exchange of information between tax authorities of the EU member states, no longer applies to VAT.[15]

(6) As regards England and Wales, Police and Criminal Evidence Act 1984 applies to VAT in a modified form.[16] Corresponding legislation applies in Scotland[17] and Northern Ireland.[18] This legislation is supplemented by Summary Jurisdiction (Process) Act 1881 and Criminal Justice and Public Order Act 1994 ss 136–139 in relation to cross-border matters.

(7) FA 2007 and FA 2008 replace a number of administrative and penalty provisions specific to VAT with similar provisions common to a number of direct and indirect taxes and duties.[19]

EU regulations are directly applicable and form part of UK law. EU customs regulations apply in a modified form in relation to the charge to VAT on goods imported from third countries.[20] The exchange of information between the tax authorities of member states in relation to VAT now takes place in accordance with regulations on administrative cooperation.[21] Directive 2006/112/EEC is interpreted in accordance with a regulation laying down implementing measures,[22] which came into force on 1 July 2006.

The principles of legitimate expectations and legal certainty do not preclude a member state from giving retrospective effect to amending legislation if taxpayers are warned of the impending change, and its retrospective effect, in a way that enables them to understand how they are affected.[23]

De Voil Indirect Tax Service V1.235–236, 240.

---

[1] VATA 1994, s 97(1) as amended by Transfer of Functions and Revenue and Customs Appeals Order, SI 2009/56, Sch 2, para 226.

Administration [63.03]

2   For examples of statutory provisions authorising the publication of a notice, see VATA 1994, Sch 6, para 11 (values expressed in foreign currency) and VAT Regulations, SI 1995/2518, reg 67(1) (supplies by retailers). The relevant parts of the notices issued under statutory authority are listed in Notice No 747. However, this notice was issued in June 2003 and has not been updated.

3   As regards an early edition of what is now Notice No 727, where this was not done, see Woolf J in *GUS Merchandise Corpn Ltd v Customs and Excise Comrs* [1980] STC 480 at 486.

4   Comprising CEMA 1979, Customs and Excise Duties (General Reliefs) Act 1979, Alcoholic Liquor Duties Act 1979, Hydrocarbon Oil Duties Act 1979 and Tobacco Products Duties Act 1979 and any other enactments for the time being in force relating to customs or excise: CEMA 1979, s 1(1).

5   Postal Packets (Customs and Excise) Regulations, SI 1986/260; Postal Packets (Revenue and Customs) Regulations, SI 2007/2195.

6   VATA 1994, s 16(1)(*a*) and (2). For excluded and modified UK legislation, see SI 1995/2518, regs 118, 119, 121 as amended by SI 2000/634. For modifications in relation to the channel tunnel, see Channel Tunnel (Customs and Excise) Order, SI 1990/2167.

7   For untrue declarations, see CEMA 1979, s 167(1)–(4) (as amended by Criminal Justice Act 1982, ss 37, 38, 46 and Police and Criminal Evidence Act 1984, s 114(1)). For counterfeited documents, see CEMA 1979, s 168 (as amended by Police and Criminal Evidence Act 1984, s 114(1)).

8   VATA 1994, s 16(1) ("where the contrary intention appears") overrides the specific exclusion in VAT Regulations, SI 1995/2518, reg 118(*d*). For the orders having effect, see Customs and Excise (Personal Reliefs for Special Visitors) Order, SI 1992/3156; Customs and Excise Duties (Personal Reliefs for Goods Permanently Imported) Order, SI 1992/3193 (as most recently amended by SI 2004/1002); Travellers Allowances Order, SI 1994/955 (as most recently amended by SI 2004/1002, SI 2008/3058).

9   For the system of civil penalties, see FA 2003, ss 24–41 as amended by SI 2009/56; Finance Act 2003, Part 3 (Appointed Day) Order, SI 2003/2985; Customs (Contravention of a Relevant Rule) Regulations, SI 2003/3113; Export (Penalty) Regulations, SI 2003/3102 as amended by SI 2008/56.

10 Isle of Man Act 1979, ss 8, 9 do not apply to VAT charged on imported goods: VAT Regulations, SI 1995/2518, reg 118(*e*).

11 VAT (Isle of Man) Order, SI 1982/1067; VAT (Isle of Man) (No 2) Order, SI 1982/1068.

12 As amended by SI 2008/2871 and extended by FA 2004, s 322 (customs union with the Principality of Andorra).

13 Recovery of Duties and Taxes Etc Due in Other Member States (Corresponding UK Claims, Procedure and Supplementary) Regulations, SI 2004/674 as amended by SI 2005/1709, SI 2007/3508.

14 For the mutual assistance directives, see supra, § **63.02**.

15 VAT was removed from the scope of Directive 77/799/EEC with effect from 1 January 2004 by Directive 2003/93/EC arts 1(3), 3. FA 2003, s 197 was amended accordingly by the Mutual Provisions Order, SI 2003/3092, art 3.

16 The 1984 Act is amended, modified and supplemented from 1 December 2007 by FA 2007, ss 82, 84; Finance Act 2007 (Sections 82 to 84 and Schedule 23) (Commencement) Order, SI 2007/3166; Police and Criminal Evidence Act 1984 (Application to Revenue and Customs) Order, SI 2007/3175.

[63.03] Introduction

[17] From 1 December 2007, see the amendments to Scottish law made by FA 2007, s 85 and Sch 23; Finance Act 2007 (Sections 82 to 84 and Schedule 23) (Commencement) Order, SI 2007/3166.

[18] From 1 December 2007, see Police and Criminal Evidence (Northern Ireland) Order, SI 1989/1341 (NI 12) as amended, modified and supplemented by FA 2007, ss 83, 84; Finance Act 2007 (Sections 82 to 84 and Schedule 23) (Commencement) Order, SI 2007/3166; Police and Criminal Evidence (Application to Revenue and Customs) Order (Northern Ireland), SR 2007/464.

[19] In particular, see: (1) FA 2007, Sch 24 (penalties for errors) and Finance Act 2007, Schedule 24 (Commencement and Transitional Provisions) Order, SI 2008/568, which replaced VATA 1994, ss 60, 61, 63, 64 in accordance with arts 2–4 of the 2008 Order; (2) FA 2008, s 113 and Sch 36 (information and inspection powers) and Finance Act 2008, Schedule 36 (Appointed Day and Savings) Order, SI 2009/404, which replaced VATA 1994, Sch 11, paras 7(2)–(9), 10(1)–(2A) and FA 1999, s 13(5)(c) with effect from 1 April 2009; (3) FA 2008, s 114 (computer records), which replaced FA 1985, s 10 with effect from 21 July 2008 (Royal Assent); (4) FA 2008, s 115 and Sch 37, para 10 (record-keeping) and Finance Act 2008, Schedule 37 (Appointed Day) Order, SI 2009/402, which amended FA 1999, s 13(6) from 1 April 2009; and (5) FA 2008, s 123 and Sch 41 (penalties for failure to notify and improperly issuing VAT invoices) and Finance Act 2008, Schedule 41 (Appointed Day and Transitional Provisions) Order, SI 2009/511, which replace VATA 1994, s 67 with effect from 1 April 2010.

[20] VATA 1994, s 16(1)(b). The relevant regulations are Regulation (EEC) No 2568/87 (tariff and statistical nomenclature and the common customs tariff), Regulation (EEC) No 2913/92 (the Community Customs Code) and Regulation (EEC) No 2454/93 (implementing the Community Customs Code). For the provisions excluded or modified, see SI 1995/2518, regs 117(11), 120(2), (3), 121B, 121C, 121D as amended or inserted by SI 2000/634, SI 2001/630, SI 2003/2318, SI 2004/1082, SI 2006/587. Regulation (EEC) 918/83 (conditional reliefs on final importation of goods) does not apply: see SI 1995/2518, reg 120(1).

[21] Regulation (EC) No 1798/2003 (as last amended by Regulation (EC) No 885/2004).

[22] Regulation (EC) No 1777/2005.

[23] *Stichting Goed Wonen v Staatssecretaris van Financiën* (case C-376/02) [2005] ECR I-3445, [2005] STC 833, ECJ.

Extra-statutory concessions

[63.04] An extra-statutory concession is a relaxation which gives the taxpayer a reduction in tax liability to which he is not entitled under the strict letter of the law.[1] Concessions are announced by the Commissioners from time to time and periodically consolidated in a notice.[2] The Commissioners' responsibility for the collection and management of VAT[3] allows them to deal pragmatically with "minor or transitory anomalies, cases of hardship at the margins or cases in which a statutory rule is difficult to formulate or its enactment would take up a disproportionate amount of parliamentary time". However, it does not allow them to go beyond "mere management of the efficient collection of the revenue".[4] These comments have given rise to the the enactment of FA 2008, s 160 and a review of the exisiting extra-statutory

Administration [63.04]

concessions. The legislation allows the Treasury to make orders giving effect to any existing concession. The review has resulted in an order giving effect to a number of concessions,[5] legislation giving effect to concessions under other powers[6] and announcements that others have been withdrawn.[7]

It has been said that a VAT and duties tribunal has no jurisdiction in relation to concessions in any circumstances.[8] This has been held to be so in relation to the circumstances in which the Commissioners waive their right to assess on the grounds of genuine misunderstanding or misleading advice[9] and in relation to refunds allowed under extra-statutory provisions,[10] but not in a case where the Commissioners' refusal to allow a concession resulted in a liability to pay VAT.[11] However, a taxpayer can apply for judicial review in those circumstances where the tribunal has no jurisdiction.[12] The relevant principle is that a concession is available to those who fall clearly within its terms.[13]

In *R (on the application of Greenwich Property Ltd) v Customs and Excise Comrs*,[14] Collins J said:

> The language of concession is not that of a statute and should not be construed as if it was. But if a concession is published to all who might benefit from it, they are entitled to arrange their affairs in reliance on it, provided that what they do falls clearly within the terms of the concession. . . . I am prepared to accept that . . . the taxable person must demonstrate that he has acted strictly in accordance with what the concession permits and has complied with all the conditions necessary to obtain relief. Any doubt should be resolved in favour of the tax being payable according to the statutory provision since, if there is doubt, or the language of the concession is ambiguous, the taxpayer should enquire of the Commissioners whether what he intends to do falls within the concession.

De Voil Indirect Tax Service V1.239.

---

1. Explanatory memorandum placed in the House of Commons library on 16 March 1985.
2. For the text of concessions currently in force, see Notice No 48 (July 2009).
3. VATA 1994, Sch 11, para 1.
4. Per Lord Hoffmann in *R (on the application of Wilkinson) v Inland Revenue Comrs* [2005] UKHL 30, [2006] STC 270, HL at [21].
5. See Enactment of Extra-Statutory Concessions Order, SI 2009/730, art 17.
6. See VAT (Place of Supply of Goods) Order, SI 2009/215 and VAT (Input Tax) (Amendment) Order, SI 2009/217.
7. See, for example, Revenue and Customs Brief 15/09, 27 March 2009 (concession no longer necessary as "it has been overtaken by other published guidance").
8. See Lord Murray in *Customs and Excise Comrs v United Biscuits (UK) Ltd* [1992] STC 325 at 328; Hidden J in *Customs and Excise Comrs v Arnold* [1996] STC 1271 at 1275. Cf *Greenwich Property Ltd v Customs and Excise Comrs* (2000) VAT decision 16746.
9. *Customs and Excise Comrs v Arnold* [1996] STC 1271, where the contrary decision in *British Teleflower Services Ltd v Customs and Excise Comrs* [1995] V & DR 356 was overruled. See also *Mitzi (a firm) v Customs and Excise Comrs* (1986) VAT decision 2233. For misunderstanding, see Notice No 48 (July 2009) para 3.4. For misleading advice, see Revenue and Customs Brief 15/09, 27 March 2009 and the current guidance referred to therein.
10. *Customs and Excise Comrs v Arnold* [1996] STC 1271.

[63.04] Introduction

[11] *Shepherd v Customs and Excise Comrs* [1994] VATTR 47.
[12] *R v IRC, ex p Fulford-Dobson* [1987] STC 344 at 355; *R v Inspector of Taxes, ex p Brumfield* [1989] STC 151 at 155; *Customs and Excise Comrs v Arnold* [1996] STC 1271 at 1275.
[13] *R v Board of Inland Revenue, ex parte MFK Underwriting Agencies Ltd* [1989] STC 873 at 892. For the application of a concession to the facts of a case, see *R (on the application of Accenture Services Ltd) v Revenue and Customs Comrs, R (on the application of Barclays Bank plc) v Revenue and Customs Comrs* [2009] EWHC 857, [2009] STC 1503 at paras 34–36. For examples of applications for judicial review in relation extra-statutory concessions, see *R (on the application of Greenwich Property Ltd) v Customs and Excise Comrs* [2001] STC 618 *(application granted); R (on the application of British Telecommunications plc) v Revenue and Customs Comrs* [2005] EWHC 1043 (Admin), [2005] STC 1148, *R (on the application of Silicon Graphics Finance SA v Revenue and Customs Comrs* [2006] EWHC 1889 (Admin), [2008] STC 1928, *R (on the application of Accenture Services Ltd) v Revenue and Customs Comrs, R (on the application of Barclays Bank plc) v Revenue and Customs Comrs* [2009] EWHC 857, [2009] STC 1503 (applications refused).
[14] [2001] STC 618 at paras 13 and 23.

Outline

Taxation of value added

[63.05] There are four basic methods of taxing value added: the direct additive method, the indirect additive method, the direct subtractive method and the indirect subtractive method. VAT, as its name implies, is a tax on value added. However, the indirect subtractive method adopted by the EU tends to obscure this fact because tax liabilities for an accounting period are calculated without ascertaining the underlying value added. The relationship between tax liabilities and value added is further obscured by:

(1) The use of exemptions, valuation reliefs and multiple rates.
(2) The fact that changes in stock levels are disregarded.[1]
(3) The fact that no distinction is made between capital and revenue expenditure.[2]

The interaction of these factors can give rise to the curious feature that a trader who has added value during an accounting period may nevertheless receive a repayment of tax.

De Voil Indirect Tax Service V1.101.

---

[1] However, taxable persons are entitled to input tax credit in respect of goods held in stock at the time of registration. For the relief given, see infra, § **66.04**.
[2] However, input tax on certain capital goods is adjusted over a period of adjustment. For the capital goods scheme, see infra, § **66.27**.

Taxable transactions

[63.06] VAT is a broadly based tax on goods and services. To be more specific, it is a tax charged on three classes of transaction:[1]

(1) Supplies of goods and services.
(2) A removal of goods (referred to as an "acquisition") to the UK from another EU member state.
(3) A removal of goods (referred to as an "importation") to the UK from a country (referred to as a "third country") which is not an EU member state.

VAT is charged on taxable supplies of goods and services[2] made in the course or furtherance of business[3] by traders known as "taxable persons".[4] Taxable persons periodically account to the Commissioners for the tax chargeable. This tax is referred to as "output tax".[5] Traders (referred to as "non-taxable persons") who are not taxable persons do not charge VAT on their supplies of goods and services.

The VAT chargeable on taxable acquisitions[6] is collected from the persons who acquire the goods concerned. Taxable persons periodically account to the Commissioners for the tax due on their acquisitions. This tax is also referred to as "output tax".[7] To the extent that non-taxable persons are liable to VAT on their acquisitions, they make a declaration and pay the tax chargeable direct to the Commissioners.[8]

In broad terms, the VAT on importations[9] is collected by the Commissioners at the same time, and in the same manner, as customs duties, excise duties and other charges arising on imported goods.[10]

De Voil Indirect Tax Service V3.101.

---

[1] VATA 1994, s 1(1).
[2] For supplies of goods and services, see infra, §§ **63.17–63.32**.
[3] For the activities which do, or do not, amount to the carrying on of a business, see infra, §§ **63.14–63.16**.
[4] For taxable persons, see infra, §§ **63.09–63.11**.
[5] VATA 1994, s 24(2).
[6] For acquisitions, see infra, §§ **63.33–63.37**.
[7] VATA 1994, s 24(2).
[8] For declarations and payments by non-taxable persons, see infra, §§ **67.12**.
[9] For importations, see infra, §§ **63.38–63.39**.
[10] VATA 1994, s 1(4).

Credit mechanism

[63.07] VAT is largely removed from business costs, and thereby confined to consumer expenditure, by providing taxable persons with a credit mechanism. Subject to a number of exceptions, taxable persons are entitled to recover the VAT they incur from the Commissioners. This tax is known as "input tax"[1] and represents:

(1) Tax chargeable on goods and services supplied to them by other taxable persons.

[63.07] Introduction

(2) Tax accounted for to the Commissioners on goods acquired from another EU member state.
(3) Tax paid to the Commissioners on goods imported from a third country.

In principle, non-taxable persons do not recover the VAT they incur. However, there are two important exceptions:

(1) VAT is removed from the business costs of overseas traders by a system of repayments.[2]
(2) Certain non-taxable persons are entitled to refunds of tax on strictly defined classes of expenditure.[3]

De Voil Indirect Tax Service V3.401.

[1] VATA 1994, s 24(1). For input tax, see infra, §§ **66.02–66.35**.
[2] For repayments to EU and third country traders, see infra, §§ **66.37** and **66.36** respectively.
[3] For refunds, see infra, §§ **66.39–66.41**.

Territorial considerations

[63.08] The EU common system of VAT draws a distinction between intra-EU transactions and transactions with third countries. The UK VAT legislation, in turn, draws distinctions between transactions within the UK, transactions with other EU member states and transactions with third countries. It is clearly necessary to ascertain which territories fall within each description. The task is less easy than it may appear. Although the territorial extent of the EC Treaty, and therefore of the EU, is defined in art 277 (ex 227) of the Treaty, this definition does not apply for all purposes. In particular, the relevant territories for customs, excise and VAT purposes are separately defined in terms that differ both from each other and from the position set out in the Treaty.

From 1 January 2007, the VAT territory of the EU comprises:

(1) The territory of the member states, subject to the exclusions noted:[1]
    (i) Austria,[2]
    (ii) Belgium,
    (iii) Bulgaria,
    (iv) Cyprus,[3]
    (v) the Czech Republic,
    (vi) Denmark (excluding the Faeroe Islands and Greenland),
    (vii) Estonia,
    (viii) Finland (excluding the Aland Islands),
    (ix) France (excluding the overseas departments),
    (x) Germany (excluding Heligoland and Büsingen),
    (xi) Greece (excluding Mount Athos),
    (xii) Hungary,
    (xiii) Ireland,
    (xiv) Italy (excluding Livigno, Campione d'Italia and the Italian waters of Lake Lugano),

(xv) Latvia,
(xvi) Lithuania,
(xvii) Luxembourg,
(xviii) Malta,
(xix) the Netherlands,
(xx) Poland,
(xxi) Portugal,[4]
(xxii) Romania,
(xxiii) Slovakia,
(xxiv) Slovenia,
(xxv) Spain (excluding Ceuta, Mellila and the Canary Islands),
(xxvi) Sweden, and
(xxvii) the United Kingdom.
(2) The following territories:[5]
 (i) the Isle of Man (which is treated as part of the UK),
 (ii) the UK Sovereign Base Areas in Cyprus (which are treated as part of Cyprus), and
 (iii) Monaco (which is treated as part of France).

The UK legislation arrives at the same position by a different route. It starts from the EU customs territory[6] and excludes the following territories in order to arrive at the VAT territory: the Aland Islands, Andorra, the Canary Islands, the Channel Islands, the French overseas departments, Mount Athos and San Marino.[7] This is a helpful formulation. It highlights the fact that VAT and customs rules do not coincide in relation to movements of goods to and from these territories.

Gibraltar does not form part of the EU VAT and customs territories.[8] It is therefore a third country for the purposes of both VAT and customs duties.

The United Kingdom (comprising England, Scotland, Wales and Northern Ireland) and the Isle of Man are in a customs union.[9] The Isle of Man enacted VAT under separate but almost identical legislation[10] under the terms of the customs union. The two countries are treated as a single area for VAT purposes.[11] The Isle of Man is also treated as part of the EU territory for VAT purposes.[12]

De Voil Indirect Tax Service V1.213.

---

[1] Directive 2006/112/EC art 5(2), which defines the territories of the member states by reference to the areas to which the EC Treaty applies. For the exclusions, see Directive 2006/112/EC, art 6; EC Treaty, art 299(6)(*a*) (the Faeroe Islands); Act of Accession (1994), Protocol No 2, art 2(*a*) (Finland). Greenland withdrew from the EC Treaty with effect from 1 February 1985. The national territory of a coastal member state includes its territorial sea, its bed and subsoil. This does not include the exclusive economic zone and continental shelf in respect of which the sovereignty of a member state is limited to the right of exploration and exploitation: *Aktiebolaget NN v Skatteverket* (case C-111/05) [2007] ECR I–2697, [2008] STC 32–3, ECJ.

[2] Austria includes the communes of Jungholz (which is virtually surrounded by German territory) and Mittleberg (Kleines Walsertal) (which is accessible only from Bavaria).

[63.08] Introduction

[3] The Community acquis is currently suspended in the areas over which the government does not exercise effective control: Act of Accession (2003), Protocol No 10.
[4] Portugal includes the autonomous regions of Madeira and the Azores.
[5] Directive 2006/112/EEC, art. This is given effect in the UK by VAT Regulations, SI 1995/2518, reg 139 as amended by SI 2004/1082.
[6] As defined in Regulation (EEC) No 2913/92, art 3(1), (2) as amended by the Act of Accession (2003), Annex II, Chapter 19 and Protocol No 3. This definition applies for VAT purposes by virtue of VATA 1994, s 16(1)(*b*) as interpreted in accordance with VAT Regulations, SI 1995/2518, reg 117(11) as inserted by SI 2004/1082. By inference, it is the "territory of the Community" referred to in VAT Regulations, SI 1995/2518, regs 136, 137, 139 as amended by SI 2004/1082.
[7] SI 1995/2518, regs 136, 137. Andorra and San Marino are not member states of the EU. They are, however, in customs union with the EU: see Decision 90/680/EEC (Andorra) and Decision 92/561/EEC (San Marino).
[8] EU VAT legislation does not apply to Gibraltar by virtue of the Act of Accession (1972), art 28. As a Crown Colony, Gibraltar does not form part of the territory of the UK for the purposes of Regulation (EEC) No 2193/92, art 3(1). In the absence of any specific reference to Gibraltar in that provision, it does not form part of the EU customs territory.
[9] The current agreement is Customs and Excise Agreement 1979, Cmnd 7747, which is given effect by Isle of Man Act 1979.
[10] Value Added Tax and Other Taxes Act 1973 (an Act of Tynwald). The exception relates to the taxation of gaming machine receipts: Isle of Man Act 1979, s 1(1)(*d*).
[11] Isle of Man Act 1979, s 6; SI 1982/1067; SI 1982/1068.
[12] VAT Regulations, SI 1995/2518, reg 139.

Avoidance, evasion and abuse

[63.09] It may be incautious to mention avoidance and evasion in the same breath. However, preventing possible tax evasion, avoidance and abuse is an objective recognised and encouraged by the Directive 2006/112/EC.[1] Moreover, there is one theme common to them both running through the recent legislation and case law: the opportunities posed by chains of supply.

The principle of VAT involves applying a general tax on consumption exactly proportional to the price of the goods and services whatever the number of transactions taking place in the production and distribution process.[2] The number of links from (say) manufacturer to consumer is determined partly by the nature of the goods or services concerned (window cleaning requires fewer steps than manufacturing) and partly by the manner in which businesses are organised (a trader carrying on a number of activities may do so through one company or through separate companies for each activity). The chain is clearly lengthened if businesses are fragmented or activities outsourced.

Fraud arises in many forms. Missing trader intra-Community fraud ("MTIC fraud") has posed particular problems in recent years. The Commissioners distinguish three classes: "acquisition fraud", "carousel fraud" and "contra-trading fraud". All involve one or more chains of supplies made up of both innocent and fraudulent traders.[3]

FA 2003 introduced two measures specifically designed to make traders wary of transactions that may form part of an MITC fraud. The first measure enables the Commissioners to require security in respect of tax due from another member of the chain.[4] The second measure makes traders jointly and severally liable for tax due from, but unpaid by, another member of the chain.[5] The vires of these provisions has recently been considered by the Court of Justice.[6] FA 2006 introduced three additional measures.[7] One measure provides that the customer rather than the supplier is liable to account for and pay the VAT chargeable on supplies of certain goods.[8] The other measures impose new record-keeping requirements and clarify the Commissioners' powers to inspect goods.

As the essence of MTIC fraud is a missing trader, or a trader hiding behind a false identity, the Commissioners face obvious difficulties in recovering the unpaid VAT or prosecuting the individuals behind the fraud. However, the sums at stake may justify the cost of petitioning the Court for the winding up of an insolvent company if there is evidence that funds have been improperly diverted and their destination can be traced. Whether the liquidator can prove his claim and successfully recover the funds is another matter.[9] However, he will clearly be in a position to discharge all or part of the claims made by the Commissioners and other creditors if the sums realised on liquidation exceed the costs incurred.

Traders taking part in a fraudulent chain of transactions are not immune from consequences.

(1) As regards a link in the chain consisting of a supply made to another trader in the UK repayment of the VAT credit claimed by the supplier may be delayed while his claim is investigated.[10] Input tax deducted in respect of the relevant purchase may be recovered from the trader if it is ascertained, having regard to objective factors, that he knew – or should have known – that, by his purchase, he was participating in a transaction connected with fraudulent evasion of VAT.[11]

(2) As regards a link in the chain consisting of a purported movement of goods to another member state, zero-rating may be withdrawn on similar grounds if the documentation relating to the movement does not stand up to examination.[12]

(3) Receiving or dealing with goods, and receiving services, are criminal offences if the recipient has reason to believe that VAT has been, or will be, evaded.[13]

(4) An action for damages may lie against one or more of the traders involved in the chain of supply for conspiracy to injure by unlawful means.[14]

A trader's choice between exempt transactions and taxable transactions may be based on a number of factors. These factors include tax considerations relating to the VAT system. If a taxable person chooses one of two transactions, the Sixth Directive does not require him to choose the one that involves paying the highest amount of VAT. On the contrary, taxpayers may choose to structure their businesses so as to limit their tax liability. However, EU law cannot be relied on for abusive ends, ie transactions solely for the purpose of wrongly obtaining advantages provided for by EU law, which have not been

[63.09] Introduction

carried out in the context of normal commercial operations. The principle of prohibiting abusive practices applies to VAT.[15]

The principle prohibiting the abuse of rights is intended to ensure, particularly in the field of VAT, that Community legislation is not extended to cover abusive practices by economic operators, ie transactions which are carried out solely for the purpose of wrongfully obtaining advantages provided for by Community law and which are not carried out in the context of normal commercial operations.[16]

An abusive practice exists in relation to a transaction meeting the formal conditions laid down by Directive 77/388/EEC, now Directive 2006/112/EC, and the national legislation transposing it, only if:[17]

(1) The transaction creates a tax advantage contrary to the purpose of those provisions.[18]
(2) The principal aim of the transaction is to obtain a tax advantage. This must be apparent from a number of objective factors. The national court may take account of the purely artifical nature of transactions and links of a legal, economic or personal nature between the operators involved in the scheme. However, abuse is irrelevant where the economic activity carried out may have some explanation other than the mere attainment of tax advantages.

It is for the national court to verify whether an abusive practice has taken place in the case before it.[19] In doing so, the national court is necessarily guided by any clarification of the foregoing conditions provided by the Court of Justice.[20]

The Government has reaffirmed its intention to counteract avoidance, in whatever form, on a number of occasions. Most recently, the Commissioners have started a national VAT anti-avoidance visiting programme,[21] introduced measures to block specific avoidance schemes[22] and, in a new departure, introduced[23] a requirement for taxable persons to notify[24] the Commissioners when they secure a tax advantage[25] by means of a scheme[26] falling within one or other of the following descriptions:

(1) A scheme (referred to in the legislation as a "designated scheme") of a description designated by Treasury order.[27]
(2) A scheme (referred to by the Commissioners as a "hallmarked scheme") that includes, or is associated with, a provision of a description designated by Treasury order and has as its main purpose, or one of its main purposes, the obtaining of a tax advantage by any person.[28]

De Voil Indirect Tax Service V2.210.

---

[1] *Gemeente Leusden and Holin Groep BV v Staatssecretaris van Financién* (joined cases C-487/01 and C-7/02) [2004] ECR I–5337 at para 76.
[2] Directive 2006/112/EC, art 1.
[3] For a recent outline of MITC fraud and its three variants, see in particular *R (on the application of Just Fabulous (UK) Ltd) v Revenue and Customs Comrs* [2007] EWHC 521 (Admin), [2008] STC 2123 at paras 4–10 and *Revenue and Customs Comrs v Livewire Telecom LTD* [2009] EWHC 15 (Ch) at para 1.
[4] For security in respect of another person's VAT liabilities, see infra, § **67.09**.

Administration [63.09]

5 For joint and several liability, see infra, § **67.10**.
6 *Customs and Excise Comrs v Federation of Technological Industries and others* (case C-384/04) [2006] ECR I-4191, [2006] STC 1483, ECJ.
7 See VATA 1994, ss 26AB, 55A, 69B and Sch 11 para 10(2A) as inserted by FA 2006, ss 19–21.
8 For the reverse charge on specified goods, see infra, § **65.41**.
9 For an action by the liquidator of a company to recover sums due from the customer but paid to a third party on the instructions of the company's sole director, see *Silversafe Ltd (in liquidation) v Hood* [2006] EWHC 1849 (Ch), [2007] STC 871.
10 See *R (on the application of Just Fabulous (UK) Ltd) v Revenue and Customs Comrs* [2007] EWHC 521 (Admin), [2008] STC 2123.
11 *Kittel v Belgian State; Belgian State v Recolta Recycling SPRL* (joined cases C-439/04 and C-440/04) [2006] ECR I-6161, [2008] STC 1537, ECJ For the withdrawal of input tax credit, see infra, § **66.06**.
12 For the relevant principles see infra, **69.07**.
13 VATA 1994, s 72(10).
14 *Revenue and Customs Comrs v Total Network SL* [2008] UKHL 19, [2008] STC 644, HL, where the alleged unlawful means comprised the common law offence of cheating the public revenue.
15 *Halifax plc and others v Customs and Excise Comrs* (case C-255/02) [2006] ECR I-1609, [2006] STC 919, ECJ at paras 68–70 and 73.
16 *Halifax plc and others v Customs and Excise Comrs* (case C-255/02) [2006] ECR I-1609, [2006] STC 919, ECJ at paras 69, 70 as restated in *Ampliscientifica Srl and another v Ministero dell'Economia e delle Finanze, Agenzia delle Entrate* (case C-162/07) [2008] ECR I-4109, [2008] SWTI 1387, ECJ at para 27.
17 *Halifax plc and others v Customs and Excise Comrs* (case C-255/02) [2006] ECR I-1609, [2006] STC 919, ECJ at paras 74, 75, 81 as modified in *Ministero dell'Economia e delle Finanze v Part Service Srl (in liquidation)* (case C-425/06) [2008] ECR I-897, [2008] STC 3132, ECJ at paras 42–45 and 58.
18 For the accrual of a tax advantage linked to exemption, see *Ministero dell'Economia e delle Finanze v Part Service Srl (in liquidation)* (case C-425/06) [2008] ECR I-897, [2008] STC 3132, ECJ at paras 59–61.
19 *Halifax plc and others v Customs and Excise Comrs* (case C-255/02) [2006] ECR I-1609, [2006] STC 919, ECJ at para 76. For a situation which gave rise to abuse, see *WHA Ltd and another v Revenue and Customs Comrs* [2007] EWCA Civ 728, [2008] STC 1695, CA. For a situation which did not, see *Weald Leasing Ltd v Revenue and Customs Comrs* [2008] EWHC 30 (Ch), [2008] STC 1601.
20 For guidance in relation to the deduction of input tax outside the context of normal commercial operations, see *Halifax plc and others v Customs and Excise Comrs* (case C-255/02) [2006] ECR I-1609, [2006] STC 919, ECJ at paras 77–80.
21 This programme was announced in Business Brief (Issue 14/03) 7 August 2003.
22 For recent examples, see FA 2004, ss 20 (VAT groups), 22 (private use for a nominal consideration of motor cars held as trading stock by motor dealers); VAT (Amendment) (No 5) Regulations, SI 2003/3220, reg 3 (continuous supplies of goods or services to a connected person), F(No 2)A 2005, s 1 (goods subject to a warehousing regime) and FA 2006, s 22 (face value vouchers).
23 VATA 1994, Sch 11A as inserted by FA 2004, s 19 and Sch 2; Finance Act 2004, section 19(1) and Schedule 2, (Appointed Day) Order, SI 2004/1934.
24 For the requirement to notify, see VATA 1994, Sch 11A, para 6 as inserted by FA 2004, s 19, Sch 2 and amended by F(No 2)A 2005, s 6, Sch 1. For exemption from

[63.09] Introduction

this requirement, see VATA 1994, Sch 11A, paras 6(2A), (4), (5), 7, 8 as so inserted and amended. For penalties for failure to disclose, see VATA 1994, Sch 11A, paras 10, 11 as so inserted and amended. For voluntary notifications, see VATA 1994, Sch 11A, para 9 as so inserted; VAT (Disclosure of Avoidance Schemes) Regulations, SI 2004/1929, reg 4.

25 As defined in VATA 1994, Sch 11A, para 2(1), (2) as substituted by F(No 2)A 2005, s 6 and Sch 1.
26 As defined in VATA 1994, Sch 11A, para 1 as inserted or amended by FA 2004, s 19, Sch 2 and F(No 2)A 2005, s 6, Sch 1.
27 VATA 1994, Sch 11A, paras 3, 5(1)(a) as inserted by FA 2004, s 19 and Sch 2. For the schemes designated, see VAT (Disclosure of Avoidance Schemes) Order, SI 2004/1933, Sch 1 as amended by SI 2005/1724. For the information to be notified, see VATA 1994, Sch 11A, para 6(2) as so inserted. For the time, form and manner of notification, see VAT (Disclosure of Avoidance Schemes) Regulations, SI 2004/1929, regs 2, 3.
28 VATA 1994, Sch 11A, paras 4, 5(1)(b), (2), (3) as inserted by FA 2004, s 19 and Sch 2. For the provisions designated, see VAT (Disclosure of Avoidance Schemes) Order, SI 2004/1933, Sch 2 as amended by SI 2005/1724. For the information to be notified and the time, form and manner of notification, see VAT (Disclosure of Avoidance Schemes) Regulations, SI 2004/1929, regs 2–4.

Taxable persons

Definition

[63.10] A person is a taxable person while he is, or is required to be, registered for the purposes of VAT.[1] A person is registered when his particulars are entered in the register of taxable persons maintained by the Commissioners.[2] This is done following a notification from the person that he is liable to registration or, if not liable to registration, that he wishes to be registered.[3]

A person required to be registered is a person who, being liable to registration, has failed to register. He becomes a taxable person on the date from which he should have been registered.[4] It follows that a person cannot escape his duties as a taxable person merely by disregarding the duty to register.[5]

De Voil Indirect Tax Service V2.101.

1 VATA 1994, s 3(1).
2 VATA 1994, s 3(3).
3 For liability, entitlement and eligibility for registration, see infra, § **63.10**.
4 For a registration held to be invalid when the person was registered with effect from an earlier date, see *Dyer v Customs and Excise Comrs* [2005] STC 715.
5 For the consequences of failing to register, see infra, § **64.14**.

Liability, entitlement and eligibility for registration

[63.11] A person is liable to registration if he makes taxable supplies or taxable acquisitions.

A general rule applies to any person making any taxable supplies. In principle, he is required to register if the value of his actual or expected taxable supplies exceeds the limit for the time being in force.[1] Special rules apply if the person has taken over a business as a going concern, made "direct sales" to private individuals from an EC member state, or (being an overseas trader receiving repayment of tax) he makes a taxable supply of business assets.[2] A person liable to registration under these provisions can claim exemption from registration in certain circumstances.[3]

A person making taxable acquisitions is required to register if the value of his actual or expected "relevant acquisitions" exceeds the limit for the time being in force.[4] A person liable to registration under these provisions can claim exemption from registration in certain circumstances.[5]

In broad terms, a person is entitled to registration as of right, or is eligible for registration at the Commissioners' discretion, in any of the following circumstances:[6]

(1) He makes taxable supplies or taxable acquisitions, but their value is below the registration threshold.
(2) He intends to make taxable supplies or taxable acquisitions.
(3) (If neither (1) nor (2) apply) he makes supplies outside the UK which, if made in the UK, would be taxable supplies.

De Voil Indirect Tax Service V2.134, 144, 146, 147, 190C.

---

[1] For liability to registration under this provision, see infra, §§ **64.02–64.03**.
[2] For liability to registration under these provisions, see infra, §§ **64.04, 64.10**.
[3] For exemption from registration under these provisions, see infra, §§ **64.21**.
[4] For liability to registration under this provision, see infra, § **64.12**.
[5] For exemption from registration under these provisions, see infra, § **64.23**.
[6] For entitlement to registration under these provisions, see infra, §§ **64.15–64.19**.

Persons liable, entitled or eligible for registration

[63.12] The term "person" clearly includes an individual. Under English law, it also includes a body of persons corporate or unincorporate.[1] Thus, the references to a "person" in the legislation contemplate a natural person (ie an individual),[2] a legal person (ie a body corporate), and a number of persons jointly carrying on an activity (eg the partners in a firm, the members of an unincorporated association or the trustees of a trust).

As regards the third class, the partners, members or trustees are registered collectively rather than individually. This does not confer any legal personality on a partnership. It merely reflects the joint liability of the partners for the VAT liabilities of the enterprise.[3] This appears to be what Glidewell LJ had in mind

[63.12] Introduction

when he said that a partnership is not a person within the meaning the VAT legislation.[4] A similar situation no doubt applies in relation to trusts and unincorporated associations.

A person is entitled to only one registration, and this includes all his businesses however diverse they may be.[5] There are two exceptions to this principle: a body corporate organised in divisions may apply for separate registrations for each division;[6] and limited partnerships having common partners, but different combinations of general and limited partners, are entitled to separate registrations.[7]

Bodies of natural and legal persons may be registered as a single taxable person in the following circumstances:

(1) Two or more bodies corporate eligible to be treated as members of a group may elect to be registered as a single taxable person.[8] The bodies included in the registration are frequently referred to collectively as a "VAT group".

(2) The Commissioners may serve a direction whereby the persons named therein are treated as a single taxable person carrying on the activities of a business described in the direction. A direction may be made for the purposes of preventing VAT avoidance arising from the maintenance or creation of any artificial separation of business activities carried on by two or more persons.[9] This is frequently referred to as "business splitting".

A club, association or organisation is treated as continuing notwithstanding changes in its membership.[10] A partnership is treated as continuing notwithstanding the admission of new partners or the retirement of existing partners. A partnership may be registered in the firm name.[11] The legislation is silent regarding the appointment and retirement of trustees.

Special provisions apply in determining whether a person is liable to register with the Commissioners under the UK legislation or with the Manx customs and excise service under the Isle of Man legislation.[12]

De Voil Indirect Tax Service V2.101, 103, 110, 112, 190C.

[1] Interpretation Act 1978, Sch 1.
[2] A natural person does not carry on a business independently of a company merely because he is the sole director, shareholder and member of staff of the company: see *J A van der Steen v Inspecteur van de Belastingdienst Utrecht-Gooi / kantoor Utrecht* (case C-355/06) [2007] ECR I–8863, [2007] SWTI 2406, ECJ.
[3] See *Customs and Excise Comrs v Evans* [1982] STC 342 at 348; *Scrace v Revenue and Customs Comrs* [2006] EWHC 2646 (Ch), [2007] STC 269 at paras 16, 17. For persons holding themselves out as partners in an application for registration, see *Revenue and Customs Comrs v Pal and others* [2006] EWHC 2016 (Ch), [2008] STC 2442.
[4] *Customs and Excise Comrs v Evans* [1982] STC 342 at 348
[5] *Customs and Excise Comrs v Glassborow* [1974] STC 142, [1974] 1 All ER 1041.
[6] VATA 1994, s 46(1).
[7] *Saunders v Customs and Excise Comrs* [1980] VATTR 53.
[8] For the formation and variation of VAT groups, see infra, § **66.37**.

[9] VATA 1994, Sch 1, paras 1A, 2 as inserted or amended by FA 1997, s 31.
[10] VATA 1994, s 46(3).
[11] VATA 1994, s 45(1).
[12] VAT (Isle of Man) Order, SI 1982/1067, arts 10–12.

VAT representatives

[63.13] The Commissioners face obvious difficulties in securing compliance by an overseas trader who does not have a presence in the UK.[1] The Commissioners may allow any such trader to voluntarily appoint a VAT representative. They may direct such a trader to appoint a VAT representative if, but only if, he is established in a third country which does not have mutual assistance arrangements with the UK.[2]

A VAT representative is not liable to registration,[3] but he is required to comply with specified notification requirements.[4] His rights and duties are specified and he has a personal liability for any breach of those duties so as to be liable to prosecution in certain circumstances.[5]

An overseas trader may be required to provide security if he fails to appoint a VAT representative when required to do so.[6] A VAT representative is liable to a penalty if he fails to notify his appointment or retirement to the Commissioners.[7]

[1] ie he meets the conditions in VATA 1994, s 48(1)(*a*), (*b*), (*c*) as amended by FA 2001, s 100.
[2] VATA 1994, s 48(1), (1A), (2) as amended by FA 2001, s 100.
[3] VATA 1994, s 48(4).
[4] VAT Regulations, SI 1995/2518, reg 10.
[5] VATA 1994, s 48(4), (5).
[6] VATA 1994, s 48(7).
[7] VATA 1994, s 69(1)(*b*).

Business

Importance

[63.14] Whether or not an activity amounts to the carrying on of a business is of considerable importance to the scheme of VAT in the following respects:

(1) A trader is liable to register by reference to supplies made in the course or furtherance of business and goods acquired in the course or furtherance of business.[1]

(2) His supplies are charged to tax only if they are made in the course or furtherance of business.[2]

(3) Any VAT he incurs is recoverable from the Commissioners as input tax only if the goods or services concerned are used or to be used for the purposes of his business.[3]

[63.14] Introduction

De Voil Indirect Tax Service V2.201A.

1   VATA 1994, Sch 1, para 19, Sch 2, para 10(d), Sch 3, para 11(a), Sch 3A, para 9(1)(b) as inserted by FA 2000, s 136.
2   VATA 1994, s 4(1).
3   VATA 1994, s 24(1).

Meaning of 'business'

[63.15] Although the UK legislation and Directive 2006/112/EC use different terminology—"business" in the UK and "economic activity" in the directive—the UK legislation must be construed, as far as possible, to give effect to the directive.[1] In most cases, it seems likely that the terms may be regarded as synonymous. However, the UK legislation does not, in terms, reflect the special regime applicable to "states, regional and local government authorities and other bodies governed by public law" set out in Directive 2006/112/EC art 13.[2] This provision has direct effect (so that a public body can rely on it), but it is doubtful whether the UK legislation can be interpreted in a manner which gives effect to it (so that the Commissioners can enforce it against a public body).[3]

The leading UK case on the meaning of "business"[4] was decided before the Sixth Directive was adopted and many of the subsequent cases made no reference to it. These cases do not, therefore, provide an authoritative interpretation of the Sixth Directive, although they may provide useful guidelines on matters not expressly covered by it and possible answers to questions not yet considered by the Court of Justice.[5]

It has been said that it will never be possible or desirable to define the word exhaustively[6] and that it does not have the same meaning wherever used in the VAT legislation.[7] Moreover, similar activities carried on by different persons may amount to a business in some cases but not in others.[8] However, the earlier UK case law suggests that the following considerations should be taken into account in deciding whether an activity amounts to a business, although they are not principles which are conclusive in every case:

(1) Whether the activity is a "serious undertaking earnestly pursued" or "a serious occupation not necessarily confined to commercial or profit making undertakings".
(2) Whether the activity is an occupation or function actively pursued with reasonable or recognisable continuity.
(3) Whether the activity has a certain measure of substance as measured by quarterly or annual value of taxable supplies made.
(4) Whether the activity is conducted in a regular manner and on sound and recognised business principles.
(5) Whether the activity is predominantly concerned with the making of taxable supplies to consumers for a consideration.
(6) Whether the taxable supplies are of a kind which, subject to differences of detail, are commonly made by those who seek to profit by them.[9]

It has been said that a business or commercial purpose is characterised, in particular, by a concern to maximise returns on capital investment.[10] Thus, independent notaries and bailiffs carried on an economic activity in *EC Commission v Netherlands*[11] because their purpose was to cover their overheads and provide themselves with income. However, activities do not need to be carried on with the object of making a profit in order to amount to a business.[12]

An activity does not become an economic activity merely because money is paid and a benefit obtained: the activity must have some "economic" content.[13] On the other hand, supplying goods and services without charge does not amount to an economic activity.[14]

An activity does not cease to be an economic activity, if that is what it is, merely because the relevant transactions are carried out for a tax avoidance purpose,[15] or because they form part of a chain of transactions in which one or more of the participants misappropriate VAT.[16]

De Voil Indirect Tax Service V2.201–213, 231–236.

---

[1] *Institute of Chartered Accountants in England and Wales v Customs and Excise Comrs* [1999] STC 398 at 402, HL.

[2] For contrasting views on the implementation of art 4(5), see *Glasgow City Council v Customs and Excise Comrs* (1998) VAT decision 15391 and *Isle of Wight Council v Customs and Excise Comrs* (2004) VAT decision 1855 (not implemented); Business Brief (Issue 11/2003), 24 July 2003 and Business Brief (Issue 18/04), 13 July 2004 (implemented); *Rhondda Cynon Taff County Borough Council v Customs and Excise Comrs* [2000] V & DR 150 (provision applied). For the absence of proper implementation measures in Ireland, see *EC Commission v Ireland (case C-554/07)* [2009] ECR I–0000.

[3] *Customs and Excise Comrs v Isle of Wight Council* [2004] EWHC 2541 (Ch), [2005] STC 257.

[4] *Customs and Excise Comrs v Morrison's Academy Boarding Houses Association* [1978] STC 1.

[5] *Wellcome Trust Ltd v Customs and Excise Comrs* (1994) VAT decision 12206.

[6] Per Lord Emslie in *Customs and Excise Comrs v Morrison's Academy Boarding Houses Association* [1978] STC 1 at 6.

[7] *Singer & Friedlander Ltd v Customs and Excise Comrs* [1989] VATTR 27, [1989] 1 CMLR 814 (meaning in VATA 1994, s 9 differs from that given in relation to ss 24–26 in *Customs and Excise Comrs v Apple and Pear Development Council* [1986] STC 192, HL).

[8] For an example, see *University of Southampton v Revenue and Customs Comrs* [2006] EWHC 528 (Ch), [2006] STC 1389 (publicly funded research).

[9] *Customs and Excise Comrs v Lord Fisher* [1981] STC 238, [1981] 2 All ER 147.

[10] *Floridienne SA v Belgium* (case C-142/99) [2000] STC 1044 at [28], ECJ.

[11] (Case 235/85) [1987] ECR 1471, ECJ.

[12] *Customs and Excise Comrs v Morrison's Academy Boarding Houses Association* [1978] STC 1.

[13] *Institute of Chartered Accountants in England and Wales v Customs and Excise Comrs* [1999] STC 398 at 404, HL. For examples of activities lacking an economic content, see infra, § **63.17**.

[63.15] Introduction

[14] *Staatssecretaris van Financiën v Hong-Kong Trade Development Council: 89/81* [1982] ECR 1277, ECJ (providing trade information without charge).
[15] *Halifax plc v Customs and Excise Comrs* (case C-255/02) [2006] ECR I-1609, [2006] STC 919, ECJ; *University of Huddersfield Higher Education Corp v Customs and Excise Comrs* (case C- 223/03) [2006] ECR I-1751, [2006] STC 980, ECJ.
[16] *Optigen Ltd v Customs and Excise Comrs* (joined cases C-354/03, C-355/03 and C-484/04) [2006] ECR I-483, [2006] STC 419, ECJ.

Activities specifically treated as a business

[63.16] The general definition in supra. § 63.14 provides helpful guidance regarding the activities which do or do not amount to the carrying on of a business. The relevant legislation and the decided cases are more specific. A business includes, among other things:[1]

(1) Carrying on any trade, profession or vocation.[2]
(2) Exploiting tangible and intangible property for the purpose of obtaining income on a continuing basis[3], but not in the passive role of an investor.[4] A letting does not amount to exploitation of tangible property merely because the transaction takes place. The transaction must also have an economic character.[5]
(3) The provision of facilities or advantages[6] by a club, association or organisation to its members[7] for a subscription or other consideration.[8]
(4) Admitting persons to any premises for a consideration.[9]
(5) Specified activities carried on by states, regional and local government authorities, and other bodies governed by public law, unless the activities are carried out on such a small scale as to be negligible.[10]
(6) Supplies made by government departments[11] specified in a Treasury direction.[12]
(7) The activities of bodies carrying out statutory duties where supplies are made to the public[13] for a consideration.[14]

De Voil Indirect Tax Service V2.201–213, 231–236.

[1] *Customs and Excise Comrs v Morrison's Academy Boarding Houses Association* [1978] STC 1.
[2] VATA 1994, s 94(1).
[3] Directive 2006/112/EC art 9(1). Under EC law, see *Rompelman v Minister van Financiën* (case 268/83) [1985] ECR 655, ECJ (right to future transfer of property); *Van Tiem v Staatssecretaris van Financiën* (case C-186/89) [1993] STC 91, ECJ (grant of building rights); *Enkler v Finanzamt Homberg* (case C-230/94) [1996] STC 1316, ECJ (hire of goods); *Banque Bruxelles Lambert SA v Belgium* (case C-8/03) [2004] ECR I-10157, [2004] STC 1643, ECJ (open-ended investment company). In the UK, see *Adstock Ltd v Customs and Excise Comrs* (1993) VAT decision 10034 (fishing rights); *Three H Aircraft Hire v Customs and Excise Comrs* [1982] STC 653, *Coleman v Customs and Excise Comrs* [1976] VATTR 24, *Walker v Customs and Excise Comrs* [1976] VATTR 10, *Wilcox v Customs and Excise Comrs* [1978] VATTR 79 (hire of assets).

Business **[63.17]**

4   For the distinction between business and investment, see *Tarrakarn Ltd v Customs and Excise Comrs* [1996] V & DR 516. For investment, see infra, § **63.16**.
5   *Customs and Excise Comrs v Yarburgh Children's Trust* [2002] STC 207 (lease by charitable trust to playgroup not constituting an economic activity); *Laurie and Laurie v Customs and Excise Comrs* (2001) VAT decision 17219 (lease and leaseback arrangement entered into for tax avoidance purposes).
6   For "facilities" and "advantages", see *Customs and Excise Comrs v British Field Sports Society* [1998] STC 315, CA.
7   Membership involves an element of participation or belonging: *Compassion in World Farming Ltd v Customs and Excise Comrs* [1997] V & DR 281.
8   VATA 1994, s 94(2)(a). See *Eastbourne Town Radio Cars Association v Customs and Excise Comrs* [2001] UKHL/19, [2001] STC 606 (communications network for private car hire drivers); *Carlton Lodge Club v Customs and Excise Comrs* [1974] STC 507, [1974] 3 All ER 798; *Customs and Excise Comrs v British Field Sports Society* [1988] STC 315, CA (campaigning activities); *Royal Ulster Constabulary Athletic Association Ltd v Customs and Excise Comrs* [1989] VATTR 17; *Friends of the Ironbridge Gorge Museum v Customs and Excise Comrs* [1991] VATTR 97; *Northamptonshire Football Association v Customs and Excise Comrs* (1995) VAT decision 12936. This includes a consideration paid to a third party: *Lord Advocate v Largs Golf Club* [1985] STC 226. It also includes facilities or advantages provided for a consideration to non-members: *Cambuslang Athletic Club v Customs and Excise Comrs* (1984) VAT decision 1592; but not those provided without consideration: *British Olympic Association v Customs and Excise Comrs* [1979] VATTR 122.
9   VATA 1994, s 94(2)(b). See *Eric Taylor Deceased Testimonial Match Committee v Customs and Excise Comrs* [1975] VATTR 8.
10 Directive 2006/112/EC, art 13(1) and Annex I.
11 As defined in VATA 1994, s 41(6)–(8).
12 VATA 1994, s 41(2), (5). For the direction in force, see Treasury Direction dated 29 October 2008 (*London Gazette*, 10 November 2008).
13 *National Water Council v Customs and Excise Comrs* [1979] STC 157.
14 *Customs and Excise Comrs v Apple and Pear Development Council* [1986] STC 192, HL.

Activities which do not amount to a business

[63.17] The following activities do not amount to the carrying on of a business activity:

(1)   The services of employees.[1]
(2)   Activities that are no more than an activity for pleasure and social enjoyment.[2]
(3)   Activities lacking an economic content that provide a service to the community.[3]
(4)   Activities that amount to no more than holding stocks and shares for the purpose of obtaining dividends.[4]

[63.17] Introduction

(5) The mere acquisition of financial holdings in other undertakings by a holding company. However, there may be an economic activity if the holding company has a direct or indirect involvement in the management of its subsidiaries and makes taxable supplies to them, eg administrative, financial, commercial or technical services.[5]

(6) Transactions carried out in the capacity of a public authority by states, regional and local government authorities, and other bodies governed by public law—even if a charge is made—unless this would lead to a significant distortion of competition.[6]

(7) Activities of public bodies performed exclusively for ministers or other public bodies.[7]

(8) Statutory duties funded by a statutory levy and performed by a public body,[8] although this does not appear to be so if the same duties are also carried out by commercial enterprises authorised to do so in accordance with the statutory scheme.[9]

(9) The issuing of licences by a national regulatory authority.[10]

De Voil Indirect Tax Service V2.201–213, 231–236.

---

[1] Directive 2006/112/EC arts 9(1), 10. For an example, see *Dimosio v Karageorgou (joined cases C-78/02 to C-80/02)* [2003] ECR I-13295, ECJ. For the distinction between contracts of service and contracts for services in the UK, see *Berbrooke Fashions v Customs and Excise Comrs* [1977] VATTR 168; *New Way School of Motoring Ltd v Customs and Excise Comrs* [1979] VATTR 57; *Customs and Excise Comrs v Hodges* [2000] STC 262. See also *Nasim v Customs and Excise Comrs* [1987] STC 387, where the taxpayer carried out various duties in respect of a business of which she had wholly divested herself.

[2] *Customs and Excise Comrs v Lord Fisher* [1981] STC 238, [1981] 2 All ER 147 and contrast *Williams v Customs and Excise Comrs* (1996) VAT decision 14240. For racehorse breeding, training and dealing, see Notice No 700/67.

[3] *EC Commission v France* (case 50/87) [1988] ECR 4797 (lettings at low rent by local authority to associations with social objectives or undertakings establishing themselves in the locality). In the UK, see *Customs and Excise Comrs v Yarburgh Children's Trust* [2002] STC 207 (lease to playgroup with a purpose of providing day care facilities for children); *Customs and Excise Comrs v St Paul's Community Project Ltd* [2004] EWHC 2490 (Ch), [2005] STC 95 (day nursery); *Greater London Red Cross Blood Transfusion Service v Customs and Excise Comrs* [1983] VATTR 241. Contrast *Riverside Housing Association Ltd v Revenue and Customs Comrs* [2006] EWHC 2383 (Ch), [2006] STC 2072 (housing association). For the Commissioners' policy regarding non-profit making bodies, see Business Brief 2/05, 10 February 2005.

[4] *Harnas & Helm CV v Staatssecretaris van Financién* (case C-80/85) [1997] STC 384, ECJ; *The Wellcome Trust Ltd v Customs and Excise Comrs* (case C-155/94) [1996] STC 945. For holding companies, see supra, § **62.13**. In the UK, see *NSPCC v Customs and Excise Comrs* [1992] VATTR 417; Business Brief (Issue 21/96), 17 October 1996.

[5] *Polysar Investments Netherlands BV v Inspecteur der Invoerrechten en Accijnzen, Arnhem* (case C-60/90) [1993] STC 222, ECJ (holding company); *Sofitam SA v Ministre Chargé du Budget* (case C-333/91) [1997] STC 226, ECJ; *Floridienne SA v Belgium* (case C-142/99) [2000] STC 1044, ECJ; *Cibo Participations SA v*

Directeur régional des impôts du Nord-Pas-de-Calais (case C-16/00) [2002] STC 460, ECJ.

[6] Directive 2006/112/EC art 13(1); *Ufficio Distrettuale delle Imposte Dirette di Fiorenzuola d'Arda v Commune di Carpaneto Piacentino* (joined cases 231/87 and 129/88) [1991] STC 205, ECJ; *Commune di Carpaneto v Ufficio Provinciale Imposta sul Valore Aggiunto di Piacenza* (case 4/89) [1990] 3 CMLR 153, ECJ; *Finanzamt Augsburg-Stadt v Marktgemeinde Welden* (case C-247/95) [1997] STC 531, ECJ; *EC Commission v United Kingdom* (case C-359/97) [2000] STC 777, ECJ; *Fazenda Pública v Câmara Municipal do Porto (Ministério Público, third party)* (case C-446/98) [2001] STC 560, ECJ. For activities resulting in a significant distortion of competition, see *Revenue and Customs Comrs v Isle of Wight Borough Council* (case C-288/07) [2008] ECR I-0000, [2008] STC 2964, [2009] STC 1096, ECJ, The distortion of competition may be to the detriment of public authorities or their private competitors: *Finanzamt Düsseldorf-Süd v SALIX Grundstücks-Vermietungsgellschaft mbH & Co Objekt Offenbach KG* (case C-102/08) [2009] ECR I-0000, [2009] STC 1607, ECJ. In the UK, see *Institute of Chartered Accountants of England and Wales v Customs and Excise Comrs* [1999] STC 398, HL; *West Devon Borough Council v Customs and Excise Comrs* [2001] STC 1282; *Customs and Excise Comrs v Isle of Wight Council* [2004] EWHC 2541 (Ch), [2005] STC 257; *Edinburgh Telford College v R & C Comrs* [2006] CSIH 13, [2006] STC 1291; *Cambridge University v Revenue and Customs Comrs* [2009] EWHC 434 (Ch), [2009] STC 1288; *Revenue and Customs Comrs v Isle of Wight Borough Council* [2009] EWHC 592 (Ch), [2009] STC 1098 (case remitted to tribunal for rehearing); *Radio Authority v Customs and Excise Comrs* [1992] VATTR 155; *Arts Council of Great Britain v Customs and Excise Comrs* [1994] VATTR 313; *Rhonnda Cynon Taff County Borough Council v Customs and Excise Comrs* [2000] V & DR 150; *Cardiff Community Housing Association Ltd v Customs and Excise Comrs* [2000] V & DR 346; Business Brief 9/95, 18 May 1995 (supplies between local authorities).

[7] *National Water Council v Customs and Excise Comrs* [1979] STC 157.

[8] *Customs and Excise Comrs v Apple and Pear Development Council* [1986] STC 192, HL; refd. [1988] STC 221, ECJ.

[9] Building regulation fees fall within this description. For the Commissioners' views, see Business Brief (Issue 5/97) 5 March 1997.

[10] *Hutchison 3G UK Ltd v Customs and Excise Comrs* (case C-369/04) [2007] ECR I-5247, [2008] STC 218, ECJ and *T-Mobile v Austria* (case C-284/04), [2007] ECR I-5189, [2008] STC 184, ECJ (licences to use a defined part of the radio-frequency spectrum reserved for telecommunications services).,

Supplies

Introduction

[63.18] A trader may become a taxable person, and thus liable to registration, if he makes supplies. If he is a taxable person, he is required to charge tax on some or all of the supplies he makes. The supplies giving rise to registration,

[63.18] Introduction

or a charge to tax, are referred to as "taxable supplies". A supply must meet the following conditions in order to be a taxable supply:

(1) It must be made for a consideration.[1] In principle, a transaction is not a supply, and is therefore outside the scope of tax, if made without consideration. However, a number of free transactions are specifically stated to be supplies of goods, or supplies of services, so as to be charged to tax.[2]

(2) It must be a supply of goods or a supply of services.[3] A number of transactions are treated as neither a supply of goods nor a supply of services. These supplies are outside the scope of tax.

(3) It must be made in the UK.[4] A supply made outside the UK is not charged to tax in the UK. It may, however, give rise to a liability to register as a taxable person, and to charge tax, in another EC member state.

(4) It must be made in the course or furtherance of business.[5]

(5) It must not be exempted from tax.[6]

De Voil Indirect Tax Service V3.122.

[1] VATA 1994, s 5(2)(a).
[2] VATA 1994, Sch 4 para 5(1), (4). For the charge to tax on these supplies, see infra, §§ **65.28–65.31**.
[3] VATA 1994, ss 1(1)(a), 4(1), 5(1)–(3).
[4] VATA 1994, ss 1(1)(a), 4.
[5] VATA 1994, s 4(1) and Sch 1, para 19.
[6] VATA 1994, s 4(2).

Supplies

General principles

[63.19] Supply, in the enigmatic words of the parliamentary draftsman, "includes all forms of supply".[1] It is submitted that the term is no more than a generic description given to transfers in the possession or ownership of goods, the grant, assignment or surrender of rights in property and the provision of facilities or services. It thus includes transactions known by a myriad of names in everyday commercial life, eg sale, hire, loan, and so on. On this basis, "a supply" is something that is supplied.

VAT is a general tax on consumption.[2] Thus, that which is done must give rise to consumption, and this must involve either the provision of services to an identifiable consumer or the provision of a benefit capable of forming a cost component of another person's activity in the commercial chain.[3] It follows that a trader is not regarded as making a supply of goods or services merely because he receives money, goods or services from another person.[4]

It is necessary to identify the person making the supply (in order to determine who is liable to register or charge tax)[5] and the person receiving the goods or services concerned (in order to determine who is entitled to an input tax credit, repayment or refund in respect of the tax charged).[6] It is also necessary to identify the true legal description of that which has been supplied in order to determine whether it falls within the scope of tax and, if so, whether any tax is chargeable on it.[7]

The true nature of a supply or, indeed, whether a supply has been made, is necessarily resolved by reference to the contract between the parties,[8] or to the general law. In practice, contracts may be less than helpful. After all, they are concerned with the private law obligations of the parties and do not need to define the tax consequences flowing from them.[9] Moreover, a contract may be made orally and a written contract may be supplemented orally. In these cases, it may be necessary to consider what (if any) implications can be drawn from such matters as statute, custom, usage, previous dealings between the parties and so on, and how the parties gave effect to their agreement.[10] Furthermore, a contract may not tell the whole story, or be equivocal about who is supplying what to whom. In these circumstances, it is necessary to "stand back and look at the characteristics of the provision and payment in issue in a relatively robust and commonsensical way, not bound by a strict analysis of the mesh of contracts or the language used in them"[11] in order to discover what one tribunal referred to as the "real deal" between the parties.[12]

The nature of a supply is determined at the time of supply[13] and cannot be rewritten by reference to the unilateral act of one party or an agreement between both parties.[14]

The tax consequences flowing from a transaction may be affected by some impropriety arising from the nature of the goods or services supplied or the manner in which they are supplied. In principle, a transaction does not cease to be a supply merely because it is void (eg the sale of a stolen car),[15] it infringes a third party's rights (eg the sale of counterfeit perfume),[16] the conditions for carrying it out lawfully have not been met (eg the unlawful operation of a game of chance),[17] the goods and services are used by the purchaser to carry on an unlawful activity (eg table rented to a drug dealer),[18] it is carried out with the sole aim of obtaining a tax advantage without any other economic objective[19] or, although not vitiated by VAT fraud, it forms part of a chain of transactions in which one or more of the other participants misappropriates VAT without the relevant supplier knowing or having any means of knowing this.[20] However, no supply is made by the person from whom goods are stolen,[21] or if the goods or services germane to a transaction are subject to an outright ban on the supplier and recipient alike.[22]

De Voil Indirect Tax Service V3.102.

---

1   VATA 1994, s 5(2)(a).
2   Directive 67/227/EEC, art 2 (the First Directive) (repealed).
3   *Mohr v Finanzamt Bad Segeberg* (case C-215/94) [1996] STC 328, ECJ; *Landboden-Agrardienste GmbH & Co KG v Finanzamt Calau* (case C-384/95) [1998] STC 171, ECJ. For a transfer of title to goods meeting this requirement, see *Stewart (t/a GT Shooting) v Customs and Excise Comrs* [2002] STC 255, CA (compensation for firearms surrendered for destruction).
4   For examples, see *Tolsma v Inspecteur der Omzetbelasting Leeuwarden* (case C-16/93) [1994] STC 509, ECJ (donations solicited by organ-grinder); *Mohr v Finanzamt Bad Segeberg* (case C-215/94) [1996] STC 328, ECJ (grant for discon-

tinuing milk production); *Landboden-Agrardienste GmbH & Co KG v Finanzamt Calau* (case C-384/95) [1998] STC 171, ECJ (compensation for undertaking to reduce potato production under national scheme); *KapHag Renditefonds, 35 Spreecenter Berlin-Hellersdorf 3 Tranche GbR v Finanzamt Charlottenburg:* C-442/01 [2003] ECR I–6851, [2005] STC 1500, ECJ (cash contribution on admission to a partnership) and Business Brief (Issue 21/04) 10 August 2004, Business Brief (Issue 30/04) 19 November 2004 (wider implications of partnership contributions); *Kretztechnik AG v Finanzamt Linz* (case C-465/03) [2005] ECR I–4357, [2005] STC 1118, ECJ and Business Brief (Issue 21/05) 23 November 2005, Business Brief (Issue 22/05) 2 December 2005 (new shares and other securities issued by a company); *Société thermale d'Eugénie-les-Bains v Ministère de l'Économie, des Finances et de l'Industrie* (case C-277/05), [2007] ECR I–6815, [2007] SWTI 1866, ECJ (hotel deposit retained on cancellation of reservation); *Warwick Masonic Rooms Ltd v Customs and Excise Comrs* (1979) VAT decision 839 (unsolicited donation); *NDP Co Ltd v Customs and Excise Comrs* [1988] VATTR 40 (voluntary restaurant gratuity); *Hillingdon Legal Resources Centre Ltd v Customs and Excise Comrs* [1991] VATTR 39 (local authority grant); *Sleaford RFC v Customs and Excise Comrs* (1993) VAT decision 9844 (match fees).

5 For examples, see *Spearmint Rhino Venturers (UK) Ltd v Revenue and Customs Comrs* [2007] EWHC 613 (Ch), [2007] STC 1252 (whether supplies made by a club or by the women performing entertainment services for customers at the club); *Lancashire County Council v Customs and Excise Comrs* [1996] V & DR 550 (whether supplies made by school or local education authority).
6 See *Customs and Excise Comrs v Redrow Group Ltd* [1999] STC 161, HL.
7 See, for example, *Customs and Excise Comrs v Sai Jewellers* [1996] STC 269 (whether contracts for exchange or refashioning of jewellery); *Keydon Estates Ltd v Customs and Excise Comrs* (1990) VAT decision 4471 (whether trader received a share of partnership profits or consideration for supply geared to customer's actual profit).
8 For the court's approach, see in particular *Customs and Excise Comrs v Automobile Association* [1974] STC 192; *British Airports Authority v Customs and Excise Comrs* [1977] STC 36, CA; *British Railways Board v Customs and Excise Comrs* [1977] STC 221, CA; *Telewest Communications plc v Customs and Excise Comrs* [2005] EWCA Civ 102, [2005] STC 481; *Customs and Excise Comrs v Scott* [1978] STC 191; *Dyrham Park Country Club v Customs and Excise Comrs* [1978] VATTR 244. For recent examples, see *Tesco plc v Customs and Excise Comrs* [2003] EWCA Civ 1367, [2003] STC 1561, CA; *Debenhams Retail plc v Revenue and Customs Comrs* [2005] EWCA Civ 892, [2005] STC 1155, CA; *Ford Motor Company Ltd v Revenue and Customs Comrs* [2007] EWCA Civ 1370, [2008] STC 1016, CA; *MBNA Europe Bank Ltd v Revenue and Customs Comrs* [2006] EWHC 2326 (Ch), [2006] STC 2089; *Highland Council v Revenue and Customs Comrs* [2007] CSIH 36, [2008] STC 1280; *Revenue and Customs Comrs v Board of Governors of Robert Gordon University* [2008] CSIH 22, [2008] STC 1890.
9 *Customs and Excise Comrs v Reed Personnel Services Ltd* [1995] STC 588 at 595.
10 *Customs and Excise Comrs v Music and Video Exchange Ltd* [1992] STC 220 at 222-223.
11 Per Lindsay J in *Revenue and Customs Comrs v Loyalty Management UK Ltd* [2006] EWHC 1498 (Ch), [2007] STC 536 at para 78.
12 *Debenhams Retail plc v Customs and Excise Comrs* (2003) VAT decision 18169.

Supplies **[63.20]**

13 *W F Graham (Northampton) Ltd v Customs and Excise Comrs* (1980) VAT decision 908.
14 *Castle Associates Ltd v Customs and Excise Comrs* (1989) VAT decision 3497. For examples, see *Mannesmann Demag Hamilton Ltd v Customs and Excise Comrs* [1983] VATTR 156 (repossessed machine); *M E Braine (Boatbuilders) Ltd v Customs and Excise Comrs* (1989) VAT decision 3881 (boat acquired following dispute regarding repair); *Rickard v Customs and Excise Comrs* (1989) VAT decision 3711 (payment for supply treated as loan). Contrast *Kwik Fit (GB) Ltd v Customs and Excise Comrs* [1992] VATTR 427 (contractual right to return goods); *AEG (UK) Ltd v Customs and Excise Comrs* [1993] VATTR 379 (cancellation of call-out charge if appliance purchased).
15 *Customs and Excise Comrs v Oliver* [1980] STC 73, [1980] 1 All ER 353; *Libdale Ltd v Customs and Excise Comrs* [1993] VATTR 425.
16 *R v Goodwin and Unstead* [1997] STC 22, CA; refd sub nom *Criminal proceedings against Goodwin* (case C-3/97) [1998] STC 699, ECJ.
17 *Fischer v Finanzamt Donaueschingen* (case C-238/95) [1998] STC 708, ECJ. See also *R v Citrone* [1999] STC 29, CA (anabolic steroids).
18 *Staatssecretaris van Financiën v Coffeeshop Siberië* (case C-158/98) [1999] STC 742, ECJ. See also *Customs and Excise Comrs v Polok* [2002] STC 361 (escort agency).
19 *Halifax plc and others v Customs and Excise Comrs* (case C-255/02) [2006] ECR I–1609, [2006] STC 919, ECJ; *University of Huddersfield Higher Education Corpn v Customs and Excise Comrs* (case C-223/03) [2006] ECR I–1751, [2006] STC 980, ECJ.
20 *Optigen Ltd v Customs and Excise Comrs* (joined cases C-354/03, C-355/03 and C-484/03) [2006] ECR I–483, [2006] STC 419, ECJ.
21 *British American Tobacco International Ltd and another v Belgian State* (case C 435/03) [2005] ECR I 7077, [2006] STC 158, ECJ.
22 *Vereniging Happy Family Rustenburgerstraat v Inspecteur der Omzetbelasting* (case 289/86) [1989] 3 CMLR 729, ECJ (narcotic drugs); cf *Witzemann v Hauptzollamt-Munchen-Mitte* (case C-343/89) [1993] STC 108, ECJ (counterfeit currency).

Practical problems

[63.20] A number of practical problems arise in deciding whether anything has been supplied and, if so, the identity of the parties or the nature of that which was supplied.

Difficulties can arise in deciding who supplied what to whom when there are three parties to a transaction. It may be necessary to identify the relationship between the parties in order to decide what supplies have been made. For example, if X (the proprietor) operates of a hairdressing salon where a number of hairdressers (Y) perform the work done for customers (Z), X makes a supply to Z if Y are employees, but X makes a supply to Y (a chair rent) and Y makes a supply to Z (hairdressing services) if Y are independent contractors. It is necessary to determine the nature of the contractual arrangements between X, Y and Z before the VAT implications flowing from them can be determined.[1] It is immaterial whether the customer is aware of the identity of the supplier.[2]

[63.20] Introduction

There are many variations on this theme. Thus, for example, the courts have been called upon to decide:

(1) Whether Y acts as agent in relation to a transaction between X and Z.[3]
(2) Whether something passing from X to Z involves an intermediate supply so that X makes a supply to Y and Y makes a supply to Z.[4]
(3) Whether X and Y carry on a joint venture so that the supply to Z does not involve an intermediate supply by Y to X.[5]
(4) Whether X and Y both make supplies to Z.[6] An arrangement between X and Y may, in addition, involve a side payment by X to Y[7] or by Y or X.[8]
(5) Whether Y consumes something supplied by X or supplies it on to Z.[9]

Business promotion schemes have posed particular problems over the years. It is necessary to establish the identity of the parties to a particular scheme in order to determine who supplies what to whom, the nature of the supply or supplies they make, the value of those supplies and whether they are taxed or exempted from tax. The absence of specific Community legislation[10] has given rise to a rich tapestry of case law in relation to such matters as gift voucher schemes,[11] cash back schemes,[12] money-off schemes,[13] "free gift" schemes,[14] discount voucher schemes,[15] payment cards,[16] points schemes,[17] interest-free credit[18] and introductory gifts.[19]

A service performed for a customer may give rise to a number of benefits for which a single charge is made. It is necessary to decide whether the charge made represents the consideration for a single supply or for a number of different supplies.[20] In some cases, it is helpful to look at the benefits in terms of what is "principal" and what is "ancillary".[21] In other cases, it is inappropriate to analyse the benefits in this way, and it is unhelpful to strain the meaning of "ancillary" in an attempt to do so.[22] A supply comprising of two or more elements which are so closely linked that they form objectively a single indivisible economic supply is capable of attracting a different tax treatment from that which would be attracted by even the main element of the supply.[23]

Similar problems arise when separate payments are made at different times, or different matters are separately itemised on the same invoice. In either case, it is necessary to decide whether each payment or itemised amount represents the consideration for a different supply or a single consideration for one supply. It is necessary to determine how many supplies have been made before their nature, and therefore the tax consequences flowing from them, can be determined.[24] Considerations due to separate suppliers cannot be fused to make a single supply.[25] Similarly, if a supply made by X is ancillary to a supply made by Y, it does not follow that the tax treatment of the supplies should be the same.[26]

The relevant principles have been summarised by Briggs J in the following terms:[27]

(1) The identification of the taxable supply or supplies made by the taxpayer pursuant to a particular transaction is, at least where the transaction consists of a contract, limited to the goods or services provided by the taxpayer for which the payment is consideration.

(2) Prima facie every supply of a good or of a service must normally be regarded as distinct and independent.

(3) None the less the functioning of the VAT system would be distorted if what is in substance a single service from an economic point of view were artificially split.

(4) The relevant transaction must be analysed with due regard to all the circumstances in which it takes place.

(5) The essential features of the relevant transaction must be ascertained in order to determine whether the taxable person is supplying the customer, being a typical customer, with several distinct principal services or with a single service.

(6) The fact that the goods and/or services are supplied in consideration of a single price may suggest that for VAT purposes there is a single supply, but this is not decisive.

(7) Where elements of the consideration are ancillary to another element or elements which is or are identified as the principal service, then there will be a single VAT supply of the principal service, and the ancillary elements will be treated as part of that principal supply. A service will be regarded as ancillary to a principal service if it does not constitute for customers an aim in itself, but a means of better enjoying the principal service supplied.

(8) It does not follow that every distinct part of the goods or services provided pursuant to a transaction is a separate supply for VAT purposes unless it is "ancillary". Separate non-ancillary parts of the consideration provided pursuant to a transaction may be so closely linked from an economic perspective so as to constitute a single supply for VAT purposes.

(9) In circumstances where the application of the principle in (8) above leads to the identification of a single supply, its character for VAT purposes may be that of one or other of the constituent elements, if predominant. Alternatively it may have a unique character enjoyed by neither of the constituent elements.

De Voil Indirect Tax Service V3.102, 105–107.

---

[1] For examples of supplies to Z made by X (who engaged the persons who actually carried out the work), see *Cronin v Customs and Excise Comrs* [1991] STC 333 (driving school); *Customs and Excise Comrs v Jane Montgomery (Hair Stylists) Ltd* [1994] STC 256 (hairdresser); *Clark v Customs and Excise Comrs* [1996] STC 263 (bus service). For supplies to Z made by Y (the person who actually carried out the work), see for example *Customs and Excise Comrs v MacHenrys (Hairdressers) Ltd* [1993] STC 170, *Kieran Mullin Ltd* [2003] STC 274 (hairdresser renting chair in salon); *Carless v Customs and Excise Comrs* [1993] STC 632 (taxi driver); *Customs and Excise Comrs v Reed Personnel Services Ltd* [1995] STC 588 (agency nurse); *Lancashire County Council v Customs and Excise Comrs* [1996] V & DR 550 (school photographer).

[2] *Customs and Excise Comrs v MacHenrys (Hairdressers) Ltd* [1993] STC 170 at 175; *Kieran Mullin Ltd v Customs and Excise Comrs* [2003] STC 274 at [32], [33].

[3] For agency, see VATA 1994, s 47(1), (2A); *Nell Gwynn House Maintenance Fund Trustees v Customs and Excise Comrs* [1999] STC 79, HL; Notice No 700. For the

[63.20] Introduction

vires of VATA 1994, s 47(2A), see *Express Medicare Ltd v Customs and Excise Comrs* [2000] V & DR 377. For examples, see *Customs and Excise Comrs v Johnson* [1980] STC 624, QBD; *Potter v Customs and Excise Comrs* [1985] STC 45, CA; *Betterware Products Ltd v Customs and Excise Comrs* [1985] STC 648; *Customs and Excise Comrs v Paget* [1989] STC 733; *Customs and Excise Comrs v Music and Video Exchange Ltd* [1992] STC 220; *Durham Aged Mineworkers'Homes Association v Customs and Excise Comrs* [1994] STC 553; *Ringside Refreshments v Customs and Excise Comrs* [2003] EWHC 3043 (Ch), [2004] STC 426.

4. For simultaneous supplies by X to Y and Y to Z, see *Philips Exports Ltd v Customs and Excise Comrs* [1990] STC 508n and contrast *Kwik Save Group plc v Customs and Excise Comrs* [1994] VATTR 457 (sub-sale of land); *Mölnlycke Ltd v Customs and Excise Comrs* (1996) VAT decision 14641 (incontinence products).

5. For a joint venture between X (landowner) and Y (building contractor), see *Customs and Excise Comrs v Latchmere Properties Ltd* [2005] EWHC 133 (Ch), [2005] STC 731 (dwelling constructed by Y on the land owned by X, where the proceeds of the sale to Z were merely divided between X and Y with no supply made by Y to X).

6. For a sale of goods by X and card handling service by Y when Z paid for the goods by credit card, see *Debenhams Retail plc v Revenue and Customs Comrs* [2005] EWCA Civ 892, [2005] STC 1155.

7. For a payment by a sauna operator to a hostess, see *Joppa Enterprises Ltd v Revenue and Customs Comrs* [2009] CSIH 17, [2009] STC 1279 (proportion of admission charge to sauna paid by proprietor to hostess).

8. For a payment by a club hostess to a club proprietor, see *Spearmint Rhino Ventures (UK) Ltd v Revenue and Customs Comrs* [2007] EWHC 613 (Ch), [2007] STC 1252 (payments by self-employed dancer to gentleman's club where dancer's fee paid under contract between dancer and customer).

9. For examples of consumption, see *Football Association Ltd v Customs and Excise Comrs* [1985] VATTR 106; *J Hopkins (Contractors) Ltd v Customs and Excise Comrs* [1989] VATTR 107. For examples of onward supply, see *Customs and Excise Comrs v John Willmott Housing Ltd* [1987] STC 192; *Ibstock Building Products Ltd v Customs and Excise Comrs* [1987] VATTR 1; *Northern Lawn Tennis Club v Customs and Excise Comrs* [1989] VATTR 1; *Stormseal (UPVC) Window Co Ltd v Customs and Excise Comrs* [1989] VATTR 303.

10. For a consultation paper published by the Commission, see *Modernising the VAT Treatment of Vouchers and Related Issues* (Brussels, 13 November 2006).

11. *Argos Distributors Ltd v Customs and Excise Comrs* (case C-288/94) [1996] ECR I-5311, ECJ.

12. *Elida Gibbs Ltd v Customs and Excise Comrs* (case C-317/94) [1996] ECR I-5339, [1996] STC 1387, ECJ.

13. For manufacturers' schemes, see *Elida Gibbs Ltd v Customs and Excise Comrs* (case C-317/94) [1996] ECR I-5339, [1996] STC 1387, ECJ; *Commission v Germany* (case C-427/98) [2002] ECR I-8315, [2003] STC 301, ECJ; *Yorkshire Co-operatives Ltd* (case C-398/99) [2003] ECR I-427, [2003] STC 301, ECJ. For retailers' schemes, see *Boots Co plc v Customs and Excise Comrs* (case C-126/88) [1990] ECR I-1235, [1990] STC 387, ECJ.

14. *Kuwait Petroleum (GB) Ltd v Customs and Excise Comrs* (case C-48/97) [1999] STC 488, ECJ; *Total UK Ltd v Revenue and Customs Comrs* [2007] EWCA Civ 987, [2008] STC 564, CA.

Supplies [63.20]

15 *Customs and Excise Comrs v Granton Marketing Ltd* [1996] STC 1049, CA.
16 *Revenue and Customs Comrs v IDT Card Services Ireland Ltd* [2006] EWCA Civ 29, [2006] STC 1252, CA.
17 *Tesco plc v Customs and Excise Comrs* [2003] STC 396, CA; *Revenue and Customs Comrs v Loyalty Management UK Ltd* [2007] EWCA Civ 965, [2008] STC 59, CA; *Baxi Group Ltd v Revenue and Customs Comrs* [2007] EWCA Civ 1378, [2008] STC 42, CA.
18 *Primback Ltd v Customs and Excise Comrs* (case C-34/99) [2001] ECR I–3833, [2001] STC 803, ECJ.
19 *Empire Stores Ltd v Customs and Excise Comrs* (case C-33/93) [1994] ECR I–2329, [1994] STC 623, ECJ; *Bertelsmann AG v Finanzamt Wiedebbrück* (case C-380/99) [2001] ECR I–5163, [2001] STC 1153, ECJ.
20 VATA 1994, s 19(4); *Card Protection Plan Ltd v Customs and Excise Comrs* (case C-349/96) [1999] STC 270, ECJ.
21 *College of Estate Management v Customs and Excise Comrs* [2005] UKHL 62, [2005] STC 1597, HL. For examples, see *C & E Comrs v British Telecommunications plc* [1999] STC 758, HL (delivery of motor car subordinate to its sale); *Card Protection Plan Ltd v Customs and Excise Comrs* [2001] UKHL 4, [2001] STC 174, HL (peripheral parts of a package of services and goods of trivial value subordinate to the main package of insurance services); *International Masters Publishers Ltd v Revenue and Customs Comrs* [2006] EWCA Civ 1455, [2007] STC 153, CA ("CD book" where the bound text was ancillary to the CD fixed to the inside cover); *Tumble Tots (UK) Ltd v Revenue and Customs Comrs* [2007] EWHC 103 (Ch), [2007] STC 1171, [2007] SWTI 293 (membership fee including T-shirt and magazine).
22 *College of Estate Management v Customs and Excise Comrs* [2005] UKHL 62, [2005] STC 1597, HL. For examples, see *Faaborg-Gelting Linien A/S v Finanzamt Flensburg* (case C-231/94) [1996] STC 774, ECJ (restaurant meal comprising a single supply of services); *Levob Verzekeringen BV and another v Staatssecretaris van Financiën* (case C-41/04) [2005] ECR I–9433, [2006] STC 766, ECJ (supplying and customising standard software package); *Talacre Beach Caravan Sales Ltd v Customs and Excise Comrs* (case C-251/05) [2006] ECR I–6269, [2006] STC 1671, ECJ (caravan and removable contents); *Aktiebolaget NN v Skatteverket* (case C-111/05) [2007] ECR I–2697, [2007] SWTI 1167, ECJ (supply and installation of fibre-optic cable);*Dr Beynon & Partners v Customs and Excise Comrs* [2004] UKHL 53, [2005] STC 55, HL (drugs administered by the medical practitioner who dispensed them); *College of Estate Management v Customs and Excise Comrs* [2005] UKHL 62, [2005] STC 1597, HL (distance learning course); *Bryom (trading as Salon 24 v Revenue and Customs Comrs* [2006] EWHC 111 (Ch), [2006] STC 992 (room hire and other facilities supplied to masseuse).
23 See *Byrom and others (trading as Salon 24) v Revenue and Customs Comrs* [2006] EWHC 111 (Ch), [2006] STC 992 at para 46; *Holland (trading as The Studio Hair Company) v Revenue and Customs Comrs, Vigdor Ltd v Revenue and Customs Comrs* [2008] EWHC 2621 (Ch), [2009] STC 150 at para 78. A different tax treatment was applied to the single economic supply held to exist in each case.
24 For examples of separate payments, see *British Railways Board v Customs and Excise Comrs* [1977] STC 221, CA (rail card and ticket); *Revenue and Customs Comrs v Weight Watchers (UK) Ltd* [2008] EWCA Civ 715, [2008] STC 2313, CA (enrolment fee and fee for each meeting attended); *Revenue and Customs Comrs v Axa UK plc* [2008] EWHC 1137 (Ch), [2008] STC 2091 (one-off

[63.20] Introduction

fees and monthly fees); *Patrick Eddery Ltd v Customs and Excise Comrs* [1986] VATTR 30 (jockey's retainer and riding fee); *Mothercare Ltd v Customs and Excise Comrs* [1993] VATTR 391 (payments for discount card and subsequent purchases). For examples of separate invoices or an itemised invoices, see *RLRE Tellmer Property sro v Finanční v Ústí nad Labem* (case C-572/07) [2009] ECR I-0000, [2009] SWTI 1886, ECJ (apartment letting and cleaning common parts of the building); *Rowe and Maw v Customs and Excise Comrs* [1975] STC 340 (travelling expenses which were not a disbursement); *Customs and Excise Comrs v British Telecommunications plc* [1999] STC 758, HL (delivery charge for motor vehicles); *Birkdale School, Sheffield v Revenue and Customs Comrs* [2008] EWHC 409 (Ch), [2008] STC 2002 (school fee protection scheme). See also *Exeter Golf and Country Club Ltd v Customs and Excise Comrs* [1981] STC 211, CA (club subscription and benefit of interest-free loan made by member); *Muys'en De Winter's Bouw-en Aannemingsbedrijf BV Staatssecretaris van Financiën* (case C-281/91) [1997] STC 665, ECJ (interest on payment deferred until delivery of goods or services).

[25] *Nell Gwynn House Maintenance Fund Trustees v Customs and Excise Comrs* [1999] STC 79, HL.

[26] *Telewest Communications plc v Customs and Excise Comrs* [2005] EWCA Civ 102, [2005] STC 481.

[27] *Tumble Tots (UK) Ltd v Revenue and Customs Comrs* [2007] EWHC 103 (Ch), [2007] STC 1171 at para 11 (case citations omitted).

Consideration

General principles

[63.21] In principle, a transaction amounts to a supply only if a consideration is given for it.[1] However, a transfer, disposal or use of business goods or services without consideration is specifically stated to be a supply of goods or a supply of services (so as to be chargeable to tax) in specified circumstances.[2]

The meaning of the term "consideration" is a matter of EU law.[3] The essential element is a direct link between the relevant supply and whatever is alleged to have been the consideration for it.[4] This link is provided by an agreement between the person making the supply and the person receiving it so that there is a reciprocal performance of obligations. However, it appears that the agreement may be something less than a legal relationship[5] and that there is no necessity for the obligations flowing from it to be legally binding.[6]

Consideration may comprise money (ie cash), something other than money (ie a barter deal) or partly money and partly something else (eg a part exchange deal for a new motor car).[7] A consideration in something other than money must be capable of being expressed in money.[8] The money or other thing may be provided by the customer or a third party.[9] It may be paid or given to the supplier or to someone other than the supplier.[10]

It is necessary to undertake a factual investigation to determine what both sides of the relevant transaction thought they were agreeing to. In doing so, it is necessary to remember that there is a limit to the reasonable gullibility of ordinary members of the public. Thus, reasonably-minded members of the public giving the terms of a "free gift" offer any thought may reasonably believe that they are getting something free in some cases but not in others.[11]

It is necessary to identify the reason why a payment is made in order to discover whether or not it is linked to a supply of goods or services.[12] A sum of money received by a trader amounts to consideration only if there is a corresponding supply and the trader is free to deal with the sum as his own or receive some benefit from it.[13] Thus, whilst an agent makes a supply when he collects moneys due to his principal or disburses moneys on behalf of his principal, the amounts received from third parties and the amounts reimbursed by his principal do not amount to consideration for this supply.[14] It is necessary to distinguish a disbursement from an amount laid out by a trader as part of the cost of supplying goods or performing services.[15]

The consideration for a transaction is that which is given, and this is determined objectively upon the facts of the transaction by reference to the terms agreed. Thus, the fact that a trader does not obtain the best possible bargain does not mean that his forbearance to charge a higher price amounts to consideration.[16] On the other hand, the fact that a trader does not make a profit on a supply does not mean that there is no consideration for it.[17] The determining factor is whether a consideration is due, not whether it has been received.[18] Thus, cash received for a retail sale amounts to consideration whether it is placed in the till or diverted by an employee before getting as far as the till.[19]

A charge imposed under a statutory rather than a contractual obligation is not consideration where the payee receives no more than an indirect benefit from services supplied by the statutory body concerned.[20]

Transactions should not be artificially dissected so as to demonstrate that the consideration is something less, or something different, from that which is given.[21]

De Voil Indirect Tax Service V3.103, 108.

[1] VATA 1994, s 5(2)(a).
[2] The transfer, disposal or use is accordingly treated as a supply so as to be within the charging provisions of VATA 1994, s 1(1)(a). For the charge to tax, see infra, §§ 65.28–65.31.
[3] Staatssecretaris van Financiën v Coöperatieve Aardappelenbewaarplaats GA (case 154/80) [1981] ECR 445 at [9], ECJ.
[4] Staatssecretaris van Financiën v Coöperatieve Aardappelenbewaarplaats GA (case 154/80) [1981] ECR 445 at [12], ECJ; Apple and Pear Development Council v Customs and Excise Comrs (case 102/86) [1988] STC 221 at [11], [12], ECJ; Naturally Yours Cosmetics Ltd v Customs and Excise Comrs (case 230/87) [1988] STC 879 at [11], ECJ; Tolsma v Inspecteur der Omzetbelasting Leeuwarden (case C-16/93) [1994] STC 509 at [13], ECJ.
[5] Tolsma v Inspecteur der Omzetbelasting Leeuwarden (case C-16/93) [1994] STC 509 at [14], ECJ as interpreted in Customs and Excise Comrs v Church Schools Foundation Ltd [2001] STC 1661 at [31], CA.
[6] Town and County Factors Ltd v Customs and Excise Comrs (case C-498/99) [2002] STC 1263, ECJ.

[63.21] Introduction

7   VATA 1994, s 19(2), (3).
8   *Staatssecretaris van Financiën v Coöperatieve Aardappelenbewaarplaats GA* (case 154/80) [1981] ECR 445, ECJ. For an example of circumstances where this test was not met, see *Julius Fillibeck Söhne GmbH & Co KG v Finanzamt Neustadt* (case C-258/95) [1998] STC 513, ECJ (provision of free transport to employees).
9   *Lord Advocate v Largs Golf Club* [1985] STC 226. For examples, see *Keeping Newcastle Warm Ltd v Customs and Excise Comrs* (case C-353/00) [2002] STC 943, ECJ (payment under statutory grant scheme); *Customs and Excise Comrs v Professional Footballers Association (Enterprises) Ltd* [1992] STC 86, HL (awards dinner); *Customs and Excise Comrs v Telemed Ltd* [1992] STC 89 (video tapes with advertising); *Thorn plc v Customs and Excise Comrs* [1998] V & DR 383 (mobile phones).
10 *Philip Drakard Trading Ltd v Customs and Excise Comrs* [1992] STC 568.
11 See *Kuwait Petroleum (GB) Ltd v Customs and Excise Comrs* (case C-48/97) [1999] STC 488, ECJ; *Kuwait Petroleum (GB) Ltd v Customs and Excise Comrs* [2001] STC 62; *Peugeot Motor Co plc v Customs and Excise Comrs* [2003] EWHC 2304 (Ch), STC 1438.
12 See *Strathearn Gordon Associates Ltd v Customs and Excise Comrs* [1985] VATTR 79 (whether money received was share of partnership profit or consideration for supply of services fixed by reference to profit made).
13 *H J Glawe Spiel-und Unterhaltungsgeräte Aufstellungsgesellschaft mbH & Co KG v Finanzamt Hamburg-Barmbek-Uhlenhorst* (case C-38/93) [1994] STC 453, ECJ (gaming machine with reserve compartment); *Customs and Excise Comrs v Emap MacLaren Ltd* [1997] STC 490 (sponsorship money paid in full to winner of prize); *Patrick v Customs and Excise Comrs* [1994] VATTR 247 (hammer price of goods divided between auctioneer and seller).
14 For supplies deemed to be made to and by agents, see supra, § **63.18**.
15 For examples of payments that did not amount to a disbursement, see *Nell Gwynn House Maintenance Fund Trustees v Customs and Excise Comrs* [1999] STC 79, HL (service charge); *Customs and Excise Comrs v Plantiflor Ltd* [2002] STC 1132, HL (delivery charge); *Rowe & Maw (a firm) v Customs and Excise Comrs* [1975] STC 340 (travelling expenses); *Hamilton v Customs and Excise Comrs* [1984] VATTR 95 (estate agent).
16 *Exeter Golf and Country Club Ltd v Customs and Excise Comrs* [1979] VATTR 70.
17 *Heart of Variety Ltd v Customs and Excise Comrs* [1975] VATTR 103. To the same effect under EC law, see *Hotel Scandic Gåsabäck AB v Riksskatteverket* (case C-412/03) [2005], ECR I–743, [2005] STC 1311, ECJ (whether the price paid for an economic transaction is higher or lower than cost price is irrelevant to the question whether it has been supplied for consideration).
18 VATA 1994, s 25(1).
19 *Benton v Customs and Excise Comrs* [1975] VATTR 138. For till shortages, see *Courage Ltd v Customs and Excise Comrs* (1992) VAT decision 8808.
20 *Apple and Pear Development Council v Customs and Excise Comrs* (case 102/86) [1988] STC 221, ECJ.
21 *Customs and Excise Comrs v Pippa-Dee Parties Ltd* [1981] STC 495.

The time when consideration is ascertained

[63.22] Whether or not a consideration is due is determined at the time when the supply is treated as taking place for the purposes of charging tax in accordance with the agreement made between the parties.[1] Thus, if goods or services are supplied gratuitously, they cannot be turned into a supply made for a consideration by a subsequent voluntary payment.[2] Similarly, a supply made for a consideration evidenced by a tax invoice cannot be turned into a supply for no consideration merely by issuing a credit note.[3]

De Voil Indirect Tax Service V3.103, 108.

---

[1] *Potters Lodge Restaurant v Customs and Excise Comrs* (1980) VAT decision 905.
[2] *Warwick Masonic Rooms Ltd v Customs and Excise Comrs* (1979) VAT decision 839.
[3] *British United Shoe Machinery Co Ltd v Customs and Excise Comrs* [1977] VATTR 187. For credit notes, see infra, § **65.19**.

Quantum

[63.23] The amount of the consideration for a supply is determined when the price payable has been agreed by the parties. In the case of services supplied at arm's length for an as yet unascertained consideration, the amount concerned is the amount invoiced (if the customer accepts the invoice) or the amount invoiced less the amount subsequently shown on a credit note (if the customer disputes the amount charged and the credit note reduces that amount to the sum actually agreed).[1] Both supplier and customer must adjust their VAT Accounts if an increase or decrease in consideration is agreed after the end of the prescribed accounting period in which the supply was made.[2] Once the amount of the consideration for a supply has been agreed, it is fixed for VAT purposes. If the supplier thereafter unilaterally decides that the full amount of the agreed charges is not to be payable, or if both parties so contract, the value of the supply is unaffected by the decision or contract.[3] For the validity of documents issued to reflect the consideration for a supply, see infra, § **65.19**.

It is necessary to draw a distinction between a step in the calculation of a consideration and a step in the calculation of a sum payable which involves offsetting two separate considerations. In the former case, VAT is chargeable by reference to the single consideration passing.[4] In the latter case, VAT is chargeable by reference to the separate considerations passing so that net sum payable is irrelevant for VAT purposes.[5]

The consideration for a supply includes the VAT (if any) chargeable on it.[6] The amount of a consideration in money may be determined in two ways. First, the parties may agree a price to which VAT (if any) is to be added. Here, VAT is charged at the rate in force at the time of supply and the consideration is the agreed price plus the VAT (if any) charged on it.[7] Second, the parties to a contract may agree a fixed price. If so, this is the consideration and it is unaffected by any change in the rate of VAT, or the fact that VAT may become chargeable (or not chargeable), between making the contract and making the supply to which it gives rise. It may be necessary to interpret the contract in

[63.23] Introduction

order to discover which method has been adopted.[8] The second method leaves a hostage to fortune. Thus, for example, the supplier incurs a loss if he costs the price on the basis that he will make (say) a zero-rated supply and, following a change to the legislation, his supply becomes chargeable at the standard rate. Contracts should clearly state which method is being adopted in order to avoid disputes.[9]

De Voil Indirect Tax Service V3.103, 108.

---

[1] *Castle Associates Ltd v Customs and Excise Comrs* (1989) VAT decision 3497.
[2] VAT Regulations, SI 1995/2518, reg 38. For the VAT Account, see infra, § **66.30** and § **67.15**. For the customer's obligation to accept a credit note, see *Silvermere Golf and Equestrian Centre Ltd v Customs and Excise Comrs* [1981] VATTR 106.
[3] *Castle Associates Ltd v Customs and Excise Comrs* (1989) VAT decision 3497. For failed attempts to vary the agreed consideration for a supply by way of a credit note in relation to bad debts, see in particular *Peter Cripwell & Associates v Customs and Excise Comrs* (1978) VAT decision 660; *Temple Gothard & Co v Customs and Excise Comrs* (1978) VAT decision 702; *Castle Wines Ltd v Finance Board* (1982) VAT decision 1271. For the attempted variation of a management charge, see *British United Shoe Machinery Co Ltd v Customs and Excise Comrs* [1977] VATTR 187; *Larullah Ltd v Customs and Excise Comrs* (1985) VAT decision 1779; *Bury's Transport (Oxon) Ltd v Customs and Excise Comrs* LON/85/129 unreported (reduced charge); *T S Harrison & Sons Ltd v Customs and Excise Comrs* (1993) VAT decision 11043 (increased charge).
[4] See *National Coal Board v Customs and Excise Comrs* [1982] STC 863; *Goodfellow (a firm) v Customs and Excise Comrs* [1986] VATTR 119.
[5] See *Chaussures Bally SA v Ministry of Finance (Belgium)* (case C-18/92) [1997] STC 209, ECJ; *Customs and Excise Comrs v Primback Ltd* (case C-34/99) [2001] STC 803, ECJ; *Davies v Customs and Excise Comrs* [1975] STC 28; *Trafalgar Tours Ltd v Customs and Excise Comrs* [1990] STC 127, CA; *Smith and Williamson v Customs and Excise Comrs* [1976] VATTR 215.
[6] VATA 1994, s 19(2), (3).
[7] VATA 1994, s 89(1), (2).
[8] For examples, see *Hostgilt Ltd v Megahart Ltd* [1999] STC 141; *Wynn Realisations Ltd (in administration) v Vogue Holdings Inc* [1999] STC 524, CA; *Debenhams Retail plc and another v Sun Alliance and London Assurance Co Ltd* [2005] EWCA Civ 868, [2005] STC 1443, CA.
[9] For the terms of a lease, see VATA 1994, s 89(2).

Supplies of goods and services

[63.24] A supply made for a consideration may comprise a supply of goods, a supply of services, or neither a supply of goods nor a supply of services.[1] As VAT is charged on supplies of goods and services,[2] it follows that a supply is outside the scope of VAT if it comprises neither a supply of goods nor a supply of services.

Supplies are allocated under a particular heading in the following manner:

(1) Supplies relating to tangible moveable property are divided between supplies of goods and supplies of services in accordance with a statutory formula based on the interest transferred.[3]
(2) Certain supplies are stated to be supplies of goods regardless of whether or not they would normally be regarded as such.[4]
(3) Anything which does not amount to a supply of goods is stated to be a supply of services.[5]
(4) Anything which amounts to a supply of goods or a supply of services under the foregoing rules is nevertheless treated as neither a supply of goods nor a supply of services where a Treasury order is made to that effect.[6]

De Voil Indirect Tax Service V3.111.

[1] VATA 1994, s 5(3).
[2] VATA 1994, s 1(1).
[3] VATA 1994, Sch 4, para 1.
[4] VATA 1994, Sch 4, paras 2–6.
[5] VATA 1994, s 5(2)(*b*).
[6] Under VATA 1994, s 5(3).

Supplies of goods

[63.25] The following supplies amount to supplies of goods unless they are specifically excluded from this category and treated as either a supply of services or neither a supply of goods nor a supply of services:[1]

(1) Any transfer of the whole property in goods.[2]
(2) The transfer of possession[3] in goods under either an agreement for the sale of goods[4] or an agreement which expressly contemplates that the property in goods will pass at a future time specified in the agreement, eg a hire purchase agreement.
(3) The supply of any form of power, heat, refrigeration or ventilation.
(4) The granting, assignment or surrender of a major interest[5] in land.
(5) A transfer or disposal of business assets. This includes any transfer or disposal in favour of a sole proprietor.
(6) Removing goods from one EU member state to another. There are a number of exceptions to this rule.[6]
(7) The supply of water.
(8) The transfer of an undivided share in eligible goods[7] under a non-retail supply while the goods are either subject to a fiscal warehousing regime[8] at the time of supply or subsequently become so subject before they are supplied.

It appears that a transfer of the whole property in goods in 1 above comprises any transfer of tangible property that empowers the transferee to dispose of the property as if he were the owner. UK procedures relating to the transfer of ownership are irrelevant in determining whether a transfer of tangible property falls within this description.[9] Thus, it is immaterial whether or not title to the goods has passed.[10]

[63.25] Introduction

Whether or not the whole property has passed is a question of law.[11] A transfer of the whole property in goods from A to B is a supply of goods from A to B and cannot be a supply from A to any other person.[12] This is so even if the property vests in B for an infinitely short time before passing to C.[13] A transfer of the whole property in goods may amount to a composite supply of goods,[14] a composite supply of services,[15] or a contract for work and materials, in which case only the materials element comprises a supply of goods under this heading.[16]

De Voil Indirect Tax Service V3.112.

---

[1] VATA 1994, Sch 4, paras 1(1), 3, 4, 5(1), (6), 6(1); VAT (Water) Order, SI 1989/1114, art 2; VAT (Fiscal Warehousing) (Treatment of Transactions) Order, SI 1996/1225.

[2] For the theft of goods, see *British American Tobacco International Ltd and another v Belgian State* (case C-435/03) [2005] ECR I-7077, [2006] STC 158, ECJ (thief not empowered to dispose of the goods under the same conditions as their owner so that the theft does not effect a transfer from victim to thief within Directive 2006/112/EC art 14(1)).

[3] For "possession", see *Customs and Excise Comrs v Oliver* [1980] STC 73; *Creditgrade Ltd v Customs and Excise Comrs* [1991] VATTR 87.

[4] See *Astor v Customs and Excise Comrs* [1981] VATTR 174; *Creditgrade Ltd v Customs and Excise Comrs* [1991] VATTR 87. See also *Customs and Excise Comrs v Oliver* [1980] STC 73, [1980] 1 All ER 353 (stolen goods) and *Excell Consumer Industries Ltd v Customs and Excise Comrs* [1983] VATTR 94 (title to goods not formally passed).

[5] As defined in VATA 1994, s 96(1) as amended by FA 1998, s 24. The term of a time sharing arrangement is determined by the period of occupation, not the number of years for which the agreement is expressed to run: *Cottage Holiday Associates Ltd v Customs and Excise Comrs* [1983] STC 278.

[6] For the exceptions, see VATA 1994, Sch 4, para 6(2); VAT (Removal of Goods) Order, SI 1992/3111, arts 4, 5; VAT (Special Provisions) Order, SI 1995/1268, art 8; VAT (Removal of Gas and Electricity) Order, SI 2004/3150.

[7] ie goods within VATA 1994, Sch 5A (as inserted by FA 1996, Sch 3, para 18) which meet the conditions in VATA 1994, s 18B(6) (as inserted by FA 1996, Sch 3, para 5).

[8] As defined in VATA 1994, s 18F(2) (as inserted by FA 1996, Sch 3, para 5).

[9] Directive 2006/112/EC art 14(1) as interpreted in *Staatssecretaris van Financiën v Shipping and Forwarding Enterprise Safe BV* (case C-320/88) [1991] STC 627, ECJ; *Auto Lease Holland BV v Bundesamt für Finanzen* (case C-185/01) [2005] STC 598, ECJ.

[10] *Staatssecretaris van Financiën v Shipping and Forwarding Enterprise Safe BV* (case C-320/88) [1991] STC 627, ECJ; *Excell Consumer Industries Ltd v Customs and Excise Comrs* [1985] VATTR 94.

[11] *Creditgrade Ltd v Customs and Excise Comrs* [1991] VATTR 87.

[12] *Customs and Excise Comrs v Sooner Foods Ltd* [1983] STC 376.

[13] *Philips Exports Ltd v Customs and Excise Comrs* [1990] STC 508n.

[14] See *AZO-Maschinenfabrik Adolf Zimmerman GMBH v Customs and Excise Comrs* [1987] VATTR 25 (sale, installation and commissioning of a machine);

Customs and Excise Comrs v Jeffs [1995] STC 759 (joinery work carried out off site).
15 *Faaborg-Gelting Linien A/S v Finanzamt Flensburg* (case C-231/94) [1996] STC 774, ECJ (restaurant meal).
16 See *ADP Installations (Group) Ltd v Customs and Excise Comrs* [1987] VATTR 36 (installation of custom built double glazing).

Supplies of services

[63.26] Anything done for a consideration which is not a supply of goods is a supply of services[1] unless it is specifically treated as neither a supply of goods nor a supply of services. "Anything done" includes, amongst other things, the grant, assignment or surrender of any right.[2] It does not include functions which a trader is obliged to carry out on his own behalf.[3]

The following specific activities amount to a supply of services:[4]

(1) The transfer of any undivided share in the property of goods, eg if A and B jointly own an asset and A sells his share to C.
(2) The transfer of possession of goods, eg the hire, lease, rental or loan of goods.
(3) Using business goods[5] for private or non-business purposes during their economic life.[6]
(4) Exchanging reconditioned articles for unserviceable articles of a similar kind when carried out by a trader who regularly offers to provide such facilities.

De Voil Indirect Tax Service V3.113.

---

1 VATA 1994, s 5(2)(*b*).
2 VATA 1994, s 5(2)(*b*). For examples, see *Naturally Yours Cosmetics Ltd v Customs and Excise Comrs* (case 230/87) [1988] STC 879, ECJ (procuring a gathering at which goods are sold); *Customs and Excise Comrs v Tilling Management Services Ltd* [1979] STC 365 (procuring a group relief payment); *GUS Merchandise Corpn Ltd v Customs and Excise Comrs* [1981] STC 569, CA (agreeing to act as agent); *Customs and Excise Comrs v Diners Club Ltd* [1989] STC 407, CA (making payments under a credit card scheme); *Customs and Excise Comrs v High Street Vouchers Ltd* [1990] STC 575 (redeeming vouchers at a discount); *Customs and Excise Comrs v Battersea Leisure Ltd* [1992] STC 213, *Ridgeons Bulk Ltd v Customs and Excise Comrs* [1994] STC 427, (covenanting to refurbish premises); *Neville Russell (a firm) v Customs and Excise Comrs* [1987] VATTR 194 and contrast *Iliffe & Holloway v Customs and Excise Comrs* [1993] VATTR 439 (accepting a lease); *Cooper Chasney Ltd v Customs and Excise Comrs* [1990] 3 CMLR 509 (relinquishing a trade name); *Oxford Film Foundation v Customs and Excise Comrs* (1990) VAT decision 5031 (providing publicity benefits for a sponsor).
3 *National Coal Board v Customs and Excise Comrs* [1982] STC 863; *British European Breeders'Fund v Customs and Excise Comrs* [1985] VATTR 12.
4 VATA 1994, Sch 4, paras 1(1)(*a*), (*b*) and 5(4), (6); VAT (Special Provisions) Order, SI 1995/1268, arts 6, 10A as inserted by SI 2007/2923.
5 For the application of this provision to land, see VATA 1994 Sch 4 paras 9(1), (2).

[63.26] Introduction

[6] For the economic life of goods, land and buildings, see VAT Regulations, SI 1995/2518 regs 116C, 116G, 116L as inserted by SI 2007/3099.

Supplies of neither goods nor services

[63.27] The following transactions are treated as neither supplies of goods nor supplies of services and are thus outside the scope of VAT:[1]

(1) Disposal of certain goods[2] repossessed under the terms of a finance agreement[3] or taken into possession under the terms of an aircraft or marine mortgage.[4]
(2) Disposal of certain goods[5] by an insurer who has taken them in settlement of an insurance claim.
(3) Services in connection with the supply of certain goods[6] provided by an agent or auctioneer[7] acting in his own name.
(4) The sale of business assets where a business or part of a business is transferred as a going concern.[8]
(5) The assignment of rights under a hire purchase or conditional sale agreement to a financial institution.
(6) Disposal or hire of a motor car for no consideration, hire of a motor car for a consideration less than the amount payable on an arm's length transaction, or making a motor car available for private use.[9]
(7) Goods held under temporary importation arrangements supplied to a person established in a third country.[10]
(8) Inland purchases by diplomats, members of international organisations and visiting forces.
(9) The right to private use of a motor car given to an employee for a consideration comprising a salary sacrifice.[11]
(10) Certain supplies made in the course of triangular transactions or where goods are installed or assembled in the UK.
(11) The transfer of ownership in second-hand goods or works of art which are subject to temporary importation arrangements and which have been imported from a third country for sale.[12]
(12) Goods disposed of by a pawnbroker to the pawner.
(13) A removal of goods to the UK under a supply chargeable to VAT in another EU member state by reference to the profit margin.[13]

De Voil Indirect Tax Service V3.114–118.

---

[1] VATA 1994, s 14(1), (2), (6); VAT (Treatment of Transactions) Order, SI 1986/896, art 3; VAT (Treatment of Transactions) Order, SI 1992/630. VAT (Cars) Order, SI 1992/3122, art 4 as amended by SI 1995/1269, SI 1995/1667, SI 2006/874; VAT (Supply of Temporarily Imported Goods) Order, SI 1992/3130, art 2; Customs and Excise (Personal Reliefs for Special Visitors) Order, SI 1992/3156; VAT (Treatment of Transactions) Order, SI 1995/958 art 3 as amended by SI 1999/3119, SI 2006/2187; VAT (Special Provisions) Order, SI 1995/1268, arts 4, 5, 8, 9, 10 as amended by SI 1995/1385, SI 1995/1667, SI 1998/760, SI 2004/779, SI 2006/869, SI 2008/1146; Notice No 48 (July 2009) paras 2.1–2.6 and 3.26.

[2] The goods concerned are works of art, antiques, collectors' items, used motor cars and second-hand goods as defined in SI 1992/3122, art 2; SI 1995/1268, art 2.

³ For possession regained following consensual termination of a finance agreement, see *Customs and Excise Comrs v General Motors Acceptance Corpn (UK) plc* [2004] STC 577.
⁴ For "finance agreement", "aircraft mortgage" and "marine mortgage", see SI 1992/3122, art 2; SI 1995/1268, art 2 as amended by SI 2006/2187.
⁵ For the goods concerned, see supra, Note 2.
⁶ For the goods concerned, see supra, Note 2.
⁷ For "auctioneer", see SI 1992/3122, art 2; SI 1995/1268, art 2.
⁸ The transferee must intend to operate the business (or part) following the transfer rather than liquidating it and selling the stock, but he does not need to have pursued the same type of activity before the transfer: *Zita Modes SARL v Administration de l'enregistrement et des domaines* (case C-497/01) [2003] ECR I-14393, [2005] STC 1059, ECJ. For the nature of a "going concern", see *Customs and Excise Comrs v Dearwood Ltd* [1986] STC 327; *Customs and Excise Comrs v Padglade Ltd* [1995] STC 602; *Hartley Engineering Ltd v Customs and Excise Comrs* [1994] VATTR 453; *Kwik Save Group plc v Customs and Excise Comrs* [1994] VATTR 457; *Ryan & Townsend v Customs and Excise Comrs* (1994) VAT decision 12806; *Sawadee Restaurant v Customs and Excise Comrs* (1999) VAT decision 15933.
⁹ Hiring and making a motor car available in these circumstances give rise to a self-supply under the provisions described in infra, § **65.32**.
¹⁰ For the relief from tax on importation, see infra, § **63.39**.
¹¹ For a case where a salary sacrifice did not amount to consideration, see *Co-operative Insurance Society Ltd v Customs and Excise Comrs* [1992] VATTR 44.
¹² For exceptions, see VAT (Treatment of Transactions) Order, SI 1995/958 art 4 as inserted by SI 2006/2187.
¹³ The supply would otherwise be treated as a supply of goods under VATA 1994, Sch 4, para 5 or 6.

Supplies made in the UK

Goods

[63.28] Goods situated in the UK are supplied in the UK if they are neither removed to the UK nor removed from the UK in the course of their supply. The fact that goods leave and re-enter the UK in the course of their removal from one part of the UK to another is disregarded.[1]

Goods removed to the UK are supplied in the UK if:[2]

(1) they are installed or assembled in the UK;
(2) they are removed from another EU member state under a supply made to a non-taxable person for a consideration by a trader who meets the conditions for compulsory registration under VATA 1994, Sch 2;[3] or
(3) they are supplied by the person who imported from a third country.

They are supplied outside the UK in other circumstances.[4]

Goods removed from the UK are supplied outside the UK if:[5]

(1) they are installed or assembled in the country to which they are removed;

[63.28] Introduction

(2) they are removed to another EU member state and supplied to a non-taxable person in circumstances where the supplier is registered, and liable to account for output tax on the supply, in the EU member state to which the goods are removed;[6] or
(3) they are first removed to the UK.

They are supplied in the UK in other circumstances.[7] The foregoing rules are modified in relation to warehoused goods,[8] goods supplied for consumption on board an aircraft, ship or train moving from one EU member state to another,[9] supplies of gas and electricity[10] and the supply and installation of submarine cables between the UK and another country.[11]

De Voil Indirect Tax Service V3.124.

---

[1] VATA 1994, s 7(1), (8).
[2] VATA 1994, s 7(3)(a), (4), (6).
[3] This does not apply to new means of transport. For liability to registration under VATA 1994, Schs 1, 2, see infra, §§ **64.02–64.04** and § **64.10**.
[4] VATA 1994, s 7(7)(b).
[5] VATA 1994, s 7(3)(b), (5), (7).
[6] This does not apply to new means of transport. For place of supply options exercised in the UK, see VATA 1994, s 7(5); VAT Regulations, SI 1995/2518, reg 98.
[7] VATA 1994, s 7(7).
[8] For goods subject to a warehousing regime, see VATA 1994, s 18(1), (3); VAT Regulations, SI 1995/2518, reg 145K as inserted by SI 2005/2231. For goods subject to a fiscal warehousing regime, see VATA 1994, s 18B(3) as inserted by FA 1996, Sch 3, para 5.
[9] See VAT (Place of Supply of Goods) Order, SI 2004/3148, arts 4–8 as amended by SI 2009/215; *Peninsular and Oriental Steam Navigation Co v Customs and Excise Comrs* [2000] STC 488.
[10] See VAT (Place of Supply of Goods) Order, SI 2004/3148, arts 9–14.
[11] See *Aktiebolaget NN v Skatteverket* (case C-111/05) [2007] ECR I-2697, [2007] SWTI 1167, ECJ. Both member states have a right to tax the supply. The consideration for each supply is based on a pro-rata apportionment of the consideration according to the length of the cable within the territory of each member state.

Services—general rule

[63.29] In principle, the place of supply of services is determined in accordance with EC legislation as interpreted by the EC Court of Justice.[1] This provides that the place of supply is determined by applying three rules in the following order of priority:[2]

(1) The place where the supplier has established his business.
(2) The place where the supplier has a fixed establishment. This rule applies if the first rule does not lead to a rational result for tax purposes[3] or creates a conflict with another EC member state.

(3) The place where the supplier has his permanent address or usually resides. This rule applies if the supplier does not have a place of business or fixed establishment.

The place where the supplier has established his business is a matter of economic reality. The place where a company has its registered office is irrelevant. So is the location of any particular director's residence.[4]

An establishment is a "fixed establishment" for this purpose if it has "a sufficient minimum strength in the form of the permanent presence of the human and technical resources necessary for supplying specific services".[5] A trader ("X") established in one member state may act as agent for another trader ("Y") established in another member state. Y has a fixed establishment in country X if X acts as a "mere auxiliary organ" of Y and has the human and technical resources characteristic of a fixed establishment.[6]

The UK legislation is relevant when some aspects of a service are provided from the main place of business and others from a fixed establishment. The place of supply is determined by reference to the establishment which is most directly concerned with the supply.[7]

The UK legislation proceeds on a different basis. Services are supplied in the country where the supplier belongs.[8] Thus, if a supplier belongs in the UK, his services are made in the UK regardless of whether or not they are performed there. The place where the supplier belongs is determined by the location of his business establishment or some other fixed establishment[9] (if he has one) or his usual place of residence[10] (if he does not).

A trader belongs in the UK, and therefore makes supplies of services in the UK, if he meets one of the following statutory tests:[11]

(1) His only business establishment or other fixed establishment is in the UK.
(2) He has establishments both in the UK and abroad, but the UK establishment is most directly concerned with the supply.
(3) He does not have a business establishment, either in the UK or abroad, but his usual place of residence is in the UK.

De Voil Indirect Tax Service V3.124.

---

[1] *Customs and Excise Comrs v Chinese Channel (Hong Kong) Ltd* [1998] STC 347.
[2] See Directive 2006/112/EC, art 43 as interpreted in *Berkholz v Finanzamt Hamburg-Mitte-Altstadt* (case 168/84) [1985] ECR 2251, ECJ; *Customs and Excise Comrs v DFDS A/S* (case C-260/95) [1997] STC 384, ECJ; *ARO Lease BV v Inspecteur der Belastingdienst Grote Ondernemingen, Amsterdam* (case C-190/95) [1997] STC 1272.
[3] For a case where the first rule did not lead to a rational result, see *RAL (Channel Islands) Ltd v Customs and Excise Comrs* (2002) VAT decision 17914.
[4] *British United Provident Association Ltd v Customs and Excise Comrs* (2001) VAT decision 17286.
[5] *Berkholz v Finanzamt Hamburg-Mitte-Altstadt* (case 168/84) [1985] ECR 2251 at 2263, para 18, ECJ.
[6] *Customs and Excise Comrs v DFDS A/S* (case C-260/95) [1997] STC 384, ECJ.

[63.29] Introduction

[7] VATA 1994, s 9(2)(b); *Customs and Excise Comrs v Chinese Channel (Hong Kong) Ltd* [1998] STC 347.
[8] VATA 1994, s 7(10).
[9] A trader carrying on a business through a branch or agency in the UK is treated as having a business establishment here: VATA 1994, s 9(5)(a). For intermittent use of premises not attracting goodwill, see *Source Enterprise Ltd v Customs and Excise Comrs* (1992) VAT decision 7881.
[10] The usual place of residence of a body corporate is the country where it is legally constituted: VATA 1994, s 9(5)(b).
[11] VATA 1994, s 9(2).

Services—exceptions

[63.30] The general place of supply rule described in supra, § 63.28 is varied in relation to the following supplies of services:[1]
(1) Designated travel service[2] supplied by a tour operator.[3]
(2) The grant, assignment or surrender of an interest in land, right over land, personal right to call for or be granted an interest in or right over land, licence to occupy land, or other contractual right exercisable over or in relation to land.[4]
(3) Any works of construction, demolition, conversion, reconstruction, alteration, enlargement, repair or maintenance to a building or civil engineering work.
(4) Services of the kind supplied by estate agents, auctioneers, architects, surveyors, engineers and other persons involved in matters relating to land.
(5) Services consisting of the transportation of goods or passengers.[5]
(6) Services consisting of making arrangements for a supply to be made to or by another person.[6]
(7) Cultural, artistic, sporting, scientific, educational or entertainment services, and services ancillary to such services.[7]
(8) Services relating to exhibitions, conferences or meetings, and services ancillary to such services.[8]
(9) The valuation of goods.[9]
(10) Work carried out on goods.[10]
(11) The following services,[11] if supplied to a trader[12] who belongs[13] in an EU member state or any person who belongs in a third country:[14]
    (a) transfers and assignments of copyright, patents, licences, trademarks and similar rights;
    (b) advertising services;[15]
    (c) services of consultants, engineers, consultancy bureaux, lawyers, accountants and other similar services;[16]
    (d) data processing and the provision of information;[17]
    (e) accepting any obligation to refrain from pursuing or exercising all or part of any business activity, copyright, licence, trademark or similar right;
    (f) banking, financial, insurance and reinsurance services;[18]

(g) providing access to natural gas and electricity distribution systems, transport or transmission through those systems and directly linked services;
(h) the supply of staff;[19]
(i) hiring goods other than means of transport;[20]
(j) telecommunication services;
(k) radio and television broadcasting services;
(l) electronically supplied services; and
(m) procuring any of the foregoing services for another person.

(12) Electronically supplied services[21] supplied by a trader who belongs in a third country[22] to a recipient who belongs in an EU member state and receives them for non-business purposes.

(13) Telecommunication services, radio and telephone broadcasting services, electronically supplied services received for business purposes and the hire of goods where, in each case, the services are not used and enjoyed in the country where the supply is deemed to be made.[23]

(14) A right to services,[24] whether or not it is exercised.

De Voil Indirect Tax Service V3.186–196.

---

[1] VAT (Tour Operators) Order, SI 1987/1806, art 5; VAT (Place of Supply of Services) Order, SI 1992/3121, arts 5–18, 21 as amended by SI 1995/3038, SI 1996/2992, SI 1997/1524, SI 1998/763, SI 2006/1683.

[2] As defined in VAT (Tour Operators) Order, SI 1987/1806, arts 3, 16.

[3] As defined in VATA 1994, s 53(3).

[4] For fishing permits, see *Heger Rudi GmbH v Finanzamt Graz-Stadt* (case C-166/05) [2006] ECR I–7749, [2006] SWTI 2182, ECJ.

[5] See *Reisebüro Binder GmbH v Finanzamt Stuttgart-Körperschaften* (case C-116/96) [1998] STC 604, ECJ (pro rata allocation according to the distances covered in each member state); *Köhler v Finanzamt Düsseldorf Nord* (case C-58/04) [2005] ECR I–8218, [2006] STC 469, ECJ (cruise beginning and ending in ports within the EU but having an intermediate stop in a third country).

[6] See *Staatssecretaris van Financiën v Lipjes* (case C-68/03) [2004] ECR I–5879, [2004] STC 1592, ECJ.

[7] For the application of this provision, see *British Sky Broadcasting Ltd v Customs and Excise Comrs* [1994] VATTR 1 (satellite TV broadcasts). For entertainment services, see *RAL (Channel Islands) Ltd v Customs and Excise Comrs* (case C-452/03) [2005] ECR I–3947, [2005] STC 1025, ECJ (gaming machines). For ancillary services under EC law, see *Dudda v Finanzamt Bergisch Gladbach* (case C-327/94) [1996] STC 1290, ECJ. In the UK, see *Sugar and Spice On Tour Catering v Customs and Excise Comrs* (2002) VAT decision 17698.

[8] This provision implements Directive 77/388/EEC art 9(2)(c) (first indent) as interpreted in Ministre de l'Économie, des Finances dt de l'Industrie v Gillian Beach Ltd (case C-114/05) [2006] STC 1080, ECJ

[9] See *Maatschap M J M Linthorst, K G P Pouwels and J Scheres Cs v Inspecteur der Belastingdienst/Ondernemingen Roermond* (case C-167/95) [1997] STC 1287, ECJ (veterinary surgeon).

[10] See *Maatschap M J M Linthorst, K G P Pouwels and J Scheres Cs v Inspecteur der Belastingdienst/Ondernemingen Roermond* (case C-167/95) [1997] STC 1287, ECJ (veterinary surgeon).

[63.30] Introduction

[11] Listed in VATA 1994, Sch 5, paras 1–8.

[12] For "trader" in this context, see *Design Concept SA v Flanders Expo SA* (case C-438/01) [2003] STC 912, ECJ (intermediate supplier of advertising services); *Diversified Agency Services Ltd v Customs and Excise Comrs* [1996] STC 398, *Omnicom UK plc v Customs and Excise Comrs* [1994] VATTR 465 (supply to tourist board). A customer who makes carries on both business and non-business activities is regarded as a trader for the purposes of this provision: see *Kollektivavtalsstifttelsen TRR Trygghetsrådet v Skatteverket* (case C-291/07) [2008] ECR I-0000, [2009] STC 526, ECJ (consultancy services).

[13] For the place where the recipient of a supply belongs, see VATA 1994, s 9(3)–(5). These provisions are interpreted so as to comply with Directive 77/388/EEC, art 9(2)(e), now 2006/112/EC art 56(1): see *W H Payne & Co v Customs and Excise Comrs* [1995] V & DR 490; Business Brief (Issue 26/96), 19 December 1996. For individuals receiving services in a non-business capacity, see *Razzak and Mishari v Customs and Excise Comrs* [1997] V & DR 392. For a UK registered office, see *Binder Hamlyn v Customs and Excise Comrs* [1983] VATTR 171; *Vincent Consultants Ltd v Customs and Excise Comrs* [1988] VATTR 152; *Singer & Friedlander Ltd v Customs and Excise Comrs* [1989] VATTR 27; *Chantrey Vellacott v Customs and Excise Comrs* [1992] VATTR 138. For marine, aviation and transport insurance services, see Business Brief (Issue 21/93), 5 July 1993.

[14] The place of supply of services within VATA 1994, Sch 5, paras 7–7C is modified by the provisions in head 13. For the place of supply in relation to an issue of shares to a nominee acting for an overseas shareholder, see *Water Hall Group plc v Customs and Excise Comrs* (2003) VAT decision 18007; Business Brief (Issue 21/05), 23 November 2005.

[15] For advertising services, see *EC Commission v France* (case C-68/92) [1997] STC 684, ECJ; *EC Commission v Luxembourg* (case C-69/92) [1997] STC 712, ECJ; *EC Commission v Spain* (case C-73/92) [1997] STC 700, ECJ; *Syndicat des Producteurs Indépendants (SPI) v Ministère de l'Economie, des Finances et de l'Industrie* (case C-108/00) [2001] STC 523, ECJ; *International Trade and Exhibitions J/V Ltd v Customs and Excise Comrs* [1996] V & DR 165; *Austrian National Tourist Office v Customs and Excise Comrs* (1998) VAT decision 15561; *John Village Automotive Ltd v Customs and Excise Comrs* [1998] V & DR 340; *Miller Freeman World-wide plc v Customs and Excise Comrs* (1998) VAT decision 15452.

[16] See *Maatschap M J M Linthorst, K G P Pouwels and J Scheres Cs v Inspecteur der Belastingdienst/Ondernemingen Roermond* (case C-167/95) [1997] STC 1287, ECJ (veterinary surgeon); *von Hoffmann v Finanzamt Trier* (case C-145/96) [1997] STC 1321, ECJ (arbitrator); *Levob Verzekeringen BV, OB Bank NV cs v Staatssecretaris van Financiën* (case C-41/04) [2005] ECR I-9433, [2006] STC 766, ECJ (computer science); *EC Commission v Germany* (case C-401/06) [2007] SWTI 2848, ECJ (executor of will); *Hutchvision Hong Kong Ltd v Customs and Excise Comrs* (1993) VAT decision 10509. For the exclusion of services relating to land, see VATA 1994, Sch 5, para 3.

[17] For the exclusion of services relating to land, see VATA 1994, Sch 5, para 3.

[18] For financial services, see *Culverpalm Ltd v Customs and Excise Comrs* [1984] VATTR 199; *Singer & Friedlander Ltd v Customs and Excise Comrs* [1989] VATTR 27; Business Brief (Issue 20/94), 18 November 1994. For the exclusion of safe deposit facilities, see VATA 1994, Sch 5, para 5.

[19] For the supply of staff, see *Strollmoor Ltd v Customs and Excise Comrs* (1990) VAT decision 5454.
[20] For means of transport, see *Hamann v Finanzampt Hamburg-Eimsbüttel* (case 51/88) [1991] STC 193, [1990] 2 CMLR 383, ECJ.
[21] As defined in VATA 1994, Sch 5, para 5C as inserted by SI 2003/863.
[22] For the place where the supplier belongs, see supra, § **63.28**.
[23] Telecommunications services, radio and telephone broadcasting services, electronically supplied services received for business purposes and the hire of goods other than means of transport fall within VATA 1994, Sch 5, paras 7–7C as inserted or substituted by SI 2003/863. The provisions in head 11 are modified in relation to these services. The hire of new means of transport does not fall within head 11.
[24] As defined in SI 1992/3121, art 21(2). For phone cards allowing cheaper telephone call to overseas destinations, see *Revenue and Customs Comrs v Arachchige* [2009] EWHC 1077 (Ch), [2009] STC 1729.

Services—new rules applicable from 1 January 2010

[63.31] FA 2009, s 75 and Sch 36, Part 1 introduce new place of supply rules for services supplied on or after 1 January 2010.[1] The new rules give effect to Directive 2008/8/EC, art 2.[2] In brief, the new place of supply rules for services are as follows:

(1) The general rule is that:[3]
 (a) services (or a right to services) supplied to a relevant business person[4] are supplied in the country in which that person belongs,[5] and
 (b) services (or a right to services) supplied to any other person are supplied in the country in which the supplier belongs.[6]
(2) The general rule gives way to special rules applicable generally,[7] in relation to supplies made to relevant business persons[8] and to supplies made to persons who are not a relevant business person.[9]
(3) The person liable to account for VAT on a supply within head (1)(a) is the person to whom the services were supplied.[10]

---

[1] This is done by: (1) amending VATA 1994, ss 7, 8, 43, 96, 97, 98 and VAT (Tour Operators) Order, SI 1987/1806, art 5; (2) inserting a new VATA 1994, s 7A; (3) substituting a new VATA 1994, s 9; and (4) repealing VATA 1994, Sch 5. For transitional provisions, see FA 2009, Sch 36, para 19.
[2] OJ L44/11, 20.2.08. This amends Directive 2006/112/EC. Articles 3–5 of the 2008 Directive make further amendments to the 2006 Directive with effect from 1 January 2011, 1 January 2013 and 1 January 2015. The 2011 and 2013 changes are given prospective effect by FA 2009, Sch 36, Parts 2 and 3 respectively.
[3] VATA 1994, s 7A(2), (3) as inserted by FA 2009, Sch 36, para 4.
[4] As defined in VATA 1994, s 7A(4) as inserted by FA 2009, Sch 36, para 4.
[5] For the place where a relevant business person belongs, see VATA 1994, s 9(2)–(4) as substituted by FA 2009, Sch 36, para 6.
[6] For the place where a person who is not a relevant business person belongs, see VATA 1994, s 9(5), (6) as substituted by FA 2009, Sch 36, para 6.
[7] VATA 1994, s 7A(6) and Sch 4A, Part 1 (paras 1–8) as inserted by FA 2009, Sch 36, paras 4, 11.

[63.31] Introduction

[8] VATA 1994, s 7A(6) and Sch 4A, Part 2 (para 9) as inserted by FA 2009, Sch 36, paras 4, 11.
[9] VATA 1994, s 7A(6) and Sch 4A, Part 3 (paras 10–16) as inserted by FA 2009, Sch 36, paras 4, 11.
[10] Directive 2006/112/EC, art 196 as substituted by Directive 2008/8/EC, art 7. For the reverse charge adopted in the UK in relation to supplies received by UK taxable persons from overseas suppliers, see infra, § 65.38.

Supplies made in the course or furtherance of business

[63.32] Once an activity has been identified as a business,[1] any supply made while carrying it on[2] is likely to be made in the course or furtherance of business.[3] No distinction is made between capital and revenue items. Thus, a supply in the course or furtherance of business includes the disposition of the assets and liabilities of a business, the disposition of a business as a going concern and anything done in connection with the termination or intended termination of a business.[4] Similarly, no distinction is made between trading and investment activities. Thus, a firm of solicitors holding client's moneys on deposit receives the interest thereon in the course or furtherance of business.[5]

A person who accepts an office in the course or furtherance of his trade, profession or vocation is treated as supplying his services as holder of the office in the course or furtherance of his trade, profession or vocation.[6] A charity is treated as making a supply in the course or furtherance of business when it exports goods to a third country.[7]

For transactions carried out for tax avoidance purposes, or forming part of a chain of transactions in which one or more of the participants misappropriate VAT, see supra, § **63.15**.

De Voil Indirect Tax Service V2.201–213, 231–236.

[1] For the activities which do, or do not, amount to the carrying on of a business, see §§ **63.14–63.16**.
[2] For the intention to carry on an activity, see *Intercommunale voor Zeewaterontzilting (in liquidation) v Belgian State* (case C-110/94) [1996] STC 569, ECJ.
[3] For supplies made in the course or furtherance of business, see *Edward James Foundation v Customs and Excise Comrs* [1975] VATTR 61; *Ridley v Customs and Excise Comrs* [1983] VATTR 81; *Stirling v Customs and Excise Comrs* [1985] VATTR 232; *Trustees of the Mellerstain Trust v Customs and Excise Comrs* [1989] VATTR 223.
[4] VATA 1994, s 94(5), (6). See *H B Mattia Ltd v Customs and Excise Comrs* [1976] VATTR 33 and *Stirling v Customs and Excise Comrs* [1985] VATTR 232.
[5] *Hedges and Mercer v Customs and Excise Comrs* [1976] VATTR 146.
[6] VATA 1994, s 94(4). See *Gardner v Customs and Excise Comrs* [1989] VATTR 132 (whether office accepted in course of trade, etc); *Hempsons (a firm) v Customs and Excise Comrs* [1977] VATTR 73 (partner holding office).
[7] VATA 1994, s 30(5). The supply is deemed to be made in the UK.

Exempt supplies

[63.33] A supply of goods or services is an exempt supply if it is for the time being specified in VATA 1994, Sch 9.[1] As its name suggests, an exempt supply is exempt from tax. Thus, no tax is charged on it.[2]

A taxable supply is a supply of goods or services made in the UK which is not an exempt supply.[3]

De Voil Indirect Tax Service V3.121.

---

[1] VATA 1994, s 31(1). For the goods and services within VATA 1994, Sch 9, see Chapter 70. For the option to tax which overrides exemption, see infra, § **68.03**. For the difference between exempt supplies and zero-rated supplies, see infra, § **68.01**.
[2] For the effect of exempt supplies on input tax recovery, see infra, § **68.01**.
[3] VATA 1994, s 4(2).

Acquisitions

Introduction

[63.34] The abolition of frontier controls on movement of goods between EU member states from 1 January 1993 had the consequence that VAT could no longer be levied in the same manner as VAT chargeable on goods imported from third countries. A new charge to tax was accordingly introduced. It applies to "acquisitions" of goods from another EU member state.

An acquisition giving rise to registration or the charge to tax is referred to as "taxable acquisitions". The registration and charging provisions apply if a taxable acquisition is made in the UK.[1]

De Voil Indirect Tax Service V3.361, 362.

---

[1] VATA 1994, s 10(1) and Sch 3, para 11.

Meaning of 'acquisition'

[63.35] An acquisition is a supply of goods, or a transaction treated as a supply of goods,[1] which involves the removal of goods from one EU member state to another.[2] It is immaterial whether the removal is made by or under the direction of the supplier, the person who acquires the goods, or any other person.[3] The term includes a transaction where the person with the property in any goods does not change in consequence of anything which is treated as a supply of goods.[4]

The following transactions are not treated as an acquisition of goods:

(1) A central bank receiving gold from a supplier in another EU member state.[5]

[63.35] Introduction

(2) A removal of goods under a supply made to a taxable person chargeable to VAT in another EU member state by reference to the profit margin.[6]

De Voil Indirect Tax Service V3.363.

---

[1] For supplies and transactions within this description, see supra, § **63.24**.
[2] VATA 1994, s 11(1). For triangular transactions and supplies of installed goods, see infra, § **63.37**.
[3] VATA 1994, s 11(2).
[4] VATA 1994, s 11(3).
[5] VAT (Treatment of Transactions) (No 2) Order, SI 1992/3132.
[6] VAT (Special Provisions) Order, SI 1995/1268, art 7.

Taxable acquisitions

[63.36] An acquisition of goods is a taxable acquisition if meets the following conditions:[1]

(1) The goods fall within any of the following descriptions:
    (a) they comprise a new means of transport;
    (b) they are acquired in the course or furtherance of any business carried on by the person who acquires them; or
    (c) they are acquired in the course or furtherance of any non-business activity carried on by the body corporate or unincorporated association which acquires them.
(2) (In the case of goods within (b) or (c)) the supplier is a taxable person in another EU member state who acts in the course or furtherance of business in participating in the transaction.
(3) The acquisition is not an exempt acquisition. An acquisition of goods is an exempt acquisition if it is for the time being specified in VATA 1994, Sch 9.[2]

De Voil Indirect Tax Service V3.361, 362.

---

[1] VATA 1994, s 10(2), (3).
[2] VATA 1994, s 31(1). For the goods within VATA 1994, Sch 9, see Chapter 70.

The place of acquisition

[63.37] Goods are normally treated as acquired in the UK if they are removed to the UK under a transaction which does not involve their removal from the UK, ie the goods are not merely removed from EU member state X to member state Y via the UK. Goods are otherwise treated as acquired outside the UK.[1]

However, goods are treated as acquired in the UK if the person acquiring them makes use of a UK VAT registration number[2] in circumstances where no VAT is paid in another EU member state.[3] The goods are treated as acquired outside the UK if VAT is so paid[4] and the person is entitled to a refund of any UK VAT paid.[5] Thus, if X (a French supplier) sells goods to Y (a UK taxable person) but removes the goods to Germany on X's instructions, Y can elect to make an acquisition in the UK, rather than in Germany, by notifying his UK VAT registration number to X if German legislation allows him to make a tax-free acquisition in Germany.

Special place of acquisition rules apply to warehoused goods.[6]

De Voil Indirect Tax Service V3.371–383.

[1] VATA 1994, s 13(2).
[2] Assignment and use of a UK VAT registration number is determined in accordance with regulations made under VATA 1994, s 13(5)(a), (b). No regulations have been made to date.
[3] VATA 1994, s 13(3), (4).
[4] VATA 1994, s 13(4). Payment of VAT in another EU member state is determined in accordance with regulations. No regulations have been made to date.
[5] In accordance with regulations made under VATA 1994, s 13(5)(c). No regulations have been made to date.
[6] For goods subject to a warehousing regime, see VATA 1994, s 18(1), (3); VAT Regulations, SI 1995/2518, reg 145K as inserted by SI 2005/2231. For goods subject to a fiscal warehousing regime, see VATA 1994, s 18B(3) as inserted by FA 1996, Sch 3, para 5.

Triangulation

[63.38] An "acquisition" is one side of a transaction which involves the removal of goods from one EU member state to another. The other side of the transaction is a supply of goods or a transaction treated as such a supply.[1] The general principle is that the supply takes place in one EU member state and the acquisition takes place in another EU member state. Thus, if X (a French supplier) sells goods to Y (a UK customer) and the goods are removed from France to the UK, X will normally make a supply in France which is taxed or relieved from tax under French VAT law and Y will normally make an acquisition in the UK which is taxed or relieved from tax under UK VAT law. A similar situation arises when X moves his own goods from France to (say) a distribution depot in the UK without making a supply to a third party.

A more complex situation results when three or more persons are involved in a single removal of goods, eg where X sells the goods to Y (a German trader), Y sells the same goods to Z, and X removes the goods to the UK in accordance with instructions given by Y. This situation is referred to as "triangulation" and gives rise to a complex series of reliefs designed to avoid double taxation in two or more EU member states.[2]

The position is further complicated by the fact that goods are not necessarily acquired in the member state to which they are removed.[3] Thus, if X removes goods to the UK under a supply to Y, and Y is registered for VAT purposes in Germany, he can elect to make an acquisition in Germany rather than the UK by making use of his German VAT registration number.

De Voil Indirect Tax Service V3.363.

[63.38] Introduction

1   For the taxation of goods removed from the UK to another member state, see infra, § **69:07**.
2   See VATA 1994, s 14. For an example, see *EMAG Handel Eder OHG v Finanzlandesdirecktion für Kärnten* (case C-245/04) [2006] ECR I-3227, [2006] SWTI 1267, ECJ.
3   For the place of acquisition, see supra, § **63.36**.

Imported goods

Introduction

[63.39] Goods entering the territory of the EU are placed under customs supervision until such time as the customs duty (if any) is discharged or the goods are removed to a third country. Duty may be discharged in the EU member state into which the goods are imported or the member state to which they are subsequently moved. Thus, goods charged to customs duty in the UK may have arrived direct from a third country or via another EU member state.

A further level of customs supervision arises on goods subject to excise duty. Customs duty is imposed under EU legislation having direct effect throughout the EU. Excise duties are imposed under national legislation, which is partly harmonised on the basis of the EU excise directives.

Goods entering the UK directly or indirectly from a third country are charged to VAT.[1] Thus, VAT represents a third level of customs supervision. However, it is charged and payable as if it were a duty of customs.[2] In consequence, it is charged paid in accordance with customs legislation. This legislation applies in a modified form in accordance with provisions set out in the VAT legislation. In essence, this legislation provides that certain customs legislation does or does not apply, modifies some of the applicable customs legislation, and supplements the applicable customs legislation as so modified with provisions applicable solely to VAT.[3]

De Voil Indirect Tax Service V3.111.

1   See VATA 1994, s 1(1)(c). A third country is a place that does not form part of the EU VAT territory. For the extent of the VAT territory, see supra, § **63.08**. For transitional provisions in relation to the enlargement of the EU on 1 May 2004, see VAT Regulations, SI 1995/2518, reg 138 as amended by SI 2004/1082.
2   See VATA 1994, s 1(4).
3   See VATA 1994, s 16. For the legislation concerned, see supra, § **63.03**.

Goods delivered or removed without payment of duty

[63.40] Goods may be imported without payment of VAT where conditions specified in the legislation, or imposed by the Commissioners, are met. The principal purpose of these reliefs is to assist national and international trade by creating a "tax-free ring".

In broad terms, relief is available for:

(1) Goods removed to a customs or excise warehouse.[1]
(2) Goods removed to a free zone.[2]
(3) Goods temporarily imported for removal to another EU member state.[3]
(4) Temporary importations of commercial vehicles and aircraft.[4]
(5) Goods entered for transit through the UK or transhipment with a view to re-exportation.[5]

De Voil Indirect Tax Service V3.315, 331–338.

[1] CEMA 1979, s 46. For customs warehouses, see Regulation (EEC) Nos 2503/88 and 2561/90. For excise warehouses, see Excise Warehousing (etc) Regulations, SI 1988/809. VAT is charged when goods are entered for home use. For the place of supply of warehoused goods, see VATA 1994, s 18.

[2] VATA 1994, s 17(2); Free Zone Regulations, SI 1991/2727, reg 3. The following places have been designated as free zones: Liverpool (SI 2001/2881 as amended by SI 2006/1834), Port of Sheerness (SI 2004/2742 as amended by SI 2006/1834), Port of Tilbury (SI 2002/1418 as amended by SI 2006/1834), Prestwick Airport (SI 2001/2882 as amended by SI 2006/1834), Southampton (SI 2001/2880 as amended by SI 2006/1834). For the regulation of free zones, see Free Zone Regulations, SI 1984/1177 and SI 1991/2727. VAT is charged when goods are entered for home use on use or consumption in a free zone or removal therefrom, subject to relief if the goods have been supplied by a non-taxable person: Free Zone Regulations, SI 1984/1177, regs 9(7), 11, 16, 17(1), 27. For goods cleared for removal from the free zone by the customer, see Notice No 48 (July 2009) para 3.14.

[3] VAT Regulations, SI 1995/2518, reg 123.

[4] Temporary Importation (Commercial Vehicles and Aircraft) Regulations, SI 1961/1523.

[5] CEMA 1979, s 47.

Simplification schemes

Cash accounting scheme

[63.41] The cash accounting scheme, as its name suggests, is a scheme which, in broad terms, enables a trader to account for output tax and deduct input tax by reference to the time when payments are received or made.[1] A trader is entitled to begin using the scheme from the beginning of a prescribed accounting period if he meets specified conditions. In particular, he must have reasonable grounds for believing that the value of his taxable supplies for the ensuing year will not exceed £1,350,000.[2] It is not necessary to obtain prior approval.

The cash accounting scheme has proved popular because it often confers a cash flow advantage. It also avoids the need to claim bad debt relief when customers

[63.41] Introduction

pay very late—or not at all—and the requirement to pay back input tax when suppliers are paid very late. The downside is a need for parallel records if purchase and sales ledgers (or their computer equivalents) are maintained on a double entry basis.

De Voil Indirect Tax Service V2.199.

---

[1] VAT Regulations, SI 1995/2518, regs 57, 65(1). For transactions to which the scheme does not apply, see SI 1995/2518, regs 56A, 58(2) as inserted, substituted and amended by SI 1997/1614, SI 2002/1142, SI 2007/1418.

[2] For the conditions, see SI 1995/2518, reg 58(1), (4) as substituted by SI 1997/1614 and amended by SI 2001/677, SI 2004/767, SI 2007/768.

Flat-rate scheme for small businesses

[63.42] The flat-rate scheme is a simplified method of accounting for VAT. It applies to all supplies made (referred to as "relevant supplies") and to all purchases, acquisitions and importations (referred to as "relevant purchases") which fall within the scheme.[1] Instead of calculating output tax and input tax for a prescribed accounting period and deducting one from the other to arrive at the amount due to or from the Commissioners, an authorised flat-rate trader[2] calculates output tax by reference to a percentage (referred to as the "appropriate percentage")[3] of the VAT-inclusive value of his relevant supplies for the period (referred to as "relevant turnover")[4] and does not claim input tax credit in respect of his relevant purchases.[5] Output tax and input tax are calculated in accordance with the normal rules in respect of supplies, purchases, acquisitions and importations which are neither relevant supplies nor relevant purchases. For the calculation of tax due under the scheme, see infra, § **64.17**.

It will be appreciated that the scheme only approximately reflects the true liability for a prescribed accounting period. Whether a flat-rate trader saves or loses by using the scheme depends upon how closely his own business fits the profile used by the Commissioners to fix the percentage applicable to his business.

As a means of encouraging new businesses to use the scheme, the appropriate percentage is reduced during the 12-month period commencing with the effective date of registration. However, the reduction applies for only part of the period if a trader registers late (so that his effective date of registration is backdated), or if he delays applying for authorisation (so that he starts to use the scheme part way through the period).[6] The full benefit is obtained by registering on time and applying for authorisation contemporaneously.

EXAMPLE

An accountant's relevant supplies for a prescribed accounting period comprise standard rate supplies of £30,000 plus VAT thereon of £4,500 and exempt supplies of £750 in respect of insurance commission. His input tax on relevant purchases amounts to £425. His relevant turnover is £35,250. The appropriate percentage currently used by accountants is 11.5%. His output tax is therefore 11.5% of £35,250 = £4,053.75. He is not entitled to input tax credit. He therefore makes a payment of £4,053.75 to the Commissioners.

If the accountant had used the normal method of accounting, his payment to the Commissioners would have been £4,500 − £425 = £4,075. He therefore saves £21.25 by using the scheme. Moreover, once relevant turnover has been ascertained, the VAT return can be prepared in a matter of seconds.

The neutral outcome shown in the example has been contrived. An increase in exempt supplies or input tax would have resulted in a very different position. In practice, a trader should take a close look at the pattern of his purchases and sales (in order to calculate the likely financial consequences) and the complexity of his current method of VAT accounting (in order to find out whether any worthwhile administrative saving will arise) before joining the scheme. A tax review may indicate a clear tax gain or loss, but it will not necessarily do so. It may merely suggest a neutral or uncertain position. Administrative savings may be more illusory than real because some of the information no longer required for VAT accounting is nevertheless required for other purposes.[7] The scheme may release more time for leisure, increase chargeable hours or save the cost of employing an accountant. Shorter working hours and the ability to meet VAT return deadlines in a more relaxed manner may be worthwhile benefits in themselves, even if they have no monetary value. Any increase in sales or reduction in costs may outweigh any increase in VAT payments. It is necessary to weigh these factors carefully before reaching a decision.

De Voil Indirect Tax Service V2.199B.

---

[1] For relevant purchases and relevant supplies, see VATA 1994, s 26(2)(*b*) as inserted by FA 2002, s 23 and VAT Regulations, SI 1995/2518, reg 55C as inserted and amended by SI 2002/1142, SI 2007/1418.

[2] For authorisation, see VAT Regulations, SI 1995/2518, reg 55B as inserted or amended by SI 2002/1142, 2003/3220. For eligibility for authorisation, see SI 1995/2518, reg 55L as inserted or amended by SI 2002/1142, SI 2003/1069, SI 2009/586.

[3] For the appropriate percentage, see infra, § **65.21**.

[4] For relevant turnover, see VATA 1994, s 26(2)(*c*) as inserted by FA 2002, s 23 and SI 1995/2518, reg 55G as inserted by SI 2002/1142. For the "basic turnover method", "cash turnover method" and "retailer's turnover method", see Notice No 733.

[5] See infra, § **66.06**.

[6] SI 1995/2518, reg 55JB as inserted by SI 2003/3220.

[7] For the impact of the scheme on the preparation of financial statements for direct tax purposes, see *Joint statement by Customs and Inland Revenue on record keeping and the FRS* (VAT Information Sheet 17/03, Annex B).

Special accounting scheme for electronic services

[63.43] Traders making electronically supplied services[1] to non-taxable persons from a third country are deemed to supply those services in the EC member state where a non-taxable person has his permanent address or usually resides.[2] In consequence, he may make supplies in a number of member states and have a liability register in all of them. Multiple registrations are an

[63.43] Introduction

obvious inconvenience. An EC simplification scheme enables traders to register in only one member state and to account for VAT on all of his EC supplies in the member state he chooses.[3] This member state retains the VAT attributable to supplies made in the UK and distributes the balance to the other member states in which supplies have been made.[4] The manner in which the simplification scheme applies to traders choosing to register in the UK is determined in accordance with UK legislation.[5] The manner in which the scheme applies to traders choosing to register in other member states is set out in the national legislation of those member states.

The UK legislation sets out arrangements similar to, but separate from, the arrangements applicable to taxable persons. Thus, there are self-contained provisions for registration,[6] liability to pay for VAT,[7] special accounting returns,[8] payment of VAT,[9] records,[10] understatements and overstatements of VAT,[11] appeals,[12] The repayment scheme for third country traders is adapted for the purposes of the simplification scheme.[13] Third country traders cannot be required to appoint a VAT representative.[14] The common feature is that things are done electronically.

De Voil Indirect Tax Service V2.189E–189N.

---

[1] As defined in VATA 1994, Sch 5, para 7C as inserted by SI 2003/863. These services are referred to as "qualifying services" in VATA 1994, Sch 3B, para 3 as inserted by FA 2003, s 23.

[2] Directive 2006/112/EC art 56(1). For the corresponding UK provisions, see VAT (Place of Supply of Services) Order, SI 1992/3121, art 16A as inserted by SI 2003/862.

[3] For the simplification scheme, see Directive 2006/112/EC arts 357–369 as amended by Directive 2006/138/EC. This scheme expires on 31 December 2008.

[4] In accordance with Regulation (EEC) No 218/92 as amended by Regulation (EC) No 792/2002. For consequences within the UK, see VATA 1994, Sch 3B, para 21 as so inserted.

[5] VATA 1994, s 3A and Sch 3B as inserted by FA 2003, Sch 2, paras 2, 4. This Schedule may be amended by Treasury order: VATA 1994, s 3A(2), (3) as so inserted.

[6] VATA 1994, Sch 3B, paras 1–9, 17, 18 as inserted by FA 2003, Sch 2, para 4.

[7] VATA 1994, Sch 3B, para 10 as so inserted.

[8] VATA 1994, Sch 3B, paras 11, 12 as so inserted.

[9] VATA 1994, Sch 3B, para 13 as so inserted.

[10] VATA 1994, Sch 3B, paras 14, 15 as so inserted.

[11] VATA 1994, Sch 3B, para 16 as so inserted.

[12] VATA 1994, Sch 3B, para 20 as so inserted and amended by Transfer of Tribunal Functions and Revenue and Customs Appeals Order, SI 2009/56, Sch 2, para 227.

[13] VATA 1994, Sch 3B, para 22 as so inserted. For the repayment scheme, see infra, § 66.38.

[14] VATA 1994, Sch 3B, para 19 as so inserted.

Other simplification schemes

[63.44] Traders have the option to use the following special schemes:

Simplification schemes [63.44]

(1) The annual accounting scheme.[1] This scheme enables traders to prepare annual rather than quarterly VAT returns. Traders must be authorised by the Commissioners before using this scheme. A trader is eligible for authorisation if he meets specified conditions. In particular, he must have reasonable grounds for believing that the value of his taxable supplies for the ensuing year will not exceed £1,350,000. The Commissioners may refuse a request for authorisation if they consider that it is necessary to do so for the protection of the revenue.[2]

(2) The flat-rate scheme for farmers.[3] This scheme compensates unregistered farmers for the loss of input tax credits by way of a flat-rate addition charged to customers. Traders must be certified by the Commissioners before using this scheme.

(3) The special schemes for retailers.[4] These schemes enable retailers to account for output tax by reference to their aggregate takings rather than by reference to individual supplies. For the calculation of output tax under the retail schemes, see infra, § **65.22**.

De Voil Indirect Tax Service V2.191.

---

[1] See VATA 1994, Sch 11, para 2(7) and VAT Regulations, SI 1995/2518 Part VII (regs 49–55).

[2] SI 1995/2518, reg 52 as substituted by SI 1996/542 and amended by SI 2002/1142, SI 2003/1069, SI 2004/767.

[3] See VATA 1994, s 54 and SI 1995/2518 Part XXIV (regs 202–211). For examples of activities excluded from the scheme, see *Finanzamt Rendsburg v Harbs* (case C-321/02) [2004] ECR I–7101, [2006] STC 340, ECJ (rent from leasing part of the agricultural land, cattle and milk quota); *Finanzamt Arnsberg v Stadt Sundern* (case C-43/04) [2005] ECR I–4491, ECJ (grant of hunting licences).

[4] VATA 1994, Sch 11, para 2(6) and SI 1995/2518 Part IX (regs 66–75).

64

Registration

Liability to registration	PARA **64.01**
Entitlement to registration	PARA **64.15**
Exemption from registration	PARA **64.20**
VAT groups	PARA **64.24**

Liability to registration

Person making taxable supplies

Taxable supplies

[64.01] A trader is a taxable person, and is therefore required to register for the purposes of VAT, if the value of his taxable supplies exceeds one of the limits set out below.[1] Taxable supplies for this purpose means supplies other than exempt supplies made in the UK in the course or furtherance of business.[2] The value is equivalent to the consideration for those supplies since value is determined on the basis that no tax is chargeable on the supply.[3]

The values of certain self-supplies are also taken into account for registration purposes.[4] So are the values of relevant services,[5] gold,[6] and certain goods[7] supplied *to* the recipient in connection with his business.[8]

A supply of goods or services made in the course or furtherance of business is disregarded for registration purposes if the items concerned are "capital assets" of the business.[9] However, the grant of an interest in, right over or licence to occupy land is not disregarded for this purpose if it is chargeable to tax at the standard rate.[10] Goods and services supplied by a certified flat-rate farmer in the course of carrying on a designated activity and certain supplies of warehoused goods are also disregarded.[11]

De Voil Indirect Tax Service V2.134.

---

[1] A local authority which makes taxable supplies is liable to registration whatever the value of its supplies: VATA 1994, s 42.
[2] VATA 1994, s 4(2) and Sch 1, para 19. See *Trustees of the Mellerstain Trust v Customs and Excise Comrs* [1989] VATTR 223.
[3] VATA 1994, s 19(2) and Sch 1, para 16.
[4] For the self-supplies concerned, see infra, §§ **65.33–65.35**.
[5] As defined in VATA 1994, s 8(2).
[6] As defined in VATA 1994, s 55(5), as amended by FA 1996, ss 29(3), 32(1).
[7] As defined in an order made under VATA 1994, s 55A(9) as inserted by FA 2006, s 19. No order has been made to date.

[64.01] Registration

[8] VATA 1994, ss 8(1), 55(1) and 55A(3) as inserted by FA 2006, s 19. For the reverse charge on relevant services, gold and certain goods, see infra, §§ **65.38, 65.40, 65.41**.
[9] VATA 1994, Sch 1, para 1(7). For the nature of capital assets, see *Trustees of the Mellerstain Trust v Customs and Excise Comrs* [1989] VATTR 223; *Harbig Leasing Two Ltd v Customs and Excise Comrs* (2000) VAT decision 16843.
[10] VATA 1994, Sch 1, para 1(8).
[11] VATA 1994, Sch 1, para 1(9), as inserted by FA 1996, Sch 3, para 13.

Taxable supplies for the past twelve months

[64.02] An unregistered person who makes taxable supplies is liable to registration at the end of any month if the value of his taxable supplies in the period of one year then ending has exceeded £68,000.[1] However, he does not become liable to registration under this provision if the Commissioners are satisfied that the value of his taxable supplies in the period of one year then beginning will not exceed £66,000.[2] Where a trader has previously been deregistered on the basis of a full disclosure of the relevant facts, the value of taxable supplies made prior to deregistration is disregarded.[3]

A trader liable to registration under this provision must notify the Commissioners of that fact within 30 days of the end of the relevant month.[4] He must do so even if he considers that his future turnover will not exceed the stated limit. The Commissioners cannot be "satisfied" in this respect unless he does so.[5] A trader is registered with effect from the end of the month following the relevant month, or from a mutually agreed earlier date.[6] Thus, if X's turnover for the year ended 31 July 2009 is £69,000, he must notify the Commissioners by 30 August 2009, and is registered with effect from 1 September 2009, unless he satisfies the Commissioners that turnover for the year to 31 July 2010 will be less than £66,000. However, if X is also liable to registration at 31 July 2009 under some other provision, he is registered under that provison.[7]

De Voil Indirect Tax Service V2.135.

[1] VATA 1994, Sch 1, para 1(1)(*a*) as amended by SI 2009/1031.
[2] VATA 1994, Sch 1, para 1(3) as amended by SI 2009/1031. The Commissioners must be satisfied on the basis of the information available to them at the time when the registration is due to take effect. This applies whether or not the application for registration is made at the proper time: *Gray (t/a William Gray & Son) v Customs and Excise Comrs* [2000] STC 880.
[3] VATA 1994, Sch 1, para 1(4).
[4] VATA 1994, Sch 1, para 5(1), (3). Liability to registration is notified on forms VAT 1 and (in the case of a partnership) VAT 2: VAT Regulations, SI 1995/2518, reg 5(1) as substituted or amended by SI 2000/794, SI 2004/1675. For electronic notification, see SI 1995/2518 reg 5(4)–(14) as inserted by SI 2004/1675.
[5] See *Briggs v Customs and Excise Comrs* (1985) VAT decision 1813.
[6] VATA 1994, Sch 1, para 5(2).
[7] VATA 1994, Sch 1, para 8.

Taxable supplies for the next 30 days

[64.03] An unregistered person who makes taxable supplies[1] is liable to registration at any time if there are reasonable grounds[2] for believing that the value of his taxable supplies in the period of 30 days then beginning will exceed £68,000.[3] He must notify the Commissioners of that fact before the end of the 30-day period[4] and is registered with effect from the beginning of the 30-day period.[5] Thus, if X considers that turnover for the period 15 July 2009–13 August 2009 will be (say) £69,000, he must notify the Commissioners by 13 August 2009 and is registered with effect from 15 July 2009.

De Voil Indirect Tax Service V2.136.

---

[1] See *XL (Stevenage) Ltd v Customs and Excise Comrs* [1981] VATTR 192 (intending trader unaffected by this provision); *Merseyside Cablevision Ltd v Customs and Excise Comrs* [1987] VATTR 134 at 157 (term connotes some degree or regularity).
[2] For the test applied under superseded legislation, see *Bennett v Customs and Excise Comrs* [1999] STC 248; *Optimum Personnel Evaluation (Operations) Ltd v Customs and Excise Comrs* (1987) VAT decision 2334.
[3] VATA 1994, Sch 1, para 1(1)(*b*) as amended by 2009/1031.
[4] VATA 1994, Sch 1, para 6(1). Liability to registration is notified on forms VAT 1 and (in the case of a partnership) VAT 2: VAT Regulations, SI 1995/2518, reg 5(1) as substituted or amended by SI 2000/794, SI 2004/1675. For electronic notification, see SI 1995/2518 reg 5(4)–(14) as inserted by SI 2004/1675.
[5] VATA 1994, Sch 1, para 6(2).

Business transferred as a going concern

[64.04] An unregistered person is liable to registration if all or part[1] of a business carried on by a taxable person is transferred to him as a going concern in either of the following circumstances:

(1) The value of his taxable supplies in the period of one year ending at the time of transfer has exceeded £68,000.[2] However, he does not become liable to registration under this provision if the Commissioners are satisfied that the value of his taxable supplies in the period of one year then beginning will not exceed £66,000.[3] The taxable supplies taken into account include those of both vendor and purchaser.[4] Where a trader has previously been deregistered on the basis of a full disclosure of the relevant facts, the value of taxable supplies made prior to registration is disregarded.[5]

(2) There are reasonable grounds for believing that the value of his taxable supplies in the period of 30 days beginning at the time of transfer will exceed £68,000.[6]

A trader liable to registration under either provision must notify the Commissioners of that fact within 30 days of the time of transfer.[7] He is registered with effect from the time of transfer.[8] Thus, if X acquires a business as a going concern on 15 July 2009, he must notify the Commissioners by 13 August 2009 and is registered with effect from 15 July 2009.

De Voil Indirect Tax Service V2.137.

[64.04] Registration

[1] A part of a business falls within this provision only if it was transferred as a going concern pursuant to a contract entered into after 31 August 2007: see FA 2007, s 100(8), (10).
[2] VATA 1994, Sch 1, para 1(2)(a) as amended by SI 2009/1031.
[3] VATA 1994, Sch 1, para 1(3) as amended by SI 2009/1031. See *Gray (trading as William Gray & Son) v Customs and Excise Comrs* [2000] STC 880 noted at supra, § **64.02**.
[4] VATA 1994, s 49(1)(a) as amended by FA 2007, s 99.
[5] VATA 1994, Sch 1, para 1(4).
[6] VATA 1994, Sch 1, para 1(2)(b) as amended by SI 2009/1031.
[7] VATA 1994, Sch 1, para 7(1). Liability to registration is notified on forms VAT 1 and (in the case of a partnership) VAT 2: VAT Regulations, SI 1995/2518, reg 5(1) as substituted or amended by SI 2000/794, SI 2004/1675. For electronic notification, see SI 1995/2518 reg 5(4)–(14) as inserted by SI 2004/1675.
[8] VATA 1994, Sch 1, para 7(2).

Person supplying tax relieved goods in the UK

Relevant supplies

[64.05] An EC[1] or third country[2] trader entitled to receive repayment of VAT on his purchases, acquisitions or importations[3] is liable to registration if he makes or intends to make a supply of goods (referred to as a "relevant supply") in respect of which the following conditions are met:[4]

(1) The goods are assets of the trader's business.
(2) The goods are supplied in the course or furtherance of that business.
(3) The supply is a taxable supply.[5]
(4) The trader, or one of his predecessors[6] has either claimed or received a repayment, or intends to make a claim for repayment, in respect of his purchase, acquisition or importation of the goods.

De Voil Indirect Tax Service V2.189.

[1] ie a person carrying on business in an EC member state who is not established in the UK: see VAT Regulations, SI 1995/2518, regs 173, 174, 175.
[2] ie a person established in a third country who is neither established in the EC nor a taxable person in the UK: see VAT Regulations, SI 1995/2518, regs 185, 186, 188.
[3] In accordance with VAT Regulations, SI 1995/2518, regs 173–184 (EC trader) or 185–197 (third country trader).
[4] VATA 1994, Sch 3A, paras 1, 9 as inserted by FA 2000, s 136 and Sch 36.
[5] For taxable supplies, see supra, § **64.01**.
[6] As defined in VATA 1994, Sch 3A, para 9(2) as inserted by FA 2000, s 136 and Sch 36.

Liability to registration

[64.06] A person is liable to registration in either of the following circumstances:

(1) He makes relevant supplies. He must notify the Commissioners within 30 days of doing so. He is registered with effect from the beginning of the day on which his liability to registration arises.[1]
(2) There are reasonable grounds for believing that he will make relevant supplies in the next 30 days. He must notify the Commissioners before the end of the 30-day period. He is registered with effect from the beginning of the 30-day period.[2]

Liability to registration is notified on forms VAT 1C and (in the case of a partnership) VAT 2.[3]

De Voil Indirect Tax Service V2.189.

---

[1] VATA 1994, Sch 3A, paras 1(1)(*a*), 3 as inserted by FA 2000, s 136 and Sch 36.
[2] VATA 1994, Sch 3A, paras 1(1)(*b*), 4 as inserted by FA 2000, s 136 and Sch 36.
[3] VAT Regulations, SI 1995/2518, reg 5(1) as substituted or amended by SI 2000/794, SI 2004/1675. For electronic notification, see SI 1995/2518 reg 5(4)–(14) as inserted by SI 2004/1675.

Person supplying goods from another EU member state

Relevant supplies

[64.07] A supply of goods is referred to as a "relevant supply" if it is made in the following circumstances:[1]

(1) The supply is made for a consideration in the course or furtherance of business.
(2) The goods are removed to the UK from another EU member state by the supplier.
(3) The customer is not a taxable person.
(4) The customer makes an acquisition of the goods in the UK.

A trader is a taxable person, and is therefore required to register for the purposes of VAT, if he makes a relevant supply, or makes relevant supplies in excess of a specified value, of any goods other than a new means of transport or goods[2] which are installed or assembled in the UK. New means of transport are excluded because the non-taxable person makes a taxable acquisition[3] so as to be charged to tax under the provisions described in infra, § **67.12**. Thus, there is no point in registering him. Goods installed or assembled in the UK are excluded because the place of supply is the UK.[4] Thus, the supplier makes a taxable supply and may become a taxable person by reference to it under the provisions described in supra, §§ **64.02–64.04**.

Different registration provisions apply to goods which are subject to excise duty and goods which are not.

De Voil Indirect Tax Service V2.171.

[64.07] Registration

1 The common provisions of VATA 1994, Sch 2, paras 1(3)(*a*)–(*e*) and 10.
2 As defined in VATA 1994, s 95.
3 VATA 1994, s 10(2)(*a*).
4 VATA 1994, s 7(3)(*a*).

Supply of goods subject to excise duty

[64.08] A person is liable to registration if the following conditions are met:[1]

(1) He makes a relevant supply of excise goods at any time.
(2) He is neither registered nor liable to registration under the provisions described in infra, § **64.10**.

He must notify the Commissioners within 30 days of making the supply.[2] He is registered with effect from the day on which the supply was made or a mutually agreed earlier date.[3]

De Voil Indirect Tax Service V2.171.

[1] VATA 1994, Sch 2, para 1(3). For relevant supplies, see supra, § **64.06**.
[2] VATA 1994, Sch 2, para 3(1). Liability to registration is notified on forms VAT 1 and (in the case of a partnership) VAT 2: VAT Regulations, SI 1995/2518, reg 5(1) as substituted or amended by SI 2000/794, SI 2004/1675. For electronic notification, see SI 1995/2518 reg 5(4)–(14) as inserted by SI 2004/1675.
[3] VATA 1994, Sch 2, para 3(2).

Other goods affected by a place of supply option

[64.09] A person is liable to registration if the following conditions are met:[1]

(1) He makes a relevant supply of goods[2] which are not subject to excise duty.
(2) The supply is affected by a place of supply option made under the law of the EU member state where he is registered.
(3) He is neither registered nor liable to registration under the provisions described in infra, § **64.10**.

The option in head 2 is made under legislation giving effect to Directive 2006/112/EEC art 34(4). It provides that a relevant supply is treated as made in the country of arrival rather than the country of despatch. A relevant supply triggers registration in the UK if it is made at a time when the option is in force and involves a removal of goods from the EU member state where it was exercised.[3]

The person must notify the Commissioners within 30 days of making the supply.[4] He is registered with effect from the day on which the supply was made or from a mutually agreed earlier date.[5]

De Voil Indirect Tax Service V2.171.

[1] VATA 1994, Sch 2, para 1(2). For relevant supplies, see supra, § **64.07**.
[2] For supplies of warehoused goods disregarded for registration purposes, see VATA 1994, Sch 2, para 1(7), as added by FA 1996, Sch 3, para 14.

[3] VATA 1994, Sch 2, para 1(2).
[4] VATA 1994, Sch 2, para 3(1). Liability to registration is notified on forms VAT 1 and (in the case of a partnership) VAT 2: VAT Regulations, SI 1995/2518, reg 5(1) as substituted or amended by SI 2000/794, SI 2004/1675. For electronic notification, see SI 1995/2518 reg 5(4)–(14) as inserted by SI 2004/1675.
[5] VATA 1994, Sch 2, para 3(2).

Other goods unaffected by a place of supply option

[64.10] A person is liable to registration if the following conditions are met:[1]

(1) The cumulative value of his relevant supplies for the current calendar year has exceeded £70,000.[2] Certain supplies of warehoused goods are disregarded for this purpose.[3]
(2) He is neither registered under any other provision nor liable to registration under the provisions described in infra, §§ **66.02, 66.03** or **66.04**.[4]

He must notify the Commissioners within 30 days of exceeding the limit in head 1.[5] He is registered with effect from the day on which he exceeded that limit or from a mutually agreed earlier date.[6]

De Voil Indirect Tax Service V2.171.

[1] VATA 1994, Sch 2, para 1(1). For relevant supplies, see supra, § **64.07**.
[2] Value, for this purpose, represents the consideration for a supply less VAT (if any) charged under the law of another EU member state: VATA 1994, Sch 2, para 1(6).
[3] For the supplies disregarded, see VATA 1994, Sch 2, para 1(7), as added by FA 1996, Sch 3, para 14.
[4] VATA 1994, Sch 2, para 3(1). Liability to registration is notified on forms VAT 1 and (in the case of a partnership) VAT 2: VAT Regulations, SI 1995/2518, reg 5(1) as substituted or amended by SI 2000/794, SI 2005/1675. For electronic notification, see SI 1995/2518 reg 5(4)–(14) as inserted by SI 2004/1675.
[5] VATA 1994, Sch 2, para 3(1).
[6] VATA 1994, Sch 2, para 3(2).

Person making relevant acquisitions

Relevant acquisitions

[64.11] An acquisition of goods from another EU member state is a "relevant acquisition" if the following conditions are met:[1]

(1) It is a taxable acquisition[2] treated as taking place in the UK.[3]
(2) The goods acquired comprise neither a new means of transport[4] nor goods subject to excise duty.
(3) The supplier did not make a taxable supply[5] when he supplied the goods to the person who acquired them.
(4) The first relevant event[6] in relation to the acquisition occurred after 31 December 1992.

[64.11] Registration

Certain acquisitions deemed to be made in triangular transactions, and when goods are installed or assembled in the UK, are disregarded for the purposes of VATA 1994, Sch 3.[7]

De Voil Indirect Tax Service V2.181.

[1] VATA 1994, Sch 3, para 11.
[2] As defined in VATA 1994, s 10(2).
[3] For the place of acquisition, see supra, § **63.36**.
[4] As defined in VATA 1994, s 95.
[5] As defined in VATA 1994, s 4(2).
[6] As defined in VATA 1994, s 12(2).
[7] VATA 1994, s 14(1), (2).

Past acquisitions

[64.12] A person is liable to registration at the end of any month if the following conditions are met:[1]

(1) The value[2] of his relevant acquisitions[3] for the current calendar year exceeds £68,000.[4]
(2) He is neither registered under any other provision nor liable to registration under the provisions described in infra, §§ **65.06–65.08**, or **65.12–65.14**.

He must notify the Commissioners within 30 days of the end of the month when he becomes so liable.[5] He is registered with effect from the end of the month following the month at the end of which liability arose, or from a mutually agreed earlier date.[6]

De Voil Indirect Tax Service V2.181.

[1] VATA 1994, Sch 3, para 1(1) as amended by SI 2009/1031.
[2] Value for this purpose excludes any part of consideration representing VAT chargeable under the law of another EU member state: VATA 1994, Sch 3, para 1(5).
[3] For relevant acquisitions, see supra, § **64.11**.
[4] For the acquisitions of warehoused goods disregarded in determining whether a person is liable to registration, see VATA 1994, Sch 3, para 1(6), as inserted by FA 1996, Sch 3, para 15.
[5] VATA 1994, Sch 3, para 3(1)(a). Liability to registration is notified on forms VAT 1 and (in the case of a partnership) VAT 2: VAT Regulations, SI 1995/2518, reg 5(1) as substituted or amended by SI 2000/794, SI 2004/1675. For electronic notification, see SI 1995/2518 reg 5(4)–(14) as inserted by SI 2004/1675.
[6] VATA 1994, Sch 3, para 3(2), (3)(a).

Future acquisitions

[64.13] A person is liable to registration at any time if the following conditions are met:[1]

(1) There are reasonable grounds for believing that the value of his relevant acquisitions in the next 30 days will exceed £68,000.
(2) He is neither registered under any other provision nor liable to registration under the provisions described in supra, §§ **64.02–64.04**, or infra §§ **65.12–65.14**.

He must notify the Commissioners before the end of the 30-day period.[2] He is registered with effect from the beginning of the 30-day period or from a mutually agreed earlier date.[3]

De Voil Indirect Tax Service V2.181.

---

[1] VATA 1994, Sch 3, para 1(2) as amended by SI 2009/1031. For the acquisitions disregarded for this purpose, see VATA 1994, Sch 3, para 1(6), as inserted by FA 1996, Sch 3, para 15.
[2] VATA 1994, Sch 3, para 3(1)(*b*). Liability to registration is notified on forms VAT 1 and (in the case of a partnership) VAT 2: VAT Regulations, SI 1995/2518, reg 5(1) as substituted or amended by SI 2000/794, SI 2004/1675. For electronic notification, see SI 1995/2518 reg 5(4)–(14) as inserted by SI 2004/1675.
[3] VATA 1994, Sch 3, para 3(2), (3)(*b*).

Failure to notify liability to registration

[64.14] A trader who is liable to registration under the foregoing provisions is a taxable person whether or not he takes the necessary steps to register.[1] Where he is late in notifying liability to registration, his registration is backdated to the date from which he was liable to registration.[2] This has three consequences. First, he must account for output tax from the effective date of registration regardless of whether or not he has charged such tax to his customers.[3] Second, such tax may carry interest.[4] Third, the trader may be liable to penalties.

If accompanied by some other act or omission, failure to notify may amount to dishonest conduct (ie an attempt to evade payment of tax) and as such may render a person liable to criminal[5] or civil[6] penalties.

Mere failure to notify liability to registration is a default giving rise to civil penalties unless there is a reasonable excuse for the conduct or it gives rise to either of the foregoing penalties for dishonest conduct.[7]

A trader does not have a reasonable excuse[8] if the delay in notifying liability to registration arises from an insufficiency of funds to pay any tax due; reliance on any other person to perform any task;[9] any dilatoriness or inaccuracy on the part of any person relied on to perform any task;[10] ignorance of the law of registration;[11] mitigating circumstances by reason of conduct subsequent of the material event; or mere oversight unaccompanied by any other conduct.

De Voil Indirect Tax Service V5.347.

---

[1] VATA 1994, s 4(2).
[2] *Whitehead v Customs and Excise Comrs* [1975] VATTR 152.

[64.14] Registration

3   *Whitehead v Customs and Excise Comrs* [1975] VATTR 152.
4   VATA 1994, s 74. For the charge to interest, see supra, § **2A.43**.
5   VATA 1994, s 72(1)–(8); *R v McCarthy* [1981] STC 298, CA.
6   Currently VATA 1994, s 60 (repealed) by virtue of Finance Act 2007, Sch 24 (Commencement and Transitional Provisions) Order, SI 2008/568, art 4. This penalty does not apply to any registration obligation arising after 31 March 2010 giving rise to a penalty under FA 2008, Sch 41, para 1: see Finance Act 2008, Schedule 41 (Appointed Day and Transitional Provisions) Order, SI 2009/511, art 4(a)(*i*).
7   Currently VATA 1994, s 67(1), (8), (9) as amended by FA 1995, s 32, FA 1996, s 37 and FA 2000, s 136. This penalty does not apply to any registration obligation arising after 31 March 2010 giving rise to a penalty under FA 2008, Sch 41, para 1: see Finance Act 2008, Schedule 41 (Appointed Day and Transitional Provisions) Order, SI 2009/511, art 4(a)(*ii*). For penalties in respect of obligations arising after 31 March 2010, see FA 2008, Sch 41, para 1 and arts 2, 3(*a*) of the 2009 Order.
8   VATA 1994, s 71(1); *Hutchings v Customs and Excise Comrs* [1987] VATTR 58.
9   See *Customs and Excise Comrs v Harris* [1989] STC 907.
10 Cf *Frank Galliers Ltd v Customs and Excise Comrs* [1993] STC 284.
11 *Neal v Customs and Excise Comrs* [1988] STC 131. But see, for example, *Jenkinson v Customs and Excise Comrs* [1988] VATTR 45 (ignorance of detailed regulations); *Mason v Customs and Excise Comrs* (1989) VAT decision 3517 (deaf trader with reading difficulties); *Bell v Customs and Excise Comrs* (1989) VAT decision 3774 (turnover monitored by reference to incorrect periods).

Entitlement to registration

Person making or intending to make taxable supplies

[64.15] The Commissioners must register a person if the following conditions are met:[1]

(1) He satisfies them that either:
  (a) he is making taxable supplies,[2] or
  (b) he is carrying on a business and intends to make taxable supplies in the course or furtherance of that business.[3]
(2) He is neither registered nor liable to registration under any provision.
(3) He so requests.

He is registered with effect from the day on which his request is made or from a mutually agreed earlier date.[4] Retrospective registration is a matter of discretion, not an entitlement.[5]

De Voil Indirect Tax Service V2.144.

1   VATA 1994, Sch 1, para 9.
2   For taxable supplies, see supra, § **64.01**.
3   For applications by property developers, see News Release 65/90, 25 September 1990; Business Brief (Issue 8/96), 17 May 1996.

2308

[4] VATA 1994, Sch 1, para 9.
[5] For the Commissioners' policy on backdated registrations, see Business Brief (Issue 8/97) 25 March 1997.

Person making or intending to make overseas supplies

[64.16] The Commissioners must register a person if the following conditions are met:[1]

(1) He satisfies them that either:
  (a) he makes supplies outside the UK which would be taxable supplies if made within the UK,
  (b) he makes supplies of a description specified for the purposes of VATA 1994, s 26(2),[2] or
  (c) he carries on a business and intends to make supplies within (i) or (ii) in the course or furtherance of that business.
(2) He is neither registered nor liable to registration under any other provision.
(3) He either has a business establishment[3] in the UK or has his usual place of residence[4] there.
(4) He neither makes nor intends to make taxable supplies.
(5) He so requests.

He is registered with effect from the day on which his request is made or from a mutually agreed earlier date.[5]

De Voil Indirect Tax Service V2.146.

[1] VATA 1994, Sch 1, para 10 as amended by FA 1997, s 32.
[2] For the supplies concerned, see VAT (Input Tax) (Specified Supplies) Order, SI 1992/3123, art 3.
[3] This includes a branch or agency in the UK: VATA 1994, Sch 1, para 10(4)(a).
[4] As regards a body corporate, this means that the body is legally constituted in the UK: VATA 1994, Sch 1, para 10(4)(b).
[5] VATA 1994, Sch 1, para 10(1). For the Commissioners' policy on backdated registrations, see Business Brief (Issue 8/97) 25 March 1997.

Person intending to supply goods from another EU member state

[64.17] The Commissioners may register a person if the following conditions are met:[1]

(1) He satisfies them that he intends to:
  (a) exercise a place of supply option[2] and make relevant supplies[3] of goods not subject to excise duty which are affected by that option from a specified date,
  (b) make relevant supplies of goods not subject to excise duty from a specified date which will be affected by a place of supply option already made, or

[64.17] Registration

        (c)   make relevant supplies of excise goods[4] from a specified date.
(2)   He is not liable to registration under any provision.
(3)   He is not entitled to registration under the provisions described in supra, §§ **64.15–64.16**.[5]
(4)   He is not already registered.
(5)   He so requests.

The Commissioners may impose such conditions as they think fit.[6] The person is registered from a mutually agreed date.[7]

A registered person must notify the Commissioners within 30 days of exercising the option or making the supplies relevant to his registration.[8]

De Voil Indirect Tax Service V2.172.

---

[1] VATA 1994, Sch 2, para 4(1), (3).
[2] For the place of supply option, see supra, § **64.09**.
[3] For supplies within this description, see supra, § **64.07**.
[4] For supplies within this description, see supra, § **64.07**.
[5] He is registered under one of those provisions if he is so entitled: VATA 1994, Sch 2, para 4(3).
[6] VATA 1994, Sch 2, para 4(1), (2).
[7] VATA 1994, Sch 2, para 4(1). For the Commissioners' policy on backdated registrations, see Business Brief (Issue 8/97) 25 March 1997.
[8] VATA 1994, Sch 2, para 5(2).

Person making relevant acquisitions

[64.18] The Commissioners must register a person if the following conditions are met:[1]

(1)   He satisfies them that he makes relevant acquisitions.[2]
(2)   He is not liable to registration under any provision.
(3)   He is not entitled to registration under the provisions described in supra, §§ **64.15–64.16**.
(4)   He is not already registered.
(5)   He so requests.

He is registered with effect from the day on which his request is made or from a mutually agreed earlier date.[3]

De Voil Indirect Tax Service V2.181.

---

[1] VATA 1994, Sch 3, para 4(1), (4).
[2] For relevant acquisitions, see supra, § **64.11**.
[3] VATA 1994, Sch 3, para 4(1). For the Commissioners' policy on backdated registrations, see Business Brief (Issue 8/97) 25 March 1997.

Person intending to make relevant acquisitions

[64.19] The Commissioners may register a person if the following conditions are met:[1]

(1)   He satisfies them that he intends to make relevant acquisitions[2] from a specified date.
(2)   He is not liable to registration under any provision.
(3)   He is not entitled to registration under the provisions described in §§ **64.15–64.16**.
(4)   He is not already registered.
(5)   He so requests.

The Commissioners may impose such conditions as they think fit.[3] The registration takes effect from a mutually agreed date.[4]

De Voil Indirect Tax Service V2.182.

---

[1]   VATA 1994, Sch 3, para 4(2), (4).
[2]   For relevant acquisitions, see supra, § **64.11**.
[3]   VATA 1994, Sch 3, para 4(2), (3).
[4]   VATA 1994, Sch 3, para 4(2). For the Commissioners' policy on backdated registrations, see Business Brief (Issue 8/97) 25 March 1997.

Exemption from registration

Introduction

[64.20] A trader who is prima facie liable to compulsory registration may escape registration by either making use of the statutory exemption set out below or by reorganising his business affairs so that the statutory turnover limits do not apply.

Zero-rated supplies

[64.21] The Commissioners may exempt a trader from registration under the provisions described in § **64.02–64.04** if the following conditions are met:[1]

(1)   He makes, or intends to make, taxable supplies.
(2)   He satisfies the Commissioners that any such supply would be zero-rated if he were a taxable person.
(3)   He applies for exemption.
(4)   The Commissioners think fit to accept the application.

This provision enables an unregistered person to avoid registration and a registered person to be deregistered. The test to be applied by the Commissioners is whether exemption from registration is in the interests of the Revenue. This clearly applies where the trader is a repayment trader.[2]

A person remains exempted from registration until he withdraws his request or the Commissioners consider that it should no longer be acted upon.[3]

[64.21] Registration

De Voil Indirect Tax Service V2.147.

[1] VATA 1994, Sch 1, para 14(1). "Any" such supply does not mean "all" such supplies: *Fong v Customs and Excise Comrs* [1978] VATTR 75.
[2] *Fong v Customs and Excise Comrs* [1978] VATTR 75.
[3] VATA 1994, Sch 1, para 14(1).

Zero-rated supplies of tax relieved goods

[64.22] A trader making, or intending to make, relevant supplies may be exempted from registration under the provisions described in § **64.06** if the following conditions are met:[1]

(1) He satisfies the Commissioners that some or all of those supplies are chargeable at the zero rate.
(2) He requests exemption.
(3) The Commissioners think fit.

This provision enables an unregistered person to avoid registration and a registered person to be deregistered.

A person remains exempted from registration until he withdraws his request or the Commissioners consider that it should no longer be acted upon.[2]

De Voil Indirect Tax Service V2.189A.

[1] VATA 1994, Sch 3A, para 7(1) as inserted by FA 2000, s 136 and Sch 36.
[2] VATA 1994, Sch 3A, para 7(4) as inserted by FA 2000, s 136 and Sch 36.

Zero-rated acquisitions

[64.23] The Commissioners may exempt a trader from registration under the provisions described in §§ **64.12–64.13** and §§ **64.18–64.19** if the following conditions are met:[1]

(1) He makes, or intends to make, relevant acquisitions.[2]
(2) He satisfies the Commissioners that any such acquisition would be zero-rated if the goods concerned had been supplied by a taxable person.
(3) He requests exemption.
(4) The Commissioners think fit to accept his request.

This provision enables an unregistered person to avoid registration and a registered person to be deregistered.

A person remains exempted from registration until he withdraws his request or the Commissioners consider that it should no longer be acted upon.[3]

De Voil Indirect Tax Service V2.183.

[1] VATA 1994, Sch 3, para 8(1).

2   For relevant acquisitions, see supra, § **64.11**.
3   VATA 1994, Sch 3, para 8(1).

VAT groups

Eligibility for membership of a VAT group

[64.24] Two or more companies established in the UK, or having a fixed establishment in the UK, are eligible for membership of a VAT group if one of the companies controls each of the others or if one person (being either a company, an individual or two or more individuals carrying on a partnership) controls all of them.[1] A company may meet these criteria in relation to more than one VAT group. However, it can be treated as a member of only one of them.[2]

EXAMPLE

X is a person exercising control over A, B and C. A single VAT group can comprise any of the following:

(a)   XABC, if X is a company.
(b)   ABC, if X is a company and decides not to be a group member.
(c)   ABC, if X is an individual or a partnership.

In practice, many groups of companies find it convenient to form two or more VAT groups. Thus, for example, X (a holding company) and its subsidiaries (A, B and C) could form two VAT groups comprising:

(i)   XA (which is equivalent to the structure in head (a) above).
(ii) BC (which is equivalent to the structure in head (b) above).

If X forms or acquires D (a new subsidiary), D meets the criteria to join both the XA and BC VAT groups. However, D can become a member of only one of them.

In broad terms, a person controls a company if he holds a majority of the voting rights or controls the composition of its board of directors.[3] A company can also control another company if it is empowered by statute to control that company's activities.[4]

If a body corporate ("D") is a "specified body", it must meet two additional conditions (referred to as the "benefits condition" and the "consolidated accounts condition") before it is eligible for membership of a VAT group ("ABC") controlled by "X".[5]

"D" is a specified body if the following conditions are met:[6]

(1)   D carries on a "relevant business activity".[7]
(2)   One of the following conditions is met at time when D carries on this activity:
      (a)   D is not a wholly-owned subsidiary[8] of X;
      (b)   D's relevant business activity is managed by a third party;[9] or
      (c)   D is the sole general partner of a limited partnership.[10]
(3)   D does not fall within any of the following descriptions:
      (1)   another body corporate is empowered by statute to control its activities;

(2) its only activity is acting as the trustee of an occupational pension scheme[11] established under a trust; and
(3) it is a charity.
(4) Either:
(a) the value of the ABC group's supplies for the past year exceeded £10 million; or
(b) there are reasonable grounds for believing that the value of the ABC group's supplies for the coming year will exceed £10 million.

X is not a specified body. It is therefore eligible for membership of the ABC group without meeting the benefits and consolidated accounts conditions.[12]

De Voil Indirect Tax Service V2.190.

---

[1] VATA 1994, s 43A(1) as inserted by FA 1999, Sch 2, para 2.
[2] VATA 1994, s 43D(1) as inserted by FA 2004, s 20. For the effect of an application which would result in a company being treated as a member of more than one VAT group, see VATA 1994, s 43D(2)–(4).
[3] VATA 1994, s 43A(2), (3) as inserted by FA 1999, Sch 2, para 2, applying Companies Act 1985, s 736. See *Mannin Shipping Ltd v Customs and Excise Comrs* [1979] VATTR 83.
[4] VATA 1994, s 43A(2) as inserted by FA 1999, Sch 2, para 2.
[5] VAT (Groups: eligibility) Order, SI 2004/1931, art 2. For the "benefits condition" and the "consolidated accounts condition", see respectively SI 2004/1931, arts 5 and 6.
[6] SI 2004/1931, art 3(1)–(3), (4)(b)–(d) and (5)(c).
[7] As defined in SI 2004/1931, art 4.
[8] As defined in SI 2004/1931, art 3(5)(a), (b).
[9] As defined in SI 2004/1931, art 7(2).
[10] For the manner in which the legislation is modified in its application to the sole general partner of a general partnership, see SI 2004/1931, art 7(1).
[11] As defined in Pension Schemes Act 1993, s 1.
[12] SI 2004/1931, art 3(4)(a).

Formation and variation of a VAT group

[64.25] The companies are treated as members of a VAT group if an application is made to that effect.[1] The application takes effect from the date when it is received by the Commissioners or from such earlier or later date as they may allow.[2]

The VAT group may be varied or disbanded in accordance with the following provisions:

(1) An application is made for another company to become a member of the group, for an existing member of the group to be excluded, or for the companies to cease to be treated as a group. The application takes effect from the date when the Commissioners receive it or from such earlier or later date as they may allow.[3]

(2) The Commissioners make a direction varying membership of the group. The direction has effect for the period specified therein.[4]

(3) The Commissioners issue a notice terminating a company's membership of the group in order to protect the revenue.[5] Membership is terminated with effect from a day specified in the notice. This day may be no earlier the date of the notice.[6]

(4) The Commissioners issue a notice terminating a company's membership of the group on the grounds that it was not eligible to join the group. Membership is terminated with effect from a day specified in the notice. This may be no earlier than the date when the company became a member of the group.[7]

(5) The Commissioners issue a notice terminating a company's membership of the group on the grounds that it has ceased to be eligible to remain a member. The notice has effect from a day specified in the notice.[8] This may be no earlier than 1 January 2000 (if the company became a member of the group under the legislation in force prior to the enactment of FA 1999) and the date when the company ceased to be eligible for membership (in other cases).[9]

(6) A company has ceased to be eligible to remain a member. Membership of the VAT group does not automatically terminate when the company ceases to be eligible to remain a member. The company must make an application under point 1 or the Commissioners must issue a notice under point 5.[10] The Commissioners normally allow a member to leave the group from the date requested by the representative member. However, they may set a later date if VAT avoidance arises or is likely to arise.[11]

The Commissioners may refuse an application to form or extend a VAT group on the grounds that the company or companies are not eligible to be treated as members of a VAT group. If the Commissioners do so, the group is treated as if it has not been formed or extended.[12] The Commissioners may refuse any application in order to protect the revenue. If they do so, the group is treated as if it had not been formed, varied or disbanded.[13] The Commissioners have 90 days in which to make a decision.[14] A right of appeal is given against this decision.[15] An application has no effect if, or to the extent, that it would result in a company becoming a member of two or more VAT groups.[16]

A right of appeal is given against a direction given by the Commissioners under head 2[17] and against a notice terminating membership of a group under heads 3–5.[18]

De Voil Indirect Tax Service V2.190.

---

[1] VATA 1994, s 43B(1) as inserted by FA 1999, Sch 2, para 2 and amended by FA 2004, s 20. The application must nominate one of the bodies corporate as the representative member: VATA 1994, s 43B(3)(*b*) as so inserted. For applications to change the representative member, see VATA 1994, s 43B(2)(*c*), (4), (5)(*c*) as so inserted.

[2] VATA 1994, s 43B(4) as inserted by FA 1999, Sch 2, para 2.

[3] VATA 1994, s 43B(2)(*a*), (*b*), (*d*) and (4) as inserted by FA 1999, Sch 2, para 2 and amended by FA 2004, s 20.

[64.25] Registration

4   The Commissioners may make a direction if a company joins or leaves a group and the conditions in VATA 1994, Sch 9A, para 1, as inserted by FA 1996, s 31 and Sch 4, are met. In principle, the Commissioners may not make a direction if they are satisfied that the change in treatment had a genuine commercial purpose. However, this does not prevent them making a direction if change arises from a notice terminating membership on eligibility or revenue protection grounds: VATA 1994, Sch 9A, para 2 as so inserted and amended by FA 1999, Sch 2, para 5. For the form and effect of a direction, see VATA 1994, Sch 9A, para 3(1)–(3) as so inserted. For the manner in which a direction is made, varied and withdrawn, see VATA 1994, Sch 9A, paras 3(6), (7), 5(1), (3), (4), 7(2) as so inserted. For the form and effect of a direction, see VATA 1994, Sch 9A, paras 3(1)(b), (3), (4)(a), 4(3)(b) so as inserted. For time limits, see VATA 1994, Sch 9A, para 4 as so inserted. For assessment of VAT for periods prior to the making of a direction, see VATA 1994, Sch 9A, paras 3(4)(b), 6(1)–(8), (11) as so inserted. For the assessment of interest thereon, see VATA 1994, Sch 9A, para 6(9), (10) as so inserted. For the right of appeal against assessments of VAT and interest, see VATA 1994, s 83(q), (wa) as so inserted. For a statement of practice regarding the application of VATA 1994, Sch 9A, see Notice No 700/2.

5   For protection of the revenue, see *National Westminster Bank plc v Customs and Excise Comrs* [1999] V & DR 201. For the manner in which the Commissioners exercise their powers, see Business Brief, Issues 15/99 (12 July 1999), 1/01 (10 January 2001) and 30/02 (19 November 2002).

6   VATA 1994, s 43C(1), (2) as inserted by FA 1999, Sch 2, para 2.

7   VATA 1994, s 43C(3), (4)(a) as inserted by FA 1999, Sch 2, para 2 and amended by FA 2004, s 20.

8   VATA 1994, s 43C(3) as inserted by FA 1999, Sch 2, para 2 and amended by FA 2004, s 20.

9   VATA 1994, s 43C(4)(b) as inserted by FA 1999, Sch 2, para 2 and interpreted by reference to the transitional provisions in FA 1999, Sch 2, para 6.

10 *Customs and Excise Comrs v Barclays Bank plc* [2001] EWCA Civ 1513, [2001] STC 1558. It is submitted that the principle stated is unaffected by the changes introduced by FA 1999, Sch 2.

11 Business Brief 30/02, 19 November 2002.

12 VATA 1994, s 43B(5)(a), (b), (6) as inserted by FA 1999, Sch 2, para 2 and amended by FA 2004, s 20.

13 VATA 1994, s 43B(5)(c), (6) as inserted by FA 1999, Sch 2, para 2.

14 VATA 1994, s 43B(5) as inserted by FA 1999, Sch 2, para 2 and amended by FA 2004, s 20.

15 For the right of appeal, see VATA 1994, s 83(k) as inserted by FA 1999, Sch 2, para 3. For the status of an application during the appeal proceedings, see VATA 1994, s 84(4A) as inserted by FA 1999, Sch 2, para 4.

16 VATA 1994, s 43D(2)–(4) as inserted by FA 2004, s 20.

17 For the right of appeal, see VATA 1994, ss 83(wa), 84(7A) as inserted by FA 1996, s 31.

18 For the right of appeal, see VATA 1994, s 83(ka) as inserted by FA 1999, Sch 2, para 3. For the status of a notice during the appeal proceedings, see VATA 1994, s 84(4B), (4C), (4D) as inserted by FA 1999, Sch 2, para 4.

Consequences of a VAT group registration

[64.26] The effects of a group registration are as follows:[1]

(1) The VAT affairs of the group are vested in a group company known as the representative member.
(2) A supply between group companies is normally disregarded[2] (so that no VAT is charged on it and no liability to registration arises in respect of it) but it is not wholly devoid of VAT consequences (eg in relation to attribution of input tax).[3]
(3) Group companies are jointly and severally liable for tax due from the representative member.
(4) A liability to output tax or entitlement to input tax is fixed by reference to the statutory description of the relevant group company rather than that of the representative member.

De Voil Indirect Tax Service V2.190.

---

[1] VATA 1994, ss 43(1) (as amended by FA 2004, s 20), (1AA), (1AB), (2) (as inserted and amended by FA 1997, s 40), 44(5), 56(4); VAT (Cars) Order, SI 1992/3122, art 7 as amended by SI 1999/2832; VAT (Special Provisions) Order, SI 1995/1268, art 11(4); VAT (Self-supply of Construction Services) Order, SI 1989/472; *Davis Advertising Service Ltd v Customs and Excise Comrs* [1973] VATTR 16; *Customs and Excise Comrs v Kingfisher plc* [1994] STC 63; *Midland Bank plc v Customs and Excise Comrs* [1991] VATTR 525; *Triad Timber Components Ltd v Customs and Excise Comrs* [1993] VATTR 384; *Canary Wharf Ltd v Customs and Excise Comrs* [1996] V & DR 323; *Thorn plc v Customs and Excise Comrs* [1998] V & DR 80.
[2] See infra, § **64.27**.
[3] See *Customs and Excise Comrs v Svenska International plc* [1999] STC 406, HL (input tax incurred before joining a VAT group); *J P Morgan Trading and Finance v Customs and Excise Comrs* [1998] V & DR 161 (input tax incurred after leaving a VAT group).

Intra-group supplies

[64.27] In principle, a supply made by X to Y is disregarded for VAT purposes if X and Y are members of the same VAT group.[1] In consequence, the supply made by X is not chargeable to VAT. There are three important exceptions to this principle.

First, the time of supply rules can result in part of a supply being deemed to be made while the supplier and customer are members of the same VAT group and part when they are not. This would be so, for example, if X supplies goods to Y so that an initial payment is made while X and Y are members of the same group, but the goods are delivered and the balance of the consideration paid after X had left the group. The supply deemed to be made by reference to the initial payment is disregarded, but it is not permanently excluded from charge to tax. Delivery of the goods constitutes a supply of goods chargeable to tax

[64.27] Registration

by reference to the consideration for the supply. This includes both the amount paid (ie the initial payment) and the amount payable (ie the balancing payment).[2]

Second, the Commissioners may give a direction[3] which annuls the effect of this provision in relation to any supply of goods or services made by one group member to another. Where a direction is given, the representative member must account for VAT on any supply affected by the direction made on or after the day on which it is given.[4] An assessment is made in respect of any VAT for earlier times arising as a consequence of the direction.[5] This VAT carries interest,[6] which is also assessed.[7] A right of appeal is given in respect of assessments for VAT and interest.[8]

Third, a supply made by one group member (X) to another group member (Y) is not disregarded if the following conditions are met[9] in relation to a supply made after 25 November 1996:[10]

(1) Z (person belonging in the UK or elsewhere)[11] makes a supply of services to X.
(2) The services fall within VATA 1994, Sch 5, paras 1–8 but do not fall within VATA 1994, Sch 9.
(3) X belongs outside the UK at the time when the services are supplied to him,[12] eg because they are made to X's overseas branch.
(4) The services are used by X to make a supply to Y.
(5) The services fall within VATA 1994, Sch 5, but do not fall within VATA 1994, Sch 9.
(6) Y belongs in the UK at the time when the services are supplied to him.

Where the supply made by X is not disregarded, the representative member of the group XY is deemed to make a self-supply under the provisions described in infra, § **64.28**.

De Voil Indirect Tax Service V2.113.

---

[1] VATA 1994, s 43(1)(a).
[2] *Customs and Excise Comrs v Thorn Materials Supply Ltd* [1998] STC 725, HL. For disallowance of the proportion of X's input tax attributable to the prepayment, see *BUPA Purchasing Ltd v Customs and Excise Comrs* [2003] EWHC 1957 (Ch), [2003] STC 1203. *Revenue and Customs Comrs v Gracechurch Management Services Ltd* [2007] EWHC 755 (Ch), [2008] STC 795.
[3] A direction is made under VATA 1994, Sch 9A as inserted by FA 1996, s 31 and Sch 4. For the circumstances in which a direction may be given, see VATA 1994, Sch 9A, paras 1, 2, 4. For the manner in which a direction may be made, varied or withdrawn, see VATA 1994, Sch 9A, paras 3(6), (7), 5(1), (3), (4), 7(2). For the right of appeal, see VATA 1994, ss 83(*wa*), 84(7A) as inserted by FA 1996, s 31. For a statement of practice regarding the making of directions, see Notice No 700/9.
[4] VATA 1994, Sch 9A, paras 3(1)(*a*), (2), (4)(*a*), 4(3)(*b*) as inserted by FA 1996, s 31 and Sch 4.
[5] VATA 1994, Sch 9A, paras 3(4)(*b*), 6(1)–(8), (11) as inserted by FA 1996, s 31 and Sch 4. For the charge to interest, see supra, § **2A.43**.
[6] VATA 1994, Sch 9A, para 6(9), (10) as inserted by FA 1996, s 31 and Sch 4.
[7] VATA 1994, s 76(1).

8   VATA 1994, s 83(q), (wa) as inserted by FA 1996, s 31.
9   VATA 1994, s 43(2A), (2D), (2E) as inserted by FA 1997, s 41(1) and modified by s 41(4) in relation to supplies made after 19 March 1997.
10 FA 1997, s 41(2).
11 For the place where a person making a supply belongs, see supra, § **63.28**.
12 For the place where the recipient of a supply belongs, see VATA 1994, s 9(3)–(5).

Self supplies

Group supplies using an overseas member

[64.28] A supply of certain services[1] supplied by one member of a VAT group (X) to another (Y) is not disregarded for the purposes of VAT in specified circumstances.[2] Where this is so, all the same consequences follow as if the representative member of the VAT group had made a taxable supply to himself in the course or furtherance of business.[3] Thus, the representative member is liable to account for output tax on the deemed supply and is entitled to input tax credit for all or part of the VAT so accounted for. He is thus placed in the same position as if he had made a reverse charge.[4]

The supply is treated as being made when it is paid for (if made for a consideration in money) or the last day of the prescribed accounting period in which the services were performed (in other cases).[5]

The value of the supply is open market value if the Commissioners make a direction to that effect.[6] In other cases, the value of the supply is an amount equal to the consideration (if the supply was made for a consideration in money) or such amount in money as is equivalent to that consideration (in other cases).[7] By concession, this value is reduced to the cost incurred by the overseas group member in purchasing the services concerned.[8] The foregoing time of supply and valuation rules are modified in relation to telecommunication services.[9]

De Voil Indirect Tax Service V2.113.

1 ie services within VATA 1994, Sch 5 which do not fall within VATA 1994, Sch 9.
2 For the circumstances in which the supply is not disregarded, see supra, § **64.27**.
3 VATA 1994, s 43(2B) as inserted by FA 1997, s 41.
4 For the reverse charge, see infra, § **65.38**.
5 VATA 1994, s 43(2C)(c); VAT Regulations, SI 1995/2518, reg 82.
6 ie under VATA 1994, Sch 6, para 1. The Commissioners can make such a direction because X and Y are deemed to be connected persons: VATA 1994, s 43(2C)(b) as inserted by FA 1997, s 41.
7 VATA 1994, s 43(2C)(c) as inserted by FA 1997, s 41; VATA 1994, Sch 6, para 8.
8 Notice No 48 (July 2009) para 3.2. It is necessary to provide evidence of value. For the Commissioners' approach to valuation, see Business Brief (Issue 11/97) 9 May 1997.
9 See VAT (Reverse Charge) (Anti-avoidance) Order, SI 1997/1523.

Business transferred to group member as a going concern

[64.29] The representative member of a group of companies[1] is treated as making a supply in the course or furtherance of business where:[2] (a) a business or part of a business carried on by a taxable person is transferred as a going concern to a group company; and (b) the supply of assets transferred is outside the scope of VAT.[3]

The supply comprises the assets (other than capital items[4]) which would have been charged to tax at the standard rate by the transferor if the supply were not outside the scope of VAT.[5] The supply is valued at open market value.[6]

No supply is treated as taking place if:[7] (a) the representative member is entitled to credit for all input tax in both the prescribed accounting period[8] and longer period[9] in which the assets were transferred; or (b) the Commissioners are satisfied that the assets transferred were acquired by the transferor more than three years before the date of transfer.

Tax chargeable on the deemed supply is reduced if the Commissioners are satisfied that the transferor did not receive credit for the full amount of input tax when he obtained the assets,[10] eg because he is partly exempt.

De Voil Indirect Tax Service V3.246.

---

1. For group registration, see supra, §§ **64.24–64.26**.
2. VATA 1994, s 44(1), (5).
3. ie under VAT (Special Provisions) Order, SI 1995/1268, art 5(1)–(4).
4. As defined in VAT Regulations, SI 1995/2518, reg 113. For the charge to tax on capital items, see SI 1995/2518, reg 114(7).
5. VATA 1994, s 44(1)(*b*), (4), (10).
6. VATA 1994, s 44(7), (8).
7. VATA 1994, s 44(2), (3).
8. For prescribed accounting periods, see § **67.01**.
9. Defined in VAT Regulations, SI 1995/2518, reg 99.
10. VATA 1994, s 44(9).

65

The charge to tax

Introduction	PARA **65.01**
Charge I—Supplies of goods and services	PARA **65.08**
Charge II—Events treated as supplies of goods or services	PARA **65.28**
Charge III—Goods acquired from another EU member state	PARA **65.43**
Charge IV—Goods imported from a third country	PARA **65.49**

Introduction

The charge to tax

[65.01] The charge to tax,[1] as augmented by other charging provisions,[2] may be conveniently summarised in the following form. A charge to tax arises on:

(1) Supplies of goods or services made for a consideration in the UK.[3]
(2) Events (to use a neutral term) which give rise to a charge to tax as if a supply of goods or services had been made in the UK. These events are:
 (a) making transactions which, although not supplies because of the absence of consideration, are nevertheless treated as supplies of goods or supplies of services;[4]
 (b) events giving rise to a self supply under which a taxable person is treated as if he had made a supply of goods or services;[5]
 (c) events giving rise to a reverse charge where the same consequences follow as if the recipient of the supply (rather than the supplier) had made that supply;[6] and
 (d) a charge to tax on goods held when a person ceases to be a taxable person.[7]
(3) Acquisitions of goods from another EU member state made in the UK.[8]
(4) The importation of goods into the UK from a third country.[9]

[1] VATA 1994, s 1(1).
[2] VATA 1994, ss 5, 8, 9A, 18C, 44, 55, 55A, Sch 4, para 8, Sch 10, paras 1, 5, 6.
[3] For the charge to tax, see infra, §§ **65.08–65.27**.
[4] For the charge to tax, see infra, §§ **65.28–65.31**.
[5] For the charge to tax, see infra, §§ **65.32–65.37**.
[6] For the charge to tax, see infra, §§ **65.38–65.41**.
[7] For the charge to tax, see infra, § **65.42**.
[8] For the charge to tax, see infra, §§ **65.43–65.48**.
[9] For the charge to tax, see infra, §§ **65.49–65.53**.

Supplementary charge to tax

Introduction

[65.02] The Chancellor announced a temporary reduction in the standard rate of VAT in the Pre-Budget Report on 24 November 2008.[1] The Financial Secretary to the Treasury subsequently announced that anti-forestalling legislation would be introduced in FA 2009 to protect the public finances from "artificial avoidance seeking to exploit the change in VAT rates where there is no current economic activity".[2] The measures introduced take the form of a supplementary charge on supplies of goods or services meeting specified conditions where the time of supply falls before 1 January 2010. The following situations can be distinguished:

(1) Supplies consisting of the grant of a right to goods or services ("Charge 1").[3]
(2) Supplies (which do *not* consist of the grant of a right to goods or services) where the time of supply is determined by reference to the issue of a VAT invoice ("Charge 2").[4]
(3) Supplies (which do *not* consist of the grant of a right to goods or services) where the time of supply is determined by reference to the receipt of a payment ("Charge 3").[5]

---

[1] For the standard rate and the temporary change to it, see infra, § **65.06**.
[2] Written Ministerial Statement, 27 November 2008. For the text, see [2008] SWTI 2633. For an example of the sort of arrangements that the Financial Secretary no doubt had in mind, see (Case C-419/02) *BUPA Hospitals Ltd and another v Customs and Excise Comrs* [2006] STC 967, ECJ.
[3] For the supplementary charge under Charge 1, see supra, § **65.03**.
[4] For the supplementary charge under Charge 2, see supra, § **65.04**.
[5] For the supplementary charge under Charge 3, see supra, § **65.05**.

Charge 1—Grant of a right to goods or services

[65.03] A supply consisting of the grant of a right to goods or services is subject to the supplementary charge if:[1]

(1) The supply of the grant is treated as taking place between 1 December 2008[2] and 31 December 2009 inclusive.
(2) The supply is charged to VAT at the standard rate.[3]
(3) The goods or services are to be supplied at a discount or free of charge.
(4) The basic time of supply[4] for the supply of some or all of the goods or services falls after 31 December 2009.
(5) The recipient of the supply is entitled to input tax credit, repayment or refund in respect of only part (or none) of the VAT charged on the supply.
(6) The supply is not excepted from the supplementary charge.[5]
(7) One of the following conditions is met in relation to the supply of the grant:

(a) the grantor[6] and the person to whom the right is granted are connected[7] with each other at any time between the date when the supply of the grant is treated as taking place and the later of (i) 1 January 2010; and (ii) the date on which the right is entirely exercised or (if partly exercised) the first date on which the right is partly exercised;

(b) (if the supply is treated as taking place after 31 March 2009) the aggregate of the relevant consideration[8] for the following supplies exceeds £100,000: (i) the grant; (ii) every related grant;[9] and (iii) every related supply of goods or services.[10] However, no supplementary charge arises if this is the only condition met and the supply is made in accordance with normal commercial practice[11] relating to the goods and services concerned;[12]

(c) the payment made in respect of the right is financed[13] by the grantor or (if the grant is treated as taking place after 31 March 2009) by a person connected with the grantor.

The amount of the supplementary charge is the difference between the VAT actually chargeable on the grant of the right and the VAT which would have been chargeable if the rate in force had been 17.5%.[14] The supplementary charge is a liability of the grantor. It becomes due on the first occasion on which the right is exercised after 31 December 2009.[15] It is treated as if it were VAT charged in accordance with VATA 1994.[16]

---

[1] FA 2009, Sch 3, paras 1(1), (2), (4), (5), 3, 5, 11(a), (c).

[2] Although the supplementary charge applies to supplies made after 24 November 2008, the standard rate in force between 25 November 2008 and 30 November 2008 inclusive was 17.5%. There is accordingly no "difference" between the rate in force and 17.5% for the purposes of FA 2009, Sch 3, para 17(1).

[3] For the standard rate in force between 1 December 2008 and 31 December 2009, see infra, § **65.06**.

[4] As defined in FA 2009, Sch 3, paras 4(1) (general rule) and 4(2), 18, 19 (listed supplies).

[5] For the letting of assets, see FA 2009, Sch 3, para 12. Further exceptions may be specified by order. No order has been made to date.

[6] The grant may be one of a series of grants relating to the same, or substantially the same, goods or services. If each of the grants in the series was (or will) be made in the expectation that the grant subject to the supplementary charge would (or will) take place, the reference to the "grantor" includes any person who grants one of the rights in the series: see FA 2009, Sch 3, para 5.

[7] Whether persons are connected with each other is determined in accordance with TA 1988 s 839: see FA 2009, Sch 3, para 8.

[8] As defined in FA 2009, Sch 3, para 6(2).

[9] For related grants, see FA 2009, Sch 3, para 6(3), (4).

[10] For related supplies, see FA 2009, Sch 3, para 6(3), (4).

[11] As defined in FA 2009, Sch 3, para 14.

[12] FA 2009, Sch 3, para 13.

[13] As defined in FA 2009, Sch 3, para 7.

[14] FA 2009, Sch 3, para 17(2).

[65.03] The charge to tax

[15] FA 2009, Sch 3, para 16(2), (3).
[16] FA 2009, Sch 3, para 1(7).

Charge 2—Issue of a VAT invoice

[65.04] A supply of goods or services which does not consist of the grant of a right to goods or services is subject to the supplementary charge if:[1]

(1) The supply is treated as taking place between 1 December 2008[2] and 31 December 2009 inclusive by virtue of the issue of a VAT invoice.
(2) The supply is charged to VAT at the standard rate.[3]
(3) The basic time of supply[4] is after 31 December 2009.
(4) The recipient of the supply is entitled to input tax credit, repayment or refund in respect of only part (or none) of the VAT charged on the supply.
(5) The supply is not excepted from the supplementary charge.[5]
(6) One of the following conditions is met:
  (a) the supplier[6] and the person to whom the supply is made are connected[7] with each other at any time between the date when the invoice was issued and 1 January 2010;
  (b) (if the supply is treated as taking place after 31 March 2009) the aggregate of the relevant consideration[8] for the following supplies exceeds £100,000: (i) the supply; (ii) every related supply[9] of goods or services spanning 1 January 2010; and (iii) every related grant[10] of a right to goods or services spanning 1 January 2010. However, no supplementary charge arises if this is the only condition met and the supply is made in accordance with normal commercial practice[11] relating to the goods and services concerned;[12]
  (c) a prepayment[13] in respect of the supply is financed[14] by the supplier or (if the supply is treated as taking place after 31 March 2009) by a person connected with the supplier;
  (d) all or part of the amount invoiced becomes due for payment more than six months after the date on which the invoice was issued.

The amount of the supplementary charge is the difference between the VAT actually chargeable on the supply and the VAT which would have been chargeable if the rate in force had been 17.5%. An apportionment is made if the basic time of supply for some of the some of the goods or services falls before 1 January 2010.[15] The supplementary charge is a liability of the supplier. It becomes due on 1 January 2010.[16] It is treated as if it were VAT charged in accordance with VATA 1994.[17]

[1] FA 2009, Sch 3, paras 1(1), (3), (5), 2(1), (2)(a), (3)–(6), (8), 5, 11(a), (b).
[2] Although the supplementary charge applies to supplies made after 24 November 2008, the standard rate in force between 25 November 2008 and 30 November 2008 inclusive was 17.5%. There is accordingly no "difference" between the rate in force and 17.5% for the purposes of FA 2009, Sch 3, para 17(1).
[3] For the standard rate in force between 1 December 2008 and 31 December 2009, see infra, § **65.06**.

4   As defined in FA 2009, Sch 3, para 4(1) (general rule) and 4(2), 18, 19 (listed supplies).
5   For the letting of assets, see FA 2009, Sch 3, para 12. Further exceptions may be specified by order. No order has been made to date.
6   The supply may be one of a series of supplies of the same, or substantially the same, goods or services. If each of the supplies in the series was (or will) be made in the expectation that the affected supply would (or will) take place, the reference to a "supplier" includes any person who makes one of the supplies in the series: see FA 2009, Sch 3, para 5.
7   Whether persons are connected with each other is determined in accordance with TA 1988, s 839: see FA 2009, Sch 3, para 8.
8   As defined in FA 2009, Sch 3, para 6(2).
9   For related supplies, see FA 2009, Sch 3, para 6(3), (4).
10 For related grants, see FA 2009, Sch 3, para 6(3), (4).
11 As defined in FA 2009, Sch 3, para 14.
12 FA 2009, Sch 3, para 13.
13 As defined in FA 2009, Sch 3, para 2(7).
14 As defined in FA 2009, Sch 3, para 7.
15 FA 2009, Sch 3, para 17(1), (3), (4).
16 FA 2009, Sch 3, para 16(1), (3).
17 FA 2009, Sch 3, para 1(7).

Charge 3—Receipt of a payment

[65.05] A supply of goods or services which does not consist of the grant of a right to goods or services is subject to the supplementary charge if:[1]

(1)   The supply is treated as taking place between 1 December 2008[2] and 31 December 2009 inclusive by virtue of the receipt of a payment.
(2)   The supply is charged to VAT at the standard rate.[3]
(3)   The basic time of supply[4] is after 31 December 2009.
(4)   The recipient of the supply is entitled to input tax credit, repayment or refund in respect of only part (or none) of the VAT charged on the supply.
(5)   The supply is not excepted from the supplementary charge.[5]
(6)   One of the following conditions is met:
  (a)   the supplier[6] and the person to whom the supply is made are connected[7] with each other at any time between the date when the invoice was issued and 1 January 2010;
  (b)   (if the supply is treated as taking place after 31 March 2009) the aggregate of the relevant consideration[8] for the following supplies exceeds £100,000: (i) the supply; (ii) every related supply[9] of goods or services spanning 1 January 2010; and (iii) every related grant[10] of a right to goods or services spanning 1 January 2010. However, no supplementary charge arises if this is the only condition met and the supply is made in accordance with normal commercial practice[11] relating to the goods and services concerned;[12]

[65.05] The charge to tax

(c) a prepayment[13] in respect of the supply is financed[14] by the supplier or (if the supply is treated as taking place after 31 March 2009) by a person connected with the supplier.

The amount of the supplementary charge is the difference between the VAT actually chargeable on the supply and the VAT which would have been chargeable if the rate in force had been 17.5%. An apportionment is made if the basic time of supply for some of the some of the goods or services falls before 1 January 2010.[15] The supplementary charge is a liability of the supplier. It becomes due on 1 January 2010.[16] It is treated as if it were VAT charged in accordance with VATA 1994.[17]

---

[1] FA 2009, Sch 3, paras 1(1), (3), (5) 2(1), (a), (3)–(7), 5, 11(a), (b).
[2] Although the supplementary charge applies to supplies made after 24 November 2008, the standard rate in force between 25 November 2008 and 30 November 2008 inclusive was 17.5%. There is accordingly no "difference" between the rate in force and 17.5% for the purposes of FA 2009, Sch 3, para 17(1).
[3] For the standard rate in force between 1 December 2008 and 31 December 2009, see infra, § **65.06**.
[4] As defined in FA 2009, Sch 3, para 4(1) (general rule) and 4(2), 18, 19 (listed supplies).
[5] For the letting of assets, see FA 2009, Sch 3, para 12. Further exceptions may be specified by order. No order has been made to date.
[6] The supply may be one of a series of supplies of the same, or substantially the same, goods or services. If each of the supplies in the series was (or will) be made in the expectation that the affected supply would (or will) take place, the reference to a "supplier" includes any person who makes one of the supplies in the series: see FA 2009, Sch 3, para 5.
[7] Whether persons are connected with each other is determined in accordance with TA 1988 s 839: see FA 2009, Sch 3, para 8.
[8] As defined in FA 2009, Sch 3, para 6(2).
[9] For related supplies, see FA 2009, Sch 3, para 6(3), (4).
[10] For related grants, see FA 2009, Sch 3, para 6(3), (4).
[11] As defined in FA 2009, Sch 3, para 14.
[12] FA 2009, Sch 3, para 13.
[13] As defined in FA 2009, Sch 3, para 2(7).
[14] As defined in FA 2009, Sch 3, para 7.
[15] FA 2009, Sch 3, para 17(1), (3), (4).
[16] FA 2009, Sch 3, para 16(1), (3).
[17] FA 2009, Sch 3, para 1(7).

The rate of tax

[65.06] A supply is charged to tax at one or other of three rates:

(1) The zero-rate (a tax rate of nil).[1]
(2) The reduced rate (currently 5%).[2]
(3) The standard rate (currently 15%).[3]

Introduction [65.07]

In principle, the rate of tax (or exemption from tax) is determined by reference to the nature of the goods or services supplied.[4] However, this does not apply to certain classes of face value voucher. Here, the rate of tax is determined by reference to the nature of the goods or services for which the voucher can be exchanged.[5]

An acquisition or importation is either charged to tax or not. No VAT is said to be chargeable on acquisitions or importations which would have been zero-rated if they were supplies.[6] Other acquisitions and importations are charged to tax at the reduced rate (currently 5%) or standard rate (currently 15%).[7]

The difference in terminology in relation to supplies on one hand and acquisitions and importations on the other is explained by the nature of the zero rate. A supply made by a taxable person at the zero rate is a taxable supply with the consequence that any input tax attributable to it is allowable for credit.[8] Input tax is not attributed to acquisitions or importations. Thus, although a taxable person's input tax is increased by the VAT charged on them, they do not affect the proportion of input tax recoverable. It follows that the different form of words does no more than reflect the different input tax consequences of the charge to tax on supplies, acquisitions and importations. The revenue consequences in terms of tax charged are, however, the same: no tax is charged so there is no revenue.

[1] VATA 1994, s 30(1). For supplies, goods and services chargeable at the zero-rate, see Chapter 69.
[2] VATA 1994, s 29A(1) (as inserted by FA 2001, s 99). For supplies, goods and services chargeable at the reduced rate, see Chapter 70.
[3] VATA 1994, s 2(1). The standard rate was reduced from 17.5% to 15% from 1 December 2008 by VAT (Change of Rate) Order, SI 2008/3020, art 3. The 2008 Order expires on 1 January 2010 with the consequence that the 17.5% rate is restored from that date: see FA 2009, s 9(1).
[4] VATA 1994, ss 29A(1)(*a*) as inserted by FA 2001, ss 99, 30(2) and 31(1).
[5] This applies in relation to a "retailer voucher" supplied by an intermediary and to any voucher which is not a "credit voucher", "retailer voucher" or "postage stamp" supplied by anyone: VATA 1994, Sch 10A, paras 4(4) and 6(2)–(5) as inserted by FA 2003, Sch 1, para 2.
[6] VATA 1994, s 30(3). For the acquisitions and importations on which no VAT is chargeable, see Chapter 69.
[7] VATA 1994, ss 2(1) and 29A(1) as amended or inserted by FA 1995, s 21, FA 2001 s 99; VAT (Change of Rate) Order, SI 2008/3020, art 3. For acquisitions and importations chargeable at the reduced rate, see Chapter 70.
[8] For the attribution of input tax to taxable supplies, see infra, § **66.07**.

Accounting and payment

[65.07] Insofar as the liability for VAT chargeable on transactions within Charges I–III falls on a taxable person, the VAT concerned is referred to as

[65.07] The charge to tax

"output tax".[1] In principle, a taxable person liable to account for output tax does so by making an entry in his VAT Account and declaring the amount concerned on his VAT return.[2]

Insofar as the liability for VAT on acquisitions within Charge III falls on a non-taxable person, that person is required to make a declaration to the Commissioners and pay the tax due direct to them.[3]

Insofar as the liability for VAT arises on imported goods within Charge IV, the person liable is required to make a declaration to the Commissioners and pay the tax due direct to them. This applies whether or not that person is a taxable person.[4]

[1] VATA 1994, s 24(2).
[2] For the VAT account, see infra, § **67.02**.
[3] For accounting and payment, see infra, § **67.12**.
[4] For accounting and payment, see infra, § **67.14**.

Charge I—Supplies of goods and services

The charge to tax

[65.08] A supply of goods or services made for a consideration[1] is charged to tax if all of the following conditions are met:[2]

(1) The supply is made by a taxable person.
(2) The supply is made in the course or furtherance of the taxable person's business.
(3) The supply is made in the UK.

There are two exceptions to this rule. First, a supply is not charged to tax if it is an exempt supply.[3] A supply which is not an exempt supply is referred to as a "taxable supply".[4] Thus, the charge to tax is confined to taxable supplies. Secondly, a supply of goods or services is normally disregarded, so that no tax is charged on it, if both the supplier and the recipient of the supply are members of the same VAT group.[5]

A taxable supply of goods or services is chargeable to tax at the zero rate, the reduced rate or at the standard rate.[6]

[1] For supplies within this description, see supra, § **63.23–63.26**.
[2] VATA 1994, s 4(1).
[3] The charge to tax under VATA 1994, s 4(1) is confined to taxable supplies.
[4] VATA 1994, s 4(2).
[5] VATA 1994, s 43(1). For the exception to this rule, and the consequences, see supra, § **64.28**.
[6] For the rates of tax, see supra, § **65.06**.

Person liable to account for tax

[65.09] In principle, the VAT on any supply of goods or services is a liability of the person making the supply.[1] There are a number of exceptions to this rule:

(1) Certain goods and services are subject to what is referred to as a "reverse charge" under which it is the recipient of the supply, not the supplier, who is required to account for the tax chargeable on the supply.[2]

(2) If a person acting under a power (X) sells goods owned by a taxable person (Y) in satisfaction of a debt owed by Y, Y is deemed to make the supply but X is required to account for and pay the tax chargeable on it.[3]

(3) A person may be required to give security for the VAT that is, or may become, due from any other person in a chain of supply.[4] The Commissioners may offset the security against the VAT unpaid by the other persons. VAT due from the other persons in the supply chain may therefore become the liability of the person required to give security.

(4) A person may be served with a notice making him and other persons in a chain of supply jointly and severally liable for the amount of unpaid VAT specified in the notice.[5] The person served with a notice therefore assumes liability for VAT due from the other persons if he is required to make a payment in accordance with these provisions.

De Voil Indirect Tax Service V3.502.

[1] VATA 1994, s 1(2).
[2] For reverse charge on services received from abroad, gas and electricity, gold and specified goods, see infra, §§ **65.38–65.41**.
[3] VATA 1994, Sch 4, para 7; VAT Regulations, SI 1995/2518 reg 27. For the return made by the person acting under a power, see infra, §§ **67.11**.
[4] For the requirement to give security, see infra, § **67.09**.
[5] For joint and several liability, see infra, § **67.10**.

Time when the charge to tax arises

The time of supply

[65.10] A supply of goods or services is treated as taking place at the time of supply. In principle, the supply is treated as taking place on the occurrence of an event (which is frequently referred to as the "basic tax point"). The basic tax point is displaced by a different event (referred to simply as a "tax point") in prescribed circumstances.

The time of supply is important for three reasons. First, all or part of the tax due on a supply of goods or services becomes due at that time. This VAT becomes a liability of the supplier and he is required to account to the Commissioners for it.[1] Secondly, the supplier is required to issue a VAT invoice

[65.10] The charge to tax

within 30 days of the time of supply,[2] and is liable to a penalty if he does not do so.[3] Thirdly, the rate of tax is determined by reference to the legislation in force at the time of supply.[4]

De Voil Indirect Tax Service V3.131–141.

[1] VATA 1994, s 1(2).
[2] VAT Regulations, SI 1995/2518, reg 13(5).
[3] VATA 1994, s 69(1)(d).
[4] *W F Graham (Northampton) Ltd v Customs and Excise Comrs* (1980) VAT decision 908.

Basic tax points

[65.11] In principle, a supply of goods or services is treated as taking place on the occurrence of one of the following events (referred to as a "basic tax point"):[1]

(1) As regards goods removed on approval, sale or return or similar terms[2] before it is known whether a supply will take place—the time when it becomes certain that the supply has taken place or (if sooner) twelve months after removal.

(2) As regards other goods—the time when they are removed or (if not removed) the time when they are made available[3] to the recipient of the supply.

(3) As regard services—the time when the services are performed.[4]

De Voil Indirect Tax Service V3.131–141.

[1] VATA 1994, s 6(2), (3).
[2] For goods within this description, see *Diaform Ltd v Customs and Excise Comrs* (1993) VAT decision 11069; *Littlewoods Organisation plc v Customs and Excise Comrs* [1997] V & DR 408. For goods outside this description, see *Customs and Excise Comrs v Robertson's Electrical Ltd* [2005] CSIH 75, [2007] STC 612.
[3] For the time when goods are made available, see *West End Motors (Bodmin) Ltd v Customs and Excise Comrs* (1982) VAT decision 1205. As regards land, see *Cumbernauld Development Corpn v Customs and Excise Comrs* [2002] STC 226.
[4] For the time when services are performed, see *Trustees for the Greater World Association Trust v Customs and Excise Comrs* [1989] VATTR 91; *Mercantile Contracts Ltd v Customs and Excise Comrs* (1989) VAT decision 4357; *Granton Marketing Ltd and Wentwalk Ltd (No 2) v Customs and Excise Comrs* [1999] V & DR 383.

Other tax points

[65.12] The basic tax point is displaced by a different event (referred to simply as a "tax point") in accordance with the normal and special tax point rules.[1] The most important events are:

(1) The time when the trader issues a VAT invoice[2] in respect of the supply. An invoice must contain all the information required to be shown on a tax invoice before it creates a tax point.[3] It is issued when it is sent or given to a customer.[4] An invoice issued in respect of a zero-rated supply does not create a tax point.[5] A self-billed invoice does not create a tax point in specified circumstances.[6]

(2) The time when the trader receives a payment in respect of the supply. All relevant information regarding the future delivery of the goods, or future performance of the services, must be known at the time of payment, and the goods or services precisely defined at that time, if a payment on account is to create a tax point under this provision.[7] A payment relates to a specific supply if this is what the parties have agreed.[8] The recipient must demonstrate that he has received payment.[9] A payment is received by the supplier if the payment is made to him and he thereafter has no right to sue for payment,[10] even if he does not have complete freedom to draw on the moneys received.[11] A payment is deemed to be received by the supplier if it is received by the person to whom the right to receive the payment has been assigned.[12] Payment is not received or deemed to be received by the supplier if the moneys are paid to a stakeholder[13] or held in a clients account.[14]

The fact that a tax point has arisen by virtue of a VAT invoice or payment (so that VAT in respect of the supply becomes a liability of the supplier) does not create a supply where none has taken place.[15]

De Voil Indirect Tax Service V3.501.

---

[1]   For the normal and special tax point rules, see infra, §§ **66.09** and **66.10**.
[2]   For VAT invoices, see infra, § **66.04**.
[3]   *J D Fox Ltd v Customs and Excise Comrs* [1988] 2 CMLR 875. The Commissioners may waive this requirement: SI 1995/2518, reg 14(1). For the information shown on a tax invoice, see infra, § **65.18**.
[4]   *Customs and Excise Comrs v Woolfold Motor Co Ltd* [1983] STC 715.
[5]   *Double Shield Window Co Ltd v Customs and Excise Comrs* (1985) VAT decision 1771.
[6]   VAT Regulations, SI 1995/2518, reg 13(3F) as inserted by SI 2003/3220.
[7]   *BUPA Hospitals Ltd and another v Customs and Excise Comrs (case C-419/02)* [2006] ECR I–1685, [2006] STC 967, ECJ. In the UK, see *Weldons (West One) Ltd v Customs and Excise Comrs* (1980) VAT decision 984 (advance payment for goods not yet ordered); *Old Chigwellians' Club v Customs and Excise Comrs* [1987] VATTR 66 (life membership fee paid in advance by instalments); *West Yorkshire Independent Hospital (Contract Services) Ltd v Customs and Excise Comrs* [1986] VATTR 151 (imprecise contract).
[8]   *Customs and Excise Comrs v British Telecom plc* [1995] STC 239 (overpayments).
[9]   For set-off under a close-out netting agreement, see *Revenue and Customs Comrs v Enron Europe Ltd (in administration)* [2006] EWHC 824 (Ch), [2006] STC 1339. For inter-company current accounts see *Legal and Contractual Services Ltd v Customs and Excise Comrs* [1984] VATTR 85; *Schlumberger Inland Services Inc v Customs and Excise Comrs* [1985] VATTR 35; *Pentex Oil Ltd v Customs and Excise Comrs* (1992) VAT decision 7989. For deposits see *Purshotam M Pattni & Sons v Customs and Excise Comrs* [1987] STC 1; *Customs and Excise Comrs v*

[65.12] The charge to tax

Moonrakers Guest House Ltd [1992] STC 544; *Bethway & Moss Ltd v Customs and Excise Comrs* [1988] 3 CMLR 44; *Regalstar Enterprises Ltd v Customs and Excise Comrs* [1989] 1 CMLR 117. A cheque payment is received when it is met by the drawer's bank: *Rampling v Customs and Excise Comrs* [1986] VATTR 62. For loan-back schemes, see *Customs and Excise Comrs v Faith Construction Ltd* [1989] STC 539, CA; *Barratt Construction Ltd v Customs and Excise Comrs* [1989] VATTR 204.

[10] *Customs and Excise Comrs v Faith Construction Ltd* [1989] STC 539, CA.

[11] *Customs and Excise Comrs v Faith Construction Ltd* [1989] STC 539, CA (funds released on presentation of architects' certificates); *Barratt Urban Construction (Northern) Ltd v Customs and Excise Comrs* (1988) VAT decision 2723 (netting arrangements and cross guarantees on bank overdraft facilities); *Customs and Excise Comrs v Richmond Theatre Management Ltd* [1995] STC 257 (advance ticket sales).

[12] SI 1995/2518, reg 94A as inserted by SI 1999/599. This applies for the purposes of the time of supply rules in SI 1995/2518, regs 81–95.

[13] *Double Shield Window Co Ltd v Customs and Excise Comrs* (1985) VAT decision 1771.

[14] See *Ghaus v Customs and Excise Comrs* (1990) VAT decision 4999; *Nigel Mansell Sports Cars Ltd v Customs and Excise Comrs* [1991] VATTR 491.

[15] *Theotrue Holdings Ltd v Customs and Excise Comrs* [1983] VATTR 88.

The general time of supply rule

[65.13] In principle, a supply is treated as taking place at the basic tax point.[1] However, the basic tax point is displaced in the following circumstances and the date indicated is substituted:[2]

(1) As regards goods removed on approval, sale or return, or similar terms, the time of supply is the invoice date if:
    (a) a VAT invoice is issued before the basic tax point; or
    (b) a VAT invoice is issued within 14 days (or such longer period as may be specified in a direction to an individual trader) after the basic tax point.

(2) As regards other goods and services, the time of supply is:
    (a) the earlier of the invoice date or date of receipt (if a VAT invoice is issued or payment received before the basic tax point); or
    (b) the invoice date (if a VAT invoice is issued within 14 days—or such longer period as may be specified in a direction to an individual trader—after the basic tax point).

Issuing an invoice or making a payment in advance of the basic tax point have long been used as a means of avoiding or delaying tax liabilities, eg when an increase in the rate of tax is predicted or announced. The arrangements made do not always achieve their intended aim.[3]

De Voil Indirect Tax Service V3.131–141.

[1] VATA 1994, s 6(2), (3). For the basic tax point, see supra, § **65.11**.
[2] VATA 1994, s 6(4)–(8).

[3] For examples, see *Customs and Excise Comrs v Thorn Materials Supply Ltd* [1998] STC 725, HL (payer and payee members of the same VAT group); *BUPA Hospitals Ltd and another v Customs and Excise Comrs* [2006] STC 967, ECJ (list of goods, which was subject to variation by mutual agreement, from which articles could be selected, where the purchaser could unilaterally resile from the agreement and recover the unused balance of his prepayment).

Special time of supply rules

[65.14] Traders may adopt a special tax point with the consent of the Commissioners, who will then issue a direction to that effect. The time of supply may be determined by reference to some specific event or the beginning or end of a "relevant working period".[1]

The legislation sets out special time of supply rules in relation to the following supplies of goods and services. As regards points (1)–(6), the time of supply is the earlier of the time when a VAT invoice is issued and the time when a payment is received. A more complex formulation is used in the other cases.

(1) Rent in respect of a lease for a term exceeding 21 years.[2]
(2) Supplies of water, gas, power, heat, refrigeration or ventilation.[3]
(3) Continuous supplies of services,[4] eg hire charges.
(4) Retention payments.[5]
(5) Royalties and similar payments.[6]
(6) Construction industry stage payments.[7]
(7) A supply of goods which involves removing the goods from the UK to another EU member state.[8]
(8) The compulsory purchase of interests in land.[9]
(9) Freeholds granted for an undetermined future consideration.[10]
(10) Goods sold under reservation of title.[11]
(11) Services supplied by barristers and advocates.[12]
(12) Supplies of warehoused goods.[13]
(13) Coin-operated machines.[14]
(14) The place of supply of certain services[15] changes.[16]

Although a self-billed invoice is normally treated as a VAT invoice issued by the supplier, this is not always so for the purposes of determining a special tax point in relation to the foregoing goods and services.[17]

An overriding anti-avoidance rule applies in relation to a positive rate supply of the goods and services in points 1–3 to a connected person or to a fellow undertaking in a group undertaking that is not a member of the same VAT group where, in either case, all or part of the VAT chargeable on the supply is irrecoverable by the customer. To the extent that the goods or services have been provided, and that a tax point has not already arisen in respect of a taxable supply of them under any time of supply rule, the goods or services are treated as being supplied separately and successively on a specified anniversary and at the end of each subsequent period of 12 months.[18] This rule is displaced (unless the supplier elects otherwise) if a VAT invoice is issued, or a payment is received, within six months (or such other period as the Commissioners may allow) after the relevant anniversary.[19]

De Voil Indirect Tax Service V3.131–141.

[65.14] The charge to tax

1. VATA 1994, s 6(10).
2. VAT Regulations, SI 1995/2518, reg 85.
3. SI 1995/2518, reg 86.
4. SI 1995/2518, regs 90(1)–(3) (generally) and 93 (construction industry) as amended and substituted by SI 1997/2887. For supplementary provisions relating to telecommunications services, see SI 1995/2518, regs 90(4), (5), 90A and 90B as inserted by SI 1997/1525 and amended by SI 1998/765. For amounts overpaid, see *Customs and Excise Comrs v British Telecommunications plc* [1996] STC 818, CA. For recoveries in respect of pre-registration supplies, see *B J Rice & Associates v Customs and Excise Comrs* [1996] STC 581, CA.
5. SI 1995/2518, regs 89 (generally) and 93 (construction industry) as amended and substituted by SI 1997/2887, SI 2003/3220.
6. SI 1995/2518, reg 91.
7. SI 1995/2518, reg 93 as amended or substituted by SI 1999/1374, SI 2009/1967.
8. If the recipient makes an acquisition, and is charged to VAT, under the law of the member state concerned, the supply is treated as taking place on the earlier of: (a) the fifteenth day of the month following that in which the removal takes place; and (b) the day when a VAT invoice is issued: VATA 1994, s 6(7), (8). However, supplies of water, gas, power, heat, refrigeration and ventilation are treated as taking place when a tax invoice is issued: SI 1995/2518, reg 86(5).
9. SI 1995/2518, reg 84(1).
10. SI 1995/2518, reg 84(2)–(5) as amended or inserted by SI 2003/1069, SI 2003/3220, SI 2008/1146, SI 2009/1967.
11. SI 1995/2518, reg 88 as amended by SI 2003/3220.
12. SI 1995/2518, reg 92; Leaflet No700/44/93.
13. VATA 1994, s 18(4).
14. Notice No 48 (July 2009) para 3.6.
15. ie services specified in an order made under VATA 1994, s 7(11) which meet the conditions specified in VATA 1994, s 97A(1) as inserted by FA 1998, s 22. For services affected by this provision, see VAT (Place of Supply of Services) Order, SI 1992/3121, arts 17, 18 as substituted by SI 1998/763.
16. VATA 1994, s 6(14A) as inserted by FA 1998, s 22. For the special rules, see VATA 1994, s 97A(2)–(6) as inserted by FA 1998, s 22.
17. SI 1995/2518, reg 13(3F) as inserted by SI 2003/3220.
18. The end date of the subsequent periods may be varied with the Commissioners' consent.
19. SI 1995/2518, reg 94B as inserted and amended by SI 2003/3220, SI 2008/1146, SI 2009/1967.

Change in the rate or description of supply

[65.15] Traders may elect for a special tax point to apply where a change takes place in any of the following circumstances:

(1) The rate of tax changes, ie the standard rate or reduced rate is increased or decreased.
(2) A description of exempt supplies changes, ie the supplies become taxable supplies.
(3) A description of reduced rate or zero-rated supplies changes, ie they become exempt or chargeable to tax at a different rate.

Where goods or services are supplied on one side of the change (regardless of whether or not they have a basic tax point) but the tax point governing the charge to tax takes place on the other side, tax is charged by reference to the tax regime in force when the goods or services are supplied.[1] This election is not available where goods are sold in satisfaction of a debt or where a self-billing invoice is issued.[2]

EXAMPLE

X delivers goods to a customer on 1 January (the basic tax point) and issues a tax invoice on 10 January (the tax point governing the charge to tax). The rate of tax is increased on 5 January. X can elect to charge tax by reference to the rate of tax in force on 1 January.

Y hires a motor car to a customer on 1 February (no tax point arises) and is paid in arrears by standing order on the first day of each month (each payment creates a tax point). The rate of tax is increased on 15 April. X may account for tax at the old rate on one half of the 1 May payment. The other half is charged at the new rate.

De Voil Indirect Tax Service V3.131–141.

[1] VATA 1994, s 88(2) as amended by FA 2001, Sch 31, para 4; VAT Regulations, SI 1995/2518, reg 95 as amended by SI 2003/2318, SI 2004/3140.
[2] VATA 1994, s 88(6) as amended by FA 2002, s 24.

Value

General principles

[65.16] Tax is charged by reference to the value of the goods or services supplied.[1] Value is defined as the residual amount found by deducting the tax (if any) chargeable on the supply from the consideration or the amount treated as the consideration.[2] This is a useful way of looking at valuation for retailers who price their goods and services in VAT-inclusive terms. It is also useful when calculating the tax for which a trader is liable in those cases where he has failed to charge tax to his customer. In each case, the tax element of a supply chargeable is 3/23 of the consideration (if the supply is chargeable at the standard rate) or 1/21 (if it is chargeable at the reduced rate). In other cases, value is either the VAT-exclusive price fixed by the supplier or a value determined in accordance with valuation principles derived from the legislation and the case law flowing from it.

The distinction between VAT-exclusive and VAT-inclusive accounting is also relevant to the quantum of VAT charged to the customer and accounted for (in the former case) or accounted for (in the latter case). VAT-exclusive accounting involves invoicing an amount of VAT which the customer is able to pay. It therefore involves rounding on a line-by-line or invoice total basis if the amount calculated includes a fraction of a penny. As the VAT accounted for by the supplier and paid by the customer is the same, the supplier makes neither gain nor loss whatever the rounding system used. VAT-inclusive accounting, on the other hand, requires VAT to be accounted for by way of a single calculation based on total consideration for the prescribed accounting period concerned. This ensures that the VAT accounted for is exactly proportional to the consideration. Thus, although the accounting systems used by some retailers

[65.16] The charge to tax

enable them to compute VAT on a line-by-line basis, allowing them to account for VAT on this basis could produce a significant gain or loss if VAT amounts were to be consistently rounded up or down.[3]

Consideration is clearly crucial to the valuation of supplies. It is therefore necessary to identify the consideration for which individual goods or services were supplied. This may be a matter of some difficulty if a single price is charged for two or more separable supplies. It is necessary to attribute a consideration to each supply[4] on a fair and reasonable basis[5] and calculate the value from the consideration so attributed. Similarly, two or more prices charged at different times, or separately itemised on an invoice, by the same supplier[6] may represent the consideration for a single supply. Where this is so, it is necessary to aggregate the separate prices in order to ascertain the consideration for the supply. For the difficulties in determining whether the supplier has made one or more than one supply, see supra, § **63.19**.

De Voil Indirect Tax Service V3.151–166.

[1] VATA 1994, s 2(1)(a).
[2] Cf VATA 1994, s 19(2).
[3] See *J D Wetherspoon plc v Revenue & Customs Comrs* (case C-302/07) [2009] ECR I–0000, [2009] STC 1022, ECJ (rounding methods a matter for the member states and retailers not having a Community right to use the national rounding down method available to "invoice traders").
[4] VATA 1994, s 19(4); *Customs and Excise Comrs v Automobile Association* [1974] STC 192, [1974] 1 All ER 1257.
[5] *Southend United Football Club v Customs and Excise Comrs* [1997] V & DR 202. For methods suggested by the Commissioners, see Notice No 700. For an example, see *River Barge Holidays Ltd v Customs and Excise Comrs* (1978) VAT decision 572.
[6] Considerations due to separate suppliers cannot be fused in this manner to make a single supply: *Nell Gwynn House Maintenance Fund Trustees v Customs and Excise Comrs* [1999] STC 79, HL.

Valuation rules

[65.17] The value of a supply made for a consideration in money is such amount as, with the addition of VAT, equals the consideration[1] less the amount of any prompt payment discount offered.[2] Thus, if A Ltd sells goods for £100 and offers a 5% discount for prompt payment, VAT is calculated on £95 whether or not the discount is taken. "Consideration" for this purpose includes:

(1) Taxes, duties, levies and charges other than VAT.[3]
(2) Incidental expenses such as commission, packing, transport and insurance costs charged by the supplier to the customer,[4] insofar as they do not amount to separate supplies.[5]
(3) A deduction for price discounts and rebates allowed to the customer.[6]

The value of a supply in other cases is such amount in money as, with the addition of VAT, is equivalent to the consideration.[7] Monetary equivalents are determined by reference to "subjective value" or "the value for the purposes of the transaction", ie the value placed on the goods or services in the context of the particular transaction rather than some "objective" value commanded in the open market. Thus, VAT is not charged on a value exceeding the consideration actually received.[8]

Monetary equivalents are ascertained in the same manner whether goods or services have been supplied. If the parties have expressly or implicitly attributed a value to the non-monetary consideration, the monetary equivalent is that value.[9] An attributed value is frequently ascertained from the relevant documentation. If the documentation specifies different values for different circumstances, the relevant value is the one applicable in the circumstances that actually happen.[10] The other values are irrelevant.[11] If the parties have not attributed a value to the non-monetary consideration, the monetary equivalent is the price paid by the supplier for the goods or services he has supplied.[12] Any delivery costs paid are added to this sum.[13]

The Commissioners are empowered to direct traders to account for tax by reference to open market value in relation to supplies to connected persons,[14] private use of motor cars held as trading stock by motor dealers[15] and supplies made to the public through unregistered intermediaries.[16]

Traders opting to supply goods under the special scheme for works of art, antiques, collectors' items and secondhand goods are not permitted to issue VAT invoices. The VAT chargeable on an individual supply is the amount (if any) by which the price at which the goods were supplied[17] is exceeded by the price at which they were obtained,[18] both prices being determined in accordance with statutory provisions.[19]

Traders are required or permitted to use special accounting schemes in respect of retail supplies, designated travel services, works of art etc, services which have been used for business entertaining, gaming machines and fuel for private use. Traders using these schemes account for tax by reference to the value of all supplies (as opposed to individual supplies) made under the scheme during a prescribed accounting period. The basis of valuation and manner of calculating tax are described individually in infra, §§ **65.22–65.27**.

The following goods and services are valued on a special basis:[20]

(1) Stamps, tokens and vouchers (collectively referred to as "face value vouchers") in physical or electronic form representing a right to receive goods or services, or to be used in part-payment for goods or services, to the value of an amount stated on, or recorded in, them.[21]
(2) Hotel accommodation.
(3) Food and accommodation supplied to employees.[22]

De Voil Indirect Tax Service V3.151–166.

---

[1] VATA 1994, s 19(2). For the manner in which value is arrived at in practice, see infra, § **65.16**.
[2] For discounts for prompt payment, see *Gold Star Publications Ltd v Customs and Excise Comrs* [1992] STC 365; *Springfield China Ltd v Customs and Excise Comrs* (1990) VAT decision 4546.
[3] Directive 2006/112/EC art 78(*a*).

[65.17] The charge to tax

4 Directive 2006/112/EC art 78(b).
5 For transport, see *Customs and Excise Comrs v British Telecommunications plc* [1999] STC 758, HL; *Customs and Excise Comrs v Plantiflor Ltd* [2002] STC 1132, HL.
6 Directive 2006/112/EC art 79(b). For the distinction between discounts and rebates, see *Freemans plc v Customs and Excise Comrs (case C-86/99)* [2001] ECR I-4167, [2001] STC 960, ECJ at paras 22, 23. For discounts, see *Boots Co plc v Customs and Excise Comrs (case C-126/88)* [1990] ECR I-1235, [1990] STC 387, ECJ (cost of "money off" coupons borne by the retailer issuing them).
7 VATA 1994, s 19(3).
8 *Staatssecretaris van Financiën v Coöperatieve Aardappelenbewaarplaats GA (case 154/80)* [1981] ECR 445, ECJ; *Elida Gibbs Ltd v Customs and Excise Comrs (case C-317/94)* [1996] STC 1387, ECJ; *Customs and Excise Comrs v Littlewoods Organisation plc and related cases* [2001] STC 1568, CA.
9 For an exceptional case where the attributed value was nil, see *Customs and Excise Comrs v Ping (Europe) Ltd* [2002] STC 1186, CA (golf clubs infringing the rules of golf).
10 *Customs and Excise Comrs v Westmorland Motorway Services Ltd* [1998] STC 431, CA; *Customs and Excise Comrs v Littlewoods Organisation plc and related cases* [2001] STC 1568, CA.
11 For examples of alternative values, see *Rosgill Group Ltd v Customs and Excise Comrs* [1997] STC 811, CA; *Customs and Excise Comrs v Littlewoods Organisation plc and related cases* [2001] STC 1568, CA (in the *Bugeja* case).
12 *Empire Stores Ltd v Customs and Excise Comrs (case C-33/93)* [1994] STC 623, ECJ; *Customs and Excise Comrs v Littlewoods Organisation plc and related cases* [2001] STC 1568, CA; *Lex Services plc v Customs and Excise Comrs* [2003] UKHL 67, [2004] STC 73.
13 *Bertelsmann AG v Finanzamt Wiedenbrück (case C-380/99)* [2001] STC 1153, ECJ.
14 VATA 1994, Sch 6, para 1. See *Oughtred & Harrison Ltd v Customs and Excise Comrs* [1988] VATTR 140; *RBS Leasing & Services Ltd v Customs and Excise Comrs* [2000] V & DR 33.
15 VATA 1994, Sch 6, para 1A as inserted by FA 2004, s 22; Finance Act 2004, section 22(2) (Appointed Day) Order, SI 2004/3104.
16 VATA 1994, Sch 6, para 2. The validity of this provision was upheld in *Direct Cosmetics Ltd and Laughtons Photographs Ltd v Customs and Excise Comrs (joined cases 138 and 139/86)* [1988] STC 540, ECJ. For examples of directions, see *Direct Cosmetics Ltd v Customs and Excise Comrs* (1989) VAT decision 3624; *Moore v Customs and Excise Comrs* [1989] VATTR 276; *Gold Star Publications Ltd v Customs and Excise Comrs* [1992] STC 365; *Fine Arts Developments plc v Customs and Excise Comrs* [1994] STC 668, CA; *Beckbell Ltd v Customs and Excise Comrs* [1993] VATTR 212.
17 For the basis of calculation, see SI 1992/3122, art 8(5)(a), (6), (7)(a) as so substituted and amended by SI 1998/759; SI 1995/1268, art 12(5)(a), (6), (7)(a) as amended by SI 1998/760.
18 For the basis of calculation, see SI 1992/3122, art 8(5)(b), (6), (7)(b) as so substituted; SI 1995/1268, art 12(5)(b), (6), (7)(b).
19 VATA 1994, s 50A(4) as added by FA 1995, s 24. For the statutory provisions, see supra, notes 17, 18.
20 For the special basis of valuation, see VATA 1994, Sch 6, paras 9, 10.

[21] Face value vouchers, as defined in VATA 1994, Sch 10A, paras 1(1), 8(3) as inserted by FA 2003, Sch 1, para 2. For a voucher outside this description, see *Leisure Pass Group Ltd v Revenue and Customs Comrs* [2008] EWHC 2158 (Ch), [2008] STC 3340 (voucher limited by time rather than by a monetary limit). For the valuation of (1) "credit vouchers", "retailer vouchers" and postage stamps supplied by the issuer, and (2) "credit vouchers" and postage stamps supplied by an intermediary, see VATA 1994, Sch 10A, paras 3(2), 4(2) and 5 as so inserted. The consideration is the amount (if any) by which the consideration exceeds face value. For the exceptions to this rule when the person accepting the voucher in exchange for goods or services fails to account for the VAT on that supply, see VATA 1994, Sch 10A, paras 3(3), (4) and 4(3) as so inserted and by FA 2006, s 22. For face value vouchers deemed to be supplied for nil consideration when they form part of a composite transaction, see VATA 1994, Sch 10A, para 8 as so inserted.

[22] See *Goodfellow (a firm) v Customs and Excise Comrs* [1986] VATTR 119; *Glendale Social Club v Customs and Excise Comrs* [1994] VATTR 372; *Co-operative Insurance Society Ltd v Customs and Excise Comrs* [1997] V & DR 65.

VAT invoices

The duty to issue a VAT invoice

[65.18] A registered taxable person is required to issue a VAT invoice when he makes a supply to another taxable person, and must do so within 30 days (or such longer time as the Commissioners may allow) of the time when the supply is treated as taking place for the purposes of charging tax.[1] A VAT invoice for this purpose includes a document provided by a person selling someone else's goods under a power, a self-billed invoice (ie an invoice prepared by the customer) prepared under a self-billing agreement[2] and an authenticated receipt given in respect of construction industry stage payments.[3] A VAT invoice must contain specified particulars.[4]

A registered taxable person is also required to issue a VAT invoice in the following circumstances:[5]

(1) He makes a supply of goods or services to a person in another EU member state.
(2) He receives a payment on account from a person in another EU member state in respect of a supply made or intended to be made.

He must do so within 30 days (or such longer time as the Commissioners may allow) of the time when the supply is treated as taking place for the purpose of charging tax.[6] A VAT invoice must contain specified particulars.[7]

Retailers are not required to provide a VAT invoice, but must do so on request if the customer is a taxable person.[8] More generally, the requirement to issue a VAT invoice does not extend to:[9]

(1) Exempt supplies.
(2) Zero-rated supplies (unless the recipient makes an acquisition in another EU member state under a supply involving removal of the goods from the UK to another EU member state).

[65.18] The charge to tax

(3) Supplies of goods or services relieved from tax under the margin schemes.
(4) Supplies made for no consideration.

A VAT invoice may be provided electronically if both supplier and customer can guarantee the authenticity of its origin and the integrity of its contents. The supplier (or customer in the case of a self-billed invoice) must comply with any conditions imposed by the Commissioners.[10]

The consideration for a positive rate supply may be increased after the end of the prescribed accounting period in which the supply was made. If so, both the supplier and his customer must adjust their VAT Accounts accordingly.[11]

An unauthorised person[12] is liable to civil penalties[13] and interest[14] if he issues an invoice showing an amount as being VAT or as including an amount attributable to VAT. The VAT may be recovered as a debt due to the Crown.[15]

De Voil Indirect Tax Service V3.513–517.

---

[1] VAT Regulations, SI 1995/2518, reg 13(1), (1A), (5) as amended or inserted by SI 2007/2085.
[2] For self-billing agreements, see VAT Regulations, SI 1995/2518, reg 13(3A)–(3D) as inserted by SI 2003/3220. For an example under superseded legislation, see *UDL Construction plc (in administrative receivership and compulsory liquidation) v Customs and Excise Comrs* [1995] V & DR 396.
[3] SI 1995/2518, reg 13(2), (3), (3E), (4) as amended by SI 2003/3220. For credit notes (rather than self-billed invoices) issued by the recipient of a supply, see *Finanzamt Osnabrück-Land v Langhorst (case C-141/96)* [1997] STC 1357, ECJ. For the assessment of tax understated on a self-billed invoice, see VATA 1994, s 29.
[4] For the specified particulars, see SI 1995/2518, regs 14(1) (as amended by SI 1996/1250, SI 2003/3220, SI 2007/2085), (5), (6) (as inserted by SI 1995/3147) and 14SD(1) (as amended by SI 1996/1250). For documents omitting or misstating information, see *ABB Power Ltd v Customs and Excise Comrs* [1992] VATTR 491; *Finch v Customs and Excise Comrs* (1993) VAT decision 10948; *Libdale Ltd v Customs and Excise Comrs* [1993] VATTR 425.
[5] SI 1995/2518, reg 13(1) as amended by SI 2007/2085.
[6] SI 1995/2518, reg 13(5).
[7] SI 1995/2518, reg 14(1) as amended by SI 2007/2085 and modified by reg 14(2) as amended by SI 2003/3220, SI 2007/2085.
[8] SI 1995/2518, reg 16 as amended by SI 2003/3220. A simplified invoice may be provided if the consideration for the supply does not exceed £250.
[9] SI 1995/2518, regs 13(1), 20.
[10] SI 1995/2518, regs 13A, 14(7) as inserted by SI 2003/3220.
[11] VAT Regulations, SI 1995/2518, reg 38 as amended by SI 1997/1086, SI 2007/1418, SI 2009/586. The increase must be evidenced by a debit note, credit note or similar document: SI 1995/2518, reg 24; *British Telecommunications plc v Customs and Excise Comrs* (1997) VAT decision 14669. For the adjustment in respect of "specified goods", see SI 1995/2518, regs 38(1C), (3A) and 38A as inserted by SI 2007/1418. For "specified goods", see infra, § **65.41**. For the VAT Account, see infra, § **67.02**.
[12] Defined in VATA 1994, s 67(2).

[13] Currently VATA 1994, s 67(1)(c). A statutory defence of reasonable excuse is available: see VATA 1994, ss 67(8), 71(1). For an example, see *Alm v Customs and Excise Comrs* (1998) VAT decision 15863. This penalty is repealed and replaced by FA 2008, Sch 41, para 2 as regards any unauthorised issue of an invoice taking place after 31 March 2010: see FA 2008, Sch 41, para 25(f); Finance Act 2008, Schedule 41 (Appointed Day and Transitional Provisions) Order, SI 2008/511, arts 2, 3(b).

[14] VATA 1994, s 74(4). For the charge to interest, see supra, § **2A.43**.

[15] VATA 1994, Sch 11, para 5(2), (3). By concession, a deduction is made for input tax attributable to the goods or services invoiced: see Notice No 48 (July 2009) para 3.9. For recovery of tax shown on a sham invoice, see *Sandell v Customs and Excise Comrs* (1992) VAT decision 9665.

The right to issue a credit note

[65.19] A credit note is valid for VAT purposes only if it is issued under statutory authority[1] or if it is issued bona fide in order to correct a genuine mistake or overcharge or to give a proper credit.[2] A "proper credit" is one which reflects the supplier's true liability to output tax.[3] This does not include a credit note which attempts to re-write the nature of a transaction after the time of supply,[4] a credit note issued to someone other than the purchaser,[5] or a credit note which attempts to reduce the *agreed* consideration for a supply[6] (eg in the case of a bad debt).

A trader must issue a credit note if he wishes to reduce his own liability to output tax in respect of a tax invoice which he has issued.[7] A credit note may, by agreement between the parties, omit credit for tax charged in certain circumstances.[8]

A credit note may validly reduce the supplier's liability to output tax if:

(1) it cancels an invoice issued in respect of a supply which does not take place;[9]

(2) it reduces an amount invoiced in respect of a supply for an as yet unascertained consideration to the amount subsequently agreed by the parties to be payable;[10]

(3) it corrects a mistake in invoicing the agreed amount payable,[11] eg an arithmetical error;

(4) it gives effect to an election which reduces the tax chargeable on a supply consequent upon a change in the rate of tax or in the description of exempt, zero-rated or reduced-rated goods or services;[12]

(5) it is issued when goods subject to a hire purchase agreement are repossessed from someone other than a taxable person.[13]

The consideration for a positive rate supply may be decreased after the end of the prescribed accounting period in which the supply was made. If so, both the supplier and his customer must adjust their VAT Accounts accordingly.[14] However, no adjustment may be made in respect of VAT erroneously charged on an exempt or zero-rated supply. The amount charged is overpaid VAT and must be claimed accordingly.[15]

De Voil Indirect Tax Service V3.520.

[65.19] The charge to tax

1. ie under VAT Regulations, SI 1995/2518, reg 15.
2. *British United Shoe Machinery Co Ltd v Customs and Excise Comrs* [1977] VATTR 187.
3. *Securicor Granley Systems Ltd v Customs and Excise Comrs* [1990] VATTR 9.
4. See the cases cited in supra, § **63.18**.
5. *Sheepcote Commercial (Vehicles) Ltd v Customs and Excise Comrs* (1987) VAT decision 2378; *Senator Marketing Ltd v Customs and Excise Comrs* (1991) VAT decision 5598.
6. See the cases cited in supra, §§ **63.20–63.22**.
7. *Springfield China Ltd v Customs and Excise Comrs* (1990) VAT decision 4546.
8. Notice No 700 (April 2002) para 18.2.1.
9. *Securicor Granley Systems Ltd v Customs and Excise Comrs* [1990] VATTR 9 (invoices issued at beginning of hire period); *Cobojo Ltd v Customs and Excise Comrs* (1989) VAT decision 4055 (unauthorised work for which payment was refused).
10. *Castle Associates Ltd v Customs and Excise Comrs* (1989) VAT decision 3497.
11. *Castle Associates Ltd v Customs and Excise Comrs* (1989) VAT decision 3497.
12. VATA 1994, s 88; VAT Regulations, SI 1995/2518, reg 15 as amended by SI 2003/1485, SI 2008/3021.
13. Leaflet No 700/5/85.
14. VAT Regulations, SI 1995/2518, reg 38 as amended by SI 1997/1086, SI 2007/1418, SI 2009/2518. For the requirement for the decrease to be evidenced by a debit note, credit note or similar document, see SI 1995/2518, reg 24; *Customs and Excise Comrs v General Motors Acceptance Corpn (UK) plc* [2004] EWHC 192 (Ch), [2004] STC 577; *British Telecommunications plc v Customs and Excise Comrs* (1997) VAT decision 14669. For the adjustment in respect of "specified goods", see SI 1995/2518, regs 38(1C), (3A) and 38A as inserted by SI 2007/1418. For "specified goods", see infra, § **65.41**. For decreases in the consideration of supplies made by manufacturers, see *Boots Co plc v Customs and Excise Comrs (case C-126/88)* [1990] ECR I–1235, [1990] STC 387, ECJ ("money off" coupons); *Elida Gibbs Ltd v Customs and Excise Comrs (case C-317/94)* [1996] ECR I–5339, [1996] STC 1387 ("cash back" coupons); *Total UK Ltd v Revenue and Customs Comrs* [2006] EWHC 3422 (Ch), [2007] STC 564 (face value vouchers under a business promotion scheme); and contrast *Kuwait Petroleum (GB) Ltd v Customs and Excise Comrs* [2001] STC 62 (redemption goods under a business promotion scheme). For the VAT Account, see infra, § **67.02**.
15. *Customs and Excise Comrs v McMaster Stores (Scotland) Ltd (in receivership)* [1995] STC 846 (exempt supply); *Robinson Group of Companies Ltd v Customs and Excise Comrs* (1999) VAT decision 16081 (zero-rated supply). For recovery of overpaid VAT, see infra § **67.16**.

Output tax

General principles

[65.20] A taxable person is required to account for and pay output tax[1] by reference to prescribed accounting periods.[2] Thus, as a taxable person is required to issue VAT invoices in respect of supplies chargeable to tax at a positive rate,[3] his output tax for a prescribed accounting period represents the VAT shown on VAT invoices having a tax point which falls within that period.[4]

In practice, there are a number of exceptions to this principle. In particular, a trader is not required to issue VAT invoices, or is prohibited from issuing them, in respect of supplies made under special accounting schemes in respect of retail supplies, works of art etc, designated travel services, gaming machines and fuel for private use.[5] The VAT chargeable on these supplies is calculated in accordance with the terms of the individual schemes. Similarly, although a flat-rate trader[6] may or may not be required to issue VAT invoices in respect of his supplies, his output tax is calculated in accordance with the terms of the flat-rate scheme. The relevant requirements of the foregoing schemes are described in infra, §§ **65.21–65.27**.

The following provisions also represent an exception to the general principle stated above:

(1) A trader using the cash accounting scheme[7] normally accounts for output tax by reference to payments[8] received during a prescribed accounting period.[9]

(2) The Commissioners may allow a trader to estimate his output tax for a prescribed accounting period if they are satisfied that he is unable to account for the exact amount chargeable in that period.[10]

(3) The Commissioners may allow VAT chargeable in a prescribed accounting period to be treated as being chargeable in a later prescribed accounting period specified by them.[11]

De Voil Indirect Tax Service V3.521.

[1] For output tax, see supra, § **65.07**, VATA 1994, s 1(2).
[2] VATA 1994, s 25(1).
[3] VAT Regulations, SI 1995/2518, regs 13(1)(a), 20(a).
[4] In the absence of specific Community legislation, the rules for rounding VAT amounts are fixed by the member states: *Fiscale eenheid Koninklijke Ahold NV v Staatssecretaris van Financiën (case C-484/06)* [2008] SWTI 1713, ECJ. For the rules applied by the Commissioners in the UK, see Notice No 700 (April 2002), paras 17.5 and 17.6.
[5] SI 1995/2518, reg 16(1) (retailers); VAT (Cars) Order, SI 1992/3122, art 8(3)(c) and VAT (Special Provisions) Order, SI 1995/1268 art 12(4)(a)(ii) (works of art etc); Notice No 709/5/98, para 3.9 (tour operator's margin scheme).
[6] For the flat-rate scheme for small businesses, see supra, § **63.41**.
[7] For the cash accounting scheme, see supra, § **63.40**.
[8] For the meaning of "payment", see Notice No 731; *A–Z Electrical v Customs and Excise Comrs* [1993] VATTR 389. The scheme does not apply to the following payments: (a) payments relating to supplies made prior to commencing to use the scheme are excluded (the trader has already accounted for tax on these supplies); and (b) tax on supplies made under hire purchase, conditional sale and credit sale transactions, or under certain advance payment or invoicing schemes, is accounted for outside the scheme: SI 1995/2518, reg 58(2).
[9] SI 1995/2518, regs 57(a), 65(1). For the limited extent to which a flat-rate trader may use the scheme, see SI 1995/2518, reg 57A as inserted by SI 2002/1142. For the

[65.20] The charge to tax

equivalent relief available under the flat-rate scheme, see SI 1995/2518, reg 55G as so inserted.
[10] SI 1995/2518, reg 28.
[11] SI 1995/2518, reg 25(5). For the manner in which the Commissioners should exercise this power, see *Inchcape Management Services Ltd v Customs and Excise Comrs* [1999] V & DR 397.

Flat-rate scheme for small businesses

[65.21] A trader using the flat-rate scheme[1] calculates output tax by reference to a percentage (referred to as the "appropriate percentage")[2] of the VAT-inclusive value of his relevant supplies for the period (referred to as "relevant turnover")[3] and does not claim input tax credit in respect of his relevant purchases.[4] The appropriate percentage applied is determined by reference to a trader's business activity in accordance with the prescribed table:[5]

The appropriate percentages shown in the table are reduced by one (so that "accountancy", for example, is reduced from 11.5% to 10.5%) for all or part of the 12-month period commencing with the trader's effective date of registration.[6]

De Voil Indirect Tax Service V2.199B.

[1] For the flat-rate scheme generally, see supra, § 63.42.
[2] For the manner in which the appropriate percentage is applied, see VATA 1994, s 26(2)(b) as inserted by FA 2002, s 23 and VAT Regulations, SI 1995/2518, regs 55H, 55K(1)–(4) as inserted, substituted or amended by SI 2002/1142, SI 2003/3220.
[3] For relevant turnover, see VATA 1994, s 26(2)(c) as inserted by FA 2002, s 23 and SI 1995/2518, reg 55G as inserted by SI 2002/1142. For the "basic turnover method", "cash turnover method" and "retailer's turnover method", see Notice No 733.
[4] See infra, § 66.06.
[5] For the table, see SI 1995/2518, reg 55K as substituted by 2008/3021.
[6] SI 1995/2518, reg 55JB as inserted by SI 2003/3220. The reduction applies for that part of the twelve-month period commencing with the later of: (a) the day when the Commissioners received the trader's application for registration or otherwise became fully aware of his liability for registration; and (b) the day from which the trader is authorised to use the scheme.

Retail schemes

[65.22] A retail scheme is a method which enables a retailer to determine what proportion of his taxable retail sales for all or part of a prescribed accounting period is chargeable to tax at a positive rate. Most traders derive this information from invoices issued to customers. Retail schemes provide an alternative for retailers who find it difficult to issue invoices for a large number of supplies made direct to the public.[1]

A retailer may use a retail scheme only in respect of his retail supplies. Retail supplies are generally low value and made to a large number of customers in small quantities. A retailer may not use a retail scheme in respect of supplies (other than occasional cash sales) made to VAT registered traders.[2]

A retailer must keep a record of his daily gross takings. The record must include:[3]

(1) All payments for retail supplies as they are received from cash customers.
(2) The consideration for all credit and other non-cash retail sales at the time when the supply is made.
(3) Details of any adjustment made to this record.

There are five standard schemes: one point of sale scheme (PSS), two apportionment schemes (AS1 and AS2) and two direct calculation schemes (DCS1 and DCS2). In addition, there is a scheme for retail caterers (RCS).[4] These schemes are referred to below by the acronyms indicated.

The manner in which daily gross takings are apportioned between positive and zero rate supplies is briefly summarised in the following table.

Scheme	Method
PSS	All takings positive rated or takings at different rates distinguished at the point of sale.
AS1	Takings analysed in ratio to cost of positive and zero-rate purchases for resale for the period.
AS2	Calculate the retail value of positive and zero-rate purchases for resale for the period (using estimated selling prices). Analyse takings in ratio.
DCS1	Calculate the retail value of "minority goods" using estimated selling prices. Analysed takings are: (1) this value, and (2) daily gross takings minus this value.
DCS2	As DCS1 with an annual stock adjustment.
RCS	Catering takings are a percentage of daily gross takings. The percentage is derived from the results of a test period.

Output tax for a prescribed accounting period represents the tax element of standard rated daily gross takings calculated under the appropriate retail scheme. Retail chemists are required to make a special adjustment.[5]

De Voil Indirect Tax Service V3.557.

---

[1] Notice No 727 (March 2002), para 1.2. For the limited extent to which a flat-rate trader may use the retail schemes, see SI 1995/2518, reg 69A as inserted by SI 2002/1142. For the equivalent relief available under the flat-rate scheme, see SI 1995/2518, reg 55G as so inserted.
[2] Notice No 727 (March 2002), paras 2.1 and 2.4.
[3] Notice No 727 (March 2002), para 4.4. The record must be completed in accordance with checklists set out in the agreement relating to a bespoke scheme, or the separate scheme notices relating to the standard point of sale, apportionment, and direct calculation schemes: see Notice Nos 727/2, 727/3, 727/4, 727/5.

[65.22] The charge to tax

4 See Notice Nos 727 (March 2002), Section 8.
5 Notice No 727 (March 2002), Section 9.

Margin scheme for works of art, antiques, collectors' items and second-hand goods

[65.23] A trader making a supply of the following goods may opt to account for VAT by reference to his profit margin, rather than by reference to the consideration for the supply, if specified conditions are met:[1]

(1)   Works of art,[2] antiques and collectors' items.[3]
(2)   Used motor cars.[4]
(3)   Any other tangible movable property (other than precious metals and precious stones) which is suitable for further use as it is or after repair.[5] This property is referred to as "second-hand goods".

The profit margin is equal to the amount (if any) by which the price at which the goods were obtained[6] is exceeded by the price at which they were supplied,[7] both prices being determined in accordance with statutory provisions.[8]

A trader may account for VAT by reference to the total profit margin on goods supplied by him during a prescribed accounting period instead of by reference to the profit margin on individual supplies. He may do so only in relation to certain descriptions of goods[9] and only if he complies with such conditions as the Commissioners may direct by notice of otherwise.[10] This is referred to as "global accounting".[11]

The total profit margin for a prescribed accounting period is the amount (if any) by which the total selling price[12] exceeds the total purchase price,[13] such prices being determined in accordance with statutory provisions.[14] If the total purchase price exceeds the total selling price in any prescribed accounting period, the excess amount is carried forward to the following period and taken into account in calculating the total purchase price for that period.[15]

De Voil Indirect Tax Service V3.531–536.

1 VAT (Cars) Order, SI 1992/3122, art 8(1) as substituted by SI 1995/1269; VAT (Special Provisions) Order, SI 1995/1268, art 12(1),(2). For the conditions imposed, see SI 1992/3122, art 8(1)–(3) as substituted by SI 1995/1269 and amended by SI 1995/1667, SI 1997/1615, SI 1999/2832, SI 2002/1502; SI 1995/1268, art 12(1)–(4) as amended by SI 1997/1616, SI 1998/760, SI 2002/1503, SI 2006/2187; *Peugeot Motor Co plc v Customs and Excise Comrs* [1998] V & DR 1; *Wood v Customs and Excise Comrs* (2001) VAT decision 17256. For conditions imposed by notice, see Notice No 718. For relief given by concession where the prescribed records have not been kept in respect of used vehicles, see Notice No 48 (July 2009), para 3.8.
2 As defined in VATA 1994, s 21(5), by virtue of 1995/1268, art 2 as substituted by SI 1999/3120.
3 As defined in 1995/1268, art 2 as amended by SI 1999/2831, SI 1999/3120. Cf *Pressland v Customs and Excise Comrs* [1995] V & DR 432.
4 As identically defined in SI 1992/3122, art 2 and SI 1995/1268, art 2 as substituted by SI 1999/2831.

Charge I—Supplies of goods and services [65.25]

5. As defined in 1995/1268, art 2. For live animals, see *Förvaltnings AB Stenholmen v Riksskatteverket (case C-320/02)* [2004] ECR I–3509, [2004] STC 1041, ECJ (horses for training and subsequent resale).
6. For the basis of calculation, see SI 1992/3122, art 8(5)(a), (6), (7)(a) as substituted by SI 1995/1269 and amended by SI 1998/759, SI 2001/3754, SI 2002/1502; and SI 1995/1268, art 12(5)(a), (6), (7)(a) as amended by SI 1998/760, SI 2001/3753, SI 2002/1503, SI 2006/2187.
7. For the basis of calculation, see SI 1992/3122, art 8(5)(b), (6), (7)(b) as so substituted; and SI 1995/1268, art 12(5)(b), (6), (7)(b).
8. VATA 1994, s 50A(4) as added by FA 1995, s 24. For the statutory provisions, see supra, notes 3, 4.
9. Global accounting may not be used in relation to supplies of: (a) motor vehicles, (b) aircraft, (c) boats and outboard motors, (d) caravans and motor caravans, (e) horses and ponies, or (f) any individual item with a value exceeding £500: SI 1995/1268, art 13(2).
10. SI 1995/1268, art 13(1), (2). For directions made by notice, see Notice No 718.
11. See heading to SI 1995/1268, art 13.
12. Calculated in accordance with SI 1995/1268, art 13(4).
13. Calculated in accordance with SI 1995/1268, art 13(5).
14. SI 1995/1268, art 13(3) as amended by SI 1999/3120.
15. SI 1995/1268, art 13(6).

Margin scheme for services used for business entertainment

[65.24] The VAT on services purchased by a trader for the purposes of business entertainment is excluded from credit. The legislation avoids a double charge to tax on any subsequent supply of those services by providing that VAT is chargeable by reference to the profit (if any) made by the trader on his supply.[1]

The trader's profit is the amount by which the consideration for his supply exceeds the value of his purchase, acquisition or importation plus the VAT chargeable thereon.[2]

De Voil Indirect Tax Service V3.166.

1. VAT (Input Tax) Order, SI 1992/3222, art 5(2) as amended by SI 1999/2930. For the circumstances in which input tax is excluded from credit, see infra, § **66.20**.
2. SI 1992/3222, art 5(2) as amended by SI 1999/2930.

Tour operators' margin scheme

[65.25] Where a tour operator[1] supplies designated travel services[2] from a fixed establishment[3] in the UK,[4] the value of the supply is the difference between sums paid or payable to him in respect of the service and the sums paid or payable by him in respect of those services. This difference is referred to as "the margin". It is calculated in a manner specified by the Commissioners.[5]

Travel services which do not amount to designated travel services (ie because they are supplied from the tour operator's own resources rather than being

[65.25] The charge to tax

bought in) are referred to as "in house" travel services. The value of such supplies is determined in accordance with the normal valuation rules.[6]

A travel service may comprise:

(1) Wholly a designated travel service.
(2) Wholly an in house travel service. Supplies under this head are charged to tax under the tax invoice basis[7] and both purchases and sales are excluded from margin scheme calculations.
(3) Partly a designated travel service and partly an in house travel service.

A travel service within heads (1) or (3) may include elements chargeable to tax at the zero rate,[8] exempt from tax,[9] or outside the scope of tax.[10]

A fixed proportion of the value of travel services within heads (1) and (3) is charged to tax at the standard rate. A provisional percentage is applied to all such supplies made in the current year (based on data for the previous year). Output tax for each prescribed accounting period is calculated by applying this percentage to the value of supplies having a tax point falling within that period.[11] A final percentage is calculated at the end of the current year (based on data for that year). Output tax for the prescribed accounting periods is then recalculated using the final percentage. Any difference between output tax provisionally and finally calculated is adjusted in the tax payable or tax allowable portion of the trader's VAT Account for the following prescribed accounting period.[12]

De Voil Indirect Tax Service V3.591.

---

[1] As defined in VATA 1994, s 53(3). See *Beheersmaatschappij Van Ginkel Waddinxveen BV v Inspecteur der Omzetbelasting, Utrecht (case C-163/91)* [1996] STC 825, ECJ; *Customs and Excise Comrs v Madgett and Baldwin (joined cases C-308/96 and C-94/97)* [1998] STC 1169, ECJ; *Finanzamt Heidelberg v iSt Internationale Sprach- und Studienreisen GmbH (case C-200/04)* [2005] ECR I-8691, [2006] STC 52, ECJ; *Aer Lingus plc v Customs and Excise Comrs* [1992] VATTR 438, *Virgin Atlantic Airways Ltd v Customs and Excise Comrs* [1993] VATTR 136. For wholesale travel services, see *Independent Coach Travel (Wholesaling) Ltd v Customs and Excise Comrs* [1993] VATTR 357; *Norman Allen Group Travel Ltd v Customs and Excise Comrs* [1996] V & DR 405.

[2] ie a supply of goods or services acquired for the purposes of a tour operator's business and supplied by him for the benefit of a traveller without material alteration or further processing: VAT (Tour Operators) Order, SI 1987/1806, art 3(1). For supplies excluded from this description, see SI 1987/1806, arts 3(3), (4), 14.

[3] For "fixed establishment", see *Customs and Excise Comrs v DFDS A/S: C-260/95* [1997] STC 384, ECJ.

[4] SI 1987/1806, art 5(2). Supplies made from a fixed establishment in a third country do not amount to a designated travel service: SI 1987/1806, art 3(1). If a tour operator does not have a fixed establishment, his designated travel services are taxed in the EU member state where he has established his business: SI 1987/1806, art 3(1). For the place where a business is established, see *Customs and Excise Comrs v DFDS A/S: C-260/95* [1997] STC 384, ECJ. For the place of supply under EU law, see Directive 2006/112/EC art 307.

[5] SI 1987/1806, art 7. For the manner in which the margin is calculated, see Notice No 709/5; *Customs and Excise Comrs v Madgett and Baldwin (joined cases C-308/96 and C-94/97)* [1998] STC 1169, ECJ; *My Travel plc v Customs and Excise Comrs (case C-291/03)* [2005] ECR I-8477, [2005] STC 1617, ECJ; *Jenny Braden Holidays Ltd v Customs and Excise Comrs* (1993) VAT decision 10892. For overheads, see *Whittle (a firm) v Customs and Excise Comrs* [1994] VATTR 202; *Devonshire Hotel (Torquay) Ltd v Customs and Excise Comrs* (1996) VAT decision 14448. For discounts, see *Customs and Excise Comrs v First Choice Holidays plc* [2004] EWCA Civ 1044, [2004] STC 1407. For permission to use a separate calculation for third country sales, see *Customs and Excise Comrs v Simply Travel Ltd* [2002] STC 194. For directions to substitute open market value, see SI 1997/1806, art 8.
[6] ie VATA 1994, s 19 and Sch 6. See supra, §§ **65.16–65.17**.
[7] See supra, §§ **65.11–65.20**.
[8] SI 1987/1806, art 10(1). For transport services, see VATA 1994, Sch 8, Group 8. For designated travel services enjoyed outside the EU, see VATA 1994, Sch 8, Group 8, Item 12 and Note 8.
[9] SI 1987/1806, art 10(2). For insurance, see VATA 1994, Sch 9, Group 2.
[10] For in house supplies supplied outside the UK, see SI 1987/1806, art 5(3)–(6).
[11] For the time of supply, see SI 1987/1806, art 4.
[12] For the detailed computation, see Notice No 709/5/98. For the assessment of output tax arising from the end-of-year adjustment, see *Revenue and Customs Comrs v Dunwood Travel Ltd* [2008] EWCA Civ 174, [2008] STC 959.

Gaming machines

[65.26] The amount paid[1] by a person to gamble[2] by means of a gaming machine[3] is treated as the consideration for a supply of services to him.[4] The value of supplies made in any period is determined as if the amounts paid were reduced by an amount equal to the amount[5] (if any) received[6] in the period by persons playing successfully.[7]

De Voil Indirect Tax Service V3.264.

[1] For "payment", see VATA 1994, s 23(3) as amended by FA 2006, s 16 (tokens); *Feehan v Customs and Excise Comrs* [1995] STC 75 (no requirement to insert coin or token into machine).
[2] As defined in VATA 1994, s 23(6)(a) as substituted and amended by by FA 2006, s 16, SI 2006/2686.
[3] As defined in VATA 1994, s 23(4)–(6) as substituted and amended by FA 2006, s 16, SI 2006/2686.
[4] VATA 1994, s 23(1) as amended by FA 2006, s 16.
[5] For tokens, see VATA 1994, s 23(3) as amended by FA 2006, s 16.
[6] See *Feehan v Customs and Excise Comrs* [1995] STC 75 (no requirement for coin or token to be ejected by machine).
[7] VATA 1994, s 23(2) as amended by FA 2006, s 16; cf. *H J Glawe Spiel und Unterhaltungsgeräte Aufstellungsgesellschaft mbH & Co KG v Finanzamt Hamburg-Barmbek-Uhlenhorst (case C-38/93)*, [1994] STC 543, ECJ.

Fuel for private use

[65.27] Fuel is provided or appropriated for private use in a vehicle[1] by a taxable person[2] if:[3]

(1) He purchased, acquired, imported or manufactured the fuel in the course of his business.
(2) The fuel is provided to an employee, officer or partner, or appropriated by a sole proprietor, for private use.[4]
(3) The private use is either in a vehicle allocated to an employee or officer,[5] or in an employee, officer, partner or sole proprietor's own vehicle.[6]
(4) (In the case of an employee or officer) the fuel is provided by reason of his employment.[7]

Fuel is not provided for private use if it is supplied at a price which is not less than the purchase price or cost of manufacture.[8]

A taxable person is deemed to make a supply in the course or furtherance of business at the time when fuel is put into the fuel tank of the relevant vehicle.[9] If one or more such supplies are made to an individual in a prescribed accounting period, the consideration for all such supplies made to him in respect of any one vehicle in that period is determined in accordance with one of the following scales.[10]

(1) A scale determined by reference to the vehicle's CO_2 emissions figure, expressed in grams per kilometre driven.[11] This scale applies if the vehicle's CO_2 emissions figure is specified in an EC certificate of conformity[12] or a UK approval certificate.[13] If more than one CO_2 emissions figure is specified, the relevant figure is determined in accordance with statutory rules.[14]
(2) A scale determined by reference to the vehicle's cylinder capacity.[15] This scale applies in other cases.

The scale consideration is time apportioned if fuel is successively supplied in respect of two or more vehicles in a prescribed accounting period.[16]

By concession, a taxable person is not deemed to make a supply if he disclaims input tax on all his purchases of road fuel.[17]

De Voil Indirect Tax Service V3.266.

---

[1] As defined in VATA 1994, s 56(10). A van is outside the scope of this definition by virtue of the terms of Decision 86/356/EEC: see Customs and Excise Press Notice No 24/87 dated 25 March 1987. For the term "company cars" used in Decision 86/356/EEC, see *Kimber v Customs and Excise Comrs* (1993) VAT decision 10469. Decision 86/356/EEC is repealed on 30 April 2007 and replaced by Decision 2006/659/EC. This uses the term "business cars".
[2] For groups of companies, see VATA 1994, s 56(4).
[3] VATA 1994, s 56(1), (3), (10).
[4] For the distinction between business use and private use, see *McLean Homes Midland Ltd v Customs and Excise Comrs* (1990) VAT decision 5010.
[5] For vehicles within this description, see VATA 1994, s 56(3)(*d*), (9).
[6] For vehicles within this description, see VATA 1994, s 56(3)(*c*); *Kimber v Customs and Excise Comrs* (1993) VAT decision 10469.

[7] For fuel deemed to be so provided, see VATA 1994, s 56(3)(e).
[8] VATA 1994, s 56(2).
[9] VATA 1994, s 56(6).
[10] VATA 1994, ss 56(7), 57(1)–(3) as amended by FA 1995, s 30 and SI 2006/868.
[11] VATA 1994, s 57(3), Table A and Notes 1, 2, 5 as inserted or substituted by SI 2007/966, 2009/1030.
[12] As defined in VATA 1994 s 57(9) as inserted by SI 2007/966.
[13] As defined in VATA 1994 s 57(9) as inserted by SI 2007/966.
[14] VATA 1994, s 57(3), Table A and Notes 1, 3–5 as inserted or substituted by SI 2007/966, SI 2008/722.
[15] VATA 1994, s 57(3), Table A and Note 6 as inserted, substituted or amended by SI 2007/966, 2008/722, 2009/1030.
[16] VATA 1994, ss 56(8), 57(5), (6) as amended by SI 2007/966.
[17] Notice No 48 (July 2009), para 3.1.

Charge II—Events treated as supplies of goods or services

Supplies made for no consideration

Transfer or disposal of goods

[65.28] Where goods forming part of the assets of a business[1] are transferred or disposed of by or under the directions of the person carrying on a business, and the goods cease to form part of those assets, the transfer or disposal is treated as a supply of goods despite the absence of consideration.[2] The goods are also supplied where an individual who carries on a business makes the transfer or disposition in favour of himself personally.[3] Thus, a licensee who drinks a pint of beer and a furnisher who furnishes his home from business stock are both deemed to make supplies of goods and must account to the Commissioners for output tax thereon. The same consequences follow when an interest in, right over or licence to occupy land forming part of the assets of a business is granted, assigned or surrendered without consideration.[4] It follows that such a transfer or disposal is treated as a supply if it does not otherwise amount to a supply.

The following transactions are not treated as a supply of goods under the foregoing provisions and are thus outside the scope of VAT:[5]

(1) A transfer or disposal of goods which, when purchased, acquired or imported by the trader or any of his predecessors,[6] did not give rise to an entitlement to input tax credit or a repayment of tax. Thus, for example, the disposal without charge of a computer purchased wholly for use in a non-business activity gives rise to neither an input tax credit nor a charge to tax under this provision.[7] A transfer or disposal is wholly or partly charged to tax in other circumstances.[8] This charge extends to anything incorporated in the goods since their purchase, acquisition or importation.[9]

[65.28] The charge to tax

(2) A gift[10] of goods made in the course or furtherance of business. The cost of acquiring or producing the goods (whether incurred by the donor or one of his predecessors)[11] must not exceed £50. Moreover, if any other such gifts have been made to the same person in the previous 12 months, the aggregate cost of the gift and the previous gifts must not exceed £50.

(3) The gift of a sample. Relief is restricted to one of a number of similar samples given at the same time or the first of a series of similar samples given on different occasions.

The supply is treated as taking place when the goods are transferred or disposed of or the grant is made.[12] The value of the supply for tax purposes is the money consideration (excluding VAT) which would be payable for identical or similar goods or, failing that, the cost of producing the goods concerned.[13] However, the value is nil if the supply comprises food or beverages supplied to employees in the course of catering.[14]

De Voil Indirect Tax Service V3.211.

---

[1] For goods forming part of a non-business activity, see Business Brief (Issue 19/05), 10 October 2005.

[2] VATA 1994, Sch 4, para 5(1). For examples, see *Kuwait Petroleum (GB) Ltd v Customs and Excise Comrs (case C-48/97)* [1999] STC 488, ECJ (gifts under a sale promotion scheme); *Customs and Excise Comrs v West Herts College* [2001] STC 1245 (college prospectuses); *Church of England Children's Society v Revenue and Customs Comrs* [2005] EWHC 1692 (Ch), [2005] STC 1644 (newsletter distributed free to regular givers). A supply made for a consideration is charged to tax under Charge I. For private use of vehicle fuel, see supra, § **65.27**. For meals provided on company premises for staff and business contacts, see *Danfoss A/S and another v Skatteministeriet* (case C-371/07) [2008] ECR I–0000, [2009] STC 701, ECJ.

[3] VATA 1994, Sch 4, para 5(6)(a).

[4] VATA 1994, Sch 4, para 9 as amended by FA 2007, s 98. See *De Jong v Staatssecretaris van Financiën (case C-20/91)* [1995] STC 727, ECJ.

[5] VATA 1994, Sch 4, para 5(2), (2ZA), (3), (5) as inserted or amended by FA 1996, s 33, FA 2000, s 136, FA 2003, s 21 and SI 2001/735.

[6] As defined in VATA 1994, Sch 4, para 5(5A) as inserted by FA 1998, s 21.

[7] Cf *Vereniging Noordelijke Land- en Tuinbouw Organisatie v Staatssecretaris van Financiën* (case C515/07) [2009] ECR I–0000, [2009] STC 935, ECJ.

[8] For the charge to tax where input tax has been wholly or partly deducted, see *Bakcsi v Finanzamt Fürstenfeldbruck (case C-415/98)* [2002] STC 802, ECJ. For examples of a charge to tax at the zero-rate, see *C & E Comrs v West Herts College* [2001] STC 1245 (course prospectus); *Church of England Children's Society v Revenue and Customs Comrs* [2005] EWHC 1692 (Ch), [2005] STC 1644 (newsletter sent to donors making monthly contributions).

[9] For the charge to tax where component parts have been incorporated in goods since purchase, see *Finanzamt Burgdorf v Fischer; Finanzamt Düsseldorf-Mettmann v Brandenstein (joined cases C-322/99 and C-323/99)* [2001] STC 1356, ECJ

[10] For "gifts", contrast *Mitrolone Ltd v Customs and Excise Comrs* LON/88/1335 unreported and *Cartlidge v Customs and Excise Comrs* LON/91/546 unreported. For "gifts" under a business promotion scheme, see *Kuwait Petroleum (GB) Ltd v*

Customs and Excise Comrs [2001] STC 62.
[11] The cost to a predecessor is included if the goods, or anything comprised in them, were transferred to the donor without payment of tax on the transfer of a business as a going concern: VATA 1994, Sch 4, para 5(2A) as inserted by FA 1998, s 21.
[12] VATA 1994, s 6(12).
[13] VATA 1994, Sch 6, para 6. For the valuation of component parts incorporated in goods, see *Finanzamt Burgdorf v Fischer; Finanzamt Düsseldorf-Mettmann v Brandenstein (joined cases C-322/99 and C-323/99)* [2001] STC 1356, ECJ.
[14] VATA 1994, Sch 6, para 10.

Use of business assets for private or non-business purposes

[65.29] In principle, a supply of services takes place—regardless of the fact that no consideration is given for it—where, by or under the direction of a person carrying on a business, land or goods held or used for the purposes of a business are put to any private use, used for any purpose other than a purpose of the business, or made available to any person for use for any purpose other than a purpose of the business.[1] A supply also takes place where land or goods are used or made available for use personally by an individual who carries on a business.[2] There is one precondition: a supply of services is made only if the trader or his predecessor(s)[3] is entitled to input tax credit or a repayment of tax in respect of all or part of the VAT incurred on his purchase, acquisition or importation of the goods concerned.[4] Thus, for example, the use for private purposes by an employee, without payment, of a computer purchased wholly for use in a non-business activity gives rise to neither an input tax credit nor a charge to tax under this provision.

In principle, a trader makes a supply of services, and must account to the Commissioners for output tax thereon, if, for example, he allows an employee to use an asset for private purposes or loans an asset to (say) an associated company. However, this principle is modified in relation to motor cars. Certain use gives rise to a charge to tax by way of self supply rather than by way of a deemed supply of services.[5]

The supply is treated as taking place when the land or goods are appropriated for use.[6] The value of the supply for tax purposes is the full cost of providing the services.[7] However, the value is nil if the supply comprises accommodation for employees in a hotel, inn, boarding house or similar establishment.[8]

De Voil Indirect Tax Service V3.212.

[1] VATA 1994, Sch 4, paras 5(4), 9 as amended by FA 2007, s 98. Under EC law, see *Julius Fillibeck Söhne GmbH & Co KG v Finanzamt Neustadt (case C-258/95)* [1998] STC 513, ECJ (free transport to employees). Under UK law, see *Wimpey Group Services Ltd v Customs and Excise Comrs* [1984] VATTR 66. A supply within this description made for a consideration is charged to tax under Charge I. For private use of vehicle fuel, see supra, § **65.27**. For meals provided on company premises for staff and business contacts, see *Danfoss A/S and another v Skatteministeriet* (case C-371/07) [2008] ECR I-0000, [2009] STC 701, ECJ.
[2] VATA 1994, Sch 4, paras 5(6)(*b*), 9 as amended by FA 2007, s 98.
[3] As defined in VATA 1994, Sch 4, para 5(5A) as inserted by FA 1998, s 21.

[65.29] The charge to tax

4   VATA 1994, Sch 4, para 5(5) as amended by FA 1998, s 21. Cf *Kühne v Finanzamt München III (case 50/88)* [1990] STC 749, [1990] 3 CMLR 287, ECJ; *Finanzamt München III v Mohsche (case C-193/91)* [1997] STC 195, ECJ; *Allied Lyons plc v Customs and Excise Comrs* [1994] VATTR 361.
5   For the interaction of the two provisions, see infra § **65.32**.
6   VATA 1994, s 6(13).
7   VATA 1994, Sch 6, para 7(*b*); see *Enkler v Finanzamt Homburg (case C-230/94)* [1996] STC 1316, ECJ, *Hausgemeinschaft Jörg und Stefanie Wollny v Finanzamt Landshut (case C-72/05)* [2006] ECR I-8297, [2008] STC 1618, ECJ; *Customs and Excise Comrs v Teknequip Ltd* [1987] STC 664. For the calculation of "full cost" from 1 November 2007, see VAT Regulations, SI 1996/2518 regs 116E-116M as inserted by SI 2007/3099. For guidance and worked examples, see VAT Information Sheet 14/07 (November 2007). For prior periods, see Business Brief (Issue 15/05), 9 August 2005.
8   VATA 1994, Sch 6, para 10.

Services used for private or non-business purpose

[65.30] A person is deemed to make a supply services in the course or furtherance of business if the following conditions are met:[1]

(1)   A supply of services has been made to the person or his predecessor.
(2)   He or his predecessor has or will become entitled to input tax credit for all or part of the input tax chargeable on that supply.
(3)   The subject matter of that supply is used for a private or non-business purpose, or made available for use by another person,[2] without consideration.
(4)   The use comprises neither employee accommodation in a hotel, inn, boarding house or similar establishment nor the hire of a motor for which input tax credit was restricted to one half.[3]
(5)   Output tax on any previous supply of the same services does not exceed the input tax to which the person or his predecessor has or will become entitled in respect of his purchase of them.

A sole proprietor is deemed to make such a supply if he uses the services personally or makes them available for his personal use.[4] If input tax has been apportioned between business and other use,[5] a supply is deemed to be made only in respect of the business portion.[6]

The services are deemed to be supplied on the last day of the prescribed accounting period in which the services are performed.[7] The value of the supply is that part of the value of the services supplied to the person which fairly and reasonably represents the cost to him of providing the services.[8] This value is reduced if output tax on this and any previous supply would exceed the input tax to which the person was entitled when the services were supplied to him.[9]

De Voil Indirect Tax Service V3.216.

1   VAT (Supply of Services) Order, SI 1993/1507, arts 3, 6-9 as amended and inserted by SI 1995/1668, SI 1998/762, SI 2002/2918. SI 1993/1507, arts 3A, 3B were revoked with effect from 1 September 2007 by SI 2007/2173.

² For an example of non-business use, see *Telecential Communications Ltd v Customs and Excise Comrs* (1998) VAT decision 15361 (free telephone line rental and cable television provided to employees by telecommunications supplier).
³ For the circumstances in which one-half of the input tax is excluded from credit, see infra, §§ **66.17–66.18**.
⁴ SI 1993/1507, art 4.
⁵ ie under VATA 1994, s 24(5).
⁶ SI 1993/1507, art 6 as amended by SI 1995/1668, SI 1998/762.
⁷ VAT Regulations, SI 1995/2518, reg 81(2).
⁸ SI 1993/1507, art 5. This value displaces the amount prescribed by VATA 1994, Sch 6, para 7 by virtue of the power conferred by VATA 1994, s 5(8). See Business Brief (Issue 17/94), 12 September 1994.
⁹ SI 1993/1507, art 7 as amended by SI 1998/762.

Goods removed to another EU member state

[65.31] A person is deemed to make a supply of goods if he removes goods forming part of the assets of his business from one EU member state to another in the course or furtherance of business.[1] However, this does not apply if[2] goods are removed from one part of member state X to another part via member state Y, or if goods are removed from a third country to member state Y via member state X without being put into free circulation in member state X. Nor does it apply to removals of a description specified by Treasury order.[3]

A special time of supply rule applies if the goods are removed from the UK and the recipient is charged to VAT on an acquisition in another EU member state. The goods are supplied on the earlier of[4] the 15th day of the month following that in which the removal takes place;[5] and the day when a VAT invoice is issued in respect of the supply. The normal time of supply rules[6] apply in other cases.

The supply is valued at the current purchase price (excluding VAT) of identical or similar goods or, failing that, the current cost of producing the same goods.[7]

De Voil Indirect Tax Service V3.213.

1 VATA 1994, Sch 4, para 6(1).
2 VATA 1994, Sch 4, para 6(2).
3 VATA 1994, s 5(3). For the removals concerned, see VAT (Removal of Goods) Order, SI 1992/3111; *Centrax Ltd v Customs and Excise Comrs* [1998] V & DR 369.
4 VATA 1994, s 6(7), (8).
5 This does not apply if the supply comprises water (other than water of a description in VAT Regulations, SI 1995/2518, reg 86(1)(*a*)(i), (ii)), coal gas, water gas, producer gases or similar gases, or any form of power, heat, refrigeration or ventilation: SI 1995/2518, reg 86(5).
6 For the time of supply, see supra, § **65.11–65.15**.
7 VATA 1994, Sch 6, para 6.

[65.32] The charge to tax

Self-supplies

Motor cars

[65.32] A trader is deemed to supply a motor car[1] in the course or furtherance of his business if:[2]

(1) He produces,[3] purchases, acquires or imports the motor car, or obtains it when a business is transferred to him as a going concern.
(2) He or (in the case of a business transferred as a going concern) one of his predecessors[4] was entitled to credit for all or part of the VAT incurred in producing, purchasing, acquiring or importing the motor car.
(3) He has not supplied the motor car in the course or furtherance of his business.
(4) He uses the motor car.
(5) Input tax would be wholly excluded from credit[5] if he purchased a motor car for that use.

The motor car is deemed to be supplied when it is appropriated for its new use.[6] The value of the supply is the money consideration (excluding VAT) which would be payable for an identical or similar car or, failing that, the cost of producing the car concerned.[7]

The trader is also deemed to supply the motor car to himself.[8] The condition in point (5) indicates that the trader is not entitled to input tax credit in respect of his deemed purchase.

The private use of a motor car normally gives rise to a self supply. In consequence, no charge to tax arises under the provisions described in supra, § **65.29**.[9] However, the position is reversed if a motor car forms part of the stock in trade of a motor manufacturer or motor dealer. Input tax is not excluded from credit in respect of motor cars held in stock by motor manufacturers and motor dealers[10] and motor cars retain their status as stock if they are temporarily used for private purposes.[11] As the private use is a use giving rise to a continued entitlement to input tax credit, the test in point (5) above is not met and no self supply takes place. The private use is instead charged to tax under the provisions described in supra, § **65.29**.

De Voil Indirect Tax Service V3.242.

---

[1] As defined in VAT (Cars) Order, SI 1992/3122, art 2 as amended by SI 1999/2832. It is the physical attributes of a vehicle, and nothing else, which determines whether a vehicle falls within this definition: *Customs and Excise Comrs v Jeynes* [1984] STC 30; *Withers of Winsford Ltd v Customs and Excise Comrs* [1988] STC 431. For vehicles constructed or adapted for the carriage of passengers, see *Chartcliffe Ltd v Customs and Excise Comrs* [1976] VATTR 165; *A L Yeoman Ltd v Customs and Excise Comrs* (1990) VAT decision 4470. For vehicles with roofed accommodation behind the driver's seat, contrast *John Beharrel Ltd v Customs and Excise Comrs* [1991] VATTR 497 and *County Telecommunications Systems Ltd v Customs and Excise Comrs* (1993) VAT decision 10224.

[2] SI 1992/3122, art 5(1), (2),(3) as amended and substituted by SI 1999/2832.

[3] For motors cars produced by converting another vehicle, see *GA Security Systems Ltd v Customs and Excise Comrs* (1993) VAT decision 1527; *Direct*

Link Couriers (Bristol) Ltd v Customs and Excise Comrs (1986) VAT decision 2105.
4   As defined in VAT (Cars) Order, SI 1992/3122, art 5(2A) as substituted by SI 1999/2832.
5   For the circumstances in which input tax is wholly excluded from credit, see infra, §§ **66.15–66.17**.
6   VATA 1994, s 6(11). For appropriation, see *A and B Motors (Newton-le-Willows) Ltd v Customs and Excise Comrs* [1981] VATTR 29.
7   VATA 1994, Sch 6, para 6.
8   VAT (Cars) Order, SI 1992/3122, art 5(3) as substituted by SI 1999/2832.
9   SI 1992/3122 art 4A.
10 VAT (Input Tax) Order, SI 1992/3222, art 7(2)(*a*) as inserted by SI 1999/2930. "Motor dealer". "motor manufacturer" and "stock in trade" are defined in SI 1992/3222, art 2 as inserted by SI 1999/2930.
11 Definition of "stock in trade" in SI 1992/3222, art 2 as inserted by SI 1999/2930.

Stationery

[65.33] In principle, the self-supply charge for printed matter[1] produced for internal use[2] does not apply after 31 May 2002. However, as an anti-avoidance measure to counter prepayment schemes, it continues to apply in relation to goods purchased before 1 June 2002 if they were collected or delivered after 31 May 2002.[3]

De Voil Indirect Tax Service V3.243.

1   As defined in VAT (Special Provisions) Order, SI 1995/1268, art 2 (revoked by SI 2002/1280).
2   See SI 1995/1268, art 11 (revoked by SI 2002/1280). For the self-supply charge, see the 19th Edition of this work, para 64.28.
3   VAT (Special Provisions) (Amendment) Order, SI 2002/1280 art 1(2).

Construction services

[65.34] This provision applies to the following services:[1] (a) constructing a building or civil engineering work; (b) increasing the floor area of a building by 10% or more; and (c) demolition works carried out in connection with (a) or (b). However, a charge to tax arises only where the value of the services is £100,000 or more and they would have been charged to tax at the standard rate if supplied to a third party.[2]

The foregoing services are deemed to be supplied by a trader in the course or furtherance of business when he performs them for the purpose of his business and otherwise than for a consideration[3], eg where a developer constructs a factory on his own land using in-house labour. The value of the supply is the open market value of those services performed on or after 1 April 1989.[4] The time of supply appears to be the time when the services are performed.[5]

The services are deemed to be supplied to the trader for the purpose of his business.[6]

De Voil Indirect Tax Service V3.244.

[65.34] The charge to tax

1 VAT (Self-supply of Construction Services) Order, SI 1989/471, art 3(1).
2 SI 1989/471, art 3(2).
3 SI 1989/471, art 3(1). For companies in a group registration, see SI 1989/471, art 3(3).
4 SI 1989/471, art 4.
5 VATA 1994, s 6(3).
6 VAT (Self-supply of Construction Services) Order, SI 1989/472, art 3(1).

Building—change of use

[65.35] A person intending to use a building for a relevant residential[1] or charitable[2] purpose may receive a supply zero-rated under VATA 1994, Sch 8, Group 5[3] if he purchases the freehold, leases the building for a term exceeding 21 years, or engages a building contractor to construct the building on land in which he has a freehold, lease or licence. This provision creates a charge to tax where the building ceases to be used for its intended purpose.[4]

A trader is deemed to supply his interest in the building in the course or furtherance of business if he ceases to use the building for a relevant residential or charitable purpose during the ten year period following completion of the building.[5] Part of the interest is deemed to be supplied if only part of the building ceases to be so used.[6] The supply is treated as taking place on the day when the building (or part) is first used for the new purpose.[7] The value of the supply is calculated by reference to the VAT that would have been charged on the supplies received if they had not been zero-rated. This value is reduced by 10% for each whole year expired since the date when the building was completed. The supply is chargeable to tax at the relevant positive rate.[8]

The interest (or part of the interest) is deemed to be supplied to the trader for the purpose of his business.[9]

De Voil Indirect Tax Service V3.248.

1 As defined in VATA 1994, Sch 8, Group 5, Notes 4, 5, 12.
2 As defined in VATA 1994, Sch 8, Group 5, Notes 6, 12; Notice No 48 (July 1009) para 3.29.
3 See infra, §§ **69.17–69.21**.
4 For the circumstances in which the charge to tax is waived, see Revenue and Customs Brief 29/07, 27 March 2007 (unexpected reduction in charitable use of building which benefited from the concession in Notice No 48 (July 2009) para 3.29).
5 VATA 1994, Sch 10, para 37(1)–(3) as inserted by SI 2008/1146. For the time when a building is completed, see VATA 1994, Sch 9, Group 1, Note 2 by virtue of Sch 10, para 39 as so inserted.
6 VATA 1994, Sch 10, para 37(2) as inserted by SI 2008/1146.
7 VATA 1994, Sch 10, para 37(3)(*b*) as inserted by SI 2008/1146.
8 VATA 1994, Sch 10, para 37(4)–(7) as inserted by SI 2008/1146.
9 VATA 1994, Sch 10, para 37(3)(*a*) as inserted by SI 2008/1146.

Services relating to warehoused goods

[65.36] A person may receive a supply of services which is zero-rated under VATA 1994, s 18C(1).[1] This is referred to as a "zero-rated supply of services". The recipient of a zero-rated supply of services is deemed to make an identical supply unless[2] the goods to which the goods relate are supplied and the material time[3] for that supply occurs while the goods are subject to a warehousing regime[4] or fiscal warehousing regime[5] and after the material time for the zero-rated supply of services. The identical supply is deemed to be made in the course or furtherance of the recipient's business.[6]

The supply is deemed to be made on the earlier of[7] the time when the goods are removed from the warehousing or fiscal warehousing regime, and the duty point.[8]

The supply has the same value as the zero-rated supply of services.[9]

The supply is deemed to be a taxable supply chargeable to VAT at a positive rate.[10] VAT is chargeable on the supply whether or not the recipient of the zero-rated supply of services is a taxable person.[11] In principle, VAT is payable at the time of supply by either the person who removes the goods or (where excise duty is payable on the goods concerned) the person who is required to pay the duty.[12] However, a registered person may defer payment if he has been approved under Excise Duties (Deferred Payment) Regulations, SI 1992/3152.[13] Any VAT due, but unpaid, when the goods are removed for a warehousing or fiscal warehousing regime may be assessed.[14] The assessment carries interest.[15] Interest is assessed.[16] A right of appeal is given in respect of the VAT and interest assessed.[17]

De Voil Indirect Tax Service V3.383.

---

[1] For services zero-rated under this provision, see infra, § **69.06**.
[2] VATA 1994, s 18C(2), (3)(*a*).
[3] As defined in VATA 1994, s 18F(1).
[4] As defined in VATA 1994, s 18(7).
[5] As defined in VATA 1994, s 18F(2).
[6] VATA 1994, s 18C(3)(*a*).
[7] VATA 1994, s 18C(3)(*a*).
[8] As defined in VATA 1994, s 18(6).
[9] VATA 1994, s 18C(3)(*b*).
[10] VATA 1994, s 18C(3)(*c*).
[11] VATA 1994, s 18C(3)(*d*).
[12] VATA 1994, s 18D(2). For payment, see VAT Regulations, SI 1995/2518, reg 145J.
[13] VAT Regulations, SI 1995/2518, reg 43.
[14] VATA 1994, s 73(7B), as inserted by FA 1996, Sch 3, para 10.
[15] VATA 1994, s 74(1). For the charge to interest, see supra, § **2A.43**.
[16] VATA 1994, s 76(1).
[17] VATA 1994, s 83(*p*), (*q*), as amended by FA 1996, Sch 3, para 12.

Withdrawal from the flat-rate scheme

[65.37] A flat-rate trader is deemed to supply capital expenditure goods in the course or furtherance of business if the following conditions are met:[1]

[65.37] The charge to tax

(1) He continues to be a taxable person when he ceases to be authorised for the purposes of the flat-rate scheme.
(2) He claimed input tax to which he was entitled in respect of the goods while authorised for the purposes of the scheme.
(3) He did not make a supply of those goods whilst so authorised.

The supply is treated as taking place on the day after his end date.[2] The value of the supply is open market value.[3]

The flat-rate trader is deemed to supply the goods to himself for the purposes of his business.[4] An entitlement to input tax credit may therefore arise.

De Voil Indirect Tax Service V2.199B.

---

[1] VAT Regulations, SI 1995/2518, reg 55R(1), (2) as inserted by SI 2002/1142.
[2] SI 1995/2518, reg 55R(2) as inserted by SI 2002/1142. For the end date, see SI 1995/2518, reg 55Q as so inserted.
[3] VATA 1994, Sch 6, para 1 by virtue of SI 1995/2518, reg 55R(3) as inserted by SI 2002/1142. For open market value, see VATA 1994, s 19(5).
[4] SI 1995/2518, reg 55R(2) as inserted by SI 2002/1142.

Reverse charge

Services received from abroad

[65.38] Partly exempt traders could reduce their irrecoverable input tax by obtaining services from overseas traders (who would not charge tax on the supply)[1] rather than UK traders (who would). This would both cause distortions in trading patterns and result in a reduction in VAT revenues. These consequences are avoided by making the recipient liable to account for the tax chargeable if he is a taxable person. The value of the supplies received by a non-taxable person is taken into account in determining whether he is liable to registration.

A person belonging in the UK[2] who receives a relevant supply of services[3] is treated as if he had supplied them in the UK in the course or furtherance of his business if the following conditions are met:[4]

(1) The services are supplied by a person who belongs in a country other than the UK.[5]
(2) The recipient uses the services for the purposes of his business.

The supply is treated as taking place on either the date when the supply is paid for (where there is a consideration in money) or the last day of the prescribed accounting period in which the services were performed (where the consideration is not in money).[6]

The value of the supply for tax purposes is the money consideration for which it is made (if there is one) or such amount in money as is equivalent to that amount (in other cases).[7]

The foregoing rules are modified in relation to telecommunication services.[8] They do not normally apply to flat-rate traders.[9]

The change to the place of supply rules for services taking effect from 1 January 2010[10] gives rise to a consequential modification to the reverse charge.[11] From that date, a distinction is drawn between:[12]

(1) The services listed in VATA 1994, Sch 4A, Parts 1 and 2.[13] The reverse charge gives rise to a charge to VAT only if the recipient is registered for the purposes of VAT; and
(2) Other services. The reverse charge gives rise to a charge to VAT if the recipient is registered for the purposes of VAT. If the recipient is not registered, but is nevertheless a taxable person within the meaning of Directive 2006/112/EC, art 9,[14] the value of the supplies is taken into account in determining whether or not he is liable to registration.

The modified reverse charge does not apply to services if they are exempt from VAT[15] or received wholly for private purposes.[16]

De Voil Indirect Tax Service V3.231.

1 Under UK law, the services are supplied in the country where the supplier belongs. The place of supply does not become the UK by virtue of VAT (Place of Supply of Services) Order, SI 1992/3121, art 16 because the recipient is liable to the reverse charge.
2 For the place where the recipient belongs in relation to services within VATA 1994, Sch 5, paras 1–9, see VATA 1994, s 9(4) and Sch 5, para 10. For the relationship between VATA 1994, s 9(4) and Directive 2006/112/EC art 56, see *Zurich Insurance Company v Revenue and Customs Comrs* [2006] EWHC 593 (Ch), [2006] STC 1694, affd sub nom *Revenue and Customs Comrs v Zurich Insurance Company* [2007] EWCA Civ 218, [2007] STC 1756, CA (UK branch of a company established in a third country)
3 A relevant supply of services is a supply of a description in VATA 1994, Sch 5 as amended by SI 1997/1523, SI 2003/863, SI 2004/3149 which is not an exempt supply. For advertising services, see *EC Commission v France (case C-68/92)* [1997] STC 684, ECJ; *EC Commission v Luxembourg (case C-69/92)* [1997] STC 712, ECJ; *EC Commission v Spain (case C-73/92)* [1997] STC 700, ECJ; *Syndicat des Producteurs Indépendants (SPI) v Ministère de l'Economie, des Finances et de l'Industrie (case C-108/00)* [2001] STC 523, ECJ; *International Trade and Exhibitions J/V Ltd v Customs and Excise Comrs* [1996] V & DR 165; *Austrian National Tourist Office v Customs and Excise Comrs* (1998) VAT decision 15561; *John Village Automotive Ltd v Customs and Excise Comrs* [1998] V & DR 340; *Miller Freeman World-wide plc v Customs and Excise Comrs* (1998) VAT decision 15452. For services within Sch 5, para 3, see *Maatschap M J M Linthorst, K G P Pouwels and J Scheres Cs v Inspecteur der Belastingdienst/Ondernemingen Roermond (case C-167/95)* [1997] STC 1287, ECJ (veterinary surgeon); *von Hoffmann v Finanzamt Trier (case C-145/96)* [1997] STC 1321, ECJ (arbitrator); *Levob Verzekeringen BV, OB Bank NV cs v Staatssecretaris van Financiën (case C-41/04)* [2005] ECR I-9433, [2006] STC 766, ECJ (computer science); *EC Commission v Germany* (case C-401/06) [2007] SWTI 2848, ECJ (executor of will); *Hutchvision Hong Kong Ltd v Customs and Excise Comrs* (1993) VAT decision 10509. For financial services, see *Culverpalm Ltd v Customs and Excise Comrs* [1984] VATTR 199; *Singer & Friedlander Ltd v Customs and Excise Comrs* [1989] VATTR 27; Business Brief (Issue 20/94), 18 November 1994. For the supply of staff, see

[65.38] The charge to tax

    Strollmoor Ltd v Customs and Excise Comrs (1990) VAT decision 5454. For means of transport, see *Hamann v Finanzampt Hamburg-Eimsbüttel (case 51/88)* [1991] STC 193, [1990] 2 CMLR 383, ECJ.

4   VATA 1994, s 8(1). The supply is deemed to be make in the UK in order to bring it within the charge to tax in VATA 1994, s 4(1) because it is actually made outside the UK: see Note 1 above. The supply is deemed to be made in the course or furtherance of business in order to bring it within the charge to tax.

5   For the place where the supplier belongs, see VATA 1994, s 9(2).

6   VAT Regulations, SI 1995/2518, reg 82. Special transitional rules apply when the place of supply of certain services is changed: see VATA 1994, s 6(14A) as inserted by FA 1998, s 22. For the special rules, see VATA 1994, s 97A(2)–(6) as inserted by FA 1998, s 22. The services affected are those specified in an order made under VATA 1994, s 7(11) which meet the conditions specified in VATA 1994, s 97A(1) as inserted by FA 1998, s 22. For services specified, see VAT (Place of Supply of Services) Order, SI 1992/3121, arts 17, 18 as substituted by SI 1998/763. For similar provisions relating to telecommunication services, see VAT (Reverse Charge) (Anti-Avoidance) Order, SI 1997/1523.

7   VATA 1994, Sch 6, para 8 as amended by F(No 2)A 2005, s 5. For conversion of foreign currency amounts, see VATA 1994, Sch 6, para 11.

8   See VAT (Reverse Charge) (Anti-avoidance) Order, SI 1997/1523.

9   See SI 1995/2518, reg 55U as inserted by SI 2002/1142.

10   For the new place of supply rules, see supra, § **63.31**.

11   VATA 1994, s 8 is modified by VATA 1994, Sch 5 and repealed by FA 2009, Sch 36, paras 5, 12.

12   See VATA 1994, s 8(2) (proviso) as substituted by FA 2009, Sch 36, para 5(2).

13   As inserted by FA 2009, Sch 36, para 11.

14   A trader within this meaning is a "relevant business person" so as to fall within the scope of the reverse charge: see VATA 1994, s 7A(4)(a) as substituted by FA 2009, Sch 36, para 4.

15   VATA 1994, s 8(4A) as inserted by FA 2009, Sch 36, para 5(2).

16   A trader is not a "relevant business person" in relation to these services: see VATA 1994, s 7A(4) (proviso) as inserted by FA 2009, Sch 36, para 4.

Gas and electricity

[65.39] The cross-border distribution of gas and electricity gives rise to practical difficulties in connection with the place of supply and the invoicing of transmission costs.[1] As regards the wholesale distribution network, these difficulties have been overcome by changing the place of supply and the person liable to account for VAT. From 1 January 2005,[2] the place of supply is determined by reference to the customer's location and he (rather than the supplier) becomes responsible for payment of output tax.

The following consequences arise if a person outside the UK[3] supplies "relevant goods" (ie gas through the natural gas distribution network, or electricity) to a registered taxable person:[4]

(1)   The registered taxable person is deemed to make the supply.

(2)   This supply is deemed to be a taxable supply made in the course or furtherance of business. Thus, the taxable person is required to account for VAT on the supply.

(3) The taxable person is entitled to credit for input tax in respect of the supply he is deemed to have made.
(4) The supply is excluded from the pro-rata calculation of unattributed input tax for the purposes of the standard partial exemption method.[5]

The place of supply differs according to whether the relevant goods are supplied to a dealer[6] or to some other person who does,[7] or does not,[8] use and consume[9] the goods.

The supply is treated as taking place on either the date when the goods are paid for (where there is a consideration in money) or the last day of the prescribed accounting period in which the goods are removed or made available (in other cases).[10]

The value of the supply is the money consideration for which the goods were supplied (if there is one) or such amount in money as is equivalent to that consideration (in other cases).[11]

By implication, the supply actually made by the person outside the UK is disregarded for VAT purposes in the UK. Thus, the overseas supplier is neither liable to account for VAT in the UK on his supply (if he is a taxable person in the UK) nor liable to registration in respect of his supply (in other cases).

De Voil Indirect Tax Service V3.232.

[1] See the Explanatory Memorandum to the European Commission's proposal for Directive 2003/92/EC in COM (2002) 688, para 2.
[2] FA 2004, s 21(2).
[3] As defined in VAT (Place of Supply of Goods) Order, SI 2004/3148, art 14.
[4] VATA 1994, s 9(1) (5) as inserted by FA 2004, s 21.
[5] For the standard method, see infra, § **66.08**.
[6] As defined in SI 2004/3148, art 9(b). For the place of supply, see art 10.
[7] For the place of supply, see SI 2004/3148, art 11(a).
[8] For the place of supply, see SI 2004/3148, art 11(b).
[9] For effective use and consumption in relation to onward supplies and supplies to a member of a VAT group, see SI 2004/3148, arts 12, 13.
[10] VAT Regulations, SI 1995/2518, reg 82A as inserted by SI 2004/3140.
[11] VATA 1994, Sch 6, para 8 as amended by F(No 2)A 2005, s 5. For conversion of foreign currency amounts, see VATA 1994, Sch 6, para 11.

Gold

[65.40] If a person (X) makes a supply of gold[1] to another person (Y), the supply is treated for registration purposes as a supply made by both X and Y. The supply by Y is deemed to be made in the course or furtherance of Y's business. It is not disregarded for registration purposes on the grounds that the gold is a capital asset of Y's business.[2] A supply is brought within this provision only if it is a taxable supply chargeable to tax at a positive rate.[3]

If a taxable person (X) makes a supply of gold to another taxable person (Y) to be used in connection with the business carried on by Y, Y is required to account for and pay tax on X's behalf.[4]

[65.40] The charge to tax

The foregoing provisions apply to supplies of investment gold excluded from exemption[5] on the grounds that only one of the parties to the transaction is a member of the London Bullion Market Association.[6]

---

1. As defined in VATA 1994, s 55(5).
2. ie by virtue of VATA 1994, Sch 1, para 1(7).
3. VATA 1994, s 55(1).
4. VATA 1994, s 55(2).
5. ie excluded from exemption under VATA 1994, Sch 9, Group 15 by virtue of Note 4(b) to that Group.
6. VAT (Terminal Markets) Order, SI 1973/173, art 5.

Specified goods

[65.41] A new reverse charge takes effect in relation to supplies made after 31 May 2007.[1] It applies if the aggregate value[2] of specified goods[3] supplied to a person (Y) in a month by one or more suppliers (X) exceeds £1,000. The supplies made by X are deemed to have been made by both X and Y. The value of the supplies deemed to have been made by Y is taken into account in determining whether he is liable to registration. For this purpose, Y's supplies are deemed to be made in the course or furtherance of business if the goods were supplied to him for business purposes.[4] They are not disregarded for registration purposes on the grounds that the goods are a capital asset of Y's business.[5]

If a taxable person (X) makes a supply of specified goods to another taxable person (Y) to be used in connection with the business carried on by Y, Y is required to account for and pay tax on X's behalf. The amount due from Y is recoverable as a debt due to the Crown.[6]

A person must notify the Commissioners of the first supply of specified goods made by him after 31 May 2007. He must do so within 30 days using the on-line portal provided by the Commissioners.[7]

Having made his first supply of specified goods, a taxable person must submit a statement (referred to as a "reverse charge sales list") to the Commissioners in respect of that prescribed accounting period, and every successive period, setting out prescribed information. This requirement continues until the taxable person notifies the Commissioners that he has ceased to supply specified goods and that he does not intend to restart doing so.[8]

A supply of specified goods falls within the foregoing provisions only if it is chargeable to tax at a positive rate and it is not an excepted supply.[9]

---

1. FA 2006, s 19(1), (4), (8); Finance Act 2006, section 19, (Appointed Day) Order, SI 2007/1419. This measure derogates from Directive 2006/112/EC in accordance with the authorisation granted by Decision 2007/250/EC.
2. As defined in VATA 1994, s 55A(5) as inserted by FA 2006, s 19.
3. ie goods of a description specified in VAT (Section 55A) (Specified Goods and Excepted Supplies) Order, SI 2007/1417 art 3 (mobile telephones and integrated circuit devices).

Charge II [65.42]

4   VATA 1994, s 55A(1)–(3) as inserted by FA 2006, s 19.
5   VATA 1994, s 55A(4) as inserted by FA 2006, s 19. For the exclusion that would otherwise apply, see VATA 1994, Sch 1, para 1(7).
6   VATA 1994, s 55A(6)–(8) (as inserted by FA 2006, s 19) and Sch 11 para 5(1).
7   VAT Regulations, SI 1995/2518, reg 23B as inserted by SI 2007/1418.
8   SI 1995/2518, reg 23C as inserted by SI 2007/1418. For the information to be provided, see SI 1995/2518, reg 23C(1)(a)–(c) and (4) as so inserted. Reverse charge sales lists are submitted electronically in accordance with VAT Information Sheet 8/07 (May 2007) para 14: see SI 1995/2518, reg 23C(1) as so inserted. For the notification made when ceasing to make specified supplies, see SI 1995/2518, reg 23D, as inserted by SI 2007/1599. For the notification made if the person subsequently recommences making specified supplies, see SI 1995/2518, reg 23D, as inserted by SI 2007/1599.
9   VATA 1994 s 55A(1)(a), (b) as inserted by FA 2006 s 19. For excepted supplies, see VAT (Section 55A) (Specified Goods and Excepted Supplies) Order, SI 2007/1417 arts 4, 5.In particular, a supply is an excepted supply if the value of the supply is less than £5,000: SI 2007/1417 art 4(a).

Goods held at date of deregistration

[65.42] This provision is enacted to secure equity between traders who carry on trading after deregistration and traders who have not been registered. A trader in the former category is deemed to supply any land or goods then forming part of the assets of his business. The supply is deemed to be made in the course or furtherance of business, takes place immediately before he ceases to be a taxable person[1] and is valued for tax purposes at the money consideration (excluding VAT) which would be payable for identical or similar goods or, failing that, the cost of producing the goods concerned.[2] In effect, therefore, input tax credits previously claimed are clawed back by the deemed supply and the trader is placed in the same position as if he had acquired them after deregistration.[3]

There are three exceptions:

(1)   In principle, no supply takes place in relation to goods which did not give rise to input tax credit when they were acquired. However, this does not apply if the goods were acquired by the trader when all or part of a business was transferred to him as a going concern by another taxable person.[4]
(2)   All goods are exempted from charge if:
    (a)   the business is transferred to another taxable person;
    (b)   the taxable person has died or become bankrupt or incapacitated and the business is carried on by some other person; or
    (c)   tax on the deemed supply does not exceed £1,000.[5]
(3)   No supply takes place if the trader ceases to be a taxable person following certification for the purposes of the flat-rate scheme for farmers.[6]

De Voil Indirect Tax Service V3.261.

[1] VATA 1994, Sch 4, paras 8(1), 9 as amended by FA 2007, s 98.
[2] VATA 1994, Sch 6, para 6.
[3] The trader may not, however, claim input tax credit under the provisions described in infra, § **66.04** if he subsequently re-registers: *Haugh v Customs and Excise Comrs* (1997) VAT decision 15055.
[4] VATA 1994, Sch 4, para 8(2) as amended by FA 2007 s 99.
[5] VATA 1994, Sch 4, para 8(1) as amended by SI 2000/266.
[6] VATA 1994, Sch 4, para 8(3).

Charge III—Goods acquired from another EU member state

The charge to tax

[65.43] VAT is charged on an acquisition of goods[1] within any of the following descriptions:[2]

(1) An acquisition of *any* goods made in the UK by a taxable person if the transaction giving rise to the removal of the goods to the UK is not a taxable supply.
(2) An acquisition of goods subject to excise duty[3] made in the UK by a non-taxable person of a specified description[4] if the transaction giving rise to the removal of the goods to the UK is not a taxable supply.
(3) An acquisition of new means of transport[5] by any non-taxable person.

In principle, an acquisition is chargeable to tax at either the reduced rate or the standard rate.[6] However, no tax is charged on an acquisition if:

(1) It is an exempt acquisition.[7] (An acquisition is an exempt acquisition if the goods are acquired in pursuance of an exempt supply.)[8]
(2) The legislation specified that no tax is charged on it.[9]

An acquisition which is not an exempt acquisition is referred to as a "taxable acquisition".[10] This applies whether or not any tax is charged on it.

Although a non-taxable person does not make taxable acquisitions in respect of goods other than new means of transport and goods subject to excise duty, the acquisitions may be "relevant acquisitions"[11] so that their value is taken into account in determining whether he is liable to registration.[12]

De Voil Indirect Tax Service V3.366–371.

[1] For the transactions which amount to an acquisition of goods, see supra, § **63.34**.
[2] VATA 1994, s 10(1). For the place of acquisition, see supra, § **63.36**.
[3] For the goods subject to excise duty, see Alcoholic Liquor Duties Act 1979, Hydrocarbon Oil Duties Act 1979 and Tobacco Products Duty Act 1979.
[4] ie (a) any person carrying on a business acquiring the goods in the course or furtherance of that business, and (b) any body corporate or unincorporated body acquiring the goods in the course or furtherance of a non-business activity: VATA 1994, s 10(3)(*a*), (*b*).

5   As defined in VATA 1994, s 95; VAT Regulations, SI 1995/2518, reg 147.
6   For the rates of tax, see supra, § **65.06**.
7   An exempt acquisition is not a taxable acquisition: VATA 1994, ss 10(2)(*b*). As the charge to tax is confined to taxable acquisitions by VATA 1994, s 10(1)(*a*), it follows that an exempt acquisition is not chargeable to tax and that no tax is therefore chargeable on it.
8   VATA 1994, s 31(1).
9   For the acquisitions specified, see infra, § **69.09**.
10   VATA 1994, s 10(2).
11   VATA 1994, Sch 3, para 11(*a*).
12   For liability to registration in respect of acquisitions, see supra, § **64.12**.

Persons liable to account for tax

[65.44] VAT on an acquisition is a liability of the person who acquires the goods. Subject to provisions about accounting and payment, the VAT becomes due at the time of acquisition.[1]

De Voil Indirect Tax Service V3.366–371.

1   VATA 1994, s 1(3). For accounting and payment, see infra, § **65.46**. For the time of acquisition, see infra, § **65.44**.

The time of acquisition

[65.45] An acquisition is normally treated as taking place on the earlier of:[1]

(1)   The fifteenth day of the month following that in which the goods are first removed under the transaction concerned.
(2)   The date on which an invoice is issued. The invoice must constitute a VAT invoice under the law of the EU member state concerned.[2]

Special time of acquisition rules apply to: warehoused goods[3] and water,[4] coal gas, water gas, producer gases or similar gases, or any form of power, heat, refrigeration or ventilation.[5]

De Voil Indirect Tax Service V3.388.

1   VATA 1994, s 12(1), (2); VAT Regulations, SI 1995/2518, reg 83 as amended by SI 2003/3220.
2   For tax invoices under UK law, see supra, § **65.18**.
3   For goods subject to a warehousing regime, see VATA 1994, s 18. For goods subject to a fiscal warehousing regime, see VATA 1994, s 18B.
4   But not water within SI 1995/2518, reg 86(1)(*a*)(i), (ii).
5   SI 1995/2518, reg 87 as amended by SI 2003/3220.

Value

[65.46] The value of an acquisition is the value of the transaction under which the goods were acquired.[1] This is determined as follows:[2]

(1) A transaction for a money consideration has a value equal to the consideration.[3] However, open market value[4] is used if the Commissioners make a direction to that effect.[5]

(2) A transaction wholly or partly for a non-money consideration has a value of such amount in money as is equivalent to the consideration.[6]

(3) The value in (1) or (2) is increased, in accordance with regulations,[7] by UK excise duty or EU customs duty or agricultural levy chargeable when the goods are removed to the UK.[8]

(4) A transfer, disposal or removal of goods forming part of the assets of a business made without consideration has a value of the current purchase price (excluding VAT) of identical or similar goods or, failing that, the current cost of producing the same goods.[9]

A money consideration is apportioned if it relates to more than one transaction.[10] Foreign currency amounts relevant to valuation are converted into sterling at the market rate. However, a trader may elect to use the customs period rate of exchange or a method specified in a notice published by the Commissioners.[11]

De Voil Indirect Tax Service V3.166, 390–393.

---

[1] VATA 1994, s 20(1).
[2] VATA 1994, s 20(2).
[3] VATA 1994, s 20(3).
[4] As defined in VATA 1994, Sch 7, para 1(4).
[5] For the circumstances in which a direction may be made, see VATA 1994, Sch 7, para 1. For the right of appeal, see VATA 1994, s 83(w).
[6] VATA 1994, s 20(4).
[7] See VAT Regulations, SI 1995/2518, regs 96, 97.
[8] VATA 1994, Sch 7, para 2.
[9] VATA 1994, Sch 7, para 3. For the supply of goods made, see supra, §§ **65.28** and **65.31**.
[10] VATA 1994, s 20(5).
[11] VATA 1994, Sch 7, para 4.

Accounting

Taxable persons

[65.47] VAT chargeable on an acquisition made by a taxable person is output tax.[1] VAT on dutiable goods subject to a warehousing regime is paid under a special accounting procedure.[2] VAT on other goods is accounted for in the same manner as other output tax, save that the amount concerned is disclosed as a separate item on the trader's periodic tax return.[3]

Where the time of acquisition[4] is determined by reference to a tax invoice issued under the law of another EU member state, VAT is accounted for and paid only on so much of the value of the acquisition as is shown on the invoice.[5]

De Voil Indirect Tax Service V3.396.

[1] VATA 1994, s 24(2).
[2] See VAT Regulations, SI 1995/2518, reg 41.
[3] See SI 1995/2518, Sch 1, Form Nos 4, 5.
[4] For the time of acquisition, see supra, § **65.44**.
[5] SI 1995/2518, reg 26.

Non-taxable persons

[65.48] A non-taxable person making a taxable acquisition of goods subject to excise duty is required to notify the Commissioners in writing at the later of the time of acquisition[1] and the date when the goods arrive in the UK. The VAT due must be paid no later than the due date for notification and is normally payable when the notification is made.[2]

A non-taxable person making a taxable acquisition of a new means of transport is required to notify the Commissioners in writing within seven days. The VAT due must be paid at the time of notification or within 30 days of a written demand.[3]

An acquisition of goods subject to a fiscal warehousing regime[4] is disregarded in determining whether a person is liable to registration.[5] However, the person is liable to account for VAT on the acquisition if he would be a taxable person but for the fact that such acquisitions were disregarded.[6] VAT is accounted for and paid in accordance with a prescribed procedure.[7]

De Voil Indirect Tax Service V3.396.

[1] For the time of acquisition, see supra, § **65.44**.
[2] For notifications and payment, see VAT Regulations, SI 1995/2518, reg 36.
[3] For notifications and payment, see VAT Regulations, SI 1995/2518, reg 148; Notice No 728.
[4] ie under VATA 1994, s 18B(4).
[5] VATA 1994, Sch 1, para 1(9); Sch 2, para 1(7); Sch 3, para 1(6).
[6] VATA 1994, s 18B(5).
[7] VATA 1994, s 18D; VAT Regulations, SI 1995/2518, reg 145J.

Charge IV—Goods imported from a third country

The charge to tax

[65.49] VAT is chargeable on the importation of goods into the UK from a third country.[1] In principle, imported goods are chargeable to tax at either the reduced rate or the standard rate.[2] However, no tax is charged where the legislation so specifies.[3]

De Voil Indirect Tax Service V3.312.

---

[1] VATA 1994, s 1(1)(c). But see *Einberger v Hauptzollamt Freiburg (case 294/82)* [1984] ECR 1177, ECJ (prohibited narcotics); *Witzemann v Hauptzollamt Munchen-Mitte (case C-343/89)* [1993] STC 108, ECJ (counterfeit money).
[2] For the rate of tax, see supra, § **65.06**.
[3] For the goods on which no tax is charged, see infra, §§ **69.10** and **69.11**.

Person responsible for payment of tax

[65.50] VAT on the importation of goods is charged and payable as if it were a duty of customs.[1] The person responsible for payment of VAT appears to be the person who imports the goods. This is the person who is liable to discharge the customs debt (if any) on the goods.[2] The person required to discharge a customs debt is determined in accordance with EU customs legislation.[3]

De Voil Indirect Tax Service V3.312.

---

[1] VATA 1994, s 1(4).
[2] VATA 1994, s 15(2)(b). This defines the person treated as importing the goods for VAT purposes rather than the person responsible for payment. For customs practice in relation to customs debt, see Notice No 199.
[3] VATA 1994, s 96(3). For the relevant EU customs legislation, see Council Regulation (EEC) No 2913/92, arts 201–206 (OJ L302/1, 19.10.92); Commission Regulation (EEC) No 2454/93, arts 859–867 (OJ L253/1, 11.10.93).

Time when the charge to tax arises

[65.51] For VAT purposes, goods are not treated as being imported into the UK until such time as a customs debt is incurred (or would be incurred if the goods were chargeable to customs duty) in respect of their entry into the territory of the EU.[1] The time when a customs debt arises, or would arise, is determined in accordance with EU customs legislation.[2] It follows that VAT becomes due for payment at, or after, the time when the customs debt is (or would be) incurred.

De Voil Indirect Tax Service V3.312.

---

[1] VATA 1994, s 15(2)(a).

[2] VATA 1994, s 96(3). For the relevant EU customs legislation, see Council Regulation (EEC) No 2913/92, arts 201–206 (OJ L302/1, 19.10.92); Commission Regulation (EEC) No 2454/93, arts 859–867 (OJ L253/1, 11.10.93).

Value

[65.52] Imported goods are valued in accordance with EU customs rules.[1] This value includes, if not already included, the following:[2]

(1) All foreign taxes, duties and other charges.
(2) All UK import duties other than VAT.
(3) All commission, packing, transport, insurance and other incidental expenses incurred up to the first place of destination[3] in the UK.[4]
(4) (If a further place of destination within the EU is known at the time of importation) incidental expenses associated with transporting the goods to that destination.

Any discount for prompt payment earned under the contract is deducted from this value unless the contract provides for payment by instalments.[5]

Valuation reliefs apply in respect of: works of art, antiques and collectors' pieces;[6] goods re-imported after receiving a treatment or process abroad;[7] and goods removed from the Isle of Man which, exceptionally, give rise to a charge to VAT in the UK.[8]

De Voil Indirect Tax Service V3.314, 321–329.

[1] VATA 1994, s 21(1). For EU customs rules, see Regulation (EEC) Nos 2913/92 (OJ L302/1, 19.10.92) and 2454/93 (OJ L253/1, 11.10.93). For the application of those rules, see *Dolland & Aitchison Ltd v Customs and Excise Comrs (case C-491/04)* [2006] ECR I–2129, [2006] SWTI 531, ECJ (single price for goods imported from the Channel Islands and services subsequently supplied in the UK).
[2] VATA 1994, s 21(2) as amended by FA 2006, s 18.
[3] As defined in VATA 1994, s 21(2) as amended by FA 2006, s 18.
[4] For a simplified system of flat rates, see Business Brief (Issue 6/96), 30 April 1996. For an exception in relation to works of art, antiques, collections and collectors' pieces imported under temporary import arrangements for sale by auction after 31 August 2006, see VATA 1994, s 21(2A), (2B) as inserted by FA 2006, s 18; Finance Act 2006, section 18, (Appointed Day) Order, SI 2006/2149.
[5] VATA 1994, s 21(3).
[6] VATA 1994, s 21(4)–(7) as amended by FA 1999, s 12 and (between 1 December 2008 and 31 December 2009 inclusive) by FA 2009, s 9(1) and VAT (Change of Rate) Order, SI 2008/3020, art 4. The value of the goods is reduced so as to charge VAT at an effective rate of approximately 5%. The standard rate in force between 1 December 2008 and 31 December 2009 inclusive is 15%; the value of the goods is accordingly reduced by 66.66%. The standard rate in force from 1 January 2010 is 17.5%; the value of the goods is accordingly reduced by 71.42%. For an extra-statutory concession, see Notice No 48 (July 2009), para 3.36. For the standard rate, see supra, **§ 65.06**.

[65.52] The charge to tax

7 VAT Regulations, SI 1995/2518, reg 126.
8 VAT (Isle of Man) Order, SI 1982/1067, art 3(2).

Accounting and payment

[65.53] VAT on the importation of goods is charged and payable as if it were a duty of customs.[1] In principle, therefore, VAT is accounted for at the same time, and in the same manner, as customs duty, ie it is payable direct to the Commissioners (by reference to a customs declaration known as an "entry" or by personal declaration at the place where a passenger enters the UK) or to the Post Office (in the case of postal importations).[2] However, special accounting arrangements apply in relation to goods are subject to a warehousing regime,[3] and to certain goods imported by post.[4]

1 VATA 1994, s 1(4).
2 For payment of VAT on imported goods, see infra, § 67.13.
3 See VATA 1994, s 18.
4 See VAT Regulations, SI 1995/2518 reg 122.

66

Tax credits, repayments and refunds

Introduction	PARA 66.01
Nature of input tax	PARA 66.02
Input tax credit	PARA 66.06
Input tax excluded from credit	PARA 66.16
Deduction and variation of input tax credit	PARA 66.22
Repayments of tax	PARA 66.36
Refunds	PARA 66.39

Introduction

[66.01] A person may pay, or be required to pay, VAT on the goods and services he purchases, acquires or imports. A taxable person may also be required to account for VAT under the self-supply or reverse charge arrangements. It is necessary to decide whether this VAT can be recovered and, if so, from whom.

In principle, VAT is recoverable from the Commissioners only if it is chargeable under the UK legislation. VAT chargeable under the legislation of another EU member state is recoverable, if at all, from the tax authorities of that member state in accordance with the legislation of that member state giving effect to the Eighth Directive.[1]

VAT is recoverable from the Commissioners under three different systems: input tax credit, repayments and refunds. The three systems may be summarised in broad terms as follows:

(1) The VAT incurred by a taxable person is referred to as "input tax" if the goods or services concerned are used, or to be used, for the purposes of a business he carries on or intends to carry on. A taxable person recovers input tax by deducting the amount claimed on his VAT return.[2]

(2) The VAT incurred by overseas traders is recoverable in accordance with legislation giving effect to the Eighth and Thirteenth Directives.[3] The recoveries are referred to as "repayments". Repayments are claimed from the Commissioners in accordance with statutory rules.[4]

(3) In principle, persons are unable to recover VAT unless they are taxable persons or overseas traders. However, certain non-taxable persons are entitled to recover VAT incurred in respect of certain activities and taxable persons are entitled to recover certain VAT which is not input tax. The recoveries are referred to as "refunds". Refunds are claimed from the Commissioners in accordance with statutory rules.[5] Non-taxable persons claim refunds direct from the Commissioners. Taxable persons claim refunds by deducting the amount claimed on their VAT returns.

[66.01] Tax credits, repayments and refunds

De Voil Indirect Tax Service V3.401–405.

[1] Directive 79/1072/EEC. Refund applications are sent to the tax authorities of the member state concerned. The 1979 Directive is replaced by Directive 2008/9/EC in relation to refund applications made after 31 December 2009. From 1 January 2010, applications must be sent electronically to the Commissioners under arrangements to be made in accordance with VATA 1994, s 39A as inserted by FA 2009, s 77(3).
[2] For input tax, see infra, §§ **66.02–66.35**.
[3] Directives 79/1072/EEC and 86/560/EEC respectively. Directive 79/1072/EEC is replaced by Directive 2008/9/EC in relation to refund applications made after 31 December 2009.
[4] For repayments, see infra, §§ **66.36–66.38**.
[5] For refunds, see infra, §§ **66.39–66.41**.

Nature of input tax

Definition

[66.02] VAT chargeable under the UK or Isle of Man legislation is referred to as "input tax" if it is incurred by a taxable person in respect of goods and services used (or to be used) for the purpose of a business carried on (or to be carried on) by him.[1]

De Voil Indirect Tax Service V3.402.

[1] VATA 1994, s 24(1).

Transactions on which VAT is chargeable

[66.03] Input tax is incurred by a taxable person if it becomes chargeable on any of the following transactions:[1]

(1) A supply[2] made to him[3] by another taxable person on which VAT is chargeable.[4]
(2) A supply made to him by another person upon which he is required to account to the Commissioners for the VAT chargeable under the reverse charge arrangements.[5]
(3) A supply which he is treated as making to himself under the self-supply provisions.[6]
(4) An acquisition of goods from another EU member state upon which he is required to account to the Commissioners for the VAT chargeable.[7]
(5) An importation of goods upon which he is required to pay the VAT chargeable.[8]

A flat-rate trader is entitled to a credit for input tax in respect of goods held in stock when he ceases to be authorised to use the flat-rate scheme if he continues to be a taxable person thereafter.[9]

De Voil Indirect Tax Service V3.421–429.

---

[1] VATA 1994, s 24(1).
[2] Goods are supplied to a person if he obtains possession or control so as to be able to use them immediately: *W Puddifer (Jun) Ltd v Customs and Excise Comrs* [1996] V & DR 237. A tax point does not create a supply where none has taken place: *Theotrue Holdings Ltd v Customs and Excise Comrs* [1983] VATTR 88; *Northern Counties Co-operative Enterprises Ltd v Customs and Excise Comrs* [1986] VATTR 250. A documented transaction is deprived of its VAT consequences if it is a sham: see *McNicholas Construction Co Ltd v Customs and Excise Comrs* [2000] STC 553 (fictitious supply); *Revenue and Customs Comrs v Dempster (trading as Boulevard)* [2008] EWHC 63 (Ch), [2008] STC 2079 (misdescription of supply). Thus, input tax credit does not arise merely because a tax invoice has been issued or a payment made: *Genius Holding BV v Staatssecretaris van Financiën (case 342/87)* [1991] STC 239, ECJ.
[3] For the person to whom the supply was made, see *Customs and Excise Comrs v Redrow Group Ltd* [1999] STC 161, HL; *WHA Ltd v Customs and Excise Comrs* [2004] EWCA Civ 559, [2004] STC 1081, CA. For examples, see *British Airways plc v Customs and Excise Comrs* [2000] V & DR 74 (food for passengers at airport restaurant); *Revenue and Customs Comrs v Jeancharm Ltd (trading as Bever International)* [2005] EWHC 839 (Ch), [2005] STC 918 (employee's defence costs). Input tax credit does not arise in respect of supplies made to someone other than the person who claims credit: see, for example, *Turner (t/a Turner Agricultural) v Customs and Excise Comrs* [1992] STC 621 (payment of other party's costs in legal proceedings); *Customs and Excise Comrs v Pennystar Ltd* [1996] STC 163 (financing transaction between third parties). For input tax credit in respect of reimbursements by employers in respect of the business element of road fuel delivered to, and paid for by, employees acting in the employer's name and on his behalf, see VAT (Input Tax) (Reimbursement by Employers of Employees' Business Use of Road Fuel) Regulations, SI 2005/3280. For exact reimbursements to employees: Notice No 700 (April 2002) para 19.7.5. For agency supplies, see VATA 1994, s 47(3). See also *Leesportefeuille Intiem CV v Staatssecretaris van Financiën (case 165/86)* [1989] 2 CMLR 856, ECJ.
[4] Input tax credit is limited to the amount which is properly due: *Podium Investments Ltd v Custom and Excise Comrs* [1977] VATTR 121. Thus, the tax is erroneously charged on a supply is not input tax: see, for example, *Advanced Business Technology Ltd v Customs and Excise Comrs* (1983) VAT decision 1488 (tax erroneously charged on assets of business sold as going concern).
[5] For the VAT accounted for on goods and services subject to the reverse charge, see supra, §§ **65.38–65.41**. For input tax where the reverse charge is assessed, or voluntarily disclosed, after the prescribed accounting period in which it arose, see *Ecotrade SpA v Agenzia Entrate Ufficio Genoa 3* (joined cases C-95/07 and C-96/07); [2008] SWTI 1327, ECJ.
[6] For the VAT accounted for on self-supplies, see supra, §§ **65.32–65.37**.
[7] For the VAT accounted for on acquisitions, see supra, § **65.45**.
[8] For the VAT accounted for on imported goods, see supra, § **65.51**.

[66.03] Tax credits, repayments and refunds

⁹ For the amount of the claim, see VAT Regulations, SI 1995/2518, reg 55S as inserted by SI 2002/1142 and Notice No 733. For the flat-rate scheme, see SI 1995/2518, regs 55A–55V as so inserted.

Transactions by a taxable person

[66.04] Input tax, by definition, is VAT incurred by a taxable person.[1] Since a taxable person is a trader who is, or is required to be, registered for the purposes of VAT,[2] it follows that VAT is input tax only if it is chargeable on goods and services purchased, acquired or imported on or after the date from which a trader is, or should have been, registered.[3] It also follows that a right to input tax credit ceases to apply in respect of goods and services supplied after the date from which he is deregistered. These general propositions are subject to two exceptions.

First, a taxable person is permitted to count tax incurred prior to becoming a taxable person as if it were input tax. A body corporate is similarly permitted to count tax incurred prior to the incorporation as if it were input tax. In broad terms, the tax relates to unsold goods, and to services, purchased respectively in the four-year or six-month period prior to the relevant date.[4] However, no claim may be made in respect of goods or services used to make a supply which, under the legislation in force at the time of purchase, would have been an exempt supply.[5]

Secondly, a trader is entitled to a refund in respect of certain VAT which becomes chargeable after he ceases to be a taxable person.[6]

De Voil Indirect Tax Service V3.431, 432.

---

[1] VATA 1994, s 24(1).
[2] VATA 1994, s 3(1).
[3] See *Schemepanel Trading Ltd v Customs and Excise Comrs* [1996] STC 871; cf *Charles-Greed v Customs and Excise Comrs* (1992) VAT decision 7790.
[4] VAT Regulations, SI 1995/2518, reg 111(1)–(4) as amended by SI 1997/1086, SI 2009/586.
[5] See *C Jeffrey Black (Opticians) Ltd v Customs and Excise Comrs* (1989) VAT decision 4072; *Douros v Customs and Excise Comrs* (1994) VAT decision 12454; *Byrd v Customs and Excise Comrs* (1994) VAT decision 12675; *Gulland Properties v Customs and Excise Comrs* (1996) VAT decision 13955; *Jenkins v Customs and Excise Comrs* (1997) VAT decision 14784; Business Brief (Issue 30/93) 24 September 1993.
[6] For refunds under this provision, see infra, § **66.40**.

Goods and services used for business purposes

[66.05] The VAT chargeable on a supply, acquisition or importation is input tax only if the goods or services are used or to be used for the purposes of any business carried on or to be carried on by the trader.[1] Goods or services meet this test if they are received in connection with the trader's business activities for the purposes of being incorporated within his economic activities.[2] An activity for this purpose includes an activity preparatory to the carrying on of an economic activity.[3]

A subjective test is applied in deciding the purpose for which goods or services were obtained.[4] This is applied by ascertaining what was in the mind or minds of the person or persons who took the decision[5] and is adjudged at the time of supply or importation[6] (in the case of a purchase) or in each prescribed accounting period of use[7] (in the case of continuous supplies such as rental agreements). However, there must be a clear nexus between the matter giving rise to the expenditure and the business itself.[8]

Goods and services purchased, acquired or imported by a company are not treated as being used for business purposes[9] if they are used or to be used in connection with the provision of accommodation used, or to be used, for domestic purposes[10] by a director of the company or a person connected with him.[11]

VAT incurred on goods or services to be used for the purposes of somebody else's business is not input tax[12] unless both parties benefit[13] or the trader is deemed to make an onward supply of the goods or services concerned, eg where he acts as a buying agent in his own name.[14]

In principle, VAT incurred on goods or services wholly for private or non-business purposes is not input tax.[15] VAT is apportioned if the goods or services are used partly for business purposes and partly for other purposes and only that part which relates to the business purpose is treated as input tax.[16] However, fuel for private use is treated as input tax if the trader accounts for output tax by reference to a scale charge.[17]

Under EC law, a trader is given a choice in relation to capital items used for both business and private purposes:[18]

(1)　He may allocate the item wholly to the assets of his business. The consequence of this option is that the VAT incurred is input tax. However, any transfer or disposal of the goods, and any private or non-business use of the goods, services or land, is charged to tax under the provisions described in supra, §§ **65.28–65.30**.

(2)　He may retain the item wholly within his private assets. The consequence of this option is that the item is entirely excluded from the VAT system. Thus, no input tax is deducted in respect of the item and no VAT becomes chargeable on its use or disposal. Moreover, as there is no initial deduction of input tax, there can be no subsequent adjustment under the capital goods scheme.[19]

(3)　He may integrate the item in his business only to the extent that the item is actually used for business purposes.[20] The consequence of this option is that only part of the VAT incurred is input tax. On the other hand, only the business proportion is charged to tax when the item is transferred or disposed of.

De Voil Indirect Tax Service V3.406–410.

---

[1]　VATA 1994, s 24(1), (2).

[66.05] Tax credits, repayments and refunds

2   *Customs and Excise Comrs v Redrow Group plc* [1999] STC 161, HL.
3   *Rompelman and Rompelman-van-Deelen v Minister van Finaciën (case 268/83)* [1985] 3 CMLR 202, ECJ; *Intercommunale voor Zeewaterontzilting (in liquidation) v Belgian State (case C-110/94)* [1996] STC 569, ECJ; *Merseyside Cablevision Ltd v Customs and Excise Comrs* [1987] VATTR 134. This does not include a share issue to raise initial working capital: *Park Commercial Developments plc v Customs and Excise Comrs* [1990] VATTR 99. In the UK, it has been held that an activity does not amount to a business until such time as it is possible to forecast making taxable supplies in the course of it in the reasonably foreseeable future: see *K & K Thorogood Ltd v Customs and Excise Comrs* (1984) VAT decision 1595 and the cases cited therein.
4   *National Water Council v Customs and Excise Comrs* [1979] STC 157.
5   *Ian Flockton Developments Ltd v Customs and Excise Comrs* [1987] STC 394. The credibility of a witness with regard to evidence of intention may be tested by the standards and thinking of an ordinary businessman standing in the taxpayer's shoes.
6   *Sisson v Customs and Excise Comrs* (1981) VAT decision 1056.
7   *Denmor Investments Ltd v Customs and Excise Comrs* [1981] VATTR 66.
8   *Customs and Excise Comrs v Rosner* [1994] STC 228 (legal costs incurred in defending criminal prosecution).
9   VATA 1994, s 24(3). For employees occupying accommodation as a term of their contracts of employment, see *Dean and Chapter of Hereford Cathedral v Customs and Excise Comrs* [1994] VATTR 159.
10 For domestic purposes, see *Suregrove Ltd v Customs and Excise Comrs* (1993) VAT decision 10740; *R S & E M Wright Ltd v Customs and Excise Comrs* (1995) VAT decision 12984.
11 As defined in VATA 1994, s 24(7).
12 See *Ashtree Holdings Ltd v Customs and Excise Comrs* [1979] STC 818; *Jackson (a firm) v Customs and Excise Comrs* (1985) VAT decision 1959; *Bird Semple & Crawford Herron v Customs and Excise Comrs* [1986] VATTR 218.
13 For work done to property, see *Burntisland Golf House Club v Customs and Excise Comrs* (1991) VAT decision 6340; *Thorpe Architecture Ltd v Customs and Excise Comrs* (1992) VAT decision 6955. For expenditure by an agent on behalf of his principal, who repudiated liability, see *Scott v Customs and Excise Comrs* (1992) VAT decision 6922. See also *Kelly (a firm) v Customs and Excise Comrs* (1987) VAT decision 2452.
14 VATA 1994, s 47.
15 Under EC law, see *De Jong v Staatssecretaris van Financiën (case C-20/91)* [1995] STC 727, ECJ; *Finanzamt Uelzen v Armbrecht (case C-291/92)* [1995] STC 997, ECJ.
16 VATA 1994, s 24(5). VAT may be apportioned in accordance with an agreement between the trader and the Commissioners: see *Labour Party v Customs and Excise Comrs* (2001) VAT decision 17034. For apportionments where some activities amount to a business and some do not, see *Customs and Excise Comrs v Apple and Pear Development Council* [1986] STC 192, HL; *Whitechapel Art Gallery v Customs and Excise Comrs* [1986] STC 156; *Victoria and Albert Museum Trustees v Customs and Excise Comrs* [1996] STC 1016; *Church of England Children's Society v R & C Comrs* [2005] STC 1644; see also Business Brief (Issue 19/05), 10 October 2005 and Notice No 701/5. For apportionment between business and private expenditure, see *Ballacmaish Farms Ltd v HMTrea-*

sury (1987) VAT decision 2364. For farmhouses, see *F & M Mounty & Sons v Customs and Excise Comrs* [1995] V & DR 128; Business Brief (Issue 18/96), 27 August 1996.

[17] VATA 1994, s 56(5). For the scale charge, see supra, § **65.26**. For input tax credit in relation to motor expenses generally, see Notice No 700/64.

[18] See *Finanzamt Uelzen v Armbrecht* (case C-291/92) [1995] STC 997, ECJ; *Bakcsi v Finanzamt Fürstenfeldbruck* (case C-415/98) [2001] ECR I–1831, ECJ; *Seeling v Finanzamt Starnberg* (case C-269/00) [2003] STC 805, ECJ; *Finanzamt Bergisch Gladbach v HE* (case C-25/03) [2005] ECR I–3123, [2005] SWTI 864, ECJ; *Charles v Staatssecretaris van Financiën* (case C-434/03) [2005] ECR I–7037, [2005] SWTI 1258, ECJ; *Sandra Puffer v Unabhängiger Finanzsenat, Außenstelle Linz* (case C-460/07) [2009] ECR I–0000, [2009] STC 1693, ECJ.

[19] See *Lennartz v Finzanzamt München III (case C-97/90)* [1995] STC 514, ECJ. For an example, see *Waterschap Zeeuws Vlaanderen v Staatssecretaris van Financiën (case C-378/02)* [2005] ECR I–4685, [2005] STC 1298, ECJ. For the capital goods scheme, see infra, § **66.26**.

[20] For the deductible proportion in relation to a jointly owned property where only one of the joint owners was a taxable person, see *Finanzamt Bergisch Gladbach v HE (case C-25/03)* [2005] ECR 1-3123, [2005] SWTI 864, ECJ.

Input tax credit

Allowable input tax

[66.06] In principle, a taxable person is entitled, at the end of each prescribed accounting period, to credit for so much of his input tax as is allowable.[1] Input tax is allowable if it is attributable to specified supplies[2] made by a taxable person in the course or furtherance of his business.[3] The manner in which input tax is attributed to these supplies is determined in accordance with regulations.[4] The position is summarised in the following table.

	Specified supplies	Attribution method (SI 1995/2518)	Commentary
(1)	Taxable supplies:		
	standard method	Reg 101	66.08
	special method	Reg 102	66.09
(2)	Supplies outside the UK which would have been taxable supplies if made in the UK	Reg 103(a)	66.10
(3)	Services supplied to a person who belongs in a third country	Reg 103(b)	66.11

[66.06] Tax credits, repayments and refunds

(4)	Services directly linked to the export of goods to a third country	Reg 103(b)	66.11
(5)	Intermediary services relating to a transaction in heads (3) or (4).	Reg 103(b)	66.11
(6)	Supplies, wherever made, which fall within VATA 1994, Sch 9, Group 15, Items 1 or 2	Reg 103A	66.12
(7)	Both a supply with heads (1)–(5) and a supply within VATA 1994, Sch 9, Group 5, Items 1 or 6	Reg 103B	66.13

Input tax is not allowable (and may thus be said to be disallowed) if it is attributable to any other supplies. Input tax is not normally recoverable from the Commissioners in these circumstances.[5]

The principle that a taxable person is entitled to input tax credit is subject to three important exceptions. First, as a general principle, a flat-rate trader[6] is not entitled to input tax credit.[7] However, an exception is made in relation to the following classes of expenditure where the input tax is not excluded from credit.[8]

(1) Any relevant purchase[9] of capital expenditure goods[10] with a value (together with the VAT chargeable) exceeding £2,000. The whole of the input tax is treated as being attributable to taxable supplies so as to be allowable.

(2) Any purchase, acquisition or importation that is not a relevant purchase.

Second, a trader's deduction of input tax credit may be withdrawn if: (a) he exercised the deduction fraudulently; or (b) he knew (or should have known) that, by purchasing the relevant goods or services, he was taking part in a transaction connected with fraudulent evasion of VAT.[11] On the other hand, his deduction is unaffected if he did not know, and no means of knowing, the intentions of other traders in the chain or the possible fraudulent nature of other transactions in the chain.[12]

Third, a trader's deduction of input tax may be withdrawn if has been exercised abusively. The amount to be repaid is reduced by the amount of any output tax for which the trader became artificially liable under the scheme.[13]

---

[1] VATA 1994, s 25(2).
[2] The specified supplies are listed in VATA 1994, s 26(2) and VAT (Input Tax) (Specified Supplies) Order, SI 1999/3121, arts 2–4.
[3] VATA 1994, s 26(1).
[4] VATA 1996, s 26(1). For the regulations made, see VAT Regulations, SI 1995/2518, regs 101–103B.
[5] For an exception, see infra, §§ **66.14** and **66.15** (de minimis provisions).
[6] ie a person for the time being authorised to use the flat-rate scheme for small businesses: VAT Regulations, SI 1995/2518, reg 55A(1) as inserted by SI

2002/1142. For the flat-rate scheme, see supra, § **63.41**.
[7] VATA 1994, s 26B(5) as inserted by FA 2002, s 23.
[8] SI 1995/2518, reg 55E as inserted by SI 2002/1142.
[9] As defined in SI 1995/2518, regs 55A(1) and 55C(1), (3), (5) as inserted by SI 2002/1142.
[10] As defined in SI 1995/2518, reg 55A(1) as inserted by SI 2002/1142.
[11] *Kittel v Belgian State, Belgian State v Recolta Recycling SPRL* (joined cases C-439/04 and C-440/04) [2006] SWTI 1851, ECJ.
[12] *Optigen Ltd v C & E Comrs; Fulcrum Electronics Ltd v C & E Comrs; Bond House Systems Ltd v C & E Comrs* (joined cases C-354/03, C-355/03 and C-484/03) [2006] ECR I–483, [2006] STC 419, ECJ.
[13] *Halifax plc and others v C & E Comrs* (case C-255/02) [2006] ECR I–1609, [2006] STC 919, ECJ. For abusive practices, see supra, § **63.09**.

Attribution of input tax

[66.07] Input tax is attributed to a supply if the goods and services are used, or to be used, in making that supply. It is necessary to decide whether goods or services are used, or to be used, in making supplies of a particular description or supplies of two or more descriptions. The relevant test has been expressed in two different ways in relation to taxable supplies (head 1 above). First, there must be a direct and immediate link between the input tax and the taxable supplies.[1] Secondly, the expenditure must form part of the cost components of the taxable supply.[2] There is no material difference between these two tests. It is necessary to take account of all the circumstances of the transaction at issue. It is not permissible to look beyond the purposes of the particular transactions by having regard to some ultimate aim. The quest is not for the closest link, but for a sufficient link.[3] It is submitted that this test is equally applicable to the other circumstances.

Where there is mixed use, it is necessary to decide the extent to which the goods or services are "used or to be used" in making a particular class of supplies. As regards taxable supplies, the manner of calculating "the extent" of this use is prescribed by the legislation in relation to the standard method[4] and authorised or directed by the Commissioners in relation to a special method[5]. However, the legislation does not prescribe the means by which "the extent" is calculated. It appears that the extent of the use or intended use of the relevant goods or services should be calculated in a manner which gives a credible result in economic terms. A credible result may be derived from a calculation based on physical use (eg by reference to time, space or population). However, it does not necessarily do so.[6]

Input tax is attributed in accordance with the nature[7] and tax status of the supply intended to be made by the trader[8] in accordance with the rules in force at the time when the right to deduct arose.[9] Whether the intended supply is taxable or exempt is determined by reference to the legislation and, where appropriate, the effect of any option to tax, in force at that time.

Input tax arising on a self-supply is not attributed to the supply deemed to be made by the trader.[10]

[66.07] Tax credits, repayments and refunds

A freehold sale or letting may amount to a taxable supply if the option to tax has been exercised in respect of the relevant land or building.[11] Thus, input tax incurred in respect of it is attributable to a taxable supply and is apparently deductible. However, the right to deduct does not arise until the election has effect,[12] ie a deduction may not be made in contemplation of an election being made and having effect. Moreover, deduction may be restricted if the input tax concerned was incurred before the election has effect.[13]

De Voil Indirect Tax Service V3.461.

---

[1] *BLP Group plc v Customs and Excise Comrs (case C-4/94)* [1995] STC 424, ECJ.
[2] *Midland Bank plc v Customs and Excise Comrs (case C-98/98)* [2000] STC 501, ECJ.
[3] *Dial-a-Phone Ltd v Customs and Excise Comrs* [2004] EWCA Civ 603, [2004] STC 987 at paras 28, 71, 73, 74.
[4] For the standard method, see infra, § **66.08**.
[5] For special methods, see infra, § **66.09**.
[6] *St Helen's School Northwood Ltd v Revenue and Customs Comrs* [2006] EWHC 3306 (Ch), [2007] STC 633. In this case, the standard method reflected economic use more accurately than the trader's proposed special method based on time. For the contrast between "physical use" and "economic use", see paras 63, 75, 76 of the judgment.
[7] For examples, see *Neuvale Ltd v Customs and Excise Comrs* [1989] STC 395, CA (buildings refurbished for letting); *Sheffield Co-operative Society Ltd v Customs and Excise Comrs* [1987] VATTR 216; *Wigan Metropolitan Development Co (Investment) Ltd v Customs and Excise Comrs* (1990) VAT decision 4993; *Clovelly Estate Co Ltd v Customs and Excise Comrs* [1991] VATTR 351; *Imperial War Museum v Customs and Excise Comrs* [1992] VATTR 346. For shares, see *Customs and Excise Comrs v C H Beazer (Holdings) Ltd* [1989] STC 549 and *BLP Group Ltd v Customs and Excise Comrs (case C-4/94)* [1995] STC 424, ECJ (shares); *Polysar Investments Netherlands BV v Inspecteur der Invoerrechten en Accijnzen (case C-60/90)* [1993] STC 222, ECJ (holding companies); *Customs and Excise Comrs v Deutsche Ruck UK Reinsurance Co Ltd* [1995] STC 495 (legal costs); *Customs and Excise Comrs v Harpcombe Ltd* [1996] STC 726 (caravan park).
[8] See *Customs and Excise Comrs v Briararch Ltd* [1992] STC 732; *Key v Customs and Excise Comrs* (1998) VAT decision 15354.
[9] *Perna v Customs and Excise Comrs* [1990] VATTR 106. For the time when the right to deduct arises in respect of VAT incurred prior to registration, see *St George's Home Co Ltd v Customs and Excise Comrs* (1993) VAT decision 10213.
[10] VAT Regulations, SI 1995/2518, reg 104.
[11] VATA 1994, Sch 10, para 2(1)–(3).
[12] *Lawson Mardon Group Pension Scheme v Customs and Excise Comrs* (1993) VAT decision 10231. *Hi-Wire Ltd v Customs and Excise Comrs* (1991) VAT decision 6204.
[13] VATA 1994, Sch 10, para 2(4). This provision does not contravene EC law: *Newcourt Property Fund v Customs and Excise Comrs* (1991) VAT decision 5825; *Trustees for Taylor Dyne Ltd Pension Fund v Customs and Excise Comrs* [1992]

VATTR 315; *Acre Friendly Society v Customs and Excise Comrs* [1992] VATTR 308.

Attribution methods

Standard method

[66.08] Subject to relief under the de minimis rule,[1] the amount of input tax attributable to taxable supplies[2] is determined as follows:[3]

(1) Importations and acquisitions by, and supplies to, the taxable person in the period are identified.

(2) Input tax may be deducted in full in respect of goods and services *exclusively* used or to be used[4] in making:[5]
  (a) taxable supplies[6] – there must be a direct and immediate link between the input tax and the taxable supplies.[7] The expenditure must form part of the cost components of the taxable supply.[8] There is no material difference between these two tests. It is necessary to take account of all the circumstances of the transaction at issue. It is not permissible to look beyond the purposes of the particular transactions by having regard to some ultimate aim. The quest is not for the closest link, but for a sufficient link;[9]
  (b) supplies made outside the UK which would be taxable supplies if made in the UK;
  (c) the insurance and financial services of a specified description[10] which are supplied to a person who belongs in a third country, directly linked to an export of goods to a third country or comprise intermediary services in relation to either of those transactions.

(3) Input tax may not be deducted in respect of:
  (a) goods and services *exclusively* used or to be used in making exempt supplies; or
  (b) goods and services exclusively used or to be used in carrying on an activity which does not give rise to taxable supplies.[11]

(4) A proportionate deduction is made in respect of:
  (a) goods and services used or to be used partly for the purposes of a business activity and partly for the purposes of a non-business activity.[12] The business proportion must be calculated in a "fair and reasonable" manner;[13]
  (b) goods and services used or to be used wholly or partly in making supplies of a specified description[14] within or outside the UK. The input tax is attributed to taxable supplies on the basis of the extent to which the goods or services are used or to be used in making taxable supplies;[15]

[66.08] Tax credits, repayments and refunds

       (c)   goods and services used or to be used wholly or partly in making supplies from an establishment outside the UK. The input tax is attributed to taxable supplies on the basis of the extent to which the goods or services are used or to be used in making taxable supplies.[16]

(5)   Input tax incurred in respect of other goods and services is apportioned is referred to as "relevant residual input tax."[17] Relevant residual input tax may arise in either of the following circumstances.[18] First, it has a direct link, and is therefore attributable, to *both* taxable and exempt supplies.[19] Secondly, it has a direct link to neither taxable nor exempt supplies.[20] In principle, input tax in the second class has a direct and immediate link with the whole activity carried on by the taxable person. The following apportionment exercise ensures that a deduction arises in respect of input tax in either class only if one or more taxable supplies are made in the relevant accounting period.

    A proportionate deduction is made in accordance with one or other of three prescribed methods (referred to here as "Method 1", "Method 2" and "Method 3"). The options available to a taxable person are as follows:[21]

       (a)   he may use Method 1 (the default method) or Method 2 if he has an immediately preceding longer period. If Method 1 is adopted, it must be used in all the prescribed accounting periods falling within the same longer period;

       (b)   he may use Method 2 (the default method) or Method 3 if he does not have an immediately preceding longer period.

Method 1 provides that input tax is attributed to taxable supplies by reference to the percentage recovery rate for the immediately preceding longer period.[22]

Method 2 provides that input tax is attributed to taxable supplies according to the ratio of taxable supplies to total supplies[23] made in the accounting period expressed as a percentage. This percentage is rounded up to the next whole number (if the input tax incurred does not exceed £400,000) or to two decimal places (in other cases).[24]

Method 3 provides that input tax is attributed to taxable supplies by reference to the extent to which the goods or services are used or to be used in making taxable supplies.[25]

Input tax on goods and services may fall within head 5 above in either of the following circumstances.[26] First, it has a direct link, and is therefore attributable, to *both* taxable and exempt supplies.[27] Secondly, it has a direct link to neither taxable nor exempt supplies.[28] In principle, input tax in the second class has a direct and immediate link with the whole activity carried on by the taxable person. The apportionment exercise ensures that a deduction arises in respect of input tax in either class only if one or more taxable supplies are made in the relevant accounting period.

A taxable person may make a provisional deduction in respect of the input tax attributed to taxable supplies.[29] This does not mean that a change of circumstances results in the withdrawal of a deduction which has been properly made.[30] However, it does mean that the amount deducted may be varied in accordance with a statutory scheme.[31]

De Voil Indirect Tax Service V3.461, 464, 465.

1. For the de minimis rule, see infra, § **66.14**.
2. As defined in SI 1995/2518, reg 101(7) as inserted by SI 2009/820.
3. VAT Regulations, SI 1995/2518, reg 101(2), (4), (5) as inserted or amended by SI 1996/1250, SI 2005/763, SI 2009/820.
4. For "use", see *Wigan Metropolitan Development Co (Investment) Ltd v Customs and Excise Comrs* (1990) VAT decision 4993 (repair of property prior to re-letting); *Imperial War Museum v Customs and Excise Comrs* [1992] VATTR 346 at 354 (overheads); *Kwik-Fit (GB) Ltd v Customs and Excise Comrs* [1998] STC 159 at 169, Ct of Sess (intra-group supplies). For the relevance of intention, see *BUPA Hospitals Ltd v Customs and Excise Comrs* (2002) VAT decision 17588 (intention to purchase and supply prepaid goods only if the legislation changed so that the onward supplies would be exempt from tax).
5. SI 1995/2518, reg 101(2)(*b*) and (7) as inserted by SI 2009/820.
6. For recent examples, see *Abbey National plc v Customs and Excise Comrs (case C-408/98)* [2001] STC 297, ECJ, *Finanzamt Offenbach am Main-Land v Faxworld Vorgründungsgesellschaft Peter Hünninghausen und Wolfgang Klein GbR (case C-137/02)* [2004] ECR I–5547, [2005] STC 1192, ECJ (business or part of business transferred as going concern); *Midland Bank plc v Customs and Excise Comrs (case C-98/98)* [2000] STC 501, ECJ (expenditure arising as a consequence of making the taxable supplies); *Investrand BV v Staatssecretaris van Financiën (case C-435/05)* [2007] ECR I–1315, [2008] STC 518, ECJ (costs of arbitration proceedings relating to sale of share predating commencement of the business); *Royal and Sun Alliance Insurance Group plc v Customs and Excise Comrs* [2003] STC 832, HL (sub-letting of empty property); *RAP Group plc v Customs and Excise Comrs* [2000] STC 980 (acquisition of subsidiary and issue of shares); *Southampton Leisure Holdings plc v Customs and Excise Comrs* (2002) VAT decision 17716 and Business Brief (Issue 23/2003), 20 August 2002 (exchange of shares); *Customs and Excise Comrs v Southern Primary Housing Association* [2004] STC 209, CA (separate contracts for the sale of land and construction of buildings); *Dial-a-Phone Ltd v Customs and Excise Comrs* [2004] STC 987, CA (advertising and marketing costs); *J P Morgan Trading and Finance v Customs and Excise Comrs* [1998] V & DR 161 (goods and services used to make both intra-group supplies and taxable supplies).
7. *BLP Group plc v Customs and Excise Comrs (case C-4/94)* [1995] STC 424, ECJ.
8. *Midland Bank plc v Customs and Excise Comrs (case C-98/98)* [2000] STC 501, ECJ.
9. *Dial-a-Phone Ltd v Customs and Excise Comrs* [2004] EWCA Civ 603, [2004] STC 987 at paras 28, 71, 73, 74.
10. The description is specified in VAT (Input Tax) (Specified Supplies) Order, SI 199/3121, art 3.
11. For supplies made outside the UK, see *Customs and Excise Comrs v Liverpool Institute for Performing Arts* [1999] STC 424, CA affd; [2001] STC 891, HL. For examples of non-business activities, *Customs and Excise Comrs v Apple and Pear Development Council* [1986] STC 192, HL, *Neuvale Ltd v Customs and Excise Comrs* [1989] STC 395, CA; *Whitechapel Art Gallery v Customs and Excise Comrs* [1986] STC 156.
12. For the proportion attributable to business use: see *Securenta Göttinger Immobilienanlagen und Vermögensmanagement AG v Finanzamt Göttingen* [2008]

[66.08] Tax credits, repayments and refunds

SWTI 939, ECJ.
[13] See Notice No 706 (December 2006), para 33.4. No method is prescribed, but an example of an apportionment method is set out in Notice No 706 (December 2006) para 33.5.
[14] The descriptions are specified in VATA 1994, Sch 9, Group 5, Item 1 (money, securities for money or notes or orders for the payment of money) or 6 (securities and secondary securities).
[15] SI 1995/2518, reg 101(8)(a) as inserted by SI 2009/820.
[16] SI 1995/2518, reg 101(8)(a) as inserted by SI 2009/820.
[17] SI 1995/2518, reg 101(9)(c) as inserted by SI 2009/820.
[18] *Mayflower Theatre Trust Ltd v Revenue and Customs Comrs* [2006] EWCA Civ 116, [2007] STC 880, CA at para 26.
[19] For recent examples, see *Dial-a-Phone Ltd v Customs and Excise Comrs* [2004] STC 987, CA (advertising and marketing costs); *Mayflower Theatre Trust Ltd v R & C Comrs* [2006] EWCA Civ 116, [2007] STC 880, CA (theatre production costs).
[20] For recent examples, see *Abbey National plc v Customs and Excise Comrs (case C-408/98)* [2001] STC 297, ECJ (costs of transferring all or part of a business as a going concern); *Kretztechnik AG v Finanzamt Linz(case C-465/03)* [2005] ECR I–4357, [2005] STC 1118, ECJ (costs relating to an issue of shares).
[21] SI 1995/2518, reg 101(2)(d)–(g) as amended or inserted by SI 2009/820.
[22] SI 1995/2518, reg 101(2)(f) as inserted by SI 2009/820.
[23] For supplies disregarded in calculating taxable supplies and total supplies, see VATA 1994, ss 8(3), 44(6); SI 1995/2518, reg 101(3), (6) as inserted and amended by SI 2007/768, SI 2009/820. In relation to capital goods, see *Nordania Finas A/S and another v Skatteministeriet* (case C-98/07) [2008] SWTI 433, ECJ (vehicles acquired for hire and sale at the end of the hire period). For incidental financial transactions, see *Empresa de Desenvolvimento Mineiro SA v Fazenda Pública (case C-77/01)* [2004] ECR I–4295, [2005] STC 65, ECJ. *In relation to specific situations, see Customs and Excise Comrs v Liverpool Institute for Performing Arts* [2001] STC 891, HL (treatment of supplies made outside the UK); *Sofitam SA v Ministre Chargé du Budget (case C-333/91)* [1997] STC 226, ECJ (dividends received by holding company); *António Jorge Lda v Fazenda Pública (case C-536/03)* [2005] ECR I–4463, [2005] SWTI 1017, ECJ (work in progress).
[24] SI 1995/2518, reg 101(5).
[25] SI 1995/2518, reg 101(2)(e) as inserted by SI 2009/820.
[26] *Mayflower Theatre Trust Ltd v Revenue and Customs Comrs* [2006] EWCA Civ 116, [2007] STC 880, CA at para 26.
[27] For recent examples, see *Dial-a-Phone Ltd v Customs and Excise Comrs* [2004] STC 987, CA (advertising and marketing costs); *Mayflower Theatre Trust Ltd v R & C Comrs* [2006] EWCA Civ 116, [2007] STC 880, CA (theatre production costs).
[28] For recent examples, see *Abbey National plc v Customs and Excise Comrs (case C-408/98)* [2001] STC 297, ECJ (costs of transferring all or part of a business as a going concern); *Kretztechnik AG v Finanzamt Linz(case C-465/03)* [2005] ECR I–4357, [2005] STC 1118, ECJ (costs relating to an issue of shares).
[29] VAT Regulations, SI 1995/2518, reg 101(1) as amended by SI 2004/3140, SI 2009/820.
[30] *Intercommunale voor Zeewaterontzilting (in liquidation) v Belgium (case C-110/94)* [1996] STC 569, ECJ (intended economic activity did not come to

fruition); *Belgium v Ghent Coal Terminal NV (case C-37/95)* [1998] STC 260, ECJ (intended use prevented by circumstances beyond the trader's control).
31 *Belgium v Ghent Coal Terminal NV (case C-37/95)* [1998] STC 260, ECJ. For statutory schemes, see infra, § **66.23**.

Special method

[66.09] The Commissioners may allow,[1] or direct,[2] a trader to use a method other than the standard method.[3] Such a method is referred to as a "special method". An approval or direction is given in writing.[4] The relevant document has effect only if specifies that it is an approval or direction[5] and sets out the terms of the method clearly and unambiguously.[6] These terms may be agreed centrally between the Commissioners and a trade association,[7] or individually between the Commissioners and a trader. The terms of the method may incorporate an attribution of input tax that would otherwise have to be made separately under the method described in infra, §§ **66.10** and **66.11**.[8] The manner in which a percentage recovery rate is to be rounded may be specified. This may lawfully diverge from the system of rounding specified for the purposes of the standard method.[9] The value of certain supplies is disregarded in calculating the proportion of input tax attributable to taxable supplies. This overrides any contrary provision of the document setting out the terms of the method.[9]

A special method may fail to prescribe how all or part of the input tax is to be attributed (eg because the nature of the business has changed since the method was approved or directed) and may not fall to be attributed under the methods described in infra, §§ **66.10** and **66.11**. If so, the input tax (or the part of the input tax) concerned is attributed to taxable supplies by reference to the extent that the goods or services are used (or to be used) in making taxable supplies. This use (or proposed use) is expressed as a proportion of the whole use.[10] Thus, if the use (or proposed use) in making taxable supplies is (say) 15% of the whole use, 15% of the input tax is allowable.

A trader must continue to use a special method until the Commissioners allow or direct otherwise.[11] The consequence of the Commissioners so allowing or directing is that the trader commences to use either the standard method or a new special method. The terms of the new special method may be agreed by the parties or imposed by the Commissioners.

The Commissioners have discretion whether or not to terminate the use of a special method. However, their discretion must be exercised in a manner that secures, or better secures, a fair and reasonable attribution of input tax. Thus, in the absence of an alternative special method to replace the existing one, the Commissioners should compare the results of the existing method and the standard method before making a direction so as to avoid replacing an unsatisfactory method with one that is even less satisfactory.[12]

The reasons for changing the terms of the method may be various. The Commissioners, for example, may consider that the existing method overstates the trader's entitlement to input tax. The trader, on the other hand, may consider the reverse, or may merely find that the existing method is cumbersome to operate. Whatever the reason, practical experience suggests that a lengthy

[66.09] Tax credits, repayments and refunds

period may elapse before there is a meeting of minds regarding the terms of the new method. In the meantime, input tax continues to be calculated in accordance with the existing method to the dissatisfaction of either party. The Commissioners can wholly or partly alleviate the adverse consequences for a trader by backdating an approval. However, they cannot backdate a direction.

This situation has long been unsatisfactory. It has now been remedied in those cases where a special method does not fairly and reasonably reflect the extent to which goods or services are used by a trader to make taxable supplies. Either party may now serve a notice to this effect on the other setting out their reasons.[13] The consequence of a notice is that the trader is required to calculate deductible input tax twice—once according to his existing method (£x) and then according to the extent to which he uses (or intends to use) goods or services to make taxable supplies (£y). He calculates the difference between the two (£x − £y = £z). He deducts £x and makes a tax adjustment in respect of £z. He does this in respect of:

(1) The next prescribed accounting period commencing on or after the date of the notice (or any later date specified therein).
(2) The longer period (if any) that straddles the relevant date in point (1). He does so in relation to the period commencing on this date and ending on the last day of the longer period.
(3) Every subsequent prescribed accounting period or longer period unless or until the Commissioners approve or direct otherwise.[14]

A trader can appeal against: (a) a direction requiring him to use a special method, or (b) (if using a special method) a direction requiring him to use the standard method or a new special method.[15]

De Voil Indirect Tax Service V3.462.

---

[1] When requesting approval, a trader must make a declaration that, to the best of his knowledge and belief, the method fairly and reasonably represents the extent to which goods or services are used (or to be used) by him in making taxable supplies and that he has taken reasonable steps to ensure that he is in possession of all the relevant information. The declaration must be made in writing and signed: VAT Regulations, SI 1995/2518, reg 102(9), (10) as inserted by SI 2007/768. For the consequences of making an incorrect declaration, see SI 1995/2518, reg 102(11)–(17) as inserted by SI 2007/768.

[2] A direction takes effect from the date on which it is given or a later specified date: SI 1995/2518, reg 102(4).

[3] SI 1995/2518, reg 102(1) as amended by SI 2004/3140. The method may incorporate a method for apportioning input tax between business and non-business use: *Labour Party v Customs and Excise Comrs* (2001) VAT decision 17034. For retrospective approval, see *Barrett (provisional liquidator for Rafidain Bank) v Customs and Excise Comrs* (1993) VAT decision 11016.

[4] SI 1995/2518, reg 102(1A)(a) as inserted by SI 2007/768.

[5] SI 1995/2518, reg 102(5) as inserted by SI 2005/762.

[6] *Kwik-Fit (GB) Ltd v Customs and Excise Comrs* [1998] STC 159, CA.

[7] For agreements with trade bodies, see Notice No 700/57.

[8] SI 1995/2518, reg 102(1A)(*b*) as inserted by SI 2007/768. For Class 2, see infra, § **66.10**.
[9] *Royal Bank of Scotland plc v HMRC* (case C-488/07) [2008] ECR I-0000, [2009] STC 461, ECJ. For rounding for the purposes of the standard method, see supra, § **66.08** ("Method 2").
[9] SI 1995/2518, reg 102(2) as amended by SI 2007/768, SI 2009/820.
[10] SI 1995/2518, reg 102(6)–(8) as inserted by SI 2005/762.
[11] SI 1995/2518, reg 102(3). A direction takes effect from the date on which it is made or a later specified date: SI 1995/2518, reg 102(4).
[12] *Banbury Visionplus Ltd v Revenue and Customs Comrs* [2006] EWHC 1024 (Ch), [2006] STC 1568; *MBNA Europe Bank Ltd v Revenue and Customs Comrs* [2006] EWHC 2326 (Ch), [2006] STC 2089.
[13] For the circumstances in which the Commissioners expect to serve a notice, see Business Brief (Issue 27/03), 10 December 2003.
[14] SI 1995/2518, regs 102A–102C as inserted and amended by SI 2003/3220, SI 2007/768.
[15] VATA 1994, s 83(*e*). For the tribunal's jurisdiction on appeal, see *Banbury Visionplus Ltd v Revenue and Customs Comrs* [2006] EWHC 1024 (Ch), [2006] STC 1568; *St Helen's School Northwood Ltd v Revenue and Customs Comrs* [2006] EWHC 3306 (Ch), [2007] STC 633.

Overseas supplies which would be taxable if made in the UK

[66.10] Input tax is allowable, so that a taxable person is entitled to credit in respect of it if the goods or services are used or to be used in making supplies outside the UK which, if made in the UK, would be taxable supplies. All of the input tax is allowable if the goods or services are wholly used or to be used. A proportion of the input tax is allowable in other cases. The allowable proportion is the use made (or to be made) of the goods or services expressed as a percentage of the whole use made of them.[1]

The foregoing attribution of input tax is subsumed in the standard method[2] and may be subsumed in the special method used by an individual trader.[3] It follows that this provision supplements special methods which do not make provision for attribution in this manner.

De Voil Indirect Tax Service V3.464.

[1] VAT Regulations, SI 1995/2518, reg 103(*a*) as renumbered by SI 2004/3140.
[2] SI 1995/2518, reg 101(7) as inserted by SI 2009/820.
[3] SI 1995/2518, regs 102(1A)(*b*), 103 as inserted and amended by SI 1999/3114, SI 2004/3140, SI 2007/768, SI 2009/820.

Insurance and financial services

[66.11] Input tax is allowable, so that a taxable person is entitled to credit in respect of it if the goods or services are used or to be used in making any of the following insurance and financial services:[1]

(1) Services supplied to a person who belongs in another EU member state.
(2) Services directly linked to the export of goods to a third country.

[66.11] Tax credits, repayments and refunds

(3) Intermediary services[2] in relation to a transaction within heads 1 or 2.

It is a condition that the supply is either exempt from tax or would have been so exempt if made in the UK.[3]

All of the input tax is allowable if the goods or services are wholly used or to be used in making the foregoing supplies. A proportion of the input tax is allowable in other cases. The allowable proportion is the use made (or to be made) of the goods or services expressed as a percentage of the whole use made of them.[4]

The foregoing attribution of input tax is subsumed in the standard method[5] and may be subsumed in the special method used by an individual trader.[6] It follows that this provision supplements special methods which do not make provision for attribution in this manner.

De Voil Indirect Tax Service V3.464.

---

[1] VAT Regulations, SI 1995/2518, reg 103(b) as amended or renumbered by SI 1999/3114, SI 2004/3140; VAT (Input Tax) (Specified Supplies) Order, SI 1999/3121, art 3.
[2] ie services within VATA 1994, Sch 9, Group 2, Item 4 (insurance) or Group 5, Item 5 (financial services).
[3] VAT (Input Tax) (Specified Supplies) Order, SI 1999/3121, art 3. The exemption must arise under VATA 1994, Sch 9, Group 2 (insurance) or Group 5, Items 1–6 and 8 (financial services).
[4] SI 1995/2518, reg 103 as amended or renumbered by SI 1999/3114, SI 2004/3114.
[5] SI 1995/2518, reg 101(7) as inserted by SI 2009/820.
[6] SI 1995/2518, regs 102(1A)(b), 103 as inserted and amended by SI 1999/3114, SI 2004/3140, SI 2007/768, SI 2009/820.

Investment gold

[66.12] Input tax incurred by a taxable person in any prescribed accounting period is allowable[1] if it arises in either of the following circumstances:[2]

(1) The goods or services fall within any of the following descriptions and were purchased, acquired or imported by the taxable person in order to make supplies of investment gold:[3]
   (a) investment gold purchased by him under a supply chargeable to tax at the standard rate;[4]
   (b) investment gold acquired by him;
   (c) gold (other than investment gold) purchased, acquired or imported by him for transformation into investment gold; and
   (d) services (comprising a change of form, weight or purity of gold) purchased by him.
(2) (If the taxable person produces investment gold or transforms gold investment gold) goods or services purchased, acquired or imported by him if the goods or services are linked to the production or transformation of gold into investment gold.

De Voil Indirect Tax Service V3.465A.

[1] ie because it is attributable to supplies within VATA 1994, s 26(2)(c); VAT (Input Tax) (Specified Supplies) Order, SI 1999/3121, art 4; VAT Regulations, SI 1995/2518, reg 103A(1) as inserted by SI 1999/4114.
[2] VAT Regulations, SI 1995/2518, reg 103A(2), (3) as inserted by SI 1999/4114. For apportionments, see SI 1995/2518, reg 103A(4)–(6).
[3] ie supplies of a description within VATA 1994, Sch 9, Group 15, Items 1 or 2. For supplies within this description, see infra, § **68.31**.
[4] ie because the supplier has exercised the option to tax or because one of the parties to the transaction was a member of the London Bullion Market Association and the other was not.

Professional services

[66.13] A taxable person may incur input tax during a prescribed accounting period on certain services[1] and related goods in circumstances where the services and related goods are used (or to be used) to make both:

(1)   A relevant supply[2] incidental to one or more of his business activities.
(2)   One or more other supplies.

Input tax is attributed to taxable supplies[3] by reference to the extent to which the services or related goods are used (or to be used) in making the incidental relevant supply expressed as a proportion of the whole use or intended use.[4]

This method overrides the terms of any special method which the taxable person is required or allowed to use.[5]

De Voil Indirect Tax Service V3.464.

[1] The services concerned are listed in VAT Regulations, SI 1995/2518, reg 103B(4) as inserted by SI 2004/3140.
[2] ie a supply of a description within VATA 1994, Sch 9, Group 5, Items 1 or 6 made in the UK or in another EU member state: SI 1995/2518, reg 103B(3)(a) as inserted by SI 2004/3140. For the supplies concerned, see infra, § **68.16**.
[3] As defined in SI 1995/2518, reg 103B(3)(b) as inserted by SI 2004/3140.
[4] SI 1995/2518, reg 103B(2) as inserted by SI 2004/3140.
[5] SI 1995/2518, reg 103B(2) as inserted by SI 2004/3140, SI 2009/820.

De minimis provisions

Prescribed accounting periods

[66.14] Input tax for a prescribed accounting period is deductible, so that a taxable person is entitled to credit in respect of it, if the following conditions are met:[1]

(1)   The prescribed accounting period forms part of a longer period.
(2)   The goods or services are used or to be used by the taxable person in making exempt supplies or supplies that would have been exempt supplies if they had been made in the UK (so that the input tax is not allowable under the methods described in supra §§ **66.08–66.10**).

[66.14] Tax credits, repayments and refunds

(3) The input tax is not allowable under Classes 3, 4 or 5.
(4) The input tax is less than both £625 per month on average and 50% of total input tax for the period.

Input tax for a prescribed accounting period is deductible, so that a taxable person is entitled to credit in respect of it, if the following conditions are met:[2]

(1) The prescribed accounting period does not form part of a longer period.
(2) The taxable person has made a provisional attribution of input tax under the standard method (so that an adjustment may arise under the provisions described in infra, § **66.25**).
(3) The goods or services are used or to be used in making exempt supplies or supplies that would have been exempt supplies if they had been made in the UK (so that the input tax is not allowable under Classes 1 or 2).
(4) The input tax is not allowable under the methods described in supra, §**66.11**.
(5) The aggregate of input tax for the period and the amount of the adjustment (if any) is less than both £625 per month on average and 50% of total input tax incurred for the period.

De Voil Indirect Tax Service V3.465.

[1] VAT Regulations, SI 1995/2518, reg 106(1), (3) as substituted or amended by SI 2002/1074, SI 2004/3140.
[2] SI 1995/2518, reg 106A(1), (2) as inserted or amended by SI 2002/1074, SI 2004/3140. For accounting, see SI 1995/2518, reg 106A(3), (5) as inserted by SI 2002/1074. For the clawback of any relief claimed under SI 1995/2518, reg 106(1), (3) as substituted or amended by SI 2002/1074, SI 2002/1074, see reg 106A(4), (5) as inserted by SI 2002/1074.

Longer periods

[66.15] Input tax for a longer period is deductible, so that a taxable person is entitled to credit in respect of it, if the following conditions are met:[1]

(1) The taxable person has used a special method to calculate the input tax to which he is provisionally entitled for the prescribed accounting periods included in the longer period.
(2) The goods or services are used or to be used in making exempt supplies or supplies that would have been exempt supplies if they had been made in the UK (so that the input tax was not allowable under the methods described in supra, §§ **66.08–66.10** when calculating the provisional entitlement to input tax credit for each prescribed accounting period).
(3) The input tax is not allowable under the method described in supra, §§ **66.11**.
(4) The input tax is less than both £625 per month on average and 50% of total input tax incurred for the period.

Input tax for a longer period is deductible, so that a taxable person is entitled to credit in respect of it, if the following conditions are met:[2]

(1) The taxable person has made an attribution of input tax under the standard method (so that an adjustment may arise under the provisions described in infra, § **66.25**).
(2) The goods or services are used or to be used in making exempt supplies or supplies that would have been exempt supplies if they had been made in the UK (so that the input tax was not allowable under Classes 1 or 2 when calculating the provisional entitlement to input tax credit for each prescribed accounting period).
(3) The input tax is not allowable under the method described in supra, § **66.11**.
(4) The aggregate of input tax and the amount of the adjustment (if any) is less than both £625 per month on average and 50% of total input tax incurred for the period.

De Voil Indirect Tax Service V3.465.

---

1 VAT Regulations, SI 1995/2518, reg 106(1), (3) as substituted by or amended by SI 2002/1074, SI 2004/3140.
2 SI 1995/2518, reg 106(1), (3) as substituted or amended by SI 2002/1074, SI 2004/3140.

Input tax excluded from credit

Introduction

[66.16] Input tax incurred in respect of the certain goods and services is not available for credit. This tax described as being "excluded from credit".[1] Input tax is wholly or partly excluded from credit if the relevant goods or services fall within one of the following descriptions:

(1) Leased motor cars;[2]
(2) Motor cars which are not leased;[3]
(3) Goods installed in buildings;[4]
(4) Business entertainment;[5]
(5) Works of art, antiques, collectors' items and secondhand goods;[6]

---

1 VATA 1994, s 25(7).
2 For leased motor cars, see infra, § **66.17**.
3 For motor cars which are not leased, see infra, § **66.18**.
4 For goods installed in buildings, see infra, § **66.19**.
5 For business entertainment, see infra, § **66.20**.
6 For works of art, antiques, collectors' items and second-hand goods, see infra, § **66.21**.

[66.17] Tax credits, repayments and refunds

Leased motor cars

[66.17] In principle, one half of the input tax on a hired motor car[1] is excluded from credit.[2] As an exception to this principle, no input tax is excluded from credit in any of the following circumstances:[3]

(1) The motor car is a qualifying motor car,[4] or a motor car treated as a qualifying motor car by virtue of an election made by a taxable person,[5] which is either:[6]
 (a) intended to be used exclusively for the purposes of the trader's business;[7] or
 (b) intended to be used primarily for hire with the services of a driver, for self-drive hire[8] or for giving driving instruction.
(2) The motor car is not a qualifying motor car. However, the 50% deduction applies if the car is not a qualifying car solely by reason of the fact that the trader re-hired the car to another person before 1 August 1995.
(3) The motor car has been hired in the following circumstances:
 (a) the motor car is unused;
 (b) the trader's business is predominantly concerned with hiring motor vehicles to handicapped persons under a zero-rated supply;[9] and
 (c) the motor car is hired from a taxable person whose only taxable supplies comprise hiring motor cars to such traders.

De Voil Indirect Tax Service V3.443.

---

[1] For "motor car", see VAT (Input Tax) Order, SI 1992/3222, art 2 as amended by SI 1999/2930, SI 2009/217.
[2] SI 1992/3222, art 7(1), (2H) as amended and inserted by SI 1995/281 and SI 1995/1666.
[3] SI 1992/3222, art 7(2)(*a*), (*b*), (*d*) as inserted by SI 1995/1666.
[4] As defined in SI 1992/3222, art 7(2A)(*a*), (2C) as inserted by SI 1995/1666. For motor cars hired before 1 August 1995, see *Customs and Excise Comrs v BRS Automotive Ltd* [1998] STC 1210, CA (lessee) and Business Brief (Issue 21/95), 8 October 1995 (lessor).
[5] For the making of elections, see SI 1992/3222, art 7(2A)(*b*), (2B), (2D) as inserted by SI 1995/1666.
[6] SI 1992/3222, art 7(2E), (2F) as inserted by SI 1995/1666.
[7] As defined in SI 1992/3222, art 7(2G) as inserted by SI 1995/1666. For lettings on hire, see *Tamburello Ltd v Customs and Excise Comrs* [1996] V & DR 268. For cars made available for private use, see *Customs and Excise Comrs v Upton (t/a Fagomatic)* [2002] STC 640.
[8] As defined in SI 1992/3222, art 7(3)(*b*).
[9] ie under VATA 1994, Sch 8, Group 12, Item 14, as to which see infra, §§ **69.34–69.36**.

Input tax excluded from credit [66.18]

Motor cars which are not leased

[66.18] In principle, the whole of the input tax on a motor car[1] which is not hired is excluded from credit.[2] As an exception to this principle, no input tax is excluded from credit in any of the following circumstances:[3]

(1) The motor car is a qualifying motor car,[4] or a motor car treated as a qualifying motor car by virtue of an election made by a taxable person,[5] which is either:[6]
   (a) intended to be used exclusively[7] for the purposes of the trader's business; or
   (b) intended to be used primarily for hire with the services of a driver, for self-drive hire[8] or for giving driving instruction.
(2) The motor car forms part of the trading stock of a motor manufacturer or motor dealer.[9]
(3) The motor car has been purchased, acquired or imported in the following circumstances:
   (a) the motor car is unused; and
   (b) the trader's only taxable supplies comprise hiring motor cars to taxable persons whose business is predominantly concerned with hiring motor vehicles to handicapped persons under a zero-rated supply.[10]

De Voil Indirect Tax Service V3.443.

---

[1] For "motor car", see supra, § 65.32, note 1. For vehicles equipped for carrying wheelchair passengers treated as if they were suitable for carrying more than 12 persons, see Notice No 48 (July 2009) para 3.12. For delivery charges, see *Customs and Excise Comrs v British Telecommunications plc* [1999] STC 758, HL. For optional extras, contrast *Turmeau v Customs and Excise Comrs* (1981) VAT decision 1135 and *Broadhead Peel & Co v Customs and Excise Comrs* [1984] VATTR 195.

[2] SI 1992/3222, art 7(1) as amended and inserted by SI 1995/281 and SI 1995/1666. For motor cars purchased under the margin scheme, see infra, § 66.21.

[3] SI 1992/3222, art 7(2)(a), (aa), (c) as inserted by SI 1995/1666, SI 1999/2930.

[4] As defined in SI 1992/3222, art 7(2A)(a), (2C) as inserted by SI 1995/1666. For motor cars hired before 1 August 1995, see *Customs and Excise Comrs v BRS Automotive Ltd* [1998] STC 1210, CA (lessee) and Business Brief (Issue 21/95), 8 October 1995 (lessor).

[5] For the making of elections, see SI 1992/3222, art 7(2A)(b), (2B), (2D) as inserted by SI 1995/1666.

[6] SI 1992/3222, art 7(2E), (2F) as inserted by SI 1995/1666.

[7] For exclusive business use in relation to cars hired at an undervalue, see SI 1992/3222, art 7(2G)(a) as inserted by SI 1995/1666; *Tamburello Ltd v Customs and Excise Comrs* [1996] V & DR 268. For exclusive business use in relation to sole traders and partnerships, see SI 1992/3222, art 7(2G)(b) as so inserted; *Customs and Excise Comrs v Upton (t/a Fagomatic)* [2002] STC 640, CA; *Customs and Excise Comrs v Skellett (t/a Vidcom Computer Services)* [2004] STC 201; *Customs and Excise Comrs v Robbins* [2004] EWHC 3573 (Ch), [2005] STC 1103; *Shaw v Revenue and Customs Comrs* [2007] EWHC 3699 (Ch), [2007] STC 1525. In the *Shaw* case (at paras [33], [34]), Lindsay J drew attention to "a sort of Catch-22

[66.18] Tax credits, repayments and refunds

position" which makes it "difficult to see how a sole trader could ever pass the [statutory] test": For the steps available to companies in order to demonstrate exclusive business use of company cars, contrast *Thompson v Customs and Excise Comrs* [2005] EWHC 342 (Ch), [2005] STC 1777 (cars made available for private use) and *Customs and Excise Comrs v Elm Milk Ltd* [2006] EWCA Civ 164, [2006] STC 792, CA (car not made available for private use).

[8] As defined in SI 1992/3222, art 7(3)(*b*).
[9] "Stock in trade", "motor manufacturer" and "motor dealer" are defined in SI 1992/3222, art 2 as amended by SI 1999/2930.
[10] ie under VATA 1994, Sch 8, Group 12, Item 14, as to which see infra, §§ 69.34–69.36.

Goods installed in buildings

[66.19] A taxable person constructing or refurbishing a building for the purpose of granting a major interest[1] in all or part of it, or its site, may incorporate goods in the building or its site. If so, VAT on the goods is excluded from credit unless they comprise building materials.[2]

De Voil Indirect Tax Service V3.444.

[1] As defined in VATA 1994, s 96(1). For the vires of this provision, cf *McCarthy & Stone plc v Customs and Excise Comrs* [1992] VATTR 198.
[2] VAT (Input Tax) Order, SI 1992/3222, art 6 as substituted by SI 1995/281. For "building materials", see SI 1992/3222, art 2 as so substituted.

Business entertainment

[66.20] In principle, VAT incurred on goods and services is excluded from credit if the purchaser uses the goods or services to provide entertainment[1] in connection with a business carried on by him.[2] Such entertainment is referred to as "business entertainment". Entertainment provided for non-business purposes is not business entertainment. VAT incurred in respect of it is not input tax[3] so the question of exclusion from credit does not arise.

The essence of business entertainment is that the recipient enjoys it free of charge.[4] Thus, VAT is not excluded from credit if entertainment or hospitality is provided in return for cash, goods or services under the terms of a contract between the parties[5] or in accordance with the terms of a reciprocal arrangement which is binding on the parties.[6]

It is necessary to identify who receives the entertainment where three parties are involved. For example, X may organise an exhibition, letting stands to exhibitors (Y) and admitting members of the public (Z) to the venue without charge. X supplies business entertainment as he provides free refreshments to Z and is accordingly not entitled to input tax deduction in respect of the food and drink he purchases.[7] However, if X supplies the food and drink to Y, who provides them free to Z, X makes a supply in the course of catering (so as to be entitled to input tax deduction) whereas Y provides business entertainment

Input tax excluded from credit [66.20]

to Z (so that Y is not entitled to deduct input tax in respect of the supply made to him by X).[8] Neither X nor Y appear to provide business entertainment if Z is admitted to the exhibition for a consideration.[9]

In principle, VAT is not excluded from credit if the entertainment is provided for employees,[10] the directors or managers of a body corporate,[11] partners (if their presence is incidental to, and part of, the entertainment of employees),[12] or amateur sports persons or committee members (if the entertainment is provided by a representative sporting body).[13] However, VAT is excluded from credit in respect of entertainment provided for employees, directors or managers if the entertainment is incidental to its provision for others.[14]

Input tax is apportioned if it relates only partly to a business entertainment purpose. Input tax is deducted to the extent that it relates to a business purpose other than business entertainment.[15]

De Voil Indirect Tax Service V3.446.

---

[1] Entertainment includes hospitality of any kind: VAT (Input Tax) Order, SI 1992/3222, art 5(3). For examples, see *Customs and Excise Comrs v Shaklee International* [1981] STC 776, CA (food and accommodation); *British Car Auctions v Customs and Excise Comrs* [1978] VATTR 56 (racehorses); *William Matthew Mechanical Services Ltd v Customs and Excise Comrs* [1982] VATTR 63 (theatre). Contrast *WR Ltd v Customs and Excise Comrs* (1992) VAT decision 6968.

[2] SI 1992/3122, art 5(1), (3) as amended by SI 1995/281.

[3] VATA 1994, s 24(1). A determination by the Commissioners under VATA 1994, s 84(4) is relevant to this class of entertainment; see *Ernst & Young v Customs and Excise Comrs* [1997] V & DR 183. For non-business entertainment of partners and employees, see *Ernst & Young v Customs and Excise Comrs* [1997] V & DR 183.

[4] *Celtic Football and Athletic Co Ltd v Customs and Excise Comrs* [1983] STC 470; *BMW (GB) Ltd v Customs and Excise Comrs* [1997] STC 824.

[5] *Customs and Excise Comrs v Kilroy Television Co Ltd* [1997] STC 901 (contributors taking part in a television programme provided with transport and buffet). For examples, see *DPA (Market Research) Ltd v Customs and Excise Comrs* (1997) VAT decision 14751 (product trial); *Ernst & Young v Customs and Excise Comrs* [1997] V & DR 183 (staff Christmas party for which a charge was made).

[6] *Celtic Football and Athletic Co Ltd v Customs and Excise Comrs* [1983] STC 470. See also *Football Association Ltd v Customs and Excise Comrs* [1985] VATTR 106; *Ibstock Building Products Ltd v Customs and Excise Comrs* [1987] VATTR 1; *Northern Lawn Tennis Club v Customs and Excise Comrs* [1989] VATTR 1.

[7] For examples of situations where X provides hospitality to Z, see *BMW (GB) Ltd v Customs and Excise Comrs* [1997] STC 824; *Evensis Ltd v Customs and Excise Comrs* (2001) VAT decision 17218.

[8] For an example of the situation where X makes a supply of catering and Y provides hospitality, see *Webster Communications International Ltd v Customs and Excise Comrs* [1997] V & DR 173.

[9] For an example of the situation where Z makes a payment, see *Board of Trade, City of Chicago v Customs and Excise Comrs* (1992) VAT decision 9114.

[10] SI 1992/3222, art 5(3)(a). This does not extend to: (a) self-employed persons: *Customs and Excise Comrs v Shaklee International* [1981] STC 776, CA; or (b)

guests of employees who are admitted free or for a nominal charge: *KPMG (a firm) v Customs and Excise Comrs* [1997] V & DR 192 (free admission); *Ernst & Young v Customs and Excise Comrs* [1997] V & DR 183 (charge less than cost price).

[11] SI 1992/3222, art 5(3)(b).
[12] *Ernst & Young v Customs and Excise Comrs* [1997] V & DR 183.
[13] Notice No 48 (July 2009), para 3.10.
[14] SI 1992/3222, art 5(3).
[15] *Thorn EMI plc v Customs and Excise Comrs* [1995] STC 674, CA.

Works of art, antiques, collectors' items and second-hand goods

[66.21] Input tax is excluded from credit if it arises in respect of:

(1) Works of art, antiques, collectors' items or second-hand goods (including motor cars)[1] purchased under a supply on which VAT was charged by reference to the profit margin.[2]

(2) A work of art, antique or collector's item imported by the trader himself if his onward supply is to be charged to VAT by reference to the profit margin.[3]

(3) A work of art purchased or acquired from its creator, or his successor in title, if the trader's onward supply is to be charged to VAT by reference to the profit margin.[4]

[1] For goods within these descriptions, see VAT (Input Tax) Order, SI 1992/3222, art 2 as amended by SI 1995/1267, SI 1999/2930 and SI 1999/3118.
[2] SI 1992/3222, art 4(1), (2), (3)(a).
[3] SI 1992/3222, art 4(1), (2), (3)(b), (4) as inserted by SI 1995/1267; VAT (Special Provisions) Order, SI 1995/1268, art 12(8), (9).
[4] SI 1992/3222, art 4(1), (2), (3)(c), (4) as inserted by SI 1995/1267; VAT (Special Provisions) Order, SI 1995/1268, art 12(8), (9).

Deduction and variation of input tax credit

Claim for deduction of input tax credit

[66.22] A taxable person is entitled to deduct so much of his input tax as is allowable.[1] This entitlement cannot be withdrawn merely because the relevant purchase forms part of a chain of transactions vitiated by VAT fraud, at some earlier or later stage, of which the purchaser has no knowledge and no means of knowledge.[2] However, no right to deduct arises in respect of the relevant purchase if the transactions giving rise to that right constitute an abusive practice.[3]

A deduction must be claimed. In principle, two conditions must be met.[4] First, deduction must be claimed for the prescribed accounting period in which the tax became chargeable.[5] Secondly, the taxable person must hold specified documents at the time when he makes a claim.[6] However, these conditions are subject to a number of exceptions:

(1) A taxable person must necessarily hold over all or part of his claim to a later period if one or more documents are unavailable at that time. Deduction is claimed in the period in which he receives the documents.[7]
(2) A trader using the cash accounting scheme[8] normally claims deduction by reference to the time when he makes a payment in respect of the goods or services concerned.[9]
(3) The Commissioners may direct that all or part of a trader's claim is made in a different period.[10]
(4) One or more of the documents required to be held by a trader may be missing[11] or deficient in some respect.[12] The Commissioners may make a direction requiring a trader to hold such alternative evidence of the charge to VAT as they may specify.[13]
(5) The Commissioners may allow an estimate to be used. An adjustment is made in the next period where this is done.[14]

The input tax allowable to a taxable person must be recorded in the VAT allowable portion of his VAT Account for the prescribed accounting period concerned.[15]

---

[1] VATA 1994, s 25(2).
[2] *Optigen Ltd v Customs and Excise Comrs (joined cases C-354/03, C-355/03 and C-484/03)* [2006] ECR I–483, [2006] STC 419, ECJ.
[3] *Halifax plc and others v Customs and Excise Comrs (case C-255/02)* [2006] ECR I–1609, [2006] STC 919. For abusive practices, see supra, § **63.09**. For the recovery of input tax where an abusive practice is found to exist, see infra, § **66.33**.
[4] For the position under EU legislation, see *Reisdorf v Finanzamt Köln-West (Case C-85/95)* [1997] STC 180, ECJ; *Finanzamt Gummersbach v Bockemühl (Case C-90/02)* [2004] ECR I–3303, [2005] STC 934, ECJ.
[5] VAT Regulations, SI 1995/2518, reg 29(1) as amended by SI 2009/586.
[6] SI 1995/2518, reg 29(2). For the documents concerned, see SI 1995/2518, reg 29(2)(a)–(f). For import documents, see Notice No 702 (October 2006), Section 8.
[7] SI 1995/2518, reg 29(1) as amended by SI 2009/586. See *Terra Baubedarf-Handel GmbH v Finanzamt Osterholz-Scharmbeck (case C-152/02)* [2004] ECR I–5583, [2005] STC 525; *Local Authorities Mutual Investment Trust v Customs and Excise Comrs* [2003] EWHC 2766 (Ch), [2004] STC 246; Notice No 700 (April 2002), para 10.5.1. The Commissioners may allow or direct otherwise. In doing so, they must require the deduction to be made no later than the fourth anniversary of the due date for filing the return for the prescribed accounting period in which the taxable person was entitled to claim the deduction. This prescribed accounting period must end after 31 March 2006: SI 1995/2518, reg 29(1A), (1B) as inserted or amended by SI 1997/1086, SI 2009/586.
[8] For the cash accounting scheme, see supra, § **63.40**.
[9] SI 1998/2518, reg 65(2). The trader may make claims in a later period if the Commissioners so agree: ibid.
[10] SI 1995/2518, reg 29(1) as amended by SI 2009/586. The Commissioners may not allow or direct the deduction to be made later than the fourth anniversary of the due

[66.22] Tax credits, repayments and refunds

date for filing the return for the prescribed accounting period in which the taxable person was entitled to claim the deduction. This prescribed accounting period must end after 31 March 2006: SI 1995/2518, reg 29(1A), (1B) as inserted or amended by SI 1997/1086, SI 2009/586. For a direction made in respect of second-hand goods, works of art, antiques and collectors' items, see Information Sheet 11/95, para 4.

[11] For lost documents, see *Vaughan v Customs and Excise Comrs* [1996] V & DR 95.

[12] For VAT invoices showing an insufficient description of the goods or services supplied, see *Revenue and Customs Comrs v Dempster (trading as Boulevard)* [2008] EWHC 63 (Ch), [2008] STC 2079.

[13] SI 1995/2518, reg 29(2) (proviso) as amended by SI 2003/11. For business telephone calls, coin-operated machines and parking charges, see Notice No 700 (April 2002), para 19.7.5. For VAT shown on an invoice issued by an unregistered trader in respect of a supply that has taken place, see Notice No 48 (July 2009), para 3.9. For the manner in which the Commissioners intend to exercise their discretion to accept alternative evidence of the charge to VAT, see Input tax without a valid VAT invoice: Statement of Practice (HM Customs and Excise (March 2007)); cf *Kohanzad v Customs and Excise Comrs* [1994] STC 967.

[14] SI 1995/2518, reg 29(3).

[15] SI 1995/2518, reg 32(4)(a). For the VAT Account, see infra, § **67.02**.

Variation of input tax deductions

Circumstances giving rise to variation

[66.23] The input tax deducted (or not deducted) in a prescribed accounting period may be varied in accordance with a number of statutory schemes. In consequence, the input tax deducted may be increased, decreased or withdrawn and an entitlement may arise in respect of input tax not previously deducted. A variation arises in the following circumstances:

(1) A "longer period" expires.[1]
(2) The standard method does not produce a fair and reasonable attribution of input tax.[2]
(3) Goods or services intended for use in making one class of supply are used in making a different class of supply.[3]
(4) The taxable use of a "capital item" changes during the period of adjustment.[5]
(5) The option to tax has been exercised.[16]
(6) The Commissioners make a determination that goods or services are something in the nature of a luxury, amusement or entertainment.[7]
(7) The supplier claims bad debt relief in respect of unpaid amounts due to him.[8]
(8) The purchaser fails to pay all or part of the consideration for a supply made to him.[9]
(9) The consideration for a supply is varied.[10]
(10) The deduct arose from a transaction constituting an abusive practice.[14]
(11) The deduction arose from participation in a fraudulent chain of transactions.[15]

(12) The transfer, disposal or use of goods.[16]

De Voil Indirect Tax Service V3.401.

[1] See infra, § **66.24**.
[2] See infra, § **66.25**.
[3] See infra, § **66.26**.
[5] See infra, § **66.27**.
[16] See infra, § **66.28**.
[7] See infra, § **66.29**.
[8] See infra, § **66.30**.
[9] See infra, § **66.31**.
[10] See infra, § **66.32**.
[14] See infra, § **66.33**.
[15] See infra, § **66.34**.
[16] See infra, § **66.35**.

Longer periods

[66.24] A taxable person who incurs exempt input tax[1] during a tax year[2] or registration period[3] normally has a "longer period" applied to him.[4] A longer period is normally a period of 12 months ending on 31 March, 30 April or 31 May according prescribed accounting periods allocated to him.[5]

The recoverable proportion of relevant residual input tax may vary from one prescribed accounting period to another as a result of seasonal fluctuations, or an abnormal transaction, with the consequence that the provisional deduction made in a particular prescribed accounting period does not secure a fair and reasonable attribution of input tax. The risk of this outcome is reduced, but not entirely eliminated, by adjusting the deductions made in individual prescribed accounting periods by reference to a longer period.

The calculation proceeds as follows:

(1) Determine the amount of input tax attributable to taxable supplies for the longer period. In principle, the input tax attributable to taxable supplies is determined in accordance with the method used in the prescribed accounting period,[6] ie the standard method or a special method. However, the standard method is modified in the manner described in point (2).

(2) As regards the standard method, the method[7] used to calculate the proportion of relevant residual input tax attributed to taxable supplies is determined as follows:
    (a) the trader may have had an immediately preceding longer period. Here, the default method for provisionally attributing relevant residual input tax in a prescribed accounting period is Method 1, with an option to use Method 2:[8]
        (i) if the trader used Method 1, he must use Method 2 in the longer period;[9]
        (ii) if the trader opted to use Method 2,[10] he must use the same method in the longer period;[11]

[66.24] Tax credits, repayments and refunds

    (b)   the trader did not have an immediately preceding longer period. Here, the default method for provisionally attributing relevant residual input tax in a prescribed accounting period is Method 2, with an option to use Method 3:[12]

        (i)   if the trader used Method 2, he may use either Method 2 or Method 3 in the longer period;[13]

        (ii)   if the trader opted to use Method 3,[14] he must use the same method in the longer period.[15]

(3)   Test whether all input tax in the longer period is treated as being attributable to taxable supplies.[16]

(4)   Calculate the difference between:

    (a)   the amount of input tax attributable to taxable supplies for the longer period in accordance with points (1)–(3); and

    (b)   the amounts of input tax (if any) deducted in the trader's returns for the prescribed accounting periods falling within the longer period.

(5)   The amount calculated in point (4) represents an over-declaration or under-declaration of input tax. The amount concerned must be included in the trader's tax return.[17]

De Voil Indirect Tax Service V3.466.

---

[1] As defined in VAT Regulations, SI 1995/2518, reg 99(1)(a) as substituted and amended by SI 2002/1074, SI 2004/3140.

[2] As defined in SI 1995/2518, reg 99(1)(d) as amended by SI 2000/794.

[3] As defined in SI 1995/2518, reg 99(1)(e) as amended by SI 2000/794.

[4] SI 1995/2518, reg 99(4), (5). For the exception, see the proviso to SI 1995/2518, reg 99(4).

[5] SI 1995/2518, reg 99(1), (4). For the exceptions, see SI 1995/2518, reg 99(4)–(7).

[6] SI 1995/2518, reg 107(1)(a).

[7] For this purpose, a "method" is one of calculations prescribed by SI 1995/2518, regs 101(2)(f) ("Method 1"), 101(2)(d) ("Method 2") and 101(2)(e) ("Method 3"). For the scope and use of these methods, see infra, § **66.08**.

[8] Method 1 is the default method if the trader has an immediately preceding longer period: see SI 1995/2518, reg 101(2)(f).

[9] SI 1995/2518, reg 107(1)(a), (f).

[10] For the option to use Method 2, see SI 1995/2518, reg 101(2)(g).

[11] SI 1995/2518, reg 107(1)(a).

[12] Method 2 is the default method if the trader does not have an immediately preceding longer period: see SI 1995/2518, reg 101(2)(d).

[13] SI 1995/2518, reg 107(1)(a), (c).

[14] For the option to use Method 3, see SI 1995/2518, reg 101(2)(e).

[15] SI 1995/2518, reg 107(1)(a), (b).

[16] For the tests applied, see supra, § **66.15**.

[17] For the return used, see SI 1995/2518, reg 107(1)(g), (2), (3).

Retrospective recalculation under the standard method

[66.25] The partial exemption methods prescribed in regulations are required to secure a fair and reasonable attribution of input tax.[1] The standard method[2] does not necessarily meet this requirement. There are two reasons. First, as regards goods and services used (or to be used) in making both taxable and exempt supplies, a simple ratio of taxable turnover and total turnover does not necessarily reflect the degree of taxable use with any degree of accuracy. Secondly, the method takes no account of the transferee's circumstances if all or part of the business is to be transferred to another person.

These deficiencies give rise to avoidance opportunities. Although the Commissioners can direct a trader to use a special method,[3] this only applies to the future.[5] In consequence, it cannot affect earlier attributions of input tax with a consequent loss to the revenue. This situation is counteracted by a new adjustment having effect in relation to input tax incurred after 17 April 2002.[6]

A taxable person using the standard method must make the necessary calculations in order to determine whether an adjustment is necessary. He must do so at the end of a prescribed accounting period (if the period does not form part of a longer period)[7] or at the end of a longer period (if the de minimis provisions do not apply in that period).[8]

The calculation in each case proceeds on the following lines:[9]

(1) Determine the following amounts:
   (a) input tax wholly attributed taxable supplies for the period. Call this sum £a.
   (b) input tax partly attributable to both taxable supplies and exempt supplies for the period. Call this sum £b.
(2) Attribute £a and £b to taxable supplies in accordance with the standard method. Call the sum attributed £x. This is the input tax provisionally attributed to taxable supplies for the prescribed accounting period (in relation to a prescribed accounting period which does not fall within a longer period) or the aggregate amount of input tax provisionally so attributed in the prescribed accounting periods falling within the longer period (in relation to a longer period).
(3) Determine whether £x exceeds £25,000 per annum on average (in the case of a group undertaking)[10] or £50,000 per annum on average (in other cases). No adjustment is made if £x falls below the relevant threshold.
(4) Reattribute £a and £b according to the use made or to be made of the goods and services concerned by the taxable person or his successor.[14] Call this sum £y.
(5) Calculate the difference between £x (see head 2) and £y (see head 4). Call this sum £z.
(6) Determine whether £z exceeds either:
   (a) £50,000, or
   (b) both 50% of £b (see head 1) and £25,000.
(7) An adjustment is made if £z exceeds either or both of the thresholds in head 6.[15] No adjustment is made in other cases.

De Voil Indirect Tax Service V3.461, 465.

---

[1] VATA 1994, s 26(3).
[2] For the standard method, see supra, § **66.08**.

[66.25] Tax credits, repayments and refunds

[3] For special methods, see supra, § **66.09**.
[5] VAT Regulations, SI 1995/2518 reg 102(4).
[6] VAT (Amendment) Regulations, SI 2002/1074, reg 1.
[7] SI 1995/2518, reg 107A(1) as inserted by SI 2002/1074.
[8] SI 1995/2518, reg 107B(1) as inserted by SI 2002/1074.
[9] SI 1995/2518, regs 107A–107E as inserted by SI 2002/1074.
[10] As defined in SI 1995/2518, reg 107E(2) as inserted by SI 2002/1074.
[14] As defined in SI 1995/2518, reg 107D as inserted by SI 2002/1074.
[15] For the manner in which the adjustment is made, see SI 1995/2518, regs 107A(2), (3) and 107B(2)(*b*), (3) as inserted by SI 2002/1074.

Appropriation for different use

[66.26] A taxable person must make an adjustment if:[1]

(1) He has deducted input tax on the basis that he intended to use the goods or services wholly or partly in making taxable supplies.[2]
(2) He modifies his intention[3] so that all or part of the input tax deducted becomes attributable to exempt supplies.[5]
(3) The change takes place during the six-year period commencing on the first day of the prescribed accounting period in which the attribution was determined.

The trader must account for such proportion of the input tax deducted which has ceased to be attributable to taxable supplies.[6]

A trader is entitled to a repayment of tax in the reverse circumstances.[7] He must make a claim in such form and manner as the Commissioners may direct and give such particulars as they may direct.[8]

The amounts paid to or by a trader in the foregoing circumstances are adjusted where the goods or services concerned are for use in making overseas supplies.[9]

De Voil Indirect Tax Service V3.467.

[1] VAT Regulations, SI 1995/2518, reg 108(1), (3). See *Cooper & Chapman (Builders) Ltd v Customs and Excise Comrs* [1993] STC 1; *Customs and Excise Comrs v Briararch Ltd* [1992] STC 732.
[2] As defined in SI 1995/2518, reg 110(1)(b), (2)(b) as substituted or amended by SI 1999/3114, SI 2004/3140.
[3] For force majeure, see *Belgium v Ghent Coal Terminal NV (case C-37/95)* [1998] STC 260, ECJ.
[5] As defined in SI 1995/2518, reg 110(1)(a), (2)(a) as substituted by SI 1999/3114. See *Customs and Excise Comrs v Svenska International plc* [1999] STC 406, HL (intended taxable supply made after the parties became members of a VAT group); *Gulland Properties Ltd v Customs and Excise Comrs* (1996) VAT decision 13955 (intended exempt supply became taxable following a change in the legislation); *Tremerton Ltd v Customs and Excise Comrs* (1998) VAT decision 15590 (land sold before intended development carried out).
[6] SI 1995/2518, reg 108(2). For the entry made in the trader's VAT Account, see infra, § **67.02**.
[7] For an example, see *Community Housing Association Ltd v Customs and Excise Comrs* [2009] EWHC 455 (Ch), [2009] STC 1324 (assignment of benefits of

contracts relating to construction projects). For a case where no entitlement to a repayment arose, see *Royal and Sun Alliance Insurance Group plc v Customs and Excise Comrs* [2003] STC 832, HL (rent on empty property).
8   SI 1995/2518, reg 109. For claims, see Notice No 706 (March 2002), para 9.2.2.
9   For the restriction made, see SI 1995/2518, reg 110(4) as substituted or amended by SI 1999/3114, SI 2004/3140.

Capital items

[66.27] The proportion of "total input tax"[1] ultimately deducted in respect of a "capital item"[2] is determined by reference to a period of adjustment comprising five or ten "intervals".[3] The first interval normally ends on the last day of the registration period,[4] first tax year[5] or tax year[6] in which the trader purchases, imports or first uses the capital item.[7] Each subsequent interval normally corresponds with the trader's longer period[8] (if he has one) or his tax year (if he does not).[9] An adjustment is made in a subsequent interval if the taxable use (if any) for the prescribed accounting period in which the right to deduction arose[10] changes[11] in a subsequent interval.[12] This change, expressed as a percentage, is known as the "adjustment percentage".[13] The adjustment may give rise to an additional deduction of input tax or to a payment to the Commissioners.

The adjustment is calculated as follows:[14]

$$\text{Adjustment} = \frac{\text{Total input tax on the capital item}}{\text{Number of intervals}} \times \text{Adjustment percentage}$$

Special provisions apply if:[15] (a) the capital item is sold during the period of adjustment;[16] (b) the owner is deregistered during the period of adjustment; (c) the capital item is lost, stolen or destroyed during the period of adjustment; or (d) a capital item comprising a lease expires during a period of adjustment.

The amount of an adjustment is normally shown on the trader's tax return for the second prescribed accounting period next following the interval to which the amount relates.[17] The amount is also shown in the trader's VAT Account.[18]

De Voil Indirect Tax Service V3.470–476.

1   As defined in VAT Regulations, SI 1995/2518, reg 115(5).
2   As defined in SI 1995/2518, regs 112(2), 113 as amended by SI 1997/1614, SI 2008/1146. For refurbishment and fitting out, see Notice No 48 (July 2009) para 3.22.
3   SI 1995/2518, reg 114(3) as amended by SI 1997/1614, SI 2008/1146.
4   As defined in SI 1995/2518, regs 99(1)(*e*), 112(1) as substituted by SI 1999/3114.
5   As defined in SI 1995/2518, regs 99(1)(*d*)(i), 112(1) as substituted by SI 1999/3114.
6   As defined in SI 1995/2518, regs 99(1)(*d*)(ii), 112(1) as substituted by SI 1999/3114.
7   SI 1995/2518, reg 114(4), (5B) as amended and inserted by SI 1997/1614.
8   As defined in SI 1995/2518, regs 99(3)–(7), 112(1) as substituted by SI 1999/3114.
9   SI 1995/2518, reg 114(5) as amended by SI 1997/1614. For the exceptions, see SI 1995/2518, reg 114(5A), (5B).

[66.27] Tax credits, repayments and refunds

[10] As determined in accordance with the partial exemption rules: SI 1995/2518, reg 115(5) as amended by SI 1999/599, SI 2008/1146.
[11] For the manner of ascertaining taxable use in a subsequent interval, see SI 1995/2518, reg 116 as amended by SI 1995/3147, SI 1997/1614.
[12] SI 1995/2518, reg 115(1), (2) as amended by SI 1999/599.
[13] SI 1995/2518, reg 115(5) as amended by SI 1999/599, SI 2008/1146.
[14] SI 1995/2518, reg 115(1), (2), (5) as amended by SI 1999/599, SI 2008/1146. For the right to make an adjustment, see *Lennartz v Finanzamt M ünchen III (case 97/90)* [1995] STC 514, ECJ.
[15] SI 1995/2518, reg 115(3), (3A), (3B), (4) as amended and inserted by SI 1997/1614, SI 2000/258; statement of practice in Business Brief (Issue 30/97) 19 December 1997.
[16] For the disposal of an interest in a building by granting a long lease to X and selling the freehold reversion to Y, see *Centralan Property Ltd v Customs and Excise Comrs (case C-63/04)* [2006] SWTI 158, ECJ; Business Brief (Issue 17/06) 22 December 2006.
[17] SI 1995/2518, reg 115(6), (7) as amended and inserted by SI 1997/1086, SI 1997/1614. For the extent to which the Commissioners may allow otherwise, see SI 1995/2518, reg 115(8)–(10) as substituted by SI 2009/586. For bodies corporate ceasing to be members of a group, see SI 1995/2518, reg 115(6) proviso (*a*). For businesses transferred as a going concern, see SI 1995/2518, reg 115(6) proviso (*b*).
[18] For the entry made, see infra, § **67.02**.

Option to tax exercised

[**66.28**] Input tax attributable to an intended freehold sale or letting is allowable (because it is attributable to an intended taxable supply) once an option to tax[1] has effect in relation to the land or building concerned. Input tax incurred before the option has effect becomes allowable as a consequence of the option if the input tax was incurred after 31 July 1989 and the option became effective from a day falling after 31 December 1991.[2]

The legislation does not lay down any method for recovering input tax incurred before the election had effect. As the input tax was disallowed when incurred because the intended use of the goods or services was to make exempt supplies,[3] the making of an election appears to be treated as a change of intended use so that a claim for repayment arises under the provisions described in infra, § **68.26**.[5] However, this does not appear to be so in all circumstances or in respect of all input tax incurred prior to time when the election has effect.[16]

[1] For the option to tax in respect of land and buildings, see infra, §§ **68.03** and **68.04**.
[2] VATA 1994, Sch 10, para 2(4), (8). Under EU law, see *Proceedings brought by Uudenkaupungin kaupunki (case C-184/04)* [2006] ECR I–3039, [2006] SWTI 1145, ECJ. It is observed that no provision is made for deduction in respect of goods acquired from an EU member state after 31 December 1992. On the other hand, the term "importation" is not confined to goods imported from third countries as happens elsewhere in the legislation. The parliamentary draftsman seems to have overlooked VATA 1994, Sch 10, para 2(8) when amending the legislation to give effect to Directive 91/680/EEC in FA 1992, s 14 and Sch 3.

Deduction and variation of input tax credit **[66.30]**

Different rules applied in relation to elections having effect on 1 August 1989 and those having effect between 2 August 1989 and 31 December 1991: see VATA 1994, Sch 10, para 2(4), (5), (6), (9); *Lawson Mardon Group Pension Scheme v Customs and Excise Comrs* (1993) VAT decision 10231.

[3] *Lawson Mardon Group Pension Scheme v Customs and Excise Comrs* (1993) VAT decision 10231; *Hi-Wire Ltd v Customs and Excise Comrs* (1991) VAT decision 6204.

[5] This appears to be the effect of Notice No 742A (March 2002) para 9(2).

[16] This was so in *Royal and Sun Alliance Insurance Group plc v Customs and Excise Comrs* [2003] STC 832, HL.

Luxury, amusement or entertainment

[66.29] The Commissioners may make a determination that there is no entitlement to input tax credit on the grounds that the goods or services are something in the nature of a luxury, amusement or entertainment.[1]

De Voil Indirect Tax Service V5.404.

[1] VATA 1994, s 84(4). See *John Price Business Courses Ltd v Customs and Excise Comrs* [1995] V & DR 106; *Myatt & Leason (a firm) v Customs and Excise Comrs* [1995] V & DR 440; *Ernst & Young v Customs and Excise Comrs* [1997] V & DR 183.

Bad debt relief

[66.30] In principle, the VAT charged on a supply of goods and services is input tax whether or not the purchaser pays for them.[1] However, the purchaser ceases to be entitled to input in respect of the goods or services if all or part of the consideration for them is unpaid at the "relevant date". This is the later of the time of supply[2] and the due date for payment.[3]

The purchaser is required to make a negative entry in the VAT allowable portion of his VAT Account for the prescribed accounting period in which the relevant date falls. The amount of the entry is the input tax credit (if the whole consideration is unpaid) or an aliquot part (if only part is unpaid).[4]

The purchaser is required to make a positive entry in the VAT allowable portion of his VAT Account if all or part of the unpaid consideration is paid in a subsequent prescribed accounting period.[5]

This provision applies to supplies made on or after 1 January 2003.[6] It has no application to purchasers using the cash accounting scheme.[7]

De Voil Indirect Tax Service V3.404.

[1] VATA 1994, s 24(1) is silent on the question of payment.
[2] As defined in VATA 1994, s 26A(6) as inserted by FA 2002, s 22.
[3] VATA 1994, s 26A(1)–(3) as inserted by FA 2002, s 22. For bad debt relief, see supra, § **65.42**.
[4] VAT Regulations, SI 1995/2518, reg 172H(1), (2) as inserted by SI 2002/3027. For the identification of payments for this purpose, see reg 172J as so inserted. For the VAT Account, see infra, § **67.02**.

[66.30] Tax credits, repayments and refunds

5. For the entry made and the amount thereof, see SI 1995/2518, regs 172I and 172J as inserted by SI 2002/3027.
6. FA 2002, s 22(3); Finance Act 2002 section 22 (Appointed Day) Order, SI 2002/3028. For supplies made before this date, see VATA 1994, s 36(4A) as inserted by FA 1997, s 39; SI 1995/2518, regs 166A, 172(ZC)–172E as inserted or amended by SI 1997/1086, SI 2002/3027 and the 20th edition of this work.
7. SI 1995/2518, reg 172H(5) as inserted by SI 2002/3027. For the cash accounting scheme, see supra, § **63.40**.

All or part of the consideration for a supply is unpaid

[66.31] In principle, the VAT charged on a supply of goods and services is input tax whether or not the purchaser pays for them.[1] Thus, insofar as the input tax is allowable,[2] the purchaser is entitled to input tax credit in respect of it. However, this entitlement is wholly or partly withdrawn if all or part of the consideration for the supply remains unpaid six months after the time of supply or, if later, six months after the due date for payment.[3] The purchaser is required to make a negative entry in the VAT allowable portion of his VAT Account for the prescribed accounting period in which the six month period ends. The relevant amount is calculated by reference to the proportion of the consideration for the supply that is unpaid.[4]

All or part of the input tax credit is restored if all or part of the consideration is paid after the relevant six-month period has expired. The purchaser is required to make a positive entry in the VAT allowable portion of his VAT Account for the period in which the payment is made. The relevant amount is calculated by reference to the proportion of the unpaid consideration that has now been paid.[5]

De Voil Indirect Tax Service V5.156, 157.

1. VATA 1994, s 24(1) is silent on the question of payment.
2. For "allowable" input tax, see supra, § **66.06**.
3. VATA 1994, s 26A(1), (2) as inserted by FA 2002, s 22; Finance Act 2002 Section 22 (Appointed Day) Order, SI 2002/3028.
4. VATA Regulations, SI 1995/2518, reg 172H as inserted by SI 2002/3027. For the corresponding entry made to the VAT payable portion of the VAT Account in relation to specified goods subject to the reverse charge, see: VATA 1994, s 26AB(2), (3) as inserted by FA 2006, s 19; SI 1995/2518, reg 172L as inserted by SI 2007/313. For the reverse charge on specified goods, see supra, § **65.41**.
5. SI 1995/2518, reg 172I as inserted by SI 2002/3027. For the corresponding entry made to the VAT payable portion of the VAT Account in relation to specified goods subject to the reverse charge, see: SI 1995/2518, reg 172M as inserted by SI 2007/313. For the reverse charge on specified goods, see supra §**65.41**.

Variation in the consideration for a supply

[66.32] A trader must adjust his VAT Account if:[1]
(1) There is an increase or decrease in the consideration for a supply.
(2) The increase or decrease includes an amount of tax.

(3) The increase or decrease occurs no more than three years[2] after the end of the prescribed accounting period in which the supply was made.
(4) The increase or decrease is evidenced by a debit note,[3] credit note[4] or other document having the same effect.

De Voil Indirect Tax Service V5.156.

---

[1] VAT Regulations, SI 1995/2518, regs 24 and 38 as amended by SI 1997/1086. For the VAT Account, see infra, § **67.02**.
[2] For exceptions, see SI 1995/2518, reg 38(1B) as inserted by SI 1997/1086; Business Brief (Issue 9/97) 27 March 1997.
[3] For VAT invoices, see supra, § **65.18**.
[4] For credit notes, see supra, § **65.19**.

Transactions constituting an abusive process

[66.33] No right to input tax credit arises in respect of a purchase if the transactions giving rise to that right constitute an abusive practice.[1] A finding that an abusive practice has taken place creates an obligation to make a repayment to the Commissioners. The amount to be repaid is determined as follows:[2]

(1) Redefine the transactions involved in the abusive process in order to re-establish the situation that would have prevailed in the absence of the abusive practice. This establishes the identity of taxable persons liable to make a repayment, and the transactions giving rise to an adjustment. How the "situation that would have prevailed" is to be determined is an open question.
(2) The amount to be repaid by a taxable person is the difference between: (a) input tax on the transactions in respect of which he exercised the right to deduct abusively, and (b) the tax (if any) for which he was artificially liable in respect of a supply made by him under the scheme.
(3) The input tax deducted by a taxable person is unaffected if, under the "situation that would have prevailed", he would have benefited from the first transaction that did not constitute an abusive practice.

De Voil Indirect Tax Service V3.407.

---

[1] For abusive practices, see supra, § **63.09**. For the absence of a right to deduct, see supra, § **63.09**.
[2] *Halifax plc and others v Customs and Excise Comrs (case C-255/02)* [2006] ECR I-1609, [2006] STC 919, ECJ.

Fraudulent chain of transactions

[66.34] Input tax deducted in respect of a purchase may be disallowed if it is subsequently ascertained, having regard to objective factors, that the trader knew – or should have known – that, by his purchase, he was participating in a transaction connected with the fraudulent evasion of VAT.[1] On the other hand, his right to deduct is unaffected if he is unaware of the fraud and had no means of knowing of it.[2]

[66.34] Tax credits, repayments and refunds

These principles have been developed in a number of cases. Lewison J has summarised the current state of the jurisprudence in the following manner:[3]

(1) The objective of preventing evasion of VAT is an objective encouraged by the Sixth Directive (now Directive 2006/112/EC).

(2) This objective precludes the recovery of input tax where the tax is evaded by the taxable person himself. In such cases, where the right to deduct has been exercised fraudulently, the deduction may be retrospectively disallowed.

(3) This objective sometimes justifies stringent requirements as regards suppliers' obligations, but any sharing of risk must be compatible with the principle of proportionality.

(4) It is disproportionate and contrary to Community law to require a person who is a careful and honest trader to assume liability for the frauds of others.

(5) It is also disproportionate to hold a taxable person liable for fraudulent acts of third parties over whom he has no influence.

(6) A trader who does take every precaution that could reasonably be required of him, and does not realise that he is participating in VAT fraud, must be entitled to rely on the legality of his own transaction.

(7) A person who knew, or should have known, that by his purchase he was taking part in a transaction connected with the fraudulent evasion of VAT is to be treated in the same way as a person who fraudulently exercises the right to deduct.

(8) It is not contrary to Community law to require a supplier to take every step that could reasonably be required of him to satisfy himself that the transaction which he is effecting does not result in his participation in tax evasion.

(9) Likewise, a taxable person can be expected to act with all due diligence and care.

(10) Whether a taxable person knew or should have known that he was participating in a transaction connected with the fraudulent evasion of VAT must be determined having regard to objective facts or factors.

(11) Community law does not prohibit presumptions, but presumptions must be rebuttable by evidence.

De Voil Indirect Tax Service V3.000.

---

[1] *Axel Kittel v Belgian State, Belgian State v Recolta Recycling SPRL* (joined cases C-439/04 and C-440/04) [2006] ECR I–6161, [2008] STC 1537, ECJ. For the scope of this test in relation to missing trader intra-Community fraud, see most recently *Revenue and Customs Comrs v Livewire Telecom Ltd, Revenue and Customs Comrs v Olympia Technology Ltd* [2009] EWHC 15 (Ch), [2009] STC 643; *Mobilx Ltd (in administration) v Revenue and Customs Comrs* [2009] EWHC 133 (Ch), [2009] STC 1107; *Blue Sphere Global Ltd v Revenue and Customs Comrs* [2009] EWHC 1150 (Ch), [2009] SWTI 1792; *Calltel Telecom Ltd and another v Revenue and Customs Comrs* [2009] EWHC 1081 (Ch), [2009] SWTI 1798.

[2] *Optigen Ltd v Customs and Excise Comrs, Bond House Systems Ltd v Customs and Excise Comrs* (joined cases C-354/03, C-355/03 and C-484/03) [2006] ECR I–483, [2006] STC 419, ECJ.

[3] *Revenue and Customs Comrs v Livewire Telecom Ltd, Revenue and Customs Comrs v Olympia Technology Ltd* [2009] EWHC 15 (Ch), [2009] STC 643 at para 76 (case citations omitted).

Charge to tax on subsequent transfer, disposal or use

[66.35] A taxable person is charged to output tax rather than having his input tax deduction adjusted or withdrawn in the following circumstances:

(1) Goods are transferred or disposed of for no consideration.[1]
(2) The goods or services are used for private or non business purposes for no consideration.[2]
(3) The transfer, disposal or use is a chargeable event for the purposes of the self-supply arrangements.[3]

De Voil Indirect Tax Service V5.156.

[1] For the deemed supply made, see supra, § **65.28**.
[2] For the deemed supply made, see supra, §§ **65.29** and **65.30**.
[3] For the deemed supply made, see supra, §§ **65.32–65.36**.

Repayments of tax

Introduction

[66.36] The UK has implemented the Eighth and Thirteenth Directives[1] so as to make provision for repayment to certain overseas traders without imposing a requirement for them to register for the purposes of VAT.[2] As the traders necessarily make supplies outside the UK in order to qualify for repayments, they are entitled to register for VAT purposes if they so wish.

Where the Commissioners repay tax in error under these provisions, they may issue an assessment to the person to whom the repayment was made.[3] The tax assessed is treated as an amount of tax due from him and is thus recoverable as a debt due to the Crown.[4] Alternatively, the amount overpaid may be deducted from a subsequent repayment claimed by the trader.[5] The Commissioners may refuse to pay claims for a two-year period if a false or altered document is submitted in support of a claim.[6]

De Voil Indirect Tax Service V5.156.

[1] Directives 79/1072/EEC and 86/560/EEC.
[2] For the traders concerned, see infra, §§ **66.37** and **66.38**.
[3] VATA 1994, s 73(2)(*a*), (6A) as inserted by FA 2008, s 120; VAT Regulations, SI 1995/2518 regs 181, 194.
[4] VATA 1994, s 73(2), Sch 11, para 5(1).
[5] VAT Regulations, SI 1995/2518 regs 183, 196.
[6] VAT Regulations, SI 1995/2518 regs 184, 197.

[66.37] Tax credits, repayments and refunds

Repayments to EC traders

[66.37] In principle, a person carrying on business in another EC member state is entitled to a repayment of the following tax:[1]

(1) VAT charged on imported goods in respect of which no other relief is available.
(2) VAT on goods and services purchased for business purposes which would be input tax of his, and not excluded from credit, if he were a taxable person.[2]

However, the person is ineligible for relief if he is established in the UK[3] during the claim period or (subject to specified exceptions) he supplies goods or services in the UK during that period.[4]

VAT is excluded from relief if goods or services have been purchased or imported in order to make supplies in the UK or (in the case of goods) in order to remove them to another EC member state or export them to a third country.[5]

De Voil Indirect Tax Service V5.151

---

[1] VAT Regulations, SI 1995/2518, regs 174, 175, 177(1)(a) as amended by SI 2004/3140. For a repayment refused on the grounds that the goods had not been supplied in the course or furtherance of business, so that no VAT was chargeable on them, see *Blackqueen Ltd v Customs and Excise Comrs* (2002) VAT decision 17680 (supplies made in the course of a tax avoidance scheme). For transactions carried out for tax avoidance purposes, see supra, § 63.15. For undue VAT invoiced in error, see *Reemtsma Cigarettenfabriken GmbH v Ministero delle Finanze (case C-35/05)* [2007] ECR I–2425, [2007] SWTI 543, ECJ.
[2] For the exception in relation to supplies made to a travel agent, see SI 1995/2518, reg 190(1)(a), (2).
[3] As defined in SI 1995/2518, reg 173(2), (3).
[4] SI 1995/2518, reg 175 as amended by SI 2004/3140.
[5] SI 1995/2518, reg 176.

Repayments to third country traders

[66.38] In principle, a person carrying on business in a third country is entitled to a repayment of the following tax:[1]

(1) VAT charged on imported goods in respect of which no other relief is available.
(2) VAT on goods and services purchased for business purposes which would be input tax of his, and not excluded from credit, if he were a taxable person.[2]

However, the person is ineligible for relief if he is a taxable person, established in another EU member state[3] during the claim period or (subject to specified exceptions) he supplies goods or services in the UK during that period.[4] If the third country has a comparable system of turnover taxes, it must provide reciprocal arrangements for refunding tax to taxable persons established in the UK.[5]

VAT is excluded from relief if goods or services have been purchased or imported in order to make supplies in the UK or (in the case of goods) in order to export them from the UK.[6]

De Voil Indirect Tax Service V5.152.

[1] VAT Regulations, SI 1995/2518, reg 186.
[2] For the exceptions, see SI 1995/2518, reg 190(1)(b), (c) as inserted by SI 2004/3140.
[3] As defined in VAT Regulations, SI 1995/2518, regs 185(2), (3).
[4] SI 1995/2518, regs 185(1), 188(2), 190(1)(a).
[5] SI 1995/2518, reg 188(1).
[6] SI 1995/2518, reg 189.

Refunds

Introduction

[66.39] The general scheme of VAT is such that only taxable persons are allowed a credit mechanism whereby they recover all or part of the input tax they incur. The strict application of this principle can lead to a number of difficulties. The legislation therefore makes provision for refunds of VAT in certain situations[1] to alleviate anomalies, avoid hardship or comply with treaty obligations.

The legislation also makes provision for refund of output tax where bad debts have been incurred.[2]

Grant aid is available under two schemes administered by the Department for Culture, Media and Sport. These schemes apply to:

(1) VAT incurred in respect of repairs or maintenance carried out to listed places of worship.[3]
(2) VAT incurred by charities and religious groups in respect of the construction, renovation and maintenance of memorials.[4]

De Voil Indirect Tax Service V5.153–166.

[1] Listed in infra, § **66.40**.
[2] For bad debt relief, see infra § **66.41**.
[3] For guidance notes and an application form, see www.lpwscheme.org.uk
[4] For guidance notes and an application form, see www.memorialgrant.org.uk. The scheme applies to costs incurred after 15 March 2005.

Refunds of VAT incurred

[66.40] The following persons are entitled to a refund of VAT incurred on the purchase, acquisition or importation of goods and services subject to the restrictions imposed by the legislation under which the individual reliefs are conferred:

[66.40] Tax credits, repayments and refunds

(1) Persons constructing[1] or converting[2] certain buildings otherwise than in the course or furtherance of business.[3]
(2) Diplomats, international organisations and visiting forces.[4]
(3) Traders who have ceased to be taxable persons.[5]
(4) Taxable persons importing goods for non-business purposes.[6]
(5) Government departments,[7] to the extent specified by Treasury direction.[8]
(6) Local authorities[9] and public bodies[10] in respect of their non-business activities.[11]
(7) Bodies providing free admission to a relevant museum or gallery.[12]
(8) Designated EU bodies.[13]
(9) Non-taxable persons removing a new means of transport to another EU member state.[14]
(10) Taxable persons acquiring the same goods in the UK and another EU member state.[15]

Where the Commissioners repay tax in error under one of the foregoing provisions, they may issue an assessment to the person to whom the repayment was made.[16] The tax assessed is treated as an amount of tax due from him and is thus recoverable as a debt due to the Crown.[17]

A person is liable to a penalty if he carelessly or deliberately makes a false or inflated claim for repayment of VAT.[18]

A local authority, public body or other body within point (5) above may be entitled to repayment supplement if the repayment is delayed.[19] A person within any other description may be entitled to interest if the repayment is delayed due to an error on the part of the Commissioners.[20] Overpaid interest is recovered by assessment[21] and carries interest.[22]

De Voil Indirect Tax Service V5.153–166.

---

[1] For works amounting to construction, see *Customs and Excise Comrs v Arnold* [1996] STC 1271.
[2] For the conversion of a building containing both residential and non-residential parts, see *Customs and Excise Comrs v Blom-Cooper* [2003] STC 669, CA; *R & C Comrs v Jacobs* [2005] EWCA Civ 930, [2005] STC 1518, CA.
[3] VATA 1994, s 35 as amended by FA 1996, s 30 and SI 2001/2305; VAT Regulations, SI 1995/2518, regs 200, 201 and 201A as amended or inserted by SI 2009/1967.
[4] Consular Relations Act 1968, s 8; International Organisations Act 1968, Sch 1, paras 6, 7 and 12; Diplomatic and Other Privileges Act 1979, s 1; CEMA 1979, Sch 4, para 12; FA 1972, s 55(5); Customs and Excise (Personal Reliefs for Special Visitors) Order, SI 1992/3156.
[5] VAT Regulations, SI 1995/2518, reg 111(5)–(8) as amended by SI 1997/1086, SI 2009/586. Claims are made on form VAT 427. For the recovery of VAT on post-cessation rent paid in respect of the former business premises, see *I/S Fini H v Skatteministeriet (case C-32/03)* [2005] ECR I–1599, [2005] STC 903, ECJ.
[6] VATA 1994, s 27. See Notice No 702 (October 1998), para 2.8. Applications are made by way of correspondence.
[7] Defined in VATA 1994, s 41(6)–(8).

[8] VATA 1994, s 41(3), (4). For the direction currently in force, see Treasury direction dated 2 December 2002 (London Gazette, 10 January 2003, and correction on 15 January 2003).
[9] Defined in VATA 1994, s 96(1), (4).
[10] Listed in VATA 1994, s 33(3); VAT (Refund of Tax) (No 2) Order, SI 1973/2121; VAT (Refund of Tax) Order, SI 1976/2028; VAT (Refund of Tax) Order, SI 1985/1101; VAT (Refund of Tax) Order, SI 1986/336; VAT (Refund of Tax) (No 2) Order, SI 1986/532; VAT (Refund of Tax) Order, SI 1989/1217; VAT (Refund of Tax) Order, SI 1995/1978; VAT (Refund of Tax) (No 2) Order, SI 1995/2999; VAT (Refund of Tax) Order, SI 1997/2558; VAT (Refund of Tax) Order, SI 1999/2076; VAT (Refund of Tax) Order, SI 2000/1046; VAT (Refund of Tax) (No 2) Order, SI 2000/1515; VAT (Refund of Tax) (No 3) Order, SI 2000/1672; VAT (Refund of Tax) Order, SI 2001/3453; VAT (Refund of Tax) Order, SI 2006/1793; VAT (Refund of Tax to Charter Trustees and Conservators) Order, SI 2009/1177.
[11] VATA 1994, ss 33(1), 41(3); *Haringey London Borough Council v Customs and Excise Comrs* [1995] STC 830.
[12] VATA 1994, s 33A as inserted by FA 2001, s 98 and amended from 1 April 2009 by FA 2008, Sch 39, para 33 and Finance Act 2008, Schedule 39 (Appointed Day, Transitional Provision and Savings) Order, SI 2009/403, art 2(1). The bodies, museums and galleries are specified in VAT (Refund of Tax to Museums and Galleries) Order, SI 2001/2879 as amended by SI 2004/1709, SI 2008/1339.
[13] The European Communities (Privileges of the European School) Order, SI 1990/237; The European Bank for Reconstruction and Development (Immunities and Privileges) Order, SI 1991/757.
[14] VATA 1994, s 40; VAT Regulations, SI 1995/2518.
[15] VATA 1994, s 13(5). No regulations have been made to date.
[16] VATA 1994, s 73(2)(a), (6A) as inserted by FA 2008, s 120.
[17] VATA 1994, s 73(2), Sch 11, para 5(1).
[18] FA 2007, s 97 and Sch 24, para 1; Finance Act 2007, Schedule 24 (Commencement and Transitional Provisions) Order, SI 2008/568, arts 2, 3.
[19] See VATA 1994, s 79(1) (as amended by FA 2001, s 98); VAT Regulations, SI 1995/2518.
[20] See VATA 1994, s 78; *National Council of YMCA's Inc v Customs and Excise Comrs* [1993] VATTR 299. For interest, see supra, § **2A.43**.
[21] VATA 1994, s 78A as inserted by FA 1997, s 45.
[22] VATA 1994, s 78A(6), (7) as inserted by FA 1997, s 45. For the charge to interest, see supra, § **2A.43**.

Bad debt relief

[66.41] A person[1] is entitled to a refund in respect of bad debts incurred by him if the following conditions are met:[2]

(1) He has supplied goods or services.[3]
(2) The value of the supply[4] does not exceed open market value.
(3) He has accounted for, and paid, tax on the supply.
(4) He has written off all or part of the consideration in his accounts[5] as a bad debt.
(5) A period of six months has elapsed since the time of supply.[6]

[66.41] Tax credits, repayments and refunds

(6) He has not claimed a refund under repealed provisions.[7]
(7) He makes a claim.[8]

The same conditions apply to flat-rate traders.[9] Although flat-rate traders using the cash turnover method do not meet the condition in point 3 above, they are entitled to make a special claim.[10]

All or part of a refund must be repaid if[11]

(1) A subsequent payment is received in respect of the relevant supply.
(2) A subsequent payment is treated as attributed to the relevant supply.[12]
(3) The consideration for the relevant supply is subsequently reduced.
(4) The claimant failed to comply with the terms of the refund scheme.

De Voil Indirect Tax Service V5.156.

---

[1] For companies leaving a group registration after the supply was made, see *Triad Timber Components Ltd v Customs and Excise Comrs* [1983] VATTR 384.

[2] VATA 1994, s 36(1) (as amended by FA 1998, s 22), (2), (4) (as amended by FA 1997, s 39) and Sch 13, para 9(2). For supplies made for a non-money consideration prior to the enactment of FA 1998, s 23, see *Goldsmiths (Jewellers) Ltd v Customs and Excise Comrs (case C-330/95)* [1997] STC 1073, ECJ; Business Brief (Issue 21/97), 3 October 1997.

[3] For debts passing on the novation of a contract for the domestic supply of gas or electricity, see the Extra-statutory Concession set out in Business Brief (Issue 20/04), 2 August 2004.

[4] For the value of a supply made wholly or partly for something other than money, see VATA 1994, s 36(3A) as inserted by FA 1998, s 23.

[5] A trader writes off consideration by making an entry in his Refunds for Bad Debts Account. An entry is validly made in this account if the consideration first became payable more than six months previously: VAT Regulations, SI 1995/2518, regs 168(3) and 172(1), (1A), (2) as substituted or amended by SI 1996/2960, SI 1997/1086. For the entry made, see SI 1995/2518, reg 168(2) as amended by SI 1997/1086.

[6] For the time of supply, see supra, §§ **66.07–66.12**.

[7] ie VATA 1983, s 22 (repealed) as saved by VATA 1994, Sch 13, para 9(1) (repealed by FA 1997, s 39(5) and Sch 18, Part IV(3)) and VAT Regulations, SI 1995/2518, regs 156–164 (revoked by SI 1997/1086).

[8] For claims, see SI 1998/2518, regs 165A, 166, 167, 168 as inserted or amended by SI 1997/1086, SI 2002/3027, SI 2009/586. For the attribution of payments, see regs 170, 170A and 172J as inserted, substituted or amended by SI 2002/3027, SI 2007/313; cf *Abbey National plc v C & E Comrs* [2005] EWHC 1187 (Ch), [2006] STC 1 (finance agreement). For margin scheme supplies, see regs 172A and 172B as inserted by SI 1997/1086.

[9] For the flat-rate scheme for small businesses, see supra, § **63.41**.

[10] For the claim made, see SI 1998/2518, reg 55V as inserted by SI 2002/1142.

[11] SI 1995/2518, reg 171 as amended by SI 1999/3029, SI 2002/3027, SI 2007/313.

[12] ie in accordance with SI 1995/2518, regs 170 (payment received in respect of two or more supplies) or 170A (payment received under a credit agreement) as substituted or amended by SI 2002/3027, SI 2007/313.

67

Accounting and payment

VAT returns	PARA **67.01**
Other accounting systems	PARA **67.11**
Correction of errors	PARA **67.15**

VAT returns

Prescribed accounting periods

[67.01] A taxable person is required to account for and pay tax by reference to "prescribed accounting periods".[1] A prescribed accounting period is a period of one month, three months or such other period as the Commissioners may determine in particular cases.[2] In practice, one month periods are available to repayment traders other than those who register voluntarily.[3] A taxable person authorised under the annual accounting scheme[4] has a prescribed accounting period of 12 months which commences on the date specified in his authorisation or an anniversary thereof.[5]

Prescribed accounting periods end on the dates specified in a trader's registration certificate.[6] The last period ends on the date from which his registration is cancelled. A period is artificially brought to an end if a liquidator, receiver or trustee in bankruptcy is appointed.[7]

De Voil Indirect Tax Service V5.101–107.

---

[1] VATA 1994, s 25(1).
[2] VAT Regulations, SI 1995/2518, reg 25(1). See *Spillane v Customs and Excise Comrs* [1990] STC 212; *Bjellica v Customs and Excise Comrs* [1995] STC 329, CA; *Leonidas and Leonidas v Customs and Excise Comrs* [2000] V & DR 207.
[3] Notice No 700 (April 2002), para 20.5.2.
[4] For the annual accounting scheme, see supra, § **63.42**.
[5] SI 1995/2518, reg 49 as substituted by SI 1996/542 and amended by SI 2002/1142. A transitional accounting period applies for the period commencing on the date from which his authorisation becomes effective and ending on the day preceding the date specified in his authorisation.
[6] Traders are allocated to "stagger groups". For the Commissioners' policy, see Business Brief (Issue 12/05), 15 June 2005; *R (on the application of BMW AG and others) v Revenue and Customs Comrs* [2009] EWCA Civ 77, [2009] STC 963, CA.
[7] SI 1995/2518, reg 25(1), (3), (5).

[67.02] Accounting and payment

The VAT Account

[67.02] A taxable person is required to keep a "VAT Account" for each prescribed accounting period.[1] He must preserve this record for six years or such lesser period as the Commissioners may allow.[2]

The VAT Account is divided into a "tax payable portion" and a "tax allowable portion".[3] The aggregate of entries in each portion is included respectively in Boxes 1 and 2 (output tax) and 4 (input tax) of the trader's tax return for the period concerned.[4]

De Voil Indirect Tax Service V5.211.

---

[1] VAT Regulations, SI 1995/2518, reg 32(1).
[2] SI 1995/2518, reg 31(1).
[3] SI 1995/2518, reg 32(2). For the information recorded in the tax payable and tax allowable portions, see SI 1995/2518, reg 32(3), (4) as amended by SI 2007/1418.
[4] SI 1995/2518, reg 39(1)–(3). For the tax return, see infra, § **67.03**.

The VAT return

[67.03] A taxable person is required to furnish a VAT return on the prescribed form to the controller of VAT Central Unit (or such specified address as the Commissioners may allow or direct) in respect of each prescribed accounting period. The prescribed forms are VAT 100 (normal return) and VAT 193 (final return). A return must be furnished two calendar months after the end of the prescribed accounting period to which it relates (in the case of traders authorised under the annual accounting scheme) or one month after such period (in other cases).[1] This time limit is extended by up to seven days if returns and related payments are made under the electronic return system.[2] A trader may furnish tax returns in this manner if the Commissioners authorise him to do so.[3]

The following accounting information is shown on a tax return:

(1) Tax due in the period on sales and other outputs.
(2) Tax due in the period in respect of acquisitions.
(3) Tax claimed in the period on purchases and other inputs.
(4) The net amount of tax due to the Commissioners or repayable by them.[4]

The information in points (1)–(3) is derived from the tax payable and tax allowable portions of the trader's VAT Account.[5] The Commissioners may allow traders to estimate part of their output tax or input tax.[6]

A number of consequences follow if a trader fails to furnish a tax return by the due date. In particular, the Commissioners may estimate the tax due and assess him accordingly. No appeal can be entertained in respect of such an assessment until the outstanding return has been furnished.[7] The Commissioners may also issue a surcharge liability notice, or assess default surcharge.[8]

De Voil Indirect Tax Service V5.101–107.

[1] SI 1995/2518, regs 25, 50(b) as substituted by SI 1996/542. For the time when a tax return is furnished, see *Aikman v White* [1986] STC 1; *Hayman v Griffiths, Walker v Hanby* [1987] STC 649; *Richard Costain Ltd v Customs and Excise Comrs* [1988] VATTR 111.
[2] For the electronic return system, see SI 1995/2518, reg 25(4A)–(4M) as inserted, amended or substituted by SI 2000/794, SI 2004/1676.
[3] For authorisations, see SI 1995/2518, reg 25(4G).
[4] SI 1995/2518, reg 25(1), (4) and Sch 1, Form Nos 4, 5.
[5] SI 1995/2518, reg 39.
[6] SI 1995/2518, regs 28, 29(3).
[7] VATA 1994, ss 73(1), (8) and 83(p)(i).
[8] For default surcharge, see infra, § **67.08**.

Payment of tax due to the Commissioners

[**67.04**] A tax return may show an amount of tax due to the Commissioners. If so, the tax due must be paid within the same time limits applicable to tax returns, ie normally within one month after the end of the prescribed accounting period concerned.[1] Traders furnishing returns using the electronic return system[2] must pay tax by electronic means acceptable to the Commissioners.[3] The acceptable means specified by the Commissioners are Bankers Automated Clearing System (BACS), Bank Giro Credit Transfer and Clearing House Automated Payment System (CHAPS).[4] The normal time limit for payment is extended[5] if the payment is actually made by one of these methods.

Other traders may make payments by cheque, postal order, credit card or the foregoing acceptable electronic means. Payments by credit card give rise to a fee if authorisation is given by telephone[6] or via the internet.[7] A direction made by the Commissioners extend the additional due date for the payment if payments are made by electronic communications.[8]

Traders are required to make payments on account if they have an annual tax liability exceeding £2,000,000[9] or if they are authorised to use the annual accounting scheme.[10]

Failure to pay tax by the due date may lead to the issue of a surcharge liability notice or an assessment for default surcharge.[11] Any tax unpaid is recoverable as a debt due to the Crown.[12] It may be recovered by set off against amounts due to the trader,[13] by distraint,[14] or by recovery proceedings.[15]

De Voil Indirect Tax Service V5.109, 111.

[1] VAT Regulations, SI 1995/2518, regs 25(1). For payment under the annual accounting scheme, see SI 1995/2518 reg 50(b) as substituted by SI 1996/542.
[2] For the electronic return system, see supra, § **67.03**.
[3] SI 1995/2518, reg 40(2A) as inserted by SI 2000/258. For the electronic return system, see supra, § **67.03**. For the fee payable on credit card payments made by telephone, see FA 2008, s 136; The Taxes (Fees for Payment by Telephone) Regulations, SI 2008/1948, which came into force on 13 August 2008.
[4] Notice No 700 (April 2002) para 21.3.2.

[67.04] Accounting and payment

5   For the extended time limit, see Notice No 700 (April 2002) para 21.3.1 (seven days unless the seventh day falls on a weekend or Bank Holiday).
6   See FA 2008, s 136; The Taxes (Fees for Payment by Telephone) Regulations, SI 2008/1948 (fee of 0.91% added to the payment made).
7   For acceptable means of electronic communications and the extended time limit applicable thereto, see Notice No 700 (April 2002) para 21.3.1 This is described as a concession rather than a direction.
8   SI 1995/2518, reg 40(4) as inserted by SI 2004/1675. For acceptable means of electronic communications and the extended time limit applicable thereto, see Notice No 700 (April 2002) para 21.3.1 This is described as a concession rather than a direction.
9   VATA 1994, s 28 as amended by FA 1996, s 34 and FA 1997, s 43; VAT (Payments on Account) Order, SI 1993/2001 as amended by SI 1995/291, SI 1996/1196, SI 2007/1420; SI 1995/2518, regs 40A (as inserted by SI 1996/1198) and 44–48. For the right of appeal, see VATA 1994, s 83(*fa*) as inserted by SI 1997/2542. For payments on account under EC law, see *Balocchi v Ministero delle Finanze dello Stato* (case C-10/92) [1997] STC 640, ECJ.
10 SI 1995/2518, regs 50, 51 as substituted by SI 1996/542 and amended by SI 2002/1142.
11 For default surcharge, see infra, § **67.08**.
12 VATA 1994, Sch 11, para 5(1); *Customs and Excise Comrs v International Language Centres Ltd* [1986] STC 279.
13 VATA 1994, s 81(3), (3A) as inserted by FA 1997, s 48.
14 Distress for Customs and Excise Duties and Other Indirect Taxes Regulations, SI 1997/1431.
15 For proceedings in the UK, see Crown Proceedings Act 1947, ss 13–15. For proceedings in another EU member state, see Directive 76/308/EEC (as amended).

Payment of VAT credit by the Commissioners

[67.05] A tax return may show an amount due from Commissioners. This is known as a "VAT credit".[1] The Commissioners are required to pay the amount of a VAT credit to the trader concerned subject to the following qualifications:[2]

(1) No repayment is made if the sum due is less than £1.[3]
(2) The Commissioners are empowered to withhold payment if a tax return for a prior period is outstanding.[4]
(3) The Commissioners may require a trader to produce evidence of input tax credit as a condition for allowing repayment.[5]
(4) The Commissioners may require a trader to give security for the amount of the payment if they consider this necessary for the protection of the revenue.[6] An appeal lies to a tribunal in respect of a requirement for security.[7]

The right to payment of a VAT credit arises when the claim is admitted or established.[8] Thus, the Commissioners have discretion to withhold payment of all or part of a VAT credit if they dispute the amount claimed.[9] However, they must investigate disputed claims expeditiously and proportionately. They have power to make interim payments. Subject to exercising any right of set off, they must pay claims promptly once they have been admitted.[10] The Commissioners do not have a general power to pay interest on delayed payments. Thus, traders are entitled only to repayment supplement or to a payment of interest under statutory rules.[11]

An assessment is necessary only if the Commissioners consider that the trader has a liability to pay tax rather than receive a VAT credit. The amount assessed is limited to the amount payable.[12] This amount is recoverable as a debt due to the Crown.[13]

De Voil Indirect Tax Service V5.109, 111.

---

[1] VATA 1994, s 25(3).
[2] VATA 1994, s 25(3), (6). For conditions imposed, see *Hordern v Customs and Excise Comrs* [1992] VATTR 382.
[3] VATA 1994, Sch 11, para 2(13).
[4] VATA 1994, s 25(5).
[5] VATA 1994, Sch 11, para 4(1) as substituted by FA 2003, s 17.
[6] VATA 1994, Sch 11, para 4(1A) as inserted by FA 2003, s 17. For the Commissioners' practice, see Notice No 700/52 (April 2003), Section 2.
[7] VATA 1994, s 83(ra) as amended by FA 2003, s 17.
[8] *R (on the application of UK Tradecorp Ltd) v Customs and Excise Comrs* [2004] EWHC 2515 (admin), [2005] STC 138.
[9] *Capital One Developments Ltd v Customs and Excise Comrs* [2002] EWHC 197 (Ch), [2002] STC 479.
[10] *R (on the application of UK Tradecorp Ltd) v Customs and Excise Comrs* [2004] EWHC 2515 (admin) [2005] STC 138.
[11] *R (on the application of UK Tradecorp Ltd) v Customs and Excise Comrs* [2004] EWHC 2515 (amin) [2005] STC 138; *R (on the application of Elite Mobile plc) v Customs and Excise Comrs* [2004 EWHC 2923 (admin), [2005] STC 275. For repayment supplement, see infra, § **67.06**. For statutory interest, see VATA 1994, s 78 (official error); Supreme Court Act 1981, s 35A (proceedings for recovery of a debt).
[12] VATA 1994, s 73(1); *International Language Centres Ltd v Customs and Excise Comrs* [1982] VATTR 172; affd [1983] STC 394; *Potter (a firm) v Customs and Excise Comrs* [1983] VATTR 108; on appeal [1984] STC 290; revsd [1985] STC 45, CA.
[13] VATA 1994, s 73(9), Sch 11, para 5(1). See *Customs and Excise Comrs v Fine Art Developments plc* [1988] STC 178, [1988] 2 All ER 70, CA. For tax recoverable as a debt due to the Crown, see infra, § **67.07**.

Repayment supplement on delayed payment of VAT credits

[67.06] In principle, the Commissioners are required to pay repayment supplement in respect of VAT credits shown on a return received[1] no later than the due date.[2] However, no supplement is due unless the Commissioners fail to issue[3] a written instruction directing payment[4] within the relevant period[5] and (if the VAT credit has been overstated) the amount of the overstatement does not exceed the greater of £250 or 5% of the amount due. Supplement is the greater of £50 and 5% of the VAT credit.[6]

De Voil Indirect Tax Service V5.109, 111.

[67.06] Accounting and payment

1. "Received" means physical receipt by the Commissioners: *Customs and Excise Comrs v W Timms & Son (Builders) Ltd* [1992] STC 374.
2. For the due date, see supra, § **67.03**. In relation to traders normally making payments and using the credit transfer arrangements to do so, see *Refrigeration Spares (Manchester) Ltd v Customs and Excise Comrs (2002) VAT decision 17603*.
3. A written instruction is "issued" when it is received by the trader or his agent: *Aston v Customs and Excise Comrs* [1991] VATTR 170.
4. ie a cheque or payment order: *Aston v Customs and Excise Comrs* [1991] VATTR 170.
5. As defined in VATA 1994, s 79(2A) as inserted by FA 1999, s 19. For the days left out of account in determining this 30-day period, see VATA 1994, s 79(4); VAT Regulations, SI 1995/2518, regs 198, 199.
6. VATA 1994, s 79. For the "tax due", see *British Steel Exports Ltd v Customs and Excise Comrs (1992) VAT decision 7562*.

Assessment of VAT credits incorrectly paid

[67.07] All or part of a VAT credit[1] paid to a trader may subsequently prove not to have been due to him. Where this is so, the amount overpaid is treated as an amount of tax due from the trader for the prescribed accounting period in which the payment was made to him and assessed accordingly.[2] The amount assessed is recoverable as a debt due to the Crown.[3] It carries interest.[4]

De Voil Indirect Tax Service V5.109, 111.

1. For VAT credits, see supra, § **67.05**.
2. VATA 1994, s 73(2), (3), (6A) as inserted by FA 2008, s 120. See *Customs and Excise Comrs v Laura Ashley Ltd* [2003] EWHC 2832 (Ch), [2004] STC 635; *Farm Facilities (Fork Lift) Ltd v Customs and Excise Comrs* [1987] VATTR 80.
3. VATA 1994, Sch 11, para 5(1).
4. VATA 1994, s 74. For the charge to interest, see supra, § **2A.43**.

Default surcharge

[67.08] A trader is liable to default surcharge if he fails to furnish a VAT return, or pay any tax shown to be due thereon, in respect of a prescribed accounting period falling within a "surcharge period" notified to him in a surcharge liability notice.[1] Default surcharge is the greater of £30 and a percentage of outstanding tax,[2] the rate being governed by the number of previous failures to pay tax during the surcharge period.[3] The specified percentages are: 2% (no previous failures), 5% (one previous failure), 10% (two previous failures) and 15% (three or more previous failures).

Default surcharge is assessed.[4] The amount assessed is treated as an amount of tax due from the trader and is thus recoverable as a debt due to the Crown.[5] A right of appeal is given in respect of any liability to surcharge, or the amount thereof.[6]

A trader is not liable to default surcharge in either of the following circumstances. First, if payment of all or part of the tax due is deferred by reason of circumstances arising from a disaster or emergency.[7] Secondly, if the trader satisfies the Commissioners or, on appeal, a VAT and duties tribunal, that:

(1) He did not receive a surcharge liability notice.[8]
(2) The surcharge liability notice is invalid.[9]
(3) He posted his return and remittance before the due date.[10]
(4) He has a reasonable excuse for the failure.[11]

De Voil Indirect Tax Service V5.371–380.

[1] VATA 1994, s 59(1)–(3). These provisions apply in a modified form if the trader is liable to make payments on account: see VATA 1994, s 59A, added by FA 1996, s 35(2). For the relationship between VATA 1994, ss 59 and 59A, see s 59B, added by FA 1996, s 35(2).
[2] As defined in VATA 1994, s 59(6).
[3] VATA 1994, s 59(4), (5).
[4] VATA 1994, s 76(1).
[5] VATA 1994, s 76(9), Sch 11, para 5(1).
[6] VATA 1994, s 83(n), (q). For the tribunal's jurisdiction, see *Dollar Land (Feltham) Ltd v Customs and Excise Comrs* [1995] STC 414.
[7] For the circumstances in which payment may be deferred, see FA 2008, s 135; Finance Act 2008 Section 135 (Disaster or Emergency) Order, SI 2008/1936.
[8] See *Customs and Excise Comrs v Medway Draughting and Technical Services Ltd* [1989] STC 346; *Eidographics Ltd v Customs and Excise Comrs* [1991] VATTR 449.
[9] See *Dow Chemical Co Ltd v Customs and Excise Comrs* [1996] V & DR 52.
[10] VATA 1994, s 59(7)(a). See, for example, *Halstead Motor Co v Customs and Excise Comrs* [1995] V & DR 201. For payment by credit transfer, see *Barney & Freeman v Customs and Excise Comrs* [1990] VATTR 19.
[11] VATA 1994, s 59(7)(b). For reasonable excuse, see VATA 1994, s 71(1); *Customs and Excise Comrs v Palco Industry Co Ltd* [1990] STC 594; *Customs and Excise Comrs v Salevon Ltd* [1989] STC 907; *Customs and Excise Comrs v Steptoe* [1992] STC 757, CA; *Dollar Land (Feltham) Ltd v Customs and Excise Comrs* [1995] STC 414; *Profile Security Services Ltd v Customs and Excise Comrs* [1996] STC 808; *CMS Peripherals Ltd v Revenue and Customs Comrs* [2007] EWHC 1128 (Ch), [2008] STC 985.

Security

[67.09] The Commissioners may require a taxable person to give security, or further security, for the payment of any tax[1] which is, or may become, due from him or from any other person in a chain of supply[2] in which the taxable person is involved.[3] However, the taxable person can be required to give security for tax due from another person only if both persons are jointly and severally liable for that tax.[4]

A trader faced with a notice of requirement has three options:

[67.09] Accounting and payment

(1) He may provide security. The Commissioners determine both the amount of the security and the manner in which it is given.[5] They normally accept cash, a bankers draft, a bank or building society guarantee, or a joint bank or building society account.[6]
(2) He may appeal to a tribunal[7] and submit that the call should be modified or withdrawn.
(3) If neither of the foregoing options succeeds, he must cease receiving or making taxable supplies. Failing to do so is a criminal offence.[8]

A requirement for security has been described as a draconian provision which can effectively put a trader out of business.[9] Thus, there must be safeguards. The following can be identified:

(1) A trader should normally be given an opportunity to explain his conduct before a requirement for security is made.[10]
(2) The requirement must be necessary for the protection of the revenue.[11] Traders have most frequently been required to give security in respect of their own VAT in so-called "phoenix syndrome" situations[12] and cases where traders have previously been involved in the management of an insolvent business. Calls have occasionally been made on the sole ground of persistent failure to furnish returns and pay tax.[13] The stated purpose of making requirements in respect of another person's VAT is "to tackle serious cases of VAT evasion where several businesses act together to attack the tax system". It is considered necessary because, in certain types of fraud, "the business with the greatest tax liability will often quickly disappear or become insolvent, resulting in serious revenue loss". Thus, the intention is to protect "the total tax at risk in a VAT supply chain".[14]
(3) On appeal against a requirement for security in respect of another person's VAT, the Commissioners must satisfy the tribunal that evasion, or an attempt to evade, has taken place somewhere in the chain of supply or that, in the absence of security, it is likely that evasion will take place.[15] It follows that the Commissioners should be similarly satisfied at the time when the notice of requirement is issued.
(4) The Commissioners have indicated that a trader may be required to give security if he has "previously been engaged in one or more supply chains involving businesses or individuals who evade substantial VAT payments" and he is unable to show that he has taken "reasonable steps to establish the business credentials of [his] suppliers and customers".[16]
(5) The Commissioners have indicated that a warning will be given before security is required.[17]

On appeal, a tribunal must decide whether, in deciding to issue a notice of requirement, the Commissioners have acted unreasonably, taken account of irrelevant matters or disregarded any matter which should have been given weight.[18] In doing so, the court takes account of the facts known or ascertainable by the Commissioners at the time when the trader challenges their decision.[19]

De Voil Indirect Tax Service V5.186.

VAT returns [67.10]

1 ie output tax less input tax: *Colette Ltd v Customs and Excise Comrs* [1992] VATTR 240.
2 For chains of supply, see supra, § **63.08**.
3 VATA 1994, Sch 11, para 4(2) as substituted by FA 2003, s 17.
4 *Customs and Excise Comrs v Federation of Technological Industries and others* (case C-384/04) [2006] ECR I–4191, [2006] STC 1483, ECJ. For joint and several liability, see infra, § **67.10**.
5 VATA 1994, Sch 11, para 4(4) as inserted by FA 2003, s 17.
6 Notice No 700/52 (April 2003), para 4.5.
7 VATA 1994, s 83(*l*). He should apply for an extension of any time limit imposed by the Commissioners when serving notice of appeal: *Gayton House Holdings Ltd v Customs and Excise Comrs* [1984] VATTR 11. For the Commissioners' statement of case, see *M & S Services Ltd v Customs and Excise Comrs* [1995] V & DR 512.
8 VATA 1994, s 72(11) as amended by FA 2003, s 17.
9 *Evans v Customs and Excise Comrs* [1979] VATTR 194. This was said in relation to a requirement for the trader to give security for his own VAT.
10 *Restorex v Customs and Excise Comrs* (1997) VAT decision 15014.
11 VATA 1994, Sch 11, para 4(2). See *Rosabronze Ltd v Customs and Excise Comrs* (1984) VAT decision 1668; also *Anglo Associates (Tyres and Exhausts) Ltd v Customs and Excise Comrs* LON/84/154 unreported.
12 See Report of the Committee on Enforcement Powers of the Revenue Departments, Cmnd. 8822, para 24.4.
13 For examples, see *Longsight Cricket Club v Customs and Excise Comrs* (1989) VAT decision 4064; *Cameron v Customs and Excise Comrs* (1998) VAT decision 15779.
14 Budget Notice CE 14, 9 April 2003, paras 3, 4.
15 VATA 1994, s 84(4E) as inserted by FA 2003, s 17. "Evading VAT" in this context includes obtaining a VAT credit to which a person is not entitled or a VAT credit in excess of the amount due: VATA 1994, s 84(4F) as so inserted.
16 Notice No 700/52 (April 2003), para 4.2. "Evasion" in this context means: (1) deliberately using the VAT registration of another trader without his knowledge, (2) going missing, or (3) becoming insolvent owing VAT. It is difficult to reconcile "insolvency" with "evasion" unless some element of dishonesty is involved.
17 Notice No 700/52 (April 2003), para 4.3. The letter will state that the trader is considered to have been involved in a supply chain where tax has been evaded. It will alert the trader to the steps he can take to help avoid dealing with high risk businesses or individuals in the future. These steps are set out in Section 6 of the Notice.
18 *John Dee Ltd v Customs and Excise Comrs* [1995] STC 941, CA.
19 *Lomond Services Ltd v Customs and Excise Comrs* (1998) VAT decision 15451.

Joint and several liability

[67.10] Joint and several liability for another person's VAT liabilities is a long-established feature of the VAT legislation. It applies automatically in relation to VAT groups (where all members of the group are jointly an severally liable for any VAT due from the representative member)[1] and traders subject to a disaggregation direction (where each of the constituent members is jointly and severally liable for any VAT due from the single taxable person).[2] The

[67.10] Accounting and payment

common feature is a financial, economic or organisational link between the persons having joint and several liability.

This feature is absent from a recent measure introduced as part of the Government's strategy for tackling missing trader fraud.[3] This enables the Commissioners to serve a notice on any taxable person in a chain of supply[4] making that person jointly and severally liable for unpaid VAT incurred by any other person in the chain[5] if the following conditions are met:[6]

(1) A taxable supply of goods has been made to the taxable person.
(2) The goods fall within one or more of three descriptions, which can be broadly stated as telephones,[7] computers[8] and electronic equipment for use by individuals for the purpose of leisure, amusement or entertainment.[9]
(3) At the time of supply, the taxable person knew, or had reasonable grounds to suspect, that some or all of the VAT payable in respect of any supply in the chain would go unpaid.

Whether or not a person has "reasonable grounds" appears to be a question of fact. However, a person is deemed to have "reasonable grounds" if he purchased the goods for less than their open market value, or for less than the price paid by an earlier supplier in the chain, unless he can prove that the low price payable was unconnected with the failure to pay VAT.[10] It is for the UK courts to decide whether this presumption complies with the general principles of EU law.[11]

The notice must specify the amount of unpaid VAT concerned. It must also state the effect of the notice.[12] A right of appeal lies to a tribunal against any liability arising from the notice.[13]

The vires of these provisions has been challenged in judicial review proceedings and a reference made to the Court of Justice.[14]

De Voil Indirect Tax Service V3.502.

---

[1] VATA 1994, s 43(1) as amended by FA 1995, s 25 and FA 1999 s 16, Sch 2, para 1. For VAT groups, see supra, §§ **64.24–64.29**.
[2] VATA 1994, Sch 1, para 2(7)(d). For disaggregation directions, see supra, § **63.11**.
[3] See *Tackling Indirect Tax Fraud* (HM Customs and Excise, November 2001), paras 4.1–4.7; *Protecting Indirect Tax Revenues* (HM Customs and Excise, November 2002); *Joint and Several Liability – Consultation on Reasonable Checks* (HM Customs and Excise, April 2003), paras 1–4.
[4] For chains of supply, see supra, § **63.08**.
[5] VATA 1994, s 77A(2), (3) as inserted by FA 2003, s 18. VAT counts as unpaid only to the extent that it exceeds the amount of any refund due: VATA 1994, s 77A(10)(b) as so inserted,
[6] VATA 1994, s 77A(1), (2), (6), (10)(a) as inserted by FA 2003, s 18. The description of goods in head (2) may be changed by Treasury order: VATA 1994, s 77A(9) as substituted by FA 2007, s 97.
[7] As defined in VATA 1994, s 77A(1)(a) as substituted by SI 2007/939.
[8] As defined in VATA 1994, s 77A(1)(b) as substituted by SI 2007/939.
[9] As defined in VATA 1994, s 77A(1)(c) as substituted by SI 2007/939.
[10] VATA 1994, s 77A(6)–(8) as inserted by FA 2003, s 18.

[11] *Federation of Technological Industries and others v Customs and Excise Comrs* (case C-384/04) [2006] ECR I–4191, [2006] STC 1483, ECJ..
[12] VATA 1994, s 77A(2) as inserted by FA 2003, s 18.
[13] VATA 1994, s 83(ra) as inserted by FA 2003, s 18.
[14] See supra, § **63.09**.

Other accounting systems

Goods sold under a power

[67.11] Special accounting arrangements apply where a person acting under a power (eg a bailiff or a receiver acting on behalf of a debenture holder) sells a trader's goods, in satisfaction of a debt,[1] The person selling the goods, or the auctioneer (if any) acting on behalf of such a person, is required to render a special return (form VAT 833) to VAT Central Unit within 21 days of the sale.[2] He is also required to account to the Commissioners for the tax, provide the trader with a copy of the return, and issue a document in lieu of a tax invoice to the purchaser.[3]

De Voil Indirect Tax Service V5.142.

[1] VATA 1994, Sch 4, para 7. The same consequences follow when an interest in, right over or licence to occupy land is granted by the person acting under a power in relation to land forming part of the trader's business assets: VATA 1994, Sch 4, para 9.
[2] VAT Regulations, SI 1995/2518, reg 27.
[3] SI 1995/2518, regs 13(2), 29.

Acquisitions by non-taxable persons

[67.12] The legislation sets out an accounting and payment procedure for the declaration and payment of VAT by non-taxable persons in respect of the following acquisitions:

(1) New means of transport.[1]
(2) Goods subject to excise duty.[2]
(3) Goods subject to a fiscal warehousing regime.[3]

De Voil Indirect Tax Service V5.109, 111.

[1] VAT Regulations, SI 1995/2518, reg 148; Notice No 728.
[2] SI 1995/2518, reg 36.
[3] SI 1995/2518, reg 145J as inserted by SI 1996/1250.

[67.13] Accounting and payment

Imported goods

[67.13] In principle, import duties (and therefore VAT[1]) are due for payment when a customs debt is incurred.[2] This is normally the time when an entry is made for customs purposes. In principle, goods may not be delivered or removed until the VAT due has been paid.[3] These general principles are modified in the following circumstances:

(1) Where a charge to tax arises on postal imports, the amount due is either collected by the Post Office when the postal packet is delivered[4] or accounted for under the postponed accounting system.[5]

(2) Where no entry is required on importation (eg on passenger's baggage) VAT is charged when the goods physically arrive in the UK (eg when an airline passenger walks through the red channel in the customs hall of an airport).[6]

(3) Approved importers may account for VAT by direct debit on a monthly basis under the duty deferment system.[7]

De Voil Indirect Tax Service V5.115–122.

[1] VATA 1994, s 16(1).
[2] VATA 1994, s 15(2)(*a*). For customs debts, see VATA 1994, s 96(3)(*b*).
[3] CEMA 1979, s 43(1). For payments by shipping agents and forwarding agents on behalf of an insolvent importer, see Notice No 48 (July 2009), para 3.13.
[4] See Postal Packet (Customs and Excise) Regulations, SI 1986/260 as amended by SI 1986/1019, SI 1992/3224, SI 2001/1149.
[5] See VAT Regulations, SI 1995/2518, reg 122. Datapost packets and goods valued at £2,000 or more are excluded from this relief.
[6] See CEMA 1979, ss 37, 78. For deferment, see Customs and Excise (Deferred Payment) (RAF Airfields and Offshore Installations) (No 2) Regulations, SI 1988/1898.
[7] See Customs Duties (Deferred Payment) Regulations, SI 1976/1223 (as amended), Excise Duties (Deferred Payment) Regulations, SI 1992/3152. See Notice No 101.

Electronic services

[67.14] Third country traders using the simplified scheme for electronic services supplied in the EU[1] are required to submit a special accounting return[2] for each reporting period.[3] Returns must be submitted electronically within 20 days after the end of the reporting period.[4] The tax shown to be due on the return must be paid in sterling at the time when the return is submitted.[5]

[1] For the special scheme, see supra, § **63.42**.
[2] For the information to be shown, see VATA 1994, Sch 3B, para 11(4) as inserted by FA 2003, Sch 2, para 4.
[3] For reporting periods, see VATA 1994, Sch 3B, para 11(2) as so inserted.
[4] VATA 1994, Sch 3B, para 12(3) as so inserted.
[5] VATA 1994, Sch 3B, para 13(1) as so inserted.

Correction of errors

Correcting the VAT Account

[67.15] A trader may correct his VAT Account[1] if he discovers understatements or overstatements of input tax or output tax during a prescribed accounting period. Two conditions must be met if understatements or overstatements are discovered during a prescribed accounting period ending after 31 March 2006.[2] First, the prescribed accounting period to which the understatements or overstatements relate must end less than four years before the first day of the prescribed accounting period in which the discovery was made. Secondly, the net underdeclaration or net overdeclaration must be:

(1) £10,000 or less (if the value of outputs included in Box 6 of the trader's VAT return[3] for the period is £1,000,000 or less).
(2) Not more than 1% of the value of outputs included in Box 6 (if the value of those outputs is between £1,000,000 and £5,000,000 exclusive).
(3) Not more than £50,000 (in any other case).

Output tax for the current prescribed accounting period is increased by the net amount of output tax understated in prior periods or decreased by the net amount of output tax overstated. Each entry is cross-referenced to the return(s) and document(s) to which it relates.[4]

Input tax for the current prescribed accounting period is increased by the net amount of input tax understated in prior periods or decreased by the net amount of input tax overstated. Each entry is cross-referenced to the return(s) and document(s) to which it relates.[5]

De Voil Indirect Tax Service V3.419, 506.

---

[1] For the VAT Account, see supra, §§ **67.02**.
[2] VAT Regulations, SI 1995/2518, reg 34(1), (1A), (1C), (2), (3), (7) as inserted or amended by SI 1997/1086, SI 2008/1482, SI 2009/586.
[3] For the forms used, see supra, § **67.03**.
[4] SI 1995/2518, reg 34(4), (6).
[5] SI 1995/2518, reg 34(5), (6).

Credit for output tax not due

[67.16] The Commissioners are liable to credit a person in either of the following circumstance:[1]

(1) The person has accounted to the Commissioners for VAT in respect of a prescribed accounting period and, in doing so, has overstated the amount of output tax due. The person must claim the credit no later than four years after the end of the prescribed accounting period in which the disclosure was made (if an error was made in a voluntary disclosure) or four years after the end of the prescribed accounting period in which the output tax was accounted for (in other cases).

[67.16] Accounting and payment

(2) The Commissioners have assessed the person to VAT for a prescribed accounting period and, in doing so, have overstated the amount of output tax due from him. The person must claim the credit no later than four years after the end of the prescribed accounting period in which the disclosure was made (if the assessment was made on the basis of an erroneous voluntary disclosure) or four years after the end of the prescribed accounting period in which the assessment was made (in other cases).

The Commissioners have a defence against a claim if the claimant would be unjustly enriched[4] by the credit.[5] In principle, a trader is regarded as being unjustly enriched if he has been passed on the VAT at issue to another person. However, this not so if he demonstrates that his business has suffered loss or damage as a result of the error. In this situation, the credit given is the lower of the VAT claimed and an amount shown by the trader to represent appropriate compensation for the loss or damage incurred.[6] The onus of demonstrating that VAT has been passed on – and, if so, the extent to which it has been passed on – lies with the Commissioners.[7] Once established, the fact that VAT has been passed on may give rise to an inference that no loss or damage has occurred. The trader must produce some material in order to displace this inference. In the absence of relevant facts or figures, he must justify his inability to produce them.[8]

A trader is not unjustly enriched if he enters into a reimbursement arrangement in prescribed terms and his claim is supported by written undertakings given to the Commissioners no later than the time when the claim is made.[9]

A claim for credit must be made in writing. It must state the amount claimed and the method used to calculate that amount.[10] Any amounts due to the Commissioners are set off against the credit due to the claimant and the balance is paid or repaid to him.[11] The amount paid or repaid carries interest if the overstatement resulted from an error made by the Commissioners.[12] A right of appeal is given in relation to claims.[13]

If the amount credited by the Commissioners exceeds the amount for which they are liable, the Commissioners may assess the excess.[14] The amount assessed carries interest.[15]

De Voil Indirect Tax Service V5.159.

---

1 VATA 1994, s 80(1), (1A), (2), (4), (4ZA), (4ZB) as inserted, substituted or amended by F(No 2)A 2005, s 3; FA 2008, Sch 39, para 36; Finance Act 2008, Schedule 39 (Appointed Day, Transitional Provision and Savings) Order, SI 2009/403, art 2(1). For prescribed accounting periods ending on or before 31 March 2006, see art 6 of the 2009 Order. For voluntary disclosures, see infra, § **67.19**. For rights to credit transferred from one person to another, see *Midlands Co-operative Society Ltd v Revenue and Customs Comrs* [2008] EWCA Civ 305, [2008] STC 1803 (transfer of engagements from one industrial and provident society to another). For set-off where rights to credit are so transferred, see FA 2008, s 133.

4 For a review of the case law on "unjust enrichment" see *Baines & Ernst Ltd v Customs and Excise Comrs* [2006] EWCA Civ 1040, [2006] STC 1632, CA. In

order to comply with Community law, the principle prohibiting unjust enrichment must be implemented in accordance with principles such as that of equal treatment: see *Marks and Spencer v Customs and Excise Comrs* (case C-309/06) [2008] STC 1408, ECJ at para 41.
5   VATA 1994, s 80(3) as amended by F(No 2)A 2005, s 3.
6   VATA 1994, s 80(3A)–(3C) as inserted or amended by FA 1997, s 46 and F(No 2)A 2005, s 3.
7   *Baines & Ernst Ltd v Customs and Excise Comrs* [2006] EWCA Civ 1040, [2006] STC 1632, CA; see also *Marks and Spencer plc v Customs and Excise Comrs* [1999] STC 205.
8   *Baines & Ernst Ltd v Customs and Excise Comrs* [2005] EWHC 2300 (Ch), [2006] STC 653 at para 24.
9   VATA 1994, s 80A as inserted or amended by FA 1997, s 46 and F(No 2) A 2005, s 4; SI 1995/2518, regs 43B, 43C, 43G as inserted, renumbered and amended by SI 1998/59, SI 1999/438, SI 2005/2231. The trader has 90 days to pass on the tax and interest credited to him. Any balance which has not been disbursed at that time must be notified to the Commissioners and repaid without prior demand: SI 1995/2518, reg 43D as substituted by SI 2005/2231. For the records to be kept, see SI 1995/2518, reg 43E as inserted and renumbered by SI 1998/59, SI 1999/438. For the production of records, see 1995/2518, reg 43F as inserted, renumbered and amended by SI 1998/59, SI 1999/438, SI 2005/2231. For assessments in respect of reimbursement arrangements, see VATA 1994, s 80B(1), (1B) as inserted by FA 1997, s 46 and F(No 2)A 2005, s 4. For the right of appeal in relation to these assessments, see VATA 1994, s 83(*ta*) as inserted or amended by FA 1997, s 46 and F(No 2)A 2005, s 4. The amounts assessed carry interest: VATA 1994, s 80B(1E), (2) as inserted by FA 1997, s 46 and F(No 2)A 2005, s 4.
10 VATA 1994, s 80(6); VAT Regulations, SI 1995/2518, reg 37. Form VAT 652 can be used, but its use is not compulsory.
11 VATA 1994, s 80(2A) as inserted by F(No 2)A 2005, s 3.
12 VATA 1994, s 78 as amended by F(No 2)A 2005, s 4. For interest, see supra, § **2A.43**.
13 VATA 1994, s 83(*t*) as amended by F(No 2)A 2005, s 4.
14 VATA 1994, s 80(4A) as substituted by F(No 2)A 2005, s 3. A right of appeal is given in relation to assessments: VATA 1994, s 83(*t*) as amended by F(No 2)A 2005, s 4.
15 VATA 1994, s 80(4C) as inserted or amended by FA 1997, s 47 and FA 2008, s 120.

Repayment of VAT not due

[67.17] The Commissioners are liable to make a repayment to a person if all of the following conditions are met:[1]

(1) The person has paid an amount of VAT to them for a prescribed accounting period.[2]

(2) The VAT comprised neither output tax (for which a claim is made under the provisions described in infra, § **67.16**) nor input tax (to which the provisions described in infra, § **67.18** apply).

(3) The VAT was not due to the Commissioners.

[67.17] Accounting and payment

(4) The person makes a claim for this purpose no later than four years after the date on which the payment was made.

A claim for repayment must be made in writing. It must state the amount claimed and the method used to calculate that amount.[3] The amount repaid carries interest if the overstatement resulted from an error made by the Commissioners.[4] A right of appeal is given in relation to claims.[5]

If the amount repaid by the Commissioners exceeds the amount for which they are liable, the Commissioners may assess the excess.[6] The amount assessed carries interest.[7]

De Voil Indirect Tax Service V5.159.

---

[1] VATA 1994, s 80(1B), (2), (4), (4ZA) as inserted or substituted by F(No 2)A 2005 s 3; FA 2008, Sch 39, para 36; Finance Act 2008, Schedule 39 (Appointed Day, Transitional Provision and Savings) Order, SI 2009/403 art 2(1). For payments made before 31 March 2006, see art 6 of the 2009 Order. For rights to repayment transferred from one person to another, see *Midlands Co-operative Society Ltd v Revenue and Customs Comrs* [2008] EWCA Civ 305, [2008] STC 1803, CA (transfer of engagements from one industrial and provident society to another). For set-off where rights to repayment are so transferred, see FA 2008, s 133.

[2] For the circumstances in which a payment is made to the Commissioners, see *R (on the application of Cardiff City Council) v Customs and Excise Comrs* [2003] EWCA Civ 1456, [2004] STC 356.

[3] VATA 1994, s 80(6); VAT Regulations, SI 1995/2518, reg 37. Form VAT 652 can be used, but its use is not compulsory.

[4] VATA 1994, s 78 as amended by F(No 2)A 2005, s 4.

[5] VATA 1994, s 83(*t*) as amended by F(No 2)A 2005, s 4.

[6] VATA 1994, s 73(2), (6A) as inserted by FA 2008, s 120. A right of appeal is given in relation to such an assessment: see VATA 1994, s 83(*p*).

[7] VATA 1994, s 74.

Input tax unclaimed or understated

[67.18] A trader may understate, or fail to claim, input tax on his VAT return. In principle, it appears that:

(1) Input tax previously unclaimed by a trader is relieved by way of a deduction on his current VAT return.[1] A deduction is made in such manner as the Commissioners allow or direct.[2] As the Commissioners have discretion whether or not to allow or direct a deduction, it appears that a voluntary disclosure is necessary unless the circumstances fall within the terms of a general direction.[3]

(2) An understatement in a previous claim for input tax is relieved by way of either an adjustment to the trader's VAT Account[4] or a voluntary disclosure.[5] It appears that the Commissioners' response to a voluntary disclosure is to make a direction for the error to be corrected in such manner as they require.[6]

De Voil Indirect Tax Service V5.159.

1   ie under VAT Regulations, SI 1995/2518, reg 29(1). See *University of Sussex v Customs and Excise Comrs* [2003] EWCA Civ 1448, [2004] STC 1.
2   SI 1995/2518, reg 29(1). In principle, an authorisation or direction may not permit a claim for deduction more than three years after the due date for filing the return for the prescribed accounting period in which the VAT was incurred: see SI 1995/2518, reg 29(1A) as inserted by SI 1997/1086. However, the three-year time limit does not apply to claims made before 1 April 2009 if: (1) the VAT was incurred in a prescribed accounting period ending before 1 May 1997; and (2) the claimant held the required evidence in an accounting period ending before that date: FA 2008, s 121(2).
3   For the scope of the Commissioners' discretion, see *University of Sussex v Customs and Excise Comrs* [2003] EWCA Civ 1448, [2004] STC 1 at [158]. For voluntary disclosures, see infra, § **67.19**. A deduction is allowed if the trader did not hold evidence to support a claim for deduction in his VAT return for the prescribed accounting period in which the VAT became chargeable: see Notice No 700/45 (March 2002), para 6.1.
4   ie under SI 1995/2518, reg 34. For corrections to the VAT Account, see supra, § **67.15**.
5   Notice No 700/45 (March 2002), Section 6. For voluntary disclosures, see infra, § **67.19**.
6   ie in accordance with SI 1995/2518, reg 35.

Voluntary disclosure

[67.19] The Commissioners have introduced an extra-statutory procedure for making voluntary disclosures. A trader necessarily uses this procedure if the net underdeclaration exceeds £2,000.[1] A voluntary disclosure is made on form VAT 652 or by letter. An unprompted disclosure[2] reduces the amount of any penalty to which a person may be liable in respect of the underdeclaration.[3]

The amount disclosed carries interest from the reckonable date[4] until the date on which it was paid.[5] However, interest is assessed only if it represents commercial restitution.[6]

De Voil Indirect Tax Service V5.144, 343, 344.

1   Net underdeclarations of £2,000 or less can be corrected through the VAT Account under the provisions described in supra, § **67.15**.
2   Defined in FA 2007, Sch 24, para 9(2)(*a*).
3   For penalties in respect of careless or deliberate understatements of a person's liability to VAT, see FA 2008, Sch 24, para 1.
4   Defined in VATA 1994, s 74(5)(*a*), (*b*).
5   VATA 1994, s 74(2).
6   Customs and Excise Press Notice No 30/94 dated 7 September 1994.

68

Exemption

Introduction	PARA **68.01**
The option to tax	PARA **68.03**
Exempt supplies	PARA **68.11**

Introduction

The nature of exemption

[68.01] Exemption from tax is confined to supplies.[1] It has no application to acquisitions and importations. The purpose of exemption is to exclude supplies from the charge to tax. The legislation does this in a circuitous manner: it provides that VAT is charged on taxable supplies[2] and that a taxable supply is a supply which is not an exempt supply.[3] As an exempt supply is not a taxable supply, and only taxable supplies are charged to tax, it follows that exempt supplies are not charged to tax.

Exempt supplies have one point of similarity with zero-rated supplies: no tax is charged on them. The difference lies in the fact that a zero-rated supply, unlike an exempt supply, is treated in all respects as if it were a taxable supply.[4]

The consequences of exemption are as follows:

(1) A person is neither liable nor entitled to registration by reference to the exempt supplies he makes. This arises from the fact that it is taxable supplies which are taken into account for registration purposes.[5] In principal, therefore, a trader is unable to become registered if his supplies consist wholly of exempt supplies.[6]

(2) A taxable person is not normally entitled to credit for input tax attributable to an exempt supply.

(3) An acquisition is not a taxable acquisition, and is therefore excluded from the charge to tax, if the goods were supplied under an exempt supply.[7]

There are two exceptions to the general rule that input tax is irrecoverable if it is attributable to an exempt supply. First, the legislation provides that a taxable person is entitled to input tax credit in respect of some, but not all, input tax attributable to exempt supplies of investment gold.[8] To this extent, the manner in which exemption operates is more akin to zero-rating. Secondly, the legislation provides that a taxable person is entitled to input tax credit for certain input tax (referred to as "exempt input tax") attributable to exempt supplies if the input tax falls below a specified de minimis threshold.[9]

[68.01] Exemption

Exemption has one further peculiarity. A trader is entitled or permitted to make an election (referred to as the "option to tax") in relation to land and investment gold whereby supplies cease to be exempt from tax and instead become chargeable to VAT at a positive rate.[10]

The charging provisions do not assign any territorial limit on exempt supplies and it is therefore arguable that supplies are exempt, and therefore affect recovery of input tax, whether they are made in the UK or elsewhere.[11] However, other provisions proceed on the basis that only supplies made in the UK are exempt from tax[12] and, since the Commissioners have yet to argue otherwise, it is reasonable to assume for all practical purposes that exemption applies only to supplies made in the UK. A taxable person is entitled to input tax credit in respect of VAT attributable to certain supplies which, if made in the UK, would be exempt supplies.[13]

De Voil Indirect Tax Service V4.101–103.

1. VATA 1994, s 31(1).
2. VATA 1994, s 4(1).
3. VATA 1994, s 4(2).
4. VATA 1994, s 30(1).
5. VATA 1994, Sch 1, paras 1(1), (2) and 9.
6. A person may be registered by reference to his acquisitions under see VATA 1994, Sch 3 or his overseas supplies under VATA 1994, Sch 1, para 10.
7. VATA 1994, s 31(1).
8. VAT Regulations, SI 1995/2518, reg 103A as inserted by SI 1999/3114.
9. SI 1995/2518, reg 106.
10. For elections to waive exemption, see infra, § **68.05**.
11. VATA 1994, s 4(2) does no more than provide that a supply of a description for the time being in VATA 1994, Sch 9 (ie an exempt supply) made in the UK is not a taxable supply. This is not the same thing as providing that a supply made in the UK is an exempt supply if it is of a description for the time being in VATA 1994, Sch 9.
12. ie VAT (Input Tax) (Specified Supplies) Order, SI 1999/3121, art 3 (proviso).
13. SI 1999/3121, art 3.

Legislation

[68.02] VATA 1994, s 31(1) and Sch 9 exempt a wide range of goods and services. Schedule 9 may be varied by statutory instrument.[1] It is divided into 15 groups, each of which is subdivided into one or more items. These items are interpreted in accordance with the notes to each group.[2]

The provisions of Sch 9 are briefly described under broad headings in the following paragraphs.

A person is liable to civil penalties if he gives an incorrect certificate to a supplier which results in a supply to him being improperly exempted from tax under VATA 1994, Sch 9, Group 1.[3]

De Voil Indirect Tax Service V4.101–103.

[1] VATA 1994, s 31(2).
[2] VATA 1994, s 96(9) as amended by FA 2001, Sch 31, para 5.
[3] VATA 1994, s 62, as amended by FA 1996, Sch 3, para 8 and FA 2001, Sch 31, para 3.

The option to tax

Land

Exercising the option to tax

[68.03] The option to tax may be exercised[1] in respect of:[2]

(a) specified land;[3] or
(b) a specified building[4] or part of a building.[5]

The option has effect from the later of:

(i) the start of the day on which the option is exercised; or
(ii) the start of the day specified in the option.[6]

It must be notified to the Commissioners in writing within a period of 30 days or such longer period as the Commissioners may allow.[7] The Commissioners may publish a notice specifying that the notification must contain prescribed information and be given in a prescribed form.[8]

In principle, a person must obtain the Commissioners' prior permission in writing before exercising an option to tax if:

(a) he made, makes or intends to make an exempt supply in the ten-year period ending on the day from which the option is to take effect; and
(b) the supply arises from a grant of the land to which the option is to apply.[9]

The Commissioners must satisfy themselves that relevant input tax[10] would be fairly and reasonably attributed to relevant supplies[11] before giving permission.[12] However, the option to tax may be exercised without prior permission if specified conditions are met.[13]

Construction[14] of a building[15] may commence[16] on land in respect of which the option to tax has been exercised. The whole of the building and all the land within its curtilage may be excluded from the option provided none of the land within the curtilage of the new building falls within the curtilage of an existing building.[17] In principle, notification of the exclusion must be given to the Commissioners no later than 30 days after the time from which it is to have effect. The Commissioners may extend this period in an individual case.[18]

An option may be revoked by the taxpayer during a six-month "cooling off" period[19] or at any time after the twentieth anniversary of the day from which the option took effect[20] if specified conditions are met. In principle, an option is deemed to have been revoked if the taxpayer does not have a relevant interest[21] in the land or building throughout a continuous six-year period beginning at any time after the day from which the option has effect.[22]

---

1. For the manner in which the option to tax is exercised, see *Marlow Gardner & Cooke Ltd Directors' Pension Scheme v Revenue and Customs Comrs* [2006] EWHC 1612 (Ch), [2006] STC 2014. For the Commissioners' guidance, see Notice No 742A (June 2008) para 4.1.
2. VATA 1994, Sch 10, para 18(2) as inserted by SI 2008/1146.
3. For the extent to which the option extends to a building constructed, or to be constructed, on the land, see VATA 1994, Sch 10, para 18(3), as inserted by SI 2008/1146.
4. A building for this purpose includes an enlarged or extended building, an annexe to a building and a planned building: VATA 1994, Sch 10, para 18(6) as inserted by SI 2008/1146. For the extent to which buildings and complexes are treated as a single building, see VATA 1994, Sch 10, para 18(4), (5) as so inserted. The option has effect in relation to the whole of the building and all the land within its curtilage: VATA 1994, Sch 10, para 18(2) as so inserted.
5. The option has effect in relation to the whole of the building and all the land within its curtilage: VATA 1994, Sch 10, para 18(2) as inserted by SI 2008/1146. For land which has been built on, see *Finanzamt Goslar v Breitsohl* (case C-400/98), [2001] STC 355, ECJ.
6. VATA 1994, Sch 10, para 19(1) as inserted by SI 2008/1146.
7. VATA 1994, Sch 10, paras 20(1)(a), (2) and 34(1) as inserted by SI 2008/1146.
8. VATA 1994, Sch 10, para 20(1)(b), (3) as inserted by SI 2008/1146. Notice No 742A (June 2008) paras 4.2.2 and 4.2.3 are largely drafted in the form of guidance. Notification may be given on Form 1614A.
9. VATA 1994, Sch 10, paras 28(1), (2)(b) and 34(1) as inserted by SI 2008/1146. For applications, see VATA 1994, Sch 10, para 29 as so inserted; Notice No 742A (June 2008) para 5.5. Form 1614H must be used.
10. Ie input tax incurred or likely to be incurred in relation to the land: see VATA 1994, Sch 10, para 28(4) as inserted by SI 2008/1146.
11. Ie any supplies which arise from a grant relating to the land and which would be taxable if the option had effect: see VATA 1994, Sch 10, para 28(4) as inserted by SI 2008/1146.
12. For the factors to be taken into account by the Commissioners when making a decision, see VATA 1994, Sch 10, para 28(5), (6) as inserted by SI 2008/1146.
13. VATA 1004, Sch 10, paras 28(2)(a) and 34(3) as inserted by SI 2008/1146. For the conditions, see Notice No 742A (June 2008) para 5.2.
14. As defined in VATA 1994, Sch 10, para 27(6) as inserted by SI 2008/1146.
15. As defined in VATA 1994, Sch 10, paras 18(4)–(6) and 27(5) as inserted by SI 2008/1146.
16. For the time when construction commences, see VATA 1994, Sch 10, para 27(7) as inserted by SI 2008/1146; Notice No 742A (June 2008) para 2.6.4.
17. VATA 1994, Sch 10, para 27(1), (2) as inserted by SI 2008/1146.
18. For notification, see VATA 1994, Sch 10, paras 27(4) and 34(1) as inserted or amended by SI 2008/1146, SI 2009/1966; Notice No 742A (June 2008) para 2.6.3. Form 1614F is used.
19. See VATA 1994, Sch 10, para 23 as inserted by SI 2008/1146; Notice No 742A (June 2008) paras 8.1.2, 8.1.3 and 8.1.5. Notifications and applications are made

on Form 1614C.
[20] See VATA 1994, Sch 10, para 25 as inserted or amended by SI 2008/1146, SI 2009/1966; Notice No 742A (June 2008) paras 8.3.2, 8.3.3 and 8.3.5. Notifications and applications are made on Form 1614J.
[21] As defined in VATA 1994, Sch 10, para 24(3) as inserted by SI 2008/1146.
[22] See VATA 1994, Sch 10, para 24(1), (2) as inserted by SI 2008/1146. For the exception, see VATA 1994, Sch 10, paras 24(4) as so inserted and 26 as so inserted and amended by SI 2009/1966.

Making a real estate election

[68.04] A real estate election may be made in relation to relevant interests[1] in any land or building acquired[2] after the election is made.[3] In principle, the effect of an election is that the person making it is deemed to exercise an option to tax whenever he subsequently acquires a relevant interest in land, a building or part of a building.[4] The option is deemed to be made on the day on which the relevant interest is acquired and has effect from the beginning of that day.[5]

A real estate election must be notified to the Commissioners in writing within a period of 30 days or such longer period as the Commissioners may allow.[6]

A real estate election may be revoked by the Commissioners if the taxpayer fails to provide specified information.[7] The election may not be revoked in any other circumstances.[8] If an election is revoked, another election can be made only with the Commissioners' prior permission.[9]

[1] As defined in VATA 1994, Sch 10, para 21(12) as inserted by SI 2008/1146.
[2] For the time when a relevant interest is acquired, see VATA 1994, Sch 10 para 21(13), (14) as inserted by SI 2009/1966.
[3] VATA 1994, Sch 10, para 21(1)(a) as inserted by SI 2008/1146. As regards an election made by a member of a VAT group, the election has effect in relation to land and buildings acquired while the body corporate is a member of the VAT group.
[4] VATA 1994, Sch 10, para 21(2)(a) as inserted by SI 2008/1146. For the exceptions, see VATA 1994, Sch 10, para 21(3)–(5) as so inserted.
[5] VATA 1994, Sch 10, para 21(2)(b) as inserted by SI 2008/1146.
[6] VATA 1994, Sch 10, paras 21(7)(a) and 34(1) as inserted by SI 2008/1146. For notification, see VATA 1994, Sch 10, para 21(7)(b) and (c) as so inserted; Notice No 742A (June 2008) para 14.8. Form 1614E is used.
[7] See VATA 1994, Sch 10, para 21(9) as inserted by SI 2008/1146. For the information concerned, see VATA 1994, Sch 10, para 21(8) as so inserted; Notice No 742A (June 2008) para 14.11.
[8] VATA 1994, Sch 10, para 21(10) as inserted by SI 2008/1146.
[9] VATA 1994, Sch 10, para 21(11) as inserted by SI 2008/1146.

[68.05] Exemption

Consequences of exercising the option to tax
General rule
[68.05] In principle, a grant does not fall within VATA 1994, Sch 9, Group 1 if the following conditions are met:[1]

(1) a person exercises the option to tax in relation to the land;
(2) a grant is made in relation to the land at a time when the option to tax it has effect; and
(3) the grant is made by either the person who exercising the option or (in relation to a body corporate) a relevant associate.[2]

A grant made in relation to land before the option to tax is exercised in respect of it may give rise to supplies which are treated as taking place after the option has effect. For the purposes of (2) above, the option has effect in relation to those supplies as if the grant had been made at a time when the option had effect.[3] Thus, for example, if an office lease is granted on 1 January, an option in respect of the building has effect from 1 March and a periodic rent (ie a supply arising from the grant) is invoiced or paid on 25 March, the supply made on 25 March is deemed to arise from a grant made on or after 1 March so as to be a taxable supply by virtue of the option.

In principle, VAT may be added to the rent reserved in a lease or tenancy once the option to tax has been exercised in respect of the land, building or part concerned. However, this does not apply if the agreement specifies otherwise.[4] For input tax incurred before the option is exercised, see supra, § **68.04**.

---

[1] VATA 1994, Sch 10, para 2(1), (2) as inserted by SI 2008/1146. For the exceptions, see infra, § **68.06**.
[2] As defined in VATA 1994, Sch 10, para 3(2) as inserted by SI 2008/1146. For the circumstances in which a body corporate ceases to be a relevant associate, see VATA 1994, Sch 10, paras 3(3)–(5), 4 as so inserted; Notice No 742A (June 2008) para 6.3.5, 6.3.6 and 6.3.8. Applications and notifications in respect of relevant associates are made on Form 1614B.
[3] VATA 1994, Sch 10, para 31 as inserted by SI 2008/1146.
[4] VATA 1994, s 89. For arbitration in respect of a variation of rent in relation to an agricultural holding following the making or withdrawal of an option to tax, or a change in the rate of VAT, see Agricultural Holdings Act 1986, s 12 and Sch 2, para 4 as amended by FA 2009, s 78.

Exceptions
[68.06] An option to tax has no effect in relation to a grant made in the following circumstances.

(1) It is made in relation to a building or part of a building designed or adapted for use as one or more dwellings.[1] The building or part must be intended for that use.[2]
(2) It is made in relation to a building or part of a building designed or adapted for use solely for a relevant residential purpose.[3] The building or part must be intended for that use.[4] The recipient must provide the grantor with a certificate to that effect.[5]

The option to tax [68.06]

(3) It is made to a person ("the recipient") in relation to any building or part of a building intended for use as one or more dwellings.[6] The recipient must give a certificate to this effect.[7] He may do so only if:[8]
   (a) he intends to use the building or part as a dwelling or number of dwellings;
   (b) he intends to convert the building or part with a view to its being used as one or more dwellings;[9] or
   (c) he is a relevant intermediary.[10]

(4) It is made to a person ("the recipient") in relation to a building or part of a building intended for use solely for a relevant residential purpose.[11]. The recipient must give a certificate to this effect.[12] He may do so only if:[13]
   (a) he has the relevant conversion intention;[14] or
   (b) he is a relevant intermediary.[15]

(5) It is made to a person ("the recipient") in relation to a building or part of a building. The recipient must intend that the building or part will be used solely for a relevant charitable purpose,[16] other than as an office.[17] The recipient must provide the grantor with a certificate to that effect.[18]

(6) It is made in relation to a pitch for a residential caravan.[19]

(7) It is made in relation to facilities for mooring, anchoring or berthing a residential houseboat.[20]

(8) It is made to a relevant housing association[21] which certifies[22] that the land is to be used to construct one or more buildings for use as one or more dwellings[23] or solely for a relevant residential purpose.[24]

(9) It is made to an individual in the following circumstances:[25]
   (a) the land is to be used for the construction of a building;
   (b) the building is intended for use by the individual as a dwelling; and
   (c) the construction is not carried out in the course or furtherance of a business carried on by the individual.

(10) The anti-avoidance provisions in infra, § **68.07–68.09** apply.

---

[1] As defined in VATA 1994, Sch 8, Group 5, Note 2.
[2] VATA 1994, Sch 10, paras 5(1)(a), 33 as inserted by SI 2008/1146. For intention, see Notice No 742A (June 2008) para 3.2.
[3] As defined in VATA 1994, Sch 8, Group 5, Notes 4, 5.
[4] VATA 1994, Sch 10, para 5(1)(*b*) as inserted by SI 2008/1146.
[5] VATA 1994, Sch 10, paras 5(2) and 33 as inserted by SI 2008/1146. For the certificate to be provided, see VATA 1994, Sch 8, Group 5 Note 12(b). Notice No 742A (June 2008) para 3.3 does not mention this certification requirement.
[6] VATA 1994, Sch 10, para 6(1)(*a*) as inserted by SI 2008/1146. For buildings designed as one or more dwellings, see VATA 1994, Sch 8, Group 5, Note 2 by virtue of VATA 1994, Sch 10, para 33 as so inserted. For the circumstances in which a building or part is not regarded as being intended for use as one or more dwellings, see VATA 1994, Sch 10, para 6(8) as so inserted.
[7] For certificates, see VATA 1994, Sch 10, para 6(2), (6), (10) as inserted by SI 2008/1146; Notice No 742A (June 2008) paras 3.4.2 and 3.4.3. Form 1614D must be used.
[8] VATA 1994, Sch 10, para 6(3) as inserted by SI 2008/1146.

[68.06] Exemption

[9] As defined in VATA 1994, Sch 10, para 6(7) as inserted by SI 2008/1146.
[10] As defined in VATA 1994, Sch 10, para 6(4), (5), (7) as inserted by SI 2008/1146.
[11] VATA 1994, Sch 10, para 6(1)(a) as inserted by SI 2008/1146. For use for a relevant residential purpose, see VATA 1994, Sch 8, Group 5, Notes 4, 5 by virtue of VATA 1994, Sch 10, paras 6(9), 33 as so inserted.
[12] For certificates, see VATA 1994, Sch 10, para 6(2), (6), (10) as inserted by SI 2008/1146; Notice No 742A (June 2008) paras 3.4.2 and 3.4.3. Form 1614D must be used.
[13] VATA 1994, Sch 10, para 6(3) as inserted by SI 2008/1146.
[14] As defined in VATA 1994, Sch 10, para 6(7) as inserted by SI 2008/1146.
[15] As defined in VATA 1994, Sch 10, para 6(4), (5), (7) as inserted by SI 2008/1146.
[16] As defined in VATA 1994, Sch 8, Group 5, Notes 6, 12; Notice No 48 (July 2009) para 3.29.
[17] VATA 1994, Sch 10, para 7(1) as inserted by SI 2008/1146.
[18] VATA 1994, Sch 8, Group 5, Note 12(b) by virtue of VATA 1994, Sch 10, paras 7(2) and 33 as inserted by SI 2008/1146. Notice No 742A (June 2008) para 3.5 does not mention this certification requirement.
[19] VATA 1994, Sch 10, para 8(1) as inserted by SI 2008/1146. For the circumstances in which a caravan is not a residential caravan, see VATA 1994, Sch 10, para 8(2) as so inserted.
[20] VATA 1994, Sch 10, para 9(1) as inserted by SI 2008/1146. For houseboats, see VATA 1994, Sch 8, Group 9, Item 2. For the circumstances in which a houseboat is not a residential houseboat, see VATA 1994, Sch 10, para 9(2) as so inserted.
[21] As defined in VATA 1994, Sch 10, para 10(3) as inserted by SI 2008/1146.
[22] For the certificate to be given, see VATA 1994, Sch 10, para 10(2), (5) as inserted by SI 2008/1146; Notice No 742A (June 2008) paras 3.6.2 and 3.6.3. Form 1614G must be used.
[23] As defined in VATA 1994, Sch 8, Group 5, Note 2 as substituted by SI 1995/280.
[24] VATA 1994, Sch 10, para 10(1) as inserted by SI 2008/1146. For relevant residential purpose, see VATA 1994, Sch 8, Group 5, Notes 4, 5 by virtue of VATA 1994, Sch 10, paras 10(4) and 33 as so inserted.
[25] VATA 1994, Sch 10, para 11 as inserted by SI 2008/1146.

The anti-avoidance provisions

The general rule

[68.07] A supply is not a taxable supply as a result of an option to tax if the following conditions are met.

(1) The grant giving rise to the supply was made by a person ("the grantor") after 25 November 1996 otherwise than in pursuance of a written agreement entered into before 30 November 1999 giving effect to terms fixed before 26 November 1996.[1]
(2) One or other of the following conditions was met at the time when the grant was made by the grantor:[2]
  (a) the land was a capital item[3] for the purposes of the capital goods scheme;[4]

(b) the grantor or a development financier[5] intended or expected that the land, a building or part of a building on the land, or a building or part of a building to be constructed on the land, would become a capital item of the grantor or a relevant transferee[6] for the purposes of the capital goods scheme.
(3) The grant giving rise to the supply was made before the end of the period of adjustment[7] for the purposes of the capital goods scheme.[8]
(4) At the time when the grant was made, the grantor or a development financier[9] intended or expected that, whether or not as a result of the grant, the following conditions would be met:[10]
  (a) the grantor, a development financier or a person connected[11] with either would continue, for a period at least, to occupy[12] the land or (if not already in occupation) would immediately or eventually begin to do so;
  (b) the occupation would take place during the period of adjustment applicable to the land for the purposes of the capital goods scheme;
  (c) at the time of occupation, the grantor, development financier or connected person would fall within one or other of the following descriptions:[13]
    (i) he is not a taxable person, a local authority or public body entitled to refunds,[14] or a government department;[15]
    (ii) (if a taxable person, local authority, public body or government department) he would not occupy the land wholly, or substantially wholly,[16] for an eligible purpose.[17]

---

[1] VATA 1994, Sch 10, para 12(8) as inserted by SI 2008/1146.
[2] VATA 1994, Sch 10, paras 12(1)(a), 13(2)(a), (3), (4), (8), (9) as inserted by SI 2008/1146.
[3] For land, buildings and parts of a building regarded as a capital item for the purposes of the capital goods scheme, see VAT Regulations, SI 1995/2518, reg 113.
[4] For the capital goods scheme, see supra, § **66.27**.
[5] As defined in VATA 1994, Sch 10, paras 12(4) and 14(2)–(7) as inserted by SI 2008/1146.
[6] As defined in VATA 1994, Sch 10, para 13(5) as inserted by SI 2008/1146.
[7] For the period of adjustment applicable to land, see VAT Regulations, SI 1995/2518, reg 114(3)(a), (b).
[8] VATA 1994, Sch 10, paras 12(1)(a) and 13(2)(b), (6), (9) as inserted by SI 2008/1146.
[9] As defined in VATA 1994, Sch 10, para 14(1), (3), (7) as inserted by SI 2008/1146.
[10] VATA 1994, Sch 10, paras 12(1)(b), (2), (3), 13(9), 15(2), (3), (4) as inserted by SI 2008/1146.
[11] In principle, any question whether a person is connected with another person is decided in accordance with TA 1988, s 839: see VATA 1994, Sch 10, para 34(2) as inserted or amended by SI 2008/1146, SI 2009/1966. For the exceptions, see VATA 1994, Sch 10, para 34(2A), (2B) as inserted by SI 2009/1966.
[12] For "occupation", see *Revenue and Customs Comrs v Principal and Fellows of Newnham College in the University of Cambridge* [2008] UKHL 23, [2008] STC

1225, HL.
[13] VATA 1994, Sch 10, para 16(1)–(7) as inserted by SI 2008/1146.
[14] For refunds to local authorities and public bodies, see infra, § **66.27**.
[15] As defined in VATA 1994, s 41(6)–(8).
[16] For the criteria used in deciding whether land is occupied wholly or substantially wholly used for an eligible purpose, see VATA 1994, Sch 10, para 15(5) as inserted by SI 2008/1146; Notice No 742A (June 2008) para 13.10.1.
[17] For eligible purposes, see VATA 1994, Sch 10, para 16(3)–(7) as inserted by SI 2008/1146 (taxable person making creditable supplies; non-business activities of a local authority or public body; any occupation by a government department; and occupation arising because an automatic teller machine is fixed to the land).

Grants made between 19 March 1997 and 9 March 1999

[68.08] The general rule[1] is modified in relation to a grant made between 19 March 1997 and 9 March 1999 inclusive.[2] The grant is treated as if it had been made on 10 March 1999[3] if the following conditions were met at the time when the grant was actually made[4]:

(1) the grantor or a development financier[5] intended or expected that the land, a building or part of a building on the land, or a building or part to be constructed on the land would become a capital item[6] in relation to the grantor or any relevant transferee;[7] and
(2) the land, building or part had not become a capital item[8] for the purposes of the capital goods scheme.[9]

[1] See supra, § **68.07**.
[2] VATA 1994, Sch 10, para 12(7) as inserted by SI 2008/1146.
[3] VATA 1994, Sch 10 para 17(1) as inserted by SI 2008/1146.
[4] VATA 1994, Sch 10, para 17(2) as inserted by SI 2008/1146.
[5] As defined in VATA 1994, Sch 10, paras 12(4) and 14(2)–(7) as inserted by SI 2008/1146.
[6] As defined in VATA 1994, Sch 10, para 13(8) as inserted by SI 2008/1146.
[7] As defined in VATA 1994, Sch 10, para 13(5) as inserted by SI 2008/1146.
[8] For land, buildings and parts of a building regarded as a capital item for the purposes of the capital goods scheme, see VAT Regulations, SI 1995/2518, reg 113.
[9] For the capital goods scheme, see supra, § **66.27**.

Supply made by someone other than the grantor

[68.09] A supply arising from the grant may be made by someone other than the grantor, eg where the grant comprises a lease and the grantor assigns the lease to another person. The general rule[1] applies with the following modifications in these circumstances.

(1) The grant giving rise to the supply is deemed to have been made by the person ("the deemed grantor") who made the supply.[2]
(2) The grant is deemed to have been made at the time when the first supply arising from the grant is made by the deemed grantor,[3] eg the tax point of the first periodic rent received or invoiced by him.

The option to tax [68.10]

(3) In determining whether the deemed grantor is a developer of the land,[4] it is irrelevant whether or not the period of adjustment[5] for the purposes of the capital goods scheme[6] has expired at the time when the deemed grantor makes his first supply.[7]

[1] See supra, § **68.07**.
[2] VATA 1994, Sch 10, para 12(6)(*a*) as inserted by SI 2008/1146.
[3] VATA 1994, Sch 10, para 12(6)(*b*) as inserted by SI 2008/1146.
[4] As defined in VATA 1994, Sch 10, para 13 as inserted by SI 2008/1146.
[5] For land, buildings and parts of a building regarded as a capital item for the purposes of the capital goods scheme, see VAT Regulations, SI 1995/2518, reg 113.
[6] For the capital goods scheme, see supra, § **66.27**.
[7] VATA 1994, Sch 10, para 13(7). This overrides the requirement in VATA 1994, Sch 10, para 13(2)(b).

Investment gold

[**68.10**] A taxable person who produces or transforms gold may exercise the option to tax. The option has effect in relation to an exempt supply[1] of investment gold[2] made to another taxable person. It has effect from the day on which it is made. A taxable person making a supply in respect of which an election has effect must comply with conditions. The consequence of exercising the option is that the supply is excluded from exemption and is consequently chargeable to tax at the standard rate.[3]

A taxable person who supplies gold for industrial purposes in the normal course of his business may be permitted to make an election in accordance with a notice published by the Commissioners. An election has effect from the day on which it is made. It has effect in relation to an exempt supply of investment gold made to another taxable person. A taxable person making a supply in respect of which an election has effect must comply with conditions. The consequence of an election is that the supply is excluded from exemption and is consequently chargeable to tax at the standard rate. The Commissioners may cancel an election in order to protect the revenue. Where they do so, the election ceases to have effect from the date specified in the notification given by the Commissioners.[4]

An agent acting for a disclosed principal may make an election. The election has effect in relation to agency services[5] directly linked to a supply of investment gold made by his principal and chargeable to tax by virtue of an election made by his principal. A taxable person making a supply in respect of which an election has effect must comply with conditions. The consequence of an election is that the agent's supply is excluded from exemption and is consequently chargeable to tax at the standard rate.[6]

De Voil Indirect Tax Service V4.186.

[1] ie a supply exempt from tax by virtue of VATA 1994, Sch 9, Group 15, Items 1, 2. For supplies within this description, see infra, § **68.31**.
[2] As defined in VATA 1994, Sch 9, Group 15, Note 1.

[68.10] Exemption

[3] VAT (Investment Gold) Order, SI 1999/3116, SI 1999/3116, arts 1(2), 3(1), (2). (7).
[4] SI 1999/3116, arts 1(2), 3(3), (4), (8).
[5] ie services within VATA 1994, Sch 9, Group 15, Item 3.
[6] SI 1999/3116, art 3(5), (7).

Exempt supplies

Group 1—land

The general rule

[68.11] Subject to the exceptions set out below,[1] a grant[2] of any of the following is exempt from tax:[3]

(1) Any interest in or right over land.[4]
(2) Any personal right to call for, or be granted, any interest in or right over land in Scotland.[5]
(3) Any licence to occupy land.[6] A licence which falls short of a licence to occupy land is always chargeable to tax at the standard rate.[7]

A grant may be described as the supply made by a person with an interest, right, personal right or licence in the land when he transfers all or part of his interest, right, personal right or licence to another person.

A person clearly makes a grant if, for example, he sells the freehold or leases the land. He also makes a grant if he assigns or surrenders his interest etc in the land.[8] He is treated as making a grant if he makes a "reverse surrender",[9] but not if he makes what may be described as a "reverse assignment".[10] What may be described as a "reverse grant" may give rise to a supply chargeable to tax or to no supply at all.[11] The variation of an existing lease,[12] the lifting of a restrictive covenant,[13] the grant of an option,[14] the grant of a milk quota,[15] the virtual assignment of a lease[16] and the treatment of a service charge as rent[17] all give rise to their own particular problems.

De Voil Indirect Tax Service V4.111–113.

[1] For the exceptions, see infra, § **68.12**.
[2] For "grant", see VATA 1994, s 96(10A) as inserted or amended by FA 1997, s 35, SI 2008/1146. For the person making, or deemed to make, a grant, see VATA 1994, Sch 10, para 8. For private use of a dwelling forming part of the business assets, see *Seeling v Finanzamt Stamberg (case C-269/00)* [2003] STC 805, ECJ.
[3] VATA 1994, Sch 9, Group 1, Item 1.
[4] For interests and rights, see *Trewby v Customs and Excise Comrs* [1976] STC 122, [1976] 2 All ER 199. For land, see *Brodrick, Wright & Strong Ltd v Customs and Excise Comrs* (1987) VAT decision 2347.
[5] For the position prior to 1 January 1992, see *Margrie Holdings Ltd v Customs and Excise Comrs* [1991] STC 80.
[6] The meaning of the term "licence to occupy land" is no wider than the words "letting of immovable property" derived from Directive 77/388/EEC art 13B(b),

Exempt supplies **[68.11]**

now Directive 2006/112/EC art 135(1)(l): *Customs and Excise Comrs v Sinclair Collis Ltd* [2001] STC 989, HL. For the nature of a letting of immovable property under Community law, see *Staatssecretaris van Financiën v Coffee Shop Siberië vof (case C-158/98)* [1999] STC 742; *EC Commission v United Kingdom (case C-359/97)* [2000] STC 777; *Sweden v Stockholm Lindöpark AB (case C-150/99)* [2001] STC 103; *Customs and Excise Comrs v Sinclair Collis Ltd (case C-275/01)* [2003] STC 898, ECJ; *Belgium v Temco Europe SA (case C-284/03)* [2004] ECR I–11237, [2005] STC 1451, ECJ; *Gabriele Walderdorff v Finanzamt Waldviertel* (case C-451/06) [2007] SWTI 2850, ECJ. For a summary of the principles derived from these cases, see *Revenue and Customs Comrs v Denyer* [2007] EWHC 2750 (Ch), [2008] STC 633 at [19]. For the Commissioners' practice, see Business Brief 21/99, 7 September 1999.

[7] See in particular *Trewby v Customs and Excise Comrs* [1976] STC 122 (admission charge); *Revenue and Customs Comrs v Denyer* [2007] EWHC 2750 (Ch), [2008] STC 633 (hairdressers' hair renting agreement); *British Airports Authority (No 3) v Customs and Excise Comrs* (1975) VAT decision 147 (airport transfer desk); *South Glamorgan County Council v Customs and Excise Comrs* (1985) VAT decision 1956 (swimming pool); *Z Cars v Customs and Excise Comrs* BIR/76/194 unreported (taxi radio service). For bridge tolls, see *EC Commission v United Kingdom (case C-359/97)* [2000] STC 777, ECJ; Business Brief (Issue 3/03), 28 March 2003.

[8] VATA 1994, Sch 9, Group 1, Note 1. In the case of an assignment, the tenant assigning his lease to another person both makes the supply and receives the consideration. In the case of surrender, the tenant surrendering his lease to his landlord both makes the supply and receives the consideration. For surrender, see *Lubbock Fine & Co v Customs and Excise Comrs (case C-63/92)* [1994] STC 101, ECJ.

[9] A "reverse surrender" takes place when a tenant makes a payment to his landlord when he surrenders his lease. This payment is consideration for a supply made by the landlord: VATA 1994, Sch 9, Group 1, Notes 1, 1A. For a reverse surrender, see *AA Insurance Services Ltd v Customs and Excise Comrs* [1999] V & DR 361.

[10] See *Customs and Excise Comrs v Cantor Fitzgerald International (case C-108/99)* [2001] STC 1453, ECJ. A "reverse assignment" (a non-statutory term) takes place when a tenant assigning his lease to another person ("the new tenant") makes a payment to the new tenant. A payment may be necessary, for example, to induce the new tenant to accept an onerous lease. The payment is consideration for a supply made by the new tenant.

[11] See *Customs and Excise Comrs v Mirror Group plc (case C-409/98)* [2001] STC 1453, ECJ (payment to anchor tenant). A "reverse grant" (a non-statutory term) takes place when a landlord makes a payment to a new tenant as an inducement to accept the lease.

[12] See Business Brief (Issue 16/94), 25 July 1994.
[13] See Business Brief (Issue 17/94), 12 September 1994.
[14] See *Customs and Excise Comrs v Mirror Group plc (case C-409/98)* [2001] STC 1453, ECJ.
[15] See Business Brief (Issue 17/94), 12 September 1994.
[16] See *Revenue and Customs Comrs v Abbey National plc* [2006] EWCA Civ 886, [2006] STC 1961, CA. The "virtual assignment" of a lease is a transfer of the economic benefits and burdens of the lease without conferring a legal or equitable interest in the property.

[68.11] Exemption

[17] See *Nell Gwynn House Maintenance Fund Trustees v Customs and Excise Comrs* [1999] STC 79, HL; Notice No 48 (July 2009) para 3.18; cf *Globe Equities Ltd v Customs and Excise Comrs* [1995] V & DR 472.

Exceptions

[68.12] The following supplies are excluded from exemption:[1]

(1) The freehold of a new[2] or partly completed[3] building[4] which is neither designed as one or more dwellings[5] nor intended for use solely for a relevant residential[6] or charitable[7] purpose.

(2) The freehold of a new[8] or partly completed[9] civil engineering work.[10]

(3) A supply made before 1 June 2020[11] pursuant to a lease of, or licence to occupy, a building or civil engineering work if the lease or licence is deemed to be self-supplied before 1 March 1997 by virtue of construction, reconstruction, enlargement or extension works commenced after 31 December 1991.[12]

(4) The grant of any interest, right or licence consisting of a right to take game or fish[13] unless the freehold is transferred to the grantee at the same time.

(5) Accommodation[14] in a hotel, inn, boarding house or similar establishment.[15]

(6) The freehold, lease or licence of holiday accommodation[16] or a dwelling excluded from zero-rating,[17] subject to specified exceptions[18] in respect of buildings which are not new.[19]

(7) A lease or licence which permits the grantee to erect and occupy holiday accommodation.[20]

(8) Seasonal pitches[21] for caravans and facilities provided in connection with them.[22]

(9) Pitches for tents and camping facilities.

(10) Facilities for parking a vehicle.[23]

(11) Rights to fell and remove standing timber.

(12) Facilities for housing or storing aircraft.

(13) Facilities for mooring or storing a ship, boat or vessel.[24]

(14) Rights to occupy accommodation at a place of entertainment.[25]

(15) Facilities for playing sport and participating in physical recreation.[26]

(16) The grant of any right[27] to call for or be granted an interest or right within points (1) or (3)–(15).

A grant may be chargeable to tax at the standard rate if the option to tax has been exercised in respect of the land concerned.[28]

A major interest in a building or its site is zero-rated when granted by a person constructing or (in certain circumstances) substantially reconstructing a building.[29] A building zero-rated on the ground that it was intended solely for relevant residential or charitable use may cease to be used, or wholly used, for that purpose during the ten year period following completion of the building by virtue of the grant of an interest, right or licence in the building to another person. All or part of the supply is charged to tax at a positive rate if the purchaser, tenant or licensee intends to use all or part of the building for another purpose.[30]

Exempt supplies [68.12]

A grant of a description within heads 1, 2, 4, 6 or 10–16 may give rise to a succession of supplies following the grant. As regards a grant of a description within heads 1 or 2, the supplies are excluded from exemption whether the building or civil engineering work is new or partly completed at the time of supply or whether it is no longer new at that time. As regards any grant of a description within heads 4, 6 or 10–16, the supplies are excluded from exemption only if they fall within the relevant description at the time of supply.[31]

De Voil Indirect Tax Service V4.113.

---

1. VATA 1994, Sch 9, Group 1, Item 1(a)–(n).
2. As defined in VATA 1994, Sch 9, Group 1, Note 4.
3. For the time when a building is completed, see VATA 1994, Sch 9, Group 1, Note 2.
4. For buildings completed before 1 April 1989, see VATA 1994, Sch 9, Group 1, Notes 5, 6.
5. As defined in VATA 1994, Sch 8, Group 5, Note 2.
6. As defined in VATA 1994, Sch 8, Group 5, Note 3.
7. As defined in VATA 1994, Sch 8, Group 5, Note 4; Notice No 48 (July 2009) para 3.29.
8. As defined in VATA 1994, Sch 9, Group 1, Note 4.
9. For the time when a civil engineering work is completed, see VATA 1994, Sch 9, Group 1, Note 2.
10. For civil engineering works completed before 1 April 1989 see VATA 1994, Sch 9, Group 1, Notes 5, 6.
11. VATA 1994, Sch 9, Item 1(b) and Note 7 are repealed in relation to supplies made after 31 May 2020: see VAT (Buildings and Land) Order, SI 2008/1146, arts 1(3), 4 and Sch 2, para 10.
12. For the tenant's obligation to notify a self-supply, see VATA 1994, Sch 10, para 7(1). For the apportionment of the consideration for the supply in specified circumstances, see VATA 1994, Sch 10, para 7(2).
13. An apportionment is made where an interest in, right over or licence to occupy land includes a valuable right to take game or fish: VATA 1994, Sch 9, Group 1, Note 8. For rights considered to be "valuable", see Leaflet No 742/2/92, para 2. The grant of a right to fish waters for a term of years does not amount to a "leasing or letting of immovable property" for the purposes of Directive 2006/112/EC, art 135(1)(l) if the grantor retains a right to fish in common with the person to whom the right was granted: see *Gabriele Walderdorff v Finanzamt Waldviertel* (case C-451/06) [2007] ECR I-10637, [2008] STC 3079. For the nature of admission charges, see *Chalk Springs Fisheries (a firm) v Customs and Excise Comrs* (1987) VAT decision 2518.
14. As defined in VATA 1994, Sch 9, Group 1, Item 1(d) and Note 9. For rooms provided for the purpose of a supply of catering, see *Camilla Enterprises Ltd v Customs and Excise Comrs* (1993) VAT decision 10426; *Packford v Customs and Excise Comrs* (1994) VAT decision 11626.
15. For the nature of a "similar establishment", see most recently *Dinaro Ltd v Customs and Excise Comrs* (2001) VAT decision 17148.
16. As defined in VATA 1994, Sch 9, Group 1, Note 13. See *Poole Borough Council v Customs and Excise Comrs* [1992] VATTR 88.

[68.12] Exemption

17 As defined in VATA 1994, Sch 9, Group 1, Note 11(a). For the vires of this provision, see *Ashworth v Customs and Excise Comrs* [1994] VATTR 275.
18 Set out in VATA 1994, Sch 9, Group 1, Note 12.
19 As defined in VATA 1994, Sch 9, Group 1, Note 4.
20 As defined in VATA 1994, Sch 9, Group 1, Note 13.
21 As defined in VATA 1994, Sch 9, Group 1, Note 14. For covenants, statutory planning consents and similar permissions, see *Revenue and Customs Comrs v Tallington Lakes Ltd* [2007] EWHC 1955 (Ch), [2008] STC 2734.
22 For the vires of this provision, see *Colaingrove Ltd v Customs and Excise Comrs* [2003] STC 680.
23 See *Skatteministeriet v Henriksen (case 173/88)* [1990] STC 768, ECJ; *Customs and Excise Comrs v Trinity Factoring Services Ltd* [1994] STC 504; *Customs and Excise Comrs v Venuebest Ltd* [2003] STC 433.
24 See *Strand Ship Building Co Ltd v Customs and Excise Comrs* (1984) VAT decision 1651; *Fisher v Customs and Excise Comrs* (1975) VAT decision 179; *Roberts v Customs and Excise Comrs* [1992] VATTR 30. For exclusion from exemption under EU law, see *Fonden Marselisborg Lystbödehavn v Skatteministeriet (case C-428/02)* [2005] ECR I–1525, [2005] SWTI 360, ECJ.
25 An apportionment is necessary if the accommodation can be occupied outside the times when the entertainment takes place: see *Southend United Football Club v Customs and Excise Comrs* [1997] V & DR 202 (box at football ground).
26 Subject to the exceptions set out in VATA 1994, Sch 9, Group 1, Note 16. See *Queens Park Football Club Ltd v Customs and Excise Comrs* [1988] VATTR 76.
27 This includes an equitable right, a right under an option or right of pre-emption or, in relation to land in Scotland, a personal right.
28 See supra, § **68.04**.
29 See infra, § **69.17** and § **69.22**.
30 VATA 1994, Sch 10, para 36 as inserted by SI 2008/1146.
31 FA 2003, s 20(2); VATA 1994, s 96(10A), (10B) as inserted or amended by FA 1997, s 35, FA 2003, s 20(1), SI 2008/1146. For an example of supplies relating to a grant within head 1 made before 9 April 2003, see *RBS Property Development Ltd and Royal Bank of Scotland Group plc v Customs and Excise Comrs* (VAT decision 17789) [2003] SWTI 312.

Group 2—insurance

[68.13] The following services are exempt:

(1) Insurance[1] and re-insurance transactions.[2]
(2) The following services when related[3] to an insurance or reinsurance transaction and performed by an insurance broker or insurance agent[4] acting in an intermediary capacity:[5]
    (a) bringing together persons seeking and providing insurance or reinsurance with a view to the insurance or reinsurance of risks;[6]
    (b) carrying out work preparatory to the conclusion of insurance or reinsurance contracts;[7]
    (c) providing assistance in the administration and performance of insurance or reinsurance contracts;[8] and
    (d) collecting premiums.[9]

Exempt supplies [68.14]

De Voil Indirect Tax Service V4.121–124.

1   For "insurance", see *Card Protection Plan Ltd v Customs and Excise Comrs (case C-349/96)* [1999] STC 270, ECJ; *European Commission v Hellenic Republic (case C-13/06)* [2006] ECR I–11563, [2007] STC 194, ECJ. Cf *Co-operative Wholesale Society Ltd v Customs and Excise Comrs* [2000] STC 727, CA.
2   VATA 1994, Sch 9, Group 2, Item 1 as substituted or amended by SI 2001/3649, SI 2004/3083. For the parties to the transaction, see *Re Forsakringsaktiebolaget Skandia (publ)* (case C-240/99) [2001] STC 754, ECJ (management of insurance subsidiary not an exempt insurance transaction). For the exemption of insurance provided under a block insurance policy by a person not authorised to carry on insurance business in the UK, see *Card Protection Plan Ltd v Customs and Excise Comrs* [2001] UKHL 4, [2001] STC 174, HL.
3   Services are related to insurance if there is a close nexus between the service and the insurance transaction concerned; *Century Life plc v Customs and Excise Comrs* [2001] STC 38, CA. It is immaterial whether or not a contract is finally concluded: VATA 1994, Sch 9, Group 4, Item 4(a).
4   For the identification of a trader as an insurance broker or insurance agent, see *Staatssecretaris van Financiën v Arthur Andersen & Co Accountants* (case C-472/03) [2005] ECR I–1719, [2005] STC 508, ECJ; *JCM Beheer BV v Staatssecretaris van Financiën* (case C-124/07) [2008] ECR I–2101, [2008] STC 3360, ECJ; *InsuranceWide.com Services Ltd v Revenue and Customs Comrs* [2009] EWHC 999 (Ch), [2009] SWTI 1724.
5   VATA 1994, Sch 9, Group 2, Item 4 and Note 1(a) as substituted or amended by FA 1997, s 38, SI 2001/3649 and SI 2004/3083. For excluded services, see VATA 1994, Sch 9, Group 2, Notes 7–10. For back office activities, see *Staatssecretaris van Financiën v Arthur Andersen & Co Accountants* (case C-472/03) [2005] ECR I–1719, [2005] STC 508, ECJ. For the review of pension policies by a third party insurance broker, see *Century Life plc v Customs and Excise Comrs* [2001] STC 38, CA.
6   VATA 1994, Sch 9, Group 2, Item 4 and Note 1(a). For the requirements to be met when insurance is arranged in connection with the supply of goods or services, see VATA 1994, Sch 9, Group 2, Notes 4, 5; Notice No 701/36 (May 2002) para 11.3; *R Smith Glaziers (Dunfermline) Ltd v Customs and Excise Comrs* [2003] STC 419, HL. For internet services, see *InsuranceWide.com Services Ltd v Revenue and Customs Comrs* [2009] EWHC 999 (Ch), [2009] SWTI 1724. For call centres, see *Teletech UK Ltd v Customs and Excise Comrs* (2003) VAT decision 18080.
7   VATA 1994, Sch 9, Group 2, Item 4 and Note 1(b).
8   VATA 1994, Sch 9, Group 2, Item 4 and Note 1(c).
9   VATA 1994, Sch 9, Group 2, Item 4 and Note 1(d).

Group 3—postal services

[68.14] The following postal services are exempt:[1]

(1)   Postal packets conveyed by the post office company.[2]
(2)   Services supplied by the post office company in connection with conveying postal packets.

De Voil Indirect Tax Service V4.126.

[68.14] Exemption

---

1. VATA 1994, Sch 9, Group 3, Items 1, 2 and Notes 1, 2. For the scope of the exemption conferred by Directive 2006/112/EC art 132(1)(a), see *R (on the application of TNT Post UK Ltd) v Customs and Excise Comrs* (case C-357/07) [2009] ECR I–0000, [2009] STC 1464, ECJ.
2. As defined in VATA 1994, s 96(1).

Group 4—betting, gaming and lotteries

[68.15] The following services are exempt:[1]

(1) Providing facilities for placing bets.[2]
(2) Providing facilities for playing games of chance[3] for a prize.[4]
(3) Granting a right to take part in a lottery.[5]

However, exemption does not extend to:[6]

(1) admission charges;
(2) subscriptions; and
(3) the provision of a gaming machine.[7]

De Voil Indirect Tax Service V4.131.

---

1. VATA 1994, Sch 9, Group 4, Items 1, 2. For the extent to which member states can impose limitations and conditions on the exemptions conferred by Directive 77/388/EEC art 13B(f), now Directive 2006/112/EC art 135(1)(i), see *Finanzamt Gladbeck v Linneweber; Finanzamt Herne-West v Akritidis* (joined cases C-453/02 and C-462/02) [2005] ECR I–1131, [2008] STC 1069, ECJ. For unlawful games of chance, see *Fischer v Finanzamt Donaueschingen* (case C-283/95) [1998] ECR I–3369, ECJ. For the right to take part in gaming, see *Rum Runner Casino Ltd v Customs and Excise Comrs* (1981) VAT decision 1036; *WMT Entertainments Ltd v Customs and Excise Comrs* (1992) VAT decision 9385; *Lee and Sarrafan v Customs and Excise Comrs* (1998) VAT decision 15563.
2. For outsourced services excluded from exemption, see *United Utilities plc v Customs and Excise Comrs (case C-89/05)* [2006] ECR I–6813, [2006] STC 1423, ECJ (call centre).
3. As defined in VATA 1994, Sch 9, Group 4, Notes 2, 3 as inserted by SI 2006/2685. For examples of exempt facilities, see *Grantham (a firm) v Customs and Excise Comrs* (1979) VAT decision 853; *J Seven Ltd v Customs and Excise Comrs* [1986] VATTR 42. For services excluded from exemption, see *Customs and Excise Comrs v Annabel's Casino Ltd* [1995] STC 225.
4. VATA 1994, Sch 9, Group 4, Note 4 as inserted by SI 2006/2685.
5. See *McCann v Customs and Excise Comrs* [1987] VATTR 101.
6. VATA 1994, Sch 9, Group 4, Note 1 as amended by SI 2006/2685, FA 2009, s 112(1)–(3).
7. As defined in VATA 1994, s 23(4)–(6) as substituted and amended by FA 2006, s 16(5), SI 2006/2686. For gaming machines, see *H J Glawe Spiel-und Unterhaltungsgeräte Aufstellungsgesellschaft mbH & Co KG v Finanzamt Hamburg-Barmbek-Uhlenhorst (case C-38/93)* [1994] STC 543, ECJ; *R v Ryan* [1994] STC

446, CA; *Feehan v Customs and Excise Comrs* [1995] STC 75; *McCann v Customs and Excise Comrs* [1987] VATTR 101.

Group 5—finance

[68.16] The following services are exempt:[1]

(1) Transactions with money,[2] any security for money,[3] or any note or order for the payment of money. This does not include preparatory services.[4]
(2) Making an advance.
(3) Granting credit.
(4) Providing instalment credit finance under a hire purchase, conditional sale or credit sale agreement.[5]
(5) Services comprising administrative arrangements, documentation and transfer of title in connection with the provision of instalment credit finance within point 4.[6]
(6) Transactions with any security or secondary security.[7]
(7) Intermediary services[8] relating to a transaction within points 1–6 by a person acting in an intermediary capacity.[9]
(8) Underwriting an issue within point 1.
(9) Underwriting a transaction within point 6.
(10) The management of credit by a person granting credit.
(11) Operating any current, deposit or savings account.
(12) Management[10] of an authorised open-ended investment company,[11] an authorised unit trust scheme,[12] a Gibraltar collective investment scheme,[13] an individually recognised overseas scheme,[14] a recognised collective investment scheme,[15] or a closed-ended collective investment undertaking.[16]

The foregoing descriptions include services supplied to merchants,[17] and services (including the management of credit) supplied to cardholders,[18] by persons carrying on credit card, charge card and similar payment card operations.[19]

The transactions in points 1 and 6 include an "issue". The UK courts and tribunals have proceeded on the basis that an issue of shares by a company is a supply of services so as to be exempt from tax under point 6.[20] The Court of Justice has now held otherwise.[21] This judgment raises the question whether any issue within points 1 and 6 is a supply, let alone an exempt one. The Commissioners have now issued guidance on this question.[22]

De Voil Indirect Tax Service V4.136–136J.

---

[1] VATA 1994, Sch 9, Group 5, Items 1–10 as amended by SI 1997/510, SI 1999/594, SI 2003/1568, 2003/1569, SI 2008/1892, SI 2008/2547. For the exclusion of debt collection and factoring from exemption under EU law, see *Finanzamt Groß-Gerau v MKG-Kraftfarzeuge-Factory GmbH (case C-305/01)* [2003] STC 951, ECJ. For outsourced financial services, see *Sparekassernes Datacenter (SDC) v Skatteministeriet (case C-2/95)* [1997] STC 932, ECJ; *Customs and Excise Comrs v FDR Ltd* [2000] STC 672, CA; *Customs and Excise Comrs v Electronic Data Systems Ltd*

[68.16] Exemption

[2003] STC 688, CA; *Nightfreight plc v Customs and Excise Comrs* (1998) VAT decision 15479; *Prudential Assurance Co Ltd v Customs and Excise Comrs* (2001) VAT decision 17030; *Abbey National plc v Customs and Excise Comrs* (2002) VAT decision 17506.

2   For coins and banknotes supplied as a collectors' piece or investment article, see VATA 1994, Sch 9, Group 5, Note 2; *Milk Marketing Board v Customs and Excise Comrs* (1989) VAT decision 3389. For the transfer of money by means of a book entry in the accounts of payee and payor, see *Customs and Excise Comrs v FDR Ltd* [2000] STC 672, CA (payment card acquirer). For clearing house schemes involving the physical transfer of funds, see *Revenue and Customs Comrs v Axa UK plc* [2008] EWHC 1137 (Ch), [2008] STC 2091 (collection of dental fees from patients); *British Hardware Federation v Customs and Excise Comrs* [1975] VATTR 172 (payment of sums due by retailers). For the services of booking agents accepting payment by credit card, see *Bookit Ltd v Revenue and Customs Comrs* [2006] EWCA Civ 550, [2006] STC 1367, CA; *Scottish Exhibition Centre Ltd v Revenue and Customs Comrs* [2006] CSIH 42, [2008] STC 967. For the mere transit of cash, contrast *Williams & Glyn's Bank Ltd v Customs and Excise Comrs* [1974] VATTR 262.

3   See *MBNA Europe Bank Ltd v R & C Comrs* [2006] EWHC 2326 (Ch), [2006] STC 2089 at para 28; *Dyrham Park Country Club v Customs and Excise Comrs* [1978] VATTR 244.

4   VATA 1994, Sch 9, Group 5, Note 1A as inserted by SI 1999/594.

5   A separate charge must be made for the facility and disclosed to the customer: VATA 1994, Sch 9, Group 5, Item 3. For the information to be disclosed, see *Freight Transport Leasing Ltd v Customs and Excise Comrs* [1991] VATTR 142.

6   The consideration must not exceed £10 and must be specified in the agreement: VATA 1994, Sch 9, Group 5, Item 4. For administration fees on conditional sale agreements, see *Wagon Finance Ltd v Customs and Excise Comrs* (1999) VAT decision 16288. For option fees on hire purchase agreements, see *General Motors Acceptance Corpn (UK) plc v Customs and Excise Comrs* [1999] V & DR 456 (fee for right to secure ownership excluded from exemption).

7   See *Singer & Friedlander Ltd v Customs and Excise Comrs* [1989] VATTR 27, [1989] 1 CMLR 814 (arranging and underwriting issue of shares); *Ivory & Sime Trustlink Ltd v Customs and Excise Comrs* [1998] STC 597, Ct of Sess (initial charge for personal equity plan).

8   As defined in VATA 1994, Sch 9, Group 5, Notes 5, 5B as inserted by SI 1999/594. For "negotiation" within Directive 77/388/EEC art 13B(d)(1)–(5), now Directive 2006/112/EC art 135(1)(b)–(f), see *CSC Financial Services Ltd v Customs and Excise Comrs (case C-235/00)* [2002] STC 57, ECJ; *Volker Ludwig v Finanzamt Lukenwalde (case C-453/05)* [2007] ECR I-5083, [2008] STC 1640, ECJ. For intermediary services in the UK, see *Customs and Excise Comrs v Civil Service Motoring Association* [1988] STC 111, CA; *Customs and Excise Comrs v BAA plc* [2003] STC 35. For outsourced debt collection services, see *HBOS plc v Revenue and Customs Comrs* [2008] CSIH 69, [2009] STC 486.

9   As defined in VATA 1994, Sch 9, Group 5, Notes 5A, 5B as inserted by SI 1999/594.

10 For "management", see *Abbey National plc and another v Customs and Excise Comrs (case C-169/04)* [2006] ECR I-4027, [2006] STC 1136, ECJ.

11 As defined in Financial Services and Markets Act 2000, s 237(3).

12 As defined in Financial Services and Markets Act 2000, s 237(3).

[13] As defined in VATA 1994, Sch 9, Group 5, Item 9(c),(d) and Notes 6, 6A.
[14] As defined in VATA 1994, Sch 9, Group 5, Item 9(e) (f) and Notes 6, 6A.
[15] As defined in VATA 1994, Sch 9, Group 5, Item 9(g)–(j) and Notes 6, 6A.
[16] As defined in VATA 1994, Sch 9, Group 5, Note 6.
[17] VATA 1994, Sch 9, Group 5, Note 4. The payment card operator appears to transfer funds from cardholder to merchant so that exemption in this respect also arises under VATA 1994, Sch 9, Group 5, Item 1.
[18] VATA 1994, Sch 9, Group 5, Item 2 and Note 2A. The payment card operator appears to supply management services if the cardholder pays on time and grant credit if he does not.
[19] For payment card operations, see *Customs and Excise Comrs v Diners Club Ltd* [1989] STC 407, CA (issuer); *Customs and Excise Comrs v FDR Ltd* [2000] STC 672, CA (acquirer). For affinity and co-branded credit cards, see *Customs and Excise Comrs v BAA plc* [2003] STC 35, CA. For cheque trading companies, see *Kingfisher plc v Customs and Excise Comrs* [2000] STC 992.
[20] This was specifically held to be so in *Trinity Mirror plc (formerly Mirror Group Newspapers Ltd) v Customs and Excise Comrs* [2001] EWCA Civ 65, [2001] STC 192.
[21] *Kretztechnik AG v Finanzamt Linz (case C-465/03)* [2005] ECR I–4357, [2005] STC 1118, ECJ.
[22] See Business Brief (Issue 21/05), 23 November 2005.

Group 6—education

Education

[68.17] The following supplies are exempt from tax:[1]

(1) The provision of education[2] by an eligible body.[3]
(2) The supply of any goods or services (other than examination services)[4] closely related thereto[5] if the supply is made by the eligible body providing the education and the goods or services are directly used by the pupil or student receiving the education.
(3) The provision of education, and any goods or services essential thereto[6] supplied by the person providing the education, if the consideration for the training, goods or services is ultimately a charge on funds provided by the Learning and Skills Council for England or the National Council for Education and Training for Wales.

De Voil Indirect Tax Service V4.141.

[1] VATA 1994, Sch 9, Group 5, Items 1(*a*), 4, 5A as inserted by Learning and Skills Act 2000, Sch 9, para 47.
[2] For "education", see *Stichting Regionaal Opleidingen Centrum Noord-Kennemerland/West-Friesland (Horizon College) v Staatssecretaris van Financiën (case C-434/05)* [2007] ECR I–4793, [2008] STC 2145, ECJ; *North of England Zoological Society v Customs and Excise Comrs* [1999] STC 1027; *Revenue and Customs Comrs v Board of Governors of Robert Gordon University* [2008] CSIH 22, [2008] STC 1890; *Phillips v Customs and Excise Comrs* [1992] VATTR 77;

[68.17] Exemption

    Oxford Open Learning (Systems) Ltd v Customs and Excise Comrs (2000) VAT decision 16890.

[3]   As defined in VATA 1994, Sch 9, Group 5, Note 1. For a "college, institution, school or hall" of a "UK university" within Note 1(b), see *Customs and Excise Comrs v University of Leicester Students' Union* [2001] EWCA Civ 1972, [2002] STC 147; *Customs and Excise Comrs v School of Finance and Management (London) Ltd* [2001] STC 1690. For the teaching of English as a foreign language by an eligible body within Note 1(f), see Note 2; *Pilgrims Language Courses Ltd v Customs and Excise Comrs* [1999] STC 874, CA.

[4]   For the exemption of examination services, see infra, § **68.18**.

[5]   For goods and services "closely related" to education, see *Stichting Regionaal Opleidingen Centrum Noord-Kennemerland/West-Friesland (Horizon College) v Staatssecretaris van Financiën (case C-434/05)* [2007] ECR I–4793, [2007] SWTI 1735, ECJ.

[6]   For "essential", see VATA 1994, Sch 9, Group 5, Note 5A as inserted by Learning and Skills Act 2000, Sch 9, para 47.

Examination services

[68.18] The following supplies are exempt from tax:[1]

(1)   The provision of examination services by an eligible body[2] to anyone.
(2)   The provision of examination services by anyone to:
    (a)   an eligible body;
    (b)   a person receiving education, private tuition or vocational training which is exempt from tax;[3] or
    (c)   a person receiving education or vocational training[4] provided otherwise than in the course or furtherance of business.

De Voil Indirect Tax Service V4.141.

[1]   VATA 1994, Sch 9, Group 5, Item 3 as amended by Learning and Skills Act 2000, Sch 9, para 47.
[2]   As defined in VATA 1994, Sch 9, Group 5, Note 1. For supplies by eligible bodies within Note 1(f), see Note 2.
[3]   ie under the provisions in supra, § **68.17** and infra, § **68.19** and § **68.21** respectively.
[4]   As defined in VATA 1994, Sch 9, Group 5, Note 3.

Private tuition

[68.19] Private tuition[1] in a subject ordinarily taught in a school or university[2] is exempt from tax[3] if supplied by an individual teacher acting independently[4] of an employer.

De Voil Indirect Tax Service V4.141.

[1]   For the nature of private tuition, see *Werner Haderer v Finanzamt Wilmersdorf (case C-445/05)* [2007] ECR I–4841, [2008] STC 2171, ECJ; *Revenue and Customs Comrs v Empowerment Enterprises Ltd* [2006] CSIH 46, [2008] STC 1835; *Clarke (a firm) v Customs and Excise Comrs* (1997) VAT decision 15201.

² For "school or university education", the term used in Directive 2006/112/EC art 132(1)(j), see *Werner Haderer v Finanzamt Wilmersdorf (case C-445/05)* [2007] ECR I-4841, [2008] STC 2171, ECJ at para 26.
³ VATA 1994, Sch 9, Group 5, Item 2.
⁴ For examples of independence, see *Ellicott v Customs and Excise Comrs* (1993) VAT decision 11472 (licensee); *Clarke (a firm) v Customs and Excise Comrs* (1997) VAT decision 15201, Business Brief (Issue 1/98) 7 January 1998 (partner).

Research

[68.20] The following supplies are exempt from tax:[1]

(1) The provision of research by one eligible body[2] ("Y") to another ("Z").
(2) The supply of any goods or services (other than examination services)[3] closely related thereto if the supply is made by X (another eligible body) to Y or by Y to Z.

De Voil Indirect Tax Service V4.141.

[1] VATA 1994, Sch 9, Group 5, Items 1(*b*), 4.
[2] As defined in VATA 1994, Sch 9, Group 5, Note 1. For supplies by eligible bodies within Note 1(*f*), see Note 2.
[3] For the exemption of examination services, see supra, § **68.18**.

Vocational training

[68.21] The following supplies are exempt from tax:[1]

(1) The provision of vocational training[2] by an eligible body.[3]
(2) The supply of any goods or services (other than examination services)[4] closely related thereto if the supply is made by the eligible body providing the vocational training and the goods or services are directly used by the trainee receiving the training.
(3) The provision of vocational training, and any goods or services essential thereto[5] supplied by the person providing the training, if the consideration for the training, goods or services is ultimately a charge on:
   (a) funds provided pursuant to arrangements made under Employment and Training Act 1973, s 2;[6]
   (b) funds provided by the Learning and Skills Council for England; or
   (c) funds provided by the National Council for Education and Training for Wales.

De Voil Indirect Tax Service V4.141.

[1] VATA 1994, Sch 9, Group 5, Items 1(*c*), 4, 5, 5A as inserted by Learning and Skills Act 2000, Sch 9, para 47.
[2] As defined in VATA 1994, Sch 9, Group 5, Note 3. See *Harrowgate Business Development Centre Ltd v Customs and Excise Comrs* (1998) VAT decision 15565.
[3] As defined in VATA 1994, Sch 9, Group 5, Note 1. For supplies by eligible bodies within Note 1(*f*), see Note 2.

[68.21] Exemption

⁴ For the exemption of examination services, see supra, § **68.18**.
⁵ For "essential", see VATA 1994, Sch 9, Group 5, Notes 5, 5A as inserted by Learning and Skills Act 2000, Sch 9, para 47.
⁶ In Scotland, see Enterprise and New Towns (Scotland) Act 1990, s 2. In Northern Ireland, see Employment and Training Act (Northern Ireland) 1950, s 1A. For funds provided by the Further Education Funding Council, see Business Brief (Issue 13/96), 1 July 1996.

Youth clubs

[68.22] The following supplies are exempt from tax:[1]

(1) The provision of facilities by a youth club[2] to its members.
(2) The provision of facilities by an association of youth clubs[3] to its members.
(3) The provision of facilities by an association of youth clubs to members of a youth club which is a member of that association.

De Voil Indirect Tax Service V4.141.

[1] VATA 1994, Sch 9, Group 5, Item 6.
[2] As defined in VATA 1994, Sch 9, Group 5, Note 6.
[3] For an organisation outside this description, see *World Association of Girl Guides and Girl Scouts v Customs and Excise Comrs* [1984] VATTR 28.

Group 7—health and welfare

[68.23] The following goods and services are exempt:[1]

(1) Medical care[2] supplied by specified medical and para-medical practitioners,[3] dentists and dental care professionals,[4] and pharmaceutical chemists.[5]
(2) Any services supplied by a dental technician.[6]
(3) Dental prostheses supplied by dentists and dental care professionals in head (1), and by dental technicians in head (2).
(4) Care,[7] medical treatment[8] or surgical treatment provided in any hospital or state-regulated[9] institution whether by legal persons or natural persons.[10]
(5) Providing a doctor's deputising service.
(6) Human blood, products derived therefrom, and human organs and tissues for specified purposes.
(7) Welfare services[11] and goods supplied in connection therewith, provided by a charity,[12] state-regulated private welfare institution or agency,[13] or public body.[14]
(8) Goods and services incidental to the provision of spiritual welfare supplied by a religious community to a resident member on a non-profit making basis.
(9) Transport services for sick and injured persons in specially designed vehicles.

De Voil Indirect Tax Service V4.146.

Exempt supplies [68.23]

1   VATA 1994, Sch 9, Group 7, Items 1–11 as amended or inserted by SI 2002/762, SI 2003/24, SI 2007/206. For cases decided under Directive 77/388/EEC art 13A(1)(g), now Directive 2006/112/EC art 132(1)(g), see *Yoga for Health Foundation v Customs and Excise Comrs* [1984] STC 630; *International Bible Students Association v Customs and Excise Comrs* [1988] STC 412; *Westminster City Council v Customs and Excise Comrs* [1989] VATTR 71, [1990] 2 CMLR 81; *Central YMCA v Customs and Excise Comrs* [1994] VATTR 146.

2   The services must comprise diagnosing, treating and (if possible) curing diseases and health disorders: see *Ambulanter Pflegedienst Kugler GmbH v Finanzamt für Körperschaften I in Berlin (case C-141/00)* [2002] ECR I–6833, ECJ; *d'Abrumenil v Customs and Excise Comrs (case C-307/01)*, *Unterpertinger v Pensionsversicherungsanstalt der Arbeiter (case C-212/01)* [2005] STC 650, ECJ. For medico-legal services, see *D v W (Österreichischer Bundesschatz intervening) (case C-384/98)* [2002] STC 1200, ECJ; *d'Abrumenil v Customs and Excise Comrs (case C-307/01)* [2003] ECR I–13989, [2005] STC 650; *Unterpertinger v Pensionversicherungsanstalt der Arbeiter (case C-212/01)* [2003] ECR I–13859, [2005] STC 650, ECJ.

3   Listed in VATA 1994, Sch 9, Group 7, Items 1(*a*)–(*e*) as amended by SI 1998/1294, SI 1999/1575, SI 2002/253 (see *The London Gazette*, 21 July 2004), SI 2002/254, SI 2002/762. For the register in Item 1(c), see Health Professions (Parts of and Entries in the Register) Order in Council, SI 2003/1571, Sch 1 as amended by SI 2009/1182. For the hire of goods in connection with services, see Note 1 and contrast *Aslan Imaging Ltd v Customs and Excise Comrs* [1989] VATTR 54 and *Cleary (a firm) v Customs and Excise Comrs* (1992) VAT decision 7305. For services supplied by unregistered persons (eg a company) but wholly performed or directly supervised by certain registered practitioners, see Note 2; *Elder Home Care Ltd v Customs and Excise Comrs* (1994) VAT decision 11185; *Land v Customs and Excise Comrs* (1998) VAT decision 15547; News Release 23/96, 11 April 1996. For drugs dispensed and administered by medical practitioners, see *Dr Beynon & Partners v Customs and Excise Comrs* [2004] UKHL 53, [2005] STC 55. For dispensing opticians, see *Customs and Excise Comrs v Leightons Ltd* [1995] STC 458; Business Brief (Issue 31/93) 30 September 1993.

4   Listed in Item 2(*a*), (*b*) as amended by SI 2005/2011 (see *The London Gazette*, 21 July 2006). For services supplied by unregistered persons (eg a company) but wholly performed or directly supervised by certain registered practitioners, see Note 2.

5   Listed in Item 3. For services supplied by unregistered persons (eg a company) but wholly performed by registered pharmaceutical chemists, see Note 2A as inserted by SI 1996/2949. For the hire of goods, see Note 3.

6   For dental technicians, see *VDP Dental Laboratory NV v Staatssecretaris van Financiën (case 401/05)* [2006] ECR I–12121, [2007] SWTI 108, ECJ; *Bennett v Customs and Excise Comrs* (1979) VAT decision 865.

7   For "care", see *Christoph-Dornier-Stiftung für Klinische Psychologie v Finanzamt Gießen (case C-45/01)* [2003] ECR I–12911, [2005] STC 228, ECJ; *Diagnostikon & Therapeftikon Kentron Athino–Ygeia AE v Ipourgos Ikonomikon (joined cases C-394/04 C-395/04)* [2005] STC 1349, ECJ; *Customs and Excise Comrs v Kingscrest Associates Ltd* [2002] EWHC 410 (Ch), [2002] STC 490. Care outside this description may comprise welfare services within head 7. For food and accommodation for a child patient's parent, see *Nuffield Nursing Homes Trust v*

[68.23] Exemption

  Customs and Excise Comrs [1989] VATTR 62. For intermediaries, see *Staatssecretaris van Financiën v Stichting Kinderopvang Enschede (case C-415/04)* [2006] ECR I–1365, [2007] STC 294, ECJ.

8 For medical tests carried out by a third party, see *LuP GmbH v Finanzamt Bochum-Mitte (case C-106/05)* [2006] ECR I–5123, [2006] SWTI 1620, ECJ.
9 As defined in VATA 1994, Sch 9, Group 7, Note 8 as inserted by SI 2002/762.
10 *Gregg v Customs and Excise Comrs (case C-216/97)* [1999] STC 934, ECJ.
11 As defined in VATA 1994, Sch 9, Group 7, Note 6 as substituted by SI 2002/762. For "care", see *Viewpoint Housing Association Ltd v Customs and Excise Comrs* (1995) VAT decision 13148; *Watford and District Old People's Housing Association Ltd v Customs and Excise Comrs* (1998) VAT decision 15660; Business Brief 4/99, 15 February 1999. For accommodation and catering, see VATA 1994, Sch 9, Group 7, Note 7; *Viewpoint Housing Association Ltd v Customs and Excise Comrs* (1995) VAT decision 13148; *Trustees for the MacMillan Cancer Trust v Customs and Excise Comrs* [1998] V & DR 289. For adoption services, see *Parents and Children Together v Customs and Excise Comrs* (2001) VAT decision 17283; Business Brief (Issue 21/01), 21 December 2001. For a supply of staff, see *Revenue and Customs Comrs v K & L Childcare Service Ltd* [2005] EWHC 2414 (Ch), [2006] STC 18.
12 For "charity", see *Kingscrest Associates Ltd and Montecello Ltd v Customs and Excise Comrs (case C-498/03)* [2005] ECR I–4427, [2005] STC 1547, ECJ (term having its own independent meaning in EC law and not precluding bodies having a profit-making aim).
13 For "state regulated" in relation to a private welfare institution or agency, see VATA 1994, Sch 9 Group 7, Note 8; *Revenue and Customs Comrs v K & L Childcare Service Ltd* [2005] EWHC 2414 (Ch), [2006] STC 18. For private welfare agencies, see Business Brief (Issue 1/03), 20 January 2003; Business Brief (Issue 5/05), 3 March 2005. For a partnership registered under the Care Standards Act 2000, see *Kingscrest Associates Ltd and Montecello Ltd v Customs and Excise Comrs (case C-498/03)* [2005] ECR I–4427, [2005] STC 1547, ECJ.
14 For "public body", see VATA 1994, Sch 9, Group 7, Note 5; *Prospects Care Services Ltd v Customs and Excise Comrs* [1997] V & DR 209.

Group 8—burial and cremation

[68.24] The following supplies are exempt:[1]

(1) Burial and cremation.[2]
(2) Funeral arrangements.[3]

De Voil Indirect Tax Service V4.151.

---

1 VATA 1994, Sch 9, Group 8, Items 1, 2.
2 See *UFD Ltd v Customs and Excise Comrs* [1981] VATTR 199; *CJ Williams' Funeral Service of Telford v Customs and Excise Comrs* [1999] V & DR 318.
3 See *Network Insurance Brokers Ltd v Customs and Excise Comrs* [1998] STC 742; *Co-operative Wholesale Society Ltd v Customs and Excise Comrs* [2000] STC 727, CA.

Group 9—trade unions, professional and other public interest bodies

[68.25] Services (and related goods) are exempt when supplied by any of the following non-profit-making organisations to its members in return for a subscription. The services and related goods must be referable to the aims of the organisation. Exemption does not extend to rights of admission if non-members are admitted to the premises, event or performance concerned for a consideration.[1] The organisations are:

(1) A trade union[2] or similar organisation of persons.
(2) A professional association which restricts membership to individuals seeking an appropriate professional qualification.[3]
(3) An association for advancing a particular branch of knowledge, or fostering professional expertise connected with members' professions or employments, which restrict membership to individuals having professions or employments directly connected with the association's purposes.[4]
(4) An association making representations to Government on public matters affecting members' business or professional interests which restricts membership to individuals or corporate bodies having business or professional interests directly connected with the association's purposes.[5]
(5) A body with objects in the public domain[6] of a political[7], religious, patriotic, philosophical, philanthropic[8] or civic[9] nature.
(6) An organisation of organisations within points (1)–(5).

De Voil Indirect Tax Service V4.156.

---

[1] See VATA 1994, Sch 9, Group 9, Item 1 (as amended by SI 1999/2844) and Notes 1, 3, 4, 5.

[2] As defined in VATA 1994, Sch 9, Group 9, Note 2. For the nature of a trade union, see *Institute of the Motor Industry v Customs and Excise Comrs (case C-149/97)* [1998] STC 1219, ECJ.

[3] For bodies within this description, see *Allied Dancing Association v Customs and Excise Comrs* [1993] VATTR 405; *Institute of Chartered Shipbrokers v Customs and Excise Comrs* (1997) VAT decision 15033.

[4] For bodies within this description, see *British Organic Farmers v Customs and Excise Comrs* [1988] VATTR 64; *British Association for Counselling v Customs and Excise Comrs* (1994) VAT decision 11855.

[5] For bodies within this description, see *Bee Farmers Association v Customs and Excise Comrs* (1984) VAT decision 1565.

[6] For objects in the public domain, see *English Speaking Union of the Commonwealth v Customs and Excise Comrs* [1980] VATTR 184.

[7] For objects of a political nature, see *British Association for Shooting and Conservation Ltd v Revenue and Customs Comrs* [2009] EWHC 399 (Ch), [2009] STC 1421.

[8] For bodies within this description, see *Rotary International v Customs and Excise Comrs* [1991] VATTR 177.

[9] For bodies within this description, see *Expert Witness Institute v Customs and Excise Comrs* [2001] EWCA Civ 1882, [2002] STC 42, CA; *British Association for*

[68.25] Exemption

Shooting and Conservation Ltd v Revenue and Customs Comrs [2009] EWHC 399 (Ch), [2009] STC 1421.

Group 10—sport and physical education

[68.26] Certain competition[1] entry fees are exempt[2] if either of the following conditions are met:

(1) The fees are wholly allocated towards the provision of prizes.
(2) The fees are charged by a non-profit-making[3] body established for sport or recreation.

Services[4] supplied by a non-profit making body[5] to an individual are exempt if:[6] (a) the services are closely linked with, and essential to, the sporting or physical education activity in which the individual is taking part[7]; and (b) (if the body operates a membership scheme)[8] the individual is a member.[9] Services supplied to bodies corporate and unincorporated associations are covered by this exemption if the true beneficiaries of the services are persons taking part in sport.[10]

De Voil Indirect Tax Service V4.161.

---

[1] ie in sport or physical recreation.
[2] VATA 1994, Sch 9, Group 10, Items 1, 2 as amended by SI 1999/1994.
[3] A body is "non-profit-making" only if: (1) it meets prescribed conditions relating to the distribution of profits; (2) it applies the profits from its exempt sports supplies in maintaining or improving the facilities used in making those supplies or in supporting a non-profit-making body; and (3) it is not subject to a commercial influence. In broad terms, a body is subject to a commercial influence if: (1) it purchases or agrees to purchase specified goods or services from an officer or shadow officer of the body, an intermediary for making supplies to the body, or a person connected with any of those persons; or (2) it pays or agrees to pay emoluments to such a person: see VATA 1994, Sch 9, Group 10, Notes 2A–2C and 4–17 as inserted by SI 1999/1994. In relation to Directive 77/388/EEC art 13A(1)(m), now Directive 2006/112/EC art 132(1)(m), see *Kennemer Golf and Country Club v Staatssecretaris van Financiën (case C-174/00)* [2002] STC 502, ECJ. For an example of a body that was not "non-profit making", see *Messenger Leisure Developments Ltd v Revenue and Customs Coms* [2005] EWCA Civ 648, [2005] STC 1078 (wholly-owned subsidiary of commercial parent).
[4] Excluding accommodation, catering or transport: VATA 1994, Sch 9, Group 10, Note 1 as amended by SI 1999/1994.
[5] A body specified in VATA 1994, Sch 9, Group 10, Note 3 as amended by SI 1999/1994 is outside this description.
[6] VATA 1994, Sch 9, Group 10, Item 3 as amended by SI 1999/1994. For a case decided under Directive 2006/112/EC art 132(1)(m), see *British Association for Shooting and Conservation Ltd v Revenue and Customs Comrs* [2009] EWHC 399 (Ch), [2009] STC 1421.
[7] For persons taking part in an activity, see *Swansea Yacht and Sub Aqua Club v Customs and Excise Comrs* [1996] V & DR 89, *Royal Pigeon Racing Association v Customs and Excise Comrs* (1996) VAT decision 14006.

[8] For membership schemes, see *Basingstoke and District Sports Trust Ltd v Customs and Excise Comrs* [1995] V & DR 405; Business Brief (Issue 3/96), 16 February 1996.
[9] An individual is considered to be a member only if he is granted membership for a period of three months or more: VATA 1994, Sch 9, Group 10, Note 2 as amended by SI 1999/1994.
[10] *Canterbury Hockey Club and another v Revenue and Customs Comrs* (case C-253/07) [2008] ECR I–0000, [2008] STC 3351, ECJ

Group 11—works of art, etc

[68.27] Certain heritage objects[1] are exempt[2] when supplied by way of private treaty sale to a heritage body,[3] or transfer to the Revenue in lieu of duty, in circumstances where:

(1) No estate duty is chargeable.
(2) No inheritance tax is chargeable.
(3) Any gain arising is exempt from capital gains tax.

De Voil Indirect Tax Service V4.166.

[1] ie works of art, pictures, prints, manuscripts, scientific collections and other objects which, in each case, are of national, scientific, historic or artistic interest; and objects historically associated with a building of outstanding historic or architectural interest.
[2] VATA 1994, Sch 9, Group 11, Items 1–4.
[3] ie The National Gallery, British Museum, Royal Scottish Museum, National Museum of Wales, Ulster Museum and certain similar bodies.

Group 12—fund-raising events

[68.28] A supply of goods or services in connection with an event[1] is exempt if it meets any of the following conditions:[2]

(1) The event is organised by one or more charities for the primary purpose of raising money for charitable purposes and must be promoted as such. The supply must be made by a charity.[3]
(2) The event is organised for the primary purpose of raising money for the body's benefit and must be promoted as such. The supply must be made by a qualifying body.[4]
(3) The event is organised jointly by a qualifying body and one or more charities exclusively for charitable purposes, exclusively for the body's own benefit, or for a mixture of those purposes, and must be promoted as such. The supply must be made by a charity or qualifying body.

Supplies are excluded from exemption if:[5]

(1) More than fifteen[6] events of the same kind[7] are held in the same financial year.

[68.28] Exemption

(2) The supply comprises accommodation provided by the organiser of the event or a connected charity[8] which is not incidental[9] to the event.
(3) The supply distorts competition so as to place a commercial enterprise at a disadvantage.

De Voil Indirect Tax Service V4.171.

---

[1] As defined in VATA 1994, Sch 9, Group 12, Note 1 as inserted by SI 2000/803.
[2] VATA 1994, Sch 9, Group 12, Items 1–3 as inserted by SI 2000/803.
[3] As defined in VATA 1994, Sch 9, Note 2 as inserted by SI 2000/803.
[4] As defined in VATA 1994, Sch 9, Note 3 as inserted by SI 2000/803.
[5] VATA 1994, Sch 9, Notes 4, 8, 11 as inserted by SI 2000/803.
[6] This number is proportionately increased or decreased if the financial period is longer or shorter than twelve months: VATA 1994, Sch 9, Note 6 as inserted by SI 2000/803. Events are excluded for this purpose (so that exemption applies) if they take place in the same week and the aggregate gross takings from them do not exceed £1,000: VATA 1994, Sch 9, Note 5 as inserted by SI 2000/803.
[7] As defined in VATA 1994, Sch 9, Note 7 as inserted by SI 2000/803.
[8] As defined in VATA 1994, Sch 9, Note 10 as inserted by SI 2000/803.
[9] As defined in VATA 1994, Sch 9, Note 9 as inserted by SI 2000/803.

Group 13—cultural services

[68.29] The supply of a right of admission is exempt if the following conditions are met:[1]

(1) The supply is made by a public body[2] or eligible body.[3]
(2) The supply is unlikely to create distortions of competition which place commercial enterprises at a disadvantage.[4]
(3) Admission is granted to either:
   (a) a museum,[5] gallery, art exhibition or zoo; or
   (b) a theatrical, musical or choreographic performance of a cultural nature.
(4) (In the case of eligible bodies) the performance in point 3(a) is provided exclusively by one or more public bodies, eligible bodies or both.

De Voil Indirect Tax Service V4.176.

---

[1] VATA 1994, Sch 9, Group 13, Items 1, 2 and Notes 3, 4 as inserted by SI 1996/1256.
[2] As defined in VATA 1994, Sch 9, Group 13, Note 1 as inserted by SI 1996/1256.
[3] As defined in VATA 1994, Sch 9, Group 13, Note 2 as inserted by SI 1996/1256. For management and administration on a voluntary basis, see *Customs and Excise Comrs v Zoological Society of London (case C-267/00)* [2002] STC 521, ECJ; *Bournemouth Symphony Orchestra v Customs and Excise Comrs*, [2006] EWCA Civ 1281, [2007] STC 198, *Longborough Festival Opera v Revenue and Customs Comrs* [2006] EWHC 40 (Ch), [2006] STC 818, [2007] STC 198, CA.
[4] Current policy is not to insist upon exemption where this would be financially disadvantageous: see News Release 33/96, 3 June 1996.

[5] See *Dean and Canons of Windsor v Customs and Excise Comrs* (1998) VAT decision 15703.

Group 14—Goods where input tax is irrecoverable

[68.30] A supply of goods made by a trader (referred to as the "relevant supplier") is exempt from tax if all of the following conditions are satisfied:[1]

(1) The relevant supplier or one of his predecessors[2] incurs[3] VAT (other than VAT incurred on a self-supply) in respect of his purchase, acquisition or importation of:
   (a) (if the supply of goods is the grant, assignment or surrender of a major interest in land)[4] any supply consisting in or arising out his acquisition of the major interest and any goods used in the construction of a building or civil engineering work which became part of the land; or
   (b) (in other cases) the goods supplied and any goods comprised in them used in producing them.
(2) The VAT in point (1) is not deductible as input tax by the relevant supplier or predecessor because:
   (a) it was not allowable,[5] or was allowable merely because it was attributed to taxable supplies under the de minimis rule,[6] when the VAT was incurred and does not subsequently become allowable;[7]
   (b) it was excluded from credit;[8] or
   (c) it would have fallen within (a) or (b) if the relevant supplier or predecessor had been a taxable person at the time when the VAT was incurred.
(3) (If the supply comprises the grant, assignment or surrender of a major interest) no option to tax[9] has effect in relation to the land.

VAT is not non-deductible input tax for the purpose of point (2) if it has been repaid or refunded to a local authority, statutory body, museum or gallery, government department or overseas trader.[10]

De Voil Indirect Tax Service V4.181.

[1] VATA 1994, Sch 9, Group 14, Item 1, Notes 1–8, 10 as inserted by SI 1999/2833.
[2] As defined in VATA 1994, Sch 9, Group 14, Notes 11–15 as inserted by SI 1999/2833.
[3] A person incurs VAT for this purpose whether or not he is a taxable person at the time when it is incurred and whether the VAT is incurred at the time when the goods are purchased, acquired or imported or at a later time.
[4] The grant, assignment or surrender of a major interest in land is a supply of goods: see supra, § **63.24**.
[5] For the circumstances in which input tax is allowable, see supra, § **66.07**.
[6] For the de minimis rule, see supra, § **66.13**.
[7] For the circumstances in which input tax is adjusted after the initial deduction (if any) is made, see supra, § **66.22**.
[8] For input tax excluded from credit, see supra, §§ **66.17–66.21**.

[68.30] Exemption

⁹ For the option to tax land, see supra, §§ **68.03–68.04**.
¹⁰ VATA 1994, Sch 9, Group 14, Note 9 as amended by FA 2001, s 98.

Group 15—investment gold

[68.31] The following supplies are exempt from tax:[1]

(1) The supply of investment gold.[2]
(2) The grant, assignment or surrender of any interest in, right over, or claim to, investment gold. The right, interest or claim must be a right to the transfer or possession of investment gold or confer a right to such a transfer. The grant of an option is not exempt from tax. Nor is the assignment or surrender of a right under an option if the assignment or surrender takes place before the option has been exercised.
(3) The services of an agent acting in the principal's name in relation to the purchase or sale (or intended purchase or sale) of the goods and services in heads (1) or (2).

A supply is excluded from exemption, and chargeable to tax at the zero-rate, if the parties are members of the London Bullion Market Association.[3] A supply is also excluded from exemption if one of the parties is a member and the other is not.[4] The supply is charged to tax at the standard rate and special accounting and record-keeping requirements apply.[5]

A supply is also excluded from exemption if the option to tax has been exercised in relation to it.[6]

De Voil Indirect Tax Service V4.186.

---

[1] VATA 1994, Sch 9, Group 15, Items 1–3 and Note 3 as inserted by SI 1999/3116.
[2] As defined in VATA 1994, Sch 9, Group 15, Note 1 as inserted by SI 1999/3116.
[3] VATA 1994, Sch 9, Group 15, Note 4(a) as inserted by SI 1999/3116; VAT (Terminal Markets) Order, SI 1973/173, art 4 as inserted by SI 1999/3117. For the zero-rating of such supplies, see infra, § **69.04**.
[4] VATA 1994, Sch 9, Group 15, Note 4(b) as inserted by SI 1999/3116.
[5] VAT (Terminal Markets) Order, SI 1973/173, arts 5–7 as inserted by SI 1999/3117.
[6] For elections to waive exemption in respect of investment gold, see supra, § **68.10**.

69

The zero rate

Introduction	PARA **69.01**
Specific provisions	PARA **69.03**
Common provisions	PARA **69.12**

Introduction

Nature of zero-rating

[69.01] The legislation[1] relieves a wide range of goods and services from VAT. It does so by providing that the relevant supplies, acquisitions and importations are not charged to tax.[2] The supplies (but not the acquisitions and importations) are said to be "zero-rated". They are treated as if they were taxable supplies chargeable to tax at a nil rate.[3] This distinguishes them from exempt supplies: exempt supplies are not charged to tax but, by definition, they are not taxable supplies.[4] Zero-rating takes priority over both exemption and a charge to tax at the standard or reduced rate.[5]

A number of consequences flow from a zero-rated supply being treated as a taxable supply. In particular, it is taken into account in determining whether a trader is liable or entitled to registration[6] and any VAT attributable to it is allowable for input tax credit.[7]

A trader can claim exemption from registration if some or all of his supplies are zero-rated.[8] He can also claim exemption from registration if he makes an acquisition which "would be zero-rated if it were a taxable supply".[9] An acquisition is within this description if no tax is charged on it.

---

[1] For the legislation, see infra, § **69.02**.
[2] VATA 1994, s 30(1)(a), (3).
[3] VATA 1994, s 30(1).
[4] VATA 1994, s 4.
[5] VATA 1994, s 30(1); *CGI Pension Trust Ltd v Customs and Excise Comrs* (1999) VAT decision 15926.
[6] VATA 1994, Sch 1, paras 1, 9.
[7] VATA 1994, s 26(1), (2)(a).
[8] VATA 1994, Sch 1, para 14.
[9] VATA 1994, Sch 3, para 8.

[69.02] The zero rate

Legislation

[69.02] The legislation governing the zero-rating of supplies, and the acquisition and importation of goods without payment of tax, is set out in VATA 1994, ss 17(2), 18C(1), 30(2), (2A), (3), (6) and Sch 8; Customs and Excise Duties (General Reliefs) Act 1979 ss 8, 9(*b*); orders made under VATA 1994 ss 37(1), 50(1)(*a*) and Customs and Excise Duties (General Reliefs) Act 1979 ss 7, 13; and regulations made under ss 17(4)(*a*), 30(8), (8A), (9) and 38. A number of extra-statutory concessions are currently in force.[1]

A person is liable to civil penalties if he gives an incorrect certificate to a supplier which results in a supply to him being improperly zero-rated under VATA 1994, s 18C(1) or Sch 8, Groups 5 and 6.[2] Goods found in the UK after their supposed export are liable to forfeiture.[3]

The legislation specific to supplies, acquisitions or importations is separately described in infra, §§ **69.03–69.08** (supplies), § **69.09** (acquisitions) and §§ **69.10–69.11** (importations). VATA 1994, Sch 8 (which is common to all three) is described in infra, §§ **69.12–69.42**.

De Voil Indirect Tax Service V3.316, 387, V4.207.

---

[1] For concessions, see Notice No 48 (July 2009).
[2] VATA 1994, s 62 as amended by FA 1996, Sch 3, para 8 and FA 1999, s 17.
[3] VATA 1994, s 30(10). For forfeiture, see CEMA 1979, s 139 and Sch 3.

Specific provisions

Supplies of goods and services chargeable at the zero rate

Application of the common provisions

[69.03] A supply of goods or services is zero-rated if a description of the supply, goods or services is for the time being specified in VATA 1994, Sch 8.[1] If a person produces goods by applying a treatment or process to another person's goods, his supply of services is zero-rated if a description of the supply or goods is for the time being specified in VATA 1994, Sch 8.[2]

De Voil Indirect Tax Service V4.210.

---

[1] VATA 1994, s 30(2).
[2] VATA 1994, s 30(2A) as inserted by FA 1996, s 29.

Terminal markets

[69.04] The following supplies of goods and services are zero-rated when they take place in the course of dealings on a specified terminal market:[1]

(1) The sale of any goods (other than investment gold) ordinarily dealt with on the market. The sale must be made to or by a member of the market. Specified conditions[2] must be met.

Specific provisions [69.06]

(2) A supply of investment gold.[3] The parties to the transaction must be members of the London Bullion Market Association.

(3) The grant of a right to acquire goods (other than investment gold) ordinarily dealt with on the market. The grant must be made to or by a member of the market. Specified conditions[4] must be met.

(4) The grant, assignment or surrender of any right (or any interest or claim conferring a right) to the transfer of possession of investment gold. This does not include either the grant of an option or the assignment or surrender of a right under an option at a time before the option is exercised. The parties to the transaction must be members of the London Bullion Market Association.

(5) Agency services relating to transactions in points (1)–(4) and to certain investment gold transactions excluded from exemption.[5]

De Voil Indirect Tax Service V4.208.

---

[1] VAT (Terminal Markets) Order, SI 1973/173, arts 3(1), 4 as amended and inserted by SI 1999/3117. For the specified terminal markets, see SI 1973/173, art 2 as amended by SI 1975/385, SI 1980/304, SI 1981/338, SI 1984/202, SI 1987/806, SI 1997/1836, SI 1999/3117.

[2] For the conditions, see SI 1993/173, art 3(2).

[3] As defined in VATA 1994, Sch 9, Group 15, Note 1 as inserted by SI 1993/3116.

[4] For the conditions, see SI 1993/173, art 3(3).

[5] ie the transactions in VATA 1994, Sch 9, Group 15, Items 1 and 2 as inserted by SI 1993/3116. Transactions between members of the London Bullion Market and non-members are excluded from exemption by VATA 1994, Sch 9, Group Note 4(b) as inserted by SI 1993/3116.

Stores for use in ships, aircraft and hovercraft

[69.05] Goods are zero-rated if the Commissioners are satisfied that the person supplying them has shipped them for use as stores (other than stores on a private voyage or flight to be made by the customer) or retail merchandise on a voyage or flight to a destination outside the UK.[1] Any conditions specified in regulations[2] or imposed by the Commissioners must be met.

De Voil Indirect Tax Service V4.322, 323.

---

[1] VATA 1994, s 30(6)(b), (7). For fuel oil, kerosene and marked gas oil, see Notice No 48 (July 2009), para 9.2.

[2] No regulations have been made to date.

Services relating to warehoused goods

[69.06] A supply of specified services[1] by a taxable person is zero-rated if the following conditions are met:[2]

(1) The services are wholly performed on, or in relation to, goods subject to a warehousing regime[3] or fiscal warehousing regime.[4]

[69.06] The zero rate

(2) (If the services comprise carrying out operations on the goods) the recipient of the supply gives the supplier a certificate in the prescribed form[5] that the service is wholly performed on goods subject to a warehousing or fiscal warehousing regime.

(3) The services would be chargeable to VAT at a positive rate but for this relief.

(4) The supplier issues an invoice in the prescribed form[6] to the recipient of the supply.

De Voil Indirect Tax Service V3.332.

---

[1] As defined in VATA 1994, s 18C(4).
[2] VATA 1994, s 18C(1).
[3] As defined in VATA 1994, s 18(7).
[4] As defined in VATA 1994, s 18F(2).
[5] See VAT Regulations, SI 1995/2518, reg 145C.
[6] See SI 1995/2518, reg 145D.

Goods removed to another EU member state

[69.07] A supply is zero-rated if the Commissioners are satisfied that goods are removed from the UK to another EU member state in the following circumstances:

(1) The goods are removed under a supply made to a person who is a taxable person in another EU member state.[1] The Commissioners may impose conditions.[2]

(2) The goods are removed in accordance with Excise Goods (Holding, Movement, Warehousing and REDS) Regulations, SI 1992/3135 under a supply made in the UK to a customer who is not a taxable person in another EU member state.[3]

(3) A new means of transport[4] supplied to a customer who is not a taxable person in another EU member state is to be removed within two months of the date of the supply.[5]

The customer may arrange the removal of the goods from the UK. In these circumstances, the supplier must rely on the evidence of removal provided by the customer. This evidence may prove to be false. The Commissioners cannot withdraw zero-rating if: (a) the supplier has acted in good faith; (b) at first sight, the evidence establishes the supplier's right to zero-rating; (c) the supplier's involvement in the tax evasion is not established; and (d) the supplier took every reasonable measure in his power to ensure that the supply did not lead to his participation in tax evasion. The fact that the customer accounts for VAT on his acquisition in another member state may constitute evidence that the goods have been removed from the UK, but this evidence is not conclusive.[6]

The Commissioners are not required to request the tax authorities of the destination member state to provide information in order to support the supplier's claim that goods have been removed to another member state.[7]

De Voil Indirect Tax Service V4.351, 352, 356.

1   A supply is not zero-rated under this provision if the supplier has opted to charge VAT by reference to the profit margin on the supply.
2   VAT Regulations, SI 1995/2518, reg 134. For the conditions imposed, see Notice No 725; *Customs and Excise Comrs v Musashi Autoparts Europe Ltd (formerly TAP Manufacturing Ltd)* [2003] EWCA Civ 1738, [2004] STC 220; *JP Commodities Ltd v Revenue and Customs Comrs* [2007] EWHC 2474 (Ch), [2008] STC 816. For a condition held to be incompatible with Directive 77/388/EEC, now Directive 2006/112/EC, see *Centrax Ltd v Customs and Excise Comrs* [1998] V & DR 369. For evidence which is not produced in good time in respect of a supply which has actually taken place, see *Albert Collée v Finanzamt Limburg an der Lahn* (case C-146/05) [2007] ECR I-7861, [2008] STC 757, ECJ.
3   VAT Regulations, SI 1995/2518, reg 135. For the conditions imposed, see Notice No 725. A supply is not zero-rated under this provision if the supplier has opted to charge VAT by reference to the profit margin on the supply. For the option see supra, § **65.23**.
4   As defined in VATA 1994, s 95.
5   VAT Regulations, SI 1995/2518, reg 155. For the conditions imposed, see Notice No 728.
6   *R (on the application of Teleos plc and others) v Customs and Excise Comrs* (case C-409/04) [2007] ECR I-7797, [2008] STC 706, ECJ. For a case where zero-rating was withdrawn, see *N2J Ltd v Revenue and Customs Comrs* [2009] EWHC 1596 (Ch), [2009] SWTI 2091 (condition (d) not met).
7   See *Twoh International BV v Staatssecretaris van Financiën* (case C-184/05) [2007] ECR I-7897, [2008] STC 740, ECJ.

Goods exported to a third country

[69.08] A supply of any goods is zero-rated if the goods are exported to a third country by the person who supplied them.[1] This applies whether or not the supply falls within a description in VATA 1994, Sch 8.[2] The legislation also allows a supply to be zero-rated in the following circumstances where the goods are removed to a third country by the customer:

(1)   A freight container[3] intended for export to a third country.[4]
(2)   Any goods intended for export to a third country supplied to an overseas resident, an overseas authority[5] or a trader who does not have a business establishment in the UK from which taxable supplies are made.[6]
(3)   Goods (other than a motor vehicle or boat intended to exported under its own power) supplied to an overseas visitor[7] who intents departing for a destination in a third country taking the goods with him.[8]
(4)   A motor vehicle supplied by a registered taxable person to a person intending to leave the EU for a prescribed minimum period within a specified time limit.[9]
(5)   A boat supplied to a UK resident for export to a third country within two months of delivery.[10]

De Voil Indirect Tax Service V4.311, 323, 326, 331, 334.

[69.08] The zero rate

1. VATA 1994, s 30(6)(*a*). For goods exported in contravention of an export ban, see *Lange v Finanzamt Fürstenfeldbruck (case C-111/92)* [1997] STC 564, ECJ. For conditions, see Notice No 703.
2. For VATA 1994, Sch 8, see infra, §§ **69.12–69.42**.
3. As defined in VAT Regulations, SI 1995/2518, reg 117(2).
4. VAT Regulations, SI 1995/2518, reg 128. For conditions, see Notice No 703.
5. As defined in VAT Regulations, SI 1995.2518, reg 117(7).
6. SI 1995/2518 reg 129(1). For conditions, see Notice No 703.
7. As defined in SI 1995/2518, reg 117(7A), (7B), (7C), (7D) as inserted by SI 1999/438.
8. SI 1998/2518, regs 117(4) (as inserted by SI 1996/210), 131(1). The goods must be produced for inspection before they leave the EU. For conditions, see Notice No 704. For forged documents provided by customers, see *Netto Supermarkt GmbH & Co OHG v Finanzamt Malchin* (case C-271/06) [2008] SWTI 315, ECJ.
9. SI 1995/2518, regs 132, 133 as amended by SI 2000/258. The customer must apply for relief under this provision. For conditions, see Notice No 705.
10. This relief is granted by concession. For the terms of the concession and the conditions to be met, see Notice No 48 (July 2009) para 8.1.

Acquisitions not charged to tax

[69.09] In principle, an acquisition of goods is not charged to tax if the goods (or a description of a supply of the goods) is for the time being specified in VATA 1994, Sch 8.[1] However, goods within VATA 1994, Sch 8, Group 5 (land and buildings), Group 10 (gold held in the UK) and Group 12 Items 1 and 1A (qualifying goods as defined in VATA 1994, Sch 8 Group 12, Note 2A) are not excluded from the charge to tax,[2] and goods within Group 12, Items 2–20 are excluded from the charge to tax only if they are acquired by a handicapped person or charity.[3]

An acquisition of goods may be wholly or partly relieved from tax in a like manner to goods imported from a third country in accordance with an order made by the Treasury.[4] No orders have been made to date.

De Voil Indirect Tax Service V3.387.

1. VATA 1994, s 30(3).
2. VATA 1994, s 30(3) and Sch 8, Group 5 Note 24 as substituted by SI 1995/280, Group 10, Note 2, Group 12, Note 1 as amended by SI 1995/652.
3. VATA 1994, Sch 8, Group 12, Note 1 as amended by SI 1995/652.
4. VATA 1994, s 36A as inserted by FA 2000, s 25.

Importations not charged to tax

Application of the common provisions

[69.10] In principle, an importation of goods is not charged to tax if the goods (or a description of a supply of the goods) is for the time being specified in VATA 1994, Sch 8.[1] However, goods within VATA 1994, Sch 8, Group 5 (land and buildings), Group 10 (gold held in the UK) and Group 12, Items 1 and 1A (qualifying goods as defined in VATA 1994, Sch 8 Group 12, Note 2A) are not excluded from the charge to tax.[2]

Goods within Group 12, Items 2–20 are excluded from the charge to tax only if they are imported by a handicapped person or charity.[3]

De Voil Indirect Tax Service V3.316.

[1] VATA 1994, s 30(3).
[2] VATA 1994, s 30(3) and Sch 8, Group 5, Note 24 as substituted by SI 1995/280, Group 10, Note 2, Group 12, Note 1 as amended by SI 1995/652.
[3] VATA 1994, Sch 8, Group 12, Note 1 as amended by SI 1995/652.

Goods not charged to tax or relieved from payment of tax

[69.11] A wide range of goods are relieved from payment of tax on importation. The goods concerned are stated below under broad descriptive headings: the legislation imposes conditions and creates exceptions in many instances.

Relief is available for:

(1) Specific goods produced by the United Nations and UN organisations.[1]
(2) Goods relieved from import duties under corresponding EC provisions.[2]
(3) Gold and gold coins imported by a central bank.[3]
(4) Investment gold.[4]
(5) Gas and electricity.[5]
(6) Gifts under a specified value consigned by one private individual to another for personal use.[6]
(7) Returned goods.[7]
(8) Goods imported by a person who became entitled to them as legatee.[8]
(9) Miscellaneous reliefs conferred by order[9] made under Customs and Excise Duties (General Reliefs) Act 1979, s 13.
(10) Trade samples, labels and awards for distinction.[10]
(11) Goods imported for business purposes by Manx taxable persons.[11]
(12) Goods imported for diplomats, international organisations and visiting forces.[12]

De Voil Indirect Tax Service V3.316, 341–347.

[1] VAT (Imported Goods) Relief Order, SI 1984/746, art 4 and Sch 1 implementing Directive 83/181/EEC, art 79(8).
[2] VAT (Imported Goods) Relief Order, SI 1984/746, arts 5, 8 and Sch 2 as amended by SI 1995/3222, implementing Directive 83/181/EEC Titles III–XI. For corresponding reliefs, see Regulation (EEC) No 918/83.
[3] VAT (Imported Gold) Relief Order, SI 1992/3124.
[4] VAT (Importation of Investment Gold) Relief Order, SI 1999/3115.
[5] VAT (Imported Gas and Electricity) Relief Order, SI 2004/3147. Gas must be imported through the natural gas distribution network.

[69.11] The zero rate

6 VAT (Small Non-Commercial Consignments) Relief Order, SI 1986/939.
7 Regulation (EEC) Nos 2913/92 (arts 185–197) and 2454/93 (arts 844–856, 882) as modified by VAT Regulations, SI 1995/2518, reg 121D as inserted by SI 2006/587. These provisions replace the reliefs previously conferred by SI 1995/2518, regs 124 (revoked), 125(revoked).
8 Customs and Excise Duties (General Reliefs) Act 1979, s 7; Customs and Excise Duties (Personal Reliefs for Goods Permanently Imported) Order, SI 1992/3193, art 21 as interpreted in accordance with SI 2004/1002 art 6 and SI 2006/3158 art 2.
9 See: (a) Customs and Excise Duties (Personal Reliefs for Goods Permanently Imported) Order, SI 1992/3193; (b) Notice No 48 (July 2009) paras 9.3–9.7 (concessions in respect of art 11 of the 1992 Order); (c) Travellers' Allowances Order, SI 1994/955 as amended by SI 1995/3044, SI 2008/955 and interpreted in accordance with SI 2004/1002 art 6.
10 Customs and Excise Duties (General Reliefs) Act 1979, ss 8, 9(b).
11 VAT (Isle of Man) Order, SI 1982/1067, art 4(b).
12 Customs and Excise (Personal Reliefs for Special Visitors) Order, SI 1992/3156 as amended by SI 2007/5; Notice No 48 (July 2009), paras 2.1–2.5.

Common provisions

Introduction

[69.12] The legal basis of VATA 1994, Sch 8 arises partly under Directive 2006/112/EC art 110 and partly under art 169. Article 110 authorises member states to maintain national provisions enacted for clearly defined social reasons and for the benefit of final consumers if they comply with Community law. Article 169 provides an entitlement to input tax deduction in respect of goods and services used for the purposes making specified exempt transactions. These exemptions are referred to as "exemptions with refund". In UK terms, they are zero-rated.

The legal basis of the zero-rated descriptions, and the amendments made to them from time to time, affect both the nature of the rights they confer and the manner in which the legislation is interpreted. The distinction between the two legal bases is therefore a matter of some importance. Ascertaining the proper legal basis of a particular description entails researching the legislative history. This is a matter of some difficulty.[1] Although many modern directives require member states to make reference to the directive they are implementing, the manner of doing so is left to the member states. In the UK, the relevant information may be set out in the legislation, an explanatory note to a statutory instrument, a transposition note or in some other manner.[2] Unfortunately, the information provided may be something less than comprehensive.[3] Moreover, the preparation of correlation tables becomes increasing difficult as directives, statutes and statutory instruments are amended, consolidated or recast.

The legal basis for zero rating in the UK is Directive 2006/112/EEC art 110. This permits member states to apply "exemptions with refund" if first, they were in force at 1 January 1991; secondly, they were adopted for clearly defined social reasons and for the benefit of final consumers; and thirdly, they are in accordance with Community law. The UK provisions in force at 1 January 1991 complied with Community law if either of the following conditions was met:

(1) They were originally adopted for clearly defined social reasons and for the benefit of final consumers, and they were in force at 31 December 1975; or
(2) They implemented an exemption conferred by the 2006 Directive which gives rise to the right to deduct input tax.

A description meeting the first test neither implements Directive 2006/112/EC nor gives rise to a directly enforceable Community-law right to have the relevant supplies taxed at the zero rate. However, the principles governing the common system of VAT (which include the principle of fiscal neutrality) apply. Those principles may, if necessary, be relied on by a taxable person if the UK description, or its application, fails to have regard to them.[4]

A description meeting the firs test may be wider than a Community exemption with refund enacted at some later date. The description cannot be construed as if it implemented the new Community provision in the absence of some positive action. The fact that the description exists, and that it includes the subject-matter of the Community provision, is insufficient. As the description was not enacted to give effect to the Community provision, its legal basis continues to be art 110.[5]

A description meeting the first test may have been amended on one or more occasions since 1975. The consequences of an amendment appear to be as follows:

(1) A description may be amended in a manner which reduces the scope of zero-rating. This does not appear to affect its compliance with Community law.[6]
(2) A description may be restated. There are grounds for supposing that the new description complies with Community law if it is substantially the same as one it replaces.[7]
(3) A description may be amended in a manner which increases the scope of zero-rating. This is prima facie a breach of Community obligations giving grounds for infraction proceedings.[8] The manner in which the UK courts and tribunals deal with the matter appears to be governed by the nature of the description. The following situations can be distinguished:
  (a) Although originally deriving its legal basis from art 110, a description may be similar to an exemption with refund which the UK would otherwise be obliged to apply.[9] If so, the courts and tribunals apply the principle of conforming interpretation so as to construe the UK description by reference to the Community provision.[10] It follows that a trader does not derive any benefit from the infraction.
  (b) In other circumstances, the courts and tribunals apply the offending description as a matter of UK law until such time as it is amended.[11]

[69.12] The zero rate

A description meeting the second test is intended to implement a provision of the 2006 Directive. In appropriate circumstances, therefore, the courts and tribunals interpret the UK description in accordance with the principle of conforming interpretation and, if necessary, apply the Community description under the principle of direct effect.[12]

VATA 1994, Sch 8 is divided into 17 groups, each of which is subdivided into one or more items. These items are interpreted in accordance with the notes to each group.[13]

---

[1] For an example of the extensive research which may be necessary, see *Revenue and Customs Comrs v Stone* [2008] EWHC 1249 (Ch), [2008] STC 2501, where a full historical account of VATA 1994, Sch 8, Group 6, Item 1 is set out at para 33.

[2] In *Revenue and Customs Comrs v EB Central Services Ltd* [2008] EWCA Civ 486, [2008] STC 2209, CA, the Court referred to the Explanatory Memorandum submitted to the Select Committee on Statutory Instruments in relation to the amendments made by VAT (Transport) Order, SI 1990/752.

[3] In referring to four orders amending FA 1972, Sch 4 to implement Directive 77/388/EEC from 1 January 1998, Customs and Excise Press Notice No 482, 10 November 1977 merely stated that "the opportunity has also been taken to make a number of incidental changes and to consolidate certain existing legislation". It is not readily apparent which of the orders, or which parts of them, implemented the 1977 Directive.

[4] *Marks and Spencer plc v Customs and Excise Comrs* (case C-309/06) [2008] STC 1408, ECJ at paras 24, 33, 34.

[5] See *Revenue and Customs Comrs v Stone* [2008] EWHC 1249 (Ch), [2008] STC 2501 at paras 36–46.

[6] The scope of the legislation at issue in *Revenue and Customs Comrs v Stone* [2008] EWHC 1249 (Ch), [2008] STC 2501 was reduced in scope prior to enactment of the Community provision giving rise to the Commissioners' disputed decision.

[7] Cf *Direct Cosmetics Ltd v Customs and Excise Comrs* (case 5/84) [1985] ECR 617, [1985] STC 479, ECJ at para 25 in relation to a derogation under what is now Directive 2006/112/EC art 394.

[8] EC Treaty, art 226 (ex art 169).

[9] In accordance with Directive 2006/112/EC art 169(b), (c).

[10] This was done in *Revenue and Customs Comrs v EB Central Services Ltd* [2008] EWCA Civ 486, [2008] STC 2209, CA. The court held that, in so far as VATA 1994, Sch 8, Group 8, Item 11(a) amounts to a derogation, the amendment made by VAT (International Services and Transport) Order, SI 1992/3223 was not permissible. Item 11(a) was construed in accordance with Directive 77/388/EEC art 15, and in particular with art 15(13).

[11] See *Revenue and Customs Comrs v Stone* [2008] EWHC 1249 (Ch), [2008] STC 2501 at para 48.

[12] This was done in *Revenue and Customs Comrs v EB Central Services Ltd* [2008] EWCA Civ 486, [2008] STC 2209, CA (VATA 1994, Sch 8, Group 8, Item 6(b) amended to comply with Directive 77/388/EEC arts 15(9) and (13) and construed accordingly).

[13] VATA 1994, s 96(9) as amended by FA 2001, Sch 31, para 5.

Group 1—food

[69.13] The following supplies are zero-rated[1] unless the goods fall within one of the excepted items:[2]

(1) Food[3] of a kind used for human consumption[4] unless it is supplied in the course of catering.[5] Food is deemed to be supplied in the course of catering (if it would not otherwise be regarded as such) if: (a) it is supplied for consumption on the premises where the supply takes place,[6] or (b) it is supplied hot for consumption off the premises.[7]
(2) Animal[8] feeding stuffs.[9].
(3) Seeds and plants providing food for human consumption or use as animal feeding stuffs.
(4) Live animals[10] of a kind generally used as food for human consumption (eg as meat), to yield food for human consumption (eg milk), or to produce food for human consumption (eg honey).

De Voil Indirect Tax Service V4.221–228.

1 VATA 1994, Sch 8, Group 1, Items 1–4.
2 As defined in VATA 1994, Sch 8, Group 1, Excepted Items 1–7; Items overriding the Exceptions 1–6; Notes 4–6.
3 As defined in VATA 1994, Sch 8, Group 1, Note 1.
4 For fish used as bait, see *North Isles Shellfish Ltd v Customs and Excise Comrs* [1995] V & DR 415.
5 VATA 1994, Sch 8, Group 1, para (a). For the nature of a supply in the course of catering, see *Compass Contract Services UK Ltd v Revenue and Customs Comrs* [2006] EWCA Civ 730, [2006] STC 1999, CA; *Customs and Excise Comrs v Cope* [1981] STC 532; *Customs and Excise Comrs v Safeway Stores plc* [1997] STC 163; *Whitbread Group plc v Customs and Excise Comrs* [2005] EWHC 418 (Ch), [2005] STC 539; *DCA Industries Ltd v Customs and Excise Comrs* [1983] VATTR 317.
6 VATA 1994, Sch 8, Group 1, Note 3(a). See *Revenue and Customs Comrs v Compass Contract Services UK Ltd* [2006] EWCA Civ 730, [2006] STC 1999, CA; *Customs and Excise Comrs v Cope* [1981] STC 532; *R v Customs and Excise Comrs, ex p Sims* [1988] STC 210.
7 VATA 1994, Sch 8, Group 1, Note 3(b) as amended by SI 2004/3343. See *John Pimblett & Sons Ltd v Customs and Excise Comrs* [1988] STC 358, CA; *Greenhalgh's Craft Bakery Ltd v Customs and Excise Comrs* (1993) VAT decision 10955; Business Brief (Issue 9/05), 4 April 2005.
8 As defined in VATA 1994, Sch 8, Group 1, Note 2.
9 See *Fluff Ltd (t/a Mag-It) v Customs and Excise Comrs* [2001] STC 674; *Smith v Customs and Excise Comrs* MAN/87/321 unreported; *Chapman & Frearson Ltd v Customs and Excise Comrs* (1989) VAT decision 4428; *North Isles Shellfish Ltd v Customs and Excise Comrs* [1995] V & DR 415; *Marczak (a firm) v Customs and Excise Comrs* (1995) VAT decision 13141.
10 See *Customs and Excise Comrs v Lawson-Tancred* [1988] STC 326n

[69.14] The zero rate

Group 2—sewerage services and water

[69.14] The following supplies are zero-rated:[1]

(1)　The reception, disposal or treatment of foul water or sewage in bulk.
(2)　Emptying cesspools, septic tanks and similar receptacles which are not used in carrying on a relevant industrial activitiy.[2]
(3)　Water[3] which is not used in a relevant industrial activity.

De Voil Indirect Tax Service V4.271.

---

[1]　VATA 1994, Sch 8, Group 2, Items 1 and 2 as amended by SI 1996/1661.
[2]　Defined in VATA 1994, Sch 8, Group 2, Note.
[3]　This excludes water of a description in VATA 1994, Sch 8, Group 2, Item 2(a)–(c) as amended by SI 1996/1661. See *Mander Laundries Ltd v Customs and Excise Comrs* [1973] VATTR 136; *Scott-Morley v Customs and Excise Comrs* (1981) VAT decision 1097.

Group 3—books, etc

[69.15] Supplies[1] of the following articles are zero-rated:[2]

(1)　Books,[3] booklets, brochures,[4] pamphlets[5] and leaflets.[6]
(2)　Newspapers, journals and periodicals.[7]
(3)　Children's picture books and painting books.
(4)　Sheet music, maps, charts[8] and topographical plans.[9]
(5)　Covers, cases, etc supplied with the foregoing and not separately accounted for.[10]

De Voil Indirect Tax Service V4.273.

---

[1]　Including services defined in VATA 1994, Sch 8, Group 3, Note (b).
[2]　VATA 1994, Sch 8, Group 3, Items 1–6.
[3]　See *Customs and Excise Comrs v Colour Offset Ltd* [1995] STC 85; *W F Graham (Northampton) Ltd v Customs and Excise Comrs* (1980) VAT decision 908; *City Research Associates Ltd v Customs and Excise Comrs* [1984] VATTR 189; *GUS Catalogue Order Ltd v Customs and Excise Comrs* (1988) VAT decision 2598; *International Master Publishers Ltd v Customs and Excise Comrs* (1992) VAT decision 8807. For printed matter published in instalments, see Notice No 48 (July 2009), para 3.15.
[4]　See *Betty Foster (Fashion Sewing) Ltd v Customs and Excise Comrs* [1976] VATTR 229; *Schusman v Customs and Excise Comrs* [1994] VATTR 120; *Full Force Marketing Ltd v Customs and Excise Comrs* (1997) VAT decision 15270.
[5]　See *Pace Group (Communications) Ltd v Customs and Excise Comrs* (1978) VAT decision 510.
[6]　See *Cronsvale Ltd v Customs and Excise Comrs* [1983] VATTR 313; *Multiform Printing Ltd v Customs and Excise Comrs* [1996] V & DR 580.
[7]　See *Geoffrey E Snushall (a firm) v Customs and Excise Comrs* [1982] STC 537; *Stilwell Darby & Co Ltd v Customs and Excise Comrs* [1973] VATTR 145; *Emap Consumer Magazines Ltd v Customs and Excise Comrs* (1995) VAT decision 13322.

[8] See *Brooks Histograph Ltd v Customs and Excise Comrs* [1984] VATTR 46.
[9] Other than plans and drawings specified in VATA 1994, Sch 8, Group 3, Note (*a*).
[10] See *Odhams Leisure Group Ltd v Customs and Excise Comrs* [1992] STC 332; *Fabbri & Partners Ltd v Customs and Excise Comrs* [1973] VATTR 49.

Group 4—talking books and wireless sets

[69.16] The following goods are zero-rated[1] in the stated circumstances:

(1) Talking books, transfer, copying and rewinding machines, recording equipment, magnetic tape, spoken recordings and accessories[2] supplied to the Royal National Institute for the Blind, the National Listening Library and similar charities.
(2) Wireless receiving sets and cassette recorders supplied to a charity for an onward gratuitous loan to the blind.

De Voil Indirect Tax Service V4.262.

[1] VATA 1994, Sch 8, Group 4, Items 1, 2 and Note.
[2] As defined in VATA 1994, Sch 8, Group 4, Item 1(*a*)–(*i*).

Group 5—buildings and civil engineering works

Grant of a major interest

[69.17] The first grant[1] of a major interest[2] in all or part of a building[3] or its site by the following persons is zero-rated:[4]

(1) A person constructing a building designed as one or more dwellings.[5]
(2) A person constructing a building to be used solely for a relevant residential purpose.[6]
(3) A person constructing a building to be used solely for a relevant charitable purpose.[7]
(4) A person converting a non-residential building, or a non-residential part of a building, into a building designed as one or more dwellings.[8]
(5) A person converting a non-residential building, or a non-residential part of a building, into a building to be used solely for a relevant residential purpose.[9]

As regards leases, zero-rating extends only to the premium payable (if there is one) or the first rent payable (if there is not).[10] The consideration for a grant is apportioned if part of a building falls within one of the foregoing descriptions and part does not.[11]

A person constructing a building is a person who is constructing, or has constructed, a building.[12] A person does not normally construct a building if he merely converts, reconstructs, alters, enlarges or extends an existing building[13] or constructs an annex thereto.[14]

A building intended solely for relevant residential or charitable use may cease to be used, or wholly used, for that purpose during the ten year period

[69.17] The zero rate

following completion of the building. The benefit of zero-rating is wholly or partly reversed by way of a self-supply charge if all or part of the building begins to be used for another purpose.[15] If an interest, right or licence is granted in the building, all or part of the supply is charged to tax at a positive rate if the purchaser, tenant or licensee intends to use all or part of the building for another purpose.[16]

De Voil Indirect Tax Service V4.233–235.

---

[1] For "grant", see VATA 1994, s 96(10A) as inserted or amended by FA 1997, s 35, SI 2008/1146. "Grant" includes assignment or surrender: VATA 1994, Sch 8, Group 5, Note 1. For the first grant in relation to VAT groups, see Business Brief (Issue 11/03), 24 July 2003.

[2] ie the fee simple or a lease for a term of not less than 20 years (land held on feudal tenure in Scotland) or a term exceeding 21 years (other leases): VATA 1994, s 96(1) as amended by FA 1998, s 24. For the term of a lease, see *Cottage Holiday Associates Ltd v Customs and Excise Comrs* [1983] STC 278. For short-term lettings prior to the grant of a major interest, see Revenue and Customs Brief 44/08, 16 September 2008 (adjustment of input tax already deducted). For the grant of a major interest to a connected person who then grants short-term lettings, see Revenue and Customs Brief 54/08, 28 October 2008 (grant of the major interest not normally regarded as an abusive practice).

[3] For "buildings", see *Walle v Customs and Excise Comrs* [1976] VATTR 101; *Smith v Customs and Excise Comrs* (1991) VAT decision 5579. Cf *Maierhofer v Finanzamt Augsburg-Land* (case C-315/00) [2003] STC 564, ECJ (building constructed from prefabricated components).

[4] VATA 1994, Sch 8, Group 5, Item 1.

[5] For buildings "designed" as one or more dwellings, see VATA 1994, Sch 8, Group 5, Note 2; *Whiteley v Customs and Excise Comrs* [1993] VATTR 248; *Thompson v Customs and Excise Comrs* (1998) VAT decision 15834. For "dwelling", see VATA 1994, Sch 8, Group 5, Note 3. The purchaser or tenant must be entitled to reside in the dwelling throughout the year and use it as his principal private residence: VATA 1994, Sch 8, Group 5, Note 13.

[6] For "relevant residential purpose", see VATA 1994, Sch 8, Group 5, Note 4. For the certificate to be provided by the purchaser or tenant, see VATA 1994, Sch 8, Group 5, Note 12(*b*); Notice No 708 (August 1997), Annex A. For groups of buildings, see VATA 1994, Sch 8, Group 5, Note 5.

[7] For "relevant charitable purpose", see VATA 1994, Sch 8, Group 5, Note 6; Notice No 48 (March 2002) para 3.29. For the certificate to be provided by the purchaser or tenant, see VATA 1994, Sch 8, Group 5, Note 12(*b*); Notice No 708 (August 1997), Annex A.

[8] For "non-residential", see VATA 1994, Sch 8, Group 5, Notes 7 (as substituted by SI 2001/2305), 8; *Calam Vale Ltd v Customs and Excise Comrs* (2000) VAT decision 16869. If the building contains both a residential part and a non-residential part, the conversion of the non-residential part must create one or more additional dwellings: VATA 1994, Sch 8, Group 5, Note 9; cf *Customs and Excise Comrs v Blom-Cooper* [2003] STC 669, CA. For "dwelling", see VATA 1994, Sch 8, Group 5, Note 3.

[9] For the certificate to be provided by the purchaser or tenant, see VATA 1994, Sch 8, Group 5, Note 12(*b*); Notice No 708 (August 1997), Annex A.

[10] VATA 1994, Sch 8, Group 5, Note 14.
[11] VATA 1994, Sch 8, Group 5, Note 10.
[12] *Customs and Excise Comrs v Link Housing Association Ltd* [1992] STC 718. For the works to be carried out, see *Monsell Youell Developments Ltd v Customs and Excise Comrs* [1978] VATTR 1 (infrastructure works); *Hulme Trust Educational Foundation v Customs and Excise Comrs* [1978] VATTR 179 (construct or order construction); *Stapenhill Developments Ltd v Customs and Excise Comrs* [1984] VATTR 1 (unnecessary for construction to have been completed).
[13] For the circumstances in which a building ceases to be an existing building, see VATA 1994, Sch 8, Group 5, Note 18.
[14] VATA 1994, Sch 8, Group 5, Note 16. For the exceptions, see VATA 1994, Sch 8, Group 5, Notes 16(b), 17 as amended by SI 2002/1101.
[15] VATA 1994, Sch 10, para 37 as inserted by SI 2008/1146; see supra, § **65.35**.
[16] VATA 1994, Sch 10, para 36 as inserted by SI 2008/1146.

Construction of buildings

[69.18] A supply of services[1] made in the course of[2] constructing a building[3] is zero-rated[4] if it is related to either a building designed as one or more dwellings[5] or a building intended to be used solely for a relevant residential purpose[6] or solely for a relevant charitable purpose.[7]

A building is under construction for this purpose if the work commenced at a greenfield site; the site of a building which has been demolished completely to ground level;[8] or the site of a building which has been demolished to a single facade (or double facade on a corner site) retained as a condition of statutory planning consent or similar permission.[9]

In principle, a building is not constructed if an existing building is converted, reconstructed, altered, enlarged or extended, or an annexe constructed.[10] However, by way of exception, the following works to an existing building amount to the construction of a building:

(1) Enlarging an existing building to create one or more additional dwellings.[11]

(2) Constructing an extension to an existing building which creates one or more additional dwellings.[12]

(3) Constructing an annexe[13] to an existing building where all or part of the annexe is intended to be used solely for a relevant residential purpose.[14]

Part of a building may be designed as one or more dwellings and part may not. Similarly, part may be intended to be used for a relevant residential or charitable purpose and part may not. A supply relating to both parts is apportioned to determine the extent to which the supply is zero-rated.[15]

A building intended solely for relevant residential or charitable use may cease to be used, or wholly used, for that purpose during the ten year period following completion of the building. The benefit of zero-rating is wholly or partly reversed by way of a self-supply charge if all or part of the building begins to be used for another purpose.[16] If an interest, right or licence is granted in the building, all or part of the supply is charged to tax at a positive rate if the purchaser, tenant or licensee intends to use all or part of the building for another purpose.[17]

[69.18] The zero rate

De Voil Indirect Tax Service V4.238.

1. The services must comprise something other than the services of an architect, surveyor, consultant or supervisor; the transfer of possession of goods (eg plant hire); or the use of business assets for non-business or private purposes (eg plant used by the proprietor for work to his private residence). The services must be related to the construction works concerned. If necessary, an apportionment is made to determine the extent to which the services are zero-rated: VATA 1994, Sch 8, Group 5, Item 2 and Notes 11, 20.
2. For the period during which a building is in the course of construction, see *Customs and Excise Comrs v St Mary's RC High School* [1996] STC 1091; *Lamberts Construction Ltd v Customs and Excise Comrs* (1992) VAT decision 8882. For phased developments, see *Bruce v Customs and Excise Comrs* [1991] VATTR 280 and contrast *Whiteley v Customs and Excise Comrs* [1993] VATTR 248, *Brahma Kumaris World Spiritual University v Customs and Excise Comrs* (1995) VAT decision 12946. For site clearance and landscaping, see *Gazzard v Customs and Excise Comrs* (1991) VAT decision 6029; *Rialto Homes plc v Customs and Excise Comrs* (1999) VAT decision 16340.
3. For "building", see *Walle v Customs and Excise Comrs* [1976] VATTR 101 *Smith v Customs and Excise Comrs* (1991) VAT decision 5579.
4. VATA 1994, Sch 8, Group 5, Item 2(*a*). For connection to gas or electricity mains supply, see Notice No 48 (July 2009) para 3.16.
5. For "dwellings", see VATA 1994, Sch 8, Group 5, Note 3. For buildings "designed" as one or more dwellings, see VATA 1994, Sch 8, Group 5, Note 2; *Whiteley v Customs and Excise Comrs* [1993] VATTR 248.
6. For "relevant residential purpose", see VATA 1994, Sch 8, Group 5, Notes 4, 5; *R (on the application of Greenwich Property Ltd) v Customs and Excise Comrs* [2001] EWHC Admin 230, [2001] STC 618 (concession for university student accommodation); *Riverside School (Whassett) Ltd v Customs and Excise Comrs* [1995] V & DR 186; *Urdd Gobaith Cymru v Customs and Excise Comrs* [1997] V & DR 273; *Denman College v Customs and Excise Comrs* [1998] V & DR 399; *General Healthcare Group Ltd v Customs and Excise Comrs* (2001) VAT decision 17129. For "hospital, prison or similar institution", see *R & C Comrs v Fenwood Developments Ltd* [2005] EWHC 2954 (Ch), [2006] STC 644 (mental home). The services must be supplied to the person intending to use the building for that purpose: VATA 1994, Sch 8, Group 5, Note 12(*a*). For the certificate to be provided by that person, see VATA 1994, Sch 8, Group 5, Note 12(*b*); Notice No 708 (August 1997), Annex A. For groups of buildings, see VATA 1994, Sch 8, Group 5, Note 5.
7. For "relevant charitable purpose", see VATA 1994, Sch 8, Group 5, Note 6; Notice No 48 (July 2009) para 3.29; *Jubilee Hall Recreation Centre Ltd v Customs and Excise Comrs* [1999] STC 381, CA; *Customs and Excise Comrs v Yarburgh Children's Trust* [2002] STC 207; *Riverside Housing Association Revenue and Customs Comrs* [2006] EWHC 2383 (Ch), [2006] STC 2072. For examples, see *Shinewater Association Football Club v Customs and Excise Comrs* (1995) VAT decision 12938; *Ormiston Charitable Trust v Customs and Excise Comrs* [1995] V & DR 180; *Newtownbutler Playgroup Ltd v Customs and Excise Comrs* (1995) VAT decision 13741; *Bennachie Leisure Centre Association v Customs and Excise Comrs* (1996) VAT decision 14276; *Cardiff Community Housing Associa-*

tion Ltd v Customs and Excise Comrs [2000] V & DR 346. The services must be supplied to the person intending to use the building for that purpose: VATA 1994, Sch 8, Group 5, Note 12(*a*). For the certificate to be provided by that person, see VATA 1994, Sch 8, Group 5, Note 12(*b*); Notice No 708 (August 1997), Annex A.
[8] Cf VATA 1994, Sch 8, Group 5, Note 18(*a*).
[9] Cf VATA 1994, Sch 8, Group 5, Note 18(*b*).
[10] VATA 1994, Sch 8, Group 5, Note 16.
[11] VATA 1994, Sch 8, Group 5, Note 16(*b*).
[12] VATA 1994, Sch 8, Group 5, Note 16(*b*).
[13] For "annexe", see *Chantrell (trading as Foxearth Lodge Nursing Home) v Customs and Excise Comrs (No 2)* [2003] STC 486.
[14] VATA 1994, Sch 8, Group 5, Notes 16(*c*), 17 as amended by SI 2002/1101. Both buildings must be capable of functioning independently, and must have separate entrances so that the sole or main means of access is not via the other building.
[15] VATA 1994, Sch 8, Group 5, Note 10. For communal areas in blocks of flats, see Business Brief (Issue 11/03), 24 July 2003.
[16] VATA 1994, Sch 10, para 37 as inserted by SI 2008/1146; see supra, § **65.35**.
[17] VATA 1994, Sch 10, para 36 as inserted by SI 2008/1146.

Construction of civil engineering works

[69.19] A supply of services is zero-rated if it is made in the course of constructing a civil engineering work necessary for the development of a permanent park for residential caravans.[1]

The services must comprise something other than:[2]

(1) The services of an architect, surveyor, consultant or supervisor.
(2) Services comprising the conversion, reconstruction, alteration or enlargement of a civil engineering work.
(3) A transfer of possession of goods (eg plant hire).
(4) The use of business goods for non-business or private purposes.

De Voil Indirect Tax Service V4.237.

[1] VATA 1994, Sch 8, Group 5, Item 2(*b*). For "civil engineering work", see *GKN Birwelco Ltd v Customs and Excise Comrs* [1983] VATTR 128; *UFD Ltd v Customs and Excise Comrs* [1981] VATTR 199. For "residential caravan", see VATA 1994, Sch 8, Group 5, Note 19.
[2] VATA 1994, Sch 8, Group 5, Item 2 and Notes 15, 20. For "conversion, reconstruction, alteration or enlargement", see supra, § **69.17**.

Conversion of buildings and parts of buildings

[69.20] A supply of services is zero-rated[1] if it is made in the course of converting a non-residential[2] building, or a non-residential part of a building, into either:

(1) A building or part designed as one or more dwellings.[3]
(2) A building or part intended for use solely for a relevant residential purpose.[4]

[69.20] The zero rate

The services must be supplied to a relevant housing association.[5] They must relate to the conversion[6] and comprise something other than:[7] the services of an architect, surveyor, consultant or supervisor; a transfer of possession of goods (eg plant hire);[8] or the use of business assets for non-business or private purposes.[9]

Part of a building may be designed as one or more dwellings and part may not. Similarly, part may be intended to be used for a relevant residential purpose and part may not. A supply relating to both parts is apportioned to determine the extent to which the supply is zero-rated.[10]

De Voil Indirect Tax Service V4.234.

---

[1] VATA 1994, Sch 8, Group 5, Item 3.
[2] For "non-residential", see VATA 1994, Sch 8, Group 5, Notes 7A (as substituted by SI 2001/2305), 8; *Look Ahead Housing Association v Customs and Excise Comrs* (2000) VAT decision 16816.
[3] For "dwellings", see VATA 1994, Sch 8, Group 5, Note 3. For buildings "designed" as one or more dwellings, see VATA 1994, Sch 8, Group 5, Note 2. Note 2 does not make any reference to a "part" of a building designed as one or more dwellings. If a building contains both a residential part and a non-residential part, the conversion of the non-residential part must create one or more additional dwellings: VATA 1994, Sch 8, Group 5, Note 9. For examples, see *Customs and Excise Comrs v Blom-Cooper* [2003] STC 669, CA; *Calam Vale Ltd v Customs and Excise Comrs* (2000) VAT decision 16869.
[4] For "relevant residential purpose", see VATA 1994, Sch 8, Group 5, Note 4. For the certificate to be provided by the housing association, see VATA 1994, Sch 8, Group 5, Note 12(*b*); Notice No 708 (August 1997), Annex A.
[5] VATA 1994, Sch 8, Group 5, Item 3 as amended by SI 1997/50. For "relevant housing association", see VATA 1994, Sch 8, Group 5, Note 21 as substituted by SI 1997/50.
[6] VATA 1994, Sch 8, Group 5, Item 3. An apportionment is made if necessary to determine the extent to which the services are zero-rated: VATA 1994, Sch 8, Group 5, Note 11.
[7] VATA 1994, Sch 8, Group 5, Item 3 and Note 20.
[8] For transfers amounting to supplies of goods and supplies of services, see respectively supra, §§ **63.24–63.25**.
[9] For services within this description, see supra, § **65.29**.
[10] VATA 1994, Sch 8, Group 5, Note 5.

Goods supplied with services

[69.21] A supply of building materials[1] is zero-rated if:[2]

(1) The supplier makes a supply of services to a person.
(2) The services are zero-rated under the provisions described in supra, §§ **69.18–69.19**.
(3) The supplier supplies the building materials to the same person,
(4) The supplier incorporates the building materials into the building or site concerned.

De Voil Indirect Tax Service V4.242.

[1] For "building materials", see VATA 1994, Sch 8, Group 5, Notes 22, 23. For fitted furniture, see *Customs and Excise Comrs v McLean Homes Midland Ltd* [1993] STC 335; *Edmond Homes Ltd v Customs and Excise Comrs* (1993) VAT decision 11567; *Wade v Customs and Excise Comrs* (1995) VAT decision 13164; *Moores Furniture Group Ltd v Customs and Excise Comrs* (1997) VAT decision 15044; Business Brief (Issue 12/97) 5 June 1997. For goods prefabricated off site, see *Customs and Excise Comrs v Jeffs* [1995] STC 759.
[2] VATA 1994, Sch 8, Group 5, Item 4.

Group 6—protected buildings

Grant of a major interest

[69.22] The first grant[1] of a major interest[2] in all or part of a building or its site is zero-rated if the following conditions are met:[3]

(1) The building is a listed building[4] or scheduled monument.[5]
(2) It has been substantially reconstructed.[6]
(3) It is designed to become, or remain as, one or more dwellings[7] or is intended to be used solely for a relevant residential[8] or charitable[9] purpose following the reconstruction.
(4) The grant is made by the person who substantially reconstructed the building.

If the major interest is a lease or tenancy, the grant is zero-rated only to the extent that it is made for a consideration in the form of the premium (if a premium is payable) or the first payment of rent due (in other cases).[10]

Part of the building may have been designed to become, or remain as, one or more dwellings and part may not. Similarly, part may be intended for use for a relevant residential or charitable purpose, and part may not. A grant relating to both parts is apportioned to determine the extent to which the grant is zero-rated.[11]

De Voil Indirect Tax Service V4.235.

[1] For "grant", see VATA 1994, s 96(10A) as inserted or amended by FA 1997, s 35, SI 2008/1146. "Grant" includes assignment or surrender: VATA 1994, Sch 8, Group 5, Note 1 and Group 6, Note 3.
[2] ie the fee simple or lease for a term of not less than 20 years (land held on feudal tenure in Scotland) or a term exceeding 21 years (other leases): VATA 1994, s 96(1) as amended by FA 1998, s 24. See *Cottage Holiday Associates Ltd v Customs and Excise Comrs* [1983] STC 278.
[3] VATA 1994, Sch 8, Group 6, Item 1.
[4] As defined in VATA 1994, Sch 8, Group 6, Note 1. For buildings immune from listing treated as a listed building, see News Release 22/96, 22 April 1996.
[5] As defined in VATA 1994, Sch 8, Group 6, Note 1.
[6] ie the work done meets either or both the tests in VATA 1994, Sch 8, Group 6, Note 4. See *Barraclough v Customs and Excise Comrs* (1987) VAT decision 2529.
[7] ie it meets the tests in VATA 1994, Sch 8, Group 6, Note 2. The purchaser or tenant must be entitled to reside in the dwelling throughout the year and use it as his

[69.22] The zero rate

principal private residence: VATA 1994, Sch 8, Group 5, Note 13 and Group 6, Note 3.
[8] For "relevant residential purpose", see VATA 1994, Sch 8, Group 5, Note 4 and Group 6, Note 3. For the certificate to be provided by the purchaser or tenant, see VATA 1994, Sch 8, Group 5, Note 12(b) and Group 6, Note 3; Notice No 708 (August 1997), Annex A.
[9] For "relevant charitable purpose", see VATA 1994, Sch 8, Group 5, Note 6 and Group 6, Note 3. For the certificate to be provided by the purchaser or tenant, see VATA 1994, Sch 8, Group 5, Note 12(b) and Group 6, Note 3; Notice No 708 (August 1997), Annex A.
[10] VATA 1994, Sch 8, Group 5, Note 14 and Group 6, Note 3.
[11] VATA 1994, Sch 8, Group 6, Note 5.

Approved alterations

[69.23] Services are zero-rated[1] if they are supplied in the course of carrying out an "approved alteration" of a building, being a listed building or scheduled monument,[2] which is designed to become, or remain as, one or more dwellings;[3] or is intended to be used solely for a relevant residential[4] or charitable[5] purpose. In the latter case, the services must be supplied to the person intending to use the building for the purpose concerned.[6] A service may relate only partly to an approved alteration. Where this is so, an apportionment is made to determine the extent to which the supply is zero-rated.[7]

The services must comprise something other than:[8] the services of an architect, surveyor, consultant or supervisor; a transfer of the possession of goods; or the use of business goods for non-business or private purposes. Part of the building may have been designed to become, or remain as, one or more dwellings and part may not. Similarly, part may be intended for use for a relevant residential or charitable purpose, and part may not. A supply relating to both parts is apportioned to determine the extent to which the supply is zero-rated.[9]

The works comprising an "approved alteration" are specifically defined in relation to ecclesiastical buildings, scheduled monuments in Northern Ireland and buildings subject to a Crown or Duchy interest.[10] The following conditions must be met in other cases:[11]

(1) The works must comprise alterations[12] as opposed to works of repair or maintenance,[13] or reconstruction which does not amount to alteration.[14]
(2) The works must not comprise an incidental alteration to the fabric of the building that results from carrying out repairs.[15]
(3) The works must not comprise the construction of a separate[16] building within the curtilage of a listed building.
(4) To the extent that the works amount to an alteration within the meaning of points (1)–(3),[17] they must affect the character of the building (ie its character as a building of special architectural or historic interest)[18] so as to require listed building consent.[19]
(5) Listed building consent must have been given before the works commenced.[20]
(6) The works must have been executed in accordance with the terms and conditions of the consent.[21]

A listed building may have a structure fixed to it or have a structure within its curtilage that has formed part of the land since 1 July 1948. These structures are treated as part of the building for the purposes of determining whether listed building consent is necessary in order to carry out works to them.[22] However, works carried out to these structures are *not* regarded as works carried out to the listed building.[23] Thus, works carried out to one of these structures cannot be an approved alteration unless, following completion of the works, the structure comprises one or more dwellings or a building for relevant charitable or residential use.

De Voil Indirect Tax Service V4.239.

1 VATA 1994, Sch 8, Group 6, Item 2.
2 As defined in VATA 1994, Sch 8, Group 6, Note 1.
3 ie it meets the tests in VATA 1994, Sch 8, Group 6, Note 2.
4 For "relevant residential purpose", see VATA 1994, Sch 8, Group 5, Note 4 by virtue of Group 6, Note 3.
5 For "relevant charitable purpose", see VATA 1994, Sch 8, Group 5, Note 6 by virtue of Group 6, Note 3.
6 VATA 1994, Sch 8, Group 5, Note 12(*a*) by virtue of Group 6, Note 3. For the certificate to be provided, see VATA 1994, Sch 8, Group 5, Note 12(*b*) by virtue of Group 6, Note 3; Notice No 708 (August 1997), Annex A.
7 VATA 1994, Sch 8, Group 6, Note 9.
8 VATA 1994, Sch 8, Group 6, Item 2 and Note 11.
9 VATA 1994, Sch 8, Group 6, Note 5.
10 VATA 1994, Sch 8, Group 6, Notes 6(*a*)–(*c*), 7, 8.
11 VATA 1994, Sch 8, Group 6, Notes 3, 10; Planning (Listed Buildings and Conservation Areas) Act 1990, ss 7, 8.
12 In *Customs and Excise Comrs v Morrish* [1998] STC 954, Moses J said that an alteration "probably" means a structural alteration, but did not decide the point. He disapproved two previous contrasting lines of authority: (1) *Evans v Customs and Excise Comrs* (1989) VAT decision 4415 and later cases (word construed by reference to *ACT Construction Co Ltd v Customs and Excise Comrs* [1982] STC 25, HL and *Customs and Excise Comrs v Viva Gas Appliances Ltd* [1983] STC 819, HL); and (2) *Wrencon Ltd v Customs and Excise Comrs* (1996) VAT decision 13968 (word construed in accordance with relevant planning law).
13 For "repair or maintenance", see *Wrencon Ltd v Customs and Excise Comrs* (1996) VAT decision 13968; *Parochial Church Council of St Andrew's Church, Eakring v Customs and Excise Comrs* (1998) VAT decision 15320.
14 *Customs and Excise Comrs v Morrish* [1998] STC 954.
15 For incidental alterations, see *Wrencon Ltd v Customs and Excise Comrs* (1996) VAT decision 13968.
16 For separate buildings, see *Customs and Excise Comrs v Arbib* [1995] STC 490.
17 This test determines whether listed building consent is necessary. It does not affect the question whether or not the works amount to an alteration: *Customs and Excise Comrs v Morrish* [1998] STC 954.
18 For works affecting the character of a building, see *Walsingham College (Yorkshire Properties) Ltd v Customs and Excise Comrs* [1995] V & DR 141 (drainage system).

[69.23] The zero rate

[19] A tribunal is not bound by the views of the local planning authority regarding the necessity for listed building consent: *Evans v Customs and Excise Comrs* (1989) VAT decision 4415. Thus, work covered by consent can amount to an approved alteration only if consent was required: *Gibbs v Customs and Excise Comrs* (1990) VAT decision 5596.

[20] *Wells v Customs and Excise Comrs* (1997) VAT decision 15169, *Alan Roper & Sons Ltd v Customs and Excise Comrs* (1997) VAT decision 15260 (works authorised by written consent for retention of the works under Planning (Listed Buildings and Conservation Areas) Act 1990, s 8(3), which become authorised from the date of the consent, do not amount to an approved alteration).

[21] For variations from the terms of a listed building consent held to be de minimis, see *Walsingham College (Yorkshire Properties) Ltd v Customs and Excise Comrs* [1995] V & DR 141.

[22] Planning (Listed Buildings and Conservation Areas) Act 1990, s 1(5).

[23] *Customs and Excise Comrs v Zielinski Baker & Partners Ltd* [2004] UKHL 7, [2004] STC 456, HL. For an example, see *Revenue and Customs Comrs v Tinsley* [2005] EWHC 1508 (Ch), [2005] STC 1612 (construction of terrace).

Goods supplied with services

[69.24] A supply of building materials[1] is zero-rated if:[2] (a) the supplier makes a zero-rated supply of services to a person in the course of an approved alteration to a protected building;[3] (b) he supplies the building materials to the same person; and (c) he incorporates the building materials into the building or site concerned.

De Voil Indirect Tax Service V4.242.

[1] For "building materials", see VATA 1994, Sch 8, Group 5, Notes 22, 23 and Group 6, Note 3.

[2] VATA 1994, Sch 8, Group 6, Item 3.

[3] ie a supply under supra, § **69.23**.

Group 7—international services

[69.25] The following services are zero-rated:[1]

(1) Work carried out within the EU on goods to be exported to a third country.
(2) Agency services for a named principal in arranging:
  (a) the export of goods to a third country;
  (b) a supply of services within head (1); or
  (c) any supply of services made in a third country.[2]

De Voil Indirect Tax Service V4.246.

[1] VATA 1994, Sch 8, Group 7, Items 1, 2.

[2] For the place of supply of services, see supra, §§ **63.28** and **63.29**.

Group 8—transport

Ships and aircraft

[69.26] The following supplies are zero-rated:[1]

(1) The supply, charter,[2] hire, repair or maintenance, modification or conversion of qualifying ships[3] and qualifying aircraft.[4] The legal basis for this provision is Directive 2006/112/EC art 110.[5]
(2) Parts and equipment of a kind ordinarily installed or incorporated in the propulsion, navigation or communications systems of qualifying ships and aircraft, or in their general structure.
(3) Safety equipment for use in a qualifying ship or aircraft.
(4) Handling any ship or aircraft in a port, customs and excise airport or outside of the UK.
(5) Surveying any ship or aircraft.
(6) Classifying any ship or aircraft for the purposes of any register.
(7) Agency services.

De Voil Indirect Tax Service V4.251.

---

[1] VATA 1994, Sch 8, Group 8, Items 1, 2, 2A, 2B, 6(a), 9, 10 and Notes 1, 2, 2A (as inserted by SI 1995/3039), 5, 6 (as amended by SI 2002/1173), 7.
[2] For partial charter, see *Navicon SA v Administración del Estado* (case C-97/06) [2007] ECR I–8755, [2007] SWTI 2405, ECJ (national court must decide whether the contract is for the charter of a ship or aircraft or for the carriage of goods).
[3] For an example of services which do not consist of "making arrangements", see *Société Internationale de Télécommunications Aéronautiques v Customs and Excise Comrs* [2004] EWHC 3039 (Ch), [2004] STC 950 (means of communication).
[4] As defined in VATA 1994, Sch 8, Group 8, Note A1(b) as inserted by SI 1995/3039.
[5] *Revenue and Customs Comrs v Stone* [2008] EWHC 1249 (Ch), [2008] STC 2501.

Passenger transport

[69.27] The following passenger transport[1] services are zero-rated[2] subject to specified exceptions[3] and modifications:[4]

(1) Transport in a vehicle,[5] ship or aircraft designed or adapted to carry 10 or more passengers.[6]
(2) Transport by the Post Office company.
(3) Transport on any scheduled flight.
(4) Transport to or from a place outside the UK[7] (to the extent that it is supplied in the UK).
(5) Agency services.[8]

De Voil Indirect Tax Service V4.251.

---

[1] For "transport", see *Customs and Excise Comrs v Blackpool Pleasure Beach Co* [1974] STC 138, [1974] 1 All ER 1011 ("big dipper"); *Faulkner (a firm) v Customs and Excise Comrs* (1992) VAT decision 7597 (balloon flights); *Quarry Tours Ltd v Customs and Excise Comrs* [1984] VATTR 238 (tour of slate cavern); *Naro-*

[69.27] The zero rate

gauge Ltd v Customs and Excise Comrs (1997) VAT decision 14680 (narrow-gauge railway); *Customs and Excise Comrs v Peninsular and Oriental Steam Navigation Co* [1996] STC 698; *Virgin Atlantic Airways Ltd v Customs and Excise Comrs* (1996) VAT decision 13840, Business Brief (Issue 14/96), 15 July 1996 (cruises).

[2] VATA 1994, Sch 8, Group 8, Items 4 (as amended by the Postal Services Act 2000, s 127 and Sch 8, para 22), 10.

[3] See VATA 1994, Sch 8, Group 8, Notes 4A, 4B, 4C.

[4] Points (1), (2) and (3) are modified in relation to designated travel services supplied by a tour operator by VAT (Tour Operators) Order, SI 1987/1806, art 10(1), (1A).

[5] For "vehicles", see *Quarry Tours Ltd v Customs and Excise Comrs* [1984] VATTR 238; *Llandudno Cabinlift Co Ltd v Customs and Excise Comrs* [1973] VATTR 1.

[6] For determining how many passengers a ship is designed to carry, see *Cirdan Sailing Trust v C & E Comrs* [2005] EWHC 2999 (Ch), [2006] STC 185. For vehicles equipped for carrying wheelchair passengers treated as if they were suitable for carrying more than ten persons, see VATA 1994, Sch 8, Group 8, Note 4D as inserted by SI 2001/753.

[7] See *Virgin Atlantic Airways v Customs and Excise Comrs* [1995] STC 341, Business Brief (Issue 4/96), 13 March 1996.

[8] For an example of services which do not consist of "making arrangements", see *Société Internationale de Télécommunications Aéronautiques v Customs and Excise Comrs* [2003] EWHC 3039 (Ch), [2004] STC 950 (means of communication).

Freight transport

[69.28] The following freight transport services are zero-rated:[1]

(1) Transporting goods from the UK to a third country (including intermediate transport to the place of exportation).
(2) Transporting goods from a third country to the UK (including subsequent transport from the place of importation).
(3) Intra-Community transport services[2] to, from or between the Azores and Madeira.[3]
(4) Handling or storing[4] goods. The legal basis for this provision is Directive 2006/112/EC art 148(g) (as regards VATA 1994, Sch 8, Group 8, Item 6(b)) and art 146(1)(e) (as regards VATA 1994, Sch 8, Group 8, Item 11(a)).[5]
(5) Agency services.

De Voil Indirect Tax Service V4.251.

[1] VATA 1994, Sch 8, Group 8, Items 5, 6(b) (as amended by SI 2002/1173), 10 (as amended by SI 2002/456), 11(a), 13 and Notes 5, 6 (as amended by SI 2002/1173).

[2] As defined in VATA 1994, Sch 8, Group 8, Note 9.

[3] VATA 1994, Sch 8, Group 8, Item 13.

[4] For the storage of passengers' luggage at an airport, see *Revenue and Customs Comrs v EB Central Services Ltd* [2008] EWCA Civ 486, [2008] SWTI 1361, CA.

[5] *Revenue and Customs Comrs v EB Central Services Ltd* [2008] EWCA Civ 486, [2008] STC 2209, CA.

Miscellaneous transport related services

[69.29] The following supplies are zero-rated:[1]

(1) Supplies made to sea-rescue charities in connection with lifeboats,[2] associated equipment and slipways.
(2) Pilotage, air navigation,[3] salvage and towage services.
(3) Designated travel services[4] for enjoyment outside the EU.

De Voil Indirect Tax Service V4.251.

---

[1] VATA 1994, Sch 8, Group 8, Items 3 (as amended by SI 2002/456, SI 2006/1750), 6A, 7, 8, 12 and Notes 2, 3, 6A, 8.
[2] As defined in VATA 1994, Sch 8, Group 8, Note 4.
[3] As defined in Civil Aviation Act 1982, s 105(1).
[4] As defined in VAT (Tour Operators) Order, SI 1987/1806, arts 3, 14.

Services to overseas traders

[69.30] The following services supplied to traders belonging outside the UK[1] are zero-rated:[2]

(1) Handling any ship or aircraft.
(2) Air navigation services.[3]
(3) Surveying and classifying any ship or aircraft.
(4) Making arrangements for the supply of any ship or aircraft.
(5) Making arrangements for the supply of space in any ship or aircraft.

De Voil Indirect Tax Service V4.251.

---

[1] For the country where the recipient of a supply belongs, see VATA 1994, s 9(3), (4).
[2] VATA 1994, Sch 8, Group 8, Item 11(*b*) and Note 7.
[3] As defined in VATA 1994, Sch 8, Group 8, Note 6A; Civil Aviation Act 1982, s 105(1).

Group 9—caravans and houseboats

[69.31] The supply[1] of a "mobile home" caravan[2] or houseboat[3] is zero-rated.[4] Removable contents are zero-rated only if they comprise building materials.[5] The provision of accommodation is excluded from zero-rating.[6]

De Voil Indirect Tax Service V4.275.

---

[1] This includes: (a) hire, (b) use for private or non-business purposes, and (c) transfer of an undivided share. The reference to VATA 1994, Sch 4, para 5(3) in Sch 8, Group 9, Item 3 should be a reference to para 5(4).
[2] ie exceeding 7 metres in length or 2.3 metres in breadth, excluding tow bars and similar attachments: VATA 1994, Sch 8, Group 9, Item 1; Road Vehicles (Construction and Use) Regulations, SI 1986/1078.
[3] As defined in VATA 1994, Sch 8, Group 9, Item 2.
[4] VATA 1994, Sch 8, Group 9, Items 1, 2, 3. For connection to gas or electricity mains supply, see Notice No 48 (July 2009), para 3.16.

[69.31] The zero rate

[5] VATA 1994, Sch 8, Group 9, Note (a). See *Talacre Beach Caravan Sales Ltd v Customs and Excise Comrs* (case C-251/05) [2006] ECR I–6269, [2006] STC 1671, ECJ. For building materials, see supra, § **68.32**. VATA 1994, Sch 8, Group 5, Item 3 was re-enacted as Item 4 by SI 1995/280.

[6] VATA 1994, Sch 8, Group 9, Item 3 and Note (b).

Group 10—gold

[69.32] A supply[1] of gold[2] held in the UK is zero-rated. The parties to the transaction must be either two Central Banks or a Central Bank and a member of the London Gold Market.[3]

De Voil Indirect Tax Service V4.277.

[1] For supplies included, see VATA 1994, Sch 8, Group 10, Note 3.
[2] As defined in VATA 1994, Sch 8, Group 10, Note 1.
[3] VATA 1994, Sch 8, Group 10, Items 1, 2.

Group 11—bank notes

[69.33] A note payable to bearer on demand issued by a bank is zero-rated.[1]

De Voil Indirect Tax Service V4.279.

[1] VATA 1994, Sch 8, Group 11, Item 1. For a supply outside this description, see *Royal Bank of Scotland Group plc v Customs and Excise Comrs* [2002] STC 575.

Group 12—drugs, medicines, aids for the handicapped, etc

Drugs and appliances

[69.34] Goods (other than hearing aids, dentures, spectacles and contact lenses) designed or adapted for use in connection with any medical or surgical treatment are zero-rated if supplied or hired by:[1]

(1) A registered pharmacist. The goods must be dispensed[2] on prescription[3] given by a registered medical practitioner or dentist for the personal use[4] of an individual.

(2) A registered medical practitioner who is authorised or required to dispense such goods.[5]

De Voil Indirect Tax Service V4.281.

[1] VATA 1994, Sch 8, Group 12, Items 1 (as amended by SI 1997/2744), 1A (as inserted by SI 1995/652 and amended by SI 1997/2744) and Notes 2A (as inserted by SI 1997/2744), 5 (as amended by SI 1995/652). See *Bio Oil Research Ltd v Customs and Excise Comrs* (1994) VAT decision 12252. For medicinal products supplied to certain charities, see infra, § **68.40**.

2   For "dispensed", see *Bio Oil Research Ltd v Customs and Excise Comrs* (1994) VAT decision 12252.
3   For "prescription", see *Bio Oil Research Ltd v Customs and Excise Comrs* (1994) VAT decision 12252.
4   ie use at a time when the individual is not receiving medical treatment, surgical treatment or care as an in-patient, resident or out-patient of a private hospital or nursing home: see VATA 1994, Sch 8, Group 12, Notes 5A and 5I both as inserted by SI 1997/2744. For a concession, see Notice No 48 (July 2009) para 3.29.
5   A medical practitioner makes a single supply of services when he administers the drugs he dispenses. This service comprises medical treatment and is exempt from tax under the provisions described in supra, § **68.23**: see *Dr Beynon & Partners v Customs and Excise Comrs* [2004] UKHL 53, [2005] STC 55, HL.

Supplies to handicapped persons

[69.35] The following supplies made to a handicapped person[1] are zero-rated:

(1) The supply or hire of specified goods[2] for domestic or personal use[3] by him.[4]
(2) The supply or hire of a qualifying motor vehicle.[5] The handicapped person must usually use a wheelchair or be carried in a stretcher.[6]
(3) Adapting goods to suit his condition, including goods used therein.[7]
(4) Installing a lift in his private residence.[8]
(5) Supplying an alarm system directly connected to a specified person or control centre.[9]
(6) Repair or maintenance of the goods in points 1–5 above.[10]
(7) Installing the goods in point 1 and parts and accessories therefor.[11]
(8) Constructing ramps or widening doorways or passages in his private residence.[12]
(9) Providing, extending or adapting a bathroom, washroom or lavatory in his private residence.[13]
(10) Hiring an unused motor vehicle to him for a minimum term of three years.[14]

De Voil Indirect Tax Service V4.281.

1   As defined in VATA 1994, Sch 8, Group 12, Note 3. See *Tempur Pedic (UK) Ltd v Customs and Excise Comrs* (1995) VAT decision 13744 (long-term pain).
2   ie the goods specified in VATA 1994, Sch 8, Group 12, Item 2(a)–(i) as amended by SI 2001/754 and Note 4(a)–(c) as amended by SI 1997/2744. These goods do not include hearing aids (other than hearing aids designed for the auditory training of deaf children), dentures, spectacles and contact lenses. For Item 2(a), see *Customs and Excise Comrs v Wellington Private Hospital Ltd* [1997] STC 445, CA; *Neen Design Ltd v Customs and Excise Comrs* (1994) VAT decision 11782; Business Brief (Issue 4/94), 21 February 1994. For Item 2(b), see *Niagara Holdings Ltd v Customs and Excise Comrs* [1993] VATTR 503. For Item 2(g), see *Princess Louise Scottish Hospital v Customs and Excise Comrs* [1983] VATTR 191; *Kirton Designs Ltd v Customs and Excise Comrs* (1987) VAT decision 2374; *Softley Ltd v Customs and Excise Comrs* (1997) VAT decision 15034; *Boys' and Girls' Welfare Society v Customs and Excise Comrs* (1997) VAT decision 15274.

[3] ie use at a time when the handicapped person is not receiving medical treatment, surgical treatment or care as an in-patient, resident or out-patient of a private hospital, nursing home or institution: see VATA 1994, Sch 8, Group 12, Notes 5B and 5I both as inserted by SI 1997/2744. This definition applies to: (a) any supply or hiring of specified goods (other than a supply of the goods listed in VATA 1994, Sch 8, Group 12, Note 5C(*b*), (*c*) as so inserted) made by a relevant institution (as defined in VATA 1994, Sch 8, Group 12, Note 5I as so inserted), and (b) a supply of the specified goods listed in VATA 1994, Sch 8, Group 12, Note 5D(*a*)–(*c*) as so inserted made by someone other than a person within VATA 1994, Sch 8, Group 12, Note 5H as so inserted and amended by SI 2000/503, SI 2002/2813.

[4] VATA 1994, Sch 8, Group 12, Item 2 and Note 5. For any agreement, arrangement or understanding relating to the supply, see VATA 1994, Sch 8, Group 12, Notes 5E(*a*), 5F(*a*) both as inserted by SI 1997/2744. For payments relating to the supply, see VATA 1994, Sch 8, Group 12, Notes 5E(*b*), 5F(*b*) both as so inserted. For a concession, see Notice No 48 (July 2009), para 3.24.

[5] As defined in VATA 1994, Sch 8, Group 12, Note 5L as inserted by SI 2001/754.

[6] VATA 1994, Sch 8, Group 8, Item 2A and Note 5 as inserted by SI 2001/754.

[7] VATA 1994, Sch 8, Group 12, Items 3, 6. For apportionment, see VATA 1994, Sch 8, Group 12, Note 8.

[8] VATA 1994, Sch 8, Group 12, Items 16, 18. See *Brian Perkins & Co Ltd v Customs and Excise Comrs* (1989) VAT decision 3885.

[9] VATA 1994, Sch 8, Group 12, Item 19. For "specified person or control centre", see VATA 1994, Sch 8, Group 12, Note 9.

[10] VATA 1994, Sch 8, Group 12, Items 5, 6.

[11] VATA 1994, Sch 8, Group 12, Item 7.

[12] VATA 1994, Sch 8, Group 12, Items 8, 13. See *Flather v Customs and Excise Comrs* (1994) VAT decision 11960 (goods supplied in connection with services).

[13] VATA 1994, Sch 8, Group 12, Items 10, 13 and Note 5K (as inserted by SI 2000/805). See *Mid-Derbyshire Cheshire Home v Customs and Excise Comrs* (1990) VAT decision 4512 (washroom); *Flather v Customs and Excise Comrs* (1994) VAT decision 11960 (goods supplied in connection with services).

[14] VATA 1994, Sch 8, Group 12, Item 14 and Notes 6, 7.

Supplies for the benefit of handicapped persons

[69.36] The following supplies are zero-rated:

(1) Goods and services supplied to a charity for the benefit of handicapped persons.[1] (The supplies are similar to those listed in supra, § **69.35**, points 1–9.)

(2) The sale of a motor vehicle which has been hired to a handicapped person under a zero-rated supply.[2] The sale must be the first supply of the vehicle following the end of the hire period.[3]

(3) Services necessarily performed by a control centre[4] in receiving and responding to calls from an alarm system.[5]

De Voil Indirect Tax Service V4.281.

[1] VATA 1994, Sch 8, Group 12 Items 2 (as amended by SI 2001/754), 2A (as inserted by SI 2001/754), 4, 5, 6, 9, 11 (as substituted by SI 2000/805), 12, 13, 17, 18, 19

Common provisions [69.39]

and Notes 3, 4 (as amended by SI 1997/2744), 5 (as amended by SI 1995/652, SI 2001/754), 5E (as inserted by SI 1997/2744), 5J (as inserted by SI 2000/805), 5K (as inserted by SI 2000/805), 5L (as inserted by SI 2001/754), 8, 9. For "day centre", see *Union of Students of the University of Warwick v Customs and Excise Comrs* [1995] V & DR 519.
[2] ie a supply zero-rated under VATA 1994, Sch 9, Group 12, Item 14. For the supply made, see supra, § **69.35**, point 9.
[3] VATA 1994, Sch 8, Group 12, Item 15.
[4] As defined in VATA 1994, Sch 8, Group 12, Note 9.
[5] VATA 1994, Sch 8, Group 12, Item 20.

Group 13—imports, exports, etc

[69.37] The following supplies are zero-rated:[1]

(1) Imported goods supplied before an entry has been delivered.[2]
(2) Goods and services supplied to or by certain bodies[3] managing international defence projects.[4]
(3) Specified goods[5] supplied to specified overseas persons[6] for use in the UK solely for the manufacture of goods for export to a third country.

De Voil Indirect Tax Service V4.283.

[1] VATA 1994, Sch 8, Group 13, Items 1–3.
[2] For delivery of an entry, see Customs Controls on Importation of Goods Regulations, SI 1991/2724, reg 5.
[3] Defined in VATA 1994, Sch 8, Group 13, Notes 2–4.
[4] Defined in VATA 1994, Sch 8, Group 13, Item 2 and Note 1.
[5] Defined in VATA 1994, Sch 8, Group 13, Item 3. See *Technicolor Ltd v Customs and Excise Comrs* (1997) VAT decision 14871.
[6] Defined in VATA 1994, Sch 8, Group 13, Notes 2–5.

Group 14—tax-free shops

[69.38] Goods supplied in a tax-free shop, or on board a ship or aircraft, ceased to be zero-rated after 30 June 1999.[1]

De Voil Indirect Tax Service V4.210.

[1] VATA 1994, Sch 8, Group 14 was repealed by VAT (Abolition of Zero-Rating for Tax-Free Shops) Order, SI 1999/1642.

Group 15—charities, etc

Supplies made by charities

[69.39] A sale or letting of goods[1] by a charity is zero-rated[2] if the goods were donated to the charity for sale, letting[3] or export. The goods must be made

[69.39] The zero rate

available to handicapped persons, to persons entitled to one or more specified benefits,[4] or to the general public prior to the sale or letting. The supply is not zero-rated if the goods have been used by the charity or if arrangements have been entered into by the donor, the charity or the recipient of the supply. Sales and lettings by a "profits to charity person"[5] are zero-rated under similar conditions.[6]

Goods exported from the UK to a third country by a charity are zero-rated.[7]

De Voil Indirect Tax Service V4.266.

---

[1] As defined in VATA 1994, Sch 8, Group 15, Note 1F (as substituted by SI 2000/805).
[2] VATA 1994, Sch 8, Group 15, Items 1(as substituted by SI 2000/805), 3 and Notes 1, 1B, 1C (as substituted or inserted by SI 2000/805).
[3] As defined in VATA 1994, Sch 8, Group 15, Note 1A (as substituted by SI 2000/805).
[4] ie the benefits listed in VATA 1994, Sch 8, Group 15, Note 1D (as substituted by SI 2000/805).
[5] As defined in VATA 1994, Sch 8, Group 15, Note 1E (as substituted by SI 2000/805).
[6] VATA 1994, Sch 8, Group 15, Item 1A and Notes 1, 1B, 1C (as substituted or inserted by SI 2000/805).
[7] VATA 1994, Sch 8, Group 15, Item 3; *International Planned Parenthood Federation v Customs and Excise Comrs* (2000) VAT decision 16922. The goods are deemed to be supplied in the UK in the course or furtherance of a business carried on by the charity if this would not otherwise be the case, eg in relation to gifts of goods for disaster relief: VATA 1994, s 30(5).

Supplies made to charities

[69.40] The following goods and services are zero-rated when supplied to the persons stated.[1] Other goods and services supplied to charities are zero-rated under other groups.[2]

(1) Goods[3] donated to a charity or "profits-to-charity person"[4] for sale, letting[5] or export.
(2) The following supplies made to any charity, insofar as the goods and services are not used to create or update the charity's web site:
    (a) promulgating an advertisement to the public at large (as opposed to selected individuals) by means of a medium of communication;
    (b) supplying goods closely related to a supply in point 2(a) (but not goods and services directly used by the charity to design or produce an advertisement);
    (c) the right to promulgate an advertisement in point 2(a);
    (d) designing or producing an advertisement (but not goods and services directly used by the charity to design or produce an advertisement).
(3) Medicinal products[6] supplied to a medical or veterinary charity solely for care, treatment or research.

(4)   Substances[7] supplied to any charity for synthesis or testing in medical or veterinary research.

De Voil Indirect Tax Service V4.266.

---

[1]   VATA 1994, Sch 8, Group 15, Items 2, 8–8C (as substituted by SI 2000/805), 9, 10 and Notes 10A–10C (as substituted by SI 2000/805), 11, 12.
[2]   See supra, §§ **69.16, 69.29** and **69.36**. For buildings used for charitable purposes, see supra, §§ **69.17–69.24**.
[3]   As defined in VATA 1994, Sch 8, Group 15, Note 1F (as substituted by SI 2000/805).
[4]   ie a taxable person as defined in VATA 1994, Sch 8, Group 15, Note 1E (as substituted by SI 2000/805).
[5]   As defined in VATA 1994, Sch 8, Group 15, Note 1A (as substituted by SI 2000/805).
[6]   Defined in VATA 1994, Sch 8, Group 15, Note 11.
[7]   Defined in VATA 1994, Sch 8, Group 15, Note 12.

Relevant goods

[69.41] The following supplies are zero-rated if the funds used to pay for them are contributed by a charity or raised by voluntary contributions:[1]

(1)   A supply or hire of any relevant goods[2] to an intermediary for donation to a nominated eligible body.[3]
(2)   A supply or hire of any relevant goods to an eligible body.
(3)   The provision of computer software to an eligible body. The software must be solely for use in medical research, diagnosis or treatment.
(4)   The repair or maintenance of relevant goods owned by, or in the possession of, an eligible body.
(5)   A supply of goods in connection with a supply described in point 4.

Relief is given in a more restricted form[4] if the recipient of the supply is a charitable institution providing care,[5] medical treatment or surgical treatment for handicapped persons[6] in a relevant establishment[7] where most of the patients are such persons.[8] As a charity, the institution can make a contribution to the funds used to pay for the supply.[9]

De Voil Indirect Tax Service V4.266.

---

[1]   VATA 1994, Sch 8, Group 15, Items 4–7 and Note 8(*a*), 9, 10. The eligible body can make a contribution to these funds only if it is a charity: Notes 6, 7, 8(*b*).
[2]   As defined in VATA 1994, Sch 8, Group 15, Note 3. For goods within Note 3(*a*), see *Customs and Excise Comrs v David Lewis Centre* [1995] STC 485. For goods within Note 3(*c*), see *Royal Midland Counties Home for Disabled People v Customs and Excise Comrs* [2002] STC 395. For goods within Note 3(*e*), see *Customs and Excise Comrs v Help the Aged* [1997] STC 406. For concessions, see Notice No 48 (July 2009), para 3.25 (resuscitation training models).
[3]   As defined in VATA 1994, Sch 8, Group 15, Note 4 (as amended by SI 2000/503, SI 2002/2813). For concessions, see Notice No 48 (July 2009), para 3.19 (charities providing care or transport services).

[69.41] The zero rate

4   The relevant goods must be for use in the relevant establishment used to provide the care or treatment or (if the goods are relevant goods within VATA 1994, Sch 8, Group 15, Note 3(*a*), or are parts or accessories for them so as to be relevant goods within VATA 1994, Sch 8, Group 15, Note 3(*c*)), for use in, or in connection with, the provision of medical care to handicapped persons in their own homes: VATA 1994, Sch 8, Group 15, Notes 5A, 5B as inserted by FA 1997, s 34.

5   For "care", see *Customs and Excise Comrs v Help the Aged* [1997] STC 406; *Medical Care Foundation v Customs and Excise Comrs* [1991] VATTR 28.

6   As defined in VATA 1994, Sch 8, Group 15, Note 5.

7   As defined in VATA 1994, Sch 8, Group 15, Note 4B as inserted by FA 1997, s 34.

8   ie the recipient is an eligible body within VATA 1994, Sch 8, Group 15, Note 4(*f*) as defined by Note 4A as inserted by FA 1997, s 34.

9   VATA 1994, Sch 8, Group 15, Notes 6, 8(*b*).

Group 16—clothing and footwear

[69.42] The following supplies[1] are zero-rated:[2]

(1)   Clothing, headgear[3] and footwear for young children[4] which are neither suitable for older persons[5] nor (with exceptions[6]) made of fur skin.[7]

(2)   Protective boots and helmets for industrial use manufactured to specified standards.[8]

(3)   Protective motor cycle and pedal cycle helmets manufactured to specified standards.

De Voil Indirect Tax Service V4.287.

1   Including services defined in VATA 1994, Sch 8, Group 16, Note 5.

2   VATA 1994, Sch 8, Group 16, Items 1–3 and Notes 1, 4 (amended by SI 2001/732), 4A (as inserted or amended by SI 2000/1517, SI 2001/732), 5.

3   See *Cassidy v Customs and Excise Comrs* (1991) VAT decision 5760.

4   See *Walter Stewart Ltd v Customs and Excise Comrs* [1974] VATTR 131; *Jeffrey Green & Co Ltd v Customs and Excise Comrs* [1974] VATTR 94; *VF Corpn (UK) Ltd v Customs and Excise Comrs* (1980) VAT decision 898; *Customs and Excise Comrs v Ali Baba Tex Ltd* [1992] STC 590; *H & M Hennes Ltd v C & E Comrs* [2005] EWHC 1383 (Ch), [2005] STC 1749.

5   See *Jeffrey Green & Co Ltd v Customs and Excise Comrs* [1974] VATTR 94; *Walter Stewart Ltd v Customs and Excise Comrs* [1974] VATTR 131; *Brays of Glastonbury Ltd v Customs and Excise Comrs* (1978) VAT decision 650; *Charles Owen & Co (Bow) Ltd v Customs and Excise Comrs* [1993] VATTR 514; *Dauntgate Ltd v Customs and Excise Comrs* (1994) VAT decision 11663.

6   Defined in VATA 1994, Sch 8, Group 16, Note 2(a)–(d).

7   Defined in VATA 1994, Sch 8, Group 16, Note 3.

8   Supplies to employers for use by employees are excluded from zero-rating under this head: VATA 1994, Sch 8, Group 16, Note 5.

Group 17–emissions allowances

[69.43] The following supplies are zero-rated:[1]

(1) A community tradeable emissions allowance;[2]
(2) A unit[3] issued pursuant to the Kyoto Protocol;[4]
(3) Any option relating to an allowance in (1) or a unit in (2).

---

[1] VATA 1994, Sch 8, Group 17, Item 1 and Note 1 as inserted by SI 2009/2093. Zero-rating applies to supplies made after 30 July 2009.
[2] As defined in FA 2007, s 16(6).
[3] As defined in VATA 1994, Sch 8, Group 17, Note 4 as inserted by SI 2009/2093.
[4] As defined in VATA 1994, Sch 8, Group 17, Note 3 as inserted by SI 2009/2093.

70

The reduced rate

| Introduction | PARA **70.01** |
| Common provisions | PARA **70.04** |

Introduction

Rate of tax

[70.01] The reduced rate of tax was introduced by FA 1995, s 21 and has effect in relation to supplies, acquisitions and importations taking place after 31 March 1995. The rate of tax was originally set at 8%.[1] This was reduced to 5% with effect from 1 September 1997.[2]

The rate of tax can be varied by order.[3]

---

[1] VATA 1994, s 2(1A) (repealed) as inserted by FA 1995, s 21.
[2] VATA 1994, s 2(1A) (repealed) as amended by F(No 2)A 1997, s 6. The same rate continues to apply from 1 November 2001 in accordance with VATA 1994, s 29A(1) as inserted by FA 2001, s 99(4).
[3] VATA 1994, s 2(2).

Legislation

[70.02] The supplies, acquisitions and importations for the time being charged to tax at the reduced rate are described in VATA 1994, Sch 7A.[1] These descriptions can be varied by Treasury order.[2]

VATA 1994, Sch 7A is divided into eleven groups, each of which is sub-divided into one or more items. These items are interpreted in accordance with the notes to each group.[3]

A person is liable to civil penalties if he gives an incorrect certificate which results in a supply made to him being improperly charged at the reduced rate under VATA 1994, Sch 7A.[4]

---

[1] As inserted by FA 2001 s 99(5) and Sch 31 with effect from 1 November 2001 (Groups 1–7), SI 2006/1472 with effect from 1 July 2006 (Groups 8 and 9) and SI 2007/1601 with effect from 1 July 2007 (Groups 10 and 11).
[2] VATA 1994, s 29A(3) as inserted by FA 2001, s 99(4).
[3] VATA 1994, s 96(9) as amended by FA 2001, Sch 30, para 5.

[70.02] The reduced rate

[4] VATA 1994, s 62 as amended by FA 1996, Sch 3, para 8 and FA 2001, Sch 31, para 3. For the requirement to issue a certificate, see VATA 1994, Sch 7A, Note 8(2)(*b*).

Application to supplies, acquisitions and importations

[70.03] The reduced rate is charged on:[1]

(1) Any supply for the time being falling within VATA 1994, Sch 7A.
(2) Any acquisition of goods from another EU member state if a supply of the goods would be a supply falling within VATA 1994, Sch 7A.
(3) Any importation of goods from a third country if a supply of the goods would be a supply falling within VATA 1994, Sch 7A.

[1] VATA 1994, s 29A(1), (2) as inserted by FA 2001, s 99(4).

Common provisions

Group 1—Fuel and power

[70.04] The following are charged at the reduced rate[1] when supplied[2] for domestic use[3] or use by a charity for non-business purposes:[4]

(1) Solid fuel and material for kindling fires.
(2) Coal gas, water gas, producer gases and similar gases other than road fuel gas.[5]
(3) Hydrocarbon gases other than road fuel gas.
(4) Fuel oil,[6] gas oil,[7] and kerosene.[8]
(5) Electricity,[9] heat and air conditioning.

De Voil Indirect Tax Service V4.406.

[1] VATA 1994, s 29A(1) and Sch 7A, Group 1, Item 1 and Note 1 as inserted by FA 2001, s 99 and Sch 31 and amended by SI 2008/2676 art 2.
[2] For equivalent acquisitions and importations, see supra, § **69.03**.
[3] For domestic use, see VATA 1994, Sch 7A, Group 1, Notes 3(*a*), 4–7 as inserted by FA 2001, s 99 and Sch 31.
[4] For charitable use, see VATA 1994, Sch 7A, Group 1, Notes 3(*b*), 4 as inserted by FA 2001, s 99 and Sch 31.
[5] As defined in Hydrocarbon Oil Duties Act 1979, s 5.
[6] As defined in VATA 1994, Sch 7A, Group 1, Note 2(1) as inserted by FA 2001, s 99 and Sch 31. For supplies of fuel oil which are not taxed at the reduced rate, see VATA 1994, Sch 7A, Group 1, Note 1(3) as amended by SI 2008/2676.
[7] As defined in VATA 1994, Sch 7A, Group 1, Note 2(2) as inserted by FA 2001, s 99 and Sch 31. For supplies of gas oil which are not taxed at the reduced rate, see VATA 1994, Sch 7A, Group 1, Note 1(3) as amended by SI 2008/2676.

[8] As defined in VATA 1994, Sch 7A, Group 1, Note 2(3) as inserted by FA 2001, s 99 and Sch 31. For supplies of kerosene which are not taxed at the reduced rate, see VATA 1994, Sch 7A, Group 1, Note 1(3) as amended by SI 2008/2676.
[9] See *Dyrham Park Country Club v Customs and Excise Comrs* [1978] VATTR 244; *Mander Laundries v Customs and Excise Comrs* [1978] VATTR 136; *CMC (Preston) Ltd v C & E Comrs* (1989) VAT decision 3858.

Group 2—Energy-saving materials

[70.05] The following supplies are charged at the reduced rate:[1]

(1) Installing (or both supplying and installing) energy saving materials[2] in residential accommodation.[3]
(2) Installing (or both supplying and installing) energy saving materials in a building used for a relevant charitable purpose.[4]

De Voil Indirect Tax Service V4.409.

[1] VATA 1994, s 29A(1) and Sch 7A, Group 2, Items 1, 2 as inserted by FA 2001, s 99 and Sch 31.
[2] As defined in VATA 1994, Sch 7A, Group 2, Note 1 as inserted by FA 2001, s 99 and Sch 31 and amended by SI 2004/777, SI 2005/726, SI 2005/3329.
[3] As defined in VATA 1994, Sch 7A, Group 2, Note 2 as inserted by FA 2001, s 99 and Sch 31.
[4] As defined in VATA 1994, Sch 7A, Group 2, Note 3 as inserted by FA 2001, s 99 and Sch 31.

Group 3—Heating equipment, security goods and gas supply

[70.06] The following supplies are charged at the reduced rate:[1]

(1) Installing (or both supplying and installing) heating appliances[2] in the sole or main residence of a qualifying person.[3]
(2) Connecting or reconnecting a mains gas supply to a qualifying person's sole or main residence.
(3) Installing, maintaining or repairing a central heating system[4] in a qualifying person's sole or main residence.
(4) Lease and subsequent supply of goods forming all or part of a central heating system installed in a qualifying person's sole or main residence.
(5) Installing, maintaining or repairing a renewable source heating system[5] in a qualifying person's sole or main residence.
(6) Installing (or both supplying and installing) qualifying security goods[6] in a qualifying person's sole or main residence.

The consideration for a supply in points 1–6 must be funded by a grant made under a relevant scheme[7] or (in the case of a subsequent supply in point 4) represent a payment becoming due on termination of the lease. An apportionment is necessary if the grant is made in respect of both a supply in points 1–6 and other matters.[8]

[70.06] The reduced rate

De Voil Indirect Tax Service V4.407, 408, 416.

[1] VATA 1994, s 29A(1) and Sch 7A, Group 3, Items 1–10 as inserted by FA 2001, s 99 and Sch 31 and SI 2002/1100.
[2] As defined in VATA 1994, Sch 7A, Group 3, Note 4 as inserted by FA 2001, s 99 and Sch 31 and amended by SI 2002/1100.
[3] As defined in VATA 1994, Sch 7A, Group 3, Note 6 as inserted by FA 2001, s 99 and Sch 31.
[4] As defined in VATA 1994, Sch 7A, Group 3, Note 4A as inserted by SI 2002/1100.
[5] As defined in VATA 1994, Sch 7A, Group 3, Note 4B as inserted by SI 2002/1100.
[6] As defined in VATA 1994, Sch 7A, Group 3, Note 5 as inserted by FA 2001, s 99 and Sch 31.
[7] As defined in VATA 1994, Sch 7A, Group 3, Note 2 as inserted by FA 2001, s 99 and Sch 31.
[8] VATA 1994, Sch 7A, Group 3, Notes 1, 3 as inserted by FA 2001, s 99 and Sch 31.

Group 4—Women's sanitary products

[70.07] Women's sanitary products[1] are charged at the reduced rate.[2]

De Voil Indirect Tax Service V4.417.

[1] As defined in VATA 1994, Sch 7A, Group 4, Note 1 as inserted by FA 2001, s 99 and Sch 31.
[2] VATA 1994, Sch 7A, Group 4, Item 1 as inserted by FA 2001, s 99 and Sch 31.

Group 5—Children's car seats

[70.08] The following are charged at the reduced rate:[1]

(1) A safety seat.[2]
(2) A related base unit[3] for a safety seat.
(3) A child's pushchair where the seat, when detached from the related wheeled framework,[4] is a safety seat.
(4) A booster seat.[5]
(5) A booster cushion.[6]

De Voil Indirect Tax Service V4.418.

[1] VATA 1994, s 29A(1) and Sch 7A, Group 5, Item 1 and Note 1(1) as inserted by FA 2001, s 99 and Sch 31 and amended by SI 2009/1359.
[2] As defined in VATA 1994, Sch 7A, Group 5, Note 2 as inserted by FA 2001, s 99 and Sch 31 as amended by SI 2009/1359.
[3] As defined in VATA 1994, Sch 7A, Group 5, Note 2A as inserted by FA 2001, s 99 and Sch 31 and amended by SI 2009/1359.
[4] As defined in VATA 1994, Sch 7A, Group 5, Note 3 as inserted by FA 2001, s 99 and Sch 31.
[5] As defined in VATA 1994, Sch 7A, Group 5, Note 4 as inserted by FA 2001, s 99 and Sch 31.

[6] As defined in VATA 1994, Sch 7A, Group 5, Note 5 as inserted by FA 2001, s 99 and Sch 31.

Group 6—Residential conversions

[70.09] A supply of qualifying services[1] is charged at the reduced rate[2] if it is made in the course of carrying out any of the following works:

(1) Converting a building or part of a building which is designed[3] for occupation by a single household and which is not used for a relevant residential purpose[4] (referred to as a "single occupancy dwelling") into two or more single occupancy dwellings. Thus, for example, a house may be converted into flats or a flat sub-divided into (say) two flats.

(2) Converting a building or part of a building comprising two or more single occupancy dwellings into a different number of single occupancy dwellings. Thus, for example, a block of four flats may be converted into a house, and two of the flats may be merged into one flat or sub-divided into three flats.

(3) Converting a building or part of a building which is not a single occupancy dwelling into one or more single occupancy dwellings. Thus, for example, an office may be converted into a house or into flats.

(4) Converting a building or part of a building into one or more dwellings designed for occupation by persons not forming a single household (referred to as "multiple occupancy dwellings") which are not intended to be used wholly or partly for a relevant residential purpose after the conversion. The building or part must not contain any multiple occupancy dwellings prior to the conversion. Thus, for example, a house or office may be converted into bed-sits.

(5) Converting premises[5] that are not being used for a relevant residential purpose into premises that are intended to be used solely for a relevant residential purpose after the conversion. If the intended relevant residential purpose is an institutional purpose,[6] the premises must form the entirety of an institution after the conversion. The customer must be the person intending to use the premises for a relevant residential purpose after the conversion. He must give the supplier a certificate in the prescribed form[7] before the supply is made.

(6) Garage works[8] carried out at the same time as a conversion in heads 1–5 where the resulting garage is intended to be occupied with the single household dwelling (heads 1, 2 or 3), multiple occupancy dwelling (head 4) or institution or other accommodation (head 5) resulting from the conversion.

To the extent that a building or part is a single household dwelling or multiple occupancy dwelling before or after the conversion, it must meet specified conditions.[9] In all cases, any statutory planning consent or building control approval needed for the conversion must have been granted.[10] An apportionment is made if a supply of services consists partly of qualifying services and partly of other services.[11]

A supply of building materials[12] is charged at the reduced rate if the materials are supplied by the person carrying out qualifying services and incorporated in

[70.09] The reduced rate

the building or its immediate site by him in the course of carrying out the conversion or garage works concerned.[13]

De Voil Indirect Tax Service V4.411.

[1] As defined in VATA 1994, Sch 7A, Group 6, Note 11 as inserted by FA 2001, s 99 and Sch 31.
[2] VATA 1994, s 29A(1) and Sch 7A, Group 6, Item 1 and Notes 2–9 as inserted by FA 2001, s 99 and Sch 31 and amended by SI 2002/1100.
[3] As defined in VATA 1994, Sch 7A, Group 6, Note 4(4) as inserted by FA 2001, s 99 and Sch 31.
[4] As defined in VATA 1994, Sch 7A, Group 6, Note 6 as inserted by FA 2001, s 99 and Sch 31.
[5] The premises may consist of a building, a part of a building, or either in combination with all or part of one or more other buildings.
[6] As defined in VATA 1994, Sch 7A, Group 6, Note 7(7) as inserted by FA 2001, s 99 and Sch 31.
[7] For the form and content of certificates, see VATA 1994, Sch 7A, Group 6, Note 8(3) as inserted by FA 2001, s 99 and Sch 31.
[8] As defined in VATA 1994, Sch 7A, Group 6, Note 9(2) as inserted by FA 2001, s 99 and Sch 31.
[9] The conditions are specified in VATA 1994, Sch 7A, Group 6, Note 4(3) as inserted by FA 2001, s 99 and Sch 31.
[10] VATA 1994, Sch 7A, Group 6, Note 10 as inserted by FA 2001, s 99 and Sch 31.
[11] VATA 1994, Sch 7A, Group 6, Note 1 as inserted by FA 2001, s 99 and Sch 31.
[12] As defined in VATA 1994, Sch 7A, Group 6, Note 12 as inserted by FA 2001, s 99 and Sch 31.
[13] VATA 1994, Sch 7A, Group 6, Item 2 as inserted by FA 2001, s 99 and Sch 31.

Group 7—Residential renovations and alterations

[70.10] Qualifying services[1] are charged at the reduced rate if they are supplied in the course of carrying out the following works:[2]

(1) The renovation or alteration[3] of a single household dwelling.[4] One of the following conditions must be met:
    (a) the dwelling was not lived in during the two-year period immediately preceding commencement of the relevant works;[5] or
    (b) the relevant works were carried out within one year of a major interest[6] in the dwelling being granted or assigned (either alone or jointly with another person) to a person ("the customer") living there. The dwelling must have been empty, and not have been renovated or altered, during the two-year period immediately preceding the grant or assignment. If the customer started to live there after the time when interest was granted or assigned, the dwelling must have remained empty until he did so.

(2) The renovation or alteration of a multiple occupancy dwelling.[7] It is a condition that the dwelling was not lived in during the three-year period immediately preceding commencement of the works.

(3) The renovation or alteration of a building (or part of a building) which, when last lived in, was used for a relevant residential purpose and which, following the renovation or alteration, is intended to be used for a relevant residential purpose. The customer must give the supplier a certificate to that effect before the supply takes place. It is a condition that the dwelling was not lived in during the two-year period immediately preceding commencement of the works.

(4) The renovation or alteration of a building (or part of a building) which, when last lived in, was one of a number of buildings on the same site used together as a unit for a relevant residential purpose and which, following the renovation or alteration, is intended to be used for a relevant residential purpose. The customer must give the supplier a certificate to that effect before the supply takes place. It is a condition that neither the building (or part) nor any of the other buildings forming part of that unit were lived in during the two year period immediately preceding commencement of the works.

(5) Constructing a garage at the same time as a renovation or alteration to premises within heads 1–4 takes place. There must be an intention for the garage to be occupied with the premises.

(6) Converting a building (or part of a building) to a garage at the same time as a renovation or alteration to premises within heads 1–4 takes place. There must be an intention for the garage to be occupied with the premises.

(7) Renovating or altering a garage at the same time as a renovation or alteration to premises within heads 1–4 takes place. There must be an intention for the garage to be occupied with the premises.

Any statutory planning consent or building control approval needed for the conversion must have been granted.[8] An apportionment is made if a supply of services consists partly of qualifying services and partly of other services.[9]

A supply of building materials[10] is charged at the reduced rate if the materials are supplied by the person carrying out qualifying services and incorporated in the dwelling or its immediate site by him in the course of carrying out the renovation or alteration concerned.[11]

De Voil Indirect Tax Service V4.413.

---

[1] As defined in VATA 1994, Sch 7A, Group 7, Note 5 as inserted by FA 2001, s 99 and Sch 31 and amended by SI 2002/1100.

[2] VATA 1994, s 29A(1) and Sch 7A, Group 7, Item 1 and Notes 2(1)–(3), 3(1)–(3), 3A, 4A as inserted, amended or substituted by FA 2001, s 99 and Sch 31, SI 2002/1100, SI 2007/3448.

[3] As defined in VATA 1994, Sch 7A, Group 7, Note 2(1) as substituted by SI 2002/1100.

[4] As defined in VATA 1994, Sch 7A, Group 6, Note 4(1) by virtue of Group 7, Note 2(4) as substituted by SI 2002/1100.

[5] As defined in VATA 1994, Sch 7A, Group 7, Note 3(4) as inserted by FA 2001, s 99 and Sch 31.

[6] As defined in VATA 1994, s 96(1).

[7] As defined in VATA 1994, Sch 7A, Group 6, Note 4(2) by virtue of Group 7, Note 2(4) as substituted by SI 2002/1100.

[70.10] The reduced rate

8 VATA 1994, Sch 7A, Group 7, Note 4 as inserted by FA 2001, s 99 and Sch 31.
9 VATA 1994, Sch 7A, Group 7, Note 1 as inserted by FA 2001, s 99 and Sch 31.
10 As defined in VATA 1994, Sch 7A, Group 7, Note 6 as inserted by FA 2001, s 99 and Sch 31.
11 VATA 1994, Sch 7A, Group 7, Item 2 as inserted by FA 2001, s 99 and Sch 31.

Group 8—Contraceptive products

[70.11] Contraceptive products[1] are charged at the reduced rate[2] unless provided in connection with care, medical treatment or surgical treatment in a hospital or state regulated institution.[3]

De Voil Indirect Tax Service V4.420.

1 As defined in VATA 1994, Sch 7A, Group 8, Note 1 as inserted by SI 2006/1472.
2 VATA 1994, Sch 7A, Group 8, Item 1 as inserted by SI 2006/1472.
3 VATA 1994, Sch 7A, Group 8, Note 2 as inserted by SI 2006/1472. Contraceptive products provided in this manner are exempted from tax by VATA 1994, Sch 9, Group 7, Item 4, as to which see supra, § **68.23**.

Group 9—Welfare advice or information

[70.12] Subject to specified exceptions,[1] welfare advice or information[2] supplied by a charity or state-regulated[3] private welfare institution is charged at the reduced rate.[4]

De Voil Indirect Tax Service V4.419.

1 Listed in VATA 1994, Sch 7A, Group 9, Note 3 as inserted by SI 2006/1472.
2 As defined in VATA 1994, Sch 7A, Group 9, Notes 1 as inserted by SI 2006/1472.
3 As defined in VATA 1994, Sch 9, Group 7, Note 8 (see VATA 1994, Sch 7A, Group 8, Note 2 as inserted by SI 2006/1472).
4 VATA 1994, Sch 7A, Group 8, Item 1 as inserted by SI 2006/1472.

Group 10—Mobility aids for the elderly

[70.13] A supply is charged at the reduced rate if it comprises installing, or both supplying and installing, mobility aids[1] in domestic accommmodation[2] for use by a person who, at the time of supply, has attained the age of 60.[3]

De Voil Indirect Tax Service V4.422.

1 As defined in VATA 1994, Sch 7A, Group 10, Note 1 as inserted by SI 2007/1601.
2 As defined in VATA 1994, Sch 7A, Group 10, Note 2 as inserted by SI 2007/1601.
3 VATA 1994, Sch 7A, Group 10, Items 1, 2 as inserted by SI 2007/1601.

Group 11—Smoking cessation products

[70.14] Supplies of pharmaceutical products designed to help stop people smoking tobacco are charged at the reduced rate.[1]

De Voil Indirect Tax Service V4.421.

---

[1] VATA 1994, Sch 7A, Group 11, Item 1 as inserted by SI 2007/1601. This provision continues to have effect in relation to supplies made after 30 June 2008: see VAT (Reduced Rate) (Smoking Cessation Products) Order, SI 2008/1410, art 3.

Table of Cases

Decisions of the European Commission of Human Rights and European Court of Human Rights are included in the main table of cases, and also listed separately after the main table, following which there appears a numerical table of decisions of the European Court of Justice.

A

A (Application to vary the undertakings of), Re [2005] STC (SCD) 103 .... 44:28
A v R & C Comrs (2007) SpC 650 .... 2A:68
A and B Motors (Newton-le-Willows) Ltd v Customs and Excise Comrs [1981] VATTR 29 .... 65:32
A Firm v Honour [1997] STC (SCD) 293 .... 8:70
AA Insurance Services Ltd v Customs and Excise Comrs [1999] V & DR 361 .... 68:11
AB (a firm) v Revenue and Customs Comrs [2007] STC (SCD) 99 .... 8:100
AB Bank v Inspector of Taxes [2000] STC (SCD) 229 .... 8:105
ABB Power Ltd v Customs and Excise Comrs [1992] VATTR 491 .... 65:18
ACT Construction Ltd v Customs and Excise Comrs [1982] 1 All ER 84, [1981] 1 WLR 1542, [1982] STC 25, [1981] TR 489, HL 69:23
ADP Installations (Group) Ltd v Customs and Excise Comrs [1987] VATTR 36 ...... 63:25
AEG (UK) Ltd v Customs and Excise Comrs [1993] VATTR 379 .... 63:19
AP, MP and TP v Switzerland (1997) 26 EHRR 541, [1998] EHRLR 88, EC of HR 1:22, 2:118
ARO Lease BV v Inspecteur der Belastingdienst Grote Ondernemingen, Amsterdam: C-190/95 [1997] STC 1272, ECJ 63:01, 63:29
A-Z Electrical v Customs and Excise Comrs [1993] VATTR 389 .... 65:20
AZO-Maschinenfabrik Adolf Zimmerman GmbH v Customs and Excise Comrs [1987] VATTR 25 .... 63:25
Abacus Trust Co (Isle of Man) Ltd v National Society for the Prevention of Cruelty to Children [2001] STC 1344, [2001] 35 LS Gaz R 37, (2001) Times, 25 September, [2001] All ER (D) 207 (Jul) 2A:71
Abbey National plc v Customs and Excise Comrs: C-408/98 [2001] All ER (EC) 385, [2001] 1 WLR 769, [2001] STC 297, ECJ 66:08
Abbey National plc v Customs and Excise Comrs: C-169/04 [2006] ECR I-4027, [2006] STC 1136, (2006) Times, 6 June, [2006] All ER (D) 44 (May), ECJ 68:16
Abbey National plc v Revenue and Customs Comrs [2006] EWCA Civ 886, [2006] NLJR 1100, 150 Sol Jo LB 892, [2006] STC 1961, [2006] All ER (D) 336 (Jun) 68:11
Abbott v Albion Greyhound (Salford) Ltd [1945] 1 All ER 308, 26 TC 390, 173 LT 82, 24 ATC 25 .... 8:73
Abbott v IRC [1996] STC (SCD) 41n 8:95
Abbott v Philbin [1961] AC 352, [1960] 2 All ER 763, 39 TC 82, [1960] TR 171, HL 7:42, 7:44, 7:58, 7:66, 37:32
Abbott Laboratories Ltd v Carmody [1968] 2 All ER 879, 44 TC 569, [1968] TR 75, 47 ATC 88 .... 9:13
Aberdeen Construction Group Ltd v IRC [1977] STC 302, 52 TC 281, [1977] TR 87; on appeal [1978] 1 All ER 962, [1978] STC 127, 52 TC 281, [1978] TR 25, HL . 3:23, 16:02, 16:19, 17:10
Able (UK) Ltd v Revenue and Customs Comrs [2006] EWHC 3046 (Ch), [2006] SWTI 2345, [2007] RVR 101, [2006] All ER (D) 241 (Oct) 8:81
Absalom v Talbot [1944] AC 204, [1944] 1 All ER 642, 26 TC 166, 23 ATC 137, HL 8:148
Acadia Forest, The. See Wirth Ltd v SS Acadia Forest and Lash Barge CG 204, The Acadia Forest

2511

Table of Cases

Accountant v Inspector of Taxes [2000] STC (SCD) 522; affd sub nom R (on the application of Murat) v IRC [2005] STC 184 .... 2A:68
Acre Friendly Society v Customs and Excise Comrs (1992) VAT decision 7649 .... 66:07
Adams, Re, Bank of Ireland Trustee Co Ltd v Adams Hutchings and Parker [1967] IR 424 .... 33:19
Adamson (Joseph) & Co v Collins [1938] 1 KB 477, [1937] 4 All ER 236, 21 TC 400, 16 ATC 355 8:101
Addiscombe Garden Estates Ltd v Crabbe [1958] 1 QB 513, [1957] 3 All ER 563, [1957] 3 WLR 980, CA 57:25
Adstock Ltd v Customs and Excise Comrs (1993) VAT decision 10034 .... 63:16
Advanced Business Technology Ltd v Customs and Excise Comrs (1983) VAT decision 1488 .... 66:03
Advocate, Lord v Countess of Moray [1905] AC 531, 74 LJPC 122, 93 LT 569, 21 TLR 715, HL 1:28, 46:12
Advocate, Lord v Edinburgh Corpn (1905) 7 F (Ct of Sess) 1972, 42 Sc LR 691, 13 SLT 241 .... 11:40
Advocate, Lord v Gordon (1901) 8 SLT 439 .... 56:31
Advocate, Lord v Hay (1924) 21 ATC 146 .... 32:27
Advocate, Lord v Largs Golf Club [1985] STC 226 .... 63:16, 63:21
Advocate, Lord v McKenna [1989] STC 485, 61 TC 688, 1989 SLT 460 .... 23:29
Aer Lingus plc v Customs and Excise Comrs [1992] VATTR 438 .... 65:25
Agassi v Robinson (Inspector of Taxes) [2004] EWHC 487 (Ch), [2004] STC 610, (2004) Times, 1 April, [2004] All ER (D) 319 (Mar); revsd [2004] EWCA Civ 1518, [2005] 1 WLR 1090, [2005] STC 303, [2004] NLJR 1789, (2004) Times, 27 November, [2004] All ER (D) 322 (Nov); revsd [2006] UKHL 23, [2006] 3 All ER 97, [2006] 1 WLR 1380, [2006] NLJR 880, 150 Sol Jo LB 671, [2006] All ER (D) 240 (May) 2:22, 36:11
Agassi v Robinson (Inspector of Taxes) (Bar Council intervening) [2005] EWCA Civ 1507, [2006] 1 All ER 900, [2006] STC 580, [2005] NLJR 1885, (2005) Times, 22 December, 150 Sol Jo LB 28, [2005] SWTI 1994, [2005] All ER (D) 40 (Dec) 2:22
Aiken Industries v Comr 56 TC (US) 925 (1971) 37:36
Aikin v Macdonald's Trustees (1894) 32 Sc LR 85, 3 TC 306 .... 13:13
Aikman v White [1986] STC 1 .... 67:03
Ainslie v Buckley [2002] STC (SCD) 132 .... 7:01, 10:03
Ainsworth, Re, Finch v Smith [1915] 2 Ch 96, 84 LJ Ch 701, 113 LT 368, 31 TLR 392 .... 11:41
Airfix Footwear Ltd v Cope [1978] ICR 1210, [1978] IRLR 396 .... 49:03
Albert Collée v Finanzamt Limburg an der Lahn: C-146/05 [2007] ECR I-7861, [2008] STC 757, ECJ 69:07
Alexander v IRC [1991] STC 112, 23 HLR 236, [1991] 2 EGLR 179, CA 45:02
Al Fayed v Advocate General for Scotland (representing the IRC) [2002] STC 910, 2003 SC 1, 2003 SLT 745; affd [2004] STC 1703, Inner House 1:21, 2:03, 2:07
Alherma Investments Ltd v Tomlinson [1970] 2 All ER 436, 48 TC 81, [1970] TR 15, 19 ATC 15 .... 25:15
Alianza Co Ltd v Bell [1906] AC 18, 75 LJKB 44, 5 TC 172, HL 8:127
Aktiebolaget NN v Skatteverket: C-111/05 [2007] 2 CMLR 1021, [2008] STC 3203, [2007] All ER (D) 478 (Mar), ECJ 63:08, 63:20, 63:28
Allan v IRC [1994] STC 943, 66 TC 681 .... 7:17, 7:30, 7:33
Allen v Farquharson Bros & Co (1932) 17 TC 59, 11 ATC 259 .... 8:131
Allen v Revenue and Customs Comrs [2005] STC (SCD) 614 .... 33:21
Allen (Norman) Group Travel Ltd v Customs and Excise Comrs [1996] V & DR 405 .... 65:25
Allen-Meyrick's Will Trusts, Re, Mangnall v Allen-Meyrick [1966] 1 All ER 740, [1966] 1 WLR 499 .... 42:07
Allhusen v Whittell (1867) LR 4 Eq 295, 36 LJ Ch 929, 16 LT 695 .... 42:11
Alliance and Leicester plc v Hamer [2000] STC (SCD) 332 .... 8:114
Allied Dancing Association v Customs and Excise Comrs [1993] VATTR 405 .... 68:25
Allied Lyons plc v Customs and Excise Comrs [1994] VATTR 361 .... 65:29
Allison v Murray [1975] 3 All ER 561, [1975] 1 WLR 1578, [1975] STC 524, 51 TC 57 .... 16:21, 20:20

Table of Cases

Alloway v Phillips [1980] 3 All ER 138, [1980] STC 490, 53 TC 372, [1980] TR 111, CA 12:08, 12:12
Allum v Marsh (Inspector of Taxes) [2004] STC 147 ..... 29:14
Alm v Customs and Excise Comrs (1998) VAT decision 15863 ..... 65:18
Alongi v IRC [1991] STC 517 ..... 8:05
Ambulanter Pflegedienst Kügler GmbH v Finanzamt für Körperschaften I in Berlin: C-141/00 [2002] ECR I-6833, [2004] 3 CMLR 1175, ECJ 68:23
American Leaf Blending Co Sdn Bhd v Director General of Inland Revenue [1979] AC 676, [1978] 3 All ER 1185, [1978] STC 561, [1978] TR 243 ... 22:10, 25:43, 44:02, 44:08
American Thread Co v Joyce (1911) 6 TC 1 ..... 33:29, 35:04
Amis v Colls (1960) 39 TC 148, [1960] TR 213, 53 R & IT 539, 39 ATC 249 ..... 2:27
Ammonia Soda Co v Chamberlain [1918] 1 Ch 266, [1916–17] All ER Rep 708, 87 LJ Ch 193, 118 LT 48, CA 8:110, 22:04
Ampliscientifica Srl and another v Ministero dell'Economia e delle Finanze, Agenzia delle Entrate: C-162/07, [2008], ECR 1–4109, [2008] SWTI 1387, ECJ 63:09
Amurta v Inspecteur van de Belastingdienst: C-379/05 [2008] STC 2851 .. 1: 14, 1:17, 1:18
An application by R & C Comrs to serve a TMA 1970 s 20(3) notice on plc and a s 20(1) notice on its subsidiary company, Re (2007) SpC 647 ..... 2:111
Anand v IRC [1997] STC (SCD) 58 ..... 40:04
Anders Utkilens Rederi A/S v O/Y Lovisa Stevedoring Co A/B and Keller Bryant Transport Co Ltd [1985] 2 All ER 669, [1985] STC 301 ..... 18:14
Anderson v IRC [1939] 1 KB 341, [1938] 4 All ER 491, 108 LJKB 41, 106 LT 127 ..... 56:12
Anderton v Lamb [1981] STC 43, 55 TC 1, [1981] TR 393 ..... 22:12, 44:13
Andrew v Taylor (1965) 42 TC 569, [1965] TR 355, CA 8:19
Andrews v Astley (1924) 8 TC 589, 3 ATC 366 ..... 7:125
Andrews v King [1991] ICR 846, [1991] STC 481 ..... 7:08
Ang v Parrish [1980] 2 All ER 790, [1980] 1 WLR 940, [1980] STC 341, 53 TC 304 ..... 15:01
Anglo Associates (Tyres and Exhausts) Ltd v Customs and Excise Comrs LON/84/154 unreported 67:09
Anglo-French Exploration Co Ltd v Clayson [1956] 1 All ER 762, [1955] 1 WLR 325, 36 TC 545, [1956] TR 37, CA 8:87
Anglo Persian Oil Co Ltd v Dale [1932] 1 KB 124, [1931] All ER Rep 725, 16 TC 253, 10 ATC 149, CA 8:95, 8:110, 8:118, 8:120
Ansell v IRC [1929] 1 KB 608, 98 LJKB 384, 143 LT 437 ..... 56:15
Ansell Computer Services Ltd v Richardson [2004] STC (SCD) 472 ..... 7:11, 8:26
Antelope v Ellis [1995] STC (SCD) 297 ..... 7:17
Apple and Pear Development Council v Customs and Excise Comrs. See Customs and Excise Comrs v Apple and Pear Development Council
Apthorpe v Peter Schoenhofen Brewing Co Ltd (1899) 80 LT 395, 15 TLR 245, 4 TC 41, CA 35:03
Archer-Shee v Baker. See Baker v Archer-Shee
Argos Distributors Ltd v Customs and Excise Comrs: C-288/94, [1996] ECR I-5311, ECJ 63:20
Argosam Finance Co Ltd v Oxby [1965] Ch 390, [1964] 3 All ER 561, 42 TC 86, [1964] TR 255, CA 2:11
Arkwright (Williams' Personal Representatives) v IRC [2004] STC (SCD) 89; revsd [2004] EWHC 1720 (Ch), [2005] 1 WLR 1411, [2004] STC 1323 ..... 12:17, 45:10
Armitage v Moore [1900] 2 QB 363, 69 LJQB 614, 4 TC 199 ..... 8:31
Arnander (executors of McKenna, decd) v Revenue and Customs Comrs [2006] STC (SCD) 800 ..... 44:14
Arnold (Inspector of Taxes) v G-Con Ltd [2006] EWCA Civ 829, [2006] STC 1516, (2006) Times, 9 June, [2006] SWTI 1517, [2006] All ER (D) 189 (May) 2A:19
Arranmore Investment Co Ltd v IRC [1973] STC 195, 48 TC 623, 52 ATC 192, [1973] TR 151, NI CA 2A:69
Arts Council of Great Britain v Customs and Excise Comrs [1994] VATTR 313 ..... 63:02, 63:17
Aschrott, Re, Clifton v Strauss [1927] 1 Ch 313, 96 LJ Ch 205 ..... 45:02
Ashby v Comr of Succession Duties (1942) 67 CLR 284, ALR 44, 16 ALJ 259 ..... 57:06

Table of Cases

Asher v London Film Productions Ltd [1944] KB 133, [1944] 1 All ER 77, 113 LJKB 149, 22 ATC 432, CA 7:30, 8:07, 11:28
Ashley v R & C Comrs (2007) SpC 633 .... 31:15
Ashton Gas Co v A-G [1906] AC 10, 75 LJ Ch 1, 93 LT 676, 70 JP 49, HL 8:108
Ashtree Holdings Ltd v Customs and Excise Comrs [1979] STC 818, [1980] TR 253 .... 66:05
Ashworth v Customs and Excise Comrs [1994] VATTR 275 .... 68:12
Aslan Imaging Ltd v Customs and Excise Comrs [1989] VATTR 54 .... 68:23
Aspden v Hildesley [1982] 2 All ER 53, [1982] 1 WLR 264, [1982] STC 206, 55 TC 609 .... 16:41, 16:44, 18:10
Aspinall (executors of Postlethwaite, decd) v Revenue and Customs Comrs [2007] STC (SCD) 83, [2007] SWTI 346, SCD 39:14, 39:23
Asscher v Staatssecretaris van Financiën: C-107/94 [1996] All ER (EC) 757, [1996] ECR I-3089, [1996] 3 CMLR 61, [1996] STC 1025, ECJ 1:09
Associated London Properties Ltd v Henriksen (1944) 26 TC 46 .... 8:06
Associated Portland Cement Manufacturers Ltd v Kerr [1946] 1 All ER 68, 27 TC 103, 24 ATC 272, CA 7:29, 8:68, 8:129
Association of British Travel Agents v IRC [2003] STC (SCD) 194 .... 35:66
Astall v HMRC [2008] SpC 628, [2008] STC (SCD) 142 .... 3:03, 3:24
Astley v IRC [1975] 3 All ER 696, [1975] STC 557, [1975] TR 137, CA 41:27
Aston v Customs and Excise Comrs [1991] VATTR 170 .... 67:06
Aston Cantlow and Wilmcote with Billesley Parochial Church Council v Wallbank (2000) 81 P CR 165, [2000] 2 EGLR 149; on appeal [2001] EWCA Civ 713, [2002] Ch 51, [2001] 3 All ER 393, [2002] STC 313; revsd [2003] UKHL 37, [2004] 1 AC 546, [2003] 3 All ER 1213 .... 1:01, 1:21, 1:23
Astor v Customs and Excise Comrs [1981] VATTR 174 .... 63:25
Astor v Perry [1935] AC 398, [1935] All ER Rep 713, 19 TC 255, 14 ATC 22, HL 15:09
Astrawall Ltd v Waters [1995] STC 1n, 67 TC 145 .... 8:110
Atherton v British Insulated and Helsby Cables Ltd. See British Insulated and Helsby Cables Ltd v Atherton
Athill, Re, Athill v Athill (1880) 16 Ch D 211, 50 LJ Ch 123, 43 LT 581, CA 4:10
Atkinson (HM Inspector of Taxes) v Dancer (1988) 22:33
Attenborough (George) & Son v Solomon [1913] AC 76, 82 LJ Ch 178, 107 LT 833, HL 14:03
A-G v Alexander (1874) LR 10 Exch 20, 44 LJ Ex 3, 31 LT 694 .... 33:28
A-G v Boden [1912] 1 KB 539, 81 LJKB 704, 105 LT 247 .... 22:44, 39:14, 42:02
A-G v Brown (1849) 3 Exch 662, 18 LJ Ex 336, 13 LTOS 121 .... 57:07
A-G v Cohen [1937] 1 KB 478, [1937] 1 All ER 27, 106 LJKB 262, 156 LT 130, CA 57:16
A-G v Coote (1817) 4 Price 183, 2 TC 385 .... 33:02
A-G v Eyres [1909] 1 KB 723, 78 LJKB 384, 100 LT 396, 25 TLR 298 .... 7:08
A-G v Jameson [1905] 2 IR 218, 38 ILTR 117 .... 7:57, 45:02, 45:06
A-G v Johnstone (1926) 10 TC 758, 136 LT 31, 5 ATC 730 .... 2:28
A-G v Lamplough (1878) 3 Ex D 214, 47 LJQB 555, 38 LT 87, 42 JP 356, CA 56:02, 57:15
A-G v Midland Bank Executor and Trustee Co Ltd (1934) 19 TC 136, 13 ATC 602 .... 2:28
A-G v Murray [1904] 1 KB 165, 73 LJKB 66, 89 LT 710, CA 17:01
A-G v National Provincial Bank Ltd (1928) 14 TC 111, 44 TLR 701, 7 ATC 294 .... 2:11
A-G v Potter. See Potter v IRC
A-G v Prince Ernest Augustus of Hanover [1957] AC 436, [1957] 1 All ER 49, [1957] 2 WLR 1, HL 1:27
A-G v Quixley (1929) 98 LJKB 652, [1929] All ER Rep 696, 141 LT 288, CA 38:20
A-G v Seccombe [1911] 2 KB 688, 80 LJKB 913, 105 LT 18 .... 41:06
A-G v Wiltshire United Dairies (1921) 37 TLR 884 .... 1:01
A-G v Worrall [1895] 1 QB 99, 64 LJQB 141, 59 JP 467, 71 LT 807, CA 41:06
A-G for Canada v William Schulze & Co (1901) 9 SLT 4 .... 34:02
A-G for Northern Ireland v Heron [1959] TR 1, 38 ATC 3, NI CA 43:03
A-G of Ceylon v Mackie [1952] 2 All ER 775, 31 ATC 435, [1952] TR 431 .... 45:02

Attwood v Anduff Car Wash Ltd [1996] STC 110, 69 TC 575; affd [1997] STC 1167, 69
   TC 575, CA 9:26, 9:29, 9:30
Auckland Gas Co Ltd v IRC [2000] 1 WLR 1783, [2000] STC 527, 73 TC 266 ..... 8:110
Australia (Commonwealth) Taxation Comr v Squatting Investment Co Ltd [1954] AC
   182, [1954] 1 All ER 349, [1954] 2 WLR 186, [1954] TR 37 .... 8:75
Austrian National Tourist Office v Customs and Excise Comrs (1998) VAT decision
   15561 .... 63:30; 65:38
Auto Lease Holland BV v Bundesamt für Finanzen: C-185/01 [2003] ECR I-1317,
   [2005] STC 598, ECJ 63:25
Autologic Holdings plc v IRC [2005] UKHL 54, [2006] 1 AC 118, [2005] 4 All ER
   1141, [2005] 3 WLR 339, [2005] STC 1357, 77 TC 504, [2005] NLJR 1277, (2005)
   Times, 1 August, [2005] SWTI 1336, [2005] All ER (D) 424 (Jul) 2A:70
Automatic Self Cleansing Filter Syndicate Co Ltd v Cunninghame [1906] 2 Ch 34, 75 LJ
   Ch 437, 94 LT 651, CA 33:29
Aviation and Shipping Co Ltd v Murray [1961] 2 All ER 805, [1961] 1 WLR 974, 39
   TC 595, [1961] TR 133, CA 8:52
Axel Kittel v Belgian State: C-439/04 [2006] ECR I-6161, [2008] STC 1537, ECJ ... 66:34
Ayerst v C and K (Construction) Ltd [1975] 1 All ER 162, [1975] 1 WLR 191, [1975]
   STC 1, CA; affd [1976] AC 167, [1975] 2 All ER 537, [1975] STC 345, 50 TC
   651, HL 21:18, 28:21, 60:03
Ayrshire Employers Mutual Insurance Association Ltd v IRC [1946] 1 All ER 637, 175
   LT 22, 27 TC 331, 25 ATC 103, HL 8:40
Ayrshire Pullman Motor Services and Ritchie v IRC (1929) 14 TC 754, 8 ATC 531
   .... 4:01

B

BFP Holdings Ltd v IRC (1942) 24 TC 483 .... 25:35
BLP Group Ltd v Customs and Excise Comrs [1992] VATTR 448; on appeal [1994] STC
   41; revsd [1994] STC 41, CA; refd C-4/94: [1995] All ER (EC) 401, [1995] ECR I-
   983, [1995] STC 424, ECJ 66:07, ... 66:08
BMBF (No 24) Ltd v IRC [2002] EWHC 2466 (Ch), [2002] STC 1450; affd [2003]
   EWCA Civ 1560, [2004] STC 97, 147 Sol Jo LB 1309 .... 9:46, 9:52, 56:29
BMW (GB) Ltd v Customs and Excise Comrs [1997] STC 824 .... 66:20
BP (Australia) Ltd v Taxation Comr [1966] AC 224, [1965] 3 All ER 209, [1965] TR
   317, 44 ATC 312 .... 8:130
BSC Footwear Ltd v Ridgway [1971] Ch 427, [1970] 1 All ER 932, 47 TC 495; on
   appeal [1972] AC 544, [1971] 2 All ER 534, 47 TC 495, [1971] TR 121, HL . 8:68, 8:163,
   8:164
BSM (1257) Ltd v Secretary of State for Social Services [1978] ICR 894 .... 7:11, 49:03
BUPA Hospitals Ltd v Customs and Excise Comrs (2002) VAT Decision 17588 ...... 1:13
BUPA Hospitals Ltd v Customs and Excise Comrs: C-419/02 [2006] ECR I-1685, [2006]
   Ch 446, [2006] 2 WLR 964, [2006] STC 967, [2006] All ER (D) 278 (Feb), ECJ 1:13,
   63:15, 65:12
BUPA Hospitals Ltd and Goldsborough Developments Ltd v Customs and Excise Comrs
   [2006] STC 967 .... 65:13, 66:08
BUPA Purchasing Ltd v Customs and Excise Comrs [2003] EWHC 1957 (Ch), [2003]
   STC 1203 .... 64:27
Baars v Inspecteur der Belastingen Particulieren/Ondernemingen Gorinchem: C-251/98
   [2000] ECR I-2787, ECJ 1:07
Bachmann v Belgium: C-204/90 [1992] ECR I-249, [1993] 1 CMLR 785, [1994] STC
   855, ECJ 1:11, 1:12
Bacon v Simpson (1837) 3 M & W 78, Murp & H 309, 7 LJ Ex 34 .... 56:14
Baines & Ernst Ltd v Customs and Excise Comrs [2005] EWHC 2300 (Ch), [2006] STC
   653, [2005] SWTI 1775, [2005] All ER (D) 289 (Oct); revsd sub nom Baines &
   Ernst Ltd v Revenue and Customs Comrs [2006] EWCA Civ 1040, [2006] STC 1632,
   [2006] All ER (D) 351 (Jul) 67:16
Baird v Williams [1999] STC 635, 71 TC 390 .... 7:137, 7:139
Baird's Executors v IRC [1991] 1 EGLR 201, [1991] 09 EG 129, 10 EG 153, 1991 SLT
   (Lands Tr) 9 .... 39:20, 44:25

2515

Table of Cases

Bakcsi v Finanzamt Furstenfeldbruck: C-415/98 [2002] QB 685, [2001] ECR I-1831, [2002] 2 CMLR 1397, [2002] STC 802, ECJ 66:05
Baker v Archer-Shee [1927] AC 844, 96 LJKB 803, 137 LT 762, 43 TLR 758, 71 Sol Jo 727; sub nom Archer-Shee v Baker 11 TC 749, HL 13:15, 13:17, 35:10, 62:29
Baker v Cook [1937] 3 All ER 509, 21 TC 337, 16 ATC 248 .... 8:34
Baker v Dale (1858) 1 F & F 271 .... 56:29
Baldwins Industrial Services plc and Barr Ltd, Re [2002] EWHC 2915 (TCC), [2003] CILL 1949 .... 9:46
Balen v IRC [1978] 2 All ER 1033, [1978] STC 420, 52 TC 406, [1978] TR 181, CA 4:18
Ball v Johnson (1971) 47 TC 155, [1971] TR 147, 50 ATC 178 .... 7:25
Ball v Phillips [1990] STC 675 .... 7:65
Ball's Settlement, Re [1968] 2 All ER 438, [1968] 1 WLR 899 .... 39:15
Ballacmaish Farms Ltd v HM Treasury (1987) VAT decision 2364 .... 66:05
Balocchi v Ministero delle Finanze dello Stato: C-10/92 [1993] ECR I-5105, [1997] STC 640, ECJ 67:04
Bambridge v IRC [1955] 3 All ER 812, [1955] 1 WLR 1329, 36 TC 313, [1955] TR 295, HL 35:31
Bambro (No 2) Pty Ltd v Comr of Stamp Duties (1964) 8 WN (NSW) 1142 .... 56:14
Bamford v ATA Advertising Ltd [1972] 3 All ER 535, 48 TC 359, [1972] TR 69, 51 ATC 81 .... 8:113, 8:131
Banbury Visionplus Ltd v Revenue and Customs Comrs [2006] EWHC 1024 (Ch), (2006) Times, 12 June, [2006] SWTI 1511, [2006] All ER (D) 105 (May) 66:09
Banca popolare di Cremona Soc Coop arl v Agenzia Entrate Ufficio Cremona: C-475/03 [2007] 1 CMLR 863, [2006] All ER (D) 19 (Oct), ECJ 1:06
Bancroft v Crutchfield [2002] STC (SCD) 347 .... 2A:44
Bank Line Ltd v IRC [1974] STC 342, 49 TC 307, [1974] TR 115, 53 ATC 114 ..... 6:23, 25:23
Bank of Ireland Britain Holdings Ltd v Revenue and Customs Comrs SpC 544 [2006] STC (SCD) 477, [2008] EWCA Civ 58 .... 4:12
Bank voor Handel en Scheepvaart NV v Administrator of Hungarian Property [1954] AC 584, [1954] 1 All ER 969, [1954] 2 WLR 867, 35 TC 311, [1954] TR 115, HL 49:03
Banning v Wright [1972] 2 All ER 987, [1972] 1 WLR 972, 48 TC 421, [1972] TR 105, HL 10:22
Banque Bruxelles Lambert SA v Belgium: C-8/03 [2004] STC 1643, ECJ 63:16
Barber v Guardian Royal Exchange Assurance Group: C-262/88 [1991] 1 QB 344, [1990] 2 All ER 660, [1991] 2 WLR 72, [1990] ICR 616, ECJ 32:29
Barbier (Heirs of) v Inspecteur van de Belastingdienst Particulieren/Ondernemingen buitenland te Heerlen: C-364/01 [2004] 1 CMLR 1283, ECJ 1:10, 1:11
Barclays Bank Ltd v Naylor [1961] Ch 7, [1960] 3 All ER 173, 39 TC 256, [1960] TR 203 .... 7:23
Barclays Bank Trust Co Ltd v IRC [1998] STC (SCD) 125 .... 44:04
Barclays Mercantile Business Finance Ltd v Mawson [2002] EWHC 1527 (Ch), [2002] STC 1068, 76 TC 446; on appeal [2002] EWCA Civ 1853, [2003] STC 66, 76 TC 446; affd [2004] UKHL 51, [2005] 1 AC 684, [2005] 1 All ER 97, [2004] 3 WLR 1383, [2005] STC 1, 76 TC 446 .. 1:13, 1:24, 3:01, 3:02, 3:12, 3:16, 3:17, 3:18, 3:20, 3:21, 3:23, 9:23, 9:46
Barclays Mercantile Industrial Finance Ltd v Melluish [1990] STC 314 .... 9:14, 9:24
Barker (Christopher) & Sons v IRC [1919] 2 KB 222, 88 LJKB 947, 121 LT 123, 35 TLR 443 .... 8:07
Barnes, Re [1939] 1 KB 316, [1938] 4 All ER 870, 108 LJKB 232, CA 45:27
Barnes (Inspector of Taxes) v Hilton Main Construction Ltd [2005] EWHC 1355 (Ch), [2005] STC 1532, 77 TC 255, [2005] SWTI 834, [2005] All ER (D) 200 (Apr) 2A:19
Barnett v Brabyn [1996] STC 716, 69 TC 133 .... 7:08, 7:11, 8:10
Barney & Freeman v Customs and Excise Comrs [1990] VATTR 19 .... 67:08
Barr Crombie & Co Ltd v IRC 1945 SC 271, 1945 SLT 234, 26 TC 406, 24 ATC 55 .... 8:88
Barr's Trustees, v IRC 1943 SC 157, 1943 SLT 173, 25 TC 72, 22 ATC 83 .... 15:14
Barraclough v Customs and Excise Comrs (1987) VAT decision 2529 .... 69:22
Barratt Construction Ltd v Customs and Excise Comrs [1989] VATTR 204 .. 2A:67, 65:12

Table of Cases

Barratt Urban Construction (Northern) Ltd v Customs and Excise Comrs (1988) VAT decision 2723 .... 65:12
Barrett (HM Inspector of Taxes) v Powell (1998) 22:33
Barrett (provisional liquidator for Rafidain Bank) v Customs and Excise Comrs (1993) VAT decision 11016 .... 66:09
Barron v Littman. See Littman v Barron
Barry (Inspector of Taxes) v Cordy [1946] 2 All ER 396, 28 TC 250, 90 Sol Jo 528, 62 TLR 614, sub nom Cordy v Barry (Inspector of Taxes) 176 LT 111, CA 8:49
Barson v Airey (1925) 134 LT 586, 42 TLR 145, 10 TC 609, CA 7:03
Barty-King v Ministry of Defence [1979] 2 All ER 80, [1979] STC 218 .... 40:06
Basingstoke and District Sports Trust Ltd v Customs and Excise Comrs [1995] V & DR 405 .... 68:26
Bassett Enterprises Ltd v Petty (1938) 21 TC 730 .... 8:113
Bates v IRC [1968] AC 483, [1967] 1 All ER 84, [1967] 2 WLR 60, [1966] TR 369, sub nom IRC v Bates 44 TC 225 .... 15:28
Batey v Wakefield [1982] 1 All ER 61, [1981] STC 521, 55 TC 550, [1981] TR 251, CA 23:06
Batley, Re, Public Trustee v Hert (No 2) [1952] Ch 781, [1952] 2 All ER 562, [1952] TR 389, 31 ATC 410, CA 11:43
Battersby v Campbell [2001] STC (SCD) 189 .... 7:11, 8:26
Battle Baptist Church v IRC and Woodham [1995] STC (SCD) 176n 6:36
Batty, Re, Public Trustee v Bell [1952] Ch 280, [1952] 1 All ER 425, [1952] 1 TLR 412 .... 11:43
Baxendale v Murphy [1924] 2 KB 494, [1924] All ER Rep 754, 9 TC 76, 3 ATC 518 .... 11:27
Baxi Group Ltd v Revenue and Customs Comrs [2007] EWCA Civ 1378, [2008] STC 42, CA 63:20
Bayley v Rogers [1980] STC 544, 53 TC 420, [1980] TR 245 .... 18:01, 23:21
Baylis v Gregory [1986] 1 All ER 289, [1986] 1 WLR 624, [1986] STC 22, 62 TC 1; on appeal [1989] AC 398, [1987] 3 All ER 27, [1987] 3 WLR 660, [1987] STC 297, 62 TC 1, CA; affd [1989] AC 398, [1988] 3 All ER 495, [1988] 3 WLR 423, [1988] STC 476, 62 TC 1, HL 2A:48, 3:18
Baytrust Holdings Ltd v IRC [1971] 3 All ER 76, [1971] 1 WLR 1333, [1971] TR 111, 50 ATC 136 .... 60:03, 62:18
Beak v Robson [1943] AC 352, [1943] 1 All ER 46, 112 LJKB 141, 25 TC 33, HL 7:29
Bean v Doncaster Amalgamated Collieries Ltd [1944] 2 All ER 279, 27 TC 296, 23 ATC 264, CA; affd sub nom Doncaster Amalgamated Collieries Ltd v Bean [1946] 1 All ER 642, 27 TC 296, 25 ATC 15, HL 2:19, 8:114, 8:118
Beare v Carter [1940] 2 KB 187, 109 LJKB 701, 23 TC 353, 19 ATC 206 .... 12:08
Beattie v Jenkinson [1971] 3 All ER 495, [1971] 1 WLR 1419, 47 TC 121, [1971] TR 97 .... 18:21
Beatty's (Earl) Executors v IRC (1940) 23 TC 574, 19 ATC 419 .... 35:31, 35:32, 35:33
Beauchamp v F W Woolworth plc [1987] STC 279, 61 TC 542; revsd [1989] 1 WLR 50, [1988] STC 714, 61 TC 542, CA; on appeal [1990] 1 AC 478, [1989] 3 WLR 1, [1989] STC 510, 61 TC 542, HL 7:11, 8:68, 8:110, 8:114, 8:117, 8:130, 8:131
Beautiland v Comr of Inland Revenue [1991] STC 467 .... 8:21
Beauty Consultants Ltd v Inspector of Taxes [2002] STC (SCD) 352 .... 8:96
Beazer (C H) (Holdings) plc v Customs and Excise Comrs [1987] VATTR 164; affd sub nom Customs and Excise Comrs v C H Beazer (Holdings) plc [1989] STC 549 ...... 66:07
Bebb v Bunny (1854) 1 K & J 216, 1 Jur NS 203 .... 11:12
Beckbell Ltd v Customs and Excise Comrs [1993] VATTR 212 .... 65:17
Becker v Finanzamt Münster-Innenstadt: 8/81 [1982] ECR 53, [1982] 1 CMLR 499, ECJ 63:02
Becker v Wright [1966] 1 All ER 565, [1966] 1 WLR 215, 42 TC 591, [1965] TR 411: 15:20, 33:01
Beckman v IRC [2000] STC (SCD) 59 .... 44:04
Bee Farmers Association v Customs and Excise Comrs (1984) VAT decision 1565 .... 68:25
Beecham Group Ltd v Fair [1984] STC 15, 57 TC 733 .... 10:04
Begg-MacBrearty v Stilwell [1996] 4 All ER 205, [1996] 1 WLR 951, [1996] STC 413, 68 TC 426 .... 18:40

Table of Cases

Beharrell (John) Ltd v Customs and Excise Comrs [1991] VATTR 497 .... 65:32
Beheersmaatschappij Van Ginkel Waddinxveen BV v Inspecteur der Omzetbelasting, Utrecht: C-163/91 [1996] STC 825, ECJ 65:25
Belfort, The (1884) 9 PD 215, 53 LJP 88, 51 LT 271, 33 WR 171 .... 56:29
Belfour v Mace (1928) 138 LT 338, 13 TC 539, 7 ATC 1, CA 36:05
Belgian State v Recolta Recycling SPRL: C-440/04 [2006] ECR I-6161, [2006] SWTI 1851, [2008] STC 1537, ECJ 63:09, 66:06, 66:34
Belgium v Ghent Coal Terminal NV: C-37/95 [1998] All ER (EC) 223, [1998] 1 CMLR 950, [1998] STC 260, ECJ 66:08, 66:26
Belgium v Temco Europe SA: C-284/03 [2004] ECR I-11237, [2004] STC 1451, ECJ 68:11
Beliot Technologies Inc v Valmet Paper Machinery Inc [1995] RPC 705 .... 63:02
Bell v Customs and Excise Comrs (1989) VAT decision 3774 .... 64:14
Bell v Kennedy (1868) LR 1 Sc & Div 307, 5 SLR 566, 6 Macq 69, HL 33:02, 33:19, 33:23
Bell v National Provincial Bank [1904] 1 KB 149, 73 LJKB 142, 5 TC 1, CA 8:57
Bell's Executors v IRC [1987] SLT 625 .... 57:25
Ben Nevis v IRC [2001] STC (SCD) 144 .... 7:137
Ben-Odeco Ltd v Powlson [1978] 2 All ER 1111, [1978] 1 WLR 1093, [1978] STC 460, 52 TC 459, HL 9:04
Bendit (Julius) Ltd v IRC (1945) 27 TC 44 .... 8:157
Beneficiary v IRC [1999] STC (SCD) 134 .... 35:29
Benendoun v France (Application 12547/86) 2:118
Benham's Will Trusts, Re [1995] STC 210 .... 43:31
Bennachie Leisure Centre Association v Customs and Excise Comrs (1996) VAT decision 14276 .... 69:18
Bennet v Underground Electric Railways Co of London Ltd [1923] 2 KB 535, 92 LJKB 909, 8 TC 475 .... 30:04
Bennett, Re, Jones v Bennett (1896) 1 Ch 778 .... 13:13
Bennett v Customs and Excise (1979) VAT decision 865 .... 68:23
Bennett v Customs and Excise Comrs [1999] STC 248 .... 64:03
Bennett v Customs and Excise Comrs (No 2) [2001] STC 137 .... 2:07, 2A:67
Bennett v IRC [1995] STC 54 .... 43:04
Bennett v Marshall [1938] 1 KB 591, [1938] 1 All ER 93, 107 LJKB 391, 22 TC 73, CA 7:11
Bennett v Ogston (1930) 15 TC 374, 9 ATC 182 .... 5:14, 11:05
Benson v Counsell [1942] 1 KB 364, [1942] 1 All ER 435, 24 TC 178, 21 ATC 23 .... 12:11
Benson v Yard Arm Club Ltd [1979] 2 All ER 336, [1979] STC 266, 53 TC 67, [1979] TR 1, CA 9:30
Bentley v Pike [1981] STC 360, 53 TC 590, [1981] TR 17 .... 16:02, 16:08, 35:46
Bentleys, Stokes and Lowless v Beeson [1952] 2 All ER 82, [1952] 1 TLR 1529, 33 TC 491, [1952] TR 239, CA 8:96, 8:101
Benton v Customs and Excise Comrs [1975] VATTR 138 .... 63:21
Berbrooke Fashions v Customs and Excise Comrs [1977] VATTR 168 .... 63:17
Berkholz v Finanzamt Hamburg-Mitte-Alstadt: 168/84 [1985] ECR 2251, [1985] 3 CMLR 667, ECJ 63:29
Bernard & Shaw Ltd v Shaw [1951] 2 All ER 267, [1951] TR 205, 30 ATC 187 ..... 7:144
Berry v Warnett [1982] 2 All ER 630, [1982] 1 WLR 698, [1982] STC 396, 55 TC 92, HL 18:14, 18:34, 20:10
Bertelsmann AG v Finanzamt Wiedenbrück: C-380/99 [2001] ECR I-5163, [2001] 3 CMLR 271, [2001] STC 1153, ECJ 63:20; 65:17
Bestway (Holdings) Ltd v Luff [1997] STC (SCD) 87; affd [1998] STC 357, 70 TC 512 .... 9:12
Bethway & Moss Ltd v Customs and Excise Comrs [1988] 3 CMLR 44 .... 65:12
Betterware Products Ltd v Customs and Excise Comrs [1985] STC 648 .... 63:20
Betts Brown's Trustees v Whately Smith 1941 SC 69 .... 46:22
Bevins v McLeish [1995] STC (SCD) 342n 7:122
Beynon (T) & Co Ltd v Ogg (1918) 7 TC 125 .... 8:15, 8:17

Beynon (Dr) & Partners v Customs and Excise Comrs [2002] EWHC 518 (Ch), [2002] STC 699; on appeal [2002] EWCA Civ 1870, [2003] STC 169; revsd [2004] UKHL 53, [2004] 4 All ER 1091, [2005] 1 WLR 86, [2005] STC 55 .... 68:23, 69:34
Bhadra v Ellam [1988] STC 239, 60 TC 466 .... 7:126
Biehl v Administration des Contributions du Grand-Duch de Luxembourg: C-175/88 [1990] ECR I-1779, [1990] 3 CMLR 143, [1991] STC 575, ECJ 1:08
Billam v Griffith (1941) 23 TC 757, 20 ATC 42 .... 8:07
Billingham v Cooper. See Cooper v Billingham
Billows v Hammond [2000] STC (SCD) 430 .... 45:02
Binder Hamlyn v Customs and Excise Comrs [1983] VATTR 171 .... 63:30
Bio Oil Research Ltd v Customs and Excise Comrs (1994) VAT decision 12252 ...... 69:34
Birch v Treasury Solicitor [1951] Ch 298, [1950] 2 All ER 1198, [1951] 1 TLR 225, CA 56:09
Birchall v Bullough [1896] 1 QB 325, 65 LJQB 252, 74 LT 27, 44 WR 300 .... 56:29
Bird v IRC [1985] STC 584, 61 TC 238; on appeal [1987] STC 168, 61 TC 238, CA; on appeal [1989] AC 300, [1988] 2 All ER 670, [1988] 2 WLR 1237, [1988] STC 312, 61 TC 238, HL 4:18, 4:19, 4:25, 4:28
Bird v Martland [1982] STC 603, 56 TC 89 .... 7:24
Bird Semple and Crawford Herron v Customs and Excise Comrs [1986] VATTR 218
.... 66:05
Bird Precision Bellows Ltd, Re [1986] Ch 658, [1985] 3 All ER 523, [1986] 2 WLR 158, [1985] BCLC 493, [1986] PCC 25, 130 Sol Jo 51, [1986] LS Gaz R 36, CA 45:02
Birkbeck Freehold Land Society, ex p (1883) 24 Ch D 119, 52 LJ Ch 777, 49 LT 265, 31 WR 716 .... 56:33
Birkdale School, Sheffield v Revenue and Customs Comrs [2008] EWHC 409 (Ch), [2008] STC 2002 .... 63:20
Birmingham and District Cattle By-Products Co Ltd v IRC (1919) 12 TC 92, 1 ATC 345 .... 8:49
Birmingham Corpn v Barnes [1935] AC 292, [1935] All ER Rep 533, 19 TC 195, 14 ATC 33, HL 9:04
Bishop v Finsbury Securities Ltd [1966] 3 All ER 105, [1966] 1 WLR 1402, 43 TC 591, [1966] TR 275, HL 4:01
Bispham v Eardiston Farming Co (1919) Ltd [1962] 2 All ER 376, [1962] 1 WLR 616, 40 TC 322, [1962] TR 73, [1962] BTR 255 .... 8:42
Bjellica v Customs and Excise Comrs [1994] 1 CMLR 437, [1993] STC 730 .... 67:01
Black (C Jeffrey) (Opticians) Ltd v Customs and Excise Comrs (1989) VAT decision 4072 .... 66:04
Black Nominees Ltd v Nicol [1975] STC 372, 50 TC 229 .... 1:07, 4:30, 12:03
Blackburn v Close Bros Ltd (1960) 39 TC 164, [1960] TR 161, 39 ATC 274 ... 7:15, 7:16
Blackburn v Keeling [2003] EWHC 754 (Ch), [2003] STC 639; revsd [2003] EWCA Civ 1221, [2003] STC 1162, 75 TC 608 .... 7:144
Blackburn & Anor v R & C Comrs [2008] EWHC 266 (Ch) 31:14
Blackpool Marton Rotary Club v Martin [1988] STC 823; affd [1990] STC 1, CA
.... 25:03
Blackqueen Ltd v Customs and Excise Comrs (2002) VAT decision 17680 ...... 1:12, 1:13, 66:37
Blackwell v Mills [1945] 2 All ER 655, 26 TC 468, 24 ATC 233 .... 7:138
Blakiston v Cooper [1909] AC 104, [1908–10] All ER Rep 682, 5 TC 347, HL 7:25
Blausten v IRC [1972] Ch 256, [1972] 1 All ER 41, 47 TC 542, 50 ATC 273, CA
.... 42A:44
Blendett v IRC [1984] STC 95, CA 57:10, 57:27, 57:29, 62:10
Bloom v Kinder (1958) 38 TC 77, [1958] TR 91, 51 R & IT 336, 37 ATC 158 ..... 12:06, 12:09
Blount v Blount [1916] 1 KB 230, [1914–15] All ER Rep 680, 85 LJKB 230, 114 LT 176 .... 11:42
Bluck v Salton [2003] STC (SCD) 439 .... 7:36
Blue Sphere Global Ltd v Revenue and Customs Comrs [2009] EWHC 1150 (Ch), [2009] SWTI 1792 .... 66:34
Blyth v Birmingham Waterworks Co (1856) 20 JP 247, 25 LJ Ex 212, 11 Exch 781, 2 Jur NS 333, 4 WR 294, 156 ER 1047, [1843–60] All ER Rep 478, 26 LTOS 261 .... 2A:81
Boacke Allen and other v HMRC [2007] UKHL 25; [2007] STC 1265 .... 1:12

Table of Cases

Bolam v Barlow (1949) 31 TC 136, [1949] TR 65, 28 ATC 10 ...... 7:141
Bolam v Muller (1947) 28 TC 471, 26 ATC 417 ...... 7:34
Bolam v Regent Oil Co Ltd (1956) 37 TC 56, [1956] TR 403, 50 R & IT 79, 35 ATC 499 ...... 8:130
Bolson (J) & Son Ltd v Farrelly (1953) 34 TC 161, [1953] TR 89, 32 ATC 80, [1953] 1 Lloyd's Rep 258, CA 8:13, 8:25, 23:02
Bolton v Halpern & Woolf (a firm) [1979] STC 761, 53 TC 445, [1979] TR 269; revsd [1981] STC 14, 53 TC 445, [1980] TR 367, CA 8:95
Bolton v International Drilling Co Ltd [1983] STC 70, 56 TC 449 ...... 8:110, 8:116, 9:25
Bomford v Osborne [1942] AC 14, [1941] 2 All ER 426, 23 TC 642, 20 ATC 77, HL 8:42
Bond v Pickford [1982] STC 403, 57 TC 301; affd [1983] STC 517, 57 TC 301, CA 20:05, 20:11
Bone (Peter) Ltd v IRC [1995] STC 921 ...... 2:89, 56:26, 57:18, 62:04
Bonner v Basset Mines Ltd (1912) 108 LT 764, 6 TC 146 ...... 8:114
Bookit Ltd v Revenue and Customs Comrs [2006] EWCA Civ 550, [2006] SWTI 1513, [2006] All ER (D) 151 (May) 63:02, 68:16
Booth v Booth [1922] 1 KB 66, 91 LJKB 127, 126 LT 342 ...... 11:42
Booth v Ellard [1980] 3 All ER 569, [1980] 1 WLR 1443, [1980] STC 555, 53 TC 393, CA 20:06, 20:08, 20:09
Booth v Mirror Group Newspapers plc [1992] STC 615 ...... 7:18, 7:144
Booth (E V) (Holdings) Ltd v Buckwell [1980] STC 578, 53 TC 425, [1980] TR 249 ...... 16:11
Bootle v Bye [1996] STC (SCD) 58 ...... 7:17
Boots Co plc v Customs and Excise Comrs: C-126/88 [1990] ECR I-1235, [1990] 2 CMLR 731, [1990] STC 387, ECJ 63:20, 65:17, 65:19
Boparan v Revenue and Customs Comrs [2007] STC (SCD) 297 ...... 22:18
Bosal Holdings BV v Staatssecretaris van Financien: C-168/01 [2003] All ER (EC) 959, [2003] 3 CMLR 674, [2003] STC 1483, ECJ 1:10, 1:12
Bott (E) Ltd v Price [1987] STC 100, 59 TC 437 ...... 8:113
Bouanich v Skatteverket C-265/04: [2006] SWTI 203, [2006] All ER (D) 103 (Jan), ECJ 1:07, 1:12
Bourne v Norwich Crematorium Ltd [1967] 2 All ER 576, [1967] 1 WLR 691, 44 TC 164, [1967] TR 49 ...... 9:12
Bourne and Hollingsworth Ltd v Ogden (1929) 45 TLR 222, 14 TC 349, 8 ATC 13 ...... 8:101
Bournemouth Symphony Orchestra v Customs and Excise Comrs [2006] EWCA Civ 1281, [2007] STC 198, (2006) Times, 9 November, 150 Sol Jo LB 1431, [2006] SWTI 2299, [2006] All ER (D) 101 (Oct) 68:29
Bowater Paper Corpn Ltd v Murgatroyd [1970] AC 266, [1969] 3 All ER 111, 46 TC 37, [1969] TR 251, HL 37:21
Bowden v Russell and Russell [1965] 2 All ER 258, [1965] 1 WLR 711, 42 TC 301, [1965] TR 89 ...... 8:97, 8:98, 8:102
Bower & Anor (Exors of Bower, dec'd) v R & C Comrs (2008) SpC 665 ...... 45:02
Bowers v Harding [1891] 1 QB 560, 60 LJQB 474, 3 TC 22 ...... 7:137
Bowie (or Ramsay) v Liverpool Royal Infirmary [1930] AC 588, [1930] All ER Rep 127, 99 LJPC 134, 143 LT 388, 46 TLR 465 ...... 33:21
Bowles v Bank of England [1913] 1 Ch 57, 82 LJ Ch 124, 6 TC 136 ...... 1:25, 1:32
Boyce v Whitwick Colliery Co Ltd (1934) 151 LT 464, 18 TC 655, CA 8:114
Boyd (T L) & Sons Ltd v Stephen [1926] WN 102, 10 TC 698, 5 ATC 247 ...... 36:09
Boys' and Girls' Welfare Society v Customs and Excise Comrs (1997) VAT decision 15274 ...... 69:35
Bradbury v Arnold (1957) 37 TC 665, [1957] TR 333, 36 ATC 332 ...... 12:06, 12:08
Braden (Jenny) Holidays Ltd v Customs and Excise Comrs (1993) VAT decision 10892 ...... 65:25
Bradford Corpn v Pickles [1895] AC 587, [1895-9] All ER Rep 984, 64 LJ Ch 759, HL 1:12, 1:13
Bradley v London Electricity plc [1996] STC 1054, 70 TC 155 ...... 9:26
Bradshaw v Blunden (1956) 36 TC 397, [1956] TR 81, 35 ATC 109 ...... 8:19
Bradshaw v Pawley [1979] 3 All ER 273, [1980] 1 WLR 10, 40 P & CR 496, 124 Sol Jo 31, 253 Estates Gazette 693 ...... 62:11

Table of Cases

Brahma Kumaris World Spiritual University v Customs and Excise Comrs (1995) VAT decision 12946 .... 69:18
Braine (M E) (Boatbuilders) Ltd v Customs and Excise Comrs (1989) VAT decision 3881 .... 63:19
Brander & Ors v R & C Comrs (2007) SpC 610 .... 7:36
Bray v Best [1986] STC 96; on appeal [1988] 2 All ER 105, [1988] 1 WLR 784, [1988] STC 103, CA; affd [1989] 1 All ER 969, [1989] 1 WLR 167, [1989] STC 159, HL 5:14, 7:22, 35:16
Brays of Glastonbury Ltd v Customs and Excise Comrs (1978) VAT decision 650, 102 Taxation 218 .... 69:42
Brennan v Deanby Investment Co Ltd [2001] STC 536, 73 TC 455, NI CA 29:10
Briararch Ltd v Customs and Excise Comrs [1991] VATTR 127; affd sub nom Customs and Excise Comrs v Briararch Ltd [1992] STC 732 .... 66:07, 66:26
Bridges v Bearsley [1957] 2 All ER 281, [1957] 1 WLR 674, 37 TC 289, 50 R & IT 397, CA 7:18
Bridges v Watterson [1952] 2 All ER 910, [1952] 2 TLR 850, 34 TC 47, [1952] TR 441 .... 32:27
Bridgett and Hayes Contract, Re [1928] Ch 163, [1927] All ER Rep 191, 97 LJ Ch 33, 138 LT 106 .... 46:14
Briggs v Customs and Excise Comrs (1985) VAT decision 1813 .... 64:02
Brighton College v Marriott [1926] AC 192, [1925] All ER Rep 600, 10 TC 213, 5 ATC 32, HL 13:23
Brighton Convent of the Blessed Sacraments v IRC (1933) 18 TC 76 .... 13:23
Bristol (Marquess) v IRC [1901] 2 KB 336, 70 LJKB 759, 65 JP 360, 84 LT 659 .... 57:07
British Airports Authority v Customs and Excise Comrs [1977] 1 All ER 497, [1977] 1 WLR 302, [1977] STC 36, CA 63:19
British Airports Authority (No 3) v Customs and Excise Comrs (1975) VAT decision 147, 95 Taxation 151 .... 68:11
British Airways plc v Customs and Excise Comrs [2000] V & DR 74 .... 66:03
British American Tobacco International Ltd v Belguim: C-435/03 [2005] ECR I-7077, [2006] STC 158, [2005] SWTI 1256, [2005] All ER (D) 225 (Jul), ECJ 63:19, 63:25
British Association for Counselling v Customs and Excise Comrs (1994) VAT decision 11855 .... 68:25
British Association for Shooting and Conservation Ltd v Revenue and Customs Comrs [2009] EWHC 399 (Ch), [2009] STC 1421 .... 68:25, 68:26
British-Borneo Petroleum Syndicate Ltd v Cropper [1969] 1 All ER 104, [1968] 1 WLR 1701, 45 TC 201, [1968] TR 255 .... 8:74
BBC v Johns [1965] Ch 32, [1964] 1 All ER 923, 41 TC 471, [1964] TR 45, CA 8:35
British Car Auctions Ltd v Customs and Excise Comrs [1978] VATTR 56 .... 66:20
British Commonwealth International Newsfilm Agency Ltd v Mahany [1963] 1 All ER 88, [1963] 1 WLR 69, 40 TC 550, [1962] TR 383, HL 8:89, 8:91
British Electric Traction Co v IRC [1902] 1 KB 441, 71 LJKB 92, 66 JP 83, 85 LT 663, CA 57:28
British European Breeders' Fund v Customs and Excise Comrs [1985] VATTR 12 .... 63:26
British Hardware Federation v Customs and Excise Comrs [1975] VATTR 172 ...... 68:16
British Insulated and Helsby Cables Ltd v Atherton [1926] AC 205, 95 LJKB 336, 4 ATC 47, sub nom Atherton v British Insulated and Helsby Cables Ltd (1926) 10 TC 155, HL 8:84, 8:105, 8:110
British Mexican Petroleum Co Ltd v Jackson (1932) 16 TC 570, HL 2A:69
British Olympic Association v Customs and Excise Comrs [1979] VATTR 122 .... 63:16
British Olympic Association v Winter [1995] STC (SCD) 85 .... 8:12
British Organic Farmers v Customs and Excise Comrs [1988] VATTR 64 .... 68:25
British Railways Board v Customs and Excise Comrs [1977] 2 All ER 873, [1977] 1 WLR 588, [1977] STC 221, CA 63:19, 63:20
British Salmson Aero Engines Ltd v IRC [1938] 2 KB 482, [1938] 3 All ER 283, 22 TC 29, 17 ATC 187, CA 8:131
British Sky Broadcasting Ltd v Customs and Excise Comrs [1994] VATTR 1 .... 63:30
British Steel Exports Ltd v Customs and Excise Comrs (1992) VAT decision 7562 ... 67:06
British Sugar Manufacturers Ltd v Harris [1938] 2 KB 220, [1938] 1 All ER 149, 21 TC 528, 16 ATC 421, CA 8:106

Table of Cases

British Telecom Pension Scheme Trustees v Clarke [1998] STC (SCD) 14; on appeal sub nom Clarke v British Telecom Pension Scheme Trustees [1998] STC 1075; revsd [2000] STC 222, CA 1:17, 2:19, 8:23, 12:06, 12:07
British Telecommunications plc v Customs and Excise Comrs (1997) VAT decision 14669 .... 65:18, 65:19
British Telecommunications plc v Revenue and Customs Comrs [2006] STC (SCD) 347 .... 18:07
British Teleflower Service Ltd v Customs and Excise Comrs [1995] V & DR 356 .... 63:04
British Tenpin Bowling Association v Customs and Excise Comrs [1989] 1 CMLR 561, [1989] VATTR 101 .... 63:02
British Transport Commission v Gourley [1956] AC 185, [1955] 3 All ER 796, [1955] TR 303, 34 ATC 305, HL 10:04
British United Shoe Machinery Co Ltd v Customs and Excise Comrs [1977] VATTR 187 .... 63:22, 63:23, 65:19
Briton Ferry Steel Co Ltd v Barry [1940] 1 KB 463, [1939] 4 All ER 541, 23 TC 414, 18 ATC 318, CA 8:60
Britto v Secretary of State for the Home Department [1984] Imm AR 93, IAT 33:14
Broadbridge v Beattie (1944) 26 TC 63, 23 ATC 118 .... 8:165, 23:02
Broadhead Peel & Co v Customs and Excise Comrs [1984] VATTR 195 .... 66:18
Brocklesby v Merricks (1934) 18 TC 576, CA 12:06
Brodie's Will Trustees v IRC (1933) 17 TC 432, 12 ATC 140 .... 11:30, 13:21
Brodrick, Wright & Strong Ltd v Customs and Excise Comrs (1987) VAT decision 2347 .... 68:11
Brokaw v Seatrain UK Ltd [1971] 2 QB 476, [1971] 2 All ER 98, [1971] TR 71, CA 34:04
Brooklands Selangor Holdings Ltd v IRC [1970] 2 All ER 76, [1970] 1 WLR 429, [1969] TR 485 .... 25:19, 60:03, 62:18
Brooks Histograph Ltd v Customs and Excise Comrs [1984] VATTR 46 .... 69:15
Brotherton v IRC [1977] STC 73, 52 TC 137, [1976] TR 299; revsd [1978] 2 All ER 267, [1978] 1 WLR 610, [1978] STC 201, 52 TC 137, [1977] TR 317, CA 13:16
Brown v Brown (1981) 3 FLR 212, CA 33:19
Brown v Bullock [1961] 1 All ER 206, [1961] 1 WLR 53, 40 TC 1, [1960] TR 303; affd [1961] 3 All ER 129, [1961] 1 WLR 1095, 40 TC 1, [1961] TR 173, CA 7:49, 7:138, 7:139, 7:141
Brown v Burt (1911) 81 LJKB 17, 5 TC 667, CA 33:03
Brown v IRC (1900) 84 LT 71, 17 TLR 177, CA 59:08
Brown v IRC (1965) 42 TC 583, [1965] TR 391, 44 ATC 399 .... 2:27
Brown v National Provident Institution [1919] 2 KB 497, 88 LJKB 1201, 8 TC 57; on appeal [1920] 3 KB 35, 89 LJKB 866, 8 TC 57, CA; varied [1921] 2 AC 222, 90 LJKB 1009, 125 LT 417, 8 TC 57, HL 5:17, 11:15
Brown v Richardson [1997] STC (SCD) 233 .... 6:27, 10:15
Brown & Root McDermott Fabricators Ltd's Application, Re [1996] STC 483 ...... 56:29, 62:05
Brown's Executors v IRC [1996] STC (SCD) 277 .... 44:04
Bruce v Customs and Excise Comrs [1991] VATTR 280 .... 69:18
Brumby v Milner [1975] 2 All ER 773, [1975] 1 WLR 958, [1975] STC 215, [1974] TR 397; on appeal [1975] 3 All ER 1004, [1976] 1 WLR 29, [1975] STC 644, CA; affd [1976] 3 All ER 636, [1976] 1 WLR 1096, [1976] STC 534, 5 ITC 583, [1976] TR 249, HL 7:17
Buccleuch (Duke) v IRC [1966] 1 QB 851, [1965] 3 All ER 458, [1965] TR 263, CA; affd [1967] 1 AC 506, [1967] 1 All ER 129, [1966] TR 393, 45 ATC 472, HL 45:01, 45:02, 45:04, 45:16
Buchanan (Peter) Ltd and MacHarg v McVey [1954] IR 89 .... 34:03, 34:04
Buckingham v Securitas Properties Ltd [1980] 1 WLR 380, [1980] STC 166, 53 TC 292, [1979] TR 415 .... 9:12
Building and Civil Engineering Holidays Scheme Management Ltd v Clark (1960) 39 TC 12, [1960] TR 1, 53 R & IT 141, 39 ATC 105 .... 8:11
Bull v Bull [1955] 1 QB 234, [1955] 1 All ER 253, [1955] 2 WLR 78, CA 42:08
Bullivant Holdings Ltd v IRC [1998] STC 905, 71 TC 22 .... 18:33
Bulloch v IRC [1976] STC 514, 51 TC 563, [1976] TR 201 .... 8:61
Bullock v Unit Construction Co Ltd. See Unit Construction Co Ltd v Bullock

Bullrun Inc v Inspector of Taxes [2000] STC (SCD) 384 .... 8:119
Bulmer v IRC [1967] Ch 145, [1966] 3 All ER 801, 44 TC 1, 45 ATC 293, [1966] TR 257 .... 15:02
Bulmer (H P) Ltd v J Bollinger SA [1974] Ch 401, [1974] 2 All ER 1226, [1974] 3 WLR 202, [1974] FSR 334, CA 63:02
Burca v Parkinson. See Editor v Inspector of Taxes
Burden v United Kingdom (Application 13378/05) [2007] STC 252, [2008] STC 1305, [2007] 1 FCR 69, 21 BHRC 640, [2007] SWTI 106, [2006] All ER (D) 160 (Dec), ECtHR 1:21
Burdge v Pyne [1969] 1 All ER 467, [1969] 1 WLR 364, 45 TC 320, [1968] TR 385 .... 12:05
Burkinyoung v IRC [1995] STC (SCD) 29 .... 44:04
Burmah Steamship Co Ltd v IRC 1931 SC 156, 1931 SLT 116, 16 TC 67, 9 ATC 482 .... 8:81, 8:84
Burman v Hedges & Butler Ltd [1979] 1 WLR 160, [1979] STC 136, 52 TC 501, [1978] TR 409 .... 28:23, 28:25
Burman v Thorn Domestic Appliances (Electrical) Ltd [1982] STC 179, 55 TC 493 .... 8:89
Burman v Westminster Press Ltd [1987] STC 669, 60 TC 418 .... 22:03
Burntisland Golf House Club v Customs and Excise Comrs (1991) VAT decision 6340 .... 66:05
Burrell v Burrell [2005] EWHC 245 (Ch), [2005] STC 569, [2005] SWTI 278, [2005] All ER (D) 351 (Feb) 2A:71
Burroughes v Abbott [1922] 1 Ch 86, [1921] All ER Rep 709, 91 LJ Ch 157, 126 LT 354 .... 2A:71, 11:42
Burrows v Matabele Gold Reefs and Estates Co Ltd [1901] 2 Ch 23, 70 LJ Ch 434, 49 WR 500, 84 LT 478, CA 61:11
Burton v Rednall (1954) 35 TC 435, [1954] TR 329, 33 ATC 337 .... 7:125
Bury's Transport (Oxon) Ltd v Customs and Excise Comrs LON/85/129 unreported 63:23
Businessman v Inspector of Taxes [2003] STC (SCD) 403; affd sub nom Weston v Garnett [2005] STC 617 .... 2:17, 17:12
Butler v Butler [1961] P 33, [1961] 1 All ER 810, [1961] TR 19, 40 ATC 19, CA 11:38
Butler v Wildin [1989] STC 22, 61 TC 666 .... 15:05
Butt v Haxby [1983] STC 239, 56 TC 547 .... 6:21
Butter v Bennett [1963] Ch 185, [1962] 3 All ER 204, [1962] 3 WLR 874, 40 TC 402, [1962] TR 257, CA 7:49, 7:102
Buxton v Public Trustee (1962) 41 TC 235 .... 2:11
Bye v Coren [1985] STC 113, 60 TC 116; affd [1986] STC 393, 60 TC 116, CA 8:02
Byrd v Customs and Excise Comrs (1994) VAT decision 12675 .... 66:04
Byrom and others (trading as Salon 24) v Revenue and Customs Comrs [2006] EWHC 111 (Ch), [2006] STC 992, [2006] All ER (D) 75 (Feb) 63:20

C

CGI Pension Trust Ltd v Customs and Excise Comrs (1999) VAT decision 15926 .... 69:01
CMC (Preston) Ltd v Customs and Excise Comrs (1989) VAT decision 3858 .... 70:04
CMS Peripherals Ltd v Revenue and Customs Comrs [2007] EWHC 1128 (Ch), [2007] SWTI 1563, [2007] All ER (D) 204 (May) 67.08
CSC Financial Services Ltd v Customs and Excise Comrs. See Customs and Excise Comrs v CSC Financial Services Ltd.
CVC/Opportunity Equity Partners Ltd v Demarco Almeida [2002] UKPC 16, [2002] 2 BCLC 108 .... 45:03
Cable's (Lord) Will Trusts, Garret v Walters [1976] 3 All ER 417, [1977] 1 WLR 7 .... 34:05
Cadbury Schweppes plc and Cadbury Schweppes Overseas Ltd v IRC: C-196/04 [2004] 3 CMLR 325, [2004] SWTI 1496, SCD 1:04, 1:06, 1:07, 1:13, 1:15

Table of Cases

Cadbury Schweppes plc v Revenue and Customs Comrs: C-196/04 [2007] Ch 30, [2007] All ER (EC) 153, [2006] STC 1908, [2006] 3 WLR 890, [2007] 1 CMLR 43, [2006] SWTI 2201, (2006) Times, 20 September, [2006] All ER (D) 48 (Sep), ECJ 1:11, 1:13, 1:15, 1:19, 35:65, 35:66
Cadbury Schweppes plc v Williams [2002] STC (SCD) 115 .... 8:117
Cadbury Schweppes plc v Williams [2005] STC (SCD) 151 .... 11:08
Caglar v Billingham [1996] STC (SCD) 150 .... 5:18
Caillebotte v Quinn [1975] 2 All ER 412, [1975] 1 WLR 731, [1975] STC 265, 50 TC 222 .... 8:102
Cairns v MacDiarmid [1982] STC 226, 56 TC 556, [1981] TR 499; affd [1983] STC 178, 56 TC 556, CA 6:45, 11:05, 11:12
Calam Vale Ltd v Customs and Excise Comrs (2000) VAT decision 16869 .... 69:17
Calcutta Jute Mills Co Ltd v Nicholson (1876) 1 Ex D 428, [1874–80] All ER Rep 1102, 45 LJQB 821, 1 TC 83, Ex D 33:25
Caldicott v Varty [1976] 3 All ER 329, [1976] STC 418, 50 TC 222, [1976] TR 173 .... 7:01
Caledonian Paper plc v IRC [1998] STC (SCD) 129 .... 8:110
Caledonian Rly Co v Banks (1880) 1 TC 487, 18 Sc LR 85 .... 9:26
California Oil Products Ltd v FCT (1934) 52 CLR 28 .... 8:88
Californian Copper Syndicate Ltd v Harris (1904) 6 F (Ct of Sess) 894, 5 TC 159 .... 8:151
Calkin v Commissioner of Inland Revenue [1984] 1 NZLR 440, NZ CA 29:10
Calltel Telecom Ltd and another v Revenue and Customs Comrs [2009] EWHC 1081 (Ch), [2009] SWTI 1798 .... 66:34
Calvert v Wainwright [1947] KB 526, [1947] 1 All ER 282, 27 TC 475, 26 ATC 13 .... 7:20, 7:25
Camas plc v Atkinson [2004] EWCA Civ 541, [2004] STC 860, 148 Sol Jo LB 571 .... 30:03
Cambridge University v Revenue and Customs Comrs [2009] EWHC 434 (Ch), [2009] STC 1288 .... 63:17
Cambuslang Athletic Club v Customs and Excise Comrs (1984) VAT decision 1592 .... 63:16
Camcrown Ltd v McDonald [1999] STC (SCD) 255 .... 25:35
Camden London Borough v Customs and Excise Comrs [1993] VATTR 73 .... 2:49
Cameron v Customs and Excise Comrs (1998) VAT decision 15779 .... 67:09
Cameron, Re, Kingsley v IRC [1967] Ch 1, [1965] 3 All ER 474, 42 TC 539, [1965] TR 271 .... 11:43
Cameron v Cameron 1996 SLT 306 .... 33:14
Cameron v Prendergast. See Prendergast v Cameron
Camilla Enterprises Ltd Customs and Excise Comrs (1993) VAT decision 10426 ..... 68:12
Campbell v Hall (1774) 1 Cowp 204, Lofft 655, 20 State Tr 239, 98 ER 1045, [1558–1774] All ER Rep 252 .... 2A:70
Campbell v IRC [1967] Ch 651, [1967] 2 All ER 625, 45 TC 427, [1967] TR 9, CA; affd [1970] AC 77, [1968] 3 All ER 588, 45 TC 427, [1968] TR 327, HL .. 11:28, 11:29, 13:23
Campbell v IRC [2004] STC (SCD) 396 .... 3:01, 3:05, 3:21, 7:60, 11:17
Campbell v Mirror Group Newspapers Ltd [2004] UKHL 22, [2004] 2 AC 457, [2004] 2 All ER 995, [2004] 2 WLR 1232, [2004] IP & T 764, [2004] 21 LS Gaz R 36, [2004] NLJR 733, (2004) Times, 7 May, 148 Sol Jo LB 572, [2005] 1 LRC 397, 16 BHRC 500, [2004] All ER (D) 67 (May) 1.21
Campbell Connelly & Co Ltd v Barnett [1992] STC 316, 66 TC 380; affd [1994] STC 50, 66 TC 380, CA 22:16
Canada Permanent Mortgage Corpn v IRC 1932 SC 123, 1932 SLT 169, 1931 SN 118 .... 59:08
Canada Safeway Ltd v IRC [1973] Ch 374, [1972] 1 All ER 666, [1972] 2 WLR 443, [1971] TR 411 .... 60:02
Canadian Eagle Oil Co Ltd v R [1946] AC 119, [1945] 2 All ER 499, 27 TC 205, 24 ATC 156, HL 11:23
Canary Wharf Ltd v Customs and Excise Comrs [1996] V & DR 323 .... 64:26
Cando 70 v Customs and Excise Comrs [1978] VATTR 211 .... 2:16
Cannon Industries Ltd v Edwards [1966] 1 All ER 456 [1966] 1 WLR 580, 44 ATC 391, 42 TC 625 .... 8:50

Table of Cases

Cannop Coal Co Ltd v IRC (1918) 12 TC 31 .... 8:49
Canterbury Hockey Club and another v Revenue and Customs Comrs (case C-253/07) [2008] ECR I–0000, [2008] STC 3351, ECJ 68:26
Cantor Fitzgerald International v Customs and Excise Comrs: C-108/99 [2002] QB 546, sub nom Customs and Excise Comrs v Cantor Fitzgerald International [2001] ECR I-7257, [2001] 3 CMLR 1441, [2001] STC 1453, ECJ 68:11
Capcount Trading v Evans [1993] 2 All ER 125, [1993] STC 11, 65 TC 545, CA ... 16:08, 35:46
Cape Brandy Syndicate v IRC [1921] 1 KB 64, 90 LJKB 113, 12 TC 358; affd [1921] 2 KB 403, 90 LJKB 461, 12 TC 358, CA 1:24, 8:15, 8:17, 8:20
Capital and National Trust Ltd v Golder [1949] 2 All ER 956, 31 TC 265, 28 ATC 326, 42 R & IT 576, [1949] TR 395, CA 30:06
Capital One Developments Ltd v Customs and Excise Comrs [2002] EWHC 197 (Ch), [2002] STC 479 .... 67:05
Card Protection Plan Ltd v Customs and Excise Comrs [1994] 1 CMLR 756, [1994] STC 199, CA; on appeal (15 October 1996, unreported), HL; refd: C-349/96 [1999] 2 AC 601, [1999] All ER (EC) 339, [1999] 3 WLR 203, [1999] 2 CMLR 743, [1999] STC 270, ECJ; apld [2001] UKHL 4, [2002] 1 AC 202, [2001] 2 All ER 143, [2001] 1 All ER (Comm) 438, [2001] STC 174 .... 63:20, 68:13
Cardiff Community Housing Association Ltd v Customs and Excise Comrs [2000] V & DR 346 .... 63:17, 69:18
Carless v Customs and Excise Comrs [1993] STC 632 .... 63:20
Carlill v Carbolic Smoke Ball Co [1892] 2 QB 484, 61 LJQB 696; on appeal [1893] 1 QB 256, [1891–94] All ER Rep 127, CA 56:09
Carlisle and Silloth Golf Club v Smith [1913] 3 KB 75, 82 LJKB 837, 108 LT 785, 6 TC 198, CA 8:35
Carlton Lodge Club v Customs and Excise Comrs [1974] 3 All ER 798, [1975] 1 WLR 66, [1974] STC 507 .... 63:16
Carmichael v National Power plc [1999] 4 All ER 897, [1999] 1 WLR 2042, [1999] ICR 1226, [2000] IRLR 43, HL 2:20
Carney v Nathan [2003] STC (SCD) 28 .... 8:102
Carnoustie Golf Course Committee v IRC 1929 SC 419, 1929 SLT 366, 14 TC 498, 8 ATC 201 .... 8:35
Carpet Agencies Ltd v IRC (1958) 38 TC 223, 37 ATC 331, 52 R & IT 27, [1958] TR 341 .... 30:05
Carr v Armpledge Ltd [2000] STC 410, 72 TC 420, CA 1:24, 9:07
Carr v Sayer [1992] STC 396, 65 TC 15 .... 9:12, 9:29, 9:30
Carreras Group Ltd v Stamp Comr [2004] UKPC 16, [2004] STC 1377 .... 3:08
Carrimore Six Wheelers Ltd v IRC [1944] 2 All ER 503, 26 TC 301, 172 LT 11, 61 TLR 64, CA 2A:69
Carson v Cheyney's Executors [1959] AC 412, [1958] 3 All ER 573, 38 TC 240, [1958] TR 349, HL 5:14
Carter v Sharon [1936] 1 All ER 720, 20 TC 229 .... 35:17
Carter v Wadman (1946) 176 LT 206, 28 TC 41, 25 ATC 420, CA 7:35
Carter (Joseph) & Sons Ltd v Baird [1999] STC 120n, 73 TC 303 .... 22:12, 22:16
Cartlidge v Customs and Excise Comrs (1992) VAT decision 7152 .... 65:28
Carver v Duncan [1985] AC 1082, [1985] 2 All ER 645, [1985] 2 WLR 1010, [1985] STC 356, 59 TC 125, HL 13:11, 13:13
Carvill v IRC [2000] STC (SCD) 143 .... 35:26
Carvill v IRC (No 2) [2002] EWHC 1488 (Ch), [2002] STC 1167 .... 35:26
Casdagli v Casdagli [1919] AC 145, [1918–19] All ER Rep 462, 120 LT 52, HL 33:15, 33:24
Cassidy v Customs and Excise Comrs (1991) VAT decision 5760 .... 69:42
Cassidy v Ministry of Health [1951] 2 KB 343, [1951] 1 All ER 574, [1951] 1 TLR 539, CA 49:03
Castle Associates Ltd v Customs and Excise Comrs (1989) VAT decision 3497 ...... 63:19, 63:23, 65:19
Castle Wines Ltd v Finance Board (1982) VAT decision 1271 .... 63:23
Castleton Management Services Ltd v Kirkwood [2001] STC (SCD) 95 .... 29:15, 31:12

2525

Table of Cases

Caton's Administrators v Couch [1995] STC (SCD) 34; on appeal sub nom Couch v Caton's Administrators [1996] STC 201, 70 TC 10; affd sub nom Caton's Administrators v Couch [1997] STC 970, 70 TC 10, CA 17:30, 45:02
Cayzer and Irvine & Co v IRC (1942) 24 TC 491 .... 8:15
Cecil v IRC (1919) 36 TLR 164 .... 8:07
Cedar plc v Inspector of Taxes [1998] STC (SCD) 78 .... 4:19, 4:22
Celtic Football and Athletic Co Ltd v Customs and Excise Comrs [1983] STC 470 .... 66:20
Cenlon Finance Co Ltd v Ellwood [1962] AC 782, [1962] 1 All ER 854, 40 TC 176, [1962] TR 1, HL 2A:74
Central and District Properties Ltd v IRC [1966] 2 All ER 433, [1966] 1 WLR 1015, [1966] TR 147, HL 57:08
Central YMCA v Customs and Excise Comrs [1994] VATTR 146 .... 68:23
Centralan Property Ltd v Customs and Excise Comrs: C-63/04 [2006] SWTI 158, [2006] 03 EG 120 (CS), [2005] All ER (D) 238 (Dec), ECJ 66:27
Centrax Ltd v Customs and Excise Comrs [1998] V & DR 369 .... 65:31, 69:07
Centros Ltd v Erhvervs-Og Selskabsstyrelsen: C-212/97 [2000] Ch 446, [2000] All ER (EC) 481, [1999] ECR I-1459, [1999] 2 CMLR 551, [2000] 2 BCLC 68, ECJ ... 1:12, 1:13
Century Life plc v Customs and Excise Comrs [2001] STC 38, CA 63:02, 68:13
Cerberus Software Ltd v Rowley [2001] EWCA Civ 78, [2001] ICR 376, [2001] IRLR 160 .... 50:13
Cesena Sulphur Co Ltd v Nicholson (1876) 1 Ex D 428, [1874–80] All ER Rep 1102, 45 LJQB 821, 1 TC 88, Ex D 33:25
Chadwick v Pearl Life Insurance Co [1905] 2 KB 507, 74 LJKB 671, 93 LT 25, 54 WR 78 .... 11:34
Chalk Springs Fisheries (a firm) v Customs and Excise Comrs (1987) VAT decision 2518 .... 68:12
Chamberlain v IRC [1943] 2 All ER 200, 25 TC 317, 22 ATC 111, HL 15:06, 15:12
Chambers (G H) (Northiam Farms) Ltd v Watmough [1956] 3 All ER 485, [1956] 1 WLR 1483, 36 TC 711, [1956] TR 247 .... 9:08
Chaney v Watkis [1986] STC 89, 58 TC 707 .... 16:19
Channel 5 TV Group Ltd v Morehead [2003] STC (SCD) 327 .... 50:04
Chantrey Vellacott v Customs and Excise Comrs [1992] VATTR 138 .... 63:30
Chapman & Frearson Ltd v Customs and Excise Comrs (1989) VAT decision 4428 .... 69:13
Chapman (A W) Ltd v Hennessey [1982] STC 214, 55 TC 516 .... 28:06
Charge Card Services Ltd, Re [1989] Ch 497, [1988] 3 All ER 702, [1988] 3 WLR 764, [1988] BCLC 711n, CA 50:07
Charles v Staatssecretaris van Financien: C-434/03 [2005] SWTI 1258, [2005] All ER (D) 200 (Jul), ECJ 66:05
Charles-Greed v Customs and Excise Comrs (1992) VAT decision 7790 .... 66:04
Chartcliffe Ltd v Customs and Excise Comrs [1976] VATTR 165 .... 65:32
Charter Reinsurance Co Ltd v Fagan [1997] AC 313, [1996] 3 All ER 46, [1996] 2 WLR 726, [1996] 2 Lloyd's Rep 113, HL 3:05
Chartered Accountant v Inspector of Taxes [2003] STC (SCD) 166 .... 2A:19
Chartered Institute of Bankers v Customs and Excise Comrs (1998) VAT decision 15648 .... 2A:43
Chaussures Bally SA v Ministry of Finance (Belgium): C-18/92 [1993] ECR I-2871, [1997] STC 209, ECJ 63:23
Cheatle v IRC [1982] 1 WLR 834, [1982] STC 376, 56 TC 111 .... 61:11
Cheney v Conn [1968] 1 All ER 779, [1968] 1 WLR 242, 44 TC 217, [1967] TR 177 .... 1:01
Chesterfield Brewery Co v IRC [1899] 2 QB 7, 68 LJQB 204, 79 LT 559, 47 WR 320 .... 57:18, 58:10
Chetwode (Lord) v IRC [1977] 1 All ER 638, [1977] 1 WLR 248, [1977] STC 64, 51 TC 647, HL 35:32, 35:37
Chevron Petroleum (UK) Ltd v BP Petroleum Development Ltd [1981] STC 689, 57 TC 137 .... 11:05
Chibbett v Robinson (1924) 132 LT 26, 9 TC 48, 3 ATC 521 .... 7:30
Chicago (City) Board of Trade v Customs and Excise Comrs (1992) VAT decision 9114 .... 66:20

Table of Cases

Chicago Railway Terminal Elevator Co v IRC (1891) 75 LT 157 .... 59:08
Chick v Stamp Duties Comr [1958] AC 435, [1958] 2 All ER 623, [1958] 3 WLR 93, 37 ATC 250 .... 41:03, 41:04, 41:05
Chilcott v IRC [1982] STC 1, 55 TC 446 .... 23:37
China Navigation Co Ltd v A-G [1932] 2 KB 197, [1932] All ER Rep 626, 101 LJKB 478, 147 LT 22, CA 1:01
Chinn v Collins [1981] 1 All ER 189, [1981] STC 1, 54 TC 311, [1980] TR 467, HL 15:02, 15:05, 15:08, 20:16
Cholmondeley v IRC [1986] STC 384 .... 42:58
Christensen v Vasili. See Vasili v Christensen
Christie v IRC (1866) LR 2 Exch 46, 4 H & C 664, 36 LJ Ex 11, 15 LT 282 .... 57:07
Christoph-Dornier-Stiftung fur Klinische Psychologie v Finanzamt Giessen: C-45/01 [2003] ECR I-12911, [2004] 1 CMLR 991, [2005] STC 228, ECJ 68:23
Church of England Children's Society v Revenue and Customs Comrs [2005] EWHC 1692 (Ch), [2005] STC 1644, (2005) Times, 21 September, [2005] All ER (D) 481 (Jul) 65:28, 66:05
Cibo Participations SA v Directeur régional des impôts du Nord-Pas-de-Calais: C-16/00 [2001] ECR I-6663, [2002] 1 CMLR 688, [2002] STC 460, ECJ 63:17
Ciola v Land Vorarlberg: C-224/97 [1999] ECR I-2517, [1999] 2 CMLR 1220, ECJ 1:06
Cirdan Sailing Trust v Customs and Excise Comrs [2005] EWHC 2999 (Ch), [2006] STC 185 .... 69:27
City of London Contract Corpn Ltd v Styles (1887) 2 TC 239 .... 8:49
City Permanent Building Society v Miller [1952] Ch 840, [1952] 2 All ER 621, [1952] 2 TLR 547, CA 10:19, 42:10
City Research Associates Ltd v Customs and Excise Comrs [1984] VATTR 189 .... 69:15
Civil Engineer v IRC [2002] STC (SCD) 72 .... 33:23
Claimants under Loss Relief Group Litigation Order, Re. See Loss Relief Group Litigation, Re
Clark v Customs and Excise Comrs [1996] STC 263 .... 63:20
Clark v Green [1995] STC (SCD) 99 .... 45:02
Clark v IRC [1979] 1 All ER 385, [1978] STC 614, 52 TC 482, [1978] TR 335 .... 4:28
Clark v Oceanic Contractors Inc [1983] 2 AC 130, [1983] 1 All ER 133, [1983] STC 35, 56 TC 183, HL 7:148, 33:34
Clark and another (exors of Clark dec'd) v Revenue and Customs Comrs [2005] STC (SCD) 823 .... 44:04
Clarke, Re (1906) 40 ILTR 117 .... 22:44
Clarke v British Telecom Pension Scheme Trustees. See British Telecom Pension Scheme Trustees v Clarke
Clarke (a firm) v Customs and Excise Comrs (1997) VAT decision 15201 .... 68:19
Clarke v United Real (Moorgate) Ltd [1988] STC 273, 61 TC 353 .... 10:17, 23:23
Clarke Chapman-John Thompson Ltd v IRC [1976] Ch 91, [1975] 3 All ER 701, [1976] 2 WLR 1, [1975] STC 567, CA 60:04
Classicmoor Ltd v Customs and Excise Comrs [1995] V & DR 1 .... 2A:67
Clayton v Lavender (1965) 42 TC 607, [1965] TR 461, 44 ATC 477 .... 7:08, 7:33
Cleary (a firm) v Customs and Excise Comrs (1992) VAT decision 7305 .... 68:23
Cleary v IRC [1968] AC 766, [1967] 2 All ER 48, 44 TC 399, [1967] TR 57, HL 1:25, 4:19, 4:26
Clements v Revenue & Customs Comrs (2008) SpC 677 .... 53:15
Cleveleys Investment Trust Co v IRC 1971 SC 233, 47 TC 300, [1971] TR 205, 50 ATC 230 .... 16:22, 17:10, 21:19
Cleveleys Investment Trust Co v IRC [1975] STC 457, 51 TC 26, [1975] TR 209 .... 17:01
Clibbery v Allan [2002] EWCA Civ 45, [2002] Fam 261, [2002] 1 All ER 865, [2002] 2 WLR 1511, [2002] 1 FCR 385, [2002] 1 FLR 565 .... 2:17
Clifford v IRC [1896] 2 QB 187, 65 LJQB 582, 74 LT 699, 45 WR 14, 14 TC 189 .... 56:18
Clinch v IRC [1974] QB 76, [1973] 1 All ER 977, [1973] STC 155, 49 TC 52 ...... 35:35
Clixby v Pountney [1968] Ch 719, [1968] 1 All ER 802, 44 TC 515, [1967] TR 383 .... 2:27
Clore (No 3), Re, IRC v Stype Trustees (Jersey) Ltd [1985] 2 All ER 819, [1985] 1 WLR 1290, [1985] STC 394 .... 2A:09

Table of Cases

Clore's Settlement Trusts, Re, Sainer v Clore [1966] 2 All ER 272, [1966] 1 WLR 955 .... 35:63
Clovelly Estate Co Ltd v Customs and Excise Comrs [1991] VATTR 351 .... 66:07
Coalite and Chemical Products Ltd v Treeby (1971) 48 TC 171, [1971] TR 425 ...... 8:76
Coates v Arndale Properties Ltd [1984] 1 WLR 537, [1984] STC 124, 59 TC 516, CA; revsd [1985] 1 All ER 15, [1984] 1 WLR 1328, [1984] STC 637, 59 TC 516, HL 4:08, 22:06, 28:27
Coats (J & P) Ltd v IRC [1897] 2 QB 423, [1895–9] All ER Rep 744, 66 LJQB 423, 77 LT 270, CA 57:07, 59:04
Cobojo Ltd v Customs and Excise Comrs (1989) VAT decision 4055 .... 65:19
Cohan's Executors v IRC (1924) 12 TC 602, 131 LT 377, CA 8:28
Cohen v Customs and Excise Comrs [1994] VATTR 290 .... 64:14
Cohen & Moore v IRC [1933] 2 KB 126, [1933] All ER Rep 950, 102 LJKB 696, 149 LT 252, 26 TC 471 .... 56:09, 58:06
Colaingrove Ltd v Customs and Excise Comrs [2000] V & DR 82 .... 68:12
Cole Bros Ltd v Phillips [1981] STC 671, 55 TC 188, CA; affd [1982] 2 All ER 247, [1982] STC 307, 55 TC 188, HL 9:29, 9:30
Coleman v Customs and Excise Comrs [1976] VATTR 24 .... 63:16
Colette Ltd v Customs and Excise Comrs [1992] VATTR 240 .... 67:09
Collard's Will Trusts, Re, Lloyds Bank Ltd v Rees [1961] Ch 293, [1961] 1 All ER 821, [1961] TR 325 .... 35:63
Collector of Stamp Revenue v Arrowtown Assets Ltd [2003] FACV No 4 of 2003, HK CA 3:09, 3:19, 3:21, 56:10
College of Estate Management v Customs and Excise Comrs [2005] UKHL 62, [2005] STC 1597 .... 63:20
Collins v Addies [1991] STC 445, 65 TC 190; affd [1992] STC 746, 65 TC 190, CA 29:12
Collins v Joseph Adamson & Co [1938] 1 KB 477, [1937] 4 All ER 236, 21 TC 400, 16 ATC 355 .... 8:129
Collins (Edward) & Sons Ltd v IRC 1925 SC 151, 12 TC 773, 4 ATC 179 .. 8:147, 8:149, 8:160
Collis v Hore (Inspector of Taxes) (1949) 31 TC 173, 28 ATC 8, 42 R & IT 187, [1949] TR 67, L(TC) 1480 .... 7:129
Coloroll Pension Trustees Ltd v Russell: C-200/91 [1995] All ER (EC) 23, [1994] ECR I-4389, [1995] ICR 179, [1994] IRLR 586, ECJ 32:29
Colquhoun v Brooks (1889) 14 App Cas 493, [1886–90] All ER Rep 1063, 2 TC 490, HL 1:27, 11:39, 12:12, 35:02
Coltness Iron Co v Black (1881) 6 App Cas 315, 51 LJQB 626, 1 TC 311, HL 9:01
Columbus Container Services BVBA & Co v Finanzamt Bielefeld-Innenstadt: C-298/05 [2007] ECR I-10451, [2009] 1 CMLR 241, [2008] STC 2554, [2007] SWTI 2846, [2007] All ER (D) 80 (Dec) 1:12
Coman v Governors of the Rotunda Hospital Dublin [1921] 1 AC 1, 89 LJPC 162, 123 LT 529, 7 TC 517, HL 10:07, 12:11, 13:23
Commercial Union Assurance Co plc v Shaw [1998] STC 386, 72 TC 101; affd [1999] STC 109, 72 TC 101, CA 8:98, 37:19
Commission v Germany: C-427/98, [2002] ECR I–5311, [2003] STC 301 .... 63:20
Commissioner of Inland Revenue v Challenge Corpn Ltd [1987] AC 155, [1987] 2 WLR 24, [1986] STC 548 .... 3:11, 39:35
Commissioner of Inland Revenue v Hang Seng Bank Ltd [1991] AC 306, [1990] 3 WLR 1120, [1990] STC 733 .... 35:02
Commissioner of Inland Revenue v New Zealand Forest Research Institute Ltd [2000] 1 WLR 1755, [2000] STC 522, 72 TC 628 .... 8:113
Commissioner of Inland Revenue v Secan Ltd (2000) 74 TC 1, HK CA 8:67
Community Housing Association Ltd v Customs and Excise Comrs [2009] EWHC 455 (Ch), [2009] STC 1324 .... 66:28
Compagnie de Saint-Gobain v Finanzamt Aachen-Innenstadt: C-307/97 [2000] STC 854, [1999] ECR I-6161, [2001] 3 CMLR 708, ECJ 1:07, 1:10, 25:45
Company A v R & C Comrs (2007) SpC 602 .... 7:57
Compass Contract Services UK Ltd v Revenue & Customs Comrs [2006] EWCA Civ 730, [2006] STC 1999, [2006] SWTI 1622, [2006] All ER (D) 74 (Jun) 69:13

Table of Cases

Compassion in World Farming Ltd v Customs and Excise Comrs [1997] V & DR 281 .... 63:16
Comune di Carpaneto Piacentino v Ufficio Provinciale Imposta sul Valore Aggiunto di Piacenza: C-4/89 [1990] 3 CMLR 153, ECJ 63:17
Condé Nast Publications Ltd v Revenue and Customs Comrs [2006] EWCA Civ 976, [2006] STC 1721, [2006] All ER (D) 130 (Jul) 66:22
Congreve v IRC [1946] 2 All ER 170, 30 TC 163, 25 ATC 171; revsd [1947] 1 All ER 168, 30 TC 163, 25 ATC 328, CA; on appeal [1948] 1 All ER 948, [1948] LJR 1229, 30 TC 163, 27 ATC 102, HL 35:26, 35:31, 35:32, 35:36
Conn v Robins Bros Ltd (1966) 43 TC 266, [1966] TR 61, 45 ATC 59 ...... 8:122, 8:123
Conn (Mervyn) Organisation Ltd v Customs and Excise Comrs (1990) VAT decision 5205 .... 2A:67
Connell Estate Agents (a firm) v Begej [1993] 2 EGLR 35, [1993] 39 EG 123, CA 57:20
Connelly (C) & Co v Wilbey [1992] STC 783, 65 TC 208 .... 8:51
Connor v Connor [1974] 1 NZLR 632 .... 34:02
Conservative and Unionist Central Office v Burrell [1982] 2 All ER 1, [1982] 1 WLR 522, [1982] STC 317, 55 TC 671, CA 25:03
Consolidated Goldfields plc v IRC [1990] 2 All ER 398, [1990] STC 357 .... 2:20
Constable v Federal Taxation Comr (1952) 86 CLR 402 .... 7:23
Consultant Psychiatrist v Revenue and Customs Comrs [2006] STC (SCD) 653 ...... 7:137
Continuum (Europe) Ltd v Customs and Excise Comrs [1998] V & DR 70 .... 68:16
Cook v Billings [2001] STC 16, CA 31:11
Cook (Watkins' Executors) v IRC [2002] STC (SCD) 318 .... 40:21
Cook v Knott (1887) 4 TLR 164, 2 TC 246 .... 7:125
Cook (Thomas) (New Zealand) Ltd v IRC [2004] UKPC 53, [2005] STC 297 .... 8:143
Cooke v Beach Station Caravans Ltd [1974] 3 All ER 159, [1974] STC 402, 49 TC 514, [1974] TR 213 .... 9:30
Cooke v Blacklaws [1985] STC 1, 58 TC 255 .... 7:08
Cooke v Haddock (1960) 39 TC 64, [1960] TR 133, 39 ATC 244 .... 8:25
Cooke v Quick Shoe Repair Service (1949) 30 TC 460, [1949] TR 87, 28 ATC 24 .... 8:116
Cooksey and Bibbey v Rednall (1949) 30 TC 514, [1949] TR 81, 28 ATC 41 .... 8:22
Cooper v Billingham [1999] STC (SCD) 176; on appeal sub nom Billingham v Cooper [2000] STC 122, 74 TC 139; affd [2001] EWCA Civ 1041, [2001] STC 1177, 74 TC 139 .... 35:56
Cooper v C & J Clark Ltd [1982] STC 335, 54 TC 670 .... 8:79, 28:01
Cooper v Cadwalader (1904) 7 F (Ct of Sess) 146, 42 Sc LR 117, 5 TC 101 .... 33:03
Cooper v Flynn (1841) 3 ILR 472 .... 56:15
Cooper v Stubbs [1925] 2 KB 753, [1925] All ER Rep 643, 10 TC 29, 4 ATC 373, CA 12:05
Cooper & Chapman (Builders) Ltd v Customs and Excise Comrs [1991] VATTR 135; affd [1993] STC 1 .... 66:26
Cooper Chasney Ltd v Customs and Excise Comrs [1990] 3 CMLR 509 .... 63:26
Co-operative Insurance Society Ltd v Customs and Excise Comrs [1991] 3 CMLR 10, [1992] VATTR 44 .... 63:27
Co-operative Insurance Society Ltd v Customs and Excise Comrs [1997] V & DR 65 .... 65:17
Co-operative Wholesale Society Ltd v Customs and Excise Comrs [1999] STC 1096; affd [2000] STC 727, CA 68:13, 68:24
Copeman v Coleman [1939] 2 KB 484, [1939] 3 All ER 224, 108 LJKB 813, 22 TC 594, 18 ATC 109 .... 15:02
Copeman v William J Flood & Sons Ltd [1941] 1 KB 202, 110 LJKB 215, 24 TC 53, 19 ATC 521 .... 8:98
Copol Clothing Co Ltd v Hindmarch [1982] STC 421, 57 TC 575, 126 Sol Jo 313; affd [1984] 1 WLR 411, [1984] STC 33, 57 TC 575, CA 9:12
Corbally-Stourton v HMRC (2008) SpC 692 .... 2A:62
Corbett v Duff [1941] 1 KB 730, [1941] 1 All ER 512, 23 TC 763, 20 ATC 51 . 7:25, 7:26
Corbett v IRC [1938] 1 KB 567, [1937] 4 All ER 700, 21 TC 449, 16 ATC 389, CA 13:03, 14:03

2529

Table of Cases

Corbett's Executrices v IRC [1943] 2 All ER 218, 169 LT 166, 25 TC 305, 22 ATC 160, CA 35:32
Cordova Union Gold Co, Re [1891] 2 Ch 580, 60 LJ Ch 701, 39 WR 536, 64 LT 772 .... 29:11
Cordy v Barry (Inspector of Taxes). See Barry (Inspector of Taxes) v Cordy
Coren v Keighley [1972] 1 WLR 1556, 48 TC 370, [1972] TR 75, 51 ATC 88 ...... 16:07, 16:13
Corinthian Securities Ltd v Cato [1970] 1 QB 377, [1969] 3 All ER 1168, 46 TC 93, [1969] TR 401, CA 11:12
Cormack (Inspector of Taxes) v CBL Cable Contractors Ltd [2005] EWHC 1294 (Ch), [2006] STC 38, 77 TC 239, [2005] SWTI 1170, [2005] All ER (D) 258 (Jun) 2A:19
Cory (Wm) & Son Ltd v IRC [1964] 3 All ER 66, [1964] 1 WLR 1332, [1964] 2 Lloyd's Rep 43, 43 ATC 215, [1964] TR 231, 108 Sol Jo 579, CA; revsd [1965] AC 1088, [1965] 1 All ER 917, [1965] 2 WLR 924, [1965] TR 77 . 56:11, 57:04, 57:07, 57:18
Costain (Richard) Ltd v Customs and Excise Comrs [1988] VATTR 111 .... 67:03
Cottage Holiday Associates Ltd v Customs and Excise Comrs [1983] QB 735, [1983] 2 WLR 861, [1983] STC 278 .... 63:25, 69:17, 69:22
Cottingham's Executors v IRC [1938] 2 KB 689, [1938] 3 All ER 560, 22 TC 344, 17 ATC 293 .... 35:29
Cottle v Coldicott [1995] STC (SCD) 239 .... 18:14
Couch v Caton's Administrators. See Caton's Administrators v Couch
Countess Warwick Steamship Co Ltd v Ogg [1924] 2 KB 292, 93 LJKB 736, 131 LT 348, 8 TC 652 .... 8:118
Country Pharmacy Ltd v Revenue and Customs Comrs [2005] STC (SCD) 729 ...... 7:115
County Telecommunications Systems Ltd v Customs and Excise Comrs (1993) VAT decision 10224 .... 65:32
Courage Ltd v Customs and Excise Comrs (1992) VAT decision 8808 .... 63:21
Courtaulds Investments Ltd v Fleming [1969] 3 All ER 1281, [1969] 1 WLR 1683, 46 TC 111, [1969] TR 345 .... 35:10
Courts plc v Customs and Excise Comrs [2003] EWHC 2541 (Ch), [2004] STC 690 .... 2A:67
Coventry City Council v IRC [1979] Ch 142, [1978] 1 All ER 1107, [1978] 2 WLR 857, [1977] TR 267 .... 56:18, 57:28
Cowan v Seymour [1920] 1 KB 500, 89 LJKB 459, 7 TC 372, CA 7:20, 7:24
Cowcher v Richard Mills & Co Ltd (1927) 13 TC 216, 6 ATC 996 .... 8:119
Crabb v Blue Star Line Ltd [1961] 2 All ER 424, [1961] 1 WLR 1322, 39 TC 482, [1961] TR 69 .... 8:81
Crabtree v Hinchcliffe [1972] AC 707, [1971] 3 All ER 967, 47 TC 419, [1971] TR 321, HL 17:26
Craddock v Zevo Finance Co Ltd [1944] 1 All ER 566, 27 TC 267, CA; affd [1946] 1 All ER 523, 174 LT 385, 27 TC 267, 25 ATC 58, HL 8:151, 8:157, 8:164
Craignish, Re, Craignish v Hewitt [1892] 3 Ch 180, 67 LT 689, 8 TLR 451, CA 33:24
Cramer v Cramer [1987] 1 FLR 116, [1986] Fam Law 333, CA 33:23
Crane Fruehauf Ltd v IRC [1975] 1 All ER 429, [1975] STC 51, [1974] TR 389, 53 ATC 403, CA 56:11, 62:18
Craven v White [1985] 3 All ER 125, [1985] 1 WLR 1024, [1985] STC 531; on appeal [1989] AC 398, [1987] 3 All ER 27, [1987] 3 WLR 660, [1987] STC 297, CA; affd [1989] AC 398, [1988] 3 All ER 495, [1988] 3 WLR 423, [1988] STC 476, HL 3:17, 3:18, 4:01, 37:36, 39:39
Craven's Mortgage, Re, Davies v Craven [1907] 2 Ch 448, 76 LJ Ch 651, 97 LT 475 .... 11:12
Creditgrade Ltd v Customs and Excise Comrs [1991] VATTR 87 .... 63:25
Creed v H and M Levinson Ltd [1981] STC 486, 54 TC 477, [1981] TR 77 .... 8:87
Criminal proceedings against Goodwin. See R v Goodwin
Cripwell (Peter) & Associates v Customs and Excise Comrs (1978) VAT decision 660, 102 Taxation 250 .... 63:23
Crole v Lloyd (1950) 31 TC 338, [1951] TR 105, 30 ATC 65 .... 2:28
Cronin (t/a Cronin Driving School) v Customs and Excise Comrs [1991] STC 333 .... 8:21, 63:20
Cronsvale Ltd v Customs and Excise Comrs [1983] VATTR 313 .... 69:15
Crookston Bros v Furtado (1910) 5 TC 602 .... 36:06

Case	Reference
Crosby (Trustees) v Broadhurst [2004] STC (SCD) 348	17:07
Crossland v Hawkins [1961] Ch 537, [1961] 2 All ER 812, 39 TC 493, 40 ATC 126, CA	4:30, 15:07, 15:31
Crowe v Appleby [1975] 3 All ER 529, [1975] 1 WLR 1539, [1975] STC 502, 51 TC 451; affd [1976] 2 All ER 914, [1976] 1 WLR 885, [1976] STC 301, 51 TC 451, CA	20:05, 20:06, 20:16
Crown Bedding Co Ltd v IRC [1946] 1 All ER 452, 34 TC 107, CA	4:05
Croydon Hotel and Leisure Co Ltd v Bowen [1996] STC (SCD) 466	8:110
Crusabridge Investments Ltd v Casings International Ltd (1979) 54 TC 246, [1980] LS Gaz R 596	9:12
Culverpalm Ltd v Customs and Excise Comrs [1984] VATTR 199	63:30; 65:38
Cumbernauld Development Corpn v Customs and Excise Comrs [2002] STC 226, 2002 SLT 146	65:11
Cunard's Trustees v IRC [1946] 1 All ER 159, 174 LT 133, 27 TC 122, 24 ATC 317, CA	11:23, 13:21
Cunliffe v Goodman [1950] 2 KB 237, [1950] 1 All ER 720, 66 (pt 2) TLR 109, CA	39:14
Curnock v IRC [2003] STC (SCD) 283	39:01
Currie v IRC [1921] 2 KB 332, 90 LJKB 499, 12 TC 245, CA	8:07
Curtis-Brown Ltd v Jarvis (1929) 14 TC 744	12:12, 12:13
Curzon Offices Ltd v IRC [1944] 1 All ER 163	60:04
Customs and Excise Comrs v Ali Baba Tex Ltd [1992] 3 CMLR 725, [1992] STC 590	69:42
Customs and Excise Comrs v Annabel's Casino Ltd [1995] STC 225	68:15
Customs and Excise Comrs v Apple and Pear Development Council [1985] STC 383, CA; on appeal [1986] STC 192, HL; refd sub nom Apple and Pear Development Council v Customs and Excise Comrs: 102/86 [1988] 2 All ER 922, [1988] STC 221, ECJ	63:15, 63:16, 63:17, 63:21, 66:05, 66:08
Customs and Excise Comrs v Arbib [1995] STC 490	69:23
Customs and Excise Comrs v Arnold [1996] STC 1271	2:16, 63:04, 66:40
Customs and Excise Comrs v Automobile Association [1974] 1 All ER 1257, [1974] 1 WLR 1447, [1974] STC 192, [1974] TR 165	63:19, 65:16
Customs and Excise Comrs v BAA plc [2002] EWHC 196 (Ch), [2002] STC 327; affd [2002] EWCA Civ 1814, [2003] STC 35, [2003] 1 CMLR 703	68:16
Customs and Excise Comrs v BRS Automotive Ltd [1997] STC 336; on appeal [1998] STC 1210, CA	66:17, 66:18
Customs and Excise Comrs v Barclays Bank plc [2000] STC 665; revsd [2001] EWCA Civ 1513, [2002] 1 CMLR 73, [2001] STC 1558	64:25
Customs and Excise Comrs v Battersea Leisure Ltd [1992] STC 213	63:26
Customs and Excise Comrs v Blackpool Pleasure Beach Co [1974] 1 All ER 1011, [1974] 1 WLR 540, [1974] STC 138, [1974] TR 157	69:27
Customs and Excise Comrs v Blom-Cooper [2002] EWHC 1421 (Ch), [2002] STC 1061; revsd [2003] EWCA Civ 493, [2003] STC 669	66:40
Customs and Excise Comrs v Briararch Ltd. See Briararch Ltd v Customs and Excise Comrs	
Customs and Excise Comrs v British Field Sports Society [1997] STC 746; affd [1998] 2 All ER 1003, [1998] 1 WLR 962, [1998] STC 315, CA	63:16
Customs and Excise Comrs v British Telecom plc [1995] STC 239; affd [1996] 1 WLR 1309, [1996] STC 818, CA	65:12, 65:14
Customs and Excise Comrs v British Telecommunications plc [1997] STC 475; revsd [1998] STC 544, CA; on appeal [1999] 3 All ER 961, [1999] 1 WLR 1376, [1999] STC 758, HL	63:20, 65:17, 66:18
Customs and Excise Comrs v Bugeja [2000] STC 1; revsd [2001] EWCA Civ 1542, [2001] STC 1568	65:17
Customs and Excise Comrs v C H Beazer (Holdings) plc. See Beazer (C H) (Holdings) plc v Customs and Excise Comrs	
Customs and Excise Comrs v CSC Financial Services Ltd: C-235/00 [2002] All ER (EC) 289, [2002] 1 CMLR 715, sub nom CSC Financial Services Ltd v Customs and Excise Comrs [2002] 1 WLR 2200, [2002] STC 57, ECJ	68:16
Customs and Excise Comrs v Cantor Fitzgerald International. See Cantor Fitzgerald International v Customs and Excise Comrs	

Table of Cases

Customs and Excise Comrs v Chinese Channel (Hong Kong) Ltd [1998] STC 347 .... 63:02, 63:29
Customs and Excise Comrs v Church Schools Foundation Ltd [2000] STC 651; revsd [2001] EWCA Civ 1745, [2001] STC 1661 .... 63:21
Customs and Excise Comrs v Civil Service Motoring Association Ltd [1998] STC 111, CA 68:16
Customs and Excise Comrs v Colour Offset Ltd [1995] STC 85 .... 69:15
Customs and Excise Comrs v Cope [1981] STC 532, [1982] TR 273 .... 69:13
Customs and Excise Comrs v Croydon Hotel and Leisure Co Ltd [1996] STC 1105, CA 2A:67
Customs and Excise Comrs v DFDS A/S: C-260/95 [1997] All ER (EC) 342, [1997] 1 WLR 1037, [1997] STC 384, ECJ 63:29, 65:25
Customs and Excise Comrs v DFS Furniture Co plc [2003] EWHC 857 (Ch), [2003] STC 739; revsd [2004] EWCA Civ 243, [2004] 1 WLR 2159, [2004] STC 559 ...... 2A:43
Customs and Excise Comrs v David Lewis Centre [1995] STC 485 .... 69:41
Customs and Excise Comrs v Dearwood Ltd [1986] STC 327 .... 63:27
Customs and Excise Comrs v Deutsche Ruck UK Reinsurance Co Ltd [1995] STC 495 .... 66:07
Customs and Excise Comrs v Diners Club Ltd [1988] 2 All ER 1016, [1988] STC 416; affd [1989] 2 All ER 385, [1989] 1 WLR 1196, [1989] STC 407, CA 63:26, 68:16
Customs and Excise Comrs v Elm Milk Ltd [2006] EWCA Civ 164, [2006] STC 792, CA 66:18
Customs and Excise Comrs v Emap MacLaren Ltd [1997] STC 490 .... 63:21
Customs and Excise Comrs v Evans (t/a The Grape Escape Wine Bar) [1982] STC 342 .... 63:12
Customs and Excise Comrs v FDR Ltd [2000] STC 672, CA 68:16
Customs and Excise Comrs v Faith Construction Ltd [1989] QB 179, [1988] 1 All ER 919, [1988] 3 WLR 500, [1988] STC 35; affd [1990] 1 QB 905, [1989] 2 All ER 938, [1989] 3 WLR 678, [1989] STC 539, CA 65:12
Customs and Excise Comrs v Federation of Technological Industries: C-384/04 [2006] ECR I-4191, [2006] 3 CMLR 337, [2006] STC 1483, (2006) Times, 29 May, [2006] SWTI 1514, [2006] All ER (D) 159 (May), ECJ 67:09, 67:10
Customs and Excise Comrs v Fine Art Developments plc [1988] QB 895, [1988] 2 All ER 70, [1988] 2 WLR 795, [1988] STC 178, CA; revsd [1989] AC 914 [1989] 1 All ER 502, [1989] 2 WLR 369, [1989] STC 85, HL 67:05
Customs and Excise Comrs v First Choice Holidays plc [2004] EWCA Civ 1044, [2004] 3 CMLR 1002, [2004] STC 1407 .... 65:25
Customs and Excise Comrs v General Motors Acceptance Corpn (UK) plc [2004] EWHC 192 (Ch), [2004] STC 577 .... 65:19
Customs and Excise Comrs v Glassborow [1975] QB 465, [1974] 1 All ER 1041, [1974] STC 142, [1974] TR 161 .... 63:12
Customs and Excise Comrs v Granton Marketing Ltd [1996] STC 1049. CA 63:20
Customs and Excise Comrs v Han. See Han v Customs and Excise Comrs
Customs and Excise Comrs v Harpcombe Ltd [1996] STC 726 .... 66:07
Customs and Excise Comrs v Harris [1989] STC 907 .... 64:14
Customs and Excise Comrs v Help the Aged [1997] STC 406, [1998] RTR 120 ... 69:41
Customs and Excise Comrs v High Street Vouchers Ltd [1990] STC 575 .... 63:26
Customs and Excise Comrs v Hodges [2000] STC 262 .... 63:17
Customs and Excise Comrs v International Language Centres Ltd [1986] STC 279 .... 67:04
Customs and Excise Comrs v Isle of Wight Council. See Isle of Wight Council v Customs and Excise Comrs
Customs and Excise Comrs v Jane Montgomery (Hair Stylists) Ltd [1994] STC 256 .... 63:20
Customs and Excise Comrs v Jeffs (t/a J & J Joinery) [1995] STC 759 ...... 63:25, 69:21
Customs and Excise Comrs v Jeynes [1984] STC 30 .... 65:32
Customs and Excise Comrs v John Willmott Housing Ltd [1987] STC 692 .... 63:20
Customs and Excise Comrs v Johnson [1980] STC 624 .... 63:20
Customs and Excise Comrs v Kilroy Television Co Ltd [1997] STC 901 .... 66:20
Customs and Excise Comrs v Kingfisher plc [1994] STC 63, [1991] VATTR 47 ... 64:26

2532

Customs and Excise Comrs v Kingscrest Associates Ltd (t/a Kingscrest Residential Care Homes) [2002] EWHC 410 (Ch), [2002] STC 490 .... 68:23
Customs and Excise Comrs v Latchmere Properties Ltd [2005] EWHC 133 (Ch), [2005] STC 731 .... 63:20
Customs and Excise Comrs v Laura Ashley Ltd [2003] EWHC 2832 (Ch), [2004] STC 635 .... 67:07
Customs and Excise Comrs v Lawson-Tancred [1988] STC 326n 69:13
Customs and Excise Comrs v Leightons Ltd [1995] STC 458 .... 65:23, 68:23
Customs and Excise Comrs v Link Housing Association Ltd. See Link Housing Association Ltd v Customs and Excise Comrs
Customs and Excise Comrs v Littlewoods Organisation plc [2000] STC 588; revsd [2001] EWCA Civ 1542, [2001] STC 1568 .... 65:17
Customs and Excise Comrs v Liverpool Institute for Performing Arts [1998] STC 274; on appeal [1999] STC 424, CA; affd [2001] UKHL 28, [2001] 1 WLR 1187, [2001] 3 CMLR 75, [2001] STC 891 .... 66:07, 66:08
Customs and Excise Comrs v Lord Fisher [1981] 2 All ER 147, [1981] STC 238 .... 63:15, 63:17
Customs and Excise Comrs v MacHenrys (Hairdressers) Ltd [1993] STC 170 .... 63:20
Customs and Excise Comrs v McLean Homes Midland Ltd [1993] STC 335 .... 69:21
Customs and Excise Comrs v McMaster Stores (Scotland) Ltd (in receivership) [1995] STC 846 .... 65:19
Customs and Excise Comrs v Madgett and Baldwin. See Madgett and Baldwin (t/a Howden Court Hotel) v Customs and Excise Comrs
Customs and Excise Comrs v Medway Draughting and Technical Services Ltd [1989] STC 346 .... 67:08
Customs and Excise Comrs v Midland Bank plc: C-98/98 [2000] All ER (EC) 673, [2000] ECR I-4177, [2000] 3 CMLR 301, sub nom Midland Bank plc v Customs and Excise Comrs [2000] 1 WLR 2080, [2000] STC 501, ECJ 66:08
Customs and Excise Comrs v Mirror Group plc. See Mirror Group plc v Customs and Excise Comrs
Customs and Excise Comrs v Moonrakers Guest House Ltd [1992] STC 544 .... 65:12
Customs and Excise Comrs v Morrish [1998] STC 954 .... 69:23
Customs and Excise Comrs v Morrison's Academy Boarding Houses Association 1977 SLT 197, [1978] STC 1 .... 63:15, 63:16
Customs and Excise Comrs v Musashi Autoparts Europe Ltd (formerly TAP Manufacturing Ltd) [2003] STC 449; affd [2003] EWCA Civ 1738, [2004] STC 220 .... 69:07
Customs and Excise Comrs v Music and Video Exchange Ltd. See Music and Video Exchange Ltd v Customs and Excise Comrs
Customs and Excise Comrs v National Westminster Bank plc [2003] EWHC 1822 (Ch), [2003] STC 1072 .... 2:16
Customs and Excise Comrs v Oliver [1980] 1 All ER 353, [1980] STC 73, [1980] TR 423 .... 63:19, 63:25
Customs and Excise Comrs v Padglade Ltd [1995] STC 602 .... 63:27
Customs and Excise Comrs v Paget [1989] STC 733 .... 63:20
Customs and Excise Comrs v Palco Industry Co Ltd [1990] STC 594 .... 67:08
Customs and Excise Comrs v Parkinson. See Parkinson v Customs and Excise Comrs
Customs and Excise Comrs v Pegasus Birds Ltd [2003] EWHC 2552 (Ch), [2004] STC 262; on appeal [2004] EWCA Civ 1015, [2004] STC 1509 .... 2A:67
Customs and Excise Comrs v Peninsular and Oriental Steam Navigation Co [1994] STC 259. See P and O Ferries v Customs and Excise Comrs
Customs and Excise Comrs v Peninsular and Oriental Steam Navigation Co [1996] STC 698 .... 69:27
Customs and Excise Comrs v Pennystar Ltd [1996] STC 163 .... 66:03
Customs and Excise Comrs v Ping (Europe) Ltd [2001] STC 1144; affd [2002] EWCA Civ 1115, [2002] STC 1186 .... 65:17
Customs and Excise Comrs v Pippa-Dee Parties Ltd [1981] STC 495, [1982] TR 243 .... 63:21
Customs and Excise Comrs v Plantiflor Ltd [1999] STC 51; on appeal [2000] STC 137, CA; revsd [2002] UKHL 33, [2002] 1 WLR 2287, [2002] STC 1132 .... 63:21, 65:17
Customs and Excise Comrs v Polok [2002] EWHC 156 (Ch), [2002] STC 361 .... 63:19

Table of Cases

Customs and Excise Comrs v Primback Ltd: C-34/99 [2001] All ER (EC) 714, [2001] ECR I-3833, [2001] 2 CMLR 1032, [2001] STC 803, sub nom Primback Ltd v Customs and Excise Comrs [2001] 1 WLR 1693, ECJ 63:20, 63:23
Customs and Excise Comrs v Professional Footballers Association (Enterprises) Ltd. See Professional Footballers Association (Enterprises) Ltd v Customs and Excise Comrs
Customs and Excise Comrs v Redrow Group Ltd [1996] STC 365; revsd [1997] STC 1053, CA; on appeal [1999] 2 All ER 1, [1999] 1 WLR 408, HL, [1999] STC 161, HL 63:19, 66:03, 66:05
Customs and Excise Comrs v Reed Personnel Services Ltd [1995] STC 588 ... 63:19, 63:20
Customs and Excise Comrs v Richmond Theatre Management Ltd [1995] STC 257 .... 65:12
Customs and Excise Comrs v Robertson's Electrical Ltd [2005] CSIH 75, [2007] STC 612 .... 65:11
Customs and Excise Comrs v Rosner [1994] STC 228 .... 66:05
Customs and Excise Comrs v Safeway Stores plc [1997] STC 163 .... 69:13
Customs and Excise Comrs v Sai Jewellers [1996] STC 269 .... 63:19
Customs and Excise Comrs v St Mary's Roman Catholic High School [1996] STC 1091 .... 69:18
Customs and Excise Comrs v St Paul's Community Project Ltd [2004] EWHC 2490 (Ch), [2005] STC 95 .... 63:17
Customs and Excise Comrs v Salevon Ltd [1989] STC 907 .... 67:08
Customs and Excise Comrs v School of Finance and Management (London) Ltd [2001] STC 1690 .... 68:17
Customs and Excise Comrs v Scott [1978] STC 191 .... 63:19
Customs and Excise Comrs v Shaklee International [1981] STC 776, CA 66:20
Customs and Excise Comrs v Shingleton [1988] STC 190 .... 64:14
Customs and Excise Comrs v Sinclair Collis Ltd [1998] STC 841; affd [1999] STC 701, CA; revsd [2001] UKHL 30, [2001] 3 CMLR 86, [2001] STC 989 .... 68:11
Customs and Excise Comrs v Skellett (t/a Vidcom Computer Services) [2004] STC 201 .... 66:18
Customs and Excise Comrs v Sooner Foods Ltd [1983] STC 376 .... 63:25
Customs and Excise Comrs v Steptoe [1991] STC 302; affd [1992] STC 757, CA 67:08
Customs and Excise Comrs v Svenska International plc [1997] STC 958, CA; on appeal [1999] 2 All ER 906, [1999] 1 WLR 769, [1999] STC 406, HL 64:26, 66:26
Customs and Excise Comrs v Teknequip Ltd [1987] STC 664 .... 65:29
Customs and Excise Comrs v Telemed Ltd [1992] STC 89 .... 63:21
Customs and Excise Comrs v Thorn Materials Supply Ltd and Thorn Resources Ltd [1996] STC 1490, CA; affd [1998] 3 All ER 342, [1998] 1 WLR 1106, [1998] STC 725, HL 64:27, 65:13
Customs and Excise Comrs v Tilling Management Services Ltd [1979] STC 365, [1978] TR 287 .... 63:26
Customs and Excise Comrs v Top Ten Promotions Ltd [1969] 3 All ER 39, [1969] 1 WLR 1163, HL 1:25
Customs and Excise Comrs v Total Network SL [2007] EWCA Civ 39, [2007] 2 WLR 1156, [2007] STC 1005, (2007) Times, 6 February, [2007] SWTI 291, [2007] All ER (D) 309 (Jan), [2008] UKHL 19, [2008] STC 644, HL 1:01, 63:09
Customs and Excise Comrs v Trinity Factoring Services Ltd [1994] STC 504, 1995 SLT 1136 .... 68:12
Customs and Excise Comrs v United Biscuits (UK) Ltd (t/a Simmers) [1992] STC 325, 1992 SLT 781 .... 63:04
Customs and Excise Comrs v University of Leicester Students' Union [2001] STC 550; affd [2001] EWCA Civ 1972, [2002] STC 147 .... 68:17
Customs and Excise Comrs v Upton (t/a Fagomatic) [2001] STC 912; affd [2002] EWCA Civ 520, [2002] STC 640 .... 66:17, 66:18
Customs and Excise Comrs v Viva Gas Appliances Ltd [1984] 1 All ER 112, [1983] 1 WLR 1445, [1983] STC 819, HL 69:23
Customs and Excise Comrs v W Timms & Son (Builders) Ltd [1992] STC 374 ...... 67:06
Customs and Excise Comrs v Wellington Private Hospital Ltd. See Wellington Private Hospital Ltd v Customs and Excise Comrs
Customs and Excise Comrs v West Herts College [2001] STC 1245 .... 65:28

Customs and Excise Comrs v West Yorkshire Independent Hospital (Contract Services) Ltd. See West Yorkshire Independent Hospital (Contract Services) Ltd v Customs and Excise Comrs
Customs and Excise Comrs v Westmorland Motorway Services Ltd [1997] STC 400; affd [1998] STC 431, [1998] RTR 440, CA 65:17
Customs and Excise Comrs v Wiggett Construction Ltd [2001] STC 933 .... 66:08
Customs and Excise Comrs v Woolfold Motor Co Ltd [1983] STC 715 .... 65:12
Customs and Excise Comrs v Yarburgh Children's Trust [2002] STC 207 .... 63:16, 63:17, 69:18
Customs and Excise Comrs v Zielinski Baker & Partners Ltd [2004] UKHL 7, [2004] 2 All ER 141, [2004] 1 WLR 707, [2004] STC 456 .... 69:23
Customs and Excise Comrs v Zoological Society of London (21 June 2000, unreported), QBD; refd C-267/00: [2002] QB 1252, [2002] All ER (EC) 465, [2002] 2 CMLR 261, [2002] STC 521, ECJ 68:29
Cyganik v Agulian [2006] EWCA Civ 129, [2006] 1 FCR 406, [2006] All ER (D) 372 (Feb) 33:21

D

D v Inspecteur van de Belastingdiest/Particulieren/Ondernemingen buitenland te Heerlen: C-376/03 [2005] SWTI 1233, [2005] All ER (D) 41 (Jul), ECJ 1:07, 1:11
DCA Industries Ltd v Customs and Excise Comrs [1983] VATTR 317 .... 69:13
DPA (Market Research) Ltd v Customs and Excise Comrs (1997) VAT decision 14751 .... 66:20
DTE Financial Services Ltd v Wilson [1999] STC (SCD) 121; on appeal [1999] STC 1061, 74 TC 14; affd [2001] EWCA Civ 455, [2001] STC 777, 74 TC 14 . 3:05, 3:06, 7:47, 7:144, 7:146, 50:35
D'Abreu v IRC [1978] STC 538, 52 TC 352, [1978] TR 129 .... 15:08
D'Abrumenil and Dispute Resolution Services Ltd v Customs and Excise Comrs (1999) VAT decision 15977 .... 68:23
D'Ambrumenil v Customs and Excise Comrs: C-307/01 [2004] QB 1179, [2003] ECR I-13989, [2004] 2 CMLR 396, [2005] STC 650, ECJ 68:23
D'Arcy v Revenue and Customs Comrs [2006] SWTI 1856, SCD 4:12
Dale v De Soissons [1950] 2 All ER 460, 32 TC 118, [1950] TR 221, CA 7:33
Dale v IRC [1951] Ch 893, [1951] 2 All ER 517, 34 TC 468, [1951] TR 209; on appeal [1952] Ch 704, [1952] 2 All ER 89, 34 TC 468, [1952] TR 249, CA; revsd [1954] AC 11, [1953] 2 All ER 671, 34 TC 468, [1953] TR 269, HL 1:27, 5:22, 7:08, 11:27
Dale v Johnson Bros (1951) 32 TC 487 .... 9:12
Danfoss A/S and another v Skatteministeriet: C-371/07 [2008] ECR I-0000, [2009] STC 701, ECJ 65:32, 65:33
Danner (proceedings brought by): C-136/00 [2002] ECR I-8147, [2002] 3 CMLR 823, [2002] STC 1283, ECJ 1:06
Danubian Sugar Factories Ltd v IRC [1901] 1 KB 245, 70 LJQB 211, 84 LT 101, 65 JP 212, CA 58:02
Dass v Special Comr [2006] EWHC 2491 (Ch), [2007] STC 187, [2006] SWTI 2298, [2006] All ER (D) 152 (Oct) 8:110
Dauntgate Ltd v Customs and Excise Comrs (1994) VAT decision 11663 .... 69:42
Davenport v Chilver [1983] STC 426, 57 TC 661 .... 18:03, 18:16
Davies v Braithwaite [1931] 2 KB 628, 100 LJKB 619, 18 TC 198, 10 ATC 286 ..... 7:08, 7:10, 7:11
Davies v Customs and Excise Comrs [1975] 1 All ER 309, [1975] 1 WLR 204, [1975] STC 28, [1974] TR 317 .... 63:23
Davies v Hicks. See Hicks v Davies
Davies v Powell [1977] 1 All ER 471, [1977] 1 WLR 258, [1977] STC 32, 51 TC 492 .... 17:01, 18:03, 18:16
Davies v Premier Investment Co Ltd [1945] 2 All ER 681, 27 TC 27, 24 ATC 213 .... 11:05
Davies v Presbyterian Church of Wales [1986] 1 All ER 705, [1986] 1 WLR 323, [1986] ICR 280, [1986] IRLR 194, HL 2:20, 49:03

Table of Cases

Davies v Shell Co of China Ltd (1951) 32 TC 133, [1951] TR 121, 44 R & IT 379, 30 ATC 117, CA 8:78
Davies v Whiteways Cyder Co Ltd [1975] QB 262, [1974] 3 All ER 168, [1974] STC 411, [1974] TR 177 .... 40:15
Davies, Jenkins & Co Ltd v Davies [1968] AC 1097, [1967] 1 All ER 913, 44 TC 273, [1967] TR 65, HL 1:27
Davis Advertising Service Ltd v Customs and Excise Comrs [1973] VATTR 16 .... 64:26
Dawson v Counsell [1938] 3 All ER 5, 22 TC 149, 159 LT 176, CA 10:07
Dawson v IRC [1987] 1 WLR 716, [1987] STC 371; on appeal [1988] 3 All ER 753, [1988] 1 WLR 930, [1988] STC 684, CA; affd [1990] AC 1, [1989] 2 All ER 289, [1989] 2 WLR 858, [1989] STC 473, HL 13:08, 13:09
Dealler v Bruce (1934) 19 TC 1 .... 11:23
Dean v Prince [1953] Ch 590, [1953] 2 All ER 636; revsd [1954] Ch 409, [1954] 1 All ER 749, 47 R & IT 494, CA 45:02
Dean and Canons of the Chapel and College of St George, Windsor v Customs and Excise Comrs (1998) VAT decision 15703 .... 68:29
De Beers Consolidated Mines Ltd v Howe [1906] AC 455, 75 LJKB 858, 5 TC 198, HL 33:25
Debenhams Retail plc v Customs and Excise Comrs [2004] EWHC 1540 (Ch), [2004] STC 1132, [2004] NLJR 1106; revsd sub nom Debenhams Retail plc v Revenue and Customs Comrs [2005] EWCA Civ 892, [2005] STC 1155, ... 63:19, 63:20
Debenhams Retail plc and another v Sun Alliance and London Assurance Co Ltd [2005] EWCA Civ 868, [2006] 1 P & CR 123, [2005] STC 1443, [2005] 32 LS Gaz R 32, [2005] 30 EG 89 (CS), (2005) Times, 29 September, [2005] All ER (D) 272 (Jul) 63:23
Deddington Steamship Co Ltd v IRC [1911] 2 KB 1001, 81 LJKB 75, 105 LT 482, 18 Mans 373, CA 56:13, 56:34
Dee (John) Ltd v Customs and Excise Comrs [1995] STC 265; affd [1995] STC 941, CA 2:16, 67:09
Deeny v Gooda Walker Ltd (in voluntary liquidation) (IRC third party) [1995] STC 439; on appeal [1996] STC 39, CA; affd sub nom Deeny v Gooda Walker Ltd (in liquidation) (No 2) [1996] 1 All ER 933, [1996] 1 WLR 426, [1996] STC 299, HL 7:37, 8:81
de Groot (FWL) v Staatssecretaris van Financiën: C-385/00 [2002] ECR I-11819, ECJ 1:09
De Jong v Staatssecretaris van Financiën: C-20/91 [1992] 3 CMLR 260, [1995] STC 727, ECJ 65:28, 66:05
Delage v Nuggett Polish Co Ltd (1905) 92 LT 682, 21 TLR 454 .... 11:28
Delaney v Staples (t/a De Montfort Recruitment) [1991] 2 QB 47, [1991] 1 All ER 609, [1991] ICR 331, [1991] IRLR 112, CA; affd [1992] 1 AC 687, [1992] 1 All ER 944, [1992] 2 WLR 451, [1992] ICR 483, HL 50:11
De Lasala v De Lasala [1980] AC 546, [1979] 2 All ER 1146 .... 18:10
De Lasteyrie v Ministère de l'Economie, des Finances et de l'Industrie: C-9/02 [2004] ECR I-2409, [2004] 3 CMLR 847, [2005] STC 1722, [2004] All ER (D) 240 (Mar), [2004] SWTI 890, ECJ 1:10, 1:14
Delian Enterprises (a partnership) v Ellis [1999] STC (SCD) 103 .... 6:25, 6:26
Demibourne Ltd v HMRC (2005) SpC 486 .... 2:23
Denekamp v Pearce [1998] STC 1120, 71 TC 213 .... 2:20, 45:02
Denkavit Internationaal BV v Ministre de l'Economie, des Finances et de l'Industrie: C-170/05 [2007] STC 452, [2007] 1 CMLR 1235, [2007] SWTI 109, [2006] All ER (D) 222 (Dec), ECJ 1:17
Denman College v Customs and Excise Comrs [1998] V & DR 399 .... 69:18
Denmor Investments Ltd v Customs and Excise Comrs [1981] VATTR 66 .... 66:05
Denny v Reed (1933) 18 TC 254, 12 ATC 433 .... 7:20, 7:24
Dent v Moore (1919) 26 CLR 316 .... 56:29
Derby (Earl) v Aylmer [1915] 3 KB 374, 84 LJKB 2160, 6 TC 665 .... 9:26
Derby (Earl) v Bassom (1926) 135 LT 274, 42 TLR 380, 10 TC 357, 5 ATC 260 .... 12:11
De Rothschild v Lawrenson [1994] STC 8; affd [1995] STC 623, CA 20:02
Design Concept SA v Flanders Expo SA: C-438/01 [2003] ECR I-5617, [2003] STC 912, ECJ 63:30

Deutsche Morgan Grenfell Group plc v IRC [2006] UKHL 49, [2007] 1 AC 558, [2007] 1 All ER 449, [2006] 3 WLR 781, [2007] STC 1, [2007] 1 CMLR 429, (2006) Times, 26 October, 150 Sol Jo LB 1430, [2006] All ER (D) 298 (Oct) 1:02, 2A:70
Devai v IRC [1997] STC (SCD) 31 .... 37:30
De Vigier v IRC [1964] 2 All ER 907, [1964] 1 WLR 1073, 42 TC 24, [1964] TR 239, HL 15:24, 15:29
Devonshire Hotel (Torquay) Ltd v Customs and Excise Comrs (1996) VAT decision 14448 .... 65:25
Dewar v Dewar [1975] 2 All ER 728, [1975] 1 WLR 1532 .... 18:01
Dewar v IRC [1935] 2 KB 351, [1935] All ER Rep 568, 19 TC 561, 14 ATC 329, CA 5:15, 14:05
Diaform Ltd v Customs and Excise Comrs (1993) VAT decision 11069 .... 65:11
Diagnostiko & Therapeftiko Kentro Athinon-Ygeia AE v Ipourgos Ikonomikon: C-394/04 and C-395/04 [2005] STC 1349, [2005] All ER (D) 09 (Dec), ECJ 68:23
Dial-a-Phone Ltd v Customs and Excise Comrs [2004] EWCA Civ 603, [2004] STC 987 .... 66:07, 66:08
Diamond v Campbell-Jones [1961] Ch 22, [1960] 1 All ER 583, [1960] TR 131, 53 R & IT 502 .... 8:82
Dickinson v Abel [1969] 1 All ER 484, [1969] 1 WLR 295, 45 TC 353, [1968] TR 419 .... 12:09
Dickson v Dickson 1990 SCLR 692 .... 33:14
Dimosio v Karageorgou: C-78/02 to C-80/02 [2003] ECR I-13295, [2003] All ER (D) 87 (Nov), [2003] SWTI 1937, ECJ 63:17
Dinaro Ltd (t/a Fairway Lodge) v Customs and Excise Comrs (2001) VAT decision 17148 .... 68:12
Di Paolo v Office National de l'Emploi: 76/76 [1977] ECR 315, [1977] 2 CMLR 59, ECJ 54:15
Direct Cosmetics Ltd v Customs and Excise Comrs [1983] VATTR 194, [1984] 1 CMLR 99 .... 63:02
Direct Cosmetics Ltd v Customs and Excise Comrs: 5/84 [1985] ECR 617, [1985] STC 479, [1985] 2 CMLR 145, ECJ 63:02
Direct Cosmetics Ltd v Customs and Excise Comrs (1989) VAT decision 3764 .... 65:17
Direct Cosmetics Ltd and Laughtons Photographs Ltd v Customs and Excise Comrs: 138, 139/86 [1988] STC 540, ECJ 65:02, 65:17
Direct Link Couriers (Bristol) Ltd v Customs and Excise Comrs (1986) VAT decision 2105 .... 65:32
Ditchfield v Sharp [1982] STC 124, [1981] TR 457, 57 TC 555; affd [1983] STC 590, 57 TC 555, CA 11:15
Diversified Agency Services Ltd v Customs and Excise Comrs [1996] STC 398 .... 63:30
Dixon v Fitch's Garage Ltd [1975] 3 All ER 455, [1976] 1 WLR 215, [1975] STC 480, 50 TC 509 .... 9:30
Dixon v IRC [2002] STC (SCD) 53 .... 44:11, 44:14
Dolland & Aitchison Ltd v Revenue and Customs Comrs: C-491/04 [2006] ECR I-2129, [2006] SWTI 531, [2006] All ER (D) 327 (Feb), ECJ 65:52
Dollar v Lyon [1981] STC 333, 54 TC 459, [1981] TR 27 .... 8:96, 8:102
Dollar Land (Feltham) Ltd v Customs and Excise Comrs [1995] STC 414 .... 67:08
Dominion Tar and Chemical Co Ltd, Re [1929] 2 Ch 387, [1929] All ER Rep 279, 98 LJ Ch 448, 142 LT 15 .... 26:01
Don Francesco v De Meo (1908) 45 SLR 13, 1908 SC 7, 15 SLT 387 .... 56:29
Doncaster Amalgamated Collieries Ltd v Bean. See Bean v Doncaster Amalgamated Collieries Ltd
Donnelly v Williamson [1982] STC 88, 54 TC 636, [1981] TR 433 .... 7:24
Donoghue v Stevenson. See M'Alister (or Donoghue) v Stevenson
Dott v Brown [1936] 1 All ER 543, 154 LT 484, 15 ATC 147, CA 11:31, 11:34
Double Shield Window Co Ltd v Customs and Excise Comrs (1985) VAT decision 1771 .... 65:12
Dougal, Re (Cowie's Trustees) [1981] STC 514 .... 46:15
Douros v Customs and Excise Comrs (1994) VAT decision 12454 .... 66:04
Dow Chemical Co Ltd v Customs and Excise Comrs [1996] V & DR 52 .... 67:08
Down v Compston [1937] 2 All ER 475, 157 LT 549, 21 TC 60, 16 ATC 64 .... 12:05
Dowse v Customs and Excise Comrs (1973) VAT decision 46, 92 Taxation 242 ...... 68:12

Table of Cases

Doyle v Revenue and Customs Comrs [2005] STC (SCD) 775 ...... 2A:52
Dragonfly Consultancy Ltd v Revenue and Customs Comrs [2008] EWHC 2113 (Ch), [2008] STC 3030, [2008] All ER (D) 17 (Sep) 8.27
Drakard (Philip) Trading Ltd v Customs and Excise Comrs [1992] STC 568 ...... 63:21
Drevon v Drevon (1864) 34 LJ Ch 129, 10 Jur NS 717, 4 New Rep 316 ...... 33:15
Dreyfus v IRC (1963) 41 TC 441, [1963] TR 461, 42 ATC 513 ...... 13:16
Dreyfus (Camille and Henry) Foundation Inc v IRC [1956] AC 39, [1955] 3 All ER 97, 36 TC 126, HL 56:37, 62:22
Drummond v Austin Brown [1983] STC 506, 58 TC 67; affd [1986] Ch 52, [1984] 2 All ER 699, [1984] 3 WLR 381, [1984] STC 321, 58 TC 67, CA 18:03, 18:16
Drummond v Collins [1913] 3 KB 583, 83 LJKB 111, 6 TC 525; affd [1914] 2 KB 643, 83 LJKB 729, 6 TC 532, CA; on appeal [1915] AC 1011, 84 LJKB 1690, 6 TC 525, HL 7:23, 11:23, 13:09, 13:19
Drummond v R & C Comrs (2007) SpC 617 ...... 16:16
Duchy Maternity Ltd v Hodgson [1985] STC 764, 59 TC 85 ...... 2A:74
Duckering v Gollan [1965] 2 All ER 115, [1965] 1 WLR 680, 42 TC 333, [1965] TR 129, HL 37:19
Du Cros v Ryall (1935) 19 TC 444 ...... 7:34, 50:11
Dudda v Finanzamt Bergisch Gladbach: C-327/94 [1996] ECR I-4595, [1996] 3 CMLR 1063, [1996] STC 1290, ECJ 63:30
Duff v Barlow (1941) 23 TC 633, 20 ATC 33 ...... 7:34
Duffy, Re [1949] Ch 28, [1948] 2 All ER 756, [1949] LJR 133, [1948] TR 317, CA 57:06
Dumbarton Harbour Board v Cox 1919 SC 162, 56 Sc LR 122, 7 TC 147 ...... 9:26, 9:59
Duncan's Executors v Farmer 1909 SC 1212, 5 TC 417 ...... 11:23
Dunk v General Comrs for Havant [1976] STC 460n, [1976] TR 213 ...... 2:11
Dunmore v McGowan [1978] 2 All ER 85, [1978] 1 WLR 617, [1978] STC 217, 52 TC 307, [1978] TR 35, CA 5:15
Dunstall (Paul) Organisation Ltd v Hedges [1999] STC (SCD) 26 ...... 7:144
Dunstan v Young Austen Young Ltd [1989] STC 69, 61 TC 448, CA 21:12
Duomatic Ltd, Re [1969] 2 Ch 365, [1969] 1 All ER 161, [1969] 2 WLR 114 ...... 50:32
Duple Motor Bodies v Ostime [1961] 2 All ER 167, [1961] 1 WLR 739, 39 TC 537 ...... 8:166, 8:167
Durham Aged Mineworkers' Association v Customs and Excise Comrs [1994] STC 553 ...... 63:20
Dyer v Customs and Excise Comrs [2005] STC 715, 2005 SLT 255 ...... 63:10
Dyrham Park Country Club v Customs and Excise Comrs [1978] VATTR 244 ...... 63:19, 68:16, 70:04

E

EC Commission v Belgium: C-478/98 [2000] ECR I-7587, [2000] 3 CMLR 1111, [2000] STC 830, ECJ 1:07
EC Commission v EU Council: C-533/03 [2006] SWTI 234, [2006] All ER (D) 199 (Jan), ECJ 1:04
EC Commission v France: 50/87[1988] ECR 4797, ECJ 63:17
EC Commission v France: C-68/92 [1993] ECR I-5881, [1997] STC 684, ECJ 63:30; 65:38
EC Commission v France: 270/83 [1986] ECR 273, ECJ 1:08
EC Commission v Germany: C-401/06 [2007] SWTI 2848, ECJ 63:30; 65:38
EC Commission v Ireland: C-554/07 [2009] ECR I-0000 ...... 63:15
EC Commission v Luxembourg: C-69/92 [1993] ECR I-5907, [1997] STC 712, ECJ 63:30; 65:38
EC Commission v Netherlands: 235/85 [1987] ECR 1471, [1988] 2 CMLR 921, ECJ 63:15
EC Commission v Spain: C-73/92 [1993] ECR I-5997, [1997] STC 700, ECJ . 63:30; 65:38
EC Commission v United Kingdom: 353/85 [1988] 2 All ER 557, [1988] STC 251, ECJ 63:02
EC Commission v United Kingdom: 416/86 [1990] 2 QB 130, [1989] 1 All ER 364, [1988] 3 WLR 1261, [1988] STC 456, ECJ 63:02; 69:12

Table of Cases

EC Commission v United Kingdom: C-359/97 [2000] 3 CMLR 919, [2000] STC 777, ECJ 68:11, 63:17
EC Commission v United Kingdom: C-33/03 [2005] ECR I–1865, [2005] STC 582 .... 63:02
ECC Quarries Ltd v Watkis [1975] 3 All ER 843, [1975] STC 578, 51 TC 153, [1975] TR 185 .... 8:115
EDI Services v Revenue and Customs Comrs SpC 539 [2006] STC (SCD) 392 .... 50:35
EMAG Handel Eder OHG v Finanzlandesdirektion fur Karnten: C-245/04 [2006] ECR I-3227, [2006] SWTI 1267, [2006] All ER (D) 85 (Apr), ECJ 63:38
EMI Group Electronics Ltd v Coldicott. See Thorn EMI Electronics Ltd v Coldicott
EYL Trading Co Ltd v IRC [1962] 3 All ER 303, [1962] 1 WLR 1072, 40 TC 386, 41 ATC 275, [1962] TR 253, CA 30:05
Eagerpath Ltd v Edwards [1999] STC 771, 73 TC 427; affd [2001] STC 26, 73 TC 427, CA 2A:65
Eagles v Levy (1934) 19 TC 23, 13 ATC 349 .... 7:141
Eagleton v Gutteridge (1843) 11 M & W 465, 2 Dowl NS 1053, 12 LJ Ex 359, 8 JP 643 .... 57:25
Eames v Stepnell Properties Ltd [1967] 1 WLR 593, 43 TC 678, [1966] TR 67, 45 ATC 65; affd [1967] 1 All ER 785, [1967] 1 WLR 593, 43 TC 678, [1966] TR 347, CA 8:14, 8:22
Earlspring Properties Ltd v Guest [1993] STC 473; affd [1995] STC 479, 67 TC 259, CA 8:98, 8:102
Eastbourne Town Radio Cars Association v Customs and Excise Comrs [1996] STC 1469; revsd [1998] STC 669, CA; on appeal [2001] UKHL 19, [2001] 2 All ER 597, [2001] 1 WLR 794, [2001] STC 606 .... 63:16
Eastern National Omnibus Co Ltd v IRC [1939] 1 KB 161, [1938] 3 All ER 526, 108 LJKB 167, 160 LT 270 .... 56:10, 57:06
Eastham v Leigh, London and Provincial Properties Ltd [1971] Ch 871, [1971] 2 All ER 887, 46 TC 687, [1971] TR 33, CA 18:09
Ebrahimi v Westbourne Galleries Ltd [1973] AC 360, [1972] 2 All ER 492, [1972] 2 WLR 1289,HL 45:02, 45:03
Eckel v Board of Inland Revenue [1989] STC 305, 62 TC 331 .... 8:49
Eclipse Film Partners No 35 LLP v Revenue and Customs Comrs [2009] SWTI 627 .... 2A:52
Ecotrade SpA v Agenzia Entrate Ufficio Genoa 3: Joined cases C-95/07 and C-96/07, [2008] SWTI 1327, ECJ 66:03
Eddery (Patrick) Ltd v Customs and Excise Comrs [1986] VATTR 30 .... 63:20
Ede v Wilson and Cornwall [1945] 1 All ER 367, 26 TC 381, 24 ATC 116 .... 7:43
Edgelow v MacElwee [1918] 1 KB 205, 87 LJKB 738, 118 LT 177 .... 29:10
Edinburgh's Telford College v Customs and Excise Comrs [2006] CSIH 13, [2006] STC 1291 .... 63:17
Editor v Inspector of Taxes [2000] STC (SCD) 377; affd sub nom Burca v Parkinson [2001] STC 1298 .... 17:01
Edmond Homes Ltd v Customs and Excise Comrs (1993) VAT decision 11567 ...... 69:21
Edmunds v Coleman [1997] STC 1406, 70 TC 322 .... 8:50
Edwards v Bairstow and Harrison [1956] AC 14, [1955] 3 All ER 48, 36 TC 207, [1955] TR 209, HL 2:19, 8:03, 8:19, 9:29, 10:07, 33:02, 49:03, 54:02
Edwards v Clinch [1981] Ch 1, [1980] 3 All ER 278, [1980] STC 438, 56 TC 367, CA; affd [1982] AC 845, [1981] 3 All ER 543, [1981] 3 WLR 707, [1981] STC 617, 56 TC 367, HL 7:08, 49:01
Edwards v Walters [1896] 2 Ch 157, [1895–9] All ER Rep 767, 65 LJ Ch 557, 74 LT 396, CA 39:04
Edwards v Warmsley, Henshall & Co [1968] 1 All ER 1089, 44 TC 431 .... 8:97
Egerton v IRC [1982] STC 520 .... 42:57
Egyptian Hotels Ltd v Mitchell [1915] AC 1022, 84 LJKB 1772, 6 TC 542, HL 35:04
Eidographics Ltd v Customs and Excise Comrs [1991] VATTR 449 .... 67:08
Eilbeck v Rawling [1980] 2 All ER 12, [1980] STC 192, 54 TC 101, [1980] TR 13, CA; affd [1982] AC 300, [1981] 1 All ER 865, [1981] STC 174, 54 TC 101, HL .. 5:23, 16:22, 17:17
Einberger v Hauptzollamt Freiburg: 294/82 [1984] ECR 1177, ECJ 65:49
Elder Home Care Ltd v Customs and Excise Comrs (1994) VAT decision 11185 ..... 68:23

Table of Cases

Elderkin v Hindmarsh [1988] STC 267, 60 TC 651 .... 7:122, 7:138
Electronics Ltd v Inspector of Taxes [2005] STC (SCD) 512 .... 25:24
Ellicott v Customs and Excise Comrs (1994) VAT decision 11472 .... 68:19
Ellis v Lucas [1967] Ch 858, [1966] 2 All ER 935, 43 TC 276, [1966] TR 87 .... 7:08
Elliss v BP Oil Northern Ireland Refinery Ltd [1987] STC 52, 59 TC 474, CA 9:07
Elmdene Estates Ltd v White [1960] AC 528, [1960] 1 All ER 306, [1960] 2 WLR
  359, HL 10:17, 50:21
Elson v James G Johnston Ltd (1965) 42 TC 545, [1965] TR 333, 44 ATC 327 ...... 8:88
Elson v Price's Tailors Ltd [1963] 1 All ER 231, [1963] 1 WLR 287, 40 TC 671, [1962]
  TR 359 .... 8:90, 8:147
Elwood v Utitz (1965) 42 TC 482, [1965] TR 201, 44 ATC 193, CA .. 7:138, 7:139, 7:141
Emanuel (Lewis) & Son Ltd v White (1965) 42 TC 369, [1965] TR 99, 44 ATC 84
  .... 8:04, 8:22
Emap Consumer Magazines Ltd v Customs and Excise Comrs (1995) VAT decision
  13322 .... 69:15
Embleton's Will Trusts, Re, Sodeau v Nelson [1965] 1 All ER 771, [1965] 1 WLR 840,
  [1965] TR 83, 44 ATC 69 .... 46:24
Emery v IRC [1981] STC 150, 54 TC 607, [1980] TR 447 .... 4:19, 4:25, 4:26
Emery (J) & Sons Ltd v IRC [1937] AC 91, 105 LJPC 95, 20 TC 213, HL 8:165
Emmerson v Computer Time International Ltd [1976] 2 All ER 131, [1976] 1 WLR 749,
  [1976] STC 111, 50 TC 628; affd [1977] 2 All ER 545, [1977] 1 WLR 734, [1977]
  STC 170, 50 TC 628, CA 16:19, 16:21
Empire Stores Ltd v Customs and Excise Comrs [1992] VATTR 271; refd C-33/93:
  [1994] 3 All ER 90, [1994] STC 623, ECJ 63:20; 65:17
Empresa de Desenvolvimento Mineiro SGPS SA v Fazenda Pública (Ministério Público
  intervening): C-77/01 [2004] ECR I-4295, [2005] STC 65, ECJ 66:08
Emro Investments Ltd v Aller (1954) 35 TC 305, [1954] TR 91, 33 ATC 277 .... 8:22
Engel v Netherlands (Applications 5100/71, 5101/71, 5102/71) (1976) 1 EHRR 647, E
  Ct HR 2:118
Engineer v IRC [1997] STC (SCD) 189 .... 25:03
English and Scottish Joint Co-operative Wholesale Society Ltd v Assam Agricultural
  IT Comr [1948] AC 405, [1948] 2 All ER 395, 27 ATC 332 .... 8:35, 8:39
English Electric Co Ltd v Musker. See Musker v English Electric Co Ltd
English-Speaking Union of the Commonwealth v Customs and Excise Comrs [1980]
  VATTR 184, [1981] 1 CMLR 581 .... 63:02, 68:25
Enkler v Finanzamt Homburg: C-230/94 [1996] ECR I-4517, [1997] 1 CMLR 881,
  [1996] STC 1316, ECJ 3:15, 65:29
Ensign Tankers (Leasing) Ltd v Stokes [1989] 1 WLR 1222, [1989] STC 705; revsd
  [1991] 1 WLR 341, [1991] STC 136, CA; on appeal [1992] 1 AC 655, [1992]
  2 All ER 275, [1992] 2 WLR 469, [1992] STC 226, HL . 3:11, 3:12, 3:14, 3:19, 4:08, 6:25,
  8:11, 9:05
Entergy Power Development Corpn v Pardoe [1999] STC (SCD) 165; affd sub nom
  Pardoe v Entergy Power Development Corpn [2000] STC 286, 72 TC 617 ..... 4:31, 23:29
Enterprise Safety Coaches v Customs and Excise Comrs [1991] VATTR 74 .... 2A:44
Enterprise Zone Syndicate v Inspector of Taxes [1996] STC (SCD) 336 .... 9:15
Erichsen v Last (1881) 8 QBD 414, 51 LJQB 86, 4 TC 422, CA 8:03, 36:03
Ernst & Young v Customs and Excise Comrs [1997] V & DR 183 .... 66:20, 66:29
Escoigne Properties Ltd v IRC [1957] 1 All ER 291, [1957] 1 WLR 174, [1956] TR
  453, CA; on appeal [1958] AC 549, [1958] 1 All ER 406, [1958] 2 WLR 336, [1958]
  TR 37, HL 60:03, 60:04
Esdaile v IRC (1936) 20 TC 700, 15 ATC 330 .... 13:20
Esplen (William) & Son and Swainston Ltd v IRC [1919] 2 KB 731, 89 LJKB 29, 121 LT
  614 .... 29:15
Esquire Nominees (1971) 129 CLR 173 .... 33:25
Essex (Somerset's Executors) v IRC [2002] STC (SCD) 39; on appeal sub nom IRC v
  Eversden (Greenstock's Executors) [2002] EWHC 1360 (Ch), [2002] STC 1109, 75
  TC 340; affd [2003] EWCA Civ 668, [2003] STC 822, 75 TC 340 .... 41:01, 41:12
Essex County Council v Ellam [1988] STC 370; affd [1989] 2 All ER 494, [1989] STC
  317, CA 11:28
Esslemont v Marshall [1994] STC 813n; affd [1996] STC 1086n, CA 2:20, 7:01

Euro Hotel (Belgravia) Ltd, Re [1975] 3 All ER 1075, [1975] STC 682, 51 TC 293 .... 11:05
Eurofood IFSC Ltd, Re: C-341/04 [2006] All ER (EC) 1078, [2006] 3 WLR 309, [2006] All ER (D) 20 (May), ECJ 1:15
Europa Oil (NZ) Ltd v IRC [1976] 1 All ER 503, [1976] 1 WLR 464, [1976] STC 37 .... 8:99
European Commission v Germany: C-318/05 [2007] ECR I-6957, [2008] All ER (EC) 556, [2007] 3 CMLR 1283, [2008] STC 1357, (2007) Times, 11 October, [2007] SWTI 2188, [2007] All ER (D) 52 (Sep) 1:03
European Commission v Hellenic Republic: C-13/06 [2007] STC 194, [2006] SWTI 2747, ECJ 68:13
European Commission v Kingdom of Sweden: C-104/06 [2007] ECR I-671, [2007] 2 CMLR 153, [2008] STC 2546, [2007] SWTI 194 .... 1.20
European Commission v Republic of Austria C-128/05 [2006] ECR I-9265, [2006] SWTI 2259, ECJ 63:01
European Investment Trust Co Ltd v Jackson (1932) 18 TC 1, 11 ATC 425, CA 8:131
Europeenne et Luxembourgeoise d'investissements SA (ELISA) v Directeur general des impots and another: C-451/05 [2007] ECR I-8251, [2008] 1 CMLR 276, [2008] STC 1762, [2007] SWTI 2399, [2007] All ER (D) 153 (Oct) 1:11
Evans v Customs and Excise Comrs [1979] VATTR 194 .... 67:09
Evans v Customs and Excise Comrs (1989) VAT decision 4415 .... 69:23
Evans v Wheatley (1958) 38 TC 216, [1956] TR 273, 51 R & IT 530, 37 ATC 212 .... 8:130
Evans Medical Supplies Ltd v Moriarty [1957] 3 All ER 718, [1958] 1 WLR 66, 37 TC 540, 51 R & IT 49, HL 8:76
Evans (Lloyd), Re, National Provincial Bank v Evans [1947] Ch 695, [1948] LJR 498, 177 LT 585 .... 33:17
Eve, Re, National Provincial Bank Ltd v Eve [1956] Ch 479, [1956] 2 All ER 321, [1956] 3 WLR 69 .... 46:23
Evensis Ltd v Customs and Excise Comrs (2001) VAT decision 17218 .... 66:20
Eves, Re, Midland Bank Executor and Trustee Co Ltd v Eves [1939] Ch 969, 108 LJ Ch 374, 161 LT 270, 18 ATC 401 .... 11:43
Ewart v Taylor [1983] STC 721, 57 TC 401 .... 15:02, 20:05, 20:11
Excell Consumer Industries Ltd v Customs and Excise Comrs [1985] VATTR 94 ..... 63:25
Executive Network (Consultants) Ltd v O'Connor [1996] STC (SCD) 29 .... 8:96
Exeter Golf and Country Club Ltd v Customs and Excise Comrs [1979] VATTR 70; on appeal [1980] STC 162, [1979] TR 471; affd [1981] STC 211, [1981] TR 53,CA ... 63:20, 63:21
Expert Witness Institute v Customs and Excise Comrs [2001] EWCA Civ 1882, [2002] 1 WLR 1674, [2002] 1 CMLR 1082, [2002] STC 42 .... 68:25
Express Medicare Ltd v Customs and Excise Comrs [2000] V & DR 377 .... 63:20
Eyre, Re [1907] 1 KB 331, 76 LJKB 227, 96 LT 236 .... 41:28
Eyres v Finnieston Engineering Co Ltd (1916) 7 TC 74 .... 8:106

F

F v IRC [2000] STC (SCD) 1 .... 33:23
FA and AB Ltd v Lupton [1972] AC 634, [1971] 3 All ER 948, 47 TC 580, [1971] TR 285, HL 4:08, 4:28, 6:25, 8:11, 8:131
F S Consulting Ltd v McCaul [2002] STC (SCD) 138 .... 7:11, 8:26
Faaborg-Gelting Linien A/S v Finanzamt Flensburg: C-231/94 [1996] All ER (EC) 656, [1996] ECR I-2395, [1996] STC 774, ECJ 63:20, 63:25
Fabbri & Partners Ltd v Customs and Excise Comrs [1973] VATTR 49 .... 69:15
Fairrie v Hall [1947] 2 All ER 141, 177 LT 600, 28 TC 200, 26 ATC 102 .... 8:105
Fall v Hitchen [1973] 1 All ER 368, [1973] 1 WLR 286, [1973] STC 66, 49 TC 433 .... 7:11
Fallon (Morgan's Executors) v Fellows [2001] STC 1409, 74 TC 232 .. 21:20, 21:24, 25:19
Falmer Jeans Ltd v Rodin [1990] STC 270 .... 8:60, 25:27
Family Golf Centres Ltd v Thorne [1998] STC (SCD) 106 .... 9:29, 9:30
Farm Facilities (Fork Lift) Ltd v Customs and Excise Comrs [1987] VATTR 80 ...... 67:07

Table of Cases

Farmer (Farmer's Executors) v IRC [1999] STC (SCD) 321 .... 44:04
Faulconbridge v National Employers Mutual General Insurance Association Ltd (1952) 33 TC 103, [1952] TR 7, 31 ATC 28, [1952] 1 Lloyd's Rep 17 .... 8:35, 8:36
Faulkner (a firm) v Customs and Excise Comrs (1992) VAT decision 7597 .... 69:27
Faulkner (Adams's Trustee) v IRC [2001] STC (SCD) 112 .... 42:10
Faye v IRC (1961) 40 TC 103, 40 ATC 304, [1961] TR 297 .... 33:19
Fazenda Pública v Cámara Municipal do Porto (Ministério Público, third party): C-446/98 [2001] STC 560, [2000] ECR I-11435, ECJ 63:17
Federal Comr of Taxation v Cooke and Sherden (1980) 29 ALR 202, 10 ATR 696 .... 8:150
Federal Comr of Taxation v Myer Emporium Ltd (1987) 18 ATR 693, 163 CLR 199, 71 ALR 28, Aust HC 3:07
Feehan v Customs and Excise Comrs [1995] 1 CMLR 193, [1995] STC 75 ... 65:26, 68:15
Fellowes-Gordon v IRC (1935) 19 TC 683, 14 ATC 262 .... 35:19
Fengl v Fengl [1914] P 274, 84 LJP 29, 112 LT 173, 31 TLR 45 .... 56:29
Fenston v Johnstone (1940) 23 TC 29, 19 ATC 62 .... 3:13, 8:61
Fenston Will Trusts (Trustees of) v Revenue and Customs Comrs [2007] STC (SCD) 316, [2007] SWTI 556, SCD 16:16
Ferguson v Donovan [1929] IR 489 .... 35:04
Ferguson v IRC [1970] AC 442, [1969] 1 All ER 1025, 46 TC 15, 48 ATC 50, HL 11:42
Ferguson v IRC [2001] STC (SCD) 1 .... 7:47
Ferrazzini v Italy [2001] STC 1314, E Ct HR 1:22
Fetherstonaugh v IRC. See Finch v IRC
Fidium Finanz AG v Bundesanstalt Fur Finanzdienstleistungsaufsicht C-452/04: [2006] ECR I-9521, [2007] All ER (EC) 239, [2007] 1 CMLR 489 .... 1:11
Fielder v Vedlynn Ltd [1992] STC 553, 65 TC 145 .... 16:05
Figael Ltd v Fox [1990] STC 583, 64 TC 441; affd [1992] STC 83, 64 TC 441, CA 7:144
Figg v Clarke [1997] 1 WLR 603, [1997] STC 247, 68 TC 645 .... 20:16
Figgis, Re, Roberts v MacLaren [1969] 1 Ch 123, [1968] 1 All ER 999, [1968] 2 WLR 1173 .... 40:04
Fillibeck (Julius) Söhne GmbH & Co KG v Finanzamt Neustadt: C-258/95 [1998] All ER (EC) 466, [1998] 1 WLR 697, [1998] STC 513, ECJ 63:21, 65:29
Finanzamt Arnsberg v Stadt Sundern: C-43/04 [2005] ECR I-4491, ECJ 63:44
Finanzamt Augsburg-Stadt v Marktgemeinde Welden: C-247/95 [1997] All ER (EC) 665, [1997] STC 531, ECJ 63:17
Finanzamt Bergisch Gladbach v HE: C-25/03 [2005] SWTI 864, [2005] All ER (D) 304 (Apr), ECJ 66:05
Finanzamt Bergisch Gladbach v Skripalle: C-63/96 [1996] STC 1035, ECJ 63:02
Finanzamt Düsseldorf-Süd v SALIX Grundstücks-Vermietungsgellschaft mbH & Co Objekt Offenbach KG: C-102/08 [2009] ECR I–0000, [2009] STC 1607, ECJ 63:17
Finanzamt fur Korperschaften III in Berlin v Krankenheim Ruhesitz am Wannsee-Seniorenheimstatt GmbH: C-157/07 [2009] All ER (EC) 513, [2009] STC 138, [2008] All ER (D) 255 (Oct) 1:14
Finanzamt Gladbeck v Linneweber: C-453/02 [2008] STC 1069, [2005] All ER (D) 254 (Feb), ECJ 68:15
Finanzamt Goslar v Breitsohl: C-400/98 [2001] STC 355 .... 68:03
Finanzamt Gummersbach v Bockemühl: C-90/02 [2004] ECR I-3303, [2005] STC 934, ECJ 66:22
Finanzamt Herne-West v Akritidis: C-462/02 [2008] STC 1069, [2005] All ER (D) 254 (Feb), ECJ 68:15
Finanzamt Köln-Altstadt v Schumacker: C-279/93 [1996] QB 28, [1995] All ER (EC) 319, [1995] STC 306, ECJ 1:09
Finanzamt München III v Möhsche: C-193/91 [1993] ECR I-2615, [1997] STC 195, ECJ 65:29
Finanzamt Offenbach am Main-Land v Faxworld Vorgründungsgesellschaft Peter Hünninghausen und Wolfgang Klein GbR: C-137/02 [2004] ECR I-5547, [2004] 2 CMLR 637, [2005] STC 1192, ECJ 66:08
Finanzamt Osnabrück-Land v Langhorst: C-141/96 [1998] All ER (EC) 178, [1998] 1 CMLR 673, [1997] STC 1357, ECJ 65:18

Table of Cases

Finanzamt Rendsburg v Detlev Harbs: C-321/02 [2004] ECR I-7101, [2006] STC 340, [2004] All ER (D) 262 (Jul), ECJ 63:44
Finanzamt Uelzen v Armbrecht: C-291/92 [1995] All ER (EC) 882, [1995] ECR I-2775, [1995] STC 997, ECJ 66:05
Finch v Customs and Excise Comrs (1993) VAT decision 10948 ..... 65:18
Finch v IRC [1983] 1 WLR 405, [1983] STC 157; revsd [1985] Ch 1, [1984] 3 WLR 212, sub nom Fetherstonaugh v IRC [1984] STC 261, CA 1:20, 1:27
Findlay v Findlay 1994 SLT 709 ..... 33:14
Fine Arts Developments plc v Customs and Excise Comrs [1991] VATTR 9; on appeal [1993] STC 29; revsd [1994] STC 668, CA; revsd [1996] 1 All ER 888, [1996] STC 246, HL 65:17
Fini H I/S v Skatteministeriet: C-32/03 [2005] STC 903, [2005] All ER (D) 62 (Mar), ECJ 66:40
Firestone Tyre and Rubber Co Ltd v Lewellin [1957] 1 All ER 561, [1957] 1 WLR 464, 37 TC 111, [1957] TR 19, HL 3:13, 36:05, 36:06
Fiscale eenheid Koninklijke Ahold NV v Staatsecretaris van Financien C-484/06: [2008] SWTI 1713 ..... 65:20
Fischer v Finanzamt Donaueschingen: C-283/95 [1998] QB 883, [1998] All ER (EC) 567, [1998] ECR I-3369, [1998] 3 CMLR 1055, [1998] STC 708, ECJ 63:19, 68:15
Fisher v Customs and Excise Comrs (1975) VAT decision 179, 95 Taxation 391 ..... 68:12
Fisher (Donald) (Ealing) Ltd v Spencer [1989] STC 256, CA 8:82
Fitch Lovell Ltd v IRC [1962] 3 All ER 685, [1962] 1 WLR 1325, [1962] TR 129, 41 ATC 228 ..... 56:15, 56:21, 57:07, 57:13, 58:10
Fitton v Gilders and Heaton (1955) 36 TC 233, [1955] TR 197, 48 R & IT 516, 34 ATC 215 ..... 9:09
Fitzpatrick v IRC [1991] STC 34, 1991 SLT 841 ..... 2:20
Fitzpatrick v IRC (No 2) [1992] STC 406, 66 TC 407; on appeal [1994] 1 All ER 673, [1994] 1 WLR 306, [1994] STC 237, 66 TC 407, HL 2:20, 2:21, 7:137
Fitzwilliam (Countess) v IRC [1990] STC 65; on appeal [1992] STC 185, CA; affd [1993] 3 All ER 184, [1993] 1 WLR 1189, [1993] STC 502, HL 3:20, 15:07, 15:14, 21:03, 39:35, 39:36, 39:39, 42:04
Flather v Customs and Excise Comrs (1994) VAT decision 11960 ..... 69:35
Fleetwood-Hesketh v IRC [1936] 1 KB 351 ..... 57:23
Fleming v Associated Newspapers Ltd [1973] AC 628, [1972] 2 All ER 574, 48 TC 382, [1972] TR 87, HL 8:133, 8:134
Fleming (t/a Bodycraft) v Revenue and Customs Comrs [2006] EWCA Civ 70, [2006] 10 LS Gaz R 25, (2006) Times, 1 March, [2006] SWTI 457, [2006] All ER (D) 199 (Feb), [2008] UKHL 2, [2008] STC 324 ..... 63:02, 66:22
Fleming v London Produce Co Ltd [1968] 2 All ER 975, [1968] 1 WLR 1013, 44 TC 582, [1968] TR 97 ..... 2A:65, 36:09
Fletcher v IT Comr [1972] AC 414, [1971] 3 All ER 1185, [1971] TR 385 ..... 8:38
Fletcher v Thompson [2002] EWHC 1552 (Admin), [2002] STC 1149, 74 TC 710 ..... 31:14
Flockton (Ian) Developments Ltd v Customs and Excise Comrs [1987] STC 394 ..... 66:05
Floor v Davis [1978] Ch 295, [1978] 2 All ER 1079, [1977] STC 436, 52 TC 609, CA; affd [1980] AC 695, [1979] 2 All ER 677, [1979] STC 379, 52 TC 609, [1979] TR 163, HL 1:24, 18:01, 18:47
Floridienne SA v Belgium: C-142/99 [2001] All ER (EC) 37, [2000] ECR I-9567, [2001] 1 CMLR 689, [2000] STC 1044, ECJ 63:15, 63:17
Fluff Ltd (t/a Mag-it) v Customs and Excise Comrs [2001] STC 674 ..... 69:13
Flynn, Re, Flynn v Flynn [1968] 1 All ER 49, [1968] 1 WLR 103 ..... 33:15, 33:19
Flynn, Re, Flynn v Flynn (No 2) [1968] 112 Sol Jo 804 ..... 33:15
Flynn, Re, Flynn v Flynn (No 3) [1969] 2 All ER 557 ..... 33:15
Foley v Fletcher and Rose (1858) 3 H & N 769, 28 LJ Ex 100, 33 LTOS 11, 22 JP 819 ..... 11:20, 11:32, 11:35
Fonden Marselisborg Lystbadehavn v Skatteministeriet: C-428/02 [2005] ECR I-1525, [2005] SWTI 360, [2005] All ER (D) 63 (Mar), ECJ 68:12
Fong v Customs and Excise Comrs [1978] VATTR 75 ..... 64:21
Football Association Ltd v Customs and Excise Comrs [1985] VATTR 106 ... 63:20, 66:20
Forbes v Director of the Assets Recovery Agency [2007] STC (SCD) 1 ..... 8:09

Table of Cases

Ford Motor Co Ltd v Revenue and Customs Comrs [2007] EWCA Civ 1370, [2007] All ER (D) 280 (Mar), [2008] STC 1016, CA 63:19
Försäkringsaktiebolaget Skandia (publ), Re: C-240/99 [2001] 1 All ER (EC) 822, [2001] 1 WLR 1617, [2001] STC 754, ECJ 68:13
Försäkringsaktiebolaget Skandia (publ) v Riksskatteverket: C-422/01 [2003] All ER (EC) 831, [2003] ECR I-6817, [2003] STC 1361, ECJ 1:10
Forth Conservancy Board v IRC [1931] AC 540, [1931] All ER Rep 679, 16 TC 103, 10 ATC 203, HL 12:11
Forthright (Wales) Ltd v Davies [2004] EWHC 524 (Ch), [2004] STC 875 .... 31:07
Förvaltnings AB Stenholmen v Riksskatteverket: C-320/02 [2004] All ER (EC) 870, [2004] ECR I-3509, [2004] 2 CMLR 1307, [2004] STC 1041, ECJ 65:23
Foster v Williams [1997] STC (SCD) 112 .... 21:27
Foster (Betty) (Fashion Sewing) Ltd v Customs and Excise Comrs [1976] VATTR 229 .... 69:15
Foster (John) & Sons Ltd v IRC [1894] 1 QB 516, 63 LJQB 173, 69 LT 817, 58 JP 444, CA 57:04
Fothergill v Monarch Airlines Ltd [1981] AC 251, [1980] 2 All ER 696, [1980] 3 WLR 209, HL 8:40
Foulds v Clayton (1953) 34 TC 382, [1953] TR 203, 32 ATC 211 .... 8:13, 23:02
4Cast Ltd v Mitchell [2005] STC (SCD) 287 .... 31:12
Fox (J D) Ltd v Customs and Excise Comrs [1988] 2 CMLR 875 .... 65:12
Frampton (Trustees of the Worthing Rugby Football Club) v IRC. See Worthing Rugby Football Club Trustees v IRC
Frankland v IRC [1996] STC 735; affd [1997] STC 1450, CA 40:21
Fraser v Canterbury Diocesan Board of Finance [2001] Ch 669, [2001] 2 WLR 1103, 82 P CR 145, CA 16:48
Fredensen v Rothschild [1941] 1 All ER 430 .... 2A:71
Freeman v Evans [1922] 1 Ch 36, 91 LJ Ch 195, 125 LT 722, CA 57:25
Freeman v IRC (1871) LR 6 Exch 101, 40 LJ Ex 85, 24 LT 323, 19 WR 591 .... 56:15
Freemans plc v Customs and Excise Comrs: C-86/99 [2001] ECR I-4167, [2001] 1 WLR 1713, [2001] 2 CMLR 1166, [2001] STC 960, ECJ 65:17
Freight Transport Leasing Ltd v Customs and Excise Comrs [1991] VATTR 142 ..... 68:16
French v Macale (1842) 2 Dr & War 269 .... 57:28
Friends of the Ironbridge Gorge Museum v Customs and Excise Comrs [1991] VATTR 97 .... 63:16
Frost v Feltham [1981] 1 WLR 452, [1981] STC 115, 55 TC 10, [1980] TR 429 .... 23:10
Fry, Re, Chase National Executors and Trustees Corpn Ltd v Fry [1946] Ch 312, [1946] 2 All ER 106, 115 LJ Ch 225 .... 18:05
Fry v Salisbury House Estate Ltd. See Salisbury House Estate Ltd v Fry
Fry v Shiels' Trustees 1915 SC 159, 6 TC 583 .... 5:24
Fuge v McClelland (1956) 36 TC 571, [1956] TR 245, 35 ATC 274 .... 7:08
Fuld's Estate (No 3), Re, Hartley v Fuld [1968] P 675, [1965] 3 All ER 776, [1966] 2 WLR 717 .... 33:15, 33:21, 3:21
Full Force Marketing Ltd v Customs and Excise Comrs (1997) VAT decision 15270 .... 69:15
Fuller v Evans [2000] 1 All ER 636, [2000] 1 FCR 494, [2000] 2 FLR 13 .... 35:63
Fuller v Fenwick (1846) 3 CB 705, 1 New Pract Cas 592, 16 LJCP 79, 8 LTOS 162 .... 57:28
Fullwood Foundry Ltd v IRC (1924) 9 TC 101, 4 ATC 127 .... 8:50
Fundfarms Development Ltd v Parsons [1969] 3 All ER 1161, [1969] 1 WLR 1735, 45 TC 707 .... 8:06
Funke v France [1993] 1 CMLR 897, 16 EHRR 297, E Ct HR 1:14, 1:22
Furness v IRC [1999] STC (SCD) 232 .... 44:04
Furniss v Dawson [1982] STC 267; affd [1984] AC 474, [1983] STC 549, 55 TC 324, CA; revsd [1984] AC 474, [1984] 1 All ER 530, [1984] STC 153, 55 TC 324, HL 2:20, 3:14, 3:17, 3:18, 4:01, 4:18, 4:28, 13:24, 16:02, 17:29, 18:07, 56:10
Futura Participations SA v Administrations des Contributions: C-250/95 [1997] ECR I-2471, [1997] STC 1301, ECJ 1:12
Future Online Ltd v Faulds [2004] STC (SCD) 237; affd [2004] EWHC 2597 (Ch), [2005] STC 198 .... 7:11, 8:26

Fynn v IRC [1958] 1 All ER 270, [1958] 1 WLR 585, 37 TC 629, [1957] TR 323 .... 35:38

G

G v G (financial provision: equal division) [2002] EWHC 1339 (Fam), [2002] 2 FLR 1143, [2003] Fam Law 14 .... 8:38, 31:22
GA Security Systems Ltd v Customs and Excise Comrs (1983) VAT decision 1527 ... 65:32
GC Trading Ltd v Revenue & Customs Comrs (2007) SpC 630 .... 31:07
GCA International Ltd v Yates [1991] STC 157 .... 37:07
GHR Co Ltd v IRC [1943] KB 303, [1943] 1 All ER 424, 112 LJKB 311, 169 LT 206 .... 57:24
GKN Birwelco Ltd v Customs and Excise Comrs [1983] VATTR 128 .... 69:19
GUS Catalogue Order Ltd v Customs and Excise Comrs (1988) VAT decision 2598 .... 69:15
GUS Merchandise Corpn Ltd v Customs and Excise Comrs [1978] VATTR 28; on appeal [1980] 1 WLR 1508, [1980] STC 480, [1980] TR 135; affd [1981] 1 WLR 1309, [1981] STC 569, [1981] TR 321, CA 63:03, 63:26
Gabem Management Ltd v Revenue and Customs Comrs [2007] STC (SCD) 247 .... 2A:40
Gable Construction Co Ltd v IRC [1968] 2 All ER 968, [1968] 1 WLR 1426 . 57:28, 57:35
Gabriele Walderdorff v Finanzamt Waldviertel: C-451/06 [2007], ECR I–10637, [2008] STC 3079, ECJ 68:11, 68:12
Gaines-Cooper v Revenue and Customs Comrs [2007] STC (SCD) 23, [2007] EWHC 2617 (Ch) 33:06, 33:09, 33:14, 33:21
Gale (Elias) Racing v Customs and Excise Comrs [1999] STC 66 .... 2A:67
Gallagher v Jones [1993] STC 199; revsd [1994] Ch 107, [1994] 2 WLR 160, [1993] STC 537, CA 8:64, 8:68, 8:105, 8:147, 8:149, 8:161
Galliers (Frank) Ltd v Customs and Excise Comrs [1993] STC 284 .... 64:14
Gamble v Rowe [1998] STC (SCD) 116; affd [1998] STC 1247, 71 TC 190 .... 6:21
Gardner v Customs and Excise Comrs [1989] VATTR 132 .... 63:32
Garforth v Newsmith Stainless Ltd [1979] 2 All ER 73, [1979] 1 WLR 409, [1979] STC 129, 52 TC 522, [1978] TR 477 .... 50:32
Garforth v Tankard Carpets Ltd [1980] STC 251, 53 TC 342, [1980] TR 29 ... 8:98, 8:116
Garland v Archer-Shee [1931] AC 212, 100 LJKB 170, 15 TC 693, 9 ATC 516, HL 35:10, 62:29
Garnac Grain Co Inc v HMF Faure and Fairclough Ltd and Bunge Corpn [1966] 1 QB 650, [1965] 3 All ER 273, [1965] 3 WLR 934, [1965] 2 Lloyd's Rep 229, CA; affd [1968] AC 1130n, [1967] 2 All ER 353, [1967] 3 WLR 143n, [1967] 1 Lloyd's Rep 495, HL 3:14
Garner v Pounds [2000] 3 All ER 218, [2000] 1 WLR 1107, [2000] STC 420, 72 TC 561, HL 16:19, 18:24
Garnett v IRC (1899) 81 LT 633, 48 WR 303 .... 57:07
Garston Overseers v Carlisle [1915] 3 KB 381, 84 LJKB 2016, 113 LT 879, 6 TC 659 .... 11:12
Gartside v IRC [1968] AC 553, [1968] 1 All ER 121, 41 TC 92, [1967] TR 309, HL 1:27, 20:19, 41:12
Garty v The Queen 94 DTC 1947 (TCC) 8:49
Gascoine v Wharton [1996] STC 1481, 69 TC 147 6:21
Gascoines Group Ltd v Inspector of Taxes [2004] EWHC 640 (Ch), [2004] STC 844 .... 25:44
Gaspet Ltd v Elliss [1985] 1 WLR 1214, [1985] STC 572, 60 TC 91; affd [1987] 1 WLR 769, [1987] STC 362, 60 TC 91, CA 9:62, 16:20
Gasque v IRC [1940] 2 KB 80, 109 LJKB 769, 23 TC 210, 19 ATC 201 .... 33:33
Gayton House and Holdings Ltd v Customs and Excise Comrs [1984] VATTR 11 ... 67:09
Gazelle v Servini [1995] STC (SCD) 324 .... 8:98
Gazzard v Customs and Excise Comrs (1991) VAT decision 6029 .... 69:18
Gemeente Leusden and Holin Groep BV v Staatssecretaris van Financien: C-487/01 and C-7/02 [2004] ECR I-5337, [2004] All ER (D) 351 (Apr), [2004] SWTI 1199, ECJ 63:09

Table of Cases

General Accident Assurance Corpn Ltd v IRC (1906) 8 F (Ct of Sess) 477, 43 Sc LR 368, 13 SLT 903 .... 56:13
General Healthcare Group Ltd v Customs and Excise Comrs (2001) VAT decision 17129 .... 69:18
General Motors Acceptance Corpn (UK) plc v Customs and Excise Comrs [1999] V & DR 456 .... 68:16
General Motors Acceptance Corpn (UK) Ltd v IRC [1985] STC 408, 59 TC 651; affd [1987] STC 122, 59 TC 651, CA 8:25, 8:73
General Reinsurance Co Ltd v Tomlinson [1970] 2 All ER 436, [1970] 1 WLR 566, 48 TC 81, [1970] TR 15 .... 8:25, 8:79, 25:45
Genius Holding BV v Staatssecretaris van Financiën: 342/87 [1989] ECR 4227, [1991] STC 239, ECJ 66:03
Genovese v Revenue and Customs Comrs [2009] STC (SCD) 373 .... 33.14
George v Ward [1995] STC (SCD) 230 .... 7:36, 7:39
Georgiou (t/a Mario's Chippery) v United Kingdom [2001] STC 80, E Ct HR 1:14
Gerritse v Finanzamt Neukölln-Nord: C-234/01 [2003] ECR I-5933, ECJ 1:10
Ghaidan v Godin-Mendoza [2004] UKHL 30, [2004] 2 AC 557, [2004] 3 WLR 113, [2004] 2 FCR 481, [2004] 2 FLR 600, [2004] Fam Law 641, [2004] HLR 827, [2004] 27 LS Gaz R 30, [2004] NLJR 1013, (2004) Times, 24 June, 148 Sol Jo LB 792, [2004] All ER (D) 210 (Jun), sub nom Ghaidan v Mendoza [2004] 3 All ER 411, [2005] 1 LRC 449 .... 1:01, 1:21, 1:22
Ghaus v Customs and Excise Comrs (1990) VAT decision 4999 .... 65:12
Ghosh v Robson [1993] BTR 496 .... 11:28
Gibbs v Customs and Excise Comrs (1991) VAT decision 5596 .... 69:23
Gibbs (Elida) Ltd v Customs and Excise Comrs: C-317/94 [1996] ECR I–5339, [1997] QB 499, [1997] All ER (EC) 53, [1996] STC 1387, ECJ 63:20; 65:17, 65:19
Gilly v Directeur des Services Fiscaux du Bas-Rhin: C-336/96 [1998] All ER (EC) 826, [1998] ECR I-2793, [1998] 3 CMLR 607, [1998] STC 1014, ECJ 1:07, 1:12; 37:01
Gilmore v Inspector of Taxes [1999] STC (SCD) 269 .... 8:142
Girls' Public Day School Trust Ltd v Ereaut [1931] AC 12, 99 LJKB 643, 15 TC 529, 9 ATC 293, HL 13:22
Girobank plc v Clarke [1996] STC 540; affd [1998] 4 All ER 312, [1998] 1 WLR 942, [1998] STC 182, 70 TC 387, CA 9:12
Girvan v Orange Personal Communications Services Ltd [1998] STC 567, 70 TC 602 .... 5:15
Gittos v Barclay [1982] STC 390, 55 TC 633 .... 5:03, 8:42, 10:07
Glantre Engineering Ltd v Goodhand [1983] 1 All ER 542, [1983] STC 1, 56 TC 165 .... 7:28, 7:144, 50:16
Glasgow City Council v Customs and Excise Comrs (1998) VAT decision 15391 .... 63:15
Glass v IRC 1915 SC 449 .... 45:05
Glawe (H J) Spiel- und Unterhaltungsgeräte Aufstellungsgesellschaft mbH & Co KG v Finanzamt Hamburg-Barmbek-Uhlenhorst: C-38/93 [1994] ECR I-1679, [1994] STC 543, ECJ 63:21, 65:26, 68:15
Glaze & Frame Ltd v Revenue and Customs Comrs [2005] STC (SCD) 757 .... 2A:19
Glenboig Union Fireclay Co Ltd v IRC 1922 SC 112, 59 Sc LR 162, 12 TC 427, 1 ATC 142, HL 8:83, 8:84, 8:130
Glendale Social Club v Customs and Excise Comrs [1994] VATTR 372 .... 65:17
Glenrothes Development Corpn v IRC [1994] STC 74 .... 57:09
Glessing v Green [1975] 2 All ER 696, [1975] 1 WLR 863, CA 56:33
Gliksten (J) & Son Ltd v Green [1929] AC 381, [1929] All ER Rep 383, 14 TC 364, 8 ATC 46, HL 8:82
Global Plant Ltd v Secretary of State for Social Services [1972] 1 QB 139, [1971] 3 All ER 385, 11 KIR 284 .... 7:11
Globe Equities Ltd v Customs and Excise Comrs [1995] V & DR 472 .... 68:11
Gloucester Railway Carriage and Wagon Co Ltd v IRC [1925] AC 469, 94 LJKB 397, 12 TC 720, 4 ATC 150, HL 8:16
Glowacki (dec'd) v R & C Comrs (2007) SpC 631 .... 40:22
Glyn v IRC [1948] 2 All ER 419, 30 TC 321, 27 ATC 190 .... 15:13
Godden v Wilson's Stores (Holdings) Ltd (1962) 40 TC 161, [1962] TR 19, 41 ATC 25 .... 8:56

Table of Cases

Goff v Osborne & Co (Sheffield) Ltd (1953) 34 TC 441, [1953] TR 265, 32 ATC 262 .... 8:52
Gold v Inspector of Taxes [1998] STC (SCD) 222 .... 7:111
Gold Coast Selection Trusts Ltd v Humphrey [1948] AC 459, [1948] 2 All ER 379, 30 TC 209, 27 ATC 149, HL 8:149
Gold Fields Mining and Industrial Ltd v GKN (UK) plc [1996] STC 173 .... 9:46
Gold Star Publications Ltd v Customs and Excise Comrs [1992] STC 365, [1992] 3 CMLR 1 .... 65:17
Golden Horseshoe (New) Ltd v Thurgood [1934] 1 KB 548, [1933] All ER Rep 402, 18 TC 280, 12 ATC 551, CA 8:110, 22:04
Golder v Great Boulder Proprietory Gold Mines Ltd [1952] 1 All ER 360, [1952] 1 TLR 306, 33 TC 75, [1952] TR 25 .... 8:105
Golding v Kaufman [1985] STC 152, 58 TC 296 .... 18:26
Goldsmiths (Jewellers) Ltd v Customs and Excise Comrs: C-330/95 [1997] 3 CMLR 978, [1997] STC 1073, ECJ 66:41
Gooch, Re [1929] 1 Ch 740, [1929] All ER Rep 394, 98 LJ Ch 285, 141 LT 150 .... 42:03
Goodbrand v Loffland Bros North Sea Inc. See Loffland Bros North Sea v Goodbrand
Goodfellow (a firm) v Customs and Excise Comrs [1986] VATTR 119 .... 63:23, 65:17
Goodson's Settlement, Goodson v Goodson [1943] Ch 101, [1943] 1 All ER 201, 112 LJ Ch 158, 22 ATC 67 .... 1:42
Goodwin, Criminal proceedings against. See R v Goodwin and Unstead
Goodwin v Brewster (1951) 32 TC 80, [1951] TR 1, 30 ATC 1, CA 7:08
Goodwin v Curtis [1998] STC 475, 70 TC 478, CA 23:06
Gordon v IRC [1991] STC 174, 64 TC 173 .... 22:10
Gordon and Blair Ltd v IRC (1962) 40 TC 358, [1962] TR 161, 41 ATC 111 .... 6:19
Goslings and Sharpe v Blake (1889) 23 QBD 324, 58 LJQB 446, 2 TC 450, 51 LT 311, CA 11:12
Government of India v Taylor [1955] AC 491, [1955] 1 All ER 292, [1955] TR 9, 34 ATC 10, HL 34:02
Governments Stock and Other Securities Investment Co Ltd v Christopher [1956] 1 All ER 490, [1956] 1 WLR 237 .... 61:11
Grace v R & C Comrs (2008) SpC 663 .... 33:03, 33:05, 33:08, 33:14
Graham v Arnott (1941) 24 TC 157, 20 ATC 211 .... 8.07, 12.05
Graham v Green [1925] 2 KB 37, [1925] All ER Rep 690, 9 TC 309, 4 ATC 232 .... 8:07, 12:05
Graham v White [1972] 1 All ER 1159, [1972] 1 WLR 874, 48 TC 163, [1971] TR 477 .... 7:03
Graham (W F) (Northampton) Ltd v Customs and Excise Comrs (1980) VAT decision 908, 105 Taxation 452 .... 3:18, 65:10, 69:15
Grainger & Son v Gough [1896] AC 325, 65 LJQB 410, 3 TC 462, HL 36:04, 36:06
Gramophone and Typewriter Ltd v Stanley [1908] 2 KB 89, [1908–10] All ER Rep 833, 77 LJKB 834, 5 TC 358, CA 35:03
Grange (S J) Ltd v Customs and Excise Comrs [1979] 2 All ER 91, [1979] STC 183, [1978] TR 251; affd [1979] 2 All ER 99, [1979] 1 WLR 239, [1979] STC 183, [1978] TR 423, CA 2A:67
Granite Supply Association Ltd v Kitton (1905) 43 Sc LR 65, 5 TC 168 .... 8:114, 8:115
Grant v Watton [1999] STC (SCD) 330; on appeal [1999] STC 330, 71 TC 333 ..... 7:111
Grant (Andrew) Services Ltd v Watton [1999] STC 330, 71 TC 333 .... 29:11
Grantham (a firm) v Customs and Excise Comrs (1979) VAT decision 853, 104 Taxation 566 .... 68:15
Granton Marketing Ltd and Wentwalk Ltd v Customs and Excise Comrs (No 2) [1999] V & DR 383 .... 65:11
Gray (t/a William Gray & Son) v Customs and Excise Comrs [2000] STC 880 ...... 64:02, 64:04
Gray v Matheson [1993] 1 WLR 1130, [1993] STC 178, 65 TC 577 .... 2A:65
Gray v Seymours Garden Centre (Horticulture) (a firm) [1995] STC 706, CA 9:29
Gray and Gillitt v Tiley (1944) 26 TC 80 .... 23:02
Great Northern Rly Co v IRC [1901] 1 KB 416, 70 LJKB 336, 65 JP 275, 84 LT 183, CA 57:14

Table of Cases

Great Western Rly Co v Bater [1920] 3 KB 266, 8 TC 231; on appeal [1921] 2 KB 128, 90 LJKB 550, 8 TC 231, CA; revsd [1922] 2 AC 1, 91 LJKB 472, 8 TC 231, 1 ATC 104, HL 7:08
Greater London Red Cross Blood Transfusion Service v Customs and Excise Comrs [1983] VATTR 241 .... 63:17
Greater World Association Trust (Trustees for) v Customs and Excise Comrs [1989] VATTR 91 .... 65:11
Green v Cobham [2002] STC 820 .... 2A:71, 33:40
Green v Favourite Cinemas Ltd (1930) 15 TC 390, 9 ATC 166 .... 10:16
Green v IRC [1975] STC 633, 50 TC 688, [1975] TR 201, CA 4:19
Green v IRC [1982] STC 485, 56 TC 10 .... 23:06
Green v IRC [2005] 1 WLR 1722. See St Barbe Green v IRC
Green (Jeffrey) & Co Ltd v Customs and Excise Comrs [1974] VATTR 94 .... 69:42
Greenberg v IRC [1972] AC 109, [1971] 3 All ER 136, [1971] 3 WLR 386, 47 TC 240, [1971] BTR 1319, HL .... :25, 4:20, 4:25
Greene King No 1 Ltd v Adie [2005] STC (SCD) 398 .... 27:01, 29:12
Greenhalgh's Craft Bakery v Customs and Excise Comrs (1993) VAT decision 10955 .... 69:13
Greenwich Property Ltd v Customs and Excise Comrs (2000) VAT decision 16746 .... 63:04
Greenwood v F L Smidth & Co. See Smidth (F L) & Co v Greenwood
Gregg v Customs and Excise Comrs: C-216/97 [1999] All ER (EC) 775, [1999] STC 934, [1999] ECR I-4947, [1999] 3 CMLR 343, ECJ 68:23
Greig v Ashton [1956] 3 All ER 123, [1956] 1 WLR 1056, 36 TC 581, [1956] TR 289 .... 5:14, 8:149, 17:01, 37:12
Grenfell v IRC (1876) 1 Ex D 242, 45 LJQB 465, 34 LT 426, 24 WR 582 .... 59:08
Gresham Life Assurance Society v Bishop [1902] AC 287, 71 LJKB 618, 4 TC 464, HL 35:20
Gresham Life Assurance Society v Styles [1892] AC 309, 62 LJQB 41, 3 TC 185, HL 8:131
Grey (Earl) v A-G [1900] AC 124, 69 LJQB 308, 82 LT 62, HL 41:06
Grey v IRC [1958] Ch 690, [1958] 2 All ER 428, CA; affd [1960] AC 1, [1959] 3 All ER 603, HL 57:06, 58:10
Grey v Tiley (1932) 16 TC 414, CA 12:06, 12:07, 12:13
Greycon Ltd v Klaentschi [2003] STC (SCD) 370 .... 8:84
Greyhound Racing Association (Liverpool) Ltd v Cooper [1936] 2 All ER 742, 20 TC 373, 15 ATC 436 .... 8:81
Griffin v Craig-Harvey [1994] STC 54, 66 TC 396 .... 23:11
Griffiths v J P Harrison (Watford) Ltd. See Harrison (J P) (Watford) Ltd v Griffiths
Griffiths v Jackson [1983] STC 184, 56 TC 583 .... 5:03, 6:02, 10:07, 22:15
Griffiths v Mockler [1953] 2 All ER 805, [1953] 1 WLR 1123, 35 TC 135, [1953] TR 287 .... 7:138, 7:139
Grimwood-Taylor (Mallender's Executors) v IRC [2000] STC (SCD) 39 ...... 44:02, 44:04, 44:09
Grosvenor Place Estates Ltd v Roberts [1961] Ch 148, [1961] 1 All ER 341, 39 TC 433, [1960] TR 391, CA 11:40
Grove v Young Men's Christian Association (1903) 88 LT 696, 67 JP 279, 4 TC 613, 19 TLR 491 .... 8:35
Gschwind v Finanzamt Aachen-Aussenstadt: C-391/97 [1999] ECR I-5451, [2001] 1 CMLR 36, [2001] STC 331, ECJ 1:09
Gubay v Kington [1983] 2 All ER 976, [1983] 1 WLR 709, [1983] STC 443, 57 TC 601, CA; revsd [1984] 1 All ER 513, [1984] 1 WLR 163, [1984] STC 99, 57 TC 601, HL 1:24, 16:43, 23:11
Guild v IRC [1991] STC 281, 1991 SLT 855, Ct of Sess; revsd [1992] 2 AC 310, [1992] 2 All ER 10, [1992] 2 WLR 397, [1992] STC 162, HL 43:17
Gulland Properties Ltd v Customs and Excise Comrs (1996) VAT decision 13955 .... 66:04, 66:26
Gunsbourg, Re (1919) 88 LJKB 562, [1918–19] B & CR 108 .... 56:29
Gurney v Richards [1989] 1 WLR 1180, [1989] STC 682, 62 TC 287 .... 7:115
Guyer v Walton [2001] STC (SCD) 75 .... 2A:68

H

H & M Hennes Ltd v Customs and Excise Comrs [2005] EWHC 1383 (Ch), [2005] STC 1749, (2005) Times, 10 May, [2005] SWTI 866, [2005] All ER (D) 327 (Apr) 69:42
HM Customs & Excise v Barclays Bank plc [2006] UKHL 28 .... 2:23
HBOS plc v Revenue and Customs Comrs [2008] CSIH 69, [2009] STC 486 .... 68:16
HMRC v Household Estate Agents Limited [2007] EWHC 1684 (Ch) 2A:74
HSBC Life (UK) Ltd v Stubbs [2002] STC (SCD) 9 .... 27:01, 27:02
Haddock v Wilmot Breeden Ltd. See Wilmot Breeden Ltd v Haddock
Haderer v Finanzamt Wilmersdorf: C-445/05 [2007] ECR I-4841, [2008] STC 2171, [2007] All ER (D) 141 (Jun), ECJ 68:19
Hadgett v IRC (1877) 3 Ex D 46, 37 LT 612, 42 JP 216, 26 WR 115 .... 56:15
Hadlee v Commissioner of Inland Revenue [1993] AC 524, [1993] STC 294, 65 TC 663 .... 15:30, 18:50, 22:43
Hafton Properties Ltd v McHugh [1987] STC 16, 59 TC 420 .... 11:14
Hagart and Burn-Murdoch v IRC [1929] AC 386, 98 LJPC 113, 141 LT 97, 14 TC 433, HL 8:131
Hague v IRC [1969] 1 Ch 393, [1968] 2 All ER 1252, 44 TC 619, [1968] TR 193, CA: 4:26
Haig's (Earl) Trustees v IRC 1939 SC 676, 22 TC 725 .... 12:08, 12:11
Hale v Shea [1965] 1 All ER 155, [1965] 1 WLR 290, 42 TC 260, [1964] TR 413 .... 5:22
Halifax plc v Customs and Excise Comrs: C-255/02 [2006] ECR I-1609, [2006] STC 919, ECJ 1:12, 1:13, 63:09,3:14, 63:19, 66:06, 66:22
Halifax plc v Davidson [2000] STC (SCD) 251 .... 8:114
Hall v IRC [1997] STC (SCD) 126 .... 44:04
Hall v Lorimer [1992] 1 WLR 939, [1992] ICR 739, [1992] STC 599; affd [1994] 1 All ER 250, [1994] 1 WLR 209, [1994] STC 23, CA 7:08, 7:11, 49:03
Hall v Marians (1935) 19 TC 582 .... 35:22
Hall & Co v Pearlberg [1956] 1 All ER 297, [1956] 1 WLR 244 .... 10:04
Hall (J P) & Co Ltd v IRC [1921] 3 KB 152, 90 LJKB 1229, 12 TC 382, CA 8:144
Halliburton Services BV v Staatssecretaris van Financiën: C-1/93 [1994] ECR I-1137, [1994] STC 655, ECJ 1:10
Halstead v Condon (1970) 46 TC 289, [1970] TR 91, 49 ATC 99 .... 7:137, 7:141
Halstead Motor Co v Customs and Excise Comrs [1995] V & DR 201 .... 67:08
Hamann v Finanzamt Hamburg-Eimsbüttel: 51/88 [1991] STC 193, [1990] 2 CMLR 383, ECJ 63:30; 65:38
Hamblett v Godfrey [1987] 1 All ER 916, [1987] 1 WLR 357, [1987] STC 60, 59 TC 694, CA 7:17, 7:28, 50:01
Hamerton v Overy (1954) 35 TC 73, [1954] TR 61, 33 ATC 64 .... 7:141
Hamilton v Customs and Excise Comrs [1984] VATTR 95 .... 63:21
Hamilton Finance Co Ltd v Coverley Westray Waltaum & Toseti Ltd [1969] 1 Lloyd's Rep 53 .... 56:29
Hamilton-Russell's Executors v IRC [1943] 1 All ER 474, 22 ATC 107, sub nom IRC v Hamilton-Russell's Executors 25 TC 200, CA 13:08, 13:16
Hammond Engineering Co Ltd v IRC [1975] STC 334, 50 TC 313, [1975] TR 89, 54 ATC 92 .... 8:116
Han v Customs and Excise Comrs [2001] EWCA Civ 1040, [2001] 4 All ER 687, [2001] 1 WLR 2253, sub nom Customs and Excise Comrs v Han [2001] STC 1188 ... 1:22, 2:118
Hanbury, Re, Comiskey v Hanbury (1939) 38 TC 588, 20 ATC 333, CA 11:26
Hancock v Austin (1863) 14 CBNS 634, 32 LJCP 252, 8 LT 329 .... 2:38
Hancock v General Reversionary and Investment Co Ltd [1919] 1 KB 25, 88 LJKB 248, 7 TC 358, 119 LT 737 .... 8:113
Hand v Hall (1877) 2 Ex D 355, 46 LJQB 603, 36 LT 765, 42 JP 133, CA ... 57:26, 58:05
Handley-Page v Butterworth (1935) 19 TC 328, 153 LT 34 .... 57:06
Hankinson v HMRC (2007) SpC 649 .... 2A:62
Hannay's Executors v IRC (1956) 37 TC 217, [1956] TR 461, 35 ATC 476 .... 15:13
Hanson (Lord) v Mansworth [2004] STC (SCD) 288 .... 7:49
Harbig Leasing Two Ltd v Customs and Excise Comrs (2000) VAT decision 16843 .... 64:01
Hardcastle (Vernede's Executors) v IRC [2000] STC (SCD) 532 .... 45:20

Table of Cases

Harding v Revenue and Customs Comrs [2008] EWHC 99 (Ch) 21:21
Haringey London Borough Council v Customs and Excise Comrs [1994] VATTR 70; on appeal [1995] STC 830 .... 66:40
Harmel v Wright [1974] 1 All ER 945, [1974] 1 WLR 325, [1974] STC 88, 49 TC 149 .... 35:20
Harnas & Helm CV v Staatssecretaris van Financiën: C-80/95 [1997] All ER (EC) 267, [1997] STC 364, ECJ 63:17
Harper v Director of Assets Recovery Agency [2005] STC (SCD) 874 .... 2:35
Harris (John M) (Design Partnership) Ltd v Lee [1997] STC (SCD) 240 .... 25:43
Harrison v Harrison [1953] 1 WLR 865, 97 Sol Jo 456 .... 33:21
Harrison (T S) & Sons Ltd v Customs and Excise Comrs (1993) VAT decision 11043 .... 63:23
Harrison (J P) (Watford) Ltd v Griffiths (1960) 40 TC 281, [1960] TR 265, 53 R & IT 739, 39 ATC 287; on appeal (1961) 40 TC 281, [1961] TR 121, 40 ATC 132, CA; affd sub nom Griffiths v J P Harrison (Watford) Ltd [1963] AC 1, [1962] 1 All ER 909, 40 TC 281, [1962] TR 33, HL 4:01, 4:08, 8:11
Harrods (Buenos Aires) Ltd v Taylor-Gooby (1964) 41 TC 450, [1964] TR 9, 43 ATC 6, CA 8:108
Harrogate Business Development Centre Ltd v Customs and Excise Comrs (1998) VAT decision 15565 .... 68:21
Harrold v IRC [1996] STC (SCD) 195 .... 44:11
Harrop v Gilroy [1995] STC (SCD) 294 .... 7:122
Harthan v Mason [1980] STC 94, 53 TC 272, [1979] TR 369 .... 20:21
Hartland v Diggines [1926] AC 289, [1926] All ER Rep 573, 10 TC 247, 5 ATC 114, HL 2A:76, 7:23, 50:08, 50:21, 50:33, 57:04
Hartley Engineering Ltd v Customs and Excise Comrs [1994] VATTR 453 .... 63:27
Harvey v Caulcott (1952) 33 TC 159, [1959] TR 101, 31 ATC 90 .... 8:14
Harvey v Williams [1995] STC (SCD) 329 .... 7:111
Hasloch v IRC (1971) 47 TC 50, [1971] TR 45, 50 ATC 65 .... 4:28, 4:29
Hastings-Bass, Re, Hastings-Bass v IRC [1975] Ch 25, [1974] 2 All ER 193, [1974] STC 211, CA 2A:71, 33:40
Hatch, Re, Hatch v Hatch [1919] 1 Ch 351, [1918–19] All ER Rep 357, 88 LJ Ch 147, 120 LT 694 .... 11:41
Hatrick v IRC [1963] NZLR 641 .... 57:07
Hatt v Newman [1999] STC (SCD) 171; on appeal [2000] STC 113, 72 TC 462 ...... 2:23, 18:09, 22:15
Hatton v IRC [1992] STC 140, 67 TC 759 .... 39:35, 42:04, 47:15
Haugh v Customs and Excise Comrs (1997) VAT decision 15055 .... 65:42
Hausgemeinschaft Jorg und Stefanie Wollny v Finanzamt Landshut: C-72/05 [2006] ECR I-8297, [2006] SWTI 2205, [2006] All ER (D) 77 (Sep), ECJ 65:29
Hawkings-Byass v Sassen [1996] STC (SCD) 319 .... 45:02
Hawkins, Re, Hawkins v Hawkins [1972] Ch 714, [1972] 3 All ER 386 .... 11:05
Hayes v Duggan [1929] IR 406 .... 8:09
Hayman v Griffiths [1988] QB 97, [1987] 3 WLR 1125, [1987] STC 649 .... 67:03
Heart of Variety Ltd v Customs and Excise Comrs [1975] VATTR 103 .... 63:21
Heastie v Veitch & Co Ltd [1934] 1 KB 535, 103 LJKB 492, 150 LT 228, 18 TC 305, CA 8:100, 8:106
Heather v G & J A Redfern & Sons (1944) 171 LT 127, 26 TC 119, 23 ATC 71 .... 8:165
Heather v P E Consulting Group [1973] Ch 189, [1973] 1 All ER 8, 48 TC 293, 51 ATC 255, CA 8:64, 8:68, 8:109, 8:113
Heaton v Bell [1970] AC 728, [1969] 2 All ER 70, 46 TC 211, [1969] TR 77, HL 7:42, 7:43, 7:119, 51:14
Hedges and Mercer v Customs and Excise Comrs [1976] VATTR 146 .... 63:32
Heger Rudi GmbH v Finanzamt Graz-Stadt: C-166/05 [2006] ECR I-7749, [2006] SWTI 2182, [2006] All ER (D) 24 (Sep), ECJ 63:30
Helstan Securities Ltd v Hertfordshire County Council [1978] 3 All ER 262, 76 LGR 104 .... 7:43
Hempsons (a firm) v Customs and Excise Comrs [1977] VATTR 73 .... 63:32
Hemsworth v Hemsworth [1946] 1 KB 431, [1946] 2 All ER 117, 115 LJKB 422, 25 ATC 465 .... 11:41

Table of Cases

Henderson v Henderson [1967] P 77, [1965] 1 All ER 179, [1965] 2 WLR 218 ..... 33:17, 33:24
Hendy v Hadley [1980] 2 All ER 554, [1980] STC 292, 53 TC 353, [1980] TR 133 .... 6:40
Henke v Revenue and Customs Comrs [2006] STC (SCD) 561 .... 23:07
Henley v Murray [1950] 1 All ER 908, 31 TC 351, [1950] TR 25, 29 ATC 35, CA 7:20, 7:33, 7:34
Henriksen v Grafton Hotel Ltd [1942] 2 KB 184, [1942] 1 All ER 678, 24 TC 453, 21 ATC 87, CA 8:129
Henry v Foster (1931) 16 TC 605, CA 7:31, 7:33
Henty & Constable (Brewers) Ltd v IRC [1961] 3 All ER 1146, [1961] 1 WLR 1504, sub nom IRC v Henty & Constable (Brewers) Ltd [1961] TR 389, 40 ATC 422, CA 57:24
Herbert v McQuade [1902] 2 KB 631, 71 LJKB 884, 4 TC 489, CA 7:25
Hereford Cathedral (Dean and Chapter of) v Customs and Excise Comrs [1994] VATTR 159 .... 66:05
Herman v Revenue and Customs Comrs [2007] SWTI 1441, SCD 35:58
Hertford (Ninth Marquess) (Executors of the Eighth Marquess of Hertford) v IRC [2005] STC (SCD) 177 .... 44:01
Hewitt v Kaye (1868) LR 6 Eq 198, 37 LJ Ch 633, 32 JP 776 .... 39:01
Hibernian v Macuimis [2000] TR 75 .... 30:06
Hicks v Davies [2005] STC (SCD) 165; affd sub nom Davies v Hicks [2005] EWHC 847 (Ch), [2005] STC 850 .... 21:03, 35:55
Higginson's Executors v IRC [2002] STC (SCD) 483 .... 44:14
Higgs v Olivier [1952] Ch 311, [1952] 1 TLR 441, 33 TC 136, [1952] TR 57, CA 8:80, 18:20
Higgs v Wrightson [1944] 1 All ER 488, 171 LT 185, 26 TC 73 .... 8:89
Highland Council v Revenue and Customs Comrs [2007] CSIH 36, [2008] STC 1280 .... 63:19
Highland Rly Co v Balderston (1889) 26 Sc LR 657, 2 TC 485 .... 8:122, 8:124
Hill v Booth [1930] 1 KB 381, [1929] All ER Rep 84, 99 LJKB 49, 142 LT 80, CA 57:28
Hillenbrand v IRC (1966) 42 TC 617, [1966] TR 201, 45 ATC 224 .... 2A:19
Hillerns and Fowler v Murray (1932) 146 LT 474, 17 TC 77, 11 ATC 31, CA .. 8:04, 8:33
Hillingdon Legal Resources Centre Ltd v Customs and Excise Comrs [1991] VATTR 39 .... 63:19
Hillyer v Leake [1976] STC 490, 51 TC 90, [1976] TR 215 .... 7:139
Hinsley v Revenue and Customs Comrs [2007] STC (SCD) 63 .... 7:122
Hinton v Maden & Ireland Ltd [1959] 3 All ER 356, [1959] 1 WLR 875, 38 TC 391, [1959] TR 233, HL 8:126, 9:26
Hirsch v Crowthers Cloth Ltd [1990] STC 174 .... 22:01
Hitch's Executors v Stone [1999] STC 431, 73 TC 600; revsd [2001] EWCA Civ 63, [2001] STC 214, 73 TC 600 .... 3:14
Hi-Wire Ltd v Customs and Excise Comrs (1991) VAT decision 6204 .... 66:07, 66:28
Hoare Trustees v Gardner [1979] Ch 10, [1978] 1 All ER 791, [1978] STC 89, 52 TC 53 .... 20:12
Hobbs v Hussey [1942] 1 KB 491, [1942] 1 All ER 445, 24 TC 153, 21 ATC 78 ... 12:06, 12:08
Hobbs v United Kingdom (Applications 63469/00, 63475/00, 63484/00, 63684/00) [2008] STC 1469, (2006) Times, 28 November, [2006] SWTI 2506, [2006] ECHR 63684/00, [2006] All ER (D) 178 (Nov) 1.21
Hochstrasser v Mayes [1959] Ch 22, [1958] 1 All ER 369, 38 TC 673, [1957] TR 365; on appeal [1959] Ch 22, [1958] 3 All ER 285, 38 TC 673, [1958] TR 237, CA; affd [1960] AC 376, [1959] 3 All ER 817, 38 TC 673, [1959] TR 355, HL ... 7:01, 7:17, 7:18, 7:19, 7:20, 7:40, 50:01, 50:08
Hodgson v De Beauchesne (1858) 12 Moo PCC 285, 7 WR 397, 33 LTOS 36 .... 33:24
Hoechst AG v IRC and A-G: C-410/98 [2001] Ch 620, [2001] All ER (EC) 496, [2001] STC 452, ECJ 1:02, 1:10, 1:11, 1:12
Hoechst Finance Ltd v Gumbrell [1983] STC 150, 56 TC 594 .... 30:04
Hofman v Wadman (1946) 27 TC 192, 25 ATC 457 .... 7:33
Holden (Isaac) & Sons Ltd v IRC (1924) 12 TC 768, 3 ATC 633 .... 8:75, 8:144

Table of Cases

Holdings Ltd v IRC [1997] STC (SCD) 144 .... 30:03
Holland v Geoghegan [1972] 3 All ER 333, [1972] 1 WLR 1473, 48 TC 482, [1972] TR 141 .... 7:34
Holland v IRC [2003] STC (SCD) 43 .... 1:21, 43:06
Holland (trading as The Studio Hair Company) v Revenue and Customs Comrs, Vigdor Ltd v Revenue and Customs Comrs [2008] EWHC 2621 (Ch), [2009] STC 150 .... 63:20
Holliday v De Brunner [1996] STC (SCD) 85 .... 6:15
Holly v Inspector of Taxes [2000] STC (SCD) 50 .... 2A:48
Holman v Johnson (1775) 1 Cowp 341, [1775–1802] All ER Rep 98 .... 34:03, 35:63
Holmes v Cowcher [1970] 1 All ER 1224, [1970] 1 WLR 834, 21 P & CR 766 .... 17:01
Holmes v Mitchell [1991] STC 25, [1991] FCR 512 .... 6:07
Holmleigh (Holdings) Ltd v IRC (1958) 46 TC 435, [1958] TR 403, 37 ATC 406 .... 2:89, 56:26, 60:02, 60:03, 60:04
Holt v Federal Taxation Comr (1929) 3 ALJ 68 .... 12:05
Holt v IRC [1953] 2 All ER 1499, [1953] 1 WLR 1488, [1953] TR 373, 32 ATC 402 .... 45:02, 45:03, 45:04
Honour v Norris [1992] STC 304, 64 TC 599 .... 23:06
Hood Barrs v IRC [1946] 2 All ER 768, 27 TC 385, 25 ATC 375, CA 15:07
Hood Barrs v IRC (No 2) [1957] 1 All ER 832, [1957] 1 WLR 529, 37 TC 188, [1957] TR 47, HL 8:127
Hood (John) & Co Ltd v Magee [1918] 2 IR 34, 7 TC 327 .... 33:25, 33:29
Hopes v Hopes [1949] P 227, [1948] 2 All ER 920, 113 JP 10, 46 LGR 538, CA 6:05
Hopkins v Hopkins [1951] P 116, [1950] 2 All ER 1035 .... 33:14
Hopkins (J) (Contractors) Ltd v Customs and Excise Comrs [1989] VATTR 107 .... 63:20
Hopwood v C N Spencer Ltd (1964) 42 TC 169, [1964] TR 361, 43 ATC 334 .... 8:127
Horan v Williams [1997] STC (SCD) 112 .... 21:27
Hordern v Customs and Excise Comrs [1992] VATTR 382 .... 67:05
Horne, Re, Wilson v Cox Sinclair [1905] 1 Ch 76, 74 LJ Ch 25, 92 LT 263, 53 WR 317 .... 11:41
Horner v Hasted [1995] STC 766n 7:36
Horton v Young [1972] Ch 157, [1971] 3 All ER 412, 47 TC 60, [1971] TR 181, CA 8:103
Hostgilt Ltd v Megahart Ltd [1999] STC 141 .... 63:23
Hotel Scandic Gasaback AB v Riksskatteverket: C-412/03 [2005] ECR I-743, [2005] STC 1311, ECJ 63:21
Hotung v Collector of Stamp Revenue [1965] AC 766, [1965] 2 WLR 546, [1965] TR 69, 44 ATC 57 .... 57:08
Housden v Marshall [1958] 3 All ER 639, [1959] 1 WLR 1, 38 TC 233, [1958] TR 337 .... 12:06, 12:08, 12:11
House (t/a P & J Autos) v Customs and Excise Comrs [1992] VATTR 11; on appeal [1994] STC 211; on appeal [1996] STC 154, CA 2A:67
Household v Grimshaw [1953] 2 All ER 12, [1953] 1 WLR 710, 34 TC 366, [1953] TR 147 .... 7:11
Howard (Alexander) & Co Ltd v Bentley (1948) 30 TC 334, 41 R & IT 483, 27 ATC 162 .... 8:118
Howard de Walden (Lord) v IRC [1942] 1 KB 389, [1942] 1 All ER 287, 25 TC 121, CA 4:01, 35:33
Howden Boiler and Armaments Co Ltd v Stewart (1924) 9 TC 205 .... 8:50
Howe v IRC [1919] 2 KB 336, [1918–19] All ER Rep 1088, 7 TC 289, 88 LJKB 821, CA 11:26
Howell v Trippier. See Red Discretionary Trustees v Inspector of Taxes
Howells v IRC [1939] 2 KB 597, [1939] 3 All ER 144, 22 TC 501, 18 ATC 205 .... 11:38
Howson v Monsell [1950] 2 All ER 1239, 31 TC 529, [1950] TR 333, 29 ATC 313 .... 12:08, 18:20
Hozee v Netherlands (1998) unreported 1:22
Hudson v Humbles (1965) 42 TC 380, [1965] TR 135, 44 ATC 124 .... 2:26
Hudson v Wrightson (1934) 26 TC 55, 13 ATC 382 .... 8:19, 23:02
Hudson Contract Services Ltd v Revenue and Customs Comrs [2005] STC (SCD) 740, [2007] EWHC 73 (Ch) 2A:19
Hudson's Bay Co Ltd v Stevens (1909) 5 TC 424, 101 LT 96, CA 8:17

Hugh v Rogers (1958) 38 TC 270, 37 ATC 412, 52 R IT 140, 1958 TR 369 .... 12:06
Hulme Trust Educational Foundation v Customs and Excise Comrs [1978] VATTR
 179 .... 69:17
Humbles v Brooks (1962) 40 TC 500, [1962] TR 297, 41 ATC 309 .... 7:137
Humphries (George) & Co v Cook (1934) 19 TC 121, 13 ATC 649 .... 8:50
Hunt v Henry Quick Ltd [1992] STC 633, 65 TC 108 .... 9:29, 9:30
Hunter v Dewhurst (1932) 16 TC 605, 146 LT 510, 9 ATC 574, HL 7:20, 7:34
Huntington v IRC [1896] 1 QB 422, 65 LJQB 297, 74 LT 28, 44 WR 300 ... 57:07, 57:11
Hurley v Taylor [1998] STC 202, 71 TC 268; revsd [1999] STC 1, 71 TC 268, CA
 .... 2:28; 2A:74
Hutchings v Customs and Excise Comrs [1987] VATTR 58 .... 64:14
Hutchison 3G UK Ltd v Revenue and Customs Comrs: C-369/04 (2007) Times, 3 July,
 [2007] All ER (D) 305 (Jun), ECJ, [2007] ECR I–5247, [2008] STC 218 .... 63:17
Hutchinson & Co (Publishers) Ltd v Turner [1950] 2 All ER 633, 31 TC 495, [1950] TR
 285, 29 ATC 210 .... 8:101
Hutchvision Hong Kong Ltd v Customs and Excise Comrs (1993) VAT decision
 10509 .... 63:30; 65:38

I

Ibe v McNally [2005] EWHC 1551 (Ch), [2005] STC 1426 .... 2:17, 7:33
Ibstock Building Products Ltd v Customs and Excise Comrs [1987] VATTR 1 . 63:20, 66:20
Iliffe and Holloway v Customs and Excise Comrs [1993] VATTR 439 .... 63:26
Impact Foiling v Revenue and Customs Comrs [2006] STC (SCD) 746 .... 7:118
Imperial Chemical Industries of Australia and New Zealand v Taxation Comr of
 the Commonwealth of Australia (1970) 120 CLR 396 .... 9:29
Imperial Chemical Industries plc v Colmer [1992] STC 51; affd [1993] 4 All ER 705,
 [1993] STC 710, CA; on appeal [1996] 2 All ER 23, [1996] 1 WLR 469, [1996] STC
 352, HL; refd C-264/96: [1998] All ER (EC) 585, [1999] 1 WLR 108, [1998] STC
 874, ECJ; apld [2000] 1 All ER 129, [1999] 1 WLR 2035, [1999] STC 1089, HL 1:06,
 1:08, 1:09, 1:10, 1:11, 1:14, 1:20, 28:01, 28:11
Imperial Tobacco Co (of Great Britain and Ireland) Ltd v Kelly [1943] 2 All ER 119, 169
 LT 133, 25 TC 292, 22 ATC 137, CA 8:78
Imperial War Museum v Customs and Excise Comrs [1992] VATTR 346 ..... 66:07, 66:08
Inchcape Management Services Ltd v Customs and Excise Comrs [1999] V & DR 397
 .... 65:20
Inchiquin v IRC (1948) 31 TC 125, 27 ATC 338, CA 33:03
Inchyra v Jennings [1966] Ch 37, [1965] 2 All ER 714, 42 TC 388, [1965] TR 141
 .... 35:10
IT Comrs Bihar and Orissa v Singh [1942] 1 All ER 362 .... 8:116
IT Comrs for General Purposes (City of London) v Gibbs [1942] AC 402, [1942]
 1 All ER 415, 24 TC 221, HL 1:27
IT Special Purposes Comrs v Pemsel [1891] AC 531, [1891–4] All ER Rep 28, 61 LJQB
 265, 3 TC 53, HL 1:21, 1:27, 16:46
Independent Coach Travel (Wholesaling) Ltd v Customs and Excise Comrs [1993]
 VATTR 357 .... 65:25
Independent Television Authority and Associated Rediffusion Ltd v IRC [1961] AC 427,
 [1960] 2 All ER 481, [1960] 3 WLR 48, [1960] TR 137, HL 56:18
Indian Radio and Cable Communications Co Ltd v IT Comr, Bombay Presidency and
 Aden [1937] 3 All ER 709 .... 8:106
Indo China Steam Navigation Co, Re [1917] 2 Ch 100, 86 LJ Ch 723, 117 LT 212
 .... 56:29
Indofood International Finance Ltd v JP Morgan Chase Bank NA [2006] EWCA Civ
 158, [2006] STC 1195, [2006] SWTI 582, [2006] All ER (D) 18 (Mar) 37:33
Indofood International Ltd v JP Morgan Chase Bank, NA, London Branch [2006] STC
 192 .... 37:33
Inglewood v IRC [1983] STC 133, [1983] 1 WLR 366, CA 42A:44
Ingram v IRC [1986] Ch 585, [1986] 2 WLR 598, [1985] STC 835 .... 56:10

Table of Cases

Ingram v IRC [1995] 4 All ER 334, [1995] STC 564; on appeal [1997] 4 All ER 395, [1997] STC 1234, CA; revsd [2000] 1 AC 293, [1999] 1 All ER 297, [1999] STC 37, HL 12:20, 18:01, 18:05, 39:35, 41:06, 41:08, 41:10, 57:25
Ingram (J G) & Son Ltd v Callaghan [1969] 1 All ER 433, [1969] 1 WLR 456, 45 TC 151, [1968] TR 363, CA 8:52
IRC v Adam 1928 SC 738, 1928 SLT 476, 14 TC 34, 7 ATC 393 .... 8:119, 16:14
IRC v Aken [1988] STC 69, 63 TC 395; affd [1990] 1 WLR 1374, [1990] STC 497, 63 TC 395, CA 2:23, 8:09, 12:10, 18:08
IRC v Alexander von Glehn & Co Ltd [1920] 2 KB 553, 89 LJKB 590, 123 LT 338, 12 TC 232, CA 8:09
IRC v Anchor International Ltd [2005] STC 411, 2004 SCLR 1045 .... 9:28
IRC v Angus (1889) 23 QBD 579, 61 LT 832, 38 WR 3, 5 TLR 697, CA 57:18
IRC v Ayrshire Employers Mutual Insurance Association Ltd [1946] 1 All ER 637, 175 LT 22, 27 TC 331, 25 ATC 103, HL 1:25
IRC v Ballantine (1924) 8 TC 595, 3 ATC 716 .... 11:06
IRC v Barclay, Curle & Co Ltd [1969] 1 All ER 732, 45 TC 221, 48 ATC 17, HL 9:12, 9:26, 9:29
IRC v Bernstein [1961] Ch 399, [1961] 1 All ER 320, 39 TC 391, CA 15:13
IRC v Berrill [1982] 1 All ER 867, [1981] 1 WLR 1449, [1981] STC 784, 55 TC 429 .... 13:11
IRC v Biggar [1982] STC 677, 56 TC 254 .... 8:80
IRC v Botnar [1998] STC 38, 72 TC 205; affd [1999] STC 711, 72 TC 205, CA 35:33
IRC v Bowater Property Developments Ltd [1985] STC 783; on appeal [1989] AC 398, [1987] 3 All ER 27, [1987] 3 WLR 660, [1987] STC 297, CA; affd [1989] AC 398, [1988] 3 All ER 495, [1988] 3 WLR 423, [1988] STC 476, HL 3:18
IRC v Brackett [1986] STC 521, 60 TC 134 .... 25:49, 35:27, 35:30, 35:33, 36:05
IRC v Brander and Cruickshank [1971] 1 All ER 36, [1971] 1 WLR 212, 46 TC 574, [1970] TR 353, HL 7:11, 7:12, 7:15, 7:37
IRC v Brebner [1967] 2 AC 18, [1967] 1 All ER 779, 43 TC 705, [1967] TR 21, HL 4:20, 4:29, 62:16
IRC v British Salmson Aero Engines Ltd [1938] 2 KB 482, [1938] 3 All ER 283, 22 TC 29, 107 LJKB 648 .... 11:30
IRC v Brown (1926) 11 TC 292, 6 ATC 65 .... 33:02, 33:03, 33:06
IRC v Brown [1971] 3 All ER 502, [1971] 1 WLR 1495, 47 TC 236, [1971] TR 185, CA 4:24
IRC v Buchanan [1914] 3 KB 466, [1914–15] All ER Rep 882, 83 LJKB 1425, CA 45:05
IRC v Buchanan [1958] Ch 289, [1957] 2 All ER 400, 37 TC 365, [1957] TR 43, CA 15:04, 15:07, 15:08, 39:04
IRC v Bullock [1976] 3 All ER 353, [1976] 1 WLR 1178, [1976] STC 409, 51 TC 522, CA 33:17, 33:22, 33:23
IRC v Burmah Oil Co Ltd [1980] STC 731, 54 TC 200, [1980] TR 397, Ct of Sess; revsd [1982] STC 30, 54 TC 200, HL 3:12, 3:16, 21:14
IRC v Burrell [1924] 2 KB 52, [1924] All ER Rep 672, 93 LJKB 709, 9 TC 27, CA 8:31, 26:01
IRC v Carron Co 1968 SC 47, 1968 SLT 305, 45 TC 18 [1968] TR 173, HL 8:110, 8:115, 8:121
IRC v Chubb's Settlement Trustees (1971) 47 TC 353, [1971] TR 197, 50 ATC 221 .... 16:17
IRC v Church Comrs for England [1977] AC 329, [1976] 2 All ER 1037, [1976] STC 339, 50 TC 516, HL 11:30, 11:31, 11:33, 11:35
IRC v City of Glasgow Police Athletic Association [1953] AC 380, [1953] 1 All ER 747, 34 TC 76, [1953] TR 49, HL 13:22
IRC v Clay [1914] 3 KB 466, [1914–15] All ER Rep 882, 83 LJKB 1425, CA 45:02, 45:05
IRC v Cock Russell & Co Ltd [1949] 2 All ER 889, 65 TLR 725, 29 TC 387, [1949] TR 367 .... 8:164
IRC v Coia (1959) 38 TC 334, [1959] TR 15 .... 8:130
IRC v Collco Dealings Ltd [1962] AC 1, [1961] 1 All ER 762, 39 TC 509, [1961] TR 49, HL 37:33, 37:35
IRC v Combe (1932) 17 TC 405, 11 ATC 486 .... 33:03

Table of Cases

IRC v Commerzbank AG [1990] STC 285, 63 TC 218 .... 1:10, 37:05, 37:33, 37:41
IRC v Cook [1946] AC 1, [1945] 2 All ER 377, 26 TC 489, 24 ATC 174, HL 11:43
IRC v Cornish Mutual Assurance Co Ltd [1926] AC 281, 95 LJKB 446, 12 TC 841, HL 8:36
IRC v Cosmotron Manufacturing Co Ltd [1997] 1 WLR 1288, [1999] STC 1134, 70 TC 292 .... 8:56
IRC v Crawley [1987] STC 147, 59 TC 728 .... 11:38
IRC v Crossman [1937] AC 26, [1936] 1 All ER 762, 105 LJKB 450, HL ... 45:01, 45:02, 45:05, 45:06
IRC v Desoutter Bros Ltd [1946] 1 All ER 58, 174 LT 162, 62 TLR 110, 29 TC 155, CA 8:76
IRC v Donaldson's Trustees 1963 SC 320, 41 TC 161, [1963] TR 237 .... 8:29
IRC v Dowdall O'Mahoney & Co Ltd [1952] AC 401, [1952] 1 All ER 531, 33 TC 259, [1952] TR 85, HL 8:108
IRC v Duchess of Portland [1982] Ch 314, [1982] 1 All ER 784, [1982] STC 149, 54 TC 648 .... 33:19, 33:20, 33:22
IRC v Duke of Westminster [1936] AC 1, [1935] All ER Rep 259, sub nom Duke of Westminster v IRC 19 TC 490, HL .. 3:12, 3:15, 3:19, 3:21, 4:01, 7:18, 7:28, 11:28, 11:30, 35:03
IRC v Eccentric Club Ltd [1924] 1 KB 390, 93 LJKB 289, 12 TC 657, 3 ATC 17, CA 8:35
IRC v Educational Grants Association Ltd [1967] Ch 993, [1967] 2 All ER 893, 44 TC 93, [1967] TR 79, CA 13:23
IRC v Europa Oil (NZ) Ltd [1971] AC 760, [1971] 2 WLR 55 .... 8:99
IRC v Eversden (Greenstock's Executors). See Essex (Somerset's Executors) v IRC
IRC v Falkirk Ice Rink Ltd [1975] STC 434, 51 TC 42, [1975] TR 223 .... 8:75
IRC v Falkirk Iron Co Ltd 1933 SC 546, 1933 SLT 283, 17 TC 625, 12 ATC 235 .... 8:119
IRC v Fisher [1926] AC 395, 95 LJKB 487, 134 LT 681, 10 TC 302, HL 4:01
IRC v Fleming & Co (Machinery) Ltd 1952 SC 120, 33 TC 57, [1951] TR 415 . 3:14, 8:88
IRC v Forth Conservancy Board [1931] AC 540, [1931] All ER Rep 679, 16 TC 103, 10 ATC 203, HL 8:35, 12:06
IRC v Fraser 1942 SC 493, 24 TC 498, 1942 SLT 280, 21 ATC 223 .... 8:16
IRC v Gardner, Mountain and D'Ambrumenil Ltd [1947] 1 All ER 650, 177 LT 16, 29 TC 69, 26 ATC 143, HL 8:144
IRC v Garvin [1981] 1 WLR 793, [1981] STC 344, 55 TC 24, HL .. 4:18, 4:19, 4:25, 4:26
IRC v Gaunt [1941] 2 All ER 82, 24 TC 69, 20 ATC 19; affd [1941] 1 KB 706, [1941] 2 All ER 662, 24 TC 69, 20 ATC 128, CA 15:14
IRC v George (Stedman's Executors). See Stedman's Executors v IRC
IRC v Glasgow and South Western Rly (1887) 12 App Cas 315, 56 LJPC 82, 57 LT 570, HL 57:07
IRC v Glasgow Musical Festival Association 1926 SC 920, 1926 SLT 604, 11 TC 154, 5 ATC 668 .... 13:23
IRC v Goodwin [1976] 1 All ER 481, [1976] 1 WLR 191, [1976] STC 28, 50 TC 583, HL 4:28
IRC v Gordon [1952] 1 All ER 866, 33 TC 226 .... 35:22
IRC v Granite City Steam Ship Co Ltd 1927 SC 705, 1927 SLT 495, 13 TC 1, 6 ATC 678 .... 8:124
IRC v Gray (Executor of Lady Fox) [1994] STC 360, [1994] RVR 129, CA .. 45:01, 45:02
IRC v Great Wigston Gas Co (1946) 176 LT 97, 62 TLR 623, 29 TC 197, 25 ATC 161, CA 8:126
IRC v Hague [1969] 1 Ch 393, [1968] 2 All ER 1252, [1968] 3 WLR 576, 44 TC 619 .... 4:29
IRC v Hamilton-Russell's Executors. See Hamilton-Russell's Executors v IRC
IRC v Hang Seng Bank Ltd [1991] 1 AC 306, [1990] STC 733 .... 37:07
IRC v Hawley [1928] 1 KB 578, 97 LJKB 191, 13 TC 327, 6 ATC 1021 .... 14:05
IRC v Hay 1924 SC 521, 61 Sc LR 375, 8 TC 636, 3 ATC 661 .... 11:12
IRC v Helen Slater Charitable Trust Ltd [1982] Ch 49, [1981] 3 All ER 98, [1981] STC 471, SS TC 230, CA 13:22, 13:26, 16:45
IRC v Henderson's Executors 1931 SC 681, 1931 SLT 496, 16 TC 282, 10 ATC 292 .... 14:01, 40:05

Table of Cases

IRC v Herd [1992] STC 264, Ct of Sess; revsd [1993] 3 All ER 56, [1993] 1 WLR 1090, [1993] STC 436, HL 7:21, 7:145
IRC v Herdman [1969] 1 All ER 495, [1969] 1 WLR 323, 45 TC 394, [1969] TR 1, HL 35:29, 35:31
IRC v Hinchy [1960] AC 748, [1960] 1 All ER 505, 38 TC 625, [1960] TR 33, HL 1:20, 1:24
IRC v Hogarth 1941 SC 1, 1940 SLT 458, 23 TC 491 .... 11:31, 11:32, 11:34
IRC v Holmden [1968] AC 685, [1968] 1 All ER 148, [1967] TR 323, 46 ATC 337, HL 20:12
IRC v Horrocks [1968] 3 All ER 296, [1968] 1 WLR 1809, 44 TC 645, [1968] TR 233 .... 4:26
IRC v Hyndland Investment Co Ltd (1929) 14 TC 694, 8 ATC 378 .... 2:20
IRC v Iles [1947] 1 All ER 798, 177 LT 284, 29 TC 225 .... 8:76
IRC v Jay's the Jewellers Ltd [1947] 2 All ER 762, 29 TC 274 .... 8:90
IRC v John Lewis Properties plc. See Lewis (John) Properties plc v IRC
IRC v John M Whiteford & Son (1962) 40 TC 379, [1962] TR 157, 41 ATC 166 .... 9:59
IRC v Joiner [1975] 3 All ER 1050, [1975] 1 WLR 1701, [1975] STC 657, 50 TC 419, HL 1:27, 4:20, 4:21
IRC v Kent Process Control Ltd [1989] STC 245 .... 60:06, 62:18
IRC v Kleinwort Benson Ltd [1969] 2 Ch 221, [1969] 2 All ER 737, 45 TC 369, [1969] TR 455 .... 4:23, 4:29
IRC v Korean Syndicate Ltd [1921] 3 KB 258, 90 LJKB 1153, 12 TC 181, CA 8:22
IRC v Korner [1969] 1 All ER 679, [1969] 1 WLR 554, 45 TC 287, 1969 SC (HL) 13, 1969 SLT 109 .... 44:14
IRC v Laird Group plc. See Laird Group plc v IRC
IRC v Lambhill Ironworks Ltd 1950 SC 331, 1950 SLT 251, 31 TC 393, [1950] TR 145 .... 9:12
IRC v Land Securities Investment Trust Ltd [1969] 2 All ER 430, [1969] 1 WLR 604, 45 TC 495, [1969] TR 173, HL 3:13
IRC v Lebus' Executors [1946] 1 All ER 476, 27 TC 136, 25 ATC 1 .... 5:15
IRC v Leckie 1940 SC 343, 23 TC 471, 19 ATC 109 .... 7:23
IRC v Leiner (1964) 41 TC 589, 43 ATC 56, [1964] TR 63 .... 12:17, 15:02
IRC v Levy [1982] STC 442, 56 TC 68 .... 15:05
IRC v Liquidators of City of Glasgow Bank (1881) 8 R 389, 18 SLR 242 .... 57:11
IRC v Lithgows 1960 SC 405, 39 TC 270 .... 25:15, 25:43
IRC v Littlewoods Mail Order Stores Ltd. See Littlewoods Mail Order Stores Ltd v IRC
IRC v Livingston 1927 SC 251, 11 TC 538, 1927 SLT 112, 6 ATC 397 .... 8:20
IRC v Lloyds Private Banking Ltd. See Lloyd's Private Banking v IRC
IRC v London Corpn [1953] 1 All ER 1075, [1953] 1 WLR 652, 34 TC 293, [1953] TR 123, HL 11:25
IRC v Longmans Green & Co Ltd (1932) 17 TC 272, 11 ATC 244 .... 1:27
IRC v Lysaght [1928] AC 234, [1928] All ER Rep 575, sub nom Lysaght v IRC 13 TC 511, HL 33:02, 33:03, 33:05, 33:06, 33:14, 54:02
IRC v McGuckian [1994] STC 888, 69 TC 1, NI CA; revsd [1997] 3 All ER 817, [1997] 1 WLR 991, [1997] STC 908, 69 TC 1, HL ... 1:24, 2:21, 2A:52, 2A:53, 3:07, 3:12, 3:21, 4:11, 4:18, 35:26, 39:35
IRC v McIntosh 1956 SLT 67, 36 TC 334, [1955] TR 333, 34 ATC 345 ..... 13:01, 13:02
IRC v McNaught's Executors (1964) 42 TC 71, [1964] TR 163, 43 ATC 139 .... 35:19
IRC v Macpherson [1989] AC 159, [1988] 2 WLR 1261, sub nom Macpherson v IRC [1988] 2 All ER 753, [1988] STC 362, HL 39:28
IRC v Mallaby-Deeley [1938] 3 All ER 463, 23 TC 153; revsd [1938] 4 All ER 818, 55 TLR 293, 23 TC 153, CA 3:13, 13:35
IRC v Mallender (Drury-Lowe's Executors) [2001] STC 514 .... 44:04
IRC v Mann [1937] AC 26, [1936] 1 All ER 762, 105 LJKB 450, HL 45:05, 45:06
IRC v Maple & Co (Paris) Ltd. See Maple & Co (Paris) Ltd v IRC
IRC v Mardon (1956) 36 TC 565, [1956] TR 237, 35 ATC 219 .... 14:07
IRC v Marr's Trustees (1906) 44 SLR 647, 14 SLT 585 .... 45:03, 45:04
IRC v Maxse [1919] 1 KB 647, 88 LJKB 752, 12 TC 41, CA 8:07
IRC v Metrolands (Property Finance) Ltd [1981] 2 All ER 166, [1981] STC 193; affd [1982] STC 259, 54 TC 679, HL 1:27

Table of Cases

IRC v Miller [1930] AC 222, [1930] All ER Rep 713, 15 TC 25, 9 ATC 73, HL 7:23, 7:41, 13:16
IRC v Mills [1973] Ch 225, [1972] 3 All ER 977, [1973] STC 1, [1972] TR 245, CA; revsd [1975] AC 38, [1974] 1 All ER 722, [1974] STC 130, 49 TC 367, HL .. 4:30, 15:03, 15:07, 15:08
IRC v Montgomery [1975] Ch 266, [1975] 1 All ER 664, [1975] STC 182, 49 TC 679 .... 18:03
IRC v Morris (1967) 44 TC 685, [1967] TR 431 .... 7:24
IRC v National Book League [1957] Ch 488, [1957] 2 All ER 644, 37 TC 455, [1957] TR 141, CA 11:28
IRC v National Federation of Self Employed and Small Businesses Ltd [1982] AC 617, [1981] 2 All ER 93, [1981] STC 260, 55 TC 133, HL 2:07
IRC v North British Rly Co (1901) 4 F (Ct of Sess) 27, 39 Sc LR 17, 9 SLT 209 ..... 57:11
IRC v Northfleet Coal and Ballast Co Ltd (1927) 12 TC 1102, 6 ATC 1030 .... 8:82
IRC v Oban Distillery Co Ltd 1933 SC 44, 1933 SLT 78, 18 TC 33, 11 ATC 466 .... 8:31
IRC v Oldham Training and Enterprise Council [1996] STC 1218, 69 TC 231 .... 16:46
IRC v Olive Mill Ltd [1963] 2 All ER 130, [1963] 1 WLR 712, 41 TC 77, [1963] TR 59 .... 21:18
IRC v Oswald [1945] AC 360, [1945] 1 All ER 641, 26 TC 448, 24 ATC 120, HL 11:38
IRC v Oughtred. See Oughtred v IRC
IRC v Paget [1938] 2 KB 25, [1938] 1 All ER 392, 107 LJKB 657, 21 TC 677, CA 11:07
IRC v Parker [1966] AC 141, [1966] 1 All ER 399, 43 TC 396, [1966] TR 1, HL 4:19, 4:20, 4:26
IRC v Patrick Thomson Ltd (1956) 37 TC 145, [1956] TR 471, 35 ATC 487 .. 8:56, 8:113
IRC v Payne (1940) 110 LJKB 323, 23 TC 610, 19 ATC 505, CA 15:02
IRC v Pearlberg [1953] 1 All ER 388, [1953] 1 WLR 331, 34 TC 57, CA 2:39
IRC v Pilcher [1949] 2 All ER 1097, 31 TC 314, [1949] TR 405, 28 ATC 385, CA 8:127
IRC v Plummer [1980] AC 896, [1979] 3 All ER 775, [1979] STC 793, 54 TC 1, HL 11:21, 11:38m 11:45, 12:17, 15:02, 15:05
IRC v Potts [1951] AC 443, [1951] 1 All ER 76, 32 TC 211, [1950] TR 379, HL 15:23
IRC v Pratt [1982] STC 756, 57 TC 1 .... 35:26
IRC v Priestley [1901] AC 208, 70 LJPC 41, 84 LT 700, 49 WR 657, HL 1:27
IRC v Regent Trust Co Ltd [1980] 1 WLR 688, [1980] STC 140, 53 TC 54, [1979] TR 401 .... 13:11
IRC v Reinhold 1953 SC 49, 34 TC 389, [1953] TR 11, 32 ATC 10 . 8:14, 8:17, 8:21, 8:22
IRC v Rennell [1964] AC 173, [1963] 1 All ER 803, [1963] TR 73, 42 ATC 55, HL 1:26
IRC v Richards' Executors [1971] 1 All ER 785, [1971] 1 WLR 571, 46 TC 626, [1971] TR 221, HL 16:21, 16:22, 19:06
IRC v Schroder [1983] STC 480, 57 TC 94 .... 35:33
IRC v Scottish and Newcastle Breweries Ltd [1982] 2 All ER 230, [1982] 1 WLR 322, [1982] STC 296, 55 TC 252, HL 9:29, 9:30
IRC v Scottish Provident Institution [2004] UKHL 52, [2005] 1 All ER 325, [2004] 1 WLR 3172, [2005] STC 15, 76 TC 538 .... 3:01, 3:03, 3:18, 3:24
IRC v Soul (1976) 51 TC 86 .... 2:39
IRC v South Behar Rly Co Ltd [1925] AC 476, 94 LJKB 386, 12 TC 657, 4 ATC 139, HL 33:26
IRC v Spencer-Nairn [1991] STC 60 .... 39:14, 41:04
IRC v Spirax Manufacturing Co Ltd (1946) 29 TC 187 .... 8:60
IRC v Stannard [1984] 2 All ER 105, [1984] 1 WLR 1039, [1984] STC 245 .... 46:03
IRC v Stenhouse's Trustees [1992] STC 103 .... 45:01
IRC v Stonehaven Recreation Ground Trustees 1930 SC 206, 1930 SLT 141, 15 TC 419, 8 ATC 523 8:35
IRC v Stype Investments (Jersey) Ltd [1981] Ch 367, [1981] 2 All ER 394, [1982] STC 310, [1981] TR 115; on appeal [1982] Ch 456, [1982] 3 All ER 419, [1982] STC 625, CA 46:02, 46:03

2557

Table of Cases

IRC v Thomas Nelson & Sons Ltd 1938 SC 816, 22 TC 175, 17 ATC 408 .... 11:05
IRC v Thompson [1937] 1 KB 290, [1936] 2 All ER 651, 20 TC 422 .... 8:31
IRC v Titaghur Jute Factory Co Ltd 1978 SC 96, 1978 SLT 133, [1978] STC 166, 53 TC 675 .... 8:148
IRC v Trustees of Sema Group Pension Scheme [2002] EWHC 94 (Ch), [2002] STC 276, 74 TC 593; revsd [2002] EWCA Civ 1857, [2003] STC 95, 74 TC 593 .... 4:19
IRC v Ufitec Group Ltd [1977] 3 All ER 924, [1977] STC 363 .... 62:18
IRC v Universities Superannuation Scheme Ltd [1997] STC 1, 70 TC 193 .... 4:19, 4:22
IRC v Vas [1990] STC 137 .... 37:30
IRC v Von Glehn & Co Ltd [1920] 2 KB 553, 89 LJKB 590, 12 TC 232, 123 LT 338, CA 8:105
IRC v Wachtel [1971] Ch 573, [1971] 1 All ER 271, 46 TC 543, [1970] TR 195 ... 15:14, 15:23
IRC v Watson 1943 SC 115, 1943 SLT 164, 25 TC 25, 21 ATC 341 .... 11:40
IRC v Wattie [1999] 1 WLR 873, [1998] STC 1160, 72 TC 639 .... 8:135
IRC v Wesleyan and General Assurance Society [1948] 1 All ER 555, [1948] LJR 948, 30 TC 11, 27 ATC 75, HL 11:21, 31:28, 31:30
IRC v West 1950 SC 516, 1950 SLT 337, 31 TC 402, [1950] TR 165 .... 9:40
IRC v West [1991] STC 357n, 64 TC 196, CA 2A:65
IRC v Wiggins [1979] 2 All ER 245, [1979] STC 244, 53 TC 639, [1978] TR 393 .... 4:18
IRC v Wilkinson [1992] STC 454, 65 TC 28, CA 8:02, 23:29
IRC v William Grant & Sons Distillers Ltd [2005] CSIH 63, [2006] STC 69, [2005] SWTI 1647 .... 8:64, 8:127
IRC v William Sharp & Son (1959) 38 TC 341, [1959] TR 21, 38 ATC 18 .... 8:119
IRC v Willoughby [1995] STC 143, 70 TC 57, CA; on appeal [1997] 4 All ER 65, [1997] 1 WLR 1071, [1997] STC 995, 70 TC 57, HL 3:11, 35:26
IRC v Wolfson [1949] 1 All ER 865, 31 TC 158, [1949] TR 121, HL 15:12
IRC v Woollen [1992] STC 944, CA 2:28
IRC v Zorab (1926) 11 TC 289, 6 ATC 68 .... 33:03
Innocent v Whaddon Estates Ltd [1982] STC 115, 55 TC 476, [1981] TR 379 ...... 28:21
Institute of Chartered Accountants of England and Wales v Customs and Excise Comrs [1996] STC 799; affd [1998] 4 All ER 115, [1997] STC 1155, CA; on appeal [1999] 2 All ER 449, [1999] STC 398, HL 63:15, 63:17
Institute of Chartered Shipbrokers v Customs and Excise Comrs (1997) VAT decision 15033 .... 68:25
Institute of the Motor Industry v Customs and Excise Comrs: C-149/97 [1998] ECR I-7053, [1998] STC 1219, ECJ 68:25
InsuranceWide.com Services Ltd v Revenue and Customs Comrs [2009] EWHC 999 (Ch), [2009] SWTI 1724 .... 68:13
Intercommunale voor Zeewaterontzilting (in liquidation) v Belgium: C-110/94 [1996] ECR I-857, [1996] STC 569, ECJ 63:32, 66:05, 66:08
International Bible Students Association v Customs and Excise Comrs [1988] STC 412 .... 68:23
International Language Centres Ltd v Customs and Excise Comrs [1982] VATTR 172; revsd [1983] STC 394 .... 2A:67, 67:05
International Master Publishers Ltd v Customs and Excise Comrs (1992) VAT decision 8807 .... 69:15
International Masters Publishers Ltd v Revenue and Customs Comrs [2006] EWHC 127 (Admin), [2006] STC 1450, [2006] SWTI 205, [2006] All ER (D) 123 (Jan); affd sub nom R (on the application of International Masters Publishers Ltd) v Revenue and Customs Comrs [2006] EWCA Civ 1455, [2007] STC 153, [2006] NLJR 1766, [2006] SWTI 2454, [2006] All ER (D) 90 (Nov) 63:20
International Planned Parenthood Federation v Customs and Excise Comrs (2000) VAT decision 16922 .... 69:39
International Trade and Exhibitions J/V Ltd v Customs and Excise Comrs [1996] V & DR 165 .... 63:30; 65:38
Inverclyde's (Lord) Trustees v Millar [1924] AC 580, 93 LJPC 266, 9 TC 14, 3 ATC 706, HL 14:02
Investrand BV v Staatssecretaris van Financien: C-435/05 [2007] ECR I–1315, [2007] All ER (D) 113 (Feb), ECJ, [2008] STC 518 .... 66:08

Table of Cases

Inzani (Peter) v Revenue & Customs Comrs (SpC 529) [2006] STC (SCD) 279 ...... 51:05
Irvine v Irvine [2006] EWHC 583 (Ch), [2006] 4 All ER 102, [2007] 1 BCLC 445, (2006) Times, 21 April, 150 Sol Jo LB 433, [2006] All ER (D) 346 (Mar) 45:02
Irving v Tesco Stores (Holdings) Ltd [1982] STC 881, 58 TC 1 .... 28:01, 28:09
Isle of Wight Council v Customs and Excise Comrs (2004) VAT decision 18557; revsd sub nom Customs and Excise Comrs v Isle of Wight Council [2004] EWHC 2541 (Ch), [2005] STC 257, [2007] EWHC 219 (Ch), [2008] STC 614 ..... 63:02, 63:15, 63:17
Isle of Wight Council and others v Revenue and Cutsoms Comrs (2006) VAT decision 19427 .... 63:17
Iswera v Ceylon Commissioners of Inland Revenue [1965] 1 WLR 663, [1965] TR 159, 44 ATC 157 .... 8:21, 23:02
Iveagh v IRC [1930] IR 386; revsd [1930] IR 431 .... 33:03
Ivory & Sime Trustlink Ltd v Customs and Excise Comrs [1998] STC 597 .... 68:16

J

J A Van der Steen v Inspecteur van de Belastingdienst Utrecht-Gooi/ kantoor Utrecht: Case C-355/06, [2007] ECR I-8863, [2007] SWTI 2406, ECJ 63:12
JCM Beheer BV v Staatssecratarais van Financiën: C-124/07 [2008] SWTI 1144, ECJ 68:13
JD Wetherspoon plc v R & C Comrs (2008) SpC 665 .... 9:30, 9:37
JD Wetherspoon plc v Revenue & Customs Comrs: C-302/07 [2009] ECR I–0000, [2009] STC 1022, ECJ 65:20
JJ v Netherlands (1998) 28 EHRR 168, E Ct HR 1:14
JP Commodities Ltd v Revenue and Customs Comrs [2007] EWHC 2474 (Ch), [2008] STC 816 .... 69:07
JP Morgan Fleming Claverhouse Investment Trust plc v Comrs of HM Revenue and Customs C-363/05, [2007] ECR I–5517, [2008] STC 1180, [2007] All ER (D) 368 (Jun), ECJ 68:16
Jacgilden (Weston Hall) Ltd v Castle [1971] Ch 408, [1969] 3 All ER 1110, [1969] 3 WLR 839, 45 TC 685 .... 8:157
Jackman v Powell. See Powell v Jackman
Jackson v Customs and Excise Comrs (1985) VAT decision 1959 .... 66:05
Jackson v Laskers Home Furnishers Ltd [1956] 3 All ER 891, [1957] 1 WLR 69, 37 TC 69, [1956] TR 391 .... 8:125
Jacobs v IRC (1925) 10 TC 1 .... 29:10
Jacques v Revenue and Customs Comrs [2006] STC (SCD) 40 .... 2A:68
Jade Palace v Revenus and Customs Comrs [2006] STC (SCD) 419 .... 2A:70
Jaggers (t/a Shide Trees) v Ellis [1997] STC 1417, 71 TC 164 .... 8:42
James (Edward) Foundation v Customs and Excise Comrs [1975] VATTR 61 .... 63:32
Janes' Settlement, Re, Wasmuth v Janes [1918] 2 Ch 54, 87 LJ Ch 454, 119 LT 114 .... 11:12, 11:24
Janson v Driefontein Consolidated Mines [1902] AC 484, [1900–3] All ER Rep 426, 71 LJKB 857, 87 LT 372, HL 33:01
Jarmin (HM Inspector of Taxes) v Rawlings (1994) 22:33
Jarrold v Boustead [1964] 3 All ER 76, [1964] 1 WLR 1357, 41 TC 701, [1964] TR 217, CA 7:21, 7:28, 17:01, 18:04
Jarrold v John Good & Sons Ltd [1963] 1 All ER 141, [1963] 1 WLR 214, 40 TC 681, [1962] TR 371, CA 9:26, 9:29
Jaworski v Institution of Polish Engineers in Great Britain Ltd [1951] 1 KB 768, [1950] 2 All ER 1191, [1950] TR 399, 29 ATC 386, CA 7:23
Jays the Jewellers Ltd v IRC [1947] 2 All ER 762, 29 TC 274, 41 R & IT 125 .... 2A:69
Jefferson v Jefferson [1956] P 136, [1956] 1 All ER 31, [1955] TR 321, 36 ATC 320, CA 11:43
Jefford v Gee [1970] 2 QB 130, [1970] 1 All ER 1202, [1970] 2 WLR 702, [1970] 1 Lloyd's Rep 107, CA 11:12
Jeffries v Stevens [1982] STC 639, 56 TC 134 .... 10:06
Jeffs v Ringtons Ltd [1986] 1 All ER 144, [1986] 1 WLR 266, [1985] STC 809, 58 TC 680 .... 8:110
Jenkins v Brown [1989] 1 WLR 1163, [1989] STC 577 .... 20:06, 20:09, 23:04

Table of Cases

Jenkins (t/a Lifetime Financial Services) v Customs and Excise Comrs (1997) VAT decision 14784 .... 66:04
Jenkins Productions Ltd v IRC [1943] 2 All ER 786, 29 TC 142; on appeal [1944] 1 All ER 610, 29 TC 142, 22 ATC 42, CA 25:35
Jenkinson v Customs and Excise Comrs [1988] VATTR 45 .... 64:14
Jenkinson v Freedland (1961) 39 TC 636, [1961] TR 181, 40 ATC 190, CA 8:20
Jenks v Dickinson [1996] STC (SCD) 299 .... 21:21
Jenners Princes Street Edinburgh Ltd v IRC [1998] STC (SCD) 196 ..... 8:67, 8:122, 10:08
Jennings v Barfield and Barfield [1962] 2 All ER 957, [1962] 1 WLR 997, 40 TC 365, [1962] TR 187 .... 8:131
Jennings v Kinder [1959] Ch 22, [1958] 1 All ER 369, 38 TC 673, [1957] TR 365; on appeal [1959] Ch 22, [1958] 3 All ER 285, 38 TC 673, [1958] TR 237, CA ... 7:19, 7:101
Jennings v Middlesbrough Corpn [1953] 2 All ER 207, [1953] 1 WLR 833, 34 TC 447, 51 LGR 622 .... 10:07
Jennings v Westwood Engineering Ltd [1975] IRLR 245 .... 7:23
Jerome v Kelly [2001] STC (SCD) 170; on appeal [2002] EWHC 604 (Ch), [2002] STC 609; revsd [2002] EWCA Civ 1879, [2003] STC 206, [2003] 24 EG 163; revsd [2004] UKHL 25, [2004] 2 All ER 835, [2004] 1 WLR 1409, [2004] STC 887 .... 1:28, 18:06
Jervis v Howle and Talke Colliery Co Ltd [1937] Ch 67, [1936] 3 All ER 193, 106 LJ Ch 34, 80 Sol Jo 875, 155 LT 572 .... 2A:71
Joachimson v Swiss Bank Corpn [1921] 3 KB 110, [1921] All ER Rep 92, 90 LJKB 973, 26 Com Cas 196, CA 8:143
Johansson v US 336 F 2d 809 (1964) 37:36
John Village Automotive Ltd v Customs and Excise Comrs [1998] V & DR 340 ..... 63:30
Johnson v Edwards [1981] STC 660, 54 TC 488, [1981] TR 269 .... 18:11
Johnson v Holleran [1989] STC 1, 61 TC 428 .... 50:05
Johnson v Johnson [1946] P 205, [1946] 1 All ER 573, 175 LT 252, 62 TLR 333, CA 11:41
Johnson v W S Try Ltd [1946] 1 All ER 532, 174 LT 399, 27 TC 167, 25 ATC 33 .... 8:144
Johnston v Britannia Airways Ltd [1994] STC 763, 67 TC 99 .... 8:64, 8:147, 8:148
Johnston v Heath [1970] 3 All ER 915, [1970] 1 WLR 1567, 46 TC 463, [1970] TR 183 .... 8:03, 8:15
Johnston Publishing (North) Ltd v Revenue and Customs Comrs [2008] EWCA Civ 858 .... 28:21
Jones, Re, Jones v Jones [1933] Ch 842, [1933] All ER Rep 830, 102 LJ Ch 303, 21 ATC 595 .... 11:43
Jones v Borland 1969 (4) SA 29 .... 34:04, 69:34
Jones v Garnett [2005] STC (SCD) 9; on appeal [2005] EWHC 849 (Ch) 2A:74, 15:30, 15:31
Jones v Garnett (Inspector of Taxes) [2005] STC 1667, (2005) Times, 17 May, [2005] SWTI 903, [2005] All ER (D) 396 (Apr); revsd [2005] EWCA Civ 1553, [2006] 2 All ER 381, [2006] 1 WLR 1123, [2006] STC 283, [2006] ICR 690, [2006] 2 FCR 294, [2006] NLJR 22, (2006) Times, 3 January , 150 Sol Jo LB 95, [2005] All ER (D) 224 (Dec), [2007] UKHL 35, [2007] STC 1536 .... 3:01, 15:15, 15:30, 15:31
Jones v Garnett (Inspector of Taxes) [2007] UKHL 35, (2007) Times, 9 August, [2007] All ER (D) 390 (Jul) 15:31
Jones v IRC [1920] 1 KB 711, [1920] All ER Rep 138, 7 TC 310, 89 LJKB 129 ...... 11:34
Jones v Leeming. See Leeming v Jones
Jones v Mason Investments (Luton) Ltd (1966) 43 TC 570, [1966] TR 335, 45 ATC 413, [1967] BTR 75 .... 2A:62
Jones v Wright (1927) 139 LT 43, 44 TLR 128, 13 TC 221, 6 ATC 895 .... 11:27
Jones (Samuel) & Co (Devonvale) Ltd v IRC 1952 SC 94, 32 TC 513, [1951] TR 411, 30 ATC 412 .... 8:123
Jopp v Wood (1865) 4 De GJ & Sm 616, 34 LJ Ch 212, 11 Jur NS 212, 12 LT 41 .... 33:22
Joppa Enterprises Ltd v Revenue and Customs Comrs [2009] CSIH 17, [2009] STC 1279 .... 63:20
Jordan v Customs and Excise Comrs [1994] VATTR 286 .... 64:14
Jorge (Antonio) Lda v Fazenda Publica: C-536/03 [2005] SWTI 1017, [2005] All ER (D) 426 (May), ECJ 66:08

Table of Cases

Joscelyne v Nissen [1970] 2 QB 86, [1970] 1 All ER 1213, [1970] 2 WLR 509, 114 Sol Jo 55, CA 2A:71
Jowett v O'Neill and Brennan Construction Ltd [1998] STC 482, 70 TC 566 .... 25:43
Joynson's Wills Trusts, Re, Gaddum v IRC [1954] Ch 567, [1954] 2 All ER 294, [1954] TR 141, 33 ATC 126 .... 1:24
Jubb, Re, Neilson v King (1941) 20 ATC 297 .... 11:43
Jubilee Hall Recreation Centre Ltd v Customs and Excise Comrs [1997] STC 414; revsd [1999] STC 381, CA 69:18

K

KPMG (a firm) v Customs and Excise Comrs [1997] V & DR 192 .... 66:20
Kahler v Midland Bank Ltd [1950] AC 24, [1949] 2 All ER 621, [1949] LJR 1687, HL 34:02
KapHag Renditefonds 35 Spreecenter Berlin-Hellersdorf 3 Tranche GbR v Finanzamt Charlottenburg: C-442/01 [2003] ECR I-6851, [2003] All ER (D) 362 (Jun), ECJ 63:19
Kato Kagaku Co Ltd v Revenue and Customs Comrs [2007] STC (SCD) 412, [2007] SWTI 1181, SCD 8:110
Kauri Timber Co Ltd v I T Comr [1913] AC 771, 83 LJPC 6, 109 LT 22 .... 8:127
Keene, Re [1922] 2 Ch 475, [1922] All ER Rep 258, 91 LJ Ch 484, 127 LT 831 .... 57:06
Keeping Newcastle Warm Ltd v Customs and Excise Comrs: C-353/00 [2002] All ER (EC) 769, [2002] 2 CMLR 1359, [2002] STC 943, ECJ 63:21
Kelly (a firm) v Customs and Excise Comrs (1987) VAT decision 2452 .... 66:05
Kelsall v Stipplechoice Ltd [1995] STC 681, CA 25:35
Kelsall Parsons & Co v IRC 1938 SC 238, 1938 SLT 239, 21 TC 608, 17 ATC 87 .... 7:37, 8:87, 8:88
Kempton v Special Comrs and IRC [1992] STC 823, 66 TC 249 .... 2:07
Kenmare v IRC [1958] AC 267, [1957] 3 All ER 33, 37 TC 383, [1957] TR 215, HL 15:11, 15:12
Kennemer Golf and Country Club v Staatssecretaris van Financiën: C-174/00 [2002] QB 1252, [2002] All ER (EC) 480, [2002] 2 CMLR 237, [2002] STC 502, ECJ 68:26
Kerr v Brown [2002] STC (SCD) 434 .... 7:125
Kerr v Brown (No 2) [2003] STC (SCD) 266 .... 7:125
Keston v IRC [2004] EWHC 59 (Ch), [2004] STC 902 .... 57:13
Key v Customs and Excise Comrs (1998) VAT decision 15354 .... 66:07
Keydon Estates Ltd v Customs and Excise Comrs (1990) VAT decision 4471 .... 63:19
Khan v Director of Assets Recovery Agency [2006] STC (SCD) 154 .... 2:35
Khan v Miah [2001] 1 All ER 20, [2001] 1 All ER (Comm) 282, [2000] 1 WLR 2123, [2000] 45 LS Gaz R 41, [2000] NLJR 1658, 144 Sol Jo LB 282, [2001] 2 LRC 332, [2000] All ER (D) 1647, HL 8:49
Kildrummy (Jersey) Ltd v IRC [1990] STC 657, 1992 SLT 787 .... 57:25
Kimber v Customs and Excise Comrs (1993) VAT decision 10469 .... 65:27
Kimbers & Co v IRC [1936] 1 KB 132, [1935] All ER Rep 609, 105 LJKB 97, 154 LT 305 .... 57:16, 58:03, 62:05
King, Re, Barclays Bank Ltd v King [1942] Ch 413, [1942] 2 All ER 182 .... 46:25
King v United Kingdom (Application No 13881/02) [2005] STC 438, 76 TC 699, E Ct HR 1:13
King v Walden [2001] STC 822, 74 TC 45 .... 1:22, 2A:82
Kingcome, Re, Hickley v Kingcome [1936] Ch 566, [1936] 1 All ER 173, 105 LJ Ch 209, 15 ATC 237 .... 11:43
Kingfisher plc v Customs and Excise Comrs [2000] STC 992 .... 68:16
Kingscrest Associates Ltd v Customs and Excise Comrs: C-498/03 [2005] ECR I-4427, [2005] STC 1547, [2005] All ER (D) 404 (May), ECJ 68:23
Kinloch v IRC (1929) 14 TC 736, 8 ATC 469 .... 33:03
Kirby v Thorn EMI plc [1986] 1 WLR 851, [1986] STC 200, 60 TC 519; revsd [1988] 2 All ER 947, [1988] 1 WLR 445, [1987] STC 621, 60 TC 519, CA 18:03, 18:06
Kirk & Randall Ltd v Dunn (1924) 8 TC 663, 131 LT 288, 3 ATC 185 ... 8:49, 8:50, 8:52
Kirkby v Hughes [1993] STC 76, 65 TC 532 .... 8:21, 8:49
Kirkham v Williams [1989] STC 333; revsd [1991] 4 All ER 240, [1991] 1 WLR 863, [1991] STC 342, CA 8:21

Table of Cases

Kirkness v John Hudson & Co [1955] AC 696, [1955] 2 All ER 345, [1955] TR 145, HL 57:07
Kirkwood v Evans [2002] EWHC 30 (Ch), [2002] 1 WLR 1794, [2002] STC 231, 74 TC 481 .... 7:129, 7:135
Kirton Designs Ltd v Customs and Excise Comrs (1987) VAT decision 2374 .... 69:35
Kittel v Belgian State: C-439/04 [2006] ECR I-6161, [2008] STC 1537, ECJ .. 63:09, 66:06
Kleinwort Benson Ltd v Lincoln City Council [1999] 2 AC 349, [1998] 4 All ER 513, [1998] 3 WLR 1095, [1998] RVR 315, HL 7:144, 11:41
Knapp v Morton [1999] STC (SCD) 13 .... 7:126
Kneen v Martin [1935] 1 KB 499, [1934] All ER Rep 595, 19 TC 33, 13 ATC 454, CA 35:19
Knight v Parry [1973] STC 56, 48 TC 580, [1972] TR 267, 51 ATC 283 ...... 8:97, 8:105
Knight v Taxation Comr (1928) 28 SR NSW 523 .... 12:05
Kodak Ltd v Clark [1903] 1 KB 505, 72 LJKB 369, 4 TC 549, CA 35:03
Koenigsberger v Mellor [1993] STC 408, 67 TC 280; affd [1995] STC 547, 67 TC 280, CA 5:23
Koeppler Will Trusts, Re, Barclays Bank Trust Co Ltd v Slack [1986] Ch 423, [1985] 2 All ER 869, [1985] 3 WLR 765, CA 25:03
Kohanzad v Customs and Excise Comrs [1994] STC 967 .... 66:22
Kohler v Finanzamt Dusseldorf-Nord: C-58/04 [2006] STC 469, [2005] All ER (D) 82 (Sep), ECJ 63:30
Koitaki Para Rubber Estates Ltd v Federal Comr of Taxation (1940) 64 CLR 15 .... 33:28
Kollektivavtalsstiftelsen TRR Trygghetsrådet v Skatteverket: C-291/07 [2008] ECR I-0000, [2009] STC 526, ECJ 63:30
Kretztechnik AG v Finanzamt Linz: C-465/03, [2005] ECR I-4357, [2005] STC 1118, ECJ 63:19, 66:08, 68:16
Kühne v Finanzamt München III: 58/88 [1990] STC 749, [1989] ECR 1925, [1990] 3 CMLR 287, ECJ 65:29
Kuwait Petroleum (GB) Ltd v Customs and Excise Comrs: C-48/97 [1999] All ER (EC) 450, [1999] ECR I-2323, [1999] 2 CMLR 651, [1999] STC 488, ECJ . 63:20, 63:21, 65:28
Kuwait Petroleum (GB) Ltd v Customs and Excise Comrs [2001] STC 62; affd [2001] EWCA Civ 1542, [2001] STC 1568 .... 63:21, 65:19, 65:28
Kwik Fit (GB) Ltd v Customs and Excise Comrs [1992] VATTR 427 .... 63:19
Kwik-Fit (GB) Ltd v Customs and Excise Comrs [1998] STC 159, 1998 SC 139 ..... 66:08
Kwik Save Group plc v Customs and Excise Comrs [1994] VATTR 457 ...... 63:20, 63:27

L

LCC v Edwards (1909) 100 LT 444, 73 JP 213, 5 TC 383 .... 8:122, 9:26
LM Tenancies 1 plc v IRC [1996] STC 880; affd [1998] STC 326, CA .. 2:89, 56:18, 56:26
LuP GmbH v Finanzamt Bochum-Mitte: C-106/05 [2006] SWTI 1620, [2006] All ER (D) 40 (Jun), ECJ 68:23
Labour Party v Customs and Excise Comrs (2001) VAT decision 17034 . 2:07, 66:05, 66:09
Lace v Chandler [1944] KB 368, [1944] 1 All ER 305, 113 LJKB 282, 170 LT 185, CA 57:26
Lack (Frederick) Ltd v Doggett (1970) 46 TC 524, [1970] TR 123, 49 ATC 136, CA 2:27
Laidler v Perry [1965] Ch 192, [1964] 3 All ER 329, 42 TC 351, [1964] TR 213, CA; affd [1966] AC 16, [1965] 2 All ER 121, 42 TC 351, [1965] TR 121, HL 7:17, 7:19, 7:24, 7:25, 7:44
Laird Group plc v IRC [1999] STC (SCD) 86; revsd sub nom IRC v Laird Group plc [2002] EWCA Civ 576, [2002] STC 722; on appeal [2003] UKHL 54, [2003] 4 All ER 669, [2003] 1 WLR 2476, [2003] STC 1349, 75 TC 399 .... 4:20, 4:28
Lake v Lake [1989] STC 865 .... 2A:71, 40:21
Lamberts Construction Ltd v Customs and Excise Comrs (1992) VAT decision 8882 .... 69:18
Lamport and Holt Line Ltd v Langwell (1958) 38 TC 193, [1958] TR 209, 37 ATC 224, [1958] 2 Lloyd's Rep 53, CA 8:74, 56:29
Lancashire County Council v Customs and Excise Comrs [1996] V & DR 550 ...... 63:19, 63:20

Lancaster v IRC [2000] STC (SCD) 138 .... 6:41
Land (t/a Crown Optical Centre) v Customs and Excise Comrs (1998) VAT decision
    15547 .... 68:23
Land Management v Fox [2002] STC (SCD) 152 25:43
Landboden-Agrardienste GmbH & Co KG v Finanzamt Calau: C-384/95 [1998] STC
    171, ECJ 63:19
Lander, Re, Lander v Lander [1951] Ch 546, [1951] 1 All ER 622, [1951] TR 93, 30
    ATC 93 .... 46:23
Landes Bros v Simpson (1934) 19 TC 62 .... 8:78
Lang v Rice [1984] STC 172, 57 TC 80 .... 8:82, 18:03
Lange v Finanzamt Fürstenfeldbruck: C-111/92 [1993] ECR I-4677, [1997] STC
    564, ECJ 69:08
Langham v Veltema [2002] EWHC 2689 (Ch), [2002] STC 1557; revsd [2004] EWCA
    Civ 193, [2004] STC 544 .... 2A:48, 2A:74
Langley v Appleby [1976] 3 All ER 391, [1976] STC 368 .... 22:12, 44:13
Lankhorst-Hohorst GmbH v Finanzamt Steinfurt: C-324/00 [2002] ECR I-11779,
    [2003] 2 CMLR 693, [2003] STC 607, ECJ 1:10, 1.19, 25:45
Larullah Ltd v Customs and Excise Comrs (1985) VAT decision 1779 .... 63:23
Lasertec v Finanz amt Emmingem: C-429/04 .... 1:19
Last v London Assurance Corpn (1885) 10 App Cas 438, 55 LJQB 92, 2 TC 100, HL
    .... 8:36
Latilla v IRC [1943] AC 377, [1943] 1 All ER 265, 25 TC 107, 22 ATC 23, HL 4:01,
    35:32, 35:37
Laurie and Laurie (t/a Peacock Montessori Nursery) v Customs and Excise Comrs (2001)
    VAT decision 17219 .... 63:16
Law Shipping Co Ltd v IRC 1924 SC 74, 12 TC 621, 3 ATC 110 .... 8:124
Lawrence v Lawrence [1985] Fam 106, [1985] 1 All ER 506, [1985] 2 WLR 86, [1984]
    FLR 949; affd [1985] Fam 106, [1985] 2 All ER 733, [1985] 3 WLR 125, [1985] FLR
    1097, CA 33:17
Lawrie v IRC 1952 SC 394, 1952 SLT 413, 34 TC 20, [1952] TR 305 .... 8:122
Lawson v Brooks [1992] STC 76, 64 TC 462 .... 6:40
Lawson v Johnson Matthey plc [1990] 1 WLR 414, [1990] STC 149; affd [1991] 1 WLR
    558, [1991] STC 259, CA; revsd [1992] 2 AC 324, [1992] 2 All ER 647, [1992] 2
    WLR 826, [1992] STC 466, HL 8:98, 8:110, 8:116
Lawson v Rolfe [1970] Ch 612, [1970] 1 All ER 761, 46 TC 199, [1969] TR 537,
    [1970] BTR 142 .... 13:21, 35:10
Lawson Mardon Group Pension Scheme v Customs and Excise Comrs (1993) VAT
    decision 10231 .... 66:07, 66:28
Laycock v Freeman, Hardy and Willis Ltd [1939] 2 KB 1, [1938] 4 All ER 609, 22 TC
    288, 17 ATC 450, CA 8:57, 8:60
Lazard Bros & Co v Midland Bank Ltd [1933] AC 289, [1932] All ER Rep
    571, 102 LJKB 191, 148 LT 242, HL 33:33
Leach v Pogson (1962) 40 TC 585, [1962] TR 289, 41 ATC 298 .... 8:13, 27:32
Leather Cloth Co v American Leather Cloth Co (1865) 11 HL Cas 523, 6 New Rep 209,
    35 LJ Ch 53, 12 LT 742, HL 57:06
Lee v IRC (1941) 24 TC 207 .... 35:33
Lee v Jewitt [2000] STC (SCD) 517 .... 16:21
Lee v Lee's Air Farming Ltd [1961] AC 12, [1960] 3 All ER 420, [1960] 3 WLR 758
    .... 7:08
Lee and Sarrafan (t/a Regal Sporting Club) v Customs and Excise Comrs (1998) VAT
    decision 15563 .... 68:15
Leeds Permanent Building Society v Procter [1982] 3 All ER 925, [1982] STC 821, 56
    TC 293 .... 9:28, 9:30
Leeland v Boarland [1946] 1 All ER 13, 27 TC 71, 24 ATC 313 .... 7:34
Leeming v Jones [1930] 1 KB 279, 99 LJKB 17, 15 TC 333, 141 LT 472, 8 ATC
    307, CA; affd (1970) 15 TC 333, sub nom Jones v Leeming [1930] AC 415,
    [1930] All ER Rep 584, 99 LJKB 318, 143 LT 50, 46 TLR 296, 74 Sol Jo 247, 9 ATC
    134, HL 5:17, 8:04, 12:03, 12:04
Leesportefeuille 'Intiem' CV v Staatssecretaris von Financiën: 165/86 [1988] ECR 1471,
    [1989] 2 CMLR 856, ECJ 66:03

Table of Cases

Legal and Contractual Services Ltd v Customs and Excise Comrs [1984] VATTR 85 .... 65:12
Legal and General Assurance Society v Thomas [2005] STC (SCD) 350 .... 37:12, 37:27
Leigh v IRC [1928] 1 KB 73, 96 LJKB 853, 11 TC 590, 6 ATC 514 .... 5:15, 12:13
Leigh's Will Trusts, Re, Handyside v Durbridge [1970] Ch 277, [1969] 3 All ER 432 .... 42:11
Leisure Pass Group Ltd v Revenue and Customs Comrs [2008] EWHC 2158 (Ch), [2008] STC 3340 .... 65:21
Lennartz v Finanzamt München III: C-97/90 [1991] ECR I-3795, [1995] STC 514, ECJ 66:05, 66:27
Lenz v Finanzlandesdirektion für Tirol: C-315/02; [2004] ECR I-7063 .... 1:18
Leonidas and Leonidas v Customs and Excise Comrs [2000] V & DR 207 .... 67:01
Leroux v Brown (1852) 12 CB 801, 22 LJCP 1, 20 LTOS 68 .... 17:01
Lessex Ltd v Spence [2004] STC (SCD) 79 .... 2A:91
Letts v IRC [1956] 3 All ER 588, [1957] 1 WLR 201, [1956] TR 337, 35 ATC 367 .... 57:04
Leur-Bloem v Inspecteur der Belastingdienst/Ondernemingen Amsterdam 2: C-28/95 [1998] QB 182, [1997] All ER (EC) 738, [1998] 1 CMLR 157, [1997] STC 1205, ECJ 25:47
Levene v IRC [1928] AC 217, [1928] All ER Rep 746, 13 TC 486, HL . 4:01, 33:03, 33:05, 33:06, 33:14, 54:02
Levob Verzekeringen BV, OB Bank NV cs v Staatssecretaris van Financien: C-41/04 ECR I-9433, [2006] STC 766, [2005] All ER (D) 328 (Oct), ECJ 63:20, 63:30; 65:38
Lewis v IRC [1999] STC (SCD) 349 .... 4:28
Lewis v Lady Rook [1990] STC 23, 64 TC 567; revsd [1992] 1 WLR 662, [1992] STC 171, 64 TC 567, CA 23:06
Lewis v Walters [1992] STC 97, 64 TC 489, 24 HLR 427 .... 23:19, 23:21
Lewis (John) Properties plc v IRC [2000] STC (SCD) 494; on appeal sub nom IRC v John Lewis Properties plc [2001] STC 1118, [2002] 1 WLR 35; affd [2002] EWCA Civ 1869, [2003] Ch 513, [2003] STC 117, [2003] 2 WLR 1196 . 3:07, 8:119, 10:16, 62:03
Lex Services plc v Customs and Excise Comrs [2003] UKHL 67, [2004] 1 All ER 434, [2004] 1 WLR 1, [2004] STC 73 .... 65:17
Libdale Ltd v Customs and Excise Comrs [1993] VATTR 425 .... 63:19, 65:18, 66:22
Lidl Belgium GmbH & Co KG v Finanzamt Heilbronn: C-414/06 [2008] 3 CMLR 31, [2008] STC 3229, [2008] All ER (D) 187 (May) 1.14
Lilley v Harrison (1951) TC 344, [1951] TR 11, 30 ATC 10, CA; affd [1952] WN 383, 33 TC 344, [1952] TR 333, 31 ATC 365, HL 12:12
Lime-IT Ltd v Justin [2003] STC (SCD) 15 .... 7:11, 8:26
Limmer Asphalte Paving Co Ltd v IRC (1872) LR 7 Exch 211, 41 LJ Ex 106, 26 LT 633, 20 WR 610 .... 56:13, 57:10
Lincolnshire Sugar Co Ltd v Smart [1937] AC 697, [1937] 1 All ER 413, 106 LJKB 185, 20 TC 643, HL 8:89
Lindman, Re: C-42/02 [2004] 1 CMLR 1220, ECJ 1:07
Lindsay v IRC 1933 SC 33, 18 TC 43 .... 8:08
Lindsay v IRC (1952) 34 TC 289, [1953] TR 5, 46 R & IT 146, 32 ATC 1 .... 9:59
Lindsay, Woodward and Hiscox v IRC 1933 SC 33, 1933 SLT 57, 18 TC 43 .... 8:09
Lindus and Hortin v IRC (1933) 17 TC 442, 12 ATC 140 .... 11:23, 13:15, 13:21
Link Housing Association Ltd v Customs and Excise Comrs [1991] VATTR 112; affd sub nom Customs and Excise Comrs v Link Housing Association Ltd [1992] STC 718 .... 69:17
Lion Ltd v Inspector of Taxes [1997] STC (SCD) 133 .... 28:01
Lions Ltd v Gosford Furnishing Co and IRC 1962 SC 78, 1962 SLT 138, 40 TC 256, [1961] TR 395 .... 8:160
Lipkin Gorman (a firm) v Karpnale Ltd [1991] 2 AC 548, [1992] 4 All ER 512, [1991] 3 WLR 10, [1991] NLJR 815, 135 Sol Jo LB 36, HL 2A:70
Little Olympian Each Ways Ltd, Re [1994] 4 All ER 561, [1995] 1 WLR 560, [1995] 1 BCLC 48, 1994] BCC 959 .... 33:32, 33:25
Littlewoods Mail Order Stores Ltd v IRC [1961] Ch 597, [1961] 3 All ER 258, [1961] TR 161, 40 ATC 171, CA; affd sub nom IRC v Littlewoods Mail Order Stores Ltd [1963] AC 135, [1962] 2 All ER 279, [1962] TR 107, 41 ATC 116, 45 TC 519, HL 57:07, 57:24, 57:25, 60:04

Littlewoods Organisation plc v Customs and Excise Comrs [1997] V & DR 408 ..... 65:11
Littman v Barron [1951] Ch 993, [1951] 2 All ER 393, 33 TC 373, [1951] TR 141, CA;
  affd sub nom Barron v Littman [1953] AC 96, [1952] 2 All ER 548, 33 TC 373,
  [1952] TR 363, HL 1:24, 12:13
Liverpool and London and Globe Insurance Co v Bennett [1913] AC 610, 82 LJKB
  1221, 6 TC 327, HL 8:91
Liverpool Corn Trade Association Ltd v Monks [1926] 2 KB 110, 95 LJKB 519, 10 TC
  442, 5 ATC 228 .... 8:39
Llandudno Cabinlift Co Ltd v Customs and Excise Comrs [1973] VATTR 1 .... 69:27
Lloyd v R & C Comrs (2008) SpC 671 .... 4:29
Lloyd v Sulley (1884) 11 R (Ct of Sess) 687, 21 Sc LR 482, 2 TC 37 .. 33:02, 33:04, 54:02
Lloyd v Taylor (1970) 46 TC 539, [1970] TR 157 .... 1:01
Lloyds Private Banking v IRC [1997] STC (SCD) 259; revsd sub nom IRC v Lloyds
  Private Banking Ltd [1998] STC 559, [1998] 2 FCR 41, [1999] 1 FLR 147 .... 42:08
Lloyds TSB (Personal Representative of Antrobus, dec'd) v IRC [2002] STC (SCD)
  468 .... 44:14, 44:16
Lloyds TSB Private Banking plc v Twiddy (Inland Revenue Capital Taxes)
  [2006] 1 EGLR 157, [2006] RVR 138, Land Trib 44:14
Lloyds UDT Finance Ltd v Chartered Finance Trust Holdings plc (Britax
  International GmbH, Pt 20 defendants) [2002] EWCA Civ 806, [2002] STC 956, 74
  TC 662 .... 9:50
Local Authorities Mutual Investment Trust v Customs and Excise Comrs [2003] EWHC
  2766 (Ch), [2004] STC 246 .... 66:22
Lochgelly Iron and Coal Co Ltd v Crawford 1913 SC 810, 1913 1 SLT 381, 6 TC
  267 .... 8:101
Loffland Bros North Sea v Goodbrand [1997] STC 102, sub nom Goodbrand v Loffland
  Bros North Sea Inc 71 TC 57; affd [1998] STC 930, 71 TC 57, CA 16:02, 16:07
Lomax v Newton [1953] 2 All ER 801, [1953] 1 WLR 1123, 34 TC 558, [1953] TR
  283 .... 7:136, 7:138
Lomax v Peter Dixon & Son Ltd [1943] KB 671, [1943] 2 All ER 255, 25 TC
  353, CA 11:05
Lomond Services Ltd v Customs and Excise Comrs (1998) VAT decision 15451 ...... 67:09
London and Brighton Rly Co v Fairclough (1841) 2 Man & G 674, 2 Ry & Can Cas
  544, Drinkwater 196, 3 Scott NR 68 .... 56:14
London and Thames Haven Oil Wharves Ltd v Attwooll [1967] Ch 772, [1967]
  2 All ER 124, 43 TC 491, [1967] TR 411, CA 8:82
London Cemetery Co v Barnes [1917] 2 KB 496, 86 LJKB 990, 7 TC 92, 15 LGR
  543 .... 8:148
London Recruitment Services Ltd v Revenue and Customs Comrs [2006] STC (SCD)
  502 .... 2A:19
Long v Belfield Poultry Products Ltd (1937) 21 TC 221, 16 ATC 277 .... 8:155
Long v Clark [1894] 1 QB 119, [1891–4] All ER Rep 1145, 63 LJQB 108, CA 2:38
Longborough Festival Opera v Revenue and Customs Corms [2006] EWHC 40 (Ch),
  [2006] STC 818, (2006) Times, 6 February, [2006] SWTI 237, [2006] All ER (D) 206
  (Jan) 68:29
Longsight Cricket Club v Customs and Excise Comrs (1989) VAT decision 4064 ..... 67:09
Longson v Baker [2000] STC (SCD) 244 .... 23:07
Look Ahead Housing Association v Customs and Excise Comrs (2000) VAT decision
  16816 .... 69:20
Loquitar Ltd, Re, IRC v Richmond [2003] EWHC 999 (Ch), [2003] STC 1394, 75 TC
  77, [2003] 2 BCLC 442 .... 22:11
Lord v Tustain [1993] STC 755, 65 TC 761 .... 6:41
Loss Relief Group Litigation, Re [2004] EWHC 3588 (Ch), [2004] STC 594; revsd sub
  nom Re Claimants under Loss Relief Group Litigation Order [2004] EWCA Civ 680,
  [2004] STC 1054 .... 2:11
Lothian Chemical Co Ltd v Rogers (1926) 11 TC 508, 6 ATC 823 .... 8:64
Lowe v J W Ashmore Ltd [1971] Ch 545, [1971] 1 All ER 1057, 46 TC 597, [1970] TR
  209 .... 8:91, 10:04, 10:06
Lubbock Fine & Co v Customs and Excise Comrs: C-63/92 [1994] QB 571, [1994]
  3 All ER 705, [1993] ECR I-6665, [1994] STC 101, ECJ 68:11
Lucas v Cattell (1972) 48 TC 353, [1972] TR 83, 51 ATC 97 .... 7:139

Table of Cases

Lucy & Sunderland Ltd v Hunt [1961] 3 All ER 1062, [1962] 1 WLR 7, 40 TC 132, [1961] TR 305 .... 8:21, 8:34
Ludwig v Finanzamt Luckenwalde: C-453/05 [2007] ECR I–5083, [2008] STC 1640, [2007] All ER (D) 237 (Jun), ECJ 68:16
Luke v IRC [1963] AC 557, [1963] 1 All ER 655, 40 TC 630, [1963] TR 21, HL 7:102, 7:108, 7:110
Lunt v Wellesley (1945) 27 TC 78, 24 ATC 293 .... 8:105
Lupton v Potts [1969] 3 All ER 1083, [1969] 1 WLR 1749, 45 TC 643, [1969] TR 295 .... 7:137, 7:141
Lurcott v Wakely and Wheeler [1911] 1 KB 905, [1911–13] All ER Rep 41, 80 LJKB 713, 104 LT 290, CA 8:123
Lutchumun v Director General of the Mauritius Revenue Authority [2008] UKPC 53 .... 8:83
Lynall, Re [1969] 1 Ch 421, 47 TC 375; on appeal [1970] Ch 138, [1969] 3 All ER 984, [1969] TR 353, CA: revsd sub nom Lynall v IRC [1972] AC 680, [1971] 3 All ER 914, 47 TC 375, [1971] TR 309, HL 45:02, 45:03, 45:05, 45:06, 45:10
Lynch v Edmondson [1998] STC (SCD) 185 .... 23:02
Lyon v Pettigrew [1985] STC 369, 58 TC 452 .... 18:02
Lyons, Re, Barclays Bank Ltd v Jones [1952] Ch 129, [1952] 1 All ER 34, [1951] TR 407, 30 ATC 377, CA 11:43
Lyons v Cowcher (1926) 10 TC 438 .... 12:06
Lyons (J) & Co Ltd v A-G [1944] Ch 281, [1944] 1 All ER 477, 113 LJ Ch 196, 170 LT 348 .... 9:29
Lysaght v Edwards (1876) 2 Ch D 499, 45 LJ Ch 554, 3 Char Pr Cas 243 .... 18:06
Lysaght v IRC. See IRC v Lysaght

M

M & S Services Ltd v Customs and Excise Comrs [1995] V & DR 512n 67:09
MBNA Europe Bank Ltd v Revenue and Customs Comrs [2006] EWHC 2326 (Ch), [2006] STC 2089, [2006] 39 LS Gaz R 34, [2006] SWTI 2234, [2006] All ER (D) 104 (Sep) 66:09, 68:16
MEPC Holdings Ltd v Taylor [2000] STC (SCD) 504; on appeal sub nom Taylor v MEPC Holdings Ltd [2002] STC 430; affd [2002] EWCA Civ 883, [2002] STC 997; revsd [2003] UKHL 70, [2004] 1 All ER 536, [2004] 1 WLR 82, [2004] STC 123, 75 TC 632 .... 16:02, 25:02, 28:13
Maatschap MJM Linthorst, KGP Pouwels and J Scheres cs v Inspecteur Der Belastingdienst/Ondernemingen Roermond: C-167/95 [1997] 2 CMLR 478, [1997] STC 1287, ECJ 63:30, 65:38
Mac, The (1882) 7 PD 126, 51 LJP 81, 4 Asp MLC 555, 46 LT 907, CA 9:44
M'Alister (or Donoghue) v Stevenson [1932] AC 562, 101 LJPC 119, 37 Com Cas 350, 48 TLR 494, 1932 SC (HL) 31 sub nom Donoghue (or M'Alister) v Stevenson 3:23
McBride v Blackburn [2003] STC (SCD) 139 .... 7:25
McBurnie v Tacey [1984] 1 WLR 1019, [1984] FLR 730, [1984] STC 347, 58 TC 139: 11:29
McCall & Ors (PRs of McClean, dec'd) v Revenue & Customs Comrs (2008) SpC 678 .... 44:04
McCann v Customs and Excise Comrs [1987] VATTR 101 .... 68:15
McCarthy & Stone plc v Customs and Excise Comrs [1992] VATTR 198 .... 66:19
McCash and Hunter v IRC (1955) 36 TC 170, [1955] TR 117, 34 ATC 113 .... 8:70
McClelland v Taxation Comr of Australian Commonwealth [1971] 1 All ER 969, [1971] 1 WLR 191, [1970] TR 281, 49 ATC 300 .... 23:32
McClure v Petre [1988] 1 WLR 1386, [1988] STC 749, 61 TC 226 .... 10:06
McClymont v Glover [2004] STC (SCD) 54 .... 8:111
McCrone v IRC 1967 SC 192, 1967 SLT 198, 44 TC 142, [1967] TR 95 .... 15:24
McCullough v Ahluwalia [2004] EWCA Civ 889, [2004] STC 1295 .... 2:19, 2:23, 2:37
MacDonald v Dextra Accessories Ltd [2003] EWHC 872 (Ch), [2003] STC 749, [2003] 25 LS Gaz R 47; revsd [2004] EWCA Civ 22, [2004] STC 339, 148 Sol Jo LB 150 .... 7:22

Table of Cases

MacDonald (Inspector of Taxes) v Dextra Accessories Ltd [2005] UKHL 47, [2005] 4 All ER 107, [2005] STC 1111, (2005) Times, 11 July, [2005] All ER (D) 85 (Jul) 3:01, 8:104
MacDonald v IRC [1940] 1 KB 802, 109 LJKB 609, 23 TC 449, 19 ATC 161 .... 35:29
McDougall v Sutherland (1894) 3 TC 261 .... 7:41
McDowall v IRC [2004] STC (SCD) 22 .... 43:03
Macedo v Stroud [1922] 2 AC 330, 91 LJPC 222, 128 LT 45 .... 18:34
Macfarlane v IRC 1929 SC 453, 1929 SLT 395, 14 TC 532, 8 ATC 227 .... 13:17
McGowan v Brown and Cousins [1977] 3 All ER 844, [1977] 1 WLR 1403, [1977] STC 342, 52 TC 8 .... 8:75
McGregor v Adcock [1977] 3 All ER 65, [1977] 1 WLR 864, [1977] STC 206, 51 TC 692 .... 25:19
McGregor v Randall [1984] 1 All ER 1092, [1984] STC 223, 58 TC 110 .... 7:28, 7:34
McGregor v United Kingdom (Application No 30548/96) (3 December 1997, unreported), E Ct HR 1:21
McGregor (HM Inspector of Taxes) v Adcock (1977) 22:33
McGuckian, Re [2000] STC 65, sub nom R v Dickinson, ex p McGuckian 72 TC 343, NI CA 1:25, 2:26
McIntosh v Manchester Corpn [1952] 2 All ER 444, [1952] WN 390, 33 TC 428, [1952] TR 341, CA 9:11
Macken v Hamilton [2003] STC (SCD) 286 .... 7:129
MacKenzie, Re [1941] Ch 69, [1940] 4 All ER 310, 110 LJ Ch 28, 19 ATC 399 .... 33:03
Mackenzie v Customs and Excise Comrs (1993) VAT decision 11597 .... 2:49
McKie v Warner [1961] 3 All ER 348, [1961] 1 WLR 1230, 40 TC 65, 40 ATC 226, [1961] TR 231 .... 7:49
MacKinlay v Arthur Young McClelland Moores & Co [1986] 1 WLR 1468, [1986] STC 491; on appeal [1989] Ch 454, [1988] 2 All ER 1, [1988] 2 WLR 1117, [1988] STC 116, CA; revsd [1990] 2 AC 239, [1990] 1 All ER 45, [1989] 3 WLR 1245, [1989] STC 898, HL 8:100, 8:106
McKinlay v H T Jenkins & Son Ltd (1926) 10 TC 372, 5 ATC 317 .... 8:78
McKnight v Sheppard [1997] STC 846, CA; affd [1999] STC 669, [1999] 3 All ER 491, [1999] 1 WLR 1333, HL 8:96, 8:105
Maclaine & Co v Eccott [1926] AC 424, 95 LJKB 616, 10 TC 481, 5 ATC 237, HL 36:04, 36:05
McLaren v Mumford [1996] STC 1134, 69 TC 173 .... 8:96
Maclean v Revenue and Customs Comrs [2007] STC (SCD) 350 .... 22:12
Maclean v Trembath [1956] 2 All ER 113, 36 TC 653, [1956] TR 73, 35 ATC 76 .... 7:138
McLean Homes Midland Ltd v Customs and Excise Comrs (1990) VAT decision 5010 .... 65:27
McLeish v IRC (1958) 38 TC 1, [1958] TR 1, 37 ATC 3 .... 7:101
McLellan Rawson & Co Ltd v Newall (1955) 36 TC 117, [1955] TR 175, 34 ATC 160 .... 8:14
Maclennan, Re, Few v Byrne [1939] Ch 750, [1939] 3 All ER 81, 108 LJ Ch 364, 18 ATC 121, CA 11:43
Macleod v IRC (1885) 12 R (Ct of Sess) 105 .... 57:07
McLoughlin v Revenue and Customs Comrs [2006] STC (SCD) 467 .... 7:24
MacMahon and MacMahon v IRC (1951) 32 TC 311, 30 ATC 74, [1951] TR 67 .... 23:02
McMann v Shaw [1972] 3 All ER 732, [1972] 1 WLR 1578, 48 TC 330, [1972] TR 47 .... 32:25, 50:05
McManus v Griffiths [1997] STC 1089, 70 TC 218 .... 7:08
McMeekin, Re [1974] STC 429, 48 TC 725 .... 18:22
McMenamin v Diggles [1991] 4 All ER 370, [1991] 1 WLR 1249, [1991] STC 419 .... 7:08, 7:11, 49:19
McMichael v United Kingdom (Application 16424/90) (1995) 20 EHRR 205, [1995] 2 FCR 718, [1995] Fam Law 478, ECtHR 1:21
McMillan v Guest [1942] AC 561, 1942] 1 All ER 606, 24 TC 190, 21 ATC 73, HL 7:08
MacMillan Cancer Trust v Customs and Excise Comrs [1998] V & DR 289 .... 68:23
McMullen v Wadsworth (1889) 14 App Cas 631, 59 LJPC 7, 61 LT 487 .... 33:24

Table of Cases

McNeill, Re, Royal Bank of Scotland v Macpherson [1958] Ch 259, [1957] 3 All ER 508, [1957] TR 313, 36 ATC 301, CA 46:19
McNicholas Construction Co Ltd v Customs and Excise Comrs [2000] STC 553 .... 66:03
McNiven v Westmoreland Investments Ltd [1997] STC 1103, 73 TC 1; on appeal sub nom Westmoreland Investments Ltd v MacNiven [1998] STC 1131, 73 TC 1, CA; affd sub nom MacNiven v Westmoreland Investments Ltd[2001] UKHL 6,, [2003] 1 AC 311, [2001] 1 All ER 865, [2001] 2 WLR 377, [2001] STC 237, 73 TC 1 . 3:01, 3:01, 3:04, 3:11, 3:15, 3:16, 3:17, 3:18, 3:19, 3:20, 3:21, 3:23, 6:45, 18:01, 21:03,39:28, 39:35, 56:10
Maco Door and Window Hardware (UK) Ltd v Revenue and Customs Comrs [2006] STC (SCD) 1, [2008] UKHL 54 .... 9:12
Macpherson v Bond [1985] 1 WLR 1157, [1985] STC 678, 58 TC 579 .... 5:15
Macpherson v IRC. See IRC v Macpherson
McVeigh v Arthur Sanderson & Sons Ltd [1969] 2 All ER 771, [1969] 1 WLR 1143, 45 TC 273, [1968] TR 451, [1969] BTR 130 .... 9:26
Madgett and Baldwin (t/a Howden Court Hotel) v Customs and Excise Comrs [1996] STC 167; refd sub nom Customs and Excise Comrs v Madgett and Baldwin: C-308/96, C-94/97 [1999] 2 CMLR 392, [1998] STC 1189, ECJ 65:25
Madley and another v Revenue and Customs Comrs [2006] STC (SCD) 513 .... 7:123
Madras Electric Supply Corpn Ltd v Boarland [1955] AC 667, [1955] 1 All ER 753, 35 TC 612, [1955] TR 57, HL 1:26
Magnavox Electronics Co Ltd v Hall [1985] STC 260, 59 TC 610; affd [1986] STC 561, 59 TC 610, CA 18:07
Magraw v Lewis (1933) 18 TC 222, 12 ATC 424 .... 35:16
Maidment v Kibby [1993] STC 494, 66 TC 137 .... 8:50
Mairs v Haughey [1992] STC 495, 66 TC 273, NI CA; affd [1994] 1 AC 303, [1993] 3 All ER 801, [1993] STC 569, 66 TC 273, HL . 7:01, 7:17, 7:28, 7:30, 7:33, 7:102, 50:10, 50:11
Major v Brodie [1998] STC 491, 70 TC 576 .... 6:41
Makins v Elson [1977] 1 All ER 572, [1977] 1 WLR 221, [1977] STC 46, 51 TC 437 .... 23:06
Malik (t/a Hotline Foods) v Customs and Excise Comrs [1998] STC 537 .... 69:13
Mallaby-Deeley v IRC [1938] 3 All ER 463, 23 TC 153; on appeal [1938] 4 All ER 818, 55 TLR 293, 23 TC 153, CA 11:30, 11:32
Mallalieu v Drummond [1981] 1 WLR 908, [1981] STC 391, 57 TC 330, [1981] TR 105; affd [1983] 1 All ER 801, [1983] 1 WLR 252, [1983] STC 124, 57 TC 330, CA; revsd [1983] 2 AC 861, [1983] 2 All ER 1095, [1983] 3 WLR 409, [1983] STC 665, 57 TC 330, HL 7:97, 7:133, 8:96, 8:97, 9:23
Mallandain Investments Ltd v Shadbolt (1940) 23 TC 367 .... 8:82
Mallett v Staveley Coal and Iron Co Ltd [1928] 2 KB 405, [1928] All ER Rep 644, 13 TC 772, 7 ATC 139, CA 8:119
Mamor Sdn Bhd v Director General of Inland Revenue [1985] STC 801 .... 8:16
Mander Laundries Ltd v Customs and Excise Comrs [1973] VATTR 136 ..... 69:14, 70:04
Mangin v IRC [1971] AC 739, [1971] 1 All ER 179, [1970] TR 249 .... 1:25
Mankowitz v Income Tax Special Comrs and IRC (1971) 46 TC 707, 50 ATC 75, [1971] TR 53 .... 2A:16
Mann v Nash [1932] 1 KB 752, [1932] All ER Rep 956, 16 TC 523, 11 ATC 94 ..... 8:09
Mann Crossman and Paulin Ltd v IRC [1947] 1 All ER 742, 28 TC 410, 40 R & IT 235, 26 ATC 60 .... 8:122
Mannesman Demag Hamilton Ltd v Customs and Excise Comrs [1983] VATTR 156 .... 63:19
Mannin Shipping Ltd v Customs and Excise Comrs [1979] VATTR 83 .... 64:24
Manninen, Re: C-319/02 [2005] Ch 236, [2005] All ER (EC) 465, [2005] 2 WLR 670, [2004] 3 CMLR 881, [2004] STC 1444, ECJ 1:11, 1:12
Mannion (HM Inspector of Taxes) v Johnst (1988) 22:33
Mansell v Revenue and Customs Comrs [2006] STC (SCD) 605 .... 8:49
Mansell (Nigel) Sports Cars Ltd v Customs and Excise Comrs [1991] VATTR 491 .... 65:12
Mansworth v Jelley [2002] EWHC 442 (Ch), [2002] STC 1013; affd [2002] EWCA Civ 1829, [2003] STC 53 .... 7:91, 16:06, 18:28
Maple & Co (Paris) Ltd v IRC [1906] 2 KB 834, CA; affd sub nom IRC v Maple & Co (Paris) Ltd [1908] AC 22, 77 LJKB 55, 97 LT 814, 24 TLR 140, HL 56:07

Table of Cases

Maples v IRC [1914] 3 KB 303, 83 LJKB 1647, 111 LT 764 .... 57:13
Marczak (a firm) v Customs and Excise Comrs (1995) VAT decision 13141 .... 69:13
Margerison v Tyresoles Ltd (1942) 25 TC 59, 21 ATC 357 .... 8:80
Margrett v Lowestoft Water and Gas Co (1935) 19 TC 481, 14 ATC 237 .... 8:123
Margrie Holdings Ltd v Customs and Excise Comrs [1991] STC 80, 1991 SLT 38 .... 68:11
Marine Investment Co v Haviside (1872) LR 5 HL 624, 42 LJ Ch 173, HL 56:28
Market Investigations Ltd v Minister of Social Security [1969] 2 QB 173, [1968] 3 All ER 732, [1969] 2 WLR 1 .... 7:11, 49:03
Markey v Sanders [1987] 1 WLR 864, [1987] STC 256 2 .... 2:06
Marks v McNally [2004] STC (SCD) 503 .... 6:34
Marks & Spencer plc v Customs and Excise Comrs [1997] V & DR 85; on appeal [1999] 1 CMLR 1152, [1999] STC 205; on appeal [2000] 1 CMLR 256, [2000] STC 16, CA; refd C-62/00: [2003] QB 866, [2002] ECR I-6325, [2002] 3 CMLR 213, [2002] STC 1036, ECJ 2:16, 67:16
Marks & Spencer plc v Customs and Excise Comrs: C-309/06 [2008] STC 1408, ECJ 69:12
Marks & Spencer plc v Halsey [2003] STC (SCD) 70; refd C-319/02 (unreported), ECJ 1:03, 1:07, 1:11
Marks & Spencer plc v Halsey (Inspector of Taxes): C-446/03 [2006] Ch 184, [2006] All ER (EC) 255, [2006] 2 WLR 250, [2006] STC 237, (2005) Times, 15 December, [2005] All ER (D) 174 (Dec), ECJ 1:12, 1:14,28:01, 28:08
Marks & Spencer plc v Revenue and Customs Comrs [2005] UKHL 53, [2005] STC 1254, [2005] SWTI 1338, [2005] All ER (D) 442 (Jul) 67:16
Marleasing SA v La Comercial Internacional de Alimentacion SA: C-106/89 [1990] ECR I-4135, [1992] 1 CMLR 305, [1993] BCC 421, ECJ 63:02
Marlow Gardner & Cooke Ltd Directors' Pension Scheme v Revenue & Customs Comrs [2006] EWHC 1612 (Ch), [2006] STC 2014 .... 68:03
Marren v Ingles [1979] STC 58, [1978] TR 233; on appeal [1979] STC 637, 54 TC 76, CA; affd [1980] 3 All ER 95, [1980] STC 500, 54 TC 76, HL 16:02, 16:05, 16:09, 16:10, 17:09, 18:03, 18:14, 21:23
Marsh v IRC [1943] 1 All ER 199, 29 TC 120, [1943] TR 13, 22 ATC 31 .... 7:11
Marshall, Re, Marshall v Marshall [1914] 1 Ch 192, [1911–13] All ER Rep 671, 83 LJ Ch 307, 109 LT 835, CA 20:16
Marshall v Kerr [1991] STC 686; revsd [1993] STC 360, CA; on appeal [1994] 3 All ER 106, [1994] STC 638, HL 1:27, 19:03, 40:21
Marshall Hus & Partners Ltd v Bolton [1981] STC 18, 55 TC 539, [1980] TR 371 .... 25:35
Marshall's Executors, Hood's Executors and Rogers v Joly [1936] 1 All ER 851, 20 TC 256 .... 8:05, 8:30
Marson v Marriage [1980] STC 177, 54 TC 59, [1979] TR 499 .... 16:09, 21:23
Marson v Morton [1986] 1 WLR 1343, [1986] STC 463, 59 TC 381 ..... 8:18, 8:25, 23:02
Martin v IRC [1995] STC (SCD) 5 .... 44:04
Martin v Lowry [1926] 1 KB 550, 95 LJKB 497, 11 TC 297, CA; affd [1927] AC 312, 96 LJKB 379, 11 TC 297, HL 1:23, 1:27, 8:16, 8:17
Martin v O'Sullivan [1984] STC 258n 52:05
Marwood Homes Ltd v IRC [1997] STC (SCD) 37 .... 4:28
Marwood Homes Ltd v IRC [1998] STC (SCD) 53 .... 4:18
Marwood Homes Ltd v IRC [1999] STC (SCD) 44 .... 4:28
Marx v Estates and General Investments Ltd [1975] 3 All ER 1064, [1976] 1 WLR 380, [1975] STC 671 .... 56:22, 56:29
Mary Clark Home Trustees v Anderson [1904] 2 KB 645, 73 LJKB 806, 5 TC 48, 91 LT 547 .... 13:22
Mason v Customs and Excise Comrs (1989) VAT decision 3517 .... 64:14
Mason v Innes [1967] Ch 1079, [1967] 2 All ER 926, 44 TC 326, [1967] TR 135, CA 8:156, 8:157
Mason v Motor Traction Co [1905] 1 Ch 419, 74 LJ Ch 273, 92 LT 234, 21 TLR 238 .... 56:29
Mason v Tyson [1980] STC 284, 53 TC 333, [1980] TR 23 .... 8:102
Massey v Massey [1949] WN 422 .... 11:42

Table of Cases

Matrix-Securities Ltd v IRC [1994] 1 All ER 769, [1994] STC 272, 66 TC 587, HL 1:30, 2:07
Matson v Booth (1816) 5 M & S 223 .... 56:14
Matthew (William) Mechanical Services Ltd v Customs and Excise Comrs [1982] VATTR 63 .... 66:20
Matthews v Martin [1991] STI 418 .... 40:21
Matthews v Martin [1991] BTC 8048 .... 2A:71
Mattia (H B) Ltd v Customs and Excise Comrs [1976] VATTR 33 .... 63:32
Mayflower Theatre Trust Ltd v Revenue and Customs Comrs [2007] EWCA Civ 116, [2007] STC 880, (2007) Times, 16 March, [2007] SWTI 413, [2007] All ER (D) 281 (Feb) 66:08
Measures Bros Ltd v IRC (1900) 82 LT 689 .... 57:06
Medical Care Foundation v Customs and Excise Comrs [1991] VATTR 28 .... 69:41
Meilicke v Finanzamt Bonn-Innenstadt: C-292/04 [2007] ECR I-1835, [2007] 2 CMLR 469, [2008] STC 2267, 9 ITLR 834, [2007] SWTI 484, [2007] All ER (D) 75 (Mar) 1:18
Mellerstain Trust (Trustees of) v Customs and Excise Comrs [1989] VATTR 223 .... 63:32, 64:01
Mellor v Gurney [1994] STC 1025n, 67 TC 217 .... 2:23
Melluish v BMI (No 3) Ltd [1995] Ch 90, [1994] STC 315; revsd [1995] Ch 90, [1994] STC 802, CA; on appeal [1996] AC 454, [1995] 4 All ER 453, [1995] STC 964, HL 9:25
Melville v IRC [2000] STC 628, 74 TC 372; affd [2001] EWCA Civ 1247, [2002] 1 WLR 407, [2001] STC 1271, 74 TC 372 .... 38:20, 39:07
Memec plc v IRC [1996] STC 1336, 71 TC 77; affd [1998] STC 754, 71 TC 77, CA 35:10, 37:20, 37:33
Mercantile Contracts Ltd v Customs and Excise Comrs (1989) VAT decision 4357 .... 65:11
Merchant (Peter) Ltd v Stedeford (1948) 30 TC 496, 42 R & IT 28, 27 ATC 342, CA 8:148
Merchiston Steamship Co Ltd v Turner [1910] 2 KB 923, 80 LJKB 145, 5 TC 520, 102 LT 363 .... 8:52
Mercury Tax Group Limited v Revenue and Customs Commissioners (2008) SpC 737 .... 2A:05
Meredith-Hardy v McLellan [1995] STC (SCD) 270 .... 15:15
Mersey Docks and Harbour Board v Lucas (1883) 8 App Cas 891, 53 LJQB 4, 2 TC 25, HL 8:12
Merseyside Cablevision Ltd v Customs and Excise Comrs [1987] VATTR 134 .... 63:02, 64:03, 66:05
Mesco Properties Ltd, Re [1980] 1 All ER 117, [1980] 1 WLR 96, [1979] STC 788, 54 TC 238, CA 25:04
Mesher v Mesher and Hall (1973) [1980] 1 All ER 126n, CA 16:44
Messenger Leisure Developments Ltd v Revenue and Customs Comrs [2005] EWCA Civ 648, [2005] STC 1078 .... 68:26
Messina v Smith [1971] P 322, [1971] 2 All ER 1046, [1971] 3 WLR 118 .... 33:17
Metal Industries (Salvage) Ltd v S T Harle (Owners) 1962 SLT 114 ..... 34:02, 54:14
Metallgesellschaft Ltd v IRC and A-G: C-397/98 [2001] Ch 620, [2001] All ER (EC) 496, [2001] STC 452, ECJ 1:02, 1:06, 1:12, 1:18
Metropolitan Boot Co Ltd v IRC. See Holmleigh (Holdings) Ltd v IRC
Micklethwaite, Re (1855) 11 Exch 452, 25 LJ Ex 19 .... 1:24
Mid-Derbyshire Cheshire Home v Customs and Excise Comrs (1990) VAT decision 4512 .... 69:35
Midland Bank plc v Customs and Excise Comrs [1991] VATTR 525 .... 64:26
Midland Bank plc v Customs and Excise Comrs: C-98/98. See Customs and Excise Comrs v Midland Bank plc
Midlands Co-operative Society Ltd v Revenue and Customs Comrs [2008] EWCA Civ 305, [2008] STC 1803 .... 67:16, 67:17
Miesegaes v IRC (1957) 37 TC 493, [1957] TR 231, 36 ATC 201, CA 33:03
Milk Marketing Board v Customs and Excise Comrs (1989) VAT decision 3389 ..... 68:16
Miller v IRC [1930] AC 222, 15 TC 25 .... 13:16
Miller v IRC [1987] STC 108 .... 42:07

Table of Cases

Miller v Tebb (1893) 9 TLR 515, CA 2:38
Miller v The Queen 2001 CanLII 593 (TCC) 8:49
Miller Freeman World-wide plc v Customs and Excise Comrs (1998) VAT decision 15452 .... 63:30; 65:38
Mills (John) Productions Ltd v Mathias (1964) 44 TC 441, [1964] TR 285, 43 ATC 262 .... 8:31, 8:86, 8:88
Milroy v Lord (1862) 4 De GF & J 264, [1861–73] All ER Rep 783, 31 LJ Ch 798 .... 18:34
Minister dell'Economia e delle Finanze v Part Service Srl (in liquidation): C-425/06, [2008] ECR I–0000, [2008] SWTI 315, ECJ 63:09
Milton v Chivers [1996] STC (SCD) 36 .... 22:16
Mimtec Ltd v IRC [2001] STC (SCD) 101 .... 7:01
Minden Trust (Cayman) Ltd v IRC [1984] STC 434 .... 47:09
Minister of Finance v Smith [1927] AC 193, 95 LJPC 193, 136 LT 175, 42 TLR 734 .... 8:09
Minister of National Revenue v Anaconda American Brass Ltd [1956] AC 85, [1956] 1 All ER 20, [1955] TR 339, 34 ATC 330 .... 8:161
Ministero dell'Econimia e delle Finanze v Part Service Srl (in liquidation): C-425/06 [2008] ECR 1–897, [2008] STC 3132, ECJ 63:09
Ministre des Finances v Weidert: C-242/03 [2004] 3 CMLR 374, [2005] STC 1241, [2004] SWTI 1657, [2004] All ER (D) 281 (Jul), ECJ 1:07
Ministre de l'Economie, des Finances dt de l'Industrie v Gillian Beach Ltd: C-114/05 [2006] STC 1080, ECJ 63:30
Ministry of Health v Simpson [1951] AC 251, [1950] 2 All ER 1137, HL 11:41
Ministry of Housing and Local Government v Sharp [1970] 2 QB 223, [1969] 3 All ER 225 .... 7:08
Mink v Inspector of Taxes [1999] STC (SCD) 17 .... 11:12
Minsham Properties Ltd v Price [1990] STC 718 .... 11:12, 11:38
Mirror Group plc v Customs and Excise Comrs: C-409/98 [2002] QB 546, sub nom Customs and Excise Comrs v Mirror Group plc [2001] ECR I-7175, [2001] 3 CMLR 1417, [2001] STC 1453, ECJ 68:11
Mitchell v B W Noble Ltd [1927] 1 KB 719, [1927] All ER Rep 717, 11 TC 372, 6 ATC 173, CA 8:118, 8:120, 35:04
Mitchell and Edon v Ross [1960] Ch 145, [1959] 3 All ER 341, 40 TC 11, [1959] TR 225; affd [1960] Ch 498, [1960] 2 All ER 218, 40 TC 11, [1960] TR 79, CA; on appeal [1962] AC 814, [1961] 3 All ER 49, 40 TC 11, [1961] TR 191, HL 5:03, 7:08, 7:11, 7:14, 7:15, 7:40, 7:141
Mitchell Bros v Tomlinson (1957) 37 TC 224, [1957] TR 63, 36 ATC 55, CA .. 8:21, 8:24, 8:49
Mitrolone Ltd v Customs and Excise Comrs (1989) VAT decision 4301 .... 65:28
Mitzi (a firm) v Customs and Excise Comrs (1986) VAT decision 2233 .... 63:04
Mobilx Ltd (in administration) v Revenue and Customs Comrs [2009] EWHC 133 (Ch), [2009] STC 1107 .... 66:34
Mohr v Finanzamt Bad Segeberg: C-215/94 [1996] All ER (EC) 450, [1996] ECR I-959, [1996] STC 328, ECJ 63:19
Mölnlycke Ltd v Customs and Excise Comrs (1996) VAT decision 14641 .... 63:20
Momin & Others v R & C Comrs [2007] EWHC 1400 (Ch) 2A:74
Momm v Barclays Bank International Ltd [1976] 3 All ER 588 .... 11:38
Monro v Revenue and Customs Comrs [2007] EWHC 114 (Ch), [2007] SWTI 290, [2007] All ER (D) 08 (Feb), [2008] EWCA Civ 306 .... 1:02, 2A:69, 2A:70, 18:28
Monsell Youell Developments Ltd v Customs and Excise Comrs [1978] VATTR 1 ... 69:17
Moodie v IRC [1990] 1 WLR 1084, [1990] STC 475; revsd [1991] 1 WLR 930, [1991] STC 433, CA; on appeal [1993] 2 All ER 49, [1993] 1 WLR 266, [1993] STC 188, HL 15:05
Moody v Tyler [2000] STC 296 .... 26:24
Moore v Customs and Excise Comrs [1989] VATTR 276 .... 65:17
Moore v Griffiths [1972] 3 All ER 399, [1972] 1 WLR 1024, 48 TC 338, [1972] TR 61 .... 7:20, 7:25, 7:26
Moore v R J Mackenzie & Sons Ltd [1972] 2 All ER 549, [1972] 1 WLR 359, 48 TC 196, [1971] TR 457 .... 8:157, 8:168
Moore v Thompson [1986] STC 170, 61 TC 15 .... 23:06

Table of Cases

Moore and Osborne v IRC. See Trafford's Settlement, Re, Moore v IRC
Moore's Executors v IRC [2002] STC (SCD) 463n 33:23
Moores Furniture Group Ltd v Customs and Excise Comrs (1997) VAT decision 15044 .... 69:21
Moorhouse v Dooland [1955] Ch 284, [1955] 1 All ER 93, 36 TC 1, [1954] TR 393, CA 7:25, 7:26
Morgan v Cilento [2004] EWHC 188 (Ch), [2004] All ER (D) 122 (Feb) 33:23
Morgan v Tate & Lyle Ltd [1955] AC 21, [1954] 2 All ER 413, 35 TC 367, [1954] TR 189, HL 8:101, 8:104, 8:109, 8:116, 16:21
Morgan (J P) Trading and Finance v Customs and Excise Comrs [1998] V & DR 161 .... 64:26, 66:08
Morley v Hall (1834) 2 Dowl 494 .... 56:02
Morley v Lawford & Co (1928) 14 TC 229, 140 LT 125, 7 ATC 428, CA 8:105
Morley v Pincombe (1848) 18 LJ Ex 272, 2 Exch 101 .... 2:38
Morley v Tattersall [1938] 3 All ER 296, 108 LJKB 11, 22 TC 51, 17 ATC 164, CA 8:90
Morning Post Ltd v George (1941) 23 TC 514, 19 ATC 428 .... 8:52
Morris & Anor v R & C Comrs [2007] EWHC 1181 (Ch) 2A:48
Morse v Stedeford (1934) 18 TC 457, 13 ATC 68 .... 8:115
Moss Empires Ltd v IRC [1937] AC 785, [1937] 3 All ER 381, 21 TC 264, 15 ATC 178, HL 5:17, 8:89, 11:24
Mothercare Ltd v Customs and Excise Comrs [1993] VATTR 391 .... 63:20
Mount Edgcumbe (Earl) v IRC [1911] 2 KB 24, 80 LJKB 503, 105 LT 62, 27 TLR 298 .... 57:10, 57:26
Mounty (F & M) & Sons v Customs and Excise Comrs [1995] V & DR 128 .... 66:05
Mudd v Collins (1925) 133 LT 186, 41 TLR 358, 9 TC 297, 4 ATC 176 .... 7:24
Muir v IRC [1966] 1 All ER 295, [1966] 1 WLR 251, 43 TC 367, [1965] TR 375 .... 15:14, 20:02
Muir (or Williams) v Muir [1943] AC 468, 112 LJPC 39, 1943 SC (HL) 47, 1944 SLT 67, HL 23:13
Muller & Co's Margarine Ltd v IRC [1900] 1 QB 310, 69 LJQB 291, 81 LT 667, 16 TLR 72, CA 58:02
Multiform Printing Ltd v Customs and Excise Comrs [1996] V & DR 580 .... 69:15
Munby v Furlong [1977] Ch 359, [1977] 2 All ER 953, 50 TC 501, [1977] STC 232, [1977] TR 121, CA 9:26
Mundial Invest SA v Moore [2005] EWHC 1735 (Ch), [2006] STC 412, [2005] SWTI 278, [2005] All ER (D) 353 (Feb) 2A:19
Municipal Mutual Insurance Ltd v Hills (1932) 16 TC 430, 147 LT 62, 48 TLR 301, 11 ATC 66, HL 8:35, 8:36, 8:37, 8:39
Munro v Munro (1840) 7 Cl & Fin 842, HL 33:17
Munro v Stamp Duties Comr [1934] AC 61, [1933] All ER Rep 185, 103 LJPC 18, 150 LT 145 .... 22:38, 41:05
Murat v IRC [2004] EWHC 3123 (Admin), [2005] STC 184, [2004] All ER (D) 333 (Oct) 1:21
Murat v Ornoch [2004] STC (SCD) 115 .... 2A:68
Murgatroyd v Evans-Jackson [1967] 1 All ER 881, [1967] 1 WLR 423, 43 TC 581, [1966] TR 341, [1967] BTR 285 .... 8:102
Murray v Goodhews [1978] 2 All ER 40, [1978] 1 WLR 499, [1978] STC 207, 52 TC 104, CA 8:75
Murray v Imperial Chemical Industries Ltd [1967] Ch 1038, [1967] 2 All ER 980, 44 TC 175, [1967] TR 129, CA 8:80
Murray v IRC 1926 SLT 714, 11 TC 133, 5 ATC 607 .... 13:17
Murray v IRC (1951) 32 TC 238, [1951] TR 61, 44 R & IT 270, 30 ATC 53 .... 8:127
Musgrave, Re, Machell v Parry [1916] 2 Ch 417, 85 LJ Ch 639, 115 LT 149 .... 11:41
Music and Video Exchange Ltd v Customs and Excise Comrs [1990] VATTR 26; sub nom Customs and Excise Comrs v Music and Video Exchange Ltd [1992] STC 220 .... 63:20
Musker v English Electric Co Ltd (1964) 41 TC 556, [1964] TR 129, 43 ATC 119, HL 8:76, 57:06
Muys' en De Winter's Bouw-en Aannemingsbedrijf BV v Staatssecretaris van Financiën: C-281/91 [1993] ECR I-5405, [1997] STC 665, ECJ 63:20

2572

Myatt & Leason (a firm) v Customs and Excise Comrs [1995] V & DR 440 .... 66:29
MyTravel plc v Customs & Excise Comrs: C-291/03 [2005] STC 1617, [2005] SWTI 1679, [2005] All ER (D) 53 (Oct), ECJ 65:25

N

N Ltd v Inspector of Taxes [1996] STC (SCD) 346 .... 22:06
N2J Ltd v Revenue and Customs Comrs [2009] EWHC 1596 (Ch), [2009] SWTI 2091 .... 69:07
NAP Holdings UK Ltd v Whittles [1994] STC 979, 67 TC 166, HL 28:21
NDP Co Ltd v Customs and Excise Comrs [1988] VATTR 40 .... 63:19
NMB Holdings Ltd v Secretary of State for Social Security (2000) 73 TC 85 ... 3:05, 50:35
Nadin v IRC [1997] STC (SCD) 107 .... 43:04
Namecourt Ltd v Customs and Excise Comrs [1984] VATTR 22 .... 68:12
Nargett v Nias (1859) 1 E & E 439, 28 LJQB 143 .... 2:38
Narich Pty Ltd v Pay-roll Tax Comr [1984] ICR 286 .... 49:03
Narogauge Ltd v Customs and Excise Comrs (1997) VAT decision 14680 .... 69:27
Nasim v Customs and Excise Comrs [1987] STC 387 .... 63:17
National Association of Local Government Officers v Watkins (1934) 18 TC 499, 13 ATC 268 .... 8:35
National Bank of Greece SA v Westminster Bank Executor and Trustee Co (Channel Islands) Ltd. See Westminster Bank Executor and Trustee Co (Channel Islands) Ltd v National Bank of Greece SA
National Coal Board v Customs and Excise Comrs [1982] STC 863 .... 63:23, 63:26
National Council of YMCAs Inc v Customs and Excise Comrs [1993] VATTR 299 .... 2A:43
National Smokeless Fuels Ltd v IRC [1986] STC 300, [1986] 3 CMLR 227 .... 63:02
National Society for the Prevention of Cruelty to Children v Customs and Excise Comrs [1992] VATTR 417 .... 63:17
National Water Council v Customs and Excise Comrs [1979] STC 157, [1978] TR 307 .... 63:16, 63:17, 66:05
National Westminster Bank plc v Customs and Excise Comrs [1999] V & DR 201 .... 64:25
National Westminster Bank plc v IRC [1994] STC 184, [1994] 2 BCLC 30; affd [1995] 1 AC 119, [1994] 3 All ER 1, [1994] STC 580, [1994] 2 BCLC 239, HL 31:07, 60:02, 61:11
Naturally Yours Cosmetics Ltd v Customs and Excise Comrs [1987] VATTR 45; refd 230/87: [1988] ECR 6365, [1988] STC 879, ECJ 63:02, 63:21, 63:26
Naval Colliery Co Ltd v IRC (1928) 12 TC 1017, 138 LT 593, 7 ATC 48, HL 8:147
Navicon SA v Administración del Estado: C-97/06 [2007] ECR I-8755, [2007] SWTI 2405, ECJ 69:26
Neal v Customs and Excise Comrs [1988] STC 131 .... 64:14
Neeld, Re, Carpenter v Inigo-Jones [1964] 2 All ER 952n, [1965] 1 WLR 73, [1964] TR 437, 43 ATC 397, CA 46:25
Neen Design Ltd v Customs and Excise Comrs (1994) VAT Decision 11782 .... 69:35
Neil Martin Ltd v R & C Comrs [2007] EWCA Civ 1041 .... 2:24
Nell Gwynn House Maintenance Fund Trustees v Customs and Excise Comrs [1994] STC 995; revsd [1996] STC 310, CA; on appeal [1999] 1 All ER 385, [1999] 1 WLR 174, [1999] STC 79, HL 63:20, 63:21, 65:16, 68:11
Nelson Dance Family Settlement, Re; Trustees of the Nelson Dance Family Settlement v Revenue and Customs Comrs (2008) SpC 682, [2008] STC (SCD) 792 .... 44:01
Nerva v United Kingdom (2002) 36 EHRR 31, [2002] IRLR 815, 13 BHRC 246, E Ct HR 50:04
Netherlane Ltd v York [2005] STC (SCD) 305 .... 8:26
Nethermere (St Neots) Ltd v Gardiner [1984] ICR 612, [1984] IRLR 240, CA 49:03
Netlogic Consulting Ltd v Revenue and Customs Comrs [2005] STC (SCD) 524 ..... 25:23
Netto Supermarkt GmbH & Co OHG v Finanzamt Malchin: C-271/06 [2008] SWTI 315, ECJ 69:08
Network Insurance Brokers Ltd v Customs and Excise Comrs (1996) VAT decision 14755 .... 68:24

Table of Cases

Neubergh v IRC [1978] STC 181, 52 TC 79, [1977] TR 263 .... 33:10
Neuvale Ltd v Customs and Excise Comrs [1989] STC 395, CA 66:07, 66:08
New Angel Court Ltd v Adam [2003] EWHC 1876 (Ch), [2003] STC 1172, [2003] 38 LS Gaz R 35; revsd [2004] EWCA Civ 242, [2004] 1 WLR 1988, [2004] STC 779 .... 21:25, 28:27
New Way School of Motoring Ltd v Customs and Excise Comrs [1979] VATTR 57 .... 63:17
New World Medical Ltd v Cormack [2002] EWHC 1787 (Ch), [2002] STC 1245 ..... 2:11
New York Life Insurance Co v Styles (1889) 14 App Cas 381, 59 LJQB 291, 5 TLR 621, 2 TC 460, HL 8:37, 8:39
New Zealand Forest Products (1995) 17 NZTC 12, 073 .... 33:25
New Zealand Shipping Co Ltd v Thew (1922) 8 TC 208, 1 ATC 90, HL 33:28
Newbarns Syndicate v Hay (1939) 22 TC 461, 18 ATC 80, CA 8:30, 8:28, 8:29
Newcourt Property Fund v Customs and Excise Comrs (1991) VAT decision 5825 .... 66:07
Newhill Compulsory Purchase Order 1937, Re, Payne's Application [1938] 2 All ER 163, 102 JP 273, sub nom Payne v Minister of Health 36 LGR 280, 158 LT 523 .... 23:07
Newidgets Manufacturing Ltd v Jones [1999] STC (SCD) 193 .... 2A:65
Newlin v Woods (1966) 42 TC 649, [1966] TR 29, 45 ATC 29 .... 7:137
News Datacom v Atkinson [2006] STC (SCD) 732 .... 33:25
Newsom v Robertson [1953] Ch 7, [1952] 2 All ER 728, 33 TC 452, [1952] TR 401, CA 8:103
Newstead v Frost [1978] 2 All ER 241, [1978] 1 WLR 511, [1978] STC 239, 53 TC 525, [1977] TR 301; affd [1979] 2 All ER 129, [1978] 1 WLR 1441, [1979] STC 45, 53 TC 525, [1978] TR 221, CA; on appeal [1980] 1 All ER 363, [1980] 1 WLR 135, [1980] STC 123, 53 TC 525, HL 29:15, 35:22
Newton v Pyke (1908) 25 TLR 127 .... 29:10
Newtownbutler Playgroup Ltd v Customs and Excise Comrs (1995) VAT decision 13741 .... 69:18
Niagara Holdings Ltd v Customs and Excise Comrs [1993] VATTR 503 .... 69:35
Nichols v Gibson [1994] STC 1029; affd [1996] STC 1008, 68 TC 611, CA 7:36
Nichols v IRC [1975] 2 All ER 120, [1975] 1 WLR 534, [1975] STC 278, [1974] TR 411, CA 39:28, 41:05
Nicholson v Morris [1976] STC 269, 51 TC 95, [1976] TR 87; affd [1977] STC 162, 51 TC 95, [1977] TR 1, CA 2A:19
Nicoll v Austin (1935) 19 TC 531, 14 ATC 172 .... 7:23, 7:44
Nielsen, Andersen & Co v Collins [1928] AC 34, 97 LJKB 267, 13 TC 91, 6 ATC 851, HL 36:03
Nightfreight plc v Customs and Excise Comrs (1998) VAT decision 15479 .... 68:16
Nightingale Ltd v Price [1996] STC (SCD) 116 .... 13:26
Nixon v Albion Marine Insurance Co (1867) LR 2 Exch 338, 36 LJ Ex 180, 16 LT 568, 15 WR 964 .... 56:29
Nixon v Freeman (1860) 5 H & N 647, [1843–60] All ER Rep 750, 29 LJ Ex 271 .... 2:38
Noble (B W) Ltd v Mitchell (1926) 43 TLR 102, 11 TC 372 .... 8:82
Nolder v Walters (1930) 46 TLR 397, 15 TC 380, 9 ATC 251 .... 7:128, 7:129, 7:141
Nordania Finas A/S and another v Skatteministeriet: C-98/07, [2008] SWTI 433, ECJ 66:08
Norman v Evans [1965] 1 All ER 372, [1965] 1 WLR 348, 42 TC 188, [1964] TR 373 .... 12:06, 12:11
Norman v Golder [1945] 1 All ER 352, 114 LJKB 108, 26 TC 293, 23 ATC 362, CA 8:102
Normanton (Earl) v Giles [1980] 1 All ER 106, [1980] 1 WLR 28, HL 44:11
North East Media Development Trust Ltd v Customs and Excise Comrs [1995] V & DR 240 .... 2A:43
North Isles Shellfish Ltd v Customs and Excise Comrs [1995] V & DR 415 .... 69:13
North of England Zoological Society v Customs and Excise Comrs [1999] STC 1027 .... 68:17
Northamptonshire Football Association v Customs and Excise Comrs (1995) VAT decision 12936 .... 63:16

Table of Cases

Northend v White, Leonard and Corbin Greener [1975] 2 All ER 481, [1975] 1 WLR 1037, [1975] STC 317, 50 TC 121 .... 5:24
Northern Counties Co-operative Enterprises Ltd v Customs and Excise Comrs [1986] VATTR 250 .... 66:03
Northern Ireland Comr of Valuation v Fermanagh Protestant Board of Education [1969] 3 All ER 352, [1969] 1 WLR 1708, 133 JP 637, HL 22:12, 44:13
Northern Lawn Tennis Club v Customs and Excise Comrs [1989] VATTR 1 .. 63:20, 66:20
Northern Rock plc v Thorpe [2000] STC (SCD) 317 .... 8:114
Norton v Frecker (1737) 1 Atk 524 .... 45:27
Nuclear Electric plc v Bradley [1995] STC 285; on appeal [1995] STC 1125, 68 TC 670, CA; affd [1996] 1 WLR 529, [1996] STC 405, 68 TC 670, HL 6:19, 6:23, 8:79, 25:23, 27:05
Nuffield Nursing Homes Trust v Customs and Excise Comrs [1989] VATTR 62 68:23

O

Oakes v Stamp Duties Comr of New South Wales [1954] AC 57, [1953] 2 All ER 1563 .... 41:06, 41:07
O'Brien v Benson's Hosiery (Holdings) Ltd [1979] Ch 152, [1978] 3 All ER 1057, [1978] STC 549, 53 TC 241, CA; revsd [1980] AC 562, [1979] 3 All ER 652, [1979] STC 735, 53 TC 241, HL 17:01, 18:04
Oce van Grinten NV v IRC: C-58/01 [2003] 3 CMLR 1104, [2003] STC 1248, ECJ 26:16
O'Connor v Hume [1954] 2 All ER 301, [1954] 1 WLR 824 .... 10:16
Odeon Associated Theatres Ltd v Jones [1973] Ch 288, [1972] 1 All ER 681, 48 TC 257, 50 ATC 398, CA 8:64, 8:125, 16:17
Odhams Leisure Group Ltd v Customs and Excise Comrs [1992] STC 332 .... 69:15
Ogilvie v Kitton 1908 SC 1003, 5 TC 338 .... 35:02
O'Grady v Bullcroft Main Collieries Ltd (1932) 17 TC 93, 11 ATC 181 ...... 8:122, 8:123
O'Grady v Wilmot [1916] 2 AC 231, 85 LJ Ch 386, 114 LT 1097, 32 TLR 456, HL 46:09
O'Kane (J & R) & Co Ltd v IRC (1922) 12 TC 303, 126 LT 707, HL ... 3:13, 8:32, 8:168
O'Keeffe v Southport Printers Ltd [1984] STC 443, 58 TC 88 .... 8:56, 8:99
O'Kelly v Trusthouse Forte plc [1984] QB 90, [1983] 3 All ER 456, [1983] 3 WLR 605, [1983] ICR 728, [1983] IRLR 369, CA 7:11, 49:03
Old Chigwellians' Club v Customs and Excise Comrs [1987] VATTR 66 .... 65:12
O'Leary v McKinlay [1991] STC 42, 63 TC 729 .... 5:22, 7:17
Olin Energy Systems Ltd v Scorer [1982] STC 800, 58 TC 592 .... 8:99, 25:26
Omega Group Pension Scheme (Trustees) v IRC [2001] STC (SCD) 121 .... 4:19
Omnicom UK plc v Customs and Excise Comrs [1994] VATTR 465 .... 63:30
O'Neill v IRC [1998] STC (SCD) 110 .... 38:20, 40:04
Onslow v IRC [1891] 1 QB 239, 60 LJQB 138, 64 LT 211, 39 WR 373, CA 57:06
Open University v Customs and Excise Comrs [1982] 1 VATTR 29, [1982] 2 CMLR 572 .... 63:02
Oppenheimer, Re, Tyser v Oppenheimer [1948] Ch 721, [1948] LJR 1553, 50 TC 159, [1948] TR 369 .... 46:25
Optigen Ltd v Customs and Excise Comrs: C-354/03, C-355/03 and C-484/03 [2006] ECR I-483, [2006] STC 419, ECJ 63:15, 66:06, 66:22, 66:34
Optimum Personnel Evaluation (Operations) Ltd v Customs and Excise Comrs (1987) VAT decision 2334 .... 64:03
Optos plc v Revenue and Customs Comrs [2006] STC (SCD) 687 .... 31:12, 31:14
Oram v Johnson [1980] 2 All ER 1, [1980] 1 WLR 558, [1980] STC 222, 53 TC 319 .... 8:65, 8:166, 16:17
Orchard Wine and Spirit Co v Loynes (1952) 33 TC 97, [1952] TR 33, 31 ATC 46 .... 8:74
Ormiston Charitable Trust Ltd v Customs and Excise Comrs [1995] V & DR 180 .... 69:18
O'Rourke v Binks [1991] STC 455, 65 TC 165; revsd [1992] STC 703, 65 TC 165, CA: 18:15, 21:17
Osborne v Dickinson [2004] STC (SCD) 104 .... 2A:48, 2A:62

2575

Table of Cases

Ostime v Australian Mutual Provident Society [1960] AC 459, [1959] 3 All ER 245, 38 TC 492, [1959] TR 211, HL 37:33
Ostime v Duple Motor Bodies Ltd [1961] 2 All ER 167, [1961] 1 WLR 739, 39 TC 537, [1961] TR 29, HL 68, 8:147, 8:164
O'Sullivan v O'Connor [1947] IR 416 .... 8:78
Oughtred v IRC [1958] Ch 678, [1958] 2 All ER 443; sub nom IRC v Oughtred [1958] TR 177, 37 ATC 148, CA; on appeal sub nom Oughtred v IRC [1960] AC 206, [1959] 3 All ER 623, [1959] 3 WLR 898, [1959] TR 319, HL 56:10, 58:10
Oughtred & Harrison Ltd v Customs and Excise Comrs [1988] VATTR 140 .... 65:17
Ounsworth v Vickers Ltd [1915] 3 KB 267, 84 LJKB 2036, 113 LT 865, 6 TC 671 .... 8:111, 8:114, 8:123
Overseas Containers Finance Ltd v Stoker [1989] 1 WLR 606, [1989] STC 364, 61 TC 473, CA 8:11
Overy v Ashford, Dunn & Co Ltd (1933) 17 TC 497, 49 TLR 230, 12 ATC 102 .... 8:106
Owen, Re, Owen v IRC [1949] 1 All ER 901, [1949] TR 189, [1949] LJR 1128 .... 39:01
Owen v Burden [1972] 1 All ER 356, 47 TC 476, 50 ATC 176, CA 7:138
Owen v Elliott [1989] 1 WLR 162, [1989] STC 44; revsd [1990] STC 469, CA 23:09
Owen v Pook [1970] AC 244, [1969] 2 All ER 1, 45 TC 571, [1969] TR 113, HL 7:01, 7:24, 7:90, 7:125,7:126, 7:127, 7:128, 50:06
Owen (Charles) & Co (Bow) Ltd v Customs and Excise Comrs [1993] VATTR 514 .... 69:42
Owers, Re, Public Trustee v Death [1941] Ch 17, [1940] 4 All ER 225, 110 LJ Ch 22, CA 46:25
Oxford Film Foundation v Customs and Excise Comrs (1990) VAT decision 5031 .... 63:26
Oxford Open Learning (Systems) Ltd v Customs and Excise Comrs (2000) VAT decision 16890 .... 68:17
Oy AA, Proceedings brought by: C-231/05 [2007] ECR I-6373, [2007] All ER (EC) 1079, [2009] 3 CMLR 1, [2008] STC 991, [2007] SWTI 1863, [2007] All ER (D) 283 (Jul) 1.14

P

P and O Ferries v Customs and Excise Comrs [1991] VATTR 327, [1991] 3 CMLR 683; revsd sub nom Customs and Excise Comrs v Peninsular and Oriental Steam Navigation Co [1994] STC 259, CA 2:49
PM v United Kingdom (App No 6638/03) [2005] STC 1566, [2005] 3 FCR 101, (2005) Times, 15 September, [2005] SWTI 1480, [2005] All ER (D) 255 (Jul), ECtHR 1:21
Pace Group (Communications) Ltd v Customs and Excise Comrs (1978) VAT decision 510, 101 Taxation 81 .... 69:15
Packford v Customs and Excise Comrs (1994) VAT decision 11626 .... 68:12
Padmore v IRC [1987] STC 36; affd [1989] STC 493, CA 33:38, 37:33, 37:35
Padmore v IRC (No 2) [2001] STC 280, 73 TC 470 .... 37:33
Page v Lowther [1983] STC 61, 57 TC 199; affd [1983] STC 799, 57 TC 199, CA 23:29, 23:34
Page v Pogson (1954) 35 TC 545, [1954] TR 359, 33 ATC 363 .... 8:16, 8:24
Paget v IRC [1938] 2 KB 25, [1938] 1 All ER 392, 21 TC 677, 17 ATC 1, CA 4:11
Palmer, Re, Palmer v Palmer [1916] 2 Ch 391, [1916–17] All ER Rep 892, 85 LJ Ch 577, CA 46:21
Palmer v Maloney and Shipleys [1998] STC 425, 71 TC 183; revsd (1999) 71 TC 502, sub nom Palmer v Moloney [1999] STC 890, CA 1:24
Paradise Motor Co Ltd, Re [1968] 2 All ER 625, [1968] 1 WLR 1125, CA 18:01
Pardoe v Entergy Power Development Corpn. See Entergy Power Development Corpn v Pardoe
Parents and Children Together v Customs and Excise Comrs (2001) VAT decision 17283 .... 68:23
Parikh v Sleeman [1988] STC 580, 63 TC 75; affd [1990] STC 233, 63 TC 75, CA 7:126
Parinv (Hatfield) Ltd v IRC [1996] STC 933; affd [1998] STC 305, CA 56:08, 56:29, 58:10

Park, Re, IRC v Park (No 2) [1972] Ch 385, [1972] 1 All ER 394, [1972] TR 229, CA 43:05
Park Commercial Developments plc v Customs and Excise Comrs [1990] 2 CMLR 746, [1990] VATTR 99 .... 66:05
Parker v Batty (1941) 23 TC 739, 20 ATC 38 .... 8:34
Parker-Jervis, Re, Salt v Locker [1898] 2 Ch 643, 67 LJ Ch 682, 79 LT 403 .... 46:20
Parkfield Trust Ltd v Dent [1931] 2 KB 579, [1931] All ER Rep 720, 101 LJKB 6, 146 LT 90 .... 56:29
Parkin v Cattell (1971) 48 TC 462, [1971] TR 177, 50 ATC 204, CA 2A:74
Parkinson v Customs and Excise Comrs [1985] VATTR 219; affd sub nom Customs and Excise Comrs v Parkinson [1989] STC 51 .... 63:02
Parkside Leasing Ltd v Smith [1985] 1 WLR 310, [1985] STC 63, 58 TC 282 ... 5:14, 5:15
Parry v Deere (1836) 5 Ad & El 551, 6 LJKB 47, 2 Har & W 395, 1 Nev & PKB 47 .... 57:08
Partridge v Mallandaine (1886) 18 QBD 276, 56 LJQB 251, 2 TC 179 .. 8:07, 8:09, 12:05, 18:08
Parway Estates Ltd v IRC (1958) 45 TC 135, [1958] TR 193, 37 ATC 164, CA 60:02, 60:03
Passant v Jackson [1985] STC 133, 59 TC 230; affd [1986] STC 164, 59 TC 230, CA: 16:21, 19:05
Paterson Engineering Co Ltd v Duff (1943) 25 TC 43, 22 ATC 62 .... 8:131
Paterson's Will Trusts, Re, Lawson v Payn [1963] 1 All ER 114, [1963] 1 WLR 623, [1962] TR 389, 41 ATC 412 .... 46:24
Patrick v Burrows (1954) 35 TC 138, [1954] TR 73, 33 ATC 71 .... 7:24
Patrick v Customs and Excise Comrs [1994] VATTR 247 .... 63:21
Pattison v Marine Midland Ltd [1982] Ch 145, [1981] 3 WLR 673, [1981] STC 540, 57 TC 219; on appeal [1983] Ch 205, [1983] 2 WLR 819, [1983] STC 269, 57 TC 219, CA; affd [1984] AC 362, [1984] 2 WLR 11, [1984] STC 10, 57 TC 219, HL 8:64, 8:78, 8:110, 8:117, 16:08, 22:04
Pattullo's Trustees v IRC (1955) 36 TC 87, [1955] TR 105, 34 ATC 101 .... 8:29
Patuck v Lloyd (1944) 171 LT 340, 26 TC 284, 23 ATC 357, CA 35:19
Paul v Paul 1936 SC 443 .... 57:16
Pawlowski v Dunnington [1999] STC 550, CA 7:144
Payne v Deputy Federal Comr of Taxation [1936] AC 497, [1936] 2 All ER 793, 15 ATC 345 .... 5:14, 35:16
Payne v Minister of Health. See Newhill Compulsory Purchase Order 1937, Re, Payne's Application
Payne (W H) & Co v Customs and Excise Comrs [1995] V & DR 490 .... 63:30
Peakviewing (Interactive) Ltd v Secretary of State for Culture, Media and Sport [2002] EWHC 1531 (Admin), [2002] STC 1226 .... 9:54
Pearn v Miller (1927) 11 TC 610, 6 ATC 519 .... 12:07
Pearson v IRC (1868) LR 3 Exch 242, 37 LJ Ex 171, 18 LT 570 .... 57:28
Pearson v IRC [1981] AC 753, [1980] 2 All ER 479, [1980] STC 318, [1980] TR 177, HL 41:12, 42:07, 42:08
Pegasus Birds Ltd v Customs and Excise Comrs [1999] STC 95; affd [2000] STC 91, CA 2A:67
Pegg and Ellam Jones Ltd v IRC (1919) 12 TC 82 .... 8:106
Peirse-Duncombe Trustees v IRC (1940) 23 TC 199, 19 ATC 216 .... 13:20
Pendleton v Mitchells and Butlers Ltd [1969] 2 All ER 928, 45 TC 341, [1968] TR 461, 47 ATC 498 .... 8:115
Peninsular and Oriental Steam Navigation Co v Customs and Excise Comrs [2000] STC 488, [2000] 3 CMLR 1104 .... 63:28
Pentex Oil Ltd v Customs and Excise Comrs (1992) VAT decision 7989 .... 65:12
Pepper v Hart [1991] Ch 203, [1990] 1 WLR 204, [1990] STC 6; affd [1991] 2 All ER 824, [1991] ICR 681, [1991] IRLR 125, [1990] STC 786, CA; on appeal [1993] AC 593, [1993] 1 All ER 42, [1992] STC 898, HL 1:26, 7:107
Pepper (HM Inspector of Taxes) v Daffurn (1993) 22:33
Peracha v Miley [1989] STC 76, 63 TC 444; affd [1990] STC 512, 63 TC 444, CA 5:15
Perkins (Brian) & Co Ltd v Customs and Excise Comrs (1989) VAT decision 3885 .... 69:35

Table of Cases

Perna v Customs and Excise Comrs [1990] VATTR 106 .... 66:07
Perrin v Dickson [1930] 1 KB 107, [1929] All ER Rep 685, 14 TC 608, 8 ATC 367, CA 11:21, 31:30
Perrons v Spackman [1981] 1 WLR 1411, [1981] STC 739, 55 TC 403 .... 7:24
Perry v IRC [2005] STC (SCD) 474 .... 40:04
Petch v Gurney [1994] 3 All ER 731, [1994] STC 689, 66 TC 743, CA 2:99
Pettifor's Will Trusts, Re, Roberts v Roberts [1966] Ch 257, [1966] 1 All ER 913, [1966] 2 WLR 778 .... 20:16
Pettit, Re, Le Fevre v Pettit [1922] 2 Ch 765, [1922] All ER Rep 163, 91 LT Ch 732, 127 LT 491 .... 11:43
Peugeot Motor Co plc v Customs and Excise Comrs [1998] V & DR 1 .... 65:23
Peugeot Motor Co plc v Customs and Excise Comrs [2003] EWHC 2304 (Ch), [2003] STC 1438 .... 63:21
Pexton v Bell [1976] 2 All ER 914, [1976] 1 WLR 885, [1976] STC 301, 51 TC 457, [1976] BTR 257, CA 18:21, 20:20
Philippi v IRC [1971] 3 All ER 61, [1971] 1 WLR 1272, 47 TC 75, [1971] TR 167, CA 35:29
Philips Exports Ltd v Customs and Excise Comrs [1990] STC 508n 63:20, 63:25
Phillips v Customs and Excise Comrs [1992] VATTR 77 .... 68:17
Phillips v Hamilton [2003] STC (SCD) 286 .... 7:129
Phillips (executors of Phillips, deceased) v Revenue and Customs Comrs [2006] STC (SCD) 639D 29:14, 44:04
Phillips v Whieldon Sanitary Potteries Ltd (1952) 33 TC 213, [1952] TR 113, 31 ATC 82 8:123
Philson & Partners Ltd v Moore (1956) 167 Estates Gazette 92 .... 7:144
Phipps v Boardman [1967] 2 AC 46, [1966] 3 All ER 721, [1966] 3 WLR 1009, HL 57:06
Phizackerley (personal representative of Phizackerley, decd) v Revenue and Customs Comrs [2007] STC (SCD) 328 .... 45:23
Pickford v Quirke (1927) 138 LT 500, 13 TC 251, 6 ATC 779, CA 8:05, 8:13
Pilgrim's Language Courses Ltd v Customs and Excise Comrs [1998] STC 784; revsd [1999] STC 874, [2000] ELR 18, CA 68:17
Pilkington v IRC [1964] AC 612, [1962] 3 All ER 622, 40 TC 416, [1962] TR 265, HL 15:13, 42A:44
Pilkington v Randall (1965) 42 TC 662, [1965] TR 241; affd (1966) 42 TC 662, CA 8:21
Pilkington Bros Ltd v IRC [1981] 1 WLR 781, [1981] STC 219, 55 TC 705, [1980] TR 483; revsd [1982] 1 All ER 715, [1982] 1 WLR 136, [1982] STC 103, 55 TC 705, HL 1:25, 25:30, 28:09
Pimblett (John) & Sons Ltd v Customs and Excise Comrs [1988] STC 358, CA 69:13
Pimm, Re, Sharpe v Hodgson [1904] 2 Ch 345, 73 LJ Ch 627, 91 LT 190 .... 46:25
Pinnel's Case (1602) 5 Co Rep 117a, [1558–1774] All ER Rep 612, 77 ER 237 ..... 39:04
Pipe & Ors v R & C Comrs [2008] EWHC 646 (Ch) 2A:61, 2A:90
Piratin v IRC [1981] STC 441, 54 TC 730, [1981] TR 93 .... 15:24
Pirelli Cable Holding NV v IRC [2003] EWHC 32 (Ch), [2003] 2 CMLR 722, [2003] STC 250; affd [2003] EWCA Civ 1849, [2004] STC 130 .... 1:10
Pirelli Cable Holding NV v Revenue and Customs Comrs [2006] UKHL 4, [2006] 1 WLR 400, (2006) Times, 13 February, 150 Sol Jo LB 226, [2006] SWTI 381, [2006] All ER (D) 101 (Feb), sub nom Pirelli Cable Holding NV v IRC [2006] 2 All ER 81, [2006] STC 548, 77 TC 409, [2006] 09 LS Gaz R 27 .... 1:10
Pirelli Cable Holdings NV v Revenue & Customs Comrs [2008] EWCA Civ 70, [2008] 2 CMLR 552, [2008] STC 508, 79 TC 232, (2008) Times, 27 February, [2008] SWTI 276, [2008] All ER (D) 191 (Feb) 1:10
Pitt v Castle Hill Warehousing Co Ltd [1974] 3 All ER 146, [1974] 1 WLR 1624, [1974] STC 420, 49 TC 638 .... 8:114, 8:116
Plumbly (personal representatives of Harbour's Estate) v Spencer [1997] STC 301, 71 TC 399; revsd [1999] STC 677, 71 TC 399, CA 1:27
Pobjoy Mint Ltd v Lane [1984] STC 327, 58 TC 421; affd [1985] STC 314, 58 TC 421, CA 25:29
Podium Investments Ltd v Customs and Excise Comrs [1977] VATTR 121 .... 66:03

Table of Cases

Polysar Investments Netherlands BV v Inspecteur der Invoerrechten en Accijnzen: C-60/90 [1991] ECR I-3111, [1993] STC 222, ECJ 63:15, 63:17, 66:07
Pommery and Greno v Apthorpe (1886) 56 LJQB 155, 56 LT 24, 2 TC 182 .... 36:04
Pontypridd and Rhondda Joint Water Board v Ostime [1946] AC 477, [1946] 1 All ER 668, 115 LJKB 343, 28 TC 261, HL 8:89
Pool Shipping Co Ltd, Re [1920] 1 Ch 251, 89 LJ Ch 111, 122 LT 338, 36 TLR 53 .... 57:04
Poole Borough Council v Customs and Excise Comrs [1992] VATTR 88 .... 68:12
Pope v Beaumont [1941] 2 KB 321, [1941] 3 All ER 9, 24 TC 78, 20 ATC 154 ...... 8:39
Porter v Revenue and Customs Comrs [2005] STC (SCD) 803 .... 7:36
Portman (Viscount), Re, Portman v Portman [1924] 2 Ch 6, 93 LJ Ch 362, 132 LT 440 .... 46:20
Potel v IRC [1971] 2 All ER 504, 46 TC 658, [1970] TR 325, 49 ATC 355 .. 14:01, 26:04
Potter (a firm) v Customs and Excise Comrs [1983] VATTR 108; on appeal [1984] STC 290; revsd [1985] STC 45, CA 63:20, 67:05
Potter v IRC (1854) 10 Exch 147, 23 LJ Ex 345, sub nom Re Stamp Duty on Potter's Deed 2 CLR 1131, sub nom A-G v Potter 23 LTOS 269 .... 57:06
Potters Lodge Restaurant v Customs and Excise Comrs (1980) VAT decision 905, 105 Taxation 421 .... 63:22
Potts' Executors v IRC [1951] AC 443, [1951] 1 All ER 76, 32 TC 211, 44 R & IT 136, [1950] TR 379, HL 12:17
Poulter v Gayjon Processes Ltd [1985] STC 174, 58 TC 350 .... 8:89
Powell v IRC [1997] STC (SCD) 181 .... 44:04
Powell v Jackman [2002] STC (SCD) 488; revsd sub nom Jackman v Powell [2004] EWHC 550 (Ch), [2004] STC 645 .... 7:125, 8:103
Powell-Cotton v IRC [1992] STC 625 .... 39:27
Powlson v Welbeck Securities Ltd [1986] STC 423, 60 TC 269; affd sub nom Welbeck Securities Ltd v Powlson [1987] STC 468, 60 TC 269, CA 18:03, 18:26
Pratt v Strick (1932) 17 TC 459 .... 8:61
Prendergast v Cameron [1939] 1 All ER 223, 23 TC 122, 18 ATC 21, CA; on appeal sub nom Cameron v Prendergast [1940] AC 549, [1940] 2 All ER 35, 23 TC 122, 19 ATC 69, HL 7:21, 7:28, 7:34
Pressland v Customs and Excise Comrs [1995] V & DR 432 .... 65:23
Prest v Bettinson [1980] STC 607, 53 TC 437, [1980] TR 271 .... 14:03, 19:10
Price (John) Business Courses Ltd v Customs and Excise Comrs [1995] V & DR 106 .... 66:29
Primback Ltd v Customs and Excise Comrs. See Customs and Excise Comrs v Primback Ltd
Prince v Mapp [1970] 1 All ER 519, [1970] 1 WLR 260, 46 TC 169, [1969] TR 443 .... 8:102, 8:131
Princess Louise Scottish Hospital v Customs and Excise Comrs [1983] VATTR 191 .... 69:35
Principal and Fellows of Newnham College in the University of Cambridge v Revenue and Customs Comrs [2006] EWCA Civ 285, [2006] STC 1010, 150 Sol Jo LB 435, [2006] All ER (D) 368 (Mar) 29:14
Prior v Saunders [1993] STC 562, 66 TC 210 .... 8:97
Pritchard v Arundale [1972] Ch 229, [1971] 3 All ER 1011, 47 TC 680, [1971] TR 277 .... 7:18, 7:28, 50:116
Professional Footballers Association (Enterprises) Ltd v Customs and Excise Comrs [1989] VATTR 84; on appeal sub nom Customs and Excise Comrs v Professional Footballers Association (Enterprises) Ltd [1990] STC 742; on appeal [1992] STC 294, CA; affd [1993] 1 WLR 153, [1993] STC 86, HL 63:21
Profile Security Services Ltd v Customs and Excise Comrs [1996] STC 808 .... 67:08
Property Co v Inspector of Taxes [2005] STC (SCD) 59 .... 5:03, 10:04
Prospects Care Services Ltd v Customs and Excise Comrs [1997] V & DR 209 ...... 68:23
Prudential Assurance Co Ltd v Customs and Excise Comrs (2001) VAT decision 17030 .... 68:16
Prudential Assurance Co Ltd v IRC [1935] 1 KB 101, [1934] All ER Rep 515, 104 LJKB 195, 152 LT 214 .... 56:14
Prudential Assurance Co Ltd v IRC [1993] 1 WLR 211, [1992] STC 863 ..... 58:04, 62:05

2579

Table of Cases

Prudential Mutual Assurance Investment and Loan Association v Curzon (1852) 8 Ex 97, 22 LJ Ex 85, 19 LTOS 257 .... 56:22
Prudential plc v Revenue and Customs Comrs [2008] EWHC 1839 (Ch), [2008] STC 2820, [2008] SWTI 1919, [2008] All ER (D) 424 (Jul) 3:24
Puddifer (W) (Jun) Ltd v Customs and Excise Comrs [1996] V & DR 237 .... 66:03
Punjab Co-operative Bank Ltd v Amritsar IT Comr Lahore [1940] AC 1055, [1940] 4 All ER 87, 19 ATC 533 .... 8:25
Purchase v Tesco Stores Ltd [1984] STC 304, 58 TC 46 .... 25:29
Purshotam M Pattni & Sons v Customs and Excise Comrs (1984) VAT decision 1658; affd [1987] STC 1 .... 65:12
Purves (HM Inspector of Taxes) v Harrison (2000) 22:33
Puttick v A-G [1980] Fam 1, [1979] 3 All ER 463, [1979] 3 WLR 542, 10 Fam Law 51 .... 33:17, 33:22
Pym v Campbell (1856) 6 E & B 370 .... 18:09
Pyrah v Annis & Co Ltd [1956] 2 All ER 858, 37 TC 163, [1956] TR 193, 35 ATC 230; affd [1957] 1 All ER 196, 37 TC 163, [1956] TR 423, 35 ATC 431, CA 8:110, 8:115

Q

QRS 1 Aps v Frandsen [1999] 3 All ER 289, [1999] STC 616, 71 TC 515, CA 34:02
Quarry Tours Ltd v Customs and Excise Comrs [1984] VATTR 238 .... 69:27
Queens Park Football Club Ltd v Customs and Excise Comrs [1988] VATTR 76 ..... 68:12
Quietlece v IRC [1984] STC 95, CA 57:10, 57:27, 57:29, 62:10

R

R v Allen [2000] QB 744, [2000] 3 WLR 273, [1999] STC 846, [2000] 1 Cr App Rep 203, CA; affd [2001] UKHL 45, [2002] 1 AC 509, [2001] 4 All ER 768, [2001] STC 1537 .... 1:21, 1:22, 7:48, 7:100, 47:08
R v Asif (1985) 82 Cr App Rep 123, CA 2:34
R v A-G, ex p ICI plc [1985] 1 CMLR 588, 60 TC 1; on appeal [1987] 1 CMLR 72, 60 TC 1, CA 2:07
R v Birmingham (West) Rent Tribunal, ex p Edgbaston Investment Trust Ltd [1951] 2 KB 54, [1951] 1 All ER 198, 115 JP 45 .... 23:23
R (on the application of BMW AG and others) v Revenue and Customs Comrs [2009] EWCA Civ 77, [2009] STC 963, CA 2:23, 67:01
R v Board of Inland Revenue, ex p MFK Underwriting Agencies Ltd [1990] 1 All ER 91, sub nom R v IRC, ex p MFK Underwriting Agencies Ltd [1990] 1 WLR 1545, [1989] STC 873 .... 1:30, 2:23; 63:04
R v British Columbia Fir and Cedar Lumber Co Ltd [1932] AC 441, [1932] All ER Rep 147, 101 LJPC 113, 15 ATC 624 .... 8:82
R v Brown (Mark Michael) noted in Inland Revenue Tax Bulletin, February 2004, p 1096 .... 2:107
R v Chief Metropolitan Stipendiary Magistrate, ex p Secretary of State for the Home Department [1989] 1 All ER 151, [1988] 1 WLR 1204 .... 34:04
R v Choudhury [1996] STC 1163, [1996] 2 Cr App Rep 484, CA 2:34
R v Citrone [1999] STC 29, CA 63:19
R v Collier [1997] SWTI 474, CA 2:34
R (on the application of British Sky Broadcasting Group plc) v Customs and Excise Comrs [2001] EWHC Admin 127, [2001] STC 437 .... 2:07
R (on the application of Cardiff City Council) v Customs and Excise Comrs [2003] EWCA Civ 1456, [2004] STC 356, 147 Sol Jo LB 1240 .... 67:17
R v Customs and Excise Comrs, ex p EMU Tabac SARL (Imperial Tobacco intervening): ...... C-296/95 [1998] QB 791, [1998] All ER (EC) 402, [1998] ECR I-1605, [1998] 2 CMLR 1205, ECJ 1:12, 1:13
R (on the application of British Telecommunications plc) v Revenue & Customs Comrs [2005] EWHC 1043 (Admin), [2005] STC 1148 .... 63:04

R (on the application of Elite Mobile plc) v Customs and Excise Comrs [2004] EWHC
2923 (Admin), [2005] STC 275 .... 67:05
R (on the application of Federation of Technological Industries) v Customs and
Excise Comrs [2004] EWHC 254 (Admin), [2004] STC 1008; on appeal [2004]
EWCA Civ 1020, [2004] STC 1424 .... 2:23, 63:09
R (on the application of Freeserve.com plc) v Customs and Excise Comrs (America
Online Inc, interested party) [2003] EWHC 2736 (Admin), [2004] STC 187 .... 2:07
R (on the application of Greenwich Property Ltd) v Customs and Excise Comrs [2001]
EWHC Admin 230, [2001] STC 618 .... 63:04, 69:18
R v Customs and Excise Comrs, ex p Lunn Poly Ltd [1998] 2 CMLR 560, [1998] STC
649; affd [1999] 1 CMLR 1357, [1999] STC 350, CA 1:04
R (on the application of Sagemaster plc) v Customs and Excise Comrs [2004] EWCA Civ
25, [2004] 2 CMLR 141, [2004] STC 813 .... 2:23
R (on the application of Silicon Graphics Finance SA) v Revenue and Customs Comrs
[2006] EWHC 1889 (Admin), [2008] STC 1928 .... 63:04
R v Customs and Excise Comrs, ex p Sims [1988] STC 210 .... 69:13
R (on the application of Teleos) v Customs and Excise Comrs [2004] EWHC 1035
(Admin), [2004] All ER (D) 73 (May) 69:07
R (on the application of TNT Post UK Ltd) v Customs and Excise Comrs [2009] ECR
I-0000, [2009] STC 1464, ECJ 68:14
R (on the application of UK Tradecorp Ltd) v Customs and Excise Comrs [2004] EWHC
2515 (Admin), [2005] STC 138 .... 67:05
R v Dealy [1995] 1 WLR 658, [1995] STC 217, [1995] 2 Cr App Rep 398, CA 2:34
R v Department of Social Security, ex p Overdrive Credit Card Ltd [1991] 1 WLR 635,
[1991] STC 129 .... 50:08, 50:21
R v Dickinson, ex p McGuckian. See McGuckian, Re
R v Dimsey [2000] QB 744, [2000] 3 WLR 273, [1999] STC 846, [2000] 1 Cr App Rep
203, CA; affd [2001] UKHL 46, [2002] 1 AC 509, [2001] 4 All ER 786, [2001] STC
1520 .... 1:21, 35:26
R v Fisher [1989] STI 269, CA 2:34
R v Fulham, Hammersmith and Kensington Rent Tribunal, ex p Zerek [1951] 2 KB 1,
[1951] 1 All ER 482, 115 JP 132, [1951] 1 TLR 423 .... 56:29
R (on the application of Accenture Services Ltd) v Revenue and Customs Comrs, R (on
the application of Barclays Bank plc) v Revenue and Customs Comrs [2009] EWHC
857, [2009] STC 1503 .... 63:04
R (on the application of Cook) v General Commissioners of Income Tax [2009] EWHC
590 (Admin), [2009] SWTI 683, [2009] All ER (D) 12 (Mar) 2.10
R (on the application of Corr) v General Comrs of Income Tax [2006] STC 709 .... 2A:19
R v Gill [2003] EWCA Crim 2256, [2003] 4 All ER 681, [2004] 1 WLR 469, [2003]
STC 1229, [2004] 1 Cr App Rep 214 .... 1:14, 1:22, 2:32, 2A:75
R v Goodwin and Unstead [1997] STC 22, CA; refd sub nom Criminal proceedings
against Goodwin: C-3/97 [1998] All ER (EC) 500, [1998] STC 699, ECJ 63:19
R (on the application of Davies) v HMRC [2008] EWCA Civ 933 .... 2:24, 33:08
R v HM Treasury, ex p Daily Mail and General Trust plc [1987] STC 157; refd 81/87:
[1989] QB 446, [1989] 1 All ER 328, [1989] 2 WLR 908, [1988] STC 787, ECJ 1:12,
33:36
R v HM Treasury, ex p Service Authority for National Crime Squad [2000] STC 638
.... 2:07
R v Howard [1990] STI 351, CA 2:34
R v Hudson [1956] 2 QB 252, [1956] 1 All ER 814, 36 TC 561, [1956] TR 93, CCA
.... 56:29
R v Hunt [1994] STC 819, 68 TC 132, CA 2:31
R v Ike [1996] STC 391, [1996] Crim LR 515, CA 2:34
R v IT Special Purposes Comrs, ex p Dr Barnado's Homes National Incorporated
Association [1920] 1 KB 26, 89 LJKB 194, 7 TC 646; revsd [1920] 1 KB
468, 89 LJKB 194, 7 TC 646, CA; on appeal [1921] 2 AC 1, 90 LJKB 545, 7 TC
666, HL 14:03
R v IRC, ex p Bishopp [1999] STC 531, 72 TC 322 .... 1:30
R v IRC, ex p Camacq Corpn [1990] 1 All ER 173, [1990] 1 WLR 191, [1989] STC
785, CA 1:30

2581

Table of Cases

R (on the application of Carvill) v IRC (No 2) [2003] EWHC 1852 (Admin), [2003] STC 1539, 75 TC 477 .... 35:26
R (on the application of Churchhouse) v IRC [2003] EWHC 681 (Admin), [2003] STC 629, 75 TC 231 .... 2:25
R v IRC, ex p Commerzbank AG [1991] 3 CMLR 633, [1991] STC 271, 68 TC 252; refd C-330/91 [1994] QB 219, [1993] STC 605, 68 TC 252, ECJ; apld (1995) 68 TC 252 .... 1:10, 25:40, 37:03
R v IRC, ex p Cook [1987] STC 434, 60 TC 405 .... 7:144
R v IRC, ex p Fulford-Dobson. See R v Inspector of Taxes, Reading, ex p Fulford-Dobson
R v IRC, ex p Howmet Corpn [1994] STC 413n 1:40
R v IRC, ex p J Rothschild Holdings plc [1986] STC 410, 61 TC 178; affd [1987] STC 163, 61 TC 178, CA 1:30, 2:07
R v IRC, ex p Kaye [1992] STC 581, 65 TC 82 .... 1:30
R v IRC, ex p MFK Underwriting Agencies Ltd. See R v Board of Inland Revenue, ex p MFK Underwriting Agencies Ltd
R v IRC, ex p McVeigh [1996] STC 91, 68 TC 121 .... 7:144
R (on the application of Mander) v IRC [2001] EWCA 358 (Admin), [2002] STC 631 .... 32:13
R v IRC, ex p Mead and Cook [1992] STC 482, 65 TC 1 .... 2:27
R (on the application of Murat) v IRC. See Accountant v Inspector of Taxes
R v IRC, ex p Newfields Developments Ltd [1999] STC 373, 73 TC 532; on appeal [2000] STC 52, 73 TC 532, CA; revsd [2001] UKHL 27, [2001] 1 WLR 1111, [2001] STC 901, 73 TC 532 .... 12:17, 25:44
R v IRC, ex p Preston [1983] 2 All ER 300, [1983] STC 257, 59 TC 1; on appeal [1985] AC 835, [1984] 3 All ER 625, [1984] STC 579, 59 TC 1, CA; affd [1985] AC 835, [1985] 2 All ER 327, [1985] STC 282, 59 TC 1, HL 2A:66, 2:20, 4:18
R (on the application of Professional Contractors Group Ltd) v IRC [2001] EWHC Admin 236, [2001] STC 629, 74 TC 393; affd [2001] EWCA Civ 1945, [2002] STC 165, 74 TC 393 .... 1:03, 1:08, 1:12, 49:03
R (on the application of Professional Contractors Group) v IRC [2001] EWCA Civ 1945, [2002] STC 165, 74 TC 393, [2002] 09 LS Gaz R 31, 146 Sol Jo LB 21, [2001] All ER (D) 356 (Dec) 1:21
R v IRC, ex p Roux Waterside Inn Ltd [1997] STC 781, 70 TC 545 32:13
R v IRC, ex p Sims [1987] STC 211, 60 TC 398 .... 7:144
R (on the application of Wilkinson) v IRC [2002] EWHC 182 (Admin), [2002] STC 347; affd [2003] EWCA Civ 814, [2003] 3 All ER 719, [2003] 1 WLR 2683, [2003] STC 1113, [2003] 2 FCR 558 .... 1.22, 1:30
R (on the application of Wilkinson) v IRC [2005] UKHL 30, [2006] 1 All ER 529, [2005] 1 WLR 1718, [2006] STC 270, 77 TC 78, (2005) Times, 6 May, 149 Sol Jo LB 580, [2005] SWTI 904, [2005] All ER (D) 68 (May) 1:21, 1:30, 2:07, 2A:77
R v Immigration Appeal Tribunal, ex p Siggins [1985] Imm AR 14 .... 33:14
R v Inspector of Taxes, ex p Bass Holdings Ltd [1993] STC 122, 65 TC 495 . 2A:65, 2A:71
R v Inspector of Taxes, ex p Brumfield [1989] STC 151, 61 TC 589 .... 1:30, 63:04
R v Inspector of Taxes, Reading, ex p Fulford-Dobson [1987] QB 978, [1987] 3 WLR 277, 60 TC 168, sub nom R v IRC, ex p Fulford-Dobson [1987] STC 344 .... 1:30, 16:39, 33:10, 35:46, 63:04
R v Lovitt [1912] AC 212, 81 LJPC 140, 105 LT 650, 28 TLR 41 .... 47:06
R v McCarthy [1981] STC 298, CA 2:34, 64:14
R v Mavji [1986] STC 508, CA 2:34, 56:29
R v Melford Developments Inc (1982) 139 DLR (3d) 577, 82 DTC 6281 .... 37:33
R v Mulligan [1990] STC 220, CA 56:29
R (on the application of Westminster City Council) v National Asylum Support Service [2002] UKHL 38, [2002] 4 All ER 654, [2003] LGR 23, [2002] HLR 1021, (2002) Times, 18 October, [2002] All ER (D) 235 (Oct)
R v Redford [1988] STC 845, 89 Cr App Rep 1, CA 2:34, 56:29
R (on the application of BMW AG & Ors) v R & C Comrs [2008] EWHC 712 (Admin), [2009] EWCA Civ 77, [2009] STC 963, CA 2:23, 67:01
R (on the application of Bamber) v R & C Comrs [2007] EWHC 798 (Admin) 2:23

2582

Table of Cases

R (on the application of International Masters Publishers Ltd) v Revenue and Customs Comrs. See International Masters Publishers Ltd v Revenue and Customs Comrs
R (on the application of Just Fabulous (UK) Ltd) v Revenue and Customs Comrs [2007] EWHC 521 (Admin), [2008] STC 2123, [2007] All ER (D) 271 (Mar) 63:09
R (on the application of Software Solutions Partners Ltd) v R & C Comrs [2007] EWHC 971 .... 2:23
R (on the application of Wilkinson) v IRC [2005] UKHL 30, [2006] 1 All ER 529, [2005] 1 WLR 1718, [2006] STC 270, 77 TC 78, (2005) Times, 6 May, 149 Sol Jo LB 580, [2005] SWTI 904, [2005] All ER (D) 68 (May) 2:01
R v Ridgwell (1827) 6 B & C 665, 9 Dow & Ry KB 678, 4 Dow & Ry MC 459, 5 LJOSMC 67 .... 57:04
R v Ryan [1994] 2 CMLR 399, [1994] STC 446, CA 68:15
R v Secretary of State for the Home Department, ex p Chugtai [1995] Imm AR 559 .... 33:14
R v Special Comr of Income Tax, ex p IRC [2000] STC 537, 73 TC 209 .... 2:115
R (on the application of Morgan Grenfell & Co Ltd) v Special Comr of Income Tax [2001] 1 All ER 535, [2000] STC 965, 74 TC 511, DC; affd [2001] EWCA Civ 329, [2003] 1 AC 563, [2002] 1 All ER 776, [2002] 2 WLR 255, [2001] STC 497, 74 TC 511; on appeal [2002] UKHL 21, [2003] 1 AC 563, [2002] 3 All ER 1, [2002] 2 WLR 1299, [2002] STC 786, 74 TC 511 .... 1:21
R v W [1998] STC 550, CA 2:27
R v Williams [1942] AC 541, [1942] 2 All ER 95 .... 47:05
RAL (Channel Islands) Ltd v Customs and Excise Comrs (2002) VAT decision 17914 .... 63:29
RAL (Channel Islands) Ltd v Customs and Excise Comrs: C-452/03 [2005] ECR I-3947, [2005] STC 1025, ECJ 63:30
RAP Group plc v Customs and Excise Comrs [2000] STC 980 .... 66:08
RBS Leasing and Services Ltd v Customs and Excise Comrs [2000] V & DR 33 ..... 65:17
RBS Property Development Ltd and Royal Bank of Scotland Group plc v Customs and Excise Comrs (VAT decision 17789) [2003] SWTI 312 .... 68:12
RCI (Europe) Ltd v Woods [2003] STC (SCD) 128; affd [2003] EWHC 3129 (Ch), [2004] STC 315 .... 50:09
RMSG (a partnership) v Customs and Excise Comrs [1994] VATTR 167 ...., 2:49
RTZ Oil and Gas Ltd v Elliss [1987] 1 WLR 1442, [1987] STC 512, 61 TC 132 .... 8:114
Racal Group Services Ltd v Ashmore [1994] STC 416; affd [1995] STC 1151, 68 TC 86, CA 2A:71, 40:21
Radcliffe v Holt (1927) 11 TC 621, 6 ATC 618 .... 7:20, 7:24
Radio Authority v Customs and Excise Comrs [1992] VATTR 155 .... 63:17
Rae v Lazard Investment Co Ltd [1963] 1 WLR 555, 41 TC 1, [1963] TR 149, [1963] BTR 121 .... 35:10
Raffenel's Goods, Re (1863) 32 LJPM & A 203, 9 Jur NS 386, 1 New Rep 569, 3 Sw & Tr 49 .... 33:19
Rahman (t/a Khayam Restaurant) v Customs and Excise Comrs (No 2) [2002] EWCA Civ 1881, [2003] STC 150 .... 2A:67
Raja's Commercial College v Gian Singh & Co Ltd [1977] AC 312, [1976] 2 All ER 801, [1976] STC 282 .... 10:04
Ralli Bros Trustee Co Ltd v IRC [1968] Ch 215, [1967] 3 All ER 811, [1967] TR 279, 46 ATC 300 .... 39:08
Ram Rattan v Parma Nand (1945) LR 173 Ind App 28 .... 56:29
Rampling v Customs and Excise Comrs [1986] VATTR 62 .... 65:12
Ramsay v IRC (1935) 154 LT 141, 20 TC 79 .... 11:32
Ramsay (W T) Ltd v IRC [1979] 3 All ER 213, [1979] STC 582, 54 TC 101; affd [1982] AC 300, [1981] 1 All ER 865, [1981] STC 174, 54 TC 101, HL .. 1:24, 3:01, 3:08, 3:15, 3.16, 3:21, 3:22, 16:02, 17:10, 17:17, 18:01, 18:47, 32:13, 44:03, 50:35
Ramsden v IRC (1957) 37 TC 619, [1957] TR 247, 36 ATC 325 .... 35:33
Rand v Alberni Land Co (1920) 7 TC 629 .... 8:19
Randall v Plumb [1975] 1 All ER 734, [1975] STC 191, 50 TC 392 ... 16:12, 16:13, 18:24
Rangatira Ltd v IRC [1997] STC 47 .... 8:10, 23:02
Rank Xerox Ltd v Lane [1981] AC 629, [1979] 3 All ER 657, [1979] STC 740, 53 TC 185, HL 17:11

Table of Cases

Rankine (D and G R) v IRC (1952) 32 TC 520, [1952] TR 1, 1952 SC 177, 1952 SLT 153 .... 8:70
Ransom v Higgs [1974] 3 All ER 949, [1974] 1 WLR 1594, [1974] STC 539, 50 TC 1, HL 2:20, 3:13, 4:01, 8:03, 8:06, 8:15, 8:19, 23:29
Ratcliffe, Re, Holmes v McMullan [1999] STC 262 .... 43:31
Razzack and Mishari v Customs and Excise Comrs [1997] V & DR 392 .... 63:30
Ready-Mixed Concrete (South East) Ltd v Ministry of Pensions [1968] 2 QB 497, [1968] 1 All ER 433 .... 7:08, 7:11, 49:03
Red Discretionary Trustees v Inspector of Taxes [2004] STC (SCD) 132; affd sub nom Howell v Trippier [2004] EWCA Civ 885, [2004] STC 1245, 76 TC 415 ..... 13:11, 26:18
Redkite Ltd v Inspector of Taxes [1996] STC (SCD) 501 .... 8:96
Redundant Employee v McNally [2005] STC (SCD) 143 .... 2:17
Reed v Clark [1986] Ch 1, [1985] 3 WLR 142, [1985] STC 323, 58 TC 528 . 33:03, 33:14, 35:47
Reed v Nova Securities Ltd [1982] STC 724, 59 TC 516; affd [1984] 1 WLR 537, [1984] STC 124, 59 TC 516, CA; on appeal [1985] 1 All ER 686, [1985] 1 WLR 193, [1985] STC 124, 59 TC 516, HL 22:06, 28:27
Reed v Young [1985] STC 25, 59 TC 196, CA; affd [1986] 1 WLR 649, [1986] STC 285, 59 TC 196, HL 3:13, 6:18
Reemtsma Cigarettenfabriken GmbH v Finance Minister: C-35/05 [2007] 2 CMLR 874, [2007] SWTI 543, [2007] All ER (D) 266 (Mar), ECJ 66:37
Refrigeration Spares (Manchester) Ltd v Customs and Excise Comrs (2002) VAT decision 17603 .... 67:06
Refson v R & C Comrs [2008], unreported 2:23
Regalstar Enterprises Ltd v Customs and Excise Comrs [1989] 1 CMLR 117 .... 65:12
Regazzoni v KC Sethia (1944) Ltd [1958] AC 301, [1957] 3 All ER 286, HL 34:04
Regent Oil Co Ltd v Strick [1966] AC 295, [1965] 3 All ER 174, 43 TC 1, [1965] TR 277, HL 3:07, 8:110, 8:112, 8:117, 8:128, 8:129, 8:130
Reid, Re (1970) 17 DLR (3d) 199 .... 34:04, 34:05
Reid v IRC 1926 SC 589, 1926 SLT 365, 10 TC 673, 5 ATC 357 .... 54:02
Reid's Trustees v IRC 1929 SC 439, 1929 SLT 372, 14 TC 512, 8 ATC 213 .. 13:08, 13:15
Reisdorf v Finanzamt Köln-West: C-85/95 [1997] 1 CMLR 536, [1997] STC 180, ECJ 66:22
Reisebüro Binder GmbH v Finanzamt Stuttgart-Körperschaften: C-116/96 [1998] 2 CMLR 61, [1998] STC 604, ECJ 63:30
Religious Tract and Book Society of Scotland v Forbes (1896) 60 JP 393, 3 TC 415 .... 8:12, 13:24
Rendell v Went [1964] 2 All ER 464, [1964] 1 WLR 650, 41 TC 641, [1964] TR 133, HL 7:102, 7:109
Renfrew Town Council v IRC 1934 SC 468, 1934 SLT 426, 19 TC 13 .... 11:44
Rennell v IRC [1964] AC 173, [1963] 1 All ER 803, [1963] TR 73, 42 ATC 55, HL 43:05
Restorex Ltd v Customs and Excise Comrs (1997) VAT decision 15014 .... 67:09
Revell v Elsworthy Bros & Co Ltd (1890) 3 TC 12, 55 JP 392 .... 7:125
Revelstoke (Lord) v IRC [1898] AC 565, 67 LJQB 855, 79 LT 227, 62 JP 740, HL 59:08
Revenue and Customs Comrs v Arachchige [2009] EWHC 1077 (Ch), [2009] STC 1729 .... 63:30
Revenue and Customs Comrs v Axa UK plc [2008] EWHC 1137 (Ch), [2008] STC 2091 .... 63:20; 68:16
Revenue and Customs Comrs v Bank of Ireland Britain Holdings Ltd [2007] EWHC 941 (Ch), [2008] STC 253, [2007] SWTI 1397, [2007] All ER (D) 273 (Apr) 3:25
Revenue and Customs Comrs v Board of Governors of Robert Gordon University [2008] CSIH 22, [2008] STC 1890 .... 63:19; 68:17
Revenue and Customs Comrs v D'Arcy [2007] EWHC 163 (Ch), [2008] STC 1329, [2007] SWTI 337, [2007] All ER (D) 91 (Feb) 3:25
Revenue and Customs Comrs v Decadt (2007) Times, 4 June, [2007] SWTI 1434, [2007] All ER (D) 139 (May) 7:136
Revenue and Customs Comrs v Dempster (trading as Boulevard) [2008] EWHC 63 (Ch), [2008] STC 2079 .... 66:03, 66:22

Table of Cases

Revenue and Customs Comrs v Deyner [2007] EWHC 2750 (Ch), [2008] STC 633 .... 68:11
Revenue and Customs Comrs v EB Central Services Ltd (formerly known as Excess Baggage plc) [2007] EWHC 201 (Ch), [2007] SWTI 342, [2007] All ER (D) 137 (Feb), [2008] EWCA Civ 486, [2008] STC 2209 .... 69:12, 69:28
Revenue and Customs Comrs v Empowerment Enterprises Ltd [2006] CSIH 46, 2007 SC 123, [2008] STC 1835 .... 68:19
Revenue and Customs Comrs v Enron Europe Ltd [2006] EWHC 824 (Ch), [2006] STC 1339 .... 65:13
Revenue and Customs Comrs v Facilities Maintenance Engineering Ltd [2006] EWHC 689 (Ch), [2006] STC 1887, 77 TC 575, (2006) Times, 18 April, [2006] SWTI 1149, [2006] All ER (D) 481 (Mar) 2A:19
Revenue and Customs Comrs v Grace [2008] EWHC 2708 (Ch), [2009] STC 213, [2008] SWTI 2503, [2008] All ER (D) 90 (Nov) 33:10
Revenue and Customs Comrs v Gracechurch Management Services Ltd [2007] EWHC 755 (Ch), 151 Sol Jo LB 507, [2008] STC 795, [2007] All ER (D) 30 (Apr) 64:27
Revenue and Customs Comrs v IDT Card Services Ireland Ltd [2006] EWCA Civ 29, [2006] STC 1252, [2006] All ER (D) 220 (Jan) 63:01, 63:02, 63:20
Revenue and Customs Comrs v Isle of Wight Borough Council: C-288/07 [2008] ECR I-0000, [2008] STC 2964, [2009] STC 1096, [2009] STC 1098, ECJ, EWHC 592 (Ch) 63:17
Revenue and Customs Comrs v Jeancharm Ltd (t/a Beaver International) [2005] EWHC 839 (Ch), [2005] STC 918, [2005] All ER (D) 86 (May) 66:03
Revenue and Customs Comrs v K&L Childcare Service Ltd [2005] EWHC 2414 (Ch), [2006] STC 18, [2005] All ER (D) 65 (Nov) 68:23
Revenue and Customs Comrs v Khawaja [2008] EWHC 1687 (Ch), [2009] 1 WLR 398, [2008] STC 2880, [2008] NLJR 1076, (2008) Times, 20 October, [2008] SWTI 1748, [2008] All ER (D) 227 (Jul) 2A:04
Revenue and Customs Comrs v La Senza Ltd [2006] EWHC 1331 (Ch), [2007] STC 901, [2005] SWTI 1148, [2006] All ER (D) 455 (Mar) 2A:08
Revenue and Customs Comrs v Livewire Telecom Ltd [2009] EWHC 15 (Ch), [2009] STC 643 .... 63:09, 66:34
Revenue and Customs Comrs v Loyalty Management UK Ltd [2006] EWHC 1498 (Ch), [2007] STC 536, [2006] SWTI 1792, [2006] All ER (D) 256 (Jun), [2007] EWCA Civ 965, [2008] STC 59, CA 63:19, 63:20
Revenue and Customs Comrs v Muco Door and Window Hardware (UK) Ltd [2006] SWTI 1919 .... 9:12
Revenue and Customs Comrs v Oriel Support Ltd [2006] EWHC 3217 (Ch), [2007] STC 1148, [2007] SWTI 111, [2006] All ER (D) 223 (Dec) 2A:19
Revenue and Customs Comrs v Pal and others [2006] EWHC 2016 (Ch), [2008] STC 2442 .... 63:12
Revenue and Customs Comrs v Principal and Fellows of Newnham College in the University of Cambridge [2008] UKHL 23, [2008] STC 1225, HL 68:07
Revenue and Customs Comrs v Prizedome Ltd and Limitgood Ltd [2008] EWHC 19 (Ch) 3:24, 28:14
Revenue and Customs Comrs v Salaried Persons Postal Loans Ltd [2006] STC 1315 .... 25:47
Revenue and Customs Comrs v Smallwood. See Smallwood v Revenue and Customs Comrs
Revenue and Customs Comrs v Smith [2007] SWTI 537 .... 2A:19
Revenue and Customs Comrs v Stone [2008] EWHC 1249 (Ch), [2008] STC 2501 .... 69:12, 69:26
Revenue and Customs Comrs v Tallington Lakes Ltd [2007] EWHC 1955 (Ch), [2008] STC 2734 .... 68:12
Revenue and Customs Comrs v Trustees of the Peter Clay Discretionary Trust [2007] EWHC 2661 (Ch) 13:13
Revenue and Customs Comrs v Tinsley [2005] EWHC 1508 (Ch), [2005] STC 1612, [2005] SWTI 1063, [2005] All ER (D) 72 (Jun) 69:23
Revenue and Customs Comrs v Vodafone 2 [2006] EWCA Civ 1132, [2006] STC 1530, (2006) Times, 8 August, [2006] All ER (D) 425 (Jul) 2A:52

Table of Cases

Revenue and Customs Comrs v Weight Watchers (UK) Ltd [2008] EWCA Civ 715, [2008] STC 2313, CA 63:20
Revenue and Customs Comrs v William Grant & Sons Distillers Ltd [2007] UKHL 15, [2007] 2 All ER 440, [2007] 1 WLR 1448, [2007] STC 680, (2007) Times, 2 April, [2007] SWTI 1165, [2007] All ER (D) 459 (Mar) 8:64, 8:127, 25:05
Revenue and Customs Comrs v Wright [2007] EWHC 526 (Ch), [2007] STC 1684, [2007] SWTI 337, [2007] All ER (D) 68 (Feb) 2:21
Revenue and Customs Comrs v Zurich Insurance Co. See Zurich Insurance Co v Revenue and Customs Comrs
Rewe Zentralfinanz eG v Finanzamt Koln-Mitte: C-347/04 [2007] ECR I-2647, [2007] 2 CMLR 1111, [2008] STC 2785, [2007] SWTI 1169, [2007] All ER (D) 497 (Mar) 1:14
Reynaud v IRC [1999] STC (SCD) 185 .... 39:28
Reynolds' Executors v Bennett (1943) 25 TC 401, 22 ATC 233 .... 8:21, 23:02
Reynolds, Sons & Co Ltd v Ogston (1930) 15 TC 501, 9 ATC 8, CA 8:57, 8:60
Rhodes v Customs and Excise Comrs [1986] VATTR 72 .... 64:14
Rhodesia Railways Ltd v Bechuanaland Protectorate IT Collector [1933] AC 368, 102 LJPC 72, 149 LT 3, 12 ATC 223 .... 8:122, 8:123
Rhokana Corpn Ltd v IRC [1937] 1 KB 788, [1937] 2 All ER 79, 21 TC 552, 16 ATC 12, CA; revsd [1938] AC 380, [1938] 2 All ER 51, 21 TC 552, 17 ATC 71, HL 11:38
Rhondda Cynon Taff County Borough Council v Customs and Excise Comrs [2000] V & DR 150 .... 63:15, 63:17
Rialto Homes plc v Customs and Excise Comrs (1999) VAT decision 16340 .... 69:18
Rice (B J) & Associates v Customs and Excise Comrs [1994] STC 565; revsd [1996] STC 581, CA 65:14
Richardson v Delaney [2001] STC 1328, 74 TC 167, [2001] IRLR 663 .... 7:33
Richardson v Jenkins [1995] STC 95n 6:15
Richardson v Worrall [1985] STC 693, 58 TC 642 .... 7:23, 7:24, 7:44, 50:07, 50:08
Riches v Westminster Bank Ltd [1947] AC 390, [1947] 1 All ER 469, 28 TC 159, 26 ATC 85, HL 11:05, 11:06
Rickard v Customs and Excise Comrs (1989) VAT decision 3711 .... 63:19
Ricketts v Colquhoun [1925] 1 KB 725, 94 LJKB 340, 10 TC 118, 4 ATC 32, CA; affd [1926] AC 1, 95 LJKB 82, 10 TC 118, 4 ATC 565, HL . 7:122, 7:125, 7:126, 7:127, 7:128, 7:137, 7:138, 7:141, 50:06
Ridge Nominees v IRC [1962] Ch 376, [1961] 2 All ER 354, [1961] TR 61, 40 ATC 72 .... 57:07
Ridge Securities Ltd v IRC [1964] 1 All ER 275, [1964] 1 WLR 479, 44 TC 373, [1963] TR 449 .... 8:154, 11:05, 11:23
Ridgeons Bulk Ltd v Customs and Excise Comrs [1994] STC 427 .... 63:26
Ridley v Customs and Excise Comrs [1983] VATTR 81 .... 63:32
Riley v Coglan [1968] 1 All ER 314, [1967] 1 WLR 1300, 44 TC 481, [1967] TR 155 .... 7:28
Ringside Refreshments v Customs and Excise Comrs [2003] EWHC 3043 (Ch), [2004] STC 426 .... 63:20
Ritter v Finanzamt Gemersheim, Van Raad: C-152/03 .... 1:11
River Barge Holidays Ltd v Customs and Excise Comrs (1978) VAT decision 572, 101 Taxation 375 .... 65:16
River Thames Conservators v IRC (1886) 18 QBD 279, 56 LJQB 181, 56 LT 198, 35 WR 274 .... 57:06
Riverside Housing Association Ltd v Revenue and Customs Comrs [2006] EWHC 2383 (Ch), [2006] STC 2072, (2006) Times, 1 November, [2006] SWTI 2277, [2006] All ER (D) 20 (Oct) 63:17
Riverside School (Whassett) Ltd v Customs and Excise Comrs [1995] V & DR 186 .... 69:18
RLRE Tellmer Property sro v Finanèní v Ústí nad Labem: C-572/07 [2009] ECR I–0000, [2009] SWTI 1886, ECJ 63:20
Robb (W M) Ltd v Page (1971) 47 TC 465, [1971] TR 265, 50 ATC 302 .... 8:25
Roberts v Customs and Excise Comrs [1992] VATTR 30 .... 68:12
Roberts v Customs and Excise Comrs (1998) VAT decision 15759 .... 2A:67
Roberts v Granada TV Rental Ltd [1970] 2 All ER 764, [1970] 1 WLR 889, 46 TC 295, [1970] TR 73 .... 9:50

Table of Cases

Robertson v IRC [2002] STC (SCD) 182 .... 2A:09
Robertson v IRC (No 2) [2002] STC (SCD) 242 .... 2A:09
Robinson, Re, McLaren v Public Trustee [1911] 1 Ch 502, [1911–13] All ER Rep 296, 104 LT 331, 80 LJ Ch 381 .... 11:41
Robinson v Scott Bader Co Ltd [1980] 2 All ER 780, [1980] 1 WLR 755, [1980] STC 241, 54 TC 757; affd [1981] 2 All ER 1116, [1981] STC 436, 54 TC 757, CA . 8:98, 22:16
Robinson Group of Companies Ltd v Customs and Excise Comrs (1999) VAT decision 16081 .... 65:19
Robroyston Brickworks Ltd v IRC (1976) 51 TC 230 .... 8:52
Robson v Dixon [1972] 3 All ER 671, [1972] 1 WLR 1493, 48 TC 527, [1975] BTR 466 .... 7:03
Robson v Mitchell [2005] EWCA Civ 585, [2005] STC 893 .... 17:07
Roebank Printing Co Ltd v IRC 1928 SC 701, 13 TC 864 .... 8:131
Rogers v IRC (1879) 16 Sc LR 682, 1 TC 225 .... 33:03
Rolfe v Nagel [1982] STC 53, 55 TC 585, CA 8:75
Rolfe v Wimpey Waste Management Ltd [1988] STC 329, 62 TC 399; affd [1989] STC 454, 62 TC 399, CA 8:114, 8:130
Rolls-Royce Ltd v Jeffrey [1962] 1 All ER 801, [1962] 1 WLR 425, 40 TC 443, [1962] TR 9, HL 8:76
Rolls-Royce Motors Ltd v Bamford [1976] STC 162, 51 TC 319, [1976] TR 21 ...... 8:51, 8:52, 8:56
Rompelman v Minister van Financiën: 268/83 [1985] ECR 655, [1985] 3 CMLR 202, ECJ 63:16, 66:05
Roome v Edwards [1979] 1 WLR 860, [1979] STC 546, 54 TC 359, [1979] TR 87, [1979] BTR 261; affd [1980] Ch 425, [1980] 1 All ER 850, [1980] 2 WLR 156, [1980] STC 99, 54 TC 359, [1979] TR 451, CA; revsd [1982] AC 279, [1981] 1 All ER 736, [1981] STC 96, 54 TC 359, HL 3:10, 20:05, 20:11, 20:12, 33:40
Roper (Alan) & Sons Ltd v Customs and Excise Comrs (1997) VAT decision 15260 .... 69:23
Rosabronze Ltd v Customs and Excise Comrs (1984) VAT decision 1668 .... 67:09
Rose, Re, Midland Bank Executor and Trustee Co Ltd v Rose [1949] Ch 78, [1948] 2 All ER 971, [1949] LJR 208 .... 18:05, 39:05
Rose, Re, Rose v IRC [1952] Ch 499, [1952] 1 All ER 1217, [1952] TR 175, 31 ATC 138, CA 18:34, 56:11
Rose v Director of the Assets Recovery Agency [2006] SWTI 1631, SCD 2:35
Rose v Trigg (1963) 41 TC 365, [1963] TR 357, 42 ATC 377 .... 31:31
Rose & Co (Wallpaper and Paints) v Campbell [1968] 1 All ER 405, [1968] 1 WLR 346, 44 TC 500, [1967] TR 259 .... 9:04
Rosemoore Investments v Inspector of Taxes [2002] STC (SCD) 325 .... 8:10
Rosette Franks (King Street) Ltd v Dick (1955) 36 TC 100, [1955] TR 133, 34 ATC 130 .... 2:28
Rosgill Group Ltd v Customs and Excise Comrs [1995] V & DR 155; affd [1997] 3 All ER 1012, [1997] STC 811, CA 65:17
Roskams v Bennett (1950) 32 TC 129, [1950] TR 343, 29 ATC 281 .... 7:138, 7:141
Rossano v Manufacturers' Life Insurance Co Ltd [1963] 2 QB 352, [1962] 2 All ER 214, [1962] 3 WLR 157 .... 34:04
Rosser v IRC [2003] STC (SCD) 311 .... 44:14
Rotary International v Customs and Excise Comrs [1991] VATTR 177 .... 68:25
Rothschild (J) Holdings plc v IRC [1988] STC 645, 61 TC 188; affd [1989] STC 435, CA 2:89, 56:26
Rowan v Rowan [1988] ILRM 65 .... 32:16, 33:19
Rowe and Maw v Customs and Excise Comrs [1975] 2 All ER 444, [1975] 1 WLR 1291, [1975] STC 340 .... 63:20, 63:21
Rowland v Revenue and Customs Comrs [2006] STC (SCD) 536 .... 2A:44
Royal and Sun Alliance Insurance Group plc v Customs and Excise Comrs [2000] STC 933; on appeal [2001] EWCA Civ 1476, [2001] STC 1476; revsd [2003] UKHL 29, [2003] 2 All ER 1073, [2003] STC 832 .... 66:08, 66:28
Royal Antediluvian Order of Buffaloes v Owens [1928] 1 KB 446, 97 LJKB 210, 13 TC 176, 6 ATC 920 .... 13:22
Royal Bank of Canada v IRC [1972] Ch 665, [1972] 1 All ER 225, 47 TC 565, [1972] TR 197 .... 11:14, 35:35

Table of Cases

Royal Bank of Scotland v Greece: C-311/97 [2000] STC 733, [1999] ECR I-2651, [1999] 2 CMLR 973, ECJ 1:06, 1:08
Royal Bank of Scotland Group plc v Customs and Excise Comrs [2002] STC 575, 2000 SLT 664 .... 69:33
Royal Bank of Scotland plc v HMRC: C-488/07 [2008] ECR I–0000, [2009] STC 461, ECJ 66:09
Royal College of Veterinary Surgeons v Meldrum [1996] STC (SCD) 54 .... 2A:71
Royal Insurance Co v Watson [1897] AC 1, 66 LJQB 1, 3 TC 500, HL 8:113
Royal Insurance Co Ltd v Stephen (1928) 14 TC 22, 44 TLR 630, 7 ATC 307 .... 8:149
Royal Midland Counties Home for Disabled People v Customs and Excise Comrs [2002] STC 395 .... 69:41
Royal Pigeon Racing Association v Customs and Excise Comrs (1996) VAT decision 14006 .... 68:26
Royal Ulster Constabulary Athletic Association Ltd v Customs and Excise Comrs [1989] VATTR 17 .... 63:16
Ruhamuh Property Co Ltd v FCT (1928) 41 CLR 1648 .... 8:22
Rum Runner Casino Ltd v Customs and Excise Comrs (1981) VAT decision 1036, 108 Taxation 532 .... 68:15
Russell v Aberdeen Town and County Bank (1888) 13 App Cas 418, 58 LJPC 8, 2 TC 321, HL 5:06, 8:64
Russell v IRC [1988] 2 All ER 405, [1988] 1 WLR 834, [1988] STC 195 .... 40:21, 43:24, 44:01
Russell (Neville) (a firm) v Customs and Excise Comrs [1987] VATTR 194 .... 63:26
Rutledge v IRC 1929 SC 379, 14 TC 490, 8 ATC 207 .... 8:16
Rutter v Charles Sharpe & Co Ltd [1979] 1 WLR 1429, [1979] STC 711, 53 TC 163, [1979] TR 225 .... 8:95
Ryall v Hoare [1923] 2 KB 447, [1923] All ER Rep 528, 8 TC 521, 2 ATC 137 ..... 5:17, 12:03, 12:06 12:10
Ryan v Asia Mill Ltd (1951) 32 TC 275, [1951] TR 181, 30 ATC 110, HL 8:162
Ryan v Crabtree Denims Ltd [1987] STC 402, 60 TC 183 .... 8:89
Ryan and Townsend v Customs and Excise Comrs (1994) VAT decision 12806 ...... 63:27
Rydon's Settlement, Re [1955] Ch 1, [1954] 3 All ER 1, CA 42:03
Rye v Rye [1962] AC 496, [1962] 1 All ER 146, [1962] 2 WLR 361, HL 57:25
Rye and Eyre v IRC [1935] AC 274, [1935] All ER Rep 897, 19 TC 164, 14 ATC 38, HL 11:38
Rysaffe Trustee Co (CI) Ltd v IRC [2001] STC (SCD) 225; on appeal [2002] EWHC 1114 (Ch), [2002] STC 872; affd [2003] EWCA Civ 356, [2003] STC 536 ... 39:29, 39:33

S

S v S (No 2) [1997] STC 759 .... 2:28
SCA Packaging Ltd v Revenue and Customs Comrs [2006] STC (SCD) 426 .... 7:36
SGS Holdings UK Ltd v Customs and Excise Comrs (1996) VAT decision 13918 ...... 2:49
Sabine v Lockers Ltd (1958) 38 TC 120, [1958] TR 213, 37 ATC 227, CA 8:86
Sainsbury (J) plc v O'Connor [1990] STC 516; affd [1991] 1 WLR 963, [1991] STC 318, CA 28:01, 28:09, 31:07, 60:03
St Andrew's Church, Eakring (Parochial Church Council) v Customs and Excise Comrs (1998) VAT decision 15320 .... 69:23
St Aubyn v A-G [1952] AC 15, [1951] 2 All ER 473, 30 ATC 193, HL 41:05
St Barbe Green v IRC [2005] EWHC 14 (Ch), [2005] STC 288, sub nom Green v IRC [2005] 1 WLR 1722 .... 42:07, 45:20
St Dunstan's v Major [1997] STC (SCD) 212 .... 6:36
St George's Home Co Ltd v Customs and Excise Comrs (1993) VAT decision 10213 .... 66:07
St Helen's School Northwood v Revenue and Customs Comrs [2006] EWHC 3306 (Ch), [2007] STC 633, [2007] SWTI 117, [2006] All ER (D) 316 (Dec) 66:07, 66:09
St John's School (Mountford and Knibbs) v Ward [1974] STC 69, [1973] TR 267; affd [1975] STC 7, 49 TC 524, [1974] TR 273, CA 9:30
Salaried Persons Loans Ltd v Revenue and Customs omrs [2005] STC (SCD) 851 .... 25:43

Salisbury House Estate Ltd v Fry [1930] 1 KB 304, 15 TC 266, 45 TLR 562, CA; affd sub nom Fry v Salisbury House Estate Ltd [1930] AC 432, 99 LJKB 403, 15 TC 266, HL 5:03, 5:06, 10:07
Salt v Chamberlain [1979] STC 750, 53 TC 143, [1979] TR 203 .... 8:25
Salt v Fernandez [1997] STC (SCD) 271 .... 8:07
Salt v Golding [1996] STC (SCD) 269 .... 9:62
Salter v Minister of National Revenue (1947) 2 DTC 918 .... 5:15
Salvesen's Trustees v IRC (1930) 9 ATC 43, 1930 SLT 387 .... 45:02
Samuel v Salmon & Gluckstein Ltd [1946] Ch 8, [1945] 2 All ER 520, 115 LJ Ch 103, 173 LT 358 .... 57:28
San Paulo (Brazilian) Rly Co Ltd v Carter [1896] AC 31, 65 LJQB 161, 3 TC 407, HL 33:28, 35:02, 35:04
Sandell v Customs and Excise Comrs (1992) VAT decision 9665 .... 65:18
Sanderson v Durbidge [1955] 3 All ER 154, [1955] 1 WLR 1087, 36 TC 239, [1955] TR 221 .... 7:137
Sandra Puffer v Unabhängiger Finanzsenat, Außenstelle Linz: C-460/07 [2009] ECR I-0000, [2009] STC 1693, ECJ 66:05
Sansom v Peay [1976] 3 All ER 375, [1976] 1 WLR 1073, [1976] STC 494, 52 TC 1 .... 20:14, 23:13
Sargaison v Roberts [1969] 3 All ER 1072, [1969] 1 WLR 951, 45 TC 612, 48 ATC 149 .... 1:28
Sargent v Barnes [1978] 2 All ER 737, [1978] 1 WLR 823, [1978] STC 322, 52 TC 335 .... 8:103
Sargent v Eayrs [1973] 1 All ER 277, [1972] 1 WLR 236, [1973] STC 50, 48 TC 573 .... 8:103
Sarsfield v Dixons Group plc [1997] STC 283, 71 TC 121; revsd [1998] STC 938, 71 TC 121, CA 9:12
Sassoon v IRC (1943) 25 TC 154, 22 ATC 57, CA 35:29
Saunders, Re, Saunders v Gore [1898] 1 Ch 17, 67 LJ Ch 55, 77 LT 450, CA 46:24
Saunders v Customs and Excise Comrs [1980] VATTR 53 .... 63:12
Save and Prosper Securities Ltd v IRC [2000] STC (SCD) 408 .... 59:19, 61:09, 61:10
Sawadee Restaurant v Customs and Excise Comrs (1999) VAT decision 15933 .... 63:27
Saxone Lilley and Skinner (Holdings) Ltd v IRC [1967] 1 All ER 756, [1967] 1 WLR 501, 44 TC 122, [1967] TR 17, HL 9:12
Saywell v Pope [1979] STC 824, 53 TC 40, [1979] TR 361 .... 8:61
Scales v George Thompson & Co Ltd (1927) 13 TC 83, 138 LT 331, 6 ATC 960 ..... 8:50
Scappaticci v A-G [1955] P 47, [1955] 1 All ER 193n, [1955] 2 WLR 409 .... 33:15
Scrace v Revenue and Customs Comrs [2006] EWHC 2646 (Ch), [2007] STC 269, [2006] SWTI 1886, [2006] All ER (D) 195 (Jul) 63:12
Schaffer v Cattermole [1980] STC 650, 53 TC 499, [1980] TR 331, CA 11:07
Schemepanel Trading Ltd v Customs and Excise Comrs [1996] STC 871 .... 66:04
Schemp v Finanzamt Munchen V: C-403/03 [2005] STC 1792, [2005] SWTI 1255, [2005] All ER (D) 147 (Jul), ECJ 1:09
Schioler v Westminster Bank Ltd [1970] 2 QB 719, [1970] 3 All ER 177, [1970] TR 167 .... 35:16
Schlumberger Inland Services Inc v Customs and Excise Comrs [1985] VATTR 35; affd [1987] STC 228 .... 65:12
Schmid, Re: C-516/99 [2002] ECR I-4573, ECJ 1:06
Schnieder v Mills [1993] 3 All ER 377, [1993] STC 430 .... 19:03, 40:21
Schofield v R and H Hall Ltd [1975] STC 353, 49 TC 538, CA 9:30
Schouten and Meldrum v Netherlands (Applications 19005/91 and 19006/91) (1994) 19 EHRR 432, E Ct HR 1:22
Shove v Lingfield Park 1991 Ltd [2003] EWHC 1684 (Ch), [2003] STC 1003, [2003] 35 LS Gaz R 38; affd [2004] EWCA Civ 391, [2004] STC 805, 148 Sol Jo LB 537 .... 9:29, 9:30
Schuldenfrei v Hilton [1998] STC 404, 72 TC 167; affd [1999] STC 821, 72 TC 167, CA 2A:65
Schusman v Customs and Excise Comrs [1994] VATTR 120 .... 69:15
Schwarz v Finanzamt Bergisch Gladbach: C-76/05 [2007] ECR I-6957, [2008] All ER (EC) 556, [2007] 3 CMLR 1283, [2008] STC 1357, (2007) Times, 11 October, [2007] SWTI 2188, [2007] All ER (D) 52 (Sep) 1.03

Table of Cases

Scorer v Olin Energy Systems Ltd [1984] 1 WLR 675, [1984] STC 141, 58 TC 592, CA; affd [1985] AC 645, [1985] 2 All ER 375, [1985] 2 WLR 668, [1985] STC 218, 58 TC 592, HL 2A:65
Scott v Customs and Excise Comrs (1992) VAT decision 6922 .... 66:05
Scott v Ricketts [1967] 2 All ER 1009, [1967] 1 WLR 828, 44 TC 303, [1967] TR 123, CA 12:09
Scott-Morley v Customs and Excise Comrs (1981) VAT decision 1097 .... 69:14
Scottish and Canadian General Investment Co Ltd v Easson 1922 SC 242, 1922 SLT 216, 8 TC 265 .... 8:149
Scottish and Universal Newspapers Ltd v Fisher [1996] STC (SCD) 311 .... 28:09
Scottish Exhibition Centre Ltd v Revenue and Customs Comrs [2006] CSIH 42, [2006] SWTI 1918, [2008] STC 967 .... 63:02; 68:16
Scottish Insurance Corpn Ltd v Wilsons and Clyde Coal Co Ltd [1949] AC 462, [1949] 1 All ER 1068, [1949] LJR 1190, 93 Sol Jo 423, 65 TLR 354, 1949 SC (HL) 90, 1949 SLT 230, HL 15:31
Scottish Investment Trust Co v Forbes (1893) 21 R (Ct of Sess) 262, 3 TC 231, 31 Sc LR 219 .... 8:160
Scottish National Orchestra Society Ltd v Thomson's Executors 1969 SLT 325 ...... 34:05
Scottish Provident Institution v Farmer 1912 SC 452, 6 TC 34 .... 12:03, 35:16
Scottish Widows plc v HMRC (2008) SpC 664 .... 3:24
Seaham Harbour Dock Co v Crook (1931) 96 JP 13, 48 TLR 91, 16 TC 333, 10 ATC 350, HL 8:89
Seaman v Tucketts Ltd (1963) 41 TC 422, [1963] TR 419, 42 ATC 461 .... 8:50
Sebright, Re, Public Trustee v Sebright [1944] Ch 287, [1944] 2 All ER 547, 23 ATC 190 .... 46:24
Secretan v Hart [1969] 3 All ER 1196, [1969] 1 WLR 1599, 45 TC 701, 48 ATC 314 .... 62:05
Secretary of State in Council of India v Scoble [1903] AC 299, 72 LJKB 617, 4 TC 618, HL 3:13, 11:31, 11:35
Securenta Göttinger Immobilienanlagen und Vermögensmanagement AG v Finanzamt Göttingen [2008] SWTI 939, ECJ 66:08
Securicor Granley Systems Ltd v Customs and Excise Comrs [1990] VATTR 9 ...... 65:19
Seeling v Finanzamt Starnberg: C-269/00 [2003] ECR I-4101, [2004] 2 CMLR 757, [2003] STC 805, ECJ 66:05
Seldon v Croom-Johnson [1932] 1 KB 759, 101 LJKB 358, 16 TC 740, 11 ATC 126 .... 8:50
Self-assessed v Inspector of Taxes [1999] STC (SCD) 253 .... 2A:49
Sempra Metals Ltd (formerly Metallgesellschaft Ltd) v IRC [2004] EWHC 2387 (Ch), [2004] STC 1178; affd [2005] EWCA Civ 389, [2005] STC 687 ..... 1:02, 1:06, 1:10, 1:12
Senator Marketing Ltd v Customs and Excise Comrs (1991) VAT decision 5598 ..... 65:19
Set, Deuce v Ball v Robinson [2003] STC (SCD) 382 .... 2:22
Seven (J) Ltd v Customs and Excise Comrs [1986] VATTR 42 .... 68:15
Seymour v Reed [1927] AC 554, [1927] All ER Rep 294, 11 TC 625, 6 ATC 433, HL 7:25, 7:26
Seymour v Seymour (1989) Times, 16 February 2A:71
Shadford v H Fairweather & Co Ltd (1966) 43 TC 291, [1966] TR 75, 45 ATC 78 .... 8:16
Shah v Barnet London Borough Council [1983] 2 AC 309, [1983] 1 All ER 226, [1983] 2 WLR 16, 81 LGR 305, HL 33:14
Sharkey v Revenue and Customs Comrs [2006] EWHC 300 (Ch), [2006] STC 2026, 77 TC 484, [2006] SWTI 455, [2006] All ER (D) 147 (Feb) 1:22
Sharkey v Wernher [1956] AC 58, [1955] 3 All ER 493, 36 TC 275, [1955] TR 277, HL6:38, . 8:08, 8:49, 8:78, 8:92, 8:141, 8:151, 8:154, 8:157, 8:168, 8:166, 22:07, 28:27
Sharman's Will Trusts, Re, Public Trustee v Sharman [1942] Ch 311, [1942] 2 All ER 74 .... 42:20
Sharp, Re, Rickett v Rickett [1906] 1 Ch 793, 75 LJ Ch 458, 95 LT 522, 22 TLR 368 .... 11:40
Sharpless v Rees (1940) 23 TC 361, 19 ATC 212 .... 8:16
Shaw, Re, ex p Official Receiver (1920) 90 LJKB 204, [1920] B & CR 156 .... 56:29
Shaw v Revenue and Customs Comrs [2007] EWHC 3699 (Ch), [2007] STC 1525 .... 66:18

Table of Cases

Shaw v Vicky Construction Ltd [2002] EWHC 2659 (Ch), [2002] STC 1544, 75 TC 26 .... 2A:19
Sheepcote Commercial (Vehicles) Ltd v Customs and Excise Comrs (1987) VAT decision 2378 .... 65:19
Sheffield Co-operative Society Ltd v Customs and Excise Comrs [1987] VATTR 216 .... 66:07
Shepherd, Re, Public Trustee v Henderson [1949] Ch 116, [1948] 2 All ER 932, [1949] LJR 205, [1948] TR 379 .... 46:24
Shepherd v Customs and Excise Comrs [1994] VATTR 47 .... 2:16, 63:04
Shepherd v Law Land plc [1990] STC 795, 63 TC 692 .... 28:09
Shepherd v Lyntress Ltd [1989] STC 617, 62 TC 495 .... 39:35
Shepherd v Revenue and Customs Comrs Spc 484 [2005] STC (SCD) 644 ... 33:03, 33:05, 33:08, 33:14
Shepherd v Revenue and Customs Comrs [2006] EWHC 1512 (Ch), [2006] STC 1821, [2006] SWTI 1518, [2006] All ER (D) 191 (May) 33:03
Sheppard (Trustees of the Woodlands Trust) v IRC (No 2) [1993] STC 240, 65 TC 724 .... 4:19
Sherdley v Sherdley [1986] 2 All ER 202, [1986] 1 WLR 732, [1986] STC 266, CA; revsd [1988] AC 213, [1987] 2 All ER 54, [1987] 2 WLR 1071, [1987] STC 217, HL 3:14
Sherwin v Barnes (1931) 16 TC 278, 10 ATC 256 .... 12:10
Shilton v Wilmshurst [1989] 1 WLR 179, [1988] STC 868; on appeal [1990] 1 WLR 373, [1990] STC 55, CA; revsd [1991] 1 AC 684, [1991] 3 All ER 148, [1991] 2 WLR 530, [1991] STC 88, HL 7:17, 7:19, 7:28, 7:33, 7:35, 50:16
Shinewater Association Football Club v Customs and Excise Comrs (1995) VAT decision 12938 .... 69:18
Shipstone (James) & Son Ltd v Morris (1929) 14 TC 413, 8 ATC 256 .... 8:58
Shipway v Skidmore (1932) 16 TC 748, 11 ATC 223 .... 7:24
Shokar v Customs and Excise Comrs [1998] V & DR 301 .... 2:49
Shop and Store Developments Ltd v IRC [1967] 1 AC 472, [1967] 1 All ER 42, [1966] TR 357, 45 ATC 435, HL 15:02, 60:04
Short Bros Ltd v IRC (1927) 12 TC 955, 136 LT 689, 6 ATC 126, CA 8:82, 8:86
Shove v Dura Manufacturing Co Ltd (1941) 23 TC 779, 20 ATC 22 .... 8:87
Sidey v Phillips [1987] STC 87, 59 TC 458 .... 7:10, 7:11
Significant Ltd v Farrel [2005] EWHC 3434 (Ch), [2006] STC 1626, [2005] SWTI 1097, [2005] All ER (D) 161 (Jun) 1:22
Silk v Fletcher [1999] STC (SCD) 220 .... 8:98
Silk v Fletcher (No 2) [2000] STC (SCD) 565 .... 8:98
Sillars v IRC [2004] STC (SCD) 180 .... 38:20, 40:04
Silva v Charnock [2002] STC (SCD) 426 .... 7:97, 8:139
Silvermere Golf and Equestrian Centre Ltd v Customs and Excise Comrs [1981] VATTR 106 .... 63:23
Simmons v IRC [1980] 2 All ER 798, [1980] 1 WLR 1196, [1980] STC 350, 53 TC 461, HL 8:04, 8:49
Simpson v John Reynolds & Co (Insurances) Ltd [1975] 2 All ER 88, [1975] 1 WLR 617, [1975] STC 271, 49 TC 693, CA 8:75
Simpson v Jones [1968] 2 All ER 929, [1968] 1 WLR 1066, 44 TC 599, [1968] TR 107 .... 8:142
Simpson v Tate [1925] 2 KB 214, 94 LJKB 817, 9 TC 314, 4 ATC 187 .... 7:143
Sinclair v IRC (1942) 24 TC 432, 21 ATC 333 .... 56:11, 56:29
Sinclair v Lee [1993] Ch 497, [1993] 3 All ER 926, [1994] 1 BCLC 286 .... 13:15
Singer & Friedlander Ltd v Customs and Excise Comrs [1989] 1 CMLR 814, [1989] VATTR 27 .... 63:15, 63:30, 65:38, 68:16
Singh v Ali [1960] AC 167, [1960] 1 All ER 269 .... 34:04
Singh v Williams [2000] STC (SCD) 404 .... 7:143
Sisson v Customs and Excise Comrs (1981) VAT decision 1056 .... 66:05
Siwek v IRC [2002] STC (SCD) 247 .... 2A:56
Skandinavia Reinsurance Co of Copenhagen v Da Costa [1911] 1 KB 731 .... 56:29
Skatteministeriet v Henriksen: 173/88 [1990] STC 768, [1990] 3 CMLR 558, ECJ 68:12

2591

Table of Cases

Skatteverket v A: C-101/05 [2008] All ER (EC) 638, [2009] 1 CMLR 975, [2009] STC 405, [2008] SWTI 991:11
Skinner, Re, Milbourne v Skinner [1942] Ch 82, [1942] 1 All ER 32, 111 LJ Ch 73, 58 TLR 77 .... 11:43
Skinner v Berry Head Lands Ltd [1971] 1 All ER 222, [1970] 1 WLR 1441, 46 TC 377, [1970] TR 219 .... 8:154
Slaney v Starkey [1931] 2 KB 148, 100 LJKB 341, 16 TC 45, 10 ATC 100 .... 7:25
Slater v Commissioner of Inland Revenue [1996] 1 NZLR 759 .... 8:49
Slater v IT General Comrs for Beacontree (No 2) [2002] EWHC 2676 (Ch), [2004] STC 1342 .... 2A:90
Slater Ltd v IRC [2002] EWHC 2676 (Ch), [2004] STC 1342 .... 2A:90
Sleaford Rugby Football Club v Customs and Excise Comrs (1993) VAT decision 9844 .... 63:19
Slocock's Will Trusts, Re [1979] 1 All ER 358 .... 2A:71
Small (Inspector of Taxes) v Mars UK Ltd [2005] EWHC 553 (Ch), [2005] STC 958, (2005) Times, 11 May, [2005] SWTI 833, [2005] All ER (D) 103 (Apr) . 8:64, 8:127, 25:05
Small (Inspector of Taxes) v Mars UK Ltd [2007] UKHL 15, [2007] 2 All ER 440, [2007] 1 WLR 1448, [2007] STC 680, (2007) Times, 2 April, [2007] SWTI 1165, [2007] All ER (D) 459 (Mar) 25:05
Smallwood v Revenue and Customs Comrs [2005] SWTI 1998, SCD; affd [2006] EWHC 1653 (Ch), (2006) Times, 23 August, [2006] SWTI 1852, [2006] All ER (D) 70 (Jul); affd [2007] EWCA Civ 462, (2007) Times, 7 June, [2007] SWTI 1562, [2007] All ER (D) 297 (May) sub nom Revenue and Customs Comrs v Smallwood [2006] STC 2050 .... 22:01, 22:02
Smallwood v Revenue and Customs Comrs [2009] EWHC 777 (Ch), [2009] STC 1222, 11 ITLR 943, [2009] 17 LS Gaz R 15, [2009] All ER (D) 122 (Apr) 35.62
Smart v Lowndes [1978] STC 607, 52 TC 436, [1978] TR 203 .... 8:06
Smidth (F L) & Co v Greenwood [1921] 3 KB 583, 37 TLR 949, 8 TC 193, CA; affd sub nom Greenwood v F L Smidth & Co [1922] 1 AC 417, 91 LJKB 349, 8 TC 193, 1 ATC 95, HL 36:03, 36:04, 36:05, 37:07
Smith v Abbott [1992] 1 WLR 201, [1991] STC 661; on appeal [1993] 2 All ER 417, [1993] STC 316, CA; on appeal [1994] 1 All ER 673, [1994] STC 237, HL .. 7:137, 7:138
Smith v Customs and Excise Comrs MAN/87/321 unreported 69:13
Smith v Customs and Excise Comrs (1991) VAT decision 5579 .... 69:17, 69:18
Smith v Incorporated Council of Law Reporting for England and Wales [1914] 3 KB 674, 83 LJKB 1721, 111 LT 848, 6 TC 477 .... 8:113
Smith v Lion Brewery Co Ltd [1911] AC 150, 80 LJKB 566, 5 TC 568, HL 8:108
Smith v Schofield [1990] 1 WLR 1447, [1990] STC 602, 65 TC 669; on appeal [1992] 1 WLR 639, [1992] STC 249, 65 TC 669, CA; revsd [1993] 1 WLR 399, [1993] STC 268, 65 TC 669, HL 16:02, 23:20, 24:23
Smith v Smith [1923] P 191, [1923] All ER Rep 362, 92 LJP 132, 130 LT 8 .. 11:23, 11:24
Smith v Stages [1989] AC 928, [1989] 1 All ER 833, [1989] 2 WLR 529, [1989] ICR 272, [1989] IRLR 177, HL 7:125
Smith (Herbert) (a firm) v Honour [1999] STC 173, 72 TC 130 ..... 8:65, 8:67, 8:90, 8:147
Smith (John) & Son v Moore [1921] 2 AC 13, 90 LJPC 149, 12 TC 266, 3 ATC 369, HL 8:128
Smith (Rose) & Co Ltd v IRC (1933) 17 TC 586 .... 2A:69
Smith and Williamson v Customs and Excise Comrs [1976] VATTR 215 .... 63:23
Smith & Ors v Revenue and Customs Comrs [2007] EWHC 2304 (Ch) 39:40
Smith Barry v Cordy (1946) 28 TC 250 .... 8:15
Smiths Potato Estates Ltd v Bolland [1948] 2 All ER 367, 30 TC 267 .... 8:109
Smyth, Re, Leach v Leach [1898] 1 Ch 89, 67 LJ Ch 10, 77 LT 514 .... 47:06
Smyth v Revenue Comrs [1931] IR 643 .... 45:02
Smyth v Stretton (1904) 5 TC 36, 20 TLR 443 .... 50:34
Snell v Revenue and Customs Comrs [2006] STC (SCD) 296, [2007] SWTI 115 ..... 21:25
Snell v Rosser Thomas & Co Ltd [1968] 1 All ER 600, [1968] 1 WLR 295, 44 TC 343, [1967] TR 193 .... 8:25
Snook v London and West Riding Investments Ltd [1967] 2 QB 786, [1967] 1 All ER 518, [1967] 2 WLR 1020, CA 3:14
Snook (James) & Co Ltd v Blasdale (1952) 33 TC 244, [1952] TR 233, 31 ATC 268, CA 8:105

Table of Cases

Snowdon v Charnock [2001] STC (SCD) 152 .... 7:137
Snushall (Geoffrey E) (a firm) v Customs and Excise Comrs [1982] STC 537 .... 69:15
Société Internationale de Télécommunications Aéronautiques v Customs and Excise Comrs [2003] EWHC 3039 (Ch), [2004] STC 950 .... 69:26, 69:27
Société Thermale d'Eugénie-les-Bains v Ministere de l'Economie, des Finances et de l'Industrie C-277/05, [2007] ECR I–6415, [2007] SWTI 1866, ECJ 63:19
Sofitam SA (formerly Satam SA) v Ministre chargé du Budget: C-333/91 [1993] ECR I-3513, [1997] STC 226, ECJ 63:17, 66:08
Softley Ltd (t/a Softley Kitchens) v Customs and Excise Comrs (1997) VAT decision 15034 .... 69:35
Sokoya v Revenue and Customs Comrs [2008] EWHC 2132 (Ch), [2008] SWTI 1641, [2008] All ER (D) 297 (Jun) 2A:68
Sotgiu v Deutsche Bundespost: 152/73 [1974] ECR 153, ECJ 1:10
Sothern-Smith v Clancy [1941] 1 KB 276, [1941] 1 All ER 111, 24 TC 1, 19 ATC 443, CA 11:21, 31:30
Soul v Caillebotte (1966) 43 TC 662, [1966] TR 391, 45 ATC 471 .... 11:01
Source Enterprise Ltd v Customs and Excise Comrs (1992) VAT decision 7881 ...... 63:29
South Behar Rly Co Ltd v IRC [1925] AC 476, 94 LJKB 386, 12 TC 657, 4 ATC 139, HL 8:52
South Glamorgan County Council v Customs and Excise Comrs (1985) VAT decision 1956 .... 68:11
South Shore Mutual Insurance Co Ltd v Blair [1999] STC (SCD) 296 .... 28:01
Southend on Sea Corpn v Hodgson (Wickford) Ltd [1962] 1 QB 416, [1961] 2 All ER 46, [1961] 2 WLR 806, 125 JP 348 .... 2:07
Southend United Football Club v Customs and Excise Comrs [1997] V & DR 202 .... 65:16, 68:12
Southern v AB [1933] 1 KB 713, [1933] All ER Rep 916, 18 TC 59, 12 ATC 203 .... 8:09
Southern v Borax Consolidated Ltd [1941] 1 KB 111, [1940] 4 All ER 412, 23 TC 597, 19 ATC 435 .... 8:84, 8:116
Southern v Watson [1940] 3 All ER 439, 23 TC 566, 19 ATC 358, CA 8:34
Southern Counties Agricultural Trading Society Ltd v Blackler [1999] STC (SCD) 200 .... 8:110
Southern Rly Co's Appeals, Re. See Westminster City Council v Southern Rly Co, Railway Assessment Authority and W H Smith & Son Ltd
Southern Railway of Peru Ltd v Owen [1957] AC 334, [1956] 2 All ER 728, 37 TC 602, [1956] TR 197, HL 8:68, 8:148
Southwell v Savill Bros Ltd [1901] 2 KB 349, 70 LJKB 815, 4 TC 430, 65 JP 649 .... 8:68
Soutter's Executry v IRC [2002] STC (SCD) 385 .... 40:22
Sparekassernes Datacenter (SDC) v Skatteministeriet: C-2/95 [1997] All ER (EC) 610, [1997] STC 932, ECJ 68:16
Spearmint Rhino Ventures (UK) Ltd v Revenue and Customs Comrs [2007] EWHC 613 (Ch), [2007] STC 1252, [2007] All ER (D) 387 (Mar) 63:19, 63:20
Spectros International plc v Madden [1997] STC 114, 70 TC 349 .... 16:05
Spectrum Computer Supplies Ltd & Kirkstall Timber Ltd v Revenue and Customs Comrs (unreported) 50:35
Spence v Spence 1995 SLT 335 .... 33:17, 33:24
Spencer (James) & Co v IRC 1950 SC 345, 32 TC 111 .... 8:147
Spens v IRC [1970] 3 All ER 295, [1970] 1 WLR 1173, 46 TC 276, [1970] TR 85 .... 13:15, 14:05
Speyer Bros v IRC [1908] AC 92, [1908–10] All ER Rep 474, 77 LJKB 302, 98 LT 286, HL 56:12
Spillane v Customs and Excise Comrs [1990] STC 212 .... 67:01
Spilsbury v Spofforth [1937] 4 All ER 487, 21 TC 247, 16 ATC 274 .... 11:44
Spiro v Glencrown Properties Ltd [1991] Ch 537, [1991] 1 All ER 600, [1991] 2 WLR 931, 62 P & CR 402, [1990] NPC 90, 134 Sol Jo 1479, [1991] 1 EGLR 185, [1990] NLJR 1754, [1991] 02 EG 167 .... 8:49
Spofforth and Prince v Golder [1945] 1 All ER 363, 173 LT 77, 26 TC 310 .... 8:105
Sportsman v IRC [1998] STC (SCD) 289 .... 37:12, 37:33, 36:47

Table of Cases

Spring Salmon and Seafood Ltd v Revenue and Customs Comrs [2005] STC (SCD) 830 .... 1:28, 2A:68
Springfield China Ltd v Customs and Excise Comrs (1990) VAT decision 4546 ...... 65:17, 65:19
Staatssecretaris van Financien v Arthur Andersen & Co Accountants: C-472/03 [2005] ECR I-1719, [2005] STC 508, ECJ 68:13
Staatssecretaris van Financiën v BGM Verkooijen: C-35/98 [2002] ECR I-4071, [2002] 1 CMLR 1379, [2002] STC 654, ECJ 1:11, 26:15
Staatssecretaris van Financiën v Coffeeshop Siberië vof: C-158/98 [1999] All ER (EC) 560, [1999] 2 CMLR 1239, [1999] STC 742, ECJ 63:19, 68:11
Staatssecretaris van Financiën v Coöperatieve Vereniging 'Coöperatieve Aardappelen-bewaarplaats GA': 154/80 [1981] ECR 445, [1981] 3 CMLR 337, ECJ . 1:11, 63:21, 65:17
Staatssecretaris van Financiën v Hong Kong Trade Development Council: 89/81 [1982] ECR 1277, [1983] 1 CMLR 73, ECJ 1:11, 63:15
Staatssecretaris van Financien v Lipjes: C-68/03 [2004] 2 CMLR 1016, [2004] STC 1592, ECJ 63:30
Staatssecretaris van Financiën v Shipping and Forwarding Enterprise Safe BV: C-320/88 [1990] ECR I-285, [1993] 3 CMLR 547, [1991] STC 627, ECJ 63:25
Staatssecretaris van Financien v Stichting Kinderopvang Enschede: C-415/04 [2007] STC 294, [2006] SWTI 385, [2006] All ER (D) 130 (Feb), ECJ 68:23
Stafford Coal and Iron Co Ltd v Brogan [1963] 3 All ER 277, [1963] 1 WLR 905, 41 TC 305, [1963] TR 287, HL 8:41
Stainer's Executors v Purchase [1952] AC 280, [1951] 2 All ER 1071, 32 TC 367, [1951] TR 353, HL 5:14
Stamp Comr v Carreras Group Ltd [2004] UKPC 16, [2004] SWTI 990, 148 Sol Jo LB 473, [2004] All ER (D) 35 (Apr) 56:10
Stamp Duties Comr (Queensland) v Hopkins (1945) 71 CLR 351 .... 56:11
Stamp Duties Comr (Queensland) v Livingston [1965] AC 694, [1964] 3 All ER 692, [1964] TR 351, 43 ATC 325 .... 14:03, 42:11
Stamp Duties Comr of New South Wales v Pendal Nominees Pty Ltd (1989) 167 CLR 1 .... 56:15
Stamp Duties Comr of New South Wales v Permanent Trustee Co of New South Wales [1956] AC 512, [1956] 2 All ER 512, [1956] 3 WLR 152, [1956] TR 209, ... 41:03
Stamp Duties Comr of New South Wales v Perpetual Trustee Co Ltd [1943] AC 425, [1943] 1 All ER 525, 112 LJPC 55, 168 LT 414 .... 41:07
Stamp Duty on Potter's Deed, Re. See Potter v IRC
Stamps Comrs v Queensland Meat Export Co Ltd [1917] AC 624, 86 LJPC 202 .... 57:06
Standard Chartered Bank Ltd v IRC [1978] 3 All ER 644, [1978] 1 WLR 1160, [1978] STC 272, [1978] TR 45 .... 47:05
Stanley v IRC [1944] KB 255, [1944] 1 All ER 230, 26 TC 12, 23 ATC 13, CA 13:15, 13:18, 14:07
Stanton v Drayton Commercial Investment Co Ltd [1981] 1 WLR 1425, [1981] STC 585, 55 TC 286, CA 16:05, 17:06
Stanmore and another (exors of Dickinson, decd) v IRC [2001] STC (SCD) 199 ..... 17:28
Stapenhill Developments Ltd v Customs and Excise Comrs [1984] VATTR 1 .... 69:17
Staples v Secretary of State for Social Services (15 March 1985, unreported), QBD 49:06
Starke v IRC [1994] 1 WLR 888, [1994] STC 295; affd [1996] 1 All ER 622, [1995] 1 WLR 1439, [1995] STC 689, CA 44:14
State of Norway's Application, Re [1990] 1 AC 723, [1989] 1 All ER 745, [1989] 2 WLR 458, HL 34:02
Stauder v City of Ulm: 29/69 [1969] ECR 419, [1970] CMLR 112 .... 1:12, 1:13
Steadman v Steadman [1976] AC 536, [1974] 2 All ER 977, [1974] 3 WLR 56, HL 33:17
Stedeford v Beloe [1931] 2 KB 610, 16 TC 505, CA; affd [1932] AC 388, 101 LJKB 268, 16 TC 505, 11 ATC 132, HL 11:23
Stedman's Executors v IRC [2002] STC (SCD) 358; on appeal sub nom IRC v George (Stedman's Executors) [2003] EWHC 318 (Ch), [2003] STC 468; revsd [2003] EWCA Civ 1763, [2004] STC 147 .... 29:14, 44:04
Steel Barrel Co Ltd v Osborne (No 2) (1948) 30 TC 73, [1948] TR 11, 41 R & IT 225, 27 ATC 196, CA 8:164

Table of Cases

Steele v EVC International NV (formerly European Vinyls Corpn (Holdings) BV) [1996] STC 785, CA 25:43
Steibelt v Paling [1999] STC 594, 71 TC 376 .... 1:30, 2:23, 22:12, 22:21
Stenhouse's Trustees v Lord Advocate [1984] STC 195, 1984 SC 12, 1986 SLT 73 .... 42:07
Stephens v T Pittas Ltd [1983] STC 576, 56 TC 722 .... 7:111, 29:11
Stephenson v Barclays Bank Trust Co Ltd [1975] 1 All ER 625, [1975] 1 WLR 882, [1975] STC 151, 50 TC 374 .... 20:06, 20:16
Sterling Trust Ltd v IRC (1925) 12 TC 868, CA 7:06
Stern v IRC (1930) 15 TC 148, HL 13:15
Stevenson v Wishart [1986] 1 All ER 404, [1986] STC 74, 59 TC 740; affd [1987] 2 All ER 428, [1987] STC 266, 59 TC 740, CA 13:12, 13:21
Stevenson, Jordan and Harrison Ltd v Macdonald and Evans [1952] 1 TLR 101, 69 RPC 10, CA 7:08, 49:03
Stewart (t/a GT Shooting) v Customs and Excise Comrs [2001] EWCA Civ 1988, [2002] STC 255 .... 63:19
Stewart (Walter) Ltd v Customs and Excise Comrs [1974] VATTR 131 .... 69:42
Stichting 'Goed Wonen' v Staatssecretaris van Financien: C-376/02 [2005] ECR I-3445, [2005] STC 833, ECJ 63:03
Stichting Regionaal Opleidingen Centrum Noord-Kennemerland/West Friesland (Horizon College) v Staatssecretaris van Financien: C-434/05 [2007] ECR I-4793, [2008] STC 2145, [2007] All ER (D) 132 (Jun), ECJ 68:17
Stilwell Darby & Co Ltd v Customs and Excise Comrs [1973] VATTR 145 6 .... 8:15
Stirling v Customs and Excise Comrs [1985] VATTR 232 .... 63:32
Stockham v Wallasey UDC (1906) 95 LT 834, 71 JP 244, 5 LGR 200 .... 8:58
Stockler Charity (a firm) v R & C Comrs [2007] EWHC 2967 (Ch) 2:24
Stokes v Bennett [1953] Ch 566, [1953] 2 All ER 313, 34 TC 337, [1953] TR 255 .... 11:38, 11:39
Stokes v Costain Property Investments Ltd [1984] 1 All ER 849, [1984] STC 204, 57 TC 688, CA 9:25, 9:49
Stone v Yeovil Corpn (1876) 1 CPD 691, 45 LJQB 657; on appeal (1876) 2 CPD 99, 46 LJQB 137, 42 JP 212, CA 1:24
Stone & Temple Ltd v Waters [1995] STC 1n, 67 TC 145 .... 8:110
Stoner and another (exors of Dickinson, dec'd) v IRC [2001] STC (SCD) 199 .... 45:16
Stones v Hall [1989] STC 138 .... 7:50
Stormseal (UPVC) Window Co Ltd v Customs and Excise Comrs [1989] VATTR 303 .... 63:20
Stott v Hoddinott (1916) 7 TC 85 .... 8:04, 8:24
Stovin v Wise [1996] AC 923 .... 2:24
Stradasfalti Srl v Agenzia delle Entrate – Ufficio di Trento: C-228/05 [2007] STC 508, [2006] All ER (D) 68 (Sep), ECJ 63:01
Strahan v Wilcock [2006] EWCA Civ 13, [2006] 2 BCLC 555, [2006] 06 LS Gaz R 30, [2006] All ER (D) 106 (Jan) 45:02
Straits Settlements Comr of Stamps v Oei Tjong Swan [1933] AC 378, 102 LJPC 90, 149 LT 145, 49 TLR 428 .... 1:27
Strand Futures and Options Ltd v Vojak [2002] STC (SCD) 398; on appeal [2003] EWHC 67 (Ch), [2003] STC 331; revsd [2003] EWCA Civ 1457, [2004] STC 64 ... 26:20, 26:30
Strand Ship Building Co Ltd v Customs and Excise Comrs (1984) VAT decision 1651 .... 68:12
Strange v Openshaw [1983] STC 416, 57 TC 544 .... 18:24
Stratford v Mole and Lea (1941) 165 LT 37, 24 TC 20, 20 ATC 66 .... 8:127
Strathearn Gordon Associates Ltd v Customs and Excise Comrs [1985] VATTR 79 .... 63:21
Strick v Longsdon (1953) 34 TC 528, [1953] TR 293, 32 ATC 317 .... 5:14
Strollmoor Ltd v Customs and Excise Comrs (1990) VAT decision 5454 ...... 63:30; 65:38
Strong v Bird (1874) LR 18 Eq 315, [1874–80] All ER Rep 230, 43 LJ Ch 814, 30 LT 745 .... 38:20
Strong & Co of Romsey Ltd v Woodifield [1906] AC 448, [1904–7] All ER Rep 953, 5 TC 215, HL 8:95, 8:104, 8:105, 8:131

Sturge (John & E) Ltd v Hessel [1975] STC 573, 51 TC 183, [1975] TR 205, 54 ATC 245, CA 8:76
Sugarwhite v Budd [1988] STC 533, CA 23:32
Sugden v Kent [2001] STC (SCD) 158 .... 13:12, 13:21
Sulley v A-G (1860) 5 H & N 711, 29 LJ Ex 464, 2 TC 149n 35:02, 36:03
Sun Alliance Insurance Ltd v IRC [1972] Ch 133, [1971] 1 All ER 135, [1970] TR 411, 49 ATC 430 .... 57:05, 57:07
Sun Insurance Office Ltd v Clark [1912] AC 443, [1911–13] All ER Rep 495, 6 TC 59, HL 8:64
Sun Life Assurance Co of Canada v Pearson [1984] STC 461, 59 TC 250; affd [1986] STC 335, 59 TC 250, CA 37:33
Sun Life Assurance Society v Davidson [1958] AC 184, [1957] 2 All ER 760, 37 TC 330, [1957] TR 171, HL 30:03
Suregrove Ltd v Customs and Excise Comrs (1993) VAT decision 10740 .... 66:05
Surveyor v IRC [2002] STC (SCD) 501 .... 33:23
Svenska Management Grupen v Sweden (Application No 11036/84) 45 DR 211 (1985), EC of HR 1:13
Swales v IRC [1984] 3 All ER 16, [1984] STC 413 .... 42:07, 42:49
Swan (Hellenic) Ltd v Secretary of State for Social Services (18 January 1983, unreported) 7:11
Swansea Yacht and Sub Aqua Club v Customs and Excise Comrs [1996] V & DR 89 .... 68:26
Swayne v IRC [1900] 1 QB 172, 69 LJQB 63, 81 LT 623, 48 WR 197, CA 57:11
Sweden v Stockholm Lindöpark AB: C-150/99 [2001] ECR I-493, [2001] 3 CMLR 319, [2001] STC 103, ECJ 63:02, 68:11
Swedish Central Rly Co Ltd v Thompson [1924] 2 KB 255, [1924] All ER Rep 710, 9 TC 342, CA; affd [1925] AC 495, [1924] All ER Rep 710, 9 TC 342, 4 ATC 163, HL 33:26, 35:04
Swinburne, Re, Sutton v Featherley [1926] Ch 38, [1925] All ER Rep 313, 95 LJ Ch 104, 134 LT 121, CA 39:01
Swires v Renton [1991] STC 490, 64 TC 315 .... 20:12
Swithland Investments Ltd v IRC [1990] STC 448 .... 60:06, 62:18
Sycamore plc and Maple Ltd v Fir [1997] STC (SCD) 1 .... 8:64
Symons v Weeks [1983] STC 195, 56 TC 630 .... 2A:69, 8:68, 8:142
Synaptek Ltd v Young [2003] EWHC 645 (Ch), [2003] STC 543, 75 TC 51, [2003] ICR 1149 .... 2:20, 7:11, 8:26
Syndesmos ton en Elladi Touristikon Kai Taxidiotikon Grafeion v Ypourgos Ergasias: C-398/95 [1997] ECR I-3091, [1998] 1 CMLR 420, ECJ 1:12
Syndicat des Producteurs Indépendants (SPI) v Ministère de l'Economie des Finances et de l'Industrie: C-108/00 [2001] All ER (EC) 564, [2001] ECR I-2361, [2001] 2 CMLR 903, [2001] STC 523, ECJ 63:30; 65:38
Sywell Aerodrome Ltd v Croft [1942] 1 KB 317, [1942] 1 All ER 110, 24 TC 126, CA: 8:42, 10:07

T

T's Settlement, Re (6 February 2002, unreported), Royal Court of Jersey (Samedi Division) 34:06, 35:63
T and E Homes Ltd v Robinson [1976] STC 462; revsd [1979] 2 All ER 522, [1979] 1 WLR 452, [1979] STC 351, 52 TC 567, [1979] TR 19, CA 10:04, 57:28
T-Mobile v Austria: C-284/04 [2007] All ER (D) 308 (Jun), ECJ, [2007] ECR I-5189, [2008] STC 184, ECJ 63:17
Talacre Beach Caravan Sales Ltd v Customs and Excise Comrs: C-251/05 [2006] ECR I-6269, [2006] 3 CMLR 919, [2006] STC 1671, [2006] SWTI 1855, [2006] All ER (D) 66 (Jul), ECJ 63:20, 69:31
Talotta v Belgium: C-383/05 [2007] 2 CMLR 931, [2008] STC 3261, [2007] SWTI 1053, [2007] All ER (D) 364 (Mar) 1:06
Tamburello Ltd v Customs and Excise Comrs [1996] V & DR 268 .... 66:17, 66:18
Tanfield Ltd v Carr [1999] STC (SCD) 213 .... 8:74
Tapemaze Ltd v Melluish [2000] STC 189, 73 TC 167 .... 8:67, 8:74

Table of Cases

Tarmac Roadstone Holdings Ltd v Williams [1996] STC (SCD) 409 .... 17:10
Tarrakarn Ltd v Customs and Excise Comrs [1996] V & DR 516 .... 63:16
Tatham, Re, National Bank Ltd and Mathews v Mackenzie [1945] Ch 34, [1945]
   1 All ER 29, 114 LJ Ch 9, 23 ATC 283 .... 11:43
Taw and Torridge Festival Society Ltd v IRC (1959) 38 TC 603, [1959] TR 291, 38 ATC
   414, [1960] BTR 61 11:28
Taxation Comr (Victoria) v Phillips (1937) 55 CLR 144 7:30
Taxation Comrs v Kirk [1900] AC 588, 83 LT 4 .... 36:03
Taxes Comr v Nchanga Consolidated Copper Mines Ltd [1964] AC 948, [1964]
   1 All ER 208, [1964] TR 25, 46 ATC 20 .... 8:84, 8:110, 8:111, 8:128, 8:129
Taylor v Clatworthy [1996] STC (SCD) 506 .... 8:96
Taylor v Cox [1998] STC (SCD) 179 .... 2:17
Taylor v Good [1973] 2 All ER 785, [1973] 1 WLR 1249, [1973] STC 383, 49 TC 277;
   on appeal [1974] 1 All ER 1137, [1974] 1 WLR 556, [1974] STC 148, 49 TC
   277, CA 8:20, 8:49, 23:02
Taylor v IRC [1946] 1 All ER 488n, 27 TC 93, 25 ATC 155, CA 15:11
Taylor v MEPC Holdings Ltd. See MEPC Holdings Ltd v Taylor
Taylor v Provan [1973] Ch 388, [1973] 2 All ER 65, [1973] STC 170, 49 TC 579, CA;
   revsd [1975] AC 194, [1974] 1 All ER 1201, [1974] STC 168, 49 TC 579, HL . 7:03, 7:24,
                                                    7:122, 7:125, 7:126, 7:127, 7:128, 7:138
Taylor v Taylor [1938] 1 KB 320, [1937] 3 All ER 571, 107 LJKB 340, 16 ATC
   218, CA 11:41
Taylor Clark International Ltd v Lewis [1997] STC 499, 71 TC 226; on appeal [1998]
   STC 1259, 71 TC 226, CA 17:06, 17:10
Taylor (Eric) Deceased Testimonial Match Committee v Customs and Excise Comrs
   [1975] VATTR 8 .... 63:16
Taylor Dyne Ltd Pension Fund Trustees v Customs and Excise Comrs [1992] VATTR
   315 .... 66:07
Tebrau (Johore) Rubber Syndicate Ltd v Farmer 1910 SC 906, 5 TC 658 .... 8:20
Technicolor Ltd v Customs and Excise Comrs (1997) VAT decision 14871 .... 69:37
Tee v Inspector of Taxes [2002] STC (SCD) 370; revsd sub nom West v Trennery [2003]
   EWHC 676 (Ch), [2003] STC 580, [2003] 23 LS Gaz R 39; revsd [2003] EWCA Civ
   1792, [2004] STC 170, 148 Sol Jo LB 56; revsd [2005] UKHL 5, [2005] 1 All ER 827,
   [2005] STC 214 .... 3:01, 20:04, 35:58
Tee v Tee [1973] 3 All ER 1105, [1974] 1 WLR 213, 118 Sol Jo 116, CA 33:19
Telecential Communications Ltd v Customs and Excise Comrs (1998) VAT decision
   15361 .... 65:30
Telent Plc v HMRC (2007) SpC 632 .... 50:05
Telewest Communications plc v Customs and Excise Comrs [2003] EWHC 3176 (Ch),
   [2004] STC 517; revsd [2005] EWCA Civ 102, [2005] STC 481 .... 63:19, 63:20
Temperley v Smith [1956] 3 All ER 92, [1956] 1 WLR 931, 37 TC 18, [1956] TR
   275 .... 8:75
Temperley v Visibell Ltd [1974] STC 64, 49 TC 129, 52 ATC 308 .... 22:16
Temple Gothard & Co v Customs and Excise Comrs (1978) VAT decision 702, 102
   Taxation 388 .... 63:23
Templeton v Jacobs [1996] 1 WLR 1433, [1996] STC 991 .... 7:41
Templeton (Inspector of Taxes) v Transform Shop Office and Bar Fitters Ltd [2005]
   EWHC 1558 (Ch), [2006] STC 900, (2005) Times, 20 September, [2005] SWTI 1261,
   [2005] All ER (D) 229 (Jul) 2A:19
Tempur Pedic (UK) Ltd v Customs and Excise Comrs (1995) VAT decision 13744 ... 69:35
Tenbry Investments Ltd v Peugeot Talbot Motor Co Ltd [1992] STC 791,
   [1993] 1 EGLR 71 .... 10:12, 11:41
Tennant v Smith [1892] AC 150, 61 LJPC 11, 3 TC 158, HL . 1:24, 7:41, 7:43, 7:44, 7:49,
                                                                        7:99, 7:102
Terra Baubedarf-Handel GmbH v Finanzamt Osterholz-Scharmbeck: C-152/02
   [2004] ECR I-5583, [2004] 3 CMLR 1021, [2005] STC 525, ECJ 66:22
Terrapin International Ltd v IRC [1976] 2 All ER 461, [1976] 1 WLR 665, [1976] STC
   197 .... 56:11
Terry and Terry (t/a C & J Terry & Sons) v Revenue and Customs Comrs [2005] STC
   (SCD) 629 .... 8:127

2597

Table of Cases

Tesco plc v Customs and Excise Comrs [2003] EWCA Civ 1367, [2003] STC 1561, [2003] 42 LS Gaz R 32 .... 63:19
Tesco plc v Customs and Excise Comrs [2003] STC 396 .... 63:20
Test Claimants in Class IV of the ACT Group Litigation v IRC: C-374/04 [2007] All ER (EC) 351, [2007] 1 CMLR 1111, [2007] STC 404, [2006] SWTI 2748, [2006] All ER (D) 157 (Dec), ECJ 1:16, 1:17
Test Claimants in the FII Group Litigation v IRC: C-446/04 [2008] EWHC 2893 (Ch), [2007] 1 CMLR 1021, [2007] STC 326, [2006] SWTI 2750, [2006] All ER (D) 168 (Dec), ECJ 1:11, 1:12, 1:18, 26:15
Teward v IRC [2001] STC (SCD) 36 .... 7:17
Theotrue Holdings Ltd v Customs and Excise Comrs [1983] VATTR 88 ...... 65:12, 66:03
Thin Cap Group Litigation (Test Claimants in the) v IRC: C-524/04 [2007] 2 CMLR 765, [2007] STC 906, [2007] SWTI 538, [2007] All ER (D) 219 (Mar), ECJ 1:16, 1:19
Thomas v Marshall [1953] AC 543, [1953] 1 All ER 1102, 34 TC 178, [1953] TR 141, HL 15:21
Thomas v Reynolds [1987] STC 135, 59 TC 502 .... 9:30
Thomas v Richard Evans & Co Ltd [1927] 1 KB 33, 95 LJKB 990, 11 TC 790, 5 ATC 551, CA 8:36, 8:41
Thompson v Customs and Excise Comrs (1998) VAT decision 15834 .... 69:17
Thompson v Customs and Excise Comrs [2005] EWHC 342 (Ch), [2005] STC 1777, [2005] All ER (D) 202 (Mar) 66:18
Thompson v Giles (1824) 2 B & C 422, 3 Dow & Ry KB 733, 2 LJOSKB 48 .... 11:15
Thompson v Hart [2000] STC 381, 72 TC 543 .... 31:07
Thompson v Magnesium Elektron Ltd [1944] 1 All ER 126, 26 TC 1, 22 ATC 369, CA 8:80
Thompson v Minzly [2002] STC 450, 74 TC 340 .... 2A:44
Thompson v Salah [1972] 1 All ER 530, 47 TC 559, [1971] TR 401 .... 18:08
Thompson v Trust and Loan Co of Canada [1932] 1 KB 517, [1932] All ER Rep 647, 16 TC 394, 11 ATC 8 .... 4:09, 8:91
Thompson (George) & Co Ltd v IRC (1927) 12 TC 1091, 6 ATC 965 ... 8:77, 8:78, 8:128
Thompson (Joseph L) & Sons Ltd v Chamberlain (1962) 40 TC 657, [1962] TR 327, 41 ATC 371 .... 8:101
Thomson v Bensted (1918) 56 Sc LR 10, 7 TC 137 .... 35:17
Thomson v Minister of National Revenue [1946] SCR 209 .... 33:03
Thomson v Moyse [1961] AC 967, [1960] 3 All ER 684, 39 TC 291, [1960] TR 309, HL 7:103, 35:20, 35:22
Thomson v White (1966) 43 TC 256, [1966] TR 51, 45 ATC 48 .... 50:06
Thomson and Balfour v Le Page 1924 SC 27, 8 TC 541, 61 Sc LR 35 .... 8:57, 8:59
Thorn EMI Electronics Ltd v Coldicott [1996] STC (SCD) 455; affd sub nom EMI Group Electronics Ltd v Coldicott [1997] STC 1372, 71 TC 455; affd [2000] 1 WLR 540, [1999] STC 803, 71 TC 455, CA 7:31, 50:13
Thorn EMI plc v Customs and Excise Comrs [1994] STC 469; affd [1995] STC 674, CA 66:20
Thorn plc v Customs and Excise Comrs [1998] V & DR 80 .... 64:26
Thorn plc v Customs and Excise Comrs [1998] V & DR 383 .... 63:21
Thorne v Sevenoaks General Comrs and IRC [1989] STC 560, 62 TC 341, [1989] 25 LS Gaz R 44 .... 2A:44
Thornley, Re (1928) 7 ATC 178 .... 45:02
Thorogood (K & K) Ltd v Customs and Excise Comrs (1984) VAT decision 1595 ... 66:05
Thorpe Architecture Ltd v Customs and Excise Comrs (1992) VAT decision 6955 .... 66:05
Three H Aircraft Hire v Customs and Excise Comrs [1982] STC 653 .... 63:16
Three Rivers District Council v Bank of England [2003] 2 AC 1, [2000] 3 All ER 1, [2000] 2 WLR 1220, [2000] 3 CMLR 205, HL 1:12, 1:13
Tilbury Consulting Ltd v Gittins [2004] STC (SCD) 72 .... 7:11, 8:26
Tilcon Ltd v Holland [1981] STC 365, 54 TC 464, [1981] TR 39 .... 28:01
Tilley v Wales. See Wales v Tilley
Timbrell v Lord Aldenham's Executors [1947] LJR 1234, 176 LT 413, 28 TC 293, 26 ATC 42, CA 35:18
Times Newspapers Ltd v IRC [1973] Ch 155, [1971] 3 All ER 98, [1971] TR 57 .... 60:04
Timpson's Executors v Yerbury [1936] 1 KB 645, [1936] 1 All ER 186, 20 TC 155, 15 ATC 1, CA 35:17

Table of Cases

Tippett v Watton [1995] STC (SCD) 17; on appeal sub nom Watton v Tippett [1996] STC 101, 69 TC 491; affd [1997] STC 893, 69 TC 491, CA ... 22:11, 22:13, 22:22, 23:38
Tod v South Essex Motors (Basildon) Ltd [1988] STC 392, 60 TC 598 .... 2A:65
Todd v Egyptian Delta Land and Investment Co Ltd [1929] AC 1, 98 LJKB 1, 14 TC 119, 7 ATC 355, HL 33:03, 33:27
Tollemache (Lord) v IRC (1926) 96 LJKB 766, 136 LT 144, 11 TC 277, 6 ATC 71 .... 11:23, 13:15
Tolsma v Inspecteur der Omzetbelasting Leeuwarden: C-16/93 [1994] ECR I-743, [1994] STC 509, ECJ 63:19, 63:21
Tomlinson v Glyns Executor and Trustee Co [1970] Ch 112, [1970] 1 All ER 381, 45 TC 600, [1969] TR 211, CA 20:07
Torbell Investments Ltd v Williams [1986] STC 397, 59 TC 357 .... 8:11, 8:99
Toronto-Dominion Bank v Oberoi [2002] EWHC 3216 (Ch), [2004] STC 1197, 75 TC 244 .... 2A:71, 7:51, 10:17
Torrens v IRC (1933) 18 TC 262, 12 ATC 613 .... 11:15
Toshoku Finance UK plc, Re [2000] 3 All ER 938, [2000] 1 WLR 2478, [2000] STC 301, [2000] 1 BCLC 683, CA; affd [2002] UKHL 6, [2002] 3 All ER 961, [2002] 1 WLR 671, [2002] STC 368, [2002] 1 BCLC 598 2A:20, 25:46, 27:13
Total UK Ltd v Revenue and Customs Comrs [2006] EWHC 3422 (Ch), [2007] STC 564, (2006) Times, 8 December, [2006] SWTI 2457, [2006] All ER (D) 47 (Nov), [2007] EWCA Civ 987, [2008] STC 564 .... 63:20; 65:19
Tower Mcashback LLP v Revenue and Customs Comrs [2008] EWHC 2387 (Ch), [2008] STC 3366, [2008] All ER (D) 105 (Oct) 2:11
Town and Country Factors Ltd v Customs and Excise Comrs [1998] STC 225 .... 63:21
Townsend v Grundy (1933) 18 TC 140, 12 ATC 293 .... 12:03, 12:05
Trafalgar Tours Ltd v Customs and Excise Comrs [1990] 3 CMLR 68, [1990] STC 127, CA 63:23
Trafford's Settlement, Re, Moore v IRC [1985] Ch 32, [1984] 1 All ER 1108, [1984] STC 236 .... 42:07
Transco plc v Dyall [2002] STC (SCD) 199 .... 8:110
Trautwein v Federal Taxation Comr (1936) 56 CLR 196 .... 12:05
Tremerton Ltd v Customs and Excise Comrs (1998) VAT decision 15590 .... 66:26
Trenchard v Bennet (1933) 17 TC 420, 49 TLR 226, 12 ATC 1 .... 12:10
Trend Properties Ltd v Crutchfield [2005] STC (SCD) 534 .... 27:07
Trevor Smallwood and Mary Caroline Smallwood (Trustees of the Trevor Smallwood Trust) v R & C Comrs (2008) SpC 669 .... 35:62
Trewby v Customs and Excise Comrs [1976] 2 All ER 199, [1976] 1 WLR 932, [1976] STC 122 .... 68:11
Triad Timber Components Ltd Customs and Excise Comrs [1993] VATTR 384 ..... 64:26, 66:41
Triage Services Ltd v Revenue and Customs Comrs [2006] STC (SCD) 85 .... 8:127
Trinity Mirror plc (formerly Mirror Group Newspapers Ltd) v Customs and Excise Comrs [2001] EWCA Civ 65, [2001] 2 CMLR 759, [2001] STC 192 .... 68:16
Trustees Executors and Agency Co Ltd v IRC [1973] Ch 254, [1973] 1 All ER 562, [1973] STC 96, [1972] TR 339 .... 47:06
Trustees of BT Pension Scheme v Revenue and Customs Comrs [2005] EWHC 3088 (Ch), [2006] STC 1685, [2005] All ER (D) 244 (Nov) 2:11
Tryka Ltd v Newall (1963) 41 TC 146, [1963] TR 297, 42 ATC 293, [1964] BTR 286 .... 8:52
Tucker (a bankrupt), Re, ex p Tucker [1990] Ch 148, [1988] 1 All ER 603, CA 34:02
Tucker v Granada Motorway Services Ltd [1979] 2 All ER 801, [1979] 1 WLR 683, [1979] STC 393, 53 TC 92, HL 8:110, 8:119, 8:129
Tullet and Tokyo Forex International Ltd v Secretary of State for Social Security (25 May 2000, CO/2038/1999) 50:18
Tumble Tots (UK) Ltd v Revenue and Customs Comrs [2007] EWHC 103 (Ch), [2007] STC 1171, [2007] SWTI 293, [2007] All ER (D) 274 (Jan) 63:20
Turmeau v Customs and Excise Comrs (1981) VAT decision 1135 .... 66:18
Turnbull v Foster (1904) 7 F (Ct of Sess) 1, 42 Sc LR 15, 6 TC 206 .... 33:03
Turner (t/a Turner Agricultural) v Customs and Excise Comrs [1992] STC 621 ...... 66:03
Turner v Follett [1973] STC 148, 48 TC 614, CA 18:01, 18:33
Turner v Last (1965) 42 TC 517, [1965] TR 249, 44 ATC 234 .... 8:14

Table of Cases

Turner (Thomas) (Leicester) Ltd v Rickman (1898) 4 TC 25 .... 36:04
Turpeinen (Civil proceedings concerning): C-520/04 [2006] ECR I-10685, [2008] All ER (EC) 725, [2007] 1 CMLR 783, [2008] STC 1, [2006] SWTI 2458, [2006] All ER (D) 106 (Nov) 1:02
Turton v Cooper (1905) 92 LT 863, 5 TC 138 .... 7:25
Turvey v Dentons (1923) Ltd [1953] 1 QB 218, [1952] 2 All ER 1025, [1952] TR 471, 31 ATC 470 .... 11:41
Twiss, Re, Barclays Bank Ltd v Pratt [1941] Ch 141, [1941] 1 All ER 93, 57 TLR 146 .... 11:43
Twoh International BV v Staatssecrataris van Financiën: C-184/05 [2007] ECR I–7897, [2008] STC 740, ECJ 69:07
Tyrer v Smart [1976] 3 All ER 537, [1977] 1 WLR 1, [1976] STC 521, 52 TC 533; on appeal [1978] 1 All ER 1089, [1978] 1 WLR 415, [1978] STC 141, 52 TC 533, CA; revsd [1979] 1 All ER 321, [1979] 1 WLR 113, [1979] STC 34, 52 TC 533, HL 7:17

U

UDL Construction plc v Customs and Excise Comrs [1995] V & DR 396 .... 65:18
USB v Revenue and Customs Comrs [2005] STC (SCD) 589 .... 36:33
UFD Ltd v Customs and Excise Comrs [1981] VATTR 199, [1982] 1 CMLR 193 ... 63:02, 68:24, 69:19
Udny v Udny (1869) LR 1 Sc & Div 441, 7 Macq 89, HL 33:17, 33:18, 33:19, 33:23
Ufficio Distrettuale delle Imposte Dirette di Fiorenzuola d'Arda v Comune di Carpaneto Piacentino: 231/87 [1991] STC 205, ECJ 63:17
Ufficio Provinciale Imposta sul Valore Aggiunto di Piacenza v Comune di Rivergaro: 129/88 [1991] STC 205, ECJ 63:17
Ulverstone and Lancaster Rly Co v IRC (1864) 2 H & C 855, sub nom Furness Rly Co v IRC 33 LJ Ex 173, 10 Jur NS 1133, 10 LT 161 .... 57:08
Uudenkaupungin kaupunki, Re: C-184/04 [2006] ECR I-3039, [2006] SWTI 1145, [2006] All ER (D) 447 (Mar), ECJ 66:28
Underground Electric Railways v IRC [1906] AC 21, 75 LJKB 117, 93 LT 819, 54 WR 381, HL 56:18, 57:08, 57:10
Underground Electric Railways v IRC [1914] 3 KB 210, 84 LJKB 115, 111 LT 759; affd [1916] 1 KB 306, 85 LJKB 356, 114 LT 111, CA 56:18, 57:08
Underwood v R & C Comrs [2008] EWHC 108 (Ch) 18:11
Unilever (UK) Holdings Ltd v Smith [2002] STC 113; affd [2002] EWCA Civ 1787, [2003] STC 15 .... 21:12
Union Cold Storage Co Ltd v Adamson (1931) 16 TC 293, 146 LT 172, 10 ATC 345, HL 8:106
Union Corpn v IRC [1952] 1 All ER 646, 34 TC 207, [1952] TR 69, CA; affd [1953] AC 482, [1953] 1 All ER 729, 34 TC 207, [1953] TR 61, HL 33:32
Union of Students of the University of Warwick v Customs and Excise Comrs [1995] V &DR 519 .... 69:36
Union Texas Petroleum Corpn v Critchley [1988] STC 691, 63 TC 244; affd sub nom Union Texas International Corpn v Critchley [1990] STC 305, 63 TC 244, CA 37:33
Unit Construction Co Ltd v Bullock [1960] AC 351, [1959] 3 All ER 831, [1959] TR 345, sub nom Bullock v Unit Construction Co Ltd (1959) 38 TC 712, HL ... 33:25, 33:29
United Dominions Trust Ltd v Kirkwood [1966] 1 QB 783, [1965] 2 All ER 992, [1965] 3 WLR 817; on appeal [1966] 2 QB 431, [1966] 1 All ER 968, [1966] 2 WLR 1083, CA 11:14
United Steel Companies Ltd v Cullington [1940] AC 812, [1940] 2 All ER 170, 23 TC 71, 19 ATC 132, HL 8:129
United Utilities plc v Customs and Excise Comrs: C-89/05 [2006] ECR I-6813, [2006] STC 1423, ECJ 68:15
University Court of the University of Glasgow v Customs and Excise Comrs [2003] STC 495, 2003 SLT 472 .... 2A:67
University of Huddersfield Higher Education Corpn v Customs and Excise Comrs: C-223/03 [2006] ECR I-1751, [2006] STC 980, ECJ 1:12, 63:15, 63:19
University of Southampton v Revenue and Customs Comrs [2006] EWHC 528 (Ch), (2006) Times, 26 April, [2006] SWTI 622, [2006] All ER (D) 273 (Mar) 63:15

Table of Cases

University of Sussex v Customs and Excise Comrs [2003] EWCA Civ 1448, [2004] STC 1 .... 67:18
Unmarried Settlor v IRC [2003] STC (SCD) 274 .... 15:15, 20:02
Untelrab Ltd v McGregor (Inspector of Taxes) [1996] STC (SCD) 1, SCD 33:25
Unterpertinger Pensionsversicherungsanstalt der Arbeiter: C-212/01 [2005] STC 650, ECJ 68:23
Urdd Gobaith Cymru v Customs and Excise Comrs [1997] V & DR 273 .... 69:18
Usher's Wiltshire Brewery Ltd v Bruce [1915] AC 433, 84 LJKB 417, 112 LT 651, 6 TC 399, HL 8:95, 8:104
Utol Ltd v IRC [1944] 1 All ER 190, 25 TC 517 .... 8:106
Utting (B G) & Co Ltd v Hughes [1940] AC 463, [1940] 2 All ER 76, 23 TC 174, HL 8:165

V

V (a minor) (abduction: habitual residence), Re [1996] 3 FCR 173, [1995] 2 FLR 992, [1996] Fam Law 71 .... 33:14
VDP Dental Laboratory NV v Staatssecretaris van Financien: C-401/05 [2007] STC 474, [2007] SWTI 108, [2006] All ER (D) 212 (Dec), ECJ 68:23
VF Corpn (UK) Ltd v Customs and Excise Comrs (1980) VAT decision 898, 105 Taxation 244 .... 69:42
VGM Holdings Ltd, Re [1942] Ch 235, [1942] 1 All ER 224, 111 LJ Ch 145, CA 45:15, 61:01
Vallambrosa Rubber Co Ltd v Farmer 1910 SC 519, 5 TC 529 .... 8:105, 8:111, 8:147
Van Arkadie v Sterling Coated Materials Ltd [1983] STC 95, 56 TC 479 .... 9:04
Van den Berghs Ltd v Clark [1935] AC 431, [1935] All ER Rep 874, 19 TC 390, 14 ATC 62, HL 7:37, 8:85, 8:86, 8:87, 8:88, 8:110
Vandenberg v Taxation Comr New South Wales (1933) ATD 343 .... 12:05
Van der Linde v Van der Linde [1947] Ch 306, [1947] LJR 592, 91 Sol Jo 131, 176 LT 297 .... 2A:71
Van der Mussele v Belgium (Application 8919/80) (1983) 6 EHRR 163, ECtHR 1:21
Vandervell v IRC [1967] 2 AC 291, [1967] 1 All ER 1, 43 TC 519, [1966] TR 315, HL 58:10
Van Dijk's Boekhuis BV v Staatssecretaris van Financiën: 139/84 [1986] 2 CMLR 575, ECJ 1:11, 1:20
Van Duyn v Home Office: 41/74 [1975] Ch 358, [1975] 3 All ER 190, [1974] ECR 1337, [1975] 1 CMLR 1, ECJ 63:02
van Hilten-van der Heijden v Inspecteur van de Belastingdienst/Particulieren/Ondernemingen buitenland te Heerlen: C-513/03 [2006] SWTI 535, [2006] All ER (D) 349 (Feb), ECJ 1:11
Van Tiem v Staatssecretaris van Financiën: C-186/89 [1990] ECR I-4763, [1993] STC 91, ECJ 63:16
Varnam v Deeble [1984] STC 336, 58 TC 501 .... 6:11
Varty v British South Africa Co [1966] AC 381, [1965] 2 All ER 395, 42 TC 406, [1965] TR 163, HL 8:149
Varty v Lynes [1976] 3 All ER 447, [1976] 1 WLR 1091, [1976] STC 508, 51 TC 419 .... 23:07
Vasili v Christensen [2003] STC (SCD) 428; revsd sub nom Christensen v Vasili [2004] EWHC 476 (Ch), [2004] STC 935 .... 7:116
Vassis, Re (1986) 64 ALR 407, Aus FC 33:14
Vastaberga Taxi v Sweden (Application 36985/97) 2:118
Vaughan v Archie Parnell and Alfred Zeitlin Ltd (1940) 23 TC 505, 19 ATC 463 ..... 8:82
Vaughan v Customs and Excise Comrs [1996] V & DR 95 .... 66:22
Vaughan-Neil v IRC [1979] 3 All ER 481, [1979] 1 WLR 1283, [1979] STC 644, 54 TC 223 .... 7:28, 7:29
Venables v Hornby [2002] EWCA Civ 1277, [2002] STC 1248, [2003] ICR 186; revsd [2003] UKHL 65, [2004] 1 All ER 627, [2003] 1 WLR 3022, [2004] STC 84, [2004] ICR 42, ... 2:23, 32:10
Verbond van Nederlandse Ondernemingen v Inspecteur der Invoerrechten Accijnzen: 51/76 [1977] ECR 113, [1977] 1 CMLR 413, ECJ 63:02

Table of Cases

Vereniging Happy Family Rustenburgerstraat v Inspecteur der Ometbelasting: 289/86 [1988] ECR 3655, [1989] 3 CMLR 729, ECJ 63:19
Vereniging Noordelijke Land- en Tuinbouw Organisatie v Staatssecretaris van Financiën: C-515/07 [2009] ECR I–0000, [2009] STC 935, ECJ 65:32
Vernon, Re, Edwards v Vernon (1946) 175 LT 421 .... 11:38
Vertigan v Brady [1988] STC 91 .... 7:49
Vestey v IRC [1962] Ch 861, [1961] 3 All ER 978, 40 TC 112, [1961] TR 289 ..... 11:31, 11:35
Vestey v IRC [1980] AC 1148, [1979] 3 All ER 976, [1980] STC 10, 54 TC 503, HL 1:24, 1:25, 1:27, 2:07, 15:08, 35:26, 35:28
Vestey's (Lord) Executors v IRC [1949] 1 All ER 1108, 31 TC 1, [1949] TR 149, HL 15:14, 15:15, 35:27, 35:30, 35:33
Vibroplant Ltd v Holland [1982] 1 All ER 792, [1982] STC 164, 54 TC 658, CA 9:12
Vickerman v Personal Representatives of Mason [1984] 2 All ER 1, [1984] STC 231, 58 TC 39 .... 2A:74
Victoria and Albert Museum Trustees v Customs and Excise Comrs [1996] STC 1016 .... 66:05
Viewpoint Housing Association Ltd v Customs and Excise Comrs (1995) VAT decision 13148 .... 68:23
Village (John) Automotive Ltd v Customs and Excise Comrs [1998] V & DR 340 ... 65:38
Vincent Consultants Ltd v Customs and Excise Comrs [1989] 1 CMLR 374, [1988] VATTR 152 .... 63:30
Virgin Atlantic Airways Ltd v Customs and Excise Comrs [1993] VATTR 136; revsd [1995] STC 341 .... 65:25, 69:27
Virgin Atlantic Airways Ltd v Customs and Excise Comrs (1996) VAT decision 13840 .... 69:27
Vodafone Cellular Ltd v Shaw [1995] STC 353, 69 TC 376; revsd [1997] STC 734, 69 TC 376, CA 8:96, 8:98, 8:112
Vodafone 2 v Her Majesty's Revenue and Customs: C-203/05 .... 1:15
Vodafone 2 v R & C Comrs (2007) SpC 622 .... 35:66
Vodafone 2 v Revenue and Customs Comrs [2009] EWCA Civ 446, [2009] STC 1480, (2009) Times, 26 June, [2009] SWTI 1795, [2009] All ER (D) 209 (May) 1:02, 1:15
Von Ernst & Cie SA v IRC [1980] 1 All ER 677, [1980] 1 WLR 468, [1980] STC 111, [1979] TR 461, CA 16:45, 47:09
Von Hoffmann v Finanzamt Trier: C-145/96 [1997] All ER (EC) 852, [1998] 1 CMLR 99, [1997] STC 1321, ECJ 63:30; 65:38

W

WHA Ltd v Customs and Excise Comrs [2003] EWHC 305 (Ch), [2003] STC 648; on appeal [2004] EWCA Civ 559, [2004] STC 1081 .... 1:12, 1:13, 66:03
WHA Ltd and another v Revenue and Customs Comrs [2007] EWCA Civ 728, [2008] STC 1695, CA 63:09
WMT Entertainments Ltd v Customs and Excise Comrs (1992) VAT decision 9385 .... 68:15
WN v Staatsecretaris van Financin: C-420/98 2000 ECR I-2847, 2001 STC 974, ECJ 1:05
WR Ltd v Customs and Excise Comrs (1992) VAT decision 6968 .... 66:20
Wade v Customs and Excise Comrs (1995) VAT decision 13164 .... 69:21
Wadsworth Morton Ltd v Jenkinson [1966] 3 All ER 702, [1967] 1 WLR 79, 43 TC 479, [1966] TR 289 .... 8:52, 28:21
Wagon Finance Ltd v Customs and Excise Comrs (1999) VAT decision 16288 .... 68:16
Wain v Cameron [1995] STC 555 .... 8:07
Wakefield v Inspector of Taxes [2005] STC (SCD) 439 .... 22:29
Wakeling v Pearce [1995] STC (SCD) 96 .... 23:07
Walcot-Bather v Golding [1979] STC 707, 52 TC 649, [1979] TR 249 .... 6:40
Waldie (James) & Sons Ltd v IRC 1919 SC 697, 1919 SLT 176, 12 TC 113 .... 8:131

Wales v Tilley [1942] 2 KB 169, [1942] 2 All ER 22, 25 TC 136, 21 ATC 117, CA; on appeal sub nom Tilley v Wales [1943] AC 386, [1943] 1 All ER 280, 25 TC 136, 22 ATC 74, HL 7:01, 7:21, 7:28, 7:32, 7:34, 7:35
Walker v Carnaby, Harrower, Barham and Pykett [1970] 1 All ER 502, [1970] 1 WLR 276, 46 TC 561, [1969] TR 435 .... 8:75
Walker v Cater Securities Ltd [1974] 3 All ER 63, [1974] 1 WLR 1363, [1974] STC 390, 48 TC 495 .... 8:116
Walker v Centaur Clothes Group Ltd [2000] 2 All ER 589, [2000] 1 WLR 799, [2000] STC 324, 72 TC 379, HL 1:27
Walker v Customs and Excise Comrs [1976] VATTR 10 .... 63:16
Walker v R & C Comrs (2007) SpC 626 .... 2A:62
Walker v Hanby [1988] QB 97, [1987] 3 WLR 1125, [1987] STC 649 .... 67:03
Walker v Joint Credit Card Co Ltd [1982] STC 427, 55 TC 617 .... 8:110, 8:116
Walker (A W) & Co v IRC [1920] 3 KB 648, 90 LJKB 287, 12 TC 297 .... 8:106
Walker's Executors v IRC [2001] STC (SCD) 86 .... 44:01
Wall v IRC [2002] STC (SCD) 122 .... 2A:65
Walle v Customs and Excise Comrs [1976] VATTR 101 .... 69:17, 69:18
Walls v Livesey [1995] STC (SCD) 12 .... 6:25, 6:26, 23:05
Walsh v Lord Advocate [1956] 3 All ER 129, [1956] 1 WLR 1002, 1956 SLT 283, HL 49:09
Walsh v Randall (1940) 23 TC 55, 19 ATC 92 .... 35:19
Walsh v Taylor [2004] STC (SCD) 48 .... 6:26
Walsingham College (Yorkshire Properties) Ltd v Customs and Excise Comrs [1995] V & DR 141 .... 69:23
Walters v Tickner [1992] STC 343; affd [1993] STC 624, 66 TC 174, CA 5:18, 7:144
Walton v IRC [1996] STC 68, [1996] RVR 55, [1996] 1 EGLR 159, CA 45:05
Wang v Commissioner of Inland Revenue [1994] 1 WLR 1286, [1994] STC 753 ...... 2:23
Wannell v Rothwell [1996] STC 450, 68 TC 719 .... 6:25, 8:15
Ward, Re, Harrison v Ward [1922] 1 Ch 517, 91 LJ Ch 332, 126 LT 628 .... 46:29
Ward v Anglo-American Oil Co Ltd (1934) 19 TC 94, 13 ATC 560 .... 11:12
Ward v Dunn [1979] STC 178, 52 TC 517, [1978] TR 375 .... 7:139
Wardhaugh v Penrith Rugby Union Football Club [2002] EWHC 918 (Ch), [2002] STC 776, 74 TC 499 .... 22:13
Waring v Ward (1802) 7 Ves 332 .... 18:21
Warner v Prior [2003] STC (SCD) 109 .... 7:128
Warren v Warren (1895) 72 LT 628, 43 WR 490, 11 TLR 355, 13 R 485 .... 11:41
Warwick Masonic Rooms Ltd v Customs and Excise Comrs (1979) VAT decision 839, 104 Taxation 503 .... 63:19, 63:22
Wase (HM Inspector of Taxes) v Bourke (1995) 22:33
Waterloo Main Colliery Co Ltd v IRC (1947) 29 TC 235, 40 R & IT 425, 26 ATC 56 .... 8:86
Waterloo plc v IRC [2002] STC (SCD) 95 .... 7:76
Waterschap Zeeuws Vlaanderen v Staatssecretaris van Financiën: C-378/02 [2005] STC 1298, ECJ 66:05
Watford and District Old People's Housing Association Ltd (t/a Watford Help in the Home Service) v Customs and Excise Comrs (VAT decision 15660) [1998] SWTI 1529 .... 68:23
Watkis v Ashford Sparkes & Harward (a firm) [1985] 2 All ER 916, [1985] 1 WLR 994, [1985] STC 451, 58 TC 468 .... 8:96, 8:97, 8:131
Watney & Co v Musgrave (1880) 5 Ex D 241, 49 LJQB 493, 1 TC 272 .... 8:105
Watney Combe Reid & Co Ltd v Pike [1982] STC 733, 57 TC 372 ...... 8:75, 8:99, 8:114
Watson v Sandie and Hull [1898] 1 QB 326, 67 LJQB 319, 77 LT 528, 3 TC 611 .... 35:03
Watson v Watson 1934 SC 374 .... 56:29
Watson Bros v Hornby [1942] 2 All ER 506, 168 LT 109, 24 TC 506, 21 ATC 279 .... 8:151, 8:153, 8:154
Watson Bros v Lothian (1902) 4 TC 441, 10 SLT 49 .... 8:57
Watton v Tippett. See Tippett v Watton
Watts v Hart [1984] STC 548, 58 TC 209 .... 8:52
Way v Underdown (No 2) [1974] 2 All ER 595, [1974] STC 293, 49 TC 215; affd [1975] 2 All ER 1064, [1975] STC 425, 49 TC 648, [1975] TR 91, CA 5:14

2603

Table of Cases

Waylee Investment Ltd v Comr of Inland Revenue [1990] STC 780, 63 TC 684 .... 8:21
Weald Leasing Ltd v Revenue and Customs Comrs [2007] SWTI 1368, VAT & D Trib, [2008] EWHC 30 (Ch), [2008] STC 1601 .... 63:09
Webb v Conelee Properties Ltd [1982] STC 913, 56 TC 149 .... 8:42, 10:07, 25:05
Webster Communications International Ltd v Customs and Excise Comrs [1997] V & DR 173 .... 66:20
Weigall's Will Trusts, Re, Midland Bank Executor and Trustee Co Ltd v Weigall [1956] Ch 424, [1956] 2 All ER 312, [1956] TR 113, 35 ATC 91 .... 46:21
Weight v Salmon (1935) 19 TC 174, 153 LT 55, 14 ATC 47, HL ... 7:44, 7:54, 7:64, 7:65, 8:113
Weiner's Will Trusts, Re, Wyner v Braithwaite [1956] 2 All ER 482, [1956] 1 WLR 579 .... 20:16
Weir and Pitt's Contract, Re (1911) 55 Sol Jo 536 .... 56:33
Weisberg's Executrices v IRC (1933) 17 TC 696, 12 ATC 192 .... 8:28
Welbeck Securities Ltd v Powlson. See Powlson v Welbeck Securities Ltd
Weldons (West One) Ltd v Customs and Excise Comrs (1980) VAT decision 984, 107 Taxation 202 .... 65:12
Wellcome Trust Ltd v Customs and Excise Comrs (1994) VAT decision 12206; refd C-155/94: [1996] All ER (EC) 589, [1996] ECR I-3013, [1996] 2 CMLR 909, [1996] STC 945, ECJ 63:15, 63:17
Wellington v Reynolds (1962) 40 TC 209, [1962] TR 57, 41 ATC 90 .... 2:26
Wellington Private Hospital Ltd v Customs and Excise Comrs [1993] VATTR 109; on appeal sub nom Customs and Excise Comrs v Wellington Private Hospital Ltd [1995] STC 628; revsd [1997] STC 445, CA 69:35
Wells v Customs and Excise Comrs (1997) VAT decision 15169 .... 69:23
Wells v Gas Float Whitton No 2 (Owners) [1897] AC 337, 66 LJP 99, 8 Asp MLC 272, 76 LT 663, HL 9:44
Wensleydale's Settlement Trustees v IRC [1996] STC (SCD) 241 .... 33:25, 33:39
Werle & Co v Colquhoun (1888) 20 QBD 753, 57 LJQB 323, 2 TC 402, CA 36:04, 36:05
West v Crossland [1999] STC 147, 71 TC 314 .... 7:111
West v Phillips (1958) 38 TC 203, [1958] TR 267, 37 ATC 270 .... 8:19, 8:21
West v Trennery. See Tee v Inspector of Taxes
West Devon Borough Council v Customs and Excise Comrs [2001] STC 1282 .... 63:17
West End Motors (Bodmin) Ltd v Customs and Excise Comrs (1982) VAT decision 1205 .... 65:11
West London Syndicate Ltd v IRC [1898] 2 QB 507, 67 LJQB 956, 79 LT 289, 47 WR 125 .... 57:07, 57:18
West Somerset Railway plc v Chivers [1995] STC (SCD) 1 .... 9:26
West Yorkshire Independent Hospital (Contract Services) Ltd v Customs and Excise Comrs [1986] VATTR 151; affd sub nom Customs and Excise Comrs v West Yorkshire Independent Hospital (Contract Services) Ltd [1988] STC 443; on appeal [1990] 1 QB 905, [1989] 2 All ER 938, [1989] 3 WLR 678, [1989] STC 539, CA
.... 65:12
Westall v McDonald [1985] STC 693, 58 TC 642 .... 7:42
Westbourne Supporters of Glentoran Club v Brennan [1995] STC (SCD) 137 .... 8:36
Westcott v Bryan [1969] 2 Ch 324, [1969] 3 All ER 564, 45 TC 476, [1969] TR 195, CA 7:109
Westcott v Woolcombers Ltd [1986] STC 182, 60 TC 575; affd [1987] STC 600, 60 TC 575, CA 1:27, 28:21
Western Abyssinian Mining Syndicate v IRC (1935) 46 TC 407, 14 ATC 286 .... 57:06
Western United Investment Co Ltd v IRC [1958] Ch 392, [1958] 1 All ER 257, [1958] 2 WLR 192, [1957] TR 351 .... 56:11, 56:18, 57:08, 57:10
Westminster (Duke) v IRC. See IRC v Duke of Westminster
Westminster Bank Executor and Trustee Co (Channel Islands) Ltd v National Bank of Greece SA [1970] 1 QB 256, [1969] 3 All ER 504, 46 TC 472, [1969] TR 221, CA; affd sub nom National Bank of Greece SA v Westminster Bank Executor and Trustee Co (Channel Islands) Ltd [1971] AC 945, [1971] 1 All ER 233, 46 TC 472, [1969] BTR 415, HL 11:05, 11:39
Westminster Bank Ltd v Osler [1933] AC 139, [1932] All ER Rep 917, 17 TC 381, 11 ATC 413, HL 8:149

Table of Cases

Westminster City Council v Customs and Excise Comrs [1989] VATTR 71, [1990] 2 CMLR 81 .... 68:23
Westminster City Council v Southern Rly Co, Railway Assessment Authority and W H Smith & Son Ltd [1936] AC 511, [1936] 2 All ER 322, 105 LJKB 537, sub nom Re Southern Rly Co's Appeals 100 JP 327, 155 LT 33, HL 10:07
Westmoreland Investments Ltd v MacNiven. See McNiven v Westmoreland Investments Ltd
Weston v Garnett. See Businessman v Inspector of Taxes
Weston v Hearn [1943] 2 All ER 421, 25 TC 425, 22 ATC 240 .... 7:20, 7:24
Weston (Weston's Executors) v IRC [2000] STC (SCD) 30; affd [2000] STC 1064 ... 44:04, 44:11
Wheatley v IRC [1998] STC (SCD) 60 .... 44:11
Whelan v Dover Harbour Board (1934) 151 LT 288, 18 TC 555, 12 ATC 123, CA 8:125
Whimster & Co v IRC 1926 SC 20, 1925 SLT 623, 12 TC 813, 4 ATC 570 . 8:128, 8:147, 8:159, 8:160
Whitbread Group plc v Customs and Excise Comrs [2005] EWHC 418 (Ch), [2005] STC 539 .... 69:13
White v Franklin [1965] 1 All ER 692, [1965] 1 WLR 492, 42 TC 283, [1965] BTR 152, CA 5:22
White v G & M Davies (a firm) [1979] STC 415, 52 TC 597, [1979] TR 105 .... 8:80
White v Higginbottom [1983] 1 WLR 416, [1983] STC 143, 57 TC 283 .... 9:23
White v IRC [2003] STC (SCD) 161 .... 7:22
Whitechapel Art Gallery v Customs and Excise Comrs [1986] STC 156 .... 66:05, 66:08
Whitehead v Customs and Excise Comrs [1975] VATTR 152 .... 64:14
Whitehead v Tubbs (Elastics) Ltd [1984] STC 1, 57 TC 472, CA 8:110, 8:121
Whiteley v Customs and Excise Comrs [1993] VATTR 248 .... 69:17, 69:18
Whiteside v Whiteside [1950] Ch 65, [1949] 2 All ER 913, [1949] TR 457, 28 ATC 479, CA 2A:71, 11:42
Whiting to Loomes (1881) 17 Ch D 10, 50 LJ Ch 463, 44 LT 721, 29 WR 435, CA 56:33
Whitney v IRC [1926] AC 37, 95 LJKB 165, 10 TC 88, 4 ATC 551, HL 33:01
Whittaker v Kershaw (1890) 45 Ch D 320, sub nom Kershaw, Re, Whittaker v Kershaw 60 LJ Ch 9, 39 WR 22, 63 LT 203, CA 29.11
Whittle (a firm) v Customs and Excise Comrs [1994] VATTR 202 .... 65:25
Whittles v Uniholdings Ltd (No 3) [1995] STC 185; revsd [1996] STC 914, 68 TC 528, CA 3:22, 16:02, 16:22
Whitworth Park Coal Co Ltd v IRC [1961] AC 31, [1959] 3 All ER 703, 38 TC 531, [1959] TR 293, HL 11:24, 11:25
Whyte v Clancy [1936] 2 All ER 735, 20 TC 679, 15 ATC 393 .... 12:10
Wicker v Fraser [1982] STC 505, 55 TC 641 .... 2:85
Wicks v Firth [1982] Ch 355, [1982] 2 All ER 9, [1982] 2 WLR 208, [1982] STC 76, 56 TC 318, CA; revsd [1983] 2 AC 214, [1983] 1 All ER 151, [1983] 2 WLR 34, [1983] STC 25, 56 TC 318, HL 7:19, 7:23, 7:102, 7:103, 7:120
Wielockx v Inspecteur der Directe Belastingen: C-80/94 [1995] All ER (EC) 769, [1996] 1 WLR 84, [1995] ECR I-2493, [1995] STC 876, ECJ 1:12
Wienand v Anderton [1977] 1 All ER 384, [1977] STC 12, 51 TC 570, [1976] TR 275 .... 7:36
Wigan Metropolitan Development Co (Investment) Ltd v Customs and Excise Comrs (1990) VAT decision 4993 .... 66:07, 66:08
Wigmore v Thomas Summerson & Sons Ltd [1926] 1 KB 131, 94 LJKB 836, 9 TC 577, 4 ATC 487 .... 4:09, 11:07
Wilcock v Eve [1995] STC 18, 67 TC 223 .... 7:19, 7:64
Wilcock v Pinto & Co [1925] 1 KB 30, 94 LJKB 101, 9 TC 111, 3 ATC 585, CA 36:09
Wilcox v Customs and Excise Comrs [1978] VATTR 79 .... 63:16
Wilcox v Smith (1857) 4 Drew 40, 26 LJ Ch 596, 29 LTOS 235, 5 WR 667 .... 1:24
Wild v Madame Tussauds (1926) Ltd (1932) 17 TC 127 .... 8:60
Wildin & Co (a firm) v Jowett [2002] STC (SCD) 390 .... 8:93
Wilkie v IRC [1952] Ch 153, [1952] 1 All ER 92, 32 TC 495, [1951] TR 371 .... 33:04, 33:09

Table of Cases

Wilkins v Rogerson [1961] Ch 133, [1961] 1 All ER 358, 39 TC 344, [1960] TR 379, CA 7:23, 7:44, 7:45
Williams v Customs and Excise Comrs (1996) VAT decision 14240 .... 63:17
Williams v Davies [1945] 1 All ER 304, 26 TC 371, 24 ATC 1 .... 8:06
Williams v Evans [1982] 1 WLR 972, [1982] STC 498, 59 TC 509 .... 22:12
Williams v IRC [1980] 3 All ER 321, [1980] STC 535, 54 TC 257, [1980] TR 347, HL 4:21, 4:27
Williams v Merrylees [1987] 1 WLR 1511, [1987] STC 445, 60 TC 297 .... 23:06
Williams (personal representative of Williams, dec'd) v Revenue and Customs Comrs [2005] STC (SCD) 782 .... 44:15
Williams v Simmonds [1981] STC 715, 55 TC 17 .... 7:33
Williams v Singer [1921] 1 AC 65, 89 LJKB 1151, 123 LT 632, 7 TC 387, HL 13:08, 13:09
Williams v Todd [1988] STC 676 .... 7:111
Williams & Glyn's Bank v Customs and Excise Comrs [1974] VATTR 262 .... 68:16
Williams' Executors v IRC [1942] 2 All ER 266, 26 TC 23, 167 LT 272; affd [1943] 1 All ER 318, 112 LJKB 259, 26 TC 23, CA; on appeal [1944] 1 All ER 381, 26 TC 23, 60 TLR 255, HL 8:82
Williams' (C J) Funeral Service of Telford v Customs and Excise Comrs [1999] V & DR 318 .... 68:24
Williamson v Dalton [1981] STC 753, 55 TC 575, [1981] TR 337 .... 7:66
Williamson v Ough [1936] AC 384, 105 LJKB 193, 20 TC 194, 15 ATC 38, HL 13:20
Willingale v International Commercial Bank Ltd [1976] 2 All ER 468, [1976] 1 WLR 657, [1976] STC 188, [1976] TR 77; affd [1977] Ch 78, [1977] 2 All ER 618, [1977] STC 183, [1977] TR 33, CA; on appeal [1978] AC 834, [1978] 1 All ER 754, [1978] STC 75, 52 TC 242, HL 8:64, 8:68, 8:73, 8:160, 11:15
Willingale v Islington Green Investment Co [1972] 1 All ER 199, 48 TC 547, [1971] TR 271, 50 ATC 309 .... 29:04
Willis v Peeters Picture Frames Ltd [1983] STC 453, 56 TC 436, CA 25:29, 25:42
Wills v Bridge (1849) 4 Exch 193, 18 LJ Ex 384 .... 56:15
Willson v Hooker [1995] STC 1142 .... 36:09
Wilson v Bye [1996] STC (SCD) 58 .... 7:17
Wilson v Clayton [2004] EWHC 898 (Ch), [2004] STC 1022, [2004] IRLR 611; affd [2004] EWCA Civ 1657, [2005] STC 157, [2005] IRLR 108 .... 7:17, 7:36
Wilson v Customs and Excise Comrs [1977] VATTR 225 .... 68:12
Wilson v First County Trust Ltd [2003] UKHL 40, [2004] 1 AC 816, [2003] 4 All ER 97, [2003] 2 All ER (Comm) 491, [2003] 3 WLR 568, [2003] 35 LS Gaz R 39, (2003) Times, 11 July, 147 Sol Jo LB 872, [2004] 2 LRC 618, [2003] All ER (D) 187 (Jul) 1:26
Wilson v Mannooch [1937] 3 All ER 120, 21 TC 178, 16 ATC 121 .... 12:11
Wilson (Thomas) (Keighley) Ltd v Emmerson (1960) 39 TC 360, [1960] TR 273 .... 8:122
Wilson and Barlow v Chibbett (1929) 14 TC 407 .... 8:60
Wilson Box (Foreign Rights) Ltd v Brice [1936] 3 All ER 728, 20 TC 736 .... 8:31
Wimpey (George) & Co Ltd v IRC [1975] 2 All ER 45, [1975] 1 WLR 995, [1975] STC 248, [1975] TR 39, CA 57:06, 58:02
Wimpey (George) International Ltd v Rolfe [1989] STC 609, 62 TC 597 ...... 37:07, 37:19
Wimpey Group Services Ltd v Customs and Excise Comrs [1984] VATTR 66 .... 65:29
Wimpy International Ltd v Warland [1988] STC 149, 61 TC 51; affd [1989] STC 273, 61 TC 51, CA 9:26, 9:29
Winans v A-G [1904] AC 287, [1904–7] All ER Rep 410, 73 LJKB 613, 90 LT 721, HL 33:15, 33:17, 33:22, 33:24
Wing v O'Connell [1927] IR 84 .... 8:07
Wing Hung Lai v Bale [1999] STC (SCD) 238 .... 2A:48
Winterton v Edwards [1980] 2 All ER 56, [1980] STC 206, 52 TC 655, [1979] TR 475 .... 23:30
Wirth Ltd v SS Acadia Forest and Lash Barge CG 204, The Acadia Forest [1974] 2 Lloyd's Rep 563 .... 9:44
Wisdom v Chamberlain [1969] 1 All ER 332, [1969] 1 WLR 275, 45 TC 92, [1968] TR 345, CA 8:13, 8:18, 8:21, 8:25, 8:78
Wiseburgh v Domville [1956] 1 All ER 754, 36 TC 527, [1956] TR 29, CA 1:27, 8:84
Withers of Winsford Ltd v Customs and Excise Comrs [1988] STC 431 .... 65:32

Table of Cases

Witzemann v Hauptzollamt München-Mitte: C-343/89 [1990] ECR 4477, [1993] STC 108, ECJ 63:19, 65:49
Wood v Black's Executor (1952) 33 TC 172, [1952] TR 123, 31 ATC 74 ..... 8:29
Wood v Holden [2005] EWHC 547 (Ch), [2005] STC 789 ..... 33:25
Wood v Holden (Inspector of Taxes) [2006] EWCA Civ 26, [2006] 1 WLR 1393, [2006] STC 443, (2006) Times, 20 February, 150 Sol Jo LB 127, [2006] SWTI 236, [2006] All ER (D) 190 (Jan) 33:25
Wood (A) & Co Ltd v Provan (1968) 44 TC 701, [1968] TR 141, 47 ATC 166, CA 9:09
Wood Preservation Ltd v Prior [1968] 2 All ER 849, [1968] TR 37; affd [1969] 1 All ER 364, [1969] 1 WLR 1077, 45 TC 112, [1968] TR 353, CA 25:28, 28:01, 60:03
Woodcock v IRC [1977] STC 405, 51 TC 698, [1977] TR 147 ..... 7:139
Woodend (KV Ceylon) Rubber and Tea Co Ltd v Comr of Inland Revenue [1971] AC 321, [1970] 2 All ER 801, [1970] TR 115 ..... 37:33
Woodhall (Woodhall's Personal Representative) v IRC [2000] STC (SCD) 558 ..... 42:08
Woods (Inspector of Taxes) v Lightpower Ltd [2005] EWHC 1799 (Ch), [2006] STC 759, [2005] SWTI 1169, [2005] All ER (D) 234 (Jun) 2A:19
Woolwich Equitable Building Society v IRC [1993] AC 70, [1991] 4 All ER 577, [1991] STC 364, CA; affd [1993] AC 70, [1992] 3 All ER 737, [1992] STC 657, HL .. 1:01, 1:21, 51:12
Woolwich plc v Davidson [2000] STC (SCD) 302 ..... 8:114
World Association of Girl Guides and Girl Scouts v Customs and Excise Comrs [1984] VATTR 28 ..... 68:22
Worsley Brewery Co Ltd v IRC (1932) 17 TC 349, 11 ATC 340, CA 8:109
Worthing Rugby Football Club Trustees v IRC [1985] 1 WLR 409, [1985] STC 186, 60 TC 482; affd [1987] 1 WLR 1057, 60 TC 482, sub nom Frampton (Trustees of the Worthing Rugby Football Club) v IRC [1987] STC 273, CA 20:09, 25:03
Wrencon Ltd v Customs and Excise Comrs (1996) VAT decision 13968 ..... 69:23
Wright v Boyce [1958] 2 All ER 703, [1958] 1 WLR 832, 38 TC 160, [1958] TR 225, CA 7:25
Wright (R S & E M) Ltd v Customs and Excise Comrs (1995) VAT decision 12984 ..... 66:05
Wynn Realisations Ltd (in administration) v Vogue Holdings Inc [1999] STC 524, CA 63:23
Wynne-Jones v Bedale Auction Ltd [1977] STC 50, 51 TC 426, [1976] TR 293 ..... 8:123

X

X plc v Roe [1996] STC (SCD) 139 ..... 28:29
XL (Stevenage) Ltd v Customs and Excise Comrs [1981] VATTR 192 ..... 64:03

Y

Yarmouth v France (1887) 19 QBD 647, 57 LJQB 7, 36 WR 281, 4 TLR 1 ..... 9:26
Yates v GCA International Ltd [1991] STC 157 ..... 37:12, 37:38
Yenidje Tobacco Co Ltd, Re [1916] 2 Ch 426, [1916–17] All ER Rep 1050, 86 LJ Ch 1, CA 45:02, 45:03
Yeoman (A L) Ltd v Customs and Excise Comrs (1990) VAT decision 4470 ..... 65:32
Yewens v Noakes (1880) 6 QBD 530, 50 LJQB 132, 44 LT 128, 45 JP 8, 1 TC 260, CA 49:03
Yoga for Health Foundation v Customs and Excise Comrs [1984] VATTR 297; revsd [1984] STC 630, [1985] 1 CMLR 340 ..... 63:02, 68:23
Yorkshire Co-operatives Ltd: C-398/99, [2003] ECR I-427, [2003] STC 301, ECJ 63:20
Young v Pearce [1996] STC 743, (1996) 70 TC 331 ..... 15:06, 15:15, 15:30, 15:31
Young v Phillips [1984] STC 520, 58 TC 232 ..... 3:20, 47:05
Young v Racecourse Betting Control Board [1959] 3 All ER 215, [1959] 1 WLR 813, 38 TC 426, [1959] TR 249, HL 8:107

Table of Cases

Young v Sealey [1949] Ch 278, [1949] 1 All ER 92, [1949] LJR 529 .... 40:04
Young (J H) & Co v IRC 1926 SC 30, 1925 SLT 628, 12 TC 827, 4 ATC 579 ...... 8:147
Young & Woods Ltd v West [1980] IRLR 201, CA 49:03
Yuill v Fletcher [1984] STC 401, 58 TC 145, CA 23:37
Yuill v Wilson [1979] 2 All ER 1205, [1979] 1 WLR 987, [1979] STC 486, [1978] TR 451, CA; revsd [1980] 3 All ER 7, [1980] 1 WLR 910, [1980] STC 460, 52 TC 674, HL 12:17, 23:37

Z

Z Cars v Customs and Excise Comrs BIR/76/194 unreported 68:11
Zim Properties Ltd v Procter [1985] STC 90, 58 TC 371 ...... 17:01, 17:02, 18:03, 18:12, 18:14, 18:16
Zita Modes SARL v Administration de l'enregistrement et des domaines: C-497/01 [2003] ECR I-14393, [2004] 2 CMLR 533, [2005] STC 1059, ECJ 63:27
Zurich Insurance Co v Revenue and Customs Comrs [2006] EWHC 593 (Ch), (2006) Times, 26 April, [2006] STC 1694, [2006] All ER (D) 357 (Mar); affd sub nom Revenue and Customs Comrs v Zurich Insurance Co [2007] EWCA Civ 218, [2007] 2 CMLR 1491, (2007) Times, 5 April, [2007] STC 1756, [2007] All ER (D) 269 (Mar) 65:38
Zurstrassen v Administration des Contributions Directes: C-87/99 [2000] ECR I-3337, [2001] 3 CMLR 1715, [2001] STC 1102, ECJ 1:09

Decisions of the European Commission of Human Rights and European Court of Human Rights are listed below. These decisions are also included in the preceding table.

AP, MP and TP v Switzerland (1997) 26 EHRR 541, [1998] EHRLR 88, EC of HR 1:14, 2:118
Benendoun v France (Application 12547/86) 2:118
Engel v Netherlands (Applications 5100/71, 5101/71, 5102/71) (1976) 1 EHRR 647, E Ct HR 2:118
Ferrazzini v Italy [2001] STC 1314, E Ct HR 1:14
Georgiou (t/a Marios Chippery) v United Kingdom [2001] STC 80, E Ct HR .. 1:22, 2:118
Hozee v Netherlands (1998) unreported 1:14
JJ v Netherlands (1998) 28 EHRR 168, E Ct HR 1:22
McGregor v United Kingdom (Application No 30548/96) (3 December 1997, unreported), E Ct HR 1:13
National and Provincial Building Society v United Kingdom [1997] STC 1466, E Ct HR 1:21
Nerva v United Kingdom (2002) 36 EHRR 31, [2002] IRLR 815, 13 BHRC 246, E Ct HR 50:04
Schouten and Meldrum v Netherlands (Applications 19005/91 and 19006/91) (1994) 19 EHRR 432, E Ct HR 1:14
Svenska Management Grupen v Sweden (Application No 11036/84) 45 DR 211 (1985), EC of HR 1:13
Van der Mussele v Belgium (Application 8919/80) (1983) 6 EHRR 163, ECtHR 1:13
Vastaberga Taxi v Sweden (Application 36985/97) 2:118

Decisions of the European Court of Justice are listed below numerically. These decisions are also included in the preceding alphabetical table.

29/69: Stauder v City of Ulm [1969] ECR 419, [1970] CMLR 112 .... 1:12
152/73: Sotgiu v Deutsche Bundespost [1974] ECR 153, ECJ 1:10
41/74: Van Duyn v Home Office [1975] Ch 358, [1975] 3 All ER 190, [1974] ECR 1337, [1975] 1 CMLR 1, ECJ 63:02
51/76: Verbond van Nederlandse Ondernemingen v Inspecteur der Invoerrechten en Accijnzen [1977] ECR 113, [1977] 1 CMLR 413, ECJ 63:02
76/76: Di Paolo v Office National de l'Emploi [1977] ECR 315, [1977] 2 CMLR 59, ECJ 54:15

Table of Cases

154/80: Staatssecretaris van Financiën v Coöperatieve Vereniging 'Coöperatieve Aardappelenbewaarplaats GA' [1981] ECR 445, [1981] 3 CMLR 337, ECJ ... 1:11, 63:21, 65:17
8/81: Becker v Finanzamt Münster-Innenstadt [1982] ECR 53, [1982] 1 CMLR 499, ECJ 63:02
89/81: Staatssecretaris van Financiën v Hong Kong Trade Development Council [1982] ECR 1277, [1983] 1 CMLR 73, ECJ 1:11, 1:20, 63:15
294/82: Einberger v Hauptzollamt Freiburg [1984] ECR 1177, ECJ 65:49
268/83: Rompelman v Minister van Financiën [1985] ECR 655, [1985] 3 CMLR 202, ECJ 63:16, 66:05
5/84: Direct Cosmetics Ltd v Customs and Excise Comrs [1985] ECR 617, [1985] 2 CMLR 145, [1985] STC 479, ECJ 63:02; 69:12
139/84: Van Dijk's Boekhuis BV v Staatssecretaris van Financiën [1986] 2 CMLR 575, ECJ 1:11, 1:20
168/84: Berkholz v Finanzamt Hamburg-Mitte-Alstadt [1985] ECR 2251, [1985] 3 CMLR 667, ECJ 63:29
235/85: EC Commission v Netherlands [1987] ECR 1471, [1988] 2 CMLR 921, ECJ 63:15
353/85: EC Commission v United Kingdom [1988] 2 All ER 557, [1988] STC 251, ECJ 63:02
102/86: Apple and Pear Development Council v Customs and Excise Comrs [1988] 2 All ER 922, [1988] STC 221, ECJ 63:15, 63:16, 63:17, 63:21, 66:05, 66:08
138, 139/86: Direct Cosmetics Ltd and Laughtons Photographs Ltd v Customs and Excise Comrs [1988] STC 540, ECJ 63:02, 65:17
165/86: Leesportefeuille 'Intiem' CV v Staatssecretaris van Financiën [1988] ECR 1471, [1989] 2 CMLR 856, ECJ 66:03
289/86: Vereniging Happy Family Rustenburgerstraat v Inspecteur der Ometbelasting [1988] ECR 3655, [1989] 3 CMLR 729, ECJ 63:19
416/86: EC Commission v United Kingdom [1990] 2 QB 130, [1989] 1 All ER 364, [1988] 3 WLR 1261, [1988] STC 456, ECJ 63:02; 69:12
50/87: EC Commission v France [1988] ECR 4797, ECJ 63:17
81/87: R v HM Treasury, ex p Daily Mail and General Trust plc [1989] QB 446, [1989] 1 All ER 328, [1989] 2 WLR 908, [1988] STC 787, ECJ 1:12, 33:36
230/87: Naturally Yours Cosmetics Ltd v Customs and Excise Comrs [1988] ECR 6365, [1988] STC 879, ECJ 63:02, 63:21, 63:26
231/87: Ufficio Distrettuale delle Imposte Dirette di Fiorenzuola d'Arda v Comune di Carpaneto Piacentino [1991] STC 205, ECJ 63:17
342/87: Genius Holding BV v Staatssecretaris van Financiën [1989] ECR 4227, [1991] STC 239, ECJ 66:03
50/88: Kúhne v Finanzamt München III [1990] STC 749, [1989] ECR 1925, [1990] 3 CMLR 287, ECJ 65:29
51/88: Hamann v Finanzamt Hamburg-Eimsbüttel [1991] STC 193, [1990] 2 CMLR 383, ECJ 63:30; 65:38
126/88: Boots Co plc v Customs and Excise Comrs [1990] ECR I-1235, [1990] 2 CMLR 731, [1990] STC 387, ECJ 63:20; 65:17, 65:19
129/88: Ufficio Provinciale Imposta sul Valore Aggiunto di Piacenza v Comune di Rivergaro [1991] STC 205, ECJ 63:17
173/88: Skatteministeriet v Henriksen [1990] STC 768, [1990] 3 CMLR 558, ECJ 68:12
C-175/88: Biehl v Administration des Contributions du Grand-Duch de Luxembourg [1990] ECR I-1779, [1990] 3 CMLR 143, [1991] STC 575, ECJ 1:08
C-262/88: Barber v Guardian Royal Exchange Assurance Group [1991] 1 QB 344, [1990] 2 All ER 660, [1991] 2 WLR 72, [1990] ICR 616, ECJ 32:29
C-320/88: Staatssecretaris van Financiën v Shipping and Forwarding Enterprise Safe BV [1990] ECR I-285, [1993] 3 CMLR 547, [1991] STC 627, ECJ 63:25
C-4/89: Comune di Carpaneto Piacentino v Ufficio Provinciale Imposta sul Valore Aggiunto di Piacenza [1990] 3 CMLR 153, ECJ 63:17
C-106/89: Marleasing SA v La Comercial Internacional de Alimentacion SA [1990] ECR I-4135, [1992] 1 CMLR 305, [1993] BCC 421, ECJ 63:02
C-186/89: Van Tiem v Staatsssecretaris van Financiën [1990] ECR I-4363, [1993] STC 91, ECJ 63:16

Table of Cases

C-213/89: R v Secretary of State for Transport, ex p Factortame Ltd (No 2) [1991] 1 AC 603, [1991] 1 All ER 70, [1990] 3 CMLR 1, ECJ; apld [1991] 1 AC 603, [1991] 1 All ER 70, [1990] 3 CMLR 375, HL 1:02
C-343/89: Witzemann v Hauptzollamt München-Mitte [1990] ECR 4477, [1993] STC 108, ECJ 63:19, 65:49
C-60/90: Polysar Investments Netherlands BV v Inspecteur der Invoerrechten en Accijnzen [1991] ECR I-3111, [1993] STC 222, ECJ 63:17, 66:07
C-97/90: Lennartz v Finanzamt München III [1991] ECR I-3795, [1995] STC 514, ECJ 66:05, 66:27
C-204/90: Bachmann v Belgium [1992] ECR I-249, [1993] 1 CMLR 785, [1994] STC 855, ECJ 1:11, 1:12
C-20/91: De Jong v Staatssecretaris van Financiën [1992] 3 CMLR 260, [1995] STC 727, ECJ 65:28, 66:05
C-163/91: Beheersmaatschappij Van Ginkel Waddinxveen BV v Inspecteur der Omzetbelasting, Utrecht [1996] STC 825, ECJ 65:25
C-169/91: Stoke-on-Trent City Council v B & Q plc [1993] AC 900, [1993] 1 All ER 481, [1992] ECR I-6635, ECJ; apld [1993] AC 900, [1993] 2 All ER 297n, 91 LGR 237, HL 1:02
C-193/91: Finanzamt München III v Möhsche [1993] ECR I-2615, [1997] STC 195, ECJ 65:29
C-200/91: Coloroll Pension Trustees Ltd v Russell [1995] All ER (EC) 23, [1994] ECR I-4389, [1995] ICR 179, [1994] IRLR 586, ECJ 32:29
C-281/91: Muys' en De Winter's Bouw-en Aannemingsbedrijf BV v Staatssecretaris van Financiën [1993] ECR I-5405, [1997] STC 665, ECJ 63:20
C-330/91: R v IRC, ex p Commerzbank AG [1994] QB 219, [1993] STC 605, 68 TC 252, ECJ; apld (1995) 68 TC 252 .... 1:10, 25:40, 37:03
C-333/91: Sofitam SA (formerly Satam SA) v Ministre chargé du Budget [1993] ECR I-3513, [1997] STC 226, ECJ 63:17, 66:08
C-10/92: Balocchi v Ministero delle Finanze dello Stato [1993] ECR I-5105, [1997] STC 640, ECJ 67:04
C-18/92: Chaussures Bally SA v Ministry of Finance (Belgium) [1993] ECR I-2871, [1997] STC 209, ECJ 63:23
C-63/92: Lubbock Fine & Co v Customs and Excise Comrs [1994] QB 571, [1994] 3 All ER 705, [1993] ECR I-6665, [1994] STC 101, ECJ 68:11
C-68/92: EC Commission v France [1993] ECR I-5881, [1997] STC 684, ECJ 63:30; 65:38
C-69/92: EC Commission v Luxembourg [1993] ECR I-5907, [1997] STC 712, HL 63:30; 65:38
C-73/92: EC Commission v Spain [1993] ECR I-5997, [1997] STC 700, ECJ . 63:30; 65:38
C-111/92: Lange v Finanzamt Fürstenfeldbruck [1993] ECR I-4677, [1997] STC 564, ECJ 69:08
C-291/92: Finanzamt Uelzen v Armbrecht [1995] All ER (EC) 882, [1995] ECR I-2775, [1995] STC 997, ECJ 66:05
C-1/93: Halliburton Services BV v Staatssecretaris van Financiën [1994] ECR I-1137, [1994] STC 655, ECJ 1:10
C-16/93: Tolsma v Inspecteur der Omzetbelasting Leeuwarden [1994] ECR I-743, [1994] STC 509, ECJ 63:19, 63:21
C-33/93: Empire Stores Ltd v Customs and Excise Comrs [1994] 3 All ER 90, [1994] STC 623, ECJ 63:20; 65:17
C-38/93: H J Glawe Spiel- und Unterhaltungsgeräte Aufstellungsgesellschaft mbH & Co KG v Finanzamt Hamburg-Barmbek-Uhlenhorst [1994] ECR I-1679, [1994] STC 543, ECJ 63:21, 65:26, 68:15
C-279/93: Finanzamt Köln-Altstadt v Schumacker [1996] QB 28, [1995] All ER (EC) 319, [1995] STC 306, ECJ 1:09
C-4/94: BLP Group Ltd v Customs and Excise Comrs [1995] All ER (EC) 401, [1995] ECR I-983, [1995] STC 424, ECJ 66:07, 66:08
C-55/94: Gebhard [1996] ECR I-1416 .... 1:07
C-80/94: Wielockx v Inspecteur der Directe Belastingen [1995] All ER (EC) 769, [1996] 1 WLR 84, [1995] ECR I-2493, [1995] STC 876, ECJ 1:12
C-107/94: Asscher v Staatssecretaris van Financiën [1996] All ER (EC) 757, [1996] ECR I-3089, [1996] 3 CMLR 61, [1996] STC 1025, ECJ 1:09

Table of Cases

C-110/94: Intercommunale voor Zeewaterontzilting (in liquidation) v Belgium [1996] ECR I-857, [1996] STC 569, ECJ 63:32, 66:05, 66:08

C-155/94: Wellcome Trust Ltd v Customs and Excise Comrs [1996] All ER (EC) 589, [1996] ECR I-3013, [1996] 2 CMLR 909, [1996] STC 945, ECJ 63:15, 63:17

C-215/94: Mohr v Finanzamt Bad Segeberg [1996] All ER (EC) 450, [1996] ECR I-959, [1996] STC 328, ECJ 63:19

C-288/94: Argos Distributors Ltd v Customs and Excise Comrs [1996] ECR I–5311, ECJ 63:20

C-230/94: Enkler v Finanzamt Homburg [1996] ECR I-4517, [1997] 1 CMLR 881, [1996] STC 1316, ECJ 63:16, 65:29

C-231/94: Faaborg-Gelting Linien A/S v Finanzamt Flensburg [1996] All ER (EC) 656, [1996] ECR I-2395, [1996] STC 774, ECJ 63:20, 63:25

C-317/94: Elida Gibbs Ltd v Customs and Excise Comrs [1996] ECR I–5339, [1997] QB 499, [1997] All ER (EC) 53, [1996] STC 1387, ECJ 63:20; 65:17

C-327/94: Dudda v Finanzamt Bergisch Gladbach [1996] ECR I-4595, [1996] 3 CMLR 1063, [1996] STC 1290, ECJ 63:30

C-2/95: Sparekassernes Datacenter (SDC) v Skatteministeriet [1997] All ER (EC) 610, [1997] STC 932, ECJ 68:16

C-28/95: Leur-Bloem v Inspecteur der Belastingdienst/Ondernemingen Amsterdam 2 [1998] QB 182, [1997] All ER (EC) 738, [1998] 1 CMLR 157, [1997] STC 1205, ECJ 25:47

C-37/95: Belgium v Ghent Coal Terminal NV [1998] All ER (EC) 223, [1998] 1 CMLR 950, [1998] STC 260, ECJ 66:08, 66:26

C-80/95: Harnas & Helm CV v Staatssecretaris van Financiën [1997] All ER (EC) 267, [1997] STC 364, ECJ 63:17

C-85/95: Reisdorf v Finanzamt Köln-West [1997] 1 CMLR 536, [1997] STC 180, ECJ 66:22

C-167/95: Maatschap MJM Linthorst, KGP Pouwels and J Scheres cs v Inspecteur Der Belastingdienst/Ondernemingen Roermond [1997] 2 CMLR 478, [1997] STC 1287, ECJ 63:30, 65:38

C-190/95: ARO Lease BV v Inspecteur der Belastingdienst Grote Ondernemingen, Amsterdam [1997] STC 1272, ECJ 63:01, 63:29

C-247/95: Finanzamt Augsburg-Stadt v Marktgemeinde Welden [1997] All ER (EC) 665, [1997] STC 531, ECJ 63:17

C-250/95: Futura Participations SA v Administrations des Contributions [1997] ECR I-2471, [1997] STC 1301, ECJ 1:12

C-258/95: Julius Fillibeck Söhne GmbH & Co KG v Finanzamt Neustadt [1998] All ER (EC) 466, [1998] 1 WLR 697, [1998] STC 513, ECJ 63:21, 65:29

C-260/95: Customs and Excise Comrs v DFDS A/S [1997] All ER (EC) 342, [1997] STC 384, ECJ 63:29, 65:25

C-283/95: Fischer v Finanzamt Donaueschingen [1998] QB 883, [1998] All ER (EC) 567, [1998] ECR I-3369, [1998] 3 CMLR 1055, [1998] STC 708, ECJ 63:19, 68:15

C-296/95: R v Customs and Excise Comrs, ex p EMU Tabac SARL (Imperial Tobacco intervening) [1998] QB 791, [1998] All ER (EC) 402, [1998] ECR I-1605, [1998] 2 CMLR 1205, ECJ 1:12

C-330/95: Goldsmiths (Jewellers) Ltd v Customs and Excise Comrs [1997] 3 CMLR 978, [1997] STC 1073, ECJ 66:41

C-384/95: Landboden-Agrardienste GmbH & Co KG v Finanzamt Calau [1998] STC 171, ECJ 63:19

C-398/95: Syndesmos ton en Elladi Touristikon Kai Taxidiotikon Grafeion v Ypourgos Ergasias [1997] ECR I-3091, [1998] 1 CMLR 420, ECJ 1:12

C-63/96: Finanzamt Bergisch Gladbach v Skripalle [1996] STC 1035, ECJ 63:02

C-116/96: Reisebüro Binder GmbH v Finanzamt Stuttgart-Körperschaften [1998] 2 CMLR 61, [1998] STC 604, ECJ 63:30

C-141/96: Finanzamt Osnabrück-Land v Langhorst [1998] All ER (EC) 178, [1998] 1 CMLR 673, [1997] STC 1357, ECJ 65:18

C-145/96: Von Hoffmann v Finanzamt Trier [1997] All ER (EC) 852, [1998] 1 CMLR 99, [1997] STC 1321, ECJ 63:30; 65:38

C-264/96: Imperial Chemical Industries plc v Colmer [1998] All ER (EC) 585, [1999] 1 WLR 108, [1998] STC 874, ECJ; apld [2000] 1 All ER 129, [1999] 1 WLR 2035, [1999] STC 1089, HL 1:06, 1:08, 1:12, 1: 20, 28:01

Table of Cases

C-308/96, C-94/97: Customs and Excise Comrs v Madgett and Baldwin [1999] 2 CMLR 392, [1998] STC 1189, ECJ 65:25
C-336/96: Gilly v Directeur des Services Fiscaux du Bas-Rhin [1998] All ER (EC) 826, [1998] ECR I-2793, [1998] 3 CMLR 607, [1998] STC 1014, ECJ 1:07, 1:12; 37:01
C-349/96: Card Protection Plan Ltd v Customs and Excise Comrs [1999] 2 AC 601, [1999] All ER (EC) 339, [1999] 3 WLR 203, [1999] 2 CMLR 743, [1999] STC 270, ECJ; apld [2001] UKHL 4, [2002] 1 AC 202, [2001] 2 All ER 143, [2001] 1 All ER (Comm) 438, [2001] STC 174 .... 63:20, 68:13
C-3/97: Criminal proceedings against Goodwin [1998] All ER (EC) 500, [1998] STC 699, ECJ 63:19
C-48/97: Kuwait Petroleum (GB) Ltd v Customs and Excise Comrs [1999] All ER (EC) 450, [1999] ECR I-2323, [1999] 2 CMLR 651, [1999] STC 488, ECJ . 63:20, 63:21, 65:28
C-400/98 Finanzamt Goslar v Breitsohl [2001] STC 355 .... 68:03
C-149/97: Institute of the Motor Industry v Customs and Excise Comrs [1998] ECR I-7053, [1998] STC 1219, ECJ 68:25
C-212/97: Centros Ltd v Erhvervs-Og Selskabsstyrelsen [2000] Ch 446, [2000] All ER (EC) 481, [1999] ECR I-1459, [1999] 2 CMLR 551, [2000] 2 BCLC 68, ECJ ... 1:12, 1:13
C-216/97: Gregg v Customs and Excise Comrs [1999] All ER (EC) 775, [1999] ECR I-4947, [1999] 3 CMLR 343, [1999] STC 934, ECJ 68:23
C-224/97: Ciola v Land Vorarlberg [1999] ECR I-2517, [1999] 2 CMLR 1220, ECJ 1:06
C-307/97: Compagnie de Saint-Gobain v Finanzamt Aachen-Innenstadt [2000] STC 854, [1999] ECR I-6161, [2001] 3 CMLR 708, ECJ 1:07, 1:10; 25:45
C-311/97: Royal Bank of Scotland v Greece [2000] STC 733, [1999] ECR I-2651, [1999] 2 CMLR 973, ECJ 1:04, 1:06
C-359/97: EC Commission v United Kingdom [2000] 3 CMLR 919, [2000] STC 777, ECJ 63:17, 68:11
C-391/97: Gschwind v Finanzamt Aachen-Aussenstadt [1999] ECR I-5451, [2001] 1 CMLR 36, [2001] STC 331, ECJ 1:09, 1:12
C-35/98: Staatssecretaris van Financiën v BGM Verkooijen [2000] ECR I-4071, [2002] 1 CMLR 1379, [2002] STC 654, ECJ 1:07, 26:15
C-98/98: Customs and Excise Comrs v Midland Bank plc [2000] All ER (EC) 673, [2000] ECR I-4177, [2000] 3 CMLR 301, sub nom Midland Bank plc v Customs and Excise Comrs [2000] 1 WLR 2080, [2000] STC 501, ECJ 66:07, 66:08
C-158/98: Staatssecretaris van Financiën v Coffeeshop Siberië vof [1999] All ER (EC) 560, [1999] 2 CMLR 1239, [1999] STC 742, ECJ 63:19, 68:11
C-251/98: Baars v Inspecteur der Belastingen Particuliere/Ondernemingen Gorinchem [2000] ECR I-2787, ECJ 1:11
C-397/98: Metallgesellschaft Ltd v IRC and A-G [2001] Ch 620, [2001] All ER (EC) 496, [2001] STC 452, ECJ 1:02, 1:06, 1:12, 1:16, 1:18
C-408/98: Abbey National plc v Customs and Excise Comrs [2001] All ER (EC) 385, [2001] 1 WLR 769, [2001] STC 297, ECJ 66:08
C-409/98: Mirror Group plc v Customs and Excise Comrs [2002] QB 546, sub nom Customs and Excise Comrs v Mirror Group plc [2001] ECR I-7175, [2001] 3 CMLR 1417, [2001] STC 1453, ECJ 68:11
C-410/98: Hoechst AG v IRC and A-G [2001] Ch 620, [2001] All ER (EC) 496, [2001] STC 452, ECJ 1:02, 1:10, 1:11, 1:12, 1:16
C-415/98: Bakcsi v Finanzamt Furstenfeldbruck [2002] QB 685, [2001] ECR I-1831, [2002] 2 CMLR 1397, [2002] STC 802, ECJ 66:05
C-420/98: WN v Staatsecretaris van Financin [2000] ECR I-2847, [2001] STC 974, ECJ 1:05
C-427/98: Commission v Germany [2002] ECR I-5311, [2003] STC 301 .... 63:20
C-446/98: Fazenda Pública v Càmara Municipal do Porto (Ministério Público, third party) [2001] STC 560, [2000] ECR I-11435, ECJ 63:17
C-478/98: EC Commission v Belgium [2000] ECR I-7587, [2000] 3 CMLR 1111, [2000] STC 830, ECJ 1:11
C-34/99: Customs and Excise Comrs v Primback Ltd [2001] All ER (EC) 714, [2001] ECR I-3833, [2001] 2 CMLR 1032, [2001] STC 803, sub nom Primback Ltd v Customs and Excise Comrs [2001] 1 WLR 1693, ECJ 63:20, 63:23
C-86/99: Freemans plc v Customs and Excise Comrs [2001] ECR I-4167, [2001] 1 WLR 1713, [2001] 2 CMLR 1166, [2001] STC 960, ECJ 65:17

Table of Cases

C-87/99: Zurstrassen v Administration des Contributions Directes [2000] ECR I-3337, [2001] 3 CMLR 1715, [2001] STC 1102, ECJ 1:09
C-108/99: Cantor Fitzgerald International v Customs and Excise Comrs [2002] QB 546, sub nom Customs and Excise Comrs v Cantor Fitzgerald International [2001] ECR I-7257, [2001] 3 CMLR 1441, [2001] STC 1453, ECJ 68:11
C-142/99: Floridienne SA v Belgium [2001] All ER (EC) 37, [2000] ECR I-9567, [2001] 1 CMLR 689, [2000] STC 1044, ECJ 63:15, 63:17
C-150/99: Sweden v Stockholm Lindöpark AB [2001] ECR I-493, [2001] 2 CMLR 319, [2001] STC 103, ECJ 63:02, 68:11
C-240/99: Re Försäkringsaktiebolaget Skandia (publ) [2001] All ER (EC) 822, [2001] 1 WLR 1617, [2001] STC 754, ECJ 68:13
C-380/99: Bertelsmann AG v Finanzamt Wiedenbrück [2001] ECR I-5163, [2001] 3 CMLR 271, [2001] STC 1153, ECJ 63:20; 65:17
C-398/99: Yorkshire Co-operatives Ltd [2003] ECR I–427, [2003] STC 301, ECJ 63:20
C-516/99: Re Schmid [2002] ECR I-4573, ECJ 1:06
C-16/00: Cibo Participations SA v Directeur régional des impôts du Nord-Pas-de-Calais [2001] ECR I-6663, [2002] 1 CMLR 688, [2002] STC 460, ECJ 63:17
C-62/00: Marks & Spencer plc v Customs and Excise Comrs [2003] QB 866, [2002] ECR I-6325, [2002] 3 CMLR 213, [2002] STC 1036, ECJ 2:16
C-108/00: Syndicat des Producteurs Indépendants (SPI) v Ministère de l'Economie des Finances et de l'Industrie [2001] All ER (EC) 564, [2001] ECR I-2361, [2001] 2 CMLR 903, [2001] STC 523, ECJ 63:30; 65:38
C-136/00: Proceedings brought by Danner [2002] ECR I-8147, [2002] 3 CMLR 823, [2002] STC 1283, ECJ 1:06
C-141/00: Ambulanter Pflegedienst Kügler GmbH v Finanzamt für Körperschaften I in Berlin [2002] ECR I-6833, [2004] 3 CMLR 1175, ECJ 68:23
C-174/00: Kennemer Golf and Country Club v Staatssecretaris van Financiën [2002] QB 1252, [2002] All ER (EC) 480, [2002] 2 CMLR 237, [2002] STC 502, ECJ 68:26
C-235/00: Customs and Excise Comrs v CSC Financial Services Ltd [2002] All ER (EC) 289, [2002] 1 CMLR 715, sub nom CSC Financial Services Ltd v Customs and Excise Comrs [2002] 1 WLR 2200, [2002] STC 57, ECJ 68:16
C-267/00: Customs and Excise Comrs v Zoological Society of London [2002] QB 1252, [2002] All ER (EC) 465, [2002] 2 CMLR 261, [2002] STC 521, ECJ 68:29
C-269/00: Seeling v Finanzamt Starnberg [2003] ECR I-4101, [2004] 2 CMLR 757, [2003] STC 805, ECJ 66:05
C-324/00: Lankhorst-Hohorst GmbH v Finanzamt Steinfurt [2002] ECR I-11779, [2003] 2 CMLR 693, [2003] STC 607, ECJ 1:010, 1.19, 25:49
C-353/00: Keeping Newcastle Warm Ltd v Customs and Excise Comrs [2002] All ER (EC) 769, [2002] 2 CMLR 1359, [2002] STC 943, ECJ 63:21
C-385/00: FWL de Groot v Staatssecretaris van Financiën [2002] ECR I-11819, ECJ 1:09
C-436/00: X and Y v Riksskatteverket [2002] ECR I–10829 .... 1:11
C-45/01: Christoph-Dornier-Stiftung fur Klinische Psychologie v Finanzamt Giessen [2003] ECR I-12911, [2004] 1 CMLR 991, [2005] STC 228, ECJ 68:23
C-58/01: Oce van Grinten NV v IRC [2003] 3 CMLR 1104, [2003] STC 1248, ECJ 26:16
C-77/01: Empresa de Desenvolvimento Mineiro SGPS SA v Fazenda Pública (Ministério Público intervening [2004] ECR I-4295, [2005] STC 65, ECJ 66:08
C-168/01: Bosal Holdings BV v Staatssecretaris van Financien [2003] All ER (EC) 959, [2003] 3 CMLR 674, [2003] STC 1483, ECJ 1:10
C-185/01: Auto Lease Holland BV v Bundesamt für Finanzen [2003] ECR I-1317, [2005] STC 598, ECJ 63:25
C-186/01: Bosal Holding BV v Staatssecrataris van Financien [2003] STC 1483 . 1:10, 1:12
C-212/01: Unterpertinger Pensionsversicherungsanstalt der Arbeiter [2005] STC 650, ECJ 68:23
C-234/01: Gerritse v Finanzamt Neukölln-Nord [2003] ECR I-5933, ECJ 1:07, 1:10
C-307/01: D'Ambrumenil v Customs and Excise Comrs [2004] QB 1179, [2003] ECR I-13989, [2004] 2 CMLR 396, [2005] STC 650, ECJ 68:23
C-364/01: Heirs of Barbier v Inspecteur van de Belastingdienst Particulieren/Ondernemingen buitenland te Heerlen [2004] 1 CMLR 1283, ECJ . 1:10, 1:11

Table of Cases

C-422/01: Försäkringsaktiebolaget Skandia (publ) v Riksskatteverket [2003] All ER (EC) 831, [2003] ECR I-6817, [2003] STC 1361, ECJ 1:10
C-438/01: Design Concept SA v Flanders Expo SA [2003] ECR I-5617, [2003] STC 912, ECJ 63:30
C-442/01: KapHag Renditefonds 35 Spreecenter Berlin-Hellersdorf 3 Tranche GbR v Finanzamt Charlottenburg [2003] ECR I-6851, [2003] All ER (D) 362 (Jun), ECJ ... 63:19
C-487/01 and C-7/02: Gemeente Leusden and Holin Groep BV v Staatssecretaris van Financien [2004] ECR I-5337, [2004] All ER (D) 351 (Apr), [2004] SWTI 1199, ECJ 63:09
C-497/01: Zita Modes SARL v Administration de l'enregistrement et des domaines [2003] ECR I-14393, [2004] 2 CMLR 533, [2005] STC 1059, ECJ 63:27
C-9/02: De Lasteyrie v Ministère de l'Economie, des Finances et de l'Industrie [2004] ECR I-2409, [2004] 3 CMLR 847, ECJ 1:10
C-42/02: Lindman, Re [2004] 1 CMLR 1220, ECJ 1:06
C-78/02 to C-80/02: Dimosio v Karageorgou [2003] ECR I-13295, [2003] All ER (D) 87 (Nov), [2003] SWTI 1937, ECJ 63:17
C-90/02: Finanzamt Gummersbach v Bockemühl [2004] ECR I-3303, [2005] STC 934, ECJ 66:22
C-137/02: Finanzamt Offenbach am Main-Land v Faxworld Vorgründungsgesellschaft Peter Hünninghausen und Wolfgang Klein GbR [2004] ECR I-5547, [2004] 2 CMLR 637, [2005] STC 1192, ECJ 66:08
C-152/02: Terra Baubedarf-Handel GmbH v Finanzamt Osterholz-Scharmbeck [2004] ECR I-5583, [2004] 3 CMLR 1021, [2005] STC 525, ECJ 66:22
C-255/02: Halifax plc v Customs and Excise Comrs [2006] ECR I-1609, [2006] STC 919, ECJ 1:12, 63:09, 63:15, 63:19, 66:06, 66:22, 66:33
C-315/02: Lenz v Finanzlandesdirektion für Tirol; [2004] ECR I-7063 .... 1:18
C-319/02: Manninen, Re [2005] Ch 236, [2005] All ER (EC) 465, [2005] 2 WLR 670, [2004] 3 CMLR 881, [2004] STC 1444, ECJ 1:11
C-319/02: Marks & Spencer plc v Halsey (unreported), ECJ 1:03, 1:07, 1:11
C-320/02: Förvaltnings AB Stenholmen v Riksskatteverket [2004] All ER (EC) 870, [2004] ECR I-3509, [2004] 2 CMLR 1307, [2004] STC 1041, ECJ 65:23
C-321/02: Finanzamt Rendsburg v Detlev Harbs [2004] ECR I-7101, [2006] STC 340, [2004] All ER (D) 262 (Jul), ECJ 63:44
C-376/02: Stichting 'Goed Wonen' v Staatssecretaris van Financien [2005] ECR I-3445 890, [2005] STC 833, ECJ 63:03
C-378/02: Waterschap Zeeuws Vlaanderen v Staatssecretaris van Financiën [2005] STC 1298, ECJ 66:05
C-419/02: BUPA Hospitals Ltd v Customs and Excise Comrs [2006] ECR I-1685, [2006] Ch 446, [2006] 2 WLR 964, [2006] STC 967, [2006] All ER (D) 278 (Feb), ECJ 1:13, 63:15, 65:12
C-428/02: Fonden Marselisborg Lystbadehavn v Skatteministeriet [2005] ECR I-1525, [2005] SWTI 360, [2005] All ER (D) 63 (Mar), ECJ 68:12
C-442/02: Caixa-Bank v Ministère de l'Économie, des Finances et de l'Industrie [2004] ECR I-8961 .... 1:07
C-453/02: Finanzamt Gladbeck v Linneweber [2008] STC 1069, [2005] All ER (D) 254 (Feb), ECJ 68:15
C-462/02: Finanzamt Herne-West v Akritidis [2008] STC 1069, [2005] All ER (D) 254 (Feb), ECJ 68:15
C-8/03: Banque Bruxelles Lambert SA v Belgium [2004] STC 1643, ECJ 63:16
C-25/03: Finanzamt Bergisch Gladbach v HE [2005] SWTI 864, [2005] All ER (D) 304 (Apr), ECJ 66:05
C-32/03: Fini H I/S v Skatteministeriet [2005] STC 903, [2005] All ER (D) 62 (Mar), ECJ 66:40
C-68/03: Staatssecretaris van Financien v Lipjes [2004] 2 CMLR 1016, [2004] STC 1592, ECJ 63:30
C-152/03: Ritter v Finanzamt Gemersheim, Van Raad 1:11
C-223/03: University of Huddersfield Higher Education Corpn v Customs and Excise Comrs [2006] STC 980, ECJ 1:12, 1.13, 63:15, 63:19
C-242/03: Ministre des Finances v Weidert [2004] 3 CMLR 374, [2005] STC 1241, [2004] SWTI 1657, [2004] All ER (D) 281 (Jul), ECJ 1:11
C-253/03: CLT-UFA SA v Finanzamt. Köln-West [2007] STC 1303 .... 1:10

Table of Cases

C-284/03: Belgium v Temco Europe SA [2004] ECR I-11237, [2004] STC 1451, ECJ 68:11

C-291/03: MyTravel plc v Customs & Excise Comrs [2005] STC 1617, [2005] SWTI 1679, [2005] All ER (D) 53 (Oct), ECJ 65:25

C-354/03, C-355/03 and C-484/03: Optigen Ltd v Customs and Excise Comrs [2006] ECR I-483, [2006] STC 419, ECJ 63:15, 66:06, 66:22, 66:34

C-376/03: D v Inspecteur van de Belastingdiest/Particulieren/Ondernemingen buitenland te Heerlen [2005] SWTI 1233, [2005] STC 1211, [2005] All ER (D) 41 (Jul), ECJ 1:07, 1:11

C-403/03: Schemp v Finanzamt Munchen V [2005] STC 1792, [2005] SWTI 1255, [2005] All ER (D) 147 (Jul), ECJ 1:09

C-412/03: Hotel Scandic Gasaback AB v Riksskatteverket [2005] ECR I-743, [2005] STC 1311, ECJ 63:21

C-434/03: Charles v Staatsssecretaris van Financien [2005] SWTI 1258, [2005] All ER (D) 200 (Jul), ECJ 66:05

C-435/03: British American Tobacco International Ltd v Belguim [2005] ECR I-7077, [2006] STC 158, [2005] SWTI 1256, [2005] All ER (D) 225 (Jul), ECJ 63:19, 63:25

C-446/03: Marks & Spencer plc v Halsey (Inspector of Taxes) [2006] Ch 184, [2006] All ER (EC) 255, [2006] 2 WLR 250, [2006] STC 237, (2005) Times, 15 December, [2005] All ER (D) 174 (Dec), ECJ 1:12, 1:14, 28:01, 28:08

C-452/03: RAL (Channel Islands) Ltd v Customs and Excise Comrs [2005] ECR I-3947, [2005] STC 1025, ECJ 63:30

C-465/03: Kretztechnik AG v Finanzamt Linz [2005] ECR I-4357, [2005] STC 1118, ECJ 63:19, 66:08, 68:16

C-472/03: Staatssecretaris van Financien v Arthur Andersen & Co Accountants [2005] ECR I-1719, [2005] STC 508, ECJ 68:13

C-475/03: Banca popolare di Cremona Soc Coop arl v Agenzia Entrate Ufficio Cremona [2007] 1 CMLR 863, [2006] All ER (D) 19 (Oct), ECJ 1:06

C-498/03: Kingscrest Associates Ltd v Customs and Excise Comrs [2005] ECR I-4427, [2005] STC 1547, [2005] All ER (D) 404 (May), ECJ 68:23

C-513/03: van Hilten-van der Heijden v Inspecteur van de Belastingdienst/Particulieren/Ondernemingen buitenland te Heerlen [2006] SWTI 535, [2006] All ER (D) 349 (Feb), ECJ 1:11

C-533/03: European Commission v EU Council [2006] SWTI 234, [2006] All ER (D) 199 (Jan), ECJ 1:04

C-536/03: Antonio Jorge Lda v Fazenda Publica [2005] SWTI 1017, [2005] All ER (D) 426 (May), ECJ 66:08

C-41/04: Levob Verzekeringen BV, OB Bank NV cs v Staatssecretaris van Financien ECR I-9433, [2006] STC 766, [2005] SWTI 1777, [2005] All ER (D) 328 (Oct), ECJ 63:20, 63:30; 65:38

C-43/04: Finanzamt Arnsberg v Stadt Sundern [2005] ECR I-4491, ECJ 63:44

C-58/04: Kohler v Finanzamt Dusseldorf-Nord [2006] STC 469, [2005] All ER (D) 82 (Sep), ECJ 63:30

C-63/04: Centralan Property Ltd v Customs and Excise Comrs [2006] SWTI 158, [2006] 03 EG 120 (CS), [2005] All ER (D) 238 (Dec), ECJ 66:27

C-169/04: Abbey National plc v Customs and Excise Comrs [2006] ECR I-4027, [2006] STC 1136, (2006) Times, 6 June, [2006] SWTI 1493, [2006] All ER (D) 44 (May), ECJ 68:16

C-184/04: Uudenkaupungin kaupunki, Re [2006] ECR I-3039, [2006] SWTI 1145, [2006] All ER (D) 447 (Mar), ECJ 66:28

C-196/04: Cadbury Schweppes plc and Cadbury Schweppes Overseas Ltd v IRC [2004] 3 CMLR 325, [2004] SWTI 1496, SCD 1:06, 1:07, 1:10, 1:15, 1:19

C-196/04: Cadbury Schweppes plc v Revenue and Customs Comrs [2007] Ch 30, [2007] All ER (EC) 153, [2006] STC 1908, [2006] 3 WLR 890, [2007] 1 CMLR 43, [2006] SWTI 2201, (2006) Times, 20 September, [2006] All ER (D) 48 (Sep), ECJ 1:13, 1:15, 1:19, 35:65, 35:66

C-245/04: EMAG Handel Eder OHG v Finanzlandesdirektion fur Karnten [2006] ECR I-3227, [2006] SWTI 1267, [2006] All ER (D) 85 (Apr), ECJ 63:38

C-284/04: T-Mobile v Austria [2007] All ER (D) 308 (Jun), ECJ, [2007] ECR I–5189, [2008] STC 184, ECJ 63:17

2615

Table of Cases

C-292/04: Meilicke v Finanzamt Bonn-Innenstadt [2007] ECR I-1835, [2007] 2 CMLR 469, [2008] STC 2267, 9 ITLR 834, [2007] SWTI 484, [2007] All ER (D) 75 (Mar) 1:18
C-341/04: Eurofood IFSC Ltd, Re [2006] All ER (EC) 1078, [2006] 3 WLR 309, [2006] All ER (D) 20 (May), ECJ 1:15
C-347/04: Rewe Zentralfinanz eG v Finanzamt Koln-Mitte [2007] ECR I-2647, [2007] 2 CMLR 1111, [2008] STC 2785, [2007] SWTI 1169, [2007] All ER (D) 497 (Mar) 1:14
C-369/04: Hutchison 3G UK Ltd v Revenue and Customs Comrs [2007] SWTI 1764, (2007) Times, 3 July, [2007] All ER (D) 305 (Jun), ECJ, [2007] ECR I-5247, [2008] STC 218 .... 63:17
C-374/04: Test Claimants in Class IV of the ACT Group Litigation v IRC [2007] All ER (EC) 351, [2007] 1 CMLR 1111, [2007] STC 404, [2006] SWTI 2748, [2006] All ER (D) 157 (Dec), ECJ 1:16, 1:17
C-384/04: Customs and Excise Comrs v Federation of Technological Industries [2006] ECR I-4191, [2006] 3 CMLR 337, [2006] STC 1483, (2006) Times, 29 May, [2006] SWTI 1514, [2006] All ER (D) 159 (May), ECJ 67:09, 67:10
C-394/04 and C-395/04: Diagnostiko & Therapeftiko Kentro Athinon-Ygeia AE v Ipourgos Ikonomikon [2005] STC 1349, [2005] All ER (D) 09 (Dec), ECJ 68:23
C-415/04: Staatssecretaris van Financien v Stichting Kinderopvang Enschede ECR I-1365, [2007] STC 294, [2006] SWTI 385, [2006] All ER (D) 130 (Feb), ECJ 68:23
C-429/04: Lasertec v Finanz amt Emmingem 1:19
C-439/04: Axel Kittel v Belgian State [2006] ECR I-6161, [2008] STC 1537, ECJ ... 66:34
C-439/04: Kittel v Belgian State [2006] ECR I-6161, [2006] SWTI 1851, ECJ . 63:09, 66:06
C-440/04: Belgian State v Recolta Recycling SPRL [2006] ECR I-6161, [2006] SWTI 1851, [2008] STC 1537, ECJ 63:09, 66:06, 66:34
C-446/04: Test Claimants in the FII Group Litigation v IRC [2008] EWHC 2893 (Ch), [2007] 1 CMLR 1021, [2007] STC 326, [2006] SWTI 2750, [2006] All ER (D) 168 (Dec), ECJ 1:11, 1:12, 1:18, 26:15
C-452/04: Fidium Finanz AG v Bundesanstalt Fur Finanzdienstleistungsaufsicht [2006] ECR I-9521, [2007] All ER (EC) 239, [2007] 1 CMLR 489 .... 1:11
C-491/04: Dolland & Aitchison Ltd v Revenue and Customs Comrs [2006] ECR I-2129, [2006] SWTI 531, [2006] All ER (D) 327 (Feb), ECJ 65:52
C-513/04: Kerckhaert, Morres v. Beligische Staat 1:18
C-520/04: Turpeinen (Civil proceedings concerning) [2006] ECR I-10685, [2008] All ER (EC) 725, [2007] 1 CMLR 783, [2008] STC 1, [2006] SWTI 2458, [2006] All ER (D) 106 (Nov) 1:02
C-35/05: Reemtsma Cigarettenfabriken GmbH v Finance Minister [2007] 2 CMLR 874, [2007] SWTI 543, [2007] All ER (D) 266 (Mar), ECJ 66:37
C-72/05: Hausgemeinschaft Jorg und Stefanie Wollny v Finansamt Landshut [2006] ECR I-8297, [2006] SWTI 2205, [2006] All ER (D) 77 (Sep), ECJ 65:29
C-76/05; Schwarz v Finanzamt Bergisch Gladbach [2007] ECR I-6957, [2008] All ER (EC) 556, [2007] 3 CMLR 1283, [2008] STC 1357, (2007) Times, 11 October, [2007] SWTI 2188, [2007] All ER (D) 52 (Sep) 1.03
C-89/05: United Utilities plc v Customs and Excise Comrs [2006] ECR I-6813, [2006] STC 1423, ECJ 68:16
C-101/05: Skatteverket v A [2008] All ER (EC) 638, [2009] 1 CMLR 975, [2009] STC 405, [2008] SWTI 991:11
C-106/05: LuP GmbH v Finanzamt Bochum-Mitte [2006] ECR I-5123, [2006] SWTI 1620, [2006] All ER (D) 40 (Jun), ECJ 68:23
C-111/05: Aktiebolaget NN v Skatteverket [2007] ECR I-2697, [2008] STC 3203, [2007] All ER (D) 478 (Mar), ECJ 63:08, 63:20, 63:28
C-114/05: Ministre de l'Economie, des Finances dt de l'Industrie v Gillian Beach Ltd [2006] STC 1080, ECJ 63:30
C-146/05: Albert Collée v Finanzamt Limburg an der Lahn [2007] ECR I-7861, [2008] STC 757, ECJ 69:07
C-166/05: Heger Rudi GmbH v Finanzamt Graz-Stadt [2006] ECR I-7749, [2006] SWTI 2182, [2006] All ER (D) 24 (Sep), ECJ 63:30
C-170/05: Denkavit Internationaal BV v Ministre de l'Economie, des Finances et de l'Industrie [2007] STC 452, [2007] 1 CMLR 1235, [2007] SWTI 109, [2006] All ER (D) 222 (Dec), ECJ 1:17

Table of Cases

C-184/05: Twoh International BV v Staatssecrataris van Financiën [2007] ECR I–7897, [2008] STC 740, ECJ 69:07
C-203/05: Vodafone 2 v Her Majesty's Revenue and Customs 1:15
C-228/05: Stradasfalti Sri v Agenzia delle Entrate – Ufficio di Trento [2007] STC 508, [2006] All ER (D) 68 (Sep), ECJ 63:01
C-231/05: Oy AA, Proceedings brought by [2007] ECR I-6373, [2007] All ER (EC) 1079, [2009] 3 CMLR 1, [2008] STC 991, [2007] SWTI 1863, [2007] All ER (D) 283 (Jul) 1.14
C-251/05: Talacre Beach Caravan Sales Ltd v Customs and Excise Comrs [2006] ECR I-6269, [2006] 3 CMLR 919, [2006] STC 1671, [2006] SWTI 1855, [2006] All ER (D) 66 (Jul), ECJ 63:20, 69:31
C-277/05: Société Thermale d'Eugénie-les-Bains v Ministere de l'Economie, des Finances et de l'Industrie [2007] ECR I–6415, [2007] SWTI 1866, ECJ 63:19
C-298/05: Columbus Container Services BVBA & Co v Finanzamt Bielefeld-Innenstadt [2007] ECR I-10451, [2009] 1 CMLR 241, [2008] STC 2554, [2007] SWTI 2846, [2007] All ER (D) 80 (Dec) 1:12, 1:15
C-318/05: European Commission v Germany [2007] ECR I-6957, [2008] All ER (EC) 556, [2007] 3 CMLR 1283, [2008] STC 1357, (2007) Times, 11 October, [2007] SWTI 2188, [2007] All ER (D) 52 (Sep) 1:03
C-363/05: JP Morgan Fleming Claverhouse Investment Trust plc v Revenue and Customs Comrs [2007] ECR I–5517, [2008] STC 1180, [2007] All ER (D) 368 (Jun), ECJ 68:16
C-379/05: Amurta v Inspecteur van de Belastingdienst [2008] STC 2851 ... 1:14, 1:17, 1:18
C-383/05: Talotta v Belgium [2007] 2 CMLR 931, [2008] STC 3261, [2007] SWTI 1053, [2007] All ER (D) 364 (Mar) 1:06
C-434/05: Stichting Regionaal Opleidingen Centrum Noord-Kennemerland/West Friesland (Horizon College) v Staatssecretaris van Financien [2007] ECR I–4793, [2008] STC 2145, [2007] All ER (D) 132 (Jun), ECJ 68:17
C-435/05: Investrand BV v Staatssecretaris van Financien [2007] SWTI 340, [2007] All ER (D) 113 (Feb), ECJ 66:08
C-445/05: Haderer v Finanzamt Wilmersdorf [2007] ECR I–4841, [2008] STC 2171, [2007] All ER (D) 141 (Jun), ECJ 68:19
C-451/05: Européenne et Luxembourgeoise d'investissements SA (ELISA) v Directeur general des Impôts and Another 1:11
C-453/05: Ludwig v Finanzamt Luckenwalde [2007] ECR I–5083, [2008] STC 1640, [2007] All ER (D) 237 (Jun), ECJ 68:16
C-13/06: European Commission v Hellenic Republic [2006] ECR I-11563, [2007] STC 194, [2006] SWTI 2747, ECJ 68:13
C-97/06: Navicon SA v Administración del Estado [2007] ECR I–8755, [2007] SWTI 2405, ECJ 69:26
C-104/06: European Commission v Kingdom of Sweden [2007] ECR I-671, [2007] 2 CMLR 153, [2008] STC 2546, [2007] SWTI 194 .... 1.20
C-271/06: Netto Supermarkt GmbH & Co OHG v Finanzamt Malchin [2008] SWTI 315, ECJ 69:08
C-309/06: Marks & Spencer plc v Customs and Excise Comrs [2008] STC 1408, ECJ 69:12
C-355/06: J A Van der Steen v Inspecteur van de Belastingdienst Utrecht-Gooi/ kantoor Utrecht [2007] ECR I–8863, [2007] SWTI 2406, ECJ 63:12
C-401/06: EC Commission v Germany [2007] SWTI 2848, ECJ 63:30; 65:38
C-414/06: Lidl Belgium GmbH & Co KG v Finanzamt Heilbronn [2008] 3 CMLR 31, [2008] STC 3229, [2008] All ER (D) 187 (May) 1.14
C-425/06: Ministero dell'Econimia e delle Finanze v Part Service Srl (in liquidation) [2008] ECR 1–897, [2008] STC 3132, ECJ 63:09
C-451/06: Gabriele Walderdorff v Finanzamt Waldviertel [2007] ECR I–10637, [2008] STC 3079, ECJ 68:11, 68:12
C-484/06: Fiscale eenheid Koninklijke Ahold NV v Staatsecretaris van Financien [2008] SWTI 1713 .... 65:20
C-95/07 and C-96/07 (Joined cases): Ecotrade SpA v Agenzia Entrate Ufficio Genoa 3 [2008] SWTI 1327, ECJ 66:03
C-98/07: Nordania Finas A/S and another v Skatteministeriet [2008] SWTI 433, ECJ 66:08

Table of Cases

C-105/07: Lammers v Van Cleeff 1:19
C-124/07: JCM Beheer BV v Staatssecrataris van Financiën [2008] SWTI 1144, ECJ 68:13
C-157/07: Finanzamt fur Korperschaften III in Berlin v Krankenheim Ruhesitz am Wannsee-Seniorenheimstatt GmbH [2009] All ER (EC) 513, [2009] STC 138, [2008] All ER (D) 255 (Oct) 1:14
C-162/07: Ampliscientifica Srl and another v Ministero dell'Economia e delle Finanze, Agenzia delle Entrade [2008] ECR I–4109, [2008] SWTI 1387, ECJ 63:09
C-253/07: Canterbury Hockey Club and another v Revenue and Customs Comrs [2008] ECR I–0000, [2008] STC 3351, ECJ 68:26
C-288/07: Revenue and Customs Comrs v Isle of Wight Borough Council [2008] ECR I–0000, [2008] STC 2964, [2009] STC 1096, ECJ 63:17
C-291/07: Kollektivavtalsstifttelsen TRR Trygghetsrådet v Skatteverket [2008] ECR I–0000, [2009] STC 526, ECJ 63:30
C-302/07: JD Wetherspoon plc v Revenue & Customs Comrs [2009] ECR I–0000, [2009] STC 1022, ECJ 65:20
C-357/07: R (on the application of TNT Post UK Ltd) v Customs and Excise Comrs [2009] ECR I–0000, [2009] STC 1464, ECJ 68:14
C-371/07: Danfoss A/S and another v Skatteministeriet [2008] ECR I–0000, [2009] STC 701, ECJ 65:32, 65:33
C-460/07: Sandra Puffer v Unabhängiger Finanzsenat, Außenstelle Linz [2009] ECR I–0000, [2009] STC 1693, ECJ 66:05
C-488/07: Royal Bank of Scotland plc v HMRC [2008] ECR I–0000, [2009] STC 461, ECJ 66:09
C-515/07: Vereniging Noordelijke Land- en Tuinbouw Organisatie v Staatssecretaris van Financiën [2009] ECR I–0000, [2009] STC 935, ECJ 65:32
C-554/07: EC Commission v Ireland [2009] ECR I–0000 .... 63:15
C-572/07: RLRE Tellmer Property sro v Finanèní v Ústí nad Labem [2009] ECR I–0000, [2009] SWTI 1886, ECJ 63:20
C-102/08: Finanzamt Düsseldorf-Süd v SALIX Grundstücks-Vermietungsgellschaft mbH & Co Objekt Offenbach KG [2009] ECR I–0000, [2009] STC 1607, ECJ 63:17

Table of Statutes

Bill of Rights 1689
   art 4 .... 2A:70
Stamp Duty Act 1694
   .... 2A:01; 56:01
Property and Income Tax Act 1797
   .... 5:04
Accumulation Act 1800 (Thellusson Act)
   .... 13:15
Finance Act 1803 .... 5:03
Income Tax Act 1842
   .... 5:03; 10:06
Leasehold Conversion Act 1849
   s 1 .... 42:10
   37 .... 42:10
Succession Duty Act 1857
   .... 1:28
Crown Private Estates Act 1862
   .... 5:18
Consecration of Churchyards Act 1867
   s 6 .... 56:35
Employers' Liability Act 1880
   .... 9:26
Customs and Inland Revenue Act 1881
   s 38 (2) 41:02
Summary Jurisdiction (Process) Act 1881
   .... 63:03
Bills of Exchange Act 1882
   .... 1:28
Customs and Inland Revenue Act 1889
   s 11 .... 41:02
Inland Revenue Regulation Act 1890
   .... 1:30, 56:07
   s 1 .... 2:01
   13 .... 2:01
   39 .... 2:01
Partnership Act 1890
   .... 1:28; 8:70; 10:09; 62:27
   s 1 (1) 6:02
   24 (1) 22:39
Stamp Act 1891 .... 56:01
   s 1 .... 56:02, 56:07, 56:09
   2 .... 59:19
   3 (2) 56:14
   4 .... 56:06, 56:15
      (b) 56:16
   5 . 2A:95; 56:19, 56:20, 56:21, 56:32; 57:15
   6 .... 57:08
   11 .... 56:23
   12 .... 2A:28; 60:16
      (2) 56:19, 56:21
      (6) 56:21

Stamp Act 1891 – *cont.*
   s   (b) 56:22
   12a 2A:28
      a (2) 56:21, 56:30
   13 .... 56:26
      (4) 2A:95; 56:30
   13a 2A:95; 56:07, 56:26, 56:30
   14 (1) 56:29
      (4) 56:08, 56:29
   15 .... 56:30; 62:25
      (1) 56:11
      (2) (a) 2A:39; 56:30
      (3) 2A:39; 56:30
   15a (1) (b) 56:23
      a (2) 2A:39; 56:30
      b (4), (5) 2A:95; 56:30
   17 .... 2A:95; 56:29, 56:32, 56:33; 59:04
   41 .... 56:09; 57:34
   54 .... 57:05
   55 . 57:07; 58:10; 59:02, 59:04, 59:14
   56 .... 57:10, 57:29
   57 .... 56:05; 57:07, 57:11
   58 (1), (2) 57:12
      (3) 56:17; 57:12
      (4) 57.13, 57:22; 62:30
      (5) 57:13
   59 .... 59:14
      (3) 56:23
   60 .... 57:13
   61 .... 57:12
   72 .... 56:23
   73 .... 57:19
   77 .... 56:15
      (1), (2) 57:28
      (5) 57:28, 57:35
   117 .... 56:33
   122 .... 56:11; 57:05
      (1) 56:09; 61:14
   Sch 1 .... 56:04, 56:05; 57:19
Stamp Duties Management Act 1891
   .... 56:01, 56:07
   s 2 (1) 56:31
   9 .... 56:27
      (7) 56:10
   10 .... 56:27
   12a 56:28
   27 .... 56:11
Sale of Goods Act 1893
   s 8 .... 8:153
Finance Act 1894
   s 3 (1) 22:44

Table of Statutes

Finance Act 1894 – *cont.*
  s 5 (2) 42:25
    6 (5) 45:19
    7 (3) 45:02
Finance Act 1895
  s 12 .... 56:35; 57:05
Finance Act 1898
  s 6 .... 57:05, 57:07
Finance Act 1900
  s 10 .... 57:28; 58:03
Limited Partnerships Act 1907
  .... 59:18; 62:27
National Insurance Act 1907
  .... 2A:01; 48:05
Finance Act 1909 .... 1:32
  s 8 .... 57:28
Finance Act 1910 .... 1:32
Finance Act 1911 .... 1:32
Official Secrets Act 1911
  s 2 .... 2:06
Parliament Act 1911
  s 1 .... 1:01
Finance Act 1914
  s 5 .... 37:02
Finance (No 2) Act 1915
  .... 33:27
  s 39 (c) 29:15
    47 .... 47:08
Income Tax Act 1918
  .... 1:23; 11:36; 35:10
  Sch 1
    r 7 .... 33:27
Finance Act 1920
  s 30 (1) (c) 13:23
War Pensions Act 1920
  s 10 .... 56:36
Finance Act 1921 .... 32:08
Finance Act 1923
  s 24(2) 2A:69
Administration of Estates Act 1925
  s 1 .... 39:15
    22 (1) 46:14
    34 (3) 46:15
    36 .... 58:13
    46 .... 13:06
    47 (1) 13:06
    47a 42:22
  Sch 1
  Pt II
    para 8 .... 46:15
Land Registration Act 1925
  s 14 (3) 56:33
    130 .... 56:35
Law of Property Act 1925
  s 52 .... 18:05
    (1) 56:09
    53 (1) (b) 56:09
       (c) 56:09; 58:10

Law of Property Act 1925 – *cont.*
  s 72 (3), (4) 57:25
    149 .... 10:18; 20:19
      (3) 57:27
      (6) 42:10
    205 .... 62:03
Settled Land Act 1925
  .... 20:05; 42:09, 42:10
Trustee Act 1925
  s 31 .... 13:11, 13:18; 18:40; 42:49
    (1) (ii) 42:07; 42:51
    (2) 42:51
    32 .... 2A:71
    33 .... 42:57
    40 .... 56:09
Agricultural Credits Act 1928
  s 8 .... 56:35
Finance Act 1930
  s 42 .... 56:21, 56:35; 57:25, 57:29;
                                  59:20; 60:04
    (1) 60:01
    (2) 60:01; 62:16
      (a) 60:03
    (2a), (2b) 60:02
    (3)–(6) 60:02
Finance Act 1931
  s 22 .... 47:08
    28 .... 56:24; 57:30
  Sch 2 .... 56:24
Finance Act 1933
  s 31 .... 8:40
Foreign Judgments (Reciprocal
    Enforcement) Act 1933
  s 1 (2) (b) 34:02
Law Reform (Miscellaneous Provisions)
    Act 1934
  s 3 .... 11:06
Government of India Act 1935
  s 273 .... 40:08
Finance Act 1936 .... 15:02
  s 21 .... 15:30
Housing Act 1936
  s 75 .... 23:07
Finance Act 1937
  s 12 .... 4:10
Finance Act 1938
  s 24 .... 4:11
    50 (1) (a), (b) 60:04
  Sch 4
  Pt I (ss 1–6) 60:02
Emergency Powers (Defence) Act 1939
  s 1 (3) 1:01
    2 .... 1:01
Finance Act 1939
  s 30 (3) 39:04
    31 .... 45:23
Finance (No 2) Act 1939
  s 12 .... 8:40

2620

Table of Statutes

Finance Act 1940
  s 13–18 .... 5:06
Finance Act 1941
  s 35 .... 4:05
Disabled Persons (Employment) Act 1944
  .... 50:03
Finance (No 2) Act 1945
  s 29 .... 8:40
  54 .... 47:18
Income Tax Act 1945
  .... 9:01
Finance Act 1946 .... 8:40
  s 50 .... 17:15; 56:36
  51 .... 17:15
  52 .... 56:35
  54 (1) 59:14
  57 (1) 59:14
National Insurance Act 1946
  .... 2A:01
Crown Proceedings Act 1947
  s 13–15 .... 2:37; 67:04
Finance Act 1947
  s 19 .... 32:10
  57 .... 56:35
Companies Act 1948
  s 55 .... 61:11
  209 .... 57:07
Finance Act 1948 .... 7:100
Landlord and Tenant (Rent Control) Act 1949 .... 10:17
Lands Tribunal Act 1949
  s 1 (5) 56:26
Employment and Training Act (Northern Ireland) 1950
  s 1a 68:21
Finance Act 1950
  s 16 .... 7:29
  34 (4) (a) 7:29
  36 .... 37:06
Income Tax Act 1952
  .... 1:23
Landlord and Tenant Act 1954
  .... 18:03; 23:21
Finance Act 1956
  s 10 .... 7:01
Finance Act 1957
  s 38 .... 41:13
Finance Act 1958
  s 35 (1) 57:28
Variation of Trusts Act 1958
  .... 15:08; 39:15; 44:32; 56:21
Finance Act 1960
  s 28 .... 62:16
  32 .... 5:14
  74 .... 56:36
Land Compensation Act 1961
  s 31 (3) 8:81

Finance Act 1962
  s 30 (1) 59:14
Finance Act 1963
  s 55 .... 57:02, 57:03
  59 .... 57:33; 59:08
  60 (3) 56:21
  65 (3) 56:35
  67 .... 57:13
Continental Shelf Act 1964
  s 1 (7) 54:07
Diplomatic Privileges Act 1964
  .... 38:22
  s 4 .... 5:18
Finance Act 1964
  s 23 .... 56:35
Perpetuities and Accumulations Act 1964
  s 3 (1) 15:14
  13 (1) 13:15
Finance Act 1965 .... 3:17; 16:02; 23:20; 24:13
  s 81 .... 8:40
  90 .... 56:11, 56:21; 57:07
  (3), (5) 57:17
Solicitors Act 1965
  s 8 (2) 5:24
Finance Act 1966
  s 40 .... 37:20
Cayman Islands Trust Act 1967
  s 75 (3) 35:33
Finance Act 1967
  s 27 (3) (a), (b) 60:04
General Rate Act 1967
  s 23 .... 7:50
Leasehold Reform Act 1967
  .. 23:07, 23:19, 23:21, 23:38; 44:29
Capital Allowances Act 1968
  s 73 .... 9:07
Consular Relations Act 1968
  .... 38:22
  s 8 .... 66:40
Finance Act 1968
  s 15 .... 6:01
International Organisations Act 1968
  .... 38:22
  Sch 1
    para 6, 7 .... 66:40
    12 .... 66:40
Provisional Collection of Taxes Act 1968
  .... 56:07
  s 1 .... 1:32
Theft Act 1968 .... 2:34
  s 32 (1) 2:27
    (a) 2:34
Family Law Reform Act 1969
  .... 18:40
  s 1 .... 13:18
  9 .... 7:133

Table of Statutes

Finance Act 1969
  s 31 .... 4:30
    32 .... 23:29
    Sch 16 .... 4:30
Finance Act 1970
  s 33 .... 60:12
  Sch 5 .... 32:27
Income and Corporation Taxes Act 1970
  .... 1:23
  s 30 .... 11:08
    52 (1) (a) 11:40
    122 (2) (b) 5:24
    144 .... 8:156
    516 .... 8:108
    244 .... 25:27
    258 .... 60:03
    303 (3) (c) 29:04
    403, 404 .... 31:28
    430 .... 45:19
    460 .... 62:16
    478 .... 3:21
  Sch 1
  Pt III 34:08
Taxes Management Act 1970
  .... 2:31, 2:32; 2A:95; 56:32; 61:01
  s 1 .... 1:30; 2:01; 5:03
    2 (1) 2:36
    7 (1) 2A:02; 14:10
      (8) 2A:02
    8 .... 5:14; 14:10
      (1) 2A:02, 2A:03
      (1b), (1c) 8:43
    8a 2A:02
    9 .... 14:10
      (1) 2A:48
        (a) 2A:02
      (2) 2A:03, 2A:16
      (3) 2A:16
      (4) (b) 2A:04
    9za 2A:68; 35:13
    9a 2A:03; 2A:04; 10:08, 10:69
      a (1) 2A:47, 2A:49
      a (2) 2A:47, 2A:48
      a   (a) 2A:62; 14:10
    9d 8:91
    11b (1) 2A:49
    12 .... 17:30
    12a 33:43
    12aa 2A:02; 8:43
    12aba 2A:68
    12ac 2A:03, 2A:48
      (1) 2A:49
    12b 2A:56
      b (1) (a) 2A:49
      b (2), (3) 2A:49
    19a 1:22; 2A:54, 2A:56
      (1) 2A:50
      (2) 2A:49, 2A:50
        (a) 2A:56
      (2a) 2A:49
      (3) 2A:49

Taxes Management Act 1970 – *cont.*
  s 19a (6) 2:11
    20(1) 2A:54
    20a, 20b 2:30
    23 .... 61:25
    25, 26 .... 61:25
    28a (1) 2A:51
      (4) 2A:52
      (6) 2:11; 2A:52
      (7) 2A:62
    28b 2A:51
      (4) 2A:52
      (7) 2A:52
    28c (3) 2A:85
    29 .... 2A:47
      (1) (b) 2A:63
      (2)–(4) 2A:62
      (5) 2A:48, 2A:62
      (8) 2A:62, 2:11
    31 (1) 2:11
    32 .... 2A:63, 2:11
    33 .... 2A:65, 2A:70
      (1) 2A:69
      (2A) (a), (b) 2A:69
        (c) 35:13
    34 .... 2A:48, 2A:66
    36 (1) 2A:66
      (3) 2A:66
    40 (1) 14:01
    42 .... 6:12, 6:13
      (2) 16:33
    43 .... 18:39
      (1) 6:13; 22:25
      (2) 6:13
    43a, 43b 2A:62
    44 (1) 1:28
    46 .... 1:28
    46c (1) (a) 33:15
    49(2)–(6) 2:84
    49a 2:11, 2.12
    49b 2.12
      (2) 2:11
      (5) 2:11
    49c 2.12
      (2), (3) 2:11
    49c (6) 2:11
    49d 2.12
    49e 2.12
      (5) 2:11
    49f 2:11, 2.12
    49g 2.12
      (3) 2:11
    49h 2:11, 2.12
    49i 2.12
    50 (6) 2A:62
    54 .... 2A:65
      (6) 2:21
    56d 1:29
    59 (3) (b) 2A:14
    59a (1) (c) 2A:17
      (2) 2A:17, 2A:32

Taxes Management Act 1970 – cont.
  s 59a (4), (5) 2A:17
    59b (1) 2A:14, 2A:62
        (b) 2A:17
        (3) 2A:32
        (b) 2A:14
        (4) 2A:14, 2A:32; 13:11
        (8) 2A:15
    59c (2)–(4) 2A:44
        (6) 2A:32
        (9) (a) 2A:44
    59d 2A:20
    59e 2A:21, 2A:34
    60 .... 61:31
    61 .... 61:31
        (1), (2) 2:38
    65 .... 61:31
        (1) 2:37
    66 .... 2:37; 61:31
    68 .... 2:37; 61:31
    69 .... 61:31
    71 .... 61:31
        (1) 34:06
    72 .... 13:01; 61:31
        (1) 13:02, 13:03
        (2) 13:02
    73 .... 13:02; 61:31
    74 .... 14:01; 61:31
    76 .... 13:09
    78 .... 34:02; 61:31
    79 .... 36:05
    82 (1) 35:15
    83 .... 61:31
    86 .... 6:49; 18:36; 61:31
        (2) (a), (b) 2A:32
    87 .... 2A:34
    87a 2A:34
    90 .... 61:31
        (2) 2A:06
    93 .... 2A:02, 2A:95; 61:18
        (1) (a) 2:28; 2A:90
        (b) 2A:90
    94 (6) 28:20
    95 .... 1:22; 2A:93, 2A:95; 61:18
        (1) 2A:04
        (2) 2A:90
    97 .... 2A:95, 2:27; 61:18
    97aa 1:22; 2A:90
    98 .... 2A:21; 33:36; 61:25
        (1) (i), (ii) 2A:90
        (2) 2A:90
    98a 8:26
        (3) 2A:90
        (4) 51:10
    98c 2A:05
        (1) 55:07
        (3) 55:07
    99 .... 2:30; 2A:90, 2A:95; 61:18
    100 ...... 2A:05, 2A:95; 61:18, 61:25
    100a 2:27
    101 .... 2A:95; 61:18, 61:25

Taxes Management Act 1970 – cont.
  s 102 ...... 2:07; 2A:90, 2A:91, 2A:95;
                        2:27; 61:18, 61:25
    103 .... 2:27; 2A:95; 61:18, 61:25
    103a 2A:32, 2A:90
    104 .... 2A:95; 61:18, 61:25
    105 .... 2:27; 2A:95; 61:18, 61:25
        (1) 2:28
    106 (1) 11:37
        (2) 11:42
    108 .... 61:25
        (2), (3) 25:03
    111 .... 61:25
    114 ...... 2: 53; 2A:65, 2A:90; 61:25
        (1), (2) 2A:61
    118 (1) 13:02
        (2) 2A:95; 61:18, 61:25
  Sch 1
    Pt III 34:08; 34:01
  Sch 1a 6:12
    para 5 .... 2A:49
  Sch 1b 6:12
    para 3, 4 .... 5:15; 6:49
  Sch 3
    para 4(3) 1:28
Atomic Energy Authority Act 1971
  s 22 .... 56:35
Diplomatic and other Privileges Act 1971
  .... 56:36
Finance Act 1971 .... 6:01
  s 32 (1) 5:20
    56 (1) 16:01
    59 .... 16:01
    64 .... 56:18; 57:28, 57:42
        (1) (a) (i) 57:35
  Sch 10 .... 18:11
European Communities Act 1972
  s 2 .... 1:02
    (1) 63:02
    (2) 3:03
    3 (1) 63:02
Finance Act 1972
  Pt I (ss 1–51) 63:01
  s 55 (5) 66:40
  Sch 1–5 .... 63:01
Domicile and Matrimonial Proceedings Act 1973
  s 1 .... 33:15
    (1), (2) 33:20
    3 (1) 33:20
    4 (1) 33:20
Finance Act 1973
  s 47, 48 .... 59:07
    50 .... 1:32; 56:07
  Sch 19 .... 59:07
Matrimonial Causes Act 1973
  s 16 .... 43:13
    23 (5) 18:10
    24 (3) 18:10

2623

Table of Statutes

Overseas Pensions Act 1973
  s 2 .... 40:08
Value Added Tax and Other Taxes Act 1973 .... 63:08
Consumer Credit Act 1974
  .... 27:29
  s 14 .... 7:45
Finance Act 1974
  s 18 .... 7:100
  Sch 4 .... 69:12
    11
    para 9 .... 56:04
Finance Act 1975
  s 49 (1) 42:27
    (4) 44:34
  Sch 5
    para 11 (4) 42:30
    15 (3) 42:50
  Sch 12
    para 16 (2) 45:19
Finance (No 2) Act 1975
  s 69 .... 2A:19
Inheritance (Provision for Family and Dependants) Act 1975
  .... 19:09; 40:34
  s 2 .... 19:04
    10 .... 40:20
    19 (1) 19:04, 19:05; 40:26
    (2) (c) 40:26
Social Security Act 1975
  .... 52:05
  s 4 (2) 50:09
Social Security Pensions Act 1975
  .... 48:05
  s 5 .... 53:07
Adoption Act 1976
  .... 5:18
  s 39 .... 15:21
    (1) 33:18
    (5) 33:18
Development Land Tax Act 1976
  s 13 .... 1:24
Finance Act 1976
  s 1–51 .... 2A:01
    62 (5) 7:110
    87, 88 .... 40:29
    127 .... 56:35
    131 .... 47:08
  Sch 5
    para 23 .... 25:29
Income Tax Act 1976
  s 99 .... 3:11
Finance Act 1977
  s 11 .... 1:05
    14 .... 63:01
    33 (4) 7:49
    35 (3) 7:100
    38 .... 44:32
  Sch 6 .... 63:01

Adoption (Scotland) Act 1978
  .... 5:18
Finance Act 1978
  s 23 .... 7:100
    31 .... 1:21
Interpretation Act 1978
  .... 9:28
  Sch 1 ...... 12:17; 23:01; 25:34; 63:12
Theft Act 1978 .... 2:34
Alcoholic Liquor Duties Act 1979
  .... 63:03; 65:43
  s 1 .... 50:25
Capital Gains Tax Act 1979
  .... 1:23; 16:01
  s 14 .... 35:22
    21 .... 17:03
    29a 21:28
    31 (2) 22:01
    41 .... 16:13
    45 .... 16:41
    60 .... 22:47
    68 .... 21:05
    89, 90 .... 21:13
    101 .... 23:11
    117 .... 24:12
  Sch 5
    para 2 (2) 21:09
Customs and Excise Management Act 1979
  .... 2:01, 2:31
  s 1 (1) 63:03
    37 .... 67:13
    43 (1) 67:13
    46, 47 .... 63:40
    78 .... 67:13
    139 .... 69:02
    148 .... 2:35
    152 .... 2:07, 2:34
    167 .... 2:34
    (1)–(4) 63:03
    168 .... 2:34; 63:03
    171 (4) 2:34
  Sch 3 .... 69:02
  Sch 4
    para 12 .... 66:40
Customs and Excise Duties (General Reliefs) Act 1979
  s 7 .... 63:03; 69:02, 69:11
    8 .... 69:02, 69:11
    9 (b) 69:02, 69:11
    13 .... 63:03; 69:02, 69:11
    13a 63:03
Diplomatic and Other Privileges Act 1979
  s 1 .... 66:40
European Assembly (Pay and Pensions) Act 1979
  s 3 .... 5:18
Hydrocarbon Oil Duties Act 1979
  .... 63:03; 65:43
  s 5 .... 70:04

Table of Statutes

Isle of Man Act 1979
  s 1 (1) (d) 63:08
    6 .... 63:03, 08
      (1) 1:01; 2:04
      (2) (f), (g) 2:04
    8, 9 .... 63:03
Tobacco Products Duties Act 1979
  .... 63:03; 65:43
Finance Act 1980
  s 79 .... 16:24; 24:12
    82 .... 44:32
    83 .... 22:01
    97 .... 57:25
      (2), (4) 57:32
    98 .... 56:21
    102 .... 56:21; 57:07, 57:11
Housing Act 1980
  s 56 .... 9:22
Limitation Act 1980
  s 2 .... 1:02
    9 (1) 2A:73
    29 (5) 2A:73
    32 .... 1:02; 2A:73
      (1) (c) 1:02; 2A:70
    37 (2) (a) 2A:73
Betting and Gaming Duties Act 1981
  s 26a–26m 68:15
British Nationality Act 1981
  s 51 (2) 54:11
Companies Act 1981
  s 45 .... 26:20
    46 .... 26:20
Finance Act 1981
  s 32 .... 32:04
    53 .... 31:06
    71 .... 7:45
    107 .... 57:08, 57:13
    108 .... 57:32
    111 .... 1:06
Supreme Court Act 1981
  s 35a 67:05
    116 .... 46:14
Civil Aviation Act 1982
  s 59 .... 56:35
    105 (1) 69:29, 69:30
Criminal Justice Act 1982
  s 37 .... 63:03
    38 .... 63:03
    46 .... 63:03
Finance Act 1982 .... 24:11
  s 45 .... 7:45
    86 .... 16:01
    89 .... 21:08
    92 (1), (3) 43:10
    129 .... 56:21, 56:37
  Sch 13
    para 3 .... 24:05
      5 .... 24:07
      7 .... 24:09

Finance Act 1982 – *cont.*
  Sch 13 – *cont.*
    para 9 .... 21:09
Industrial Development Act 1982
  .... 9:04
Insurance Companies Act 1982
  s 151 (1a) 60:16
  Sch 2c 60:16
Finance Act 1983
  s 34 .... 21:10
    46 .... 56:21
      (3) 56:37
  Sch 6 .... 21:10
Finance (No 2) Act 1983
  s 15 .... 56:35
Matrimonial Homes Act 1983
  .... 17:01
Mental Health Act 1983
  .... 13:05
National Heritage Act 1983
  .... 56:37
Value Added Tax Act 1983
  .... 1:04, 1:23; 63:01
  s 3 .... 8:159
    22 .... 66:41
County Courts Act 1984
  s 40 (2) 2:37
    41 (1) 2:37
    79 .... 56:35
Finance Act 1984 .... 31:19; 38:02
  s 2 (1) (c) 41:02
    6 (1) 42:27
    7 (5) 42:27; 45:16
    7 (6) 42:27
    18 .... 1:21
    48 (4) (b) 47:09
    83 (3) 35:65
    109 .... 57:02; 59:14
    110 .... 57:08, 57:13
    111 (2) 56:23; 57:30
      (3) 56:23
    112 (1) 57:13
Income Tax Conventions Interpretation Act
  1984 .... 37:33
Industrial and Development Act 1984
  .... 8:89
Inheritance Tax Act 1984
  ... 1:23; 12:17; 38:01, 38:02; 45:10
  s 1 .... 39:01; 41:11
    2 .... 39:15
      (1) 38:06, 38:11, 39:01; 41:11
      (2) 39:01
    3 .... 35:59
      (1) 1:28; 38:20, 39:06; 42:42
      (2) 1:28; 33:16; 38:21, 39:01,
                   39:12; 41:11; 47:11
      (3) 39:04, 39:08, 39:10; 42:42
      (4) 38:06; 42:15; 43:03
    3a 38:09; 42:05, 42:58; 44:27
      a (1) 39:01, 39:02; 43:06

2625

Table of Statutes

Inheritance Tax Act 1984 – *cont.*
  s 3a   (c) 42:14
    a   (b) 39:02
    a (4) 39:03
    a (5) 38:19; 39:03
    a (6) 39:02, 39:21; 42:13
    a (7) 39:02
  3b, 3c 44:27
  4 . 40:01, 40:06, 40:07, 41:11; 42:13;
                                42:49
    (1) 38:08, 38:20; 42:58; 45:10
    (2) 40:05
  5 (1) 33:16; 38:20, 38:21; 39:12;
                  40:08; 42:27, 42:58
    (2) .... 38:20, 40:02, 4);04
    (3) 45:20
    (4) 45:28
    (5) 45:21; 46:10
  6 .... 41:11; 47:11, 47:12
    (1) 33:16; 38:21; 40:08; 47:16
    (1a) 47:11
    (2) 42:47; 47:07, 47:08, 47:11
    (3) 47:07, 47:08, 47:11
  7 (1) 38:18
    (2) 38:07, 38:08; 40:15
    (4) 40:15, 40:16
    (5) 40:15
  8A 38:14
  10 .... 8:157; 39:01, 39:10, 39:15,
        39:20, 39:27, 39:28, 39:33; 42:02,
        42:15, 42:23, 42:33, 42:42; 46:10
    (1) 39:14; 43:10
  11 .... 12:20; 42:19; 43:34
    (6) 39:15
  12 .... 43:34
    (2) 39:20
    (2b) 40:35
    (2d) 40:35
  13 .... 39:20; 43:20, 43:34
  14, 15 .... 39:20; 43:34
  16 .... 39:20, 39:33
  17 .... 40:21, 40:23, 40:25
  18 . 38:14; 40:34, 41:01, 41:12; 43:06
    (1) 18:44; 39:15; 43:10, 43:11,
                              43:12
    (2) 33:16; 43:10, 43:11, 43:12
    (3) (a) 43:07
       (b) 43:08
  19 .... 12:20; 39:13
    (1) 38:09
    (2), (3) 43:01
    (3a) (a) 43:01
       a (b) 39:02; 43:01
    (5) 43:01
  20 .... 12:20; 41:01; 43:34
    (3) 43:02
  21 .... 40:11; 43:04
    (1) 43:03
       (a) 43:05
    (3) 43:03
  22 .... 41:01

Inheritance Tax Act 1984 – *cont.*
  s 22 (1) (b) 43:05
    (2), (4) 43:05
    (6) 43:05
  23 .... 40:34, 41:01; 43:14, 43:17
    (1) 43:17
    (2) (a)–(c) 43:15
    (3) 43:15
    (4) 41:13; 43:16
    (5) 43:15
    (6) 43:17
  24 .... 18:40; 40:34; 41:01; 42:44;
                        43:14, 43:18
  24a 41:01; 42:44; 43:14, 43:19
  25 .... 40:34; 42:44; 43:14
  26 .... 18:40; 40:34; 41:01; 43:19
    (2) 17:15
  26a 44:27
  27 . 18:40; 41:01; 43:20, 40:34; 44:32
  28 .... 39:20; 40:34; 41:01
    (2) 43:20
    (3) 43:05
  29a (1)–(3) 40:34
    a (4) (b) (i), (ii)
                  .... 40:34
    a (10) 40:34
  30 .... 17:16; 18:40
    (3) 44:27
    (3ba) 44:28
  31 (1) 44:28
      (b)–(e) 44:29
    (4) 44:29
    (4fa) 44:28
    (5) 44:28
  32 (4), (5) 44:28
  33 (1) (a) 44:30
      (b) (i), (ii) 44:30
    (2), (3) 44:30
    (5)–(8) 44:30
  34 (1)–(4) 44:31
  35 .... 44:27
  35a (2) (c) 44:28
  37 (1), (2) 43:30
  38 (2) 43:29
    (3) 43:27
    (4), (5) 43:28
    (6) 43:24
  39a (2)–(5) 43:33
  40 .... 43:22
  41 .... 43:31
  42 (1) 43:23, 43:24
    (2) 43:25
    (3) 43:26
    (4) 43:24
  43 (1) 42:02
    (2) 47:15
    (3) 42:10, 42:23
    (4) 42:02
    (5) 42:02, 42:10
  44 .... 15:07
    (2) 42:03, 42:04; 47:15

Inheritance Tax Act 1984 – *cont.*
s 45 .... 42:04
  46 .... 42:07
  47 .... 42:23
  47a 38:20; 39:07
  48 (1) 38:21; 42:23
    (c) 42:10
    (3) 33:16; 38:21; 42:02; 42:30:
                          47:13, 47:16
      (a) 12:22; 41:11; 42:04
    (3a) 47:13
    (4) 42:03; 47:07, 47:08, 47:13
    (5), (6) 42:03
  49 .... 12:23; 19:01; 42:01
    (1) 33:16; 38:20; 41:12; 42:08,
         42:09, 42:27, 42:58; 44:33; 45:08,
                                  45:20
    (1a) 43:06
    (b) 42:01
    (2), (3) 42:14
  49a 42:05
  49c 42:05, 42:17
  49d 42:05
  50 (1)–(3) 42:09
    (5) 42:09
    (6) 42:10
  51 .... 42:12, 42:14
    (1b) 42:13
    (1) 39:15
    (2) 39:15; 42:19
  52 ...... 42:12, 42:13, 42:16, 42:24,
                        42:49; 43:09
    (1) 39:27; 42:04
    (2) 42:14
    (3) 42:15
    (4) (b) 42:16
  53 (1) 38:0
    (2) 40:23; 42:16
    (2A) 42:16
    (3) 12:23; 40:08; 42:04, 42:17
    (4) 12:23; 42:04, 42:18
    (5) 40:08; 42:18
      (a), (b) 42:17
  54 .... 42:17
    (1) 12:23; 40:08
    (2) 12:23; 40:08
      (a) 42:24
    (3) 40:08
  54a (1), (2) 42:24
    a (5), (6) 42:24
  54b (1)–(6) 42:24
  55 .... 39:14
    (1) 42:23; 43:09
    (2) 42:23
  55a 38:20; 39:07
  56 (1) 43:09
    (2) 43:09, 43:16
    (3) 43:16
  57 (2) 43:05
  57a 18:40; 44:32
  58 .... 42:01, 42:32, 42:49

Inheritance Tax Act 1984 – *cont.*
s 58 (1) 42:28
  59 .... 42:01
    (1) 38:11
  60 .... 42:01, 42:31
  61 .... 42:01, 42:33
  62 .... 42:01, 42:29
  63 .... 42:01
  64 . 39:29; 42:01, 42:05, 42:33, 42:37
  65 ...... 39:15; 42:01, 42:37, 42:40,
                        42:46, 42:55
    (1) (a) 42:05, 42:41, 42:50
      (b) 42:42
    (2) (a) 42:41
    (3) 42:41
    (4) 42:42
    (5) 42:41, 42:42
    (6) 42:42
    (7), (8) 42:43; 47:13
  66 .... 42:01, 42:39, 42:46
    (2) 42:33, 42:38, 42:41
    (4) 42:35, 42:36
    (5) 42:36; 44:27
    (6) 42:37
  67 .... 42:01
    (2)–(3) 42:39
    (4) 42:39, 42:40
    (5) 42:39
    (6) 42:40
  68 .... 42:01, 42:41
    (1)–(5) 42:45
  69 .... 42:01, 42:41
    (1) 42:46
    (2) (b) 42:46
    (3), (4) 42:46
  70 (2) 42:53, 42:54
    (5) (b) 42:53
    (6) 42:53
    (8) 42:53
  71 .... 39:02
      (a) 42:49, 42:50
      (b) 42:50, 42:51
    (2) 42:50, 42:51, 42:52
      (a), (b) 42:53
    (3) 42:49
    (4) 18:40; 42:49
    (6) (a)–(c) 42:53
  71a 42:05
  71d 42:05
  71f 42:05
  72 .... 42:55
  75 .... 42:44, 42:55
  76 (1) 42:54
    (3) 42:44
    (8) 42:50
  77 .... 42:44; 44:32
  78 .... 44:27
    (1) 18:40
    (1a) 44:28
    (4) 44:31
  79 (3)–(4) 44:27

Table of Statutes

Inheritance Tax Act 1984 – *cont.*
s 79 (5) 43:02; 44:27
    (6)–(10) 44:27
  80 .... 42:33, 42:47
  81 .... 42:03, 42:41
    (2), (3) 42:30
  82 .... 38:21; 42:30, 42:47
  84 .... 42:29
  86 .... 43:20
    (4) (b) 42:55
  87 .... 42:55
  88 .... 42:57
  89 .... 42:01, 42:05, 42:17
    (1) 42:58
    (2) 42:04; 42:58
    (4) 42:58
  90 .... 40:08; 42:21
  91 .... 42:11; 47:06
  92 .... 42:11
  93 .... 42:20
  94 .... 39:15, 39:26; 43:01, 43:02
    (1) 39:14, 39:21; 40:18
    (5) 43:01
  95, 96 .... 39:24
  97 .... 28:23; 39:24
    (1) 39:23
  98 .... 39:20, 39:26
    (1) 39:15, 39:25; 40:18
    (3) 39:02, 39:25
  99, 100 .... 39:26
  101 (1) 39:27
  103 .... 44:01, 44:33
    (3) 44:02
  104 (1) 44:01
  105 (1) (a) 44:01
      (bb) 44:01
      (b) 44:01, 44:03
      (cc), (d), (e)
    .... 44:01
    (3) ... 29:14; 44:02, 44:04, 44:08
    (4) (a) 44:04
    (5) 44:09
    (7) 44:04
    (12a) 44:01
  106 .... 44:05
  107 (1) (b) 44:07
    (2) 44:07
    (4) 44:05
  108 .... 44:05
  109 .... 44:06
  110 (b) 44:04
  111 .... 44:09
  112 .... 44:08
    (2) 44:09
    (5) 44:09
  113 .... 44:01
  113a 44:10
    a (3) (a), (b) 44:10
    a (4) 44:10
    a (6) 44:10
    a (8) 44:10

Inheritance Tax Act 1984 – *cont.*
  s 113b 2A:24
    b (2) (a) 44:10
    b (4) 44:10
    b (5) (b) 44:10
  114 (2) 44:34
  115 (1) 44:11
    (2) ... 44:12, 44:14, 44:33; 44:15,
                           44:16
    (3) 44:11, 44:16
    (4) 44:11
    (5) 44:11
  116 (1) 44:16, 44:26
    (2) (a)–(c) 44:18
    (3) 44:16
    (4) 44:18
    (6), (7) 44:18
  117 .... 44:20
  118 (1) 44:22
  119 .... 44:21
  120 .... 42:47
    (1) 44:21
    (2) 44:21
  121 (2), (3) 44:23
  122 .... 44:11, 44:21
    (1) (a) 44:17
  124 .... 44:11
    (1) 44:14
  124a 44:11
    a (3) (a)–(c) 44:24
    a (4), (6) 44:24
    a (8) 44:24
  124b 2A:24
    b (2) (a) 44:24
    b (3) 44:24
    b (5) (b) 44:24
  125 .... 44:33
    (1) 44:34
  126 .... 44:34
    (1) 44:35
  127 .... 44:34
    (2) 44:33
  128 .... 44:35
  130 .... 44:35
  131 (2a), (3) 40:17
  132 .... 40:17
  133 (1) 40:18
  134, 135 .... 40:18
  136 (2)–(4) 40:18
  137 .... 4:16
    (2) 40:19
  138 .... 40:19
  139 (4) 40:19
  140 (2) 40:17
  141 .... 40:28, 40:30
  142 .... 19:03; 40:22
    (1) 40:21; 41:11
    (2)–(4) 40:21
    (5) 41:13; 42:20
  143 .... 40:25
    (1) 42:05

Inheritance Tax Act 1984 – *cont.*

s 144 (3)	40:24
145	40:23; 42:22
146	19:05; 40:20, 40:26, 40:34
147	4:16; 39:15; 40:27, 40:31
148	40:29, 40:31
(2) (a)	39:08
149	40:29
(5) (a)	39:08
150	42:10
(1), (2)	39:13
151	32:20; 40:35
(2)	40:08
(4)	46:06
151a (3) (a), (b)	40:35
(4)	40:35
151b (5)	40:35
151c	40:35
152	40:08; 42:13
153	47:08
(2)	40:08
154 (1)	40:06
155	47:08
157 (1) (a), (b)	47:10
158	47:01, 47:08
(1a)	34:08
(6)	47:17
159 (2)–(5)	47:20
(7)	47:19
160	45:01, 45:03
161	38:09; 45:08, 45:10
(1)	45:10
(2) (a)	45:10
(3)	45:07, 45:10
(4), (4)	45:07
162 (1)	45:27
(2)	45:29
(3)	45:26; 46:09
(4)	45:22
(5)	47:21
163	45:06
164, 165	45:28
166	45:18
168	57:08
(5)	40:34
169 (1)	44:03
170	42:10
171	40:07; 45:10
172	45:30
173	47:21
174 (2)	45:28
176	40:17
176 (1) (a), (b)	45:09
177 (1)–(4)	44:25
Pt VI Ch III (ss 178–189)	45:12
s 178 (2)	45:12
(4)	45:14
(5)	45:13
179 (1)	45:12, 45:13, 45:14
180 (1), (3)	45:15

Inheritance Tax Act 1984 – *cont.*

s 181, 182	45:13
183, 184	45:15
186	45:13
186a	45:12
a (2)	45:13
186b	45:12
b (3)	45:13
188	45:13
189	45:12
190 (1)	45:16
(4)	45:16
191 (1)	45:16
(1) (b)	17:28
192 (4)	45:17
193–196	45:17
197	45:16
197a	45:16
a (3)	45:17
198	45:16
199 (1)	46:01
(a)	39:04
(2)	40:15; 46:01, 46:03, 46:05
(4)	1:28; 42:04; 46:02
(5)	46:01
200	46:03, 46:04
(1)	43:31
(c)	45:14
(4)	42:04
201 (1) (d)	42:04; 47:13
(2)	46:02, 46:05
(3), (3a)	46:02
202 (1)	39:22
(3)	46:05
203	46:13
(1), (2)	46:01
204 (1)	46:04
(2)	42:04, 46:04
(3)	46:04
(4)	46:05
(5)	46:01, 46:04
(6)–(8)	46:01
(9)	41:13; 46:01
207	44:28; 46:05, 46:16
208	46:05
211 (1)	43:31; 46:14, 46:15; 47:22
(b)	46:14
(2)	46:15
(3)	46:14; 47:22
212	46:17, 46:19
(1)	46:09, 46:10, 46:11, 46:13
(2)	46:12
213, 214	46:14
216	2A:07
(1) (b)	42:04
(bb)–(bd)	2A:09
(2)	2A:08
(3)	2A:08, 2A:09
(6) (aa), (ab)	2A:09

2629

Table of Statutes

Inheritance Tax Act 1984 – *cont.*
- s 218 .... 2A:72
  - (1), (2) 4:01
- 218a 2A:92
- 219 (1a) 2A:72
- 219a, 219b 2A:72
- 222 (2) 44:04
  - (3) 44:04
  - (4a) 45:10
- 226 (1) 2A:22
  - (2) 2A:01, 2A:22
  - (3a) 2A:22
  - (3b) 42:36
- 227 (1) 46:03
  - (1a) 2A:24
  - (1aa) 2A:25
  - (1b) 2A:24
- 228 (3a) 2A:24
  - (5) 2A:25
- 229 .... 2A:24
- 230 .... 2A:72; 17:15; 44:27, 44:28
- 233 .... 2A:35
  - (1) 2A:36
  - (1a) 2A:72
- 234 (1)–(4) 2A:36
- 236 (1a) 42:36
  - (2) 19:05; 40:26
  - (3) 39:13; 40:26
  - (4) 40:27
- 237 .... 46:06; 46:14
  - (3) 46:06
  - (3a) (a), (b) 46:06
  - (3c) 44:28; 46:06
  - (4) 46:14
- 238 .... 46:06
- 239 .... 46:07
- 242 .... 2A:72
- 245 (2) (a), (b) 2A:92
  - (3) 2A:92
  - (4) (b) 2A:92
  - (7) 2A:92
- 245a (1a), (1b) 2A:92
- 247 (1) 2A:09
  - (2), (3) 2A:92
- 249 .... 44:09
- 256 .... 2A:09
- 262 .... 39:11
- 263 .... 40:12
- 264 (3)–(6) 46:08
- 265 .... 38:15; 42:24
- 266 (1) 38:17
- 267 .... 12:22; 33:16; 41:11; 42:43
  - (1) (b) 47:07
  - (2) 47:07, 47:08
  - (3) 47:13
  - (4) 47:07
- 268 .... 39:33, 39:39; 41:06
  - (1) 39:28, 39:35
    - (a) 39:29
    - (b) 39:29, 39:31
  - (2), (3) 39:35

Inheritance Tax Act 1984 – *cont.*
- s 269 (1) 44:17
- 270 .... 12:20; 39:19
- 271 .... 38:20
- 272 .... 18:50; 18:28, 18:31; 39:07, 39:14, 39:25, 39:28, 39:31; 40:18; 44:01; 45:12, 45:22, 45:23
- Sch 1 .... 38:07
- Sch 2
- para 2 .... 40:15
  - 3 .... 42:46
  - 4 .... 44:35
- Sch 3 .... 17:15; 16:46; 43:19; 44:27
- Sch 4 .... 42:44; 43:20
- para 8 .... 42:56
  - 11–13 .... 42:56
  - 15a 42:56
  - 16–18 .... 44:32
- Sch 6
- para 1 .... 46:24
  - 2 .... 40:08; 42:25
  - 3 .... 42:26

Police and Criminal Evidence Act 1984
.... 1:22; 2:33; 63:03
- s 8 .... 2:31
- 14a, 14b 2:31
- 67 (8), (9) 2:32
  - (10) (b) 2:32
  - (11) 2:32
- 78 .... 2:32
- 104 .... 2:32
- 114 .... 2:32
  - (1) 63:03
  - (2) 2:31

Companies Act 1985
- s 14 .... 29:11
- 22 .... 26:08
- 59 (1) 61:11
- 60 (1) 61:11
- 88 .... 59:02
- 130 .... 26:10
- 135 .... 28:29
- 159–162 .... 26:20
- 169 (1) 61:21
  - (1b) 61:21
- 311 .... 7:23
- 425 .... 25:19; 28:29
- 459 .... 15:31
- 652 .... 26:01
- 691 (1) 54:05
- 718 .... 51:04
- 735 (1) 51:04
- 736 .... 64:24
- 741 .... 7:23

Films Act 1985
- Sch 1
- para 9 .... 9:54

Finance Act 1985 .... 4:13; 12:11; 21:05
- s 10 .... 63:03
- 63 .... 9:62

Finance Act 1985 – *cont.*
  s 73–75 .... 11:08
   82 . 56:05, 56:21, 56:35; 57:17, 57:42
   83 (1) 56:05
     (a)–(c) 58:15
     (2) 56:05; 58:15
   84 .... 56:21
     (1) 56:05; 58:14
     (2)–(3) 58:14
     (4) 56:05; 58:13
     (5) 56:05
     (7), (8) 56:05
   85 .... 57:42; 58:07, 09
   86 .... 57:42
   87 .... 56:05
   88 .... 57:08
   89 .... 56:24, 56:25
   94 .... 44:29
   96 .... 56:35; 59:12
  Sch 19
   Pt II 24:11
   para 15 .... 24:09
  Sch 24 .... 57:42; 58:07, 58:09
  Sch 26 .... 44:29
  Sch 27 .... 57:42
   Pt IX 57:17
Housing Act 1985 .... 57:32
  Pt V (ss 118–188) 57:31
Housing Associations Act 1985
  .... 9:22; 18:37
Landlord and Tenant Act 1985
  s 11 .... 7:110
   16 .... 7:110
   36 .... 7:110
Social Security Act 1985
  .... 32:04, 32:05
Agricultural Holdings Act 1986
  .... 18:03
  s 12 .... 68:05
  Sch 2
   para 4 .... 68:05
Building Societies Act 1986
  s 109 .... 56:35
Finance Act 1986 .... 32:28; 41:04
  s 66 .... 59:06; 61:21
   67 .... 59:13; 60:14
     (6) 61:15
   68 .... 59:13; 60:14
   69–72 .... 60:14
   72a 60:14
   73 .... 60:08
   75 . 56:21, 56:35; 59:20; 60:09; 62:16,
                                   62:17
     (1)–(3) 60:06
     (4) 60:06; 62:18
     (5), (5a) 60:06
     (6), (7) 60:07
   76 .... 56:21, 56:35; 59:20; 60:08,
                              60:09; 62:19
     (1)–(3) 60:08

Finance Act 1986 – *cont.*
  s 76 (3a) 60:08
     (4)–(7) 60:08
   77 .... 56:21, 56:35; 59:20; 60:08,
                              60:09; 62:21
     (3), (3a) 60:07
     (4), (5) 60:07
   79 .... 56:35; 59:05
     (2) 59:05; 61:13
     (3)–(4) 59:05
     (5), (6) 59:05; 61:13
     (7) 59:05
     (7A), (7B), (8)
     .... 59:05
   80a 56:35
     (7) 60:10
   80b 56:35; 60:10
   80c 56:35; 60:07, 60:11
   80d 60:11
   81 .... 60:10
   83 (2), (3) 60:12
   84 (4)–(6) 60:13
  Pt IV (ss 86–99) ... 56:09; 61:01, 61:27
  s 86 (2), (4) 61:01
   87 . 61:11, 61:19, 61:21, 61:23, 61:26
     (1) 61:16, 61:18, 61:27
     (3) 61:21
     (6) 61:02
     (7) 61:01
     (7a) 61:03
     (7b) 61:23
   88 (1) (aa)–(b) 61:24
     (1a)–(1d) 61:24
     (4) 61:24
     (5) 61:03, 61:24
     (5a), (6) 61:24
   88a (2) 61:06
   89 .... 61:18
   89a (1) 61:11
     (2) 61:01, 61:11
     (3), (4) 61:11
   89aa 61:07, 61:11
   89ab 61:07
   90 (1) 61:08
     (3) (b) 59:12
     (3a)–(3f) 59:12
     (4)–(6) 61:14
     (7) 61:12
     (7a) 61:14
     (8), (9) 59:12
   91 .... 61:02, 61:16
   92 .... 61:03, 61:24, 61:30
     (1) 61:21
     (1a)–(1d) 61:21
     (2), (3) 61:21
     (7) 61:23
   93 .... 61:04, 61:05
     (1) (b) 61:01
     (8)–(10) 61:16
     (7) 61:04
     (9), (10) 61:04

Table of Statutes

Finance Act 1986 – *cont.*
  s 94 (1) 61:04
    95 (1) 61:15
      (2) (a), (b) 61:15
      (2a)–(2d) 61:15
      (3)–(6) 61:15
    95a 61:15
    96 (1) (b) 61:01
      (4) 61:04
      (5) 61:04
      (6)–(8) 61:16
    97 .... 61:15
    97a 61:04
    97b 61:15
    98 (1) 61:01
    99 (1a) 61:15
      (3) 61:05
      (4)–(6) 61:05
      (6a), (6b) 61:05
      (7) 61:05
      (10)–(12) 61:05
    100 (1) (a) 2A:01; 38:01
          (b) 46:24
    101 .... 38:18
    102 .... 12:15; 12:19; 40:04, 40:32,
                       40:33; 41:01, 41:08
      (1) 41:02
         (b) 41:13
      (3) 41:12, 41:13
      (4) 40:32; 41:13; 43:01
      (5) .. 41:01, 41:13; 43:02, 43:03,
                                43:05
         (a) 41:12
      (5a)–(5c) 41:12
      (6), (7) 41:13
    102a 12:20; 41:04
      a (1) 41:09
      a (2)–(3) 41:09, 41:10
      a (4) (a) 41:09
    102b 41:09
      b (4) 12:21; 41:10
    102c (2) 41:10
      (3) (a), (b) 41:10
      (4) 41:10
      (5) 41:10
      (7) 41:10
    102za 41:02
    103 .... 40:30; 43:24
      (1) (a), (b) 45:23
      (2) (a), (b) 45:24
      (3), (4) 45:23
      (5) 40:33; 45:25
      (6) 40:33; 45:23
      (7) 40:10
    104 (1) 41:12
        (a) 40:30
        (b) 40:32
        (d) 40:31
      (2) 41:01
      (5) 41:12
    108 .... 1:01

Finance Act 1986 – *cont.*
  s 114 .... 56:35
  Sch 19 .... 38:18
  para 43 .... 42:46
      46 .... 39:02; 44:34
  Sch 20
  para 2 .... 41:10
      (2), (4), (5) 41:13
      3–4 .... 41:13
      6 (1) (a) 41:04
         (b) 12:21; 41:04, 41:10
         (c) 41:06
      8 .... 44:05, 44:21
  Sch 23
  Pt IX 56:35
Financial Services Act 1986
           6:34; 50:23, 50:27; 60:12
  s 43 .... 18:23
    78 .... 61:09
  Sch 1
  Pt I 7:47
Insolvency Act 1986
                            8:142
  s 110 .... 62:17
    190 .... 56:35
    339, 340 .... 39:13
    378 .... 56:35
    423 .... 39:13
  Sch 6
  para 1–7 .... 2:37
                            32:05
Social Security Act 1986
  s 12 .... 32:30
Tax Reform Act 1986
                            33:31
Debtors (Scotland) Act 1987
                             2:38
Finance Act 1987
  s 49 .... 57:42
    50 .... 56:35
    52 .... 60:14
    54 .... 57:32
    55 .... 56:36
  Sch 7
  para 5 .... 61:14
      6 .... 61:12
      7 .... 61:22
  Sch 8
  para 17 .... 45:12
  Sch 16
  Pt III 8:40
Finance (No 2) Act 1987
      32:03, 32:14, 32:15, 32:16, 33:31
  s 31 .... 52:06
    95 (2) 2A:01
    98 (4) 40:08
    97 .... 2A:72
    99 .... 56:35
  Sch 7
  para 2 .... 43:09

Table of Statutes

Housing (Scotland) Act 1987
.... 57:31
Interpretation Act 1987
  Sch 1 .... 23:38
Landlord and Tenant Act 1987
  s 42 .... 25:02
  43 (2) (b) 10:08
Copyright, Designs and Patents Act 1988
  s 90 (3) 18:05
Finance Act 1988 . 7:66, 7:71; 11:01,
                    11:37; 16:02; 21:05;
                    22:44; 24:12
  s 38 .... 6:54
  42 .... 8:69, 8:70, 8:154
  43 .... 10:08
  46 (3) 7:103
    (4), (5) 7:24
  55 .... 49:06
  63 .... 10:28
  65 .... 5:13
  66 (1) 33:28, 33:30
  72 .... 8:134
  73 (2) 10:08
  75 .... 8:136
  76 .... 10:08
  78 .... 7:70
  83 (4) 7:63
  90 (3) (a) 61:13
    (3a)–(3f) 61:13
  95 (5) 24:03
  96 .... 16:01
    (5) 21:05
  98 .... 16:01
  102 .... 8:69
  137 .... 43:18
  140 .... 59:14, 59:15
  141 .... 59:01, 59:07
  143 .... 56:35; 59:12, 59:13
    (1)–(7) 59:13
  144 (2), (4), (5) 61:05
  145 .... 56:35
  178 .... 2A:33
  Sch 6 .... 5:13; 8:69
  para 2 .... 10:28
    (1) 8:70
    3(2) 8:42
    4(4)–(6) 8:70
    5 .... 8:70
    6 .... 8:70
    7 .... 8:70
    (b) 8:70
  Sch 12
  para 8 .... 56:35
  Sch 14
  Pt VIII 4:19
  Sch 15
  para 1(1) 8:69
Housing Act 1988
  Pt I (ss 1–45) 9:22
  s 95 (4) 9:22

Income and Corporation Taxes Act 1988
.... 1:09, 1:23; 6:51; 61:11
  s 1 .... 5:30
    (1) 5:03
    (2) 5:05
  1a 4:16
  2 (2) 1:24
  5 (1) 5:13
  6 .... 25:01; 36:01
    (1) 8:64; 35:01
  7 .... 35:05
  8 (2) 8:62
    (6) 1:32
  9 .... 10:08
    (1) 35:01
    (4) 13:22
  11 .... 36:01
    (1) 25:45
  12 (4) 24:39
    (8) 25:35, 25:38, 25:39
  13 .... 24:48; 29:13
    (1) (b) 29:14
    (2) 24:36
    (3) 25:41, 25:42
    (4) 25:43
    (4A)–(4C) 25:44
    (6) 25:41
    (7) 25:40
  13a 29:13
    a (1) 29:14, 29:15
    a (2) (a)–(d) 29:14
    a (3)–(4) 29:14
  14 .... 2A:70
    (2) (a), (b) 26:03
  15 .... 5:11; 10:01, 10:23
    (1) 8:64
    para 1 (1)
.... 10:03, 10:07
    (2)
.... 10:03, 10:24
    (4)
.... 10:03, 10:04
    2 (1)
.... 10:05
    (2)
.... 10:05
    (a), (b)
.... 10:07
    (3)
.... 10:05
    3 .... 10:02
    4 .... 10:03, 10:13
    (1)
.... 10:07
  16 .... 5:13
    (6) 8:42
  17 .... 5:13
  18 .... 5:01; 8:91; 11:01, 11:39
    (1) 8:64
    (a) (i) 12:11

2633

Table of Statutes

Income and Corporation Taxes Act 1988 – cont.
s 18 (3) 8:01; 10:05, 10:29; 12:01, 12:02
19 ...... 7:18, 7:21, 7:25, 7:28, 7:64; 33:14
　(1) 7:17, 7:31, 7:34
20 (2) 26:12
21 .... 28:37
　(5) 10:01
21a 10:02
　a (1) 5:20; 10:08
　a (2)–(4) 10:08
21b 10:08
24 (1), (2) 10:17
　(4) 10:17
29 .... 11:08
31a, 31b 9:33
31za 9:33; 10:10, 10:13
31zb, 31zc 9:33; 10:10, 10:13
32 .... 9:24
34 . 6:46; 8:130; 10:06, 10:07, 10:16, 10:24, 10:26; 23:36
　(1) 10:04, 10:08, 10:18, 10:19, 10:25, 10:27
　(2), (3) 10:20
　(4) 10:21, 10:23, 10:27
　　(b) 10:22
　(5) 10:23, 10:27
　　(b) 10:22
　(6) 10:19
　(7) 10:22
　(7a) 10:22
　(8) 10:19
35 .... 10:06, 10:08, 10:16, 10:24, 10:25, 10:27; 23:36
　(2) 10:23
36 .... 10:06, 10:08, 10:16, 10:25, 10:26; 23:36
　(1) 10:24
　(2) (a) 10:24
　　(b) 10:27
　(3), (4) 10:24
37 .... 10:16, 10:24
　(2) 10:25
　(4) 10:26
　(5), (7) 10:25
37a (1) 10:26
38 .... 10:16; 23:19; 57:27
　(1) 9:14
　(2) 9:14; 10:18
　(3)–(4) 9:14
　(6) 9:14
39 .... 10:16
　(2) 10:22
42 .... 6:46; 8:68
42a (1) 36:10
43a 3:07; 10:16
　a (2), (4) 8:66
43b–43g 3:07; 10:16
47 .... 47:08

Income and Corporation Taxes Act 1988 – cont.
s 53 (1) 8:42
　(2) 8:42
　(3) 8:42
54 .... 8:42
55 .... 8:42, 8:171; 17.01
56 .... 36:02
　(5) 12:14
56a 12:14
60 .... 10:09
　(5) 5:16
61 .... 6:21; 8:56; 10:09
62 .... 8:48, 8:56; 10:09, 54, 55
63 .... 8:47, 8:56; 10:09
63a 10:09
　a (1) 37:17
　a (3) 8:47
64 .... 11:01
65 .... 7:01
　(4) 12:12; 16:32; 33:15
　(5) (b) 35:22
70 (1) 11:01
　(2) 35:12
70a 10:03; 35:07
72 .... 10:08
　(2) 12:13; 25:35
Pt IV Ch V (ss 74–99)
.... 10:07; 13:08
s 74 .... 8:64, 8:68, 8:95, 8:118, 8:131; 10:07
　(1) 8:122
　(a) .. 8:96, 8:102, 8:104, 8:128, 8:131, 8:134; 10:11; 13:22; 32:22
　(b) 8:102, 8:131
　(c) 8:103, 8:131
　(d) 8:126, 8:131; 10:08
　(da) 9:31
　(e) 8:104, 8:131
　(f)–(h) 8:131
　(j) 7:22; 8:131, 8:146
　(k)–(l) 8:131
　(m) 8:131
　(n)–(o) 8:131
　(p) 8:131
　(q) 8:131
75 .... 10:08; 27:06
　(3) 25:26
76 .... 10:08
77 .... 10:08
78 .... 10:07
79 .... 8:101, 8:139; 10:08
79a 8:101, 8:139
79b 8:101, 8:139
80, 81 .... 10:08
82 .... 10:08
83 .... 8:139; 10:08
83a 8:158
　a (3) (a) 8:141
84 .... 8:158; 10:08

Table of Statutes

Income and Corporation Taxes Act 1988 – cont.

s 84 (2)	8:141
(3) (a)	8:141
84a	8:139
85	8:106, 8:139; 10:08
85a	8:139
86	10:08; 13:22
(1)	7:08; 8:139
86a	8:139
87	8:139; 10:08, 10:25, 10:27
88, 89	10:08
90	8:53; 10:08
91	8:139; 10:07
91a, 91b	8:114
92	10:07
93	8:89; 10:07
94	8:93; 10:07
95	8:91; 10:07
96	10:07
97	10:07
98	8:139; 10:07
99	10:07
(2), (3)	10:27
100	7:141; 8:142, 8:157, 8:161; 22:07; 25:19
(1) (b)	8:168
(1a) (b)	8:168
(1b)–(1f)	8:168
(2)	8:73
101	8:142
(1), (2)	8:168
102	8:161
(?)	8:168
103	5:14; 8:168; 10:08
(1)	8:142
(2) (a)	8:142
(3)	8:142
(4) (b)	8:142
104	8:156, 8:168; 10:08
105	8:139, 8:142; 10:08
106	10:08
a (7)	25:32
110	10:08
110a	8:47
112 (4), (5)	33:38; 37:35
113	8:41, 8:50
114	8:62, 8:63
115	8:62
116	25:31
117	8:63
118za–118zc	8:63
118zd	8:63
118ze–118zk	8:63
118l	8:63
119	8:171; 11:01
120	10:03
(2)	10:05
(1)	8:171
(4)	23:28
123	5:30

Income and Corporation Taxes Act 1988 – cont.

s 125	1:30; 7:117
126	7:117
128 (1)	12:11
132 (4) (a)	31:01
(5)	35:22
134 (5) (c)	49:06
135	7:85, 7:87
136 (4)	7:65
138	7:71
140a (2)	7:69
148	7:24, 7:31, 7:36; 16:14
(5) (b)	7:36
149 (6)	25:49
153	7:41, 7:127, 7:137
154	7:19, 7:25, 7:41, 7110
(4) (a)	7:49
155	7:41
155a (7)	7:91
156	7:41
(2)	7:109
(5) (b)	7:110
157	7:41; 51:14
158, 159	7:41
160	7:41, 7:64
(5) (b)	7:113
161	7:41
162	7:41, 7:64
163–167	7:41
168a (3)	7:107
185	7:65
(4)	7:15, 7:24
193	50:02
198	7:24, 7:99, 7:137
198a	7:129
201	7:99, 7:102
203	2A:18
(2) (dd)	2A:32
203f	3:03
f (3)	37:32
203fb	37:32
208	1:17, 1:18; 25:23; 26:30; 32:08; 35:71; 39:23
209	28:37
(1)	21:11; 26:01, 26:02
(2) (a)	26:04
(b)	21:11; 26:02, 26:05, 26:20
(c)	26:06
(d)	4:12; 26:07, 26:08
(da)	4:12; 26:07
(e)	26:08
(iii)	26:07
(vii)	26:09
(4)	26:02, 26:08
(5)	26:05, 26:08; 28:04
(6)	26:02, 26:05, 26:08
(7)	28:04
(9)–(11)	26:09
210	26:06; 28:41

Table of Statutes

Income and Corporation Taxes Act 1988 – cont.
- s 210 (2) 26:11
- (3) 26:11; 29:01
- 211 .... 26:06, 26:11; 28:41
- (2) 26:10; 29:01
- (3) 26:10
- (5)–(7) 26:10
- 212 (1) 25:14; 26:08
- 213 .... 26:02
- (2) 28:38, 28:39, 28:40
- (3) (a) 28:38
- (b) 28:38, 28:39
- (4) 28:37
- (5) 28:37, 28:38, 28:40
- (6) 28:37
- (a) 28:38
- (b) 28:38
- (7) 28:38
- (8) (a) 28:37, 28:38, 28:39
- (b) 28:37, 28:38, 28:39, 28:40
- (c), (d) 28:39, 28:40
- (e) 28:40
- (9) 28:39
- (10)–(11) 28:37
- (12) 28:38
- 214 .... 8:94; 28:37
- (1) (a)–(d) 28:41
- (2) (c) 28:41
- (3) 28:41
- 215–217 .... 28:37
- 218 (1) 28:37, 28:38
- 219 .... 21:11; 26:02, 26:21
- (1) 26:21
- (a) 26:23; 29:14
- (b) 26:28
- (2) 26:28
- 220 .... 26:02, 26:24
- (5) 26:23, 26:25
- (6) 16:43; 26:25
- (7)–(9) 26:25
- 221 .... 26:02
- (2) 26:26
- (4)–(8) 26:26
- 222 .... 26:02
- (2), (3) 26:26
- (6) 26:26
- 223 .... 26:26
- (1) 26:27
- (2) 26:27
- 224 .... 26:02, 26:26
- 225 .... 1:30; 26:29
- 227 .... 26:26
- 228 .... 26:27
- 229 .... 26:02, 26:22
- (1) (a) 26:21
- 231a 32:24
- 232 (1) 26:13
- 233 .... 1:17
- 239, 240 .... 2A:70

Income and Corporation Taxes Act 1988 – cont.
- s 242 .... 26:20
- 245 (4) (a)–(d) 2A:22
- 246a 26:20
- 247 .... 2A:70; 25:40
- 251 (1) (a) 26:18
- (c) 26:18
- 254 (1) 26:05, 26:06; 28:04
- (2)–(4) 28:04
- (8) 28:04
- Pt VII Ch I(ss 256–278) 5:32
- s 257aa 6:51
- 259 .... 1:21
- 262 .... 1:21
- 263 .... 39:19
- 266 .... 31:31
- (2) (b) 31:28
- 273 .... 31:31
- 277 .... 8:62
- 278 .... 6:04; 26:13; 33:01
- (a) 6:10
- 282 .... 16:42; 23:11
- 282b 16:42
- b (5) 6:02
- 289 (1) (a) 31:14
- (2) (a) 29:15
- (c) 31:12
- (7) 22:28; 31:08
- 289a (1a) 22:28
- (7) 22:28
- 290 .... 22:28; 31:08
- 291 .... 22:28; 31:08
- (1) (b) 22:24
- (2) 7:08
- 291a 7:08
- 292 .... 22:28; 31:08
- 293 .... 31:08
- (2) 22:28
- (6a) 22:28
- 294–295 .... 22:28; 31:08
- 296 .... 22:28; 31:08
- 297 .... 22:28; 31:08
- (2) (h), (j) 31:12
- 298 .... 22:28; 31:08
- 299 ...... 21:05, 21:06; 22:28; 31:08
- (6) 22:31
- 300 .... 31:08
- 301 .... 22:28; 31:08
- 302 .... 22:28; 31:08
- 303 .... 22:28; 31:08
- 304 .... 22:28; 31:08
- 304a 22:30
- 305 .... 22:28; 31:08
- 306 .... 22:28; 31:08
- 307 .... 22:28; 31:08
- 308 .... 22:28; 31:08
- 309 .... 22:28; 31:08
- 310 .... 22:28; 31:08
- 311 .... 22:28; 31:08

Table of Statutes

Income and Corporation Taxes Act 1988 – cont.
```
s 312 ................... 22:28; 31:08
   (1) ....................... 22:29
  313 ..................... 7:27, 7:29
  314 ......................... 7:08
  326 ........................ 47:11
  326a ........................ 1:06
  331 .. 7:23, 7:97, 7:102, 7:103, 7:120
  333 ......................... 5:18
  334 ........................ 33:03
  335 ......................... 7:03
  336 ........................ 33:03
Pt VIII (ss 337–347)
s 337 ......................... 8:41
   (1) ................. 8:168; 10:08
  338 ................... 3:04; 27:06
   (2) ........................ 30:09
  338a ........................ 25:21
  339 ............. 6:37; 13:22; 25:21
   (4) ........................ 26:01
   (7aa) ........ 13:22; 25:22; 26:01
  340 (1) (b) .................. 31:25
  342a (2) ..................... 25:34
    a (5) ...................... 25:37
    a (6) ...................... 25:35
  343 ........ 8:54, 8:60; 25:30, 25:31
   (1) ........................ 25:27
   (2) ................. 25:27; 33:31
   (3), (4) .................... 25:27
   (6)–(9) ..................... 25:27
  343ZA ....................... 25:31
  344 (1) ..................... 25:28
   (4) ........................ 25:28
   (5), (6) .................... 25:27
  347 (1) (b) ................... 1:21
  347a ..... 11:01, 11:03; 11:32; 43:03
    a (2) ............... 8:131; 11:23
    a (6) ...................... 11:03
  347b ........................ 11:01
    b (1) ....................... 1:21
  348 ..... 4:16, 4:22; 7:16, 7:29; 8:91,
        8:131, 8:171; 11:41, 11:70, 11:72,
        11:73, 11:74, 11:75, 11:78; 13:15;
                    14:07; 26:14; 29:12
   (d) ............. 11:68, 11:69
   (4) (e) ............. 14:07
  349 .... 4:16, 4:22; 7:16; 8:91, 8:131,
        8:171; 9:63; 11:39,11:65, 11:74,
        11:75, 11:77, 11:78; 13:15; 14:08;
                                29:12
   (1) ........................ 28:41
   (2) (c) ..................... 11:12
  349b (2) ..................... 25:49
  350 ......................... 8:91
  353 .................. 7:111;11:05
   (1AA), (4), (5)
   ............................ 6:44
  356, 357 .................... 8:133
  362 (1) ...................... 8:63
  365 (1) (aa) ................. 6:44
```

Income and Corporation Taxes Act 1988 – cont.
```
s 365   (d) ....................... 6:44
   (1aa) ....................... 6:44
   (1ab)–(1ad) ............ 6:44, 6:45
   (1a), (1b) .................. 6:44
Pt X Ch I (ss 379a–392)
  ............................ 10:15
s 380 .. 6:29; 7:01; 10:77; 11:43; 22:09
  381 ............. 9:24, 9:40; 10:14
  384 (6)–(8) ................... 9:48
  385 .................... 6:29;11:43
  386 ........................ 22:10
  387 ........................ 52:06
  392 ................. 11:32; 23:36
Ch II (ss 392a–396)
  ............................ 10:15
s 392a .................. 10:02; 27:06
    a (1), (2) .................. 25:32
  392b ........................ 25:32
  393 ...... 13:24; 25:17, 25:29; 28:10,
                        28:13; 37:30
   (1) ................. 25:27, 25:52
   (2a)–(2b) ................... 25:24
   (8) ................. 25:23; 37:24
   (9) ........................ 25:26
  393a ..... 13:24; 25:27, 25:29; 27:06;
                               37:30
    a (1) ...................... 25:27
    a   (a), (b) ................ 25:24
    a (2) ...................... 25:24
    a (3), (4) .................. 25:25
    a (9) ...................... 25:24
  395 (4), (5) .................. 25:31
  396 ........................ 25:32
  397 ........................ 25:25
  401 ......................... 8:49
   (1) ........................ 10:08
  402 ................... 1:10; 60:03
   (2a), (2b) .................. 28:01
   (3) ........................ 28:11
   (3b) ....................... 28:08
   (4) ........................ 28:11
   (6) ........................ 28:20
  403 ........................ 10:01
   (1) ................. 28:10, 28:13
    (a) ............. 27:05; 28:13
    (b) ............ 10:02; 28:13
   (3) ........................ 28:13
   (4), (5) .................... 30:09
   (7) ........................ 28:06
   (8) ................. 16:02; 28:10
   (9), (10) ................... 28:10
  403a, 403b .................. 28:10
  403c (2), (3) ................. 28:11
  403za (3) .................... 28:13
  403zb ....................... 28:13
  403zc .............. 27:05; 28:13
  404 (1), (2) .................. 33:31
   (6) ........................ 33:31
  405 (6) ...................... 28:12
```

Table of Statutes

Income and Corporation Taxes Act 1988 – cont.
- s 406 (4) 28:12
- (7), (8) 28:12
- 407 .... 28:13
- 410 (1)–(4) 28:09
  - (5) 28:09; 62:16
  - (6) 28:09
- 413 .... 1:10; 60:03
  - (3) 28:08
    - (b), (c) 28:11
  - (4) 28:08
  - (5) 28:08, 28:11
  - (6) 28:11
  - (7) 28:09
  - (10) 28:09, 28:11
- 414 (1) 29:02, 29:07
  - (2) 29:02
  - (2a)–(2d) 29:02
  - (4) 29:07
  - (5) (a), (b) 29:07
  - (6) 29:02; 29:07
- 415 .... 29:12; 35:72
  - (2) 29:08
  - (6) (a) 29:08
- 416 ..... 2A:22; 7:132; 25:44; 26:10, 26:11; 28:25; 29:12; 49:12, 49:24; 60:08; 62:17, 62:19, 62:20
  - (2) 25:43; 29:03
    - (c) 29:07
  - (3) 25:43; 29:04
  - (4) 29:02
  - (5), (6) 25:44; 29:02, 29:04
- 417 .... 29:12
  - (1) 29:04
  - (3) 29:04; 49:24
    - (a) 25:44
    - (b) 25:44; 29:04
    - (c) (i), (ii)
    .... 29:04
  - (4) 29:04; 49:24
  - (5) 29:04
  - (6) 29:04
  - (7)–(9) 29:04; 62:21
- 418 .... 26:02; 29:12
  - (2)–(8) 29:09
- 419 ..... 2A:21; 2A:06; 15:26; 35:59
  - (1) 29:10
  - (2) 29:11
  - (3) 29:10
  - (4) 15:25; 29:10, 29:12
  - (4a) 29:10
- 420 .... 29:12
  - (1), (2) 29:11
- 421 .... 29:12
  - (2)–(4) 29:10
- Pt XII (ss 431–519)
  .... 31:05
- s 431 (4) 32:24
- 433 .... 8:36
- 436 .... 37:30

Income and Corporation Taxes Act 1988 – cont.
- s 440 (4) 27:17
- 441 (8) 35:45
- 442 (3) 25:49
- 445 .... 37:33
- 447 .... 15:14
- 459, 460 .... 25:03
- 461–461D 31:05
- 462 (1), (1a) 31:05
- 463 (1) 31:05
- 464 .... 31:05
- 467 .... 25:03
- 468 .... 25:03; 30:18; 59:19
  - (1) 4:29
  - (2) 30:15
  - (6) 30:14
- 468a 30:18
- 468e (2) 30:15
- 469 .... 30:14
- 473 .... 8:149
- 486 (9) 26:01
- 488 .... 9:22; 25:03
- 490 .... 8:36; 26:01
- 491 (4) 8:41
- 494a 10:01
- 503 .... 10:15
  - (3) (a) 10:14
- 504 .... 5:20
  - (2) 6:27
  - (3) 10:15
- 504a 10:15
- 505 (1) 13:22; 16:45
  - (i), (ii)
  .... 8:94
  - (f) 8:94; 13:24
- 506 (1) 16:45, 16:46
- 508 .... 25:03
- 509 .... 8:139
- 510a (2) 33:43
  - (3) (b) 22:47; 33:43
  - (4), (5) 33:43
  - (6) 16:39; 22:47
- 516 .... 5:18; 25:03
- 517 .... 25:03
- 517A 5:18
- 519 (1) (b) 5:18
- 519a 16:46
- 526 .... 8:139
- 531 (1) 8:76
  - (2) 17:01
  - (3) 8:76
  - (7) 9:09
- 532 (5) (b) 9:09
- 534 .... 8:158
- 539 (3) 31:05
- s 540 (1) (a) (v) 31:23
- 541 .... 16:14
  - (3) 4:04
  - (4a), (4b) 31:26
- 547 .... 8:94

Table of Statutes

Income and Corporation Taxes Act 1988 – cont.
s 547 (1) (a) 31:26
       (b) 31:26
       (d) 31:26
548 (2) 31:28
    (3) (a) (ii) 7:107
551 .... 31:26
553 (3) 31:23
554 .... 31:28
555 .... 36:11
    (1) 36:11
556 .... 2:22; 36:11
557, 558 .... 36:11
559 .... 8:26
560 .... 8:26
    (1) 2A:19
    (2) (a) 2A:19
       (f) 2A:19
561 .... 8:26
    (9) 2A:19
562 .... 2A:19; 8:26
563 .... 8:26
564 .... 2A:19; 8:26
565 .... 8:26
    (2) (a) 2A:19
566 .... 2A:19; 8:26
    (1a) 8:131
567 .... 8:26
568 .... 8:139
572 .... 8:139
573 .... 4:33; 30:04
574 .... 16:04
577 ... 4:02; 8:68, 8:97; 10:08; 13:22
    (1) (a) 8:133
    (2) 8:134
    (5) 130, 8:134
    (7) 8:134
    (8) 8:133
       (b) 8:134
    (9) 8:133, 8:134; 13:22
    (10) 8:134
577a 5:19; 8:09; 10:08
579 .... 10:08
    (2) 8:139
580 .... 10:08
584 .... 35:68
587b 8:141; 16:49
587c 8:141
588 .... 7:97; 8:139; 10:08
    (6), (7) 7:86
589 .... 10:08
589a 10:08
    a (8) 8:139
589b 10:08
Part XIV Ch I, II, VI
    .... 32:09
590 (2) 32:11, 32:12
    (3) 32:11, 32:12
    (4c) 32:02
590a 32:12

Income and Corporation Taxes Act 1988 – cont.
s 590b 32:12
590c (1)–(6) 32:12
591 (1) 32:13
    (2) 32:13, 32:18
       (g) 32:04
591d (6) 32:20
592 (1) 32:18
    (2) 8:23; 32:24
    (3) 8:23
    (4) 8:139
    (7) 7:110
    (8) 32:23
593 .... 5:18
594 .... 7:110; 32:08
598 (2) 32:27
601 .... 32:28
602 (4) 32:28
603 .... 32:28
611aa 32:11
612 .... 32:20; 50:05
    (1) 32:19
617 (5) 52:06
619 .... 5:14, 5:31; 40:08
    (1) (a) 7:110
    (2) 12:07
620, 621 .... 40:08
623 .... 31:31
624 (1) 32:20
630 .... 40:08
631 .... 40:08
632 .... 40:08
633 .... 40:08
634 .... 40:08
635 .... 40:08
636 .... 40:08
    (3a) 40:08
637 .... 40:08
638 .... 40:08
    (7a) 32:35
639 .... 5:31; 40:08
    (5a) 32:32
640 .... 5:14; 40:08
    (1) (b) 12:07
641 .... 40:08
642 .... 40:08
643 .... 40:08
644 .... 40:08
    (4) (a) 50:22
645 .... 40:08
646 .... 40:08
647 .... 40:08
648 .... 40:08
649 .... 40:08
650 .... 40:08
651–654 .... 40:08
655 .... 40:08
656 .... 5:26; 11:20, 11:31; 16:14
657 .... 16:14

Table of Statutes

Income and Corporation Taxes Act 1988 – cont.
Pt XV Ch I–III (ss 660–682a)
.... 14:02
s 660a 18:50
s 660a (2) 15:13; 20:02
    a (4), (5) 15:23
  660b 39:04
    b (1) (a) 40:21
  660c 12:02
    (1) 40:21
  663 .... 15:04, 15:08
    (2) 35:45
  673 .... 15:05, 15:13, 15:14
  674a 15:06
  677 .... 15:26
  678 (7) 15:26
  683 .... 15:01
  686 . 5:02; 13:12; 15:22; 25:02, 26:18
    (1a) (b) 5:17; 13:17
      a (b) 13:08
    (2) (b) 13:14, 13:19; 15:19
      (c) (i) 32:20
    (2a) 5:02
  687 .... 13:21; 15:17
    (3) 35:45
      (a) 13:11
  691 (2) 23:16
  694 .... 44:32
  695 .... 14:06
    (2), (3) 14:07
    (5) 14:07
  696 (3) 14:08
    (3a) 14:08
    (3b) 14:08
    (5)–(7) 14:08
  697 (1), (1a) 14:08
    (2) 14:08
  698 (1) 14:09
    (1a), (1b) 14:09
    (2) 14:09
    (3) 14:09; 14:08
  699 .... 40:05; 45:19
  699a (1a) 14:07, 14:08
    a (2) (b) 14:07
    a (3) 14:07, 14:08
    a (4) 14:07
    a (6) 14:08
  700 (5), (6) 14:07, 14:08
  701 (2) 14:08
    (3) 14:07
    (3a) (b) 14:07, 14:08
    (5), (6) 42:11
    (9)–(10a) 14:04
    (12) 14:07, 14;08
Pt XVII (ss 703–787)
.... 23:29
s 703 ..... 4:03, 4:14, 4:18, 4:19, 4:23;
                8:94; 25:51; 29:01
    (1) 4:28
    (2) 4:20

Income and Corporation Taxes Act 1988 – cont.
s 703 (7) 4:19
    (12) 4:29
  704 .... 4:18; 26:10, 26:11
  704A 4:22
  704B 4:23
  704C 4:24
  704D 4:26; 29:01
  704E 4:27
  705A 4:18
    B 4:18
  706 .... 4:18, 4:28
  707 .... 1:30; 4:18; 62:16
  709 .... 27:04
    (1) 11:18
    (2) 4:20
    (4), (6) 4:22
  710 .... 3:24; 21:05
    (3) (da) 12:14
  729 .... 4:10, 4:13, 4:29
  730 .... 4:11, 4:17
  730a 3:24; 4:17
  731 .... 4:13
  732 .... 4:13
    (1a) 4:15
  733 .... 4:13
  734 .... 4:13; 27:15
  736 .... 4:14; 28:29
  737a 3:24; 4:17
  739 ... 1:21; 3:11; 4:11; 11:46; 12:20;
      25:51; 32:20; 33:39; 35:37, 35:66;
                35:39, 35:64; 36:05
    (1a) (a) 35:26
    (2) 35:31
    (3) 35:29
  740 .... 11:17; 35:26
    (2) (a) 35:56
    (6) (a) 35:56
  741 .... 3:11; 35:26, 35:29
  742 .... 33:39
  743 .... 33:39
  744 .... 33:39
  745 .... 33:39
  746 .... 33:39
  747 .... 2A:06, 2A:52
    (1) (c) 35:67
    (4) (a), (b) 35:64
    (5) (b) 35:64
  748 .... 2A:52
    (1) (d) 35:64
    (3) 35:66
  748a 2A:52; 35:70
  749 .... 2A:52; 32:20; 35:64
    (1)–(6) 35:67
    (8), (9) 35:67
  749a 2A:52
    (1) (b) 35:67
  750 .... 2A:52; 35:64
    (1), (1a) 35:67
  751 .... 2A:52; 35:64

Table of Statutes

Income and Corporation Taxes Act 1988 – cont.
s 751a (2)	35:65
751b	35:65
752–753	2A:52; 35:64
754	2A:52; 35:64
(2)	35:64
755	2A:52; 35:64
754a	2A:52; 35:64, 35:67
754b	2A:52; 35:64, 35:67
755c	2A:52; 35:67
756	2A:52; 21:05; 35:64
757	19:01; 21:28; 21:05; 32:20
(1)	35:40
(2), (3)	35:41
(5), (6)	35:41
758	21:05, 21:28; 35:40
759	21:05, 21:28; 35:40
(1)–(6)	35:42
760	21:05, 21:28; 35:40
(2)	35:43
761	12:02; 21:28
(1)	13:08; 15:22; 35:45
(6)	35:45
762	21:28; 35:40, 35:45
762a	35:44
763	21:28; 35:40, 35:45
(6a)	35:44
764	21:28; 35:40, 35:45
765	25:20
(1) (a)–(d)	33:36
765a	33:36
766 (2)	33:36
767a (1)	2A:22
a (2) (a), (b)	2A:22
a (4)–(10)	2A:22
767aa (2)–(10)	2A:22
767b (2)	2A:22
b (5)–(9)	2A:22
767c (2), (3)	2A:22
768	3:04; 25:52, 25:33
(2)–(6)	25:29
(8)	2A:22; 25:29
(9)	25:29
768a (2), (3)	25:29
768b	30:10, 30:11
768c	30:10
768d	10:01
769 (1)	33:25
(2a)	2A:22
(6)–(6c)	25:29
(8), (9)	2A:22
770	8:153
770a	8:92, 8:151
773 (4)	7:76
774	25:15, 25:43
774A–774G	3:08
775	4:03; 8:156
776	2A:63; 4:03; 8:94; 22:02, 23:07, 23:32, 23:36
(2)	23:37

Income and Corporation Taxes Act 1988 – cont.
s 776 (2) (a)	23:34
(c)	23:29, 23:34
(3) (b)	23:29, 23:33
(4)	18:01; 23:31
(5)	23:31
(7)	23:34
(8)	23:29, 23:33
(9)	23:35
(10)	23:35
(13)	23:30
(14)	23:29
777 (2)	18:01; 23:31
(3)	18:01; 23:31
(5)	23:30
(8)	23:29
(9)	23:29
(12)	23:29
(13)	23:29
779	8:135, 8:136
780	8:135
(5)	8:136
781, 782	8:137
785A–785E	10:03
786	6:45
787	6:45
Pt XVIII (ss 788–816)	15:22; 35:69
s 788	6:35; 8:94; 37:21, 37:29
(1)	37:03, 37:12
(2)	34:08
(3)	37:03, 37:06, 37:33
(5)	37:13
789	37:29
790	6:35; 8:94; 37:11; 37:29
(1)	37:03
(3)	37:20
(4)	37:07, 37:08, 37:19, 37:20
(5) (c)	37:08
(6)	37:20, 37:38
(7)–(10)	37:20
(10a)–(10c)	37:13
(12)	37:06
(a), (b)	37:07
791	37:29
792	37:03, 37:09, 37:10, 37:20, 37:29
(1)	37:12, 37:33
793	37:03, 37:09, 37:29
(1)	37:15
793a	37:06
794	37:03, 37:08, 37:09, 37:11, 37:15, 37:29
795	37:03, 37:09, 37:29
(4)	37:14
795a	37:12
a (3)	37:10
796	37:03, 37:09, 37:29
(1)–(3)	37:18
797	37:03, 37:09, 37:25, 37:29

2641

Table of Statutes

Income and Corporation Taxes Act 1988 – cont.
```
s 797 (3) ........................ 37:19
     (3a), (3b) ................. 37:19
  797a ........................... 37:19
  798    37:03, 37:09, 37:27, 37:29
  798a–798c .................... 37:27
  799 ...... 37:03, 37:09, 37:21, 37:29
     (1a), (1b) ................. 37:23
     (2a) ................. 37:23; 37:34
  800 ...... 37:03, 37:09, 37:20, 37:29
  801 ...... 36:44; 37:03, 37:08, 37:09
     (2a), (2b) ................. 37:27
     (5) ........................... 37:25
  801c ................... 35:71; 37:25
  802, 803 ........ 37:03, 37:09, 37:29
  803a ........................... 37:12
     a (2), (3) ................... 37:22
  804 ........ 8:94; 37:03, 37:09, 37:29
     (1) ................... 8:47; 37:17
     (5a) .................. 8:47; 37:17
     (5b) (a), (b) ......... 8:47; 37:17
     (5c) ........................ 37:17
  804za–804zc .................... 37:27
  805 ...... 37:03, 37:05, 37:09, 37:29
  806 .................... 37:03, 37:29
     (1) ........................... 37:09
     (3)–(6) ..................... 37:12
  806a (2) ............ 37:24, 37:25
     (4), (5) .................... 37:25
  806b ........................... 37:24
     b (2)–(7) .................... 37:25
  806c (1), (2) .................. 37:25
  806d–806f .................... 37:26
  806h ........................... 37:25
  806j ........................... 37:25
  806k–806m ................... 37:28
  807 ........................... 11:09
  808 ........................... 37:30
  808a (4), (5) ................. 37:34
  808b ........................... 37:34
  810 ........................... 37:14
  811 ............. 8:108; 37:05, 37:23
     (4)–(10) .................... 37:03
  812–815 ....................... 37:09
  815a ........... 21:26; 25:49; 37:12
  815c (1) ....................... 34:08
  817 ........................... 8:95
  824 (3) (b) ................... 2A:33
  825 ........................... 37:03
     (4) (c) (i) .................. 25:24
        (b) ..................... 29:12
  826 (4) ........................ 29:10
        (c) (ii) .................. 25:24
     (5a) ........................ 2A:06
     (7b) ........................ 37:28
  827 ........................... 8:138
     (1) ........................ 8:104
  829 (2) ........................ 5:18
  831 ..................... 1:27; 8:03
     (1) ........................ 33:04
```

Income and Corporation Taxes Act 1988 – cont.
```
s 832 ..................... 1:27; 8:03
     (1) .... 9:09; 10:03; 12:05; 21:20;
           22:28; 25:03, 25:20; 28:01;
                                   33:04
     (2) .................. 25:03; 33:04
     (5) ........................... 15:21
  833 ........................... 10:01
     (4) ........................... 5:21
     (5), (6) ....................... 5:21
     (5a) ........................ 32:32
  834 (1) ................. 25:02, 25:34
     (3) ........................... 26:04
  835 ........................... 15:05
     (5) ........................... 5:32
  836b ...... 8:94; 12:06, 13:22, 13:25
  837a ........................... 9:62
     a (2) ................. 8:66, 8:140
  838 (1) ........................ 28:01
     (3) ........................... 28:01
     (5)–(10) ..................... 62:15
  839 ...... 7:112; 8:135; 9:09; 10:17,
           10:24; 12:20; 25:31; 49:24; 57:12;
           60:09; 62:09; 65:03, 65:04, 65:05;
                                   68:07
     (3) ........................... 62:08
     (5) ........................... 9:48
  840 ............. 5:15; 60:02; 62:16
  840a ........................... 27:29
  841 ........................... 18:23
     (1) ........................... 26:21
  842 (1) (e) .................... 30:12
     (2a)–(2c) .................... 30:12
  842a ........................... 25:03
  844 ........................... 5:20
Sch 4
  para 1 ........................ 21:05
     12 ........................... 21:05
Sch 5
  para 1 (1) ..................... 8:169
     7 ........................... 8:169
     8 (2), (3) ................... 8:169
     9 (1) ....................... 8:169
        (4) (b) ................... 8:169
        (5) ....................... 8:169
Sch 5aa
  para 8 ........................ 35:38
Sch 5c
  para 39 ........................ 6:41
Sch 12
  para 3 ........................ 37:30
Sch 15
  3–6 ........................... 31:05
Sch 16 ................. 13:24; 25:02
Sch 18 .......... 25:29; 28:23, 28:44
  para 1 (5) ..................... 17:12
     (5e)–(5i) .................... 28:09
  5 ........................... 28:09
     (3) ................. 60:02; 62:15
  5a ........................... 60:02
```

Table of Statutes

Income and Corporation Taxes Act 1988 – cont.
Sch 18 – cont.
  para 5b 60:02; 62:15
       b (9) 28:09
      5c–5e 60:02; 62:15
Sch 18a 1:14; 28:08
  para 5–7 .... 28:04
Sch 20
  para 10 (d) 13:26
Sch 22
  para 2 .... 32:28
      3 (2) (b) 32:28
      7 .... 32:28
Sch 23 .... 32:14
Sch 23a
  para 7a (1) (b) 4:16
Sch 24
  para 1–3 .... 35:68
      4 (2) 35:68
      5–8 .... 35:68
      9 (4) 35:68
      10 .... 35:68
      12 .... 35:68
Sch 25
  para 1 .... 35:71
      2 (1a), (1b) 35:71
         (4) (b) 35:71
      3 .... 35:71
      4 (1a) 35:71
      5 .... 35:73
      6 (4) 35:73
      7 .... 35:73
      8 (5) 35:64
      9 .... 35:73
      10–12 .... 35:73
      16 (2) (b) 35:66
Pt III 35:72
Sch 26
  para 1 .... 35:68
      16–19 .... 35:66
Sch 27 .... 21:28; 35:40
  para 1(1) 35:43
      (2) (b) 35:43
      4 .... 35:43
      5(2) 35:43
Pt II
    14 .... 35:43
Sch 28 .... 21:28; 35:40
  para 2–5 .... 35:45
Pt II 35:45
Sch 28a 30:11
Sch 28aa 4:04; 7:76; 8:151; 25:07;
            27:04, 27:15, 27:26, 27:34
  para 1a (7) 25:14
    1b 25:14
      (6) 25:14
    5b 8:152
      (4) 25:10
      (5) 25:08
    5c 8:152

Income and Corporation Taxes Act 1988 – cont.
Sch 28aa – cont.
  para 5e 25:10
    6 .... 25:13
    6c 25:14
    7a 25:13
Sch 29
  para 26 .... 32:24
Sch 30
  para 6 (2) (b) 1:01
    21 .... 1:01
Sch 31 .... 5:20
Local Government Finance Act 1988
  s 43 (5), (6) 13:22
    45 (5), (6) 13:22
    47 (2) 13:22
Road Traffic Act 1988
  s 192 (2) 7:132
Electricity Act 1989
  s 4 (4) 57:18
Finance Act 1989 . 7:84, 7:96; 21:21;
              32:07, 32:15, 32:16
  s 18 .... 57:25
    36 (3) 35:16
    43 .... 7:22; 8:113; 10:07
    45 .... 7:22
    59 .... 11:28
    67 .... 7:96
      (2) 8:139
    68 .... 7:96
      (2) 13:08
    69 (1) 7:95
      (c) 7:96
      (2), (3) 7:95, 7:96
      (3a) 7:96
      (4)–(12) 7:96
    70 .... 7:96
    71 .... 7:96
      (4) 13:08
    72 (2) 7:96
    73 .... 7:93
    76 .... 10:07
    83 .... 3:24
    100 .... 24:33
    102 (1)–(8) 28:20
    110 .... 13:08; 35:55
      (2), (3), (4) 33:59
    111 .... 33:42
    112, 113 .... 8:102
    114 .... 8:48
    115 .... 37:35
    135–138 .... 28:30
    140 .... 18:01
    165(1) 2A:93
    173 .... 57:42
    178 ..... 2A:34, 2A:39, 2A:96; 51:10;
                56:30; 61:21; 62:25
    182 .... 56:07; 61:01
      (1) 2:06

Table of Statutes

Finance Act 1989 – *cont.*
  s 182 (5) 2:06
      (8) 2:06
  Sch 3 .... 57:25
  Sch 5
    para 2, 3 .... 7:95
      3a–3c 7:95
      4 .... 7:95
      5 (2) (c), (d) 7:95
      6 (3) 7:95
      7–10 .... 7:95
      16 .... 7:95
  Sch 6
    para 20 .... 32:15
      23 .... 32:15
      28, 29 .... 32:15
  Sch 12
    para 1–4 .... 29:02
  Sch 17
    Pt VII 45:28
Law of Property (Miscellaneous Provisions) Act 1989 .... 58:10
  s 1 .... 56:11
    2 .... 57:23
Capital Allowances Act 1990
  s 24(1) 3:02
    28 .... 27:06
    50 (2) 9:52
    61 (2) 10:12
    137 .... 16:20
    155 (6) 9:04
Enterprise and New Towns (Scotland) Act 1990
  s 2 .... 68:21
Finance Act 1990 .... 32:24
  s 25 .... 8:141; 11:28; 25:22
    77 .... 7:08
    78 .... 8:114
    100 .... 61:01
    107, 108 .... 56:01; 57:43
    111 .... 61:01
    112 .... 59:12, 59:13
    113 .... 61:05
    124 (3) 2A:70
    125 .... 1:05
    126 .... 42:32
      (4) 9:04
  Sch 13
    para 7 .... 9:22
Planning (Listed Buildings and Conservation Areas) Act 1990
  s 1 (5) 69:23
    7 .... 69:23
    8 (3) 69:23
Social Security Act 1990 .... 32:05, 32:17
  s 11 (3) 32:29
    17 (7) 51:10
  Sch 5 .... 51:10
Finance Act 1991 .... 20:25

Finance Act 1991 – *cont.*
  s 71 .... 16:04
    (3) 22:09
    (4) 22:09;
    99 (2) 21:05, 21:06
    110–114 .... 56:01; 57:43
    116 .... 60:13, 60:15; 61:14, 61:24
    117 .... 60:13; 61:14, 61:24
    121 .... 42:32
      (2) 8:139
Social Security (Contributions) Act 1991 .... 51:14
Finance Act 1992
  s 14 .... 66:28
  Sch 1
    para 6 (2), (3) 2A:32
  Sch 3 .... 66:28
Finance (No 2) Act 1992 .... 31:05
  s 14 .... 63:01
    24 .... 60:03
    25 (2) 28:25
    38 .... 31:06
    41 (3), (4) 9:54
    61 .... 1:06
    209 (10) 26:09
  Sch 3 .... 63:01
  Sch 6
    para 2 .... 60:03
  Sch 8
    para 5 .... 12:14
  Sch 10
    para 5 (4) 23:09
  Sch 13 .... 9:12
Social Security Administration Act 1992 .... 48:14
  s 19 .... 49:13
    113, 114 .... 2:40
    114 (2) 51:05
    121c 2.12, 2:40; 51:05
    122 (3) (b) 2:06
    141, 142 .... 48:06
    143 (4) (b) 52:05
    188 (1), (2) 56:36
Social Security (Consequential Provisions) Act 1992
  Sch 4
    para 8 .... 52:05
Social Security Contributions and Benefits Act 1992 .... 48:14; 50:09
  s 1 (6) (a), (b) 54:01
    2 (1) (a) .. 48:08; 49:01; 50:01; 51:14; 54:07
      (b) .. 2A:10; 49:01; 50:01; 52:01
      (2) (b) 49:04
    3 (1) 50:01
      (a) ... 50:06, 50:10, 50:19, 50:21
    4 (1) (a), (b) 50:01
      (4) (a), (b) 50:01
    5 (2), (3) 51:02

Table of Statutes

Social Security Contributions and Benefits Act 1992 – *cont.*
s 6 (1) 50:09, 50:24, 50:21
    (a), (b) 51:01
    (2) 51:01
  7 .... 48:08
    (1) (a), (b) 49:23
    (2) 49:23
  8 (1) (b) 51:01
  10 .... 48:09
    (1) (a)–(c) 51:14
    (2) (a), (b) 51:14
    (3) 51:14
    (5) 51:14
    (6) 51:14
      (b) 51:16
    (7) 51:14
    (8) 51:14
      (b) 51:17
    (9) 51:14, 51:17
  10a 48:10
  a (2), (6) 51:19
  11 .... 2A:10; 48:11
    (1), (2) 52:01
    (4) 52:02
  12 (2) 53:13
    (3) 52:01; 53:13
s 13 .... 48:12
    (1) 2A:10
    (4) 53:14
    (6), (7) 53:14
  14 .... 53:08
  15 .... 2A:02; 48:13
    (1) 52:05
      (b) 52:06
    (2) 2A:10; 52:05
    (3) 52:05
      (a) 52:05, 52:06
      (b) 52:05
    (3za) 52:05
    (5) 52:05, 52:06
  55 .... 6:06; 7:02
  112 .... 50:14
  132a (7) 55:06
Sch 1
para 1 (1) (a), (b) 51:07
    3 .... 50:36
      (1) 51:09
      (3) 51:09
    3a, 3b 50:29
    5 .... 51:14
    6 .... 51:18
    7 (11) (a) 51:18
    8 .... 52:02
      (1) (a) 51:18
        (b) 51:14
        (l) 51:18
        (m) 51:18
Sch 2
para 2 (a) 52:06
    3 (1) (a) 52:06

Social Security Contributions and Benefits Act 1992 – *cont.*
Sch 2 – *cont.*
para 3   (c), (d) 52:06
    (2) (a), (b) 52:06
      (d)–(g) 52:06
    (3) 52:06
    (5) 52:06
  5 (a), (b) 52:05
  6–8 .... 52:05
Sch 4
para 16 .... 2A:93
Sch 5 .... 6:06; 7:02
Taxation of Chargeable Gains Act 1992
                                             1:23
s 1 .... 16:04
    (1) 1:32; 33:16
    (2) (a) 6:17
  2 (1) 16:43; 16:39; 32:45; 33:14; 35:57
    (2) (a) 16:27
      (b) 16:28
    (5) 20:02; 35:62
    (6) 20:02
  2a 18:38; 22:13;
  a (2) 16:26
  a (6) 16:26
  3 .... 20:13
    (3) 16:40; 20:01
      (a) 16:40
    (5) (b) 16:28
    (7) 19:10
  3a 2A:03
  4 (1a) 16:40
    (1aa) 32:20
      (b) 19:10
    (1ab) 16:40
    (1b) 16:40
    (3a), (3b) 16:40
  8 .... 25:17; 28:22
    (1) 25:33; 26:30
      (b) 25:02
    (2) 4:33; 16:26
    (2a) 4:33
  9 (3) 35:46
  10 .... 16:39; 35:57
    (1) 12:12; 16:31; 35:46
    (2) 35:46
    (3) 22:27; 25:48; 35:46
    (5) 22:48; 35:46
  10A 16:39; 35:23
    a (1) 35:47; 37:35
    a (2)–(5) 35:47
    a (7)–(9) 35:47
  10b (1) 25:45
  12 .... 35:48
    (1) 16:32; 33:16; 35:12
  13 .... 33:40; 35:47; 35:52
    (4) 35:53, 35:54
    (5a) 35:54
    (5b) (b) 35:54

Table of Statutes

Taxation of Chargeable Gains Act 1992 – cont.

s 13 (7), (8)	35:54
(9)	35:53
(11)	35:54
14	35:54
Pt II (ss 15–57)	16:02
s 16 (2)	16:26
(3)	16:31
(4)	16:32; 35:49
16a	16:26
(2)	4:33
16ZA (3)	35:49
16ZB	35:49
16ZC (2)	35:49
17	18:03, 18:29, 18:33, 18:48, 18:52; 19:02; 21:28; 28:21
(1)	16:43; 22:48; 23:24
(a)	21:16; 22:44
(b)	16:06, 16:44; 22:44
(2)	18:16, 18:49
18	62:05
(1)	18:51
(2)	16:43
(3)	16:30; 18:49, 18:52
(4)	16:30; 18:27
(5), (6)	18:52
19 (1), (2)	17:29
(5), (6)	17:29
20 (3)	17:29
(4) (a), (b)	17:29
(6)–(9)	17:29
21 (1)	16:09; 17:01, 18:06
(a)	18:23
(2)	18:11
(a)	18:14
22	8:82; 17:01, 17:02, 18:03, 18:04, 18:07; 44:28
(1)	16:09; 18:06, 18:17, 18:26
(d)	23:27
(2)	18:12
(b)	18:14
23	17:03; 18:16; 35:47; 44:28
(1)–(3)	18:19
(4), (5)	24:12
(6)–(8)	18:19
24	16;33, 16:34; 18:16; 44:28
(1)	16:04; 18:12
(2)	16:35; 21:01; 28:29, 28:47
(a)	16:34, 16:36
25 (1)	22:48; 35:46
(2)	35:46
(3)	22:48; 25:46, 25:52; 35:46
(3a)	25:19
(6), (7)	35:46
26 (1)–(3)	18:21
27	18:02
28	18:05, 18:11; 28:43
(1)	18:06; 23:23
(2)	18:27
(4)	16:16

Taxation of Chargeable Gains Act 1992 – cont.

s 29	16:44; 18:47; 39:20, 39:23
30	4:14; 16:44; 17:17; 28:25, 28:30, 28:32, 28:33, 28:34, 28:35
(2) (a)–(c)	28:36
(5)	28:30
(8)	28:30, 28:31
31	17:17; 28:30; 28:31, 28:33, 28:36
(3) (a), (b)	28:32
(4)–(7)	28:32
(8)	28:32, 28:33
(9) (a)–(c)	28:32
(10) (a), (b)	28:32
(11)	28:31
31a	28:30, 28:35
a (4)–(10)	28:33
32	17:17; 28:30, 28:31
(2)–(5)	28:34
33	17:17; 28:30; 28:32
(2)–(4)	28:32
(8)	28:32
(9), (10)	28:30
33a	28:30
34	17:17; 28;31, 28:35
35	16:04; 21:09, 21:20; 24:10
(1)	24:11
(3)	21:05
(d)	28:28
(5)	21:05; 24:03, 24:11
(6)	22:37
35A	16:43; 24:05
37	16:04, 16:15
(1)	16:14; 23:24; 26:30
(2)	16:14
(a)	22:01
(3)	22:45
38	16:03
(1) (b)	16:16, 16:19, 16:21
(2)	16:18
(b)	16:16; 17:30
(3), (4)	16:17
39	16:04, 16:15
39 (1), (2)	16:17
(1)	22:01
(3)	22:01
(4)	9:22; 22:01
(5)	22:04
42	21:04; 23:24; 24:12
(4)	18:13
43	23:21
44	16:25; 20:21; 23:18
(1) (a)	23:01
(c)	16:25; 17:18
(3)	16:25
45	17:05
(1)	16:25; 17:18
(2)	16:25; 17:18; 22:03
(3), (4)	16:25; 17:18
(5)	17:18
46	18:26, 18:31; 22:03

Table of Statutes

Taxation of Chargeable Gains Act 1992 – *cont.*

s 46 (2) (b)	16:25
47 (1)	20:16; 22:03
48	16:07, 16:10; 21:23; 24:08
49	15:13
(2)	16:12
50	16:17
51 (2)	8:08
52 (1)	16:17
(4)	16:11, 16:22
53	22:01
(1) (b)	21:27
(1a)	23:09; 25:17
(2) (a), (b)	24:03
(2a)	16:26
(3)	23:20; 24:04
54 (2)	24:03
(3)	21:07
(4)	24:03
(8)	24:03
55 (1), (2)	24:03
(4)	24:03
(5), (6)	24:05
(7)	16:43
(8)	24:05
56 (1)	24:04
(2)	15; 16:43; 23:14; 24:05
(3)	15; 16:43; 24:05
57	24:06
(2), (3)	18:27
58	17:05; 24:05, 24:12; 35:47; 43:13
(1)	16:43; 22:08; 23:14
(2) (a)	22:08
59	22:20, 22:36, 22:37, 22:47; 35:46
(b)	18:50
60	16:42; 18:01; 20:08, 20:21
(1)	18:06; 20:06
(2)	20:06, 20:16
62	17:05; 22:07; 40:21
(1)	19:01
(a)	19:11
(b)	16:29
(2)	16:29; 19:08
(3)	35:48
(4)	19:01, 19:05
(a), (b)	19:12
(5)	18:33; 19:02, 19:09
(6)	19:03; 40:21
(a)	18:01
(7)	19:03
(8)	19:03
(9)	19:03
(10)	16:20; 19:02, 19:09
64 (1)	20:16
(b)	20:17
(2)	19:01, 19:02, 19:05
65	33:40
(1)	19:10
66	18:22; 20:05
67	20:18

Taxation of Chargeable Gains Act 1992 – *cont.*

s 67 (1)	16:24
(3)	16:24
68	20:05, 20:21
68a	15:08; 42:04
(1)–(4)	20:03
69	26:24
(1)	20:01; 33:39, 33:40, 35:55, 35:57, 39:59
(2)	33:39, 33:40
(3)	20:01, 20:05
70	18:01; 20:10
71	16:49; 20:06, 20:07
(1)	20:16, 20:21
(2) (b) (ii)	20:17
(2a), (2b)	20:17
(2d) (a), (c)	20:17
(2i)	20:17
(3)	20:16
72	19:01
(1) (a), (b)	19:07, 20:18
(3)	20:19; 20:21
(4)	20:21
73	19:01; 20:16, 20:18; 24:12; 35:47
(1) (b)	20:12
74	18:44; 19:01, 19:07, 20:16, 20:18
76	35:61
(1)	20:01, 20:21
(2)	20:12, 20:21
77	12:19; 16:10; 20:04; 35:62
(1)	20:24
(2)	20:02
(3) (a)	15:15; 20:02
(6)	20:02
78	20:24
79 (1), (2)	20:24
(3), (4)	20:02, 20:24
(5)	20:24
(5a)	20:24
(7), (8)	20:24
79a	20:17
a (1)	20:22
79b	35:53
80	20:21, 20:25; 21:01, 21:03
(1)–(7)	35:55
81	20:25
(1)	35:55
(3)–(7)	35:55
82	20:25
(3)	35:55
(b)	17:10
83, 84	20:25; 35:55
85	20:25; 35:55
(1)	20:01, 20:21; 35:61
(3)–(8)	35:61
(10), (11)	35:61
86	12:19; 16:10; 20:04, 20:25; 21:03; 34:06; 35:47
(1)	35:62
(3)	35:62

2647

Table of Statutes

Taxation of Chargeable Gains Act 1992 – cont.
s 86 (4)	35:62, 35:63
(5)	35:62
87	16:10; 20:04, 20:25; 35:47, 35:56, 35:57; 37:35
(1)	35:56, 35:57
(4)	35:56
(5)	35:56
(7)	35:56
88	20:25
(1)	35:56
89	20:25; 35:57
(2)	16:10; 35:56, 35:61
90	20:25; 35:57
91	20:25
(2)–(4)	35:56
(5) (b)	35:56
(6)	35:56
92	20:25
(4)	35:56
93	20:05, 20:25
(2)–(5)	35:56
94, 95	20:25; 34:5
96	20:25
(11)	35:56
97	20:25
(1) (b)	35:56
(2)	35:56
(4)	35:56
(6), (7)	35:56
(8)–(10)	35:56
98	20:25
99	22:01
(1)	20:05
100 (1)	16:39; 30:12, 30:15
(2)	30:14
101a–101c	28:20
102	18:01
104	21:02, 21:05; 24:11
(1)	17:04; 21:01, 21:05
(2) (aa)	30:17
(4)	21:05
105	21:05
(1) (b)	21:02
(2)	21:01, 21:02, 21:05
105a	21:01
106	21:02; 21:03
106a	21:04; 35:55
a (1)	21:03
a (5)	21:01; 21:03
a (5a)	21:03
107 (3)	21:02, 21:05
107 (4)–(6)	21:02, 21:05
107 (7)–(9)	21:02, 21:05
108	21:05
(4), (5)	21:08
(7)	21:08
109 (1)	21:05, 21:09; 24:11
(2)–(3)	21:09
(4)	21:05

Taxation of Chargeable Gains Act 1992 – cont.
s 110	21:05
(2), (3)	21:07
(4)	21:09
(6), (6a)	21:07
(7)	21:07
(8) (a)–(d)	21:07
(10), (11)	21:07
112	21:10
(4)	21:17
113	21:15
(1) (b)	24:07
114	21:05, 21:07; 24:09
115	17:05
(1)	17:12
(3)	18:32
116	17:12; 21:21; 35:47
(10), (11)	24:12
(13)	18:15
117	17:12
(1)	21:21
(6a)	21:21
120	2A:69
122	21:16, 21:19; 26:01; 28:38, 28:39
(1)	21:11
(2)	18:15, 21:17
(5)	21:17
(b)	21:11
123	21:16; 27:45
126	21:14; 44:10
(3)	21:12
127	7:87; 17:05; 21:12, 21:13; 28:21, 28:35, 28:45; 40:18; 44:10
128	7:87; 44:10
(1), (2)	21:14
(3)	21:12; 28:35
129	7:87; 44:10
(1)	21:15
130	7:74, 87; 44:10
(2)	21:15
131	21:14; 24:07
132	17:07; 21:14, 21:22
(1)	21:19
(2) (b)	17:10
(3)	17:10; 28:32
133	21:19
(2)	18:15
134	17:10; 24:12; 35:47
(2)	18:32
(4), (5)	21:19
135	17:12; 28:21, 28:45; 35:41
(1)	7:96
(c)	21:20, 21:26
(3)	28:35
(4), (5)	21:20
136	21:20, 21:24, 21:26; 25:19; 27:25; 28:39, 28:45; 35:41
137	21:25, 21:26; 27:25; 62:16
(4)	2A:22; 21:25

Taxation of Chargeable Gains Act 1992 – cont.
```
s 138 ............... 1:30; 21:25; 21:26
    (2)–(5) ............. 25:48, 25:49
    138a .................... 16:07, 16:10
      a (1) ....................... 21:23
      a (2) (c) ................... 21:23
      a (3) ....................... 21:23
      a (4) (b) ................... 21:23
      a (6) (b) ................... 21:23
      a (7)–(10) ................. 21:23
    139 ............................. 28:39
      (1a) ....................... 25:19
      (2) ......................... 25:19
      (4) ......................... 25:19
      (5) ................. 1:30; 25:19
      (7) ................. 2A:22; 25:19
    140 ..................... 25:20, 25:49
      (6a) ....................... 25:20
    140a ..... 21:26; 22:48; 25:49, 25:50;
                                  27:25
      a (2), (3) ................. 25:48
      a (4) (b) .................. 25:48
      a (5), (6) ........... 25:47, 25:48
      a (7) ....................... 25:47
    140b .................. 25:48; 27:25
    140c ........... 21:26; 25:20, 25:50
      (1) (e) .................... 25:49
      (3) ......................... 25:49
      (4) ................. 25:20, 25:49
      (5) ......................... 25:49
      (6), (7) ................... 25:47
      (8) ......................... 25:49
      (9) ................. 24:43; 25:47
    140d ............................ 21:26
      d (2) ....................... 25:49
    141 ............................. 21:13
    142 ..................... 17:05; 21:13
    143 (8) .......................... 18:31
    144 ............................. 23:01
    144 (1) ......... 18:24, 18:27, 18:30
      (2) ................. 18:29, 18:30
        (a), (b) ................. 18:27
      (3) ................. 16:25; 21:07
        (b) ....................... 18:27
      (4) ................. 18:03, 18:26
        (b) ....................... 18:31
      (6) ......................... 18:30
      (7) ......... 18:11, 18:26, 18:30
      (8) (a), (b) ................ 18:23
        (c) ....................... 18:23
          (ii) .................... 18:31
    144a ............................ 18:27
    144za ........................... 18:29
    144zb ........................... 18:29
    144zc ........................... 18:29
    145 ..................... 18:27; 24:09
    146 ............................. 18:26
      (1) (c) .................... 18:31
      (2) ......................... 18:31
      (4) (b) .................... 18:31
```

Taxation of Chargeable Gains Act 1992 – cont.
```
s 148 ................... 18:25, 18:31
    150 ..................... 21:05, 21:06
      (2), (3) .................... 17:24
    150a (1) ............... 17:05, 17:23
      a (2) ......... 17:23; 22:31; 31:13
      a (2a) . 17:05, 17:23; 22:31; 31:13
      a (8a), (8b) ................ 17:23
    151 ............................. 31:01
    151a ............................ 17:22
    152 ...... 16:44; 22:13, 22:15, 22:46;
          23:05, 23:38; 25:20; 28:25; 35:47;
                                  44:10
      (1) ... 22:12, 22:16, 22:18, 22:24
      (3) ... 22:12, 22:21, 22:22, 22:23
      (4) ......................... 22:12
      (6) ................. 22:12, 22:14
      (7) ................. 22:12, 22:14
      (8) ......... 22:12, 22:16, 22:18
      (9) ......................... 22:14
    153 ...... 22:14, 22:16, 22:46, 23:05,
                                  23:38; 28:25
      (1) ......................... 22:34
    153a (1) ........................ 22:23
      a (3) (b) ................... 25:04
      a (4) ....................... 22:23
      a (5) (b) ................... 25:04
    154 ...... 22:16, 22:46, 23:05; 28:25;
                                  35:47
      (2) ......................... 24:12
      (6) ......................... 22:17
    155 ...... 22:12, 22:16, 22:18, 22:23,
          22:34, 22:46, 23:05; 27:22; 28:25
    156 ...... 22:12, 22:15, 22:16, 22:46,
                                  23:05; 28:25
    157 ...... 22:12, 22:16, 22:46, 23:05;
                                  28:25
      (b) ......................... 22:18
    158 ............ 22:16, 22:46; 28:25
      (1) (a)–(b) ................. 22:15
        (c) ................. 22:15, 22:19
        (e) ....................... 22:15
      (2) ......................... 22:12
    159 (1) ................. 22:48; 35:46
      (2) ......................... 35:46
      (3) ................. 22:48; 35:46
      (4) ......................... 35:46
    161 .............................. 8:49
      (1) ......................... 22:06
      (2) ......................... 22:07
      (3) ... 22:06, 22:08; 27:20; 28:27
      (4) ......................... 22:06
    162 ...... 22:10, 22:34, 24:12; 35:47
    162a .................... 22:10, 22:34
    164a (1) ........................ 22:24
      a (2) (a) .................. 22:24
    164b–164n ....................... 22:24
    165 ...... 16:24; 17:05, 18:51; 20:02,
          20:15, 20:16; 23:05; 24:12; 26:42;
                                  28:43; 42:06
```

Table of Statutes

Taxation of Chargeable Gains Act 1992 – cont.
- s 165 (1) 18:39
  - (a) 18:38
  - (1) (b) 18:44
  - (2) 18:44
    - (a) 18:41
    - (b) (i), (ii) 18:41
  - (3) 18:41
  - (6) 18:44
  - (6a) 18:41
  - (7) 18:42
  - (8) (a) 18:41
  - (9) 18:41
  - (10), (11) 16:24
- 167 .... 18:39
- 168 .... 24:12; 33:40
- 169b 20:02
  - b (1) 18:44
- 169c 18:44
- 169f (1) 20:02
- 169f (2) 20:02
  - (b) 18:44
- 169g 18:44
- 169I (1)–(4), (6)–(8) 22:33
- 169J (1)–(6) (b) 22:33
- 169K 22:33
- 169M (3) 22:33
- 169N 17:05
  - (2), (3) 22:33
- 169S (1), (3) 22:33
- 170 .... 3:24; 25:03, 25:20; 27:24; 28:30
  - (2)–(7) 28:23
  - (10) 28:23, 28:24
  - (11) 28:23
- 171 .... 16:45, 17:05; 25:17, 25:20, 25:27; 28:14, 28:23, 28:25, 28:29, 28:32, 28:34; 39:25
  - (1) 28:22, 28:36
  - (1a) 25:46; 35:46
  - (2) 33:31
    - (c) 28:21
    - (cc), (cd) 28:21
    - (da) 28:21
  - (3) 28:21
  - (4) 28:21
- 171a 3:24; 25:17, 25:33; 28:22
  - a (2) 28:22; 39:25
  - a (4) 28:22
  - a (5) 28:22; 39:23
- 172 .... 22:48
- 173 (2) 28:27
- 174 (4) 28:22
- 175 (1) 28:28
  - (1a) 28:28
  - (2) 28:28; 33:31
  - (2a) 28:28
    - a (b) 22:18
  - (2aa) 28:28

Taxation of Chargeable Gains Act 1992 – cont.
- s 175 (2b) 22:15; 28:28
  - (2c) 28:28
  - (3) 28:28
- 175 .... 35:51
- 176 .... 28:34
  - (3), (4) 28:29
  - (6) 28:29
  - (8) 28:29
- 177 .... 4:14; 28:29
- 177a 28:14
- 178 .... 28:32, 28:38
  - (3) 24:12; 28:25
- 179 .... 27:24; 28:23, 28:36, 28:39, 28:40, 28:41, 28:43
  - (1) 28:24, 28:25
  - (2) 28:21, 28:25
  - (2a) 28:24, 28:25
  - (2b) (b), (c) 28:25
  - (2c) 28:25
  - (3) 28:24, 28:25
  - (4) 28:24
  - (6)–(9) 28:25
  - (10) (b), (c) 28:25
- 179a (3) 28:24
  - a (11) 28:24
- 179b 28:24
- 181 .... 28:25
- 184a 28:29
  - (1) (c) 28:17
- 184b 28:17, 28:29
- 184g 28:29
- 185 .... 25:17
  - (4) 25:46
- 187 .... 24:42, 24:39; 25:44, 27:27
- 188 .... 33:31
- 189 .... 2A:22
- 190 .... 2A:22; 28:22
  - (3), (4) 28:24
  - (7) 28:24
  - (11) 28:24
- 192 (3) 28:25, 28:38, 28:39, 28:40
  - (4) 28:38, 28:39, 28:40, 28:41
- 199 .... 35:46
- 201 (1) 23:27
- 204 .... 17:05, 17:13
- 205 .... 16:17
- 206 .... 20:06
- 210 .... 31:19
- 213 .... 28:18
- 222 .... 16:44; 17:05; 19:03; 23:02, 23:06, 23:08
  - (5) (a) 19:10; 23:11
    - (b) 23:11
  - (6) 16:43; 23:11
  - (7) 23:08, 23:11
    - (a) 19:05; 23:14
  - (8), (9) 23:10
- 223 (1) 23:08, 23:10
  - (2) 23:08

2650

Table of Statutes

Taxation of Chargeable Gains Act 1992 – *cont.*

s 223 (3)	23:10
(4) (b)	23:09
(7)	23:08, 23:10
224 (1)	23:08
(3)	23:07
225	20:14; 23:13, 23:14, 23:16
225a (1)	19:10; 23:11
(3), (4)	23:15
(5) (b)	23:15
(6)	23:15
226	23:09, 23:12
226a	18:44; 23:16
226b	23:16
227–235	7:96
236a	17:05
237 (c)	17:11
241	22:15
(2)	23:05
(3)	18:41
(b)	23:05
(3a)	23:05
242 (1) (a)	18:15
(3) (a)	18:15
243 (1) (a)	18:15
(5)	23:38
244	18:15
245, 246	18:01
247	24:12; 35:47
(1)	23:38
(2) (b)	23:38
(5) (h)	23:38
(8)	23:38
247a	22:23; 25:04
248 (1)	23:38
(3)	24:12
250	17:05, 17:14
251	12:14; 17:05, 17:09
(1)	17:06, 17:10
(2)–(4)	17:06
252	17:06
253	17:05; 23:05
(3a)	17:07
(4) (b)	17:08
(6)	17:07
254	21:21
256	13:22; 16:46
(1)	13:26; 16:45
(2)	16:48; 20:15
257	17:05
(1) (b)	16:46
(2), (3)	16:49
258 (1)	17:15
(2)	17:05
(a), (b)	17:15
(3)	17:16
(4)	35:48
(5)	17:16
259	18:37

Taxation of Chargeable Gains Act 1992 – *cont.*

s 260	17:05; 18:38, 18:40, 18:42, 18:44; 19:07; 20:02, 20:10, 20:15, 20:16; 39:07; 42:06
(1)	18:40
(2) (a), (b)	18:40
(d)	18:40
(7), (8)	16:24
261b, 261c	6:17
262 (1)	17:19; 18:18, 18:35
(2)–(3)	17:19
(4)	17:21
(5)	17:20; 22:03
(8)	17:19
263	17:05
264	17:05
265	17:05; 59:12
266	17:05
270	17:05
271 (5)–(8)	17:05
272	7:57; 62:08
(2)	17:25; 45:01
(3)	17:26
273	17:05; 62:08
(3)	7:57; 45:02
274	17:28; 19:01, 19:02, 19:11; 62:08
275	35:51
(1)	23:01
(2)	23:01; 35:51
276 (7)	7:148
277	16:23; 35:48; 37:03, 37:18, 37:29, 37:38
278	16:23; 35:48, 37:03
279	35:54
(3) (a)	35:52
280	16:07, 16:38
281 (1) (b) (ii)	16:38
(3)	18:36
(7) (b)	18:36
282 (1), (2)	18:35
284a, 284b	16:01; 22:12, 22:13, 22:15
286	18:29, 18:51; 22:48
(2)	16:43; 18:50
(3), (3a)	18:50
(4)	18:50; 22:43, 22:44, 22:46
(5)	18:50
(b)	18:49
(6), (7)	18:50
(8)	39:19
286a, 286b	23:21
287	18:31
(4)	17:12
288 (1)	18:23; 23:01
(3)	23:11
(6)	18:23
Sch A1	23:05; 24:02
para 15	23:14
Sch 1	11:09; 20:13

Table of Statutes

Taxation of Chargeable Gains Act 1992 – cont.
Sch 1 – cont.
para 1 (6) 20:01
para 2 .... 20:01
Sch 2
para 1 (1) (a), (b) 24:13
9 .... 24:13
16 .... 23:20
(4)–(7) 24:14
(9), (10) 24:14
17 (1) 24:13
19 (1) 24:13
20 .... 22:02
21 .... 22:10
Sch 3
para 1 ..... 16:43; 22:40; 24:05, 24:12
3 .... 22:02
4 .... 18:13; 24:12
5 .... 24:12
Sch 4
para 1 .... 24:12
2 .... 22:10, 22:13; 24:12
3 .... 24:12
4 .... 24:12
(5) 21:19; 22:17
5 .... 18:45
9 .... 24:12
(1) (b), (c) 18:45
Sch 4a 19:20, 20:21
para 1 .... 20:22
4 (1) 35:61
5–7 .... 35:61
7 .... 20:22
8 (1), (2) 20:22
11 .... 20:22
12 (2) (a) 35:61
13 (2) (b) 35:61
Sch 4b 35:57, 35:59
para 1 (1) (b) 20:04
2 .... 20:04
6–8 .... 20:04
10 (1) 20:04
14 .... 35:57
Sch 4c
para 8 .... 35:56
(3) 35:61
9 (3) (b) 35:57
Sch 5 .... 32:20
para 2 (1)–(3) 35:62
(4)–(6) 35:62
3–5 .... 35:62
6 .... 34:06
(2) 35:63
7–9 .... 35:62
9 (10a) (b)–(d)
.... 35:62
10 .... 35:62
10a 35:62
14 .... 35:62

Taxation of Chargeable Gains Act 1992 – cont.
Sch 5aa 20:34; 21:20, 21:24; 25:19; 28:21; 62:18
para 1–5 .... 25:19
Sch 5b 31:08
para 1 .... 31:14
para 1 (1) (a) 22:26
(c) 22:24; 31:08
(d) 22:26
(2) (a) 22:24; 31:08
(b) 31:08
(e) 22:24
(3) 22:25
(4) 22:26
1a (2) 22:30
2 (1), (3) 22:25
3 (1) 22:29
(a) 22:25, 22:30
(c) 22:26
(d) 22:25
(3) 22:26
(5) 22:25
4 .... 22:24, 22:29
(1) 22:30
(a) 22:25
13 .... 22:29
(2) 31:14
13a 22:29
16 (2), (4) 31:15
17 (2) 20:14
(a), (b)
.... 22:26
(8) 20:14
19 .... 20:24
(1) 22:28, 22:29; 31:08
Sch 5ba
para 3–5 .... 22:32
Sch 5c
para 1 (3) 17:22
2 .... 17:22
3 (1) 17:22
(2) 31:17
4 (2) 17:22
Sch 7
para 1 (1) 18:41
2 (2) (a) (ii) 18:44
(b) 18:44
3 .... 21:20
4 .... 16:38
5 .... 16:38
(1), (2) 18:43
6 .... 16:38
(1), (2) 18:43
7 .... 16:38; 18:43
Sch 7a 21:20; 24:33
para 1 (1) 28:14
(2) (a), (b) 28:14
(3), (4) 28:14
(6) 3:24; 28:14
2 .... 28:18

Taxation of Chargeable Gains Act 1992 – *cont.*
Sch 7a – *cont.*
 para 2 (1)–(6) 28:15
  (6a), (6b) 28:15
  (7), (8) 28:15
 3 .... 28:15
 5 (8) 28:15
 6 (1) 28:16
 7 (1)–(3) 28:16
 8 .... 28:19
 9 (6) 28:19
 10–12 .... 28:19
Sch 7aa 24:33
 para 1–7 .... 28:18
Sch 7ab 28:24
Sch 7ac 17:05; 21:02; 23:05; 28:38
 para 1, 2 .... 28:43
  (7) 28:43
 4 .... 28:43
 5 (2) 28:43
 6 .... 28:43
 7 .... 28:45
 8 .... 28:44
 9–17 .... 28:45
 18 .... 28:46
  (1) (a) 29:15
 19 .... 28:46
  (2) 29:15
 20 (2) (c) 28:46
 21–23 .... 28:46
 24 (1) 28:46
 26 (4), (5) 28:45
 30 .... 28:43
 32 .... 28:42
 33 .... 16:37; 28:47
 34, 35 .... 28:47
 36–38 .... 28:43
Sch 7c 17:05; 21:20
Sch 8
 para 1 .... 40:19
  (1) 23:20
  (5) 23:18
  (6) 23:22
 2 (2) 23:24
  (11) 23:24
 3 (2) (a) 23:23
  (3) (a) 23:23
  (7) 16:45; 23:23
 4 .... 23:24
  (2) (a), (b) 23:25
  (3) 23:25
 5 (1), (2) 23:25
 7a 35:07
 8 (2)–(6) 23:19
 9 (3) 23:19
 10 (2), (3) 23:23
Sch 9
 para 1 .... 17:12
 Pt II 17:12
Sch 11

Taxation of Chargeable Gains Act 1992 – *cont.*
Sch 11 – *cont.*
 para 13, 14 .... 17:01
Finance Act 1993 .... 31:05; 33:08
 s 83 .... 16:40
 s 86 (2) 22:12
 92 .... 8:64, 8:78; 25:54
 93 .... 8:64, 8:78
 93a 8:64
 94 .... 8:64, 8:78
 94a 8:64
 109 .... 8:48; 57:25
 110 .... 8:114
 118 .... 13:15
 171 (2) 35:16; 36:02
 198 .... 45:13
 199 (1) (b) 45:16
 201 .... 57:02
 202, 203 .... 57:31
 204 .... 56:20
Leasehold Reform, Housing and Urban Development Act 1993
 .... 44:29; 57:31
Pension Schemes Act 1993
 s 1 .... 64:24
 104 .... 32:28
Social Security Act 1993
 .... 48:06
Trade Union Reform and Employment Rights Act 1993 .... 51:18
Criminal Justice and Public Order Act 1994
 s 136–139 .... 2:31; 63:03
Finance Act 1994 ... 3:24; 7:47, 7:84; 50:27
 s 5 (2) 40:08
 7 .... 2:14
 93 .... 16:33
 102 .... 7:95
 107 .... 32:04
 119 (2) 2A:33
 128 .... 7:146
 144 (1) 8:146
 150a (1) 3:03
 165 .... 27:15
 168 .... 26:45
 178 .... 2A:01
 196 .... 2:37
 201 .... 8:44
 217 (3) 37:17
 222, 223 .... 42:32
 239 .... 56:11
 240 .... 62:33
  (2) 57:25
  (4) 56:23
 240a 56:23
 241 ...... 57:19, 57:29; 62:05, 62:12
 242 .... 56:18, 56:19
  (2) 57:28
  (3) 57:29

Table of Statutes

Finance Act 1994 – *cont.*
s 242 (3) (a) 57:28
    243 .... 57:23
    244, 245 .... 56:24, 56:25
    248 (2) 42:32
    249 ...... 22:48; 33:25, 33:30; 35:26
    251 (10) 33:31
  Sch 16 .... 1:18
Social Security (Contributions) Act 1994
  s 3 .... 52:06
Value Added Tax Act 1994
    ... 1:02, 1:23; 63:01, 63:02; 65:03,
                    65:04, 65:05
  s 1 .... 1:32
    (1) 63:06, 63:24; 65:01
      (a) 63:18, 63:21
      (c) 63:39; 65:49
    (2) 65:09, 65:10, 65:20
    (3) 65:44
    (4) 63:06, 63:39; 65:50, 65:53
  2 (1) 65:06
    (a) 65:16
  (1a) 70:01
    (2) 70:01
  3 .... 8:157
    (1) 63:10; 66:04
    (3) 63:10
  3a (2), (3) 63:43
  4 .... 69:01
    (1) 63:14, 63:18; 65:08, 65:38;
                          68:01
    (2) 63:18, 63:33; 64:01, 64:11,
                64:14; 65:08; 68:01
  5 .... 8:157; 65:01
    (1) 63:18
    (2) (a) 63:18, 63:19, 63:21
      (b) 63:24, 63:26
    (3) 63:17, 63:24; 65:31
    (8) 65:30
  6 (2) 65:11, 65:13
    (3) 65:11, 65:13, 65:34
    (4)–(6) 65:13
    (7), (8) 65:13, 65:14, 65:31
    (9) 65:13
    (11) 65:32
    (12) 65:28
    (13) 65:29
    (14a) 65:14, 65:38
  7 .... 63:31
    (1) 63:28
    (3) (a) 63:28; 64:07
      (b) 63:28
    (4)–(6) 63:28
    (7) (b) 63:28
    (8) 63:28
    (10) 63:29
    (11) 65:14, 65:38
  7a (2), (3) 63:31
    (4) 63:31
      (a) 63:35
  8 .... 63:31

Value Added Tax Act 1994 – *cont.*
s 8 (1) 64:01; 65:38
    (2) 64:01; 65:38
    (4a) 65:38
  9 .... 63:15
    (1) 65:39
    (2) 65:38, 65:39
    (b) 63:29
    (3) 63:30; 64:27; 65:39; 69:30
    (4) 63:30; 64:27; 65:38, 65:39;
                          69:30
    (5) 63:30; 63:31; 64:27
    (a), (b) 63:29
    (6) 63:31; 65:39
  9a 65:01
  10 (1) 63:34
    (a) 65:43
    (2) 63:36; 64:11
    (a) 64:07
    (b) 65:43
    (3) 63:36
    (a), (b) 65:43
  11 (1)–(3) 63:35
  12 (1) 65:45
    (2) 64:11, 65:45
  13 (2)–(4) 63:37
    (5) 66:40
    (a)–(c) 63:37
  14 .... 63:38
    (1), (2) 63:27; 64:11
    (6) 63:27
  15 (2) (a) 65:51; 67:13
    (b) 65:50
  16 .... 63:39
    (1) 67:13
    (a) 63:03
    (b) 63:03, 63:08
    (2) 63:03
  17 (2) 63:40; 69:02
    (4) (a) 69:02
  18 . 63:28, 63:37, 63:41; 65:45, 65:53
    (1) 63:28
    (3) 63:28
    (4) 65:14
    (6) 65:36
    (7) 65:36; 69:06
  18b 63:28, 63:37; 65:45
    b (3) 63:37
    b (4), (5) 65:48
    b (6) 63:25
  18c 65:01
    (1) 69:02, 69:06
    (2) 65:36
    (3) (a)–(d) 65:36
    (4) 69:06
  18d 65:48
    d (2) 65:36
  18f (1) 65:36
    f (2) 65:36; 69:06
    f (6) 63:25
  19 .... 57:09; 65:25

Table of Statutes

Value Added Tax Act 1994 – *cont.*
s 19 (2) 63:21, 63:23; 64:01; 65:16, 65:17
  (3) 63:21, 63:23; 65:17
  (4) 63:20; 65:16
20 (1)–(5) 65:46
21 (1)–(4) 65:52
  (5) 65:23, 65:52
  (6)–(7) 65:52
  (2a), (2b) 65:52
23 (1)–(3) 65:26
  (4) 65:26; 68:15
  (5), (6) 68:15
24 (1) 63:07, 63:14; 66:02, 66:03, 66:04, 66:05, 66:20, 66:30, 66:31
  (2) 63:06; 65:07, 65:46; 66:05
  (3) 66:05
  (4) 66:03
  (5) 65:30; 66:05, 66:08
  (7) 66:05
25 (1) 63:21; 65:20; 67:01
  (2) 66:06, 66:22
  (3) 67:05
  (5), (6) 67:05
  (7) 66:06, 66:16
26 (1) 66:06, 66:07; 69:01
  (2) 64:16; 66:06
    (a) 66:07; 69:01
    (b) 63:42; 65:21; 66:07
    (c) . 63:42; 65:21; 66:07, 66:12
  (3) 66:25
26a (1), (2) 66:30, 66:31
s 26a (3) 66:30
  a (6) 66:30
26ab 63:09
  (2), (3) 66:31
26b (5) 66:06
27 .... 66:40
28 .... 67:04
29a (1) ... 70:01, 70:03, 70:04, 70:05, 70:06, 70:08, 70:10
  a (a) 65:06
  a (2) 70:03
  a (3) 70:02
30 (1) 65:06; 68:01
  (a) 69:01
  (2), (2a) 69:02, 69:03
  (3) 65:06; 69:01, 69:02, 69:09, 69:10
  (5) 63:32; 69:39
  (6) 69:02
    (a) 69:08
    (b) 69:05
  (7) 69:05
  (8), (8a) 69:02
  (9), (10) 69:02
31 .... 64:27
  (1) 63:33, 63:36; 65:43; 68:01, 68:02
  (2) 68:02
33 .... 2:62

Value Added Tax Act 1994 – *cont.*
s 33 (1) 66:40
  (3) 66:40
33a 66:40
35 .... 66:40
36 (1) 66:41
  (2) 66:41
  (3a) 66:41
  (4) 66:41
  (4a) 66:30
36a 69:09
37 (1) 69:02
38 .... 69:02
39a 66:01
40 .... 66:40
41 (2) 63:16
  (3) 66:40
  (4) 66:40
  (5) 63:16
  (6)–(8) 63:16; 66:07, 66:40
42 .... 64:01
43 .... 63:31
  (1) 64:26; 65:08; 67:10
  (a) 64:27
  (1aa), (1ab) 64:26
  (2) 64:26
  (2a) 64:27
  (2b) 64:28
  (2c) (b), (c) 64:28
  (2d) 64:27
  (2e) 64:27
43a (1)–(3) 64:24
43b (1) 64:25
  b (2) (a)–(d) 64:25
  b (3) (b) 64:25
  b (4) 64:25
  b (5) (a)–(c) 64:25
  b (6) 64:25
43c (1)–(3) 64:25
  (4) (a), (b) 64:25
43d (1) 64:24
  d (2)–(4) 64:24, 64:25
44 .... 65:01
  (1) (b) 64:29
  (2)–(4) 64:29
  (5) 64:26, 64:29
  (7)–(10) 64:29
45 (1) 63:11
46 (1), (3) 63:12
47 .... 66:05
  (1) 63:20
  (2a) 63:20
  (3) 66:03
48 (1) (a)–(c) 63:13
  (1a) 63:13
  (2) 63:13
  (4), (5) 63:13
  (7) 63:13
50 (1) (a) 69:02
50a (4) 65:17, 65:23
53 (3) 63:30

2655

Table of Statutes

Value Added Tax Act 1994 – *cont.*
- s 54 .... 63:44; 65:25
- 55 .... 65:01
  - (1) 64:01; 65:40
  - (2) 65:40
  - (5) 64:01; 65:40
- 55a 63:09; 65:01
  - a (1) (a), (b) 65:41
  - a (2) 65:41
  - a (3) 64:01; 65:41
  - a (4)–(8) 65:41
  - a (9) 64:01
- 56 (1), (2) 65:27
  - (3) (c)–(e) 65:27
  - (4) 64:26; 65:27
  - (5) 66:05
  - (6)–(10) 65:27
- 57 (1)–(3) 65:27
  - (9) 65:27
- 59 (1)–(3) 2A:45; 67:08
  - (4)–(6) 67:08
  - (7) (a), (b) 67:08
- 59a, 59b 67:08
- 60 .. 1:22; 2A:97; 63:03; 64:14; 66:40
  - (1) (b) 2:61
  - (2), (3) 2:61
  - (6), (7) 2:61
- 61 .... 2A:97; 63:03
  - (1) (b) 2:61
  - (2), (3) 2:61
  - (5), (6) 2:61
  - (8) 2:61
- 62 .... 68:02; 69:02; 70:02
  - (1) 2A:97
- 63 .... 1:22; 2A:97; 63:03; 67:19
  - (1) 2:62
  - (2), (3) 2:62, 2:63
  - (4) (a) 2:62
  - (5) 2:62, 2:63
  - (6) 2:62
  - (8) 2:62, 2:63
  - (9) 2:62; 66:40
  - (9a) 66:40
  - (10) (a) 2:62
    - (b) 2:62; 67:19
  - (11) 2:62
- 64 .... 2A:97; 63:03
  - (1) 2:63
  - (2) (b) 2:63
    - (d) 2:63
  - (3) 2:63
  - (4) 2:63; 66:40
  - (5) 2:63
    - (b) 67:19
  - (6) 2:63
  - (6a) (a), (b) 2:63
- 65 (1) 2A:97
  - (7) 2A:97
- 66 (3) 2A:97
  - (10) 2A:97
- 67 .... 63:03

Value Added Tax Act 1994 – *cont.*
- s 67 (1) 64:14
  - (a), (b) 2A:97
  - (c) 2A:97; 65:18
  - (2) 64:14; 65:18
  - (3), (4) 64:14
  - (8) 64:14; 65:18
  - (9) 64:14
- 68 .... 2:38
  - (3) 2A:97
- 69 (1) 2A:97
  - (b) 63:13
  - (d) 65:10
- 69a(2) 2A:97
- 69b 63:09
  - (1) 2A:97
- 70 .... 2:61, 2:62, 2:63; 64:14
- 71 (1) 2:62; 64:14; 65:18; 67:08
- 72 (1)–(8) 2:34; 64:14
  - (9) 2:34
  - (10) 2:34; 63:09
  - (11) 2:34; 67:09
  - (12) 2:07, 2:34
- 73 (1) 2A:42, 2A:67; 67:03, 67:05
  - (2) 67:07, 67:17
  - (a) 66:36, 66:40
  - (3) 67:07
  - (6) 2A:67
  - (6A) ... 66:36, 66:40; 67:07, 67:17
  - (7b) 65:36
  - (8) 67:03
  - (9) 2A:67; 67:05
- 74 .... 64:14; 67:07, 67:17
  - (1) 65:36
  - (a)–(c) 2A:42
  - (2) 2A:42; 67:19
  - (3) 2A:42
  - (4) 2A:42; 65:18
  - (5) 2A:42
  - (a), (b) 67:19
  - (7) 2A:42
- 76 .... 66:40
  - (1) 64:14, 64:27; 65:36; 67:08
  - (a) 2:61, 2:62, 2:63
  - (b) 2A:42, 2A:97
  - (3) (c) 2:62, 2:63
  - (d) 2A:42
  - (4) 2A:42, 2:62, 2:63
  - (7), (8) 2A:42
  - (9) 2A:42, 2A:97, 2:61, 2:62,
              2:63; 66:40; 67:09
- 77 (1) 2A:42, 2:61, 2:62, 2:63
  - (a) 2A:67
  - (2), (3) 2A:42, 2:61, 2:62, 2:63
  - (4) 2A:42, 2:61, 2A:67
  - (5) 2A:42, 2:61
  - (a) 2:62, 2:63
  - (b) 2A:67
  - (6) 2A:67
- 77a (1) (a)–(c) 67:10
- s 77a (2), (3) 67:10

2656

Value Added Tax Act 1994 – *cont.*
　s 77a (6)–(9) 67:10
　　a (10) (b) 67:10
　　78 .... 66:40; 67:05, 67:16, 67:17
　　　(1) (a), (b) 2A:43
　　　(3) 2A:43
　　　(4), (5) 2A:43
　　　(8)–(11) 2A:43
　　78a (1)–(4) 2A:43
　　　a (6) 2A:43; 66:40
　　　a (7) 66:40
　　　a (8) 2A:43
　　79 (1) 66:40
　　　(2a), (4) 67:06
　　80 (1), (1a) 67:16
　　　(1b) 67:17
　　　(2) 67:16, 67:17
　　　(2a) 67:16
　　　(3) 67:16
　　　(4) 67:16, 67:17
　　　(4za) 67:16, 67:17
　　　(4zb) 67:16
　　　(3a)–(3c) 67:16
　　　(4) 67:16
　　　(4a) 67:16
　　　(6) 67:16, 67:17
　　80a 67:16
　　80b (1), (1b) 67:16
　　　b (1e) 67:16
　　　b (2) 67:16
　　81 (3), (3a) 67:04
　　83 .... 2:16
　　　(a) 2:14
　　　(c) 2:14
　　　(e) 66:09
　　　(f) 67:16
　　　(g) (1), (3)–(6)
　　　　............................... 2:14
　　　(l) 67:09
　　　(k) 64:25
　　　(ka) 64:25
　　　(n) 2A:97, 2:61, 2:62, 2:63;
　　　　　　　　　　　　 64:14; 67:08
　　　(p) 65:36; 67:17
　　　　(i) 67:03
　　　(q) 2A:42, 2A:97, 2:61, 2:62,
　　　　2:63; 64:14, 64:25, 64:27; 65:36;
　　　　　　　　　　　　　　　 67:08
　　　(r) 2A:42
　　　(ra) 67:05, 67:10
　　　(s) 2A:43
　　　(t) 67:16, 67:17
　　　(ta) 67:16
　　　(w) 65:46
　　　(wa) 64:25, 64:27
　　84 (2), (3) 2:17
　　　(4) 66:20, 66:29
　　　(4a) 2:16; 64:25
　　　(4b)–(4d) 64:25
　　　(4e)–(4f) 67:09
　　　(5) 2A:67

Value Added Tax Act 1994 – *cont.*
　s 84 (6) 2A:42, 2:61, 2:62, 2:63
　　　(7a) 64:25, 64:27
　　　(8) 2:93
　　　(10) 2:16
　　85 .... 2:93
　　88 .... 65:19
　　　(2), (6) 65:15
　　89 .... 68:05
　　　(1), (2) 63:23
　　94 .... 50:03
　　　(1) 63:16
　　　(2) (b) 63:16
　　　(4)–(6) 63:32
　　95 .... 64:07, 64:11; 65:43; 69:07
　　96 .... 63:31
　　　(1) 63:25; 66:19, 66:40; 68:14;
　　　　　　　　　　 69:17, 69:22; 70:10
　　　(3) 65:50, 65:51
　　　(4) 66:40
　　　(9) 68:02; 69:12; 70:02
　　　(10a) .. 68:11, 68:12; 69:17, 69:22
　　　(10b) 68:12
　　97 .... 63:31
　　　(1) 63:03
　　97a (1)–(6) 65:14, 65:38
　　98 .... 63:31
　　Sch 1 .... 63:27
　　para 1 .... 69:01
　　　(1) 68:01
　　　　(a) 64:02
　　　　(b) 64:03
　　　(2) 68:01
　　　　(a), (b) 64:04
　　　(3), (4) 64:02, 64:04
　　　(7) 64:01; 65:40, 65:41
　　　(8) 64:01
　　　(9) 64:01; 65:48
　　　1a 63:12
　　　2 .... 63:12
　　　(7) (d) 67:10
　　　5 (1)–(3) 64:02
　　　6 (1), (2) 64:03
　　　7 (1), (2) 64:04
　　　8 .... 64:02; 69:01
　　　9 .... 64:15; 68:01; 69:01
　　　10 .... 68:01
　　　(1) 64:16
　　　(4) (a), (b)
　　　　............................. 64:16
　　　14 .... 69:01
　　　(1) 64:21
　　　16 .... 64:01
　　　19 .... 63:14, 63:18; 64:01
　　Sch 2 .... 63:27
　　para 1 (1) 64:10
　　　(2) 64:09
　　　(3) 64:08
　　　　(a)–(e) 64:07
　　　(6) 64:10
　　　(7) 64:09, 64:10; 65:48

2657

Table of Statutes

Value Added Tax Act 1994 – *cont.*
  Sch 2 – *cont.*
    para 3 (1), (2) 64:08, 64:09, 64:10
        4 (1)–(3) 64:17
        5 (2) 64:17
       10 .... 64:07
          (d) 63:14
  Sch 3 .... 64:11; 68:01
    para 1 (1) 64:12
       (2) 64:13
       (5) 64:12
       (6) 64:12, 64:13, 65:48
      3 (1) (a) 64:12
        (b) 64:13
       (2) 64:12, 64:13
       (3) (a) 64:12
        (b) 64:13
      4 (1) 64:18
       (2), (3) 64:19
       (4) 64:18, 64:19
      8 (1) 64:23
     11 .... 63:34; 64:11
       (a) 63:14; 65:43
  Sch 3a
    para 1 .... 64:05
       (1) (a), (b) 64:06
      3, 4 .... 64:06
      7 (1) 64:22
       (4) 64:22
      9 (1) (b) 63:14
       (2) 64:05
  Sch 3b
    para 1–10 .... 63:43
      11 .... 63:43
       (2), (4) 67:14
      12 .... 63:43
       (3) 67:14
      13 .... 63:43
       (1) 67:14
     14–22 .... 63:43; 67:14
  Sch 4
    para 1 (1) 63:25
       (a), (b) 63:26
      2 .... 63:24
      3, 4 .... 63:24, 63:25
      5 .... 63:24, 63:27
       (1) 63:18, 63:25; 65:28
       (2), (2a) 65:28
       (2za) 65:28
       (3) 65:28; 69:31
       (4) .. 63:18, 63:26; 65:29; 69:31
       (4a) 65:29; 66:05
       (5), (5a) 65:28, 65:29
       (6) 63:25, 63:26
        (a) 65:28
        (b) 65:29
      6 .... 63:24, 63:27; 65:40
       (1) 63:25; 65:31
       (2) 63:25; 65:31
      7 .... 67:11
      8 .... 65:01

Value Added Tax Act 1994 – *cont.*
  Sch 4 – *cont.*
    para 8 (1)–(3) 65:42
      9 ..... 65:28, 65:29, 65:41, 65:42;
                                          67:11
       (1), (2) 63:26
  Sch 4a
    Pt 1 (paras 1–8) 63:31; 65:38
    Pt 2 (para 9) 63:31, 65:38
    Pt 3 (paras 10–16)
                   .... 63:31
  Sch 5 .... 63:31; 64:28; 65:38
    para 1–5 .... 63:30; 64:27; 65:38
      5c 63:30
      6, 7 .... 63:30; 64:27; 65:38
      7a–7b 63:30
      7c 63:30, 63:43
      8 .... 63:30; 64:27; 65:38
      9–10 .... 65:38
  Sch 5a 63:25
  Sch 6 .... 65:25
    para 1 .... 64:28; 65:17, 65:37
      1a 65:17
      2 .... 65:17
      6 ..... 65:28, 65:31, 65:32, 65:41;
                                          65:42
      7 .... 65:30
      8 .... 64:28; 65:38, 65:39
      9 .... 65:17
      10 .... 65:17, 65:28, 65:29
      11 .... 63:03, 65:38, 65:39
  Sch 7
    para 1 (4) 65:46
      2–4 .... 65:46
  Sch 7a 70:03
  Group 1
    item 1 .... 70:04
    note 1 (3) 70:04
      2 (1)–(3) 70:04
      3 (a), (b) 70:04
      4–7 .... 70:04
  Group 2
    item 1, 2 .... 70:05
    note 1–3 .... 70:05
  Group 3
    item 1–10 .... 70:06
    note 1–4 .... 70:06
      4a, 4b 70:06
      5, 6 .... 70:06
  Group 4
    item 1 .... 70:07
    note 1 .... 70:07
      2–5 .... 70:08
  Group 5
    item 1 .... 70:08
    note 1 (3) 70:08
  Group 6
    item 1, 2 .... 70:09
    note 1 .... 70:09
      2, 3 .... 70:09
      4 (1) 70:10

Value Added Tax Act 1994 – *cont.*
  Sch 7a – *cont.*
    note 4 (2) 70:09, 70:10
        (4) 70:09
      5, 6 .... 70:09
      7 (7) 70:09
      8 (3) 70:09
      9 (2) 70:09
      10–12 .... 70:09
  Group 7
    item 1 .... 70:10, 70:11
       2 .... 70:10
    note 1 .... 70:10, 70:11
       2 .... 70:10, 70:11
        (1)–(3) 70:10
      3 (1)–(4) 70:10
      3a 70:10
      4 .... 70:10
      4a 70:10
      5, 6 .... 70:10
      8 .... 70:11
  Group 10
    item 1, 2 .... 70:13, 70:14
    note 1, 2 .... 70:13
  Sch 8 ...... 69:02, 69:03, 69:08, 69:10,
                           69:12
  Group 1
    para (a) 69:13
    item 1–4 .... 69:13
    excepted Item 1–7 .... 69:13
    exception 1–6 .... 69:13
    note 1, 2 .... 69:13
       3 (a), (b) 69:13
       4–6 .... 69:13
  Group 2
    item 1 .... 69:14
       2 (a)–(c) 69:14
    note 69:14
  Group 3
    item 1–6 .... 69:15
    note (a), (b) 69:15
  Group 4
    item 1 (a)–(i) 69:16
       2 .... 69:16
    note 69:16
  Group 5 .... 65:35; 69:02, 69:09, 69:10
    item 1 .... 69:17
       2 (a) 69:18
        (b) 69:19
       3 .... 69:20, 69:31
       4 .... 69:21, 69:31
    note 1 .... 69:17, 69:22
       2 ..... 68:06, 68:12, 68:22; 69:18,
                                69:20
       3 ...... 68:12, 68:22; 69:18, 69:20
       4 ..... 65:35; 68:06, 68:12, 68:22;
                   69:18, 69:20, 69:22, 69:23
       5 ...... 68:06, 68:22; 69:18, 69:20
       6 ..... 65:35; 68:06, 68:22; 69:18,
                            69:22, 69:23
       7 .... 69:17

Value Added Tax Act 1994 – *cont.*
  Sch 8 – *cont.*
    note 7a 69:20
       8, 9 .... 69:17, 69:20
       10 .... 69:17, 69:18
       11 .... 69:18, 69:20
    note 12 .... 66:06
       (a) 69:18, 69:23
       (b) 68:06, 69:17, 69:18,
                      69:20, 69:22, 69:23
      13, 14 .... 69:17, 69:22
      15 .... 69:19
      16 (a) 69:18
        (b) 69:17, 69:18
        (c) 69:18
      17 .... 69:17, 69:18
      18 .... 69:17
        (a), (b) 69:18
      20 .... 69:18, 69:19, 69:20
      21 .... 69:20
      22, 23 .... 69:21, 69:24
      24 .... 69:09, 69:10
  Group 6 .... 69:02
    item 1 .... 69:12, 69:22
       2 .... 69:23
       3 .... 69:24
    note 1 .... 69:22, 69:23
       2 .... 69:22, 69:23
       3 .... 69:22, 69:23, 69:24
       4 .... 69:22
       5 .... 69:22, 69:23
       6 (a)–(c) 69:23
       7–11 .... 69:23
  Group 7
    item 1, 2 .... 69:25
  Group 8
    item 1 .... 69:26, 69:31; 70:11
       2 .... 69:26, 69:31
       2a 69:26, 69:35
       2b 69:26
       3 .... 69:29, 69:31
       4 .... 69:27
       5 .... 69:28
       6 (a) 69:26
        (b) 69:12, 69:28
       6A 69:29
       7, 8 .... 69:29
       9 .... 69:26
       10 .... 69:26, 69:27, 69:28
       11 (a) 69:12, 69:28
        (b) 69:30
       12 .... 65:25; 69:29
       13 .... 69:28
    note a1 .... 69:26
       1 .... 69:26
       2 .... 69:26, 29; 70:11
       2a 69:26
       4 .... 69:29
       4a–4d 69:27
       5 .... 69:28, 69:35
       6 .... 69:28

Table of Statutes

Value Added Tax Act 1994 – *cont.*
Sch 8 – *cont.*
  note 6A 69:29, 69:30
    7 .... 69:30
    8 .... 65:25; 69:29
    9 .... 69:28
  Group 9
    item 1 .... 69:31
      2 .... 68:06, 69:31
      3 .... 69:31
    note (a), (b) 69:31
      1 .... 70:11
      3 .... 70:11
  Group 10 .... 69:09, 69:10
    item 1, 2 .... 69:32
    note 1 .... 69:32
      2 .... 69:09, 69:10
      3 .... 69:32
  Group 11
    item 1 .... 69:33
  Group 12
    item 1, 1a 69:09, 69:10, 69:34
      2 ...... 69:09, 69:10, 69:35, 69:36
        (a)–(i) 69:35
      2a 69:36
      3 .... 69:09, 69:10, 69:35
      4 .... 69:09, 69:10, 69:36
      5, 6 ... 69:09, 69:10, 69:35, 69:36
      7, 8 .... 69:09, 69:10, 69:35
      9 .... 69:09, 69:10, 69:36
      10 .... 69:09, 69:10, 69:35
      11, 12 .... 69:09, 69:10, 69:36
      13 .... 69:09, 69:10, 69:35, 69:36
      14 .... 66:17, 66:18; 69:09, 69:10, 69:35
      15 .... 69:09, 69:10, 69:36
      16 .... 69:09, 69:10, 69:35
      17 .... 69:09, 69:10, 69:36
      18, 19 . 69:09, 69:10, 69:35, 69:36
      20 .... 69:09, 69:10, 69:36
    note 1 .... 69:09, 69:10
      2a 69:09, 69:10, 69:34
      3 .... 69:35, 69:36
      4 .... 69:36
        (a)–(c) 69:35
      5 .... 69:34, 69:35, 69:36
      5a 69:34
      5b 69:35
      5c (b), (c) 69:35
      5d (a)–(c) 69:35
      5e 69:36
        (a), (b) 69:35
      5f (a), (b) 69:35
      5h 69:35
      5i 69:34, 69:35
      5j 69:36
      5k, 5l 69:35, 69:36
      6, 7 .... 69:35
      8, 9 .... 69:35, 69:36
  Group 13
    item 1–3 .... 69:37

Value Added Tax Act 1994 – *cont.*
Sch 8 – *cont.*
  note 1–5 .... 69:37
  Group 14 .... 69:38
  Group 15 .... 13:22
    item 1, 1a 69:39
    item 2 .... 69:40
      3 .... 69:39
      4–7 .... 69:41
      8–8c 69:40
      9, 10 .... 69:40
    note 1 .... 69:39
      1a 69:39, 69:40
      1b–1d 69:39
      1e, 1f 69:39, 69:40
      3 (a) 69:41
        (c) 69:41
      4 (f) 69:41
      4a, 4b 69:41
      5 .... 69:41
      5a, 5b 69:41
      6, 7 .... 69:41
      8 (a), (b) 69:41
      9, 10 .... 69:41
      10a–10c 69:40
      11, 12 .... 69:40
  Group 16
    item 1–3 .... 69:42
    note 1 .... 69:42
      2 .... 65:35
        (a)–(d) 69:42
      3 .... 69:42
      4, 4a 69:42
      5 .... 69:42
  Group 17
    item 1 .... 69:43
    note 1, 3, 4 .... 69:43
  Sch 9 ...... 63:33, 63:36; 64:27, 64:28; 68:01
  Group 1 .... 68:02, 68:05
    item 1 .... 68:11
      (a)–(n) 68:12
      1a 68:11
    note 1 .... 68:11
      2 .... 65:35; 68:12
      4–6 .... 68:12
      7–9 .... 68:12
      11 (a) 68:12
      12–14 .... 68:12
      16 .... 68:12
  Group 2 .... 65:25; 66:11
    item 1–3 .... 68:13
      4 .... 66:11; 68:13
    note 1, 4, 5, 7–10 .... 68:13
  Group 3
    item 1, 2 .... 68:14
    note 1, 2 .... 68:14
  Group 4
    item 1, 2 .... 68:15
    item 4(a) 68:13
    note 1–10 .... 68:15

Value Added Tax Act 1994 – *cont.*
Sch 9 – *cont.*
Group 5
 item 1 ..... 66:07, 66:08, 66:11, 66:13; 68:16
  item 1 (a) 68:17
   (b) 68:20
   (c) 68:21
  2 .... 66:11; 68:16, 68:19
  3 .... 66:11; 68:16, 68:18
  4 ..... 66:11; 68:16, 68:17, 68:20, 68:21
  5 .... 68:16, 68:21
  5a 68:17, 68:21
  6 ..... 66:07, 66:08, 66:11, 66:13; 68:16, 68:22
  7 .... 68:16
  8 .... 66:11; 68:16
  9 (c)–(j) 68:16
  10 .... 68:16
 note 1 ...... 68:17, 68:18, 68:20, 68:21
  1a, 2 .... 68:16
  2a, 2b 68:16
  3 .... 68:18, 68:21
  4, 5 .... 68:16
  5a 68:16, 68:17
  5b 68:16
  6 .... 68:16, 68:22
  6a 68:16
  8–10 .... 68:16
Group 7
 item 1 (a)–(e) 68:23
  2 (a)–(c) 68:23
  3 .... 68:23
  4 .... 70:11
  5–11 .... 68:23
 note 1–8 .... 68:23
Group 8
 item 1, 2 .... 68:24
Group 9
 item 1 .... 68:25
 note 1–5 .... 68:25
Group 10
 item 1–3 .... 68:26
 note 1 .... 68:26
  2 .... 68:26
  2a–2c 68:26
  3–17 .... 68:26
Group 11
 item 1–4 .... 68:27
Group 12
 item 1–3 .... 68:28
  14 .... 69:36
 note 1–11 .... 68:28
Group 13
 item 1, 2 .... 68:29
 note 1–4 .... 68:29
Group 14
 item 1 .... 68:30
 note 1–15 .... 68:30
Group 15

Value Added Tax Act 1994 – *cont.*
Sch 9 – *cont.*
 item 1, 2 .. 66:07, 66:12; 68:10, 68:31; 69:04
 item 3 .... 68:10, 68:31
 note 1 ...... 66:07; 68:10, 68:31; 69:04
  3 .... 68:31
  4 (a) 68:31
   (b) 65:40; 68:31; 69:04
Sch 9a 64:27
para 1, 2 .... 64:25, 64:27
 3 (1) (a) 64:27
  (b) 64:25
  (2) 64:25, 64:27
  (3) 64:25
  (4) (a), (b) 64:25, 64:27
  (6), (7) 64:25, 64:27
 4 (3) (b) 64:25, 64:27
 5 (1), (3) 64:25, 64:27
  (4) 64:25
 6 (1)–(11) 64:25, 64:27
 7 (2) 64:25, 64:27
Sch 10
para 1 .... 65:01
 2 .... 62:05
  (1)–(2) 66:07; 68:05
  (3) 66:07
  (4) 66:07, 66:28
  (5), (6) 66:28
  (8) 66:28
  (9) 66:28
  (2)–(5) 68:05
  a (7) 29:14
 5 .... 65:01
  (1) (a), (b), (2)
.... 68:06
 6 .... 65:01
  (1) (a), (2), (3)–(10)
.... 68:06
 7 (1), (2) 68:06, 68:12
 8 .... 68:11
  (1), (2) 68:06
 9 (1), (2) 68:06
 10 (1)–(5) 68:06
 11 .... 68:06
 12 (1) (a), (b), (2)–(3)
.... 68:07
  (4) 68:07, 68:08
  (6) (a), (b)
.... 68:09
  (7) 68:08
  (8) 68:07
 13 .... 68:09
  (2) (a) 68:07
   (b) 68:07, 68:09
  (3)–(4) 68:07
  (5) 68:07, 68:08
  (6) 68:07
  (7) 68:09
  (8) 68:07, 68:08
  (9) 68:07

Table of Statutes

Value Added Tax Act 1994 – *cont.*
Sch 10 – *cont.*
para 14 (1) 68:07
       (2)–(7) 68:07, 68:08
  15 (2)–(5) 68:07
  16 (1)–(7) 68:07
  17 (1), (2) 68:08
  18 (2)–(6) 68:03
  19 (1) 68:03
  20 (1) (a), (b), (2), (3)
.... 68:03
  21 (1) (a), (2) (a), (b), (7) (a)–(c), (8)–(14) 68:04
  23 .... 68:03
  24 (1)–(4) 68:03
  25 .... 68:03
  26 .... 68:03
  27 (1), (2), (4)–(7)
.... 68:03
  28 (1), (2) (a), (b), (4)—(6)
.... 68:03
  29 .... 68:03
  31 .... 68:05
  33 .... 68:06
  34 (1) 68:03, 68:04
    (2), (2A), (2B)
.... 68:07
    (3) 68:03
  36 .... 68:12; 69:17, 69:18
  37 .... 69:17, 69:18
    (1)–(2) 65:35
  37 (3) (a), (b)
.... 65:35
  37 (4)–(7)
  39 .... 65:35
Sch 10a
para 1 (1) 65:17
  3 (2), (3), (4) 65:17
  4 (2), (3) 65:17
    (4) 65:06
  5 .... 65:17
  6 (2)–(5) 65:06
  8 (3) 65:17
Sch 11
para 1 .... 2:07; 63:04
    (1) 04
  2 (6), (7) 63:44
    (13) 67:05
  4 (1), (1a) 67:05
    (2) 67:09
    (4) 67:09
  5 (1) ... 2A:42, 2A:97, 2:61, 2:62,
      2:63, 2:37; 65:41; 66:36, 66:40;
      67:04, 67:05, 67:07, 67:08
    (2), (3) 65:18
  7 (2)–(9) 63:03
  10 (1)–(2A) 63:03
Sch 11a
para 1 .... 63:09
  2(1), (2) 63:09
  3, 4 .... 63:09

Value Added Tax Act 1994 – *cont.*
Sch 11a – *cont.*
para 5 (1) (a), (b) 63:09
    (2), (3) 63:09
  6(2a) 63:09
    (4), (5) 63:09
  7–11 .... 63:09
  10(2a) 63:09
Sch 12
para 9, 10 .... 63:03
Sch 13
para 9 (1), (2) 66:41
Vehicle Registration Act 1994
.... 7:107
Disability Discrimination Act 1995
.... 7:58
Finance Act 1995 . 1:19; 10:04 10:09;
              32:07; 60:01, 60:02
  s 21 .... 65:06; 70:01, 70:02
  24 .... 65:17, 65:23
  25 .... 67:10
  30 .... 65:27
  32 .... 64:14
  39 .... 12:13
  41 (8) 6:31
  43 .... 7:41; 51:14
  45 (2) 7:113
    (5) 7:113
  54 .... 31:05
  55 .... 2A:19
  56 .... 2A:19; 31:21
  57 .... 2A:19
  79 .... 4:17
  94–98 .... 9:45
  117 .... 8:43
  120 .... 8:48
  121 .... 24:38
  123 .... 60:02
  124 .... 8:47
  125 (3) 33:38
  126 .... 36:08
    (2) 26:13
    (c) 22:48
  127 .... 22:48; 26:13
    (1) (a)–(d) 36:09
    (2) 36:09
    (e) 36:02
    (3) 36:09
    (4)–(12) 36:09
    (18) 36:09
  128 ..... 11:02; 26:16; 33:10; 36:02
    (1), (2) 26:13
    (3) (a) 26:13
  137 .... 1:06
  139 .... 2A:19
  140 .... 8:168
  149 .... 60:02
  151 .... 56:21, 56:35; 57:29
  151 (2) 60:01
    (d) 60:04
    (3),(4) 60:04

Table of Statutes

Finance Act 1995 – *cont.*
  s 151 (5) 60:01
      (7) 60:02
      (9), (10) 60:02
    152 .... 30:18; 59:20; 61:10
    154 .... 8:42; 17:14; 22:15
      (2) 44:11, 44:34
  Sch 8 .... 2A:19
  Sch 10 .... 31:05
  Sch 22
    para 3–5 .... 8:48
      14–17 .... 8:48
  Sch 23 .... 22:48
  Sch 29 .... 2A:19
  Pt VIII (3) 7:113
  Sch 36
    para 4 .... 35:71
Jobseekers Act 1995
  s 27 .... 2.12
Pensions Act 1995 .... 32:03, 32:08
  s 37 .... 32:28
  51 .... 32:29
Chunnel Tunnel Rail Link Act 1996
  .... 23:38
Employment Rights Act 1996
  s 139 (1) 50:10
Finance Act 1996 ...... 3:03; 4:13; 7:64;
                     8:23; 12:06; 25:05;
                                34:76
  s 29 .... 69:03
    (3) 64:01
  31 .... 64:25, 64:27
  32 (1) 64:01
  33 .... 65:28
  34 .... 67:04
  35 (2) 67:08
  36 (1) 2:63
  37 .... 64:14
  41 .... 22:11
  50 (1) 27:03
  79 .... 10:29
  80 .... 8:62, 8:64; 17:12; 35:43
    (5) 37:14
  81 .... 8:62, 8:64; 17:12; 35:43
  82 .... 8:62, 8:64; 17:12; 35:43
  83 .... 8:62, 8:64; 17:12; 35:43
    (3a) 27:06
  84 .... 8:62, 8:64; 17:12; 35:43
  85 .... 8:62, 8:64; 17:12; 35:43
  86 .... 8:62, 8:64; 17:12; 35:43
  87 .... 8:62, 8:64; 17:12; 35:43
  88 ...... 8:62, 8:64; 17:12; 27:07; 35:43
  89 .... 8:62, 8:64; 17:12; 35:43
  90 .... 8:62, 8:64; 35:43
  91 .... 8:62, 8:64; 35:43
  91a–91e 35:74
  92 .... 8:62, 8:64; 35:43
  93 .... 8:62, 8:64; 35:43
  93c 27:07
  94 .... 8:62, 8:64; 35:43

Finance Act 1996 – *cont.*
  s 95 .... 8:62, 8:64; 35:43
  96 .... 8:62, 8:64; 27:08; 35:43
  97–99 .... 8:62, 8:64; 35:43
  100 .... 8:62, 8:64; 35:43
    (1a) 27:31
    (2) 11:12
    (3a) 27:31
    (4) 2A:06; 11:12
  101, 102 .... 8:62, 8:64; 35:43
  103 .... 8:62, 8:64; 35:43
  104, 105 .... 8:62, 8:64; 35:43
  133 .... 6:12
  134 .... 16:22
  146 .... 6:10
  148 .... 5:18, 11:10; 11:05; 32:05
  184 (3) 44:05
  185 (5), (6) 44:18
  186 .... 56:35; 59:04; 61:24
  187 .... 61:01
  188 .... 61:01
    (2) 61:24
  189 .... 61:24
  190 (1) 61:24
    (3) 61:24
  192 (4) 61:21
  196 (3) (b) 61:04
    (5), (6) 61:05
  197 (5) 2A:42, 2A:43
  201 .... 56:28
  Sch 3
    para 5 .... 63:25
      8 .... 68:02; 69:02; 70:02
      10, 12 .... 65:36
      13 .... 64:01
      14 .... 64:09, 64:10
      15 .... 64:12, 64:13
      18 .... 63:25
  Sch 4 .... 64:27
  Sch 7
    para 4 .... 5:13
      (2) 10:29
  Sch 8 .... 35:43
  Sch 9 .... 35:43
  para 12 .... 28:26
  Sch 10 .... 35:43
  Sch 11 .... 35:43
  Sch 13 .... 17:12
  para 3 .... 3:24
  Sch 14
  para 21 .... 33:31
  Sch 17
  para 2 (2) 16:33
  Sch 19 .... 6:12
  Sch 23
  para 1, 2 .... 36:08
    4 .... 36:08
    6 .... 36:08
  Sch 26 .... 5:18
  Sch 35 .... 9:45
  Sch 36

Table of Statutes

Finance Act 1996 – *cont.*
  Sch 36 – *cont.*
    para 4 (6) 34:76
  Sch 39
    para 4 .... 16:37
    para 10 (3) 56:28
Trusts of Land and Appointment of Trustees Act 1996
  s 12 .... 35:59
    (1)–(2) 45:10
    13 (1), (2) 45:10
    (7) 45:10
Finance Act 1997 .... 9:37
  s 31 .... 63:12
    32 .... 64:16
    34 .... 69:41
    35 .... 68:11, 68:12; 69:17, 69:22
    39 .... 66:30
    40 .... 64:26
    41 .... 64:28
      (1), (2) 64:27
      (4) 64:27
    43 .... 67:04
    45 .... 67:18
    46 .... 67:16
    48 .... 67:04
    52 .... 2:38
    68 .... 28:11
    81 (2) 35:26
    88 .... 21:22
    95 (1)–(6) 59:19
    96 .... 56:21, 56:35; 62:17
      (1) 60:16
      (3)–(5) 60:16
      (7) 60:16
      (9), (10) 60:16
    97 .... 56:35
    98 .... 56:35
    100 (1), (2) 61:09
    101 (1) 61:09
      (2) (a) 61:09
      (3) 61:09
    105 .... 59:12; 61:13
    106 (2) 61:03
      (8) 61:23
  Sch 18
Finance (No 2) Act 1997
  s 6 .... 70:01
    24 .... 8:91
    35 (2) 13:22
    36 (3) 26:20
    48 (2) (a) 9:54
    49 .... 57:02
Finance Act 1998 .... 10:04, 10:23; 20:25
  s 15 (1) 61:15
    21 .... 65:28, 65:29
    22 .... 65:14, 65:38
    23 .... 66:41
    24 .... 63:25; 69:17, 69:22

Finance Act 1998 – *cont.*
  s 26 .... 1:21
    33, 34 .... 2A:34
    36 .... 2A:21, 2A:22; 28:03
    42 .... 8:65, 8:143; 10:08
      (1) 8:166
    44 .... 10:07
    46 (1), (2) 10:08
    49 .... 50:29
    58 .... 7:38
    63 .... 7:05; 50:02
    75 .... 31:01
    76 (1) (a) 31:01
    99 .... 35:38
    111 .... 57:02
    120 (4) 35:54
    121 .... 16:01
    127 .... 33:10
      (4) 35:47
    135 (3) 28:18
      (3b) 28:18
      (4) 28:18
    143 (1) 43:19
    149 .... 57:02
    150 .... 56:08
    151 (2) 61:15
    163 .... 25:54
  Sch 3
    para 24 .... 29:10
  Sch 5
    para 29 .... 10:01
  Sch 6 .... 10:07
    2 (2) (a) 8:71
    4 .... 8:71
  Sch 10 .... 8:103
  Sch 17
    para 12 .... 35:64
  Sch 18 .... 2A:01, 2A:54
    para 2 .... 2A:06, 2A:91; 28:03
    3 .... 2A:06
    5 (2) 2A:06
    7 .... 28:03
      (1) 2A:06
    8 .... 29:10; 35:64
    9, 10 .... 2A:06
    14 .... 2A:06
    15 .... 2A:20; 28:07
    16 .... 2A:06
    17 .... 2A:91
    18 (2) (a), (b)
      .... 2A:91
    20 .... 2A:91
    24 .... 2A:06, 2A:48
    25–32 .... 2A:06
    33 .... 2A:06
    34, 35 .... 2A:06
  Pt IV 9:06
    para 41 .... 2A:62, 28:07
    42–45 .... 2A:62
    51 (1) (c) 1:02; 2A:69

Table of Statutes

Finance Act 1998 – *cont.*
  para 51 (3) (a), (b)
    .... 1:02; 2A:69
    52 (4) 8:94
    66 .... 28:03
    67 .... 2A:68; 28:03, 28:07
    68 .... 28:03, 28:07
    69 .... 28:03
      (2) 28:07
    70 .... 28:03
      (5) 28:07
    72 .... 28:03, 28:07
    73 .... 2A:68; 28:03, 28:07
    74 .... 28:03, 28:07
      (1) 2A:68; 28:07
      (2) 28:07
    75 .... 28:03, 28:07
    75a 28:07
    76 .... 28:03, 28:07
    77 .... 28:03
    77a 28:03
  Pt IX
    para 82 .... 9:37
Human Rights Act 1998
    . 1:01, 1:22, 1:30; 2:23, 6:10; 8:102
  s 3 .... 1:01, 1:21, 1:27; 2A:44
    4 .... 1:01, 1:21; 2:07
    6 (1), (2) 1:21
    8 .... 1:21
  Sch 1 .... 1:21; 2A:19
Late Payment of Commercial Debts (Interest) Act 1998
    .... 11:12
Petroleum Act 1998
  s 11 (2) 54:07
Scotland Act 1998
  s 73–80 .... 1:01
Social Security Act 1998
  .... 48:01
  s 48 .... 50:05
    50 .... 50:29
      (1) 50:01
      (3) 50:01
    57 .... 2:40
    64 .... 51:05
Finance Act 1999 ... 1:13; 6:44; 7:69; 16:40; 41:04; 56:01, 56:07; 62:25; 64:25
  s 7 .... 32:02
    13 (5) (c) 63:03
    16 .... 67:10
    17 .... 69:02
    19 .... 67:06
    31 .... 6:05
    42 (2) 7:69
    54 .... 10:06; 23:26
      (2) 8:135
    60 .... 5:18
    64 (5) 15:21
    65 .... 11:18

Finance Act 1999 – *cont.*
  s 84 .... 22:12
    89 .... 2A:21
    99 (9), (9A) 61:05
    103 .... 8:135; 22:12
    107 (1) 46:06
    109 .... 56:30
      (1) 56:11; 62:25
      (3) 56:22
    110 .... 56:26, 56:30
    112 .... 56:04
      (3) 56:09
    114 .... 2A:95; 56:32
    116, 117 .... 59:12; 61:15
    118 (1) 61:15
      (3) 61:15
    119 .... 61:01, 61:15
    121 .... 61:01
    122 .... 57:39; 59:14; 61:08
  Sch 2
    para 1 .... 67:10
      2 .... 64:24, 25
      3–6 .... 64:25
  Sch 6 .... 10:06; 23:26
    para 1 (7) 8:135
      2 (2), (3) 8:135
      3 (1) 8:135
        (4) 8:135
      4, 5 .... 8:135
      7 .... 8:135
  Sch 10
    para 18 .... 32:02
  Sch 12 .... 56:22
    para 1 .... 56:19, 56:21
      2 .... 56:26
      4 .... 56:23; 57:25
  Sch 13 ..... 56:04, 56:09; 57:01, 57:02
  Pt I 56:02, 57:07
    para 1 .... 57:18; 58:02
      (2) 57:04, 57:05
      (3) 59:06
      (3A) 57:16; 59:04, 59:06
      (4)–(6) 59:06
      3 .... 59:04
      4 .... 57:02, 57:03
      6 .... 57:15, 57:21
      (2) 57:16
      7 .... 58:06; 59:02, 59:04
      (1) 57:18; 58:02
      (3), (4) 56:23; 57:18
      9 .... 56:27
  Pt II 56:02, 56:07
    para 12 (3) 57:25
      13 .... 57:27
      14 (2) 57:30
      15 .... 57:26
  Pt III 56:02, 56:07
    para 17 .... 57:36; 58:12
      19 .... 56:23
      (2), (3) 57:37
      20 .... 57:28, 57:35

Table of Statutes

Finance Act 1999 – *cont.*
    para 21 .... 57:38
          22 .... 57:40
          23 .... 57:41
    Pt IV 56:34
    para 24 (a) 59:12
    Sch 14
    para 20 (3) 61:24
    Sch 15 ..... 57:01, 57:33; 61:13; 62:33
    para 1, 2 .... 59:08
         4–6 .... 59:09
         7, 8 .... 59:10
         12A 59:09
    Pt II
    para 13 .... 59:11
         16 .... 59:12; 61:15
         17 .... 59:11, 59:12, 59:13; 61:13,
                                                 61:15
         21 .... 56:21; 59:11
            (2) 56:23
         22 .... 59:11
    Sch 16
    para 6 .... 61:13
         7 .... 61:15
         9 .... 61:15
         11 (4) 59:13
    Sch 17 .... 56:32
    Pt III 2A:95; 56:32
    Sch 19 ..... 57:39; 59:14, 59:20, 59:21;
                                     61:08, 61:10
    Pt III
    para 2–4 .... 59:16
         13 .... 59:20; 61:10
Social Security Contributions (Transfer of Functions, etc) Act 1999
    .... 50:36
    s 1 .... 55:01
      2 .... 55:01; 55:03
      3 .... 55:03
      5 .... 2:06
      8 .... 2.12; 49:02
     11 .... 2.12; 49:02
     12 .... 49:02
    Sch 3 .... 55:03
Welfare Reform and Pensions Act 1999
    .... 32:02
    s 75, 76 .... 1:21
Child Support, Pensions and Social Security Act 2000 .... 32:06; 51:14
Finance Act 2000   . 1:12; 2A:60; 3:07;
                   6:44; 7:74, 7:75,
                   7:111; 9:23, 9:45,
                  9:54; 10:16, 10:30;
                  15:05; 28:21; 35:53,
                  35:57, 35:60, 35:73;
                  36:44; 37:06, 37:08,
                  37:37, 37:38; 57:20,
                                57:29
    s 25 .... 69:09
      38 .... 9:25

Finance Act 2000 – *cont.*
    s 41 .... 11:01
     46 (1) 8:94
       (2) 8:94
       (2a) 8:94; 12:02
       (4) 8:94
     47 .... 31:02
     60 .... 1:21
     63 .... 30:06; 31:16
     73 .... 9:24
     75 .... 1:10
     74 (5) 9:37
     76 (2) 8:169
     79 (2) 22:27
     86 .... 26:07
     95 (5) 35:61
     97 .... 1:10; 28:01
     104 .... 1:06; 12:20
     110 .... 8:66
     114 .... 57:03
     115 .... 57:25
     116 .... 57:27
     117 .... 56:07
     118–119 .... 57:20
     120 .... 57:20
       (5) 62:08
     121 .... 57:20, 57:29
     122 .... 59:04
     123 .... 60:01, 60:02
     125 .... 57:29
     126 .... 57:07; 59:02
     127 .... 60:06, 60:08
     128 .... 57:23
     129 .... 56:35; 58:16
     130 .... 56:38
     133 .... 59:05
     134 .... 60:14
       (3) 61:15
     136 ...... 63:14, 63:23; 64:05, 64:06,
                   64:14, 64:22; 65:28
     144 ... 2:25, 2:29, 2:34; 2A:76; 62:26
     156 .... 7:103
    Sch 2
    para 2–4 .... 24:42
       6 .... 24:42
    Sch 8 .... 31:02; 59:18
    para 88 .... 7:75, 7:88
       98 .... 7:75
       99 .... 7:91
       101 (1) 7:91
       104 .... 7:91
       105–113 .... 7:94
    Sch 12 .... 1:21; 2A:18; 8:140
    Sch 13 .... 8:140
    Sch 14 .... 8:140
    para 56–58 .... 7:87
    Sch 15 .... 30:06
    para 1–6 .... 31:16
       11 .... 31:16
       23 .... 31:16
       67–72 .... 31:16

Table of Statutes

Finance Act 2000 – *cont.*
Sch 15 – *cont.*
  para 73 .... 31:16
       (3) 22:27
    74 .... 31:16
       (1), (2) 22:27
    75 .... 31:16
    76 .... 31:16
       (1) 22:27
    77 .... 31:16
    78 .... 31:16
       (1) 22:27
    79 .... 31:16
       (2) 22:27
    83 (2) 22:27
Sch 16 .... 30:06; 31:16
Sch 17
  para 4 (1) 31:07
Sch 19
  para 1 .... 8:66
Sch 20
  para 1 (1) 8:140
    2 (1) 8:140
    4 (1) 8:140
    6 .... 8:140
    15 .... 8:140
Sch 21
  para 3 (2) 9:62
Sch 22 .... 9:01
  para 4 .... 25:16
    7–12 .... 25:16
    13 .... 25:16
    14 .... 25:16
    89–102 .... 9:01
Sch 27 .... 28:23
Sch 28 .... 2A:22
  para 2–4 .... 25:46
Sch 30
  para 7 .... 37:19
    19 .... 37:03
Sch 32 .... 57:27
Sch 33 .... 56:07
Sch 34
  para 2, 3 .... 58:16
    4 .... 57:16; 58:16
Sch 36 .... 64:05, 64:06, 64:22
Financial Services and Markets Act 2000
.. 18:31; 35:42; 59:20; 61:10; 62:08
  s 235 .... 68:16
    236 .... 62:28; 68:16
    237 .... 59:18
      (2), (3) 68:16
    243 .... 30:14; 59:19
Learning and Skills Act 2000
.... 7:98
Sch 9
  para 47 .... 68:17, 68:18, 68:21
Limited Liability Partnerships Act 2000
.... 62:27
  s 1, 10 .... 8:63

Postal Services Act 2000
  s 127 .... 69:27
Sch 8
  para 22 .... 69:27
Capital Allowances Act 2001
.... 1:23; 25:27
  s 2 (1) 9:07
    3 (2), (3) 9:07
    4 .... 9:06, 9;33
      (2) (a) 9:04
    5 .... 9:37
      (1)–(3) 9:06
      (4) (c) 9:06
      (5) 9:06
      (6) 9:09
    6 (1)–(6) 9:07
    7–9 .... 9:07, 9:26
    10 (2) 9:07, 9:26
    11 (4) 3:02; 9:23, 9:40, 9:47
    13 (2)–(5) 9:23
      (7) 9:23
    14 (2), (3) 9:23
      (5) 9:23
    15 .... 5:11
      (1) (a) 9:23
      (e) 9:51
      (i) 7:01
    19 .... 9:23, 9:37
    20 (1) 7:01
      (2) 7:01; 9:51
    21 (3) 9:28, 9:29
    22 (3) (b) 9:28
      (3b) 9:23
    23 (1)–(3) 9:28
      (4) 9:26, 9:29
    24 .... 9:28
    25, 26 .... 9:37
    28 .... 9:23
    30, 31 .... 9:12, 9:23
    32 .... 9:12
    33 .... 9:23
    33A 9:31
    33B (4) 9:31
    35 .... 9:46
      (2) 10:13
    36 .... 7:132
      (2) 7:01; 9:51
    38A 9:01, 9:36
    38A (4) 9:36
    38B 9:36
Pt I Ch IV (ss 39–50)
.... 9:23
  s 39 .... 9:01, 9:32
    45a 9:32, 9:34
      (1) (c) 9:33
    45b 9:33
    45d 9:32, 9:50
    45h, 45i 9:32, 9:34
    45j 9:34
    46 (2) 9:23, 9:32, 9:46
    51A 9:01

Table of Statutes

Capital Allowances Act 2001 – *cont.*
- s 51A (4), (5) 9:36
- s 51B 9:01, 9:36
- 51C–51E 9:01, 9:36
- 51F 9:01
- 51G 9:01, 9:36
- 51H–51I 9:01
- 51J 9:01, 9:36
- 51N 9:01
- 53 .... 9:37
- 56 (3) 9:37
- (7) 9:40
- 56A 9:39
- 58 (4) 9:24
- 60 .... 9:40
- 61 .... 8:141
- (2) 9:40
- 62 (2), (3) 9:40
- 64a 9:23
- 65 (1) 9:46
- (2) 9:42, 9:50
- 67 .... 9:30
- (1)–(3) 9:48
- (4) 9:40, 9:45
- 68 (1), (2) 9:40
- (4) 9:40
- 69 .... 9:37, 9:45
- 70 .... 9:37
- (1)–(5) 9:49
- 71 (1), (2) 9:27
- 72 .... 9:37, 9:42
- (3) 9:27
- 73 .... 9:40
- (1)–(3) 9:27
- 74 .... 9:37
- (1) 9:50
- 75–78 .... 9:23, 9:37, 9:50
- 79 .... 9:51
- 80 .... 7:01; 9:52
- 81 .... 9:36, 9:37, 9:50
- 82 (2)–(4) 9:50
- 83 .... 9:37, 9:42
- (2a) 9:23
- 84 .... 9:37, 9:42
- 85 (1)–(4) 9:42
- 86 (1)–(4) 9:42
- 87 (1) 9:42
- (c) 9:52
- (2) 9:42
- 88, 89 .... 9:42
- 90–95 .... 9:43
- 97–100 .... 9:43
- 104A—104B 9:38
- 104C, 104D 9:37, 9:38
- 105 .... 9:23, 9:37, 9:52
- (2), (3) 9:53
- 107 (2) 9:37
- 109 (2) 9:52, 9:53
- 110–113 .... 9:52
- 114 (1)–(4) 9:52
- 115–120 .... 9:52

Capital Allowances Act 2001 – *cont.*
- s 123 (1)–(4) 9:53
- 127 .... 9:37
- 129 .... 9:44
- 130 (1) 9:44
- (3)–(5) 9:44
- 131 (1), (2) 9:44
- (4) 9:44
- 132 .... 9:44
- (1) (b) 9:53
- 133 .... 9:44
- 145, 146 .... 9:44
- 147 (1) 9:44
- 148 .... 9:44
- 151, 152 .... 9:44
- 153 .... 9:04, 9:44
- 154 .... 9:44
- 167–170 .... 9:25
- 172 .... 9:47
- (1) 9:25
- (5) 9:25
- 173 (1) 9:25
- 174 .... 9:25, 9:47
- 175 (2) 9:25
- 175a 9:25, 9:33
- 176 .... 9:25
- 177 (1)–(3) 9:25
- (5) 9:25
- 179 (1), (2) 9:25
- 180 (1)–(3) 9:25
- 180a 9:33
- 181, 182 .... 9:25
- 182a 9:25, 9:33
- 183–186 .... 9:25
- 188 .... 9:25
- 190–192 .... 9:25
- 192a 9:33
- 195a 9:33
- 196–198 .... 9:25
- 200 .... 9:24
- 203 (1)–(4) 9:25
- 205 .... 9:23, 9:36, 9:37
- 208 .... 9:23, 9:37
- 213 .... 9:09, 9:47, 9:53
- (1), (2) 9:23
- 214–218 .... 9:23
- 219 .... 9:62
- 220, 221 .... 9:47
- 222 (4) 9:47
- 223–225 .... 9:47
- 226 .... 9:47, 9:62
- 227, 228 .... 9:47
- 228B–228H 9:47
- 229 (3) 9:48
- 235 .... 9:06, 9:37
- 236 .... 9:06
- 238 .... 9:06, 9:40
- 239 .... 9:06, 9:40
- 240 .... 9:06
- 247 .... 8:43; 9:03, 9:07
- 250 .... 35:07

Capital Allowances Act 2001 – *cont.*
s 251 .... 7:01
258 .... 9:14
    (4) 9:46, 9:48
259 .... 9:14
260 .... 9:14
    (7) 9:48
262 .... 7:01, 7:110; 9:07
265 .... 9:40
266 .... 33:31
    (1)–(7) 9:40
267 .... 33:31
268 (5)–(7) 9:40
269 (1) 8:133
270 (1), (2) 9:23
271 .... 9:11
    (1) 9:12, 9:16
    (3) 9:14, 9:16
272 (1) 9:11
273 (1) 9:11
274 .... 9:59
    (1) 9:12, 9:14
277 (1) 9:12
    (5) 9:12
278 .... 9:14
279 (1) 9:21
    (9) 9:21
280 .... 9:12
282 .... 9:12
283 (1), (2) 9:13
285 (1), (2) 9:16
286 .... 9:14
288 (1) 9:14
289, 290 .... 9:14
291 (1) 9:14
    (3), (4) 9:14
294, 295 .... 9:12
296 .... 9:12, 9:21
298, 299 .... 9:12
302 .... 9:12
305 .... 9:01
    (1), (2) 9:11, 9:14
306 .... 9:01
    (4) 9:08
307 .... 9:01, 9:12
308 .... 9:01
309 .... 9:11
310 .... 9:11
    (1) 9:16, 9:21
    (2) 9:16
311 (1) 9:11, 9:21
    (2) 9:10, 9:11, 9:21
    (3) 9:11, 9:21
312 .... 9:11
313 .... 9:11
313A 9:20
314–326 .... 9:17, 9:60
342 (1) 9:14
346 .... 9:06
    (1)–(3) 9:11
    (5) 9:11

Capital Allowances Act 2001 – *cont.*
s 347 .... 9:06
    (1)–(3) 9:11
348 .... 9:06
349 .... 9:06
    (1), (2) 9:11
350, 351 .... 9:06
352 .... 9:14
    (1), (2) 9:07
353 .... 9:14
    (2) 9:07
353 (3)–(4) 9:07
359 (1)–(5) 9:14
360a 9:66
360b (1) 9:66
360c (1), (2) 9:66
360d (1) 9:66
360e–360z 9:66
361 .... 9:59
362 (1) (a) 9:59
363 .... 9:60
369 (1)–(5) 9:59
370 .... 9:59
371 .... 9:59
373 (1) 9:59
392 .... 9:59
393 (3) (a) 9:65
    (d) 9:65
393a 9:64
393b (1) (a)–(c) 9:64
    (4) 9:64
393c 9:64
393d (1) (a) 9:64
    (c), (d) 9:64
    (g), (h) 9:64
    (3) 9:64
393e (2) (d) 9:64
    (5) 9:64
393f 9:64
393g (1) (d) 9:64
    (2) 9:64
393h (1)–(3) 9:64
393i 9:64
393j (4) 9:64
393k (1) 9:64
393l 9:64
393m (1) (b) 9:64
    (4) 9:64
393n (1) (b), (c) 9:64
    (e), (f) 9:64
393o (1) 9:64
393p (1), (2) 9:64
393q–393w 9:64
396 (2)–(3) 9:55
399 (2)–(6) 9:55
400 .... 9:55
    (2) 9:56
401, 402 .... 9:55
404 .... 9:57
407, 408 .... 9:57
409 (1) 9:57

2669

Table of Statutes

Capital Allowances Act 2001 – *cont.*
s 410 .... 9:57
411 (3) 9:57
412 .... 9:57
415, 416 .... 9:55
417, 418 .... 9:56
421–423 .... 9:56
424 .... 9:57
426, 427 .... 9:56
428 (1)–(3) 9:56
430 (1) 9:56
431–433 .... 9:56
437 (2) 9:62
438 .... 9:62
439 (1) 9:62
(4) 9:62
440 .... 9:62
441 (1), (2) 9:62
442 .... 9:62
443 (4) 9:62
444 .... 9:62
447 (3) 9:62
449 .... 9:62
450 .... 9:07
451 .... 9:62
454–457 .... 9:63
458 .... 9:63; 27:22
459–462 .... 9:63
468–471 .... 9:63
472 .... 9:63; 27:22
484 (3), (4) 9:58
485 (1) 9:58
487 (1), (2) 9:58
488 (1)–(5) 9:58
490 (2)–(4) 9:22
491 (1)–(3) 9:22
501 .... 9:22
502, 503 .... 9:22, 9:23
504 (1) 9:22
505 (1) 9:22
(3) 13:26
506, 507 .... 9:22
508 (1), (2) 9:22
509, 510 .... 9:22
511 .... 9:40
(2) 9:22
512–522 .... 9:22
532–536 .... 9:04
537 .... 9:04, 9:14, 9:25
538 (3) 9:04
539–541 .... 9:04
547–551 .... 9:06
557 .... 8:54
561 .... 9:10
(1)–(3) 25:50
562 .... 9:09, 9:40
(3) 9:33
563, 564 .... 9:40
566 .... 9:07
567 .... 9:20
569 .... 9:09

Capital Allowances Act 2001 – *cont.*
s 569 (3) 9:62
(4) 9:09, 9:62
(7) 9:09
570 (1) 9:09
(2) 9:09; 33:31
(3)–(4) 9:09
570a 9:41
571 (1) 9:23
574 .... 9:09
577 (1) 9:62; 33:31
Sch A1 .... 0:35
2
para 30 .... 9:48
52 .... 9:50
82 .... 9:54
Sch 3
para 17 .... 9:37, 9:49
20 .... 9:43
23 .... 9:53
46 (2) 9:04, 9:06
47 (6) 9:37
52 .... 9:40
57 .... 9:14
59 .... 9:13
64 .... 9:11, 9:14
75, 76 .... 9:11
89 .... 9:62
92–100 .... 9:63
103 .... 9:59
Criminal Justice and Police Act 2001
.... 2:32
s 50 .... 2:31
Pt 2 (ss 51–70) 2:31
s 67 .... 2:31
Finance Act 2001 .... 2A:51; 9:24; 35:71
s 30 (2) 65:06
31 (1) 65:06
59 .... 7:01, 7:132; 9:50
(1), (2) 9:51
70 .... 8:139
85 .... 24:34
92 .... 10:42; 56:35
(4) 62:14
(9) 62:14
92a, 92b 56:35; 62:14
93 .... 59:21
94 .... 56:35; 59:21
95 .... 56:35
98 .... 68:30
99 . 65:06; 70:04, 70:05, 70:06, 70:07, 70:08, 70:09, 70:10
(4) 70:01, 70:02, 70:03
(5) 70:02
100 .... 63:13
106 .... 39:25
110 .... 7:01
Sch 13
para 3 .... 7:94
Sch 22

Finance Act 2001 – *cont.*
Sch 22 – *cont.*
  para 1 (1) (a) 9:65
  para 1 (3) 9:65
    (5) 8:139
  para 2 (2)–(8) 9:65
    (11) 9:65
  para 5 (3), (4) 9:65
  7 .... 9:65
  10 .... 9:65
    (2) 9:65
  13 .... 8:139; 9:65
  16 .... 8:139
Sch 23 .... 8:139
  para 1 .... 9:65
Sch 25 .... 8:63
Sch 30 .... 56:35; 62:14
  para 3 .... 57:16
  5 .... 70:02
Sch 31 ..... 70:04, 70:05, 70:06, 70:07,
              70:08, 70:09, 70:10
  para 3 .... 68:02; 70:02
  4 .... 65:15
  5 .... 68:02; 69:12
Social Security Contributions (Share Options) Act 2001
s 1 (6) 50:29
Adoption of Children Act 2002
s 2 (6), (7) 5:18
  4 .... 5:18
Sch 4
  para 3 (1) 5:18
Employee Share Scheme Act 2002
s 1 (3), (4) 7:75
  (6) 7:75
  3 (1) 7:89
  (2), (3) 7:75
Enterprise Act 2002
s 251 .... 2:37
Finance Act 2002 ...... 1:02; 6:37; 8:66;
              16:10; 16:22, 16:25;
              27:05, 28:13
s 22 .... 66:31
  (3) 66:30
  23 .... 63:42; 65:21; 66:06
  30 .... 24:43
  48 (3) 22:09
  52 .... 40:21
  55 .... 8:141, 8:158
  62 .... 9:33
  64 .... 10:08
  69 .... 27:04
  76 .... 2A:01
  88 (2) (b) 37:03
  (3) 37:03
  89 .... 35:70
  97 .... 16:49
  99 (1) 9:54
  110 (1) 62:14
  (6) 62:14

Finance Act 2002 – *cont.*
s 111 .... 56:21; 60:01,60:05
  112 .... 60:08
  113 .... 56:21; 60:08
  114 .... 56:30
  115 ...... 40:21; 57:13, 57:18; 58:02
  (2) 56:23
  (4) 56:23
  116 .... 56:35
  120 .... 19:03
  133 .... 24:43
  134 .... 2:38; 24:43; 63:03
  (2), (6) 34:01
Sch 12 .... 8:140
Sch 13, 14 .... 8:140
Sch 20 .... 9:32
Sch 22 .... 10:08
  para 1 .... 9:32
  2 .... 8:71; 9:32
  3 .... 7:59; 9:32
  4 .... 8:71; 9:32
  (2) 8:65
  (a), (b) 8:71
  5 .... 8:71; 9:32
  (1) 8:71
  6–11 .... 9:32
  13 (2) (a) 8:71
Sch 23
  para 11 (1)–(2) 27:11
  (4)–(6) 27:11
Sch 26 .... 8:64; 35:43
Sch 28
Sch 29
  para 3 (1) 27:03
  104 .... 26:53
Sch 33 .... 31:17
Sch 34 .... 60:05
Sch 35 .... 60:08
Sch 36 .... 57:13
  para 3 .... 57:13
  5, 6 .... 57:13, 57:18
Sch 37 .... 2:38
  para 3 .... 57:16
Sch 39 .... 63:03
  para 2 (1) (a) 34:01
  (2) 34:01
  3 (4), (5) 34:01
Proceeds of Crime Act 2002
.... 2:31; 2A:60
s 2 (1) 2:36
  232 (1)–(3) 2:36
  317 (1) (a), (b) 2:36
  (2), (3) 2:36
  319 (1) 2:36
  323 (1) 2:36
Tax Credits Act 2002
.... 2:31
s 1 (1) 6:51
  (3) 6:51
  3 .... 6:52
  (3) (a), (aa) 6:51

Table of Statutes

Tax Credits Act 2002 – *cont.*
s 5 .... 6:51
  6 .... 2A:11; 6:51
  7 .... 6:51
    (2) 6:53
  8 (1) 6:52
  14 (1) 2:13
    (2) 2A:47
    (3) 2A:11
  15 (1) 2:13
    (2) 2A:47
  16 (1) 2:13
    (2), (3) 2A:47
  17 .... 2A:11, 2A:94; 6:51
  18 .... 2:13; 2A:11; 6:51
  19 .... 2A:47
    (2) (a), (b) 2A:49
    (3) 2:13
    (4) (a), (b) 2A:48
    (8) 2A:51
    (10) 2:13
  20 .... 2A:47
    (1) 2:13; 2A:62
    (3) 2A:62
    (4) 2:13; 2A:62
    (5) 2A:62
  21 .... 2:13; 2A:65
  22 (1) (b) 2A:11
  24 (4) 6:51
  28 (1) 6:53
    (5) 6:53
  29, 30 .... 6:53
  31 .... 2A:94
    (3) 2A:94
  33 .... 2A:94
  35 .... 2:34
  37 .... 2A:38
    (1) 2:13
  38 .... 2:13
    (1) 2A:51
  39 (1) 2:13
  42 .... 6:52
  63 .... 6:51
Sch 2
  para 1 .... 2:13
Sch 5 .... 2:06
Criminal Justice Act 2003
.... 2:32
Finance Act 2003 .... 5:03; 11:17;
                56:01, 56:02, 56:07,
                56:35; 57:18; 58:02
  s 17 .... 2.23; 67:05, 67:09
  18 .... 2.23
  20 (1), (2) 68:12
  21 .... 65:28
  23 .... 63:43
  24–41 .... 63:03
Pt IV (ss 42–124) 62:02
  s 42 .... 62:02
  43 .... 62:04
    (1), (2) 62:03

Finance Act 2003 – *cont.*
s 43 (3) (d) 62:03
    (4)–(6) 62:03
  44 .... 62:33
    (1) 62:04
    (2) 62:04, 62:10
    (3)–(5) 62:04
    (6) 62:04, 62:10
    (7) (b) 62:04
    (8) 62:04
    (9) 62:10
  44a 62:03, 62:24, 62:30
    a (3) 62:23
  45 .... 62:13
    (1), (2) 62:30
    (3) 62:30, 62:34
    (5a) (b) 62:30
  45a 62:30
  46 (1) 62:32
    (3) 62:32
  47 (1)–(4) 62:31
  48 .... 62:04
    (1) (a) 62:29
    (2) 62:10
  49 .... 62:23
  50 .... 62:05
  51 (1)–(3) 62:06
  52 .... 62:10
    (1)–(3) 62:07
    (5)–(7) 62:07
  53 (1), (1a) 62:08
    (4) 62:08
  54 (2)–(4) 62:08
  55 .... 62:05
    (1), (2) 62:09
    (4), (5) 62:09
  56 .... 62:09, 62:11
  57 .... 62:13, 62:14
  57a 62:12, 62:13
  58 .... 62:14
  58A 62:13
  58B–58C 62:13
  59 .... 62:14
  60, 61 .... 62:13, 62:14
  62 .... 62:13
    (3) 62:15
  63–64 .... 62:13
  64a 62:13, 62:28
  65 .... 62:13, 62:25
  66–67 .... 62:13
  68 .... 62:13, 62:22
  69–72 .... 62:13
  73 .... 62:13, 62:30
    (3) 62:34
  74, 75 .... 62:09, 62:13
  75A 62:01, 62:02, 62:05, 62:23
    (2) 62:34
  75b, 75c 62:01, 62:34
  76 .... 62:04
    (1) 62:23
    (3) 62:23

Table of Statutes

Finance Act 2003 – *cont.*
  s 77 (1) 62:04, 62:23
      (2) 62:04, 62:23
      (2a) 62:23
      (3) 62:04, 62:23
      (4) 62:04
      (5), (6) 62:23
  77A 62:23
  80 .... 2A:41; 62:23, 62:25
      (4a) 62:10
  81 .... 62:23
  81A 62:11, 62:23
  81B 62:23
  82 .... 62:23
  82A 62:23
  83 .... 62:23
  86 .... 2A:30
      (1), (2) 62:25
  87 (3) (b) 62:06
      (5) 2A:41; 62:06, 62:25
      (6) 2A:41, 2A:96; 62:06, 62:25
  88, 89 .... 2A:96; 62:25
  90 .... 2A:41; 62:06, 62:25
      (7) 62:11
  91, 92 .... 62:25
  93–95 .... 2:29; 2A:76; 6:26
  96 .... 6:26
  101 (1)–(4) 62:28
      (7) 62:28
  102 .... 62:28
  103 .... 62:09
      (2) (c) 62:25
  106 .... 62:29
  107 .... 62:13
  108 .... 62:09
  114 .... 7:85
  116 .... 62:09, 62:14
  117 .... 62:23, 62:31
  118 .... 62:08
  119 .... 62:04
  120 .... 62:10
  125 .... 56:35; 62:01
      (1) 62:33
      (5) (b) 62:33
      (8) 62:33
  126 .... 60:05
  127 .... 60:08
  131 .... 5:01
      (1) (a) 5:02
  134 .... 24:37
  137 .... 7:123
  138 .... 7:115
  141 .... 7:75
  142 .... 25:06
  144 .... 7:47
  148 .... 11:02
      (1)–(5) 25:45
      (5a) 27:30
  150 (1) 36:07
      (2) (a), (b) 36:07
      (6) 25:45

Finance Act 2003 – *cont.*
  s 151 .. 5:01, 5:18; 11:02; 26:16; 36:02
  157 .... 16:14, 16:15
  161 .... 21:23
  162 .... 16:10
  175 .... 5:18
  179 .... 26:42
  185 (4) 41:12
  186 (2) 47:11
      (3) 47:13
  195 .... 62:29
      (2) 26:20
      (8) (a) 26:20
  195 (11) 26:20
  197 .... 34:01; 63:03
      (3) 34:08
  198 .... 62:29
  199 .... 34:08
  203 .... 7:144
Sch 1
para 2 .... 65:07
Sch 2
para 2 .... 63:43
    4 .... 63:43; 67:14
Sch 3 .... 62:23
para 1 .... 62:08, 62:13
    2 .... 62:13
    3 .... 62:13
      (a)–(d) 62:21
    3a 62:13
    4 .... 62:13, 62:21
Sch 4
para 1 .... 62:05
    2 .... 62:05, 62:10
    3 .... 62:05
    4 (3) 62:05
    5 .... 62:12
    6, 7 .... 62:05
    8 (1a), (1b) 62:05
    9 .... 62:05
    10 (2a) 62:05
      (3) (b) 62:05
    11, 12 .... 62:05
    13 .... 62:10
    16 .... 62:05
    16a 62:05
    17 .... 62:05
Sch 5
para 2 (3), (5) 62:11
    3 .... 62:11
    5 .... 62:11
    6 (3) 62:10
    9A 62:09
Sch 6 .... 9:60
para 1, 2 .... 62:14
    13 .... 62:23
Pt II 62:14
Pt III 62:14
Sch 6a 62:13
Sch 7 .... 62:13
para 1 .... 62:18

Table of Statutes

Finance Act 2003 – *cont.*
  Sch 7 – *cont.*
    para 1 (1)–(6) 62:15
        2 (1) 62:16
          (2) (a), (b) 62:16
          (3a) 62:16
          (4a) 62:16
          (5) 62:16
        3 .... 62:15, 62:20
          (1), (2) 62:17
          (4) 62:17
        4 (4) 62:17
          (6)–(7) 62:17
        4a (6a) 62:17
          (1)–(4) 62:17
        5 .... 62:18
          (1), (2) 62:17
          (3) (a) 62:17
        6 (1), (2) 62:17
          (5) 62:17
        7 (1) 62:17, 62:18
          (2)–(4) 62:18
        8 (1)–(4) 62:19
          (5) (a) 62:19
          (5a)–(5c) 62:19
        9 (1) 62:20
          (4) 62:20
          (5) (a)–(c) 62:20
        10 .... 62:21
        11 (1)–(3) 62:21
          (5) 62:21
        12 (1)–(3) 62:20
  Sch 8 .... 62:13
  para 1 (1)–(4) 62:22
        3 .... 62:22
  Sch 10 .... 62:23
  para 1 (1) (c) 62:23
        (2)–(4) 62:23
        1A 62:23
        6–9 .... 62:23
        28–30 .... 2A:62
  Pt III–VI 62:23
  Pt VII 62:23
  para 39, 40 .... 62:25
  Sch 11A 62:23
  Sch 12 .... 62:25
  Sch 13 .... 2:29, 2:31; 2A:76
  Sch 15 .... 62:01, 62:33
  para 1–5 .... 62:27
        6 (2) 62:25
        7 (1), (1a) 62:25
  Pt III 57:01; 62:27
  para 9, 10 .... 62:25
        11 .... 62:25, 62:27
        12 .... 62:25
        13 .... 62:25
          (2) 62:33
        16–19 .... 62:27
        25–28 .... 62:27

Finance Act 2003 – *cont.*
  para 36 .... 62:27
  Sch 16
  para 1 (1) 62:07, 62:29
        (3) 62:07, 62:29
        2 .... 62:29
        3 .... 62:08, 62:29
        4 .... 62:29
        5 (1) 62:25
          (3) 62:25
        7 .... 62:29
  Sch 17a
  para 1 .... 62:11
        2, 3 .... 62:11
        5 .... 62:10, 62:11
        6 .... 62:11
        7 (3) 62:10
          (5) 62:11
        7a 62:11
        8 .... 62:11
        9 .... 62:10, 62:11
        9a 62:11
        10 .... 62:05
          (1) (e) 62:11
        12a 62:10
          (2) 62:23
        12b 62:30
        13–15 .... 62:11
        15a 62:03
        16 .... 62:12
        18 .... 62:12
        18a 62:10
  Sch 19 .... 62:33
  para 2 (1) 62:33
        3 (1) 62:33
          (3) (c) 62:33
        4 .... 62:33
        5 (1) 62:33
        8 .... 62:33
        9 (1), (2) 62:33
  Sch 20 .... 62:33
  Pt I 57:12
  Pt II
  para 3 .... 57:02
  Sch 21
  para 2 .... 7:88
  Sch 22 .... 7:54; 50:29
  para 2 .... 7:55, 7:56
        4 .... 7:61
        10 .... 7:58
        15 .... 7:63
  Sch 23 .... 7:75
  Sch 28
  para 1 .... 2:07
  Sch 31
  para 2 .... 8:140
  Sch 32 .... 9:01; 25:16
  Sch 40
  para 4 .... 61:21

Income Tax (Earnings and Pensions) Act
2003 .... 1:23, 2:36; 3:13; 5:01, 5:03,
5:05; 7:116,7:37, 7:40, 7:147;
8:170; 12:02; 33:14; 35:01; 50:01;
51:17
Pt II (ss 3–61) 7:01
s 1 (1) 5:21
4, 5 .... 7:08
6 .. 5:09; 7:01, 7:02, 7:06, 7:17, 7:21,
7:32; 7:36; 49:01
(1) (a) 7:30, 7:33, 7:36
(b) 7:30
(5) 7:08
7 .. 7:01, 7:02, 7:17, 7:21, 7:24, 7:29,
7:45, 7:47, 7:69, 7:72, 7:73, 7:66,
7:78, 7:81, 7:89, 7:93, 7:96, 7:102,
7:103, 7:104, 7:130; 8:133, 8:139; 10;
11:46; 29:10; 32:10, 32:19; 40:08,
49:01
(2) 5:22; 32:32
(3) 50:01
Ch III–VI (ss 9–43)
.... 7:02
s 9 .... 7:02, 7:17, 7:30
(2) 7:36
(3)–(5) 7:49
10 . 7:01, 7:02, 7:17, 7:21, 7:66, 7:69,
7:72, 7:73, 78, 81; 32:10, 32:19;
49:01
11 .... 7:02
(1) 7:123
12 .... 7:02
(1) 7:123
15 .... 7:02, 7:04, 7:22; 49:01
(2) 5:16
16 .... 7:04, 7:48
17 .... 5:05, 5:14; 7:04, 22
18 .... 7:04; 7:22, 51:04
19 .... 7:04, 7:22
21 ...... 7:02, 7:06, 7:07, 7:21, 7:22;
35:15; 49:01
(2) 5:16
22 ..... 7:02, 7:22, 7:23, 7:53; 35:12,
35:15; 49:01
(3) 35:16
23 .... 7:06, 7:07
(3) 35:15
24 .... 7:07
25 ...... 7:02, 7:03, 7:06, 7:22; 49:01
(2) 5:16
26 ...... 7:02, 7:06, 7:22, 7:53; 49:01
27 .... 7:02, 7:03, 7:22; 49:01
(2) 5:16
28 .... 7:03
29 .... 7:07
30 .... 5:05, 5:14; 7:07, 7:22
31 .... 7:07; 7:22, 51:04
32 .... 7:07, 7:22
33 .... 7:07, 7:22
(4) 35:15
34 .... 7:07, 7:22; 35:15

Income Tax (Earnings and Pensions) Act
2003 – cont.
s 35–37 .... 35:25
38 .... 6:12
39 .... 7:03
Pt II Ch 5A (ss 41A–41E)
.... 35:15
44 .... 7:01, 7:144; 49:06
45–46 .... 49:06
47 .... 7:01, 7:75; 49:06
48 (2) (aa) 7:09, 8:26
49 .... 8:26
(1) (c) 7:09
50 .... 7:09; 8:26
51–60 .... 7:09; 8:26
Pt III Ch I (ss 61–62)
.... 5:22
s 61 .... 7:09; 8:26
61a 8:26
61b 8:26
(1) 8:27
(2) 8:27; 49:24
(3) 8:27
61c 8:26
61d 8:26
(1), (2) 8:27
61e, 61f 8:26
61g 8:26
(1) 8:27
(3) 49:24
61h–61j 8:26
62 ..... 7:17, 7:23, 7:30, 7:33, 7:102;
8:27
(2) 7:54
(3) 7:01
(b) 7:43
Pt III Ch II (ss 63–69)
.... 7:102; 50:22
s 64 .... 7:102
65 .... 7:100, 7:101, 7:135
67 .... 7:48, 7:121
70 ..... 7:19, 7:24, 7:89, 7:90, 7:130;
8:133
71 .... 7:101
Ch III (ss 70–72) 7:01, 7:53, 7:127;
50:22
s 70 .... 7:137
(2) 7:101
72 ... 7:24, 7:89, 7:130, 7:140; 8:133
(3) 7:24
Ch IV (ss 73–76) ... 7:47, 7:102; 50:22
s 73 .... 7:45, 7:47
74–80 .... 7:47
81 .... 7:45
(2) 7:47
82 .... 7:45, 7:47, 7:89, 7:103, 7:105,
7:130
83 .... 7:47
84 .... 7:45, 7:47
(2a) 7:46
85 .... 7:47

Table of Statutes

Income Tax (Earnings and Pensions) Act
2003 – *cont.*

s 86	7:45, 7:47
87	7:46, 7:47, 7:89, 7:105, 7:130
(2) (b)	7:45
88	7:45, 7:47, 7:89, 7:105, 7:130
89	7:45, 7:47
90	7:45, 7:47, 7:89, 7:118, 7:130
91–93	7:45, 7:47
94	7:89, 7:130
(2)	7:47
(b)	7:45
(3)	7:45
95	7:47, 7:89, 7:105, 7:130
(3a)	7:46
96	7:47
Ch V (ss 97–113)	7:102; 50:22
s 97	7:110
(2)	7:48
98	7:48
99	6:12; 7:110; 22:12
(1), (2)	7:49
100	7:50, 7:110
103	7:50
105	7:47, 7:51; 47:08
(2) (b)	7:50
(3), (4)	7:50
106	7:47, 7:51; 47:08
107 (3), (4)	7:51
110	7:50
Ch VI (ss 114–172)	7:01, 7:102, 7:118; 50:22
s 115	7:115
116	7:117
119	7:41, 7:119
121	7:117
(1)	7:115
122–124	7: 115, 7:117
124a	7:115
125 (2) (c)	7:115, 7:117
126	7:115
(4) (b)	7:117
127–131	7:115, 7:117
132	7:116, 7:117
143	7:115
144	7:105, 7:116
145	7:115
147	7:116
(1)	7:117
(3)–(7)	7:117
149–153	7:118
155 (3) (a)	7:119
(4), (5)	7:119
156–159	7:119
160 (1)	7:119
161b	7:119
161–164	7:119
167	6:12; 7:116
168 (4)	7:93
169	7:116
169a	7:119

Income Tax (Earnings and Pensions) Act
2003 – *cont.*

s 170	7:105, 7:117
171	7:105
(1)	7:115
(2)	7:117
172	7:115, 7:117
Ch VII (ss 173–191)	7:102, 7:111; 50:22
s 174	7:102, 7:113; 29:10
(5) (b)	7:111
(6)	7:111
175	7:62, 7:111
(4)	7:112
176 (6)	7:111
(8), (9)	7:111
177	7:112
178	7:62, 7:111
179	7:111
180	6:12; 7:62, 7:103, 7:111
181	12:18
(2)	7:112
182, 183	7:62, 7:112
184	7:62, 102
(2)	7:111
(5)	7:111
185	7:62, 7:112
186	7:112
187	7:62, 7:111
188 (2), (3)	7:113
190 (2)	7:113
Ch VIII (ss 192–197)	7:102; 50:22
s 192	7:87, 7:91, 7:104
193, 194	7:87, 7:114
195	7:69, 7:87, 7:86, 7:114
196	7:87, 7:114
197	7:74, 7:87, 7:104, 7:114
Ch IX (ss 198–200)	7:102; 50:22
s 198	7:91, 7:114
199	7:114
200	7:114
Ch X (ss 201–215)	7:01, 7:102; 50:22
s 201	7:01, 7:25, 7:53, 7:68, 7:93, 7:96, 7:103, 7:110, 7:130
(3)	7:102
202	7:93, 7:102
203	7:01, 7:102, 7:93, 7:109, 7:110
204	7:107, 7:109
205	7:10, 7:109
(3) (b)	7:108
(4) (a)	7:110
206 (2)–(5)	7:108
207	7:108
209	7:102
210	7:93
211	7:23
212	7:102
213	7:120

Table of Statutes

Income Tax (Earnings and Pensions) Act 2003 – *cont.*
s 215 .... 7:120
Ch XI (ss 216–220)
.... 7:100; 50:22
s 216 (3) 7:100
218–220 .... 7:100
221 .... 7:102
222 .... 7:47, 7:146
223 .... 7:23
(5), (6) 7:121
(8) 7:121
224 .... 40:08
225 .. 7:28, 7:29; 8:139; 11:46; 50:01
Pt IV (ss 227–326)
.... 7:01
s 228 .... 5:18; 7:20, 50:02
s 229 .... 7:132
230 .... 8:103
(3)–(5) 7:132
231 .... 7:132
232 .... 7:110, 7:132
233, 234 .... 7:132
235 (5) 7:132
236 (1) 7:132
237 .... 7:23, 7:24, 7:103, 7:131
(3) (a) 7:119
240 .... 7:103, 7:135
(1) 7:130
(4)–(6) 7:130
241 .... 7:103, 7:130
242 .... 7:103
(1) (a)–(c) 7:131
(2), (3) 7:131
243 .... 7:103, 7:131
244 .... 7:103
(5) 7:131
245–247 .... 7:125
248 (3) 7:125
248a (3), (4) 7:115
249 .... 7:131
250 .... 7:97, 7:98; 8:139
251, 252 .... 7:97
253, 254 .... 7:97, 7:98
255 .... 7:98
256 .... 7:97
257 .... 7:97, 7:98
258–260 .... 7:97, 7:98
261 (4)–(6) 7:105
262 (1) (a) (i) 7:105
263 .... 7:105
264 .... 7:24, 7:103
265 .... 7:103
266 .... 7:17; 7:23, 7:24, 7:45, 7:105
(2) 7:131
267 .... 7:45
268 .... 7:130, 7:135
270 .... 7:45, 7:103
270a 7:104
(8), (9) 7:46

Income Tax (Earnings and Pensions) Act 2003 – *cont.*
Ch VII (ss 271–289)
.... 7:52
s 271 .... 7:51
s 271 (2) 7:53
272 (1) 7:52
(3) (a), (b) 7:52
273 (2)–(4) 7:52
274–285 .... 7:52
286 (1), (2) 7:52
287, 288 .... 7:53
289 .... 7:53
291 .... 5:18; 7:36
292 .... 7:123; 50:02
293 .... 7:123
294 .... 7:123; 50:02
295 .... 7:123
296 .... 7:103
299–303 .... 5:18
304 .... 5:18; 7:03
305 .... 5:18; 7:125
306, 307 .... 5:18; 7:103
308 .... 5:18; 8:139; 32:35; 40:08
309 .... 5:18; 7:30, 7:33; 10:08
310 .... 5:18
(1)–(6) 7:30
311 .... 5:18; 7:97; 10:08
312 .... 5:18; 7:98; 10:08
(4), (5) 7:97
313 .... 5:18
(2) (a) 7:110
314 .... 5:18; 7:49
315 .... 5:18
(5) 7:110
316 .... 5:18; 7:103
(2)–(4) 7:106
(5) (a), (b) 7:106
316a 7:123, 7:136; 8:102
317 .... 5:18; 7:17, 7:103
318 .... 5:18; 7:46, 7:102; 8:102
(1) 7:104
(3) 7:104
(4) (a), (b) 7:104
(5)–(8) 7:104
318a 7:102
(c) 7:104
318b 7:102
(2), (3) 7:104
318c 7:102
(2) (b) 7:104
(3)–(5) 7:104
318d 7:102
319 .... 5:18; 7:93, 7:103
320 .... 5:18; 7:42, 7:103
321 .... 5:18; 7:17, 7:24
322 .... 5:18; 7:17, 7:24
323 .... 5:18; 7:20, 7:24
324 .... 5:18; 7:25, 7:45, 7:103
325 .... 5:18; 7:103
326 .... 5:18; 7:107

2677

Table of Statutes

Income Tax (Earnings and Pensions) Act
  2003 – *cont.*
  Pt V (ss 327–385) .. 7:01, 7:110, 7:122
  s 327 .... 5:18; 7:01, 7:101
  s 328 ..... 5:18; 6:30; 7:01, 7:08, 7:45,
              7:89, 7:100, 7:129; 8:103, 8:133;
              9:24; 11:03; 50:02
    (ff) 8:133
  329 .. 5:18; 6:30; 7:01, 45, 89, 7:140;
         8:103, 8:128, 8:133; 11:03; 50:02
    (4) 7:122
    (6) 7:122
  330 ...... 5:18; 6:30; 7:01, 89; 8:103,
                            8:133; 50:02
  331 .... 5:18; 6:30; 7:129; 8:103
  332 .... 5:18; 8:103
Ch II (ss 333–360)
  .... 7:14, 7:50, 7:122
  s 333 .... 5:18; 6:30; 7:01, 7:89; 8:103,
                                   8:133
  334 ... 6:30; 7:01, 7:122, 7:89; 8:103,
                            8:133; 11:03
  335 .... 6:30, 6:125; 7:122, 7:129;
  336 ... 6:30; 7:01, 7:89, 7:122, 7:136,
         7:137, 7:141, 7:142; 8:103, 8:133;
                      50:02, 50:06, 51:14
    (1) (b) 7:133
  337 ... 6:30; 7:01, 7:122, 7:125, 7:89,
                7:132, 7:131; 8:103, 8:133
    (1) (b) 7:133
  338 ... 6:30; 7:01, 7:89, 7:122, 7:124,
                    7:132; 8:103, 8:133
    (1) (b) 7:129
    (2)–(4) 7:129
  339 .... 7:122, 7:132
    (2), (3) 7:129
    (5) 7:129, 7:135
  340 ...... 7:122, 7:124, 7:129, 7:132
  341 ...... 7:122, 7:129, 7:132, 7:133
  342 .... 7:122, 7:129; 50:02
    (8) 7:133
  343 .... 7:89, 7:143; 50:03
  344 .... 7:89, 7:143
  345 .... 7:143
  346 .... 50:03
    (2) 7:140
    (3) (b) 7:140
  348–350 .... 7:140
  351 .... 7:122, 7:123
  352 .... 7:08, 7:123, 7:137
  353 .... 7:45
  355 .... 7:134; 11:03
  356 .... 5:19; 8:131
  357 .... 8:131
  359 .... 7:132; 50:02
  362, 363 .... 7:45
  364 .... 7:50, 7:53
  367 .... 7:141
  368 .... 7:141; 50:02
Ch V (ss 369–377)
  .... 7:50

Income Tax (Earnings and Pensions) Act
  2003 – *cont.*
  s 369 .... 7:133
  s 370 .... 7:129, 7:133
  371 .... 7:129, 7:130
    (1) 7:133
    (3) 7:133
  372 .... 7:129, 7:133
  373 .... 7:129
    (1) (b) 7:133
  374 .... 7:129, 7:130
    (1) (b) 7:133
  375 .... 7:129, 7:133
  376 .... 7:129, 7:130, 7:133
    (3) 7:133
Ch VI (ss 378–385)
  .... 7:05
  s 378 .... 7:03, 7:05
Pt VI (ss 386–416)
  .... 7:01, 7:30
  s 386 .... 32:10, 32:19
  s 386 (ff) 32:08
    (1) (a) 7:38
  388 .... 32:19
  393–394 .... 32:10, 32:19
  395 .... 32:19, 32:20
  396 .... 32:19
  397 .... 32:19, 32:20
  398 .... 32:10, 32:19
  400 .... 32:10, 32:19
  401 ..... 7:15, 7:28, 7:30, 7:33, 7:36,
                      7:37; 32:19, 32:26
    (3) 7:36
  402 .... 7:36
  403 ..... 5:15; 7:15, 7:17, 7:31, 7:36,
                             7:39; 32:26
    (1) 7:25, 7:36
    (2) 7:22
    (4) 7:36
  404 .... 7:15, 7:36; 32:26
  412–414 .... 7:36
  415 .... 7:36; 32:10, 32:19
  416 .... 7:36
Pt VII (ss 417–554)
  .... 7:01
  s 417 .... 7:54
  418 .... 7:54; 29:09
  419 .... 7:54
  420 .... 7:54, 7:55, 7:86
    (8) 50:29
  421 .... 7:54
  421b (1) 7:56
    (2) (b) 7:56
    (3) 7:56; 50:2
  421j 7:63
Pt VII Ch 2 (ss 422–434)
  422 .... 7:54, 7:69
  423 .... 7:54, 7:69, 7:70
  424 .... 7:54, 7:69
  425 .... 7:54
    (2), (3) 7:59

Table of Statutes

Income Tax (Earnings and Pensions) Act 2003 – *cont.*
s 426 .... 7:54, 7:69
    (2), (3) 7:59
427 .... 7:54, 7:69
    (3) (a)–(c) 7:59
428 .... 7:54, 7:69
428a 7:63
429 .... 7:54, 7:69, 7:70, 7:86
430–431 .... 7:54
432 .... 7:54, 7:69
433 .... 7:54
434 .... 7:54, 7:69, 7:70
Pt VII Ch 3 (ss 435–446)
.... 35:15
435 .... 7:54, 7:70
436 .... 7:54, 7:69, 7:70
437 .... 7:54, 7:61
438 .... 7:54
    (2) 7:61
439 .... 7:54, 7:70, 7:87
    (3) (a)–(d) 7:61
440 .... 7:54, 7:70
    (1)–(3) 7:61
441 .... 7:54
442 .... 7:54, 7:70
442a 7:63
443 .... 7:54
444 .... 7:54, 7:70
445 .... 7:54
Pt VII Ch 3C (ss 446Q–446W)
.... 35:15
446s 7:62
Pt VII Ch 3D (ss 446X–446Z)
.... 35:15
446Y 7:57
Pt VII Ch 4 (ss 447–450)
.... 35:15
447 .... 7:54, 7:71, 7:72
448 .... 7:54, 7:72
449 .... 7:54, 7:71, 7:72, 7:86
450 .... 7:54, 7:72
Pt VII Ch 4A (ss 451–460)
.... 35:15
451 .... 7:54, 7:59, 7:72
452 .... 7:54, 7:59, 7:71, 7:72
453 ...... 7:54, 7:59, 7:71, 7:72, 7:73
454, 455 .... 7:54, 7:59, 7:73
456 .... 7:54, 7:59, 7:71, 7:73
457, 458 .... 7:54, 7:59, 7:74
459 .... 7:59
460 .... 7:54, 7:59, 7:74
464 .... 7:54, 7:72
465–466 .... 7:54
467 .... 7:54, 7:73
468 .... 7:54
469 .... 7:54, 7:72, 7:74
470 .... 7:54
Pt VII Ch 5 (ss 471–484)
.... 35:15

Income Tax (Earnings and Pensions) Act 2003 – *cont.*
s 471 ..... 7:65, 7:66, 7:67, 7:69, 7:73; 50:01
    (3) 7:58
472 .... 7:54; 50:01
473 .... 7:54, 7:66; 50:01
474 .... 7:65; 50:01
475 .... 7:54, 7:66; 50:01
    (1) 7:65, 7:58
476 .... 7:54; 50:01
477 .... 7:65, 7:66, 7:58; 50:01
478 .... 7:65, 7:66; 60:01
479 .... 7:65, 7:66, 7:69; 50:01
480 .... 7:65, 7:66, 7:58
    (1)–(6) 50:01
481–482 .... 7:54; 50:01
483 .... 7:54, 7:55; 50:01
484 .... 7:65; 50:01
488 .... 7:68, 7:88
498 .... 7:89
505 .... 7:89, 7:93
517 .... 7:66
519–521 .... 21:13
522 .... 7:66; 21:13
523–525 .... 21:13
526 .... 7:58
528 .... 7:85
529 .... 7:84, 7:87
530, 531 .... 7:85
532 .... 7:86
534 .... 7:86, 7:87
535–539 .... 7:86
540 .... 7:87
541 .... 7:86, 7:87
542–547 .... 7:64
549–554 .... 7:84
Pt VIII (ss 555–564)
.... 7:140
s 555 (2) 7:140
    (6) 7:140
558 (2) 7:140
    (3) (b) 7:140
559–561 .... 7:140
Pt IX–X (ss 565–681)
.... 7:01
s 566 .... 32:25
    (2) 5:23
567 .... 32:25
    (3) 7:123
569 .... 32:19
570 .... 5:25; 10:52; 32:25
575 (2) (a) 7:01
580 .... 32:25
601 .... 40:08
619 (3) 8:27
633 .... 5:25
637 .... 32:19
641, 642 .... 5:18
645 .... 11:29
657 (2) 5:23

Table of Statutes

Income Tax (Earnings and Pensions) Act
2003 – *cont.*
s 658 (3) 7:123
Pt XI (ss 682–712)
.... 7:144
s 683 .... 7:144
684 .... 7:01, 7:36, 7:96; 32:35
686 .... 7:22, 7:144; 51:04
687 .... 5:15; 7:146
689 .... 7:148
690 .... 7:149
691 .... 7: 146
693 .... 7:47
694 (4) 7:47
695 .... 7:47
696 .... 7:47, 7:144
  (1) 7:63
702 .... 7:47
  (5a) 7:63; 50:29
  (5b) 7:63
703 .... 7:144
709 .... 7:144
710 .... 7:47, 7:146
712 (4), (5) 7:103
Pt XII (ss 713–715)
.... 7:123
713 .... 6:36; 7:123; 13:22; 50:02
714, 715 .... 50:02
716 .... 7:130
717 .... 7:83
718 . 7:72, 7:103, 7:112; 32:10, 32:19
719 .... 7:83, 7:87
721 .... 7:36, 7:94; 7:133
722 .... 49:01
Sch 2
para 2–4 .... 7:88
  7–10 .... 7:88
  14, 15 .... 7:88
  18a (1) 7:88
  19–30 .... 7:88
  32 .... 7:88
  37 .... 7:89
  39–42 .... 7:89
  58–61 .... 7:93
  62 .... 7:90
  64 .... 7:90
  65 .... 7:90, 7:95
  66–69 .... 7:90
  71–75 .... 7:89
  76 .... 7:89, 7:94
  77 .... 7:89
  78 .... 7:89, 7:91
  79–80 .... 7:89
  81, 82 .... 7:88
  90 .... 7:89
  99 .... 7:88, 7:89
Sch 3
para 12–16 .... 7:67
Sch 5
para 4 .... 7:83
  5–7 .... 7:83, 7:84

Income Tax (Earnings and Pensions) Act
2003 – *cont.*
Sch 5 – *cont.*
para 8–23 .... 7:83, 7:84
  24–33 .... 7:84
  35–37 .... 7:84
  39–50 .... 7:87
Sch 6
para 169 .... 49:01
  171 .... 49:01
Sch 7
para 8 (4) 7:01
  14 .... 7:144
  16 .... 7:132
  20 .... 7:132
  21 .... 7:50
  25 .... 7:103
    (1) 7:111
    (2) 7:113
  28 .... 7:104
  55 .... 7:71
  57 .... 7:71
Civil Partnership Act 2004
.... 6:01; 6:51
Finance Act 2004 . 1:19; 5:02; 12:04;
                    23:13, 23:16, 23:17;
                    32:41; 62:01
s 19 .... 63:09
  20 .... 63:09; 64:25, 64:26
  21 (2) 65:39
  22 .... 63:09; 65:17
  23 .... 5:01
  30 .... 25:07
  31 .... 25:07, 25:11
    (3) 8:152
  32 .... 25:07
  33 .... 25:07, 25:12
  34 .... 25:07
    (7) 25:14
  35 .... 25:07
  36 .... 25:07
  37 .... 25:07
    (4) 8:152
  38 (1) 30:02
  50 .... 8:65; 30:07
  53 .... 8:110, 8:140
  57, 58 .... 2A:18, 2A:19
  59–77 .... 2A:19
  78 .... 7:45
  79 .... 7:42, 7:109
  80 .... 8:65
  81 .... 7:115; 8:65
  82 .... 8:65
  83 .... 8:65
  84 .... 8:65
  91 .... 6:02
  96 .... 7:83
  97–106 .... 1:05; 11:13
  107–115 .... 37:06
  134 .... 9:48
  135 .... 10:03

Finance Act 2004 – *cont.*
s 141 .... 8:140
143 (1) 9:34; 10:13
Pt IV (ss 149–284)
.... 32:16; 50:02
s 150 (5) 32:16
(6) 32:16
154 .... 32:16
165 (1) 32:34, 32:36
166 .... 32:36
167 (1) 32:36
181a (1) 32:36
193 .... 5:31
194 .... 5:31
197 (1)–(3) 32:22
(6)–(10) 32:22
Ch 5 (ss 204–242)
.... 32:42
s 204–215 .... 5:21
216 .... 5:21
(1) 32:26, 32:27
217–242 .... 5:21
270 .... 32:16
270 (3) 32:16
279 (1) 32:34
293 .... 2:16
306 .... 2A:05; 4:32; 35:74
(1) (a) 4:01
307 ...... 2A:05; 4:01, 4:32; 35:74
308 .... 4:01, 4:32; 35:74
(3)–(5) 2A:05
309 ...... 2A:05; 4:01, 4:32; 35:74
310 ...... 2A:05; 4:01, 4:32; 35:74
314 ...... 2A:05; 4:01, 4:32; 35:74
315 .... 4:01, 4:32; 35:74
(2), (3) 2A:05
316 .... 2A:05; 4:32; 35:74
Pt VII (ss 317–319)
.... 62:01
s 317 ..... 2A:05; 4:01, 4:32; 35:74
318 .... 4:01, 4:32; 35:74
(1) 2A:05
319 .... 4:01, 4:32; 35:74
320 .... 1:02; 2A:70
Sch 2 .... 63:09
Sch 5
Sch 10
para 1–45 .... 27:15
Sch 11 .... 2A:19
Sch 12 .... 2A:19
Sch 13
para 4 .... 13:10
Sch 14 .... 7:102, 7:119
Sch 15 .... 12:15
para 1 .... 12:17, 12:19; 41:14
2 (2) (b) 12:17
3 (1) (a) 12:16
(2) (a) (ii) 12:17
(b) 12:20
(3) 12:17
4 (3) 12:17

Finance Act 2004 – *cont.*
Sch 15 – *cont.*
para 4 (6) 12:17
5 .... 12:17
6 .... 12:16, 12:18
(2) (b) 12:20
8 (1) 12:16
(a), (b) 12:19
9 (1) 12:19
10 (1) (a) (i) 12:20
(2) (c) 12:20
(10) (a) (ii)
.... 12:20
11 (1) 12:21
(4) 12:21
(5) (a) 12:19
(c), (d)
.... 12:21
(11) 12:23
12 (1)–(4) 12:22
(a) 12:23
13 (1), (2) 12:21
21, 22 .... 12:21
22 (2) (b) (iii)
.... 12:23
23 (1)–(3) 12:21
Sch 16 .... 7:63
Sch 18
para 6 (3) 31:14
Sch 21 .... 20:02
para 4 .... 18:44
Sch 23 .... 9:47
Sch 26 .... 35:43
Sch 28
para 11 .... 32:36
12 (2), (3) 32:36
13–15 .... 32:36
Sch 29
para 1 .... 32:26
4, 5 .... 32:27
10 .... 32:35
(6) 32:36
18, 19 .... 32:36
Sch 32 .... 32:26
para 15 .... 32:27
Sch 33
para 2 .... 50:05
Sch 39
para 12 .... 62:33
National Insurance Contributions
and Statutory Payments Act 2004
.... 50:36
s 3, 4 .... 50:29
Pensions Act 2004 . 6:06; 7:02; 49:24
Tribunals, Courts and Enforcement Act
2007 .... 1:28; 2:09
s 15 .... 2:23
Commissioners for Revenue and Customs
Act 2005
s 4 .... 55:01

Table of Statutes

Commissioners for Revenue and Customs Act 2005 – *cont.*
s 5(1) 2:03, 2:07
  (3) 2:01
 11 .... 2:01
 16a 2:08
 34 .... 2:05
 35 .... 2:01, 2:05
 53 .... 2:01
Sch 4
  para 13 .... 34:01, 34:08
Constitutional Reform Act 2005
.... 2:18
Finance Act 2005 .... 62:01
 s 14 .... 5:02
  (1) 13:10
 15 .... 7:104
 20 (1) 7:59
 21 .... 7:59
 23–29 .... 13:04; 20:23
 30 .... 13:04, 20:23
  (1) (c) 20:23
 31 .... 13:04; 20:23
  (2) (a) 19:24
 32, 33 .... 13:04; 20:23
 34 .... 13:04, 13:05; 20:23
 35 .... 13:04; 20:23
  (2) (a), (b) 13:06
  (3) 13:06
 36 .... 13:04; 20:23
 37 .... 13:04; 20:23
  (1) 13:07
  (2) 13:07
   (b) 13:04
  (4) 13:07
 38 .... 13:04, 13:05; 20:23
 39 .... 13:04; 20:23
  (1) (a) 13:06
 40–45 .... 13:04; 20:23
 46 (2) 27:29
 47 (1) 27:30
  (2) (a) 27:29
  (8) 27:30
 47a 27:33
 48 (1) 27:30
 48A 61:05
 49 .... 27:30
  (1) 27:31
 49a (1) (a) 27:32
 51 (1) 27:31
 52 .... 27:34
 58–71 .... 9:54
 85 .... 37:23
 86 .... 37:27
 95 .... 57:02
 96 .... 62:14
 98 .... 38:13
Pt VII (ss 104–106)
.... 5:18
Sch 9 .... 62:15

Finance (No 2) Act 2005
.... 18:28; 62:01
s 1 .... 63:09
 3, 4 .... 67:16
 5 .... 65:38, 65:39
 6 .... 63:09
 7 .... 5:21
  (2) (b) 6:06; 7:02; 59:11;61:05
 17–22 .... 30:18
 24 .... 4:32
  (4)–(6) 35:74
 25–31 .... 4:32
 30 (2) 35:74
 32 .... 35:47
 33 .... 35:56
 36 .... 28:22
 51–56 .... 25:47
 57 .... 25:47
  (1) 61:05
 58 .... 25:47
  (3) (a) 59:11
 59–65 .... 25:47
 68 .... 1:05; 34:08
Sch 1 .... 63:09
Sch 2 .... 7:54; 50:36
 para 3–7 .... 7:60
   8–11 .... 7:61
Sch 3
 para 1–11 .... 35:74
Sch 5 .... 18:27
Sch 7 .... 35:74
 para 1 .... 10:16
   2 .... 4:11
   6 .... 4:15
  10 .... 35:74
Sch 8 .... 27:01
Sch 10
 para 2 .... 62:30
   6 .... 62:17
   9 .... 62:20
  10 .... 62:27
  11 .... 62:07, 62:08, 62:29
  13 .... 62:03
  19 .... 62:16
  21 .... 62:27
  33 .... 62:27
Sch 13 .... 4:32
Income Tax (Trading and Other Income) Act 2005 ...... 1:23, 5:01,5:03, 5:05;
         12:02, 12:09; 27:31; 35:02
s 1 (1) 5:21
 2 .... 33:16
Pt II (ss 3–259) . 3:13; 5:10, 5:14; 8:01,
         8:02, 8:03, 8:07, 8:08,
         8:23; 10:11; 12:10; 32:32
s 3 .... 7:10
 4 (1), (2) 8:91
Ch II (ss 5–23) 52:05, 52:06, 52:05
 s 5 .... 8:01, 8:64
 6 .... 33:16
  (1) 8:02

Income Tax (Trading and Other Income) Act 2005 – cont.
- s 6 (2) 36:03
- 8 .... 5:05; 13:03; 52:05
- 9 (1) 6:29; 8:42
- (2) 8:42
- 10 (1) 8:42
- 11 .... 8:42
- 12 .... 8:42; 8:171
- (4) 10:01
- 16 (4) 33:16
- 17 .... 8:47
- 19 .... 8:139
- 20 .... 8:42; 10:04
- 21 .... 10:27
- 24 .... 7:10, 8:01
- 25 ... 8:66, 8:68, 8:143, 8:154, 8:166; 10:08
  - (1) 8:65
- 26 .... 10:08
- 27 .... 10:08
- 28 .... 32:32
- 30 (1) (a) 8:169
  - (4) 8:01
- Ch IV (ss 32–55) 8:131
- s 33 .... 8:122, 8:131; 10:08
- 34 .... 8:68, 8:95, 8:96, 8:102, 8:104, 8:133, 8:134; 10:08, 10:11; 13:22; 32:22
  - (1) 8:64
  - (2) 8:103, 8:131
- 35 .... 8:131, 8:146; 10:08
- 36 .... 8:113; 10:08; 31:24
- 37–44 .... 10:08
- 45 ..... 4:02; 5:19; 8:30, 8:68, 8:101, 8:134; 10:08; 13:22
  - (4) (b) 8:131, 8:133
- 46 .... 10:08
- 47 .... 10:08
  - (2) 8:133
  - (3) 8:131, 8:133, 8:134
    - (b) 8:133
  - (5) 8:131, 8:133, 8:134
    - (a) 13:22
- 48–50 .... 10:08
- 51 .... 8:131; 10:08
- 52 .... 10:08
- 53 .... 10:08; 36:02; 52:01
- 54 .... 8:105, 8:138; 10:08
- 55 .... 8:09; 10:08
  - (2) 5:19
- 55A 9:31
- Ch V (ss 56–94) 8:131; 18:50
- s 57 .... 8:49; 10:08
- 58 .... 8:117
  - (1) 8:139
- 58, 59 .... 10:08
- 60 .... 10:25, 10:27
- 61 .... 10:25, 10:27
  - (1) 8:139
- 62 .... 10:25, 10:27

Income Tax (Trading and Other Income) Act 2005 – cont.
- s 62 (4) (d) 15:15
- 63 .... 10:25, 10:27
- 64 .... 10:25, 10:27
  - (3) 8:139
- 65 .... 10:25, 10:27
- 66 .... 10:25, 10:27
  - (2) 10:07
- 67 .... 10:25, 10:27
- 68 .... 8:126; 10:08
  - (2) 8:131
- 69 .... 10:08; 33:16
- 70 .... 13:22
  - (2) 8:139
- 72, 73 .... 8:139
- 74 (1) 8:139
- 77 (2) 8:139
- 79 .... 8:53
  - (3) 8:139
- 82 .... 8:101
  - (2) 8:139
- 89, 90 .... 8:139
  - (2) 35:09
- 92 (3) (a) 35:07
- 93 .... 35:07, 35:09
- 97 .... 8:93
- 99 (4) 8:135
- 100 .... 8:159; 11:13
  - (1)–(3) 8:135
- 101 (1)–(3) 8:135
- 102 (2), (3) 8:135
- 104 .... 8:41
- 106 .... 8:131
- 108 .... 8:158
  - (1) (a), (b) 8:141
  - (2) 6:38
- 109 (1) 8:141
- Ch VIII (ss 111–129)
  - 12:06
- 111 (3) 8:169
- 112 (1) (c) 8:169
  - (3) 8:169
  - (7) (b) 8:169
- 150 .... 8:149
- 158 .... 10:27
- 160 (1) 8:70
  - (2) 8:70
  - (3) 8:70
  - (4) 8:70
  - (5) 8:70
  - (6) 8:70
- 162 (3) 8:139
- 165 (2) 8:114
- 168 (2) 8:114
- 170 .... 8:139
- Ch XIA (ss 172A–172F)
  - 8:08, 8:141, 8:151, 8:154
- Ch XII (ss 173–186)
  - 8:142, 8:157, 8:161, 8:168
- s 173 .... 8:73

Table of Statutes

Income Tax (Trading and Other Income) Act 2005 – *cont.*
- s 173 (4) 8:170
- 174 .... 8:73
- 175 .... 22:07
  - (3), (4) 8:168
- 176, 177 .... 8:168; 22:07
- 178 .... 22:07
  - (1)–(5) 8:168
- 179 .... 8:168
- 180 .... 8:168
- 182 (3) 8:168
- 184 (2) 8:168
- 185 .... 8:168
- 192 .... 9:63
- 193 (2), (3) 8:76
- Ch XV (ss 196–220)
  .... 10:08
- s 197 (1) 5:16
- 198 .... 8:44
  - (1) 5:16; 8:43; 12:07
- 199 .... 8:49, 8:54, 8:55, 8:56
- 200 .... 8:44, 8:49
- 202 .... 8:53, 8:54
  - (1) 8:47
- 205 .... 8:47, 8:63
- 207 (2) 5:25
- 209 .... 8:44
- 215 .... 8:45
- 216 .... 8:45
  - (4) 5:16
- 217 (2) 8:45
  - (6) (b) 8:45
- 218 (3) (a), (b) 8:45
- 220 .... 8:46
- Ch XVI (ss 221–225)
  .... 6:49
- s 221 .... 6:46
  - (2) (a)–(c) 6:47
  - (3) 6:48
- 222 (4) (a) 6:47
- 223 .... 5:15; 6:47
- 224 (4) 6:49
- Ch XVII (ss 226–240)
  .... 8:71
- s 227 .... 6:46; 35:12
- 228 (3) 8:71
- 229 .... 8:65
- 230 .... 13:08
- 231 .... 8:71, 8:72
- 232 (4) 8:71
- 233 .... 8:71
- 238 (2) 8:70
  - (4), (5) 8:70
- 239 .... 8:70
- 240 (3) 8:70
- Ch XVIII (ss 241–257)
  .... 8:155, 8:168
- s 242 .... 8:142
- 245 .... 13:08
- 249 (1) (c) 8:142

Income Tax (Trading and Other Income) Act 2005 – *cont.*
- s 249 (2) 8:142
- 252, 253 .... 8:142
- 254 .... 8:139
  - (2) 8:142
- 256 .... 10:02
- 257 .... 8:142
- Pt III (ss 260–364)
  .... 5:11; 8:23, 8:171; 10:01, 10:08
- s 260 (1) 5:11
  - (c) 10:01
- 261 .... 8:91
- 263 .... 35:07
- 264 .... 10:02; 35:07
  - (a), (b) 10:03
- 265 .... 5:11; 35:07
- 266 .... 35:07
  - (1) 10:03, 10:07
  - (3) 10:03
- 267 .... 10:07; 35:07
  - (a)–(c) 10:05
- 268 .... 6:32; 8:64; 10:08; 35:07
  - (2), (3) 35:07
- 270 .... 5:16; 35:07
  - (1) 10:02, 10:08
- 271 . 5:05; 10:08; 13:08; 13:03; 35:07
- 272 ...... 8:131; 10:02; 13:22; 35:07
  - (1) 10:03, 10:08
  - (2) 35:07
- 273 .... 10:07; 35:07
  - (2) 10:05
- 274, 275 .... 35:07
- Ch IV (ss 276–307)
  .... 10:16
- s 276 ...... 5:11; 10:06; 13:08; 35:07
  - (1) 10:19
- 277 ...... 6:46; 8:130; 10:06, 10:24, 10:25, 10:26, 10:27; 13:08; 35:07
  - (1) (a) 10:18
  - (3) 10:08, 10:19
  - (4) 10:19
- 278 ...... 10:06, 10:24, 10:25, 10:26, 10:27; 13:08; 35:07
  - (4), (5) 10:20
- 279 ...... 10:06, 10:21, 10:23, 10:24, 10:25, 10:26, 10:27; 13:08; 35:07
  - (2) 10:19
  - (3) 10:22
- 280 ...... 10:06, 10:23, 10:24, 10:25, 10:26, 10:27; 13:08; 35:07
  - (3) 10:22
- 281 ...... 10:06, 10:23, 10:24, 10:25, 10:26, 10:27; 13:08; 35:07
  - (1) (b) 10:22
  - (3) 10:22
- 282 ...... 10:06, 10:23, 10:24, 10:25, 10:26, 10:27; 13:08; 35:07
  - (3) 10:08, 10:23
  - (4) 10:23
- 283 ...... 10:06, 10:27; 13:08; 35:07

Income Tax (Trading and Other Income) Act 2005 – *cont.*
- s 284 ...... 10:06, 10:24, 10:25, 10:26, 10:27; 13:08; 35:07
  - (1) (b) 10:24
  - (2) 10:24
  - (3) 10:08, 10:24
- 285 ...... 10:06, 10:23, 10:25, 10:26, 10:27; 13:08; 35:07
  - (2) 10:24
- 286 .... 10:06; 13:08; 35:07
- 287 ...... 10:06, 10:25; 13:08; 35:07
- 288 .... 10:06; 13:08; 35:07
  - (2)–(4) 10:25
- 289–290 .... 10:06; 13:08; 35:07
- 291 ...... 10:06, 10:26; 13:08; 35:07
- 292–298 .... 10:06; 13:08; 35:07
- 299 ...... 10:06, 10:19; 13:08; 35:07
- 300 .... 10:06; 13:08; 35:07
- 301, 302 . 10:06, 10:27; 13:08; 35:07
- 303 ...... 10:06, 10:18; 13:08; 35:07
- 304 .... 10:06; 13:08; 35:07
  - (1) 10:18
- 305 .... 10:06; 13:08; 35:07
- 306 .... 10:06; 13:08; 35:07
  - (1)–(3) 10:17
- 307 .... 10:06; 13:08; 35:07
  - (1) 10:17
- 308 ...... 10:04, 10:07, 10:13; 35:07
- 309 .... 35:07
- 310 .... 10:08; 35:07
- 311 .... 10:06; 35:07
- 312 .... 9:33; 10:10, 10:13; 35:07
- 313 .... 35:07
- 314 .... 35:07
  - (1) 10:10
- 315–321 .... 35:07
- 323 .... 10:15; 23:05
  - (2) 6:27
- 324–325 .... 10:15
- 326 .... 6:12; 10:15; 23:05
- 329–231 .... 10:08
- 332 .... 10:08; 13:08
- 333, 334 .... 10:08
- 337 .... 8:171
- 338 .... 13:08
- 340 .... 8:171
- 345 .... 10:03, 10:05
- 348 .... 13:08
- 349 .... 10:02, 10:08
- 350 .... 10:08
- 351 .... 10:08
- 352 .... 10:08; 13:08
- 353–356 .... 10:08
- 357, 358 .... 35:07
- 359 .... 35:07
- 360 .... 13:08; 35:07
- 361 .... 10:08
- Pt IV (ss 365–573)
  - 5:12; 11:01
- s 365 (1) (a) 5:13

Income Tax (Trading and Other Income) Act 2005 – *cont.*
- s 366 .... 26:01
  - (1) 8:91; 26:29
- 367 .... 26:01
- 368 .... 10:03; 33:16
- Ch II (ss 369–381)
  - 5:27
- s 369 .... 5:13, 5:27; 36:02
- 370 .... 5:16, 5:27
  - (1) 11:01
- 371 .... 5:05, 5:27; 13:08; 35:26
- 379 .... 26:01
- 382 .... 25:01
- 383 ...... 14:07; 25:01; 26:01; 36:02
- 384 .... 5:16; 25:01
- 385 .... 13:08; 25:01
  - (1) (b) 35:26
- 386–396 .... 25:01
- 397 .... 25:01; 35:37
  - (1) 5:26; 26:13
- s 397A 35:08
- s 397C 35:08
- 398 .... 25:01
  - (1) 5:30
- 399–401 .... 25:01
- 404 (1) 13:08
- Ch VII (ss 422–426)
  - 5:27
- s 410 (3) 26:19
  - (4) 14:07; 26:19
- 412 (1) 26:19
- 419 (2) 14:07
- 422 .... 5:27
- 423 .... 5:27; 31:31
- 424 .... 5:27
  - (1) 11:01
- 425 .... 5:27; 13:08
- 426 .... 5:27
- Ch VIII (ss 427–460)
  - 5:27
- s 427 .... 5:27; 11:17
- 428 .... 5:27
  - (1) 11:01
- 429 .... 5:27; 13:08
- 430 .... 5:27
  - (1) 11:18
- 431 .... 5:27
  - (1) 11:18
  - (2) (b), (c) 11:18
  - (3) 11:18
  - (5) 11:18
- 432 .... 5:27
  - (1) (a)–(d) 11:18
  - (4) 11:18
- 433 .... 5:27
  - (1) 11:18
- 434 .... 5:27; 11:18
- 435 .... 5:27
  - (1) 11:18
- 436 .... 5:27; 11:18

Table of Statutes

Income Tax (Trading and Other Income) Act 2005 – cont.
- s 437 .... 5:27
  - (1) (c) 11:17
  - (3) 11:17
- 438 .... 5:27; 11:17
- 439 .... 5:27
  - (4) 11:17
- 440 .... 5:27
  - (1) 11:17
  - (2) (b), (c) 11:17
  - (4) 11:17
- 441 .... 5:27
- 442 .... 5:27; 11:18
- 443, 444 .... 4:12; 5:27; 11:18
- 445–448 .... 4:12; 5:27
- 449 .... 4:12; 5:27
  - (1), (2) 11:19
- 450 .... 4:12; 5:27; 11:17
  - (1) 11:19
- 451, 452 .... 4:12; 5:27
- 453 .... 5:27
- 454 .... 5:27; 11:17
- 455 .... 5:27
- 456 .... 5:27
- 457 .... 5:27
- 458 .... 5:27
- 459 .... 5:27; 11:17

Ch IX (ss 460–546)
.... 8:94
- s 460 .... 5:27
  - (2) 11:18
- 461 .... 5:27; 6:08; 6:46; 12:19
- 462–465 .... 5:27; 6:08; 12:19
- 466 .... 5:27; 6:08; 12:19
  - (2) 14:07
- 467 .. 5:27; 6:08; 12:19; 13:08; 31:20
- 468 .... 5:27; 6:08; 12:19
- 469–480 .... 5:27; 6:08
- 481 .... 5:27; 6:08; 31:20
- 482–483 .... 5:27; 6:08
- 484 .... 5:27; 6:08; 6:46; 31:22
- 485–490 .... 5:27; 6:08
- 491 .... 5:27; 6:08; 6:50; 31:23
- 492 .... 5:27; 6:08
- s 493 .... 5:27; 6:08
  - (6) 31:23
- 494–499 .... 5:27; 6:08
- 500–501 .... 5:27; 6:08; 31:22
- 502 .... 5:27; 6:08
- 503 .... 5:27; 6:08
  - (2), (3) 31:28
- 504–506 .... 5:27; 6:08
- 507 .... 5:27; 6:08; 31:22
  - (2), (4)–(5) 31:23
- 508–521 .... 5:27; 6:08
- 522 .... 5:27; 6:08; 31:27
- 523–529 .... 5:27; 6:08
- 530 .... 5:27; 6:08
  - (1) 31:20
- 531 .... 5:27; 6:08

Income Tax (Trading and Other Income) Act 2005 – cont.
- s 531 (1), (3) 31:29
- 532 .... 5:27; 6:08; 31:22
- 533–534 .... 5:27; 6:08
- 535 .... 5:27; 6:08; 31:24
- 536 .... 5:27; 6:08
  - (7) 31:24
- 537–538 .... 5:27; 6:08
- 539 .... 5:27; 6:08; 31:24
- 540 .... 5:27; 6:08
- 541 .... 5:27; 6:08
- 541a 5:27; 6:08
  - (2)–(4) 31:23
- 542–546 .... 5:27; 6:08

Ch X (ss 547–551)
.... 11:03
- s 549 .... 13:08
- 551 .... 12:14
- 552 .... 36:02
  - (1) (c) 12:14
- 554 .... 13:08
- 557 .... 13:08
- 568 .... 13:08
- 569 .... 35:38
- 573 .... 13:08

Pt V (ss 574–689)
- s 575 (1) 8:91
- 577 .... 33:16
- 579 .... 11:03
- 581 .... 13:08
- 587 .... 9:63
- 590 .... 9:63
- 600 .... 8:139
- 611 .... 13:08

Ch IV (ss 614–618)
.... 11:03
- s 616 .... 13:08

Ch V (ss 619–648)
.... 11:17
- s 619 .... 13:14; 15:01; 15:18
- 620 .... 15:01; 15:18; 42:04
  - (1) 15:02; 15:07
  - (2), (3) 15:07
  - (5) 15:18
- 621 .... 15:01; 15:18
- 622 .... 15:01; 15:18
- 623 .... 15:01; 15:18
  - (2) 15:25
- 624 ...... 6:03; 14:03; 15:01; 15:10,
  15:14, 15:16, 15:17, 15:20, 15:21,
  15:22, 15:18
  - (1) 12:19; 15:15, 15:31
  - (b) 15:10
- 625 .... 12:19; 15:01, 15:14, 15:18
  - (1) ... 15:10, 15:13, 15:15, 15:30
  - (2) 15:16, 15:23
  - (3) 15:16
  - (4) 15:15
- 626 ...... 12:19; 15:01, 15:30, 15:31,
  15:18

Table of Statutes

Income Tax (Trading and Other Income) Act 2005 – *cont.*

s	(1)	6:03
	(4)	15:15
	627	12:19; 15:01, 15:18
	(1)	15:15
	(2) (c)	6:03
	628	15:01, 15:18
	(1)	15:17
	(4), (5)	15:17
	629	6:01; 11:21; 15:01, 15:04, 15:08, 15:22, 15:30, 15:18
	(1) (b)	15:21
	(3)	15:21
	(7) (a)–(c)	15:21
	630	15:01, 15:05, 15:18
	(1)	15:17
	(3), (4)	15:17
	631	15:01, 15:18
	(1)–(5)	15:22
	(5) (d)	15:22
	(6), (7)	15:22
	632	15:01, 15:22, 15:18
	633	15:01, 15:24, 15:25, 15:26, 15:27, 15:28, 15:18
	(1)	15:23
	634	15:01, 15:18
	(1) (a)	15:23
	(b) (ii)	15:23
	(3) (a), (b)	15:23
	(5)	15:23
	(7)	15:23
	635	15:01, 15:23, 15:25, 15:18
	636, 637	15:01, 15:18
	638	15:01, 15:18
	(1)	15:24
	(4), (5)	15:24
	639	15:01, 15:18
	640	15:01, 15:18
	(2)	15:27
	641	15:01, 15:18
	(1) (b)	15:26
	642	15:01, 15:26, 15:18
	643	15:01, 15:18
	(2)	15:26
	644	15:01, 15:18
	(1)	14:06, 15:08
	(3)	15:08
	(a), (b)	15:06
	(4)	15:08, 15:09
	(5)	15:09
	645	15:01, 15:18
	(1)	15:06
	(c)	15:08
	(2)	15:08
	(4)	15:06, 15:08
	646	15:01, 15:18
	646a	15:17, 15:18
	647	15:01, 15:18
	648	15:01, 15:18
	(1) (a)	15:09

Income Tax (Trading and Other Income) Act 2005 – *cont.*

s 648 (2) (3)		15:09
650 (1)		14:08
(2)		14:07
(5)		14:09
651 (1)		14:04
(4)		14:04
654 (3), (4)		14:07
655		14:08
657		14:07
(3), (4)		14:08
660 (1)		14:08
661 (1)		14:06, 14:07
662		14:09
663		14:07
665		14:09
(1)–(3)		14:08
666 (1)		14:08
(2) (d)		14:08
(6), (5)		14:08
668		14:08
669		14:01
671–674		14:09
674 (4), (5)		14:07
675		14:09
679 (3), (4)		14:07
680		14:08
(3) (a), (b)		14:07
(4), (5)		14:07
680A		14:09
681		14:07, 14:08
682		14:08
Ch VII (ss 683–686)		
	3:12; 11:03; 11:24, 11:25, 11:27, 11:30, 11:36	
s 683		5:17; 11:04; 13:15
(1), (2)		11:27
685		13:08
686		13:15
Ch VIII (ss 687–689)		
	23, 53; 11:24; 12:01	
s 687		5:17; 6:31
(1)		12:02
688		6:31; 12:02, 12:12
(1)		12:07
689		6:31; 11:04; 12:02; 13:08
691		31:04
692		5:18; 31:04
693		31:04
694		31:01
697		31:01
702		5:18
Ch V (ss 709–713)		
	8:94	
Ch VI (ss 717–726)		
	31:31	
s 717		5:25; 11:31
718		31:31
719 (3), (4), (8)		31:31
720 (3)		31:31

2687

Table of Statutes

Income Tax (Trading and Other Income) Act 2005 – *cont.*
s 721 (3)	31:31
724	31:31
727	11:03
(1) (a)	11:23
728–729	11:03
732	5:18
734	5:18
735	5:18; 11:04
736	11:04
737–740	11:04
744	5:18
751	5:18; 11:06
753	5:18
756a(1)	5:18
757	11:13
758 (2)–(5)	11:13
759, 760	11:13
761	5:18; 11:13
763–765	11:13
768 (1)	8:42
769	5:18
776	5:18
779 (1)	12:11
781, 782	5:18
785 (1),(b)	10:14
786 (1), (2)	10:14
788 (1)	10:14
789 (3), (4)	10:14
790 (2)	10:14
795–800	10:14
830	11:09
(2)	33:04
(o)	12:12
831	12:12; 33:16
(5)	35:12
832	5:26, 5;28; 11:09; 33:16, 33:41; 35:05, 35:12, 35:16
(1)	33:15
832A	35:23
833	35:21, 35:22
834	35:21
835–837	35:25
839 (5), (6)	11:03
841	35:24
842	6:12; 35:24
843–845	35:24
847 (2)	8:62
848, 849	8:62
850 (2)	8:62
851	10:09
852	8:43
(1)	8:63
(2) (a), (b)	8:62
(4)	8:62
854	8:62; 10:08, 10:09, 11:01; 35:06
855	10:08, 10:09, 11:01; 35:06
856	10:08, 10:09, 11:01
857, 858	33:38; 35:46
860 (2)	8:50

Income Tax (Trading and Other Income) Act 2005 – *cont.*
s 860 (4)	8:71
863	8:63
867	5:19; 8:133; 33:38
(3)	8:42
870 (3)	5:19
878 (5)	10:17
Sch 1	
para 7	35:01
Sch 2	
para 28	8:135
52 (2)	8:48
12	31:27

Companies Act 2006
s 112	26:01
555	59:02
684–686	26:20
Pt 18, Ch 4 (ss 690–708)	26:20
s 707	59:06
724	61:14
728	59:06
730	59:06
830	4:24
841(2)	4:24
899	57:05
900	56:21
974	57:07
981	57:07
1000	26:01

Finance Act 2006
	38:13
s 17 (1)	9:33
19 (1)	65:41
(4)	65:41
22	63:09
26	25:41
28	8:140
64(2)	5:18
65	5:18
68	5:18
69	16:26; 28:17
70, 71	28:17
73	17:13
74 (5), (6)	21:03
77	27:26
80 (8)	12:23
92	50:36
97	27:33
98	27:28
103–146	31:33
111 (1)	31:33
(4)	31:33
112 (3)	31:33
122 (2) (a)	31:33
134 (2)	31:33
146 (1)	31:33
155 (3), (4)	38:07
156	38:13
165	62:29
189 (2)	62:29

Table of Statutes

Finance Act 2006 – *cont.*
  Sch 1 .... 10:02
  Sch 12
    para 1 .... 20:03
  Sch 14
    para 1 (1) 31:12
  Sch 15
    para 1 (5) 8:72
    para 2 (2) 8:72
        (4) 8:72
       4 .... 8:72
       7 (2), (3) 8:72
  Sch 16, 17 .... 31:33
  Sch 20
    para 2–4 .... 42:01
      14 (3) 42:16
      27 .... 40:24
      33 .... 41:02
National Assurance Act 2006
  s 7 .... 2A:05
National Insurance Contributions Act 2006
  .... 50:36
  s 6 .... 55:04
Finance Act 2007 .... 1:31; 9:01
  s 1 (b) 5:26
    4 .... 38:07
      (1), (2) 38:13
    16 (6) 69:43
    18 (3) 10:10
    24 .... 25:01
    25 .... 49:24
      (2) 7:09
    27 (2), (3) 16:26
    28 (3) 31:23
    36 .... 9:14
      (1) 9:01, 9:17
      (2), (3) 9:10
      (5) 9:60
      (7) 9:10, 9:17, 9:59, 9:60
    73 .... 60:10; 61:06
    76 .... 62:02
    80 .... 62:23
    81 .... 2:31
    82 .... 2:31; 63:03
    83 .... 63:03
      (1)–(3) 2:31
    84 .... 63:03
    85 .... 2:31; 63:03
    86 .... 2:31
    96 .... 2A:78
      (2)–(4) 2A:97
    97 .... 64:14; 66:40; 67:19
    100 (8), (10) 64:04
  Sch 3 .... 49:24
    para 3 .... 7:09
  Sch 11
  Sch 13 .... 4:12
  Sch 21 .... 60:10; 61:61:06
  Sch 22
    para 2–5 .... 2:31
      8 .... 2:31

Finance Act 2007 – *cont.*
  Sch 22 – *cont.*
    para 14–16 .... 2:31
  Sch 23 .... 63:03
  Sch 24 .... 2A:04, 2A:78, 2A:97; 63:03
    para 1 ..... 2A:79, 2A:99; 66:40; 67:19
    Table 2A:83
      1(4) 2A:79
      1 a 2A:99
        (1)–(3) 2A:84
      2 .... 2A:85
      3 (1) 2A:81
        (2) 2A:82
      4 (1a) 2A:87
      5 .... 2A:86
      7 (5) 2A:86
      8 .... 2A:86
      9 (1) 2A:87
        (2) 2A:87
        (a) 67:19
      10 .... 2A:87
      14(1) 2A:88
        (3) 2A:88
    29 .... 66:40; 67:19
      (d) 64:14
  Sch 25
    para 6 .... 62:11
      8 .... 35:72
Income Tax Act 2007
  .... 1:23; 5:01, 5:22
  s 3 .... 5:03; 13:08
    (1) 5:05
    4 .... 1:23; 1:31; 13:08
    6 .... 13:08, 13:11
    7 .... 11:01; 13:08
    8 ... 5:26; 11:01; 13:08; 14:07; 14:07
    (1), (2) 5:02
    9 .... 5:02; 13:08; 36:12
    (a), (b) 13:11
    10 .... 13:08
      (2) 5:26
    11 .... 13:08; 14:02
      (1) 12:23
    12 .... 5:02, 5:26; 13:08
      (10) 11:01
    13 .... 13:08; 35:12
      (1) (c) 5:26
      (2) 5:26
    14 .... 5:26; 13:08; 14:07
    16 .... 5:26; 11:01
      (3) 26:12
    17 .... 13:08
    18 .... 5:26; 13:08
      (2) (b) 5:28
      (3) (d) 11:08
    19 .... 13:08
      (3) 5:26
    20 .... 13:08
    21 .... 5:02; 13:08
    23 ...... 5:07, 5:26, 5:30, 5:31; 6:09;
                               11:01; 13:08

Table of Statutes

Income Tax Act 2007 – *cont.*
- s 25 (2) 5:32
- 35 .... 6:12; 13:08
- 36 .... 6:06, 6:12; 13:08
  - (2) 6:08
- 37 .... 6:06; 13:08
- 38 .... 6:09, 6:12; 13:08; 52:06
  - (4) 6:09
- 42 .... 6:07
- 43 .... 11:45
- 45 .... 6:12, 6:35
  - (1) 6:07
  - (2) (a) 6:07
- 46 .... 6:12
  - (2) (a) 6:07
  - (e) 6:07
  - (4) 6:07
- 47 (1) 6:07
- 48 .... 6:07
- 50 (2) (b) 6:07
- 55 (2) 6:06
- 56 (3) 6:10, 6:12; 35:08
- 57 .... 6:04
- 58 .... 6:06, 6:08

Part IV (s 59–155)
- 31:13
- 59–61 .... 10:15
- 62 .... 6:24, 6:28; 10:15
- 63 .... 10:15
- 64 .... 6:12, 6:15; 9:48; 10:15; 13:24; 52:06
  - (1) 5:07
- 65 .... 10:15
- 66 .... 6:25, 6:26; 10:15; 13:24
- 67 .... 6:29; 10:15
- 69, 70 .... 10:15
- 71 .... 6:12, 6:15, 6:17; 10:15
- 72 ..... 6:12, 6:15, 6:21; 9:48; 10:15; 13:24
- 73 .... 10:15
- 74 .... 6:26; 10:15; 52:06
- 74A 6:18
- 75 .... 10:15
- 76–80 .... 10:15
- 81 .... 6:25; 10:15
- 82 .... 10:15
- 83 ... 6:12, 6:15; 10:15; 13:24; 52:06
  - (4) 6:19
- 84 .... 10:15
- 85 .... 6:19; 10:15
- 86 .... 10:15
  - (3) 6:20
- 88 .... 52:06
- 89 .... 6:12, 6:15, 6:24; 10:15
- 90 .... 10:15
  - (1) 6:22
- 91 .... 6:22; 10:15
- 92 .... 6:23; 10:15
- 93 .... 10:15
- 94 .... 10:15; 52:06
- 95 .... 6:31; 10:15

Income Tax Act 2007 – *cont.*
- s 96 .... 6:12; 10:15
- 97–103 .... 10:15
- 104 .... 6:21; 10:15
- 105 .... 10:15
- 106 .... 10:15; 13:25
- 107 .... 6:19; 10:15
- 108 .... 10:15
- 109 .... 6:25; 10:15
- 110–112 .... 6:21; 10:15
- 113, 114 .... 10:15
- 115 .... 6:19; 10:15
- 116 .... 10:15
- 117 .... 6:31; 10:15
- 118 .... 5:11; 6:31, 6:32; 10:15
- 119 .... 10:15
- 120 .... 5:11; 10:15
  - (1) 6:32
  - (2) (b) 6:32
- 121 .... 10:15
- 122 .... 10:15
  - (2) 6:32
- 123 .... 10:15
  - (2), (3) 6:32
  - (5) (a), (b) 6:32
- 124 .... 10:15
- 125 .... 6:12; 10:15
- 126 .... 10:15
- 127 .... 5:20; 6:27, 6:32
  - (4) 10:15
  - (7) 10:15
- 128 .... 6:30
- 131 .... 22:31; 31:13
  - (3) 6:34
- 132 .... 6:34
- 133 .... 4:33; 6:34
- 134–151 .... 6:34
- 152 .... 6:31; 23:36
  - (2) 12:07
  - (3) 12:13
- 153 .... 6:31

Part V (s 156–257)
- 31:06, 31:13
- s 157 (1) 31:11
  - (2) 31:07
- 158 (1) 31:09, 31:15
  - (2) 31:07, 31:09
  - (5) 31:07
- 159 .... 31:10
  - (2), (3) 31:11
- 163 .... 31:11
- 164 .... 31:06
  - (2) 31:10
- 168 (1)–(4) 31:11
- 169 .... 31:11
- 170 (9), (10) 31:11
- 171 .... 31:11
- 173 (2) 31:07
  - (3) 31:07, 31:12
- 174 .... 31:15
- 175 .... 31:07, 31:15

Table of Statutes

Income Tax Act 2007 – *cont.*
- s 176 (7) (2) 31:12
- 179 .... 31:12
- 181 (2) 31:12
- 182 (4) 31:12
- 184 .... 31:12
- 185 .... 31:12
- 186 .... 31:12
- 189 (1) (a) 31:12
- 190 .... 31:12
- 192 (1) 31:12
- 193–199 .... 31:12
- 201 (2)–(5), (7) 31:09
- 202 (1) (a), (b) 31:15
- 204 .... 6:12
- 205 .... 6:12
- 205 (4) 31:15
- 209 (2), (3) 31:13
- 210 .... 31:13
- 212 .... 31:13
- 213 .... 31:14
- 214 .... 31:14
- 215 (2) 31:14
- 216 (2) (b) 31:14
- 218 (2) 35:26
- 221 .... 31:14
- 222 (4) 31:14
- 223–231 .... 31:14
- 232 (1)–(3) 31:14
- 234 (2) 31:15
- 235 .... 6:05
- 239–244 .... 31:15
- 246 (6) 31:13
- 251 (3) 31:07
- 253 .... 31:10
- 255 .... 31:09
- Part VI (s 238–332)
  - 31:17
- 262 (3) 31:17
- 263 (2) 31:17
- 277 .... 6:46
- 286 .... 31:17
- 288 .... 31:18
- 289 .... 31:18
- 297 .... 31:17
- 299 (4) 31:13
- 303 (1) (ia)–(ic) 31:18
- 304–313 .... 31:18
- 326 .... 31:17
- 329 .... 31:17
- 330 .... 31:17
- 383 .... 5:32; 6:39
- 384 .... 6:40
- 388 .... 6:38
- 390 .... 6:38, 6:41
- 392 .... 6:38
  - (3) 6:42
- 393, 394 .... 6:42
- 396 .... 6:38, 6:42
- 398 .... 6:38, 6:42
- 401 .... 6:38

Income Tax Act 2007 – *cont.*
- s 403 .... 6:38, 6:43; 14:02
- 405 .... 14:02
- 407 .... 6:42
- 411 (1) 6:42
- 414 .... 6:11
  - (1) 6:36
  - (2) (b) 6:36; 12:21
- 415 .... 6:36
- 416 (1), (2) 6:36
  - (7) 6:36
- 418 .... 6:37
- 420 (4) 6:37
- 423 (5) 6:36
- 424 (1) 6:36
- 426 (6), (7) 6:36
- 429 .... 6:36
- 430 (1) 11:28
  - (d) 6:36
- 431, 432 .... 6:38
- 434 (1) 6:38
- 436, 437 .... 6:38
- 448 .... 10:01; 11:37
  - (5) 11:39, 11:40
- 449 .... 10:01
- 453 .... 6:35; 35:12
  - (3) 11:45
- 454 .... 35:12
  - (3) 6:35; 11:45
- 455–459 .... 35:12
- 463 (1) 13:11
- 464 (1), (2) 13:15
- 467 .... 15:07; 42:04
- 479 .... 5:02; 13:11, 13:14, 13:19; 14:02
- 480 .... 13:11, 13:19
  - (1) 13:14; 15:17
  - (3) (a) 13:14; 15:17
- 482 .... 11:17; 13:08
- 483 .... 14:02; 14:07
- 484 .... 5:02; 13:17
  - (1), (2) 13:13
  - (5) 13:08, 13:11
  - (b) 13:13
  - (6) 13:08
- 485 .... 13:11
- 486 .... 13:08, 13:11, 13:17
- 487 .... 36:12
  - (4) 13:11
- 491 .... 13:10
- 492 (1), (2) 13:10
- 493 (1) (b) 36:12
- 494 (2) 36:12
- 505 (1) (aa) 13:22
- 518 .... 5:21
- 519 .... 5:21; 16:46
- 520 .... 5:21
  - (1) 6:36; 15:17
  - (2) 13:22; 15:17
- 521 .... 5:21
- 522 .... 5:21; 13:22
- 523, 524 .... 5:21

Table of Statutes

Income Tax Act 2007 – *cont.*
- s 525 .... 5:21
  - (4) 13:23
- 526 .... 5:21
- 527 .... 5:21
  - (1) 13:25
  - (2) 12:02
  - (e) 12:07
  - (4), (5) 13:25
- 528 .... 5:21; 12:07
  - (1) (b) 13:25
  - (6) 13:25
- 529 .... 5:21
- 530 .... 5:21
  - (1) 13:22
- 531 .... 5:21; 12:06
  - (2a) 13:22
- 532 .... 5:21; 13:22
- 533, 534 .... 5:21
- 535 .... 5:21; 13:22
- 536 .... 5:21; 12:06
  - (3) 12:07
- 537–539 .... 5:21
- 540–542 .... 5:21; 13:26
- 543 .... 5:21; 13:27
  - (1) (i) 13:26
- 544–548 .... 5:21
- 549 .... 5:21
  - (2) 13:27
- 551 .... 5:21
  - (1) 13:27
- 554 .... 5:21
  - (1)–(3) 13:27
- 555 .... 5:21
  - (1) 13:27
- 556, 557 .... 5:21
- 558, 559 .... 5:21; 13:26
- 560–560 .... 5:21
- 562, 563 .... 5:21; 13:26
- 564 .... 5:21
- 569 (4) 4:12
- 573 .... 4:15, 4:16
- 575 .... 4:12
- 578 .... 4:15, 4:16
  - (3) 4:12
- 581 .... 4:15, 4:16
- 582 .... 4:15
- 583–585 .... 4:16
- 593, 594 .... 4:12, 4:16, 4:17
- 596 .... 4:15
- 601–605 .... 4:15
- 607 .... 4:12
- 612 (1) 4:17
- 615 .... 11:08, 11:09
- 616–618 .... 4:10, 4:13; 5:21, 5:27; 11:08
- 619 .... 4:10, 4:13; 5:21, 5:27
  - (1), (2) 11:08
- 620, 621 ...... 4:10, 4:13; 5:21, 5:27; 11:08, 11:09
- 622 ...... 4:10, 4:13; 5:21, 5:27; 11:08

Income Tax Act 2007 – *cont.*
- s 623, 624 ...... 4:10, 4:13; 5:21, 5:27; 11:08, 11:09
- 625, 626 ...... 4:10, 4:13; 5:21, 5:27; 11:08
- 627 .... 4:10, 4:13; 5:21, 5:27; 11:08, 11:09
- 628 ..... 4:10, 4:13; 5:21, 5:27; 11:08
  - (5) 13:08
- 629 ..... 4:10, 4:13; 5:21, 5:27; 11:08
- 630 ..... 4:10, 4:13; 5:21, 5:27; 11:08
  - (2) 13:08
- 631, 632 ...... 4:10, 4:13; 5:21, 5:27; 11:08
- 633 .... 4:10, 4:13; 5:21, 5:27
  - (5) 11:08
- 634 ..... 4:10, 4:13; 5:21, 5:27; 11:08
- 635 .... 4:10, 4:13; 5:21, 5:27; 11:08, 11:09
- 636 ..... 4:10, 4:13; 5:21, 5:27; 11:08
- 637 .... 4:10, 4:13; 5:21, 5:26
  - (2) 11:08
- 638–642 ...... 4:10, 4:13; 5:21, 5:27; 11:08, 11:09
- 643 .... 4:10, 4:13; 5:21, 5:27; 11:08, 11:09
  - (3) 11:09
- 645, 646 ...... 4:10, 4:13; 5:21, 5:27; 11:08, 11:09
- 647 ..... 4:10, 4:13, 4:15; 5:21, 5:27; 11:08, 11:09
- 648–652 ...... 4:10, 4:13; 5:21, 5:27; 11:08
- 653 .... 4:10, 4:13; 5:21, 5:27; 11:08, 11:09
- 654 ..... 4:10, 4:13, 4:17; 5:21, 5:27; 11:08, 11:09
- 655–658 ...... 4:10, 4:13; 5:21, 5:27; 11:08
- 659 .... 4:10, 4:13; 5:21, 5:27; 11:08, 11:09
- 660–667 ...... 4:10, 4:13; 5:21, 5:27; 11:08
- 668, 669 ...... 4:10, 4:13; 5:21, 5:27; 11:08, 11:09
- 670–672 ...... 4:10, 4:13; 5:21, 5:27; 11:08
- 673 ..... 4:10, 4:13; 5:21, 5:27; 11:09
  - (1) (b) 11:08
- 674, 675 ...... 4:10, 4:13; 5:21, 5:27; 11:08
- 676 .... 4:10, 4:13; 5:21, 5:27; 11:08, 11:09
- 677 ..... 4:10, 4:13; 5:21, 5:27; 11:08
- 678, 679 .... 4:10
- 680 .... 4:10, 4:22
- 681 .... 4:10
- Part 13, Ch 1 (s 682–713) 2A:05
- 682, 683 .... 4:18; 5:21
- 684 .... 4:18; 5:21

Income Tax Act 2007 – *cont.*
s   (3) 4:20; 5:21
   685 .... 4:18, 4:28; 5:21
   686 .... 4:18, 4:28; 5:21
   687 .... 4:18, 4:23, 4:28; 5:21
   688 .... 4:18, 4:24, 4:28; 5:21
   689 .... 4:18, 4:26, 4:28; 5:21
   690 .... 4:18, 4:30, 4:28; 5:21
   691 .... 4:18, 4:28; 5:21
   692 .... 4:18, 4:22, 4:28; 5:21
   693 .... 4:18, 4:28; 5:21
   694 .... 4:18, 4:22, 4:28; 5:21
   695–697 .... 4:18, 4:28; 5:21
   698 .... 4:18, 4:28, 4:29; 5:21
   699–712 .... 4:18, 4:28; 5:21
   713 .... 4:18, 4:20, 4:28; 5:21
   714 .... 5:21; 12:19; 35:26
       (4) 35:27
   715 .... 5:21; 35:26
   716 .... 5:21; 35:26
       (2) 35:27, 35:30
   717 .... 5:21; 35:26, 35:27
       (a) 35:30
   718 .... 5:21
       (2) (a) 35:26
   719 .... 5:21; 35:25
   720 .... 3:11; 5:21; 35:26
   721 .... 5:21; 35:26, 35:27, 35:33
   722 .... 5:21; 35:26
       (4) (b) 35:33
   723 .... 5:21; 35:26, 35:33
   724, 725 .... 5:21; 35:26
   726 .... 5:21; 35:26, 35:36
   727 .... 5:21; 35:26
   728 .... 5:21; 35:26, 35:28
   729 .... 5:21; 35:26
       (1) (a) (iii) 35:28
           (b) 35:28
       (2) 35:28
       (3) (a), (b) 35:28
       (4) 35:28
   730 .... 5:21; 35:26
   731 .... 5:21; 35:26, 35:39
   732 .... 5:21; 35:26
   733 .... 5:21; 35:26
       (1) 35:39
   734 .... 5:21; 35:26
   735 .... 5:21; 35:26, 35:39
   736 .... 5:21; 35:26
   737 .... 5:21; 35:26
       (2), (3) 35:29
       (4) (a) 35:29
   738 .... 5:21; 35:26
   739 .... 3:11; 5:21; 35:26
       (1) 35:29
       (3), (4) 35:29
   740, 741 .... 5:21; 35:26
   742 .... 5:21; 35:26
       (2), (3) 35:29
   743–745 .... 5:21; 35:26
   746 .... 5:21; 35:26

Income Tax Act 2007 – *cont.*
s   (2) 35:37
   747 .... 5:21; 35:26
   748 .... 5:21; 35:26
       (4) 35:35
   749 .... 5:21; 35:26, 35:35
   750 .... 5:21; 35:26, 35:35
   751 .... 5:21; 35:26
   Part 13, Ch 3 (s 752–772)
       .... 23:02
   752–754 .... 5:21; 13:08
   755 . 5:21; 12:06, 12:12; 13:08; 23:35
   756 .... 5:21; 13:08; 23:29
   757–764 .... 5:21; 13:08
   765–767 .... 5:21; 13:08; 35:29
   768–772 .... 5:21; 13:08
   773, 774 .... 4:30; 5:21
   775 .... 4:30; 5:21
       (b) 4:31
   776, 777 .... 4:30, 4:31; 5:21
   778 .... 4:30, 4:31; 5:21; 35:29
   779 .... 4:30, 4:31; 5:21
   780–783 .... 4:30; 5:21
   784 .... 4:30; 5:21
       (4) 4:31
   785–789 .... 4:30; 5:21
   790–809A 5:21
   809B . 5:21; 6:12; 35:12, 35:16, 35:49
       (3) 35:13
   809C–809D 5:21; 35:12
   809E–809F 5:21
   809G 5:21
       (2), (4), (5)
       .... 35:13
   809H–809I 5:21; 35:14
   809J 5:21
   809K 5:21; 35:21
       (2)–(5) 35:16
   809L 5:21; 35:16
   809M 5:21
   809N–809R 5:21; 35:16
   809S 5:21
       (2) 35:16
   809T 5:21; 35:16
   809U 5:21
       (1), (3)–(4)
       .... 35:16
   809V 5:21
       (3), (4), (5), (9)
       .... 35:16
   809W 5:21
       (2)–(8) 35:16
   809X 5:21
       (3), (4) 35:16
   809Y–809ZD 5:21
   811 .... 11:02
   829 .... 33:03
   830 .... 33:13
   831 (1) 33:04, 33:06, 33:08
       (1B) 33:09
   832 .... 4:31

Table of Statutes

Income Tax Act 2007 – *cont.*
s 832 (1) 33:08
    (6) 33:09
836 (2), (3) 6:02
837 .... 6:02
838 .... 5:18
839 .... 5:18
841 .... 5:18
848 .... 11:37
    (1) 5:15
851 (2) 5:26
853 .... 11:13
854 (2) 11:13
856–859 .... 11:13
860, 861 .... 11:13
863 (1) 11:13
864, 865 .... 11:13
866 (2) 11:13
Part 15 (s 847–987)
.... 2A:18; 11:01, 11:37, 11:40, 11:42,
11:43, 11:44, 33:43
867–870 .... 11:13
874 .... 5:04; 11:14
    (1) 11:12
874 .... 11:14
885 (1) 11:14
900 .... 13:21
    (2) 11:37
    (3) 11:14
901 .... 13:21
    (3) (a) 11:37
    (4) 11:37
    (5) (a) 11:14, 11:37
    (6) (a) 11:37
902 (2) 11:14
    (4) 11:14
903 .... 11:36
911, 912 .... 11:14
930 .... 11:14
931 (1) 11:14
933 .... 11:14
935 .... 11:14
937 .... 11:14
944 .... 4:31
947 .... 11:14
952 .... 11:37
964 .... 11:14
965–970 .... 2A:18
971 .... 2A:18; 10:12
972 .... 2A:18
979 .... 5:18
993 .... 10:24; 35:16
1005 .... 13:26
1011 .... 6:07
1026 .... 14:07, 14:08
1374 .... 6:35
Sch 1
para 40 .... 6:10
309 .... 6:34
Pensions Act 2007 .... 51:02

Finance Act 2008 ... 2:63, 2:84; 4:13,
4:14, 4:24; 5:18,
5:28;6:38; 7:36, 7:49,
7:83, 7:115; 8:78,
8:140, 8:157;9:01,
9:29, 9:32, 9:35, 9:36,
9:37, 9:39,
9:50;10:04; 13:22;
24:05, 24:10; 25:17,
25:31;31:05, 31:09,
31:16; 33:08; 35:07,
35:22;42:05, 42:16
s 2 (1) (a) 6:06
    (b) 6:06
5 .... 25:01
6 .... 25:02
65 (1) 5:26
80 .... 9:43
82 (2) 9:18
    (3) 9:18, 9:61
    (4) 9:18
    (6), (7) 9:61
83 .... 9:19
94 .... 62:23
98 .... 59:04
101 .... 59:05
113 .... 63:03
114 .... 63:03
115 .... 63:03
118 .... 67:16, 67:17
120 ...... 66:36, 66:40; 67:07, 67:16,
67:17
121 (1) 67:16, 67:17
    (2) 66:22; 67:18
    (3)–(4) 66:22
122 .... 63:03
123 .... 63:03
    (2) 64:14
133 .... 67:16, 67:17
135 .... 67:08
136 .... 67:04
154 .... 1:30
160 .... 2:01; 63:04
Sch 1
para 5 .... 5:26
Sch 3
para 6 .... 22:33
Sch 4 .... 38:14
7 .... 5:05
para 4ZA (4) 62:17
Sch 19 .... 6:36
31 .... 62:27
32
para 5 .... 59:06
10 (2) 59:06
11 .... 59:09
22 .... 56:01; 57:40, 57:42; 58:06,
58:12
Sch 36 .... 2A:53; 63:03
para 1 .... 2A:50
2 .... 2A:57

Table of Statutes

Finance Act 2008 – *cont.*
  Sch 36 – *cont.*
    para 3 .... 2A:56
      (1) 2A:57
      4 .... 2A:57
      5(3) 2A:57
      10(2) 2A:58
      12, 12a 2A:58
      13 .... 2A:58
      21(1), (2) 2A:55
        (4)–(6) 2A:55
      29(1)–(3) 2A:56
      30(1)–(3) 2A:57
      31 .... 2A:57
      39, 40 .... 2A:59
      45 .... 2A:59
      47 .... 2A:59
      62 .... 2A:56
      63 .... 2A:46
      64(1)(a)–(c) 2A:54
      37
    para 10 .... 63:03
  Sch 39
    para 36 .... 67:16, 67:17
      40 .... 63:03
      41 .... 63:03
    para 1 .... 2A:89, 2A:99; 64:14
      2 .... 65:18
      5, 6 .... 2A:89
      12, 13 .... 2A:89
      20 .... 2A:89
      25 .... 64:14
        (f) 65:18
National Insurance Contributions Act 2008
  .... 51:02
Corporation Tax Act 2009
  .... 1:23; 30.07
  s 2 (1) 25:02, 25:34
    (2) 25:17
    (4) 25:02, 25:05
    3 .... 25:02, 25:05
    4 .... 25:02
    5 (1) 25:04, 25:05
      (2) 25:45
      (3) 25:05
    6 (1) 25:04
      (2) 25:02, 25:04
    7 .... 25:02, 25:04
    8 (2) 25:05, 25:34
      (5) 25:05
    9 (1) 25:36
        (a) 25:05
      (2) 25:36
      (3) 25:39
    10 (1) (d) 25:05
        (j) 25:37
    11 (3) 25:38
    12 (2) 25:36, 25:38
    19 (2), (3) 25:45
    21 .... 25:45
    29 .... 25:45

Corporation Tax Act 2009 – *cont.*
  Pt 3 (ss 34–201) 25:53
  s 46 .... 25:06
  s 52 (3) 25:35
    89 .... 27:22
    107 .... 25:06
    130 .... 26:01, 26:29
    132 .... 26:01
    153 .... 25:03
  Pt 4 (ss 202–291) 25:32
  s 209 .... 25:04
    250–291 .... 27:07
  Pt 5 (ss 292–476) 27:01
  s 292–296 .... 27:07
    297 .... 27:01, 27:05, 27:07
    298 .... 27:07
      (1) 27:05
    299, 300 .... 27:07
    301 .... 27:01, 27:05, 27:07
    302 .... 27:02, 27:07
    303 .... 27:07
      (1)–(4) 27:02
    304 .... 27:03, 27:07; 28:26
    305, 306 .... 27:07
    307 .... 27:01, 27:07
      (4) 27:03; 30:04
    308 .... 27:07
      (1) 27:03
    309 .... 27:03, 27:07
    310 .... 27:07
    311 .... 27:04, 27:07
    312 .... 27:07
    313, 314 .... 27:07
    315–318 .... 27:03, 27:07
    319, 320 .... 27:07
    321 .... 27:03, 27:04, 27:07
    322–326 .... 27:07
    327 .... 27:04, 27:07
    328 .... 27:07, 27:11, 27:15
    329 .... 27:03, 27:07
    330 .... 27:07
      (3)–(5) 27:05
    331 .... 27:07
    332 .... 27:03, 27:07
    333–340 .... 27:07
    341 .... 27:07, 27:17; 28:26
    342, 343 .... 27:07
    344, 345 .... 27:07; 28:26
    346–352 .... 27:07
    355 .... 27:07
    361 .... 27:07
    372, 373 .... 27:07
    378 .... 27:07
  Pt 5, Ch 9 (ss 380–385)
  .... 27:01
  s 399, 400 .... 27:09
    401 (2)–(7) 27:10
    403za 28:13
    406, 407 .... 27:07
    409 .... 27:07
    415 .... 27:09

2695

Table of Statutes

Corporation Tax Act 2009 – *cont.*
  s 441 (4), (5) 27:04
    444, 445 .... 27:04
    447 .... 27:11
    453 .... 27:07
    454 .... 25:04
    457 .... 25:05
    459 .... 25:05
      (3) 25:06
    460 (1) 25:05
    461 .... 25:05
    462 (2) 25:06
    463 (1)–(3) 25:06
    463 (5) 25:05, 25:06
    468–470 .... 27:07
    473 .... 27:07
    479 (2) 27:31
    481 .... 27:12
    482 (1) 27:12
    483 .... 27:12
    486 (1)–(4) 27:12
  Pt 6, Ch 2a (ss 486a–486e)
    .... 27:04
  Pt 6, Ch 2b (ss 486f, 486g)
    .... 27:04
  s 498 .... 25:04
  Pt 6, Ch 6 (ss 501–521)
    .... 27:28
  s 502, 503 .... 27:29
    504 .... 27:33
    505 (1) 27:31
    506 (1) (a) 27:32
    508 .... 27:34
    509 .... 27:03
    510 (3) 27:03
      (4) 27:32
    511 .... 27:29
  Pt 6, Ch 6a (ss 521a–521f)
    .... 27:04
  s 522–533 .... 27:02
  Pt 7 (ss 570–710) 27:14
  s 573, 574 .... 27:15
    579 (1), (2) 27:14
    580 (1) 27:13
      (3), (4) 27:13
    581 (3), (4) 27:13
    582 (3), (4) 27:13
    583 .... 27:14
    587 .... 27:19
    589 (3) 27:14
    590, 591 .... 27:14
    593 .... 27:13, 27:20
    596 .... 27:15
    601, 602 .... 27:19
    604 .... 27:15
    609–611 .... 27:15
    630–632 .... 27:17
    633, 634 .... 27:19
    636 .... 27:17
    637, 638 .... 27:19

Corporation Tax Act 2009 – *cont.*
  Pt 7, Ch 7 (ss 639–659)
    .... 27:15
  s 661, 662 .... 27:20
  s 684 .... 27:17
    690 .... 27:16
    691 (1)–(6) 27:16
    692 .... 27:16
    694, 695 .... 27:15
    696 (1)–(4) 27:18
    697 (1)–(4) 27:18
    701 .... 27:14
      (3) 27:14
    710 .... 27:14
  Pt 8 (ss 711–906) 27:21
  s 712 (2) 27:21
      (3) (c) 27:21
    713 .... 27:21
      (3), (4) 27:23
  Pt 8, Ch 2 (ss 720–725)
    .... 27:23
  s 721 .... 27:23
    723, 724 .... 27:23
  Pt 8, Ch 3 (ss 726–732)
    .... 27:23
  s 728–732 .... 27:23
  Pt 8, Ch 4 (ss 733–741)
    .... 27:23
  s 741 .... 27:24
  Pt 8, Ch 5 (ss 742–744)
    .... 27:23
  s 747 .... 27:23
    751 .... 27:23
    753 .... 28:13
      (3) 27:23
    754–759 .... 27:24
    761 .... 27:24
  Pt 8, Ch 8 (ss 764–773)
    .... 27:23
  s 775 .... 27:25
    777–779 .... 27:25
    783–787 .... 27:25
    791 .... 27:24, 27:25
    792, 793 .... 27:25
    794 .... 27:24, 27:25
    795–799 .... 27:25
    803 .... 27:25
    805 .... 27:25
    806 .... 27:25, 27:27
    807 .... 27:25
    809–815 .... 27:25
    816 (4) 27:25
    818 (3) 27:25
    819, 820 .... 27:25
    822 .... 27:25
    824–826 .... 27:25
    827–829 .... 27:25
    832 .... 27:25
    835–837 .... 27:26
    845–847 .... 27:26
    850 .... 27:26

Table of Statutes

Corporation Tax Act 2009 – *cont.*
s 852, 853	27:27
854	27:25, 27:27
855	27:27
858–864	27:27
866–870	27:27
Pt 8, Ch 15 (ss 871–879)	27:23
Pt 8, Ch 16 (ss 880–900)	27:27
s 884	27:22
896	27:22
898, 899	27:23
900, 901	27:23
902 (3)	27:25
904	27:25
906	27:03
Pt 9 (ss 907–931)	27:25
Pt 9a (ss 931a–931w)	25:23; 26:15
s 931b, 931c	26:15
931e, 931i	26:15
931p–931r	26:15
Pt 10 (ss 932–982)	25:32, 25:53
s 979 (2) (b)	25:03
Pt 12, Ch 2 (ss 1006–1013)	25:06
s 1007 (2)	25:06
1008, 1009	25:06
Pt 12, Ch 3 (ss 1014–1024)	25:06
Pt 12, Ch 4 (ss 1025–1029)	25:06
s 1038 (2)	25:06
(5)	25:06
1218	30:01, 30:05
Pt 16, Ch 2 (ss 1219–1231)	30:01
s 1219	30:02
(1)	30:09
(3)	30:03, 30:06
1221 (1)	30:06
(2)	30:08, 30:09
(3)	30:08
1232	30:03
1249, 1250	30:04
1262	25:40
1265	25:40
1285	26:15, 26:30
(1)–(4)	26:01
1290	25:06
1305	25:05; 26:15
1307 (4)	25:05, 25:35
1311	25:34
Sch 1	
para 100	26:01
227	27:19
257–259	27:25
367	27:02

Finance Act 2009 .... 2:41;2A:02, 2A:06, 2A:46, 2A:58, 2A:78; 6:16; 9:23, 9:32; 25:20; 44:11, 44:33; 62:09; 65:02
s 1 (1)	5:01
6	25:40
8 (1) (a)	25:40
(2) (a)	25:41
9 (1)	65:05
10	62:11
23	25:24
25	27:08
35	28:05
75	63:31
92	2:08
94 (1) (b)	2A:98
(2) (a)–(d)	2A:99
(4)	2A:98
(6), (7)	2A:100
(8), (9)	2A:101
(10)	2A:99
(11)	2A:100
122	62:13
Sch 1	6:10
Sch 3	
para 1 (1)	65:03, 65:04, 65:05
(2)	65:03
(3)	65:04, 65:05
(4)	65:03
(5)	65:03, 65:04, 65:05
(7)	65:03, 65:04
2 (1)	65:05
(2) (a)	65:04, 65:05
(3)–(7)	65:04, 65:05
(8)	65:04
3	65:03
4 (1), (2)	65:03, 65:04, 65:05
5	65:03, 65:04, 65:05
6 (2)–(4)	65:03, 65:04, 65:05
7	65:03, 65:04, 65:05
8	65:03, 65:04, 65:05
11 (a)	65:03, 65:04, 65:05
(b)	65:04, 65:05
(c)	65:03
12	65:03, 65:04, 65:05
13–14	65:03, 65:04, 65:05
16 (1)	65:04, 65:05
(2)	65:03
(3)	65:03, 65:04, 65:05
17 (1)	65:03, 65:04, 65:05
(2)	65:03
(3), (4)	65:04, 65:05
18, 19	65:03, 65:04, 65:05
Sch 6	25:24
15	27:08; 28:05
25	27:04
Sch 28	
para 2	7:115
Sch 36	
Pt 1 (para 1–15)	63:31

Table of Statutes

Finance Act 2009 – *cont.*
  Sch 36 – *cont.*
    para 19 .... 63:31
  Sch 46 .... 2.41
    para 1(1), (2) 2:42
    para 2(1), (2) 2:42
      (3)(b) 2:42
    3 .... 2:45
    4 .... 2:46
    5(1)(a), (b) 2:46

Finance Act 2009 – *cont.*
  Sch 46 – *cont.*
    para 5(4) 2:46
    7 .... 2:46
    10 .... 2:46
    14 .... 2:42
    15(2)–(4) 2:44
      (8) 2:44
    16(1), (2) 2:43
  Sch 61 .... 63:13

Index

Accommodation, *see* LIVING ACCOMMODATION
Accountability, *see* INHERITANCE TAX
Accumulation and maintenance settlement
    meaning, 42.50
    special treatment, 42.49–42.52
    tapered charge, 42.53
Administration
    assessment, *see* ASSESSMENT
    estate in course of, *see* ESTATE IN COURSE OF ADMINISTRATION
    HM Revenue and Customs, duties of, 2.01
    stamp duty, *see* STAMP DUTY
    stamp duty reserve tax, 61.01, 61.20, 61.25–61.28
    value added tax, *see* VALUE ADDED TAX
Advance corporation tax, *see* CORPORATION TAX
Advantage
    surrender of—
        generally, 7.27
        restrictive covenant, 7.29
        reward for services distinguished from compensation, 7.28
Adventure in the nature of trade, *see* TRADE
Agency
    contract, trading receipts, 8.87–8.88
Agreement
    stamp duty, *see* STAMP DUTY
Agricultural property
    business property, as, 44.26
    company owning, shares of, 44.17
    conditions, 44.20–44.23
    generally, 44.11–44.19
    relief—
        buildings attracting, 44.15
        dwelling house, for, 44.12–44.14
        generally, 43.33
        planning, 43.32
        rate of, 44.18
        value qualifying for, 44.16
    tenancy, Scottish, 44.25
Aids
    handicapped, for, value added tax, 69.35, 69.36

Aircraft
    capital allowances, 9.53
    leased on charter, 9.53
    stores for use in, value added tax, 69.05
    value added tax, 69.26
Airmen
    national insurance, 54.07
Allowable expenditure
    capital gains tax computation, *see* CAPITAL GAINS TAX
Allowances
    capital, *see* CAPITAL ALLOWANCES
    personal reliefs, *see* INCOME TAX
Animal
    farm, treatment of, 8.169
Annual payment
    trading receipt cannot be, 11.26
Annuities
    advances, and, 11.21
    consideration for land consisting of, 62.08
    deferred contracts, disposal of, 16.14
    land, purchase of life annuity secured on, 6.44
    life annuity contract, 31.29
    meaning, 11.20
    purchased, 31.30–31.31
    retirement—
        retiring partner, for, 22.45
    stamp duty, *see* STAMP DUTY
    trustee, of, 42.21
Anti-avoidance, *see* TAX AVOIDANCE
Appeal
    amendment of self-assessment, against, 2A.51
    appellate court, function of, 2.19
    assessment, against, 2.09–2.19
    conduct of hearings, 2.17
    costs, 2.15
        higher courts, in, 2.22
    direct taxes, as to, 2.11
    European law, ruling on, 2.11
    group litigation order, 2.11
    HMRC decisions, against, 2.09
    internal reviews, 2.10

2699

Index

Appeal – *cont.*
  issue of fact or law, on, 2.20
  national insurance, 2.12
  order of court, 2.21
  stamp duty, 56.26
  tax credits, 2.13
  taxpayer notice, against, 2A.56
  tribunal, 2.09
    appeal from, 2.18
    function, 2.19
  VAT and Duties Tribunal, to, *see* VAT AND DUTIES TRIBUNAL
Apportionment
  expenses, 8.98
  only or main residence, capital gains tax, 23.08–23.11
Appreciation
  sporting achievement, for, 7.26
Armed forces
  death, transfers on, 40.06
Arrangement, *see* SETTLEMENT
Art, *see* WORKS OF ART
Assessment
  appeal against, 2.09–2.19
  discharging, 2A.65
  discovery, 2A.62
  discrepancies, 2A.61
  disturbing, 2A.65
  estimated, 2A.63
  making, 2A.01, 2A.60
  minor discrepancies, 2A.61
  self-assessment, *see* SELF-ASSESSMENT
  time limit for, 2A.66
  validity, challenging, 2.39
  value added tax, *see* VALUE ADDED TAX
Assets
  business—
    disposal of, *see* VALUE ADDED TAX
    replacement of, rollover relief, *see* CAPITAL GAINS TAX
    trading receipts, 8.74
  capital allowances, *see* CAPITAL ALLOWANCES
  capital gains tax, *see* CAPITAL GAINS TAX
  leased overseas, 9.52
  sale and leaseback—
    assets other than land, 8.137
    land, 8.136
  transfer abroad, attribution of income, *see* FOREIGN INCOME
  wasting, *see* WASTING ASSETS
Assets Recovery Agency
  prosecution by, 2.36

Associated operations
  disposition by, 39.28–39.34
  meaning, 39.29
Association
  value added tax, 63.12
Attorney, *see* POWER OF ATTORNEY
Authorship
  casual, 12.08
Averaging
  creative works, for, 6.47
  farmers, for, 6.47-6.48
  generally, 6.46
  relief, obtaining, 6.49
Avoidance, *see* TAX AVOIDANCE
Bankruptcy
  capital gains tax, 18.22
Banks
  notes, value added tax, 69.33
Bare trust
  absolute entitlement to, 20.07
  co-owners, 20.09
  nature of, 20.06
  settled property distinguished, 20.08
Bearer instrument
  stamp duty—
    amount of, 59.10
    charge, 59.08
    chargeable instruments, 59.08
    head of charge, 57.33
    not chargeable, 59.12
    paired shares, on, 59.13
    penalties, 59.11
    procedures, 59.11
    rate of, 59.09
    reserve tax, 61.13
Beneficiary
  charity, from, *see* CHARITY
  close company as, 39.27
  death, income arising after—
    foreign estates, 14.04
    generally, 14.03
    non-residuary beneficiary, 14.05
    residuary beneficiary—
      absolute interests, 14.08
      accrued income, 14.06
      limited interest, 14.07
      other, 14.09
    UK estates, 14.04
  inheritance tax, incidence of, *see* INHERITANCE TAX
Benefits in kind
  agricultural workers, board and lodging for, 7.49
  child care facilities, 7.46, 7.102, 7.104

Index

Benefits in kind – *cont.*
  Code, 7.102
  convertibility—
    generally, 7.42–7.43
    liability, extent of, 7.44
  credit tokens, 7.45
  director, *see* DIRECTOR
  duties of employment, minor benefits derived in performing, 7.106
  expenses, *see* EXPENSES
  generally, 7.40–7.41
  higher paid employee, *see* EMPLOYEE EARNING £8500 PER ANNUM OR MORE
  living accommodation, *see* LIVING ACCOMMODATION
  PAYE, extension of, 7.47
  profit-sharing schemes, *see* PROFIT-SHARING SCHEMES
  relocation benefits and expenses, 7.52–7.53
  securities given to employees, *see* SECURITIES
  share incentive schemes, *see* SHARE INCENTIVE SCHEMES
  share option schemes, *see* SHARE OPTION SCHEMES
  sports facilities, 7.105
  tradeable assets, 7.47
  training schemes, 7.97
  travelling expenses, *see* TRAVELLING EXPENSES
  vouchers, 7.45
Betting
  value added tax, 68.15
Bill of sale
  stamp duty, 57.34
Blind person
  personal reliefs, 6.09
Board and lodging
  foreign expenses, 7.133
Bonds
  stamp duty, 57.35
Bonus
  sporting achievement, for, 7.26
Books
  talking, 69.16
  value added tax, 69.15, 69.16
Building
  agricultural, capital allowances, 9.59–9.60
  change of use, value added tax, 65.35
  industrial, *see* INDUSTRIAL BUILDINGS
  value added tax—
    election to waive exemption, 66.28
    grant of major interest, 69.17, 69.22

Building society
  shares in, 21.27
Burial
  value added tax, 68.24
Business
  activities, restriction of, trading receipts, 8.80
  assets, *see* ASSETS
  capital allowances, *see* CAPITAL ALLOWANCES
  capital expenditure, *see* CAPITAL EXPENDITURE
  capital gains tax, *see* CAPITAL GAINS TAX
  contract relating to structure of, trading receipts, 8.85–8.86
  entertainment, value added tax, 65.24, 66.20
  gifts, prohibited expenditure, 8.133
  incorporation of, corporation tax, 25.51
  meaning, 44.02
  property—
    agricultural property, as, 44.26
    companies, special rules, 44.09
    excepted assets, 44.08
    period of ownership, 44.05
    relevant, 44.01
    relief—
      excluded business, 44.04
      generally, 43.33
      planning, 43.32
      potentially exempt transfers, 44.10
    shares, meaning, 44.03
    scope of, 10.03
    succession, 44.06
  sale of, stamp duty, 58.01
  trading receipts, 8.74
  trading stock—
    appropriation from trade, 22.07
    appropriation to trade, 22.06
    rules for, 22.05
    transfer to company, 22.10
Business expansion scheme
  capital gains tax exemption, 17.24
  replacement of, 31.06
Calculation of tax
  income tax, *see* INCOME TAX
  value added tax, *see* VALUE ADDED TAX
Capital
  movement of, 1.11
  payments, emoluments, as, 7.21
Capital allowances
  agricultural land and buildings, 9.59–9.60
  anti-avoidance legislation, 9.09

2701

Index

Capital allowances – *cont.*
  balancing charge or allowance, amount of, 9.09
  business, for, 22.01–22.02
  business premises, conversion to flats, 9.64
  capital expenditure, *see* CAPITAL EXPENDITURE
  capital gains tax—
    calculation of gain or loss, 22.02
    generally, 22.01
    renewals allowance, 22.04
    sale proceeds less than £6,000, 22.03
  contaminated land, remediation of, 9.65
  current year basis of tax, 9.06
  deductible expense, differing from, 9.08
  disadvantaged areas, renovation of business premises in, 9.66
  dredging, 9.58
  expenditure, incurring, 3.02, 9.06
  film production, for, 3.19
  generally, 9.01–9.03
  industrial buildings, *see* INDUSTRIAL BUILDINGS
  know-how, 9.63
  methods of giving, 9.07
  mining, *see* MINING
  patents, 9.63
  plant and machinery, *see* PLANT AND MACHINERY
  research and development, 9.62
  succession, 9.10
  transfer of trade, 25.50
Capital distribution
  liquidation, 21.18
  meaning, 21.10
  reorganisation—
    bonus issues, 21.13
    computation, 21.15
    generally, 21.12
    rights issue, 21.14
    scrip issues, 21.13
  rights issue, sale of rights under, 21.16
  small distributions, 21.17
Capital duty
  abolition, 59.07
Capital expenditure
  allowable, 8.126
  business—
    acquisition of, 8.113
    expansion of, 8.115
    facilities for, 8.114
    maintenance of, 8.115
    reorganisation of, 8.114
    running, 8.113
  capital, preservation of, 8.116

Capital expenditure – *cont.*
  ending onerous obligations and restrictions, 8.118–8.121
  improvements, 8.122
  initial repairs, 8.124–8.125
  non-recourse loans, 9.05
  petrol ties, 8.130
  profits, not-deductible from, 8.110
  renewals, 8.123
  renewals basis, 8.126
  repairs, 8.122–8.125
  revenue distinguished, 8.110–8.112
  trading arrangements, 8.129
  trading stock, 8.127–8.128
  when incurred, 9.04
Capital gains
  corporation, of, *see* CAPITAL GAINS TAX
  estimating, 2A.04
  reporting, 2A.03
Capital gains tax
  annual exempt amount, 16.40
  assets—
    anti-avoidance, 17.17
    exempt, 17.05
    generally, 17.01
    held on 6 April 1965—
      calculation of gain, 24.14
      indexation allowance, 24.13
      time apportionment, 24.13, 24.15
    held on 31 March 1982—
      holdover relief, 18.45
      rebasing, 24.10
      rollover, 24.12
    negligible value, of—
      backdated claims, 16.37
      claims, 16.33
      land and buildings, 16.36
      meaning, 16.34
      partnership goodwill written off, 16.35
    pooling, 17.04
    receipt and underlying asset, link between, 17.02
    Revenue concession, 17.03
    right of action, disposal of, 17.03
    rollover relief—
      assets for which available, 22.15
      deferral relief, interaction with, 22.34
      depreciating asset, investment in, 22.17
      intellectual property, 27.24
      operation of, 22.13
      outline, 22.11
      partnership, assets held by, 22.20
      partial, 22.14

Capital gains tax – *cont.*
  assets— – *cont.*
    rollover relief— – *cont.*
      payment of tax, deferring, 22.23
      persons claiming, 22.15
      same asset, reinvestment in, 22.22
      taper relief, 24.02
      time limit, 22.21
      trade—
        asset used in, 22.16
        company, of, 22.18
        employment, of, 22.19
        meaning, 22.15
    valuation—
      basic rule, 17.25
      costs of, 17.30
      inheritance tax, for, 17.28
      quoted securities, of, 17.26
      rebasing, market value for, 33.46
      Revenue agreement to, 17.31
      series of transactions, disposal in, 17.29
      unquoted securities, of, 17.27
    value shifting, 17.17
    wasting, 17.18
  basic elements of, 16.03
  business—
    assets, *see* ASSETS, *above*
    spouses and civil partners, disposals between, 22.08
    renewals allowance, 22.04
    rollover relief, *see* ASSETS, *above*
    stock in trade, 22.05–22.07
    transfer to company, 22.10
    trading losses, 22.09
  capital allowances, *see* CAPITAL ALLOWANCES
  capital distribution—
    liquidation, 21.18
    meaning, 21.10
    reorganisations—
      bonus issues, 21.13
      computation, 21.15
      generally, 21.12
      rights issues, 21.14
      scrip issues, 21.13
    rights issue, sale of rights under, 21.16
    small distributions, 21.17
  charities. *See* CHARITIES
  chattels sold for £6,000 or less—
    anti-avoidance provisions, 17.20–17.21
    generally, 17.19
    part disposal, 17.20–17.21

Capital gains tax – *cont.*
  company—
    amalgamation—
      anti-avoidance, 21.25
      securities, exchange of, 21.20–21.23
    reconstruction—
      anti-avoidance, 21.25
      schemes of, 21.24
      securities, exchange of, 21.20–21.23
  computation—
    allowable expenditure—
      acquisition cost—
        generally, 16.16
        incidental, 16.18
      apportionment of, 16.22
      improvements, 16.16, 16.19–16.20
      not deductible, 16.17
      person other than taxpayer, by, 16.20
      preservation of title, 16.21
      revenue expenditure, 16.17
    consideration—
      apportionment, 16.11
      contingent liability, 16.12, 16.13
      deferred, 16.07
      deferred annuity contracts, 16.15
      foreign currency, in, 16.08
      generally, 16.05
      income tax, liable to, 16.14
      liabilities, allowance for, 16.13
      life assurance policies, 16.15
      right, consisting of, 16.09
      unascertainable, loss on, 16.10
      valuation, incapable of, 16.09
    foreign taxes, 16.23
    inheritance tax, charge of, 16.24
    wasting assets, 16.25
  death—
    acquisition on, 19.02
    cost of probate, allowance for, 19.06
    disposal—
      administration, during, 19.10
      deed of variation, 19.03
      legatee, to, 19.05
    family provision, 19.04
    generally, 19.01
    life tenant, of, 19.07
    losses in year of death, 19.08
    no charge on, 19.01
    personal representatives—
      disposals in course of administration—
        assessment, 19.10
        beneficiaries, transfer to, 19.12

Index

Capital gains tax – *cont.*
  death– – *cont.*
    personal representatives– – *cont.*
      disposals in course of administration– – *cont.*
        chargeable gain, calculation of, 19.10, 19.11
        transfer to, 19.09
  dependent relative, residence of, 23.12
  deemed disposal, *see* DISPOSAL, *below*
  deferral relief—
    clawback, 22.30
    Enterprise Investment Scheme relief¾
      disposal of shares, 22.29
      interaction with, 22.31
    history of, 22.24
    interaction of reliefs, 22.34
    investment, 22.28
    operation of, 22.25
    qualifying investor¾
      companies, 22.27
      individuals and trustees, 22.26
    reorganisations and takeovers, 22.30
    trustees, for, 20.14, 22.26
  disposal—
    acquisition, without, 18.03
    bankruptcy, 18.21–18.22
    compensation payments—
      generally, 18.16
      use of assets, for, 18.20
    connected persons—
      definition, 18.50
      disposals between, 18.52
      holdover election, 18.51
      persons being, 18.50
      treatment of, 18.49
    deemed—
      generally, 20.15
      life interest, termination on death, 20.18–20.20
      losses, transfer to beneficiary, 20.17
      property vesting in beneficiary, 20.16
    forfeiture or surrender of rights, 18.04
    gifts—
      date of, 18.34
      disposal, as, 18.33
      donee, recovery of tax from, 18.35
      holdover relief, 18.38–18.39
      housing association, to, 18.37
      inheritance tax, subject to, 18.40
      instalments, payment of tax by, 18.36
      market value rule, 18.33
      exclusion of, 18.48
    gratuitous transfers of value, 18.47

Capital gains tax – *cont.*
  disposal— – *cont.*
    identification of, 16.02
    insurance receipts—
      generally, 18.17
      replacement or repair, not used for, 18.18
      restoration or replacement, used for, 18.19
    meaning, 18.01
    mortgages, 18.21–18.22
    options—
      abandonment, 18.26
      definition, 18.23
      disposal of, 18.25
      employee share, 18.28–18.29
      exercise of, 18.27
      financial, 18.31
      gilt edged securities and qualifying bonds, over, 18.32
      grant of, 18.24
      traded, 18.31
      transactions other than sale or purchase, binding grantor to, 18.30
      types of, 18.23
      wasting asset rules, application of, 18.31
    part—
      generally, 18.13
      lease, 18.17
      meaning, 18.14
    sale at undervalue, 18.42
    small, 18.15
    time of—
      consent order, under, 18.10
      contract—
        conditional, 18.09
        date of, 18.06
        generally, 18.06
        unenforceable, 18.08
        whether made, 18.07, 18.11
      generally, 18.05
      loss or destruction, where, 18.12
  entrepreneurs' relief, for, 22.32, 22.33
  European Economic Interest Grouping, treatment of, 22.47
  exemptions—
    business expansion scheme, 17.24
    conditional, 17.16
    covenants, 17.11
    debts, 17.06–17.10
    enterprise investment scheme, 17.23
    exempt assets, 17.05
    Government stock, 17.12

Capital gains tax – *cont.*
  exemptions– – *cont.*
    guarantees, 17.08
    insurance policy, disposal of interest in, 17.13
    loans to traders, 17.07
    qualifying corporate bonds, 17.12
    tangible movable property, 17.18
    venture capital trusts, 17.22
    wasting assets, 17.18
    woodlands, 17.14
    works of art, 17.15
  gain—
    chargeable, 16.04
    meaning, 16.02
  hire purchase transaction, 18.02
  history of, 16.01
  holdover relief—
    assets held at 31 March 1982, 18.45
    assets qualifying, 18.41
    claiming, 18.38
    connected person, disposal to, 18.51
    gifts, 18.38
    interest in possession trust, 42.06
    no formal valuation, election for, 18.46
    partial, 18.43
    principal private residence relief, effect on, 23.16-23.17
    property in trust, 18.44
    sale at undervalue, 18.42
    settlement, creation of, 20.14
    taper relief, 24.02
    types of, 18.38
  indexation allowance—
    calculation, 24.03
    calls on shares, 24.08
    company, disposal by, 24.03
    generally, 24.03
    introduction, 24.01
    no gain/no loss, 24.05
    options, 24.09
    part disposal, 24.04
    relevant receipts, 24.06
    reorganisations, 24.07
  international dimension—
    delayed remittances, 35.52
    generally, 35.46
    non-resident companies, attribution of gains by, 35.53-35.54
    overseas trusts, 35.55-35.63
    remittance basis, 35.48-35.51
    temporary non-residence, 35.47
  land, *see* LAND

Capital gains tax – *cont.*
  lease—
    duration, 23.19
    extensions, 23.21
    grant of—
      freehold or long lease, from, 23.24
      premium, definition, 23.23
      wasting lease, from, 23.25
    mergers, 23.21
    mineral royalties, 23.27–23.28
    reverse premium, 23.26
    rules as to, 23.18
    wasting assets, not treated as, 23.22
    writing down expenditure, 23.20
  legislation, 16.01
    interpretation, 16.02
  losses—
    computation of, 16.26
    death, on, 19.08
      carry back, 16.29
    disposal to connected person, on, 16.30
    non-domiciled person, of, 16.32
    non-resident, of, 16.31
    relief—
      carry forward against gains of later years, 16.28
      set off, by, 16.27
  nature of, 16.01
  non-residents trading in the UK, 22.48
  only or main residence—
    apportionment, 23.08–23.11
    deemed residence, periods of, 23.10
    election for, 23.11
    generally, 23.06
    grounds, 23.07
    letting, period of, 23.09
  options, 24.09
    abandonment, 18.26
    definition, 18.23
    disposal of, 18.25
    employee share, 18.28–18.29
    exercise of, 18.27
    financial, 18.31
    gilt edged securities and qualifying bonds, over, 18.32
    grant of, 18.24
    traded, 18.31
    transactions other than sale or purchase, binding grantor to, 18.30
    types of, 18.23
    wasting asset rules, application of, 18.31
  outline, 16.04
  overpaid, interest on, 2A.33

Index

Capital gains tax – *cont.*
  partnership—
    asset distributed amongst partners, 22.39
    capacity in which asset held, 22.37
    disposal of assets, 22.38
    mergers and demergers, 22.46
    one or more partners, asset passed to, 22.39
    profit sharing ratios, changes in, 22.40–22.44
    retiring partner, annuity purchased for, 22.45
    statutory provision, 22.36
  payment by instalments, 16.38
  penalties, 2A.78, 2A.90
  personal representative, sale of dwelling house by, 23.15
  persons chargeable, 16.39
  rates of tax, 16.40
  rebasing, 24.10–24.15
  reinvestment relief, replacement of, 22.24
  rollover relief, *See* ASSETS, *above*
  securities—
    bed and breakfasting, 21.03
    conversion of, 21.19
    identification—
      companies, rules for, 21.02
      pool of 6 April 1985—
        generally, 21.08
        parallel pooling, 21.10
        pre 6 April 1982 acquisitions, 21.09
      s 104 pool, 21.05, 21.06
    pooling—
      acquisition before 6 April 1965, 21.05
      acquisitions before 6 April 1982, 21.05
      acquisitions since 5 April 1982, 21.05
      capital gains tax and the s 104 pool, 21.06
      generally, 21.01
      identification rules, 21.01–21.02
      identifying pool of 6 April 1985—
        generally, 21.08
        parallel pooling, 21.10
        pre 6 April 1982 acquisitions, 21.09
      indexation, and, 21.07
      transfers between spouses and civil partners, 21.04
  settled property—
    annual exempt amount, 20.01

Capital gains tax – *cont.*
  settled property— – *cont.*
    bare trust—
      absolute entitlement to, 20.07
      co-owners, 20.09
      distinguished, 20.08
      nature of, 20.06
    beneficial interests, disposal of, 20.21, 35.60
    beneficiary's interest, sale of, 20.22
    deemed disposals—
      generally, 20.15
      life interest, termination on death, 20.18–20.20
      losses transferred to beneficiary, 20.17
      property vesting in beneficiary, 20.16
    disposal by trustees, rate of tax and annual exempt amount, 20.01
    exemptions available to trustees, 20.14
    generally, 20.01–20.02
    life tenant, death of, 19.07
    meaning, 20.05–20.12
    non-resident trust, *see* TRUSTS
    property declared to be, 20.05
    settlor, identification of, 20.03
    settlor retaining interest in, 20.02
      charge, avoiding, 20.04
    settlor with interest, attribution of gains to, 35.62
    transfer into trust, 20.10
      one trust or two, 20.11
      other settlement, to, 20.12
    trust period, disposals during, 20.13
  spouses and civil partners—
    dwelling house, transfer between, 23.14
    inter-spousal transfers, 16.43–16.44
    joint property, 16.42
    matrimonial home, transfer after separation, 16.44
    separate computation, 16.41
    separate taxation, 16.41
  spouses, transfer of dwelling house between, 23.14
  stock in trade, 22.05
  substantial shareholdings, disposal of¾
    definition, 28.44
    earlier reorganisations, etc, gain or loss held over from, 28.47
    events before 1 April 2002, 28.47
    exemptions, 28.43
    negligible value claims, 28.47
    period of ownership, 28.45
    relief on, 28.42
    trading company, requirement for, 28.46

Index

Capital gains tax – *cont.*
  taper relief—
    availability of, 24.02
    deferred gains, 24.02
    held over and rolled over gains, 24.02
    introduction, 24.01
    relevant period of ownership, 24.02
    rollover relief, 24.02
    transfers between spouses and civil partners, 21.04
  trading losses set against, 6.16
  trustee, dwelling house held by, 23.13
  unpaid, interest on, 2A.32
  valuation¾
    basic rule, 17.25
    costs of, 17.30
    inheritance tax purposes, for, 17.28
    quoted securities, of, 17.26
    Revenue agreement to, 17.31
    series of transactions, disposal in, 17.29
    unquoted securities, of, 17.27
  value shifting—
    application of provisions, 28.31
    basic scheme, 28.30
    distributions followed by disposal of shares, 28.32
    non-resident company, transfers to, 28.33
    reduction in value followed by disposal of shares, 28.36
    reorganisation of share capital, transaction treated as, 28.35
    transfer followed by disposals of shares, 28.34
  vulnerable beneficiary, trust with, 20.23-20.24

Capital transfer tax, *see* INHERITANCE TAX

Car
  accessories, 7.117
  capital allowances, 9.50
  class 1A contributions, 48.09, 51.13–51.18
  director, 7.115–7.118
  employee contributing to cost of, 7.116
  employee earning £8,500 or more, 7.115–7.118
  fuel, 7.118
  price of, 7.115
  private motoring, free petrol for, 7.118
  value added tax, 65.32, 66.17–66.18
  vans, 7.119

Caravan
  value added tax, 69.31

Cases
  precedents, 1.29

Cases – *cont.*
  settlements, on, 15.03–15.06

Cash
  investment of, trading receipts, 8.79

Cashbacks
  tax treatment, 8.170

Causation test
  emoluments—
    consequences, 7.18–7.19
    generally, 7.17

Certificates of Deposit
  profit arising, 12.14

Chargeable transfer, *see* INHERITANCE TAX

Charges on income, *see* INCOME

Charity
  capital gains tax—
    definition of charity, 16.46
    exemption, 16.45
      restriction of, 16.47
    generally, 16.45
    gifts, 16.49
    property ceasing to be held on charitable trust, 16.48
  covenanted donations to, 25.22
  corporation tax, 25.03
  definition, 16.46
  exempt trading income, 8.94
  Gift Aid, 6.36
    benefit received, 6.37
  gift of trading stock to, 8.158
  land, gifts of, 6.38
  loans to, 15.18
  non-charitable purpose, 13.26
  shares and securities, gifts of, 6.38
  single gift to, relief for, 6.36, 13.22
  small receipts, relief for, 13.25
  stamp duty, 56.37
  stamp duty reserve tax, 61.12
  substantial donor, transaction with, 13.27
  transfer to, inheritance tax, 43.17
  trust—
    gifts from, 15.17
    relief—
      generally, 13.22
      restriction of, 13.26, 13.27
    small receipts, 13.25
    trading income, 13.23–13.24
  value added tax, 69.39–69.41

Chattels
  pre-owned, charge to tax, 12.18
  sold for £6,000 or less, capital gains tax exemption—
    anti-avoidance provisions, 17.20–17.21

2707

Index

Chattels – *cont.*
  sold for £6,000 or less, capital gains tax exemption– – *cont.*
    generally, 17.19
    part disposal, 17.20–17.21
  valuation, 45.04
Child
  car seats, value added tax, 70.08
  legitim, 40.28
  maintenance, disposition for, 39.16–39.18
Civil engineering works
  value added tax, 69.17, 69.19
Clearing house
  transfers to, stamp duty, 60.13
Close company
  acquisition of interest in, interest relief, 6.42
  inheritance tax—
    beneficiary, close company as, 39.27
    exemptions, 39.23–39.24
    generally, 39.21
    liability, 39.22
    settled property trustees as participators, 39.26
    share rights, alteration in, 39.25
  investment-holding—
    defining, 29.14
    restriction of tax credit, 29.13
  life assurance policy held by, 31.26
  transfers of value,
    beneficiary, close company as, 39.27
    exemptions, 39.23–39.24
    generally, 39.21
    liability for, 39.22
    settled property trustees as participators, 39.26
    share rights, alteration in, 39.25
    spouse exemption, 39.23
Clothing
  value added tax, 69.42
Club
  taxation of, 2A.06
  value added tax, 63.12
Commission
  tax treatment, 8.170
Community charge
  employer, payment by, 7.23
Company
  acquisitions, 25.52
  amalgamation—
    anti-avoidance, 21.25
    corporation tax, 25.19
    exchange of securities, 21.20–21.23
    associated, 25.42–25.44

Company – *cont.*
  bridge, 8.28.23
  capital distribution, *see* CAPITAL DISTRIBUTION
  capital gains tax, *see* CAPITAL GAINS TAX
  close, *see* CLOSE COMPANY
  controlled foreign, resident in low tax areas—
    apportionment process, 35.68
    EU subsidiary of, 35.65
    freedom of establishment, abuse of, 1.15
    generally, 35.64
    lower level of taxation, 35.68
    meaning, 35.64
    motive test, 35.66
    place of residence, 35.67
    rules, challenge to, 1.15
    territory, classification by—
      acceptable distribution policy, 35.71
      acceptable level of taxation, 35.69
      exempt activities, 35.73
      public quotation condition, 35.72
      unacceptable level of taxation, 35.70
  disposals, 25.53
  domicile, 33.33
  employee-controlled, acquisition of interest in, interest relief, 6.42
  group—
    corporation tax, *see* CORPORATION TAX
  insurance, *see* INSURANCE COMPANY
  intermediate, payment of fees through, 7.09, 8.26
  investment, 30.01–30.11. *See also* INVESTMENT COMPANY
  issue of shares by, 21.28
  loan relationships, *see* LOAN RELATIONSHIPS
  non-resident—
    capital gains tax, 35.53–35.54
    corporation tax, 25.45
    Treasury General Consents, 33.37
  ordinary residence, 33.32
  profits, reporting, 2A.06
  reconstruction—
    anti-avoidance, 21.25
    corporation tax, 25.19
    European Community Directive, 21.26
    exchange of securities, 21.20–21.23
    schemes of, 21.24
  residence of—
    certification, 33.35
    change of, 25.46, 33.36
    common law test, 33.25–33.28

Index

Company – *cont.*
  residence of– – *cont.*
    dual, 33.26–33.28
    dual resident investing, 33.31
    ordinary residence, 33.32
    relevant control, 33.29
    statutory test, 33.30
    tax presence, 33.34
  sale of business, 25.53, 30.01
  shares, *see* SHARES
  stamp duty, *see* STAMP DUTY
  taxation, *see* CORPORATION TAX
  trading, losses on unquoted shares in, 6.34
  see also CORPORATION TAX
Compensation
  advantage, surrender of, 7.28
  employer, payment for claim against, 7.30–7.39
  payment—
    capital gains tax—
      generally, 18.16
      use of assets, for, 18.20
    employer, claim against, 7.30–7.39
    trading receipts—
      agency contracts, 8.87–8.88
      business, contract relating to structure of, 8.85–8.86
      generally, 8.81–8.88
      subsidies, 8.89
Competition
  sports, value added tax, 68.26
Computation
  capital gains tax, *see* CAPITAL GAINS TAX
  corporation tax, *see* CORPORATION TAX
  land, artificial transactions in, 23.36
  profits of foreign taxpayer, *see* NON-RESIDENT
  reorganisation, 21.15
  residual income, 12.13-12.14
Computer software
  capital allowances, 9.27
Connected persons
  capital gains tax—
    definition, 18.50
    disposals between, 18.52
    holdover election, 18.51
    persons being, 18.50
    treatment of, 18.49
  meaning, 18.50
Connecting factors
  domicile, 33.15-33.24; *see also* DOMICILE
  generally, 33.01

Connecting factors – *cont.*
  residence, *see* RESIDENCE
Consideration
  capital gains tax computation, *see* CAPITAL GAINS TAX
  stamp duty, *see* STAMP DUTY
  value added tax, 63.21–63.23
Consortium
  consortium relief, 28.11-28.12
  meaning, 28.02
Construction industry
  tax deduction scheme, 2A.19
Construction services
  value added tax, 69.18
Containers
  export of, value added tax, 69.08
Contaminated land
  remediation of, 9.65
Continental Shelf
  workers, national insurance, 54.07
Contraceptive products
  value added tax, 70.11
Contract
  agency, trading receipts, 8.87–8.88
  capital gains tax—
    hire purchase, 18.02
    joint interests, exchange of, 23.04
    time of disposal—
      conditional, 18.09
      generally, 18.06
      unenforceable, 18.08
      whether made, 18.07, 18.11
  life annuity, surrender of, 31.29
  stamp duty, *see* STAMP DUTY
  structure of business, relating to, trading receipts, 8.85–8.86
  trading stock, for supply of, trading receipts, 8.76
Control, *see* VALUE ADDED TAX
Conveyance
  stamp duty, *see* STAMP DUTY
Co-operative
  acquisition of interest in, interest relief, 6.42
Corporate bonds, *see* QUALIFYING CORPORATE BONDS
Corporate venturing scheme
  investment in, 31.16
Corporation, *see* COMPANY
Corporation tax
  accounting periods, 25.34–25.39
  advance—
    abolition, 25.01
    shadow, 26.17
    waived dividend, on, 26.04

Index

Corporation tax – *cont.*
  capital allowances, *see* CAPITAL ALLOWANCES
  charge, 25.01, 25.02
  close company—
    control—
      directors, by, 29.05
      exceptions, 29.07–29.08
      generally, 29.03
      participators, by, 29.06
      who has, 29.04
    distribution—
      expense on participator or associate, 29.09
      quasi—
        loans to participators, 29.10–29.12
        release as distribution, 29.12
    generally, 29.01
    investment-holding, charge to tax, 29.13
    profession, carrying on, 29.15
    tests, 29.02
  company—
    associated, 25.42–25.44
    change of residence, 25.46
    meaning, 25.03
    non-resident, 25.45
  computation—
    allowable deductions, 25.06
    capital gains—
      company—
        amalgamation, 25.19
        non-resident, transfer of assets to, 25.20
        reconstruction, 25.19
        shareholder, and, 25.18
      generally, 25.17
    charges on income—
      charity, covenanted donations to, 25.22
      generally, 25.21
      meaning, 25.21
    generally, 25.04
    income—
      generally, 25.05
      transactions between dealing and associated non-dealing company, 25.15
    losses—
      capital, 25.33
      charges on income as, 25.26
      other, 25.32
      restrictions—
        change in ownership and change in trade, 25.29
        groups, 25.30

Corporation tax – *cont.*
  computation— – *cont.*
    losses— – *cont.*
      restrictions— – *cont.*
        plant and machinery, 25.30
        reconstruction without change of ownership, 25.27–25.28
        successor companies, 25.30
      trading—
        future trading income, set off against, 25.23
        general profits, set off against, 25.24
        non-allowable, 25.25
      transfers of trade: balancing allowances, 25.31
  distribution—
    advance corporation tax, shadow, 26.17
    assets, from, 26.05
    bonus shares, issue of, 26.11
    capital, out of, 26.10
    close company, *see* CLOSE COMPANY, *above*
    companies resident in UK, 26.15
    debt, and, 26.09
    dividends, 26.04
    foreign, 35.08
    generally, 26.01
    interest as, 26.07, 26.08
    meaning, 26.04–26.06
    non-qualifying, 26.02, 26.03
    non-resident companies, 26.16
    premiums, 26.10
    purchase by company of own shares, 26.20–26.30
    qualifying and non-qualifying, 26.02
    redeemable share capital, issue of, 26.06
    share capital, repayment of, 26.10
    stock dividends, 26.18–26.19
    tax credit—
      entitlement to, 26.12
      non-residents, non-entitlement of, 26.13, 26.14
  financial years—
    accounting periods, 25.34–25.39
    period of account, 25.38
  generally, 25.01
  groups—
    company or group—
      anti-avoidance—
        company leaving group, 28.24–28.25
        depreciatory transactions, losses attributable to, 28.29
        value shifting, 28.30–28.32

Index

Corporation tax – *cont.*
  groups— – *cont.*
    company or group— – *cont.*
      distributions, 28.04
      generally, 28.03
      group finance costs, restriction on, 28.05
      group relief—
        charges of surrendering company, 28.13
        consortium, 28.02, 28.11–28.12
        generally, 28.06
        group, 28.08–28.09
        management expenses, 28.13
        minor capital allowances, 28.13
        overlapping periods, 28.10
        pre-entry gains, 28.18
        pre-entry losses and gains, 28.14-28.18
        self assessment, 28.07
        trading losses, 28.12
      intra-group transfers of capital assets—
        anti-avoidance, 28.29–28.36
        business assets relief, 28.28
        company tax refund, transfer of, 28.20
        computation, 28.22
        disposal outside group, 28.22
        group, 28.23
        loans, transfer of, 28.26
        notional transfer, 28.22
        postponement of liability, 28.24
        tax neutrality, 28.21
        trading stock, 28.27
    demergers—
      anti-avoidance, 28.37
      generally, 28.37
      subsequent payments, 28.41
      subsidiaries, of, 28.38
      three party, 28.39–28.40
    generally, 28.01
  incorporation of business, 25.51
  loan relationships, *see* LOAN RELATIONSHIPS
  loss relief, EC non-discrimination, 1.14
  Mergers Directive, 25.47
  other company's, liability for, 2A.22
  payment¾
    date for, 2A.20
    quarterly instalments, by, 2A.21
  penalties, 2A.91
  rate of, 25.01
  shipping company, measurement of liability by reference to tonnage, 25.16

Corporation tax – *cont.*
  small profits relief, 25.40–25.41
  transfer of UK trade, 25.48
  treaty relief by credit, 37.19
  unit trust, on, 30.15
  unpaid and overpaid, interest on, 2A.34
Court order
  payment free of tax, 11.44
Covenant
  capital gains tax, exemption from, 17.11
  restrictive, 7.29
  settlement of income by, 15.30
  stamp duty, 57.35
Credit
  treaty relief by, *see* DOUBLE TAXATION RELIEF
Credit tokens
  benefit in kind, as, 7.45
Cremation
  value added tax, 68.24
Cultural services
  value added tax, 68.29
Currency, *see also* FOREIGN CURRENCY
  accounts, of, 25.54
  contracts, *see* INTEREST RATE AND CURRENCY CONTRACTS
  trading income, for, 25.54
Customs and Excise Commissioners, *see* HM REVENUE AND CUSTOMS
Damages
  interest and, 11.06
Death
  capital gains tax—
    acquisitions, 19.02
    cost of probate, allowance for, 19.06
    deed of variation, 19.03
    disposal—
      administration, during, 19.10
      legatee, to, 19.05
    family provision, 19.04
    generally, 19.01
    life tenant, of, 19.07
    losses in year of death, 19.08
    personal representatives—
      disposals in course of administration, 19.10
      transfer to, 19.09
  income arising after—
    accrued interest, 11.10
    beneficiary—
      foreign estates, 14.04
      generally, 14.03
      non-residuary, 14.05
      residuary—
        absolute interests, 14.08

Index

Death – *cont.*
  income arising after— – *cont.*
    beneficiary— – *cont.*
      residuary— – *cont.*
        accrued income, 14.06
        limited interest, 14.07
        other, 14.09
      UK estates, 14.04
      personal representative—
        duties of, 14.10
        liability of, 14.02
      tax return, 14.10
  transfer, *see* INHERITANCE TAX
Debts
  bad, value added tax relief. *see* VALUE ADDED TAX
  capital gains tax—
    debt on a security, 17.10
    exemption from, 17.06
    loans to traders, 17.07
    meaning of debt, 17.09
  discharge of, as consideration, 57.11
  distributions, and, 26.09
  equitable liability, 2A.77
  foreign, 47.21
  location of, 47.04
  meaning, 17.09
  perpetual, 26.09
  release, 8.93
  security, on, 17.10
  valuation, *see* INHERITANCE TAX
Deceased person
  estate of, *see* ESTATE IN COURSE OF ADMINISTRATION
Decorations
  valour, for, inheritance tax relief, 43.21
Deductions
  income tax, *see* INCOME TAX
Deed
  variation, of, stamp duty, 58.14
Deemed disposals, *see* CAPITAL GAINS TAX
Demergers
  anti-avoidance, 28.37
  generally, 28.37
  partnership, capital gains tax, 22.46
  subsequent payments, 28.41
  subsidiaries, of, 28.38
  three party, 28.39–28.40
Department of Social Security
  national insurance, formerly administering, 55.01
Dependent relative
  maintenance, disposition for, 39.19

Deposit
  rights in respect of, 12.14
Deregistration, *see* VALUE ADDED TAX
Derivative contracts
  accounting standards, 27.13
  apportionments, 27.20
  change of status, 27.20
  definitions, 27.13
  groups, treatment of, 27.17
  non-residents, with, 27.18
  special savings vehicles, 27.19
  subject matter, 27.14
  tax treatment, 27.15
  unallowable purposes, 27.16
Director
  benefits in kind—
    apportionment, 7.109
    asset remaining property of employer, 7.108
    child care facilities, 7.102
    exceptions, 7.103
    expense allowances, 7.101
    expenses, payments for, 7.101
    extent of charge, 7.107–7.108
    generally, 7.99–7.100, 7.102–7.102
  cars, 7.115–7.118
  fuel, 7.118
  living accommodation, 7.110
  loan—
    cash equivalent, 7.111
    low interest, 7.111–7.112
    waivers, 7.113
  national insurance, 51.04
  private motoring, free petrol for, 7.118
  relocation benefits and expenses, 7.52–7.53
  scholarships, 7.120
  share purchase schemes, 7.114
  sports facilities, 7.105
  tax paid by employer, 7.121
  vans, 7.119
Disabled person
  aids for, value added tax, 69.34–69.36
  trust for, 13.05, 42.58
Discontinuance
  trade, of—
    effects of, 8.53
    generally, 8.51–8.52
  valuation of trading stock on, 8.168
Discount
  company, *see* CORPORATION TAX
  tax treatment, 8.170
Discs
  capital allowances, 9.54

Disposal, *see* CAPITAL GAINS TAX
Disposition
  conveyance or transfer by way of, *see* STAMP DUTY
  transfer of value by, *see* INHERITANCE TAX
Distress
  tax, for, 2.38
Distributions, *see* CORPORATION TAX
Dividends, *see* SHARES
Document
  stamp duty, *see* STAMP DUTY
Domicile
  choice, of, 33.21
    actual residence requirement, 33.22
    intention to remain permanently, 33.23, 33.24
  company, of, 33.33
  deemed, 47.07
  dependency, of, 33.20
  difficulty of, 33.15
  fact, question of, 33.15
  importance of, 33.15, 33.16
  meaning, 33.15
  origin, of, 33.18
    reversion to, 33.19
  rules of, 33.17
  trust, of, 33.41
Double taxation relief
  employment income exempted, 37.31
  exemption, by, 37.30
  expense, foreign tax as, 37.05
  generally, 37.01
  inheritance tax—
    credit, 47.20
    generally, 47.17–47.18
    unilateral relief, 47.19
  methods, 37.02–37.03
  planning—
    generally, 37.35
    particular, 37.36–37.41
  reform—
    generally, 37.35
    particular, 37.36–37.41
  share options, 37.32
  60 day rule, 37.31
  treaty relief by credit—
    capital gains, 37.18
    credit, 37.15–37.17
    foreign tax, 37.10, 37.12–37.13
    generally, 37.09
    limitation on credit, 37.10
    permanent establishments, rules for, 37.28
    reform, 37.37–37.43

Double taxation relief – *cont.*
  treaty relief by credit— – *cont.*
    relief—
      corporation tax, 37.19
      dividends, 37.20, 37.27
      group, foreign tax paid on basis of, 37.22
      income tax, 37.18
      mechanics of, 37.25
      pioneer, 37.13
      relevant profits, 37.21
      relievable tax, 37.24
      underlying tax, 37.20–37.28
    residence, 37.11
    restrictions, 37.27
    set-off rules, 37.26
    tax sparing, 37.13
    UK income, 37.14
  treaty shopping, 37.36
  UK resident, available to, 37.04-37.08
  UK treaty relief—
    changes, 37.35
    effect, 37.33
    international payment, determining nature of, 37.34
    treaty shopping, 37.36
  unilateral tax credit—
    amount of, 37.07,
    capital gains, 37.29
    generally, 37.06
    treaty relief, differing from, 37.08
    use of, 37.06
Dredging
  capital allowances, 9.58
Drugs
  value added tax, 69.34
Dwelling house
  assured tenancy, 9.22
  capital allowances, 9.22
    business premises, conversion to flats, 9.64
  personal representative, sale by, 23.15
  spare rooms, renting out, 10.14
  spouses and civil partners, transfer between, 23.14
  trustees, held by, 23.13
  value added tax¾
    goods installed, on, 66.19
    renovations and alterations, on, 70.10
    residential conversions, on, 70.09
Earned income
  investment income distinguished from, 5.20
  meaning, 5.21–5.24

2713

Index

Education
  gifts to, 8.141
  scholarships, benefit in kind, as, 7.120
  value added tax, 68.17
    examination services, 68.18
    private tuition, 68.19
    research, 68.20
    vocational training, 68.21

Electricity supply
  cross-border, 65.39

Employee
  controlled company, acquisition of interest in, interest relief, 6.42
  double taxation relief, 37.31
  employment income, see EMPLOYMENT INCOME
  higher paid, see EMPLOYEES EARNING £8,500 PER ANNUM OR MORE
  national insurance, see NATIONAL INSURANCE
  pension scheme, contribution to, 32.08, 32.23
  seconded to work in UK, 7.135
  self-employed distinguished, 49.02–49.03
  share schemes, see EMPLOYEE SHARE SCHEMES; SHARE INCENTIVE SCHEMES
  trust, 42.55, 43.20

Employee share schemes, see also SHARE INCENTIVE SCHEMES
  Approved Profit Sharing Schemes, 7.78
  Company Share Option Schemes, 7.81
  Discretionary Share Option Schemes, 7.80
  Savings-related Share Option Schemes, 7.79
  Share Incentive Plan,
    capital gains tax treatment, 7.91
    cash dividends, reinvestment of, 7.90
    costs, deduction of, 7.94, 25.06
    free share plan, 7.89
    introduction of, 7.88
    matching shares, 7.93
    partnership share plan, 7.92
  types of, 7.77

Employees earning £8,500 per annum or more
  benefits in kind—
    apportionment, 7.109
    asset remaining property of employer, 7.108
    child care facilities, 7.102
    exceptions, 7.103
    expense allowances, 7.101
    expenses, payments for, 7.101

Employees earning £8,500 per annum or more – *cont.*
  benefits in kind— – *cont.*
    extent of charge, 7.107–7.108
    generally, 7.99–7.100, 7.102
    cars, 7.115–7.118
    fuel, 7.118
    living accommodation, 7.110
    loan—
      cash equivalent, 7.112
      low interest, 7.111–7.112
      waivers, 7.113
    private motoring, free petrol for, 7.118
    relocation benefits and expenses, 7.52–7.53
    scholarships, 7.120
    share purchase schemes, 7.114
    sports facilities, 7.105
    tax paid by employer, 7.121
    vans, 7.119

Employee Share Ownership Plans
  consequences of, 7.96
  legislation, 7.95

Employer
  compensation payment for claim against, 7.30–7.36
  pension scheme, contribution to, 32.08, 32.10, 32.22
  plant and machinery, interest relief for purchase of, 6.41
  tax paid by—
    benefit in kind, as, 7.121
    director, 7.121
    employee earning £8,500 or more, 7.121

Employment income
  advantage, surrender of—
    generally, 7.27
    restrictive covenants, 7.29
    reward for services distinguished from compensation, 7.28
  benefits in kind, see BENEFITS IN KIND
  capital, 7.21
  causation test—
    consequences, 7.18–7.19
    generally, 7.17
  charge to tax, 7.01
  chargeable overseas earnings, 7.06–7.07
  charging base—
    income, 7.02
    place of performance of duties, meaning, 7.03
  compensation—
    claims against employers, payments for, 7.30–7.39
    surrender of advantage, 7.28

2714

Index

Employment income – *cont.*
earned, previous charge to tax on, 5.20–5.21
earnings¾
  charge to tax, generally, 7.04
  seafarers, 7.05
  employees not resident in UK, of, 7.07
  employees resident and ordinarily resident but not domiciled in UK, of, 7.06
  employees resident but not ordinarily resident in UK, of, 7.06
  meaning, 7.01
employment—
  consequences, 7.12–7.16
  definition, 5.22
  illegal contract, under, 7.08
  IR35 rules, 7.09, 8.26
  managed service company, 7.09, 8.27
  meaning, 7.08
  profession, and, 7.10
  secondment, effect of, 7.08
  self-employment, or, 7.11
examples, 7.24
income declared to be, 5.24
loss relief, 6.30
meaning, 7.08
money's worth, discharge of employee's obligation, 7.23
office, meaning, 7.08
pensions, *see* PENSIONS
profit related pay, *see* PROFIT RELATED PAY
relocation expenses, 7.19
services—
  gift on personal grounds, 7.25
  past, 7.20
  payment for, distinguished from gift on personal grounds, 7.25
  reward for, whether compensation, 7.28
  sporting achievements, 7.26
  suggestion scheme, payments under, 7.17
  technical colleges, schemes at, 7.97
  termination payments—
    compensation, 7.30–7.38
    continuing benefits, provision of, 7.39
    employee and trader contrasted, 7.37
    non-approved retirement benefits scheme, payments to, 7.38
    payments in lieu of notice, 7.31–7.35
    special scheme of taxation, 7.36
  timing rules, 7.22
  training schemes, exemption for, 7.97
  university, schemes at, 7.97

Energy-saving materials
value added tax, 70.05
Enterprise Investment Scheme
business expansion scheme, replacing, 31.06
capital gains tax exemption, 17.23
connected persons, 31.11
disposal of shares, 31.13
deferral relief, 22.29
extension to, 31.08
investor, requirements as to, 31.11
qualifying company, 31.12
qualifying trade, 31.12
relief—
  claims for, 31.15
  deferral relief, interaction with, 22.29, 22.31
  eligibility for, 31.07
  form of, 31.09
  loan backs, prohibition, 31.10
  loss of, 31.14
  withdrawal of, 31.15
Entertainment
business, value added tax, 65.24, 66.20
Entertainment expenses
prohibited expenditure—
  exceptions, 8.134
  generally, 8.133
Entitlement trust, *see* INHERITANCE TAX
Equity notes
interest on, 26.09
Estate
meaning, 38.20
see also INHERITANCE TAX
Estate duty
pre-1975 election to defer, 42.27
purchasers of reversionary interests, saving for, 42.26
surviving spouse relief, 42.25
Estate in course of administration
death, income arising after—
  beneficiary—
    foreign estates, 14.04
    generally, 14.03
    non-residuary, 14.05
    residuary—
      absolute interests, 14.08
      accrued income, 14.06
      limited interest, 14.07
      other, 14.09
    UK estates, 14.04
  personal representatives—
    duties of, 14.10
    liability of, 14.02

Index

Estate in course of administration – *cont.*
  deceased's income, 14.01
  disposals, capital gains tax, 19.10
    deed of variation, 19.03
  inheritance tax, 42.11
  tax return, 14.10
European Community, *see* EUROPEAN UNION
European Economic Area
  treaty establishing, 54.13
European Economic Interest Grouping
  capital gains tax treatment, 22.47
  charge to tax, 33.43
  use of, 33.43
European Union
  abuse of rights, 1.13
  Commission, role of, 1.20
  Court of Justice, non-discrimination case law of, 1.08–1.12
  corporate reorganisation directive, 21.26
  cross-frontier workers, 1.09
  Directives, 1.02
  dividend cases, 1.16–1.18
  freedom of establishment, 1.10
  freedom of movement of capital, 1.11
  human rights, 1.01, 1.21–1.22, 1.27
  implementation of legislation, 1.05
  interpretation of law, 1.20
  law, breach of, 1.01, 1.09, 1.12
  Mergers Directive, 25.47
  national insurance, and, 54.12–54.16
  non-discrimination, principle of, 1.06–1.12
  power to tax, 1.01
  recovery of tax, mutual assistance, 34.01
  state aid, 1.03
  statutes, interpretation of, 1.01
  supreme law, Treaty as, 1.02
  tax competition, 1.20
  territory of, 63.08
  thin capitalisation, 1.19
  Treaty provisions, 1.04
  value added tax, directives on, 63.02
Evasion, *see* TAX EVASION
Exempt transfer, *see* INHERITANCE TAX
Exempt transferee, *see* INHERITANCE TAX
Expenses
  apportionment, 8.98
  basic rules, 7.122
  benefits in kind—
    directors, 7.101
    generally, 7.136
    employee earning £8,500 or more, 7.101
  capital expenditure, *see* CAPITAL EXPENDITURE

Expenses – *cont.*
  charities, gifts to, 8.141
  duality, 8.98–8.101
  educational establishments, gifts to, 8.141
  employee seconded to work in UK, 7.135
  entertainment, *see* ENTERTAINMENT EXPENSES
  express deductions, 7.123
  foreign, 7.133
  foreign emoluments, corresponding payments, 7.134
  funeral, 45.30
  generally, 8.95
  homeworking, unreimbursed, 7.142
  in performance of duties, 7.137
  incidental overnight, 7.130
  liability insurance, 7.140
  necessarily incurred, 7.138
  partnership, of, 8.100
  permitted expenditure, 8.139
  personal expenditure, 8.102
  professional subscriptions, 7.143
  profits—
    division of, 8.106–8.109
    earning—
      expense of, 8.106–8.109
      purpose of, 8.104–8.105
  prohibited expenditure—
    business gifts, 8.133
    entertainment—
      exceptions, 8.134
      generally, 8.133
    generally, 8.131
    interest, 8.132
    other deductions, 8.138
    reverse premiums, 8.135
    sale and leaseback—
      land, leaseback of, 8.136
      leased assets other than land, 8.137
  property income, 10.08
  remoteness, 8.96–8.97
  research and development, enhanced allowance for, 8.140
  subscriptions, 8.101
  summary, 7.141
  travelling, *see* TRAVELLING EXPENSES
  uninsured liabilities, 7.140
  wholly and exclusively incurred, 7.139, 8.96–8.97
Exports, *see* VALUE ADDED TAX
Family
  disposition for maintenance of, 39.15–39.19, 42.19
  foreign travel, 7.133

Index

Farm animals
special rules for, 8.169
Farmer
averaging for, 6.47-6.48
Farming
hobby, trading losses, 6.29
Fees
introduction, 12.09
Films
capital allowances, 9.54
Finance
value added tax, 68.16
Food
value added tax, 69.13
Footwear
value added tax, 69.42
Foreign currency
consideration in, computation of capital gain, 16.08
trading receipts, 8.78
Foreign element, *see* INTERNATIONAL DIMENSION
Foreign emoluments
chargeable overseas earnings, 7.06
corresponding payments, 7.134
Foreign exchange
gains and losses on accounting periods on or after 1 October 2002¾
exceptions to general rule, 27.11
generally, 27.11
money debts, treatment of, 27.12
Foreign income
foreign law rule, 35.10
generally, 35.01
offshore income gains—
charge to tax, 35.45
disposals, 35.41
distributing funds, 35.43
exchanges within offshore fund, 35.44
generally, 35.40
material interests, 35.42
non-qualifying offshore funds, 35.43
place of trade, 35.02-35.04
remittance basis—
application of, 35.12
claims, 35.13
employment income, 35.15
income of taxpayer, 35.17-35.19
nominated income, 35.14
remittance—
avoiding liability, 35.22
meaning, 35.16
money, of, 35.20-35.21
rules from 2008-09, 35.16

Foreign income – *cont.*
tax arbitrage, 35.74
trading income—
foreign dividends, distributions and interest, 35.08
income, meaning, 35.10
overseas property, income from, 35.07
partnership, overseas income, 35.06
transparent overseas business entities, 35.11
travel expenses, 35.09
transfer of assets abroad, attribution of income—
charge, 35.36-35.37
defences, 35.29
elements, 35.30-35.35
generally, 35.26-35.28, 35.39
limitations, 35.38
unremittable, relief for, 35.24-35.25
Foreign revenue laws
enforcement of—
evasion, countering, 34.07
exchange of information, 34.08
foreign jurisdiction, consequences in, 34.06
generally, 34.02-34.03
UK, consequences in, 34.04, 34.05
Foreign tax
capital gain, on, 16.23
expense, treatment as, 37.05
recovery, mutual assistance, 34.01
tax credit, limitation on, 37.10
Foreign taxpayer, *see* NON-RESIDENT
Fraud
assessment in case of, 2.25-2.26
nature of, 2.26
Freight containers
export of, value added tax, 69.08
Friendly society
exemption from tax, 31.05
Fuel and power
value added tax, 70.04
see also PETROL
Fund-raising events
value added tax, 68.28
Funeral expenses
allowance for, 45.30
Furnished lettings
holiday, 10.15
capital gains tax treatment, 23.05
definition, 23.05
loss relief, 6.27
charge to tax, 10.13-10.15
Futures markets
stamp duty, 60.15

2717

Index

Gambling
  charge to tax, outside, 12.05
Gaming
  value added tax, 68.15
Gaming machines
  value added tax, 65.26
Gas supply
  value added tax, 65.39, 70.06
Gift
  business, prohibited expenditure, 8.133
  capital gains tax, see CAPITAL GAINS TAX
  charity, to, 5.28–5.30, 8.141, 13.22
  educational establishments, to, 8.141
  inheritance tax, see INHERITANCE TAX
  marriage, 43.05
  normal expenditure out of income, 43.03–43.04
  not exceeding £3,000, 43.01
  personal grounds, on, payment for services distinguished from, 7.30
  small, to same person, 43.02
Gilt strips
  loan relationship regime, 27.10
  tax avoidance schemes, 11.19
Gold
  investment—
    exemption from VAT, 68.31
    election to waive, 68.10
    input tax, attribution of, 66.12
  value added tax, 65.40, 69.32
Goods
  supplies of, see VALUE ADDED TAX
Government document
  stamp duty, 56.36
Government stock
  capital gains tax, exemption from, 17.12
Group of companies
  corporation tax, see CORPORATION TAX
Handicapped person, see DISABLED PERSON
Health
  value added tax, 68.23
Heating equipment
  value added tax, 70.06
Heritage property
  inheritance tax—
    beneficiaries, position of, 46.16
    charge, 44.30
    designated objects, 44.28
    generally, 44.27
    land, 44.29
    maintenance fund, 44.32
    transferor's cumulative total, 44.31

Heritage property – *cont.*
  maintenance fund for, 42.56, 44.32
Higher paid employee, see EMPLOYEE EARNING £8,500 PER ANNUM OR MORE
Hire purchase
  capital allowances, 9.45
  contract, capital gains tax, 18.02
HM Revenue and Customs
  amounts collected, 2.02
  back duty powers, 2.28
  Charter, 2.08
  contract settlement, 2.28
  decisions, challenging, 2.09, see also APPEAL
  Director of Revenue and Customs Prosecutions, 2.05
  documents, power to call for, 2A.49
  enforcement powers—
    court proceedings, 2.37
    distraint, 2.38
  exchange of information, 2.06
  fairness, duty of, 2.07
  information powers, 2.06
  informers, payments to, 2.25
  inheritance tax, powers, see INHERITANCE TAX
  inspection powers, 2A.58
  local offices, 2.04
  naming and shaming by, 2A.89
  national insurance system, administering, 55.01–55.03
  practice, 1.30
  Prosecution Office, 2.05
  prosecution powers—
    contract settlement, 2.28
    direct taxes, 2.27
    stamp duty land tax, 2.29
  remedies against, 2.24
  responsibility of, 2.01
    direct taxes, 2.03
    indirect taxes, 2.04
  serious fraud—
    documents held by tax accountants, 2.30
    human rights provisions, 2.33–2.34
    PACE, procedure in, 2.32
    statutory powers, 2.31
  taxpayer notices—
    appeals, 2A.56
    issue of, 2A.54
    penalties, 2A.59
    self-assessment, interaction with, 2A.55
  third party notice—
    issue of, 2A.54

Index

HM Revenue and Customs – *cont.*
  third party notice— – *cont.*
    penalties, 2A.59
Hobby farming
  trading losses, 6.29
Holiday
  furnished lettings, 10.15
Hotel
  capital allowances, 9.21
House, *see* DWELLING HOUSE
Houseboat
  value added tax, 69.31
Housing association
  gift to, capital gains tax, 18.37
Hovercraft
  stores for use in, value added tax, 69.05
Human rights
  criminal offences, prosecution of, 2.34
  statutes, interpretation of, 1.27
  tax law, relevance to, 1.21-1.22
Identification, *see* CAPITAL GAINS TAX
Imported goods, *see* VALUE ADDED TAX
Improvements
  capital expenditure, 8.122
  capital gains tax, 16.16, 16.19–16.20
Incentive, *see* SHARE INCENTIVE SCHEMES
Income
  charges on—
    corporation tax computation, *see* CORPORATION TAX
    personal reliefs, 6.11
  company, *see* CORPORATION TAX
  derived from personal activities, sale of, 4.30–4.31
  earned, *see* EARNED INCOME
  employment, *see* EMPLOYMENT INCOME
  estate in course of administration, *see* ESTATE IN COURSE OF ADMINISTRATION
  foreign, *see* FOREIGN INCOME
  spouses and civil partners, of, 6.02-6.03
  investment, *see* INVESTMENT INCOME
  non-taxable, 5.17–5.18
  property, *see* PROPERTY INCOME
  savings, *see* SAVINGS INCOME
  schedule, falling within, 5.06-5.07
  total—
    deductions in calculating, 5.31-5.32
    inclusions in, 5.30
    meaning, 5.30
  trust, *see* TRUST
  undistributed, *see* SETTLEMENT

Income tax
  accounting date, 5.16
  averaging—
    creative works, for, 6.47
    farmers, for, 6.47-6.48
    generally, 6.46
    relief, obtaining, 6.49
  basis period, 5.16
  benefits in kind, *see* BENEFITS IN KIND
  calculation of—
    generally, 5.29
    total income—
      deductions, 5.31-5.32
      inclusions, 5.30
      meaning, 5.30
  capital allowances, *see* CAPITAL ALLOWANCES
  charity, gift to, 6.36–6.38; 13.22
  employment income, *see* EMPLOYMENT INCOME
  enterprise investment scheme, 31.06–31.15
  estate in course of administration, *see* ESTATE IN COURSE OF ADMINISTRATION
  exceptions from liability to, 5.18
  foreign income, *see* FOREIGN INCOME
  interest relief—
    anti-avoidance, 6.45
    close company, acquisition of interest in, 6.42
    co-operative, acquisition of interest in, 6.42
    employee-controlled company, acquisition of interest in, 6.42
    generally, 6.39, 6.40
    inheritance tax, payment of, 6.43
    land, purchase of life annuity secured on, 6.44
    partnership, acquisition of interest in, 6.42
    plant and machinery, purchase of, 6.41
  investment relief—
    enterprise investment scheme, 31.06–31.15
  loss relief—
    employment losses, 6.30
    foreign trade, 6.31
    generally, 6.15
    interest of dividend income, 6.33
    miscellaneous income, 6.31
    property income, 6.32
    temporary extension, 6.16
    trading company, unquoted shares in, 6.34
    trading losses, *see* TRADING LOSSES

Income tax – *cont.*
  non-resident, 36.01
    limits on chargeable income, 36.02
  non-taxable income, 5.17–5.18
  ordinary rate, 5.02
  overpaid, interest on, 2A.33
  Pay As You Earn, 7.144–7.149
    compliance rules, 51.10
    cumulative withholding under, 7.147
    determination, 2A.64
    earnings, applied to, 7.147
    intermediaries, payments by, 7.146
    national insurance, harmonisation with, 50.37
    non-resident employee, 7.149
    obligation to operate, 7.148
    overseas employer, 7.148
    system of, 7.144
    underpayments, 2A.15
    unrealised gains, deductions for, 7.145
  penalties, 2A.78, 2A.90
  personal reliefs—
    age allowance, 6.06, 6.08
    blind person's, 6.09
    charges on income, 6.11
    generally, 6.04-6.05
    independent taxation, 6.01
    married couples' allowance for persons born before 6 April 1935, 6.07
    non-residents, 6.10
  pre-owned assets, charge on, 41.14
    categories of asset, 12.16
    chattels, 12.18
    excluded transactions, 12.20
    exemptions, 12.21
    intangible property, 12.19
    land, 12.17
    non-domiciled taxpayer, 12.22
    rationale, 12.15
    reverter to settlor trust, 12.23
  profession, *see* PROFESSION
  prohibited deductions, 5.19
  property income, *see* PROPERTY INCOME
  provisional collection, 1.32
  rate structure, 5.02
  reliefs, claiming—
    appeals, 6.14
    procedure, 6.12
    time limit, 6.13
  remittance basis, *see* FOREIGN INCOME
  residual charge to¾—
    annual profits, 12.03
    casual authorship, 12.08

Income tax – *cont.*
  residual charge to¾ – *cont.*
    Certificates of Deposit, 12.14
    computation—
      deposits, rights in respect of, 12.14
      machinery, 12.13
    foreign element—
      generally, 12.12
      offshore income gain, *see* OFFSHORE INCOME GAIN
    gambling transactions, 12.05
    generally, 12.01
    income eiusdem generis, 12.04
    introduction fees, 12.09
    loss relief, 6.31
    miscellaneous, 12.10
    premiums, *see* PREMIUMS
    property, analogy of income from, 12.11
    trading profits, profits analogous to, 12.06–12.07
    winnings, 12.05
  savings and investment income, 5.12
  schedular system—
    generally, 5.03–5.07
    history of, 5.04–5.05
    imposition of, 5.01
    Schedule D, 5.10
    Schedule E, 5.09
  settlement, *see* SETTLEMENT
  starting rate, 5.02
  tax unit, 6.01
  timing, 5.14–5.15
  top slicing, 6.50
  trade, *see* TRADE
  trading income, 5.10
  treaty relief by credit, 37.19
  trust income, *see* TRUST
  unpaid, interest on, 2A.32
  vocation, *see* VOCATION
Incumbrances
  valuation, *see* INHERITANCE TAX
Indexation
  capital gains tax computation, 24.03–24.09, *see also* CAPITAL GAINS TAX
  share pooling and, 21.07
Individual
  residence, of, *see* RESIDENCE
Individual Learning Account
  statutory establishment of, 7.98
  tax exemption, 7.98
Individual savings account
  life assurance component, 31.03
  scheme, 31.01
  stocks and share component, 31.02

Index

Industrial buildings
  capital allowances—
    assured tenancies, 9.22
    balancing allowance and charge, 9.17
    dwelling houses, 9.22
    generally, 9.11–9.13
    hotel buildings and extensions, 9.21
    initial, 9.15
    person claiming, 9.14
    part of building, for, 9.13
    transitional measures before 2011—
      anti-avoidance measures connected with transitional rules, 9.20
      writing down allowances, 9.18, 9.19, 9.61
    writing down, 9.16, 9.18, 9.19, 9.61
  definition, 9.12

Inheritance tax
  abatement, 43.30
  accountability—
    liability for—
      certificate of settlement of liabilities, 46.07
      death, on, 46.03
      Inland Revenue charge, 46.06
      lifetime transfers, 46.01
      limitations of liability, 46.04
      settled property, 46.02
      special cases, 46.05
    reporting transfer—
      death, 2A.08
      excepted estate, 2A.09
      late, 46.08
      lifetime dispositions, 2A.07
  agricultural property—
    business property, as, 44.26
    company owning, shares of, 44.17
    conditions, 44.20–44.23
    dwelling house, qualification of, 44.12-44.14
    generally, 44.11–44.19
    relief, 43.33
    replacement of, 44.24
  alternatives to, 38.05
  associated operations, disposition by¾
    consequences of, 39.30-39.33
    disposition, definition, 39.32
    government statement on, 39.34
    meaning, 39.29
    operation, meaning, 39.28
  burden of tax, 43.31
  business property—
    agricultural property as, 44.26
    business, meaning, 44.02
    companies, special rules for, 44.09

Inheritance tax – *cont.*
  business property— – *cont.*
    control of, 44.01
    excepted assets, 44.08
    excluded business, 44.04
    generally, 44.01
    period of ownership, 44.05
    potentially exempt transfer, 44.10
    relevant, 44.01
    relief, 43.33
    replacement of, 44.07
    shares, meaning, 44.03
    succession, 44.06
  calculation of tax—
    aggregation—
      exemptions from, 38.16
      generally, 38.15
    cumulation, 38.18–38.19
    estate, meaning, 38.20
    excluded property, meaning, 38.21
    exempt persons, meaning, 38.22
    nil rate band, transfer of, 38.14
    potentially exempt transfers, 39.02
    property, meaning, 38.20
    rates, 38.13
    transfer of nil rate band, 38.14
    transfers on same day, 38.17
  charities, transfers to, 43.17
  close company—
    beneficiary, as, 39.27
    exemptions, 39.23–39.24
    generally, 39.21
    liability, 39.22
    settled property trustees as participators, 39.26
    share rights, alteration in, 39.25
  death, transfer at—
    abatement of exemptions, 40.35
    armed forces, member of, 40.06
    estate, valuation, 40.07
    events after death, *see* EVENTS AFTER DEATH, *below*
    exemption, 40.06
    40.generally, 40.01
    joint assets, 40.02–40.04
    pension fund, of, 40.36
    posthumous acquisition, 40.05
  disposal for capital gains tax purposes, chargeable on, 16.24
  disposition—
    associated operations, by, 39.28–39.34
    definition, 39.28
    Fitzwilliam case, 39.36–39.39
    payable on, 38.07

Index

Inheritance tax – *cont.*
  disposition— – *cont.*
    transfer of value by—
      associated operations, disposition by, 39.28–39.34
      chargeable, 38.11
      close company, to, *see* CLOSE COMPANY
      disposition, meaning, 39.04
      events treated as, 38.08, 38.09
      excluded property, disposition of, 39.12
      exempt beneficiary, disposal to settle claim by, 40.35
      exempt lifetime transfers—
        annual exemption, 43.01
        marriage gifts, 43.05
        normal expenditure out of income, 43.03–43.04
        small gifts to same person, 43.02
        transfers not exceeding £3,000, 43.01
      future payments, 39.11
      generally, 39.01
      gifts with reservations—
        consequences, 41.13
        excluded property, 41.11
        exclusion of benefit to donor, 41.06, 41.07
        generally, 41.01
        inter-spouse and civil partners transfer, 41.12
        land, gift of, 41.08–41.10
        meaning, 41.02–41.07
        right over land, donor enjoying, 41.09, 41.10
        transfer of same property, and, 40.33
      matters not transfers of value—
        maintenance of family, disposition for, 39.15–39.19
        other, 39.20
        transaction with no intent to give, 39.14
      omission to exercise right, 39.10
      potentially exempt transfers, 39.02, 39.03
      pre-owned assets, income tax charge, 41.14
      timing, 39.05
      value transferred, 39.06–39.09
      voidable transfers, 39.13
  donee-based, move to, 38.02–38.04
  donor-based, defence of, 38.03
  due date for payment, 2A.23

Inheritance tax – *cont.*
  estate—
    changes in realised value after death, 40.09
    exclusions, 40.08
    valuation on death, 40.07–40.09
  estate duty surviving spouse relief, 42.25
  events after death—
    beneficiary, death of during administration, 40.23
    disclaimer, 40.22
    family provision, 40.27
    legitim, 40.28
    property settled by will, payment out of, 40.25
    rearrangements, 40.22
    statutory provisions, 40.27
    surviving spouse, election to redeem life interest, 40.24
    testator's wishes, carrying out, 40.26
  exempt transfers—
    employee trust, to, 43.20
    gifts for public purposes, 43.14–43.19
    partly exempt transfers, allocation of relief, 43.22–43.33
    spouses and civil partners, transfers between, 43.06–43.13
    valour, decorations for, 43.21
  foreign element—
    administration expenses, 47.21
    double taxation relief, 47.17–47.20
    foreign debts, 47.21
    foreign property—
      excluded, 47.11-47.16
      individual, owned by, 47.11-47.12
      settled property, 47.13–47.16
    liability, 47.22
    location of assets, 47.02–47.07
    property in UK, 47.08–47.10
    territorial limits, 47.01
  generally, 38.01
  gift and loanback, on, 40.34
  gifts for public purposes, 43.14–43.19
  heritage property—
    charge, 44.30
    designated objects, 44.28
    generally, 44.27
    land, 44.29
    maintenance funds, 44.32
    transferor's cumulative total, 44.31
  incidence—
    accounting parties, position of—
      discretionary beneficiaries, 46.13
      limited owners, 46.12
      personal representatives, 46.14

Index

Inheritance tax – *cont.*
  incidence— – *cont.*
    accounting parties, position of— – *cont.*
      transferees, 46.10
      transferors, 46.09
      trustees, 46.11
    beneficiaries, position of—
      annuitant and remainderman, 46.19–46.21
      apportionment of tax, 46.17–46.18
      deceased person, estate of, 46.15
      life tenant of part, death of, 46.22
      works of art and heritage property, 46.16
    foreign element, 47.22
    option, person exercising, 46.23
    variation by will or other document, 46.24–46.25
  instalments, payment by, 2A.24-2A.25
    interest on, 2A.36
  interest, recovery of, 2A.23, 2A.35
  lease for life—
    interest in possession, 42.10
    matrimonial home, 42.08
    potentially exempt transfer, special rate of charge on, 42.24
    reversionary interests—
      generally, 42.23
      purchasers, 42.26
    rules applying to, 38.10
    settlement—
      creation of—
        generally, 42.05
        interest in possession, 42.07
      generally, 42.02–42.03
      meaning, 42.02
      settlor, meaning, 42.04
    survivorship clauses, 42.11
    transfers of—
      depreciatory transactions, 42.15
      disposal, 42.14
      exceptions—
        beneficiary becoming entitled to property, 42.16
        disclaimer, 42.20
        family maintenance, disposition to provide, 42.19
        intestacy, redemption of life interest on, 42.22
        property reverting to settlor, 42.17
        settlor's spouse or civil partner, transfer on termination to, 42.18
        trustee's annuities, 42.21

Inheritance tax – *cont.*
  life policies—
    associated operations, 40.12-40.14
    estate, valuation of, 40.10
    generally, 40.10
    premiums as transfers of value, 40.11
  lifetime transfers—
    accountability, 46.01
    chargeable, 40.16
    death within 3 years, 40.16
    death within 7 years, 40.16–40.17
    decline in value between transfer and death, relief for, 40.18
    restrictions on reliefs, altered property—
      land, 40.20
      other property, 40.20
      shares, 40.19
    tapering relief, 40.16
    transfer undone by court order, 40.21
  location of assets—
    debts, 47.04
    deemed domicile, 47.07
    generally, 47.02, 47.06
    land, 47.03
    securities, 47.05
    stocks and shares, 47.05
  mutual transfers, 40.30
  outline of—
    calculation of tax, *see* CALCULATION OF TAX, *above*
    charge to, 38.06-38.11
    exemptions, 38.12
    reliefs, 38.12
  payment of, interest relief, 6.43
  penalties, 2A.92
  planning, 43.32
  political parties, gifts to, 43.18
  potentially exempt transfer—
    beneficial interests in possession, of, 41.01
    liability for tax, 46.02
    same property, of, 40.31
    special rate of charge, 42.24
    taxation of, 39.03
  public benefit, property given for, 43.19
  public purposes, gifts for, 43.14–43.19
  quick succession relief, 40.29
  rates, 38.13
  recovery, proceedings for, 2A.72
  same property, transfer of—
    chargeable, 40.32
    death, on, 40.31–40.32
    gift with reservation, 40.33
    potentially exempt, 40.31

Index

Inheritance tax – *cont.*
  same property, transfer of— – *cont.*
    same transferor, by, 40.30
  Scottish agricultural tenancies, 44.25
  settled property—
    accountability, 46.02
      generally, 42.12
      termination, 42.13
    estate in course of administration, 42.11
    excluded and non-excluded, mixture of, 47.14
    excluded settlement, addition of property to, 47.15
    interest in possession—
      creation of settlement, 42.07
      entitlement trust—
        extent of entitlement, 42.09
        lease for lives, 42.10
      gain, holding over, 42.06
  special occasions of charge—
    close company, 39.21–39.27
    transfers reported late, 46.08
  specified bodies, gifts to, 43.19
  spouses and civil partners, transfers between, 43.06–43.13
  territorial limits, 47.01
  timber, 44.33–44.35
  transfers of value, matters not being, 43.34
  transfers reported late, 46.08
  valuation—
    accrued income to date of transfer, 45.19
    case law, 45.02
    debts due to transferor, 45.18
    fiscal and commercial, 45.03
    generally, 45.01
    land—
      adjustments, 45.17
      restrictions, 45.17
      sales at loss following transfer on death, 45.16
    liabilities—
      debts—
        estate, due from, 45.29
        generally, 45.26
        non-deductible, 45.27
        unenforceable, 45.27
      estate immediately before death, 45.23–45.25
      funeral expenses, 45.30
      generally, 45.20
      incumbrances, 45.26
      interaction of taxes, 45.28
      jointly owned property, 45.10
      other taxes, 45.28

Inheritance tax – *cont.*
  valuation— – *cont.*
    liabilities— – *cont.*
      transferor—
        incumbrances created by, 45.22
        incurred by, 45.21
      particular assets, sales at loss following transfer on death, 45.11–45.15
    related property—
      generally, 45.07–45.08
      undoing after death, 45.09–45.10
    restrictions on sale, 45.06
    special purchaser, 45.05
  works of art—
    charge, 44.30
    designated objects, 44.28
    generally, 44.27
    maintenance fund, 44.32
    transferor's cumulative total, 44.31
Inland Revenue, *see* HM REVENUE AND CUSTOMS
Input tax, *see* VALUE ADDED TAX
Instrument
  stamp duty, *see* STAMP DUTY
Insurance
  liability, relief for, 7.140
  non-life, disposal of interest in, 17.13
  permanent health, 11.04
  receipts, capital gains tax—
    generally, 18.17
    replacement or repair, not used for, 18.18
    restoration or replacement, used for, 18.19
  value added tax, 68.13
  see also LIFE ASSURANCE
Insurance company
  demutualisation, 60.16
Intangible assets
  chargeable, 27
  pre-owned, 12.19
Intellectual property
  acquired or created after 1 April 2002, 27.23
  acquired or created before 1 April 2002, 27.22
  chargeable intangible assets, 27
  excluded assets, 27.25
  fungible assets, 27
  grants and contributions, treatment of, 27
  meaning, 27.21
  related parties, transactions between, 27.26
  rollover relief, 27.24
  sale or disposition, stamp duty exemption, 58.16

Intellectual property – *cont.*
  tax treatment, 27.21
Interest
  distribution, as, 26.07, 26.08
  foreign, 35.08
  inheritance tax, on, 2A.23, 2A.35, 2A.36
  meaning, 11.05
  National Insurance contributions, on, 2A.37
  overpaid tax credits, on, 2A.38
  prohibited expenditure, 8.132
  property income, deductions, 10.11
  relief—
    anti-avoidance, 6.45
    close company, acquisition of interest in, 6.42
    co-operative, acquisition of interest in, 6.42
    employee-controlled company, acquisition of interest in, 6.42
    generally, 6.39, 6.40
    inheritance tax, payment of, 6.43
    land, purchase of life annuity secured on, 6.44
    partnership, acquisition of interest in, 6.42
    plant and machinery, purchase of, 6.41
  savings income, *see* SAVINGS INCOME
  stamp duty, on, 2A.39
  stamp duty land tax, on, 2A.41
  stamp duty reserve tax, on, 2A.40
  unpaid or overpaid tax, on, 2A.32–2A.43
  value added tax, on, 2A.42
Interest in possession, *see* INHERITANCE TAX
International dimension
  capital gains tax, *see* CAPITAL GAINS TAX
  connecting factors—
    domicile, 33.15-33.24, *see also* DOMICILE
    generally, 33.01
    residence, *see* RESIDENCE
  controlled foreign companies resident in low tax areas, *see* COMPANY
  discretionary trust, 42.43
  double taxation relief, *see* DOUBLE TAXATION RELIEF
  foreign revenue laws, enforcement of—
    evasion, countering, 34.07
    exchange of information, 34.08
    foreign jurisdiction, consequences in, 34.06
    generally, 34.02–34.03
    mutual assistance, 34.01

International dimension – *cont.*
  foreign revenue laws, enforcement of— – *cont.*
    UK, consequences in, 34.04, 34.05
  inheritance tax, *see* INHERITANCE TAX
  national insurance, 54.01–54.17
  residual income, 12.12
International services
  value added tax, 69.25
Intestacy
  redemption of life interest on, 42.22
  stamp duty, 58.13–58.14
Introduction fees
  charge to tax, 12.09
Investment
  cash, of, trading receipts, 8.79
Investment company
  management expenses¾
    commissions, 30.04
    depreciation, 30.08
    disbursement, 30.07
    generally, 30.06
    investment business, relief for, 30.05
    meaning, 30.02, 30.03
    not qualifying for relief, 30.04
    relief for, 30.09-30.11
    Revenue view, 30.05-30.06
    total profits, set against, 30.01
  open-ended, 30.18
    stamp duty, 59.20
    stamp duty land tax, 62.28
    stamp duty reserve tax, 61.10
  significant increase in capital, 30.11
Investment income
  earned income distinguished from, 5.20
  franked, *see* CORPORATION TAX
  surplus franked, *see* CORPORATION TAX
Investment intermediaries
  investment company, 30.01–30.11, *see also* INVESTMENT COMPANY
  investment trust, 30.12
  unit trust, 30.13–30.16
Investment relief
  enterprise investment scheme, 31.06–31.15
Investment trust
  real estate, 31.33
  taxation, 30.12
Islamic finance
  diminishing musharaka, 27.33
  financial institutions, 27.29
  Modaraba, 27.31
  Morabaha, 27.30
  overview, 27.28

2725

Index

Islamic finance – *cont.*
  provisions not at arm's length, 27.34
  Wakala, 27.32
Judicial review
  challenging decisions by, 2.23
  stamp duty, 56.26
Know-how
  capital allowances, 9.63
  trading receipts, 8.76
Land
  agricultural, capital allowances, 9.59–9.60
  artificial transactions in—
    exceptions—
      clearance, 23.36
      compulsory purchase, 23.38
      computation, 23.36
      generally, 23.35
      losses, 23.36
      Yuill v Wilson, 23.37
    generally, 23.29
    situations—
      land developed to realise gain, 23.34
      land held as trading stock, 23.33
      land or property deriving value from land—
        disposal, 23.31
        land or property, 23.30
        object, 23.32
  capital allowances, 9.59–9.60
  charity, gifts to, 6.38
  definition, 23.01
  disposal of interest in—
    capital gain or trading transaction, as, 23.02
    joint interests, exchange of, 23.04
    part disposal, 23.03
  furnished holiday lettings, *see* FURNISHED LETTINGS
  gains in respect of, *see* PROPERTY INCOME
  heritage property, 44.29
  life annuity secured on, interest relief for purchase of, 6.44
  lifetime transfer, 40.20
  location of, 47.03
  pre-owned, charge to tax, 12.17
  profits in respect of, *see* PROPERTY INCOME
  sale and leaseback, 8.136
  stamp duty, *see* STAMP DUTY
  trading income, 8.42
  valuation, 45.16–45.17
  value added tax, 68.11–68.12

Lease
  capital allowances, *see* PLANT AND MACHINERY
  capital gains tax, *see* CAPITAL GAINS TAX
  income tax, *see* PROPERTY INCOME
  lives, for, *see* INHERITANCE TAX
  part disposal, 18.17
  premium, *see* PREMIUM
  sale and leaseback—
    assets other than land, 8.137
    land, 8.136
  stamp duty, *see* STAMP DUTY; STAMP DUTY LAND TAX
Legatee
  disposal to, capital gains tax, 19.05
Letter of allotment
  stamp duty, 59.12
Life annuity contract
  surrender of, 31.29
Life assurance
  policy—
    associated operations, 40.12–40.14
    disposal of, gain on, 16.15
    excess liability charge—
      non-qualifying policies, 31.20–31.24
      qualifying policies, 31.25–31.26
    generally, 31.19, 40.10
    life annuity contracts, 31.29
    loans, 31.28
    personal portfolio bonds, 31.27
    premiums as transfers of value, 40.11
    top slicing, 6.50
    special treatment, 31.19
Life interest
  meaning, 20.19
  part of settled property, in, 20.20
  termination of, 20.18–20.20
Lifetime transfer, *see* INHERITANCE TAX
Liquidation
  capital distribution, 21.18
  trade, sale of, 8.31
Living accommodation
  additional charge, 7.51
  basic charge, 7.50
  benefit in kind, as, 7.48–7.51
  director, 7.110
  employee earning £8,500 or more, 7.110
  exceptions, 7.49
  generally, 7.48
  non beneficial occupation, 7.49
Loan
  charity, to, 16.18
  capital, costs of, 8.117

Index

Loan – *cont.*
  life assurance policy, 31.28
  low interest—
    cash equivalent, 7.112
    director, 7.111–7.112
    employee earning £8,500 or more, 7.111–7.112
    settlor, to, 16.24
  share purchase scheme—
    director, 7.114
    employee earning £8,500 or more, 7.114
  waiver—
    director, 7.113
    employee earning £8,500 or more, 7.113
Loan relationships
  anti-avoidance, 27.04
  connected party transactions, 27.07
  debits and credits, recognition of, 27.03
  deficits, 27.05
  definition, 27.02
  excluded securities, 27.09
  gilt strips, 27.10
  group finance costs, restriction on, 27.08
  losses—
    carry back, 27.06
    relief, 27.05
  regime, 27.01
Loss relief
  income tax, *see* INCOME TAX
Losses
  capital gains tax, *see* CAPITAL GAINS TAX
  capital, manufactured, 4.33
  company, *see* CORPORATION TAX
Lotteries
  value added tax, 68.15
Low tax areas
  controlled foreign companies resident in, *see* COMPANY
Machinery, *see* PLANT AND MACHINERY
Main residence, *see* RESIDENCE
Maintenance
  accumulation and maintenance settlement, 42.49–42.53
  family, of, disposition for, 39.15–39.19, 42.19
Maintenance fund
  heritage property, 42.56, 44.32
  works of art, 44.32
Maintenance payment
  qualifying, 11.03
  relief for, 6.35, 11.45
Managed service company
  deemed employment payment by, 7.09, 8.27

Mariners
  national insurance, 54.07, 54.15
Market value
  capital gains tax—
    basic valuation rule, 17.25
    exclusion of rule, 18.48
    gratuitous transfers of value, 18.47
  death, acquisition on, 19.02
  trading receipts, 8.92
  trading stock, *see* TRADING STOCK
Marriage
  breakdown, incidence of stamp duty, 58.16
  gift, 43.05
Medicines
  value added tax, 69.34
Mergers
  Directive, 25.47
Mining
  capital allowances—
    allowance, 9.56
    qualifying expenditure—
      generally, 9.55
      limitations of, 9.57
  income from, 8.171
Mobile home
  value added tax, 69.31
Money's worth
  employee's obligation, discharge of, 7.23
Mortgage
  capital gains tax, 18.21–18.22
Motor vehicle, *see* CAR
National insurance
  administration—
    Department for Work and Pensions, 55.01
    HM Revenue and Customs, 55.01–55.03
    secondary legislation, 55.03
  airmen, 54.07
  annual maximum contributions, 51.08
  anti-avoidance rules, 51.06
  appeals, 2.12
  benefits, interaction with—
    credits—
      early retirement, 53.07
      education and training, 53.05
      meaning, 53.02
      non-working periods, for, 53.04
      unemployment or sickness, 53.03
      working tax credit, 53.06
    earnings factor, 53.01
    voluntary contributions, 53.08
  class 1 contributions—
    collection of, 2A.73, 51.09–51.11

Index

National insurance – *cont.*
  class 1 contributions– – *cont.*
    generally, 48.08, 51.01
    late payment of, 53.12
    liability for, 54.06
  class 1A contributions–
    basic scheme, 51.14
    cars and fuel, relating to, 51.15
    collection, 51.18
    generally, 48.09
    introduction of, 51.13
    liability for, 54.06
    mileage threshold, 51.16
    special cases, 51.17
  class 1B contributions–
    generally, 48.10
    liability for, 54.06
    PAYE Settlement Agreement, on payment into, 51.19
  class 2 contributions–
    exceptions from liability, 52.02
    generally, 48.11, 52.01
    late payment of, 53.13, 53.15
    liability for, 54.06
    receipt of benefits, 52.04
    spare time employment exception, 52.03
  class 3 contributions
    generally, 48.12, 53.08
    late payment of, 53.14–53.15
    liability for, 54.06
  class 4 contributions–
    computation of profits for, 52.06
    generally, 48.13, 52.05
  collection of, 2A.73
  company directors, 51.04
  continental shelf workers, 54.07
  contribution scheme–
    classes, 48.07–48.13
    employee or self-employed, 49.02–49.03
    generally, 48.01–48.04
    legislation, 48.14
  contributions–
    arrears, liability of director for, 51.05
    conditions, general rules, 53.10
    deferment, 53.11
    enforcement, 2.40
    late paid, 53.09
    non-payment of, 2A.73
    overdue, interest on, 2A.37
  earnings limit, 51.02
  earnings period, 51.03
  EC law, 54.12–54.16
  employed earner–
    actors, musicians and performers, 49.10

National insurance – *cont.*
  employed earner– – *cont.*
    agency workers, 49.06, 49.16
    airmen, 54.07
    barristers' clerk, 49.19
    determinations, 49.13
    entertainers, 49.22
    examiners, 49.11
    lecturers, 49.08, 49.20
    mariners, 54.07
    meaning, 49.01
    ministers of religion, 49.09, 49.21
    non-earners' employment, 49.12
    office cleaners, 49.05, 49.15
    regulations, categorisation by, 49.04–49.13
    secondary contributor, 49.14–49.23
    spouse or civil partner, employment by, 49.07, 49.17
    voluntary liquidation, company in, 49.18
  employment earnings–
    back pay, 50.15
    current account, payment of bills charged to, 50.18
    deductions not allowed, 50.02
    definition, 50.01
    earnings, meaning, 50.01–50.03
    employee trusts, 50.04
    employment rights payments, 50.14
    ex gratia payments, 50.12
    gratuities, 50.04
    inducement payments, 50.16
    loans written off, 50.19
    loss of employment, compensation for, 50.11
    notice, pay in lieu of, 50.13
    options, 50.29
    PAYE, harmonisation with, 50.37
    payments excluded, 50.03
    payments in kind–
      assets exchangeable for cash, 50.31
      blocking measures, 50.23–50.28
      cash equivalent, statement of, 50.34
      cash sum, entitlement to, 50.32
      employer, liability of employee discharged by, 50.33
      scope, 50.22
      shares, securities and options, 50.29
      status of exclusion, 50.21
      traps, 50.30–50.34
    pension payments, 50.05
    petrol allowances, 50.07, 50.08
    Ramsay principle, application of, 3.15, 3.16, 50.35

Index

National insurance – *cont.*
employment earnings– – *cont.*
redundancy pay, 50.10
reimbursements, 50.06
retrospective liability on earnings, 50.36
special cases, 50.17–50.20
staff suggestion schemes, 50.20
termination payments, 50.11
Employers' Guides, 55.02
European Economic Area, 54.13
fund, 48.06
Great Britain, going to and from, 54.08–54.10
international transport undertakings, workers in, 54.15
liabilities, reporting, 2A.10
mariners, 54.07, 54.15
more than one employment, effect of, 51.07
offences, 2.40
ordinary residence, 54.04
overpayment of contributions, 51.12
payment, 2A.26
penalties and interest, 2A.93, 51.06
person both employed and self-employed, 52.07
personal service companies and other intermediaries, 49.24
place of business, 54.05
planning considerations, 54.17
presence in UK, 54.03
rates of, 51.02
reciprocal agreements, 54.11
residence, 54.02
self-employed persons, 48.03
students temporarily in Great Britain, 54.10
tax purposes, differing status for, 52.07
taxation distinguished, 48.01
territorial scope, 54.01
thresholds, 51.02
voluntary contributions, 53.08
National savings
exemption from tax, 31.04
Negligent conduct
assessment in case of, 2.26
nature of, 2.26
Newspaper
trust, 42.55
Non-resident
capital gains tax, 22.48
temporary non-residence, 35.47
capital losses, 16.31
company—
capital gains tax, 35.53–35.54

Non-resident – *cont.*
company– – *cont.*
change of residence, 25.46
corporation tax, 25.45
distributions, 26.16
derivative contract with, 27.18
entertainers, 36.11
income chargeable to tax, limits on, 36.02
income tax, 36.01
interest income received by, 11.02
landlords, 36.10
permanent establishment, trade carried on through, 36.07, 36.08
personal reliefs, 6.10
place of trade, 36.03–36.06
pre-owned assets regime, not subject to, 12.22
sportsmen, 36.11
supplies to, value added tax, 69.08
trustees, 36.12
UK representative—
persons not treated as, 36.09
responsibilities of, 36.08
Non-residuary beneficiary, *see* BENEFICIARY
Northern Ireland
tax law, application of, 1.28
Office
employment income, *see* EMPLOYMENT INCOME
meaning, 7.08
Offshore income gain
charge to tax, 35.45
disposals, 35.41
distributing funds, 35.43–35.44
material interests, 35.42
non-qualifying offshore funds, 35.43
residual income, 12.12
Schedule D, Case VI, 35.40
Only or main residence, *see* RESIDENCE
Options
capital gains tax—
abandonment, 18.26
definition, 18.23
disposal of, 18.25
exercise of, 18.27
financial, 18.31
gilt edged securities and qualifying bonds, over, 18.32
grant of, 18.24
traded, 18.31
transactions other than sale or purchase, binding grantor to, 18.30
types of, 18.23
wasting asset rules, application of, 18.31

Index

Options – *cont.*
  share option schemes, *see* SHARE OPTION SCHEMES
Organisation
  value added tax, 63.12
Output tax, *see* VALUE ADDED TAX
Overseas person, *see* NON-RESIDENT
Parent
  unmarried minor children, settlement on, 15.21–15.22
Part disposal, *see* CAPITAL GAINS TAX
Partial exemption, *see* VALUE ADDED TAX
Partnership
  acquisition of interest in, interest relief, 6.42
  capital gains tax—
    asset distributed amongst partners, 22.38
    capacity in which asset held, 22.37
    disposal of assets, 22.38
    mergers and demergers, 22.46
    one or more partners, asset passed to, 22.39
    profit sharing ratios, changes in, 22.40–22.44
    retiring partner, annuity purchased for, 22.45
    rollover relief, 22.20
    statutory provision, 22.36
  expenses, deduction of, 8.100
  film, 6.18
  generally, 8.61
  goodwill written off, 16.35
  land transactions, 62.27
  limited liability, 8.63
  loss relief, 6.28
  overseas income, 35.06
  partners, liability of, 8.62
  plant and machinery, interest relief for purchase of, 6.41
  profits, taxation of, 8.62
  property income, 10.09
  trading losses, 6.18
  value added tax, 63.12
Patents
  capital allowances, 9.63
Pay As You Earn
  compliance rules, 51.10
  court, approach of, 7.145
  cumulative withholding under, 7.147
  earnings, applied to, 7.147
  intermediaries, payments by, 7.146
  non-resident employee, 7.149
  obligation to operate, 7.148
  overseas employer, 7.148

Pay As You Earn – *cont.*
  self-assessment, and, 7.150
  system of, 7.144
  unrealised gains, deductions for, 7.145
Payment
  annual, *see* ANNUAL PAYMENT
  compensation, *see* COMPENSATION
  trading receipts, *see* TRADING RECEIPTS
Payment of tax
  account, on, calculation, 2A.17
  accounting for, 2A.18
  capital gains tax, 2A.14
  income tax, 2A.14
  self-assessment, under, 2A.17
  surcharges, 2A.44
  unpaid or overpaid tax, interest on, 2A.32–2A.43
  value added tax, 67.04–67.05
Penalties
  administrative fines, replacement of, 2A.95
  amount of, 2A.86
  corporation tax, 2A.91
  errors due to third parties, for, 2A.84
  errors on tax return, for, 2A.79–2A.83
  incorrect return or accounts, for, 2A.78, 2A.90
  inheritance tax, 2A.92
  late stamping, 2A.39
  national insurance, 2A.93, 51.10
  provision for, 2.27
  range, 2A.87
  stamp duty and stamp duty reserve tax, 2A.95
    administrative offences, 2A.95, 56.32
  stamp duty land tax, 2A.96
  suspension, 2A.88
  tax credits, 2A.94
  under-assessment, in case of, 2A.85
  unified regime, 2A.78
  value added tax, *see* VALUE ADDED TAX
Pensions
  additional voluntary contributions, 32.30
  alternatively secured, 32.36
  approved occupational schemes—
    approval, new code of, 32.08
    conditions for approval pre 6 April 2006, 32.11
    discretionary approval—
      pre 6 April 2006, 32.13
      subject to FA 1989 changes, 32.15
      subject to F(No 2)A 1987 changes, 32.14
    employee's contributions, 32.23
    employer's contributions, 32.22

Index

Pensions – *cont.*
  approved occupational schemes— – *cont.*
    exempt, 32.08
      pre 6 April 2006, 32.18
    fund, taxation of, 32.24
    mandatory approval pre 6 April 2006, 32.12
    non-approval or non-registration, consequences of, 32.10
    registered schemes, 32.16
    retirement benefits scheme, meaning, 32.09
    small self-administered schemes, 32.17
  available schemes, 32.07
  commissions, cashbacks and discounts, 8.170
  death, transfer of remaining fund on, 40.36
  divorce, sharing on, 32.02
  earlier developments, 32.03–32.06
  early leaver's disability, 32.05
  Employer Financed Retirement Benefits Schemes, 32.21
  equality of treatment, 32.29
  funded unapproved scheme under trust (FURBS), 32.20
  income, definition, 5.23
  individual pension accounts¾
    units and shares in, stamp duty reserve tax exemption, 59.21
  meaning, 32.25
  money purchase, 32.31
  personal, 32.32
    contracting out of S2P, 32.33
    secured and unsecured income, 32.35
  preservation of, 32.04
  registered schemes, 32.16
    secured and unsecured income, 32.35
    unauthorised payments, 32.42
  retirement age, 32.34
  stakeholder, 32.01
  state earnings related pensions scheme, 32.06
  state scheme, increasing cost of, 32.06
  surpluses, correction of, 32.28
  taxation of benefits—
    generally, 32.25
    lump sums, 32.26
    refunds, 32.27
    special commutation payments, 32.27
  transitional protection—
    enhanced, 32.39
    options for, 32.37
    primary, 32.38
    registration, 32.41

Pensions – *cont.*
  transitional protection— – *cont.*
    tax-free lump sums, rights to, 32.40
  unapproved schemes, 32.19
  unregistered schemes, 32.19
Personal activities
  sale by individual of income derived from, 4.30–4.31
Personal expenditure
  expenses, as, 8.102
Personal grounds
  gift on, payment for services distinguished from, 7.25
Personal reliefs, *see* INCOME TAX
Personal representative
  death, income arising after, 14.02
  disposals in course of administration, capital gains tax—
    assessment, 19.10
    beneficiaries, transfer to, 19.12
    chargeable gain, calculation of, 19.10, 19.11
  duties of, 14.10
  dwelling house, sale of, 23.15
  inheritance tax, 46.14
  residence of, 33.42
  trade, sale of, 8.28–8.30
  transfer to, 19.09
Petrol
  employee earning £8,500 or more, 7.118
  ties, capital expenditure, 8.130
  value added tax, 65.27
Place of trade
  foreign income, 35.02–35.04
  foreign taxpayer, 36.03–36.06
Planning, *see* TAX PLANNING
Plant and machinery
  capital allowances—
    annual investment allowance, 9.36
    apparatus, 9.30
    backdating claims, 9.24
    balancing charge, anti-avoidance, 9.41
    building—
      apparatus distinguished, 9.30
      exclusion of expenditure on provision of, 9.28
    computer software, 9.27
    discs, 9.54
    disposal value, 9.40
    employee, for, 9.51
    films, 9.54
    first year, 9.32
      energy efficient plant and machinery, for, 9.33

Index

Plant and machinery – *cont.*
  capital allowances— – *cont.*
    first year, 9.32 – *cont.*
      environmentally beneficial plant and machinery, for, 9.34
    first year tax credits, 9.35
    generally, 9.23
    hire purchase, 9.45
    integral features, 9.31
    leasing—
      aircraft, 9.53
      assets leased overseas, 9.52
      generally, 9.46
      lessee's expenditure, 9.49
      motor vehicles, 9.50
      operating lease and finance lease distinguished, 9.47
      restrictions, 9.48
      ships, 9.53
    long life assets, 9.43
    non-pooling option, 9.42
    ownership of asset, 9.25
    ships, 9.44
    short life assets, 9.42
    small pools allowance, 9.39
    special rate expenditure, 9.38
    structure, definition, 9.28
    tapes, 9.54
    writing down, 9.37
  meaning, 9.26
  plant, meaning, 9.29
  purchase of, interest relief, 6.41
  setting—
    case law principles, 9.29–9.30
    statutory prescription, 9.28

Political party
  gift to, inheritance tax, 43.18

Pooling, *see* CAPITAL GAINS TAX

Postal services
  value added tax, 68.14

Power, *see* FUEL AND POWER

Power to tax
  European Community, 1.01–1.07
  generally, 1.01
  planning, *see* TAX PLANNING

Premiums
  definition, 23.23
  income, as—
    anti-avoidance provisions—
      assignment of lease granted at undervalue, 10.23
      commutation of rent, 10.21
      improvements, 10.20
      sale with right of reconveyance, 10.24

Premiums – *cont.*
  income, as— – *cont.*
    anti-avoidance provisions— – *cont.*
      surrender of lease, 10.21
      variations, 10.22
      waivers, 10.22
    franking on sublease, 10.25
    generally, 10.16
    interaction with trading income, 10.27
    lease, duration of, 10.18
    reduction, 10.19
    set off against rent, 10.26
    taxation, 10.19
  meaning, 10.17
  reverse, 8.135, 23.26
  stamp duty, *see* STAMP DUTY

Profession or vocation
  basis of assessment, *see* TRADES, PROFESSIONS AND VOCATIONS, INCOME FROM
  expenses, *see* EXPENSES
  income from, *see* TRADES, PROFESSIONS AND VOCATIONS, INCOME FROM
  meaning, 8.07
  partnership, *see* PARTNERSHIP
  trade distinguished from, 8.08
  trading income, former distinction, 8.01

Professional bodies
  value added tax, 68.25

Professional services
  input tax, attribution of, 66.12

Profit-sharing schemes
  approved, 7.78

Profits
  annual, 12.03
  division of, 8.106–8.109
  earning—
    expense of, 8.106–8.109
    purpose of, 8.104–8.105
  foreign taxpayer, of, *see* NON-RESIDENT
  profit-sharing schemes, *see* PROFIT-SHARING SCHEMES

Property
  agricultural, *see* AGRICULTURAL PROPERTY
  business, *see* BUSINESS
  excluded, meaning, 38.21
  management companies, taxation of, 2A.06
  settled, *see* SETTLED PROPERTY
  stamp duty, *see* STAMP DUTY
  tangible movable, capital gains tax, exemption from, 17.18
  trader, of, trading receipts, 8.90

Property – *cont.*
  transfer of value, *see* INHERITANCE TAX
Property income
  basis of charge, 10.02
  business, 10.09
  calculation of, 10.08–10.09
  capital expenditure on energy saving items, deduction for, 10.10
  charge to tax, 10.02
  computation, rules for, 10.02
  former Schedule A, 5.08
  former Schedule D Case VI, analogy, 12.11
  exclusions from charge, 10.05
  furnished lettings, 10.13
    holidays, 10.15
    rent a room, 10.14
  interest, calculation of, 10.11
  loss relief, 6.32
  non-resident landlord, payments to, 10.12
  overseas property, from, 35.07
  partnership issues, 10.09
  premiums, *see* PREMIUMS
  rent, meaning, 10.04
  scope of, 5.08
  tax on, 10.06
  trading income, borderline with, 10.07
  trading partnership, of, 10.09
Prosecution
  Assets Recovery Agency, by, 2.36
  HM Revenue and Customs Prosecution Office, 2.05
  serious fraud, procedures in, 2.32-2.33
  Scotland, in, 2.35
  VAT offences, 2.34–2.35
Protective trust
  special treatment, 42.57
Public benefit
  property given for, inheritance tax, 43.19
Public purposes
  gifts for, 43.14–43.19
Purchased annuities, *see* ANNUITIES
Qualifying corporate bonds
  capital gains tax, exemption from, 17.12
Rates of tax
  capital gains tax, 16.40
  inheritance tax, 38.13
  stamp duty—
    ad valorem, 56.03
    fixed, 56.04
  trustees¾
    dividends, 13.12
    effect of, 13.12
    first £1,000 of income, 13.10
    income in excess of £1,000, 13.11

Reconstruction, *see* COMPANY
Registered social landlord
  transfers to, stamp duty exemption, 56.38
Registration for VAT, *see* VALUE ADDED TAX
Relief
  agricultural, 43.33
  business, 43.33
  charity, *see* CHARITY
  double taxation, *see* DOUBLE TAXATION RELIEF
  interest, *see* INTEREST
  investment—
    enterprise investment scheme, 31.06–31.15
  loss, *see* INCOME TAX
  personal, *see* INCOME TAX
  quick succession, 40.29
Renewals
  capital expenditure, 8.123
Rent
  income tax, *see* PROPERTY INCOME
  meaning, 10.04
  spare rooms, for, 10.14
  stamp duty, *see* STAMP DUTY
  trading stock, 8.165
Reorganisation
  capital gains tax, *see* CAPITAL GAINS TAX
Repairs
  capital expenditure, 8.122–8.125
  initial, 8.124–8.125
Repayment
  settlor, to, 15.24
  stamp duty reserve tax, of, 61.21–61.22
  value added tax, 66.36–66.38
Representative, *see* PERSONAL REPRESENTATIVE
Research and development
  enhanced allowance for, 8.140
  scientific, capital allowances, 9.62
Reserve tax, *see* STAMP DUTY RESERVE TAX
Residence
  corporation, of—
    certification of, 33.35
    change of, 25.46, 33.36
    common law test, 33.25-33.28
    dual, 33.26–33.28
    dual resident investing, 33.31
    ordinary residence, 33.32
    relevant control, 33.29
    statutory test, 33.30
    tax presence, 33.34
  dependent relative, of, 23.12

Index

Residence – *cont.*
 double taxation relief, 37.11
 individual, of—
  accompanying spouse or civil partner, of, 33.13
  actual residence, 33.04
  available accommodation, 33.08
  change during tax year, 33.10–33.11
  coming to UK, 33.07
  days of arrival and departure, 33.09
  extended presence as residence, 33.04
  generally, 33.02–33.03
  giving up residence, 33.11–33.12
  habitual and substantial visits, 33.05–33.06
  return visits, 33.12
  working abroad, 33.11
 national insurance, for, 54.02, 54.04
 only or main—
  apportionment, 23.08–23.11
  deemed residence, periods of, 23.10
  election for, 23.11
  generally, 23.06
  grounds, 23.07
  holdover relief, effect of claim for, 23.16-23.17
  letting, period of, 23.09
 ordinary, 33.14
 personal representatives, of, 33.42
 trading partnership, of, 33.38
 trustee, of, 33.34, 33.40
Residuary beneficiary, *see* BENEFICIARY
Restrictive covenant
 advantage, surrender of, 7.29
Retail schemes, *see* VALUE ADDED TAX
Retirement
 benefits scheme, *see* PENSIONS
 income, 5.34
 trading stock, disposal of, 8.32–8.34
Revocable settlement, *see* SETTLEMENT
Sale
 leaseback, and, *see* LEASE
Sanitary products
 value added tax, 70.07
Savings
 friendly societies, 31.05
 income, *see* SAVINGS INCOME
 individual savings account, *see* INDIVIDUAL SAVINGS ACCOUNT
 life assurance, *see* LIFE ASSURANCE
 national, 31.04
 pensions, *see* PENSIONS
 purchased annuities, *see* ANNUITIES
 savings-related share option schemes, 7.79

Savings income
 lower rate, taxed at, 5.26
 meaning, 5.27
 remittance basis, taxed on, 5.28
 annual payments—
  exclusion of deduction of, 11.03
  other, *see* OTHER ANNUAL PAYMENT, *below*
 annuity—
  advances, and, 11.21
  generally, 11.20
 deduction at source, 11.36–11.41
 discounts—
  deeply discounted securities—
   definition, 11.18
   gilt strips, removal from definition, 11.19
   transfer or redemption of, 11.17
  generally, 11.15–11.16
 generally, 11.01–11.03
 income received by non-resident, exclusion of, 11.02
 interest—
  accrued, 11.07–11.11
  Accrued Income Scheme, 11.08–11.10
  damages, and, 11.06
  death, charge at, 11.10
  generally, 11.05–11.06, 11.14
  meaning, 11.05
  relevant deposits, on, 11.13
  yearly, 11.12-11.14
 loss relief, 6.33
 maintenance payments, *see* MAINTENANCE PAYMENTS
 other annual payment—
  capital or income, 11.28–11.31
  generally, 11.22
  income of payee, 11.29
  obligation, 11.23
  principles, 11.32–11.35
  profession, receipt of, 11.27
  pure income profit, 11.25–11.28
  recurrence, 11.24
 payments free of tax—
  court orders, construction of, 11.44
  rule in *Re Pettit*, 11.43
  validity of agreements, 11.42
 payments within scheme—
  failure to deduct—
   parties inter se, 11.41
   Revenue and parties, 11.40
  generally, 11.36
  payer, 11.38
  permanent health insurance, for, 11.04
  tax deducted, 11.39

Savings income – *cont.*
  qualifying maintenance payments, 11.03
  corporation tax property rules, 10.01
  former charge, 5.08
Schedule D
  Case VI, former charge under, 12.02
  former charge, 5.10
Schedule F
  former charge under, 5.12
  loss relief, 6.33
Scholarships
  benefit in kind, as, 7.120
  director, 7.120
  employee earning £8,500 or more, 7.120
Scotland
  tax law, application of, 1.28
Seamen
  duties performed overseas, 7.05
Securities
  capital gains tax, *see* CAPITAL GAINS TAX
  charity, gifts to, 6.38
  conversion of, 21.19
  employees, given to—
    acquisition, notional loan on, 7.62
    convertible, 7.61
    employment, by reason of, 7.56
    general principles, 7.54
    market value, 7.57
    meaning, 7.55
    options, 7.58
    PAYE, within scope of, 7.63
    restricted, 7.59-7.60
  exchange of, 21.20–21.23
  location of, 47.05
  meaning, 4.21
  quoted, valuation of, 17.26
  deeply discounted—
    definition, 11.18
    gilt strips, removal from treatment, 11.19
    transfer or redemption of, 11.17
  transactions in, cancellation of tax advantages—
    defences, 4.28–4.29
    five sets of circumstances, 4.22–4.27
    generally, 4.18
    securities, meaning, 4.21
    tax advantage, meaning, 4.19
    transaction, meaning, 4.20
  unquoted valuation of, 17.27
Security
  commissioners' power to call for, 67.09

Security goods
  value added tax, 70.06
Self-assessment
  amendment of return by taxpayer, 2A.68
  appeals, 2A.51
  balancing payment, 2A.14–2A.16
  capital gains, reporting, 2A.03
    estimate, 2A.04
  company profits, reporting, 2A.06
  discrepancies, 2A.61
  enquiries, 2A.48-2A.52
  generally, 2A.01
  group relief, 28.07
  income and gains, reporting, 2A.02
  NIC liabilities, 2A.10
  notices requiring documents, 2A.50
  PAYE, and, 7.150
  PAYE underpayments, 2A.15
  purpose, 2A.47
  rectification, 2A.71
  relief for overpaid tax—
    restitution, 2A.70
    statutory, 2A.69
  taxpayer notice, interaction with, 2A.55
Self-employed person
  IR35 rules, 7.09, 8.26
Services
  past, emoluments, as, 7.20
  payment for, gift on personal grounds distinguished from, 7.25
  reward for, surrender of advantage, 7.28
  supplies of, *see* VALUE ADDED TAX
Settled property
  capital gains tax, *see* CAPITAL GAINS TAX
  foreign, 47.13–47.16
  inheritance tax, *see* INHERITANCE TAX
Settlement
  accumulation and maintenance, 15.22, 42.49–42.52
  beneficiary's interest, sale of, 20.22
  bounty, element of, 15.05
  charge—
    income arising, on—
      inter-spousal gifts, 15.15
      meaning, 15.09
      parental settlement on unmarried minor children, 15.21–15.22
      settlor retaining interest in settled property, 15.10–15.20
    undistributed income, on—
      capital sums paid to settlor—
        charge, 15.25–15.29
        generally, 15.23
        loans, 15.24

Index

Settlement – *cont.*
  charge— – *cont.*
    undistributed income, on— – *cont.*
      capital sums paid to settlor— – *cont.*
        repayments, 15.24
  covenants, *see* COVENANT
  discretionary trust, *see* DISCRETIONARY TRUST
  income, of¾
    covenant, by, 15.30
    spouse or civil partner, diversion to, 15.30-15.31
  inheritance tax, *see* INHERITANCE TAX
  meaning, 15.02, 42.02
  property comprised in, determining, 15.06
  settlor—
    capital sums paid to, 15.23-15.29
    identification of, 20.03
    interest retained by, 13.14
      any circumstances, in, 15.13-15.14
      avoidance of charge, 20.04
      cases on, 15.03-15.06
      chargeable gains, 20.02
      charging provision, 15.10
      effect of charge, 15.20
      generally, 15.01
      inter-spousal gifts, 15.15
      permitted interests, 15.16
      purpose of provisions, 15.01
      rates of tax, 15.19
      revocable, 15.11-15.12
    meaning, 15.07, 42.04
    more than one person as, 15.08
  transfer into, 20.10
  see also TRUST
Settlor, *see* SETTLEMENT; TRUST
Sewerage services
  value added tax, 69.14
Share incentive schemes, *see also* EMPLOYEE SHARE SCHEMES
  company, taxation of, 7.75
  conditional acquisition, 7.69
  convertible shares, charge on conversion, 7.70
  Employee Share Ownership Plans, 7.95-7.96
  Share Incentive Plan—
    capital gains tax treatment, 7.91
    cash dividends, reinvestment of, 7.90
    costs, deduction of, 7.94, 25.06
    free share plan, 7.89
    introduction of, 7.88
    matching shares, 7.93
    partnership share plan, 7.92
    generally, 7.68

Share incentive schemes, *see also* EMPLOYEE SHARE SCHEMES – *cont.*
  growth in value charge, 7.71
  shares acquired by reason of employment, charges, 7.72-7.74
Share option schemes
  company, 7.81
  discretionary, 7.80
  double tax relief, 37.32
  employee, 18.28-18.29
  enterprise management incentives—
    application of scheme, 7.83
    disqualifying events, 7.86
    eligible employees, 7.84
    income tax treatment, 7.85
    main features, 7.82
    purpose of, 7.83
    rules applying to, 7.87
  history, 7.64
  internationally mobile employees, for, 7.76
  options to acquire shares, 7.65-7.66
  planning, 7.67
  savings-related, 7.79
Share purchase scheme
  director, 7.114
  employee earning £8,500 or more, 7.114
Shares
  anti-avoidance legislation—
    bond washing, 4.09
    dividend stripping, 4.08, 4.14
    generally, 4.07
    manufactured dividends, 4.15-4.17
    repo transactions, 4.09
    right to dividends, sale of, 4.08
    sale and repurchase, 4.07-4.10
    value of holding, reduction of, 4.14
  building societies, in, 21.27
  bonus issues, 21.13
  calls on, 24.08
  charity, gift to, 6.38
  dividend¾
    ECJ, cases in, 1.16-1.18
    foreign, 35.08
    inbound, 1.18
    outbound, 1.17
    trust, received by, 13.12
  employee schemes, *see* EMPLOYEE SHARE SCHEMES
  identification, *see* CAPITAL GAINS TAX
  incentive schemes, *see* SHARE INCENTIVE SCHEMES
  lifetime transfer, 40.19
  location of, 47.05
  option schemes, *see* SHARE OPTION SCHEMES

Index

Shares – *cont.*
  paired, stamp duty on, 59.13
  pooling, *see* CAPITAL GAINS TAX
  purchase of own—
    corporate shareholder, position of, 26.30
    disposal, treated as, 26.29
    liability to IHT, discharging, 26.28
    minimum holding requirements, 26.25
    provision for, 26.20
    purpose of, 26.23
    residence requirements, 26.24
    scheme or arrangement, as part of, 26.27
    trading company or holding company, by, 26.22
    unquoted company, by, 26.21
    vendor's interest in company, 26.26
  purchase scheme, *see* SHARE PURCHASE SCHEME
  rights issues, 21.14, 21.16
  small distributions, 21.17
  stamp duty, *see* STAMP DUTY
  treaty relief by credit, 37.20
  unquoted trading company, losses in, 6.34
  valuation, 45.11
Ship
  capital allowances, 9.44, 9.53
  leased on charter, 9.53
  stores for use in, value added tax, 69.05
  value added tax, 69.26
Shipping company
  liability to corporation tax, measurement by reference to tonnage, 25.16
Special trust, *see* DISCRETIONARY TRUST
Sporting achievement
  bonus distinguished from appreciation, 7.26
Sport and physical education
  value added tax, 68.26
Spouses and civil partners
  capital gains tax—
    dwelling house, transfer between, 23.14
    joint property, 16.42
    matrimonial home, transfer after separation, 16.44
    separate computation, 16.41
    separate taxation, 16.41
    transfers between spouses and civil partners, 16.43, 16.44, 21.04
  death transfer, *see* INHERITANCE TAX
  discretionary trust, 42.47
  income from property derived from other spouse or civil partner, 6.03
  inheritance tax, effect of transfers, 41.12
  maintenance, disposition for, 39.15

Spouses and civil partners – *cont.*
  property jointly owned by, 6.02
  settlor, spouse or civil partner of, 15.15
  transfers between¾
    both spouses and civil partners domiciled within UK, 43.06
    conditions, 43.07-43.09
    spouse and civil partner, meaning, 43.13
    spouses and civil partners with separate domiciles, 43.10-43.12
Stamp duty
  abolished heads of charge, 57.42
  action for recovery of, 56.31
  administration—
    adjudication—
      appeals following, 56.26
      generally, 56.21
      judicial review, 56.26
      limits of, 56.22
      stamp, 56.21
    appeals following adjudication, 56.26
    denoting stamp, 56.23
    generally, 56.07
    lost or spoiled instruments, 56.28
    produced stamp, 56.24
    spoiled stamps, 56.28
    stamping, methods of, 56.20
  basic principles, 56.09
  building plot, conveyance and lease of, 58.04
  business, sale of, 58.01
  consideration—
    unascertainable, 56.19
    uncertain value, of, 56.18
  contingency principle, 56.18–56.19
  conveyance on sale duty, relief from—
    associated bodies corporate, transfers between—
      associate status, 60.02
      beneficial interest, transfer of, 60.03
      conditions, 60.02–60.03
      exemption, 60.01
      restriction of relief, 60.04
      withdrawal of relief, 60.05
    company reconstructions, on—
      acquisition reliefs—
        further relief provisions, 60.08
        schemes of reconstruction, 60.06
        target company's share capital, 60.07
      procedure, 60.09
    property subject to debt, 57.11
  delivery of documents for stamping, 2A.12
  documents stamped according to legal effect, 56.10

Index

Stamp duty – *cont.*
　duties on documents, as, 56.09
　exemptions—
　　charities, 56.37
　　Crown documents, 56.36
　　Finance and other Acts and Orders, under, 56.35
　　general, 56.34
　　government documents, 56.36
　　instruments, 56.05–56.06
　　intellectual property, transfers relating to, 58.16
　　registered social landlords, transfers to, 56.38
　failure to stamp, consequences of, 2A.74
　form, 56.02
　futures markets, 60.15
　general background, 56.01–56.06
　heads of charge—
　　bearer instruments, 57.34, 59.08–59.11
　　　See also BEARER INSTRUMENT
　　bills of sale, 57.34
　　bonds, 57.35
　　conveyance or transfer on sale—
　　　agreements for sale, 57.18
　　　agreements to surrender lease, 57.23
　　　certificate of value, 57.15–57.16, 57.21
　　　consideration—
　　　　apportionment, 57.12
　　　　discharge of debts and liabilities as, 57.11
　　　　generally, 57.08
　　　　periodical payments as, 57.10
　　　　value added tax, 57.09
　　　conveyance or transfer in contemplation of sale, 57.17
　　　exchanges deemed to be sales, 57.19–57.22
　　　instrument, 57.05
　　　on sale, 57.07
　　　property, meaning, 57.06
　　　property subject to debt, 57.11
　　　rates of duty, 57.02–57.03
　　　sale of annuity, 57.14
　　　sub-sales, 57.13, 57.22
　　　threshold, 57.03, 57.21
　　　transactions structured as sales, 57.20
　　　transfer, meaning, 57.04
　　counterpart, 57.37
　　covenants, 57.35
　　declaration of trust, 57.36
　　duplicate, 57.37
　　exchange, 57.19
　　generally, 57.01

Stamp duty – *cont.*
　heads of charge— – *cont.*
　　lease or tack—
　　　charge, 57.25
　　　lease—
　　　　agreement for, 57.30
　　　　charge, 57.25
　　　　duration, 57.26
　　　　premium, duty on, 57.29
　　　　rent—
　　　　　duty on, 57.27
　　　　　generally, 57.28
　　　　rent to mortgages scheme, 57.3
　　　　shared ownership leases, 57.32
　　　miscellaneous fixed transfer duty, 57.24
　　　overlapping, 56.12
　　　partition, 57.38
　　　release, 57.40
　　　renunciation, 57.40
　　　surrender, 57.41
　　　unit trust, 57.39
　instruments—
　　administrative offences, penalties for, 56.32
　　exemptions, 56.05–56.06, 56.25
　　lost or spoiled, 56.28
　　not properly stamped—
　　　admissibility, 56.29
　　　fines, replacement of, 56.32
　　　generally, 56.33
　　　interest, 2A.39
　　　money received and not appropriated, 56.31
　　　penalties for late stamping, 2A.39
　intestacy, 58.13–58.14
　land—
　　covenant to improve property, 58.03
　　distributions, 58.08
　　leases, 58.05
　　revocation, 58.09
　　sale of, 58.02
　land tax, *see* STAMP DUTY LAND TAX
　leading and principal object, 56.13–56.17
　marriage, transfer of property on break-up of, 58.15
　open-ended investment companies, 59.20
　paired shares, 59.13
　payment of, 2A.28
　penalties, 2A.95–2A.96
　potential abolition, 57.43
　rates of—
　　ad valorem, 56.03
　　fixed, 56.04

2738

Index

Stamp duty – *cont.*
  reliefs—
    clearing houses, transfer to, 60.13
    composition agreements, 60.12
    depositary receipts, 60.14
    insurance companies, demutualisation, 60.16
    intermediaries, sale to, 60.10
    repurchases, 60.11
    stock lending, 60.11
  rent to mortgages scheme, 57.31
  reserve tax, *see* STAMP DUTY RESERVE TAX
  self-assessment, 2A.01
  share transactions—
    company formation, 59.01
    issue of shares—
      cash, for, 59.01
      consideration other than cash, for, 59.02
    loan capital, transfer of, 59.05
    other issues, 59.03
    purchase by company of own shares, 59.06
    transfer of shares, 59.04
  stamp—
    adjudication, 56.21
    denoting, 56.23
    produced, 56.24
      exempt instruments, 56.25
    spoiled, 56.28
  stamping, methods of, 56.20
  territorial limits, 56.08
  time of execution governs, 56.11
  trust—
    assignment of interests under, 58.10
    declaration of, 58.06
    instrument creating, 58.12
    trustee, change of, 58.07
    variation of, 58.11–58.12
  unit trust, 57.39, 59.14–59.19
  variation, deed of, 58.14
  will, 58.13–58.14

Stamp duty land tax
  amount chargeable, as percentage of consideration, as, 62.09
  anti-avoidance, 62.34, 62.35
  compliance, 62.26
  connected company, purchase of chargeable interest from, 62.08
  documents and information, power of HM Revenue and Customs to call for, 2.29, 2A.76
  fraudulent evasion of, 2.29, 2A.110

Stamp duty land tax – *cont.*
  land transactions, on, 62.02-62.03
    certificates, 62.24
    chargeable consideration, 62.05-62.09
    contract for, 62.04
    exchanges, 62.31
    open-ended investment companies, of, 62.28
    options, 62.32
    partnership, by, 62.27
    registration, 62.24
    sub-sales, 62.30
    trusts, by, 62.29
    unit trust schemes, of, 62.28
  late payment, interest on, 2A.41
  lease, on¾
    agreement for, 62.10
    charge of, 62.10
    rent, consideration as, 62.11
    sale and leaseback, 62.12
    surrender and regrant, 62.12
    term of, 62.11
  legislation, 62.01
  liability to, 62.25
  notifiable transactions, 62.23
  offences, 62.26
  partnership, transactions by, 62.27
  payment, 2A.30, 62.25
  penalties, 2A.96
  reliefs¾
    acquisition, 62.19
      charities, by, 62.22
      not withdrawn, 62.21
      withdrawal, 62.20
    disadvantaged areas, for, 62.14
    group, 62.15
      clawback, 62.17
      restriction on, 62.16
      withdrawal, 62.17
    list of, 62.13
    reconstruction, 62.18
      not withdrawn, 62.21
      withdrawal, 62.20
  returns, 62.23
  scope of charge, 62.02-62.04
  stamp duty on land, replacing, 62.01
  sub-sales, on, 62.30
  transitional provisions, 62.33
  VAT, treatment of, 62.10

Stamp duty reserve tax
  accountability, 61.18
    relief from, 61.19
  administration, 61.01, 61.20
    information, power to require, 61.25

Index

Stamp duty reserve tax – *cont.*
  administration, 61.01, 61.20 – *cont.*
    notice of determination, 61.27
    records, inspection of, 61.26
    service of documents, 61.28
  cancellation, 61.21
  charge to, 61.01
    agreement to transfer chargeable securities, 61.02
    execution and stamping not cancelling, 61.24
    sub-sales, 61.03
  chargeable securities, 61.05
  clearance services, 61.04
  depositary receipts, 61.04
  determinations—
    appeals, 61.29
    notice of, 61.21
  exceptions—
    authorised unit trusts, mergers of, 61.09
    bearer instruments, 61.13
    charities and institutions, 61.12
    general, 61.14
    higher rate charge, from, 61.15
    Individual Pension Accounts, unit trusts and shares held in, 59.21
    intermediaries, 61.06
    open-ended investment companies, 61.10
    public issues, 61.11
    repurchases, 61.07
    stock lending, 61.07
    unit trusts, 61.08
  higher rate charge, 61.04
    exceptions, 61.15
  incidence of liability, 61.16
  late payment, interest on, 2A.40
  overpayments, 61.30
  payment, 61.20
  penalties, 2A.95
  purchase with loan transactions, 61.23
  recovery of, 2A.75, 61.31
  repayment, 61.21
    interest, exemption from income tax, 61.22
  sub-sales, 61.03
  surrender of units, on, 59.16
  time for payment, 2A.29
  underpayments, 61.30
Stationery
  value added tax, 65.33
Statutes
  interpretation of, 1.23–1.27
  Scotland and Northern Ireland, application in, 1.28

Stock dividends
  corporation tax, 26.18–26.19
Stocks, *see* SHARES
Stores
  aircraft, for use in, 69.05
  hovercraft, for use in, 69.05
  ships, for use in, 69.05
Subcontractors
  tax deduction scheme, 2A.19
Subscriptions
  professional, 7.143
Subsidies
  trading receipts, 8.89
Succession
  business property, transfer of, 44.06
  capital allowances, 9.10
  trade, to—
    generally, 8.54
    new trader, effects on, 8.55
    old trader, effects on, 8.56
    part of trade, to, 8.58
    rules to determine, 8.55–8.60
Supplies, *see* VALUE ADDED TAX
Survivorship clauses
  inheritance tax, 42.11
Talking books
  value added tax, 69.16
Tangible movable property
  capital gains tax, exemption from, 17.18
Taper relief, *see* CAPITAL GAINS TAX
Tapes
  capital allowances, 9.54
Tax advantage
  cancellation of, *see* SECURITIES
Tax avoidance
  authority for decisions, 3.01
  Barclays Mercantile Business Finance case, 3.01, 3.02
  Burmah Oil case, 3.16
  Campbell v IRC, 3.01
  capital allowances, 3.02, 9.09
  capital gains tax, 17.17, 17.20–17.21
  company reconstructions and amalgamations, 21.25
  Craven v White, 3.18
  current cases, 3.24–3.26
  DLT fragmentation scheme, 3.18
  Ensign Tankers case, 3.19
  evasion distinguished from, 2.25, 3.10
  Fitzwilliam case, 3.20
  Furniss v Dawson, 3.17
  generally, 3.10–3.21
  Hong Kong case, 3.26
  improvements, 10.20

Index

Tax avoidance – *cont.*
  interpretation, 1.25
  land, artificial transactions in, *see* LAND
  lease—
    granted at undervalue, assignment of, 10.23
    sale with right of reconveyance, 10.24
    surrender of, 10.21
    variations, 10.22
    waivers, 10.22
  legislation—
    artificial transactions in land, *see* LAND
    bond-washing, 4.09
    cancellation of tax advantages, transactions in securities, *see* SECURITIES
    generally, 4.01–4.06
    manufactured dividends, 4.15–4.17
    personal activities, sale by individual of income derived from, 4.30–4.31
    shares, specific provisions relating to, *see* SHARES
  loan relationships, 3.03
  McGuckian case, 3.21
  MacNiven case, 3.04-3.05
    principle, application of, 3.06-3.09
  mitigation, and, 3.11
  new approach—
    authority for, 3.22
    cases, 3.15–3.21
    conclusions, 3.23
    inheritance tax cases, 39.35–39.39
    statutory construction, 3.21-3.22
  Ramsay principle, 3.15, 3.16
  rent, commutation of, 10.21
  Revenue defeats, 3.25
  Revenue victories, 3.24
  schemes—
    disclosure, 55.04–55.07
    penalties, 55.07
    reference numbers, 55.06
    reporting, 2A.05-2A.06
    tests and hallmarks, 55.05
  Scottish Provident, 3.01, 3.03
  settlement, *see* SETTLEMENT
  sham transactions, 3.14
  stamp duty land tax—
    general rule for, 62.34
    schemes, disclosure of, 62.35
  tax arbitrage, 35.74
  tax mitigation, distinguished from, 3.11
  Westminster doctrine, 3.12–3.14
  whole, treatment of scheme as, 3.20
Tax credits
  administration, 6.51

Tax credits – *cont.*
  appeals, 2.13
  award notice, 2A.11
  benefits, integrating, 6.51
  calculating, 6.52
  claiming, 2A.11
  enquiries, 2A.48-2A.52
  income, calculating, 6.54
  overpaid, interest on, 2A.38
  payment of, 2A.27
  penalties, 2A.94
  qualifying conditions, 6.52
  unit of claim, 6.51
  working tax credit, 53.06
Tax evasion
  avoidance distinguished from, 2.25, 3.10
  powers as to, 2.25
Tax free shops
  value added tax, 69.38
Tax mitigation
  meaning, 3.11
  scheme, disclosure of, 4.32
Tax planning
  agricultural relief, 43.33
  Burmah Oil case, 3.16
  business relief, 43.33
  Craven v White, 3.18
  discretionary trust, 42.48
  double taxation relief, 37.37-37.43
  Furniss v Dawson, 3.17
  generally, 3.10
  Ramsay principle, 3.15, 3.16
  share option schemes, 7.67
  Westminster doctrine, 3.12–3.14
Tax returns
  duty to make, 2A.02
  equitable liability, 2A.77
  penalties, 2A.78–2A.84
  self-assessment, *see* SELF-ASSESSMENT
  value added tax, 67.01–67.03, 67.05
  verification, 2A..46-2A.52
Tax unit
  choice of, 6.01
Tax year
  meaning, 1.31
Taxpayer
  assessment by, 2A.01
  income and gains, reporting, 2A.02
Tenancy
  assured, dwelling house, of, 9.22
  Scottish agricultural, 44.25
Terminal markets
  value added tax, 69.04

Index

Territorial limits
  inheritance tax, 47.01
  stamp duty, 56.08
Timber, *see* WOODLANDS
Timing
  capital gains tax—
    consent order, under, 18.10
    contract—
      conditional, 18.09
      generally, 18.06
      unenforceable, 18.08
      whether made, 18.07, 18.11
    generally, 18.05
    loss or destruction, where, 18.12
  earnings basis—
    contingent liabilities, 8.148
    generally, 8.143
    liabilities, 8.147
    payment in advance, 8.145
    receipts in kind, 8.149–8.150
    relating forward, 8.145
  emoluments, 7.22
  income tax, 5.14–5.15
  inheritance tax, 39.05
Title
  preservation of, capital gains tax, 16.21
Trade
  adventure in nature of—
    charitable endeavour, and, 8.12
    example, 8.18
    profit, purpose of, 8.11, 8.12
    scope, 8.10
  badges of¾
    employment generated, 8.25
    frequency of transactions, 8.13
    income provided, 8.25
    intention to resell, 8.21-8.24
    list of, 8.10
    lots, breaking purchase into, 8.20
    manner of transaction, 8.17
    other activities of taxpayer, 8.15
    repeated actions, 8.13-8.14
    source of finance, 8.18
    subject matter, 8.16
    work done, 8.19
  basis of assessment, *see* TRADES, PROFESSIONS AND VOCATIONS, INCOME FROM
  charity carrying on, 13.22–13.24
  currency of accounts, 25.54
  earned income, 5.92
  expenses, *see* EXPENSES
  generally, 8.03–8.04
  illegal trading, 8.09

Trade – *cont.*
  income from, *see* TRADES, PROFESSIONS AND VOCATIONS, INCOME FROM
  intermediate company, establishment of, 8.26
  land, use of, 8.42
  liability, 8.05, 8.06
  liquidator, sales by, 8.31
  managed service company, 8.27
  meaning, 8.03
  mutual—
    generally, 8.35–8.39
    legislation, 8.40–8.41
  non-UK, transfer of, 25.49
  partnership, *see* PARTNERSHIP
  personal representative, sales by, 8.28–8.30
  profession distinguished from, 8.08
  profession or vocation, former distinction, 8.01
  profit, with view to, 6.26
  retirement, 8.32–8.34
  terminal losses, 6.22
  trading receipts, *see* TRADING RECEIPTS
  UK, transfer of, 25.48
  use of, 8.42
  who is trading, 8.05, 8.06
Trade union
  value added tax, 68.25
Trader
  property of, trading receipts, 8.90
  value added tax, *see* VALUE ADDED TAX
Trades, professions and vocations, income from
  basis of assessment—
    commencement of trade—
      generally, 8.49
      new trade or development of existing one, 8.50
    continuing business—
      cessation, 8.47
      change of accounting date, 8.45
      commencement, 8.44
      deemed overlap profit, 8.48
      generally, 8.43
      overlap profit relief, 8.46
    discontinuance—
      effects of, 8.53
      generally, 8.51–8.52
    succession—
      generally, 8.54
      new trader, effects on, 8.55
      old trader, effects on, 8.56
      part of trade, to, 8.58
      rules to determine, 8.57–8.60

Index

Trades, professions and vocations, income from – *cont.*
  conventional basis, accounts on, 8.70
  earnings basis—
    accounting policy, change of, 8.71–8.72
    changes to, 8.139
    computation, 8.139
    receipts after discontinuance, 8.142
    timing—
      contingent liabilities, 8.148
      contract, provisions of, 8.144
      debtor, default of, 8.146
      generally, 8.143
      liabilities, 8.147
      payment in advance, 8.145
      receipts in kind, 8.149–8.150
      relating forward, 8.145
  expenses, *see* EXPENSES
  measure of —
    accounting practice, 8.65–8.68
    generally, 8.64
  partnerships, *see* PARTNERSHIP
  premium, deduction of portion of, 10.27
  property income, borderline with, 10.07
  spreading adjustments—
    change from cash basis to earnings basis, 8.70
    change of accounting policy, 8.69, 8.71–8.72
  taxation, 5.10
Trading company
  losses on unquoted shares in, 6.34
Trading income
  individual, trade carried on by, 5.24
Trading losses
  capital gains, relief against, 6.17
  furnished holiday lettings, 6.27
  hobby farming, 6.29
  limited partnership, of, 6.18
  meaning, 6.25
  opening years, carry-back of losses in, 6.21
  partnership, 6.28
  profit, view to, 6.26
  rolling forward—
    business, incorporation of, 6.20
    generally, 6.19
  set off against general income, 6.16
  temporary extension, 6.16
  terminal losses, 6.22–6.24
Trading receipts
  annual payment, cannot be, 11.26
  business, 8.74
  business assets, 8.74
  cash, investment of, 8.79

Trading receipts – *cont.*
  compensation payments—
    agency contracts, 8.87–8.88
    business, contract relating to structure of, 8.85–8.86
  capital, as, 8.84
  contract—
    agency, 8.87–8.88
    structure of business, relating to, 8.85–8.86
    generally, 8.81–8.84
    subsidies, 8.89
  debt, release of, 8.93
  foreign currency, 8.78
  know-how, 8.76
  market value, 8.92
  mining, 8.171
  non-trade purposes, payment for, 8.75
  payment—
    falling under different heading, 8.91
    incidental—
      cash, investment of, 8.79
      foreign currency, 8.78
      generally, 8.76
      know-how, 8.76
      trading stock, contract for supply of, 8.77
    non-trade purposes, for, 8.75
  restriction of activities, 8.80
  subsidies, 8.89
  trader, property of, 8.90
  trading stock, *see* TRADING STOCK
Trading stock
  appropriation from trade, 22.07
  appropriation to trade, 22.06
  capital expenditure, 8.127–8.128
  charities, gift to, 8.158
  contract for supply of, 8.77
  end of year valuations—
    cost, 8.162
    formula applied, 8.164
    generally, 8.159–8.161
    market value, 8.163
  ground rents, 8.165
  land held as, artificial transactions, 23.33
  market value, substitution of—
    generally, 8.151
    limits of rule, 8.155–8.157
    Sharkey v Wernher, 8.154
    transfer-pricing, 8.152
    Watson Bros v Hornby, 8.153
  rentcharges, 8.165
  rules for, 22.05

2743

Index

Trading stock – *cont.*
  trading receipts—
    farm animals, 8.169
    generally, 8.74
  valuation, 8.168
  work in progress, 8.166–8.167
Transactions
  land, in, *see* LAND
  securities, in, *see* SECURITIES
Transfer of value, *see* INHERITANCE TAX
Transfer on sale
  stamp duty, *see* STAMP DUTY
Transfer pricing
  arm's length price, substitution of, 8.152
  balancing payments, 25.13
  compensating adjustments, 25.13
  connected persons not at arms' length, transactions between¾
    application of regime, 25.07
    medium-sized enterprise exemption, 25.11
    penalties, 25.12
    related parties, 25.08
    relevant transactions, 25.09
    small-sized enterprise exemption, 25.10
  returns, 25.13
  thin capitalisation, 25.14
Transport
  value added tax, 69.08, 69.26–69.30
Travelling expenses
  alternative explanation, 7.128
  cycle equipment, 7.131
  foreign, 7.133-7.134, 35.09
  generally, 7.124
  incidental overnight expenses, 7.130
  mileage allowances, 7.132
  parking spaces, 7.131
  performance of duties, travelling in, 7.125–7.128
    dual place of employment, 7.128
    personal qualifications of taxpayer, 7.127
    temporary workplace, to, 7.129
  public bus transport service, support for, 7.131
  wholly and exclusively incurred, 8.103
  works bus service, provision of, 7.131
Treaty relief, *see* DOUBLE TAXATION RELIEF
Trust
  allowable management expenses, 13.13
  bare—
    absolute entitlement, 20.07

Trust – *cont.*
  bare– – *cont.*
    co-owners, 20.09
    nature of, 20.06
    settled property distinguished, 20.08
  beneficial interest, disposal of, 35.60
  beneficiary—
    income accruing to, 13.09
    whether taxable—
      accumulations, 13.18–13.19
      generally, 13.15
      grossing up, 13.17
      no vested right in income, 13.18–13.19
      vested rights in income, 13.16
  capital as income, 13.21
  categories of, 42.05
  charities—
    gifts to, 15.17
    reliefs—
      generally, 13.22
      restriction of, 13.26, 13.27
    small receipts, 13.25
    trading income, 13.23–13.24
  declaration of, stamp duty, 57.36, 58.06
  disabled person, for, 13.05, 42.58
  discretionary, for disabled person, 42.58
  domicile, 33.41
  employee, 42.55
  entitlement, *see* INHERITANCE TAX
  generally, 13.01
  investment, 30.12
  loans, treatment of, 13.20
  newspaper, 42.55
  non-resident—
    settlor's right to reimbursement, 35.63
  overseas¾
    beneficial interests, disposal of, 35.60
    beneficiaries, capital gains charged on, 35.56, 35.58
    Revenue practice, 35.61
    transfer of value, 35.59
    trustees, CGT charge on, 35.55, 35.57
  protective, 42.57
  rates of tax¾
    dividends, 13.12
    effect of, 13.12
    first £1,000 of income, 13.10
    income in excess of £1,000, 13.11
  reverter to settlor, 12.23
  revocation, 58.09
  settlor-interested, 13.14
    rates of tax, 15.19 .

Trust – *cont.*
  special, *see* DISCRETIONARY TRUST
  specially favoured—
    accumulation and maintenance settlement, 42.49–42.52
    employee trusts, 42.55
    heritage property, funds for maintenance of, 42.56
    newspaper trusts, 42.55
    problems, 42.51–42.52
    protective trust, 42.57
    tapered charge, 42.53
    temporary charitable trust, 42.54
  stamp duty, *see* STAMP DUTY; STAMP DUTY LAND TAX
  trustee, *see* TRUSTEE
  unit, 30.13–30.17, 57.39, 59.14–59.19
  variation, 58.11–58.12
  vulnerable beneficiary, with¾
    capital gain, taxation of, 20.24
    disabled person, 13.05
    election for application of regime, 13.07, 20.23
    minor, 13.06
    new tax regime, 13.04, 20.23
  see also SETTLEMENT

Trustee
  annuity of, 42.21
  bare, 13.02-13.03
  capital gains tax, 20.01, 35.55, 35.57
    annual exempt amount, 20.01
    exemptions available, 20.14
    rate of tax on disposal, 20.01
  change of, stamp duty, 58.07
  domicile, 33.41
  dwelling house held by, 23.13
  foreign, 36.12
  income accruing to beneficiary, exception to liability, 13.09
  inheritance tax, 42.01, 46.11
  generally, 13.08
  life assurance policy held by, 31.26
  minor or incapacitated person, for, 13.02
  overseas—
    appointment of, 35.55
    overseas gains charged on, 35.57
  relevant property, charge to tax—
    exclusions, 42.32
    generally, 42.28
    meaning, 42.28
    other occasions of charge—
      before first ten year anniversary, 42.45
      between ten year anniversaries, 42.46
      ceasing to be relevant property, 42.41

Trustee – *cont.*
  relevant property, charge to tax— – *cont.*
    other occasions of charge— – *cont.*
      disposition by trustees, loss to trust—
        foreign element, 42.43
        generally, 42.42
        other exclusions, 42.44
      exit charge, 42.41
      initial interest of settlor or spouse, 42.47
      planning, 42.48
    qualifying interest in possession, 42.28
    principal occasion of charge—
      added property, 42.39–42.40
      property relevant property for only part of period, 42.38
      rate of tax on—
        trust created after 26 March 1974, 42.34–42.36
        trust created before 27 March 1974, 42.37
      ten year anniversary, 42.33
    settlement—
      commencement of, 42.31
      property moving between settlements, 42.30
      related, 42.29
  residence of, 33.39, 33.40
  taxation, recasting of regime, 13.01

Ultra vires
  decisions, challenging, 2.23

Unilateral tax credit, *see* DOUBLE TAXATION RELIEF

Unincorporated association
  taxation of, 2A.06

Unit trust
  authorised—
    capital gains tax computation, 30.17
    corporation tax, 25.03
    distribution of income, options, 30.16
    mergers, 59.19, 61.09
    taxation treatment, 30.15
  corporation tax rate, 30.15
  generally, 30.13
  land transactions, 62.27
  not authorised, treatment of, 30.14
  stamp duty, 57.39, 59.14–59.19
  surrender of units, stamp duty reserve tax on, 59.16
  taxation, 30.14–30.16

Used goods schemes, *see* VALUE ADDED TAX

Valuation
  inheritance tax, *see* INHERITANCE TAX
  trading stock, *see* TRADING STOCK

Index

Valuation – *cont.*
  value added tax, *see* VALUE ADDED TAX
Value added tax
  Account—
    correction of, 67.15
    requirement to keep, 67.02
    tax allowable portion, 67.02
    tax payable portion, 67.02
  acquisitions not charged to, 69.09
  administration, 2.04, 63.01
  annual accounting scheme, 63.44
  assessments, 2A.67
  assurance visits, 2A.53
  avoidance, 63.09
  bad debt relief—
    claiming, 66.30
    refund, entitlement to, 66.41
  business—
    activities amounting to carrying on of, 63.14
    activities not amounting to carrying on of, 63.17
    activities treated as, 63.16
    meaning, 63.15
    supplies in course or furtherance of, 63.31
  business entertainment, services used for, 65.24
  cash accounting scheme, 63.41
  charge to tax—
    EC acquisitions, on—
      excise duty, goods subject to, 65.48
      fiscal warehousing regime, goods subject to, 65.48
      generally, 63.34, 65.43
      liability to account, 65.44
      meaning of acquisition, 63.35
      non-taxable persons, 65.48
      output tax, 65.47
      place of acquisition, 63.37
      taxable persons, 65.47
      time of acquisition, 65.45
      value, 65.46
    goods imported from third countries—
      accounting and payment, 65.53
      charge to tax, 65.49
      delivered or removed without payment of duty, 63.40
      generally, 63.39
      payment, responsibility for, 65.50
      relief, 69.11
      time when arising, 65.51
      valuation of imported goods, 65.52

Value added tax – *cont.*
  charge to tax— – *cont.*
    reverse—
      aggregate value exceeding £1000, 65.41
      gas and electricity, cross-border distribution, 65.39
      gold, 65.40
      services received from abroad, 65.38
      specified goods, 65.41
    supplementary—
      amount of, 65.04
      introduction of, 65.02
      measures, 65.02
      payment, receipt of, 65.05
      right to goods or services, grant of, 65.03
      VAT invoice, issue of, 65.04
  supplies—
    abusive process, transactions constituting, 66.33
    consideration—
      general principles, 63.21
      quantum, 63.23
      time for ascertaining, 63.22
      unpaid, 66.31
      variation, 66.32
    course or furtherance of business, in, 63.31
    events treated as—
      another member state, goods removed to, 65.27
      building, change of use of, 65.35
      construction services, 65.34
      disposal of business assets, 65.28–65.29
      goods held at date of deregistration, 65.42
      group company, business transferred as going concern to, 64.29
      group supplies using overseas members, 64.28
      no consideration, made for, 65.28–65.31
      motor cars, 65.32
      self-supplies, 65.32–65.36
      services received from abroad, 65.38
      stationery, 65.33
      use of business assets, 65.29–65.30
      warehoused goods, services relating to, 65.36
    exempt, 63.33
    generally, 63.18, 63.19
    goods, of, 63.24, 63.25, 63.28

Index

Value added tax – *cont.*
  charge to tax— – *cont.*
    supplies— – *cont.*
      intra-group, disregard of, 64.27
      meaning, 63.19
      neither goods nor services, 63.27
      outside scope of VAT, 63.27
      place of, 63.30
      practical problems in identifying, 63.20
      services, of, 63.24, 63.26, 63.29–63.31
      taxable—
        supplies made in UK, 63.28–63.30
        supplies made in course or furtherance of business, 63.32
      UK, made in—
        goods, 63.28
        services, 63.29–63.31
  control, prosecution, 2.34–2.35
  credit—
    delayed payment, repayment supplement on, 67.06
    incorrectly paid, assessment of, 67.07
    payment of, 67.05
  credit note, right to issue, 65.19
  default surcharge, 2A.45, 67.08
  EC acquisitions, on—
    excise duty, goods subject to, 65.48
    fiscal warehousing regime, goods subject to, 65.48
    generally, 65.43
    liability for, 65.44
    meaning of acquisition, 63.35
    non-taxable, 65.48
    output tax, 65.47
    place of acquisition, 63.37
    taxable, 63.36
    time of acquisition, 65.45
    triangulation, 63.38
    value, 65.46
  electronic services, special accounting scheme for, 63.43, 67.14
  enforcement—
    default surcharge, 67.08
    security, 67.09
  errors, correction of—
    Account, correcting, 67.15
    credit for output tax not due, 67.16
    input tax unclaimed or understated, 67.18
    voluntary disclosure, 67.19
  European Union, territory of, 63.08
  evasion, 63.09

Value added tax – *cont.*
  exemption—
    betting, 68.15
    burial, 68.24
    consequences of, 68.01
    cremation, 68.24
    cultural services, 68.29
    education, 68.17–68.22
    election to waive—
      investment gold, 68.10
    examination services, 68.18
    finance, 68.16
    fund-raising events, 68.28
    gaming, 68.15
    health, 68.23
    input tax irrecoverable, where, 68.30
    insurance, 68.13
    investment gold, 68.31
      election to waive exemption, 68.10
    land, 68.03–68.12
    legislation, 68.02
    lotteries, 68.15
    nature of, 68.01
    postal services, 68.14
    private tuition, 68.19
    professional bodies, 68.25
    public interest bodies, 68.25
    real estate, 68.04
    research, 68.20
    sport and physical education, 68.26
    the option to tax, 68.03–68.10
    trade unions, 68.25
    vocational training, 68.21
    welfare, 68.23
    works of art, 68.27
    youth clubs, 68.22
  flat-rate scheme¾
    farmers, for, 63.44
    small businesses, for, 63.42, 65.21
    withdrawal from, 65.37
  goods sold under a power, accounting for, 67.11
  history of, 63.01
  imports, on, 63.39, 67.13
    goods delivered or removed without payment of duty, 63.40
    goods not charged—
      common provisions, application of, 69.10
      relief from payment, 69.11
  input tax—
    attribution of—
      capital items, 66.27
      de minimis provisions, 66.14-66.15

Index

Value added tax – *cont.*
  input tax— – *cont.*
    attribution of— – *cont.*
      different use, appropriation for, 66.26
      exempt supplies, 66.14-66.15
      generally, 66.07
      insurance and financial services, 66.11
      investment gold, supplies of, 66.12
      overseas supplies taxable if made in UK, 66.10
      professional services, supplies of, 66.13
      special method, 66.09
      standard method, 66.08
    credit—
      deduction of, 66.22
      exclusion from, 66.16-66.21
      luxury, amusement of entertainment, goods for, 66.29
      nature of, 66.06
      variation of deductions, 66.23-66.32
    definition, 66.02
    election to waive exemption, 66.28
    goods and services used for business, on, 66.05
    subsequent transfer, disposal or use of goods, 66.35
    tax excluded from credit—
      business entertainment, 66.20
      election to waive exemption, 66.28
      goods installed in buildings, 66.19
      margin scheme for goods, 65.23
      motor cars, 66.17-66.18
      works of art, antiques, collectors' items and secondhand goods, 66.21
    taxable person, incurred by, 66.04
    transactions on which chargeable, 66.03
    unclaimed or understated, 67.18
  legislation—
    EU directives, 63.02
    extra-statutory concessions, 63.04
    generally, 63.03
  liability for, 65.07
    joint and several, 67.10
  missing trader intra-Community fraud, 63.09
  non-taxable persons, acquisitions by, 67.12
  outline—
    credit mechanism, 63.07
    taxable transactions, 63.06
    taxation of value added, 63.05
  output tax—
    fuel for private use, 65.27
    gaming machines, 65.26

Value added tax – *cont.*
  output tax— – *cont.*
    generally, 65.07, 65.20
    retail schemes, 65.22
    tour operators, margin scheme for, 65.25
    used goods, margin scheme for, 65.23
  overpayment due to official error, interest on, 2A.43
  payment—
    duties of, 2A.31
    imported goods, 67.13
    tax returns, 67.04
  penalties, civil—
    interest on, 2A.42
    misdeclarations, generally, 2A.97
  prescribed accounting periods, 67.01
  private or non-business purposes, services used for, 65.30
  prosecutions, 2.34-2.35
  rate of, 65.06
  reduced rate—
    charge of, 70.02-70.03
    children's car seats, on, 70.08
    contraceptive products, on, 70.11
    energy-saving materials, on, 70.05
    fuel and power, on, 70.04
    gas supply, on, 70.06
    generally, 65.06, 70.01
    heating equipment, on, 70.06
    legislation, 70.02
    mobility aids for the elderly, on, 70.13
    renovation and alteration of dwellings, on, 70.10
    residential conversions, on, 70.09
    security goods, on, 70.06
    smoking cessation products, on, 70.14
    welfare advice or information, on, 70.12
    women's sanitary products, on, 70.07
  refunds—
    bad debt relief, 66.41
    principle, 66.39
    VAT incurred, of, 66.40
  registration—
    associations, 63.12
    bodies corporate, 63.12
    clubs, 63.12
    deemed partnership, 63.12
    entitlement to, 63.11, 63.12
      goods from another EU state, intention to supply, 64.17
      overseas supplies, persons making or intending to make, 64.16
      relevant acquisitions—
        persons intending to make, 64.19

Value added tax – *cont.*
registration— – *cont.*
  entitlement to, 63.11, 63.12 – *cont.*
    relevant acquisitions— – *cont.*
      persons making, 64.18
      taxable supplies, persons making or intending to make, 64.15
  exemption from—
    generally, 64.20
    zero-rated acquisitions, 64.23
    zero-rated supplies, 64.21, 64.22
  failure to notify liability to, 64.14
  liability to—
    generally, 63.11, 63.12
    going concern, business transferred as, 64.04
    persons supplying tax relieved goods in UK, 64.05
    relevant acquisitions, persons making, 64.11
    relevant supplies, making, 64.06
    supply of goods from another EU state¾
      goods subject to excise duty, 64.08
      place of supply option, goods affected by, 64.09
      place of supply option, goods not affected by, 64.10
      relevant supplies, 64.07
    taxable supplies, making¾
      next 30 days, for, 64.03
      past twelve months, for, 64.02
  organisations, 63.12
  VAT group—
    eligibility for membership, 64.24
    formation and variation, 64.25
    intra-group supplies, 64.27
    registration, consequences of, 64.26
    self supplies using an overseas member, 64.28
    transfer of business to member as going concern, 64.29
  VAT representatives, 63.13
  relevant acquisitions, persons making—
    conditions, 64.13
    entitlement to registration, 64.18–64.19
    past acquisitions, 64.12
    registration, failure to notify liability to, 64.14
  relevant supplies, persons making, meaning, 64.07
repayment—
  EC traders, to, 66.37
  provision for, 66.36
  tax not due, of, 67.17

Value added tax – *cont.*
repayment— – *cont.*
  third country traders, to, 66.38
retailers' schemes, 63.44
security for, 67.09
stamp duty, and, 57.09
supplies of goods and services, on—
  accounting for tax, person liable, 65.09
  basic tax point, 65.11
  charge to tax, 65.08
  no consideration, made for—
    another EU state, removal to, 65.31
    private or non-business purposes, for, 65.29–65.30
    transfer or disposal, 65.28
  rate or description, change in, 65.15
  reporting, 2A.13
  tax points, 65.11–65.13
  time of, 65.10
    special rules, 65.14
  time when charge arising, 65.10
tax invoice, duty to issue, 65.18
tax returns—
  amount of tax due, showing, 67.04
  generally, 67.03
  prescribed accounting periods, 67.01
  repayment supplement, 67.06
  VAT credit, showing, 67.05
taxable persons—
  definition, 63.10
  liability, 63.11, 63.12
taxable supplies, person making—
  entitlement to registration, 64.14
  meaning, 64.01
  registration, liability to, 64.02–64.04
territorial considerations, 63.08
value of goods and services—
  general principles, 65.16
  meaning, 65.16
  valuation rules, 65.17
VAT representatives, 63.13
works of art, etc, margin scheme for, 65.23
zero-rating—
  aids for handicapped, 69.35, 69.36
  bank notes, 69.33
  books—
    generally, 69.15
    talking, 69.16
  buildings—
    approved alterations, 69.23
    construction, 69.17–69.21
    conversion, 69.20
    goods supplied with services, 69.21, 69.24

Index

Value added tax – *cont.*
  zero-rating— – *cont.*
    buildings— – *cont.*
      major interest, grant of, 69.17, 69.22
      protected, 69.22–69.24
    caravans, 69.31
    charities, 69.39–69.41
    civil engineering works, 69.17, 69.19
    clothing, 69.42
    common provisions, application of, 69.03
    drugs, 69.34
    exports, 69.37
    food, 69.13
    footwear, 69.42
    gold, 69.32
    goods exported to third countries, 69.08
    goods removed to another EU member state, 69.07
    houseboats, 69.31
    imports, 69.37
    international services, 69.25
    legislation, 69.02
    medicines, 69.34
    nature of, 69.01
    sewerage services, 69.14
    ships, aircraft and hovercraft, stores for use in, 69.05
    tax free shops, 69.38
    terminal markets, 69.04
    transport, 69.26–69.30
    warehoused goods, services relating to, 69.06
    water, 69.14
    wireless sets, 69.16
VAT and Duties Tribunal
  appeal to, 2.14
  costs, 2.15
  .establishment of, 2.14
  jurisdiction, 2.16
Vehicle, *see* CAR
Venture capital trusts
  capital gains tax exemption, 17.22
  excluded activities, 31.18
  investment in, 31.17
Vocation
  basis of assessment, *see* TRADES, PROFESSIONS AND VOCATIONS, INCOME FROM
  expenses, *see* EXPENSES

Vocation – *cont.*
  income from, *see* TRADES, PROFESSIONS AND VOCATIONS, INCOME FROM
  meaning, 8.07
  trading income, former distinction, 8.01
Voluntary registration, *see* VALUE ADDED TAX
Vouchers
  benefit in kind, as, 7.45
  childcare, 7.46
Wasting assets
  capital gains tax—
    computation, 16.25
    exemption from, 17.18
Water
  value added tax, 69.14
Welfare advice or information
  value added tax, 70.02
Wife, *see* SPOUSES AND CIVIL PARTNERS
Will
  stamp duty, 58.13–58.14
  variation, deed of, 58.14
  variation of incidence of inheritance tax by, 46.24–46.25
Winnings
  charge to tax, 12.05
Wireless sets
  value added tax, 69.16
Woodlands
  capital gains tax, exemption from, 17.14
  inheritance tax, 44.33–44.35
Work in progress
  trading stock, 8.166–8.167
Works of art
  capital gains tax, exemption from, 17.15
  inheritance tax–
    beneficiaries, position of, 46.16
    charge, 44.30
    designated objects, 44.28
    generally, 44.27
    maintenance fund, 44.32
    transferor's cumulative total, 44.31
  maintenance fund, 44.32
  value added tax, 68.27
    credit, exclusion from, 66.21
    margin scheme, 65.23
Writing down allowances, *see* CAPITAL ALLOWANCES
Youth clubs
  value added tax, 68.22
Zero–rating, *see* VALUE ADDED TAX